WORLD RADIO TV HANDBOOK

WRTH

THE DIRECTORY OF GLOBAL BROADCASTING

2013

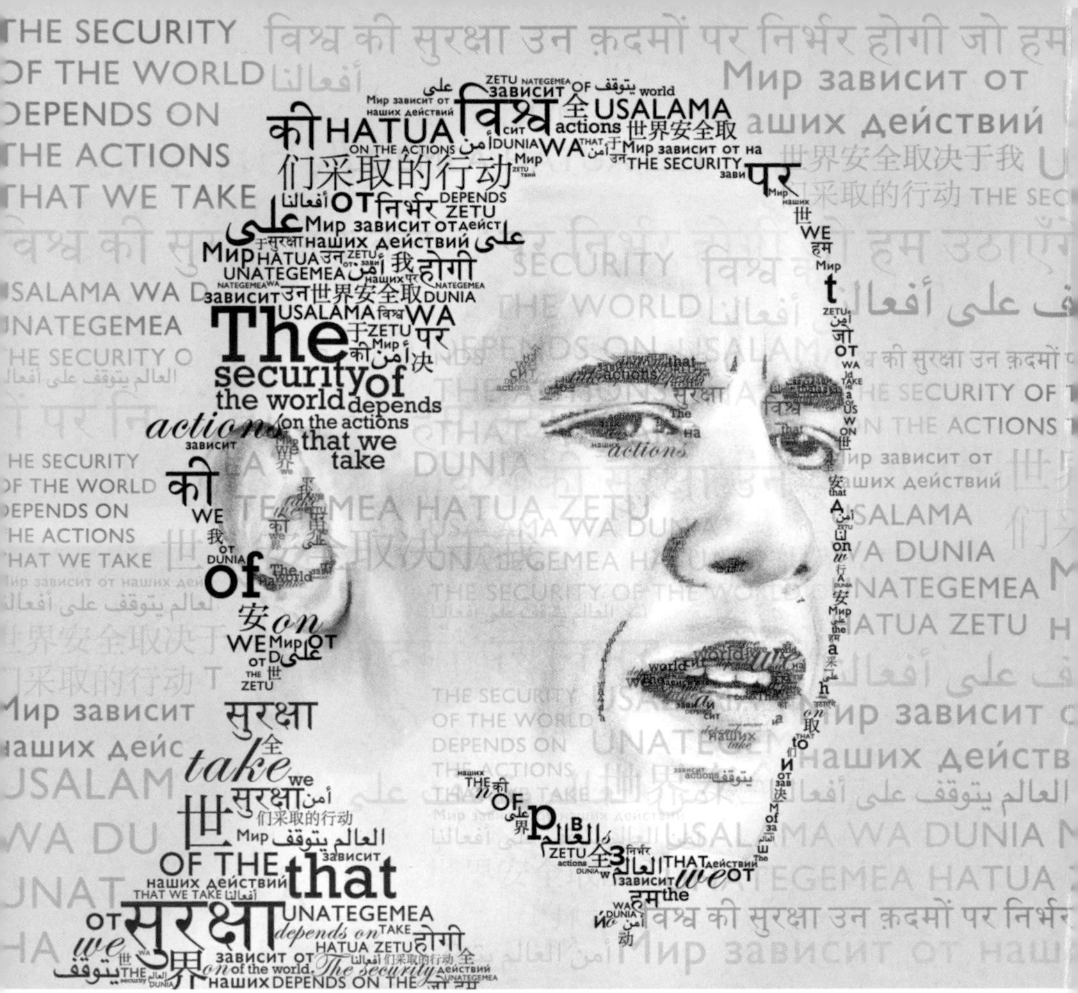

THE NEWS DOESN'T ALWAYS
HAPPEN IN YOUR LANGUAGE

That's why BBC World Service speaks yours
Available in 27 languages

BBC
WORLD
SERVICE

bbcworldservice.com/languages

中文网   MUNDO   عربي   INDONESIA   हिन्दी   BRASIL   TIẾNG VIỆT

9001169312

WORLD RADIO TV HANDBOOK

WRTH

THE DIRECTORY OF GLOBAL BROADCASTING

VOLUME 67 – 2013

Publisher
Nicholas Hardyman

International Editor
Sean Gilbert

'A' Schedule & Web Updates Editor
Mauno Ritola

Television Editor
Bernd Trutenau

Technical Editor
John Nelson

Contributing Editors
George Jacobs
Bengt Ericson
Dave Kenny
Mauno Ritola
Bernd Trutenau
Torgeir Woxen

Cover Design
Richard Boxall Design Associates

Published in the UK by:
WRTH Publications Limited
PO Box 290
Oxford OX2 7FT
United Kingdom
Tel: +44 (0) 1865 339355
Fax: +44 (0) 1865 339301
Email: wrth@wrth.com
Web: www.wrth.com
ISBN 978-0-9555481-5-4

Distributed in the USA by:
Innovative Logistics
575 Prospect St.
Lakewood, NJ 08701
USA
Web: www.innlog.net
Email: lsucar@innlog.net
Tel: US toll free: 866-289-2088
Fax: US toll free: 877-372-8892
ISBN 978-0-9555481-5-4

Printed and bound in the UK by CPI William Clowes, Beccles NR34 7TL

WORLD RADIO TV HANDBOOK

CONTENTS

Section Contents

Features & Reviews

National Radio

International Radio

Frequency Lists

Terrestrial Television

Reference

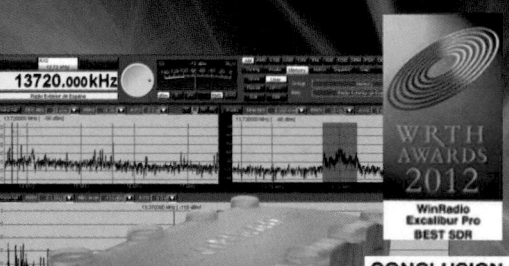
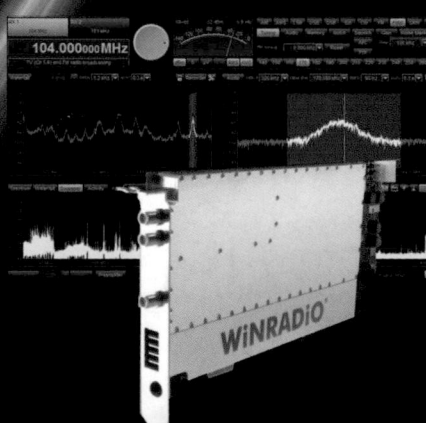

Editorial

NEW WAVES

Welcome to the 67th edition of *WRTH*. We are proud to bring you the most comprehensive and up-date information on global broadcasting available anywhere in the world. This book is the result of the hard work and dedication of our team of editors and contributors without whom the compilation and correction of this data would not be possible. In 2012 we were sorry to say farewell to Christer Brunström who editied Spain and the Central American countries. The updating of these countries has been split between Mauno Ritola, Dario Monferini and Dave Kenny.

We are very pleased this year to welcome Wake Island back as a radio country in *WRTH*. The last station on the island, KEAD 1490 AM, closed 30 years ago, and the creation of the new FM station is testament to the ease with which a small FM station can now be put on air. We also welcome the Pitcairn Islands as they make their first appearance as a radio country.

This year has seen little development in the desktop receiver market, with only variants of existing receivers appearing. We were, however, delighted to review the first capable standalone DRM receiver we have seen, in the form of the Newstar DR111, and have also enjoyed examining some interesting new SDR receivers.

HF BROADCASTING

Whilst editing the maps at the end of this section, it was our melancholy duty this year to remove many shortwave transmitter sites. This is the first year that the number of sites being dismantled outweighed the number of new sites created. The uncertain outlook for HF broadcasting was also evident in many of the comments made at the August 2012 HFCC meeting but some positive factors were also highlighted.

The continuing high usage of the Sentech shortwave site in South Africa, the management buy-out of the famous RNW site at Talata Volonondry on Madagascar and the result of the recent Trans World Radio survey to determine whether people were still listening to them on shortwave, confirms that HF in Africa is still an important delivery system. This highlights the fact that the global decline in HF transmissions does not mean that there is no place for HF broadcasting, and we are sure that it will continue to have a part to play for many years to come. However we are now convinced that this decline will accelerate until HF is beamed only to those places where economic or political conditions, or challenging terrain make its use necessary.

Radio broadcasting is generally in very good health. This year the BBC celebrated the 90th anniversay of its first transmision with a simultaneous global broadcast called Radio Reunited, and at its 67th session the General Assembly of the United Nations approved the idea of a World Radio Day to be held on 13 February each year. We see this as a very fitting tribute to this great medium of communication.

WRTH FREQUENCY BARGRAPH

The bargraph frequency CDs we produced in the past year for the B11 and A12 seasons proved increasingly popular and we will be producing them again for the B12 and A13 seasons. It remains our intention to provide them also as downloads which we feel will be even more useful to our readers. The CDs and the downloads will only be available from our website.

WEBSITE UPDATES

We will be uploading pdf updates to our website. Updates to the B12 season will be available in February 2013. The full schedules for the A13 season will be posted in May 2012 with an update in July 2013. We will also continue to provide updates to the National Radio section on the *WRTHmonitor* page on our website.

PRIZE DRAW RESULTS

These winners were again drawn by members of the British DX Club.

RESULTS OF THE
WRTH 2012 PRIZE DRAW

First prize: the Tecsun PL-660

FIRST PRIZE
J. Gimenez Gandia, Spain

RUNNERS-UP PRIZES (copies of WRTH 2013)
K. M. Vyas, India
D. Artz, USA
S. Höfig, Germany
B. Allen, UK
P-L. Brochier, Canada

I hope you will enjoy reading and using this new edition of *WRTH*

Nicholas Hardyman
Publisher

WRTH Contributors 2013

The *WRTH* contributors come from all walks of life; yet share a common fascination with all aspects of global broadcasting. Each year we profile one of the people whose dedicated enthusiasm makes possible the enormous task of updating *WRTH* each year. This year it is the turn of Karel Honzík, our contributor for some of the countries of Central Europe, who gives us an insight into what makes a *WRTH* contributor.

Karel Honzík at his favourite receiving location

We have heard and read many times that today's DXers became interested in radio waves in their childhood through their parents' radio receivers. It was the same with me. I added a few metres of wire to our simple kitchen receiver, hung the wire out of the window, and I was listening to my first shortwave stations from around the world. There I heard the first mentions of DXing and SWLing on Radio Canada International and Radio Australia. At that time I knew medium waves a bit more because already for some time I had been listening not only to the Voice of America and Radio Free Europe but also to musical pirate stations broadcasting from the waters close to the UK coast. Night time and early mornings were the best times for reception. It was the second half of the 1960s.

Later, during my two-year army service, I managed to get to a radio receiver too. At that time, in Czechoslovakia ruled by communists, soldiers were not allowed to have their own receivers in barracks but there was a big luxury table receiver in our commander's office. From autumn to spring the office was open during the night because the night guard was ordered to heat the office. So I had access to this extraordinary receiver with many bands once or twice a week during my night guard.

In the middle of the 1970s we established an unofficial Czechoslovak DX Circle with about 20 members. At that time it was forbidden to establish such clubs officially. We were publishing a monthly DX bulletin circulated in one copy among members of the circle. Our activity was interrupted in 1980 after a series of investigations by the StB (Czechoslovak State Security, and a branch of the well known Soviet KGB). I still remember very well my interrogation in January 1980 when two StB agents picked me up in the morning at my workplace and interrogated me in their office from 10 am to 4 pm.

Our public activity sank to zero, but privately everyone of us spent his daily hours by his radio. Usually we were meeting once a year on so-called Field Days in a cottage somewhere in the country with a plenty of receivers and antennas. It is necessary to mention at this point the support we were given by fellow DXers abroad. Above all it was Bernd Trutenau, a German DXer, today one of the contributing editors of *WRTH*, who was getting printed DX materials for us from abroad. He was also helping us to subscribe to foreign DX clubs and, from time to time, he visited our country. I think that he has not yet been given enough thanks for his praiseworthy and brave activity.

At the end of 1989, when the age of the East European block of countries ruled by the Soviet Union came to its bitter end, we immediately started thinking about establishing an official DX club. It was in January 1990 when the Czechoslovak DX Club (ČSDXC: www.dx.cz) was established in Prague. Right from the beginning we started publishing a printed monthly DX bulletin entitled *DX Revue*, later renamed as *Radio Revue*.

Because I had participated in writing and publishing the former unofficial DX bulletin, and I had access to printing equipment and DTP, I was "appointed" editor-in-chief of DX Revue and I have been doing this work until today when we are in the 22nd year of publishing. In 2010 we converted to an electronic version in PDF which allows for a larger A4 format and colour layout which was unaffordable for us in the previous printed form.

During my DX years I changed my receivers several times, from German WWII military receivers over Russian military receivers to newer civil communication receivers. Later I had also Grundig Satelits, Drake, Lowe, AOR. . . . Today it is Perseus and its FM downconverter marked FM+. Some role is still played by an excellent 16 year old AOR AR7030.

I run away from the big city noise to a quiet forest environment with my receivers and antennas. I spend about a half of every month in a former gamekeeper's lodge, three miles from the nearest village. In this electrically quiet place, my antennas bring DX signals from my favourite medium waves and tropical bands, occasionally also from the longwave portion of the NDB band. I spend some time also in the FM band where I have discovered a possibility of reception of stations from distances of 500 km or more.

About five years ago one short wave listener asked me, "Is it wise to buy a communications receiver now when it is known that everything is going to be digital even on short waves?" I told him at that time that he will surely make use of his receiver until the end of its lifetime. And still today I am quite sure that we will have the opportunity to listen to interesting DX stations for many years.

Karel Honzík

Official *WRTH* contributor for Austria, The Czech Republic and Slovakia

A large project such as *WRTH* could not be produced without the help of many people from all over the world. The following organisations and publications give invaluable help:

Asian Broadcasting Institute, BC-DX Top, British DX Club, Danish Shortwave Club International, DX-Listening Digest, DX Mix News, Electronic DX Press, Grupo Radioescucha Argentino, National Radio Club Inc (USA listings), Radio Heritage Foundation

our Country Contributors provide us with updated entries for the countries for which they are responsible:

Herman Boel, Luis Carvalho, Swopan Chakroborty, Svotomir Cuckovic, Alan Davies, Alok Dasgupta, Bengt Ericson, David Foster, Stig Hartvig Nielsen, István Hegedüs, Karel Honzík, Jose Jacob, Richard Jary, Dave Kenny, Tetsuya Kondo, Vashek Korinek, Kai Ludwig, Dario Monferini, Andy Reid, David Ricquish, Mauno Ritola, Tony Rogers, Roberto Scaglione, Bernd Trutenau, Max van Arnhem, Thierry Vignaud, Tore B Vik, Torgeir Woxen

they and we are greatly aided by our other major contributors:

Carlos Benoit, Erich Bergmann, Dino Bloise, Héctor García Bojorge, Jordi Brunet, Mustafa Cancurt, Alfredo Cañote, Marcelo A. Cornachioni, Patricio R. de los Rios, Samir Elahcene, Jack FitzSimons, José Días Gómez, Victor Goonetilleke, Noel Green, Chris Greenway, Rudolf Walter Grimm, Alokesh Gupta, Wolf Harranth, Glenn Hauser, Aslam Javaid, Hans Johnson, Anatoly Klepov, Sergey Kolesov, Andrej Kuznecov, Miller Liu, James MacDonell, Alexander Mak, Cláudio Rótolo de Moraes, Adán Mur, Michael Nevradakis, Horacio Nigro, Alexey Osipov, Samuel Ouma, Anker Petersen, Mieczyslaw Pietruski, Arnulf Piontek, Rimantas Pleikys, Patrick Robic, Rafael Rodríguez, Célio Romais, Daniel Rosenzweig, Ibrahim Rustamov, Victor Rutkovsky, Jari Savolainen, David Sharp, Zhang ShiFeng, Paulo Roberto e Souza, David Stanley, Numan Vasquez, Tarek Zeidan

We thank them, and also all our readers who have written or emailed us with useful ideas and information. Please keep sending your thoughts and updates to:

wrth@wrth.com

or write to:
WRTH Publications Limited, PO Box 290, Oxford OX2 7FT, UK

WRTH Receiver Reviews 2013

Yet again it is our sad duty to report further closures of HF broadcast services. Although local FM and AM broadcasting will undoubtedly persist in the medium term, it is now abundantly clear that in time the internet and cellular radio handsets will ultimately become the bearers of choice as far as international broadcast television and radio 'reception' is concerned. As we said last year, where that leaves international broadcasting will continue to be an open question for the foreseeable future but the omens are not good.

In the meantime it seems that the disciplines of the radio and broadcast engineer will continue to be steadily displaced by those appropriate to networks and IT. We have referred before to what has become a large-scale uptake of techniques such as streaming and podcasting. Tablet computers and handsets have proliferated along with 3G and 4G mobile and wi-fi networks, and some form of wireless coverage is now available in some of the most remote places in the world.

REVIEWS

New receivers were a little thin on the ground this year and it is striking that almost all the stand-alone units were SDRs of one sort or another. The two main exceptions were 'internet radios' – for want of a better description although there is obviously no 'radio' involved – which also offered off-air DAB and FM reception facilities. Both were very impressive. The availability and performance of home and business broadband connections has steadily advanced in recent years and a very high proportion of premises in the developed world now have some form of broadband service based on ADSL, fibre, cable or indeed cellular radio. Consequently the internet has steadily become a mainstream method of reception for many. The modern table-top internet radio is an easy-to-use 'black box' about the size of most mains radios but offering immediate access to thousands of outlets from mainstream international broadcasters to tiny niche operators as well as small conventional radio stations. Perhaps the most significant points are that little or no technical knowledge is required to use an internet radio except for the initial setting-up and that the audio quality is generally very good.

Another interesting newcomer was the Newstar DR111, offering DRM in addition to conventional AM and FM. We were not very impressed with this receiver when it first arrived but a firmware update addressed many of its issues and it turned out to be a respectable performer if perhaps slightly expensive. We still tend towards the view that DRM30 will not now find a place as a mass-market mode, not because there is anything intrinsically wrong with it but because the era of long-distance HF broadcasting is passing. So whether anyone other than a radio enthusiast *per se* would purchase a DRM-capable radio is somewhat open to question. But we would be very pleased to be proved wrong.

Small and very capable software-defined radios were our main preoccupation this year. In their different ways the Afredi, the Bonito and the CrossCountry all exemplify the modern approach to obtaining high performance and versatility from receivers taking advantage of the enormous processing power available in modern personal computers. Whilst we still have issues with the ergonomics of many SDRs, there is little doubt that spectacularly high performance is now available to the enthusiast at very reasonable prices.

We have not reviewed small portables this year. A few new models from Tecsun and others have appeared in the marketplace but they seemed to be variations on a theme already discussed comprehensively in these pages rather than harbingers of anything particularly new. There were also no large table-top receivers offering the usual feature set and functionality hitherto associated with this product class. In fact it is notable that many of the major players appear to have pulled out of this market sector altogether, which may be another sign that the SDR is beginning to dominate. The primary driver for this is undoubtedly financial. A large proportion of the cost of any conventional radio is associated with the design, manufacture and installation of the cabinet, controls and display. In hardware terms, however, a software-defined receiver consists of a printed-circuit board in a simple box and the user's computer does the rest.

ABOUT THE AUTHOR

John Nelson is an author, editor and consultant specialising in audio, radio and communications technology. After graduation in 1974, John worked for the BBC and the Radio Society of Great Britain before forming his own company in 1986 and has written, edited and contributed to a wide variety of publications. He is now the managing director of Crew Green Consulting Ltd, which specialises in electronic and communications systems design and assessment for an international client base.

John's amateur radio callsign GW4FRX is often heard on the HF bands – where he currently has 323 DXCC countries confirmed – and on 144MHz. In his remaining spare time he enjoys aviation, music, literature and architecture. He lives in east Wales.

Newstar DR111

US$140   £140   €175

OVERVIEW

In the 2008 edition of *WRTH* we looked at DRM-capable receivers from Morphy Richards and Himalaya and were unimpressed by both. Since then both have disappeared from the market and there have been no sign of replacements. It is therefore pleasant to be able to record that for the first time in the recent history of this publication we have received a stand-alone radio for review which has a band selector button marked 'DRM'. The Newstar DR111 is manufactured by Chengdu NewStar Electronics and distribution is in the hands of Peter Senger, who was at one time chairman of the DRM Consortium.

The DR111 covers 150-288 and 522-1710kHz (the latter with selectable step sizes of 9 or 10kHz) and 2300kHz to 27MHz for AM and DRM reception together with 87.5-108MHz for FM. The manual indicates that the latter offers some RDS functionality but in practice this appeared to be confined to presentation of the PS name and programme type. On DRM the stated functions are station name, programme information, Journaline and alternative-frequency switching. There are quite comprehensive alarm and timer facilities. In appearance the DR111 might be described as Seventies-retro. Its white plastic cabinet measures 280 x 120 x 100mm with an inset upper section carrying the angled lime-green-backlit display. Mode-selector and other control function buttons together with six station presets are mounted on the top of this section. Eighteen DRM, 18 AM and 12 FM station frequencies can be preset. The buttons all exhibit a combination of long travel and moderately high breakout force which makes them feel 'heavy' in operation.

FEATURES

Two speakers of about 50mm diameter are mounted on the front, as is a combined volume and tuning control at upper right. This latter is rather non-intuitive in operation and requires a little patience; we tend to think that more conventional tuning and volume controls would have been a distinct improvement! There is no numeric keypad, which implies that tuning takes place either by means of the rotary knob (pushing it in invokes tuning and pushing it again re-selects volume) or by a rather long-winded process using the info and cursor keys. There is a scan mode but this seemed to be somewhat erratic in our sample at least and did not appear to work at all on DRM stations. All in all, tuning and frequency selection are decidedly tedious process in the DR111 and its ergonomics are unimpressive

A telescopic antenna is mounted on the rear drop together with a socket for an external antenna on the right-hand side. This works on SW and FM and an internal ferrite antenna is used for LW and MW reception. Sockets for power and headphones together with an SD-card slot and a USB port are located on the left-hand side. The supplied 'wall wart' PSU had a two-pin Continental mains plug and its temperature rose to a slightly alarming level during extended operation of the receiver. As with many PSUs of Chinese origin, its size and rating suggested a transformer core dimensioned for 60Hz operation rather than 50Hz. Neither the adaptor nor the radio itself carried CE marking or FCC approval. Incidentally some internet forum users have mentioned that the receiver is very sensitive to its supply voltage and can be damaged if more than 5V is applied. There is no provision for operation from batteries.

The SD card slot can be used for music playback or firmware updates and indeed an updated firmware version (790) became available in early August 2012. We had used the DR111 for a short period prior to the arrival of this update and frankly we were less than impressed with it; major elements of its functionality did not work well and its performance in several areas was poor. It is fair to say that the upgraded firmware transformed the DR111 into a very much more respectable receiver which was considerably less awkward to use. We would imagine that all current production receivers have the revised firmware incorporated but purchasers should check to see whether this is the case. There does not appear to be a method of checking the installed version by key presses but one obvious clue is that the lower end of the volume-control range was extremely abrupt in the original version. This has been successfully addressed in the newer firmware, as has a mute-during-tuning issue which was exceedingly irritating. Upgrading is simple, requiring only the downloading of a zipped archive file from the manufacturer's web site and the copying of the files on to the root directory of the SD card.

There is no information in the literature about the DR111's internal architecture. In performance terms the receiver was generally reasonable. FM sensitivity was fair although the audio quality was not particularly good, with a marked lack of treble. On certain programme material there was a sense of just-audible peak distortion of the sort that used to be associated with slight mistuning of an elderly non-synthesized FM receiver. On conventional AM the sensitivity seemed to be usefully high after the firmware upgrade had been carried out and results were generally good. On occasion the receiver exhibited quite marked distortion when first switched on and tuned to an AM channel. The cure seemed to be to switch off, unplug the PSU and switch on again. This was also the cure for an occasional loss of ability to switch modes. No doubt these are minor firmware 'bugs' which will be fixed in the next release. Measurements suggested that the AM sensitivity varied somewhat with frequency but was generally around -116dBm for 20dB SINAD.

PERFORMANCE

The majority of the DR111's potential purchasers will have its DRM reception capability principally in mind and we spent much time investigating this. In general terms it performed quite well and the unit is certainly better than anything else that has yet appeared in its price class. Using the receiver's own telescopic antenna the BBC transmissions from Woofferton on 5875 were consistently well received at the test site, as was the 7355 outlet. This latter often provided solid copy for almost the entire transmission period. Other transmissions which were usually audible for long periods included REE on 9780 and VoR on 6155, which during the evening was very strong. Several comparison tests were made using a Wellbrook loop, which was – not surprisingly –

considerably better than the DR111's own antennas and here again the overall results were generally good. It was noted that on occasions the audio from the DR111 would mute for periods of several seconds even when the incoming RF level was quite high, presumably due to interference. That said, on several occasions when we were carrying out direct comparisons against a WinRadio Excalibur Pro using the Wellbrook antenna and Marconi coupler, the latter did not mute when the DR111 did. More surprisingly there were occasions on which several DRM stations were audible at good strength on the WinRadio which the DR111 resolutely refused to decode at all. There was no common pattern to this and the reason remains something of a mystery. Obviously the comparison is rather unfair in that the WinRadio is by far the best DRM receiver we have ever tested and also costs ten times more than the DR111, but it would be interesting to establish the reason.

A salient point about the DR111 is that its pricing is likely to be central to its marketplace viability. In the UK the receiver costs £139.99 and in the USA it is about $140.00. This is not a negligible amount of money – one could buy a very respectable internet radio for rather less – and one is in effect being invited to pay a considerable premium for the inclusion of DRM. A mains-powered AM/FM radio with the overall quality and functionality of the DR111 would be expected to cost somewhere between £30 and £50 in the UK, which implies that the DRM function is costing a further £90-110. Our guess is that this is rather more than the non-specialist radio user will be willing to pay for what is at best a marginal enhancement in functionality.

CONCLUSION

But the DR111 works well enough to be interesting to the enthusiast and it is good to see DRM receiver finally coming to market. We look forward to a Mk II version with better ergonomics (and a numeric keypad), slightly more consistent performance and perhaps a lower price.

Rating table for Newstar DR111

Constructional quality	★★★
Sensitivity	★★★★
Dynamic range	★★★
RF intermodulation	★★★
Audio quality	★★★
Versatility	★★★
VFM	★★★

Overall rating   ★★★

Key:
★ = Poor   ★★ = Fair   ★★★ = Average
★★★★ = Good   ★★★★★ = Excellent
VFM = Value for money

Cross Country Wireless SDR-4+

US$270   £170   €210

Cross Country Wireless is a small but extremely capable UK-based company which specialises in RF products and software for the amateur and professional markets. Its new SDR-4+ is a direct-conversion SDR developed from an earlier product which was very useful either as a VHF/UHF panadaptor or a 6-15MHz crystal-controlled fixed-frequency receiver. The SDR-4+ covers 850kHz-40MHz and makes an interesting comparison with the Afredi reviewed on page 16. It uses a Silicon Labs Si570 10MHz-1.4GHz programmable VCXO as the basis of its synthesiser. This very advanced IC uses some remarkable and innovative techniques to achieve very high performance, including running its reference oscillator at frequencies well into the GHz region. The receiver also embodies relay-switched bandpass filtering which in principle should give it good strong-signal performance.

Realised as a small aluminium box measuring 188 x 110 x 30mm, the block diagram of the SDR-4+ shows an antenna isolation transformer with 50 or 450 ohm inputs (on BNC female and 2mm jack sockets respectively) for use with coax-fed or random-wire antennas. This is followed by bandpass filters for 1-4, 4-8, 8-16 and 16-30MHz which are relay-switched on both ports; the switching is carried out by a section of the Si570 and a BCD converter. The filter output passes through 500kHz high-pass and 40MHz low-pass filters, an E-PHEMT RF amplifier and thence to a species of Tayloe mixer/detector using what are described as 'precision low-noise op-amps'. When correctly implemented this type of detector should give very good intermodulation performance. There is a built-in USB stereo 'soundcard' and a 3.5mm I-Q audio output for connection to an external high sampling-rate card if one is available or required. The maximum frequency display is 48kHz using the internal card and up to 192kHz with an external card. Two USB sockets are provided for connections and the receiver is powered via the USB port. Current consumption is 320mA which in principle should not unduly tax even a laptop although for some reason our sample refused to work at all with a powered USB hub and much preferred direct connection to the office PC. Cross Country Wireless claims an MDS of -135dBm although the bandwidth at which this applies is not stated; our testing suggested that it was met at 1kHz, which is in line with expectation and a good performance. The stated 'clipping level' is -13dBm and the input IP_3 given as +14.5dBm measured with two -20dBm carriers with 5kHz spacing at 14MHz.

In general terms the performance was very good and more than good enough for general listening around the MF and HF bands. A few odd glitches and freezes were noted from time to time and for some reason there were occasional bursts of noise when retuning the receiver. A review in a UK magazine suggested that this may be inherent in the design of the Si570 but it is certainly not an issue in day-to-day use and is noted here only for completeness. Strong night-time 6/7MHz signals from our reference dipole occasionally overloaded the receiver, which was to be expected, and there were odd instances of breakthrough from other services whilst listening to weak MW stations. As with the Afredi receiver this should be very easy to address if required by the addition of an external low-pass filter.

Our overall impression of the Cross Country Wireless SDR-4+ is of a very competent low-cost SDR which offers good performance. As with the Afredi it is not perhaps for the complete novice. However, for those considering dipping a toe into the waters of software-defined receivers and who are reasonably fluent with personal computers, the SDR-4+ would be a very good choice.

Internet Radio

INTRODUCTION

In 2009 we took our first look at the world of internet radio and assessed some early 'receivers'. Of course, as we observed at the time, 'internet radio' is a contradiction in terms; the essence of the method is that the programme content is not used to modulate a radio-frequency transmitter but instead converted into a *stream* of data transmitted via the internet. This is decoded and reassembled either by a personal computer or a stand-alone device which can use either a wired or a wireless connection to the internet.

A very high proportion of premises in the developed world now have some form of broadband service based on ADSL, fibre or cable. Consequently internet radio has become a mainstream method of reception for many. At the time of writing it was estimated that there were about 30,000 internet radio 'channels' available worldwide, of which some 8,000 originated in the USA alone. They range from international broadcasters almost literally to one man in a garden shed.

For this years' *WRTH* we have looked at two stand-alone 'receivers'. These combine conventional DAB and FM reception capabilities with the ability to handle internet radio streams. Given the price/performance ratio of these and similar items, it is abundantly clear that the age of the internet radio has well and truly arrived. If you have reasonable broadband access and your main interest is in listening to international radio stations rather than DXing, it is our considered opinion that there is nowadays no reason at all to consider buying any other species of 'receiver'.

PURE 'ONE FLOW'

The Pure 'One Flow' is an internet radio offering L-band and Band III DAB and FM reception facilities. The firmware also supports DAB+ and DMB-R. The 'One Flow' measures 210 x 145 x 65mm and has a matt rubberized finish. The display is a yellow OLED type and five push-buttons are located below it, three of which are context-sensitive. There are two rotary controls, one for volume and the other acting as a multi-purpose rotary and push-button selector. The supported codecs include various flavours of MPEG and WMA together with AAC and Real Audio. Media streaming is also available via a UPnP media server or a PC or Mac running UPnP server software. The unit runs from a 5.5V DC mains adaptor. An optional 'ChargePAK' rechargeable battery set can be fitted if required but there is no facility for using conventional primary cells.

The front-mounted speaker has a diameter of 3in and the audio output is a claimed 2.5W RMS.

Pure 'One Flow'
US$118   £75   €100

A stereo headphone output is provided on one side together with an auxiliary input, a standby/on button and a mini-USB connector. The latter can in principle be used for a wired Ethernet connection but a suitable adaptor is not supplied with the radio. Consequently the 'One Flow' relies as standard on its in-built 802.11b/g wireless link for connection with a router. Both WEP and WPA/WPA2 encryption are automatically detected. Pure recommends a minimum broadband speed of 0.5 Mb/s. A telescopic antenna is provided for DAB and FM reception.

Setting-up wireless access was very simple and all that is required is entry of the selected WEP or WPA key. As usual with Pure products, the unit is remarkably intuitive in operation and hardly needs a manual; a quick-reference card is included and is perfectly adequate. Once the connection has been made and the list of available stations downloaded, the radio is ready for operation. There are 30 station presets available on DAB and ten on FM, together with what is in essence an unlimited set of internet radio favourites available at the Pure portal. We did not find this particularly easy to navigate at first and some persistence was necessary to find and allocate the required stations. In this respect we preferred the Frontier Silicon portal with its much freer menu structure.

Once selected, most internet stations took only a short time to appear. Many connections were fairly stable but the impression was gained over time that the 'One Flow' dropped-out or disconnected rather more often than the Stream 83i. It was initially thought that this might be due to the wireless link but using the unit within a metre or so of the router did not improve the performance. On DAB the 'One Flow' was noticeably less sensitive than the Stream 83i and also exhibited abrupt transitions between producing good audio and no audio at all when reception was arranged to be marginal. FM sensitivity appeared reasonable. In terms of sound quality we have noted previously that Pure seems to have adopted a policy of rolling-off the treble response slightly earlier than strictly necessary in many of its recent radios. This is also the case with the 'One Flow' and the result is mildly 'boomy' speech and less 'sparkle' to music. There are no adjustable tone controls. We were interested to find when listening via a high-quality headset that there was essentially no audible difference between the same programme material via FM and DAB but that on occasion the streaming audio sounded better than both!

All in all, the Pure 'One Flow' offers plenty of functionality for a low price and is recommended.

ROBERTS STREAM 83i

Whilst not perhaps the best-looking electronic device ever reviewed by *WRTH*, the Stream 83i is beautifully finished in black lacquer and exceedingly solidly built. The cabinet measures 240 x 160 x 100mm. Two 34mm speakers are mounted at left and right operating in conjunction with a 76mm rear-mounted subwoofer; the audio performance of the Stream 83i is excellent, assisted by comprehensive equalisation. The blue backlit display at centre is commendably clear. A multi-purpose knob to its right handles most selection

Roberts Stream 83i

US$210   £120   €150

functions with a matching volume control to the left. There are five station presets and a row of seven small function buttons beneath the display.

The Stream 83i offers DAB, FM and internet radio. Its chipset appears to be from Frontier Silicon and it uses the latter's portal for access. Supported formats are AAC, FLAC, LPCM, MP3, RealAudio, WAV and WMA. The unit can also connect to Windows Shares or UPnP servers, implying that in addition to its internet radio functionality the Stream 83i can replay music or sound files stored on an associated computer. In practice this feature worked very well. The Stream 83i has both a wired Ethernet port with the standard RJ-45 connector and an IEEE

802.11b/g wireless facility which supports both WPA/WPA2 and WEP encryption. On the rear of the Stream 83i is the Ethernet RJ-45 port, a USB connector and 3.5mm jacks for auxiliary input, line output and headphones. A telescopic antenna caters for DAB and FM reception and the curved upper handle (very reminiscent of the 'snooze handle' on many Pure radios) appears to be the wi-fi antenna. A remote-control unit is supplied and is simple and effective.

Roberts Stream 83i

BEST INTERNET RADIO

Setting-up is straightforward, especially if a wired Ethernet connection to the router is used. Making a wireless connection is almost as simple and only requires entry of a WEP or WPA passkey. When the connection has been made, the radio automatically downloads a list of the available stations via the Frontier Silicon portal. It then offers a main menu giving easy access to favourite stations, system settings and a main menu. Sequential presses of the mode button select internet radio, DAB, FM, a proprietary feature called last.fm (which we did not test) auxiliary in and the UPnP music player. The internet radio menu allows selection by location or genre in the usual way. The portal is easy to use and allows customisation via definable sub-menus.

Extensive testing of the Stream 83i suggested that it produced consistently good-quality audio and we experienced very few instances of poor quality or dropping-out. Those which did occur were probably due to shortcomings of the broadband connection rather than the radio. The test location is decidedly rural and the maximum speed achievable on a daily basis is only about 1.3Mb/s. Both DAB and FM reception were extremely good. A few Stream 83i users have reported poor FM reception but our sample exhibited excellent sensitivity and noise performance together with very low distortion. Almost all DAB radios have struggled to produce usable audio in certain areas of the test location but the Stream 83i was certainly not one of them; in fact it is possibly the best semi-portable DAB receiver we have trialled to date. One minor drawback is that there are no stop, pause and repeat controls for the 'listen again' feature.

Overall, the Stream 83i is an excellent product which can be confidently recommended. The quality of construction and finish is exemplary and the functionality is excellent. The ergonomics are the best of any internet radio we have yet encountered and the audio quality is splendid.

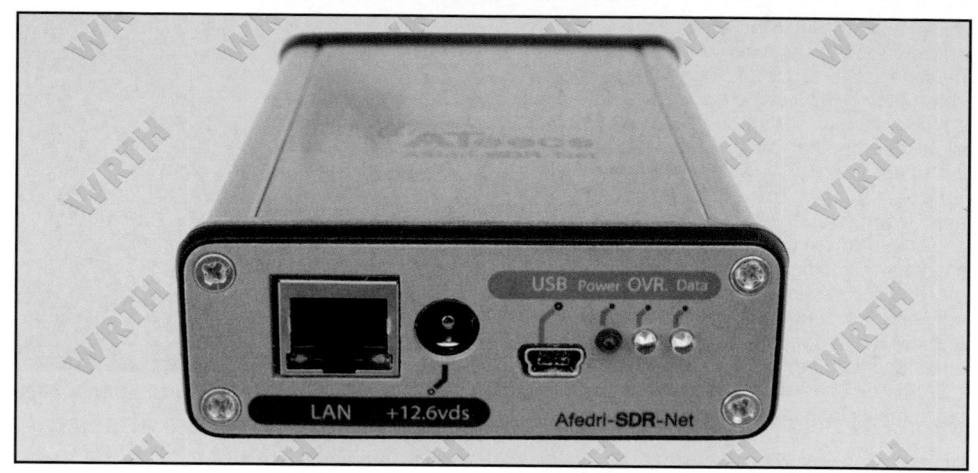

Afedri SDR-Net

US$249   £155   €190

A relatively new arrival on the SDR scene, the Afedri is a direct-sampling software-defined digital down-conversion receiver covering 100 kHz-30MHz. It was designed by Alex Trushkin whose amateur callsign is 4Z5LV and is available either in the form of a stand-alone unit in small but very substantial aluminium box measuring 135 x 82 x 30mm overall or as an assembled and tested bare printed-circuit board for incorporation into other equipment or one's own casework.

The Afedri has a standard LAN socket on its front panel together with a mini-USB port and a coaxial connector for DC power. The receiver can run either from an external DC source of between 7.5 and 14V or the USB port. Interestingly (and with refreshing honesty) the web site advises that the internal switched DC/DC converter will produce some interference on 930kHz and its harmonics and that for best results on MF and LF the mini-USB power supply should be used. Three status LEDs indicate power, overload and data. Rather unusually an SMA connector is provided on the rear drop for the antenna input although suitable adaptors for other RF connectors such as BNC are widely available.

The receiver is stated to be compatible with Linrad, Winrad, HDSDR, WRPlus and SDR Console and all our testing was carried out with Winrad 1.6.1 since this is the software with which we are most familiar. We had no difficulty running the unit on an ordinary office-type PC with a 1.6GHz dual-core processor under WinXP SP3.

The Afedri makes use of the eponymous Burr-Brown/TI 8201 80Ms/s 12-bit analogue/digital converter IC, the name being supposedly an acronym for 'Analogue Front End Device Radio Interface'. At first sight this may appear to be a retrograde step insofar as the best modern SDRs use 16-bit ADCs. However all these are a great

deal more expensive than the Afredi. A minor limitation of the receiver is that apart from a 30MHz low-pass filter there is no band-pass filtering provided. When connected to large antennas there is consequently some danger of overload, especially for short-wave listeners living near high-power medium-wave transmitters. The Afredi is certainly not short of basic sensitivity; the manufacturer claims -133dBm in a 500Hz bandwidth and this is approximately correct but there is a caveat. The unit has an internal variable-gain amplifier with gain controllable between -10 and +35dB. The claimed sensitivity is certainly met at the higher setting but the overload margin is decidedly low and issues were clearly setting in at around -30dBm during laboratory testing. Using either the Wellbrook loop or a 6/7MHz dipole at our test site there are at least 20 stations which exceed this level and in off-air testing it was seldom feasible to use VGA settings in excess of about +12dB. At this the MDS was about -93dBm, which is not sufficient for reception of weak signals. Some form of front-end filtering will be necessary if the potential performance of the Afredi is to be realised in practice but several companies manufacture suitable components and it is also not difficult to make one's own. A bare-board version with relay-switched bandpass filtering would make a very capable low-cost home-brewed receiver. The recording and processing bandwidth is 1.25MHz and since this is very similar to the width of the MW broadcast band the Afedri has already begun to find favour with the MW DX fraternity.

We liked the Afredi. It does not pretend to offer the last word in state-of-the-art SDR performance but it does provide a great deal of performance for the price. In certain respects it gives little away to its competitors costing four or five times more.

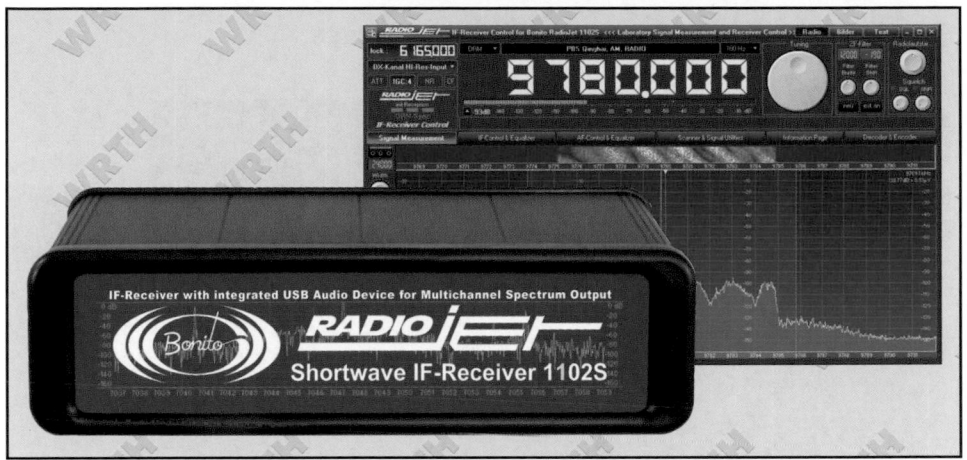

Bonito 1102S Radiojet

US$679   £599   €499

The Bonito 1102S RadioJet is a software-defined receiver although one with slightly unusual architecture. It is realised as an aluminium case measuring 115 x 90 x 32mm and devoid of any connections apart from a BNC antenna socket and a USB port. In fact the Bonito is not quite an SDR in the conventional sense and its configuration is perhaps more reminiscent of an early DSP radio. Coverage is 40kHz-30MHz and its front end is essentially that of a classical up-converting double superheterodyne with a first IF of 45MHz and a second IF of 12kHz. Thereafter the circuitry becomes rather innovative. If we have understood the description correctly, the down-converted signal is split and passed to a two-channel 16-bit analogue/digital converter. One channel of this (the 'RX Channel') is directly fed but the signal fed to the other (the 'DX Channel') is amplified by 27dB beforehand. Some very clever processing then takes place involving selection (and on occasions cascading) of the ADC channels according to parameters defined in the software. There is no AGC in the conventional sense and also no wide I-Q output. Many contemporary SDRs can record large segments of the radio spectrum but the RadioJet can only cater for 24kHz. This appears to be a deliberate design choice in which signal quality and handling have been given precedence over recording ability.

Installation of the Bonito receiver was simple. No drivers as such are provided or required, and under Windows XP the device was found as soon as it was connected. At first sight the interface looks complex and rather daunting, partly because it offers a great deal of scope for customisation. The upper portion of the screen is chiefly concerned with frequency and mode selection and the main spectrum display sits beneath. To the right are various controls for IF and audio gain and a rather small frequency-entry keypad. Available modes are USB, LSB, CW, AM FM and DRM, the latter being built-in; there is no requirement for entry of a licence key. It should be said at this point that the Bonito proved extremely good at DRM reception. Real-time comparison tests against a WinRadio Excalibur Pro using a Wellbrook ALA-1530 loop and Marconi 3dB coupler in conjunction with two separate PCs suggested that the Bonito was very nearly as good as the WinRadio, and that is high praise indeed since the latter is superb. In fact the excellent DRM performance of the Bonito might constitute a very good reason for buying it, although the receiver also excelled itself in more conventional reception.

In use, the Bonito proved to be generally very competent. The 'DX Channel' seemed to provide better signal/noise ratios on weaker signals whereas the 'RX Channel' provided better overall results on strong stations. We tended to prefer switching manually between these modes although the Bonito is quite capable of making its own decisions. One minor drawback of the Bonito's architecture is that SSB and CW reception was made rather difficult by the lack of conventional AGC, especially if signals were subject to fading. However, manual gain control (called IGC) is provided in the software and works well.

The Bonito RadioJet 1102S is a fine example of a modern HF receiver combining tried and trusted techniques with modern digital methods. Its basic RF performance is excellent and its software, while not entirely bug-free, is thoroughly comprehensive and reasonably easy to use. Perhaps aimed more at the broadcast listener than the general shortwave listener (especially if DRM reception is a priority) the Bonito Radiojet SDR is well worth consideration.

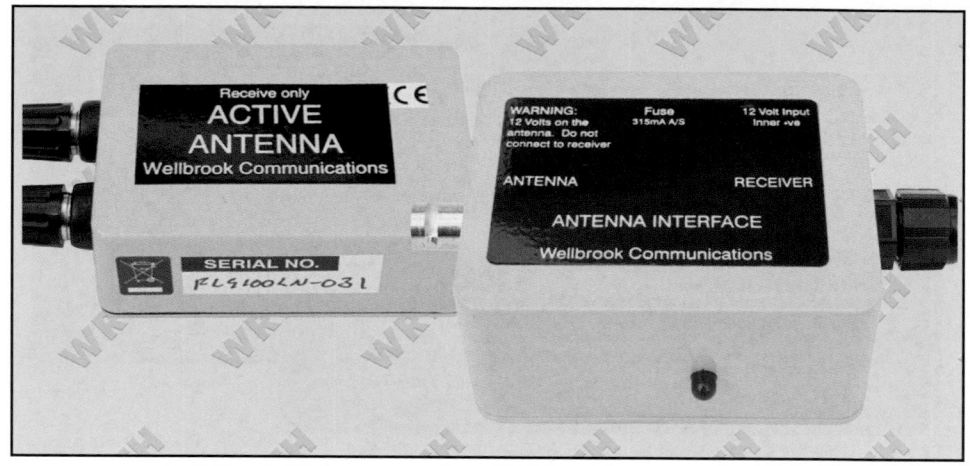

Wellbrook FLG100LN

US$255   £159   €198

In previous years we have reviewed several products from Wellbrook Communications including their deservedly famous loop antennas. Wellbrook also has considerable expertise in other areas and one of its new products is specifically designed for a particular type of small directive antenna which appeared some years ago. Variants of these are known to enthusiasts and radio amateurs by names such as Waller loop, Flag, EWE, Pennant, KAZ, DKAZ and DHDL and – to summarise a somewhat complex picture in one sentence – the salient feature of all of them is that they can offer a considerable degree of directivity at low frequencies. Regular readers will know that this normally requires physically very large antennas and the trade-off for their small size is that in general terms all these antennas have relatively low output. All therefore require a high-gain low-noise preamplifier to be located close to the antenna.

Wellbrook's FLG100LN deals effectively with both these requirements. It uses no less than eight JFETs in parallel push-pull with feedback to give about 22dB gain at 1MHz together with antenna-to-feedline isolation equivalent to about 10pF and a noise figure of about 1dB. A low-capacitance 4:1 antenna matching transformer galvanically isolates the antenna from the feeder. The amplifier itself is supplied as an encapsulated box measuring 70 x 48 x 28mm and there is an accompanying power interface box which is slightly larger. A substantial 12V 'wall wart' power supply is provided and is connected to the interface box. The antenna terminals are 4mm banana plugs and the output is via a BNC female socket; a weatherproofing 'boot' is provided.

We could perhaps best sum up this review by saying that we thoroughly enjoyed ourselves trying out different forms of loop antenna hooked up to the Wellbrook amplifier, including one or two for which it was not really designed but with which it worked brilliantly. The stated frequency response is 100kHz to 10MHz but our sample at least was still going strong at 24MHz or thereabouts. As we were part-way through our testing an email from Wellbrook mentioned that the amplifier could form the basis of an active vertical by connecting one end to a ground rod and the other to an antenna 4-10m in length. This technique was tried with several different ground systems and lengths of wire and worked exceedingly well. It was fascinating to compare the differences in directivity and noise performance between the verticals and the loop antennas, the vertical of course being non-directional. A Flag-type antenna connected to the FLG100LN with its output taken to a Racal RA1778 proved capable of hearing every operational NDB in the UK in daylight together with several in continental Europe and Scandinavia, two in Greenland and one in Iceland. This was an astonishing and entirely unprecedented performance.

Measurements suggested that on 198kHz our sample exhibited about 24dB gain and this was maintained up to about 6MHz after which there was a gentle reduction. Wellbrook claims an IPI_2 of +90dBm and an IPI_3 of +42dB for the FLG100LN and both figures are frankly much too high for us to be able to measure with any accuracy; knowing the company's claims to be generally conservative we have not the slightest reason to doubt them. No trace of anything resembling intermodulation was noted during the test period, even when we were experimenting with very large verticals and a 12m loop.

The FLG100LN is a fine product which will be indispensable to the low-band DXer and enthusiast interested in experimenting with antennas.

WRTH HF Receiver Guide 2013

Budget, Hand-held & Travel Portables

Maker	Model	Size	SEL	DR	OV	US$	£	€
AOR	AR8200 MkIII	H	****	***	***	800	500	620
Degen	DE-1103	S	***	***	**	79	50	60
Kchibo	KK-D6110	S	***	***	***	49	32	38
Roberts	R861	M	****	***	****	280	175	215
Roberts	R9914	S	****	***	****	175	110	135
Sangean	ATS-404	S	***	***	***	80	52	60
Sangean	ATS-909X	S	****	****	****	260	165	200
Sony	ICF-SW11	S	***	***	***	95	58	70
Sony	ICF-SW35	S	***	***	****	140	85	105
Sony	ICF-SW7600GR	S	****	****	****	170	185	175
Tecsun	PL-310	S	****	****	*****	55	35	45
Tecsun	PL-380	S	****	****	*****	50	45	55
Tecsun	PL-660	S	***	****	****	120	95	120

SDRs, DRM, Serious Shortwave & Semi-pro Receivers

Maker	Model	Size	SEL	DR	OV	US$	£	€
Afedri	SDR-Net	C	***	***	***	249	155	190
Alinco	DX-R8E	M	****	****	****	450	500	620
AOR	AR5001D	M	*****	****	****	4300	3750	4650
AOR	AR8600	L	**	***	***	1120	700	870
Bonito	1102S Radiojet	C	****	****	****	679	599	499
Cross Country	SDR-4+	C	****	****	****	270	170	210
Elad	FDM77	C	****	****	****	640	400	480
Etón	Satellit 750	L	***	***	***	300	260	360
FlexRadio	FLEX-1500	C	****	****	***	600	580	715
FlexRadio	FLEX-5000A	C	*****	*****	*****	3400	2450	2620
Icom	IC-718	L	***	****	****	740	570	699
Icom	IC-7000	M	*****	****	*****	1300	1100	1300
Icom	IC-7600	L	*****	****	****	3750	3300	3800
Icom	IC-R9500	L	*****	*****	*****	13300	10000	12000
Medav	LR2	C	*****	*****	***	4680	2900	3600
Microtelecom	Perseus	C	*****	*****	*****	1000	700	670
Newstar	DR111	D	****	***	***	140	140	175
Palstar	R30	M	*****	*****	****	740	500	620
Pappradio		C	****	***	*****	85	52	65
Reuter Elektronik	RDR54C	M	*****	*****	*****	3850	2400	2950
RFSpace	SDR-IQ	C	****	****	****	500	490	610
Ten-Tec	RX320	C	***	***	***	380	240	295
Ten-Tec	RX340	L	*****	*****	*****	4450	3900	4800
WinRadio	G31 Excalibur	C	*****	****	*****	950	585	710
WinRadio	G33 Excalibur Pro	C	*****	*****	*****	1800	1600	1900
WinRadio	G313i	C	*****	****	*****	1200	925	1020
WinRadio	G313e	C	*****	*****	*****	1120	925	1020
WinRadio	G305e	C	****	****	****	750	580	640

KEY: SEL = Selectivity, DR = Dynamic Range, OV = Overall Value. C = SDR, D = DRM, H = Hand-held, L = Large, table top use, M = Medium, suitcase size, S = Small, easily portable.　　* = Avoid ** = Poor *** = Fair **** = Good ***** = Outstanding.
NOTE: Prices vary due to exchange rate fluctuations. Some models may be unavailable in certain markets.

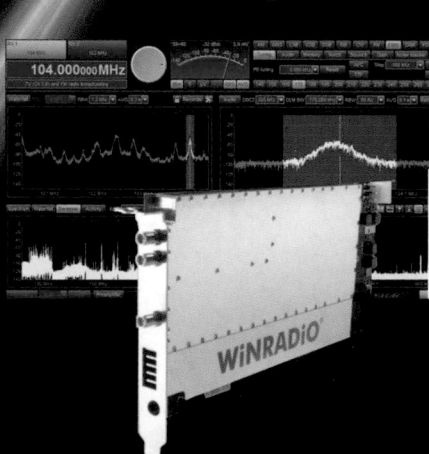

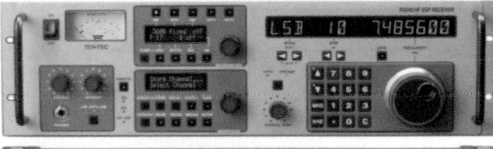

Classic 1990s DSP Receivers

Over the last few years we have published features on some classic professional and military receivers. This year we look at some classic DSP receivers.

The scale of change in electronic design and manufacturing techniques over the last forty years or so has been nothing short of revolutionary. This applies as much to military and professional HF receivers as any other electronic product. Consider a Racal RA17 of 1958 and a Racal RA3791 of 1998, which at their respective dates of manufacture probably cost approximately similar amounts in real terms. The first is founded on a substantial die-cast aluminium chassis and weighs about 35kg. Its internal circuitry makes use of thermionic techniques which although very advanced for their day are largely intelligible to the interested layman; in essence the receiver is clearly a classical superheterodyne, albeit one with a novel form of drift-cancelling local oscillator. Many elements of its architecture can be inferred from inspection. Its tuning mechanism makes extensive use of precision-machined gears and pulleys and the frequency readout is by means of a film strip backlit by small tungsten-filament lamp bulbs which habitually fail. The receiver has perhaps three or four switchable IF bandwidths, each one of which is defined by an impressive-looking and very expensive filter element approximately the size of a modern SDR. Its power consumption is a little short of 200W and it runs decidedly warm, partly due to its large and heavy mains transformer and also to several of its valves which become uncomfortably hot in use. Its mean time between failures is probably measured in tens of hours and its performance inevitably deteriorates over time because of slow changes in valve and component characteristics and the effects of thermal cycling. In the workshop of a large-scale user such as BBC Monitoring there will always be several RA17s undergoing routine maintenance, alignment and general mechanical fettling, and several highly skilled individuals will be working on them.

The RA3791 weighs 5.5kg and it can easily be lifted and carried in one hand. Internally its slender casework contains two large and inscrutable printed-circuit boards. One has several well-screened sections which may be presumed to handle RF signals. The other carries a myriad of complex integrated circuits. Nothing about the receiver's internal appearance gives a clue to its functionality and there are probably not more than a handful of individuals in the world who could claim to understand its inner workings in detail. Even its power supply – a small anonymous box containing nothing so obvious and tra-

ditional as a mains transformer – is something of an enigma to the average electronic engineer, so-called 'switched-mode' supplies being perceived as something of a black art. The receiver's power consumption is a few watts and it runs essentially cold. There are no visible IF filters but in essence there are about 100 discrete filter bandwidths, all implemented in software. Its frequency readout and other indications use backlit liquid-crystal displays. The mean time between failures of this receiver is probably expressed in thousands of hours and 'maintenance' as such is unknown. A failure is dealt with by replacement of either the main PCBs or the PSU and subsequent return to the manufacturer for repair. A built-in test facility will indicate where the fault lies and no technical knowledge will be required to deal with it. Since there are practically no internal adjustments, no 'alignment' in the classical sense is possible or necessary.

These two Racal receivers stand at the beginning and end of the company's involvement in high-grade HF receiver production. As such, both remain highly desirable to the radio enthusiast and collector. At one level the gulf between them is clearly enormous. There is probably not a single component common to the RA17 and RA3791 and the latter offers far more functionality with much less mechanical complexity than the RA17. Practically all the RA3791's massive abilities are embodied in its firmware and the enormous processing power inherent in its DSP architecture. This receiver is (and will undoubtedly remain) much more reliable and a good deal more efficient than its therminoic ancestor.

And yet in another sense these receivers are remarkably alike despite the forty-year separation between them. In the hands of a reasonably skilled operator and assuming that the RA17 was a well-maintained example in good condition, both would be expected to recover usable audio or copy from signals whose strength was comparable with the local noise floor. Both would also be expected to cope with strong unwanted local transmissions without prejudice to their ability to hear wanted weak signals. We have not carried out this particular comparison but we would be very surprised if the RA3791 was consistently able to copy a signal which was could not also be copied on the RA17. In fact we would imagine that a three-cornered contest involving a modern software-defined radio would produce a similar result. To put the point the other way round, we

Racal RA3791

In 1987 Racal replaced the successful RA1792 with the RA370x family of which there were four main models. The RA1792 had used an early integrated-circuit microprocessor with firmware stored in EPROMs and the RA370x used similar architecture but with more modern (and robust) devices in a modular layout. RA370x receivers were quite widely used but by the mid-1990s it was becoming evident that most of Racal's competitors were espousing digital signal processing. In 1996 the company introduced the DSP-based RA379x family, again consisting of four main models with variants for remote and diversity operation. The RA3791 was the basic receiver covering 10kHz to 30MHz in 1Hz steps and providing AM, FM, CW, SSB, ISB and optionally FSK. The RA3792 was a version with two independent HF receivers with a common chassis, PSU and front panel. The RA3793 was a remote-control version of the RA3791 and the RA3794 was the remote version of the RA3792.

Perhaps it is not surprising that the RA3791 is the variant usually encountered in the marketplace. At first glance it is almost indistinguishable from an RA3701 but contains very different technology within. There are two main printed-circuit boards, one for the RF section and the other for digital control. The latter features no fewer than three Motorola DSP ICs together with an unpopulated socket for what appears to be a fourth.

Racal manuals and literature were – to put it kindly – never the company's strong point and board-level information on any of the RA379x family is exceedingly difficult to obtain but the general consensus is that the spare socket is for an automatic notch filter. It is sometimes stated that the overall design and architecture of the RA379x is generally similar to that of the Watkins Johnson 8711A and variants but the performance and functionality of the Racal is considerably superior in some areas, notably phase noise and reciprocal mixing.

Apart from its excellent performance, the RA379x family is notable for the fact that they were the last conventional receivers to be built by Racal before the company's absorption into the Thales group in 2000 and the subsequent disappearance of its product line. In fact late examples of the RA3791 carry Thales branding on the rear. The RA379x is thus the culmination of an unbroken sequence of thoroughbred HF receivers which began with the iconic RA17 of 1955. Production quantities for many Racal radios are difficult to establish with certainty but on balance it would seem that relatively few of any of the RA379x variants were manufactured, chiefly because by the turn of the century many long-standing Racal users had migrated to other systems or abandoned HF altogether. For all these reasons any RA379x is prized by collectors.

could compare the RA17 or the RA3791 with any of the generally competent radios we have tested over the years. In our view it is unlikely that there would be major differences between them except in extreme circumstances. For example the Racal receivers would undoubtedly work perfectly well with electrically very large antennas whereas a consumer-grade receiver might well exhibit symptoms of overloading such as RF intermodulation or cross-modulation.

So why might one want a radio of this type? At one level, of course, there is simple pleasure

in ownership. A vintage Rolls-Royce is not perhaps necessary for collection of the weekly shopping but is (presumably) a pleasant machine for high days and holidays. More seriously, many high-grade receivers exhibit excellent ergonomics and to the enthusiast can offer a sensual pleasure all their own. However stellar its performance, no software-defined receiver can in our opinion come near something like an RA1778 or a W-J 8711A for sheer enjoyment.

In our 2009 feature on classic receivers from the 1980s we remarked that they represented the apotheosis of what might be thought of as the "conventional" superheterodyne design. All featured extensive internal digital memory and processing circuitry or microprocessor control. The four receivers in this years' collection date from a slightly later period – broadly speaking the last ten years of the twentieth century – and represent arguably the apex of conventional receiver technology before the software-defined receiver began to dominate in professional and military applications. As well as conferring excellent performance, the inclusion of what by earlier standards was a massive amount of processing power and memory space makes DSP receivers of this era astonishingly versatile and configurable. Functions such as noise reduction, notch filtering, highly adjustable AGC with individually selectable attack and release times, infinitely configurable filter parameters, variable tuning-step sizes and passband tuning/IF shift are all perfectly feasible and universally incorporated. Although in principle these features are fairly simple to use, there is so much functionality available that the 'learning curve' is fairly steep. A potential purchaser should always ensure that a copy of the operating manual is supplied.

Marconi H2550

The name of Marconi is synonymous with the history of radio. The history of the Marconi company is complex and convoluted but the UK business division was acquired by English Electric in 1946. After a complex set of mergers and buyouts in the 1960s and again in 1987 it emerged as GEC-Marconi, the defence subsidy of the massive GEC conglomerate. In 1989 GEC-Marconi in turn acquired some divisions of the Plessey company and inherited much of the latter's work-in-progress. At this distance it is difficult to establish the facts with certainty but it seems that at the time of the takeover Plessey had been working on a high-performance HF receiver intended to meet a Royal Navy requirement and that this became a Marconi project. By this time high-performance digital signal-processing technology was beginning to become feasible and was incorporated into the new design. The result was the H2550 which appeared in 1994 and was one of the last HF receivers to bear the Marconi name. Much of its architecture was similar to that in the Racal 379x family; a conventional up-converting front end and high-performance IF analogue-to-digital converter was followed by digital conversion to baseband I and Q signals. As an IEEE paper of the time put it, "This avoids the limitation on I/Q orthogonality and poor response in the region of the carrier found with the baseband zero IF technique which adopts analogue I/Q conversion to baseband followed by independent analogue-to-digital conversion of the baseband I and Q signals." An unusual form of digital feed-forward AGC was employed in the H2550 and was one of its best features, with a control range around 110dB according to one contemporary report.

It is not clear how many H2550 receivers were manufactured or who their end users were although the Royal Navy are believed to have employed them at several of their shore-based radio sites. Extant serial numbers suggest that about 350 examples were manufactured and several have found their way into private collections. Unfortunately maintenance documentation for the H2550 seems to be extremely elusive (even original copies of the operator's manual are rare) and fault-finding and rectification are consequently difficult. To make matters worse the receiver employed several custom-manufactured ICs together with some from the Plessey SL family; sadly replacements for the latter in particular are nowadays somewhere between exceedingly difficult and impossible to obtain. Nevertheless the Marconi name and logo on the front panel and the generally very good performance of the receiver have made examples of the H2550 highly desirable to collectors.

STC STR8212

The story of Standard Telephones and Cables is almost as convoluted as that of Marconi but STC was a major UK telecommunications company for much of the last century and by the mid-1980s it was Britain's second-largest electronics group. It has been stated that the genesis of the STR8212 was a requirement on the part of the UK Independent Broadcasting Authority for a broadcast monitor receiver. This may be so although it is not clear why the IBA would have required an HF monitoring capability; it did not undertake HF broadcasting and did not have or require a capability equivalent to that of BBC Monitoring at Caversham. It seems reasonable to assume that STC had other markets in mind.

Designed in the late 1980s the STR8212 was an up-converting double superheterodyne with a first IF of 70.05MHz. This was followed in conventional fashion by a roofing filter and down-conversion to a second IF, after which it was digitised in the usual way for processing. The Northern Telecom analogue-to-digital converter in the STR8212 was implemented in two custom ICs and said to possess "…far greater resolution, linearity and accuracy than conventional ADCs" and to employ a pulse-density modulator "designed specifically for radio" although the precise meaning of this is unclear. A third DSP board could be fitted for what were coyly referred to as "special modes". The receiver catered for AM, FM, USB, LSB, ISB and data; in a rather

similar way to the Watkins-Johnson 8711A there were default filter bandwidth settings for each mode which could be varied as required and subsequently stored. Filter bandwidths between 320Hz and 15kHz were available, the former being perhaps slightly wider than is ideal for CW reception. Up to 99 frequencies could be stored together with the applicable mode, bandwidth, BFO setting, AGC time constant and RF attenuator setting. All control functions were handled by a 16-bit microprocessor and an optional IEEE488 interface board could be fitted.

The operating manual is written in such a way as to make operation of the STR8212 sound complicated but in practice the receiver is very easy to use. Comprehensive built-in test facilities are provided and work well. Its only real drawbacks are a lack of maintenance information (although the operator's manual is available on-line) and the fact that the two cooling fans on its rear drop are rather noisy. The receiver runs warm despite their assistance and obstructing the lower-cover air vents is not a good idea!

Only about 200 examples of the STR8212 were manufactured and they are consequently quite rare and sought-after. Often neglected by historians, the STC product is a fine receiver which should not be overlooked by those considering a classic although by all accounts its appetite for tantalum capacitors is second only to that of the contemporary Racal RA1792.

Our four featured receivers offer RF performance levels which are more or less on a par with those of the best modern SDRs although of course they require a very different operating technique. But the world has moved on. In general terms you can now buy one of these radios for something like a tenth of the original purchase price. Such a level of depreciation reflects many things including the fact that professional and military operations now use the HF bands in ways which are fundamentally different from those of ten or fifteen years ago. Modern HF communications almost invariably involve automatic link sys-

tems which can easily and quickly find the 'best' frequency for the propagation path involved. These often operate in conjunction with very complex and resilient techniques for data transmission incorporating comprehensive and reliable error detection and correction. In effect these requirements have driven modern professional HF receiver design down a different and very largely software-defined path, and one where an individual 'receiver' is merely part of a complex and highly integrated communications system.

Other erstwhile users of high-grade HF receivers have either changed their methodology

Rohde & Schwarz EK 085

Founded in 1933 by Dr Lothar Rohde and Dr Hermann Schwarz, the German company remains a major player in many fields of radio and telecommunications. It has an illustrious history of high-grade receiver design and development and is still very much in business today. The legendary Rohde & Schwarz EK 07 of the 1960s was a classic which managed the considerable feat of being even larger and heavier than its Collins and Racal competition.

Rather more modern in appearance than its EK 070 predecessor but just as expensive at a reported price of some $30,000, the newer receiver was similarly a double-conversion design covering 10kHz-30MHz. There were 100 memories and mode and bandwidth information was stored in each channel. Very comprehensive scanning facilities were provided and dwell times could be set between 20mS and 99s. Capable of handling CW, MCW, FSK, AM, USB and LSB in standard form and with other options available, the EK 085 was also widely used by European news agencies for facsimile reception. For its era the remote-control facilities available as options were very comprehensive. A large number of different options and configurations were available thanks to the receiver's modular construction

and it is said that no two EK 085s are alike. Employing a double-conversion architecture with IFs of 80.64 and 1.44MHz and with microprocessor control, the EK 085 is unarguably one of the best of the era immediately prior to the advent of DSP-based receivers.

As always with Rohde & Schwarz products the EK 085 is mechanically exquisite and every element of its signal path is designed with extraordinary attention to detail; as an object lesson in how to design a conventional superheterodyne for optimum performance the EK 085 remains unexcelled. Even without the optional preselector the claimed IPI_3 was +35dBm and those who have measured it confirm that this is correct.

Ergonomically no Rohde & Schwarz receiver known to us could be described as user-friendly but as precision instruments they are unexcelled. The EK 085 is no exception. The bright and clear LED display is ideal for lengthy periods of operating, the audio is pleasant and the AGC performance is excellent. All in all, the EK 085 is highly desirable and it is not surprising that they are much prized and somewhat difficult to find. The last one we saw on an internet auction site was sold for just under €2,700 and we suspect that future examples will cost at least that.

or seen their capability lapse. From what we can gather of the shadowy world of HF signals intelligence (SIGINT) this has changed beyond recognition insofar as it still exists at all. It seems that there are nowadays no highly skilled operators sitting at banks of racked receivers and that remotely located SDRs under computer control have entirely replaced them. For concerns such as BBC Monitoring at Caversham, a long-standing requirement to be able to listen in depth to the HF broadcast bands has very nearly disappeared. And the once-extensive networks of world-wide diplomatic communications which relied on HF as their main bearers have almost entirely migrated to the internet and elsewhere.

All in all we doubt that the contemporary equivalents of any of our four receivers will be featuring on internet auction sites ten years from now because the world of HF communications has inexorably changed. At some stage in the not-too-distant future the stand-alone high-grade professional HF receiver will become the electronic equivalent of the steam railway locomotive; fondly regarded and cherished by enthusiasts but essentially irrelevant to modern operations.

The author would like to acknowledge the invaluable assistance of Andy Cygan, Pat McAlister and David Schofield in the preparation of this feature.

Children's Radio Foundation

Africa is the youngest continent, with half of its population under the age of 25. But how often are young people in Africa given a platform to share their experiences and views?

Keith records ambient sound in Manenberg for a radio show about his neighbourhood, Cape Town (South Africa)

It's an uncomfortably hot February day in Mongu, Zambia. The whirring of the fan is overpowered by the chatter of 15 young people from Zambia as they plan a "show clock" for their first radio show. They have chosen the theme of Child Rights and are now deciding how the different elements of the broadcast will fit together.

It's a pivotal moment in the radio training they have undertaken, bringing together all they have learned in the past four days, so that they can produce their first radio show.

They decide that the most important elements of the programme are to ask people in the community what they know or understand about Child Rights, and to share youth opinions on the topic. As they develop their show clock the young reporters realise how much more they want to say, and decide to make their first show an Introduction to Children's Rights.

These young people are receiving training from the Children's Radio Foundation (CRF), a not-for-profit organisation based in Cape Town, South Africa. CRF provides the skills and tools to make the voices of African youth heard and to

start dialogues about important issues with their peers and the wider community.

Young people have a lot to think about, but they do not have many outlets through which they can speak about their challenges, voice their concerns, or share their triumphs and strategies for success. A simple idea powers the Children's Radio Foundation: impart the tools and skills needed to express ideas and share stories through radio and you will give them a springboard to a world of wider opportunities.

Working directly with community radio stations and local organisations, CRF uses the needs and strengths of the different communities they work in to create sustainable youth media projects. Each place and its people have specific needs and abilities which provide the framework for designing the projects.

CRF has active youth radio networks across Tanzania, Zambia, the Democratic Republic of the Congo, Liberia and South Africa. This means that collectively there are over 1000 youth reporters on air in Africa. Sixteen-year-old Bianca Mwela from Lusaka in Zambia reflected on her

Joyce and Amanda practice how to use the audio recorder, Kakata (Liberia)

radio training experience, "This has taught me that as young people we can use radio to express ourselves and I can now help other young people and my community share their points of view and get it out there for everyone to hear."

Young people need opportunities to tell their own stories and to learn from the experiences of others. CRF uses radio broadcasts as a "tool for talk". CRF's radio workshops allow young people not only to gain technical and IT skills, but also to reflect on their world. It is a chance for them to interview their peers, family and community members. It allows listeners to hear directly from young people about the issues that matter to them, such as domestic violence and sexual abuse, HIV and AIDS, poverty and malnutrition, gender inequality and access to education. Through youth-produced broadcasts they are able to break the traditional media stereotype that frames the young as victims of social issues and, at the same time, redressing the dominant adult point of view.

CRF youth reporters interview a community member on the rights of a child, Mongu (Zambia)

CRF also trains adults from community organisations and local radio stations to mentor youth radio projects. Alphonso Wright, a local trainer from Liberia says, "This is actually a new phenomenon in media activities in Liberia: working with young people and bringing them into the media field where they can run their own programmes and feel a part of the development process of our country."

What resonates most for young journalists from Libera to South Africa is the impact the radio training has on their ability to express themselves confidently and to engage constructively with their community. Fifteen-year-old Bronwyn is from Manenberg, a neighborhood in Cape Town, South Africa which suffers from many social problems. She spoke of her experience with CRF, "Through the workshops I learnt more about my community and I got more clever asking questions to other people. Through radio, I learnt how to speak out loudly, more openly, so I think teenagers will find a way to talk through radio."

Creating platforms for young people to be able to express themselves and engage with their counterparts as well as the larger community allows them to be seen as more than just characters to substantiate news. Young people experience many issues featured in the media and fill diverse roles in their communities – they offer valuable perspectives and experiences.

Radio gives them a chance to tell their own stories. It's about time we started to listen.

To find out more about the Children's Radio Foundation, to become a Member or make a donation, please visit our website at:

www.childrensradiofoundation.org

Listening on Curaçao

WRTH contributor and well-known DXer Max van Arnhem reflects on the political and radio changes in a small Caribbean island which became a new radio country in 2010.

The waterfront at Willemstad, Curaçao

Readers of *World Radio TV Handbook* 2011 will have noticed the absence of a familiar country name, that of The Netherlands Antilles.

Originally a country within The Netherlands, The Netherlands Antilles consisted of the islands of Aruba, Bonaire, Curaçao, Sint Maarten, Saba and Sint Eustatius. In January 1986 the island of Aruba seceded from The Netherlands Antilles and officially became a separate country, with a special status (*status aparte*) within the kingdom of the Netherlands. On 10 October 2010 the existence of The Netherlands Antilles ended and Curaçao and Sint Maarten, like Aruba, were granted a special status within the kingdom, while the islands of Bonaire, Sint Eustatius and Saba (the *BES* Islands) became special municipalities of The Netherlands.

Aruba, Bonaire and Curaçao (the *ABC* islands) are positioned just off the coast of Venezuela, while Sint Maarten, Sint Eustatius and Saba are located about 900 kilometres north of the ABC islands and to the east of Puerto Rico. Bonaire is also known as 'flamingo island' because of the many flamingos living in and around the salt lakes on the island.

On the ABC islands the languages spoken are Papiamento and Dutch, Papiamento being a mixture of Spanish, Portuguese, English and Dutch.

On Sint Maarten, Saba and Sint Eustatius, English and Dutch are spoken.

There is a broad spectrum of political sentiment on the islands. On one side the wish to be a completely independent country (Aruba, Curaçao and Sint Maarten) and on the other side the wish to be part of the kingdom of The Netherlands (Bonaire, Sint Eustatius and Saba).

I paid my first visit to Bonaire and Curaçao in 1983 and have visited Aruba, Bonaire and Curaçao frequently in the past ten years. During my travels I paid visits to several radio stations on Curaçao such as Radio Korsou FM, CUROM, Radio Hoyer and Hit 100.3FM. On Aruba I was welcomed at Radio Kelkboom, at that time still on 1440 kHz on the mediumwave band. On Bonaire I received a very friendly reception at Voz di Bonaire which was then broadcasting on 1400 kHz, but is now heard only on FM.

Of course, during all these journeys I took my portable radio with me to explore the radio scene on the islands.

As everywhere in the world, a lot of things have changed on the islands during the past 30 years. Radio used to be the main source of news, music and entertainment on Curaçao, but now many people, and especially the young, are increasingly turning to the internet as their main source of domestic and foreign news, and music. Despite this, the island has today an enormous amount of commercial newsmedia: 28 radio stations and nine newspapers for a population of fewer than 150,000 inhabitants. Many of the radio stations broadcast religious programmes.

When I visited the area in 1983, only 13 stations were active on all the islands of The Netherlands Antilles, and many of these were medium wave stations. On Curaçao two stations were on FM, and all other stations were on medium wave. Radio Hoyer had two medium wave frequencies, one broadcasting in Papiamento and the other in Dutch. Bonaire was the home of the well-known shortwave station Trans World Radio (TWR) and the Radio Netherlands shortwave relay station. There is no shortwave transmitted from Bonaire any longer, and TWR has the only mediumwave station on the island, the widely heard station PJB on 800 kHz.

Nowadays Aruba has 19 radio stations, Curaçao 28, Bonaire eight, St. Maarten nine and St. Eustatius and Saba each have one station. But apart from TWR on Bonaire, Radio 1270 AM on Aruba and CUROM Radio Z86 on Curaçao, still transmitting on 860 kHz on mediumwave, all other stations are only on FM.

Since I started DXing in 1969, the local stations of The Netherlands Antilles haven't been on shortwave. I recall only one exception, in April 1972, when CUROM from Curaçao was audible on 17513 kHz. This freak reception was the result of radiation in the station of Landsradio en Telefoniedienst, the government radiotelephone-line to The Netherlands.

Radio Hoyer and Radio Kelkboom were often heard by DXers in Europe when these stations were still on medium wave. The names Hoyer and Kelkboom are the family names of the founders and their direct decendants are still the owners of the stations. Founder and owner of Radio Korsou FM, Hans Oosterhof, was once the programme director and also a radio presenter on the famous

The imposing sign of Radio Direct, Curaçao

Radio Hoyer, Curaçao

1960s offshore radio station Radio Veronica.

Radio Hoyer is still audible on two frequencies but these are on FM. Located on top of Tafelberg, the highest hill on the eastern part of Curaçao, is Radio Hoyer's FM transmitting tower. The power source for the transmitters is what gives Radio Hoyer FM its claim to fame. The two commercial FM radio stations that broadcast from this site are the world's first to be fully solar powered. The system was put into operation in March 1984.

The radio scene changes frequently on FM. The national TV station Telecuraçao has recently started a radio station, Telecuraçao FM, broadcasting on 93.3 MHz which was the frequency of the defunct Radio Top FM.

Because of the few stations left on medium wave it will be almost impossible in future for DXers to log one of the islands, apart of course for the powerful transmitter of TWR Bonaire.

As the ABC islands lie just off the coast of Venezuela, one can imagine that DXing from one of these islands can be very interesting. Some years ago, while on Curaçao, I concentrated on listening to the tropical bands and it was a nice surprise to hear stations not only from South and Central America, but also from Indonesia and the Solomon Islands. These stations were generally heard at local dawn.

Now, however, many stations have unfortunately left the tropical bands and so, on my most recent visits, I concentrated on medium wave and FM transmission. During daytime, because of the short distance to Venezuela, many Venezuelan stations are audible with good reception quality. The Venezuelan government would like to exercise a high degree of influence over broadcasting and, in 2009, announced the closure of some 240 AM and FM stations for failure to comply with licensing requirements. At the time of editing

Trans World Radio, Bonaire

WRTH 2013 these measures had only been partially implemented although some stations such as Radio Guadalupana, Coro and CBN Valencia have left the airwaves.

On the 2nd of December 2011 all the Venezuelan stations I could hear were carrying a live transmission of the summit of Latin American and Caribbean States taking place in Caracas. Long speeches were heard by President Hugo Chavez of Venezuela. There are some easy ways to identify that a transmission is from Venezuela. It is very common in the local afternoon for many stations to carry the same programme of Radio Nacional de Venezuela and there are frequent references to "*el comandante*" Hugo Chavez. The programmes or slogans of the stations also often refer to the government. Examples of this are 1070 Mundial Zulia: "*Mundial Zulia revolución con impacto social de la mano con el pueblo*" and 1280 Radio Trujillo "*Trujillo socialista en la calle*". It is also possible to identify Venezuelan stations from the announcement of the classification of a following programme, such as: "*El siguiente programa recreativo informativo contiene elementos de lenguaje, tipo A . . .*"

Call signs are heard less frequently than in the past. Station identifications can often be heard during programmes, but not especially at the top of the hour which in Venezuela is at hh+30.

Because of the many stations from Venezuela that fill the airwaves, hearing stations from other countries needs some more effort. But transmissions from Anguilla, The Bahamas, Colombia, Cuba, The Dominican Republic, Nevis and Puerto Rico can also be heard.

FM reception from Venezuela is also possible on the ABC islands, especially stations from Coro, which are heard daily. The Venezuelan Rumbera Network also has its own station on Curaçao on 107.9 MHz.

Telling the difference between stations from Venezuela and, say, Colombia is possible from announcements, as Venezuela has a local time of UTC minus four-and-a-half hours while Colombia has UTC minus five hours

Every time I have been on the islands I have hoped for Sporadic E FM reception, but I have never been fortunate enought to experience this type of propagation on the islands.

Listening on Curaçao presents many opportunities. You are in the Caribbean and also have South America at your feet. So, if you are fortunate enough to visit this special island, don't forget to bring your receiver so that you can do some interesting listening to the local stations as well as the many stations from Venezuela.

The beach at Curaçao

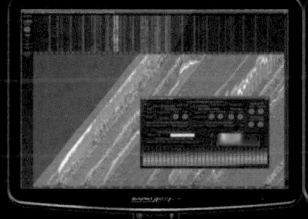

Digital Update

*Our regular round-up of what has been happening in the world of digital radio and TV
over the past year*

Firstly an obituary. The 1worldspace network appears to be defunct. Its two satellites (AfriStar and AsiaStar) are approaching the end of their twelve-year design lives; the first was launched in 1998 and the second in 2000. There have been occasional reports of audible transmissions from both satellites, some from the erstwhile Maestro channel together with Indian religious outlets. But it seems safe to say that Noah Samara's vision has been extinguished, which is regrettable since it held great promise. As we went to press there were rumours of a relaunch under the auspices of the Indian group Timbre Media but the company appeared to be concentrating on the provision of private and corporate internet radio services. A quasi-revival of 'WorldSpace Radio' under the auspices of Vodafone India took place recently in which 10 channels of genre broadcasting would be available via mobile handsets but this is rather outside the scope of *WRTH*.

One of our readers took us gently to task last year for not discussing IBOC or HD Radio in more detail. HD Radio is in fact a trademark owned by iBiquity and used for its in-band on-channel – hence IBOC – digital system. Memorably referred to recently by a senior BBC research engineer in a seminar as "junk engineering", IBOC was selected by the Federal Communications Commission in October 2002 as the approved terrestrial digital audio broadcasting method for the USA. Unlike DAB in the UK and parts of Europe which is multiplexed and used as the basis of single-frequency networks in dedicated bands, IBOC is transmitted in conjunction with existing AM and FM broadcasts. The latest statistics suggest that about 2,200 broadcasting stations in the USA have added HD to their outlets, some using additional 'streams' called HD-2 and HD-3 which are not simultaneously transmitted as analogue. This represents about 15% of the total number of stations in the USA.

In hindsight it was perhaps unfortunate that the FCC chose to adopt a proprietary technology which involved very high licensing and royalty fees together with not inconsiderable transmitter conversion charges. Radio manufacturers are also required to pay fees to incorporate HD Radio into their products. Other digital radio standards adopted elsewhere in the world have not involved proprietary systems.

Originally the IBOC specification called for the use of OFDM in conjunction with an audio compression technique called *perceptual audio coding* (PAC). In principle this was intended to provide what was called 'near-CD' quality on AM and FM but it was found that in certain circumstances the audio quality was not at all good. In 2003 iBiquity began using an additional technique known as *spectral band replication* (SBR) which was intended to improve the audio quality at lower bit-rates. Many early receivers did not work well and proved both insensitive and prone to interference. It was originally thought that the digital component of the signal would provide similar coverage to the existing analogue transmissions using about 20dB less power but this has proved to be very optimistic and many stations are operating at RF levels between -14 and -10dB. This in turn has exacerbated some interference problems experienced by some listeners to the FM analogue component. In principle an HD radio will fall back to the analogue signal if the digital transmission becomes unusable for some reason. In practice this often fails to work well, and the feature is not of course available with HD-2 and HD-3 streams. On the AM bands it now seems to be generally accepted that in certain propagation circumstances IBOC generates intolerable levels of interference. At the time of writing there were about 300 AM stations with an HD capability but most do not use it at night to avoid the problem.

It is difficult to foresee the future of HD Radio with any certainty. The technology has found

> *"In hindsight it was perhaps unfortunate that the FCC chose to adopt a proprietary technology . . ."*

some take-up in car radios and some OEMs currently supply vehicles whose radios have an HD capability. A recent report suggested that this market was forecast to grow by about 5% per year. According to iBquity the mode is or will be available on radios in 28 different brands of new vehicles during 2012-13. Also in its favour is the fact that HD Radio is subscription-free unlike the output from the satellite broadcaster SiriusXM Radio. At the time of writing the latter had 22.9m subscribers and operated 135 channels of programming receivable in principle anywhere in the

USA, which arguably makes it the most powerful single player in the industry apart from ClearChannel. However, it is subscription-based. For mobile applications the advent of large-area wireless internet connections – particularly with the rapid spread of 4G cellular systems – will probably have some additional effect on the uptake of HD Radio but at this stage of development it would be foolish to attempt an estimate.

DRM staggers on. The latest emphasis of the DRM Consortium seems to be on energy efficiency, which is undoubtedly a worthwhile feature of the mode but not perhaps when the lack of available receivers in the marketplace renders the issue academic. At IBC this year the Consortium launched its "DRM Introduction and Implementation Guide". This turned out to be quite an interesting publication insofar as it combines a good technical description of the system with a rather peculiar appraisal of the effects of the lack of receivers, which it defines as a 'marketing problem'. Apparently one DRM broadcaster ". . . proposed purchasing 500,000 receivers, and free-issuing to taxi-cabs, retails outlets and domestic consumers". We also enjoyed the proposal for 'Trojan Horse' marketing. According to this extract:

The 'Trojan Horse' approach to digital migration has the potential to seed the market with digital radios ahead of a formal digital radio service. This serves as a catalyst to the launch process and boots the positive feedback loop described earlier. The technique is simply to introduce and market new 'analogue' receivers which include some new or distinctive features which are either intrinsic to the radio itself (e.g. recording-to-memory, radical styling), and/ or can be readily supported by existing broadcasts (some RDS or AMSS data service etc.). These new radios also support DRM, but initially this is not the key feature used for marketing; the DRM function is 'hidden', and hence the term 'Trojan Horse'. In this scenario, it is clearly vital to have a medium-term strategy agreed and co-ordinated with the receiver manufacturers. Once sales have reached some target, digital services can be launched to an audience that is ready-equipped with receivers.

We considered awarding a prize for renditions of this into intelligible English but decided that there was some danger of the task inducing psychological disturbance in those with enough courage to undertake it.

In the meantime, several more DRM30-capable transmitters have been installed in various parts of the world and to our knowledge no new receivers capable of handling either DRM30 or DRM+ have appeared although bullish noises continue to emerge from the usual quarters. It gives us no pleasure whatsoever to repeat verbatim our observation last year that given the con-tinuing decline in international HF broadcasting we see no mainstream future for DRM30. This is particularly unfortunate given that both modes and DRM+ in particular are arguably the most attractive of the current digital radio systems proposed for future use in terms of spectrum efficiency. Eight channels of CD-equivalent quality audio transmitted via DRM+ could be fitted into the same amount of spectrum that one such

". . . both modes and DRM+ in particular are arguably the most attractive of the current digital radio systems . . ."

channel currently requires in DAB. It is even more striking that there could be enough space for an additional lower-quality channel depending on the engineering assumptions made.

Indeed DAB could also be used more effectively. A recent EBU paper pointed out that DMB is actually transmitted over a DAB transmitter network and is in essence DAB with an HE AAC audio codec and better error correction. Broadcasters who have DAB transmitter networks could continue to use them for DMB but much more efficiently, because somewhere between six and 10 stations could be carried on the existing multiplex for every one currently transmitted. Transmitter conversion costs would be relatively low and there would in principle be no issues of backward compatibility. It will be interesting to see whether this radical proposition ever comes to anything like fruition.

Yet another interesting and relevant issue is the future of the increasing amount of spectrum being freed by the gradual abandonment of terrestrial analogue television broadcasting. Much of this is likely to be absorbed by what seems to be an exponentially increasing requirement for mobile cellular telephony, and in particular the advent of what has come to be known as '4G' or LTE systems. Earlier systems operated on the basis of globally agreed specifications and frequency bands but this is emphatically not the case for LTE. As far as we can see 36 different bands have been allocated worldwide and within them are different and incompatible modulation systems. It seems to us that if 4G delivers on its promise of very high-speed data and ways can be found to deal with its lack of worldwide compatibility, a very large and exponentially increasing number of current 'broadcast' services are likely to become available via this means.

All in all, it would be a very brave person who claimed to be able to predict the future shape and development of digital radio with any accuracy. It is unfortunate that the special *WRTH* crystal ball remains stubbornly cloudy.

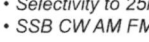

Khmer Post Radio

Hans Johnson explains why newly-founded clandesine station, Khmer Post Radio, chooses to send its message via the short waves

Sovannara Meach of Khmer Post Radio against a backdrop of a strangler fig at Ta Prohm temple, Angkor Wat

Press Release 4 June 2012. "*Radio Voice of Democracy was yesterday banned from broadcasting election news by the Ministry of Information. This is the first such instance of total censorship during polling day. Both Radio Sarika stations – FM 106.5 in Phnom Penh and FM 95.5 in Siem Reap – were shut down at intervals during the day: the Phnom Penh-based station was allowed to broadcast only music programs*" — Cambodian Center for Independent Media

Sovannara Meach of Khmer Post Radio had to make an important communications decision. Given the poor state of press freedom in Cambodia, Khmer Post wanted to reach as many Cambodians as possible with its message. "Many Cambodians cannot receive the truth because many news sources favour or are controlled by the government. We want to report the actual news about the people and the government," explains Meach. "Local stations are controlled by the government and we cannot say what we want," he adds. Khmer Post Radio needed a solution that was affordable, a long way from the control of the Cambodian authorities, and capable of reaching their target audience.

One might naturally think that the solution would have been the internet and social media but this was not the case. "People in the capital, Phnom Penh, can listen on the internet, but the majority of the people live in the countryside," explains Meach. They are poor, subsistence farmers living in remote, rural areas. Access to electricity is very low in Cambodia where barely a quarter of the population has it. So simply using the internet and social media is out. Nor did it make any sense to use television given the scarcity of electricity. Television is also very expensive to produce, especially when it comes to filling several hours a day on an international satellite television channel.

So Khmer Post decided upon radio. "Radio can reach more people in Cambodia," says Meach. But what type of radio broadcasts? FM offered high fidelity, but its local reach mean that any station used would have to be in Cambodia or near an adjacent country's border. Even if stations were found, it would take a lot of them to cover a nation the size of Cambodia. High-powered medium-wave stations are few and far between and since they require more power, they are more expensive than shortwave.

The Royal Palace of Phnom Penh is a popular attraction in the Cambodian capital

"We did some searching and talked with some friends and learned that we could broadcast on shortwave," explains Meach. He chose the facilities of T8WH in Palau, an island in the Western Pacific and well beyond the reach of the agencies of the Cambodian government.

T8WH is owned by World Harvest Radio of Indiana, USA. World Harvest operates T8WH as a brokered station, selling airtime to a variety of programmers as well as transmitting their own productions. Meach is in good company on this shortwave station, as organizations such as Radio Australia and Radio Free Asia are also using the facility. Programmers are not required to buy all the time on one of the station's two transmitters, but only what they need. Those starting out or with smaller budgets do not even have to broadcast daily. Khmer Post Radio, for instance, is on from Tuesdays through Fridays from 1200-1300 UTC on 9960 kHz. "Shortwave is what we can afford at the moment", Meach says.

Khmer Post Radio created a studio and purchased the equipment to create their radio programme. Once the recording is completed, the station's programmes are then delivered to T8WH via a file sharing service. Listeners are adults from 18 years old to the elderly. Shortwave sets are readily available in Cambodia, and Khmer Post Radio bought hundreds of shortwave radios locally and is donating them to listeners too poor to purchase one of their own.

Meach explains that Khmer Post Radio is funded through outright donations and via fundraisers conducted all over the world. With sufficient funds "we eventually plan to go on for an hour or two every day", says Meach.

A flower market in Phnom Penh

Since 1998 Hans Johnson has represented hundreds of clients broadcasting on shortwave, AM, and television. He makes his home in Naples, Florida and can be reached at hans_johnson@rocketmail.com

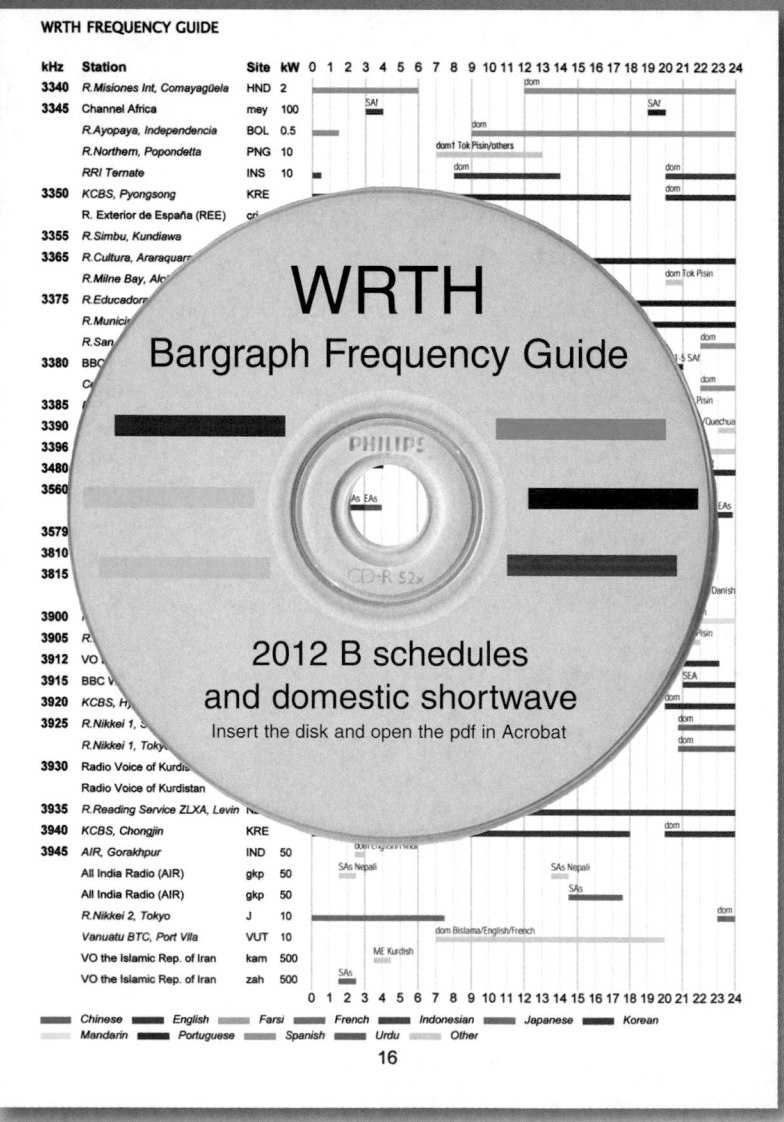

HF BROADCASTING RECEPTION CONDITIONS EXPECTED DURING 2013

George Jacobs, P.E. MSEE, Life Fellow IEEE (USA), Fellow Radio Club of America,
Dean of WRTH Contributing Editors, analyses likely listening conditions in the coming year

CYCLE 24 REACHES ITS PEAK

Sunspot cycle 24 rising towards its peak, combined with an expected record low interference level between stations , bids well for 2013 being an exceptionally good year for reception on the HF broadcasting bands.

The current sunspot cycle is the 24th observed since 1756, when telescopic observation of the sun began. *Fig. 1*, provided by NASA, charts the complete previous Cycle 23 and the progression of Cycle 24. NASA scientists estimate that the peak intensity of solar activity will range between the smoothed sunspot numbers of approximately 80 and 100.

Ultraviolet radiation associated with sunspots

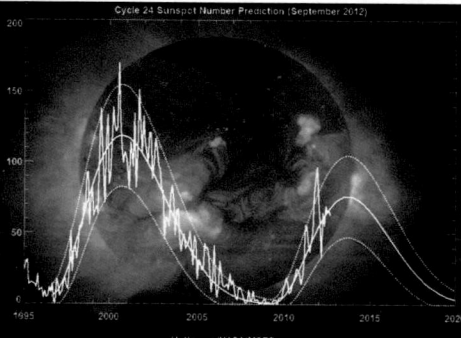

Fig. 1 Sunspot Cycles 23 and 24

forms the ionosphere, that gaseous region which begins approximately 100 miles above the earth. It is the ionosphere that reflects HF radio waves over great distances. As the solar cycle reaches its peak, the ionosphere correspondingly reaches its strongest reflective level. Expected peak ionospheric conditions should result in reception conditions in the HF bands being at their best during 2013. Reception should be more stable, with an increased number of broadcasters using the 17 19 and 21 MHz bands during the daylight hours, with the 11, 9, 7, 6 and 5 MHz bands being most popular during night time hours.

LESS INTERFERENCE

The HFCC is a sector member of the International Telecommunication Union in Geneva. Since 1990 it has been responsible for helping ITU members carry out an effective internationally agreed coordinated frequency assignment plans for reducing interference between broadcast stations, thus improving reception conditions for HF broadcasts worldwide.

At its beginning the HFCC faced severe

TABLE 1			
MHz	m.	%	Reception Characteristics
26	11	*	No significant HF broadcasting
21/19	13	9	Day: long distance, all seasons
17	16	9	Day: mid and long distance, all seasons
15	19	15	Day: mid and long distance, all seasons
13	22	12	Day: mid and long distance, all seasons
			Eve: mid and long distance, not local winter
11	25	13	Day: short and mid distance, all seasons
			Eve: mid and long distance, not winter
9	31	14	Day: short and mid distance, all seasons
			Eve: mid and long distance, all seasons
			Night: mid and long distance, all seasons
7	41	14	Day: short and mid distance, all seasons
			Night: mid and long distance, all seasons
6/5	49	12	Day: short and mid distance, all seasons
			Night: mid and long distance, all seasons
4/3	75	2	Day: short distance, all seasons
			Night: short and mid distance, all seasons

m. = Metre Bands % = % of total band usage
* = used for local digital broadcasting in Europe
Short-distance: up to *c.* 1200 miles (2000 km)
Mid-distance: c. 1000-2400 miles (1600-4000 km)
Long-distance: over 2400 miles (4000 km)

crowding in the HF broadcast bands. There were, on average, more than two stations operating on each available frequency, causing a high level of mutual interference severely affecting the grade of reception. With the HFCC acting as a legal focal point for direction and services, and with the cooperation of the ITU members using the HF broadcasting bands, two seasonal coordinated frequency schedules have been issued annually since 1990. With each passing year the HFCC reports mutual interference has been progressively reduced and a stabilized pattern of usage has evolved which only varies slowly with propagation and programme requirements. While there is still some overcrowding in the HF broadcasting bands, 2013 is expected to be a year with the benfits of greatly minimized mutual interference and a continuity of frequency usage. This should result in an improved grade of service for the world wide HF broadcast audience.

Good listening on the HF broadcast bands in 2013.

ABOUT THE AUTHOR

Engineer, diplomat, journalist, George Jacobs is the *WRTH* Dean of Contributing Editors, this being his 51st year of writing for the Handbook. He is a world-renowned innovative engineer and diplomat with a fierce belief in the free flow of information. George is a legend in the field of HF broadcasting, with 2013 marking his 73rd year of practice. He can be reached by email at b17nav8af@gmail.com.

Most Suitable Frequencies 2013

Prepared by Prof. Dr. rer. nat. Ulf-Peter Hoppe, Chief Scientist
E-mail: ulf-peter.hoppe@tveco.net
Web: www.mn.uio.no/fysikk/english/people/aca/uph/index.html

TRANSMITTING STATION LOCATION

Each period column lists 8 sub-values in the order: **EUR/NAF · N.AM(E) · N.AM(W) · C/S.AM · C/S.AF · ME/S.AS · E.AS · AUS/NZ**

LISTENER'S AREA	LOCAL TIME	APPROX. UTC TIME	JAN/FEB & NOV/DEC	MAR/APR & SEPT/OCT	MAY-AUGUST
EUROPE AND NORTH AFRICA	00:00-04:00	23:00-03:00	7 7 11 9 9 7 9 -	7 9 11 11 9 9 11 -	9 9 15 9 9 9 15 17
	04:00-08:00	03:00-07:00	6 7 9 9 7 15 15 21	/ / 11 13 / 17 17 -	13 9 15 11 9 17 17 17
	08:00-12:00	07:00-11:00	13 9 11 15 21 21 15 21	15 11 - 17 21 21 21 25	17 13 - 17 21 21 17 21
	12:00-16:00	11:00-15:00	15 17 - 21 21 15 11 17	15 17 15 25 25 21 15 17	17 17 17 21 17 17 17 -
	16:00-20:00	15:00-19:00	9 15 15 21 13 9 7 15	11 21 21 25 17 11 15 15	15 17 17 21 15 13 13 13
	20:00-00:00	19:00-23:00	7 9 - 11 11 7 9 11	9 13 17 11 9 9 11 11	11 13 17 11 9 11 9 11
NORTH AMERICA (EAST)	22:00-02:00	03:00-07:00	6 7 6 7 9 17 15 -	7 7 9 9 15 15 17 17	9 9 9 9 11 - 17 17
	02:00-06:00	07:00-11:00	7 6 6 7 9 - 15 11	9 7 6 11 13 - 15 13	11 7 7 9 15 - 17 11
	06:00-10:00	11:00-15:00	13 11 7 17 21 17 9 11	15 13 7 17 21 17 15 15	17 13 9 21 21 17 17 15
	10:00-14:00	15:00-19:00	15 15 17 17 21 13 13 17	21 17 17 21 21 17 15 -	17 15 21 25 17 21 17 -
	14:00-18:00	19:00-23:00	7 13 17 15 13 11 9 15	11 15 17 17 15 15 13 17	17 15 21 15 13 17 17 21
	18:00-22:00	23:00-03:00	7 9 9 9 9 11 15 -	9 11 11 13 9 13 17 25	9 11 11 11 9 17 17 21
NORTH AMERICA (WEST)	00:00-04:00	08:00-12:00	9 7 7 9 - 15 9 11	9 7 7 11 - 17 9 11	11 7 7 13 - 17 13 11
	04:00-08:00	12:00-16:00	13 11 7 21 - 11 9 9	15 7 21 21 13 11 13 15	15 15 11 17 21 15 15 13
	08:00-12:00	16:00-20:00	15 17 13 21 25 13 9 15	17 15 25 21 15 17 25 -	17 13 13 21 21 15 15 -
	12:00-16:00	20:00-00:00	9 15 13 17 21 13 13 17	15 15 13 21 21 15 17 25	17 15 13 21 17 17 17 25
	16:00-20:00	00:00-04:00	9 9 9 13 17 17 11 11	11 11 9 11 17 13 15 11	11 9 9 13 13 - 17 15
	20:00-00:00	04:00-08:00	6 7 7 7 9 17 11 15	9 9 7 13 11 - 13 15	11 9 9 13 13 - 17 15
CENTRAL AND SOUTH AMERICA	00:00-04:00	04:00-08:00	7 7 7 9 - 15 17 -	9 9 9 11 11 - 21 17	11 9 11 9 9 - 21 13
	04:00-08:00	08:00-12:00	13 7 9 7 17 25 15 13	17 9 13 9 17 25 17 13	17 9 11 9 15 21 17 11
	08:00-12:00	12:00-16:00	21 17 15 21 21 25 - -	21 17 21 21 25 25 - -	21 15 21 21 21 25 21 -
	12:00-16:00	16:00-20:00	17 25 21 17 21 - - -	21 21 25 25 21 21 - -	21 17 21 21 15 21 - -
	16:00-20:00	20:00-00:00	9 13 17 17 11 15 9 21	11 15 21 21 13 17 13 21	13 13 21 17 9 15 17 17
	20:00-00:00	00:00-04:00	9 7 9 11 9 11 15 21	15 9 11 15 11 15 17 25	11 11 13 11 7 17 21 17
CENTRAL AND SOUTH AFRICA	00:00-04:00	22:00-02:00	9 13 17 9 9 11 - -	9 17 9 9 9 17 - -	9 11 15 7 7 13 9 -
	04:00-08:00	02:00-06:00	7 11 11 9 9 15 17 17	9 13 15 7 9 17 21 17	9 11 13 7 9 17 21 15
	08:00-12:00	06:00-10:00	21 - 15 17 17 25 21 -	17 15 - 15 17 21 25 25	21 15 - 13 17 21 25 17
	12:00-16:00	10:00-14:00	21 21 - 21 21 17 17 17	21 25 - 25 21 21 17 21	21 21 - 21 17 17 25 -
	16:00-20:00	14:00-18:00	17 25 25 25 15 13 11 13	21 25 25 25 17 15 15 11	17 21 17 17 15 13 13 9
	20:00-00:00	18:00-22:00	11 17 21 13 11 11 11 11	11 17 25 11 13 13 9 -	11 21 21 9 9 9 15 9
MIDDLE EAST AND SOUTH ASIA	00:00-04:00	21:00-01:00	7 11 13 15 9 7 7 15	9 13 15 17 11 9 9 15	11 17 17 13 9 9 11 11
	04:00-08:00	01:00-05:00	7 9 13 11 7 13 17 25	7 13 17 15 9 15 17 21	11 15 17 15 11 17 17 21
	08:00-12:00	05:00-09:00	17 - - 17 21 21 21 25	17 - 17 21 25 25 21 -	17 - - 21 21 17 21 -
	12:00-16:00	09:00-13:00	17 13 - 17 21 21 17 17	21 17 - 25 25 21 17 17	17 17 - 25 21 21 17 15
	16:00-20:00	13:00-17:00	13 17 11 25 21 11 15 11	15 21 15 25 21 15 15 11	13 21 17 15 11 15 11 11
	20:00-00:00	17:00-21:00	7 13 - 21 11 9 7 11	9 15 - 21 13 11 9 11	13 21 17 15 9 11 11 11
EAST ASIA AND FAR EAST	00:00-04:00	16:00-20:00	11 13 9 - 11 9 6 9	11 - 11 - 15 11 11 9	15 17 15 17 17 13 11 7
	04:00-08:00	20:00-00:00	9 15 17 13 11 7 7 15	11 21 21 15 9 9 17 -	15 15 17 17 13 11 11 15
	08:00-12:00	00:00-04:00	9 15 17 17 17 17 25 -	17 13 15 17 25 25 21 -	15 15 21 - 21 21 17 -
	12:00-16:00	04:00-08:00	11 9 9 15 21 21 17 21	17 13 15 17 25 25 21 -	17 15 21 21 17 21 17 -
	16:00-20:00	08:00-12:00	15 9 7 13 - 15 9 13	17 11 7 21 25 17 11 11	17 11 9 17 21 17 15 9
	20:00-00:00	12:00-16:00	9 11 7 - 9 7 11	15 13 9 - 17 11 9	17 9 21 21 15 13 9
AUSTRALIA AND NEW ZEALAND	00:00-04:00	14:00-18:00	15 17 15 - 13 11 9 9	17 - 13 - 13 9 11 9	15 - 15 - 11 9 9 7
	04:00-08:00	18:00-22:00	9 17 17 13 17 11 9 11	13 25 21 17 11 11 11 9	13 21 21 11 9 9 9 -
	08:00-12:00	22:00-02:00	- 25 25 21 21 15 21 17	- 25 25 17 21 21 21 -	17 21 25 17 13 17 17 -
	12:00-16:00	02:00-06:00	- 11 21 - 21 17 17 -	21 - 21 - 21 25 21 17	17 17 21 15 - 21 25 9
	16:00-20:00	06:00-10:00	25 11 11 17 - 21 17 9	25 13 11 13 25 21 13 -	21 13 11 9 21 15 9 -
	20:00-00:00	10:00-14:00	21 11 11 17 13 13 13 11	11 11 11 15 - 11 13 9	- 13 11 11 - 11 9 7

**Band selections have been made according to predicted propagation conditions. Also check neighbouring bands of the most suitable bands shown here.
A '-' means there is no reliable propagation in any frequency band.**

How to use *WRTH*

ORGANISATION OF THE BOOK

The book consists of three main areas: **Features**, consisting of equipment reviews, broadcasting predictions and informative radio-related articles; **Directory**, which is further divided into *National Radio*, *International Radio* (including Clandestine and Other Target Broadcasts), *Frequency Lists* (which includes Mediumwave lists by region, Shortwave Stations of the World, International Broadcasts in selected languages and International DRM broadcasts), and *Terrestrial Television*; and finally **Reference** where a full country index, abbreviations used in WRTH and transmitter site location tables, as well as other useful information related to the world of radio broadcasting can be found.

Each section is identified by a unique 'side-bar', which can be found both on the main contents page and on each individual page throughout the book. Each section starts with an alphabetical country listing.

In the Directory, countries are listed alphabetically within each section so that they may be easily located by flicking forward to the relevant location. Alternatively, the index in the Reference section may be used to find the exact page number for a specific country of interest.

Under each country in the National Radio section, state broadcasters are listed first followed by major networks and then other stations. Armed forces stations and local relays of international stations are at the end of the entry. For all stations, mediumwave is listed first, followed by shortwave and finally FM. Many stations now only broadcast on FM. Details are given of digital radio multiplexes where appropriate.

OPERATING TECHNIQUES

When operating their receivers, the majority of listeners tend to operate in one of two main modes, switching between them as and when they deem appropriate. One method is to 'target' a given station or country by monitoring known frequencies and the other is simply to 'cruise' a specific band and identify each station as they occur (known as 'band scanning'). We have designed WRTH in such a way that either of these methods can be accommodated.

When operating in the targeting mode there are two ways to find a particular country. The first option is to go to the main contents page and use the section 'side-bars' to direct you to the right area of the book. Once there, you then only have to flick forward a few pages to locate the country of interest. Alternatively you can use the country index at the back of the book, which will tell you the precise page number. As you develop a 'feel' for the book and get used to the alphabetical layout, you will probably find that the side-bar method is simpler and quicker than using the country index.

Should you prefer to use band-scanning, there are listings of both medium wave and international short-wave broadcasts available in the Frequency Listings. These can also be useful for casual listening, but in either case can help to identify a station by frequency – whereupon further details can be obtained using the country entry to identify alternative frequencies for the station of interest.

UTC

UTC (Coordinated Universal Time) is the current time standard used throughout the world by broadcasters and many other organisations. UTC replaced Greenwhich Mean Time, GMT, as the world time standard some years ago. UTC, like its predecessor, is based on the Greenwich meridian at 0 degrees longitude (in London, England). To find out how many hours ahead or behind UTC your location is, refer to the World Time Table elsewhere in this section. If your location is ahead of UTC (indicated by a '+' sign in the table) you will need to add that number of hours to the time shown in the schedules. Likewise, if your location is behind UTC (indicated by '-'), you will need to subtract that many hours from the time shown in the schedules in order to find out at what time the broadcast can be heard at your location.

RECEPTION REPORTS

When requesting a verification of the reception report you sent (commonly referred to as a QSL-card), it is important that you include details of the programming heard (over a period of time, usually at least 15 minutes wherever possible); The date and time, in UTC (as explained above); how well you heard the broadcast and what receiver/antenna you were using. Where possible, try to use the language of the broadcast, rather han English, as there may be no English speakers available at the station. Be polite and do not demand a QSL card - stations on a tight budget may not have the resources to print QSL cards, but may send you promotional items and a verification letter instead.

It is courteous to enclose return postage when writing to small domestic broadcasters. This can be in the form of an International Reply Coupon (IRC) available from post offices. In all cases, when writing to radio stations you must write clearly. Remember, if the station cannot read your address, then you cannot expect to receive a reply!

Local Time, with respect to UTC — Population — Country

ANGOLA — Principal Language(s)

L.T: UTC +1h — **Pop:** 10 million — **Pr.L:** Portuguese + ethnic — **E.C:** 50Hz, 220V — **ITU:** AGL — Electricity supply (Electric Current)

Country Code

RÁDIO NACIONAL DE ANGOLA (RNA) — Telephone & Fax

Address — ✉ Rua Rainha Jinga, CP. 1329, Luanda ☎ +244 2 323172/321258

Mediumwave Stations — 📠 +244 2 324647/391234 **W:** www.rna.ao **E:** dgeral@rna.ao **LP:** DG: Filipe Diatezua. PD: Júlio Mendonça. TD: Sândido R. Pinto. — Leading Personnel

Web & email

MW:				
Location	kHz	kW	Prgr.	H. of tr.
Mulenvos	1088	25	A	24h

SW Stations

SW:				
Location	kHz	kW	Prgr.	H. of tr.
Mulenvos	4950	25	A	24h
Mulenvos	7217v	15	N/A	24h

Frequency in kiloHertz

FM Stations — **FM** (MHz): Luanda (4kW): 93.5 (A), 94.5 (5), 96.5MHz (FME), 99.9 (RL), 101.4MHz (N). — Hours of Transmission

Power in kiloWatts

Announcement — **Ann:** "Rádio Nacional de Angola". **F.PI:** new 100kW tx on MW.

Prgrs: A=Canal A in Portuguese (general coverage): 24h. **N:** on the h. **N**=Rádio N'Gola Yetu (ethnic): 0000-2000. **N:** rel. Canal A. — Programme

Programme decode — **FME**=Rádio FM Estéreo (music): 1000-2400. **RL**=Rádio Luanda (capital channel): 24h. **5**=Rádio 5 (sports): 0500-2300. — Future Plans (F.PI)

NB: Not all entries are in the same format, example above is given for guidance and should cover most entries. If a country observes Daylight Savings Time/Summer Time, the effective dates are shown after the local time (**L.T**).

International Frequency Allocation Chart

0–10 MHz

Band	Frequency
LW	
MW	1
160m	2
120m	
90m	3
80m (NA)	
80m (EU)	4
←75m	
60m	5
49m	6
41m EU	7
40m	
41m	
31m	8
	9
	10

10–20 MHz

Band	Frequency
←30m	10
25m	11
	12
	13
22m	14
20m	
19m	15
	16
16m	17
	18
←17m	19
←15m	20

20–30 MHz

Band	Frequency
15m	20
13m	21
	22
	23
	24
←12m	25
11m	26
	27
	28
10m	29
	30

■ = Broadcast Band
■ = Radio Amateur Band
■ = Utility · Other Services
⊕ = Standard Time & Frequency Transmission

Top face of each bar shows regional differences where appropriate

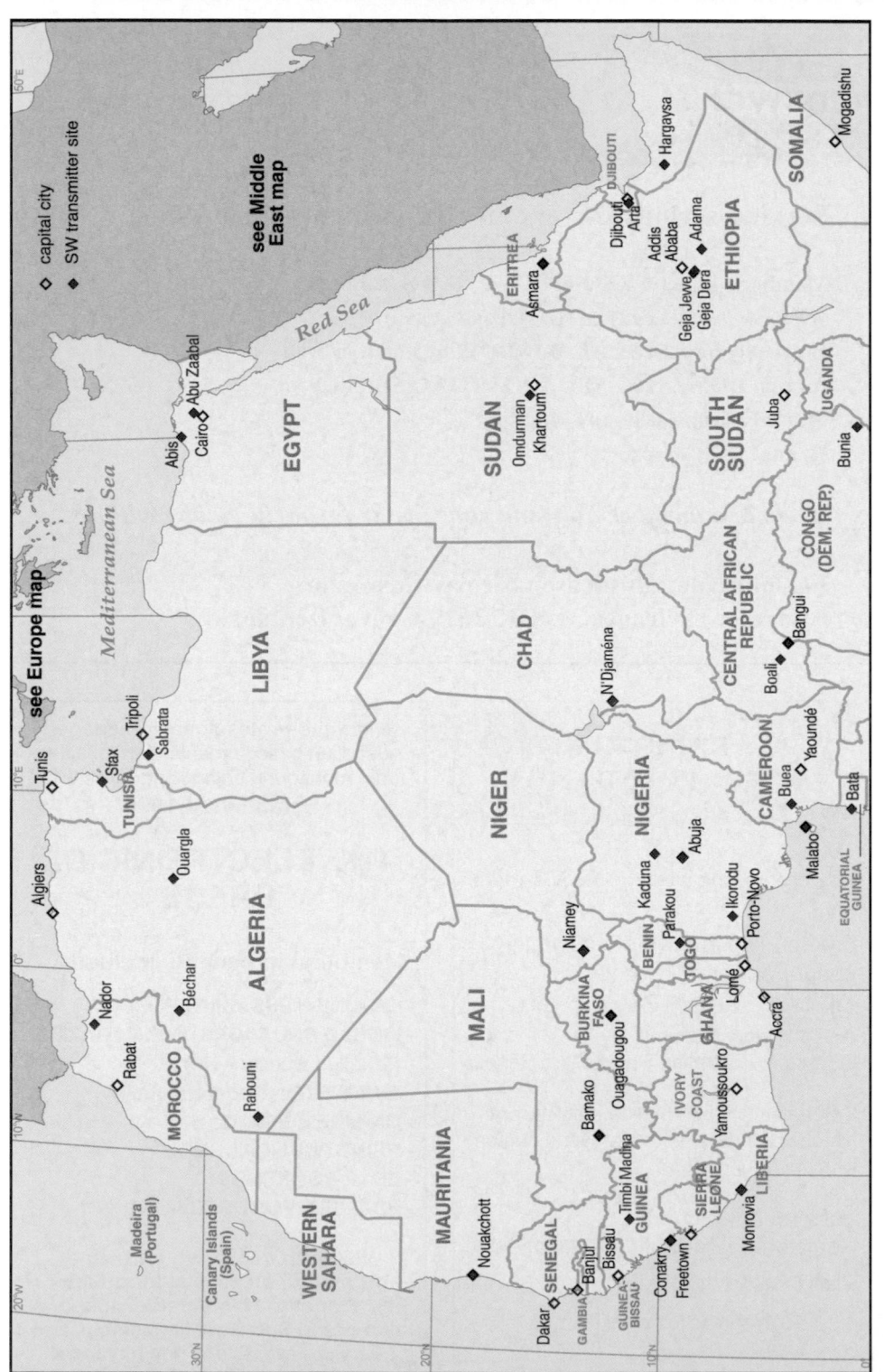

◇ capital city
◆ SW transmitter site

see Middle
East map

see Europe map

Mediterranean Sea

Red Sea

Madeira
(Portugal)

Canary Islands
(Spain)

WESTERN
SAHARA

MOROCCO

Rabat
Rabouni
Nador
Béchar

ALGERIA

Algiers

Ouargla

Tunis
TUNISIA
Sfax
Sabrata
Tripoli

LIBYA

EGYPT

Abis
Cairo
Abu Zaabal

Omdurman
Khartoum

SUDAN

SOUTH
SUDAN

Juba

CENTRAL AFRICAN
REPUBLIC

Boali
Bangui

CONGO
(DEM. REP.)

Bunia

UGANDA

SOMALIA

Mogadishu

Hargaysa

ETHIOPIA

DJIBOUTI
Djibouti
Arta
Addis
Ababa
Adama
Geja Jewe
Geja Dera

ERITREA
Asmara

CHAD

N'Djaména

NIGER

MALI

Bamako
Timbi Madina
GUINEA

MAURITANIA

Nouakchott

Dakar
SENEGAL
Banjul
GAMBIA
Bissau
GUINEA-
BISSAU

Conakry
Freetown
SIERRA
LEONE

Monrovia
LIBERIA

IVORY
COAST
Yamoussoukro

GHANA
Accra
Lomé
TOGO

BURKINA
FASO
Ouagadougou

Niamey

BENIN
Kaduna
Parakou
Porto-Novo
Ikorodu
Abuja
NIGERIA

CAMEROON
Buea
Yaoundé
Malabo
Bata
EQUATORIAL
GUINEA

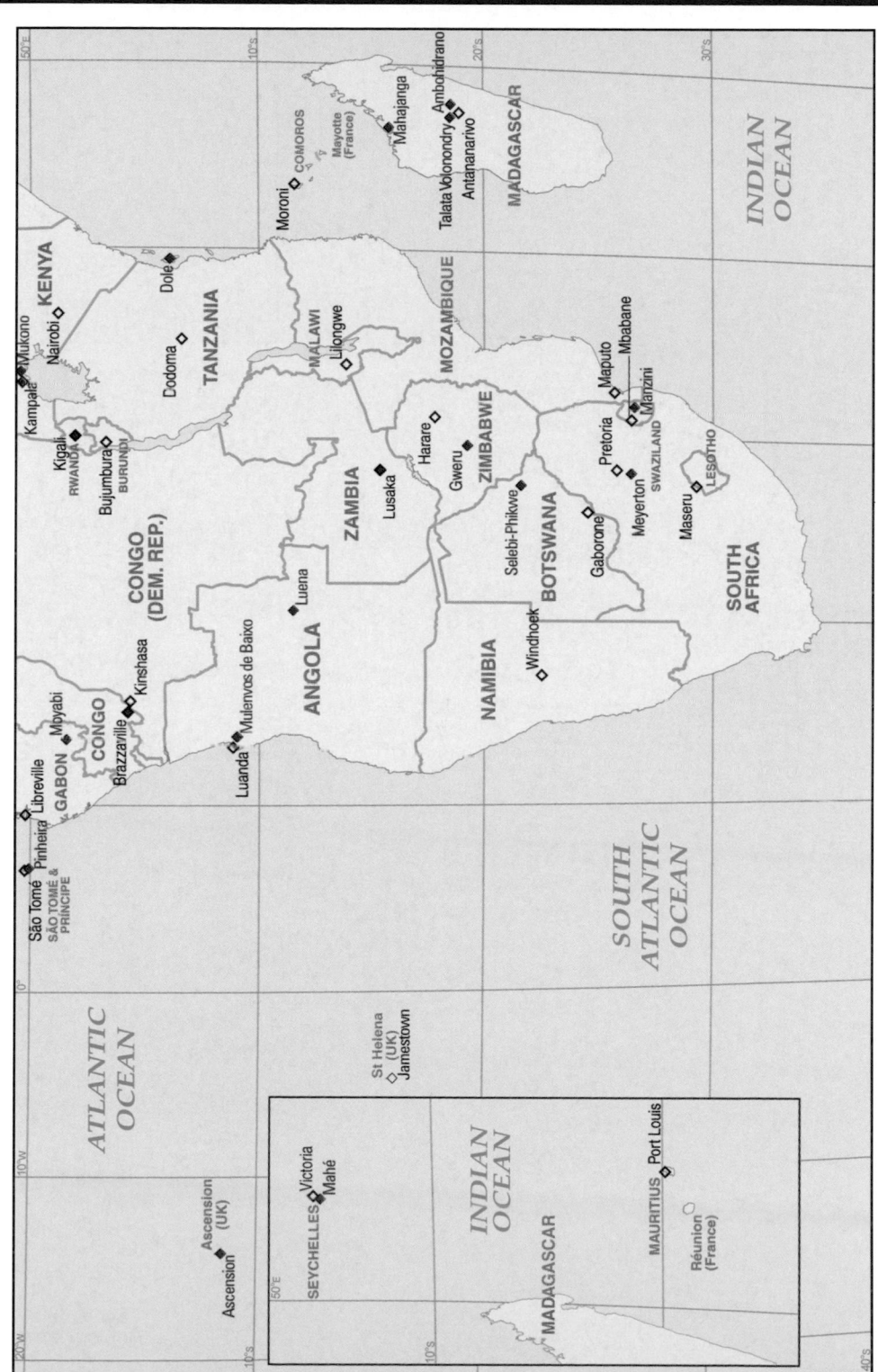

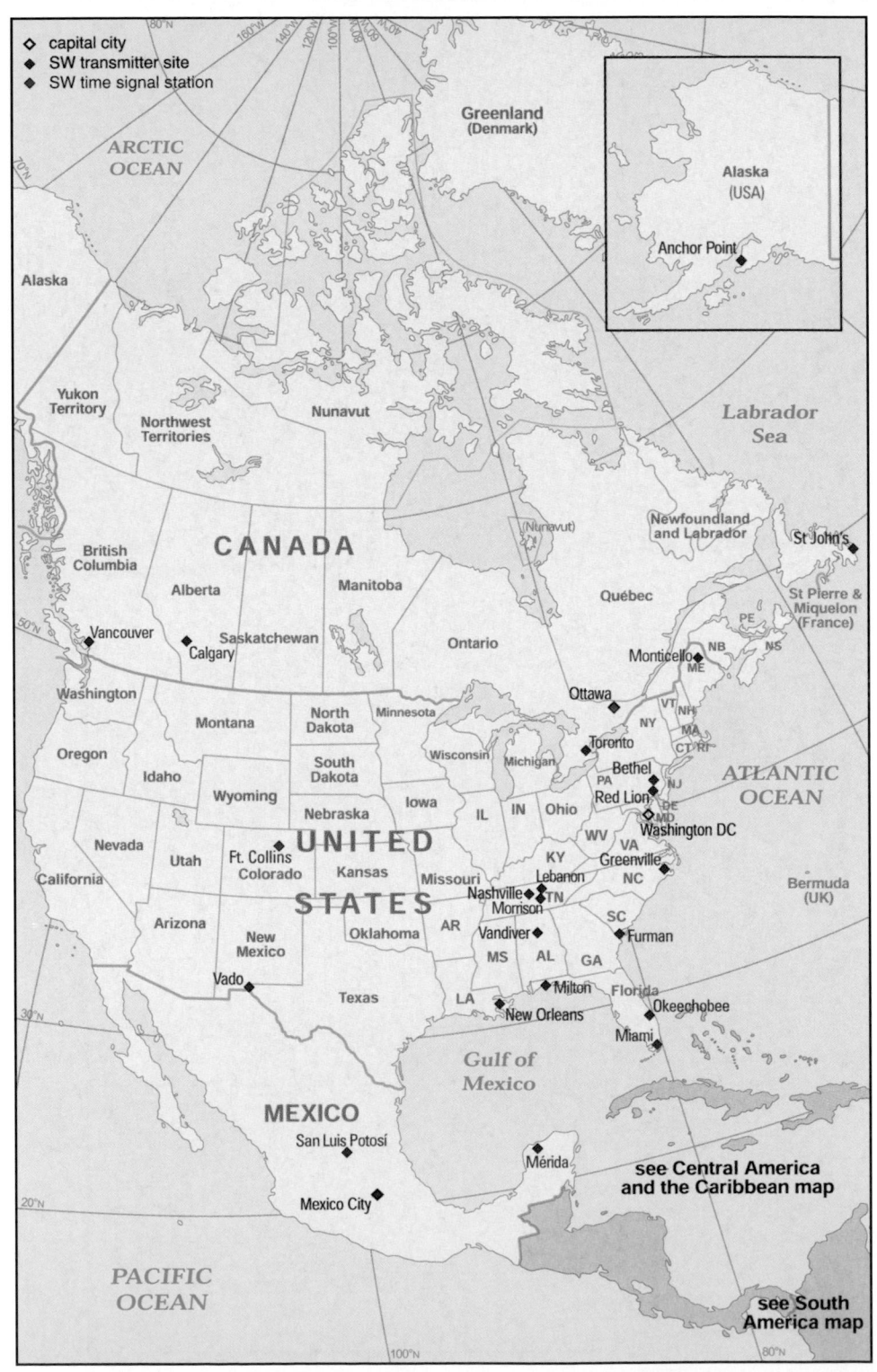

◇ capital city
◆ SW transmitter site
◆ SW time signal station

ARCTIC
OCEAN

Greenland
(Denmark)

Alaska
(USA)

Anchor Point ◆

Alaska

Yukon
Territory

Northwest
Territories

Nunavut

Labrador
Sea

British
Columbia

CANADA

Newfoundland
and Labrador

St John's ◆

Alberta

Manitoba

Québec

St Pierre &
Miquelon
(France)

Saskatchewan

Ontario

PE

NS

Vancouver ◆

Calgary ◆

Monticello ◆
ME
NB

Washington

Montana

North
Dakota

Minnesota

Ottawa ◆

NY

VT
NH
MA
CT RI

Oregon

Idaho

Wyoming

South
Dakota

Wisconsin

Michigan

Toronto ◆

PA

Bethel ◆

ATLANTIC
OCEAN

Nevada

Utah

Ft. Collins ◆
Colorado

UNITED

Nebraska

Iowa

IL

IN

Ohio

WV

Red Lion ◆
NJ
DE
MD
Washington DC ◇

Kansas

Missouri

KY

VA

Greenville ◆

Bermuda
(UK)

California

Arizona

New
Mexico

STATES

Oklahoma

AR

Lebanon ◆
Nashville ◆
Morrison ◆
TN

Vandiver ◆

NC

SC

Furman ◆

Vado ◆

Texas

MS

AL

GA

LA

Milton ◆

Florida

New Orleans ◆

Okeechobee ◆

Miami ◆

Gulf of
Mexico

MEXICO

San Luis Potosí ◆

Mérida ◆

see Central America
and the Caribbean map

Mexico City ◆

PACIFIC
OCEAN

see South
America map

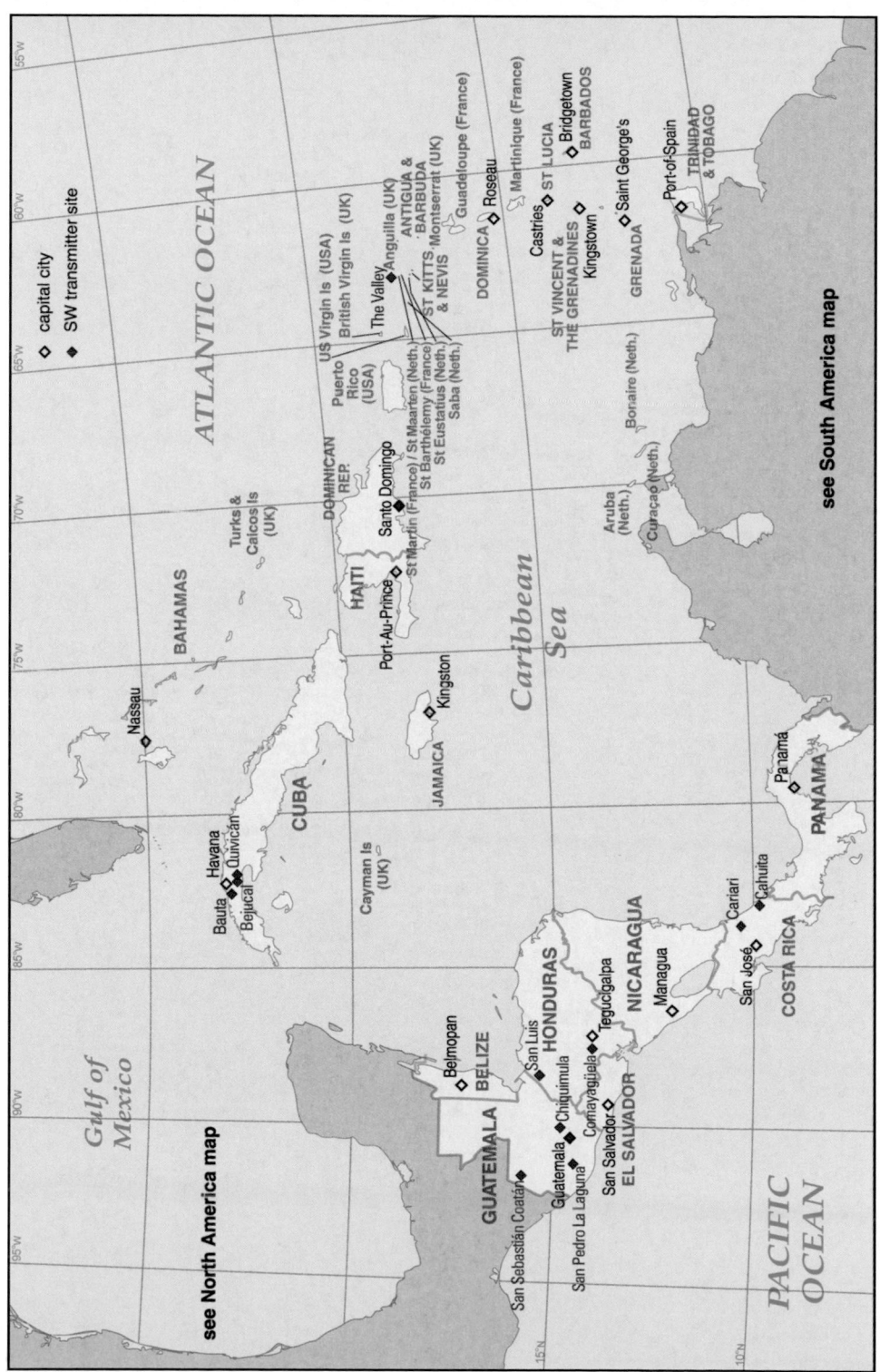

MAPS

Central America

ATLANTIC OCEAN

◇ capital city

◆ SW transmitter site

55 w

60 w

65 w

70 w

75 w

80 w

86 w

90 w

96 w

Gulf of Mexico

PACIFIC OCEAN

Caribbean Sea

see North America map

see South America map

BAHAMAS

Nassau

CUBA

Bauta

Havana

Quivicán

Bejucal

Cayman Is (UK)

JAMAICA

Kingston

Turks & Caicos Is (UK)

DOMINICAN REP.

Santo Domingo

HAITI

Port-Au-Prince

St Martin (France) / St Barthélemy (France)

Puerto Rico (USA)

US Virgin Is (USA)

British Virgin Is (UK)

Anguilla (UK)

The Valley

ANTIGUA & BARBUDA

ST KITTS & NEVIS

Montserrat (UK)

St Maarten (Neth.)

St Eustatius (Neth.)

Saba (Neth.)

Guadeloupe (France)

DOMINICA

Roseau

Martinique (France)

ST LUCIA

Castries

ST VINCENT & THE GRENADINES

Kingstown

BARBADOS

Bridgetown

Saint George's

GRENADA

Port-of-Spain

TRINIDAD & TOBAGO

Boraire (Neth.)

Aruba (Neth.)

Curaçao (Neth.)

BELIZE

Belmopan

GUATEMALA

San Luis

HONDURAS

Chiquimula

Comayagüela

Tegucigalpa

Guatemala

San Pedro La Laguna

San Salvador

EL SALVADOR

San Sebastián Coatán

NICARAGUA

Managua

Cariari

COSTA RICA

San José

Cahuita

PANAMA

Panamá

South America – Features map

- ◇ capital city
- ◆ SW transmitter site
- ◆ SW time signal station

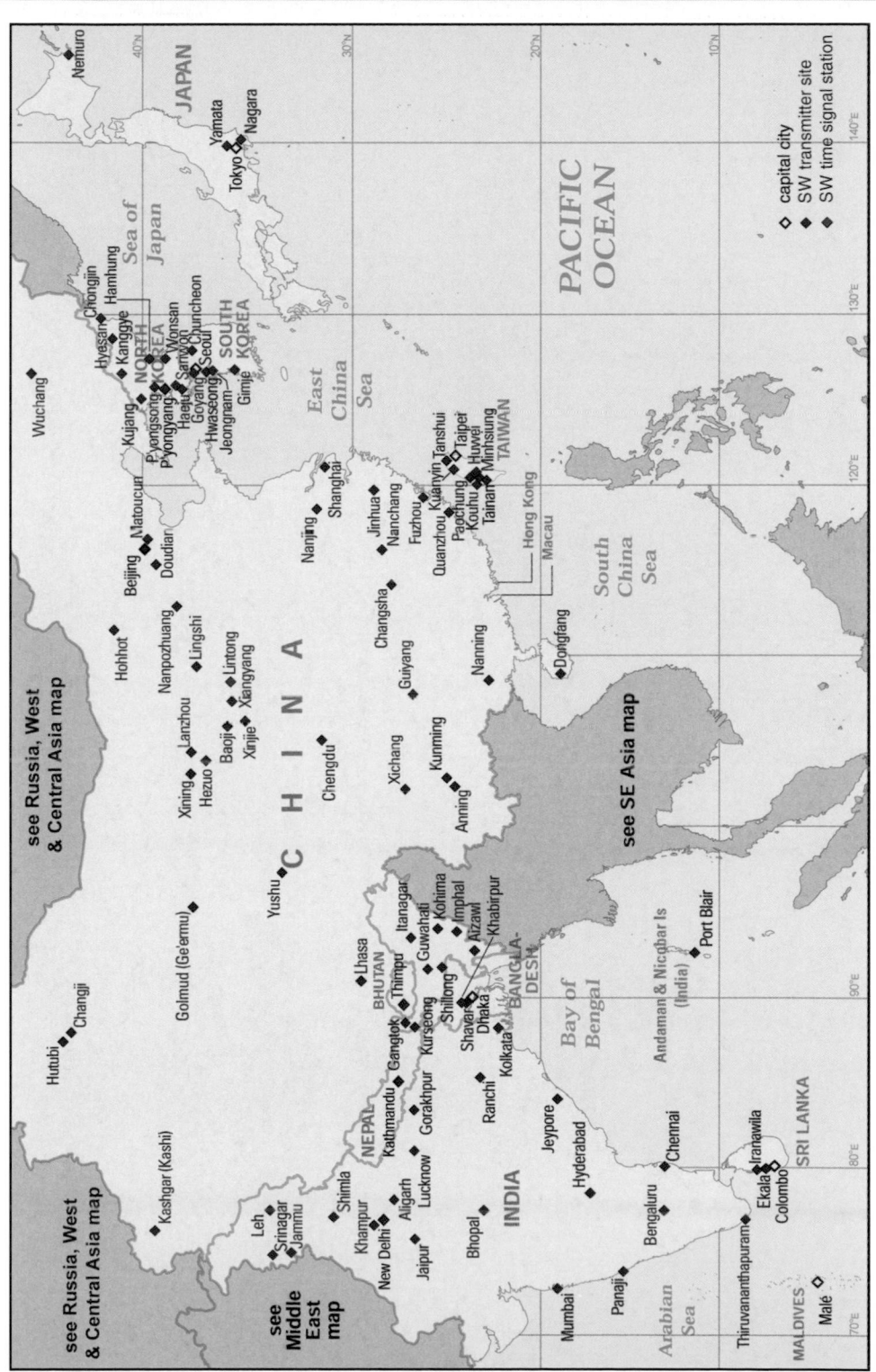

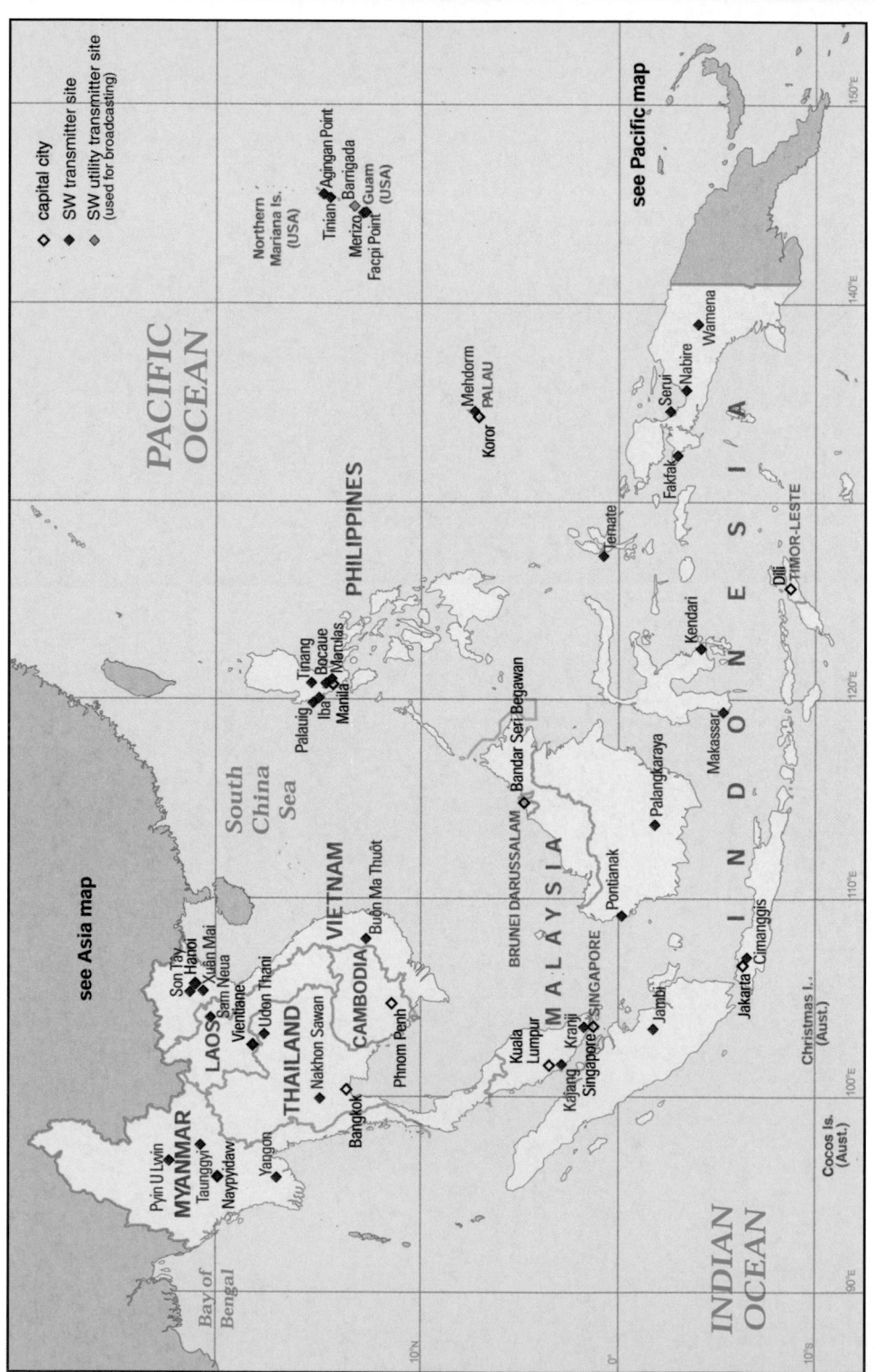

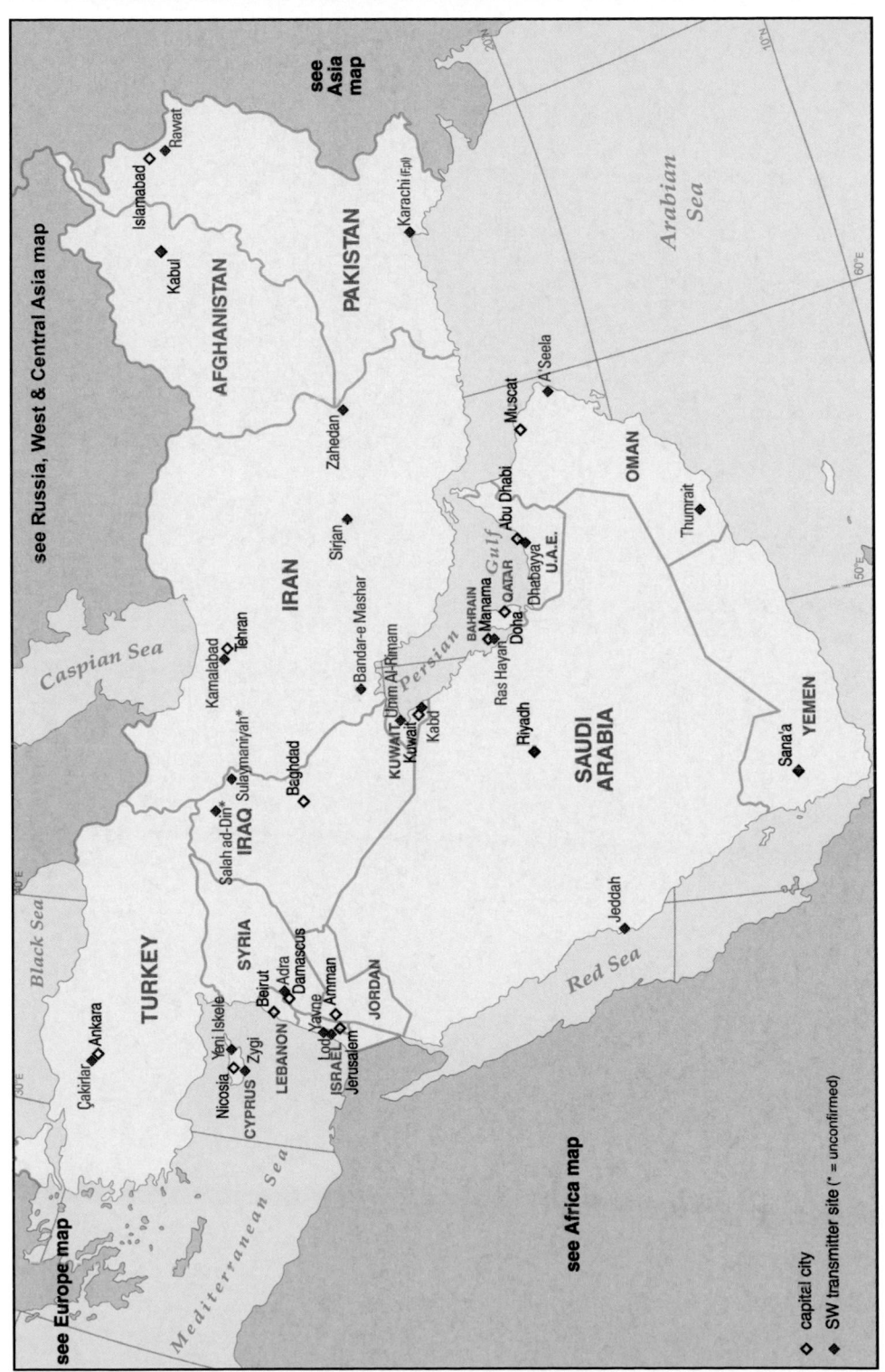

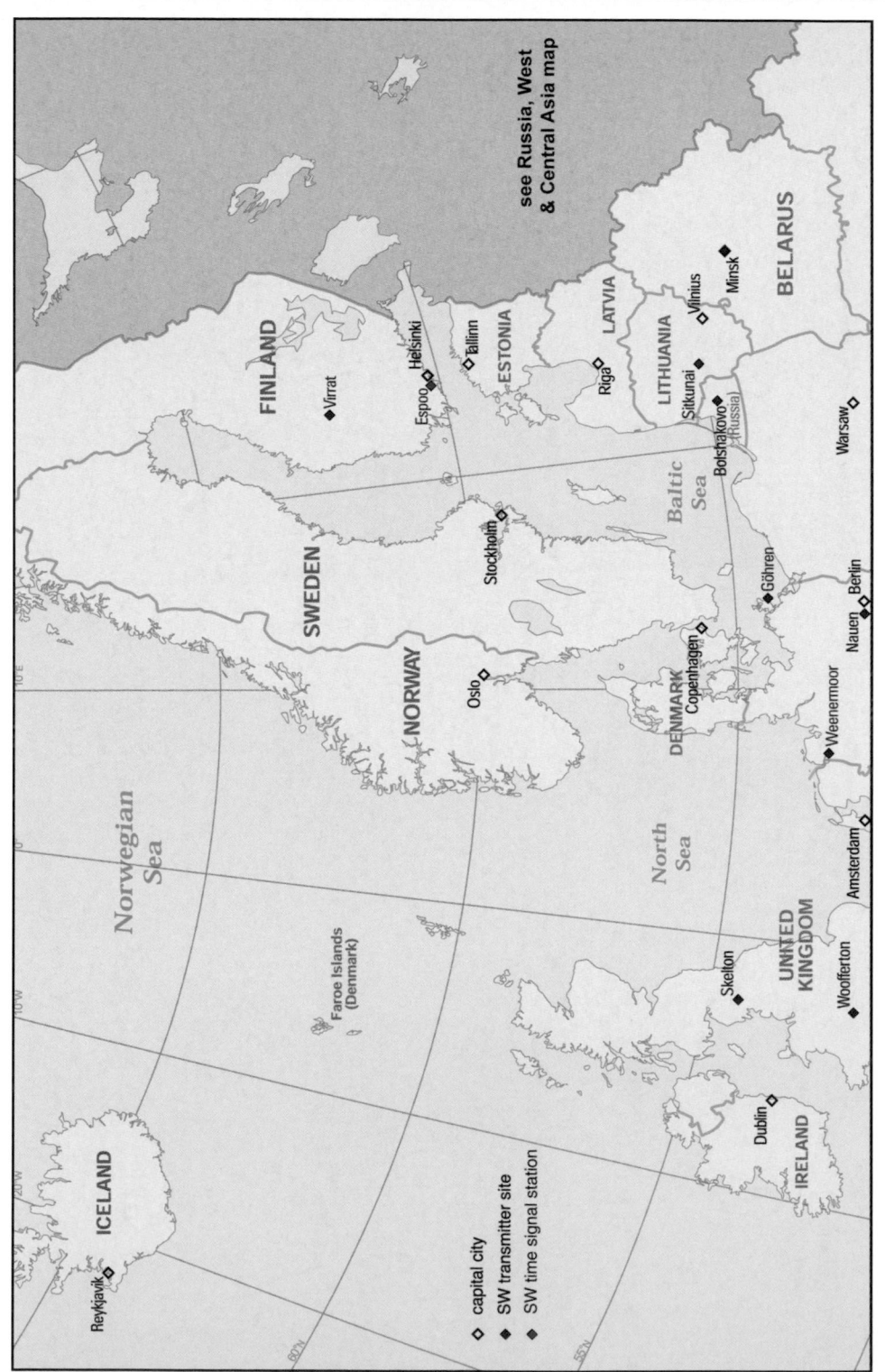

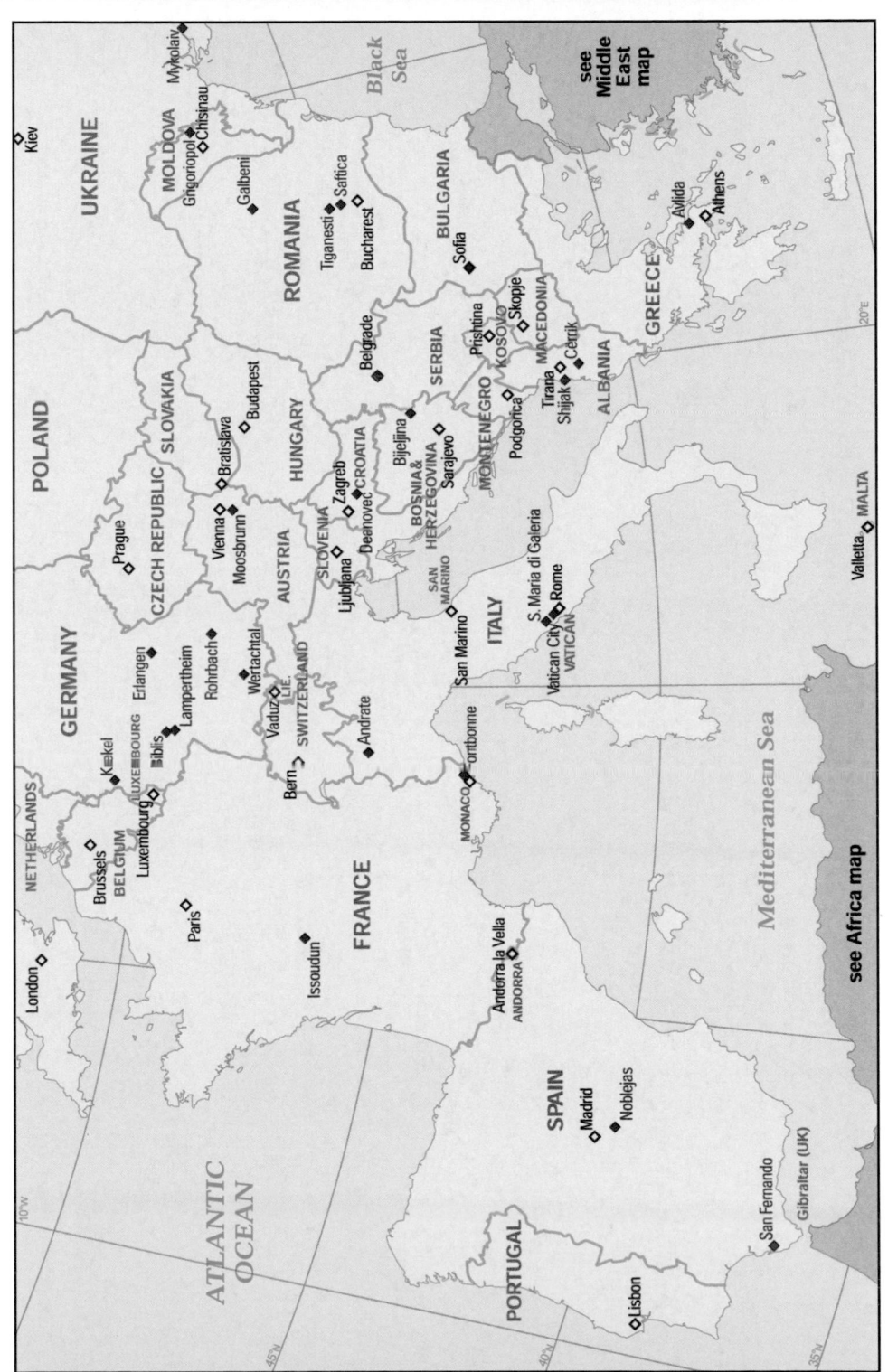

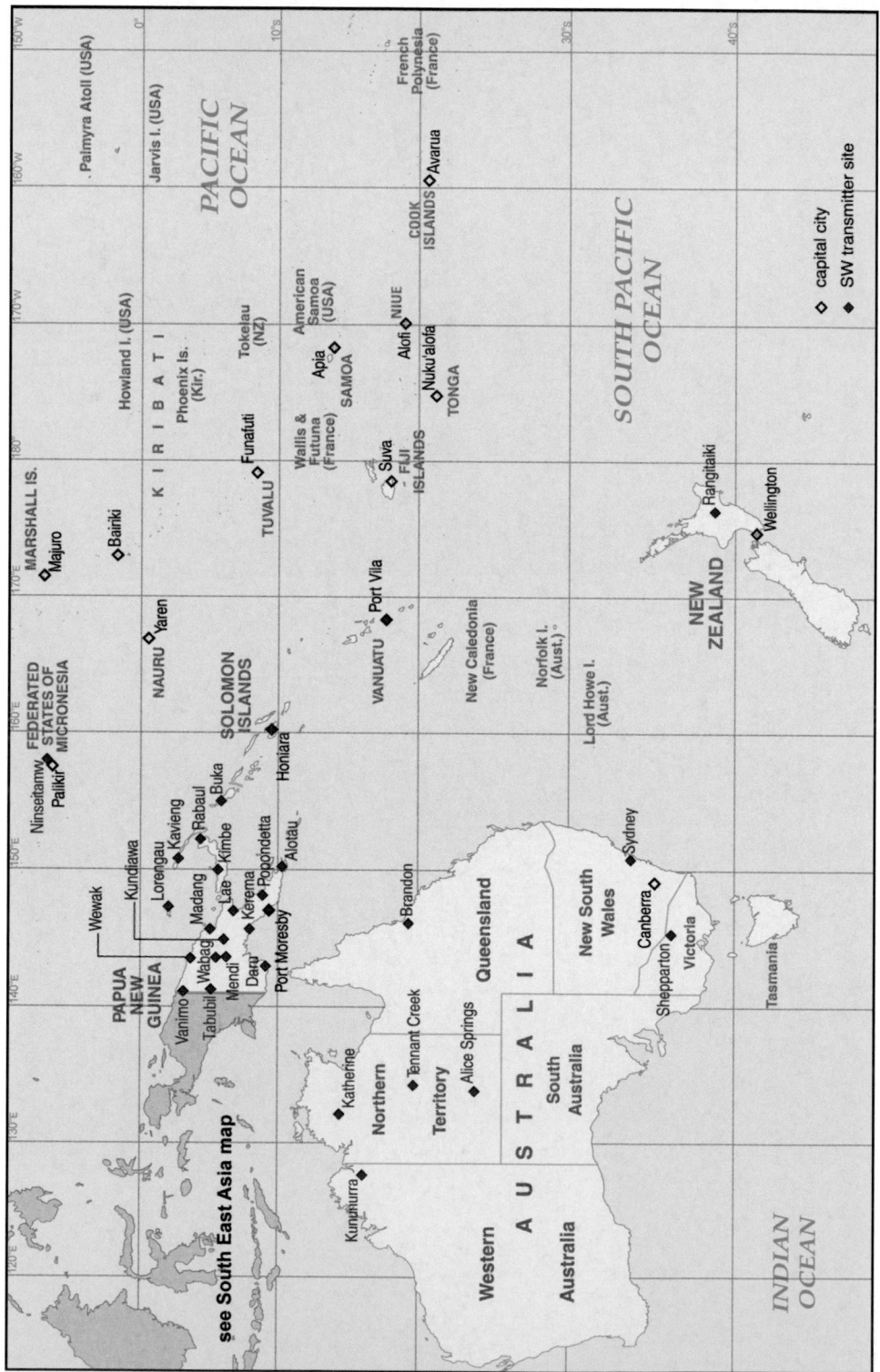

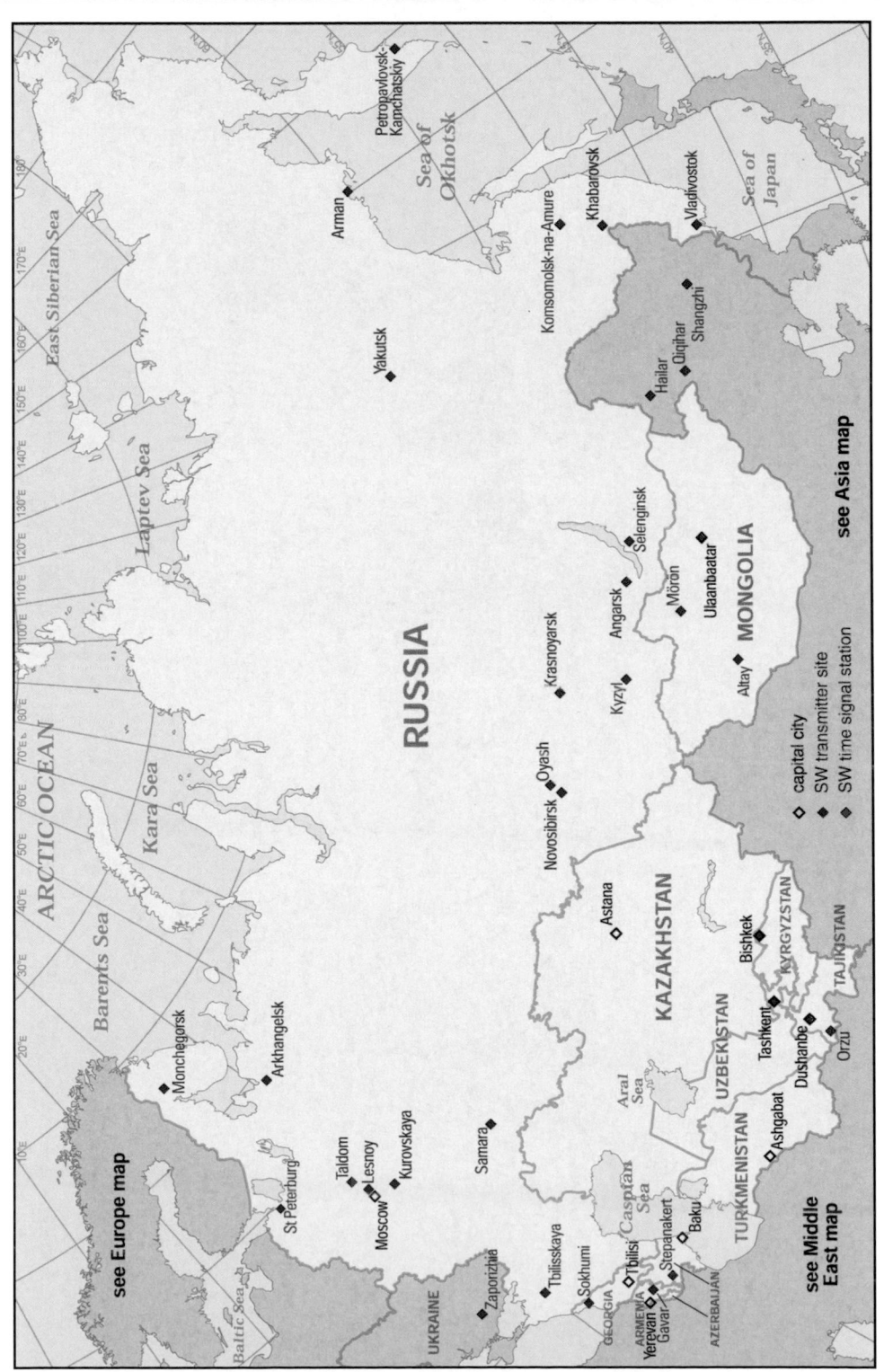

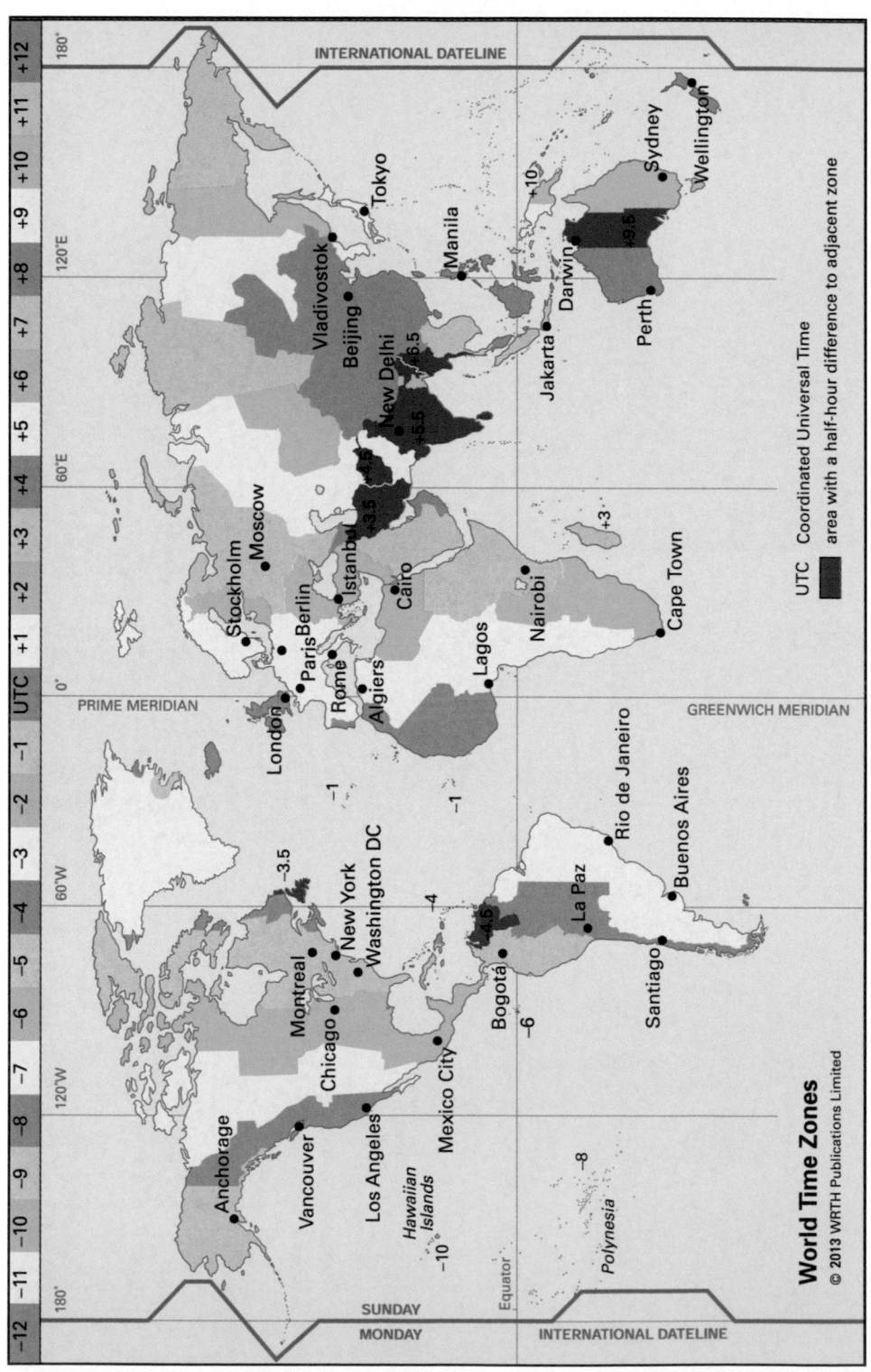

World Time Zones
© 2013 WRTH Publications Limited

UTC — Coordinated Universal Time

area with a half-hour difference to adjacent zone

WORLD TIME TABLE

Differences marked + or - show the number of hours ahead, or behind, UTC. Variations from Standard Time for part of the year (referred to as DST or Summer Time) are shown below; see the various country sections for the dates of operation. *) DST2013-2014 subject to confirmation
N=Normal (Standard) Time; **D**=Daylight Saving Time (DST) **¹**) in parts of the territory **²**) for other regions, see country section **°**) subj. to confirm

Country	N	D
Afghanistan	+4½	+4½
Alaska	−9	−8
Aleutian Is	−10	−9
Albania	+1	+2
Algeria	+1	+1
American Samoa	−11	−11
Andorra	+1	+2
Angola	+1	+1
Anguilla	−4	−4
Antarctica		
(Argentine)	−3	−3
(Chilean)	−4	−3
(McMurdo)	+12	+13
Antigua	−4	−4
Argentina (B.Aires)²	−3	−3
Armenia	+4	+4
Aruba	−4	−4
Ascension I.	UTC	UTC
Australia		
We. Australia	+8	+8
No. Territory	+9½	+9½
So. Australia	+9½	+10½
Queensland	+10	+10
VIC, NSW, TAS	+10	+11
Austria	+1	+2
Azerbaijan (Baki)²	+4	+5
Azores	−1	UTC
Bahamas	−5	−4
Bahrain	+3	+3
Bangladesh	+6	+6
Barbados	−4	−4
Belarus	+3	+3
Belgium	+1	+2
Belize	−6	−6
Benin	+1	+1
Bermuda	−4	−3
Bhutan	+6	+6
Bolivia	−4	−4
Bonaire	−4	−4
Bosnia & Herzegovina	+1	+2
Botswana	+2	+2
Brazil (Brasília)²	−3	−2
British Ind. Oc. Terr.	+6	+6
British Virgin Is	−4	−4
Brunei	+8	+8
Bulgaria	+2	+3
Burkina Faso	UTC	UTC
Burundi	+2	+2
Cambodia	+7	+7
Cameroon	+1	+1
Canada		
NL (SE Labr. & Is)	−3½	−2½
NL¹, NB, NS, PE, QC¹	−4	−3
QC¹	−4	−4
NT¹, NU¹, ON¹, QC¹	−5	−4
NU¹	−5	−5
MB, NU¹, ON¹	−6	−5
SK¹	−6	−6
AB, BC¹, NT, NU¹, SK¹	−7	−6
BC¹	−7	−7
BC¹, YT	−8	−7
Canary Is	UTC	+1
Cape Verde	−1	−1
Cayman Is	−5	−5
Ce. African Rep.	+1	+1
Chad	+1	+1
Chile	−4	−3
China (P.R.)	+8	+8
Christmas Is	+7	+7
Cocos (Keeling) Is	+6½	+6½
Colombia	−5	−5
Comoros	+3	+3
Congo (Kinshasa)²	+1	+1

Country	N	D
Congo (Rep.)	+1	+1
Cook Is	−10	−10
Costa Rica	−6	−6
Côte d'Ivoire	UTC	UTC
Croatia	+1	+2
Cuba	−5	−4
Curaçao	−4	−4
Cyprus	+2	+3
Akrotiri & Dhekelia	+2	+3
Czech Rep.	+1	+2
Denmark	+1	+2
Djibouti	+3	+3
Dominica	−4	−4
Dominican Rep.	−4	−4
Easter I.	−6	−5
Ecuador	−5	−5
Egypt	+2	+2
El Salvador	−6	−6
Equatorial Guinea	+1	+1
Eritrea	+3	+3
Estonia	+2	+3
Ethiopia	+3	+3
Falkland Is*	−4	−3
Faroe Is	UTC	+1
Fiji	+12	+13
Finland	+2	+3
France	+1	+2
French Guiana	−3	−3
French Poly.(Tahiti)²	−10	−10
French So.& Ant. L.	+5	+5
Gabon	+1	+1
Galapagos Is	−6	−6
Gambia	UTC	UTC
Georgia	+4	+4
Germany	+1	+2
Ghana	UTC	UTC
Gibraltar	+1	+2
Greece	+2	+3
Greenland (Nuuk)²	−3	−2
Grenada	−4	−4
Guadeloupe	−4	−4
Guam	+10	+10
Guatemala	−6	−6
Guinea	UTC	UTC
Guinea-Bissau	UTC	UTC
Guyana	−4	−4
Haiti	−5	−5
Hawaii	−10	−10
Honduras	−6	−6
Hong Kong	+8	+8
Hungary	+1	+2
Iceland	UTC	UTC
India	+5½	+5½
Indonesia (Jakarta)²	+7	+7
Iran	+3½	+4½
Iraq	+3	+3
Ireland	UTC	+1
Israel	+2	+3
West Bank & Gaza	+2	+3
Italy	+1	+2
Jamaica	−5	−5
Japan	+9	+9
Jordan	+2	+3
Kazakhstan (Astana)²	+6	+6
Kenya	+3	+3
Kiribati	+12	+12
Korea (North, DPR)	+9	+9
Korea (South, Rep.)	+9	+9
Kosovo	+1	+2
Kuwait	+3	+3
Kyrgyzstan	+6	+6
Laos	+7	+7
Latvia	+2	+3

Country	N	D
Lebanon	+2	+3
Lesotho	+2	+2
Liberia	UTC	UTC
Libya	+2	+2
Liechtenstein	+1	+2
Lithuania	+2	+3
Lord Howe I.	+10½	+11
Luxembourg	+1	+2
Macau	+8	+8
Macedonia	+1	+2
Madagascar	+3	+3
Madeira	UTC	+1
Malawi	+2	+2
Malaysia	+8	+8
Maldives	+5	+5
Mali	UTC	UTC
Malta	+1	+2
Marshall Is	+12	+12
Martinique	−4	−4
Mauritania	UTC	UTC
Mauritius	+4	+4
Mayotte	+3	+3
Mexico (Mexico City)²	−6	−5
Micronesia		
Chuuk, Yap	+10	+10
Kosrae, Pohnpei	+11	+11
Moldova	+2	+3
Monaco	+1	+2
Mongolia	+8	+8
Montenegro	+1	+2
Montserrat	−4	−4
Morocco*	UTC	+1
Ceuta & Melilla	+1	+2
Mozambique	+2	+2
Myanmar	+6½	+6½
Namibia	+1	+2
Nauru	+12	+12
Nepal	+5¾	+5¾
Netherlands	+1	+2
New Caledonia	+11	+11
New Zealand	+12	+13
Nicaragua	−6	−6
Niger	+1	+1
Nigeria	+1	+1
Niue	−11	−11
Norfolk I.	+11½	+11½
No. Mariana Is	+10	+10
Norway	+1	+2
Oman	+4	+4
Pakistan	+5	+5
Palau	+9	+9
Panama	−5	−5
Papua N. Guinea	+10	+10
Paraguay	−4	−3
Peru	−5	−5
Philippines	+8	+8
Pitcairn Is	−8	−8
Poland	+1	+2
Portugal	UTC	+1
Puerto Rico	−4	−4
Qatar	+3	+3
Réunion	+4	+4
Romania	+2	+3
Russia (Moscow)²	+3°	+3°
Rwanda	+2	+2
Saba	−4	−4
Samoa	+13	+14
San Marino	+1	+2
São Tomé & Prínc.	UTC	UTC
Saudi Arabia	+3	+3
Senegal	UTC	UTC
Serbia	+1	+2
Seychelles	+4	+4

Country	N	D
Sierra Leone	UTC	UTC
Singapore	+8	+8
Slovakia	+1	+2
Slovenia	+1	+2
Solomon Is	+11	+11
Somalia	+3	+3
South Africa	+2	+2
South Sudan	+3	+3
Spain	+1	+2
Sri Lanka	+5½	+5½
St. Barthélemy	−4	−4
St. Eustatius	−4	−4
St. Helena	UTC	UTC
St. Kitts & Nevis	−4	−4
St. Lucia	−4	−4
St. Martin	−4	−4
St. Pierre & Miq.	−3	−2
St. Vincent & Gren.	−4	−4
Sudan	+3	+3
Suriname	−3	−3
Swaziland	+2	+2
Sweden	+1	+2
Switzerland	+1	+2
Syria	+2	+3
Taiwan	+8	+8
Tajikistan	+5	+5
Tanzania	+3	+3
Thailand	+7	+7
Timor-Leste	+9	+9
Togo	UTC	UTC
Tokelau	+13	+13
Tonga	+13	+13
Trinidad	−4	−4
Tristan da Cunha	UTC	UTC
Tunisia	+1	+1
Turkey	+2	+3
Turkmenistan	+5	+5
Turks & Caicos Is	−5	−4
Tuvalu	+12	+12
Uganda	+3	+3
Ukraine	+2	+3
United Arab Em.	+4	+4
United Kingdom	UTC	+1
Uruguay	−3	−2
USA		
Eastern Time (CT, DE, FL, GA, IN¹, KY, MA, MD, ME, MI, NC, NH, NJ, NY, OH, PA, RI, SC, VA, VT, WV)	−5	−4
Central Time (AL, AR, IA, IL, IN¹, KS, LA, MN, MO, MS, ND, NE, OK, SD, TN, TX, WI)	−6	−5
Mountain Time^a (N-E AZ, CO, ID, MT, NM, UT, WY)	−7	−6
a) exc. most of AZ	−7	−7
Pacific Time (CA, NV, OR, WA)	−8	−7
Uzbekistan	+5	+5
Vanuatu	+11	+11
Vatican City State	+1	+2
Venezuela	−4½	−4½
Vietnam	+7	+7
Virgin Is	−4	−4
Wake I.	+12	+12
Wallis & Futuna	+12	+12
Yemen	+3	+3
Zambia	+2	+2
Zimbabwe	+2	+2

NATIONAL RADIO

Section Contents

Initial entries for each letter,
see Main Index for full details

Features & Reviews

National Radio

International Radio

Frequency Lists

Terrestrial Television

Reference

AFGHANISTAN

L.T: UTC +4½h — **Pop:** 33 million — **Pr.L:** Dari, Pashto, Turkmen, Uzbek — **E.C:** 50Hz, 220V — **ITU:** AFG

AFGHANISTAN TELECOM REGULATORY AUTHORITY (ARTA) ⌖ Moh. Jan Khan Watt 10th floor MoCIT Building, Kabul
☎+93 20 2105361 **W:** atra.gov.af

RADIO TELEVISION AFGHANISTAN (RTA, Gov.)
⌖ PO Box 544, Mohammad Akbar Khan Street 13, Kabul ☎+93 20 2102487 **W:** rta.org.af **E:** info@rta.org.af
L.P: DG Radio: Abdul Ghaney Mudaqiq. Dir. Eng: Mr. Zarin Anzor.
MW: Kabul (Pol-e-Charkhi) 1107kHz 400kW.
FM: Kabul 93.0 1kW, 105.2MHz 30W.
D.Prgr: 0100-1930. Main **N:** Pashto 1430, Dari 1530. **Ann:** "Radyo Afghanistan, Kabul". For Foreign Sce. see International Radio Section. Relayed also on 93.0MHz for Kabul.

PROVINCIAL STATIONS
R. Badakhshan, Faizabad: 584kHz‡ 5kW, 105.1MHz‡ 30W – **R. Badghis,** Qalay-e Naw: 1500kHz 6kW, 91.4MHz 250W. 0130-0330, 1330-1630, times vary – **R. Baghlan,** Pol-e-Khomri 103.0MHz, Baghlan: 106.6MHz 250W – **R. Balkh,** Mazar-e-Sharif: 1584kHz 10kW, 105.1MHz 0.1kW. In Dari/Pashto/Tajik/Uzbek: 0230-0430 (Fri 0430-0730), 1230-1530 – **R. Bamyan:** 96.0MHz – **R. Day Kundi:** Nili 1200kHz‡ 0.5kW, 103.2MHz 30W, Qalat 99.0MHz 0.5kW – **R. Farah,** Farah: 1044kHz‡ 7kW, 88.5MHz 1kW (F.P.I.). 0300-0430 – **R. Faryab,** Maimana: 594kHz 5kW, 104.3MHz 30W. 1230-1430 – **R. Ghazni:** 1017kHz 10kW, 92.4MHz 30W. 0230-0330, 1130-1530 – **R. Ghor,** Chaghcharan: 1584kHz 0.5kW, 93.4MHz – **R. Helmand,** Lashkar Ga: 999kHz‡ 5kW, 96.1MHz 1kW. 0330-0730, 1130-1430 – **R. Herat:** 1550kHz 0.1kW, 95.5MHz 250W. 0300-0500, 1130-1330 – **R. Jowzjan,** Sheberghan 106.6MHz 250W – **R. Kandahar:** 1305kHz 10kW, 90.6MHz 1kW. 0230-1430 – **R. Kapisa,** Mahmud-e-Raqi: 101.1MHz 600W – **R. Khost:** 1602kHz 10kW, 91.2MHz 1kW. 0230-0630, 1130-1530 – **R. Kunar,** Asadabad: 1575kHz 10kW, 100.5MHz 1kW.0330-0530, 0930-1500 – **R. Kunduz:** 909kHz 10kW, 94.4MHz 250W – **R. Laghman,** Mehtarlam: 88.2MHz‡ 0.5kW – **R. Logar,** Pol-e-Alam: 92.7MHz – **R. Nangarhar,** Jalalabad: 1440kHz 10kW, 93.5MHz 250W. 0230-0730, 1030-1130 **R. Nimroz,** Zaranj: 1584kHz 2kW, 90.0MHz 1kW. 0330-0530, 1230-1500 (Fri 1930) – **R. Nuristan,** Nuristan: 1500kHz 0.1kW, 88.5MHz 300W – **R. Paktia,** Gardez: 909kHz 50W, 104.2MHz 0.5kW – **R. Paktika,** Zareh Sharan: 93.2MHz – **R. Paktin Voice** (semi-gov), Shakin 1386kHz 5kW, 89.8MHz 150W. 0230-1730. W: paktinvoice.com – **R. Panjshir,** Bazarak: 88.0MHz 0.1kW – **R. Parwan,** Charikar: 88.9MHz – **R. Samangan,** Aybak: 1500kHz‡ 0.1kW, 90.4MHz‡ 150W – **R. Sar-e-Pol:** 89.9MHz – **R. Takhar,** Taloqan: 91.2MHz 30W – **R. Uruzgan,** Tarin Kowt: 93.0MHz 50W – **R. Wardak,** Meydan Shahr: 88.9MHz – **R. Zabul,** Qalat: 936kHz 10kW, 88.9MHz.
‡ = inactive

BBG–R. FREE AFGHANISTAN / R. MASHAAL / VOA ASHNA & DEEWA R. (US Gov.)
R. Free Afghanistan & VOA Ashna R: MW: Kabul (Pol-e-Charkhi) 1296kHz 400kW. **FM:** Herat/Jalalabad/Kabul/Kandahar/Mazar-e-Sharif 100.5MHz. 24h in Dari/Pashto/E.
R. Mashal & VOA Deewa R: MW: Khost 621kHz 0100-1900. **FM:** Asadabad/Gardez/Khost 100.5MHz.
For SW broadcasts & more details see International R. section (USA).

Independent commercial stations:
Arman FM ⌖ P.O. Box 1045, Central PO, Kabul **W:** arman.fm **E:** info@arman.fm **L.P:** Dir: Saad Mohseni. **FM:** 98.1MHz in Kabul (2kW)/Ghazni/Herat/Jalalabad/Kandahar/Konduz/Lashkar Ga/ Mazar-e-Sharif – **Ariana R.** ⌖ Darlaman St. (near Ministry of Trade), Kabul ☎+93 70 151515 **W:** arianatelevision.com **E:** marketing@arianatelevision.com **L.P:** Dir: Ahmad Zubair. **FM:** Kabul: 93.5MHz – **R. City** ⌖ Karte 3, District 6, Street 3, House no. 96, Kabul ☎+93 0 2100995/77 7955955 **W:** citymedia.af **E:** info@citymedia.af **L.P:** Saleem Totakhil, CEO. **FM:** Kabul/Mazar-i-Sharif 95.5MHz 3.5/1kW – **R. Killid** ⌖ The Killid Group, House No. 442, Street No. 6, Chardehi Watt, Near to Uzbekha Mosque, Karta-e-sea, Kabul 442 ☎+93 77 1088888 **W:** tkg.af **E:** info@killid.org **L.P:** Dir: Najiba Ayubi. **FM:** Kabul 88.0MHz 4kW, Herat 88.0MHz 2kW, Khost 88.2MHz. **Kabul Rock R:** 108.0MHz – **R. Maiwand,** Kabul: 92.7MHz 1.5kW – **Nawa R:** sabacent.org **L.P:** Dir: Mohammad Waqfi. **FM:** Kabul/Ghazni/Herat/Jalalabad/Kandahar/Konduz/Mazar e-Sharif/Paktia: 103.1MHz.

Other stations (powers 50-500W if not stated otherwise, frqs in MHz): **Ayna R,** Shahrak-e Shirpoor: 88.0 – **ERTV R,** (UNESCO), Kabul: 96.8

– **Gorbat FM,** Kabul: 91.8 – **R. Abasin,** Jalalabad: 93.7 – **R. Adib,** Shahr-e Jadid: 89..7 – **R. Aliksiz,** Kabul: 90.0 – **R. Amo,** Faizabad: 88.7 – **R. Amozgar,** Kabul: 101.3 – **R. Arghawan,** Ada-e Kabul: 90.1 – **R. Arkozia,** Charahi: 90.3 – **R. Armaghan,** Sheberghan: 89.9 – **R. Arya,** Kabul: 100.2 – **R. Arzu,** Mazar-e-Sharif: 91.8 – **R. Arzu ha FM,** Jada-e Sahat: 88.1 – **R. Aye Khanum,** Shahr-e Taliqan: 88.9 – **R. Azad Afgan,** Kandahar: 88.1 – **R. Azad Paktia Ghagh,** Gardez: 94.2 – **R. Armaghan,** Sheberghan: 89.9 – **R. Bakhtar,** Kabul: 99.2 – **R. Baran,** Herat: 98.4 1kW – **R. Biltoon,** Kabul: 104.9 – **R. Bustan,** Andkhoy: 87.7 – **R. Charchino,** Uruzgan prov: 88.1 – **R. Cheragh,** Kunduz: 87.4 – **R. Dahwat,** Kabul: 102.5 – **R. Daikundi,** Shahr-e Nili: 88.5 – **R. Darman,** Aqcha: 89.5 – **R. Dehkada,** Shahr-e Naw: 91.6 – **R. Dehrawod,** Uruzgan: 87.5 – **R. De Helo Karwan,** Khost: 90.6 – **R. Dunya,** Parwan: 88.8 – **R. Ejtima,** Logar: 88.5 – **R. Ertibat,** Malistan: 88.3 – **R. Faryad,** Herat: 87.8 – **R. Ghaznawiyan,** Ghazni: 89.3 – **R. Hamdard,** Ghazni prov: 94.9 – **R. Hamisha Bahar,** Nangarhar: 90.6 – **R. Hanzala,** Qalay-e Naw: 91.4 – **R. Humsada,** Takhar: 89.6 – **R. Istiqlal,** Baraki-Barak: 89.6 – **R. Jaghori,** Ghazni prov.: 90.9 – **R. Jaihoon,** Imam Shahib: 88.0 – **R. Javan,** Ghazni: 96.6 – **R. Jawanan,** Kabul: 97.5 – **R. Jurm,** Badakhsan prov: 98.0 – **R. Kaihan,** Tahmirat-e Spinzar: 88.4 – **R. Kalagush,** Nuristan prov: 90.0 – **R. Kawoon Voice,** Meterlam: 90.1 – **R. Khorasan,** Rokha: 91.3 – **R. Khushi,** Baghlan prov: 89.2 – **R. Kokcha,** Badakshan: 96.0 – **R. Meher,** Dasht-e Shor: 99.3 – **R. Milli e-Paygham,** Mohammad Agha: 94.5 – **R. Mirman,** Kandahar: 92.0 – **R. Mowj,** Kabul: 105.5 1kW – **R. Muram,** Nangarhar: 97.8 – **R. Muzdah,** Herat: 91.5MHz – **R. Nargis,** Jalalabad: 88.6 – **R. Nan:** Ghani Khel: 89.1 – **R. Naw-e-Bahar,** Balkh: 87.9 – **R. Nedaye Afghan,** Kabul: 99.6 – **R. Nedaye Solh,** Ghoreyan: 90.4 – **R. Nedaye Subh,** Ghoryan: 90.0 – **R. Nehad,** Mazar-e Sharif: 90.4MHz – **R. Nida,** Kabul: 97.2 – **R. Nin,** Khost: 89.1 – **R. Omid-e Jawan,** Ghazni: 96.9 – **R. Paiwastoon,** Terinkot: 89.9 – **R. Paktika Voice,** Zareh Sharan: 92.9 – **R. Payman,** Baghlan: 90.0 – **R. Pashtun Voice,** Shahr-e Sharan: 89.4 – **R. Payam,** Faizabad: 94.7 – **R. Qarabagh,** Kabul prov: 94.8 – **R. Qoyash,** Maimana: 89.0 – **R. Rabia-e Balkhi,** Mazar-e-Sharif: 89.7 – **R. Rah-e Farda,** Kabul: 92.0 – **R. Roshani,** Kunduz: 89.0 – **R. Rustam,** Aibak: 88.1 – **R. Sabawoon,** Lashkar Ga: 88.0 0.6kW – **R. Sadat,** Ghazni: 90.9 – **R. Safa,** Nangarhar prov: 89.7 – **R. Sahar,** Herat: 88.7 – **R. Samun,** Lashkar Ga: 88.6 – **R. Sana,** Pol-e Khumri: 87.8 – **R. Setara,** Kabul: 87.2 – **R. Setara-e Sahar,** Balkh: 91.3 – **R. Shahr,** Kabul: 95.5 – **R. Shahrwand,** Samangan prov: 87.8 – **R. Sharq,** Jalalabad: 91.3 – **R. Solh-e Paygham,** Khost: 88.8 – **R. Spin Ghar,** Ghani Khel: 89.4 – **R. Tahlim ul-Salaam,** Kandahar: 94.6 – **R. Takharistan,** Taloqan: 93.2 – **R. Tamana,** Faryab: 89.6 – **R. Tanin,** Shindan: 89.7 – **R. Tiraj Mir,** Pol-e Khumri: 89.4 – **R. Waranga,** Kandahar: 95.2 0.6kW – **R. Watan** Kabul: 100.8 – **R. Watandar:** Herat/Kabul 87.5 0.5/1kW – **R. VO Adalat,** Chagcharan: 90.3 – **R. VO Baharistan,** Baharak: 95.3 – **R. VO Haqiqat,** Aibaq: 90.0 – **R. VO Islam,** Kabul: 104.3 – **R. VO Jawan,** Herat University: 92.3 – **R. VO Kishm,** Badakhshan prov: 90.3 – **R. VO Najrab,** Kapisa prov: 96.0 – **R. VO Peace,** Naray: 94.0 – **R. VO Peace,** Jabul Saraj: 96.7 – **R. VO Wolas,** Khost: 96.4 – **R. Yawali Voice,** Sayedabad: 94.4 – **R. Zafar,** Paghman: 96.5 – **R. Zala Kunar,** Azadabad: 89.2 – **R. Zalah,** Kunduz prov.: 106.6 0.6kW – **R. Zhwandoon,** Kabul: 107.0 – **R. Zohra,** Kunduz: 89.8 – **R. Zrak,** Kunduz: 96.9 – **R. Zuhal,** Herat prov: 90.0 – **Rana FM,** Kandahar: 88.5. W: www.ranafm.org – **Salam Watandar,** Kabul: 98.9 1kW. W: salamwatandar.com – **Shamshad FM,** Ghanikhel: 101.1 – **Spogmai R,** Kabul: 102.2 – **University R.** (UNESCO), Kabul: 106.7 1.2kW, Herat 92.3 – **VO Afghan Women** (UNESCO), Kabul 96.3 10kW, Herat 88.7 – **Zala FM,** Naray: 89.2 600W – **Zawon Voice R,** Khost: 99.7 – **Zenat R,** Pol-e Alam: 105.7.
NB: many stations are Internews affiliates and relay their news prgr: "Salam Watandar". **W:** internews.org

Military stations and International relays
American Forces Network: (powers 50-500W, fqs in MHz) Kabul 104.6/105.8MHz, Adraskan/Bagram/Jalalabad/Mazar-e-Sharif/Nangarhar/Paktika/Shindad/Wardak 94.1/96.1/98.1, Kunar/Khost/Logar 94.1MHz, Garm Ser: 94.5MHz Kandahar: 91.1/92.1/97.5/98.1. **W:** afrts.dodmedia.osd.mil
BBC World Sce: in English/Pashto/Dari/Uzbek/Farsi: Kunar 87.5, Gardez 87.9, Konduz 88.1, Ghazni/Saloquan/Taloqan 88.3, Ghazni 88.3, Faizabad 88.4, Kabul/Bamian/Jalalabad/Pol-e-Khomri/Sheberghan/Zareh Sharan 89.0, Herat/Lashkar-Ga/Mazar-e-Sharif 89.2, Kandahar 90.0, Khost 90.1, Maimana 92.1, Jabal-os-Saraj 92.2, Kabul 101.6.
BFBS R: Kabul 101.5/103.7/104.0/105.8, Lashkar Ga: 101.5/103.7, Nad' Ali: 101.5/103.7, Nahr-e Saraj 101.5/103.7, Now Zad 101.5/103.7, Chakhansur: 101.5/103.7, Dand 101.5/103.7, Wasner 101.5/103.7, Gurkha R: Kabul 107.5, Lashkar Ga 106.3, Nad' Ali 106.3, Nahr-e Saraj 106.3, Now Zad 106.3, Chakhansur 106.3, Dand 106.3, Wasner 106.3. **W:** bfbs.com/radio
R Andernach: Feyzabad/Hazrar e-Sultan/Kabul/Kunduz/Mazar-e-Sharif/Talah wa Barfak 103.7, Feyzabad/Kunduz/Mazar-e-Sharif 94.0, Feyzabad 107.5. **W:** radio-andernach.bundeswehr.de

Radio Bayan: Kabul 88.5 1kW, 98.3MHz 3kW, Eastern Provinces 93.8/95.8/98.3/98.6/99.3/101.1/102.8/103/107.1 0.6-3kW, Southern Provinces 93.8/98.6/99.3/100.1/100.5/101.1/101.6/102.8/103.4/10 3.7/104.1/105.9/106.3/106.6/107.5/107.7 0.7-3kW, South-western Provinces 93.8/97.4/100.5 3kW, Western Provinces 94.7/95.5/97.0/97.5/107.1 3kW. **Commando R:** Kabul/Jalalabad/Gardez/Mazar-e-Sharif/ Kandahar/Helmand,/Herat: 95.1 3kW.
R. Zet: Ghazni 102.8/106.3 100W. **W:** radiozet.pl
Deutsche Welle/Monte-Carlo Doualiya: Kabul: 90.5 1kW.
R. France Int: Kabul 89.5 0.2kW.
Many stns supporting the former Taliban gov. rep. to be in operation.

ALASKA (USA)

L.T: UTC -9h (10 Mar-3 Nov -8h). Aleutian Is. UTC -10h (10 Mar-3 Nov -9h) — **Pop:** 627,000 — **Pr.L:** English — **E.C:** 60Hz, 120/240V — **ITU:** ALS

FEDERAL COMMUNICATIONS COMMISSION (FCC)
see USA for details

ALASKA BROADCASTERS ASSOCIATION
700 W 41st Ave, Anchorage AK 99503 ☎+1 907 258 2424
W: alaskabroadcasters.org

MW	kHz	Call	kW	N	Location
2)	550	KTZN	3.1/5		Anchorage
3)	560	KVOK	1		Kodiak
4)	580	KRSA	5	d	Petersburg
5)	590	KHAR	5		Anchorage
6)	620	KGTL	5		Homer
7)	630	KJNO	5/1		Juneau
8)	630	KIAM	10/3.1		Nenana
9)	640	KYUK	10		Bethal
2)	650	KENI	50		Anchorage
11)	660	KFAR	10		Fairbanks
12)	670	KDLG	10		Dillingham
13)	680	KBRW	10		Barrow
14)	700	KBYR	10		Anchorage
15)	720	KOTZ	10		Kotzebue
5)	750	KFQD	50		Anchorage
17)	770	KCHU	9.7		Valdez
18)	780	KNOM	25/14		Nome
19)	790	KCAM	5		Glennallen
7)	800	KINY	10/7.6		Juneau
11)	820	KCBF	10		Fairbanks
22)	830	KSDP	1		Sand Point
24)	850	KICY	50	*	Nome
25)	870	KSKO	10		McGrath
26)	890	KBBI	10		Homer
27)	900	KZPA	5	r	Fort Yukon
28)	910	KIYU	5		Galena
29)	920	KSRM	5		Soldotna
30)	930	KTKN	5/1		Ketchikan
12)	930	KNSA	4.2	r	Unalakleet
32)	950	KSEW	1		Seward
33)	970	KFBX	10		Fairbanks
34)	1020	KOAN	10	d	Eagle River
34)	1080	KUDO	10		Anchorage
35)	1110	KAGV	10		Big Lake
29)	1140	KSLD	10		Soldotna
37)	1170	KJNP	50/21		North Pole
38)	1230	KIFW	1		Sitka
39)	1230	KVAK	1		Valdez
7)	1330	KXXJ	10/3		Juneau
41)	1430	KWAP	1		Wasilla
42)	1450	KLAM	0.25		Cordova

d=directional *=directional 0800-1200 r=relay +=F.Pl.

FM	Call	MHz	kW	Location	FM	Call	MHz	kW	Location
	KAKL	88.5	11	Anchorage	2)	KASH-FM	107.5	100	Anchorage
	KATB	89.3	4.9	Anchorage		KJNR	91.9	3	Bethel
	KNBA	90.3	100	Anchorage	8)	KYKD	100.1	12	Bethel
	KSKA	91.1	100	Anchorage		KCUK	88.1	6	Chevak
	KFAT	92.9	10	Anchorage		K220CL	91.9	1	Chignik
	KAFC	93.7	27	Anchorage	11)	KTDZ	103.9	3	College
5)	KEAG	97.3	55	Anchorage	42)	KCDV	100.9	1.2	Cordova
34)	KLEF	98.1	25	Anchorage		KRUP	99.1	6	Dillingham
2)	KYMG	98.9	100	Anchorage		KDJF	93.5	20.5	Ester
2)	KBFX	100.5	25	Anchorage	27)	KUAC	89.9	38	Fairbanks
2)	KGOT	101.3	26	Anchorage		KSUA	91.5	3	Fairbanks
	KDBZ	102.1	23	Anchorage	11)	KXLR	95.9	25	Fairbanks
5)	KMXS	103.1	100	Anchorage		KYSC	96.9	5.8	Fairbanks
5)	KBRJ	104.1	50	Anchorage		KWLF	98.1	28	Fairbanks
34)	KNLT	105.7	51	Anchorage	33)	KAKQ-FM	101.1	50	Fairbanks
5)	KWHL	106.5	100	Anchorage	33)	KIAK-FM	102.5	100	Fairbanks

FM	Call	MHz	kW	Location	FM	Call	MHz	kW	Location
33)	KKED	104.7	50	Fairbanks	3)	KRXX	101.1	3.1	Kodiak
	KEUL	88.9	1.4	Girdwood	8)	KAKN	100.9	3	Naknek
19)	KCAM-FM	88.7	2	Glennallen		KXBA	93.3	50	Nikiski
17)	KXGA	90.5	3.2	Glennallen	18)	KNOM-FM	96.1	1	Nome
	KHNS	102.3	3	Haines	24)	KICY-FM	100.3	1	Nome
	KHGO	89.9	3	Homer	37)	KJNP-FM	100.3	25	North Pole
6)	KWVV-FM	103.5	100	Homer		KFSK	100.9	2	Petersburg
37)	KJHA	88.7	1	Houston		KIBH-FM	91.7	1	Seward
	KBBO-FM	92.1	10	Houston		KSBZ	103.1	3.1	Sitka
34)	KZND-FM	94.7	15	Houston		KCAW	104.7	3.6	Sitka
	KXLW	96.3	10	Houston	29)	KKIS-FM	96.5	10	Soldotna
	KCAI	88.1	1.7	Juneau	6)	KPEN-FM	101.7	25	Soldotna
	KLSF	89.7	1.7	Juneau		KUHB-FM	91.9	15	St. Paul
	KXLL	100.7	6	Juneau		KWMD	90.1	1.2	Sterling
	KRNN	102.7	6	Juneau	34)	KMVV	104.9	45	Sterling
	KTOO	104.3	1.4	Juneau	32)	KKNI	105.3	7	Sterling
7)	KTKU	105.1	3.8	Juneau		KTNA	88.9	7.2	Talkeetna
20)	KSUP	106.3	10	Juneau		K220AD	91.9	1.1	Valdez
	KABN-FM	88.9	3.2	Kasilof	39)	KVAK-FM	93.3	1.2	Valdez
29)	KFSE	106.9	8	Kasilof	41)	KMBQ-FM	99.7	51	Wasilla
	KDLL	91.9	4.9	Kenai		KAYO	100	50	Wasilla
29)	KWHQ-FM	100.1	25	Kenai		KSTK	101.7	3	Wrangell
	KRBD	105.3	3.4	Ketchikan		NB: Txs below 1kW not listed			

Addresses:
2) 800 E Dimond Blvd, Ste. #3-370, Anchorage AK 99515-2058 – **3)** Box 708, Kodiak AK 99615-0708 – **4)** Box 650, Petersburg AK 99833-0650 – **5)** 301 Arctic Slope Ave #200, Anchorage AK 99518-3035 – **6)** Box 109, Homer AK 99603-0109 – **7)** 3161 Channel Dr #2, Juneau AK 99801-7815 – **8)** Box 474, Nenana AK 99760-0474 – **9)** Box 468, Bethal AK 99559-0468 – **11)** 819 1st Ave #A, Fairbanks AK 99701-4449 – **12)** Box 670, Dillingham AK 99576-0670 – **13)** Box 109, Barrow AK 99723-0109 – **14)** 833 Gambell St, Anchorage AK 99501-3756 – **15)** Box 78, Kotzebue AK 99752-0070 – **17)** Box 467, Valdez AK 99686-0467 – **18)** Box 988, Nome AK 99762-0988 – **19)** Box 249, Glennallen AK 99588-0249 – **22)** Box 328, Sand Point AK 99661 – **24)** Box 820, Nome AK 99762-0820. Russian 0800-1300 (Summer -1h) – **25)** Box 70, McGrath AK 99627-0070 – **26)** 3913 Kachemak Way, Homer AK 99603-7618 – **27)** Box 50, Fort Yukon AK 99740-0050 – **28)** Box 165, Galena AK 99741-0165 – **29)** 40960 Kalifornsky Beach Rd, Kenai AK 99611-6445 – **30)** 526 Stedman St, Ketchikan AK 99901-6629 – **32)** Box 2414, Seward AK 99664-2414 – **33)** 548 9th Ave, Fairbanks AK 99701-4902 – **34)** 4700 Business Park Blvd #E-44A, Anchorage AK 99503-7176 – **35)** 4723 King David St, Houston Park AK 99694 – **37)** Box 56359, North Pole AK 99705-1359 – **38)** 611 Lake St, Sitka AK 99835-7402 – **39)** Box 367, Valdez AK 99686-0367 – **41)** 2200 E Parks Hwy, Wasilla AK 99654-7355 – **42)** Box 60, Cordova AK 99574-0060

EXTERNAL SERVICE: Radio Station KNLS
see International Broadcasting section

ALBANIA

L.T: UTC +1h (31 Mar-27 Oct +2h) — **Pop:** 3.6 million — **Pr.L:** Albanian — **E.C:** 50Hz, 220V — **ITU:** ALB

KËSHILLI KOMBËTAR I RADIOS DHE TELEVIZIONIT (KKRT) (NATIONAL COUNCIL OF RADIO & TELEVISION)
Rruga "Abdi Toptani", Ish Hotel Drini, Tirana. ☎+355 4 2233326
+355 4 2226287 **W:** kkrt.gov.al **E:** kkrt@kkrt.gov.al **LP:** Chairman: Mesila Doda. Tech. Dir: Pirro Koci.

RADIOTELEVIZIONI SHQIPTAR (RTSH) ALBANIAN RADIO & TELEVISION (Pub.)
Rruga Ismail Qemali 11, Tirana ☎ +355 4 2256059 +355 4 2227745 **W:** rtsh.al **E:** marketing@rtsh.al **L.P:** DG: Petrit Beci. Tech. Dir: Agron Aranitasi, Dir Stns: Eng. Arben Mehillu.

FM	MHz	kW	Ch	FM	MHz	kW	Ch
Llogora	88.3	1		Cervenake	99.1	1	1
Korce	89.5	1	2	Tirana(Dajt)	99.5	10	1
Tarabosh	91.0	1	1	Zvernec	99.8	3	1
Shkodra	92.0	2	R	Erseke	100.2	1	1
Mile	93.0	1	1	Kukesi	100.4	1	R
Ishem	95.4	1	1	Qafe Prush	100.7	1	1
Petresh	95.4	1		Homesh	102.2	1	1
Tirana(Dajt)	95.8	2	2	Gjirokastra	102.5	0.3	R
Mide	96.0	3	1	Sopot	107.0	1	1

+11 more txs under 1kW.
D.Prgr: 1st Ch.: 24h, **2nd Ch.:** 24h, **Regional Ch.:** 0600-2000.

EXTERNAL SERVICES: R. Tirana + relays (CRI & TWR) on MW 1215/1395/1458kHz and SW: see International Broadcasting section.

Nationwide Private FM Stations:
+2 RADIO
Rr. Aleksandër Moisiu Nr 76/1, ish kinostudjo Shqipëria e Re, Tirana ☎+355 4 2368490 **W:** plus2radio.com.al **E:** info@plus2radio.com.al **LP:** Mgr: Leonard Gremi.

FM	MHz	kW	FM	MHz	kW
Fushe Dajt	89.8	63	Zvernec	96.3	0.3
Cervenake	90.3	4	Gllave	97.6	3
Mide	94.3	6	Tirana/Dajt	101.6	89

TOP ALBANIA RADIO
Piramida QNK, Blvd. Dëshmorët e Kombit, Tirana. ☎+355 4 2247592 ◫ +355 4 2247493 **W:** topalbaniaradio.com **E:** contact@topalbaniaradio.com

FM	MHz	kW	FM	MHz	kW
Kerculle	93.0	1	Sarande	100.6	1
Shkoder	94.1	2	Mide	101.3	15
Korce	95.0	2	Elbasan	102.2	2
Gllave	96.0	1	Sopot	104.0	5
Dürres	99.0	1	Lezhe	104.3	1
Tirana/Dajt	100.0	15	Ardenice	104.5	2

Other Private FM Stations

FM Station	MHz	kW	FM Station	MHz	kW
1) R. Ngjallja	88.5	6	1) R. Koha	98.1	2
1) R. New Planet	89.0	3	1) R. Aldo 03	98.8	2
1) R. Kontakt	89.3	2	1) R. Super Star	99.0	-
1) AMC Love R.	90.7	2	16) R.Armonia	99.2	0.4
2) R. Alfa	90.9	1	10) R. Saranda	100.0	0.5
3) R. Argjiropoli	91.0	1	1) R. Club FM	100.4	13
1) R. Skorpion	91.4	0.3	11) R. E Pare	100.4	0.1
4) R. +3	91.6	1	12) R. Prespa	100.8	0.3
1) R. Italia	92.4	0.4	1) R. Top Gold	100.8	56
5) R. Planet	93.0	2	1) R. Boom Boom	101.2	38
1) R. Nacional AH	93.4	1	1) R. Alfa & Omega	102.6	6
6) R. Klea	93.9	1	14) R. Val e Kalter	103.3	2
7) R. Alpo	94.1	0.1	1) R. Club FM	104.3	1
1) R. Eurostar	94.5	2	1) R. Rock	104.6	25
6) R. Fantasy	94.7	0.3	1) R. Perla	105.0	1
8) R. Ruzvelt	94.8	0.1	1) R. Ime	105.4	0.5
9) R. Emanuel	95.7	4	4) R. Star	105.5	2
1) R. Oxygen	96.1	3	2) R. Club Alsion	106.3	1
1) R. Real	96.4	2	15) R. Perla	106.4	0.5
2) R. Eurostar	96.6	1	1) R. NRG	106.6	2
1) R. Rash	97.0	3	1) R. Stinet	106.9	1
1) R. Muzika Jone	97.3	2	9) R. Magic Star	107.0	4
1) R. +7	97.7	6	4) R. Fieri	107.2	1
9) R. ABC	98.0	2	1) R. House of Arts	107.7	2

Locations: 1) Fushe Dajt, 2) Petresh, 3) Kerculle, 4) Fier, 5) Tirana, 6) Kavaje, 7) Kerculle, 8) Memaliaj, 9) Korce 10) Mile 11) Burrel, 12) Prespe, 13) Shkoder, 14) Zvernec, 15) Dürres, 16) Bularat.

Other FM stations:
R. France International: Fushe Dajt/Korca 102.0MHz 1kW – **VOA Europe:** Tirana (Dajt) 107.4MHz 0.8kW – **BBC Europe:** Tirana (Dajt) 103.9MHz 2.2kW – **Deutsche Welle:** Tirana 106.0MHz 6.3kW

ALGERIA

L.T: UTC +1h — **Pop:** 35 million — **Pr.L:** Arabic, French, Berber dialects — **E.C:** 50Hz, 230V — **ITU:** ALG

TÉLÉDIFFUSION D'ALGERIE (TDA)
Direction Générale, B.P. 50, Bouzaréah, Route de Baïnam, 16340 Algér ☎+213 21 901717 ◫ +213 21 902424 **W:** tda.dz **E:** contact@tda.dz **LP:** DG: Abdelmalek Houyou. Dir. Tech. Sces: Mohamed Hacine Ladj.

RADIO ALGÉRIENNE (RA, Pub.)
DCRR, 12 Rue Shakespeare, El Mouradia, Algér ☎+213 21 230805 ◫ +213 21 694620 **W:** radioalgerie.dz **E:** radionet@radioalgerie.dz **LP:** DG: Tewfik Khelladi.

	LW/MW	kHz	kW	Pr.	Hrs.
	Béchar	153	**2000	1	24h
	Ouargla	198	**2000	1	24h
	Tipaza	252	*1500	3	24h
	F'Kirina	531	600	J	24h
	Sidi Hamadouche	549	600	J	24h
20)	Touggourt	558	10	1/L	24h
4)	Béchar	576	*400	L	24h
30)	Tindouf	666	10	1/L	24h

	LW/MW	kHz	kW	Ch.	Hrs.
	Aboudid (Ain el H.)	693	5	2	0400-2400
1)	Reggane	693	10	1/L	24h
14)	Laghouat	702	25	3/L	0500-0100
12)	In Amenas	738	5	1/L	24h
12)	Djanet	783	5	1/L	24h
24)	El Oued	783	10	1/L	24h
	Béchar	837	5	3	0500-0100
10)	Ghardaïa	873	10	1/L	24h
	Ouled Fayet	*891	600/300	1	24h
	Tamanrasset	909	10	1	24h
1)	Timimoun	927	10	1/L	24h
	Ouled Fayet	981	100	2	0400-2400
20)	Hassi Messaoud	1026	10	1/L	24h
	Illizi	1071	5	1	24h
1)	Adrar	1089	10	1/L	24h
27)	In Salah	1161	5	1/L	24h
	Ouled Fayet	1422	50	C	0400-0100

*) half-power 1900-0600. **running on low power.

FM (MHz)	1	2	3	I	J	kW(TRP)
Adrar			88.8			2
Aflou	90.7					10
Akfadou		91.8				10
Bains Romains				95.6		0.1
Bordj El Bahri	91.0		89.2	104.2		2
Chréa			88.4	101.5	94.7	10
Doukhane			91.0			2
Gara Djebilet	98.0					0.1
Kef El Akhal				87.6		10
Mahouna		97.6				2.5
M'cid		91.9				10
Mecheria	87.8					10
Meghriss	93.5					10
Nador		88.4	91.5			10
Puits des Zouaves					92.4	0.1
Tessala	102.7					2
Tiaret	89.4					2
Tizi Ouzou		88.0				0.1

FM Station, location	MHz	kW(TRP)	Ch.
14) R. Laghouat, Aflou	87.6	10	3/L
5) R. Chlef, Ain N'sour	87.7	10	3/L
28) R. Tébessa, Doukhane	87.9	2	1/L
3) R. Batna, Metlili	88.1	10	2/L
11) R. El Tarf, Oum Ali	88.3	2.5	1/L
26) R. Soummam, Akfadou	88.7	10	1/L
2) R. Annaba, M'cid	88.8	10	2/L
4) R. Béchar	89.3	5	1/L
39) R. Tipaza	89.9		1/L
9) R. Setif, Megriss	90.4	10	3/L
21) R. Rélizane, Ain N'sour	90.8	10	3/L
18) R. Naama, Mecheria	90.9	10	3/L
16) R. Djelfa, Sbaa Mokrane	91.1	2	3/L
32) R. Biskra, Metlili	91.2	10	1/L
7) R. El Bahdja, Chréa	91.5	10	L
1) R. Adrar	91.9	2	1/L
20) R. Ouargla	92.1	10	1/L
29) R. Tiaret	92.5	2	B/L
9) R. Oran, Tessala	92.7	10	3/L
44) R. Tizi Ouzou, Belloua	93.0	0.25	1/L
12) R. Illizi	93.5	0.1	1/L
6) R. Constantine, Kef El Akhal	93.9	10	1/L
7) R. El Bahdja, Bordj el Bahri	94.2	2	L
32) R. Tlemcen, Nador	94.7	10	1/L
23) R. Skikda, Filfila	94.8	2.5	1/L
25) R. Souk Ahras, M'cid	95.1	10	3/L
43) R. Aïn Defla, Anneb	95.2	0.25	1/L
36) R. Aïn Témouchent, Tessala	95.9	10	1/L
45) R. Oum el Bouaghi, Chettaia	96.4	2.5	1/L
46) R. Blida, Bordj el Bahri	97.5	2.5	1/L
10) R. Ghardaïa, El Golea	98.0	2.5	1/L
47) R. Guelma, Mahouna	97.6	2.5	1/L
24) R. El Oued, 2 locations	98.0		1/L
14) R. Laghouat, Hassi R'Mel	98.0	2.5	1/L
27) R. Tamanrasset, 4 locations	98.0	1	1/L
30) R. Tindouf	98.0	0.1	1/L
15) R. Mascara, Chareb Rih	98.5	3	1/L
37) R. Bordj Bou Arreridj, Tafartas	98.7	2.5	1/L
22) R. Sidi Bel Abbés, Tessala	99.2	10	1/L
34) R. Bouira, Dirah	99.8	2.5	1/L
8) R. El Bayadh	100.1	0.1	1/L
40) R. Médéa	100.7	0.1	1/L
41) R. Saïda	101.3	0.1	1/L

FM	Station, location	MHz	kW(TRP)	Ch.
42)	R. Boumerdes	102.6	0.1	1/L
38)	R. Mila, Kef Bouderga	102.7	2.5	1/L
13)	R. Jijel, Kern	103.0	2.5	1/L
33)	R. Tissemsilt	103.2	0.1	3/L
17)	R. Mostaganem	104.0	2.5	1/L
48)	R. M'Sila	104.5	1.5	1/L
35)	R. Khenchela, Chettaia	105.7	2.5	1/L

+25 more stations under 1kW.

D.Prgr: 1=Chaîne 1 in Arabic: 24h. Satellite Eutelsat 702MHz.
2=Chaîne 2 in Tamazight: 0400-2400. Satellite Eutelsat 728MHz.
3=Chaîne 3 in French, 0500-0100. Satellite Eutelsat 738MHz.
I=R. Algérie Internationale in Arabic, French, E. & Spanish: 0800-2300.
C= incl. **R. Koran** 0400-0800, **R. UFC** 0800-1200, **Chaîne 1** 1200-1600,
R. Culture in Arabic: 1600-2200 and Chaîne 3 2200-0100 on 1422kHz.
J: Jil FM: youth channel: 24h.
L=Local stations: times of local prgrs vary by stn (may be longer in
summer than winter), but at least between 0800-1600. Most local stns
transmit Chaîne 1 at other times (Some stations rep. also occ. with
R. Algérie Int, Koran and Culture relay). Many local stns carry Arabic
news from Chaîne 1 1100-1200 and at other times.

Addresses and other information for local stations:
1) B.P. 309, Adrar. **W:** radio-adrar.dz – **2)** 7, Boulevard Radji Mokhtar,
Quartier Annasr, Annaba. **W:** annabafm.net – **3)** B.P. 453, Batna. **W:**
radio-batna.dz – **4)** Cité Badr, B.P. 330, Béchar. **W:** saoura.radiobechar.
com – **5)** Aïn N'sour – **6)** B.P. 28B El Koudia, Constantine. **W:** radio-con-
stantine.dz – **7) W:** elbahdjafm.com – **8)** B.P. 195, El Bayadh. **W:** radio-
elbayadh.dz – **9)** B.P. 54, Aïn Tbinet, Sétif. **W:** radio-setif.dz – **10)** B.P.
17, Ghardaïa – **11)** El Tarf. **W:** eltarffm-dz.net – **12)** Route de l'aéroport,
B.P. 230, Illizi – **13)** B.P. 48, Jijel – **14)** radiolagh.voila.net – **15)** Place
Mostfa Ben Iouhami, Mascara – **16)** Djelfa – **17)** Place El Matemar, B.P.
1014, Mostaganem 027000. **W:** radiomostaganem.net – **18)** Av. du 1
Novembre, BP 223, Naama. **W:** radionaamafm.com – **19) W:** radio-oran.
dz – **20)** Hussat, B.P. 83, Ouargla. **W:** radio-ouargla.dz – **21)** 15 Rue
Ismail Mustapha, Maison de Culture, Rélizane. **W:** radiorelizane.net –
22) Ex Gare de l'État, Sidi Bel Abbés 022000 – **23)** Porte des Aurès, B.P.
55, Skikda – **24)** Cité Reml El Oued, B.P. 172, El Oued. **W:** radio-eloued.
com – **25)** Blvd. Messous Hamid, Souk Ahras – **26)** Boulevard Youcef
Bouchebah, Béjaia. **W:** radio-bejaia.com – **27)** B.P. 1080, Tamanrasset
– **28)** Unité de Tébéssa, Parc des Loisirs, Tébéssa – **29)** Rue des Fréres
Saim Tiaret, B.P. 671, Tiaret. **W:** radiotiaret.dz – **30)** B.P. 213, Agence
Enasr, Tindouf – **31)** B.P. 44K, Tlemcen – **32)** Av. Idriss Mohamed, Biskra.
W: radiobiskra.com – **33)** Tissemsilt – **34)** Bouira – **35)** Khenchela – **36)**
Aïn Témouchent. **W:** radioaintemouchent.com – **37)** Bordj Bou Arreridj.
W: radio-bordjbouarreridj.dz – **38)** Mila – **39)** Tipaza – **40)** Médéa – **41)**
Saïda. **W:** saidafm.com – **42)** Boumerdes – **43)** Aïn Defla – **44)** Tizi
Ouzou – **45)** Oum el Bouaghi. **W:** radio-oumelbouaghi.dz – **46)** Blida
– **47)** Guelma. **W:** radio-guelma.dz – **47)** M'Sila. **W:** radio-msila.dz
Ann: Chaîne 1: "Al Kanet al Oula min Idha'at al-Djazairiyah.", 2:
"Radio Isnath", 3: "Chaine Trois, Radio Algérienne", C: "Idha'atul-
Thaqafiyah", K:"Idha'atul-Koran al Karim". **IS:** Oriental Lute (Ud)

ANDORRA

L.T: UTC + 1h (31 Mar-27 Oct: + 2h) — **Pop:** 82,000 — **Pr.L:** Catalan,
French, Spanish — **E.C:** 50Hz, 230V — **ITU:** AND

ANDORRA TELECOM
Av. Meritxell 112, Andorra la Vella, AD 500 ☎+376 875000 🖷
+376 821414 **E:** comunicacio@andorratelecom.ad
W: www.andorratelecom.ad **L.P:** Admin Dir: Jaume Salvat Font. Dir.
International relations & Television: Xavier Jimenez Beltran.

FM	MHz	kW	Location	Station
22)	87.8	0.3	Pic de Carroi	R. María España (r)
1)	88.1	0.3	Pic de Carroi	Cadena Dial
2)	89.0	0.3	Pic de Carroi/Pic de Maià	R7P - RAC 1
2)	89.5	0.3	Pic de Carroi	Europa FM
2)	90.1	0.3	Bony de la Caubera	R. Tele Taxi
11)	90.7		Pas de la Casa	R. Montaillou (r)
10)	90.9		Bony de la Caubera	iCAT FM
4)	91.4	1	Pic de Maià	R. Nacional d'Andorra
1)	92.1	1	Pic de Carroi	Maxima FM
1)	92.6	1	Pic de Carroi	M80 R.
2)	93.3	0.3	Pic de Carroi	R. Valira/Onda Cero
5)	93.8	0.3	Pic de Carroi/Pic de Maià	Flaix FM
4)	94.2	1	Pic de Maià	R. Nacional d'Andorra
9)	94.6	0.3	Pic de Carroi	Pròxima FM
2)	95.0	0.3	Pic de Carroi	R. Valira/ABC Punto R.
10)	95.6		Bony de la Caubera	Catalunya Informació
5)	96.0	1	Pic de Carroi/Pic de Maià	Andorra 1/R. Flaixbac

FM	MHz	kW	Location	Station
10)	96.5		Bony de la Caubera	Catalunya Música
4)	97.0	1	Pic de Carroi/Pic de Maià	Andorra Música
3)	97.7		Sant Julià de Lòria	R. Festa Major
2)	98.1	0.1	Organyà	R. Valira/Onda Cero
2)	98.5	0.1	Pic de Carroi	R. Valira/Onda Cero
2)	98.9	1	Pic de Carroi	Kiss FM (relay)
9)	100.2		Bony de la Caubera	Pròxima FM
6)	100.6	0.3	Pic de Carroi	N.R.J. (r)
6)	101.5	1	Pic de Carroi/Pic de Maià	COPE/AD Ràdio
6)	101.8	1	Pic de Carroi/Pic de Maià	France Inter (relay)
1)	102.3	0.5	Pic de Carroi/Pic de Maià	R. SER Principat d'Andorra
6)	102.6	1	Pic de Carroi/Pic de Maià	France Musiques (r)
1)	103.3	0.3	Pic de Carroi/Pic de Maià	Los 40 Principales
6)	104.0	1	Pic de Carroi/Pic de Maià	France Culture (r)
10)	104.6	1	Pic de Carroi/Pic de Maià	Catalunya R. (r)
6)	106.0	1.2	Pic de Carroi/Pic de Maià	RNE R. 4 (r)
6)	106.8	1.2	Pic de Carroi/Pic de Maià	RNE R. 1 (r)
7)	107.5	1.2	Pic de Carroi	R. Principat/R. Estel
6)	107.9	1.2	Pic de Carroi/Pic de Maià	RNE R. 3 (r)

Addresses & other information:
1) C. Prat de la Creu, 32, AD-500 Andorra la Vella ☎ +376 808300 🖷
+376 828301 – **2)** Cadena Pirenaica de Ràdio i Televisió, SA, Av. Príncep
Benlloch 24, 200 Encamp ☎ +376 732000 🖷 +376 834831 **E:** info@
cadenapirenaica.com (R. Valira stations at C/ del Parnal 2, "Edifici Prat
de Casa de Escaldes", 500 Andorra la Vella) – **3)** Plaça Major, 9, 600
Sant Julià de Lòria ☎ +376 842601 (temporary station only broadcast
last week of July) – **4)** Baixada del Molí 24, 500 Andorra la Vella ☎
+376 873777 🖷 +376 863242 **W:** www.rtva.ad **E:** rtva@rtva.ad **L.P:**
DG: Francesc Robert Ribes – **5)** Av. Meritxell 75, 500 Andorra la Vella
☎ +376 862288 🖷 +376 862287 – **6)** Servei de Telecomunicacions
d'Andorra, Av. Meritxell 112, 500 Andorra la Vella – **7)** Passeig del Parc
16-18, 25700 Seu d'Urgell, Spain ☎ +973 354400 **E:** radio@radioprin-
cipat.com Frequent relays of R. Estel, Barcelona – **8)** Avda Bonaventura
Riberaygua, 39, 5 Pis, Edifici Alexandre, 500 Andorra la Vella ☎+376
877477 **W:** www.diariandorra.ad **E:** laradio@adradio.ad – **9)** Carrer del
Parnal 2, 700 Escaldes Engordany – **10)** Av. Diagonal 614-616, 08021
Barcelona, Spain – **11)** 09110 Montaillou - Le Village, France **E:** radio.
montaillou@orange.fr

ANGOLA

L.T: UTC +1h — **Pop:** 13 million — **Pr.L:** Portuguese + ethnic — **E.C:**
50Hz, 220V — **ITU:** AGL

MINISTÉRIO DA COMUNICAÇÃO SOCIAL (MCS)
Av. Comandante Valódia 1°&2° amdar, CP. 2608, Luanda ☎+244
22 2443495 🖷 +244 22 2392649 **W:** www.mcs.gov.ao **L.P:** Min:
Carolina Cerqueiro.

RÁDIO NACIONAL DE ANGOLA (RNA, Pub.)
Av. Comandante Gika, CP. 1329, Luanda ☎+244 22 2323172 🖷
+244 22 2324647 **W:** www.rna.ao **E:** dgeral@rna.ao **L.P:** CEO: Pedro
Cabral. PD: Júlio Mendonça. TD: Cândido R. Pinto.

MW	kHz	kW	Prgr.	H of tr
Mulenvos	945	25	N/E	24h
Mulenvos	1088	25	A	24h

SW	kHz	kW	Prgr.	H of tr.
Mulenvos	4950	25	A	24h
Mulenvos	±7217	15	N/A	24h

FM (MHz): Luanda 4kW: 93.5 (A), 94.5 (5), 96.5MHz (FME), 99.9 (RL),
101.4MHz (N).
Ann: "Rádio Nacional de Angola".
Prgrs: A=Canal A in Portuguese (general coverage): 24h. **N:**
on the h. **N=Rádio N'Gola Yetu** (ethnic): 24h. **N:** rel. Canal A.
E=External service. FME=Rádio FM Estéreo (music): 1000-2400.
RL=Rádio Luanda (capital channel): 24h. **5=Rádio 5** (sports): 0500-2300.
P=Emissora Provincial: 0400-2300, rel. A at night.

PROVINCIAL STATIONS

MW	kHz	kW	Pr	MW	kHz	kW	Pr
2) Benguela	774	50	A	16) Uíge	1296	10	P
3) Kuito	990	50	A	15) Namibe	1314	10	P
1) Mulenvos	1134	10	P	12) Saurimo	1386	10	P
17)Mbanza Congo	1152	10	P	3) Kuito	±1404	10	P
6) Huambo	1170	25	P	11) Dundo	1440	10	P
13)Malange	1197	10	P	14) Luena	±1458	10	P
7) Lubango	1233	10	P	8) Menongue	1467	10	P
9) N'dalatando	1260	10	P	10) Sumbe	±1485	10	P
4) Tenda	1278	25	A	2) Benguela	1503	10	P
17)Soyo	±*1290	1	P	4) Tenda	1530	10	P

N.B: Most transmitters r. inactive. *Reported, not confirmed.

FM	MHz	kW	Pr	FM	MHz	kW	Pr
9) Dondo	88.8	0.5	P	3) Kuito	91.0	4	A
2) Benguela	90.4	1	5	16) Uíge	91.0	4	P
7) Lubango	91.1	4	P	2) Lobito	93.5	0.25	P
4) Cabinda	91.3	4	P	13) Malange	93.7	4	P
1) Caxito	91.5	4	P	11) Xá Muteba	93.8		P
11) Capenda Cam.	91.5		A	16) Negage	94.4	0.25	P
10) Sumbe	91.7	4	P	15) Tômbwa	95.9	0.25	P
9) N'dalatando	91.8	0.15	P	14) Luena	96.0	2	P
6) Huambo	92.1	4	P	17) Mbanza Congo	96.1	2	A
5) Ondjiva	92.2	4	A	17) Mbanza Congo	97.7	0.5	P
15) Namibe	92.5	4	P	5) Ondjiva	98.0	5	P
12) Saurimo	92.5	0.25	P	9) Ambaca	98.0	0.5	P
16) Uíge	92.5	2	A	9) Golungo Alto	100.4	0.2	P
17) Soyo	92.7	0.1	P	2) Lobito	101.4	1	5
2) Benguela	92.9	4	P	2) Benguela	101.7	2	A
8) Menongue	93.1	0.25	P	2) Lobito	104.9	2	A
11) Dundo	93.3	4	P				

+30 more stations under 1kW.

Addresses & other information:
1) EP do Bengo, Caxito – **2)** EP de Benguela, C.P. 19, Benguela. Also rep. on 1200kHz – **3)** EP do Bié, C.P. 33, Kuito. Dir: Cordeiro Chimo – **4)** EP de Cabinda, Cabinda – **5)** EP de Cunene, Ondjiva – **6)** EP do Huambo, C.P. 125, Huambo – **7)** EP da Huíla, C.P. 111, Lubango – **8)** EP do Kuando-Kubango, C.P. 36, Menongue – **9)** EP do Kuanza Norte, C.P. 174, N'dalatando – **10)** EP do Kuanza Sul, C.P. 10, Sumbe – **11)** EP da Lunda Norte, Lucapa – **12)** EP da Lunda Sul, C.P. 116, Saurimo – **13)** EP de Malange, C.P. 83, Malange – **14)** EP do Moxico, C.P. 74, Luena – **15)** EP do Namibe, C.P. 174, Namibe – **16)** EP do Uíge, C.P. 140, Uíge – **17)** EP do Zaire, Mbanza Congo.
Affiliated community stations on FM in Buco Zau, Camabatela, Golungo Alto, Tombwa, Viana and Virei.

EXTERNAL SERVICE: Angolan National Radio
see International Radio section.

RÁDIO ECCLESIA (Rlg)
✉ Rua Comandante Bula 118, São Paulo, CP. 3579, Luanda ☎+244 22 2443041 🖷 +244 22 2443093 **W:** radioecclesia.org
L.P: Exec. Dir: Father Maurício Kamutu. Adm. Dir: Sister Fátima Kavate. **FM:** 97.5MHz 5kW. **D.Prgr** in Portuguese: 0500-2030.

Private station: Luanda Antena Comercial, Luanda. 95.5MHz 5kW. **W:** lacluanda.com **E:** lac@lacluanda.com

ANGUILLA (UK)

L.T: UTC -4h — **Pop**: 15,000 — **Pr.L:** English — **E.C:** 50Hz, 230V — **ITU:** AIA

RADIO ANGUILLA (Gov. Comm.)
✉ PO Box 60, The Valley ☎ +1 264 497 2218/0955 🖷 +1 264 497 5432 **E:** radioaxa@anguillanet.com **W:** www.radioaxa.com
L.P: Dir.: Farrah Banks. PM: Keithstone Greaves. Eng.: Lester Richardson **FM:** 95.5MHz, Crocus Hill. **D.Prgr:** Mon-Sat: 0925-0300, Sun: 1055-0200. N: Mon-Fri 1106 & 2306. Sat: 1106

THE CARIBBEAN BEACON (Rlg.)
✉ PO Box 690, The Valley ☎+1 264 497 4340 🖷 +1 264 497 4311
L.P: GM & CEN: Eddie Sutton
MW: 690kHz (inactive), 1610kHz 30kW
SW: 6090/11775kHz 100kW
FM: 100.1MHz 35kW
D.Prgr: 24h. Local prgrs 1000-1600 on 1610kHz
Owned by the University Network

PRIVATE FM STATIONS
KLASS FM, Wilmot Estate Rock Farm, PO Box 339, AI-2640 The Valley ☎ +1 264 497 3791 **W:** www.klass929.com **FM:** 92.9MHz – **KOOL FM**, North Side, AI-2640 The Valley ☎ +1 264 497 0103 🖷 +1 264 497 0104 **W:** www.koolfm103.com **FM:** 103.3MHz. Format: Urban Caribbean – **NEW BEGINNING 99.3 GRACE FM**, Shoal Bay, PO Box 1122, AI-2640 The Valley ☎+1 264 497 0977 🖷 +1 264 497 7977 **W:** www.nbr993.com **FM:** 99.3MHz. Format: Rlg. – **RAINBOW FM**, The Quarter, PO Box 603, The Valley ☎ +1 264 498 9305. **FM:** 93.3MHz – **UP BEAT RADIO**, Cedar Av., Rey Hill, PO Box 5045, AI-2640 The Valley ☎ +1 264 497 3354 🖷 +1 264 497 5995 **W:** www.hbr1075.com **FM:** 77.7MHz – **VOICE OF CREATION RADIO J.E.S.U.S.**, Sachasses, The Valley ☎ +1 264 497 0106 🖷 +1 264 497 0106 **FM:** 106.7MHz Format: Gospel – **VIBZ FM**, **FM:** 90.5MHz (relay Antigua) – **ZRON – TRADEWINDS RADIO**, 398 East Dania Beach Blvd. No. 210, Dania Beach, FL 33004, USA. **W:** www.tradewindsradio.com **FM:** 105.1MHz

ANTARCTICA

L.T: Antártida Argentina: UTC -3h; Antártida Chilena: UTC -4h (2 Sep 12-9 Mar 13, 13 Oct 13-8 Mar 14: -3h, subject to change); Ross Dependency (NZL)/South Pole Station: UTC +12h (30 Sep 12-7 Apr 13, 29 Sep 13-6 Apr 14: +13h) — **Pop:** 4,120 (Su), 1,066 (Wi) — **ITU:** ATA

RADIO NACIONAL ARCANGEL SAN GABRIEL
✉ LRA36 Radio Nacional Arcangel San Gabriel, Base de Ejercito Esperanza, CP 9411-Antártida Argentina, Argentina. ☎+54 2974 44 5304, +54 810 222 0776 **E:** esperanzaantar@infovia.com.ar, lra36esperanza@yahoo.com.ar **L.P:** Dir: Guillermo Bolger, Op.: Pablo González **SW:** see international section. **FM:** 97.6MHz 24h.

SOBERANIA FM, Villa Las Estrellas, Antartica Chilena, Chile. **FM:** 90.5MHz 0.1kW.
ICE FM, McMurdo Station, Ross Dependency. **FM:** 104.5MHz 0.05kW. Rel AFRTS exc. some local prgrs
KOLD, South Pole Station, Ross Dependency. **FM:** 87.5MHz
88.7 FM, McMurdo Station, Ross Dependency. **FM:** 88.7MHz
SCOTT BASE R., Scott Base, Ross Dependency. **FM:** 97.0MHz
AMERICAN FORCES ANTARCTIC NETWORK, AFAN McMurdo, US Naval Support Force Antarctica, 651 Lyons Str, Port Hueneme, CA 93043-4345, USA. **FM:** 93.9MHz 0.03kW. **D.Prgr:** 24h.

ANTIGUA & BARBUDA

L.T: UTC -4h — **Pop:** 89,000 — **Pr.L:** English — **E.C:** 60Hz, 110/220V — **ITU:** ATG

ANTIGUA & BARBUDA BROADCASTING SERVICE (Gov. Comm.)
✉ Cross Street, PO Box 590, St. John's ☎ +1 268 462 4427/0112 🖷 +1 268 462 2801 **W:** www.cmatt.com/abs.htm **L.P:** SM: Dave Lester Payne. PM: Blondell Anthony. CEN: Denis Leandro.
MW: ‡620kHz 10kW. **FM:** 90.5/101.5MHz **D.Prgr:** ABS Radio 24h

CARIBBEAN RADIO LIGHTHOUSE (Rlg.)
✉ Jolly Hill, PO Box 1057, St.John's ☎ +1 268 462 7420 🖷 +1 268 462 7420/1452 **E:** info@radiolighthouse.org **W:** www.radiolighthouse.org **L.P:** Dir: Curt Waite. Asst. Dir. & Tech. Dir: Jerry Baker. Owned by Baptist International Missions Inc.
MW: 1160kHz 10kW **FM:** 92.3MHz 2kW **D.Prgr:** MW: 0925-0145. FM: 24h

GRENVILLE RADIO LTD. (Comm.)
✉ Bird & All Saints Rd, PO Box 1100, St. John's ☎ +1 268 462 1116 🖷 +1 268 462 1101 **E:** mail@radiozdk.com **W:** www.radiozdk.com
L.P: PD: Ivor Bird
FM: Liberty Radio ZDK 97.1MHz 1kW 24h – **Power 100.1:** 100.1MHz 2.5kW 24h

OBSERVER MEDIA GROUP (Comm.)
✉ Ryans Place, High Street, PO Box 1203, St. John's ☎ +1 268 460 0911/481 9100 🖷 +1 268 725 9125 **W:** www.antiguaobserver.com
FM: Observer Radio 91.1MHz (News/talk) – **Hitz 91.9:** 91.9MHz

OTHER FM STATIONS:
ABUNDANT LIFE RADIO, Codrington Village, Barbuda ☎ +1 268 560 2676 🖷 +1 268 560 2676 **W:** www.abundantliferadio.com **E:** lifefm1031@hotmail.com **L.P:** MD: Clifton Francois. Barbuda 103.1MHz 1kW, Antigua 103.9MHz 1kW. Format: Gospel – **BBC**, Caribbean Relay Co. Ltd., PO Box 1203, St. John's ☎ +1 268 462 0994. - 89.1MHz – **CATHOLIC RADIO**, Michaels Mount, PO Box 836, St. John's ☎ +1 268 562 6868. **E:** catholicradio@candw.ag. 89.7MHz – **JAZZ FM** 97.5MHz Format: Rlg – **NICE FM**, Action Radio, All Saintes Rd, Clarkes Hill ☎ +1 268 462 4343 - 104.3MHz – **RED HOT RADIO**. Carlisle Estate ☎ +1 268 562 9805 🖷 +1 268 562 6693 **E:** redhotfm@hotmail.com – 98.5MHz – **SECOND ADVENT RADIO**, PO Box 2962, St. John's ☎ +1 268 562 1015 **W:** www.secondadventradio.com **E:** radio101.5fm@hotmail.com **L.P.:** SM Maple Lake - 101.5MHz. Format: Rlg. – **VARIETY RADIO**, Cooks Hill, Harbour View, St. John's ☎ +1 268 562 4835. **E:** varietyradio@hotmail.com **L.P:** SM: Kelvin Carter - 102.3MHz 1kW – **VIBZ FM**, Family Radio Network, Belmont School of Business, PO Box W1102, St. John's ☎ +1 268 560 7578/9 🖷 +1 268 560 7577 **W:** www.vibzfm.com - 92.9MHz

ARGENTINA

L.T: UTC -3h; exc. SC: -4h. — **Pop:** 41 million — **Pr.L:** Spanish — **E.C.:** 50Hz, 220V — **ITU:** ARG — **Int. dialling code:** +54

SECRETARIA DE COMUNICACIONES (SECOM)
✉ Tucumán 744, piso 4, (C1049AAP) Buenos Aires ☎11 5071 9412 **W:** www.secom.gov.ar

L.P: Lic. Arq.Carlos Lisandro Salas (Secretario de Comunicaciones).

COMISION NACIONAL DE COMUNICACIONES (C.N.C.)
✉ Perú 103, (C1067AAC) Buenos Aires 11 4347-9850 **W:** www.cnc.gov.ar **L.P:** Interventor: Ceferino Namuncurá

AUTORIDAD FEDERAL DE SERVICIOS DE COMUNICACIÓN AUDIOVISUAL (AFSCA)
✉ Suipacha 765, 9° piso, (C1008AAO) Buenos Aires ☎11 4320-4900 **W:** www.afsca.gov.ar **L.P:** Interventor: Lic. Juan Gabriel Mariotto. AFSCA controls certain technical aspects of broadcasting, and also controls the prgrs. trs over all kinds of broadcasting stns.

SECRETARIA DE PRENSA Y DIFUSION
Reports to the Presidencia de la Nación. Administers the media.

SISTEMA NACIONAL DE MEDIOS PÚBLICOS (SNMP)
✉ Balcarce 50, 1° piso, (C1064AAB) Buenos Aires ☎11 4344 3850 **W:** www.snmp.gov.ar **L.P:** Interventor: Tristan Bauer
All LRA stns belong to S.O.R. (incl. LRA36 in Antarctica). Common prgrs (originated from LRA1) in network called "Cadena Celeste y Blanca de Emisoras Argentinas".

° = on-air stn name not confirmed, ‡ = inactive, ± = varying freq.

MW	Call	kHz	kW	Station, location and h of tr
CF34)		530	25/5	LV de las Madres, Buenos Aires
BA119)		540		R.Italia, Villa Martelli (n.f. 1610)
SF01)	LRA14	540	25/1	R. Nal., Santa Fé: 0900-0300
SA01)	LRA25	540	5	R. Nal.,Tartagal: 1000-0400
CB04)	LU17	540	10/5	R. Golfo Nuevo, Pto. Madryn: 24h
TF03)		‡540	25/5	F.P.I.: Ushuaia
NE11)		‡550	5/0.5	F.P.I.: Neuquén
CB01)	LRA9	560	25/1	R. Nal., Esquel: 0900-0300
BA01)	LRA13	560	25/5	R. Nal., Bahia Blanca: 0900-0400
ER01)	LT15	560	10/5	R. del Litoral, Concordia: 0900-0500
SJ01)	LV1	560	25/5	R. Colón, San Juan: 24h
JU01)	LRA16	560	25/1	R. Nal., La Quiaca: 0855-0400
CF30)		570		R. Argentina, Buenos Aires
CB02)	LU20	580	10/5	R. Chubut, Trelew: 24h
CO01)	LW1	580	25/5	R. Univ. Nal. de Córdoba, Córdoba: 0800-0500
ME12)		580		R.Andina, San Rafael
CF01)	LS4	590	50	R. Continental, Buenos Aires: 24h
RN01)	LRA30	590	25/1	R. Nal., San Carlos de Bariloche: 0855-0400
TU01)	LV12	590	4	R. Independencia, San Miguel de Tucumán: 24h
NE04)	LU5	600	20/5	R. Neuquén, Neuquén: W: 0900-0300, Sat/Sun: 1100-0300
SE03)	LRK201	610	1	R. Solidaridad, Añatuya: Mon-Sat: 1000-2200, Sun 1000-2400
BA91)		610	5/1	R.General San Martin – "La Buena Radio", San Martin: 24h
ME07)	LV4	620	10/5	R. San Rafael, San Rafael: 1000-0400
SC01)	LRA18	620	25	R. Nal,. Río Turbio: 0845-0400
MS01)	LT17	620	25/5	R. Provincia de Misiones, Posadas: 0900-0500
CH03)	LRA26	620	10	R. Nal,. Resistencia: 0830-0300
CF02)	LS5	630	25/5	R. Rivadavia, Buenos Aires: 24h
JU03)	LW8	630	25/15	R. San Salvador de Jujuy: 0900-0400
CB05)	LU4	630	10/5	R. Patagonia Argentina, Comodoro Rivadavia: 0900-0500
TF01)	LRA24	640	25/5	R. Nal., Río Grande: 24h
RN02)	LU18	640	10/5	R. El Valle, "640 AM", General Roca: 0900-0300
SL01)	LV15	640	10/5	R. Villa Mercedes: 0900-0300
CF38)		650		R. Belgrano AM 650, Buenos Aires
ER04)	LT41	660	1/0.5	R. LV del Sur Entrerriano, Gualeguaychú: 0800-0300
BA36)		660		Amplitud 660, San Justo
BA68)		660		R. Popular, Claypole
BA172)		670		R. Republica, Lomas de Mirador
CB03)	LRA11	670	25/5	R. Nal., Comodoro Rivadavia: 24h
NE01)	LRA52	670	10	R. Nal., Chos Malal: 0900-0300
MS02)	LT4	670	1	R. Dif. Misiones, Posadas: 0800-0200
BA02)	LRI209	670	25/5	R. Mar del Plata, Mar del Plata: 24h
BA173)		680		R. Magna, San Martin
SF07)	LT3	680	5	R. Cerealista, Rosario: 24h
SC02)	LU12	680	25/5	R. Río Gallegos, Río Gallegos: 1000-0300
ME01)	LV6	680	25/5	R. Nihuil, Mendoza: 24h
CF45)		690		K -24 en Radio, Buenos Aires
SA02)	LRA4	690	25/5	R. Nal. Salta: 0900-0400
RN03)	LU19	690	10/3	R. LV de Comahue, Cipolletti: 0900-0500
CB08)		700		F.P.I.: Rawson
CO05)	LV3	700	25/5	R. Córdoba – "Caden 3 Argentina": 24h
NE02)	LRA17	710	25/1	R. Nal., Zapala: 0900-0300
MS03)	LRA19	710	25/5	R. Nal., Pto. Iguazú: 0900-0300
CF13)	LRL202	710	50	R. Diez, Buenos Aires: 24h

MW	Call	kHz	kW	Station, location and h of tr
SC03)	LRA59	720	25/1	R. Nal., Gobernador Gregores: 1100-2300
ME02)	LV10	720	25/5	R. de Cuyo, Mendoza: 24h
LP01)	LRA3	730	20/5	R. Nal., Santa Rosa: 0900-0300
SC04)	LU23	730	10/1	R. Lago Argentino, El Calafate:1000-0300
CA01)	LRA27	730	10/5	R. Nal., Catamarca: 24h
CF27)		730	10/5	Concepto AM, Gregorio de Laferrere: 24h
CB07)	LRA55	740	25	R. Nal., Alto Río Senguer: 0900-0400
CF48)		740		R. Rebelde, Buenos Aires
SC05)	LRI200	740	10/1	R. Municipal: 24h
CH05)	LRH251	740	25/5	R. Chaco, Resistencia: 0800-0300
NE09)		740	5/0.5	R.Nacional, Neuquén – F.P.I.
RN13)		740	10	AM 740 La Carretera, Allen
BA207)		750	1/0.25	R. AM 7-50, Lomas de Zamora
CO02)	LRA7	750	100/10	R. Nal., Córdoba: 0900-0500
BA09)	LU6	760	25/5	Emisora Atlántica, Mar del Plata: 24h
CF21)		770	5/1	R. Cooperativa, Valentín Alsina: 24h
TF02)	LRA10	780	25/1	R. Nal., Ushuaia: 24h
CS01)	LRA12	780	5	R. Nal., Santo Tomé: 0900-0300
ME03)	LV8	780	25/5	R. Libertador, Mendoza: 0900-0500
CB06)	LRF210	780	10/5	R. Tres "Cadene Patagoni", Trelew: 24h
ME06)	LV19	790	5	R. Malargüe: 1100-0400
CF04)	LR6	790	5	R. Mitre "AM 80", Buenos Aires: 24h
JU02)	LRA22	790	25/5	R. Nal, San Salvador de Jujuy: 0945-0500
RN04)	LU15	800	24/5	R. Viedma: 0900-0300
ME04)	LV23	800	1/0.25	R. Rio Atuel, General Alvear:1000-0400
CH01)	LT43	800	1/0.25	R. Mocoví, Charata: 0900-0300
BA182)		810		R. La Gauchita, Morón
CO16)		810	10/1	R. Mitre AM 810, Córdoba
FO01)	LRA8	820	25/5	R. Nal., Formosa: 0855-0400
BA04)	LU24	820	5/1	R. Tres Arroyos : 0900-0400
BA33)	LRI208	820	5/1	Estacion 820, Lomas de Zamora
JU04)	LRK221	820	1/0.25	R. Ciudad Perico, Perico: 1000-0400
CF24)		830	5	R. Del Pueblo, Buenos Aires: 24h
SF02)	LT8	830	10/5	R. Rosario, Rosario: 24h
ME08)	LV18	830	0.25	R. Municipal, San Rafael: 1030-0230
SC06)	LU14	830	25	R. Provincia de Santa Cruz,Río Gallegos: 0900-0500
CS05)	LT21	830	1/0.5	R. Municipal, Alvear
CS02)	LT12	840	10/5	R. General Madariaga, Paso de los Libres: 0900-0300
BA05)	LU2	840	25/5	R. Bahía Blanca, Bahía Blanca: 24h
SA03)	LV9	840	25/5	R. Salta AM 840, Salta: 1000-0500
CF18)		840	3	R. General Belgrano, Buenos Aires
BA126)		850	10	LV de Amércia, San Miguel Oeste
BA139)		860		R. Digital, Lanús: 24h
SC07)	LRA56	860	25	R. Nal., Perito Moreno: 0955-0300
LR02)		‡860	5/1	R. Municipal, Chilecito: 1000-0300
CF05)	LRA1	870	100	R. Nal., Buenos Aires: 24h
BA228)		880		Radiar AM 880, Buenos Aires
RN12)		‡880		R. Provincial de Sierra Colorada, Sierra Colorada (F.P.I: move from 1580)
SC06)	LU14	880	10	R. Provincia de Santa Cruz, Las Heras (//LU14 830): 1000-0300
BA183)		890		R.Libre, San Justo
LP02)	LU33	890	25/5	Emisora Pampeana, Santa Rosa: 24h
SE01)	LV11	890	25/5	Em. Santiago del Estero, Santiago del Estero: 0900-0530
CS03)	LT7	900	25/5	R. Provincia de Corrientes, Corrientes: 0900-0300
LP05)		900	1	R. Municipal, 25 de Mayo
SJ02)	LRA23	910	50/5	R. Nal.,San Juan: 0855-0400
CF06)	LR5	910	150	R. La Red, Buenos Aires: 24h
TU02)	LV7	930	25/5	R. Tucumán, San Miguel de Tucumán: 24h
CO09)	LV28	930	5/1	R. Villa María, Villa María: 24h
BA138)		930		R. Nativa – "LV de Nuestra Gente", Ciudad Madero
SL03)	LRJ241	940	20/5	R. Dimensión, San Luís: 0900-0400
ER07)	LRH200	940	3/5	R. Chajarí, Chajarí: 0900-0300
CF07)	LR3	950	25/5	R. 9am "La Deportiva", Buenos Aires: 24h
CH04)	LT16	950	25/5	RSP - R. Sáenz Peña (Cadena Eco), Roque Saénz Peña: 0900-0300
ME05)	LRA6	960	25/5	R. Nal., Mendoza: 1000-0500
BA06)	LU13	960	10/1	R. Necochea, Necochea: 0900-0400
CF35)		970		R. Génesis, Buenos Aires
CO03)	LV2	970	25/5	R. General Paz "AM 970", Córdoba: 24h
CS07)	LT25	970	1/0.25	R. Guaraní, Curuzú Cuatiá:0900-0300
LP03)	LU37	980	3/1	R. General Pico "Radio37",: 0930-0300
BA188)		980	2/1	R. Regional, San Miguel
ER06)	LT39	980	25/5	R. Victoria, Victoria: 0900-0400
RN11)	LRG387	980	1	R. Luján AM, Valcheta
SC08)		‡980		F.P.I., Río Gallegos
CF12)	LR4	990	25/5	R. Splendid AM 990, Villa Domínico: 24h
SJ03)	LRJ201	990	1	R. Calingasta, Tamberías: 1000-0500
FO03)	LRH203	990	25/5	AM 990, Formosa
BA120)		1000		R.Sintonia, José C.Paz: 24h

MW	Call	kHz	kW	Station, location and h of tr
RN05)	LU16	1000	1/0.25	R. Río Negro, Villa Regina: 0900-0300
CS06)	LT42	1000	1/0.25	R. Del Iberá, Mercedes: 0900-0300
CH09)		‡1000	5/1	F.Pl.: Comodoro Rivadavia
CO04)	LV16	1010	20/10	R. Río Cuarto, Río Cuarto: 0830-0500
SA05)	LW2	1010	1/0.25	R. Emis. Tartagal: 1000-0300
CF15)		1010		R. Onda Latina, Buenos Aires: 24h
SJ07)	LRJ214	1020	25/5	AM Mil 20 - La R. de la Gente, San Juan
SF03)	LT10	1020	10/5	R. Univ. Nal. del Litoral, Santa Fé: 0800-0500
CH02)	LRA58	1020	1	R. Nacional, Río Mayo: 1100-2300
CF08)	LS10	1030	25/5	R. del Plata, Buenos Aires: 24h
BA206)		1050	1.3	R. General Güemes "La Radio Mundial", Villa Lynch
CO08)	LV27	1050	10	R. San Francisco – LV de San Justo, San Francisco: 0900-0300
BA186)		1060		R. Las Naciones, Monte Grande
CF09)	LR1	1070	25/5	R. El Mundo, Buenos Aires: 24h
BA08)	LU3	1080	25/5	Ondas del Sur, Bahía Blanca
BA127)		1080		R. Claridad, Monte Grande (r. 1230)
SA06)	LW4	1080	25/5	R. Orán/R.Maria: 1000-0600
BA141)		1090		R. Décadas, Hurlingham
BA79)		1090	2	R. Popular, Valentín Alsina
SF17)		1090	0.5	Libertad AM 1100, Rosario
BA66)		1100	1.3	R. Estilo, Glew: 24h
CF03)	LS1	1110	25/5	R. de la Ciudad, Buenos Aires:
BA184)		1120		R.Sudamericana, San Martin
BA198)		1120		Em. Santiago y Copla, Gregoria de Laferrere
CF33)		1120		AM Tango, Buenos Aires
SJ04)	LV5	1120	25/5	R. Sarmiento, San Juan: 0900-0400
BA229)		1130		R.Popular, Buenos Aires
SE02)	LRA21	1130	25/5	R. Nal., Santiago del Estero: 0900-0400
CF22)		1130	10	R. Cadena Vida, Buenos Aires
CF46)		‡1130		AM 1130 El Manantial, Buenos Aires
LP06)	LRG203	1130	5/1	R. Capital "Antena 10", Santa Rosa
BA12)	LU22	1140	10/1	R. Tandil, Tandil: 0830-0300
BA185)		1140		R. Independencia, Lanús
BA208)		1140		R. La Luna, El Palomar
RN06)	LRA2	1150	25	R. Nal., Viedma: 0900-0400
SJ05)	LRA51	1150	5	R. Nal., Jáchal: 1030-0300
SF04)	LT9	1150	60	R. Brigadier López, Santa Fé: 0700-0300
MS07)	LRH202	1150	10	R. Tupá Mbaé, Posadas: 0800-0300
BA154)		1150	5	R. Sagrada Familia (R.Maria), Ciudad Madero
BA56)		1160		R. Excelsior, Monte Grande
RN07)	LRA57	1160	1	R. Nal., El Bolsón: 0900-0300
MS04)	LRH253	1160	5/10	R. Cataratas, Pto. Iguazú: 1000-1600
BA10)	LU32	1160	10/2.5	R. Coronel Olavarría, Olavarría: 0900-0300
SL02)	LRA29	1170	10	R. Nal., San Luis: 1000-0500
BA77)		1170	5	R. Mi País, Hurlingham: 24h
BA155)	LRI230	1180		R. de la Sierra, Tandil
TU03)	LRA15	1190	50	R. Nal., San Miguel de Tucumán: 24h
CF10)	LR9	1190	25/5	R. América, Buenos Aires: 24h
ME11)	LRA6	1200	1	R. Nal. Mendoza (r. LRA6 960), Valle de Uspallata: 1000-0500
CB09)		‡1200		F.Pl.: Esquel
CS04)	LT6	1200	1	R. Goya, Goya: 0900-0300
TF04)		‡1200	25/5	F.Pl.: Rio Grande
BA29)	LRI229	1210	5/1	R. Las Flores, Las Flores: 24h
BA54)		1210	5	AM Doce Diez, La Tablada
BA200)		1210		R. Mailín, Gregorio de Laferrere (n.f. 1330)
BA83)	LRI224	1220	1	R. Onda Marina, Mar del Plata (Cad. Eco)
CF16)	LRL328	1220	5/1	R. Cadena Eco, Buenos Aires: 24h
CH06)		1220		LRC Radio "La Radio de Chaco", Pres. Roque Sanez Peña
SF05)	LT2	1230	25/5	R. Gen. San Martín "R.Dos", Rosario: 24h
JU05)	LW5	1230	5/1	R. Libertador, General San Martin
BA89)		1230		R. Litoral, Isidro Casanova
BA127)		1230		R. Claridad, Monte Grande (nf. 1080)
CF44)		1230		R. Creativa, CA Buenos Aires
LP07)		1230		R. La Bendición, General Pico
BA230)	LRI218	1240		R. Universidad Nal. del Sur, Bahia Blanca
CF31)		1240		R. Cadena Uno, Buenos Aires: 24h
BA31)		1250	1	R. Estirpe Nacional., San Justo: 24h
BA131)		1260	2	R. Oasis, Victoria: 24h
CF36)		1260		R. Oliva "Unicon del Cielo", Buenos Aires
CF39)		1260		R. Panamericana, CA Buenos Aires
ER02)	LT14	1260	10/5	R. General Urquiza, Paraná: 24h
NE10)		1260		R. y Television del Neuquén, Neuquén
FO02)	LRA20	1270	25/5	R. Nal., Las Lomitas: 0900-0300
BA11)	LS11	1270	100	R. Provincia de Buenos Aires, La Plata: 24h
BA15)	LU11	1280	10/5	R. Trenque Lauquén, Tr. Lauquén: 0900-0300
CF17)		1280		AM 1530, CA Buenos Aires (n.f. 1530)
BA73)		1280		R. Mística, Libertad (n.f. 1320)
CF41)		1280		R. Punto, Buenos Aires
SF11)	LRI371	1290	1	R. Amanecer, Reconquista: 0800-0400
BA72)		1290		R. Provinciana, San Miguel
BA53)		1290		R. Interactiva, Gregorio de la Ferrere
ME10)	LRJ212	1290	5/1	R. Murialdo, Villa Nueva de Guaymallén: 0900-0300
SF06)	LRA5	1300	5	R. Nal., Villa Gobernador Gálvez: 0853-0303
BA63)		1300		Plus Radio, Lanús
CF26)		1300		R. Identidad, Buenos Aires: 24h
BA199)		1310		Gesell Radio, Villa Gesell
ER03)	LRA42	1310	10	R. Nal., Gualeguaychú
NE06)		1310	1	R. Dr. Gregorio Alvarez (Cadena Eco) Piedra del Aguila: 24h
BA90)		1310		R. Imagen, Castelar
CF29)		1310	1	Rdif. Antártida Argentina, Buenos Aires: 24h
BA13)	LU10	1320	5/3	R. Azul, Azul: 0900-0300
BA43)		1320		R.Ciudad, Remedios de Escalada
BA73)		1320		R. Mística, Libertad (r. 1280)
BA187)		1320		R. Máster, Luján
BA209)		1320		R.Area Uno, Tres de Febrero
ME09)	LV24	1320	0.25	R. Manantiales, Tunuyán: 1000-0600
BA200)		1330		R. Mailín, Gregorio de Laferrere (r. 1210)
SF19)		1330	1/0.25	AM Rosario, Rosario
BA205)		1340		AM Renacer, Moreno
BA225)		1340		R.Tradicional Conurbano Norte
CS08)		‡1340	1/0.25	F.Pl.: Mercedes
ER13)		1340		R. Mediterránea, Rosario del Tala
CF11)	LS6	1350	25/5	R. Buenos Aires, Buenos Aires 24h
CH07)		1350	1/0.25	F.Pl.: Juan José Castelli
CO13)	LRJ747	1350	5/1	R. Sucesos, Villa Carlos Paz: 24h
BA38)		1360		R. Nuestra Señora de Itatí - "R. Itati", Morón
RN08)	LRA54	1370	10	R. Nal., Ingeniero Jacobacci: 0900-0300
BA76)		1370	5/3	AM Trece-70, Isidro Casanova: 24h
BA226)		‡1370		F.Pl.: Junin
SF20)		1370	1/0.25	Aire de Santa FeRafaela
BA143)		1380		R. Redentor, Claypole
BA144)		1380		R. Buenas Nuevas, Merlo
BA189)		1380		R. Los Toldos, Los Toldos
BA190)	LRI231	1380	5/1	LV del Sudeste, Necochea
BA14)	LR11	1390	10	R. Univ. Nacional, La Plata: 24h
BA216)		1390		R. General Paz, José C. Paz
NE07)	LRG202	1400	5/1	R. Cumbre, Neuquén
BA69)		1400		R. Gama, Lanús: 1000-0300
BA123)		1400		R. AM 1400, Luján
BA217)		‡1400		R.Gen. Lavalle, General Lavalle (F.Pl.)
CH08)		‡1400	1/0.25	F.Pl.: Charata
SF23)		1400		R. Malvinas Argentina, Rosario: irr
BA42)		1410	5/1	R. Folclorismo, José Léon Suárez: 1100-0100
BA214)		1410		R. Fundacion, Rafael Calzada
BA218)		1410		R.Cope, Chivilcoy (F.Pl)
SL04)		1410	1	R. María de La Paz, Villa Mercedes
BA108)		1420		R. Génesis 2000, General Conesa
CF28)	LRI220	1420	1/0.25	R. AM 1420, Buenos Aires
BA16)	LT24	1430	1/0.25	R. San Nicolás, San Nicolás: 24h
CO06)	LV26	1430	1/0.25	R. Río Tercero (Cad. 26), Río Tercero: 24h
BA17)	LRI235	1430	0.25	R. Balcarce, Balcarce: 0900-0300
BA152)		1430		R.Victoria, La Plata
BA201)		1430		R. Shekinah, Merlo
BA212)		1430		R. Cunumi Guazú
LP08)		1430	1	Red La Pampeana, General Pico
BA146)		1440		R. Cristo Viene, Mar del Plata
NE03)	LRA53	1440	1	R. Nal., San Martín de los Andes: 1000-0300
BA18)	LU36	1440	1	R. Coronel Suárez, Coronel Suárez: 1000-0300
CO07)	LV20	1440	1/0.25	R. Laboulaye, Laboulaye: 0900-0300
BA52)		1440		R. Impacto, Tapiales
SF12)	LRI221	1440	5/1	R. General Obligado, Reconquista
CF37)	LRI213	1450	5/1	R. El Sol, Porción Quilmes
CO17)		‡1450	5/1	F.Pl.: Corrientes
SJ06)	LRI211	1450	5/1	R. Las 40, Villa Aberastain
SF08)	LT29	1460	1/0.25	R. Venado Tuerto, Venado Tuerto: 24h
BA19)	LU30	1460	0.25	R. Maipú (Cad. Eco), Maipú: 0900-2400
BA20)	LU34	1460	0.1	R. Pigüé, Pigüé: 1000-0300
BA41)		1460		R. Contacto, Merlo: 24h
BA191)		1460		R. Jerusalén, Jerusalen
TU04)	LRK204	1460	1	R. 21 (Cadena Eco), Yerba Buena: 24h
BA21)	LT20	±1470	1/0.25	R. Junín: 0900-0300
BA22)	LU26	1470	0.25	Em. Coronel Dorrego "La Dorrego", Coronel Dorrego: 1030-0300 (r. 1468)
BA174)		1470		R. Lider, Mariano Acosta
BA49)		1470		R. Mburucuya, José León Suarez
BA84)		1470		Cadena 1470, Lanús: 1000-2300
ER05)	LT26	1470	1/0.25	R. Nuevo Mundo, Colón: 0900-0300
RN09)		1470	1	R. Municipal, Luis Beltrán: 1200-0100
SF09)	LT28	1470	1/0.25	R. Rafaela, Rafaela: 0900-0300
BA50)	LU27	1480	1	R. Centro, Dolores: 1100-0300

MW	Call	kHz	kW	Station, location and h of tr
BA147)		1480		R. Sensaciones, Tapiales
CO15)	LV22	1490	1	R. Huinca Renancó, Huinca Renancó: 1000-0300
BA24)	LU25	‡1490	0.1	R. Carhué, Carhué: 0900-0330
BA67)		1490		AM Vida en el Espíritu, Mar del Plata
BA169)		1490		R. Emanuel, Partido de Ezieza
BA219)		1490		R. Unidad, José Mármol
CO18)		1490		R. AM Vida, Córdoba
BA07)	LRI214	1500	5/1	R. Bonaerense, Lavallol: 0900-0300
RN10)		‡1500	1/0.25	R. Municipal, Gral. Conesa: 1000-2400
BA23)	LT34	v1500	0.25	R. Nuclear, Zárate: 0900-0000
BA34)		1510		LV del Oeste,Libertad: 24h
BA220)		1510		R. RBN "Radio de las Buenas Nuevas", Lomas de Zamora
CF20)		1510		R. Urkupiña, Buenos Aires (n.f. 1550)
BA74)		1510		R. Alabanza, Guernica
SF14)	LRI253	1510	1/0.25	R. Belgrano, Suardi: 0900-0400
ER08)	LT38	1520	0.25	R. Gualeguay, Gualeguay: 0900-0300
BA40)		1520		R. Metropolitana "R.Metro", Ciudadela
BA47)		1520		R. Cielo Nuevo, Isidro Casanova
BA92)		1520	5/1	R. Chascomús, Chascomús: 24h
BA145)		1520	3	R. Norteña, Los Polvorines
BA148)		1520		Cadena D, Monte Chingolo
BA161)		1520		R. Visión Fortaleza, Ezeiza
CF17)		1530		R. Eco, CA Buenos Aires (r. 1280)
BA192)		1530		R. Esencia "LV del Litoral", San Miguel Oeste
BA221)		1530		R. El Faro, Gregorio de Laferrere
BA222)		1530		AM 1530 Cadena UOCRA, Buenos Aires
CO12)	LRJ200	1530	1	R. Centro Morteros, Morteros: 0900-0300
BA25)	LT35	1540	0.25	R. Mon, Pergamino: 0900-0400
BA26)	LU28	1540	0.25	R. Tuyú:1000-0300
BA100)		1540		R. AM Líder, José León Suárez
BA150)		‡1540		R. Cotidiana, Merlo
BA231)		1540		R. Zorobabel, Esteban Echeverría
CF43)		1540		R. Amanecer, CA Buenos Aires
CF20)		1550		R. Urkupiña, Buenos Aires (r. 1510)
SF10)	LT23	1550	5/0.25	R. Regional, San Jenaro Norte: 0900-0300
BA27)	LT32	1550	0.25	R. Chivilcoy, Chivilcoy: 1000-0400
ER09)	LT40	1550	1	R. LV de la Paz, La Paz: 0900-0100
BA175)		1550		R. Popular, José León Suárez
BA213)		1550		R. Esperanza, Gregorio de Laferrere
ER10)	LT11	1560	2.5/1.5	R. Gral. Francisco Ramírez, Villaguay
BA28)	LT33	1560	0.25	R. Nueve de Julio, 9 de Julio: 0900-0300
BA44)		1560		R. Castañares, Ituzaingó
BA99)		1560		R. Restauración, Llavallol
BA194)		1560	0.5/0.25	AM 1560 "La R. de la Gente", Tandil
BA196)		1560	1	R. Antena Lobos, Lobos
ME13)		‡1560	1/0.25	F.PI.: Mendoza
BA55)		1570		R. Melody, Remedios de Escalada
BA71)		1570	2	R. AM Rocha, La Plata
BA162)	LRI223	1570	5/1	F.PI.: Lomas de Zamora
BA163)		1570		R. La Morena de Itati, Grand Bourg
SF22)		1570		R. Alegría Regional, Luis Palacio
ER11)	LT27	1580	1	R. LV del Montiel, Villaguay: 0900-0300
BA48)		1580		AM Tradición, San Martín
BA135)		1580	1	R. 26. de Julio, Longchamps
BA164)		1580		R. Tradición, Isidro Casanova
BA176)	LT36	1580	0.25	R. Chacabuco, Chacabuco
RN12)		1580		R. Provincial de Sierra Colorada, Sierra Colorada – F.pl. – move to 880
BA39)		‡1590		R. Cristiana Adonal, Bánfield Oeste
BA178)		1590		R. Olivera, General Rodríguez
BA223)		1590		AM 1590 La Radio de la Region, Dolores
CF49)		1590		R.Stentor, Buenos Aires
BA37)		1600	1.2	R. Armonia, Caseros: 24h
BA57)		1600		R. Metropolitana "La Radio", Luís Guillón
SF21)		1600	0.25	AM 1600 R. del Centro, Montes de Oca
BA51)		1610	0.05	R. Luz del Mundo, Rafael Calzada
BA124)		1610		R. Guabiyú, Gregorio de Laferrere
CO14)		1610	0.5	R. Regional, Laboulaye
SF18)		1610	0.2	R. Fósil, Rosario: active Sun to 2200 UTC
BA45)		1620		R. Vida, Monte Grande
BA119)		1620		R.Italia, Villa Martelli (r. 540)
BA180)		1620	10/1	AM 16-20 La Radio, Mar del Plata
BA224)		1620		R. Sentir,Merlo
BA134)		1630		R. Restauración, Hurlingham
BA179)		1630		R. AM Súper Sport, Lomas de Zamora
BA227)		1630	10	AM Diagonal, La Plata
ER12)		1630	1/0.25	R.America, San José
BA177)		1640		Hosanna AM 1640, Isidro Casanova
CF23)		1640		R. Nueva Bolivia , Buenos Aires: Irr
BA181)	LRI227	1650	1/0.5	Antares AM 1650 "La R. de la Familia", Pilar
BA195)		1650		R.Fenix. Temperley

MW	Call	kHz	kW	Station, location and h of tr
BA153)		1650		R. Guarani AM, San Justo
BA156)		1660		R. Reivir, Gregorio de la Ferrere
ER14)		‡1660	5/0.25	F.PI.: Nogoyá
CO09)		‡1660	1/0.25	F.PI.: Paso de los Libres
BA167)		±1670		R. Bethel, Banfield (r. v1672-1675)
BA166		1680		R.Hosanna Tropical, Ezeiza
BA107)		1690	1/0.25	R. Cristo la Solucuión, San Justo
CF47)		1700	5/1	R.Fantastico, Tigre
CF32)		1710	0.3	AM 1710 – R.Urquiza, Buenos Aires

SW	Call	kHz	kW	Station, location and h of tr
CF05)	LRA31	6060	30	R. Nal., Buenos Aires: 2100-1500

ASOCIACION DE RADIODIFUSORAS PRIVADAS ARGENTINAS (ARPA)

✉ Tte. Gral. Juan D. Perón 1561, Piso 3, (C1037ACB) Buenos Aires ☎11 4371 5999 🖷11 4382 4483 **W:** www.arpa.org.ar **E:** arpaorg.@ arpa.org.ar **L.P:** Presidente: Carlos Maria Molina.
ARPA is an association of privately owned commercial stns.

ASOCIACION DE RADIODIFUSORES CATOLICOS ARGENTINOS (ARCA)

✉ Av. Juan D. Perón 3461, (S2003FYC) Rosario, Santa Fe ☎341 431 2872 **E:** info@radiodelrosario.com **L.P:** Presidente: Osvaldo Bufarini

Addresses and other information:
BA00) BUENOS AIRES (PROV.):
BA01) Moreno 30, 1° Piso, (B8000FWB) Bahía Blanca ☎ 291 453 2700 **W:** www.nacionalbahiablanca.com.ar **E:** bahiablanca@radionacional. gov.ar **– FM:** 99.3MHz **– BA02)** Hipólito Yrigoyen 2641, (B7600DPG) Mar del Plata ☎223 494 7700 🖷223 492 2020 **W:** www.lu9mardelplata.com. ar **E:** lu9-adm@lacapitalnet.com.ar **– FM:** 103.3MHz FM 103 Universo **– BA04)** Av. Belgrano 457, (B7500EBE) Tres Arroyos ☎2983 42 3504 🖷2983 42 7000 **W:** www.radiotresarroyos.com **E:** lu24@lu24.com.ar **– FM:** 95.3MHz FM Ilusiones **– BA05)** Rodriguez 55 (B8000HSA) Bahía Blanca ☎291 459 0002 🖷291 455 5556 **W:** www.lu2.com.ar **E:** radio@ lu2.com.ar **– FM:** 94.7MHz FM Ciudad **– BA06)** Calle 64 No. 2946, Gran Galería Central, EP, (B7630CIR) Necochea ☎2262 42 0100 **W:**www. radionecochea.com.ar **E:** administracion@radionecochea.com.ar **– FM:** 88.1MHz FM Oceánica **– BA07)** Doyhenard 316, (B1836EVH) Lavallol ☎11 4231 3225 **W:** www.am1500.com.ar **E:** radiobonarense@yahoo. com **– BA08)** Av. Lamadrid 116, (B8000FKD) Bahía Blanca ☎291 452 0382 **W:** www.lu3am1080.com.ar **E:** radiolu3@yahoo.com.ar **– FM:** 94.3MHz FM Ondas **– BA09)** Córdoba 1865, (B7600DVM) Mar del Plata ☎223 491 7047 🖷223 491 2355 **W:** www.lu6.com.ar **E:** radioa@lu6. com.ar **– FM:** 93.3MHz **– BA10)** Alsina 3377, (B7400COW) Olavarría ☎2284 41 0911 **W:** www.lu32.com.ar **E:** administracion@lu32.com.ar **– FM:** 98.7MHz FM Cristal **– BA11)** Calle 53 No. 810, (B1900BBQ) La Plata ☎221 424 9713 **W:** www.amprovincia.com.ar **E:** secretaria@ amprovincia.com.ar **– FM:** 97.1MHz FM Provincia **– BA12)** Gral. Rodriguez 762, PA, (B7000AOP) Tandil ☎249 442 7493 **W:**www.lu22radiotandil.com.ar **E:** radiotandil@arnet.com.ar **– FM:** 97.1MHz **– BA13)** Av. Bartolomé Mitre 819/21, (B7300IKQ) Azul ☎2281 42 5628 **E:** lu10radioazul@latinmail.com **– FM:** 89.5MHz FM Celestial **– BA14)** Plaza Rocha 133, 2°Piso, (B1900DVA) La Plata ☎221 422 0330 🖷221 422 4165 **W:** www.lr11.com.ar **E:**secretaria@lr11.com.ar **– FM:** 107.5MHz **– BA15)** Av. Pedro García Salinas 1815, (B6400EIF) Trenque Lauquen ☎2392 42 5454 **W:** www.radiotrenquelauquen.com.ar **E:** radiolu11@speedy.com.ar or radiolu11@ciudad.com.ar **– FM:** 88.5MHz **– BA16)** Av. Moreno 124, (B2900GPO) San Nicolás ☎336 442 5222 🖷336 442 4479 **W:** www. lt24online.com.ar **E:** lt24@cablenet.com.ar **– FM:** 88, 88.3MHz **– BA17)** Av. San Martin 2700, (B7620) Balcarce ☎2266 43 0780 🖷2266 43 0779 **W:** //radiobalcarce.blogspot.com **E:** radiobalcarce@telefax.com.ar **– FM:** 89.7MHz **– BA18)** Garibaldi 71, (B7540DQA) Coronel Suárez ☎2926 43 2706 **W:** www.1440am.com.ar **E:** produccion@1440am.com.ar **– FM:** 100.5MHz "Frecuencia 36" **– BA19)** Lavalle Sud 312, (B7160BAH) Maipú ☎2268 42 1774 **W:** www.lu30radiomaipu.com.ar **E:** lu30radiomaipu@ hotmail.com **– BA20)** Lavalle 210, (B8170CHF) Pigüé ☎2923 47 2205 **W:** www.radiopigue.com.ar **E:** radiolu34@s8.coopenet.com.ar **– FM:** 96.3MHz **– BA21)** Hipólito Yrigoyen 86, (B6000DDB) Junín ☎236 444 3610 🖷236 444 3474 **W:**www.lt20radiojunin.com.ar **E:** oyentes@lt20radiojunin.com.ar **– FM:** 89.1MHz **– BA22)** Uslenghi 592, 1° Piso, (B8150EGD) Coronel Dorrego ☎2921 45 3456 **W:** www.ladorrego.com. ar **E:** info@ladorrego.com.ar **– BA23)** Independencia 501, (B2800JIG) Zárate ☎3487 42 3116 🖷3487 43 9500 **W:** www.radionuclear.com.ar **E:** radionuclear@delta.com.ar **– FM:** 90.1MHz **– BA24)** Av. Colón 985, (B6430BHF) Carhué ☎2936 43 2560 🖷2936 43 2955 **E:** radiocarhue@ yahoo.com.ar **– BA25)** Dr. Alem 340, (B2700LHH) Pergamino ☎2477 42 4022 **W:**www.lt35radiomon.com.ar **E:** lt35radiomon@speedy.com.ar **– FM:** 90.3MHz FM Mágica **– BA26)** Av. San Martín 366, (B7163EGQ) General Madariaga ☎ 2267 55 1540 **W:**www.radiotuyu.blogspot.com **E:** radiotuyu@telpin.com.ar **– FM:** 92.5MHz R.Tuy **– BA27)** Av. Mitre 924.

(B6620BMW) Chivilcoy ☎2346 43 0690 **E:** radiochivilcoy@speedy.com - **FM:** 101.1MHz FM Sónica – **BA28)** Pte. Hipólito Yrigoyen 969, (B6500DJQ) 9 de Julio ☎2317 52 1560 **W:** www.cadenanueve.com.ar **E:** imagen@cadenanueva.com.ar - **FM:** 89.9MHz Maxima FM – **BA29)** Av. Avellaneda 773, (B7200AOH) Las Flores **W:** www.radiolasflores.com. ar **E:** am1210@multimediolasflores.com.ar ☎2244 45 2320 - **FM:** 89.7MHz FM Condor – **BA31)** Juan Florio 3579, (B1754AJK) San Justo ☎11 4441 1400 **W:** www.estirpe1250.com.ar **E:** estirpe1250@yahoo. com.ar – **BA33)** Antonio Sáenz 572, 2° piso, (B1832HUL) Lomas de Zamora ☎11 4243 7891 ▤11 4292 5559 **W:** www.radioestacion820. com **E:** 820am@speedy.com.ar – **BA34)** Isla Soledad 205 =ex 2560=, (B1716NXB) Libertad ☎220 494 1300 **W:** www.lavozdeloeste1510.com. ar **E:** oyentes@lavozdeloeste1510.com.ar - **FM:** 91.9MHz – **BA36)** Dr. Ignacio Arieta 3950 (B1754AQT) San Justo ☎11 4651 0193 **W:** www. radioamplitud.com.ar **E:** amplitud@radioamplitud.com.ar – **BA37)** Wenceslao Paunero 2915, (B1678DSG) Caseros ☎11 4716 6495 **W:** www.am1600armonia.com.ar **E:** armoniaam1600@arnet.com.ar – **BA38)** San Luís 989, (B1708JUE) Morón ☎11 4627 7439 – **BA39)** Arroyo Santa Catalina 4067, Barrio Juan Manuel de Rosas, (B1828) Bánfield Oeste ☎11 4693 2789 **W:** //radioadonay.ohlog.com **E:** radioadonay@yahoo. com.ar – **BA40)** Julio A. Roca 3414, (B1702BCL) Ciudadela ☎11 4488 3644. ▤11 4657 4098 **W:** www.radiometro1520.com.ar **E:** amradiometro@yahoo.com.ar – **BA41)** Correa 275, (B1718BSE) San Antonio de Padua ☎220 482 4526 **W:** www.amcontacto.blogspot.com **E:** contacto1460@gmail.com – **BA42)** Lacroze 1871, (B1655LVS) José León Suárez ☎11 4720 2688 **W:** www.radiofolclorisimo.com.ar **E:** info@ radiofolclorisimo.com.ar – **BA44)** 33 Orientales 1033, Villa Ariza, (B1714NOS) Ituzaingó ☎11 4623 4549 **W:** //radioam1560.blogspot. com.ar – **BA45)** Mariano Alegre 23, (B1842FSA) Monte Grande ☎11 4281 4094 **W:** www.radiovidaam.com.ar **E:** contacte@radiovidaam.com.ar - **FM:** 104.9MHz – **BA47)** Juan Jofré 4243, (B1765MOY) Isidro Casanova ☎11 4694 8131 **W:** www.radiocielonuevo.com.ar **E:** radiocielonuevo@ hotmail.com – **BA48)** Pueyrredón 3846, (B1650CVP) San Martín ☎11 4754 8784. ▤11 4713 2517 **W:** amtradicion.com.ar **E:** amtradicion@ gmail.com – **BA49)** Santa Cruz 1312, (B1655IHD) José León Suárez ☎11 4720 0059.- **W:** www.radioam1470.com.ar **E:** radiomb@arnet.com.ar – **BA50)** Bartolomé Mitre 317, B7100BNG) ☎2245 44 2175 **W:** www. radiocentrodolores.com.ar **E:** radiocentro97@yahoo.com.ar - **FM:** 97.1 MHz R.Centro – **BA51)** Catamarca 2560, (B1847CXH) Rafael Calzada ☎11 4219 1150 **W:** www.radioluzdelmundo.com.ar **E:** radioluzdelmundo@hotmail.com– **BA52)** Juncal 12, 1° Piso, Of. "3", (B1770AOB) Tapiales ☎11 4442 6333 **W:** www.am-1440.com.ar **E:** impactoam@ hotmail.com – **BA53)** Mariquita Sánches de Thompson 1850, (B1768BDP) Ciudad Madero ☎11 4622 1570 **W:** www.radiointeractiva.com.ar – **BA54)** Av.General Paz 13869, Villa Insuperable, (B1751BRG) Lomas del Mirador ☎11 4454 7799 **W:** www.amdocediec.com.ar **E:** comercial@ amdocediez.com.ar – **BA55)** Las Piedras 2447, (B1826DJO) Remedios de Escalada ☎11 4249 6047 **W:** www.radiomelody1570.com.ar **E:** melody1570@hotmail.es – **BA56)** Gral. Martin Rodríguez 377, (B1842DIG) Monte Grande ☎11 4290 5245 **W:**www.amexcelsior1160.com.ar **E:** radioexcelsior@ciudad.com.ar - **FM:** FM Malvinas 91.7MHz – **BA57)** Robertson 1249, 1° Piso "3", (B1838AIE) Luis Guillón ☎11 4296 3396 **W:** www.netmetro.com.ar **E:** am1600@netmetro.com.ar - **FM:** 96.9MHz FM Metro – **BA63)** Calle Eva Perón 1169, (B1824IBI) Lanús ☎11 4427 3106 **W:** www.plusradio.com.ar **E:** plusradio1300@hotmail. com – **BA66)** Florencio Sánchez 119, Barrio Los Alamos, (B1856FXE) Glew ☎11 4233 1323 **W:** www.am1100estilo.com **E:** amestilo@hotmail.com – **BA67)** Gascón 6343, (B7604BGA) Mar del Plata ☎223 478 2947 **W:** www.radioamvidaenelespiritu.com **E:** radioamvidaenelspiritu@hotmail.com – **BA68)** Potrerillos 1246, (B1849DVX) Claypole ☎11 4219 3850 **W:** www.am660popular.com.ar **E:** am660popular. com.ar - **FM:** 89.1MHz – FM Popular – **BA69)** Choele Choel 1233, (B1822DPY) Valentín Alsina ☎11 4218 4860 **W:** www.gama1400.com **E:** radiogama@hotmail.com – **BA71)** Calle 39 No. 256, (B1902APL) La Plata ☎221 427 3360 **W:** www.radiorocha.com.ar **E:** director@radiorocha.com.ar – **BA72)** Domingo F.Sarmiento 2220, (B1663GFX) San Miguel ☎11 4667 4460 **W:** www.radioproviniciana.com **E:** radioprovinciaanaam1290@ hotmail.com – **BA73)** Congresales 570, 1° piso, (B1716) Libertad ☎220 495 0245 **E:** chmistica@hotmail.com – **BA74)** Santiago del Estero 73, (B1862SCA) Guernica ☎2224 47 6963 **W:** www.amradioalabanzas.com. ar **E:** info@ amradioalabanzas.com.ar – **BA76)** Cristianía 3049, (B1765HOG) Isidro Casanova ☎11 4694 5434 ▤11 4694 7222 **W:**www. la1370.com.ar **E:** landproducciones@hotmail.com.ar - **FM:** 92.1MHz R.Cosmos – **BA77)** Jauretche 1052, 1° Piso "B", (B1686FCD) Hurlingham ☎11 4662 9534 **W:** radiompais1170.com.ar **E:** radiompais1170. com.ar – **BA79)** Av. José María Moreno 1443, 1° Piso "A-B", (C1424ABB) CA Buenos Aires ☎11 4296 1623 **W:**www.radio1090.com.ar **E:** mensajes@radio1090.com.ar – **BA83)** España 468, (B7600CXJ), Mar del Plata ☎223 475 1365 **W:** www.cadenaeco.com.ar **E:** radio@cadenaeco. com.ar **FM:** 89.1MHz – **BA84)** Carlos Gardel 599. (B1824NTK) Lanús ☎11 4225 7304 **W:** www.cadenaam1470.com **E:** info@cadenaam1470.

com - – **BA89)** José P. de Lafayette 549, (B1765GXC) Isidro Casanova ☎11 4485 7376 ▤11 4485 6516 **W:** www.litoral1230am.com.ar **E:** info@litoral1230am.com.ar – **BA90)** Madrid 3987, Barrio San Juan, (B1712NMO) Castelar ☎11 4692 4412 – **BA91)** Av. General Paz 3755, (B1672AMA) Villa Lynch ☎11 4755 9061 **W:** www.radioam610.com.ar **E:** radio610@gmail.com – **BA92)** Libres del Sur 128, (B7130ACD) Chascomús ☎2241 42 5367 **W:** www.rchradiochascomus.com.ar **E:** rch@radiochascomus.com.ar - **FM:** 90.9MHz – **BA99)** Av. Alte. Francisco Seguí 1059, (B1836BYK) Llavallol ☎11 4293 9904 **W:** www.restaurandote.com **E:** radioytv@restaurandote.com.ar – **BA100)** Av. Santa Fe 2470, 1° piso, (B1640IFY) Martinez ☎11 5788 2223 **W:** www.amlider.com.ar **E:** info@amlider.com.ar - **FM:** 99.3MHz – **BA107)** Av. Brig. Gral. Juan Manuel de Rosas 4357, (B1754FVB), San Justo ☎11 4484 4517 **W:** www.cristolasolucionsj.com.ar **E:** contacto@cristolasolucionsj.com.ar - **FM:** 90.7MHz – **BA108)** Manuel Dorrego 292, (B7101) General Conesa ☎2245 49 2140 **W:** www.am1420.com.ar – **BA119)** Gral. Martín Miguel de Güemez 5025, (B1603CUE) Villa Martelli ☎11 4709 1172 **W:** www.amitalia.com.ar **E:** radioitalia.am@gmail.com – **BA120)** Domingo F.Sarmiento 4154, (B1665KON) José C.Paz ☎2320 42 3306 **W:** www. sintonia1000.com.ar **E:** info@sintonia1000.com.ar – **BA123)** 25 de Mayo 579, (B6700ALK) Luján ☎2323 44 2020 **E:** am1400lujan@yahoo.com.ar - **FM:** 91.1MHz FM Fantástica – **BA124)** Soberanía Nacional 2945, (B1757KHY) Gregorio de Lafferrere ☎11 4457 3674 **W:** www.guabiyu1610.com.ar **E:** radioguabiyuam1610@hotmail.com – **BA126)** Maestro Ferreyra 175, Barrio Trujui, (B1663CHC) San Miguel ☎11 4455 1408 – **BA127)** Vicente López 235 2° Piso, (B1842AUE) Monte Grande ☎11 4284 3186 **W:** www.radioclaridad.com.ar **E:** radio@radioclaridad.com.ar – **BA131)** Av. Pte. Juan D. Perón 2514, (B1644CYP) Victoria ☎11 4746 6856 **W:**www.radiooasis.com.ar **E:** radiooasis@mixmail.com - **FM:** 92.5MHz – **BA134)** Av.Gral. Pedro Diaz 1460, (B1686IQH) Hurlingham ☎11 4662 6387 **W:** www.radiorestauracion.com.ar **E:** restauracionam@ hotmail.com – **BA135)** San Martin 513 (B1854FEM) Longchamps ☎11 4233 5560 **W:** www.radio26.com.ar **E:** radio26dejulio@gmail.com – **BA138)** Santander 5714, 2° Piso "D" (C1439ASZ) CA Buenos Aires ☎11 4602 8553 **W:**www.amnativa.com.ar **E:** info@amnativa.com.ar – **BA139)** Fray Mamerto Esquiú 1161, (B1842BFQ) Lanús ☎11 4225 2256 **W:** www.digital860.99k.org **E:** digital860@hotmail.com – **BA141)** Jauretche 1052, 1° Piso "C", (B1686FCD) Hurlingham ☎11 4452 8688 **W:** decadasam1090.com.ar **E:** info@decadasam1090.com.ar – **BA143)** Av.Monteverde 8158, (B1849HAX) Claypole ☎11 4238 8427 **W:** www.radioredentoram1380. com.ar **E:** radioredentoram1380@hotmail.com – **BA144)** Santa Fe 2540, (B1722BGZ) Merlo ☎220 485 6696 **W:**buenasnuevasradio.com.ar **E:** radiobuenasnuevasama1380@yahoo.com.ar – **BA145)** Ex. Combatientes de Malvinas 2053, (B1613ECO) Los Polvorines ☎2320 44 7711 **W:** www. santiaguenañorteña.com.ar **E:** info@santiaguenanortena.com.ar – **BA146)** Jujuy 2928, (B7602BKD) Mar del Plata ☎223 475 1365 **E:** sensacionesam@yahoo.com.ar – **BA148)** Victor Hugo 647, (B1825FBI) Monte Chingolo ☎11 4220 6822 **W:** www.logdesignmedia.com.ar/ socalo_am1520.swf or www.am1520.tk **E:** am1520_suma@yahoo.com. ar - **FM:** 106.1MHz – **BA150)** San Martin 1337, (B1722LTK) Merlo ☎220 482 1760 **E:** radiocotidiana@hotmail.com – **BA152)** Diagonal 74 No 1357, (B1900BZG) La Plata ☎221 427 3227 **W:** //radiovictorialaplata. blogspot.com – **BA153)** Dr. Ignacio Arieta 3950, (B1754AQT) San Justo ☎11 4482 2597 **W:** www.radio-guarani.com.ar **E:** info@radio-guarani. com.ar – **BA154)** Salta 2641, (B1754IQS) San Justo ☎11 4441 8196 - **FM:** 104.5MHz FM Sintonia – **BA155)** Gral. Belgrano 531, (B7000GEK) Tandil ☎249 444 6383 **W:** www.am1180.com.ar **E:** am1180@speedy. com.ar - **FM:** 99.5MHz – **BA156)** Juan Sebastian Bach 3687, (B1756KKM) Isidro Casanova ☎11 4694 6470 **W:** www.radiorevivir.com **E:** radio@ radiorevivir.com - **FM:** 99.7MHz – **BA161)** 12 de Octubre 537, (B1804AAC) Ezeiza ☎11 4232 9739 – **BA162)** Lomas de Zamora – **BA163)** Juan F.Segui 895, (B1615MNA) Grand Bourg ☎23 2041 4426 - **FM:** 105.3MHz – **BA164)** Elías Bedoya 2020/4, (B1765LXH) Isidro Casanova ☎11 4669 4925 **E:** stcom@uolsinectis.com.ar – **BA166)** Reconquista 27, (B1804CFA) Ezeiza ☎11 4232 0321 **W:** www.radiohosanna1660.com.ar **E:** canaachanel@hotmail.com – **BA167)** Benito Pérez Galdós 688, Villa Fiorito, (B1821EON) Banfield ☎11 4276 5194 – **BA169)** Calle Yatay 628, (B1804CMH) Ezeiza ☎11 4232 7070 **W:** www.radiodifusoraemanuel.com.ar **E:** radiodifusoraemanuel@hotmail.com – **BA172)** Juan Florio 3579, (B1754AJK) San Justo ☎11 4441 8200 **W:** www.radiorepublica.com.ar – **BA173)** Belgrano 4033, (B1650CCS) San Martin ☎11 4713 8808 **W:** www.radio-atlantico.com.ar – **BA174)** Heredia 920, Augstín Ferrari, (B1724ETO) Mariano Acosta ☎220 498 1498 – **BA175)** Av. Brigadier Juan Manuel de Rosas 2468, (B1655MSS) José León Suárez ☎11 4729 1545 **W:** www.popular1550.com.ar **E:** radio1550popular@hotmail.com – **BA176)** Almirante Brown 135, (B6740DRB) Chacabuco ☎2352 43 1136 **W:**lt36radiochacabuco.com.ar **E:** radiochacabuco@topmail.com.ar - **FM:** 91.7 MHz FM Universal – **BA177)** Zufriategui 871, (B1765CKQ) Isidro Casanova ☎11 4467 2468 **W:** www. radiohosannaam1640.com **E:** hosannaam1640@hotmail.com – **BA178)**

Pedro Laurenz 237, Las Malvinas (B1748), General Rodríguez ☎237 487 3200 **W:** wwwradioolivera.tk **E:** radioolivera@hotmail.com – **BA179)** Bombero Ariño 1150, (B1834IAX) Temperley ☎11 5290 0075 **W:**www. lasupersport.com.ar **E:** lasuper@lasupersport.com.ar – **BA180)** Hipólito. Yrigoyen 2629, (B7600DPG) Mar del Plata ☎22 3494 1428 **W:** www.1620laradio.com.ar **E:** am1620@1620laradio.com – **BA181)** Cjal. Manuel Martitegui 598, Fátima, (B1629JGL) Pilar ☎ 230 444 9899 **W:** www.am1650antares.com.ar **E:** info@1650antares.com.ar – **BA182)** Salta 138, 2° Piso "C", (B1708JOD) Morón ☎11 4489 2024 **W:** www. lagauchita810.com.ar **E:** lagauchita810@hotmail.com – **BA183)** Juan Florio 3573, (B1754AJK) San Justo ☎11 4651 1694 **W:** www.am890. com.ar **E:** radio@am890.com.ar – **BA184)** Santa Rosalía 1465 (B1651CXE) San Justo ☎11 4752 3245 **W:** www.sudamericana1120. com.ar **E:** info@sudamericana1120.com.ar – **BA185)** Fray Mamerto Esquiú 2855, (B1826GBO) Remedios de Escalada ☎11 4225 3198 **W:** www.radioindependencia.com.ar **E:** radioindependencia@hotmail.com – **BA186)** Calle Angel Rotta 168, (B1842AED) Monte Grande ☎11 4296 0771 **W:** www.lasnaciones.org/radio.html – **BA187)** Las Heras 1478, (B6700AUO) Luján ☎2323 42 9595 **W:** www.radiomasterradioluan. com.ar – **BA188)** Av. Pte. Juan Domingo Perón 1774, (B1663GHT) San Miguel ☎11 4664 0077 **E:** rafolk@yahoo.com.ar – **FM:** 99.3 MHz FM Integracion – **BA189)** Paso 1943, (B6015ASC) Los Toldos ☎2358 44 3954 – **BA190)** Avenida 59 N° 2465, 1° Piso, (B7630GYJ) Necochea ☎2262 52 0003 **W:** www.am1380.com.ar **E:** contacto@am1380.com.ar – **FM:** 103.9 MHz FM R.10 – **BA191)** Fragate Heroína 2035, (B1842FQI) Monte Grande ☎11 4284 2830 **W:** www.jerusalenradio.com **E:** info@ jerusalenradio.com – **BA192)** Paula Albarracin 3957, Barrio Sarmiento (B1663CPE) San Miguel Oeste ☎2320 46 0649 **W:** www.amesencia. com **E:** radioesencia@live.com.ar – **BA194)** Av. Aristóbulo del Valle 1202 (B7000HLN) Tandil **W:**www.lavozdetandil.com.ar **E:** 1560@lavozdetandil. com.ar – **BA195)** Coronel Suárez 554, (B1034GHL) Temperley ☎11 4244 1843 **W:** www.fenix1650.com.ar **E:** amradiofenix@hotmail.com – **BA196)** Aristóbulo del Valle 23, (B7240IXA) Lobos ☎2227 42 1211 **W:** www.amradioantena.com.ar **E:** info@amradioantena.com.ar – **BA198)** Luis Vernet 6654, (B1757MOB) Gregorio de Laferrere ☎11 4467 4224 **W:** www.santiagoycopla.com.ar **E:** santiagoycopla@hotmail.com – **BA199)** Av. Buenos Aires 735, Galeria Pinar, Local 11, (B7165JCH) Villa Gesell ☎2255 47 6749 **W:** www.am1310gesell.com.ar **E:** am1310gesell@hotmail.com – **FM:** 89.9MHz – FM Plus – **BA200)** Fournier 4075, (B1757IDW) Gregorio de Laferrere ☎11 4457 7204 **W:** www.am1330radiomailin.com.ar **E:** radiomailin@am1330radiomailin. com.ar – **BA201)** Burela 560, Barrio Pompeya (B1722PHL) Merlo ☎220 489 1727 **W:** www.radioshekinah **E:** am1430shekinah@hotmail.com – **BA205)** Dr. Eugenio Asconape 371, (B1744FIG) Moreno ☎237 460 0878 **W:** www.radiorenaceram1340.com.ar – **BA206)** Av. General Paz 3755, (B1672AMA) Villa Lynch ☎11 4755 0479 **W:** www.730am.com.ar **E:** guemes730am@gmail.com – **BA207)** Venezuela 370, 2° piso, (C1095AAH) CA Buenos Aires ☎11 5354 6651 **W:** www.radioam750. com.ar **E:** web@radioam750.com.ar – **BA208)** Ramón L.Falcón 2193, (B1685BDY) El Palomar ☎11 4443 7424 **W:** www.radiolaluna.com.ar – **FM:** 90.5 MHz – **BA209)** Dr.Rebizzo- (Calle 626) – No 3917 (B1678BCC) Caseros ☎11 4578 5130 **W:** www.area1am1320.com.ar **E:** radioarea1@ gmail.com – **BA212)** Marcelo T.de Alvear 650 (B1755JMN) Rafael Castillo ☎11 4697 4919 **W:** www.cunumiguasu.com.ar **E:** cunumiquasu@hotmail.com – **BA213)** Mñor. López May 3372, (B1757DHJ) Gregorio de Laferre ☎11 4467 3600 **W:** //radiooficialdelaferrere.blogspot.com **E:** radioesperanza@gmail.com – **FM:** 88.3 MHz – **BA214)** Calle Gen. Lavalle 2307, (B1847BQW) Rafael Calzada ☎11 4219 1903 **W:** www. radiofundacion.org.ar **E:** contacto@radiofundacion.org.ar – **BA216)** José C. Paz ☎2320 59 9321 **W:** www.generalpazam1390.com – **BA217)** Pedro Luro 1296, (B7103AYJ) General Lavalla ☎2252 49 1126 – **BA218)** Av. Ceballos 241 (CB6620HQ) Chivilcoy ☎2346 42 4532 **E:** cope1410@ gmail.com – **BA219)** Juan Carlos Molina 830, (B1846BEL) José Mármol ☎11 4291 2544 **W:** //radiounidad.com.ar **E:** radiounidad941@yahoo. com.ar – **FM:** 94.1MHz – **BA220)** Ejército de los Andes 5, Villa Florito, (B1821BWA) Banfield Oeste ☎11 4276 2423 **W:** www.rbn1510am.com. ar **E:** rbn.am1510@hotmail.com – **BA221)** Fardman 4640, (B1757IIJ) Gregorio de Laferrere ☎11 4626 7749 **E:** am1530laroca@hotmail.com. es – **BA222)** Camino Costanero Almirante Brown, Columna 273 (B1931), Punta Lara ☎221 410 4915 **W:** www.fmfuertebarragan.com.ar **E:** info@ fmfuertebarragan.com.ar – **FM:** 89.3 MHz – **BA223)** Faustino Brughetti 1392, (B7100) Dolores ☎2245 44 3131 **W:** www.laregionhoy.com.ar **E:** radiodsentires@hotmail.com – **FM:** 97.1 MHz R.Dolores – **BA224)** Merlo ☎220 470 4265 **W:** www.radiosentires.com **E:** sentires1620@hotmail.com – **BA225)** Aristtóbulo del Valle 1582, X° Piso, (B1602EIB) Florida **W:** www.amradiotradicional.jimdo.com.ar **E:** amradiotradicional@ yahoo.com.ar – **BA226)** Remedios de Escalada de San Martin 65, PB "1", (B6000CZA) Junin ☎236 444 4450 – **FM:** 96.5MHz – **BA227)** La Plata ☎221 410 4800 **W:** www.diagonal1630.com.ar **E:** diagonal@ diagonal1630.com.ar – **BA228)** Buenos Aires – **BA229)** Buenos Aires – **BA230)** Avenida Colón 80, (B8000FTN) Bahía Blanca ☎291 459 5058

E: radio@.uns.edu.ar – **BA231)** 9 de Abril, Barrio La Victoria, Partido de Esteban Echeverría ☎15 4977 2740

CA00) CATAMARCA
CA01) Chacabuco 762, (K4700BTP) S.F. del Valle de Catamarca ☎3833 42 4223 🖷3833 42 2251 **W:** www.lra27.com.ar **E:** catamarca@radionacional.gov.ar - **FM:** 103.3MHz

CB00) CHUBUT
CB01) Av. Alvear 1180, (U9200AXY) Esquel ☎2945 45 1900 **W:** www. lra9.com.ar **E:** esquel@radionacional.gov.ar - **FM:** 88.7MHz – **CB02)** Av. Hipólito Yrigoyen 1735, (U9102BGM) Trelew ☎280 443 0580 🖷280 442 5457 **W:** www.radiochubut.com.ar **E:** lu20@speedy.com.ar or info@ lu20radiochubut.com.ar - **FM:** 95.7MHz Galaxia – **CB03)** 25 de Mayo 453, (U9000CXC) Comodoro Rivadavia ☎297 447 2125 🖷297 446 2564 **E:** administracionlra11@radionacional.gov.ar - **FM:** 94.7MHz – **CB04)** Estivariz 226, (U9120KEF) Puerto Madryn ☎280 445 1600 **W:** www. lu17.com **E:** lu17@patagonia.net - **FM:** 100.3MHz – **CB05)** Av. Rivadavia 198, (U9000AKP) Comodoro Rivadavia ☎297 447 6561 **W:** www. lu4radio.com.ar **E:** direccion@lu4radio.com - **FM:** 101.7MHz FM Alfa – **CB06)** 25 de Mayo 740, (U9100BRP) Trelew ☎280 443 5221 **W:** www. radio3cadenapatagonia.com.ar **E:** radiotres@speedy.com.ar – **CB07)** Av. Comandante Fontana y Dr. Mariano Moreno, (U9033) Alto Rio Senguer ☎2945 49 7050 **E:** directorlra55@radionacional.gov.ar - **FM:** 93.5MHz – **CB08)** Rawson – **CB09)** Esquel.

CF00) CIUDAD AUTÓNOMA DE BUENOS AIRES (BUENOS AIRES)
CF01) Rivadavia 835, (C1002AAG) CA Buenos Aires ☎11 4999 1500 🖷11 4338 4250 **W:** www.continental.com.ar **E:** info@continental.com. ar – **CF02)** Arenales 2467, (C1124AAM) CA Buenos Aires ☎11 5219 4744 🖷11 5219 4760 **W:** www.rivadavia.com.ar **E:** info@rivadavia.com. ar – **CF03)** Sarmiento 1551, 8° Piso, (C1042ABC) CA Buenos Aires ☎11 5371 4646 🖷11 5371 4613 **W:** www.radiodelaciudad.gov.ar **E:** ciudadam1110@gmail.com – **CF04)** Gral. Mansilla 2668, 1° piso (C1425BPD) CA Buenos Aires ☎11 5777 1500 🖷11 5777 1504 **W:** www.cienradios.com.ar/argentina/mitre-am790 **E:** info@radiomitre.com.ar – **CF05)** Maipú 555, (C1006ACE) CA Buenos Aires ☎11 4327 3021. 🖷11 4325 9433 **W:** www.radionacional.com.ar **E:** buenosaires@radionacional. gov.ar - **International Sce:** see International Broadcasting section – **CF06)** Fitz Roy 1460, (C1414CHT) CA Buenos Aires ☎11 5032 0400 **W:** www.radiolared.multimediosamerica.com.ar **E:** info@radiolared. com.ar – **CF07)** Pedro Conde 935, (C1426AYS) CA Buenos Aires ☎11 4546 0633 **W:** www.radio9am.com **E:** contacto@radio9am.com – **CF08)** José Ignacio Gottiti 5963, (C1414BKK) CA Buenos Aires ☎11 4556 9000 🖷11 4556 9056 **W:** www.amdelplata.com – **CF09)** Rivadavia 825, (C1002AAG) CA Buenos Aires ☎11 4121 8900 **W:** www.radioelmundo. com.ar **E:** info@radioelmundo.com.ar – **CF10)** José de Amenábar 23, (C1426AIA) CA Buenos Aires ☎11 4778 8500 **W:** www.estoesamerica. com **E:** contacto@amradioamerica.com – **CF11)** Av. Entre Ríos 1931, (C1133AAH) CA Buenos Aires ☎11 4307 2200 **W:** www.radiobuenosaires.com.ar **E:** am1350@radiobuenosaires.com.ar – **CF12)** San Martín 569, 2° piso "6", (C1004AAK) CA Buenos Aires ☎11 4893 1701 **W:** www.splendid990.com.ar **E:** info@splendid990.com.ar – **CF13)** Fitz Roy 1940, (C1414CID) CA Buenos Aires ☎11 4535 4000 **W:** www.infobae. com or www.radio10.com **E:** radio10@infobae.com – **CF15)** Sarmiento 1586, 6° Piso "E", 2° Cuerpo, (C1042ABD) CA Buenos Aires ☎11 4372 2841 **W:** www.am1010ondalatina.com.ar **E:** contactoam1010@yahoo. com.ar – **CF16)** Av. Rivadavia 10561, 3° piso, (C1408AAF) CA Buenos Aires ☎11 5631 1000 🖷11 5631 1001 **W:** www.cadenaeco.com. ar **E:** radio@cadenaeco.com.ar – **CF17)** Av.Rivadavia 10561, 3° Piso, (C1408AAF) CA Buenos Aires ☎11 5631 1000 🖷11 5631 1001 **W:** www. cadenaeco.com.ar **E:** am1530@cadenaeco.com.ar – **CF18)** Traful 3834, (C1437HML) CA Buenos Aires ☎11 4912 0497 **W:** www.am840generalbelgrano.com.ar **E:** am840generalbelgrano@hotmail.com – **CF20)** Av. Saénz 459, (B1437DNE) CA Buenos Aires ☎11 4912 0819 **W:** www. radiourkupina.com.ar **E:** info@sergiocorrea.com.ar – **CF21)** Cerrito 422, PB "B", (C1010AAF) CA Buenos Aires ☎11 5252 0741 **W:** www.am740. com.ar **E:** direccíon@radiocooperativa.com.ar – **CF22)** Av. San Juan 2461, (C1232AAG) CA Buenos Aires ☎11 4942 6913 **W:** www.radioaleluya.com.ar – **CF23)** Av. Int. Francisco Rabanal 1465, PA, (C1437FPB) CA Buenos Aires ☎11 4919 2994 **W:** www.radiobolivia.net **E:** radioboliviafm@hotmail.com – **CF24)** Montevideo 497, 3° Piso "B", (C1019ABI) CA Buenos Aires ☎11 4371 2597 **W:** www.amradiodelpueblo.com. ar **E:** gerencia@amradiodelpueblo.com.ar – **CF26)** Bonpland 1114, (C1414CMJ) CA Buenos Aires ☎11 4856 8819 **W:** www.radioidentidad.com.ar **E:** radioidentidad@radioidentidad.com.ar – **CF27)** Maipu 267 7° Piso, (C1084ABE) CA Buenos Aires ☎11 4136 1050 **W:** www. conceptoam.com.ar **E:** radio@conceptoam.com.ar – **CF28)** Salguero 2745, 6° Piso, Of.. 63, (C1425DEL) CA Buenos Aires ☎11 4803 4434 🖷 11 4807 6006 **W:** www.la1420.com.ar **E:** amlamarea@amlamare.com.ar – **CF29)** Av.José María Moreno 1443, 1° piso, (C1424AAB) CA Buenos Aires ☎11 4926 0177 **W:** www.radioam1310.com **E:** radioam1310@ gmail.com – **CF30)** San Martin 569 2° piso "6", (C1004AAK) CA Buenos

Aires ☎11 4893 1701 **W:** www.am570radioargentina.com.ar **E:** info@am570radioargentina.com.ar – **CF31)** Manzanares 4006, (C1430AEN) CA Buenos Aires ☎11 4541 0303 **W:** www.cadenauno.com.ar **E:** mensajes@cadenauno.com.ar – **CF32)** Av. Triunvirato 4671, (C1431FBJ) CA Buenos Aires ☎11 4521 3931 **W:** www.am1710.com.ar **E:** mensajes@am1710.com.ar – **CF33)** Brasil 907, 1° Piso "B", (C1154AAO) CA Buenos Aires ☎11 4307 1835 **W:** www.amtango.com.ar **E:** amtango@amtango.com.ar – **CF34)** Pte. Luis Sàenz Peña 210 (C1110AAF) CA Buenos Aires ☎11 4382 9327 **W:** www.madres.org **E:** radio@madres.org – **CF35)** Av. José María Moreno 1443, 1° Piso, (C1424ABB) CA Buenos Aires ☎11 4926 1622 **W:** www.radiogenesis970.com.ar **E:** mensajes@radiogenesis970.com.ar – **CF36)** Fonrouge 76, (C1408HFB) CA Buenos Aires ☎11 3979 5663 **W:** www.radiooliva.net **E:** radiooliva2006@hotmail.com – **CF37)** Alicia Moreau de Justo 2050, 1°P, Of. "132", (C1107AFP) CA Buenos Aires ☎11 4893 7555 **W:** www.radioelsol.com.ar **E:** trd@trdpublicidad.com.ar - **FM:** 93.1MHz – **CF38)** San Martín 569, 2° Piso "6", (C1004AAK) CA Buenos Aires ☎11 4893 1701 **W:** www.reporteram650.com.ar – **CF39)** Pje. Espinillo 1449, PA "1", (C1407ISA), CA Buenos Aires ☎11 4683 3641 **W:** //radiopanamericana1260.blogspot.com – **CF41)** Rivadavia 1615, 12° Piso, Oficina 46/47 (C1033AAG) CA Buenos Aires ☎11 4383 9773 **W:** www.amradiopunto.com.ar **E:** contacto@amradiopunto.com.ar – **CF43)** Cnel. Martiniano Chilavert 5875, (C1439CLM) CA Buenos Aires ☎11 4605 4857 **W:** www.siembraelpan.com.ar/radio_amanecer.html **E:** radio_amanecer@hotmail.com – **CF44)** Av. Callao 441,17° Piso "G", (C1022AAE) CA Buenos Aires ☎11 4372 5863 **W:** www.am1230creativa.com.ar **E:** am1230creativa@yahoo.com.ar – **CF45)** Ulrico Schmidt 6057, 4° Piso, (C1440CFS) CA Buenos Aires ☎11 3530 9382 **W:** www.am690.com.ar **E:** radioam690@yahoo.com.ar – **CF46)** Av. Callao 178, 1° Piso, (C1022AAO) CA Buenos Aires ☎11 4374 2500 **W:** www.manantialdesalud.com.ar **E:** info@manantialdesalud.com.ar – **CF47)** Pje. Gibson 3999 (C11 4921 9999) CA Buenos Aires ☎11 4921 9999 **W:** www.radiofantastico.com.ar – **CF48)** Av.Pueyrrdeon 19, 2° Piso, (C1032ABA) CA Buenos Aires ☎11 4864 2230 **W:** www.amrebelde.com.ar **E:** amrebelde@hotmail.com – **CF49)** Libertad 434, 1 Subsuelo, Of. 5, (C1012AAJ) CA Buenos Aires ☎11 4381 4305 **W:** www.am1590.com.ar **E:** supersebak@gmail.com

CH00) CHACO:
CH01) Av. General Güemes 1103, (H3730AML) Charata ☎3731 42 0150 🖨 3731 42 0735 **W:** www.mocovi.com.ar **E:** am800@mocovi.com.ar - **FM:** 95.7MHz FM Lider – **CH02)** Acceso Ruta Nacional N° 40 s/n, Barrio Gendarmería, (U9030) Río Mayo ☎2903 42 0099 **E:** direccionlra58@radionacional.gov.ar - **FM:** 88.1MHz – **CH03)** Av. Sarmiento 1255, (H3502COE) Resistencia ☎362 443 2920. 🖨362 442 4937.- **W:** www.radionacional.chaco.com.ar **E:** resistencia @radionacional.gov.ar **Guaraní:** Sat. 1800 - **FM:** 96.7MHz – **CH04)** Avellaneda - Calle 19 - No 151, (H3700ASC) Presidencia Roque Sáenz Peña ☎364 442 9651 **W:** www.lt16.net **E:** lt16am950@yahoo.com.ar - **FM:** 93.3MHz – **CH05)** Córdoba 710, (H3500APP) Resistencia ☎362 442 9490 🖨362 443 3999 **W:** www.radiochaco.com.ar **E:** radiochaco740@yahoo.com.ar - **FM:** 101.5MHz FM Chaco – **CH06)** San Martin - Calle 12 - N° 1213, (H3700BJY) Presidencia Roque Sáenz Peña ☎364 442 7188 **W:** www.lrcradio.com.ar **E:** lrcradio@hotmail.com - **FM:** 101.5MHz – **CH07)** Juan José Castelli – **CH08)** Maipú 540 (H3730DPL) Charata ☎3731 42 0159 – **CH09)** Comodoro Rivadavia

CO00) CORDOBA:
CO01) Fray Miguel de Mojica 1600, Barrio Marquez de Sobremonte, (X5008CCN) Córdoba ☎🖨351 410 5000 **W:** www.580am.com.ar **E:** administracion@srtunc.com.ar - **FM:** 102.3MHz Nuestra Radio – **CO02)** Santa Rosa 241, (X5000ESE) Córdoba ☎351 422 5664 🖨351 422 5665 **W:** www.radionacionalcba.com.ar **E:** cordoba@radionacional.gov.ar - **FM:** 100.1 MHz – **CO03)** 27 de Abril 979, (X5000AES) Córdoba ☎351 526 5200 🖨351 526 5222 **W:** www.am970.com.ar **E:** info@am970.com.ar - **FM:** 99.7MHz R. Dos – **CO04)** Constitución 399, (X5800BBB) Río Cuarto ☎358 463 8255 **W:** www.lv16.com **E:** lv16@lv16.com - **FM:** 93.9, 106.9MHz – **CO05)** Alvear 139, (X5000ILC) Córdoba ☎351 526 0597 **W:** www.lv3.com.ar **E:** audencia@cadena3.com.ar - **FM:** 92.3, 100.5, 106.9MHz – **CO06)** Libertad 455 2° Piso, (X5850KNI) Río Tercero ☎3571 42 1019 **W:** www.lv26.com.ar **E:** lv26@itc.com.ar - **FM:** 94.5MHz FM Libra – **CO07)** Tucumán 159, (X6120EOC) Laboulaye ☎3385 42 6259 🖨3385 42 5848 **W:** www.radiolv20.com **E:** radiolv20.com – **CO08)** Córdoba 51,"Edifico Reggio II", (X2400PQA) San Francisco ☎3564 42 2186 **W:** www.lavozdesanjusto.com.ar **E:** lavoz@lavozdesanjusto.com.ar - **FM:** 88.7MHz FM Galaxia – **CO09)** Santa Fe 1490, (X5900DTJ) Villa María ☎353 452 2699 **W:** www.radiovillamaria.com **E:** contame@radiovillamaria.com - **FM:** 98.5 MHz FM Record – **CO12)** Blvd. 25 de Mayo 133, PB, (X2421ABB) Morteros ☎3562 42 2148 🖨3562 42 3176 **W:** www.radiomorteros.com.ar **E:** radiomorteros@yahoo.com.ar - **FM:** 90.3MHz FM Selección – **CO13)** Av. Concepción Arenal 1174, (X5004AAY) Córdoba ☎351 460 1010 **W:** www.radiosucesos.com **E:** audiencia@radiosucesos.com - **FM:** 104.7MHz – **CO14)** Pte.Gral. Julia A.Roca 36, (X6120CGB) Laboulaye ☎3385 42 5199 **W:** www.1610am.

com.ar **W:** info@1610am.com.ar **CO15)** Santa Fé 804, (X6270CWR) Huinca Renancó ☎2336 44 2007 **W:** www.lv22.com.ar **E:** lv22_1490@yahoo.com.ar – **CO16)** Av. Fernando Fader 3469, Barrio Cerro de Las Rosas, (X5009ABB) Córdoba ☎351 526 1300 **W:** www.cienradios.com.ar/argentina/mitre-cordoba - **FM:** 97.9MHz – **CO17)** Corrientes – **CO18)** Tolosa 2379, Barrio Maipú, (X5014JSE) Córdoba ☎351 411 7010 **W:** www.radioamvida.com **E:** inforadioamvida.com.ar

CS00) CORRIENTES:
CS01) Chacra 46, Km 3, La Tablada, (W3340) Santo Tomé ☎3756 42 0090 **E:** santotome@radionacional.gov.ar - **FM:** 100.5MHz – **CS02)** Juan Sitja Nin 491, (W3230GEQ) Paso de los Libres ☎3772 42 4332 **W:** www.radiolt12.com.ar **E:** contacto@radiolt12.com.ar - **FM:** 92.7MHz – **CS03)** La Rioja 743, (W3400BZG) Corrientes ☎379 442 3560 🖨379 442 3149 **W:** www@radiolt7.com **E:** info@radiolt7.com - **FM:** 95.3MHz FM Capital – **CS04)** Mariano I. Loza 231, (W3450BXE) Goya ☎3777 43 3002 **W:** www.lt6noticias.com.ar **E:** lt6radiogoya@hotmail.com.ar - **FM:** 98.3MHz FM Esplendida – **CS05)** General Paz 903, (W3344AYQ) Alvear ☎3772 47 0699 **W:** www.lt21radioalvear.com.ar **E:** lt21radiomunicipal@hotmail.com – **CS06)** Av. Atanaico Aguirre Km 2, (W3470EHA) Mercedes ☎3773 42 0087 **W:** www.radioliberia.com.ar **E:** oyentes@lt42.net.ar - **FM:** 93.5MHz – **CS07)** San Martín 1380, (W3461AKA) Curuzú Cuatiá ☎3774 42 2634 🖨3774 42 5873 **W:** www.lt25.com.ar **E:** info@lt25..com.ar - **FM:** FM Guarani 107.1MHz – **CS08)** Goya – **CO09)** Paso de los Libres

ER00) ENTRE RIOS:
ER01) San Martín 371, (E3200FUG) Concordia ☎345 421 5506 **W:** www.lt15concordia.com.ar **E:** lt15adm@arnet.com.ar - **FM:** 89.3MHz – **ER02)** Av. Rivadavia 126, (E3100GNO) Paraná ☎343 423 0101 **W:** www.lt14.com.ar **E:** lt14@radiolt14.com.ar - **FM:** 93.1MHz Baxada del Paraná (ER03) Justo José de Urquiza al Oeste, Parada 12, (E2820) Gualeguaychú ☎3446 42 6159 **E:** gualeguaychu@radionacional.gov.ar - **FM:** 98.7MHz – **ER04)** Carlos Pellegrini 106, (E2822EWD) Gualeguaychú ☎3446 43 7550 🖨3446 42 7088 **W:** www.lt41.com.ar **E:** info@radiolt41.com.ar - **FM:** 90.3 / 97.9MHz – **ER05)** Av. Pte. Juan D. Perón 117, (E3280CBS) Colón ☎3447 42 1067 **W:** www.nuevomundodigital.com.ar **E:** radionmundo@ colonred.com.ar - **FM:** 93.7MHz FM Palmares – **ER06)** Sarmiento 474, (E3153EZH) Victoria ☎3436 42 1285 **W:** www.lt39am980.com.ar **E:** gerencia@lt39am980.com.ar - **FM:** FM Victoria 90.3MHz – **ER07)** Pablo Stampa 2430, (E3228FDD) Chajarí ☎3456 42 0002 **W:** www.multimedioschajari.com.ar **E:** info@multimedioschajari.com - **FM:** 107.7MHz – **ER08)** Chacabuco 38, 1° Piso, (E2840BFB) Gualeguay ☎3444 42 4915 **W:** www.radiogualeguay.com.ar **E:** info@radiogualeguay.com.ar - **FM:** 104.3MHz R.100 – **ER09)** Roque Sáenz Peña 1082, (E3190FZJ) La Paz ☎3437 42 1568 **W:** www.lt40.com.ar **E:** info@lt40.com.ar - **FM:** 91.3MHz FM La Paz – **ER10)** Onésimo Leguizamón 269, (E3260FQE) Concepción del Uruguay ☎3442 42 5661 **W:** www.lt11.net **E:** direccion@eleteonce.com.ar - **FM:** 92.9MHz FM Arenas – **ER11)** Av. Vélez Sársfield 1111, (E3240AUL) Villaguay ☎3455 42 1717 **W:** www.lt27villaguay.com.ar **E:** lt27@clavis.com.ar - **FM:** 88.7MHz FM 27 – **ER12)** Chacabuco 1514, (E3283AWB) San José ☎3447 47 0998 **E:** danycanal@hotmail.com – **ER13)** Dr. Rozados 533, (E3174BEK) Rosario del Tala ☎344 542 3009 **W:** www.siempreprimera.com.ar **E:** frecuenciamediterranea@hotmail.com – **FM:** 102.5MHz – **ER14)** Nogoyá – **ER15)** Calle Justo de Urquiza No 607, (E3133DGM) Maria Grande ☎343 494 1464

F00) FORMOSA:
F001) Junín 655, (P3600IDM) Formosa ☎3717 42 6197 **E:** lra8@radionacional.gov.ar - **FM:** 94.1MHz – **F002)** Ruta Nacional 81 y Ruta Provincial 32, (F3630) Las Lomitas ☎3715 43 2167 **E:** laslomitas@radionacional.gov.ar - **FM:** 93.5MHz – **F003)** Av. 9 de Julio 165, (P3600BCB) Formosa ☎370 442 2590 **W:** www.am990formosa.com **E:** info@am990formosa.com - **FM:** 98.9MHz

JU00) JUJUY:
JU01) Av. España (Sur) 700, (Y4650ALN) La Quiaca ☎3885 42 2356 **E:** laquiaca@radionacional.gov.ar - **FM:** 92.5MHz – **JU02)** Rio Bermejo y Olavarria, (Y4600) San Salvador de Jujuy ☎388 422 2781 🖨388 422 6047 **E:** jujuy@radionacional.gov.ar - **FM:** 94.1MHz – **JU03)** Dr. Horacio Guzmán 496, (Y4600) San Salvador de Jujuy ☎388 423 0035 **W:** radiovisionjujuy.com.ar **E:** rvj@arnet.com.ar - **FM:** 97.7MHz FM Tropico – **JU04)** Av. Villafañe y Calilegua, (Y4608) Perico ☎388 491 1465 **W:** radiovisionjujuy.com.ar **E:** rvj@arnet.com.ar – **JU05)** Jujuy 470, (Y4512DRJ) Libertador General San Martin ☎38 8642 3399 **W:** radiovisionjujuy.com.ar **FM:** 104.5MHz

LP00) LA PAMPA:
LP01) Rivadavia 202, 4° Piso, (L6300DWF) Santa Rosa ☎2954 42 2456 🖨2954 42 5102 **E:** santarosa@radionacional.gov.ar - **FM:** 96.1MHz – **LP02)** Lisandro de la Torre 474, (L6300BQJ) Santa Rosa ☎2954 41 4003 **W:** www.lu33pampeana.com.ar **E:** publicidadlu33@yahoo.com.ar - **FM:** 103.7MHz – **LP03)** Calle 40 No 1250, (L6360EVZ) General Pico ☎2302 43 0055 **W:** www.radiolu37.com.ar **E:** radiolu37@radiolu37.com.ar - **FM:** 88.9MHz Melodiás FM – **LP05)** General Pico 610, (L8201BIL) 25 de Mayo

☎299 494 8086 **W:** www. 25demayo.gov.ar/comunicacion_y_prensa. htm **E:** radiomuni@hotmail.com - **FM:** 91.1MHz FM Rio – **LP06)** José Ingenieros 855, (L6304FBA) Santa Rosa ☎2954 42 7545 **W:** www. antena10.com.ar **E:** radioantena10@gmail.com - **FM:** 102.5MHz R.10 – **LP07)** Calle 39 No 1531, (L6360CNE) General Pico ☎2302 43 4892 **W:** www.amorymisericordia.org **E:** iglesiaamorymisericordia@gmail.com - **FM:** 106.3MHz – **LP08)** Calle 105 Bis (Oeste) No 546, (L6360FLL) General Pico ☎2302 43 2331 **W:** www.laredpampeana.com.ar **E:** contacto@ laredpampeana.com.ar – **FM:** 95.7 MHz

LR00) LA RIOJA:
LR02) Arturo Marasso 170, (F5360CPF) Chilecito ☎3825 42 5025 – **FM:** 99.3 MHz

ME00) MENDOZA:
ME01) Manuel A.Sáez 2421, (M5539HSW) Las Heras ☎261 430 1600 **W:** www.radionihuil.com.ar **E:** radionihuil@radionihuil.com.ar - **FM:** 98.9MHz – **ME02)** Rioja 1093, (M5500ALU) Mendoza ☎261 521 5100 ☐261 521 5121 **W:** www.lvdiez.com **E:** eleve10@info-via.com.ar or info@lvdiez.com.ar - **FM:** 100.9MHz Estacion del Sol – **ME03)** Rioja 1484, (M5500AMD) Mendoza ☎261 423 8872 **W:** www.amlibertador780.blogspot.com **E:** contacto@radio-libertador.com. ar - **FM:** 92.7MHz – **ME04)** Bernado de Irigoyen 17, PA (M5620BDA) General Alvear ☎2625 42 6566 **W:** www.lv23.com.ar **E:** lv23am800@ yahoo.com.ar - **FM:** 88.9MHz – **ME05)** Emilio Civit 460, (M5502GVR) Mendoza ☎261 438 0596 **W:** www.radionacionalmendoza.blogspot. com **E:** mendoza@radionacional.gov.ar - **FM:** 97.1MHz – **ME06)** Esquivel Aldao 350, (M5613AEH) Malargüe ☎260 447 1160 ☐260 447 0658 **W:** www.lv19radiomalargue.com.ar **E:** radiomalargue03@yahoo.com. ar - **FM:** 88.1MHz – **ME07)** Av. Hipólito Yrigoyen 223, (M5602HBC) San Rafael ☎260 443 0055 ☐260 443 0065 **W:** www.radiosanrafael. com **E:** lv14@radiosanrafael.com - **FM:** 97.3MHz – **ME08)** Comandante. Salas 150 1 Piso Of. 6, (M5600DJD) San Rafael ☎260 444 9342 **E:** prensalv18@sanrafael.gov.ar - **FM:** 98.7MHz – **ME09)** Av. Pellegrini 692, (M5560EMT) Tunuyán ☎2622 42 5588 **E:** lv24am1320@yahoo.com.ar - **FM:** 104.5MHz – **ME10)** Av. Bandera de los Andes 4420, (M5521AXL) Villa Nueva de Guaymallén ☎261 421 3992 **W:** www.radiomuraldo. com.ar **E:** mensajes@radionrualdo.com.ar - **FM:** 90.5MHz FM Familia. – **ME11)** Valle de Uspallata, Las Heras – **ME12)** Comandante Salas 200, (M5602AVD) San Rafael ☎260 442 4265 – **FM:** 104.5 FM Andina – **ME13)** Mendoza

MS00) MISIONES:
MS01) Cristóbal Colón 1452, (N3300LXF) Posadas ☎3752 43 3432 **W:** www.lt17.com.ar **E:** info@lt17.com.ar - **FM:** 107.3MHz FM Provincia – **MS02)** Félix de Azara 2440, (N3300LQZ) Posadas ☎3752 43 0500 **W:** www.lt4digital.com - **FM:** 104.5MHz – **MS03)** Av. Victoria Aguirre Sur 009, (N3370AYI) Puerto Iguazú ☎3757 42 0099 **E:** puertoiguazu@ radionacional.gov.ar - **FM:** 99.1MHz – **MS04)** Av. Las Calandrias y Las Golondrinas, (N3370) Puerto Iguazú ☎3757 42 0060 **W:** www.radio-cataratas.com **E:** info@radiocataratas.com - **FM:** 94.7MHz – **MS07)** Domingo F.Sarmiento 1847, 7° Piso, (N3300HUM) Posadas ☎3752 42 0203 ☐3752 42 2758 **W:**www.tupambaenoticias.com.ar **E:** tupambae@ tupambaenoticias.com.ar or tupambae@arnet.com.ar – **Guaraní:** Sun 0900-1500. - **FM:** 105.9MHz

NE00) NEUQUÉN:
NE01) Gral. Paz 536, (Q8353CGL) Chos Malal ☎2948 42 1198 **E:** chos-malal@radionacional.gov.ar - **FM:** 92.3MHz – **NE02)** Av. San Martín 324, (Q8340EYQ) Zapala ☎2942 42 2960 **E:** zapala@radionacional. gov.ar - **FM:** 93.9MHz – **NE03)** Gral. Villegas 1320, (Q8370ELB) San Martín de los Andes ☎2972 42 7766 **W:** www.radionacional.com. ar/emisoras/6-patagonia-norte/37-lra-53-radio-nacional-san-martin-de-los.html **E:** sanmartindelosandes@radionacional.gov.ar - **FM:** 92.5MHz – **NE04)** Fotheringham 445, (Q8302HBI) Neuquén ☎299 443 2772 **W:** www.lu5am.com.ar **E:** info@lu5am.com.ar - **FM:** 94.7, 102.5, 103.3MHz – **NE06)** Las Rosas 81, Barrio Jardín, (Q8315AYA) Piedra del Aguila ☎2942 49 3216 **W:** www.rga1310am.com.ar **E:** contactorga@ gmail.com - **FM:** 99.5MHz – **NE07)** Pte. Bernardino Rivadavia 609, (Q8300HDM) Neuquén ☎299 443 0249 **W:** www.cumbream.com.ar **E:** cumbre@cumbream.com.ar - **FM:** 89.9MHz FM Cumbre – **NE09)** Neuquén – **NE10)** Santa Cruz 679, (Q8300) Neuquén ☎299 449 5109 ☐299 442 1568 **W:** www.rtn.gob.ar **E:** rtnweb@neuquen.gov.ar – **NE11)** Neuquén

RN00) RIO NEGRO:
RN01) Av. 12 de Octubre 2421, (R8403AOH) San Carlos de Bariloche ☎2944 42 2457 ☐2944 42 4035 **W:** www.lra73bariloche.com.ar **E:** bariloche@radionacional.gov.ar - **FM:** 95.5MHz – **RN02)** Tucumán 1074, (R8332HQV) General Roca ☎298 443 0640 ☐298 442 6192 **W:** www. radioelvalle.com **E:** am640@radioelvalle.com - **FM:** 99.3MHz FM Color – **RN03)** Gral. Roca 365, 2° piso, (R8324BPG) Cipolletti ☎299 477 6333 ☐299 477 6800 **W:** www.lu19lavozdelcomahue.com **E:** ricardodiluca@ lu19lavozdelcomahue.com - **FM:** 102.9MHz FM 19 – **RN04)** Av. Alvaro Barros 1148, (R8500FFX) Viedma ☎2920 42 7700 **W:** www.lu15radio. com.ar **E:** gerencia@lu15radio.com.ar - **Italian:** Sat 1500-1600. - **FM:**

94.3MHz FM - Rio – **RN05)** Remedios de Escalada 52, (R8336FED) Villa Regina ☎298 446 1102 ☐298 446 2620 **W:** www.lu16radiorn. com **E:** info@lu16radio.com.ar - **FM:** FM Rio Negro 92.7MHz – **RN06)** Gral. Manuel Belgrano 710, (R8500FAP) Viedma ☎2920 43 1697 **E:** viedma@radionacional.gov.ar - **FM:** 93.5MHz – **RN07)** Av. San Martín y Salta, (R8430) El Bolsón ☎2944 49 2350 **W:** lra57.radionacional.com. ar **E:** elbolson@radionacional.gov.ar - **FM:** 92.5MHz – **RN08)** Martín Coronado y José Hernández, (R8418) Ingeniero Jacobacci ☎2940 43 2032 **E:** ingenierojacobacci@radionacional.gov.ar - **FM:** 93.5MHz – **RN09)** Casa de Tucumán 481, (R8361BKO) Luis Beltrán ☎2946 48 0180 **W:** www.lamunicipalam1470.com.ar **E:** contacto@lamunicipalam1470. com.ar - **FM:** 93.9MHz – **RN10)** Pte. Julio A. Roca 570, (R8503BHL) General Conesa ☎2931 49 8653 – **RN11)** Hipolito Yrigoyen y Remedios de Escalada, (R8536BBE) Valcheta ☎2934 49 3283 **E:** aznarezmarco@ hotmail.com - **FM:** 105.3MHz FM Alegria – **RN12)** Hipólito Yrigoyen 402, (R8534) Sierra Colorada ☎2940 49 5176 **E:** am_provincia@hotmail.com – **RN13)** Ruta Nacional N 22, Km 1200, (R8328xxxx) Allen ☎298 445 4000 **W:** //radioam740.com.ar **E:** radioam740@gmail.com

SA00) SALTA:
SA01) Ruta Nal. 34,km. 1433, (A4560CJA) Tartagal ☎3875 421600 **W:** www.radionacionaltartagal.blogspot.com **E:** tartagal@radionacional.gov.ar - **FM:** 92.3MHz – **SA02)** Dr.Carlos Pellegrini 715, 1° piso, (A4402FYO) Salta ☎387 426 0109 ☐387 427 2468 **W:** www.radionacionalsalta. blogspot.ar **E:** salta@radionacional.gov.ar - **FM:** 102.7MHz – **SA03)** Deán Funes 28 (☐ Cas. 113), (A4400EDB) Salta ☎387 431 3233 ☐378 431 1140 **W:** www.radiosalta.com **E:** contacto@radiosalta.com - **FM:** 96.9MHz FM Genesis – **SA05)** Gorriti 524, (A4560BRL) Tartagal ☎3873 42 4141 **E:** lw2@fullnet.com.ar - **FM:** 96.9MHz FM Géminis – **SA06)** 9 de Julio 163, (A4530XBF) San Ramón de la Nueva Orán ☎3878 42 1026 **W:** www.radiooran.com **E:** oranradio@yahoo.com - **FM:** 90.9MHz FM Orán

SC00) SANTA CRUZ:
SC01) Comodoro Py 342, (Z9407BFH) Río Turbio ☎☐2902 421131 **W:** www.lra18.com.ar **E:** rioturbio@radionacional.gov.ar - **FM:** 90.3MHz – **SC02)** Zapiola 25, (Z9400BCA) Río Gallegos ☎2966 42 0023 ☐2966 42 2608 **W:** www.lu12.com.ar **E:** lu12_am680@speedy.com.ar - **FM:** 92.9MHz – **SC03)** Av. San Martín 1114, (Z9311AVY) Gobernador Gregores ☎2962 49 1044 **E:** direccionlra59@radionacional.gov.ar - **FM:** 99.9MHz – **SC04)** Hermanos Vidal 261, (Z9405) El Calafate **W:** www. lu23..com.ar **E:** info@lu23.com.ar ☎2902 49 5580. - **FM:** 88.1MHz – Glaciar FM – **SC05)** Ramón Lista 36, (Z9050DLB) Puerto Deseado ☎297 487 1211 **E:** lri200@deseado.gov.ar – **SC06)** Av. Pte. Julio A. Roca 823, 1°piso, (Z9400BAH) Río Gallegos **W:** www.santacruz.gov. ar/lu14 **E:** radiolu14@santacruz.gov.ar ☎2966 42 2315 ☐2966 42 3510 - **FM:** 99.3MHz FM Provincia – **SC07)** Saavedra 1318, (Z9040BQN) Perito Moreno ☎2963 43 2233 **E:** administracionlra56@radionacional.gov.ar - **FM:** 93.5MHz – **SC08)** Rio Gallegos

SE00) SANTIAGO DEL ESTERO:
SE01) 9 de Julio 390, (G4200DEH) Santiago del Estero ☎☐385 421 3230 **W:** radiolv11.com.ar **E:** mensajeria@radiolv11.com.ar - **FM:** 88.1, 89.5MHz FM Total – **SE02)** Urquiza 332, 1° Piso, (G4300DHH) Santiago del Estero ☎385 421 2565 **E:** santiagodelestero@radionacional.gov.ar - **FM:** 93.5MHz – **SE03)** Av. 25 de Mayo sur 69, (G3760AEA) Añatuya ☎3844 42 1661 **W:** www.amradiosolidaridad.com.ar **E:** amsolidari-dad@yahoo.com.ar

SF00) SANTA FE:
SF01) Mendoza 2430, 7° piso, (S3000CHB) Santa Fé ☎342 453 3340. ☐342 452 8640 **W:** www.nacionalsantafe.comeride.gov.ar **E:** santafe@ radionacional.gov.ar - **FM:** 94.9MHz – **SF02)** Córdoba 1843, (S2000AXC) Rosario ☎341 410 0600. ☐341 410 0637 **W:** www.lt8.com.ar **E:** info@ lt8.com.ar - **FM:** 99.5MHz – **SF03)** 9 de Julio 3560, (S3002EXB) Santa Fé ☎342 452 0187 **W:** www.lt10digital.com.ar **E:** correo@lt10digital.com. ar - **FM:** 103.5MHz – **SF04)** 4 de Enero 2153, (S3000FHY) Santa Fé ☎342 410 9999 **W:** www.lt9.ceride.com.ar **E:** lt9@ceride.gov.ar - **FM:** 92.5MHz – **SF05)** Av. Pte. Juan Domingo Perón 8101, (S2010ACF) Rosario ☎341 457 5415 **W:** www.radio3.com **E:** radio2@rosario3.com - **FM:** 97.9MHz FM Vida – **SF06)** Córdoba 1331, 1° Piso, (S2000AWS) Rosario ☎341 440 2490 **W:** www.lranacionalrosario.com **E:** rosario@radionacional. gov.ar – **FM:** 104.5MHz – **SF07)** Balcarce 840, (S2000DNR) Rosario ☎341 530 1190 **W:** www.lt3.com.ar **E:** lt3@lt3.com.ar - **FM:** 102.7MHz – **SF08)** Av. Casey 642, (S2600FJN) Venado Tuerto ☎346 242 0777 **W:** www.radiovenadotuerto.com.ar **E:** lt29@radiovenadotuerto.com. ar – **FM:** 88.9MHz – **SF09)** Blvd. Lehman 245, (S2300GSC) Rafaela ☎3492 50 1470 **W:** www.lt28rafaelaargentina.com **E:** www.am1470. com.ar **E:** lt28@lt28rafaelaargentina.com - **FM:** 96.5MHz – **SF10)** Juan Chavarri 458, (S2147AUH) San Jenaro Norte ☎3401 49 3069 **W:** www. radiolt23.com **E:** lt23@co19set.com.ar - **FM:** 92.1MHz FM Concierto – **SF11)** Lucas Funes 1258, (S3560ETZ) Reconquista ☎3482 42 8945 **W:**www.radioamanecer.com.ar **E:** radioamanecer@radioamanecer.com. ar - **FM:** 92.7MHz FM Amanecer – **SF12)** Ludueña 661, (S3560EWM) Reconquista ☎3482 42 2005 **W:** www.radioobligado.com.ar **E:** info@

am1440.com.ar - **FM:** 95.7MHz – **SF14)** Belgrano 470, (S2349AJJ) Suardi ☎3562 47 7612 **W:** www.radiobelgranosuardi.com.ar **E:** belgrano@suardi.com.ar - **FM:** 104.9MHz – **SF17)** Corrientes 1172, 8° Piso "A", (S2000CTX) Rosario ☎341 558 1090 **W:** www.amlibertad.com.ar am1100@argentina.com – **SF18)** José Grevasio Artigas 253, (S2013ALA) Rosario ☎ 341 474 7584 **W:** www.radiofosil.com.ar – **SF19)** Rioja 670 (S2000AYF) Rosario ☎341 449 5040 **W:** www.mariatti.com **E:** info@mariatti.com – **SF20)** 25 de Mayo 3255, (S3000FUI) Santa Fe ☎342 410 1370 **W:** www.airedesantafe.com.ar **E:** info@airedesantafe.com.ar – **FM:** 91.1MHz – **SF21)** Ruta Provincial 28 s/n, (S2521) Montes de Oca **W:** www.am1600.com.ar – **SF22)** Av.San Martín 710, (S3142XAC) Luis Palacio ☎3476 49 9249 **W:** www.radioalegria.supersitio.net **E:** radioalegriaregional@hotmail.com.ar – **FM:** 99.3MHz – **SF23)** Casilda 5670, (S2007CKN) Rosario ☎341 437 3431

SJ00) SAN JUAN:
SJ01) Mitre 50 Oeste, (J5402CXB) San Juan ☎264 422 2344 📱264 421 4950 **W:** www.lv1radiocolon.com.ar **E:** colonsa@speedy.com.ar - **FM:** 105.7, 106.3MHz – **SJ02)** Av. Ignacio de la Roza 293 Este, 2° Piso, (J5402DBC) San Juan ☎264 421 4149. 📱264 421 4264 **E:** sanjuan@ radionacional.gov.ar - **FM:** 91.3MHz – **SJ03)** Av. Belgrano y San Martin, (J5405AAA) Barreal ☎2648 44 1260 - **FM** Nuestra 103.5MHz – **SJ04)** Mendoza 452 Sur, (J5402GUJ) San Juan ☎264 420 4028 **W:** www. lv5radiosarmiento.com.ar **E:** lv5@radiolv5.com - **FM:** 102.3, 103.7, 104.3, 104.7MHz Sarmiento FM – **SJ05)** General Paz 631, (J5460BBM) San José de Jáchal ☎2647 42 0028. 📱2647 42 0561 **E:** jachal@radionacional.gov.ar - **FM:** 102.7MHz – **SJ06)** Mitre 11 este, (J5402CWA) San Juan ☎264 427 2740. - **FM:** 105.1 – **SJ07)** Santa Fe 681 oeste, (J5402ACM) San Juan ☎264 422 4646 📱264 421 2443 **W:** www. am1020sj.com.ar **E:** info@am1020sj.com.ar - **FM:** 96.3

SL00) SAN LUIS:
SL01) Lavalle 291, Planta Alta, (D5732AEE) Villa Mercedes ☎📱2657 42 4400 **W:** www. radiolv15.com.ar **E:** lv15@speedy.com.ar - **FM:** 95.5MHz FM Unica – **SL02)** Av. Lafinur 488, (D5700DCR) San Luís ☎264 443 1318 **E:** sanluis@radionacional.gov.ar - **FM:** 96.7MHz – **SL03)** Ruta Provincial No 3 s/n, Extremo Sur, (D5700) San Luís ☎266 445 8100 **W:** www.am940dimension.com.ar **E:** info@am940dimension.com.ar - **FM:** Maxima FM 92.5/102.5MHz – **SL04)** General Paz 1078, (D5732AGJ) Villa Mercedes ☎2657 43 7734 **W:** www.mariadelapazradio.com.ar – **FM:** 105.3 MHz

TU00) TUCUMAN:
TU01) Lapride 530, (T4000IFL) San Miguel de Tucmán ☎381 484 5100 **W:** www. lv12.com.ar **E:** radiolv12@yahoo.com.ar - **FM:** 99.1MHz – **TU02)** Mendoza 273, (T4000DAE) San Miguel de Tucumán ☎381 497 5080 **W:** www.lv7.com.ar**E:** lv7@lv7.com.ar - **FM:** 102.7MHz – **TU03)** San Martín 251, 4 Piso, (T4000CVE) San Miguel de Tucumán ☎381 431 0131 📱381 430 2409 **E:** tucuman@radionacional.gov.ar - **FM:** MHz – **TU04)** San Martín 610, Piso 6 "6", (T4000CVN) San Miguel de Tucumán ☎381 400 0247 **W:** www.radio21tucuman.com.ar **E:** info@ radio21tucuman.com.ar

TF00) TIERREA DEL FUEGO:
TF01) Leonardo Rosales 490, (V9420CMJ) Río Grande ☎2964 42 2176 📱2964 43 0763 **W:** www.nacionalriogrande.com.ar **E:** direccion@ nacionalriogrande.gov.ar - **FM:** 88.1MHz – **TF02)** Av. San Martín 331, (V9410BFD) Ushuaía ☎2901 42 1670 **W:** www.mracionalushuaia.com.ar **E:** lra10@radionacional.gov.ar **FM:** 92.1MHz – **TF03)** Ushuaia – **TF04)** Río Grande

FM in Buenos Aires: CF05) 93.7 R.Pop Nac – 96.7 FM Clásica Nacional – 98.7 Folclórica FM – **CF22)** 89.1 – **CF28)** 89.9 FM La Isla – **CF16)** 90.3 Eco Radio, 91.1 R.Abierta, 92.1 Mambo, 92.3 La Radio – **CF03)** 92.7 La Ciudad, 93.7, FM Federal – **CF09)** 94.3 Disney, 94.7 FM Palermo – **CF08)** 95.1 La Metro – **CF12)** 95.9 Rock & Pop, 96.3 R.Jai – **CF05)** 96.7 Clásica, 97.1 FM Europa, 97.3 Contacto FM, 97.9 R.Cultura – **CF13)** 98.3 Mega – **CF05)** 98.7 FM Folklorica, 99.1 Cadena 3 Argentina – **CF04)** 99.9 Cadena 100, 100.3 FM Cultural Musical – **CF07)** 100.7 Blue FM, 101.1 La Ciento Uno – **CF06)** 101.5 Pop Radio – **CF10)** 102.3 Aspen Classic – **CF02)** 103.1 R. Uno, 103.7 Amadadeus FM – **CF01)** 104.3 – **CF01)** 105.5 FM Hit – **CF11)** 106.3 R.Alfa, 106.7 X4, 107.3 Milenium, 107.9 Kabul Rock.
In the city area there are over 150 unlicensed LP FM stns, about 900 in the rest of the country.
FM in Córdoba: 88.1 FM Láser, 90.1FM Sur – **CO02)** 91.3 R.Nacional, 91.9 Hot FM – **CO05)** 92.3 R.Popular, 92.9 FM Logos, 93.7 R.Vital, 94.3 R.Universidad, 95.1 Radiocentro Bar, 96.1 FM Shopping Classics, 96.3 FM Norte, 96.5 R.Suquia, 96.9 CNI, 98.5 FM Latinoamericana, 99.1 FM Amistad, 99.3 FM Impacto – **CO03)** 99.7 Estacion Tierra – **CO05)** 100.5 FM Córdoba, 101.5 R.Maria – **CO01)** 102.3 Power 102, 102.7 FM Vision – **CO13)** 104.7, 105.5 FM Cielo, 107.5 Box Music Station, 107.9 FM Potencia
FM in Mar del Plata: 87.7 R.Urbana, 87.9 R. 87.9, 88.1 Graffiti FM, 88.3 LV del Puerto, 88.5 Onda Cero, 88.7 DeLaAzotea, 88.9 Mediterran

– **BA83)** 89.1 Red Impacto, 89.3 Láser, 89.7 d-Rock, 90.1 R. 90.1, 90.5 Kids, 90.7 Rural, 90.9 Concierto FM, 91.3 La Red, 91.7 K.L.A., 92.1 R. María, 92.3 Nova-92, 92.7 Líder – **BA09)** 93.3 Atlantica Latina, 93.7 Lisán, 94.1 R. 94-1 – **BA105)** 94.5 Latina, 94.9 Mega, 95.3 R. Uno, 95.9 Compacto, 96.5 Residencias, 96.9 Red 92, 97.1/ 97.5 R 97-1, 97.5 Popular, 97.6 R. 97.6, 97.7 Faro, 97.9 Estación 97, 98.1 R.Disney, 98.5 Brisas, 98.9 Rock'n Pop, 99.1 R. 99.1, 99.5 Más R., 99.9 Coast, 101.1 Cadena Musica, 100.3 Cadena Latina, 100.7 Del Sol, 101.1 Red Master, 101.5 Arena Sports, 101.7 La Ola, 101.9 Concierto, 102.1 Bristol, 102.1 R.10, 102.3 Municipal, 102.5 Nativa, 102.9 Ferimar, 102.9 Box, 102.9 La Nueva – **BA02)**103.3 Universo, 103.7 Premium, 103.9 Canaan, 104.1 FM 104-1, 104.5 Via, 104.7 Urbana, 104.9 LV Amiga, 104.9 Cosmos, 105.1 Señal, 105.5 Inolviable, 105.9 Coast-Melody, 106.3 Five, 106.5 Argentian, 106.7 Sur, 106.9 Veronica, 107.1 Cielo, 107.5 Radioactiva, 107.7 R.107.7, 107.9 Trinidad.
FM in Rosario (Santa Fe): 89.5 R.Fisherton (CNN R.), 90.9 Uruguay – **SF05)** 92.3 FM Vida, 92.7 A-Z 927, 92.9 Radioactiva, 93.7 Cordial, 94.5 Latina, 95.5 Corazon, 96.5 Rio – **SF05)** 97.9 Vida, 98.5 Tango, 98.9 FM Si – **SF02)** 99.5 Estacion del Siglo, 100.5 Radiofónica, 100.9 Meridiano, 101.3 Hollywood – **SF02)** 102.3 FM No – **SF07)** 102.7 – **SF06)** 104.5 R.Nacional, 105.5 Tiempo Libre, 107.1 R.Universidad, 107.9 Cristal FM
FM in Santa Fe: 89.9 Federal, 90.7 Eclipse – **SF04)** 92.5 Láser, 93.1 Estacion Rock – **SF01)** 94.9 R.Nacional, 98.1 Santa Fe Capital, 101.7 Cielo, 104.3 Plenitud, 104.5 Sensación, 105.1 Hot 105, 105.5 News, 105.9 Ibiza FM – **SF03)** 107.3 FM X, 107.9 R.Antena (CNN R.)

ARMENIA

L.T: UTC +4h — **Pop:** 3.2 million — **Pr.L:** Armenian — **E.C:** 50Hz, 220V — **ITU:** ARM

NATIONAL COMMISSION ON TV AND RADIO (NCTR)
✉ Isahakyan St. 28, 0002 Yerevan ☎ +374 10 528370 📱 +374 10 539034 **E:** nctr@tvradio.am **W:** www.tvradio.am
L.P: Chmn: Grigor Amalyan
NB: NCTR is the licensing body for broadcasting.

HAYASTANI HANRAYIN RADIO (Armenian Public Radio)
✉ A.Manoogian St. 5, 0025 Yerevan ☎ +374 10 551143 📱 +374 10 554600 **E:** aa@arradio.am **W:** www.armradio.am
L.P: DG: Armen Amiryan

FM (MHz)	AR1	AR2	kW
Yerevan	107.6	103.8	1

+ nationwide netw. (AR1)
D.Prgr: AR1 (Armenian Pub. R. 1) 24h. – **AR2 (Arm. Pub. R. 2)** 24h.
External Service (Public R. of Armenia): see Int. Radio section.

OTHER STATIONS

FM	MHz	kW	Location	Station
4)	90.2	1	Yerevan	Nor Radio
5)	90.7	1	Yerevan	Ararat FM
8)	100.6	1	Yerevan	R. Aurora
2)	102.0	2	Yerevan	AR R.Intercontinental
9)	102.4	1	Yerevan	FM-102.4
3)	103.5	1	Yerevan	R. Ardzaganq
1A)	104.1	1	Yerevan	Hay FM
7)	104.9	1	Yerevan	Russkoye R.
1B)	105.5	1	Yerevan	FM-105.5
10)	106.0	1	Yerevan	City FM
6)	107.0	1	Yerevan	ArmRadio7

NB: Txs below 1kW not listed.
Addresses & other information:
1A,B) Pavstos Buzandi St. 1/3, 0010 Yerevan. **E:** info@hayfm.am. 1A) via nationwide tx network; 1B) incl. rel. Europa+ (Russia). – **2)** A.Manoogian St. 5, 0025 Yerevan. **E:** aa@arradio.am – **3)** Armeniak Armenakyan St. 250, 0047 Yerevan. **E:** ardzagank@ardzagank.com – **4)** A.Manoogian St. 5, 0025 Yerevan. **E:** info@sigmatv.am – **5)** Acharyan St. 42, 0040 Yerevan. **E:** info@araratfm.am – **6)** Yeghvard Highway 1, 0054 Yerevan. **E:** info@fm107.am – **7)** Khandjyan St. 13a, 0010 Yerevan. **E:** radio_alfa@mail.ru – **8)** Nairi Zaryan St. 22, 0051 Yerevan. **E:** radio-aurora@mail.ru – **9)** Ovsepyan St. 95, 0047 Yerevan. Rel. RFI (France), Deutsche Welle (Germany) – **10)** Yerevan.

Int. relays on MW: Gavar 864/1314/1350/1377kHz 1000kW, 1395kHz 500kW. See Int. Radio section.

ARUBA (Netherlands)

L.T: UTC -4h — **Pop:** 103,065 — **Pr.L:** Dutch (official), Papiamentu, English, Spanish — **E.C:** 50+60Hz, 127/220V — **ITU:** ABW

DIRECTIE TELECOMMUNICATIE ZAKEN

✉ Rumbastraat 19, Oranjestad ☎297-582-6069 📠 297-582-5307
E: dirtelza@setarnet.aw **W:** www.dtz.aw

MW	kHz	kW	Station, location
2)	1270	2.5	R. 1270 AM, San Nicolas
FM	**MHz**	**kW**	**Station, location**
12)	88.1	1	Mega 88FM, Oranjestad
11)	88.9	0.1	Bo Guia, Oranjestad
3)	89.9	0.25	Canal 90FM, San Nicolas
14)	90.7	0.45	Real FM, Oranjestad
7)	91.5	0.5	Rumba 91.5 FM
10)	92.3	0.1	Latina 92.3, Oranjestad
1)	93.1	0.66	R. Victoria, Oranjestad (Rlg.)
12)	94.1	1	Hit 94 FM, Oranjestad
7)	95.1	1	Top 95 FM, Oranjestad
8)	96.5	0.2	Magic 96.5 FM, Oranjestad
6)	97.9	0.25	Easy FM Aruba, Oranjestad
13)	98.9	0.3	New Cool FM 98.9, Oranjestad
9)	99.9	0.5	R. Galactica 99.9 FM, Oranjestad
16)	100.9	0.85	Hit 100.9, Oranjestad
17)	101.7	0.7	Blizz FM, Oranjestad
15)	105.3	0.5	R. Shalom, Oranjestad
4)	106.7	3	R. Kelkboom, Oranjestad
2)	107.5	0.2	Mi FM, San Nicolas

Addresses and other information

1) Washington 23A (P.O.Box 5291) Oranjestad ☎/📠 +297 587 3444 Mngr: Nico Arts. Rlg: 24h in English, Spanish, Papiamentu, Dutch, Creole, Tagalog and Cantonese **W:** www.radiovictoriaaruba.com – **2)** Balashi 62A, San Nicolas. Mi FM: ☎+297 585 8624 📠 +297 585 8622 **E:** mifmaruba@live.com Radio 1270 AM SM: J.A.C. Alders. Dir: F.A. Leauer – **3)** Van Leeuwenhoekstraat 26, Oranjestad ☎+297 582 1601 📠 +297 583 7340 **E:** canal90fm@gmail.com **W** www.canal90fm.aw **MW:** in Dutch and Spanish – **4)** Bloemond 14, Paradera, Oranjestad ☎+297 582 1899 📠 +297 584 4825 GM: Emile A.M. Kelkboom. 24h in Papiamentu, Dutch, English, Spanish **W:** under construction **E:** radiokelkboom@setarnet.aw – **6)** Sabana Basora 31-D, Oranjestad ☎+297 593 3637 📠 +297 585 2639 GM: Wouter Gesterkamp 24h in English, Papiamentu, Spanish and Dutch **E:** eaysy979fm@yahoo.com and aruba@easyfm.com **W:** under construction – **7)** Santa Cruz 110, Oranjestad ☎+297 585 9500 📠+297 585 0951 24 h in Papiamentu on Top 95 FM and 24 h in Spanish on Rumba FM **W:** www.top95fm.aw **W:** www.rumba91fm.aw Dir. Edmond Croes – **8)** L.G. Smith Boulevard 9 ☎+297 586 5353 📠 +297 586 5354 24h **W:** www.magic965.com **E:** magic965fm@hotmail.com – **9)** Macapruimstraat 1-E, Oranjestad ☎+297 588 2536 📠 +297 583 8999 Man. Dir: Richard A. Arends Stn Man.: Maikel Oduber **E:** radiogalactica@hotmail.com 24h in Papiamentu, English and Dutch – **10)** L.G. Smith Boulevard – 11 ☎+297 582 6608 📠 +297 583 3101 – **11)** Tanki Flip 26B ☎+297 587 3889 📠 +297 587 5889 **E:** radio.boguia@gmail.com – **12)** Caya Ernesto Petronia 68-A, Oranjestad. Mega FM: ☎ +297 582 6888 📠 +297 582 0494 **W:** www.mega88fm.com ; **E:** hit94@setarnet.aw ; 24h in Papiamentu, Spanish and English: Latin Caribbean R.; Hit 94 FM: ☎ +297 582 0694 and +297 583 9494 📠 +297 582 0494 **W:** www.mega88fm.com **E:** hit94@setarnet.aw 24h in Papiamentu, Spanish and English. GM: John A. Habibe – **13)** Caya Betico Croes 23 ☎+297 583 3100 + 297 583 3110 and +297 588 1495 📠+ 297 583 3101 Dir. Alexander Ponson 24 prgr in Papiamentu, Dutch and English **W:** www.coolaruba.com **E:** alex@coolaruba.com – **14)** John G. Emanstraat 124A, Oranjestad ☎+ 297 583 1434 📠+ 297 583 1515 – **15)** Cumana 20, Oranjestad ☎+297 582 5477 📠+ 297 582 5477 Rlg prgr. **W:** www.visionaruba.com – **16)** South Beach Mall, Palm Beach 51 lok. D-7 ☎+297 588 6100 **W:** http://hits100.fm **E:** contact@hits100.fm and inf@hits100.fm – **17)** Piedra Plat 44, Oranjestad ☎+297 585 9766 **E:** info@blizz.aw

ASCENSION ISLAND (UK)

L.T: UTC — **Pop:** 900 — **Pr.L:** English — **E.C:** 50Hz, 220V — **ITU:** ASC

VOLCANO RADIO (USAF)

✉ Ascension Radio Station, Ascension AAF, P.O. Box 4235, Patrick AFB, FL 32925-0235, USA.
FM: AFN, 98.7MHz 0.4kW 24h.
NB: MW service ZD8VR on 1602kHz currently inactive

BBC ATLANTIC RELAY STATION

✉ English Bay, Ascension Island, So. Atlantic.
Local Sce: FM: 93.2MHz 15W (24h relay of BBCWS in English plus occ. local prgrs).
See International section for details of SW relays.

BFBS: BFBS 1 100.9MHz & 107.3MHz, BFBS 2 97.3MHz & 105.3MHz
SAINT FM: 91.4MHz 25W, internet feed from St Helena

AUSTRALIA

L.T: See World Time Table. DST (where applicable): 7 Oct 12-7 Apr 13, 6 Oct 13-6 Apr 14 — **Pop:** 24 million — **Pr.L:** English — **E.C:** 50Hz, 240V — **ITU:** AUS

ABORIGINAL RESOURCE & DEVELOPMENT SERVICES

✉ Box 36921, Winnellie NT 0821 ☎+61 (08) 8984 4174 📠 +61 (08) 8984 4192 **W:** www.ards.com.au **E:** info@ards.com.au
MW: 1530kHz Humpty Doo 2kW

AUSTRALIAN BROADCASTING CORP. (ABC)

HQ: Ultimo Centre, 700 Harris Str, Ultimo, NSW 2007(✉ GPO Box 9994, Sydney NSW 2001) ☎+61 (02) 9333 1500 📠 +61 (02) 9333 5305
MW: N = R. National, L = Local R, P = Parliamentary & News Netw. **Call letters:** 2 = NSW (exc. Canberra = A.C.T.), 3 = Victoria, 4 = Queensland, 5 = So. Australia, 6 = We. Australia, 7=Tasmania, 8=Northern Territory.

MW	Call	kHz	kW	Netw	Location
46)	6DL	531	10	L	Dalwallinu
29)	4QL	540	10	L	Longreach
11)	2CR	549	50	L	Orange (Cumnock)
44)	6WA	558	50	L	Wagin
25)	4JK	567	10(d)	L	Julia Creek
47)	6MN	567	0.1	L	Newman
47)	6PN	567	0.1	L	Pannawonica
47)	6PU	567	0.1	L	Paraburdoo
47)	6TP	567	0.1	L	Tom Price
2)	2RN	576	50	N	Sydney
6)	6PB	585	50	P	Perth
7)	7RN	585	10	N	Hobart
42)	3WV	594	50	L	Horsham
2)	2RN	603	10(d)	N	Nowra
26)	4CH	603	10(d)	L	Charleville
47)	6PH	603	2	L	Port Hedland
4)	4QR	612	50	L	Brisbane
6)	6RN	612	10	N	Dalwallinu
3)	3RN	621	50	N	Melbourne
2)	2PB	630	10	P	Sydney
24)	4QN	630	50	L	Townsville (Brandon)
48)	6AL	630	5	L	Albany
7)	7RN	630	0.4	N	Queenstown
23)	4MS	639	1	L	Mossman
31)	5CK	639	1	L	Port Pirie (Crystal Brook)
8)	8RN	639	2	N	Katherine
14)	2NU	648	10	L	Tamworth (Manilla)
43)	6GF	648	2	L	Kalgoorlie
19)	2BY	657	10(d)	L	Byrock
8)	8RN	657	2	N	Darwin
1)	2CN	666	5	L	Canberra ACT
9)	2CO	675	10	L	Albury (Corowa)
45)	6BE	675	5	L	Broome
13)	2KP	684	10	L	Kempsey (Smithtown)
49)	6BS	684	5	L	Busselton
8)	8RN	684	1	N	Tennant Creek
34)	5SY	693	2(d)	L	Streaky Bay
2)	2BL	702	50	L	Sydney
47)	6KP	702	10	L	Karratha
26)	4QW	711	10(d)	L	Roma/St.George
16)	2ML	720	0.4	L	Murwillumbah
2)	2RN	720	0.05	N	Armidale
38)	3MT	720	2(d)	L	Omeo
23)	4AT	720	4	L	Atherton
6)	6WF	720	50	L	Perth
5)	5RN	729	50	N	Adelaide
16)	2NR	738	50	L	Grafton
49)	6MJ	738	5(d)	L	Manjimup
26)	4QS	747	50	L	Toowoomba (Dalby)
7)	7PB	747	10(d)	P	Hobart (6.3kW night)
8)	8JB	747	0.2	L	Jabiru
13)	2TR	756	2(d)	L	Taree
3)	3RN	756	10(d)	N	Wangaratta
3)	3LO	774	50	L	Melbourne
20)	8AL	783	2	L	Alice Springs
4)	4RN	792	25	N	Brisbane
23)	4QY	801	2	L	Cairns
17)	2BA	810	10	L	Bega
6)	6RN	810	10	N	Perth
14)	2GL	819	10	L	Glen Innes
45)	6KW	819	5	L	Kununurra

MW	Call	kHz	kW	Netw	Location
38)	3GI	828	10	L	Sale (Longford)
46)	6GN	828	10	L	Geraldton
21)	4RK	837	10	L	Rockhampton (Gracemore)
43)	6ED	837	1	L	Esperance
1)	2RN	846	10	N	Canberra
47)	6CA	846	2.5	L	Carnarvon
30)	4QB	855	10(d)	L	Pialba
30)	4QO	855	10	L	Eidsvold
45)	6DB	873	2	L	Derby
5)	5AN	891	50	L	Adelaide
4)	4PB	936	10	P	Brisbane
7)	7ZR	936	10(d)	L	Hobart
5)	5PB	972	2	P	Adelaide
3)	3RN	990	0.5	N	Albury-Wodonga
8)	8GO	990	0.5	L	Gove (Nhulunbuy)
10)	2NB	999	2(d)	L	Broken Hill
45)	6WH	1017	0.5	L	Wyndham
3)	3PB	1026	10	P	Melbourne
18)	2UH	1044	2(d)	L	Muswellbrook
23)	4WP	1044	0.5	L	Weipa
49)	6BR	1044	1	L	Bridgetown
23)	4TI	1062	2	L	Thursday Island
32)	5MV	1062	2	L	Renmark/Loxton
2)	2RN	1098	0.2	N	Goulburn
6)	6PNN	1152	10(d)	P	Busselton
6)	6RN	1152	10(d)	N	Manjimup
33)	5PA	1161	10(d)	L	Naracoorte
35)	7FG	1161	1(d)	L	Fingal
47)	6XM	1188	2	L	Exmouth
46)	6NM	1215	0.5	L	Northam
6)	6RN	1224	5	N	Busselton
15)	2NC	1233	10	L	Newcastle
6)	6RN	1269	5	N	Busselton
6)	6RN	1296	10	N	Wagin
5)	5RN	1305	2	N	Renmark/Loxton
11)	2LG	1395	0.2	L	Lithgow
2)	2RN	1431	2	N	Wollongong
2)	2PB	1458	2	P	Newcastle
33)	5MG	1476	1(d)	L	Mt. Gambier
2)	2RN	1485	0.1	N	Wilcannia
24)	4HU	1485	0.05	L	Hughenden
34)	5LN	1485	0.2	L	Port Lincoln
2)	2RN	1512	10	L	Newcastle
21)	4QD	1548	50	L	Emerald
30)	4GM	1566	0.2	L	Gympie
10)	2WA	1584	0.1	L	Wilcannia
31)	5WM	1584	0.05	L	Woomera
7)	7SH	1584	0.1	L	St. Helens
17)	2CP	1602	0.05	L	Cooma
41)	3WL	1602	0.25	L	Warrnambool
31)	5LC	1602	0.2	L	Leigh Creek South

FM stations (txs of greater than 1kW)
Networks: N=Radio National, L=Local Radio, FM=Fine Music Network, JJJ=Triple J Network (alternative)

FM	Area	State	N	L	FM	JJJ
5)	Adelaide	SA			103.9	105.5
5)	Adel. Foothills	SA			97.5	95.9
39)	Alexandra	VIC	104.5	102.9		
14)	Armidale	NSW		101.9	103.5	101.1
3)	Bairnsdale	VIC	106.3			
36)	Ballarat	VIC		107.9	105.5	107.1
17)	Batemans Bay	NSW	105.1	103.5	101.9	
2)	Bega/Cooma	NSW	100.9		99.3	100.1
37)	Bendigo	VIC		91.1	92.7	90.3
17)	Bombala	NSW		94.1		
2)	Bourke	NSW	101.1			
4)	Brisbane	QLD			106.1	107.7
5)	Broken Hill	NSW	102.9		103.7	102.1
6)	Broome	WA	107.7			
6)	Bunbury	WA			93.3	94.1
35)	Burnie	TAS		102.5		
23)	Cairns	QLD	105.1	106.7	105.9	107.5
23)	Cairns North	QLD	93.9	95.5	94.7	97.1
1)	Canberra	ACT			102.3	101.5
6)	Cen.Agricult	WA			98.9	98.1
23)	Cen.Table'nds	NSW	104.3		102.7	101.9
11)	Cen. Western	NSW	107.9	107.1	105.5	102.3
4)	Darling Downs	QLD	105.7		107.3	104.1
4)	Darwin	NT		105.7	107.3	103.3
2)	Deniliquin	NSW	99.3			
35)	Devonport E	TAS		100.5		
19)	Dubbo City	NSW		95.9		
4)	Emerald	QLD	93.9		90.7	
6)	Esperance	WA	106.3		104.7	

FM	Area	State	N	L	FM	JJJ
6)	Geraldton	WA	99.7		94.9	98.9
2)	Glen Innes	NSW	105.1			
22)	Gold Coast	QLD	90.1	91.7	88.5	97.7
39)	Goulburn V.	VIC		97.7	96.1	94.5
13)	Grafton/Kemp.	NSW	99.5	92.3	97.9	91.5
30)	Gympie	QLD	96.9	95.3	93.7	
9)	Hay	NSW	88.9	88.1		
7)	Hobart	TAS			93.9	92.9
12)	Illawara	NSW		97.3	95.7	98.9
2)	Jerilderie	NSW	94.1			
6)	Kalgoorlie	WA	97.1		95.5	98.7
8)	Katherine	NT		106.1		
5)	Keith	SA	96.9			
35)	King Island	TAS		88.5		
38)	Latrobe Valley	VIC		100.7	101.5	96.7
35)	Lileah	TAS	89.7	91.3		
16)	Lismore	NSW	96.9	94.5	95.3	96.1
4)	Longreach	QLD	99.1			
28)	Mackay	QLD	102.7	101.1	97.9	99.5
13)	Manning River	NSW	97.1	95.5	98.7	96.3
4)	Meandarra	QLD	104.3			
3)	Melbourne	VIC			105.9	107.5
40)	Mildura	VIC	105.9	104.3	102.7	101.1
23)	Mission Beach	QLD	90.9	89.3		
4)	Monto	QLD	101.9			
28)	Moranbah	QLD	106.5	104.9		
4)	Mossman	QLD	90.1			
25)	Mount Isa	QLD	107.3	106.5	101.7	104.1
5)	Mt Gambier	SA	103.3		104.1	102.5
39)	Murray Valley	VIC		102.1	103.7	105.3
9)	Murrumbidgee	NSW	98.9	100.5	97.3	96.5
18)	Muswellbrook	NSW		105.7		
27)	Nambour	QLD		90.3	88.7	89.5
6)	Narrogin	WA		92.5		
35)	NE Tas.	TAS	94.1	91.7	93.3	90.9
2)	Newcastle	NSW			106.1	102.1
3)	Nhill	VIC	95.7			
6)	Perth	WA			97.7	99.3
6)	Port Hedland	WA	95.7			
41)	Portland	VIC	98.5	96.9		
5)	Renmark	SA			105.1	101.9
4)	Rockhampton	QLD	103.1		106.3	104.7
6)	Roebourne	WA	107.5			
26)	Roma	QLD	107.3	105.7	97.7	
31)	Roxby Downs	SA	101.9	102.7	103.5	
6)	Salmon Gums	WA	100.7			
6)	S. Agricultural	WA	96.9		94.5	92.9
46)	South'n Cross	WA	107.9	106.3		
26)	South'n Downs	QLD	106.5	104.9	101.7	103.3
5)	Spencer Gulf N	SA	106.7		104.3	103.5
5)	Streaky Bay	SA	100.9			103.3
9)	SW Slopes	NSW	89.1	89.9	88.3	90.7
2)	Sydney	NSW			92.9	105.7
2)	Tamworth	NSW	93.9		103.1	94.7
4)	Townsville	QLD	104.7		101.5	105.5
5)	Tumby Bay	SA	101.9			
39)	Upper Murray	VIC		106.5	104.1	103.3
14)	Upper Namoi	NSW	100.7	99.1	96.7	99.9
3)	Warrnambool	VIC	101.7		92.1	89.7
42)	Western Vic.	VIC	92.5	94.1	93.3	94.9
30)	Wide Bay	QLD	100.9	100.1	98.5	99.3
4)	Winton	QLD	107.9			
5)	Wirrulla	SA	107.3			
5)	Wudinna	SA	107.7			105.3
6)	Wyndham	WA				98.9

NB: (MHz) Parliamentary News Network: 89.1 Emerald QLD (8d), 89.3 Horsham VIC (20), 89.5 Bendigo VIC (10), 89.7 Bega/Cooma NSW (112d), 90.5 Burnie TAS (1d), 90.9 Illawarra NSW (150d), 91.3 Warrnambool VIC (3.2d), 91.5 SW Slopes/E Riverina NSW (80), 91.5 Tumby Bay SA (2), 90.7 Grafton/Kemspey NSW (20d), 91.7 Tamworth NSW (10), 91.7 Western Victoria (80d), 91.9 Central Tablelands NSW (5d), 92.1 Southern Agricultural WA (80), 92.5 NE Tasmania (192d), 93.5 Inverell NSW (10), 93.9 Renmark SA (150d), 94.3 Ballarat VIC (5d), 94.3 Townsville QLD (92d), 94.5 Gympie QLD (20d), 94.7 Manning River NSW (5), 94.9 Port Hedland WA (2), 95.1 Latrobe Valley VIC (200d), 95.7 Gold Coast (26d), 95.9 Murray Valley VIC (20), 96.3 Cairns North QLD (10d), 96.3 Warwick QLD (2), 96.3 Wagin WA (5), 96.7 Toowoomba QLD (2.5d), 97.7 Portland VIC (2.6d), 97.7 Wide Bay QLD (10d), 98.1 Murrumbidgee NSW (100), 98.5 Lismore NSW (100d), 99.7 Central Agricultural WA (80), 100.3 Mildura VIC (150d), 100.3 Kalgoorlie WA (6), 100.5 Batemans Bay NSW (40d), 100.9 Deniliquin NSW (2d), 100.9 Upper Murray VIC (2), 101.1 Cairns QLD (100), 101.3 Geraldton WA (10), 101.5 Upper Namoi NSW (20d), 102.1 Devonport

East TAS (1.2), 102.5 Darwin (32d), 102.7 Armidale NSW (4), 102.7 Spencer Gulf North SA (70), 103.1 Esperance WA (5), 103.9 Canberra ACT (80), 104.1 Alice Springs NT (1), 104.3 Mackay QLD (100d), 104.5 Broken Hill NSW (4), 104.7 Colac VIC (10d), 104.9 Muswellbrook NSW (16), 104.9 Mount Isa QLD (1), 105.3 Katherine NT (1), 105.5 Rockhampton QLD (80), 105.7 Mt Gambier SA (240d), 106.3 Central West Slopes NSW (220d), 106.9 Broome WA (2), 107.7 Goulburn Valley VIC (5d), 107.9 Bairnsdale VIC (2d).

Reports for R. National, Parliament, ABC-FM and Triple J should go to the capital city ABC office in that state (Addresses 1-8)

ABC local radio addresses:
1) ABC Canberra, GPO Box 9994, Canberra ACT 2601 – **2)** ABC Sydney, GPO Box 9994, Sydney NSW 2001 – **3)** ABC Melbourne, GPO Box 9994, Melbourne VIC 3001 – **4)** ABC Brisbane, GPO Box 9994, Brisbane QLD 4001 – **5)** ABC Adelaide, GPO Box 9994, Adelaide SA 5001 – **6)** ABC Perth, GPO Box 9994, Perth WA 6848 – **7)** ABC Hobart, GPO Box 9994, Hobart TAS 7001 – **8)** ABC Darwin, PO Box 9994, Darwin NT 0801 – **9)** ABC Riverina, 100 Fitzmaurice St, Wagga Wagga NSW 2650 – **10)** ABC Broken Hill, PO Box 315, Broken Hill NSW 2880 – **11)** ABC Central West, PO Box 8549, East Orange NSW 2800 – **12)** ABC Illawarra, PO Box 973, Wollongong NSW 2520 – **13)** ABC Mid North Coast, PO Box 42, Port Macquarie NSW 2444 – **14)** ABC New England / North West, PO Box 558, Tamworth NSW 2340 – **15)** ABC Newcastle, PO Box 2205, Dangar NSW 2309 – **16)** ABC North Coast, PO Box 908, Lismore NSW 2480 – **17)** ABC South East NSW, PO Box 336, Bega NSW 2550 – **18)** ABC Upper Hunter, PO Box 400, Muswellbrook NSW 2333 – **19)** ABC Western Plains, PO Box 985, Mudgee NSW 2830 – **20)** ABC Alice Springs, PO Box 1144, Alice Springs NT 0871 – **21)** ABC Capricornia, GPO Box 911, Rockhampton QLD 4700 – **22)** ABC Gold Coast, PO Box 217, Mermaid Beach QLD 4218 – **23)** ABC Far North, PO Box 932, Cairns QLD 4810 – **24)** ABC North Queensland, PO Box 694, Townsville QLD 4810 – **25)** ABC North West Queensland, 114 Camooweal St, Mount Isa QLD 4825 – **26)** ABC Southern Queensland, PO Box 358, Toowoomba QLD 4350 – **27)** ABC Sunshine Coast, PO Box 1212, Maroochydore QLD 4558 – **28)** ABC Tropical Queensland, PO Box 127, Mackay QLD 4740 – **29)** ABC Western Queensland, PO Box 318, Longreach QLD 4730 – **30)** ABC Wide Bay, PPO Box 1152, Bundaberg QLD 4670 – **31)** ABC North and West South Australia, PO Box 289, Port Pirie SA 5540 – **32)** ABC Riverland, PO Box 20, Renmark SA 5341 – **33)** ABC Southeast, PO Box 1448, Mount Gambier SA 5290 – **34)** ABC Eyre Peninsula, PO Box 679, Port Lincoln SA 5606 – **35)** ABC Northern Tasmania, PO Box 201, Launceston TAS 7250 – **36)** ABC Ballarat, PO Box 7, Ballarat VIC 3353 – **37)** ABC Central Victoria, PO Box 637, Bendigo VIC 3550 – **38)** ABC Gippsland, PO Box 330, Sale VIC 3850 – **39)** ABC Goulburn Murray, PO Box 1063, Wodonga VIC 3690 – **40)** ABC Mildura / Swan Hill, PO Box 10083, Mildura VIC 3502 – **41)** ABC South West Victoria, PO Box 310, Warrnambool VIC 3280 – **42)** ABC Western Victoria, PO Box 506, Horsham VIC 3402 – **43)** ABC Goldfields / Esperance, PO Box 125, Kalgoorlie WA 6430 – **44)** ABC Great Southern, 58 Tudhoe St, Wagin WA 6315 – **45)** ABC Kimberley, PO Box 217, Broome WA 6725 – **46)** ABC Mid West & Wheatbelt, PO Box 211, Geraldton WA 6530 – **47)** ABC North West, PO Box 994, Karratha WA 6714 – **48)** ABC South Coast, 2 St Emilie Way, Albany WA 6330 – **49)** ABC South West, PO Box 242, Bunbury WA 6231.

EXTERNAL SERVICE: Radio Australia
See International Broadcasting section.

DAB: Now rolled out in capital cities: Channel 9A 202.928 MHz, 9B 204.64 MHz, 9C 206.352 MHz. All 50kW. Relays existing stns and some extra programming controlled by existing stns. All prgr also available at http://www.digitalradioplus.com.au/. Sydney NSW, Melbourne VIC, Brisbane QLD all 9A, 9B and 9C. Adelaide SA and Perth WA 9B and 9C. Canberra ACT and Darwin NT trials on channel 10B 211.648 MHz.

NORTHERN TERRITORY SHORTWAVE SERVICE
✉ Box 9994, Darwin, NT 0801

SW: VL8A Alice Springs: 2310kHz (0830-2130), 4835kHz (2130-0830), 3230kHz (alt. freq) – **VL8T Tennant Creek:** 2325kHz (0830-2130), 4910kHz (2130-0830), 3315kHz (alt. freq) – **VL8K Katherine:** 2485kHz (0830-2130), 5025kHz (2130-0830), 3370kHz (alt. freq). Prgrg has been known to run over designated times.

COMMERCIAL RADIO AUSTRALIA
✉ Level 5, 88 Foveaux Street, Surry Hills NSW 2010 Australia ☎ +61 2 9281 6577 🖷 +61 2 9281 6599 **CEP:** Joan Warner

Abbreviations: N-1: News on the h. N-2: News on the half h. N-3:

News on the h and half h. The numeral preceding the call letters indicates the state: 2=New South Wales,. 3=Victoria, 4=Queensland, 5=South Australia, 6=Western Australia; 7=Tasmania, 8=Northern Territory. (/t designated translator station).
News: Additional newscasts are often carried during breakfast and drive times. t=translator (relays main stn).

MW	Call	kHz	kW	Location
1)	2PM	531	5(d)	Kempsey
2)	3GG	531	5(d)	Warragul
3)	4KZ	531	5(d)	Innisfail
4)	7SD	540	5(d)	Scottsdale
5)	4AM	558	5(d)	Atherton
6)	4GY	558	5(d)	Gympie
7)	7BU	558	2	Burnie
8)	2BH	567	0.5	Broken Hill
164)	6EL	621	2	Bunbury
133)	2HC	639	5(d)	Coffs Harbour
33)	4CC(t)	666	2(d)	Biloela
103)	4LM	666	2	Mount Isa
160)	6LN	666	1	Carnarvon
105)	3AW	693	5(d)	Melbourne
9)	4KQ	693	10/5(d)	Brisbane
3)	4KZ(t)	693	0.5	Tully
103)	4LM(t)	693	0.5	Cloncurry
31)	6FMS	747	1	Exmouth
131)	6SE	747	5(d)	Esperance
166)	6TZ	756	2	Margaret River
10)	2EC	765	5(d)	Bega
73)	4GC(t)	765	0.5	Hughenden
134)	5CC	765	5(d)	Port Lincoln
88)	6SAT	765	0.1	Paraburdoo
88)	6SAT	765	0.1	Tom Price
147)	8HOT(t)	765	0.5	Katherine
4)	4TO	774	5(d)	Townsville
13)	6VA	783	2	Albany
14)	5RM	801	2	Berri
73)	4GC	828	1	Charters Towers
16)	7XS	837	0.5	Queenstown
17)	4EL	846	5(d)	Cairns
18)	4GR	864	2	Toowoomba
19)	6AM	864	2	Northam
21)	2GB	873	5	Sydney
22)	3YB	882	2(d)	Warrnambool
24)	4BH	882	5(d)	Brisbane
23)	6PR	882	10	Perth
25)	2LM	900	5(d)	Lismore
107)	2LT	900	5(d)	Lithgow
58)	6BY	900	2	Bridgetown
27)	7AD	900	2	Devonport
28)	8HA	900	2	Alice Springs
29)	2XL	918	2	Cooma
153)	4VL	918	2/2.5	Charleville
164)	6NA	918	2	Narrogin
32)	3UZ	927	5	Melbourne
33)	4CC	927	5(d)	Gladstone
69)	4HI(t)	945	1(d)	Dysart
36)	2UE	954	5	Sydney
17)	4EL(t)	954	0.35	Gordonvale
38)	2RG	963	5(d)	Griffith
37)	4WK	963	5(d)	Warwick
93)	5SE	963	5(d)	Mt. Gambier
164)	6TZ	963	2	Bunbury
86)	2DU(t)	972	0.3	Cobar
39)	2MW	972	5(d)	Murwillumbah
112)	2NM	981	5(d)	Muswellbrook
41)	3HA	981	2	Hamilton
42)	6KG	981	2	Kalgoorlie
43)	4RO	990	5(d)	Rockhampton
45)	2ST	999	5(d)	Nowra
46)	4TAB	1008	10(d)	Brisbane
49)	2KY	1017	5	Sydney
139)	4AA	1026	5(d)	Mackay
52)	6NW	1026	2	Port Hedland
53)	5AU	1044	2	Port Pirie
54)	2CA	1053	5(d)	Canberra
55)	3EL	1071	5(d)	Maryborough
4SB		1071	2	Kingaroy
151)	6WB	1071	2	Katanning
57)	2MO	1080	5(d)	Gunnedah
61)	6IX	1080	2	Perth
59)	2EL	1089	5(d)	Orange
60)	3WM	1089	5(d)	Horsham
61)	4LG	1098	2	Longreach
62)	6MD	1098	2	Merredin
156)	3AK	1116	5(d)	Melbourne

MW	Call	MHz	kW	Location
65)	4BC	1116	6.3/17(d)	Brisbane
135)	6MM	1116	2	Mandurah
113)	5MU	1125	5(d)	Murray Bridge
66)	2AD	1134	2(d)	Armidale
67)	3CS	1134	5(d)	Colac
164)	6TZ(t)	1134	2	Collie
68)	2HD	1143	2	Newcastle
69)	4HI	1143	5(d)	Emerald
70)	2WG	1152	2	Wagga Wagga
30)	4FC	1161	2	Maryborough
72)	2CH	1170	5	Sydney
75)	2NZ	1188	2	Inverell
80)	2CC	1206	5/5(d)	Canberra
78)	2GF	1206	5(d)	Grafton
69)	4HI(t)	1215	0.25	Moranbah
82)	3GV	1242	5(d)	Sale
85)	4AK	1242	2	Toowoomba
84)	5AU	1242	2(d)	Port Augusta
86)	2DU	1251	2	Dubbo
32)	3SR	1260	2	Shepparton
88)	6KA	1260	1	Karratha
89)	2SM	1269	5	Sydney
90)	3EE	1278	5	Melbourne
91)	2TM	1287	2	Tamworth
32)	3BT	1314	5(d)	Ballarat
40)	5DN	1323	2	Adelaide
98)	3SH	1332	2	Swan Hill
99)	4BU	1332	5(d)	Bundaberg
102)	2LF	1350	5(d)	Young
37)	4WK(t)	1359	0.25	Toowoomba City
104)	2GN	1368	2	Goulburn
105)	3MP	1377	5(d)	Melbourne
106)	5AA	1395	5(d)	Adelaide
108)	2PK	1404	2	Parkes/Forbes
5)	4AM(t)	1422	1(d)	Port Douglas
111)	2MG	1449	5(d)	Mudgee
32)	3ML	1467	2	Mildura
115)	4ZR	1476	2	Roma
116)	2AY	1494	2	Albury
117)	2BS	1503	5(d)	Bathurst
142)	6BAY	1512	5	Geraldton
119)	2QN	1521	2	Deniliquin
120)	2VM	1530	2	Moree
121)	2RE	1557	2	Taree
122)	3NE	1566	5(d)	Wangaratta
10)	2EC(t)	1584	0.2	Narooma
33)	4CC(t)	1584	0.5	Rockhampton
153)	4VL(t)	1584	0.2	Cunnamulla

FM stations (1kW and higher):

FM	Call	MHz	kW	Location
117)	2BS(t)	88.1	2(d)	Burraga
3)	4KZ(t)	88.5	1(d)	Mission Beach
165)	4RGC	88.5	1	Mossman
170)	8SAT	88.7	1	Hawker SA
41)	3HFM	88.9	20(d)	Hamilton
56)	4KRY	89.1	15	Kingaroy
117)	2BS(t)	89.3	1(d)	Blayney
63)	7LAA	89.3	5(d)	Launceston
46)	4TAB	89.7	5(d)	Beaudesert
71)	5CCC	89.9	6(d)	Port Lincoln
48)	7EXX	90.1	5(d)	Launceston
69)	4HIT(t)	90.3	1	Blackwater
130)	5SSA (t)	90.3	2(d)	Adelaide Foothills
154)	4SEA	90.9	25(d)	Gold Coast
170)	8SAT	90.9	4(d)	Maitland SA
168)	4MCY	91.1	10(d)	Nambour
150)	4RBL	91.1	1.5	Tara
123)	2MAC	91.3	1	Campbelltown
120)	2NOW(t)	91.3	1	Lightning Ridge
32)	3SRR(t)	91.3	1.2(d)	Mt. Buller
96)	4HIT	91.3	5	Moranbah
148)	3PTV	91.5	56(d)	Melbourne
29)	2SKI(t)	91.7	1	Bombala
45)	2ST(t)	91.7	2(d)	St Georges Basin
17)	4HOT(t)	91.7	1	Mossman
52)	6HED	91.7	2	Port Hedland
55)	3BDG	91.9	120(d)	Bendigo
18)	4RGD	91.9	2	Warwick
15)	4SEE	91.9	10(d)	Nambour
169)	5ADL	91.9	20(d)	Adelaide
150)	4BRZ	92.1	5(d)	Beaudesert
16)	7AUS	92.1	20(d)	Queenstown/Zeehan
29)	2XL(t)	92.5	1	Bombala
96)	4CCA(t)	92.5	1	Mossman
155)	4GLD	92.5	25(d)	Gold Coast

FM	Call	MHz	kW	Location
86)	2ZOO	92.7	10	Dubbo
15)	4SSS	92.7	10(d)	Nambour
29)	2SKI(t)	92.9	1	Thredbo
91)	2TTT	92.9	20(d)	Tamworth
120)	2VM(t)	92.9	1	Lightning Ridge
44)	6PPM	92.9	40(d)	Perth
143)	2GEE	93.1	10	Mudgee
70)	2WZD	93.1	80	Wagga Wagga
154)	4RGB	93.1	3(d)	Bundaberg
14)	5RIV	93.1	10(d)	Renmark/Loxton
163)	2DBO	93.5	10	Dubbo
1)	2PM(t)	93.5	3(d)	Port Macquarie
104)	2SNO	93.5	40	Goulburn
35)	3BBO	93.5	120(d)	Bendigo
43)	4ROK	93.5	1(d)	Gladstone
41)	3HFM(t)	93.7	2	Portland
87)	3SUN(t)	93.7	1(d)	Alexandra/Eildon
87)	3SUN(t)	93.7	1.2(d)	Mt. Buller
87)	3SUN(t)	93.7	1(d)	Yea
150)	4RBL	93.7	4	Tenterfield NSW
47)	6PER	93.7	40(d)	Perth
102)	2LFF	93.9	40	Young
101)	3BAY	93.9	55(d)	Geelong
99)	4RUM	93.9	3.2(d)	Bundaberg
83)	2BDR	94.1	1(d)	Falls Creek VIC
2)	3SEA(t)	94.3	7	Warragul
60)	3WWM(t)	94.5	2	Nhill/Lawloit
79)	6MIX	94.5	40(d)	Perth
29)	2SKI(t)	94.7	2	Jindabyne
69)	4HIT	94.7	5	Emerald
45)	2WSK	94.9	50(d)	Nowra
141)	4MIX	94.9	50(d)	Ipswich
88)	6KAN	94.9	5	Katanning
75)	2GEM	95.1	10	Inverell
43)	4RGK	95.1	1(d)	Gladstone
115)	4ROM	95.1	1	Roma
145)	2PTV	95.3	150(d)	Sydney
32)	3SRR	95.3	100(d)	Shepparton
162)	3YFM	95.3	20(d)	Warrnambool
13)	6AAY	95.3	50(d)	Albany
170)	8SAT	95.3	2(d)	Karoonda SA
108)	2ROK	95.5	2(d)	Parkes/Forbes
101)	3CAT	95.5	55(d)	Geelong
170)	8SAT	95.5	3(d)	Kingscote (SA)
151)	6BUN	95.7	40(d)	Bunbury
73)	4CHT	95.9	1.5	Charters Towers
12)	2ONE	96.1	5	Katoomba
6)	4NNN	96.1	5(d)	Gympie
150)	4RBL	96.1	1	Weipa
93)	5SEF	96.1	20	Mount Gambier
125)	6NOW	96.1	40(d)	Perth
29)	2XL(t)	96.3	2(d)	Jindabyne
8)	2HIL	96.5	4(d)	Broken Hill
95)	2UUL	96.5	40(d)	Wollongong
142)	6GGG	96.5	30(d)	Geraldton
19)	6NAM	96.5	10	Northam
170)	8SAT	96.5	4(d)	Pinnaroo (SA)
40)	5ADD(t)	96.7	2(d)	Adelaide Foothills
161)	2SYD	96.9	150(d)	Sydney
118)	3SUN	96.9	100(d)	Shepparton
14)	5RIV	97.1	2.5(d)	Morgan
159)	4BFM	97.3	12	Brisbane
150)	4RBL	97.3	1	Inglewood
135)	6CST	97.3	5(d)	Mandurah
57)	2GGG	97.5	20(d)	Gunnedah
29)	2SKI	97.7	50(d)	Cooma
170)	8SAT	97.7	5(d)	Birchip VIC
170)	8SAT	97.7	3(d)	Coonalpyn SA
136)	3RMR	97.9	12(d)	Mildura
5)	4AMM	97.9	5(d)	Atherton
42)	6KAR	97.9	6	Kalgoorlie
170)	8SAT	97.9	1.3(d)	Roxby Downs SA
112)	2VLY	98.1	20(d)	Muswellbrook
123)	2WIN	98.1	40(d)	Wollongong
142)	6BAY	98.1	30(d)	Geraldton
120)	2NOW	98.3	100(d)	Moree
11)	4TOO	98.3	2(d)	Bowen
3)	4ZKZ	98.3	20(d)	Innisfail
77)	5MMM(t)	98.3	2(d)	Adelaide Foothills
60)	3WWM(t)	98.5	2(d)	Ararat
98)	3SHI(t)	98.7	1	Kerang
158)	4RGM	98.7	100(d)	Mackay
113)	5EZY	98.7	20(d)	Murray Bridge
170)	8SAT	98.9	10(d)	Minlaton SA
169)	5ADL(t)	99.1	2(d)	Adelaide Foothills

FM	Call	MHz	kW	Location
117)	2BXS	99.3	10	Bathurst
170)	8SAT	99.3	4	Streaky Bay (SA)
150)	4RBL	99.4	2(d)	Mt. Tamborine
114)	3MDA	99.5	20(d)	Mildura
82)	3TFM	99.5	20(d)	Sale
150)	4RBL	99.5	1	Meandarra
157)	4RGC	99.5	10(d)	Cairns
170)	8SAT	99.5	1(d)	Kapunda SA
38)	2RGF	99.7	50	Griffith
113)	5EZY	99.7	1	Victor Harbour
132)	6CAR	99.7	5	Carnarvon
154)	7RGS	99.7	5(d)	Scottsdale
82)	3TFM(t)	99.9	5(d)	Bairnsdale
69)	4HI(t)	100.1	1(d)	Rolleston Mine
147)	8HOT	100.1	15(d)	Darwin
66)	2NEB	100.3	10	Armidale
121)	2RE(t)	100.3	1.6	Forster
172)	3MEL	100.3	56(d)	Melbourne
51)	4MKY	100.3	100(d)	Mackay
113)	5EZY(t)	100.3	1	Mount Barker
170)	8SAT	100.3	5(d)	Padthaway East (SA)
116)	2AAY(t)	100.5	1(d)	Falls Creek VIC
88)	6BET	100.5	5	Bridgetown
164)	6NAN	100.5	5	Narrogin
150)	4BRZ	100.6	2(d)	Mt. Tamborine
1)	2PQQ	100.7	20(d)	Port Macquarie
18)	4RGD	100.7	10(d)	Toowoomba
11)	4RGR	100.7	100(d)	Townsville
25)	2ZZZ	100.9	32(d)	Lismore
144)	7TTT	100.9	36	Hobart
50)	3TTT	101.1	56(d)	Melbourne
140)	2CFM	101.3	16	Gosford
60)	3WWM	101.3	20(d)	Horsham
52)	6HED	101.3	2	Broome
170)	8SAT	101.5	5(d)	Lake Cargellico NSW
43)	4RGK	101.5	10	Rockhampton
81)	2UUS	101.7	150(d)	Sydney
33)	4CCC	101.7	2	Charleville
20)	7HHO	101.7	36	Hobart
27)	7SEA(t)	101.7	20(d)	Burnie
120)	2NOW(t)	101.9	1	Collarenebri
126)	3FOX	101.9	56(d)	Melbourne
149)	4CEE	101.9	10(d)	Maryborough
139)	4MMK	101.9	100(d)	Mackay
122)	3NNN	102.1	25(d)	Wangaratta
1)	2ROX	102.3	20	Port Macquarie
94)	3RBA	102.3	20(d)	Ballarat
11)	4TOO	102.3	100(d)	Townsville
40)	5ADD	102.3	20(d)	Adelaide
131)	6SEA	102.3	5	Esperance
10)	2EEE	102.5	5	Bega
119)	2MOR	102.5	50	Deniliquin
150)	4BRZ	102.5	4	Tenterfield NSW
150)	4BRZ	102.5	1	Childers
170)	8SAT	102.5	3	Bourke
96)	4CCA	102.7	10(d)	Cairns
75)	2GEM	102.9	2	Warialda
109)	2KKO	102.9	20(d)	Newcastle
45)	2ST	102.9	2	Bowral
76)	4HTB	102.9	25(d)	Gold Coast
52)	6NW	102.9	2	Broome
94)	3BBA	103.1	20(d)	Ballarat
34)	4RAM	103.1	100(d)	Townsville
120)	2VM(t)	103.5	1	Collarenebri
96)	4HOT	103.5	10(d)	Cairns
149)	4MBB	103.5	10(d)	Maryborough
78)	2GF(t)	103.9	5(d)	Maclean
128)	2DAY	104.1	150(d)	Sydney
39)	2MW(t)	104.1	1(d)	Gold Coast QLD
10)	2EEE	104.3	20(d)	Batemans Bay/Moruya
25)	2LM(t)	104.3	1(d)	Kyogle
74)	3KKZ	104.3	56(d)	Melbourne
171)	2GOS	104.5	16	Gosford
61)	4LRE	104.5	1(d)	Longreach
127)	4MMM	104.5	12	Brisbane
78)	2CLR	104.7	20(d)	Grafton
138)	2ROC	104.7	20	Canberra
77)	5MMM	104.7	20(d)	Adelaide
116)	2AAY	104.9	100(d)	Albury
129)	2MMM	104.9	150(d)	Sydney
150)	4RBL	104.9	3	Bourke NSW
146)	8MIX	104.9	30(d)	Darwin
120)	2NOW(t)	105.1	1	Walgett
59)	2OAG	105.1	5	Orange
1)	2ROX	105.1	10(d)	Kempsey

FM	Call	MHz	kW	Location
124)	3MMM	105.1	56(d)	Melbourne
62)	6MER	105.1	10	Merredin
139)	2NEW	105.3	20(d)	Newcastle
92)	4BBB	105.3	12	Brisbane
133)	2CSF	105.5	15	Coffs Harbour
10)	2EC(t)	105.5	1	Eden
120)	2VM(t)	105.5	1	Mungindi
83)	2BDR	105.7	100(d)	Albury
167)	6IX(t)	105.7	4(d)	Wanneroo
10)	2EC(t)	105.9	20(d)	Batemans Bay/Moruya
59)	2GZF	105.9	5	Orange
84)	5AUU	105.9	20	Spencer Gulf North
170)	8SAT	106.1	3	Ceduna/Smoky Bay (SA)
137)	1CBR	106.3	20	Canberra
133)	2CFS	106.3	15	Coffs Harbour
67)	3CCS	106.3	10(d)	Colac
11)	4RGT	106.3	100(d)	Townsville
64)	2WFM	106.5	150(d)	Sydney
88)	6RED	106.5	1	Karratha
1)	2PQQ	106.5	10(d)	Kempsey
45)	2ST(t)	106.7	1.6	Ulladulla
120)	2VM(t)	106.7	1	Walgett
150)	4RBL	106.7	1	Childers
100)	2XXX	106.9	20(d)	Newcastle
26)	4BNE	106.9	12	Brisbane
170)	8SAT	106.9	2	Minnipa SA
146)	8MIX	106.9	1	Katherine
120)	2NOW(t)	107.1	1	Mungindi
130)	5SSA	107.1	20(d)	Adelaide
121)	2MVB	107.3	10(d)	Taree
150)	4BRZ	107.3	1	Bourke (NSW)
152)	7XXX	107.3	36	Hobart
170)	8SAT	107.3	2(d)	Kingston SE (SA)
97)	2GGO	107.5	16	Gosford
98)	3SHI	107.7	10	Swan Hill
27)	7DDD	107.7	7(d)	Devonport
107)	2ICE	107.9	10(d)	Lithgow
34)	4RAM(t)	107.9	2(d)	Bowen
43)	4ROK	107.9	10	Rockhampton

Addresses and other information (ARN: Australian Radio Network). **NB:** The term midnight-to-dawn refers to local time. Exact hrs vary from stn to stn

1) PO Box 1161, Port Macquarie NSW 2444 (DMG). Supplementary stn. on 102.3MHz and 105.1MHz – **2)** PO Box 253, Warragul Vic. 3820. (N-2) – **3)** PO Box 19, Innisfail, Qld. 4860 **E:** zedamfm@4kz.com.au (N-1): Translators: Tully 693kHz 0.5kW, Dunk Island 88.5MHz 0.5kW – **4)** PO Box 189, Scottsdale, TAS. 7254 (N-1).Part of TASmanian Broadcasting Network – **5)** PO Box 177, Mareeba, QLD 4880 (N-1) Translators: Port Douglas 1422kHz, Weipa 97.7MHz – **6)** PO Box 42, Gympie QLD 4370 (N-1) – **7)** PO Box 120, Burnie, TAS. 7320 (N-1) – **8)** 25 Garnet St, Broken Hill, NSW 2880 (N-3). Supplementary stn on 106.9MHz – **9)** PO Box 693, Newstead, QLD 4006 (N-1) – **10)** PO Box 471, Bega, NSW 2550. Translators: 1584=Narooma, 105.9MHz = Batemans Bay – **11)** PO Box 986, Townsville, QLD 4810 **E:** fourto@ultra.net.au **W:** www.ozemail.com.au/~asichter (N-1:) – **12)** PO Box 145, Penrith, NSW 2750 (N-1) – **13)** PO Box 293, Albany, WA 6330. (N-1) – **14)** PO Box 321, Berri SA 5343 **E:** fiverm@riverland.net. au **W:** www.riverland.net.au /~fiverm/ (N-1) – **15)** PO Box 828, Nambour, QLD 4560 (N-1) – **16)** PO Box 315, Queenstown, TAS 7467 (N-3). Translators at Strahan 105.1MHz 25w & Rosebery 107.1MHz 0.3kW – **17)** PO Box 6110, Cairns, QLD 4870. (N-1: Sky Radio) – **18)** PO Box 111, Toowoomba, QLD 4350 (N-1) – **19)** PO Box 256 Northam, WA 6401 – **20)** GPO Box 542F, Hobart, TAS 7001 (N-3) – **21)** GPO Box 4290, Sydney 2001 (N-1) – **22)** PO Box 485, Warrnambool, Vic. 3280 – **23)** GPO Box 6072, Perth, W.A. 6000 (N-1) – **24)** GPO Box 906, Brisbane, QLD 4001 (N-1) – **25)** PO Box 44, Lismore, NSW 2480. (N-1) – **26)** Locked Bag 1069, Fortitude Value BC, QLD 4006 – **27)** PO Box 635, Launceston TAS 7310 – **28)** PO Box 2106, Alice Springs 0871 (N-1).Translator at Yularaon 100.5MHz with 100w. Supplementary st. 8SUN on 96.9MHz with 300w at Alice Springs – **29)** PO Box 651, Cooma, NSW 2630 (N-1) Relays 2UE 9:00-10:00 and AUSTEREO 16:00-18:00. Translators: Thredbo 92.1MHz 1kW, Jindabyne 96.3MHz 2kW and Perisher 98.7MHz 1kW – **30)** 625 Wyndham St, Shepparton, VIC 3630 – **31)** PO Box 665, Carnarvon WA 6701 – **32)** 3UZ Pty Ltd, PO Box 927, Carlton, VIC 3053 (N-1) ID's as "Sport 927" – **33)** PO Box 420, Gladstone, QLD 4680. (N-1). Translator at Rockhampton on 1584 with 500w and at Biloela on 666kHz with 2.5 Kw – **34)** PO Box 986, Townsville, QLD 4810 (FM **E:** hotfm@ultra.net.au) (N-1). 4RR: Racing format, prgrs 8.00-24.00, also relays 4TAB 1408. 4RAM: Translator at Mt Stuart 107.9MHz 1kW, ID's as "103.1 Hot FM" – **35)** PO Box 108, Golden Square, Vic. 3555 (N-1) – **36)** PO Box 950, North Sydney, NSW 2059 (N-3) – **37)** PO Box 195, Warwick, QLD 4370 (N-1) Rel 2TM 1287

7:00pm to 6:00am. Translator: Toowoomba 1359kHz 0.3kW – **38)** PO Box 493, Griffith, NSW 2680 (N-10) – **39)** PO Box 97, Coolangatta, QLD 4225 (N-1). Ids as "Radio 97" – **40)** 201 Tynte St, Nth Adelaide SA 5006. **W:** www.5dn.com.au (N-1) – **41)** PO Box 981, Hamilton, VIC 3300 (N-1) – **42)** PO Box 440, Kalgoorlie, WA 6430 (N-1) – **43)** PO Box 159, Rockhampton, QLD 4700 (N-1) – **44)** PO Box 157, Subiaco, WA 6008 (N-1) – **45)** PO Box 540, Nowra 2540 (N-1). Translators: Uladulla 106.7MHz. Supplementary St. on 94.9MHz. (N-1) – **46)** Radio 4TAB, PO Box 275, Albion, QLD 4010. Racing format – **47)** Level 1, 464 Hay St, Subiaco, WA 6008 – **48)** G.PO Box 572F, Hobart, TAS 7001 on 1008kHz & 1080kHz, 87.6MHz 1W narrowcast throughout Queenstown, Strahan, Zeehan, Roseberry, Tullah, Stanley& Smithton (N-1:Sky Radio). Racing format. Rel 2UE M-F – **49)** PO Box 1303, Parramatta, NSW 2150 (N-3) Provides relays to over 100 NSW stns carrying racing: – **50)** Private Bag 1011, Richmond Vic. 3121 (N-1) – **51)** PO Box 183, Mackay, QLD 4740 (N-1). Airlie Beach on 94.7MHz. Bowen on 107.9MHz – **52)** PO Box 2216, South Hedland, WA 6722 – **53)** PO Box 481, Pt. Pirie, SA 5540 (N-1) – **54)** G.PO Box 163, Canberra City, ACT 2601 **W:** www.2ca.village.com.au (N-3) – **55)** PO Box 178, Bendigo VIC 3550 – **56)** PO Box 305, Kingaroy, QLD 4610 (N-1) ID's as "1071AM" and "Classic Gold" – **57)** PO Box 62, Gunnedah 2380 – **58)** 3 Gommes Lane, Yornup WA 6256 – **59)** PO Box 88, Orange, NSW 2800. (N-1:Sky Radio) – **60)** PO Box 606, Horsham, VIC 3400. (N-1) – **61)** PO Box 20, Longreach, QLD 4730 – **62)** PO Box 264, Merredin, WA 6415. (N-1) – **63)** PO Box 835G, Launceston, TAS 7250 (N-3) – **64)** PO Box 1107, Neutral Bay NSW 2089 (N-1). ID's as "Mix 106.5 FM" – **65)** G.PO Box 95, Brisbane, QLD 4001 (N-1) – **66)** PO Box 270, Armidale, NSW 2350. **E:** 2AD@mpx.com.au (N-1 – **67)** PO Box 63, Colac, Vic. 3250 (N-1) – **68)** PO Box 19, Mayfield, NSW 2304 (N-3) – **69)** PO Box 267, Emerald, QLD 4720. (N-1). Translators: 945kHz 1kW, 1215kHz 0.1kW, 88.1MHz 30W, 92.5MHz 10W, 98.2MHz 0.1kW, 102.1MHz 0.25kW. Rel 4AM 558kHz, 4ZR 1476kHz, 4CC 927kHz – **70)** PO Box 480, Wagga Wagga, NSW 2650. (N-1). Translator at Tumut on 107.9MHz with 10w. Supplementary Stn. on 93.1MHz. Both stns – **71)** PO Box 143, Maryborough, QLD 4650. (N-1) – **72)** GPO Box 2516, Nth Sydney, NSW 2001 (N-1) – **73)** PO Box 381, Charters Towers, QLD 4820 Translator: Hughenden 765kHz 0.5kW – **74)** Private Bag 1043, Richmond Vic. 3121 ID's as "Gold FM" – **75)** PO Box 770, Inverell, NSW 2360. (N-3) – **76)** PO Box 10290, Southport BC, QLD 4215 – **77)** PO Box 1047, Unley, SA 5061 (N-1) Translator in Adelaide on 98.3MHz 0.5kW – **78)** PO Box 276, Grafton, NSW 2460. (N-1) – **79)** PO Box 945, Subiaco, WA 6008 (N-1: BBC) – **80)** PO Box 1499, Canberra City, ACT 2601 (N-1) – **81)** PO Box 234, Seven Hills, NSW 2147 (N-1 – **82)** PO Box 160, Sale, Vic. 3850 (N-1) – **83)** 490 David Street, Albury NSW 2640 – **84)** PO Box 496, Port Augusta, SA 5700 (N-1) – **85)** PO Box 783, Toowoomba, QLD 4350 (N-1) – **86)** PO Box 1221, Dubbo, NSW 2830 **E:** 2du@lisp.com.au. (N-1) FM station "ZOO FM" Dubbo 92.7MHz, Cobar 103.7MHz – **88)** PO Box 153, Karratha, WA 6714. (N-1) – **89)** 8 Jones Bay Road, Pyrmont NSW 2009 **E:** contact@kick-am.com.au. **W:** www.kick-am.com.au/ (N-1) ID's as "Kick AM" – **90)** GPO Box 369F, Melbourne 3001 **W:** www.3aw.com.au/ – **91)** PO Box 497, Tamworth, NSW 2340 (N-1). Supplementary stn. on 92.9MHz – **92)** PO Box 105, Albion, QLD 4010 (N-1) ID's as "B105" – **93)** PO Box 500, Mt. Gambier, SA 5290 (N-1) – **94)** PO Box 360, Ballarat, VIC 3350. (N-1) – **95)** PO Box 1234, Wollongong, NSW 2500 **E:** mike@w151.aone.net.au (N-1) – **96)** 58 Abbott St Cairns QLD 4870 – **97)** PO Box 564, Gosford, NSW 2250 (N-1) – **98)** PO Box 504, Swan Hill, VIC 3585 (N-1) – **99)** PO Box 1059, Bundaberg, QLD 4670 (N-1) – **100)** PO Box 97, Charlestown, NSW 2290 (N-1) – **101)** PO Box 9550, Geelong, VIC 3220 **E:** krock@slanreach.au (N-1). ID's as "K-Rock" – **102)** PO Box 31, Young, NSW 2594 (N-1) – **103)** PO Box 780, Mount Isa, QLD 4825 (N-1). Relays to 4GC 828. Translator: Cloncurry 693kHz. Supplementary FM license at Mt. Isa. (N-1) – **04)** PO Box 115, Goulburn, NSW 2580 (N-1: Sky Radio) – **105)** PO Box 75, Frankston, Vic. 3199 **E:** magic@magic.com.au (N-1). 3EE ID's as "Magic" – **106)** GPO Box 5AA, Adelaide SA 5001 (N-1) – **107)** Mailbag 90, Lithgow, NSW 2790 **E:** 2lt@lisp.com.au. (N-1) (for QSL'ing purposes) c/o John Wright, 15 Olive Cres, Peakhurst NSW 2210 – **108)** PO Box 295, Parkes, NSW 2870. (N-1) – **109)** PO Box 606, Charlestown, NSW 2290. (N-1) – **111)** PO Box 17, Mudgee, NSW 2850 – **112)** PO Box 600, Muswelbrook, NSW 2333 (N-1) 2VLY 98.1 ID's as "Power FM" – **113)** PO Box 470, Murray Bridge, SA 5253 (N-1). Serves Murray Bridge, The Coorong and Meninge – **114)** PO Box 539, Mildura, VIC 3500 (N-1). 3MA 99.5 ID's as "Today's Music 99.5FM" – **115)** PO Box 22, Roma, QLD 4455. (N-1:Sky Radio) – **116)** PO Box 670, Albury, NSW 2640 **W:** www.albury.net.au/radio.albury.wodonga/2ay.html (N-1). Supplementary stn. on FM – **117)** PO Box 310, Bathurst, NSW 2795 **E:** stereo@2bs.ix.net.au or 2bs@csu.edu.au **W:** www.2bs.ix.net.au (N-1) FM service on 99.3MHz – **118)** PO Box 195, Shepparton, Vic. 3630 – **119)** PO Box 312, Deniliquin, NSW 2710. (N-1) 2MOR 102.5 ID's as "Classic Rock 102.5" – **120)** PO Box 389, Moree, NSW 2400. (N-1). Supplementary license on 98.3MHz. Translator on 88.7MHz with 250w r. (N-1) – **121)** PO Box 275, Taree, NSW 2430 (N-1). Translator: Gloucester 100.1MHz and Forster

MW	Call	Location	kHz	kW

on 100.3MHz – **122)** PO Box 449, Wangaratta, VIC 3677 (N-1). 3NE Translators: Mt. Hotham 89.3MHz 0.02kW, Mt. Buffalo 105.3MHz 0.2kW, Mt. Beauty 90.3MHz 10w. 3NNN ID's as "Edge FM" – **123)** Locked Bag 6198 Sth Coast Mail Centre NSW 2521 (N-1) ID's as "98FM" – **124)** GPO Box 105, Melbourne, VIC (N-1) – **125)** 111 Wellington Str, East Perth, WA 6004. (N-1) – **126)** PO Box 1019, St. Kilda, Vic. 3182 (N-1) – **127)** GPO Box 1041, Brisbane, QLD 4001. (N-1) – **128)** PO Box 920, Crows Nest, NSW 2065 **W:** www.2dayfm.com.au (N-1) – **129)** GPO Box 442, Sydney, NSW 2001 (N-1). **W:** www.mrock.com.au – **130)** PO Box 1071, Unley, SA 5061.24h (N-1) Translator South Tce, Adelaide on 91.1MHz 1kW. ID's as "SAFM" – **131)** PO Box 527, Esperance, WA 6450. N-1. Rel. 6PPM-FM 1000-2200 – **132)** PO Box 665, Carnarvon, WA 6701. 2200-1500 (N-1). Translator: Exmouth – **133)** PO Box 1950, Coffs Harbour, NSW 2450 (N-1). Rp – **134)** PO Box 483, Port Lincoln, SA 5606. (N-1) – **135)** 141 Mandurah Tce, Mandurah, WA 6210 (N-1) – **136)** GPO Box 163, Canberra, ACT 2601. Belongs to 54). **F.PI:** translator for Tuggeranong area – **137)** PO Box 106, Dickson, ACT 2602. (N-1) ID's as "Mix 106.3" – **138)** GPO Box 163, Canberra, A.C.T. 2601 (N-1) – **139)** PO Box 185, Mackay QLD 4740 – **140)** PO Box 2101, Gosford, NSW 2250 (N-1) – **141)** PO Box 7, Ipswich, QLD 4305 (N-1) ID's as "Mix 106.9 QFM" – **142)** PO Box 128 Geraldton, WA 6530. 24h (N-1) – **143)** 15 Puttabucca Rd, Mudgee NSW 2850 – **144)** G.PO Box 1800, Hobart, TAS. 7001 (N-1) – **145)** Locked Bag 5000, Broadway NSW 2007 – **146)** GPO Box 2510, Darwin NT 0801 – **147)** 4 Peary St., Darwin, NT 0800 (N-1) Translators: Katherine 765kHz 0.5kW – **148)** 678 Victoria St, Richmond VIC 3121 – **149)** 403 The Esplanade, Torquay QLD 4655 – **150)** PO Box 332, Beaudesert QLD 4285 – **151)** PO Box 148, Bunbury WA 6231 – **152)** GPO Box 1345, Hobart TAS 7001 – **153)** PO Box 84, Charleville, QLD 4470 (N-1) ID's as "Outback Radio". Translator: Cunnamulla 1584kHz 0.2kW – **154)** PO Box 5910 Gold Coast Mail Centre Bundall QLD 4217 r. (N-1) – **155)** Private Bag 925 Gold Coast Mail Centre QLD 4215. (N-1) – **156)** Paul Taylor, 41 Allards Crt., Clifton Springs VIC 3222 – **157)** Sea FM, 320 Sheridan St Cairns QLD 4870 – **158)** Sea FM, Suncorp/Metway Building Suite 3, Level 3, 123 Victoria St Mackay QLD 4740 – **159)** 444 Logan Rd, Stones Corner QLD 4120 – **160)** PO Box 665 Carnarvon WA 6701 – **161)** 33 Saunders Road, Pyrmont NSW 2009 – **162)** Regional Communications Pty Ltd, PO Box 7515, St Kilda Road VIC 3004 – **163)** 47 Wingewarra St Dubbo NSW 2830 – **164)** DMG Regional Radio, Locked Bag 5000, Broadway NSW 2007 – **165)** 68 Aboott St, Cairns QLD 4870 – **166)** PO Box 112, Bunbury WA 6230 – **167)** PO Box 33, Tuart Hill WA 6060 **168)** cnr Plaza Pde & Carnaby St, Maroochydore QLD 4558 – **169)** Locked Bag 919, Adelaide SA 5001 – **170)** PO Box 579, Lilydale VIC 3140 – **171)** PO Box 3535, Erina NSW 2250, - **172)** Level 2, 678 Victoria Street, Richmond, Vic, 3121.

COMMUNITY BROADCASTING ASSOCIATION OF AUSTRALIA

Suite One, Level Three, 44-54 Botany Rd. Alexandria, NSW 2015
+61 (2) 9310 2999 +61 (2) 9319 4545
PRN: Public Radio Network, CBAA: Community Broadcasting Association of Australia. CBAA provides ComRadSat.

PUBLIC BROADCASTING STATIONS

MW	Call	Location	kHz	kW
1)	2WEB	Bourke	585	10(d)
2)	6WR	Kununurra	693	5
3)	3CR	Melbourne	855	2(d)
4)	7RPH	Hobart	864	2
15)	6FX	Fitzroy Crossing	936	5
220)	6RPH	Perth	990	5
7)	1RPH	Canberra	1125	2(d)
9)	3RPH	Melbourne	1179	5
8)	4BI	Brisbane	1197	0.5/1
10)	5RPH	Adelaide	1197	2
11)	2RPH	Sydney	1224	5(d)
6)	4MW	Thursday Is.	1260	2
18)	4RPH	Brisbane	1296	5(d)
193)	3KND	Melbourne	1503	5(d)

FM	Call	MHz	kW	Location
151)	3MFM	88.1	2(d)	Leongatha
9)	3BPH	88.7	6.6	Bendigo
176)	3RUM	88.7	1	Walwa/Jingellic
13)	2RBR	88.9	1(d)	Coraki
14)	2YOU	88.9	1(d)	Tamworth
112)	7DBS	88.9	1(d)	Lileah
217)	4CCR	89.1	2(d)	Cairns
148)	5BBB	89.1	1	Barossa Valley
17)	4CRB	89.3	25(d)	Gold Coast
16)	4SDB	89.3	2	Warwick
149)	5EFM	89.3	1	Victor Harbour

FM	Call	MHz	kW	Location	FM	Call	MHz	kW	Location
150)	5GFM	89.3	10(d)	Arthurton	215)	4ACR	99.7	1	Woorabinda
151)	3MFM	89.5	1(d)	Foster	169)	4RED	99.7	2(d)	Redcliffe
218)	2HIM	89.7	1	Tamworth	71)	6GME	99.7	2	Broome
19)	2TEN	89.7	4	Tenterfield	170)	2BAY	99.9	3	Byron Bay
147)	5TCB(t)	89.7	1.5	Naracoorte	72)	2PMQ	99.9	3	Port Macquarie
158)	6TCR	89.7	2(d)	Wanneroo	73)	3BBB	99.9	3	Ballarat
152)	3TSC	89.9	56(d)	Melbourne	74)	4TCB	99.9	20	Townsville
20)	5DDD	89.9	2	Dalby	171)	5MBS	99.9	2(d)	Adelaide Foothills
153)	5GSFM	90.1	1	Victor Harbour	75)	2BCB	100.1	10	Bathurst
153)	3SYN	90.7	56(d)	Melbourne	9)	3SPH	100.1	10(d)	Shepparton
21)	4CSB	90.7	5	Wondai	172)	4RIM	100.1	1	Boonah
22)	5KIX	90.7	3(d)	Kangaroo Island	214)	5GTR	100.1	1	Mt. Gambier
23)	1CMS	91.1	20	Canberra	5)	6NR	100.1	6.5(d)	Perth
24)	2CBD	91.1	5	Deepwater	76)	2TLC	100.3	1	Maclean
1)	2WEB(t)	91.1	1(d)	Coonamble	216)	2YAS	100.3	2	Yass
25)	2MAX	91.3	10(d)	Narrabri	77)	4BAY	100.5	4(d)	Wynnum/Redlands
102)	4BRR	91.5	1	Gayndah	11)	2RPH	100.5	4	Newcastle
26)	4GCR	91.5	1	Gympie	11)	2RPH	100.5	1(d)	Sydney Eastern Suburbs
27)	1WAY	91.9	20	Canberra	1)	2WEB	100.7	1(d)	Nyngan
28)	4RGL	91.9	1	Gladstone	78)	3CH	100.7	1(d)	Woodend
37)	2ARM	92.1	2	Armidale	79)	4US	100.7	1	Rockhampton
30)	2MFM	92.1	6	Sydney	211)	2PSR	100.9	1(d)	Port Stephens
31)	6RTR	92.1	10(d)	Perth	80)	6CRA	100.9	10	Albany
33)	2MCE	92.3	1	Bathurst	166)	6NME	100.9	16(d)	Perth
34)	3ZZZ	92.3	56(d)	Melbourne	81)	4CBL	101.1	4(d)	Logan
35)	1ART	92.7	20	Canberra	82)	3WPR	101.3	1	Wangaratta
155)	5FBI	92.7	20(d)	Adelaide	83)	2GLA	101.5	10(d)	Forster
36)	2NCR	92.9	6	Lismore	230)	3BBS	101.5	1	Bendigo
147)	5TCB	92.9	2	Kingston SE	174)	4BSR	101.5	1	Beaudesert
38)	2BBB	93.3	3.2	Dorrigo	84)	4OUR	101.5	3(d)	Caboolture
156)	2MNO	93.3	2	Monaro	185)	5UV	101.5	20(d)	Adelaide
157)	2SNR	93.3	2	Gosford	9)	2APH	101.7	2	Albury
9)	3RPH	93.5	1	Warragul	231)	6SEN	101.7	8(d)	Perth
39)	2BAR	93.7	1(d)	Bega	177)	2PAR	101.9	1	Ballina
212)	2LND	93.7	50(d)	Sydney	86)	4ZZZ	102.1	12	Brisbane
40)	5DDD	93.7	6.3	Adelaide	87)	6WR	102.1	1	Wyndham
226)	2CCM	94.1	2	Gosford	88)	2NIM	102.3	1	Nimbin
41)	2LIV	94.1	4(d)	Wollongong/Nowra	89)	2MBS	102.5	50(d)	Sydney
42)	4JAZ	94.1	25(d)	Gold Coast	90)	3RRR	102.7	56(d)	Melbourne
43)	2DCB	94.3	10	Dubbo	178)	4DDB	102.7	4	Toowoomba
213)	2FBI	94.5	150(d)	Sydney	91)	2CVC	103.1	1	Grafton
9)	3RPH	94.5	5(d)	Warrnambool	92)	2WET	103.1	1	Kempsey
44)	5CCR	94.5	1	Ceduna/Smoky Bay	210)	3BBR	103.1	1	Warragul
45)	8KNB	94.5	15	Darwin	93)	5EBI	103.1	20(d)	Adelaide
33)	2MCE	94.7	1(d)	Orange	94)	2CBA	103.2	50(d)	Sydney
228)	3PLS	94.7	56(d)	Geelong	95)	2TLP	103.3	3(d)	Taree
47)	4BCR	94.7	3(d)	Bundaberg	97)	2CCB	103.5	5	Orange
194)	2GCB	94.9	2	Gosford	98)	3MBR	103.5	4.8	Murrayville
160)	2MIA	95.1	5	Griffith	99)	3MBS	103.5	56(d)	Melbourne
229)	2TRR	95.3	2	Coolah	100)	2NUR	103.7	10(d)	Newcastle
161)	6EBA	95.3	16(d)	Perth	53)	3WAY	103.7	5	Warrnambool
162)	7HRT	95.7	1(d)	Nthn Midlands	101)	4MBS	103.7	12	Brisbane
12)	4BVR	95.9	1	Esk	179)	7LTN	103.7	3.2	Launceston
229)	2TRR	96.1	1	Dunedoo	103)	2WAY	103.9	3	Port Macquarie
32)	7THE	96.1	3(d)	Hobart	104)	3BGR	103.9	3	Ballarat
48)	2CCC	96.3	2	Gosford	209)	3GCB	103.9	10(d)	Latrobe Valley
49)	3GGR	96.3	56(d)	Geelong	105)	4TTT	103.9	20	Townsville
50)	2CHR	96.5	2(d)	Cessnock/Maitland	106)	6ESP	103.9	5	Esperance
51)	3EON	96.5	1(d)	Bendigo (city)	107)	2CHY	104.1	5	Coffs Harbour
52)	4FRB	96.5	1	Brisbane	108)	8TOP	104.1	16	Darwin
46)	4RFM	96.9	5	Moranbah	69)	2UUU	104.5	2(d)	Nowra
219)	7MID	97.1	2	Oatlands	147)	5TCB	104.5	1.6	Keith
159)	2MAQ	97.3	1	Lake Macquarie	180)	8KIN	104.5	1	Katherine
54)	3HCR	97.3	1	Omeo	109)	2BOB	104.7	5	Taree
165)	7TAS	97.7	1	Tasman Peninsula	110)	3GCR	104.7	7.9(d)	Latrobe Valley
55)	8GGG	97.7	15	Darwin	111)	3GRR	104.7	5(d)	Echuca
56)	2LVR	97.9	4	Parkes/Forbes	112)	7DBS	104.7	2	Devonport
57)	6DBY	97.9	2	Derby	181)	4SFM	104.9	3	Nambour
58)	4EB	98.1	12	Brisbane	182)	5RCB	104.9	20	Mt. Gambier
59)	1XXR	98.3	20	Canberra	113)	4WBR	105.1	10(d)	Maryborough
60)	6MKA	98.3	1	Meekatharra	201)	5TRX	105.1	5	Port Pirie
61)	2OOO	98.5	25(d)	Sydney	114)	7WAY	105.3	3.2	Launceston
62)	3ONE	98.5	10(d)	Shepparton	115)	4MET	105.7	10(d)	Gold Coast
167)	4YOU	98.5	1	Rockhampton	24)	2CBD	105.9	3	Glen Innes
147)	5TCB	98.5	2	Padthaway	116)	2NVR	105.9	2(d)	Nambucca Heads
63)	6SON	98.5	16(d)	Perth	175)	4MUR	105.9	1	Mackay
64)	2KRR	98.7	1	Kandos	147)	5TCB	106.1	1.6	Bordertown
65)	4CIM	98.7	10(d)	Cairns	112)	7DBS	106.1	10(d)	Wynyard
66)	4AAA	98.9	9.5	Brisbane	117)	2CUZ	106.5	10	Bourke
29)	3SFM	99.1	1	Swan Hill	183)	4CLG	106.5	3	Nambour
67)	3RPC	99.3	2(d)	Portland	96)	7HFC	106.5	36	Hobart
168)	7EDG	99.3	1	Hobart South	227)	3HOT	106.7	1	Mildura
68)	2RFM	99.7	10(d)	Newcastle	118)	3PBS	106.7	56(d)	Melbourne
69)	2UUU	99.7	1	Ulladulla	119)	2VOX	106.9	2(d)	Wollongong
70)	3MCR	99.7	1	Mansfield	120)	3UGE	106.9	1	Alexandra/Eildon

FM	Call	MHz	kW	Location
4)	7RPH	106.9	3.2	Launceston
121)	4KIG	107.1	16	Townsville
122)	2REM	107.3	2	Albury
123)	2SER	107.3	14	Sydney
124)	4CAB	107.3	10(d)	Gold Coast
125)	2EAR	107.5	1.6(d)	Moruya
173)	2OCB	107.5	5	Orange
9)	3MPH	107.5	1	Mildura
126)	4CRM	107.5	1	Mackay
176)	3RUM	107.7	1	Tumbarumba NSW
127)	2AIR	107.9	5	Coffs Harbour
128)	2COW	107.9	1	Casino
129)	5RAM	107.9	20(d)	Adelaide
130)	6CCR	107.9	1(d)	Fremantle

HIGH POWER OPEN NARROWCAST STATIONS

These stns are licensed for a specific market such as horseracing or certain local audience that cannot be filled by commercial or other stns. Official callsigns are not issued for these stns but may be used. **NB:** many expanded band (1611-1701kHz) stns are licensed but may not be on air. Confirming their status is difficult.

MW	Call	kHz	kW	Location
188)	5RTI	531	0.5	Adelaide
141)	6RF	657	2	Perth
141)	2RF	801	5(d)	Gosford
189)	4AY	873	2	Innisfail
138)	4TAB	891	5(d)	Townsville
146)	3UZ	945	2	Bendigo
190)	2TAB	1008	0.3	Canberra
232)	7TAB	1008	5(d)	Launceston
132)	6TAB	1017	1	Bunbury
141)	4RF	1053	0.5	Brisbane
191)	7TAB	1080	5(d)	Hobart
132)	6TAB	1206	2	Perth
190)	2TAB	1215	0.35	Bowral
140)	8TAB	1242	2	Darwin
190)	2TAB	1314	5(d)	Wollongong
220)	1——	1323	0.4(d)	Canberra
190)	2TAB	1341	5(d)	Newcastle'
192)	3CW	1341	5(d)	Geelong
146)	3UZ	1359	0.2	Mildura
132)	6TAB	1404	4	Busselton
164)	3UCB	1413	0.5(d)	Shepparton
195)	3XY	1422	5	Melbourne
200)	6GS	1422	2	Wagin
132)	6TAB	1431	2	Kalgoorlie
132)	6TAB	1449	2	Mandurah
186)	2KA	1476	0.18(d)	Penrith
187)	2RF	1539	1	Sydney
139)	5TAB	1539	5(d)	Adelaide
139)	5TAB	1557	0.5(d)	Renmark/Loxton
187)	2RF	1575	5(d)	Wollongong
154)	2TAB	1593	0.2	Murwillumbah
187)	3RG	1593	5(d)	Melbourne
196)	2NTC	1611	0.4	Grafton
233)	2_	1611	0.05	Wee Waa
164)	2UCB	1611	0.4	Western Sydney
196)	2NTC	1611	0.4	Tamworth
187)	2RG	1611	0.4	Griffith
199)	3_	1611	0.4	Mildura
164)	3UCB	1611	0.4	Hoppers Crossing
197)	4KIK	1611	0.05	Croydon
197)	4KZ	1611	0.4	Karumba
164)	5UCB	1611	0.4	Adelaide
164)	6UCB	1611	0.4	Margaret River
200)	6GS	1611	0.4	Wagin
187)	6RF	1611	0.4	Esperance
187)	7RF	1611	0.4	Devonport
187)	7RF	1611	0.4	Launceston
187)	8RF	1611	0.4	Darwin
187)	1RF	1620	0.4	Canberra
190)	2KM	1620	0.4	Sydney
202)	3CW	1620	0.4	Melbourne
187)	3RF	1620	0.4	Wangaratta
197)	4KZ	1620	0.4	Taylors Beach
203)	2HRN	1629	0.1	Newcastle
205)	2MM	1629	0.4	Nowra
196)	2NTC	1629	0.4	Bathurst
196)	2NTC	1629	0.4	Dubbo
202)	3CW	1629	0.4	Melbourne
187)	3RF	1629	0.4	Shepparton
187)	5RF	1629	0.4	Adelaide
187)	5RF	1629	0.4	Mount Gambier
234)	6ABN	1629	0.4	Busselton

MW	Call	kHz	kW	Location
187)	6RF	1629	0.4	Albany
187)	6RF	1629	0.4	Busselton
187)	1RF	1638	0.4	Canberra
222)	2ME	1638	0.4	Sydney
196)	2NTC	1638	0.4	Armidale
222)	3ME	1638	0.4	Melbourne
220)	4_	1638	0.4	Brisbane
222)	8ME	1638	0.4	Darwin
220)	1_	1647	0.4	Canberra
222)	4ME	1647	0.4	Brisbane
198)	4UCB	1647	0.4	Mackay
205)	2MM	1656	0.4	Sydney
223)	4_	1656	0.4	Brisbane
222)	6ME	1656	0.4	Perth
206)	2MM	1665	0.4	Sydney
198)	3UCB	1665	0.4	Melbourne
225)	3_	1674	0.4	Melbourne
207)	2_	1683	0.4	Sydney
198)	4UCB	1692	0.4	Nanango
241)	2_	1701	0.4	Sydney
224)	3VMV	1701	0.4	Somerton
208)	4_	1701	0.1	Brisbane

SW	Call	kHz	kW	Location
85)	2——	2368.5	1	Sydney

FM	MHz	kW	Location
131)	88.7	2(d)	Atherton QLD
132)	89.5	1.2	Esperance WA
187)	90.3	1	Griffith NSW
142)	90.5	1(d)	Barossa Valley SA
133)	90.5	1(d)	Tamworth NSW
232)	90.5	5(d)	Perth WA
134)	90.9	1	Mossman QLD
133)	90.9	1	Mudgee NSW
135)	91.5	1	Toowoomba QLD
154)	91.9	1(d)	Latrobe Valley VIC
136)	92.3	10(d)	Maryborough QLD
132)	92.5	2	Port Hedland WA
133)	92.7	1	Inverell NSW
133)	92.7	3(d)	Port Macquarie NSW
164)	93.7	50(d)	Albany WA
133)	94.3	1	Goulburn NSW
137)	94.9	4	Broken Hill NSW
133)	95.5	10(d)	Wagga Wagga NSW
138)	95.5	3(d)	Bundaberg QLD
138)	95.5	4.5(d)	Emerald QLD
139)	95.5	5(d)	Renmark/Loxton SA
133)	95.9	20(d)	Gunnedah NSW
140)	95.9	1	Alice Springs NT
163)	96.5	1	Katherine NT
133)	96.9	1(d)	Cooma NSW
164)	97.5	2(d)	Bairnsdale VIC
138)	97.5	1	Blackwater QLD
165)	97.7	1(d)	Burnie TAS
136)	98.1	1	Inglewood QLD
184)	98.7	1	Alice Springs NT
141)	99.1	2(d)	Atherton QLD
133)	99.9	10	Parkes/Forbes NSW
138)	99.9	1	Rockhampton QLD
133)	100.5	4	Broken Hill NSW
132)	100.5	1	Wyndham WA
133)	100.9	10	Bathurst NSW
142)	101.1	10(d)	Nowra NSW
143)	101.3	2	Devonport TAS
133)	101.5	1	Grafton NSW
133)	101.5	1	Kempsey NSW
132)	101.7	1	Karratha WA
164)	102.1	1	Hamilton VIC
133)	102.7	2(d)	Jindabyne NSW
164)	102.9	2	Horsham VIC
133)	103.3	1	Muswellbrook NSW
138)	103.5	100(d)	Mackay QLD
133)	103.7	1	Moree NSW
133)	103.7	2(d)	Nowra NSW
140)	103.7	1	Katherine NT
133)	104.3	10	Armidale NSW
143)	104.3	10(d)	Cairns QLD
164)	105.3	1	Portland NSW
144)	105.3	2(d)	Wollongong NSW
145)	105.7	5	Taree NSW
133)	106.1	1	Deniliquin NSW
133)	106.7	5	Orange NSW
146)	106.9	10	Swan Hill VIC
133)	107.1	1	Eden NSW
133)	107.5	3	Glen Innes NSW

NB FM stns below 1kW are not mentioned. There have been allocations for a number of years for HF outlets but only one has any ever made it to air.

Addresses and other information

1) Western Region Educational Broadc. Co. Ltd, PO Box 426, Bourke NSW 2840. Plus 5 FM translators. – **2)** Radio Station 6WR. PO Box 162 Kununurra WA 6743. (N-1:CBAA) Aboriginal prgrs from National Indigenous Radio Service – **3)** Community R. Federation Ltd, PO Box 277, Collingwood VIC 3066. Various foreign languages – **4)** Radio 7RPH Broadcasting Services for Handicapped Inc. 136 Davey st Hobart TAS. 7000. Information and reading service format. Relays BBCWS 11:00pm to 10:00am Mon-Sat, Sunday – **5)** Curtin Univ of Technology, GPO Box U1987, Perth WA 6001.. Rel. CBAA Network at times and BBCWS overnight – **6)** PO Box 385, Thursday Island QLD 4875 – **7)** Print-Handicapped Radio of ACT Inc, Barton Highway, Gungahlin, ACT 2912 – relays BBCWS Mon-Fri 1:00pm to 6:00pm SA noon to Su 9:30am – **8)** Switch FM, PO Box 173, Fortitude Valley QLD, 4006 – **9)** Assoc. for the Blind, 454 Glenferrie Rd, Kooyong 3144. Relays BBCWS overnight – **10)** Radio 5RPH, 231 Morphett St. Adelaide SA 5000. Relays BBCWS overnight – **11)** R. for the Print-Handicapped (NSW) Co-op Ltd, 2/252 Illawarra Rd, Marrickville NSW 2204 – **12)** PO Box 148, Toogoolawah QLD 4313 – **13)** 50 Houghwood Rd, Bora Ridge NSW 2471 – **14)** PO Box 998, Tamworth NSW 2340 – **15)** PO Box 52, Fitzroy Crossing WA 6765 – **16)** Rainbow FM, PO Box 473 WArwick QLD 4370 – **17)** PO Box 86, Burleigh Heads QLD 4220 – **18)** Unit 3/17 Henry Street, Spring Hill QLD 4000 – **19)** PO Box 93, Tenterfield NSW 2372 – **20)** PO Box 483, Dalby QLD 4405 – **21)** Crow FM, PO Box 171, Emerald QLD 4606 – **22)** PO Box 90, Kingscote SA 5223 – **23)** PO Box 3882, Weston ACT 2611 (Ethnic) – **24)** Gough St, Deepwater NSW 2371 – **25)** PO Box 94, Narrabri NSW 2390 – **26)** The Positive Alternative, PO Box 774, Gympie QLD 4570 (Christian) – **27)** Canberra Christian Radio, PO Box 927, Fyshwick ACT 2609 (Christian) – **28)** 257 Goondoon St WArwick QLD 4680 (Christian) – **29)** PO Box 998, Swan Hill VIC 3585 – **30)** Muslim Community Radio, PO Box 969, Bankstown NSW 1885 (Ethnic) **31)** Arts Radio, PO Box 949, Nedlands WA 6009 – **32)** GPO Box 1324, Hobart TAS 7001 – **33)** Charles Sturt University, Locked Bag 30, Bathurst NSW 2795 – **34)** PO Box 1106, Collingwood VIC 3066 (Ethnic) – **35)** Artsound, PO Box 87, Curtin ACT 2605 – **36)** PO Box 5123, East Lismore NSW 2480 – **37)** PO Box 707, Armidale NSW 2350 – **38)** PO Box 304, Dorrigo NSW 2454 – **39)** Edge FM, PO Box 771, Bega NSW 2550 – **40)** 48 Nelson St, Stepney SA 5069 – **41)** Living Sound Broadcasters, PO Box 7, Coniston NSW 2500 (Christian) – **42)** Radio Hope Island, PO Box 16 SAnctuary Cove QLD 4212 – **43)** Radio Rhema, PO Box 1502, Dubbo NSW 2830 (Christian) – **44)** PO Box 271, Ceduna SA 5690 – **45)** Radio Larrakia, Shop 2, Alawa Shops, Alawa NT 0810 (Aboriginal) – **46)** PO Box 597, Moranbah QLD 4744 – **47)** PO Box 2678, Bundaberg QLD 4670 – **48)** PO Box 19, Gosford NSW 2250 – **49)** Rhema FM, PO Box 886, Belmont VIC 3216 (Christian) – **50)** PO Box 421, Cessnock NSW 2325 – **51)** Radio KLFM, PO Box 2997, Bendigo Delivery Centre VIC 3554 – **52)** Family Radio, PO Box 1700, Milton QLD 4064 – **53)** PO Box 752 WArrnambool VIC 3280 – **54)** PO Box 86, Omeo VIC 3898 – **55)** Darwin Christian Broadcasters, PO Box 43146, Casaurina NT 0810 (Christian) – **56)** Parkes Road, Forbes NSW 2871 – **57)** PO Box 655, Derby WA 6728 – **58)** 140 Main St, Kangaroo Point QLD 4169 – **59)** 2XX, GPO Box 812, Canberra ACT 2601 – **60)** PO Box 259, Meekatharra WA 6642 – **61)** Radio 2000, 2/25 Belmore Rd, Burwood NSW 2134 (Ethnic) – **62)** PO Box 6824, Shepparton VIC 3630 – **63)** Sonshine FM, PO Box 6340, Morley WA 6062 (Christian) – **64)** PO Box 99, Kandos NSW 2848 – **65)** PO Box 1856, Cairns QLD 4870 (Aboriginal) – **66)** Box 6229, Fairfield Gardens QLD 4103 (Aboriginal) – **67)** PO Box 450, Portland VIC 3305 – **68)** Rhema FM, PO Box 2000, Dangar NSW 2309 (Christian) – **69)** PO Box 884, Nowra NSW 2541 – **70)** PO Box 667, Mansfield VIC 3724 – **71)** PMB Turkey Creek, via Kununurra WA 6743 (Aboriginal) – **72)** Radio Rhema, PO Box 1537, Port Macquarie NSW 2444 (Christian) – **73)** Voice FM, PO Box 149, Ballarat VIC 3350 – **74)** Live FM, PO Box 332, Aitkenvale QLD 4814 (Christian) – **75)** Radio Rhema, PO Box 615, Bathurst NSW 2795 (Christian) – **76)** PO Box 210, Yamba NSW 2464 – **77)** PO Box 1003, Cleveland QLD 4163 – **78)** Central Highlands Broadc. Inc, PO Box 966, Woodend VIC 3442 – **79)** PO Box 663, Rockhampton QLD 4700 (Aboriginal) – **80)** 211-217 North Road, Albany WA 6330 – **81)** PO Box 2101, Logan City DC QLD 4114 – **82)** PO Box 605 Wangaratta VIC 3676 – **83)** PO Box 1015, Tuncurry NSW 2428 – **84)** PO Box 418, Caboolture QLD 4510 – **85)** Radio Symban, 867 New Canterbury Rd, Hurlstone Park NSW 2193 – **86)** PO Box 509, Fortitude Valley QLD 4006 – **87)** PO Box 815, Kununurra WA 6743 (Aboriginal) – **88)** PO Box 522, Nimbin NSW 2480 – **89)** 76 Chandos St, St Leonards NSW 2065 – **90)** PO Box 304, Fitzroy VIC 3065 – **91)** PO Box 115, Grafton NSW 2460 (Christian) – **92)** PO Box 200, West Kempsey NSW 2440 – **93)** 10 Byron Pl, Adelaide SA 5000 (Ethnic) – **94)** PO Box 54, Five Dock NSW 2046 – **95)** Ngarralinyi, The Listening Place, PO Box 657, Taree NSW 2430 (Aboriginal) – **96)** PO Box 1033, New Town TAS 7008 – **97)** Radio

Rhema, PO Box 974, Orange NSW 2800 – **98)** PO Box 139, Murrayville VIC 3512 – **99)** 146 Cotham Road, Kew VIC 3101 – **100)** University Dr, Callaghan NSW 2308 – **101)** 384 Old Cleveland Rd, Coorparoo QLD 4151 – **102)** PO Box 915, Gayndah QLD 4625 – **103)** PO Box 603, Port Macquarie 2446 – **104)** Good News Radio, PO Box 312, Ballarat VIC 3350 – **105)** PO Box 1033, Townsville QLD 4810 – **106)** PO Box 2154, Esperance WA 6450 – **107)** PO Box J233, Coffs Harbour NSW 2450 – **108)** PO Box 40146, Casaurina NT 0810 – **109)** PO Box 400, Taree NSW 2430 – **110)** PO Box 579, Morwell VIC 3840 – **111)** 1/15 Matong Rd, Echuca VIC 3564 – **112)** PO Box 333, Wynyard TAS 7325 – **113)** Rhema FM, PO Box 384, Hervey Bay QLD 4655 (Christian) – **114)** 93 Reatta Rd, Trevallyn TAS 7250 (Christian) – **115)** Radio Metro, PO Box 6530, GCMC QLD 9726 – **116)** PO Box 69, Bowraville NSW 2449 – **117)** PO Box 363, Bourke NSW 2840 (Aboriginal) – **118)** PO Box 2917, Fitzroy VIC 3065 – **119)** PO Box 1663, Wollongong NSW 2500 – **120)** PO Box 270, Alexandra VIC 3714 – **121)** PO Box 5483, Townsville QLD 4810 (Aboriginal) – **122)** Garland Ave, North Albury NSW 2640 – **123)** PO Box 123, Broadway NSW 2007 – **124)** Life FM, PO Box 948, Southport QLD 4125 (Christian) – **125)** PO Box 86, Moruya NSW 2537 – **126)** PO Box 1075, Mackay QLD 4740 – **127)** PO Box 2028, Coffs Harbour NSW 2450 – **128)** PO Box 1149, Casino NSW 2470 – **129)** Radio Alta Mira, PO Box 1079, North Adelaide SA 5006 (Christian) – **130)** Unit 4, 153 Rockingham Rd, Hamilton Hill WA 6163 – **131)** KIK FM, PO Bpx 1434, Edge Hill QLD 4870 – **132)** TAB WA, 14 Hasler Rd, Osborne Park WA 6017 – **133)** PO Box 1303, Parramatta NSW 2150 – **134)** 90.9 FM, Mossman & Port Douglas PO Box 383, Whakatane NEW ZEALAND – **135)** PO Box 111, Toowoomba QLD 4350 – **136)** PO Box 1059, Bundaberg QLD 4670 – **137)** Cross FM, Broken Hill Church of Christ, 232 Lane St, Broken Hill NSW 2880 – **138)** Radio 4TAB, PO Box 275, Albion QLD 4010 – **139)** GPO Box 5AA, Adelaide SA 5001 – **140)** NT Racing Commission, PO Box 3170, Darwin NT 0800 – **141)** Rete Italia, PO Box 159, Clifton Hill VIC 3068 – **142)** Ambersky, PO Box 540, Nowra NSW 2541 – **143)** PO Box 5109, GCMC, Bundall QLD 9726 – **144)** 63 Minimbah Rd, Northbridge NSW 2063 **145)** Rich Rivers Radio, PO Box 312, Deniliquin NSW 2710 – **146)** PO Box 927, Carlton VIC 3053 – **147)** PO Box 526, Bordertown SA 5268 – **148)** PO Box 654, Tanunda SA 5352 – **149)** PO Box 591 Victor Harbour SA 5211 – **150)** PO Box 390, Kadina SA 5554 – **151)** PO Box 144, Inverloch NSW 3996 – **151)** PO Box 899, Mont Albert VIC 3127 – **152)** PO Box 999 VICtor Harbour SA 5211 – **153)** PO Box 12013, A'Beckett St, Melbourne VIC 3000 – **154)** PO Box 5910 Gold Coast Mail Centre Bundall QLD 4217 – **155)** Level 2, 230-232 Angas St, Adelaide SA 5000 – **156)** PO Box 28, Nimmitabel NSW 2631 – **157)** PO Box 2050, Gosford NSW 2250 – **158)** PO Box 281 WAnneroo WA 6946 – **159)** 30 Pillapai Rd, Brightwaters NSW 2264 – **160)** PO Box 2122, Griffith NSW 2680 – **161)** PO Box 1005, Subiaco WA 6904 – **162)** c/- PO, Gordon St, Poatina TAS 7302 – **163)** PO Box 79, Earlwood NSW 2206 – **164)** Vision FM, Locked Bag 3, Springwood QLD 4127 – **165)** GPO Box 1345, Hobart TAS 7001 – **166)** PO Box 105, Bentley WA 6102 – **167)** PO Box 5035, North Rockhampton MC QLD 4701 – **168)** GPO Box 252-44, Hobart TAS 7001 – **169)** PO Box 139, Redcliffe QLD 4020 – **170)** PO Box 440, Byron Bay NSW 2481 – **171)** PO Box 7016, Hutt St, Adelaide SA 5000 – **172)** PO Box 243, Boonah QLD 4310 – **173)** PO Box 1031, Orange NSW 2800 – **174)** PO Box 235, Beaudesert QLD 4285 – **175)** PO Box 5337, Mackay MC QLD 4741 – **176)** 55 Main St WAlwa VIC 3709 – **177)** PO Box 612, Ballina NSW 2478 – **178)** PO Box 400, Toowoomba QLD 4350 – **179)** 43 Tamar St, Launceston TAS 7250 – **180)** CAAMA, PO Box 2608, Alice Springs NT 0871 – **181)** 5 Desiree Cl, Buderim QLD 4556 – **182)** Radio Rhema, PO Box 1465, Mt. Gambier SA 5290 – **183)** Radio Rhema, PO Box 200, Woombye QLD 4559 – **184)** 17 North St, Frewville SA 5063 – **185)** 228-230 North Tce, Adelaide SA 5000 – **186)** PO Box 186, Kingswood NSW 2747 – **187)** c/- John Wright, 29 Milford Rd, Peakhurst NSW 2210 – **188)** GPO Box 1329, Adelaide SA 5001 (Italian) – **189)** PO Box 19, Innisfail QLD 4860 – **190)** 2MORO, Suite 1B, 9 Burwood Rd, Burwood NSW 2134 – **191)** GPO Box 527F, Hobart TAS 7001 – **192)** PO Box 9550, Geelong VIC 3220 – **193)** 48 Mary Street, Preston VIC 3072 –**194)** Radio Rhema, Suite 4, 162 The Entrance Road, Erina NSW 2250 – **195)** Radio Hellas, Level 2, 280 William St, Melbourne VIC 3000 – **196)** 5 Phoenix St, Castle Hill NSW 2154 – **197)** PO Box 177, Mareeba QLD 4880 – **198)** 46 Ord St, West Perth WA 6005 – **199)** Gold AM, PO Box 1251, Mildura VIC 3502 – **200)** PO Box 280, Wagin WA 6315 – **201)** Box 887, Port Pirie SA 5540 – **202)** PO Box 2160, Bayswater VIC 3153 – **203)** Hospital Radio Network, 70 Dawson St, Cooks Hill NSW 2300 – **204)** PO Box 163, Dulwich Hill NSW 2203 – **205)** 1 Woodley Close, Kariong NSW 2250 – **206)** Locked Bag 888, St. Peters NSW 2044 – **207)** 4/9 Mavis St, Revesby NSW 2212 – **208)** PO Box 187, Oxley QLD 4075 – **209)** PO Box 124 Sale VIC 3853 – **210)** PO Box 995, Drouin VIC 3818 – **211)** PO Box 22 SAlamander Bay NSW 2317 – **212)** PO Box 966, Strawberry Hills NSW 2012 – **213)** PO Box 1962, Strawberry Hills NSW 2012 – **214)** PO Box 2161, Mt Gambier SA 5290 – **215)** Rankin St, Woorabinda QLD 4702 – **216)** PO Box 51, Yass NSW 2582 – **217)** PO Box 891, Manunda QLD 4870 – **218)** PO Box 1527,

Tamworth NSW –**219)** PO Box 21, Oatlands TAS 7120 – **220)** China Radio International, email:beyondbeijing@cri.com.cn – **221)** 12 Pickering Close Hoppers Crossing VIC 3029 – **222)** 5 Phoenix St, Castle Hill NSW 2154 – **223)** Suite 46-48, Pacific Centre,.223 Calam Rd, Sunnybank Hills QLD 4109 – **224)** PO Box 20, Cambellfield VIC 3061 – **225)** Surfside Radio, 9 Overton Rd, Frankston VIC 3199 – **226)** PO Box 1042, Gosford NSW 2250 (country format) – **227)** PO Box 1067, Mildura VIC 3502 – **241)** Voice of Charity, 22 Frank St, Mt. Druitt NSW 2770 – **228)** 68-70 Little Ryrie Street, Geelong VIC 3220 – **229)** PO Box 1000, Dunedoo NSW 2844 – **230)** PO Box 1206, Bendigo Central VIC 3552 – **231)** PO Box 1388, Booragoon WA 6954 – **232)** 15 Peneral Way, Bulleen VIC 3105 – **233)** PO Box 1921, Southport BC QLD 4125 – **234)** PO Box 752, Morrisset NSW 2264.

SPECIAL BROADCASTING SERVICE (SBS)

✉ Locked Bag 028, Crows Nest, NSW 2065 ☎+61 (02) 9430 2828 📠 +61 (02) 9430 3700

MW	Call	kHz	kW	Service
1) Wollongong	2EA	1035	2	National Prgr
1) Sydney	2EA	1107	5	Sydney 1
1) Melbourne	3EA	1224	5(d)	Melbourne 1
1) Newcastle	2EA	1413	5(d)	National Prgr
1) Canberra	1SBS	1440	2	National Prgr
1) Shellharbour	2EA	1485	0.15	Sydney
FM	**Call**	**MHz**	**kW**	**Service**
1) Cairns	4SBS	90.5	1(d)	National Prgr
1) Griffith	2SBS	92.7	1	National Prgr
2) Melbourne	3SBS	93.1	100	Melbourne 2
1) Brisbane	4SBS	93.3	96	National Prgr
1) Adel. Hills	5SBS	95.1	2(d)	National Prgr
2) Ballarat	3SBS	95.9	1	National Prgr
1) Perth	6SBS	96.9	100	National Prgr
1) Sydney	2SBS	97.7	150(d)	Sydney 2
1) Lismore	2SBS	98.9	1	National Prgr
1) Wondai	4SBS	98.9	2	National Prgr
1) Renmark	5SBS	99.1	1	National Prgr
1) Darwin	8SBS	100.9	32(d)	National Prgr
1) Sapphire	4SBS	103.5	1	National Prgr
1) Canberra	2SBS	105.5	80	National Prgr
1) Hobart	7SBS	105.7	56	National Prgr
1) Adelaide	5SBS	106.3	32	National Prgr

Addresses and other information
1) Locked Bag 028, Crows Nest, NSW 2065
2) PO BOX 294, South Melbourne VIC 3205

AUSTRIA

L.T: UTC +1h (31 Mar-27 Oct: +2h) — **Pop:** 7.8 million — **Pr.L:** German — **E.C:** 50Hz, 230V — **ITU:** AUT

ORF - ÖSTERREICHISCHER RUNDFUNK
✉ ORF-Funkhaus, Argentinierstr. 30A, 1040 Wien ☎+43 1 50101 18699 📠 +43 1 50101 82500 **W:** www.orf.at
L.P: DG: Dr. Alexander Wrabetz MD: Bettina Roither-Epp Tech. Dir.: Michael Götzhaber

FM (MHz)	Ö-1	Ö-Reg	Ö-3	FM4	kW
Bad Gleichen		94.9a	6		
Bludenz	87.6	96.0h	98.8		4
Bregenz	93.3	98.2h	89.6	102.1	50
Bruck/Mur	87.6	93.2f	98.7		20
Graz	91.2	95.4f	89.2	101.7	67
Innsbruck	92.5	96.4g	88.5	101.4	45
Klagenfurt	92.8	97.8b	90.4	102.9	100
Kufstein	97.5	95.4g	103.9	99.9	5
Lienz	89.3	93.8b	99.3	101.0	2.6
		95.9g			2.6
Linz	97.5	95.2d	88.0	104.0	100
		90.1c			10
Mattersburg	89.0	96.2a	100.9	0.6/3/0.6	
Rechnitz	90.6	93.5a	87.9	97.4	6
		100.1f			3
Salzburg	90.9	94.8e	99.0	104.6	100
		101.2d			7
St. Pölten	97.0	91.5c	89.4	98.8	100
Schärding	92.5	99.5d	88.2		3/4/3
Schladming	94.3	96.3f	101.3	103.3	3
Semmering	97.9	95.8c	88.2	92.4	9
Spittal/Drau	91.6	100.4b	87.9	103.6	3
Weitra	92.7	95.7c	98.1	101.4	2
Wolfsberg	96.7	94.5b	99.5	102.3	1.5
Wien	92.0	89.9i	99.9	103.8	100
		97.9c			100
		94.7a			2.4

+ more than 500 low power txs

Österreich-1 (Ö1): 24h. **N:** on the h
Österreich 2 (Ö2): Regional services
a) Burgenland – Buchgraben 51, 7001 Eisenstadt. **W:** burgenland.orf.at **b)** Kärnten – Sponheimerstr. 13, 9010 Klagenfurt **W:** kaernten.orf.at **c)** Niederösterreich – Radioplatz 1, 3100 St. Pölten **W:** noe.orf.at **d)** Oberösterreich – Europaplatz 3, 4010 Linz **W:** ooe.orf.at **e)** Salzburg – Nonntaler-Haupstr. 49d, 5020 Salzburg **W:** salzburg.orf.at **f)** Steiermark – Marburgerstr. 20, 8042 Graz **W:** steiermark.orf.at **g)** Tirol – Rennweg 14, 6010 Innsbruck. **W:** tirol.orf.at **h)** Vorarlberg – Höchsterstrasse 38, 6851 Dornbirn **W:** vorarlberg.orf.at **i)** Wien – Argentinierstr. 30a, 1040 Wien **W:** wien.orf.at
Österreich 3 (Ö3): 24h. **N:** on the h.
FM4: Prgrs in English (0000-1300), otherwise in German **W:** http://fm4.orf.at
Ann: "Österreich 1", "Ö2 (Wien, Niederösterreich, Tirol)", "Ö3"
IS: Österreich 1: composition by Werner Pirchner. Ö2: Composition by Bert Breit. Ö3: Electronic Music.
F.PI: Permission to use the following freq for commercial radio (kHz): 585, 630, 774, 891, 963, 1026, 1125, 1143, 1314, 1458, 1485, 1548 & 1602.

EXTERNAL SERVICES: Radio Ö1 International
see international radio section

PRIVATE STATIONS
KRONEHIT
Nationwide network with regional news windows
✉ Daumegasse 1, A-1100 Wien **W:** www.kronehit.at

FM	MHz	kW	FM	MHz	kW
Weitra	90.2	3	Schärding	104.9	8
Linz	92.6	14	St. Pölten	105.3	100
Semmering	102.9	8	Schladming	105.6	2
Bad Gleichenberg	103.2	8.5	Wien	105.8	100
Mattersburg	103.4	1	Innsbruck	106.5	32
Klagenfurt	103.7	1	Lienz	107.1	1
Rechnitz	104.1	6	Graz	107.5	1

+ 40 txs below 1kW

Other Private Stations by Area - FM (MHz):
BURGENLAND: HiT FM, 106.3 Mattersburg, 1kW; 105.5 Rechnitz, 1kW + 1rly
KÄRNTEN (Carinthia): Antenne Kärnten, 104.9 Klagenfurt, 100kW; 107.4 Spittal a.d.Drau, 3kW; 104.3 Wolfsberg, 2kW + 4rly – **Radio Dva (ORF)-Agora** (German/Slovenian progr), 105.5 Klagenfurt, 10kW; 106.8 Wolfsberg, 1kW + 7rly – **Radio Harmonie,** 95.2 Klagenfurt, 1kW + 4rly – **Radio Maria,** 99.3 Spittal a.d. Drau, 0.2kW – **Lokalradio Spittal a.d.Drau,** 101.6 Spittal a.d.Drau, 1kW (F.PI.)
NIEDERÖSTERREICH (Lower Austria): HiT FM, 104.9 Weitra, 1kW; Nebelstein, 3kW; 103.3 Melk, 3kW; 100.8 St. Pölten, 2kW; 106.7 Hornstein, 1kW; 101.6 Horn 1kW + 9rly – **Campus Radio 94.4,** 94.4 St. Pölten, 0.2kW – **Radio Ypsilon Live,** 94.5 Hollabrunn, 0.1kW + 1rly – **Radio Maria,** 95.5 St. Pölten, 0.2kW; 104.7 Waidhofen a.d.Ybbs, 0.5kW – **Radio Arabella 99.4,** 99.4 Tulln-Judenau, 0.3kW + 1rly – **Radio Arabella 96.5,** 96.5 Ybbs a.d. Donau, 2kW + 2rly – **Antenne Wien,** 96.3 St.Pölten, 1kW
OBERÖSTERREICH (Upper Austria): Life Radio, 100.5 Linz, 100kW; 102.6 Schärding, 3kW; 102.2 Bad Ischl, 0.4kW + 7rly – **Welle 1 Music Radio** (Linz), 91.8 Linz, 0.3kW – **Welle 1 Music Radio** (Steyr), 102.6 Steyr, 1.4kW; 98.3 Wels, 0.1kW + 3 rly – **R. Arabella 96.7,** 96.7 Linz, 4kW – **Radio FRO,** 105.0 Linz, 0.3kW – **LoungeFM,** 102.0 Linz, 2.2kW; 95.8 Ried im Innkreis, 1kW (F.PI.); 95.8 Schärding, 1kW (F.PI.) + 2rly – **Freies Radio Salzkammergut,** 100.2 Bad Ischl, 1kW; 107.3 Gmunden, 0.1kW + 4rly – **FR 107,1 Freies Radio Freistadt** 107.1 Freistadt, 0.6kW + 1rly
SALZBURG: Antenne Salzburg, 101.8 Salzburg/Gaisberg, 10kW; 105.9 Zell am See, 1kW; 102.5 St. Michael i. Lungau, 0.5kW + 15rly – **Welle 1 Salzburg LIVE,** 106.2 Salzburg/Gaisberg, 2kW; 107.1 Zell am See, 0.3kW; 107.5 St. Johann Pongau, 0.2kW – **Radiofabrik,** 107.5 Salzburg-Maria Plain, 0.5kW – **R. Arabella 102.5,** 102.5 Salzburg/Högl (D), 0.3kW; **Energy 94,0 Salzburg,** 94.0 Salzburg/Gaisberg, 0.3kW
STEIERMARK (Styria): Antenne Steiermark, 99.1 Graz/Schöckl, 80kW; 105.7 Bruck a.d. Mur, 20kW; 92.0 Schladming, 2kW; 106.1 Rechnitz, 3kW + 17rly – **Soundportal,** 100.4 Bad Gleichenberg 1.3kW; 97.9 Graz, 1kW + 5rly – **Radio Helsinki,** 92.6 Graz, 0.3kW – **Radio Eins,** 98.9 Bruck a.d. Mur 8kW + 106.3 Schladming 2kW + 4rly – **Radio Grün-Weiss,** 106.6 Bruck a.d.Mur 1.2kW + 3rly – **Radio West,** 107.3 Köflach, 0.1kW + 1rly – **Radio Freequenns,** 100.8 Liezen/Salberg, 1kW – **Radio Maria 92.4 Graz,** 0.5kW – **Welle 1 Graz,** 104.6 Graz, 0.5kW – **Lokalradio Schladming,** 88.5 Schladming, 3kW (F.PI.)
TIROL (Tyrol): Life Radio Tirol, 103.4 Inzing, 8kW; 101.8 Innsbruck, 1kW; 100.4 Lienz, 1kW; 105.4 Haiming, 1kW; 106.0 Landeck, 1kW; 106.8 Kufstein, 1kW + 8rly – **Antenne Tirol,** 100.8 Zirog (Italy), 1kW; 105.1 Innsbruck, 0.2kW; 106.4 Lienz 0.5kW; 104.6 Jenbach 0.2kW;

+ 4rly – **Welle 1 Innsbruck**, 92.9 Innsbruck, 0.3kW – **Welle 1 Oberland**, 103.9 Haiming (Telfs), 0.5kW; 104.3 Inzing, 0.4kW; 107.1 Landeck, 0.4kW + 5rly – **Welle 1 Ausserfern**, 104.0 Reutte, 0.3kW + 2rly – **Radio U1 Tirol**, 89.2 Jenbach, 0.4kW; 97.0 Innsbruck, 1kW + 8rly – **Radio Freirad**, 105.9 Innsbruck, 0.3kW – **Radio Osttirol**, 101.7 Matrei-Hopfgarten, 0.7kW; 107.8 Lienz, 0.4kW; + 6rly – **Energy Innsbruck**, 99.9 Innsbruck 0.3kW – **Klassik Radio**, 95.5 Innsbruck, 0.3kW – **Radio Maria**, 91.1 Innsbruck, 0.4kW; 107.9 Jenbach 0.2kW; 96.0 Mayrhofen 0.2kW – **Lokalradio Lienz**, 107.1 Lienz, 1kW (F.Pl.)
VORARLBERG: Antenne Vorarlberg, 106.5 Bregenz/Pfänder, 50kW; 101.1 Bludenz, 1.5kW; 105.1 Feldkirch 0.2kW + 2rly – **Radio Proton 104,6**, 104.6 Bludenz, 0.5kW; 95.9 Bregenz, 0.3kW; 104.3 Feldkirch 0.2kW – **Lokalradio Bregenz**, 103.2 Bregenz/Pfänder, 1kW (F.Pl.)
WIEN (Vienna): Radio 88.6, 88.6 Wien/Kahlenberg, 10kW – **Antenne Wien 102.5**, 102.5 Wien/Kahlenberg, 10kW – **R. Arabella 92.9**, 92.9 Wien-Donauturm, 3kW – **Energy Wien**, 104.2 Wien/RiFu-Arsenal, 1kW – **R. Stephansdom**, 107.3 Wien-Donauturm, 2kW – **R. Orange 94,0**, 94.0 Wien/Donauturm, 1kW; **98.3 superfly**, 98.3 Wien/Donauturm, 2kW – **LoungeFM**, 103.2 Wien/Raiffeisenhaus, 0.3kW

AZERBAIJAN

L.T: UTC +4h (31 Mar-27 Oct: +5h, except Mountainous Karabagh) — **Pop:** 9.2 million — **Pr.L:** Azeri, Armenian — **E.C:** 50Hz, 220V — **ITU:** AZE

MILLI TELEVIZIYA VÄ RADIO SURASI (MTRS)
(National TV & Radio Council)
✉ Nizami küç. 105, AZ 1000 Baki ☎ +994 12 5983659 🖷 +994 12 4987668 **E:** office@ntrc.gov.az **W:** www.ntrc.gov.az
L.P: Chmn: Nusirävan Mähärrämov
NB: MTRS is the licensing body for broadcasting.

AZÄRBAYCAN TELEVIZIYA VÄ RADIO VERILISLÄRI
QSC (Azerbaijan TV and Radio Broadcasting CJSC) (Gov)
✉ Mehdi Hüseyn küç. 1, AZ 1011 Baki ☎ +994 12 4923807 🖷 +994 12 4972020 **E:** info@aztv.az **W:** www.aztv.az
L.P: Chmn: Arif Alisanov

MW	kHz	kW	Prgr	MW	kHz	kW	Prgr
Gäncä	549	70	AzR	Haciqabul*	1296	75	F
Haciqabul	801	150	AzR	Sixli	1476	1	AzR
Baki	891	30	AzR				

F=External Service *= location/power unconfirmed

FM (AzR)	MHz	kW	FM (AzR)	MHz	kW
Gülüstan	88.0	5	Danaçi	103.0	2
Astara	90.0	1	Ordubad*	103.0	1
Poylu	90.0	5	Säki	104.0	1
Daskäsän	101.5	2	Babäk*	104.5	1.5
Lerik	101.5	2	Särur*	105.0	1
Yergüc	101.5	2	Baki	105.0	5

NB: Txs below 1kW not listed.*) situated in the Naxçivan exclave
D.Prgr: AzR (R. Respublika) 24h.
External Service (Voice of Azerbaijan): see Int. Radio section.

ICTIMAI TELEVIZIYA VÄ RADIO YAYIMLARI SIRKETI
(Public TV and Radio Broadcasting Co.)
✉ Särifzadä küç. 241, AZ 1012 Baki ☎ +994 12 4313968 🖷 +994 12 4302958 **E:** info@itv.az **W:** www.itv.az **L.P:** Dir: Ismayil Ömärov

FM	MHz	kW	FM	MHz	kW
Daskäsän	88.3	1	Danaçi	100.6	1
Lerik	88.3	1	Gülüstan	102.5	5
Yergüc	88.3	1	Poylu	103.0	5
Baki	90.0	5	Babäk*	103.0	1
Säki	91.6	1			

NB: Txs below 1kW not listed.*) situated in the Naxçivan exclave
D.Prgr: Ictimai R. 24h.

OTHER STATIONS

FM	MHz	kW	Location	Station
1)	88.6	1	Danaçi	Bürc FM
7)	89.0	1	Gäncä	Xäzär FM
7)	89.0	1	Lerik	Xäzär FM
1)	91.0	1	Gülüstan	Bürc FM
3)	92.0	1	Lerik	R. ANS-ÇM
2)	100.0	1	Poylu	R. Antenn
2)	100.0	1	Lerik	R. Antenn
1)	100.7	1	Quba	Bürc FM
2)	101.2	1	Baki	R. Antenn
2)	101.2	1	Gülüstan	R. Antenn
3)	102.0	1	Baki	R. ANS-ÇM
3)	102.0	1	Säki	R. ANS-ÇM
1)	102.8	1	Lerik	Bürc FM

FM	MHz	kW	Location	Station
7)	103.0	2	Baki	Xäzär FM
4)	104.0	2	Baki	R. Space
3)	104.5	1	Xizi	R. ANS-ÇM
6)	105.0	1	Gäncä	Lider Jazz FM
2)	105.3	2	Daskäsän	R. Antenn
8)	105.5	2.5	Baki	Media FM
5)	106.3	2	Baki	R. Azad Azärbaycan
6)	107.0	1	Baki	Lider Jazz FM
6)	107.0	1	Imisli	Lider Jazz FM

NB: Txs below 1kW not listed.
Addresses & other information:
1) Atatürk pr. 28, AZ 1069 Baki – **2)** Azadliq pr. 189, AZ 1130 Baki. **E:** info@antenn.az – **3)** Keçid 1128, 504-cü mähällä, AZ 1073 Baki. **E:** info@ansradio.ws – **4)** C.Cabbarli küç. 33, AZ 1009 Baki. **E:** radio@spacetv.az – **5)** A.Abbaszadä küç. 8, AZ 1001 Baki. **E:** info@atv.az – **6)** S. Mehtiyev küç. 83/23, AZ 1141 Baki. **E:** radio@lidertv.az – **7)** Atatürk pr. 28, AZ 1069 Baki. **E:** info@xazar.tv – **8)** Teymur Äliyev küç. 25A, AZ 1130 Baki. **E:** mediafm@mediafm.az

MOUNTAINOUS KARABAGH

LERNAYIN GHARABAGH
HANRAYIN HERUSTARADIOYIN KERUTYUN
(Public Radio & TV Co. of Mountainous Karabagh)
✉ Tigran Mets St. 23a, Stepanakert ☎ +374 47 945261 **E:** artv_or@ktsurf.net
L.P: Chmn: Norek A. Gasparyan
FM: Stepanakert 102.1MHz. **D.Prgr:** 0500-1700 in Armenian.

OTHER STATIONS

SW	kHz	kW	Location	Station
1)	9677±	5	Stepanakert	Adalätin Säsi

FM	MHz	kW	Location	Station
6)	101.8	-	Stepanakert	Ekho Moskvy
4)	103.0	-	Stepanakert	R. Novaya volna
3)	104.3	-	Stepanakert	R. Pace
5)	105.0	-	Stepanakert	Mix FM
2)	105.5	-	Stepanakert	R. Hay
7)	107.5	-	Stepanakert	R. Vem

Addresses & other information:
1) Tigran Mets St. 23a, Stepanakert. In Azeri, Armenian, Russian: Wed/Sat 0600-0630, Tue/Fri 1400-1430 (times may vary). **E:** justice@ktsurf.net – **2)** Azatamartikneri St. 18a, Stepanakert. Rel. Hay (Armenia) – **3)** Vazgen Sarkisyan St. 25, Stepanakert. **E:** pace@nk.am – **4)** A.Akopyan 30, Stepanakert. In Russian – **5)** Azatamartikneri St. 18a, Stepanakert. **E:** radio@mix.am – **6)** Stepanakert. Rel. Ekho Moskvy (Russia) – **7)** Stepanakert. Rel. R. Vem (Armenia).

AZORES (Portugal)

L.T: UTC -1h (31 Mar-27 Oct: UTC) — **Pop:** 245,000 — **Pr.L:** Portuguese — **E.C:** 50Hz, 220/380V — **ITU:** AZR

ANACOM-Autoridade Nacional de Comunicações, Delegação dos Açores
✉ Rua dos Valados 18, 9500-652 Relva (São Miguel) ☎+351 296 30 20 40 🖷 +351 291 30 20 41

RDP-RADIODIFUSÃO PORTUGUESA, S.A - Centro Regional da RDP-Açores
✉ Rua de Castelo Branco, 9500-761 Ponta Delgada ☎+351 296 201100 🖷 +351 296 201120 **E:** rdp.acores@rtp.pt **W:** www.rtp.pt
L.P: Dir: Pedro Bicudo
RDP Antena 1 Açores

MW	kHz	kW	Island
Santa Bárbara	693	a10	Terceira
Monte das Cruzes	828	1	Flores

a=r. currently running at 3kW

FM (MHz)	Ant. 1	Ant. 2	Ant. 3	kW
Arrife	94.5	97.5		0.3
Cabeço Gordo	88.9	105.8		9.1
Cabeço Verde	98.1			1
Cascalho Negro	92.2			1
Espalamaca	93.8	101.4	102.7	0.03/0.5/1
Fajãzinha	100.4	103.7		1
Furnas	93.6			0.5
Lajes das Flores	102.6	97.0		0.2/0.5
Lajes do Pico	96.5	93.5		1
Macela	87.6	93.2		1
Monte das Cruzes	99.8	97.4		1
Morro Alto	93.5	91.9		1
Nordeste	104.6			0.1

FM (MHz)	Ant. 1	Ant. 2	Ant. 3	kW
Nordestinho	103.7	91.8		1
Pico Alto Sta. Maria	96.7			10
Pico Bartolomeu	92.7	89.9		0.5
Pico da Barrosa	97.9	101.7	87.7	33/33/30
Pico das Éguas	89.5			10
Pico do Geraldo	103.7	107.5		1
Pico do Jardim	97.0			0.9
Pico São Mateus	103.4			0.1
Ponta Delgada	94.1	100.8		0.3/1.3
Povoação	102.8	97.2		0.5
Santa Bárbara	90.5	98.9	103.0	35/35/30
Serra do Cume	99.7	89.2	103.9	0.9

D.Prgrs: all networks 24h
V: by QSL card via RDP in Lisboa
Prgr: RDP Antena 1 Açores carries its own prgrs M-F 0730-0200, Sat. 0700-0200, Sun. 0800-0200 LT; Antena 2 relays Lisboa 24h
DAB: RDP halted T-DAB broadcasts in June 2011. There are no current plans to reactivate this service, which does not mean that it will not be restored in future.

COMMERCIAL STATIONS:
RÁDIO RENASCENÇA – Emissora Católica Portuguesa (Rlg/Comm)
✉ (see Portugal) - **FM:** Pico da Barrosa 95.2MHz 50kW (RR), 100.0MHz 50kW (RFM)
Private stations (only active on FM, but owning MW licences):

RÁDIO CLUBE DE ANGRA – "A VOZ DA TERCEIRA" (Comm.)
✉ Av. Tenente Coronel José Agostinho, 4, 9700 Angra do Heroismo ☎+351 295 21 31 01 ⊞ +351 295 21 31 02 **E:** administrativo@rcangra.com direccao@rcangra.com **W:** www.rcangra.com
FM: Santa Bárbara 101.1MHz 0.4kW, Serra do Cume (Terceira island) 94.7MHz 0.05kW

ESTAÇÃO EMISSORA DO CLUBE ASAS DO ATLÂNTICO (Comm.)
✉ Aeroporto de Santa Maria, Apartado 545, 9580-908 Vila do Porto ☎+351 296 88 64 68 /+351 296 820 720/1 ⊞+351 296 88 64 59 **E:** geral@asasdoatlantico.pt, radio@asasdoatlantico.pt **W:** www.asasdoatlantico.pt
FM: Pico Alto, 103.2MHz, 2kW **D.Prgr:** 24h

Other Stations

FM	Island	MHz	kW	Station, location
8)	São Miguel	88.5	3	R. Atlântida, Ponta Delgada
11)	São Miguel	91.0	0.5	R. Povoação/Canal FM, Pico Bartolomeu
3)	Faial	91.3	0.5	Antena Nove, Horta
9)	São Miguel	99.4	3	R. Comercial dos Açores/TSF, Ponta Delgada
6)	Pico	100.2	0.5	R. Pico, Madalena do Pico
2)	São Jorge	100.5	0.5	Canal FM, Calheta (Macelinha)
10)	São Miguel	102.4	0.5	Top FM, Pico da Barrosa (Ponta Delgada)
1)	Terceira	104.4	1	R. Horizonte Açores, Angra do Heroismo
15)	Flores	104.5	0.5	Canal FM, Santa Cruz das Flores
4)	Pico	104.7	0.5	R. Clube das Lajes do Pico, "A Voz da Montanha", Lajes do Pico
18)	São Miguel	105.0	0.5	R. Vila Franca, Pico da Barrosa
13)	São Miguel	105.5	2	R.Nova Cidade,Ribeira Grande
7)	São Miguel	106.0	0.5	R. Nordeste FM, Nordeste
16)	Pico	106.1	0.5	Top FM, São Roque do Pico
12)	Terceira	106.6	1	Top FM - Praia da Vitória, Santa Bárbara
17)	São Jorge	107.1	0.5	R. Lumena, Pico Rebineu
5)	São Miguel	107.2	1	R. Insular, Lagoa
14)	Graciosa	107.9	0.5	R.Graciosa, Serra Branca

+ 16 relays of 50W used by 9 stns

Addresses & other information (add +351 to tel/fax nos):
1) Caminho do Meio, nº 51, S. Carlos, 9700 Angra do Heroismo ☎295-216011/2/3/4 ⊞295- 216015 **E:** comercial@horizonteacores.com **W:** www.horizonteacores.com – **2)** Rua Manuel Augusto Amaral 1-D 2-Direito 9500-222 Ponta Delgada ☎296- 307 470 ⊞296- 307 479 **E:** radio@canal.fm **W:** www.canal.fm – **3)** Rua de São João, 38-B, 9900-129 Horta ☎292-29 33 90, ⊞ 292-39 16 02 **E:** antenanove@iol.pt **W:** www.antenanove.com – **4)** R. S. Pedro, 9, 9930-129 Lajes do Pico ☎292-672950 ⊞292 - 672950 **E:** radiomontanha@iol.pt – **5)** (relays R. Horizonte Açores 104.4) ☎296- 653 911/2/3/4 ⊞ 296- 653 910 **E:** horizonte2@horizonteacores.com **W:** www.horizonteacores.com – **6)** Avenida Machado Serpa nº 54 9950-321 Madalena do Pico ☎292- 622 727 ⊞292- 622 874 **E:** geral@radiopico.com , radiopico@sapo.pt **W:** www.radiopico.com – **7)** Rua Manuel João da Silveira nº 1A 9630-142 Nordeste ☎296- 098 480 **E:** nordeste.fm@gmail.com **W:** www.radionordeste.fm – **8)** Rua Bento José Morais 23 - 5º Sul, 9500-772 Ponta Delgada ☎296 201 910 ⊞296 629 856 **E:** webmaster@radioatlantida.net, director@radioatlantida.net **W:** www.radioatlantida. net – **9)** (relays TSF Lisboa) Rua Dr. Bruno Tavares Carreiro 34 - 2º - 9500 Ponta Delgada ☎296-202800 ⊞296-202825 **E:** radioacores@acoriano-

oriental.pt **W:** www.acorianooriental.pt/noticias/tsf/ – **10)** Caminho do Meio, n.º 51, 9700-222 Angra do Heroísmo ☎295 216 011/13 ⊞295 216 015 **E:** geral@mytop.fm **W:** www.mytop.fm – **11)** (Relays Canal FM) R. Manuel Augusto Amaral, 1 D - 2º Dto. 9500-222 Ponta Delgada ☎296 307470, ⊞296 307 479 **E:** radio@canal.fm **W:** www.canal.fm – **12)** (see 10) – **13)** R. Adolfo Coutinho de Medeiros, 24 (Apartado 007), 9600-516 Ribeira Grande ☎296 472738/296 472802 ⊞296 472654 **E:** radionovacidade@gmail.com **W:** www.radionovacidade.pt – **14)** R. do Corpo Santo, 37, 9880-368 Santa Cruz da Graciosa ☎295-732536 ⊞295 712768 **E:** geral@radiograciosa.com **W:** www.radiograciosa.com – **15)** (see 2) – **16)** Largo do Museu da Indústria da Baleia ☎292 642930 ⊞ 292 642934 **E:** cais@mytop.fm **W:** www.mytop.fm – **17)** Rua Cunha da Silveira, 25, Apartado 8, 9800-531 Velas ☎295 412575/295 412819 ⊞295 412810 **E:** radiolumena@iol.pt **W:** www.radiolumena.com – **18)** R. Nova Misericórdia, 271-R/C 9500-336 Vila Franca do Campo ☎296 654112/296 653053 ⊞296 653053 **E:** clubedamusica@105fmazores. com **W:** www.105fmazores.com

Military Stations:
RÁDIO LAJES – A VOZ DA FAP-FORÇA AÉREA PORTUGUESA (The Voice of the Portuguese Air Force)
✉ Comando da Zona Aérea dos Açores, 9760-290 Lajes, Terceira ☎+351 295 540891/2/3 ⊞ +351 295 540791 **E:** fap.radiolajes@emfa.pt **W:** www.radiolajes.pt **LP:** Dir.: Tenente-Coronel Carlos Mendes
MW to be reactivated on the new freq. of 1530kHz (ex-648) 1kW
FM 93.5MHz 150W **F.P.I.:** 500W 24h.
UNITED STATES AFRTS
✉ Lajes, Terceira, 9760 Praia da Vitoria ☎+351 295 57 34 97 **W:** www.lajes.af.mil
MW 1503kHz 100W (1kW nominal). **FM** 96.1MHz 150W
D.Prgr: Locally produced & relays of AFRTS

BAHAMAS

L.T: UTC -5h (10 Mar–3 Nov: -4h) — **Pop:** 316,000 — **Pr.L:** English — **E.C:** 60Hz, 120/220V — **ITU:** BAH

ZNS – THE BROADCASTING CORPORATION OF THE BAHAMAS (Comm., Gov.)
✉ Harcourt 'Rusty' Bethel Drive, Third Terrace, Centreville, PO Box N-1347, Nassau ☎ +1 242 502 3800 ⊞ +1 242 322 6598 **W:** www.znsbahamas.com **E:** info@znsbahamas.com
L.P: GM: Edwin Lightbourn. CEN: Donald Rolle
MW: ZNS1 Nassau 1540kHz 8kW **ZNS2** Freeport ‡1240kHz 1kW, – **ZNS3** 810kHz 1kW
FM: ZNS-Power FM: 104.5MHz 10kW – **ZNS1:** 107.1MHz 0.3kW So. Bahamas/107.7MHz 0.3kW No. Bahamas/107.9 0.3kW So. Bahamas
D.Prgr 24h. **N.** (ZNS1): 0800, 1300, 1830, 0000, 0300.
Ann. ZNS1: "This is Radio Bahamas" or "National Voice of Bahamas". ZNS2: "Inspiration 1240". ZNS3: This is Northern Service, Radio Bahamas". ZNS-FM: "Power 104.5"

TRIBUNE MEDIA GROUP (Comm.)
✉ Radio House, PO Box N-3207, Nassau ☎ +1 242 328 0950 ⊞ +1 242 356 5343 **W:** www.100jamz.com **L.P:** PD Eric Ward
Stations: Cool 96 FM: Yellow Pine Street, PO Box F-40773, Freeport ☎ +1 242 352 7440 ⊞ +1 242 352 8709 **W:** www.cool96fm.com **L.P:** GM: Andrea Gottlieb. **FM:** 96.1MHz – **100 Jamz FM:** Nassau 100.3, Freeport 100.3, Abaco: 100.1 and Coopers Town: 100.5MHz – **Joy FM,** PO Box N-1807, Nassau +1 242 356 5110. L.P.: Steven Haughey. **FM:** Nassau 101.9MHz – **Y98.7, FM:** Nassau 98.7MHz

THE NASSAU GUARDIAN (Comm.)
✉ Carter St, PO Box N-3011, Nassau ☎ +1 242 302 2300/328 6868 ⊞ +1 242 328 5311 **W:** www.guardiantalkradio.com, www.hot917fm.com & www.star106fm.com
Stations: Guardian Radio: FM 96.1MHz – **Hot 91.7:** FM 91.7MHz – **Star 106.5:** FM 106.5MHz

OTHER STATIONS:
Radio Abaco, Dundas Town, Mars Harbour, P.O. Box AB-20418, Abaco ☎ +1 242 367 4935 **FM:** 93.5MHz – **Breeze FM,** Georgetown, Exuma. ☎ +1 242 358 7221 **L.P:** CEO Dwight Hart. **FM:** 98.3MHz – **Gems Radio,** 57 Sears Hill, PO Box SS-6094, Nassau ☎ +1 242 326 4381 ⊞ +1 242 326 4371 **L.P.:** CEO Deborah Bartlett. **FM:** Nassau: 105.9MHz – **Global 99.5 FM**, Christie St., Nassau ☎ +1 242 326 0270. **FM:** Nassau: 99.5MHz – **Island FM,** Dowdeswell St, PO Box N-1807, Nassau ☎ +1 242 3322 8826 **W:** www.islandfmonline.com **FM:** Nassau 102.9MHz – **Love-97 FM,** East St North, PO Box N-3909, Nassau ☎ +1 242 356 2555 ⊞ +1 242 356 7256 **FM:** Nassau 97.5MHz – **Mix 102.1**, 31 Bishops Place, PO Box F-44008, Freeport ☎ +1 242 373 2275 ⊞ +1 242 373 2271

L.P.: GM: Don Martin. **FM:** Freeport 102.1MHz 5kW – **More 94 FM**, Carmiohael Rd, PO Box CR54245, Nassau ☎ +1 242 361 2447 🖹 +1 242 361 2448 **W:** www.more94fm.com **FM:** Nassau 94.9MHz – **Splash FM**, Spirit Gospel, PO Box EL-27495, Spanish Wells, Eleuthera ☎ +1 242 333 4638 🖹 +1 242 333 4693 **W:** www.splash899fm.com L.P.: Chris Forsythe **FM:** Eleuthera: 89.9MHz, Nassau: 92.5MHz (Spirit Gospel), Abaco 95.5MHz, South Eleuthera 98.5MHz – **Star 106**, 4 Carter St, Oakes Field, PO Box N-3011, Nassau ☎ +1 242 302 2300 🖹 +1 242 328 5311 **W:** www.star106fm.com **FM:** Nassau 106.5MHz

BAHRAIN

L.T: UTC +3h — **Pop:** 700,000 — **Pr.L:** Arabic — **E.C:** 50Hz, 230V(60/110 at Awala) — **ITU:** BHR

BAHRAIN RADIO & TV CORPORATION (BRTC, Gov.)
🖃 P.O.Box 1075, Manama ☎+973 17780780 🖹 +973 17780911 **W:** www.radiobahrain.fm **E:** info@bahrainradio.com **L.P:** CEO: Ahmed Najim. Dir. of Bc: Hamad Al-Manai. Act. Dir. Tech: Abdulla Ahmed Al-Balooshi.
General Prgr. in Arabic: 24h on **MW:** 801kHz 100kW, 1458kHz 10kW. **FM:** 90.9MHz 3kW – **Quran Prgr. in Arabic:** Quran recitations & religious affairs 0300-2100 on **MW:** 612kHz 100kW. **FM:** 106.1MHz.
– **Songs Prgr. in Arabic** : 0500-1700 on **MW:** 1521kHz 10kW. **FM:** 93.3MHz 3kW – **Prgr. for the Indian community:** 24h on **FM:** 104.2MHz – **English Sce (R. Bahrain):** 0300-2100 on **MW:** 1584kHz 1kW. **FM:** 96.5MHz 2.5kW. 1600-2100 on 99.5MHz 0.5kW – **Shabab FM**(Youth prgr.): Manama 98.4MHz.
Ann: As "Idha'atul-Bahrain". E: "Radio Bahrain".
IS: Local composition on guitar and violin.
Relays for abroad on shortwave: see International Radio section.

Other stations:
Sawt el-Ghad, Manama: 94.8MHz. **W:** sawtelghad.com
Voice FM, Manama: 104.2MHz. **W:** radiovoice.bh
Emarat FM, Manama: 92.3MHz. See main entry under UAE.
Panorama FM, Manama 103.0MHz. See main entry under UAE.
BBC World Sce, Manama: English 101.0MHz, Arabic 103.8MHz.
Deutsche Welle/Monte Carlo Doualiya, Manama: 90.9MHz 1kW.
R. Sawa, Manama 89.2MHz 1kW. 24h in Arabic

BANGLADESH

L.T: UTC +6h — **Pop:** 158 million — **Pr.L:** Bengali — **E.C:** 50Hz, 220/440V — **ITU:** BGD

BANGLADESH BETAR (Gov.)
🖃 National Broadcasting Authority, NBA House, 121 Kazi Nazrul Islam Ave, Dhaka-1000 ☎ +880 2 ,8625538 8625904 🖹 +880 2 8612021 **E:** rrc@dhaka.net **W:** www.betar.org.bd
L.P: DG: Kazi Akhter Uddin Ahmed DDG (News) Narayan Chandra Sheel : Chief Engineer: Dulal Chandra Pal Sr. Engineer & Project Director: Md. Nazmul Islam Sr. Engineer (Research): Zia Hassan Dy.Station Engineer: Muzibur Rahman Asst. Radio Engineer: Golam Suklain

MW	kHz	kW	Times
Khulna	558	100	0030-0400, 0600-1710
Dhaka-B	630	100	0000-0145, 0300-1710, 1800-2100
Dhaka-A	693	1000	0030-0610, 0830-1730
Rajshahi	846	100	0030-0400, 0600-1710
Chittagong	873	100	0030-0400, 0600-1710
Sylhet	963	20	0030-0400, 0800-1710
Thakurgaon	999	10	0950-1710
Rangpur	1053	20	0030-0400, 0800-1710
Rajshahi	1080	10	0030-0400 0600-1710
Rangamati	1161	10	0530-1030
Dhaka-C	1170	10	0900-1100
Barishal	1287	10	0445-1115
Cox's Bazar	1314	10	0545-1045
Comilla	1413	10	1000-1710
Bandorban	1431	10	0530-1030

SW	kHz	kW	Times
Shavar	4750	100	0600-1715

NB: Relays Dhaka A prog. Sign on/off varies due to special prgr relay

FM	MHz	kW	Rel	Times
Chittagong	105.4	2	c,b,d,j	0030-0400, 1300-1710
Comilla	101.2	2	b, d,j	0030-0400 1100-1710
Dhaka	97.6	5	c,d,j	0200-0600 0930-1330
Dhaka	103.2	5		0030-0400 1300-1710
Dhaka 100	100.0	3	b	0700-1000 1800-2100
Khulna	102.0	1	b, d.j	0030-0400, 1300-1710

FM	MHz	kW	Rel	Times
Rajshahi	104.0	5		0030-0400 1300-1710
Rajshahi	105.0	1	b, d,j	0030-0400 1300-1710
Rangpur	105.4	1	b, d,j	0030-0400 1300-1710
Sylhet	105.0	1	b, d,j	0030-0400, 1300-1710
Thakurgaon	92.0	5		1000-1710
Traffic Channel	88.8	10		0200-1400

b) Rel. BBC World Service 0030-0100, 0130-0200, 1330-1400, 1630-1700. d) Rel. Deutsche Welle 0200-0230, 1400-1430. j) Radio Japan 1500-1545 c) China R Int. 1300-1400
N. in English: 0200, 1100, 1530, 1805. **N. in Bengali:** 0100, 0300, 0400, 0500, 0600, , 0900, 1000, 1200, 1430, 1600, 1700 **SAARC N. in Bengali:** 1235 **SAARC N. in English:** 1250 Every Mon
F.PI: Establishment of countrywide FM network (2nd phase), Establishment of new FM stations located in Gopalganj & Mymensingh, 100kW tx at Chittagong to be replaced. Replacement of 100kW tx at Dhaka B. One standby 100kW tx for Dhaka B. Introduction of new MW frequency 819 kHz. 2 x 10kW Medium Wave AM Transmitter at Barisal.

EXTERNAL SERVICE: BANGLADESH BETAR
See International Radio section.

OTHER STATIONS:
RADIO TODAY
🖃 Radio Broadcasting FM (Bangladesh) Co. Ltd Awal Centre (13th & 19th floor), Kamal Atraturk Avenue, Banani, Dhaka 1213 ☎ +880 2 8829293 8836491, 8836492 🖹 +880 2 8836494
E: info@radiotodaybd.fm **W:** www.radiotodaybd.fm
FM: 89.6MHz 10kW Dhaka Chittagong

RADIO FOORTI
🖃 Radio Foortii Limited Landmark (8th flr), 12-14 Gulshan-2 North C/A, Dhaka 1212 ☎ +880 2 8835747 8835748 **E:** info@radiofoorti.fm **W:** www.radiofoorti.fm **FM:** 88.0MHz 20kW Dhaka 24h, Chjittagong, Sylhet, Mymensingh, Rajshahi, Barishal, Khulna, Cox's Bazar

UNIWAVE BROADCASTING COMPANY LTD
L.P: CEO: Zulfiker Ahmed Uniwave Broadcasting Company Limited, Silver Tower (12th Floor), 52, Gulshan Avenue, Gulshan- 1, Dhaka-1212 ☎ +880 2 9886800, 9861133, 8832989 **E:** info@radioaamar.com **W:** www.radioaamar.com **FM:** Radio Aamar 24h 88.4MHz Dhaka

AYENA BROADCASTING CORPORATION
🖃 Dhaka Trade Centre, 99 Kazi Nazrul Islam Avenue, Kawran Bazar, Dhaka **W:** www.abcradiobd.fm
L.P: Man. Dir.: Matiur Rahman Choudhury. **FM:** 89.2MHz 24h in Dhaka.

DHAKA FM
🖃 Navana Tower (15th floor), Navana Tower (15th Floor) 45, Gulshan South, Circle-1 Dhaka-1212, ☎ +880 2 8811720-21, 🖹: +880 2 8811722 **E:** admin90.4@dhakafm904.com
FM: Dhaka, 90.4 MHz 24h

PEOPLES RADIO
🖃 41, Samsuddin Mashon, Gulshan-2 Dhaka ☎ +880 2 9890952-3 🖹 +880 2 9570757 **E:** mnhbabu@peoplesradio.fm - **FM:** 91.6Mhz

F.PI: License to be issued for new pvt. FM stns: Media City Ltd, Asiatic Marketing Communication, Ayurvedio Pharmacy (Dhaka) Ltd, Next Wave Broadcasting Co. Ltd, Asian Radio Ltd, and Gunchil Ltd

Community R Stations
R Chilmari, Kurigram - **FM:** 99.2MHz – R Mukti, Bogra - **FM:** 99.2MHz – Barendra R, Naogaon - **FM:** 90.2MHz – R Mahananda, Chapai Nawabganj - **FM:** 98.8MHz – R Padma, Rajshahi - **FM:** 99.2MHz – R Jhenuk, Jhenidah - **FM:** 99.2MHz – R Nalta, Satkhira - **FM:** 99.2MHz R Sundarban, Khulna - **FM:** 98.8MHz – Loko Betar, Barguna - **FM:** 99.2MHz – Krishi R, Barguna - **FM:** 98.8MHz – R Naf, Cox's Bazar - **FM:** 99.2MHz – R SagorGiri, Chittagong - **FM:** 99.2MHz – R Bikrampur, Munsiganj - **FM:** 99.2MHz – R Pallikantho, Moulavi Bazar - **FM:** 99.2MHz

BARBADOS

L.T: UTC -4h — **Pop:** 288,000 — **Pr.L:** English — **E.C:** 50Hz 110V — **ITU:** BRB

CARIBBEAN BROADCASTING CORP. (Gov. Comm.)
🖃 The Pine, Wildey, St.Michael ☎ +1 246 429 2041 🖹 +1 246 429 4795 **W:** www.cbc.bb **L.P:** Chrmn: Leroy Parris. GM: Vacant. Head of R.: Pearson Bowen

MW: FM 94,7: 900kHz 5kW: 24h
FM: FM 94.7: 94.7MHz 5kW: 24h – **98.1 FM The One**: 98.1MHz 5kW: 24h – **Quality/Q FM 100.7** 100.7MHz 5kW

BARBADOS BROADCASTING SERVICE (Comm.)
✉ Astoria, St George ☎ +1 246 437 9550 🖷 +1 246 437 9203
L.P: MD: Anthony T. Brian. GM: Shery Anne Padmore.
FM: BBS-FM 90.7MHz: 24h – **Faith FM** (Rlg.) 102.1MHz: 24h

STARCOM NETWORK INC. (Comm.)
✉ River Road, PO Box 1267, Bridgetown ☎ +1 246 430 7300 🖷 +1 246 426 5377 **W:** www.starcomnetwork.net & www.vob929.com
L.P: CEO: Victor Fernandez. Mgr Ops: Lennox Edwards. PM (R.): Patrick Gollop
FM: CSS Caribbean SuperStation: 97.5MHz (relay Trinidad) – **VOB Voice of Barbados** (Gospel: 2215-0400 exc. Mon): 92.9MHz – **HOTT 95.3 FM**: 95.3MHz – **LOVE 104.1 FM**: 104.1MHz All stns: 24h

Other Stations:
BBC: FM 92.1. 24h relay of BBC World Service – **Christ is the Answer R.** (Rlg.): ✉ Bishop's Court Hill, BB46307, St. Michael ☎ +1 246 430 3599 **W:** www.citaradio.com **FM:** 90.1MHz – **Educational Radio 91.1 FM** ✉ Elsie Payne Complex, Constitution Rd., St. Michael **FM:** 91.1MHz. **D.Prgr:** Mon-Fri 0900-1213, Tue + Thu 1400-1500 during school terms only and irr. at other times – **Mix 96.9 (Comm.)** ✉ Garden House, Upper Bay St., St. Michael ☎ +1 246 228 4183 🖷 +1 246 228 3550 **W:** www.mix969fm.com/new/privacy.cfm. **L.P:** MD: Scott Weatherhead. **FM:** 96.9MHz – **Radio Ged** (Educ.) ✉ Barbados Community College, General Education Dept., Eyrie Howells Cross Road, St. Michael ☎ +1 246 426 3312 🖷 +1 246 429 5935 **FM:** 106.1MHz (0.02kW) **D.Prgr:** 1500-1900MF during school terms only – **Slam FM (Comm.)**: ✉ Hagget Hall, St. Michael ☎ +1 246434 1011 🖷 +1 246 437 7526. **FM:** 101.1MHz

BELARUS

L.T: UTC +3h — **Pop:** 9.5 million — **Pr.L:** Belarusian, Russian — **E.C:** 50Hz, 220V — **ITU:** BLR

MINISTERSTVA KULTURY (Ministry of Culture)
✉ pr. Peramozcaú 11, 220004 Minsk ☎ +375 17 2037574 **E:** ministerstvo@kultura.by **W:** www.kultura.by **L.P:** Minister: Pavel Latuška
NB. The Ministry of Culture is issuing broadcasting licenses.

NACYJANALNAJA DZIARZAÚNAJA TELERADYJO-KAMPANIJA RESPUBLIKI BELARUS (BELTELE-RADYJOKAMPANIJA) (Gov)
(State TV & Radio Co. of Belarus)
✉ vul. Makajonka 9, 220807 Minsk ☎ +375 17 3896352 🖷 +375 17 2678182 **E:** pr@tvr.by **W:** www.tvr.by
✉ **Belaruskaje Radyjo (BR):** vul. Cyrvonaja 4, 220807 Minsk; exc. **Radyus FM:** vul. Cyhunacnaja 27/2, 220014 Minsk.
L.P: Chmn: Genadz Davydznka

LW/MW	kHz	kW	Prgr	MW	kHz	kW	Prgr
Sasnovy	279	500	BR1	Sasnovy	1170	800	F, BR1
SW	kHz	kW					
Minsk (a)	6080	150	(a) Kalodzišcy F=External Service				

BR1 rel. on SW for listeners in Russia: see Int. Radio section

FM (MHz)	*BR1	BR2	*BR1	BR2	RS	RFM	kW
Asipovicy	67.46d	71.69	91.0d	107.7	72.47	104.9	2x4/1/3x2
Asveja	-	-	103.5e	106.0	-	-	4
Babrujsk	71.45d	68.96	101.6d	106.0	73.01	104.1	2x4/2x2/4/2
Berazino	70.79	-	94.7	104.7	67.07	100.7	3x1/0.25/1
Brahin	67.37b	68.30	103.3b	105.8	69.11	100.8	2x4/2/2x4/2
Braslaú	69.08e	71.99	105.7e	107.7	73.49	102.3	2x4/2/2x4/2
Brest	70.91a	71.69	100.0a	88.5	72.47	103.7	2x4/2x1/2x4
Drahicyn	72.14a	-	101.8a	-	69.80	102.4	0.5/1/0.5/1
Heraniony	72.32c	68.39	105.8c	102.2	69.26	103.3	2x4/2/1/4/2
Homiel	67.76b	69.26	105.1b	91.5	66.20	100.1	2x2/2x1/21
Hrodna	66.98c	66.20	103.0c	95.0	68.90	100.5	3x4/1/4/2
Kapyl	-	70.97	102.3	101.6	73.22	103.9	01/4/05/01/05
Kascjukovicy	66.47	68.03	104.7	107.2	69.38	102.2	2x4/2/1/4/2
Krupki	-	103.8	-	106.3	-	-	4
Luki	-	-	90.6c	94.7	-	104.3	1
Mahilioú	72.74d	71.96	105.9d	99.1	71.18	100.9	2x4/2/1/4/1
Miadziel	68.69	70.31	106.4	104.9	66.86	103.9	2x4/2x2/2x4
Minsk	71.33	70.43	106.2	102.9	72.89	103.7	2x4/2/1/2x4
Minsk	-	-	-	105.1	72.11	1/4	
Mscislaúl	66.89d	-	106.7d	101.7	73.73	102.9	3x1/0.25/1
Pinsk	66.32a	67.10	104.5a	106.8	67.88	102.0	2x4/2/3x4

FM (MHz)	*BR1	BR2	*BR1	BR2	RS	RFM	kW
Salihorsk	70.22	72.23	100.3	106.7	68.57	102.8	2x1/4/2/1/4
Slonim	66.56c	67.34	106.5c	97.3	-	104.0	3x4/1/4
Smarhon	67.97c	70.13	103.6c	-	66.38	101.4	2x2/3x1
Smiatanicy	67.22b	68.00	106.3b	104.6	70.28	103.8	4
Staryja Darohi	-	-	100.6	103.1	-	-	1
Svislac	-	66.08	105.9c	98.9	68.72	96.7	2x4/0.5/4/0.1
Trokeniki	-	70.76	104.5c	-	-	-	0.5/1
Ušacy	72.65e	66.74	106.7e	101.7	70.94	102.7	3x4/1/2x4
Vasilievicy	-	-	102.0b	106.5	73.19	-	1
Viciebsk	70.67e	69.92	100.5e	99.3	72.26	105.5	2x4/2x2/2x4
Vorša	67.85e	69.14	107.0e	105.0	73.82	100.2	2/4/3x1/2
Zlobin	69.68b	71.03	105.5b	101.0	71.81	100.5	3x2/1/2x2

NB. Sites with only txs below 1kW not listed. *) incl. reg. prgrs
D.Prgr: BR1 (Peršy nacyjanalny kanal): 24h in Belarusian, Russian on FM; limited schedule on LW/MW/SW. Most FM txs are shared with regional broadcasting stations (see below). Txs that do not carry reg. prgrs, relay instead R. Stalica at 0340-0400 (W), 1500-1600 (W). – **BR2 (Kanal Kultura):** 0300-2300 in Belarusian – **RS (Radyjo Stalica):** 0300-2300 in Belarusian. – **RFM (Radyus FM):** 0400-2300 mainly in Russian.

External Service (Radio Belarus): see Int. Radio section. On FM: Brest 96.4 (0.5kW), Hrodna 96.9 (1kW), Heraniony 99.9 (1kW), Svislac 100.8 (1kW), Miadziel 102.0 (4kW), Braslaú 106.6 (1kW).

BELTELERADYJOKAMPANIJA REGIONAL STATIONS
D.Prgr: In addition to the services shown below, all stns broadcast reg. prgrs via BR1 txs (see tx table above) at 0340-0400 (W), 1500-1600 (W). All stns broadcast in Belarusian and Russian. TRK = teleradyjokampanija.
a) TRK "Brest", vul. Kujbyšava 64, 224030 Brest. **E:** radiobrestgosti@tut.by. "R. Brest" 24h on 69.08 (Pinsk 4kW), 69.44 (Slonim 4kW), 69.68 (Brest 4kW), 94.6 (Pinsk 1kW), 101.1 (Baranavicy 0.5kW), 102.5 (Stolin 0.5kW), 104.2 (Drahicyn 2kW), 104.8 (Brest 2kW), 105.6 (Pruzany 0.1kW). – **b) TRK "Homiel"**, vul. Puškina 8, 246050 Homiel. **E:** radio@tvrgomel. by. "Homiel FM" 0200-0100 on 66.44 (Smiatanicy 4kW), 66.98 (Homiel 2kW), 68.45 (Zlobin 2kW), 69.92 (Brahin 4kW), 101.3 (Homiel 2kW), 103.0 (Zlobin 2kW), 105.3 (Brahin 1kW), 107.8 (Vasilievicy 1kW). – **c) TRK "Hrodna"**, vul. Horkaha 85, 230015 Hrodna. **E:** radio@tvr.grodno.by. "R. Hrodna" 24h on 67.76 (Hrodna 4kW), 68.12 (Slonim 4kW), 68.48 (Masty 0.5kW), 71.54 (Heraniony 4kW), 72.80 (Trokeniki 0.5kW), 101.2 (Hrodna 1kW), 101.8 (Luki 1kW), 102.5 (Slonim 1kW), 102.8 (Smarhon 1kW), 104.4 (Svislac 4kW), 107.8 (Heraniony 1kW). – **d) TRK "Mahilioú"**, vul. Peršamajskaja 83, 212030 Mahilioú. **E:** radiomogilev@tut.by. "R. Mahilioú" 0340-1900 on 66.02 (Babrujsk 4kW), 67.25 (Kascjukovicy 4kW), 70.10 (Mahilioú 4kW), 70.91 (Asipovicy 2kW), 96.4 (Mahilioú 1kW), 99.4 (Kascjukovicy 1kW), 100.0 (Krycaú 0.5kW), 100.4 (Mscislaúl 0.25kW), 102.3 (Asipovicy 1kW), 106.6 (Babrujsk 1kW). – **e) TRK "Viciebsk"**, vul. Kamunistycnaja 8, 210602 Viciebsk. **E:** info@radio. vitebsk.by. "R. Viciebsk" 24h on 67.64 (Miadziel 4kW), 68.30 (Ušacy 4kW), 71.48 (Viciebsk 2kW), 91.2 (Viciebsk 2kW), 100.6 (Hara 1kW), 102.0 (Asveja 1kW), 102.4 (Vorša 2kW), 104.0 (Bycycha 0.5kW), 104.6 (Braslaú 1kW), 105.2 (Sianno 1kW), 107.8 (Ušacy 4kW).

OTHER REGIONAL STATIONS (Gov)
Minskaya volna: vul. Ckalova 5, 220039 Minsk. "MV-Radyjo" in Russian, Belarusian 0400-2200 on 97.4 (Minsk 2kW), 102.4 (Miadziel 1kW), 102.6 (Krupki 0.5kW), 104.2 (Barysaú 0.5kW), 104.8 (Kapyl 1kW), 105.3 (Salihorsk 2kW), 105.5 (Berazino 1kW), 105.6 (Staryja Darohi 1kW), 107.4 (Maladzecna 2kW).

OTHER STATIONS
FM	MHz	kW	Location	Station
1A)	91.0	1	Homiel	R. BA
5)	92.2	1	Viciebsk	Pilot FM
15)	92.4	2	Minsk	R. Minsk
5)	93.2	1	Mahilioú	Pilot FM
1A)	95.7	1	Hrodna	R. BA
1B)	96.2	1	Minsk	Melodii veka
7)	97.8	1	Viciebsk	Evropa plus Vitebsk
9)	98.4	1	Minsk	Novoye R.
11)	98.6	1	Mahilioú	Nashe R.
7)	98.7	1	Viciebsk	Novoye R.
3)	98.9	2	Minsk	Russkoye R.
6)	99.5	2	Minsk	R. Unistar
13)	100.4	1.5	Minsk	Hit FM
4)	100.8	2	Brest	Alfa-Radio
2)	101.2	1	Brest	R. ROKS
5)	101.4	1	Minsk	Pilot FM
1A)	101.5	1	Slonim	R. BA
8)	101.8	1	Viciebsk	R. Mir Belarus

FM	MHz	kW	Location	Station
5)	102.1	1	Hrodna	Pilot FM
2)	102.1	1	Minsk	R. ROKS
6)	102.3	1	Brest	R. Unistar
2)	102.6	1	Homiel	R. ROKS
5)	102.9	1	Brest	Pilot FM
2)	103.0	1	Viciebsk	R. ROKS
2)	103.4	1	Mahilioú	R. ROKS
8)	103.6	1	Babrujsk	R. Mir Belarus
1A)	104.5	1	Mahilioú	R. BA
12)	104.6	4	Viciebsk	Retro FM
1A)	104.6	4	Minsk	R. BA
16)	105.1	1	Hrodna	Hrodna Plyus
10)	106.1	1	Pinsk	Svaje R.
1A)	106.2	4	Brest	R. BA
15)	106.4	1	Viciebsk	R. Minsk
8)	106.6	1	Brest	R. Mir Belarus
9)	106.7	1	Homiel	Novoye R.
2)	106.9	1	Hrodna	R. ROKS
8)	107.1	4	Minsk	R. Mir Belarus
4)	107.6	1	Viciebsk	Alfa-Radio
8)	107.8	4	Mahilioú	R. Mir Belarus
4)	107.9	2	Minsk	Alfa-Radio

NB: Txs below 1kW not listed.

Addresses & other information:
1A,B) vul. Surhanova 26, 220010 Minsk. **E:** radioba@list.ru – **2)** vul. Starazoúskaja 8a, 220002 Minsk. **E:** radio@roks.com. In Russian. – **3)** vul. Starazoúskaja 8a, 220002 Minsk. **E:**info@rusradio.by. In Russian. – **4)** pr. Nezaleznasci 181, 220125 Minsk. **E:** alpha@alpha.by In Russian. – **5)** vul. K.Marksa 40, 220030 Minsk. **E:** pilot-fm@mail.ru – **6)** pr. Nezaleznasci 4, 220050 Minsk. **E:** radio@unistar.by. In Russian. – **7)** Maskaúski pr. 10, 210015 Viciebsk. In Russian. – **8)** vul. Kamunistycny 17, 220029 Minsk. **E:** info@radiomir.by. In Russian. – **9)** pr. Puškina 39, 220092 Minsk. **E:** reklama@novoeradio.by In Russian. – **10)** vul. Karasiova 6, 225710 Pinsk. **E:** v_vizit@varjag.net. In Russian. – **11)** vul. Caljuskincaú 105, 212003 Mahilloú. **E:** nashe_mogilev@mall.ru – **12)** vul. Hoholia 11, 210601 Viciebsk. Rel. Retro FM (Russia). – **13)** vul. Kamunistycny 6a, 220029 Minsk. Rel. Hit FM (Russia). – **14)** vul. Kamunistycny 6, 220029 Minsk. **E:** fm@ont.by – **15)** zav. Kaliningradski 20a, 220012 Minsk. **E:** radio924fm@gmail.com. In Russian. – **16)** pl. Saveckaja 6, 230025 Hrodna. **E:** grodnoplustv@gmail.com

Radio via DTT: see TV section

BELGIUM

L.T: UTC +1h (31 Mar-27 Oct: +2h) — **Pop:** 10.9 million — **Pr.L:** Flemish, French, German — **E.C:** 50Hz, 230V — **ITU:** BEL

FLANDERS Pop: 6.4 million — **Pr.L:** Flemish

VLAAMSE RADIO EN TELEVISIEOMROEP (VRT)
(Pub) Flemish (Dutch) Language Network
Public Sce. grants by Flemish government.
VRT, August Reyerslaan 52, B-1043 Brussels ☎+32 2 741 3111 ▤ +32 2 734 9351 **W:** www.vrt.be **E:** info@vrt.be
L.P: General Director Media: Leo Hellemans; Radiomanager: Els Van de Sijpe

Regional Centres Radio 2:
Antwerpen: Jan Van Rijswijcklaan 157, 2018 Antwerpen ☎+32 3 2479111 ▤ +32 3 2378282 **E:** redactieantwerpen@radio2.be
Vlaams-Brabant: Dikke Lindelaan 2, 1020 Brussels ☎+32 2 7414111 ▤ +32 2 4780800 **E:** redactievlaamsbrabant@radio2.be
Oost-Vlaanderen: Martelaarslaan 232, 9000 Gent ☎+32 9 2247256 ▤ +32 9 2254903 **E:** redactieoostvlaanderen@radio2.be
West-Vlaanderen: Doorniksesteenweg 241B, 8500 Kortrijk ☎+32 56 247311 ▤ +32 56 221358 **E:** redactiewestvlaanderen@radio2.be
Limburg: Via Media 2, 3500 Hasselt ☎+32 11 249611 ▤ +32 11 242436 **E:** redactielimburg@radio2.be

FM (MHz)	R1	R2	RK	SB	M	kW
Antwerpen	-	-	92.0	-	-	1
Brussegem	-	90.7	-	-	-	2
Brussels	-	-	-	-	88.3	1
Diest	-	92.4	-	-	-	1
Egem O.+W.-VI.	95.7	-	90.4	102.1	101.5	50/50/50/40
Egem O.-VI	-	98.6	-	-	-	50
Egem W.-VI.	-	-	-	100.1	-	50
Genk	99.9	97.9	89.9	101.4	102.0	20/20/20/40/40
	-	-	-	-	93.0	3
Gent	-	-	-	94.5	-	0.5
Leuven	-	-	-	88.0	-	0.5/0.5
N'kerken Waas	-	89.8	-	-	-	1
Schoten	94.2	97.5	96.4	100.9	89.0	20/20/3/40/20

FM (MHz)	R1	R2	RK	SB	M	kW
St-Pieters-Leeuw	91.7	93.7	89.5	100.6	97.0	50/50/50/50/2
Veltem	-	88.7	-	-	94.8	1/1

+3 txs under 1kW

R1=Radio Een (information and music), **R2**=Radio Twee (light & popular music), **RK**=Radio Klara (classical music), **SB**=Studio Brussel (youth stn), **M**=MNM (hit music stn)
Radio 2 Regional prgrs: 0500-0700 (M-F), 1100-1200 (M-F), 1500-1700 (daily) on FM
Sporza: replaces normal R.1 prgrs during sports events **W:** www.sporza.be
D.Prgr: Night prgr on all frequencies.
DAB: 223.936MHz all services plus Sporza, MNM Hits, Klara continuo, and Nieuws+.
Ann: R1:"Radio Een", R2: "Radio Twee", RK: "Radio Klara", SB: "Studio Brussel", M: "MNM"

COMMERCIAL NETWORKS:
NB: For further information on all radio stns in Flanders visit **W:** www.radioinvlaanderen.info

FM	Mhz	kW	Location	Station
1)	87.6	3	Oostende	Nostalgie
1)	88.0	2	Kortrijk	Nostalgie
1)	88.1	1	Brugge	Nostalgie
2)	88.3	1	Oost-Vleteren	QMusic
2)	88.6	3	Gent	QMusic
4)	88.9	1	Diksmuide	Club FM
3)	89.1	1	Tongeren	Joe FM
5)	89.6	2	Brugge	VBRO
3)	90.6	5	Turnhout	Joe FM
6)	91.3	3	Brugge	Topradio
3)	92.2	3	Dendermonde	Joe FM
2)	92.2	1	Herentals	Qmusic
7)	92.7	2	Kortrijk	Radio Maria
3)	92.8	1	Gent	Joe FM
1)	92.8	1	Beringen	Nostalgie
3)	93.5	2	Sint-Niklaas	Joe FM
3)	93.5	2	Geel	Joe FM
3)	93.5	1	Bree	Joe FM
4)	93.6	5	Egem	Club FM
8)	95.1	1	Turnhout	RGR FM
3)	95.5	1	StPietersLeeuw	Joe FM
3)	95.6	1	Brussegem	Joe FM
2)	95.8	1	Veltem	Qmusic
7)	96.3	2	Gent	Radio Maria
3)	96.7	2	Mechelen	Joe FM
1)	96.9	1	Sint-Truiden	Nostalgie
10)	98.0	1	Antwerpen	Minerva
1)	98.1	10	Brussel	Nostalgie
1)	98.2	3	Egem	Nostalgie
11)	98.8	3	Brussel	FM Brussel
12)	99.0	1	Mechelen	Randstad
2)	99.2	10	Antwerpen	Qmusic
13)	99.3	1	Bree	Hit FM
6)	99.4	4	Gent	Topradio
3)	99.7	1	Leuven	Joe FM
2)	100.0	1	Wuustwezel	Qmusic
9)	100.2	2	Antwerpen	FG DJ Radio
1)	101.0	20	Oost-Vleteren	Nostalgie
2)	102.5	1	Brussel	QMusic
2)	102.5	50	Genk	Qmusic
13)	102.6	2	Leuven	Hit FM
14)	102.6	1	Eeklo	Family Radio
15)	102.7	3	Aalst	City Music
16)	102.7	2	Brugge	Exclusief
4)	102.8	1	Brussel	Club FM
17)	102.8	1	Gent	Zen FM
1)	102.9	50	Schoten	Nostalgie
2)	103.0	20	Egem	Qmusic
1)	103.0	1	Bree	Nostalgie
2)	103.1	50	StPietersLeeuw	Qmusic
3)	103.3	1	Diest	Joe FM
2)	103.3	1	Brugge	Qmusic
3)	103.4	10	Brussel	Joe FM
3)	103.4	5	Antwerpen	Joe FM
3)	103.4	20	Genk	Joe FM
1)	103.5	20	Gent	Nostalgie
4)	103.6	1	Oostende	Club FM
3)	103.7	1	Wuustwezel	Joe FM
3)	103.7	3	Lommel	Joe FM
1)	103.7	2	Sint-Niklaas	Nostalgie
1)	103.8	3	Leuven	Nostalgie
15)	103.8	2	Gent	City Music
8)	103.8	1	Geel	RGR FM
14)	103.8	1	Hasselt	Family Radio

FM	Mhz	kW	Location	Station
3)	104.1	50	Egem	Joe FM
4)	104.1	2	Hasselt	Club FM
7)	104.2	5	Leuven	Radio Maria
3)	104.2	1	Aalst	Joe FM
18)	104.2	1	Antwerpen	Crooze FM
1)	104.2	1	Overpelt	Nostalgie
5)	104.5	1	Oostende	VBRO
6)	104.5	1	Poperinge	Topradio
1)	104.5	1	Mechelen	Nostalgie
1)	104.5	1	Turnhout	Nostalgie
1)	104.6	2	Geel	Nostalgie
7)	104.6	2	Antwerpen	Radio Maria
6)	104.7	1	Hasselt	Topradio
1)	104.8	3	Aalst	Nostalgie

+ 273 stns below 1kW

Addresses and other information
1) Katwilgweg 2, 2050 Antwerpen **W:** www.nostalgie.eu – **2)** Medialaan 1, 1800 Vilvoorde **W:** www.qmusic.be – **3)** Medialaan 1, 1800 Vilvoorde **W:** www.joe.be – **4)** Stationsstraat 68, 9900 Eeklo **W:** www.clubfm.be – **5)** Jan Miraelstraat 24, 8000 Brugge **W:** www.vbro.be – **6)** Nekkerputstraat 150, 9000 Gent **W:** www.topradio.be – **7)** Postbus 5045, 5201 GA 's-Hertogenbosch, Netherlands **W:** www.radiomaria.be – **8)** Postbus 77, 3000 Leuven 3 **W:** www.rgrfm.be – **9)** Koningin Astridplein 38 bus 3 - 2000 Antwerpen **W:** www.radiofg.com – **10)** Wandeldijk 20, 2050 Antwerpen **W:** www.radio-minerva.be – **11)** Eugène Flageyplein 18 bus 18, 1050 Elsene **W:** www.fmbrussel.be – **12)** Hogeweg 211 2800 Mechelen **W:** www.randstad.fm – **13)** KAAI.16, Scheepvaartkaai 16 A bus 8, 3500 Hasselt **W:** www.hitfm.be – **14)** Leopoldlaan 98c, 9900 Eeklo **W:** www.familyradio.be – **15)** Geraardsbergsestraat 21, 9300 Aalst **W:** www.city-music.be – **16)** Emile Bethunelaan 5, 8200 Brugge – **17)** Einde Were 150, 9000 Gent **W:** www.zenfm.be – **18)** Diksmuidelaan 173, 2600 Berchem **W:** www.crooze.fm

WALLONIA Pop: 4 million — **Pr.L:** French, German

RADIO-TÉLÉVISION BELGE DE LA COMMUNAUTE FRANCAISE (R.T.B.F.) (Pub.)
French Language Network
Public sce. Grants by French Parliament.
✉ Cité de la Radio-Television, B-1044 Brussels ☎+32 2 737 2111 🖷 +32 2 737 4357 **W:** www.rtbf.be
L.P: Admin. Gen: Jean-Paul Philippot. Dir. Radio: Francis Goffin
Regional & Local Centres: Bruxelles: Reyerslaan 52, 1044 Brussel **Charleroi:** Passage de la Bourse, 6000 Charleroi **Liège:** Palais des congrès, 4020 Liège **Hainaut:** Rue du gouvernement 15, 7000 Mons **Namur-Brabant-Wallon:** Av. Golenvaux 8, 5000 Namur **Verviers:** Rue de Verviers 203, 4821 Andrimont **Luxembourg:** Parc des Expositions, 6700 Arlon

MW	kHz	kW	Prgr	MW	kHz	kW	Prgr
Wavre	621	300	Ext.Svce	Houdeng	1125	9	2

FM (MHz)	1	2	3	4	5	kW
Anderlues	93.4	92.3		99.1	96.6	0.6/40/40/40
Bruxelles		99.3	91.2	93.2	88.8	3/40/1/?
Léglise	96.4	91.5	94.1	87.6		10/10/10/10
Liège	96.4	90.5	99.5	95.6	92.5	5/40/40/13/0.1
Malmédy	89.2	91.6				1/0.1
Marche	93.3	95.2				0.5/4
Profondeville	102.7			92.8	90.8	25/10/10
Tournai	106.0	101.8	102.6	104.6	90.6	25/30/30/30/?
Verviers	91.3	103.0			87.9	1/3/0.1
Wavre	96.1	97.3			101.1	10/35/50

+ many txs under 1kW

Network 1 (Première – information & musique)
Network 2 (Vivacité – light music)
Reg. Prgrs: W 0530-0800, 1200-1300, 1600-1800; Fri 1800-2100 – R. Hainaut (Mons) on 92.3/101.8MHz – R. Liège 90.5/103.0/94.6/89.1/89.4MHz – R. Namur on 93.2/92.8/89.3/91.5/89.4/90.2MHz – R. Bruxelles on 93.2MHz
Local Prgrs: R. Verviers (Radiolène) on 103.0MHz
Network 3 (Musique 3 – classical music)
Network 4 (Classic 21 – oldies & rock classics)
Network 5 (Pure FM – youth stn)
DAB: 225.648MHz
Ann: "Vous écoutez La Première, Vivacité, Musique trois, Radio 21, Pure FM, Classic 21"

EXTERNAL SERVICE: RTBFi
See International Broadcasting section

BELGISCHES RUNDFUNK-UND FERNSEHZENTRUM DER DEUTSCHSPRACHIGEN GEMEINSCHAFT (BRF)
German Language Network (Pub)
Grants by RDG-Rat (German speaking community council)
✉ Kehrweg 11, B-4700 Eupen ☎+32 87 59 1111 🖷+32 87 591199 **W:** www.brf.be **E:** info@brf.be
Regional: ✉ Blvd. Reyers 52, B-1044 Brussels – Malmedyer Str. 25, B-4780 St. Vith **L.P:** Dir. of BRF: A. Spoden

FM	MHz	kW	FM	MHz	kW
Lüttich	88.5	50	Brussel*	95.2	2
Auel	92.2	0.16	Eupen	98.4	1
Recht	94.9	5	Recht	104.1	20

*: broadcasts joined prgrs of Deutschlandfunk and BRF
Ann: "Hier ist der Belgischer Rundfunk"

COMMERCIAL NETWORKS:
NB: For further information on all radio stns in Wallonia visit **W:** www.tuner.be/tuner.asp?content=radio

FM	Mhz	kW	Location	Station
14)	87.6	1	Ath	Sud Radio
14)	88.2	1	Charleroi	Sud Radio
11)	88.3	5	Bouillon	NRJ
11)	88.7	1	Arsimont	NRJ
1)	88.9	1	Fauquez	Bel RTL
10)	89.2	1	La Louvière	Radio Nostalgie
1)	90.0	1	Tournai	Sud Radio
10)	92.3	1	Verviers	Radio Nostalgie
11)	92.7	1	Malmédy	NRJ
7)	92.9	1	Bastogne	Fun Radio
2)	94.4	1	Bütgenbach	100.5 Das Hitradio
9)	94.7	5	Bouillon	Must FM
10)	95.0	1	Liège	Radio Nostalgie
15)	95.6	1	Houdeng	Twizz
7)	97.1	4	Bouillon	Radio Contact
14)	97.6	1	Braine-le-cte	Sud Radio
12)	98.0	2	Bütgenbach	Radio Contact (DE)
1)	99.0	2	Bouillon	Bel RTL
7)	99.0	1	Liège	Fun Radio
10)	100.0	5	Brussel	Radio Nostalgie
4)	100.1	1	Liège	Equinoxe FM
1)	100.2	1	Limal	Bel RTL
10)	100.4	4	Namur	Radio Nostalgie
2)	100.5	20	Eupen	100.5 Das Hitradio
10)	100.5	2	Couvin	Radio Nostalgie
10)	100.7	2	Dinant	Radio Nostalgie
8)	100.9	2	Liège	Maximum FM
1)	101.6	5	Marche	Bel RTL
12)	101.6	1	Verviers	Radio Contact
1)	101.7	2	Namur	Bel RTL
1)	101.7	1	Couvin	Bel RTL
1)	101.8	50	Meix Le Tige	Bel RTL
1)	101.9	1	Dinant	Bel RTL
14)	102.0	2	Mons	Sud Radio
12)	102.2	10	Brussel	Radio Contact
12)	102.2	5	Charleroi	Radio Contact
12)	102.2	1	Liège	Radio Contact
12)	102.3	5	Mons	Radio Contact
12)	102.4	1	Arlon	Radio Nostalgie
12)	102.5	1	Houffalize	Radio Contact
11)	103.2	10	Vlessart	NRJ
15)	103.2	2	Liège	Twizz
1)	103.4	5	Mons	Bel RTL
7)	103.5	1	Charleroi	Fun Radio
1)	103.6	1	Ath	Bel RTL
1)	103.6	50	Liège	Bel RTL
11)	103.7	1	Brussel	NRJ
6)	104.0	1	Brussel	Foo Rire
1)	104.0	2	Charleroi	Bel RTL
10)	104.1	1	Huy	Radio Nostalgie
1)	104.3	15	Brussel	Bel RTL
11)	104.3	5	Namur	NRJ
12)	104.5	1	Wavre	Radio Contact
12)	104.6	1	Marche	Radio Contact
7)	104.7	1	Brussel	Fun Radio
12)	104.7	2	Malmédy	Radio Contact
12)	104.7	5	Namur	Radio Contact
2)	104.8	3	Sankt Vith	100.5 Das Hitradio
12)	104.8	2	Virton	Radio Contact
7)	105.5	1	Louvain-L-N	Fun Radio
12)	106.2	1	Florzé	Radio Ourthe Amblève
3)	106.3	2	Tubize	Radio Antipode
11)	106.7	1	Bastogne	NRJ
5)	106.8	1	Malmédy	Est FM
8)	106.9	1	Aywaille	Maximum FM
10)	100.2	50	Saint-Hubert	Radio Nostalgie
11)	104.5	5	Liège	NRJ

FM	Mhz	kW	Location	Station
12)	107.0	1	Eupen	Radio Contact (DE)
7)	107.5	1	Arlon	Fun Radio
2)	107.6	1	Honsfeld	100.5 Das Hitradio
10)	107.6	5	Bouillon	Radio Nostalgie
11)	107.7	1	Tournai	NRJ
12)	107.8	1	Libramont	Radio Contact

+ many stns below 1kW

Addresses:
1) Avenue Georgin 2, 1030 Bruxelles 02-3376911 W: www.belrtl.be – 2) Kehrweg 11, B-4700 Eupen +32 87 591259 ☒ +32 87 591249 W: www.hitradioworld.fm – 3) Boîte postale 2, 1348 Louvain-La-Neuve ☎ 010-451110 ☒ 010-451717 W: www.antipode.be – 4) Rue Montagne St Walburge, 261, 4000 Liège W: www.equinoxefm.be – 5) – – 6) Avenue d'Hougoumont, 2, 1180 Bruxelles W: www.foorirefm.be – 7) Av. Telemaque 33, 1190 Bruxelles ☎ 02-3457575 W: www.funradio.be – 8) 22 Rue de la Chaudronnerie, 4030 Grivegnée W: www.maximumfm.be – 9) BP20, 1360 Perwez ☎ 081-655469 W: www.mustfm.be – 10) Quai au Foin 55, 1010 Bruxelles ☎ 02-2270450 ☒ 02-2231455 W: www.nostalgie.eu – 11) Chaussèe de Louvain 467, 1030 Bruxelles ☎ 02-5137575 ☒ 02-5114859 W: www.nrj.be – 12) Avenue des Croix de Guerre 94, 1120 Bruxelles 02-2442711 ☒ 02-2442710 W: www.radiocontact.be and www.derbestemix.be (DE) – 13) Rue Armand Binet 35B, 4140 Rouvreux (Sprimont) – 14) 42, rue de la chaussée de Mons, 7000 Mons ☎ 065-401010 ☒ 065-401011 W: www.sudradio.net – 15) Rue des Francs, 79, 1040 Bruxelles W: www.twizz.be

Military Stations:
AMERICAN FORCES NETWORK, SHAPE
☒ Box 7, 7010 SHAPE. (APO AE 09700) ☎+32 65 44 41 21
L.P: Officcr in chargc: Cpt. G. Martel. Broadc. Superv: SFC C. Kubicek. Chief Eng: René Libre
Stations: Kleine Breugel 106.2MHz 0.1kW, Brussels 101.7MHz 0.9kW, SHAPE 104.2/106.5MHz 4kW, Florennes 107.7MHz 0.1kW, Chievres 107.9.
D.Prgr: 24h on 101.7/104.2/107.7MHz. Own prgrs Mon-Fri 0500-0800, 1400-1700; Sat 0800-1200. Other times rel. AFN Europe.
AFN-2: 24h easy listening stereo prgr on 106.5MHz
BRITISH FORCES BROADCASTING SERVICE
Stations: SHAPE BFBS 1, Casteau, 107.7MHz 0.05kW
☒ Wentworth B., Listnstr., D-32049 Herford, Germany
D.Prgr: rel. BFBS Germany

BELIZE

L.T: UTC -6h — **Pop:** 301,000 — **Pr.L:** English, Spanish — **E.C:** 60Hz, 110/220V — **ITU:** BLZ

PUBLIC UTILITIES COMMISSION (PUC)
☒ PO Box 300, 41 Gabourel Lane, Belize City ☎+501 2234938 ☒ +223 2236818 W: puc.bz E: info@puc.bz L.P: Chairman: John Avery. Dir. Telecomm: Kingsley Smith.

FM	MHz	kW	Name and loc. (Hrs of tr usually 24h)
5)	88.9	40	Love FM, Ladyville
1)	90.5	0.25	Positive Vibes R, Belize City
6)	91.1	13	Krem FM, Ladyville
2)	92.3		Reef R, San Pedro
8)	93.7	0.5	My Refuge Christian R, Roaring Creek
3)	94.3		Our Lady of Mount Carmel R, Benque Viejo
4)	94.5		People's R. (Da Beat), Belize City
5)	95.1		Love FM, Belize City
5)	95.9		Estéreo Amor, Belize City
6)	96.5	6	Krem FM, Belize/Carmelita/Cattle Landing
7)	97.1		Integrity R., Belize City
7)	97.5		Estéreo Amor, Belize City
5)	99.5		More FM, Belize City
8)	100.5	0.2	My Refuge Christian R, Belize City
6)	101.1	1	Krem FM, Dangriga
9)	101.3		R. Emanuel, San Pedro
1)	102.9		Positive Vibes R, Belmopan
10)	104.5		Faith FM, Pine Ridge
10)	104.5		Faith FM, Punta Gorda
11)	105.9		Wave 105.9, Belmopan
5)	107.1		More FM, Belmopan

+ several other local FM stns

Addresses and other information:
1) Belize City. E: vibesradiogm@gmail.com – 2) San Pedro W: www.threeefradio.com – 3) Our Lady of Mount Carmel High School, Benque Viejo del Carmen. W: www.carmelradio.org F.Pl: 1 kW FM transmitter at Pine Ridge – 4) 3321 Central American Boulevard, Belize City

E: modulation945@yahoo.com – 5) 7145 Slaughterhouse Road, PO Box 1865, Belize City. FM: Belize City 95.1MHz + 9 FM repeaters. W: www.lovefm.com – 6) 3304 Partridge Str, c/o P.O. Box 15, Belize City. W: krembz.com – 8) P. O. Box 275, Belmopan. W: myrefugebelize.org – 9) San Pedro, Ambergris Caye – 10) PO Box 145, Santa Elena, Cayo District. W: faithfmbelize.com – 11) Belmopan E: waveradio105_9@yahoo.com

BENIN

L.T: UTC +1h — **Pop:** 9 million — **Pr.L:** French + 18 ethnic — **E.C:** 50Hz, 220V — **ITU:** BEN

HAUTE AUTORITÉ DE L'AUDIOVISUEL ET DE LA COMMUNICATION (HAAC)
☒ BP 3567, Ave. de la Marina, Face Hôtel du Port, 01 Cotonou +229 21311743 ☒ +229 21311742 W: haacbenin.org

OFFICE DE RADIODIFFUSION ET TÉLÉVISION DU BENIN (ORTB, Gov.)
☒ 01 B.P. 366, Cotonou +229 21360047 W: www.ortb.bj E: ortb@intnet.bj L.P: DG: Hamado Ouangraoua. Chief Tech. Sces: Anastase Adjoko. **Regional** ☒ B.P. 128, Parakou ☎+229 23611096
FM: Cotonou 94.7 10kW, Parakou 89.4/92.5MHz 7kW
Radio Nationale: from Cotonou in French/ethnic.
N. in French: 0615MF, 0800SS, 1200SS, 1215MF, 1930, 2115.
R. Regionale Parakou: in French/ethnic.
(Cotonou & Parakou carry the same programme between 1900-2000).
Atlantic FM, Cotonou: 0700-2300 on 92.2MHz.
Ann: "Ici R. Bénin, Office de Radiodiffusion et Télévision du Bénin, émettant de Cotonou". "Ici Parakou, Office de Radiodiffusion et Télévision du Bénin, station regionale" **IS:** Bénin Tam-Tam

Other stations:
R. Adja Ouèrè FM, Cotonou: 92.6/100/100.6/107.6MHz – **R. Afrique Espoir**, Porto-Novo: 99.1MHz – **Benin Culture**, Porto-Novo: 93.4MHz – **CAPP FM**, Cotonou: 99.6MHz – **R. Carrefour**, Cotonou: 90.4MHz – **Cité Savalou Culture FM**, Cotonou: 87.8MHz – **Deeman R**, Parakou: 90.2MHz – **FM Ahémé**, Possotome: 99.6MHz – **FM Alakétou**, Ketou: 95.8MHz – **FM Monts Kouffé**, Bassila: 103MHz – **FM Noon Sina**, Bembereke: 90.8MHz – **FM Oré Ofé**, Tchetti: 102.1MHz – **Gerddes FM**, Cotonou: 89.5 MHz – **Golfe FM**, Cotonou: 105.7MHz W: eit.to/golfefm.htm – **La Voix de la Lama**, Porto-Novo: 103.8MHz – **La Voix de l'Islam**, Cotonou: 91.2MHz – **R. Immaculee Conception** (Rlg.): Djougou 89.1MHz, Natitingou 93.1MHz, Parakou 93.3MHz, Cotonou 98.7MHz, Bembèrèkè 100.8MHz, Bohicon 100.9MHz, Allada 101.3MHz, Dassa-Zoumey 107.3MHz – **R. Liéma**, Cotonou: 104MHz – **R. Planète**, Cotonou: 95.7MHz – **R. Maranatha**, Cotonou: 103.1MHz W: eit.to/RadioMaranatha.htm – **R. Allodalome**, Cotonou: 97.4MHz – **R. Star**, Cotonou: 94.3/96.3MHz – **R. Tokpa**, Cotonou: 104.3MHz – **R. Tonassé**, Covè: 107.6MHz – **R. Wekè**, Cotonou: 107MHz – **R. Rurale** stns in Tanguiéta 90, Ouessè 97.7, Dogbo 100, Ouaké 101 & Banikoara 104.2MHz – **Africa No 1**: Porto-Novo 102.6MHz (see main entry under Gabon) – **BBC African Service:** Cotonou 101.7MHz – **RFI Afrique:** Cotonou 90MHz, Parakou 106.1MHz.
Trans World R, Parakou: 1566kHz 100kW 0315-0555, 1725-2230. (For details see International Radio section)

BERMUDA (UK)

L.T: UTC -4h (10 Mar-3 Nov: - 3h) — **Pop:** 69,000 — **Pr.L:** English — **E.C:** 60Hz, 115/230V — **ITU:** BER

BERMUDA BROADCASTING CO. LTD. (Comm.)
☒ 4 Fort Hill Road, Prospect, Devonshire DV 02, P.O. Box HM 452, Hamilton HM BX ☎ +1 441 295 2828 ☒ +1 441 295 4282 W: www.power95.bm. PM: CE: Ulric P Richardson. PM: Darlene Ming. News Dir: Jannell Ford. CEN: Earlston Chapman
Gov. Emergency Broadc. Stn: MW: 1610kHz FM: 100.1MHz
FM: ZBM: 89.1MHz 15kW – **Power 95 FM:** 94.9MHz 1kW – **Spirit FM/Moody Radio (Rlg.):** 105.1MHz

DEFONTES BROADCASTING CO. LTD. (Comm.)
☒ P.O. Box HM 1450 (**studios:** 94 Reid Str.) Hamilton HM FX ☎ +1 441 292 0050 ☒ +1 441 295 1658 E: vsbnews@ibl.bm W: www.vsb-bermuda.com L.P: CEO: Kenneth De Fontes. SM: Mike Bishop. N. Dir: Chris Lodge. TD: Ed. Tucker & Fred Blanchette
MW: 1450 AM Gold 1450kHz 1kW 24h (oldies) – **Bible Broadcasting Network** 1280kHz 1kW 24h (rlg.) – **BBC World Service** 1160kHz 1kW 24h. Rel. BBCWS except for special event prgrs
FM: Mix 106.1: 106.1MHz 2.5kW: 24h (CHR)

INTER-ISLAND COMMUNICATIONS (Comm.)
✉ 49 Union Square Mall, Hamilton ☎ +1 441 297 1076 🖷 +1 441 296 7680 E: feedback@hott1075bermuda.bm W: www.hott1075.com
L.P: CEO: Glenn Blakeney
FM: Magic 102.7: 102.7MHz – Hott 107.5 107.5MHz

LTT BROADCASTING LTD. (Comm.)
✉ P.O. Box 1564 HMGX, Hamilton HMEX ☎ +1 441 700 9810 🖷 +1 441 292 1593 W: www.irie.bm L.P: Leo Trott
FM: Irie FM: 98.3MHz

VIBE 103 FM (Comm.)
✉ Somerset, Sandys ☎ +1 441 297 1076 🖷 +1 441 232 0699 E: info@vibe103.com W: www.vibe103.com
FM: Vibe 103 FM: 103.3MHz

BHUTAN

L.T: UTC +6h — Pop: 2 million — Pr.L: Dzongha, Sharchopkha, Lhotsam(Nepali), English — E.C: 50Hz, 220V — ITU: BTN

BHUTAN BROADCASTING SERVICE (Corp.)
✉ P.O. Box 101, Thimphu ☎ +975 2 322866/322533/323071 🖷 +975 2 323073 W: www.bbs.com.bt E: request@bbs.com.bt
L.P: Exec. Dir: Sonam Tshong.Tech. MD: Pema Choden, Dir: Dorji Wangchuk. Prgr. Dir: Tashi Dhendup. News Dir: Thinley Tobgye
SW: 6035kHz 10/100kW D.Prgr: 0000-0700, 0800-1400 (Irr. Usually 0100/0300-1300/1330 and using 10kW at press date).
FM(MHz): 88.1 & 96.0 Thimphu, 92.0 Phuentsholing, 92.0 Paro, 93.0 Trongsa, 98.0 Chhukha, 90.0 Trashigang, also Samtse, Haa & Tsirang
D.Prgr: 24h English: Daily 0500-0600, 0800-0900, 1500-1700. N: Daily: 0500, 0800, 1500 (15/20'); English Music: 1600-1700;UN Radio Prgr: Thurs 0520, Bhutan This week: Fri 0820; Dzongkha: Daily 0000-0300,0700-0800,1100-1500,1700-2400 (N:0100,0200,0700, 1100,1200,1300,1400; Music: 1700-2000, Repeat b'cast: 2000-2400) Sharchhop: 0300-0400, 0600-0700,0900-1000 (N:0300,0600,0900), Lhotsam (Nepali): Daily 0400-0500, 1000-1100 (N:0400,1000);
V. by QSL card. 15 min prgr details req. Rp. (2 IRCs)

Other FM Stations
Kuzoo FM, ✉ P.O. Box 419, Thimphu W: www.kuzoo.net DPrgr: 24h in English on 104.0MHz and Dzongkha on 105.0MHz – Radio Valley, ✉ P.O. Box 224/225, Thimphu W: www.radiovalley.bt DPrgr: 0200-1630 in E on 99.9MHz – Sherbutse FM 94.7MHz – Centennial Radio Thimphu 101.0 MHz – Radio High Thimphu 92.7 MHz (alliance with India's Big FM netw.) – Radio Waves Thimpu 88.8 MHz (Music Stn) – Sherubtse FM 94.7MHz (College Campus) 1300-1500

BOLIVIA

L.T: UTC -4h — Pop: 9.7 million — Pr.L: Spanish, Quechua, Aymara — E.C: 50Hz, La Paz 110/220V, Santa Cruz 220/380V — ITU: BOL — Int. dialling code: +591

AUTORIDAD DE FISCALIZACIÓN Y CONTROL SOCIAL DE TELECOMUNICACIONES Y TRANSPORTES (ATT)
Dirección Oficina Central: ✉ Calle 13 Calacote No. 8260 La Paz ☎ 2 2772266 🖷 2 2772299 E: informaciones@att.gov.bo W: www.att.gob.bo L.P: Superintendente: Lic. Jóse Antonio MoralesOffice in Santa Cruz: Calle Prolongación No 29, Edifico Bicenteario Tercer Piso, Santa Cruz de la Sierra ☎3 120587 🖷3 1220978
Office in Cochabamba: Av. Ayacucho No 460, enter Calama y Jordan, edifico Santa Isabel Piso 3, Cochabamba ☎4 458182
Office in Tarija: Calle General Trigo No 474, Edifico Colonial Center Piso 1, Of. 7-8-9, Tarija ☎4 4666484
NB: ‡ = inactive, ± = varying freq., † = irregular

MW	kHz	kW	Station, location, h of tr
LP77)	540		Radiodifusora Victoria, La Paz
LP03)	‡560	15	R. El Mundo, La Paz
LP01)	580	10	R. Panamericana, La Paz: 1000-0300 (Sun 1100-0100)
CH01)	600	10	R. ACLO, Sucre: 0800-0200
LP35)	600	1	Radioemisoras del Recobro, La Paz
LP02)	620	10	R. San Gabriel, El Alto
TA12)	640		R. ALCO, Sucre: 0850-0130
LP11)	640	15	R. Dif. Integración, El Alto: 0900-0130
SC10)	660	1	R. ABC, Santa Cruz: 0900-0100
PO28)	680		R. ACLO, Potosi: 0850-0130
LP27)	680	5	R. Andina, La Paz: 0900-0300
LP116)	700		R. Pacha Qamasa, El Alto: 0955-0100,

MW	kHz	kW	Station, location, h of tr
			Sat: -1805, Sun: - 1615
OR17)	720	10	R. Pío XII, Siglo Veinte: 0830-0230
LP06)	720	10	R. La Cruz del Sur, La Paz: Sat:1300-2100, Sun: 1200-2100
LP05)	720	2.5	R. Yungas, Chulumani: 0900-1700, 2000-0100
CO56	760		R. Casachun Coca, Lauca N
LP07)	760	50	R. Fides, La Paz: 1000 (Sun 1100-0300, Sat -0500
CO02)	760	5	R. Cosmos, Cochabamba: 1100-0300
SC44)	780		R. Sol, Santa Cruz: 24h
LP08)	‡800	5	R. Libertad, La Paz: 1000-0200 (Sun 2400)
LP10)	820	10	R. Altiplano, La Paz: 24h
LP75)	840	3	R. Atipiri, El Alto
SC03)	850	5	R. María, Montero: 0900-0100
LP12)	860	10	R.Nuava America, La Paz
LP42)	880		R. Inca, El Alto: 0900-0100
SC39)	880		Rdif. Oriente, Santa Cruz[sic]
TA01)	900	0.25	R. LV Nacional, Tarija: 0100-2300
LP36)	900	5/0.1	R. Popular, La Paz: 1000-0100
CO33)	‡902	1	R. Central Misionera, Cochabamba:1100-0100
CH11)	920	3	R. Encuentro, Sucre: 0900-0400 Sun: 1100-2200
LP65)	920	1	R. San Andres de Topohoco, Topohoco: 0900-0330
LP88)	920		R. Bartolina Sisa, El Alto
SC46)	920		R. El Mana, Santa Cruz
CH13)	940	1	R. Chuquisaca XXI, Sucre
LP13)	940		R. Metropolitana, La Paz: 0900-0500
PO02)	960	1	R. Kollasuyo, Potosí: 1000-0400 (Sun 1000-0200)
SC04)	960	10	R. Santa Cruz, Santa Cruz
LP43)	962	1	R. Huayna Potosí, Milluni
LP14)	980	2.5	R. Mar, La Paz: 1000-0200
CH26)	980		R. La Bohemia, Sucre
CO04)	980	3	R. Esperanza, Aiquile: 0900-0100(Fri -0400), Sat 1000-0300(Sun -2230)
SC33)	1000	1	Rdif. Oriente, Santa Cruz: 0930-0400, Sat 1000(Sun 1130)-0330
OR03)	1000	10	R. Bahá'í de Bolivia, Caracollo: 0800-0200
LP115)	1000		R. LV del Arrebatamiento, Guaqui
LP44)	1000	1	R. Mística, La Paz
LP15)	1020	10	R. Illimani - R.Patria Nueva, La Paz: 0900-0400
CO57)	1020		R. Illimani - R.Patria Nueva, Cochabamba
CO58)	1020		R. Illimani - R.Patria Nueva, Aiquila
CO59)	1020		R. Illimani - R.Patria Nueva, Valle Alto
CO60)	1020		R. Illimani - R.Patria Nueva, Tarata
CO61)	1020		R. Illimani - R.Patria Nueva, Chapare
BE21)	1020		R. Illimani - R.Patria Nueva, Trinidad
BE22)	1020		R. Illimani - R.Patria Nueva, San Borja
PA07)	1020		R. Illimani - R.Patria Nueva, Potosi
PA08)	1020		R. Illimani - R.Patria Nueva, Catavi
SC40)	1020		R. Illimani - R.Patria Nueva, Santa Cruz
SC41)	1020		R. Illimani - R.Patria Nueva, Vallegrande
SC42)	1020		R. Illimani - R.Patria Nueva, Camiri
SC43)	1020		R. Illimani - R.Patria Nueva, Yapacani
CO62)	1020		R. Illimani - R.Patria Nueva, Kami
CH21)	1020		R. Illimani - R.Patria Nueva, Sucre
TA13)	1020		R. Illimani - R.Patria Nueva, Tarija
TA14)	1020		R. Illimani - R.Patria Nueva, Bermejo
OR29)	1020		R. Illimani - R.Patria Nueva, Oruro
LP89)	1020		R. Illimani - R.Patria Nueva, Achacachi
LP90)	1020		R. Illimani - R.Patria Nueva, Carabuco
LP91)	1020		R. Illimani - R.Patria Nueva, Copacabana
LP92)	1020		R. Illimani - R.Patria Nueva, Caranavi
LP93)	1020		R. Illimani - R.Patria Nueva, Chulumani
LP94)	1020		R. Illimani - R.Patria Nueva, Guaqui
CH19)	1030		R. Comunitaria Mojocoya (RPO), Mojocoya:1000-0200
OR26)	1030	3	R. Comunitaria Orinaca (RPO), Orinaca
CO51)	1030		R. Totora (RPO) Totora
CO48)	1030	3	R. Independencia, Ayopaya (RPO)
PO27)	1030		R. Comunitaria Colquechaca (RPO), Colquechaca
BE20)	1030	3	R. Comunitaria Riberalte (RPO), Riberalta
CH18	1040		R. 12 de Marzo (RPO), Tarabuco
OR28)	1040		R. Comunitaria Qaqachaca (RPO), Qaqachaca
CO20)	1040	0.25	R. Sipe Sipe, Quillacollo: 1000-0300 (Sun 1100-0400)
TA11)	1040		R. Comunitaria Libertad (RPO), Villamontes
SC37)	1040		R. Nanduti (RPO), Camiri
SC38)	1040		R. Comunitaria San Juan (RPO), San Julián
SC30)	1040		R. San José (RPO), San José de Chiquitos
LP45)	1040	1	R. Bolivianíssima, La Paz
OR14)	1040	0.25	R. Atlántida, Oruro: 1100-2400
CO52)	1050		R. Em.Comunitaria (RPN), Independencia
OR27)	1050	3	R. Sabaya (RPN) Sabaya
PO26)	1050		R. Comunitaria Caiza (RPO), Caiza D
LP95)	1060		R. Quana, Caranavi
OR01)	1060	1.5	R. Noticias, Oruro: 1000-2200, 0200-0600

MW	kHz	kW	Station, location, h of tr
CH02)	1060	1	R. Dif. Colosal, Sucre: 0900-0300
LP38)	1060	10	R. Eco Loyola, La Paz: 1100-0100
LP76)	1080		LV de la Mayoria, Caranavi
CO06)	1090	3	R. Cultura, Cochabamba: 0900-0400 (Sun 1200-2300)
CO63)	1090		R. Cliza (RPN), Cliza
LP110)	1090		R. Comunitaria Pachakuti
OR06)	1100		R. Universidad de Oruro: 1100(Sun 1200)-2300 (n.f.: 620)
LP29)	1100		R. Cultural Chaka, Pucarani: 0900-1300, 2030-0130
CO53)	1120		R. El Porvenir, Tiquipaya
LP96)	1120		R. Celestial El Milagro, El Alto
LP97)	1120		R. Wiñay Khantatt, Tiahuanacu
SC09)	1120	1.5	R. Norte, Montero: 0930-0200
LP49)	1140	2	R. Pico Verde, Chulumani
LP98)	1140		R. Sol Poder de Dios, La Paz: 24h
LP99)	1140		R. Sol Poder de Dios, Huanca: 24h
LP50)	1150	0.3	R. Guaqui, Puerto de Guaqui
SC11)	1160	5	R. Centenario "La Nueva", Sta. Cruz
CO08)	1160	3/1	R. RTC, Cochabamba: 1030-2400
CH03)	1160	1	R. Nuevo Mundo, Sucre: 1000-0300
LP33)	1160	10	R. Continental, La Paz: 0930-0400
LP18)	1180	1	R. Ingavi, Viacha: 1000-0200 (Sun 1100-2400)
CO09)	1180	1	R. Independencia, Quillacollo
LP100)	1200		Cuarzo Comunicaciones, La Paz
LP115)	1200		R. Carlos Palenque, La Paz
LP117)	1200		R. Maria de la Candelaria, Copacabana
SC12)	1200	5	R. Oriental, Santa Cruz: 0930-0200
CO10)	1200	0.25	R. 24 de Noviembre, Arani: 1030-0400
CH10)	1200		R. Mauro Nuñes, Villa Serrano
OR31)	1200		R. Capital, Oruro
LP19)	1220	1	R. Splendid, La Paz: 0900-0100
OR09)	1220	1	R. Batallón Topáter, Oruro: 1000-0200 (Sat 1000-2300, Sun 1100-2300)
PO29)	1240		R. Indoamerica, Potosi
TA03)	1240	2	R. Los Andes, Tarija: 1000-2200
LP51)	1240		Rdif. Achocalla, Achocalla
PA01)	1250	0.1	R. Frontera, Cobija: 1000-1800
CH04)	1250	2.5	R. La Plata, Sucre: 1000-0200
CO54)	1260		R. LV de la Esperanza, Quillacollo
OR20)	1260	10	R. Nacional de Huanuni, Hunanuni: 0930-0200, Sat 1100-1800(Sun -1600)
PO05)	1265	0.4	R. Uncía, Uncía: 1100-0300
LP68)	1280		R. Ondas del Titicaca, Huarina
OR12)	1290	1	Radiodifusoras Minería, Oruro: 1000-2400
CH05)	1300	2.5	R. Loyola, Sucre: 1000-2400, Sun 1015-0200
SC16)	1300	1	R. Fuerzas Armadas, Sta. Cruz: 0930-0230
LP23)	1300	15/6	R. Sol, "Poder de Diós", El Alto 24h
BE18)	1300	5	R. Bandera Beniana, Trinidad
CO14)	1310	10	R. San Rafael, Cochabamba: 0900-0200
CH25)	1320		R. Sucre, Sucre
LP53)	1320		R. Tawantinsuyo, Taraco
LP111)	1320		R. Em. Septima Voz, Achocalla
LP119)	1320		R. Taipichullo, Taraco
LP121)	1320		R.Comunitaria La Lumberia, La Paz
SC17)	±1340	1	R. Grigotá, Santa Cruz: 1000 (Sun 1100)-0100v
LP39)	1340	0.5	R. Copacabana, Copacabana: 0500(SS 0600)-2100
LP40)	1340	0.5	R. Jach'a Suyu, Corocoro: 1000-1630, 2000-0100
LP102)	1340		R. Comunitario Taipichullo
CH06)	1350	1	R. America, Sucre: 1000-0400(SS -1400)
LP113)	1350		R. Comunitario Inti, Contorno/Viacha
CO15)	±1355	0.25	R. Armonía, Cliza (n.f.: 1350)
CH27)	1360		R. Instituto Politécnico Tomás Katari, Sucre
CO05)	1360	2.5	R. Cochabamba "CBA", Cochabamba: 1030-0200
LP16)	1360	5	Radiodifusoras Jiménez, El Alto: 0800-0100
LP103)	1360		R. Em. Tunupa, Tiahuanacu
OR32)	1360		R. Coral, Oruro
SC47)	1360		R. 24 de Septiembre, Santa Cruz
CO16)	1370	0.15	R. Libertad, Cliza: 0930-0300
CH22)	1380		R. Global, Sucre
LP104)	1380		R. Maria, La Paz
CO34)	1380	1.5	R. Bandera Tricolor, Cochabamba: 1100-0300
OR33)	1380		R. Horizontes, Huanuni
TA06)	1380	0.5	R. Luis de Fuentes, Tarija: 0930-0400
CO50)	1390		R. Andina (CEPRA), Pongo K´asa
CH20)	1400		R. Antena 2000, Sucre
LP25)	1400	5	R. Nacional de Andina, La Paz: 0900-0200
LP1059)	1420		R. Omasuyos Andina, Achacachi
LP114)	1420		R. Creo en Milagros, Murillo
TA05)	1420	1.5	R. Guadalquivir, Tarija: 0900-0100
CO18)	1420	1	R. Centro, Cochabamba: 1030-2300 (Sun 1100-0000)
CH15)	1420	1	R. Real Audiencia, Sucre: 0900-0200

MW	kHz	kW	Station, location, h of tr
LP26)	1440	1	R. Batallón Colorados, La Paz: 1100-0100(Sun -2400)
SC21)	1440	2/1	R. Yaguary, Vallegrande: 1000- 0200
CO42)	‡1440	0.25	R. Bolivia, Cochabamba: 1000-1830, 2200-0200
BE24)	1440		R. Dif. Tropico, Trinidad
OR13)	1440	1	R. Em. Bolivia, Oruro: 0900-0130
LP118)	1450		R. Litoral, Guaqui
CO39)	1455	0.5	R. Magnal, Capinota: 1600-2400 (Sun 1000-1800)
LP106)	1460		R. Plenitud de Vida, El Alto
CO44)	1460		R. Morochata (CEPRA), Morochata
CH29)	1470	1	R. Integración, Padilla
LP109)	1470		R. Em. Ayni, Corapata
CH24)	1480		R. Charcas, Sucre
LP108)	1480		LV de los Andes, Carabuco
PO12)	1480	0.1	R. Patrimonio del Sur, Potosí: 0950-0100
CO32)	1480	1/0.8	R. Chiwalaki, Vacas: 0900-1400, 2100-0100
CO40)	1480		R. Domingo Savio, Villa Independencia
LP58)	1480		R. Amor de Diós, El Alto
LP107)	1480		R. Comunitaria Waley, Saguadero
OR15)	1480	1	R. San José, San José, Oruro: 1000-1300, 0000-0400 (Sun 1200-1300)
SC25)	1500	1	R. Sagrado Corazón, Mineros
LP31)	‡1500	5/1	R. Chuquisaca, El Alto
CO64)	1520	1	R. la Chiwana, Cochabamba
LP59)	1520		R. La Luz del Tiempo, El Alto
LP120)	1520		R. San Pedro, Tiahuanacu
PO10)	1520	0.25	R. Litoral, Llica
BE07)	1530	0.5	R. Em. Ballivián, San Borja 1030-0100
LP34)	1540	0.8	R. Sariri, Escoma: 1000-1300, 2200-0200
LP112)	1540		R. Comunitario Tutuka, Vilaque
LP67)	1540		R. Bendita Trinidad y Espirito Santo, El Alto
LP28)	1550	10	R. Caranavi, Caranavi: 0930 1800, 2200 0200
OR19)	1560	1	R. Occidental, Oruro: 0930-2400
CO27)	1560	0.5	R. Urkupiña, Quillacollo: 1000-2400
BE23)	1570		R. Pedro Ignacio Muiba
LP101)	1570		R. Comunitaria Tawantinsuyo, Taraco
CH28)	1580		R. Contacto, Sucre
SC29)	1580	1	R. Adonai, Santa Cruz: 1000-0300
LP62)	1580		R. El Fuego del Espíritu Santo, El Alto: 1000-2400
TA07)	1580	3	R. Bermejo, Bermejo: 0930-0100
CO24)	1590	1	R. Wayana Songo, Pongo K´asa
LP61)	1580		R. Kollasuyo Marka, Tiawanaku
CO28)	1600	0.5	R. Continental, Punata: 1000-0200

SW	kHz	kW	Station, location, h of tr
CO29)	3310	10	R. Mosoj Chaski, Cochabamba: 0900-1300, 2100-0100
CH08)	3390	1	R. Em. Camargo "LV del Valle Cinteño", Camargo
PO22)	4111	0.5	R. Virgen de los Remedios, Tupiza (r)
BE10)	4409	0.5	R. Eco, Reyes
BE04)	4451	1	R. Santa Ana, Santa Ana del Yacuma
BE08)	±4699		R. San Miguel, Riberalta: 1030-0330
PO15)	±4717	1	R. Yatun Ayllu Yura, Yura (n. 4715)
LP74)	4782		R. Tacana, Tumupasa
PO19)	±4796		R. López, Uyuni: 1000-2330
SC36)	4865	5	R. Logos, Santa Cruz
SC30)	5580	0.25	R. San José, San José de Chiquitos: 1100-1700, 2100-0200±
LP01)	5765	10	R. Panamericana, La Paz: (r.)
OR17)	±5952	5	R. Pío XII, Siglo Veinte: (n. 5955)
LP15)	6025	10	R. Illimani - R. Patria Nueva, La Paz: 0930-0300
SC02)	±6054	3	R. Cultural Juan XXIII, San Ignacio de Velasco: 1030-2300 (n. 6055)
CO56)	‡6075		R. Kawasachun Coca, Lauca Ñ
LP01)	±6105	10	R. Panamericana, La Paz (r. 5765)
SC04)	6135	10	R. Santa Cruz, Santa Cruz: 1100-0200
LP07)	6155	10	R. Fides, La Paz: †
SC36)	6165	1	R. Logos, Santa Cruz

NB: RPN = Red Patira Nueva. RPO = Radioemisoras de los Pueblos Originarios

Addresses and other information
NB: Whenever listed, Casilla addresses should preferably be used for mailing purposes.
ERBOL (Educación Radiofónica de Bolivia), Calle Ballivián 1323, 4° piso (Cas. 5946), La Paz ☎ 2 232 4606, 232 4768 🖷 2 239 1985
W: www.erbol.combo – Pte.: Jorge Trias S.J. Secr. Ejecutivo: Jorge Aliaga Murillo
UNESBO (Unión de Emisoras Sindicales de Bolivia), Yanacocha 689, La Paz ☎1 234 1881 Pte: Jorge Bustillo Burgos.
BE00 (BENI)
BE04) Calle Sucre 250, Santa Ana de Yacuma – **BE06)** Sucre 320, Guayaramerín – **BE07)** Oruro 52, San Borja ☎3 848 3020 – **BE08)** Calle Tomás Daney s/n, Barrio San José, Riberalta ☎591 3952 3363

591 3852 3268 - **FM:** 99.1MHz "Centenario" – **BE09)** Av Selim Majuli (Correo Central), San Borja, Pcia BalliviáN – **BE10)** Reyes, Pcia Ballivián **E:** gonzaloeco@hotmail.com – **BE12)** Calle Nicanor Gonzalo Salvatierra 249, Riberalta - **FM:** 91.1MHz – **BE13)** Ballivián s/n, San Ignacio de Moxos – **BE14)** Cas 395, Guayaramerín – **BE15)** Calle Beni s/n, Guayaramerín – **BE16)** Plaza Fr Martín Baltasar de Espinosa, Santa Ana del Yacuma – **BE18)** Calle Santa Cruz esq Mamoré s/n, Trinidad – **BE19)** Avenida Primero de Mayo esquina Loreto, Guayaramerin **E:E:** ninafelima@hotmail.com – **BE20)** Riberalta, Prov Vaca Diez – **BE21)** Trinidad – **BE22)** San Borja – **BE23)** Calle Isiboro esquina Machupo, Trinidad - **FM:** 89.5 MHz – **BE24)** Avenida Panamericana km 2½ - EPARU, Trinidad ☎3 46 35300 ☐3 46 35058 **W:** www.facebook. com/difusoras.tropico **E:** radiotropico1440@hotmail.com

CH00 (CHUQUISACA)

CH01) Guillermo Loayza No 274 esq Vicente Donso (Zona Mercado Campesino), (or Cas 538), Sucre ☎46460422 Prgrs in **Quechua** except **Spanish** 1330-2030 0900-0200 **W:** www.aclo.org.bo **E:** aclochuqui-saca@aclo.org.bo **FM:** 101.5 MHz – **CH02)** Cas 335, Sucre - **FM:** 90.7MHz – **CH03)** Cas 25, Sucre – **CH04)** Abaroa 422, Cas 276, Sucre ☎4 645 3231 - **FM:** 92.1MHz – **CH05)** Calle Ayacucho 161, Sucre ☎4 645 3677 ☐4 644 2555 **W:** www.radioloyola.com **E:** loyola@radiofides. com - **FM:** 98.3MHz "Onda Joven" – **CH06)** Calle Guillermo Loayza 377, Mercado Campesino, Sucre ☎4 464 46574 ☐4 464 44445 – **W:** www. radioamericatk.com.bo **E:** info@radioamericatk.com.bo - **FM:** 97.5 MHz – **CH08)** Cas 09, Camargo, Pcia Nor Cinti **W:** www.radiocamargo. cjb.net - **FM:** 100.0MHz – **CH09)** Alcaldía Municipal, Padilla – **CH10)** CEDEC, Cas 196, Sucre ☎4 645 5008 ☐4 646 2628 **E:** chober_in@ yahoo.es - **FM:** 103.1MHz – **CH11)** Calle Loa No 41, Sucre ☎6 441 300 **W:** www.encuentroradio.com – **FM:** 95.9MHz – **CH13)** Calle Kantuta 3, Barrio Ferroviario, Zona San Matias, Sucre – **CH15)** Calle Avarioa 537, Sucre – **CH16)** Sucre – **CH17)** Sucre – **CH18)** Comunidad de Tarabco, Prov Yamparáez – **CH19)** Comunia de Mojocoya, Prov Zudáñez – **CH20)** Calle Lima Pampa No 72, Sucre ☎6 440 606 – **CH21)** Sucre – **CH22)** Sucre **W:** www.radioglobalbolivia.com – **CH23)** Calle Eduardo Berdecio No 568, Sucre. **W:** www.radiohorizonte.boliviastreaming.com - **FM:** 91.1 MHz – **CH24)** Calle Eduardo Berdecio No 522, Sucre ☎6 461 112 – **CH25)** Sucre **W:** http://radiosucre1320.com – **CH26)** Sucre – **CH27)** Sucre – **CH28)** Sucre – **CH29)** Padilla

C000 (COCHABAMBA)

CO02) Av Heroinas O-467, Zona Sur, (Cas 1092), Cochabamba ☎4 425 0422 ☐4 425 1173 **Quechua:** 0930-1030, 0000-0200 1100-0300 - FM: 95.1MHz "Fides" – **CO04)** Calle Loa Final s/n, Ivirganzana, (Cas 5716), Cochabamba. ☎4 115 030 **E:** aiquile@pino.cbb.entelnet. bo **Quechua:** 8 hours daily **W:** www.radioesperanza.com.bo - **FM:** 100.3MHz – **CO05)** Calle 25 de Mayo 230 entre Bolívar y Sucre (Cas 5500), Cochabamba ☎4 425 1504 ☐4 425 1561 **E:** ragarobol@ yahoo.es - **FM:** 104.3MHz "Gaviota" – **CO06)** Santiváñez 172 Casi Junín (cas 719), Cochabamba **Aymara & Quechua:** 1130-1300 – **CO07)** Cochabamba – **CO08)** Lanza esq Ecuador N-0261 (Cas 846), Cochabamba ☎4 425 7289 ☐4 424 1414 – **CO09)** Cochabamba esq Heroes del Chaco, Quillacollo (or Cas 108), Cochabamba – **CO10)** Arani – **CO14)** Calle Calama E- 0315 (Cas 546), Cochabamba ☎4 4256 563 ☐4 250 522 **Quechua/Aymara:** 0900-0200 - **FM:** 92.1MHz – **CO15)** Calle 6 de Agosto 11, Cliza – **CO16)** Calle Santa Cruz 4, Cliza – **CO18)** Calle Ecuador casi Avenida Ayacucho No 115 (Cas 839), Cochabamba ☎4 4251 434 **W:** www.grupocentro.com.bo **E:** contactos@grupo-centro.com.bo - **FM:** 96.3 & 106.7 MHz – **CO20)** Plaza de Granos 44, Quillacollo - **FM:** 99.1MHz **CO24)** Cas 1151, Cochabamba ☎4 811 9295 Prgrs in Sp, **Aymara & Quechua W:** www.sdb.bo **E:** japaricio@ sdb.bo – **CO27)** Plaza Bolivar 25 Acera Oeste, Quillacollo ☎4 260 661 – **CO28)** Ayacucho 138, Punata – **CO29)** Calle Abaroa S-0254 (Cas 4493), Cochabamba **E:** rmchaski@bo.net ☎4 422 0651 ☐4 425 1041 – **CO32)** Misuk'ani (Cas 80), Vacas, Prov. de Arani ☎4 223 089 ☐4 255 390 **W:** www.aler.org/lpi/fscommand/lpi/chiwalaki/ficha/index.htm **E:** chiwalak@entelnet.bo Prgrs mainly in **Quechua** 0900-1400, 2100-0100 – **CO33)** Av Petrolera Km 0.5, Cochabamba – **CO34)** Av. Oquendo No 560 entre Paccieri y Federeico Blanco (Cas 3655), Zona Muyurina, Cochabamba **E:** latripple999@yahoo.com 323 **Quechua:** 1000-1200 - **FM:** 99.9MHz "La Triple" – **CO39)** Augusto Larrain, Capinota. **W:** www.radiomagnal.ondalocal.org.bo – **CO40)** Villa Independencia, Prov. Ayopaya (Av. Papa Paulo No 0982, Muyurina, Cochabamba) **W:** http://radiosavio.galeon.com **E:** radioisavio@hotmail.com - **FM:** 98.1 MHz – **CO42)** Calle Calama 0-0135, Cochabamba – **CO43)** Calle Junín 309, Tiraque, Prov Arani – **CO44)** Calle Tumusla esquina Ecuador No 310, Plazuela Cobija, area Oeste (Casilla 1986) Cochabamba ☎4 589 366 ☐4 589 377 **W:** http//ceprabolivia.org **E:** cepra@supernet.– **CO48)** Provincia de Ayaypoya – **CO50)** Calle Tumusla esquina Ecuador No 310, Plazuela Cobija, area Oeste (Cas. 1986) Cochabamba ☎4 589 366 ☐4 589 377 **W:** http//ceprabolivia.org **E:** cepra@supernet.com.bo – **CO51)** Totora, Prov Carrasco – **CO52)** Comunidad de Independencia, Prov de Ayopaya – **CO53)** Calle Pablo Jaimes 188, Tiquipaya, Prov

Quillacollo – **FM:** 90.5MHz – **CO54)** Quillacollo – **CO56)** km 182 Lauca-Eñe, Shinahota ☎44 135860 **W:**www.radiokawsachuncoca.com **E:**radiokawsachuncoca@gmail.com or rkc_radionacional@hotmail.com – **FM:**99.7MHz – **CO57)** Cochabamba – **CO58)** Aiquile – **CO59)** Valle Alto – **CO60)** Tarata – **CO61)** Chapare – **CO62)** Kami – **CO63)** Cliza – **CO64)** Junin casi Aroma, Edif. De la Federacion de Campesinos - 5° piso, Cochabamba **W:** www.radiolachiwana.org - **FM:** 107.9 MHz

LP00 (LA PAZ)

LP01) Av 16 de Julio, Edificio 16 de Julio, Of 902, El Prado, La Paz **W:** www.panamericana-bolivia.com **E:** pana@panamericana.bo ☎2 233 4271 **N:** «El Panamericano» relayed by many stns – **LP02)** Av. Bolivia Pza de la Cruz No 100 Camina a Villa Adela, Puchucollo Bajo, El Alto ☎2 832 544 Prgrs in **Aymara** exc Sp & Quechua 1400-1430, Sat 2100-2130 – **LP03)** Av. La Bandera No 1462, V.Pabón, La Paz – **LP05)** Calle Nuñez del Prado s/n, Chulumani (Cas 4535, La Paz) ☎2220 3672 **Aymara:** 0930-1130, 2230-0030 0900-1700, 2000-0100 **W:** www. qhana.org.bo **E:** radioyungas@qhana.org.bo - **FM:** 92.1MHz – **LP06)** Calle Nicaragua 1759(Cas 1408), La Paz ☎2 220541 ☐2 243337 **W:** www.radiocruzdelsur.com **E:** contactos@radiocruzdelsur.com – **LP07)** Calle Jenaro Sanjinés 799, Centro (Cas 9143), La Paz ☎2 240 6363 ☐2 240 6332 **W:** www.radiofides.com **E:** sistemas@radiofides.com - **N:** «La hora del país», relayed by many stns, at 1100, 1630, 2230, 0130 – **LP08)** Av Sánchez Lima 2278, 3° piso (entre Fernando Guachalla y Rosendo Guttierez), Sopocachi, (Cas. 5324) La Paz ☎ 2 236 1591 ☐ 2 236 3069 **Aymara:** 0945-1015 1000-0200 (SS 2400) – **LP10)** Calle Abdon Saavedra N° 2110 casi esquina Fernando Guachalla, (Cas 8631), Sopocachi) La Paz ☎2 426 742 **W:** altiplanoadvenir.org – **LP11)** Calle 2 No 95 P.3 entre Av. 6 de Marzo y Jorge Carrasco, Ceja, El Alto (Cas. 312472, La Paz) ☎2 810048 ☐2 813424 **E:** integracionam@yahoo.es **Aymara:** 0830-1200 0900-0100 – **LP12)** Calle Abdón Saavedra 1990 (or Cas 2431), La Paz ☎2 235 6622 – **LP13)** Juan de la Riva 1527 (Cas 8704), Zona Santa Bárbara, La Paz ☎2 203 339 ☐2 201 559 **E:** metropolitana@rtpbolivia.com Aymara: 0900-1000 – **LP14)** Calle Jenaro Sanjinés 799 esqquina Calle Sucre, Centro, La Paz ☎2 406 590 **E:** editor@radiofides.com – **LP15)** Av Camacho 1485, Edificio Ministerio Informaciones P 6, Centro, La Paz ☎2 220 0282 **W:** www. patrianueva.bo **E:** illimani@comunica.gov.bo – **LP16)** Av Panamericana 93, Zona Alpacoma, El Alto (or Cas 6412, La Paz) ☎2 310 796 – **LP18)** Calle General Lanza 93, Viacha, Provincia Ingavi – **LP19)** Calle Tumusla No 765 Edifico Rios P1C, Zona 14 de Septiembre (Cas 1539), La Paz. ☎2 452 422 Prgr in **Aymara** 0900-0100 – **LP23)** Calle Calama s/n entre Humahuca y Montenegro, Zona Norte, La Paz ☎2 283 124 **W:** www.poderdedios.com **E:** radiosol@poderdedios.com - **FM:** 90.1 MHz – **LP25)** Av. Tumusla No 639, 4° piso (or Cas 2532), Zona 14 de Septiembre, La Paz. ☎2 453 945 ☐2 454 211 – **LP26)** Av. Saavedra del Ejército, Zona Miraflores, La Paz ☎2 149 439 **Aymara:** 1100-1200 – **LP27)** Calle Francisco de Chirino No 1080, Miraflores (Cas. 12413), La Paz– **LP28)** Liga de Oración en Misión Mundial, Av Civica S/N, Caranavi, (Cas. 266, La Paz) ☎8 233 018 **E:** rtc@megalink.com **LP29)** Casilla 204, Colegio Don Bosco, Pucarani Prgrs mainly in **Aymara**, but also in Spanish 0900-1300, 2030-0130 – **LP31)** Ave. Saavedra No 1145, Edif. Holanda P10 Of. 1002, Zona Miraflores (Cas 3123), La Paz ☎2 246 158 – **LP33)** Av República 870 Esq. Quintanilla Zuazo, Estacion Central, La Paz ☎2 453 573 – **LP34)** Colegio Don Bosco, Parroquia Escoma, Escoma (Cas 204, La Paz) **E:** escoma@caoba.entelnet.bo ☎2 213 5336 - **FM:** 104.7MHz – **LP35)** Calle Murillo 1379, La Paz ☎2 235 0588 – **LP36)** Calle Cuba 1845, Zona Miraflores, La Paz ☎2 222 368 **W:** www.radiogentelapaz.com **E:** sistemapopular@hotmail.com – **LP38)** Plaza Alonso de Mendoza 500 5° piso del Edificio Santa Anita, Ofic 501 (or Cas 4973), La Paz ☎2 239 0542 **W:** www.loyola.edu.bo/ radio/ **E:** radioeco@loyola.edu.bo – **LP39)** Callle Gral. Hugo Ballivián No 11 Copacabana, Prov. Manco Capac ☎2 341 920 **W:** www.apcbo-livia.org/Medios/copacabana.aspx – **FM:** 95.1 MHz – **LP40)** Plaza 15 de Agosto, Corocoro, Prov Pacajes **E:** tricolor-jachasuyu@hotmail.com ☎2 283 0192 Prgr In **Aymara & Sp** 1000-1630, 2000-0100 – **LP42)** Av Patriotica No 3048, Entre C.Topáter y Héroes del Acre , Zona Bolívar Municipal P 1, El Alto ☎2 282 1675 – **LP43)** Avenida del Ejercito No 30, Zona Central, La Paz – **LP44)** Calle Heroínas 1010 esq 10 de Julio, El Alto, la Paz – **LP45)** Calle Viacha # 360 e/ Avenida Manco Kapac y Av. América, Barrio Churubamba I, La Paz – **LP46)** Comunidad Contorno Letania, Camino a Collana 30, Letania, Prov Ingavl – **LP47)** Av Manco Kapac 50, Tiawanaku, Prov Ingavi – **LP49)** Plaza Libertad s/n, Chulumani, Prov Ingavi ☎2 366 259 ☐2 226 536 – **LP50)** Calle Costa Rica No 1229, Miraflores, la Paz ☎2 220 401 – **LP51)** Av. Franco Valle No 87, Achocalla, Prov. de Murillo – **LP53)** Plaza 16 de Julio s/n, Cantón Taraco, Taraco, Prov Ingavi – **LP54)** Calle Noel Kempf 140, El Alto, La Paz – **LP55)** Tiawanaku, Prov Ingavi – **LP56)** Calle Yanacocha 70, Achacanti – **LP57)** Plaza 4 de Octubre, Rosario, Corapata, Prov Los Andes – **LP58)** Calle Noaviri 2105, Zona Amor de Dios, El Alto ☎2 223 916 – **LP59)** Raúl Salmón 92 entre Calle 4 y 5, Zona Ceja, El Alto (Cas. 8631, Murillo, La Paz) ☎2 282 5169 **E:** radiomisionglobal@

yahoo.es– **LP60)** Plaza Principal, Cantón Villa Iquiaca, Vilaque, Prov Los Andes – **LP61)** Calle C No 57, Zona V. Tejda, El Alto ☎2 822 470 – **LP62)** Avenida Panoramica No. 5018, Zona Faro Murillo , El Alto ☎2 281 3504 **W:** www.cesi.pastoralcl – **LP64)** Calle Topater 830, La Paz – **LP65)** Plaza Principal, Topohoco, Prov. Pacajes – **LP66)** Calle Jotan Save 3132 entre Bluniel, Zona 16 de Julio, La Paz – **LP67)** Calle Pascue #2614-B, Zona 16 de Julio, El Alto ☎2 284 4210 – **LP68)** Calle Batalla de Huarina No 255, Huarina ☎71 977 644 – – **LP74)** Tumupasa, Prov de Iturralde – **LP75)** Av. Grigota No 1514, Urb. Atipiris Sector Senkata El Alto, El Alto ☎2 288 2066 **W:** http://radioatipiri. blogspot.com – **LP76)** Caranavi, Prov Caranavi – **LP77)** Calle 11 de Calacote No 7837, La Paz. – **LP88)** Calle S.Rodriguez No 1155, Zona 16 de Febrero, Distrito 4 Carretera a Laja antes del Puente Seke, Zona 16 de Febrero ☎7 3700 079 **E:** bartolinasisa920am@gmail.com – **LP89)** Achacanhi – **LP90)** Carabuco – **LP91)** Copacabana – **LP92)** Caranavi – **LP93)** Chulumani – **LP94)** Guaqui – **LP95)** Av Cívica frente Estadio orlando quiroga, Caranavi ☎2 824 3810 **W:** www.qhana.org.bo **E:** rqamazonia@qhana.org.bo – **FM:** 90.3 MHz – **LP96)** Pza. Ballivian No 525, 16 de Julio, El Alto ☎2 844 344 – **LP97)** Av.Manco Kapaca No 50, Tiahuanacu ☎2 597 357 **LP98)** Calla Calama, entre Humahuca y Montenegro , Zona Norte, La Paz ☎2 286 983 **W:** www.poderdedios. com **E:** radiosol@poderdedios.com – **FM:** 90.5 MHz – **LP99)** Huancane **W:** www.poderdedios.net – **LP100)** Calle Topáter # 830 Zona Norte, La Paz – **LP101)** Laja, Prov. de Los Andes – **LP102)** Taipichullo, Prov. de Rin Abajo – **LP103)** Av. Manco Kapac, Tiahuanacu ☎2 898 541 – **LP104)** Av 16 de Julio int. Colegio Don Bosco, Centro, La Paz ☎2 317 072 **W:** www.radiomaria.org.bo **E.** info.bol@radiomaria.org – **LP105)** Calle Bolivar No 249, Achacachi – **LP106)** Av. Chacaltaya, calle Tiquina Nº 6580 Alto Lima primera sección (Cas.8628), El Alto ☎2 284 2492 **W:** www.plenituddevida.net **E:** plenituddevida@net – **LP107)** Ave. Cornelio Saavedra No 2875 esq. Kantuta, Desaguadero ☎2 730 628 – **LP108)** Batallas, Prov. Los Andes – **LP109)** Corapata, Prov. De Los Andes – **LP110)** Letania, Prov. de Ingavi – **LP111)** Achocalla, Prov. de Murillo – **LP112)** Villa Iquiaca, Prov. de Los Andes – **LP113)** Contorno/ Viacha, Prov. de Ingavi – **LP114)** Av.Eduardo 1168, Zona Los Andes, Murillo ☎2 2458 567 **E:** jorgetito@redcotel.bo – **LP115)** Av. Illimani No 1938, Miraflores, La Paz. ☎2 240 420 **W:** www.redpalenque.com E**palenque_radiotv@yahoo.com – **LP116)** Plaza Avaroa Nº 105, Villa Avaroa, El Alto. ☎2 825 504 ☐2 821 007 **W:** www.cea.edu.bo/radio. html **E:** pachaqamasa700@yahoo.es – **LP117)** Plaza 2 de Febrero, Ed. Municipal, Copacabana – **LP119)** Plaza 16 de Julio, Taraco ☎8 114 157 – **FM:** 105.3 MHz – **LP118)** Calle Eduardo Avaroa No 70, Guaqui. ☎2 135 325 – **LP120)** Unidad Académica Campesina de Tiahuanacu, Tiahuanacu ☎2 898 542 – **LP121)** Iglesia Bautista la Lumbrera, Av. Mecapaca No 6735, Zona Obrajes, La Paz ☎2 786947

R00 (ORURO)
OR01) Calle Ayacucho 785 (Alto) (Cas 670), Oruro ☎2 525 3500 ☐2 525 2500 **E:** cpi@coteor.net.bo **Aymara & Quechua:** 1130, 0230 – 1000-2200, 0200-0600 – **OR03)** Cas 1019, Oruro ☎2 511 2259 **W:** www.bahai.org.bo/oportunidades/servicio.htm **E:** radbahia@nogal. oru.entelnet.bo **Aymara & Quechua:** 11 hours daily – **OR05)** Oruro – **OR06)** Calle Cochabamba esquiina 6 de Octubre (Cas 49), Oruro ☎2 525 0004 ☐2 524 2215 — **OR09)** Calle Junín y 6 de Agosto, Oruro ☎2 526 0200 **Aymara & Quechua:** 1000-1100 - **FM:** 98.3MHz – **OR12)** San Felipe 493 entre Tarapacá y Tejerina (Cas 247), Oruro **Aymara:** 2200-2400 - **FM:** 107.7MHz – **OR13)** Av Velasco Galvarro entre León y Rodriguez 1551, Oruro – Prgrs in **Sp., Aymara, Aymara & Poquina** - **FM:** 105.1MHz – **OR14)** Linares 1160 entre Cochabamba y Caro, Oruro – **OR15)** Caro 235 entre Pagador y Av Velasco Galvarro, Oruro – **OR17)** Campamento Siglo XX, Llallagua (or Cas 434, Oruro) **W:** www. radiopio12.org **E:** rpiodoce@ entelnet.bo – ☎2 582 0250 ☐ 2 582 0554 **Aymara & Quechua** 6 hrs daily – **FM:** 99.9MHz –: **OR19)** Av Bakovic 1027 entre Caro y Montecinos, (Cas 326), Oruro **Aymara & Quechua:** 0930-1030 - **FM:** 93.1MHz – **OR20)** Calle Sucre, Huanuni (Cas 681), Oruro ☎2 552 0421 **W:** www.nacionaldehuanuni.com **E:** nacionaldehuanuni@gmail.com – **OR24)** Calle Adolfo Mier 1231, Oruro – **OR25)** Huanuni – **OR26)** Orinoca, Prov Sud Carangas – **OR27)** Sabaya, Prov Sabaya – **OR28)** Comunidad de Oaqahaca, Prov Eduardo Abaroa – **OR29)** Oruro – **OR31)** Calle 6 de Octubre # 6160, Oruro ☎5 275 344 **E:** radiocapitaloruro@hotmail.com – **FM:** 102.7 MHz – **OR32)** Avenida 6 de Octubre y Montecinos 1042, Oruro ☎5 254 143 ☐5 276 645 **W:** www.coralbolivia.com – **OR33)** Centro de Apoyo a la Educación Popular (CAEP), Huanuni – **OR34)** Oruro

PA00 (PANDO)
PA01) Av. Tcnl. Cornejo No 62(Cas 179), Cobija ☎8 422 200 – **PA07)** Potosi – **PA08)** Catavi

P000 (POTOSI)
PO02) Calle Cobija 15, Zona Central, Potosí ☎62 22680 ☐62 26210 **W:** www.radiokollasuyo.net – **FM:** 105.1MHz –**PO05)** Cas 15, Uncía – **PO10)** Llica, Pcia Daniel Campos 1400-0300 – **PO12)** Victor Flores 410, Potosi – **PO14)** Campamento Minero Tazna, Pcia Nor Chichas

– **PO15)** Cas 326, Yura, Prov Antonio Quijarro **E:** radioyura@hotmail. com – **PO16)** Dtto Minero de Animas – **PO19)** Calle Final Uruguay s/n (Cas 16), Uyuni, Prov Antonio Quijarro ☎2 693 2145 **E:** max_nelson_t@hotmail.com **PO22)** Casa Parroquial de Tupiza (Cas 198),Tupiza **E:** radiovirgenderemedios@hotmail.com ☎2 694 4662 - **FM:** 89.5MHz – **PO26)** Comunidad de Caiza, Prov Chayanta – **PO27)** Comunidad de Colquechaca, Prov de José María Linares. – **PO28)** Av. Cívica 739 (Cas. 538), Potosi. ☎2 62223660 **W:** www.aclo.org.bo/bolivia/ **E:** aclopotosi@aclo.org.bo;– **FM:** 106.7 MHz – **PO29)** Calle Matos No 107 Cas.472), Potosi. ☎6 223 936 **E:** info@indoamericafn.com
SC00 (SANTA CRUZ)
SC02) Plaza 31 de Julio, San Ignacio de Velasco ☎3 962 2188 **W:** www.sanignacio-diocesis.com/ **E:** radiojuan@hotmail.com - **FM:** 100.3MHz – **SC03)** Calle Potosí s/n (or Cas 38), Montero ☎4647 2469 **E:** ramacon@cotas.com.br - **FM:** 105.5MHz "Concierto" – **SC04)** Calle Mario Flores esquina Güendá No 20 Cas 672 or 3213), Santa Cruz **W:** www.irfabolivia.org **E:** direccion@irfabolivia.org ☎3353 1817 ☐3353 2257 **Guarani:** 1830-1900 - **FM:** 92.3MHz – **SC09)** Warnes 195, Altos Cine Escorpio, Montero ☎☐3 992 0970 **E:** http://radionorteamfrn.com – **FM:** 99.9MHz – **SC10)** Warnes 334 (Cas 629), Santa Cruz ☎3 336 3990 ☐3 336 3992 - **FM:** 92.7MHz – **SC11)** Av. Grigota s/n, B.Matpetrol (2Cdra. Antes del 4to Anillo) Cas 818), Santa Cruz ☎3352 9265 ☐3352 4747 **E:** mision.eplabol@scbbs-bo.com **Quechua & Guarani:** 0900-0945 - **FM:** 90.7MHz "R Super Color" – **SC12)** Independencia 372 (Cas 186), Santa Cruz ☎3333 7194 ☐3333 5778 - **FM:** 96.3MHz – **SC16)** Av Charcas 1051 lado octava División del Ejército, Santa Cruz ☎3 336 0447 ☐3 337 2242 - **FM:** 98.1MHz – **SC17)** Calle Colón 58, piso 5 Of 501-2, Cas 1399, Santa Cruz ☎3 332 2142 - **FM:** 90.3MHz – **SC21)** Florida esq Montes Claros 143, Vallegrande ☎3 942 2033 – **SC25)** Cas 507, Santa Cruz - **FM:** 89.5MHz. Prgrs also in **Quechua** – **SC29)** Calle España 572, 2°piso, Santa Cruz - **FM:** 97.9MHz – **SC30)** Cas 15, Santa Cruz de Chiquitos (Santa Cruz) – **SC33)** Cas 1766, Santa Cruz **W:** http://difusorasdeloriente.galeon.com **E:** verdeyblanco5@hotmail.com – **SC35)** Calle Quijarro 74 esq Av Uruguay. Santa Cruz - **FM:** 105.5MHz – **SC36)** Santa Cruz – **E:** relacionespublicas@radiologosnetwork.com – **SC37)** Comunidad de Camiri, Prov Cordillera – **SC38)** Comunidad de San Julián, Prov Nuflo de Chávez – **SC39)** Santa Cruz – **SC40)** Santa Cruz – **SC41)** Vallegrande – **SC42)** Camiri – **SC43)** Yapacani – **SC44)** Santa Cruz – **W:** www.poderdedios.net **E:** radiosol@poderdedios.com - **FM:** 105.5 MHz – **SC45)** Calle Lanza No 84 entre La Paz y Oruro, Santa Cruz ☎4 4526 100 ☐4 4681 178 **W:** www.radiomaria.org.bo **E:** info. bol@radiomaria.org – **SC46)** Santa Cruz – **SC47)** Santa Cruz
TA00 (TARIJA)
TA01) Calle Virginio Lema 788 (Cas 404), Tarija ☎4664 3890 – **TA03)** Av Las Américas 963, Edif Radiofónico Los Andes (Cas 344), Tarija ☎6 642 800 - **FM:** 103.1MHz – **TA05)** Calle Bolivar esq. Méndez No 327 piso 1 Tarija ☎4663 4444 ☐4663 5555 **W:** www.radioguadalquivir.com - **FM:** 91.5MHz – **TA06)** Bolívar 376, Edificio Borda (Cas 125), Tarija - **FM:** 93.1MHz – **TA07)** Av Barrientos esq Ameller, Bermejo ☎☐4 696 1584 - **FM:** 99.1MHz – **TA10)** Av Bolívar 608, Bermejo – **TA11)** Comunidad de Villamontes, Prov Gran Chaco – **TA12)** Calle Oruro E-1458 Esq. España (Cas. 1003), Tarija ☎4 6643425 **W:** www.aclo. org.bo/bolivia/ **E:** aclotarija@aclo.org.bo – **FM:** 101.5 MHz – **TA13)** Tarija – **TA14)** Bermejo

FM in La Paz (MHz): 87.7 87.7 FM – 25) 88.5 Doble 8 Latina – 88.9 Gente – 89.3 Sistema Cristiano de Comunicaciones – 89.7 Salesiana – 16) 90.1 Caliente FM – 90.5 Panamericana Classica – 90.9 PCM – 91.3 Ciudad – 91.7 El Comercio – 92.1 Estudio 92 FM – 92.5 Estelar – 92.9 Galáctica – 93.3 Melodia – 93.7 Chacaltaya – 94.1 R La Voz de Bolivia – 94.5 Red Nuevo Tiempo – 94.9 Gigante – LP06) 95.3 – 95.7 Digital Sur – 1) 96.1 – 96.5 R.Panamericana – 96.9 Diferente – 97.3 Stereo 97 – 6) 97.7 – 11) 98.1 Láser – 98.5 Andina – 98.9 Restauración – 25) 99.3 Melodía – 99.7 Cristo Viene – 41) 100.1 FM Cien – 100.5 Constelación – 100.9 R. Color – LP07) 101.3 – 101.7 Graffiti – 102.1 RRB – 102.5 Sintonia – 102.9 Cristal – 103.3 R. Deseo – 103.7 San Francisco de Asis – 104.1 Cadena CNT – 104.5 RCN – 104.9 Fantástica – 105.3 Nuevo Amanacer – 105.7 Majestad – 106.1 Pachamama – 17) 106.5 – 106.9 Paris-La Paz – 107.3 Nueva Cosmos – 107.7 Central FM

BONAIRE (Netherlands)

L.T: UTC -4h — **Pop:** 10,100 — **Pr.L:** Dutch (official), Papiamentu, English — **E.C:** 50Hz, 127/220V — **ITU:** BES

BUREAU TELECOMMUNICATIE EN POST
✉ Kaya Grandi 69, P.O. Box 791, Bonaire ☎ + 599 717 3140 ☐ +599 717 3554 **W:** www.BTnP.org **E:** gen.affairs@burtel.an

MW	Call	kHz	kW	Station, location
1)	PJB	800	100	Trans World R., Kralendijk

FM	MHz	kW	Station, location
1)	89.5		Trans World R., Kralendijk
5)	91.1		R. Digital FM, Kralendijk
2)	93.1		Alpha FM 93.1, Kralendijk
2)	94.7	1	Radiodif. Boneriano, Voz di Bonaire, Kralendijk
3)	97.1	5	R. Energia Boneiru, Kralendijk
4)	97.5		Dolfijn FM, Kralendijk
2)	101.1	0.4	Mega Hit FM, Kralendijk
6)	102.7		Bon FM, Kralendijk

Addresses and other information

1) Kaya Gob. N Debrot 64, Kralendijk, Bonaire (PO Box 388, Kralendijk) ☎ +599 717 8800 📠 +599 717 8808 **W**: www.twrbonaire.com **E**: 800am@twr.org, 895fm@twr.org – **2)** Radiodifushon Boneriano NV, Kaya Gobernador N. Debrot 2, Kralendijk, Bonaire Voz di Bonaire : ☎ +599 717 5947 📠 +599 717 8220 **W**: www.vozdibonaire.com **E**: vozdibonaire@gmail.com Mega Hit FM: www.megahitfm.com ☎ +599 717 7220 📠 +599 717 2101 **E**: info@megahitfm.com – **3)** Kaya Grandi 8, Bonaire ☎ +599 717 0971 **W**: www.radioenergiabonaire.com – **4)** Sea Aquarium Beach, Bapor Kibra z/n, Willemstad, Curacao ☎ +599 9 465 9975 📠 599 9 461 9975 **Dir.** Enrico Stenacker and Egon Sybrandy **DPr.** 24 hours in Dutch **E**: info@dolfijnfm.com **W**: www.dolfijnfm.com – **5)** Kaya Grandi 49 , Kralendijk, Bonaire ☎ +599 717 9911 **W**: www.digital91fm.net – **6)** Kaya Irlanda 11, Kralendijk ☎ +599 717 2102 📠 +599 717 2002 **LP:** GM: Carmo Cecilia. 24h in Papiamentu, news in Dutch and a music prgr in English **W**: www.bonfm.com **E**: bonfm@hotmail.com

TRANS WORLD RADIO (Rlg. Cult. Educ.)
see International Broadcasting section

BOSNIA & HERZEGOVINA

L.T: UTC +1h (31 Mar-27 Oct: +2h) — **Pop:** 3.8 million — **Pr.L:** Bosnian, Croatian, Serbian — **E.C:** 50Hz, 220V — **ITU:** BIH

REGULATORNA AGENCIJA ZA KOMUNIKACIJE (RAK)
✉ Mehmeda Spahe 1, 71000 Sarajevo ☎ +387 33 250600 📠 +387 33 713080 **E:** info@rak.ba **W:** www.cra.ba
LP: DG: Kemal Huseinovic
NB. RAK is the licensing body for broadcasting.

RADIO-TELEVIZIJA BOSNE I HERCEGOVINE (BHRT) (Pub)
✉ Bulevar Meše Selimovica 12, 71000 Sarajevo ☎ +387 33 461101 📠 +387 33 464061 **E:** sanja.sehagic@bhrt.ba **W:** www.bhrt.ba
LP: DG: Muhamed Bakarevic

FM	MHz	kW	FM	MHz	kW
Capljina	87.8	-	Fortica	97.3	0.5
Ivovik	88.1	30	Blagaj	99.5	-
V. Gomila	88.8	30	Lisin	100.3	30
Lipik	93.7	30	Hum	101.7	10
Leotar	94.1	30	Kozara	103.1	30
Drvar	94.7	5	Trebevic	103.7	0.4
Marijin	96.2	-	Hadzica Brdo	107.3	0.4
Vlašic	97.0	100			

D.Prgr: BH Radio 1 in Bosnian, Croatian, Serbian: 24h.

FEDERACIJA BOSNE I HERCEGOVINE

RADIO-TELEVIZIJA FEDERACIJE BOSNE I HERCEGOVINE (RTV FBiH) (Pub)
✉ Bulevar Meše Selimovica 12, 71000 Sarajevo ☎ +387 33 461539 📠 +387 33 461539 **E:** press@rtvfbih.ba **W:** www.rtvfbih.ba
LP: DG: Dzemal Šabic

FM	MHz	kW	FM	MHz	kW
Drvar	88.2	-	Lisin	94.5	30
Tuzla	88.5	10	Dreznica	95.7	-
Capljina	89.1	-	Hum	95.7	10
Vlašic	89.3	100	V. Gomila	95.7	30
Jablanica	90.0	-	Lipik	98.9	30
Fortica	91.7	30	Hadzica Brdo	99.5	5
Tušnica	92.5	30	Marijn	102.5	-
Kladanj	94.5	-	Blagaj	103.5	5

D.Prgr: Radio FBiH in Bosnian, Croatian: 24h.

OTHER STATIONS

MW	kHz	kW	Location	Station
15)	774	2	Tuzla	R. 7
22)	792	1	Banovici	R. Banovici
23)	1503	1	Zavidovici	R. 1503 Zavidovici
24)	1584	1	Bos. Petrovac	R. Bosanski Petrovac

FM	MHz	kW	Location	Station
16)	88.2	2	Drvar	R. Drvar
7)	90.3	5	Posušje	R. Livno
7)	90.8	5	Glamoc R.	R. Livno
13)	90.9	1	Sarajevo	R. Stari Grad
7)	91.5	5	Bos. Grahovo	R. Livno
5)	91.5	4	Sarajevo	R. Kalman
6)	91.8	2	Gradacac	R. Kameleon
20)	92.0	1.5	Sarajevo	R. Kometa
2)	93.1	5	Posušje	R. Široki Brijeg
18)	94.7	1	Bihac	R. Bihac
1)	96.2	4	Bihac	R. USK
4)	96.2	1.5	Mostarsko Blato	R. Dobre vibracije
15)	96.5	3	Majevica Lipik	R. 7
13)	97.5	3.5	Zenica	R. Stari Grad
14)	97.6	2	Glamoc R.	R. Studio N
11)	98.1	30	Bjelašnica	R. Herceg-Bosne
8)	98.7	1	Sarajevo	R. M
3)	99.3	2.5	Zenica	R. BM
7)	100.9	1	Livno	R. Livno
19)	101.5	1	Gorazde	R. Gorazde
7)	101.8	1	Bugojno	R. Livno
4)	102.5	1.5	Neum	R. Dobre vibracije
10)	103.7	2	Osjecenica	R. Sana
11)	103.9	30	Velez	R. Herceg-Bosne
13)	104.3	16.5	Bjelašnica	R. Stari Grad
1)	105.1	31.5	Plješivica B.	R. USK
9)	105.2	1	Fojnica	R. Q
12)	105.6	1	Sarajevo	R. Istocno Sarajevo
21)	106.6	10	Zenica Lisac	R. Zenica
17)	106.7	3	Bosanska Dubica	R. Mir Medjugorje
17)	107.8	50	Bihac	R. Mir Medjugorje
17)	107.8	5	Petricevac	R. Mir Medjugorje

NB: Txs below 1kW not listed.

Addresses & other information:
1) Dom Kulture, 77000 Bihac. **E:** rtvuskbi@bih.net.ba – **2)** Trg Gojka Suška 5c, 88220 Široki Brijeg. **E:** radio-sirokibrijeg@tel.net.ba – **3)** Talica brdo br.11 i 13, 72000 Zenica. **E:** urednik@bmradio.info – **4)** Kralja P. Krešimira IV, 88000 Mostar. **E:** rdv@rdv.ba – **5)** Varazdinska 18, 71000 Sarajevo. **E:** redakcija@kalmanradio.ba – **6)** Dr. Milana Jovanovica 6, 75000 Tuzla. **E:** kameleon@kameleon.ba – **7)** Kneza Mutimira 29, 80101 Livno. **E:** radio.livno@tel.net.ba – **8)** Fra Andjela Zvizdovica 1, 71000 Sarajevo. **E:** hitradio@radiom.net – **9)** Donje Rosulje 59, 71300 Visoko. **E:** radioq@bih.net.ba – **10)** Banjalucka 2, 75260 Sanski Most. **E:** radiosana@yahoo.com – **11)** Kralja Petra Krešimira IV bb, 88000 Mostar. **E:** radiohb@tel.net.ba – **12)** Stefana Nemanje 8, 71123 Srpsko Sarajevo. **E:** radiois@sarajevo-rs.com – **13)** Urijan Dedina 7, 71000 Sarajevo. **E:** rsg@rsg.ba – **14)** Splitska bb., 80101 Livno. **E:** studio.n@tel.net.ba – **15)** Mirze Delibašica 4, 75000 Tuzla. **E:** rtv7tuzla@gmail.com – **16)** Ante Bruno Bušic 4, 80260 Drvar. – **17)** Gospin Trg 1, 88266 Medugorje. **E:** radio-mir@medjugorje.hr – **18)** Krupska bb, 77000 Bihac. **E:** rtvbihac@bih.net.ba – **19)** Zaima Imamovica 2, 73100 Gorazde. **E:** martvgo@bih.net.ba – **20)** Dedijerova 12, 71123 Istocno. **E:** kometa@paleol.net – **21)** Bulevar Kralja Tvrtka I bb., 72000 Zenica. **E:** info@rtvze.com – **22)** 7 novembra 4, 75290 Banovici. **E:** radiobanovici@yahoo.com – **23)** Maršala Tita 10, 72220 Zavidovici. **E:** info@zdiciradio.com – **24)** Bosanska 134, 77250 Bosanski Petrovac.

REPUBLIKA SRPSKA

RADIO TELEVIZIJA REPUBLIKE SRPSKE (RTRS) (Pub)
✉ Trg Republike Srpske 9, 78000 Banja Luka ☎ +387 51 339900 📠 +387 51 301922 **E:** radio@rtrs.tv **W:** www.rtrs.tv
LP: DG: Dragan Davidovic

FM	MHz	kW	FM	MHz	kW
Kmur	87.3	1	Banja Luka	90.9	1
Trebevic	88.7	10	Kozara	92.7	30
Udrigovo	89.9	30	Leotar	92.8	30
Veliki Zep	90.3	30	Petrovo	93.5	-
Duge Njive	90.7	5			

D.Prgr: Radio RS in Serbian: 24h.

OTHER STATIONS

FM	MHz	kW	Location	Station
9)	87.7	5	Sarajevo	Nes R.
5)	88.4	6	Ugljevik	RTV Step
6)	89.9	2	Bosanska Dubica	R. Vikom
12)	93.6	5	Banja Luka	Big R. 1
10)	94.3	2.5	Gracanica	Obiteljski R. Valentino
3)	94.7	10	Bosanska Dubica	R. Feniks
11)	95.3	23	Kozara	Bobar R.
1)	95.6	1	Banja Luka	R. Balkan

FM	MHz	kW	Location	Station
2)	96.3	2	Doboj	R. Doboj
9)	99.3	2	Velika Kladuša	Nes R.
4)	99.9	9	Banja Luka	BN R.
11)	100.9	30	Majevica	Bobar R.
8)	102.7	3	Banja Luka	Hard Rock R.
11)	102.8	8	Trebevic	Bobar R.
11)	104.7	30	Vlašic	Bobar R.
6)	105.3	3	Banja Luka	R. Vikom
11)	105.4	4.5	Tušnica	Bobar R.
11)	105.5	22	Leotar	Bobar R.
11)	105.9	39	Velez	Bobar R.
9)	106.4	22.5	Kozara	Nes R.
7)	106.7	1	Drvar	TMK R.
11)	107.3	12.5	Trovrh	Bobar R.
11)	107.8	77	Plješivica B.	Bobar R.

NB: Txs below 1kW not listed.
Addresses & other information:
1) Kralja Petra I Karadordevica 113-115, 78000 Banja Luka. **E:** balkan@radio-balkan.com – **2)** Kneza Lazara 8, 74000 Doboj. **E:** rdoboj@doboj.net – **3)** Svetosavska bb., 79240 Kozarska Dubica. **E:** feniksfm@teol.net – **4)** Laze Kostica 146, 76320 Bijeljina. **E:** urednik@radiobn.net – **5)** Naselje Gojsovac bb., 76320 Dvorovi. – **6)** Srpska 2/II, 78000 Banja Luka. **E:** vikom@vikom.tv – **7)** Bul. Vojvode Petra Bojevica bb., 70000 Banja Luka. **E:** tmk.oksigen@gmail.com – **8)** P.C. Krajina, Vidovdanska bb., 78000 Banja Luka. **E:** hardrockradio@blic.net – **9)** Brace Pišteljic 1, 78000 Banja Luka. **E:** nesradio@teleklik.net – **10)** Kolodvorska 108 a, 76204 Bijela. **E:** desk@valentinobh.com – **11)** Filipa Višnjica 211, 76320 Bijeljina. **E:** rbobar@teol.net – **12)** Vuka Karadzica 6, 78000 Banja Luka. **E:** redakcija@bigradiobl.com

BOTSWANA

L.T: UTC +2h — **Pop:** 2 million — **Pr.L:** Setswana, English — **E.C:** 50Hz, 220V — **ITU:** BOT

NATIONAL BROADCASTING BOARD (NBB)
206/207 Independence Ave, Private Bag 00495, Gaborone ☎+267 3957755 +267 3957976 **W:** www.bta.org.bw/nbb.htm **E:** info@bta.org.bw **L.P:** Chairman: Dr. Masego Mpotokwane.

RADIO BOTSWANA (Pub, Comm.)
Private Bag 0060, Gaborone ☎+267 3653000 **W:** www.dib.gov.bw **E:** Rbeng@info.bw **L.P:** Dir. Broadc. Sces: Habuji Sosome. Chief Broadc. Officer: Mrs Banyana Segwe. CE: Kingsley Reetsang. Mgr RB: Margaret Modise.

MW	kHz	kW	MW	kHz	kW
Maun	531	50	Mmathethe	945	25
Muchenje	558	50	Sebele‡	972	50
Selebi-Phikwe	621	100	Jwaneng	1071	25
Mopipi	648	50	Mahalapye	1215	50
Shakawe	693	25	Tshabong	1350	50
Gantsi	873	50	‡inactive		

FM(MHz)	RB1	RB2	kW	FM(MHz)	RB1	RB2	kW
Bobonong	95.9	102.7	0.5	Mabule	92.3	105.9	
Charleshill	93.5	103.5		Mabutsane	94.2	104.6	
Francistown	103.6	90.5	3	Mahalapye	96.6	107.0	2.5
Gaborone	89.9	103.0	5	Maun	94.2	104.6	0.5
Gantsi	94.0	100.8	0.1	Olifant's Drift	88.0	104.7	
Good Hope	94.6	101.6	0.5	Orapa	89.9	98.6	0.1
Hukuntsi	89.9	96.2	0.5	Palapye	91.5	101.5	0.5
Jwaneng	99.2	106.3	0.5	Sekakangwe Hill	91.9	101.9	2
Kanye	89.0	95.3	0.5	Selebi-Phikwe	94.2	104.6	0.1
Kang	89.3	98.9		Serowe	99.4	92.9	1
Kasane	94.4	104.8	0.5	Sojwe	87.7	90.7	
Lobatse	94.5	107.5	1	Tsabong	96.6	107.0	0.5

National Sce. (RB1) in Setswana/English on MW/FM: 24h.
N. in English: on the hour exc. **in Setswana:** 1100, 1600, 1900.
Commercial Sce. (RB2): 24h. **N:** rel. RB1.
Ann: E: "This is R. Botswana broadcasting from Gaborone", "RB", "RB1", "RB2". Setswana: "Se Ke Seromamowa Sa Botswana mo Gaborone".
IS: RB1: Bird chirps and first bars of the National Anthem.

Other stations (all MHz):
Duma FM: Gaborone 93.0, Francistown 93.6 – **Gabz FM**, Private Bag BO 319, 2nd Floor, Beta House, Plot 17954, Old Lobatse Rd, Gaborone. **W:** www.gabzfm.com **FM:** Maun/Selebi-Phikwe 91.0, Mahalapye 93.4, Lobatse 94.1, Palapye 94.7, Serowe 96.1, Gaborone 93.2, Francistown 96.8 – **Yarona FM:** Francistown 100.1, Gaborone: 106.6. **W:** www.yaronafm.co.bw
Voice of America relay station (MW):
Selebi-Phikwe, Moepeng Hill: 909kHz 600kW 0300-0700 ,1600-2200 & SW. For further details see International Radio section (USA)

BRAZIL

L.T: PE (Fernando de Noronha only): UTC -2h. AL, AP, BA, CE, DF*, ES*, GO*, MA, MG*, PA, PB, PE, PI, PR*, RJ*, RN, RS*, SC*, SP*, TO*: UTC -3h (*=DST: -2h). AC, AM, MS*, MT*, RO, RR: UTC -4h (*=DST: -3h). *) DST: 21 Oct 12-16 Feb 13, 20 Oct 13-15 Feb 14 — **Pop:** 199 million — **Pr.L:** Portuguese — **E.C:** 60Hz, 220V — **ITU:** B — **Int. dialling code:** +55

AGÊNCIA NACIONAL DE COMUNICAÇÕES (ANATEL)
SAS Quadra 06 Bloco H, Ed. Ministro Sérgio Motta, 2° andar, 70313-900 Brasília, DF **W:** www.anatel.gov.br
L.P: Dir. Gen. Dr. Rubens Bussacos. Dir. of Radio: Roberto Blois Montes de Souza. Dir. Dept. of Authorizations: Domingo Poty Chabalgoity.

ASSOCIAÇÃO BRASILEIRA DE EMISSORAS DE RADIO E TELEVISÃO (ABERT)
SCN Quadra 4 Bloco B-100, sala 501, Centro Empresarial Varig, 70714-900 Brasília, DF (C.P. 08780, 70312-970)
☎ 61 2104 4600 61 2104 4626 **W:** www.abert.org.br
L.P: Pres.: Paulo Machado de Carvalho Neto. Exec. Dir: Antonio Abelin

Callsign For the full callsign add ZY to the front of the calls shown. The letters preceding the stn number indicate the state or territory. ‡ = inactive ± = varying freq † = irregular
N.B: all stns carry «A Voz do Brasil» (official prgr.). Main tr. M-F 2200-2300 but stns may also transmit at other times during the day.

MW	Call	kHz	kW	Station, location, h. of tr.
BA01)	H481	540	1/0.25	R. Regional, Irecê: 24h
CE01)	H610	540	1/0.25	R. Jornal, Canindó
GO01)	H755	540	10/1	R. Riviera, Goiânia
MA01)	H894	540	1/0.25	R. Guajajara, Barra do Corda
MG151)	I331	540	1/0.5	R. Ipanema, Ipanema
PI31)	I914	540	1/0.25	R. Primeiro de Julho, Agua Branca
PR110)	J322	540	10/5	R. Nova Era, Borrazópolis: 0800-0000
RJ01)	J450	540	10/2.5	R. Fluminense, Niterói
RS01)	K226	540	1/0.5	R. Real, Canoas: 0900-0100
RS02)	K322	540	10/1	R. Sepé, Santo Ângelo: Wd: 24h Sat.: 0900-0500, Sun Silent
SC01)	J778	540	10/1	R. Mirador, Rio do Sul: 0800-0300
SE01)	J924	540	10/2.5	R. Jornal AM, Aracaju: 24h
SP01)	K697	540	10/5	R. Uirapuru, Biriguí
SP02)	K734	540	1/0.25	R. Nova Sumaré, Sumaré
CE59)	H644	550	1/0.25	R. Vale do Quincoé, Acopiara
MG01)	L225	550	5/0.5	R. Cataguases, Cataguases
MG02)	L263	550	20/5	R. Soc. Norte de Minas (RBV), M. Claros
MT29)	I429	550	10/5	R. Banda, Sinop
PE01)	I796	550	5/1	R. Meridional, Garanhuns
PI01)	I902	550	1/0.25	R. Serra da Capivara, São Raimundo Nonato
PI22)	I907	550	10/0.5	R. Globo, Parnaíba: 24h
PR139)	J331	550	10/5	R. Banda B, Curitiba
RS03)	K287	550	2.5/0.25	R. Sta. Cruz do Sul, Sta. Cruz do Sul: 24h
SP03)	K578	550	5/0.5	R. Mantiqueira, Cruzeiro: 0800-0300
SP04)	K696	550	5/0.5	R. Boa Vontade, Sertãozinho
AM09)	H289	560	1/0.25	R. Educação Rural, Coari: 1000-0100
BA02)	H456	560	5/1	R. Jornal, Itabuna
CE41)	H604	560	1/0.25	R. Educ. Jaguaribana, Limoeiro do Nte: 0700-0100, Sun 0800-2300
GO25)	H769	560	5/0.25	R. Sul Goiana, Quirinópolis: 0800-0100 (Sat -2300), Sun Silent
MA02)	H887	560	25/5	R. Educadora do Maranhão, São Luís: 0800-0300(Sat -0100), Sun 0900-0100
MG05)	L277	560	5/0.25	R. Dif., Patrocínio
MT01)	I395	560	10/2.5	R. Aruanã, Barra do Garças
MT24)	I419	560	10/1	R. Pioneira, Tangará da Serra: 0800-2200, SS: Silent
PB16)	I695	560	1/0.25	R. Maná, Mamanguape
PR01)	J214	560	1/0,5	R. Londrina Londrina
PR02)	J281	560	2.5/0.25	R. Cultura, Araraquara
RJ02)	J496	560	5/1	R. Costa do Sol, Araruama
RS04)	K231	560	5/1	R. São Francisco Sat, Caxias do Sul: 24h
SP213)	K761	560	35/1	R. Paulista, Santa Isabel
AL01)	H244	570	1/0,5	R. Novo Nordeste, Arapiraca
CE02)	H613	570	5/0.25	R. Verde Vale, Juazeiro do Norte
CE03)	H614	570	1/0.25	R. Uirapuru, Itapipoca
GO02)	H750	570	2.5/0.5	R. Cultura, Catalão: 0700-0200
MA06)	H890	570	10/1	R. Cidade Esperança, Imperatriz
MG03)	L261	570	25/5	R. Capital, Belo Horizonte: 24h
MT30)	N407	570	1/0.25	R. Jornal, São José dos Quatro Marcos: 24h
PR146)	J349	570	1/0.5	R. Continental, Palotina: 24h
RS05)	K267	570	1/0.5	R. Diário da Manhã, Passo Fundo
SC02)	J735	570	5/0.5	R. Eldorado, Criciúma

MW	Call	kHz	kW	Station, location
SC99)	J794	570	1/0.25	R. Fronteira, Dionísio Cerqueira
SP05)	K595	570	1/0.25	R. Clube de Itapeva, Itapeva: 0900-2300, Sat: 0800-0100(Sun -2200)
SP06)	K672	570	5/1	R. Dif., Taubaté
SP195)	K698	570	1/0.25	R. Jornal, Nhandeara
SP150)	K717	570	1/0.25	Bariri R. Clube, Bariri
BA03)	H477	580	1/0.25	R. Dif., Teixeira de Freitas
GO44)	H799	580	1/0.25	R. Serra Azul, Caiapônia
MG04)	L328	580	7/0.5	R. América, Uberlândia: 24h
MS01)	I387	580	25/1	R. Inmaculada Conceicao, Campo Grande
PE02)	I776	580	20/10	R. Boas Novas, Recife: 24h
PI12)	I905	580	5/1	R. Itamaraty, Piripiri
PR105)	J327	580	2/0.25	R. Pitanga, Pitanga
PR03)	J330	580	2.5/0.25	R. Grande Lago, Santa Helena: 0800-0300, Sun 0900-0100
RJ03)	J465	580	50/5	R. Relogio, Jacarepaguá: 24h
RS06)	K299	580	2/0.5	R. São Gabriel, São Gabriel: 0900-0300
RS07)	K318	580	10/5	R. Fátima, Vacaria: 24h
SP07)	K540	580	1/0.25	R. Você, Americana
SP08)	K724	580	1/0.25	R. Regional, Palmital
TO01)	H785	580	10/2	R. Tocantins, Porto Nacional
BA04)	H445	580	10/5	R. Cruzeiro da Bahia, Salvador
CE04)	H627	590	5/0.25	R. Vale do Rio Poty, Crateús
ES01)	I213	590	5/0.5	R. Tribuna, Vitória
GO03)	H798	590	10/1	R. Manchester, Anápolis
MG93)	L249	590	10/0.5	R. Cultura, João Monlevade
MT03)	I420	590	10/5	CBN Cuiabé, Cuiabá: 24h
PB25)	I692	590	5/0.25	R. Serrana, Araruna: 0730-0100
PR04)	J234	590	10/5	R. Difusora AM 590, Curitiba
PR38)	J240	590	2.7/0.75	R. Dif. Regional, Cruzeiro do Oeste
RR01)	O700	590	10	R. Dif. de Roraima, Boa Vista: 0800-0300 SS 0900-0230
RS08)	K210	590	5/0.5	R. Alegrete, Alegrete: 0830-0230
SC03)	J809	590	2/1	R. Progresso, Descanso
SP09)	K534	590	10/1	R. Atlântica, Santos: 24h
SP10)	K612	590	1/0.25	R. Clube, Mirandópolis
SP11)	K696	590	5/1	R. 79, Ribeirão Preto
AM02)	H287	600	1	R. Municipal, São Gabriel da Cachoeira: 0900-0300
BA05)	H486	600	10/1	R. Vale do Rio Grande, Barreiras
BA64)	H...	600	10/0.25	R. Dif.de Rio Real, Rio Real
CE38)	H627	600	1/0.25	R. Cultura, Aracati
MA38)	H920	600	10/1	R. Mirante, São Luís
PE03)	I789	600	1/0.25	R. Cardeal Arcoverde, Arcoverde
RS09)	K278	600	100	R. Gaúcha, Porto Alegre:24h
AL10)	H249	600	10/2	R. Imperial, Marechal Deodoro
AM18)	H321	610	10	Super R.Boa Vontade, Iranduba: 24h
GO10)	H786	610	25/0.5	R. Mega, Luziânia
MG06)	L268	610	100/25	R. Itatiaia, Belo Horizonte
MT04)	I425	610	10/5	R. Celeste, Sinop
PB01)	I678	610	1/0.25	R. Progresso, Sousa
PI02)	I899	610	10/1	R. Poty, Teresina
SC04)	J746	610	10/0.5	R. Super Condá, Chapecó
SP12)	K532	610	1/0.25	CBN, Mogi Mirim
SP13)	K577	610	1/0.25	R. Globo, Catanduva
SP14)	K589	610	1/0.25	Super R. Piratininga, Guaratinguetá
SP15)	K726	610	1/0.25	R. Paranapanema, Piraju: 0800 - 0100
SP113)	K502	610	1/0.25	R. Presidente Venceslau, Pres. Venceslau
CE05)	H590	620	10	R. Globo, Fortaleza
PR05)	J332	620	2.5/0.25	R. Jandaia, Jandaia do Sul
RS10)	K270	620	10/1	R. Pelotense, Pelotas
RS11)	K315	620	1/0.25	R. Municipal, Tenente Portela: 0830-0300 Sat 0900-0000(Sun -2200)
SC05)	J779	620	5/0.25	Super-Radio Dif. AM, Rio do Sul: 0800-0100
SP16)	K521	620	50/10	R. Jovem Pan, São Paulo
AP01)	H422	630	25/10	R. Dif. de Mapacá, Macapá: 24h
CE58)	H636	630	1/0.5	R. Cidade, Campos Sales: 0800-0300
GO04)	H777	630	10/0.5	R. Gospel 630 AM, Pires do Rio: 24h
MA16)	H924	630	10/0.5	R. Macaru, Viana
MG07)	L299	630	1/0.5	R. Jornal da Manha, Uberaba
MS32)	N603	630	10/1	R. Novo Tempo, Campo Grande
MT05)	I384	630	10/5	R. Dif. Bom Jesús, Cuiabá
PI03)	I904	630	1/0.5	R. Dif., Barras
PR06)	J284	630	10/0.5	R. Educativa, Curitiba
PR07)	J300	630	5/0.25	R. Educ. Marechal, Marechal Cândido Rondón
RJ04)	J466	630	25/10	R. Roquete Pinto, Rio de Janeiro
RS12)	K259	630	1/0.5	R. Cacique, Lagoa Vermelha: 24h
RS13)	K289	630	1/0.5	R. Santamariense, Santa Maria
SC06)	J800	630	1/0.25	R. Doze de Maio, São Lourenço d'Oeste
SE02)	J920	630	10/5	R. Aperipe, Aracaju
SP17)	K613	630	1/0.5	R. Difusora, Mirassol
SP18)	K635	630	5/0.25	R. Cidade, Presidente Prudente
BA12)	H458	640	1/0.5	R. Dif. Sul da Bahia, Itabuna: 0700-0300
ES02)	I204	640	10/0.5	R. Vitória, Vitória
GO05)	H757	640	50/5	R. Dif. Goiânia, Goiânia
MG08)	L308	640	3/0.25	R. Santa Cruz, Pará de Minas: 24h
MG125)	L320	640	10/0.25	R. Educadora, Porteirinha: 0800-0300
MT06)	I406	640	10/5	R. Progresso, Alta Floresta
MT18)	I424	640	10/1	R. Tangará, Tangará da Serra
PR08)	J262	640	20/1	Super R. Deus é Amor, Londrina
RJ05)	J489	640	5/1	R. Agulhas Negras, Resende
RN01)	J590	640	10/5	R. Globo, Natal
RS14)	K277	640	50/10	R. Bandeirantes, Porto Alegre: 24h
SP19)	K547	640	5/1	R. Morada do Sol, Araraquara
BA06)	H462	650	5/0.5	R. Clube, Valença: 24h
GO06)	H790	650	1/0.25	R. Cultural do Araguaia, Jussara
MG09)	L200	650	10/0.5	R. Vitoriosa, Lagoa Formosa
MG85)	L309	650	5/0.5	R. Globo, Unaí: 24h
MG142)	L372	650	10/1	R. Itatiaia AM Vale do Aço, Timóteo
MT19)	I414	650	5	R. Educadora, Colider
PA20)	I540	650	10/1	R. Tropical, Santarém
PB02)	I672	650	5/0.5	R. Alto Piranhas, Cajazeiras
PI26)	I925	650	10/1	R. Tapuio, Miguel Alves
PR09)	J202	650	1/0.5	R. Banda B Norte Pionerio, Cambará
PR91)	J250	650	8/1	R. Colméia, Cascavel
RS15)	K238	650	5/0.5	Radiodif. Sul Riograndense, Erechim: 0800-0300
SP20)	K508	650	1/0.25	R. Andradina, Andradina
SP22)	K518	650	5/1	R. Terra, Santos
SP21)	K524	650	5/0.8	R. Dif., Piracicaba
BA07)	H465	660	1/0.25	R. Nova Jornal, Itapetinga
BA36)	H480	660	10/0.25	R. Bom Jesus, Bom Jesus da Lapa
BA66)	H510	660	1/0.25	R. Tribuna do Vale do São Francisco, Xique-Xique
BA65)	H518	660	1/0.25	R. Planalto, Euclides da Cunha
CE06)	H619	660	1/0.25	R. Rio das Garças, Itarema (Acaraú)
GO07)	H778	660	1/0.25	R. Primavera, Itapuranga
GO51)	H794	660	1/0.25	R. Alvorada, Quirinópolis
MG11)	L206	660	10/0.25	R. Clube, Curvelo
MT07)	I401	660	10/0.5	R. Juventud, Rondonópolis
PA21)	I552	660	1/0.25	R. Xinguara, Xinguara
PE04)	I787	660	5/1	R. Jornal, Limoeiro
PE05)	I795	660	1/0.25	R. Grande Serra, Araripina
PI34)	I925	660	1/0.25	R. Tacariús, São Miguel do Tapuio
RJ06)	J472	660	5/1	R. Friburgo, Nova Friburgo: 24h
R001)	J673	660	10/5	R. Boas Novas AM, Porto Velho
RS16)	K286	660	1/0.25	R. Marajá, Rosário do Sul: 0900-2355 Sat:0830-2355
RS17)	K319	660	1/0.25	R. Esmeralda, Vacaria
SP23)	K639	660	10/0.5	R. Clube, Ribeirão Preto
SP112)	K656	°660	20/0.5	R. Mundial, São Paulo
AC11)	H...	670	0.25	R. Dif., Sena Madureira: 0900-0400
AM04)	H288	670	1	R. Mesorregional, Tabatinga: 24h
AM03)	H297	670	1/0.25	R. Vale do Rio Madeira, Humaitá: 0800-0400
AP02)	H420	670	10/1	R. CBN, Macapá: 24h
CE07)	H606	670	1/0.25	R. Cultura, Várzea Alegre: 0800-0100
GO08)	H747	670	10/1	R. São Francisco, Anápolis
MG12)	L310	670	10/2.5	R. Educadora, Montes Claros
MG126)	L347	670	1/0.25	R. Montanhesa, Ponte Nova: 24h
MG123)	L361	670	1/0.25	R.Uberaba, Uberaba
MG135)	L310	670	1/0.25	R. Cidade, Bambuí: 0800-0200
MS23)	I408	670	1/0.25	R. Patriarca, Cassilândia
MS28)	N600	670	10	Super R. Fronteira, Ponta Porã
MT16)	I422	670	6/1	R. Transpantaneira, Poconé
MT44)	I436	670	1	R. Atitude, Lucas do Rio Verde: 0900-0015 (Sat: -2300, Sun: -1700)
PA02)	I537	670	1/0.25	R. Rural, Altamira
PA22)	I539	670	5/0.25	R. Atalaia, Óbidos
PA27)	I546	670	1/0.25	R. Tropical, Paragominas
PI32)	I927	670	1/0.25	R. Livramento, José de Freitas
PR10)	J231	670	3/0.25	R. Canção Nova Esperança, Nova Esperança
PR11)	J248	670	10/2	R. Globo, Curitiba:24h
RS18)	K296	670	2.5/0.25	R. Cult. Jaguarão, Santa. Vitória do Palmar
RS19)	K370	670	10/0.5	R. Gazeta, Carazinho: 0900-0130
SE03)	J921	670	10/5	R. Cultura de Sergipe, Aracaju: 24h
SP24)	K574	670	1/0.25	R. Oceânica, Caraguatatuba
SP25)	K585	670	1/0.25	R. Centro Oeste, Garça
SP26)	K598	670	1/0.5	R. Convenção, Itu: 24h
BA08)	H471	680	10/2	R. Clube, Sto. Antônio de Jesús
GO09)	H765	680	1/0.5	R. Difusora, Jataí
GO49)	H787	680	5/1	R. Mantiqueira, Niquelândia
MA03)	H885	680	20	R. Dif. do Maranhão, São Luís: 24h
MG173)	L270	680	2/0.25	R. Difusora, Ouro Fino
MG13)	L326	680	1/0.25	R. União, João Pinheiro
MG71)	L296	680	5/0.25	R. Novo Tempo, Governador Valadares
MS02)	I389	680	5/1	R. Cultura, Campo Grande
PB26)	I683	680	2.5/0.25	R. Integração do Brejo, Bananeiras: 24h

MW	Call	kHz	kW	Station, location
PE06)	I793	680	10/1	R. Grande Rio, Petrolina: 0800-0300
PR155)	J362	680	5/0.25	R. Poema, Pitanga
RJ07)	J452	680	20/5	R. Copacabana, Rio de Janeiro
RS69)	K275	680	50	R. Farroupilha, Porto Alegre: 24h
SP27)	K576	680	1/0.25	R. Dif.680 AM, Catanduva
SP28)	K628	680	2/0.25	R. Piratininga, Piraju
BA96)	H453	690	10/1	R. Cultura, Ilhéus
CE08)	H587	690	25/10	R. Shalom, Fortaleza: 0800-0300, SS 24h
ES10)	I201	690	10/1	R. America, Vitoria
GO48)	H780	690	50/1	R. Sociedade Ceres, Ceres
MG14)	L228	690	50/5	R. Mineira, Belo Horizonte
MS03)	I402	690	5/0.25	R. Cultura, Naviraí
MT31)	I451	690	5/1	R. Parecis, Diamantino
PA03)	I532	690	20/5	R. Clube do Pará, Belém: 24h
PR13)	J229	690	5/1	R. Dif., Londrina
PR14)	J252	690	1/0.25	R. Dif., Ponta Grossa
PR143)	J360	690	5/0.25	R. Voz do Sudoeste, Coronel Vivida: 24h
RS21)	K252	690	5/0.5	R. Progresso, Ijuí: 0800-0400(SS -0300)
SC07)	J772	690	5/1	R. Clube, Lages
SP29)	K561	690	1/0.25	R. Bebedouro, Bebedouro: 0800-2300
SP30)	K588	690	1/0.25	R. Clube, Guaratinguetá
SP31)	K625	690	1/0.25	R. Cidade, Pereira Barreto: 24h Sun: 0900-0300
SP220)	K646	690	1/0.25	R. Brasil, Santa Bárbara d'Ueste
TO12)	N661	690	25/1.5	R. Canção Nova do Coração de Jesus, Palmas: 24h
BA10)	H500	700	25/1	R. Cultura, Feira de Santana
GO47)	H801	700	25/0.5	R. Pouso Alto, Piracanjuba
MT21)	I428	700	25/1	R. Sorriso, Sorriso
PI04)	I890	700	10/5	R. Globo, Teresina
PR92)	J225	700	10/0.25	R. Capital do Papel, Telêmaco Borba: 24h
RJ56)	J507	700	5/0.4	R. Aliança, Itatuva: 0800-2300, (SS -2230)
RS123)	K247	700	1/0.25	R. Sideral, Getúlio Vargas: 24h
RS22)	K356	700	1/0.25	R. Batovi, São Gabriel
SP32)	K686	700	50	R. Estado ESPN, São Paulo
AL02)	H240	710	5/1	R. Jornal, Maceió
BA46)	H490	710	10/0.25	R. 21 News, Eunápolis:24h
CE09)	H628	710	1/0.25	R. Asa Branca, Boa Viagem
DF07)	H710	710	10/2.5	R. Aliança, Brasília: 24h
MA12)	H891	710	1	R. Verdes Campos, Pinheiro: 0800-0100
MA27)	H910	710	10/0.5	R. Verdes Vales, Grajaú
MG/9)	L219	710		R. Cancella, Ituiutaba
MG15)	L258	710	20/0.5	R. Manhuaçu, Manhuaçu: 24h
MG80)	L319	710	2/0.25	R. Planeta, Carmo do Paranaíba
MG16)	L333	710	2/0.25	R. Dif., Pouso Alegre: 24h
MT08)	I386	710	5/0.5	R. Cultura, Cuiabá
MT23)	I436	710	5/1	R. Nova Xavantina, Nova Xavantina
PA04)	I534	710	25/5	R. Rural, Santarém: 0800-0300
PB03)	I685	710	5/0.5	R. Educadora, Conceição
PI19)	I901	‡710	1/0.25	R. Alvorada do Sertão, São João do Piauí
PI23)	I933	710	1/0.5	R. Clube, Barras
PR141)	J328	710	1/0.25	R. Alternativa, Cândido de Abreu
RJ09)	J451	710	10	R. Sucesso AM, Rio de Janeiro:24h
SC08)	J793	710	1/0.25	R. Fraiburgo, Fraiburgo: 0800-0300
SP33)	K559	710	1/0.25	R. 710, Bauru
AC01)	H202	720	10	R. Integração, Cruzeiro do Sul: 0900-0300
AM05)	H281	720	1	R. Difusora CBN, Itacoatiara: 24h
MG28)	L330	720	2.5/0.5	R. Divinópolis, Divinópolis
MS04)	I390	720	5/1	R. Clube, Dourados
MT20)	I411	720	5/1	R. Difusora, Barra de Garças
PE07)	I770	720	100	R. Clube AM 720, Recife: 24h
RS23)	K276	720	100	R. Guaíba, Porto Alegre: 24h
SP34)	K575	720	1/0.25	R. Difusora, Casa Branca: 0800-0000 Sun 0900-2300
SP35)	K701	720	1/0.25	R. Sentinela, Ourinhos
SP36)	K718	720	1/0.25	R. RC Vale, Cruzeiro
SP37)	K722	720	1/0.25	R. Menina, Olímpia
CE45)	H640	730	1/0.5	R. Sinal, Aracati
ES16)	I217	730	10/0.5	R. SIM, Vitória
GO31)	H759	730	25/5	R. 730 do Brasil, Goiânia
MA04)	H896	730	1/0.25	R. Eldorado, Codó
MG17)	L287	730	5/1	R. Soc. Triângulo Mineiro, Uberaba
MG18)	L297	730	10/1	R. Manchester, Juiz de Fora
MS38)	I452	730	1/0.5	R. Princesa do Vale, Camapuã
MT09)	I410	730	10/2.5	R. Jornal, Cáceres
PE08)	I780	730	10/5	Em. Rural, A Voz do São Francisco, Petrolina
PR15)	J208	730	7/0.6	R. Marumby, Curitiba
PR16)	J323	730	1/0.25	R. Objetiva, Campo Mourão
PR147)	J353	730	5/0.25	R. Integraaca Metropolitana, Corbélia
RS24)	K268	730	5/1	R. Planalto, Passo Fundo: 24h
SC09)	J787	730	1	R. Tubá, Tubarão: 0800-0100
SP38)	K523	730	10/0.25	R. Cidade, Jundiaí
SP39)	K610	730	10/1	R. Dirceu, Marília
AC02)	H206	740	20/10	Super R. Alvorada, Rio Branco
BA11)	H446	740	100	R. Soc. da Bahia, Salvador: 24h
MT25)	N403	740	1/0.5	R. Cidade, Alto Araguaia
PR17)	J259	740	1/0.25	R. Goioerê, Goioerê
PR135)	J354	740	1/0.25	R. Placar, Ortigueira
RS25)	K265	740	2.5/0.25	R. Palmeira, Palmeira das Missões: 0900-0300
RS26)	K283	740	10/0.25	R. Nativa, Rio Grande
SC10)	J753	740	10/1	CBN (R. Diário da Manha), Florianópolis
SP93)	K519	740	10/1	R. Assunção, Jales
SP40)	K553	740	1/0.25	R. Cultura, Bariri: 0900-0200(Sat-2200) Sun: 1000-2200
SP41)	K650	740	25/0.5	R. Trianon, São Paulo
DF01)	H709	750	50/25	R. Jovem Pan, Brasília
MG19)	L213	750	100/5	R. América, Belo Horizonte
PA28)	I541	750	1/0.25	R. Ximango, Alenquer
PB04)	I682	750	1/0.25	R. Panati, Patos
PI05)	I897	750	1/0.25	R. Liberdade, Campo Maior
RS27)	K264	750	5/0.25	R. Osório, Osório: 1030-0200 (Sun: 2300)
SC11)	J815	750	5/0.25	R. Aliança, Concórdia
SE04)	J927	750	10/0.25	R. Progresso, Lagarto: 0800-0300
SP42)	K516	750	1/0.25	R. Clube, Osvaldo Cruz
SP43)	K642	750	12/0.5	R. CMN, Ribeirão Preto
SP44)	K661	750	2.5/0.25	R. Super Piratininga, São José dos Campos
SP283)	K696	750	5/0.5	R. Atual, Registro
TO03)	H/92	750	1/0.25	R. Tocantins, Tocantinópolis
AL12)	H252	760	1/0.25	R. Pioneir (R.Delmiro), Delmiro Gouveia
AP03)	H424	760	5	Rede Amapaense de Rdif., Macapá
BA44)	H461	760	5/0.5	R. Cidade, Vitória da Conquista (fpl 1550)
CE10)	H588	760	25/10	R. Uirapuru, Fortaleza
GO43)	H775	760	5/0.5	R. Rio Claro, Iporá
GO11)	H783	760	10/0.5	R. Pousada do Rio Quente, Caldas Novas
MG83)	I257	760	2.5/0.25	R. Difusora, Machado
MG137)	L360	760	10/0.5	R. Terra, Monte Claros
MT32)	N408	760	10/5	R. Natureza, Chapada dos Guimarães
PR12)	J343	760	10/0.25	R. Cacique, Guarapuava
RJ11)	J478	760	25/1	R. Manchete AM, Niterói: 24h
RS28)	K222	760	1/0.25	R. Princesa do Jacuí, Candelária
RS29)	K351	760	2.5/0.25	R. Ametista, Planalto: 0800-0100
SC12)	J742	760	25/2	R. Nereu Ramos, Blumenau: 0730-0100
SP149)	K541	760	1/0.25	R. Urubupungá, Andradina
SP45)	K560	760	10/0.25	R. Auri-Verde, Bauru
BA51)	H491	760	1/0.25	R. Rio Corrente, Santa Maria da Vitória
CE11)	H609	770	10/0.25	R. Vale do Salgado, Lavras da Mangabeira
ES03)	I211	770	5/0.25	R. Globo AM, Cachoeiro de Itapemirim
GO12)	H745	770	5/1	R. A Voz do Coração Imaculado, Anápolis
MA28)	H922	770	1/0.25	R. Vitória, Coelho Neto
MA41)	H902	770	10	R. Boa Noticia, Balsas
MG20)	L209	770	2.5/0.25	R. Cultura d'Oeste, Lavras: 0800-0200
MG21)	L302	770	10/0.25	R. Clube de Patos, Patos de Minas
MG108)	L315	770	5/0.5	R. Pontal do Triangulo, Iturama
MG22)	L337	770	1/0.25	R. Itabira, Itabira
MS11)	I412	770	5/0.5	R. Caiuás, Dourados
MT28)	N404	770	1	R. Cidade de Matupá, Matupá
MT45)	I434	770	5/1	R. Xavantes, Jaciara
PA29)	I557	770	10/0.25	R. Clube, Marabá
PR131)	J344	770	1/0.25	R. Cidade, Cambé
SE05)	J922	770	10/5	R. Atalaia de Sergipe, Aracaju
SP46)	K506	770	5/0.5	R. Mix, Limeira
CE55)	H657	780	10/1	R. Dif., Nova Russas
GO13)	H789	780	10/1	R. Soc. Vera Cruz, Goianésia
MA24)	H919	780	10/5	R. Alvorada, Zé Doca
MG23)	L246	780	1	R. Educadora Jovem Pan, Uberlândia
MG103)	L259	780	10/1	R. Manhumirim, Manhumirim
PE09)	I771	780	30/10	R. Jornal do Comércio, Recife: 24h
PR18)	J247	780	1/0.25	R. Porta Voz, Cianorte: 24h
PR19)	J305	780	5/0.25	R. Chopinzinho, Chopinzinho
RS30)	K229	780	5/2	R. Diário da Manhã, Carazinho
RS31)	K279	780	25	R.O´Sul, Porto Alegre: 24h //970
SC13)	J788	780	1	R. Marconi, Urussanga
SC54)	J751	780	0.5	R. Brasil Novo, Jaraguá do Sul
SP161)	K619	780	1/0.25	R. Dif., Monte Aprazível: 0800-0100
SP47)	K695	780	50/10	CBN, São Paulo
BA13)	H484	790	10/1	R. Barreiras, Barreiras
BA14)	H505	790	1/0.25	R. Regional, Brumado
CE12)	H629	790	1/0.25	R. Jornal Centro Sul, Iguatu: 24h
GO28)	H761	790	5/0.5	R. Xavantes, Ipameri: 0800-0200, Sun: 0900-0100
GO14)	H771	790	10/0.5	R. Eldorado, Mineiros
MA29)	H904	790	1/0.25	R. Rio Turiaçu, Santa Helena
MA20)	H915	790	1/0.25	R. Cultura, Açailândia
MA30)	H899	790	1/0.25	R. Rio Flores,Tuntum
MG24)	L279	790	5/0.25	R. Soc. Ponte Nova, Ponte Nova: 0800-0200
MG25)	L311	790	1/0.25	R. Treze de Junho, Mantena
MG26)	L314	790	5/1	R. Tropical, Lagoa da Prata: 24h
MT22)	I456	790	1	R. Regional, Nortelândia

MW	Call	kHz	kW	Station, location
PB05)	I679	790	2.5/1	R. Cultura 790, Guarabira: 0700-0300
PI36)	I931	790	1/0.25	R. Mafrense, Simplício Mendes
PR130)	J316	790	2.5/0.25	R. Clube, Faxinal: 0800-2400
PR20)	J337	790	10/0.25	R. RCC, Curitiba: 24h
RS32)	K285	790	1/0.25	R. Rio Pardo, Rio Pardo
SC14)	J789	790	1/0.25	R. Videira, Videira
SP48)	K538	790	1/0.25	R. Brasil, Adamantina
SP49)	K546	790	10/0.5	R. Cultura, Araraquara
SP162)	K674	790	5/0.25	R. Cultura, Taubaté
AL17)	K256	800	10	R. Palmares, Maceió
DF02)	H705	800	10/1	R. MEC, Brasília
PI08)	I921	800	10	R. Antares, Teresina: 0930-0100
RJ12)	J457	800	100	R. MEC, Rio de Janeiro
RS33)	K292	800	10	R. Universidade, Santa Maria
BA54)	H528	810	10/0.25	R. Nossa Senhora de Guadalupe, Riacho de Santana
CE13)	H589	810	50/5	R. Verdes Mares, Fortaleza
GO15)	H767	810	50/0.5	R. Alvorada, Rialma
MG27)	L202	810	1	R. Aimorés, Aimorés
MG92)	L252	810	1/0.25	R. Educadora, Ubá
MG76)	L266	810	1/0.25	R. Clube, Nepomuceno
MG138)	L354	810	1/0.25	R. Cidade, Capinópolis: 24h
MG156)	L366	810	50/5	R. Rainha de Paz, Patrocínio
MT33)	N402	810	1/0.25	R. Integração, São José do Rio Claro
MT34)	N406	810	1/0.25	R. Floresta AM, Alta Floresta
PR49)	J261	810	1/0.25	R. RCC Cornélio Procópio
PR111)	J336	810	5/0.5	R. Esperança, Prudentópolis: 0800-0300
RS136)	K324	810	1.9/0.25	R. Cinderela, Campo Bom
SP50)	K604	810	1/0.25	R. Dif. Jundiaiense, Jundiaí
SP89)	K655	810	1/0.5	R. Universal, Santos
SP51)	K732	810	1/0.5	R. Cancao Nova São José do Rio Preto
AC03)	H...	820	1/0.25	R. Educ. 6 de Agosto, Xapuri: 1000-0100
AC12)	H207	820	0.25	R. Dif. de Tarauacá, Tarauacá
AM06)	H294	820	1/0.25	R. Princesa, Manacapuru: 24h
BA15)	H534	820	20/1	R. Cultura, Utinga
CE14)	H624	820	1/0.25	R. União, Camocim
CE60)	H655	820	1/0.25	R. Sul Cearense, Brejo Santo
ES04)	I212	820	10/2.5	R. Gazeta, Vitória
GO16)	H752	820	50/5	R. Jornal, Goiânia:1000-2300
MG29)	L255	820	5/0.25	R. Globo, Barbacena
MG167)	L273	820	3/0.25	R. Bom Sucesso, Minas Movas
MG30)	L291	820	1/0.25	R. da Familia, São Sebastião do Paraíso: 24h Sat: 0800-0130(Sun -0300)
MT10)	I400	820	1/0.25	R. Dif., Cáceres: 24h
PA05)	I543	820	5/1	R. Regional, Conceição do Araguaia: 0900-2300
PE10)	I775	820	5/1	R. Universitária, Recife
PI06)	I912	820	5/0.25	R. Cacique Bruenque, Regeneração
PR21)	J238	820	10/5	R. Cultura, Foz do Iguaçu
PR150)	J357	820	1/0.25	R. Princesa, Roncador
RJ13)	J477	820	5/0.25	R. Globo, Macaé
RS34)	K241	820	5/1	R. Alto Taquari, Estrela: 0900-0200
SC15)	J738	820	10/5	CBN, Blumenau: 24h
SP52)	K542	820	10/1	R. Aparecida, Aparecida
SP53)	K602	820	1/0.25	R. Jauense, Jaú
SP54)	K622	820	0.5/0.25	R. Clube, Ourinhos
SP55)	K624	820	1/0.25	R. Difusora, Penápolis
BA67)	H506	830	5/0.25	R. Extremo Sul da Bahia, Itamaraju: 0700-0100 Sun: -0000
CE65)	H659	830	1/0.25	R. Pioneira, Forquilha
GO50)	H805	830	1/0.25	R. Sempre, Goiatuba: 24h
MA26)	H905	830	10/1	R. Mirante do Maranhão, Imperatriz
MA21)	H925	830	10/1	R. Boa Esperança, Esperantinópolis
MG31)	L244	830	50/5	R. Cultura, Belo Horizonte
MS07)	I396	830	5/0.5	R. Cidade Maracaju, Maracaju
MT26)	N401	830	10/0.25	R. Educadora, Juina: 0800-0100
PA24)	I556	830	10/1	R. Guaraní de Marajó, Soure
PI07)	I906	830	1/0.25	R. Primeira Capital, Oeiras
PI37)	I934	830	1/0.25	R. União, Parnaíba
PR22)	J224	830	7.5/0.75	R. Iguassu, Araucária
PR24)	J266	830	10/0.5	R. Tabajara - CBN, Londrina
PR23)	J311	830	1/0.25	R. Progresso, Clevelândia
RJ39)	J488	830	10/0.5	R. Tropical Solimos, Rio de Janeiro: 24h
RN02)	J595	830	1/0.25	R. Rural do Caicó, Caicó
RS35)	K332	830	5/0.25	R. Independente, Cruz Alta
SC16)	J773	830	1/0.25	R. Cruz de Malta, Lauro Müller
SE06)	J926	830	20/1	R. Princesa da Serra, Itabaiana
SP56)	K681	830	10/1	R. Lider, Votuporanga
SP227)	K746	830	5/1	R. Novo Tempo, Nova Odessa
AM07)	H298	840	1/0.25	R. Rio Madeira, Manicoré
BA16)	H447	840	25/5	R. Excelsior da Bahia, Salvador
CE51)	H648	840	1/0.5	R. Campo Maior, Quixeramobim: 0800-2200
PI38)	I930	840	1/0.25	R. Ribeirão, Demerval Lobão
PI39)	I937	‡840	1/0.25	R. Vitória, Batalha
PR75)	J320	840	10/1.2	R. Inconfidência, Umuarama: 1000-2200 (Sat 1400-2200 Sun 1530-1600)
RS36)	K248	840	10	R. Capital, Porto Alegre
SC17)	J750	840	10/1	R. Rural, Concórdia
SP57)	K687	840	100/50	R. Bandeirantes, São Paulo
BA17)	H474	850	5/0.25	R. Caraiba, Senhor do Bonfim
CE15)	H599	850	1	R. Iracema, Juazeiro do Nte
GO17)	H776	850	5/1	R. Tropical, Porangatu: 0900-0300
MA31)	H923	850	10/0.5	R. Cidade, Vitória do Mearim
MG32)	L233	850	1/0.25	R. Difusora Formiguense, Formiga
MG33)	L254	850	10/0.5	R. Por um Mundo Melhor, Governador Valadares
MG34)	L295	850	5/0.25	R. Tupaciguara, Tupaciguara: 0900-0300
MS30)	I438	850	1/0.25	R. Difusora Nor'estado, São Gabriel
MT02)	I416	850	10/2	R. Sulmatogrossense, Poxoréo
PA17)	I538	850	10/1	R. Itacaiúnas, Marabá
PA06)	I555	850	1/0.25	R. Tocantins, Cametá
PA18)	I557	850	5/1	R. Itaituba, Itaituba
PB22)	I693	850	5/1	R. Rural, Guarabira
PI30)	I909	850	1/0.25	R. Grande Picos, Picos
PR50)	J254	850	5/0.25	R. Dif. Colméia, Campo Mourão: 24h
PR86)	J291	850	2/0.25	R. Alvorada do Sul, Rebouças: 24h
RJ31)	J470	850	10/0.5	R. Dif., Campos dos Goytacazes: 24h
RO03)	J675	‡850	5/1	R. Ariquemes, Ariquemes
SC20)	J808	850	2.5/0.25	R. Cidade, Brusque
SC102)	J807	850	1/0.25	R. Atalaia, Campo Erê
SP59)	K563	850	1/0.5	R. Nova Clube, Biriguí
SP58)	K644	850	2.5/0.25	R. Jornal, Rio Claro
CE16)	H592	860	25/10	R. Cidade, Maracanaú
RJ14)	J459	860	100	R. CBN, Rio de Janeiro
RS37)	K288	860	10/1	R. Guarathan, Santa Maria
AL03)	H245	870	5/1	R. Educ. Sampaio, Palmeira dos Indios
AM19)	H322	870	1/0.25	R. Cidade, Manacapuru: 1000-0200
BA18)	H457	870	12/0.25	R. Nacional, Itabuna
BA84)	H499	870	5/1	R. Cidade, Juazeiro
CE17)	H591	870	1/0.25	R. Liberdade, Iguatu
CE66)	H658	870	1/0.25	R. Tabajara, São Benedito
ES20)	I...	870	5/0.25	R. Globo. Linhares: 24h
GO18)	H749	870	5/0.5	R. Lago Dourado, Uruaçu
GO32)	H754	870	1/0.25	R. Universitária, Goiânia
MA05)	H903	870	10/0.5	R. Mirante, Codó
MG78)	L304	870	10/0.5	R. Juriti, Paracatu
MG38)	L318	870	1/0.5	R. Cultura, Diamantina
MG66)	L324	870	5/0.25	R. Sacramento, Sacramento
MG128)	L349	870	5/0.25	R. Atividade Muriaé
MG127)	L350	870	5/0.25	R. Voz, Pioneira do Vale
MT35)	N409	870	1/0.5	R. RGB (Garça Branca), Guiratinga: 0830-2100
PA11)	I547	870	1/0.25	R. Marajó, Breves
PR25)	J243	870	5/0.25	R. Nova Ingá, Maringá: 0800-0100
SC96)	J784	870	12/0.25	R. São Francisco, São Francisco do Sul
SP60)	K620	870	1/0.25	R. Novo Horizonte, Novo Horizonte
SP61)	K705	870	5/1	R. Central, Campinas
TO04)	H762	870	5/0.25	R. Anhanguera, Araguaína
MG35)	L275	880	100	R. Inconfidência, Belo Horizonte: 24h
PB18)	I680	880	1/0.25	R. Maringá, Pombal
RS38)	K249	880	10/2.5	R. Itaí, Porto Alegre
RS87)	K317	880	2.5/0.25	R. São Miguel, Uruguaiana
RS20)	K363	880	8/0.25	R. Seberi, Seberi: 24h
CE46)	H642	890	1/0.25	R. Itatiaia, Santa Quitéria
DF03)	H706	890	50/2.5	R. Clube AM 890, Brasília
MG36)	L250	890	10/1	R. Santa Cruz, Jequitinhonha: 0900-2300(Sun -1500)
MG154)	L370	890	5/0.25	R. Clube, Inhapim
MS33)	I453	890	10/0.5	R. Guaicurus, Fátima do Sul
PA13)	I536	890	5/1	R. Ponta Negra, Santarém
PE11)	I772	890	20/10	R. Tamandaré, Recife: 24h
PR117)	J287	890	5/0.25	R. Ubá, Ivaiporã
PR26)	J338	890	5/0.25	R. Super Itapuã, Pato Branco
RJ59)	J499	890	10/0.5	R. Musical, Cantagalo
RS39)	K215	890	5/0.25	R. Difusora, Bento Gonçalves: 24h
RS40)	K295	890	2/0.5	R. Noroeste, Santa Rosa
SC52)	J745	890	5/0.25	R. Clube, Canoinhas: 0700-0300
SC18)	J755	890	1/0.25	R. Santa Catarina, Florianópolis
SP62)	K690	890	50/10	R. Gazeta, São Paulo
SP127)	K703	890	2.5/0.25	R. Cidade, Matão: 24h
SP178)	K562	890	1/0.25	R. Imaculada Conceicao, Bilac
BA19)	K488	900	1	R. Sisal, Conceição do Coité
GO41)	H768	900	10/1	R. Rio Verde AM, Rio Verde: 0945-0300
MG86)	L207	900	5/0.25	R. Imbiara, Araxá
MG148)	L311	900	2.5/0.25	R. Onda Viva, Carangola
MG124)	L338	900	1/0.25	R. Vinícola, Andradas
MT36)	I455	900	10/2.5	R. Difusora Arco-Iris, Araputanga
MT41)	I431	900	5/1	R. Integração, Primavera do Leste
PA10)	I533	900	25/5	R. Liberal - CBN, Belém: 24h

MW	Call	kHz	kW	Station, location
PR27)	J272	900	5/0.25	R. Sant'Ana, Ponta Grossa: 24h
PR28)	J295	900	5/0.25	R. União, Toledo
RJ15)	J454	900	50/10	R. Tamoio, Rio de Janeiro: 24h
RN03)	J591	900	10	R. Nordeste Evangélica, Nata: 24h
RO04)	J672	900	5/1	R. Alvorada de Rondônia, Ji-Paraná
RS41)	K211	900	2.5/0.5	R. Aratiba, Aratiba: 24h
RS179)	K263	900	5/0.5	R. ABC 900, Nôvo Hamburgo: 24h
RS164)	K303	900	1/0.25	R. Municipal, São Pedro do Sul: 0900-0130
SP63)	K511	900	5/0.25	R. Difusora, Presidente Prudente
SP64)	K664	900	10/0.8	R. Jovem Pan, São José do Rio Preto
SP65)	K742	900	1/0.25	R. Globo, Itapetininga
CE61)	H645	910	4/0.25	R. Caiçari, Sobral
GO20)	H763	910	5/0.25	R. Paranaíba, Itumbiara
GO23)	H804	910	10/0.5	R. Cidade, Jaraguá
MG37)	L292	910	1/0.25	R. Teófilo Otoni, Teófilo Otoni
MG132)	L346	910	1/0.25	R.Gospel CRN, Nova Serrana
MG149)	N206	910	5/1	R. Globo, Juiz de Fora
PE12)	I785	910	5/1	R. Super Liberdade, Caruaru
PI41)	I935	910	10/1	R. CBN, Teresina
PR29)	J207	910	1/0.25	R. Nova AM, Apucarana
RS43)	K320	910	5/0.5	R. Venâncio Aires, Venâncio Aires: 0800-0300
SC19)	J811	910	4/0.5	R. Difusora, Içara
SC90)	J824	910	1/0.25	R. Rainha das Quedas, Abelardo Luz: 0800-0300
SP66)	K536	910	5/0.25	R. Onda Livre, Piracicaba: 24h
SP228)	K763	910	1/0.25	R. Princesa, Monte Azul Paulista
BA42)	H476	920	5/0.25	R. Educ. Santana de Caetité, Caetité: 24h
BA57)	H519	920	25/2	R. Novo Tempo, Salvador
ES05)	I207	920	10/5	R. Cultura, Linhares
GO33)	H788	920	5/1	R. Vale da Serra, São Luís de Monte Belos
MG39)	L271	920	5/0.5	R. Cultura, Visconde do Rio Branco
PB31)	I697	920	5/0.5	R.CBN, João Pessoa
PI09)	I895	920	1/0.25	R. Difusora, Picos
PI11)	I893	920	19/0.5	R. Educadora, Parnaíba
RJ41)	J494	920	1/0.5	R. Sociedade, Volta Redonda
RN04)	J600	920	1/0.25	R. Currais Novos, Currais Novos
RS44)	K348	920	20/2	R.Tramandaí, Tramandaí
SP67)	K584	920	10/0.25	R. Imperador, Franca
SP222)	K769	920	1/0.25	R. Bandeirantes, Penápolis
SP221)	K775	920	40/1	R. Nacional Gospel, Cotia
AM16)	H240	930	10	R. Boas Novas, Manaus: 24h
CE18)	H605	930	1/0.25	R. Cetama, Barbalha
CE52)	H646	930	7/0.25	R. Metropolitana, Fortaleza
MG41)	L220	930	2.5/0.25	R. Clube, Campo Belo
MG42)	L229	930	10/5	R. Vitoriosa, Araguari
MG87)	L237	930	20/1	R. Globo, Governador Valadares: 24h
MS05)	I454	930	1/0.25	R. Capital, Campo Grande: 0900-0200
MT12)	I423	930	10/0.5	R. Clube, Rondonópolis: 0800-0200
MT37)	N400	930	1/0.25	R. Jornal, Pontes e Lacerda
PA07)	I600	930	5/1	R. Liberal, Castanhal
PR30)	J227	930	1/0.25	R. Cultura, Rolândia
PR31)	J232	930	10/1	R. Cultura, Curitiba
PR69)	J235	930	10/1	R. Princesa, Francisco Beltrão
RS45)	K230	930	20/2.5	R. Caxias, Caxias do Sul:24h
RS46)	K298	930	1/0.25	R. Santo Ângelo, Santo Ângelo: 0800(Sun 1010)-0300
SE07)	J923	930	20/5	R. 930AM - Liberdade AM, Aracaju
SP71)	K500	930	1/0.25	R. Dinâmica de Santa Fe, Santa. Fé do Sul
SP68)	K503	930	1/0.25	R. Clube, Itapira
SP69)	K652	930	10/1	R. Cultura, Santos
SP70)	K713	930	5/1	R. Canção Nova, Agudos
SP214)	K717	930	1/0.25	R. Jóia, Adamantina
AC04)	H204	940	10/1	R. Verdes Florestas, Cruzeiro do Sul: 0930-0200
PI25)	I911	940	10/0.25	R. AM 7 Cidades, Piracuruca
RJ16)	J453	940	100	Super R. Brasil (RBV), Rio de Janeiro
BA50)	H489	950	1/0.25	R. Bahia Noroeste, Paulo Afonso
CE19)	H593	950	5/1	R. Educadora do Nordeste, Sobral
GO21)	H764	950	5/0.25	R. Dif., Itumbiara: 0800(Sun 1000)-0300
MA17)	H916	950	10/0.5	R. Dif. Karajás, João Lisboa
MG43)	L212	950	25/10	R. Atalaia, Belo Horizonte
MG44)	L281	950	7/0.5	R. Indy, Bueno Brandão
MT17)	I439	950	5/1	R. Tucunaré, Juara
PB17)	I681	950	1/0.25	R. Jornal (Radio News), Sousa
PE13)	I782	950	25/5	R. Planalto, Carpina: 24h
PI20)	I915	950	10/0.25	R. São José dos Altos, Altos
PI42)	I923	950	1/0.25	R. Boa Esperança, Padre Marcos
PR114)	J239	950	1/0.25	R. Difusora, Irati
RS47)	K260	950	10/0.25	R. Independente, Lajeado: 24h
SC21)	J736	950	1/0.25	R. Vale, Tijucas
SP72)	K510	950	5/0.25	R. 950, Vera Cruz
AL04)	H241	960	10	R. Difusora de Alagoas, Maceió: 24h
CE37)	H618	960	1/0.25	R. Cultura dos Inhamuns, Tauá
ES15)	I216	960	25/0.25	R. Diocesana, Cachoeiro de Itapemirim
GO45)	H802	960	50/1	R. Caraíba, Aparecida de Goiânia: 24h
MS61)	N609	960	5	R. Globo, Corumbá
PA26)	I551	960	5/1	R. Clube, Itaituba
PR109)	I217	960	2.5/0.25	R. Legendária, Lapa
PR32)	J257	960	1/0.25	R. Difusora, Maringá
RS48)	K291	960	10/1	R. Imembuí, Santa Maria
SC22)	J733	960	5/0.25	R. Guarujá, Orleães: 0800-0100 Sun: 2400
SC23)	J813	960	8/0.25	R. Super Difusora, Xanxerê
SP73)	K689	960	50/10	R. São Paulo, São Paulo
TO09)	H793	960	25/5	R. Jovem Palmas, Palmas
BA20)	H451	970	10/5	R. Sociedade, Feira de Santana
CE20)	H612	970	5/0.25	R. Monólitos, Quixadá
MG45)	L243	970	5/0.25	R. Caratinga, Caratinga
MG46)	L285	970	2.5/0.25	R. São João Del Rey, São João Del Rey
MG47)	L321	970	5/0.25	R. Central, Monte Alegre de Minas
MS18)	I399	970	5/0.5	R. Vale do Taquari, Coxim
PB06)	I684	970	1/0.25	R. Princesa Isabel, Princesa Isabel
PI43)	I910	970	10/0.5	R. Vale do Parnaíba, Luzilândia
PR33)	J260	970	7.5/1	R. Alvorada, Londrina
PR34)	J277	970	10/0.25	R. Difusora do Paraná, Marechal Cândido Rondón: 0800-0300
RS49)	K201	970	50/10	R. Pampa, Porto Alegre //780: 24h
RS50)	K349	970	1/0.5	R. Alto Uruguai, Humaitá: 0800(Sun 0900)-0200 (Sat -0100)
SC24)	J730	970	5/0.25	R. Araguaia, Brusque: 24h
SP74)	K505	970	5/0.25	R. Transamerica, Itapetininga
SP75)	K529	970	1/0.25	R. Piratininga, São João da Boa Vista
SP76)	K684	970	5/0.25	R. Hertz, Franca
SP215)	K744	970	5/0.25	R. Alvorada, Estrela d'Oeste: 24h
DF04)	H707	980	50/300	R. Nacional, Brasília: 24h
AM23)	H299	990	1	R. Independência, Maués: 0900-0200
BA21)	H483	990	1/0.25	R. Alvorada Gospel, Caravelas
PI44)	I922	990	1/0.25	R. Vale do Canindé, Oeiras
PR128)	J293	990	1/0.25	R. Najuá, Irati
PR121)	J321	990	5/0.25	R. Capital, Cianorte: 24h
RJ53)	J461	990	100/10	R. Record, Rio de Janeiro: 24h
RN05)	J596	990	10/1	R. Rural, Mossoró
RS51)	K314	990	2.5/0.5	R. Tupã, Tupanciretã: 0900-0300
RS52)	K335	990	2.5/0.25	R. Sananduva, Sananduva: 0900-0100
RS154)	K360	990	1/0.25	R. Clube, Pedro Osório
SC25)	J763	990	1/0.25	R. Itapiranga, Itapiranga
SP239)	K579	990	10/0.25	R. Cultura Regional, Dois Córregos
PB30)	I698	1000	2.5/0.5	R. Oeste da Paraíba, Cajazeiras
PE14)	I791	1000	1/0.25	R. Princesa Serrana, Timbaúba: 0800-0300
SP77)	K522	1000	200	R. Record, São Paulo
BA22)	H448	1010	25/5	R. Bahia, Salvador
CE21)	H625	1010	12.5/2.5	R. CBN, Fortaleza
GO39)	H772	1010	10/0.5	R. Santelenense, Sta. Helena de Goiás
MG50)	L230	1010	10/1	R. Educadora, Coronel Fabriciano
MG48)	L264	1010	5/0.5	R. Solar, Juiz de Fora
MG49)	L325	1010	5/0.25	R. Estância, Jacutinga
MT13)	I421	1010	5/1	R. Dif., Mirassol d'Oeste: 0800-0200
PR35)	J263	1010	25/5	R. Celinauta, Pato Branco
RS53)	K232	1010	7.5/0.75	R. 1010, Caxias do Sul
RS54)	K344	1010	3/1	R. Missioneira, São Luíz Gonzaga: 0730-0200 (SS 0900-0200)
SC71)	J764	1010	10/0.3	R. Jaraguá, Jaraguá do Sul: 24h
SC75)	J758	1010	1/0.25	R. Bandeirantes, Imbituba
SP151)	K507	1010	5/0.5	R. Difusora, Lençóis Paulista
SP78)	K556	1010	1/0.5	R. Independente, Barretos
SP79)	K611	1010	1/0.25	R. Diario, Martinópolis
AL05)	H247	1020	25/1	R. Jovem Pan, Maceió
AP04)	H423	1020	1/0.25	R. Porto, Santana
CE22)	H600	1020	5/1	R. Educadora Cariri, Crato: 24h
CE79)	H664	1020	1/0.25	R. Macambira, Ipueiras: 0800-0100
ES06)	I205	1020	10/0.4	R. Difusora, Colatina
GO52)	H781	1020	10/0.5	R. Boas Novas, Firminópolis
MG55)	L224	1020	10/1	R. Congonhas, Congonhas: 0800-0100 Sun 0800-2400
MG51)	L260	1020	10/0.25	R. Cultura, Uberlândia
MS06)	I381	1020	10/0.25	R. Independente, Aquidauana
PB19)	I686	1020	5/0.5	R. Cenecista, Picuí: 0900-2300
PR36)	J244	1020	10/0.25	R. Super Colombo, Curitiba:24h
PR37)	J307	1020	1/0.25	R. Independência, Medianeira
PR142)	J359	1020	1/0.25	R. Campo Aberto, Laranjeiras do Sul
RJ42)	J484	1020	5/0.25	R. Canção Nova, Salvador Campos dos Goytacazes
RO02)	J680	1020	5/1	R. Educadora, Rolim de Moura
RR04)	J702	1020	10/5	R. Folha, Boa Vista: 0800-0300, (Sun 0400-2200)
RS49)	K202	1020	25/5	R. Caiçara, Porto Alegre
SC27)	J805	1020	2.5/0.25	R. Continental, Coronel Freitas
SP80)	K513	1020	10/0.25	R. Canção Nova, Cachoeira Paulista
SP81)	K515	1020	5/0,25	R. Cultura, Assis: 0900-0300

MW	Call	kHz	kW	Station, location
SP82)	K531	1020	2.5/0.5	R. Educadora, Limeira
SP83)	K600	1020	5/0.25	R. Cultura, Jales
BA40)	H475	1030	10/1	R. Bahiana, Itaberaba
GO22)	H746	1030	10/1	R. Imprensa, Anápolis
MA07)	H892	1030	10/1	R. Jainara, Bacabal
PE15)	I777	1030	20/5	R. Olinda, Olinda
PR39)	J271	1030	5/0.25	R. Atalaia, Londrina
PR120)	J312	1030	2.5/0.25	R. Clube, Realeza: 0830-0300
PR40)	J329	1030	1/0.25	R. Dif. do Xisto, São Mateus do Sul
RJ18)	J467	1030	100/5	R. Capital, Rio de Janeiro
RN31)	J612	1030	1/0.25	R. Em. Vale do Apodi, Apodi
RO10)	J683	1030	5/1	R. Rondônia, Ariquemes
RS129)	K224	1030	1/0.25	R. Cultura, Canguçu: 0900-0100
RS55)	K253	1030	10/0.5	R. Repórter, Ijuí: 0800-2200
SC28)	J771	1030	2.5/0.5	R. Princesa, Lages
SP84)	K525	1030	5/0.25	R. Difusora, Franca
SP85)	K554	1030	1/0.25	R. Emissora da Barra, Barra Bonita
SP86)	K606	1030	1/0.25	Lins Rádio Clube, Lins
TO05)	H791	1030	1/0.25	R. Colinas, Colinas do Tocantins
SP87)	K537	1040	200/100	R. Capital, São Paulo
BA47)	H494	1050	25/0.75	R. Noticias, Camaçari: 24h
CE54)	H647	1050	10/0.5	R. Primeira Capital, Aquiraz
ES07)	I203	1050	100/1	R. Capixaba, Vitória
GO40)	H760	1050	1/0.25	R. Jornal, Inhumas
MG52)	L236	1050	1/0.25	R. Rural, Tupaciguara
MS20)	I391	1050	10/0.5	R. Dif. Paranaibense, Paranaíba
PB07)	I676	1050	5/1	R. Caturité, Campina Grande
PR66)	J226	1050	1/0.25	R. Dif. Platinense, Sto. Antônio da Platine
PR99)	J286	1050	5/0.25	R. Club de Palmas, Palmas: 0900-0300, (Sat 1030-0100)
RJ19)	J497	1050	10/0.5	R. Angra, Angra dos Reis
SC26)	J867	1050	7/0.25	R. Verde Vale, Braço do Norte: 0725-0300
SP160)	K601	1050	10/0.5	R. Show Jardinópolis
BA23)	H460	1060	5/1	R. Clube de Conquista, Vitória da Conquista
BA68)	H520	1060	2.5/0.25	R. Clube, Itapicuru
MG53)	L278	1060	100/5	R. Grande Belo Horizonte "R. Grande Be Aga", Pedro Leopoldo
MG54)	L306	1060	1/0.25	R. Itajubá, Itajubá
MS39)	N604	1060	5/1	R. Imaculada Conceiçoa, Dourados
PR42)	J246	1060	10/0.5	R. Evangelizar, Curitiba
PR43)	J298	1060	1/0.25	R. Colorado, Colorado: 0830-2200(Sat -2345)
PR44)	J306	1060	10/0.5	R. Educadora, Francisco Beltrão
RJ20)	J495	1060	30/1	R. Cancao Nova, Miguel Pereira
RN06)	J597	1060	5	R. Tapuyo, Mossoró (RPC)
RS56)	K220	1060	5/0.25	R. Camaqüense, Camaquã
RS57)	K302	1060	2/0.25	R. São Luís, São Luís Gonzaga: 0800-0300
RS81)	K307	1060	2/0.5	R. Cristal, Soledade: 24h
SC103)	J830	1060	2/0.4	R. Mais Alegria, Florianópolis
SP88)	K533	1060	5/0.25	R. Educadora, Piracicaba
SP229)	K765	1060	5/0.25	R. Universitária, Garça
BA48)	H492	1070	5/0.5	R. Rural "R. Tropical", Ipiaú
MG56)	L316	1070	1/0.25	R. do Povo, Muzambinho
MG150)	L355	1070	5/0.25	Super R. Patos, Patos de Minas
MT14)	I427	1070	10/2.5	R. Industrial, Cuiaba: 24h
PB08)	I673	1070	20/2.5	R. Dif. Cajazeiras, Cajazeiras: 0800-0300
PR45)	J203	1070	5/0.25	R. Difusora União, União da Vitória
PR46)	J319	1070	1/0.25	R. Guaraniaçu (Super RG), Guaraniaçu
RJ21)	J483	1070	10/0.25	R. Record, Campos dos Goitacazes
RS58)	K218	1070	2/0.25	R. Caçapava, Caçapava do Sul
RS59)	K343	1070	1/0.25	R. Metrópole, Crissiumal: 0830-0200 (Sat: -0000 Sun 0900-0000)
RS60)	K357	1070	1/0.25	R. Bento, Bento Gonçalves
SC91)	J747	1070	1/0.25	R. Gralha Azul, Urubici
SP91)	K603	1070	1/0.25	R. Nova Piratininga, Jaú
SP145)	K615	1070	10/0.25	R. Metropolitana, Mogi das Cruzes
SP92)	K633	1070	10/1	R. Presidente Prudente, P. Prudente: 1000-2000
SP212)	K758	1070	1/0.25	R. Jornal, Barretos
BA24)	H470	1080	10/0.5	R. Subaé, Feira de Santana
BA25)	H485	1080	5/1	R. Fascinação, Itapetinga: 0800-0230
CE82)	H670	1080	2.5/0.25	R. Cultura, Quixadá: 0800-0100, (Sat 0800-2130 Sun 1500-2130)
DF05)	H708	1080	25/5	R. Capital, Brasília
MG109)	L232	1080	2.5/0.5	R. Cultura, Dores do Indaiá
MG57)	L251	1080	25/0.7	R. Capital, Juiz de Fora
MT27)	I437	1080	1/0.25	R. Gaspar, Itiquira
PA32)	I540	1080	15/5	R. Novo Tempo, Belém
PE16)	I784	1080	10/0.5	R. Jornal do Comercio, Caruaru: 24h
PR47)	J201	1080	2.5/0.5	R. Clube Pontagrossense, Ponta Grossa: 24h
PR48)	J203	1080	1/0.25	R. Cultura do Norte, Paranavaí
RS61)	K254	1080	3/0.25	R. Marabá, Iraí: 0830-0130
RS62)	K280	1080	10	R. da Universidade, Porto Alegre
SC29)	J759	1080	2/1	R. Clube, Indaial: 0800-0200
SP94)	K557	1080	5/1	R. Difusora, Batatais
SP95)	K607	1080	1/0.25	R. Alvorada, Lins
SP96)	K669	1080	10/1	R. Boa Nova, Sorocaba
SP97)	K704	1080	1/0.25	R. Monumental, Aparecida
SP190)	K710	1080	1/0.25	R. Alvorada, Cardoso
AL15)	H254	1090	5/0.5	R. Gazeta, Pão de Açucar
BA26)	H455	1090	1/0.25	R. Santa Cruz, Ilhéus
GO24)	H758	1090	25/1	R. 1090, Goiânia
MA08)	H893	1090	10	R. Rio Balsas, Balsas
MG145)	L357	1090	1/0.25	R. Catuaí, Manhuaçu
PR51)	J283	1090	2.5/0.25	R. Vicente Palotti, Coronel Vivida
PR171)	J345	1090	1/0.25	R. Banda 1, Sarandi
RJ22)	J468	1090	25/5	R. Metropolitana, Rio de Janeiro: 24h
RN07)	J592	1090	10/5	R. Rural, Natal
RS63)	K216	1090	5/0.25	R. Cachoeira, Cachoeira do Sul
RS64)	K262	1090	1/0.25	R. Sallette, Marcelino Ramos: 0900-0100
RS65)	K341	1090	1/0.25	R. Giruá, Giruá: 0800-0300(Sun -2200)
SC30)	J732	1090	1/0.25	R. Colón, Joinville
SC31)	J786	1090	5/0.5	R. Bandeirantes, Tubarão
SP98)	K609	1090	3/0.5	R. Clube, Marília: 24h
SP99)	K618	1090	1/0.25	R. Cultura, Monte Alto
SP233)	K768	1090	1/0.25	R. Canção Nova da Divina Providência, Paulína
CE67)	H638	1100	1/0.25	R. Dif. dos Inhamuns, Tauá: 0730-0030 (Sun 0800-0030)
CE73)	H668	1100	1/0.25	R. Difusora do Vale Acaraú, Acaraú
RN18)	J607	1100	1/0.25	R. Seridó, Caicó
SP100)	K694	1100	150/50	R. Globo, São Paulo: 24h
CE32)	H620	1110	5/0.25	R. Litoral, Cascavel
GO46)	H782	1110	25/2	R. Redentor, Sto. Antônio do Descoberto
MG58)	L205	1110	1/0.25	R. Planalto, Araguari
MG59)	L267	1110	1	R. Aurilândia, Nova Lima
MS08)	I392	1110	1	R. Ponta Porã, Ponta Porã
PB09)	I678	1110	20/10	R. Tabajara, João Pessoa
PR52)	J241	1110	10/1	R. Paiquerê, Londrina
PR151)	J356	1110	1/0.25	R. Clube, Ubiratã
RJ23)	J471	1110	50/5	R. Cultura, Campos dos Goitacazes
RS66)	K257	1110	2.5/0.25	R. Cultura Jaguarão, Jaguarão
RS67)	K306	1110	1/0.25	R. Sobradinho, Sobradinho
RS68)	K325	1110	2.5/0.25	R. Cruzeiro do Sul, Itaqui: 0830-0200 (Sun 0900-0300)
RS152)	K364	1110	1/0.25	R. Solaris, Antônio Prado: 0900-0300
SC74)	J743	1110	1/0.25	R. Caçanjure, Caçador: 0900-0300
SC32)	J752	1110	1/0.5	R. Cultura, Florianópolis: 0800-0300 (Sun:1000-0100)
SC33)	J812	1110	1/0.25	R. São Carlos, São Carlos
SP101)	K544	1110	1/0.25	R. Jovem Luz, Araçatuba: 1000-0000
SP102)	K592	1110	1/0.25	R. Ibitinga, Ibitinga
SP103)	K617	1110	1/0.25	R. Cultura, Mogi Mirim
BA72)	H658	1120	5/0.5	R. Belo Campo, Belo Campo
BA79)	H511	1120	0.25	R. Jornal, Souto Soares: 0900-0100
CE23)	H598	1120	5/1	R. Tupinambá, Sobral: 0800-0100, (Sat 0800-2100, Sun 0900-2200)
ES14)	I215	1120	10/1	R. Sim, São Mateus
MG10)	L272	1120	2.5/0.5	R. Itatiaia, Ouro Preto
MG60)	L301	1120	5/1	R. Sete Colinas, Uberaba
MG61)	L332	1120	1/0.25	R. Serra AM, Boa Esperança: 24h
MS40)	N606	1120	25/1	R. Concordia, Campo Grande
PB10)	I687	1120	5/1	R. Independência, Catolé do Rocha
PE17)	I778	1120	5/1	R. Relógio Musical, Recife
PR53)	J253	1120	25/1	R. Mais, São José dos Pinhais: 24h
PR85)	J285	1120	5/0.5	R. Educadora, Laranjeiras do Sul
RS191)	K274	1120	50	R. Rural, Porto Alegre
RS156)	K367	1120	10/0.6	R. Querência, Santo Augusto: 0800-0300
SP104)	K631	1120	1/0.25	R. Nova Porto, Porto Feliz: 0900-0230 (Sat 0900-2300 Sun 1000-2300)
SP105)	K660	1120	10/1	R. Cidade, São José dos Campos
SP106)	K671	1120	1/0.25	R. Clube Imperial, Taquaritinga: 0800-0000(Sun -2105)
CE72)	H667	1130	10/0.25	R. Patu, Senador Pompeu
PA08)	I531	1130	10	R. Marajoara, Belém: 24H
PE18)	I783	1130	5/1	R. Cultura do Nordeste, Caruaru
PR55)	J220	1130	5/1	R. Castro, Castro: 0800-0300
PR54)	J333	1130	5/0.25	R. Ingamar, Marialva: 0900-2300(Sun -2100)
RJ17)	J460	1130	100/50	R. Nacional, Rio de Janeiro: 24h
RO06)	J677	1130	5/0.25	R. Ji-Parana, Ji-Paraná: 24h
RS70)	K290	1130	5/1	R. Medianeira, Santa Maria
SC34)	J790	1130	5/1	R. Princesa d'Oeste, Xanxerê
SP107)	K676	1130	1/0.25	R. Tupã, Tupã: 0800-0500, Sat: 24h
BA81)	H449	1140	10	R. Cultura da Bahia, Salvador: 24h
CE24)	H607	1140	5/1	R. Progresso, Russas
GO26)	H751	1140	1/0.25	R. Formosa, Formosa
MG62)	L204	1140	5/0.25	R. Minas, Divinópolis
MG63)	L248	1140	1/0.25	R. Doicesana, Campanha: 1100-0300
MG64)	L253	1140	8/0.5	R. Muriaé, Muriaé: 0800-0300
MG129)	L362	1140	5/0.5	R. Clube, Bocaiuva
MS22)	I398	1140	10/0.5	R. Globo, Fátima do Sul

MW	Call	kHz	kW	Station, location
MS36)	I398	1140	5/0.25	R. Cidade, Fatima do Sul
MT47)	I435	1140	1/0.25	R. Dif. Juara, Juara
PR144)	J352	1140	1/0.25	R. Difusora America, Chopinzinho: 0830-0300, Sat 1015-0300
RS71)	K228	1140	2/0.25	R. Cruz Alta, Cruz Alta
RS72)	K316	1140	5/0.7	R. Charrua, Uruguaiana: 0900-2200
RS73)	K330	1140	2/0.5	R. e Jornal Sobral, Butiá: 1000-2200
SC35)	J748	1140	10/0.5	R. Coroado, Curitibanos
SP108)	K550	1140	10/0.5	R. Difusora, Assis
SP109)	K555	1140	2/0.5	R. Barretos, Barretos
SP110)	K645	1140	1/0.25	R. Educação e Cultura, Rio Claro
SP111)	K709	1140	5/0.25	R. Costa Azul, Ubatuba
SP273)	K708	1140	1/0.25	R. Nova Regional, Registro: 24h
AL11)	H250	1150	20/1	R. Cultura, Arapiraca
CE47)	H643	1150	5/0.5	R. Cultura, Paracuru: 24h
MG65)	L283	1150	50/10	R. Globo, Belo Horizonte
PI10)	I891	1150	5/0.5	R. Pioneira, Teresina: 24h
RJ24)	J456	1150	10/0.5	R. Três Rios, Três Rios
RN25)	J617	1150	5/0.5	R. Cabugi do Seridó, Jardim do Seridó: 0800-0100
SP232)	K656	1150	100/50	R. Tupi, São Paulo: 24h
AM24)	H323	1160	1/0.25	R. Soc. TV Manauara, Boca do Acre
BA94)	H...	1160	5/0.25	R. São José Canção Nova, Itabuna
CE62)	H652	1160	1/0.25	R. Vale do Coreaú, Granja
CE80)	H660	1160	1/0.25	R. Montevidéo, Cedro: 0800-0200
DF09)	H714	1160	30/0.5	R. Globo Gama: 24h
ES08)	I202	1160	50/10	R. Espírito Santo, Vitória
G042)	H784	1160	5/0.25	R. Silvestre, Itaberaí: 0900-0100
MT15)	I385	1160	10/5	R. A. Voz d'Oeste, Cuiabá
PA30)	I558	1160	5/1	R. Guamá, São Miguel do Guamá
PB11)	I674	1160	1	R. Cariri, Campina Grande
PR56)	J258	1160	10/1	R. Manchete, Londrina: 0915-2315
RS74)	K242	1160	9/1	R. Miriam, Farroupilha: 0830-2100
RS75)	K245	1160	5/1	R. Luz e Alegria, Frederico Westphalen
RS76)	K256	1160	2.5/0.35	R. Jaguari, Jaguari: 0800-0230
RS77)	K273	1160	2.5/1	R. Universidade Católica, Pelotas: 0900-0300
SC36)	J741	1160	9/0.7	R. Itaberá, Blumenau: 0900-0300
SC37)	J767	1160	1/0.25	R. Dif. Laguna: 0800-(Sun:0700-)0000
SP114)	K517	1160	5/0.25	R. Cacique, Sorocaba
SP124)	K558	1160	2.5/1	R. Bandeirantes, Bauru
SP115)	K582	1160	5/0.25	R. Difusora, Fernandópolis
SP237)	K673	1160	1/0.25	R. Cacique, Taubaté
SP116)	K685	1160	1/0.25	R. Boa Nova, Mococa: 24h
AC15)	H205	1170	1/0.25	R. Dif. de Feijó, Feijó
AM08)	H284	1170	5/2.5	R. Guaranópolis, Maués: 1000-0200
BA27)	H473	1170	1/0.25	R. Jornal, Eunápolis
MG152)	L234	1170	1/0.25	R. Clube Fronteira
MG104)	L269	1170	5/0.25	R. Sociedade, Oliveira
MG75)	L327	1170	10/0.25	R. Vanguarda, Ipatinga
MG67)	L336	1170	5/0.25	R. Cidade, Araxá
PR57)	J273	1170	20/10	R. Atalaia, Curitiba
PR90)	J334	1170	2.5/0.45	R. Entre Rios, Sto. Antônio do Sudoeste: 0800:2300 (Sun -2200)
PR154)	J363	1170	8/1	R. Colméia, Mandaguaçu
RJ49)	J498	1170	5/0.25	R. Bom Jesus, Bom Jesus de Itabapoana: 0800-0300
RN08)	J598	1170	10/1	R. Difusora, Mossoró
RS78)	K207	1170	1/0.25	R. Itapuí, Santo Antônio da Patrulha: 0900-0300
RS79)	K213	1170	5/1	R. Dif. A Voz de Bagé, Bagé: 0900-0300
RS80)	K359	1170	5/0.6	R. Uirapuru, Passo Fundo: 24h
RS155)	K380	1170	2/1	R. Pitangueira, Itaqui:24h
SP117)	K569	1170	10/5	R. Bandeirantes, Campinas
AL06)	H248	1180	1/0.25	R. Correio do Sertão, Santana do Ipanema
AM20)	H280	1180	10/2.5	R. Dif. do Amazonas, Manaus: 24h
MA09)	H889	‡1180	10/5	R. Capital, São Luís
MG118)	L203	1180	10/0.25	R. Cultura, Alfenas
MS34)	I602	1180	10	R. Ativa, Campo Grande
MT38)	N405	1180	5/0.25	R. Enauan, Guarantã do Norte
PB20)	I690	1180	1/0.25	R. Bonsucesso, Pombal: 0830-0100 Sun: 0930-2100
PE19)	I797	1180	1/0.25	R. Cultural, Vitória de Sto. Antão
PR126)	J223	1180	2.5/0.5	R. Atalaia, Guarapuava
PR58)	J237	1180	10/0.5	R. Guaçu, Toledo: 0800-0200
PR81)	J314	1180	1/0.25	R. Educadora, São João do Ivaí: 0800-0100
RJ25)	J463	1180	50/10	R. Mundial (IMPD), Rio de Janeiro
RS128)	K340	1180	10/0.5	R. Gazeta, Santa Cruz do Sul
SC39)	J737	1180	1/0.25	R. Integração d'Oeste, São José do Cedro: 0830-1000
SC72)	J770	1180	1/0.5	R. Guri, Lages
SP260)	K567	1180	1/0.25	R. Brotense, Brotas
SP179)	K647	1180	2/0.5	R. Super Nova Difusora, Santa Cruz do Rio Pardo: 0800-0100
SP217)	K749	1180	5/0.25	R. Nova, Bebedouro

MW	Call	kHz	kW	Station, location
BA28)	H459	1190	10/1	R. Juazeiro, Juazeiro: 0800-2300 (Sat -1930, Sun -1800)
CE68)	H663	1190	1/0.25	R. Guaraciaba, Guaraciaba do Norte: 24h
GO35)	H800	1190	10/0.25	R. Rio Vermelho, Silvânia
MG68)	L221	1190	10/1	R. Guarani, Belo Horizonte
MG40)	L276	1190	10/0.25	R. Mineira do Sul, Passa Quatro
PR59)	J309	1190	1/0.25	R. Pontal, Nova Londrina
PR136)	J355	1190	5/0.4	R. Cidade, Palmital
RN09)	J594	1190	10/1	CBN, Natal: 24h
RS82)	K234	1190	5/0.5	R. Cerro Azul, Cerro Largo
RS102)	K301	1190	2.5/0.25	R. São Lourenço, São Lourenço do Sul: 0900-0200
RS83)	K354	1190	2.5/1	R. Rosário, Serafina Corrêa: 1000-0100
SC40)	J783	1190	1/0.25	R. Clube, São João Batista: 24h
SC87)	J817	1190	1/0.25	R. Planalto, Major Vieira: 24h
SC41)	J820	1190	2.5/0.25	R. Clube, São Domingos
SP199)	K512	1190	2.5/0.25	R. Clube Marconi, Paraguaçu Paulista
SP118)	K700	1190	5/0.25	R. Cidade, Votuporanga
SP119)	K729	1190	10/0.25	R. 31 de Março, Sta. Cruz das Palmeiras
SP120)	K741	1190	1/0.5	R. Regional, Taquarituba: 0800-0200
AL14)	H251	1200	50/1	R. Correio, Maceió
BA29)	H482	1200	5/0.5	R. Clube Rio do Ouro, Jacobina: 24h
CE26)	H585	1200	10	R. Clube, Fortaleza: 24h
RS84)	K239	1200	5/1	R. Erechim, Erechim: 0900-0300
RS85)	K342	1200	1/0.5	R. Fundação Cotrisel, São Sepé: 0800-0200(SS -0100)
SP121)	K520	1200	100/20	R. Cultura, São Paulo
BA30)	H452	1210	10/1	R. Povo, Feira de Santana
BA58)	H498	1210	10/0.25	R. Canção Nova, Vitória da Conquista
CE50)	H637	1210	5/0.25	R. Príncipe Imperial, Crateús
CE48)	H641	1210	5/0.25	R. Boa Esperança, Barro: 0800-2100, (Sun 1000-2200)
DF08)	H711	1210	50/2.5	Super R. Brasília (RBV), Brasília
ES09)	I200	1210	25/1	R. Sim Cachoeiro, Cachoeiro de Itapemirim: 24h
MG69)	L238	1210	10/0.5	R. Clube, Varginha: 0800-0300
PE20)	I786	1210	10/1	R. Jornal, Garanhuns: 24h
PR60)	J219	1210	10/5	Super Rádio Deus é Amor, Curitiba
PR140)	J325	1210	1/0.5	R. Brotense, Porecatu
RN29)	J620	1210	5/0.5	R. Vale do Potengi, São Paulo do Potengi
RS86)	K240	1210	10/5	R. Record, Porto Alegre
RS88)	K353	1210	1/0.5	R. Blau Nunes, Santa Bárbara do Sul
SC42)	J785	1210	10/0.5	R. Super Santa, Tubarão
SP122)	K509	1210	10/1	R. Vida Nova, Jaboticabal
SP123)	K545	1210	5/0.25	R. Bandeirantes, Araçatuba
SP125)	K668	1210	5/0.25	R. Vanguarda, Sorocaba: 24h
RJ25)	J458	1220	150	R. Globo, Rio de Janeiro: 24h
BA59)	H532	1230	1/0.25	R. Povo, Ubatã
GO27)	H756	1230	10/2.5	R. Daqui, Goiânia
MA23)	H896	1230	1/0.25	R. Alecrim, Caxias
MG105)	L208	1230	5/0.25	R. Correio da Serra, Barbacena
MG102)	L216	1230	2.5/0.25	R. Passos, Passos
MG176)	N203	1230	10/0.7	R. Estrela de Ibiúna, Campina Verde
PB12)	I670	1230	10/1	R. Correio Jovem Pan, João Pessoa
PR170)	J350	1230	1/0.25	R. Nova Mensagem, Telêmaco Borba
RS146)	K297	1230	1/0.25	R. Santiago, Santiago: 0800-0300, (Sun 0900-2200)
RS89)	K326	1230	2/0.25	R. Clube Nonoai, Nonoai: 1000-0000 (Sat 1900-0000 Sun 1000-1900)
RS90)	K333	1230	2.3/0.35	R. Prata, Nova Prata: 0800-0100(SS -2200)
RS91)	K352	1230	1/0.25	R. Encruzilhadense, Encruzilhada do Sul
SC38)	J776	1230	5/0.65	R. Dif. Colméia, Porto União
SC88)	J816	1230	10/1	R. Guararema, São José: 24h
SP126)	K573	1230	1/0.25	R. Cacique, Capão Bonito
SP258)	K637	1230	10/0.25	R. Difusora, Rancharia
SP128)	K716	1230	5/0.5	R. Jequitibá, Campinas
SP266)	R212	1230	50/10	Super R. Boa Vontade, São Paulo
BA31)	H463	1240	10/0.5	R. Nova AM 1240, Alagoinhas: 0900-0200(Sat -1900) Sun 1000-2200
CE49)	H654	1240	1/0.25	R. São Francisco, Canindé
MG97)	L294	1240	5/0.25	R. Cl. Três Pontas, Três Pontas
MG84)	L298	1240	1/0.25	R. Ubaense, Ubá
MG72)	L303	1240	10/0.35	R. Globo, Ituiutaba
MG116)	L317	1240	5/0.25	R. Pirapora AM, Pirapora: 24h
MS09)	I388	1240	5/1	R. Dif. Pantanal, Campo Grande: 24h
PE21)	I774	1240	5	R. Capibaribe, Recife
PR112)	J215	1240	1/0.25	R. Arapongas, Arapongas: 24h
PR61)	J280	1240	2/0.25	R. Matelândia, Matelândia
RS92)	K200	1240	1/0.25	R. Aparados da Serra, Bom Jesus
RS93)	K251	1240	1/0.25	R. Ibirubá, Ibirubá: 0800-0100
RS94)	K355	1240	1/0.25	R. São Jerônimo, São Jerônimo
SC43)	J774	1240	5/0.5	R. São José, Mafra: 24h
SC44)	J810	1240	1/0.25	R. Iracema, Cunhe Porã
SP129)	K565	1240	10/0.25	R. Municipalista, Botucatu: 0830-0200
SP130)	K621	1240	5/0.25	Orlândia R. Clube, Orlândia

MW	Call	kHz	kW	Station, location
SP131)	K653	1240	10/2.5	R. Clube, Santos
SP132)	K711	1240	1/0.25	R. Vale do Tietê, José Bonifácio: 24h
CE27)	H594	1250	1	R. Educadora, Crateús
CE69)	H669	1250	1/0.25	R. Liberdade, Itarema
ES18)	I218	1250	10/1	R. CBN, Vitória
GO29)	H748	1250	1/0.25	R. Coração Fiel, Ceres
MG73)	L282	1250	5	R. Difusora, Poços de Caldas
MG153)	L367	1250	20/0.25	R. Metropolitana, Vespasiano
MS10)	I394	1250	1/0.25	R. Difusora, Três Lagoas
MS11)	I412	1250	5/0.5	R. Caiuás, Dourados
PB27)	I701	1250	1/0.25	R. Sociedade de Soledade, Soledade
PI47)	I932	1250	1/0.25	R. João de Paiva, Altos
PR62)	J211	1250	5/0.5	R. Difusora, Guarapuava
PR63)	J233	1250	5/0.4	R. Paranavaí, Paranavaí: 0800-0300, (Sat 1200-0300, Sun 1030-0100)
PR64)	J313	1250	1/0.25	R. Danúbio Azul, Sta. Isabel do Oeste: 24h
RJ50)	J500	1250	10/0.5	R. Litoral, Casimiro de Abreu
RS95)	K233	1250	10/0.5	R. Difusora Caxiense, Caxias do Sul
RS96)	K272	1250	1	R. Tupanci, Pelotas: Wd: 0800-1830
RS142)	K361	1250	5/0.6	R. Aguas Claras, Catuípe: 0800-0200 (Sat 0800-0100 Sun 1000-2200)
SC45)	J766	1250	5/0.25	R. Cultura, Joinville
SE08)	J925	1250	10/1	R. Esperança, Estância
SP133)	K702	1250	5/0.5	R. Canção Nova, Caçapava
AL07)	H242	1260	50/5	R. Gazeta de Alagoas, Maceió: 24h
CE28)	H596	1260	1/0.25	R. Vale do Jaguaribe, Limoeiro do Nte: 0730-0100
RO09)	J670	1260	5	R. Educação, Guajará Mirim: 0900-0300
RS97)	K204	1260	1	R. Cultura, São Borja: 24h
RS98)	K327	1260	5/0.25	R. Fandango, Cachoeira do Sul: 0830-0100 (Sat 0900-0100 Sun 1000-0100)
RS99)	K345	1260	1/0.25	R. Gaurama, Gaurama
SC46)	J740	1260	5/0.5	R. Arca da Aliança, Blumenau
SP257)	K629	1260	1/0.25	Pirajau R. Clube, Pirajuí: 24h
SP134)	K688	1260	100/40	R. Morada do Sol, São Paulo
AM10)	H271	1270	5	R. Educ. Rural, Tefé: 0900-0100(Sun -0000)
GO30)	H753	1270	100/10	R. Brasil Central, Goiânia
MG74)	L227	1270	5/1	R. Carijós, Conselheiro Lafaiete
MG107)	L300	1270	2.5/0.5	R. Estância, São Lourenço
MG155)	L240	1270	5/1	R. Globo, Ipatinga
PA09)	I530	1270	10/2.5	R. Boas Novas, Belém
PB28)	I696	1270	5/0.25	R. Cidade, Sumé: 0800-0100, (Sat 0800-0000 Sun 0900-2100)
PR65)	J222	1270	5/0.5	R. Guairacá, Mandaguari: 0800-0100, (Sat 0800-2300 Sun 0900-2300)
PR67)	J236	1270	10/1	R. Continental, Curitiba: 24h
PR68)	J289	1270	5/0.5	R. Globo (R.Cidade), Cascavel: 24h
RJ26)	J474	1270	5/0.5	R. Continental, Campos dos Goitacazes: 0800-0045
RN10)	J593	1270	5/0.5	R. Clube AM 1270, Natal: 24h
RS131)	K206	1270	5/0.5	R. América, Montenegro: 24h
RS101)	K250	1270	5/0.5	R. Vera Cruz, Horizontina: 0800-0300
SC47)	J765	1270	12/0.25	R. Catarinense, Joaçaba
SC48)	J768	1270	1/0.25	R. Garibaldi, Laguna: 0830-0200 (Sun 1045-1600)
SP136)	K678	1270	5	R. Brasil, Campinas: 24h
SP274)	K640	1270	10/0.5	R. Bandeirantes, Ribeirao Preto
PB21)	I688	1280	10/5	R. Sanhauá, Bayeux
RJ27)	J455	1280	100	R. Tupi, Rio de Janeiro
AM11)	H286	1290	10/2.5	R. Rio Mar, Manaus: 0900-0300
BA32)	H450	1290	10/1	R. Metropole, Salvador
ES24)		1290	1	R.Vila, Vila Velha
MA10)	H888	1290	50/5	R. Timbira do Maranhão, São Luís: 0800-0300
MG77)	L273	1290	25/5	R. Uberlandia, Uberlandia
MG164)	L345	1290	5/0.25	R. Cidade, Arcos
PR73)	J310	1290	10/0.73	R. Brasil Sul, Londrina
RN26)	J619	1290	5/0.25	R. Caicó, Caicó: 0600-0100 (Sun 0700-2300)
RS103)	K331	1290	5/2	R. Planetário, Espumoso
SC81)	J734	1290	5/1	R. Araranguá, Araranguá:0800-0200
SC49)	J804	1290	5/1	R. Camboriú, Balneário Camboriú: 0800-0300
SP240)	K662	1290	5/0.5	R. Difusora, São José do Rio Pardo
SP137)	K663	1290	5/1	R. Novo Tempo, São José do Rio Preto:24h
SP216)	K745	1290	1/0.5	R. Eldorado, São dos Campos: 24h
CE29)	H586	1300	10	R. Iracema, Fortaleza
ES11)	I210	1300	5/0,25	R. Novo Tempo, Afonso Cláudio
MG143)	L339	1300	5/1	R. Eldorado, Sete Lagoas
PE22)	I799	1300	5/1	R. Guarany, Camaragibe
PR71)	J278	1300	1/0.25	CBN, Ponta Grossa
PR127)	J288	1300	5/0.25	R. Educadora, Dois Vizinhos
RS104)	K203	1300	50/13	Super R.Boa Vontade, Porto Alegre: 24h
RS105)	K337	1300	5/0.5	R. Regional, Santo Cristo: 0800-0200
RS106)	K347	1300	5/0.5	R. Maratan, Santana do Livramento: 24h
SC89)	J819	1300	1/0.25	R. Alvorada, Santa Cecília: 0900-0130
				(Sun 1000-0130)
SP138)	K535	1300	50/1	R. Universo, São Bernardo do Campo
SP252)	K649	1300	30/0,25	R. Onda Viva, Santo Anastácio: 0855-2200
SP226)	K762	1300	1/0.25	R. Realidade, São Carlos
AP05)	H422	1300	1/0.25	R. Mazagão, Mazagão
BA33)	H454	1310	1/0.25	R. Bahiana, Ilhéus: 0800-0300 (SS 0900-0100)
BA63)	H501	1310	5/0.25	R. Jaraguar, Jacobina: 0700-0200, (Sat 0800-0000 Sun: 24h)
CE30)	H602	1310	1	R. Progresso de Juazeiro, Juazeiro do Nte: 0800-2400, Sat 0900-0100 Sun 0830-2300
CE63)	H656	1310	1/0.25	R. Liberdade, Boa Viagem
MG144)	L359	1310	1/0.25	R. Montanheza, Vazante
MG168)	L351	1310	10/0.25	R. Difusora, Salinas
MS31)	I426	1310	5/1	R. Pindorama, Sidrolândia
PB23)	I691	1310	10/0.5	R. Cidade Esperança, Esperança
PR70)	J274	1310	10/0.5	R. Atalaia, Maringá
RJ28)	J504	1310	1/0.25	R. Coroados, São Fidélis
RO17)	J684	1310	10/5	R. Tropical, Porto Velho
RS107)	K305	1310	10/1	R. Sarandi, Sarandi: 0900-0100
RS124)	K329	1310	5/0.45	R. Integração, Restinga Seca
RS160)	K371	1310	5/0.5	R. Horizonte, Capão da Canoa. 0900-0300 (Sun 0100-0300)
SC85)	J801	1310	10/0.5	R. Sintonia, Ituporanga
SP141)	K566	1310	10/0.25	R. Bragança, Bragança Paulista
SP139)	K596	1310	2/1	R. Difusora, Itápolis
AL08)	H243	1320	10/0.25	R. Imaculada Conceicao, Maceió
BA69)	H503	1320	5/0.5	R. Regional, Cícero Dantas
CE31)	H597	1320	1	R. Regional, Sobral: 0700-0100 (Sat: 0800-2100 Sun: 0900-2100)
CE70)	H672	1320	1/0.5	R. Moriá, Aracati: 24h
MG136)	L322	1320	1/0.25	R. Mucuri, Teófilo Otoni
PE31)	I823	1320	1/0.25	R. Cultura, São José do Egito
PR72)	J255	1320	12/0.5	R. Tropical, Curitiba: 24h
PR145)	J351	1320	5/0.5	CBN, Foz do Iguaçu: 24h
RJ29)	J475	1320	25/5	R. Boas Novas, Petropólis: 24h
RS108)	K223	1320	1/0.25	R. Clube, Canela
RS109)	K266	1320	3/0.25	R. Sulbrasileira, Panambi
RS110)	K271	1320	5/1	R. Cultura, Pelotas
SC68)	J762	1320	1/0.25	R. Litoral, Imaruí
SC104)		1320	5/0.45	R. Vitória, Videira
SP140)	K630	1320	1/0.25	R. Difusora, Pirassununga
SP241)	K675	1320	1/0.25	R. Clube, Tupã
BA34)	H468	1330	5/1	R. Continental, Serrinha
MS54)	N610	1330	1/0,25	R. Pantanal, Coxim
PR74)	J264	‡1330	10/0.5	R. Jaguariaíva, Senges
RN27)	J621	1330	10/0.5	R. Eldorado, Natal
RS111)	K236	1330	1/0.25	R. Upacaraí, Dom Pedrito: 0900-0300
RS112)	K323	1330	1/0.5	R. Diplomata, São Marcos: 0800-0200 (Sun 0800-0100)
SC50)	J739	1330	5/0.5	R. Clube, Blumenau: 0800(Sun 0900)-0100
SC51)	J749	1330	5/1	R. Chapecó, Chapecó
SP142)	K638	1330	30/0.25	R. Paulista, Regente Feijó
SP143)	K641	1330	5/1	R. Cultura, Ribeirão Preto
SP187)	K736	1330	50/10	R. Terra, Osasco: 24h
CE71)	H661	1340	2.5/0.25	R. Pitaguary, Maracanaú: 0800-0300
MA11)	H886	1340	10/2	R. Cl. de São Luís, São Luís
MG81)	L241	1340	10/5	R. Cultura, Itabirito
MG139)	L352	1340	1/0.5	R. Globo, Passos: 24h
MS12)	I380	1340	3/0.25	R. Dif. 1340, Aquidauana
PB13)	I671	1340	5/1	R. Correio, João Pessoa
PR76)	J205	1340	2.5/0.25	R. Difusora, Rio Negro
PR77)	J249	1340	5/0.25	R. Cultura, Arapongas
PR41)	J368	1340	5/0.25	CBN, Cascavel
RJ40)	J490	1340	5/0.5	R. Tupi, Rio Bonito
RS113)	K227	1340	25/4	R. Educadora - CBN,Porto Alegre
RS173)	K377	1340	10/4	R. Journal da Manhã, Ijui
SP144)	K543	1340	5/1	R. Cultura, Araçatuba
SP203)	K571	1340	5/0.25	R. Em. Campos do Jordão, Campos do Jordão (fpl. 1560)
SP146)	K738	1340	1/0.25	R. Nova Canoa Grande, Igaraçu do Tietê
AC05)	H201	1350	50/5	R. Capital (RBV), Rio Branco
BA70)	H520	1350	50/10	Super R. Cristal, Salvador
CE56)	H662	1350	5/0.5	R. Liberal Jagoaribana, Morada Nova: 0800-2300 (SS 0830-2200)
MG82)	L214	1350	10/5	R. Cultura, Poços de Caldas
PB14)	I675	1350	5/0.5	R. Clube AM 1350, Campina Grande
RS114)	K205	1350	2.5/0.25	R. Aurora, Guaporé: 0100(SS 0900)-0100
RS115)	K313	1350	5/1	R. Difusora, Três Passos
RS116)	K336	1350	1/0.25	R. Agudo, Agudo: 0900-0200
SC53)	J760	1350	1/0.25	R. Clube Bandeirantes, Itajaí
SP265)	K692	1350	10/0,25	R. Excelsior, Ibiúna
BA35)	H469	1360	10/1	R. Cultura, Paulo Afonso
CE57)	H650	1360	5/0.25	R. Iracema, Ipu: 0900-0200, (Sat -2100, Sun -1300)

MW	Call	kHz	kW	Station, location
MS61)	I383	1360	2	R. Difusora, Corumbá
PR165)	J265	1360	10/0.25	R. Cidade, Pato Branco: 0800-0300
PR78)	J268	1360	1/0.25	R. Lider, Assaí
RJ30)	J464	1360	50/10	R. Bandeirantes, Rio de Janeiro
RN11)	J605	1360	1/0.5	R. Ouro Branco, Currais Novos
RS117)	K261	1360	5/0.5	R. Alvorada, Marau:24h
RS151)	K281	1360	3/0.25	R. Navegantes, Porto Lucena
SC69)	J757	1360	25/0.4	R. Belos Vales, Ibirama
SP147)	K581	1360	5/1	R. Aguas Quentes, Fernandópolis: 24h
SP148)	K739	1360	5/0.25	R. Regional, Dracena: 24h
SP235)	K759	1360	1/0.25	R. Luzes da Ribalta, Santa Bárbara d'Oeste
BA82)	H555	1370	0.25	R.Jornal Grande, Monte Santo: 0800-0300
CE81)	H628	1370	1/0.25	R. Vanguarda, Caridade
PE34)	I800	1370	1/0.25	R. Vale do Capibaribe, Sta. Cruz do Capibaribe
PI13)	I892	1370	10/1	R. Difusora, Teresina
PR80)	J267	1370	50/7	R. Canção Nova, Curitiba: 1000-0200
RN28)	J618	1370	2.5/0.25	R. Difusora,São Miguel
RS173)	K374	1370	2/0.25	R. Jornal da Manhã, Ijuí: 24h
RS118)	K243	1370	25/0.5	R. Mãe de Deus, Flores da Cunha: 0800-0300, (SS 24h)
RS119)	K334	1370	1/0.25	R. Gazeta, Alegrete: 24h
SC55)	J782	1370	10/0.5	R. Peperí AM, São Miguel do Oeste
SE09)	J929	1370	5/0.5	R. Capital do Agreste, Itabaiana: 0700-0300
SP223)	K766	1370	100/20	R. Iguatemi, São Paulo
AM12)	H283	1380	5/1	R. Alvorada, Parintins: 0900-0200
BA83)	H495	‡1380	5/0.25	R. União, Gandu
ES21)	I...	1380	10/1	R. Itaí de Rio Claro, Iúna
MG172)	L218	1380	5/0.25	R. Cidade, Brasópolis
MG120)	L284	1380	5/0.25	R. Paranaíba, Rio Paranaíba: 0900-0100
MG130)	L323	1380	1/0.25	R. Gorutubana, Janaúba
PA11)	I547	1380	1/0.25	R. Marajó, Breves
PE23)	I773	1380	10/5	R. Continental – Novas de Paz, Recife
PR122)	J276	1380	2/0.25	R. Bom Jesus, Siqueira Campos: 0730-0200
PR152)	J367	1380	1/0.25	R. Integração, Toledo
RS120)	K293	1380	1/0.25	R. Cultura, Santana do Livramento
RS134)	K311	1380	1/0.25	R. Maristela, Torres: 24h
RS121)	K350	1380	6/0.25	R. Cultura, Tapera
RS165)	K372	1380	6/0.25	R. Chiru, Palmitinho: 24h, Sat 0800-2100(Sun -1600)
SC56)	J821	1380	6/0.25	R. Cidade, Itaiópolis
SC93)	J827	1380	6/0.25	R. Barriga Verde, Capinzal
SC105)	J831	1380	1/0.25	R. Freguencia, Garopaba
SP152)	K616	1380	1/0.5	R. Difusora, Mogi Guaçu
SP247)	K623	1380	1/0.25	R. Cultura, Pederneiras
SP224)	K751	1380	5/0.25	R. Globo, Presidente Prudente
SP234)	K772	1380	1/0.25	R. República, Morro Agudo
ES13)	I209	1390	5/0.25	R. Educadora, Afonso Cláudio: 0700-0100
MG157)	L358	1390	2.5/0.25	R. Ouro Verde, São Sebastião do Paraíso
MG178)	L305	1390	10/0.5	R.Vitoriosa, Uberlândia
PA12)	I535	1390	10/1	R. Educadora, Bragança: 0830-0300, (Sun 1400-0200)
PE24)	I788	1390	5/1	R. Jornal, Pesqueira
PR82)	J242	1390	10/1	R. Cultura, Maringá
PR83)	J335	1390	1/0.25	R. Independência, Salto do Lontra
RJ32)	J473	1390	5/0.5	R. Sul Fluminense, Barra Mansa
RN32)	J599	1390	5/0.25	R. Farol, Touros
RO18)	J687	1390	5/1	R. Planalto, Ji-Paraná: 0800-0300, (Sat 0800-2100, Sun: Silent)
RR02)	O701	1390	10/5	R. Roraima, Caracaraí
RS122)	K209	1390	10	R. Esperança, Porto Alegre: 24h
RS166)	K368	1390	8/0.25	R. Atlântica, Constantina: 0900-0200 (Sun: -0000)
SC57)	J769	1390	7.5/0.65	R. CBN, Lages
SP153)	K570	1390	5/0.25	R. Globo, Campinas: 24h
SP154)	K636	1390	1/0.25	R. Cultura, Promissão
SP2859	K594	1390		R.Anchieta, Itanhaém
AC06)	H200	1400	10/1	R. Dif. Acreana, Rio Branco: 0900-0400
BA71)	H529	1400	1/0.25	R. Vasa-Barris, Jeremoabo
PB15)	I677	1400	5/1	R. Espinharas, Patos
PI27)	I926	1400	1/0.25	R. Cantagalo, Jaicós
PR84)	J256	1400	1/0.25	R. Globo, Londrina
PR87)	J299	1400	1/0.25	R. Fronteira d'Oeste, Terra Roxa
PR119)	J339	1400	10/1	R. Ágape, Balsa Nova
PR148)	J346	1400	2/0.45	R. Jornal São Miguel, São Miguel do Iguaçu: 0800-0200
RJ33)	J462	1400	50/5	R. Rio de Janeiro "R. Rio AM", Rio de Janeiro
RS192)	K376	1400	1/0,4	R. Educadora, São João da Urtiga: 0800-0130
SC58)	J775	1400	5/0.35	R. Entre Rios, Palmitos: 0800-0200, (Sun 0900-2300)
SP155)	K527	1400	1/0.25	R. Difusora, Lucélia
SP156)	K658	1400	5/0.25	R. Clube, São Carlos
SP157)	K682	1400	5/0.25	R. Metrópole AM, São José do Rio

MW	Call	kHz	kW	Station, location
				Preto: 0900-2300
TO08)	N660	1400	5/1	Radiodifusão Guaraí, Guaraí
BA37)	H467	1410	10/0.5	R. Planeta, São Gonçalo dos Campos: 0800-2000(SS -0000)
CE25)	H639	1410	10/1	R. Boa Nova, Pacajus
GO19)	H803	1410	30/0.85	R. Bandeirantes, Santo Antônio do Descoberto
MS14)	I382	1410	5/1	Nova R. Clube, Corumbá: 0700-2200, (Sat 0700-0100)
RJ34)	J486	1410	10/0.5	R. Itaperuna, Itaperuna: 24h
RN21)	J614	1410	1/0.5	R. Santa Cruz, Santa Cruz: 0800-0200 (Sun 0900-0100)
RS137)	K246	1410	5/1	R. Garibaldi, Garibaldi: 24h
RS125)	K284	1410	1/0.25	R. Minuano, Rio Grande: 24h
RS126)	K294	1410	5	R. Santa Rosa, Santa Rosa
SC100)	J799	1410	2/0.5	R. Nambâ, Ponte Serrada
SP158)	K691	1410	50/25	R. América, São Paulo: 24h
SP264)	K683	1410	2.5/0.5	R. Excelsior, Rio Claro
BA60)	H504	1420	1/0.25	R. Cidade, Irecê: 24h
MG88)	L286	1420	1/0.25	R. Difusora, São João Nepomuceno
MG89)	L288	1420	5/1	R. Cultura, Sete Lagoas
MG90)	L313	1420	1/0.25	R. Montanhês Botelhos, Botelhos
MS16)	I397	1420	1/0.25	R. Difusora Cacique, Nova Andradina
PR88)	J269	1420	5/0.25	R. Cult, Umuarama: 0900(Sun:1000)-2105
PR89)	J282	1420	1/0,25	R. Educadora, Jacarezinho
RN12)	J609	1420	1/0.25	R. Farol, Alcxandria (RPC)
RS149)	K258	1420	10/0.25	R. 14 de Julho, Júlio de Castilhos
RS171)	K308	1420	0.5	R. Tapense, Tapes
SC60)	J744	1420	6/0.5	R. Cultura, Campos Novos: 0855-0100
SC59)	J754	1420	5/2.5	R. Guarujá, Florianópolis
SP159)	K597	1420	1/0.5	C.R.N., Itatiba: 24h
SP163)	K733	1420	1/0.25	R. Nova São Manuel, São Manuel
MG91)	L239	1430	1/0.25	R. Clube, Guaxupé
MG158)	L371	1430	1/0.25	R. Planalto, Perdizes
PE32)	I826	1430	5/0.25	R. Independência, Goiana
PR134)	J200	1430	50/10	R. B2, Curitiba: 24h
RN13)	J604	1430	10/0.5	R. Libertadora Mossoroense, Mossoró
RO11)	J671	1430	10	R. Caiari, Porto Velho: 24h
RS167)	K366	1430	1/0.25	R. Guarita, Coronel Bicaco: 0900-2310 (Sun 0900-0100)
RS198)	K379	1430	1	R. AM 1430, Portão
SP164)	K666	1430	1/0.25	R. Serra Negra, Serra Negra
SP275)	K707	1430	25/0.25	R. Imaculada Conceição, São Roque
AM13)	H285	1440	10	R. Baré, Manaus: 24h
BA38)	H466	1440	50/1	R. Independência, Santo Amaro
CE33)	H603	1440	10/1	R. Araripe, Crato
MG159)	L365	1440	1/0.25	R. Som 2000, Santa Vitória: 24h
MS41)	I407	1440	1/0.25	R. Bela Vista, Bela Vista
RJ35)	J469	1440	20/5	R. Livre, Rio de Janeiro: 24h
RS168)	K221	1440	1/0.5	R. Ceres, Naõ Me Toque
RS130)	K328	1440	5/0.3	R. Excelsior, Gramado
RS153)	K362	1440	2.5/0.25	R. Caibaté, Caibaté: 0830-0200
SC61)	J792	1440	2.5/0.25	R. Difusora, Maravilha: 24h
SC82)	J797	1440	10/0,35	R. Educadora, Taió
SE11)	J930	1440	5/0.25	R. Educadora, Freí Paulo: 0700-0300
SP253)	K568	1440	1/0.25	R. Eldorado Centro Norte Paulista, Cajuru
SP165)	K634	1440	5/0.25	R. Comercial, Presidente Prudente: 24h
SP218)	K752	1440	1/0.25	R. Azul Celeste, Americana
SP284)		1440	2.5/0.5	R.Clarim de Palmas, Itaí
BA73)	H531	1450	1/0.25	R. Ipirá, Ipirá
CE34)	H601	1450	1/0.25	R. Difusora Cristal, Quixeramobim
CE35)	H623	1450	1/0.25	R. Pinto Martins, Camocim
CE99)		1450		R. Carinhosa, Acopiara: 0800-0200
ES12)	I208	1450	1/0.5	R. Sim (R.Gaeta), Guaraparí
MA32)	H900	1450	1/0.25	R. Boa Esperança, São João dos Patos
MA13)	H901	1450	1/0.25	R. Cultura, Pedreiras
MG94)	L312	1450	10/0.25	R. Diamante, Coromandel
MS13)	I417	1450	1/0.25	R. Difusora, Rio Brilhante: 0800-0100
PA33)	I559	1450	1/0.25	R. Juruá, São Felix do Xingu
PB29)	I699	1450	1/0.25	R. Certao, Patos: 0800-0100
PE25)	I794	1450	1/0.25	R. Cultura, Palmares: 24h
PI21)	I908	1450	1/0.25	R. Cultura do Gurguéia, Bom Jesus
PI35)	I917	1450	1/0.25	R. Confederação Valenciana "R. Valenciana", Valença do Piauí
PR93)	J279	1450	1/0.25	R. Cabiúna, Bandeirantes
PR95)	J317	1450	1/0.25	R. Rainha de Altônia, Altônia
PR162)	J364	1450	1/0.25	R. Clube, Mallet
PR179)	J302	1450	1/0.25	R. Dif. Ubiratanense, Ubiratã
RJ36)	J480	1450	1/0.25	R. Comércio, Barra Mansa
RJ37)	J503	1450	1/0.25	R. Feliz, Santo Antônio de Pádua: 0800-0100, Sun 1030-0030
RO12)	J674	1450	1/0.25	R. Vilhena, Vilhena
RR03)	O701	1450	1/0.25	R. Transamérca Hits, Alto Alegre
RS132)	K346	1450	5/0.6	R. Cassino, Rio Grande
RS177)	K338	1450	1/0.25	R. Cultura, Arvorezinha

MW	Call	kHz	kW	Station, location
SC62)	J802	1450	1/0.25	R. São Bento, São Bento do Sul: 0800-0200
SC63)	J822	1450	10/0.25	R. Hulha Negra, Criciúma
SC97)	J828	1450	5/0.25	R. Belos Montes, Seara
SE12)	J932	1450	10/0.5	R. Abais, Estância
SP238)	K526	1450	2.5/0.25	R. Cultura, Ituverava: 24h
SP166)	K587	1450	1/0.25	R. Difusora, Guararapes: 0900-2400
SP167)	K591	1450	50/5	R. Boa Nova, Guarulhos
SP168)	K657	1450	1/0.25	R. São Carlos, São Carlos
AL13)	H253	1460	10/0.25	R. Canaviero, União dos Palmares
AM17)	H300	1460	5	R. Clube, Parintins: 0830-0200
BA39)	H472	1460	1	R. Povo, Jequié
BA85)	H523	1460	1/0.25	R. Ferro Doido, Morro do Chapéu
BA74)	H536	1460	1/0.25	R. Alvorada, Cruz das Almas
CE53)	H595	1460	1/0.25	R. Ressurreição, Sobral: 0845-2200
CE36)	H616	1460	1/0.25	R. Uirapuru, Morada Nova
GO34)	H766	1460	1/0.25	R. Morrinhos, Morrinhos
MA33)	H917	1460	1/0.25	R. Vanguarda, Santa Luzia
MG95)	L201	1460	1/0.25	R. Cultura do Porto Novoa, Além Paraíba: 0800-0300
MG161)	L356	1460	5/0.25	R. Buritis, Buritis
MG131)	L363	1460	1/0.25	R. Entre Rios, Raul Soares
MS56)	I....	1460	1/0.25	R. Globo, Costa Rica: 0700-0100(Sun -0400)
PI14)	I903	1460	1/0.25	R. Cultura, Amarante
PI28)	I924	1460	1/0.25	R. Cruzeiro, Pedro II: 0800-2300, (Sun 0900-2100)
PR96)	J204	1460	2/0.25	R. Difusora, Paranaguá
PR97)	J228	1460	1/0.25	R. Central do Paraná, Ponta Grossa
PR98)	J251	1460	1/0.25	R. Cultura, Apucarana
PR100)	J297	1460	1/0.25	R. Guaíra, Guaíra
PR101)	J308	1460	5/0.25	R. Ampere, Ampere
PR102)	J318	1460	1/0.25	R. Guadalupe AM, Loanda: 24h
RN20)	J615	1460	10/0,25	R. Agreste, Santo Antônio
RS133)	K214	1460	1/0.25	R. Cultura, Bagé: 0830(Sun 1000)-0200
RS135)	K312	1460	1/0.25	R. Colonial, Três de Maio: 0800-0300
RS175)	K373	1460	1/0.25	R. Campinas, Campinas do Sul
RS176)	K378	1460	1/0.25	R. Mostardas, Mostardas: 24h
RS199)	K......	1460	1	R. Litoral, Imbé: 24h
SC64)	J756	1460	1/0,25	R. Sentinela do Vale, Gaspar
SP242)	K548	1460	5/0.5	R. Clube Ararense, Araras
SP170)	K608	1460	1/0.25	R. Cultura, Lorena: 24h
TO02)	H774	1460	1/0.25	R. Independência do Tocantins, Paraíso do Tocantins
BA86)	H509	1470	0.25	R. Morro Verde, Mairi
CE64)	H665	1470	1/0.25	R. Guanancés de Itapajé, Itapajé: 0800-0100
ES17)	I214	1470	1/0.25	R. Globo, Barra de São Francisco
GO36)	H773	1470	10/0.25	R. Dif. Serra dos Cristais, Cristalina
GO37)	H779	1470	1/0.25	R. Cidade, Goiás
MA34)	H908	1470	1/0.25	R. Paranoá, Presidente Dutra
MA39)	H901	1470	1/0.25	R. Urbano Santos,Urbano Santos
MG96)	L247	1470	1/0.25	R. Dif., Ituiutaba: 0800-0300(Sun -0100
MS29)	I413	1470	1/0.25	R. Alvorada, Dourados
PA25)	I548	1470	5/1.5	R. Moreno Braga, Vigia
PA56)		1470	1	R.Paranaense, Castanhal
PE35)	I822	1470	1/0.25	R. Educadora de Belém, Belém de São Francisco: 24h
PE37)	I827	1470	1/0,25	R. Papacaça, Bom Conselho: 0730-0300, (Sun 0800-0100)
PI15)	I900	‡1470	1/0.25	R. Difusora Vale do Uruçuí, Uruçuí
PI24)	I913	1470	1/0.25	R. Ingazeira, Paulistana
PI33)	I928	1470	1/0.25	R. Cidade, Castelo do Piauí
PR103)	J294	1470	1/0.25	R. Educadora, Ibaiti: 24h
PR104)	J304	1470	5/0.25	R. Jornal, Assis Chateaubriand
PR172)	J...	1470	1/0.25	R. Panorama, Itapejara d'Oeste: 0800-0300(Sat -0100) Sun 1130-0300
PR173)	J...	1470	3/0.25	R. Tradição, Rio Branco do Sul
RJ08)	J476	1470	1/0.25	R. Absoluta, Campos dos Goitacazes
RJ38)	J481	1470	1/0.25	R. Barra do Pirai, Barra do Pirai
RN23)	J616	1470	1/0.25	R. Rural de Parelhas, Parelhas: 0800-0100 (SS 0900-0100)
RO05)	J676	1470	1/0.25	R. Rondônia, Cacoal
RS169)	K219	1470	1/0.25	R. Cultura, Cacequi
SC65)	J781	1470	10/1	R. Record, São José
SC66)	J798	1470	1/0.25	R. Líder, Herval d'Oeste
SP172)	K586	1470	1/0.25	R. Cultura, Guaíra
SP173)	K599	1470	1/0.25	R. Mensagem, Jacareí
SP174)	K632	1470	1/0.25	R. Primavera, Porto Ferreira
SP175)	K712	1470	1/0.25	R. Jornal, Indaiatuba: 24h
SP243)	K771	1470	1/0.25	R. Bastos AM, Bastos
BA61)	H508	1480	5/1	R. Alvorada, Guanambi
BA75)	H524	1480	1/0.25	R. Santana, Santana
CE74)	H671	1480	1/0.25	R. Princesa do Norte, Morrinhos
MA14)	H897	1480	1/0.25	R. Itapecuru, Colinas
MG98)	L235	1480	1/0.25	R. Nova Frutal AM, Frutal
MG99)	L265	1480	5/0.25	R. Difusora, Nanuque
MG100)	L307	1480	2.5/0.25	R. Emboabas, Tiradentes: 0900-2200 (Sun -1530)
MS17)	I393	1480	1/0.25	R. Caçula, Três Lagoas
PE26)	I790	1480	1/0.25	R. A Voz do Sertão, Serra Talhada: 0800-2300
PE36)	I825	1480	5/0.25	R. Canção Nova, Gravatá
PI29)	I929	1480	1/0.25	R. Vale do Coroatá, Elesbão Veloso
PR79)	J302	1480	5/0.25	R. Cultura, Iporá
PR153)	J221	1480	1/0.25	R. Brotas, Piraí do Sul
PR106)	J230	1480	1/0.25	R. Astorga, Astorga
PR107)	J270	1480	1/0.25	R. Educadora, União da Vitória: 0900-0200
PR174)	J370	1480	1/0.25	R. Pérola, Pérola d'Oeste
RJ55)	J485	1480	10/0.5	R. Popular, Duque de Caxias
RN14)	J601	1480	1/0.25	R. Princesa do Vale, Açu
RO15)	J681	1480	1/0.25	R. Rondônia, Pimenta Bueno
RS100)	K244	1480	2.5/0.25	R. São Roque, Faxinal do Soturno
RS127)	K321	1480	5/0.25	R. Veranense, Veranópolis: 24h
RS178)	K255	1480	0.5/0.25	R. Guaramano, Guarani das Missões: 0900-0200(Sun -0100)
SC67)	J731	1480	1/0.25	R. Arca da Aliança, Joinville
SC94)	J826	1480	1/0.25	R. Caibi, Caibi
SE10)	J928	1480	1/0.25	R. Nova Cidade, Simão Dias: 24h
SP176)	K539	1480	1/0.25	R. Clube, Altinópolis
SP177)	K551	1480	1/0.25	R. Atibaia, Atibaia
SP255)	K767	1480	0.5/0.25	R. Nova America, Boituva: 0800-0000, (Sat 0800-0200, Sun 0830-1800)
TO06)	H795	1480	1/0.25	R. Cultura, Miracema do Tocantins
AL09)	H246	1490	5/1	Em. Rio São Francisco, Penedo
BA41)	H478	1490	1/0.25	R. Educadora, Ipiaú: 0800-0300, (SS 0900-2100)
BA77)	H507	1490	1/0.25	R. Rio São Francisco, Bom Jesus da Lapa
BA87)	H512	1490	0.25	R. Planalto d'Oeste, Correntina
MG162)	L231	1490	0.25	R. Onda Viva, Araguari: 0900-2400(Sat -2000)
MG163)	L274	1490	1/0.25	R. Paraisópolis, Paraisópolis
MG165)	L353	1490	1/0.25	R. Pirapetinga, Pirapetinga
MS19)	I404	1490	1/0.25	R. Nova Paiaguás, Glória de Dourados
MT53)		1490	1/0,25	R. Vila, Vila Rica
PI40)	I918	1490	1/0.25	R. Lagoa, Buriti dos Lopes
PR108)	J210	1490	1/0.25	R. Cornélio, Cornélio Procópio
PR149)	J347	1490	1/0.25	R. Dif., São Jorge do Oeste: 0900-0100
RS138)	K208	1490	25/0.25	R. Assisense, São Francisco de Assis
RS140)	K309	1490	1/0.25	R. Taquara, Taquara: 0830-0200
SC70)	J791	1490	2.5/0.25	R. Cultura, Xaxim
SP180)	K530	1490	1/0.25	R. Difusora, Olímpia
SP181)	K580	1490	1/0.25	R. Globo, Dracena: 24h
SP182)	K583	1490	1/0.25	R. Educadora Santa Rita, Fernandópolis
SP244)	K680	1490	1/0.25	R. Cult., Vargem Grande do Sul: 0900-0100
SP183)	K764	1490	25/0.5	R. Imaculada Conceição, Mauá
BA49)	H487	1500	5/0.5	R. Jacuípe, Riachão do Jacuípe: 0800-2000
CE39)	H615	1500	2.5/0.25	R. Macico, Baturité
MG101)	L215	1500	5/0.25	R. Montanhesa, Viçosa
MG140)	L340	1500	1/0.25	R. Aparecida do Sul, Ilicínea: 0900-2200
PA19)	I542	1500	1/0.25	R. Floresta, Tucuruí
PE27)	I779	1500	1/0.25	R. Pajeu, Afogados da Ingazeira: 0800-0200
PI46)	I919	1500	1/0.25	R. Voz do Longa, Esperantina
PR163)	J366	1500	2.5/0.25	R. Aracauria, Margueirinha
RS139)	K225	1500	1/0.25	R. Liberdade, Canguçu: 0900-0100
RS161)	K365	1500	3/0.25	R. Simpatia, Chapada: 0900-0100
SC06)	J......	1500	1	R.Catolica, Balneário Camboriú
SP184)	K549	1500	2.5/0.25	R. Fraternidade, Araras
SP185)	K626	1500	1/0.25	R. Difusora, Pindamonhangaba
SP186)	K706	1500	1/0.25	R. Vale do Rio Grande, Miguelópolis
SP211)	K773	1500	1/0.25	R. Cumbica, Guarulhos
SP236)	K776	1500	1/0.25	R. Cidade, Apiaí
BA52)	H493	1510	5/0.5	R. Dif. do Descobrimento, Porto Seguro
CE40)	H608	1510	1/0.25	R. Nova Plan, São Benedito
CE84)	H630	1510	0.25	R. Trapiá, Pedra Branca: 0800-0100, (SS 0900-2100)
GO38)	H770	1510	1/0.25	R. Goiatuba, Goiatuba
PA01)	I544	1510	10/0.25	R. Oriente de Redenção, Redenção
PI16)	I894	1510	1/0.25	R. Difusora, Floriano
PI17)	I896	‡1510	1/0.25	R. Progresso, Corrente
PI49)	I...	1510	1/0.25	R. Nordeste, Picos
PR113)	J216	1510	1/0.25	R. Educadora, Venceslau Bráz
PR115)	J326	1510	1/0.25	R. União, Céu Azul
RJ43)	J492	1510	1/0.25	R. Teresópolis, Teresópolis: 0900-0100 (Sat 0900-0100, Sun 0900-2400)
RN15)	J602	1510	1/0.25	R. Centenário, Caraúbas (RPC)
SC73)	J795	1510	1/0.25	R. Centro Oeste, Pinhalzinho: 0800-2300
SP188)	K654	1510	10/1	R. Cacique, Santos
SP189)	K665	1510	1/0.25	R. Clube Regional, São Manuel: 0700-2200
SP256)	K770	1510	0.5/0.25	R. Vale do Tietê, Salto
SP230)	K...	1510	1/0.25	R. Rural, Rinópolis
SP269)	K...	1510	1/0.25	R. Athenas Paulista, Jaboticabal: 0800-0300
BA78)	H530	1520	5/1	R. Povo, Poções

MW	Call	kHz	kW	Station, location
CE75)	H635	1520	1/0.25	R. Regional, Ipu: 0800-0300
CE83)	H653	1520	1/0.25	R. Cachoeira, Solonópole
GO53)	H806	1520	1/0.25	R. Nova RCB, Campos Belos: 0800-0300 (Sat 1000-1900, Sun 1500-1700)
MA15)	H899	1520	1/0.25	R. Mirante, Pindaré-Mirim
MA35)	H928	1520	1/0.25	R. Mirante AM, Chapadinha
MG174)	L223	1520	0.25	R. Cultura, Cássia
MG106)	L245	1520	2.5/0.25	R. Clube, Itaúna
MS21)	I405	1520	1/0.25	R.Globo, Amambaí: 24h
MS42)	N605	1520	1/0.25	R. Campo Alegre, Rio Verde de Mato Grosso
PE28)	I801	1520	1/0.25	R. Surubim, Surubim
PR116)	J218	1520	2.5/0.25	R. Serra do Mar, Antonina: 0900-2100, (Sat 0900-0100 Sun 0900-2300)
PR118)	J292	1520	1/0.25	R. Nova Cultura, Cândido
PR132)	J340	1520	1/0.25	R. Internacional, Quedas do Iguaçu
PR156)	J358	1520	1/0.25	R. Guairacá, Terra Rica
RJ44)	J491	1520	10/0.5	R. Continental, Rio de Janeiro: 24h
RJ10)	J499	1520	1/0.25	R. Musical, Cantagalo
RN22)	J610	1520	1/0.25	R. Salinas, Macau
RS141)	K217	1520	1/0.25	R. Vale do Jacui, Cachoeira do Sul
SC76)	J806	1520	2.5/0.25	R. Cultura, Timbó: 0800-0200
SE13)	J931	1520	1/0.25	R. Ilha AM, Tobias Barreto
SP191)	K614	1520	10/1	R. Iguatemi, Mogi das Cruzes
SP192)	KG27	1520	1/0.25	Pinhal R. Clube, Espírito Sto. do Pinhal
SP275)	K760	1520	1/0.25	R. Manchester, Sorocaba
SP270)	K...	1520	1/0.25	R. Torre Forte, Buritama (Rede Amiga)
TO07)	H797	1520	1/0.25	R. Cristal, Cristalândia
BA43)	H479	1530	10/0.5	R. Cultura, Guanambi
CE76)	H666	1530	1/0.25	R. Tres Fronteiras, Campos Sales: 0800-0000
MG175)	L262	1530	0.25	R. Progresso, Monte Santo de Minas
MG110)	L280	1530	1/0.25	R. Clube, Pouso Alegre
MT42)	I432	1530	1/0.25	R. Atual, Peixoto de Azevedo
PE29)	I781	1530	1/0.25	R. Bitury, Belo Jardim
PR157)	J348	1530	1/0.25	R. Vale do Iguaçu, Verê
RJ57)	J482	1530	1/0.25	R. Búzios, Cabo Frio
RJ45)	J502	1530	1/0.25	R. Princesinha do Norte, Miracema: 0800-0100
RN16)	J603	1530	1/0.25	R. Curimataú, Nova Cruz
RO16)	J685	1530	5/1	R. Planalto, Vilhena: 0900-0330
RS143)	K235	1530	1/0.25	R. Sulina, Dom Pedrito: 0830-0300, (SS 0900-2400)
RS144)	K300	1530	5/0.25	R. Progresso, São Leopoldo: 1000-0000
RS145)	K304	1530	1/0.25	R. Tapejara, Tapejara: 24h
SC77)	J761	1530	1/0.25	R. Dif., Itajaí: 0800-0300, Sun:1000-0000
SC78)	J780	1530	2.5/0.25	R. Difusora, São Joaquim: 0900-0200
SC79)	J796	1530	1/0.25	R. Porto Feliz, Mondaí
SP193)	K677	1530	1/0.25	R. Difusora Digital, Tupi Paulista
SP194)	K699	1530	1/0.25	R. Noticias, Tatuí
SP231)	K755	1530	1/0.25	R. Universal, Teodoro Sampaio
BA89)	H...	1540	0.25	R. Sociedade, Itiruçu
CE42)	H611	1540	1/0.5	R. Sant'Ana, Tianguá
CE77)	H631	1540	1/0.25	R. Sertões, Mombaça
CE78)	H629	1540	1/0.25	R. Aratanha, Pacatuba
ES19)	I206	1540	0.25	R. Agricultura, Santa Teresa
MA36)	H921	1540	1/0.25	R. Santa Maura, Lago da Pedra
MG111)	L217	1540	1/0.25	R. Bomdespachense, Bom Despacho
MG112)	L226	1540	1/0.25	R. Globo, Conselheiro Lafaiete
MG113)	L293	1540	1/0.25	R. Tropical, Três Corações: 24h
MS35)	N601	1540	1/0.5	R. Nova Piravevê, Ivinhema
PA14)	I545	1540	1/0.25	R. Boa Vista, São Sebastião da Boa Vista
PB24)	I694	1540	1/0.5	R. Santa Maria, Monteiro
PE33)	I824	1540	1/0.25	R. Voluntários da Pátria, Ouricuri
PR168)	J306	1540	0.25	R. Litorânea, Guaratuba
RJ54)	J508	1540	1/0.25	R. Clube, Paraíba do Sul: 0900-0300
RN30)	J611	1540	1/0.25	R. Baixa Verde, João Câmara
RS157)	K282	1540	1/0.25	R. Quaraí, Quaraí
SC80)	J803	1540	5/0.25	R. Capinzal, Capinzal
SP245)	K514	1540	1/0.25	R. Cultura, Leme
SP196)	K564	1540	2/0.5	R. Em. Botucatu, Botucatu
SP197)	K723	1540	50/1	R. Nova Difusora, Osasco
SP246)	K737	1540	0.5/0.25	R. Central, Pompéia
BA80)	H518	1550	5/0.25	R. Independencia do São Francisco, Juazeiro
MA37)	H926	1550	1/0.25	Sistema Janaina de Radiodifusão, Vargem Grande
MG114)	L211	1550	1/0.25	R. Cultura, Monte Carmelo
MG169)	L222	1550	1/0.25	R. Difusora, Carmo do Rio Claro
MG115)	L289	1550	1/0.25	R. Difusora Santarritense, Santa Rita do Sapucaí: 24h
MG195)	N211	1550		R. Cidade, Guanhães: 24h
PA34)	I550	1550	1/0.25	R. Cabano, Maracanã
PB32)	I700	1550	10/0.25	R. Jardim, Areia: 0800-0200
PR133)	J213	1550	1/0.25	R. Ipiranga, Palmeira: 24h
PR123)	J303	1550	1/0.25	R. Pioneira, Formosa do Oeste: 0800-2300 (SS 0900-2200)
PR124)	J315	1550	1/0.25	R. Cristal, Marmeleiro
PR169)	J217	1550	1/0.25	R. Itay, Tibagi
PR185)	J371	1550	1	R. Norte Sul, Jacarezinho
RJ46)	J479	1550	1/0.25	R. Imperial, Petrópolis
RN19)	J606	1550	1/0.25	R. Ivipanin, Areia Branca (RPC)
RO23)	J...	1550	0.25	R. Suprema, Cacoal: 24h
RS162)	K377	1550	1/0.25	R. Opinião Gospel, Capão do Leão
RS159)	K375	1550	1/0.25	R. Soledad, Soledade: 0800-0300 (Sun -2000)
SC92)	J814	1550	5/0.25	R. Imigrantes, Turvo: 0800-0100
SP198)	K501	1550	1/0.25	R. Clube, Itararé
SP259)	K528	1550	1/0.25	R. Tambaú, Tambaú: 24h
SP200)	K572	1550	1/0.25	R. Cacique, Capivari
SP201)	K590	1550	10/1	R. Guarujá AM, Guarujá
SP202)	K659	1550	1/0.5	R. São Joaquim, São Joaquim da Barra
SP219)	K740	1550	1/0.25	R. Nova Difusora, Auriflama
SP281)	K59	1550	1/0.25	R. Lidersom, Orlândia
AL16)	H257	1560	1/0.25	R. Princesa das Matas, Viçosa: 0830-0200, SS: 24h
BA90)	H526	1560	0.25	R. Povo Pombal, Ribeira do Pombal
CE43)	H622	1560	1/0.25	R. Difusora Vale de Curu, Pentecoste: 0800-0100, Sun 0900-0000
MA18)	H903	1560	1/0.25	R. Agua Branca, Vitorino Freire
MG117)	L256	1560	1/0.25	R. Jornal, Leopoldina
MT56)	I...	1560	1/0.25	R. Paranaita. Paranaita
PR125)	J275	1560	1/0.25	R. Capanema, Capanema
PR161)	J361	1560	0.25	R. Cultura Serpin, Ribeirão do Pinhal
PR184)		1560	10/0.25	R. Barigui, Almirante Tamandaré
RJ47)	J501	1560	5/0.25	R. Grande Rio, Itaguaí: 24h
RN17)	J608	1560	1/0.25	R. Cultura do Oeste, Pau dos Ferros
RS158)	K310	1560	2.5/0.25	R. Açoriana, Taquari
RS172)	K369	1560	5/0.25	R. Poata, São José do Ouro
SC95)	J825	1560	1/0.25	R. Cidade, São Miguel d'Oeste
SP261)	K593	1560	1/0.25	R. Show, Igarapava: 24h
SP248)	K679	1560	1/0.25	R. Valparaíso, Valparaíso
SP249)	K725	1560	0.25	R. Regional AM, Pedreira
SP250)	K778	1560	1/0.25	R. Vale do Rio Paraná, Presidente Epitácio
BA56)	H496	1570	1/0.25	R. Povo, Jaguaquara
BA91)	H533	1570	1/0.25	R. Lider, Central
CE44)	H621	1570	1/0.25	R. Sertão Central,Senador Pompeu
MA22)	H907	1570	10/0.5	R. Cultura do Rio Jordão, Coroatá
MG146)	L242	1570	0.25	R. Unifei, Itajubá
MG141)	L344	1570	1/0.25	R. Cidade, Corinto
MG170)	L364	1570	10/0.25	R. Difusora, Piranga
MS24)	I409	1570	1/0.25	R. Nova Difusora, Caarapó
MS55)	I418	1570	1/0.25	R. Cidade, Aparecida do Taboado
PE30)	I798	1570	5/1	R. Asa Branca, Salgueiro
PR158)	J324	1570	0.25	R. Nova Brasileira, Bela Vista do Paraíso
PR137)	J341	1570	1/0.25	R. Club, Nova Aurora
PR159)	J365	1570	1/0.25	R. Arapoti Popular, Arapoti
PR166)	J209	1570	1/0.25	CBN, Paranaguá
RJ48)	J493	1570	1/0.25	R. Cultura, Valença: 24h
RO19)	J678	1570	5/0.25	R. Soc. Espigão, Espigão d'Oeste
RS147)	K358	1570	1/0.25	R. Metrópole, Cachoeirinha: 24h
SC83)	J777	1570	1/0.25	R. Rio Negrinho, Rio Negrinho
SC98)	J829	1570	1/0.25	R. Modelo, Modelo
SC107)	J...	1570	1/0.25	R. Tangrá, Tangará
SP204)	K552	1570	1/0.25	R. Avaré, Avaré
SP205)	K605	1570	1/0.25	R. Junqueirópolis, Junqueirópolis: 0900-2300, SS 0900-2200
SP262)	K648	1570	1/0.25	R. Zequinha de Abreu, Santa Rita do Passa Quatro
SP206)	K651	1570	10/0.25	R. ABC, Santo André: 0800-0000
SP207)	K667	1570	1/0.25	R. Socorro, Socorro
SP208)	K670	1570	1/0.25	R. Clube, Tanabi
TO10)	N665	1570	1/0.25	R. Rio Bonito, Gurupi
BA53)	H497	1580	2.5/0.25	R. BM, Barra do Mendes
BA62)	H502	1580	1/0.25	R. Atalaia, Canavieiras
MG119)	L210	1580	1/0.25	R. Liberdade, Itapecirica
MG121)	L290	1580	1/0.25	R. Cultura, Santos Dumont: 24h (Sun 0900-1500)
MG122)	L329	1580	1/0.25	R. Educadora, Espinosa
MG133)	L335	1580	1/0.25	R. Nova Guaranésia, Guaranésia
MS25)	I415	1580	1/0.25	R. Laguna, Jardim: 0800(Sat 0900)-0200
MS43)	N611	1580	1/0.25	R. Difusora, Ivinhema
PI18)	I898	1580	1/0.25	R. Santa Clara, Floriano
PR164)	J342	1580	2.5/0.25	R. São João do Sudoeste, São João
RJ51)	J487	1580	1/0.25	R. Popular Fluminense, Conceição de Macabu
RJ52)	J506	1580	5/0.25	R. Resende AM, Resende
RJ58)	J505	1580	0.25	R. Geração 2000, Teresópolis
RN24)	J613	1580	1/0.25	R. Verdade, Ceará Mirim
RS148)	K237	1580	1/0.25	R. Encantado AM, Encantado

MW	Call	kHz	kW	Station, location
RS150)	K339	1580	1/0.25	R. Dif. Fronteira, Arroio Grande: 24h
SC84)	J818	1580	1/0.25	R. Pomerode, Pomerode
SP251)	K504	1580	1/0.25	R. Difusora, Amparo: 24h
SP209)	K743	1580	0.25	R. Pedra Bonita, Itaporanga
BA55)	H...	1590	0.25	R. Vale do Jiquiriçá, Jiquiriça
CE80)	H660	1590	1/0.25	R. Montevidéu, Cedro
CE100)	H...	1590	1	R. Veneza, Eusébio
ES22)	I...	1590	1/0.25	R. Sim Tupi, Cachoeiro de Itapemirim
MG171)	L368	1590	1/0.25	R. Cidade Carinho, Ubá
MG134)	L369	1590	10/1	R. Guaicuí, Várzea da Palma
MG193)	N207	1590	0.25	R. Globo, Lambari
MS26)	I403	1590	1/0.25	R. Independência, Eldorado
PB34)	I703	1590	1/0.25	R. Correio do Vale, Itaporanga
PE40)	I...	1590	1/0.25	R. Dif. Rainha do Céu, Bezerros
PE41)	I...	1590		R. Restauração, Caruaru
PR129)	J290	1590	1/0.25	R. Nova Cultura, Andirá
PR160)	J296	1590	1/0.25	R. Havaí, Capitão Leônidas Marques
RS174)	K212	1590	0.25	R. Clube, Bagé
SC101)	J823	1590	10/0.5	R. Clube, Joinville
SP254)	K774	1590	10/0.5	R. Japi, Cabreúva
BA45)	H464	1600	10/1	R. Nova Voz, Muritiba
SP263)	K779	1600	100/20	R. Nove de Julho, São Paulo: 24h

SW	Call	kHz	kW	Station, location, h. of tr.
SP82)	G852	2380	0.25	R. Educadora, Limeira
AC02)	F204	2460	1	Super R. Alvorada, Rio Branco: 1000-2200
SP98)	G860	3235	0.5	R. Clube, Marilia
SP112)	G867	3325	2.5	R. Mundial, Guarulhos†
AC03)	F...	3355	1	R. Educ. 6 de Agosto, Xapuri: 1000-0100
SP49)	G855	3365	1	R. Cultura, Araraquara
AM02)	F276	3375	1	R. Municipal, São Gabriel da Cachoeira
RO09)	G792	3375	5	R. Educadora, Guajará Mirim: 0900-1300, 2100-0130
MS01)	F904	4755	10	R. Imaculada Conceição, Campo Grande
PA04)	G363	4765	5	R. Rural, Santarem
MG55)	G207	4775	1	R. Congonhas, Congonhas
RO11)	G790	4785	10	R. Caiari, Porto Velho
SP136)	G857	4785	1	R. Brasil, Campinas
AM20)	F273	4805	10/5	R. Dif. do Amazonas, Manaus: 0930-1330, 1500-1800, 2000-0100
PR13)	G640	4815	10	R. Dif. Londrina
SP80)	G868	4825	10	R. Canção Nova, Cachoeira Paulista
PA12)	G364	4825	5	R. Educadora, Bragança: 0830-0300
SP102)	G869	4845	1	R. Meteorologia Paulista, Ibitinga: (r R. Ternura FM)
AM14)	F278	4845	10	R. Cultura, Manaus: 1000-0400
AC04)	F203	4865	5	R. Verdes Florestas, Cruzeiro do Sul: 0930-0200
PR33)	G641	4865	5	R. Alvorada, Londrina
RR01)	G810	4878	10	R. Roraima, Boa Vista: 0800-0300 (SS 0900-0230) r on 4878
GO12)	F692	4885	1	R. Maria, Anápolis
AC06)	F201	4885	10	R. Dif. Acreana, Rio Branco: 0900-0400
PA03)	G362	4885	5	R. Clube do Pará, Belém: 24h
AM13)	F274	‡4895	5	R. Baré, Manaus
MS32)	R200	4895	5	R. Novo Tempo, Campo Grande
TO04)	F693	4905	1	R. Anhanguera, Araguaína
AP01)	F360	4915	25	R. Dif. Macapá, Macapá: 24h
GO27)	F691	4915	10	R. Daqui, Goiânia
AM10)	F282	4925	5	R. Educação Rural, Tefé: 1000-1400, 2000-0100
ES07)	F641	4935	1	R. Capixaba, Vitória
AM12)	ZYF275	4965	5	R. Alvorada, Parintins: 2200- 0200
SP223)	G865	4975	1	R. Iguatemi, São Paulo
GO30)	F690	4985	10	R. Brasil Central, Goiânia
SP52)	G853	5035	10	R. Aparecida, Aparecida
AM09)	F272	5035	5	R. Educação Rural, Coari: 1000-0100†
SP201)	G850	5045	0.25	R. Guaruja Paulista, Guarujá†
PA16)	G360	5045	10	R. Cultura do Pará, Belém: 24h
MT10)	F901	5055	10	R. Difusora, Cáceres
SC86)		5940	1	R. Voz Missionario, Camboriú
SP62)	E965	5955	10	R. Gazeta, São Paulo
SP280)	E858	5965	7.5	R. Trans Mundial, Santa Maria
MG06)	E523	5970	10	R. Itatiaia, Belo Horizonte
SC59)	E891	5980	10	R. Guarujá, Florianópolis
DF10)	E773	5990	250	R. Senado, Brasília
RS23)	E850	6000	10	R. Guaíba, Porto Alegre
MG35)	E521	6010	10	R. Inconfidência, Belo Horizonte
RS09)	E850	‡6020	10	R. Gaúcha, Porto Alegre
PR60)	E726	6060	10	Super Rádio Deus é Amor, Curitiba
RJ18)	E765	6070	7.5	R. Capital, Rio de Janeiro
GO27)	E441	6080	5	R. Daqui, Goiânia
PR15)	E726	6080	10	R. Marumby, Curitiba
SP57)	E956	6090	10	R. Bandeirantes, São Paulo
PR138)	E728	6105	5	R.Cultura Filadélfia, Foz do Iguaçu: 24h

SW	Call	kHz	kW	Station, location, h. of tr.
SP80)	E971	6105	5	R. Canção Nova, Cachoeira Paulista
PR60)	E968	6120	10	Super Rádio Deus é Amor, Sao Paulo
SP52)	E954	6135	25	R. Aparecida, Aparecida
SP77)	E950	6150	7.5	R. Record, São Paulo
AM11)	E245	6160	10	R. Rio Mar, Manaus: 1000-2100
RS104)	E854	6160	1	Super Rede Boa Vontade, Porto Alegre
DF06)	E365	6180	250	R. Nal. da Amazônia, Brasília
SP77)	E951	9505	7.5	R. Record, São Paulo
PR15)	E726	9515	10	R. Marumby, Curitiba
SP280)	E858	9530	10	R. Trans Mundial, Santa Maria
RS104)	E855	9550	10	Super Rede Boa Vontade, Porto Alegre
PR60)	E727	9565	20	Super Rádio Deus é Amor, Curitiba
PR60)	E969	9585	10	Super Rádio Deus é Amor, Sao Paulo
SP52)	E954	9630	10	R. Aparecida, Aparecida:
SP57)	E957	9645	7.5	R. Bandeirantes, São Paulo
SC86)	E890	9665	10	R. Voz Missionária, Camboriú
SP80)	E971	9675	10	R. Canção Nova, Cachoeira Paulista
SP62)	E963	9685	7.5	R. Gazeta, São Paulo
AM11)	E245	9695	7.5	R. Rio Mar, Manaus: 1000-2100
SP263)	E...	9820	10	R. Nove de Julho, São Paulo: 24h
PR15)	E726	11725	10	R. Marumby, Curitiba
SP280)	E858	11735	50	R. Trans Mundial, Santa Maria
SC86)		11760	1	R. Voz Missionária, Camboriú
PR60)	E726	11765	20	Super Rádio Deus é Amor, Curitiba
DF06)	E365	11780	250	R. Nal. da Amazônia, Brasília
RS23)	E853	11785	7.5	R. Guaíba, Porto Alegre
PR60)	E776	11805	10	Super Rádio Deus é Amor, Rio de Janeiro
GO30)	E440	11815	7.5	R. Brasil Central, Goiânia
GO27)	E441	11830	10	R. Daqui, Goiânia
SP52)	E954	11855	1	R. Aparecida, Aparecida
RS104)	E856	11895	10	Super Rede Boa Vontade, Porto Alegre
RS09)	E851	11915	10	R. Gaucha, Porto Alegre
SP57)	E958	‡11925	10	R. Bandeirantes, São Paulo:
MG35)	E622	15190	5	R. Inconfidência, Belo Horizonte
SP121)		26045		R. Cultura, São Paulo - DRM

RADIO NETWORKS

There are several radio networks. Below are listed just some of them. The affiliated outlets are often subject to alteration.

CENTRAL BRASILEIRA DE NOTICIAS – CBN: W: www.radioclick.globo.com/cbn

IGREJA PENTECOSTAL DEUS È AMOR: W: www.ipda.com.br

IGREJA UNIVERSAL DO REINO DE DEUS: W: www.igrejauniversal.org.br

JOVEM PAN ⌨ Av. Paulista 807, 24° andar, 01311-915 São Paulo, SP **W:** www.jovempan.uol.com.br

RADIO BANDEIRANTES W: www.radiobandeirantes com.br

RADIO GLOBO: W: www.radioclick.globo.com

REDE BOA VONTADE - LBV ⌨ Legião da Boa Vontade, Rua Doraci 90, Bairro Bom Retiro, 01134-020 São Paulo, SP **W:** www.redeboavontada.com

REDE BOAS NOVAS – RBN: W: www.rbn.org.br

REDE CANÇÃO NOVA DE RÁDIO ⌨ Rua João Paulo II s/, Alto da Bela Vista, 12630-000 Cachoeira Paulista, SP **W:** www.cancanova.com **E:** radio@cancanova.com

REDE CATÓLICA DE RÁDIO – RCR: ⌨ União de Radiodifusão Católica, Rua Vergueiro 3086, Conj. 91, Vila Mariana, 04102-001 São Paulo, SP **W:** www.rcrunda.com.br **E:** rcr@rcrunda.com.br

REDE DO ESTADO DE SÃO PAULO: W: www.redecbs.com.br

REDE GAÚCHA SAT ⌨ Av. Erico Veríssimo 400, Edificio Maurício Sirotsky Sobrinho, 90169-900 Porto Alegre, RS **W:** www.rbs.clicrbs.com.br

REDE ESPERANÇA: W: www.redeesperança

REDE ITATIAIA: W: www.itatiaia.com.br/rede

REDE MILICIA SAT: W: www.milicia.org.br

REDE MINERIA DE RADIO: W: www.redemineriaderadio.com.br

REDE NOVO TEMPO: W: www. novotempo.org.br

REDE PAULUS SAT: ⌨ Rua Doutor Pinto Ferraz 183, Vila Mariana, 04117-900 São Paulo, SP **W:** www.radioamericasp.com.br/paulussat.htm

REDE POTGUAR DE COMUNICAÇÃO (RPC): W: www.redepotiguar.com

REDE SUL DE RÁDIO: W: www.saofrancisco.am.br

REDE TRANSMARICA: W: www.transanet.uol.com.br

SISTEMA GLOBO DE RADIO: W: www.radioclick.globo.com/globobrasil

SISTEMA GUAÍBA SAT: ⌨ Rua Caldas Jr. 219, 2° andar, 90019-900 Porto Alegre, RS **W:** www.guaiba.com.br

REDE SOMZOOM SAT: ⌨ Av. Herois do Acre 590, Passaré, 60743-760 Fortaleza, CE **W:** www.somzoom.com.br **E:** somzoomsat@somzoom.com.br

Addresses and other information

AC00) ACRE

AC01) Rua de Alagoas, 270 - Colégio, 69980-000 Cruzeiro do Su ☎68 3322 4637 I **E:** radiointegracao@hotmail.com - **FM:** 99.9MHz – **AC02)** Rua Marechal Deodoro, 197 sala 210 – Galeria Rio Branco, 69900-210 Rio Branco ☎68 3223 2239 **W:** www.radioalvoradaac.com.br **E:** katia-na_adm@radioalvoradaac.com.br – **AC03)** Rua Coronel Brandão, 1665 - Bairro Aeroporto, 69930-000 Xapuri ☎68 3542 2830 **E:** raimari.cardo-so@hotmail.com – **AC04)** Travessa Mário Lobão 81, 69980-000 Cruzeiro do Sul ☎68 3322 3309 **E:** verdesflorestas@yahoo.com.br – **AC05)** Rua Epaminondas Jacome, 3121 - Base, 69908-420 Rio Branco ☎68 3224 2380 **W:** www.radiocapitalacre.com.br – **AC06)** Rua Benjamin Constant 1232, 69900-161 Rio Branco ☎68 3223 9696 **E:** comercial. difusora@ac.gov.br – **AC07)** Av Castelo Branco 329, 69925-000 Senador Guiomard – **AC08)** Rua Genni Assis s/n, 69932-000 Brasiléia – **AC10)** Governo do Estado doAcre, 69960-000 Fejo – **AC11)** Av Brasil, 1800 – Jorge Alves Jr., 69940-000 Sena Madureira ☎68 3612 2626 **E:** rivaldosevero@hotmail.com – **FM:** 105.9MHz – **AC12)** Rua Nilo Freire de Albuquerqe, Lotamente SEHAB Lotes 1 2 11 E 12 QD 16, 69970-000 Tarauacá **E:** railtonrodrigues@ac.gov.br – **AC15)** Travasse Diamantino Macedo s/n, 69960-000 Feijo **E:** jocivaldogomes@bol.com.br

AL00) ALAGOAS

AL01) Av Coronel Wilson Santa Cruz 6, 57314-000 Arapiraca ☎82 3521 0570 **W:** www.novonordeste.com **E:** am@novonordeste.com – **AL02)** Via Expressa 4360, Serraria, 57080-000 Maceió – **AL03)** Rua José Maria Passos 25, 57600-030 Palmeiras dos Indios - **FM:** 92.5MHz – **AL04)** Rua Barão José Miguel, 400 - Farol, 57055-160 Maceió 82-315 1960 **W:** www.izp.al.gov.br **E:** ascom@izp.al.gov.ar – **AL05)** Rua Miguel Palmeira 1513, 7° andar, Farol, 57055-330 Maceió – **AL06)** Praça Senador Eneas Araújo 61, 57500-000 Santana do Ipanema – **AL07)** Rua Saldanha da Gama s/n, Farol, 57051-580 Maceió ☎82 4009 7070 ▤82 4009 7719 **W:** http://gazetaWglobo.com/v2/radioga-zeta/ 24h - **FM:** 94.1MHz – **AL08)** Rua Vila Kennedy 45, Ponta Grosse, 57014-630 Maceió **AL09)** C.P 6, 57201-970 Penedo - **AL10)** Quadra A lote 04, 57160-000 Marechal Deodoro – **AL11)** Rua Porcos s/n, 57300-000 Arapiraca – **AL12)** Praça Manoel Monteiro 72, 57480-000 Delmiro Gouveia – ☎82 3641 4047 ▤82 3641 4061 **W:** www.radiodelmiro. com.br - **FM:** 89.9MHz – **AL13)** BR-104 Km 36, Bairro Roberto Correia de Arajuó, 57800-000 União dos Palmares – **AL14)** Rua Pedro Olivério Rocha 784, 3 AND SL 01, Farol, 57075-560 Maceió ☎82 4009 0009 **W:** www.radiocorreio.com.br – **AL15)** Av Braulio Cavalcante 415, 57400-000 Pão de Açucar ☎82 3624 1238 – **AL16)** Rua Mota Lima, 19 – Centro, 57100-000 Viçosa ☎82 3283 1842 **W:** www.princesadasma-tas.com – **AL17)** 57100-000 Maceió

AM00) AMAZONAS

AM02) Av Alvaro Maia s/n, 69750-000 São Gabriel da Cachoeira ☎97 3471 1768 – **AM03)** Rua Júlio de Oliveira, 1323 – São Pedro, 69800-000 Humaitá ☎97 3373 3946 **W:** www.radiovrm.com.br radiovrm@bol.com.br – **AM04)** A/C Prefeitura Municipal de Tabatinga (✉C.P. 31), 69640-000 Tabatinga ☎97 3412 4078 **W:**www.ebc.com. br/ebc/canais/radios/radio-nacional-do-alto-solimoes **E:** lana.micol@ radiobras.gov.br – **FM:** 96.1 MHz – **AM05)** Rua Solimões 809, Centro, 69100-000 Itacoatiara ☎92 3521 1635 **E:** radiodifusora_ita@hotmail. com - **FM:** 94.5MHz – **AM06)** Rua Joana D'Angelo s/n, Bairro Biribiri, 69400-000 Manacapuru ☎92 3361 2042 **E:** gadelha.silva@redeama-zonica.com.br – **AM07)** Av Major Santana 2502, 69280-000 Manicoré – **AM08)** Estrada dos Morais 1455, 69190-000 Maués ☎92 3542 2264 **E:** radioguaranopolis@hotmail.com – **AM09)** Praça São Sebastião 228, 69460-000 Coari ☎97 3561 2474 **W:** //radiocoariamot.blospot.com.br **E:** radiocoari@hotmail.com – **AM10)** Praça Santa Tereza 283, 69470-000 Tefé ☎97 3343 3017 ▤97 3343 2663 **W:** www.radiorualtefe.com. br **E:** rert@osite.com.br – **AM11)** Rua José Clemente, 500 - Centro, 69010-070 Manaus ☎92 3633 2599 ▤92 3232 7763 **W:**www.roderio-mar.com.br **E:** contato@rederiomar.com.br – **AM12)** Rua Governador Leopoldo Neves 516, 69151-460 Parintins ☎92 3533 3097 ▤92 3533 2004 **W:** www.alvoradaparintins.com.br **E:** contato@alvoradaparintins. com.br - **FM:** 100.1MHz – **AM13)** Av Tefe, 3025 – Japiim, 69078-000 Manaus ☎92 2101 5500 **W:** www.radiobare.com.br – **AM14)** Rua Barcelos, s/n Praça 14, 69020-200 Manaus ☎92 3215 4743 ▤92 3215 4759 **W:** www.tvcultura.am.gov.br/site/pagina/radio-cultura **E:** radio-cultura@tvcultura.am.gov.br or radiocultura@hotmail.com – **AM16)** Av General Rodrigo Jordão Ramos, 1655 Anexo 3 - Japiim, 69077-000 Manaus ☎92 3614 0007 **W:** www.rbn.org.br **E:** contato@rbn.org. br - **FM:** 100MHz – **AM17)** Av Amazonas 1958, 69151-000 Parintins ☎92 3533 1564 ▤92 3533 2456 – **W:** www.radioclubeparintinsam. com.br **E:** contato@radioclubeparintinsam.com.br – **AM18)** Rodovia Manoel Urbano, km 2, 69405-000 Iranduba **W:** www.redeboavontade. com – **AM19)** Boulevard Pedro Rate, 176 - São José, 69640-000 Manacapuru ☎ 92 3361 2192 ▤ 92 3361 2453 – **AM20)** Av Eduardo Ribeiro 639, Ed Palácio do Comércio, 20° andar, Centro, 69010-001 Manaus ☎92 3622 2310 ▤ 92 3234 3750 **W:** www.difusoramanaus.

com.br **E:** garotinho@radiodifusora.com.br - **FM:** 96.9MHz – **AM21)** Estrada do Gavião, km 05 andar, 69500-000 Carauari – **AM23)** Praça Coronel João Vercosa, 47 - Centro, 69190-000 Maués ☎92 3542 1897 – **AM24)** Av Leopoldo Nelves 360, 69850-000 Bôca do Acre – **AM25)** Rua Anori/Anama 327, 69440-000 Anori – **AM26)** Praça Eduardo Ribeiro 2058, 69151-271 Parintins – **AM27)** 69670-000 Fonte Boa – **AM28)** 69140-000 Nhamundá – **AM29)** 69200-000 Borba – **AM30)** 69630-000 Benjamin Constant – **AM31)** 69750-000 Saó Gabriel da Cachoeira – **AM32)** 69680-000 Santo Antonio do Iça

AP00) AMAPÁ

AP01) Rua Cândido Mendes, 525 – Centro, 68900-100 Macapá ☎96 3131 2716 **W:** www.difusora.ap.gov.br **E:** rdm@rdm.ap.gov.br – **AP02)** Rua Eliezer Levy, 684 -Trem, 68901-090 Macapá ☎96 3222 3111 **E:** equatorialfm@uol.com.br – **FM:** 94.5MHz – **AP03)** Av Nações Unidas 256, 68906-100 Macapá – **AP04)** 68925-000 Santana – **AP05)** Rua Hildemar Maia 1000, 68940-000 Mazagão ☎96 3271 1227 – **AP06)** Oiapoque.

BA00) BAHIA

BA01) Praça Mario Dourado 78-A, 44900-000 Irecê ☎74 3641 3717 **W:**www.regionalam.com.br **Emai.:** contato@regionalam.com.br – **BA02)** Av. Itajuipe No 1789, Bairro Santo Antonio, 45602-380 Itabuna. ☎73 3211 2385 **W:** www.radiojornaldeitabuna.com.br – **BA03)** Praça da Independência 244, 45995-000 Teixeira de Freitas – **BA04)** Estrada Liberdade, N° 214 – Edif Dois Corações, Liberdade, 40375-016 Salvador ☎71 3326 3551 **W:** www.sistemacruzeiro.com.br – **BA05)** Rua Luis Augusto Fernandes Borges 306, 47800-000 Barreiras ☎77 3611 3570 **W:** www.radiovale.com.br **E:** Av Aurelino Ribeirao Noaves s/n, Graça, 45400-000 Valença ☎75 5575 3641 **W:** www.radioclubedeva-lenca.com.br **E:** clube@radioclubedevalenca.com.br – **BA07)** Praça Duque Caxias 3, 45700-000 Itapetinga **W:** www.novajornal.com.br – **BA08)** Rua Marieta Martins, 336 - São Benedito, 44573-250 Santo Antônio de Jesus ☎75 3631 5680 **W:** www.radioclube680.com.br **E:** contato@radioclube680.com.br – **BA10)** Rua Germiniano Costa 47, 44025-070 Feira de Santana – **BA11)** Rua Jardim Federação 81, Federação, 40231-060 Salvador ☎71 3486 3201 ▤71 3486 3214 **W:** www.radiosociedadeam.com.br **E:** comercial@radiosociedadeam.com. br – **BA12)** Av. Cinquenteário 1429, 45600-006 Itabuna ☎73 3215 2271 **W:**www.difusorabahia.com.br – **BA13)** Marechal Deodoro 639, 47800-000 Barreiras ☎77 3611 4545 **W:** www.rb.am.br – **BA14)** Praça Luiz Nogueira 385, 48700-000 Serrinha – **BA15)** Rua Antonio Neto No 27, 46810-000 Utinga ☎75 3337 1011 **W:** www.radiocultura820.com. br **E:** comercial@radiocultura820.com.br – **BA16)** Fundação Dom Avelar Brandão, Rua Martin Afonso de Souza, 270 - Garcia, 40100-050 Salvador ☎71 3328 5088 **W:** www.am840.com.br**E:** comercial@ am840.com.br – **BA17)** Av Visconde do Rio Branco. 68 - Centro, 48970 000 Senhor do Bonfim ☎74 3541 4617 **W:** www.radiocaraiba.com.br – **BA18)** Travessa da Catedral s/n, 45600-000 Itabuna ☎73 3215 0909 **W:** www.radionacionalitabuna.com.br or contato@radionacionalitabu-na.com.br – **BA19)** Rua Wercelêncio da Mota 81, Centro, 48730-000 Conceição do Coité ☎75 3262 1010 **W:** www.radiosisal.com – **BA20)** Rua Frei Hermenegildo, 300 – Capuchinos (C.P. 1525), 44050-000 Feira de Santana ☎75 2101 9700 **W:** www.sociedadedefeiraam.com.br-**FM:** 96.9MHz – **BA21)** Gleba Fazenda Ouro Verde, 45900-000 Caravelas ☎73 3011 1299 **W:** www.radioalvoradagospel.com.br **E:** diretoria@ radioalvoradogospel.com.br – **BA22)** Rua Gabriel Soares 23, 40060-040 Salvador – **BA23)** Praça Barão do Rio Branco 42, 45100-000 Vitória da Conquista **W:** www.96fmconquista.com.br – **BA24)** Av Maria Quitéria, 223 - Mar da Tranguilidad, 44062-630 Feira de Santana 75 3623 1080 75 3623 2851 **W:** www.radiosubaeam.com.br **E:** radio@radiosubaeam. com.br - **FM:** 95.3MHz Nordeste FM – **BA25)** Rua José Bonifacio No 17 2° andar, Centro, 45700-000 Itapetinga ☎77 3261 2610 **W:** www. radiofascinacao.com.br **E:** comercial@radiofascinacao.com.br – **BA26)** Rua Marquês de Paranaguá 259, 45660-000 Ilhéus ☎73 3231 3612 **W:** www.santacruzam.com.br **E:** contato@santacruzam.com.br – **BA27)** C.P 29, 45825-000 Eunápolis – **BA28)** Rua Cel. Aprigio Duarte N 05, 48900-000 Juazeiro ☎76 3611 7435 **W:** www.radiojuazeiro.com.br **E:** radiojuazeiro@hotmail.com – **BA29)** Rua Senador Pedro Lago, 54 - Centro, 44700-000 Jacobina ☎74 3621 9150 **W:** www.radiocluberio-dooruro.com.br **E:** radio@radiocluberiodoouro.com.br – **BA30)** Rua Monte Castelo,45, Sobradinha, 44018-210 Feira de Santana ☎75 3221 8815 **W:** www.radiopovo.com.br **E:** cariocapovo@veloxmail.com.br– **BA31)** Rua Dom Pedro II 98, 48100-000 Alagoinhas **W:** www.nova-am1240.com.br **E:** oliveirafm@oliveirafm.com.br – **BA32)** Rua Cde Pereire Carneiro, 226 -Pernambués,41100-010 Salvador ☎71 3505 5000 ▤71 3505 5040 **W:** www.radiometropole.com.br – **FM:** 101.3MHz – **BA33)** Av. Itabuna, 63 – Centro, 45653-160 Ilhéus ☎73 3231 5462 **E:** radiono-vabahianadeilheus@bol.com.br or clinton.alves@hotmail.com – **BA34)** Praça Luiz Nogueira 385, 48700-000 Serrinha **W:** www.continentalam. com.br **E:** continentalam@continentalam.com.br – **BA35)** Rua São Francisco 159 -163A, 48600-000 Paulo Afonso ☎73 3281 1266 **W:** www.redecultura.com.br **E:** redecultura@redecultura.com.br – **FM:**

92.7MHz – **BA36**) Praça da Bandeira s/n, Centro, 47600-000 Bom Jesus da Lapa ☎77 3481 5179 **W:** www.radiobomjesusam.com.br – **BA37**) Av Getúlio Vargas 394, 44330-000 São Gonçalo dos Campos – ☎77 3481 6161 **W:**www.planeta1410.com.br – **BA38**) Rua Coronel Francisco Pinto, 44200-000 Santo Amaro ☎75 3241 4665 📠75 3241 1602 **W:** www.radioindependenciabahia.com.br – **BA39**) Rua 2 de Julho 20, 45200-000 Jequié ☎73 3527 4114 **W:** www.radiopovo.com.br **E:** radiopovojequie@gmail.com – **BA40**) Rua Sítio Escurinha s/n, BR-242, km 90, 46880-000 Itaberaba – **BA41**) Praça Virgilio Damasio, 140b 1° andar – Centro, 45570-000 Ipiaú ☎73 3531 3441 📠73 3531 3419 **W:** www.radioeducadoradeipiau.com.br **E:** contato@radioeducadoradei-piau.com.br – **BA42**) Av. Dom Manuel Raimundo de Mello, 607 - Bairro São José, 46400-000 Caetité ☎77 3454 1819 **W:** www.educadorasan-tana.com **E:** educadora@educadorasantana.com.br – **BA43**) Rua Otavio Mangabeira 1026, Bela Vista, 46430-000 Guanambi ☎77 3451 1348 **W:** www.radioculturagbi.com.br **E:** radioculturagbi@hotmail.com – **BA44**) Av Ascendino Melo 297, 267 – Sis 106/107, Shopping Itatiaia, Recreio, 45020-908 Vitória da Conquista ☎77 3472 0760 **W:** www.radiocidadeconquista.com.br **E:** radiocidade@clubenet.com.br – **BA45**) Tv Virgillo Gonzalves Pereira 196, Centro, 44340-000 Muritiba ☎73 3424 2048 – **BA46**) Av Porto Seguro 718, 1° andar, Centro, 45820-006 Eunápolis. ☎73 3281 5594 – **BA47**) Rua da Bandeira 27, 42800-000 Camaçari – **BA48**) Travessa do Contorno 26, 45570-000 Ipiaú – **BA49**) Rua Padre Argemiro Guimarães, 32 - Centro, 44640-000 Riachão do Jacuípe ☎75 3264 2189 **W:** www.radiojacuipeam.com.br **E:** radioja-cuipe@yahoo.com.br – **BA50**) Av Getúlio Vargas 43, 48601-000 Paulo Afonso ☎75 3281 3009 **W:** www.radiobahianordeste.com.br **E:** rbm@radiobahianordeste.com.br – **BA51**) Rua Rio Corrente s/n, 47640-000 Santa Maria da Vitória – **BA52**) Rua Saldanha Marinho 30 Sala 23/24, Mesmo, 45810-000 Porto Seguro ☎73 3288 2136 **E:** radioguadalupe-am@yahoo.com.br – **BA53**) Rua Alvaro Campos 83, 44990-000 Barra do Mendes **W:** www.rbm.am.br **E:** rbm@holistica.com.br – **BA54**) Av Dom Avelar Brandão Vilella s/n, Sítio São Félix, 46470-970 Riacho de Santana **W:** www.micks.com.br/guadalupe **E:** guadalupe@micks.com. br – **BA55**) Rua Coronel Vicente s/n, 45470-000 Jiquiriça – **BA56**) Loteamento Nova Jaguaquara, Arco Iris, 45345-000 Jaguaquara ☎73 3534 2328 **W:** www.radiopovo.com.br/povojaguaquara **E:** educadora-am1570@hotmail.com – **BA57**) Rua Gamboa de Cima, 18 - Campo Grande, 40060-008 Salvador **W:** www.novotemposalvador.com.br **E:** novotemposalvador@terre.com.br – **BA58**) Av Regis Pacheco 534, Centro, 45100-000 Vitória da Conquista **W:** www.cancaonova.com **E:** radioconquista@cancaonova.com.br – **BA59**) Rua Gonçalo Martins 19, 45550-000 Ubatã ☎73 3245 1233 **E:** povoam@gmail.com – **BA60**) Rua Antônio Otaviano Dourado 91,Centro, 44900-000 Irecê ☎74 3641 3111 **W:**www.programacao10cidade.com.br **E:** minhoekaren@hotmail.com – **BA61**) C.P 45, 46430-000 Guanambi ☎ 77 3451 1596 **W:** www. radioalvoradaam.com.br **E:** alvorada@alvoradaam.com.br – **BA62**) Rua General Pederneiras 62, 45860-000 Canavieiras – **BA63**) Rua Mario Luis Vieira, 100, Centro, 44700-000 Jacobina ☎74 3621 7474 **W:** www.radiojaraguar.com.br **E:** jaraguar.am@gmail.com – **BA64**) Rua Farias Goes 164, 48330-000 Rio Real **W:** www.radiofusora600.com.br **BA65**) Rua Manoel Conselho Campos, 135 – Centro,, 48500-000 Euclides da Cunha ☎75 3271 1652 – **BA66**) Rua Rui Barbosa 119, 47400-000 Xique-Xique – **BA67**) Rua Jose de Anchita, 128 - 2° andar - Centro, 45836-000 Itamaraju. ☎73 3294 5455 **W:** www.extremosulam. com.br – **BA68**) Av José Candido dos Santos 20, Centro, Lagos Redonda, 49300-000 Itapicuru ☎79 3541 1067 **W:** www.rci1060am. com.br – **BA69**) Rua Frei Apolônio de Todi 10, 48410-000 Cícero Dantas **E:** regional@fallnet.com.br – **BA70**) Terreiro de Jesus 13, Centro Histórico, 40025-010 Salvador **W:**www.radio.boavontade.com/ba – **BA71**) Rua Vicente Paula Costa 16, 48540-000 Jeremoabo **W:** http:// radiovazabarris.com.br/ – **BA72**) Rua 2 de Julho s/n, Centro, 45160-000 Belo Campo ☎ 773437 2233 – **BA73**) Praça São José 279 44600-000 Ipirá – **BA74**) Rua Desidério Brandão, 15 – Centro, 44380-000 Cruz das Almas ☎📠 75 3621 2716 **W:** www.radioalvoradaam1460.com.br **E:** alvoradaamcomercial@hotmail.com – **BA75**) Rua Teixeira de Freitas s/n, 47700-000 Santana – **BA76**) 47400-000 Xique-Xique – **BA77**) Rua Barão do Rio Branco s/n, 47600-000 Bom Jesus da Lapa – **BA78**) Rua Dulce Pazzi 6, Alto da Bela Vista, 45260-000 Poções ☎77 3431 1848 **W:** www.radiopovo.com.br **E:** povopocoes@hotmail.com – **BA79**) Rua Idalina Pinto 169, 46990-000 Souto Soares ☎75 3339 2328 **W:** www. radiojornal1540.com.br **E:** comercial@radiojornal1540.com.br – **BA80**) Rua José Inácio 31, 48700-000 Juazeiro – **BA81**) Rua Carlos Gomes 980, Centro, 40285-280 Salvador ☎71 3329 7463 **W:** www.cultura-1140am.com.br **E:** contato@cultura1140am.com.br – **BA82**) Rua Élcio Cardoso de Matos s/n, Centro, 48800-000 Monte Santo ☎75 3275 1212 **W:** www.grupopiquaraca.com.br – **BA83**) Parque Emilia Costa s/ n, 45450-000 Gandu – **BA84**) Praça da Bandeira 47, 3° andar, Centro, 48900-000 Juazeiro ☎74 3611 5533 **W:** www.radiocidadeam870.com. br **E:** contato@radiocidadeam870.com.br – **BA85**) Rua Coronel Dias Coelho 249, 44850-000 Morro do Chapéu – **BA86**) Travessa Juracy

Magalhães 4, 2° andar, 44630-000 Mairi **W:** www.radiomorroverde. com.br **E:** adm@radiomorroverde.com.br – **BA87**) Rua Dr Guerra 91, 47650-000 Correntina **W:** www.radioplanaltodooeste.com.br **E:** conta-to@radioplanaltodooeste.com.br – – **BA89**) Rua João Brandão 233, Centro, 45350-000 Itiruçu – **BA90**) Praça Getúlio Vargas 211, 48400-000 Ribeira do Pombal ☎75 3276 1164 **W:**www.radiopovopombal.com **E:** educadorapombalgerencia@hotmail.com – **BA91**) Rua do Comércio 31, 44940-000 Central – **BA94**) 45600-000 Itabuna – **BA96**) Rua Juana Angélica, 125 – Centro, 45653-640 Iléhus ☎73 3634 6640 📠73 3634 2465 **W:** www.radioculturadeilheus.com.br **E:**site@radioculturadei-lheus.com.br – **BA97**) 46100-000 Brumado

CE00) CEARÁ
CE01) Rua Romeu Martins, Centro S/N, Ed 29 de Julho, 62700-000 Canindé ☎85 3343 2233 📠 85 3343 1602 **W:** www.radiojornal540.com **E:** admin@radiojornal540.com – **CE02**) Rua São Pedro 918, 63010-010 Juazeiro do Norte **W:** www.verdaodocairi.com.br/radio.php **E:** raimun-dodantas10@yahoo.com.br – **CE03**) Av Monsenhor Tabosa, 2514 – Bairro das Madalenas, 62500-000 Itapipoca ☎88 3631 2173 📠88 3631 0469 **W:** www.radiouirapurudeitapipoca.com.br **E:** ribamar.p@bol.com. br – **CE04**) Rua Carlos Rolim/Praça da Matriz, 63700-000 Crateús – **CE05**) Av.Rui Barbosa, 1901 - Aldeota, 60115-221 Fortaleza ☎85 3224 2340 **W:** http://radioglobofortaleza.com.br – **CE06**) Praça da Matriz s/n, 62590-000 Itarema – **CE07**) Rua Dep. Luiz Otacílio Correia, 221 - Centro, 63540-000 Várzea Alegre ☎88 3541 1055 📠88 3541 1072 **W:** www. radiocultura670.com **E:** radiocultura@radiocultura670.com – **CE08**) Shalom da Paz, Rua Maria Tomásia, 72 – Aldeota, 60150-170 Fortaleza ☎85 3261 4444 **W:** www.radioasabranca.com.br **E:** benfeitordapaz@comshalom.org **FM:** 89.1 MHz – **CE09**) Rua Agronomando Rangel 475, 63870-000 Boa Viagem **W:** www.radioasabranca.com.br **E:** asabran-ca@radioasabranca.com.br ☎88 3427 1104 📠88 3427 1456 – **CE10**) Rua Marcondes Pereira, 426-Joaquim Távora, 60130-060 Fortaleza ☎88 3272 3733 📠88 3272 3749 – **CE11**) Rua Hilda Augusto 201, 63300-000 Lavras da Mangabeira ☎88 3536 1257 **W:** www.radiovale-dosalgado.com.br **E:** contato@radiovaledosalgado.com.br – **CE12**) Rua Floriano Peixoto 351, Cento, 63500-000 Iguatu ☎88 3581 1402 📠88 3581 0828 **W:** www.jornalam.com.br **E:** contato@jornalam.com.br – **CE13**) Praça de Imprensa s/n (C.P. 851, 60001-970), ☎60135-900 Fortaleza 📠85 3266 9776 **W:** www.verdesmares.com.br – **CE14**) Praça Vicente Aguilar 16, Centro, 62400-000 Camocim ☎88 3621 1395 **W:** www.deputadosergioaguiar.com.br – **CE15**) Rua São Luís 68, 62040-450 Juazeiro do Norte ☎88 3512 3581 📠88 3511 5387 **W:** www. radioiracema.hpg.ig.com.br **E:** radioiracema@ig.com.br – **CE16**) Av Senador Virgilio Tavoar 2279, 60170-251 Fortaleza **W:** www.cidade-am860.com.br **Email** comercial860@yahoo.com.br - **CE17**) Rua Floriano Peixoto 358, 63500-000 Iguatu **W:** www.radioliberdadeam.com.br **E:** contato@radioliberdadeam.com.br – **CE18**) Rua Totonho Figueiras 244, 63180-000 Barbalha **W:** www.radiocetama.com.br – **CE19**) Praça Quirino Rodrigues 76/3, 62011- 280 Sobral. 88 3611 1550 **W:** www. educadora950.com **E:** radioeducadora@sobral.org – **CE20**) Rua Tabelião Enéas, 495 - 2° Andar – Centro, (✉ C.P 87, 63901-970) 63900-000 Quixadá ☎88 3414 5970 📠88 3412 0554 **W:** www.sistemamonolitos. com.br **E:**contato@sistemamonolitos.com.br – **FM:** 105.9 MHz – **CE21**) Av. Almirante Tamandaré 19, Praia de Icarema, 60060-200 Fortaleza ☎85 3066 4000 – **CE22**) Rua Coronel Antônio Luiz 1068, Bairro do Pimenta, 63100-000 Crato ☎88 3523 3198 **W:** www.radioeducado-ra1020.com.br **E:** comercial@radioeducadora1020.com.br – **CE23**) Travessa Crateús 46, Centro, 62010-560 Sobral ☎88 3614 8282 **W:** www.radiotupinamba.com – **CE24**) Rua Raul Vieira 562, 62900-000 Russas – **CE25**) Rodovia BR 116 s/n km 54/Fazende Guarani, Zona Rural 62870-000 Pacajús ☎85 3348 0725 **W:** www.comshalom.org/radio **E:** boanova1410@yahoo.com.br – **CE26**) Av Senador Virgilio Távora 2279, Dionisio Torres, 60170-251 Fortaleza. ☎85 3264 2944 **W:** www.radio-clubece.com.br **E:** fransilveira@gmail.com – **CE27**) Rua Coronel Zezé 1158, 63700-000 Crateús – **CE28**) Rua Luis Vicente Ferreira Lima 222, Bairro Populares, 62930-000 Limoeiro do Norte – ☎88 3423 4100 📠88 3423 2440 **W:** www.radiovaledojaguaribe.com.br **E:** comercial@radio-vale.com – **CE29**) Av Gal Osóri Paiva, 7235 – Canindezinho, 60731-000 Fortaleza ☎ 85 3498 4796 **W:** www.ipda.com.br – **CE30**) Rua Sáo Francisco 374, 63010-210 Juazeiro do Norte ☎88 3511 2404 **W:** www. radioprogressoam.com.br – **CE31**) Rua Cel Joaquim Ribeiro405, sala 04 - Centro, 62011-020 Sobral ☎88 3611 7888 **W:** www.radioregionalso-bral.com/ **E:** radioregional1320@hotmail.com – **CE32**) Av Dr Pedro de Queiroz Ferreira 2129, 62850-000 Cascavel – **CE33**) Rua São Francisco 139, 63100-000 Crato – **CE34**) Rua Monsenhor Salviano Pinto 71, 63800-000 Quixeramobim ☎88 3441 0014 **W:** contato@difusoracris-tal.com.br **E:** contato@difusoracristal.com.br – **CE35**) Praça Pinto Martins 260, 62400-000 Camocim – **CE36**) Av Manoel Castro 815, 62940-000 Morada Nova – **CE37**) Av. Moacir Pereira Gondim 333, Planalto dos Colibris, 63660-000 Tauá ☎88 3437 1345 **W:** www. cultura960am.com.br **E:** cultura960am@hotmail.com– **CE38**) Rua Coronel Alexanzito 835, 62800-000 Aracati – **CE39**) Rua Hildo Furtado

s/n, 62760-000 Baturité – **CE40**) Rua Italiano Júlio Filizola 551, 62370-000 São Benedito ☎88 3626 2142 **W:** www.novaplan.am.br – **CE41**) Rua Coronel Antônio Joaquim 2143, 62930-000 Limoeiro do Norte ☎88 3423 4225 **W:** www.radioeducadora.com.br **E:** educadora560@yahoo.com.br – **CE42**) Av. Pref. Jaques Nunes 648, Centro, 62320-000 Tianguá ☎88 3671 1322 – **CE43**) Rua João Verçosa s/n, 62640-000 Pentecoste ☎85 3352 2554 **W:** www.radiovaledocuru.com – **CE44**) Rua Santos Dumont, 414 - Centro, 63600-000 Senador Pompeu ☎88 3449 0206 **W:** www.radiosertaocentralam.com.br **E:** radiocertaocentral@hotmail.com – **CE45**) Praça Adolfo Caminha 247, 62800-000 Aracati – **CE46**) Maria de Lourdes 545, 62280-000 Santa Quitéria – **CE47**) São João Evangeliste, 655 Campo de Aviação, 62680-000 Paracuru ☎58 3269 1469 **W:** www.deuseespirito.org **E:** pr.francisco.oliveira@hotmail.com – **CE48**) Rua Justino Alves Feitosa, 364 - centro, 63380-000 Barro ☎88 3554 1166 **W:**www.rbe1210.com **E:** radioboaesperance1210am@hotmail.com – **CE49**) Rua Simão Barbosa,1290 - Centro, 62700-000 Canindé – ☎ 85 3343 0403 ▤85 3343 0574 **E:** rsf@sentralnet.com.br – **CE50**) Rua Coronel Lucio 489, 63700-000 Crateús ☎88 811 0060 – **CE51**) Rua Monsenhor Salviano Pinto 507, 63800-000 Quixeramobim ☎88 3441 0263 ▤88 3441 1209 **W:** www.sistemamaior.com.br/radio_campomaior **E:** contatomaior@sistemamaior.com.br – **CE52**) Rua Juaci Sampaio Pontes 695 – salas 25/56 2° andar, 61600-150 Caucaia ☎85 3342 1230 **W:** www.lamb.com.br **E:** radiometropolitana@fortalnet.com.br – **CE53**) Rua da Ressurreição, 929 - Rairro Pe Ibiapina, 62000-000 Sobral ☎88 3611 3349 **W:** www.rrsobral.com.br **E:** radloressurreicao@oi.com.br – **CE54**) Rua Tibúrcio Targino 155, 61700-000 Aquiraz – **CE55**) Rua Dr Almir Farias 446, 62200-000 Nova Russas- **W:** www.rd780.com **E:** – **CE56**) Rua Raimundo Nonato 81 – Centro, 62940-000 Morada Nova ☎88 3422 2561 **W:** www.portalliberal.com.br – **CE57**) Rua Dr Chagas Pinto, 3510 - Centro, 62250-000 Ipu ☎88 3683 2186 **W:** www.radioiracemadeipu.com.br **E:** radioiracemaipu@hotmail.com – **CE58**) Rua Francisco Gomes de Souza, 198 - Centro, 63150-000 Campos Sales. ☎88 3533 1188 **W:** www.cidadeam630.com.br **MSN:** r.cidade@hotmail.com – **CE59**) Rua Cazuzinha Marques, 87 - Centro, 63560-000 Acopiara ☎88 3565 0063 **W:** www.radiovaleacopiara.am.br **E:** contato@radiovaleacopiara.am.br – **CE60**) Rua Manoel Inacio de Lucena, 249 an 2 - Centro, 63260-000 Brejo Santo ☎88 3531 1093 **W:** www.radiosulcearense.com.br – **CE61**) Av. Mons Aloísio Pinto, 100 Dom Expedito, 62050-999 Sobral ☎88 3614 4043 **W:** www.radiocaicara.com **E:** radio@radiocaicara.com – **CE62**) Av. Senador Esmerino Arruda s/n, 62430-000 Granja ☎88 3624 1106 **W:** http://radiovaleam.com.br **E:**contato@radiovaleam.com.br – **CE63**) Rua Antônio Queiroz, 343 - Centro, 63870-000 Boa Viagem ☎88 3427 1064 **W:** www.amliberdade.com.br **E:** radioliberdadebv@yahoo.combr – **CE64**) Rua Major Barreto, 3000 - Centro, 62600-000 Itapajé ☎85 9104 5447 **W:** www.radioguanaces.com.br **E:** kekpubli@hotmail.com – **CE65**) Loteamento Pioneiro, Estrada Sobral Santa Quitéria km 03, 62115-000 Forquilha – **CE66**) Rua Capitão Carapeba 67, Centro, 62370-000 São Benedito **E:** radiotabajara1@hotmail.com ☎88 3626 2266 ▤88 3626 2166 – **CE67**) Rua Monsenhor Joviniano Barreto 22, 2° andar, Centro, 63660-000 Tauá ☎88 3437 1509 **W:** www.difusorataua.com.br **E:** contato@difusorataua.com.br – **CE68**) Rua Monsenhor Furtado, 149 - Centro, 62380-000 Guaraciaba do Norte ☎88 3652 2112 **W:** www.somzoom.com.br – **CE69**) Av Rios 92, 62590-000 Itarema – **CE70**) Av Coronel Alexanzito 369, 62800-000 Aracati 88 3421 3033 **W:** www.redemoria.com **E:** contato@redemoria.com **FM:** 105.3MHz – **CE71**) Av.7 N 260 Altos Conj. Jereissati - Maracanau, 61900-320 Maracanaú ☎85 3382 2222 **W:** www.radiopitaguaryam.com.br **E:** radiopitaguaryam@ibest.com.br – **CE72**) Rodovia BR-226 km 20, Distrito de Bonfim, 63600-000 Senador Pompeu – **CE73**) Avenida José Júlio Lousada 312, Centro, 62580-000 Acaraú ☎88 36611280 **W:** www.difusoraacarau.com – **CE74**) Avenida Alcides Rocha s/n, Bairro São Luis, 62550-000 Morrinhos ☎88 3665 1194 **W:** www.princesaam.com **E:** djmairton@hotmail.com – **CE75**) Rua Cel. José Lourenço, 97 – Altos,, 62250-000 Ipu ☎88 3683 1204 **W:** www.radioregionaldeipu.com.br **E:** radioregional1520am@hotmail.com – **CE76**) Rua Joaquim Távora, 363 - Centro, 63150-000 Campos Sales ☎88 3533 1530 **W:** www.tresfronteirasam.com.br **E:** tresfronterasam@gmail.com – **CE77**) Rua Manoel Alencar 35, 63610-000 Mombaça – **CE79**) Rua Caio Prado 406 – Centro, 61800-000 Pacatuba – **CE79**) Rua Raul Catunda Fontenele 61, Centro, 62230-000 Ipueiras ☎88 3685 1368 **W:** www.radiomacambira.com.br – **CE80**) Rua Raimundo Guedes Martins 25, Centro,, 63400-000 Cedro ☎88 3564 1075 **W:** www.radiomontevideoam.com.br – **CE81**) Ro BR 020 s/n, Zona Rural, 62730-000 Caridade ☎85 3324 1292 – **CE82**) Rua Francisco Brasileiro 213, Centro, 63900-000 Quixadá ☎88 3412 3047 **W:** www.radioculturaquixada.com.br **E:** radioculturaquixada@gmail.com – **CE83**) Av. Rabelo, s/n – Alto Vistoso, 63620- 000 Solonópole ☎88 3518 1520 **W:** www.radiocachoeiraam.com.br **E:** radio.cachoeira.am@hotmail.com – **CE84**) Rua Augusto Vieira, 32-Centro, 63630-000 Pedro Branca ☎88 3515 2121 **W:** www.amtrapia1510.com.br **E:**contato@amtrapia1510.com.br – **CE86**) 63140-000 Assaré – **CE88**) 63170-

000 Araripe – **CE89**) 624000-000 Camocim – **CE98**) 61760-000 Eusebio – **CE99**) Rua Afonso Pena 109, 63560-000 Acopiara ☎88 3565 0214 **W:** www.carinhosaam.com.**br E:** contato@carinohsaam.com.br – **CE100**) Rua Mário Perdigão 130, 61760-000 Eusébio ☎85 3361 2755 **W:** www.redeaquiraz.com **E:** redeaquiraz104@gmail.com

DF00) DISTRITO FEDERAL

DF01) SRTS, Qd 701, Ed Assis Chateaubriand, Bl 2, salas 701 a 716, 70340-906 Brasília ☎61 9316 9530 ▤61 9223 0532 – **DF02**) Setor de Rádio e TV Sul, Palácio do Rádio, Bloco 1 6° andar, 70340-901 Brasília **W:** www.radiomec.com.br – **DF03**) Sig Quadra.02 Lt 340 Bl.02, 1° andar,(✉ C.P. 8042, 70673-1080) 70610-901 Brasília ☎61 3214 1019 **W:** www.clube.am– **DF04**) SCRN 702/03, B1 «B», Edificio Radiobrás, 70710-750 Brasília ☎-61 3327 4260 **W:** www.radiobras.gov.br – **DF05**) SRTV/Sul, Q-701, bloco E, Térreo, 70340-000 Brasília – **DF06**) C.P 258, 70359-970 Brasília **W:** www.am.com.br **E:** amazoniabrasileira@ebc.com.br – **DF07**) SRTV-Sul, Q 701, Conj «E», Bloco 2 e 4, sala 316, 70340-902 Brasília ☎-61 2103 0710 **W:** www.novaalianca.org.br – **FM:** 103.3MHz – **DF08**) SCS-Quadra 05, Bl B, Lotes 47 a 57, Ns 39/40, 70340-000 Brasília ☎61 3245 3747 **W:** www.redeboavontade.com – **DF09**) C – 01, Lotes 1/12 – Ed. Taguatinga Trade Center, Sala 1025, 72010-010 Taguatinga ☎61 3451 3700 **W:** www.radioglobobrasilia.com.br – **DF10**) Senado Federal, Praça dos Tres Poderes, Anexo II, Bloco B -Térreo, 70165-900 Brasília ☎61 3311 4691 ▤61 3311 4238 **W:** www.senado.gov.br/radio **E:** radio@senado.gov.br

ES00) ESPÍRITO SANTO

ES01) Rua Joaquim Plácido da Silva, 225, Ihla de Santa Maria, 29051-070 Vitória ☎27 3331 9000 ▤27 3223 7340 **W:** www.redetribuna.com.br/radio/am – **FM:** 99.1MHz – **ES02**) C.P 700, 29001-970 Vitória **W:** www.vitoria640am.com.br – **ES03**) Praça Hilda Calazans dos Santos 4, Barrio Gilberto Machada, 29303-275 Cacheiro de Itapemirim – **ES04**) Rua Chafic Murad 902, Ilha de Monte Belo, 29050-901 Vitória **W:** http://gazetaonline.globo.com - **FM:** 92.5MHz «Antena Um», 102.3MHz «Litoral FM» – **ES05**) C.P 125, 29900-971 Linhares - **FM:** 98.7MHz – **ES06**) C.P 178, 29700-971 Colatina ☎27 3721 1506 **W:** www.difusoracolatina.com.br **Email** radio@difusoracolatina.com.br – **ES07**) Av Santo Antônio, 366 al Caratoira, 29025-645 Vitória ☎27 3222 4376 ▤27 3222 7747 **W:** www.radiocapixaba.com.br – **ES08**) Av NS da Penha 2141, Bairro Santa Luzia, 29045-403 Vitória ☎27 3137 2900 **W:** www.rtv.es.gov.br **E:** falecom@radioespiritosanto.com.br – **ES09**) Rua Bernardo Horta 324, Guandu, 29300-782 Cachoeiro de Itapemirim ☎28 3517 9696 **W:** www.radiosimcachoeiro.com.br – **ES10**) Rua Alberto de Oliveira Santos 42, 19° andar, salas 1916-1920, Centro, 29010-901 Vitória **W:** www.redeamericaes.com.br **E:** america@ebr.com.br ☎ 27 3222 2365 - **FM:** 101.5MHz «Cidade» – **ES11**) Rua José Cupertino 120, 29600-000 Afonso Cláudio **W:** www.novotempo.com/radio – **ES12**) Rua da Matriz 85, 29200-000 Guarapari **W:** www.simamguarapari.com.br – **ES13**) Av Presidente Vargas 449, Centro, 29600-000 Afonso Cláudio ☎27 2735 1120 **W:** www.educadoraafonsoclaudio.com.br – **ES14**) C.P 132, 29930-000 São Mateus **W:** www.redesimsat.com.br/radio – **ES15**) Rua Costa Pereira 37, Centro, 29300-090 Cachoeiro de Itapemirim **W:** www.radiodiocesana com. br **E:** radio@radiodiocesana.com.br ☎27 3521 1960 – **Italian:** Sun 1300-1600 – **ES16**) Rua Graciano Neves 250, 29156-050 Cariacica **W:** www.redesimsat.com.br – **ES17**) Rua Astrogildo Romão dos Anjos 277, 29800-000 Barra de São Francisco **W:** www.radiosaofranciscoam.com **E:** contato@radiosaofranciscoam.com – **ES18**) Rua Chafic Murad 302, Bento Ferreira,29500-660 Vitória ☎27 3331 8397 **FM:** 93.5 MHz – **ES19**) 29650-000 Santa Teresa – **ES20**) Av João Felipe Calmon, 819 – Centro, 29900-010 Linhares ☎22 3372 3100 **W:** www.globolinhares.com.br **E:** diretoria@globolinhares.com.br– **ES21**) Rodovia Mickel Chequer – Fazenda Vargem Alegre S/N. 293900-000 Iúna – **ES22**) 29300-000 Cachoeiro de Itapemirim **W:** www.radiosimtupi1590.com – **ES23**) Baixo Guandu. – **ES24**) Rua Dr Moacir Veloso, 63 – Gloria, 29122-610 Vila Velha ☎27 3319 1069 **W:** www.redesimsat.com.br

GO00) GOIÁS

GO01) Av. Goiás Q 10, 636 - Centro, 74010-010 Goiânia ☎62 3212 7872 **W:** http://radioriviera.webnode.com **E:** radioam.riviera@gmail.com – **GO02**) Av. João XXIII, 381 - Centro, 75702-130 Catal ão ☎64 3441 2700 **W:** www.radioculturaonline.com.br **E:** radioculturaonline.com.br – **GO03**) Rua Rui Barbosa, 420 – Central, 75025-060 Anápolis **W:** www.radiomanchester.com.br **E:** fm@radiomanchester.com.br – **FM:** 93.3 MHZ – **GO04**) Av Egídio Francisco Rodrigues 54, Centro, 75200-000 Pires do Rio ☎64 3461 7346 **W:**www.gospelam.com.br **E:** am630gospel@hotmail.com - **FM:** 102.3MHz «Rio FM» – **GO05**) Av 24 de Outobro 1854, Campinas, 74505-016 Goiânia ☎62 3233 4000 **W:** www.difusora.am.br **E:** difusora@netgo.com.br – **GO06**) Av Marechal Rondón, Q 18 Lote 9, 76270-000 Jussara – **GO07**) Rua 48, 1254 – Joaquim da Silva Moreira,, 76680-000 Itapuranga ☎62 3312 1548 **W:** www.radioprimavera.net **E:** radioprimavera@radioprimavera.net – **GO08**) Av 1° de Maio, 30 - Centro, 75001-970 Anápolis ☎62 3328 1641 **W:** www.radiosaochico.com.br **E:** contato@radiosaochico.

com.br - **FM:** 96.3MHz – **GO09)** Rua José de Carvalho, 542 - Centro, 75800-447 Jataí – ☎64 3631 1245 **W:** www.difusoraonline.com.br **E:** contato@difusoraonline.com.br – **GO10)** Rua Evangelino Meireles 26, 72800-000 Luziânia – **GO11)** Rua Coronel Gonzaga, 540 – Centro, 75690-000 Caldas Novas ☎64 3435 1100 **W:** www.radiopousada.com.br/cont/cont.php **E:** rpousada@itcn.com.br – **GO12)** Rua Br Cotegipe s/n, S.Central, 75025-010 Anápolis ☎62 3098 3977 **W:** www.radiovozimaculada.franciscanosdaimaculada.org **E:** frastan@hotmail.com – **R. Maria.:** Qna 05 Lote 20. 72110-050 Taguatinga Norte, DF ☎ 61 3562 8888 **W:** www.radiomaria.net.br **E:** radiomaria@radiomaria.net.br – **GO13)** Rua 29 234, Camilho, 76380-000 Goianésia ☎62 3353 3355 **W:** www.rvc780.com.br – **FM:** 96 MHz – **GO14)** Av. Antônio C. Paniago, 1, S. Pecuári, 75830-000 Mineiros ☎62 3661 1316 **W:** www.eldoradomineiros.com.br **E:** radio@eldoradomineiros.com.br – **GO15)** Av Bernardo Sayao 371, 76310-000 Rialma – **GO16)** Rua Teixeira de Freitas Qd. 04 Lt 26, Setor Serrinha 74835-180 Goiânia ☎62 3945 3820 **W:** www.820am.com.br **E:** internet@820am.com.br – **GO17)** Av Belém Brasilia Q5 10 lt 4, S Central, 76550-000 Porangatu ☎62 3362 4085 **W:** www.radiotropical850am.com.br **E:** contato@radiotropical850am.com.br – **GO18)** Av Tocantins N° 65 1° andar, Centro, 76400-000 Uruaçu ☎62 3357 6626 **W:** www.radiolagodourado.com.br **E:** contato@radiolagodourado.com.br – **GO19)** SBS Qd 2 Bl Q, s/n lt3 an 15, 70070-120 Brasilia ☎61 3325 6775 – **GO20)** Rua Minas Gerais, 135 - Central, 75503-190 Itumbiara – ☎64 3431 8485 **W:** radioparanaiba.com.br - **FM:** 92.3MHz – **GO21)** Rua Uberaba, 9, 75500-000 Itumbiara ☎64 3431 7400 **W:** www.difusoraitumbiara.com.br **E:** contato@difusoraitumbiara.com.br – **GO22)** C.P 501, 75001-970 Anápolis– **GO23)** Rua do Contorno 702, 76330-000 Jaraguá ☎64 F-52 Qd. 164 Lt 5/18 No 120, Faiçalville IV, 74350450 Goiânia ☎62 3254 1082 **W:** www.redefonte.com.br **E:** supervisao@redefonte.com – **GO25)** Rua Freio João Batista 76, Centro, 75860-000 Quirinópolis. ☎64 3651 1452 **W:** www.sulgoiana.com **E:** quirinopolis@hotmail.com – **GO26)** Rua Herculano Lobo 80, 12573800-000 Formosa **E:** radioformosaam@brturbo.com – **GO27)** Rua Thomaz Edson Qd 07, St. Serrinha, 74835- 130 Goiânia - **FM:** 92.7MHz «Executiva FM» and 97.1 «Araguaia» – **GO28)** Av. Br. Rio Branco, 1 – S. Central, (✉C.P 34, 75781-970) 75780-000 Ipameri ☎64 3491 1657 **W:** www.xavantes.net **E:** radio_xavantes@hotmail.com – **GO29)** Rua 42, 50 – Rialma II,76310-000 Rialma ☎62 3397 2175 **W:** www.coracaofiel.com.br **E:**radio@coracaofiel.com.br – **GO30)** Rua SC-01 No 299, Parque Santa Cruz, 74860-270 Goiânia ☎62 3201 7685 **W:** www.radiobrsilcentral.com.br **E:** rbc@agecom.go.gov.br or fernandocozacam@yahoo.com.br - **FM:** 90.1MHz – **GO31)** Av Goiás 174, Ed.São Judas Tadeu, 16° andar, Centro 74010-010 Goiânia ☎62 3216 0730 ▤62 3521 0412 **W:** www.radio730.com.br – **GO32)** Alameda das Rosas 2200, Setor Oeste, 74126-010 Goiânia ☎62 3521 1707 **W:** www.radio.ufg.br **E:** tro@radio.ufg.br– **GO33)** Av Amazonas, 367 – S.Central, 76100-000 São Luís de Montes Belos ☎64 3671 1621 **W:**www.valedaserraam.com.br **E:** radiovaleamfm@hotmail.com **FM:** 102.5MHz – **GO34)** Rua Barão do Rio Branco, 989, - www.radiovale-amfm.com.brwww Centro, 75650-000 Morrinhos **W:** www.intergracaofm.com.br - **FM:** 94.5MHz «Integração FM»– **GO35)** Praca Rui Barbosa, 471 - Centro, 75180-000 Silvânia **W:** www.radioriovermelho.com.br **E:** atendimento@radioriovermelho.com.br – **GO36)** Rua Kisleu Maciel 113, 73850-000 Cristalina ☎61 3612 2929 **W:** www.radioserradoscristais.com.br **E:**contato@radioserradoscristais.com.br – **GO37)** C.P 60, 76601-970 Goiás.- **W:**www.cidadeam.com.br **E:** radiocidade@virtnet.com.br– **GO38)** C.P 70, 75601-970 Goiatuba – **GO39)** Praça Pres Médici, s/n, Central, 75920-000 Santa Helena de Goiás **W:**www.radiosantelenense.com.br **E:** radiosantelenense@globo.com – **GO40)** C.P 117, 75401-970 Inhumas **W:** www.rjiam.com.br **E:** jornalam@hotmail.com – **GO41)** Av. Pauzanes Carvalho Q 25,s/n lt 7/9, S.Pauzanes (✉C.P 131, 75901-970) 75930-000 Rio Verde – ☎64 3621 4433 **W:** www.rioverdeam.com.br - **FM:** 95.3MHz – **GO42)** Rua Benedito Lemes, 45 – S Centro, 76630-000 Itaberaí. ☎62 3375 2901 **W:** www.radiosilvestream.com.br **E:** joãosilvestre@radiosilvestream.com.br **FM:** 87.9MHz – **GO43)** Rua Catalão 182, 76200-000 Iporá **W:** www.rioclaroamfelicidadefm.com.br **E:** contato@rioclaroamfelicidadefm.com.br – **GO44)** Rua 23 Q 1 s/n lt 3, S.Andrade, 75850-000 Caiapônia ☎64 3363 1219 – **GO45)** Rua Lazer Q82, s/n lt 2 Res Village Garavelo, 74900-000 Aparecida de Goiânia ☎62 3283 1040 **W:** www.radiocaraibagoiania.com.br– **GO46)** Quadra 33, Lotes 23/24, 72900-000 Santo Antônio do Descoberto (C.P 06-799, 71701-970 Brasília, DF) ☎61 3202 1110 **W:** www.radioredentor.com.br **E:** comercial@radioredentor.com.br– **GO47)** Rua 22, 150 – St.Aeroporto, 75640-000 Piracanjuba 64 3405 1919 **W:** www.radiopousoalto.com.br **E:** contato@radiopousoalto.com – **GO48)** Rua 49 Q 53, 218 (✉C.P 185, 76301-970) 76300-000 Ceres ☎62 3307 3042 **W:** www.radiosociedadeceres.com.br – **GO49)** Praça Silva Junior, 184, Centro76420-000 Niquelândia ☎62 3354 1430 **W:** www.radiomantiqueiraam.com.br **E:** radiomantiqueira@uol.com.br – **GO50)** Rua Amazonas 1355, 75600-000 Goiatuba ☎64 3495 7556 **W:** www.radiosempre.com.br **E:** contato@radiosempre.com.br – **GO51)**

Rua Francisco Corra Neves 100 – 2° andar, 75860-000 Quirinópolis – ☎ 64 3651 2106 **W:** www.radioalvoradaam.com.br **E:** radioalvorada@cultura.com.br **GO52)** Av Joaquim David Ferreira 1390, 76105-000 Firminópolis ☎64 3681 1217 **W:** http://radioboasnovas1020am.com.br – **GO53)** Av Santana, Qd 55, lote 01, Sector Vila Baiana, 73840-000 Campas Belos ☎62 3451 1209 **W:** www.rcbam.com.br – **GO54)** 78505-000 Caçu – **GO55)** 73900-000 Posse

MA00) MARANHÃO

MA01) Av Eliézer Moreira s/n, Incra, 65950-000 Barra do Corda – **MA02)** Rua Frei Querubim, 57 – Apicum – Centro, 65025-420 São Luís ☎98 3878 5707 ▤ 98 3214 3600 **W:** www.educadora560.com.br– **MA03)** Av Camboa do Mato, 120 - Camboa, 65020-260 São Luís – ☎98 3214 3000 **W:** www.difusora680.com.br - **FM:** 94.3MHz – **MA04)** Rua Henrique de Figueiredo 485, 65400-000 Codó – **MA05)** Av São Benedito 1075, Bairro São Benedito, 65400-000 Codó – **MA06)** Rua Simplicio Moreira 1686, 1° andar, Centro, 65901-490 Imperatriz **W:** www.apazdosenhor.org.br **E:** radioimp@aeronet.com.br – **MA07)** Rua Manoel Alves de Abreu 373, 65700-000 Bacabal – **MA08)** Av Coronel Fonseca 200, 65400-000 Balsas – **MA09)** Av Cel Colares Moreira, 1000 s11, Calhua, 65075-440 São Luís ☎98 3235 7676 – **MA10)** Rua Montanha Russa, s/n Centro, 65010-400 Sao Luis – ☎98 2108 2329 **W:** www.ma.gov.br/timbira **E:** timbira@secom.ma.gov.br – **MA11)** Av dos Africanos, 77 - Areinha, 65031-410 São Luís ☎98 2109 7777 **W:** www.grupozildenifalco.com.br **E:** opecsaoluis@yahoo.com.br – **FM:** 102.5MHz – **MA12)** Rua 30 de Março, 627 - Centro, 65200-000 Pinheiro ☎98 3381 3215 **W:** www.sistemapericuma.com.br **E:** rvc@sistemapericuma.com.br – **MA13)** Av Rio Branco, 670,, 65725-000 Pedreiras – **MA14)** Av Keened, 65690-000 Colinas – **MA15)** Av. Ans Jansen 200, 65076-902 São Luis ☎98 3235 3013 – **MA16)** Fazenda São João, BR-14 Km 37, 65215-000 Viana – **MA17)** Rua Guarani s/n QD 03 LOTE 09, Caicara, 65922-000 João Lisboa – **MA18)** Rua A Bandeira 831, 65320-000 Vitorino Freire – **MA20)** Rua Piauí 895, 65930-000 Açailândia – **MA21)** C Carneiro 177, 65750-000 Esperantinópolis – **MA22)** Travessa Tiradentes 338, Centro, 65415-000 Coroatá – **MA23)** Rua Aarão Reis s/n, 65604-060 Caxias – **MA24)** Av Coronel Stanley Fortes Batista 454, 65365-000 Zê Doca – **MA25)** 65278-000 Turiau – **MA26)** Rua Alagoas 497, 65900-490 Imperatriz **W:** www.imirante.globo.com/miranteam/paginas/emisoras.asp **E:** centralam@mirante.am **FM:** 96.1 MHz – **MA27)** Av Amaral Raposo s/n, 65940-000 Grajaú – **MA28)** Rua Rui Barbosa s/n, 65620-000 Coelho Neto – **MA29)** Rua Dr Paulo Ramos 495, 65208-000 Santa Helena ☎98 3382 1196 **W:** www.radiorioturiacuam.com.br – **MA30)** Rua Frederico Coelho esquina com Av Frei Aniceto, 65763-000 Tuntum – **MA31)** Rua do Puraqueu s/n, 65350-000 Vitória do Mearim – **MA32)** Parque da Bandeira 222, Edificio Ariana, Centro, 65665-000 São João dos Patos – **MA33)** Praça de Guarim s/n, 65390-000 Santa Luzia – **MA34)** Rua Terra esquina com Rua Jupiter s/n, 65760-0000 Presidente Dutra – **MA35)** Praça Coronel Luis Vieira 25, 65500-000 Chapadinha – **MA36)** Rua Cel Pedro Bogéa 227, Centro, 65715-000 Lago de Pedra – **MA37)** Rua Hemeterio Leitão 103, 65430-00 Vargem Grande – **MA38)** Av Ana Jansen 200, 65000-000 São Luís ☎98 3215 5124 **W:**http://imirante.globo.com/miranteam/_index.asp **E:** comercialam@mirante.am **FM:** 96.1MHz – **MA39)** 65530-000 Urbano Santos – **MA40)** 65600-000 Caxias – **MA41)** Praça Roosevelt Moreira, S/N° - Centro, 65800-000 Balsas ☎99 3541 2999 ▤99 3541 7308 **W:** www.radioboanoticia.com.br **E:** radio@radioboanoticia.com.br

MG00) MINAS GERAIS

MG01) Rua Rabelo Horta, 39 - Centro, (C.P 123, 36771-970) 36770-064 Cataguases ☎32 3422 1724 **W:** www.radiocataguases.com **E:** contato@radiocataguases.com- **FM:** 89.5MHz – **MG02)** Rua General Carneiro 10, Edificio Milinardo, s 200 à 305, 39400-095 Montes Claros – **MG03)** Rua Romero Gomes Vieira 1200, Cj. Hab Vila de Jatobá, 30666-330 Belo Horizonte ☎31 3382 1157 – **MG04)** Praça Nossa Senhora Aparecida 134, Bairro Aparecida, 38400-726 Uberlândia **E:** america@radioamerica.com.br **W:** www.radioamerica.com.br ☎34 3292 0400 ▤34 3292 0412 - **FM:** 98.7MHz – **MG05)** Av Padre Matias, 1089 - Bairro Marciano Brandão, 38740-000 Patrocínio ☎34 3839 9880 **W:** www.sistemadifusoraderadio.com.br- **FM:** 98.9MHz – **MG06)** Rua Itatiaia 117, Bairro Bonfim, 31210-170 Belo Horizonte ☎31 3421 3588 ▤31 3422 8588 **E:** itatiaia@itatiaia.com.br **W:** www.itatiaia.com.br **FM:** 95.7MHz – **MG07)** Av. Dr. Fidélis Reis 820, Centro,, 38010-030 Uberaba. ☎34 3331 7900 ▤34 3321 8200 **W:** www.jmonline.com.br **E:** jmonlin@emonline.com.br – **MG08)** Av Presidente Vargas, 372 - Centro, 35661-000 Pará de Minas ☎37 3232 1588 **W:** www.santacruzam.com **E:** contato@padregabriel.com.br – **MG09)** Rua Euripides Ribeiro, 739 - Centro, 38720-000 Lagoa Formosa ☎34 3824 2628 **W:** www.radiovitoriosa.com.br – **MG10)** Rua Xavier de Veiga 85, 35400-000 Ouro Preto ☎31 3551 2166 ▤31 3551 2325 **W:** www.itatiaia.com.br/ouropreto/ **E:** ouropreto@itatiata.com.br – **MG11)** C.P 30, 35791-970 Curvelo – **MG12)** Rua Prof Monteiro Fonseca 119, 39400-149 Montes Claros **MG13)** Praça Coronel Hermógenes 292, 38770-000 João Pinheiro – **MG14)** Rua Entre Rios 33, Bairro Carlos Prates, 30710-

080 Belo Horizonte ☎31 3231 7151 **W:** www.radiomineira.com **E:** contato@radiomineria.com – **MG15**) Praça 15 de Novembro, 339 - 5° andar - Centro, 36900-000 Manhuaçu ☎33 3332 4080 **W:** www. am710.com.br **E:** contato@am710.com.br - **FM:** 88 MHz – **MG16**) Rua Cel. José Inácio, 96 - Centro, 37550-000 Pouso Alegre ☎35 3423 1488 **W:** www.difusora710am.com.br **E:** difusora@tcnet.com.br – **MG17**) Rua Guilherme Ferreira 650, salas 81/82, 38022-200 Uberaba **E:** socie-dade@ldc.com.br – **MG18**) Rua Dr João Penido Filho 269, 36021-600 Juiz de Fora – **MG19**) Av Itaú, 515, Dom Cabral, 30730-910 Belo Horizonte **W:** www.americabh.com.br **E:** radioamerica-diretoria@ puc-minas.br ☎31 3469 2500 ▤31 3469 2551 – **MG20**) Praça Leonardo Venerando Pereira 200 - Centro, 37200-000 Lavras ☎35 3822 5000 **W:** www.radiocultura770.com.br – **MG21**) Avenida Getúlio Vargas, 142 Centro, 38700 128 Patos de Minas ☎34 3823 1100 **W:** www.clubeam. com **E:** clubeam@clubeam.com – **MG22**) Rua dos Cravos, 467 – Bairro São Pedro,(C.P 10, 35901-970) 35900-125 Itabira ☎31 3831 4106 **W:** www.radioitabira.com.br **E:** euclideseder@yahoo.com.br - **FM:** 93.3MHz – **MG23**) Av Prof José Ignácio de Souza 2710, Umuarama, 38405-330 Uberlândia ☎34 3222 0780 **W:** www.ameducadora.com.br or www.educadorajp.com.br – **FM:** 100.7 MHz – **MG24**) Rua Reporter Luiz Quirino No. 100, 35430-017 Ponte Nova ☎31 3817 1025 **W:** www. radiopontenova.com **E:** diretoria@radiopontenova.com.br – **MG25**) Rua Margarida Monteiro 125 (C.P 153), 35290-000 Mantena ☎33 3241 1559 **W:** www.radio13dejunho.com.br **E:** radio13dejunho@ralnet.com. br – **MG26**) Rua Luz 235, Américo Silva, 35590 000 Lagoa da Prata. ☎37 3261 4500 **W:** www.tropical790.com **E:** tropical@tropi-cal790.com – **MG27**) Rua Esposalina Leal, 141 - Centro, 35200-000 Almorés ☎33 3267 1021 **W:** www.radioam810.org.br - **FM:** 90.3MHz – **MG28**) Rua Maranhao 400, 35500-066 Divinópolis ☎37 3222 7070 **W:** www.divinopolisvirtual.com.br - **FM:**100.5MHz – **MG29**) Praça Dom Pedro Teixeira 49 - 5° andar, 36200-001 Barbacena **E:** rbq@prower.com. br – **MG30**) Rua Dos Antunes, 1175, Ed São Sebastião (C.P 36), 37950-000 São Sebastião do Paraíso ☎35 3531 2396 ▤35 3531 2332 **W:** www.radiodafamilia.com.br – **MG31**) Rua Itatiaia 117, Bairro Bonfim, 31210-170 Belo Horizonte **W:** www.culturabh.com.br – **MG32**) Rua Barão de Piunhi 31, 35570-000 Formiga ☎37 3322 2565 **W:** www. difusoraformiga.com.br – **MG33**) Av Brasil, 2770 2° andar, Centro, 35020-070 Governador Valadares. ☎33 3271 7322 **W:** www.radiomun-domelhor.com.br **E:** radiomundomelhor@wkve.com.br - **FM:** 97.7MHz – **MG34**) Rua Coronel Joaquim Mendes 19 Ed Cine T Helena, 38430-000 Tupaciguara ☎34 3281 4050 **W:** www.radiotupaciguara.com.br direcao@radiotupaciguara.com.br - **FM:** 91.9MHz – **MG35**) Av Raja Gabáglia, 1666 – Gutierrez, 30441-194 Belo Horizonte ☎31 3298 3401 ▤31 3298 3403 **W:** www.inconfidencia.com.br **E:** inconfidencia@ inconfidencia.com.br or diretoria@ inconfidencia.com.br – **FM:** 100.9 MHz – **MG36**) Rua Dr Olinto Martins 207, 39960-000 Jequitinhonha ☎33 3741 1521 **W:** www.santacruz890.com.br – **MG37**) Av Getúlio Vargas, 420 Centro, 39800-015 Teófilo Otoni ☎33 3522 3635 **W:** www. radioteofilotoni.com.br **E:** vanessa@radioteofilotoni.com.br – **MG38**) Praça Dom João 122, Centro, 39100-000 Diamantina ☎38 3531 1408 – **MG39**) Praça 28 de Setembro 95, 36520-000 Visconde do Rio Branco – **MG40**) Rua Tenente Viotti, 131 - Centro, 37460-000 Passa Quatro ☎35 3371 3301 **W:** www.mineiradosul.com.br **E:** contato@mineirado-sul.com.br – **MG41**) Av Afonso Pena, 795 2° andar - Centro, 37270-000 Campo Belo **W:** www.radioclubecampobelo.com.br **E:** radioam@ clubecampobelo.com.br ☎35 3832 2700 – **MG42**) Av Teodolino Pereira de Araújo 731, 38440-000 Araguari **W:** www.radiovitoriosa. com.br – **MG43**) Av Ferroviaria s/n, 30520-480 Belo Horizonte ☎31 3361 0205 – **MG44**) Av Bom Jesus, Centro - 464, 37578-000 Bueno Brandão ☎35 3463 1006 **W:** www.radioindy.com.br **E:** comercial@ radioindy.com.br – **MG45**) Rua Radialista Hamilton Macedo, 204 - Limoero, 35300-000 Caratinga ☎33 3329 0112 **W:** www.radiocaratin-ga.com.br **E:** contato@radiocaratinga.com.br – **MG46**) Av Tirandentes, 209 - Centro, 36307-346 São João del Rei – ☎32 3317 7777 **W:** www. radiosaojoaodelrei.am.br **E:** contato@radiosaojoaodelrei.am.br – **MG47**) Rua Rio Barbosa 259, 38420-000 Monte Alegre de Minas ☎34 3281 2100 – **MG48**) Rua Espírito Santo, 95 – Poco Rico, 36420-000 Juiz de Fora ☎32 3215 1620 ▤32 3215 4360 **W:** www.radiosola-ram.com.br **E:** solarfm@radiosolar.com.br - **FM:** 88.9MHz – **MG49**) Rua Afonso Pena, 340 - Centro, 37590-000 Jacutinga ☎35 3443 2121 ▤35 3443 1625 **W:** www.radiojacutinga.com.br **E:** joao@radiojacutinga. com.br – **MG50**) Rua Manoel Joaquim Pires 63, 35170-082 Coronel Fabriciano ☎31 3842 1400 **W:** www.educadoramg.com.br **E:** educado-ra@usinet.com.br – **FM:** 107.1MHz – **MG51**) Rua Rio Grande do Norte, 1096, Marta Helena, (C.P 557, 38409-970) 38402-016 Uberlândia ☎34 3291 5500 **W:** www.radiocultura.am.com.br - **FM:** 95.1MHz– **MG52**) Rua Bueno Brandão 26, 38430-000 Tupaciguara – **MG53**) Rua Tamoios 200, 21° andar, 30120-050 Belo Horizonte.– **MG54**) Rua Olegário Maciel 200, Rua Vila Podis, 37500-000 Itajubá ☎35 3623 2471 **W:** www.radioitajuba-am.com.br **E:** radioitajubaam1060@yahoo.com.br – **MG55**) Praça da Basílica 130 (✉ CP 05) 36415-000 Congonhas ☎31▤31

3731 4217 **W:** www.radiocongonhas.com.br **E:** gerencia@radiocongo-nhas.com.br – **MG56**) Av Dr Américo Luz 153, 37890-000 Muzambinho ☎35 3571 2399 **W:** www.radiodopovo.com.br **E:** radiodopovoam@ yahoo.com.br – **MG57**) Rua Halfeld 744 Sl 401, Centro,36010-003 Juiz de Fora ☎32 3215 4477 **W:** www.radiocapitaljuizdefora.com.br **E:** contato@radiocapitaljuizdefora. com.br – **MG58**) C.P 85, 38441-970 Araguari ☎34 3241 3030 **W:** www.radioplanalto.com.br **E:** planalto-am@netsite.com.br – **MG59**) Rua Areião do Matadouro s/n, Parque da California, 34000-000 Nova Lima – **MG60**) Rua França, 506 – Boa Vista, (✉C.P 253), 38001-970 Uberaba ☎34 3313 3400 **W:** www.setecoli-nas.com.br **E:** contato@setecolinas.com.br - **FM:** 98.1MHz – **MG61**) Av Juscelino Kubstchek 740, 37170-000 Boa Esperança ☎35 831 1000 ▤35 851 1475 **W:** www.radioserra.com.br **E:** radioserra@yahoo. com.br – **MG62**) Av Antonio Olímpio de Morais 545, Centro, 35500-005 Divinópolis **W:** www.radiominasam.com.br **E:** sistemampa@radio-94FM.com.br ☎37 3222 0001 ▤37 3222 0009 - **FM:** 95.3MHz – **MG63**) Rua João Bressane 1, 37400-000 Campanha ☎35 3261 1229 **W:** www. radiodiocesanaam.com.br **E:** radiocesana@yahoo.com.br – **MG64**) Av Constantino Pinto, 90 - Centro, 36880-000 Muriaé ☎32 3729 2929 **W:** www.radiomuriae.com.br **E:** diretoria@radiomuriae.com.br - **FM:**) 96.3MHz «R 96» – **MG65**) Av Raja Gabáglia 3502, 4° andar, Estoril, 30350-540 Belo Horizonte ☎31 3298 9303 ▤31 3298 9305 **W:**http:// radioclick.globo.com/globobrasil/ – **MG66**) Rua do Rádio 60, Bairro Pepétuo Socorro, 38190-000 Sacramento E: radiosac@sacranet.com.br ☎34 3351 1735 ▤34 3351 1432 – **MG67**) Rua Cassiano Lemos, 87 - Centro, 38180-000 Araxá ☎34 3661 2844 **W:** www.cidadeamfm.com. br **E:** cidade@radiocidadedearaxa.com.br - **FM:** 94.5 MHz – **MG68**) Av Assis Chateaubriand 499, Floresta, 30150-101 Belo Horizonte **W:** www. guarani.com.br ☎31 3237 6000 ▤31 3237 6699 – **MG69**) Praça Cleber de Holanda 111, Sion, 37048-370 Varginha ☎35 3222 8288 ▤35 3212 2722 **W:** www.sistemaclube.com **E:** sac@sistcmaclubc.com.br - **FM:** 99.3MHz – **MG71**) Rua Barao do Rio Branco 461, Conj 901 – Edifico Rio Branco, 35010-030 Governador Valadares **W:** www.novotempo.com/ radio – **MG72**) Av. 13, 658 6° andar, Edifico Ituiutaba, Centro, (✉C.P 110), 38300-140 Ituiutaba ☎34 3271 7400 **W:** www.sistemacancella. com.br – **MG73**) Rua Rio Grande do Sul, 631- Centro, 37701-001 Poços de Caldas **W:** www.difusorapocos.com.br **E:** comercial@difusorapocos. com.br ☎35 3722 1530 - **FM:**104.1MHz – **MG74**) Pc. Getúlio Vargas, 81 - Centro, 36400-000 Conselheiro Lafaiete **W:** www.radiocarijjos. com.br ☎31 3763 1470 - **FM:** 89.9MHz – **MG75**) Rua Itajubá 80, 35160-035 Ipatinga **W:** www.vanguardaam.com.br **E:** producao@van-guardaam.com.br – **MG76**) Rua Ernane Vilela Lima, 114 - Centro, 37250-000 Nepomuceno ☎35 3861 1278 **W:** www.radioam810.com.br **E:** folha@agyonet.com.br – **MG77**) Rua Duque de Caxias 450, 16° andar, Edificio Chams, 38400-066 Uberlândia – **MG78**) Rua Alexandre Silva, 295 - Centro, 38600-000 Paracatu – ☎38 3671 3047 **W:** www. radiojuriti.com.br **E:** radiojuriti@ada.com.br – **MG79**) Av 13 No 658, 6° andar, Edifício Ituiutaba, Centro, 38300-140 Ituiutaba **W:** www.siste-macancella.com.br **E:** radiocancella@mgt.com.br ☎34 3268 1813 ▤34 3251 7071 - **FM:** 93.7MHz – **MG80**) Av Costa Junior, 467 Centro, 38840-000 Carmo do Paranaíba ☎34 3851 2066 **W:** www.sistemapla-neta.net **E:** rplaneta@sistemaplaneta.net – **MG81**) Rua José Benedito 441, Santa Efigenia, 35450-000 Itabirito – **MG82**) Av João Pinheiro 596, 1° andar (C.P 143), 37701-386 Poços de Caldas **W:** www.radiocultura-pocos.com.br **E:** cultura@radioculturapocos.com.br ☎35 3722 1687 ▤35 3722 2687 – **MG83**) Rua Cel José Paulino 257, Centro, 37750-000 Machado ☎35 3295 1361 **W:** www.difusoramachado.com.br **E:** gil-son0408@gmail.com – **MG84**) Praça Guido Marliere 30, 36500-000 Ubá **W:** www.radioubaense.com.br – **MG85**) Rua Calixto Martins de Melo, 391, Centro, 38610-000 Unaí ☎38 3676 1490 **W:** www.radiove-redas.com.br/globo **E:** contato@radioveredas.com.br - **FM:** 98.0MHz – **MG86**) Rua Calimeiro Guimarães 308, 38180-000 Araxá – **MG87**) Rua Antônio Dias Adorno. 1290 – Vila Rica, 35045-040 Governador Valadares ☎33 3275 0930 **W:** www.radiogloboygv.com.br **E:** comer-cial@radioglobogv.com.br - **FM:** 100.1MHz «Imparsom» – **MG88**) Rua Dr Péricles de Mendonça 91, 36680-000 São João Nepomuceno **W:** www.difusorasjn.com.br – **MG89**) Rua Niquel 457, 35701-107 Sete Lagoas ☎31 3773 3694 **W:** www.culturasl.com.br **E:** musirama@ mrnet.com.br - **FM:** 92.1MHz «Musirama» – **MG90**) Av Major Antônio Alberto Fernandes 445, 37720-000 Botelhos – **MG91**) Av Conde Ribeirão do Vale 661, 37800-000 Guaxupé.– ☎35 3551 1245 **W:** amclu-be.com.br **E:** amclube@amclube.com.br – **MG92**) Rua XV de Novembro 62, 36500-000 Ubá ☎32 3531 1830 **W:** http://am.educadora.com.br - **FM:** 94.5MHz – **MG93**) Praça Minas Gerais 50, Satélite, 35930-259 João Monlevade ☎31 3851 6001 **W:** www.cultura590.com.br **E:** rcul-tura@robynet.com.br – **MG94**) Rua Gerson Coutinho da Silva 1001, 38550-000 Coromandel – **MG95**) Rua Juliano Marques Duarte 110, Iha Gama Cerqueira, 36660-000 Além Paraíba ☎32 3462 7400 **W:** www. culturadeportonovo.com.br **E:** sistemahf@gmail.com - **FM:** 95.5MHz «Juventude» – **MG96**) Av 15 895, 10° andar Sala 1002 e 1005, Edifico Executivo» 38300-000 Ituiutaba ☎34 3261 7118 **W:** www.difusoraituiutaba.com.br **E:** administracao@difusoraituiutaba.com.br – **MG97)** Av. Iparanga, 198 - Centro, 37190-000 Três Pontas ☎35 3265 2252 – **MG98)** Rua Coronel Domiciano Ferreira 314, 38200-000 Frutal– **MG99)** Av Belo Horizonte 108, 39860-000 Nanuque – **MG100)** Praça Dr. Antônio das Chagas Viegas, 130 2° andar - Centro, 36300-000 São João del Rei ☎32 3371 8394 ▤32 3371 8025 **W:** www.emboabasfm.com.br – **FM:** 96.9 MHz– **MG101)** Rua Floriano Peixoto, 31 - Centro, 36570-000 Viçosa ☎31 3891 1500 ▤31 3891 1242 **W:** www.montanhesa.am.br **E:** montanhesavicosa@montanhesa.am.br - **FM:** 97.9MHz – **MG102)** C.P 28, 37901-970 Passos **W:** www.radiopassos.com.br – **MG103)** Rua Nunes Roas, Centro (▢C.P 61, 36971-970), 36970-000 Manhumirim ☎33 3341 1491 **W:** www.radiomanhumirim.com.br – **MG104)** Rua Dr Coelho de Moura 158, Centro, 35540-000 Oliveira **W:** www.radiosociedade.com.br **E:** geral@radiosociedade.com.br ☎37 3331 1170 ▤37 3331 1510 – **MG105)** Rua 13 de Maio 425, 36200-000 Barbacena ☎32 3332 5299 **W:** www.correiodaserra.com.br **MG106)** Praça Dr Augusto Gonçalves 146, salas 411/412, Centro, 35680-054 Itaúna ☎37 3742 1910 **W:** www.clubeamfm.com.br **E:** comercial@clubeamfm.com.br – **FM:** 93.5 MHz – **MG107)** Alameda Monteiro Lobato, Solar Lagos, 37470-000 São Lourenço ☎35 3332 4333 **W:** www.radioestancia.com. br **E:** estancia@radioestancia.com.br - **FM:** 94.3MHz – **MG108)** Av Juscelino Kubtschek, 1016 – Bairro Boa Vista, (C.P 99) 38280-000 Iturama 34 3411 3388 **W:** www.radiopontal.com **E:** contato@radiopontal.com – **MG109)** Av Magalhães Pinto 829, 35610-000 Dores do Indaiá ☎37 551 1622 – **MG110)** Rua Cel Otávio Meyer, 150 s 507 - Centro, 37550-000 Pouso Alegre ☎35 3423 6566 **W:** www.radioclubepousoalegre.com.br **E:** radioclube@tcnet.com.br – **MG111)** Rua Dr José Gonçalves 17, 35600-000 Bom Despacho – **MG112)** Praça Getúlio Vargas 81 / 1 andar, (C.P 123) Centro 36400-000 Conselheiro Lafaiete ☎31 3763 2466 **W:** www.radiocarijos.com.br/1540.html – **MG113)** Rua Casemiro Avelar Filho 143, Centro, 37410-000 Três Corações ☎35 231 1000 **W:** www.radiotropical.net - **FM:** 95.5MHz – **MG114)** Praça Nossa Senhora do Carmo 224, 38500-000 Monte Carmelo – **MG115)** Rua Sancho Viderla 19, Centro, 37540-000 Santa Rita do Sapucaí ☎35 3473 4400 **W:** www.difusora1550.com.br **E:** comercial@difusora1550. com.br - **FM:** 95.3MHz – **MG116)** Av Brasil 508, Centro, 39270-000 Pirapora ☎38 3741 1400 ▤38 3741 2981 **W:** www.radiopirapora.com. br **E:** pirapora@piraporo.com.br – **MG117)** Praça João XXIII 15, salas 303/307/308, 36700-000 Leopoldina ☎32 3441 4260 **W:** www.radiojornalam.net – **MG118)** Rua Bias Fortes, 191 - Centro, 37410-000 Alfenas ☎35 3299 3887 ▤35 3299 3891 **W:** www.radioculturaalfenas. com.br **E:** radiocultura@unifenas.br – **MG119)** Rua JK 108, 35500-000 Itapecerica paranaiba@paranaibamaximus.com **FM:** 101.3MHz – **MG120)** Rua Anastácio José Gonçalves, 139 - Centro, 38810-000 Rio Paranaíba ☎34 3855 1433 **W:** www.paranaibamaximus.com.br **E:** rcultura@sdnet.com.br – **FM:** 101.5 MHz – **MG121)** Rua Sérgio Neves, 63/Sala 103 – Centro, 36240-000 Santos Dumont ☎32 3251 6534 **W:** www.radioculturasd.com.br **E:** contato.cultura@radiomineira.com – **MG122)** Av Minas Gerais 584, 39510-000 Espinosa – **MG123)** Praça Nossa Senhora da Abadia 490, Abadia, 38025-430 Uberaba ☎34 3322 6200 ▤34 3322 6430 **W:**www.redevitoriosa.com.br – **MG124)** Av Hermenegildo Donatti 199, Jd. Nova Andrades, 37795-000 Andradas ☎35 3731 2291 **W:** www.radiovinicola.com.br **E:** vinicola@andradasnet.com.br - **FM:** 94.9MHz – **MG125)** Praça Coronel Odilon Coelho s/n, 39520-000 Porteirinha. ☎38 3831 1228 **W:** www.educadoraam640. com.br – **MG126)** Av. Dr. Otávo Soares 108, salas 707 a 712, Palmeiras, 35430-229 Ponte Nova ☎31 3881 8831 **W:** www.montanhesa.am.br **E:** montanhesapontenova@montanhesa.am.br – **MG127)** Travessa Dona Santinha, 20 - Centro, 39480-000 Januária ☎38 3621 1856 **W:** www. alternativafm.com **Email.:** alternativa@comnt.com.br – **FM:** 90.7 MHz – **MG128)** Rua Benedito Valadares, 423 - Barra, 36880-000 Muriaé ☎32 3729 4800 **W:** www.redeatividade.com/radioam - **FM:** 94.7 MHz – **MG129)** Rua Padre Pedro 53, Bonfim, 39390-000 Bocaiúva ☎38 3251 1995 **W:** www.radioclubebocaiuva.com.br – **MG130)** Rua Kil Barbosa 74, 39440-000 Janaúba – **MG131)** Av Getúlio Vargas 205, Centro Shopping Luziana, 35350-000 Raul Soares – **MG132)** Praça José Batista de Frieitas 78, 3° andar, 35519-000 Nova Serrana – **MG133)** Av. Deputada Humborta de Almeida 60, Centro, 37810-000 Guaranésia ☎35 3555 1350 ▤35 3555 2150 **W:** www.radioam1580guaranesia. com.br **E:** radioam1580@guaranesia.com.br – **MG134)** BR-496 Km 33, 39260-000 Várzea da Palma – **MG135)** Rua Getúlio Vargas, 4 - Centro, 38900-000 Bambuí ☎37 3431 3290 **W:** www.cidadeambambui.com – **MG136)**Rua Jair Werneck, 330, Cidade Alta, 39800-000 Teófilo Otoni **W:** www.radiomucuri.com.br – **MG137)** Rua Major Honor Sarmento, 393 - São João, 39400-533 Montes Claros ☎38 3223 5666 ▤38 3221 5590 – **MG138)** Rua 102 No 498, 38360-000 Capinópolis ☎34 3263 1481 **W:** www.radiocidade810.com.br – **MG139)** Avenida Dr. Breno Soares Maia 493, Belo Horizonte, 37900-110 Passos ☎35 3529 8261 **W:** www.globopassos.com.br **E:** contato@globopassos.com.br – **MG140)** Rua Tiradentes 784, Nova Horizonte, 37175-000 Ilicínea ☎35 3854 1342 **W:** www.radioaparecidadosulam **E:** apdosulam@

gmail.com – **MG141)** Rua Astor Goulart de Moura 51, 39200-000 Corinto ☎38 3751 1858 **W:** www.radiocidadecorinto.com.br **E:**radiocidadadecorinto@futuretec.com.br – **MG142)** Rodovia BR-381 Km 195, Bairro Cachoeira do Vale, 35180-001 Timóteo ☎31 3849 4000 **W:** www.itatiaia.com.br/valedoaco/ **E:** valedoaco@itatiaia.com.br - **FM:** 95.7MHz – **MG143)** Rua Coronel Américo Teixeira Guimarães 38, Centro, 35700-181 Sete Lagoas ☎31 3772 0244 **W:** www.eldorado1300.com.br **E:** comercial@eldorado1300.com.br – **MG144)** Rua 1° de Janeiro, N° 382 Serra Dourada, 38780-000 Vazante ☎34 3813 1113 **W:** www.montanheza.com.br **E:** radio@montanheza.com.br – **MG145)** Rua Leandro Gonçalves 88, 3° andar, 36900-000 Manhuaçu – **MG146)** Rua Coronel Rennó 7, 37500-000 Itajubá – **MG148)** Praça Getúlio Vargas, 108 – Triângulo, 36800-000 Carangola ☎34 3241 5823 **W:** www.ondavivaaraguari.com.br **E:** comercial@radioondaviva.com.br - **FM:** 102.7MHz «Caparaó» – **MG149)** Rua Oscar Vidal, 416 - Centro, 36016-290 Juiz de Fora ☎32 2102 9500 **W:** www.radioglobojf.com.br **E:** atendimento@radioglobojf.com.br – **MG150)** Rua Getúlio Vargas, 254 - Centro, 38700-128 Patos de Minas ☎34 3823 1070 **W:** www. radiopatos.com.br **E:** radiopatos@radiopatos.com.br – **MG151)** Av 7 de Setembro 55-A, 36950-000 Ipanema – **MG152)** Rua Julio Cosi 5, 38230-000 Fronteira ☎34 3428 2099 – **MG153)** Av Francisco Epifâno Fagundes, 161, Fagundes, 33200-000 Vespasiano ☎31 3621 3811 – **MG154)** Rua Padre Vigilato, s/n Centro, 35330-000 Inhapim ☎33 3315 1299 **W:** www.radioclubedeinhapim.com.br **E:** radio890@radioclubedeinhapim.com.br – **MG155)** Rua Guaribus 73, Horto, 35160-300 Ipatinga – **MG156)** Rua GervásioMarques da Silveira, 1498 – Barrio Marthina, 38740-000 Patrocínio ☎34 3831 7244 **W:** www.radiorainhadapaz.com.br **E:** contato@radiorainhadapaz.com.br – **MG157)** Praça Comendador José Honorio 100, 37950-000 São Sebastião do Paraiso – **MG158)** Rua Pref Terêncio Pereira Vale 10, 38170-000 Perdizes - **FM:** 96.1MHz – **MG159)** Av Joaquim Ribeiro de Gouveia, 1651 - Centro, 38320-000 Santa Vitória ☎34 3251 2000 **W:** www.radiosom2000.com. br **E:** radiosom2000@mgt.com – **MG161)** Rua das Acacias, 672 - Canaã, 38660-000 Buritis ☎38 9966 2412 **W:** www.radioburitis.com.br **E:**radioburitis@hotmail.com – **MG162)** Rua Silvino Brandão, 164 – Aeroporto, 38440-170 Araguari ☎34 3241 5823 **W:** www.ondavivaaraguari.com.br **E:** comercialmaisfm@yahoo.com.br - **FM:** 93.5 MHz – **MG163)** Travessa Cônego Benedito Profício, 95 - Centro, 37660-000 Paraisópolis.**W:** www.paraisopolisam.com.br – **MG164)** Av Progresso 177, Olaria, 35588-000 Arcos ☎37 3351 2100 **W:** www.radiocidadearcos.com.br **E:** radiocidadeam@gmail.com – **MG165)** Rua Antônio Ribeiro da Costa Junior 16, 36730-000 Pirapetinga – **MG167)** Praça Dr Badaró 112, 36900-000 Minas Novas ☎33 3764 1181 ▤33 3764 1185 **W:** www.radiobomsucesso.com **E:** lalado@radiobomsucesso.com.br – **MG168)** Rua Marcos Vinícius Ferreira 226, São Miguel, 39560-000 Salinas ☎38 341 1060 **W:** www.radiodifusoradesalinas.com.br **E:** programacao@radiodifusoradesalinas.com.br – **MG169)** Av Rondón Pacheco, 450 – Santo Antônio, 37150-000 Carmo do Rio Claro ☎35 3561 1967 **W:** www.radiodifusoram.com.br **E:** contato@radiodifusoram.com.br – **MG170)** Rua Vereador Maria Anselmo 33, 36480-000 Piranga – **MG171)** Rua Coronel Carlos Brandão 98, sala 07/08, 36500-000 Ubá – **MG172)** Av Dr Pedro Rosa s/n, 37530-000 Brasópolis ☎35 3641 1317 – **MG173)** Rua Silviano Brandão, 795, Centro, (C.P 100) 37570-000 Ouro Fino **W:** www.difusoraourofino.com.br **E:** radio@difusoraourofino.com.br ☎35 3441 1433 ▤35 3441 1800 – **MG174)** Praça Vital Brasil 56, 37980-000 Cássia – **MG175)** Praça Coronel Silverio de Melo 172, 37958-000 Monte Santo de Minas – **MG176)** Rua Artur de Vasconcelos 18, Centro, 37958-000 Campina Verde – **MG178)** Av. Brasil, 4460 Umuarama, 38405-312 Uberlândia ☎34 3212 0855 **W:** www.radiovitoriosa.com.br **E:** triangulo@itatiaia.com.br – **MG181)** 39270-000 Pirapoar– **MG182)** 39900-000 Almenara – **MG183)** 39740-000 Guanhães – **MG186)** 38240-000 Itapagipe – **MG193)** Rua Rua Coronel Ferraz 135, 37470-000 São Lourenço ☎35 3332 6646 **W:** www. globolambari.com.br – **MG194)** 36820-000 Divino – **MG195)**Av. Gov. Milton Campos, 2232 sl 201- Centro, 39740 000 Guanhães ☎33 3421 3503 **W:** www.cidadeam1550.com.br

MS00) MATO GROSSO DO SUL
MS01) Av Mato Grosso 530, Centro, 79002-233 Campo Grande **W:** www.miliciadaimaculada.org.br/v2/Rural580.asp **E:** 580am@miliciadaimaculada.org.br – **MS02)** Av Senador Felinto Müller 59, 79080-190 Campo Grande **W:** www.culturaam680.com.br – **MS03)** Rua Jamil Selem N° 27(C.P 104 79951-970) 79950-000 Naviraí **W:** www.cultura.com.br **E:** culturanav@terra.com.br – **MS04)** Rua Ciro Melo 2045, 79805-000 Dourados **W:** www.radioclubeam720.com.br – **MS05)** Rua Anchieta 871, Bairro Parati, 79081-180 Campo Grande ☎67 3346 2686 **W:** www.amcapital.com.br **E:** contato@amcapital. com.br – **MS06)** Rua 15 de Agosto 98, 79200-000 Aquidauana **W:** www.pantanalnews.com.br/radioindependente – **MS07)** Rua Melanio Garcia Barbosa 749, 79150-000 Maracaju **W:** www.rcmdigital.com. br **E:** rcmdigital@terra.com.br – **MS08)** Rua Joaquim Pereira Teixeira 135, 79900-000 Ponta Porã – **MS09)** Rua 15 de Novembro 2649,

Jardim dos Estados, 79020-300 Campo Grande ☎67 3349 1240 **W:** www.difusorapantanal.com.br **E:** contato@difusorapantanal.com. br – **MS10**) Rua Plinio Alarcon, 901(C.P 37, 79601-970) 79630-213 Três Lagoas ☎67 3524 2129 **W:** www.radiodifusora1250.com.br **E:** radiodifusora1250@radiodifusora1250.com.br – **MS11**) Av Marcelino Pires 1404, 79801-002 Dourados – **MS12**) Rua Marechal Deodoro, 504, Bairro Guanandy, 79200-000 Aquidauana ☎67 3241 3957 **W:** www.difusora1340.com.br – **MS13**) Rua Antônio Lino Barbosa 961, 79130-970 Rio Brilhante **W:** www.difusorarb.com.br ☎67 3452 7451 – **MS14**) Rua Dom Pedro II No 26, Previsul, 79300-000 Corumbá ☎67 3232 3135 **W:** www.novaclubeam.com **E:**novaclube1410am@ gmail.com – **MS15**) Rua Delmare 1274, Centro 793330-040 Corumbá **MS16**) Av Antonio Joaquim de Moura Andrade, 145 - Centro, 79750-000 Nova Andradina ☎67 3441 2136 **W:** www.radiocacique.com **E:** falecom@radiocacique.com – **MS17**) Av Aldair Rosa de Oliveira 1045, 79640-100 Três Lagoas – **MS18**) Rua Ferreira 69 B, Piracema, 79400-000 Coxim **W:** www.radiovaledotaquari.com.br – **MS19**) Rua Angélica 455, Centro, 79730-000 Glória de Dourados ☎63 3466 2040 **W:** www.paiaguas.grupofeitosa.com.br – **MS20**) Rua Visconde de Taunay 895, 79500-000 Paranaíba **W:** www.radiodifusoraam.com **E:** difusoraparanaiba@hotmail.com – **MS21**) Rua General Câmara,1296 - Centro, 79990-000 Amambaí ☎67 3481 1373 ▤67 3481 1391 **W:** www.radiojornalamambai.com.br – **FM:** 102.5MHz – **MS22**) Rua Severino Araújo, 1375 - Centro, 79700-000 Fátima do Sul ☎67 3467 1833 **W:** www.globnfatimadosul.com.br – **MS23**) C.P 200, 79541-970 Cassilândia – **MS24**) Av Presidente Vargas, 669 - Centro, 79940-000 Caarapó ☎67 3453 1810 **W:** www.difusora.grupofeitosa.com.br– **MS25**) Rua/Av.Ra 7 de Setembro,740, Centro, 79240-000 Jardim ☎67 3251 1531 **W:** www.radiolaguna.com.br – **MS26**) Rua Rui Barbosa 753, 79970-000 Eldorado – **MS27**) C.P 129, 79301-970 Corumbá – **MS28**) C.P 199, 79901-970 Ponta Porã – **MS29**) C.P 68, 79804-970 Dourados – **MS30**) Rua São Paulo 1359, 79490-000 São Gabriel d'Oeste **W:** www.difusora850.com.br – **MS31**) Rua Thomás Cáceres 349, Bairro São Bento, 79170-000 Sidrolândia ☎67 3272 1541 **W:** www.pindorama.grupofeitosa.com.br – **MS32**) 135 Rua Amando de Oliveria, 135 - Bairro Amambai, 79005-380 Campo Grande (C.P.146 79002-970 Campo Grande) ☎67 3324 0630 **W:** www.radionovotempo.org.br **E:** ellen@radionovotempo.org.br – **MS33**) Rua Severino de Araujo Ferreira 1375, 79700-000 Fátima do Sul **W:** www.radioguaicurus.com.br – **MS34**) Rua 26 de Agosto 384 an7, Amambai, 79012-003 Campo Grande ☎67 3384 6647 – **MS35**) Av Costa Rica 654, 79740-000 Ivinhema ☎67 3442 1450 **W:** www.radioatual1530.com.br – **MS36**) Rua Severino Araújo, 1375 - Centro, 79700-000 Fatima do Sul – **MS38**) Rua Candido Severino 462, 79420-000 Camapuã ☎67 286 1366 ▤67 286 1239 – **MS39**) Rua 01 No 1550, Altos do Indaiá, 79823-500 Dourados **E:** tepims@menthor.com. br - **Spanish & Guaraní:** Sat 1400-1600 – **MS40**) Rua José Antônio Pereira 1488, sala 23, 79010-190 Campo Grande – **MS41**) Rua Antônio Maria Coelho 289, Centro, 79260-000 Bela Vista ☎67 3439 1243 **W:** radiobelavista.com.br **E:** vozdoapa@vsp.com.br – **MS42**) Rua Porfirio Gonçalves 1240, 79480-000 Rio Verde de Mato Grosso ☎67 3292 1561 **W:** www.radiocampoalegre.com – **MS43**) Rua Atilio Reginato 355, 79740-000 Ivinhema – **MS46**) 79935-000 Sete Quedas – **MS47**) 79430-000 Bandeirantes.– **MS48**) 79780-000 Bataguassu.– **MS53**) 79100-000 Campo Grande – **MS54**) Av.Federal 69 – Piracema, 79400-000 Coxim – **MS55**) Av.Joao Pedro Pedrossian 4058, 79570-000 Aperecida do Taboado ☎67 3565 1075 **W:**– **MS56**) Av José Ferreira da Costa, 771, 79550-000 Costa Rica ☎67 3247 2007 **W:** www.globocostarica.com.br **E:** radioglobo@globocostarica.com.br – **MS57**) 79560-000 Chapadao do Sul – **MS58**) 79220-000 Nivague – **MS59**) 79180-000 Ribas do Rio Pardo - **MS59**) 79220-000 Nioaque – **MS60**) 79180-000 Ribas do Rio. – **MS61**) Rua 15 de Novembro, 564 – Sala 2, 79300-000 Corumbá ☎67 3231 1060

MT00) MATO GROSSO

MT01) Rua Boróros, 45 - Centro, 78600-000 Barra do Garças ☎66 3401 1345 **W:** www.radioaruana.com.br – **MT02**) Av Brasil 27, 78600-000 Poxoréo **W:** www.radiosulmatogrossense.com.br – **MT03**) Professora Tereza Lobo 30, Concil, 78048-700 Cuiabá ☎65 3612 6530 **W:** www.cbncuiaba.com.br **E:** equipedeouro@gazetadigital.com.br – **MT04**) Rua das Primaveras 3971A, 78550-000 Sinop **W:** www.radioceleste.com.br **E:** administracao@radioceleste.com.br – **MT05**) Praça do Seminário 239, 78015-140 Cuiabá ☎65 3617 7917 **W:** www.arquidiocesecuiaba.org.br**E:** producaocuiaba@cancaonoca.com – **MT06**) Av Ludovico de Riva Netto, 3724 - Centro, 78580-000 Alta Floresta **W:** www.radioprogresso640.com **E:** contato@radioprogresso640.com.br – **MT07**) Rua JoÃo Pessao 453, Cebtro (C.P 401, 78700-970) 78700-080 Rondonópolis ☎66 3422 9894 – **MT08**) Rua Joaquim Murtinho, 1456, Centro,Centro Sul, 78025-000 Cuiabá **W:** www.radioculture-cuiaba.com.br – **MT09**) Rua São Pedro 806, 78200-000 Cáceres ☎65 223 1663 – **MT10**) Rua Tiradentes 979, Centro, 78200-000 Cáceres ☎65 3223 3820 **W:** www.difusoracaceres.com.br – **FM:** 102.3MHz – **MT12**) Av Cuiabá 829, Edifício Mikerinos, 12° andar, 78700-090

Rondonópolis ☎66 3423 3666 **W:** www.radioclubemt.com.br – **MT13**) Rua 28 de Outobro N° 3391, 78280-000 Mirassol d'Oeste ☎65 3241 1288 ▤65 3241 1770 **W:** www.difusoramirassol.com.br – **MT14**) Av. Governador Júlio Campos 311, Jardim Glória, 78140-400 Várzea Grande ☎65 3682 2525 **W:** www.industrial1070.com.br **E:** radioindustrial@industrial1070.com.br – **MT15**) Rua Zulmira Canavarros 285, 78005-390 Cuiabá – **MT16**) Rua 2 No 32, 78175-000 Poconé – **MT17**) Rua Sorocaba 716 B, 78575-000 Juara **W:** www.radiotucunare.com. br – **MT18**) Rua Brasil 780, 78300-000 Tangará da Serra ☎65 3326 2080 **W:** www.radiotangara.com.br **E:** radiotangara@radiotangara.com.br – **MT19**) Av T Neves 1682, 78500-000 Colider – **MT20**) Tv Pref Alexandrina Gomes 87, Centro, 78600-000 Barra do Garças ☎65 3401 6155 **W:** www.radiodifusorabarra.com.br**E:** radiodifusoramt@hotmail.com – **MT21**) Rua Criciúma 165, 78890-000 Sorriso **W:** www.radiosorriso.com.br – **MT22**) Praça Edgar de Araujo, Cx Postal 40, Centro, 78430-000 Nortelândia ☎65 3346 1729 **W:** www.radioregionalnortelandia.com.br **E:** edivaldodesa@reporternews.com.br – **MT23**) Av Mato Grosso 133, 78690-000 Nova Xavantina ☎65 3438 1218 **W:** www.radionx.com.br **E:** webmaster@radionx.com – **MT24**) Rua 6 No - Manoel D Sobrino 498, 78300-000 Tangará da Serra ☎65 3326 3131 **W:** www.radiopioneira.tk – **MT25**) Rua Benjamim Constant s/n, 78780-000 Alto Araguaia – **MT26**) Av Holmis Ioris 429, 78320-000 Juina ☎66 3566 1505 ▤66 3566 1228 **W:** www.rej.am.br **E:** rej@juina-fox.com.br – **MT27**) Av Mario Correa 350, 78790 000 Itiquira – **MT28**) Rua 01, 600, 78525-000 Matupá ☎66 3595 1144 **W:** anoticiadigital.com.br **E:** radiocidade@vsp.com.br – **MT29**) Rua das Aroeiras, 1557 – Setor Comercial, 78550-000 Sinop ☎66 3531 3550 **W:** www.bandsinop.com.br – **MT30**) Avenida Luiz Barbosa esq. c/ Sete de Setembro No 477, 78285-000 São José dos Quatro Marcos ☎65 3251 1062 **W:** www.radiojornal570.com.br **E:** radiojornal@vsp.com.br – **MT31**) Rua 6 s/n, 78400-000 Diamantino ☎65 736 1316 – **MT32**) Rua Perimetral s/n, Bairro Bom Clima, 78195-000 Chapada dos Guimarães – **MT33**) Av Roberto Valdecir Briante 99, Centro, 78435-000 São José do Rio Claro ☎66 3386 2216 **W:** www.integracao810.com.br – **MT34**) Rua U-2 s/n – Canteiro Central, 78580-000 Alta Floresta **W:** www.sistemarainha.com.br/radiofloresta/ – **MT35**) Rua Jovino Lopes 1292, 2° andar, Bairro Santa Maria Bertila, 78760-000 Guiratinga ☎66 9615 9449 **W:** www.radiogarcabrancaam.com.br **E:** radiorgb@hotmail.com or radiorgb@uol.com – **MT36**) Rua Joaquim Nabuco 450, 78640-000 Araputanga **W:** www.radioarcoiris.com.br **E:** radioarcoiris@terra.com.br – **MT37**) Rua São Paulo 1440, 78250-000 Pontes e Lacerda – **MT38**) Rua do Burtis s/n, 78520-000 Guarantã do Norte ☎66 3552 1114 **W:** www.anoticiadigital.com.br **E:** enauen@vsp.com.br – **MT39**) Rua Dom Antônio Malan 674, 78015-600 Cuiabá – **MT40**) Rua Carajás 69, 76800-000 Barra do Garças – **MT41**) 78850-000 Primavera do Leste – **MT42**) Rua Filinto Muller, 1804 Morada do Sol, 78043-500 Cuiaba ☎66 3575 2842 **W:** www.anoticiadigital.com.br **E:** radioatual_brasil1530am@hotmail.com.br – **MT44**) Av Universitária 504W, 78405-000 Lucas do Rio Verde ☎65 3212 0300 **W:** www.atitudeam.com.br**E:** atendimento@atitude-am.com.br – **MT45**) Rua Potiguaras, 809 – Centro Edifico Santa Fé - 2° andar, (✉ C.P. 227), 78820-000 Jaciara ☎66 3461 1966 **W:** www.radioxavantes.com.br **E:** radioxavantes@vsp.com.br or radioxavantes@hotmail.com – **MT46**) 78700-000 Rondónopolis – **MT47**) Rua Araçuaí 1105, Centro, 78575-000 Juara ☎66 3556 1478 **W:** www.difusorajuara.com.br **E:** difusoraaovivo@hotmail.com – **MT50**) 78635-000 Água Boa. – **MT51**) 78785-000 Alto Taquari – **MT52**) 78325-000 Aripuanã – **MT53**) Rua São Salvador 1, Barrio Inconfidencia, 78645-000 Vila Rica ☎66 3554-1723 **W:** www.radiovilaam.com.br **E:** am@radiovilaam.com.br – **MT54**) 78505-000 Terra Nova do Norte – **MT55**) 78390-000 Barra do Bugres – **MT56**) 78590-000 Paranaita – **MT62**) 78840-000 Campo Verde – **MT63**) 78625-000 Novo São Joaquim – **MT64**) Campo Novo do Parecis

PA00) PARÁ

PA01) Av Araguaia 247, 68551-000 Redenção **E:** roriente@realonline.com.br – **PA02**) C.P 119, 68371-970 Altamira – **PA03**) Av Almirante Barroso 2190 3° andar, Marco, 66095-000 Belém **W:** www.radioclubedopara.com.br **E:** timaocampeao@radioclubedopara.com.br – **PA04**) Av São Sebastião, 622-A Bloco A - Centro, 68005-090 Santarém ☎93 3523 1066 ▤93 3523 2685 **W:** www.radiouraldesantarem.com.br **E:** rural@radiouralsantarem.com.br or edilrural@gmail.com.br – **PA05**) Av. Juscalino Kubitschek Oliveira s/n, Centro, 68540-000 Conceição do Araguaia ☎94 3421 1576 **W:** www.radioregionaldoaraguaia.com.br – **PA06**) Praça dos Notáveis 1006, 68400-000 Cametá – **PA07**) Rodovia BR-316 Km 58, 68741-740 Castanhal – **PA08**) Travessa Campos Sales 370, 66019-050 Belém ☎91 4005 4400 **W:** www.supermarajoara.com.br **E:** contacto@supermarajoara.com.br - **FM:** 100.9MHz – **PA09**) Travessa Vileta 2193, 66093-380 Belém **W:** www.rbn.org.br **E:** rbncontato@rbn.org.br – **PA10**) Av Bráz de Aguiar, No 351, Nazaré, 66035-000 Belém ☎91 3213 1000 **W:** www.radioliberal.com.br **E:** dirgel@radioliberal.com.br **FM:** 97.5MHz – **PA11**) C.P 038, 68801-970 Breves – **PA12**) Praça das Bandeiras, s/n - Centro, 68600-000 Bragança ☎91

3425 1774 **W:** www.fundacaoeducadora.com.br **E:** contato@fundaca-oeducadora.com.br - **FM:** 106.7MHz – **PA13)** Av Mendonça Furtado, 1481 Santa Clara 68005-100 Santarém **W:** www.rtvpontanegra.com.br **E:** am890@rtvpontanegra.com.br **☎**93 3523 3348 – **PA14)** Av Coronel Monfredo 42, 68820-000 São Sebastião da Boa Vista – **PA16)** Av Almirante Barroso 735, 66093-020 Belém **☎**91 4005 7700 **W:** www.portalcultura.com.br **E:** radiocultura@gmail.com - **FM:** 93.7MHz – **PA17)** Rod. Transamazonica Km, 4 Rua das TV´s, Folha Industrial Qd. 05 Lt 06, 68507-765 Marabá **☎**94 3322 2200 **W:** www.itacaiunasam.com **E:** itacaiunas@tveldoradosbt.com.br – **PA18)** Rodovia Transamazonica Km 01, 68180-010 Itaituba – **PA19)** Rua Lauro Sodré 722, Centro, 68456-000 Tucuruí **☎**94 3787 1288 **W:** www.sistemafloresta.com.br **E:** contato@sistemafloresta.com.br – **PA20)** Av Rui Barbosa 825, 68005-080 Santarém – **PA21)** Av Xingu s/n, Centro, 68555-010 Xinguara **☎**94 3426 1008 **W:** www.radioxinguaraam.com.br **E:** grupo.sh@bol.com.br – **PA22)** Travessa E Simões 230, 68250-000 Óbidos **W:** www.kaleb.hpg.ig.com.br **☎**93 3547 1699 – **PA24)** Travessa 18 No 1863, entre 4 e 5 ruas, 68870-000 Soure – **PA25)** Av Visconde de Sousa Franco 116, Centro, 68780-000 Vigia – **PA26)** Av.Fernando Guilhon, 358 Bela Vista, 68180-000 Itaituba **☎**93 3518 4169 **W:** www.radioclubedeitaituba.com.br **E:** www.radioclubedeitaituba.com.br – **PA27)** Av Tropical s/n, 68625-000 Paragominas – **PA28)** Rua 2 de Outobro s/n, 68200-000 Alenquer – **PA29)** Rodovia Transamazonica Km 04, 68502-290 Marabá – **PA30)** Rodovia BR-010 Km 09, Bairro Industrial, 68660-000 São Miguel do Guamá – **PA32)** Travessa Mauriti 1006, Bairro da Pedreira, 66080-650 Belém **W:** www.novotempo.com/radio – **PA33)** Av Antonio Marques Ribeiro, 242, 68380-000 São Felix do Xingu **☎**91 4351 1243 – **PA34)** Av Augusto Montenegro s/n, 68710-000 Maracanã – **PA35)** Rua Barao Rio Branco 1562, 68440-000 Abaetetuba – **PA36)** 68230-000 Almeirim – **PA37)** 68430-000 Igarapé Miri – **PA40)** 68220-000 Monte Alegre – **PA41)** 68300-000 Gurupa – **PA42)** 68620-000 Visen – **PA47)** 68530-000 Rio Maria – **PA48)** Oriximineã – **PA49)** Tailândie – **PA50)** Portel – **PA51)** Prainha – **PA52)** Barcarena – **PA53)** Beiao – **PA54)** Almeirien – **PA55)** Tomé Açu – **PA56)** Rua do Contorno s/n,68746-475 Castanhal **☎**91 3711 0053 **W:** www.radioparanaenseam.com.br **E:** contato@radioparaenseam.com.br

PB00) PARAÍBA
PB01) Rua Pres. João Pessoa 25, 58800-010 Sousa **☎**83 3521 2116 **W:** www.portalprogresso.com – **PB02)** C.P 26, 58900-970 Cajazeiras **W:** www.diariodosertao.com.br **E:** diariodosertao@gmail.com 📧83 3531 1334 – **PB03)** Rua Padre Manoel Otaviano 340, 58970-000 Conceição **W:** www.radioeducadoradeconceicao.com – **PB04)** Rua Presidente Epitácio Pessoa 242, 58700-020 Patos **☎**83 3421 3932 **W:** www.radiopanati.com.br – **PB05)** Rod PB 075 s/n km 1,25, Zona Rural (📧C.P 40, 58200-970) 58200-000 Guarabira **W:** www.cultura790.com.br – **PB06)** Praça Pres Epitácio Pessoa 167, 58755-000 Princesa Isabel – **PB07)** Rua Joao Pessoa 313 1° andar (📧 C.P 134 58100-970), Campina Grande **☎**83 3349 2101 **W:** www.radiocaturite.com.br **E:** radiocaturite@radiocaturite.com.br – **PB08)** Rua Coronel Juvêncio Carneiro, 160 - Centro, 58900-000 Cajazeiras **☎**83 3531 4530 **W:** www.radiocajazeiras.com.br **E:** radiocajazeiras@hotmail.com – **PB09)** Av D.Pedro II s/n, Torre, (C.P 1089, 58001-970) 58013-420 João Pessoa **☎**83 3218 7900 **W:** www.radiotabajara.pb.gov.br – **PB10)** Rua Manoel Pedro s/n, 58884-000 Catolé do Rocha **☎**83 3441 2013 **W:** www.portalprogresso.com **E:** portalprogreso@yahoo.com **PB11)** Rua XV de Novembro 162, Palmeira, 58101-200 Campina Grande **☎**83 3342 0046 **W:** www.radiocaririam.com.br – **PB12)** Av Pedro II 523, Centro, 58013-420 João Pessoa **☎**83 3216 5044 **W:** www.correiosat.com.br/?radio=3 – **PB13)** Rua das Trincheiras 198, Centro, 58011-000 João Pessoa – **PB14)** Rua Venâncio Neiva 287, Centro, 58400-090 Campina Grande **☎**83 3349 2910 **W:** www.db.com.br/clubeAM – **PB15)** Rua Rui Barbosa, 53 – Centro (📧C.P 57, 58700-970) 58700-060 Patos **W:** www.radioespinharas.com.br **E:** contato@radioespinhares.com.br **☎**83 3421 3791 📧83 3221 3795 – **PB16)** Rua Orlando Soares de Oliveira 299 Bairro Miramar, 58032-083 Joao Pessoa **☎**83 3426 2876 **W:** www.comunidademana.com.br **E:** mana@comunidademana.com.br – **PB17)** Rua Dr Carlos Pires 17, Centro, 58804-200 Sousa **☎**83 3522 1525 **W:** www.950news.com.br **E:** contato@950news.com.br – **PB18)** Rua Monsenhor Valeriano s/n, 58840-000 Pombal – **FM:** 98.7 MHz **PB19)** Rua Antônio Firmino 344, 58187-000 Picuí **☎**83 3371 2400 **W:** www.radiocenecistapicui.com.br – **PB20)** Rua Cândido de Assis 421, Centro, 58840-000 Pombal **☎**83 3431 3558 **W:** www.bonsucessoam.com.br **E:** contactos@bonsucessam.com.br – **PB21)** Rua Conselheiro Henrique, 17 – Centro, 58010-690 Joao Pessoa **☎**83 3241 5657 **W:** www.portalsanhaua.com.br **E:** radioshanua@ig.com.br – **PB22)** Rua Epitácio Pessoa, 8 - Centro,·58200-000 Guarabira **☎**83 3321 8437 **W:** www.radiorualam850.com.br **E:** radio.rural@ol.com.br – **PB23)** Rua Monsenhor Palmeira 471, Centro, 58135-000 Esperança **☎**83 3322 6327 **W:** www.redeesperanca.com **E:** contato@redeesperanca.com – **PB24)** Rua Getúlio Vargas 129, 58500-000 Monteiro **☎**83

3351 2612 **W:** www.correiosat.com.br/?radio=9 – **PB25)** Rua Coronel Pedro Targino s/n, 58233-000 Araruna **☎**83 3370 1102 📧83 3370 1104 **W:** www.radioserrana590.com **E:** radioserrana@gmail.com or radioserranaam@hotmail.com – **PB26)** Rod. PB 105, 105 km 33, Zona Rural Solânea, 58220-000 Bananeiras **☎**83 3363 2488 **W:**www.radiointe-gracaodobrejo.com.br **E:**radioinetgracao@hotmail.com – **PB27)** Rua Gouveia Nobrega 34, 58155-000 Soledade **☎**83 3383 1229 **W:** www.sociedadeam.amaiouvida.com.br – **PB28)** Rua João Sabiá 56, 58540-000 Sumé **☎**83 3353 2566 **W:** www.radiocidadesume.com.br – **PB29)** Praça Frei Martinho s/n, 1° andar - Centro, 58700-100 Patos **☎**83 3421 3704 **W:** www.radiosertaoam.com.br **E:** marketing@radioserta-oam.com.br - **FM:** 102.9MHz – **PB30)** Rua Cel Guimarães, 6 - Centro, 58900-000 Cajazeiras **☎**83 3531 3715 **W:** www.oeste1000.com.br **E:** oesteam@hotmail.com – **PB31)** Rua Orlando Soares de Oliveira 299, Bairro Miramar, 58032-083 Joao Pessoa **☎**83 2108 0121 **W:** www.cbnjoaopessoa.com.br – **FM:** 107.7 MHz –**PB32)** Rua Epitácio Pessoa, 184 - Centro, 58397-000 Areia **☎**63 3362 2778 **W:** www.radiojardim.com.br **E:** radiojardim@hotmail.com – **PB34)** Av Ananias Conserva 18, Centro, 58780-000 Itaporanga **☎**83 3451 3879 **W:** www.correiosat.com.br/?radio=5 – **PB35)** 58100-000 Campina Grande.

PE00) PERNAMBUCO
PE01) Av Santo Antônio 324, 55290-000 Garanhuns – **PE02)** Rua Floriano Peixoto 780, São José, 50020-060 Recife **☎**81 3799 9512 📧81 3797 9511 **W:** www.redebrasildecomunicacao.com.br **E:** boas-novas@radioboasnovas.net – **PE03)** AJoaquim Nabuco 322, São Crístovah,56503-150 Arcoverde **☎**87 3821 0664 **W:** www.radiocardealam.com.br **E:** rcardeal@arconet.com.br **MSN:** cardealam@hotmail.com – **PE04)** Praça da Bandeira s/n, 55700-000 Limoeiro – **PE05)** Rodovia Araraipina – Picos Km 3, 56280-000 Araripina **☎**87 3873 1366 **W:** www.radiograndeserra.com.br **FM:** 94MHz – **PE06)** Av Sete de Setembro s/n, Bairro Km 02, 56300-000 Petrolina **☎**87 3861 4744 **W:** www.granderioam.com.br **E:** granderioam@uol.com.br – **PE07)** Rua do Veiga 590, Santo Amaro, 50040-915 Recife **☎**81 3421 4244 **W:** www.radioclubeam.com.br **E:** carlos.miguel@radioclubeam.com.br – **PE08)** Praça Maria Auxiliadora, 205 - Centro, 56302-335 Petrolina **☎**87 3862 1522 **W:** www.emissorarural.com.br - **F.PI:** FM – **PE09)** Rua Capitão Lima 250, Santo Amaro, 50040-080 Recife **☎**81 3413 6353 **W:** www.radiojornal.com – **PE10)** Av.Norte, 68 – Santo Amaro, 50040-200 Recife **☎**81 2126 8063 **W:** www.tvu.ufpe.br **E:** radioam@ufpe.br– **PE11)** Av Pres Kennedy 3092, Peixinhos, 53260-640 Olinda **☎**81 3444 8282 **W:** www.radiotamandare.com.br – **PE12)** Rua da Conceição 16/22, 2° andar, Centro, 55000-000 Caruaru **☎**81 3722 5201 **W:** www.liberdade.com.br **E:** programalcaoam@liberdade.com.br - **FM:** 94.7MHz – **PE13)** Av Padre Rocha s/n, 55810-000 Carpina **W:** www.radioplanaltoam950.com.br – **PE14)** Av Maria Emília Cavalcanti 570, 55870-000 Timbaúba **☎**81 3631 2229 **W:** www.princesa1000am.com.br **E:** falecom@princesa1000am.com.br – **PE15)** Estrada do Passarinho 1415, Caixa D´água, 53170-110 Olinda **☎**81 3444 7855 📧81 3444 7858 **W:** www.radioolindaam.com.br **E:** comercial@radioolindaam.com.br – **PE16)** C.P 88, 55001-970 Caruaru – **PE17)** Rua Floriano Peixoto 780, 1° andar, 50020-060 Recife **W:** http://jc3.uol.com.br/radiojor-nal/canal.php?canal=49 **E:** gus@jc.com.br – **PE18)** Av Rui Barbosa, 65 - Divinópolis, 55010-540 Caruaru **W:** www.radioculturadonordeste.com.br **E:** jornalismo@radioculturadonordeste.com.br – **PE19)** Rua Prefeito José Joaquim Silva 50 an 2, Livramento, 55602-150 Vitória de Santo Antão **☎**81 3523 2003 – **PE20)** Av. Rui Barbosa 1236, Heliopólis 55293-300 Garanhuns **☎**87 3762 7244 **W:** http://jc3.uol.com.br/radiojornal – **PE21)** Rua Coronel Urbano Ribeiro de Sena 956, Cajueiro, 52221-000 Recife **☎**55 3444 2566 **W:** www.radiocapibaribe.com.br **E:** radiocapibarid@radiocapibaribe.com.br – **PE22)** Av. Timbi, 672 - Timbi, 54765-240 Camarajibe **☎**81 3485 1322 **W:** www.radiogua-rany.com.br – **PE23)** Rua Pajussara, 225 Jardim São Paulo, 50920-120 Recife **☎**81 3252 5868 **W:** www.radionovasdepaz.com.br – **PE24)** Av F Pessoa de Queiróz s/n, 55200-000 Pesqueira **W:** radiojornal.com.br – **PE25)**Rodovia BR101 Sul s/n km 117, Newton Cameiro, 55540-000 Palmares **☎**81 3662 1288 **W:**www.rcpalmares.com.br **E:** rcpalmares@yahoo.com.br **PE26)** Rua Inocencio Gomes de Andrade, 619 - Centro, 56903 906 Serra Talhada **☎**83 3831 1700 **W:** www.radioavozdosertao.com – **PE27)** Rua Newton César de Macedo, 5 - Centro, 56800-000 Afogados da Ingazeira **☎**87 3838 2790 **W:** www.radiopajeu.com.br **E:** contato@radiopajeu.com.br – **PE28)** Rua Benjamim Constant 16, 55750-000 Surubim – **PE29)** Rua José Lopes da Silva s/n, São Pedro, 55150-000 Belo Jardim – **PE30)** Rua Antônio Figueira Soares s/n, 56000-000 Salgueiro **W:** www.asabranca.com.br **E:** asabranca@asabranca.com.br – **PE31)** Rua Jão Pessoa, 25 - Centro, 56700-000 São José do Egito **☎**87 3844 1024 **W:** www.cultura.am.br **Email:** cultura@cultura.am.br – **PE32)** Praça Duque de Caxias 818, 55900-000 Goiana – **PE33)** Av Fernando Bezerra 1123, Centro, 56200-000 Ouricuri **☎**87 3874 1559 **W:** www.voluntariosdapatriaam.com – **PE34)** Rua Maria Santina 200, Bela Vista, 55190-000 Santa Cruz do Capibaribe **☎**81 3731 4033 **W:** www.radiovaleam.com **E:** radio.vale.am@hotmail.

com – **PE35**) Av Coronel Trapia, s/n – Centro,, 56440-000 Belém de São Francisco ☎87 3876 1380 **W:**www.radioeducadoradebelem.com. br **E:** educadoradebelem@yahoo.com – **PE36**) Rua São Francisco de Assis s/n, Centro, 55641-190 Gravatá (C.P 64, 55641-970) ☎81 3533 4764 **W:** www.cancaonova.com or blog.cancaonova.com/gravata **E:** radiogravata@cancaonova.com – **PE37**) Rodovia PE 218 km 46, 654 – Lagoa do Jacu, 55330-000 Bom Conselho ☎87 3771 1231 ▤87 3771 1262 **W:** www.radiopapacaca.com.br **E:** radiopapacaca@hotmail.com – **PE38**) 56460-000 Petrolândia – **PE39**) 56180-000 Cabrobó – **PE40**) 55660-000 Bezerros – **PE41**) Comunidade Restauração Casa-Mae, 55000-000 Caruaru ☎81 3721 7915 **W:** http://comunidadecr.blogspot. no **E:** radiorestauracao_am1590@hotmail.com

PI00) PIAUÍ
PI01) Trav Franisco Antônio da Silva, N° 115, Centro, 64770-000 São Raimundo Nonato ☎89 3582 1497 ▤89 3582 1649 **W:** www. radioserradacapivara.com.br **E:** capivara550@yahoo.com.br – **PI02**) Rua Alvaro Mendes 972, 64000-060 Teresina - **FM:** 94.1MHz – **PI03**) Rua Taumaturgo de Azevedo 995, 64100-000 Barras – **PI04**) Av Valter Alencar 2120, Monte Castelo, 64076-410 Teresina ☎86 2107 6600 **W:** http://portaldaclube.globo.com/am_clube.html - **FM:** 99.1MHz – **PI05**) Av Heróis do Jenipapo 37, 64280-000 Campo Maior – **PI06**) Praça Pres Kennedy 233, 64490-000 Regeneração – **PI07**) Praça do Comércio 400, 1° andar, 64500-000 Oeiras – **PI08**) Av.Prof Valter Alencar 2021, Monte Castelo, 64019-625 Teresina ☎86 3216 5056 **W:** www.fundacaoan-tares.org **E:** antres@fundacaoantares.org – **PI09**) Av. Valter Alencar 2021, Monte Castillo, 64019-625 Teresina. ☎86 3216 5056 **W:** www. fundacaoantares.org **E:** antares@fundacaoantares.org – **PI10**) Rua 24 de Janeiro, 150, Sul, 64001-230 Teresina **W:** www.radiopioneira. am.br **E:** rosemiro@radiopioneira.am.br ☎86 2107 8121 ▤86 2107 8122 – **PI11**) Av. Presidente Getúlio Vargas 266, 64200-000 Parnaíba – **PI12**) Rua 18 de Setembro 678, 64260-000 Piripiri ☎86 3276 1304 **E:** itamaraty_am@hotmail.com – **PI13**) Rua Proffesor Magalhães 4190, Recanto das Palmares, 64045-750 Teresina ☎86 3232 5411 **W:** www.portaldifusora.com – **PI14**) Av Prefeito J de Carvalho, 64400-000 Amarante – **PI15**) Av Rio Branco 314, 64860-000 Uruçuí – **PI16**) Rua Clementino Ribeiro 56, 2° andar, Centro, 64490-000 Regeneração ☎89 3522 1207 **W:**www.difusorafloriano.com.br– **PI17**) Praça Emilio Cavalcante 29, 64980-000 Corrente – **PI18**) Rua Clementino Ribeiro, 187 – Centro, 64800-000 Floriano ☎86 3522 1504 ▤89 3522 1713 **W:** www. radiosantaclara.com **E:** radiosantaclara@veloxmail.com.br – **PI19**) Rua Sabino Paulo 696, 64760-000 São João do Piauí – **PI20**) Av João de Paiva 94, 64290-000 Altos – **PI21**) Av Dr Raimundo Santos, 537 – Centro, 64900-000 Bom Jesus – **PI22**) Praca Sto. Antônio, 1019 ap 101, Ed. Lise Center, 64200-361 Parnaíba ☎86 3322 3550 **W:** www.radio-globoparnaiba.com.br – **PI23**) Rua General Taumaturgo de Azevedo 800, 64100-000 Barras – **PI24**) Av Marechal Deodoro, 203, 64750-000 Paulistana – **PI25**) Av. São Vicente Paula, s/n – Centro, 64240-000 Piracuruca ☎86 3343 1107 – **PI26**) Av José de Deus Lacerda 584, 64130-000 Miguel Alves – **PI27**) Av Governador Chagas Rodrigues s/n, 64575-000 Jaicós – **PI28**) Rua Corinto Andrade, s/n - Centro, 64255-000 Pedro II ☎86 3271 1186 **W:** www.radiocruzeiroam.com.br **E:** radiocruzeirop2@hotmail.com – **PI29**) Praça da Independência 69, 64325-000 Elesbão Veloso – **PI30**) Rua Joaquim Baldoíno 48, 64600-000 Picos - **FM:** 94.5MHz – **PI31**) Av João Ferreira 199, 64460-000 Agua Branca – **PI32**) Rua Hugo Napoleão 940, 64110-000 José de Freitas – **PI33**) Rua Pedro II 695, 64340-000 Castelo do Piauí – **PI34**) Rua Pedro II s/n, 64330-000 São Miguel do Tapuio – **PI35**) Rua Padre Joaquim Nonato s/n, 64390-000 Demerval Lobão – **PI36**) Rua Coronel Messeas Melo s/n, 64190-000 Batalha – **PI41**) Av Antonino Freire 1356, 64001-040 Teresina – **PI42**) Praça Waldemar Leal 42, 64680-000 Padre Marcos – **PI43**) Rua Sete de Setembro 471, 64160-000 Luzilândia – **PI44**) Praça da Bandeira 93, 64500-000 Oeiras – **PI45**) Rua Prof Alceu Brandão 2397, Barrio Monte Castelio, 64016-150 Teresina – **PI46**) Rua Coronel José Fortes 549, 64180-000 Esperantina – **PI47**) Rodovia BR-343 s/n, 64290-000 Altos – **PI48**) Av Professor Alceu Brandão 2750, 64016-150 Teresina **W:** radioclick.globo.com - **FM:** 91.1MHz – **PI49**) Rua São VicenteS/N, Bomba, 64600-000 Picos ☎89 3415 900 ▤89 3415 5152 **W:** www.grnordeste.com.br/radionordeste

PR00) PARANÁ
PR01) Rua Quintino Bocaiuva, 41 - Centro, 86020-100 Londrina ☎43 3344 2038 **W:** www.radiolondrina.com.br **E:** radiolondrina@onda.com. br – **PR02**) Rua XV do Novembro 7466, Centro, 85010-000 Guarapuava **E:** cultura@gol.psi.br **W:** www.centralcultura.com.br ☎42 3623 6423 ▤42 3723 7269 - **FM:** 93.7MHz – **PR03**) Av Brasil, 1720(✉C.P 10, 85892-970), 85892-000 Santa Helena **W:** www.radiograndelago.com.br **E:** grandelago@rgl.com.br ☎45 3268 1212 ▤ 45 3268 1135 – **PR04**) Rua Mal Humberto de Alencar Castelo Branco 590, Cristo Rei 82530- 195 Curitiba ☎41 3263-3311 **W:** www.difusoraam590.com.br

– **PR05**) Praça de Café N° 1100, 86900-000 Jandaia do Sul ☎43 3432 9797 **W:** www.radiojandaia.com.br **E:** contato@radiojandaia.com.br **FM:** 103.3MHz – **PR06**) Rua Julio Perneta, 695, Mercês, 80810-110 Curitiba ☎41 3331 7400 ▤41 3331 7449 **W:** www.pr.gov.br/rtve/ – **PR07**) Rua 7 de Setembro, 520, Centro, (C.P 1026), 85960-000 Marechal Cândido Rondón **W:** www.radioeducadora.com **E:** educado-ra@rondonet.com.br ☎45 3284 1212 – **PR08**) Rod João Carlos Strass s/n, Heimtal (✉C.P. 337, 86001-970) 86084-610 Londrina ☎43 3339 6244 **W:** www.superradiodeuseamor.com.br – **PR09**) Rua António Costa N° 529, Bairro Bela Vista Alegre das Mercás, 86390-000 Cambará ☎41 3240 7500 **W:** www.radiobandab.com.br/norte_pioneiro.php **E:** nortepioneiro@radiobandab.com.br ☎ ▤43 3532 4050 – **PR10**) Rua Lord Lovat 497, Centro, 87600-000 Nova Esperança ☎44 3252 4533 **W:** www.cancaonova.com **E:** radionovaesperanca@cancao-nova.com – **PR11**) Rua Oyapock, 649, Cristo Rei, 80050-450 Curitiba ☎41 3318 5860 **W:** www.radioglobocuritiba.com.br – **PR12**) Rua Saldanha Marinho 1581, Apto B - Ventro, 85010-290 Guarapuava ☎42 3035 7010 **W:** www.radiocaciqueam.com.br **E:** comercialcacique@ brturbo.com.br – **PR13**) Rua Sergipe, 843 - sala 05, (C.P 916) 86010-380 Londrina **W:** www.radiodifusoradelondrina.com.br **E:** radiodifuso-ra690@aol.com ☎43 3324 7369 – **PR14**) Rua 15 de Novembro 433, Contorno, 84053-320 Ponta Grossa. ☎42 3225 9150 **W:** www.difuso-ra690.com **Email.** suporte@difusora690.com – **PR15**) Av Paraná 1885, Bairro Boa Vista, 82510-000 Curitiba ☎41 3251 2410 **W:**http://radioe-vangelismo.com.br **E:** radio@radioevangelismo.com – **PR16**) Av. Capitão Índio Bandeira, 1400 5° Andar – Centro Empresarial Antares, 87300-005 Campo Mourão ☎44 3017 0013 **W:** www.radioobjetiva.com.br – **PR17**) Av 19 de Agosto 522, 1° andar, 87360-000 Goio-Erê ☎44 3522 7777 ▤44 3522 1162 **W:** www.radiogoioere.com.br **E:** rgam@goioere. com.br – **PR18**) Av. Maranahão 62, Shopping Urbano 2° Andar – Sala 21, Centro, 87200-000 Cianorte ☎44 3629 1514 **W:** www.radiopor-tavozam.com.br **E:** radioportavoz@irapida.com.br – **PR19**) Rua Frei Everaldo 445, 85560-000 Chopinzinho **W:** www.radiochopinzinho.com. br **E:** radiochopinzinho@chnet.com.br – **PR20**) Rua Bruno Filgueira 1210, 80440-220 Curitiba ☎42 3623 7565 **W:** www.centralcultura. com.br - **FM:** 93.7 – **PR21**) Rua Marechal Floriano Peixoto 1123, 85851-020 Foz do Iguaçu **W:** www.equipelegal.com.br – **PR22**) Rodovia do Xisto BR 475 Km 20 No 2018, Centro, 83700-000 Araucária ☎41 3642 1010 **W:** www.radioiguassu.com.br – **PR23**) Rua Coronel Manoel Ferreira Bello 64, 85530-000 Clevelândia **W:** www.rdprogresso.com.br **E:** rdprogresso@pinet.com.br – **PR24**) –Rua Machado de Assis 25, Jd. Shangri-Lá, 86070-820 Londrina ☎43 3032 1500 **W:** www.cbnlondrina. com.br **E:** cbnlondrina@cbnlondrina.com.br **FM:** 93.5MHz – **PR25**) Av. Euclides Cunha 455, Zona 04, 87015- 180 Maringá ☎44 3225 8050 **W:** www.novainga.com.br **E:**comercial@pingafogo.com.br – **PR26**) Rua Iguaçu 808, Centro, 85501-270 Pato Branco ☎46 3220 0890 **W:** www. radioitapua.com.br – **PR27**) Praça Marechal Floriano Peixoto 581 - 3° andar, (C.P 090 84001-970) 84010-910 Ponta Grossa ☎42 3025 1900 ▤42 3027 2112 **W:** www.radiosantana.com.br **E:** adm@radiosantana. com.br – **PR28**) Av Largo São Vicente de Paulo 1085, 85900-215 Toledo **W:** www.radiouniaodetoledo.com.br **E:** contato@radiouniaodetoledo. com.br ☎45 3055 2841 ▤45 3055 2488 – **PR29**) Rua Sao Paulo, 910 - Centro, 86808-070 Apucarana **W:** www.novaam.com.br **E:** novaam@ uol.com.br ☎43 3423 1100 – **PR30**) C.P 178, 86600-970 Rolândia **E:** radiocultura@onda.com.br – **PR31**) Rua João Negrão 558, 80010-200 Curitiba ☎41 3339 2900 **W:** www.radiocultura930.com.br **E:** radiocul-tura@radiocultura930.com.br – **PR32**) Rua Joubert de Carvalho 623, 87013-200 Maringá – **PR33**) Rua Dom Bosco, 145 – Jardim Dom Bosco, 86060-340 Londrina **W:** www.radioalvoradadelondrina.com.br **E:** radio-alvoradalondrina@gmail.com ☎43 3347 0606 ▤43 3347 0303 – **PR34**) Rua Santa Catarina 970, 85960-000 Marechal Cândido Rondón ☎45 3284 8080 **W:** www.radiodifusora.com.br **E:** comercial@radiodifusora. net - **FM:** 95.1 MHz – **PR35**) Rua Araribóia 1909, 85505-030 Pato Branco **W:** www.radiocelinauta.com.br **E:**comercial@redecelinauta. com.br **German:** Sun 2200-2300 – **PR36**) Praça Generoso Marques 90,, Galeria Andrade, Ed Claudia 1° andar, Centro, 80020-230 Curitiba ☎41 3322 8483 **W:** www.radiocolombo.com.br – **PR37**) Av Pedro Soccol 542, São Cristovão, 85884-000 Medianeira **W:** www.independenciaam. com.br **E:** contato@independenciaam.com.br – **PR38**) Rua Paraná 650, Centro, 874-000 Cruzeiro do Oeste ☎44 3676 1184 **W:** www.difusora-regional.com.br **E:** alodifusora@bol.com.br – **PR39**) Rua Visconde de Mauá 123, Jardim Shangrilá, 86070-540 Londrina ☎43 3328 1030 – **PR40**) Rua Ulisses Faria 1077, 83900-000 São Mateus do Sul – **PR41**) Rua Maranhão, 2955 – Alto Alegre, 85805-220 Cascavel ☎45 3321 7000 ▤45 3226 5565 **W:** www.cbncascavel.com.br **E:** cbncas-cavel.com.br - **FM:** 102.7MHz – **PR42**) Praça Senador Corrêa 128 (✉ CP 20548, 81810-980 Curitiba), 80230-130 Curitiba ☎41 3221 6070 **W:** www.padrereginaldomanzotti.org.br – **PR43**) Rua Bahia 667, 86690-000 Colorado ☎44 3323 1003 **W:** www.coloradoam.com.br – **PR44**) Rua Porto Alegre 21, 1° andar, 85601-480 Francisco Beltrão **W:** www. radioeducadorafb.com.br **E:** comercialeducadora@wmail.com.br ☎ 46

3524 2255 – **PR45**) Rua Dario Antônio Bordin, 313 - Centro, 84600-000 União da Vitória ☎42 3522 3596 **W:** www.radiouniaoam.com.br **E:** gerente@radiouniaoam.com.br – **PR46**) Av Ivan Ferreira do Amaral, 331-Centro,85400-000 Guaraniaçu ☎45 3232 2722 **W:** www.superrg. com.br **E:** superrg@superrg.com.br – **PR47**) Rua 15 de Novembro 344, Centro, 84010-020 Ponta Grossa **W:** www.prj2.com.br – **PR48**) Rua Edson Martins, 1935, Esquina c/Avenida Parigot de Souza - Centro, 87703-420 Paranavaí ☎44 3423 6565 **W:** www.culturaparanavai.com. br **E:** am@culturaparanavai.com.br – **PR49**) C.P 101, 86300-000 Cornélio Procópio **E:** educa1080@uol.com.br – **PR50**) Av Brasil 1407, 87302-230 Campo Mourão ☎44 3525 1413 **W:** www.radiocolmeiaam. com.br – **PR51**) Rua das Américas 255, 85550-000 Coronel Vivida ☎46 3232 1398 **W:** www.radiovicentepallotti.com.br **E:** atendimento@radiovi-centepallotti.com.br – **PR52**) Av Higienópolis 2100, 86015-905 Londrina **W:** www.paiquere.com.br **E:** paiquere@paiquere.com.br ☎43 3323 5500 ▤43 3339 1175 - **FM:** 98.9MHz – **PR53**) Quince de Novembro 2175 - 8° andar, 83005-000 São José dos Pinhais ☎41 3568 1718 **W:** www.radiomaisam1120.com.br **E:** radio@radiomais.am.br - **FM:** 97.9MHz – **PR54**) Av Cristóvão Colombo 1055, 86990-000 Marialva ☎44 3232 1115 **W:** www.ingamar.com.br **E:** empresamartiniradio@ hotmail.com – **PR55**) Praça Manoel Ribas 112, Centro, 84165-510 Castro ☎42 3232 2224 **W:** www.radiocastro.com.br **E:** radiocastro@ convoy.com.br – **PR56**) Rua Fidelcino Dourado, 225, Centro, 86200-000 Londrina **W:** www.radiomanchetelondrina.com.br – **PR57**) Rua João Negrão 595, Centro, 80010-200 Curitiba – **PR58**) Rua Raimundo Leonardi 1301, 85900-110 Toledo ☎45 3378 3161 **W:** www.radio-guacu.com.br **E:** radioguacu@uol.com.br – **PR59**) Av Londrina 500, 87970-000 Nova Londrina **E:** Rua João Negrão 595, Centro, 80010-200 Curitiba ☎41 3324 3849 **W:** www.superradiodeuseamor. com.br – **PR61**) Av Paraná 596, 85887-000 Matelândia **E:** radiomatelan-dia@matelnet.com.br – **PR62**) Rua Afonso Alves de Camargo 1175. Alta da XV, 85010-320 Guarapuava ☎42 3035 8000 **W:** www.difusora-guarapuava.com.br **E:** difusora@mattosleao.com.br – **PR63**) Av Paeaná, 271 an 1, 87704-100 Paranavaí ☎44 3422 3322 **W:** www.radioparana-vai.com.br **E:** contato@radioparanavai.com.br – **PR64**) Av. Dos Pineiros s/n, 85650-000 Santa Isabel do Oeste ☎46 3542 1239 **W:** www. radiodanubioazul.com.br **E:** contato@radiodanubioazul.com.br – **PR65**) Rua José Ferreira 262, 86975-000 Mandaguari ☎44 3233 1180 **W:** www.radioguairaca.com.br **E:** guairaca@bwnet.com.br – **PR66**) Rua Marchal Deodora 172, Centro, (✉ C.P 91, 86430-970) 86430-000 Santo Antônio da Platina ☎43 3534 4321 **W:** www.difusoraplatinense.com. br **E:** radiofmvaledosol@bol.com.br - **FM.:** 100.5MHz – **PR67**) Rua Pedro Eloy de Souza 51, 82820-130 Curitiba ☎41 3270 9000 **W:** www. grpcom.com.br/continental **E:** continental@grpcom.com.br – **PR68**) Rua Rio Grande do Sul 1110, 85806-010 Cascavel ☎45 3224 2717 **W:** www.radiogloboscascavel.com.br **E:** radiocidade@certto.com.br – **PR69**) Rua Ponta Grossa 1682 1 Andar (✉ C.P. 71), 85601-600 Francisco Beltrão ☎46 3524 3518 **W:** www.seleski@seleski. com.br - **FM:** 105.1MHz «FM Super Jovem» – **PR70**) Av Pedro Taques 1864, Jardin Alvorada (✉C.P. 1300, 87001-970) 87033-000 Maringá ☎44 3267 3000 **E** radioatalaia@turbo.com – **PR71**) Rua XV de Novembro, 591, Centro, 84010-020 Ponta Grossa ☎42 3028 1300 **W:** www.cbnpg.com.br **E:** cbnpg@cbnpg.com.br – **PR72**) Rua Desembargador Westphalen 295, 80010-110 Curitiba ☎41 3366 5657 **W:** www.tropicalam1320.com.br **E:** tropicalam1320@tropicalam1320. com.br – **PR73**) Rua Ébio de Carvalho, 699 – Jardim Montecatine, 86031-720 Londrina ☎43 3378 2100 **W:** www.radiobrasilsul.com.br **E:** brasilsul@radiobrasilsul.com.br – **PR74**) Rua XV de Novembre 1299, Centro, 84220-000 Cidade Sengés ☎43 3535 1144 **W:** www.radioja-guariaiva.com.br – **PR75**) Rua Doutor Camargo 5152, 87502-010 Umuarama ☎44 3622 5033 **W:** www.radioinconfidenciaam.com.br **E:**nova@radioinconfidenciaam.com.br – **PR76**) Rua Exp Adir Jorge 511, Centro, 83880-000 Rio Negro ☎47 3642 3969 **W:** www.difusorarione-gro.com.br – **PR77**) Rua Flamingos 357, 86701-390 Arapongas **W:** www.transnorte.com – **PR78**) Av Paul Harris, 50 – Conjunto Paraiso, 86220-000 Assaí ☎43 3262 1367 **W:** www.radiolideram.blogspot.com **E:** contato@lideram.com.br – **PR79**) Rua Pedro Alvares Cabral 1609, 87560-000 Iporã – **PR80**) Av. Marechal Floriano Peixa 4809, Vila Hauer, 80050-150 Curitiba ☎41 3091 1370 **W:** http://blog.cancaonova.com/ curitiba **E:** radiocuritiba@cancaonova.com.br – **PR81**) Rua Paraiba 168, Centro, 86930-000 São João do Ivaí ☎43 3477 1117 **W:**www.educa-dora1180.com.br**E:** radioeducadora@ligbr.com.br – **PR82**) Av.Mauá 1988, Vila Operária, 87050-020 Maringa (C.P 76, 87001-970 Maringá) ☎44 3221 3221 ▤44 3222 4969 **W:** www.culturamaringa.com.br **E:** radio@culturamaringa.com.br - **FM:** 102.5MHz – **PR83**) Av Bertino Warmling, 1110 sala 02 - Centro, 84050-000 Salto do Lontra ☎46 3538 1320 **W:** www.rinet.com.br **E:** ri_ouvinte@slnet.com.br – **PR84**) Rua Pref Hugo Cabral, 192 - Centro, 86200-110 Londrina **W:** www.radioglo-bolondrina.com.br **E:** radioglobolondrina@radioglobolondrina.com.br ☎43 3373 5500 – **PR85**) Av Dep Ivan Ferreira do Amaral Filho, 86 - Centro, 85301-070 Laranjeiras do Sul ☎42 3635 1396 **W:** www.

radioeducadora1120.com.br **E:** comercial@radioeducadora1120.com.br – **PR86**) Rua Simão Domingues, 26 - Centro, 84550-000 Rebouças ☎42 3457 1150 **W:** www.alvoradanoar.com.br **E:** comercial@alvora-danoar.co.br – **PR87**) Rua Azauri Guedez Pereira n°1351, 85990-000 Terra Roxa ☎44 3645 1135 **W:** www.radiofronteiradoeste.com **E:** radiofronteiraam@hotmail.com – **PR88**) Rua Nicanor dos Santos Silva 4465,, 87501-120 Umuarama ☎44 3624 4664 **W:** www.culturaumua-rama.com.br – **PR89**) Rua Antônio Lemos, 807 - Centro, 86400-000 Jacarezinho **W:** www.centraldoparana.com.br **E:** educadora@uol.com. br ☎43 3525 0773 ▤43 3527 2029 – **PR90**) Rua Dom Pedro I 420, 85710-000 Santo Antônio do Sudoeste **W:** www.radioentrerios1170. com.br **E:** contato@radioentrerios1170.com.br ☎46 3563 1541 – **PR91**) Rua Mato Grosso 2229, (C.P 66) 85812-020 Cascavel ☎45 3220 1717 **W:** www.radiocolmeia.com.br **E:** radiocolmeia@brturbo.com – **PR92**) Rua V Pref V Pref Reginaldo G Nocera 335, Centro84261-020 Telêmaco Borba ☎42 3272 9000 - **FM:** 92.9MHz – **PR93**) Rua Vicente Inácio Filho 241, 86360-000 Bandeirantes ☎43 3542 3233 **W:** www. radiocabiuna.com.br – **PR95**) Rua Mal Deodoro da Fonseca 717,(✉C.P 171, 87550-970) 87550-000 Altônia ☎44 3659 3444 **W:** www.radio-rainha.com.br **E:** contato@radiorainha.com.br – **PR96**) Rua Prof Cleto, 281 - Centro, 83221-320 Paranaguá ☎41 3423 4322 **W:** www.difu-soraam1460.com.br **E:** administracao@difusoraam1460.com.br – **PR97**) Rua XV de Novembro 522, 84010-908 Ponta Grossa ☎42 3225 2144 ▤3222 7115 **W:** www.centraldoparana.com.br **E:** central@centraldopa-rana.com 24h – **PR98**) Rua Sao Paulo, 910 – Vila Feliz (✉C.P 777 86800-970), 86808-070 Apucarana ☎43 3033 2216 **W:** www.radiocul-turaapucarana.com.br **E:** contato@radioculturaapucarana.com.br or amcultura@net21.com.br – **PR99**) Rua Jesuino Alves da Rocha Loures 1764 (C.P 66) 85555-000 Palmas ☎46 3263 1818 **W:** www.redebomje-sus.com.br **E:** radioclubeamfm.com.br 9000-0300 Sat.:1030-0100 - **FM:** 96.5MHz «Horizonte» – **PR100**) Rua Acácio Nunes 1065, 85980-000 Guaíra ☎44 3642 2068 **W:** www.radioguaira.com.br **E:** alterar@alterar.com.br – **PR101**) Rua Londrina 410, 85640-000 Ampére **W:** www.ampernet.com.br **E:** radioampere@ampernet.com.br – **PR102**) Av. Belo Horizonte 497,87900-00 Loanda ☎44 3425 5252 **W:** www. guadalupeam.com.br **E:** guadelupeam@guadelupeam.com.br – **PR103**) Rua Nilo Sampaio 531, Centro, 84900-000 Ibaiti ☎43 3546 1291 **W:** www.radioeducadora1470.com – **PR104**) Praça Nossa Senhora do Carmo 99 (C.P 54), 85935-000 Assis Chateaubriand ☎44 3528 4477 **E:** radiojornal@visaonet.com.br **E:** radiojornalam.com.br – **PR105**) Rua Ébano Pereira 157, 85200-000 Pitanga ☎43 3641 1739 **W:** www. radiopitanga.com.br – **PR106**) C.P 45, 86730-970 Astorga – **PR107**) Rua Ipiranga 91, 84600-000 União da Vitória ☎42 3522 1098 **W:** www. educadora-uv.com.br **E:** contato@educadora-uv.com.br – **PR108**) Rua João Carlos Farias 85, (✉C.P 26), 86300-000 Cornélio Procópio ☎43 3524 2333 **W:** www.radiocornelio.com.br **E:** contato@radiocornelio. com.br – **PR109**) Rua 7 de Setembro 42, 83750-000 Lapa **W:** www. legendaria.am.br **W:** www.am960@matrix.com.br ☎41 3622 1918 ▤41 3622 1428 – **PR110**) Avenida Paraná,540, 86925-000 Borrazópolis ☎43 3425 1233 **W:** www.radionovaera.com.br **E:** radionovaera@brturbo. com.br – **PR111**) Av, São João No. 1952 (✉C.P 121, 84400-970) 84400-000 Prudentópolis ☎42 3446 1547 **W:** www.radioesperan-caam.com.br **E:** radioesperancaam@hotmail.com – **PR112**) Rua Rouxinol 752, 86701-150 Arapongas ☎43 3055 4535 ▤43 3055 2133 **W:** www.radioarapongas.com.br**E:** radio@arapongas.com.br – **PR113**) Rua João Ramos Piedad 120, 84950-000 Venceslau Brás ☎43 3528 1105 **W:** www.educadoraonline.com - **FM:**95.7MHz – **PR114**) Rua Dr Correis, 289, Centro, 84500-000 Irati ☎43 3423 2533 **W:** www.radio-difusoradeirati.com **E:** difusoraam@hotmail.com – **PR115**) Rua Florianópolis 1636, 85840-000 Céu Azul **E:** uniao@netceu.com.br – **PR116**) Travessa Vale Porto 240, 83370-000 Antonina ☎41 3432 1362 **W:** www.serradomaram1520.com.br **E:** radioserradomar@yahoo.com. br – **PR117**) Av Souza Naves 1265, 86870-000 Ivaiporã – **PR118**) Rua 5 de Julho 1065, 85950-000 Palotina – **PR119**) Rua Dom Pedro II 1889, Vila Dom Pedro II, 834608-380 Campo Largo ☎41 3392 1111 **W:**www. radioagapeam.com.br **E:**radioagapeam@brturbo.com.br – **PR120**) Rua Mauá 2518, (C.P. 66), 85770-000 Realeza ☎46 3543 1196 **W:** www. radiocluberza.com **E:** radioclube@wln.com.br – **PR121**) Rua Florianópolis 1813, Zona 02, 87200-000 Cianorte ☎44 3629 1317 **W:** www.radiocapital990.com.br **E:** adm@radiocapital990.com.br – **PR122**) Praça Alfredo João Lazzarotto, s/n° (Caixa Postal 61), 89490-000 Siqueira Campos ☎43 3571 1125 **W:** www.radiobomjesus.com.br **E:** bomjesus@hotmail com – **PR123**) Av. Redife, 434, 43485830-970 Formosa do Oeste ☎41 3243 0950 **W:** www.pioneiraam.com.br – **PR124**) Av Dambros e Pava, 946(C.P 10, 85615-970) 85615-000 Marmeleiro ☎46 3525 1183 ▤46 3525 1142 **W:** www.cristal.seleski. com.br **E:** radiocristal@wln.com.br – **PR125**) Av Brasil 502, 85760-000 Capanema – **PR126**) Rua Senador Pinheiro Machado 1536, Centro, 85010-100 Guarapuava ☎42 3035 8000 **W:** http://difusoraguarapuava. com.br/atalaia **E:** atalaia@mattosleao.com.br – **PR127**) Rua do Comércio 654, 85660-000 Dois Vizinhos **W:** www.educadoradv.com.br

E: radio@educadoradv.com.br ☎46 3536 3131 ▤46 3536 3003 – **FM:** 100.7MHz «Vizinhança» – **PR128**) Rua Benjamin Constant, 440 - Centro, 84500-000 Irati ☎42 3423 1331 **W:** www.radionajua.com.br **E:** radionajua@radionajua.com.br **FM:** 106.9MHz – **PR129**) Rua Sao Paulo 180, 86380-000 Andirá ☎43 3538 4150 **W:** www.culturaandira.com.br **E:** comercial@culturaandira.com.br – **PR130**) Rua São Paulo 489, 86840-000 Faxinal ☎▤43 3461 1129 **W:** www.radioclubdefaxinal.com.br **E:** radioclub@folnet.com.br – **PR131**) Rua Noruega 98, 86182-000 Cambé – **PR132**) Praça São Pedro 999, 85460-000 Quedas do Iguaçu ☎46 3532 1416 **W:** www.radiointernacional.com.br **E:** ademir@radiointernacional.com.br – **PR133**) Praça Marechal Floriano 108, 84130-000 Palmeira ☎42 3252 3669 **W:** www.radioipiranga.com.br **E:** radioipiranga@br10.com.br – **PR134**) Rua Amauri Lange Silvéro, No 270 - Pilarzinho, 82120-000 Curitiba ☎41 3271 4700 **W:** www.clubeb2.com. br **E:** grupolumen@grupolumen.com.br – **FM:** 101.5MHz – **PR135**) Av Brasil 740, 84350-000 Ortigueira – **PR136**) Av Maximiliano Vicentin 240, 85270-000 Palmital ☎42 3657 1442 **W:** www.radiocidadepalmital.com.br **E:** radiopalmital@hotmail.com – **PR137**) Rua Melissa 520, 85410-000 Nova Aurora **E:** raclubna@sercopa.com.br – **PR138**) Avenida Brasil 531, Sala 74, Centro, 85851-000 Foz do Iguaçu ☎45 3572 2410 **W:** www.radiofiladelfia.com.br **E:** radioculturamorenafiladelfia@gmail.com – **PR139**) Rua Antônio Costa, 529-Vista Alegere das Mercês, 80820-020 Curitiba **W:** www.radiobandab.com.br **E:** bandabad@radiobandab.com.br ☎41 3240 7000 – **PR140**) Rua Urbano Lunardelli 875, 86160-000 Porecatu **E:** radiohrotense@com.br – **PR141**) Av Paraná, 220 - Centro, 84470-000 Cândido de Abreu **W:** www.alternativa710.com.br **E:** radio@alternativa710.com.br ☎▤43 3476 1244 – **PR142**) Av Santos Dumont, 2505-Centro, 85301-040 Laranjeiras do Sul **W:** www.radiocampoaberto.com.br **E:** rca@radiocampoaberto.com.br – **PR143**) Av Genoroso Marques 599, 2° andar, Centro, 85550-000 Coronel Vivida ☎46 3732 1191 **W:** www.radiovozdosudoeste.com.br/2008 **E:** radiovoz@win.com.br – **PR144**) Rua Sete de Setembro 3910, 85560-000 Chopinzinho ☎46 3242 1435 **W:** www.redebomjesus.com.br **E:** difusoraamerica@chnet.com.br – **FM:** 98.7MHz – **PR145**) Av Paraná, 201 – Jardim Itajubá, 85857-970 Foz do Iguaçu **W:** www.cbnfoz.com. br**E:** jorgepedroso@cbnfoz.com.br ☎45 3523 2211 – **PR146**) Av Presidente Kennedy, 170 - Norte, 85950-000 Palotina ☎44 3649 7700 ▤44 3649 7713 **W:** www.radiocontinentalam.com.br **E:** comercialmidia@gmail.com 24h – **FM:** 93.5MHz – **PR147**) Av. Minas Gerais, 31-Centro, 85420-000 Corbélia ☎45 3242 1799 **W:** www.radiointegracao.net **E:** integracao@realplus.com.br – **PR148**) Rua Farroupilha 80, 2° andar, 85877-000 São Miguel do Iguaçu ☎43 3565 1033 **W:** www.radiojornalsaomiguel.com.br **E:** rjcomercial@brturbo.com.br – **PR149**) Av Iguaçu, 288 - Centro, 85575-000 São Jorge d'Oeste ☎46 3534 1184 **W:** www.difusorasaojorge.com.br **E:** radiodifusora1490@hotmail.com – **PR150**) Av Santo Antônio 826, 87320-000 Roncador **W:** www.princesa820.com.br – **PR151**) Av Yolanda Loureiro de Carvalho 1021, 87350-000 Ubiratã – **PR152**) Rua Dom Pedro II, 1581 – Conjunto Residensia, 85901-270 Toledo. ☎45 3252 7095 **W:** www.radiointegracaoam.com.br **E:** contato@radiointergracaoam.com.br – **PR153**) Rua Perfeito Pedro Rolim de Moura 104, 84240-000 Piraí do Sul – **PR154**) Rua Sao Vicente 83, (C.P 20) 87160-000 Mandaguaçu **W:** www.colmeia1170am.com **E:** contribuinto@colmeia1170am.com ☎44 3245 1776 – **PR155**) Rua Rosalvo Petrechem 551, 85200-000 Pitanga 42 3646 3366.**W:** www.radiopoema.com.br **E:** radiopoema@radiopoema. com.br – **PR156**) Av Euclides da Cunha s/n, 87890-000 Terra Rica **E:** guairaca@vsp.com.br – **PR157**) Av Iguaçu 858, Ed Fabiane, 85585-000 Verê **E:** rvaledoiguacu@gualinet.com.br – **Italian:** Sat mornings – **PR158**) Rua Independência s/n, Prox Escola de Aplica, 86130-000 Bela Vista do Paraíso – **PR159**) Rua Luiz Pinheiro 1446, 84990-000 Arapoti – **PR160**) Av Iguaçu 366, 85790-000 Capitão Leônidas Marques **E:** hawai@certto.com.br – **PR161**) Rua Antonio Rosa 1170, 86490-000 Ribeirão do Pinhal **E:** am@radioserpin.com.br – **PR162**) Rua Vicente Machado 385, 84570-000 Mallet ☎42 3542 2004 **W:** www.radioclubemallet.com.br **E:** contato@radioclubemallet.com.br – **PR163**) Rua Marechal Deodoro 22, 85540-000 Mangueirinha ☎46 3243 1417 **W:** www.radioaraucaria.com.br **E:** radioaraucaria@qualinet.com.br – **PR164**) Rua São Miguel 577 (✉ C.P. 1), 85570-000 São João ☎46 3533 1474 **W:** www.radiosaojoao.com.br **E:** radiosj@sudonet.com.br – **PR165**) Rua Guarani 829, sala 01, Centro, 85501-050 Pato Branco ☎46 3225 4000 **W:** www.radiopatobranco.com.br **E:** ouvinte@radiopatobranco.com.br – **PR166**) Av.Artur de Abreu 29, Ed Palácio do Café, 11° andar, conj 6, Centro, 83203-480 Paranaguá ☎41 3218 5800 – **PR167**) 85850-000 Foz do Iguau – **PR168**) Rua Guilherme Pequeno 413, Centro, 83230-000 Guaratuba ☎41 3472 3275 ▤41 3472 3019 **W:** www.radiolitoranea.com.br **E:** amlitorane@onda.com.br – **PR169**) Rua Ana Beje, 84300-000 Tibagi – ☎42 3275 3247 **W:** www.radioitay.com.br **E:** radioitay@radioitay.com.br – **PR170**) Av Vice-Prefeito Reginaldo Guedes Nocera 84260-000 Telêmaco Borba – **PR171**) Av Londrina, 523, Centro, 87111-220 Sarandi ☎44 3035 7476 **W:** www.banda1am.com. br – **PR172**) Rua José M.Soares 104, 85580-000 Itapejara d'Oeste

☎46 3526 1926 **W:** www.panoramam.com.br **E:** radiopanorama@brturbo.com.br – **PR173**) 83540-000 Rio Branco do Sul – **PR174**) Rua Parigot de Souza, 47, Centro, 86740 Pérola d´Oeste ☎46 3556 1048 **W:** www.radioperola.com.br **E:** admin@radioperola.com.br – **PR175**) 87530-000 Icaraíma – **PR176**) 86180-000 Cambé – **PR178**) 84430-000 Imbituva – **PR179**) Rua Pedro de Oliveira 938, 85440-000 Ubiratã ☎▤44 3543 1717 **W:** www.radiodifusoraubirata.com.br **E:** rdifusora@gmail.com – **PR182**) 86400-000 Jacarezinho – **PR183**) 86400-000 Jacarejinho – **PR184**) Rua José Carlos Colodel 306 cj 5, Vila Santa Terezina 306, 83501-140 Almirante Tamandaré **W:** www.radiobarigui. com.br – **PR185**) Rua Dom Pedro I, 643 conj. 84 - Vila Moraes, 19900-214Ourinhos/SP or Rua Santos Dumont, 268 - Centro – 86400-000 Jacarezinho/ PR ☎14 3325 2085 or 43 3525 1088 **W:** www.radionortesul.com.br **E:** contato@radionortesul.com.br

RJ00) RIO DE JANEIRO

RJ01) Rua Benedito Hipolito 1, Centro, 20211-130 Niterói ☎21 2509 6525 ☎21 2245 2028 **W:** www.ofluminense.com.br – **RJ02**) Rua Costa Rica 151, Parque Hotel, 28970-000 Araruama ☎22 2665 4119 **W:** www.radiocostadosol560.com **E:** radiocostadosol@araruama.com.br – **RJ03**) Av. dos Bandeirantes, 1000 – Taquara, 20040-009 Jacarepaguá ☎21 2461 0580 – **RJ04**) Av.Erasmo Brage 118, 11° andar, Centro 20020-000 Rio de Janeiro – **FM:** 94.1 MHz – **RJ05**) Rodovia Presidente Dutra Km 303, Fazenda Barra, 27365-000 Resende – ☎24 3544 1222 ▤24 3355 0733 **W:** www.radioagulhasnegras.com.br **E:**agulhasnegrasam@resenet. com.br - **FM:** 93.9MHz – **RJ06**) Praça Demerval Barbosa Moreira 28, Centro, 28610-160 Nova Friburgo ☎22 2523 3034 **W:** www.radiofriburgoam.com.br **E:** contato@novafriburgoam.com.br – **RJ07**) Av Dom Helder Camara 4242, 20771-000 Rio de Janeiro – **RJ08**) Av Deputado Alair Ferreira 201 A, Parque Turf Club, 28024-600 Campos dos Goitacazes – ☎22 2723 8989 **W:** www.radioabsoluta.com.br – **RJ09**) Rua México 111 slj, Centro, 20031-145 Rio de Janeiro ☎21 2220 3656 **W:** www.redesucesso.com – **RJ10**) Av Djalma Beda Coube 719, 28500-000 Cantagalo ☎22 2555 4458 – **RJ11**) Rua de Assembléia, 10/3401- Centro, 20011-901 Rio de Janeiro ☎21 2531 0070 **W:** www.radiomanchete.com.br **E:** comercial@radiomanchete.com.br 24h – **RJ12**) Praça da República 141-A, 3° andar, sala 306, Centro 20211-350 Rio de Janeiro ☎21 2508 8295 **W:** www.radiomec.com.br – **RJ13**) Av Rui Barbosa 749, 3° andar, 27910-361 Macaé ☎22 3311 3145 **W:** www.radioglobomacae.com.br **E:** comercial@radioglobomacae.com.br – **RJ14**) Rua do Russel 434, Glória, 22210-010 Rio de Janeiro ☎21 2555 8282 – **FM:** 92.5 MHz – **RJ15**) Av Portugal 96, Urca, 22291-050 Rio de Janeiro ☎21 4002 3599 **W:** www.radiotamoio.com.br – **RJ16**) Av. Marchal Floriano, 114 - Centro, 20080-002 Rio de Janeiro **W:** www.redeboavontade.com.br – **RJ17**) Rua de Relação, 18 – Lapa, 20231 110 Rio de Janeiro ☎21 2117 6209 **W:** www.ebc.com.br/canais/radios/radio-nacional-am-rio-de-janeiro – **RJ18**) Av. Venezuela, 27 8 andar, Saúde,, 20081-311 Rio de Janeiro ☎21 2223 3153 **W:** www.radiocapitalrio.com.br – **RJ19**) Travessa Santa Luiza 91, 23900-900 Angra dos Reis ☎24 3365 1352 E: jangra@uol.com.br – **RJ20**) Rua Buenos Aires N° 68, 19° andar, Centro, 20070-020 Rio de Janeiro ☎21 3171 1067 **W:** http://blog.cancaonova.com/riodejaneiro **E:** radioespiritosanto@cancaonova.com – **RJ21**) Av Alberto Torres 164, 28035-582 Campos dos Goitacazes ☎22 2733 1082 – **RJ22**) Estrada Adhemar Bebiano (ex-Estr. Velha da Pavuna) 3517Inhaúma, 20765-170 Rio de Janeiro ☎21 2176 8276 **W:** www.metropolitana1090.com.br **E:** contato@metropolitana1090.com.br – **RJ23**) Av Alair Ferreira, 201 Turf-Club, 28022-000 Campos dos Goitacazes ☎22 2728 1110 **W:** www.radiorecordcampos.net **E:** radiorecordcampos@r7.com – **RJ24**) Rua Presidente Vargas, 1215, Centro, 25802-200 Três Rios ☎▤24 2252 1797 **W:** www.radiotresrios.com.br **E:** rtr@radiotresrios.com.br – **FM:** 89.7MHz – **RJ25**) Rua do Russel 426/434, Glória, 22210-010 Rio de Janeiro **W:** www.mundial.am.br – **RJ26**) Rua dos Andrades, 109 - 3° andar, Centro, 28010-300 Campos dos Goitacazes ☎22 2722 5699 **W:** www.radiocontinentalam. com.br **E:** continental@viacabo.com.br – **RJ27**) Rua do Livramento 189, 8° andar, 20221-191 Rio de Janeiro ☎21 2126 2421 **W:** www.tupi.am – **RJ28**) Rua Alberto Torres 410, 3° andar, Centro, 28400-000 São Fidelis ☎22 2758 1275 **W:** http://radiocoroadosam.com **E:** radiocoroadosam1310@hotmail.com – **RJ29**) Av 28 de Setembro, 258 – Loja 01 - Vila Isabel, 20551-031 Rio de Janeiro ☎21 2576 9739 **W:** www.radioboasnovas.com.br**E:** comercial@radioboasnovas.com.br – **RJ30**) Rua Alvaro Ramo, 350, Botafogo, 22280-110 Rio de Janeiro ☎21 2586 9400 – **RJ31**) Rua Carlos de Lacerda 52, 2° andar, 28013-030 Campos de Goytacazes ☎22 2733 0102 **W:** www.radiocamposdifusora.com.br **E:** angeladifusra@yahoo.com.br – **RJ32**) Av.Joaquim Leite 465, 1° andar, 27345-391 Barra Mansa ☎24 3323 3300 **W:** www.sulfluminense.com.br – **FM:** 99.3MHz – **RJ33**) Estrada do Dendê, 659, Tauá, Ilha do Governador, 21920-000 Rio de Janeiro ☎21 3396 5252 **W:** www.radioriodejaneiro. am.br **E:** marketing@radioriodejaneiro.com.br – **Esperanto:** Wed 2330, Sun 1100 – **RJ34**) Av Cardoso Moreira 422, Sobrado, Centro, 28300-000 Itaperuna ☎24 3824 1410 **W:** www.itaperunaam.com.br **E:** thiago@radioitaperunaam.com.br or radioitaperunaam@gmail.com – **RJ35**) Rua do Mercado 34 Grupo 802, Praça XV, 20010-120 Rio de Janeiro ☎21

2203 2288 **W:** www.radiolivre1440.com.br **E:** contato@radiolivre1440.com.br – **RJ36**) Av Joaquim Leite, 279 - Centro, 27330-042 Barra Mansa **W:** www.radiodocomercio.com.br **E:** atendimento@radiodocomercio.com.br ☎24 3323 3848 – **RJ37**) Rua Dr Temistocles de Almeida 97, 28470-000 Santo Antônio de Pádua ☎22 3853 3173 **W:** www.radiofeliz.com.br **E:** directoria@radiofeliz.com.br – **RJ38**) Rua Ana Nery, 120 9° andar Centro, 27123-150 Barra do Piraí ☎24 2443 1470 **W:** www.rbpfm.com.br **E:** rbpam@terra.com.br **FM:** 89.9MHz – **RJ39**) Rua Senador Dantas 117, cob 02, Nova Iguaçú ☎21 2767 3333 **W:** www.tropical830am.com.br **E:** tropical@tropical830am.com.br – **RJ40**) Rodovia BR-101 s/n km 270, Zona Rural, 28800-000 Rio Bonito ☎21 2734 8688 **W:** http://tupi1340.blogspot.com.br – **RJ41**) Av.Fransisco Torres 12, 27286-440 Volta Redonda **E:** diretoria105fm@aleluianet.com.br – **RJ42**) Rua Cardoso 357, 28013-460 Campos dos Goytacazes ☎22 2733 9072.– **RJ43**) Rua Nilza Chiapeta Fadigas, 275 Sobrado - Várzea, 25963-150 Teresópolis ☎21 2742 1040 ▤21 2742 1920 **W:** www.radioteresopolis.com.br **E:** radioter-esopolisam@gmail.com – **RJ44**) Rua Carolina Machado, 173 - Madureira (✉ CP 17030, Madureira, 21310-971), 21351-021 Rio de Janeiro ☎21 3390 1422 **W:** www.continental1520.com.br http://continental1520.com.br**E:** contatos@continental1520.com.br – **RJ45**) Rua Paulino Padilha 80, 28460-000 Miracema – ☎22 3852 0899 **W:**www.princesinhaam.com.br – **RJ46**) Rua Marechal Deodoro 46, 9° andar, 25620-150 Petrópolis ☎24 2237 6000 - **FM:** 88.5MHz – **RJ47**) Rua Vereador D.Teixeira Fontes 556, 23815-270 Itaguaí ☎21 3395 1560 **W:** www.radiogranderio1560.com.br – **RJ48**) Rua Carneiro de Mendonça 29-A, Centro, 27600-000 Valença ☎24 2453 4418 **W:** www.radioculturadovale.com.br – **RJ49**) Rua Tenente José Teixeira 147, 28360-000 Bom Jesus do Itabapoana ☎22 3831 1570 ▤22 3831 1295 **W:** www.bomjesusam.com.br **E:** radiobjam@acessototal.com.br – **RJ50**) Av Amaral Peixoto 366, 28860-000 Casimiro de Abreu **W:** www.radiolitoralam.com.br **E:** jornalismo@radiolitoralam.com.br – **RJ51**) Rua Frei Valerio 58, 28740-00 Conceição de Macabu ☎22 2779 2100 **W:** www.popularfluminens.com.br **E:** radiopopular@facilite.com.br – **RJ52**) Rua Nilo Peçanha 329, 3° andar, 27542-210 Resende ☎24 3355 2266 – **RJ53**) Rua Gal.Gustavo C.Farias 84, 20910-220 Rio de Janeiro **W:** www.radiorecordrj.com – **RJ54**) Rua Barao Piabanha, 107 - Centro, 25850-000 Paraíba do Sul ☎24 2263 2343 **W:** www.radioclube1540.com.br – **RJ55**) Rua Gal Dionísio, 327 - Guaratiba, 23025-330 Duque de Caxias ☎21 3652 1480 **W:** www.radiopopularam.com.br **E:** rdcradio@yahoo.com.br – **RJ56**) Rua Figueiras de Barros 100, 28210-000 Italva ☎22 2783 1777 **W:** www.aliancaam.com.br **E:** superaliancaam@bol.com.br – **RJ57**) Praça Porto Rocha 56, Apt 102, Centro, 28905-250 Cabo Frio ☎22 2645 4000 **W:** www.cabofriobuzios.com.br **E:** radiocabofrio@mar.com.br – **RJ58**) Rua Coronel Santiago 250, 25950-000 Teresópolis – **RJ59**) Av.Djalma Beda Combe 719, 28500-000 Cantagalo ☎22 2555 4455 – **RJ60**) 28400-000 São Fidelis

RN00) RIO GRANDE DO NORTE
RN01) Av Duque de Caxias, 106 - Ribeira, 59010-200 Natal **W:** www.radioglobonatal.com.br **E:** rcmidia@terra.com.br ☎84 4006 6186 ▤84 4006 6178 – **RN02**) Praça Dom José de Madeiros Delgado s/n, 59300-000 Caicó **W:** www.radiorural.com **E:** comercial@radiorural.com ☎84 3421 2270 ▤84 3421 1229 - **FM:** 95.0MHz – **RN03**) Rua Luiz XV, Bairro Nordeste, 59042-070 Natal ☎84 3653 3780 **W:** www.nordesteevangelica.com.br **E:** sthenio@nordesteevangelica.com.br 24h – **RN04**) Rua João Pessoa 22, 1° andar, Centro, 59380-000 Currais Novos ☎84 3431 1720 **W:** www.radiocurraisnovosam.com – **RN05**) Rua Vigário Antonio Joaquim 39, Centro, 59600-160 Mossoró ☎84 3314 7256 **E:** rrural@serv2000.com.br – **RN06**) Rua Prof Antonio Campos, s/n, Pres Costa e Silva, 59619-218 Mossoró ☎84 3312 4618 **W:** www.redepotiguar.com **E:** boanoite@rederpc.com.br **RN07**) Rua Açú 335, Tirol, 59020-110 Natal ☎84 3201 1690 **W:** http://blog.cancanova.com/natal **E:** radionatal@cancaonova.com – **RN08**) Rua Dr Cunha Mota, s/n - Pereiros, 59600-160 Mossoró ☎84 3317 6167 **W:** www.difusoramossoro.com **E:** gravacao@difusoramossore.com – **RN09**) Rua Romualdo Galvão, 973 - Lagoa Seca, 59056-100 Natal **E:** cbn@redetropical.com **W:** www.redetropical.com.br ☎84 3211 6400 **FM:** 103.9MHz – **RN10**) Av Deodoro 245, 59012-600 Natal **W:** www.clube.am **E:** nilsonpinheiro.rn@diariosassociados.com.br – **RN11**) Praça Des Tomáz Salustino, 42, Centro, 59380-000 Currais Novos ☎84 3431 1266 **W:**www.radioourobrancoam.com.br **E:** radioourubrancoam@hotmail.com – **RN12**) Rua Francisca Delfina 30, Centro, 59860-620 Alexandria ☎84 3381 2320 **W:** www.redepotiguar.com **E:** rpcfarol@risanet.com.br – **RN13**) Praça Bento Praxedes, 104 - Centro, 59600-620 Mossoró – **RN14**) Rua Otávio Amorim 643, 59650-000 Açu ☎84 3331 1222 **W:** www.radioprincesadovale.com.br – **RN15**) Rua Nero Nazareno Fernandes, 250 - Centro, 59780-300 Caraúbas ☎84 3337 2297 **W:** http://radiocentenarioam.blogspot.com.br **E:** centenario@brisanet.com.br – **RN16**) Rua Frei Alberto Cabral 08 - Centro, 59215-000 Nova Cruz ☎84 3281 2123 – **RN17**) Rua Getúlio Vargas, 1296-Centro, 59900-000 Pau dos Ferros ☎84 3351 2388 – **RN18**) Rua Augusto Monteiro999 c415A, 59300-000 Caicó ☎84 3421 1988 **W:** www.radioserido.com.br **E:** seridoaovivo@hotmail.com – **RN19**)

Rua Avinida Rio Branco, 173 - Centro, 59655-000 Areia Branca ☎84 3312 4618 **W:** www.redepotiguar.com **E:** comecial@rederpc.com.br – **RN20**) Rua Ana de Pontes 419, 59255-000 Santo Antônio ☎84 3282 2347 ▤84 3282 2346 – **RN21**) Rua Odorico Ferreira de Souza 70, Bairro DNR, 59200-000 Santa Cruz **W:** www.radiosantacruzam.com.br **E:** contato@radiosantacruzam.com.br ☎84 3291 2300 ▤84 3291 2201 – **RN22**) Rua Experidião Coimbra, 22 - Centro, 59500-000 Macau ☎84 3521 1765 **W:** www.redetropical.com.br – **RN23**) Rua Cícero Tomáz de Azevedo 1052, Cruz do Monte, 59360-000 Parelhas ☎84 3471 2401 **W:** www.ruralam.com.br **E:** ruraldeparelhas@hotmail.com – **RN24**) Rua Bela Vista 1420, Centro, 59570-000 Ceará Mirim ☎84 3274 2794 ▤84 3274 2119 – **RN25**) Rua Sebastião Guilherme Caldas, s/n – Bairro Baixa da Beleza Jardim do Seridó, 59343-000 Jardim do Seridó ☎84 3472 2587 **W:** www.cabugidoserido.br **E:** cabugidoserido@hotmail.com or cabugidoserido@yahoo.com.br – **RN26**) A. Cel Martiniano, 1077 - Centro, 59300-000 Caicó ☎84 3421 4181 ▤84 3417 1112 **W:** www.radiocaico.com.br **E:** suerdamedeiros@uol.com.br **RN27**) Rua São Jorge 1290, Vale Dourado, 59104-200 Natal ☎84 3664 1330 – **RN28**) Rua Padre Cosme 45, Centro, 59930-000 São Miguel ☎84 3353 2166 ▤84 3353 2112 – **RN29**) Rua Coronel Freire 242, Centro, 59460-000 São Paulo do Potengi ☎84 3251 2263 ▤84 3251 2381 – **RN30**) Av 21 de Abril 460, BR-460, 59550-000 João Câmara ☎84 3262 2189 – **RN31**) Rua Joel do Amaral Gurgel s/n, Bairro Cohab, 59700-000 Apodi ☎84 3333 2528 – **RN32**) Rua do Chafariz 1390, Bairro Novo Horizonte, 59584-000 Touros ☎84 3263 2121 ▤84 3263 2526

RO00) RONDÔNIA
RO01) Rua Joaquim Nabuco 1573, 79815-350 Porto Velho ☎69 3224 1081.– **RO02**) Av Rondônio s/n, 78987-000 Rolim de Moura – **RO03**) Av Jamari 4218, 78932-000 Ariquemes ☎69 3536 3385 **W:** www.radioariquemes.com **E:** amauri@ariquemes.com.br – **RO04**) Rua Dom Augusto, 1491 - Centro, 78961-380 Ji-Paraná **W:** www.sgcrondonia.com.br **E:** rd-alvorada@ulbrajp.com.br ☎69 3421 5068 – **RO05**) Rua Rui Barbosa 3375, Bairro Floresta, 78975-000 Cacoal ☎69 3441 2122 **W:** www.radiorondonia.com.br – **RO06**) Rua Feijo, 2930 Cafézinho, 78963-085 Ji-Paraná ☎69 3424 0406 **W:** www.radiojiparana.com.br **E:** radiojiparana@uol.com.br – **RO08**) Rua Ricardo Catanhede esquina com a Rua Goiás s/n, 78941-000 Jaru – **RO09**) Praça Mário Correa 90, Cristo Rei, 76850-000 Guajará Mirim ☎69 3541 6333 **W:** www.radioeducadoraam.com.br **E:** adm@radioeducadoraam.com.br - **FM:** 93.7MHz – **RO10**) Rua Dourados 4, Setor Industriales, 78930-000 Ariquemes ☎69 3535 3000 **W:** www.radiorondonia.com – **RO11**) Rua das Crianças, 4646 - Areal da Floresta, 78912-210 Porto Velho ☎69 3210 3621 **W:** www.radiocaiari.com **E:** radiocaiari@gmail.com SW: 0900-1400, 1900-0300 – **RO12**) Rua Princesa Isabel 128, 78995-000 Vilhena ☎69 3321 3309 **W:** www.radiovilhena.com.br **E:** radiovilhena@brturbo.com.br – **RO14**) Loteamento Monte Alegre, Quadras 35, 36, 38, 39, 41 e 42, 78987-000 Rolim de Moura – **RO15**) Rua Carlos Doneje 1304, Ctg, 78984-000 Pimenta Bueno ☎69 3222 5308 **W:** www.radiorondonia.com **E:** comercialpb@radiorondonia.com – **RO16**) Rua 1005, Lote, Quadra 3 Setor 10, 1522, (✉ C.P. 105), 78995-000 Vilhena ☎69 3322 2589 **W:** www.plansol.com **E:** plansol@hotmail.com – **RO17**) Rua Miguel Chakian 1300, Bairro Embratel, 78906-300 Porto Velho – **RO18**) Rua 6 de Maio No 1811, Bairro Casa Preta(✉ C.P. 163), 76980-000 Ji-Paraná ☎69 3421 1390 **W:** www.plansol.com.br – **RO19**) Rua Sergipe 1766, Morada do Sol, 78983-000 Espigão d'Oeste ☎69 3481 3348 **W:** www.radiosociedadeespigao.com.br **E:** radio@radiosociedadeespigao.com.br – **RO20**) 78949-000 Ouro Preto do Oeste – **RO21**) 78941-000 Jaru – **RO22**) 78984-000 Pimenta Bueno – **RO23**) Rua Anel Viario, 1782, Parque Brizon, 78975-000 Cacoal ☎69 3443 2928 **W:** www.radiosuprema.com.br **E:** estudio@radiosuprema.com.br – **RO24**) 78900-000 Porto Velho.

RR00) RORAIMA
RR01) Av Capitão Ene Garcez, 888 - São Francisco, 69301-160 Boa Vista ☎95 3623 2259 **E:** direcao@radiororaima.com.br **W:** www.radiororaima.com.br – **RR02**) Rua Sebastião Diniz 363, 69360-000 Caracaraí – **RR03**) 69350-000 Alto Alegre – **RR04**) Rua Lobo D´Almada, 43 - Sao Francisco, 69035-050 Boa Vista ☎95 3623 8801 **W:** www.folhabv.com.br **E:**radiofolha@folhabv.com.br - **FM:** 91.9MHz – **RR05**) 69380-000 Bonfim.

RS00) RIO GRANDE DO SUL
RS01) Av Victor Barreto 3056, Conj 207, 92010-901 Canoas ☎51 3059 5677 ▤51 3476 5077 **W:** www.radiorealam.com.br **E:** comercial@radiorealam.com.br – **RS02**) Av Antunes Ribas 1535, 98801-630 Santo Angelo ☎55 3313 3666 **W:** www.radiosepe.com.br **E:** contato@radiosepe.com.br – **RS03**) Rua Marechal Deodoro 1157, 96810-110 Santa Cruz ☎51 3711 3908 **W:** www.radiosantacruz.com.br **E:** gerencia@radiosantacruz.com.br – **RS04**) Rua General Sampaio, 161 - Bairro Rio Branco, 95097-000 Caxias do Sul **W:** www.redsul.com.br **E:** redsul@saofrancisco.am.br ☎ 54 3220 9400 ▤54 2101 5236 - **FM:** 98.5MHz – **RS05**) Av. Sete de Setembro 509, 99010-121 Passo Fundo ☎54 3311 7756 ▤54 3314 3280 **W:** www.diario570am.com.br **E:**

diretoria@diariodamanha.net – **RS06**) Rua Mascarenhas de Morães 586, Centro, 97300-000 São Gabriel **W:** www.redetche.com.br/saogabriel/ **E:** radiosaogabriel@redetche.com ☎55 3232 6336 – **RS07**) Avenida Moreira Paz 726 (✉ C.P. 67), 95200-000 Vacaria ☎54 3231 7500 **W:** www.radiopelotense.com.br/index.php?emissora=29 **E:** gerente@fatima.am.br – **FM:** 101.5MHz «R Mais Nova FM» – **RS08**) Praça Oswaldo Aranha 39, Centro, 97541-540 Alegrete ☎55 3422 1600 **W:** www.redetche.com.br/alegrete **E:** joaoulisses@radioalegrete.com.br – **RS09**) Av Ipiranga, 1075/2° andar-Azenha, 90160-093 Porto Alegre **E:** gaucha@rdgaucha.com.br **W:** www.clicrbs.com.br ☎51 3218 6600 📠51 3218 6680 - Satellite signal downlinked via 165 stns in southern Brazil forming Rede Gaúcha Sat - **FM:** 93.7 MHz – **RS10**) Rua Andrade Neves, 2316-Centro (C.P 284, 96001-970) 96020-080 Pelotas ☎53 3222 7407 **W:** www.radiopelotense.com.br **E:** radiopelot@terra.com.br – **RS11**) Rua Suécia 255, 98500-000 Tenente Portela ☎55 3551 1395 📠55 3551 1211 **W:** www.radiomunicipal.com.br **E:** municipal@uol.com.br – **RS12**) Rua 14 de Julho, 588 – Centro, (✉ C.P 54), 95300-000 Lagoa Vermelha ☎54 3358 1788 **W:** www.redesul.am.br/Cacique-AM **E:** cacique@cacique.am.br – **RS13**) Rua Paul Harris, 02, 97015-480 Santa Maria ☎55 3220 2131 **W:** www.radiosantamariense.com.br **E:** radiosantamariense@terra.com.br – **RS14**) Rua Delfino Riet, 183 - Santo Antonio, 90660-120 Porto Alegre ☎51 3218 2100 **E:** direcaogeral@bandrs.com.br **W:** www.bandrs.com.br – **RS15**) Av Mauricio Cardoso 88, 1° andar, Centro, 99700-000 Erechim ☎55 3222 6868 **W:** www.radiosantamariense.com.br **E:** comercial@radiosantamariense.com.br – **Italian:** Sat. 1300-1400 - FM: 94.9MHz – **RS16**) Rua Voluntários da Patria 1432, 97590-000 Rosário do Sul ☎55 3231 2533 📠55 3231 4141 **W:** www.radiomaraja.com **E:** contacto@radiomaraja.com – **RS17**) Rua Ramiro Barcelos 800, sala 201, Centro, 95200-000 Vacaria **W:** www.radioesmeralda.com.br **E:** comercial@radioesmeralda.com.br **FM:** 93.1MHz – **RS18**) Rua Neita Ramos 217, 96230-000 Santa Vitória do Palmar ☎53 3263 1660 **W:** www.redemeridional.com/sta.html **E:** culturasantavitoria@redemeridional.com – **RS19**) Rua Domingos Secchi 35, Bairro Boa Vista, 99500-000 Carazinho **W:** www.gazeta670.com.br **E:** comercial@gazeta670.com.br ☎54 3330 3143 📠54 3330 2800 – **RS20**) Travessa 4 de Junho 84, 98380-000 Seberi ☎55 3746 1040 📠55 3746 1033 **W:** www.seberiam.com.br **E:** diretor@seberiam.com.br – **RS21**) Rua XV de Novembro 275, 9° andar, Edifico Panorama, Centro 98700-000 Ijuí **E:** contato@radioprogresso.com.br **W:** rpi.iju@terra.com.br ☎55 3332 9999 – **RS22**) Rua Mascarenhas de Morães 298, 97300-000 São Gabriel ☎55 3232 2244 📠55 3232 5920 **W:** www.radiobatovi.com.br **E:** radiobatovi@terra.com.br – **RS23**) Rua Caldas Jr., 219- 2° andar-Centro, 90010-260 Porto Alegre **E:** diretor@radioguaiba.com.br **W:** www.radioguaiba.com.br ☎51 3215 6333 📠51 3215 6337 - **FM:** 101.3MHz – **RS24**)Rua Coronel Chicuta 436, 5° andar,- Ed Nossa Senhora Aparecida - Centro, 99010-051 Passo Fundo ☎54 3045 3088 **W:** www.rplanalto.com **E:** comercial@rplanalto.com - **FM:** 105.9MHz – **RS25**) Av Júlio de Castilhos, 435 - Bairro Vista Alegre, 98300-000 Palmeira das Missões **W:** www.radiopalmeira.com.br **E:** direcao@radiopalmeira.com.br ☎55 3742 1082 📠55 3742 2255 - **FM:** 101.7MHz – **RS26**) Av Silva Paes 363-A, 96200-340 Rio Grande ☎53 3232 2303 **W:** radionativa.com.br **E:** radionativa@vetorial.net – **RS27**) Av Marechal Floriano 920, Sala 301, 95520-000 Osório **W:** www.radioosorio.com.br **E:** radioosorio@terra.com.br ☎51 3663 3435 – **RS28**) Rua Botucaraí 911, 96930-000 Candelária **E:** radioprincesa@terra.com.br ☎51 3743 1900 – **RS29**) Av Gal Daltro Filho 1000, 98470-000 Planalto ☎55 3794 1025 **W:** www.radioametista.com.br **E:** radioametista@hotmail.com – **RS30**) Rua Pedro Vargas 846, 99500-000 Carazinho ☎54 3331 5250 **W:** www.diarioam780.com.br **E:** radio2@dariodamanha.net – **RS31**) Rua Orfanatrófio 711, 90840-440 Porto Alegre **W:** www.pampa.com.br/radiosul **E:** princesaam@pampa.com.br ☎51 3218 2525 – **RS32**) Rua São João 485, 96640-000 Rio Pardo ☎57 3731 1390 **W:** redecartario.com.br/rccam790 **E:** contatosam790@redecartario.com.br ☎51 3731 2199 📠51 3731 1390 – **RS33**) Prédio da Reitoria, 10° andar, Campus Universitário de Camobi, 97105-900 Santa Maria ☎51 3220 8550 📠51 3220 8390 **W:** celsofranzen@smail.ufsm.br **E:** radio800am@ahoo.com.br – **RS34**) Rua Fernando Abott 427, 2° andar, Centro, 95880-000 Estrela ☎51 3720 5076 📠51 3712 1259 **W:** www.radioaltotaquari.com.br **E:** administracao@radioaltotaquari.com.br – **RS35**) Av Presidente Vargas 892, 98005-160 Cruz Alta ☎55 3322 6499 📠55 3322 6100 **E:** radioindependente@diarioserrano.com.br – **RS36**) Rua Silveiro 1321, 90850-000 Porto Alegre ☎51 3227 6809 **E:** radiorec@terra.com.br – **RS37**) Caladão Salvador Isaia 1330 - 3° andar 97010-902 Santa Maria **W:** www.guarathan.com.br **E:** guarathan@terra.com.br ☎51 3284 0777– **RS38**) Rua Correa Lima 1831, 90850-250 Porto Alegre ☎51 3024 7421 **W:** www.radioitai.com.br **E:** radioitairs@gmail.com – **RS39**) Rua Osvaldo Aranha, 808 Sala 102B – Bairro Juventud, 95700-000 Bento Gonçalves ☎54 3452 7777 **W:** www.difusora890.com **E:** contato@difusora890.com.br – **FM:** 94.5MHz – **RS40**) Praça da Bandeira 36, conj. 2° andar, Centro, (✉ C.P. 1021) 98900-000 Santa Rosa **W:** www.jornalnoroeste.com **E:** faleconosco@

jornalnoroeste.com.br ☎55 3512 5757 – **FM:** 97.7 Guaira – **RS41**) Rua XV de Novembro 336, 99770-000 Aratiba ☎54 3376 1170 **W:** www.radioaratiba.com.br **Emai:** radioaratiba@aratibars.com.br – **RS43**) Rua 7 de Setembro, 1441 - Centro, 95800-000 Venâncio Aires ☎51 3741 2000 📠51 3741 2130 **W:** www.radiovenancioaires.com.br **E:** rva@radiovenancioaires.com.br - **FM:** 105.1MHz – **RS44**) Av.Fernandes Bastos 1049 - Sobreloja, Centro, 95590-000 Tramandai 📠51 36615657 **W:** www.radiotramandai.com.br **E:** radiotramandai@yahoo.com.br – **RS45**) Rua Garibaldi 789-21° andar, Ed. Estrela, Centro, 95084-900 Caxias do Sul ☎54 3289 3000 📠54 3289 3030 **W:** www.radiocaxias.am.br **E:** radiocaxias@radiocaxias.am.br – **RS46**) Av. Brasil, 523 - Centro, 98801-590 Santo Ângelo **W:** www.radiosantoangelo.com.br **E:** radiosan@radiosantoangelo.com.br ☎55 3313 2440 – **RS47**) Av Alberto Müller 242, 95900-000 Lajeado **W:** www.independiente.com.br **E:** comercial@independente.com.br – **RS48**) Av. Walter Jobim, 222 s 106 – Patronato, 97020-425 Santa Maria ☎55 3212 6700 **W:** www.imembui.com.br **E:** radioimembui@via-rs.nrt – **RS49**) Rua Orfanatrófio 711, Alto Teresópolis, 90840-440 Canoas **E:** pampa@pampa.com.br **W:** www.radiopampa.com.br ☎51 3218 2522– **RS50**) Av Getúlio Vargas 412, 98670-000 Humaitá **W:** www.radioaltouruguai.com.br **E:** 970am@radioaltouruguai.com.br ☎55 3525 1212 📠55 3525 1222 – **FM:** 92.5 MHz – **RS51**) Rua Otacílio Tupanciretã de Azevedo 2, 98170-000 Tupanciretã ☎55 3272 1763 📠55 32721763 **W:** www.tupa.am.br **E:** contato@tupa,am.br - **FM:** 92.5MHz – **RS52**) Rua Fiorentino Bachi 791, 99840-000 Sananduva ☎54 3343 1438 **W:** www.radiosananduva.com.br **E:** contato@radiosananduva.com.br - **FM:** 97.7MHz – **RS53**) Rua Garibaldi 789, 21° andar - Centro, 95084-900 Caxias do Sul ☎54 3289 3000 **W:** www.radio1010.am.br **E:** 1010@radio1010.am.br – **RS54**) Rua Julio de Castilhos, 2236 - Centro, 97800-000 São Luís Gonzaga **W:** www.radiomissioneira.com.br **E:** missioneira@viacom.com.br ☎55 3352 4141 – **RS55**) Av David José Martins 1206, 98700-000 Ijuí **W:** www.radioreporter.com.br **E:** atendimento@radioreporter.com.br 📠55 3332 8000 - **FM:** 101.5MHz «Iguatemi» – **RS56**) Rua General Zeca Netto 1396, 96180-000 Camaquã ☎51 3671 0962 **W:** www.redemeridional.com **E:** radiocamaquense@redemeridional.com – **RS57**) Rua São João, 1894-Centro, 97800-000 São Luís Gonzaga **W:** www.radiosaoluiz.com **E:** ouvinte@radiosaluiz.com ☎55 3352 4444 – **RS58**) Rua XV de Novembro 236, 96570-000 Caçapava do Sul ☎55 3281 1495 **W:** www.redemeridional.com/cacapava.html **E:** radiocacapava@redemeridional.com – **RS59**) Rua Tucunduva 758, 98640-000 Crissiumal **W:** www.metropole1070.com.br **E:** contato@radiometropolo.com.br ☎55 3524 1212 📠55 3524 1223 – **RS60**) Rua Marechal Deodoro 101,Galeria Central, 7° andar, 95700-000 Bento Gonçalves **E:** re.bg@gruporscom.com.br ☎54 3455 3999 - **FM:** 92.5MHz «Serrana» – **RS61**) Rua João Carlos Machado 645, 98460-000 Iraí **W:** www.radiomaraba.com.br **E:** maraba@speedrs.com.br ☎55 3745 1444 – **RS62**) Rua Sarmento Leite 426, Bairro Farrouphia, 90050-170 Porto Alegre **W:** www.ufrgs.br/radio **E:** radio@ufrgs.br ☎51 3316 3435 📠51 3316 3192 24h - **Spanish:** Fri 2400 – **RS63**) Rua Ramiro Barcelos 2092, 96508-070 Cachoeira do Sul **W:** www.radiocachoeira.com.br **E:** radiocachoeira@radiocachoeira.com.br ☎51 3722 4022 - **German & Italian:** 3h weekly – **RS64**) Praça Padre Basso 95, 99800-000 Marcelino Ramos ☎54 3372 1389 **W:** www.radiosalette.com.br **E:** radiosalette@terra.com.br – **RS65**) Av Bento Gonçalves 733, 98870-000 Giruá ☎55 3361 2020 📠55 3361 3320 **W:** www.radiogirua.com **E:** radiogirua@terra.com.br – **RS66**) Rua Osvaldino Barbosa Silveira, prolongamento da Júlio de Castilhos 2470, 96300-000 Jaguarão ☎55 3261 2933 **W:** www.redemeridional.com/jaguarao.html **E:** culturajaguarao@redemeridional.com – **FM:** 92.9 MHz – **RS67**) Rua Padre Oswaldo Stracke 56, 96900-000 Sobradinho ☎51 3742 1089 📠51 3742 1833 **W:** www.radiosobradinho.com.br **E:** recepcao@radiosobradinho.com.br - **FM:** 97.3MHz "R.Jacuí" – **RS68**) Rua Borges do Canto 1056, 97650-000 Itaqui ☎55 3433 8409 **W:** www.radiocruzeirodosul.com.br **E:** radiocruzeiro@terra.com.br – **RS69**) Rua Corrêa Lima, 1960 – Morro Santa Tereza, 90850-250 Porto Alegre **W:** www.rdfarroupilha.com.br **E:** farroupilha@rdfarroupilha.com.br ☎51 3218 5781 📠51 3218 5789 – **RS70**) Av Rio Branco 809, 97010-423 Santa Maria ☎55 3221 2695 📠55 3222 9500 **W:** www.radiomedianeiraam.com.br **E:** ouvinte@radiomedianeira.com.br **FM:** 100.9 – **RS71**) Rua Pinheiro Machado 628 2° andar, 98005-000 Cruz Alta **W:** www.radiocruzalta.com **E:** gravadora-rca@comnet.com.br ☎55 3322 7222 📠55 3322 7292 - **FM:** 105.1MHz – **RS72**) Rua Domingos de Almeida 2194, 97500-004 Uruguaiana ☎55 3412 1731 📠55 3412 3046 **W:** www.radiocharrru.com.br **E:** amfm@radiocharru.com.br **FM:** 97.7MHz – **RS73**) Travess Victor Hugo Demaman Tomé, 02 – Centro, 96750-000 Butiá, **W:** www.radiojornalsobral.com.br **E:** radiosob@terra.com.br ☎51 3652 1140 – **RS74**) Rua Rui Barbosa 96, 95180-000 Farroupilha **W:** www.radiomiriam.com.br **E:** radiomiriam@radiomiriam.com.br ☎54 3261 2121 – **RS75**) Rua Tenente Lira 950 (C.P. 74), 98400-000 Frederico Westphalen **W:** www.luzealegriaam.com.br **E:** radioluzealegriaam@hotmail.com ☎55 3744 3500 - **Italian & Polish:** Sun 0930 & 1600 - FM: 95.9MHz – **RS76**) Rua General Osório, 1160 -

Centro, 97760-000 Jaguari **W:** www.radiojaguari.com.br **E:** radio-jaguari@brturbo.com.br ☎55 3255 1474 – **RS77)** Rua Félix da Cunha 328, 3° andar, 96010-000 Pelotas **W:** www.radiouniversidadeam.com.br **E:** opecalfa@via-rs.net ☎53 3222 1160 – **RS78)** Av Coronel Victor Villa Verde 491, Bairro Pitangueiras, 95500-000 Santo Antônio da Patrulha ☎513662 1255 **W:** www.radioitapui.com.br **E:** itapui@radioitapui.com.br – **RS79)** Av 7 de Setembro 1115, 96400-001 Bagé.- **W:** www.difusorabage.com.br **E:** difusora@difusorabage.com.br ☎53 3242 5211- **FM:** 99.7 FM Delta – **RS80)** Rua 7 de Setembro, 366 – Centro,(C.P 326) 99010-121 Passo Fundo ☎54 2104 1600 ☎54 2104 1612 **W:** www.radiouirapuru.com.br **E:** uirapuru@rduirapuru.com.br – **RS81)** Av Maurício Cardoso 697, 99300-000 Soledade ☎54 3381 1144 ☎54 3381 1781 **W:** www.redesul.am.br/index.php?emissora=24**E:** gerente@cristal.am.br - **FM:** 99.1MHz – **RS82)** Rua da Anunciação, 480 - Morro do Convento, 97900-000 Cerro Largo – ☎55 3359 2022 **W:** www.radiocerroazul.com.br **E:** radiocerroazul@via-rs.net - **FM:** 105.9MHz «Shamballa» – **RS83)** Rua Mons. Scalabrini, s/n - Centro, 99250-000 Serafina Corrêa ☎54 3361 1455 **W:** www.rsradios.com.br **E:** sarandi.comercial@rsradio.com.br– **RS84)** Rua Paulino de Medeiros 14, José Bonifácio,, 99700-000 Erechim ☎54 3522 1289 **W:** www.redetche.com.br/erechim**E:** administracao@radioerechim.com.br – **RS85)** BR 392 - Km 232(✉ C.P. 130), 97340-000 São Sepé **W:** www.radiocotrisel.com.br **E:** radiocotrisel@radiocotirsel.com.br ☎55 3233 1113 ☎55 3233 1163 – **RS86)** Travessa Francisco de Leonardo Truda 40, 90010-050 Porto Alegre ☎51 3221 8711 ☎51 3221 2752 **E:** radiorec@zaz.com.br – **RS87)** Rua General Canabarro 1450, Bairro Fracisca Tarragaô, 97500-003 Uruguaiana ☎55 3412 1217 ☎55 3412 3046 **W:** www.radiosaomiguel.com.br **E:** contato@radiosaomiguel.com.br – **RS88)** Rua Coronel Vitor Dumoncel 1756, Centro, 98240-000 Santa Bárbara do Sul **W:** www.radioblaununes.com.br **E:** radioblaununes@radioblaununes.com.br ☎55 3372 1435 ☎55 3372 1136 – **RS89)** Rua Rui Barbosa 373, Centro, 99600-000 Nonoai **W:** www.cluberadio.com.br **E:** radionnoai@slavenet.com.br ☎54 3362 1384 – **FM:** 89.7 MHz – **RS90)** Av Adolfo Schneider No 85 - 2° andar, Ed Elías, Centro, 95320-000 Nova Prata **W:** www.radioprata.com.br **E:** radioprata@radioprata.com.br ☎54 3242 1648 – **RS91)** Praça Silvestre Corréa 77, Centro, 96610-000 Encruzilhada do Sul ☎51 3733 1157**W:** www.radioencruzilhadense.com.br **E:** faleconosco@radioencruzilhadense.com.br – **RS92)** Rua Júlio de Castilhos 605 2° andar, 95290-000 Bom Jesus **E:** radioaparados@m2net.com.br ☎54 3237 1247 54 3237 1755 – **RS93)** Rua General Osório, 1134 – Centro (C.P. 11), 98200-000 Ibirubá **W:** www.sistemaepu.com.br **E:** ibiruba@sistemaepu.com.br ☎54 3324 1758 ☎54 3324 1083 – **FM:** 96.6MHz – **RS94)** Rua Ponciano Ramos 74, 96700-000 São Jerônimo **E:** radio.saojeronimo@terra.com.br ☎51 3651 4228 – **RS95)** Av Júlio de Castilhos 1511-8° andar, salas 81/84, Centro, 95010-003 Caxias do Sul **W:** www.radiodifusoracaxiense.com.br **E:** radio@ radiodifusoracaxiense.com.br – **RS96)** Rua 15 de Novembro 717, 96015-000 Pelotas **W:** www.radiotupanci.com.br **E:** tupanci@terra.com.br ☎53 3225 0930 ☎53 3222 6167 – **RS97)** Rua Riachuelo, 928 - Centro, 97670-000 São Borja ☎55 3431 2244 ☎55 3431 1993 **W:** www.radioculturaam1260.com.br **E:** radio@gpsnet.com.br – **FM:**97.1MHz "Radio Fronteira" – **RS98)** Rua Moron, 1520 - Centro, 96500-000 Cachoeira do Sul ☎51 3722 3033 ☎51 3722 3622 **W:** www.radiofandango.com.br **E:** radiofandango.com.br - **FM:** 102.5MHz – **RS99)** Rua José Sponchiado 418, 99830-000 Gaurama **E:** radiogaurama@awo.com.br ☎54 3391 1134 - **Italian & Polish:** 1300-1400 – **RS100)** Rua Benjaim Santo Zago 601, 97220-000 Faxinal do Soturno ☎55 3263 1021 ☎55 3263 1335 **W:** www.radiosaoroque.com.br **E:** falecom@radiosaoroque.com.br – **RS101)** Rua Balduino Schneider, 254-Horizontina, Horizontina **W:** www.radioveracruz.com.br **E:** radio@radioveracruz.com.br ☎55 3537 1212 ☎55 3537 1414 – **RS102)** Rua Dr Pio Ferreira, 453, Centro, 96170-000 São Lourenço do Sul ☎53 3251 1303 **W:** www.radiosaolourenco com br **E:** radio.sls@vetorial.net – **German:** Sun 1100 – **RS103)** Av Angelo Macalós 246, 99400-000 Espumoso **W:** www.radioplanetario.com.br **E:** falecom@radioplanetario.com.br ☎54-3383 1082 - **German:** Sun 1600 - **FM:** 95.3MHz – **RS104)** Av São Paulo 72, 3° andar, Bairro São Geral, 90230-160 Porto Alegre **W:** www.boavontade.com **E:** veraquednau@hotmail.com ☎51 3325 7000 – **RS105)** Rua 25 de Julho 39, Centro, 98960-000 Santo Cristo ☎55 3541 1188 **W:** www.radioregional1300.com.br – **RS106)** Rua dos Andrades, 663 - Centro, 97573-000 Santana do Livramento **W:** radiomaratan.webnode.com **E:** estudiomaratan@hotmail.com ☎55 3241 1300 – **RS107)** Av Duque de Caxias 1320, 99560-000 Sarandi ☎54 3361 1455 **W:** www.rsradios.com **E:** sarandi.radio@viaradiointernet.com.br – **RS108)** Av Júlio de Castilhos 232, 95680-000 Canela ☎54 3282 8822 ☎54 3282 2000 **W:** www.radioclubedecanela.com.br **E:** radioclube@pdh.net.br **FM:** 88.5MHz – **RS109)** Rua General Osório 1276, 98280-000 Panambi ☎55 3375 3600 **W:** www.radiosulbrasileira.com.br **E:**comercial@radiosulbrasileira.com.br – **RS110)** Rua Sete de Setembro 353, 96015-300 Pelotas **E:** radiopel.sul@terra.com.br ☎53 3229 3174 ☎53 3227 2382

– **RS111)** Av Rio Branco 401, 96450-000 Dom Pedrito ☎53 3243 1225 ☎53 3243 1257 **W:** www.radioupacarai.com.br **E:** upacarai@radioupacarai.com.br – **RS112)** Rua Pe Feijo 833 s42, Centro, 95190-000 São Marcos **W:** www.radiodiplomata.am.br **Emai:** diplomata@radiodiplomata.am.br ☎54 3291 2422 – **FM:** 99.7 – **RS113)** Av. Ipiranga 1075, Praia de Bela, 90160-093 Porto Alegre ☎51 3218 6751 **W:** www.rbs.com.br **E:** cbn@rbsradios.com.br – **RS114)** Av Scalabrini 777, 99200-000 Guaporé **W:** www.rsradios.com.br **E:** radioaurora@tl.com.br ☎54 3443 4488 **Italian:** Mon 1300-1500 – **RS115)** Av Santos Dumont 240, Centro, 98600-000 Três Passos ☎55 3522 1011 **W:** www.difusoraceleiro.com.br **E:** radiodifusoratrespassos@yahoo.com – **RS116)** Av Concordia, 1480 - Centro, 96540-000 Agudo ☎55 3265 2045 **W:** www.radioagudo.com.br **E:** radioagudo@terra.com.br – **RS117)** Rua Lauro R.Bortolon 402, 99150-000 Marau **W:** www.alvorada.am.br **E:** gerencia@alvorada.am.br ☎54 3342 3300 - **FM:** 94.7MHz «Kosmos» – **RS118)** Rua John Kennedy, 2220 sala 18 CxP 199, 95270-000 Flores da Cunha ☎54 3028 8881 **W:** http://comunidadeoasis.org.br **E:** oasis@comunidadeoasis.org.br – **RS119)** Rua Gaspar Martins 55-3° andar, 97542-000 Alegrete ☎55 3422 1590 **W:** www.gazeta.vipradios.com **E:** rgta@ig.com.br – **RS120)** Rua Conde de Porto Alegre 521, 97573-581 Sant´Ana do Livramento **W:** www.culturalivramento.com.br **E:** cultura-livramento@brturbo.com.br ☎55 3242 3066 – **RS121)** Rua General Osório, 1134 – Centro, (C.P 11) 99200-000 Tapera ☎54 3385 1166 ☎54 3385 1855 **W:** www.sistemaepu.com.br **E:** cultura@sistemaepu.com.br – **FM:** 96.7MHz – **RS122)** Rua Chaves Barcellos 36, conj 1205, Centro, 90030-120 Porto Alegre ☎51 3226 1390 **W:** www.radioesperanca.com.br **E:** radioesperanca.com.br – **RS123)** Rua Pedro Toniollo, 529 - Centro, 99900-000 Getúlio Vargas **W:** www.radiosideral.com.br **E:** sideral@radiosideral.com.br ☎54 3341 1555 ☎54 3341 1554 – **RS124)** Rua Augusto Rossi 316, Centro, 97200-000 Restinga Sêca **W:** www.radiojornalintegracao.com.br **E:** radio@integracao-rs.com.br ☎55 3261 1270 ☎55 3261 1030 – **RS125)** Rua Marechal Floriano 373, 96211-380 Rio Grande ☎53 3035 3141 **W:** www.radiominuano.com.br **E:** minuano@radiominuano.com – **RS126)** Rua São Francisco 246, Cruzeiro, 98900-000 Santa Rosa ☎55 3512 5265 **W:** www.radiosantarosa.com.br **E:** estudiob107@viabrazil.com.br ☎55 3512 5265 – **RS127)** Rua 24 de Maio 671, 95330-000 Veranópolis ☎53 3441 3200 **W:** www.veranense.am.br **E:** gerencia@radioveranense.am.br – **RS128)** Rua Ramiro Barcelos 1206 - Centro, 96810-050 Santa Cruz do Sul **E:** gazetaam@gazetaan.com.br ☎51 3715 7814.- **FM:** 101.7MHz – **RS129)** Rua Teófilo Conrado de Matos 135, Centro, 96600-000 Canguçu **W:** www.radiocultura1030.com.br **E:** cultura@supersul.com.br ☎53 3252 1144 – **RS130)** Av das Hortencias 78, 95670-000 Gramado ☎54 3286 5516 ☎54 3286 1902 **W:** www.radioexcelsior.com.br **E:** excelsioram@serragaucha.com.br – **RS131)** Rua São João, 1637 - Centro, 95780-000 Montenegro ☎51 3632 1867 **W:** www.radioamerica-am.com.br **E:** radio@radioamerica-am.com.br – **RS132)** Rua Benjamin Constant 377, 96200-090 Rio Grande ☎53 3231 3048 **W:** www.radiocassino.com.br **E:** cassinoam@vetorial.net – **RS133)** Av Sete de Setembro 672, Centro, 96400-003 Bagé ☎53 3242 1471 ☎53 3242 1211 **W:** www.radioculturabage.com.br **E:** radioculturabage@hotmail.com – **RS134)** Rua Borges de Medeiros 401, 95560-000 Torres ☎51 3664 4188 **W:** www.radiomaristela.com.br **E:** administracao@radiomaristela.com.br – **RS135)** Rua Dr Bruno Dockhorn 18, 98910-000 Três de Maio **W:** www.radiocolonial.com.br **E:** colonialam@gmail.com ☎55 3535 1022 – **RS136)** Rua Santos Inacio de Loiola 253, sl 203, 93700-000 Campo Bom ☎51 3585 1470 **W:** www.radiocinderela.com.br **E:** radiocinderela@gmail.com – **RS137)** Rua Julio de Castilhos 325, 95720-000 Garibaldi **W:** www.garibaldi.am.br **E:** gerencia@garibaldi.am.br ☎54 3462 1557 - **Italian:** Sat 1800-1900, Sun 1000-1200 - **FM:** 88.1MHz – **RS138)** Rua Gabriel Machado 1590, 3° andar, 97610-000 São Francisco de Assis **E:** radiodifusão@terra.com.br ☎55 3252 1455 ☎55 3252 1166 – **RS139)** Rua General Osorio 943, 96600-000 Canguçu ☎53 3252 1515 **W:** radioliberdadeam.com.br **E:** atendimento@radioliberdadeam.com.br – **RS140)** Rua Rio Branco, 1006 - Centro, 95600-000 Taquara **W:** www.jornalpanorama.com.br **E:** radiotaquara@faccat.br ☎51 3542 2288 ☎51 3542 2222 – **RS141)** Rua São Vicente 345, 96501-180 Cachoeira do Sul ☎51 3723 7534 **W:** www.radiovaledojacui.com.br **E:** rvj@radiovaledopjacui.com.br – **RS142)** Av Rio Branco, 616 - Centro, 98770-000 Catuípe **W:** www.radioaguasclaras.com.br **E:** contato@radioaguasclaras.com.br ☎55 3336 1328 – **RS143)** Rua José Bonáfacio 1128, (✉ C.P. 144) 96450-000 Dom Pedrito ☎53 3243 3110 ☎53 3243 1434 **W:** www.radiosulina.com.br **E: radio**sulina@hotmail.com – **RS144)** Rua Marqués do Herval 840 - Centro, 93010-200 São Leopoldo ☎51 3568 8680 ☎51 3554 2894 **W:** www.redetche.com.br/progresso **E:** admin_progreso@redetche.com.br – **RS145)** Rua Cel Amâncio Cardoso 596, 99950-000 Tapejara ☎54 3344 1185 **W:** www.radiotapejara.com.br **E:** contato@radiotapejara.com.br – **RS146)** Trav Jaime Pinto 136, 97700-000 Santiago **W:** www.radiosantiago.com.br **E:** zyk297@radiosantiago.com.br ☎55 3251 2211 – **RS147)** Av Flores da Cunha, 4283 - Centro, 949150-004 Cachoeirinha

☎51 3421 1922 **W:** www.radiometropoleam.com **E:** radiometropole-am@terra.com.br – **RS148)** Rua 7 de Setembro 792, 95960-000 Encantado ☎51 3751 1903 **W:** www.rdencantado.com.b **E:** ouvinte@encantoam.com.br – **FM:** 97.7 MHz – **RS149)**Av Assis Brasil 263, 98130-000 Júlio de Castilhos **W:** www.radio14dejulho.com.br **E:** comercial@radio14dejulho.com.br ☎55 3271 1414 – **RS150)** Rua José Bonifácio 41, 96330-000 Arroio Grande **W:** www.difusora1580.com.br **E:** radiodifusoraam@terra.com.br ☎53 3262 1008 – **RS151)** Rua Paraguai 42, 98980-000 Porto Lucena **W:** www.radionavigantes.com.br **E:** radionavegantes@san.psi.br ☎55 3565 1200 ▤55 3565 1221 – **RS152)** Av Valdomiro Bocchese 872, apt 01, 95250-000 Antônio Prado **W:** www.radiosolaris.com.br **E:** radiosolaris@nol.com.br ☎54 3293 1110 ▤54 3293 1733 – **RS153)** Rua Caáro 1733, 97930-000 Caibaté **W:** www.radiocaibate.com.br **E:** radiocaibate@radiocaibate.com.br ☎55 3355 1335 – **RS154)** Rua Rui Barbosa 46, 1° andar, 96360-000 Pedro Osório. **W:** www.radioclube990.com.br – **RS155)** Av Borges de Medeiros, 1462 - Chacara, 97650-000 Itaqui **W:** www.radiopitangueira.com.br **E:** radio@pintagueira.com.br ☎56 3433 2301 ▤55 3433 2157 – **RS156)** Rua. Padre Roque Gonzáles, 08, Centro (✉C.P. 241 98590-970), 98590-000 Santo Augusto ☎55 3781 1255 **W:** www.radioquerenciaonline.com **E:** radio@querenciaonline.com – **RS157)** Rua Baltazar Brum 343, 97560-000 Quaraí **E:** quarai@terra.com.br ☎55 3423 3001 – **RS158)** Rua Osvaldo Aranha 179 (C.P 80), 95860-000 Taquari **E:** radioacoriana@taquari.com.br ☎55 3621 1900 – **RS159)** Av Maurício Cardoso, 888 - Centro 99300-000 Soledade ☎54 3381 1550 **W:** www.radiosoledade-am.com.br – **RS160)** Rua Dom Luiz Guanella N° 2313, 95555-000 Capão da Canoa ☎54 3625 2300 **W:** www.radiohorizonte.com.br **E:** radiohorizonte@radiohorizonte.com.br – **RS161)** Rua da República 220, Centro, 99530-000 Chapada ☎54 3333 1338 **W:** www.radiosimpatia.com.br **E:** simpatia@radiosimpatia.com.br – **RS162)** Av. Narciso Silva 1791, Centro, 96160-000 Capão do Leão ☎53 3227 4252 **W:** www.opiniao-gospel.com.br – **RS164)** Rua Floriano Peixoto 222, 97400-000 São Pedro do Sul ☎55 3276 1311 ▤55 3276 4335 **W:** www.saopedrodosul.org/radio-municipal **E:** saopedro900@hotmail.com – **RS165)** Rua Duque de Caxias 255, Centro Palmitinho – Apto. 302, Centro, 98430-000 Palmitinho ☎55 3791 1175 **W:** www.radiochiru.com.br **E:** radiochiru@radiochiru.com.br – **RS166)** Rua João Maffesoni, 10 - centro, 99680-000 Constantina ☎54 3363 1330 **W:** www.radioatlantica.net.br **E:** radio.atlantica@hotmail.com – **RS167)** Rua Francisco Gobbi 545, 98580-000 Coronel Bicaco. ☎55 3557 1195 ▤55 3557 1220 **W:** www.radioguarita.com.br **E:** radioguarita@yahoo.com.br – **RS168)** Av Alto Jacuí 435, Terreo, 99470-000 Não Me Toque **E:** radioceres@dgnet.com.br ☎54 3332 1488 ▤54 3332 1498 – **RS169)** Rua Brasil 806, 97450-000 Cacequi ☎55 3254 1366 ▤55 3254 1157 **E:** radioculturacacequi@yahoo.com.br – **RS170)** Rua Sanaduva 178, 99855-000 São João da Urtiga ☎54 3532 1247 – **RS171)** Rua Luiz Vieira 525, 96760-000 Tapes ☎51 3672 1031 ▤51 3672 1031 **E:** rt@conectsul.com.br – **RS172)** Av Antônio Finco 700 (C.P 19), 99870-000 São José do Ouro ☎54 3352 1008 ▤54 3352 1108 – **RS173)** Rua Albino Brendler, 122 – Centro, 98700-000 Ijuí ☎55 3331 0300 ▤55 3331 0303 **W:** www.jmijui.com.br **E:** radiojmijui@gmail.com – **RS174)** Rua Consórcio, s/n, Conj 09, 96400-970 Bagé ☎53 3242 4668 **W:** www.radioclubebage.com.br **E:** akucera@globo.com – **RS175)** Rua Pedro Alvares Cabral 164, 99660-000 Campinas do Sul **W:** www.radiocampinasdosul.com.br **E:** radiocampinas@tolrs.com.br ☎51 3366 1266 ▤54 3613 3366 – **RS176)** Rua Almirante Tamandaré 1136 cj 6,, 96270-000 Mostardas ☎51 3673 2062 **W:** www.radiomostardas.com.br **E:** daltro@radiomostardas.brtdta.com.br – **RS177)** Av Barão do Triunfo, 584 2 andar, Centro, 95995-000 Arvorezinha ☎51 3772 2443 ▤51 3772 2129 **W:** www.radiocultura.inf.br **E:** cultura@radiocultura.inf.br – **FM:** 92.3MHz – **RS178)** Av. Castelo Branco 1053, - Centro, 97950-000 Guarani das Missões **W:** www.grupoguaramano.com.br **E:** faleconosco@comunidaddeoasis.org.br or radioguaramano@brturbo.com.br ☎55 3353 1721 ▤55 3353 1722 - **FM:** 91.1 Capital FM – **RS179)** Rua Jornal NH, 99-Bairro Ideal, 93334-350 Novo Hamburgo ☎51 3593 9000 **W:** www.radioabc900.com.br **E:** radioabc@gruposinos.com.br – **RS180)** Rua 15 de Novembro 236, 96570-000 Caapava do Sul ☎55 3281 1495 **E:** radiocapava@farrapo.com.br – **RS191)** Rua Rádio e TV Gaúcha, 189 - Morro Santa Tereza, 90850-250 Porto Alegre ☎51 3218 5260 ▤51 3218 5285 **W:** www.clickrbs.com.br **E:** radiorural.am1120@rdrural.com.br – **RS192)** Rua Sananduva, 178-Centro, 99855-000 São João da Urtiga ☎54 3532 1015 **W:** www.radioeducadorartiga.com.br **E:** rdeducadora@brturbo.com.br – **RS193)** 95880-000 Estrele – **RS195)** 93180-000 Portao – **RS198)** Av. Brasil, 385 – sala 202 – Centro, 93180-000 Portão ☎55 3562 5300 **W:** www.radioam1430.com.br **RS199)** Av. Paraguassu 180/05, 95625-000 Imbé ☎51 3627 1988 **W:** www.radiolitoraljp.com.br **E:** contato@radiolitoraljp.com.br

SC00) SANTA CATARINA

SC01) Almeda Aristiliano Ramos 36 1°/2° andar (C.P 61), 89160-000 Rio do Sul **W:** www.radiomiradorr.com.br **E:** am540@radiomirador.com.br ☎47 3531 2100 ▤47 3531 2102 - **FM:** 93.3MHz – **SC02)** Av Centenario

6050, Próspera, (C.P D2, 88801-970) 88815-000 Criciúma ☎48 3439 5111 **W:** www.radioeldorado.net – **SC03)** Av Martin Piaseski 25, Centro, 89910-000 Descanso. ☎49 3623 0307 **W:** www.progresso.am.br – **SC04)** Rua Benjamin Constant 286-D, 3 e 4 andares, Centro, 89801-970 Chapecó ☎49 3332 5177 **W:** www.superconda.com.br **E:** jornalismoconda@zipway.com.br – **SC05)** Rua Carlos Gomes 12, Centro, 89160-000 Rio do Sul **W:** www.amanda.fm.brE:** difusora@superdifusora.am.br ☎47 3521 1155 - **FM:** 94.9 «Amanda FM» – **SC06)** Rua João Beux Sobredinho, 350 Centro, 89990-000 São Lourenço d'Oeste **W:** www.radiodoze.com.br **E:** radiodoze@brturbo.com.br ☎49 3344 1544 ▤49 3344 1748 – **SC07)** Rua Carlos Jofre do Amaral 67, 88501-010 Lages **E:** jota@iscc.com.br – **SC08)** Av Sete de Setembro 109, Centro, 89580-000 Fraiburgo ☎49 3256 1010 **W:** www.radiofraiburgo.com.br **E:** estudio@radiofraiburgo.am.br – **SC09)** Rua Senador Gustavo Richard, 90 - Centro, 88701-220 Tubarão ☎48 3626 5177 **W:** www.radiotuba.com.br **E:** radiotuba@radiotuba.com – **SC10)** Rua General Vieira da Rosa, 1570 – Morro da Cruz, 88020-420 Florianópolis **W:** www.rbs.com.br **E:** cbndiario@rbsradios.com.br ☎48 3216 2500 ▤48 3216 2675 – **SC11)** Rua Leonel Mosele 275, 89700-000 Concórdia ☎49 3442 1366 **W:** www.radioalianca.com.br - **Italian & German:** Sun 1130, 1600 – **SC12)** Rua Buenos Aires 145, Edifico Senador Evelásio Vieira 145, Ponta Agude, 89051-050 Blumenau ☎47 3222 9000 **W:** www.radionereuramos.com.br **E:** neruam@terra.com.br – **SC13)** Rua da Criança, 171, Centro, 88840-000 Urussanga **W:** www.radiomarconi.net **E:** radiomarconi@radiomarconi.net ☎48 3465 1055 – **SC14)** Rua Venereanos dos Passos, 385 - Centro, 89560-000 Videira **W:** www.radiovideira.com.br – **SC15)** Rua Angelo Dias 207, 6° andar, Centro, 89010-020 Blumenau **W:** www.cbnblumenau.com.br **E:** cbn@rfc.com.br ☎47 3041 8020 – **SC16)** Rua Itagiba, 215 - Centro, 88880-000 Lauro Müller **W:** www.radiocruzdemalta.com.br **E:** radiocruzdemalta@netlm.com.br ☎48 3464 3762 - **Italian:** Sat 1600 – **SC17)** Rua João Suzin Marini, 64 - Centro (C.P 71, 89700-970) 89700-000 Concórdia ☎48 3437 4602 **W:** www.radiorural.com.br/2005/ - **FM:** 96.3MHz – **SC18)** Av do Adão 1784, Morro da Cruz, 88025-150 Florianópolis **W:** www.bandeirantes890.com.br **E:** lucio.jornalismo@radiosantacatarina.com.br - **FM:** 101.7MHz «Transamérica» – **SC19)** Rua Rodovia SC 444 - km3, 88820-000 Içara ☎48 3461 0700 **W:** www.difusora910.com.br **E:** difusoranoticia@hotmail.com – **SC20)** Rua Conselheiro Rui Barbosa, 50 1° andar - Centro, 88350-000 Brusque **W:** www.radiocidadeam.com.br **E:** diretoria@radiocidadeam.com.br ☎47 3351 4611 – **SC21)** Rua Jardim Portobello, 50 - Centro, 88200-000 Tijucas ☎48 3263 0303 **W:** www.radiovaletj.com.br **E:** contato@radiovaletj.com.br – **SC22)** Rua Aristiliano Ramos, 134 Ed.Regina Sala 202 - Centro, 88870-000 Orleâns ☎48 3466 0533 **W:** www.guarujaam.com.br **E:** contato@guarujaam.com.br – **SC23)** Av.Brasil 260 Centro Comercial Tiradentes-3° andar, 89820-000 Xanxerê 49 3433 0171 **W:** www.superdifusora.com.br **E:** difusora@superdifusora.com.br – **SC24)** Rua Mathilde Hoffman 66, sala 21 e 22 (C.P 96, 88350-970), 88353-120 Brusque ☎47 3351 1744 **W:** www.araguaia970am.com.br **E:** radio@verdevaleam.com.br - **FM:** 107.7MHz – **SC25)** Rua São Bonifacio 280 89896-000 Itapiranga ☎49 3622 1877 **W:** www.peperi.com.br – **SC26)** Rua Severiano Francisco Sombrio 684, Centro (✉C.P 67), 88750-000 Braço do Norte ☎48 3658 2178 **W:** www.verdevale.com.br **E:** radio@verde-vale.com.br 0720-0300 – **SC27)** Rua Pernambuco 329, 89840-000 Coronel Freitas – **SC28)** Rua Otacilio Vieira da Costa 40, Centro, 88501-050 Lages ☎49 3222 3011 **W:** www.rfc.com.br/princesa **E:** radioprincesa@rfc.com.br – **FM:** 95.7MHz «Amizade» – **SC29)** Rua Manoel Simão, 177-Salas 24 e 25 - Bairro das Nações, 89130-000 Indaial ☎47 3333 0499 **W:** www.radioclubeindaial.com.br **E:** falecom@radioclubeindaial.com.br – **SC30)** Rua Rolf Colin 80 (C.P 25, 89201-970), 89204-070 Joinville – **SC31)** Rua Vidal Ramos 519, 88701-160 Tubarão ☎48 3626 5688 - **FM:** 98.9MHz «Band FM» – **SC32)** Rua Boucauíva 88, Centro, 88015-530 Florianopolis, (C.P 1477, 88010-900), 88015-530 Florianópolis ☎48 3201 1110 ▤48 3228 4950 **W:** www.divinooleiro.com.br **E** radio@radiocultura1110am.com.br – **SC33)** Av Santa Catarina 828, Edifico Dona Olivia - 2° andar, Centro, 89885-000 São Carlos **W:** www.radiosaocarlos.com.br **E:** am1110@sancasnet.com.br ☎49 3325 4355 ▤49 3325 4483 – **SC34)** Travessa João Winkler 15, 89820-000 Xanxerê ☎49 3433 1110 ▤49 3433 0682 **W:** www.redeprincesa.com.br **E:** studio@redeprincesa.com.br - **FM:** 101.3MHz – **SC35)** Rua Cel. Vidal Ramos, 861 - Centro, 89520-000 Curitibanos **E:** coroado@coroado.am.br **W:** www.coroado.am.br ☎49 3241 0923 ▤49 3241 0928 - **FM:** 98.9MHz – **SC36)** Rua 15 de Novembro 600, sala 401, Edifico Visconde de Maúá, 89010-000 Blumenau ☎47 3322 9773 **W:** www.radioitabera.com **E:** contato@radioitabera.com.br – **SC37)** Rua Conselheiro Jeronimo Coelho 48, Centro, 88790-000 Laguna ☎48 3644 0025 **W:** www.difusoralaguna.com.br **E:** radio_difusora@yahoo.com – **SC38)** Rua Siqueira Campos 33, 89400-000 Porto União ☎42 3522 2245 **W:** www.colmeia.com.br **E:** colmeia@colmeia.com.br – **SC39)** Rua Padre Aurélio 240, 89930-000 São José do Cedro ☎49 3643 0211 **W:** www.radiointegracaoam1180.com.br **E:** comercial@radiointegracaoam1180.

com.br – **SC40**) Rua Otavianpo Dadan, 355-Centro, 88240-000 São João Batista ☎48 3265 0222 **W:** www.radioclubeam.com **Email** contato@radioclubeam.com.br – **SC41**) Rua São Cristóvão 393 (C.P 59, 89835-970), 89835-000 São Domingos ☎49 3443 0139 **W:** www.clubesd.com.br **E:** contato@clubesd.com.br – **SC42**) Av Patricio Lima, 3073 - Bairro São Bernardo, 88708-201 Tubarão ☎48 3628 0658 ▤48 3628 1356 **W:** www.radiosc.com.br **E:** radiosc@radiosc.com.br – **SC43**) Rua Tenente Ary Rauen, 1361 - Alto, 89300-000 Mafra ☎47 3642 3955 **W:** www.saojoseam.com.br **Email.** radionovaera@netuno.com.br - **FM:** 104.5MHz «Nova Era» – **SC44**) Porã – **SC45**) Rua Nove de Março 737, 8° andar, Ed.Turim 8° andar, 89201-400 Joinville ☎47 3026 0405 **W:** www.amcultura.com.br **E:** jornalismo@jovempanjoinville.com.br – **FM:** 91.1 MHz – **SC46**) Rua Dr. Amadeu da Luz 31, sala 03, 89010-160 Bluemau ☎47 3340 1260 **W:** http://arcadaalianca.com.br/radio-blumenau **E:** fale@radioblumenau.com.br – **SC47**) Av XV de Novembro, 608-Centro, 89600-000 Joaçaba **W:** www.radiiocatarinense.com.br radiocatarinense@radiocatarinense.com.br ☎49 3551 2424 ▤49 3551 2426 – **Italian:** Sun 1215-1500 - **FM:** 92.3MHz – **SC48**) Rua Osvaldo Cabral 68 - 1° andar, Centro, 88790-000 Laguna ☎48 3646 0337. **W:** www.garibaldilaguna.com.br **E:** raduiogaribaldi@brturbo.com.br – **SC49**) Av Alvin Bauer 585, Centro, 88330-000 Balneário Camboriú ☎47 3367 1044 ▤47 3367 4949 **W:** www.radiocamboriu.com.br **E:** radiocamboriu@radiocamboriu.com.br – **SC50**) Rua Buenos Aires 145, Edifico Senador Evelásio Vieira, Ponta Aguda, 89051-050 Blumenau ☎47 3222 9070 **W:** www.radioclubeblumenau.com.br – **SC51**) Rua Marechal Floriano Peixoto, 161-0 - Centro, 89800-000 Chapecó **W:** www.radiochapeco.com.br **E:** comercial@radiochapeco.com.br ☎49 3322 0688 ▤49 3322 0429 - **FM:** 107.1MHz – **SC52**) Rua Vereador Guilherme Prust, 311 - Campo d'Água Verde, 89460-000 Canoinhas ☎47 3622 7000 **W:** www.radioclubedecanoinhas.com.br – **SC53**) Av Gov Adolfo Konder 1500, Bairro São Vicente, 88308-000 Itajaí ☎47 3248 1350 **W:** www.radioclubebandeirantes.com.br **E:** jornalismo@ radioclubebandeirantes.com.br – **SC54**) Rua Olivio D Brugnago, 181 - Vila Nova, (C.P 405, 89251-970) 89259-260 Jaraguá do Sul ☎ 47 3371 0444 **W:** www.radiobrasilnovo.com.br **E:** rbn@radiobrasilnovo.com.br – **SC55**) Rua Duque de Caxias 1302, 2° andar, 89900-000 São Miguel d'Oeste **W:** www.peperi.com.br **E:** rede@peperi.com.br ☎☎49 3622 1877 - **FM:** 104.9MHz – **SC56**) Rua José Gonçalves, 333 - Lucena, 89340-000 Itaiópolis ☎47 3652 2279 **W:** www.cidade1380.am.br – **SC57**) Rua Carlos Jofre do Amaral 34, Centro, 88501-130 Lages ☎49 3221 3110 **W:** www.cbnlages.com.br – **SC58**) Rua Visconde do Rio Branco, 1028 - Centro, 89887-000 Palmitos ☎49 3647 0292 **W:** www. radioentrerios.com.br **E:** entrerios@promitos.com.br – **SC59**) Rua Nunes Machado 94, 10° andar, 88010-460 Florianópolis ☎48 3222 5555 **W:** www.radioguaruja.com.br – **SC60**) Rua Marechal Deodoro, 298 Ed Pe Quintilio Costini - Centro, 89620-000 Campos Novos ☎49 3541 0391 **W:** www.rsradios.com.br **Email;** culturaam@rsradios.com.br – **SC61**) Rua 7 de Setembro 341, Centro, 85505-030 Maravilha ☎46 3664 0029 **W:** www.difusoramaravilha.com.br **E:** atendimento@difusoramaravilha.com.br – **SC62**) Rua Ervino Rank 37, Serra Alta, 89291-695 São Bento do Sul ☎47 3633 0572 ▤47 3634 2497 **W:** www.radiosaobento.com **E:** comercial@radiosaobento.com – **SC63**) Av Centenario, 6050 - Bairro Prospera, 88815-000 Criciúma ☎48 3478 5659 **W:** www.hulhanet.com.br – **SC64**) Rua São Pedro, 245, Centro, 89110-000 Gaspar **W:** www.sentineladovale.com.br **E:** radiosentinela@terra.com.br ☎47 3332 0783 ▤47 3332 1200 – **SC65**) Rua General Vieira da Rosa, 89020-420 Florianopolis ☎48 3244 1240 **W:** www.clickric.com.br **E:** amgazeta@hotmail.com – **SC66**) Rua Santos Dumont, 204 - Centro, 89610-000 Herval d'Oeste ☎49 3527 9013. - **Italian:** Sat 1530-1730 **W:** www.radiolider.am.br **E:** gerencia@radiolider.am.br – **SC67**) Rua Coronel Procópio Gomes 1155, 89202-300 Joinville **W:** http://arcadaalianca..com.br**E:** difusora@difusora.net – **SC68**) Rua Capitão Jerônimo Luiz de Bittencourt 103, sala 01, Centro, 88770-000 Imaruí ☎48 3643 0000 **W:** www.litoralam.com.br **E:** litoralam@litoralam.com.br – **SC69**) Rua Tiradentes, 283, sala 21, Centro, 89140-000 Ibirama – ☎47 3357 2236 **W:** www.belosvales.com.br **E:** belosvales@ibnet.com.br – **SC70**) Av Plínio Arlindo de Nes 476, 89825-000 Xaxim ☎49 3353 2425 **W:** www.radioculturaxaxim.com.br **E:** culturaxaxim@brturbo.com.br – **SC71**) Rua Max Wilhelm, 373 - Baependi, 89256-000 Jaraguá do Sul **W:** www.jaraguaam.com.br **E:** jaraguaam@jaraguaam.com.br ☎47 3371 1010 ▤47 3275 0304 – **SC72**) Av Luis de Camões 1370, 88523-000 Lages ☎43 3222 8222 **W:** www.radioguri.com.br **E:** rco@rco.com.br or faleconosco@radioguri.com.br – **SC73**) Av Belém, 500 - Centro, 89870-000 Pinhalzinho ☎49 3366 1111 **W:** www.rco.com.br – **SC74**) Rua Altamiro Guimarães 480, Centro, 89500-000 Caçador ☎49 3536 2211 **W:** www.am1110.com.br – **SC75**) Av. Dr. João Renza 797,, 88780-000 Imbituba **W:** www.bandeirantes1010.com.br – **SC76**) Rua Equador 245, 89120-000 Timbó ☎47 3382 3888 **W:** www.radioculturaam.com.br **E:** radiocultura@tpa.com.br – **SC77**) Rua Manoel Vieira Garcao 3, 88301-010 Itajaí ☎47 3348 2992 **W:** www.difusoraitajai.com.br – **SC78**) Rua Boanerges P de Medeiros 205,

2° e 3° andares, 88600-000 São Joaquim ▤49 3233 0021 **W:** www.difusora1530.com.br **E:** difusora@iscc.com.br – **SC79**) Av Porto Feliz 151,Centro, 89893-000 Mondaí ☎49 3674 0122 **W:** www.portofeliz.am.br - **German & Spanish:** Sun 1300-1400 – **SC80**) Rua Carmelo Zocoli 205, 89665-000 Capinzal ☎49 3555 1333 **W:** www.radiocapinzal.am.br **E:** radiocapinzal@radiocapinzal.am.br – **SC81**) Av Getúlio Vargas, 429 - Centro, 88900-000 Araranguá ▤48 3524 0137 **W:** www.radioararangua.com.br **E:** contato@radioararangua.com.br - **FM:** 92.5MHz – **SC82**)Rodovia SC -422 km 3 (C.P 3, 89190-970), Padre Eduardo, 89190-000 Taió ☎47 3562 1440 **W:** www.educadora.am.br **E:** comercial@educadora.am.br– **SC83**) Rua Carlos Weber 228, 89295-000 Rio Negrinho – **SC84**) Av 21 de Janeiro, 966 - Centro, 89107-000 Pomerode ☎47 3395 1580 **W:** www.radiopomerode.com.br **Email** radiopomerod@radiopomerode.com.br – **SC85**) Rua João Steffens 260 (C.P 100), 88400-000 Ituporanga ☎47 3533 8310 **W:** www.sintonia.am.br **E:** radio@sintonia.am.br – **SC86**) Rua Joaquim Nuns 244, Centro, (⌂ C.P 2004) 888340-000 Camboriú ☎47 3261 3232 **W:** www.gmuh.com.br/radio/sintonia.htm **E:** contato@gideos.com.br – **SC87**) Rua João Florentino de Souza 700, 89480-000 Major Vieira ☎47 3635 1177 **W:** www.radioplanaltodemajorvieira.com.br – **SC88**) Rua Renato Ramos da Silva 239, Barreiros, (C.P 1477, 88103-970), 88110-015 São José ☎47 3041 4103 **W:** www.radioguararema.com.br **E:** grasiele@radioguararema.com.br 24h - **FM:** 103.5/107.7MHz – **SC89**) Rua Sargento Juvenil Pereira de Souza. 476 - Centro, 89540-000 Santa Cecília ▤49 3244 2188 **W:** www.radioalvoradasc.com – **SC90**) Av Getúlio Vargas 860, Centro, 89830-000 Abelardo Luz ☎49 3445 4297 **W:** www.rainhadasquedas.com.br – **SC91**) Rua Ricardo Kruger 140, sala 02, 88650-000 Urubici – **SC92**) Rua Rui Barbosa, 1321 - Cemtro, 88930-000 Turvo **W:** www.radioimigrantes.com.br **E:** imigrantes@radioimigrantes.com.br ▤48 3525 0321 – **SC93**) Rua Professor João Sobotka 222, Bairro São Cristovão, 89665-000 Capinzal ☎ 49 3555 1799 **W:** www.radiobarrigaverde.am.br - **Italian:** Sun 1500-1600 – **SC94**) Av Progresso 569, 89888-000 Caibi **E:** radiocaibi@cbi.cpnet.com.br– **SC95**) Rua Duque de Caxias 1302, 2° andar, 89900-000 São Miguel d'Oeste **W:** www.peperi.com.br ☎49 3622 1877 – **SC96**) Rua Rafael Pardinho, 249 - Centro, 89240-000 São Francisco do Sul **W:** www.radiosaofranciscosc.com.br **E:** radio.saofrancisco@ilhanet.com.br ☎47 3444 2733 ▤47 3444 0450 – **SC97**) Rua do Comercio 215, 89770-000 Seara **W:** www.belosmontes.com.br – **SC98**) Rua Nereu Ramos 2222, Centro, 89872-000 Modelo ☎49 3365 3294 **E:** radiomodelo@mhnet.com.br – **SC99**) Rua 7 de Setembro, 496, Centro, 89950-000 Dionísio Cerqueira ☎49 3644 1042 **W:** www.radiofronteira.com.br - **FM:** 94.3 – **SC100**) Rua Marechal Floriano, 505 – Ponte Serrada, 89683-000 Ponte Serrada ☎49 3435 0171 **W:** www.radionamba.com.br **E:** atendimento@radionamba.com.br – **SC101**) Av Dr Albano Schultz, 925 - 2° andar Centro, 89201-220 Joinville ☎47 3481 3030 **W:** www.radioclubejoinville.com.br**E:** - **FM:** 103.1MHz – **SC102**) Rua Maranhão 700, sala 02, 89800-000 Campo Erê **W:** www.peperi.com.br – **SC103**) Rua Pref.Dib Cherem 3440 Salas 02/03, Capoeiras, 88090-001 Florianopolsi ☎48 3028 1240 **W:** www.radiomaisalegria.com.br - **FM:** 106.5 MHz – **SC104**) Rua XV de Novembro 495, 89560-000 Videira ☎49 3650 2500 **W:** www.vitoriaam.com.br **E:** adm@vitoriaam.com.br – **SC105**) Rua João Lino da Silva Neto 621, 88495-000 Garopaba ☎48 3254 3055 **W:** www.radiofrequencia.net **E:** frequencia@radiofrequencia.net – **SC106**) 88330-000 Balneário Cambouri **W:** http://radiocatolica1500am.blogspot.co – **SC107**) 89642-000 Tangará – **SC108**) 88950-000 Jacinte Machado.

SE00) SERGIPE

SE01) Rua Claudio Batista 334, Santo Antônio, 49060-100 Aracaju ☎79 3234 3232 **W:** www.radiojornal540.com.br **E:** jornal@radiojornal540.com.br – **SE02**) Rua Propria 124, 49010-020 Aracaju **W:** www.aperipe.se.gov.br/ - **FM:** 104.9MHz – **SE03**) Rua Simão Dias, 643 - Centro, 49010-430 Aracaju ☎79 3226 8710 **W:** www.cultura670.com.br **E:** cultura@cultura670.com.br – **SE04**) 49400-000 Lagarto ☎79 3631 8500 **W:** www.radioprogressoam.com **E:** contato@radioprogressoam.com – **SE05**) C.P 409, 49001-970 Aracaju **W:** www.amatalaia.com.br – **SE06**) Rua 13 de Maio 119, 49500-000 Itabaiana ☎79 3431 1762 **W:** www.radioprincesadaserra.com.br – **SE07**) Rua Pacatuba 254, Ed Paulo Figueiredo, sala 1116, Centro 49010-900 Aracaju ☎☎79 3213 1174 **W:** www.930am.com.br **E:** jornalismo@930am.com.br – **SE08**) Praça Coronel Gonçalo Prado s/n, Bairro Santa Cruz, 49200-000 Estância ☎79 3522 1411 ▤79 3522 2327 **W:** www.radioesperancaestancia.com.br **E:** contato@radioesperancaestancia.com.br – **SE09**) Av Dr Luíz Magalhães 346, 49500-000 Itabaiana ☎79 3431 7928 **W:** www.capitaldoagreste.com.br **E:** contato@capitaldoagreste.com.br – **SE10**) Rodovia Lourival Batista 2153, 49480-000 Simão Dias ☎79 3611 1488 **W:** www.novacidadeam.com.br **E:** novacidadeam@hotmail.com – **SE11**) Av. Napoleão Emifio Costa, 1052 — Centro,, 49514-000 Frei Paulo ☎79 3447 1745 **W:** www.radioeducadoradefreipaulo.com.br **E:** radioeducadorafreipaulo@yahooa.com.br – **SE12**) Rua Barão do Rio Branco 262, 49200-000 Estância – **SE13**) Travessa Santa Luzia 69,

49300-000 Tobias Barreto ☎79 3541 1548 **W:** www.redeilha.com **E:** am1520@redeilha.com

SP00) SÃO PAULO

SP01) Rua Padre Geraldo Goseling 798, 16200-000 Biriguí – **SP02)** Rua Antônio do Vale Mello 807, Centro, 13170-011 Sumaré ☎19 3873 2972 **W:** www.radionovasumare.com.br **E.** rns@rns.com.br– **SP03)** Av Nesralla Rubez 353, 12700-000 Cruzeiro ☎12 3144 0606 🖷12 3144 3688 **W:** www.radiomantiqueira.com.br **E:** atendimento@mantiqueira. com.br - **FM:** 100.7MHz – **SP04)** Rua José Bonini 1415, 14160-000 Sertãozinho **W:** h//radio.boavontade.com – **SP05)** Prefeito João Benedito Barbosa,161, Vila Nova, 18400-000 Itapeva ☎15 3522 2000 **W:** www.radioclubeitapeva.com.br **E:** radioclube@dioclubeitapeva. com.br- **FM:** 93.5MHz «Cristal» – **SP06)** Rua Dr Sousa Alves 960, 12020-030 Taubaté ☎12 3632 8122 **W:** www.difusora570.com.br – **SP07)** Rua Rui Barbosa, 580-Centro, 13465-280 Americana **E:** radiovoce@radiovoce.com.br **W:** www.radiovoce.com.br ☎19 3475 8801 🖷19 461 7081 - **FM:** 88.9MHz "Notícia" – **SP08)** Av Rotary 85, 19970-000 Palmital ☎18 3351 2601 **W:** www.radioregionalpalmital.com.br – **SP09)** Rua Pedro Lessa 1640, sala 809 – Embaré, 11025-002 Santos **W:** www.radioatlantica.com.br **E:** radioatlantica@radioatlantica.com.br ☎13 3273 6900 24h – **SP10)** Rua das Nações Unidas 127, 16800-000 Mirandópolis **W:** www.clubeam590.com.br **E:** clubeam@expressnet. com.br ☎18 3701 4084 🖷18 3701 4143 – **SP11)** Av Jerônimo Gonçalves 640, 14010-040 Ribeirão Preto **W:** www.radio79.com.br – **SP12)** Av Luíz Gonzaga de Amoedo Campos 28, Centro, 13800-000 Muyi Mirim ☎19 3804 3893 **W:** www.cbnmogi.com.br – **SP13)** Rua Pará 147, Centro, 15800-000 Catanduva **W:** www.goboneroestepaulista.blogspot.com - **FM:** 94.9MHz – **SP14)** Praça Conselheiro Rodrigues Alves, 104 - 3° andar - Centro, 12560-020 Guaratinguetá ☎12 3122 3155 **W:**superradiopiratininga.com.br **E:** ouvintes@superradiopiratininga.com.br – **SP15)** Av. Dr. Domingos Teodoro Galla, 528 – Centro, 18800-000 Piraju ☎14 3351 1066 **W:** www.paranapanemaam.com.br **E:** contato@paranapanemaam.com.br – **SP16)** Av Paulista 807, 24° andar, 01311-941 São Paulo **E:** info@jovempan.com.br **W:** www.jovempan.com.br – **SP17)** Rua Capitão Neves 1840, 15130-000 Mirassol ☎17 3242 2101 🖷17 3242 3076 **W:** www.difusora630.com – **SP18)** Av Marcondes Filho 1130, 19013-160 Presidente Prudente – **SP19)** Rua Nove de Julho 1300, 14804-295 Araraquara ☎16 3303 3622 🖷16 3303 0114 **E:** radiomorada@uol.com.br **W:** www.radiomorada.com.br - **FM:** 98.1MHz – **SP20)** Rua Homero Rodrigues Silva 1072, 16901-025 Andradina - **FM:** 97.9MHz – **SP21)** Praça José Bonifácio 815, 13400-340 Piracicaba ☎19 2105 6600 **W:** www.rdifusora.com.br **E:** contato@difusorapiracicaba.com.br - **FM:** 102.3MHz – **SP22)** Rua Tolentino Figueiras, 119 7° andar - cj 71/72, Gonzaga, 11060-471 Santos ☎13 3289 5259 **W:** www.criacaoconsultoria.com.br - **FM:** 105.5MHz – **SP23)** Av Nove de Julho 606, 14025-000 Ribeirão Preto **W:** www.clube. com.br - **FM:** 100.5MHz – **SP24)** Rua Teotonio Tibiriçá Pimenta, 380 - Centro, 11660-230 Caraguatatuba ☎12 3882 5000 **W:** www.radiooceanicaam.com.br **E:** radio.oceanica@uol.com.br – **SP25)** Rua Prefeito Salviano 20, 17400-000 Garça ☎14 3471 0396 **W:** www.670am.com. br **E:** estudio@670am.com.br – **SP26)** Rua Quintino Bocaiúva, 37 - Centro, 13300-135 Itu.- ☎11 4023 2363 **W:** www.radioconvencao.com. br **E:** radioconvencao@hotmail.com – **SP27)** Rua 13 de Maio 720, Centro, 15800-010 Catanduva ☎17 3522 2228 **W:** www.difusora680. com.br – **SP28)** Av Dr Alvaro Schmidt Gallo 317, 18800-000 Piraju ☎14 3351 1680 **W:** www.winf.com.br/piratininga **E:** pirat680@winf.com.br – **SP29)** Rua Francisco Inácio 257, 14700-000 Bebedouro ☎17 3342 2484 **W:** www.radiobebedouro.com.br **E:** gerencia.rb@mdbrasil.com.br – **SP30)** Praça Conselheiro Rodrigues Alves, Centro, 12500-020 Guaratinguetá **E:** rclube@provale.com.br - **FM:** 97.1MHz – **SP31)** Rua Humberto Liedtke 1936, 15370-000 Pereira Barreto ☎18 3704 6677 **W:** www.radiocidadeam690.com **E:** contato@radiocidadeam690.com.br **MSN:** radiocidadeampb@hotmail.com – **SP32)** Av.Eng Caetano Alvares, 55 – Limão, 02598-900 Sao Paulo ☎11 2108 6700 **W:** http:// radio.estado.com.br - **FM:** 92.9MHz – **SP33)** Rua 1 de Agosto 927, 17010-011 Bauru **W:** www.radio710bauru.com.br – **SP34)** Rua dos Pelegrini 11, Bairro do Desterro, 13700-000 Casa Branca ☎19 3671 2101 **W:** www.radiodifusoracasabranca.com.br – **SP35)** Rua Antonio Carlos Mori 288 (C.P 355 19900-970), 19900 080 Ourinhos – **SP36)** Rua Dr Carlos Varela 104 (✉C.P 25,12700-970),12701-301 Centro, Cruzeiro ☎12 3143 6894 **W:** www.rcvale.com.br – **SP37)** Rua Dr Antônio 227, Centro 15400-000 Olímpia ☎17 3281 3045 **W:** www.meninaam.com.br **E:** ammenina@uol.com.br – **SP38)** Rua Siqueira de Morães 578, 10° andar, Ed Marijú, 13201-803 Jundiaí **E:** cidade@radiojundiai.com.br **W:** www.radiojundiai.com.br ☎11 4586 0969 – **SP39)** Rua Coronel Galdino de Almeida, 55 - Centro, bloco 3 sala 1, (✉ C.P 324, 17500-970) 17500-100 Marília ☎14 3402 5128 🖷14 3402 5127 **W:** www.dirceu.am.br **Email:** radio@dirceu.am.br – **SP40)** Av. João Lemos. 918 - Centro, 17250-970 Bariri ☎14 3662 9191 **W:** www.radioculturadebariri.com.br – **SP41)** Av Paulista, 900 – Bela Vista, 01310-100 São Paulo ☎11 3289 3755 **W:** http://radiotrianon.tempsite.ws – **SP42)**

Rua Itapura 06, Jardim América, 17700-000 Osvaldo Cruz **W:** www. radioosvaldocruz.com.br **E:** calfm@cruz.com.br – **FM:** 97.3MHz «California FM» – **SP43)** Rua Ramos de Azevedo, 622 – Jardim Paulista, 14090-180 Ribeirão Preto ☎16 3624 2848 **W:** www.radiocmn.com.br – **SP44)** Rua Euclides Miragaia 394 – 18° andar, Centro, 12245-901 São José dos Campos ☎12 3909 8000 🖷12 3941 1999 **W:** www.superradiopiratininga.com.br **E:** ouvintes@superradiopiratininga. com.br - **FM:** 99.7MHz – **SP45)** Rua Virgilio Malta, 6-78, 17015-220 Bauru ☎14 3104 0761 **W:** www.auriverde.am.br **E:** auriverde@ auriverde.am.br **W: SP46)** Rua Santa Cruz 655, 13480-041 Limeira ☎19 3404 4000 **W:** www.mixam.com.br **E:** manoelmixregional@gmail.com - **FM:** 100.7MHz – **SP47)** Rua das Palmeiras 315, Vila Buarque, 01226-901 São Paulo ☎11 3824 3200 🖷11 3825 8844 **W:** www.radioclick. globo.com.br/cbn/ **E:** contato@globonoar.com.br – **FM:** 90.5 MHz – **SP48)** Alameda Dr Armando de Sales Oliveira, 575 – Centro, 17800-000 Adamantina 18 3521 1242 **W:** www.radiobrasilam.com.br **E:** contato@ radiobrasilam.com.br – **SP49)** Av Bento de Abreu, 789 - Fonte, (C.P 59 14801-970) 14802-396 Araraquara ☎16 3303 7799 **W:** www.radiocultura.net **E:** comercial@radiocultura.net- **FM:** 97.3MHz – **SP50)** Rua Barão de Jundiaí, 1041 – 9° andar - Centro, 13201-906 Jundiaí ☎11 4586 2020 **W:** www.radiodifusorajundiai.com.br **E:** radio@radiodifusorajundiai.com.br – **SP51)** Rua Benjamin Constanst, 3327 - Centro, 15015-600 São José do Rio Preto – **Blog:** http://blog.cancanova. com/riopreto **E:** radioriopreto@cancanova.com – **SP52)** Av Getúlio Vargas, 185 - Centro, (C.P 02, 12570-970 Aparecida) 12570-000 Aparecida **W:** www.radioaparecida.com.br ☎12 3104 4400 🖷12 3104 4451 DX-prgrm - Encontro DX, Saturdays at 22.00 UTC - **FM:** 90.9MHz – **SP53)** Rua Tenente Lopes, 191-Centro, (C.P.3) 17201-460 Jaú – ☎14 3622 2800 **W:** www.radiojauense.com.br **E:** radiojauense@netsite. com.br - **FM:** 101.1MHz – **SP54)** Rua José Galvão 359, (C.P 94) 19900-260 Ourinhos ☎14 3322 2997 🖷14 3322 6255 **W:**radioclube820.com. br **E:** clube@radioclube820.com.br – **SP55)** Av.Antonieta Vilela Ferreira 900 - Violage, 16360-000 Penápolis ☎18 3662 0027 🖷18 3652 2474 **W:** www.difusoradepenapolis.com.br **E:** difusora@difusoradepenapolis.com.br – **SP56)** Rua Sao Paulo 1091, 15500-000 Votuporanga ☎17 3422 3301 **W:** www.lider830.com.br **E:** club92fm@votuporanga.com.br - **FM:** 92.1MHz – **SP57)** Rua Radiantes 12, Morumbi, 05699-900 São Paulo **W:** www.bandeirantes.com.br **E:** rbnoar@band.com.br - **FM:** 90.9MHz – **SP58)** Av Visconde do Rio Claro 2128, 13500-580 Rio Claro – **FM:** 94.9MHz – **SP59)** C.P 154, 16200-970 Birigui – **SP60)** Rua Prudente de Morães 418, 14960-000 Novo Horizonte – **SP61)** Rua Romualdo Andreazzi 516, Jd Leonor, 13041-030 Campinas **W:**radiocentral.com.br **E:** central@radiocentral.com.br ☎19 3272 1400 - **FM:** 103.7MHz «Nova» – **SP62)** Av.Paulista, 900 4° andar, Bairro Bela Vista, 01310-940 Sao Paulo ☎11 3170 5757 🖷11 3170 5630 **W:** www.casperlibero.edu.br/ canais/index.php/radio-universitaria,c=194 **E:** hrocha@radiogazeta. com.br – **SP63)** Rua Rui Barbosa 273, 19015-000 Presidente Prudente ☎18 222 2500 **W:** www.difusoraprudente.com.br – **SP64)** Rua Siqueira Campos 3223, 15010-210 São José do Rio Preto **W:** www. machadodecarvalho.com.br - **FM:** 102.1MHz «R Onda Nova FM» – **SP65)** Rua Miguel Janez, 19 – Vila Arlindo Luz, 18212-480 Itapetininga – **SP66)** Rua Alf José Caetano 1039, 13400-120 Piracicaba ☎19 3432 3000 **W:** www.ondalivre.com.br **E:** comercial@ondalivre.com.br - **FM:** 105.3 – **SP67)** Rua Monsenhor Rosa, 1561 - Centro, 14400-670 Franca ☎16 3713 3977 🖷16 3713 3905 **W:** www.radioimperador.com.br **E:** contato@radioimperador.com.br – **SP68)** Av Brasil, 31 – Prados, (✉ C.P 52), 13973-255 Itapira **W:** www.radioclubeitapira.com.br **E:** radioclube@dglnet.com.br ☎19 3843 5198 🖷19 3813 3948 - **FM:** 91.1MHz «Clube FM» – **SP69)** Av Ana Costa 532 - 5° andar, Gonzaga, 11060-002 Santos **W:** www.radiocultura.com.br **E:** cultura@radiocultura.com.br ☎13 3289 5757 🖷13 3289 4758 - **FM:** 106.7MHz – **SP70)** Av Aviador Marques Penedo 11-13, Bairro Jardim Europa, 17045-460 Bauru ☎14 3223 9433 **W:** www.cancaonova.com **E:** radio@cancaonova.com – **SP71)** Rua Doce, 303 - Centro, 15775-000 Santa Fé do Sul ☎17 3631 4859 **W:** www.radiosantafe.com.br **E:** comercial@radiosantafe.com.br - **FM:** 104.7MHz – **SP72)** Av Sampaio Vidal, 185 - Centro, 17501-040 Marília ☎14 3301 4341 **W:** www.radio950.com.br **E:** webmaster@ radio950.com.br – **SP73)** Av João Dias 1800, Santo Amaro, São Paulo ☎11 5641 4499 – **SP74)** Rua Quintino Bocaiuva 330/340 (C.P 56, 18200-970) 18200-014 Itapetininga **W:** www.difusoratransamerica. com.br **E:** ouvintes@difusoratransamerica.com.br – **SP75)** Rua Floriano Peixoto 64, Santo André, 13870-060 São João da Boa Vista **W:** www. piratininga970am.com.br **E:** radio970@dglnet.com.br – **SP76)** Al Vicente Leporace, 4583 – Parque dos Pinhas, (C.P 34, 14400-970) 14405-610 Franca – ☎16 3724 6651 **W:** www.radiohertz.com.br – **FM:** 96.5MHz «R 10» – **SP77)** Rua da Váras, 240 –Barra Funda, 01140-080 São Paulo **W:** www.radiorecord.com.br **E:** radio@rederrecord.com. br ☎11 2184 4971 🖷11 2184 4971 – **SP78)** Praça Joel Waldo Dal Moro 1, 14781-574 Barretos ☎17 3322 9411 **W:** www.odiariodebarretos.com.br – **SP79)** Rua Kametaro Morishita, 95 – 3°andar – cidade Universitaria, 19050-700 Presidente Prudente – **SP80)** Rua João Paulo ll s/n, Alto da Bela Vista (C.P 57), 12630-000 Cachoeira Paulista **W:** www.cancaonova.com **E:** radio@cancaonova.com ☎12 3186 2600 "Além Fronteiras" (Beyond Boundaries in SS, PP and EE) Sat.: 2200-2300 - **FM:** 96.3MHz – **SP81)** Rua Benjamin Constant 33, 10° andar, Centro, 19806-130 Assis ☎18 3322 8811 🖷18 3322 1319 **W:** www. culturadeassis.com.br **E:** cultura@culturadeassis.com.br - **FM:** 100.1MHz – **SP82)** Rua Profa Aparecida M.Faveri 988, Jd.Fumagalli, 13485-316 Limeira (C.P 105, 13480-970 Limeira) **W:** www.educa-doraam.com.br **E:** radio@educadoraam.com.br ☎19 3441 3760 – **SP83)** Rua 24, 2442 (C.P 16, 15700-970), 15700-000 Jales ☎17 3622 5508 **W:** www.radioculturadejales.com.br – **SP84)** Rua Ouvidor Freire, 1986 – Centro, (CP 243), 14400-630 Franca ☎16 3713 8800 🖷16 3722 1214 **E:** administracao@comerciodafranca.com.br.com.br **W:** www. comerciodafranca.com.br – **SP85)** Av.Pedro Ometto 2420, 17340-000 Barra Bonita - **FM:** 97.7MHz – **SP86)** Rua Floriano Peixoto, 1840 - Labate, 16400-101 Lins - **FM:** 103.1MHz – **SP87)** Praça Rodrigues de Abreu, 228 - Paraiso, 04040-080 São Paulo **W:** www.radiocapital-1040. com.br **E:** administra@radiocapital.am.br ☎11 3053 1040 – **SP88)** Rua Boa Morte, 1122 - Centro, 13400-140 Piracicaba 🖷19 3422 1060 **W:** www.educadora1060.com.br **E:** ouvinte@educadora1060.com.br - **FM:** 103.1MHz – **SP89)** Av Rangel Pestana 147, 11031-551 Santos – **SP91)** Rua Marechal Bitencourt 346, 17201-430 Jaú **W:** radiopiratininga.am. br – **SP92)** Av Washington Luiz, 1250-Centro, (C.P 704, 19015-970) 19015-150 Presidente Prudente ☎81 2104 6000 **W:** www.prudente. am.br **E:** contato@fm1010fm.com.be – **FM** 101.1MHz – **SP93)** Rua 20 3011 15700-000 Jales ☎17 3622 5505 **W:** www.radioassuncao.com.br **E:** comercial@regionalfm.com.br - **FM:** 103.5MHz «Regional FM» – **SP94)** Rua Santos Dumont, 239 - Centro, 14300-000 Batatais **W:** www. difusoraam.com.br **E:** diretoria@difusoraam.com.br ☎16 3761 3600 🖷16 3761 3623 – **SP95)** Rua Olavo Bilac 693, Centro, 16400-000 Lins ☎14 3522 4644 **W:** www.radioalvoradadelins.com.br **E:** alvorada@ superig.com.br – **SP96)** C.P 565, 18001-970 Sorocaba **W:** www. radioboanova.com.br – **SP97)** Av Marginal Beira Rio, 13 - Apt 02, Ponte Alta, 12570-000 Aparecida ☎12 3105 1492 **W:** www.rmpansat.com.br **E:** rmpansat@rmpansat.com.br – **SP98)** Rua Carlos Artêncio 117 (C.P 326), 17519—255 Marília ☎ **W:** www.radioclubemarilia.com.br**E:** itaipufm@ terra.com.br – **SP99)** Rua Jeremias de Paulo Eduardo 916, 15910-000 Monte Alto – **SP100)** Rua das Palmeiras 315, 01221-010 São Paulo **W:** radioclick.globo.com/globobrasil **E:** contato@globonoar.com.br – **SP101)** Rua Marechal Deodoro da Fonseca 675, Sobre Loja, 16011-000 Araçatuba ☎18 3624 9797 **W:** www.jovemluz.com.br – **SP102)** Rua Capitão Joao Marques 89, Jardim Centenarioi – 14940-000 Ibatinga (C.P 91, 14940-970) 16 3341 9900 **W:** www.radioibitinga.com.br **E:** radio.ibatinga@ibinet.com.br - **FM:** 99.3MHz «Ternura FM» – **SP103)** Av Luíz Gonzaga de Amoêdo Campos 28, 13800-000 Mogi Mirim - **FM:** 93.9MHz – **SP104)** Rua Bandeirantes 104 18540 000Porto Feliz ☎15 3261 5003 **W:** www.radionovaporto.com.br **E:**webradio@radionova-porta.com.br – **SP105)** Av Dr Mário Galvão 463, Jardim Bela Vista, 12209-004 São José dos Campos ☎12 3941 4114 **W:** www.cidade-am1120.com.br **E:** radio@cidadeam1120.com.br - **FM:** 97.5MHz «Nativa FM» – **SP106)** Rua Duque de Caxias 260 cj 22 an 2, 15900-000 Taquaritinga ☎16 3252 2999 **W:** www.regionalfm.com.br – **SP107)** Rua Cherentes 250 – 13° andar (C.P 258, 17600-970) 17600-000 Tupã ☎14 3496 3255 🖷14 3496 6835 **W:** www.radiotupa.com.br **E:** tupaam@radiotupa.com.br - **FM:** 97.7MHz – **SP108)** Rua Gonçalves Dias 208, 19800-110 Assis ☎18 3322 3833 🖷18 3322 8477 **W:** www.difu-soraassis.com.br **E:** difusora@difusoraassis.com.br – **SP109)** Praça Joel Waldo Dal Moro 1, Centro, 14781-574 Barretos ☎17 3322 4488 – **SP110)** C.P 139, 13500-970 Rio Claro **W:** SP111) Rua Bernardino 546, (C.P 153, 11680-970) 11680-000 Ubatuba ☎12 3832 2993 **W:** www. radiocostaazul.com.br – **SP112)** Av Paulista 2198, Térreo, 01310-300, Sao Paulo **W:** www radiomundial.com **E:** radio@radiomundial.com. br **FM:** 95.7MHz – **SP113)** Rua Almirante Barroso 456, 19400-000 Presidente Venceslau ☎18 3271 1213 **W:** www.venceslauam.com.br **E:** contato@venceslauam.com.br - **FM:** 95.1MHz «R Jovem Som» – **SP114)** Rua Saldanha de Gama, 184 - Centro, 18035-040 Sorocaba ☎15 3234 3444 **W:** www.radiocacique.com.br **E:** contato@radiocaci-que.com.br - **FM:** 96.5MHz – **SP115)** Av. Manoel Marques Rosa, 1075 – Ed. Atlântis - Térreo, 15600-000 Fernandópolis ☎17 3442 2666 **W:** www.radiodifusorafernandopolis.com.br - **FM:** 99.0MHz – **SP116)** Rua Barão de Monte Santo, 1211, 3° andar, Centro, 13730-000 Mococa 2799, Jd.São Gabriel, 13044-370 Campinas ☎19 3779 7404 – **SP117)** Rua Eng Antonio Francisco de Paula Souz Rua Pernambuco 4006, (C.P 380, 15500-970), 15500-000 Votuporanga ☎17 3421 2113 **W:** www.radiocidade1190.com.br **E:** contato@radioc-idade1190.com.br – **SP119)** Av XV de Novembro 715, (C.P 75) 13650-000 Santa Cruz das Palmeiras – **SP120)** Rodovia Taquarituba Avare s/n km 384, 18740-000 Taquarituba ☎14 3762 1487 🖷14 3762 1009 **W:** www.radioregional1190.com.br **E:** regionalam@yahoo.com.br – **SP121)** Rua Vladimir Herzog, 75 - Agua Branca, 05036-900 São Paulo **W:** www. tvcultura.com.br **E:** dpt@tvcultura.com.br ☎11 2182 3080 🖷11 3611

1914 – **SP122)** Rua Rui Barbosa 546, 4° andar, 14870-000 Jaboticabal ☎16 3202 0266 **W:** www.radiovidanova.com.br **E:** falecomadiovidan-ovaam.com.br – **SP123)** Rua Tupinambás 115, Bairro São João, 16025-180 Araçatuba – **SP124)** Av Dr Nunu de Assis 550 (C.P 209, 17001-970), 17010-120 Bauru ☎14 3232 3572 – **SP125)** Av. Roberto Simonsen 280, Jd. Santa Rosalia,18090-000 Sorocaba ☎15 3224 5300 🖷15 3231 4938 **W:** www.radiovanguarda.com.br **E:** comercial@radiovanguardia. com.br - **FM:** 94.9MHz – **SP126)** Rua Floriano Peixoto 375, 18300-000 Capão Bonito – **SP127)** Av. Tiradentes 312 15990-607 Matão. ☎16 3384 6619 **W:** www.radiocidade890.am.br**E:** financeiro@radiocid-ade890.am.br – **SP128)** Rua Dr Miguel Penteado 585, Jardim Chapadão, 13073-180 Santos – **SP129)** Rua Dr. Cardoso Almeida, 1000 ap 131 – Centro,, 18600-005 Botucatu ☎14 3815 3025 **W:** www.radiomunicipal-ista.com.br – **SP130)** Rua 8 No 472, 14620-000 Orlândia ☎16 3826 3000 🖷16 3826 3006 **W:** ☎ **W:** www.orc.com.br **E:** orc@orc.com.br – **SP131)** Rua José Caballero 60, 11055-300 Santos – **SP132)** Av Nove de Julho 265, 15200-000 José Bonifácio 17 3245 1621 **W:** www. radiovaledotiete.com.br **E:** contato@radiovaledotiete.com.br – **SP133)** Rua Vilaa 195, Sala 23, Centro, 12210-000 São Jose dos Campos ☎12 3923 7000 **W:** www.cancaonova.com **E:** radiosjc@cancaonova.com – **SP134)** Av Prof Alceu Maynard Araújo, 153, 7° andar - Santo Amaro, 04726-160 São Paulo **W:** www.radiomorada.com.br **E:** radiomorada@ uol.com.br – **SP136)** Av. Benjamin Constant 1214, 5° andar, Centro, 13010-141 Campinas ☎19 3231 5322 **W:** www.brasilcampinas.com.br **E:** radio@brasilcampinas.com.br – **SP137)** Rua Jamil Khauan19A, Vila Imperial, 15015-620 São José do Rio Preto ☎17 3233 3322 **W:** www. novotempoam.com.br **E:**comercial@novotempoam.com.br – **SP138)** Rua Carina 05, 09732-060 São Bernardo do Campo **W:** www.ipda.com. br – **SP139)** Rua Barao do Rio Branco 559 (C.P 66), 14900-000 Itápolis – **SP140)** Av Cap Antonio Joaquim Mendes, 790 - Jardim Carlos Gomes, 13633-030 Pirassununga ☎19 3561 2200 **W:** www.minhacida-detem.com.br/difusora/– **SP141)** Rua Coronel Osório 84, 12900-000 Bragança Paulista ☎11 4034 0442 **W:** www.radiobraganca.com.br **E:** contato@radiobraganca.com.br – **SP142)** Rua Brigadeiro Tobias 911, 19570-000 Regente Feijó – **SP143)** Av Costabile Romano, 2201 - Ribeirania, 14096-380 Ribeirão Preto ☎16 3603 6898 – **SP144)** Rua Osvaldo Cruz 67, (C.P 246 16010-971) 16010-040 Araçatuba. ☎18 3623 8726 🖷18 3622 6024 **W:** www.culturaam1340.com.br - **FM:** 95.5MHz – **SP145)** Rua Barão de Jaceguai, 468 - Centro, 08710-905 Mogi das Cruzes ☎11 4799 2888 **W:** www.redemetropolitana.com.br – **SP146)** C.P 20, 17350-970 Igaraçu do Tietê ☎14 3644 1122 **W:** www.nova-canoa.com.br **Email:** contato@novacanoa.com.br – **SP147)** Rua Sao Paulo 1708 (✉ C.P 173, 15600-970) 15600-000 Fernandópolis ☎17 3442 6639 **W:**www.aguasquentes1360.com.br - **FM:** 90.5MHz – **SP148)** Av Orlando Fruchi No 97, Distrito Industrial, 17900-000 Dracena ☎18 3821 2593 **W:** www.radioregionaljp.com.br **E:** contato@radiore-gionaljp.com.br – **SP149)** Rua Cuiabá 2790, Centro, 16901-200 Andradina ☎18 3722 2729 – **SP150)** Av Sérgio Forein 230, 17250-000, Jardim Santa Rosa, Bariri ☎14 3662 6444 **W:** www.baririradioclube.com.br **E:** contato@baririradioclube.com.br – **SP151)** Rua Pedro Natalia Lorenzetti 172, 18680-030 Lençóis Paulista **W:** www.difusora.lpnet.com.br – **SP152)** Rua Guanabara 144, 13840-000 Mogi Guaçu – **SP153)** Av. Benjamin Constant 1214, 3° andar, 13010-141 Campinas **W:** www. globocampinas.com.br **E:** cbncampinas@globo.com ☎19 3731 5100 - **FM:** 99.1MHz – **SP154)** Rua Dr Erico de Abreu Sodré 542, 16370-000 Promissão – **SP155)** Av Brasil 1119, 17780-000 Lucélia ☎18 3551 1831 – **SP156)** Rua Salomao Shevs 670, (C.P 96, 13560-970) 13560-270 São Carlos ☎16 3375 3046 Email.: radio@clube.com.br - **FM:** 104.7MHz – **SP157)** Rua Jorge Tibiriçá, 2253 - Boavista, 15025-060 São José do Rio Preto ☎17 3212 7012 **W:** www.radiometropole1400.com.br**E:** metropoloam@terra.com.br – **SP158)** Rua Doutor Pinto Ferraz 183, Vila Mariana, 04117-900 São Paulo **W:** http://america.cancaonova.com r ☎11 5557 5100 – Satellite signal downlinked to 44 stations forming Paulus Sat Network – **SP159)** Ladeira Prof Irineu Lopes de Lima, 418 - Centro, 13250-241 Itatiba ☎11 4524 0003 **W:** www.crnitatiba.com.br **E:** crnitatiba@terra.com.br – **SP160)** Rua Cerqueira Cesar 481, 14010-130 Ribeirão Preto – **SP161)** Rua Mato Grosso 37, Vila Aparecida, 15150-000 Monte Aprazível ☎17 3275 1772 **W:** www.difusoraapare-cida.com.br **E:** difusoraaparecida@bol.com.br – **SP162)** Praça Barao do Rio Branco 30, 12010-090 Taubaté – **SP163)** Rua Coronel Joaquim Floriano 287, 18650-000 São Manuel – **SP164)** Praça Lourenço Franco de Oliveira 81, 13930-000 Serra Negra – **SP165)** Av Manoel Goulart, 291 1° andar - Centro, 19010-270 Presidente Prudente ☎18 3221 2900 **W:** www.comercialam.com.br **E:** radio@comercialam.com.br – **SP166)** Rua D Pedro, 556 – Centro, 16700-000 Guararapes ☎18 3606 1840 **W:** www.rdgguararapes.com.br – **SP167)** Fundação Espírita André Luiz, Av André Luís, 723 - Picanço, 07082-050 Guarulhos. ☎11 2458 321 🖷11 6457 8085 **W:** www.radioboanova.com.br – **SP168)** C.P 115, 13560-970 São Carlos – **SP170)** Av Peixto de Castro, 539 - Vila Celeste 12630-610 Lorena ☎🖷12 3153 1691 **W:** www.cultura1460.com.br **E:** tecnica@ cultural1460com.br – **SP172)** Av 15 No 225, 14790-000 Guaíra –

SP173) Av Rui Barbosa, 229,- Centro, 12308-520 Jacareí ☎12 3954 3000 🖹12 3954 3009 **W:** www.radiomensagem.am.br **E:** mensagem@radiomensagem.am.br – **SP174)** Rua Sao Sebastiao, 33 - Centro, 13660-000 Porto Ferreira ☎19 3581 1552 **E:** primavera@linkway.com.br – **SP175)** Rua 13 de Maio 2680, Jardim Avaí, 13333-080 Indaiatuba (C.P.297 13330-970) ☎19 3875 9141 🖹19 3875 6270 **W:** www.radiojornalindaiatuba.com.br **E:** contato@radiojornalindaiatuba.com.br – **SP176)** Rua Renato Jardim 511, 14350-000 Altinópolis **W:** www.clubregionalam.com.br – **SP177)** Rua Adolfo André 478, 2° andar, 12940-280 Atibaia – **SP178)** Praça Oswaldo Martins 218, 16210-000 Bilac – **SP179)** Rua Conselheiro Danrtas No 30, Centro, 18900-000 Santa Cruz do Rio Pardo ☎18 3372 1996 **W:** www.difusorasantacruz.com.br **E:** contato@difusorasantacruz.com.br – **SP180)** Av Governador Dr Ademar Pereira de Barros 134, 15400-000 Olímpia **W:** www.difusoraolimpia.com.br – **SP181)** Rua Monte Castelo. 941 - Centro, 17900-000 Dracena ☎18 3821 4340 **W:** www.radioglobodracena.com.br – **SP182)** Av Libero Almeida Silvares 3168, 15600-000 Fernandópolis ☎17 3442 1945 **W:** www.educadora.hd1.com.br **E:** educadorasr@acif.com.br – **SP183)** Rua Padre Moro Grande, 870 - Barrio dos Finco, 09830-670 São Bernardo do Campo ☎11 4354 0059 **W:** www.sagradocoracaojesus.com.br/radio_imaculada.php or www.miliciadaimaculada.org.br **E:** sam@miliciadaimaculada.org.br – **FM:** 107.1MHz – **SP184)** Av Guerino Turatti, 200, D.Industrial III, 13600-970 Araras ☎19 3541 8322 **W:** www.fraternidade.com.br **E:** fraternidade@fraternidade.com.br – **FM:** 97.9MHz – **SP185)** Rua Rubião Júnior, 192 - Centro, 12400-450 Pindamonhangaba ☎12 243 1566 **W:** www.rededifusora.com.br/am1500/index.htm **E:** difusorapinda@rededifusora.com.br – **SP186)** Rua Leopoldo Carlos de Oliveira 1038, 14530-000 Miguelópolis – **SP187)** Av.Paulista 2200 13 andar, Cerqueira Cesar, 01310-300 Osasco ☎11 3266 6880 **W:** www.radioterra.am.br **E:** contato@radioterra.am.br – **SP188)** Rua Silva Jardim, 480 - Macuco, 11015-020 Santos ☎13 3221 1846 **W:** www.radiocacique1510.com **E:** ouvintes@radiocacique1510.com – **SP189)** Rua Epitácio Pessoa, 440 – Centro, (C.P 13), 18650-000 São Manuel ☎14 3841 2522 **W:** www.cluberegional.com.br – **SP190)** Av Romeu Viana Romaneli 1510, 15570-000 Cardoso ☎17 3453 1330 **W:** www.radioalvoradacardoso.com – **SP191)** Rua Princesa Izabel de Braganca, 235 - çj 1401, Centro, 08710-460 Mogi das Cruzes ☎11 4796 1478 **W:** www.radioiguatemi.com.br – **SP192)** Rua Vereador Rosas, 171 - Centro, 13990-000 Espírito Santo do Pinhal ☎19 3651 4444 **W:** www.pinhalradioclube.com.br **E:** radiopinhal@dglnet.com.br – **FM:** 102.7MHz – **SP193)** C.P 125, 17930-970 Tupi Paulista – **SP194)** Rua Capitão Lisboa 1080, 18270-000 Tatuí ☎15 3251 3840 **W:** www.radionoticias.com.br **E:** ouvinte@radionoticias.com.br - **FM:** 93.9MHz «Ternura» – **SP195)** Rua Benedito Carlos dos Reis 700, 15190-000 Nhandeara – **SP196)** Rua Marechal Deodoro 320, 18600-320 Botucatu ☎14 3882 1535 **W:** www.prf-8.com.br **E:** contato@prf-8.com.br - **FM:** 93.1MHz – **SP197)** Av Diogo Antonio Feijo N° 1185, 06114-029 Osasco ☎11 3681 1134 🖹11 3683 0034 **W:** www.novadifusora.com.br **E:** faleconosco@novadifusora.com.br – **SP198)** Rua Dom José Carlos Aguirre 567, 18460-000 Itararé ☎15 3532 4050 🖹15 3532 4499 **W:** www.radioclube.cjb.net **E:** radioclubeam@terra-com.br – **SP199)** Rua Pedro de Toledo, 205 - Centro, 19700-000 Paraguaçu Paulista ☎18 3361 1268 🖹18 3361 1197 **W:** www.radiomarconi.com.br **E:** comercial@radiomarconi.com.br – **SP200)** Rua Lino Dorelli 120, 13360-000 Capivari ☎19 3491 1072 **W:** www.caciqueam.com.br – **SP201)** Rua Montenegro 196, 11410-040 Guarujá ☎13 3269 1010 **W:** www.radioguarujaam.com.br **E:** radioguarujaam@radioguarujaam.com.br - **FM:** 104.5MHz – **SP202)** C.P 135, 14600-970 São Joaquim da Barra **W:** www.radiosaojoaquim.com.br – **SP203)** Av Dr Januario Miraglia 2818, Vila Jaguaribe, 17450-000 Campos do Jordão ☎12 3662 1644 **W:** www.radiocamposdojordao1340.com.br - **FM:** 94.9MHz – **SP204)** Rua A.G Guerra 175 18700-000 Avaré – **SP205)** Rua Belo Horizonte N°930 17890-000 Junquerópolis ☎18 3841 1465 **W:** www.radiojunqueiropolis.com **E:** comercial@radiojunqueiropolis.com – **SP206)** Av Pereira Barreto, 1200 Vila Gilda, 09190-210 Santo André ☎11 4435 9000 🖹11 4435 9001 **W:** www.radioabc.com.br **E:** radioabc@radioabc.com.br – **SP207)** Rua Dr Vicente D´Anna 473, 13960-000 Socorro ☎19 3895 1444 **W:** www.radiosocorro.com.br **E:** radiosocorro@terra.com.br – **SP208)** Rua Capitão da Daniel da Cunha Morais, 344 - Centro, 15170-000 Tanabi ☎17 3272 2967 **W:** www.radioclubetanabi.com.br **E:** contato@radioclubetanabi.com.br – **SP209)** Rua Dr Felipe Vita 1616, 18480-000 Itaporanga – **SP210)** Rua José Bonifácio, 765 - Centro, 13690-000 Descalvado **E:** rscapin@gmail.com – **SP211)** Rua Joaquim Moreira, 12 Parque São Miguel, 07260-220 Guarulhos ☎11 6499 2708 **W:** www.fmrradiostationez.com/br/radiocumbica-guarulhos **E:** moacyrcustodio@radiocumbica.com.br – **SP212)** Av 17 No 560, 14780-000 Barretos – **SP213)** Av Paulista 2202, 8° andar, Conj 81/82, 01310-300 São Paulo ☎11 5543 0762 – **SP214)** Av Capitão José Antônio de Oliveira, 544 - Centro, 17800-000 Adamantina ☎18 3521 3547 **W:** www.radiojoia.com.br **E:** contato@radiojoia.com.br - **FM:** 93.7MHz «Antena 1» – **SP215)** Rua Brasil 648, 15650-000

Estrela d'Oeste ☎17 3833 1389 **W:** www.alvorada970.com.br – **SP216)** Rua Rubião Junior, 84 – Cj.89 – Shopping Centro, 12210-180 São José dos Campos ☎12 3018 4889 **W:** www.radioeldoradosjc.com.br **E:** contato@radioeldoradosjc.com.br – **SP217)** Rua Brandão Veras 1274, 14700-000 Bebedouro – **SP218)** Rua Antônio Lobo, 237 1° andar - Centro, 13465-000 Americana ☎19 3462 3992 **W:** www.azulceleste.com.br **E:** azulceleste@azulceleste.com.br– **SP219)** Estrada Serrinha Km 200, 15350-000 Auriflama – **SP220)** A Monte Castelo, 225 - Centro, 13450-285 Santa Bárbara d'Oeste ☎19 3463 5255 **W:** radiobrasilsbo.com.br - **E:** radiobrasil@radibrasilsbo.com.br – **SP221)** Rua Professor Maximo Ribeiro Nunes 75, 05535-000 Rondopolis(24h Gospel prgrs) ☎11 3721 8010 **W:** www.pazevida.com**E:** radio@nacionalgospel.com.br – **SP222)** Rua Dr Mário Sabino 131, 16300-000 Penápolis – **SP223)** Avenida Paulista 2200-5°andar, Bela Vista, 01310-300 São Paulo ☎11 3016 5998 - **W:** www.radioiguatemi.com.br **E:** radioiguatemi@radioiguatemi.com.br – **SP224)** Rua Kametaro Morishita 95, Cidade Universitária, 19050-700 Presidente Prudente ☎18 3299 0300 - **FM:** 106.7MHz – **SP225)** Rua Paula Ney 79, 18110-000 Votorantim – **SP226)** Rua Bento Carlos 61, 13560-660 São Carlos - **FM:** 96.9MHz «Jovem Pan FM» – **SP227)** Rua Duque de Caxais 33, Centro, 13460-000 Nova Odessa ☎19 3466 5127 **W:** www.novotempocampinas.com.br **E:** comercial@novotempocampinas.com.br – **SP228)** Rua Américo Vespúcio 20, 14730-000 Monte Azul Paulista ☎17 3361 2215 🖹17 3361 2717 **W:** www.radioprincesa.com.br **E:** radioprincesa@monteazul.com.br – **SP229)** Av Dr Labiano da Costa Machado 1735 (C.P 235), 17400-000 Garça **W:** www.unimidianet.com – **SP231)** Al Trifon Infante Algarim 1914, 19280-000 Teodoro Sampaio – **SP232)** Rua Vergueiro 2045, Liberdade, 04101-000 São Paulo ☎11 5081 579 **W:** www.radiotupiam.com.br **E:** comercial@radiotupiam.com.br– **SP233)** Av 9 de Julho, 304 Nova Paulina, 13140-000 Paulínia **W:** www.cancaonova.com **E:** admpaulina@cancaonova.com.br ☎19.3844.8500 – **SP234)** Rua Carlos Gomes, 534 - Centro, 14640-000 Morro Agudo ☎16 3851 2414 **W:** www.radiorepublica.com.br **E:** republica@radio4.com.br – **SP235)** Rua General Câmara 733, 2° andar, Centro, 13450-029 Santa Bárbara d'Oeste ☎19 3455 3811 **W:** www.radioluzes.com.br **E:** radioluzes@uol.com.br – **SP236)** Rua Joaquim Elizíário de Campos 126, 18320-000 Apiaí ☎15 552 1968 🖹15 552 1060 – **SP237)** Rua 5 No 170, Bairro Cristo Redentor, 12100-000 Taubaté – **SP238)** Rua Soares de Oliveira 2070, 14500-000 Ituverava ☎16 3839 7739 **W:** www.radiocultura1450.com.br **E:** radiocultura@netsite.com.br – **SP239)** Av Frederico Ozanan 554, 17300-000 Dois Córregos ☎14 3652 2166 – **SP240)** Av Olinda Naston 411B, Vila Formosa, 13720-000 São José do Rio Pardo **E:** cidlivreadm@vd.com.br - **FM:** 88.7MHz «R 88» – **SP241)** Rua Bororos 344, 17600-020 Tupã **W:** www.radioclubeshow.com.br – **SP242)** Av Washington Luíz, 214 – Centro, 13600 720 Araras ☎19 3541 1265 🖹19 3541 0477 **E:** radioclube@radioclube.com.br **W:** www.radioclube.com.br – **SP243)** Av 18 de Junho 367, 17690-000 Bastos – **SP244)** Rua Santana 440, Centro, 13880-000 Vargem Grande do Sul ☎19 3641 1152 **W:** http//radioculturaam.com **E:** r.cultura@itelefonica.com.br – **SP245)** R. Rafael de Barros, 126- Centro, 13610-120 Lemé ☎ 19 3571 4288 **W:** www.radioculturadeleme.com.br **E:** ouvinte@radioculturadeleme.com.br – **SP246)** Rua Francisco Geraldino 71, 17580-000 Pompéia ☎14 9631 0974 **W:** www.sitenc.com.br **E:** leitor@sitenc.com.br – **SP247)** Rua 7 de Setembro S-73, 17280-000 Pederneiras - **FM:** 88.3MHz – **SP248)** Rua Tenente Adolfo Padilha 157, 16880-000 Valparaíso – **SP249)** Rua 15 de Novembro 52, 13920-000 Pedreira – **SP250)** Av Presidente Vargas 2-44, 19470-000 Presidente Epitácio ☎18 3281 8333 **W:** www.radiovaledorioparana.com.br– **SP251)** Rua Com Guimarães, 25 sl 402 - Centro, 13900-470 Amparo ☎19 3807 3633 **W:** www.difusoradeamparo.com.br **E:** radio@difusoradeamparo.com.br – **SP252)** Rua Padre João Goetz 370, Jardim Esplanada, 19061-460 Presidete rudente ☎18 3918 5300 **W:** www.ondaviva.com.br **E:** radioondaviva@stetnet.com.br – **SP253)** Rua 7 de Setembro 911, 14240-000 Cajuru **W:** www.miviu.com/eldorado/index.html – **SP254)** Av São Paulo 1220, 13310-000 Cabreúva – **SP255)** Alameda dos Lírios 111, Fazenda Castelo (✉ C.P. 789), 18550-000 Boituva ☎15 3263 1010 **W:** www.radioamerica1480.com.br **E:** radionovamerica@fasternet.com.br – **SP256)** Rua José Revel 477, Centro, 13320-020 Salto – **SP257)** Rua 9 de Julho 666, 16600-000 Pirajuí ☎14 3572 1352 🖹14 3572 1941 **W:** www.pirajuiradioclube.net.br – **SP258)** Rua dos Operários 1441, Vila Guaçu, 19600-000 Rancharia – **SP259)** Rua Coronel João de Carvalho, 39 1° andar - Centro, 13710-000 Tambaú ☎19 3673 1729 **W:** www.radiotambauam.com.br – **SP260)** Av. Professor Jesuíno, 352 - Centro, 17380-000 Brotas ☎14 3653 1306 **W:** www.radiobrotense.com.br – **SP261)** Rua Benjamim Constant 543, 14540-000 Igarapava ☎16 3172 2918 **W:** www.radioshowam.com.br **E:** radioshowam@yahoo.com.br – **SP262)** Rua Inácio Ribeiro 592, 13670-000 Santa Rita do Passa Quatro – **SP263)** Rua Manoel de Arzão 85, Freguesia do Ó, 02730-030 São Paulo ☎11 3935 0108 **W:** www.radio9dejulho.com.br **E:** radio9dejulho@terra.com.br – **SP264)** Rua 6 No 1460, 4° andar-Ed São Lucas, 13500-151 Rio Claro ☎19 3532 5507

W: www.radioexcelsiorrioclaro.com.br **E:** excelsior@radioexcelsiorrio-claro.com.br – **SP265)** Av São Sebastião 162, 3° piso, sala 1, 18150-000 Ibiúna **W:** www.radioexcelsiorad.com.br – **SP266)** Legião da Boa Vontade (LBV), Rua Doraci, 90 – Bom Retiro, 01134-050 Sao Paulo **W:** www.redeboavontade.com.br – **SP267)** 14100-000 Ribeirão Preto – **SP268)** 18730-000 Itaí – **SP269)** Av Carlos Berchieri, 390 - Centro, 14870-010 Jaboticabal ☎16 3203 5355 **W:** www.radioathenas.com.br **E:** adm@radioathenas.com.br – **SP270)** Rua Dos Pereiras, 1197, Bairro Palmeiras, 15290-000 Buritama 18 3691 3279 **W:** www.radioamiga.com.br **E:** torreforteam@uol.com.br – **SP271)** 14740-000 Virdouro – **SP273)** Av Clara Gianotti de Suza 1124, 1 andar, 11900-000 Registro ☎13 3821 1606 **W:** www.radionovaregionalam.com.br **E:** niltonfran-corochaotmail.com – **SP274)** Rdv. Anel Viário Contorno Sul, 99 - City, 14021-800 Ribeirao Preto ☎16 3621 2337 **W:** www.radiobandeirantes.com.br – **SP275)** Rua Honório Mendes de Moraes 23, Esplanada Mendes Moares, 18130-760 São Roque ☎11 4712 496 **W:** www.miliciadaimaculada.org.br – **SP276)** Rua barao do Rio Branco, 18550-000 Boituva – **SP277)** Capão Bonito – **SP280)** Rua Épiró 110, (C.P 18113, 04626-970), Vila Alexandria, 04635-030 São Paulo **W:** www.transmundial.com.br **E:** rtm@transmundial.com.br – **SP281)** Rua Minas Gerais 1225, Liberson, 14620-000 Orlândia **W:** www.lidersom.com.br – **SP282)** 14160-000 Sertaozinho – **SP283)** Praca Osvaldo Cruz, 124 – Conjuto 116, 11900-000 Registro. – **SP284)** Rua Vergueiro, 2045 an4 – Moinho Velho, 04101-000 Sao Paulo ☎11 5571 3014 – **SP285)** Rua Luiza Bechelli 284, Sabaúna, 11740-000 Itanhaém ☎13 3422 1177

TO00) TOCANTINS

TO01) Av Joaquim Aires 2393, 77500-000 Porto Nacional – **TO02)** Praça José Tôrres, 3 – St Central, 77600-000 Paraíso do Tocantins 📖63 3602 1135 – **TO03)** Av Nossa Senhora de Fátima 894, 77900-000 Tocantinópolis – **TO04)** BR-157 Km 1103, Zona Rural, 77804-970 Araguaína -**FM:** 99.7MHz «Araguaia» – **TO05)** Rua Raul do Espírito Santo 1334, 77760-000 Colinas do Tocantins E: elgb@zipmail.com.br – **TO06)**Rua Justianio Borpa, 344 – Setor Santa Filomena, 77650-000 Miracema do Tocantins 📖63 3366 1264 **W:** www.rcmmiracema.com **E:** contato@rcmmiracema.com – **TO07)** Almeda João Pires Querido 07, 77490-000 Cristalândia – **TO08)** Av Bernardo Sayão 2201, 77700-000 Guaraí **W:** www.radioguaraito.com **E:** gersonnk@hotmail.com - **TO09)** 77054-970 Palmas – **TO10)** 77402-970 Gurupi – **TO11)** 77300-000 Dianópolis – **TO12)** C.P 09, 77054-970 Palmas ☎63 3218 8585 **W:** www.arquidiocesedepalmas.org.br/canais/690am/ **E:** radiopalmas@cancaonova.com – **TO13)** 77950-000 Araguatins – **TO14)** 77700-000 Guaraí.– **TO19)** 77770-000 Goiatins – **TO20)** 77700-000 Guaraí

FM stations in principal cities. All MHz.

Belo Horizonte: 88.7 Scala FM – 90.7 Cidade – 91.7 Horizontes de Minas – 94.9 Alvorada – MG06) 95.7 – MG68) 96.5 – MG53) 97.3 Altaneira FM – 98.3MHz 98 (Del Rey) – 99.9MHz Terra – MG35) 100.9–102.1 BH FM – MG06) 103.9–105.1 Antena Um – MG65) 106.1–107.5 FM
Brasília: 89.9 Brasília Super FM – 91.7 Brasília Comunicação – 93.7 Atlântida FM – DF01) 95.3 – DF04) 96.1–96.9 Dest Cámara Deputados 97.7 Manchete FM – 99.3 Antena 9 – 100.1 Transamérica – DF02) 100.9 Cultura FM – 101.7 R Jornal de Brasília – 105.5 FM 105 (Planalto) – 106.3 Sigma Radiodifusão – DF03) 107.1 Atividade.
Curitiba: PR15) 88.5 – PR139) 90.1–91.3 Transamerica Hit – 92.3 Scala FM – 93.9 Capital – 95.1 Transamérica Light – 96.3 Studio 96 – PR06) 97.1 – 97.9 Melodia – 98.7 FM 98 – PR42) 99.5 Paraná FM – 100.3 Transamérica – PR134) 101.5 – 102.3 Caioba – 103.9 Jovem Pan – 105.5 Ouro Verde – 106.5 R Novo Tempo.
Fortaleza: 88.9 FM Jangadeiro – 89.9 Capital – 92.9 Tropical – 93.9 FM 93 – 94.7 Jovem Pan – CE21) 95.5 FM do Povo – 99.1 Cidade FM – CE08) 99.9 Dragão FM – 100.9 Pajeu – 101.7 FM Casablanca – 103.9 FM O Tempo – 105.7 Atlântico Sul FM – 106.7 Hoje – 107.9 Universitária.
Porto Alegre: 89.3 Antena Um – 90.3 Transamérica FM – 92.1 Cidade – 92.9 Alegria FM – 93.7 Metropolitana – 94.3 Atlântida – 94.9 Ipanema – 95.9 Liberdade FM – 96.7 Eldorado – 97.5 Jovem Pan FM – 98.3 Continental – 99.3 Band FM – 99.9 Novo Tempo FM – 100.5 Capital – RS23) 101.3 – RS09) 102.3–104.1 FM 104 (Rede Pampa) – 106.3 Aliança – 107.7 Cultura.
Recife: 88.7 Antena Um – 90.3 J.C. FM – 91.9 Rede Aleluia – 92.7 Transamérica – 94.3 Manchete – 95.9 Cidade – 97.5 Recife FM Stereo – 99.1 Caetes – PE10) 99.9–100.7 Evangélica do Brasil – 103.9 Maranata FM – 106.9 CBN – 107.9 JMB Empreendimentos.
Rio de Janeiro: 88.5 Tribuna – RJ11) 89.3–90.3 M.P.B. FM – RJ25) 98.1 FM 98 – RJ12) 98.9 – RJ16) 99.7 – RJ35) 100.5 FM O Dia – 101.3 Transamérica – 102.1 Jovem Pan – 102.9 Cidade – 91.1 Diário – RJ25) 92.5–93.3 El Shaddai FM – RJ04) 94.1–94.9 Jovem Rio FM – 95.7 Alvorada FM – RJ27) 96.5–97.3 Melodia FM – 103.7 Antena Um – 104.5 Tropical – RJ16) 105.1 105 FM – 106.3 Universidade – 106.7 Catedral – 107.1, 107.9 Universidade.
Salvador: BA57) 90.1 Globo FM – 91.3 Itaparica – 92.3 Salvador FM

– 94.3 Piata – 95.9 FM 96 (Aratu) – 97.5 Itapuã – 99.1 Bandeirantes – 100.1 Transamérica – 101.3 BA32) Metrópole – BA04) 102.3–103.9 104 FM (R FM a Tarde) – 104.7 Manchete – BA55) 107.5.
São Paulo: SP62) 88.1–89.1 FM 89 – SP77) Nova FM 89.7 – SP47) 90.5 CBN – 91.3 Manchete FM – 92.1 Lider FM – 92.5 R.Cançao Nova FM – SP32) 92.9 – 93.7 R. USP – 94.1 Deus e Amor – 94.7 Antena Um FM – 95.3 Nativa FM – 95.7 Scala FM – SP57) 96.1 Band FM – 96.9 Cidade FM – 97.7 FM 97 – SP232) 98.1–98.5 Metropolitana FM – 99.3 99 FM – 100.1 Transamérica – SP16) 100.9–101.7 Alpha FM – 102.1 Kiss FM – 102.5 Imprensa – SP121) 103.3–104.1 Apolo FM – 104.7 Transcontinental – 105.1 105 FM – 105.7 Musical FM – SP41) 106.3 Mix FM – 106.9 Nova Omega FM – 107.3 Brasil 2000 – 107.5 Antena 1 – 107.9 Tropical FM

L.T: UTC + 6h — **Pr.L:** English — **Pop:** variable (US & British military personnel). Original population of c. 3000 was removed to Mauritius — **E.C:** 60Hz, 110/220V — **ITU:** BIO **Diego Garcia ITU:** DGA

ARMED FORCES RADIO AND TELEVISION SERVICE (U.S. Mil.)

✉ Naval Media Center Detachment-Diego Garcia, PSC 466 Box 14, FPO, AP 96595-0014. ☎+246 370 3680/3685 🖷+246 370 3681 **E:** dgar@msc.navy.mil
MW: Island Talk, 1485kHz 0.25kW, (irr.)
FM: Power 99, 99.1MHz 0.25kW, weekdays 0600-1400, rock & roll, live DJ. **Island Variety,** 101.9MHz 200W, mixture of rock, alternative, urban & country. **D.Prgr:** 24h **V.** by letter.

L.T: UTC +8h — **Pop:** 402,000 — **Pr.L:** Malay, English, Chinese, Gurkha — **E.C:** 50Hz, 240V — **ITU:** BRU

AUTHORITY FOR INFO-COMMUNICATIONS TECHNOLOGY INDUSTRY OF BRUNEI DARUSSALAM - AITI (Regulatory Body)

✉ Block B14, Simpang 32-5, Kampung Anggerek Desa, Jalan Berakas BB3713 ☎ +673 2323232 🖷 +673 2382447 **E:** info@aiti.gov.bn **W:** www.aiti.gov.bn
L.P: Chmn: Dato Paduka Hj Alaihuddin bin POKDG Haji Mohd Taha

RADIO TELEVISION BRUNEI - RTB (Gov.)

✉ Jalan Elizabeth II, Bandar Seri Begawan BS8610 ☎ +673 2243111 🖷 +673 2241882 **E:** rtbipro@brunet.bn **W:** www.rtb.gov.bn
L.P: Acting Dir: Haji Idris bin Haji Md. Ali. Acting Deputy Dir: Pg. Hj. Mahari Pg Hj Abd Rajak. Head of Radio Prgrs Div: Hajah Zalinar binti Haji Abdullah. Superintendent of Engineering: Madam Lim Soh Kwang.

FM (MHz)	RN	RPi	RPe	RH	NI	kW
1) Andulau	93.8	96.9	91.0	97.7	94.9	5
2) Bukit Subok	92.3	95.9	91.4	94.1	93.3	5/0.5

DAB: on 225.648MHz
1) Kuala Belait & Tutong areas. 2) Bandar Seri Begawan (BSB) area. **RN** = Rangkaian Nasional FM in Malay: 24h **RPi** = R. Pilihan. English: 0300-0800 (Sat 0300-0700), 1200-0100. Chinese: 0100-0300, 0800-1100. Gurkha: daily 1100-1200, Sat 0700-0800. **RPe** = Rangkaian Pelangi (Pelangi FM, prgrs for young people): 24h Additional FM freqs: 88.5MHz in BSB area, 96.3MHz in Kuala Belait area. **RH** = Rangkaian Harmoni (music sce.): 24h **NI** = Rangkaian Nur Islam (rlg. talk channel): 24h **Ann:** (RN in Malay) "Nasional FM, Radio Brunei"

KRISTAL MEDIA SDN. BHD. (subsidiary of DST Group, DataStream Technology Sdn Bhd) (Comm.)

✉ Unit 1-345, 1st Fl., Gadong Properties Centre, Gadong BE 4119 11 ☎ +673 2456828 🖷 +673 2420682 **W:** www.kristal.fm **E:** kristalfm@dst-group.com

FM (MHz)	KFM	RQ
1) Andulau	98.7	99.7
2) Bukit Subok	90.7	89.1

KFM=Kristal FM. RQ=Recital of Al-Quran. 1), 2) as above
D.Prgr: Kristal FM: 24h in English/Malay. RQ: 24h in Arabic
N: (Kristal FM) rel. RTB (0500, 0930, 1200, 1300, 2300) and BBC WS (0600, 1100)

BRITISH FORCES BROADCASTING SERVICE

✉ BFBS Brunei, BFPO 11 ☎ +673 3223424 🖷 +673 3224113 **E:** bfbsbrunei@bfbs.com **W:** www.bfbs-radio.com
L.P: Station Manager: Mr. Steve Britton **Prgr.:** 24h in English on 101.7MHz 0.25kW, in Nepali (Gurkha) on 89.5MHz 0.25kW. Location: Brunei Garrison HQ, Tuker Lines, Seria, Belait District.

BULGARIA

L.T: UTC +2h (31 Mar-27 Oct: +3h) — **Pop:** 7.4 million — **Pr.L:** Bulgarian, Turkish — **E.C:** 50Hz, 220V — **ITU:** BUL

SAVET ZA ELEKTRONNI MEDII
(Council for Electronic Media)
✉ bul. Shipchenski prohod 69, 1574 Sofiya ☎ +359 2 9708810
🖷+359 2 9733769 **E:** office@cem.bg **W:** www.cem.bg
L.P: Chmn: Georgi Lozanov
NB: The Council is the regulatory authority for broadcasting.

BALGARSKO NATSIONALNO RADIO (BNR) (Pub)
✉ bul. Dragan Tsankov 4, 1040 Sofiya ☎ +359 2 9336330 **E:** bnr@bnr.bg **W:** bnr.bg **L.P:** DG: Valeri Todorov

LW/MW	kHz	kW	Prgr	MW	kHz	kW	Prgr
Sofiya (a)	261	75	1+P	Kardzhali	963	50	1+T
Shumen	747	10	1+T	Dulovo	1161	10	1+T
Blagoevgrad	864	75	R	Targovishte	1161	10	1+T
Razgrad	864	10	1+T	(a) Vakarel			

R= Reg. Service T= Turkish minority Service P= Parliamentary Ch.

FM (MHz)	BNR1	BNR2	kW	FM	BNR1	BNR2	kW
Belogradchik	102.3	00.2	10/G	Pleven	102.7	100.2	1
Berkovitsa	101.4	99.5	10/7	Plovdiv	88.1	91.7	1
Botev vrah	100.9	92.2	10/1	Popovo	-	95.7	1
Burgas	90.2	96.1	1	Razgrad	103.5	99.4	1
Dobrich	104.3	102.3	3/1	Ruse	103.0	95.7	10/1
Dupnitsa	104.1	87.8	1	Silistra	103.3	107.2	1
Dzhebel	102.1	88.4	1	Sliven	87.8	98.7	1
Gabrovo	103.2	95.4	1	Smolyan	101.6	96.0	5/1
G.Delchev	100.3	98.5	6/1	Sofiya	103.0	92.9	10
Ivailovgrad	91.6	96.4	0.1/1	St.Zagora	-	98.3	1
Kardzhali	105.0	99.2	10	Svilengrad	99.7	94.9	3
Karnobat	103.2	95.0	1	Shumen	102.0	100.4	10/1
Kavarna	88.1	90.1	10/1	Targovishte	92.8	95.4	1/0.5
Kresna	88.8	89.7	1	Tran	97.6	90.0	1
Kyustendil	102.1	99.3	10	Tsarevo	102.2	90.8	1
M.Tarnovo	90.2	106.1	1	Varna	100.9	104.8	5/1
Nesebar	102.5	99.3	10	V.Tarnovo (a)	89.1	-	1
Nikopol	96.4	98.2	0.1/1	V.Tarnovo	96.0	99.6	1
Oryahovo	99.8	101.7	1	Yablanitsa	89.2	95.0	1

NB: Sites with only txs below 1kW not listed. (a) Arbanasi
D.Prgr: BNR1 (Horizont): 24h. — **BNR2 (Hristo Botev):** 24h. — **Parlamentaren kanal:** broadcasts from parliament Wed-Fri 0700-1200 on 261 + R. Sofiya FM txs (see below). — **Service for Turkish minority (Bulgaristan Radyosu - Türkçe Yayinlar):** 0600-0700, 1200-1300, 1800-1900, freqs see MW table.

BNR Regional Services
a) R. Blagoevgrad: ul. Ivan Mihaylov 56, 2700 Blagoevgrad. **E:** reklama@radioblg.com. On 864 + 90.9 (Yakoruda 0.1kW), 102.3 (Gotse Delchev 1kW), 103.2 (Blagoevgrad 0.25kW), 105.2 (Kresna 1kW), Kyustendil 106.6 (1kW), Dubnitsa 107.4: 0400-2200. – **b) R. Burgas:** ul. Filip Kutev 2, 8000 Burgas. On 90.2 (M.Tarnovo 1kW), 91.7 (Tsarevo 1kW), 92.5 (Burgas 1kW), 106.0 (Elhovo 0.5kW): 0600-1800. Incl. N. in English & Russian for holidaymakers during summer months. – **c) R. Plovdiv:** ul. Dondukov korsakov 2, 4000 Plovdiv. **E:** director@radioplovdiv.bg. On 88.3 (Panagyurishte 0.25kW), 94.0 (Plovdiv 1kW), 100.1 (Panaporishte 0.5kW, Velingrad 0.25kW), 100.6 (Dospat 0.25kW), 103.1 (Smolyan 1kW): 0600-2200. – **d) R. Sofiya:** bul. Dragan Tsankov 4, 1040 Sofiya. **E:** sofia@bnr.bg. On 90.4 (Svoge 0.3kW), 94.5 (Sofiya 1kW), 100.0 (Samokov 0.2kW), 104.6 (Ihtiman 0.3kW): 24h. Incl. rel. of Parlamentaren kanal. – **e) R. Stara Zagora:** ul. Knyaz Boris 75, 6000 Stara Zagora. **E:** rsz@radio-sz.net. On 88.3 (Stara Zagora 1kW), 90.0 (Kardzali 1kW), 97.2 (Sliven 1kW), 107.8 (Svilengrad 1kW): 0400-2200. – **f) R. Shumen:** ul. Dobro Voynikov 7, 9700 Shumen. **E:** news@radioshumen.net. On 87.6 (Shumen 10kW), 90.3 (Silistra 0.25kW), 97.0 (Razgrad), 104.5 (Isperih): 0400-2200. – **g) R. Varna:** bul. Primorski 12, 9000 Varna. **E:** bnr@radiovarna.com. On 88.5 (Burgas 1kW), 88.7 (Dobrich 1kW), 88.9 (Provadiya 0.1kW), 98.2 (Kavarna 0.5kW), 103.4 (Varna 1kW): 24h. – **h) R. Vidin:** ul. Gradinska 1, 3700 Vidin. **E:** office@radiovidin.com. On 94.4 (Vratsa 0.3kW), 97.1 (Vidin 0.25kW), 97.5 (Belogradchik 1kW), 113.9 (Berkovitsa 1.5kW): 0400-2200.

OTHER STATIONS

FM	MHz	kW	Location	Station
2)	87.6	1	Nesebar	R. N-Joy
1)	87.9	1	Sandanski	Darik R.
7)	89.5	1	Varna	R. Fokus
1)	89.7	2	Samokov	Darik R.
10)	90.2	1	Petrich	R. Bella
5B)	90.9	1	Smolyan	R. Vitosha

FM	MHz	kW	Location	Station
1)	91.0	1	Belogradchik	Darik R.
8)	91.1	1	Burgas	Power FM
1)	91.5	1	Shumen	Darik R.
3A)	91.9	1	Petrich	R. Vega+
1)	93.2	1	Kardzali	Darik R.
6)	94.1	1	Burgas	R. FM+
5A)	94.8	1	Burgas	R. Veselina
9)	95.7	1	Burgas	BG R.
1)	96.7	1	Yablanitsa	Darik R.
5B)	96.7	1	Burgas	R. Vitosha
7)	96.8	1	Smolyan	R. Fokus
1)	99.3	1	Kavarna	Darik R.
4A)	99.9	1	Burgas	R. Veronika
1)	100.6	1	Kyustendil	Darik R.
2)	100.6	1	Primorsko	R. N-Joy
1)	100.7	1	Silistra	Darik R.
1)	101.2	1	Sliven	Darik R.
2)	101.8	1	Burgas	R. N-Joy
3B)	103.4	1	Sandanski	R. Ultra
1)	104.0	1	Svilengrad	Darik R.
1)	104.5	1	Burgas	Darik R.
1)	105.0	2	Sofiya	Darik R.
1)	105.4	1.5	Plovdiv	Darik R.
1)	106.2	1	Goce Delchev	Darik R.
1)	106.6	1	V.Tarnovo	Darik R.
1)	106.8	1	Varna	Darik R.
1)	107.0	1	Smolyan	Darik R.
1)	107.7	1	Dobrich	Darik R.
7)	107.7	1	Vidin	R. Fokus

NB: Txs below 1kW not listed.
Addresses & other information:
1) bul. Knyaz A.Dondukov 82, 1504 Sofiya. **E:** reklama@darik.net – **2)** ul. Panayot Volov 3, 1504 Sofiya. **E:** jazzfm@netbg.com – **3A,B)** ul. Todor Aleksandrov 3, 2700 Blagoevgrad. **E:** 3A) vega_plus@abv.bg, 3B) radio_ultra@abv.bg – **4A,B)** bul. Tsar Boris III 23, 1612 Burgas. **E:** 4A) reklama@radioveronika.bg, 4B) reklama@nrj.bg – **5A,B)** ul. Srebarna 21, 1407 Sofiya. **E:** office@sbsbroadcasting.bg – **6)** bul. Erusalim 51, Zhilishen Kompleks Mladost 1, 1784 Sofiya. **E:** fmplus@fmplus.net – **7)** ul. Filip Stanislavov 6, 1505 Sofiya. **E:** focus@focus-news.net – **8)** ul. A.Bogoridi 16, 8000 Burgas. **E:** office@powerfm.bg – **9)** ul. Sofiyski geroy 3a, 1612 Sofiya. **E:** office@bgradio.net – **10)** pl. Makedoniya10, 2850 Petrich. **E:** office@radiobella.com.

Radio via DTT: see TV section

BURKINA FASO

L.T: UTC — **Pop:** 15 million — **Pr.L:** French + 16 ethnic — **E.C:** 50Hz, 220V — **ITU:** BFA

CONSEIL SUPÉRIEUR DE LA COMMUNICATION (CSC)
✉ 01 BP 6437, Ouagadougou +226 50301124 🖷 +226 50301133 **W:** csi.bf **E:** infos@csc.bf **L.P:** Dir: Luc Adolphe Diao.

RADIODIFFUSION TÉLÉVISION DU BURKINA (Gov.)
✉ BP 7029, Ouagadougou 01 ☎+226 50324302 🖷 +226 50310441 **W:** rtb.bf **E:** radio@rtb.bf **L.P:** MD: Marcel Toe. Head of Tr. Centre: Marcel Teho. Prgr.Dir: Pascal Goba.
FM: 88.5/92.0/99.9MHz 0.02kW
D.Prgr in French/Ethnic: 24h. **N.** in French: 0630MF, 1000SS + Thurs, 1245 (regional), 1300, 1900, 2200. **N. in English:** W1920 (approx). **Ann:** "RTV Burkina", "RTB". **IS:** Balafon.
Canal Arc-en-Ciel, 03 BP 7045, Ouagadougou. **L.P:** Alphousseini Bassolet. FM: Ouagadougou 96.6MHz, Bobo-Dioulasso 89.8MHz.
REGIONAL STATIONS
Radio Bobo, BP 392, Bobo-Dioulasso. **FM:** 92.0MHz 0.02kW. **D.Prgr:** MF 0600-0800, 1200-1400, 1600-2400, SS 0800-2400 – **R. Gaoua**, Gaoua. **FM:** 90.1MHz – **R. Rurale:** FM txs in Diapaga, Djibasso, Gassan, Kongoussi, Orodara & Poura.

Other stations (all MHz):
Al Houda FM, Ouagadougou: 98.5 – **Bankuy FM**, Dédougou: 107.7 – **R. Ahmadiya**, Dori: 104.6 – **R. de l'Alliance Chrétienne**, Bobo-Dioulasso: 95.9 – **R. Balafon**, Bobo-Dioulasso: 102.7 – **R. Buayaba**, Diapaga 96.2MHz – **R. FM Boulgou**, Garango: 101.1 – **R. Cascade**, Banfora: 98 – **R. Catholique Teriya**, Banfora 94.7 – **R. Djawoampo**, Bogandé 98.1 – **R. Djongo**, Pô: 106.4 – **Echo des Cotonniers**, Solenzo: 95.1 – **R. Djibasso**: 94.6 – **R. Énergie:** Kaya 92.2, Yako 94.9, Fada N'Gourma 98.8 – **R. de l'Espoir**, Réo: 102.8 – **R. Évangile Développement:** Ouagadougou 93.4, Houndé 95.5, Léo 97.8, Koudougou 101.0, Ouahigouya 104.0, Yako 105.3, Bobo-Dioulasso 106.3. W: red-burkina.org – **R. Evangile du Sud-Ouest**, Gaoua:

99.7 – **R. Eveil**, Bogandé 101.0 – **R. Fréquence Espoir**: Dédougou 96.8 1kW, Tougan 101.4 0.1kW – **R. Frontière**, Tenkodogo: 97.6 – **R. Gambidi**, Ouagadougou: 97.7 – **R. Gassan**: 105.5 – **R. Gayeri**: 91.8 – **R. Goulou**, Po 99.5 – **R. du Grand Nord**, Dori: 97.5 – **Horizon FM**: Tenkodogo 97.6, Banfora 98, Koudougou 98.7, Ouayigouya 100.4, Dédougou 102.7, Ouagadougou 104.4, Dori 104.6 – **R. Kadoadb**, Ziniare: 107.7 – **R. Kantigya**, Nouna 88.8 – **R. Kongoussi**: 93.2 – **R. Kouritta**, Koupela: 93.7 – **R. La Voix des Bales**, Boromo 103.6 – **R. La Voix du Soum**, Djibo 92.1 – **R. Lotamu**, Solenzo 101.9 – **R. LCD,** Djibo 98.6 – **R. Loudon**, Sapouy 104.9 – **R. Lumière**: Ouagadougou: 98.1 – **R. Manegda**, Kaya: 99.4 – **R. Maria**: Ouagadougou 91.6 1kW, Kaya 99.4, Koupêla 96.9 1kW. W: www.radiomaria.org – **Media Star**, Bobo-Dioulasso: 96.7 – **R. Munyu FM**, Banfora: 94.7 – **R. Naboswende**, Pouytenga: 103.7 – **R. Natigmeb Zanga**, Yako: 98.2 – **R. Nemaro**, Cassou 94.2 – **R. Nerwaya**, Kongoussi 99.7 – **R. Notre Dame de la Réconciliation** Koudougou 105.8 – **R. Nostalgie,** Ouagadougou, 94.4 – **R. Notre Dame:** Kaya 102.9, Kouhougou 105.8, Ouahigouya 102.6 – **R. Ouaga FM**, Ouagadougou: 105.2 – **R. Paglayiri**, Zabré 94.3 – **R. Palabre**, B.P. 196, Kougougou: 92.2 – **R. Pog-Neere**, Pouytenga 100.2MHz – **R. Poura**: 98.2 – **R. Pulsar**, Ouagadougou: 94.8 0.4kW – **R. Salaki,** Dedougou 101.1 – **R. Salankoloto**, Ouagadougou: 97.3 – **R. Sanmentenga**, Kaya: 96.1 – **R. Savane**, Ouagadougou: 103.4 – **R. Tin-Taani**, Kantchari 100.0 – **La Voix du Sud-Ouest**, Diébougou: 101.5 – **R. Taanba**, Fada N'Gourma: 98.8 1kW – **R. Tapao**, Diapaga: 95.8 – **R. Unitas**, Diébougou: 94.7 – **R. Vive le Paysan**, Saponé: 107.0 – **R. la Voix du Passoré**, Yako: 105.3 – **R. la Voix du Paysan**, Ouahigouya: 97.0 – **R. La Voix du Verger**, Orodara: 91.2 – **R. Zoodo**, Ouahigouya: 100.4.
Africa No. 1: Ouagadougou 90.3 (see main entry under Gabon).
BBC African Sce: Ouagadougou 99.2 4kW.
RFI Afrique: Banfora 91.5, Koudougou 93.0, Ouagadougou 94.0, Ouahigouya 94.3, Bobo-Dioulasso 99.4.
Voice of America: Ouagadougou 102.4

BURUNDI

L.T: UTC +2h — **Pop:** 9 million — **Pr.L:** Kirundi, Swahili, French, English — **E.C:** 50Hz, 220V — **ITU:** BDI

CONSEIL NATIONAL DE LA COMMUNICATION(CNC)
+257 22223742 📠 +257 22226547 **W:** www.burundi.gov.bi
L.P: Chairman: Vestine Nahimana.

RADIO-TÉLÉVISION NATIONALE DU BURUNDI (RTNB, Gov.)
📧 B.P. 1900, Bujumbura ☎ +257 22223742 📠 +257 22226547
W: rtnb.bi **E:** rtnb@cbinf.com **LP:** D.G.: Innocent Muhozi

FM(MHz)	RTNB1	RTNB2	FM(MHz)	RTNB1	RTNB2
Birime	94.2	98.9	Kaberenge	94.7	98.0
Bujumbura	102.9	92.9	Manga	95.6	98.9
Inanzerwe	88.4	91.4	Mutumba	88.8	91.9

D.Prgr: W 0300-0700 & 0900-2100, Sun 0300-2100. (RTNB1 in Kirundi, RTNB2 in French/Swahili/English). **N.** in French: 0530, 1200, 1500, 1900. **N.** in Swahili: 0630, 1245, 1800. **N.** in Kirundi: 0500, 0700, 1130, 1800, 2000. **N.** in English: 0445, 1230, 1600, 1845.
Ann: "Ici Bujumbura, Radio-Télévision Nationale du Burundi". **IS:** Drums.

Other stations (FM MHz):
Bonesha FM: Manga 87.7 20kW Bujumbura: 96.8, Jenda 102.4 – **R. CCIB FM,** Bujumbura: 99.4, nationwide 102.4 – **R. Culture**, Bujumbura: 88.2/99.9 – **R. Isanganiro:** Bujumbura 89.7, Bururi 93.3/95.1, Kirundo 90.6, Ruyigi 90.7, Manga 101.0. **W:** www.web-africa.org/isanganiro – **R. Ivyizigiro**, Bujumbura: 90.9/104.8 – **R. Public Africaine**, Bujumbura: 91.5 – **R. Renaissance**, Bujumbura 101.4 – **R. Scolaire Nderagakura**, Bujumbura 87.9 – **Rema FM**, Bujumbura: 88.6/103.6/107.5. **W:** remafm.com.
RFI Afrique: Manga 103.7 in F/E/Swahili.
BBC African Sce: Bujumbura 90.2, Manga 105.6

CAMBODIA

L.T: UTC +7h — **Pop:** 15 million — **Pr.L:** Khmer (Cambodian) — **E.C:** 50Hz, 230V — **ITU:** CBG

NATIONAL RADIO OF KAMPUCHEA (RNK)
📧 No 6 Street 19 (Corner Street 102), Sangkat Wat Phnom, Khan Daun Penh, Phnom Penh 12202 ☎ +855 23 725522 📠 +855 23 427319
W: www.rnk.gov.kh
L.P: Dir. Gen: HE Tan Yan. Dir. Radio Prg Dept: Mr Bou Vannarith. Dir. Radio Tech Dept: Oum Phin. Dep. Dir. Gen, AM 918: Som Sarun. Dep. Dir. Gen. FM 96: Touch Sareth

MW	kHz	kW
Phnom Penh [a]	918	200

[a] Location: Steung Meanchey (G.C: 11N32 104E53)
National sce AM 918: 2230v-1600 on 918kHz.
FM-96 (comm.): 📧 Steung Meanchey, Phnom Penh 12352 **FM:** 96.0MHz 10kW
Wat Phnom FM: Phnom Penh 105.75MHz 10kW. Prgrs for young people & relays of 918kHz
Cambodia-China Friendship Radio (joint service with China Radio International): 2300-1700 in Chaozhou, English, Khmer and Mandarin. **FM:** Phnom Penh 96.5MHz 10kW.
Provincial sces: Battambang 92.7MHz 2kW, Kampot 99.7MHz 2kW, Komphong Thom 98.3MHz, Kratie 98.5MHz 2kW, Pailin 90.5MHz 2kW, Pursat 98.5MHz 2kW, Siem Reap 102.9MHz, Sihanoukville 105.75MHz 2kW, Svay Rieng 98.7MHz, Takeo 98.5MHz 2kW. **Ann:** (Khmer): "Thini Sathani Vithayu Cheat Kampuchea"

Other stations

FM	Location	MHz	kW	Station
1)	Battambang	87.5		VO Koh Santepheap
2)	Phnom Penh	87.5		Daun Penh EFM
1)	Phnom Penh	87.75		VO Koh Santepheap
3)	Phnom Penh	88.0	10	Sweet FM (Chinese/Khmer)
4)	Battambang	88.0		Vayo FM
5)	Phnom Penh	88.25		R. Meanchey FM
6)	Siem Reap	88.25	2	R. Mahanakor Khemara
7)	Kompong Thom	88.5	1	Steung Sen R.
8)	Battambang	88.5		Kolyanmet R.
9)	Phnom Penh	89.5	10	VO New Life R. (Samlang Chivit Thmey)
10)	Ratanakiri	89.5	2	Provincial R.
11)	Siem Reap	89.5		R. Krong Angkor
12)	Phnom Penh	90.0	10	R. Khlaing Meoung (FM90)
13)	Battambang	90.25	1	R. Khlaing Meoung
14)	Phnom Penh	90.5	5	Ta Phrom Radio
15)	Battambang	91.0	5	R. FM Khemara
16)	Kampot	91.0	2	R. Bayon FM
16)	Kompong Thom	91.0	2	R. Bayon FM
17)	Phnom Penh	91.0		R. New Phnom Penh (Phnom Penh Thmey)
16)	Takhao	91.0		R. Bayon FM
18)	Phnom Penh	91.25		Sleuk Mas FM
10)	Oddar Meanchey	91.5	2	Provincial R.
16)	Pursat	91.5	2	R. Bayon FM
19)	Phnom Penh	92.0	10	R. France Int.
16)	Sihanoukville	92.0	3	R. Bayon FM
19)	Siem Reap	92.0	0.5	R. France Int.
19)	Stung Treng	92.0	2	R. France Int.
10)	Kompong Cham	92.5	2	Provincial R. (Sweet FM)
16)	Siem Reap	93.0	10	R. Bayon FM 93
10)	Kampot	93.25	1	Provincial R. (Sweet FM)
20)	Phnom Penh	93.5	10	FM 93.5 (Metropolitan FM)
21)	Svay Rieng	93.75	1	R. WMC
22)	Phnom Penh	93.75		DAP Radio (Doem Ampil)
16)	Banteay Meanchey	94.0	4	R. Bayon FM
19)	Battambang	94.5	0.25	R. France Int.
19)	Kompong Cham	94.5	0.25	R. France Int.
23)	Phnom Penh	94.5		ABC Traffic Radio
19)	Sihanoukville	94.5	0.5	R. France Int.
16)	Phnom Penh	95.0	10	R. Bayon FM
24)	Siem Reap	95.5	10	R. Angkor Ratha (R. Sarika Angkor)
16)	Svay Rieng	95.5	2	R. Bayon FM
25)	Phnom Penh	95.7	5	Reasmey Hang Meas FM
10)	Sisopohon	96.5	10	Banteay Meanchey Provincial R.
26)	Phnom Penh	97.0	10	R Apsara
27)	Pailin	97.5		R O Torng Pailin
3)	Phnom Penh	97.5	10	Love FM (English/Khmer)
3)	Siem Reap	97.75	1	Love FM (English/Khmer)
28)	Phnom Penh	98.0	10	FM98 (Armed Forces R.)
28)	Siem Reap	98.0	5	FM98 (Armed Forces R.)
29)	Phnom Penh	98.25		Farmers R. (Kasekor FM)
30)	Poipet	98.3		FM98.3
31)	Phnom Penh	98.5		J R.
28)	Sihanoukville	98.5	1	FM98.5 (Armed Forces R.)
32)	Phnom Penh	99.0	10	FM99
33)	Sisophon	99.0	2	Meanchey FM
10)	Preah Vihear	99.0	5	Provincial R. (Sweet FM)
17)	Kompong Chnang	99.25	10	R. New Phnom Penh (Phnom Penh Thmey)
34)	Siem Reap	99.25	1	BBC World Service (E.): 24h
35)	Koh Kong	99.5	1	FM 99.5
36)	Sisophon	99.5	1	My FM
37)	Phnom Penh	99.5	10	KRUSA FM (FEBC/Family FM)
38)	Battambang	100.0		VO Dombang Kronhoung (VOD FM)

FM	Location	MHz	kW	Station
34)	Phnom Penh	100.0	1	BBC World Service (E.): 24h
10)	Kompong Cham	100.5	1	FM 100.5
10)	Pursat	100.5	1	Provincial R. (Sweet FM)
10)	Siem Reap	100.5	1	Provincial R. (Sweet FM)
10)	Sihanoukville	100.5	1	Provincial R. (Sweet FM)
10)	Stung Treng	100.5	1	Provincial R. (Sweet FM)
39)	Phnom Penh	100.7		Cool FM
40)	Phnom Penh	101.0		Nokorwat FM
41)	Phnom Penh	101.3		Our Motherland R. (Meatophum Yoeng)
28)	Battambang	101.5	1	FM 101.5 (Armed Forces R.)
42)	Phnom Penh	101.5	1	R. Australia (E.): 24h
42)	Siem Reap	101.5	0.5	R. Australia (E.): 24h
42)	Sihanoukville	101.5		R. Australia (E.): 24h
21)	Phnom Penh	102.0	10	R. WMC
43)	Phnom Penh	102.25	5	Town FM
44)	Battambang	102.3		Star FM
45)	Phnom Penh	102.5	2	R. Tonle FM (River FM)
46)	Siem Reap	102.5	1	Sathani Vithayu Krom Siem Reap (Siem Reap City R. Stn)
4)	Sihanoukville	102.5		Vayo FM
3)	Phnom Penh	103.0	10	Municipality R. (Khmer)
10)	Battambang	103.25	1	Provincial R. (Sweet FM)
10)	Bokor Hill	103.5	1	Sweet FM (rel. Kampot)
47)	Sisophon	103.5	2.5	Sweet FM
48)	Siem Reap	103.7		Star FM
10)	Svay Rieng	103.75	10	Provincial R. (Sweet FM)
49)	Phnom Penh	104.0	10	R. Sovann Phum
21)	Kompong Thom	104.3	1	R. WMC
25)	Phnom Penh	104.5	5	R. Hang Meas FM
50)	Phnom Penh	105.0	10	Sombok Ka Mum (R. Beehive)
51)	Phnom Penh	105.25		VOY FM
4)	Phnom Penh	105.5		Vayo FM
52)	Siem Reap	105.5		R. Mongkul Sovann
53)	Phnom Penh	106.0	10	South East Asia FM
54)	Battambang	106.0		Sovann Angkor FM
55)	Siem Reap	106.25	5	R. For Buddhism
56)	Phnom Penh	106.5	10	R. Sarika FM (V of Democracy)
57)	Sisophon	106.5	1	U FM
58)	Phnom Penh	106.75		Our R.
59)	Phnom Penh	107.0	10	Khmer FM (Smile R.)
10)	Kompong Thom	107.25	1	Provincial R.
60)	Phnom Penh	107.5	5	ABC Cambodia R.
61)	Kompong Cham	107.75		Mohasal FM
62)	Phnom Penh	108.0	10	R. Solida (Soft FM)

Addresses and other information
1) No 240, Street 271, Phnom Penh 12351 – **2)** No 25B, Street 320, Phnom Penh 12304 – **3)** No 02, Confédération de la Russie, Sangkat Monorom, Khann 7 Makara, Phnom Penh. Prgr in Cham: 1300-1400 on 103.0MHz – **4)** No 13B Street 70, Phnom Penh **W:** www.vayofm.com – **5)** Thmey Village, Chamkardong, Phnom Penh 12410 – **6)** National Rd 6, Borey Seang Nam, Khnar Thmey Village, Siem Reap – **7)** Slaket Village, Prey Tahou Commune, Steung Sen District, Kompong Thom – **8)** Phum Wattamem, Khum O Dombong I, Sangke District, Battambang Province – **9)** PO Box 1426 Phnom Penh. Operated by Final Frontiers Foundation – **10)** Provincial R. Stations (Gov.): TV3 Relay Station, Battambang; Phum Andong Chen, Khum Ochar, Battambang; Phum Sovansako, Kompong Kandal, Kampot; Khum Kantout, Chamksan, Preah Vihear; Phum Mondol 2, Khum Svay Dangkhum, Siem Reap; Phum 1, Sangkat 3, Khan Mittapheap, Sihanoukville; Phum Svay Hill, Kou Than Village, O Ampil Commune, Sispohon, Banteay Meanchey Province; Phum Mepleang, Svay Rieng. NB: Most provincial stns carry local Sweet FM prgrs– **11)** Chong Kaosou Village, Siem Reap – **12)** Chamkadong, Phnom Penh 12401 –**14)** No 27B Street 472, Phnom Penh 12312. Owned by Funcinpec Party – **15)** Prek Mohatep Village, Sangkat Svay Por, Battambang – **16)** HQ: 3 Street 466, Phnom Penh 12310; Phnom Penh stn: 22 Street 106, Toul Krasang, Takhmao, Kandal; Siem Reap: Kasekam Village, Sro Nge, Siem Reap; reg. stns relay 95.0MHz **W:** www.bayontv.com.kh – **17)** 99.25MHz relays Phnom Penh 91.0MHz. English: Sat/Sun 0900-1100 – **18)** No. 227C, Trasak Paem (Street 63), Phnom Penh 12302 – **19)** Centre Culturel Français, No 218, Keo Chea (Street 184), Phnom Penh. D.Prgr: 24h in French exc.1200-1300 in Khmer – **20)** Cheung Ek Village, Phnom Penh 12415 – **21)** Women's Media Center of Cambodia, 30 Street 488, Sangkat Phsar Demthkov, Khan Chamcar Morn, Phnom Penh 12307. 94.5 & 104.3MHz mostly rel. Phom Penh 102.2MHz, with limited local prgrs at times. **W:** www.wmc.org.kh – **23)** No A73 Street 271, Phnom Penh 12306 **24)** Group 10, Chong Kaosou Village, Siem Reap – **25)** No. 132-134Eo, Okhna Tep Phan (Street 182), Sangkat Boeung Prolit, Khan 7 Makara, Phnom Penh 12258 – **26)** No 69, Street No 57 (Corner Street No 370), Phnom Penh

– **28)** Street 169, Borei Keila, Phnom Penh 12253. – Module 3 Slorkram Village, Siem Reap. Owned by the Royal Cambodian Armed Forces, operated by MICA Media Co Ltd, part of Kantana Group (Bangkok, Thailand). Sts carry prgrs of Virgin Hitz R. – **29)** Chamkar Dong (Street 217), Thmey Village, Phnom Penh 12401 – **30)** Km 4, Poipet, Banteay Meanchey Province – **31)** No 7, Monireth (Street 217), Phnom Penh 12352 – **32)** No 69, Street No 57 (Corner Street No 370), Phnom Penh – **33)** Sangkat O'Ambel, Sispohon – **36)** Kampong Svay Village, Sisophon, Banteay Meanchey Province – **37)** No 8D Street 355, Phnom Penh 12105 – **38)** Wat Leap, Wat Leap Village, Battambang **W:** www. vodfm.com – **39)** Nr Cambodian Red Cross, Street 271, Phnom Penh 12401 – **39)** No. 147-153, Preah Monivong (Street 93), corner of Kampuchea Krom (Street 128), BS Office Center Phnom Penh 12208 – **41)** Preah Monivong (corner Kampuchea Krom), Phnom Penh– **42)** No 28 Street 80, Corner of Street 75, VBNK 1st Floor, Phnom Penh – **43)** No 44A, Street 592, Phnom Penh 12152 – **44)** Romchek IV Village, Sangkat Ratana, Battambang – **45)** as stn 39) – **46)** No. 627, Street 99, Sala Kanseng Village, Sangkat Svay Dangkum, Siem Reap – **47)** West of Sispohon Market, Village 3, Sangkat Preah Ponlea, Sisophon, Banteay Meanchey Province – **48)** Chong Kaosou Village, Siem Reap, affiliated with stn 44) – **49)** Cheung Ek, Phnom Penh – **50)** No 33, Street 26BT, Thnort Chrum Village, Sangkat Boeng Thumpon, Phnom Penh 12351 **W:** www.sbk.com.kh – **51)** Thmey Village, Sangkat Dangkor, Phnom Penh 12401 – **53)** No 13B, Okhna Khleang Moeng (Street No 70), Phnom Penh 12201– **52)** National Highway 6, Ta Tean Village, Sala Kamkreuk, Siem Reap – **53)** Sleng Roleung Village, Khan Sen Sok, Phnom Penh – **54)** Romchek IV Village, Sangkat Ratana, Battambang **W:** www. sovannangkorfm106.com – **55)** Wat Bo, Sangkat Sala Kamroek, Siem Reap – **56)** No 14A, Street 392, Boeung Keng Kang 1, Khan Chamkarmorn, Phnom Penh 12302 (operated by Cambodian Center for Independent Media, CCIM) – **57)** No 208, Street 358, Tuol Svay Prey, Phnom Penh 12308 – **58)** No 18, Rd. 562, Phnom Penh 12151 – **59)** 50A Russian Boulevard, Sangkat Tektla, Khan Rusey Keo, Phnom Penh **W:** www.abccambodia.com – **60)** No 73 Street 271, Phnom Penh 12160 – **61)** Village 6, Sangkat Veal Vong, Kompong Cham – **62)** 375 Thmey Village, Phnom Penh 12401.

CAMEROON

L.T: UTC +1h — **Pop:** 19 million — **Pr.L:** French, English, ethnic — **E.C:** 50Hz, 220V — **ITU:** CME

NATIONAL COMMUNICATIONS COUNCIL (CNC)
✉ Yaoundé. **LP:** Prof. Laurent Charles Boyomo.

CAMEROON RADIO TELEVISION (CRTV, Gov.)
✉ B.P. 1634, Yaoundé +237 22214077 ▤ +237 22204340 **W:** www.crtv.cm **E:** infos@crtv.cm **LP:** DG: Amadou Vamoulke. Deputy DG: Francis Wete. Dir of Inf. Radio: Michel Ndjock Abanda.

FM (MHz):
CRTV R. Nationale: Yaoundé 88.8 10kW, Douala 89.2 10kW, Bertoua 89.8 10kW, Bafoussam 91.1 10kW, Ngaoundéré 92.5. Buéa 98.6.
Regional stations:
CRTV Yaoundé FM: 94.0, **CRTV Centre,** Yaoundé: 101.9 – **CRTV Littoral,** B.P. 986, Douala: 91.3, **Suelaba FM:** 104.9 10kW – **CRTV Sud-Ouest,** Buea 94.5, **CRTV Mont Cameroun,** Buea 98.0 – **CRTV Nord,** B.P. 103, Garoua: 101.2 10kW – **CRTV Est,** B.P. 230, Bertoua: 92.9 10kW– **CRTV Ouest,** B.P. 970, Bafoussam: 93.5 10kW, Pouala FM: 104.5 – **CRTV Nord-Ouest,** B.P. 4049, Bamenda: 93.5 10kW – **CRTV Sud,** Ebolowa 97.6 10kW, **Kaze FM** 91.1 – **CRTV Adamaoua,** Ngaoundéré: 102.5 10kW – **CRTV Extrême-Nord,** Maroua 94.8, Kousseri 95.5.

Other FM stations (MHz):
Dynamic FM, Douala: 103.9 – **Magic FM,** Yaoundé: 100.1 – **R. Bon Berger,** Kaélé 99.0 – **R. Bonne Nouvelle:** Yaoundé 97.7, Ngaoundéré 98.5, Douala 102.5, Ebolowa 102.7 – **R. Campus,** Ngaoundéré: 99.0 – **R. Environnement,** Yaoundé: 107.7 – **R. Equinoxe,** Douala: 93 W: www.lanouvelleexpression.net – **R. Le Lauréat,** Douala: 90.5 – **R. Lumière,** Yaoundé: 91.9 – **R. Noor,** Ngaoundéré: 106.1 – **R. Nostalgie,** Douala: 96 – **R. Reine:** Yaoundé 103.7 1kW, Buéa 97.7 1kW – **R. Salaaman,** Garoua: 89.0 – **R. Sawtu Linjiila,** Ngaoundéré: 95.7 1kW (SW relays see Target Broadcasts Section) – **R. Siantou,** Yaoundé: 90.5 – **R. Venus,** Yaoundé: 95.4 – **R. Veritas,** Douala: 96.8 – **R. Vie Nouvelle,** Douala: 100.5 – **Real Time Music,** Douala: 103.5, Yaoundé 106.0 – **Sky One R,** Yaoundé: 104.5, Douala 100.1. W: www.skyonecameroun.com– **Sweet FM,** Douala: 88.7 – **TBC FM,** Yaoundé: 93.0.

BBC African Sce: Garoua 94.4, Bamenda 95.7, Yaoundé 98.4, Douala 101.3.
RFI Afrique: Yaoundé 105.5, Douala 97.8, Bafoussam 101.1.
Africa No 1: Douala 102, Yaoundé 106.7 (see Gabon)

CANADA

L.T: See World Time Table (DST where applicable 10 Mar-3 Nov) — **Pop:** 33 million — **Pr.L:** English, French — **E.C:** 60Hz, 120V — **ITU:** CAN

CANADIAN RADIO-TELEVISION AND TELECOMMUNICATIONS COMMISSION - CRTC

Ottawa, ON K1A 0N2 ☎+1 819 997 0313 +1 819 994 0218 **W:** crtc.gc.ca **L.P:** Chair: Jean-Pierre Blais. Vice Chair: Broadcasting: Tom Pentefountas

The CRTC is an independent public organization that regulates and supervises Canadian broadcasting and telecommunications systems.

Provinces & Terrritories: AB=Alberta, BC=British Columbia, MB=Manitoba, NB=New Brunswick, NL=Newfoundland & Labrador, NS=Nova Scotia, NT=North West Territories, NU=Nunavut, ON=Ontario, PE=Prince Edward Island, QC=Québec, SK=Saskatchewan, YT=Yukon

CBC/RADIO-CANADA (Pub)

Box 3220 Stn C, Ottawa ON K1Y 1E4 ☎+1 613 288 6033 **W:** cbc.radio-canada.ca **L.P:** Chair, Board of Dir: Rémi Racine. Pres. and CEO: Hubert T. Lacroix. VP Brand, Comm. and Corp. Affairs: William B. Chambers. VP and CFO: Suzanne Morris. VP Real Estate, Legal Sces. and General Counsel: Maryse Bertrand. Intern VP, People and Culture: Roula Zaarour. VP and Chief Regulatory Officer: Steven Guiton. Sen. Dir. Corp. Comm: Martine Ménard.
English Networks: Box 500 Stn A, Toronto ON M5W 1E6 **W:** cbc.ca **L.P:** Exec. VP, English Sces: Kirstine Stewart. GM and Ed. in Chief, CBC News, English Sces: Jennifer McGuire. Exec. Dir. Marketing Comms, English Sces: Bridget Hoffer
French Networks: Box 6000, Montréal PQ H3C 3A8 +1 514 597 6000 **W:** radio-canada.ca **L.P:** Exec. VP, French Sces: Louis Lalande. Exec. Dir. News and Current Affairs, French Sces: Michel Cormier. Exec. Dir. Comm. and Branding: Guylaine Bergeron

English Radio

CBC Radio One: c=moving to FM *=also on SW +=F.Pl.

MW	Location	Prov.	kHz	kW	N	Call
1)	Grand Falls	NL	540	10		CBT
2)	Watrous	SK	540	50		CBK
15)	St. Anthony	NL	600	10		CBNA
4)	St. John's	NL	640	10		CBN
5)	Vancouver	BC	690	50	*	CBU
7)	Edmonton	AB	740	50		CBX
24)	Bonavista Bay	NL	750	10		CBGY
10)	Prince Rupert	BC	860	10/2.5		CFPR
11)	Inuvik	NT	860	1		CHAK
15)	Winnipeg	MB	990	50/46		CBW
16)	Corner Brook	NL	990	10		CBY
17)	Calgary	AB	1010	50		CBR
19)	Sydney	NS	1140	10		CBI
21)	Iqaluit	NU	1230	1		CFFB
11)	Yellowknife	NT	1340	2.5		CFYK
24)	Gander	NL	1400	4		CBG

SW	Location	Prov.	kHz	kW	Call	Relays
5)	Vancouver	BC	6160	0.5	CKZU	CBU
22)	St. John's	NL	6160	1	CKZN	CFGB-FM

FM	Location	Prov.	MHz	kW	N	Call
17)	Calgary	AB	99.1	7		CBR-1-FM
7)	Edmonton	AB	93.9	3.9		CBX-2-FM
17)	Lethbridge	AB	100.1	100		CBRL-FM
28}	Kamloops	BC	94.1	4.8		CBYK-FM
30)	Kelowna	BC	88.9	5.2		CBTK-FM
33)	Prince George	BC	91.5	100		CBYG-FM
5)	Vancouver	BC	88.1	97.6		CBU-2-FM
31)	Victoria	BC	90.5	6.3		CBCV-FM
16)	Brandon	MB	97.9	90		CBWV-FM
16)	Winnipeg	MB	89.3	2.8		CBW-1-FM
18)	Allardville	NB	97.9	50		CBAA-FM
14)	Fredericton	NB	99.5	3.2		CBZF-FM
18)	Moncton	NB	106.1	69.5		CBAM-FM
32)	St. John	NB	91.3	80		CBD-FM
22)	Goose Bay	NL	89.5	4.5	*	CFGB-FM
9)	Halifax	NS	90.5	91		CBHA-FM
9)	Middleton	NS	106.5	93.4		CBHM-FM
9)	Mulgrave	NS	106.7	93.4		CBHB-FM
6)	Huntsville	ON	94.3	70		CBLU-FM
6)	Kingston	ON	107.5	100		CBCK-FM
6)	Kitchener/Waterloo	ON	89.1	13.5		CBLA-FM-2
25)	Leamington	ON	91.9	10.5		CBEW-FM-1
6)	London	ON	93.5	100		CBCL-FM
12)	Ottawa	ON	91.5	84		CBO-FM

FM	Location	Prov.	MHz	kW	N	Call
6)	Peterborough	ON	98.7	19.2		CBCP-FM
20)	Sudbury	ON	99.9	50		CBCS-FM
8)	Thunder Bay	ON	88.3	23.7		CBQT-FM
6)	Toronto	ON	99.1	98		CBLA-FM
25)	Windsor	ON	97.5	19		CBEW-FM
23)	Charlottetown	PE	96.1	100		CBCT-FM
29)	Chicoutimi	QC	102.7	30		CBJE-FM
13)	Montréal	QC	88.5	25		CBME-FM
13)	Québec	QC	104.7	65.8		CBVE-FM
35)	Sept îles	QC	96.9	15		CBSE-FM
13)	Sherbrooke	QC	91.7	25		CBMB-FM
2)	Regina	SK	102.5	2.7		CBKR-FM
2)	Saskatoon	SK	94.1	4.1		CBK-1-FM
3)	Whitehorse	YT	94.5	6.3		CFWH-FM

+approx 400 relay txs **NB:** calls not announced

CBC Radio Two:

FM	Location	Prov.	MHz	kW	Call
17)	Calgary	AB	102.1	100	CBR-FM
7)	Edmonton	AB	90.9	100	CBX-FM
17)	Lethbridge	AB	91.7	100	CBBC-FM
5)	Kamloops	BC	105.3	4.8	CBU-FM-4
5)	Kelowna	BC	89.7	5	CBU-FM-3
5)	Prince George	BC	90.3	0.2	CBU-FM-5
5)	Vancouver	BC	105.7	50	CBU-FM
31)	Victoria	BC	92.1	87	CBU-FM-1
16)	Brandon	MB	92.7	90	CBWS-FM
16)	Winnipeg	MB	98.3	160	CBW-FM
32)	Fredericton/St.John	NB	101.5	81	CBZ-FM
18)	Moncton	NB	95.5	77	CBA-FM
15)	Corner Brook	NL	91.1	3	CBN-FM-2
1)	Grand Falls	NL	90.7	100	CBN-FM-1
4)	St. John's	NL	106.9	100	CBN-FM
9)	Halifax	NS	102.7	92	CBH-FM
9)	Middleton	NS	93.3	16.6	CBH-FM-1
9)	Mulgrave	NS	103.1	100	CBH-FM-2
19)	Sydney	NS	105.1	100	CBI-FM
11)	Yellowknife	NT	95.3	0.1	CFYK-FM
6)	Huntsville	ON	106.9	70	CBL-FM-1
6)	Kingston	ON	92.9	1.6	CBBK-FM
6)	Kitchener/Waterloo	ON	90.7	10.6	CBL-FM-2
6)	London	ON	100.5	22.5	CBBL-FM
12)	Ottawa	ON	103.3	84	CBOQ-FM
6)	Peterborough	ON	103.9	26	CBBP-FM
20)	Sudbury	ON	90.1	50	CBBS-FM
8)	Thunder Bay	ON	101.7	23.5	CBQ-FM
6)	Toronto	ON	94.1	38	CBL-FM
25)	Windsor	ON	89.9	100	CBE-FM
23)	Charlottetown	PE	104.7	100	CBCH-FM
13)	Montréal	QC	93.5	24.6	CBM-FM
13)	Québec	QC	96.1	0.8	CBM-FM-2
13)	Sherbrooke	QC	89.7	25	CBM-FM-1
2)	Prince Albert	SK	89.1	20	CBK-FM-1
2)	Regina	SK	96.9	100	CBK-FM
2)	Saskatoon	SK	105.5	98	CBKS-FM
3)	Whitehorse	YT	104.5	0.5	CBU-FM-8

+approx 14 relay txs **NB:** calls not announced
NB: Full list of CBC English freqs at **W:** cbc.ca/frequency

French Radio – Radio Canada

Première Chaîne:

MW	Location	Prov.	kHz	kW	N	Call
25)	Windsor	ON	540	2.5/5		CBEF
26)	New Carlisle	QC	540	10	c	CBGA-1
7)	Edmonton	AB	680	10	c	CHFA
2)	Gravelbourg	SK	690	5		CBKF-1
6)	Toronto	ON	860	50		CJBC
2)	Saskatoon	SK	860	10		CBKF-2
16)	Winnipeg	MB	1050	10		CKSB

FM	Location	Prov.	MHz	kW	Call
7)	Calgary	AB	103.9	22	CBRF-FM
7)	Edmonton	AB	90.1	100	CHFA-10-FM
5)	Vancouver	BC	97.7	100	CBUF-FM
3)	Victoria	BC	99.7	1.2	CBUF-FM-9
16)	Winnipeg	MB	90.5	2.8	CKSB-10-FM
18)	Allardville	NB	105.7	50	CBAF-FM-2
18)	Fredericton/St.John	NB	102.3	84	CBAF-FM-1
18)	Moncton	NB	88.5	50	CBAF-FM
9)	Halifax	NS	92.3	91	CBAF-FM-5
12)	Ottawa	ON	90.7	84	CBOF-FM
20)	Sudbury	ON	98.1	50	CBON-FM
25)	Windsor	ON	105.5	2.4	CBEF-2-FM
29)	Chicoutimi	QC	93.7	50	CBJ-FM
26)	Gaspe	QC	89.3	4.3	CBGA-10-FM
26)	Matane	QC	102.1	42.9	CBGA-FM

FM	Location	Prov.	MHz	kW	Call
13)	Montréal	QC	95.1	100	CBF-FM
27)	Québec	QC	106.3	52.5	CBV-FM
26)	Rimouski	QC	89.1	38.8	CJBR-FM
26)	Rivière-du-Loop	QC	89.5	100	CJBR-FM-1
36)	Rouyn-Noranda	QC	90.7	25	CHLM-FM
26)	Sept îles	QC	98.1	96.8	CBSI-FM
38)	Sherbrooke	QC	101.1	35	CBF-FM-10
37)	Trois-Rivières	QC	96.5	100	CBF-FM-8
2)	Regina	SK	97.7	13.7	CBKF-FM

+approx 150 relay txs

Espace musique:

FM	Location	Prov.	MHz	kW	Call
7)	Edmonton	AB	101.1	3.9	CBCX-FM-1
5)	Vancouver	BC	90.9	2.8	CBUX-FM
16)	Winnipeg	MB	89.9	61	CKSB-FM
18)	Allardville	NB	101.9	25	CBAL-FM-1
18)	Fredericton/St.John	NB	88.1	78.5	CBAL-FM-4
18)	Moncton	NB	98.3	77	CBAL-FM
9)	Halifax	NS	91.5	77.5	CBAX-FM
12)	Ottawa	ON	102.5	84	CBOX-FM
20)	Sudbury	ON	90.9	50	CBBX-FM
6)	Toronto	ON	90.3	10	CJBC-FM
29)	Chicoutimi	QC	100.9	50	CBJX-FM
26)	Gaspe	QC	90.1	6.2	CBFX-FM-5
26)	Matane	QC	107.5	31.7	CBRX-FM-1
13)	Montréal	QC	100.7	100	CBFX-FM
27)	Québec	QC	95.3	64.6	CBVX-FM
26)	Rimouski	QC	101.5	100	CBRX-FM
26)	Rivière-du-Loop	QC	90.7	100	CBRX-FM-3
36)	Rouyn-Noranda	QC	89.9	26.7	CBFX-FM-4
26)	Sept îles	QC	96.1	84.8	CBRX-FM-2
38)	Sherbrooke	QC	90.7	25	CBFX-FM-2
37)	Trois-Rivières	QC	104.3	100	CBFX-FM-1
2)	Regina	SK	88.9	96.4	CKSB-FM-1
2)	Saskatoon	SK	88.7	100	CKSB-FM-2

+approx 16 relay txs

NB: Full list of CBC French freqs at **W:** radio-canada.ca/radio

Addresses:
1) 2 Harris Ave, Grand Falls-Windsor NL A2A 2Y2 **W:** cbc.ca/thecentral-morningshow – **2)** 2440 Broad St, Regina SK S4P 4A1 **W:** cbc.ca/sask **W: (F):** radio-canada.ca/saskatchewan – **3)** 3103 3rd Ave, Whitehorse YT Y1A 1E5 **W:** cbc.ca/north – **4)** Box 12010 Stn A, St. John's NL A1B 3T8 **W:** cbc.ca/nl – **5)** Box 4600, Vancouver BC V6B 4A2 **W:** cbc.ca/bc **W: (F):** radio-canada.ca/colombie-britannique-et-yukon – **6)** Box 500 Stn A, Toronto ON M5W 1E6 **W:** cbc.ca/toronto **W: (F):** radio-canada.ca/ontario – **7)** Box 555, Edmonton AB T5J 2P4 **W:** cbc.ca/edmonton **W: (F):** radio-canada.ca/alberta – **8)** 213 Miles St E, Thunder Bay ON P7C 1J5 **W:** cbc.ca/thunderbay – **9)** Box 3000, Halifax NS B3J 3E9 **W:** cbc.ca/ns – **10)** Unit 1 222 3rd Ave W, Prince Rupert BC V8J 1L1 **W:** cbc.ca/daybreaknorth – **11)** Box 160, Yellowknife NT X1A 2N2 **W:** cbc.ca/north –**12)** Box 3220 Stn C, Ottawa ON K1Y 1E4 **W:** cbc.ca/ottawa **W: (F):** radio-canada.ca/ottawa-gatineau – **13)** Box 6000, Montréal QC H3C 3A8 **W:** cbc.ca/montreal **W: (F):** radio-canada.ca/montreal – **14)** Box 2200, Fredericton NB E3B 5G4 **W:** cbc.ca/informationmorningfredericton – **15)** 541 Portage Ave, Winnipeg MB R3B 2G1 **W:** cbc.ca/manitoba – **16)** Box 12010 Stn A, St. John's NL A1B 3T8 **W:** cbc.ca/thewestcoastmorningshow – **17)** Box 2640, Calgary AB T2P 2M7 **W:** cbc.ca/calgary – **18)** 250 University Ave, Moncton NB E1C 8N8 **W:** cbc.ca/informationmorningmoncton **W: (F):** radio-canada.ca/acadie – **19)** 285 Alexandra St, Sydney NS B1S 2E8 **W:** cbc.ca/informationmorningcb – **20)** 15 MacKenzie St, Sudbury ON P3C 4Y1 **W:** cbc.ca/sudbury – **21)** Box 490, Iqaluit NU X0A 0H0 **W:** cbc.ca/north – **22)** Box 12010 Stn A, St. John's NL A1B 3T8 A0P 1C0 **W:** cbc.ca/labradormorning – **23)** Box 2230, Charlottetown PE C1A 8B9 **W:** cbc.ca/pei – **24)** Box 369, Gander NL A1V 1W7 **W:** cbc.ca/thecentralmorningshow – **25)** 825 Riverside Dr W, Windsor ON N9A 5K9 **W:** cbc.ca/windsor – **26)** 273 rue Saint-Jean-Baptiste Ouest, Rimouski QC G5L 4J8 **W: (F):** radio-canada.ca/est-du-quebec – **27)** 888 rue Saint-Jean, Québec QC G1R 5H6 **W: (F):** radio-canada.ca/quebec – **28)** 218 Victoria St, Kamloops BC V2C 2A2 **W:** cbc.ca/kamloops – **29)** 500 rue des Saguenées, Chicoutimi QC G7H 6N4 **W: (F):** radio-canada.ca/saguenay-lac-saint-jean – **30)** 243 Lawrence Ave, Kelowna BC V1Y 6L2 **W:** cbc.ca/daybreaksouth – **31)** 1025 Pandora Ave, Victoria BC V8V 3P6 **W:** cbc.ca/ontheisland – **32)** Box 2358, St. John NB E2L 3V6 **W:** cbc.ca/informationmorningsaintjohn – **33)** Unit 1 890 Victoria St, Prince George BC V2L 5P1 **W:** cbc.ca/daybreaknorth – **36)** 70 avenue Principale, Rouyn-Noranda QC J9X 4P2 **W: (F):** radio-canada.ca/abitibi-temiscamingue – **37)** 225 des Forges suite 101, Trois-Rivières QC G9A 2G7 **W: (F):** radio-canada.ca/mauricie – **38)** 1335 rue King Ouest, Sherbrooke QC J1J 2B8 **W: (F):** radio-canada.ca/estrie

PRIVATE STATIONS English unless: F=French m=multilingual/ethnic c=moving to FM r=relay *=also on SW +=F.PI.
NB: Txs below 100W not listed

MW	kHz	Call	kW	N	Location, Prov.
705)	530	CIAO	1/0.25	m	Toronto, ON
701)	560	CFOS	7.5/1		Owen Sound, ON
204)	570	CKWL	1		Williams Lake, BC
500)	570	CFCB	1		Corner Brook, NL
702)	570	CKGL	10		Kitchener, ON
912)	570	CKSW	10		Swift Current, SK
100)	580	CKUA	10		Edmonton, AB
703)	580	CFRA	50/30		Ottawa, ON
706)	580	CKWW	0.5		Windsor, ON
207)	590	CFTK	1		Terrace. BC
302)	590	CFAR	10/1		Flin Flon, MB
402)	590	CJCW	1/0.25		Sussex, NB
501)	590	VOCM	20		St. John's, NL
707)	590	CJCL	50		Toronto, ON
708)	600	CKAT	10/5		North Bay, ON
900)	600	CJWW	25/8		Saskatoon, SK
101)	610	CKYL	10		Peace River, AB
209)	610	CHNL	25/5		Kamloops, BC
303)	610	CHTM	1		Thompson, MB
709)	610	CKTB	10/5		St. Catharines, ON
950)	610	CKRW	1		Whitehorse, YT
501b)	620	CKCM	10		Grand Falls-Windsor, NL
901)	620	CKRM	10		Regina, SK
102)	630	CHED	50		Edmonton, AB
711)	630	CFCO	10/6		Chatham-Kent, ON
712)	640	CFMJ	50		Toronto, ON
238)	650	CISL	10/9		Richmond/Vancouver, BC
501d)	650	CKGA	5		Gander, NL
908)	650	CKOM	10		Saskatoon, SK
108)	660	CFFR	50		Calgary, AB
305)	680	CJOB	50		Winnipeg, MB
707)	680	CFTR	50		Toronto, ON
819)	690	CKGM	50		Montréal, QC
501e)	690	CKVO	10		Clarenville, NL
716)	710	CJRN	5/2.5		Niagara Falls, ON
213)	730	CHMJ	50		Vancouver, BC
306)	730	CKDM	10/5		Dauphin, MB
804)	730	CKAC	50	F	Montréal, QC
501a)	740	CHCM	10		Marystown, NL
704)	740	CFZM	50		Toronto, ON
911)	750	CKJH	25		Melfort, SK
224a)	760	CFLD	1	r	Burns Lake, BC
103)	770	CHQR	50		Calgary, AB
104)	790	CFCW	50		Camrose, AB
500a)	790	CFNW	1	r	Port au Choix, NL
206)	800	CKOR	10/0.5		Penticton, BC
502)	800	VOWR	10/2.5		St. John's, NL
704)	800	CJBQ	10		Belleville, ON
706)	800	CKLW	50		Windsor, ON
810)	800	CJAD	50/10		Montréal, QC
902)	800	CHAB	10		Moose Jaw, SK
307)	810	CKJS	10	m	Winnipeg, MB
403)	810	CJVA	10	F	Bathurst, NB
724)	820	CHAM	50/10		Hamilton, ON
128)	830	CKKY	10/3.5		Wainwright, AB
204a)	860	CKBX	1/0.5		100 Mile House, BC
206c)	870	CKIR	1/0.25	r	Invermere, BC
224)	870	CFBV	1/0.5		Smithers, BC
500b)	870	CFSX	0.5		Stephenville, NL
102)	880	CHQT	50		Edmonton, AB
312)	880	CKLQ	10		Brandon, MB
230)	890	CJDC	10		Dawson Creek, BC
725)	900	CHML	50		Hamilton, ON
903)	900	CKBI	10		Prince Albert, SK
106)	910	CKDQ	50		Drumheller, AB
308)	920	CFRY	25/15		Portage la Prairie, MB
728)	920	CKNX	10/1		Wingham, ON
107)	930	CJCA	50		Edmonton, AB
405)	930	CFBC	50		St. John, NB
501)	930	CJYQ	25/3.5		St. John's, NL
904)	940	CJGX	50/10		Yorkton, SK
309)	950	CFAM	10		Altona, MB
406)	950	CKNB	10/1		Campbellton, NB
108)	960	CFAC	50		Calgary, AB
213)	980	CKNW	50		Vancouver, BC
731)	980	CFPL	10/5		London, ON
905)	980	CJME	10/5		Regina, SK
733)	1010	CFRB	50	*	Toronto, ON
215)	1040	CKST	50		Vancouver, BC
820)	1040	CJMS	10/5	F	Saint-Constant, QC
734)	1050	CHUM	50		Toronto, ON

MW	kHz	Call	kW	N	Location, Prov.
906)	1050	CJNB	10		North Battleford, SK
111)	1060	CKMX	50	*	Calgary, AB
220)	1070	CFAX	10		Victoria, BC
736)	1070	CHOK	10		Sarnia, ON
221)	1130	CKWX	50		Vancouver, BC
122)	1140	CHRB	50/46		High River, AB
222)	1150	CKFR	10		Kelowna, BC
724)	1150	CKOC	50		Hamilton, ON
907)	1190	CFSL	10/5		Weyburn, SK
225)	1200	CJRJ	25	m	Vancouver, BC
703)	1200	CFGO	50		Ottawa, ON
505)	1210	VOAR	10		St. John's, NL
910a)	1210	CFYM	1/0.25		Kindersley, SK
309a)	1220	CJRB	10		Boissevain, MB
209c)	1230	CJNL	1	r	Merritt, BC
500c)	1230	CFGN	0.25		Ch.-Port aux Basques, NL
223)	1240	CKMK	1		Mackenzie, BC
206b)	1240	CJOR	1		Osoyoos, BC
233)	1240	CFNI	1		Port Hardy , BC
302a)	1240	CJAR	1		The Pas, MB
501c)	1240	CKIM	1	r	Baie Verte, NL
747)	1240	CJCS	1		Stratford, ON
826)	1240	CFLM	1	F	La Tuque, QC
309b)	1250	CHSM	10		Steinbach, MB
721)	1250	CJYE	10/5		Oakville, ON
119)	1260	CFRN	50		Edmonton, AB
410)	1260	CKHJ	10		Fredericton, NB
605)	1270	CJCB	10		Sydney, NS
833)	1280	CFMB	50	m	Montréal, QC
909)	1280	CJSL	10		Estevan, SK
311)	1290	CFRW	10		Winnipeg, MB
751)	1290	CJBK	10		London, ON
753)	1310	CIWW	50		Ottawa, ON
229)	1320	CHMB	50	m	Vancouver, BC
721)	1320	CJMR	20	m	Oakville, ON
910)	1330	CJYM	10		Rosetown, SK
209a)	1340	CINL	1	r	Ashcroft, BC
210)	1340	CFKC	0.25		Creston, BC
211)	1340	CIVH	1		Vanderhoof, BC
507)	1340	CKHV	1		Happy Valley, NL
612)	1350	CKAD	1		Middleton, NS
812)	1350	CIRA-5	1/.18	F	Gatineau, QC
758)	1380	CKPC	25		Brantford, ON
109)	1400	CKSQ	1	c	Stettler, AB
209b)	1400	CHNL-1	1	r	Clearwater, BC
206a)	1400	CIOR	1	r	Princeton, BC
215)	1410	CFTE	50		Vancouver, BC
751)	1410	CKSL	10		London, ON
606)	1420	CKDY	1		Digby, NS
764)	1430	CHKT	50	m	Toronto, ON
121)	1440	CKJR	10		Wetaskiwin, AB
607)	1450	CFAB	1		Windsor, NS
834)	1450	CHOU	1	m	Montréal, QC
768)	1460	CJOY	10		Guelph, ON
234)	1470	CJVB	50	m	Vancouver, BC
912a)	1490	CJSN	1		Shaunavon, SK
772)	1510	CKOT	10/-		Tillsonburg, ON
773)	1540	CHIN	50/30	m	Toronto, ON
310)	1570	CKMW	1		Winkler, MB
835)	1570	CJLV	10	F	Laval/Montréal, QC
756)	1580	CKDO	10		Oshawa, ON
774)	1610	CHHA	6.25	m	Toronto, ON
836)	1610	CJWI	1	F	Montréal, QC
729)	1650	CINA	5/0.68	m	Mississauga, ON
837)	1650	CJRS	1	m	Montréal, QC
823)	1670	CJEU	1	F	Gatineau, QC
720)	1690	CHTO	3/1	m	Toronto, ON
831)	1690	CJLO	10		Montréal, QC

SW	kHz	Call	kW	Location	Relays
111)	6030	CFVP	0.1	Calgary, AB	CKMX
733)	6070	CFRX	1	Toronto, ON	CFRB

NB: Affiliates of stns that broadcast a common prgr during part of the day have a letter as part of the reference no.

Alberta

100) 4th flr -10526 Jasper Ave NW, Edmonton AB T5J 1Z7 – **101)** Box 300, Peace River AB T8S 1T5 – **102)** 5204 84th St NW, Edmonton, AB T6E 5N8 – **103)** Shaw Court, 105 630 - 3rd Ave SW, Calgary AB T2P 4L4 – **104)** 5708-48 Ave, Camrose AB T4V 0K1 – **106)** Box 1480, Drumheller AB T0J 0Y0 – **107)** 5316 Calgary Trail NW, Edmonton AB T6H 4J8 – **108)** 2723 37th Ave NE #240, Calgary AB T1Y 5R8 – **109)** 4812A 50 St, Stettler AB T0C 2L0 – **111)** 300-1110 Centre St NE, Calgary AB T2E 2R2. Rpt: **E:** qslcalgary@gmail.com – **119)** 100-18520 Stony Plain Rd NW, Edmonton AB T5S 2E2 – **121)** 5214A-50th Ave, Wetaskiwin AB

T9A 0S8 – **122)** 11-5th Ave SE, High River AB T1V 1G2 – **128)** 1037 2nd Ave 2nd flr, Wainwright AB T9W 1K7

British Columbia

204) 83 First Ave S, Williams Lake BC V2G 1H4. Own prgrs 1400-1800 – **204a)** Box 1834, 100 Mile House BC V0K 2E0. Own prgrs Mon-Fri 1500-2100, Sat 1500-1700, 2000-2100 – **206)** 33 Carmi Ave, Penticton BC V2A 3G4 – **206a)** Box 1400, Princeton BC V0X 1W0 – **206b)** 203 – 8309 Main St, Osoyoos BC V0H 1V0 – **206c)** Box 1403, Golden BC V0A 1H0 (Lic to Invermere) – **207)** 4625 Lazelle Ave, Terrace BC V8G 1S4 – **209)** 611 Lansdowne St, Kamloops BC V2C 1Y6 – **209a)** Ashcroft BC – **209b)** Clearwater BC – **209c)** Box 1630 Stn Main, Merritt BC V1K 1B8 – **210)** Box 310, Creston BC V0B 1G0. Own prgrs 1200-0600. Rel: CJAT-FM – **211)** Box 1370, Vanderhoof BC V0J 3A0 – **213)** 2000-700 W Georgia St, Vancouver BC V7Y 1K9 – **215)** 300-380 2nd Ave W, Vancouver BC V5Y 1C8 – **220)** 1420 Broad St, Victoria BC V8W 2B1 – **221)** 2440 Ash St, Vancouver BC V5Z 4J6 – **222)** 300-435 Bernard Ave, Kelowna BC V1Y 6N8 – **223)** 2nd flr – 1810 3rd Ave, Prince George BC V2M 1G4. Rel: CKDV-FM – **224)** Box 335, Smithers BC V0J 2N0 – **224a)** Burns Lake BC – **225)** 110-3060 Norland Ave, Burnaby BC V5B 3A6 (Lic to Vancouver) – **229)** 100-1200 73rd Ave W, Vancouver BC V6P 6G5. Mostly Chinese – **230)** 901 102nd Ave, Dawson Creek BC V1G 2B6 – **233)** 7035A Market St, Port Hardy BC V0N 2P0 – **234)** 2090 Aberdeen Centre 4151 Hazelbridge Way, Richmond BC V6X 4J7 (Lic to Vancouver). Mostly langs – **238)** #20-11151 Horseshoe Way, Richmond BC V7A 4S5

Manitoba

302) Box 430 Stn Main, Flin Flon MB R8A 1N3 – **302a)** Box 2980 Stn Main, The Pas MB R9A 1R7 – **303)** 103 Cree Rd, Thompson MB R8N 0B9 – **305)** 200-1440 Jack Blick Ave, Winnipeg MB R3G 0L4 – **306)** 27 3rd Ave NE, Dauphin MB R7N 0Y5 – **307)** 520 Corydon Ave, Winnipeg MB R3L 0P1 – **308)** 350 River Rd, Portage la Prairie MB R1N 3V6 – **309)** Box 950, Altona MB R0G 0B0 – **309a)** Boissevain MB – **309b)** 105-32 Brandt St, Steinbach MB R5G 2J7 – **310)** Box 399 Stn Main, Winkler MB R6W 4A6 – **311)** 1445 Pembina Hwy, Winnipeg MB R3T 5C2 – **312)** Box 880, Brandon MB R7A 6N6

New Brunswick

402) Box 5900 Stn Main, Sussex NB E4E 5M2 – **403)** 195 rue Main 2nd flr, Bathurst NB E2A 1A7 – **405)** Box 930 Stn Main, St. John NB E2L 1B1 – **406)** 74 Water St, Campbellton NB E3N 1B1 – **410)** 206 Rookwood Ave, Fredericton NB E3B 2M2

Newfoundland & Labrador

500) Box 570 Stn Main, Corner Brook NL A2H 6H5 – **500a)** Port au Choix NL – **500b)** 60 West St, Stephenville NL A2N 1C6. Own prgrs 0930 (Sat 1030, Sun 1630)-2130 – **500c)** Gen. Delivery, Ch.-Port aux Basques NL A0M 1C0. Own prgrs Mon-Fri 1230-2130 – **501)** Box 8590 Stn A, St. John's NL A1B 3P5 – **501a)** Box 560, Marystown NL A0E 2M0. Own prgrs 0730-1630 – **501b)** Box 620 Stn Main, Grand Falls-Windsor NL A2A 2K2. Own prgrs 0730-1630 – **501c)** Baie Verte NL – **501d)** Box 650 Stn Main, Gander NL A1V 1X2. Own prgrs 0700-1900 – **501e)** Gen. Delivery, Clarenville NL A5A 2C1. Own prgrs 0730-1630 – **502)** Box 7430 Stn C, St. John's NL A1E 3Y5 – **505)** 1041 Topsail Rd, Mt. Pearl NL A1N 5E9 (Lic to St. John's) – **507)** Box 160, Nain NL A0P 1L0 (Lic to Happy Valley)

Nova Scotia

605) Box 1270 Stn A, Sydney NS B1P 1C8 – **606)** Box 1420, Digby NS B0V 1A0 – **607)** 169-A Water St, Windsor NS B0N 2T0 – **612)** Box 550, Middleton NS B0S 1P0

Ontario

701) Box 280 Stn Main, Owen Sound ON N4K 5P5 – **702)** 305 King St W #1101, Kitchener ON N2G 4E4 – **703)** 87 George St, Ottawa ON K1N 9H7 – **704)** Box 488 Stn Main, Belleville ON K8N 5B2 – **705)** 5312 Dundas St W, Toronto ON M9B 1B3 (Lic to Brampton). Mostly langs – **706)** 1640 Ouellette Ave, Windsor ON N8X 1L1 – **707)** 777 Jarvis St, Toronto ON M4Y 3B7 – **708)** Box 3000, North Bay ON P1B 8K8 – **709)** Box 977 Stn Main, St. Catharines ON L2R 6Z4 – **711)** Box 100 Stn Main, Chatham-Kent ON N7M 5K1 – **712)** Corus Quay 25 Dockside Dr, Toronto ON M5A 0B5 (Lic to Richmond Hill) – **716)** 4668 St. Clair Ave, Niagara Falls ON L2E 6X7 – **717)** 550 Queen St E Suite 205, Toronto ON M5A 1V2 – **720)** 437 Danforth Ave Suite 204, Toronto ON M4K 1P1. Mostly Greek – **721)** 284 Church St, Oakville ON L6J 7N2 – **724)** 883 Upper Wentworth St Suite 401, Hamilton ON L9A 4Y6 – **725)** 875 Main St W #900, Hamilton ON L8S 4R1 – **728)** 215 Carling Terrace, Wingham ON N0G 2W0 – **729)** 1515 Britannia Rd Suite 315, Mississauga ON L4W 4K1. Mostly langs – **731)** Box 2580 Stn B, London ON N6A 4H3 – **733)** 2 St. Clair Ave W 2nd flr, Toronto ON M4V 1L6. Rpt: **E:** cfrx@ymail.com – **734)** 250 Richmond St W, Toronto ON M5V 1W4 – **736)** 1415 London Rd, Sarnia ON N7S 1P6 – **747)** 376 Romeo St S, Stratford ON N5A 4T9 – **751)** 743 Wellington St S, London ON N6A 6H5 – **753)** 2001 Thurston Dr, Ottawa ON K1G 6C9 – **756)** 207-1200 Airport Blvd, Oshawa ON L1J 8P5 – **758)** 571 West St, Brantford ON N3T 5P8 – **764)** 8-135 East Beaver Creek Rd, Richmond Hill ON L4B 1E2 (Lic to Toronto). Mostly

Chinese – **768)** 75 Speedvale Ave E, Guelph ON N1E 6M3 – **772)** Box 10 Stn Main, Tillsonburg ON N4G 4H3. Daytime only: Jan. 1300-2215, July 1000-0100 – **773)** 622 College St, Toronto ON M6G 1B6. Mostly Italian – **774)** 22 Wenderly Dr, Toronto ON M6B 2N9. Mostly Spanish

Québec
804) 800 rue de la Gauchetière Ouest Bureau 1100, Montréal QC H5A 1M1 – **810)** 1717 boulevard René-Lévesque Est, Montréal QC H2L 4T9 – **812)** 4020 rue St-Ambrois #199, Montréal QC H4C 2T7 (Lic to Gatineau). Rel: CIRA-FM – **819)** 300 - 1310 Greene Ave, Westmount QC H3Z 2B5 (Lic to Montréal) – **820)** 143 rue Saint-Pierre, Saint-Constant QC J5A 2G9 – **823)** 855 boul. de Gappe pièce 310, Gatineau QC J8T 8H9 – **826)** 529 rue Saint-Louis, La Tuque QC G9X 3P6 – **831)** 7141 Sherbrooke St Ouest Room CC430, Montréal QC H4B 1R6 – **833)** 35 rue York, Westmount QC H3Z 2Z5 (Lic to Montréal). Mostly langs – **834)** 11876 rue demeulles, Montréal QC H4J 2E6. Mostly langs – **835)** 2040 Autoroute Laval, Laval QC H7S 2M9 – **836)** 3733 rue Jarry E 2e etage, Montréal QC H1Z 2G1 – **837)** 4835 Côte St. Catherine Rd #2, Montréal QC H3W 1M4. Mostly langs

Saskatchewan
900) 366 3rd Ave S, Saskatoon SK S7K 1M5 – **901)** 1900 Rose St, Regina SK S4P 0A9 – **902)** Box 800 Stn Main, Moose Jaw SK S6H 4P5 – **903)** Box 900 Stn Main, Prince Albert SK S6V 7R4 – **904)** Broadc Place 120 Smith St E, Yorkton SK S3N 3V3 – **905)** 210-2401 Saskatchewan Dr, Regina SK S4P 4H8 – **906)** Box 1460 Stn Main, North Battleford SK S9A 2Z5 – **907)** Box 340 Stn Main, Weyburn SK S4H 2K2 – **908)** 715 Saskatchewan Cres W, Saskatoon SK S7M 5V7 – **909)** Box 1280 Stn Main, Estevan SK S4A 2H8 – **910)** Box 490, Rosetown SK S0L 2V0 – **910a)** Box 1330, Kindersley SK S0L 1S1 – **911)** Box 750, Melfort SK S0E 1A0 – **912)** 134 Central Ave N, Swift Current SK S9H 0L1 – **912a)** Box 1176, Shaunavon SK S0N 2M0

Yukon Territory
950) 203-4103 4th Ave, Whitehorse YT Y1A 1H6

FM	Prov.	MHz	kW		Call
Airdrie	AB	106.1	100		CFIT-FM
Athabasca	AB	94.1	9		CKBA-FM
Bonnyville	AB	99.7	50		CFNA-FM
Bonnyville	AB	101.3	27		CJEG-FM
Brooks	AB	101.1	8.6		CIXF-FM
Brooks	AB	105.7	14		CIBQ-FM
Calgary	AB	88.1	27	m	CKAV-FM-3
Calgary	AB	88.9	100		CJSI-FM
Calgary	AB	90.3	100		CKMP-FM
Calgary	AB	90.9	4		CJSW-FM
Calgary	AB	92.1	100		CJAY-FM
Calgary	AB	92.9	100		CFEX-FM
Calgary	AB	93.7	100		CKUA-FM-1
Calgary	AB	94.7	65		CHKF-FM
Calgary	AB	95.9	100		CHFM-FM
Calgary	AB	96.9	100		CJAQ-FM
Calgary	AB	97.7	100		CHUP-FM
Calgary	AB	98.5	100		CIBK-FM
Calgary	AB	101.5	100		CKCE-FM
Calgary	AB	103.1	100		CFXL-FM
Calgary	AB	105.1	100		CKRY-FM
Calgary	AB	107.3	100		CFGQ-FM
Camrose	AB	98.1	50		CFCW-FM
Cold Lake	AB	95.3	100		CJXK-FM
Drayton Valley	AB	92.9	50		CIBW-FM
Drumheller	AB	91.3	100		CKUA-FM-13
Edmonton	AB	89.3	100	m	CKAV-FM-4
Edmonton	AB	91.7	96		CHBN-FM
Edmonton	AB	92.5	100		CKNG-FM
Edmonton	AB	94.9	100		CKUA-FM
Edmonton	AB	95.7	100		CKEA-FM
Edmonton	AB	96.3	100		CKRA-FM
Edmonton	AB	97.3	100		CIRK-FM
Edmonton/Spruce Grove	AB	98.5	9.3	m	CFWE-FM-4
Edmonton	AB	99.3	100		CIUP-FM
Edmonton	AB	100.3	97		CFBR-FM
Edmonton	AB	101.7	100	m	CKER-FM
Edmonton	AB	102.3	100		CKNO-FM
Edmonton	AB	102.9	100		CHDI-FM
Edmonton	AB	103.9	98		CISN-FM
Edmonton	AB	104.9	100		CFMG-FM
Edmonton	AB	105.9	100		CJRY-FM
Edmonton	AB	107.1	40		CJNW-FM
Edson	AB	94.3	20		CFXE-FM
Fort McMurray	AB	93.3	43.5		CJOK-FM
Fort McMurray	AB	94.5	23.5	m	CFWE-FM-5
Fort McMurray	AB	97.9	43.5		CKYX-FM
Fort McMurray	AB	100.5	50		CHFT-FM
Fort McMurray	AB	103.7	50		CFVR-FM
Grande Prairie	AB	93.1	100		CJXX-FM

FM	Prov.	MHz	kW		Call
Grande Prairie	AB	96.3	70		CJGY-FM
Grande Prairie	AB	97.7	100		CFGP-FM
Grande Prairie	AB	98.9	100		CIKT-FM
Grande Prairie	AB	100.9	100		CKUA-FM-4
Grande Prairie	AB	104.7	100		CFRI-FM
High Level	AB	102.1	34		CKHL-FM
High Level	AB	106.1	34		CFKX-FM
High Prairie	AB	93.5	25		CKVH-FM
High River/Okotoks	AB	99.7	16		CFXO-FM
High River/Okotoks	AB	100.9	100		CKUV-FM
Joussard	AB	91.7	4.2	m	CFWE-FM-1
Lacombe	AB	94.1	55		CJUV-FM
Lethbridge	AB	94.1	100		CJOC-FM
Lethbridge	AB	95.5	100		CHLB-FM
Lethbridge	AB	98.1	20		CKVN-FM
Lethbridge	AB	99.3	100		CKUA-FM-2
Lethbridge/Taber	AB	106.7	100		CJRX-FM
Lethbridge	AB	107.7	100		CFRV-FM
Lloydminster	AB	95.9	100		CKSA-FM
Lloydminster	AB	106.1	100		CKLM-FM
Medicine Hat	AB	94.5	100		CHAT-FM
Medicine Hat	AB	96.1	100		CFMY-FM
Medicine Hat	AB	97.3	100		CKUA-FM-3
Medicine Hat	AB	102.1	40		CJCY-FM
Medicine Hat	AB	105.3	100		CKMH-FM
Moose Hills	AB	96.7	100	m	CFWE-FM-3
Olds	AB	96.5	35		CKLJ-FM
Olds	AB	104.5	35		CKJX-FM
Peace River	AB	96.9	100		CKUA-FM-5
Peigan/Blood River	AB	89.3	10.2	m	CFWE-FM-2
Pincher Creek	AB	92.7	6		CJPV-FM
Red Deer	AB	90.5	38		CKRD-FM
Red Deer	AB	95.5	100		CKGY-FM
Red Deer	AB	98.9	100		CIZZ-FM
Red Deer	AB	100.7	100		CKRI-FM
Red Deer	AB	101.3	50		CKIK-FM
Red Deer	AB	105.5	100		CHUB-FM
Red Deer	AB	106.7	100		CFDV-FM
Red Deer	AB	107.7	100		CKUA-FM-6
Slave Lake	AB	92.7	5		CHSL-FM
Stettler	AB	93.3	23		CKSQ-FM
St. Paul	AB	97.7	45		CHSP-FM
Suffield	AB	104.1	4.3		CKBF-FM
Taber	AB	93.3	100		CJBZ-FM
Wainwright	AB	93.7	100		CKWY-FM
Westlock	AB	97.9	48		CKWB-FM
Wetaskiwin	AB	93.5	5.1		CIHS-FM
Whitecourt	AB	96.7	9		CFXW-FM
Whitecourt	AB	105.3	42.3		CIXM-FM
Campbell River	BC	99.7	6		CIQC-FM
Chilliwack	BC	98.3	5		CKSR-FM
Courtenay	BC	97.3	11.6		CKLR-FM
Courtenay	BC	98.9	5		CFCP-FM
Duncan	BC	89.7	3.5		CJSU-FM
Fort St. John	BC	98.5	50		CHRX-FM
Fort St. John	BC	100.1	20		CKFU-FM
Fort St. John	BC	101.5	40		CKNL-FM
Gibsons	BC	107.5	4.6		CISC-FM
Houston	BC	105.5	3.5		CJFW-FM-7
Kamloops	BC	97.5	4.3		CKRV-FM
Kamloops	BC	98.3	4.3		CIFM-FM
Kamloops	BC	100.1	3.5		CKBZ-FM
Kamloops	BC	103.1	5		CJKC-FM
Kelowna	BC	96.3	31		CKKO-FM
Kelowna	BC	99.9	35		CHSU-FM
Kelowna	BC	101.5	33.3		CILK-FM
Kelowna	BC	103.1	35		CKQQ-FM
Kelowna	BC	103.9	10		CJUI-FM
Kelowna	BC	104.7	36		CKLZ-FM
Nanaimo	BC	101.7	3		CHLY-FM
Nanaimo	BC	102.3	3		CKWV-FM
Nanaimo	BC	106.9	3		CHWF-FM
Penticton	BC	100.7	14.1		CIGV-FM
Port Alberni	BC	93.3	6		CJAV-FM
Powell River	BC	95.7	5.8		CFPW-FM
Prince George	BC	94.3	11.5		CIRX-FM
Prince George	BC	97.3	12		CJCI-FM
Prince George	BC	99.3	9.3		CKDV-FM
Prince George	BC	101.3	9.1		CKKN-FM
Squamish	BC	107.1	30		CISQ-FM
Terrace	BC	103.1	3.2		CJFW-FM
Trail	BC	95.7	13.5		CJAT-FM
Vancouver	BC	93.1	8	m	CKYE-FM
Vancouver	BC	93.7	75		CJJR-FM
Vancouver	BC	94.5	90		CFBT-FM

FM	Prov.	MHz	kW	N	Call	FM	Prov.	MHz	kW	N	Call
Vancouver	BC	95.3	71.3		CKZZ-FM	Stephenville	NL	98.5	4.3		CIOS-FM
Vancouver	BC	96.1	100	m	CHKG-FM	Amherst	NS	101.7	50		CKDH-FM
Vancouver	BC	96.9	75		CKLG-FM	Amherst	NS	107.9	6.5		CFTA-FM
Vancouver	BC	99.3	100		CFOX-FM	Antigonish	NS	98.9	75.4		CJFX-FM
Vancouver	BC	100.5	11		CFRO-FM	Barrington	NS	96.3	5.5		CJLS-FM-2
Vancouver	BC	101.1	100		CFMI-FM	Bridgewater	NS	98.1	32		CKBW-FM
Vancouver	BC	102.7	70		CKPK-FM	Bridgewater	NS	100.7	10		CJHK-FM
Vancouver	BC	103.5	100		CHQM-FM	Cheticamp	NS	106.1	3	F	CKJM-FM
Vancouver	BC	104.3	10		CHHR-FM	Glace Bay	NS	89.7	6		CKOA-FM
Vancouver	BC	104.9	31		CFUN-FM-2	Halifax	NS	89.9	100		CHNS-FM
Vancouver	BC	106.3	9	m	CKAV-FM-2	Halifax/Dartmouth	NS	92.9	100		CFLT-FM
Vernon	BC	105.7	100		CICF-FM	Halifax/Dartmouth	NS	93.9	5		CJLU-FM
Vernon	BC	107.5	100		CKIZ-FM	Halifax	NS	95.7	65		CJNI-FM
Victoria	BC	91.3	3.5		CJZN-FM	Halifax	NS	96.5	100		CKUL-FM
Victoria	BC	98.5	100		CIOC-FM	Halifax	NS	100.1	100		CIOO-FM
Victoria	BC	100.3	100		CKKQ-FM	Halifax	NS	101.3	100		CJCH-FM
Victoria	BC	103.1	20		CHTT-FM	Halifax	NS	101.9	91		CHFX-FM
Victoria	BC	107.3	20		CHBE-FM	Halifax	NS	103.5	100		CKHZ-FM
Brandon	MB	91.5	100		CIWM-FM	Halifax/Dartmouth	NS	104.3	100		CFRQ-FM
Brandon	MB	94.7	100		CKLF-FM	Halifax	NS	105.1	100		CKHY-FM
Brandon	MB	96.1	88.7		CKX-FM	Inverness	NS	102.5	10		CJFX-FM-1
Brandon	MB	101.1	100		CKXA-FM	Kentville	NS	89.3	30		CIJK-FM
Portage La Prairie	MB	93.1	27		CFRY-1-FM	Kentville	NS	94.9	100		CKWM-FM
Portage La Prairie	MB	96.5	24		CJPG-FM	Kentville	NS	97.7	18		CKEN-FM
Selkirk	MB	104.1	100		CFQX-FM	Liverpool	NS	94.5	8.7		CKBW-1-FM
Selkirk	MB	105.5	100		CICY-FM	New Glasgow	NS	94.1	80		CKEC-FM
St. Boniface	MB	91.1	61	F	CKSB-FM	New Tusket	NS	93.5	3		CJLS-FM-1
Steinbach	MB	96.7	100		CILT-FM	Petit-de-Grat	NS	104.1	5.8	F	CITU-FM
Swan Lake	MB	90.5	3.7		CISF-FM	Port Hawkesbury	NS	101.5	38.1		CIGO-FM
Winkler/Morden	MB	93.5	100		CJEL-FM	Shelburne	NS	93.1	8.6		CKBW-2-FM
Winnipeg	MB	92.1	140		CITI-FM	Sydney	NS	94.9	61		CKPE-FM
Winnipeg	MB	94.3	100		CHIQ-FM	Sydney	NS	98.3	100		CHER-FM
Winnipeg	MB	95.1	100		CHVN-FM	Sydney	NS	101.9	58		CHRK-FM
Winnipeg	MB	97.5	310		CJKR-FM	Sydney	NS	103.5	26.5		CKCH-FM
Winnipeg	MB	99.1	100		CJGV-FM	Truro	NS	99.5	16.8		CKTY-FM
Winnipeg	MB	99.9	100		CFWM-FM	Truro	NS	100.9	50		CKTO-FM
Winnipeg	MB	100.7	80		CFJL-FM	Weymouth	NS	103.3	3		CKDY-1-FM
Winnipeg	MB	102.3	100		CKY-FM	Yarmouth	NS	95.5	18		CJLS-FM
Winnipeg	MB	103.1	100		CKMM-FM	Yarmouth	NS	104.1	39.3	F	CIFA-FM
Winnipeg	MB	104.7	3	m	CIUR-FM	Ajax	ON	95.9	50		CJKX-FM
Winnipeg	MB	106.1	40		CHWE-FM	Bancroft	ON	97.7	50		CHMS-FM
Winnipeg	MB	107.1	100		CFEQ-FM	Barrie	ON	93.1	100		CHAY-FM
Bathurst	NB	92.9	100	F	CKLE-FM	Barrie	ON	95.7	100		CFJB-FM
Bathurst	NB	104.9	33.5		CKBC-FM	Barrie	ON	100.3	40		CJLF-FM
Campbellton	NB	103.9	15	F	CIMS-FM	Barrie	ON	101.1	7.5		CIQB-FM
Edmundston	NB	92.7	40.8	F	CJEM-FM	Barrie	ON	107.5	50		CKMB-FM
Fredericton	NB	92.3	93		CFRK-FM	Belleville	ON	91.3	3.4		CJLX-FM
Fredericton	NB	105.3	78		CFXY-FM	Belleville	ON	95.5	64		CJOJ-FM
Fredericton	NB	106.9	78		CIBX-FM	Belleville	ON	97.1	50		CIGL-FM
Grand Falls	NB	93.5	5.3		CIKX-FM	Belleville	ON	100.1	32		CHCQ-FM
Grand-Sault	NB	105.1	3	F	CFAI-FM-1	Belleville	ON	102.3	15		CKJJ-FM
Inkerman/Pokemouche	NB	97.1	44.4	F	CKRO-FM	Bluewater	ON	91.7	6		CIBU-FM-1
Kedgwick	NB	90.1	3	F	CFJU-FM	Bracebridge	ON	99.5	12		CFBG-FM
Miramichi City	NB	93.7	11	F	CKMA-FM	Brantford	ON	92.1	80		CKPC-FM
Miramichi City	NB	99.3	17.8		CFAN-FM	Brockville	ON	103.7	100		CJPT-FM
Moncton	NB	90.7	30	F	CFBO-FM	Brockville	ON	104.9	7.7		CFJR-FM
Moncton	NB	91.9	70		CKNI-FM	Cambridge	ON	107.5	6		CJDV-FM
Moncton	NB	94.5	19		CKCW-FM	Chatham	ON	89.3	18.7		CKGW-FM
Moncton	NB	96.9	100		CJXL-FM	Chatham	ON	94.3	50		CKSY-FM
Moncton	NB	99.9	9.5	F	CHOY-FM	Chatham	ON	95.1	42		CKUE-FM
Moncton	NB	103.1	46.8		CJMO-FM	Cobourg	ON	93.3	15.5		CKSG-FM
Moncton	NB	103.9	70		CFQM-FM	Cobourg	ON	103.1	86.7		CFMX-FM
Saint John	NB	88.9	79		CHNI-FM	Cobourg	ON	107.9	20		CHUC-FM
Saint John	NB	94.1	100		CHSJ-FM	Cornwall	ON	92.1	60	F	CHOD-FM
Saint John	NB	97.3	100		CHWV-FM	Cornwall	ON	101.9	3.2		CJSS-FM
Saint John	NB	98.9	12		CJYC-FM	Cornwall	ON	104.5	28.2		CFLG-FM
Saint John	NB	100.5	100		CIOK-FM	Dryden	ON	92.7	39		CKDR-FM
Shediac	NB	89.5	38	F	CJSE-FM	Elliot Lake	ON	94.1	90		CKNR-FM
St. Stephen	NB	98.1	40		CHTD-FM	Fort Erie	ON	101.1	50		CFLZ-FM
Woodstock	NB	104.1	10		CJCJ-FM	Fort Frances	ON	93.1	21		CFOB-FM
Argentia	NL	100.3	3.7		CFOZ-FM	Gananoque	ON	99.9	4.5		CJGM-FM
Bonavista	NL	92.1	6.7		CJOZ-FM	Goderich	ON	104.9	12.6		CHWC-FM
Carbonear	NL	103.9	30		CHVO-FM	Guelph	ON	106.1	50		CIMJ-FM
Clarenville	NL	100.7	4.1		VOCM-FM-1	Haldimand	ON	92.9	10		CKJN-FM
Corner Brook	NL	92.3	50		CKOZ-FM	Haliburton	ON	93.5	6		CFZN-FM
Corner Brook	NL	103.9	40		CKXX-FM	Haliburton	ON	100.9	3.4		CKHA-FM
Gander	NL	98.7	6		CKXD-FM	Hamilton/Burlington	ON	94.7	100		CHKX-FM
Grand Falls	NL	102.3	36		CKXG-FM	Hamilton	ON	95.3	100		CING-FM
Marystown	NL	96.3	31.3		CIOZ-FM	Hamilton	ON	102.9	40.3		CKLH-FM
Rattling Brook	NL	95.9	50		CKMY-FM	Hamilton/Burlington	ON	107.9	26.1		CJXY-FM
St. John's	NL	94.7	100		CHOZ-FM	Hearst	ON	91.1	5.5	F	CINN-FM
St. John's	NL	97.5	100		VOCM-FM	Huntsville	ON	105.5	43.4		CFBK-FM
St. John's	NL	99.1	100		CKIX-FM	Kapuskasing	ON	89.7	3	F	CKGN-FM
St. John's	NL	101.1	20		CKSJ-FM	Kapuskasing	ON	93.7	3.4	F	CHYX-FM

FM	Prov.	MHz	kW	N	Call	FM	Prov.	MHz	kW	N	Call
Kapuskasing	ON	100.9	12		CKAP-FM	St. Thomas	ON	94.1	4.4		CKZM-FM
Kenora	ON	89.5	50		CJRL-FM	St. Thomas	ON	103.1	50		CFHK-FM
Kenora	ON	100.5	40		CIKN-FM	Stratford	ON	107.7	6		CHGK-FM
Kincardine	ON	95.5	5.7		CIYN-FM	Sudbury	ON	91.7	50		CICS-FM
Kingston	ON	93.5	7.5		CKXC-FM	Sudbury	ON	92.7	100		CJRQ-FM
Kingston	ON	96.3	28		CFMK-FM	Sudbury	ON	93.5	100		CIGM-FM
Kingston	ON	98.3	95.5		CFLY-FM	Sudbury	ON	95.5	8.1		CJTK-FM
Kingston	ON	98.9	15		CKLC-FM	Sudbury	ON	98.9	4.6	F	CHYC-FM
Kingston	ON	101.9	3		CFRC-FM	Sudbury	ON	103.9	100		CHNO-FM
Kingston	ON	104.3	8		CKWS-FM	Sudbury	ON	105.3	100		CJMX-FM
Kingston	ON	105.7	50		CIKR-FM	Sunderland	ON	89.9	5		CJKX-FM-1
Kirkland Lake	ON	101.5	23		CJKL-FM	Thunder Bay	ON	91.5	100		CKPR-FM
Kitchener/Waterloo	ON	91.5	10		CKBT-FM	Thunder Bay	ON	94.3	93		CJSD-FM
Kitchener	ON	96.7	100		CHYM-FM	Thunder Bay	ON	105.3	100		CKTG-FM
Kitchener/Waterloo	ON	98.5	27		CKWR-FM	Tillsonburg	ON	101.3	26		CKOT-FM
Kitchener	ON	99.5	4.3		CKKW-FM	Tillsonburg	ON	107.3	7.8		CJDL-FM
Kitchener	ON	105.3	100		CFCA-FM	Timmins	ON	92.1	40		CJQQ-FM
Kitchener/Waterloo	ON	106.7	5		CIKZ-FM	Timmins	ON	93.1	16.4		CHMT-FM
Leamington	ON	92.7	4		CJSP-FM	Timmins	ON	99.3	40		CKGB-FM
Leamington	ON	96.7	27		CHYR-FM	Timmins	ON	104.1	3.5	F	CHYK-FM
Lindsay	ON	91.9	11.4		CKLY-FM	Toronto	ON	88.9	4.2	m	CIRV-FM
Little Current	ON	100.7	27.5		CFRM-FM	Toronto	ON	89.5	15		CIUT-FM
London	ON	92.7	50		CJBX-FM	Toronto	ON	91.1	40		CJRT-FM
London	ON	94.9	6		CHRW-FM	Toronto	ON	91.9	5	m	CHIN-1-FM
London	ON	95.9	300		CFPL-FM	Toronto	ON	92.5	13		CKIS-FM
London	ON	97.5	50		CIQM-FM	Toronto	ON	93.5	3.7		CFXJ-FM
London	ON	98.1	40		CKLO-FM	Toronto	ON	96.3	60		CFMZ-FM
London	ON	102.3	100		CHST-FM	Toronto	ON	97.3	28.9		CHBM-FM
London	ON	106.9	3		CIXX-FM	Toronto	ON	98.1	44		CHFI-FM
Marathon	ON	93.1	50		CFNO-FM	Toronto	ON	99.9	40		CKFM-FM
Midland	ON	104.1	20		CICZ-FM	Toronto	ON	100.7	8.5	m	CHIN-FM
Napanee	ON	88.7	11.1		CKYM-FM	Toronto	ON	102.1	35.4		CFNY-FM
New Liskeard	ON	104.5	10		CJTT-FM	Toronto	ON	104.5	40		CHUM-FM
Newmarket	ON	88.5	30		CKDX-FM	Toronto	ON	107.1	40		CILQ-FM
Niagara Falls	ON	105.1	15		CJED-FM	Trenton	ON	107.1	15		CJTN-FM
North Bay	ON	100.5	100		CHUR-FM	Welland	ON	91.7	50		CIXL-FM
North Bay	ON	101.9	100		CKFX-FM	Windsor	ON	88.7	100		CIMX-FM
North Bay	ON	106.3	10		CFXN-FM	Windsor	ON	93.9	100		CIDR-FM
Orangeville	ON	103.5	30.7		CIDC-FM	Windsor	ON	95.9	11.8		CJWF-FM
Orillia	ON	105.9	20		CICX-FM	Windsor	ON	100.7	9		CKUE-FM-1
Oshawa	ON	94.9	50		CKGE-FM	Wingham	ON	94.5	75		CIBU-FM
Ottawa	ON	88.5	12		CILV-FM	Wingham	ON	101.7	100		CKNX-FM
Ottawa	ON	89.1	18.1		CHUO-FM	Woodstock	ON	103.9	51		CKDK-FM
Ottawa	ON	89.9	27		CIHT-FM	Woodstock	ON	104.7	20		CIHR-FM
Ottawa	ON	93.1	12		CKCU-FM	Charlottetown	PE	93.1	75		CHLQ-FM
Ottawa	ON	93.9	95		CKKL-FM	Charlottetown	PE	95.1	100		CFCY-FM
Ottawa	ON	95.7	9.1	m	CKAV-FM-9	Charlottetown	PE	100.3	88		CHTN-FM
Ottawa	ON	97.9	6.8	m	CJLL-FM	Charlottetown	PE	105.5	88		CKQK FM
Ottawa	ON	99.1	66		CHRI-FM	Elmira	PE	99.9	3.4		CHTN-FM-1
Ottawa	ON	99.7	100		CJOT-FM	Elmira	PE	103.7	3.4		CKQK-FM-1
Ottawa	ON	100.3	100		CJMJ-FM	St. Edward	PE	89.9	5		CHTN-FM-2
Ottawa	ON	101.9	5.5		CIDG-FM	St. Edward	PE	91.1	5		CKQK-FM-2
Ottawa	ON	105.3	84		CISS-FM	Summerside	PE	102.1	50		CJRW-FM
Ottawa	ON	106.1	100		CHEZ-FM	Alma	QC	95.7	100	F	CKYK-FM
Ottawa	ON	106.9	84		CKQB-FM	Alma	QC	104.5	50	F	CFGT-FM
Owen Sound	ON	92.3	9.4		CJOS-FM	Amos/Val d'Or	QC	103.5	100	F	CHOA-FM-1
Owen Sound	ON	93.7	22		CKYC-FM	Amos/Val d'Or	QC	104.3	100	F	CHGO-FM
Owen Sound	ON	106.5	28		CIXK-FM	Amos	QC	105.3	32.2	F	CHOW-FM
Paris	ON	88.3	10.6		CJIQ-FM	Amqui	QC	99.9	23.8	F	CFVM-FM
Parry Sound	ON	103.3	46.6		CKLP-FM	Asbestos	QC	99.3	11.1	F	CJAN-FM
Pembroke	ON	96.7	100		CHVR-FM	Baie-Comeau	QC	97.1	4.2	F	CHLC-FM
Pembroke	ON	99.9	7.5		CKQB-FM-1	Bécancour-Nicolet	QC	90.5	60	F	CKBN-FM
Pembroke	ON	104.9	31.6		CIMY-FM	Cabano	QC	98.3	3	F	CIEL-FM-3
Penetanguishene	ON	88.1	4.5	F	CFRH-FM	Cap-aux-Meules	QC	92.7	6.3	F	CFIM-FM
Perth	ON	88.1	5.4		CHLK-FM	Carleton	QC	94.9	37.6	F	CIEU-FM
Peterborough	ON	96.7	7		CJWV-FM	Chandler	QC	96.3	22.9	F	CFMV-FM
Peterborough	ON	99.7	11		CKPT-FM	Chibougamau	QC	93.5	56.2	F	CKXO-FM
Peterborough	ON	100.5	15		CKRU-FM	Chicoutimi	QC	94.5	100	F	CJAB-FM
Peterborough	ON	101.5	15.2		CKWF-FM	Chicoutimi	QC	96.9	100	F	CFIX-FM
Peterborough	ON	105.1	7.5		CKQM-FM	Chicoutimi	QC	98.3	100	F	CKRS-FM
Port Elgin	ON	90.9	3.1		CIYN-FM	Chicoutimi	QC	106.7	46.2	F	CION-FM-2
Port Elgin	ON	97.9	9		CFPS-FM	Chisasibi	QC	101.1	3		CHFG-FM
Renfrew	ON	96.1	7.1		CHMY-FM	Dégelis	QC	95.5	12.5	F	CFVD-FM
Renfrew	ON	98.7	20		CJHR-FM	Dolbeau	QC	100.3	50	F	CHVD-FM
Sarnia	ON	99.9	50		CFGX-FM	Drummondville	QC	92.1	3	F	CJDM-FM
Sarnia	ON	103.3	6		CKCI-FM	Drummondville	QC	105.3	5.3	F	CHRD-FM
Sarnia	ON	106.3	50		CHKS-FM	Forestville	QC	100.5	6	F	CFRP-FM
Sault Ste. Marie	ON	100.5	13.9		CHAS-FM	Fort Coulonge	QC	101.7	11.9	F	CHIP-FM
Sault Ste. Marie	ON	104.3	100		CJQM-FM	Gaspé	QC	94.5	6	F	CJRG-FM
Simcoe	ON	98.9	50		CHCD-FM	Gatineau	QC	94.9	84	F	CIMF-FM
Smiths Falls	ON	92.3	17		CJET-FM	Gatineau	QC	97.1	11.2	F	CHLX-FM
Smiths Falls	ON	101.1	100		CKBY-FM	Gatineau	QC	104.1	19	F	CKTF-FM
St. Catharines	ON	97.7	50		CHTZ-FM	Gatineau	QC	104.7	100	F	CKOF-FM
St. Catharines	ON	105.7	50		CHRE-FM	Granby	QC	104.9	4.3	F	CFXM-FM

FM	Prov.	MHz	kW		Call
Joliette	QC	103.5	4.5	F	CJLM-FM
La Baie	QC	105.7	6	F	CKGS-FM
La Pocatière	QC	97.5	25.2	F	CHOX-FM
La Sarre	QC	102.1	4.1	F	CJGO-FM
Lac-Etchemin	QC	100.5	9.6	F	CFIN-FM
Lac-Mégantic	QC	106.7	4.3	F	CJIT-FM
Lachute	QC	104.9	3	F	CJLA-FM
Les Escoumins	QC	94.9	4.7	F	CHME-FM
Longueuil	QC	98.5	40.8	F	CHMP-FM
Matane	QC	95.3	30	F	CHOE-FM
Matane	QC	105.3	30	F	CHRM-FM
Mistassini	QC	95.3	30		CINI-FM
Mont-Laurier	QC	104.7	16.9	F	CFLO-FM
Montmagny	QC	90.3	41.6	F	CIQI-FM
Montréal	QC	89.3	10	F	CISM-FM
Montréal	QC	90.3	5		CKUT-FM
Montréal	QC	91.3	36.2	F	CIRA-FM
Montréal	QC	91.9	4.7	F	CKLX-FM
Montréal	QC	92.5	41.4		CKBE-FM
Montréal	QC	94.3	41.4	F	CKMF-FM
Montréal	QC	95.9	41.2		CJFM-FM
Montréal	QC	96.9	307	F	CKOI-FM
Montréal	QC	97.7	41.2		CHOM-FM
Montréal	QC	99.5	8.7	F	CJPX-FM
Montréal/Laval	QC	105.7	41	F	CFGL-FM
Montréal	QC	107.3	42.9	F	CITE-FM
Natashquan	QC	104.1	6.6	F	CKNA-FM
New Carlisle	QC	107.1	6.5	F	CHNC-FM
Pikogan	QC	100.1	3.7	m	CKAG-FM
Port-Cartier	QC	99.1	45	F	CIPC-FM
Québec	QC	90.9	5.7	F	CION-FM
Québec	QC	91.9	31	F	CJEC-FM
Québec	QC	93.3	33	F	CJMF-FM
Québec	QC	98.1	40	F	CHOI-FM
Québec	QC	98.9	41	F	CHIK-FM
Québec/Lévis	QC	102.1	33.9	F	CFEL-FM
Québec/Lévis	QC	102.9	32.8	F	CFOM-FM
Québec	QC	107.5	37	F	CITF-FM
Rimouski	QC	96.5	6.4	F	CKMN-FM
Rimouski	QC	98.7	100	F	CIKI-FM
Rimouski	QC	102.9	33.6	F	CJOI-FM
Rivière-du-Loup	QC	103.7	60	F	CIEL-FM
Rivière-du-Loup	QC	107.1	100	F	CIBM-FM
Roberval	QC	99.5	50	F	CHRL-FM
Rouyn-Noranda	QC	88.7	3.4	F	CHIC-FM
Rouyn-Noranda	QC	95.7	44	F	CHGO-FM-1
Rouyn-Noranda	QC	96.5	61.1	F	CHOA-FM
Rouyn-Noranda	QC	98.3	3.4	F	CHUN-FM
Rouyn	QC	99.1	3	F	CJMM-FM
Saguenay	QC	92.5	14.2	F	CKAJ-FM
Sainte-Foy	QC	94.3	6	F	CHYZ-FM
Sept-Îles	QC	94.1	11.3	F	CKCN-FM
Sherbrooke	QC	93.7	25.5	F	CFGE-FM
Sherbrooke	QC	102.7	92	F	CITE-FM-1
Sherbrooke	QC	107.7	25	F	CKOY-FM
Sorel	QC	101.7	3	F	CJSO-FM
St-Gabriel-de-Brandon	QC	99.1	9.8	F	CFNJ-FM
St-Georges-de-Beauce	QC	99.7	100	F	CHJM-FM
St-Georges-de-Beauce	QC	103.5	15	F	CKRB-FM
St-Hyacinthe	QC	106.5	3	F	CFEI-FM
St-Jérôme	QC	103.9	39.3	F	CIME-FM
Ste-Marie-de-Beauce	QC	101.5	100	F	CHEQ-FM
Thetford Mines	QC	97.3	100	F	CFJO-FM
Thetford Mines	QC	105.5	6	F	CKLD-FM
Trois-Rivières	QC	89.1	3	F	CFOU-FM
Trois-Rivières	QC	89.9	6	F	CIRA-FM-2
Trois-Rivières	QC	94.7	100	F	CHEY-FM
Trois-Rivières	QC	100.1	64.1	F	CJEB-FM
Trois-Rivières	QC	102.3	5.8	F	CIGB-FM
Trois-Rivières	QC	106.9	100	F	CKOB-FM
Valleyfield	QC	103.1	3	F	CKOD-FM
Val-d'Or	QC	102.7	96	F	CJMV-FM
Ville-Marie	QC	93.1	34	F	CKVM-FM
Waskaganish	QC	92.5	7.1		CJRH-FM
Waswanipi	QC	93.9	6.2		CFNE-FM
Wemindji	QC	99.9	4.8		CHPH-FM
Dafoe	SK	100.3	100		CJVR-FM-1
Estevan	SK	102.3	100		CHSN-FM
Estevan	SK	106.1	100		CKSE-FM
Gravelbourg	SK	107.1	100		CJME-2-FM
Humboldt	SK	107.5	96		CHBO-FM
Meadow Lake	SK	102.3	45		CJNS-FM
Meadow Lake	SK	104.5	45		CJCQ-FM-1
Melfort	SK	105.1	100		CJVR-FM

FM	Prov.	MHz	kW		Call
Moose Jaw	SK	100.7	100		CILG-FM
Moose Jaw	SK	103.9	100		CJAW-FM
Nipawin	SK	94.7	14.8		CJNE-FM
North Battleford	SK	93.3	100		CJHD-FM
North Battleford	SK	95.5	28	m	CJLR-FM-6
North Battleford	SK	97.9	100		CJCQ-FM
Okanese First Nation	SK	95.3	50		CHXL-FM
Prince Albert	SK	88.1	49	m	CJLR-FM-3
Prince Albert	SK	90.1	3	F	CKSF-FM
Prince Albert	SK	99.1	100		CFMM-FM
Prince Albert	SK	101.5	100		CHQX-FM
Regina	SK	90.3	43	m	CJLR-FM-4
Regina	SK	92.1	100		CHMX-FM
Regina	SK	92.7	100		CHBD-FM
Regina	SK	94.5	100		CKCK-FM
Regina	SK	98.9	100		CIZL-FM
Regina	SK	104.9	100		CFWF-FM
Saskatoon	SK	92.9	100		CKBL-FM
Saskatoon	SK	95.1	100		CFMC-FM
Saskatoon	SK	96.3	100		CFWD-FM
Saskatoon	SK	98.3	100		CJMK-FM
Saskatoon	SK	102.1	100		CJDJ-FM
Swift Current	SK	94.1	100		CIMG-FM
Swift Current	SK	97.1	100		CKFI-FM
Swift Current	SK	101.7	100		CJME-1-FM
Wapella	SK	102.9	14		CFGW-FM-2
Waskesiu Lake	SK	106.3	11		CJVR-FM-2
Warmley	SK	107.3	100		CJME-3-FM
Weyburn	SK	103.5	100		CKRC-FM
Yorkton	SK	94.1	100		CFGW-FM
Yorkton	SK	98.5	50		CJJC-FM
Whitehorse	YT	98.1	4.3		CHON-FM

NB1: Txs below 3kW not listed

NB2: Most stns identify using a name rather than calls. Industry Canada stn list database **W:** strategis.ic.gc.ca/eic/site/smt-gst.nsf/eng/h_sf01842.html Stn history & info **W:** broadcasting-history.ca

BRITISH FORCES BROADC. SCE. Suffield AB
✉ BFBS Canada, BATUS, BFPO 14, UK ☎ +1 403 544 4104 **W:** bfbs.com/radio/stations/canada **BFBS 1: FM:** 98.1MHz, 104.1MHz

WEATHERADIO CANADA
The Meteorological Service of Canada operates a network of Weatheradio stns throughout Canada which broadcast current conditions, forecasts and alerts in English and French. Weatheradio stns broadcast on 7 freqs in the VHF 162MHz range as well as low power MW & FM. Stn lists & info **W:** ec.gc.ca/meteo-weather/default.asp?lang=En&n=8830FA44-1

CANARY ISLANDS (Spain)

L.T: UTC (31 Mar-27 Oct: +1h) — **Pop:** 2 million — **Pr.L:** Spanish — **E.C:** 50Hz, 220V — **ITU:** CNR

MW	kHz	kW	Net	Location	Island
1)	576	20	RNE-1	Las Palmas	GC
2)	621	300	RNE-1	Santa Cruz	TF
2)	720	10	RNE-5	Santa Cruz	TF
1)	747	25	RNE-5	Las Palmas	GC
3)	837	10	COPE	Las Palmas	GC
4)	882	20	COPE	La Laguna	TF r. low power
5)	1008	10	ABCPR	Las Palmas	GC
6)	1179	25	SERRC	Tenerife	TF
7)	1269	20	ECCA	Las Palmas	GC

Abbreviations: GC=Gran Canaria, GCF=Fuerteventura, GCL=Lanzarote, TF=Tenerife, TFP=Isla de la Palma, TFG=Isla de la Gomera, TFH=Hierro. (For network abbreviations refer to Spain).

Addresses and other information
1) R. Nacional de España, Av.1 de Mayo 21, 35002 Las Palmas de Gran Canaria ☎ +34 928 364 088 🖷 +34 928 362 754 – **2)** R. Nacional de España, San Martín 1, 38001 Sta. Cruz de Tenerife ☎ +34 (922) 288400 🖷 +34 922 283363 **R.1:** 24h on 621kHz **N:** On the h. **R.2:** (classical music) 24h. **R.3:** 24h. **R.5:** 24h – **3)** R. Popular de Las Palmas, Av. Escaleritas 60-1°, Las Palmas 35011 ☎ +34 928 286970 **E:** direccion. laspalmas@cadenacope.net Dir: Antonio Miguel Díaz **D.Prgr:** 24h. – **4)** R. Popular de Tenerife, Darías y Padron, 1-2°-38003 Santa Cruz de Tenerife ☎ +34 922 236900/05/09 🖷 +34 922 2369121 **E:** tenerife@cadenacope.net Dir: José Carlos Marrero Gonzales. **D.Prgr:** 24h – **5)** ANC Punto Radio Las Palmas, C/ Profesor Lozano 5, 2°, Urb. Industrial El Sebadal, 35008 Las Palmas de Gran Canaria **W:** www.radiolaspal-

mas.com **E:** informacion@radiolaspalmas.com ☎ +34 928 462052 🖥
+34 928 462057 Dir:María Enma Hernández Martín. **D.Prgr:** 24h – **6)**
R. Club Tenerife, Av. de Anaga 35, Santa Cruz de Tenerife 38001 ☎ +34
922 270400 🖥 +34 922 281043 **E:** radioclubtenerife@unionradio.es Dir:
Juan Ramon Hernandez. – **7)** Av. Escaleritas 58 bajo, 35011 Las Palmas
de Gran Canaria **W:** www.radioecca.org **E:** info@radioecca.org

Major FM Networks:
Gran Canaria (MHz): R.T. Insular 87.7 – R. Maria 87.9 – R. Marca
88.4 – RNE1 88.5 – RNE5 88.6 – Hit FM 88.9 – OCR 89.9 – ECCA 90.4
– COPE 91.0 – ABC Punto R 91.2 – Canaras R. 91.4 – C100 91.8 – R.
Top 21 92.0 – Intereconomia 92.8 – RNE1 92.8 – esRadio 93.3 – Onda
Islena 93.8 – R. Juventud 94.1 – Los 40 94.4 – RNE2 95.1 – esRadio
95.6 – Inolvidable FM 95.8 – Tamaran FM 96.2 – Los 40 96.5 – Europa
FM 98.0 – Canarias Ahora R. 98.2 – RNE3 98.5 – Intereconomia 98.8
– Rock FM 99.0 – Infierno FM 99.5 – SER Maspalomas 99.8 – SER Las
Palmas 100.3 – Global FM 100.6 – Canarias R. 100.8 – esRadio 101.1
– Dial 101.4 – Maxima FM 102.0 – SER 102.4 – Maxima FM 102.7
– Radio Canarias 103.0 – 7,7 R. Las Islas 103.8 – R. Faycan 104.2 – R.
Las Palmas 105.1 – M80 105.4 – R. Guiniguada 105.9 – RNE5 106.5
– OCR 106.8
Fuerteventura (MHz): RNE2 87.7 – R.Sintonia 88.2 – OCR 90.7
– COPE 91.2 – COPE 91.6 – R.Maxorata 92.1 – ECCA 93.0 – Atlantica
FM 94.2 – Dunas FM 94.4 – RNE1 94.6 – Europa FM 95.6 – Canarias
R. 96.9 – RNE3 100.6 – MiTierra FM 103.1 – Canarias R. 104.4 – RNE5
104.8 – R.Archipielago 105.0 – MCM Radio 106.9
Lanzarote (MHz): SER 89.7 – R. Alo FM 90.1 – COPE 90.7 – COPE 91.1
– R.Cristal 92.0 – RNE1 92.5 – ECCA 93.0 – R.Marca 93.6 – R.Maria
93.9 – RNE2 94.9 – O2 Radio 96.4 – R.Insular 96.7 – R. Las Arenas
98.6 – Onda Conejera 99.1 – RNE5 100.2 – Guapa FM 100.9 – Canarias
R. 101.2 – ABC Punto R 102.0 – Europa FM 102.5 –RNE3 102.8 – Mi
Tierra FM 103.1 – Canarias R. 103.5 – Los 40 104.0 – Cronicas R. 105.5
– C100 106.5
Tenerife (MHz): R.Decibelios FM 87.5 – Dial 87.8 – Canarias R. 88.1
– Intereconomia . 88.5 – RNE5 88.8 – Dial 88.9 – C100 89.1 – ECCA
89.6 – Marcha FM 89.8 – RNE3 90.0 – Onda 7 90.2 – MM Radio 90.6
– ABC Punto R. 90.8 – Maxima FM 91.1 – Dial 91.6 R.Atlantida 91.9
– RNE1 92.3 – ABC Punto R. 92.6 – Los 40 93.2 – OCR 94.0 R.Marca
94.5 – RNE1 94.8 – Orquestras del Atlantico R. 95.0 – RNE3 95.4
– Gente R. 95.6 – Loca Fun FM 95.8 – RNE2 96.2 – ABC Punto R.
96.5 – COPE 97.1 – R.Maria 97.5 – R.Marca 97.8 – RNE5 98.1 – Onda
Tenerife 98.5 – Los 40 99.1 – Kiss FM 99.4 – Formula Hit 99.7 – M80
100.1 – R.Pimienta 100.3 – Orquestras del Atlantico R. 100.5 – R.Taoro
100.7 – SER R.Clube Tenerife101.1 – COPE 101.4 – Astrovision
R. 101.9 – RNE2 102.1 – esRadio 102.3 – Kiss FM 102.5 – Onda
Colectiva Canaria R. 102.9 – R.Maria 103.2 – RKM R. 103.8 – RNE5
104.0 – Canarias R. 104.2 – La Mega Latina 104.5 – Canarias R. 104.7
– esRadio 104.9 – Russkoe R. 105.0 – R.Union Tenerife 105.3 – RNE1
105.6 – RNE3 105.7 – Canal 4 R. 106.1 – esRadio 106.3 – ECCA 106.6
– Exito R. 107.0– R.Realejos 107.9
Isla de la Palma (MHz): RNE5 89.6 – RNE1 90.8 – R.Murion 91.0
– Onda Cero 92.7 – Canarias R. 93.0 – COPE 95.1 – C100 95.6 – RNE2
96.7 – Los 40 97.4 – Canarias R. 97.5 – RNE5 98.4 – ECCA 99.5
– Canarias R. 100.5 – SER R.La Palma 101.6 – RNE1 102.7 – R.Maria
103.1 – Dial 104.1 – RNE2 104.5 – RNE3 106.1 – OCR 106.4 – Onda
Taburiente 107.0
La Gomera (MHz): Onda Tagoror Gomera R. 88.5 – R.CLM 90.2
– RNE5 91.7 – R.Insular de la Gomera 92.2 – R.Insular de la Gomera
92.2 – RNE1 94.3 – R.Cantera 94.7 – Canarias R. 96.7 – SER R.Garoè
98.8 – RNE2 101.8 – R.Garajonay 102.6 – ECCA 103.4 – Formula Hit
103.7 – RNE3 105.2 – R.Insular de la Gomera 105.9
El Hierro (MHz): RNE5 89.8 – ECCA 90.6 – SER R.Garoè 92.0 – RNE1
92.5 – RNE2 93.9 – RNE3 96.4 – RNE2 97.0 – RNE5 98.2 – Onda
Herrena 100.8 – RNE1 101.2 – Canarias R. 102.3 – Canarias R. 103.2
– RNE3 104.9 – Onda Herrena 107.0
There are hundreds of low power FM stns throughout the islands, for
details see **W:** www.lalistadelafm.com/canarias.htm

Tourist Radio FM Stations
These stns broadcast in German, English and other languages for tour-
ists visiting the Canary Islands. Most operate 24h
Atlantis FM (GCF) 99.3 (GCL) 101.7MHz **W:** www.atlantisfm.com
– **Buzz FM** (GCL) 88.6, 88.8MHz **W:** www.buzzfm.fm – **Coast FM**
(TF) 89.4, 102.2, 103.7MHz **W:** www.coastmusicradio.co.uk – **Express
FM** (TFG) 105.3MHz **W:** www.express-fm.net – **Happy Radio** (TF)
98.7, 102.4MHz **W:** www.happyradiotenerife.com – **Hola FM** (GCF)
95.7MHz **W:** http://www.holafm.de – **Holiday FM** (GC, TF) 95.3, 98.2,
99.0, 100.0MHz **W:** www.hollandfm.de – **Holland FM** (GC) 90.7MHz
W: www.hollandfm906.nl – **Hot FM** (GFC) 96.6, 97.4,104.6 W: www.
hotfmcanary.com – **Mix 101 FM Radio** (GC) 101.0, 104.8MHz **W:**
www.mix101.net – **Oasis FM** (TF) 101.0, 101.2, 101.9MHz **W:** www.

oasisfm.com – **On Life FM** (TF) 89.3,89.5,90.6,92.9 **W:** www.onlifefm.
es – **QFM** (TF) 94.3, 94.6MHz **W:** www.qmusica.com – **R. Europa/R.
Syd** (TF) 90.0MHz **W:** www.radiosyd.net/radioeuropa.htm – **R. Mega
Welle** (TF) 88.3, 102.0, 104.7MHz (GC) 88.3, 101.7MHz **W:** http://meg-
awelle.radio.de – **Spectrum FM** (TF) 105.3MHz **W:** www.canaries.
spectrumfm.net – **UK Away FM** (GCL) 99.4, 99.9MHz **W:** www.
ukawayfm.com

CAPE VERDE

L.T: UTC -1h — **Pop:** 400,000 — **Pr.L:** Portuguese, Crioulo — **E.C:**
50Hz, 220V — **ITU:** CPV.

AGENCIA NACIONAL DAS COMUNICAÇÕES (ANAC)
🖂 C.P. 892, Edifício MIT, Ponta Belém, Praia ☎+238 2604400 🖥 +238
2613069 **W:** www.anac.cv **E:** info.anac@anac.cv

RÁDIOTELEVISÃO DE CABO VERDE (RCV, Gov.)
🖂 Rua 13 de Janeiro 1-A, Achada de Santo António, Praia 🖂C.P. 29,
Av. Marginal, Mindelo, São Vicente 🖂 C.P. 40, Espargos, Ilha do Sal
☎🖥+238 2411444 **W:** www.rtc.cv **E:** rtc@cvtelecom.cv
L.P: Dir: Marcos Oliveira. PD: Giordano Custodio. Dir. Inf: Mario
Almeida. Dir. Tec: Francisco Lopes Monteiro.
FM: Monte Verde 87.6MHz 1kW, Morro Curral 89.7MHz 0.25kW,
Monte Tchota 91.6MHz 1kW, Mindelo 95.6MHz 0.5kW, Praia 98.1MHz
0.1kW + 12 relays below 0.1kW. **D.Prgr:** 24h.

Other stations:
R. Nova, C.P. 426, Mindelo, São Vicente. **E:** radionova@cvtelecom.
cv **FM (MHz):** Pinhão 91.8, Monte Vermelho 94.1, Cachaço 95.1,
Sal Rei 97.0, Monte Tropetona 99.1, Pedra Rachada 99.9, M. Tchota
101.6 0.25kW, Mindelo 102.3, M. Verde 104.3 0.5kW, Morro do
Curral 106.4 – **R. Comercial**: Santiago 92.9 1kW, Ponta Rachada
96.1MHz, Praia/M. Verde 99.9MHz – **R. CriToula**: M. Tchota 88.5MHz,
M. Barro/M. Verde 89.6MHz, Praia 94.9MHz, Morro Curral 98.9MHz
– **R. Educativa**: Monte Verde 101.5MHz, M. Tchota 102.3MHz,
Praia & 4 sites 103.1MHz – **Mosteiros FM**: M. Chota 96.1MHz, São
Filipe/Mosteiros 97.3MHz
RDP Africa: Monte Verde 93.9MHz 3kW, Monte Tchota/Pedra
Rachada 105.2MHz 3/1kW, Pedra Rachada 105.2MHz 1kW + 4 trs
under 1kW.
RFI Afrique, Praia/Santo Antão 99.3MHz 1kW. Fogo/Mindelo/Sal
100.7MHz 0.25kW in French and Portuguese.

CAYMAN ISLANDS (UK)

L.T: UTC -5h — **Pop:** 53,000 — **Pr.L:** English — **E.C:** 60Hz, 110V
— **ITU:** CYM

RADIO CAYMAN (Gov. Comm.)
🖂 71B Elgin Av, PO Box 1110, George Town, Grand Cayman KY1-1102
☎ +1 345 949 7799 🖥 +1 345 949 6536 **W:** www.radiocayman.gov.
ky **L.P:** Dir: Norma McField. Dep. Dir: Paulette Conolly-Bailey. CE:
Paul Dedrick
FM: R. Cayman One: Grand Cayman 89.9MHz 5kW/ Cayman Brac:
93.9MHz 0.3kW music, current affairs, news: 24h Relays BBCWS
0500-1100 – **Breeze FM:** Grand Cayman 105.3MHz 5kW/ Cayman
Brac: 91.9MHz 0.3kW music and news

CAYMAN ISLANDS WEATHER SERVICE (Gov.)
🖂 Ministry of District Adm, Works, Lands & Agriculture, Gov't Adm
Bldg, George Town, Grand Cayman KY1-9000
FM: Cayman Weather Radio: 107.9MHz 1kW

HURLEYS ENTERTAINMENT CORPORATION (Comm.)
🖂 Grand Harbour, Suite 21-22, Shamrock Rd, PO Box 30110 SMB,
George Town, Grand Cayman KY1-1201 ☎ +1 345 945 1166 🖥 +1 345
945 1006 **E:** info@z99.ky **W:** www.z99.ky and www.rooster101.ky
L.P: Pres. & GM: Randy Merren. PD (Z99): Scott Hamilton. PD (Roster
101.9): Keith Michaels
FM: Z99: George Town 99.9MHz 5kW: CHR – **Rooster 101.9:**
101.9MHz 5kW/Cayman Brac 101.9MHz 1 kW: Country

PARAMOUNT MEDIA SERVICES (Comm.)
🖂 Rankin's Plaza, 21 Eclipse Drive, PO Box 10734, George Town,
Grand Cayman KY1-1007 ☎ +1 345 949 8423 🖥 +1 345 946 9867 **E:**
info@vibefm.ky **W:** www.spinfm.ky and www.vibefm.ky
FM: Spin FM: George Town 94.9MHz 1kW: dance music – **Vibe
98.9:** George Town 98.9MHz 2kW/Cayman Brac 98.9MHz 0.3kW
urban Caribbean

ICCI-FM (Educ.)

✉ International College of the Cayman Islands, Newlands, 595 Hirst Rd, PO Box 136, Grand Cayman KY1-1501. College ☎ +1 345 947 1100 🖷 +1 809 947 1230 **L.P:** College Pres.: John Cummings
FM: 101.1MHz 0.5kW **D.Prgr:** 24h. Locally produced prgrs in E & Sp for Grand Cayman residents, or continuous music, acc. to availability of student volunteers.

DMS BROADCASTING LTD. (Comm.)

✉ 38 Godfrey Nixon Way, PO Box 31910 SMB, Grand Cayman KY1-1208 ☎ + 1 345 943 1367 🖷 +1 345 943 1368 **E:** info@dmsbroadcasting.ky
W: www.dmsbroadcasting.ky **L.P:** MD: Don Seymour. GM: Steve Jones
FM: CayRock George Town: 96.5MHz (1kW) Cayman Brac: 96.5MHz (0.3kW) – **HOT** George Town: 104.1MHz – **KISS FM** George Town 106.1MHz – **X 107.1** George Town 107.1MHz

WESTPOINT RADIO (Rlg.)

✉ Goulds Estate, PO Box 349, West Bay, Grand Cayman ☎ + 1 345.926 2100 🖷 +1 345 949 2166 **W:** www.westpointradio.ky **L.P:** MD: Locksley Gould **FM:** 94.3MHz 3kW

PRAISE 87.9 RADIO (Rlg.)

✉ 37 Barnes Rd, PO Box 152, George Town, Grand Cayman KY1-1501. **W:** www.caymanadventist.org.**FM:** 87.9MHz Adventist

CAYMAN BROADCASTING LTD. (Rlg.)

✉ 125 Eastern Av., PO Box 1336, George Town, Grand Cayman KY1-1108 **E:** info@lovefm.ky **W:** www.lovefm.ky **Love FM:** 103.1MHz 2kW

STAR 92.7 (Comm.)

✉ PO Box 976, George Town KY-11102 ☎ + 1 345 943 3700 🖷 +1 345 943 3600 **W:** www.star927cayman.ky **L.P:** John Watler. **FM:** 92.7MHz 2.5kW Urban

BIG FISH (Rlg.)

✉ PO Box 1408, Prospect KY-1501 **W:** www.bigfishradio.ky **L.P:** Pamela Norton. **FM:** 95.5MHz 3kW Contemporary Christian

CENTRAL AFRICAN REPUBLIC

L.T: UTC +1h — **Pop:** 4.5 million — **Pr.L:** French, Sango — **E.C:** 50Hz, 220V — **ITU:** CAF.

MINISTÈRE DE LA COMMUNICATION

✉ B.P. 940, Bangui ☎+236 21610437. **L.P:** Minister: Abdou Karim Meckassolia

RADIO CENTRAFRIQUE (Gov.)

✉ B.P. 940, Bangui ☎+236 75503632. **E:** radio.centrafrique@yahoo.fr **L.P:** DG: Aimé-Christian Ndotah. PD: Mrs. Pauline Gbianza.
MW: Bangui 1440kHz 50kW 0700-1700.
SW: Bangui 5035kHz 1kW 0500-2300 (inactive).
FM: 106.9MHz 1kW 24h.
D.Prgr in French/Sango: 24h. **N. in French:** 0600, 0700, 1300, 1800. **Ann:** F: "Ici Bangui, Radio Centreafricaine". **IS:** Repeated piano chord. Opens and closes with National Anthem.

RADIO ICDI (Integrated Community Development Int., Rlg)

✉ B.P. 362, Bangui **W:** icdinternational.org/radio **E:** radioicdi@gmail.com **L.P:** CPO: Richard Klopp, Coordinator: Mr. Farel Ndango
SW: Boali 6030 & ‡3390kHz 1kW. **D.Prgr:** in French, Sango, Bayaka and Fulfulde: Mon-Sat 0445-1100, daily 1445-2100 on 6030kHz. 1600-2100 on 3390kHz (3390kHz currently inactive, but expected to reactivate). **Ann:** "C'est la Radio ICDI qui émet depuis Boali sur 6030 kHz".

RADIO NDEKE LUKA

(joint initiative between the UN Development Programme, CAF government and Hirondelle Foundation)
✉ c/o PNUD, Av. de l'Indépendance, B.P. 872, Bangui ☎+236 72295252. **W:** radiondekeluka.org **L.P:** Dir: Martin Faye.
FM: Bambari/Bangui/Bouar 100.9MHz 1kW. **D.Prgr:** 24h in Sango/French. Also relayed by R. ICDI, Boali on 6030 kHz between 1700-1900.
Other stations (all MHz):
R. Be Oko, Bambari: 103.5 – **R. ESCA La Voix de la Grâce,** Bangui: 98.5 **E:** radiovoixdelagrace@yahoo.fr – **R. Évangile Néhémie,** Bangui: 104.4 – **R. Maigaro,** Bouar: 98 – **R. MKA,** Berbérati: 105.9 – **R. Ndoye,** Bossangoa: 98 1kW – **R. Notre Dame,** Bangui: 103.3 1kW – **R. Songo,** M'Baiki: 97.2 1kW – **R. Voix de la Sangha,** Nola: 98.0 **Africa No. 1,** Bangui: 94.5MHz (see main entry under Gabon).
BBC African Sce, Bangui: 90.2MHz.
RFI Afrique, Bangui: 99.8MHz.
Voice of America, Bangui: 107.1MHz

CHAD

L.T: UTC +1h — **Pop:** 10 million — **Pr.L:** French, Arabic, 8 ethnic — **E.C:** 50Hz, 220V — **ITU:** TCD

HAUT CONSEIL DE LA COMMUNICATION (HCC)

✉ N'Djamena. **L.P:** Moussa Mahamat Dago, president.

OFFICE NATIONAL DE RADIO ET TÉLÉVISION DU TCHAD (ONRTV, Gov.)

✉ B.P. 892, Av. Mobotu, N'Djamena. ☎+235 22521513 🖷 +235 22521517 **W:** onrtv.td **L.P:** Dir: Nguérébaye Adoum Saleh.
Station: N'Djamena-Gredia.
MW: 840kHz 20kW (irregular). **SW:** 6165kHz 250kW (irregular).
FM: 94.5MHz 0.1kW. **D.Prgr:** in French/Arabic/others:24h. Local prgr. for N'djamena on 92.5MHz. **Ann:** "Ici N'Djamena, Office National de Radio et Télévision du Tchad".

REGIONAL FM STATIONS

R. Moundou, B.P. 122, Moundou: 94.05/98.3MHz 200/450W – **R. Sarh,** B.P. 270, Sarh: 94MHz – **R. Abéché,** B.P. 105, Abéché: 101MHz – **R. Faya-Largeau:** 99.1MHz.
F.PI: 13 more regional stations.

Other stations:
Al-Bayan FM, N'Djamena: 93.7MHz – **Al-Nasr,** N'Djamena: 102.1MHz – **Al-Quran Al-Karim,** N'Djamena: 88.3MHz – **Dja FM,** N'Djamena: 96.9MHz 0.5kW – **R. Duji Lokar,** Mondou: 101.8MHz 0.5kW – **R. Évangile Développement,** Pala: 88.5MHz – **R. Lotiko:** Koumra 100.1MHz, Sarh 97.6MHz (also r. BBC). **W:** www.lotiko.org/fr/save/lotiko.htm **E:** lotiko@intnet.td – **R. Terre Nouvelle,** Bangor 99.4MHz 1.1kW – **La Voix du Paysan,** Doba: 96.2MHz 1kW.
Africa No. 1: N'Djamena 103MHz (see main entry under Gabon)
BBC African Sce: N'Djamena 90.6MHz
RFI Afrique: N'Djamena 100.2MHz

CHILE

L.T: UTC -4h (2 Sep 12-9 Mar 13, 13 Oct 13-8 Mar 14: -3h). Subject to change — **Pop:** 17 million — **Pr.L:** Spanish — **E.C:** 50Hz, 220V — **ITU:** CHL — **Int. dialling code:** +56

SUBSECRETARIA DE TELECOMUNICACIONES

Offices: Amunátegui 139, Santiago ✉ Clasificador 120, Correo 21, Santiago ☎ 02 672 6503 🖷 02 699 5138 **W:** www.subtel.cl **L.P:** Subsecr de Telecommunocations: Roberto Pliscoff Vásquez.

ASOCIACION DE RADIODIFUSORES DE CHILE

✉ Cas. 10476, Santiago de Chile ☎2 6398755 🖷2 6394205 **W:** www.galeon.com/redarca
L.P: Pres: César Molfino Mendoza. Dir: Alfredo Matte L.
STATIONS: MW: Call letters CA, CB, CC and CD indicate: A=No. Zone, B=Central Zone, C=So. Zone and D=Antarctic Zone. The figures indicate the freq. in kHz minus one cipher, f. inst. CB82 = Central Zone 820kHz. SW: Call letters CE are used for all zones.
° = on-air stn name not confirmed ‡ = inactive ± = varying freq.

MW	Call	kHz	kW	Station, location, h of tr
MS01	CB54	540	1	R. Ignacio Serrano, Melipilla: 1100-0400
LA02	CD55	550	1	R. LV. de la Tierra, Angol
MC01	CD59	590	10	R. Pingüino, Punta Arenas
MS03	CB60	600	10	R. Monumental, Santiago: 24h
CO01	CA62	620	1	R. Norte Verde, Ovalle: 1100-0400
BB03	CC62	620	10	R. Bío-Bío, Concepción: 24h
VA01	CC63	630	10	R. Stela Maris, Valparaíso: 1100-0500
LA03	CD64	640	10	R. Cooperativa AM, Temuco: 1030-0230
MA13	CC64	640	0.25	R. Portales, Curico
MS26	CB66	660	50	R. UC, Santiago
BB04	CC68	680	10	R. Cooperativa, Concepción
MS05	CB69	690	10	R. Santiago, Santiago: 1000-0600
LL02	CD69	690	10	R. Estrella del Mar, Ancud: 1100-0330
AT01	CA70	700	1	R. Nibsan, Copiapó: 1030-0300
LL03	CD70	700	1	R. Valdivia, Valdivia: 1030-0500
MC02	CD70	700	5	R. Magallanes, Punta Arenas
TA09	CA72	720	1	R. Portales, Iquique
VA02	CB73	730	10	R. Cooperativa AM, Valparaíso: 1000-0430
BB19	CD73	730	1	R. Angelina, Los Angeles
MS06	CB76	760	50	R. Cooperativa, Santiago: 24h
LL04	CD77	770	1	R. Cooperativa, Castro
VA03	CB80	‡800	5/1	R. Maria, Viña del Mar
CO02	CA82A	820	10/1	R. Portales, La Serena: 1000-0400
MS07	CB82	820	10/5	Radioem. Carabineros de Chile, Santiago: 24h

MW	Call	kHz	kW	Station, location, h of tr
BB05)	CC82	‡820	1	R. Maria Inmaculada, Concepción: 24h
LL06)	CC82	820	1	R. Concordia, La Unión: 1100-2330
VA04)	CB84	‡840	10	R. Portales, Valparaíso: 1000-0500
GS03)	CD84	840	10	R. Santa María, Coyhaique: 1030-0230
BB06)	CC86	‡860	10	R. Inés de Suárez, Concepción: 24h
MS08)	CB88	880	10	R. Colo Colo, Santiago: 24h
BB07)	CC89	‡890	10	R. Interamericana, Concepción: 24h
MC03)	CD89	890	20	R. Nal., Punta Arenas
VA05)	CB90	‡900	1	Cablenoticias, Valparaíso: 1100-0500
BB08)	CC90	‡900	1	R. Mayor, Chillán: 1100-0400
LL07)	CD90	900	1	R. LV de la Costa, Osorno: 1030-0400
MA14)	CC91	910	1	R.Tropical Latina (RTL), Talca
LA04)	CC92	920	1	R. 920, Temuco
MS09)	CB93	‡930	10	R. Nuevo Mundo, Santiago: 1000-0530
LL08)	CD93	930	10	R. Reloncaví, Puerto Montt: 1100-0400
VA06)	CB94	‡940	1	R. Valentín Letelier, Valparaíso
VA21)	CC94	‡940		R. Armonía, Viña del Mar
MS10)	CB96	‡960	10	R. Carrera, Santiago: 1100-0400
MC04)	CB96	960	10	R. Polar, Punta Arenas
AN04)	CA97	970	1	R. Calama, Calama: 1030-0400
MA01)	CC97	970	1	R. Lautaro, Talca: 1000-0500
GS04)	CD97A	970	1	R. Patagonia Chilena, Coyhaique: 1000-0400
LL09)	CD97	970	1	R. Austral, Valdivia: 1030-0400
VA07)	CB98	980	5	R. Agricultura, Valparaíso
MS11)	CB100	‡1000	10	BBN Radio, Santiago: 1030-0500
MC09)	CD100	1000		Nuevo Mundo, Punta Arenas
MA02)	CC102	1020	5	R. Amiga, Talca: 1000-0500
BB25)	CC103	1030		R. Chilena, Concepción: 1115-0330
MS12)	CB103	1030	1	R. Progreso, Talagante
LL10)	CD103	1030	1	R. Chiloé, Castro:1100-0330
MC05)	CD103A	1030	1	R. Payne AM, Puerto Natales
LA06)	CD104	1040	1	R. Raíces, Curacautín: 1100-0100
LL11)	CD105	1050	1	R. Armonía, Osorno: 1030-0630
MS13)	CB106	1060	50	R. Maria, Santiago
CO03)	CA108	‡1080	1	R. Río Elqui, Vicuña
LA07)	CD108	1080	1	R. Los Confines, Angol: 1100-0300
MA11)	CC1090	5/1		R. Chilena (R.Familia), Talca
VA08)	CB110	‡1100	10	BBN Radio, Viña del Mar
LA08)	CD111	1110	10	R. La Frontera, Temuco: 1000-0400
MS14)	CB114	‡1140	75	R. Nal., Santiago: 1000-0600
MA04)	CC116	1160	1	R. Ancoa, Linares: 1000-0600
CO10)	CB116	1160		R. El Espectador de America, La Serena
LA01)	CD116A	1160	1	R. Baha'i, Temuco: 1030-0230
MC06)	CD117	1170	3	R. Natales, Puerto Natales: 1200-0400
MS15)	CB118	1180	50	R. Portales, Santiago: 1030-0430
LL12)	CD121	1210	5	R. Armonia, Puerto Montt
MA05)	CC121	1210	1	R. Universidad de Talca, Talca: 1100-0400
VA20)	CB121	‡1210		R. Valparaiso, Valparaiso
LA09)	CD122	1220	10	R. Maria, Temuco
AN06)	CA124	1240	0.25	R. Principal Chuquicamata, Calama: 0950-0500
LL13)	CD125	1250	10	R. Armonía, Valdivia: 1100-0400
MA06)	CC126	1260	2	R. Condell, Curicó: 1100-0500
VA09)	CB127	±1270	10	R. Festival, Viña del Mar: 1000-0700
BB10)	CC128	1280	1	R. Arturo Prat Chacón AM, San Carlos: 1050-0405
LL14)	CD128	1280	10	R. del Sur «En Voz Alta», Osorno
AN07)	CA129	1290	0.25	R. Coya, María Elena
MS25)	CB130	1300	5	R. Tierra, Santiago: 1700-0100
AT04)	CA132	‡1320	0.25	R. Estrella del Norte, Vallenar
BB21)	CD132	1320	1	R. Lincoyan, Mulchén: 1100-0300
MS17)	CB133	1330	3	La Mexicana, Santiago: 24h
LL16)	CD133	1330	3/15	R. Vicente Pérez Rosales, Puerto Montt: 1055-0400
VA10)	CB134	1340	5	R. Colo Colo, Valparaíso: 0930-0300
BB11)	CC134	±1340	1	R. La Discusión, Chillán: 24h
LL17)	CD134	1340	1	R. Panguipulli, Panguipulli: 1200-0100
CO06)	CA135	1350	1	R. Riquelme, Coquimbo: 1030-0430
MS18)	CB138	1380	50	R. Corporación, Santiago
BB22)	CD140	1400	5	R. La Amistad, Los Angeles: 1030-0400
LL18)	CD140A	1400	5	R. Viento del Sur, Puerto Montt
VA11)	CB141	1410	3	R. Quinta Región, Valparaíso
LA12)	CC141	1410	1	R. Loncoche, Loncoche: 1100-0330
MS19)	CB142	±1420	1	R. Panamericana, Santiago: 1100-0400
MA07)	CC142	1420	1	R. Maule, Cauquenes: 1050-0430
BB13)	CC144	1440	1	R. El Sembrador, Chillán
VA12)	CB145	1450	1	R. Universidad Técnica "Federico Santa María, Valparaíso: 1100-0300
AN08)	CA146	1460	10	R. Antofagasta, Antofagasta: 1130 0300
MS20)	CB146	1460	1	R. Yungay, Santiago: 1100-0400
BB14)	CC146	1460	1	R. Armonía, Concepción
BB15)	CC148	1480	1	R. La Amistad AM, Tomé: 24h
AT06)	CA149	1490	1	R. Alicanto, El Salvador
MS21)	CB149	1490	1	R. El Canelo de Nos AM, San Bernardo: 1100-0400

MW	Call	kHz	kW	Station, location, h of tr
LA13)	CD149A	1490	5	R. Malleco, Victoria
MA09)	CC150	1500	5	R. Centenario, San Javier: 1100-0300
VA14)	CB150	1500	1	R. Trasandina, Los Andes: 1100-0400
CO09)	CA151	1510	1/0.5	R. Luís Alvarez Sierra, Illapel: 1100-0400
GB02)	CB151	1510	1	R. Poder Pentecostal, Rancagua: 24h
LA20)	CD151	1510	0.05	R. La Trompeta de Dios, Loncoche: 1100-0400
MA10)	CC152	1520	1	R. Soberanía, Linares: 1030-0430
AT05)	CA153	1530	1	R. Juan Godoy, Copiapó
VA16)	CB153	1530	1	R. Nexo, Quillota: 1100-0600
LL21)	CD153	1530	1	R. Nuvo Mundo, Puerto Montt
MS22)	CB154	1540	1	R. Sudamérica, Santiago:1200-0030
BB17)	CC154	1540	1	R. Colocolo, Chillán
LL22)	CC154	1540	1	R. San José de Alcudia, Río Bueno: 0955-0300
VA17)	CB155	1550	1	R. Provincial AM, Putaendo
GB03)	CC155	‡1550	1	R. Manuel Rodríguez, San Fernando:(r 1555): 1100-0400
TA06)	CA156	1560	5/3	R. Parinacota, Putre: 24h
MS23)	CB156	1560	1	R. Manantial, Talagante: 1100-0400
LA16)	CD156	1560	1	R. Parque Nacional, Villarrica: 1100-0400
GB04)	CC157	±1570	1	R. Niebla, Rancagua:
MA11)	CC157A	1570	7	R. Familia Chilena, Talca: 24h
GB05)	CC158	±1580	1	R. Colchagua, Santa Cruz: 1000-0400
I A18)	CD158A	±1580	0.5	R. Continental, Collipulli: 1100-0430
VA18)	CB159	±1590	1	R. Carnaval, San Felipe: 1100-0430
MS24)	CD160	1600	0.25	R. Nuevo Tiempo, Santiago
VA19)	CB160A	1600	0.25	R. Positiva, Viña del Mar
BB18)	CC160	±1600	0.25	R. Llacolén, Concepción
SW	**Call**	**kHz**	**kW**	**Station, location, h of tr**
TA06)	CE601	6010	1	R. Parinacota, Putre: 24h
LA19)	CE609	6090	10	R. Esperanza, Temuco: 24h

Addresses and other information

AN00 (ANTOFAGASTA):
AN04) Rafael Vargas 1875, Calama ☎🖷55 364353 – **FM:** 104.7MHz «Aurora FM»– **AN06)** Cas. 127, Calama ☎55 342712 **E:** socintegral@hotmail.com – **FM:** 99.7MHz "Sencación El Abra FM" – **AN07)** Of. SOQUIMICH, María Elena. – **AN08)** Gloria Postrera, Colectivo Peru, Ofic. 1, Antofagasta 🖷55 229561 **W:** www.radio-antofagasta.cl

AT00 (ATACAMA):
AT01) Vallejos 650, Departamento 11, Copiapó. ☎52 214133 – **AT04)** Cas. 13, Vallenar ☎51 913847 🖷51 613739 **E:** radioestrelladelnorte-vallenar@yahoo.es – **AT05)** Colipi 371, Copiapo ☎52 212031 – **AT06)** Av. El Tofo 535, El Salvador ☎52 475023

BB00 (BIO BIO):
BB03) O'Higgins 680, Concepción ☎41 620620 **W:** www.radiobiobio.cl **E:** biobio@laradio.cl – **FM:** 98.1MHz – **BB04)** Paicavi 119, 2° piso, (Paza Peru) (or Cas. 2337), Concepción ☎41 223207 🖷41 234697 **W:** www.cooperativa.cl **E:** cgomez@coopertaiva.cl – **BB05)** Barras Arana 544 – 3er piso, Concepción 🖷41 2626168 **W:** www.radiomi.cl **E:** radiomi@radiomi.cl – **BB06)** Castellón 477, 3° piso (Cas. 862), Concepción ☎41 2938972 **W:** www.radioinesdesuarez.cl **E:** contacto@radioinesdesuarez.cl – **BB07)** Calle Barros Arana 871, 5° piso, Of. 51, Concepción ☎41 2214450 **W:** www.radiointeramericana.net **E:** contacto@radiointeramericana.net – **BB08)** 5 de Abril 655 (Cas. 267), Chillán **W:** www.radiomayor900am.cl **E:** radiocontigo@gmail.com ☎42 237820 – **FM:** 89.7MHz "R.Nuble" – **BB09)** Aníbal Pinto 215, of 801, Concepción ☎32 259129 – **W:** www.radioagricultura.cl/ - **FM:** 90.1MHz «Galaxia», 106.5MHz «Aurora» – **BB10)** Cas. 265, San Carlos **W:** www.radiosancarlos.cl – **BB11)** 18 de Septiembre 721 (Cas. 479), Chillán **W:** www.diarioladiscusion.cl **E:** radiotv@ladiscusion.cl ☎42 211667 🖷42 213578 - **FM:** 94.7MHz – **BB13)** Arauco 447 (Cas. 336), Chillán ☎🖷42 224603 **W:** www.radioelsembrador.cl **E:** administracion@radioelsembrador.cl – **FM:** 104.7MHz «Aurora FM»– **BB14)** Av.Los Carrera N° 464, Concepcion ☎41 2854594 **W:** www.armonia.cl – **BB15)** Sotomayor 952, Tomé ☎41 2653629 🖷41 2650657 **W:** www.radiolaamistad.com **E:** contacto@radiolaamistad.com – **BB16)** Pedro Aguirre Cerda N° 377 (Cas. 66), Lota – **BB17)** Bulnes 220 (Cas. 35), Chillán ☎42 225220 **E:** radiocontigo@gmail.com – **BB18)** Colo-Colo 451 Of. 120, Nivel 2, Los Angeles ☎43 349920 **E:** contacto@radiocamila.cl – **BB21)** Gana 360, Mulchén ☎43 562739 – **BB22)** Cas. 541, Los Angeles 🖷43 313964 **E:** prensalaamistad@gmail.com – **BB25)** Arzobispado de la Santísima Concepción, Barros Arana 544, 3° piso, Concepción **W:** www.radiochilenaconcepcion.cl

CO00 (COQUIMBO):
CO01) Cas. 355, Ovalle ☎53 620359 🖷53 621509 – **CO02)** Los Carrera 525, 3° piso, Departamento C, La Serena **W:** www.radiogabrielamistad.8m.com **E:** radiogmistral@mixmail.com ☎🖷51 221659 - **FM:** 98.5MHz «Intima» – **CO03)** San Marín 14, Vicuña ☎51 412867 **W:** radiorioelquium.blogspot.com **E:** radiorioelqui108@yahoo.cl – **CO06)** Aldunate 1619, Coquimbo 🖷51 321051 **W:** www.

radioriquelme.com **E:** radioriquelme@portalquimbo.com – **CO09)** Independencia 175, Illapel 🖃53 522831 **E:** lradios@gmail.com – **FM:** 100.9MHz – **CO10)** O'Higgins No 519, Piso 2, Oficina 09, La Serena **E:** radiosamericachile@yahoo.cl

GB00 (LIBERTADOR GENERAL BERNARDO O´HIGGINS RIQUELME):
GB02) Pasaje Hoffman 61, Rancagua – ☎72 234 999 **W:** www.poderpentecostal.org – **GB03)** Chacabuco Esq. España, San Fernando 🖃72 714267 – **GB04)** Calvo 447, Rancagua – **FM:** 101.3MHz «FM San Fernando».– **GB05)** Rafael Casanova 146 (Cas.170), Santa Cruz ☎72 822193 **W:** www.radiocolchagua.com **E:** contacto@radiocolchaque.com – **FM:** 105.5MHz «Ensueño»

GS00 (GENERAL CARLOS IBANEZ DEL CAMPO):
GS03) Francisco Bilbao 691, Coyhaique ☎67 232398 🖃67 231306 **W:** www.radiosantamaria.cl **E:** contacto@radiosantamaria.cl – **FM:** 102.3MHz – **GS04)** Simón Bolívar 26, Coyhaique ☎67 232240 🖃67 233287 - **FM:** 99.3MHz «Acro Iris».

LA00 (LA ARAUCANIA):
LA01) Cas. 56-D, Temuco **E:** kalimat@telsur.cl ☎45 375142 🖃45 323657 - **Mapuche:** 1030-1400, 1600-2100, 0000-0230 – **LA02)** Av. Bernardo O'Higgins 294, piso 2 (Cas. 268), Angol **E:** vozdelatierra@123click.cl ☎45 714706 – **LA03)** Portales 775, Temuco ☎43 311015 **W:** www.cooperativa.cl **E:** cgomez@cooperativa.cl - **FM:** 93.5MHz «Temuco Rock & Pop FM» – **LA04)** Gral. Cruz 551 (Cas. 1499), Temuco ☎45 212707 – **LA06)** Cas. 136, Curacautín, Malleco – **LA07)** Lautaro 124 (Cas. 211), Angol. - ☎45 413647 - **FM:** 94.9MHz – **LA08)** Claro Solar 536, Temuco. - ☎45 213166 **E:** araucnayfrontera@entelchile.net - **FM:** 95.9MHz «La Araucana» – **LA09)** Antonio Varas 920, Temuco – **LA12)** Ignacio Serrano 264 (Cas. 61), Loncoche 🖃45 411567 **E:** radiocd141@gmail.com - **FM:** 105.9MHz «Vibración» – **LA13)** Cas. 267, Victoria – **LA16)** Vicente Reyes 753 (Cas. 110), Villarrica ☎45 411567 – **LA18)** Alcázar 1158, 2° piso, Collipulli ☎ 45 811623 – **LA19)** Luis Durand 3057 (or Cas. 830), Temuco ☎45 367070 🖃45 213790. - **English:** 0800-0830. **German:** Sun 1230-1300 – **FM:** 106.9MHz – **LA20)** Sector Elecoyan, Loncoche 🖃45 471052

LL00 (LOS LAGOS):
LL02) Ramírez 207, (Cas. 260), Ancud ☎65 622905 🖃65 622722 – **W:** www.cooperativa.cl – **LL03)** Caupolicán 597, of. 31, Valdivia – **LL04)** Thompson 255 (Cas. 174), Castro – **LL06)** Arturo Prat 466 (Cas. 312), La Unión ☎64 322275 🖃 64 322322 **E:** radioconcordia@surnet.cl – **LL07)** Cochrane 746 (Cas. 5-0), Osorno ☎64 233366 🖃64 268911 **W:** www.radiovozdelacosta.cl **E:** contacto@radiovozdelacosta.cl – **LL08)** Illapel 60 (Cas. 67), Puerto Montt **W:** www.radioreloncavi.cl **E:** radio-rr@telsur.cl ☎65 252946 🖃65 256523 – **LL09)** Arauco 363 3° piso, Valdivia ☎63 213601 **E:** radioaustral@surnet.cl – **LL10)** Bernardo O'Higgins 486 (Cas. 106), Castro 🖃65 632260 **W:** www.radiochiloe.cl **E:** gerencia@www.radiochiloe.cl - **FM:** 90.1MHz «Martin Ruiz de Gamboa» – **LL11)** Ramirez N° 816 2° piso Oficina 6, Osorno ☎64 643650 **W:** www.armonia.cl – **LL12)** La Serena 97, piso 4, Puerto Montt ☎65 254997 **W:** www.armonia.cl – **LL13)** Arauco N° 340, Valdvia ☎66 333280 **W:** www.armonia.cl – **LL14)** Patricio Lynch 1814-B, Osorno ☎64 330400 🖃64 33041 - **FM:** 101.5MHz «La Palabra» – **LL16)** Concepcion 110 (Cas. 166), Puerto Montt ☎65 258439 **E:** adona@telsur.cl – **LL17)** Bernard O'Higgins 793, Panguipulli. ☎63 310796 **E:** radio2@surnet.cl – **LL18)** Benavente 385, tercere piso, Puerto Montt ☎65 258048 **W:** www.radiovientodelsur.cl **E:** contacto@radiovientodelsur.cl - **FM:** 92.3MHz «Aurora» – **LL21)** Sector Alto Bonito, Puerto Montt – **LL22)** Pedro Lagos 295, Río Bueno ☎64 341531 **W:** www.radiosanjosedealcudia.com **E:** radio@radiosanjosedealcudia.cl

MA00 (MAULE):
MA01) 6 Oriente No 928 2 y 3 Sur (Cas. 214), Talca ☎71 231344 **W:** www.radiolautaro.cl **E:** radiolautaro@tie.cl – **MA02)** Diagonal Isidoro del Solar 285, Talca **W:** www.magica.cl **E:** chb@entelchile.net ☎73 210917 🖃73 217143 - **FM:** 100.7MHz «Futura FM», 107.1MHz «Logika FM» – **MA04)** Independencia 631 (Cas. 500), Linares **W:** www.radioancoa.cl **E:** cecili.rojas@tv5linares.com - **FM:** 90.7MHz – **MA05)** Casa 2 Norte 685, Talca ☎71 233019 **W:** http://radioemisoras.utalca.cl **E:** radioemisoras@utalca.cl - **FM:** 102.1MHz – **MA06)** Cas. 492, Curicó. - ☎75 310023 **W:** http://radiocondell.cl - **FM:** 89.9MHz «Futura – **MA07)** Claudina Urrutia 707, Interior (Cas. 196), Cauquenes ☎73 514303 - **FM:** 101.9MHz «Dinastia» – **MA09)** Cas. 18-D, San Javier ☎73 322529 🖃73 321226 - **FM:** 105.5MHz «Musical FM» – **MA10)** Diputado Dario Dueñas 340 (Cas. 67), Linares ☎73 210277 **W:** www.radiosoberania.es.tl **E:** soberania@hotmail.com – **MA11)** Poniente 1239 (Cas. 516), Talca **W:** www.radiofamiliachilena.cl **E:** radiofamilia@gmail.com ☎71 227255 – **MA13)** Villouta N° 558, Curico – **MA14)** Manuel Montt 198, Curico ☎75 328021 **W:** www.radiortl.cl

MC00 (MAGALLANES Y LA ANTARCTICA CHILENA):
MC01) Errazuriz 675, 2° piso, Punta Arenas ☎61 225958 **W:** www.elpinguino.com/radio - **FM:** 96.9MHz – **MC02)** José Nogueira 1370, Punta Arenas ☎61 243551 **W:** radiomagallanes.cl **E:** prensa@radi-omagallanes.cl – **MC03)** Rocha No 931, 2° piso, Punta Arenas. ☎ 61 617 115 **W:** www.radio-nacional.cl **E:** radionacional@tie.cl – **MC04)** Bories 871, Punta Arenas **W:** www.radiopolar.cl **E:** informaciones@radiopolar.cl ☎61 241417 🖃61 249001 - **FM:** 96.5-98.5-105.7MHz «Finísima» – **MC05)** Puerto Eberhard 229, Puerto Natales **W:** www.radiopayne.cl – **MC06)** Eberhard 212, Puerto Natales ☎61 410157 🖃61 410157 – **MC09)** Chiloe 1260, Punta Arenas ☎61 245563 **W:** www.nuevomundopatagonia.cl **E:**radio@nuevomundopatagonia.cl

MS00 (METROPOLITANA DE SANTIAGO):
MS01) Avenida Ortuzar N° 935 (Cas.110), Melipilla ☎832 3193 🖃832 34440 **E:** radioserrano@123mail.cl - **FM:** 104.5MHz «Caricia FM» – **MS03)** Av. Condell 910, Santiago ☎2 2221600 🖃2 2223093 – **W:** www.monumental.cl **E:** contacto@monumental.cl – **MS05)** Triana 868, Providencia, (Cas. 10195), Santiago ☎2 2360096 🖃2 363495 **W:** radiosantiago.cl **E:** gerenciageneral@radiosantiago.cl – **MS06)** Antonio Bellet 353, Providencia, Santiago **W:** www.cooperativa.cl **E:** info@cooperativa.cl ☎23 648000 🖃23 648010 – **MS07)** Av. Presidente Bulnes 80, Of. 127, Santiago **W:** www.carabinerosdechile.cl **E:** radio@carabineros.cl ☎02 698 8141 – **MS08)** Alameda 43623 (Cas. 56042), Santiago **W:** www.radiocolocolo.cl ☎🖃 2 6642353 – **MS09)** Estados Unidos 246, Santiago **W:** www.radionuevomundo.cl **E:** gerencia@radionuevomundo.cl ☎2 633 8957 – **MS10)** Eleodoro Flores 2475, Nunoa, Santiago ☎02 2692255 🖃02 2692257 **W:** www.nuevaradiocarrera.cl **E:** radio@radiovozdelacosta.cl – **MS11)** Av. Bulnes 120, Oficina 89 (Cas. de Correo 14351), Santiago Centro a metros de la Alameda ☎ 671 8602 **W:** www.bbnradio.org **E:** red@bbnmedia.org – **MS12)** Enrique Alcalde 1081, Talagante ☎28 151666 **W:** nuevaprogresoam@qmail.com - **FM:** 103.9MHz «Contacto» – **MS13)** Alcalde Dávalos 124 - Providencia, Santiago ☎22 7322344 – **MS14)** Cas. 244-V, Santiago – **MS15)** Fanor Velasco 11, Santiago ☎26723288 🖃26 980664 – **W:** www.radioportales.net **E:** contacto@radioportales.net – **MS17)** Los Leones 668, Providencia, Santiago ☎25 836602 **W:** www.lamexicana.cl **E:** contacto@lamexicana.cl – **MS18)** Portugal 810, Santiago ☎26 650673 🖃26 651032 **W:** www.radiocorporacion.cl – **MS19)** Gran Avenida Jose Miguel Carrera 5848, 4° piso, Santiago ☎5 242868 **W:** www.radiopanamericanadechile.cl **E:** director@radiopanamericanadechile.cl – **MS20)** Irarrazaval 2821, Of. 427, Edif. Century, Torre B Nuñoa, Santiago ☎22 746596 **E:** cb146yungay@hotmail.com – **MS21)** Av. Portales 3020 (Cas. 380), San Bernardo ☎28 414135 🖃28 571160 **W:** www.radiocanelo.cl **E:** canelo@rdc.cl – **MS22)** Cas. 1346, Santiago **W:** www.radiosudamerica.cl **E:** director@radiosudamerica.cl ☎2 527 3999 – **MS23)** Av. Lib.Bdo. O'Higginsa 854, (Cas. 223), Talagante ☎81 51374 - **FM:** 102.9MHz «Embrujo FM» – **MS24)** Los Cerezos No 6251, Peñalolén, Santiago ☎22 844921 🖃22 087252 **W:** www.nuvotiempo.cl **E:** contactos@nuevotiempo.cl – **MS25)** Purisima 251, Barrio Bellavista, Recoleta, Santiago ☎ 27 323748 **W:** www.radiotierra.com – **MS26)** Alameda 340, Santiago ☎2354 2020 🖃2354 2054 **E:** radio@uc.cl

TA00 (TARAPACA):
TA06) Calle José Miguel Carrera 350 esquina Av. Circulación O'Higgins, Putre (Cas 82, Arica) 🖃58 252803 **E:** prensaputre@hotmail.com - **FM:** 94.5MHz «FM» Iquique

VA00 (VALPARAISO):
VA01) Pedro Montt 1766 (Cas. 3304), Valparaíso ☎32 2745537 🖃 32 259 6064 **W:** www.radiostellamaris.cl **E:** direccion@radiostellamaris.cl – **VA02)** Morris No 106, Depto. 155, Piso 15, Valparaíso – **W:** www.cooperativa.cl – **VA03)** 5 Norte 168, Viña del Mar ☎32 971201 – **VA04)** Cas. 89-V, Valparaíso ☎32 258699 – **W:** www.radioportales.cl/portal **E:** radioportalsger@adsl.tie.cl - **FM:** 98.9MHz «Carolina» – **VA05)** Valparaíso 633, piso 3, Valparaíso ☎32 695485 – **VA06)** Av. Errazuriz 2120, Valparaíso **W:** www.radiovalentinletelier.cl - **FM:** 97.3MHz – **VA07)** Victoria B° 2321(Cas. 90), Valparaíso ☎39 23000 🖃39 23072 **W:** www.radioagricultura.cl **E:** director@radioagricultura.cl - **FM:** 97.3MHz – **VA08)** Plaza Vergara 172, Oficina 22, Viña del Mar ☎32 885524 **W:** www.bbnradio.org **E:** red@bbnmedia.org– **VA09)** Paseo Cousiño 8, Viña del Mar **W:** www.radiofestival.cl **E:** servicios@festival.cl – **VA10)** Plaza de la Justicia 45, Of. 702, Valparaíso ☎32 2312297 🖃32 256509 **W:** www.radiocolocolo.cl – **VA11)** Chacabuco 2370, Valparaíso ☎ 32 681756 **W:** www.radiofe.cl **E:** leopoldmoreno@hotmail.com – **VA12)** Av. España 1680, Valparaíso **W:** www.radio.utfsm.cl ☎32 654137 - **FM:** 99.7MHz – **VA14)** Papudo 155 (Cas. 307), Los Andes 🖃34 421425 **E:** gerencia@radiosaconcagua.cl – **VA16)** Cas. 529, Quillota ☎33 470003 **W:** www.radiolibra.cl/NEXO **E:** lpardo@radiolibra.cl - **FM:** 104.7MHz «Libra Stereo FM» – **VA17)** Cas. 75, Putaendo ☎34 501428 🖃34 504040 – **VA18)** Carlos Condell 731, San Felipe ☎34 510428 **W:** www.radiocarnaval.cl/sanfelipe/index.htm **E:** radio@radiocarnaval.cl - **FM:** 91.7MHz – **VA19)** Cas. 972, Viña del Mar – **VA20)** Eusebio Lillo 520, local 12, edifico Torre Valparaiso, Valparaiso ☎32 296 3793 **W:** www.radiovalparaiso.cl **E:** prensa@radiovalparaiso.cl – **VA21)** Calle Antofagasta N° 131, Paradero 2, Nueva Aurora, Viña del Mar ☎32 296 2478 **W:** www.armonia.cl

FM in Santiago (all MHz) Power 1-10kW **Slogans:** Name + «FM»:

MS26) 88.1 Aurora – 88.5 Concierto – MS14) 88.9 R. Futuro – MS13) 89.3 R.Maria – MS26) 89.7 Duna – 90.5 Pudahuel – 91.3 El Conquistador – 91.7 Amistad – 92.5 Radioactiva – 92.9 Romance – 93.3 La Cooperativa – 93.7 Universo – VA02) 94.1 Rock & Pop – 95.3 40 principales – MS25) 95.9 Tiempo – 96.5 Beethoven – 97.1 Caracol – 97.7 Zero – 98.5 FM 2 – MS08) 99.3 Carolina – 99.7 Bío Bío – MS25) 100.1 Infinita – MS26) 100.9 – 101.3 Corazón – 101.7 FM Hit – 102.1 Oasis – 102.5 Univ. de Chile – 103.3 Horizonte – 103.9 Maria – 104.1 Romantica – 104.9 Nina – 105.7 Para ti – 106.3 Armonía – MS11) 106.9 Sintonía – 107.5 Fantasía

CHINA (People's Rep. of)

L.T: UTC +8h — **Pop:** 1,346 million — **Pr.L:** Mandarin, Amoy, Cantonese, Chaozhou, Hakka, Kazakh, Korean, Mongolian, Tibetan, Uighur, Zhuang, a.o. — **E.C:** 50Hz, 220V — **ITU:** CHN

MINISTRY OF INDUSTRY AND INFORMATION TECHNOLOGY
✉ 13 Xi Chang'an Jie, Beijing 100804 **W:** www.miit.gov.cn **LP:** Minister: Li Yizhong

THE STATE ADMINISTRATION OF RADIO, FILM AND TELEVISION (SARFT) (Gov.)
✉ 2 Fuxingmenwai Dajie, Beijing 100866 or P.O.Box 4501, Beijing ☎ +86 10 6809 2707 📠 +86 10 6851 2174
W: www.sarft.gov.cn **LP:** Dir: Wang Taihua

Official P.R.C Abbreviations: The 31 regions of the People's Republic of China, with their abbreviations and names in Pinyin (Chinese Phonetic Alphabet) version followed by the old spelling in brackets: AH: Anhui (Anhwei) – BJ: Beijing M. (Peking) – CQ: Chongqing M. (Chungking) – FJ: Fujian (Fukien) – GD: Guangdong (Kwangtung) – GS: Gansu (Kansu) – GX: Guangxi Zhuang A.R. (Kwangsi) – GZ: Guizhou (Kweichow) – HAN: Hainan (Hainan) – HB: Hubei (Hupeh) – HEB: Hebei (Hopeh) – HEN: Henan (Honan) – HL: Heilongjiang (Heilungkiang) – HN: Hunan (Hunan) – JL: Jilin (Kirin) – JS: Jiangsu (Kiangsu) – JX: Jiangxi (Kiangsi) – LN: Liaoning (Liaoning) – NM: Nei Menggu A.R. (Inner Mongolia) – NX: Ningxia Hui A.R. (Ningsia) – QH: Qinghai (Tsinghai) – SC: Sichuan (Szechwan) – SD: Shandong (Shantung) – SH: Shanghai M. (Shanghai) – SN: Shaanxi (Shensi) – SX: Shanxi (Shansi) – TJ: Tianjin M. (Tientsin) – XJ: Xinjiang Uighur A.R. (Sinkiang) – XZ: Xizang A.R.(Tibet) – YN: Yunnan (Yunnan) – ZJ: Zhejiang (Chekiang).

Regional Services: Add "Renmin Guangbo Diantai" (People's Broadcasting Station) to the stn name shown in the table below to obtain the full name in Standard Chinese.
Abbreviations: 1 = 1st prgr, 2 = 2nd prgr, 3 = 3rd prgr; EBS = Economic Broadcasting Station, LBS = Literary Broadcasting Station.
Languages: Standard Chinese (Putonghua), based on the Beijing dialect, is used in broadcasts throughout China. Various dialects and minority languages are included in the relevant regional services and in broadcasts to Taiwan.
Abbreviations: Ch = Standard Chinese, Kg = Kirghiz, Ko = Korean, Kz = Kazakh, Mo = Mongolian, Tb = Tibetan, Ug = Uighur.

MW	kHz	kW	Station	Tx Location
ZJ1)	531	10	Zhejiang	Jinhua
1)	540	10	CNR 1	
NM18)	540		Genhe	
QH4)	540	10	Haixi	Da Qaidam
1)	549	1200	CNR 5	Putian, FJ
EN2)	549	25	Zhengzhou	
NM12)	549	10	Alxa	Bayanhot
NM5)	549	10	Chifeng	
EB1)	558		Hebei	Shijiazhuang
FJ1)	558	50	Fujian	Jianyang
FJ1)	558		Fujian	Putian
FJ1)	558	10	Fujian	Longyan
NM17)	558	1	Zalantun	
NM3)	558		Baotou	
XJ1)	558	120	Xinjiang	Hutubi
YN16)	558		Nujiang	Lushui
1)	567	10	CNR 1	Lianyungang, JS
EN17)	567	10	Zhoukou	
TJ1)	567	20	Tianjin	
EN4)	576	10	Luoyang	
FJ5)	576		Quanzhou	
YN1)	576	10	Yunnan	Dali/Wenshan
ZJ1)	±576		Zhejiang	Linhai
14)	585	200	Southeast BC	Fuzhou, FJ

MW	kHz	kW	Station	Tx Location
EB11)	585	10	Langfang	
EN14)	585	10	Nanyang	
EN1A)	585		Henan	Anyang
GS3)	585	3	Jinchang	
HB8)	585	10	Jingzhou	
HL3)	585		Qiqihar	
JL2)	585	10	Changchun	
JL10)	585		Yanbian	
JS1)	585	50	Jiangsu	Nanjing
JX5)	585	10	Xinyu	
LN16)	585	1	Chaoyang	Beipiao
SX6)	585		Jincheng	
SD1)	594	50	Shandong	Jinan
XZ1)	594	300	Xizang	Lhasa
13)	603		VO Pujiang	SH
AH1)	603	10	Anhui	Hefei
AH4)	603		Huaibei	
BJ1)	603	25	Beijing	
EB1)	603		Hebei	Shijiazhuang
EB12)	603		Hengshui	
EB6)	603		Zhangjiakou	
EN13)	603	10	Sanmenxia	
EN1A)	603	200	Henan	Zhengzhou
GD1)	603	10	Guangdong	Guangzhou
GZ1)	603	10	Guizhou	Guiyang
HB3)	603	10	Wuhan	
HL5)	603		Shuangyashan	
JL1)	603		Jilin	Fuyu
JL10)	603		Yanbian	Dunhua
JL3A)	603		Jilin-shi EBS	
JS1)	603		Jiangsu	Yangzhou
JS12)	603		VO Jiangnan	
JS16)	603		Suzhou	
JS9)	603	1	Nantong	
JX1)	603		Jiangxi	Shangrao/Jiujiang
JX9)	603	10	Ji'an	
LN1)	603	10	Liaoning	Dandong
LN10)	603		Yingkou	
LN7)	603		Dandong	
NM10)	603	10	Ordos BS	
NM19)	603		Morin Dawa	
NM8)	603	50	Hulun Buir	Hailar
SD1)	603	1	Shandong	Zibo
SD3)	603	10	Qingdao	
SD10)	603	10	Jining	
SD5)	603	10	Zaozhuang	
SH2)	603		Dongfang	
SN1)	603	25	Shaanxi	Xi'an
SN7)	603		Yan'an	
SX1)	603	30	Shanxi	Taiyuan
SX4)	603	1	Yangquan	
XJ10)	603		Shihezi	
XJ9)	603	1	Ili	Yining
YN1)	603		Yunnan	Zhaotong/Gejiu
ZJ1)	603		Zhejiang	Hangzhou
ZJ4)	603	10	Ningbo	
FJ1)	612	100	Fujian	Ningde
LN1)	612	10	Liaoning	Dandong
SC1)	612	10	Sichuan	Neijiang/Yibin
SD13)	612	10	Linyi	
HB9)	621	10	Yichang	
HL1)	621	200	Heilongjiang	Harbin
QH4)	621	20	Haixi	Da Qaidam
SC9)	621	3	Guangyuan	
SD1)	621	10	Shandong	Liaocheng
YN11)	621	1	Zhaotong	
1)	630	200	CNR 2	Nanchang, JX
1)	630	100	CNR 2	Yingyang, HEN
1)	639	200	CNR 1	BJ
AH3)	648	1	Huainan	
GD1)	648	150	Guangdong	Guangzhou
JL2)	648		Changchun	
LN14)	648		Liaoning	
LN16)	648	3	Chaoyang	
SH1)	648	10	Shanghai	
XJ7)	648		Kashi	
EN1)	657	300	Henan	Zhengzhou
JL7)	657	1	Baishan	
ZJ6)	657		Jiaxing	
11)	666	600	VO Strait	Fuzhou, FJ
AH2)	666	10	Hefei	
GZ5)	666	1	Anshun	

MW	kHz	kW	Station	Tx Location	MW	kHz	kW	Station	Tx Location
HL10)	666	10	Jiamusi		ZJ11)	747		Zhoushan	
JL4)	666	10	Siping		ZJ4)	747		Ningbo	
LN8)	666	2	Jinzhou		SX8)	750	1	Xinzhou	
QH1)	666	200	Qinghai	Xining	1)	756	150	CNR 1	Harbin, HL
SD10)	666	1	Jining		1)	765	600	CNR 5	Fuzhou, FJ
TJ1)	666	50	Tianjin		AH7)	765	1	Bengbu	
YN10)	666	1	Dongchuan		EN24)	765	10	Gongyi	
ZJ5)	666	7.5	Wenzhou		GD8)	765	10	Shaoguan	
JX5)	675	1	Xinyu		GZ1)	765	10	Guizhou	Zunyi
NM1)	675	200	Nei Menggu	Hohhot	GZ3)	765	1	Liupanshui	
XJ1)	675		Xinjiang	Altay	NM1)	765	10	Nei Menggu	Baotou
YN12)	675	1	Gejiu		BJ1)	774	10	Beijing	
YN15)	675	10	Diqing	Shangri-la	HB1)	774	100	Hubei	Wuhan
ZJ9)	675		Jinhua		LN8)	774		Jinzhou	
1)	684	1200	CNR 6	Putian, FJ	SX2)	774		Taiyuan	
AH1)	684		Anhui	Xuancheng	XJ6)	774	10	Hotan	
AH13)	684		Suzhou		11)	783		VO Strait	Zhangpu, FJ
EB8)	684	10	Tangshan		EB1)	783	100	Hebei	Baoding
GS1)	684		Gansu	Jinchang	EB1)	783		Hebei	Chengde/Langfang
HB2)	684	10	Chutian	Jingmen	EB1)	783		Hebei	Handan/Cangzhou
HL9)	684	50	Mudanjiang		GD10)	783		Meizhou	
LN5)	684	10	Fushun		EN19)	792	1	Xinmi	
XJ1)	684	3	Xinjiang	Hotan	GS5)	792	1	Jiayuguan	
ZJ11)	684	10	Zhoushan		GX1)	792	200	Guangxi	Nanning
HL3)	693	10	Qiqihar		LN2)	792	10	Shenyang	
SN1)	693	300	Shaanxi	Xianyang	NM10)	792		Ordos BS	Otog
2)	702		CNR DS	Zhuhai, GD	SC3)	792		Chengdu	
JL3)	702	10	Jilin-shi		SH2)	792	50	Dongfang	
JS1)	702	200	Jiangsu	Nanjing	XJ2)	792		Urumqi	
LN16)	702	3	Chaoyang	Lingyuan	AH1)	801	10	Anhui	Hefei
NM15)	702	1	Manzhouli		AH12)	801	10	Fuyang	
NM5)	702	10	VO Tongliao		AH15)	801	1	Chizhou	
NM6)	702	10	Ulanqab	Jining	EB10)	801	25	Cangzhou	
SC11)	702	1	Neijiang		EB8)	801	10	Tangshan	
XJ1)	702	10	Xinjiang	Urumqi	EN8)	801		Xinxiang	
YN5)	702	10	Honghe	Gejiu	FJ3)	801		Xiamen	
AH12)	711	3	Fuyang		GD2)	801	50	Zhujiang EBS	Maoming
AH16)	711	1	Lu'an		GS1)	801		Gansu	Lanzhou
EN2)	711	10	Zhengzhou		HB1)	801	10	Hubei	Jingmen/Macheng
QH1)	711	10	Qinghai	Golmud	HB2)	801		Chutian	Chongyang
SC5)	711	1	Panzhihua		JS1)	801	1	Jiangsu	Zhenjiang
SC8)	711	1	Mianyang		JS2)	801		Nanjing	
ZJ10)	711	3	Quzhou		JS3)	801		Xuzhou	
ZJ12)	711		Lishui		JS5)	801	10	Huai'an	
1)	720	200	CNR 2	BJ	JS7)	801		Yangzhou	
SC7)	720	1	Deyang		LN1)	801		Liaoning	Dandong/Gaizhou
AH1)	720		Anhui		LN16)	801	1	Chaoyang	Lingyuan
1)	720		CNR13		NX2)	801	10	Yinchuan	
EN16)	729	10	Shangqiu		SD10)	801	1	Jining	
JX1)	729	200	Jiangxi	Nanchang	SD14)	801	10	Liaocheng	
EN1)	738		Henan	Anyang	SD4)	801	10	Zibo	
HN1)	738	200	Hunan	Changsha	SD8)	801	10	Yantai	
JL1)	738	150	Jilin	Changchun	SN1)	801		Shaanxi	Weinan
XJ1)	738	120	Xinjiang	Hutubi	SN2)	801		Xi'an	
ZJ8)	738	5	Shaoxing		XJ7)	801		Kashi	
1)	747		CNR 12	BJ	ZJ5)	801	10	Wenzhou	
AH2)	747	1	Hefei		EN18)	810		Zhumadian	
EB1)	747		Hebei	Shijiazhuang	JL5)	810	10	Liaoyuan	
EB5)	747	10	Baoding		LN1)	810	5	Liaoning	Panjin
EB12)	747		Hengshui		LN15)	810		Tieling	
EN1)	747	25	Henan	Huangchuan	LN16)	810	10	Chaoyang	
EN5)	747	10	Pingdingshan		SN2)	810	50	Xi'an	
FJ6)	747		Longyan		ZJ1)	810	200	Zhejiang	Hangzhou
GD14)	747		Zhongshan		SX1)	819	200	Shanxi	Taiyuan
HB1)	747	10	Hubei	Qichun	XJ11)	819		Korla	
JS11)	747	3	Changzhou		XJ12)	819	1	Kuytun	
JS6)	747		Yancheng		XJ13)	819		Bayingolin	Korla
JX8)	747		Ganzhou		BJ1)	828	50	Beijing	
LN1)	747		Liaoning	Dandong	EN1)	828	10	Henan	
LN10)	747		Yingkou		EN17)	±828		Zhoukou	
LN16)	747	3	Chaoyang	Jianping	EN6)	828		Jiaozuo	
LN5)	747		Fushun		GD1)	828	50	Guangdong	Heyuan
NM4)	747	1	Wuhai		HB23)	±828	1	Xiantao	
NX1)	747	10	Ningxia	Yinchuan	HB8)	828	10	Jingzhou	
SC1)	747	200	Sichuan	Chengdu	1)	837		CNR 1	
SC14)	747		Nanchong		1)	837		CNR 5	Quanzhou, FJ
SD11)	747		Rizhao		EN15)	837		Xinyang	
SD13)	747	10	Linyi		FJ1)	837	3	Fujian	Fuding
SN1)	747	50	Shaanxi	Xianyang	FJ1)	837		Fujian	Pucheng
SN6)	747	1	Weinan		HL2)	837	20	Harbin	
TJ1)	747		Tianjin Binhai		LN14)	837	1	Liaoyang	
YN6)	747	100	Xishuangbanna	Jinghong	XJ1)	837	10	Xinjiang	Urumqi

MW	kHz	kW	Station	Tx Location
12)	846	3	Jiangsu	Nanjing, JS
2)	846	10	CRI DS 4	BJ
AH1)	846	10	Anhui	Suzhou
AH14)	846	1	Chaohu	
AH4)	846	1	Huaibei	
EB1)	846		Hebei	Hengshui/Tangshan
EB10)	846	10	Cangzhou	
EB11)	846	10	Langfang	
EB3)	846		Handan	
EN1)	846	100	Henan	Zhengzhou
EN5)	846	3	Pingdingshan	
EN7)	846		Hebi	
GD1)	846		Guangdong	
GX1)	846	10	Guangxi	Qinzhou
HB1)	846	15	Hubei	Qichun
HB2)	846	10	Chutian	Xianning/Yichang
JL1)	846	10	Jilin	Changchun
JS1)	846	3	Jiangsu	Nanjing
JS11)	846	10	Changzhou	
JS13)	846	5	Suzhou	
LN13)	846	10	Fuxin Mo BS	
LN8)	846		Jinzhou	
SD15)	846	10	Binzhou	
SD2)	846		Jinan	
SD3)	846	10	Qingdao	
SD7)	846	5	Weifang	
SD9)	846	10	Weihai	
SX1)	846	20	Shanxi	Changzhi
XJ1)	846	3	Xinjiang	Hotan
XZ1)	846	10	Xizang	Lhasa
YN1)	846		Yunnan	Longchuan/Gejiu
SX10)	846		Shuozhou	
1)	855	50	CNR 2	Anning, YN
1)	855	10	CNR13	Urumqi
AH1)	864	50	Anhui	Hefei
EB20)	864		Renqiu	
EN20)	864		Qinyang	
SD15)	864	10	Binzhou	
ZJ1)	864		Zhejiang	Ninghai
ZJ15)	864	1	Jiangshan	
15)	873	200	China Huayi BC	Xiamen, FJ
EB13)	±873		Xinji	
EN3)	±873	10	Kaifeng	
GS1)	873	50	Gansu	Lanzhou
HB3)	873	50	Wuhan	
HL1)	873	50	Heilongjiang	Harbin
SD13)	873	10	Linyi	
XJ8)	873		Changji	
ZJ7)	873		Huzhou	
EB2)	882	10	Shijiazhuang	
EN23)	882		Ruzhou	
EN9)	882		Anyang	
FJ1)	882	100	Fujian	Fuzhou
FJ1)	882		Fujian	Xiamen/Sanming
GZ6)	882	1	Qiannan	Duyun
LN1)	882	10	Liaoning	Shenyang
LN3)	882	50	Dalian	
NM2)	882	10	Hohhot	
QH3)	882	10	Yushu	
XJ4)	882		Karamay	
XJ9)	882	1	Ili	Yining
LN7)	891	1	Dandong	
NM13)	891	10	Hinggan	Ulanhot
NX1)	891	200	Ningxia	Yinchuan
SD1)	891		Shandong	Dongying
XJ10)	891		Shihezi	
1)	900	10	CNR 2	Golmud, QH
2)	900		CRI DS 5	BJ
AH1)	900		Anhui	Bengbu/Haungshan
EB1)	900		Hebei	Shijiazhuang
EB6)	900		Zhangjiakou	
EB7)	900	1	Chengde	
EB8)	900		Tangshan	
EB9)	900		Qinhuangdao	
EN1)	900	100	Henan	Zhengzhou
EN12A)	900		Luohe EBS	
FJ1)	900	1	Fujian	Yongding
FJ1)	900		Fujian	Ninghua/Youxi
GD5)	900		Shenzhen	
GD6)	900		Zhuhai	
HB1)	900	1	Hubei	Yingcheng
HB2)	900	10	Chutian	Xiangyang

MW	kHz	kW	Station	Tx Location
HL1)	900	50	Heilongjiang	Bei'an/Jiamusi
HN1)	900		Hunan	Changsha
JL16)	900	1	Yanji	
JL2)	900		Changchun	
JL4)	900	1	Siping	
JS10)	900		Zhenjiang	
JS12)	900		Wuxi	
JS2)	900		Nanjing	
JS6)	900		Yancheng Huanghai	
LN1)	900		Liaoning	Chaoyang/Huludao
LN19)	900	1	Haicheng	
LN6)	900	1	Benxi	
NM5)	900	10	Chifeng	
SD3)	900	10	Qingdao	
SN1)	900	30	Shaanxi	Xi'an
SN4)	900	1	Baoji	
SX1)	900		Shanxi	Taiyuan
SX3)	900	10	Datong	
YN9)	900	100	Dehong	Luxi
ZJ11)	900		Zhoushan	
1)	909	100	CNR 6	Quanzhou, FJ
HL8)	909	7.5	Yichun	
JL6)	909	10	Tonghua	
QH1)	909	10	Qinghai	
SC1)	909	10	Sichuan	Jiange
TJ1)	909	50	Tianjin	
XJ1)	909		Xinjiang	Bortala
XJ)	909		Xinjiang	Bole
SD1)	918	200	Shandong	Jinan
1)	927		CNR 6	Xiamen, FJ
BJ1)	927	50	Beijing	
EB4)	927	12.5	Xingtai	
EN11)	927		Xuchang	
EN14)	927	10	Nanyang	
EN16)	927	10	Shangqiu	
GD1)	927	10	Guangdong	Guangzhou
GZ1)	927	200	Guizhou	Kaili
HB1)	927	10	Hubei	Xianning
HB12)	927	1	Xiaogan	
HB2)	927	10	Chutian	Suizhou
HL1)	927	10	Heilongjiang	Shuangyashan
HL2A)	927	1	Harbin EBS	Hulan
JL19)	927	1	Hunchun	
JL3)	927	10	Jilin-shi	
JS11)	927	3	Changzhou	
JS16)	927	1	Changshu	
JS8)	927		Taizhou	
JX1)	927	10	Jiangxi	Jiujiang
LN1)	927	12.5	Liaoning	Shenyang
NM7)	927	10	Xilingol	Xilinhot
SH1)	927		Shanghai	
XJ2)	927		Urumqi	
YN1)	927		Yunnan	Kaiyuan
YN17)	927	1	Lufeng	
ZJ7)	927		Huzhou	
ZJ1)	930		Zhejiang	
AH1)	936	200	Anhui	Hefei
NM10)	936	10	Ordos BS	
1)	945	400	CNR 1	Jiaohe, JL
1)	945		CNR13	
HB2)	945	10	Chutian	Qichun
HB2)	945	10	Chutian	Jingzhou
HL1)	945	50	Heilongjiang	Harbin/Jiamusi
EB12)	954	1	Hengshui	
GS2)	954	10	Lanzhou	
HA1)	954	30	Hainan	Haikou
LN4)	954	10	Anshan	
NM8)	954	50	Hulun Buir	Hailar
SC1)	954	10	Sichuan	Chengdu
SC6)	954		Luzhou	
ZJ2)	954	25	Hangzhou	
EB3)	963	10	Handan	
HB5)	963	10	Huangshi	
LN1)	963	50	Liaoning	Dalian
XJ1)	963		Xinjiang	Gulja
ZJ1)	963	10	Zhejiang	
EN1)	972	150	Henan	Zhengzhou
HL2A)	972		Harbin EBS	
XJ1)	972		Xinjiang	Altay
1)	981	200	CNR 1	Changchun, JL
1)	981	200	CNR 1	Nanchang, JX
SD7)	981	5	Weifang	

MW	kHz	kW	Station	Tx Location	MW	kHz	kW	Station	Tx Location
EB9)	990		Qinhuangdao		ZJ1)	±1080		Zhejiang	
SH1)	990	100	Shanghai		1)	1089	600	CNR 6	Fuzhou, FJ
YN1)	990	10	Yunnan	Gejiu	HN3)	1089	1	Zhuzhou	
AH19)	999		Haozhou		LN1)	1089	200	Liaoning	Shenyang
GD1)	999	10	Guangdong	Guangzhou	AH1)	1098		Anhui	Wuhu
GZ2)	999	10	Guiyang		AH18)	1098		Dangtu Xian	
LN1)	999	200	Liaoning	Shenyang	AH7)	±1098	1	Bengbu	
SC1)	999		Sichuan	Chengdu	EB1)	1098		Hebei	Zhangjiakou
SD1)	999	10	Shandong	Jining	EN1A)	1098		Henan	Zhengzhou
XJ1)	999	10	Xinjiang	Hami	EN5)	1098		Pingdingshan	
XZ1)	999		Xizang	Lhasa	GD11)	1098	1	Huizhou	
1)	1008	200	CNR 1	Anning, YN	GD19)	1098	5	Maoming	
2)	1008		CNR DS 3	BJ	GD4)	1098		Guangzhou	
2)	1008	3	CNR DS	Urumqi, XJ	HB1)	1098	10	Hubei	Jingzhou
AH1)	1008	10	Anhui	Hefei/Wuhu	HB8)	1098	10	Xiangyang	
EB11)	1008		Langfang		HN5)	1098	10	Hengyang	
EB3)	1008	10	Handan		JS1)	1098	1	Jiangsu	Zhenjiang
EN13)	1008		Sanmenxia		JS17)	1098	10	Zhangjiagang	
EN2)	1008		Zhengzhou		JS3)	1098		Xuzhou	
FJ1)	1008	1	Fujian	Zhangping	LN8)	1098		Jinzhou	
FJ1)	1008		Fujian	Shaowu	NM1)	1098	10	Nei Menggu	
GD1)	1008		Guangdong	Guangzhou	SD12)	1098	10	Dezhou	
GD22)	1008		Chenghai		TJ1)	1098		Tianjin	
HB2)	1008	50	Chutian	Jingmen	XJ5)	1098	1	Hami	
HB22)	1008	10	Suizhou		YN1)	1098		Yunnan	Kaiyuan
HN7)	±1008	1	Yueyang		ZJ11)	1098	10	Zhoushan	
HN9)	±1008		Yiyang		1)	1098	10	CNR 11	BJ
JS12)	1008		Wuxi		AH6)	1107	1	Tongling	
JS2)	1008	10	Nanjing		EN7)	1107	10	Hebi	
NX1)	1008	1	Ningxia	Guyuan	FJ3)	1107	10	Xiamen	
SD12)	1008	10	Dezhou		HA1)	1107	10	Hainan	Wuzhishan
SD3)	1008		Qingdao		JL1)	1107	1	Jilin	Siping/Fuyu
SN1)	1008	10	Shaanxi	Hanzhong/Yan'an	JX4)	1107	1	Pingxiang	
SN1)	1008		Shannxi	Xi'an	XJ1)	1107	120	Xinjiang	Hutubi
TJ1)	1008	50	Tianjin		ZJ6)	1107	10	Jiaxing	
1)	1017		CNR 1	Dongtou, ZJ	1)	1116	120	CNR 2	Harbin, HL
1)	1017	200	CNR 8	Changchun, JL	1)	1116	600	CNR 5	Shaowu, FJ
EB5)	1017	10	Baoding		AH12)	1116	10	Fuyang	
GD1)	1017		Guangdong	Shaoguan/Shantou	HA1)	1116		Hainan	
BJ1)	1026	50	Beijing		SC1)	1116	200	Sichuan	Chengdu
GZ1)	1026	200	Guizhou	Guiyang	SD10)	1116	1	Jining	
JS14)	1026		Yizheng		EB1)	1125		Hebei	Shijiazhuang
JS6)	1026		Yancheng		HB2)	1125		Chutian	Xiantao
LN10)	1026	2	Yingkou		HB3)	±1125	50	Wuhan	Changjiang
XJ6)	1026	10	Hotan		1)	1134	1000	CNR 1	Golmud, QH
1)	1035	50	CNR 1		GD18)	1134	10	Zhanjiang	
XJ1)	1044	1	Xinjiang	Yiwu	GS9)	1134	1	Yumen	
XJ1)	1044	10	Xinjiang	Urumqi	SN3)	1134	10	Tongchuan	
YN8)	1044	1	Dali		XJ9)	1134	1	Ili	Yining
ZJ1)	1050		Zhejiang		ZJ1)	±1134		Zhejiang	Wenzhou
1)	1053		CNR 10	BJ	1)	1143	10	CNR 8	
AH2)	1053	1	Hefei		AH1)	1143		Huaibei	
EB10)	1053	10	Cangzhou		EB18)	1143	1	Dingzhou	
EB15)	1053	1	Shahe		EB8)	1143		Tangshan	
EB17)	1053	1	Zhuozhou		EN1)	1143	100	Henan	Zhengzhou
EN18)	1053	10	Zhumadian EBS		EN5)	1143	3	Pingdingshan	
EN3)	1053	10	Kaifeng		GD1)	1143		Guangdong	Zhanjiang
EN4)	1053	10	Luoyang		GS4)	1143	10	Tianshui	
HB1)	1053	50	Hubei	Qianjiang	GZ5)	1143		Anshun	
HN7)	1053		Yueyang		HA1)	1143		Hainan	Haikou
JL10)	1053	20	Yanbian	Yanji	HB1)	1143	10	Hubei	Shiyan
JS1)	1053	10	Jiangsu	Nanjing	HB2)	1143		Chutian	Chanchun
LN1)	1053	50	Liaoning	Shenyang	HL10)	1143		Jiamusi	
SD2)	1053	10	Jinan		JL1)	1143	1	Jilin	Liaoyuan
YN1)	1053		Yunnan	Zhaotong	JL17)	1143	1	Tumen	
YN4)	1053	50	Wenshan		JL3)	1143	10	Jilin-shi	
GD2)	1062	150	Zhujiang EBS	Guangzhou	JL8)	1143		Songyuan	
HL11)	1062		Qitaihe		JS11)	1143	3	Changzhou	
AH13)	1071	1	Suzhou		JS2)	1143		Nanjing	
FJ1)	±1071		Fujian		JS9)	1143		Nantong	
GX1)	1071	10	Guangxi	Ningming	LN10)	1143		Yingkou	
LN4)	1071	2	Anshan		LN14)	1143		Liaoyang	
SD16)	1071	10	Heze		LN5)	1143		Fushun	
SN4)	1071	10	Baoji		NM1)	1143		Nei Menggu	Ulanqab
TJ1)	1071	50	Tianjin		NM5)	1143		Chifeng	
XJ3)	1071		Urumqi		NM16)	1143	1	Yakeshi	
ZJ1)	1071	10	Zhejiang	Hangzhou	QH1)	1143		Qinghai	Xining
GD7)	1080	5	Shantou		SC11)	1143		Neijiang	
HL7)	1080	1	Daqing		SC16)	1143	1	Dazhou	
HL12)	1080	1	Suihua		SC9)	1143		Guangyuan	
JS13)	1080	10	Suzhou		SD13)	1143	10	Linyi	
YN1)	1080		Yunnan		SD14)	1143	10	Liaocheng	

MW	kHz	kW	Station	Tx Location
SD4)	1143	10	Zibo	
SN1)	1143		Shaanxi	Baoji
SN9)	1143	1	Yulin	
XJ1)	1143		Xinjiang	Kashi
YN1)	1143		Yunnan	Gejiu
ZJ1)	±1143		Zhejiang	Yuhuan
HN1)	1152	150	Hunan	Changde
LN3)	1152	10	Dalian	
NM11)	1152	10	Bayannur	Linhe
NM13)	1152	10	Hinggan	Ulanhot
1)	1161		CNR 1	
GD2)	1161		Zhujiang EBS	Taishan
GX1)	1161	7.5	Guangxi	Beihai
HB10)	1161	10	Jingmen	
JS12)	1161		Wuxi	
SD7)	1161	10	Weifang	
AH16)	1170		Lu'an	
AH17)	1170	3	Xuancheng	
AH2)	1170	10	Hefei	
GD)	1170		Guangzhou	
GS1)	1170		Gansu	Lanzhou
SD15)	1170	10	Binzhou	
SD5)	1170	10	Zaozhuang	
HB2)	1179	100	Chutian	Wuhan
HL5)	1179	10	Shuangyashan	
JS7)	1179		Yangzhou	
XJ4)	1179		Karamay	
EB19)	1188	1	Botou	
EB4)	1188	10	Xingtai	
JL10)	1188		Yanbian	
FJ5)	±1197		Quanzhou	
HL3)	1197	10	Qiqihar	
SD16)	1197	10	Heze	
SH1)	1197	10	Shanghai	
YN1)	1197		Yunnan	
12)	1206	1	VO Jinling	Nanjing, JS
EB10)	1206		Cangzhou	
EB3)	1206	10	Handan	
EN21)	1206	1	Huixian	
GD1)	1206		Guangdong	Shenzhen/Zhaoqing
HN1)	1206	10	Hubei	Xiangyang
JL10)	1206	150	Yanbian	Yanji
JS1)	1206	1	Jiangsu	Nanjing
NX1)	1206	1	Ningxia	Zhongning
SD9)	±1206	10	Weihai	
1)	1215	20	CNR 2	Shenyang, LN
1)	1215	50	CNR 7	Zhuhai, GD
HB1)	1215		Hubei	Yichang
HL14)	1215		Heihe	
XJ1)	1215	10	Xinjiang	Urumqi
1)	1224		CNR 6	Xiamen, FJ
GX1)	1224	100	Guangxi	Nanning
JS10)	1224	10	Zhenjiang	
HN1)	1233	10	Hunan	Yueyang
JS9)	1233	10	Nantong	
XJ1)	1233		Xinjiang	Bortala
XJ1)	1233	120	Xinjiang	Hutubi
AH16)	±1242		Lu'an	
HB20)	1242	1	Macheng	
HB24)	±1242	1	Qianjiang	
JX9)	1242		Ji'an	
LN9)	1242	1	Huludao	
YN1)	1242		Kunming	
ZJ10)	1250	1	Quzhou	
2)	1251		CRI DS 1	BJ
EB1)	1251		Hebei	Qinhuangdao
EB2)	1251	25	Shijiazhuang	
EN10)	1251	10	Puyang	
EN12)	1251	10	Luohe	
EN22)	1251	1	Yima	
EN6)	1251		Jiaozuo	
EN9)	±1251		Anyang	
HB1)	1251	5	Jingmen	
JL3A)	1251		Jilin-shi EBS	
JS12)	1251	10	Wuxi	
JS2)	1251		Nanjing	
JS4)	1251		Lianyungang	
JS5)	1251	10	Huai'an	
LN4)	1251		Anshan	
QH1)	1251	100	Qinghai	Xining
SD1)	1251		Shandong	Jinan
SD13)	1251	10	Linyi	

MW	kHz	kW	Station	Tx Location
SD18)	1251		Longkou	
SD3)	1251	10	Qingdao	
SD7)	1251		Weifang	
SN8)	1251	10	Hanzhong	
YN1)	1251		Yunnan	Kaiyuan
YN14)	1251		Yuxi	
ZJ1)	1251		Zhejiang	Jinhua
ZJ4)	1251		Ningbo	
ZJ7)	1251		Huzhou	
HN8)	1260	1	Changde	
LN1)	1260		Liaoning	Tieling
XZ3)	1260	1	Shannan	Nedong
JL18)	1269	1	Dunhua	
JS3)	1269		Xuzhou	
SX1)	1269	10	Shanxi	Xinzhou
EB1)	1278	100	Hebei	Shijiazhuang
EB1)	1278		Hebei	Handan
HL13)	1278	7.5	Daxing'anling	Jagdaqi
JX2)	1278	10	Nanchang	
1)	1287		CNR 1	
EB20)	±1287	1	Renqiu	
EN11)	1287	1	Xuchang	
GD5)	1287	30	Shenzhen	
JS12)	1287		Wuxi	
LN12)	1287	20	Fuxin	
NX1)	1287	10	Ningxia	Guyuan
SD7)	1287	5	Weifang	
YN7)	1287	10	Chuxiong	Chuxiong
ZJ1)	1287		Zhejiang	Dongtou
EB16)	1296	1	Qinhe	
LN20)	1296		Xingcheng	
LN6)	1296	10	Benxi	
SC10)	1296	1	Suining	
SH2)	1296	25	Dongfang	
SN5)	1296	10	Xianyang	
1)	1305		CNR 2	
SD2)	1305		Jinan	
CQ1)	1314	50	Chongqing	
HB14)	1314	3	Xianning	
HB6)	1314	10	Xiangyang	
JS1)	1314	10	Jiangsu	Suzhou
SD8)	1314	10	Yantai	
ZJ1)	1314		Zhejiang	
HN2)	1323	10	Changsha	
JL9)	1323	10	Baicheng	
LN17)	1323	1	Wafangdian	
SD16A)	1323	10	Mudan	Heze
SN1)	1323	10	Shaanxi	Xi'an
ZJ4)	1323	20	Ningbo	
EN1)	1332	100	Henan	Zhengzhou
EN1)	1332	10	Henan	Hebi/Luoyang
EN1)	1332		Henan	Anyang
FJ1)	1332	10	Fujian	Yunxiao
FJ2)	1332	10	Fuzhou	
GS6)	1332	10	Gannan	Hezuo
JL2)	1332	10	Changchun	
1)	1341	100	CNR 1	GD
HB19)	1341	1	Yingcheng	
HB21)	1341	1	Chibi	
HL1)	1341	100	Heilongjiang	Heihe
JS8)	1341	10	Taizhou	
LN1)	1341	10	Liaoning	Shenyang
SD12)	1341	1	Dezhou	
SD19)	1341	1	Qufu	
JX1)	±1350	50	Jiangxi	Ji'an
JX1)	1350	10	Jiangxi	Shangrao/Yichun
JX1)	1350	1	Jiangxi	Jiujiang
LN19)	1350		Haicheng	
NM9)	1350	50	Tongliao	
YN2)	1350	50	Kunming	
1)	1359		CNR 1	
YN1)	1359	1	Yunnan	Hekou
YN1)	1359		Yunnan	Baoshan/Yuxi
FJ1)	±1368	1	Fujian	Changding
HB8)	1368		Jingzhou	
HB18)	1368	1	Guangshui	
HL6)	1368	10	Jixi	
1)	1377	600	CNR 1	Yingyang, HEN
AH11)	1377	1	Chuzhou	
FJ1)	1377		Fujian	Nanping
NX5)	1377	1	Qingtongxia	
QH1)	1377		Qinghai	Xining

MW	kHz	kW	Station	Tx Location
SD3)	1377	10	Qingdao	
XZ1)	1377		Xizang	
FJ1)	1386		Fujian	Quanzhou
GX3)	1386	5	Liuzhou	
HB11)	1386	1	Ezhou	
HB17)	1386	1	Shishou	
JS15)	1386	1	Jiangyin	
SD10)	1386	1	Jining	
TJ1)	1386	50	Tianjin	
AH1)	1395	50	Anhui	Hefei
FJ1)	1395		Fujian	Hui'an/Yongchun
NM1)	1395		Nei Menggu	
NM7)	1395	10	Xilingol	Xilinhot
YN1)	1395		Yunnan	Pu'er
FJ1)	1404	50	Fujian EBS	Fuzhou
FJ1)	1404		Fujian	Fuqing/Zhangpu
FJ1)	1404		Fujian	Zhao'an/Shunchang
HB1)	1404	10	Hubei	Suizhou
LN7)	1404	10	Dandong	
ZJ1)	1404		Zhejiang	Wenling
HL4)	±1413	1	Hegang	
JS1)	1413	1	Jiangsu	Xuzhou/Yancheng
LN15)	1413		Tieling	
NX4)	1413	1	Wuzhong	
XJ1)	1413	5	Xinjiang	Kunes
1)	1422	600	CNR 1/8/13	Kashi, XJ
13)	1422	20	VO Pujiang	SH
SC4)	1422	10	Zigong	
SH2)	1422	20	Dongfang	
SX2)	1422	10	Taiyuan	
AH10)	±1431	2	Huangshan	
AH4)	±1431	10	Huaibei	
EB2)	1431	10	Shijiazhuang	
HB16)	1431	1	Danjiangkou	
HN10)	1431		Jinshi	
JL8)	1431		Songyuan	
NM14)	1431	1	Fengzhen	
GX1)	1440	50	Guangxi	Bose
LN18)	1440		Zhuanghe	
NM12)	1440	10	Alxa	Bayanhot
NM5)	1440	50	Chifeng	
FJ1)	1449		Fujian	Dongshan
JX1)	1449	20	Jiangxi	
SD11)	1449	10	Rizhao	
SD6)	1449	10	Dongying	
JS4)	1458	10	Lianyungang	
LN4)	1458		Anshan	
NM1)	1458	200	Nei Menggu	Hohhot
EB5)	1467	10	Baoding	
JX3)	1467	7.5	Jingdezhen	
SD1)	1467	1	Shandong	Dezhou
1)	1476	200	CNR 2	Shuangyashan, HL
HB15)	±1476	1	Laohekou	
HL1)	1476	50	Heilongjiang	Qiqihar/Fujin
HL9)	1476		Mudanjiang	
JL14)	1476	1	Qian Gorlos	
JX5)	1476		Xinyu	
LN7)	1476		Dandong	
QH2)	1476	10	Xining	
SC12)	1476		Leshan	
SD4)	1476	10	Zibo	
ZJ1)	1476		Zhejiang	Leqing
GS1)	1485		Gansu	
GX1)	1485	1	Guangxi	Lingshan
GX4)	1485	1	Guilin	
GX5)	1485	1	Wuzhou	
HB7)	1485	10	Shiyan	
HL6)	1485	1	Jixi	
JL11)	1485	1	Gongzhuling	
JX6)	1485	1	Jiujiang	
LN11)	1485	1	Panjin	
SC3)	1485	1	Chengdu	
SD1)	1485	1	Shandong	Weihai
SX10)	1485	1	Shuozhou	
XJ12)	1485	1	Kuytun	
XJ5)	1485	1	Hami	
YN13)	1485	1	Chuxiong	
YN5)	1485	1	Honghe	Jinping
AH5)	±1494	1	Wuhu	
FJ1)	1494	1	Fujian	Lianjiang
NM1)	1494		Nei Menggu	
XJ1)	1494	1	Xinjiang	Yiwu

MW	kHz	kW	Station	Tx Location
XJ1)	1494		Korla	
AH12)	±1503	1	Fuyang	
HN4)	1503	10	Xiangtan	
LN14)	1503		Liaoyang	
ZJ1)	1503	1	Zhejiang	Xinchang
GS7)	1512	10	Linxia	
NM5)	1512	1	Chifeng	Lindong
SD2)	1512		Jinan	
EB1)	1521		Hebei	Baoding/Xingtai
EB11)	1521		Langfang	
EN1)	1521		Henan	Zhengzhou
EN5)	1521	3	Pingdingshan	
EN8)	1521	10	Xinxiang	
FJ3)	1521		Xiamen	
GD20)	1521	1	Zhaoqing	
GZ5)	1521		Anshun	
HB25)	1521	10	Xiangyang	
HL1)	1521	1	Heilongjiang	Jingbohu
JL15)	1521	1	Taonan	
JS11)	1521	3	Changzhou	
JS12)	1521		Wuxi	
JS13)	1521		Suzhou	
JS17)	1521		Zhangjiagang	
JS5)	1521	10	Huai'an	
JS7)	1521		Yangzhou	
NM6)	1521	10	Ulanqab	Jining
SC1)	1521		Sichuan	Chengdu
SD2)	1521		Jinan	
SN1)	1521	1	Shaanxi	Shangluo
SX5)	1521	1	Changzhi	Qinxian
YN3)	1521	1	Qujing	
YN5)	1521	1	Honghe	
ZJ1)	1521		Zhejiang	
ZJ7)	1521		Huzhou	
JL1)	1530		Jilin	Yanji
SX7)	1530	1	Jinzhong	
ZJ1)	1530	50	Zhejiang	Hangzhou
1)	1539	10	CNR 1	
HN6)	1548	10	Shaoyang	
SD1)	1548	200	Shandong	Weifang
EB10)	1557	25	Cangzhou	
EB14)	1557	1	Nangong	
LN12)	1557		Fuxin	
EB6)	1566	10	Zhangjiakou	
JL10)	1566		Yanbian	Songjiang
GS8)	1566		Pingliang	
HB1)	1566		Hubei	
SD14)	1566	1	Liaocheng	
SX9)	1566	1	Yuncheng	
GX1)	1575		Guangxi	Yulin
JL12)	1575		Lishu	
LN3)	1575	2	Dalian	
AH8)	±1584	1	Ma'anshan	
AH9)	±1584	1	Anqing	
EB7)	1584	1	Chengde	
GZ4)	1584	1	Zunyi	
JL13)	1584	1	Meihekou	
NM1)	1584	1	Nei Menggu	Tongliao
SX1)	1584		Shanxi	Taiyuan
SX5)	1584	10	Changzhi	
ZJ14)	1584		Rui'an	
SX3)	1584		Datong	
1)	1593	600	CNR 1	Changzhou, JS
HL1)	1593	10	Heilongjiang	
HL12)	1593	1	Suihua	
XJ1)	1593		Xinjiang	Korla
JS1)	1602	1	Jiangsu	Hongze

SW	kHz	kW	Station	Tx Loc.	Times
13)	3280	15	VO Pujiang	Shanghai	1130-1600
NM8)	3900	10	Hulun Buir	Hailar	as 603kHz
XJ1)	‡3950	100	Xinjiang	Urumqi	Nov-Apr only
1)	3985	100	CNR 2	Golmud	1300-1605
GS6)	3990	15	Gannan	Hezuo	2220-0100, 0950-1400
XJ1)	‡3990	50	Xinjiang	Urumqi	Nov-Apr only
QH1)	4220	10	Qinghai	Xining	2250-1600
XJ1)	‡4330	100	Xinjiang	Urumqi	Nov-Apr only
XJ1)	‡4500	50	Xinjiang	Urumqi	Nov-Apr only
1)	4750	10	CNR 1	Hailar	1955-1735
QH1)	4750	50	Qinghai	Xining	2200-0200, 0900-1600
1)	4800	100	CNR 1	Golmud	1955-1735
XZ1)	4820	100	Xizang	Lhasa	2000-1800

SW	kHz	kW	Station	Tx Loc.	Times
11)	‡4900	50	VO Strait	Fuzhou	Winter only
XZ1)	4905	50	Xizang	Lhasa	2100-1805
XZ1)	4920	50	Xizang	Lhasa	2100-1805
11)	4940	50	VO Strait	Fuzhou	2230-0200, 1200-1600
13)	4950	15	VO Pujiang	Shanghai	1130-1600
XJ1)	‡4980	50	Xinjiang	Urumqi	Nov-Apr only
HN1)	‡4990	10	Hunan	Changsha	
FJ1)	‡5005	10	Fujian	Fuzhou	
FJ1)	5040	10	Fujian	Fuzhou	2245-2325, 0945-1030
11)	‡5050	50	VO Strait	Fuzhou	Winter only
XJ1)	‡5060	50	Xinjiang	Urumqi	Nov-Apr only
13)	‡5075	15	VO Pujiang	Shanghai	Winter only
XZ1)	5240	50	Xizang	Lhasa	2100-1805
12)	5860	50	VO Jinling	Nanjing	1445-1705
1)	5925	100	CNR 5	Beijing	2055-2400, 1000-1705
XZ1)	5935	100	Xizang	Lhasa	2000-1800
1)	5945	100	CNR 1	Beijing	1955-0100, 1300-1735
1)	5955	100	CNR 8	Beijing	0800-0900, 1200-1300, 2055-0100
XJ1)	5960	50	Xinjiang	Urumqi	2300-0300, 1200-1800
GS6)	5970	15	Gannan	Hezuo	2220-0100, 0950-1400
1)	5975	100	CNR 8	Beijing	2055-2300, 1100-1200
QH1)	5990	50	Qinghai	Xining	2250-1600
1)	6000	100	CNR 1	Beijing	1955-2300, 1100-1735
1)	6010	100	CNR 11	Baoji-Sif.	2155-2400, 1030-1605
XJ1)	6015	100	Xinjiang	Urumqi	2300-0300, 1200-1800
1)	6020	100	CNR 8	Beijing	1100-1200, 1300-1400
XZ1)	6025	50	Xizang	Lhasa	2050-1805
1)	6030	100	CNR 1	Beijing	1955-1735
YN1)	6035	20	Yunnan	Kunming	2230-0130, 0945-1415
1)	6040	150	CNR 2	Beijing	2055-2300
NM1)	6040	50	Nei Menggu	Hohhot	2150-1605
XZ1)	6050	100	Xizang	Lhasa	2000-1800
SC1)	6060	150	Sichuan	Xichang	2155-1515
1)	6065	150	CNR 2	Beijing	2055-2330, 1200-1605
1)	6080	100	CNR 1	Golmud	1955-2400, 1200-1735
NM8)	6080	10	Hulun Buir	Hailar	as 954kHz
1)	6090	100	CNR 2	Golmud	2055-0100, 1000-1605
XZ1)	6110	100	Xizang	Lhasa	2100-1805
11)	6115	50	VO Strait	Fuzhou	2230-1300
XJ1)	6120	50	Xinjiang	Urumqi	2300-0300, 1200-1800
1)	6125	100	CNR 1	Beijing	1955-2300, 1000-1735
1)	6125	100	CNR 1	Shijiazhuang	1955-2300, 1100-1735
XZ1)	6130	100	Xizang	Lhasa	2100-1805
1)	6140	100	CNR 8	Lingshi	1600-1705
QH1)	6145	50	Qinghai	Xining	0200-0900
1)	6155	150	CNR 2	Beijing	2055-2300, 1000-1605
1)	6165	100	CNR 6	Beijing	2155-0100, 0900-1605
1)	6175	100	CNR 1	Beijing	1955-2400, 0900-1735
15)	6185	15	China Huayi BC	Fuzhou	2230-1600
1)	6190	100	CNR 2	Golmud	2055-2300
XJ1)	6190	100	Xinjiang	Urumqi	2300-0330, 1210-1800
XZ1)	6200	100	Xizang	Lhasa	2100-1805
XJ1)	7205	50	Xinjiang	Urumqi	2300-0200, 1400-1800
YN1)	7210	20	Yunnan	Kunming	0630-0830, 1055-1500, 2255-0300
1)	7215	100	CNR 1	Shijiazhuang	1955-2400
1)	7220	100	CNR 2	Golmud	2300-1300
SC1)	7225	50	Sichuan	Xichang	2155-1515
1)	7230	100	CNR 1	Xi'an	1955-1735
XJ1)	7230	50	Xinjiang	Urumqi	2300-1800
XZ1)	7240	100	Xizang	Lhasa	2000-0200, 0900-1800
1)	7245	100	CNR 2	Beijing	2055-2300, 1300-1605
1)	7255	100	CNR 2	Baoji-Sif	2055-0100
XZ1)	7255	100	Xizang	Lhasa	2100-0200, 1000-1805
XJ1)	7260	100	Xinjiang	Urumqi	2300-1800
1)	7265	100	CNR 2	Baoji-Sif	1230-1605
NM1)	7270	50	Nei Menggu	Hohhot	2150-1605
1)	7275	100	CNR 1	Beijing	1955-2300, 1100-1735
GZ1)	7275	7.5	Guizhou	Guiyang	2150-1705
XJ1)	7275	50	Xinjiang	Urumqi	2300-1800
11)	7280	50	VO Strait	Fuzhou	2230-1130
1)	7290	100	CNR 1	Beijing	1955-2400, 1100-1735
XJ1)	7295	50	Xinjang	Urumqi	Nov.-Apr.only
1)	7305	100	CNR 1	Shijiazhuang	1955-2200, 1000-1735
XJ1)	7310	50	Xinjiang	Urumqi	2300-0200, 1400-1800
1)	7315	100	CNR 2	Xi'an	2055-0100, 1100-1605
1)	7335	100	CNR 2	Baoji-Sif.	2055-0030, 1000-1605
XJ1)	7340	100	Xinjiang	Urumqi	2300-1800
1)	7345	100	CNR 1	Beijing	1955-2400, 1100-1735
1)	7350	100	CNR 11	Baoji-Sif.	0900-1605
1)	7360	100	CNR 8	Beijing	1000-1100
1)	7360	100	CNR 11	Baoji-Sif.	2155-2400
1)	7365	100	CNR 1	Shijiazhuang	1200-1735
1)	7370	150	CNR 2	Beijing	1300-1605
1)	7375	150	CNR 2	Beijing	2055-2300, 1200-1605
XZ1)	7385	100	Xizang	Lhasa	2100-0200, 0930-1805
1)	7395	150	CNR 2	Xianyang	2055-2400
1)	7410	100	CNR 5	Beijing	0900-1705
1)	7415	100	CNR 5	Beijing	2055-2400
NM1)	7420	50	Nei Menggu	Hohhot	2150-1605
1)	7425	150	CNR 2	Xianyang	1300-1605
1)	7445	100	CNR 8	Beijing	1300-1705
XZ1)	7450	100	Xizang	Lhasa	2000-0200, 0900-1800
1)	9410	100	CNR 5	Beijing	1000-1705
1)	9420	50	CNR 6	Beijing	2155-0100, 0900-1605
1)	9420	100	CNR 13	Lingshi	1100-1805
1)	9440	100	CNR 8	Beijing	0400-0500, 0600-0700
1)	9455	100	CNR 1/8	Lingshi	1955-0200
1)	9470	100	CNR 1	Beijing	1955-2300
XJ1)	9470	100	Xinjiang	Urumqi	0300-1200
1)	9480	100	CNR 11	Baoji-Sif.	2155-0100, 0800-1605
XZ1)	9490	100	Xizang	Lhasa	0200-1000
1)	9500	100	CNR 1	Shijiazhuang	1955-1735
11)	9505	50	VO Strait	Fuzhou	0200-1200
XJ1)	9510	100	Xinjiang	Urumqi	0530-1030
1)	9515	100	CNR 2	Beijing	2055-2400, 1200-1605
NM1)	9520	50	Nei Menggu	Hohhot	2150-1605
1)	9530	100	CNR 11	Baoji-Sif.	0000-1030
XJ1)	9560	50	Xinjiang	Urumqi	0300-1200
1)	9570	100	CNR 2	Golmud	0100-1000
XZ1)	9580	100	Xizang	Lhasa	0200-0930
XJ1)	9600	50	Xinjiang	Urumqi	0200-1400
1)	9610	100	CNR 8	Beijing	0300-0500, 0600-0700
1)	9615	100	CNR 8	Beijing	1200-1300
1)	9620	150	CNR 2	Beijing	2300-1300
1)	9630	100	CNR 1	Golmud	2300-1200
1)	9630	100	CNR 1/8	Lingshi	1200-1705
1)	9645	100	CNR 1	Beijing	2330-1100
1)	9645	100	CNR 8	Beijing	1300-1705
1)	9665	50	CNR 5	Beijing	2055-0100
1)	9675	100	CNR 1	Beijing	2300-1000
1)	9685	50	CNR 5	Beijing	0000-1000
13)	9705	15	VO Pujiang	Shanghai	1130-1600
XJ1)	9705	50	Xinjiang	Urumqi	0330-0530, 1030-1230
1)	9710	100	CNR 1	Shijiazhuang	1955-2330, 1100-1735
1)	9720	150	CNR 2	Baoji-Xinjie	0000-1000
NM1)	9750	50	Nei Menggu	Hohhot	2150-1605
1)	9755	100	CNR 2	Xi'an	2055-0200, 1000-1605
1)	9775	150	CNR 1	Beijing	2055-0200, 0900-1605
QH1)	9780	50	Qinghai	Xining	0230-0900
1)	9785	100	CNR 8	Beijing	1000-1100
1)	9810	150	CNR 2	Nanning	1955-2300, 1300-1735
1)	9810	100	CNR 2	Baoji-Sif.	0100-1230
1)	9820	150	CNR 2	Xianyang	2055-0100, 1100-1605
1)	9830	100	CNR 1	Beijing	1955-0100, 0730-1735
XJ1)	9835	100	Xinjiang	Urumqi	0300-1200
1)	9845	100	CNR 1	Beijing	1955-0100, 1030-1735
QH1)	9850	15	Qinghai	Xining	0230-0830
1)	9860	100	CNR 1	Beijing	1200-1735
1)	9890	100	CNR 13	Lingshi	1400-1805
1)	11610	150	CNR 2	Beijing	2300-1300
1)	11620	50	CNR 5	Beijing	0100-1000
1)	11630	100	CNR 1/8	Lingshi	1955-2400, 0200-0700, 0800-1600
1)	11630	100	CNR 8	Beijing	0100-0200
1)	11660	150	CNR 2	Xi'an	0100-1100
1)	11670	100	CNR 2	Beijing	2330-1200
1)	11685	100	CNR 11	Baoji-Sif.	0000-0900
1)	11710	100	CNR 1	Beijing	1955-0030, 1000-1735
1)	11720	100	CNR 1	Shijiazhuang	2330-1100
1)	11740	100	CNR 2	Lingshi	2055-0100, 1100-1605
1)	11750	100	CNR 1	Shijiazhuang	2200-1000
1)	11760	100	CNR 1	Shijiazhuang	0000-1200
XJ1)	11770	50	Xinjiang	Urumqi	2300-1800
1)	11780	100	CNR 8	Beijing	0500-0600, 0700-1000
1)	11800	150	CNR 2	Beijing	2300-1200
1)	11810	100	CNR 2	Beijing	0100-0300
1)	11815	50	CNR 8	Beijing	0300-0400
1)	11835	150	CNR 2	Xianyang	0000-1300
1)	11845	150	CNR 2	Xainyang	0000-1100
XZ1)	11860	100	Xizang	Lhasa	0200-0900
XJ1)	11885	50	Xinjiang	Urumqi	2300-1800
1)	11905	100	CNR 6	Beijing	0100-0900

SW	kHz	kW	Station	Tx Loc.	Times
1)	11915	100	CNR 2	Baoji-Sif.	0030-1000
1)	11925	100	CNR 1	Lingshi	1955-2330, 0900-1735
1)	11935	100	CNR 5	Beijing	0000-0900
XZ1)	11950	100	Xizang	Lhasa	0200-0900
1)	11960	100	CNR 1	Beijing	0000-0900
XJ1)	11975	50	Xinjiang	Urumqi	0330-0530, 1030-1230
1)	12045	100	CNR 1	Beijing	2300-1200
1)	12055	100	CNR 1/8	Lingshi	0200-0600, 0700-1100
1)	12080	100	CNR 2	Baoji-Sif.	0200-1000
1)	13610	150	CNR 1	Nanning	2300-1300
XJ1)	13670	50	Xinjiang	Urumqi	0200-1400
1)	13700	100	CNR 13	Lingshi	2355-1400
1)	15270	150	CNR 1	Beijing	0200-0900
1)	15370	100	CNR 1	Shijiazhuang	0100-1100
1)	15380	100	CNR 1	Beijing	0100-1100
1)	15390	100	CNR 13	Lingshi	2355-1100
1)	15415	100	CNR 8	Beijing	0500-0600, 0700-0800, 0900-1000
1)	15480	100	CNR 1	Beijing	0100-0600, 0700-1300
1)	15500	150	CNR 2	Beijing	2300-1000
1)	15540	100	CNR 2	Lingshi	0100-1100
1)	15550	100	CNR 1	Beijing	0000-1100
1)	15570	100	CNR 11	Baoji-Sif.	0100-0800
1)	15670	100	CNR 8	Beijing.	0100-0300
1)	15710	50	CNR 6	Beijing	0100-0900
1)	17550	100	CNR 1	Beijing	0100-1030
1)	17565	100	CNR 1	Beijing	0100-0730
1)	17580	100	CNR 1	Lingshi	2330-0900
1)	17595	100	CNR 1	Shijiazhuang	2300-1100
1)	17605	100	CNR 1	Beijing	0030-1000
1)	17625	150	CNR 2	Beijing	0000-1200
1)	17725	100	CNR 1	Beijing	1000-1200
1)	17890	100	CNR 1	Beijing	0000-1000

NB: Baoji-Sif. = Baoji-Sifangshan. ‡=inactive, ±=variable

FM(MHz)	CNR 1	CNR 2	CNR 3	Prov.E	Prov.M	City.E	City.M
Beijing	106.1	96.6	90.0	-	-	107.3	97.4
Changchun	99.1	104.7	91.6	-	92.7	90.0	99.6
Changsha	95.0	87.6	107.7	90.1	97.5	-	106.1
Chengdu	103.7	-	107.6	94.0	95.5	-	105.6
Chongqing	92.0	102.9	88.9	-	-	101.5	88.1
Dalian	107.8	-	107.8	87.6	-	99.1	89.1
Daqing	103.9	96.7	-	-	102.9	-	106.0
Fuzhou	93.5	-	92.6	96.1	91.3 / 99.6a	87.6	89.3
Guangzhou	89.3	106.6	87.4	95.3 / 97.4b	99.3	-	102.7
Guilin	89.8	94.1	-	-	-	-	88.3
Guiyang	93.6	105.6	107.3	98.9	91.6	104.0	102.7
Haikou	105.8	87.8	105.8	103.8	-	-	91.6
Hangzhou	90.2	97.9	103.2	95.0	96.8	91.8	105.4
Harbin	89.9	88.1	100.9	-	95.8	92.5	98.4
Hefei	93.5	104.7	94.3	97.1	89.5	-	87.6
Hengyang	95.0	105.9	-	91.0	96.9	98.9	-
Hohhot	97.1	104.5	99.1	101.4	93.6	-	-
Jinan	95.7	96.5	95.5	96.0	99.1	90.9	88.7
Jinzhou	104.9	101.2	106.0	107.6	-	96.6	-
Kaifeng	106.3	100.8	-	-	88.1	100.2	-
Kunming	96.0	100.0	94.0	88.7	97.0	-	-
Lanzhou	94.8	90.3	88.3	93.4	-	-	99.5
Lhasa	89.2	104.0	96.1	98.0	-	-	-
Nanchang	89.1	93.8	87.2	99.2	103.4	-	95.1
Nanjing	95.8	107.5	98.9	93.7	89.7	-	105.8
Nanning	106.2	104.0	103.6	97.0	95.0	-	107.4
Ningbo	95.7	101.2	107.7	103.3	-	102.9	93.9
Qingdao	93.1	104.1	98.0	-	106.0	102.9	106.6
Qiqihar	97.7	101.8	-	-	90.4	-	-
Quanzhou	96.9	98.3	102.5	95.5	-	92.3	-
Shanghai	99.0	91.4	107.7	-	-	97.7	96.8
Shenyang	94.8	93.5	99.8	89.5	102.9	90.4	87.6
Shenzhen	95.8	-	101.2	105.7	-	-	97.1
Shijiazhuang	95.6	97.2	105.1	97.2	90.7	100.9	106.7
Suzhou	100.0	-	107.7	-	-	-	94.8
Taiyuan	97.0	99.0	89.3	95.8	101.5	104.4	-
Tangshan	93.2	107.4	-	90.8	89.5	95.5	102.0
Tianjin	102.9	98.0	92.5	-	-	101.4	99.0
Urumqi	88.7	90.6	-	92.9	94.9	97.4c	100.7
Weifang	96.7	-	-	97.9	101.1	93.3	88.7
Wenzhou	90.2	-	94.9	-	-	88.8	100.3
Wuhan	95.6	97.8	90.7	99.8	103.8 / 105.8d	100.6	101.8
Xiamen	102.6	93.5	105.2	98.6	-	107.0	90.9

FM(MHz)	CNR 1	CNR 2	CNR 3	Prov.E	Prov.M	City.E	City.M
Xi'an	96.4	103.0	95.5	89.6	98.8	-	93.1
Xining	91.6	105.6	100.6	-	97.2	-	104.3
Yinchuan	96.4	107.8	99.7	92.8	-	95.0	100.6
Zhangjiakou	88.9	-	-	-	-	98.6	100.0
Zhangzhou	102.6	98.3	-	98.6	-	-	99.1
Zhengzhou	101.2	96.7	100.2	103.2	88.1	92.6	91.8
Zhuhai	99.1	-	101.2	103.8	93.9	-	87.5

Prov.E=Provincial economic stn **Prov.M**=Provincial music stn **City. E**=City economic stn **City.M**=City music stn a) V.O. the Strait, b) Zhujiang EBS, c) Traffic music ch, d) Chutian BS
Official FM band 87.0-108.0MHz. Low power college stns exist 60-87MHz, some spread over 50-108MHz.

Addresses and other information:
1) CHINA NATIONAL RADIO (CNR)
✉ 2 Fuxingmenwai Dajie, Xicheng Qu, Beijing 100866 ☎ +86 10 8609 2636 **W:** www.cnr.cn
L.P: Gen. Dir: Wang Qiu. CE: Qian Yuelin.
V.O. China (1st Prgr "News Radio"): 24h on MW/SW(exc. Tues 0600-0850)/FM. **V.O. the Economy (2nd Prgr "China Business Radio"):** 24h on MW/SW(exc. Wed 0600-0900)/FM. **V.O. the Music (3rd Prgr "Music Radio"):** 2155-1605 (exc. Tues 0605-0855) on FM. **V.O. the City (4th Prgr "Metro Radio" "Top FM"):** Sun-Thu 2200-1700 (exc. Tues 0505-0835) Fri & Sat 2300-1600 on 101.8MHz **V.O. Zhonghua (5th Prgr "Zhonghua News Radio"):** 0055-0615, 0955-0005 on MW/SW/102.3MHz(Fuzhou). **V.O. Shenzhou (6th Prgr "Shenzhou Easy Radio")** in Ch, Amoy and Hakka: 2055-0105, 0355-1805 on MW/SW/106.2MHz(Fuzhou). **V.O. Huaxia (7th Prgr "Huaxia Radio")** for the Zhujiang Delta: Ch. on 1215kHz/87.8/92.3/104.9MHz 2055-1805 (exc. Tues 0600-0855), Bilingual Ch. on 1215kHz/104.9MHz 2055-1805 in Ch and Cantonese. **V.O. the Literary (9th Prgr "Story Radio"):** 2155-1805 (exc. Tues 0500-0900) on 106.6MHz **V.O. Old Age (10th Prgr. "Senior Citizen Radio"):** 1955-1735 (exc. Tues 0605-0855) on 1053kHz. **V.O. the Entertainment (12th Prgr "Happy Radio"):** 2055-1805 (exc. Tues 0505-0855) on 747kHz

V.O. Minorities (8th Prgr "Ethnic Minority Radio"): 2055-1705 on MW/SW/104.5MHz (Hohhot) – +) relayed by regional stns
Kazakh

0100-0200		15670, 11810, 11630, 9455, 1422, 1143
0200-0300		15670, 12055, 11810, 11630, 1422, 1143
0500-0600+	XJ	15415, 12055, 11780, 11630, 1422, 1143
0900-1000		15415, 12055, 11780, 11630, 1422, 1143
1400-1500+	XJ	11630, 9645, 9630, 7445, 1143
1500-1600		11630, 9645, 9630, 7445
1600-1705		9645, 9630, 7445, 6140

Korean

2055-2300		5975, 5955, 1143
0400-0500		9610, 9440, 1143
0600-0700		9610, 9440
1000-1100+	HL	9785, 7360, 1143, 1017
1100-1200		6020, 5975

Mongolian

2300-0100		7445, 5955, 1143
0300-0400+	NM	11815, 9610, 1143
0700-0800		15415, 11780
0800-0900		11780, 5955
1200-1300		9615, 5955, 1143
1300-1400		9645, 9630, 7445, 6020

11th Prgr. Tibetan Service 2155-1605 on MW/SW (exc. Wed 0600-0855)/105.7MHz (Lhasa)
Tibetan

2155-0000		9480, 7360, 6010, 1098
0000-0100		11685, 9530, 9480, 1098
0100-0800		15570, 11685, 9530, 1098
0800-0900		11685, 9530, 9480, 1098
0900-1030		9530, 9480, 7350, 1098
1030-1605		9480, 7350, 6010, 1098

13th Prgr. Uighur Service 2355-1805 on MW/SW (exc. Tues 0600-0855) /FM
Uighur

2355-0600		15390, 13700, 945, 855, 720
0600-0630+	XJ	15390, 13700, 945, 855, 720
0630-1100		15390, 13700, 945, 855, 720
1100-1400		13700, 9420, 945, 855, 720
1400-1700		9890, 9420, 945, 855, 720
1700-1730+	XJ	9890, 9420, 945, 855, 720
1730-1805		9890, 9420, 945, 855, 720

2) CHINA RADIO INTERNATIONAL (CRI)
(Zhongguo Guoji Guangbo Diantai)

📧 Jia 16, Shijingshan Lu, Shijingshan Qu, Beijing 100040 ☎ +86 10 6889 1001 **W:** www.chinabroadcast.cn **L.P:** Gen. Dir: Wang Gengnian

Domestic Sce:
Beijing 1 "Easy FM" (1251kHz/91.5MHz): 24h in English – **Beijing 2 "Hit FM"** (88.7MHz): 24h in English – **Beijing 3 "Round the Clock"** (1008kHz): 24h in English – **Beijing 4** (846kHz) 24h in English – **Beijing 5 "News Radio"** (900kHz/90.5MHz): 24h in Chinese – **Tianjin "Hit FM"** (105.4MHz): 24h in English – **Shanghai 1 "Hit FM"** (87.9MHz): 2200-2400, 0300-1730 – **Shanghai 2 "Easy FM"** (100.1MHz): 24h – **Hefei 1 "Easy FM"** (92.4MHz): 2200-1700 – **Hefei 2 "News Radio"** (90.1MHz): 2200-1700 – **Wuhu "News Radio"** (89.8MHz): 2200-1700 – **Xiamen "Easy FM"** (95.8MHz): 2200-1700 – **Guangzhou 1 "Hit FM"** (88.5MHz): 24h – **Guangzhou 2 "News Radio"** (702kHz/107.1MHz): 24h – **Chongqing "News Radio"** (91.2MHz): 24h – **Lhasa "Easy FM"** (100.0MHz): 1930-1600 – **Lanzhou "Easy FM"** (98.5MHz): 2200-1600 – **Urumqi "News Radio"** (1008kHz) – **Shijiazhuang** (91.5MHz)

DAB: Radio, Film & TV Bureau of Guangdong on 208.720, 209.936, 210.432, 212.144, 213.856MHz (test transmission).

EXTERNAL SERVICES: China Radio International, Voice of Beibu Bay Radio, Yunnan Broadcasting Station
See International Broadcasting section

BROADCASTS TO TAIWAN
11) Voice of the Strait (Haixia zhi Sheng), Xindian, Fuzhou or P.O.Box 187, Fuzhou, Fujian 350012. Operated by the People's Liberation Army of China **W:** www.vos.com.cn News Sce. on 666/4940/9505kHz 2230-1600 (exc. Wed 0400-0955) in Ch. English Prgr. "Focus on China": Sun1500 1505 - Automobile Life Sce. on 90.6MHz 24h in Ch - Amoy Sce. on 783/4900/6115kHz 2230-1600 (exc. Wed 0400-0953) in Amoy - City Sunshine FM: on 99.6MHz 2230-1600 – **12)** Voice of Jinling (Jinling zhi Sheng), P.O.Box 268, Nanjing, Jiangsu 210002. On 1206/5860kHz 1445-1705 - City Sce. Automobile FM: 99.7MHz 24h – **13)** Voice of Pujiang (Pujiang zhi Sheng), 1376 Hongqiao Lu, Shanghai or P.O.Box 518, Shanghai 200051 **W:** www.yicai.com/mystopic/642116. On 803//3280/4950/5075/9705kHz 1130-1600. On 1422/97.7 2200-1600 – **14)** Southeast Broadcasting Company, 2 Gutian Lu, Fuzhou, Fujian 350001 **W:** www.sebc.com.cn On 585kHz/97.6/106.2MHz 2255-1700 in Ch and Amoy – **15)** China Huayi Broadcasting Corporation, P.O.Box 251, Fuzhou, Fujian 350001 **W:** www.clibcnet.com On 873/6185kHz/ 107.1MHz for Taiwan, Hong Kong, Macao and Southeast Asia. 24h (exc. Wed 0400-0953).

ANHUI PROVINCE
AH1) Anhui Radio and TV St, 355 Tongcheng Nanlu, Hefei, Anhui 230065 **W:** www.ahradio.com.cn News General Sce. on 936/846kHz/95.5MHz 2000-1700(Tues 1500) - Economic Sce. on 864/1098kHz/97.1MHz 24h (exc. Tues 1500-2000) - Economic Sce. Fortune FM: on 98.1MHz - Travel Sce. on 900kHz/96.1/106.5MHz 2130-1700(Tues 1500) - Traffic Sce. "Automobile 908": on 90.8MHz 24h (exc. Tues 1500-2150) - Life Sce. on 603/684kHz/105.5MHz 2100-1800 (exc. Mon 1500-1800) - Farm Sce. on 720/900/1008kHz/103.6MHz on 2100-1700 (exc. Tues 1500-1950) - Music Sce. "Changxiang 895": on 801kHz/89.5MHz 24h - Novel and Storytelling Sce. on 1395kHz/102.9/107.4MHz 2030-1800 (exc. Tues 1500-1800) - Chinese Opera Sce. on 99.5MHz 24h (exc. Tues 1500-2000) - My FM: on 96.1MHz 24h – **AH2)** 114 Rongshida Dadao, Hefei, Anhui 230001. News General Sce. on 666kHz/91.5MHz 2120-1600 - Traffic Sce. on 1053kHz/102.6MHz 24h (exc. Tues 0600-0850) - Literary St. on 747kHz/87.6MHz 2200-1700 - Story Sce. on 1170kHz/98.8MHz 2100-1700 - Charm Music Sce. on 88.6MHz 2300-1700. - Hui Merchant Sce. on 100.3MHz 2200-1800 – **AH3)** 11 Dongshan Zhonglu, Huainan, Anhui 232001. News General Sce. on 648kHz/103.7MHz 2125-1500 - Traffic and Literary Sce. on 97.9MHz 2140-1500 – **AH4)** Huaibei Radio and TV St, 336 Huaihai Donglu, Xiangshan Qu, Huaibei, Anhui 235000. News Sce. on 1431kHz/94.9MHz 2115-1500 - Traffic Sce. on 100.4MHz 2150-1600 (exc. Tues 0630-0900) - City Sce. on 603kHz/89.3MHz 2110-1600. - Chinese Opera Sce. on 1143kHz - Folk Art and Story Sce. on 846kHz – **AH5)** 197 Beijing Donglu, Wuhu, Anhui 241000. News Sce. on 100.4MHz 2100-1600 - Life Sce. on 1494kHz - Traffic and Economic Sce. on 96.3MHz 2128-1630 (Sun -1600) - Music and Story Sce. on 98.2MHz 2200-1600 – **AH6)** Yi'an Beilu, Tongling, Anhui 244000. On 1107kHz/100.0MHz 2120-0005, 0155-0510, 0855-1305 - Traffic and Life Sce. on 88.7MHz 2255-1100 – **AH7)** Xuehua Shan, Shengli Donglu, Bengbu, Anhui 233000. News Sce. on 765kHz/107.9MHz 2202-1600 - Economic Sce. on 1098kHz/104.2MHz 2150-1430 - Traffic and Literary Sce. on 98.4MHz 2200-1500 – **AH8)** 46 Yushan Zhonglu, Ma'anshan,

Anhui 243011. News General Sce. on 1584kHz/105.1MHz 2150-1500 (exc. Tues 0600-0850) - Traffic and Music Sce. on 92.8MHz 2130-1500 (exc. Tues 0600-0850). - City Life Sce. on 95.4MHz 2130-1500 – **AH9)** 23 Guanyue Miao, Anqing, Anhui 246004. News General Sce. on 1584kHz/90.3MHz 2200-0530, 0930-1400 – **AH10)** 9 Tiandu Dadao, Tunxi Qu, Huangshan, Anhui 245000. On 1431kHz/87.5/93.3MHz 2200-0600, 0920-1500 - Traffic and Travel Sce. on 100.4MHz 2200-1500 – **AH11)** 225 Langxie Lu, Chuzhou, Anhui 239000. News General Sce. on 95.0/97.3MHz 2125-1440 (exc. Tues 0500-0930) - Traffic and Music Sce. on 105.4MHz 2125-1530 - Literary and Story Sce. on 1377kHz/97.0MHz 2100-1500 – **AH12)** Nan 2 Huan Lu, Fuyang, Anhui 236034. News Sce. on 1116kHz/91.6MHz 2130-1610 - Economic Sce. on 711/801/1503kHz 2145-1550 (exc. Tues 0700-0830) - Traffic Sce. on 90.0/103.5MHz 2130-1530 - Story Sce. on 94.1MHz 2120-153 – **AH13)** Baihuiyuan, Huaihai Lu, Suzhou, Anhui 234000. News General Sce. on 1071kHz/105.0MHz 1015-? - Traffic and Music St. on 96.1MHz – **AH14)** 436 Dongfeng Xilu, Juchao Qu, Chaohu, Anhui 238000. News General Sce. on 846kHz/88.1MHz 2125-1500 - City Traffic Sce. on 93.8MHz 2200-1500 – **AH15)** Qiupu Donglu, Guichi Qu, Chizhou, Anhui 247100. 2120-2325, 0315-0515, 0950-1310 – **AH16)** Meishan Nanlu, Lu'an, Anhui 237001. News General Sce. on 711/1242kHz/102.1MHz 2155-1505 - Traffic and Music Sce. on 1170kHz/96.4MHz 2155-1505 – **AH17)** 10 Zhuangyuan Lu, Xuancheng, Anhui 242000. News General Sce. on 1170kHz/100.6MHz 2155-1500 - Traffic and Literary Sce. on 106.1MHz – **AH18)** Dangtu Xian, Anhui 243100. 0250-0450 – **AH19)** 62 Renmin Zhonglu, Haozhou, Anhui 236800 - News General Sce. on 999kHz/88.2MHz 2130-1530 - Traffic and Music Sce. on 107.2MHz 2130-1530.

BEIJING MUNICIPALITY
BJ1) 14 Jianguomenwai Dajie, Chaoyang Qu, Beijing 100022 **W:** www.bjradio.com.cn News Scc. on 828kHz/100.6MHz 24h (exc. Mon 1630-2100, Thurs 0700-0800). - Public Service Sce. on 1026kHz/107.3MHz 2100-1600 (exc. Mon 1630-2130) - Sports Sce. on 102.5MHz 24h (exc. Mon 1600-2100) - Traffic Sce. on 103.9MHz 24h (exc. Mon 1500-2130) - Story Sce. on 603kHz/89.1MHz 2100-1730(Mon 1630) (exc. Thurs 0700-0800) - Foreign Language Sce. "Radio 774": on 774kHz 2200-1600 (exc. Thurs 0700-0800) - Literary Sce. on 87.6MHz 24h (exc. Mon 1630-2130) - Music Sce. on 97.4MHz 24h (exc. Mon 1600-2100) - "i Home Radio": on 927kHz 2130-1600 (exc. Thurs 0700-0800).

CHONGQING MUNICIPALITY
CQ1) 159 Zhongshan 3 Lu, Yuzhong Qu, Chongqing 400015 **W:** fm968.cbg.cnNews Sce. on 1314kHz/96.8MHz 24h - Economic Sce. on 101.5/107.7MHz 24h - Traffic Sce. on 95.5/88.9/92.7MHz 24h - City Sce. on 93.8MHz 2130-1800 - Music Sce. on 88.1MHz 24h – **CQ2)** V.O. Jialing, 6 Nanjing Lu, Beibei Qu, Chongqing 400700. On 97.4/102.1MHz 2255-1600.

HEBEI PROVINCE
EB1) 63 Yuhua Donglu, Shijiazhuang, Hebei 050012 **W:** www.hebradio.com.cn News Sce. on 1278/783kHz/FM 2030-1800 (exc. Tues 0600-0900) - Economic Sce. on 846/1098/1125/1251/1521kHz/FM 2130-1800 (exc. Tues 0530-0900) - Life Sce. on 747/783kHz/FM 24h - Traffic Sce. on 99.2MHz 2130-1700(exc. Tues 0600-0900) - Literary Sce. on 900kHz/90.7/102.2MHz 2130-1700 - Music Sce. on 102.4MHz 2130-1700 - Farmer Sce. on 558kHz/98.1/88.3MHz 2130-1800 - Travel Culture Sce. on 603/1521kHz/88.1MHz 2200-1500 - Children Music Sce. "M Radio": on 89.5MHz – **EB2)** 302 Tiyu Nan Dajie, Shijiazhuang, Hebei 050021. News Sce. on 882kHz/88.2MHz 2125-1700 - Economic Sce. on 100.9MHz 2125-1600 (exc. Tues 0600-0825). - Storytelling and Entertainment Sce. on 1431kHz 2125-1600 - Farm Sce. on 1251kHz/96.1MHz 2100-1600 - Traffic Sce. on 94.6MHz 2130-1700 - Taxi Sce. on 92.2MHz 2230-1600 – **EB3)** 246 Renmin Lu, Handan, Hebei 056002. News General Sce. on 963kHz/96.4MHz 2100-1600 - Economic Life Sce. on 1206kHz/102.8MHz 2100-1600 - Traffic Sce. on 1008kHz/106.8MHz 2100-1600. - Chinese Opera and Storytelling Sce. on 846kHz/104.8MHz 2100-1600 – **EB4)** 15 Yejin Lu, Xingtai, Hebei 054000. News General Sce. on 1188kHz/90.3MHz 2125-1600 (exc. Tues 0530-0930) - Economic Life Sce. on 927kHz/102.0MHz 2120-1500 (exc. Tues 0530-0930) - Traffic and Music Sce. on 91.8/101.2MHz 2225-1500 (exc. Tues 0630-0930) - Kuaile (Happy) Sce. on 96.8MHz – **EB5)** 1620 Yangguang Bei Dajie, Baoding, Hebei 071051. News Sce. on 1467kHz/90.9/93.7MHz 24h (exc. Tues 0600-0855) - Economic Sce. on 1017kHz/99.7MHz 2145-1600 (exc. Tues 0600-0930) - Traffic Sce. on 747kHz/104.8MHz 1850-1600 (exc. Tues 0600-0900) - City Service Sce. on 101.6MHz 2200-1400 - City and Country Alliance Sce. on 101.3/103.2/105.6MHz - Traffic and Music Ch. on 105.8MHz 2200-1630 – **EB6)** 17 Jianguo Lu, Qiaodong Qu, Zhangjiakou, Hebei 075000. News General Sce. on 1566kHz/101.0/107.4MHz 2155-1505 - Literary Sce. on 900kHz/94.5MHz 2155-1500 - V.O. the Earth: on 603kHz/103.6MHz 2155-1500 (exc. Tues 0500-0900) – **EB7)** 120 Guangdian Lu, Shuangqiao Qu, Chengde, Hebei 067000. News General Sce. on 1584kHz/93.8MHz 2155-0540, 0950-1400 - Traffic Sce. on 900kHz/97.6MHz 2255-1500.

Rel. CRI English prgr: 2300-0500, 1300-1500 - Storytelling Ch. on 105.8MHz– **EB8)** 1 Guangda Jie, Wenhua Lu, Tangshan, Hebei 063000. News General Sce. on 684kHz/91.7MHz 2030-1605 (exc. Tues 0705-0855) - Economic Life Sce. on 801kHz/95.5MHz 2130-1530 (exc. Tues 0700-0830) - Traffic and Literary Sce. on 1143kHz/96.8MHz 2135-1505 - Music Sce. on 94.0MHz 2200-1600 - "V.O. Cao Jidian" Novel Sce. on 900kHz 2200-1600 (exc. Tues 0630-0900) - Cultural and Entertainment Sce. on 105.9MHz – **EB9)** 9 Yingbin Lu, Haigang Qu, Qinhuangdao, Hebei 066000. General Sce. on 990kHz/89.1MHz 2055-1600 - V.O. Qinhuangdao: on 900kHz/103.8MHz 2055-1600 - Traffic Sce. on 99.5/100.4MHz 2155-1600 - Sports and Music Sce. on 97.3MHz 2200-? - Farm Story Sce. on 92.4MHz – **EB10)** 12 Jiefang Xilu, Cangzhou, Hebei 061001. News General Sce. on 1557kHz/97.0MHz 2057-1500 - Economic Life Sce. on 101.5MHz - Agricultural Economic Sce. on 1053kHz - Traffic Sce. on 1206kHz/93.8MHz 2200-1500 - Literary Sce. on 846kHz/103.6MHz 2200-1500 - Storytelling Sce. on 801kHz 2200-1500 – **EB11)** 8 Yongfeng Dao, Langfang, Hebei 065000. News General Sce. on 1008/846kHz/95.1MHz 2055-1700 - Storytelling Sce. on 585kHz/100.3MHz 24h - Chinese Opera Sce. on 1521kHz/105.0MHz 2055-1700 – **EB12)** 49 Hongqi Dajie, Hengshui, Hebei 053000. On 954kHz 2225-0535, 0825-1630 - Traffic and Information St. on 603kHz - Literary St. on 747kHz/87.7MHz – **EB13)** 167, Bei Duan, Xinghua Lu, Xinji, Hebei 052360. 2225-2355, 0255-0500, 1025-1250 – **EB14)** Xitou, Shengli Dajie, Nangong, Hebei 055750. 2225-0045, 1005-1400 – **EB15)** 36 Yingxin Dajie, Shahe, Hebei 054100. 2200-1600 – **EB16)** Sanyang Dongjie, Qinghe Xian, Hebei 054800. 2210-0330, 0910-1230 – **EB17)** Beiguan, Zhuozhou, Hebei 072750 – **EB18)** Zhongshan Xilu, Dingzhou, Hebei 073000. 2200-1500 – **EB19)** 393 Xiguan Xijie, Botou, Hebei 062150. 2225-2355, 0345-0450, 1025-123 – **EB20)** 12-1 Xihuan Lu, Renqiu, Hebei 062550. General Ch. on 1287kHz/92.8MHz 2225-1600, Storytelling Ch. on 864kHz 2255-1400.

HENAN PROVINCE

EN1) 2 Jing 5 Lu, 18 Zhenghua Lu, Zhengzhou, Henan 450003 **W:** www.radiohenan.com News Sce. on 657kHz/FM. 24h - Economic Sce. on 738/972/846kHz/103.2MHz 24h - Traffic Sce. on 900kHz/104.1MHz 24h - Farm Sce. on 846/107.4MHz 24h - Travel Sce. on 99.9MHz 24h - Music Sce. "Meili (charm) 881": on 88.1MHz/FM 24h - Visual Sce. "My Radio": on 1521kHz/90.0MHz 24h - Chinese Opera Sce. on 1143kHz/97.6MHz 24h - Education Sce. on 1332kHz/106.6MHz – **EN1A)** 2 Wei 1 Lu, Zhengzhou, Henan 450003. **W:** www.hnir.com Information Sce. on 603kHz/96.7MHz 24h - Infromation Sce. FM Prgr. on 585kHz/96.2/103.4/105.6MHz 24h - "Binfen 1098": on 1098kHz. 24h – **EN2)** 67 Huaihe Lu, Zhengzhou, Henan 450052. News General Sce. on 549kHz/88.9/98.6MHz 24h (exc. Tues 0600-1000, Thurs 1600-2200) - Economic Sce. on 711kHz/93.1MHz 24h - City Sce. "Automobile FM": on 91.2MHz 24h - Music Sce. "Simul Radio": on 94.4MHz 24h - Cultural and Entertainment Sce. on 1008kHz/91.8MHz 24h – **EN3)** 78 Songcheng Lu, Kaifeng, Henan 475004. General Sce. on 873kHz/98.6MHz 24h - News Sce. on 101.4MHz 2200-1530 - Economic Sce. on 100.2MHz 2155-1530 - Traffic Sce. on 105.1MHz - New Farm Sce. on 1053kHz/96.6MHz 2200-1530 (exc. Tues 0630-0955) – **EN4)** 67, Jiudu Lu, Luoyang, Henan 471009. News Sce. "V.O. Heluo": on 576kHz/88.1MHz 2150-1600 - Economic Sce. on 1053kHz/106.5MHz 2155-1600 - Traffic Sce. on 92.7MHz 2155-1600 – **EN5)** Zhong Duan, Jianshe Lu, Pingdingshan, Henan 467000. News Ch. on 747kHz/98.9MHz 2055-1500 - Economic Ch. on 1143kHz 2155-1500 - Literary Sce. on 846kHz 2200-1600, on 99.6MHz 24h - Traffic Sce. on 1521kHz/96.4MHz 24h – **EN6)** 217 Jiefang Zhonglu, Jiaozuo, Henan 454002. News General Sce. on 828kHz/103.0MHz 2200-1700 - Traffic and Travel Sce. on 99.5MHz - Life and Literary Sce. on 1251kHz/89.4MHz 2200-1700 (exc. Tues 0600-0955) – **EN7)** Zhong Duan, Huashan Lu, Hebi, Henan 458030. On 1107kHz/100.3MHz 2155-0535, 0955-1430 - Economic Ch. on 846kHz 2155-0535, 0955-1330 – **EN8)** 73 Renmin Lu, Xinxiang, Henan 453003. News General Sce. on 801kHz/92.9MHz 2125-1600 (exc. Tues 0530-0955) - Traffic Sce. on 1521kHz/99.1MHz 2155-1500 (exc. Tues 0500-0955) - Good Friends Car BS: on 90.2MHz – **EN9)** Zhong Duan, Wenfeng Dadao, Anyang, Henan 455000. News General Sce. on 882kHz/94.2MHz 2155-1530 - Traffic Sce. on 1251kHz/89.0MHz 2200-1400. - Automobile Music Sce. "i Radio": on 100.8MHz 2155-1600 – **EN10)** 379 Zhongyuan Lu, Puyang, Henan 457000. News General Sce. on 1251kHz/100.1MHz 2130-1535 (exc. Tues 0600-0900) - Economic Life Sce. on 91.0MHz 2130-1530 - Traffic and Music Sce. on 93.7MHz 2100-1600 – **EN11)** 72 Balong Lu, Xiao Nanhai, Xuchang, Henan 461000. News Sce. on 1287kHz/93.8MHz 2120-1500 - Economic and Literary Sce. on 927kHz 2200-0530, 1000-1345 - Xuchang Literary and Information BS: on 92.6MHz – **EN12)** 152 Daxue Lu, Luohe, Henan 462000. News Sce. on 1251kHz/89.0MHz 2050-1620 - Traffic and Music Sce. on 106.7MHz 2155-1600 - City Sce. on 98.1MHz 2155-1600 – **EN12A)** 1 Wenhua Lu, Luohe, Henan 462000 – **EN13)** Zhong Duan, Jianshe Lu, Sanmenxia, Henan 472000. News General Ch. on 603kHz/90.8MHz 2155-1605 (exc. Tues 0530-0955) - Literary and Traffic

Ch. on 1008kHz/104.0MHz 2255-1500 (exc. Tues 0530-1000) - Story Sce. on 100.0MHz 24h - New Farm Sce. on 98.9MHz – **EN14)** Zhong Duan, Funiu Lu, Nanyang, Henan 473056. News Ch. on 104.2MHz 2130-1605 - General Ch. on 585kHz/93.6MHz 2130-1605 - Literary and Life Ch. on 927kHz/106.0MHz 2130-1605 - Traffic and Music St. on 97.7/101.0MHz 2155-1605 – **EN15)** 19 Dongfanghong Dadao, Xinyang, Henan 464000. News Sce. on 837kHz/88.8MHz 2155-1600 - Traffic and Music Sce. on 94.8MHz - Literary Sce. on 106.8MHz – **EN16)** 35 Xinjian Nanlu, Shangqiu, Henan 476000. News Sce. on 729kHz/89.0MHz 2100-1500 - City Sce. on 927kHz/100.7MHz 2155-1605 - Traffic Sce. on 94.5MHz 2200-1700 - Music Sce. on 91.4MHz – **EN17)** 10, Dong Duan, Jianshe Lu, Zhoukou, Henan 466000. News Sce. on 828kHz 2050-1515 - Economic Life Sce. on 567kHz 2050-1600 - Traffic Sce. on 89.3MHz - Music Sce. on 96.0MHz – **EN18)** 209 Wenhua Lu, Zhumadian, Henan 463000. On 810kHz/97.2MHz 2125-? - Traffic and Travel Sce. on 102.4MHz - Zhumadian EBS: on 1053kHz – **EN19)** Qingping Lu, Xinmi, Henan 452370 – **EN20)** Lianmeng Xiaoqu, Chengguan Zhen, Qinyang, Henan 454550 – **EN21)** 25 Xi Dajie, Huixian, Henan 453600 – **EN22)** 10 Qianqiu Lu, Yima, Henan 472300 – **EN23)** 30 Guangyu Lu, Ruzhou 467500 – **EN24)** Dufu Lu, Gongyi, Henan 451200. On 765kHz/98.2MHz 2155-1600 - Sunshine Ch. on 107.5MHz 2155-1530.

FUJIAN PROVINCE

FJ1) 2 Gutian Lu, Fuzhou, Fujian 350001 **W:** www.fjgb.com News General Sce. on 558/612/837/882/900/1008/1368/1395/1404/1449/1494/5040kHz/94.4/103.6MHz 24h (exc. Tues 0630-0855) in Ch and Amoy - Private Car Sce. on 98.7/101.5MHz 24h - Traffic Sce. on 87.6/100.7MHz 24h (exc. Tues 0600-0850) - Music Sce. on 91.3MHz 24h (exc. Tues 0600-0900) - Fujian EBS "Interactive FM": on 1404kHz/96.1/98.6/103.1MHz. 24h (exc. Tues 0600-0850) in Ch and Amoy – **FJ2)** Fuzhou Radio and TV, 1 Yuanyang Lu, Fuzhou, Fujian 350004. News Sce. on 1332kHz/94.4MHz 24h (exc. Wed 0605-0925) in Ch and Fuzhou dialect - Anchorwomen BS: on 89.3MHz 24h (exc. Thurs 0600-0900) - V.O. the Traffic: on 87.6MHz 24h - V.O. Zuohai: on 90.1MHz 24h in Fuzhou dialect – **FJ3)** 123 Hubin Beilu, Xiamen, Fujian 361012. News Sce. on 1107kHz/99.6MHz 2130-1700 in Ch and Amoy - Economic and Traffic Sce. on 107.0MHz 2200-1700 (exc. Tues 0600-0900) - V.O. Minnan: on 801kHz/101.2MHz 2200-? in Amoy - Music Sce. on 90.9MHz 24h - Travel Sce. on 94.0MHz – **FJ4)** Putian PBS, 416 Puyang Lu, Chengxiang Qu, Putian, Fujian 351100. General Sce. on 93.7MHz 2155-1800 in Ch and Puxian dialect - Music St. on 103.0MHz. - Travel St. on 94.0MHz 2200-1600 – **FJ5)** 1 Guangdian Lu, Quanzhou, Fujian 362000. News Ch. on 576kHz/88.9MHz 2200-1600 - V.O. the City: on 92.3MHz 24h - V.O. the Traffic: on 90.4MHz 24h (exc. Tues 0500-0900) - V.O. the Music: on 88.1MHz - V.O. Citong: on 105.9MHz 24h in Quanzhou dialect – **FJ6)** 62 Heping Lu, Longyan, Fujian 364000. 2158-1620 (exc. Tues 0600-1000) – **FJ7)** Zhangzhou PBS, Shengli Donglu, Zhangzhou, Fujian 363000. News General Sce. on 89.6/96.2MHz 2153-1700 - Traffic Sce. on 96.6/92.7MHz - Music Sce. on 99.1MHz – **FJ8)** Sanming PBS, 32 Zhuang, Liedong Shuangyuan Xincun, Sanming, Fujian 365000. News General Ch. on 87.6/103.4MHz - City Life Ch. on 97.5MHz

GUANGDONG PROVINCE

GD1) 686 Renmin Beilu, Guangzhou, Guangdong 510012 **W:** www.rgd.com.cn Satellite Sce. (News Ch.) on 648/828/846/1017/1143/1206kHz/91.4MHz 24h - V.O. the City: on 103.6/90.0MHz 24h - Yangcheng Traffic St. on 105.2MHz 24h - Southern Life Sce. on 999kHz/93.6MHz 24h (exc. Mon 0400-1000) - Stock Sce. "Caijing 927": on 927kHz/95.3MHz 24h - V.O. the Music: on 1008kHz/99.3/93.9/96.8MHz 24h - V.O. Nanyue "Liuxing 1057": on 105.7MHz 24h - Literary and Sports Sce. on 603kHz/107.7MHz 24h – **GD2)** Zhujiang EBS, 686 Renmin Beilu, Guangzhou, Guangdong 510012. On 1062/801/1161kHz/97.4MHz 24h in Cantonese – **GD4)** 231 Huanshi Zhonglu, Guangzhou, Guangdong 510010. News Information Sce. "Fengyun 962": on 96.2MHz 24h (exc. Sun 1700-2200) in Cantonese. English Prgr: Fri 1300-1400 - Golden Hit Sce. "Jinqu 1027": on 102.7MHz 24h (exc. Sun 1600-2100) in Cantonese - Traffic Sce. "Jiaotong 1061": on 1098kHz/106.1MHz 2200-1600 (exc. Mon 1600-2200) - Youth Sce. on 1170kHz/88.0MHz 24h (exc. Mon 1600-2100) – **GD5)** 1 Pengcheng 1 Lu, Futian Qu, Shenzhen, Guangdong 518026. News Ch. on 900kHz/89.8MHz 24h (exc. Tues 0530-0930) in Ch and Cantonese - Private Car Sce. "i Radio": on 94.2MHz 24h in Ch and Cantonese - Music Ch. "Feiyang 971" on 97.1MHz 24h in Ch and Cantonese - Traffic Ch. on 106.2MHz 2230-1800 - V.O. Lingnan on 1287kHz 24h – **GD6)** 1129 Dong, Jiuzhou Dadao, Xiangzhou Qu, Zhuhai, Guangdong 519015. V.O. the City: on 95.1MHz 2225-1700 in Ch and Cantonese - Traffic Music Sce. "Feiyue 875" on 900kHz/87.5MHz 2225-1700 in Ch and Cantonese – **GD7)** Chaoshan Lu, Shantou, Guangdong 515021. News Ch. on 1080kHz/99.3MHz 2200-1600 in Ch and Chaozhou dialect - V.O. the Life and Economy: on 102.5MHz 2300-1600 - Music Ch. on 107.1MHz 24h (exc. Wed 0600-0900) – **GD8)** 57 Huimin Beilu, Shaoguan, Guangdong 512026. Chinese Ch. on 105.7MHz 2225-1600 - Cantonese Ch. "V.O. Beijiang" on 765kHz/95.2MHz 2225-1700 – **GD9)** Heyuan PBS, 1 Xingyuan Donglu, Yuancheng Qu, Heyuan,

Guangdong 517000. On 92.2/97.8MHz in Ch and Cantonese – **GD10)** 42 Dong Jiaochang Bei, Meizhou, Guangdong 514011. Life Sce. on 94.8/97.8MHz 2155-1600 in Ch and Hakka - Happy Sce. on 100.3MHz – **GD11)** Ehu Lu, Huicheng Qu, Huizhou, Guangdong 516001. News General Ch. "Sunshine 100": on 100.0/88.3MHz 2230-1630 (exc. Tues 0030-0830) in Ch and Cantonese - Environment and Traffic Sce. on 1098kHz 2230-1830. - Traffic Sce. on 98.8MHz – **GD12)** Shanwei PBS, Zhong Duan, Shanwei Dadao, Shanwei, Guangdong 516600. News Ch. on 90.0/103.5MHz 0940-? in Ch and Hakka – **GD13)** Dongguan PBS, 35 Xizheng Lu, Cheng Qu, Dongguan, Guangdong 523000. General Ch. on 100.8MHz 2225-1600 in Cantonese - Music Ch. on 106.9MHz 0100-1600 in Cantonese – **GD14)** Zhongshan PBS, 4 Xingzhong Dao, Dong Qu, Zhongshan, Guangdong 528403. General Ch. on 96.7MHz 2200-1800 in Cantonese - Environment and Travel Ch. on 747kHz/88.8MHz 2200-1800. – **GD15)** Jiangmen PBS, 19 Jianshe Lu, Jiangmen, Guangdong 529000. On 100.2MHz 2200-1600 in Cantonese - Travel and Music St. on 93.3MHz 2200-1600 – **GD16)** Foshan PBS, Jihua 6 Lu, Chancheng Qu, Foshan, Guangdong 528000. Zhen'ai Ch. (Love FM) on 94.6MHz 24h in Cantonese - Qianse Ch. (Color FM) on 98.5MHz 24h in Cantonese - Travel Ch. on 88.3MHz - Feiyue 92.4 "Simul Radio": on 92.4MHz – **GD17)** Yangjiang PBS, 114 Mojiang Lu, Jiangcheng Qu, Yangjiang, Guangdong 529500. V.O. the City: on 95.6MHz in Ch and Cantonese – **GD18)** 93 Yuejin Lu, Chikan Qu, Zhanjiang, Guangdong 524038. 1st St. on 1134kHz/95.1MHz 2220-1700 in Ch, Cantonese and Leizhou dialect - 2nd St. on 89.3MHz 2220-1700 - V.O. the Traffic and Music: on 98.1/102.4MHz - Zhanjiang EBS: on 104.6MHz 2200-0600, 0800-1600 – **GD19)** 13 Gaoliang Zhonglu, Hedong Qu, Maoming, Guangdong 525000. News St. on 106.1MHz 2230-1500 in Ch and Cantonese - Music St. on 1098kHz/96.7MHz 2230-1700 – **GD20)** Xinghu Dadao, Zhaoqing, Guangdong 526060. Information Sce. on 1521kHz/92.9MHz 2200-1600 in Ch and Cantonese - Music Sce. on 90.9MHz 2200-1600 in Ch and Cantonese – **GD21)** Qingyuan PBS, 18 Xincheng, Yinquan Lu, Qingyuan, Guangdong 511515. On 88.7/96.7MHz 2225-1600 in Ch and Cantonese – **GD22)** Wenci Donglu, Chenghai Qu, Shantou, Guangdong 515800. 2250-1600 in Ch and Chaoshan dialect – **GD23)** Jieyang PBS. Radio and TV Center, Jinxianmen Dadao, Jieyang , Guangdong 522000. 1st prgr. on 103.9MHz - 2nd prgr. on 106.5MHz – **GD24)** Jiedong PBS, Jiedong, Jieyang, Guangdong 515500. on 100.2MHz 2220-1700

GANSU PROVINCE

GS1) 561 Zhangsutan, Chengguan Qu, Lanzhou, Gansu 730010. **W:** www.gstv.com.cn News Sce. on 684/873kHz/FM 2150-1605 (exc. Tues 0600-0850) - City FM: on 102.2/106.6MHz 2200-1800 (exc. Tues 0600-0855) - Economic Sce. "V.O. Yellow River": on 801kHz/93.4MHz 2255-1700 - Traffic Sce. on 103.5/104.8MHz 2150-1800 (exc. Tues 0600-0855) - Youth Sce. "Sunshine FM": on 104.8MHz 0000-1600 - Farm Sce. "Voice of Country" on 1170kHz/92.2MHz 2225-1700 (exc. Tues 0600-0850) – **GS2)** 92 Qingyang Lu, Lanzhou, Gansu 730030. News Sce. on 954kHz/97.3MHz 2125-1700 - Traffic and Music Sce. on 99.5MHz 2200-1900 (exc. Mon 0600-1000) - Life and Literary Sce. on 100.8MHz 2230-1800 – **GS3)** 6 Yan'an Xilu, Jinchang, Gansu 737100. News General Sce. on 585kHz/101.4MHz 2150-1600 - Traffic and Literary Sce. on 103.8MHz – **GS4)** 11-5 Huancheng Zhonglu, Qincheng Qu, Tianshui, Gansu 741000. News General Sce. on 1143kHz/98.2MHz 2220-1600 - Music and Literary Sce. on 93.7MHz – **GS5)** 10 Fuqiang Xilu, Jiayuguan, Gansu 735100 – **GS6)** 49 Xi 2 Lu, Hezuo, Gansu 747000. On 1332/3990/5970kHz/97.2MHz 2220-0100, 0420-0620, 0950-1400 in Ch and Tb – **GS7)** 45 Tuanjie Lu, Linxia, Gansu 731100. 2255-0130(Sun 0230) – **GS8)** 45 Hongqi Jie, Kongtong Qu, Pingliang, Gansu 744000. 2200-1500 – **GS9)** Gongyuan Lu, Zhongping Qu, Yumen, Gansu 735000.

GUANGXI ZHUANG AUTONOMOUS REGION

GX1) 75 Minzu Dadao, Nanning, Guangxi 530022. **W:** www.gxradio.com Satellite Sce. on 792/1071/1440/1485/1575/7275kHz/FM. 24h (exc. Tues 0500-0930) - Economic Sce. on 846/1161/1224kHz/FM 24h (exc. Tues 0500-0830) in Ch and Guangxi dialect - Private Car 930: on 93.0/88.5/90.1/92.3/96.9MHz 2200-1700 (exc. Tues 0500-0930) in Ch and Zhuang - Traffic St. on 100.3/89.5/106.3MHz 2200-1700 (exc. Tues 0500-0930) - Literary Sce. on 95.0/105.0MHz 24h (exc. Tues 0500-0930) - Legend Sce. "Anchorwomen BS": on 97.0MHz 24h – **GX2)** Nanning PBS, 25 Gecun Lu, Nanning, Guangxi 530012. News General Ch. on 101.4MHz 2055-1700 in Ch and Guangxi dialect - Country and Life Sce. on 104.9MHz 2300-1700 - Traffic and Music Sce. on 107.4MHz 2240-1600 – **GX3)** 1 Guizhong Dadao, Liuzhou, Guangxi 545006. News Sce. on 1386kHz/102.9MHz 24h in Ch and Liuzhou dialect - Traffic and Life Sce. on 99.1MHz - Music Sce. on 94.5MHz – **GX4)** 1 Anxin Beilu, Xiangshan Qu, Guilin, Guangxi 541002. News General Sce. on 1485kHz/97.7MHz 2200-1600 - Travel and Music Sce. on 88.3MHz 2200-1600 – **GX5)** 69 Xinxing 3 Lu, Wuzhou, Guangxi 543002. News Sce. on 1485kHz/100.8MHz 2200-1630 in Ch and Guangxi dialect - V.O. the Music and Traffic: on 107.5MHz 2200-1300 (exc. Mon – **GX6)** Beihai PBS, 36 Guizhou Nanlu, Beihai, Guangxi 536000. On 93.5MHz

2200-1700 in Ch and Guangxi dialect – **GX7)** Qinzhou PBS, 18 Liqiao Jie, Qizhou, Guangxi 535000. News General Sce. on 98.6MHz 2220-1645 - Music Sce. on 88.9MHz 2300-1645 – **GX8)** Yulin PBS, 1 Guangdian Lu, Yulin, Guangxi 537000. News Sce. on 97.8MHz 2200-1700 (exc. Tues 0600-0900) - Traffic and Music St. on 99.2MHz 2200-1700 – **GX9)** Qiandongnan PBS, 10 Ningbo Lu, Qiandongnan Prefecture 556000, 104.0MHz 2030-1600.

GUIZHOU PROVINCE

GZ1) 302 Qingyun Lu, Guiyang, Guizhou 550002 **W:** www.gzbs.cn Satellite Sce. (General Ch.) on 765/927/1026/7275kHz/FM 2150-1705 (exc. Tues 0600-0900) - Economic Sce. on 603kHz/98.9MHz 24h (exc. Tues 0700-1000). –City Sce. "Simul Radio": on 97.2MHz 24h - Traffic Sce. on 95.2MHz 24h - Health Sce. on 106.2MHz 24h (exc. Tues 0700-1000) - Music Sce. on 91.7MHz 2300-1600 (exc. Tues 0600-0900) – **GZ2)** 15 Zunyi Lu, Guiyang, Guizhou 550002. News St. on 999kHz/88.9MHz 2150-1800 - Female Ch. on 104.0MHz 2150-1800 - Traffic and Travel Sce. on 101.1MHz 2250-1800 – **GZ3)** 31 Minghu Lu, Zhongshan Qu, Liupanshui, Guizhou 553001. News General Ch. on 765kHz/99.8MHz 2225-1800 - Traffic Sce.on 93.8MHz - Safe Traffic Ch. on 96.8MHz 2225-1800 - Star Music FM: on 102.1MHz 2225-1800 – **GZ4)** 11 Wenmiao Xiang, Fenghuang Lu, Honghuagang Qu, Zunyi, Guizhou 563000 – **GZ5)** 14 Waihuan Xinan Lu, Anshun, Guizhou 561000 – **GZ6)** Qiannan PBS, 267 Huandong Zhonglu, Duyun, Guizhou 558000. News General Ch. on 882kHz/98.0MHz 2200-1530 - Traffic and Travel Ch. on 93.3MHz/92.2MHz 2225-1600.

HAINAN PROVINCE

HA1) Hainan Radio and TV St, 61 Nansha Lu, Haikou, Hainan 570206 **W:** www.hnwtv.com News Sce. on 954/1107/1116kHz/FM 24h in Ch and Hainan dialect - Economic Sce. on 99.0/103.8/106.8MHz 2225-1705 - Traffic Sce. on 1143kHz/89.3/100.0MHz 2255-1805 – **HA2)** Haikou Radio and TV St, 15 Zhongsha Lu, Haikou, Hainan 570206. News General Sce. on 101.8MHz 2155-1800 in Ch and Hainan dialect - City and Country Sce. on 95.4MHz - Music Sce. "Simul Radio" on 91.6MHz 2155-1630 – **HA3)** Sanya PBS, Jiefang 4 Lu, Sanya, Hainan 572000. General Ch. on 104.6MHz - Traffic Ch. on 100.3MHz

HUBEI PROVINCE

HB1) 1237 Jiefang Dadao, Hankou, Wuhan, Hubei 430022 **W:** www.hbtv.com.cn News General Sce. "V.O. Hubei": on 774/1404/1566kHz/FM 2000-1730 (exc. Tues 0700-0850) - Economic Ch. on 1053/1251kHz/FM 1940-1800 - Life Ch. on 801/846/900/927/1098/1143/1215kHz/96.6MHz 2000-1800 - Private Car (Sports and Travel) Sce. on 107.8/88.0/90.4MHz 2300-1400 - Women and Children St. "Sunshine FM": on 747/1206kHz/97.1/102.6MHz 2000-1700 - Music Ch. on 103.8MHz 2000-1700 – **HB2)** Chutian BS, 1237 Jiefang Dadao, Hankou, Wuhan, Hubei 430022 **W:** www.ctbs.cn News St. on 1179/927/945/1008kHz 1955-1700 (exc. Tues 0630-0855) - Farm Sce. on 684/801/846/900/945/1125/1143kHz/FM 1955-1730 (exc. Tues 0630-0855) - Traffic and Sports St. on 92.7MHz 2125-1630 (exc. Tues 0630-0855) - Music Sce. on 105.8MHz 24h (exc. Tues 0630-0855).– **HB3)** 620 Jianshe Dadao, Hankou, Wuhan, Hubei 430015. On 873kHz/88.4MHz 2030-1700 (exc. Wed 0600-0925) - Changjiang Economic Sce. on 1125kHz/100.6MHz 2100-1700 (exc. Thurs 0600-0900) - Traffic Sce. on 603kHz/89.6MHz 2100-1700 (exc. Tues 0500-0900) - Music Sce. on 101.8MHz 2100-1700 (exc. Tues 0600-1000) - Tasting Music Sce. on 87.6MHz 2100-1600 – **HB5)** 188 Wuhan Lu, Huangshi, Hubei 435000. News St. on 963kHz/101.2/101.8MHz 2200-1600 - Traffic and Music St. on 103.3MHz 2200-1600 - V.O. Cihu (Ci Lake): on 105.0MHz 2145-1600 – **HB6)** 78 Zhongshan Houjie, Fancheng Qu, Xiangyang, Hubei 441021. News Sce. on 104.0MHz 2120-1635 (exc. Tues 0700-0830) - Economic Sce. on 1314kHz/90.9MHz 2120-1635 (exc. Tues 0700-0830). - Automobile Sce. on 1098kHz/105.3MHz 2155-1635 (exc. Tues 0700-0830) - Traffic and Music Sce. "Dongli (Power) 890": on 89.0MHz 2155-1635 (exc. Tues 0700-0830) – **HB7)** 4 Renmin Beilu, Shiyan, Hubei 442000. News St. on 1485kHz/106.2/107.3MHz 2100-1600 - V.O. Checheng (Mobile City): on 99.1MHz 2200-1600 - Music and Traffic St. on 101.9MHz 2200-1700 (exc. Tues 0600-1000) – **HB8)** 266 Jiangjin Xilu, Shashi Qu, Jingzhou, Hubei 434000. V.O. Jingzhou: on 585kHz/97.2MHz 2200-1600 - General Sce. on 828/1368kHz/98.4MHz 2030-1630 - 963 Beauty Music Sce. on 96.3MHz 2200-1700 (exc. Tues 0700-0900) - 901 Automobile Sce. on 90.1MHz 2130-1600. – **HB9)** 2 Guoyuan 1 Lu, Yichang, Hubei 443000. News General Sce. on 621kHz/95.6MHz 2100-1615 (exc. Tues 0600-0700) - Economic Life Sce. on 100.6MHz 2130-1600 (exc. Tues 0600-0700) - Traffic and Music Sce. on 105.9MHz 2225-1645 (exc. Tues 0600-0700) – **HB10)** 100 Xiangshan Dadao, Dongbao Qu, Jingmen, Hubei 448000. News and Economic St. on 1161kHz/89.7MHz 2120-1600 - Health and Music St. on 93.2MHz 2120-0500, 0930-1500 - Traffic and Literary St. on 90.3MHz 2120-1600 – **HB11)** 157 Binhu Lu, Ezhou, Hubei 436000. 2100-1600 – **HB12)** 116 Changzheng Lu, Xiaogan, Hubei 432100. News General Ch. on 927kHz/91.2MHz 2155-1530 (exc. Tues 0500-1000) - Traffic and Music Sce. on 87.7MHz 2255-1505 – **HB13)** 169 Dongmen Lu, Huangzhou Qu, Huanggang, Hubei 438000. On

91.4MHz 2220-1540 - Traffic Sce. on 107.6MHz 2220-1530 – **HB14)** 38 Wenquan Lu, Xianning, Hubei 437100. ?-0800, 0930-? – **HB15)** 32 Xuefu Lu, Laohekou, Hubei 441800. 2220-0500, 0800-1400 – **HB16)** 4 Renmin Lu, Danjiangkou, Hubei 441900. News General Ch. on 1431kHz 2220-1600 – **HB17)** 2 Shannan Xiaoqu, Shishou, Hubei 434400. 2200-0005, 0955-1235 – **HB18)** 56 Guang'an Lu, Yingshan Zhen, Guangshui, Hubei 432700. 2155-0115, 0955-1305 – **HB19)** 146 Puyang Dadao, Yingcheng, Hubei 432400. 2200-0600, 0900-1305 – **HB20)** 199 Nanhuan Lu, Macheng, Hubei 436100. Educational and Music St. on 1242kHz/92.5/105.0MHz 2155-1430 – **HB21)** 50 Chunchuan Daqiao Lu, Chibi, Hubei 437300. 0950-1340 – **HB22)** 359 Lieshan Dadao, Suizhou, Hubei 441300. News General Ch. on 1008kHz 2130-2330, 0330-0500, 1030-1305 - Traffic and Music St. on 96.2MHz – **HB23)** 117 Mianyang Dadao, Xiantao, Hubei 433000. 2130-1600 – **HB24)** 16 Jianghan Lu, Yuanlin Zhen, Qianjiang, Hubei 433100. 2205-0445, 0930-1600 – **HB25)** 201 Hangkong Lu, Xiangzhou Qu, Xiangyang, Hubei 441104. On 1521kHz/96.5MHz 2155-1600.

HEILONGJIANG PROVINCE

HL1) 333 Hanshui Lu, Nangang Qu, Harbin, Heilongjiang 150090 **W:** www.hljradio.com News St. on 621/990/927/1341/94.6MHz 24h - Life St. on 104.5MHz/FM 24h (exc. Tues 1600-2100) - Traffic St. on 99.8MHz/FM 2030-1500 - City Women St. on 102.1MHz 24h - "FM 97" on 97.0MHz 24h. - Music St. on 95.8MHz 24h (exc. Tues 1600-2100) - Country St. on 945kHz/94.3MHz 24h - University St. "Radio Young": on 99.3MHz/FM 2200-? – "873 Story Hour": on 873/1476kHz/FM - Heilongjiang Korean BS: on 873/1476kHz/FM 2100-2400, 1300-1500 in Ko. - V.O. Beidahuang (Great Northern Wilderness): on FM 2055-1600 - Sanya BS "V.O. Tianya": on 104.6MHz 2200-? – **HL2)** 1 Huashan Lu, Xiangyangg Qu, Harbin, Heilongjiang 150036. News General Sce. on 837kHz/94.1/105.6MHz 24h - Literary Sce. on 98.4/97.8MHz 24h – **HL2A)** Harbin EBS, 2 Wenzheng Jie, Dongli Qu, Harbin, Heilongjiang 150040. Economic Sce. on 972kHz. 24h (exc. Tues 0500-0900) - Traffic Sce. on 92.5/95.3MHz 24h - Music Sce. on 927kHz/88.8/90.9/103.0MHz 24h – **HL3)** 99 Yong'an Dajie, Longsha Qu, Qiqihar, Heilongjiang 161005. News Sce. on 1197kHz/87.8MHz 2000-1600(Tues 1405) - Life and Literary Sce. on 693kHz/89.4/95.3MHz 2020-1505 - Traffic Sce. on 94.1/98.0MHz 2050-1605 - Country Sce. on 585kHz/103.4MHz – **HL4)** Jiuma Lu, Xiangyang Qu, Hegang, Heilongjiang 154100. News Sce. on 1413kHz/97.2/101.4/107.6MHz 2055-1400 - Traffic and Literary Sce. on 106.1MHz 2145-1400 - Life Sce. on 93.3MHz – **HL5)** 240 Xinxing Dajie, Jianshan Qu, Shuangyashan, Heilongjiang 155100. On 1179kHz 2120-0120, 0320-0530, 0905-1230 - Traffic and Literary Sce. on 98.1MHz - Storytelling Sce. on 603kHz/88.6MHz – **HL6)** 11 Diantai Lu, Jiguan Qu, Jixi, Heilongjiang 158100. News General Sce. on 1368kHz/94.5MHz 2130-0600, 0850-1350 - Traffic Sce. on 1485kHz/95.9MHz - Literary and Life Sce. on 1143kHz/98.6MHz - Storytelling Sce. on 103.9MHz 2055-1500 – **HL7)** Jia 1, Dongfeng Lu, Sa'ertu Qu, Daqing, Heilongjiang 163311. News Sce. on 1080kHz/96.7/97.5MHz 24h - Traffic Sce. on 95.0MHz 24h - Music Sce. on 106.0MHz 1955-1600.- Storytelling Sce. on 103.9MHz 24h - V.O. Baihu: on 91.9MHz 2000-1600 – **HL8)** 16 Linshan Lu, Yichun Qu, Yichun, Heilongjiang 153000. News General Sce. on 909kHz/92.4/102.1MHz 2130-0810 (exc. Mon 0725-1000) - Traffic and Life Sce. on 98.5MHz 2200-1400 – **HL9)** 138 Taiping Lu, Mudanjiang, Heilongjiang 157000. News Sce. on 684kHz/87.9MHz 2105-1400 (exc. Tues 0800-0855) - City Life Sce. on 1476kHz/91.6MHz 2200-1530 - Traffic and Literary Sce. on 98.2MHz 2300-1300 – **HL10)** 35 Shunhe Lu, Jiamusi, Heilongjiang 154002. News General Sce. on 666kHz/101.7MHz 2055-0530, 0855-1400 - Economic Sce. on 1143kHz/95.0MHz 2055-1600 - Traffic and Literary Sce. on 98.0/93.8MHz 2225-1600 – **HL11)** 2 Shanhu Dajie, Taoshan Qu, Qitaihe, Heilongjiang 154600. News General Sce. on 1062kHz/98.8MHz 2300-1545 - Traffic Ch. on 89.1MHz – **HL12)** Xizhi Lu, Suihua, Heilongjiang 152054 - Traffic Sce. on 90.7MHz 2155-1400 - Music Sce. on 1080kHz - Storytelling Sce. on 107.0MHz – **HL13)** 2 Xing'an Dajie, Jagdaqi Zhen, Heilongjiang 165000. Peoples Sce. on 1278kHz/100.1MHz 2125-1400 (exc. Tues 0600-0955) – **HL14)** 93 Hailan Jie, Aihui Qu, Heihe, Heilongjiang 164300. On 1215kHz/103.8MHz 2100-1400.

HUNAN PROVINCE

HN1) 167 Yuhua Lu, Changsha, Hunan 410007 **W:** www.hnradio. com Satellite Sce. (News Ch) on 738/1152/1233/4990kHz/FM 2100-1700 (exc. Tues 0500-0900) - V.O. the Country "Green 938": on 900kHz/93.8/100.7MHz 2100-1705 - Economic Ch. on FM 2130-1700 (exc. Tues 0500-0900) - Literary Ch. "Kuaile (Happy) 975": on 97.5/87 .5/90.6/90.8/96.9MHz 2130-1700 (exc. Tues 0500-0900) - Traffic Sce. on FM 24h - V.O. the Music "Super 893": on 89.3/102.1MHz - Travel Sce. on 106.9MHz - Mango Radio V.O. Yongzhou on 94.8/95.8MHz 2000-1600 - V.O. Golden Hawk on 95.5MHz 24h – **HN2)** 237 Laodong Xilu, Changsha, Hunan 410015. News Sce. on 1323kHz/105.0MHz 24h (exc. Tues 0600-0900). - V.O. Jinying (Golden Vox): on 95.5MHz 24h - Economic Sce. "Kuaile (Happy) 886": on 88.6MHz 24h - Traffic and Music Sce. "i Radio": on 106.1MHz 24h - Sound of City "My

FM": on 101.7MHz 24h – **HN3)** Caotangba Xiang, Jianshe Zhonglu, Zhuzhou, Hunan 412007. News Ch. on 1089kHz/101.2MHz 2150-1600 - Traffic Ch. on 98.4MHz – **HN4)** Donghu Lu, Xiangtan, Hunan 411104. General Ch. on 1503kHz/104.2MHz 2200-1700 - V.O. the Music: on 98.6MHz – **HN5)** 114 Xianfeng Lu, Hengyang, Hunan 421001. On 1098kHz/98.9MHz 2130-1700 – **HN6)** 373 Zhangshulong, Baoqing Xilu, Daxiang Qu, Shaoyang, Hunan 422000. On 1548kHz 2225-0530, 0955-1600 - Traffic Ch. on 95.4MHz – **HN7)** Nanhu Dadao, Yueyang, Hunan 414000. News and Traffic Sce. on 1053kHz/100.1/104.1MHz 2200-0530, 0925-1340 - Music Sce. on 1008kHz/106.1MHz 2155-1700 – **HN8)** 69 Wuling Dadao, Changde, Hunan 415000. On 1260kHz 2200-2355, 0400-0500, 0925-1100 - News Ch. on 105.6MHz 2225-1705 - Traffic Ch. on 97.1MHz – **HN9)** Chaoyang Lu, Yiyang, Hunan 413000. Economic Sce. on 1008kHz/99.7MHz 2220-1600 (exc. Wed 0800-1000) – **HN10)** 51 Renmin Lu, Jinshi, Hunan 415400 – **HN11)** Chenzhou PBS, 7 Li Dadao, Chenzhou, Hunan 423000. Politics and General Ch. on 99.2/89.9MHz 2200-1700 - Music and Traffic Ch. on 102.8MHz 2225-1700 – **HN12)** Huaihua PBS, Tianxing Lu, Huaihua, Hunan 418000. News Ch. on 97.2MHz - Traffic and Literary Ch. on 103.8MHz

JILIN PROVINCE

JL1) 242 Xi'an Dalu, Changchun, Jilin 130051 **W:** jlradio.chinajilin. com.cn News General Sce. on 738/1107/1530kHz/91.6MHz 24h (exc. Tues 0500-0900) - Economic Sce. on 603/846/1143kHz/93.3MHz 24h - Health and Entertainment Sce. on 101.9MHz 24h (exc Tues 1500-1800) - Traffic Sce. on 103.8MHz 24h - Infromation Sce. on 100.1MHz 24h (exc. Tues 1500-1800) - Music Sce. on 92.7MHz 24h (exc. Tues 1500-1800) - Country Sce. on 97.6MHz/FM 24h - Story Sce. on 103.3MHz 24h - Educational Sce. on 96.3MHz 24h – **JL2)** 3 Baicao Lu, Changchun, Jilin 130061. News Sce. on 87.5/88.9MHz 24h - Passionate FM "Classic 90": on 1332kHz/90.0MHz 24h - Children and Old Life Sce. on 648kHz/105.3MHz - My FM: on 900kHz/88.0MHz 24h - V.O. the Traffic on 96.8/100.6MHz 24h - Health Life Sce. on 107.9MHz - City Music Sce. "Private Car Radio": on 106.4MHz - Country Sce. on 585kHz/99.6MHz 24h – **JL3)** 90 Jilin Dajie, Jilin-shi, Jilin 132011. V.O. the News: on 927kHz/102.6MHz 24h - Public Life St. on 702kHz 2045-1600 - Traffic St. on 105.3MHz 24h - Novel and Storytelling St. on 1143kHz. 2100-1400 - Automobile Life Sce. on 88.3MHz 24h – **JL3A)** Jilin-shi EBS, 181 Jiefang Dalu Xi, Jilin-shi, Jilin 132011. "Dushi (city) 110" St. on 1494kHz/90.3MHz 24h - "Qin'ai (dear) 603" St. on 603kHz 2020-1600. - "Luyou (Travel) 893" St. on 89.3MHz 2030-1700 - V.O. Old Friends: on 1251kHz – **JL4)** 39 Nan Xinhua Dajie, Siping, Jilin 136000. News General Ch. on 666kHz/93.9MHz 2135-1300 - Traffic and Literary St. on 99.5MHz 24h - Public Storytelling Ch. on 900kHz/90.5MHz 2155-1300 – **JL5)** 20 Hebin Lu, Longshan Qu, Liaoyuan, Jilin 136200. General Ch. on 810kHz/99.2MHz - Traffic and Literary St. on 96.2MHz 2125-1500 – **JL6)** 199 Cuiquan Lu, Longquan Jie, Tonghua, Jilin 134001. News General Sce. on 909kHz 2150-1505 (exc. Tues 0705-0855), - Urban Sce. on 90.9MHz 2200-1400 - Traffic and Literary St. on 93.8MHz 2140-1700 - Storytelling St. on 97.9MHz 2150-1400 – **JL7)** 36 Hunjiang Dajie, Badaojiang Qu, Baishan, Jilin 134302. News General St. on 657kHz/107.7MHz 2100-1530 - Traffic and Literary Sce. on 98.4MHz 2100-1500 – **JL8)** 71 Linjiang Lu, Ningjiang Qu, Songyuan, Jilin 131200. News General Ch. on 1431kHz 2100-1500 - Economic St. on 89.9MHz - Traffic St. on 1143kHz/99.9MHz 2100-1500 - Popuar Life Sce. on 98.6/96.8MHz - Storytelling and Entertainment St. on 102.5MHz 2055-1600 – **JL9)** 18 Chunyang Lu, Baicheng, Jilin 137000. News General Sce. on 1323kHz/103.0MHz 2100-1400 (exc. Tues 0630-0940) - Traffic and Literary Sce. on 96.5MHz - Life Sce. on 105.0MHz - Storytelling Sce. on 98.5MHz – **JL10)** 166 Juzi Jie, Yanji, Jilin 133000. Ch Satellite Sce. on 1053/603/1566kHz/FM 2130-1630 - Ch News Sce. on 88.2/91.7/92.2/98.3MHz - Ko News General Sce. on 1206kHz 2040-1600 (exc. Tues 0540-0900) - Ko Cultural Life Sce. on 585/1188kHz/FM 2130-1510 - Traffic and Literary Sce. on 105.9MHz 2130-1600 in Ch – **JL11)** 45 Dong Huancheng Lu, Gongzhuling, Jilin 136100. V.O. the Public: on 1485kHz 2050-1420 - V.O. the Traffic: on 101.3MHz – **JL12)** 18 Nan Dalu, Lishu Xian, Jilin 136500 – **JL13)** 70 Henan Jie, Meihekou, Jilin 135000. On 1584kHz/95.7MHz 2155-1130 – **JL14)** Yucai Jie, Qian Gorlos, Jilin 131100. On 1476kHz/91.0MHz 2125-2330, 0325-0500, 0955-1230 in Ch and Mo – **JL15)** 29 Gushu Nanjie, Taonan, Jilin 137100 – **JL16)** 7 Yongle Jie, Yanji, Jilin 133000. Ch Prgr. on 900kHz. 24h - Ko Prgr. "Arirang Radio": on 88.0MHz 2100-1700 - Yanji V.O. the Traffic BS: on 93.5MHz – **JL17)** 12 Xiangshang Jie, Tumen, Jilin 133100. 2155-2400, 0330-0500, 0855-1230 in Ch and Ko – **JL18)** 1-8 Xinhua Xilu, Dunhua, Jilin 133700. 2130-1500 in Ch and Ko – **JL19)** Jinghe Jie, Hunchun, Jilin 133300. Storytelling St. on 927kHz 2030-1530 in Ch and Ko - North East Asia V.O. Hunchun on 101.0MHz.

JIANGSU PROVINCE

JS1) Jiangsu Prov. Radio and TV Headquarters, 8 Xi Citang Xiang, Zhongshan Donglu, Nanjing, Jiangsu 210002 **W:** www.jsbc.com News General Ch. on 702/801/1314/1413/1602kHz 2000-1700 (exc. Tues/ Thurs 0600-0850) - News Sce. on 93.7MHz 2100-1600 - Home Sce.

on 107.1MHz 24h (exc. Tues 0600-0900, Wed 1700-2100) - Health Sce. on 846/603/1098kHz. 24h (exc. Tues 0600-0900) - Financial Sce. on 1206kHz/95.2MHz 2100-1600 (exc. Tues 0600-0900) - Traffic Sce. on 101.1MHz 24h (exc. Tues 1800-2000) - Story Sce. on 585kHz 2000-1700 (exc. Tues 0600-0900) - Music St. "Meili (Charm) 897": on 89.7/107.8MHz 24h (exc. Tues 0600-0900) - Classic Music St. on 97.5MHz 24h - Chinese Opera Sce. on 1053kHz 2100-1600 – **JS2)** Nanjing Radio and TV Bldg., 358 Baixia Lu, Nanjing, Jiangsu 210001. News St. on 1008kHz 1950-1800 (exc. Tues 0600-0800) - News FM: on 96.6MHz 2200-1400 - Economic St. on 900kHz. 24h - Economic St. "City FM": on 101.7MHz 2200-1600 - City Control Sce. on 1143kHz 2100-1600 - Traffic St. on 102.4MHz 2130-1800 - Music Sce. on 105.8MHz 24h - Sports Sce. on 1251kHz/104.3MHz 24h - Sports St. Entertainment Sce. "Gandong (move) 801": on 801kHz 2100-1600 (exc. Tues 0600-0800) - Private Car Sce. on 98.1MHz 24h - My FM: on 103.5MHz 24h – **JS3)** 223 Zhongshan Nanlu, Xuzhou, Jiangsu 221003. News Sce. on 1269kHz/93.0/89.3MHz 2000-1730 - Life Sce. on 801kHz/91.6MHz 2025-1730 - Traffic Sce. on 103.5MHz 2030-1700 - Literary Sce. on 1098kHz/89.6MHz 2015-1600 - Music Sce. on 99.6MHz 24h – **JS4)** 221 Jiefang Xilu, Xinpu Qu, Lianyungang, Jiangsu 222003. News Sce. on 1458kHz/98.3/102.1MHz 2100-1600 (exc. Tues 0600-0855) - Economic Sce. on 1251kHz/90.2/90.7MHz 2115-1600 - Traffic Sce. on 900kHz/92.7/96.0MHz 2155-1600 - Story Sce. on 98.1MHz – **JS5)** 6 Dazhi Lu, Huai'an, Jiangsu 223001. News General Sce. on 801kHz/94.1MHz 2000-1600 (exc. Tues 0600-0900) - Economic Life Sce. on 1251kHz/105.0MHz 2000-1600 (exc. Tues 0600-0840) - Traffic and Literary Sce. on 1521kHz/94.9MHz 2100-1600 - Public (Chengshi Guanli) Sce. on 106.7MHz 2055-1600 - Automobile Music Sce. on 104.2MHz 2100-1600 – **JS6)** Yancheng Radio and TV St, 4 Shengyuan Lu, Yancheng, Jiangsu 224001. News St. on 1026kHz/99.6MHz 2100-1600 - Economic Life Sce. on 747kHz/105.3MHz 2100-1600 - Huanghai Mingzhu (Pearl) Sce. on 900kHz/93.9MHz – **JS7)** 8 Meiling Donglu, Yangzhou, Jiangsu 225002. News Sce. on 98.5/105.3MHz 2120-1800 (exc. Tues 0600-0930) - Traffic Sce. on 1521kHz/103.5MHz 2120-1800 - Life Sce. on 801kHz/94.9MHz 2130-1600 (exc. Tues 0645-0800) - Yangsheng (Health) Sce. on 1179kHz/96.7MHz – **JS8)** 20 Qingnian Lu, Taizhou, Jiangsu 225300. News Sce. on 1341kHz/103.7/106.2MHz 2120-1525 (exc. Tues 0530-0855) - Music Sce. on 927kHz/97.3MHz 2145-1600 - Traffic Sce. on 92.1MHz 2200-1600 – **JS9)** 100 Renmin Zhonglu, Nantong, Jiangsu 226001. News Sce. on 1233kHz/97.0MHz 2130-1600 - Finacial and Economic Sce. on 603kHz/103.0/102.6MHz 2130-1600 - Traffic Sce. on 1170kHz/92.9MHz 2200-1600. - Happy Sce. on 88.5/88.3MHz 2130-1600 - Music Sce. on 91.8MHz 2130-1600 – **JS10)** 94 Zhongshan Xilu, Zhenjiang, Jiangsu 212004. News Sce. on 104.0MHz 2055-1600. - Health Life Ch. on 1224kHz/94.0MHz 2000-1800 - Traffic Sce. on 88.8MHz 2130-1600 - Music Sce. "V.O. Jinshan Lake Music": on 96.3MHz 2100-1800 - Commercial St. "City Radio": on 90.5MHz 2030-1800 - Private Car BS "Donggan 102.7": on 900kHz/102.7MHz 2130-1600 – **JS11)** Changzhou Radio and TV St, 88 Guangshi Lu, Changzhou, Jiangsu 213016. General Ch. "AM846": on 846kHz 2059-1600 (exc. Tues 0600-0850) - General Ch. "FM103.4": on 103.4MHz - Xi Drama Ch. on 1143kHz 2100-1300 - Economic Ch. "FM105.2": on 105.2MHz - Traffic Ch. on 90.0MHz 2100-1800 - Traffic and Literary Ch. on 747kHz 2110-1600 (exc. Tues 0600-0900) - Music Ch. "Aiting 935": on 1521kHz/93.5MHz 2150-1600 - Classic Music Ch. on 927kHz 2200-1600 – **JS12)** Wuxi Radio and TV St, 4 Hubin Lu, Wuxi, Jiangsu 214061. News Ch. News Sce. on 1161kHz/89.4MHz 2020-1700 (exc. Tues 0500-0900) - News Ch. Information Sce. on 93.7MHz 2020-1700 - Economic Ch. on 1251kHz/104.0MHz 2030-1800 - Story and Chinese Opera Sce. on 1008kHz 24h - Traffic Ch. on 106.9MHz 24h - Automobile Music Ch. on 900kHz/91.4MHz 2130-1800 - City Life Ch. on 1521kHz/98.7MHz 2130-1800 (exc. Tues 0500-0700) - V.O. Jiangnan: on 603kHz/92.7MHz 2100-1800 - Live Sce. on 1521kHz (exc. Tues 0500-0800) – **JS13)** Suzhou Radio and TV Headquarters, 4 Gongyuan Lu, Suzhou, Jiangsu 215006. News General Sce. on 1080kHz 2030-1600 (exc. Tues 0600-0730) in Ch and Suzhou dialect - V.O. the City "My Radio": on 91.1MHz 2030-1630 - Traffic Sce. on 1521kHz/104.8MHz 2130-1600 - V.O.Old Age: on 603kHz - Life Sce. on 96.5MHz 2130-1600(Tues 1525) - Music Sce. "Dongting 948": on 94.8MHz 24h (exc. Tues 0600-1000) - Chinese Opera Sce. on 846kHz - Automobile Sce. on 102.8MHz 2200-1600 – **JS14)** 43 Gongnong Lu, Yizheng, Jiangsu 211400. On 1026kHz/94.3MHz 2155-0535, 0725-1350 – **JS15)** 79 Zhongshan Nanlu, Jiangyin, Jiangsu 214400. Happy Life Ch. on 1386kHz/106.0MHz 2200-1530 - T Automobile Ch. on 90.7MHz 2200-1500 – **JS16)** 29 Haiyu Beilu, Changshu, Jiangsu 215500. News General Ch. on 1116kHz 2130-1400 (exc. Sat 0630-0830) - Economic Service Ch. on 927kHz 2150-1400 (exc. Sat 0630-0830) - Traffic and Music Ch. on 747kHz/100.8MHz 2130-1400 (exc. Sat 0600-0800) – **JS17)** Zhangjiagang Radio and TV St, Chenjiachang Nong, Yangshe Zhen, Zhangjiagang, Jiangsu 215600. News Sce. on 1098kHz 2140-1455 (exc. Wed 0600-0830) - Traffic Sce. on 102.0MHz 2155-1500 (exc. Wed 0530-0955) - Music Sce. on

1521kHz 2155-1500.

JIANGXI PROVINCE

JX1) 207 Hongdu Zhong Dadao, Nanchang, Jiangxi 330046 **W:** www.jxgdw.com/jxgd/jxgbdt/ News Sce. on 729/1350/1449kHz/FM 2000-1700 (exc. Tues 0600-0855) - City Sce. on 927kHz/99.2/106.5 2200-1700 (exc. Tues 0600-0900) - People Life Sce. on 603/927kHz/ 101.9/94.7/101.2MHz 2200-1600 - Scientific Education and Farm Sce. on 603kHz/98.5/88.3MHz 2200-1600 (exc. Tues 0600-0900) - Traffic Sce. "My FM": on 96.9/105.4MHz 24h - Literary and Music Ch. on 103.6/94.9/97.9/100.2/101.6/103.8/107.6MHz 24h - V.O. Poyang Lake: on 97.4MHz 24h– **JX2)** 241 Ruzi Lu, Nanchang, Jiangxi 330009. News General Ch. on 1278kHz/91.7MHz 2030-1700 (exc. Tues 0500-0900) - V.O. the Traffic and Music: on 95.1MHz 24h (exc. Tues 0500-0900) - V.O. Fortune: on 89.7MHz 24h - Joyful Music and Story Sce. "You Radio": on 84.8MHz - "Phoenix 879": on 87.9MHz 2200-1600. - V.O. Qingshan Lake on 93.4MHz – **JX3)** 1073 Cidu Dadao, Jingdezhen, Jiangxi 333000. News General Sce. on 1467kHz/96.5/107.3MHz 2200-1600 – **JX4)** Jiangwan Li, Binhe Xilu, Pingxiang, Jiangxi 337005. News General Sce. on 1107kHz/96.8/106.8MHz 2155-1500 - Traffic and Literary Ch. on 88.8MHz 24h – **JX5)** 49 Xianlai Zhong Dadao, Xinyu, Jiangxi 338000. General Ch. on 675kHz 2130-1800 - City Sce. on 585kHz/94.0MHz - Health Sce. on 1476kHz 2130-1800 - Traffic Sce. "Love Radio": on 96.2MHz 2200-1800 – **JX6)** 84 Changhong Dadao, Jiujiang, Jiangxi 332000. News General Sce. on 90.0/91.6MHz 2155-1600 - Traffic Sce. on 88.4/88.9MHz 2255-1500 (exc. Tues 0530-0855) - City Life Sce. on 1485kHz 2155-1600 – **JX7)** Yingtan PBS, 3 Jianshe Lu, Yingtan, Jiangxi 335200. V.O. Xinjiang (Xin River): on 103.2MHz 2200-1605 - V.O. the Traffic and Music: on 95.6MHz 2200-1800 – **JX8)** 58 Hongqi Dadao, Ganzhou, Jiangxi 341000. News General Ch. on 747kHz/93.7/101.8MHz 2130-1700 (exc. Tues 0600-0830) in Ch and Hakka - V.O. the City: on 94.5MHz 2200-1700 - Traffic Sce. on 99.2MHz – **JX9)** 19 Beimen Jie, Ji'an, Jiangxi 343000 - V.O. Jinggang: on 603/1242kHz/95.6/102.1MHz 2150-1600 - Traffic and Entertainment Sce. on 100.6MHz – **JX10)** Shangrao PBS, 51 Qingfeng Lu, Shangrao, Jiangxi 334000. News General Ch. on 93.4MHz 2200-1630 - Traffic and Music Ch. on 99.6MHz 2200-1630.

LIAONING PROVINCE

LN1) Liaoning Radio and TV St, 10 Guangrong Jie, Heping Qu, Shenyang, Liaoning 110003 **W:** www.lnradio.cn General Sce. on 603/612/963/1089/1260kHz/102.9MHz 24h (exc. Tues 0605-0855). - Economic Sce. on 801/900/999kHz/88.8/89.5MHz 24h (exc. Tues 0540-0855) - Country Sce. on 927kHz/96.9/103.4/107.1MHz 24h (exc. Tues 0500-0800) - Traffic Sce. on 97.5MHz 24h (exc. Tues 0540-0850) - Literary Sce. on 1053/747/801/810kHz/95.9/99.5/101.8MHz 24h (exc. Tues 0540-0900). - Live Sce. on 882kHz 24h (exc. Tues 0600-0855) City Sce. on 1341kHz/92.1/103.4MHz 24h - Music Sce. on 98.6MHz 24h (exc. Thurs 0500-0855) - Information Sce. (Dalian Blanch): on 90.6/90.4MHz 24h – **LN2)** Shenyang Radio and TV St, 89 Sanhao Jie, Heping Qu, Shenyang, Liaoning 110004. News Sce. on 792kHz/104.5/107.0MHz 24h – **LN3)** Dalian Radio and TV St, 162 Minquan Jie, Shahekou Qu, Dalian, Liaoning 116022. News Sce. on 882kHz/103.3MHz 1955-1605 (exc. Tues 0600-0800) - Financial Sce. on 93.1MHz 24h (exc. Tues 0630-0800) - Automobile Sce. on 1152kHz/99.1MHz 2025-1605 (exc. Tues 0630-0800) - Traffic Sce. on 100.8MHz 24h (exc. Tues 0600-0800) - Sports and Leisure Sce. on 105.7MHz 2025-1605 (exc. Tues 0600-0800) - New City and Country Sce. on 1575kHz/95.6MHz 24h - Children Sce. "Easy Radio": on 106.7MHz 24h (exc. Tues 0600-0800) – **LN4)** 3, 219 Lu, Tiedong Qu, Anshan, Liaoning 114002. News Sce. on 954kHz/99.5MHz 24h - Economic Sce. on 1071kHz/89.7MHz 24h - Traffic Sce. on 1458kHz/95.3MHz 24h - Music Sce. on 105.1MHz - Storytelling Sce. on 1251kHz/87.9MHz – **LN5)** Fushun Radio and TV St, 2 Hunhe Beilu, Shuncheng Qu, Fushun, Liaoning 113006. News Sce. on 684kHz/93.0/93.8MHz 2000-1500 - Traffic Sce. "i Radio": on 747kHz/ 106.1MHz 24h - Music Sce. on 100.6MHz 2030-1600 - Storytelling Sce. on 1143kHz/88.2MHz – **LN6)** 15 Tiyu Lu, Mingshan Qu, Benxi, Liaoning 117000. On 1296kHz 2125-1500 - Traffic and Economic St. on 900kHz/ 107.4MHz 2155-1600 - Life and Entertainment St. on 96.4MHz ?-1500 – **LN7)** 1 Shanshang Jie, Zhenxing Qu, Dandong, Liaoning 118000. News Ch. on 1404kHz/103.6MHz 24h - Traffic Ch. on 891kHz/101.7MHz 2000-1600 - City Ch. on 1476kHz/104.3MHz 2000-1600 - Storytelling Ch. on 603kHz/88.0MHz 2000-1500 – **LN8)** 3, 4 Duan, Beijing Lu, Jinzhou, Liaoning 121000. News Sce. Shiyuan (World Park) Ch. on 666kHz/92.7MHz 2125-1500 (exc. Tues 0530-0855) - Economic Sce. on 774kHz/96.6MHz 2125-1500 (exc. Tues 0530-0855) - Public Life Sce. on 1098kHz/90.9/97.7MHz 2125-1500 (exc. Tues 0530-0855) - Traffic Sce. on 846kHz/100.3MHz 2125-1500 (exc. Tues 0530-0855) – **LN9)** Huludao Radio and TV St, 23 Haixing Lu, Longwan Dajie, Huludao, Liaoning 125000. News General Sce. on 1242kHz/93.1/95.2MHz 2130-1535 - Economic Sce. on 106.3MHz - Traffic and Literary Sce. on 87.8MHz 2150-1330 (exc. Tues 0540-0955) – **LN10)** Yingkou Radio and TV St, 10, Dong, Bohai Dajie, Zhanqian Qu, Yingkou, Liaoning 115000. News

General Sce. on 1026kHz/88.4/106.2MHz 2055-1500 - Economic Life Sce. on 747kHz/89.0/92.8MHz 2100-1500 - Traffic and Literary Sce. on 1143kHz/95.1MHz 2130-1600 - Storytelling and Entertainment Sce. on 603kHz/94.1MHz 2125-1500 – **LN11)** Panjin Radio and TV St, 7 Shifu Dajie, Xinglongtai Qu, Panjin, Liaoning 124010. News General Sce. on 1485kHz/104.2MHz 2100-1600 - Traffic and Literary Sce. on 90.1MHz 2100-1500 - Economic Life Sce. on 97.1MHz 2100-1600 - Storytelling and Chinese Opera Sce. on 101.8MHz 2100-1550 - Music Sce. "V.O. Hexiang": on 95.3MHz – **LN12)** 61 Zhonghua Lu, Haizhou Qu, Fuxin, Liaoning 123000. On 1287kHz/100.9MHz 2115-0625, 0755-1245 - Economic and Storytelling Sce. on 1557kHz/89.3MHz 2055-1600 - Literary Sce. on 105.3MHz - Traffic Sce. on 88.7MHz – **LN13)** Fuxin Mongolian BS, 84 Shanbei Jie, Haizhou Qu, Fuxin, Liaoning 123000. 2155-0610, 1040-1300 in Mo – **LN14)** Liaoyang Radio and TV St, 59 Qingnian Dajie, Taizihe Qu, Liaoyang, Liaoning 111000. News General Sce. on 837kHz 2030-1530 (exc. Tues 0600-0800) - Life Sce. on 1143kHz/102.0MHz 2025-1530 (exc. Tues 0540-0755) - Traffic and Literary Sce. on 1503kHz/107.8MHz 2025-1430 (exc. Tues ?-0755) - Storytelling and Chinese Opera Sce. on 648kHz/106.0MHz 2030-1530 – **LN15)** Liaoning Tieling Radio and TV St, 45 Gongren Jie, Yinzhou Qu, Tieling, Liaoning 112000. V.O. Tieling: on 1413kHz/101.2MHz 2150-1300 - Traffic Sce. on 102.8MHz 2200-1300 - Country Sce. on 810kHz/90.8MHz 2130-1430 - Literary Sce. on 95.9MHz – **LN16)** Chaoyang Radio and TV St, 88, 1 Duan, Xinhua Lu, Shuangta Qu, Chaoyang, Liaoning 122000. News General Sce. on 585kHz/96.1/101.1MHz 2125-1600 - New Farm Sce. on 810/702/747kHz/99.5MHz 1955-1600 (exc. Tues 0600-0900) - Traffic and Entertainment Sce. on 93.8/103.1MHz 1955-1600 (exc. Tues 0600-0900) - Economic Life Sce. on 648/801kHz/106.5MHz 2000-1600 (exc. Tues 0600-0900) – **LN17)** 67 Jinluan Lu, Wafangdian, Liaoning 116300. News General Ch. on 1323kHz/89.8/106.2MHz 2125-1345 – **LN18)** 385, 1 Duan, Huanghai Dajie, Zhuanghe, Liaoning 116400. 2100-0100, 0855-1200 – **LN19)** Haicheng Radio and TV St, 14 Huancheng Xilu, Haicheng, Liaoning 114200. News General Sce. on 900kHz/90.4MHz 2135-1500. Traffic and Entertainment Sce. on 1350kHz/106.9MHz 2135-1500 – **LN20)** 18, 2 Duan, Xinghai Beilu, Xingcheng, Liaoning 121600 – **LN21)** 6 Qingnian Lu, Nanshan Jie, Beipiao, Liaoning 122100. V.O. Beipiao: on 91.2MHz 2125-1500 (exc. Tues 0500-0930)

NEI MENGGU AUTONOMOUS REGION

NM1) 55 Xinhua Dajie, Hohhot, Nei Menggu 010058 **W:** www.nmrb. cn Chinese News General Sce. on 675/765/1494/1584/7420/9520kHz 2150-1605 (exc. Tues 0600-0950) - Ch News Sce. on 89.0MHz 2150-1600 - Mongolian News General Sce. on 1458/1098/1143/1395/6040/7270/9750kHz/91.4MHz 2150-1605 (exc. Tues 0600-0950) - Economic Life Sce. on 101.4MHz 2150-1700 - Traffic Sce. on 89.6/89.8/90.6/95.7/101.9/105.6MHz 2155-1700 - V.O. the Music: on 93.6MHz 2150-1600 - Storytelling and Folk Art Sce. on 102.8MHz 2150-1700 - V.O. the Green Field: on 91.9MHz 2150-1605 (exc. Tues 0600-0950) - Literature Sce. on 99.8MHz 2150-1700 – **NM2)** 159 Gongyuan Xilu, Hohhot, Nei Menggu 010035. On 882kHz 2200-0130, 0150-0530, 0830-1400 in Ch and Mo - Traffic Sce. on 107.3MHz 2250-1600 - City Life Sce. on 90.1MHz 2250-1600 – **NM3)** 12 Gangtie Dajie, Hondlon Qu, Baotou, Nei Menggu 014030. News General Ch. on 558kHz/94.9MHz 2045-1600 (exc. Tues 0600-0955) - Life and Entertainment Ch. on 105.9MHz 1955-1605 (exc. Tues 0600-0915) - Traffic and Literary Ch. on 89.2MHz 24h (exc. Tues 0600-0920) - Urban and Rural Music Ch. on 100.1MHz 24h (exc. Tues 0730-0930) - Story Entertainment Ch. on 98.1MHz 2015-1750 (exc. Tues 0600-0945).– **NM4)** 17 Ordos Dongjie, Haibowan Qu, Wuhai, Nei Menggu 016000. W2225-0025, Sun0025-0515, W0325-0520, D1025-1305(SS 1405) – **NM5)** Chifeng Radio and TV St, 12, Xi Duan, Gangtie Xijie, Hongshan Qu, Chifeng, Nei Menggu 024001. Ch General Sce. on 1143/549/1512kHz/96.0MHz 1958-1730 - Mo General Sce. on 1440kHz/89.4MHz 2000-1730 - Traffic Sce. on 102.4MHz 24h - Farm and Pastoral Area Sce. on 900kHz/102.4MHz 2100-1600 - "Lark" FM Stereo Sce. on 89.4MHz 2220-1400 – **NM6)** 86 Qiaoxi Shahe Lu, Jining Qu, Ulanqab, Nei Menggu 012000. Ch News General Sce. on 702kHz/93.3/98.7MHz 2200-1600 - Mo Sce. on 1521kHz/105.3MHz 2230-1210 - Traffic Sce. on 92.3MHz in Ch 2155-1700 - Literary Sce. on 94.3MHz in Ch 2155-1600 – **NM7)** 89 Xilin Dajie, Xilinhot, Nei Menggu 026000. Ch General Sce. on 1395kHz/99.4MHz 2225-1455 - Mo General Sce. on 927kHz/107.6MHz 2220-1505 - General Literary Sce. on 106.9MHz 2255-1505 - Traffic and Literary Sce. on 97.5MHz 2225-1455 – **NM8)** 43 Manzhouli Lu, Hailar Qu, Hulun Buir, Nei Menggu 021008. Ch News General Ch. on 603/3900kHz/99.9MHz 2130-1600 (exc. Tues 0230-0855) - Mo News General Ch. on 954/6080kHz/97.3MHz 2140-1430 - City Sce. on 104.6MHz 2200-1600 (exc. Tues 0100-0830) – **NM9)** Tongliao Radio and TV St, 29 Heping Lu, Horqin Qu, Tongliao, Nei Menggu 028001. V.O. Tongliao: on 702kHz/97.2/87.8MHz 2110-1730 (exc. Tues ?-0855) - Traffic Sce. on 91.3MHz 2110-1530 (exc. Tues 0600-0855) - Literary Sce. on 1233kHz/90.4MHz 2110-1530 (exc. Tues 0600-0905) - Mo Prgr. "V.O. Horqin": on 1350kHz/93.7/100.3MHz 2110-1730 – **NM10)** Ordos BS, Manduhai Xiang, Dongsheng Qu, Ordos, Nei Menggu 017000. Ch

News General Sce. on 936/792kHz/89.6MHz 2115-1600 - Mo News General Sce. on 603kHz/93.5/97.7MHz 2220-1430 - Traffic Literary and Sports Sce. on 100.8/107.1MHz 2130-1600 - Variety Sce. on 97.3MHz 2155-1600 – **NM11)** 26 Xinhua Xijie, Linhe Qu, Bayannur, Nei Menggu 015000. News General Sce. (V.O. Hetao): on 1152kHz/107.0MHz 2000-1600 - Traffic and Literary Sce. (V.O. the Yellow River): on 97.7MHz 2200-1600 - V.O. the Traffic: on 95.8MHz 2200-1600 – **NM12)** 1 Elute Donglu, Bayanhot Zhen, Alxa Zuoqi, Nei Menggu 750306. Ch Prgr. on 549/6025kHz 2230-1600 - Mo Prgr. on 1440kHz 2230-1600 – **NM13)** 73 Hinggan Bei Dalu, Ulanhot, Nei Menggu 137400. V.O. Hinggan: on 891kHz/89.1MHz 2125-1430 in Ch - V.O. Alateng Hinggan: on 1152kHz/94.7/96.4/96.6/97.7/103.3/107.0MHz 2200-1600 in Ch (0600-0655 in Mo) - V.O. the Traffic: on 99.0MHz 2125-1500 (exc. Tues 0600-0800) - V.O. the City: on 106.8MHz 2200-1500 – **NM14)** Xuegang Shan, Xinchengwan Xiang, Fengzhen, Nei Menggu 012100. 2225-0020, 0355-0505, 0955-1215 – **NM15)** 1 Dianshi Jie, Manzhouli, Nei Menggu 021400. 2225-1500 – **NM16)** 1 Xing'an Dongjie, Yakeshi, Nei Menggu 022150 – **NM17)** 3 Shengli Lu, Shiqiao Jie, Zalantun, Nei Menggu 162650. 2155-1400 – **NM18)** Zhongyang Dajie, Genhe, Nei Menggu 022350. 2130-0700, 0900-1430 – **NM19)** 129 Nawenxi Dajie, Nirji Zhen, Morin Dawa, Nei Menggu 162850.

NINGXIA HUI AUTONOMOUS REGION

NX1) 66 Beijing Zhonglu, Jinfeng Qu, Yinchuan, Ningxia 750001 **W:** www.nxtv.cn/radio/ News Sce. on 891/1206/1287kHz/FM 2100-1700 (exc. Tues 0600-0955) - Economic Sce. on 747kHz/92.8MHz 24h - City Sce. on 103.7MHz 2215-1605 - Traffic Sce. on 98.4MHz 24h (exc. Tues 0600-0950) – **NX2)** 11 Zhongshan Beijie, Xingqing Qu, Yinchuan, Ningxia 750004. On 801kHz W2225-0145, Sun0000-0500, W0355-0530, D1025-1310(Sun 1330) - Traffic Sce. on 100.6MHz 2225-1800. Pleasure Sce. on 93.8MHz 24h – **NX2A)** Yinchuan City Economic St, 11 Zhongshan Beijie, Xingqing Qu, Yinchuan, Ningxia 750001. On 95.0MHz 0000-1705 – **NX3)** Shizuishan PBS, 363 Youyi Xijie, Dawukou Qu, Shizuishan, Ningxia 753000 – **NX4)** 54 Yumin Dongjie, Litong Qu, Wuzhong, Ningxia 751100. On 1413kHz 2230-1600 – **NX5)** Wenhua Jie, Xiaoba Zhen, Qingtongxia, Ningxia 751600.

QINGHAI PROVINCE

QH1) 81 Xiguan Dajie, Xining, Qinghai 810008 **W:** www.qhradio.com News General Ch. (Satellite Sce.) on 666/711/909/4750/6145/9780kHz/91.6MHz 2200-1605 (exc. Tues 0600-0855) - Tibetan Sce. on 1251/4220/5990/9850kHz/98.3MHz 2230-1600 - Economic Ch. on 1143kHz/107.5MHz 2255-1600 (exc. Tues 0600-0855) - Traffic and Music Sce. on 1377kHz/97.2MHz 2255-1600 - Life Sce. on 90.3MHz in Ch and Qinghai dialect – **QH2)** 43 Nanguan Jie, Xining, Qinghai 810000. News General Sce. on 1476kHz 2200-1630 - Health Sce. on 95.6MHz - Music Sce. on 104.3MHz 2230-1905 – **QH3)** 139 Hongwei Lu, Jiegu Zhen, Yushu Xian, Qinghai 815000. On 882kHz 2255-0100, 1025-1230 in Ch and Tb. Rel. CNR 1: 1135-1230 – **QH4)** Haixi PBS, 7 Changjiang Lu, Delingha, Qinghai 817000. Ch Prgr. on 621kHz. Mo/Tb Prgr. on 540kHz.

SHANDONG PROVINCE

SD1) 81 Jing 10 Lu, Lixia Qu, Jinan, Shandong 250062 **W:** www.sdgb. cn News Ch. on 603/891/918/1467/1485/1548kHz/FM 1940-1700 (exc. Tues 0530-0900). English prgr: 1650-1700 - Economic Ch. "Fortune Media" on 594kHz. 24h - Economic Ch. "FM96" on 96.0MHz 24h - Life Ch. on 105.0/88.6/104.7/104.9/107.8MHz 24h - V.O. the Traffic and Music "Love FM": on 101.1/106.0/106.9MHz 24h - Literary Ch. "Anchorwomen BS": on 97.5MHz 24h (exc. Tues 0500-0900) - Country Ch. "V.O. Green": on 1251/621/999kHz/91.9MHz 24h - Music Ch. "City FM": on 99.1/106.6/107.8MHz 24h - Sports and Leasure Sce. "Star FM": on 102.1MHz – **SD2)** 32 Jing 11 Lu, Lixia Qu, Jinan, Shandong 250014. News Sce. on 1053kHz/89.3/106.6MHz 24h (exc. Tues 0410-0850) - Economic Sce. on 846kHz/90.9/95.7MHz 2055-1700 - Traffic Sce. on 103.1/91.2MHz 24h (exc. Tues 0400-0850) - Music Sce. on 88.7/105.8MHz 24h - Literary Sce. on 1305kHz/93.6MHz 24h (exc. Tues 0400-0900) - Story Sce. on 1512kHz/101.6/104.4MHz 24h - Folk Art Sce. on 99.7MHz – **SD3)** 200 Ningxia Lu, Qingdao, Shandong 266071. News Life Prgr. on 1377kHz/97.3MHz - News Sce. on 107.6MHz 2030-1630 - Economic Sce. on 1251kHz/102.9MHz 2035-1800 - Economic Sce. "Happy 603": on 603kHz/100.7MHz 2040-1800 - Traffic Sce. on 900kHz/89.7MHz 24h - Private Car Sce. on 846/1008kHz/96.4MHz 24h - Music and Sports Sce. "Simul Radio": on 91.5MHz 24h – **SD4)** Zibo Radio and TV Headquarters, 52 Huaguang Lu, Zhangdian Qu, Zibo, Shandong 255047. News Sce. on 89.0MHz 2155-1700 - News Sce. Story Ch. on 1143kHz - Economy Sce. on 801kHz 2155-1700 - Traffic and Literary Sce. on 1476kHz/100.4MHz 2145-1700 (exc. Tues 0500-0900) - Music Sce. on 92.6MHz 2145-1700 - Private Car Sce. "Yuedong 106.7" on 106.7MHz 2045-1700 – **SD5)** 88 Guangming Xilu, Zaozhuang, Shandong 277102. News Sce. on 1170kHz/99.0MHz 2155-1600 - Life and Entertainment Sce. on 603kHz/101.4MHz 2200-1600 - Traffic and Literary Sce. on 105.2MHz 2200-1600 - Music Sce. on 100.6MHz 2200-1600 – **SD6)** 1229 Dongcheng Nan 1 Lu, Dongying, Shandong 257091.

News Ch. on 1449kHz/91.0MHz 2155-1430 - Economic Ch. on 105.3MHz 2150-1435 - Traffic and Music Ch. on 88.1MHz 2150-1435 – **SD7)** 248 Dongfeng Dongjie, Kuiwen Qu, Weifang, Shandong 261041. News Sce. on 1161kHz/100.2MHz 2055-1600 - i Home Sce. on 1287kHz/93.3MHz 2100-1700 - Traffic and Music Sce. on 846kHz/95.9MHz 24h - City Sce. on 98.3MHz 2055-1700 - Music Sce. "New Star Radio" on 90.8MHz 24h - Story Sce. on 981kHz/107.1MHz 2055-1700 - Huanle (Joy) FM: on 89.9MHz – **SD8)** Yantai Radio and TV St, 32 Wenhua Xiang, Zhifu Qu, Yantai, Shandong 264000. News Sce. on 1314kHz/101.0/94.3/98.6MHz 2055-1600. - Economic Sce. on 801kHz/105.9/102.7/104.1MHz 2055-1600 - Traffic Sce. on 103.0/102.4/95.3MHz 2055-1600 - Music Sce. "i Radio": on 91.2/90.5MHz 24h - Storytelling Sce. on 88.4/89.0MHz 2055-1800. Rel. CRI "News Radio": 2300-2330, 0400-0500, 1000-1100, 1500-1600 – **SD9)** 66 Wenhua Zhonglu, Weihai, Shandong 264200. News General Ch. on 1206kHz/99.6/105.1MHz 2100-1600 (exc. Tues 0600-0825). Ko Prgr: 0530-0600, 1430-1500 - Traffic and Literary Ch. on 846kHz/95.0/102.2MHz 2125-1500 (exc. Tues 0600-0855) - Story Ch. on 96.1MHz 2100-1600 - Music Fashion Sce. on 90.7MHz – **SD10)** 11 Hongxing Zhonglu, Jining, Shandong 272037. News Sce. on 666kHz/104.2MHz 2200-1700 - Life Sce. on 1116kHz/107.0MHz 2200-1700 - Traffic and Literary Sce. on 801kHz/101.8MHz 2200-1700 - Music and Entertainment Sce. on 1386kHz/103.1MHz 2200-1700 – **SD11)** Beishou, Yantai Lu, Rizhao, Shandong 276826. News General Ch. on 1449kHz/95.0MHz 2130-1600 (exc. Tues ?-0945) - Traffic and Life Ch. on 747kHz/88.1MHz 2130-1530 - Literary and Sports Ch. on 104.0MHz 2130-1530 – **SD12)** Dezhou Radio and TV St, 64 Dongfanghong Lu, Dezhou, Shandong 253012. News Sce. on 1098kHz/92.9MHz 2150-1600 - Traffic and Music Sce. on 1341kHz/94.1MHz 2150-1600 - Literary and Life Sce. on 1008kHz/104.1MHz 2150-1600 - Storytelling Ch. on 98.9MHz – **SD13)** Linyi Radio and TV St, 21 Jinqueshan Lu, Lanshan Qu, Linyi, Shandong 276004. News Sce. on 873kHz/97.6MHz 2125-1600 (exc. Tues 0530-1020) - Economic and Literary Sce. on 1143kHz/93.2MHz 2125-1600 - V.O. the City: on 747kHz/101.0MHz 2155-1600 - Traffic Sce. on 612kHz/89.9MHz 2155-1600 (exc. Tues 0600-0950) - Story Sce. on 1251kHz/104.5MHz 2155-1600 – **SD14)** 41 Liuyuan Beilu, Liaocheng, Shandong 252000. News Sce. on 1143kHz/96.8MHz 2125-1500. - Traffic Sce. on 1566kHz/98.9MHz 2130-1600 - Music Sce. on 801kHz/92.4MHz – **SD15)** 358 Huanghe 5 Lu, Binzhou, Shandong 256618. News Sce. on 864kHz/107.6MHz 2155-1600 - Life Sce. on 1170kHz/99.4MHz 2155-1600 - V.O. the Traffic and Music: on 93.1MHz 2150-1600 - Story Sce. on 91.6MHz – **SD16)** 28 Zhonghua Donglu, Heze, Shandong 274033. News Ch. on 1197kHz/92.7MHz 2055-1600 - Traffic Ch. on 94.8MHz 2055-1600 - Chinese Opera Ch. on 1071kHz/96.8MHz 2055-1500 – **SD16A)** Mudan PBS, 2093 Changjiang Lu, Heze, Shandong 274000. V.O. Heze on 1323kHz/97.2MHz 2155-1700 - Heze V.O. the City: on 104.0MHz 2155-1700 - Story Sce. on 88.0MHz 2300-1800 – **SD17)** Qingzhou PBS, 21 Fangongting Xilu, Qingzhou, Shandong 262500. On 95.4MHz 2125-1600 – **SD18)** Huangcheng Xihuan Lu, Longkou, Shandong 265701. On 101.6MHz - Yantai Longkou Economic and Literary BS: on 1251kHz 2228-0200, 0500-0700 – **SD19)** 4 Gulou Beijie, Qufu, Shandong 273100. On 1341kHz/98.4MHz 2155-0510(SS0450), 0955-1430(SS1410) – **SD20)** Tai'an PBS, 200 Yingxuan Dajie, Taishan Qu, Tai'an, Shandong 271000. News St. on 93.2MHz 2125-1600 - Economic St. on 90.1MHz 2130-1600 (exc. Tues 0600-1000) - Story Sce. on 91.6MHz 2130-1600 - Traffic Information Sce. on 106.2MHz 2125-1600 (exc. Tues 0600-1000) - V.O. City Music: on 104.4MHz

SHANGHAI MUNICIPALITY

SH1) Shanghai Radio and TV St, 1376 Hongqiao Lu, Shanghai 200051 **W:** www.smg.cn News Ch. on 990kHz/93.4MHz 24h (exc. Thurs 1705-2100) - Traffic Sce. on 648kHz/105.7MHz 24h (exc. Fri 1700-2100) - Chinese Opera and Folk Art Sce. on 1197kHz/97.2MHz 2150-1600 (exc. Wed 0530-0830) in Ch and Shanghai dialect - Story Sce. on 927kHz/107.2MHz 2200-1600 (exc. Wed 0530-0830) - Sports Ch. on 94.0MHz 2155-1600 – **SH2)** Shanghai Dongfang BS (Eastern Radio), 1376 Hongqiao Lu, Shanghai 200051. **W:** www.smg.cn News St. on 1296kHz/90.9MHz 24h (exc. Thurs 1600-2100) - City Sce. on 792kHz/89.9MHz 24h (exc. Thurs 1600-2100) - First Financial and Economic Ch. on 1422/603kHz/97.7MHz 2158-1600 - Popular Music Ch. "Donggan 101": on 101.7MHz 2200-1800 (exc. Fri 0600-0800) - Popular Traffic Ch. "Love Radio": on 103.7MHz 24h (exc. Thurs 1600-2200) - Classical Music Ch. on 94.7MHz 2200-1700.

SHAANXI PROVINCE

SN1) 336 Chang'an Nanlu, Xi'an, Shaanxi 710061 **W:** www.sxradio.com.cn News Sce. on 693/1008/1143/1521/6176kHz/FM 24h (exc. Tues 0600-0900) - News Prgr. on 1008kHz/101.8MHz 24h - Economic (Fortune) Sce. on 89.6MHz 1930-1830. - Traffic Sce. on 801/1323kHz/91.6MHz 24h - Farm Sce. on 900kHz 1930-1700 - Youth Sce. "My FM": on 105.5MHz 24h - Chinese Opera Sce. on 747kHz/99.4MHz 24h - Music Sce. on 98.8/94.8/97.5MHz 24h - Story Sce. on 603kHz 24h (exc. Wed 1700-1945) - Qin Melody Sce. on 101.1MHz 24h – **SN2)** 100,

Zhenxing Lu, Xi'an, Shaanxi 710068. News Sce. on 810kHz/90.4MHz 2055-1700 - Information Sce. on 106.1MHz 24h - Traffic and Travel Sce. on 104.3MHz 24h - Music Sce. on 801kHz/93.1MHz 24h - Variety Sce. on 102.4MHz 2155-1710 – **SN3)** Miaopu Lu, Hongqi Jie, Tongchuan, Shaanxi 727000. News General Sce. on 1134kHz/103.7MHz 2210-0015, 0330-0515, 0915-1405 – **SN4)** 47 Hongqi Lu, Baoji, Shaanxi 721000. On 1071kHz 2145-2400, 0325-0610, 0930-1500 - Music and Storytelling Sce. on 105.3MHz 2255-1700 - Economic and Traffic Sce. on 900kHz/102.8MHz 2155-0600, 0955-1400 – **SN5)** Nan Duan, Fu'an Lu, Xianyang, Shaanxi 712000. News General Sce. on 1296kHz/100.7/107.6MHz 2150-1740 - City Music Sce. on 99.9MHz 2200-1740 – **SN6)** Xi Duan, Dongfeng Jie, Weinan, Shaanxi 714000. News Sce. on 747kHz/101.3/102.6MHz - Traffic Sce. on 90.9MHz – **SN7)** Dongguan Jie, Yan'an, Shaanxi 716000. News Sce. on 603kHz/100.1/104.6MHz 2210-1500 (exc. Wed 0630-0910) - Traffic Sce. on 98.7MHz – **SN8)** 14 Dong Jianshe Xiang, Hanzhong, Shaanxi 723000. News Sce. on 1251kHz/95.6MHz 2130-1620 - Music St. on 97.1/99.5MHz 24h (exc. Wed 0700-0930) - Traffic and Travel Sce. on 93.0/94.3/101.8MHz – **SN9)** 7 Zhonglou Xiang, Yulin, Shaanxi 719000. News Sce. on 1143kHz/99.4MHz - Traffic and Literary Sce. on 95.9MHz – **SN10)** Ankang PBS, 113 Bashan Zhonglu, Ankang, Shaanxi 725000. News Sce. on 89.7MHz - Traffic Travel and Music Sce. on 95.9MHz 2155-1600.

SHANXI PROVINCE

SX1) Shanxi Radio and TV Headquarters, 318 Yingze Dajie, Taiyuan, Shanxi 030001 **W:** www.sxrtv.com General Sce. on 819/846/900/1269kHz/FM 2100-1600 (exc. Tues 0600-0900) - Changcheng Economic Sce. on 95.8MHz 24h (exc. Tues 0600-0900) - V.O. the Health: on 1584kHz/105.9MHz 24h (exc. Mon 0600-0900) - Traffic Sce. on 88.0MHz 24h - Farm Sce. on 603kHz 2100-1600 - Music Sce. on 94.0MHz 24h – **SX2)** 2 Yifen Jie, Taiyuan, Shanxi 030024. News Ch. on 91.2MHz 24h - V.O. Old Age: on 1422kHz 2155-1600 - Private Car Radio: on 774kHz/104.4MHz 24h - Traffic Ch. on 107.0MHz 24h – **SX3)** 178 Yingbin Xilu, Datong, Shanxi 037006. General St. on 1584kHz/103.8MHz 2200-1805 - Health St. on 91.1MHz 2200-1605 - Traffic St. on 99.6MHz 2200-1805 - Folk Art St. 900kHz/88.5MHz – **SX4)** Ningbo Lu, Yangquan, Shanxi 045000. 2150-2400, 0300-0535, 0955-1355 – **SX5)** 87 Yingxiong Zhonglu, Changzhi, Shanxi 046000. News General Sce. on 1584kHz/98.8MHz 2120-0600, 0915-1530 - Traffic and Literary Sce. on 94.9/101.1MHz 2225-1600 (exc. Tues 0500-0900) – **SX6)** Fengtai Xijie, Jincheng, Shanxi 048000. News General Sce. on 585kHz/89.8MHz 2155-1600 - Traffic and Health Sce. on 93.5MHz 2155-1600 – **SX7)** 3 Xiaoyuan Lu, Yuci Qu, Jinzhong, Shanxi 030600. On 1530kHz/92.5MHz 2200-1600 – **SX8)** Cangcheng Xijie, Xinzhou, Shanxi 034000 – **SX9)** 233 Hongqi Dongjie, Yuncheng, Shanxi 044000. News General Sce. on 1566kHz/92.3MHz 2200-1600 - Traffic and Literary Sce. on 101.9MHz 2200-1600 – **SX10)** 1 Minfu Xijie, Shuozhou, Shanxi 036002. Shuozhou General St. on 846kHz/100.9MHz – Music St. on 97.2MHz – **SX11)** Linfen PBS, 10 Guangxuan Jie, Linfen, Shanxi 041000. News General Ch. on 94.1MHz - Traffic and Literary Sce. on 88.9MHz

SICHUAN PROVINCE

SC1) 119-1 Hongxing Zhonglu, Chengdu, Sichuan 610017. News Ch. on 612/909/1116kHz/98.1/90.0/93.7/95.7/103.9/106.6MHz 24h - Economic Ch. "Times Broadcast": on 88.4/94.0MHz 2300-1700 - Economic Ch. "Public Broadcast" on 89.4MHz 24h - Traffic Sce. on 101.7MHz - V.O. the Health: on 999kHz 2200-1700 (exc. Tues 0600-0800) - City Life Sce. on 97.0MHz 2155-1705 - Minority Sce. on 954/6060/7225kHz 2155-1705 in Ch, Tb and Yi - Educational Prgr. on 1521kHz/98.1MHz 0900-1030, 1330-1500 - Minjiang Music St. on 95.5MHz 2230-1700 (exc. Tues 0700-1000) - Sound of City "City FM": on 102.6MHz 2200-1600. -Literature Ch. on 747kHz 2200-1640 (exc. Tues 0600-1000) – **SC3)** 99 Shuanglin Lu, Chengdu, Sichuan 610021. News Sce. on 792kHz/99.8MHz 2130-1700 - Traffic Sce. on 1485kHz/91.4MHz 2200-1700 (exc. Tues 0500-0800) - Music Sce. "Love Radio": on 105.6MHz 2200-1700 - Cultural and Leisure Sce. "V.O. Feiyang": on 94.6MHz – **SC4)** 1 Wenhua Lu, Huidong Xinqu, Zigong, Sichuan 643000. On 1422kHz/100.9/103.0MHz 2220-1505 (exc. Tues 0600-1000) - Yandu Music St. on 97.7MHz 2150-1530 – **SC5)** 338 Linjiang Lu, Dong Qu, Panzhihua, Sichuan 617000. On 711kHz/88.5MHz 2150-1605 – **SC6)** Datong Lu, Chengbei Xinqu, Luzhou, Sichuan 646000. News General Sce. on 954kHz/89.8/97.0MHz 2155-1600 - Traffic and Music Sce. on 96.0/100.6MHz 2155-1600 – **SC7)** 63, 1 Duan, Taishan Nanlu, Deyang, Sichuan 618000. News Sce. on 792kHz/95.9MHz 2200-1600. Music and Traffic Sce. on 107.8MHz 2300-1600 – **SC8)** 232, Nan Duan, 1 Huan Lu, Fucheng Qu, Mianyang, Sichuan 621000. News Sce. on 711kHz/96.7/102.0MHz 2200-1600 - Scientific and Life Sce. on 91.2/92.6MHz 2200-1600 (exc. Tues 0700-0900) – **SC9)** 585, Xi Duan, Hezhou Donglu, Guangyuan, Sichuan 628017. News General Ch. on 621/1143kHz/102.7MHz 2200-1700 - City and Country Ch. on 104.8MHz 2220-1600 – **SC10)** 358 Suizhou Zhonglu, Suining, Sichuan 629000. 2200-1530 – **SC11)** 33, 1 Xiang, Xianglong Lu, Neijiang, Sichuan 641000 – Economic Sce. on 1143kHz/101.4MHz – **SC12)** 300,

Nan Duan, Chunhua Lu, Shizhong Qu, Leshan, Sichuan 614000. News General Sce. on 1476kHz/102.8MHz 2225-1735 — **SC13)** Jiazhou EBS, 40 Dingdong Jie, Leshan, Sichuan 614000. On 95.7MHz 2200-1405 (exc. Wed 0500-1000) — **SC14)** 6 Sichou Lu, Nanchong, Sichuan 637000. On 747kHz 2155-0015, 0355-0520, 1155-1415 - V.O. Nanchong: on 91.5MHz — **SC15)** Yibin PBS, 106 Renmin Lu, Yibin, Sichuan 644000. News General Ch. on 92.8/97.0/101.4MHz 2210-1500 (exc. Tues 0630-1000) - Traffic and Music Ch. on 94.2/105.9MHz 2200-1700 - Farm and Literary Ch. on 104.2MHz — **SC16)** 92 Zhangjiawan, Tongchuan Qu, Dazhou, Sichuan 635000. News General Ch. on 1143kHz 2200-1600.

TIANJIN MUNICIPALITY

TJ1) 143 Weijin Lu, Heping Qu, Tianjin 300070 **W**: www.radiotj.com News FM Sce. on 97.2MHz 2055-1800(Tues 1600) - News MW Sce. on 909kHz 2055-1800(Tues 1600) - Economic Sce. on 1071kHz/101.4MHz 2055-1800(Tues 1600) - Economic Sce. "V.O. Hangu": on 567kHz 2155-1800(Tues 1600) - Traffic Sce. "Chinese Comic Dialogue": on 567kHz 2155-1800(Tues 1600) - Traffic Sce. on 106.8MHz 24h (exc. Tues 1600-2100) - Life Sce. on 1386kHz/91.1MHz 2055-1800(Tues 1600) - Literary Sce. on 1098kHz/104.6MHz 2155-1800(Tues 1600) - Music Sce. "Nice Radio": on 99.0MHz 24h (exc. Tues 1600-2055) - Music MW Sce. on 1008kHz 2055-1800(Tues 1600) - Binhai Sce. on 747kHz/92.0MHz 2055-1800(Tues 1600) - Entertainment Sce. on 87.8MHz 2155-1800(Tues 1600) - Novel Sce. on 666kHz 2200-1800(Tues 1600) - My FM: on 100.5MHz 24h

XINJIANG UIGHUR AUTONOMOUS REGION

XJ1) 84 Tuanjie Lu, Urumqi, Xinjiang 830044 **W**: www.xjbs.com.cn Chinese General Sce. on 702/738/999/1494/5960/7260/7310/9600/9835/11770kHz 2300-1800 (exc. Tues 0800-1100) - Uighur General Sce. on 558/855/1044/1413/6120/7205/7275/9560/11885/13670kHz 2300-1800 (exc. Tues 0800-1100) - Kz Prgr. on 963/1233/1107/6015/7340/9470kHz 2300-1800 (exc. Tues 0800-1100) - Mo Prgr. on 909/1233/1593/6190/7230/9510kHz 2300-0330, 0530-1030(Tues 0800), 1230-1800 - Kirghiz Prgr. on 1233/6190/7230/9705/11975kHz 0330-0530, 1030(Tues/Thurs 1100)-1230 - Ch News Sce. on 96.1MHz 2300-1800 (exc. Tues 0800-1100) - City Sce. on 837/1215kHz/92.9MHz 2300-1800 (exc. Tues 0800-1100) - Traffic Sce. on 94.9/101.8MHz 2330-1800 (exc. Tues 0800-1100) - Music Sce. "My FM": on 103.9MHz 2330-1800 - Ug Literary Sce. on 101.7MHz 2300-1800 (exc. Tues 0800-1100) - Story Sce. on 102.8MHz 2300-1800 (exc. Tues 0800-1100) — **XJ2)** 28 Xinmin Lu, Urumqi, Xinjiang 830002. News Sce. on 100.7MHz 2300-1800 - Economic Sce. on 927kHz 2300-1700 - V.O. Old Age: on 792kHz 2300-1700 - Traffic Sce. on 97.4MHz 2300-1800 - Taste (Travel and Music) Sce. on 106.5MHz 2300-1705 - Ug General Sce. on 1071kHz/104.6MHz 2300-1700. — **XJ4)** 42 Tianshan Xilu, Karamay, Xinjiang 834000. Ch News General Ch. on 1179kHz 2355-1800 - Ug Ch. on 882kHz 2355-1800 - City FM: on 92.6MHz 0000-2000 — **XJ5)** 2 Hongxing Xilu, Hami, Xinjiang 839000. Ch News Information St. on 1485kHz 2200-1800 - Ug Prgr. on 1098kHz/107.9MHz 2300-1600 - City FM: on 103.5MHz 2300-1800 — **XJ6)** 13 Urumqi Nanlu, Hotan, Xinjiang 848000. Ch Prgr. on 1026kHz - Ug Prgr. on 774kHz/92.2MHz 2300-1800 — **XJ7)** Keziduwei Lu, Kashi, Xinjiang 844000. Ch Prgr. on 648kHz 2355-0215, 0455-0710, ?-1335 - Ug Prgr. on 801kHz 2355-? — **XJ8)** 15 Nan Gongyuan Xilu, Changji, Xinjiang 831100. News General Ch. "V.O. Wuchang": on 873kHz 2300-1730 - Legal FM: on 105.3MHz — **XJ9)** Ili PBS, 1 Hongqi Lu, Yining, Xinjiang 835000. News General Sce. on 1134kHz/96.3/105.9/107.4MHz2255-1805 — Economic Sce. on 90.5MHz 2325-1835 - Traffic and Music Sce. on 100.8MHz - Ug Prgr. on 882kHz/88.4MHz 2350-0200, 0550-0700, 1150-1600 - Kz Prgr. on 603kHz/93.4MHz 2350-0200, 0550-0700, 1220-1500 — **XJ10)** 184 Bei 2 Lu, Shihezi, Xinjiang 832000. News Ch. on 891kHz/103.5MHz 0030-0730, 1130-1600 - Literary Ch. on 603kHz/89.3MHz — **XJ11)** Renmin Donglu, Korla, Xinjiang 841000 — **XJ12)** Korla Donglu, Kuytun, Xinjiang 833200. Ch Prgr. on 1485kHz W2355-0230, Sun0025-0335, Sun0528-0720, W0558-0740, D1123-1425 - Kz Prgr. on 819kHz — **XJ13)** Bayingolin PBS, 1 Jianguo Lu, Korla, Xinjiang 841000.

XIZANG AUTONOMOUS REGION

XZ1) 41 Beijing Zhonglu, Lhasa, Xizang 850000 **W**: www.tibetradio.cn Chinese News General Ch. on 999/1377/4820/5935/6050/7240/7450/11860/11950kHz/93.3MHz 2000-1800 (exc. Tues 0600-1000) - Tibetan News General Ch. on 594/846/4905/4920/5240/6110/6130/6200/7255/7385/9490/9580kHz/101.6MHz 2050-1805 (exc. Tues 0600-0855). English Prgr. "Holy Tibet": 0700-0730, 1630-1700 - Kham (Tibetan dialect) Ch. on 594kHz 2200-1605 (exc. Tues 0600-1000). Kangba (Tibetan dialect) Ch. on 100.3MHz - City Life Ch. on 98.0MHz 2300-1700 (exc. Tues 0600-1000) — **XZ2)** Lhasa PBS, Lhasa, Xizang 850000. On 91.4MHz 2350-1410 in Tb and Ch — **XZ3)** 25 Nedong Lu, Zetang Zhen, Nedong, Xizang 856000. 2335-0135, 0405-0535, 1005-1340 in Ch and Tb.

YUNNAN PROVINCE

YN1) 182 Renmin Xilu, Kunming, Yunnan 650031. News Sce. on 576/846/972/990/1080/1197/1359/1395kHz/94.4/105.8MHz 2200-1600 - "FM 99": on 99.0MHz 0100-1730 - Economic Sce. on

1143/88.7MHz 24h. Rel. CRI English prgr: 1300-1500 - Minority Sce. on 7210kHz 1055-1500 in Lahu, Jingpo, Lisu, Dehong Dai and Xishuangbanna Dai - V.O. the Traffic: on 603/1098kHz/91.8MHz 2300-1700. - Music Sce. "Binfen 97": on 846/1053/1251kHz/97.0MHz 2300-1600 (exc. Tues 0600-0900) - Educational Sce. "Xinzhi 100": on 100.0MHz 2245-1700 - Children Sce. on 101.7MHz 2250-1700 - Farm Sce. on 1242kHz 2300-1600 (exc. Tues 0600-0800) — **YN2)** 198 Danxia Lu, Kunming, Yunnan 650118. City News Sce. "Sunlight Ch." on 1350kHz/100.8MHz 24h (exc. Tues 0400-0800) - New FM: on 102.8MHz 24h — Automobile Sce. "954 Car Netw.": on 95.4MHz 24h - Happy Old Age Sce. on 105.0MHz 2100-1700 (exc. Tues 0600-0900) — **YN3)** Qilin Nanlu, Qujing, Yunnan 655000 — **YN4)** Wolong Xiaoqu, Panzhihua Zhen, Wenshan Xian, Yunnan 663000. Minority Ch. on 1053kHz 2225-0030, 0355-0530, 0955-1400 in Ch, Zhuang, Miao and Yao - News General Ch. on 103.0/105.2MHz 2220-1500 - Qihua FM: on 97.3MHz 2220-1600 — **YN5)** Honghe PBS, 31 Jianshe Donglu, Gejiu, Yunnan 661000. News General Ch. on 1521/1485kHz 2200-1800 - Minority Language Ch. on 702kHz/101.4MHz 2000-1800 in Ch, Hani and Yi - City FM: on 92.9MHz - Music Sce. on 97.5MHz 2200-1900 — **YN6)** Xishuangbanna PBS, 2 Nonglin Xilu, Jinghong, Yunnan 666100. 2210-0100, 0250-0600, 1030-1540 in Ch, Xishuangbanna Dai and Hani — **YN7)** Chuxiong Autonomous Prefecture PBS, 144 Lucheng Donglu, Chuxiong, Yunnan 675000. News General St. on 1287kHz/93.9MHz 2225-0050, 0310-0625, 0955-1355 - Economic and Music Sce. on 96.7MHz 2300-1600 — **YN8)** Wanhua Lu, Xiaguan Zhen, Dali, Yunnan 671000. News General Ch. on 1044kHz - Cang'er FM: on 99.9/105.5MHz 2200-1600 — **YN9)** Dehong PBS, 30 Yingjian Lu, Mangshi Zhen, Luxi, Yunnan 678400. Minorities Ch. on 900kHz 2230-0110, 0330-0700, 1030-1530 in Ch, Dehong Dai, Jingpo and Zaiwa - V.O. the Peacock: on 104.3MHz 2245-1600 — **YN10)** Donghuan Lu, Dongchuan Qu, Kunming, Yunnan 654100 — **YN11)** 6 Longquan Lu, Zhaotong, Yunnan 657000. News General Sce. on 621kHz 2225-1600 — **YN12)** Baohua Lu, Gejiu, Yunnan 661400 — **YN13)** 38 Xueqiao Jie, Chuxiong, Yunnan 675000. W2225-2400, Sun2325-0200, D0325-0600, D0955-1405 - Dianzhong FM: on 106.1MHz — **YN14)** 29 Guihua Lu, Yuxi, Yunnan 653100. Green FM on 1251kHz/102.4MHz 2225-1600 — **YN15)** Diqing PBS, 37 Changzheng Lu, Jiantang Zhen, Shangri-la Xian, Yunnan 674400 — **YN16)** Nujiang PBS, 96 Xiangyang Xilu, Liuku Zhen, Lushui Xian, Yunnan 673100 — **YN17)** Lufeng, Yunnan. 2225-1230.

ZHEJIANG PROVINCE

ZJ1) 111 Moganshan Lu, Hangzhou, Zhejiang 310005 **W**: www.cztv.com.cn News St. "V.O. Zhejiang": on 810kHz/88.0/101.6MHz 24h (exc. Tues 0600-0800) - Economic Ch. "Fortune Sce." on 95.0MHz 24h - V.O. the City "Private Car 107": on 1530kHz/107.0MHz 24h - V.O. the Traffic: on 93.0/93.6MHz 24h - Music FM "Moving 968": on 1071kHz/96.8/88.6/89.8MHz 24h (exc. Tues 0600-0800) - People Life Information Sce. on 930/1050/1314kHz/99.6MHz 24h - Quality Life Sce. "Anchorwomen BS": on 603/1251/1521kHz/104.5MHz 24h — **ZJ2)** 86 Moganshan Lu, Hangzhou, Zhejiang 310005. **W**: www.radiohz.com News General Ch. (Jinqiu Ch.) on 954kHz/69.0MHz 2000-1600. News Sce. on 89.0MHz 24h — **ZJ2A)** Hangzhou Traffic and Economic Sce, 5 Qingchun Donglu, Hangzhou, Zhejiang 310016. On 91.8MHz 24h — **ZJ3)** Automobile Sce. "V.O. Xihu", 86 Moganshan Lu, Hangzhou, Zhejiang 310005. On 105.4MHz 24h in Ch and Hangzhou dialect — **ZJ4)** 109 Heyi Lu, Ningbo, Zhejiang 315000. News Sce. "V.O. Ningbo": on 1323kHz/92.0MHz 2055-1610 (exc. Tues 0600-0800). English N: D1600-1610 - Sunshine FM: on 1251kHz/90.4MHz 2155-1605 (exc. Tues 0600-0900) - City Life Sce. "i Radio": on 747kHz/102.9MHz 2100-1600 (exc. Tues 0600-0730) - Traffic Sce. on 603kHz/93.9MHz 24h (exc. Tues 0500-0900) - Music Sce. "Automobile Music FM": on 98.6MHz 2300-1600 — **ZJ4A)** 36 Nan Dajie, Zhenhai Qu, Ningbo, Zhejiang 315200. Ningbo Private Car Music St. on 104.7MHz 24h (exc. Mon 0500-0830). V.O. Ning River: on 100.1MHz — **ZJ5)** Wenzhou Radio and TV Media Group, Xincheng Dadao, Lucheng Qu, Wenzhou, Zhejiang 325027. News Sce. "V.O. Wenzhou": on 666kHz/94.9/102.6MHz 24h (exc. Tues 0600-0900) in Ch and Wenzhou dialect - Economic Life Sce. on 801kHz/88.8MHz 24h - Traffic Sce. "Automobile FM": on 97.2/103.9MHz 24h - Private Car Music Sce. on 100.3MHz 24h (exc. Tues 0600-0900) - V.O. Green: on 93.8MHz 24h — **ZJ6)** Jiaxing Radio and TV Headquarters, 6 Dongsheng Lu, Jiaxing, Zhejiang 314001. News Sce. on 1107kHz/104.1MHz 2125-1505 - V.O. the Traffic: on 657kHz/92.2MHz 2130-1700 (exc. Tues 0530-0730) - Life Sce. on 88.2MHz 2130-1430 — **ZJ7)** 628 Xinhua Lu, Huzhou, Zhejiang 313000. News General Ch. on 873kHz/105.0MHz 2155-1600 (exc. Tues 0600-0730) - Traffic Sce. on 927/1521kHz/103.5MHz 2155-1600 - City Literary Ch. on 1251kHz/98.5MHz 2110-1600 — **ZJ8)** Shaoxing Radio and TV Headquarters, 508 Yan'an Donglu, Shaoxing, Zhejiang 312000. News General Sce. on 738kHz/93.6MHz 2100-1600 - Traffic Sce. on 94.1MHz 2130-1600 (exc. Tues 0600-0830) - Chinese Opera Sce. on 102.5MHz 2130-0300 - Music Sce. "i Music": on 103.5MHz 2100-1500 (exc. Tues 0600-0900) — **ZJ9)** 238 Renmin Xilu, Jinhua, Zhejiang 321000. News Sce. on 675kHz/104.4MHz 2100-1600 (exc. Tues 0600-0900) - Economic Sce. "Private Car 101": on 101.4MHz 2200-1700 - Traffic Sce. on 94.2MHz 24h – **ZJ10)** Quzhou Radio and TV Headquarters, 35 Nanjie, Quzhou, Zhejiang 324000. News Sce. "V.O. Quzhou": on 711kHz/105.3MHz 2155-1600 (exc. Tues 0500-0725) - Traffic and Music Ch. on 1250kHz/97.5MHz 2200-1700 – **ZJ11)** Zhoushan Radio and TV Headquarters, 137 Changguo Lu, Dinghai Qu, Zhoushan, Zhejiang 316000. News General Ch. on 684kHz/99.8MHz 2130-1500 (exc. Tues 0530-0855) - Traffic and Economic Sce. on 1098kHz/97.0MHz 2155-1500 (exc. Tues 0500-0900) - Automobile Music FM: on 900kHz/91.0/102.6MHz 2155-1500 (exc. Tues 0530-0855) – **ZJ12)** Lishui Radio and TV Headquarters, 2 Huayuan Lu, Liandu Qu, Lishui, Zhejiang 323000. News General Ch. on 711kHz/94.0/96.4MHz 2155-1600 - Traffic and Music Ch. on 106.9MHz 2155-1600 - New Farm Sce. on 88.3MHz 24h – **ZJ13)** Xiaoshan PBS, Nanduan, Yucai Lu, Xiaoshan Qu, Hangzhou, Zhejiang 311200. on 107.9MHz 2155-1400 – **ZJ14)** Xishan, Chengguan, Rui'an, Zhejiang 325200. on 1584kHz/91.0MHz ?-1305 – **ZJ15)** 121 Zhongshan Lu, Jiangshan, Zhejiang 324100 – **ZJ16)** Taizhou PBS, 355 Donghuan Dadao, Jiaojiang Qu, Taizhou, Zhejiang 318000. News Sce. "987 Ch.": on 98.7/87.5MHz 24h - Traffic Sce. on 102.7MHz 24h - Music St. "Easy Radio" on 100.1/104.9MHz 2200-1600.

CHRISTMAS ISLAND (Australia)

L.T: UTC +7h — **Pop:** 1,402 — **Pr.L:** English, Malay, Cantonese, Hokkien, Mandarin — **E.C:** 50Hz, 240V — **ITU:** CHR

AUSTRALIAN BROADCASTING CORP. (ABC)
See Australia for details. 24h satellite relay

MW	kHz	Call	kW	Network
	1422	6ABCRN	0.5	R. National
FM	**MHz**	**Call**	**kW**	**Network**
	97.3	6ABCRN	0.02	R. National
	100.5	6JJJ	0.02	Triple J

Other Stations

FM	MHz	Call	kW	
1)	98.9	6FMS	0.02	Red FM
2)	102.1	6RCI	0.02	R. Christmas Island
2)	105.3	6RCI	0.02	R. Christmas Island
1)	106.9	6FMS	0.04	Red FM

Addresses & other information
1) 24h satellite relay RedFM, Perth WA **W:** www.redfm.com.au – **2)** Broadcast House, Murray Road, Drumsite (PO Box 474) Christmas Island WA 6798 ☎ +61 8 9164 8316/8422 🖷 +61 8 9164 8315 Local community stn

COCOS (KEELING) ISLANDS (Australia)

L.T: UTC +6½h — **Pop:** 596 — **Pr.L:** English, Cocos Malay — **E.C:** 50Hz, 220V — **ITU:** ICO

AUSTRALIAN BROADCASTING CORP. (ABC)
See Australia for details. 24h satellite relay

FM	MHz	Call	kW	Network
	102.3	6ABCRR	0.1	ABC Local R. Kimberley

Other Stations

FM	MHz	Call	kW	
1)	96.0	6CKI	0.1	Voice of the Cocos Islands
2)	100.5	6FMS	0.1	Red FM
1)	102.7	6CKI	0.2	Voice of the Cocos Islands

Addresses & other information
1) PO Box 1093, Cocos (Keeling) Islands WA 6799 ☎+61 8 9162 6700 Local community stn. **Prgr:** 24h with local news 0700 UTC M-F – **2)** 24h satellite relay from Perth WA **W:** www.redfm.com.au

COLOMBIA

L.T: UTC -5h — **Pop:** 45 million — **Pr.L:** Spanish — **E.C:** 60Hz, 110V — **ITU:** CLM

MINISTERIO DE TECNOLOGIAS DE LA INFORMACION Y LAS COMUNICACIONES (MINTIC)
🖳 Edificio Murillo Toro, Cra 8a entre Calles 12 y 13, Bogotá, DC ☎ +57 1 344 3460 **W:** www.mintic.gov.co
Call HJ-, ° also on shortwave, ‡ = inactive, rel. = relay, ± = varying freq. The letters preceding the stn number indicate the departamento. Addresses are listed by departamento in alphabetical order. Hr of tr. usually 24h – see address section for variations.

MW	Call	kHz	kW	Station, location
DC01)	KA	540	10	R. Auténtica Básica, Bogotá
DC02)	HF	550	50	R. Nal., Marinilla (r. 570)

MW	Call	kHz	kW	Station, location
VP01)	R36	550	30	Vida AM, Mitú (r. 1130)
DC02)	GS	560	10	R. Nal., Tunja (r. 570)
GU01)	PF	560	25/10	LV de la Pampa, Maicao
DC02)	ND	570	100	R. Nal de Colombia, Bogotá
DC02)	HP	580	50/10	R. Nal., Cali (r. 570)
AN01)	CR	590	50	W Radio, Medellín
AT01)	HJ	600	50	R. Libertad, Barranquilla
NA13)	Z95	600	1	LV de los Awas, Ricaurte el Diviso
DC02)	D90	610	10	R. Nal., Uríbia
DC03)	KL	610	30	La Cariñosa, Bogotá
BO01)	VP	620	10	Colmundo, Cartagena
VA01)	EL	620	50/20	Colmundo, Cali
CL01)	FD	630	10	R. Manizales, Manizales
GN01)	E69	630	10	LV del Guainía, Puerto Inírida
MA01)	BJ	640	10	RCN, Santa Marta
DC03)	KH	650	50	RCN Antena 2, Bogotá
NS01)	QS	660	25	Colmundo, Cúcuta
VA02)	EZ	660	10	R. Auténtica, Cali
AN02)	PL	670	50	RCN Antena 2, Medellín
SS28)	R33	670	10	R. U.I.S - Universidad Industrial de Santander, Bucaramanga
DC02)	ZO	680	50	R. Nal., Barranquilla (Sabanagrande)
AN56)	Z73	690	1	LV Indígena de Uberaba, Apartadó
DC04)	CZ	690	35	R. Recuerdos, Bogotá
VA03)	CX	700	30	W Radio, Cali
AN03)	NX	710	10	R. Super, Medellín
BY14)	YD	710	1	R. La Paz, Paipa
AT01)	AN	720	30	Emisoras Unidas, Barranquilla
DC02)	ZX	‡720	50	R. Dif. Nal., Rionegro (r. 570)
QU01)	VO	720	25	Transmisora Quindío, Armenia
CO03)	TJ	730	15	R. Uno, Montería
DC05)	CU	°730	10	Melodía Stéreo, Bogotá
CE01)	NS	/40	50	R. Guatapurí, Valledupar
NA01)	HB	740	10	Ecos de Pasto, Pasto
AN01)	DK	750	50	Caracol R, Medellín
CS01)	LH	750	5	LV de Yopal, Yopal
AT02)	AJ	760	25	RCN La Radio, Barranquilla
DC03)	JX	770	100	RCN L Radio, Bogotá
GU02)	ZW	780	30	R. Almirante, Riohacha
SS30)	C21	780	10	Antena del Río, Barrancabermeja
VA04)	ZG	780	10	LV del Valle, Cali
AN01)	DC	790	15	Caracol R, Medellín
DC02)	BU	‡790	50	R. Nal., Zambrano (r. 570)
DC02)	ZR	‡790	50	R. Nal., Villavicencio (r. 570)
TO03)	NC	790	1	Ecos del Combeima, Ibagué
QU06)	JH	800	1	R. Ciudad Milagro, Armenia
SS01)	BW	800	100	RCN, Bucaramanga
DC04)	CY	810	60	Caracol R, Bogotá
BO02)	AD	820	10	R. Vigía, Cartagena
VA03)	ED	820	50	Caracol R, Cali
AN01)	DM	830	15	R. Reloj, Medellín
HU01)	KK	840	30	H J Doble K, Neiva
MA02)	BI	840	10	Ondas del Caribe, Santa Marta
DC04)	KC	850	35	W Radio, Bogotá
CE02)	NJ	860	50	W Radio, Valledupar
VA05)	DV	860	10	Voces de Occidente, Buga
AN09)	ZH	870	5	Vida AM, Medellín
AT03)	SB	870	25	R. Mar Caribe Int., Barranquilla
BY16)	GD	870	1	Em. Reina de Colombia, Chiquinquirá
TO01)	LA	870	10	LV del Tolima, Ibagué
CL04)	FH	880	10	R. Regional Independiente, Anserma
SS02)	GE	880	20	Caracol R, Bucaramanga
AT13)	HKO93	890	0.25	R. Ecos de Soledad, Soledad
DC06)	CE	890	10	R. Continental, Bogotá
MA03)	PM	890	20	R. Galeón, Santa Marta
NS02)	DD	900	10	RCN Fiesta, Cúcuta
VA04)	EY	900	10	LV de Cali, Cali
AN04)	DO	910	10	LV del Río Grande, Medellín
BY12)	TT	910	1	Ondas del Porvenir, Samacá
DC24)	S52	910	15	Colombia Estereo, Florencia
IS01)	MY	910	30	RCN, San Andrés (rel. 770 Bogotá)
BO03)	AA	920	10	Em. Fuentes, Cartagena
NA02)	JN	920	10	Ondas del Mayo, Pasto
TO02)	SJ	920	10	Colmundo, Ibagué
DC07)	CS	930	10	LV de Bogotá, Bogotá
AN59)	A76	940	5	Frecuencia U, Medellín
NS03)	TL	940	25	RCN, Cúcuta
VA04)	GB	940	10	R. Calima, Cali
BY18)	UJ	950	5	Armonías Boyacenses, Tunja
RI01)	FN	950	15	Caracol R, Pereira
BO08)	HN	960	10	Caracol R, Magangué
IS05)	R31	960	15	Candela, San Andrés: (R. Candela 101.9 Bogotá)
SS23)	HX	960	5	Candela AM, Bucaramanga
CA01)	VK	970	15	Armonías del Caquetá, Florencia
DC08)	CI	970	10	R. Super, Bogotá

MW	Call	kHz	kW	Station, location
GU03)	ME	970	10	RCN Guajira, Maicao
QU09)	HKX59	970	1	Ecos del Cacique, Calarca
NS04)	JV	980	15	Bésame, Cúcuta
VA06)	ES	980	100	RCN, Cali
AN02)	CH	990	50	RCN, Medellín
BY07)	HI	990	5	LV de Garagoa, Garagoa
BO04)	AQ	1000	15	RCN, Cartagena
DC02)	ZP	‡1000	50	R. Nal., Yopal (r. 570)
CC01)		1000	0.8	R. Panamericana, Cajibío
DC02)	JG	1000	10	R. Nal., Manizales (r. 570)
GV01)	Q98	1000	20	Vida AM, San José del Guaviare (r. 1130)
AT01)	OP	1010	10	Oxígeno, Barranquilla
CO01)	ZD	1010	10	R. Panzenú, Montería
DC04)	CC	‡1010	10	R. Reloj, Bogotá
HU02)	JR	1010	15	Caracol R, Neiva
NA03)	BN	1010	10/5	LV del Galeras, Pasto
SS03)	IX	1010	10	R. Yarima, Barrancabermeja
AN04)	DQ	1020	10	Emisora Claridad, Medellín
ME01)	KS	1020	10	LV del Llano, Villavicencio
RI02)	FQ	1020	10	RCN, Pereira
SS04)	DZ	1020	15	R. Primavera, Bucaramanga
T003)	FT	1020	10	R. Super, Ibagué
BY01)	DJ	1030	10	RCN LV de los Libertadores, Duitama
CE03)	RF	1030	15	Ondas del Cesar, Aguachica
CO02)	GX	1030	1	CARACOL, Lorica
VA06)	DT	1030	30	RCN Antena 2, Cali
VP02)		1030	5	Ondas del Vaupés, Mitú
AT01)	AI	1040	15	R. Tropical, Barranquilla
CC02)	SY	1040	10	R. 1040/La Caucana 10-40, Popayán
DC10)	CJ	1040	15	Colmundo, Bogotá
NA04)	UB	1040	15	Colmundo, Pasto
NS05)	BF	1040	15	LV del Norte, Cúcuta
QU02)	FM	1040	15	LV de Armenia, Armenia
AN04)	DR	1050	10	R. Unica, Medellín
AR01)	E73	1050	10	LV del Cinaruco/Caracol, Arauca
CE04)	BB	1050	10	Caracol R, Valledupar
CO04)	AW	1080	10	LV de Montería, Montería
CS03)	S62	1050	10	Cusiana R., Yopal
ME02)	IO	1050	5	LV de la Conquista, Granada
SS05)	GU	1050	10	R. Bucarica, Bucaramanga
T004)	FZ	1050	10	La Cariñosa del Centro, Antena 2, Espinal
VA07)	NG	1050	5	R. Palmira, Palmira
AN05)	MG	1060	1	R. Litoral, Turbo
BY02)	MV	1060	10	R. Furatena, Chiquinquirá
CL02)	FJ	1060	15	RCN Caldas, Manizales
GU04)	LY	1060	10	R. Delfín, Riohacha
HU03)	OV	1060	15	R. Surcolombiana, Neiva
SU11)	YX	1060	1	Caracoli, Sincelejo
AT06)	AH	1070	20	Em. Atlántico, Barranquilla
CC03)	VR	1070	15	R. Super, Popayán
DC11)	CG	1070	30	R. Santa Fé, Bogotá
AN01)	AX	1080	15	LV de la Nostalgia, Medellín
CL03)	JS	1080	15	R. Pontoná, La Dorada
CO04)	AW	1080	10	LV de Montería, Montería
ME03)	KT	1080	10	R. Autentica, Villavicencio
SS06)	MH	1080	10	Melodía AM, Floridablanca
VA04)	JF	1080	10	R. Eco, Cali
BO05)	OM	1090	5	Fuego AM, Cartagena (r. 1160)
BY03)	IH	1090	8	Caracol R, Sogamoso
CA02)	IG	1090	10	R. Autentica, Florencia
CL01)	IA	1090	10	Oxígeno, Manizales
NS06)	BC	1090	15	Caracol R, Cúcuta
T005)	JB	1090	10	HJ Doble K, Libano
AN06)	GQ	1100	5	Transmisora Surandes, Andes
AT04)	AT	1100	15	Caracol R, Barranquilla
CO05)	MK	1100	5	Emisora Ideal, Planeta Rica
DC27)	CN	1100	10	BBN R, Bogotá
HU04)	YZ	1100	10	R. Uno, Neiva
SS07)	GI	1100	1	LV de Colombia, Socorro
VI01)	EF	‡1100	2	LV del Vichada, Puerto Carreño
AN07)	DI	1110	9	R. Bolivariana, Medellín
AR02)	GP	1110	10	LV del Río Arauca, Arauca
IS02)	PA	‡1110	1	LV de las Islas, San Andrés
ME04)	JP	1110	10	RCN, Villavicencio
SU02)	ZE	1110	15	R. Piragua, Sincelejo
VA03)	EW	1110	10	Oxígeno, Cali
BY04)	KQ	1120	10	Bésame, Tunja
DC24)	Q92	1120	5	Colombia Mía, Yopal, CS
NS01)	TI	1120	10	Vox Dei, Cúcuta
RI03)	JC	1120	5	R. Matecaña, Pereira
SS02)	GH	1120	5	Oxígeno, Bucaramanga
AT07)	AC	1130	10	Em. Riomar, Barranquilla
BO06)	NN	1130	1	Ondas del Río, Magangué
DC09)	VA	1130	15	Vida AM, Bogotá
NA05)	QQ	1130	5	Oxígeno, Pasto
AN02)	DL	1140	10	R. Paisa "La Cariñosa de Medellín",

MW	Call	kHz	kW	Station, location
				Medellín
BO07)	KO	1140	10	R. Esperanza, Cartagena
CC12)		1140		R. Piendamo, Piendamo
CU01)	CL	1140	10	R. Panamericana, Girardot
ME05)	E67	1140	10	Caracol R, Villavicencio
SS08)	RN	1140	10	RCN, Barbosa
BY05)	GJ	1150	1	W Radio, Duitama
CH01)	TE	1150	1	LV del Chocó, Quibdó
HU05)	FP	1150	10	RCN, Neiva
NS07)	BT	1150	10	R. Catatumbo, Ocaña
QU03)	FI	1150	15	Caracol R, Armenia
AT01)	BL	1160	10	R. Aeropuerto, Barranquilla
CA03)	AU	1160	15	Ondas del Orteguaza, Florencia
CO06)	AZ	1160	5	Frecuencia Bolivariana "tu emisora", Montería
DC13)	OC	1160	15	Fuego AM, Bogotá
NA06)	ZV	1160	5	RCN R. Las Lajas, Ipiales
NS08)	EC	1160	10	R. San José de Cúcuta, Cúcuta
RI04)		1160		Ondas del Puerto, La Virginia
SS09)	S31	1160	10	Colombia Mía, Barrancabermeja
VA04)	EV	1160	10	R. Unica, Cali
AN04)	FW	1170	10	R. Nutibara, Medellín
AR04)	E74	1170	10	Meridiano 70, Arauca
BO08)	NW	1170	10	Caracol R, Cartagena
BY04)	GA	1170	10	Caracol R, Tunja
CE06)	PB	1170	10	Ondas de Macondo, Valledupar
ME01)	BX	1170	10	Ondas del Meta, Villavicencio
VA08)	JE	1170	1	RCN, Tuluá
AN08)		1180		Em. Coorpurabá, Apartadó
CL05)	FX	1180	15	Caracol R, Manizales
GV02)	WA	°1180	5	LV del Guaviare, San José del Guaviare
SS10)	GK	1180	20	R. Santander 2, Bucaramanga
T006)	JT	1180	10/5	RCN, Ibagué
AT05)	CT	1190	10	LV de la Costa, Barranquilla
DC07)	CV	1190	10	R. Cordillera, Bogotá
NA07)	KG	1190	10	R. Mira, Tumaco
VA09)	EO	1190	10	Ondas del Valle, Cartago
GU05)		1195		Ondas del Ranchería, Barrancas
AN49)	IJ	1200	15	R. 1200 "LV de la Raza", Medellín
BO17)	BV	1200	10	R. Príncipe, Cartagena
BY06)	GC	1200	10	La Cariñosa, Antena2, Sogamoso
CU02)	CD	1200	10	Em. Nueva Epoca, Fusagasugá
GU06)	BZ	1200	10	Ondas del Riohacha, Riohacha
VA10)	NF	1200	10	R. Super, Cali
HU02)	FR	1210	10	Oxígeno, Neiva
NS03)	E65	1210	10	La Cariñosa, Antena 2, Cúcuta
RI02)	BQ	1210	10	La Cariñosa, Pereira
CO07)	AV	1220	10	RCN, Montería
DC22)	KR	‡1220	10	R. María, "LV Católica de su Hogar", Bogotá
NA08)	NM	1220	10	R. Viva Cultural Bolívar, Ipiales
SS11)	MT	1220	10	RCN La Radio, San Gil
AN10)	IL	1230	10	Minuto de Dios, Medellín
BY04)	BR	1230	6	Oxígeno, Tunja
CU03)	TP	1230	1	R. Colina, Girardot
GU03)	MJ	1230	1	RCN Antena 2, Maicao
SS12)	EH	1230	15	Colmundo, Bucaramanga
VA06)	LK	1230	10	R. Calidad "La Cariñosa", Cali
AR03)	GO	1240	1	R. Caribabare, Saravena
QU04)	FG	1240	10	RCN, Calarcá
SS13)	GN	1240	5	R. Barrancabermeja, Barrancabermeja
VA11)	JA	1240	3	R. Buenaventura, Buenaventura
AT07)	OK	1250	10	Em. ABC, Barranquilla
DC14)	CA	1250	10	Capital Radio, Bogotá
NA15)	FV	1250	5	R. Viva, Pasto
NS06)	HS	1250	15	Oxígeno/W Radio, Cúcuta
SU03)	EM	1250	1	LV de Corozal, Corozal
AM01)	OU	1260	2	Ondas del Amazonas, Leticia
AN11)	DA	1260	5	R. Auténtica, Medellín
BY05)	NO	1260	5	Oxígeno, Duitama
CE08)	OH	1260	5	RCN Cesar, Valledupar
IS03)	HU	1260	1	Caracol R, San Andrés (rel 810 Bogotá)
ME06)	LX	1260	5	Minuto de Dios Eco Llanero, Villavicencio
NS10)	TM	1260	5	R. Sonar, Ocaña
T007)	CO	1260	5	Caracol R, Ibagué
VA28)	ET	1260	5	R. María, Cali
BO04)	AR	1270	2	La Cariñosa, Antena 2,Cartagena
CE05)	KJ	1270	1.5	LV de Curumaní, Curumaní
CU04)	XQ	1270	1	LV Amiga, Ubaté
DC24)	Q99	1270	5	Colombia Mía, San José del Guaviare
PU01)	SV	1270	1	LV de Orito, Orito
RI05)	IM	1270	1	Colmundo, Pereira
SS02)	TX	1270	5	Bésame, Bucaramanga
T012)	BM	1270	5	R. Internacional, Honda
AN12)	MB	1270	5	R. Suroeste, Concordia
AT01)	SO	1280	5	R. Playa Mendoza, Barranquilla
DC07)	KN	1280	5	R. Única, Bogotá

MW	Call	kHz	kW	Station, location
GU07)	HO	1280	5	Impacto Popular, San Juan del Cesar
HU06)	CM	1280	5	HJ Doble K, Pitalito
NA05)	LR	1280	5	Caracol R, Pasto
NS11)	RP	1280	5	Ecos de Tibú, Tibú
SS14)	NQ	1280	1	LV del Río Suárez, Barbosa
VA12)	TK	1280	5	R. Super, Caicedonia
AN13)	TH	1290	5	LV de las Estrellas, Medellín
DC24)	SZ	1290	5	Colombia Mía, Saravena, AR
CU05)	KY	1290	5	RCN, Girardot
MA04)	EB	1290	5	LV del Turismo, Santa Marta
ME07)	NE	1290	5	LV del Ariari, Granada
SU04)	OI	1290	5	R. Chacurí, Sampués
VA13)	MC	1290	5	R. Viva 12-90, Cali
BO10)	OG	1300	5	LV de las Antillas, Cartagena
BY08)	RB	1300	5	CRB Cadena Radial Boyacense, Tunja
CC04)	IN	1300	5	R. Eucha, Belalcázar
PU02)	UA	1300	5	R. Sindamanoy, Mocoa
RI01)	LD	1300	5	Oxígeno, Pereira
SS02)	NB	1300	5	Onda 5, Bucaramanga
TO08)	EA	1300	5	R. Lumbí, Mariquita
AN14)	LM	1310	5	R. Santa Bárbara
AN15)	IR	1310	5	RCN Urabá, Apartadó
AT08)	AK	1310	5	LV de la Patria Celestial, Barranquilla
CO08)	DG	1310	5	Caracol R, Monteria
DC20)	JZ	1310	5	Aviva 2, Bogotá
HU07)	WD	1310	5	Micrófono Cívico, Palermo
NS12)	TQ	1310	5	G12 Radio, Cúcuta (r. 1550)
AN16)	TA	1320	5	R. María, Medellín
BY09)	HT	1320	5	R. Guateque, Guateque
CU06)	NV	1320	5	La Cariñosa, Girardot
IS04)	QI	‡1320	10	R. Leda Int., San Andrés
MA05)	IV	1320	5	R. Onda Fantastica, Fundación
SS15)	MS	1320	5	La Cariñosa, Barrancabermeja
VA14)	NK	1320	1	R. Luna, Palmira
AN17)	RD	1330	1	R. Fénix de Oriente 1330 AM, El Peñol
BO02)	AP	1330	5	R. Auténtica, Cartagena
CE09)	MP	1330	1	LV de Aguachica, Aguachica (nighttime rel. R. María)
CC05)	LS	1330	5	Caracol R, Popayán
CL17)	HKR33	1330	0.25	Alcaldía de Salamina, Salamina
RI02)	FE	1330	5	Antena 2, Pereira
SS16)	NR	1330	5	La Caliente 13-30, San Gil
AN18)	NP	1340	1	R. Comunal, Nariño
AT03)	FA	1340	5	R. Alegre, Barranquilla
DC03)	FB	1340	5	Amor, Bogotá
HU05)	KD	1340	5	La Cariñosa/Antena 2, Neiva
NA10)	HA	1340	5	RCN Nariño, Pasto
NS04)	PY	1340	5	R. Lemas, Cúcuta
NS13)	VL	1340	0.5	Brisas del Catatumbo, Tibú
SS05)	NY	1340	4	R. Unica, Bucaramanga
SU05)	HY	1340	5	RCN Sucre, Sincelejo
VA15)	IS	1340	5	R. El Sol, Buenaventura
AN19)	DS	1350	5	Ondas de la Montaña, Medellín
AN20)	LO	1350	5	RCN Antena 2/La Cariñosa, Caucasia
BY10)	HW	1350	1	Em. Ecos del Río, Puerto Boyacá
CE10)	MN	1350	1	R. Perijá, Codazzi
CE12)		1350	1	R. Cultural 2001, Pailitas
MA01)	OA	1350	5	R. Uno, Santa Marta
TO09)	HL	1350	5	Oxígeno, Ibagué
VA16)	EN	1350	5	R. Armonía, Cali
AN21)	PK	1360	10/5	LV de Abejorral, Abejorral
AN22)		1360	0.5	R. Segovia, Segovia
BO08)	UO	1360	5	Oxígeno, Cartagena
RI06)	RA	1360	5	Eco 13-60 "La Superestación", Pereira (nighttime rel. R. María)
SS17)	KV	1360	1	R. Láser, Zapatoca
TO18)	MI	1360	5	R. Auténtica, Melgar
AN23)	NU	1370	2.5	RCN, Rionegro
AT09)	BO	1370	5	Minuto de Dios, Barranquilla
CC06)	EQ	1370	5	RCN Cauca, Popayán: 24h
DC01)	KI	1370	5	R. Mundial, Bogotá
NS15)	BD	1370	1	R. Guaimaral, Cúcuta
SU14)	NI	1370	1	R. Sabana, Sincelejo
VA17)	JQ	1370	1	RCN Antena 2, Zarzal
AN57)	JD	1380	3	R. Nuestra Señora del Encuentro con Dios, Medellín
BY11)	EE	1380	5	RCN, Tunja
CE13)	MM	1380	5	Vida AM, Valledupar
CL06)	LG	1380	3	LV de La Dorada, La Dorada
HU08)	ID	1380	5	R. Potencia Latina, La Plata
VA18)	EJ	1380	1	Armonías del Palmar, Palmira
AN25)		1390	0.1	R. Ciudad de Antioquia, Santa Fé de Antioquia
CL07)	FO	1390	5	Red de los Andes, La Voz de Siempre, Manizales
CU07)	YW	1390	5	R. Auténtica, Pacho
SS18)	ZY	1390	1	La Primera, Bucaramanga (nights r. R. María)
TO10)	FY	1390	5	Oxígeno, Espinal
AN26)	LL	1400	1	RCN Antena 2, Santa Bárbara
AT02)	AS	1400	5	R. Uno/RCN Antena 2, Barranquilla
CC07)	WY	1400	1	LV de los Samanes: Quilichao
CC13)		1400	0.45	R. Cañaveral, Morales
CH02)	ER	1400	1	Ecos del Atrato, Quibdó
CO09)		1400	0.25	Brisas del Sinú, Tierralta
CO10)	DF	1400	5	LV de Niquel, Montelíbano
DC16)	KM	1400	5	Em. Mariana, Bogotá
NA11)	JJ	1400	1	R. Ipiales, Ipiales
NA12)		1400	1.5	LV de Samaniego, Samaniego
NS16)	BK	1400	1	LV de la Gran Colombia, Cúcuta
QU04)	HM	1400	5	La Cariñosa de Armenia, Calarcá
SS19)	D31	1400	1	LV de Cimitarra, Cimitarra
SU12)	HKZ25	1400	0.25	Alcaldía de Ovejas, Ovejas
SU13)	HKZ22	1400	0.25	Alcaldía de Majagual, Majagual
AN27)	DU	1400	5	Em. Cultural Univ. de Antioquia, Medellín
BY17)	HKP79	1410	1	R. Universidad, Tunja
BY21)	HKP86	1410	0.25	Alcaldía de Chiquinquira, Chiquinquira
GU08)	P79	1410	2	R. Evangélica, Uribia
SS20)	TY	1410	5	Caracol R, Vélez
TO11)	FS	1410	5	RCN, Honda
VA19)	EI	1410	5	R. Guadalajara, Buga
AN28)	D23	1420	1	Ecos de Frontino, Frontino
CL05)	HK	1420	5	Vida AM, Manizales
MA06)	BH	1420	5	Caracol R/R. Magdalena, Santa Marta
SS21)	SN	1420	2	R. Lenguerque, Zapatoca
TO06)	LE	1420	1	La Cariñosa, Antena 2, Ibagué
AN29)	CK	1430	1	R. Sensación, Yarumal
AN30)	MF	1430	5	La Ribereña, Puerto Berrío
AN47)	G42	1430	0.5	R. Alejandría, Alejandría
AT10)	PW	1430	5	Colmundo, Barranquilla
CC08)	EG	1430	1	LV de Belalcázar, Popayán
CL08)	IU	1430	1	Armonías del Ingrumá, Riosucio
DC17)	KU	1430	5	1430 AM "Sonríele a Jesús R.", Bogotá
NS17)	BP	1430	2	R. Cariongo, Pamplona
PU03)	HKK38	1430	0.5	R. Manantial, Sibundoy
QU08)	X61	1430	0.25	L U FM Estéreo, Armenia
RI08)	HKX73	1430	1	R. Ciudad de Pereira, Pereira
SU07)	QX	1430	5	R. Majagual, Sincelejo
AN46)	NZ	1440	5	Colmundo, Medellín
BY06)	GM	1440	5	RCN, Sogamoso
CA04)	IB	1440	5	RCN Caquetá, Florencia
CU19)	HKT58	1440	0.25	Alcaldía de Ubala, Ubala
VA20)	EK	1440	5	Caracol R, Tuluá
CU08)		1445	0.5	Em. R. Unión, La Palma
AN31)	E20	1450	1	R. María, Urrao
AN32)		1450	0.2	R. LV del Nordeste, Remedios
BO11)	MX	1450	1	R. Mancomoján, Carmen de Bolívar:
CC09)		1450	0.5	LV del Cauca, El Bordo
CL02)	NL	1450	5	La Cariñosa, Ant. 2, Manizales
SS22)	HH	1450	5	R. Católica Metropolitana, Bucaramanga
TO13)	BY	1450	5	Oxígeno, Flandes
AN33)	TN	1450	5	R. María, Turbo
AN34)	MU	1460	1	LV de Amalfi "La Primera", Amalfi
AN45)	E26	1460	1	R. Capiro, La Ceja
AT02)	VH	1460	5	R. Uno/RCN Antena 2, Barranquilla
CL18)	HKR44	1480	5	Alcaldía de Victoria, Victoria
DC18)	JW	1460	5	Em. Nuevo Continente, Bogotá
HU09)	FL	1460	1	Agustiniano Minuto de Dios, San Agustín
NA10)	ZU	1460	5	RCN Antena 2, Pasto
NS18)	NW	1460	1	R. Monumental, Cúcuta
SS29)	HKY73	‡1460	0.25	Alcaldía de San Andrés, San Andrés
SU08)	AL	1460	1	R. Sincelejo, Sincelejo
AN04)	Il	1470	5	R. Popular, Medellín
AT14)	HKO96	1470	0.25	Alcaldía de Baranoa, Baranoa
BO12)	PX	1470	5	Colmundo, Cartagena
BY13)	HJB63	1470	1	R. Uno, Iza
CU09)	HQ	1470	5	R. Futurama, Pacho
PU04)	JIF	1470	1	R. Tres Fronteras, Puerto Asís
TO14)	TB	1470	5	Ondas de Ibagué, Ibagué (nighttime rel. R. María)
TO21)	JS20	1470	0.25	Ecos de Palo Cabildo, Palo Cabildo
VA26)	NT	1470	1	R. Huellas, Cali
AN35)	TC	1480	1	R. Sonsón, Sonsón (n.f.1490)
MA07)	OD	1480	5	R. Rodadero, Santa Marta
NS14)		1480	0.25	LV del Samán, Bochalema
RI03)	FC	1480	1	R. Unica, Honda
SS10)	TZ	1480	5	RCN Antena 2, Bucaramanga
TO15)	VB	‡1480	1	R. Guayabal, Armero, Guayabal
AT11)	AY	1490	5	R. Vida Nueva "Te acerca a Dios", Barranquilla
BO14)	J76	1490	0.2	Alcaldía de El Peñón, El Peñón
DC19)	BS	1490	4	Em. Punto Cinco, Bogotá
HU10)	E62	±1490	1	R. Garzón, Garzón

MW	Call	kHz	kW	Station, location
NA18)	HKW24	1490	0.2	Alcaldía de Guaitarilla, Guaitarilla
SU09)	JO	1490	1	LV de San Marcos, San Marcos
VA21)	ZB	1490	5	Robles 14-90, La Nueva, Tuluá
CL09)	UW	1500	5	R. María, Manizales
CU10)	TW	1500	5	R. Sumapaz, Fusagasugá
CU16)	HKT71	1500	1	Macheta
VA22)	LJ	1500	5	Sonora, La Voz de la Red, Cali
AN37)	D24	1510	5	LV de La Unión, La Unión
BY15)	A22	1510	1	LV de San Luis, San Luis de Gaceno
DC24)	HKY41	1510	1	Colombia Mía, Barrancabermeja, SS
QU07)	ZA	1510	1	R. Cristal, Armenia:
SS23)	HX	1510	1	Candela AM, Bucaramanga
TO16)		1510	0.5	LV de los Cedros, Líbano
VA29)	HKZ94	1510	0.25	Alcaldía de Buenaventura, Buenaventura
VA30)	HKZ93	1510	1	Alcaldía de Versalles, Versalles
AN38)		1520	0.3	Brisas del Palmar, Caucasia
AN39)	MA	1520	1	LV de Suroeste, Jericó
AT03)	LQ	1520	5	R. Minuto, Barranquilla
CC11)	HKS24	1520	0.5	R. Cristalares Timbío, Timbío
CL10)		1520		Sonoradio 1520 AM, Viterbo
CO12)	HKT20	1520	5	Alcaldía de Montería, Montería
CU14)	V37	1520	1	R. Pueblo Viejo, Zipacon
DC09)	LI	1520	5	Libertad, Bogotá
DC24)	T21	1520	5	Colombia Mía, Tierralta, CO
NA16)	HKW37	1520	1	R. Universidad, Pasto
NA19)	HKW43	1520	0.1	Alcaldía de Tangua, Tangua
NS19)	J98	1520	1	Em. Una Voz de la Frontera, Puerto Santander
RI07)	RL	1520	1	Antena de los Andes, Santa Rosa de Cabal
SU10)	MZ	1520	1	Ecos de la Sierra Flor, Sincelejo
TO17)	AM	1520	1	R. Altamizal, Dolores
AN58)	DN	1530	5	Yeshu'a LV de Jesucristo, Medellín
AN50)	HKN57	1530	0.25	Alcaldía de San Juan de Uraba, San Juan de Uraba
AN53)	HKN85	1530	0.25	Alcaldía de Anza, Anza
AN55)	HKN79	1530	0.25	Alcaldía de Uramita, Uramita
CE11)	HKS56	1530		Fascinación AM, Becerril
CE15)	HKS58	1530	0.1	Alcaldía de El Copey, El Copey
CC14)		1530		R. Integración, Morales
DC24)	HKN65	1530	0.25	Colombia Mía, Caucasia, AN
GU09)	OZ	1530	5	LV de la Prov. de Padilla, San Juan del Cesar
ME10)	HKV82°	1530	1	Alcaraván Radio, Puerto Lleras
VA23)	EU	1530	1	Caracol Sevilla, Sevilla
VA25)	HKR73	1530	1	Ecos del Pacífico, Guapí
AN40)		1540	0.25	LV Dorada, Segovia
AN41)	A26	1540	1	Em. Brisas del Río Chico, Belmira
BO15)	HKP50	1540	0.25	Alcaldía de Arjona, Arjona
CL11)	ZF	1540	5	R. Cóndor, Manizales
CS02)	HKR80	1540	0.15	Alcaldía de Sacama, Sacama
DC24)	HKZ52	1540	1	Colombia Mía, Chaparral, TO
NA09)	RQ	1540	2	R. Austral, Túqueres
SS24)		1540	5	R. El Sur, San Vicente de Chucurí
SS25)	HD	1540	1	LV del Petróleo, Barrancabermeja
AN36)		1550	0.5	Ondas del Nechí, Campamento
AT02)	CB	1550	5	R. El Sol "La Cariñosa", Barranquilla
CL16)	UN	1550	5	LV del Río Arma, Aguadas
DC21)	ZI	1550	5	G12 Radio, Bogotá
DC24)	HKV38	1550	1	Colombia Mía, Pitalito, HU
DC24)	HKX29	1550	5	Colombia Mía, Tibú, NS
NA20)	HKW53	1550	0.1	Alcaldía de El Tablón, El Tablón
NA21)	HKW55	1550	0.1	Alcaldía de Guachucal, Guachucal
NA22)	HKW50	1550	0.25	Alcaldía de Mallama, Mallama
QU03)	QD	1550	5	Sistema Vida, Armenia
VA31)	LT	1550	5	Em. Revivir en Cristo, Cali
AN42)		1555	0.5	R. Parroquial, Cali
AN52)	XZ	1560	5	Santa María de la Paz R., Medellín
AN54)	HKO35	1560	0.25	Alcaldía de Cañasgordas, Cañasgordas
CE07)	HKS65	1560	0.5	R. Tamalameque, Tamalameque
CE14)	PZ	1560	1	R. Codazzi, Codazzi
CU11)	CP	1560	5	RCN Antena 2, Arbelaez
ME11)	HKV90	1560	0.25	Alcaldía de Villavicencio, Villavicencio
SS26)	HE	1560	5	Voces Rovirenses, Málaga
VA08)	LP	1560	5	La Cariñosa, Antena 2, Tuluá
AN43)	HK022	1560	1	R. Ciudad Dabeiba, Dabeiba
BO16)	HKP58	1570	0.25	Alcaldía de Sta Rosa Sur, Sta Rosa Sur
BY22)	HKQ83	1570	0.25	Alcaldía de Maripi, Maripi
BY23)	HKQ82	1570	0.25	Alcaldía de Sta María, Sta María
CA05)	HKR66	1570	0.2	R. Universidad de la Amazonia, Florencia
CA06)	HJR66	1570	0.5	Timbiqui Estéreo, Timbiqui
CL12)	E70	1570	1	R. Auténtica, Manizales
CU18)	HKU42	1570	0.15	Alcaldía de Cajica, Cajica
DC22)	TG	1570	1	R. María, Macheta
DC24)	E96	1570	1	Colombia Mía, Palmira, VA
DC24)	HKX52	1570	2	Arc. Armada de Colombia, Pto Leguizamo
NS09)	‡1570			LV de Fomeque, Fomeque

MW	Call	kHz	kW	Station, location
RI09)	HKX80	1570	0.1	R. Marsella, Marsella
RI11)	HKX78	1570	0.25	Alcaldía de Balboa, Balboa
AT12)	QZ	1580	5	R. María, Barranquilla
CC16)	HKS46	1580	0.15	R. Alcaldía de Padilla, Padilla
CO11)	HKT34	1580	0.25	Alcaldía de San Antero, San Antero
CU17)	HKU42	1580	0.25	Alcaldía de Cajica, Cajica
DC25)	QT	‡1580	5	Aviva R., Bogotá
HU11)		1580		Alcaldía de Yaguará, Yaguará
MA08)	LC	1580	1	LV del Banco, El Banco
NA23)	HKW74	1580	0.1	Alcaldía de Pupiales, Pupiales
NS20)	KB	1580	1	R. Zulima, Villa del Rosario
SU01)	RM	1580	5	Caracol R, Sincelejo
TO19)	E66	1580	1	R. Miraflores, Rovira
VA24)	NA	1580	5	R. Robledo/RCN Antena 2, Cartago:
AN44)	IP	1590	5	BBN 15-90 R., Envigado
CE16)	HKS72	1590		Alcaldía de La Gloria, La Gloria
CL13)	QM	1590	1	Ecos de la Miel, Samaná
CU14)		‡1590		Ondas del Rioseco, Rioseco
SS27)	WB	1590	5	Em Nuestra Sra del Socorro, Socorro
VA25)		1590		R. Espacial, Andalucía
AN51)	HKO63	1600	0.25	Alcaldía de Jardín, Jardín
BY19)		‡1600		R. Fortaleza, Sogamoso
BY20)		‡1600		R. Bello Horizonte, Pesca
CC15)		‡1600	0.25	R. Impacto Cristiano, Popayán
CL14)		‡1600	0.25	LV de Aranzazu
CL15)	HKR52	1600	0.25	LV de Colina, Risaralda
CO13)	HKT39	1600	0.25	Alcaldía de Valencia, Valencia
CU13)	HV	1600	5	Emisora Armoniaz, Zipaquirá
CU15)		1600	1	LV del Rosario, Junín
DC24)	HJO72	1600	5	Colombia Mía, Carepa, AN
RI10)	HKX84	‡1600		Em. Mundial, Dosquebradas
RI12)	HKX83	1600	0.25	Alcaldía de La Celia, Celia
TO20)	HKZ79	1600	0.15	Alcaldía de Cajamarca, Cajamarca
TO22)	HKZ77	1600	0.15	Alcaldía de Venadillo, Venadillo
VA27)	F33	1600	0.25	R. Restauración, Cali
AN48)		‡1610		Armonías de Occidente, Medellín
RI13)		‡1610		R. Estelar, Santuario
BY24)		±1613	1	R. Ideal, Umbita (nominal 1600)

SW	Call	kHz	kW	Name and h of tr
DC26)	DH	5910	5	Alcaraván Radio, Pto Lleras: 24h (r. 1530)
DC26)	DH	6010	5	LV de tu Conciencia, Pto Lleras: 24h
GV02)	OY	6035	5	LV del Guaviare,S. José del G: 1000-0300

Major Networks:

CARACOL (Primera Cadena Radial Colombiana)
✉ Calle 67 N° 7-37, Bogotá, DC ☎ +57 1 348 7600 📠 +57 1 337 7126
W: www.caracol.com.co **E:** caracolcolombia @caracol.com.co

RCN (Radio Cadena Nacional)
✉ Cra. 13A N° 37-32, Bogotá, DC ☎ +57 1 314 7070 📠 +57 1 314 7070 **W:** www.rcn.com.co
Regularly all "La Cariñosa" stations relay sport trs from Antena 2.

SUPER RADIO
✉ Calle 39A N° 18-12 (or: Ap. 23316), Bogotá, DC ☎ +57 1 338 2166 📠 +57 1 287 8678 **W:** www.cadenasuper.com

TODELAR (Circuito Todelar de Colombia)
✉ Ap. 27344 (Av. Cra 20, N° 83-64), Bogotá, DC ☎ +57 1 621 6621 📠 +57 1 616 0056 **W:** www.todelar.com **E:** todelar@telesat.com.co

COLMUNDO
✉ Diagonal 58 N° 26A-29, Bogotá, DC ☎ +57 1 217 8911 📠 +57 1 348 2746 **W:** http://colmundoradio.com.co **E:** correo@colmundo-radio.com

CADENA RADIAL AUTENTICA DE COLOMBIA (Rlg.)
✉ Ap. 18350, (Calle 32 N° 16-12), Bogotá, DC. Carrera 38D # 1-52, Barrio Santa Isabel, Cali ☎ +57 1 285 3360 📠 +57 1 285 2505 **W:** www.cmbflorestacali.org

RTVC (Radio Televisión de Colombia) (Publ)
✉ Avenida El Dorado – CAN, Bogotá, D.C. **W:** www.rtvc.gov.co

State abbreviations: (Departamentos) AM = Amazonas, AN = Antioquia, AR = Arauca, AT = Atlántico, BO = Bolívar, BY = Boyacá, CA = Caquetá, CC = Cauca, CE = Cesar, CH = Chocó, CL = Caldas, CO = Córdoba, CS = Casanare, CU = Cundinamarca, DC = Distrito Capital, GN = Guainía, GU = Guajira, GV = Guaviare, HU = Huila, IS = Islas San Andrés y Providencia, MA = Magdalena, ME = Meta, NA = Nariño, NS = Norte de Santander, PU = Putumayo, QU = Quindío, RI = Risaralda, SS = Santander del Sur, SU = Sucre, TO = Todelar, VA = Valle del Cauca, VI = Vichada, VP = Vaupés.

N.B: These abbreviations are not officially recognized by the Colombian Post Office. Letters should therefore carry full name.

Addresses and other information:
AM00) AMAZONAS
AM01) Cra. 6A N° 10-104 (or: Ap. 236), Leticia 1100-0500.
AN00) ANTIOQUIA
AN01) Cra. 81 No. 48A-39, Medellín. **W:** lavozdelanostalgia.com

– **AN02)** Edificio Coltejer, Calle 52 #47-42, Medellín - 1100-0500 – **AN03)** Calle 50 Colomb N° 67-141, Medellín – **AN04)** Av.13 N° 84-42 (or: Ap. 1431), Medellín – **AN05)** Cra. 19 N° 20-66, Turbo – **AN06)** Ap. 1431, Andes - 1000-0200 – **AN07)** Circular 1a N° 70-01, Bloque 6, P7 U.P.B. Laureles, Medellín. W: radiobolivarianavirtual.com – **FM:** 92.4MHz – **AN08)** Apartadó. – **AN09)** Cra. 77B N° 48-144, Medellín W: vidaam.comco – **AN10)** Calle 56 N° 41-57, Medellín. W: rccradio.fm/ minutodedios – **AN11)** Calle 41 N° 80B-46, P2, Medellín – **AN12)** Cra. 3 Calles 2 y 3, Concordia – **AN13)** Ap. 4300, Medellín – **AN14)** Cra. 51 N° 51-38 (or Ap. 3854) , Medellín - 1000-0500 – **AN15)** Calle 94 N° 99-51, Apartadó – **AN16)** Calle 50 N° 67-141 (or: Ap. 65103), Medellín – **AN17)** Centro Cooperativo, Parque Principal, El Peñol – **AN18)** Cra. 11 N° 10-34, Nariño - 1100-0100 – **AN19)** Calle 44 N° 94-15, P3, Medellín. W: ondasdelamontana.net – **AN20)** Cra. 2 N° 21-54, Caucasia – **AN21)** Cra. 51 N° 50-09, Abejorral - 0900-0500 – **AN22)** Segovia - 1100-0300 – **AN23)** Cra. 51 N° 49-09, Rionegro – **AN24)** Calle 48B N° 79-38, Medellín – **AN25)** Casa Fé de Antioquia - 1100-2300 – **AN26)** Cra. Bólivar, Calle López, Santa Bárbara – **AN27)** Ap. 1226 (or: Cra. 44 N° 48-72), Medellín - 1100-0500 W: emisora.udea. edu.co - FM: 101.9MHz – **AN28)** Cra. 32 N° 30-05, Frontino. – **AN29)** Cra. 20 N° 20-21, Yarumal. – **AN30)** Calle 6 N° 1-23, Puerto Berrio. – **AN31)** Urrao - 0900-0300 – **AN32)** Remedios - 1100-2400 – **AN33)** Ap. 1289, Medellín - 1000-0400 – **AN34)** Cra. 19 Restrepo N° 19-61, Amalfi - 1000-0300 W: lavozdeamalfi.com – **AN35)** Calle 8 N° 6-60, Sonsón. – **AN36)** Casa Cural, Campamento - 1100-2300 – **AN37)** Calle 10 N° 9-37, La Unión (or: Ap. 4897, Medellín) - 1000-0200 E: emivozunion@epm.net.co – **AN38)** Batallón de Infantería N° 29 "Rifles", Barrio El Palmar, Caucasia - 1130-0400 – **AN39)** Calle 7, Cras. 3 y 4, Jericó - 1000-0300 – **AN40)** Batallón Bomboná, Segovia – **AN41)** Cra. 20 N° 20-14, Belmira – **AN42)** Parroquia de Nuestra Señora de Chiquinquirá, El Santuario - 1230-1500, 2200-2400 – **AN43)** Edif.Restrepo, P3, Plaza Principal, Dabeiba - 0900-0300 – **AN44)** Ap. 81095 (or: Cra. 44A N° 31 Sur-16,Barrio San Marcos, Medellín), Envigado – **AN45)** Calle 20 N° 27-20, La Ceja - 1100-0300 (Sun -0100) W: radiocapiro.jimdo.com – **AN46)** Cra. 80 N° 46-74, Medellín - 1100-0600 – **AN47)** Junta de Acción, Comunal Central, Alejandría – **AN48)** Calle 100 N° 14-06, Turbo – **AN49)** Cra.73 N° 47-35, Medellín – **AN50)** Palacio Municipal de San Juan de Uraba, San Juan de Uraba – **AN51)** Palacio Municipal de Jardín, Jardín – **AN52)** Calle 10 N° 42-22, Medellín W: santamariadelapaz.org – **AN53)** Palacio Municipal de Anza, Anza – **AN54)** Palacio Municipal de Cañasgordas – **AN55)** Palacio Municipal de Uramita, Uramita – **AN56)** Calle 105F No. 51-16, Barrio 20 de Enero, Apartadó – **AN57)** Calle 43 No. 67a-16, Barrio San Joaquín, Medellín. W: nseradio.com – **AN58)** Cra 81A No. 48-B – 71, Barrio Calasanz, Medellín – **AN59)** Cra 87 No. 65, Univ. de Medellín, Medellín. W: webapps.udem.edu.co/FrecuenciaU

AR00) ARAUCA
AR01) Calle 19 N° 19-62 P2, Arauca – **AR02)** Cra. 20 N° 19-09, P5, Arauca (or: Ap. 16555, Bogotá) – **AR03)** Calle 20, Cra. 27 (or: Ap. 6558), Saravena – **AR04)** Cra 20 N° 17-57, P3, Arauca W: meridiano70.net

AT00) ATLÁNTICO
AT01) Cra. 53 N° 55-166,Edificio Diario La Libertad, Barranquilla. FM: 96.9. – **AT02)** Barranquilla - 1000-0300 – **AT03)** Calle 82 N° 42H-54, 2do piso, Barranquilla - 0900-0400 W: radiominuto.org – **AT04)** Ap. 1688, Barranquilla – **AT05)** Cra. 53 N° 82-132, Barranquilla 1030-0200 **W:** emisoralavozdelacosta.net – **AT06)** Organización Radial Olímpica, Calle 72 No 48-37, Barranquilla - 1000-0500 – **AT07)** Cra. 48 N° 72-25, Ofc. 306, (or: Ap. 2010), Barranquilla - 0930-0500 – **AT08)** Cra. 45 No. 76-125, Barranquilla - 0900-0500 W: vozdelapatriacelestial1310. com – **AT09)** Calle 53 N° 50-11, P2, Barranquilla W: minutodedios.org – **AT10)** Cra. 44 N° 70-61, Barranquilla – **AT11)** Cra. 26, No 75B-07, Barranquilla - 1100-0500 W: radividanueva.net – **AT12)** Calle 60 N° 47-70, Centro Cultural Santa Catalina, Barranquilla - 0930-0130 – **AT13)** Palacio Municipal, Soledad – **AT14)** Palacio Municipal, Baranoa.

B000) BOLÍVAR
B001) Av. Venezuela, Edif. Banco Internacional, La Matuna 8B-05, Cartagena – **B002)** Calle Real 20-217, Cartagena - 1000-0500 – **B003)** Calle Mayor N° 6-34 (or: Ap. 1771), Cartagena - 1000-0420 – **B004)** Ap. 246, Cartagena. – **B005)** see DC13 – **B006)** Ap. 180, Magangué – **B007)** Calle Sta Fe, N° 13-113, Torices, Cartagena. **W:** www. radioesperanza1140.net – **B008)** Matuna, Cartagena. Av. 3 Of. 1106, Edificio Banco Popular, Cartagena – **B009)** Cra. 21 N° 29B-10, Cartagena – **B010)** Cra. 21 N° 29B-10, Cartagena – **B011)** Calle 56 N° 26-01, Carmen de Bolívar - 1030-0400 – **B012)** Av. Venezuela, Edif. Suramericana, Of. 801, Cartagena – **B013)** Palacio Municipal, El Peñon – **B015)** Palacio Municipal, Arjona – **B016)** Palacio Municipal, Sta Rosa Sur – **B017)** Manzana H, Lote 20, La Consolata, Cartagena.

BY00) BOYACÁ
BY01) Calle 16 N° 15-21, P8, Edif.Camara de Comercio, Duitama – **BY02)** Cra. 10 N° 16-36, Chiquinquirá - 0900-0600 – **BY03)** Ap. 282, Sogamoso - FM: 88.5MHz, 107.3MHz – **BY04)** Edif. Camol, Piso 11, Cra. 10 Nfby18o. 21-15, Tunja. W: besame.fm – **BY05)** Cra. 15 N° 14-47, Duitama. W: wradio.com.co – **BY06)** Ap. 019, Sogamoso - 1100-0500 - **FM:** 106.1MHz – **BY07)** Cra. 9 No. 8-65, Garagoa - 1000-0330 – **BY08)** Calle 20 N° 10-64, Tunja – **BY09)** Cra. 7 N° 9-57, Guateque (or: Ap. 17387, Bogotá) - 1000-0300 – **BY10)** Cra. 3 N° 13-74, P2, Puerto Boyacá - 0900-0400 – **BY11)** Cra. 10 N° 17-50, P5, Tunja – **BY12)** Calle 5,N° 5-25, P2, Parque Santander, Samacá. W: ondasdelporvenir.com 0900-0300 – **BY13)** Iza (or: Cra. 7 N° 17-51, Of. 610, Bogotá) – **BY14)** Cra. 6 N° 6-93, Paipa - 1000-0400 – **BY15)** Calle 6 N° 5-42, San Luis de Gaceno - 0900-0300 – **BY16)** Calle 18 N° 12-81, P2, Chiquinquirá - FM: 92.6MHz – **BY17)** Universidad Pedagogica y Técnico de Colombia, Tunja – **BY18)** Calle 20 N° 10-64, Ofc.307, Tunja W: armoniasboyacenses.com – **BY19)** Cra. 10 N° 1495, Sogamoso – **BY20)** Pesca – **BY21)** Palacio Municipal, Chiquinquira – **BY22)** Palacio Municipal, Maripi – **BY23)** Palacio Municipal, Santa María – **BY24)** Calle 16A N° 3-58, Umbita.

CA00) CAQUETÁ
CA01) Cra.14 N° 12-129, Casa Episcobal, P2 (Ap. 285), Florencia - 1000-0300 – **CA02)** Ap. 465, Florencia. – **CA03)** Calle 17 N° 10-40, P2, (Ap. 209), Florencia - 1030-0300 – **CA04)** Ap. 150, Florencia. – **CA05)** Ap. 192, Florencia W: uniamazonia.edu.co - FM: 98.1MHz – **CA06)** Timbiqui.

CC00) CAUCA
CC01) Barrio El Porvenir, Cajibío (or: Ap. 945, Popayán) - 1300-2300 – **CC02)** Cra 8 N° 3-17 (or: Ap. 1321), Popayán - 1000-0400 W: www.cau-cana1040am.com – **CC03)** Cra. 8 N° 5-41, Popayán – **CC04)** Casa Cural, Parque Principal, Belalcázar (or: Ap. 987, Bogotá) - 1000-2400 – **CC05)** Calle 5A N° 11-25, Popayán – **CC06)** Ap. 535, Popayán – **CC07)** Cra. 13 N° 9-20, Santander de Quilichao - 1100-2400 – **CC08)** Calle 2a N° 1-06 (or: Ap. 759), Popayán - 0930-0400 – **CC09)** Batallón José Hilario López, Bordo – **CC11)** Calle 15 Cra. 17 Esq. Casa de la Cultura, Timbío (or: Calle 12B N° 13B-22, Popayán) - 1200-2400 – **CC12)** Cra. 4 N° 9-42, Piendamo – **CC13)** Barrio Sagrada Familia, Cra. 3 esq., Morales - 1130-1700, 1900-2200 – **CC14)** Casa de la Cultura, Morales – **CC15)** Ap. 789, Popayán - 1000-0500 – **CC16)** Palacio Municipal, Padilla.

CE00) CESAR
CE01) Calle 17 N° 15-67, Valledupar - 0900-0300 – **CE02)** Cra. 5 N° 13-52, Valledupar. W. wradio.com.co – **CE03)** Calle 7 N° 16-39, Aguachica – **CE04)** Ap. 22, Valledupar - 0900-0500 – **CE05)** Calle 6 N° 19-66, Curumaní - 1000-0100 - FM: 95. 7MHz – **CE06)** Calle 16B N° 13-74, Valledupar – **CE07)** Casa de la Cultura, Tamalameque – **CE08)** Ap. 250, Valledupar – **CE09)** Cra. 10a N° 4-38, P2, Aguachica – **CE10)** Cra. 16 N° 11-102, Codazzi – **CE11)** Becerril – **CE12)** Pailitas – **CE13)** Cra. 9 N° 5-02, Valledupar – **CE14)** Calle 12 N° 15-08, Codazzi – **CE15)** Palacio Municipal de El Copey, El Copey – **CE16)** Palacio Municipal, La Gloria.

CH00) CHOCÓ
CH01) Calle 28 N° 1-04, P2 (or: Ap. 482), Quibdó – **CH02)** Cra. 4 N° 25-18, P2, (or: Ap. 196), Quibdó - 1000-0400 – **CH03** Choco.

CL00) CALDAS
CL01) Ap. 67, Manizales – **CL02)** Ap. 244, Manizales - 1000-0500 – **CL03)** Cra. 2 N° 13-31, P3, La Dorada - 1000-0500 – **CL04)** Cra. 4 N° 8-58, P3, Anserma - 0900-0300 – **CL05)** Ap. 2000, Manizales. – **CL06)** Calle 11 N° 3-58 (or: Ap. 34), La Dorada - 0930-0500 – **CL07)** Calle 22 N° 21-40, Plaza Bolívar, Manizales W: reddelosandes1390am. com – **CL08)** Cra. 5 N° 11-102, Av. Los Fundadores, Riosucio - 1100-0300 – **CL09)** Cra. 23 N° 71-03 (or: Ap. 990), Manizales 1015-0500 – **CL10)** Viterbo – **CL11)** Antigua Estación del Ferrocarril, Manizales - 1200-0400 W: radiocondor.fundeca.org.co – **CL12)** Cra. 23 N° 71-03, Av.Sant, Manizales. – **CL13)** C. A. M, Samaná - 1100-0100 – **CL14)** La Parroquia de Nuestra Señora del Rosario, Aranzazu - 1100-1300, 1700-1900, 2100-2300 – **CL15)** Av. Joaquín 1-09, Salida a San José, Risaralda – **CL16)** Cra. 3 N° 7-31, Aguadas - 1000-0300 – **CL17)** Palacio Municipal, Salamina – **CL18)** Palacio Municipal, Victoria.

C000) CÓRDOBA
C001) Cra. 3A N° 30-12, P2, Montería - 1000-0400 – **C002)** Av. Olaya Herrera, Edif. Jatin, Lorica - 1000-0300 – **C003)** Calle 23 N° 1-53, Montería – **C004)** Cra 2 N° 28-53, P2, (or: Ap. 497), Montería - 1000-0300 – **C005)** Cra. 8 N° 17-56, Planeta Rica – **C006)** Ap. 148, Montería – **C007)** Calle 27 N° 8-25, Montería – **C008)** Ap. 364, Montería – **C009)** Brigada N° 11, Tierralta – **C010)** Cra. 5 N° 14-85, Montelibano – **C011)** Palacio Municipal, San Antero – **C012)** Palacio Municipal, Montería – **C013)** Palacio Municipal, Valencia.

CS00) CASANARE
CS01) Calle 9 N° 22-63, Edif. Cine Casanare, P2, Yopal - 1000-0500. FM: 97.7MHz – **CS02)** Palacio Municipal, Sacama – **CS03)** Yopal.

CU00) CUNDINAMARCA
CU01) Calle 11 N° 11-23, P2, Ofc.202, Girardot – **CU02)** Av. Las Palmas N° 5-08, P5, Fusagasugá - 0900-0400 – **CU03)** Terminal de Transportes, Girardot. W: radiocolina.com – **CU04)** Cra. 6 N° 6-38, Ubaté – **CU05)** Ap. 416, Girardot – **CU06)** Calle 16 N° 10-38, P3, Girardot. W: lacarinosa.com 1030-0300 – **CU07)** Calle 7 N° 14-83,

Pacho – **CU08)** La Palma. – **CU09)** Calle 3 N° 16-39, Pacho - 0930-0400 – **CU10)** Calle 8 N° 5-59, Fasagasugá - 0900-0300 – **CU11)** Cra. 3 N° 2-36, Arbeláez (or: Av. 37 N° 75-84, Bogotá) – **CU13)** Calle 3 N° 7-56, Zipaquirá. W: armoniaz.webcindario.com/html/somos.html – **CU14)** Zipacon – **CU15)** Alcaldia Municipal, Junín – **CU16)** Macheta – **CU17)** Palacio Municipal, Cajica – **CU18)** Palacio Municipal, Cajica – **CU19)** Palacio Municipal, Ubala.

DC00) DISTRITO CAPITAL
DC01) Calle 32 N° 16-12, Bogotá – **DC02)** Cra. 45 No. 26-33, Bogotá W: radionacionaldecolombia.gov.co – **DC03)** Cra. 13A N° 37-32, Bogotá. W: amores.com.co – **DC04)** Calle 67 No. 7-37, Bogotá – **DC05)** Calle 45 N° 13-70 , Ap. 19823, Bogotá. W: cadenamelodia.com – **DC06)** Calle 48 N° 18-77, Bogotá – **DC07)** Av. 13 N° 84-42, Bogotá – **DC08)** Calle 39A N° 18-12, Bogotá – **DC09)** Avenida Calle 13 N° 79-70, Bogotá, DC - 1100-0300 W: vidaam.com.co – **DC10)** Diagonal 58 N° 26A-29, Bogotá – **DC11)** Calle 57 N° 17-48, Bogotá W: radiosantafe. com – **DC12)** Cra. 16 N° 43-09, Bogotá. W: mci12.com/noticias/108-g12-radio – **DC13)** Calle 25ª No. 32, 46 Barrio Gran América, Ap. 2086350, Bogotá D.C. W: fuegoam.com.co – **DC14)** Cra. 30 N° 91-84 (or: Ap. 250649), Bogotá – **DC15)** Ap. 9291, Bogotá – **DC16)** Calle 6 N° 7-22, (or: Ap. 3201), Bogotá. (alt.address: Calle 385 N° 75-31, Cd. Kennedy, Bogotá) - 1100-0130 W: emisoramariana.org – **DC17)** Ap. Cd. Kennedy 72825, Bogotá - 1100-0300 W: 1430amradio.com – **DC18)** Cra. 27 N° 49-48, Bogotá. – **DC19)** Av. 15 N° 123-61, Of. 408, Bogotá - 1100-2300 – **DC20) W:** avivamiento.com – **DC21)** Calle 22C N° 31-01, Bogotá. – **DC22)** Carrera 21A, No. 151-23, Bogotá W: radiomariacol.org – **DC24)** Escuela de Cadetes José María Cordoba, Calle 80 N° 38-00, Bogotá – **DC25)** Fundación Sonríele a Jesús, Calle 72a No. 86-64, Bogotá – **DC26)** Librería Colombia para Cristo, Calle 46 N° 13-56, Blg C, Ap.to 215, (or Apartado Aéreo 67751) Bogotá. (Reports c/o Rafael Rodríguez R., Apartado Aéreo 67751, Bogotá, DC. 2 IRC's required for QSL reply) **E:** libreria@fuerzadepaz.com or (for reports) rafaelcoldx@yahoo.com – **DC27)** Av. Boyacá 48 A 11, Edificio Castillo Dorado, Of. 301, Bogotá. **W:** bbnradio.org

GN00) GUAINÍA
GN01) Casa Cultura, Calle 6 con Cra. 3, Puerto Inírida – FM: 88.9MHz Super Estación.

GU00) GUAJIRA
GU01) Cra. 9 N° 12-31, Maicao - 0900-0300 – **GU02)** Cra. 8 N° 3-27, Riohacha - 1000-0300 – **GU03)** Ap. 125 & 256, Maicao – **GU04)** Calle 15, Salida a Maicao, Riohacha - 0930-0400 – **GU05)** Barrancas – **GU06)** Cra 8A N° 3-27 (or: Ap. 3), Riohacha – **GU07)** Cra N° 6-60, San Juan del César – **GU08)** Cra. 18 N° 13-54, Uribia – **GU09)** Calle 1 N° 5-63, San Juan del Cesar - 1000-0400

GV00) GUAVIARE
GV01) San José del Guaviare – **GV02)** Cra 22 con Calle 9, San José del Guaviare. E: mercorio@col3.telecom.com.co

HU00) HUILA
HU01) Calle 7 N° 10-36, Neiva - 1000-0300 – **HU02)** Ap. 150, Neiva. W: oxigeno.fm – **HU03)** Ap. 496 (or: Cra. 7, Calles 21 y 22), Neiva - 1000-0530 – **HU04)** Cra. 13 N° 3A-24, Neiva. W: radio1.com.co – **HU05)** Cra. 4 N° 2-21, Of. 501-502, Neiva. – **HU06)** Calle 6 N° 5-36, P4, Pitalito - 0900-0400 . W: sistemainrai.net/hjkk1280 – **HU07)** Cra 8 N° 8-60, P2, Palermo - 0900-0300 – **HU08)** Calle 4a N° 5-59, La Plata - 1000-0100 – **HU09)** Cra. 14 N° 2-47, San Agustín – **HU10)** Cra. 7 N° 7-05, Garzón - 1000-0300 –**HU11)** Palacio Municipal, Yaguará.

IS00) ISLAS SAN ANDRÉS Y PROVIDENCIA
IS01) Ap. 354, San Andrés Isla – **IS02)** Avenida Los Libertadores No 3a – 73, Oficina 204, San Andrés Isla – **IS03)** Edif. Bermuda, P2, Av. de las Américas, San Andrés Isla – **IS04)** Av. Providencia N° 1A-48, (or: Ap. 665), San Andrés Isla - 1100-0500 – **IS5)** San Andrés Isla.

MA00) MAGDALENA
MA01) Av. Libertadores 27-101, Santa Marta. W: radio1.com.co – **MA02)** Cra. 5 N° 18-32 (or: Ap. 757), Santa Marta 0945-0500 – **MA03)** Calle 17 N° 5-83 (or: Ap. 103), Santa Marta – **MA04)** Calle 18 N° 5-58, Santa Marta - 1000-0200 – **MA05)** Cra. 9 N° 14-13, Fundación – **MA06)** Ap. 1240, Santa Marta – **MA07)** Calle 11 C N° 18a-34, Santa Marta - 1100-0400 – **MA08)** Ap. 45, El Banco - 1000-0400

ME00) META
ME01) Calle 41B N° 30-11, Barrio La Grama, Villavicencio – **ME02)** Cra. 13 N° 15-52, Granada – **ME03)** Calle 38 N° 32-41, P7, Edif. Prollano, Ofc 702, Villavicencio W: autenticavillavicencio.com – **ME04)** Cra. 30 N° 36-14, P4, Villavicencio – **ME05)** Cra. 31 N° 37-71, Of.1001, (Ap. 2472), Villavicencio - 0900-0500 – **ME06)** Cra. 40 N° 34-34, Baltazar Alto, Villavicencio – **ME07)** Calle 13 N° 28-05 (Ap. 001), Granada – **ME10)** (See DC26). **W:** www.fuerzadepaz.com - FM: 88.8MHz Marfil Stereo. – **ME11)** Palacio Municipal, Villavicencio.

NA00) NARIÑO
NA01) Cra. 29 N° 17-30 (or: Ap. 375), Pasto - 1000-0200 – **NA02)** Cra.20A N° 16-73, P2, Pasto - 1000-0100 – **NA03)** Ap. 454, Pasto. – **NA04)** Calle 20 N° 24-73, Of 603, P6, Pasto - 0900-0500 – **NA05)**

Cra. 27 N° 19-30, Pasto**.** W: oxigeno.fm – **NA06)** Ap. 1005, Ipiales - 1100-0200 – **NA07)** Parque Colón (or: Ap. 165), Tumaco - 1100-0400 – **NA08)** Cra. 8 N° 4-48, Ipiales - 1100-0200 – **NA09)** Calle 20 N° 15-13, Túquerres - 0900-0400 – **NA10)** Ap. 516, Pasto – **NA11)** Cra. 6A N° 9-14, P2, Ipiales – **NA12)** Cra. 5 N° 3-15, Samaniego – **NA13)** Fundación Tomás Cipriano de Mosquera, Ricaurte el Diviso 1300-2300 – **NA14)** Nevado Cumbal – **NA15)** Calle 15 N° 14-24 , Pasto - 1100-0500 W. radioviva.com.co – **NA16)** Universidad de Nariño, Cra. 25 N° 19-12, Pasto – **NA17)** Cra. 1 N° 21-36, Pasto – **NA18)** Palacio Municipal, Guaitarilla. – **NA19)** Palacio Municipal, Tangua. – **NA20)** Palacio Municipal, El Tablón. – **NA21)** Palacio Municipal Guachucal. – **NA22)** Palacio Municipal, Mallama. – **NA23)** Palacio Municipal, Pupiales.

NS00) NORTE DE SANTANDER
NS01) Calle 5 N° 3-26 (or: Ap. 1650), Cúcuta – **NS02)** Centro Comercial Bolívar, Local E4 y E5, Cúcuta - 1000-0400 – **NS03)** Ap. 400, Cúcuta.– **NS04)** Calle 5A N° 0-45, Cúcuta. W: besame.fm – **NS05)** Av. O. N° 10-54, P2 (or: Ap. 624), Cúcuta – **NS06)** Ap. 519, Cúcuta. W: wradio.com.co – **NS07)** Cra. 13 N° 9-10, P7, Ocaña – **NS08)** Calle 7N N° 4-117 (or: Ap. 2284), Cúcuta – **NS09)** Cra. 4 Calle 5 junto Almacén Fotorubio, Fomeque - 1000-1700, 2200-0100 – **NS10)** Calle 11 N° 15-24, Ocaña - 1030-0300 – **NS11)** Calle 7 N° 4-50, Tibú - 1000-2400 – **NS12)** Calle 17N No. 5-101, Cúcuta W: mci12.com – **NS13)** Base Militar "San Jorge", Tibú - 1030-1700, 2100-0200 – **NS14)** Av. 2 N° 4-11, Bochalema - 1100-0500 – **NS15)** Calle 12 N° 4-19, Ofc. 214, (or: Ap. 2582), Cúcuta - 1000-0500 – **NS16)** Av. OA N° 12-75, Ofc. 101 (or: Ap. 1303), Cúcuta – **NS17)** Cra. 6 N° 4-59, P3 (or: Ap. 1074), Pamplona - 0900-0300 – **NS18)** Av. 4 N° 11-17, Ofc. 303, Cúcuta - 1000-0400 – **NS19)** Cra. 2 N° 1-10, Puerto Santander - 1000-2200 – **NS20)** Av. 5 N° 9-58, P2, Edif. Mut.Aux (or: Ap. 151), Villa del Rosario.

PU00) PUTUMAYO
PU01) Calle Principal, Orito - 1100-2300 – **PU02)** Calle 10 N° 6-01 (or: Ap. 011), Mocoa - 0900-0300 – **PU03)** 19A Barrio Oriental, Sibundoy - 1300-2300 - FM: 107.3MHz – **PU04)** Calle 11 N° 17-18 (or: Ap. 9), Puerto Asís - 1100-0200

QU00) QUINDÍO
QU01) Cra 16 N° 19-23, P10, Armenia – **QU02)** Calle 9 N° 13-50 (or Ap. 2361), Armenia – **QU03)** Ap. 2481, Armenia – **QU04)** Ap. 556, Calarcá – **QU06)** Cra. 14 N° 21-26, P2, (or: km 2 via al Aeropuerto), Armenia - 1000-0500 - FM: 104.7MHz Robles FM Stereo – **QU07)** Calle 21 N° 16-31, Ofc 702, (or: Ap. 617), Armenia – **QU08)** Universidad del Quindío, Av.Bolívar Cra.15 Calle 12 Norte, Armenia W: uniquindio. edu.co/uniquindio/laufm - FM: 102.1MHz – **QU09)** Cra.24 N° 39-52, Calarcá. – **QU10)** Palacio Municipal, Armenia.

RI00) RISARALDA
RI01) Ap. 354, Pereira – **RI02)** Ap. 045, Pereira – **RI03)** Ap. 221, Pereira - 1000-0500 – **RI04)** La Virginia – **RI05)** Crra. 7a N° 18-80, Of. 705, Edificio Centro Financiero, Pereira - 0930-0515 – **RI06)** Cra. 7 N° 15-10, P3 (or: Ap. 1262), Pereira – **RI07)** Cra. 15 N° 11-80, Santa Rosa de Cabal (or: Calle 19 N° 8-74, Pereira) - 1000-0300 – **RI08)** Palacio Municipal, Pereira – **RI09)** Calle 17 N° 9-10, Marsella – **RI10)** Centro Administrativo Municipal, Dosquebradas – **RI11)** Palacio Municipal, Balboa. – **RI12)** Palacio Municipal, La Ceila. – **RI13)** Santuario.

SS00) SANTANDER DEL SUR
SS01) Ap. 915, Bucaramanga – **SS02)** Ap. 223, Bucaramanga. W: oxigeno.fm besame.fm – **SS03)** Calle 50 N° 17-71, P3, Barrancabermeja – **SS04)** Cra. 27 N° 45-80, Bucaramanga - 0900-0400 – **SS05)** Ap. 007, Bucaramanga - 1000-0200. – **SS06)** Calle 36 N° 14-58, Ofc.707, Floridablanca – **SS07)** Calle 16 N° 15-01, Esquina, Socorro - 0930-0300 – **SS08)** Transv. 6 N° 9-56, Barbosa – **SS09)** Batallón de Artillería de Defensa Aerea N° 2 "Nueva Granada" (or: Ap. 036), Barrancabermeja – **SS10)** Ap. 1100, Bucaramanga – **SS11)** Calle 11 N° 9-80, p. 3, San Gil – **SS12)** Calle 48 N° 35A-25, Bucaramanga – **SS13)** Edif. Súper Estrellas, Ofc.409 (or: Ap. 23), Barrancabermeja - 1000-0300 – **SS14)** Calle 7 N° 17-44, Barbosa 0730-2330 – **SS15)** Ap. 578, Barrancabermeja. W: lacarinosa.com 0900-0400 – **SS16)** Calle 12 N° 10-30, Centro, San Gil - 0900-0300 W: lacaliente1330.com – **SS17)** Calle 16 N° 4-47, Zapatoca – **SS18)** Calle 35 N° 20-39 (or: Ap. 3104), Bucaramanga – **SS19)** Cra. 4 N° 4-118, P2, Cimitarra - 0900-0300 – **SS20)** Cra. 3 N° 3-42, Vélez – **SS21)** Calle 20 N° 6-36, Zapatoca – **SS22)** Av. 36, No. 19-76, Piso 9, Bucaramanga. W: rcm1450.com – **SS23)** Calle 41 N° 19-87, Bucaramanga - 1000-0500 – **SS24)** Batallón Luciano D'Ahuyar, San Vicente de Chucurí – **SS25)** Calle 12 N° 17-10, Ofc.302 (or: Ap. 250), Barrancabermeja - 1000-0400 – **SS26)** Calle 11 N° 6A-11, Edif. San Gabriel, P2, Málaga - 1000-0200 – **SS27)** Diócesis del Socorro y San Gil, Calle 13 N° 34, Esquina Socorro - 0500-2300 – **SS28)** Cra.27, Calle 9, Televis, Bucaramanga – **SS29)** Palacio Municipal, San Andrés – **SS30)** Diócesis de Barrancabermeja, Calle Octava, entre Carreras 15 y 16, Barrancabermeja.

SU00) SUCRE
SU01) Ap. 167, Sincelejo - 1000-0430 – **SU02)** Cra. 18 N° 20-48 (or: Ap. 448), Sincelejo – **SU03)** Cra. 24 N° 29-50 (or: Ap. 100), Corozal - 1100-

0500 – **SU04)** Cra. 20 N° 16-40 (or: Ap. 191), Sincelejo - 1100-0300 – **SU05)** Calle 20 N° 24-93, Av. las Penitas, Sincelejo – **SU07)** Cra. 20 N° 25-92 piso 2, Sincelejo – **SU08)** Cra. 20 N° 21-46 (or: Ap. 303), Sincelejo - 1000-0400 – **SU09)** Cra. 28 Calle 18, San Marcos – **SU10)** Calle 25A N° 18, Sincelejo - 1030-0430 – **SU11)** Cra. 20 N° 25-92, P2, Sincelejo - 1030-0200 – **SU12)** Palacio Municipal, Ovejas – **SU13)** Palacio Munivipal, Majagual – **SU14)** Calle 24 No 18-31, Sincelejo.

T000) TOLIMA
T001) Calle 12 N° 1-17, P5, Ibagué - 0900-0400 - FM: 96.3MHz – **T002)** Calle 14 N° 2A-14, P2, Ibagué – **T003)** Parque Murillo Toro N° 3-29, P4, Ibagué - 1000-0400 – **T004)** Cra 7 con Calle 10, Espinal – **T005)** Calle 11 N° 10-36, Guamo - 1100-2400. W: sistemainrai.net/hjkk1090 – **T006)** Ap. 2419, Ibagué – **T007)** Ap. 1094, Ibagué FM: 93.9MHz – **T008)** Calle 5 N° 6-25, Mariquita – **T009)** Calle 9 N° 1-17-24, P3, Ibagué. W: oxigeno. fm – **T010)** Calle 11 N° 4-26 (or: Ap. 64), Espinal - 1000-0400 – **T011)** Ap. 536, Honda – **T012)** Ap. 509, Honda - 1000-0300 – **T013)** Cra. 2 N° 11-27, Flandes – **T014)** Cra 3 N° 12-76, Ofc.801 (or: Ap. 589), Ibagué - 1000-0400 – **T015)** Armero, Guayabal – **T016)** Cra. 13 N° 5-61, Libanó - 1000-0300 – **T017)** Cra. 7a N° 5-36, Dolores - 0945-0300 – **TO 18)** Calle 7a No. 20-70, Melgar - 0900-0500 – **T019)** Cra. 2 N° 3-74, Rovira –**T020)** Palacio Municipal, Cajamarca. – **T021)** Palacio Municipal, Palo Cabildo. – **T022)** Palacio Municipal, Venadillo.

VA00) VALLE DEL CAUCA
VA01) Cra. 26 N° 5C-25, San Fernando, Cali – **VA02)** Cra. 38D Diagonal 3/A-52B/Santa Isabel, Cali – **VA03)** Ap. 1941, Cali W: wradio.com. co – **VA04)** Ap. 4666, Cali - 1100-0400 – **VA05)** Cra. 14 N° 2-25, P2 (or: Ap. 96), Buga - 1100-0500 – **VA06)** Av. 5B Norte N° 21-02, Cali – **VA07)** Cra. 33 N° 28-51 (Ap. 280), Palmira - 1000-0500. W: radiopalmira.com – **VA08)** Ap. 126, Tuluá - 1000-0300 – **VA09)** Cra. 4A N° 10-75 (or: Ap. 145), Cartago – **VA10)** Calle 21 Nte N° 3N-49, P5, Cali W: radiosupercali.com – **VA11)** Calle 12-39, Ofc 301, Edif. R.Buenaventura (Ap 383), Buenaventura 1030-0500. Rel. R. Maria 0200-1000. W: radiobuenaventura.com – **VA12)** Cra. 16 N° 6-22, P2, Caicedonia – **VA13)** Cra 19 N° 2N-29, Ofc 21B, Cali – **VA14)** Cra. 30 N° 29-09, Palmira - 1000-0400 – **VA15)** Cra 6 N° 54-08, Av. Simon Bolívar, Buenaventura – **VA16)** Carrera 66B, No. 6-68, Barrio El Limonar, Cali – **VA17)** Cra. 11 N° 11-43, P2, Zarzal – **VA18)** Cra. 29 N° 32-88/90 (or: Ap. 201), Palmira - 1130-0300 – **VA19)** Cra. 14 N° 5-77, Buga – **VA20)** Cra. 26 N° 28-72, Tuluá. W: caracol.com.co – **VA21)** Calle 27 N° 33-35, Tuluá - 1100-0500 – **VA22)** Av. Roosevelt N° 34-37, Cali W: sonora1500am.com – **VA23)** Cra. 51 N° 49-21, Sevilla – **VA24)** Calle 10 N° 6-87, P3, Cartago - 1100-0500 – **VA25)** Calle 14 N° 4A-63, Andalucía 1300-2300 – **VA26)** Calle 13, No. 19-59, Barrio Guayaquil, Cali. W: sistemahuellasinternacional.com 1100-0500 – **VA27)** Cra. 13 N° 10-58, Cali – **VA28)** Av.Roosevelt N° 28, Cali. (Or: Transversal 34 N° 149-23, Cedro Golf, Bogotá) – **VA29)** Palacio Municipal, Buenaventura. – **VA30)** Palacio Municipal, Versalles. – **VA31)** Cra. 13 N° 10-62, Cali. W: sistemahuellasinternacional.com 1100-0400.

VI00) VICHADA
VI01) Av. Orinoco, Puerto Carreño.
VP00) VAUPÉS
VP01) Mitú – **VP02)** Mitú.

FM in Bogotá (MHz): 88.9 R. Uno (RCN) – 89.9 40 Principales (Caracol) – 90.4 La UD (University) – 90.9 La Mega (RCN) – 91.9 Javeriana Estereo (University) – 92.4 Policía Nacional (Police) – 92.9 La Z (Todelar) – 93.3 Colombia Estéreo (Colombian Army) – 93.9 RCN La Radio (rel. 770) – 94.9 La FM (RCN) – 95.9 R. Nac. de Colombia (RTVC) – 96.9 Melodía FM Estéreo – 97.4 Bésame (Caracol) – 97.9 Radioactiva (Caracol) – 98.5 Universidad Nacional (University) – 99.1 Radionica (RTVC) – 99.9 W Radio (Caracol) – 100.4 Oxígeno (Caracol) – 100.9 Caracol R (rel. 810kHz) – 101.9 Candela (W Radio) – 102.9 Tropicana (Caracol) – 103.9 La X (Todelar) – 104.4 Fantástica – 104.9 Vibra Bogotá (W Radio) – 105.4 Rumba Stereo (RCN) – 105.9 Olímpica – 106.9 Universidad Jorge Tadeo Lozano (University) – 107.9 Minuto de Dios (Rlg)

COMOROS

L.T: UTC +3h — **Pop:** 700,000 — **Pr.L:** French, Comorian, Arabic — **E.C:** 50Hz, 220V — **ITU:** COM

OFFICE DE RADIO TÉLÉVISION DES COMORES (ORTC, Gov.)
BP 452, Moroni, Grand Comoro ☎+269 7732531 📠 +269 7730303 **W:** radiocomores.km **LP:** Tech. Dir: Abdulkader Radjab.
FM: Moroni, R.Studio 1 101.2MHz Nkazi, R.Nkazi 107.0MHz. 6 x 1kW, 3 x 0.5kW txs. **D.Prgr:** 0300-1900. **Ann:** F: "Ici Radio Comoro".
Other stations:
R. Dziyalandze, Anjouan: 90.0MHz (rel. RFI 1700-1030).
R. Ocean Indien, Ngazidja: 100.5MHz. W: radioceanindien.km
R. France Int: 103.0MHz

CONGO (Dem. Rep.)

L.T: Kinshasa & western part: UTC +1h, eastern part: UTC +2h — **Pop:** 67 million — **Pr.L:** French, Lingala, Swahili, Tshiluba, Kikongo — **E.C:** 50Hz, 220V — **ITU:** COD

CONSEIL SUPÉRIEUR DE L'AUDIOVISUEL ET DE LA COMMUNICATION (CSAC)
Kinshasa **L.P:** President: Jean Bosco Bahala.

RADIO-TÉLÉVISION NATIONALE CONGOLAISE (RTNC, Gov.)
B.P. 3164, Kinshasa-Gombe ☎+243 81 9970699 📠+243 81 123 7691 **W:** rtnc-rdc.com **E:** info@rtnc-rdc.com **LP:** DG: Mr. E. Kipolongwa Mukambilwa, Dep. DG: M. Makuala
FM: Kinshasa: **National channel:** 100.0MHz, **Kinshasa channel:** 91.8MHz, **Channel for national languages:** 97.0MHz.
D.Prgr: 24h in French/Swahili/Lingala/Tshiluba/Kikongo. Also relayed by other stns. **Ann:** "RTNC, Radio-Télévision Nationale Congolaise", émettant de Kinshasa".
Provincial stations:
FM: 2) 94.5MHz 3kW – 3) 88.9/92.0MHz 1.5kW – 4) 93.3MHz 1.5kW/90.0MHz 0.05kW – 5) 93.5/98.5MHz 1kW – 6) 89.1MHz 50kW – 7) 90.0MHz – 8) 92.5MHz 1kW – 9) 94.8MHz – 10) 90.1MHz – 11) 93.7MHz
Addresses: 2) B.P. 7296, Lubumbashi – 3) RTNC Kivu, B.P. 475, Bukavu – 4) B.P. 1061, Mbandaka – 5) B.P. 1232, Mbuji-Mayi – 6) B.P. 708, Kananga, Western Kasai – 7) B.P. 704, Matadi – 8) B.P. 1745, Kisangani – 9) Butembo, Nord-Kivu – 10) Goma, Nord-Kivu. **E:** rtnc-nordkivu@yahoo.fr – 11) Ulvira, Sud-Kivu.

RADIO TÉLÉ CANDIP
B.P. 373, Bunia.
SW: Bunia v5066kHz 1kW. **FM:** 98MHz 1kW.
D.Prgr in French/Ethnic: 0400-0700, 1300-1900v.

RADIO KAHUZI (Rlg)
Ave. Masikits 2, Muhumba, Bukavu or B.P. 42, Cyangugu, Rwanda. **W:** radiokahuzi.com **E:** radiokahuzi@gmail.com **LP:** Dir: Richard McDonald, St. Mgr: Barbara Smith.
SW: Bukavu 6210kHz 0.8kW. **FM:** 91.1/102.1MHz 0.2kW. **D.Prgr:** 0530-2010 (SW -1710) in French, English, Kikongo, Kinyarwanda, Lingala, Mashi, Swahili and Tshiluba. Also rel. VOA. **F.PI:** FM transmitters in Fizi, Shabunda and Wamazi.

RADIO OKAPI
(joint initiative between the UN Mission in the DRC [MONUC] and Hirondelle Foundation)
QG Monuc, 12 Av. des Aviateurs, Kinshasa-Gombe ☎+243-81-890-6747 **W:** www.radiookapi.net **E:** info@hirondelle.org
LP: Dir: Yves Laplume.
FM (MHz): (powers 1-5kW): Isiro 90.1, Beni 92.0, Butembo 92.9, Gbadolite/Kananga/Lisala 93.0, Mbuji-Mayi 93.8, Kisangani 94.8, Bukavu 95.3, Gemena 95.4, Lubumbashi 95.8, Kanyabayonga/ Mahagi 96.0, Aru 98.0, Bundundu 99.0, Matadi 102.0, Baraka/Kindu/ Mbandaka 103.0, Kikwit/Kinshasa/Mbuji Mayi 103.5, Kamina 104.3, Manono 104.5, Bunia/Walikale 104.9, Kalemie 105.0, Goma/Uvira 105.2, Shabunda 105.4, Tshomo Ini 106.5.
D.Prgr: 0430-2200 in French/Lingala/Swahili/Tshiluba.
For SW relay see Clandestines & other target broadcasts section.

Other stations (all MHz):
Business R. Africa, Kinshasa: 98.6. W: brt-africa.com – **Canal Congo pour Christ,** Bukavu: 97.3 – **Canal Futur,** Kinshasa-Gombe: 107.4 – **CEBS,** Kinshasa: 93.7 – **RATELKI,** Kinshasa: 90.2 – **R. Artemis,** Bunia: 90.2 – **R. Boboto,** Isiro: 100.6 100W – **R. Butembo:** 100 – **R. Canal CVV,** Kinshasa: 102.3 – **R. Canal Révélation,** Bunia: 100.7 0.3kW – **R. Congo FM,** Kinshasa: 96.4 – **R. ECC,** Kinshasa: 100.4 – **R. Elikya,** Kinshasa: 97.5 – **R. Liberté Kinshasa (RALIK),** 96.8 – **R. Maendeleo:** Bukavu 88.7 1kW, Chomuhini 103.3 1kW – **R. Malebo Broadcast Channel** (MBC), Kinshasa: 98.3 – **R. Maria Malkia wa Amani** (Rlg.): Bukavu 94.0 & 97.0. www.pamojanakakaluigi. org/radio_maria.htm – **R. Méthodiste Lokole,** Kinshasa-Gombe: 100.8 – **R. Moto** (Rlg.): Kivu 103 1.2kW, Butembo 106.0 – **R. Neno la Uzima,** Bukavu: 100.2 – **R. Parole Eternelle,** Kinshasa: 103.8 **R. Raga FM:** Kinshasa-Binza 90.5 4kW. W: raga.cd – **R. Rehema:** Chamuhini 89.5 0.25kW, Bukavu 99.7 1kW – **R. Réveil FM,** Kinshasa-Gombe: 103.5 W: reveilfm.itgo.com – **R. Sango Malamu:** Boma 102.5, Kinshasa 104.5 – **R. Tangazeni Kristo** (Rlg.): Bunia 88.6, Aru/Kwandruma 90.0 E: buero@diguna.de – **R. Télé Armée de l'Eternel,** Kinshasa: 94.5

– **R. Télé Amani**, Kisangani; 100.1 25W, 103.1 0.5kW. – **R. Téle Boma** (RTB), Boma: 98.0 – **R. Télé Graben**, Beni/Butembo 98 – **R. Télé Groupe l'Avenir (RTGA)**, Kinshasa 88.1 –**R. Télé Kin Malebo** (RTKM): Kinshasa 95.1, Kananga 97.5 – **R. Télé Kintuadi** (RTK): Boma 91.1, Kinshasa 97.1, Mbanza Ngungu 103.4, Matadi 107.5 – **R. Télé Message de Vie**, Kinshasa: 88.7 – **R. Télé Mosaïque**, Likasi: 88.5 – **R. Télé Puissance**, Kinshasa 101.0 – **RTV Bukavu Liberté**, Ibanda 107.3 – **RTV Mulangane**, Bukavu: 100.1 0.25kW – **R. Sentinelle**, Kinshasa: 97.1 – **R. Tomisa**, Kikwit: 97.5 0.5kW – **R. Veritas** (Rlg.), Kabinda: 105.0 – **R. Vuvu Kietu**, Mbanza Ngungu: 101.0 – **RCLS**, Kirumba: 91.0 – **REB**, Butembo: 90.7 – **RTIV**, Kisangani: 89.4 0.5kW – **Sauti ya Mkaaji**, Makongo: 87.85 – **Top Congo**, Kinshasa: 88.4.

Africa No. 1: Kinshasa 102.0 (see main entry under Gabon) – **BBC African Sce**: Kinshasa 92.7, Kisangani/Lubumbashi 92.0, Goma 93.3, Bukavu 102.2 – **RFI Afrique**: Bunia 90.2, Bukavu/Kisangani/Lubumbashi/ Matadi 98, Kinshasa 105 – **RTBFi** (Belgium), Kinshasa: 99.2

CONGO (Rep.)

L.T: UTC +1h — **Pop**: 4 million — **Pr.L**: French, Lingala, Kikongo — **E.C**: 50Hz, 230V — **ITU**: COG

CONSEIL SUPÉRIEUR DE LA LIBERTÉ DE LA COMMUNICATION (CSLC)
✉ Brazzaville. **LP**: President: Jacques Banangadzala.

TELEDIFFUSION DU CONGO - RADIO CONGO (Gov.)
✉ Direction Générale, B.P. 2912, Brazzaville ☎+242 22 2810608
L.P: DG: Jean Médard Bokatola. Dir. Radio: Sylver Sandi Ibambo.
SW: Brazzaville 6115kHz 50kW 0600-1830 (irreg.)
FM: 90.1/94/96.4MHz
National Network: 0420-2300 in French & ethnic. **N. in English**: 1900 (approx). **Ann**: "Radio Congo, Chaîne Nationale".
IS: Zansi solo. Opens and closes with National Anthem.

Other stations:
Digital R. N° 1, Brazzaville: 92.2MHz – **R. Brazzaville**: 98.0MHz –**R. Mucodec**, Brazzaville: 88.4MHz. W: mucodec.com – **R. Rurale Congolaise**, Brazzaville: 99.3MHz – **R. Liberté**, Brazzaville 106.0MHz.
Africa No. 1: Brazzaville 89.6MHz (see main entry under Gabon).
BBC African Service: 103.8MHz.
RFI Afrique: Brazzaville/Pointe-Noire 93.2MHz

COOK ISLANDS

L.T: UTC-10h — **Pop**-11,124 — **PrL**: English, Cook Island Maori — **E.C**: 50Hz, 220V — **ITU**:CKH

MW	kHz	kW	Station	Location
1)	630	2.5	R. Cook Islands AM	Rarotonga
FM	**MHz**	**kW**	**Station**	**Location**
2)	88.1		88 FM Varu Ngauru Ma Varu	Rarotonga
8)	88.1		Araura FM	Aitutaki
1)	89.0		R. Cook Islands	Mitiaro
1)	89.0		R. Cook Islands	Pukapuka
1)	89.9		R. Cook Islands AM	Rarotonga
1)	90.6		R. Cook Islands	Mangaia
1)	90.6		R. Cook Islands	Rakahanga
1)	90.6		R. Cook Islands	Palmerston
4)	91.9		Matariki FM	Rarotonga
1)	92.2		R. Cook Islands	Atiu
1)	92.2		R. Cook Islands	Penrhyn
3)	93.0		R. Australia	Rarotonga
1)	93.8		R. Cook Islands	Mauke
1)	93.8		R. Cook Islands	Nassau
1)	95.4		R. Cook Islands	Aitutaki
1)	95.4		R. Cook Islands	Manihiki
4)	96.7		Matariki FM	Rarotonga
9)	97.9		Marantha FM	Rarotonga
5)	98.7		Adventist Radio TK3ANA	Rarotonga
4)	99.9		Matariki FM	Rarotonga
1)	100.0		R. Cook Islands	Aitutaki
1)	101.1		Ocean & Earth HITZ FM	Rarotonga
6)	103.3	1	R. Ikurangi KCFM	Rarotonga
7)	105.0		R. Atiu	Atiu

Addresses & other information
1) The Voice of the Nation, Elijah Communications, PO Box 126, Avarua, Rarotonga ☎+682 29460 🖷+682 21907 **W:** www.radio.co.ck **E:** tunein@radio.co.ck **R. Cook Islands AM,** M-F 1600-0900 [Fri 1000] Sat 1600-1000 Su 1700-0900 **N:** Local news hourly M-F 1700-0200 **RNZI** 1600, 1700, 1800 M-F **Prgr:** Talkback, news, rlg srvcs and music

in English and Cook Isl Maori. **Ocean & Earth HITZ FM** 24h **Prgr:** contemporary hit music. **Outer Island Network:** Txs outside Rarotonga are owned by the Cook Islands gvmt and relay R. Cook Islands AM and in some cases also originate prgrs as local community stns – **2)** The Digital Factory, Avarua, Rarotonga ☎+682 22836/54188/ 55007 **W:** www.88fmradio.com **E:** 88fmradio@gmail.com **LP:** Nicholas Henry **ID:** '88FM Raro's Hottest Hits' 24h – **3)** 24h English for the Pacific satellite rel. – **4)** Matariki FM Ltd, PO Box 511, Avarua, Rarotonga ☎ +682 25997 **W:** www.matarikifm.co.ck **E:** onair@matarikifm.co.ck **LP:** William Framheim – **5)** PO Box 31, Avarua, Rarotonga ☎+682 22851 **E:** office@ adventist.org.ck **Prgr:** Rlg (r. temp. inactive) – **6)** Kia Orana Country R., PO Box 521, Avarua, Rarotonga ☎+682 23203 (r. temp. inactive) – **7)** Enuamanu School, Mapumai, Atiu. Mgr: Bazza Ross ☎ +682 33264 **E:** rossb@oyster.net.ck – **8)** Aitutaki. **ID:** '88FM Aitutaki's Hottest Hits' 24h. Same family ownership as #2 with joint marketing and sales with the Rarotonga stn – **9)** Rarotonga. **Prgr:** Religious

COSTA RICA

L.T: UTC -6h — **Pop:** 4.2 million — **Pr.L:** Spanish — **E.C:** 60Hz, 120V — **ITU:** CTR

CONTROL NACIONAL DE RADIO (CNR)
✉ Ministerio de Gobernación y Policia, Ap.10006, 1000 San José ☎ +506 2221 0992, 2221 9910

CAMARA NACIONAL DE RADIO (CANARA)
✉ Ap.1583, 1002 San José ☎ +506 2256 2338 🖷 +506 2255 4483
E: info@canara.org

MW	Call	kHz	kW	Station, location and h. of tr
1)	RI	‡530	10	R. Sinfonola, Cartago: (r: FM 90.3)
2)	SCL	550	5	R. Santa Clara, Cd. Quesada: 1100-0130
3)	ELR	570	5	R. Libertad, San José: 1200-0400
4)	RN	590	5	R. Nacional, San José
6)	RMV	610	15	R. María, San José
5)	ALY	640	20	R. Rica, San José: 1130-0400
7)	TNT	670	10	R. Managua, San José
12)	JC	700	10	FCNRADIO.COM, San José
68)		730	1	R. Pacífico, Puntarenas: 1400-0200
70)	HB	‡730	20	Sin Fronteras, Desamparados
9)	LX	760	5	R. Columbia, San José
10)	RA	780	10	R. América, San José: 1000-0500
8)	SD	800	3	R. La Gigante, San José
11)	GC	820	2.5	R. Centro AM, San José: 1130-0600
62)	RDR	850	2	R. Cartago, Cartago: 1100-0400
13)	UCR	870	10	R. 870 UCR, San Pedro Montes de Oca
7)	BAS	890	10	R. Heredia, Heredia
14)	UM	910	5	BBN, San José
31)	RCR	930	5	R. Costa Rica, Guadalupe
71)	SD	960	5	R. Actual 960, San José: 1100-0600
72)	RC	980	10	R. Alajuela, Alajuela: 1100-0200
17)	MIL	1000	1	100.7/Mil FM, San José
29)	TIC	‡1020	5	LV de la Liberación, San José: 1100-0500
18)	AC	1040	5	R. Fides, San José
60)	HG	1040	2	R. Nosara, Hojancha: 1100-1400, 2100-2300
9)	LX	1060	1	R. Columbia, San Isidro del General: (r: 760)
19)	FC	1080	1	Faro del Caribe, San José
69)	SBC	1100	5	R. Guápiles, Guápiles
20)	SCR	1100	5	R. Chorotega, Santa Cruz: 1315-0000
54)	ACE	1120	1	R. Miel, Alajuela
15)	DKN	1140	5	R. Nueva, Guápiles
9)	CA	1160	1	R. Columbia, Puntarenas: (r: 760)
22)	PJ	1180	5	R. Victoria, Heredia: 1100-0400
23)	TQ	1200	5	R. Cucú, San José: 1000-0600
73)	Q	1220	1	R. Fe y Poder, Limón
63)	WC	1240	1	R. Corobici, Cañas
24)	DIO	1260	5	R. Emaús, San Víto de Coto Brus: 1100-0300
25)	GV	‡1280	2	Visión 1280, San José
26)	GL	1300	1	La Fuente Musical, Cartago
9)	LX	1320	1	R. Columbia, San Carlos: (r: 760)
27)	HR	1340	5	R. Sideral, San Ramón: 1000-0400
31)	DS	1360	1	R. Radio 1360, San José
28)	MS	1380	1	R. Guanacaste, Liberia: 1000-0500
61)	GJ	1400	1	R. Sinaí, San Isidro del General: 1000-0400
33)	RPN	1420	1	R. Pampa, Liberia: 1100-0100
30)	RDVC	1430	3	R. San Carlos, Cd. Quesada: 1100-0300
9)	LX	1460	1	R. Columbia, Ciudad Quesada: (r: 760)
67)	AW	1480	2	R. El Sol, Puntarenas: 1200-0400
55)	ASF	1500	1	R. Radio1500, Sarapiqui: 1100-0300
9)	LX	1520	1	R. Columbia, Cartago: (r. 760)
52)	CUB	‡1540	1	Enlace Radio, Pavas
32)	OAR	1560	5	R. Nicoya, Nicoya: 1000-0300
44)	RCVT	1580	0.25	LV de Talamanca, Talamanca

MW Call	kHz	kW	Station, location and h. of tr
34) RCLS	1580	0.25	R. Cultural Los Santos
35) RCC	1580	0.25	R. Cultural de Corredores,
36) RCLC	1580	0.25	R. Sistema Cultural de La Cruz
37) RSCM	1580	0.25	R. Cultural Maleku
38) RCL	1580	0.25	R. Sistema Cultural de Los Chiles
45) RCP ‡1580		0.5	R. Cultural, Pérez Zeledón
46) RCS	1580	0.5	R. Cultural Santiago
47) RCT ‡1580		0.5	R. CulturalTilarán
21) LG ‡1580		1	R. Casino, Siguirres, Limón
64) LGJ	1590	1.5	R. 16, Grecia: 1100-0400
39) RSCN	1600	0.25	R. Sistema Cultural Nicoyana
40) RCT	1600	0.25	R. Cultural de Turrialba
41) RCBA	1600	0.25	R. Cultural de Buenos Aires
42) RCP v1600		0.25	R. Cultural de Pital
43) RCU	1600	0.25	R. Cultural de Upala
48) RCCH	1600	2.5	R. Cultural Chirripó
49) RCSG	1600	0.5	R. Cultural San Gabriel
50) RCPV	1600	2.5	R. Cultural Puerto Viejo
65) CC	1600	2.5	R. Radio Cima, Pto Golfito
66) MQ	1600	1.5	R. Pococí, Guápiles: 1100-0400
51) RPQ	1600	0.5	R. Quepos, Pto Quepos

Hrs of tr. 24h except where shown. Add TI– to the front of the Calls. ‡ = inactive, (r) = repeater, ± = varying fq.

Addresses and other information:
1) Interamericana Sur, Km 19, Taras, Cartago **W**: www.radiosinfonola. com **E**: rumbo@racsa.co.cr ☎+506 2537 1002 – **2)** Ap. 221, 44UU Cd. Quesada **W**: www.radiosantaclara.org **E**: radio@radiosantaclara.org ☎ +506 2460 6666 – **3)** Cadena Radial Costarricense, 100m oeste de Taca, La Uruca, 1000 San José or Ap. 301-2400 Desamparados ☎ + 506-2232 3672 🖷+506 2232 9750 – **4)** Ap. 7-1980 (or: La Uruca 1 km Oeste Parque Diversionales), 1000 San José ☎ +506 2231 3331. 🖷 +506 2231 6604 **W**: www.sinart.go.cr **E**: rnacional@sinart.go.cr **5)** Ap. 1695, 1000 San José ☎ +506 2258 5806 🖷+506 2258 5803 **E**: radiorica@racsa.co.cr – **6)** Escuela Pilar Jimenez 25 Sur, Goicoechea, 1000 San José **W**: www.radiomaria.cr **E**: info.crc@radiomaria.org ☎+506 2234 1676 - 🖷 +506 2225 5795. – **7)** Ap. 800-1000 (or: Costado Oeste del Puente Juan Pablo II), 1000 San José. **E**: carias@monumental.co.cr **W**: www.monumental.co.cr ☎ +506 2296 6093. 🖷 +506 2296 0413 – **8)** Calles 15-13, Av. 11, Barrio Aranjuez (or: Ap. 1735) 1000 San José ☎ +506 2257 3131 - 🖷+506 2221 9679 **W**: www.radiogigante800am. com–**9)** Ap. 708, 1000 San José **W**: www.columbia.co.cr – **10)** Edificio de la Prensa Libre, Calle 4, Avenida 4 (or Ap. 177-1009) San José **E**: radioamerica@780am.com ☎ +506 2255 3712 **W**: www.780america. com. – **11)** Ap. 6133, 1000 San José ☎ +506 2240 7591 🖷+506 2236 3672 **E**: info@radiocentrocr.com – **12)** Family Christian Network, Ap. 60-2020, Zapote **W**: www.fcnradio.com **E**: info@fcnradio.com 🖷+506 2293 7993– **13)** Cd. Universitaria Rodrigo Facio, San Pedro Montes de Oca, 2060-1000 San José **W**: http://radiosucr.com **E**: info@radiosucr. com ☎+506 2511 3721. 🖷 +506 2511 4832. – **14)** De la Municipalidad de Tibas 100 mtrs al Norte y 75 metrs al Oeste, casa blanca a mano derecha (Ap. 2006), 1100 San José **W**: www.bbnradio.org ☎ +506 2240 2900 – **15)** Ap. 266, 7210 Guápiles ☎ +506-2711 1140 🖷+506 2710 4011 **E**: radionueva@gmail.com – **17)** Ap. 708-1000 San José **E**: r100.7@columbia.co.cr ☎ +506 2225 1000 🖷+506 2234 6198 – **18)** Ap. 5079, 1000 San José ☎ +506 2258 1415 🖷 +506 2233 2387 **W**: www.radiofides.co.cr **E**: rafides@racsa.co.cr – **19)** Ap. 2710, 1000 San José. ☎ +506 2227 1725 **W**: www.farodelcaribe.org **E**: tifc@ farodelcaribe.org – **20)** 700 mts este de Almacén Jiménez y Chaverrí, (or Ap. 92), 5175 Santa Cruz ☎ +506 2680 0447 🖷 +506-2680 2435 **E**: ugiocr@hotmail.com – **21)** Ap. 287, 7300 Puerto Limón ☎ +506 2758 0029 🖷 +506 2758 3029 - **FM:** 98.3MHz **W**: www.radiocasinodelimon. com **E**: radiocasino@yahoo.com – **22)** Ap. 298, 3000 Heredia ☎ +506 2260 2323 🖷+506 2237 5736 **E**: gpiedra@gmail.com – **23)** Ap. 1128, 1000 San José. **E**: gerencia@radiocucu.com ☎+506-2221 8620 🖷+506 2221 8636 **W**: www.radiocucu.com – **24)** Ap.262, 8257 San Vito de Coto Brus **E**: radioemaus@racsa.co.cr ☎ +506 2773 3101 🖷 +506 2773 4035 – **25)** De la Nissan de Paseo Colón 100 al sur, (or: Ap. 1851, 4050 Alajuela) 1000 San José **W**: www.estereovision.com **E**: estereovision@racsa.co.cr ☎ +506 2256 6361 – **26)** 1 km oeste de la Basilica de los Angeles, Carr. a Paraíso, 7050 Cartago **E**: lafuentemusical@ice.co.cr ☎ +506 2553 2389 🖷 +506-2591 1090 – **27)** Ap. 73, 4250 San Ramón **E**: rsideral@ice.co.cr ☎ +506 2245 5046 🖷+506 2445 5130 – **28)** Residencial Las Brisas, Casa #11A, Buscando la quebrada (Ap. 27), 5600 Liberia, (or: Ap. 6462, 1000 San José) ☎ +506 2687 2345 🖷 +506 2235 3704. – **29)** Ap. 8130, 1002 San José **W**: www.radiosancarlos.co.cr **E**: radiosancarlos@ice.co.cr ☎ +506 2460 0339 🖷 +506 2460 0358 – **31)** Barrio Córdoba, Autos Bohío 100 sur y 100 este, 894-2200 Coronado. **W**: www.radiocr.net **E**: radiocostarica@gmail.com ☎ +506 2227 4690 – **32)** Ap. 50, 5200 Nicoya **E**: micoya1560@racsa.co.cr ☎ +506 2685 5757 🖷 +506 2685

5543. – **33)** Ap. 248, 5000 Liberia **E**: pamparamirez@costaricense. cr ☎ +506 2666 4933 🖷 +506-2666 5989 **W**: www.radiopampa.com – **34-50)** Stns are affiliated to Instituto Costarricense de Enseñanza Radiofónica, Ap.132, 2050 San Pedro Montes de Oca (Ministerio de Educación Pública) **W**: www.icer.co.cr 🖷+506 2225 9252. –**34)** Edificio Municipal, Barrio de las Tres Marías, San Marcos de Tarrazú – **35)** Frente al Parque Central, Ciudad Neilly, Corredores. – **36)** Costado sur del Comando Norte, La Cruz, Guanacaste. – **37)** Palenque Tonjibe, frente a la plaza de fútbol, Tonjibe, San Rafael de Guatuso, Prov. de Alajuela. – **38)** Costado Oeste de Edificio Municipal, Los Chiles, Prov. de Alajuela. – **39)** De la esquina noreste de la Iglesia Nueva, 200m Norte, B:o Santa Lucia, Nicoya, Prov. de Guanacaste. – **40)** Palacio Municipal, 132-2050 Turrialba, Prov. de Cartago. – **41)** 300 metros al Norte del Cuerpo de Bomberos, Buenos Aires de Puntarenas. – **42)** Edificio de la Asociación de Desarrollo, Pital, San Carlos, Prov. de Alajuela. – **43)** Frente a la Sucursal Banco Nacional de Costa Rica, Upala, Prov. de Alajuela. – **44)** Frente de la Plaza de Futbol de Amubri, Talamanca. – **45)** Pérez Zeledón, San José - **46)** Puriscal, San José – **47)** Tilarán, Guanacaste - **48)** Chirripó, Turrialba - **49)** San Gabriel de Aserrí, San José - **50)** Puerto Viejo, Cachuita, Limón – **51)** 300 metros oeste del Parque de Santa María de Dota, 2541-1707 Quepos **W**: www.radioquepos.com – **52)** Ap. 23, 1200 Pavas **W**: www.enlace.org **E**: radio@enlace.org – **54)** 300 metros Norte y 50 Oeste del Antiguo I lospital de Alajuela, Alajuela (or Ap. 233-4060, Moll International, Alajuela) **E**: nelson@enlace.org ☎ +506-2442 9764 🖷 +506 2443 9102 – **55)** Ap. 827-8000 San Isidro Pérez Zeledón ☎ + 506 2460 7900 – **60)** Casa Cultural de Hojancha, Hojancha, Guanacaste ☎ +506 2659 9028 – **61)** Ap. 262, 8000 San Isidro del General **E**: radiosinai@ice.co.cr ☎ +506 2771 4367 🖷 +506 2771 4367 – **62)** Altos de Apolo, frente al Palacio Municipal, Cartago **W**: www.radiocartago.net **E**: radiocartago@ice.co.cr ☎ +506 2591 0542 🖷+506-2552 4497 – **63)** Frente a la Central de Hielo Frío, Cañas, Guanacaste ☎ +506-2669 2023 - **64)** Centro Comercial San Francisco, Loc. 5 y 6, (or Ap. 16), 4100 Grecia ☎ +506 2494 0018 🖷 +506 2494 2031 **W**: www.radio16.com **E**: gerencia@radio16.com – **65)** Barrio El Invú, La Rotonda, Pto Golfito) ☎ +506-2775 0068 🖷 +506-2775 3303 – **66)** Costado Oeste del Estadio de Guápiles (or Ap. 160), 7210 Guápiles ☎+506 2710 1600 🖷+506 2710 9884 **E**: radiopococi@gmail. com – **67)** Ap. 421, 2020 Zapote – **68)** Puntarenas – **69)** Guápiles, Pococí, Limón – **70)** Desamparados, San José – **71)** Calle 13-15, Av. 11, (or: Ap.1735-1000), San José. – **72)** 150 metros al sur del antiguo Seguro, Alajuela. – **73)** Iglesia Maranatha, 7300 Puerto Limón **W**: www.radiofeypoder.com

FM in San José and vicinities (MHz): 88.7 Lira – 89.1 R. 89.1 La Super Estación – 89.5 Sendas de Vida – 89.9 R. 899 – 90.3 Sinfonola – 90.7 R. Ritmo 90.7 – 91.1 911 La Radio – 91.5 R. 915 – 91.9 Puntarenas – 92.3 Onda Radial – 92.7 Columbia Stereo – 93.1 Fides – 93.5 Monumental – 93.9 Sonido Latino – 94.3 Reloj – 94.7 "94.7" – 95.1 Z-FM – 95.5 95 Cinco Jazz – 95.9 R. 95.9 – 96.3 Centro – 96.7 Universidad – 97.1 Faro del Caribe – 97.5 Musical – 97.9 "979" – 98.3 R. Estéreo Visión - 98.7 Columbia – 99.1 La Mejor FM – 99.5 R. Dos – 99.9 R. Azul – 100.3 La Paz del Dial – 100.7 R.100.7 – 101.1 R. Disney – 101.5 R. Nacional FM – 101.9 "U" – 102.3 Súper – 102.7 Exa FM – 103.1 "103" – 103.5 Best FM – 103.9 Sinai – 104.3 Oxígeno – 104.7 Hit – 105.1 Omega – 105.5 Ten Fifty-Five/Omega – 105.9 Beatz 106 – 106.3 R. Peninsular – 106.7 Premium – 107.1 Estéreo Actual – 107.5 R. 107.5 Real Rock

CROATIA

L.T: UTC +2h (31 Mar-27 Oct: +3h) — **Pop:** 4.3 million — **Pr.L:** Croatian — **E.C:** 50Hz, 220V — **ITU:** HRV

HRVATSKA AGENCIJA ZA POŠTU I ELEKTRONICKE KOMUNIKACIJE (HAKOM)
🖃 Jurišiceva 13, 10002 Zagreb ☎ +385 1 4896000 🖷 +385 1 4920227 **W**: www.hakom.hr **LP:** Dir: Drazen Lucic
NB. HAKOM is the regulatory authority for broadcasting.

HRVATSKI RADIO (HR) (Pub)
🖃 Prisavlje 3, 10000 Zagreb ☎+385 1 6342634 🖷+385 1 6343712 **E**: hrt@hrt.hr **W**: www.hrt.hr **LP:** Dir (Radio): Ivan Lucev

MW	kHz	kW	Prgr		
Zadar	1134	600	F (rel. Glas Hrvatske 1700-2345)		
FM (MHz)		**HR1**	**HR2**	**HR3**	**kW**
Belje		93.3	98.1	-	50
Biokovo		89.7	98.9	-	80
Borinci		88.3	96.1	-	3
Brac		99.8	-	88.8	3
Buje		91.3	103.7	93.2	1
Celavac		95.1	98.1	-	80
Drenovci		92.1	104.4	-	3

FM (MHz)	HR1	HR2	HR3	kW
Gruda	101.7	106.1	-	2
Ivanšcica	102.4	106.4	96.1	2x15/30
Kalnik	90.8	105.8	107.8	15
Labinštica	91.3	96.1	-	30
Licka Plješivica	87.7	90.5	100.3	50
Limski kanal	90.2	102.6	-	1
Mirkovica	91.3	93.3	-	30
Pag	98.5	103.4	-	3
Papuk	94.9	106.8	97.7	10
Psunj	97.3	99.7	-	80
Pula	91.4	102.1	94.2	5
Slavonski Brod	91.3	105.1	107.9	15
Sljeme	92.1	98.5	-	120
Srdj	88.9	98.5	-	30
Stipanov Gric	102.3	97.5	89.7	15
Šubicevac	94.0	90.0	102.3	1
Ucka	99.3	105.3	100.5	80
Ugljan	91.6	87.6	-	5
Uljenje	95.1	103.0	105.6	3

NB: Txs below 1kW not listed.
D.Prgr: HR1 (Prvi program): 24h. – **HR2 (Drugi program):** 24h.
– **HR3 (Treci program):** 24h.
External Service: Voice of Croatia (Glas Hrvatske):
see International Radio section.

HR Regional Services

D.Prgr: all stns 24h (incl. rel. of HR1). **HR R. Dubrovnik:** Branitelja Dubrovnika 21, 20000 Dubrovnik. **E:** radiodubrovnik@hrt.hr. On 88.2 (Rota), 89.5 (Ilija), 97.2 (Blato), 101.1 (Vela Luka), 103.7 (Slano), 103.8 (Korcula), 105.0 (Srd), 106.2 (Lastovo), 106.5 (Lopud & Ston). – **HR R. Knin:** Kralja P. Krešimira IV 30, 23300 Knin. **E:** radio.knin@hrt.hr. On 88.1 (Šubicevac), 90.2 (Knin), 94.4 (Promina). – **HR R. Osijek:** Šamacka 13, 31000 Osijek. **E:** radioosijek@hrt.hr. On 100.0 (Psunj), 102.4 (Drenovci & Osijek), 102.8 (Beli Manastir), 105.3 (Borinci), 105.6 (Zlataravec), 105.8 (Ilok). Incl. Hungarian ("Eszéki Rádió"): 1805-1830. – **HR R. Pula:** Riva 10, 52100 Pula. **E:** radiopula@hrt.hr. On 93.9 (Novigrad), 93.9 (Limski kanal), 96.3 (Koromacno), 96.4 (Buje), 100.0 (Pula & Vrsar), 101.3 (Ucka), 103.8 (Raša). Incl. Italian ("R. Pola"): MF 1000-1005, W 1300-1305, 1530-1630. – **HR R. Rijeka:** Korzo 24, 51000 Rijeka. **E:** redakcija@radio-rijeka.com. On 94.5 (Brgud), 95.1 (Pulac), 97.9 (Cres), 98.1 (Kupjacki Vrh), 100.3 (Licka Plješivica), 101.7 (Prezid), 102.7 (Mirkovica), 104.0 (Fuzine), 104.7 (Ucka), 107.4 (Mali Lošinj II), 107.5 (Mrkopalj). Incl. Italian ("R. Fiume"): 0930-0945, 1130-1135, 1330-1345, 1500-1530. – **HR R. Sljeme:** Prisavlje 3, 10000 Zagreb. **E:** radio_sljeme@hrt.hr. On 88.1 (Ucka). – **HR R. Split:** Mazuranicevo šetalište 24a, 21000 Split. **E:** radio.split@hrt.hr. On 88.4 (Komiza), 100.2 (Hvar), 101.0 (Labinštica), 102.0 (Biokovo), 104.5 (Brac), 105.3 (Orlovaca), 105.8 (Vrlika). – **HR R. Zadar:** Poljana Šime Budinica 3, 23300 Zadar. **E:** radio_zadar@hrt.hr. On 101.8 (Ugljan), 103.0 (Celevac), 105.9 (Pag).

OTHER STATIONS

FM	MHz	kW	Location	Station
13)	87.8	1.85	Brac	R. Dalmacija
7)	88.0	3	Beli Monastir	R. Baranja
26)	88.6	3	Slavonski Brod	R. Slavonija
53)	89.0	1	Valpovo	Hrvatski R. Valpovština (HRV89)
49)	89.3	5.5	Zadar	Novi R.
25)	89.4	2	Sisak	R. Sisak
11)	89.6	1	Porec	R. Centar Porec
50)	89.7	4.7	Sljeme	Antena Zagreb
34)	90.2	1	Vinkovci	Radio postaja Vincovci
28)	90.2	1	Slavonska Pozega	R. Vallis aurea (RVA)
22)	90.3	1	Dugo Selo	R. Martin
44)	90.4	1	Vrlika	HIT R.
48)	90.5	1	Komiza	Nautic R. Vis
35)	91.0	1	Dakovo	Slavonski R.
31)	91.6	5	Vinkovci	R. VFM
19)	91.7	5	Koprivnica	R. Koprivnica (RKC)
44)	92.2	1	Krizice	HIT R.
37)	92.4	2	Alaginci	R. Pozega
2)	92.6	2	Zagreb	Otvoreni R.
32)	92.9	1.9	Virovitica	R. Virovitica
11)	93.6	7	Rusnjak	R. Centar Porec
18)	93.8	1	Jastrebarsko	R. Jaska
42)	94.4	6	Cetingrad	Hrvatski R. Karlovac
47)	94.7	1	Hvar	Megamix R. Hvar
24)	94.8	1	Rovinj	Gradski R. Rovinj
30)	94.9	5	Velika Gorica	R. Velika Gorica (RVG)
1)	95.3	3	Osijek	Narodni R.
45)	95.4	5	Drenovci	Hrvatski R. Vukovar
23)	95.4	1	Duga Resa	R. Mreznica
19)	95.5	5	Kalnik	R. Koprivnica (RKC)
3)	95.5	1	Ugljan	Hrvatski Katolicki R.

FM	MHz	kW	Location	Station
27)	95.6	2	Donja Stubica	R. Stubica
21)	96.1	1	Zagreb	R. Marija
52)	96.5	1	Rijeka	Primorski R.
4)	96.5	1	Varazdin Breg	R. 042
17)	96.9	5	Ucka	R. Istra
20)	97.6	4	Bogomolje	R. Makarska Rivijera (RMR)
3)	97.9	1	Split	Hrvatski Katolicki R.
51)	98.0	5	Zagreb	Plavi R.
17)	98.0	5	Pula	R. Istra
43)	98.1	1	Nova Gradiska	Hrvatski R. Nova Gradiska
36)	98.4	1	Rijeka	Svid R.
3)	98.6	1	Osijek	Hrvatski Katolicki R.
19)	98.5	5	Zabno	R. Koprivnica (RKC)
15)	99.1	2	Bijele Vode	R. Banovina
40)	99.1	1	Osijek	Gradski R. Osijek
33)	99.5	1	Zapresic	Hrvatski R.
41)	99.5	1	Sveta Marija	Hrvatski R. Cakovec
39)	100.1	5	Moslavacka Gora	Bjelovarsko-Bilogorski R. (BBR)
14)	100.2	1	Djakovo	R. Djakovo
35)	100.6	1	Osijek	Slavonski R.
38)	100.7	3	Zirje	R. Šibenik
46)	101.0	120	Sljeme	R. 101
1)	101.2	3	Metkovic	Narodni R.
10)	101.3	1	Slavonski Brod	R. Brod
19)	101.5	5	Sedlarica	R. Koprivnica (RKC)
22)	101.5	5	Zagreb	R. Martin
37)	102.4	2	Pakrac	R. Pozega
9)	102.7	1	Brac	R. Brac
3)	103.5	120	Sljeme	Hrvatski Katolicki R.
3)	103.9	3	Psunj	Hrvatski Katolicki R.
6)	104.0	1	Sveti Martin	R. 105
3)	104.1	1	Licka Plješivica	Hrvatski Katolicki R.
45)	104.1	1	Zupanja	Hrvatski R. Vukovar
2)	104.4	5	Papuk	Otvoreni R.
12)	104.5	1.85	Zagreb	Hit FM
38)	104.9	3	Šibenik	R. Šibenik
8)	105.5	1	Okucani	R. Bljesak
5)	105.6	1.5	Cakovec	R. 1
16)	105.7	1.5	Stipanov Gric	R. Gospic
35)	106.2	50	Beli Manastir	Slavonski R.
2)	106.5	3	Vidova Gora	Otvoreni R.
3)	106.7	3	Ucka	Hrvatski Katolicki R.
21)	106.8	1	Zagreb	R. Marija
27)	106.9	2	Ostri Hum	R. Stubica
13)	106.9	4	Labinstica	R. Dalmacija
29)	107.1	4	Varazdin Breg	R. Varazdin
2)	107.3	80	Celevac	Otvoreni R.
45)	107.2	5	Vinkovci	Hrvatski R. Vukovar
3)	107.9	80	Biokovo	Hrvatski Katolicki R.

NB: Txs below 1kW not listed.
Addresses & other information:
1) Avenija Veceslava Holjevca 29, 10000 Zagreb. **E:** redakcija@narodni.hr – **2)** Cebini 28/III, 10000 Zagreb. **E:** otvoreni@otvoreni.hr – **3)** Vocarska c. 106, 10000 Zagreb. **E:** hkr@hkr.hr – **4)** Trstenjakova 3, 42000 Varazdin. **E:** radio-042@vz.tel.hr – **5)** Trg Republike 6, 40000 Cakovec. **E:** info@radio1.hr – **6)** B. Radica 23, 40314 Selnica. **E:** info@radio105.hr – **7)** Trg slobode 32/III, 31300 Beli Manastir. **E:** radio@radio-baranja.hr – **8)** Blazenog kardinala A. Stepinca 24, 35430 Okucani. **E:** radio-bljesak@sb.t-com.hr – **9)** Mladena Vodanovica 3, 21400 Supetar. **E:** radiobrac@st.t-com.hr – **10)** Dr. Mile Budaka 1, 35000 Slavonski Brod. **E:** radio-brod@sb.t-com.hr – **11)** Vitomira Širole Paje 18, 52440 Porec. **E:** rcsp1@pu.t-com.hr – **12)** Palmoticeva 7/I, 10000 Zagreb. **E:** program@hitfm.hr – **13)** Kralja Zvonimira 14/2, 21000 Split. **E:** marketing@radiodalmacija.hr – **14)** Pape Ivana Pavle II 9, 31400 Djakovo. **E:** marketing@radio-djakovo.hr – **15)** Slatina Pokupska 80, 44400 Glina. **E:** direktor@radio-banovina.hr – **16)** Budacka 12, 53000 Gospic. **E:** radiogospic1@gs.t-com.hr – **17)** Jurja Dobrile 6, 52000 Pazin. **E:** radioistra@radioistra.hr – **18)** Trg Strossmayerov 5, 10450 Jastrebarsko. **E:** info@radio-jaska.hr – **19)** Zagrebacka b.b., 48000 Koprivnica. **E:** marketing@radio-koprivnica.hr – **20)** Don Mihovila Pavlinovica 1, 21300 Makarska. **E:** radio-makarska-rivijera@st.t-com.hr – **21)** Jordanovac 110, 10000 Zagreb. **E:** info@radiomarija.hr – **22)** Josipa Zorica 17, 10370 Dugo Selo. **E:** info@radio-martin.hr – **23)** Jozefinska c. 8, 47250 Duga Resa. **E:** marketing@mreznica.hr – **24)** Zagrebacka 12a, 52210 Rovinj. **E:** marketing@gradskiradio.net – **25)** Stjepana i Antuna Radica 2, 44000 Sisak. **E:** radio.sisak@radiosisak.hr – **26)** Mile budaka 1, 35 000 Slavonski Brod. **E:** marketing@radioslavonija.hr – **27)** Toplicka 5, 49240 Donja Stubica. **E:** radio-stubica@radio-stubica.hr – **28)** Cehovska 8/I, 34000 Pozega. **E:** rva@rva.hr – **29)** P. Preradovica 4, 42000 Varazdin. **E:** info@radio-varazdin.hr – **30)** Zagrebacka 3, 10410 Velika Gorica. **E:** rvg@rvg.hr – **31)** Trg Hansa Dietricha Genschera 2, 32100 Vinkovci. **E:** vfm@vfm.hr – **32)** F. Rusana 1/9, 33000 Virovitica. **E:** icv@icv.hr – **33)** Trg zrtava fašizma 6, 10290 Zapresic. **E:** info@radio-zapresic.

hr – **34)** Jurja Dalmatinca 29, 32100 Vinkovci. **E:** radio-vinkovci@vk.t-com.hr – **35)** Hrvatske Republike 20, 31000 Osijek. **E:** slavonski-radio@glas-slavonije.t-com.hr – **36)** Trpimirova 2, 51000 Rijeka. **E:** svid-radio@hi.t-com.hr – **37)** Matice Hrvatske 5/2, 34000 Pozega. **E:** direktor@radio-pozega.hr – **38)** Bozidara Petranovica 3, 22000 Šibenik. **E:** info@radiosibenik.hr – **39)** Trg E. Kvaternika 7a, 43000 Bjelovar. **E:** bbr@bbr.hr – **40)** Trg Ante Starcevica 7/1, 31000 Osijek. **E:** marketing@gradskiradio.hr – **41)** Trg republike 5, 40000 Cakovec. **E:** info@radio-cakovec.hr – **42)** Ambroza Vraniczanya 2, 47000 Karlovac. **E:** redakcija@hrk.hr – **43)** Gunduliceva 7, 35400 Nova Gradiška. **E:** info@radiong.hr – **44)** Glavicka 29, 21230 Sinj. **E:** hitradio@hitradio.hr – **45)** Dr. Franje Tudjmana 13, 32000 Vukovar. **E:** hrv@hrv.hr – **46)** Gajeva 10, 10000 Zagreb. **E:** marketing101@radio101.hr – **47)** Šime Ljubica 30, 21000 Split. **E:** megamix@st.t-com.hr – **48)** V. Nazora 19, 21480 Vis. **E:** nautic-radio@st.t-com.hr – **49)** Zrinsko Frankopanska 13, 23000 Zadar. **E:** marketing@noviradio.hr – **50)** Avenija Veceslava Holjevca 29, 10000 Zagreb. **E:** antena@antenazagreb.hr – **51)** Slavonska avenija 2, 10000 Zagreb. **E:** marketing@plaviradio.hr – **52)** E. Barcica 4a, 51000 Rijeka. **E:** marketing@primorski.hr. – **53)** Kralja P. Krešimira IV 1, 31550 Valpovo. **E:** hrv89@hrv89.hr.

DAB (Trial): Sljeme ch12C (227.360MHz) 0.8kW. **Operator:** OIV

CUBA

L.T: UTC -5h (7 Apr 10 Nov: -4h; subject to change); Guantánamo Bay: UTC -5h (10 Mar-3 Nov: -4h) — **Pop:** 11.4 million — **Pr. L:** Spanish — **E.C:** 60Hz, 110/120V — **ITU:** CUB

MINISTERIO DE COMUNICACIONES (MC)
Dirección General de Telecomunicaciones
✉ Plaza de la Revolución, Ciudad de la Habana

INSTITUTO CUBANO DE RADIO Y TELEVISION (ICRT)
✉ Edif.Radiocentro, Av. 23 N° 250, Vedado, Habana 4 ☎ +53 7 8324648. Radio Cubana has links to most national and local stns **W:** www.radiocubana.cu
Hrs of tr. usually 24h – see address section for variations. Call CM—

MW	Call	kHz	kW	Primary network, location
N1)	BA	530	1	R. Rebelde, Guantánamo, GU
N5)	BQ	530	10	R. Enciclopedia, HA
N1)	BA	540	10	R. Rebelde, Maisí, GU
N1)	BA	540	1	R. Rebelde, Sancti Spíritus, SS
N1)	BA	550	12	R. Rebelde, Pinar del Río, PR
N1)	BA	560	10	R. Rebelde, Ciego de Avila, CA
N1)	RA	570	1	R. Rebelde, Pilón, GR
N2)	BD	570	25	R. Reloj, Santa Clara, VC
N1)	BA	580	2.5	R. Rebelde, Mabujabo, GU
N1)	BA	590	10	R. Rebelde, Guantánamo, GU
N3)	BF	590	25	R. Musical Nacional, La Julia, MB
N1)	BA	600	50	R. Rebelde, San Germán, HO
N4)	BC	600	5	R. Progreso, Santiago de Cuba, SC
N1)	BA	610	1	R. Rebelde, Cienfuegos, CI
N1)	BA	610	10	R. Rebelde, Bueycito, GR
N1)	BA	610	10	R. Rebelde, Guane, PR
N2)	BD	610	1	R. Reloj, Trinidad, SS
N1)	BA	620	25	R. Rebelde, Colón, MA
N4)	BC	630	5	R. Progreso, Camagüey, CM
N4)	BC	640	50	R. Progreso, Guanabacoa, CH
N4)	BC	640	10	R. Progreso, Las Tunas, LT
N4)	BC	650	10	R. Progreso, Ciego de Avila, CA
N1)	BA	650	5	R. Rebelde, Stgo de Cuba, SC
N4)	BC	660	12	R. Progreso, Jovellanos, MA
N1)	BA	670	10	R. Rebelde, C. Brasil, CM
N1)	BA	670	10	R. Rebelde, Camagüey, CM
N1)	BA	670	10	R. Rebelde, Arroyo Arenas, CH
N1)	BA	670	5	R. Rebelde, Ciego de Avila, CA
N1)	BA	670	10	R. Rebelde, El Coco, HO
N1)	BA	670	10	R. Rebelde, Victoria de LT, LT
N5)	BQ	670	1	R. Enciclopedia, Cárdenas, MA
N1)	BA	670	5	R. Rebelde, Circunvalación, MA
N1)	BA	670	5	R. Rebelde, Bahía Honda, PR
N1)	BA	670	1	R. Rebelde, Los Palacios, PR
N1)	BA	670	1	R. Rebelde, Pinar del Río, PR
N1)	BA	670	1	R. Rebelde, Santa Lucía, PR
N1)	BA	670	50	R. Rebelde, Santa Clara, VC
N4)	BC	690		R. Progreso, MA
N4)	BC	690	10	R. Progreso, Santa Clara, VC
N1)	BA	710	25	R. Rebelde, Camagüey, CM
N1)	BA	710	200	R. Rebelde, Chambas, CA
N1)	BA	710	50	R. Rebelde, Cacocúm, HO
N1)	BA	710	50	R. Rebelde, Martí, MA
N1)	BA	710	50	R. Rebelde, La Julia, MB
PR01)	AM	710	10	R. Guamá, La Palma, PR

MW	Call	kHz	kW	Primary network, location
N1)	BA	710	1	R. Rebelde, Yaguajay, SS
N1)	BA	710	50	R. Rebelde, Santa Clara, VC
N1)	BC	720	2.5	R. Progreso, Mabujabo, GU
N4)	BC	730	10	R. Progreso, La Fe, IJ
HO01)	KO	740	10	R. Angulo, Sagua de Tanamo, HO
N4)	BC	750	10	R. Progreso, Palmira, CI
N4)	BC	760	10	R. Progreso, Guane, PR
N4)	BC	760		R. Progreso, Mayarí Arriba, SC
N1)	BA	770	10	R. Rebelde, Victoria de LT, LT
N2)	BD	790	10	R. Reloj, Holguín, HO
N2)	BD	790	25	R. Reloj, Pinar del Río, PR
N4)	BC	810	10	R. Progreso, Guantánamo, GU
N4)	BC	820	10	R. Progreso, Ciego de Avila, CA
CH01)	BE	820	10	R. Ciudad de la Habana, Arroyo Arenas, CH
N4)	BC	820	10	R. Progreso, Ciego de Avila, CA
N4)	BC	820	1	R. Progreso, Moa, HO
SC01)	KC	840	1	R. Revolución, Palma Soriano, SC
VC01)	HW	840	10	CMHW, Santa Clara, VC
N2)	BD	850	1	R. Reloj, Nueva Gerona, IJ
N4)	BC	850	1	R. Progreso, Trinidad, SS
N2)	BD	860	5	R. Reloj, Jovellanos, MA
N2)	BD	870	10	R. Reloj, Bueycito, GR
N2)	BD	870	10	R. Reloj, Baracoa, GU
N2)	BD	870	1	R. Reloj, Sancti Spíritus, SS
N4)	BC	880	12	R. Progreso, Mantua, PR
N2)	BD	880		R. Reloj, Mayarí Arriba, SC
N4)	BC	890	200	R. Progreso, Chambas, CA
SC01)	KC	890		R. Revolución, Santiago de Cuba, SC
N4)	BC	900	50	R. Progreso, San Germán, HO
CM01)	HA	910	25	R. Cadena Agramonte, Camagüey, CM
CH02)	BL	910	5	R. Metropolitana, V. María, CH
N2)	BD	910	5	R. Reloj, Bolondron, MA
N4)	BC	920	1	R. Progreso, Pilón, GR
CA01)	IP	930	10	R. Surco, Ciego de Avila, CA
N2)	BD	930	1	R. Reloj, Cienfuegos, CI
N2)	BD	930	1	R. Reloj, La Jaiba, MA
N2)	BD	930	1	R. Reloj, Stgo de Cuba, SC
N4)	BC	940	1	R. Progreso, Sancti Spíritus, SS
N2)	BD	950	10	R. Reloj, Camagüey, CM
N2)	BD	950	10	R. Reloj, Arroyo Arenas, HA
SC01)	KC	950	1	R. R. Revolución, Mayarí Arriba, SC
N2)	BD	960	10	R. Reloj, Guantánamo, GU
PR01)	AM	970	5	R. Guamá, Los Palacios, PR
N1)	BA	970	1	R. Rebelde, Trinidad, SS
CH03)	B	980	2.5	R. COCO, L. Cruz, CH
N2)	BD	980	1	R. Reloj, Moa, HO
PR01)	AM	990	25	R. Guamá, Pinar del Río, PR
AR01)	SW	1000	1	R. Artemisa, Artemisa, AR
GR02)	NM	1000	5	R. Granma, Media Luna, GR
PR01)	AM	1000	25	R. Guamá, Pinjar del Río, PR
AR01)	AM	1020		R. Artemisa, AR
GU01)	M	1020	10	Cadena CMKS, Baracoa, GU
N2)	BD	1020	10	R. Reloj, Victoria de LT, LT
PR01)	AM	1020	10	R. Guamá, Bahía Honda, PR
MB01)	CL	1040	10	R. Mayabeque, Güines, MB
LT01)	LL	1050	10	R. Victoria, Victoria de LT, LT
PR01)	AM	1050	1	R. Guamá, Santa Lucía, PR
MA01)	DL	1060	25	R. 26, Jovellanos, MA
GU01)	M	1070	10	Cadena CMKS, Guantánamo, GU
PR01)	AM	1070	10	R. Guamá, Guane, PR
HA01)	DY	1080	5	R. Cadena Habana, V. María, CH
LT01)	LL	1090	1	R. Victoria, Amancio, LT
HO01)	KO	1100	1	R. Angulo, Mayarí, HO
HO01)	KO	1110	10	R. Angulo, Holguín, HO
GR01)	NL	1140	1	R. Bayamo, Media Luna, GR
MA02)	DP	1140	1	R. Ciudad Bandera, Cárdenas, MA
MB01)	CL	1140	25	R. Mayabeque, La Salud, MB
N1)	BA	1140	10	R. Rebelde, Aguada, CI
N1)	BA	1140	5	R. Rebelde, Circunvalación, MA
N1)	BA	1140	25	R. Rebelde, Morón, LT
N3)	BF	1140	10	R. Musical Nacional, Santa Clara, VC
N5)	BQ	1140	1	R. Enciclopedia, Camagüey, CM
GR01)	NL	1150	10	R. Bayamo, Entronque Bueycito, GR
GR01)	NL	1160	5	R. Bayamo, Pilón, GR
GU01)	M	1170	10	Cadena CMKS, Maisí, GU
N1)	BA	1180	10	R. Rebelde, Artemisa, AR
N1)	BA	1180	10	R. Rebelde, C. Brasil, CM
N1)	BA	1180	50	R. Rebelde, Camagüey, CM
N1)	BA	1180	50	R. Rebelde, Arroyo Arenas, CH
N1)	BA	1180	50	R. Rebelde, Guanabacoa, CH
N1)	BA	1180	1	R. Rebelde, Ciego de Avila, CA
N1)	BA	1180	50	R. Rebelde, Chambas, CA
N1)	BA	1180	1	R. Rebelde, Cienfuegos, CI
N1)	BA	1180	5	R. Rebelde, Tulipán, CI
N1)	BA	1180	1	R. Rebelde, Guantánamo, GU

MW	Call	kHz	kW	Primary network, location
N1)	BA	1180	1	R. Rebelde, Mabujabo, GU
N1)	BA	1180	1	R. Rebelde, Banes, HO
N1)	BA	1180	50	R. Rebelde, Cacocúm, HO
N1)	BA	1180	1	R. Rebelde, Moa, HO
N1)	BA	1180	5	R. Rebelde, Sagua de Tánamo, HO
N1)	BA	1180	5	R. Rebelde, Nueva Gerona, IJ
N1)	BA	1180	1	R. Rebelde, Puerto Padre, LT
N1)	BA	1180	10	R. Rebelde, Victoria de LT, LT
N1)	BA	1180	5	R. Rebelde, Cárdenas, MA
N1)	BA	1180	25	R. Rebelde, Colón, MA
N1)	BA	1180	5	R. Rebelde, Ja Jaiba, MA
N1)	BA	1180	200	R. Rebelde, Martí, MA
N1)	BA	1180	10	R. Rebelde, Güines, MB
N1)	BA	1180	10	R. Rebelde, Sta Cruz del Norte, MB
N1)	BA	1180	5	R. Rebelde, Bahía Honda, PR
N1)	BA	1180	10	R. Rebelde, La Palma, PR
N1)	BA	1180	10	R. Rebelde, Los Palacios, PR
N1)	BA	1180	10	R. Rebelde, Pinar del Río, PR
N1)	BA	1180	1	R. Rebelde, San Cristóbal, PR
N1)	BA	1180	1	R. Rebelde, Santa Lucía, PR
N1)	BA	1180	1	R. Rebelde, Sancti Spíritus, SS
N1)	BA	1180	1	R. Rebelde, Mayarí Arriba, SC
N1)	BA	1180	10	R. Rebelde, Sagua la Grande, VC
N1)	BA	1180	10	R. Rebelde, Santa Clara, VC
SC04)	JD	1190	10	R. Coral/R. Revolución, Chivirico, SC
SS01)	GL	1190	1	R. Sancti Spíritus, Trinidad, SS
SS01)	GL	1200	1	R. Sancti Spíritus, Yaguajay, SS
IJ01)	BY	1220		R. Caribe, IJ
SS01)	GL	1210	10	R. Sancti Spíritus, Sancti Spíritus, SS
IJ01)	BY	1220	10	R. Caribe, La Fe, IJ
N4)	BC	1250	1	R. Progreso, La Palma, PR
GU01)	M	1250	1	Cadena CMKS, Imías, GU
N4)	BC	1260	2.5	R. Progreso, Media Luna, GR
N5)	BQ	1280	1	R. Enciclopedia, Varadero, MA
SC03)	KW	1280	1	R. Mambí, Stgo de Cuba, SC
SS02)		1280	10	R. Trinidad Digital, Sancti Spíritus, SS
HO01)	KO	1300	1	R. Angulo, Banes, HO
N5)	BQ	1310	1	R. Enciclopedia, Nueva Gerona, IJ
AR01)	CW	1320	1	R. Artemisa, Artemisa, AR
MA01)	DL	1320	1	R. 26, La Jaiba, MA
CI01)	FL	1340	10	R. Ciudad del Mar, Palmira, CI
CI01)	FL	1350	10	R. Ciudad del Mar, Aguada, CI
LT03)	LM	1350	1	R. Libertad, Puerto Padre, LT (rel. CMLL R. Victoria 0300-1200) Cfr. 1470
VC02)		1400	1	R. Sagua, Sagua la Grande, VC
LT02)	LN	1450	1	R. Maboas, Amancio Rodríguez, LT
MB01)	CL	1450	1	R. Mayabeque, Mayabeque, MB
LT03)	LM	1470	1	R. Libertad, Puerto Padre, LT (rel. R. Chaparra 1100-1600, R. Victoria 0200-1100) Cfr. 1350
HO03)	KN	1490	1	R. Mayarí, Mayarí, HO
N1)	BA	1550	5	R. Rebelde, Tulipán, CI
N1)	BA	1550	1	R. Rebelde, Guantánamo, GU
N1)	BA	1550	5	R. Rebelde, Cárdenas, MA
N1)	BA	1550	5	R. Rebelde, Circunvalación, MA
N1)	BA	1550	1	R. Rebelde, Yaguajay, SS
N1)	BA	1550	1	R. Rebelde, Sagua la Grande, VC
N1)	BA	1550	10	R. Rebelde, Santa Clara, VC
N1)	BA	1620	5	R. Rebelde, Guanabacoa, CH
N1)	BA	1620	1	R. Rebelde, Guantánamo, GU
GR01)	NL	1620		R. Bayamo, Bayamo GR

SW	Call	kHz	kW	Primary network, location
N1)	BA	5025	50	R. Rebelde, Bauta, AR

Provinces: AR=Artemisa CA=Ciego de Avila CH=Ciudad Habana CI=Cienfuegos CM=Camagüey GR=Granma GU=Guantánamo HA=Habana HO=Holguín IJ=Isla de laJuventud LT=Las Tunas MA=Matanzas MB=Mayabeque PR=Pinar del Río SC=Santiago de Cuba SS=Sancti Spíritus VC=Villa Clara

N.B.: Some stns rel. different netw. at different times of day, especially the three major netw.; Progreso, Rebelde and Reloj. R. Rebelde carries sports events which are rel. by many stns. National stns operate 24h.

FM in La Habana (MHz): 90.3 R. Progreso – 91.7 CMCK R. COCO – 93.3 R. Taíno – 94.1 R. Enciclopedia – 94.9 R.Ciudad de la Habana – 96.7 R. Rebelde – 98.3 Metropolitana – 99.1 R. Musical Nacional – 99.9 R. Cadena Habana – 100.9 Habana FM –101.5 R. Reloj – 104.7 R. Rebelde – 106.3 R. Progreso – 106.9 Habana R – 107.9 R. Rebelde.

National networks: N1) R. Rebelde, Ap. 6277, La Habana 10600 (or: Edif. Del ICRT, Av. 23 N° 258, Vedado, La Habana 10400) **W:** www. radiorebelde.cu – **N2)** R. Reloj, Ap. 6277, Ciudad de la Habana (or Ed. Radiocentro, Calle 23 No. 258, (8avo piso), entre Ly M, Vedado, La Habana 10400 **W:** www.radioreloj.cu – **N3)** R. Musical Nacional, Edificio N, Calle N, entre 23 y 21, Vedado La Habana 10400 **W:** www.cmbradio.

cu – **N4)** R. Progreso, Ap. 4042, La Habana 10300 (or Infanta 105, Esq. A 25, Centro Habnana) **W:** www.radioprogreso.cu – **N5)** R. Enciclopedia, Edificio N, Calle N, N° 266 (bajos), entre 21 y 23, Vedado, La Habana 10400 **W:** www.radioenciclopedia.cu – **N6)** R. Taíno, Ap. 6277, La Habana 10400 (or Av. 23 N° 258, Vedado, La Habana 10400) - FM only

Provincial and municipal stations
Artemisa AR01) Calle 50 No. 2310, entre 23 y 25, Artemisa 33800 **W:** www.artemisaradioweb.cu
Ciego de Ávila CA01) Ap. 183 (or Chicho Valdés 66), Ciego de Ávila 65100 **W:** www.radiosurco.cu
Ciudad de La Habana CH01) Ap. 6599, La Habana 10600 (or Calle N No. 266 (5to piso), entre 21 y 23, Vedadado, Plaza de la Revolución, La Habana 10400 **W:** www.habanaenlinea.cu **CH02)** Ed. Focsa, Calle N No. 301 (1er piso), esq. A 17, Vedado, Plaza de la Revolución, La Habana 10400 **W:** www.radiometropolitana.cu **CH03)** Ed. Focsa, Calle N No. 301, esq. A 17, Vedado, Plaza de la Revolución, La Habana 10400 **W:** www.radiococo.icrt.cu
Cienfuegos CI01) Calle 37 No. 3602, entre 36 y 38, Cienfuegos 55100 **W:** www.rcm.cu
Camagüey CM01) Calle Cisneros # 310 entre Ignacio Agramonte y General Gómez, Camagüey 70100 **W:** www.cadenagramonte.cu **CM02)** Same address as CM01.
Granma GR01) Ap. 74 (or Calle General Calixto García 156, entre Figueredo y Luz Vásquez 74) Bayamo 85100 **W:** www.radiobayamo. icrt.cu **GR02)** Ap. 220 (or Calle Martí 341, entre Quintin Banderas y León), Manzanillo 87510 **W:** www.radiogranma.co.cu
Guantánamo GU01) Ap. 96 (or Donato Mármol 409, entre José Martí y Pedro A. Pérez), Guantánamo 95100 **W:** www.radioguantanamo.cu **GU02)** Calle B No. 2050, Imías 97500. **GU03)** LV del Toa (CMDX), Martí 122, Baracoa 97310 H of tr: 1000-0200 **W:** www.radiobaracoa.icrt.cu
La Habana HA01) Calle 15, esq. a J, No. 210, Vedado, Plaza de la Revolución, La Habana 10400 **W:** www.cadenahabana.cu
Holguín HO01) Ap. 14 (or Calle Máximo Gómez 298 (3er piso) entre Frexes y Martí), Holguín 80100 **W:** www.radioangulo.cu **HO03)** Calle Martí 46, Mayarí 83000. **HO04)** Calle 9na s/no, Reparto Rolo Monterrey, Moa 83330. **HO05)** Sagua de Tánamo 83200.
Isla de la Juventud IJ01) Calle 26, entre 41 y 43, Nueva Gerona 25100 **W:** www.radiocaribe.icrt.cu
Las Tunas LT01) Ap. 211 (or Calle Colón 157, entre Julián Santana y Francisco Vega), Las Tunas 75100 **W:** www.tiempo21.cu **LT02)** Avenida Sergio Reynó 19, Amancio Rodríguez 77700 **W:** www.radi-omaboas.cu **LT03)** Ap. 45 (or Avenida de La Libertad 95), Puerto Padre 77200 **W:** www.radiolibertad.cu
Matanzas MA01) Ap. 51 (or Milanés final, esq. a Guachinango), Matanzas 40100 **W:** www.radio26.icrt.cu **MA02)** Calzada, esq. a Calvo, Cárdenas 42100
Matabeque MB01) Calle 76 No. 7707, entre 77 y 81, Güines 33900. 1000-0400 **W:** www.radioguines.icrt.cu
Pinar del Río PR01) Calle Colón 14, entre Adela Azcuy y Juan Gualberto Gómez, Pinar del Río 20100 **W:** www.rguama.icrt.cu
Santiago de Cuba SC01) Ap. 232 (or Aguilera 554, entre San Augustín y Barnada), Santiago de Cuba 90100 **W:** www.cmkc.cu **SC03)** Calle 8 No. 56, entre A e Independencia, Reparto Sueño, Santiago de Cuba 90900 **W:** www.radiomambi.icrt.cu. **SC04)** R. Coral, Calle C No. 64, Chivirico, Guamá 92800
Sancti Spíritus SS01) Circunvalación s/n, Los Olivos 1, Sancti Spíritus 60100. **W:** radiosanctispiritus.cu – **SS02)** Antonio Guiteras #226, Trinidad. **W:** radiotrinidad.cu
Villa Clara VC01) Ap. 376 (or Parque Leoncio Vidal 4, entre Martha Abreu y Pao Chao), Santa Clara 50100 **W:** www.cmhw.cu **VC02)** Libertadores 100, esq. a Carmen Ribalta, Sagua la grande, Villa Clara 52310 **W:** www.radiosagua.icrt.cu

Guantánamo Bay (leased to USA)

AFRTS (US Navy)
✉ Naval Media Center Broadcasting Detatchment, Guantánamo Bay, Cuba, PSC 1005, Box 22, FPO AE 09593, USA **E:** gitmo@mediacen. navy.mil
MW: Guantánamo Bay: 1340kHz 0.25kW
FM: 102.1MHz 0.5kW (stereo), 103.1MHz 0.5kW – D.Prgr: 24h on 1340kHz/102.1MHz. Rel AFRTS satellite sce on 103.1MHz

CURAÇAO (Netherlands)

L.T: UTC -4h — **Pop:** 133,600 — **Pr.L:** Dutch (official), Papiamentu, English, Spanish — **E.C:** 50Hz, 127/220V — **ITU:** CUW

Bureau Telecommunicatie en Post
✉ Beatrixlaan 9, Emmastad; P.O. Box 2047, Curaçao ☎ +599 9 463 1700 🖷 +599 9 736 5265 **W:** www.btnp.org **E:** gen.affairs@burtel.an

MW Call	kHz	kW	Station, location
1) PJZ-86	860	10	R. Curom, Willemstad

FM	MHz	kW	Station, location
1)	88.3		Rockorsou, Willemstad
18)	88.9		R. Vishon, Willemstad
12)	90.1		R. Krioyo, Willemstad
5)	91.5		Gold 91.5 , Willemstad
11)	92.1		Direct Life 92.1 FM, Willemstad
9)	92.7		R. Edukativo, Deltha 92, Willemstad
17)	93.3		R. Top FM, Willemstad
20)	93.3	0.5	Telecuracao FM, Willemstad
3)	93.9	20	R. Korsou FM, Willemstad
19)	94.5		Voz di Bonaire, Willemstad
8)	95.1	0.5	Clazz FM, Willemstad
1)	95.7	4	ZFM, Willemstad
13)	96.5	0.5	New Song, Willemstad
10)	97.3	1	Dolfijn FM, Willemstad
8)	97.9	0.5	Easy 97.9 FM, Willemstad
4)	98.5	2.5	R. Semiya, Willemstad
15)	99.7		R. MAS, Santa. Maria
7)	100.3		Hit 100.3, Willemstad
3)	101.1	5	Laser 101, Willemstad
2)	101.9	5	R. Hoyer 1, Willemstad
5)	103.1		Paradise FM, Willemstad
8)	103.9	0.5	R. One FM, Willemstad
14)	104.5	1	R. Active FM / Prime, Willemstad
2)	105.1	5	R. Hoyer 2, Willemstad
16)	106.3		Fiesta FM, Willemstad
11)	107.1		R. Direct, Willemstad
6)	107.9	1	Rumbera Network, Willemstad

Addresses and other information

1) Roodeweg 64, Willemstad, Curaçao ☎ +599 9 462 2020 📠 +599 9 462 5796. E: mi95@curom.com, z86@curom.com, 88rockorsou@curom.com W: www.curom.com www.rockorsou.fm – 2) Plasa Horacio Hoyer 21, Willemstad, Curaçao ☎ +599 9 461 1678 📠 +599 9 461 6528 E: sales@radiohoyer.com W: www.radiohoyer.com MD: Ms. Helen Hoyer. W, Sun: 1000-0400. R. Hoyer 1 in Papiamentu, R. Hoyer 2 in Dutch – 3) Bataljonweg 7, Willemstad, Curaçao ☎ +599 9 737 3012 📠 +599 9 737 2888. Dir Hans Oosterhof. PD: Alan H. Evertsz. 24h. N. in Dutch: 1000, 2300. N. in Papiamentu: 2200. English: Tues 0000. Portuguese: Wed 2330. Sranan Tongo: Fri 0000. Rel. Radio Nederland Wereldomroep at 09.30 W: www.korsou.com E: studio@korsou.com Separate prgrs ("Laser 101") on 101.1MHz E: studio@laser101.com – 4) Parmantiersweg 2, Willemstad, Curaçao ☎ +599 9 462 4002 📠 +599 9 462 4004. Dir: Ferris Thode. Rlg 24h programs in English and Papiamentu E: info@radiosemiyafm.net W: www.radiosemiyafm.net – 5) Carawaraweg 88, Willemstad ☎ +599 9 736 9564 📠 +599 9 461 9103 W: www. paradisefm.an www.gold915.com E: info@paradisefm. an Paradise FM: Dutch with every h and half h Dutch news. Gold 915: English non-stop The Golden Hits and English news; Owner: Cees Baas – 6) Caracasbaaiweg 194, Willemstad ☎ +599 9 465 9580 📠 +599 9 461 5028 W: www.rumberanetwork.org E: contacto@rumberanetwork.com.ve – 7) Compleho Deportivo Casa Grandi Z/N Willemstad ☎ +599 9 747 3333 📠 +599 9 747 7265. Manager: Elmer Cijntje. 24h Prgrs in Papiamentu, Spanish, Creole and English E: hit100.3fm@cura.net – 8) Arikokweg 19A, Willemstad ☎ +599 9 462 3162 and +599 9 462 2664 📠 +599 9 462 8712. GM: Quintus Fliervoet ClazzFM E: info@clazzfm. com W: www.clazzfm.com 24h light music & jazz in E, Papiamentu & Dutch, R. One FM E: info@radioone.net W: www.radioone.nl 24h dance & Top 40 music in E, & Dutch. Easy FM: www.easyfm.com E: radio@easyfm.com – 9) Suffisantweg 16, Willemstad ☎ +599 9 888 5260 +599 9 888 0155 – 10) Sea Aquarium Beach, Bapor Kibra z/n, Willemstad ☎ +599 9 465 9975 📠 599 9 461 9975 Dir. Enrico Stenacker and Egon Sybrandy DPr. 24 hoursin Dutch E: info@dolfijnfm.com W: www.dolfijnfm.com – 11) F.D Rooseveltweg 214, Tesoro Shopping Center, Willemstad Dir. Mrs. Jachmin Pinedo R. Direct: in Papiamentu and Spanish 1000-0400, other times music ☎ +599 9 888 5107 📠 +599 9 888 8407 E: studio@direct107.com W: www.direct107. com Direct Life 92.1FM in Papiamentu and Dutch 1040-1300 and 1800-2400 , other times music ☎+599 9 888 8092 📠 +599 9 888 8407 E: studio@direct107.com W: www.direct107.com – 12) Gosiewveg 133,Willemstad ☎ +599 9 736 4915 📠 +599 9 736 4914 E: radiokrioyo@live.com W: www.radiokrioyofm.com – 13) New Song Building, Muizenberg z/n ☎ +599 9 888 0965 and +599 9 888 3232 📠 +599 9 888 0561 Dir. Welton F.A. Esprit ; Proj. Man.: Johnny Angelica, Christian prgrs in English, French, Papiamentu, Dutch, Spanish, Sranang Tongo, Creole and English , news 1400-1600 hours E: info@newsong-curacao. com and rtns@newsong-curacao.com W: www.newsongcuracao. com – 14) Kaya Simon Pieters Kwiers 67, Willemstad, Curaçao ☎ +599 9 869 4109 📠 +599 9 868 4109 Dir. Arthur Zimmerman 24h inPapiamentu W: www.active.fm E: info@active.fm – 15) Fosfaatweg 8, Sta. Maria ☎+599 9 888 3997 📠 +599 9 888 6997 – 16) Fatimaweg 2, Suffisant,

Willemstad ☎+599 9 869 6606 📠 +599 9 869 6613 Dir. Carlos S. de Abreu Ribeiro E: fiesta@fiesta.fm W: www.fiesta.fm – 17) F.D. Rooseveltweg 32-w ☎+599 9 888 7933 – 18) Flamingo Broadcasting Network N, World Trade Center, Willemstad ☎+599 9 463 6111 📠 +599 9 462 4482 – 19) Radiodifushon Boneriano NV, Kaya Gob. N. Debrot 2, Kralendijk, Bonaire ☎+599 717 5947 📠 +599 717 8220 W: www.vozdibonaire.com E: vozdibonaire@gmail.com – 20) Berg Arafat z/n, Willemstad , GMr Hugo Lew Jen Tai ☎+599 9 777 1688 📠 +599 9 461 4138 W: www.telecuracao.com E: 93.3@telecuracao.fm

L.T: UTC +2h (31 Mar-27 Oct: +3h) — Pop: 800,000 — Pr.L: Greek, Turkish, Armenian — E.C: 50Hz, 240V — ITU: CYP

CYPRUS RADIO-TELEVISION AUTHORITY
📧 32 Nikis Ave, P.O.Box 23377, 1682 Nicosia ☎+357 22 512468 📠 F+357 22 512473 W: www.crta.org.cy E: crtauthority@cytanet.com.cy

CYPRUS BROADCASTING CORPORATION (semi-gov)
📧 CyBC Street, Athalassa, P.O. Box 24824, CY-1397 Nicosia ☎+357 22 862000 📠 +357 22 314050 W: www.cybc.com.cy E: rik@cybc.com. cy L.P: DG: Themis Themistocleous. Deputy DG: Michael Stylianou.

MW	kHz	kW	Ch.	MW	kHz	kW	Ch.
Paphos	558	10	1	Paphos	918	10	3
Nicosia	603	100	3	Nicosia	963	100	1
Limassol	693	10	1	Limassol	1044	10	3

FM (MHz)	Ch. 1	Ch. 2	Ch. 3	Ch.4	kW
Larnaca	90.2	92.4	96.0		7
Mt. Olympos	97.2	91.1	94.8	88.2	30
Paphos	93.3	96.5	99.8		7
Paralimni	91.4	94.2	97.9		4

Ch. 1 (Proto) in Greek: 24h – Ch. 2 (Deutero) Multilingual: 24h. Prgrs in English 1030-1040, 1500-0300; Turkish 0300-1400; Armenian 1400-1500 – Ch. 3 (Trito) in Greek: 24h – Ch. 4 (R. Love) in Greek: 24h.
Ann: Greek: "Radiofonikon Idryma Kyprou". Turkish: "Burasi Kibris Radyo Yayin Korporasyonu". IS: "Avkoritssa" (guitar).

EXTERNAL SERVICES: see International Radio section.

Other Stations (all MHz):
ANT1 FM: Larnaca 102.7, Paphos 103.7. W: www.ant1fm.com.cy – Dromos FM: Larnaca 103.0, Limassol 100.3, Nicosia 106.7. W: facebook.com/dromosfmcy – Energy 107.6: Mount Olympos 107.6. W: energy1076.com – Kanali 6: Limassol 98.6, Nicosia 106.0, Mount Phanos 107.0 W: kanali6.com.cy – Kiss FM: Limassol 88.5, Larnaca/ Nicosia/Paphos: 89.0. W: kissfm.com.cy – Klik FM: Limassol 89.6, Larnaca/Paphos 98.2, Nicosia 105.6 W: klikfm.com.cy – Logos R: Limassol 100.7, Mount Olympos 101.1, Paphos/Larnaca 101.6, Mount Kykkos 102.4. W: logosradio.com.cy – Love R: Limassol 92.8, Paphos/Larnaca 101.6, Mount loveradio.gr – Orthodox Church R: Limassol 94.5 – R. Astra: Mount Olympos 92.8, Larnaca 105.3 W: astra.com.cy – R. Athina: Limassol 88.7, Nicosia 100.7 W: radioathina.com – R. Proto: Agia Napa 89.9, Larnaca 89.4, Mount Olympos 99.3 W: www.radioproto.com.cy – R. Sfera: Paphos 96.8, Limassol 106.4, Protaras 107.9 W: www.radiosfera. com.cy – Russian Wave, Limassol: 105.6 W: russianwave.com.cy – Sports 1 R, Limassol: 93.7 W: sports1radio.net – Super FM: Larnaca 95.7, Mount Olympos 104.7 W: superfmradio.com – Super Sport FM: Limassol 100.3, Larnaca 103.0, Nicosia 106.7 W: sport-fm.com.cy

BBC World Sce: MW: 1323kHz English 0200-2300
R. Monte Carlo & Trans World R. rel. on MW: 1233kHz 0200-2115
R. Sawa: MW: 990kHz 24h.
For further details on these stns see International Radio section.

NORTHERN CYPRUS

SUPREME BROADCASTING BOARD (YYK)
📧 Memduh Asaf St. 9, Kösklüçiftlik, Lefkosa, Northern Cyprus
☎+90 392 228 1368 📠+90 392 228 1272
W: kktcyyk.org E: info@kktcyyk.org

BAYRAK RADYO TELEVIZYON KURUMU (BRTK, Gov.)
📧 BRT Sitesi, Dr. Fasil Küçük Bulvari, Lefkosa, Northern Cyprus, via Mersin 10, Turkey ☎+90 392 225 5555 📠 +90 392 225 4991
W: brtk.net E: brt@brtk.net
L.P: DG: Ahmet Okan. Head Tr. Dept: Mustafa Tosun.
MW: Iskele (Trikomo) 1098kHz 100kW.

FM	R.1	B.FM	B.Int.	Klasik	B.T.	kW
Kantara	90.6	98.1	87.8	93.4		10/10/10/1
Selvilitepe	102.0	92.1	105.0	88.4/102.5	94.6	5/5/5/5/1/5
Lefkosa		94.2				0.05

Radyo 1 in Turkish: 24h on 1098kHz & FM – **Bayrak FM** in Turkish: 24h – **Bayrak International in** Greek/English/Arabic/German: 24h – **Radyo Klasik:** 24h – **Bayrak Türk Müzigi:** 24h.

OTHER STATIONS FM (MHz):

	Station	W	E	kW	Location
1)	Odtu FM	103.1		1	Kalkanli
2)	Cool FM	92.5	97.5	1	Magosa
3)	As FM	97.7		1	Lefkosa
4)	Sim FM	98.6	89.5	1/0.3	Lefkosa
5)	Süper FM	98.9		1	Lefkosa
6)	Metro FM	104.0		1	Lefkosa
7)	Kral FM	106.9		1	Lefkosa
8)	Kibris FM	103.4	100.2	10/2.5	Lefkosa
9)	First FM	90.0	96.6	1/0.2	Lefkosa
10)	Akdeniz FM	88.6		1	Lefkosa
11)	Günes FM	91.3		1	Lefkosa
12)	R. Vatan Türkü	104.5	94.4	5/5	Lefkosa
13)	R. Nihavent	100.4	89.8	1/3	Lefkosa
14)	Dance FM	95.5	95.8	2/0.3	Lefkosa
15)	Yakin Dogu FM	88.0		1	Lefkosa
16)	Kuzey FM	106.7		2	Lefkosa
17)	Radyo T	96.65		1	Lefkosa
18)	Güven FM	90.4	90.8	5	Lefkosa
19)	Plus FM	106.2		1	Magosa
20)	Laü FM	97.4		2	Lefke
21)	Mayis FM	96.0	99.5	2/0.05	Lefkosa
22)	Gaü FM	105.8		1	Gime
23)	Ukü FM	107.2		1	Lefkosa
24)	Daü FM		106.5	2.5	Magosa
25)	Enerji FM		93.0	0.5	Lefkosa
26)	InterFirst FM	100.9		0.25	Lefkosa
27)	Güven Nostalji	102.8	91.3		Lefkosa
28)	Avrasya FM	107.9	106.7	1	Lefkosa
29)	Ada FM	96.2	93.8	1	Lefkosa

Tx sites: W (west) = Selvilitepe, E (east)= Kantara-Sinan Dagi. All stns 24h.

AKROTIRI & DHEKELIA (UK)

Pop: 15,700 — **Pr.L:** English, Greek — **E.C:** 50Hz, 240V — **ITU:** CYP

BFBS RADIO, CYPRUS (Mil.)
✉ BFBS Akrotiri, BFPO 57, UK ☎ +357 2527 8518 🖷 +357 2527 8580
W: www.ssvc.com/bfbs/radio/cyprus **E:** cyprus@bfbs.com
L.P: GM: Tess Turner; Eng Mgr: J. Dunlop

FM (MHz)	BFBS1	BFBS2	kW
Akrotiri	92.1	89.9	25
Dhekelia	99.6	95.3	25
Nicosia	91.7	89.7	1.5

D.Prgr: 24h. **Ann:** "This is BFBS Radio"

Other stations:
BBC World Sce: MW: Zakaki 639 & 720kHz: Arabic 0300-2200

CZECH REPUBLIC

L.T: UTC +1h (31 Mar-27 Oct: +2h) — **Pop:** 10.5 million — **Pr.L:** Czech — **E.C:** 50Hz, 230V — **ITU:** CZE

CESKÉ RADIOKOMUNIKACE, a.s.
✉ U nákladového nádrazí 4, 130 00 Praha 3 ☎ +420 267 005 111
Operates the TV and radio transmission facilities.

CESKY ROZHLAS (CZECH RADIO)
✉ Vinohradská 12, 120 99 Praha 2 ☎ +420 221 551 111 🖷 +420 221 551 300 **E:** info@rozhlas.cz **W:** www.rozhlas.cz
L.P: DG: Peter Duhan PD: Jan Menger TD: Ladislav Musil

LW & MW:	kHz	kW	Prgr:
Uherské Hradiste	270	650	CRo 1
Praha (Liblice)	639	1500	CRo 2 + CRo 6
Ostrava-Svinov	639	30	CRo 2 + CRo 6
Brno (Dobrochov)	954	200	CRo 2 + CRo 6
Ceské Budejovice	954	30	CRo 2 + CRo 6
Karlovy Vary	954	20	CRo 2 + CRo 6
Moravské Budejovice	1332	50	CRo 2 + CRo 6

FM (MHz)	CRo 1	CRo 2	CRo 3	CRo 5	kW
9) As	107.9			96.7	0.1/0.2
1b) Benešov				99.0	1(5)
6) Brno	95.1		102.0	106.5	72/91/72
6) Brno (city)		92.6	90.4	93.1	6/6/2
2) C. Budejovice	91.1	103.7	96.1	106.4	80/1/40/80
9) Cheb			106.2	100.8	1

FM (MHz)	CRo 1	CRo 2	CRo 3	CRo 5	kW
4) Chomutov	98.9	94.2	96.3	103.1	10
3) Domazlice	98.0			105.3	10
13) Frydlant				97.4	0.2
6) Hodonín	106.2	107.8	100.4	93.6	9/3/9
5) Hradec Králové				95.3	1
11) Hradec Králové				104.7	10
8) Hulín				101.6	1
9) Jáchymov				103.4	1
8) Jeseník	91.3	88.7	98.2	106.8	20/0.2/20/20
Jicín		106.9			1
10) Jihlava	90.7	107.1	95.4	87.9	20/10/20/10
Kaplice			105.9		0.2
9) Karlovy Vary	102.6		105.7	91.0	0.1/0.2/1
Kašperské Hory			107.2		0.5
1b) Kladno				100.5	0.2
3) Klatovy	99.8	90.3	88.6	102.4	10
1b) Kutná Hora		102.2		100.5	1/3
13) Liberec	95.9	89.9	103.9	102.3	20/20/20/1
13) Liberec				91.3	0.5
8) Lipník n.Becvou				88.7	0.1
9) Marián. Lázne	97.6			100.8	1
1b) Mladá Boleslav				100.3	0.5
Nové Hrady		102.2			1
8) Olomouc		107.2		92.8	1
7) Opava		101.7		102.6	1/0.5
7) Ostrava	101.4	101.9	104.8	107.3	43/0.5/43/3
11) Pardubice	89.7	100.1	102.7	101.0	90/90/90/1
Písek	97.0	98.9	105.2		1
Plzen (North)	89.1	101.7	95.6		80
3) Plzen (East)	99.2		93.3	106.7	10
3) Plzen (city)				91.0	1
Praha		100.7			50
1a) Praha (city)	94.6	91.2	105.0	92.6	5/3/5/7
1b) Príbram	102.2	107.0		100.0	0.4/1/1
1b) Prosec n.N.				102.3	1
1b) Rakovník				100.4	1
5) Rychnov n.K.				96.5	1
2) Slavonice		103.3		88.2	1
3) Sokolov	94.3			98.2	0.4
Sušice	90.6				1
11) Svitavy				102.4	1
3) Tachov				106.3	0.4
10) Trebíc				90.1	0.2
7) Trinec	92.1			105.3	1
5) Trutnov	88.5		101.9	90.5	10/10/20
10) Uher. Hradiste				99.1	0.2
6) Uhersky Brod	93.0			107.3	1
12) Uhersky Brod				107.3	1
4) Ustí nad Labem	90.9		104.5	88.8	80
Ustí n.L. (city)		98.6			1
11) Ustí n. Orlicí				98.6	1
7) Val. Mezirící	92.5	89.9	96.8	99.0	7/1/7/7
4) Varnsdorf			88.4	98.5	0.2
Votice	93.1	103.2			95
13 Vratislavice				91.3	0.5
7) Vrbno pod Prad.		103.6		95.5	1
7) Vsetín	92.1	102.9	98.3	89.5	0.1
12 Vsetín				89.5	0.1
3) Zelezná Ruda				95.8	0.2
6) Zlín	99.5	107.7	94.8	97.5	6
12) Zlín				97.5	6
6) Znojmo	101.2	89.6	99.2	97.3	1/3/3/1

CRo 1 (Radiozurnál): 24h (LW: Mon-Sat 0400-2300, Sun 0500-2300). **N:** on the h – **CRo 2 (Dvojka):** 24h (MW: Mon-Fri 0300-1700, Sat+Sun 0400-1700) – **CRo 3 (Vltava):** 24h – **CRo 4 (Radio Wave):** 24h (on internet only: www.rozhlas.cz/radiowave/portal) – **CRo 5 REGIONAL STATIONS** – 24h own prgrs and relays of other regional stations (esp. in the night) – **CRo 6:** 1700-2300. **N:** on the h
Addresses:
1a) CRo Regina Praha, Hybešova 10, 186 72 Praha 8 **W:** www.rozhlas. cz/regina – **1b)** CRo Region - Stoední Eechy, Hybešova 10, 186 72 Praha 8 **W:** www.rozhlas.cz/strednicechy – **2)** CRo Eeské Budijovice, U Tøí Ivù 1, 370 29 Eeské Budijovice **W:** www.rozhlas.cz/cb – **3)** ERo Plzeò, Nám. Míru 10, 320 70 Plzeò **W:** www.rozhlas.cz/plzen – **4)** CRo Sever (=North), Na schodech 10, 400 91 Ustí nad Labem **W:** www.rozhlas.cz/sever – **5)** CRo Hradec Králové, Havlíèkova 292, 501 01 Hradec Králové **W:** www. rozhlas.cz/hradec – **6)** CRo Brno, Beethovenova 4, 657 42 Brno **W:** www. rozhlas.cz/brno – **7)** CRo Ostrava, Dr. Šmerala 2, 729 91 Ostrava (Polish: Mon-Fri 1800-1900, Sun 1730-1800) **W:** www.rozhlas.cz/ostrava – **8)** CRo Olomouc, Horní námìstí 21, 771 06 Olomouc **W:** www.rozhlas.cz/ol – **9)** CRo Karlovy Vary, Zítkova 3, 360 00 Karlovy Vary: Mon-Fri 1400-1640, otherwise CRo Plzeò **W:** www.rozhlas.cz/plzen – **10)** CRo Region

- Vysoèina, Masarykovo nám 42, 586 01 Jihlava **W:** www.rozhlas.
cz/vysocina – **11)** CRo Pardubice, Sv. Anežky Èeské 29, 530 02 Pardubice
W: www.rozhlas.cz/pardubice – **12)** CRo Zlín, Osvoboditelù 187, 760 01
Zlín **W:** www.rozhlas.cz/brno – **13)** CRo Liberec, Modrá 1048, 460 06
Liberec **W:** www.rozhlas.cz/liberec/portal/

EXTERNAL SERVICE: Radio Prague
See International Broadcasting section.

MAJOR PRIVATE STATIONS/NETWORKS:
RADIO IMPULS (Comm.)
✉ Ortenovo nám. 15a, 170 00 Praha 7 ☎ +420 255 700 700 🖨 +420
255 700 727 **E:** impuls@radioimpuls.cz **W:** www.radioimpuls.cz
FM: see list below **D.Prgr:** 24h
RADIO FREKVENCE 1 (Comm.)
✉ Wenzigova 4, 120 00 Praha 2 ☎ +420 257 001 111 🖨 +420 257
314 183 **E:** frekvence1@frekvence1.cz **W:** www. frekvence1.cz
FM: see list below **D.Prgr:** 24h
EVROPA 2 (Comm.)
✉ Wenzigova 4, 120 00 Praha 2 ☎ +420 257 001 111 🖨 +420 257
001 807 **E:** info@evropa2.cz **W:** www.evropa2.cz
FM: see list below **D.Prgr:** 24h
RADIO KISS FM (Comm.)
✉ Rícanská 3, 101 00 Praha 10-Vinohrady ☎ +420 267 009 800 🖨
+420 267 009 811 **E:** radio@kiss.cz **W:** www.kiss.cz
FM: see list below **D.Prgr:** 24h
Regional branches: **R. KISS 98 FM,** ✉ Rícanská 3, 101 00 Praha
10-Vinohrady ☎ +420 267 009 800 🖨 +420 267 009 811 **W:** www.
kiss98.cz – **R. KISS Hády,** ✉ Stefánikova 38, 612 00 Brno 12 ☎
+420 541 221 143 🖨 +420 541 211 117 **W:** www.kisshady.cz – **R. KISS
Jizní Cechy** ✉ U Vystaviste 15A, 370 05 Ceské Budejovice ☎ +420
385 510 888 🖨 +420 385 510 990 **W:** www.kissjiznicechy.cz – **R. KISS
Morava** ✉ Starobelská 13, 700 30 Ostrava-Zábreh ☎ +420 596 708
401 🖨 +420 596 708 400 **W:** www.kissmorava.cz – **R. KISS ProTon**
Husova 58, 301 24 Plzen 1 ☎ +420 377 235 808 🖨 +420 377 235 810
W: www.kissproton.cz – **R. KISS Publikum** ✉ Bartošova 45, 760 01
Zlín ☎ +420 577 009 036 🖨 +420 577 009 033 **W:** www.kisspublikum.
cz – **R. KISS Delta** ✉ Jana Palacha 1025, 293 01 Mladá Boleslav 1
☎ +420 326 720 000 🖨 +420 326 721 342 **W:** www.kissdelta.cz
RADIO PROGLAS (Relg)
✉ Barvicova 85, 602 00 Brno ☎ +420 543 217 241-3 🖨 +420 543 217
245 **E:** radio@proglas.cz **W:** www.proglas.cz
FM: see list below **D.Prgr:** 24h
COUNTRY RADIO (Comm.)
✉ Ricanská 3, 101 00 Praha 10-Vinohrady ☎ +420 251 024 111 🖨
+420 251 024 224 **E:** info@countryradio.cz **W:** www.countryradio.cz
MW: Praha 1062kHz 20kW (0500-1800), 1kW (1800-0500) **FM:**
Kutná Hora 87.7, Praha 89.5, Ceské Budejovice 94.7, Beroun 98.1,
Tábor 101.8, Plzen 102.1, Ceská Lípa 102.6, Usti nad Labem 106.8.
D.Prgr: 24h

Commercial FM Stations:

MHz	kW	Station	Location
87.6	70	R. Impuls	Brno
87.8	1	R. Blaník	Praha
87.8	1	R. Cerná hora	Králíky
88.1	1	R. Evropa 2	Liberec
88.1	10	Hitrádio Orion	Jeseník
88.2	5	R. Evropa 2	Praha
88.3	10	R. Kiss Hády 88 FM	Brno
88.4	1	R. Blaník - JC	Ceské Budejovice
88.7	1	R. Proglas	Tábor
88.9	10	R. Jih	Breclav
89.0	1	R. Práchen	Písek
89.0	45	R. Impuls	Ostrava
89.3	5	R. Sázava	Benešov/Kozmice
89.5	1	R. Cas	Trinec
89.5	5	Country Radio	Praha
89.6	1	R. Frekvence 1	Plzen
89.6	7	Rock Max	Zlín
89.8	1	BBCWS/R.C.	Ceské Budejovice
90.0	1	Hitradio Dragon	Cheb
90.0	1	R. Rubi	Sumperk
90.0	10	R. Kiss ProTon	Plzen
90.2	1	R. Kiss Delta	Kutná Hora
90.3	5	R. Expres	Praha
90.3	3	R. Kiss Publikum	Zlín
90.5	1.5	R. Evropa 2	Ceské Budejovice
90.6	4	Hitrádio FM Most	Chomutov
90.6	1	R. Proglas	Bystrice pod Hostynem
91.0	70	R. Frekvence 1	Ostrava
91.0	1	R. Evropa 2	Mariánské Lázne
91.1	2	R. Kiss Delta	Pardubice

MHz	kW	Station	Location
91.4	66	R. Impuls	Plzen
91.6	1	R. Blanik - SevC	Decín
91.6	5	Fajn rádio Life	Opatovice
91.7	4	R. Zlín	Zlín
91.9	1	R. 1	Praha
92.1	10	R. Impuls	Trutnov
92.3	1	R. Relax	Kladno
92.3	5	R. Haná	Pohorany
92.5	5	R. Egrensis	Mariánské Lázne
92.8	5	R. Cas	Ostrava
92.8	1	Hitradio Magic	Náchod
92.9	1	R. Kiss Delta	Mladá Boleslav
93.2	1	R. Egrensis	Cheb
93.3	20	R. Proglas	Jeseník
93.4	20	R. Frekvence 1	Jihlava
93.5	50	R. Frekvence 1	Ustí nad Labem
93.6	1	Hitrádio Faktor	Písek
93.7	5	R. City	Praha
93.7	45	R. Hellax	Ostrava
93.8	1	R. Evropa 2	Karlovy Vary
93.9	80	R. Blaník V.Cechy	Pardubice
94.0	10	R. Impuls	Klatovy
94.1	10	R. Frekvence 1	Valašské Mezirící
94.1	50	R. Frekvence 1	Ceské Budejovice
94.3	10	Hitrádio Vysocina	Jihlava
94.7	1	R. Hey Ostrava	Ostrava
94.9	1	R. Hey Ostrava	Opava
95.0	95	R. Blaník	Votice
95.2	5	Fajn North Music	Ustí nad Labem
95.2	1	R. Sumava	Klatovy
95.3	5	R. Beat	Praha
95.7	2	R Hey	Praha
95.8	1	Hitrádio Vysocina	Trebíc
96.2	1	R. Spin	Praha
96.2	1	R. Zlín	Uherský Brod
96.4	4	Hitrádio Orion	Ostrava
96.5	1	R. Kiss Morava	Sumperk
96.6	5	R. Impuls	Praha
96.7	5	BBCWS/R.C.	Jihlava
96.8	1	R. Hey Brno	Brno
96.9	1	R. Hey Profil	Pardubice
97.1	5	R. Rubi	Pohorany
97.1	1	R. Hey! Sever	Liberec
97.2	5	Fajn rádio	Praha
97.4	50	R. Frekvence 1	Pardubice
97.7	50	R. Kiss Jizní Cechy	Votice
97.7	1	Evropa 2	Ostrava
97.9	20	R. Proglas	Liberec
98.1	1	Fajn rádio Agara	Chomutov
98.1	1	R. Kiss 98 FM	Praha
98.3	1	R. Cas	Trinec
98.4	20	R. Frekvence 1	Trutnov
98.4	5	R. Impuls	Kašperské Hory
98.6	1	BBCWS/R.C.	Plzen
98.7	1	Hitrádio Orion	Trinec
98.7	5	R. Classic FM	Praha
99.0	1	Hitradio Brno	Brno
99.1	1	BBCWS/R.C.	Pardubice
99.2	1	BBCWS/R.C.	Liberec
99.3	1	Kiss Jizní Cechy	Cesky Krumlov
99.3	10	R. Evropa 2	Jeseník
99.3	1	R.France Int./Fr. Mus.	Praha
99.5	1	R. Evropa 2	Pardubice
99.7	1	Hitradio Dragon	Karlovy Vary
99.7	5	R. Gold	Ceské Budejovice
99.7	5	R. Bonton	Praha
99.8	5	Hitradio Apollo	Valašské Mezirící
99.9	1	Hitrádio Crystal	Ceská Lípa
100.3	5	R. Impuls	Jihlava
100.5	7	R. Impuls	Valašské Mezirící
100.6	2	R. Blaník Sever	Teplice
100.8	1	R. Beat	Slavonice
100.9	20	R. Impuls	Jeseník
101.1	5	R. Kiss Morava	Frydek-Místek
101.1	3	BBCWS/R.C.	Praha
101.3	10	R. Evropa 2	Plzen
101.4	20	R. Contact (RCL)	Liberec
101.8	1	Country R.	Tábor
102.0	50	R. Impuls	Ustí nad Labem
102.5	5	R. Frekvence 1	Praha
102.8	5	Hitradio Dragon	Mariánské Lázne
102.8	1	Hitrádio FM Labe	Ustí nad Labem
102.9	50	R. Impuls	Ceské Budejovice
103.0	10	R. Krokodyl	Brno
103.4	1	R. Blaník V. Cechy	Hradec Králové

MHz	kW	Station	Location
103.4	5	R. Petrov	Brno
103.6	1	R. Hey Profil	Chotebor
103.7	1	Oldies R. Olympic	Praha
103.8	10	R. Frekvence 1	Klatovy
103.9	7	Hitrádio Orion	Valašské Mezirící
104.1	50	R. Frekvence 1	Plzen
104.2	1	R. Blanik - Jiz. Morava	Znojmo
104.3	20	R. Frekvence 1	Jeseník
104.3	32	Hitrádio Faktor	Ceské Budejovice
104.5	50	R. Frekvence 1	Brno
104.7	10	R. Blanik - Západ	Plzen
105.0	10	R. Frekvence 1	Zlín
105.3	3	R. Cerná hora	Trutnov
105.4	1	R. Rubi	Vrbno pod Pradedem
105.5	95	R. Evropa 2	Votice
105.5	1.5	R. Evropa 2	Brno
105.7	1	R. Jizera	Mladá Boleslav
105.8	8	Hitrádio FM Plus	Klatovy
105.9	1	R. Cas	Frenštát p. Radh.
106.0	50	R. Impuls	Pardubice
106.1	3	Hitrádio FM Plus	Plzen
106.3	1	BBCWS/R.C.	Ostrava
106.4	1	R. Evropa 2	Vrchlabí
106.5	10	R. Blaník - Sever	Chomutov
106.6	1	Fajn rádio	Kutná Hora
106.7	1	R. Evropa 2	Znojmo
107.2	1	R. Evropa 2	Ustí nad Labem
107.4	1	Hitrádio FM Plus	Jáchymov
107.5	3	R. Proglas	Brno
107.5	2	R. Proglas	Nové Hrady

+ more than 70 txs below 1kW

NB: BBCWS/R.C. = BBCWS (in English) + Radio Cesko (in Czech)

DENMARK

L.T: UTC +1h (31 Mar-27 Oct: +2h) — **Pop:** 5.5 million — **Pr.L:** Danish — **EC:** 50Hz, 230/380V — **ITU:** DNK

TERACOM A/S
Banestrøget 19-21, 2630 Taastrup ☎+45 70118011 🖷 +45 43711143 Teracom is responsible for the operation of txs carrying prgrs of DR, Radio 24syv and TV 2.

DR RADIO (Pub.)
DR Byen, Emil Holms Kanal 20, DK-0999 Copenhagen C ☎+45 35203040 **W:** www.dr.dk **LP:** Chairman: Michael Christiansen. DG: Maria Rørbye Rønn. Media Dir.: Gitte Rabøl. News Dir.: Ulrik Haagerup
LW: Kalundborg 243kHz 50kW.

FM	P1/P2	P3	P4	kW
Bornholm	96.2	90.0	99.3	30
Copenhagen	90.8	93.9	96.5	60
Funen	89.0	92.6	96.8	60
Holstebro	90.2	92.9	98.5	60
Nakskov	89.4	94.1	92.2	30
Næstved	94.8	99.6	97.5	100
Skamlebæk	88.4	94.3	92.0	3
So. Jutland	95.1	97.2	99.9	60
Thisted	91.4	99.2	95.6	2
Tolne, N.Jutland	91.0	96.6	94.4	4
Varde			99.0	10
Vejle	95.5	90.7	94.0	10
Ølgod	88.7	92.3	97.7	10
Aalborg	93.3	89.7	98.1	60
Aarhus	88.1	91.7	95.9	60

+ 18 FM txs below 1kW. A full list is available at http://itst.dk
DAB: DAB1: ch.12C (227.360MHz). DAB2: ch.11C (220.352MHz) on Sealand & Funen and ch.13B (232.496MHz) in Jutland.
P1 on FM (MF 0500-1700, Sat 0700-1700, Sun 0854-1700) + DAB1 (24h). **N:** on the h (except Su 0900 & 1000). N in Danish from KNR, Greenland: MF 1755-1800 – **P2 Klassisk** on FM (MF 1700-0500, Sat 1700-0700, Sun 1700-0854) + DAB1 (24h): Classical and jazz music and cultural prgrs. – **P3** on FM + DAB1: Popular music, news and sport. N: on the h. + MF: 0530, 0630, 0730 – **P4** on FM. News, entertainment and regional prgrs. N: national news on the h and regional news on the half h. – **P5** on DAB1. Music etc. for +60, at times relays P4 – **P6 Beat** on DAB1. Indie/alternative music – **P7 Mix** on DAB1. A/C chart hits – **P8 Jazz** on DAB 1. Jazz – **DR Ramasjang** on DAB1. Children's radio – **DR Mama** on DAB1. Youth radio – **DR Nyhedskanalen** on DAB2. News and sports – **DR Langbølge** on LW 243kHz. 0445-0507, 0730-0807, 1045-1135, 1645-1716. Special prgrs.: Wrp.: 0445-0500, 0745-0800,

1045-1100 & 1645-1700, gymnastics: 0730-0745 & navigational warnings (repeated twice): 1703-1719. Also news from P4 at 0500-0507, 0800-0807, 1100-1120MF/1100-1115SS & 1700-1703.
Regional stations:
MF: 0507-0600, 0607-0700, 0707-0800, 0807-0900, 1130-1132, 1403-1500, 1510-1550 & 1610-1700. Sat 0603-0700, 0707-0800, 0807-0900 & 1130-1132. Sun: 0603-0700, 0703-0800, 0807-0900 & 1130-1132. P4 Trekanten, P4 Esbjerg and P4 Nordvestsjælland are on the air at a reduced schedule. At other times national P4 prgrs are carried.
DR Nordjylland, Frederik Bajers Vej 9, 9220 Aalborg: on 89.1/94.4/96.7/98.1MHz – **DR Midt- & Vest**, Vestergade 1, 7500 Holstebro: on 95.6/ 97.7/98.5/102.2MHz – **DR Østjylland**, Olof Palmes Alle 10-12, 8200 Aarhus N: on 88.9/95.9/96.4/102.0MHz – **DR Trekanten**, Den Hvide Facet 4., 7100 Vejle: on 94.0MHz – **DR Syd**, H.P. Hansensgade 11, 6220 Aabenraa: on 94.0/96.6/99.0/99.9/103.7MHz – **DR Esbjerg**, Torvegade 8, 6700 Esbjerg: on 99.0/103.7MHz – **DR Fyn**, Lille Tornbjergvej 10, 5220 Odense S: on 96.4/96.8MHz – **DR Sjælland**, Vadestedet 1, 4700 Næstved: on 92.0/92.2/97.5MHz – **DR Nordvestsjælland**, DR Sjælland, Ahlgade 3 F, 4300 Holbæk on 92.0MHz – **DR København**, Emil Holms Kanal 20, 0999 Copenhagen: on 96.5MHz – **DR Bornholm**, Aakirkebyvej 52, 3700 Rønne: on 93.7/99.3MHz
All prgrs from DR are available on the internet. P1, P2 Klassisk, P3 & P4 København are also available via satellite **Ann:** FM: "Du lytter til P et/to/tre/fire" (1st, 2nd, 3rd & 4th prgr.). LW: "Du lytter til DRs langbølgesender på 243 kHz"

RADIO 24SYV (Pub.)
Vester Farimagsgade 41, DK-1606 Copenhagen V ☎ +45 31 247 247 **E:** kontakt@radio24syv.dk **W:** www.radio24syv.dk
L.P: Dir: Jørgen Ramskov
FM (all MHz): Nakskov 98.8 30kW, Holstebro 100.3 60kW, Funen 100.5 60kW, Tolne N. Jutland 100.7 10kW, Vejle 100.9 10kW, Skamlebæk 101.1 5kW, Thisted 101.3 3kW, Næstved 101.6 100kW, So.Jutland 102.1 60kW, Copenhagen 102.3 60kW, Ølgod 102.5 10kW, Aalborg 102.7 60kW, Aarhus 103.0 60kW, Bornholm 103.5 30kW + 4 FM tx below 1 kW. Also nationwide on DAB2
Format: News/talk

SBS RADIO (Comm.)
Mileparken 20A, DK-2740 Skovlunde ☎ +45 33376666 🖷 +45 33930807 **E:** info@thevoice.dk **W:** www.sbsradio.com/da
L.P: MD: Jim Receveur. CEN: Jan Andersen
NOVA FM: AC. Ølgod 87.8MHz 10kW, So. Jutland 89.3MHz 3kW, Copenhagen 91.4MHz 12kW, Bornholm 92.2MHz 1kW, Funen 93.4MHz 1kW, Vejle 99.3MHz 1kW, Tolne N. Jutland 102.4MHz 1kW, Holstebro 103.4MHz 60kW, Næstved 103.9MHz 100kW, Aalborg 106.0MHz 6kW + 20 stns below 1kW. Also nationwide on DAB2
THE VOICE: CHR. On 26 low power FM txs in major cities + nationwide on DAB2
POP FM: Classic hits. Copenhagen 100.0MHz 75kW, Randers 99.9MHz 0.5kW + nationwide on DAB2
RADIO 100: Hot AC: On 27 low power FM txs in some major cities + nationwide on DAB2
RADIO SOFT: A/C Soft non-stop. On 7 low power FM txs in the larger Copenhagen area
RADIO KLASSISK: Classical music. On 3 low power FM txs in the larger Copenhagen area as well as txs covering Odense, Aarhus and Haderslev.
NRJ (Comm.)
Bispevej 4, 1, DK-2400 Copenhagen NV ☎ +45 38168200 🖷 +45 28168202 **E:** info@nrj.dk **W:** www.nrj.dk **Radio Energy - NRJ:** CHR. 3 low power txs in Copenhagen & Odense.

Private Stations (all MHz):
Approx. 200 organizations are operating low-powered FM txs. (0.16kW-0.5kW at 40m. height). Currently aprox. 500 txs are on the air. Major stns in the main cities are as follows (only main frequency/frequencies mentioned):
Aabenraa: Radio Mojn, Skibbroen 6,2., 6200 Aabenraa: 102.6/104.5 – Globus Guld: 106.7
Aalborg: ANR, Box 7089, 9200 Aalborg SV: 87.6/103.2/103.8 – Radio Aura, Box 7089, 9200 Aalborg SV: 105.4/106.9 – The Voice: 100.2 – Radio Nord, Sigsgaardsvej 16, 9490 Pandrup: 95.1/98.9/102.2 – Various grassroots/community stns: 92.2/101.7/106.5/107.4
Aarhus: Radio go!FM, Vesterport 3, 4., 8000 Århus C: 92.2/94.6/106.5 – The Voice: 90.9/93.1/93.7 – Radio 100: 87.6/98.3 – Radio Klassisk: 106.2 – Øst FM/Radio Hinnerup: 95.0/105.1/107.6 – Radio ABC: 105.7/107.0 – Radio Alfa: 102.4/105.4 – Various community stns: 98.7
Copenhagen: The Voice: 96.1/104.4/104.9/105.4 – NRJ: 88.6/107.1 – Radio 100: 97.2/103.6/104.1/105.6 – Radio Soft: 95.0 – Radio Klassisk: 92.7/106.9 – Various grassroots/community stns: 87.6/90.2/

90.4/92.9/94.5/95.2/95.5/97.7/98.9/100.9/102.9/103.4/105.9/106.3/107.4

Esbjerg: Skala FM, Banegårdspladsen, 6700 Esbjerg: 101.7/106.8 – Radio 100: 106.3 – Globus Guld: 101.3 – Radio Charlie, Skt. Nikolaj Kirkeplads, 6800 Varde: 95.3 – Rlg. stations: 93.5
Frederikshavn: ANR, Tordenskjoldsgade 4, 9900 Frederikshavn: 107.5 – Radio Aura: 89.0 – Vendsyssel FM, Sønderjyllands Allé 35, 9900 Frederikshavn: 106.6
Haderslev: Skala FM: 95.8 – Radio Mojn: 97.6/107.4 – Radio Klassisk/Norea Radio: 98.6 – Globus Guld: 101.7 – Radio Globus: 104.9
Herning: Radio M, Østergade 21, 7400 Herning: 105.8 – Radio Alfa, Østergade 21, 7400 Herning: 89.5 – Radio Classic, Gl. Kirkevej 33, 7400 Herning: 96.2
Hjørring/Hirtshals: Skaga FM, P. Rimmersgade 40, 9850 Hirtshals: 105.6/106.7 – ANR: 104.7 – Radio Aura: 89.0
Holstebro: Holstebro Favorit FM, Lægårdvej 86, 7500 Holstebro: 105.1/106.2 – Radio Holstebro, Gl. Struervej 36, 7500 Holstebro: 97.4
Horsens: Radio VLR Horsens, Nørregade 42, 8700 Horsens: 91.1 – Horsens Classic: 105.3 – The Voice: 105.0
Kolding: Skala FM, Dalbygade 40, 6000 Kolding: 87.6/94.4/105.2/106.3 – VLR: 103.2/106.1 – Globus Guld: 100.3 – Radio 100: 91.3/102.7 – The Voice: 90.0
Køge: Radio Køge, Box 222, 4600 Køge: 98.2/106.2/106.8 – The Voice: 93.6
Nykøbing F: Radio Sydhavsøerne, Tværgade 18, 4800 Nykøbing Falster: 87.8
Nykøbing M/Thisted: Radio Limfjord, Gasværksvej 10, 7900 Nykøbing Mors: 104.7/106.9/107.8 – Limfjord Plus: 94.7 – ANR: 97.4 – Radio Aura: 106.7 – Radio Nord: 105.6
Næstved/Ringsted/Slagelse: Radio SLR, Dania 38, 4700 Næstved: 91.6/100.7/101.0/106.5 – The Voice: 93.6/99.1/107.5
Odense: Radio 3, Box 312, 5100 Odense C: 91.1/99.1 – The Voice: 104.2/105.1/107.6 – NRJ: 103.5 – Radio 100: 101.2 – Radio Klassisk: 106.7 – VLR: 98.4 – Various grassroots/community stations: 107.1
Randers: Radio ABC Brotoften 10, 8940 Randers SV: 95.3/105.7 – Radio Alfa, Brotoften 10, 8940 Randers SV: 91.3/102.4 – Radio ABC Solo FM: 93.5/96.4 – Radio Randers, Lorentzgade 17, 8900 Randers C: 104.9
Roskilde: The Voice: 106.6 – Radio 100: 103.6/104.3 – Radio Soft: 107.7 – Roskilde Dampradio, Box 650, 4000 Roskilde: 97.8
Rødding: Radio Globus, Herredfogedvej 2, 6630 Rødding: 104.4 – Globus Guld, Herredfogedvej 2, 6630 Rødding: 90.1/93.0
Silkeborg: Radio 1, Fredensgade 1, 8600 Silkeborg: 107.7 – Silkeborg Guld: 94.5/101.2 – Radio 100: 96.9
Skive: Radio Skive, Nordbanevej 1A, 7800 Skive: 104.0 – Radio Alfa, Nordbanevej 1A, 7800 Skive: 101.8
Svendborg: Radio Diablo, Voldgade 9,1., 5700 Svendborg: 107.7 – Radio Alfa Sydfyn: 106.5
Sønderborg: Radio Als, Peblingestien 1, 6430 Nordborg: 88.0 – Globus Guld: 95.4 – Skala FM: 104.4 – Radio Mojn: 90.1
Vejle: VLR, Bugattivej 8, 7100 Vejle: 98.8/101.7 – The Voice: 105.9
Viborg: Radio Viborg, Box 501, 8800 Viborg: 105.0 – Viborg Favorit FM: 93.8

DJIBOUTI

L.T: UTC +3h — **Pop:** 500,000 — **Pr.L:** Arabic, French (official), Somali, Afar — **E.C:** 50Hz, 220V — **ITU:** DJI

MINISTÈRE DE LA COMMUNICATION ET DE LA CULTURE CHARGÉ DES POSTES ET DE TÉLÉCOMMUNICATIONS (MCC-PT)
✉ B.P. 32, 1 Rue de Moscou, Djibouti ☎ +253 355672 🖹 +253 353957 **W:** mccpt.dj **E:** mccpt@intnet.dj **L.P:** Minister: Abdi Houssein.

RADIODIFFUSION TÉLÉVISION DE DJIBOUTI (Gov.)
✉ B.P. 97, 1 Rue St. Laurent du Var, Djibouti ☎+253 350484 🖹 +253 356502 **W:** rtd.dj **E:** rtd@intnet.dj
L.P: DG: Abdoulkader Ahmed Idriss. Dir. Tec: Mohamed Moussed Yaya. PD: Adoyata Daoud. Dir. Inf: Mr. Dini Aleo.
MW: Djibouti (Dorale) 1116kHz 50kW, 1539kHz 50kW (inactive).
SW: Djibouti (Dorale) 4780kHz 50kW.

FM (MHz)	1	2	0	kW
Ali Sabieh	90.3	94.2	103.0	0.5/0.25/-
Arta	93.5	89.5	104.0	5/3/-
Ballembaley	95.3	91.3		1/0.1
Dikhil	96.6	98.8	104.0	0.5/0.25/-
Djibouti	91.3	95.3		1/1

Channel 1 in Afar/Arabic/Somali: 0300-2100 on ‡1539 & 4780kHz + FM. **Channel 2** in Afar/French: 0300-2100 on 1116kHz & FM. French:

0700-1100 & 1400-1800. **Q**=Quran prgr. **Ann:** "Radio Djibouti".

Other stations:
BBC African Sce: Djibouti 99.2MHz 1kW.
Deutsche Welle/Monte-Carlo Doualiya: Arta 97.2MHz 5kW.
R. Sawa: MW: Djibouti (Pk 12) 1431kHz 600kW 1600-0400, **FM:** Arta 100.8MHz 5kW 24h.
Voice of America: Djibouti 102.0MHz 1kW

DOMINICA

L.T: UTC -4h — **Pop:** 73,000 — **Pr.L:** English, Creole — **E.C:** 50Hz, 240V — **ITU:** DMA

DOMINICA BROADCASTING CORP. (Gov. Comm.)
✉ Victoria Str, PO Box 148, Roseau ☎ +1 767 448 3282/3 🖹 +1 767 448 2918 **E:** dbsradio@cwdom.dm **W:** www.dbcradio.net
L.P: Chairman: Aurelius Jolly. Acting GM: Shermaine Green-Brown. CEN: Kurt Matthew
DBS Radio: Eggleston Roseau 88.1MHz 1kW, Grand Fond 88.5MHz 0.03kW, Marigot 103.5MHz 0.3kW, Petite Soufriere 103.1MHz 0.1kW, Grand Bay 103.5MHz 0.1kW, Portsmouth 104.1MHz 0.1kW. Own prgrs: 0900-0300. Creole: 1800-2000MF. BBC relay: 1200-1205 & 0300-0900.
DBS 89.5: Roseau: 89.5MHz 0.3kW. Format: Easy listening.

Other stations:
KAIRI FM (Comm.), 42 Independence St., PO Box 931, Roseau ☎ +1 767 448 7330/7331 🖹 +1 767 448 7332 **W:** www.kairifm.com **L.P:** Mgr: Steve Vidal. FM: **Kairi FM:** 88.7/93.1/107.9MHz **Hot FM:** 91.1MHz — **Q95** (Comm.), 10 Hanover Str., PO Box 861, Roseau ☎ +1 767 448 5822 🖹 +1 767 448 5828 **W:** www.q95fmradio.com **L.P:** CEO: Sheridan G. Gregoire FM: 90.5/92.3/95.1/95.7/97.5/98.3/ 105.7MHz — **VOICE OF LIFE R. - ZGBC R.** (Rlg., Comm.), PO Box 205, Madrelle, Loubiere, Roseau ☎ +1 767 448 7017 🖹 +1 767 440 0551 **W:** www.voiceoflif-eradio.dm **L.P:** SM: Clementina Munro. CEN: Kurt Matthew. **FM:** 24h: Portsmouth 90.7MHz, Roseau 102.1MHz, Marigot 106.1MHz — **R. EN BA MANGO** (Community), Grand Bay. ☎ +1 767 446 3207 **FM:** 93.5/96.5MHz. **D.Prgr:** Fr-Mo 2200-0300 — **DOMINICA CATHOLIC R.** (Rlg.), The Social Centre, Turkey Lane, Roseau ☎ +1 767 448 3002 **W:** www.dominicacatholicradio.org. **FM:** 96.1MHz (inactive) — **VIBES R.** (Comm), 36 Great George St., Roseau ☎ +1 767 440 8152 🖹 +1 767 448 7376. **E:** davibes@cwdom.dm. **W:** www.vibesradio.dm. **FM:** 90.1/93.9/94.7MHz (F.pl.)

DOMINICAN REPUBLIC

L.T: UTC -4h — **Pop:** 9.5 million — **Pr.L:** Spanish — **E.C:** 60Hz, 110V — **ITU:** DOM

INDOTEL - INSTITUTO DOMINICANO DE LAS TELECOMUNICACIONES
✉ Abrahan Lincoln N° 962, Edif. Osiris 1, Planta, 10148 Santo Domingo ☎ +1 809 732 5555 🖹 +1 809 732 3904 **W:** www.indotel.org.do **L.P:** DG: Lic. Carlos Amarante Baret.

ASOCIACION DOMINICANA DE RADIODIFUSORAS (ADORA)
✉ Calle Paul Harris No 3, Centro de Los Heroes, Santo Domingo

Hrs of tr. 24h unless otherwise stated. Call HI—

MW	Call	kHz	kW	Station, location and hr of tr.
1)	CM	540	5	R. ABC, Sto Domingo: 0900-0400
52)	MS	570	10/5	R. Crystal, Sto Domingo
71)	FS	580	5	R. Montecristi, Montecristi
4)	DV	590	10/5	R. Santa María, La Vega: 0900-0300
7)	SD	‡600		R. Santo Domingo, El Seybo (r: 620)
118)		600		Celestial 600, Santo Domingo
60)	JR	610	5	R. Amanecer, Santiago (r: 1580)
7)	SD	‡610	1	R. Santo Domingo, Pedernales: (r: 620)
7)	SD	620	10	R. Santo Domingo, Sto Domingo: 0900-0400
7)	SD	‡630	1	R. Santo Domingo, San Juan (r: 620)
7)	SD	‡640	10	R. Santo Domingo, Santiago
9)	AT	650	15/5	R. Universal, Sto Domingo
62)	AM	660	3	R. Visión Cristiana, Santiago: (r: 1330)
59)	BS	670	5	R. Dial, San Pedro de Macorís
7)	SD	‡670	1	R. Santo Domingo, Barahona (r: 620)
11)	JX	‡680	3	R. Zamba, San Ignacio de Sabaneta: 0900-0300
12)	AW	690	10	R. Guarachita "La Poderosa", Sto Domingo: 0900-0400
13)	DC	‡700	0.6	R. Mao, Mao, Valverde
119)		710		Red Nacional Cristiana, Santo Domingo
104)	P	710		Onda del Caribe, San Cristóbal
14)	AQ	720	1.5	R. Norte, Santiago: 0900-0500
87)	EF	720	5	R. Cayacoa, Higüey: 0900-0400

MW	Call	kHz	kW	Station, location and hr of tr.
15)	Z	730	10	R. HIZ/Zulu R, Sto Domingo: 1100-0500
16)	DB	750	5	R. Jesús AM, Santiago
17)	CO	‡760	5	R. Cordillera, Sto Domingo
18)	MD	770	5	R. Águila, Santiago: (limited news & sports broadc.)
19)	BO	780	0.5	R. Constanza, Constanza: 1100-0200
20)	L	790	5	R. Centro, Sto Domingo (occ r. Romántica FM 107.7)
70)	VM	800	1	R. Bonao, Bonao: 1000-0400
24)	AV	810	5	R. Salvación Internacional, Baní: 1100-0300
21)	AZ	820	3	R. Vida, Santiago
22)	JB	830	10	R. HIJB, Sto Domingo: 1100-0300
23)	AB	‡840	1	R. Isabel de Torres, Puerto Plata
72)	GA	850	5	R. Guarocuya, Barahona: 1000-0400
5)	UA	‡850	5	R. Clarín, Santiago
5)	UA	860	10	R. Clarín, Sto Domingo
25)	VG	870	4	R. La Vega, La Vega: 1000-0300
26)	OR	890	3	R. 8-90/La Consentida, Valverde: 1000-0400
27)	PJ	‡890	4/5	R. Continental, Sto Domingo: 1000-0500
28)	EN	900	5/1	R. Puerto Plata, Puerto Plata: 0900-0400
60)	FK	900		R. Amanecer, Neiba (r. 1580)
29)	LB	910	3	Tiempo 910, Bonao: 0930-0300
9)	BA	920	10	R. 9-20 AM-Stereo "Power", Sto Domingo
31)	CK	‡930	10	Ondas del Yaque, Santiago
8)	AS	‡940	3	R. Metro, Montecristi (F.Pl.)
32)	IG	950	10	R. Popular, Sto Domingo
33)	FF	960	5/1	LV del Atlántico, Puerto Plata: 1000-0500
50C)	CV	970	5/1	R. Barahona, Barahona
25)	VP	970	6	R. Olímpica, La Vega
36)	SA	990	1	R. Cibao, Santiago (irr, also r. 1510 R. Pueblo)
37)	HG	‡1000	5/1	R. Beller, Dajabón: 1000-0300
38)	JA	1010	10	R. Comercial, Sto Domingo: 1100-0600
38)	JA	1010		R. Comercial, Salcedo (r: HIJA Sto Domingo 1010)
38)	JA	1010		R. Comercial, San Juan de la Maguana (r: HIJA Sto Domingo 1010)
30)	TS	‡1020	10	R. Enriquillo, Neyba: 0900-0400
39)	DL	1030	5	R. Novedades, Santiago
40)	ON	1040	10	CDN Radio, Sto Domingo
14)	CB	1050	1.5	R. Hispaniola, Santiago
60)	AJ	1060	5	R. Amanecer, San Pedro de Macorís (r: 1580)
42)	XF	1060	1	R. Azua, Azua: 1000-0200
44)	BI	1070	5/1	HIBI R. 1070, San Francisco de Macorís: 0900-0400
45)	MC	1080	1	R. RPQ Sport, Santiago
46)	JM	1090	3	R. Amistad, Santiago
50A	RB	1100	1	R. Jimaní, Jimaní
47)	HD	1100	1	R. Oriente, San Pedro de Macorís: 0900-0400
48)	MP	1100	1	R. Ocoa, San José de Ocoa: 1200-0200
49)	PS	1100	1	R. Comercial, Nagua: 0900-0200
51)	TC	1110	2.5	R. Jarabacoa, Jarabacoa: 1000-0300
95)	OS	‡1110	1/0.5	R. Marién, Dajabón
52)	CN	1120	10	R. Metro Hit, Sto Domingo
52)	CN	1120		R. Metro Hit, Samaná (r: 1120): 1000-0400
109)		1120		R. Antillas, Barahona
40)	RL	1130	10/1	CDN Radio, Santiago (r: 1040)
55)	RA	1140	5	R. Anacaona, San Juan de la Maguana: 1100-0400
55)	AS	1150	5	Onda Musical, Sto Domingo: 1100-0500
56)	BE	1160	5	Radiolandia, Santiago (Occ r: 1180kHz): 0900-0400
110)	JS	1170		Cadena Espacial, Azua
57)	BE	1180	1	R. Mil, Sto Domingo: 1000-0500
58)	AG	‡1190	10	Azul 11-90 Bachatisima, Santiago
50B)	MR	1200	1	R. Caracol, Azua
98)	AH	1200		R. VEN - Voz Evangélica Nacional, Sto Domingo
61)	CJ	1210	5	R. Merengue, San Francisco de Macorís
100)		1220		R. HIN, Sto Domingo (rel La Z 101)
63)	PM	‡1230		R. Moca, Moca
64)	AU	1240	1	R. Vida, Puerto Plata: 0900-0300
53)		1240	1	R. María, Santo Domingo
66)	BC	1250	5	LV del Progreso, San Francisco de Macorís: 1000-0400
67)	RJ	1250	5	R. Juventud, La Romana: 0930-0430
38)	T	‡1260	1	R. Recuerdos, Sto Domingo
52)	DA	1270	1.2	R. Metro-Hit 12-70, Samaná
69)	TA	1270	1	R. Ambiente, Baní: 1000-0400
110	JH	‡1280		Cadena Espacial, Azua
6)	BD	‡1290	0.5	R. Jánico, Santiago
74)	KQ	‡1300	1	Radio Doz 1300, Sto Domingo
75)	MH	1310	1	R. Real, La Vega: 1000-0300
76)	BZ	1320	1/0.5	R. Centro, San Juan de la Maguana
62)	VC	1330	3	R. Visión Cristiana, Sto Domingo
77)	PM	1350	1	R. Rutas Musical, La Romana: 1000-0400
102)	JD	1350	1	Ondas del Yuna, Bonao
108)	XZ	1360	1	R. Tropical, Sto Domingo
79)	RP	1370	5	R. Seybo, El Seybo
80)	SC	1380	1	R. Nacional, Santiago: 1000-0300
81)	AR	1390	1	R. San Cristóbal: 1100-0300
82)	AC	1400	1	Ondas del Valle, La Vega: 1100-0200

MW	Call	kHz	kW	Station, location and hr of tr.
65)	AE	1410	1	R. Tricolor, Sto Domingo
85)	JJ	1410	1/0.5	R. Grí-Grí, Río San Juan: 1000-0300
50D)	CH	1410	3/0.5	R. 14-10 Cristiana, Barahona
86)	FD	1420	1.5	R. Oro, Cotuí
34)	JC	1430	5	R. Emanuel, Santiago
89)	AD	1440	5	R. San Juan, San Juan de la Maguana: 1000-0300
90)	AK	1440	5	R. Impactante, Sto Domingo
83)		‡1450		R. Alfa y Omega, Sto Domingo
91)	AC	1450	10	R. Util, Salcedo: 0900-0400
92)	AN	1460	0.5	R. Renacimiento, Hato Mayor del Rey
93)	DE	1470	1	LV de la Alabanza, San Francisco de Macorís: 1000-0400
50C)	CH	1470		R. Vibra "La Deportiva", Barahona
50D)	CV	1470		R. Barahona, Provincia Independencia (r: R. Barahona 970)
68)	AH°	1480	5	R. Villa, Sto Domingo: 1000-0400 (Sun 1100-2300)
96)		‡1490	3	La Voz del Cibao, Santiago
97)	PA	1500	0.5	R. Higüey, Higüey: 0900-0400
111)	RD	1500	3	R. Juan Pablo Duarte, Elías Piña
98)	BL °	1510	10/3	R. Pueblo, Sto Domingo: 1000-0400 (Sun 1100-2300)
99)	WJ	1520	1	R. Samaná "R. 15-20", Samaná: 1000-0400
112)	JN	‡1530	0.25	Canal 25, Santiago: (irr. Channel 25 UHF audio)
38)	FP	‡1540	1	R. Criolla Comercial, Sto Domingo
41)	BU	‡1540	1	LV de la Romana, La Romana: 0930-0400
50E)	PZ	1560	1/0.5	R. Pedernales, Pedernales
117)		1560	1	R. Universidad UASD, Santo Domingo (CP)
101)	GL	‡1560	1	R. Única, Santiago
60)	AJ°	1580	10	R. Amanecer, Sto Domingo: 1000-0400
50F)	PK	1580	1	R. Neiba, Neiba: 0900-0400
101)	SF	1590	1	R. Libertad, Santiago
65)	FG	1600	5	R. Revelación en América, Sto Domingo: 1200-0200
103)	SR	1620	1	R. Taina/Planeta, San Pedro de Macorís
10)	C80	1640	1/0.5	R. Juventus Don Bosco, Sto Domingo
115)		‡1650	5/3	RADECO, Santiago (CP)
116)		‡1660	5/1	Fundación Lama, Sto Domingo (CP)
114)	SV	1680	1	R. Senda 1680 AM, San Pedro de Macorís
113)		1700	5/1	R. Eternidad, Sto Domingo: 1100-2400

° = also on SW, ‡ = inactive, (r) = repeater, ± = varying fq.

SW	Call	kHz	kW	Station, location and h of tr
60)	IJ	‡6025	1	R. Amanecer Internac., Sto Domingo: 0900-0300

Addresses and other information

1) Av Rómulo Betancourt N° 2078, (or: Ap 517), Sto Domingo – 2) Calle Félix María Ruiz N° 6, La Trinitaria, (or: Ap 581), Santiago FM: 95.5MHz W: www.digital95fm.com – 4) Avenida Rivera km 1.5 (or: Ap 55), La Vega W: www.rsantamaria.com - FM: 97.9MHz – 5) Av Prolongación México, esquina Clarín,Sto Domingo – 6) Santiago - FM: 90.5MHz – 7) Ap 869 (or: Dr.Tejada Florentino N° 8), Sto Domingo W: www.certvdominicana.com E: certvdominicana@gmail.com – 8) Duarte N° 1 (or: Ap 52), Montecristi W: www.microondasnacionales.com/radi-omontecristi.htm FM: 97.1MHz – 9) Av 27 de Febrero, Edificio Kira, Sto Domingo W: www.radiouniversalfm.com - FM: 98.1MHz – 10) Calle Juan Evangelista Jiménez # 49, Barrio María Auxiliadora, (or Apartado Postal 4848), Sto Domingo W: www.radiojuventusdonbosco.com – 11) Calle Restauración N° 60 (or: Ap 2), San Ignacio de Sabaneta E: t. sabaneta@verizon.net.do - FM: 92.3MHz – 12) Calle Palo Hincado 302, Sto Domingo – 13) Calle Duarte N° 49 (or: Ap 20), Valverde FM: Ap 789, Santiago) few hours on weekends – 14) Urb Las Hortensias (or: Ap 454), Santiago – W: www.norte720.com W: www.radiohispaniola.com FM: 103.5MHz – 15) Calle El Conde Esq Sánchez, Edif Copelic (or: Ap 68), Sto Domingo W: zulurd.com – 16) Calle Sánchez Esq Pedro F Bonó, Santiago W: www.radiojesus750am.org – 17) Calle Emilio A Morel esq Luis Pérez, Ensanche La Fé, Sto Domingo – 18) Calle El Sol 51, 3a Planta, Edif Lamarche Alvarez (or: Ap 1636), Santiago. FM: 97.1MHz – 19) Calle V.M de Robiou N° 18, Constanza – 20) Abraham Lincoln N° 58 (or: Ap 335) , Sto Domingo – 21) Av Estrella Sadhalá N° 3, Plaza Alejo, 3er piso (or: Ap 282), Santiago FM: 99.1MHz W: www.radiosan-tiago820am.com – 22) Edif Teleantillas, Carr Duarte km 7.5, Sto Domingo - FM: 95.7MHz – 23) Ap 146, Puerto Plata 0930-0330 – 24) Calle Mella esquina Calle 27 de Febrero, Baní W: www.radiosalvacion.com FM 95.7 Baní FM – 25) Av Pedro A Rivera, KM 0, Grupo Medrano (or: Ap 203), La Vega W: www.radiovega.com W: www.olimpica970.com - FM: 104.9MHz – 26) Calle 27 de Febrero Esq Agustin Cabral (or: Ap 80), Valverde - FM: 106.7MHz – 27) Calle Dr Delgado N° 206 (or: Ap 156), Sto Domingo – 28) Av 26 de Agosto N° 38,, Puerto Plata - FM: 99.7MHz – 29) Calle Mella 50, Bonao W: www.radio91am.com – 30) Calle A Reyes N° 3 (or: Ap 99,) Neyba - FM: 93.7 – 31) Calle Restauración Esq 30 de Marzo (or: Ap 225), Santiago - FM: 92.1MHz – 32) Av Charles Summer N° 33, Los Prados (or: Ap 928), Sto Domingo - FM: 97.3MHz – 33) Av John F Kennedy N° (altos) Puerto Plata - FM: 97.3MHz – 34) Calle Cuba No. 46, 3ra planta, Los Pepines, (or: Apartado Postal 897) Santiago W: www.radioemanuel.com FM: 89.1MHz – 36) Av

Imbert, Gurabito (or: Ap 141), Santiago - FM: 95.1MHz – **37)** Av Pablo Reyes N° 1, Dajabón - FM: 91.7MHz – **38)** E A Morel 27 (or: Ap 1322), Sto Domingo **W:** www.radiocomercial1010.com - FM: 106.5MHz – **39)** Av Estrella Sadhalá, Plaza Alejo (3era planta) , Santiago - FM: 92.7MHz **W:** www.radionovedades.net – **40)**Calle Dr Delfilló N° 4, Los Prados, Sto Domingo **W:** www.elcaribecdn.com – **41)** Av Gregforio Luperón N° 10-A, (or: Ap 213), La Romana – **42)** Calle Emilio Prud'homme 17A, Azua - FM: 97.1MHz – **44)** Av 27 de Febrero N° 51 (or:Ap 201), San Francisco de Macorís **W:** www.hibiradioam.com - FM: 102.3MHz – **45)** Edif Jaar, Calle El Conde esq Espaillat, Sto Domingo – **46)** Av Texas Esq Calle 12, Jardines Metropolitanos (or: Ap 561), Santiago **W:** www.amistad1090.com - FM: 101.9MHz – **47)** Calle Mariano Soler Merino N° 19 (altos) (or: Ap 64), San Pedro de Macorís – **48)** Calle Canada, San José de Ocoa **W:** www.radioocoa.com – **49)** Calle Narciso Minaya N° 36, Nagua – **50A-F)** Empresas Radiofónicas SA, Ap 20339, Sto Domingo **W:** www.suprafm.com/informativo.htm 50A) 27 de Febrero 1, Jimaní; 50B Félix del Rosario 1, Azua;50C-D) Edificio Rodolfo Lama, Calle María Montés #24 (Ap 20339), Barahona; 50E) Duarte 1, Pedernales; 50F) Cambronal 8, Neiba – **51)** Calle Domingo Sabio N° 1 (or: Ap 10), Jarabacoa - FM: 98.7MHz – **52)** Urbanización Las Hortensias, Santiago **W:** www.microondasnacionales.com FM: 98.3MHz – **53)** Ave 27 de Febrero # 238, Edificio Rodríguez Sandoval, 5to piso, Santo Domingo **W:** http://radiomariadominicana.org – **54)** Calle Club de Leones N° 175 (or: Ap 37), San Juan de la Maguana – **55)** Calle Palo Incado N° 161, Sto Domingo **W:** www.ondamusical1150.com – **56)** Calle Sánchez N° 64 (or: Ap 187), Santiago - FM: 93.1MHz – **57)** Av Máximo Gómez N° 65 (or: Ap 1372), Sto Domingo - FM: 103.3MHz – **58)** Calle Restauración Esq 30 de Marzo (or: Ap 79), Santiago - FM: 94.3MHz – **59)** Av. Independencia No. 169, San Pedro de Macorís - FM: 90.7MHz Sultana + 98.7 Estéreo 98 **W:** www.radiodial670am.com.do – **60)** Juan Sánchez Ramírez #40, Gazcue (or: Ap 4680), Sto Domingo (Owned and managed by the Seventh Day Adventist Church) **W:** www.radioamanecer.org – **61)** Calle 27 de Febrero N° (or: Ap 57), San Francisco de Macorís **W:** www.circuitomerengue.com - FM: 94.7MHz – **62)** Calle Sánchez N°, Casi Esquina Calle del Sol Centro, Santiago / Calle César Dargán #26, El Vergel (Frente a la Plaza Criolla), Sto Domingo (or: P O Box 2908, Paterson, NJ 07509-2908, USA) **W:** www.radiovision.net – **63)** Ave 27 de Febrero # 265, Suite 202, Piantini, Santo Domingo– **64)** Av Circunvalación Norte, Puerto Plata – **65)** Av 25 de Febrero 144, Ensanche Las Americas, P3 Hotel Hostal Puerto Rico, Sto Domingo **W:** www.radiorevelacionenamerica.org.do – **66)** Ap 264 (or: Calle San Francisco 50), San Francisco de Macorís – **67)** Calle Santa Rosa N° 18 (or:Ap 151), La Romana FM: 107.5MHz – **69)** Sánchez esq Mella, Baní FM: 96.7MHz – **70)** Calle Libertad N° 15, , Bonao FM: 88.7MHz Latina 88 – **71)** C/ Proecto No 11, Las Colinas, Montecristi **W:** www.radiomontecristi.com – **72)** Padre Billini esq Jaime Mota, Barahona– **74)** Conde esq 19 Marzo, Edif El Palacio, Sto Domingo **W:** www.la2dehiz.com – **75)** Juan Rodríguez 76-A, La Vega **W:** www.radioreal.net – **76)** Av Anacaona N° 52 (or: Ap 65), San Juan de la Maguana **W:** www. Radiocentroam.8k.com - FM: 100.1MHz Santome FM – **77)** Calle Santa Rosa N° 25 (or: Ap 207), La Romana FM: 94 5MHz – **79)** Ap 266 (or: Libertad 9), El Seybo **W:** www.radioseibo.org - FM: 93.7MHz – **80)** Av Las Carreras, Esq Mella (4ta Planta), Santiago **W:** http://radionacional.net - FM: 106.1MHz – **81)** Calle Socorro Sánchez N° 103, San Cristóbal – **82)** Restauración 64, La Vega – **83)** Ap 2674, Sto Domingo – **84)** C/ Duarte Esq Mella, Edi Fantino 2da Pta., Santiago – **85)** Calle Sánchez N° 45 (or: Ap 003), Río San Juan FM: 105.9MHz – **86)** Calle Sánchez N° 48 , Cotuí - FM: 97.3MHz – **87)** Diócesis de la Alta Gracia, Calle General Santana 65, Higüey **W:** lavozdelaaltagracia.com – **88)** Av 27 de Febrero No 265, Suite 202, Piantini, Santo Domingo – **89)** Calle Santomé N° 27 (or Ap 88), San Juan de la Maguana FM: 90.3MHz – **90)** Ave Sarasota esquina Winston Churchill, Plaza Universitaria, Local 9B, Sto Domingo **W:** www.radioimpacto.org – **91)** Calle Mella N° 90 (altos) (or: Ap 2), Salcedo **W:** www.radioutilfm.com - FM: 106.5MHz – **92)** Calle Felipe de Castro Esq Santana N° 4, Hato Mayor del Rey – **93)** Carr.salida a Nagua al lado del Hospital del Seguro Social, San Francisco de Macorís – **95)** Pres Henríquez 53, Dajabón - FM: 105.1MHz – **96)** Plaza Alejo, Av. Estrella Sadhala, Santiago FM: Comando 88 – **97)** Calle Altagracia N° 70, Higüey – **98)** Ap 2217 (or: Avenida Leopoldo Navarro No 34 Rsq. Juan E. Dunant), Sto Domingo **W:** www.radioven.com – **99)** Av Malecón, Samaná – **100)** Sto Domingo – **101)** Ap 1091, Santiago **W:** www.radiopoder.com/index.html – **102)** Calle Duarte Esq Mella, Edif Fantino (2da planta), Bonao – **103)** Circuito Telesonido, Mella N° 177, San Pedro de Macorís – **104)** San Cristóbal – **107)** Calle Proyecto, Neiba – **108)** C/Paseo de Los Periodistas N° 52, Sto Domingo – **109)** Barahona – **110)** Av Pasteur N° 204, Sto Domingo – **111)** C/La Lira N° 18, Ens.Vergel, Elias Piña – **112)** Calle General López Esq 16 de Agosto, Santiago FM: 91.3MHz – **113)** Luís Amiama Tió # 105, Arroyo Hondo, Santo Domingo **W:** www.radioeternidad.org – **114)** Calle René del Risco Bermúdez No.17, Villa Progreso, San Pedro de Macorís **W:** www.radiosenda.net – **115)** Av San Cristóbal esq L Pérez García, Santiago – **116)**

C/Fantino Falco No 47, 1er piso, Plaza Naco, Santo Domingo – **117)** Universidad Autonoma de Santo Domingo, Alma Mater, Santo Domingo **W:** www.uasd.edu.do – **118)** Avenida Las Américas Esquina España, Santo Domingo – **119)** Avenida Lope de Vega, Santo Domingo – **W:** rednacionalcristiana.net

FM in Sto Domingo (MHz):
88.1 Primera FM – 88.5 Estudio Rock – 88.9 Escape – 89.3 Neon – 89.7 Renuevo FM – 90.1 Fuego 90 – 90.5 Estrella 90 – 90.9 Alianza Francesa - 91.3 La 91 FM – 91.7 La Roka FM – 92.1 Hits 92 – 92.5 CDN - 92.9 Pura Vida 92.9 – 93.3 Independencia FM – 93.7 Latidos FM – 94.1 Fidelity – 94.5 KQ-94.5 FM – 94.9 Kiss – 95.3 Radeco – 95.7 La Nota Diferente – 96.1 Quisqueya FM (CERTV) – 96.5 Ritmo 96 – 96.9 Espacio 96.9 FM – 97.3 Disney – 97.7 R. Higo/Emociones FM – 98.1 Universal – 98.5 Rumba FM – 98.9 Dominicana FM (CERTV) – 99.3 Sonido Suave - 99.7 Listín – 100.1 Antena 100 – 100.5 Cima – 100.9 Super Q – 101.3 Z-101 – 101.7 Supra FM – 102.1 La X 102 – 102.5 Tentación – 102.5 Vaughan Radio – 102.9 Raíces FM - 103.3 Milenium FM – 103.7 Power FM – 104.1 R. Cordillera – 104.5 ESPN R. – 104.5 Mortal FM – 105.3 ABC – 105.7 Fiesta FM – 106.1 Disco – 106.5 Zol 106.0 – 106.9 LV de las FF AA – 107.3 Cadena Espacial – 107.7 Romántica R. Millón
FM in Santiago (MHz):
88.1 Primera FM – 88.5 Comando FM – 88.9 Disco 89 – 89.3 R. Disney – 89.7 CDN – 90.1 Primor FM – 90.5 Fuego 90 – 90.9 R. Amanecer – 92.1 ZOL FM (rolay)   92.7 Lider FM (R. Novedades) – 93.1 Concierto FM – 93.7 R. Luz – 94.1 Full FM – 94.7 KV 94 – 95.1 Raices – 95.5 Digital FM – 95.9 Clave FM – 96.3 La Kalle – 97.1 Caliente – 97.5 La Ley – 98.3 Turbo 98 – 99.1 Champion FM – 100.3 R. Monumental – 101.1 Premium – 101.5 Z 101 – 101.9 Amistad FM – 103.1 Super 103 – 103.9 Super Regional – 104.7 Matrix – 105.5 Ke Buena – 105.9 La Bakana – 106.1 Criolla 106 – 106.5 Red FM R. Educativa Dominicana – 106.9 La Nueva 107 – 107.3 Suave 107 – 107.9 Mix

---

EASTER ISLAND (Chile)

L.T: UTC -6h (2 Sep 12-9 Mar 13, 13 Oct 13-8 Mar 14: -5h). Subject to change — **Pop:** 5,034 — **Pr.L:** Spanish, Rapanui — **E.C:** 50Hz, 220V — **ITU:** PAQ

FM	MHz	kW	Station	FM	MHz	kW	Station
1)	88.3	-	ADN R.	3)	104.3	-	Los 40 Principales
2)	88.9	1	R. Manukena	4)	107.3	-	R. Nuevo Tiempo

Addresses and other information
1) 24h satellite relay from Santiago **W:** www.adnradio.cl – **2)** La Misma Municipalidad de Isla de Pascua, Calle Atamu Tekena, Hangaroa. Correo Isla de Pascua, Chile **☎**+5632 255 1245 **W:** www.portalrapanui.cl/rapanui/radiomanukena **LP:** Dir: Nelson Ramon Zapata Orellana. Community radio stn **Prgr:** 24h – **3)** 24h satellite relay from Santiago. **W:** www.los40.cl – **4)** 24h satellite relay from Santiago **W:** www.nuevotiempo.com

---

ECUADOR

L.T: UTC -5h — **Pop:** 13.9 million — **Pr.L:** Spanish, Quichua — **E.C:** 60Hz, 110/127 V — **ITU:** EQA

SUPERINTENDENCIA DE TELECOMUNICACIONES DEL ECUADOR
▢ 9 de Octubre 1645 y Berlin, Quito **☎** +593 22 2221500 **W:** www.supertel.gov.ec **E:** info@supertel.gov.ec

Hrs of tr. 24h unless stated below. Call HC—

MW	Call	kHz	kW	Station, location, hr. of tr.
PI01)	DC1	530	1	R. Iris/530 AM "LV de la Comunidad", Quito: 1000-0500
GU01)	FA2	540	25	R. Tropicana "Canal 540", Guayaquil: 1100-0600
PI02)	GM1	550	50	R. Reloj "5-50", Quito: 1100-0400
GU01)	RN2	560	25	C. R. E. Satelital, Guayaquil
PI03)	CE1	570	10	R. El Sol, Quito
GU02)	PC2	580	10	R. Uno, Guayaquil
PI04)	SP1	590	10	R. Carrusel, Quito: 1100-0200
GU03)	XY2	600	50	R. Ciudadana, Guayaquil: 1100-0400
PI05)	MJ1	610	10	R. Caravana AM, Quito
LO01)	XY3	620	50	R. Ciudadana, Loja: 1100-0400
LR01)	HA2	620	10	Ondas Quevedeñas, Quevedo
PI06)	XY1	640	50	R. Ciudadana, Quito: 1100-0400
MA01)	FD4	650	5	R. Visión Manta, Manta: 0900-0500
GU05)	LG2	660	30	R. Carrusel, Guayaquil: 1200-0500 (PI04)
PI07)	FF1	670	12/5	R. Jesús del Gran Poder, Quito: 0945-0500
GU06)	VP2	680	25/12	R. Atalaya, Guayaquil: W 0900-0500, Sun 1000-0300

MW	Call	kHz	kW	Station, location, hr. of tr.
MA02)	FA4	690	5	Sucre Portoviejo, Portoviejo
PI08)	JB1	°690	50d	LV de los Andes, Quito: 1030-0500
GU07)	RS2	700	50	Sucre Guayaquil, Guayaquil
CR01)	ER5	710	8	Escuelas Radiofónicas Populares, Riobamba: 0900-0300
EO01)	UE3	720	10	R. Unica, Machala
LO02)	MO3	720	5	R. Matovelle "HCM-3", Loja: 1000-0200
MA03)	GB4	±720	10	LV de Portoviejo, Portoviejo: 1000-0400
PI09)	IC1	720	5	R. Municipal, Quito
GU08)	MG2	730	10	R. Guayaquil, Guayaquil
MA04)	SE4	±740	10	R. Libertad, Chone: 1100-0600
PI15)	GC1	740	10	R. Melodía "Canal 7-40", Quito: 1100-0400
GU09)	RC2	750	30	Caravana AM, Guayaquil
PI10)	QR1	°760	25	R. Quito "LV de la Capital", Quito
GU10)	MF2	770	25/12	R. El Telégrafo, Guayaquil: 1000-0500
PI20)	CM1	780	10/2	R. Colón AM, Quito
PI12)		790		R. Paraíso, Maldonado
IM01)		790		Su Radio 790 AM, Otavalo
GU05)	ML2	800	25	K 800, Guayaquil
PI13)	FB1	800	5	R. Sensación 800, Quito: 1000-0300
GU11)	VT2	810	5	R. Atalaya, El Milagro: 2300-0300
TU01)		810		Sucre Ambato, Ambato
CA01)	VI5	820	5	LV de Ingapirca, Cañar: 0900-0330
MA06)	RF4	820	1	Canal Manabita, Portoviejo
PI54)	UP1	820	25	R. Unión, Quito: 1100-0100
CR02)	RP5	830	4.5	R. Promoción, Riobamba: 0900-1400, 2200-0200
GU12)	RM2	830	25	R. Huancavilca, Guayaquil
MA07)	EM4	840	1	R. Costa Azul, Portoviejo: 1100-0500
PI16)	PN1	840	50	R. Vigía "LV de la Policía Nacional", Quito: 1100-0300
GU13)	VS2	±850	20/12	R. San Francisco, Guayaquil: M-F 0945-0500, Sat -0300, Sun -0100
PI17)	PC1	860	10	R. Positiva AM, Quito: 1015-0400
GU14)	NY2	870	20	R. Cristal "RCQ", Guayaquil: 1000-0600
TU02)	GS6	870	1	R. Píllaro, Píllaro: 1100-0400
PI18)	RP1	880	50/40	R. Católica Nacional, Quito: 1000-0200
CR03)	TL5	‡890	1	Ondas del Chimborazo, Riobamba: 1100-0500
EO02)	RS3	±890	25/20	R. Superior, Machala: 0900-0500
AZ01)	RR5	900	1	R. Carrusel, Cuenca: 1100-0200
MA08)	OF4	±900	5	R. Chone, Chone: 1100-0400
PI19)	VA1	±900	10	Sucre Quito, Quito: 1100-0400
CR04)	GE5	910	5	R. Mundial, Riobamba: 1000-0400
GU15)	BO2	910	2	Colón AM,Guayaquil
EO03)	RU3	920	10	CRO - Compañía Radiofónica Orense, Machala: 0930-0430
PI40)	AB1	920	1	R. Democrácia "La Cariñosa", Quito: 1000-0400
GU12)	VI2	±930	5	Canal Tropical, Guayaquil
TU03)	BA6	930	5	R. Ambato, Ambato
AZ21)		940		R. Austral del Ecuador, Cuenca
PI21)	BZ1	940	5	R. Dif. de la Casa de la Cultura Ecuatoriana, Quito: -0200
CR05)	UE5	950	3	R. Colta "LV de la Asociación", Colta: 0900-0200
GU17)	DE2	‡950	10	GRD R. Internacional, Guayaquil
IM02)		°950		Chaskis del Norte, Ibarra
AZ02)	SA5	960	1	Sono Onda Internacional, Cuenca: W 0925-0430, Sun1200-0400
PI22)	NC1	960	1	La Pantera, Quito: 1100-0500
TU04)	JX6	960	1	LV del Santuario, Baños: 1000-0300
SD01)	OT1	965	10	R. Católica Nacional, Sto Domingo de los Colorados (r: 880)
GU18)	AW2	970	20	R. Católica Nal. del Ecuador, Guayaquil: 1000-0500
IM03)	MB1	970	1	R. Imperio, Ibarra: 1030-0300
CR06)	JI5	980	1	R. El Prado, Riobamba
LO11)	CL3	980	5	R. Cariamanga, Cariamanga: 1000-0400
PI24)	GH1	990	25	R. Tarquí, Quito: 1015-0400
GU19)	EW2	990	15	Frecuencia Mil, Quito
LO03)	NT3	1000	1	Dinamita Mil AM, Catamayo: 1030-2330
AZ04)	RV5	1000	2.5	R. Visión AM, Cuenca
GU20)	RZ2	1010	3	R. Amiga, Guayaquil: 1100-0500
TU05)	NR6	1010	15	TSB R. Líder, Ambato: 0945-0300
BO01)	CR6	1020	5/3	R. Surcos, Guayaquil: 1030-0100
PI26)	HR1	1020	5	RTU (Radio y Televisión Unidas), Quito
GU21)	RF2	1030	5	R. Punto 1030/Ecuantena, Guayaquill: 1100-0500
AZ05)	EV5	±1040	10/5	R. Splendit, Cuenca
PI27)	CW1	‡1040	3	LV del Valle, Machachi: 1130-0100
TU06)	GB6	1040	3	R. Colosal, Ambato: 0930-0500
GU49)	RQ2	1050	5	R. Águila, Guayaqui: 1030-0400
IM04)	IM1	1050	5/3	LV de Imbabura, Ibarra: 1000-0100
CP01)	MG6	1050	5	R. Ecos del Pueblo, Saquisilí: 1045-0330
EO19)		1060		R. Fiesta, Machala
LR02)		1060		R. Richi, El Empalme
AZ06)	CJ5	1070	5	R. LV de Tomebamba, Cuenca: 1000-0500
PI28)	VP1	1070	1	R. Libertad, Quito
SD02)	RS1	1070	1	R. Lubakán, Santo Domingo de los Colorados: 0950-0200 (Sun -2300)
CP02)	BH6	1080	10	R. Latacunga AM, Latacunga: 0900-0230
GU22)	KD2	1080	10	Sistema 2, Guayaquil
MA11)	AB4	1080	1	R. Contacto, Manta: 0900-0300
PI30)	VI1	1090	5	R. Irfeyal "Fe y Alegría", Quito
CP03)	GR6	1100	5/2	R. Novedades, Latacunga: 1000-0500
NA02)	LE7	°1100	1.5	R. Oriental, Tena: 0900-0400
AZ07)	JC5	1110	5	R. Ondas Azuayas, Cuenca: 1100-0200
PI31)	JR1	1110	10	R. Clásica, Quito
TU07)	RP6	±1110	5	R. Pelileo, Pelileo: 1100-0400
CC01)	EB1	1120	2	Canal 1120, San Gabriel
GU24)	FV2	1120	5	Estación Intercontinental, Guayaquil: 1100-0500
PA02)	AS7	1120	3	R. Variedades del Puyo, El Puyo
EO20)		1130		Romántica AM, Machala
IM05)	RD1	1130	5/3	R. Punto, Ibarra: 1000-0400
LR03)		1130		R. Sibimbe AM, Ventanas
TU08)	PV6	°1130	5	R. Centro, Ambato
AZ08)	AZ5	1140	1	R. Alfa Musical, Cuenca: 1100-0600
GU25)	FB2	1140	1.5	R. Cóndor, Guayaquil: 1130-0500
MA12)	MF4	1140	4	R. Rumbos, Portoviejo
PI33)	IR1	1140	5	Raíz 11-40, Quito: 1130-0400
CR07)	GB5	1150	10	LV de Riobamba "Antena 1", Riobamba
LO06)	AV3	1150	5	R. Luz y Vida, Loja: 1000-0330, Sat -0400, Sun -0700
CA02)		1160		LV del Pueblo, Azoguez
CP04)	UR6	1160	1	R. Runatacuyaí "LV de la Asociación", Latacunga: W 1000-0200
EO05)	VR3	1160	2	R. Vía, Machala
MA13)	WD4	1160	1	R. Cenit, Portoviejo: 1200-0500
PI34)	CP1	‡1160	5	Super Auténtica, La Radio 11-60, Quito
CR08)	JV5	1170	5	R. Central, Riobamba: 0900-0500
GU26)	RV2	1170	5	R. Filadelfia, Guayaquil
AZ09)	DP5	1180	4	R. Cuenca "LV de los 4 Ríos", Cuenca: 1200-0900
MA26)		‡1180		LV del Volante, Portoviejo
PI35)	LR1	1180	12.5	Nueva Em. Central, Quito: 1100-0400
CP05)	RF6	1190	1	R. El Sol, Pujilí: 1100-0200
GU22)	DE2	1190	2	Estudio Universidad Católica, Guayaquil: 1100-0500
AZ10)	RM5	1200	5	R. El Mercurio, Cuenca: 0900-0500
EO07)		1200		R. U Cadena Sur, Sta Rosa
LR04)	RE2	1200	5	LV del Trópico, Quevedo: 1000-0400
PI36)	CS1	±1200	5	R. Super K, La Líder, Sangolquí: 1000-0100
GU27)	BJ2	1210	20	R. El Mundo, Guayaquil: 1200-0300, Sat -0100, Sun -0400
LO07)	VC3	°1210	10	R. Centinela del Sur "CDS", Loja: 1100-0300
TU09)	JM6	1210	3	R. Sira, Ambato: 1000-0700
BO03)	EB6	1220	3/5	Ecos de Bolívar, Guaranda: 0930-0130
PI32)	AP1	1220	10	R. Marañón, Quito: 1300-0200
AZ11)	MV5	1230	3	R. Popular, Cuenca: 1045-0500
CP06)	RL6	°1230	1	LV de Saquisilí y Libertador, Saquisilí: 1045-0300
ESO2)	FG4	1230	5	Sucre Esmeraldas, Esmeraldas
GU48)	FV2	1230	15	R. Galáctica, Guayaquil: 1000-0400
IM06)	RI1	°1230	3	CRI-Centro Radiofónico de Imbabura, Ibarra: 1100-0300
EO08)	RF3	1240	5	R. Fenix, Zaruma: 1000-0100
PI37)	PA1	1240	1	R. Metropolitana, Yaraquí: 1200-0300
CC03)	EM1	1250	10	Ondas Carchenses, Tulcán: 1000-0400
GU28)	HB2	‡1250	10	R. Tricolor, Guayaquil
SD03)	MY1	1250	3	LV del Triunfo, Sto Domingo de los Colorados: 1000-0500
AZ12)	PB5	1260	2	R. Contacto XG, Cuenca: 1100-0300
EO09)	RB3	1260	1	R. Benemérita, Sta Rosa: 1030-0100
PI39)	MO1	1260	10	LV del Santuario del Quinche, Quito: 1100-0300
TU10)	RO6	1260	3	R. Calidad, Ambato: 0930-0600
GU22)	UM2	1270	15	R. Universal, Guayaqui
MA15)	LD4	1270	3	R. Junín, Junín: 1100-0500
CR10)	NW5	1280	1	R. Canal Tropical, Riobamba: 1100-0100
MA16)	IN4	‡1280	1	LV del Sur de Manabí, Jipijapa: 1100-0500
PI61)		1280		R. Universitaria, Quito
AZ13)	JA5	1290	3	LV del Río Tarqui, Cuenca: 0900-0200
CP08)	VM6	1290	0.5	R. Once de Noviembre, Latacunga: 1200-0400
GU29)	OF2	1290	1	Canal Milagreño, El Milagro
IM07)	NS1	1290	1	R. Popular, Atuntaqui: 1100-0300
BO04)		1300		R. La Paz, Guaranda
GU30)	DC2	1300	5	R. Cenit, Guayaquil: 1200-0400
SD04)	RV1	1300	5	R. Festival, Sto Domingo de los

MW	Call	kHz	kW	Station, location, hr. of tr.
				Colorados: 0930-0300
SU02)	RS7	1300	2/1	R. Sucumbios, Nueva Loja: 1100-2400
CA03)	CI5	1310	3	T. V. O. "El Poder Mágico de la Fé", Biblián
CR20)	AI5	1310	0.5	Eco de los Andes, Cumandá: 1000-0200
EO11)	CP3	±1310	1	LV de El Oro, Pasaje
PI58)	GB1	1310	20	R. Nal. Espejo, Quito
LR05)	FR2	1320	3	R. Guayaquil, Babahoyo: 1030-0300
MA24)	VO4	1320	1	R. Stéreo Carrizal, Calceta: 1130-0300
TU11)	JD6	1320	10	R. Continental, Ambato: 0930-0400
AZ14)	LW5	1330	2	R. Visión Cristiana, Cuenca
EO12)	RV3	1330	5	Nacional El Oro, Machala: 1000-0600
GU31)		1330		Lomas Stéreo 2000, Guayaquil
PI42)		±1330	3	R. Visión Cristiana, Quito
ES03)		1340		LV de su amigo "Esté Musical", Esmeraldas
LO08)		1340		Ondas de Esperanza, Loja: 1100-0300
TU12)	RT6	1340	5	R. Paz y Bien, Ambato: 0930-0130
AZ15)	SF5	1350	2/1	LV de San Fernando, San Fernando: 1100-0300
GU47)	VP2	1350	3	Teleradio 13-50 AM Digital , Guayaquil
CR12)	RJ5	*1360	1	R. América, Riobamba: 1100-0300
EO13)	HG3	1360	5	R. Jerusalem AM, Machala
PI44)	MT	±1360	3	Oyambaro AM, Tumbaco: 1000-0300
CA04)	AO5	1370		R. El Rocio, Biblián
GU32)	VO2	1370	5	LV del Milagro, El Milagro
IM08)	JS1	1370	2	Ecos Andinos, Pimampiro
LO09)	ER3	*1370	5	R. Progreso, Loja: 1000-0315
EO14)	OA3	1380	1	La Mejor, Balsas
PI45)	CV1	1380	5	R. Cristal "RCQ", Quito: 0830-0300
TU13)		±1380	5	R. Mera, Ambato
AZ16)	EA5	1390	5	R. Tropicana "Canal 13-90", Cuenca: 1200-0300
ES04)	HE4	1390	1	LV de Esmeraldas, Esmeraldas
IM09)	IE1	1390	1.5	H. Uno, Urcuquí
CP09)		1400		Impacto 1400 AM, Latacunga
GU02)	FL2	±1400	10	R. Z Uno, Guayaquil
AZ17)	GC5	1410	1	H. Centro Gualaceo, Gualaceo
CR14)		1410	1	Ondas Cisnerinas, Riobamba: 2000-2300
ES05)	FR4	1410	1	LV de Quinindé, Quinindé
GU33)	CQ2	1410	1	R. Net AM, El Milagro
PI59)	EC1	1410	1	R. El Tiempo "Em.del Amor", Quito
CP10)	MA6	1420	1	R. Alternativa, Salcedo: 1130-0300
EO15)		1420		Corazón AM, Machala
IM10)	RN1	1420	3	R. Bahá'í, Otavalo: 0900-1500, 1930-2300
NA06)	VN7	1420		LV del Napo, Tena
BO05)	JC6	‡1430	5	R. Guaranda, Guaranda: 1100-0500
GU34)	MB2	1430	10	R. Federal, Virgen de Fátima
LO10)	CV3	1430	5	Ondas del Zamora, Canal Juvenil, Luja. 1130-0330
PI46)	GF1	1430	3.5	R. Futura 14-30, Quito: 1300-0200
CA05)	OV5	1440	2.8	Ondas del Volante, Azogues: 1000-0400
CP11)	AO6	1440	3/5	R. Fenix, Latacunga
EO10)		1440		Mi Radio AM, Machala
ES06)	DY4	1440	2.5	R. Iris, Esmeraldas; 1000-0400
IM11)	DF1	±1440	5	R. Panorama, Ibarra: 1030-0400
CR15)	SC5	1450	10	R. Calidad, Riobamba: 0800-0400
GU35)	DR	±1450	1	R. Minutera, Guayaquil
SE01)	SE2	1450	1	R. Santa Elena, Santa Elena: 2200-0200
PI47)	SC1	1450	1	AS La Radio, Tabacundo
CP12)	IC6	1460	5	R. Nuevos Horizontes, Latacunga: 1000-0200
MS04)	AA7	‡1460	5	LV de Gualaquiza, Gualaquiza: 1000-0300
GU37)	LD2	1470	1.5	R. Ecos de Naranjito, Naranjito
PI48)	JC1	1470	5	Ecos de Cayambe, Cayambe: (occ. r. Colón FM Guayaquil 92.9MHz)
CR16)	WP5	1480	3	R. Atlántida, Alausí: 1000-0400
CP13)	CY6	1480	5	R. Popular de la Maná, La Maná
EO16)	BS3	‡1480	3	Oro Radio AM, Machala
IM12)	MC1	1480	1	R. Municipal, Cotacachi
MA20)	JV4	1480	5	R. LV de Jipijapa, Jipijapa: 1100-0400
CA06)	SM5	1490	5	R. Santa María, Azogues: 0930-0330
ES07)	AE4	1490	2.5	R. Unión, Esmeraldas: 1000-0300
GU38)	VY2	1490	1	La R. Dinámica, Guayaquil
PI60)		1490		Poderosa 14-90, Quito
TU14)	AI6	1490	3	R. Moderna, Pillaro: 1300-0200
IM13)	RO1	1500	1	R. Otavalo, Otavalo: 1200-0300
LR09)	HG2	1500	5	LV del Río Vinces, Vinces: 1100-0500
BO07)	RY6	1510	1	R. Runacunapac Yachana "R. El Saber del Hombre", Simiátug
CA07)	RC5	1510	2	R. Punto C 1510 AM, Cañar: 1030-0400
GU39)	HD2	°1510	0.5	Inst. Oceanográfico de la Armada, Guayaquil: time signals 24h
PI56)		1510	5	R. Monumental, Quito: 1000-0400
SU03)	JV7	1510	5	R. Ecos del Oriente, Lago Agrio: 1030-0100
TU19)		‡1510		R. Net, Ambato
CR18)	RI5	1520	2.5	LV de Guamote, Guamote

MW	Call	kHz	kW	Station, location, hr. of tr.
GU40)	RN2	1520	1	LV de Naranjal, El Naranjal
IM14)	TI1	1520	1	R. Ibarra, Ibarra: 1000-0400
CA08)	CC5	1530	5	Ondas Cañaris AM, R. Universitaria Católica, Azogues
CR19)	VP5	±1530	3	R. LV de Pallatanga, Pallatanga: 1100-0300
SE02)	MP2	1530	5	LV de la Península, La Libertad: 1100-0300
TU15)	MZ6	1530	1	R. Deportes 15-30, Pelileo: 1130-0230
CP14)	MH	±1540	0.5	Cotopaxi Digital, Latacunga: 1000-0400
EO18)		1540		R. Flecha AM, Machala
LR10)	FM2	1540	3	R. Cristal de Ventanas, Babahoyo
MS05)	VB7	°1540	0.25	LV del Upano, Macas: 1030-0300
PI49)	DP1	1540	1	R. Caracol, Quito: 1000-0300
AZ18)	AD5	1550	5	LV de Chaguarurco, Santa Isabel: 1200-0300, Sun 1100-2300
GU42)	AD2	1550	2	LV del Triunfo, El Triunfo: 1100-0400
TU16)	EI6	1550	2	R. Montalvo, Ambato: 1130-0400
EO17)	TR3	1560	2	LV del Guabo, El Guabo: 1100-1300, 2300-0400
GU43)	CS2	1560	2	R. Sideral, Daule: 1300-0500
IM15)	ZD1	1560	1.5	Ecos Culturales de Urcuquí, Urcuquí
MA23)		1570	1	R. LV Espíritu Santo de Dios, Manta: 1100-0100
PI51)	PG1	1570	10	R. Nucanchic, Maldonado
TU20)		1570	0.5	Ondas Quereñas, Quero: 1100-0300
AZ19)	TP5	±1580	3	Ecos del Portete, Girón: 1200-0330
ES09)	VA4	1580	5	Estación de la Alegria, Esmeraldas
LO14)	AB3	‡1580	0.25	Ondas de Paltas, Catacocha
PI52)	LF1	1580	1	Ecos de Orellana, Machach: 1030-0230
SE03)	AS2	1590	0.25	R. Record, La Libertad
PI53)	RZ1	1590	1	R. Mensaje, Cayambe: 1000-1400, 2130-0130
TU17)	QT6	1590	1	R. Panamericana, Quero: 1000-0200 (Sun -2400)
BO09)		±1600		Ondas de Caluma "R.del Pueblo", Caluma
PI57)		1600		R. Ilusión 1600 AM, Puembo: 0900-0500

° = also on SW, ‡ = inactive, (r) = repeater, ± = varying fq.

SW	Call	kHz	kW	Name and h of tr
NA06)	VN7	3280	2.5	LV del Napo, Tena: 0900-1115, 1300-1400, 2200-0300 Prgrs: R. María
IM06)		‡3380	1	Centro Radiofónico de Imbabura, Ibarra
NA02)	LE7	‡4781	3	R. Oriental, Tena: irr
LO15)	AX3	4815	1	R. Buen Pastor, Saraguro: 1000-1600, 2100-0355 (occ. rel. of R. Internacional/LV de los Andes)
CP06)	RL6	‡4910	1	LV de Saquisilí y Libertador, Saquisilí: irr
IM16)		‡4910		R. Chaskis, Otavalo (rep. on 4909.3kHz)
PI10)	QR1	‡4919	12	R. Quito "LV de la Capital", Quito: irr
MS05)	VB7	‡6000		LV del Upano, Lago Agrio, Sucumbíos: irr
PI08)		6050	8	HCJB, Quito: 0830-1500, 1900-0503

Stns with a (‡) are reported to be inactive, but may occasionally be reactivated for variable periods of time.

Province-abbreviations: AZ=Azuay BO=Bolívar CA=Cañar CC=Carchi CP=Cotopaxi CR=Chimborazo EO=El Oro ES=Esmeraldas GU=Guayas IM=Imbabura LO=Loja LR=Los Ríos MA=Manabí MS=Morona Santiago,NA=Napo PA=Pastaza PI=Pichincha SD=Santo Domingo de los Tsáchilas SE=Santa Elena SU=Sucumbios TU=Tungurahua ZC=Zamora Chinchipe **N.B.:** These abbreviations are not recognized by the Ecuadorian Post Office. Letters should carry the full name.

Addresses and other information:
AZ00) AZUAY
AZ01) see PI04 — **AZ02)** Av.Remigio Crespo y Calle La Libertad, Cuenca – **AZ04)** Cas 198, Cuenca – **AZ05)** Cas 01-01-1352, Cuenca - **FM:** 90.5MHz 92.5MHz – **AZ06)** Cas 01-01-0493, Cuenca **W:** www.tomebamba.satnet.net - FM: 94.9MHz 102.1MHz – **AZ07)** Cas 01-01-4980 (or: Av Héroes de Verdeloma 9-15), Cuenca E: oazuayas@cue.satnet.net - FM: 93.7MHz Sunny – **AZ08)** Simon Bolívar 226, Cuenca – **AZ09)** Bomboiza 1-83, entre Loja-España, Cuenca – **AZ10)** Av.de las Américas, Edif.Mercurio, Cuenca – **AZ11)** La Gloria de Nanuncay, Av.Loja 2408, Cuenca – **AZ12)** J Dávila y C Merchán, Cuenca – **AZ13)** Manuel Vega 653 y Presidente Córdoba, Cuenca – **AZ14)** Edif.Alfa, P4, Gran Colombia 739 y A Borrero, Cuenca – **AZ15)** Av José María Quito y Santiago de San Fernando, San Fernando – **AZ16)** Cas 830 (or: Pumapungo 5), Cuenca – **AZ17)** Gran Colombia y 9 de Octubre 3102, Frente al Parque Central, Gualaceo – **AZ18)** Cas 01-01-46 (or: Calle Bolívar 7-64), Aperado (or: Calle 24 de Mayo y Abdon Calderón, Cuenca) E: chaguarurco60@hotmail.com – **AZ19)** Antonio Flor 6-57, Girón – **AZ21)** J Roldos 480, Edif El Consorcio, Cuenca.
BO00) BOLÍVAR
BO01) Johnson City 204 y Sucre, Parraquia San Vicente, Guaranda - FM: 97.3MHz – **BO03)** 10 de Agosto 612, Guaranda - FM: 93.9MHz – **BO04)** G Moreno y 7 de Mayo, Guaranda - FM: 93.9MHz – **BO05)** Federico Paez, Frente. al Parque Cen, (or: Cas 86), Guaranda – **BO07)** Simiátug – **BO09)** Av La Naranja 169, Atras-Coliseo, Caluma.
CA00) CAÑAR
CA01) Av Ingapirca, Cdla El Vergel, Cañar (or: Cas 01-01-0447, Cuenca)

Quichua: 0900-1300 - FM: 94.3MHz – **CA02)** General Vintimilla 1-10 y Oriente, Azogues – **CA03)** Mariscal Sucre 722 y B Ochoa, Biblián (or: Cas 729, Azogues) – **CA04)** Calle Mariscal Sucre 202 y Tarquí, Biblián – **CA05)** Bolívar y Azuay, Azogues – **CA06)** Cas 03-01-730, Azogues **W:** www.radiosantamaria.com – **CA07)** Bolívar y Borrero (Junto Parque Central), Cañar -0415 – **CA08)** Calle Rivera 613, Azogues.

CC00) CARCHI

CC01) Atahualpa 166 y Aristizava, San Gabriel – **CC03)** Olmedo 52-025 y Ayacucho (or: Cas 30), Tulcán

CP00) COTOPAXI

CP01) Imbabura 2333 y 9 de Octubre, Saquisilí – **CP02)** Cas 05-01-392 (or: Calle Quito 14-56, Pasaje La Catedral), Latacunga **E:** latacunga@andinanet.net - FM: 97.1MHz +102.1MHz – **CP03)** 2 de Mayo 438, entre Tarquí y General Maldonado, Latacunga – **CP04)** Bel.Quevedo Caserio Illuchi, Latacunga – **CP05)** B Quevedo 555, Pujilí – **CP06)** Av.24 de Mayo 669, Saquisilí – **CP08)** Calle Felix Valencia 432, Plaza El Salto, Latacunga **W:** www.radio11denoviembre.com – **CP09)** General Maldonado 379 y 2 de Mayo, Latacunga – **CP10)** Calle Bolívar 1509 y Sucre, Salcedo **W:** www.radio-alternativa.net – **CP11)** Juan Abel Echeverria 6-56 y Quito, Latacunga **E:** ehquintana@hotmail.com – **CP12)** Faustino Sarmiento 5046 y Vela, Latacunga – **CP13)** Enrique Gallo 164 y Av 19 de Mayo, La Maná – **CP14)** António Clavijo, P3, Latacunga.

CR00) CHIMBORAZO

CR01) Cas 06-01-693 (or: Juan de Velasco N° 20-60 y Guayaquil), Riobamba **W:** www.ferpe.org - FM: 91.7MHz – **CR02)** Cas 06-01-0242, Riobamba – **CR03)** Pichincha 1363 y Cardondelet, Riobamba – **CR04)** Cas 06-01-572 (or: Av.Daniel León Borja 30-44), Riobamba **E:** radiomundial@soccer.com – **CR05)** Cas.87A, Majipamba, Colta Prgrs in **Quichua** only – **CR06)** Francia 1857 y Villaroel, Riobamba – **CR07)** Cardondelet 2952 y J.Montalvo, Riobamba – **CR08)** 10 de Agosto 1742 y Benalcazar, Riobamba – **CR10)** Ayacucho 3234 (or: Cas 06-01-0471), Riobamba – **CR12)** Calle Pichincha 24-26 y Veloz (or: Cas 82), Riobamba - FM: 100.1 – **CR14)** Cas 334 (or: La Paz y México Esq.), Riobamba – **CR15)** Cas 06-01-0376, Riobamba – **CR16)** Cas 06-03-0805, Alausí – **CR18)** Comunidad Sta Cruz, Guamote – **CR19)** Panamericana y Eloy Alfaro, Pallatanga – **CR20)** 1 Constituyente y G Rendon, Cumanda.

EO00) EL ORO

EO01) Bolívar Madero 1313, via Pto Bolívar, Machala – **EO02)** Cas 221, Machala – **EO03)** Bolívar 601, Edif.Encasa, Machala – **EO05)** Cas 07-01-0086, Machala (or: 9 de Octubre y Páez), Machala – **EO07)** 9 de Octubre y 1 Diagonal, Santa Rosa – **EO08)** San Francisco 114 y Sucre, Zaruma – **EO09)** El Oro y Cuenca, Sta Rosa – **EO10)** 9 de Mayo y Rocafuerte, esq, piso 2, Machala – **EO11)** San Martín 720, Entre Municipalidad y Och, Pasaje – **EO12)** 9 de Octubre y Sta Rosa, Machala – **EO13)** Calle Pasaje s/n y Costa Oeste, Machala – **EO14)** Av 10 de Agosto 1303 y 23 de Febrero, Balsas – **EO15)** Av Buena Vista 742 y 4ta Norte, Machala – **EO16)** Machala (see also GU07) – **EO17)** Av del Ejército, El Guabo – **EO18)** Av del Periodista y Calle Jon, Machala – **EO19)** Av 9 de Octubre y 23 de Abril, Machala – **EO20)** Av 12va Norte y Buena Vista, Machala.

ES00) ESMERALDAS

ES02) Malecón 805 y Cañizares, Esmeraldas (se also GU07) – **ES03)** Manuela Cañizares y Olmedo, Esmeraldas - FM: 96.3MHz – **ES04)** Edif. Mutualisat Vargas Torres, Esmeraldas – **ES05)** Simon Plata Torres y Maclovio Velazco, Quinindé – **ES06)** Bolívar s/n, Esmeraldas – **ES07)** Gustavo Becerra y Piedrahita, Esmeraldas – **ES09)** Bolívar 513 y Piedrahita, Esmeraldas.

GU00) GUAYAS

GU01) Cas 4144 (or: Boyaca 642 y Padre Solano), Guayaquil **W:** www.cre.com.ec/cre htm - FM: 105.7 – **GU02)** Cas 2119, Guayaquil (or: Amazonas 743 y Veintemilla, P8, Quito) **W:** www.radiocadenauno.com – **GU03)** Quisquis 316 y Garaicoa, Edif Huancavelica, Guayaquil – **GU04)** Quisquis 316 y Garaicoa, Guayaquil – **GU05)** Cas 9974 (or: Av de Las Américas junto Canal 10), Guayaquil **W:** superk800.com – **GU06)** Rumichaca 934 y Velez, Guayaquil – **GU07)** Cas 11714 (or: Av.Francisco de Orellana y Juan Tanca Marengo), Guayaquil **W:** www.radiosucre.com.ec - FM: 95.3MHz – **GU08)** Cas 2440 (or: Escobedo 1504 y Aguirre, P9), Guayaquil – **GU09)** Cas 716, (or: Av Juan Tanga Marengo km 3), Guayaquil **E:** caravana@gye.satnet.net - Av: 88.1MHz – **GU10)** Cas 09-01-4203 (or: Colón 548 y Boyacá, P7), Guayaquil – **GU11)** Juan Montalvo 1042, El Milagro – **GU12)** Cas 856 (or: Edif Gran Pasaje Of 906/908), Guayaquil – **GU13)** Cas 09-01-5762, Guayaquil **E:** sanfrancisco850@hotmail.com – **GU14)** Cas 5062 (or: Laque 1407 y Antepara), Guayaquil **E:** rcristal@ecua.net.ec – **GU15)** Malecón 206 entre Juan Montalvo y Laja, Guayaquil - FM: 92.9MHz – **GU17)** García Moreno y Hurtavbo, en los Altos, Ofc.Delgado Travel P3, Guayaquil – **GU18)** 10 de Agosto 504 y Chimborazo, P3), Guayaquil **E:** servidor1000@hotmail.com – **GU19)** Urdesa, Av.Circunvalación Sur 111-B, frente al parque, Guayaquil – **GU20)** José de Antepara 4415 y Nicolas González, Guayaquil – **GU21)** Los Ríos 609, Cond Orellana, P4, Ofc 2, Guayaquil – **GU22)** Miguel H Alcivar y Luis Orrantia s/n,

Guayaquil – **GU24)** Aguirre 931 y L.de Garaycoa, Guayaquil – **GU25)** Febres Cordero 315 y Chile, Guayaquil – **GU26)** Veléz 905, Edif.Forum, P16 (or: Cas 8729), Guayaquil **E:** ife@interactive.net.ec – **GU27)** Jiguas 500 y V.Emilio Estrada, Guayaquil – **GU28)** Lorenzo de Garaycoa 2615, Guayaquil – **GU29)** Laurel y Guayacanes, El Milagro – **GU30)** Luis Urdaneta 202 y Cordoba, Guayaquil – **GU31)** Simon Bolívar, entre Gonzales y Telégrafo, Guayaquil – **GU32)** Av 17 de Septiembre, El Milagro – **GU33)** Calle García Moreno y Bolívar 1013, El Milagro – **GU34)** Km 26.5 vía Duran-Tambo, Virgen de Fátima – **GU35)** Quito 1520 entre Sucre y Colón, Guayaquil – **GU37)** Av 5 de Octubre 150, Naranjito – **GU38)** Av 25 de Julio cdla 7 Lagos C, Guayaquil – **GU39)** Cas 5940, Guayaquil **W:** www.inocar.mil.ec – **GU40)** Pastaza y 15 de Octubre, El Naranjal **E:** jpinoargote@hotmail.com – **GU42)** Jaime Roldos 700 y Av.8 de Abril, El Triunfo– **GU43)** Cdla.Belén Piedrahita y 1era, Daule – **GU47)** 9 de Octubre y Baquerizo Moreno, Edif.Plaza, P1, Guayaquil – **GU48)** Edif El Forum, P5, Ofic 508, Guayaquil – **GU49)** Eloy Alfaro Duran en la Av Samuel Cisneros, via al Secap, Guayaquil.

IM00) IMBABURA

IM01) Morales 408 y Sucre, Otavalo – **IM02)** Celiano Aguinaga y Panamericana Sur, Atuntaqui, Ibarra – **IM03)** Cas 413 (or: Olmedo 1178 y Av.Peréz Guerrero), Ibarra – **IM04)** Cas 10-01-0179 (or: Bolívar y García Moreno), Ibarra – **IM05)** António Cordero 823 y Emilio Grijalva, Ibarra - FM: 98.5MHz – **IM06)** Río Chinchipe 397 y Río Daule, Ibarra – **IM07)** Cas 3, Atuntaqui – **IM08)** Bolívar 10020 y Espejo, Pimapiro – **IM09)** Matovelle s/n, Urcuquí – **IM10)** Cas 10-02-1464, Otavalo – **IM11)** Juan José Flores 11-26 y Jaime Rivadeneira, Ibarra **W:** www.imbanet.net/panorama/panorama.html - FM: 93.7MHz – **IM12)** Av.Reales Tamarindos y Calle Tenis Club, Portoviejo – **IM13)** Rocafuerte 1-10 y Guayaquil, Otavalo – **IM14)** Calle Oviedo y Bolívar, Edif Way, P2, Ibarra – **IM15)** Antonio Ante s/n, Urcuquí – **IM16)** Jirón Roldos Aguilera y Panamericana Norte, Otavalo **E:** radiochaskis@hotmail.com

LO00) LOJA

LO01) Av.J.A Eguuigurren y Bolívar, Loja – **LO02)** Cas 474 (or: Bernardo Valdiviezo 1054, entre Miguel Riofrio y Azuay), Loja - FM: 100.3MHz – **LO03)** 24 de Mayo y Eloy Alfaro, Catamayo - FM: 93.7MHz – **LO06)** Cas 11-01-222, Loja FM: 88.3MHz **E:** Luzyvida@easynet.net.ec – **LO07)** Cas 196 (or: Olmedo 11-56 y Mercadillo), Loja - FM: 88.9MHz – **LO08)** Olmedo 1146 entre Azuay y Mercadillo, Loja – **LO09)** Av Gran Colombia 2663 y Ibarra, Loja – **LO10)** B Valdiviezo 08-59, Loja – **LO11)** Sector Colinas de San Juan, Cariamanga **E:** rcmga@loja.telconet.net – **LO14)** Coop Ahorro y Crédito 3 de Diciembre, Isidro Ayora 235, Catacocha – **LO15)** Asociación Cristiana de Indigenas Saraguros, Saraguro - FM: 93.1MHz

LR00) LOS RÍOS

LR01) 12 Calle N° 207 y 7 de Octubre, Quevedo – **LR02)** Av Manabí y Juan León Mera, El Empalme, Quevedo – **LR03)** Av Velasco Ibarra 1012, Ventanas – **LR04)** Av 7 de Octubre 727, Quevedo – **LR05)** Cdla El Mamey, Babahoyo – **LR09)** Olmedo 109, Vinces – **LR10)** 28 de Mayo 1412 y 6 de Octubre, Babahoyo.

MA00) MANABÍ

MA01) Av.10ma y Calle 17, P2, Manta – **MA02)** 10 de Agosto 609 y Olmedo, Portoviejo (see also GU07) – **MA03)** Ricaurte y P.Moreira, Portoviejo – **MA04)** Av Lascano, Chone – **MA06)** Pedro Gual, Edif. Servicentro, Portoviejo – **MA07)** Colón 180, Portoviejo – **MA08)** 18 de Octubre 404, Chone – **MA11)** 9 y Malecón, Edif "Jacob Vera", P1 Ofc 7, Manta – **MA12)** C Central, Portoviejo – **MA13)** Bolívar y Espejo, Portoviejo – **MA15)** 10 de Agosto 180 y Eloy Alfaro, Junín – **MA16)** Cas 13-04-0705 (or: 9 de Octubre en Mejía y Rocafuerte), Jipijapa – **MA20)** Noboa y Colón, Jipijapa – **MA23)** 306 Entre Las Avenidas 204 y 206, Manta **E:** diosvenami@aol.com – **MA24)** Flavio Alfaro 718 Ciudadela San Bartolo, Calceta – **MA25)** Cas 13-02-0629 (or: Montufar N° 1014 y Aguilera), Bahía de Caráquez - FM: 95.3 – **MA26)** Morales 104 y Colón, Ed Sind Choferes Man, Portoviejo.

MS00) MORONA SANTIAGO

MS04) Luia Casiragui s/n y Amazonas, Gualaquiza - FM: 91.7MHz 96.5MHz – **MS05)** Misión Salesiana de Oriente, Calle 10 de Agosto s/n, Macas **E:** radioupano@cue.eolnet.net - FM: 90.5MHz For Radio María del Ecuador address, see NA06 – **MS06)** Federación de Centros Shuar, Domingo Comín 17-38, Sucúa (or: Cas 17-01-4122, Quito).

NA00) NAPO

NA02) Cas 260 (or: Av.Jumandy 536, Barrio 2 Rios), Tena – **NA06)** Misión Josefina, Juan Montalvo s/n y P Central, Tena **E:** coljav20@yahoo.es Radio Maria del Ecuador: Calles Baquerizo Moreno 281 y Leonidas Plaza, Quito **W:** www.radiomaria ecuador.org

PA00) PASTAZA

PA02) Vía Macas km 1 5, El Puyo

PI00) PICHINCHA

PI01) Ulloa 611 y Acuña, La Fincha, P1, Quito – **PI02)** Panamericana Sur km 14.5 (teléfono 2 691 573), Quito – **PI03)** Av.Maldonado 688 y Calvas, Quito – **PI04)** Conde Ruíz de Castilla 997 y Muregeón, Quito – **PI05)** Pasaje A 689 y Vasco de Contrera, Quito **W:** www.geocities.com/

~crespo – **PI06)** Cas 60 (or: Mariano Echeverria y Brasil), Quito – **PI07)** Cuenca 477 y Sucre (El convento de San Francisco), Quito 7 – **PI08)** Cas 17-17-691(or: Villalengua 884 y Av.10 de Agosto), Quito. (6050kHz is operated by Vozandes Media and broadcasts in Cofán, Shuar, Waorani, Kechwa, Cha'paala and Spanish. Reports to the German department – return postage required). International service: See Int Broadcasting section – **PI09)** García Moreno 751 entre Sucre y Bolívar, P3, Quito **W:** www.quito.gov.ec/homequito municipio.com – **PI10)** Cas 17-21-1971 (or: La Coruña 2104 y Whimper, Edif.Aragones) Quito E: radioquito@elcomercio.com – **PI12)** Av Principal s/n, Maldonado – **PI13)** Amazonas 1638 y La Pinta, Quito – **PI15)** Panamericana Sur km 14.5 (teléfono 2 678 989), Quito – **PI16)** Ramírez Dávalos 612 y 10 de Agosto, Quito – **PI17)** Av.Amazonas y Colón, Edif.España, P4, Ofc.42, Quito – **PI18)** Cas 17-03-540 (or: Av.América 1830 y Mercadillo),Quito **W:** www.radiocatolica-ecuador.org E: buenanoticia@radiocatolica.org. ec – **PI19)** Palacio 303 y Av La Gasca, Quito (see also GU07) – **PI20)** Avellanas E5-107 y Av.Eloy Alfaro, Quito **W:** www.colonfm.com – **PI21)** Cas 17-01-67, Quito – **PI22)** Morales 1224 y García Moreno, Quito **W:** lapantera.net – **PI24)** García Moreno 1315 y Olmedo, Quito– **PI26)** Edif Sevilla, P9, J L Mera 565 y Carrión, Quito – **PI27)** García Moreno 446, Machachi – **PI28)** Tarquí 785 y Estrada,Edif.de Cosi, P2, Quito – **PI30)** Cas 17-03-31 (or: Carrión 1288 y Av 10 de Agosto), Quito E: Radioirf@ecuanex.net.ec – **PI31)** Av.América 4829 y Naciones Unidas, Quito **W:** www.radioclasica.com.ec – **PI32)** Cas 17-11-2263 (or: Bolívar 359 entre García Moreno y Venezuela), Quito – **PI33)** Cas 17-01-638 (or Av Amazonas N35 89 y Corea, P4), Quito **W:** www.radioeres.com – **PI34)** Marquesa de Solanda 722, Quito – **PI35)** Central Roca 331 y Av 6 de Diciembre, Quito – **PI36)** Cas 17-23-47 (or: Av General Enríquez N° 29-35 y Río Chinchipe), Sangolquí – **PI37)** 12 de Octubre 227, Quito – **PI39)** Cas 17-01-3386 (or: García Moreno N 11-184 y Carchi), Quito E: hcmunomat@hotmail.com – **PI40)** Edif Doral Mariscal, Of 86, Páez y Mercadillo, Quito **W:** www.radiodemocracia.com – **PI42)** Reina Victoria 447 y Roca, Quito – **PI44)** Carvajal e Interoceania, Barrio Sta Rosa, Tumbaco - FM: 104.1MHz – **PI45)** Av de la Prensa N°60-22 y Av.de la Prensa, Quito E: rcu_1380@yahoo.com – **PI46)** Av.Amazonas 3911 y Corea, Unicormio 2, P10, Ofc.1008, Quito – **PI47)** Calle Bolívar y Alfredo Boada (sobre el Banco del Pichincha), Tabacundo – **PI48)** Cas.17-25-5 (or: Terán 409 y Av 10 de Agosto, Cayambe – **PI49)** Venezuela 701 y Espejo, Quito – **PI51)** Pedro Vicente, Maldonado (or: Concejo Provincial de Pichincha, Manuel Larrea y Antonio Ante, Cas 298, Quito) – **PI52)** Luis Cordero 557 y J.Mejia, Machachi – **PI53)** Av.Natalia Jarrín 2-77 y Vivar, Cayambe E: acayambe@uio.satnet.net – **PI54)** Iñaquito 133-E2 y Unión Nacional de Periodistas, Quito – **PI56)** Manuel Cajias E 14-09 y Toribio Hidalgo, Quito – **PI57)** Pasaje Santa Rosa y Av. Interoceánica, Puembo E: radioilusion1600@hotmail.com – **PI58)** Panamericana Sur km 14.5 (teléfono 2 245 300), Quito – **PI59)** Gonzalo Díaz de Pineda 290 y Pedro del Alfaro, Quito – **PI60)** Av Colón OE3-331 y Versalles, Edificio Villarre, Quito – **PI61)** Universidad Central del Ecuador, Avenida América, Ciudadela Universitaria, Quito

SD00) SANTO DOMINGO DE LOS TSÁCHILAS
SD01) Calle Ibarra y Babahoyo esq, Sto Domingo de los Colorados – **SD02)** Guayaquil 124 y Tsáchilas, Sto Domingo de los Colorados – **SD03)** Cas 17-24-0043 (or: Ibarra 905 y Av 29 de Mayo, Edif Dueñas), Sto Domingo de los Colorados – **SD04)** Quito e Ibarra, Santo·Domingo de los Colorados

SE00) SANTA ELENA
SE01) Guayaquil s/n y 9 de Octubre, Santa Elena – **SE02)** 4a Av 619 y Robles, La Libertad E: lvp@porta.net – **SE03)** 12 de Octubre 1032, La Libertad

SU00) SUCUMBIOS
SU02) Cas 21-01-14 (or: Venezuela y Progreso), Nueva Loja E: radio-suc@andinanet.net - FM: 105.3 – **SU03)** Cas 40 (or: Mariscal Sucre y 12 de Febrero), Lagos Agrio - FM: 99.3MHz

TU00) TUNGURAHUA
TU01) Cevallos 345, Ambato (see also GU07) – **TU02)** Bolívar 537 y Fund.del Canton, Pillaro (or: Cas 18-01-244, Ambato)– **TU03)** Cas 18-01-181 (or: Sucre 09-42 y Quito), Ambato **W:** www.radioambato.com - FM: 96.7MHz R. Amor – **TU04)** 12 de Noviembre y Ambato, Edif.El Pelegrino, Baños E: radiosantuario@yahoo.es – **TU05)** Cas 18-01-0674 (or: Av.Cevallos 15-57 y Mera, P10, Ofc 1001), Ambato E: radiolider@uio. telconet.net – **TU06)** Bolívar y Martinez, Ambato – **TU07)** Cas 005, (or: Av 22 de Julio y Padre Jorge Chacón 4-47), Pelileo E: radiopelileo@hot-mail.com – **TU08)** Cas 18-01-0574 (or: Castillo entre 12 de Noviembre y Olmedo, Edif.R.Centro), Ambato - FM: 93.7MHz – **TU09)** Cevallos 1624 y Maldonado, Ambato – **TU10)** Cevallos 754 y Martinez (or: Cas 18-01-0198), Ambato – **TU11)** Cotacachi 176 e Iliniza, Ambato – **TU12)** Cas 18-01-115 (or: Fray Fausto Suárez, Francisco Flor 321), Ambato - FM: 92.9MHz 104.5MHz 106.9MHz – **TU13)** Cas 618 (or: Calle Ayllón 1753 y Darquea), Ambato – **TU14)** Barrio El Censo via San Miguelito, Píllaro – **TU15)** Av Padre Chancon s/n y Juan Velasco, Pelileo **W:** www.radiodeportesambato.com – **TU16)** Av.El Rey, Ciudadela Oriente, Ambato

– **TU17)** Montalvo 106, Quero – **TU19)** Calle Montalvo y Av Cevallos, Ambato – **TU20)** Sector Kiambe, Quero.

FM in Quito (MHz): 88.1 Latina FM – 88.5 Metro – PI08) 89.3 HCJB – 89.7 Majestad – 90.1 Tropicalida – 90.5 Disney – 90.9 Platinum – 91.3 Sabormix – PI17) 91.7 Visión – 92.1 Contacto Nuevo Tiempo – 92.5 Genial Exa FM – 92.9 Música y Sonido - PI33) 93.3 Eres 93.3 – 93.7 Galaxia – PI18) 94.1 Católica Nacional FM – 94.5 Rumba – 94.9 La Gitana – 95.3 Universal – 95.7 R. Legislativa – 96.1 Joya – 96.5 BBN - 96.9 Armónica FM – PI31) 97.3 La Otra FM – 97.7 Centro – 98.1 Proyección – 98.5 Alfa – 98.9 Colón – 99.3 La Luna – 99.7 Añoranza La Rumbera – 100.1 María – PI23) 100.5 Stereo Zaracay – 100.9 Nacional del Ecuador – R. Pública - 101.3 Onda Azul – 101.7 Sucesos – 102.1 R.La Red – PI07) 102.5 Francisco Estéreo – 102.9 Armonía – 103.3 Onda Cero FM - 103.7 Sonorama – 104.1 Cobertura - 104.5 América – 104.9 Ecuashyri – 105.3 Kiss – 105.7 CRE – 106.1 Hot 106 R. Fuego – 106.5 Canela – 106.9 R. Urbana – 107.3 JC – 107.7 Más Candela
FM in Guayaquil (MHz): 88.1 María – 88.5 Galaxia Stereo – 88.9 Di Blu – 89.3 R. City – 89.7 Punto Rojo FM – 90.1 Romance FM – 90.5 Canela – 90.9 Kiss – 91.3 Tropicalida Stereo – 91.7 Antena Tres – 92.1 Estrella – 92.5 Forever Music FM – 92.9 Colón FM – 93.3 Majestad – 93.7 Disney – 94.1 Onda Positiva – 94.5 Platinum FM – 94.9 La Otra FM – 95.3 Cupido – 95.7 Metro Stereo – 96.1 Onda Cero FM – 96.5 Pasión – 96.9 Más Candela – 97.3 Nuevo Tiempo – 98.1 Morena – 98.5 J C R – 98.9 Impacto FM – 99.3 Sabormix FM – 99.7 Elite – 100.1 R. La Prensa – 100.5 RSN FM Stereo – 100.9 Mundial – 101.3 La Estación Musical – 101.7 Telequil R. Stereo – 102.1 WQ Dos – 102.5 HCJB – 102.9 Armonía Musical – 103.3 Joya Stereo – 103.7 Sonorama FM – 104.1 Alfa Stereo – 104.5 Corazón – 104.9 Once Q FM – 105.3 Nacional del Ecuador, R. Pública – 105.7 Fabustereo – 106.1 BBN – 106.5 Fuego – 106.9 Francisco Stereo – 107.3 Rumba – 107.7 Visión FM

L.T: UTC +2h — **Pop:** 82 million — **Pr.L:** Arabic — **E.C:** 50Hz, 220V — **ITU:** EGY

EGYPTIAN RADIO & TV UNION (Gov)
P.O. Box 1186, Cairo 11511 (Street: Radio & TV Building, Cornish El Nil, Cairo) ☎ +20 2 25757715, 25789145 +20 2 25789461
E: freqmeg@yahoo.com **W:** www.ertu.org (Arabic)
L.P: Pres: Mr Tharwat Mekky, Chmn Eng. Sector: Eng. Hamdy Mounir, Chmn Broadc. Sector: Ismael al-Sheshtawy al-Iraqi

MW	kHz	kW	P	Times
Cairo	558	100	2j	1200-2400
Sohag	603	50	4	0200-2200
Batra	621	1000	6a	24h
Asswan	702	10	2e	24h
			4	0200-0400, 2000-2200
El Kharga	702	10	2h	0400-1000, 1130-2000 (Fri 0400-2000)
			4	2000-2200
			10	1000-1130 (not Fri)
Tanta	711	100	24h	
Qena	756	10	2e	0400-2200
			4	0200-0400, 2000-2200
Abis	774	500	5	24h
Batra	819	1000	1a	24h
Santah	864	500	4	24h
Matruh	882	10	1a	1100-0700 (Fri 24h)
Bawti	918	10	1a	24h
Cairo	936	50	11	1500-2000
Salum	936	10	1a	24h
Abu Simbel	981	1	1a	24h
Assiut	981	10	2d	0400-2000
			4	0200-0400, 2000-2200
Baris	981	1	1a	0300-2400
El Arish	1008	100	6b	0600-1500
El Farafra	1008	1	1a	24h
El Fayoum	1008	10	2d	0400-2000
Cairo	1071	10	1b	0300-1500
El Minya	1080	10	1a	0300-2400
Luxor	1080	10	1a	0300-2400
Tanta	1161	10	2b	0400-2200
Qena	1179	10	1a	0300-2400
Ras Gharib	1188	10	1a	0300-2400
Asswan	1278	10	1a	0300-2400
Assiut	1305	10	1a	0300-2400
Abu Simbel	1314	1	2e	0400-2000
			4	0200-0400, 2000-2200
Nag Hamadi	1314	1	1a	0300-2400
Cairo	1341	100	3c	1700-0100
			8a	0500-1700
Bawiti	1341	10	2j	1300-2000

MW

MW	kHz	kW	P	Times
			4	0200-0500, 2000-2200
			10	0500-1300
Idfu	1341	10	1a	0300-2400
Siwa	1341	10	1a	24h
Quseir	1350	10	1a	0300-2400
El Farafra	1368	1	2j	1300-2000
			4	0200-0500, 2000-2200
			10	0500-1300
El Kharga	1368	10	1a	0300-2400
Luxor	1386	10	2e	0400-2000
			4	0200-0400, 2000-2200
Ras Gharib	1422	10	2j	1300-2000
			4	0200-0500, 2000-2200
			10	0500-1300
Salum	1422	10	2i	0400-2000
			4	0200-0400, 2000-2200
El Minya	1476	10	2d	0400-2000
			4	0200-0400, 2000-2200
El Tur	1485	1	2j	1300-2000
			10	4	0200-0500, 2000-2200
			1	10	0500-1300
El Arish	1503	25	2f	0400-2200
Quseir	1575	10	2j	1300-2000
			4	0200-0500, 2000-2200
			10	0500-1300
Baris	1584	1	2h	0400-1000, 1130-2000 (Fri 0400-2000)
			4	2000-2200
			10	1000-1130 (not Fri)
Idfu	1584	10	2e	0400-2000
			4	0200-0400, 2000-2200
Matruh	1593	10	2i	0400-2000
			4	0200-0400, 2000-2200
Nag Hamadi	1602	10	2e	0400-2000
			1	4	0200-0400, 2000-2200
Siwa	1602	10	2i	0400-2000
			4	0200-0400, 2000-2200

MW Prgrs: 1a=General Prgr, 1b=Adults Prgr, 2=Local Prgrs (2b=Mid Delta, 2d= North Upper Egypt, 2e= South Upper Egypt, 2f= North Sinai, 2h=El Wady El Gadid, 2i=Matruh, 2j=Educational), 3c=Cultural Prgr, 4=Holy Koran Prgr, 5=Middle East Prgr, 6a=Voice of the Arabs, 6b=Palestine Prgr, 8a=Songs Prgr, 10=Youth & Sports Prgr, 11=Om Kalthoum Prgr.

NB: Wadi el Nil prgr r. Cairo 1071kHz 1700-2200

FM (MHz):

Site	D	E	G	K	M	N	R	S	Y
Abu			90.6						
Abh				95.7					
Alx		94.3	104.7	90.1	88.0		101.1	97.6	
Al F			98.2	88.6			91.7		
Asy	99.1	102.6	99.1	95.8	89.1			92.6	99.1
Asw	98.6	92.1	98.6	95.3	89.0				98.6
Baris				88.8					
Bawiti				87.6					
Ben					91.4				
Cairo[a]		95.4	107.4	98.2	98.8	88.7	102.2	105.8	108.0
Dahab				98.5	92.0				
Dum				93.8			87.6		
El A	87.8	94.1		87.8	90.9		97.4		87.8
El D			91.1	88.0			94.3		
El K				88.4					
El M	91.0	94.2	91.0	101.0	87.9		104.6		91.0
El Tur	89.4		95.7	89.4	92.5		99.0		89.4
El Z				88.4					
Hal				96.7		107.5			
Hga[c]	101.7	94.9	88.6	101.7				98.2	101.7
Idfu				101.7					
Ism	93.5				90.4	96.7			
Isna				90.3					
Kat			90.0	87.6					
Kom				92.8					
Lux	93.1	96.3	93.1	103.1	90.0				93.1
Mah				99.6	93.1		89.2		
Man				96.3					
Mat				99.1	95.8		102.6	92.6	
Nag			90.9	87.8			94.1		
Nuw	99.1		92.6	99.1	89.5	95.8			99.1
Pt S		98.0			101.5	91.5			
Qena	100.1		100.1	90.5	93.6		96.8	100.1	
Qus				97.2					
Rafah				103.9					
Saf			96.1	92.9				89.8	
SeS[b]	97.6		91.1	97.6	88.0		94.3		97.6
Sha			103.5	93.5					
Sid				101.2					
Siwa				90.6					
Soh	99.3		96.0	89.7	104.8		102.8	92.8	99.3
Suez		91.2		94.4	88.1				

a=Also Cultural Prgr on 91.5MHz 11.9kW and Middle East Prgr on 89.5MHz at 100kW. Voice of the Arabs r. on 106.3MHz.
b=Koran Prgr also on 101.1MHz at 0.3kW, and c=at 7.96kW.

FM Prgrs: D=Educational Prgr, E=European Prgr, G=General Prgr, K=Koran Prgr, M=Musical Prgr, N=Radio Masr, R=Regional Prgr, S=Songs Prgr, Y=Youth & Sport

Stations & powers: Abu=Abu Simbel 0.3kW, Abh=Abu Homus 4kW, Alx=Alexandria 58.6kW, Al F=Al Farfra 11.9kW/R, G 0.3kW, Asy=Assyout 11.2kW, Asw=Aswan 11.9kW, Baris 0.3kW, Bawiti 0.3kW, Ben=Beni Suef 0.3kW, Cairo 100kW, Dahab 0.3kW, Dum=Dumyat 0.3kW, El A=El Arish 54.5kW, El D=El Dakhla 4kW/K 0.3kW, El K=El Kharga 0.3kW, El M=El Minyah 18kW/S 4kW, El Tur 11.9kW, El Z=El Zayat 0.3kW, Hal=Halayeb 4kW/K 0.3kW, Hga=Hurghada 28.3kW/E, G, K 7.96kW, Idfu 0.3kW, Ism=Ismailia 61.5kW, Isna 0.3kW, Kat=Katherina 0.3kW, Kom=Kom Ombo 0.3kW, Lux=Luxor 11.7kW, Mah=Mahalla 155kW, Man=Managem Bahariya 0.3kW, Mat=Matruh 9.77kW, Nag=Nag Hamadi 10kW, Nuw=Nuweiba 9.53kW, Pt S=Port Said 10kW, Qena 28.6kW, Qus=Quseir 4kW, Rafah 0.3kW, Saf=Safaga 10kW, SeS=Sharm El Sheikh 7.41kW/K 0.3kW, Sha=Shalatin 0.3kW, Soh=Sohag 38kW/R 4kW/M 0.3kW, Sid=Sidi Barani 0.3kW, Siwa 0.3kW, Suez 8.71kW

Ann: General Prgr: "Idha'atu jumhuriya misr al'arabbiya min al-qahira". Voice of the Arabs: "Saut al-'arab, min al-qahira". Holy Koran prgr: "Idha'atu-I-Quran min al-qahira"

Other FM Stations:
Nogoom FM, Cairo 100.6MHz 100kW. Arabic music, 24h
Nile FM, Cairo 104.2MHz 100kW. Mainly English pop & rock, 24h
Web: www.nilefmonline.com
Radio Hits, Cairo, Alamein, Alexandria, Hammam, Natron, R7, R8, 88.2MHz 11.9kW
Mega FM, Cairo, Alamein, Alexandria, Hammam, Natron, R7, R8, 92.7MHz 11.9kW

F.PI.: Reports of two new FM stations: R. Drama and Comedy R.

EXTERNAL SERVICES: Radio Cairo
see International Broadcasting Section.
Other Stations
AFRTS Low-power broadcasts of NPR and AFN to US contingent of UN MFO in Sinai rep. on wide range of freqs from 92.7 to 106.1. Also 107.0 at Gebel Musa.

EL SALVADOR

L.T: UTC -6h — **Pop:** 7.1 million — **Pr.L:** Spanish — **E.C:** 60Hz, 115V — **ITU:** SLV

SUPERINTENDENCIA GENERAL DE ENERGÍA Y TELECOMUNICACIONES (SIGET)
✉ Sexta Décima Calle Poniente y 3°Av.Sur N° 2001, Colonía Flor Blanca, San Salvador ☎ +503 2257-4438 **W:** www.siget.gob.sv

ASOCIACION SALVADORENA DE RADIODIFUSION (ASDER) ✉ Calle La Ceiba # 261, Col. Escalon, San Salvador **W:** asder.com.sv

MW	Call	kHz	kW	Station, location
1)	HV	540	5	La Estación de la Palabra, San Salvador
18)	FG	550	2	R. Cristo Te Llama, Sonsonate (r: 900)
3)	KT	570	10	R. Exus "YXR Radio", San Salvador
4)	NK	‡600	3	Vox FM, San Salvador (r: 94.5)
64)	LN	630	10	R. Promesa, San Salvador: 1130-0400
7)	JW	700	12	R. Mi Gente, San Salvador: 1200-0400
7)	JW	700	12	R. Mi Gente, San Miguel
9)	RA	‡720	1	Qué Buena, San Salvador (r:88.9)
10)	KL	760	5	YSKL La Poderosa, San Miguel
10)	KL	760	1	YSKL La Poderosa, Sonsonate (r:770)
10)	KL	760		YSKL La Poderosa, Zacateluca (r: 770)
10)	KL	770	10	YSKL La Poderosa,San Salvador: 1030-0530
10)	KL	780	1	YSKL La Poderosa, Usulután (r:770)
10)	KL	780	1	YSKL La Poderosa, Sta Ana (r:770)
11)	AX	800	12	R. María El Salvador, San Salvador: 1230-0600
12)	FA	810	2	R. Lorenzana, San Vicente
44)	DA	810	1.5	R. Imperial, Sonsonate: 1100-0300
13)	PX	‡830	5	R. Pax, San Miguel

MW Call	kHz	kW	Station, location
14) FB	840	10	R. Santa Biblia, San Salvador: 1030-0300
15) RC	‡860	1	R. Tecana, Sta Ana
16) AR	870	10	R. Renacer, San Salvador
8) CD	880	1	R. Ritmo, Stgo de María
17) LA	890	3	R. Renacimiento, Sta Ana: 1000-0500
18) OJ	900	2	R. Cristo Te Llama, San Salvador
59)	930		R. Rey de Gloria, San Salvador
20) HG	950	1	R. Chaparrastique, San Miguel
21) TW	‡960	0.5	R. Centro, Sonsonate
47) MS	‡970	5	R. UTEC–R. Universidad Tecnológica, San Salvador: 1200-0400
24) HH	‡1000	1	Estación H, Sta Ana
25) CA	±1020	5	R. Int. /La Máxima, San Salvador: 1100-0300
27) RM	1030	1	R. Frontera, Ahuachapán: 1200-0400
26) AN	‡1070	1	LV de los Ausoles, Ahuachapán
61) ME	1080	6	R. CRET, San Salvador
61)	1090		R. CRET, Sta Ana
28) MG	1090	3	R. 1090, Atiquizaya
29) RF	1100	3	R. Don Bosco, San Salvador
30) CL	±1110	2.5	R. Horizonte, San Miguel (r.1160)
58) LR	1120	3	Una Voz que Clama en el Desierto, San Salvador: 1045-0500
20) LG	‡1130	1	R. Chaparrastique, San Miguel
31) AJ	1130	1	R. Moderna, Sta Ana: 1200 0400
11) CF	1150	1	R. María Zona Oriental, San Miguel (r: 800)
48) RG	‡1160	1	R. Corporación, Sta Ana
55) CR	‡1170		R. Cristo Viene, San Miguel
68) CB	1170	0.5	R. Pentecostés, Sonsonate
33) VG	1180	5	R. VEA–Voz Evangélica de América, San Salvador: 1200-2400
34) KJ	‡1200	1	R. Sirama, San Miguel
22) CG	1210	1	R. América/R. La Paz, Zacatecoluca
49) MT	1240	0.5	R. Metapán, Metapán
50) QN	1240	1	R. Norteña, San Miguel
35) AA	‡1260	12	R. Abba, San Salvador
34) QZ	‡1270	1	R. W "LV de la Verdad en Oriente", San Miguel
61) QV	‡1280	1	R. CRET, Sta Ana
57)	1280		R. Emaús, San Vicente
37) MA	1290	1	R. Chalatenango, Chalatenango: 1000-0300
38) LV	1300	6	W-LV de la Verdad, San Salvador
56) KG	1300		R. Llanera "La Campechana", San Miguel
51) RV	1310	5	R. Veritas, Stgo de María
52) AH	‡1320	1	R. Emanuel, La Unión
39) HQ	‡1330	5	R. Cristo Te Llama, San Salvador
40) XW	‡1340	1	R. Novedades, Usulután
46) FM	‡1360	5	Super Radio, San Salvador
53) KO	1370	1	R. Lluvias de Bendición, San Miguel: 1100-0300
63)	1390		R. Getsemaní, La Unión
69)	1390		R. Fraternidad de Jesucristo, Chalchuapa
41) JI	1400	1	LV del Litoral, Usulután: 1100-0400
54) KR	1450	1	R. Restauración, San Miguel: 1000-0400
67) CS	1500	1	R. Pentecostal, Usulután
60)	1550	5	R. Sanidad Divina, San Salvador: 1000-0600
65)	‡1580		R. Poder y Gloria, Santa Ana

Call YS–, ‡ = inactive, (r) = repeater, ± = varying fq

Addresses and other information:
1) Ap.2854 (or: Calle al Matazano N° 1, Final Col.Sta Lucía, Ilopango), San Salvador. **W:** elim.org.sv – **2)** Carretera a Santa Ana, Colonia Monte Carlos, Calle Principal (or Apartado Postal 10), Sonsonate – **3)** Jardines de la Cima polígono "N" Calle las Begonias, Pasaje los Lirios #14, San Salvador – **4)** Edif.TV2, Alameda Dr.Manuel E.Araujo, San Salvador – **6)** 65 Av S y Av.Olipica, 192 Edif.Corporación YSKL, San Salvador. **W:** corporacionslcom – **7)** 14 Calle Poniente, entre 43 y 45, Avenida Sur No. 2309, Col. Flor Blanca, San Salvador. **W:** radiocadenamigente.blogspot.com – **8)** 2a Av.Norte 24, Stgo de María, Usulután – **9)** Ap.720, San Salvador – **10)** 65 Av S y Av.Olimpica, 192 Edif.Corporación YSKL, San Salvador. **W:** radioyskl.com – **11)** Urb. General Escalon, Pasaje Beethoven 8/E, San Salvador. **W:** radiomaria. org.sv – **12)** Carretera a Tecoluca, Col. Najarro, San Vicente – **13)** 10 Calle Oriente 102 Bis, San Miguel – **14)** Iglesia San Pablo, Final 5a Calle Poniente, Colonia Escalón, San Salvador – **15)** Altos del Cine Tecana, Sta Ana – **16)** 27 Calle Poniente 544, San Salvador. **W:** renace. org – **17)** 4a Av.Sur, Entre 7a y 9a Calle Poniente, Edif.Plaza de Vidrio, Sta Ana – **18)** Colonia San Miguel, CI Principal Pasaje Castillo, San Ramón Mejicanos, San Salvador. **W:** cristotellama.org.sv – **19)** Calle al Trapiche, Chalchuapa, Santa Ana – **20)** 4a Av.Sur 303 bis, San Miguel – **21)** 5a Calle Oriente 44 (or Apartado Postal 115), Sonsonate – **22)** 2a Calle Poniente 22, Zacatecoluca – **24)** 9a Calle Poniente 25, Sta Ana – **25)** Av.España y 23 Calle Oriente, Ex Cine Fausto, San Salvador – **26)** Av.Morazán km 101, Ahuachapán – **27)** Av.2 de Abril y 8a Calle Poniente – **28)** 5° Calle Oriente 3-204, Atiquizaya – **29)** Edificio 2, CITT, Universidad Don Bosco, Soyapango, San Salvador. **W:** www.radio.udb.edu.sv – **31)** 8a Calle Poniente 11A, Sta Ana – **33)** Calle 5 de Noviembre y final 6 Av. Norte, Frente a Banco de Famila, San Martín, San Salvador. **W:** lacapilla.org.sv – **34)** Carr.Litoral km 134, Cantón Jalacatal, San Miguel – **35)** Col.San Benito, Pasaje Las Palmas 182, San Salvador – **37)** Calle a San Francisco Lempa, Col. Veracruz, Chalatenango. **W:** radiochalatenango.com.sv – **38)** 17 Calle Oriente 143, Barrio San Miguelito, San Salvador – **39)** Misión Evangelístyica Cristo Te Llama, Ap.855, San Salvador – **40)** 1a Oeste 18, Usulután – **41)** 12 Av.Sur y final 5a Calle Oriente, Col.Sta Rosa, Usulután. **W:** lavozdellitoral.com FM: 90.1MHz – **44)** Ap.56, Sonsonate – **46)** Boulevard de los Héroes, Edificio Los Heroes, Local 8B, San Salvador – **47)** Universidad Tecnológica, 17 Av.Norte 130, San Salvador – **48)** Sta Ana – **49)** Calle Principal, Costado Norte Centro Judical, Col Lomas de Montecristo, Metapán, Sta Ana – **50)** Col.Hirleman 14 C P Block 6 N° 9, San Miguel – **51)** Bo El Centro, C.Bolivar y 4 Av.S, Stgo de María, Usulután – **52)** La Unión – **53)** Carr.Panamericana, Crio El Alto, 300 mts al Norte, El Jalacatal, San Salvador. **W:** radiolluviasde-bendicion.com.sv – **54)** Ap.210, San Miguel – **55)** San Miguel – **56)** Col. Hirleman, 14 Calle Poniente, Bloque 6, N° 9, San Miguel – **57)** 2 Av N N° 10, San Vicente – **58)** San Salvador. **W:** radiovozquecllama. org.sv – **59)** Carretera Antigua a Plan del Pino, 1 Cuadra, Antes de la Ciudadela Don Bosco, Soyapango, San Salvador – **60)** Calle 25 de Abril Poniente, Barrio San José # 22B, San Marcos, San Salvador. **W:** radi-osanidaddivina.cp, – **61)** Barrio La Cruz, 10 Av Norte N° 203-Bis, San Miguel. **W:** radiocreт.net – **62)** Misión Evangelística Cristo Te Llama, Barrio El Calvario, 4a Av.Sur 303 bis, San Miguel – **63)** Col. La Paz, La Unión (part of Radio CRET Network) – **64)** 75 Av Norte, Prolongación Juan Pablo II, Col Jardines de Escalón, final Pasaje KL, San Salvador – **65)**Santa Ana – **67)** Kilómetro 112½, Carretera El Litoral, Frente a Desvío Esmora, Usulután – **68)** Colonia Monte Carmelo, Calle a Los Naranjos, Frente Antena de la YSU, Sonsonate – **69)** Calle al trapiche, Chalchuapa, Santa Ana

FM in San Salvador (MHz): 72.5 Metroaudio – 72.9 – R. Selectos – 87.75 Canal 6 – 88.5 Paz – 88.9 Qué Buena – 89.3 Cool – 89.7 Bautista – 90.1 Láser (español) – 90.5 Progreso – 90.9 UPA – 91.3 Exa – 91.7 YSUCA – 92.1 La Klave – 92.5 La Nueva – 92.9 Láser (inglés)– 93.3 Globo – 93.7 El Mundo – 94.1 Super Estrella – 94.5 Vox – 94.9 Astral – 95.3 R. Eco – 95.7 Verdad – 96.1 Scan – 96.5 R. Roca – 96.9 R. El Salvador – 97.3 Corazón – 97.7 Luz – 98.1 Gospel FM – 98.5 Cuscatlán – 98.9 La Mejor FM – 99.3 Mesías – 99.7 Guapa – 100.1 ABC – 100.5 Restauración – 100.9 La Chévere – 101.3 Monumental – 101.7 Mil 80 –102.1 102 Uno –102.5 Femenina – 102.9 102 Nueve – 103.3 Clásica – 103.7 Cadena Central – (6) 104.1 YSKL La Poderosa – 104.5 Sonora – 104.9 Fiesta – 105.3 UFG Radio – 105.7 YXY – 106.1 El Camino – 106.5 Ranchera – 106.9 Maya Visión – 107.3 YSU – 107.7 Fuego.
FM in San Miguel (MHz): 90.1 Stereo Caliente - 90.5 Siglo 21– 90.9 Popular – 91.7 YSUCA – 92.5 Monseñor Romero – 94.1 Cadena Central – 96.5 Agape R. – 97.3 Carnaval – 98.1 La Pantera – 99.7 Mi Consentida - 102.9 102 Nueve – 104.1 YSKL La Poderosa – 106.1 La Grande – 107.3 R. María.
FM in Santa Ana (MHz): 90.5 Supra Stereo - 91.7 YSUCA - 92.1 Fe y Alegría – 92.5 R. Doremix – 93.3 Shabach – 95.3 Amor – 97.3 Uno – 97.9 La Campirona – 99.7 R. RX FM - 102.9 Doble H – 104.1 YSKL La Poderosa – 105.3 Soda Stereo – 106.1 Bautista

EQUATORIAL GUINEA

L.T: UTC +1h — **Pop:** 600,000 — **Pr.L:** Spanish, French, ethnic — **E.C:** 50Hz, 220V — **ITU:** GNE

MINISTERIO DE INFORMACIÓN, TURISMO Y CULTURA
◻ Barrio Nzalang (antiguo África 2000), Malabo. ☎+240 333 078221 ▤ +240 333 072444. **LP:** Minister: Purificacion Opo Barila. Dir R & TV: Hermenesildo Moliko Djele.

RADIODIFUSION DE GUINEA ECUATORIAL (Gov.)
◻ Ap. 749, Bata ☎+240 333 082592 ▤ +240 333 082093 ◻ Av. 3 de Agosto 90, Ap. 195, Malabo ☎+240 333 072260 ▤ +240 333 072097

SW:	kHz	kW	Times
Bata	5005	50	0500-2100 (irregular)
Malabo(Semu)	6250	20	0530-1830 (irr, times vary)

FM: Bata 98/99.9MHz 1kW, Malabo 102MHz.
D.Prgr: in Spanish/ethnic. **N:** 0600, 1415, 2100.
Ann: "Esta es Radio Bata" or "Esta es Radio Malabo".

Other stations:
Africa No. 1: Malabo 102MHz (see main entry under Gabon).
RFI Afrique: Malabo 88/97.5MHz in French/Spanish.
R. Asonga, Malabo & Bata: freq. not known.
Rural radio: La Voz de Kie Ntem at Ebibeyín, Ecos de Wele Nzás at Mongomo and La Voz de Centro Sur at Evinayong

ERITREA

L.T: UTC +3h — **Pop:** 6 million — **Pr.L:** Afar, Amharic, Arabic, Tigrinya, Tigre, others — **E.C:** 50Hz, 230V — **ITU:** ERI.

MINISTRY OF INFORMATION
✉ P.O. Box 872, Asmara ☎+291 1 120478/201820 🖶 +291 1 126747 **W:** shabait.com **E:** nesredin@tse.com.er

VOICE OF THE BROAD MASSES OF ERITREA (Gov.)
✉ P.O. Box 242, Asmara ☎+291 1 117111/118711 🖶 +291 1 124847 **L.P:** DG: Ghirmay Berhe. TD: Mehreteab Tesfagiorgis. PD: Abdu Heji. Dir. Radio Eng.: Berhane Gerezgiher.
Station: Asmara (Selai Dairo).
MW: 837kHz 100kW (Prgr. 2), 945kHz 100kW (Prgr. 1).
SW: 7205 kHz 100kW (Prgr. 1), 7175 kHz 100kW (Prgr.2). Prgr. 2 heard also via three low power transmitters between 1500-1900 on 5060/6170/7120/9710kHz. **NB:** Frequencies highly variable to escape Ethiopian jamming.
Prgr. 1 in Tigrinya/Tigre/Kunama: 0400-1000, 1300-2000 — **Prgr. 2** in Arabic/Afar/Amharic/Oromo/Saho/Bilen: 0400-1000, 1500-2000.
Zara FM: 100MHz + others. **Numa FM:** freq. not known.
Ann: Amharic:"Yeh be Asmera ketema yemigegne yesifiw Yeritrea hezeb demts yeamarigna agelgilot new". Arabic: "Huna Asmara, Idha'at Sawt al-Jamahir al-Iritriyyah". Tigrigna: "Ezi kab Asmara Zemehalalef Medeber Radio Demtsi Hafash Eritrea Eyu".
R. Sawa, west Eritrea: **FM** (fq. not known). Op. by Sawa National Youth Training Centre.

ESTONIA

L.T: UTC +2h (31 Mar-27 Oct: +3h) — **Pop:** 1.3 million — **Pr.L:** Estonian, Russian — **E.C:** 50Hz, 230V — **ITU:** EST

KULTUURIMINISTEERIUM (Ministry of Culture)
✉ Suur-Karja 23, 15076 Tallinn ☎ +372 6282250 🖶 +372 6282200 **E:** min@kul.ee **W:** www.kul.ee
L.P: Chmn (Media Services License Commission): Ilmar Raag
NB. The Ministry of Culture issues broadcasting licenses.

EESTI RAHVUSRINGHÄÄLING (ERR) (Pub)
✉ Gonsiori 21, 15020 Tallinn ☎ +372 6284100 🖶 +372 6114457
✉ Studios (exc. ERR2): Kreutzwaldi 14, 10124 Tallinn
E: err@err.ee **W:** www.err.ee **L.P:** Chmn: Agu Uudelepp

FM (MHz)	ER1	ER2	ER3	ER4	kW
Koeru	105.1	102.6	107.6	93.4	3x30/7.8
Kohtla-Nõmme	105.4	102.9	90.4	95.3	11.2
Kuressaare	105.6	103.1	107.0	-	1
Kõrgessaare	91.2	99.1	94.9	-	1
Mõksi	-	-	-	99.9	3
Orissaare	105.9	103.4	107.8	-	20/2x10
Pärnu	104.8	102.3	107.3	94.8	10
Tallinn	104.1	101.6	106.6	94.5	30
Valga	-	-	-	92.5	1.8
Valgjärve	106.1	103.6	105.7	-	2x40/12.5
Viiratsi	105.8	103.3	107.0	95.5	1

NB. Sites with only txs below 1kW not listed.
D.Prgr: ERR1 (Vikerraadio): 24h. – ERR2 (Raadio 2): 24h. – ERR3 (Klassikaraadio): 24h. – ERR4 (Raadio 4/Radio 4) in Russian: 24h. – ERR Raadio Tallinn 103.5MHz (1kW): 24h. Own prgrs 0700-1700; 1700-0700 rel. BBC World Sce, RFI, Deutsche Welle.

OTHER STATIONS
MW	kHz	kW	Location	Station
6B)	1035	200	Tartu (a)	R. Eli

FM	MHz	kW	Location	Station
18)	87.7	1	Paldiski	Paldiski R.
3A)	88.1	2.6	Paide	Star FM
6A)	88.2	3	Kohtla-Nõmme	Tartu Pereraadio
2D)	88.2	3	Muhu	Raadio 3
1C)	88.3	2	Tallinn	Spin FM
4)	88.6	3	Pärnu	Raadio 7
5)	88.8	1.3	Tallinn	R. Mania
6A)	89.0	3	Rõõmu	Tartu Pereraadio
8)	89.0	2.4	Vanamõisa	Kuressaare Pereraadio
8)	89.4	1	Kõnnu	Kuressaare Pereraadio
6A)	89.6	1	Tallinn	Tartu Pereraadio
1B)	89.8	1.1	Vinni	Raadio Uuno
1A)	89.9	1.1	Pärnu	Raadio Kuku
12)	90.1	1	Kärdla	Raadio Kadi
1E)	90.2	1	Tallinn	DFM
12)	90.5	1	Kuressaare	Raadio Kadi
2C)	90.6	1.3	Tallinn	Russkoe R.

FM	MHz	kW	Location	Station
1B)	91.0	3	Pärnu	Raadio Uuno
7A)	91.2	6.5	Valgjärve	Raadio Elmar
7A)	91.5	1	Kuressaare	Raadio Elmar
7A)	91.7	7.5	Koeru	Raadio Elmar
7A)	92.2	3	Linnamäe	Raadio Elmar
3A)	92.2	3	Pada	Star FM
1B)	92.3	1	Parksepa	Raadio Uuno
14)	92.5	1	Vinni	Raadio Viru
11)	92.7	1.5	Seljametsa	Raadio Pärnu
3A)	92.9	3	Linnamäe	Star FM
2E)	93.2	1.5	Tallinn	Energy FM
3A)	93.3	3	Kuressaare	Star FM
2B)	93.8	3	Holsta	Sky Plus
2B)	95.2	1	Rõõmu	Sky Plus
2B)	95.4	3	Tallinn	Sky Plus
4)	96.1	3	Tamsalu	Raadio 7
2B)	96.3	1.9	Vätta	Sky Plus
3A)	96.6	1.5	Maardu	Star FM
16)	96.6	1	Sangaste	Ruut FM
2B)	96.8	1.6	Audru	Sky Plus
2B)	96.9	1.5	Palade	Sky Plus
1B)	97.2	3	Tallinn	Raadio Uuno
1B)	97.2	1	Rõõmu	Raadio Uuno
1B)	97.4	3	Sikassaare	Raadio Uuno
1B)	97.4	2.5	Koeru	Raadio Uuno
2D)	97.8	2	Tallinn	Raadio 3
2D)	98.3	1	Audru	Raadio 3
2A)	98.4	3	Tallinn	Sky Radio
2D)	98.6	2.5	Rõõmu	Raadio 3
7A)	99.0	3	Pärnu	Raadio Elmar
3A)	99.4	3	Rõõmu	Star FM
1B)	99.8	2.5	Linnamäe	Raadio Uuno
1F)	100.0	1	Narva	Narodnoe R.
7B)	100.2	2	Rõõmu	Raadio Tartu Kuku
3A)	100.3	1.9	Seljametsa	Star FM
1A)	100.5	2.2	Paide	Raadio Kuku
13)	100.7	3	Põlva	Raadio Marta
1A)	100.7	3	Tallinn	Raadio Kuku
1A)	100.8	1.5	Viljandi	Raadio Kuku
1A)	100.9	2.5	Linnamäe	Raadio Kuku
9)	101.0	3	Paide	Kuma Raadio
15)	101.7	1	Võru	Ring FM
3A)	101.9	2	Jõgeva	Star FM
3B)	102.1	1.5	Maardu	Power Hit R
3A)	103.2	3	Parksepa	Star FM
1B)	104.5	1	Liiva	Raadio Uuno
15)	104.7	1	Rõõmu	Ring FM
10)	104.9	1	Tallinn	Euro FM

NB: Txs below 1kW not listed. (a) Kavastu

Addresses & other information:
1A-F) Veerenni 58a, 11314 Tallinn. **E:** 1A) kuku@kuku.ee; 1B) uuno@uuno.ee; 1D), 1F) in Russian. – **2A-E)** Pärnu mnt. 139c, 11317 Tallinn. **E:** skymedia@sky.ee. In Russian, exc. 2B,2E. **E:** 2E) info@raadio3.ee – **3A,B)** Peterburi 81, 11415 Tallinn. **E:** 3A) starfm@starfm.ee, 3B) info@power.ee – **4)** Välja 18, 10506 Tallinn. **E:** raadio7@raadio7.ee – **5)** Tartu mnt. 80d, 10112 Tallinn. **E:** raadio@mania.ee – **6A)** Annemõisa 18, 50708 Tartu. **E:** tartu@pereraadio.ee; **6B)** Vabaduse 20, 20306 Narva. Religious prgrs in Russian (incl. TWR relays): 24h. **E:** am1035@bk.ru – **7A,B)** Õpetaja 9a, 51003 Tartu. **E:** 7A) elmar@elmar.ee; 7B) raadio@tartukuku.ee – **8)** Tallinna nt. 45, 93811 Kuressaare. **E:** kuressaare@pereraadio.ee – **9)** Pärnu nt. 57, 72712 Paide. **E:** kuma@kuma.ee – **10)** Kristiina 15, 15026 Tallinn. **E:** info@eurofm.ee – **11)** Esplanaadi 10, 80010 Pärnu – **12)** Pikk tn. 62, 93815 Kuressaare. **E:** raadio@kadi.ee – **13)** Kesk 42, 63308 Põlva. **E:** martafm@martafm.ee – **14)** Maleva 23, 31021 Kohtla-Järve. **E:** info@raadioviru.ee – **15)** Teguri 37, 50107 Tartu. **E:** info@ringfm.ee – **16)** Pikk tn. 3a, 68206 Valga. **E:** ruutfm@ruutfm.ee – **18)** Sadama 21-12, 76806 Paldiski. **E:** prl04@hot.ee

ETHIOPIA

L.T: UTC +3h — **Pop:** 83 million — **Pr.L:** Amharic, Oromo, Sidamo, Somali, Tigrinya — **E.C:** 50Hz, 220V — **ITU:** ETH

ETHIOPIAN BROADCASTING AUTHORITY (EBA)
✉ P.O. Box 43142, Hailalem Bldg. Kazanchis, Addis Ababa ☎+251 11 5538755 🖶 +251 11 5536767
W: www.eba.gov.et **E:** e.b.a1@ethionet.et

RADIO ETHIOPIA (Gov.)
✉ P.O. Box 1020, Addis Ababa ☎+251 11 5516977
W: ertagov.com **E:** info@erta.gov.et **L.P:** GM: Ato Fikadu Yimeru. **SM:** Kasa Miloko. **CE:** Kebede Gobena. Head of English Prgrs: Melesse Edea Beyi.

MW	kHz	kW	MW	kHz	kW
Bahir Dar	594	100	Dese	891	100
Metu	684	100	Robe (Bale)	972	100
Arba Minch	828	100	Addis Ababa	989	1
Harar	855	100	Mekele	1044	200
Addis Ababa	873	100			

SW: Addis Ababa (Geja): 9705kHz 100kW.
FM(MHz): Addis Ababa 93.2 2.5kW, 94.5, 96.3 3.5kW, 97.1.
National Prgr. in Amharic/Others: 0300-2100. **In English:** 1200-1300. **City FM** on 96.3MHz. **FM Addis** in English on 97.1MHz. **Reg. prgrs** and **BBC relays** at times. External Sce. relay on 989kHz. **Ann:** Amharic: "Yeh Ye-Ethiopia Radio Naw". E: "This is the English service of R. Ethiopia". **IS:** Electronic keyboard.

EXTERNAL SERVICE: see International Radio section.

FANA BROADCASTING CORPORATION - RADIO FANA (Priv.)
☑ P.O.Box 30702, near Black Lion Hospital, in front of Sweden Embassy, Addis Ababa. **W:** fanabc.com **E:** fanabc@fanabc.com **LP:** GM: Woldu Yemessel. Tech. Dir: Mulugeta Mehari.
MW: Addis Ababa 1080kHz 3kW.
SW: Addis Ababa 6110 & 7210kHz 100kW.
FM (MHz): Haromage/Mekele 94.8, Dese 96.0, Nekemit 96.1, Addis Ababa/Gonder/Jimma 98.1, Wolayita 99.9, Shashemenie 103.4.
D.Prgr. in Afar/Amharic/Oromo/Somali/Tigrinya: 0300-2100. FM transmitters carry separate programming to MW and SW.

Regional government stations:
RADIO OROMIYA (Oromiya Radio & TV Organisation, ORTO)
☑ P.O. Box 2919, Adama. **W:** www.orto.gov.et **LP:** Mr. Abarra Hailu, Mgr. Mr. Habtamu Dargie Gudeta, Head Eng. Dept.
MW: Robe (Bale) 837kHz 100kW, Adama (Nazret) 1035kHz 10kW, Nekemte 1053kHz 100kW.
SW: Addis Ababa: 6030kHz 100kW.
FM: Addis Ababa (Intoto) 92.3MHz.
D.Prgr. in Oromo: Mon-Fri 0330-0600, 0900-1100, 1530-2000, SS 0330-1900. **Ann:** Oromo: "Kun Radio Oromiya".

VOICE OF TIGRAY REVOLUTION (Gov.)
☑ P.O.Box 450, Mekele, Tigray ☎+251 34 4410544/5 **W:** www.dimtsi-woyanc.com **E:** webmaster@dimtsiwoyane.com **LP:** Dir. Abera Tesfay.
MW: Mekele 1359kHz 100kW.
SW: Addis Ababa 5950kHz 100kW.
FM: Mekele 102.2MHz 3kW.
D.Prgr in Tigrinya/Afar: MF 0300-1900, SS 0300-1730. **Ann:** Tigrinya: "Dimtsi Woyane Tigray". **IS:** Melody played on washint (Ethiopian flute).

AMHARA STATE REGIONAL RADIO (Gov.)
☑ Amhara Mass Media Agency, P.O. Box 955, Bahir Dar. **L.P:** Dir: Mr. Dereje Moges. **W:** www.amma.gov.et **E:** ammawebmaster@yahoo.com
MW: Bahir Dar 801kHz 100kW. **SW:** Addis Ababa 6090kHz 100kW. **FM:** Bahir Dar 96.9MHz. **D. Prgr:** 0300-0600, 0900-1100, 1400-1900.

SOUTH FM(Gov.)
☑ Southern Nations & Nationalities Mass Media agency, P.O. Box 1080, Awasa.
FM: Awasa 96.9MHz, Arba Minch 90.9, Bensa 92.3, Bonga 97.4, Gedio 99.4, Jinka 87.8, Mizan 104.5, Waka 94.1, Wolkitie 89.2MHz.

Addis Ababa Region R.: Addis Ababa 96.3MHz 4kW – **Debub R,** Awasa: 100.6MHz – **FM Dire:** Dire Dawa: 106.1MHz – **Harar FM:** Harar: 101.4MHz – **R. Jigjiga,** Jigjiga 95.2MHz 2.5kW. **W:** radiojigjiga.com

Other stations:
Afro FM, Addis Ababa: 105.3MHz 2.5kW. **W:** afro105fm.com – **Mekele FM,** Mekele: 104.4MHz – **Ravos FM,** Awasa: 100.9MHz – **R. Sidama,** c/o Furra Institute of Development Studies, P.O. Box 69, Yirgalem – **Sheger FM,** Addis Ababa: 102.1MHz. **W:** shegerfm.com – **Zami R,** Addis Ababa: 90.7MHz 2kW. **W:** www.zami.com.et

FALKLAND ISLANDS (UK)

L.T: UTC -4h (DST: -3h, continuous DST is currently in effect) — **Pop:** 3,100 (excl. military personnel) — **Pr.L:** English — **E.C:** 50Hz, 240V — **ITU:** FLK

FALKLAND ISLANDS RADIO SERVICE (Pub)
☑ John Str, Stanley FIQQ 1ZZ. ☎+500 27277. 🖹 +500 27279. **W:**

www.firs.co.fk **E:** cgoss@firs.co.fk **L.P:** Stn Man.: Corina Goss, Prgr Contr.: Elizabeth Elliot, Senior Reporter: Stacy Bragger
MW: 530kHz 15kW. **FM**(MHz)**:** Pt Stanley 88.3 15W, Sussex Mountains 88.0 5W, March Ridge 90.0 1kW, Sapper Hill 96.5 0.25kW, Mt Maria 102.0 2kW

BRITISH FORCES BROADCASTING SERVICE
☑ Rockhopper Road, RAF Mount Pleasant. BFPO 655. ☎+500 32179. 🖹 +500 32193. **E:** adriana@bfbs.com **L.P:** SM: Steve. Eng. Mgr: Adrian J. Almond.
MW: Bush Rincon 550kHz 4kW
FM(MHz): Byron Heights 102.4, Marsh Ridge 90.0, Mt Alice 102.4, 104.2, 106.0, Mt Kent 102.4, Mt Marie 102.0, MPA 93.8, 96.0, 98.5, Sapper Hill 91.1, 94.5, San Carlos 88.0. **D.Prgr:** 24h **N:** Every hour from Independent Radio News by satellite from London. **Ann:** "This is BFBS in the Falklands". **V.** by QSL-card. Rp

KTV RADIO
☑ KTV Ltd, 68 Dean St., Stanley. ☎+500 22349 🖹 +500 21049 **E:** kmzb@horizon.co.fk **W:** www.ktv.co.fk
MW: 530kHz **FM:** 88.3MHz, 106.5MHz (rel. BBC World Service)

Deutsche Welle rel.: 101.1MHz
Saint FM rel.: 95.5MHz. (rebroadcast from St Helena).

FAROE ISLANDS (Denmark)

L.T: UTC (31 Mar-27 Oct: +1h) — **Pop:** 49,000 — **Pr.L:** Faroese — **E.C:** 50Hz, 220/380V — **ITU:** FRO

KRINGVARP FØROYA ÚTVARPIÐ (Pub.)
☑ Norðari Ringvegur, P.O.Box 1299, FR-100 Tórshavn ☎ +298 347500 🖹 +298 347501 **W:** www.kringvarp.fo
L.P: SM: Annika Mittún Jacobsen. PD: Jógvan Arge. TD: Hans Andor Johannesen
MW: Akraberg 531kHz 25/50/100kW
FM: Tórshavn 89.9MHz 31kW, Klaksvík 94.3MHz 41kW, Hesturin Suðurðy 97.5MHz 27kW, 100.0MHz Støðulfjall 3kW + 15 lp stns
D.Prgr: 24h All prgrs are in Faroese, except wrp. in English at approx 0855 LT during four summer months. **Ann:** 'Útvarpið'

RÁS 2 (Comm.)
☑ Vágsbotnur, P.O.Box 76, FR-100 Tórshavn ☎ +298 359999 🖹 +298 359990 **E:** ras2@ras2.fo **W:** www.ras2.fo
L.P: SM: Jonhard Hammer.
FM (MHz): Tórshavn 102.0, Suðuroy 102.6, Streymoy 106.0, Skarvanes 106.3, Klaksvik: 107.0 + 9 lp stns. **D.Prgr:** 0700-2400

LINDIN KRISTILIGT KRINGVARP (Rlg.)
☑ Bøkjaragøta 9, P.O.Box 2063, FR-165 Argir (Tórshavn) ☎ +298 321377 🖹 +298 321379 **E:** lindin@lindin.fo **W:** www.lindin.fo
L.P: Chairman: Preben Hansen
FM: Streymoy 98.0MHz, Tórshavn 101.0MHz, Klaksvik: 103.0MHz, Hestin Há Vági 105.5MHz + 7 lp stns. **D.Prgr:** 24h in Faroese exc. Thu+Sat 1500 LT

FIJI

L.T: UTC +12h (21 Oct 12-7 Jan 13, 27 Oct 13-26 Jan 14: +13h); DST 2013-14 subject to confirmation — **Pop:** 944,720 — **Pr.L:** English, Fijian, Hindi — **E.C:** 50Hz, 240V — **ITU:** FJI

DEPARTMENT OF COMMUNICATIONS
☑ 1st Floor, Credit Corporation Building, Suva ☎ +679 330 0766 🖹 +679 331 5167 **LP:** Dep. Secretary: Josua Turaganivalu

FIJI BROADCASTING CORPORATION LTD (Pub)
☑ PO Box 334, Suva ☎ +679 331 4333 🖹 +679 330 1643 **W:** www.fbc.com.fj **E:** infocenter@fbc.com.fj **LP:** CEO: Riyaz Saiyed Khaiyum C.E: Apisai Bakani.
Netw.: RF1 (R.Fiji One) Fijian ☎ +679 330 2588 **W:** www.rf1.fbc.com.fj – **RF2 (R.Fiji Two)** Hindi ☎ +679 330 2588 **W:** www.rf2.fbc.com.fj – **R.Mirchi** Hindi ☎ +679 330 2588 **W:** mirchifm@fbc.com.fj – **RFGold (R.Fiji Gold)** English ☎ +679 330 4500 **W:** www.goldfm@fbc.com.fj – **Bula FM** Fijian ☎ +679 331 4211 **W:** www.bulafm@fbc.com.fj – **2dayFM** English ☎ +679 331 6415 **W:** 2dayfm@fbc.com.fj **Prgr:** All 24h

MW	kHz	kW	Netw.				
Suva	558	10	RF1				
FM	RF1	RF2	Bula FM	R.Mirchi		RFGOLD	2dayFM
1)	93.0	105.0	102.6	97.8		100.2	95.4
2)	92.8	104.8	102.4	97.6		100.0	95.2

FM	RF1	RF2	Bula FM	R.Mirchi	RFGOLD	2dayFM
3)	93.2	105.4	102.8	98.0	100.4	95.6
4)	93.4	105.4	103.0	98.2	100.6	95.8

1) Deuba, Navua, Lami, Suva, Nausori, Korovou, Nadi, Lautoka, Yasawas, Mamanuca, Savusavu, Tavenui – **2)** Coral Coast, Nabau, Serua, Ba – **3)** Tavua – **4)** Rakiraki

Private commercial network
COMMUNICATIONS FIJI LTD
231 Waimanu Road [Private Mail Bag], Suva ☎ +679 331 4766 🖷 +679 330 3748 **W:** www.fijivillage.com **E:** info@fm96.com.fj **LP:** Man. Dir: William Parkinson, GM Fiji: Ian Jackson **E:** ian@fm96.com.fj CE: Philip Wilikibau **E:** philip@fm96.com.fj

Netw.: FM96 (English) PD: Amelia Rigsby **E:** amelia@fm96.com.fj – **Legend FM** (English) PD: Charles Taylor **E:** chas@fm96.com.fj – **Viti FM** (Fijian) PD: Malakai Veisamasama **E:** mala@fm96.com.fj – **Navtarang** (Hindi) PD: Satya Nand **E:** satya@fm96.com.fj – **R. Sargam** (Hindi) PD: Vijay Verma **E:** vj@sargam.com.fj **Prgr:** All 24h

FM	FM96	Navtarang	Viti FM	Legend FM	R.Sargam
1)	96.2	101.0	92.2	98.6	103.4
2)	96.0	100.8	92.0	98.4	103.2
3)	96.6	101.4	92.6	99.0	103.8

1) Suva, Nausori, Central Division, Nadi, Lautoka, Labassa – **2)** Sigatoka, Coral Coast, Ba, Tavua, Vatukoula – **3)** Rakiraki

Other Stations:

FM	MHz	Station	Location
1)	88.2	BBC	Suva
3)	89.2	femTALK 89.2	Suva
2)	89.4	R.Pasifik	Suva
8)	89.8	Harvest R.	Suva
4)	91.8	R.France Int.	Suva
5)	93.6	MIX 94FM	Ba/Tavua/Rakiraki
5)	93.8	MIX 94FM	Suva/Lautoka/Nadi/ Mamanucas/Yasawas
6)	94.6	R. Naya Jiwan	Suva
6)	103.4	Nai Talai FM	Suva
6)	104.2	R. Light	Suva
10)	106.4	R. Australia	Ba
10)	106.6	R. Australia	Suva/Nadi/Labassa
9)	107.7	Hope FM	Suva

Addresses and other information
1) BBC Pacific Stream, 24h satellite relay from London – **2)** School of Law, Arts & Media, University of the South Pacific, Private Mail Bag, Laucala, Suva ☎ +679 3232214 🖷+679 3231500 **LP:** SM: Semi Francis, Co-Ord: Shirley Tagi **W:** www.usp.ac.fj **D:Prgr:** 24h includes prgrs in English,French,Hindi, Fijian and Mandarin – **3)** Community Media Center, 2nd Fl, Bayly Trust Bldg, 193 Rodwell Rd, Suva ☎ + 679 3318160 🖷 +679 33072707 **W:** www.femlinkpacific.org.fj **LP:** Exec.Dir Sharon Bhagwan Rolls. Also operates a mobile community radio stn for women on Viti Levu. Establishing a network of similar stns in other parts of Fiji and Tonga – **5)** 11 Nasoki St, Lautoka ☎ +679 666 8900 **W:** www. mix94.fm **E:** info@mix94.fm **ID:** "Fiji's Best Mix" 24h – **6)** Evangelical Bible Missions Trust Board, Studio:15 Tower Street, Suva. Networks: R.Light (English), R. Naya Jiwan (Hindi), Nai Talai FM (Fijian, currently inactive) ☎ +679 331 9536 – **8)** WHBN, Cnr Kings Rd & Khalsa Rd, Kinoya, Suva. PO Box 1499, Nabua, Suva ☎ +679 3396808 **W:** www. whbn.org/harvest-radio **LP:** Mktg Mgr: Rajiv Puran **D.Prgr:** 24h rlg – **9)** Seventh Day Adventist Church Mission, PO Box 297, Suva ☎ +679 336 1022 🖷 +679 336 1446 – **10)** English for the Pacific stream, 24h satellite relay from Melbourne.

FINLAND

L.T: UTC +2h (31 Mar-27 Oct: +3h) — **Pop:** 5.4 million — **Pr.L:** Finnish, Swedish — **E.C:** 50Hz, 230V — **ITU:** FIN

VIESTINTÄVIRASTO
(FICORA, Finnish Communications Regulatory Authority)
PL 313, FI-00181 Helsinki ☎+358 9 69661 🖷 +358 9 6966410 **W:** www.ficora.fi **E:** info@ficora.fi **LP:** DG: Rauni Hagman. Dir. of Radio Adm.: Kari Koho.

DIGITA OY (programme distributor)
Jämsänk. 2, FI-00520 Helsinki ☎+358 20411711 🖷 +358 204117234 **W:** www.digita.fi **E:** info@digita.fi
LP: DG: Sirpa Ojala. Vice Pres, Netw. & Site Sces: Ilari Anttila.

YLEISRADIO (YLE, Pub.)
FI-00024 Yleisradio ☎+358 9 14801 🖷 +358 9 14803216 **W:** yle.fi **E:** fbc@yle.fi **LP:** DG: Lauri Kivinen

FM (MHz)	1	2	3	4	5	6	7	kW
Aavasaksa	87.9	89.8	94.7					3
Ahvenanmaa			100.3		104.9	93.1		10/3
Anjalankoski	88.5	92.8	96.9	91.4	99.5b			30
Enontekiö	88.5	91.4	98.7	104.6			101.2	5
Espoo	87.9	91.9	94.0	103.7	98.9	101.1		60
Eurajoki	87.7	103.5	94.8	92.0	99.4	103.0		30
Fiskars	90.9	93.1	97.0	105.0	102.5	99.7		3
Haapavesi	89.0	96.1	98.4	101.9				30
Hanko					101.9			5
Hämeenlinna			99.2					1
Iisalmi	87.7	92.8	96.5	107.9				2
Ilomantsi				106.1				1
Inari	88.4	92.8	98.8	105.3			101.9	50/30
Joensuu			106.9					1
Joutseno	88.0	90.9	98.5	100.7				30
Jyväskylä	89.9	87.6	99.3	92.5	103.5			3/30
Karigasniemi	89.5	93.4	96.8	103.7			100.8	2
Kerimäki	90.5	95.8	99.1	103.2				30
			97.7	103.2				6/3
Kiihtelysvaara	88.4	94.9	97.2	100.4				5
Koli	90.2	93.4	99.6	106.4	102.4b			30/5
Kruunupyy	91.4	94.0	97.6	88.8	99.7	102.7		60/3
Kuopio	91.6	93.9	98.1	88.1	100.2b			50
Kuttanen	94.1	97.2	99.6	105.6			102.2	3
Lahti	93.2	95.5	97.9	90.5	100.6b			50/0.2
Lapua	88.2	90.1	93.1	97.5	95.2	101.5		60/2
Lohja			96.1	105.0				3
Mikkeli	88.9	92.1	94.6	101.8				30
Nilsiä				90.8				
Nuorgam	88.6	93.9	97.7	107.8			101.2	3
Oulu	90.4	93.2	97.3	107.7	100.3b			50/5
Parikkala			95.1					
Pello	90.2	97.0	99.7	103.4				3
Pernaja	89.5	92.3	95.0	96.4	102.2	98.3		3/1
Pieksämäki	89.4	95.3	97.4	104.9				2/0.5
Pihtipudas	88.6	91.1	97.0	94.7	100.8b			50/2.5
Posio	86.7	91.5	98.6	104.0				30/3
Pyhätunturi	91.0	97.6	99.9	102.4				50
Pyhävuori	88.9	91.0	94.2/97.2	96.1	98.6	102.6		30/2
Rovaniemi	88.2	94.0	96.7	106.8			103.0	30/10
Ruka	90.7	92.8	95.1	104.3				3/2
Sodankylä	87.8	90.1	94.3	106.5			101.3	3
Taivalkoski	89.2	91.9	99.2/103.6	106.5				60
Tammela	89.2	91.3	96.0	105.4				5
Tampere	90.7	93.7	99.9	88.3	102.1b			60/6
Tenola(NOR)	89.0	94.1	95.8			100.5		0.02
Tervola	88.6	92.6	95.6	101.6				30
Turku	89.8	92.6	94.3	96.7	98.2	101.4		60/6
Utsjoki	90.7	93.1	99.4	107.1			102.6	2/5
Vaasa	87.8	89.6	94.8	105.2	97.3	101.0		1
Vuokatti	92.3	94.3	98.9	101.2				60
Ylläs	92.2	95.3	98.1	100.7			103.8	50
Ähtäri	91.9	94.6	96.2	102.9				3

+30 transmitters under 1kW not mentioned.
b = "FSR Mix", mixture of FM5 & FM6.

D.Prgr: FM1 "YLE Radio 1" (classical music, culture, actualities): 24h. **N:** 0400, 0500, 0600, 0900, 1100, 1400, 1600, 1700, 2000, 2200. **N. in English:** 1525. **N. in Russian:** 2055. **N. in Latin:** Fri 0755, Sat 1055 – **FM2 "YleX"** (rock & pop culture for youth): 24h (r. FM1 W00-04).**N:** on the h – **FM3 "Radio Suomi"** (news, sports, popular music and regional prgrs): 24h. **N:** on the h – **FM4 "YLE Puhe"** (news & talk prgr.): 24h. – **FM5 "Radio Extrem"** (Swedish language prgr for young people). 24h (simultaneous night prgr with R Vega) – **FM6 "Radio Vega"** (Swedish language prgr for elderly people and regional prgrs). 24h – "FSR Mix" carries R. eXtrem MF 0400-0650, 1415-1700, 2000-2200 Sat 1500-0000 Sun 1500-2200. At other times R. Vega – **FM7 "Sámiradio"** (Sámi language network). 24h. Carries YLE, SR & NRK Sámiradio: MF: 0515-0830, 1100-1130, 1300-1630 Sat 1700-1800 Sun 1700-1830, at other times FM3 – **"YLE Mondo"** (digital network carried also via Espoo 97.5MHz 5kW): 24h.

Regional & local prgrs:
In Finnish on FM3: MF 0430-1435 excl. nationwide news on the h. – **Ylen aikainen,** Helsinki: 94.0MHz. – **R. Itä-Uusimaa,** Porvoo: 90.3/95.0MHz. (also r. 94.0MHz) – **Ylen läntinen,** Lohja: 97.0/105.0MHz. (also r. 94.0MHz) – **Tampereen R,** Tampere: 99.9MHz. – **Lahden R,** Lahti: 97.9MHz. – **R. Häme,** Hämeenlinna: 96.0/97.3/99.2/107.1MHz. – **Turun R,** Turku: 94.3/100.3/107.1MHz. – **Satakunnan R,** Pori: 94.8/97.2MHz. – **R. Keski-Suomi,** Jyväskylä: 87.6/97.0/99.3MHz. – **Kymenlaakson R,** Kouvola: 96.9MHz. – **Etelä-Karjalan R,** Lappeenranta: 89.1/97.2/98.5/103.2MHz. – **Pohjois-Karjalan R,** Joensuu: 97.2/97.7/99.6MHz. – **Etelä-Savon R,** Mikkeli: 94.6/97.4/99.1MHz. – **R. Savo,** Kuopio: 96.5/98.1MHz. – **Pohjanmaan**

R, Vaasa: 93.1/94.2/94.8/96.6MHz. – **R. Keski-Pohjanmaa,** Kokkola: 97.6MHz. – **Oulu-R,** Oulu: 95.1/97.3/98.4/99.2/102.5MHz. – **Kainuun R,** Kajaani: 98.9/103.6MHz. – **R. Perämeri,** Kemi: 94.7/95.6MHz. – **Lapin R,** Rovaniemi: 96.7MHz + 15 more freqs.
In Swedish on FM6: MF 0430-1000, 1330 & 1430. **R. Vega Mellannyland,** Helsingfors: 101.1MHz. – **R. Vega Östnyland,** Borgå: 91.4/98.3MHz. – **R. Vega Västnyland,** Ekenäs: 99.7/101.9MHz. – **R. Vega Åboland,** Åbo: 93.1/101.4/103.0MHz. – **R. Vega Österbotten,** Vasa: 101.0/101.5/102.6/102.7MHz.

Digital: YLE's digital radio broadcasts are carried on Digital Video Broadcasting (DVB) network within the digital TV multiplexes. They include Ylen 1, Ylen klassinen, YleX, R. Extrem, YLE Puhe, R. Suomi, R. Vega, YLE World, YLE Mondo, YLE Multifoorumi, YLE FSR+ and commercial channels Uusi Kiss, Iskelmä and Harju ja Pöntinen.

Other stations; main networks:

FM (MHz)	1)	2)	3)	4)	5)	6)	7)	8)	9)
Alajärvi	104.3					102.2			
Anjalankoski	105.7		102.7	90.0	89.3		104.9	96.2	
Espoo	106.2					92.5			
Eurajoki	90.4	105.1	104.5	96.5	106.0		101.7	95.7	
Forssa		98.5	103.6	107.5	103.3		90.1		
Haapavesi	104.1	100.1	96.8		105.6	93.4	106.1		
Hanko	107.5	96.2			104.5	95.7	95.3		
Harjavalta					93.9				
Heinola	87.6								
Helsinki		96.2	104.6	94.9	98.1	96.8	90.0	89.0	92.9
Huittinen		93.0							
Hyvinkää				95.7		104.0			103.4
Hämeenlinna	100.2	101.7	106.5	92.3		97.3		105.9	88.1
Iisalmi		89.5	103.1	104.7	89.1		95.6		
Ikaalinen		99.0							
Imatra	105.3					101.5	102.5		
Inari						104.1			
Inkoo							105.5		
Joensuu		92.8	87.9	103.7	102.9	96.4	101.9		
Joutseno	103.8		94.2					96.0	
Juuka		103.3							
Jyväskylä	105.8	107.1	101.6	97.7	104.9	97.3	101.0	94.1	96.2
Jämsä		100.3	94.4			88.8			
Järvenpää								101.8	
Kajaani		102.8	107.0		96.3	93.7	94.8		
Kalajoki					104.6				
Kemi			105.2	98.8					
Kemijärvi	104.7								
Kerimäki	107.7							91.3	
Kitee		102.2							
Kokkola			99.1	106.3			99.1		
Koli	104.3		95.7		94.7			107.4	
Kotka		87.7				101.5			
Kouvola		100.1				93.8	107.7	96.2	
Kristiinankaup.	105.1	93.4							
Kruunupyy	98.8		107.2		105.3	104.9		104.3	
Kuopio	106.7	96.7	93.0	100.9	107.3	101.6	89.1	106.1	94.8
Kurikka		92.3			100.1				
Köyliö						107.9			
Lahti	102.4	103.0	105.0	89.7	104.4	96.6	94.2	106.4	107.4
Lappeenranta		93.5			94.8	96.5	100.2	96.0	
Lapua	106.5	96.9	105.4	100.4					89.4
Lempäälä						102.8			
Lohja		96.5				88.8		107.2	
Loimaa		98.5							
Loviisa						104.6	105.2		
Luumäki								96.0	
Mikkeli	106.9	89.7	100.5	93.0	104.8	106.3	100.9	87.8	
Mäntsälä					103.4				
Mäntyharju				93.0					
Nilsiä					97.5				
Orivesi		103.8	101.2						
Oulu	104.8	89.4	101.4	95.8	96.4	99.1	106.2	106.9	99.6
Outokumpu		101.7							
Parkano		99.0			100.2				
Pieksämäki		102.2	101.3		103.0	96.5			
Pihtipudas	105.1	107.0	98.5		104.5	101.7	102.3		
Pohja		95.1							
Pori	91.6	100.4	104.5	96.5	90.4	98.7		95.7	
Porvoo		99.8	107.9			93.5			90.8
Pyhätunturi	105.8					106.2			
Pyhävuori	107.6								
Raahe		92.5	107.0	89.9	105.8	87.7			
Rauma	105.1	103.6				93.9			
Riihimäki			99.6			94.7			
Rovaniemi	105.5	89.3	102.0	107.0	103.3	101.1			93.4
Ruka	100.8					96.3			

FM (MHz)	1)	2)	3)	4)	5)	6)	7)	8)	9)
Ruovesi	103.8								
Salo		99.1				107.7			
Savonlinna		96.7	104.2		101.4	105.2		91.3	100.0
Seinäjoki		96.9		100.4	103.3	91.2		89.4	
Sievi		107.7							
Siilinjärvi		102.0							
Sonkajärvi		107.1							
Suomussalmi					88.8	104.5			
Sysmä	90.2	106.8	101.3				96.1	89.1	
Taivalkoski	106.5					94.6			
Tammisaari			95.1	100.2	91.4	103.2		107.0	104.3
Tampere	104.7	100.9	89.6	104.2	91.6	90.0	105.6	98.8	92.2
Tervola	107.5				96.2	100.1			
Tornio					92.0		98.3		
Turku	103.9	100.1	98.7	97.6	106.8	104.6	102.4	107.3	106.8
Uusikaupunki		96.2	91.1						
Vaasa			104.4	91.6	102.0	93.9			
Valkeakoski	95.0	94.4							90.3
Vammala	101.2	97.7			88.0				
Varkaus		92.7				91.0	105.5	102.8	
Vihti	105.6								
Vilppula		95.4							
Vuokatti	105.7						88.8		
Ylivieska			88.3						
Ylläs	107.9						91.6		
Ähtäri		97.8	102.2			104.9	98.4	105.5	

Addresses:
1) **R. Nova,** Ilmalank. 2C, PL 123, 00241 Helsinki. W: radionova.fi Powers 1-60kW – 2) **Iskelmä,** Kehräsaari B5. 33200 Tampere. W: iskelma.fi Powers 0.1-3kW – 3) **The Voice,** Tallbergink. 1C 7. krs, 00180 Helsinki W: voice.fi Powers 0.1-60kW – 4) **R. Rock,** PL 350, Tehtaankatu 27-29 A, 00151 Helsinki W: radiorock.fi Powers 0.1-4kW – 5) **R. Suomipop,** Lintulahdenk. 10, 00500 Helsinki **W:** radiosuomipop.fi Powers 0.1-3kW – 6) **R. NRJ (Energy),** Kiviaidankatu 2 i, 00210 Helsinki. **W:** nrj.fi Powers 0.1-30kW – 7) **R. Aalto,** PL 350, Tehtaankatu 27-29 A, 00151 Helsinki. **W:** radioaalto.fi Powers 0.1-10kW – 8) **R. Dei** (Rlg.), Ilmalankuja 2 i, 00240 Helsinki. **W:** radiodei.fi Powers 0.2-5kW – 9) **Rondo Classic** Ilmalankuja 2L, 00240 Helsinki. **W:** rondoclassic.fi Powers 0.2-1kW.
About 50 more stations are in operation.

ÅLAND (autonomous province)

SVERIGES RADIO cf. Sweden

FM (MHz)	P1	P2	P3	P4	kW
Mariehamn	95.0	97.1	88.6	102.3	10

Steel FM, Mariehamn: 95.9MHz 0.2kW. **W:** www.steelfm.net – **Rix FM** (cf. Sweden), Mariehamn: 101.8MHz 3kW – **R. Harmonica,** Mariehamn: 102.8MHz 1kW – **Soft FM,** Mariehamn: 107.2MHz 0.2kW. **W:** www.softfm.net – **Ålands R.,** Mariehamn: 91.3MHz 10kW. **W:** www.radiotv.aland.fi

FRANCE

L.T: UTC +1h (31 Mar-27 Oct: +2h) — **Pop:** 63 million — **Pr.L:** French — **E.C:** 50Hz, 220V — **ITU:** F

CONSEIL SUPÉRIEUR DE L'AUDIOVISUEL (CSA)
✉ 39/43 quai André Citroën, 75739 Paris cedex 15 ☎ +33 1 40583800 🖷 +33 1 45790006 **W:** www.csa.fr
LP: Pres: Michel Boyon
The CSA regulates TV and radio, and issues broadcast licenses.

TDF
✉ 106 avenue Marx Dormoy, 92541 Montrouge cedex ☎ +33 1 55951000 🖷 +33 1 55952000 **W:** www.tdf.fr
LP: DG: Olivier Huart
TDF operates the majority of radio and TV txs.

TOWERCAST
✉ 46/50 avenue Théophile Gautier, 75016 Paris ☎ +33 1 40714071
W: www.towercast.fr **LP:** Pres: Jacques Roques
Towercast operates radio and TV txs

ITAS TIM
✉ 1 rue Royale, 92213 Saint-Cloud Cedex ☎ +33 1 41122700
W: www.itastim.com **LP:** DG: Jean-Claude Duffaud
Itas Tim operates FM and TV txs.

OUTRE-MER 1ère (Pub)
✉ 35/37 rue Danton, 92240 Malakoff ☎ +33 1 55227100 **W:** www.la1ere.fr **LP:** DG: Claude Esclatine

Outre-Mer 1ère is a part of France Télévisions and produces public service prgrs (radio & TV) in the French overseas territories.

RADIO FRANCE (Pub)

✉ 116 Av. du Président Kennedy, 75220 Paris cedex 16 ☎ +33 1 56402222 **W:** www.radiofrance.fr **LP:** Pres. & DG: Jean-Luc Hess

HOME SERVICES:

LW & MW	N	kHz	kW	MW	N	kHz	kW
Allouis	A	162	*2000	Ajaccio	B+L	1404	20
Lyon	I	603	300	Brest	I	1404	20
Rennes	I	711	300	Dijon	I	1404	5
Limoges	I	792	300	Grenoble	I	1404	20
Nancy	I	837	200	Pau	I	‡1404	20
Paris	B+L	s864	300	Bastia	B+L	1494	20
Toulouse	I	945	300	Bayonne	I	1494	4
Bordeaux	I	1206	300	Besançon	I	‡1494	5
Marseille	I	1242	150	Clermont-Fd	I	1494	20
Strasbourg	B+L	1278	300	Nice	I	1557	300
Lille	I	1377	300				

N=Networks: A=France Inter, B=France Bleu, F=FIP, I= France Info, L=rel. local stns at certain times. s=AM stereo C-QUAM. *=run at 1000kW 1700-0500 (Wi. time) 1900-0400 (Su. time). ‡=inactive.

FM: Station	C	D	E	F	kW
Abbeville	93.1	97.4	89.8		2.5
Ajaccio	92.4	97.6	88.0		10
Ajaccio (La Punta)	88.6	103.9		105.6	4
Albi				105.5	1
Alençon	93.0	88.0	91.0		13
Ales	87.6	96.1	98.6	105.1	1
Amiens (St Just)	95.4	102.5	99.4		20
Amiens (Dury)	92.6	97.0	89.3	105.5	2
Angers	93.2	91.4	97.4		10
Angers (La Ballue)				105.5	1
Angoulême	92.4	87.6	95.1	105.5	2
Arcachon	88.3	97.0	91.0	105.5	1.2
Argenton sur Creuse	101.9	89.8	97.2		5
Arles				105.0	1
Arnay le Duc	94.6	90.3	100.3	105.5	3
Aurillac	94.5	98.0	91.9		7
Autun	88.1	97.3	94.1		10
Auxerre	99.5	89.5	92.8		5
Auxerre (Venoy)				105.5	1
Avallon				105.6	1
Avignon	97.4	90.7	93.2		4
Avignon (Sorgues)				105.2	2
Bar le Duc	90.9	88.4	92.7	104.5	10
Bastia	95.9	89.2	93.9	105.5	10
Bayonne	89.0	96.1	92.7	105.5	16
Beaucaire				105.2	1
Beauvais				105.5	1
Bergerac	92.3	94.0	97.1		26
Besançon (Montfaucon)	98.7	89.3	95.0		10
Besançon (Lomont)	90.0	97.7	92.9		18
Beziers				105.1	1
Bonifacio				103.2	1
Bordeaux	89.7	97.7	93.5	105.5	6
Boulogne sur Mer	103.3	99.9	89.4	106.5	1
Bourges	94.9	88.5	91.8		74
Bourges (town)				105.5	1
Brest	95.4	97.8	89.4		200
Brest (town)				105.5	3
Briançon	91.5	97.8	89.5	105.4	1
Brignoles	106.7	104.0	105.5		1.5
Caen	99.6	91.5	95.6		100
Caen (town)				105.5	1
Calais	104.7			105.6	1
Cannes				105.9	1
Carcassone	88.3	96.5	90.9		80
Castres				105.5	2
Chambéry	93.5	90.5	98.6		8
Chambéry (town)				105.1	1
Champagnole	88.5	91.7	98.3		1
Charleville-Mézières	95.8	90.1	93.5	105.9	10
Chartres	94.6	98.1	89.7		32
Chartres (town)				105.7	4
Chateaubriant				105.5	1
Châteauroux				105.5	1
Chaumont	96.5	90.4	93.3		15
Chaumont (town)				105.5	1
Cherbourg-Octeville	94.1	89.2	92.3	105.6	1
Cholet				105.9	1
Clermont-Ferrand	90.4	98.4	95.5	105.5	35
Compiègne				105.3	1
Corse (East)	968	92.3	99.8		17

FM: Station	C	D	E	F	kW
Corte	98.2	91.0	94.8		1.3
Cosne Cours s.Loire				105.3	1
Creil	87.6	93.3	91.9	105.6	1
Dijon	95.9	93.7	99.2		25
Dunkerque				106.5	1
Epinal	98.6	92.4	89.4	106.5	10
Evreux	88.5	98.9	97.3	105.5	1
Fontainebleau				105.5	2
Gap	98.3	88.5	95.3	105.5	5
Gex	94.4	96.7	89.6	101.1	25
Grenoble (Chamrousse)	99.4	88.2	91.8		1
Grenoble (T. s. Venin)	89.9	92.8	107.3	105.1	1
Guéret	100.7	98.8	90.8	105.5	12
Hirson	94.4	99.7	97.2		5
Hyères	91.6	97.5	94.5	107.1	1.5
L'île Rousse				105.2	1
Laon				105.3	1
Laval	95.1	88.3	92.1	105.5	5
La Rochelle				105.5	1
Le Havre	88.9	93.3	98.5	105.5	1
Le Mans	92.6	89.0	97.0	105.5	128
Le Puy	99.3	89.3	92.8		10
Lesparre	92.4	90.3	95.1		1.6
Lille (Bouvigny)	103.7	98.0	88.7	105.2	125
Limoges	93.0	89.5	97.5		150
Limoges (town)				105.5	2
Longwy	98.1	88.3	91.0	104.3	5
Lourdes				105.3	3.5
Lyon (Mont Pilat)	99.8	88.8	92.4	103.4	150
Lyon (Town)	101.1	94.1	98.0	105.4	1
Mantes la Jolie	95.0	92.4	97.1		5
Marseille	91.3	99.0	94.2		400
Marseille				105.3	13
Marseille (town)	91.7	98.6	94.7		1
Maubeuge				106.2	2
Melun				105.7	1
Mende	90.1	96.9	93.7		10
Menton	97.0	89.6	91.7	105.5	5
Metz	99.8	94.5	89.7	106.8	145
Millau	94.9	99.2	88.9		6
Mont de Marsan				105.5	6
Montargis	102.9	98.8	94.1	105.5	1
Montauban				105.7	1
Montereau				105.7	1
Montlieu la Garde	88.3	104.8	98.8		3.5
Montluçon				105.5	1
Montpellier	89.4	97.8	92.9		18
Montpellier (Town)	89.1		96.4	105.1	1
Morosaglia	97.1	88.8	93.4		1
Mulhouse	95.7	88.6	91.6	105.5	100
Nancy	96.9	88.7	91.7	105.9	5
Nantes	90.6	94.2	98.9	105.5	125
Neufchateau	96.3	100.3	91.5		1
Neufchatel-en-Bray	92.7	96.0	90.2		5
Nevers				105.5	1
Nice	100.2	101.9	92.2	105.7	100
Nimes	88.7			105.1	1/5
Niort	99.4	96.4	91.1		190
Niort (town)				105.5	1
Orléans	99.2	95.8	90.7		4
Orléans (town)				105.5	1
Paris	87.7	93.5	91.7	105.5	10
Parthenay	93.8	87.9	98.5	105.5	12
Pau				105.5	1
Perpignan	92.1	99.8	97.2	105.1	10
Poitiers	97.7	92.3	95.5	105.5	1
Porto Vecchio (Col de Mela)	96.8	90.8	98.9		1.5
Porto Vecchio (Punto di a Varra)	92.6	87.9	94.6		1
Privas	89.8	96.5	94.7	105.2	1
Redon				95.8	1
Reims	96.8	98.8	89.2	105.5	135
Rennes	93.5	98.3	89.9		100
Rennes (town)				105.5	1
Roanne				105.5	1
Rouen	96.5	94.0	92.0		100
Rouen (town)				105.7	2.7
Ruffec				105.2	1
Saint Brieuc				105.5	1
Saint Etienne	99.5	89.1	92.7	105.6	2
Saint-Nazaire	95.2	92.2	102.6	105.5	1.5
Saint-Quentin				105.6	1
Saint-Raphaël	96.3	88.7	99.6		40
Saint-Raphaël (town)				106.0	1
Sainte Foy la Grande				105.5	1
Sarrebourg	93.1	99.4	90.3		10

FM: Station	C	D	E	F	kW
Sens	96.3	98.5	93.8		10
Sens (town)				105.7	1.3
Soissons				105.7	1
Strasbourg	97.3	87.7	95.0	104.4	48
Toulon	92.0	97.1	94.9	105.8	5
Toulouse (town)	88.1	96.3	91.1	105.5	2
Toulouse (Pic du Midi)	87.9	95.7	91.5		72
Tours	99.9	97.8	92.2		8
Tours (town)				105.5	1
Troyes	95.3	97.9	91.4		50
Troyes (town)				105.5	1
Ussel	96.0	88.2	99.7		10
Valence				105.4	3
Vannes	88.6	96.0	91.8	105.5	20
Verdun	92.1	99.3	97.4	106.3	6
Villebon sur Yvette	95.4	98.0	97.1		1
Villers-Cotterets	91.1	89.6	92.9		13
Vittel	98.2	89.0	94.0		8
Voiron	91.5	89.2	107.2	105.4	1

+ 1481 stns under 1kW

C=France Inter (stereo), D=France-Culture (stereo), E=France-Musique (stereo), F=France Info (mono). RDS on all txs.

France Inter Network A on **LW**, C on **FM**; Allouis 162kHz; **D.Prgrs**:24h exc. Tues 0005-0358. FM txs: 24h. **N:** Hourly, plus 0430, 0530, 0630 – **France Culture** (Network D) (stereo) **D.Prgrs**:24h. **N: 0500, 0530,** 0600, 0700, 0800, 1130, 1700, 2100 – **France Musique** (Network E) (stereo): **D.Prgrs**:24h **N:** 0600, 0700, 0800, 1130, 1800 – **France Info** (Network F) News and informations **D.Prgrs**:24h

Le Mouv'

Station	MHz	kW	Station	MHz	kW
Ajaccio	92.0	4	Lyon	87.8	4
Amiens	91.0	1	Marseille	96.8	2.5
Angers	96.0	1	Marseille (town)	96.4	1
Annecy	99.4	1	Mende	107.2	0.2
Besançon	93.5	1	Montpellier	102.7	3
Bordeaux	87.7	1	Nantes	96.1	3
Brest	94.0	3	Nice	101.0	1
Caen	87.8	1	Paris	92.1	8
Cannes	101.0	0.1	Reims	101.1	0.5
Carcassonne	90.0	1	Rennes	107.3	2
Clermont-Fd	97.5	2	Rouen	95.8	1
Dijon	88.9	1	St Etienne	97.1	2
Grenoble	95.5	1	Toulouse	95.2	5
Lille	91.0	2	Tours	94.1	2
Lorient	103.3	0.5	Valence	100.7	0.5
Limoges	107.6	2			

D.Prgrs: 24h RDS on all txs. (stereo)

Local Stations "FIP"

FIP Bordeaux, 95 rue Judaïque, 33000 Bordeaux ☎ +33 5 56241313 - Bordeaux 96.7MHz 2.5kW, Arcachon 96.5 0.5 kW
FIP Nantes, 2 bis quai François Mitterrand, 44200 Nantes ☎ +33 2 40731414 - Nantes 95.7MHz 2.5kW, St Nazaire 97.2MHz 1.5kW
FIP Paris, 116 avenue du Président Kennedy, 75220 Paris Cedex 16 ☎ +33 1 42201234 - 105.1MHz 10kW
FIP Strasbourg, 4 rue Joseph Massol, 67000 Strasbourg ☎ +33 3 88352400 - 92.3MHz 4kW
Sts without local news: Marseille 90.9MHz 4kW, Montpellier 99.7MHz 1kW, Rennes 101.2MHz 1kW, Toulouse 103.5MHz 2kW RDS on all txs **D.Prgrs:** 24h. Prgrs consist of music and news.

France Bleu

🖃 116 av. du Président Kennedy, 75220 Paris Cedex 16
☎ +33 1 56401111 **D.Prgrs:** 24h uninterrupted music 0030-0400
Stations: MW: Network B + **FM**
France Bleu Local Stations (F.B = France Bleu) - At certain times, local stns relay national France Bleu prgrs.
F.B 107.1, 116 av du Président Kennedy, 75220 Paris Cedex 16 ☎ +33 1 56402222: **FM:** Paris 107.1MHz 10kW, Chartres 97.3MHz 4kW, **MW:** Paris 864kHz 300kW (C-QUAM stereo)
F.B Alsace, 4 rue Joseph Massol, 67000 Strasbourg ☎ +33 3 88762000 **FM:** Strasbourg 101.4MHz 48kW, Mulhouse 102.6MHz 100kW, **MW:** 1278kHz 300kW
F.B Armorique, 14 av Jean Janvier, 35031 Rennes Cedex ☎ +33 2 99674321 **FM:** Vannes 101.3MHz 20kW, Rennes 103.1MHz 100kW
F.B Auxerre, 12 place Saint Amâtre, B.P 101, 89002 Auxerre Cedex ☎ +33 3 86723456 **FM:** Sens 100.5MHz 10kW, Auxerre 101.3MHz 5kW, Nevers 104.0MHz 1kW
F.B Azur, 2 place Grimaldi, 06012 Nice Cedex 1 ☎ +33 4 97033636

FM: Nice 103.8MHz 100kW, Menton 94.8MHz 5kW, Saint Raphaël 100.7MHz 10kW
F.B Basse Normandie, 75 rue Basse, 14053 Caen Cedex ☎ +33 2 31471414 **FM:** Le Havre 102.2MHz 2.5kW, Caen 102.6MHz 100kW
F.B Béarn, 2 rue O'Quin, BP 211, 64002 Pau Cedex ☎ +33 5 59983030 **FM:** Oloron Sainte Marie 93.2MHz 1.5kW, Pau 102.5MHz 10kW
F.B Belfort Montbéliard, 10 rue des Capucins, 90008 Belfort Cedex ☎ +33 3 84579090 **FM:** Belfort 106.8MHz 2kW
F.B Berry, 10/12 rue de la République, 36000 Châteauroux ☎ +33 2 54606060 **FM:** Argenton 93.5MHz 5kW, Bourges 103.2MHz 19kW
F.B Besançon, 2 Place Granvelle, BP 591, 25027 Besançon Cedex ☎ +33 3 81212525 **FM:** Besançon 101.4MHz 18kW + 102.8MHz 10kW
F.B Bourgogne, 29 rue Guillaume Tell, BP 11888, 21018 Dijon Cedex ☎ +33 3 80592121 **FM:** Troyes 87.8 60kW, Arnay le Duc 103.4MHz 3kW, Dijon 103.7MHz 25kW
F.B Breizh Izel, 12 esplanade François Mitterrand, 29000 Quimper ☎ +33 2 98552929 **FM:** Brest 93.0MHz 200kW
F.B Champagne, 28 bd du Maréchal Joffre, BP 1094, 51054 Reims Cedex ☎ +33 3 26845151 **FM:** Charleville-Mézières 100.9MHz 10kW, Reims 95.1MHz 2kW, Châlons en Champagne 94.8MHz 1kW, Troyes 100.8MHz 1kW
F.B Cotentin, Hôtel Atlantique, rue Piedagnel, 50100 Cherbourg-Octeville ☎ +33 2 33885050 **FM:** Cherbourg-Octeville 100.7MHz 4kW
F.B Creuse, 7 rue de la République, 23000 Guéret ☎ +33 5 55612323 **FM:** Guéret 94.3MHz 12kW
F.B Drôme Ardèche, 7 rue Poncet, BP 519, 26005 Valence Cedex ☎ +33 4 75813333 **FM:** Valence 87.9MHz 10kW, Privas 98.4MHz 1.5kW, Vals les Bains 103.8MHz 1kW
F.B Frequenza Mora, 4 rue Favalelli, BP 130, 20289 Bastia Cedex ☎ +33 4 95329532 **FM:** Corse (east) 88.2MHz 17kW, Ajaccio 100.5MHz 10kW, + 97.0MHz 4kW + 1404kHz 20kW, Corte 100.0MHz 1.33kW, Bastia 101.7MHz 10kW + 1494kHz 20kW, Porto Vecchio 101.8MHz 1.5kW + 105.4MHz 1kW, Morosaglia 104.6MHz 1kW
F.B Gard Lozère, 10 bd des Arènes, 30020 Nîmes Cedex 1 ☎ +33 4 66363030 **FM:** Nîmes 90.2MHz 5kW, Alès 91.6MHz 2kW, Mende 104.9MHz 10kW
F.B Gascogne, 13 place Jean Jaurès, BP 289, 40005 Mont de Marsan Cedex ☎ +33 5 58854040 **FM:** Mont de Marsan 98.8MHz 20kW, Bayonne 100.5MHz 38kW, Mimizan 103.4MHz 20kW
F.B Gironde, 95 rue Judaïque, BP 585, 33006 Bordeaux Cedex ☎ +33 5 57812020 **FM:** Bordeaux 100.1MHz 6kW, Lesparre 101.6MHz 1.6kW
F.B Haute Normandie, Hangar A, quai Boisguilbert, 76000 Rouen ☎ +33 2 35073107 **FM:** Le Havre 95.1MHz 1kW, Rouen 100.1MHz 100kW, Neufchâtel en Bray 101.6MHz 5kW, Evreux 89.5MHz 1kW
F.B Hérault, 474 allée Henri II de Montmorency, 34034 Montpellier ☎ +33 4 67066565 **FM:** Montpellier 101.1MHz 18kW + 100.6MHz 1kW
F.B Isère, 27 av Félix Viallet, BP 154, 38003 Grenoble Cedex ☎ +33 4 76503838 **FM:** Chambéry 99.1MHz 5kW, Lyon 101.8MHz 25kW, Grenoble 102.8MHz 1kW + 98.2MHz 1.2kW
F.B La Rochelle, 5 av Michel Crépeau, 17025 La Rochelle Cedex 01 ☎ +33 5 46351717 **FM:** Royan 103.6MHz 1kW, Saintes 103.9MHz 60kW, Angoulême 101.5MHz 2kW, La Rochelle 98,2MHz 1kW
F.B Limousin, 23 bd Gambetta, BP 3603, 87036 Limoges Cedex 1 ☎ +33 5 55113811 **FM:** Chateauponsac 92.5MHz 1kW, Ussel 101.4MHz 10kW, Limoges 103.5MHz 150kW
F.B Loire Océan, 2 bis quai François Mitterrand, 44200 Nantes ☎ +33 2 40444546 **FM:** Saint Nazaire 88.1MHz 1.5kW, Nantes 101.8MHz 200kW, Angers 88.5MHz 1 kW
F.B Lorraine Nord, 5, rue d'Austrasie, B.P 50071, 57003 Metz cedex 03 ☎ +33 3 87682222 **FM:** Metz 98.5MHz 1kW, Sarreguemines 104 MHz 1kW
F.B. Maine, 17 rue Pierre Mendès France, 72000 Le Mans ☎ +33 2 43297272 **FM:** La Flèche 91.7MHz 1kW, Le Mans 96MHz 2.5 kW, Sablé sur Sarthe 105.7MHz 1kW
F.B Mayenne, 41 av Robert Buron, 53000 Laval ☎ +33 2 43495050 **FM:** Laval 96.0MHz 5kW
F.B Nord, 14 rue Léon Trulin, 59002 Lille Cedex 01 ☎ +33 3 20135962 **FM:** Lille (town) 87.8MHz 1kW, Lille (Bouvigny) 94.7MHz 125kW, Boulogne sur Mer 95.5MHz 2kW, Etaples 97.8MHz 2kW, Calais 106.2MHz 1kW
F.B Orléans, 8 rue d'Illiers, 45057 Orléans Cedex 1 ☎ +33 2 38714545 **FM:** Blois 93.9MHz 1kW, Orléans 100.9MHz 4kW, Montargis 106.8MHz 1kW
F.B Pays Basque, 46 allées Marines, 64116 Bayonne Cedex ☎ +33 5 59466464 **FM:** Bayonne 101.3MHz 15kW
F.B Pays d'Auvergne, 80 bd François Mitterrand, BP 277, 63008 Clermont-Ferrand Cedex 01 ☎ +33 4 73346363 **FM:** Clermont-Ferrand 102.5MHz 37kW, Aurillac 100.2MHz 1kW, Montluçon 96.7MHz 1kW
F.B Pays de Savoie, 256 rue de la République, 73000 Chambéry ☎ +33 4 79707374 **FM:** Annecy 95.2MHz 1kW, Chambéry 103.9MHz 8kW, Gex 106.1MHz 20kW

F.B Périgord, 1 cours Saint Georges, BP 3033, 24003 Périgueux Cedex ☎ +33 5 53062000 Limoges **FM:** 91.7MHz 100kW, Bergerac 99.0MHz 26kW

F.B Picardie, Rue du Maréchal de Lattre de Tassigny, 80000 Amiens ☎ +33 3 22711515 **FM:** Amiens 100.2MHz 2kW, Abbeville 100.6MHz 5kW, Hirson 101.3MHz 5kW, Sailly Saillisel 102.8MHz 15kW

F.B Poitou, 27, bd de Solférino, 86000 Poitiers ☎ +33 5 49605000 **FM:** Parthenay 106.4MHz 12kW, Niort 101.0MHz 1kW

F.B Provence, 560 av Mozart, 13617 Aix en Provence.Cedex 01 ☎ +33 4 42991313 **FM:** Brignoles 102.1MHz 1.5kW, Hyères 102.5MHz 1.5kW, Toulon 102.9MHz 5kW, Marseille 103.6MHz 200kW

F.B Roussillon, 24 av du Général Leclerc, 66000 Perpignan ☎ +33 4 68519000 **FM:** Perpignan 101.6MHz 10kW

F.B Sud Lorraine, 21/23 bd du Recteur Senn, 54042 Nancy Cedex ☎ +33 3 83195488 **FM:** Epinal 100.0MHz 1kW, Nancy 100.5MHz 5kW, Vittel 102.6MHz 1kW, Neufchateau 103.0MHz 1kW

F.B. Toulouse, 78 allée Jean Jaurès, BP 50901, 31009 Toulouse ☎ +33 5 34417000 **FM:** Toulouse 90.5MHz 2kW

F.B Touraine, place Gaston Pailhou, BP 3231, 37032 Tours Cedex 1 ☎ +33 2 47363737 **FM:** Tours 105.0MHz 8kW +98.7MHz 1kW

F.B Vaucluse, 25 rue de la République, BP 320, 84021 Avignon Cedex ☎ +33 4 90141312 **FM:** Avignon 100.4MHz 2kW

+ 327 txs less than 1kW not mentioned. Stereo and RDS on all txs.

Special Programmes (MW)
Lyon 603kHz (Rlg) Sun 1700-1800. ✉ Foyer Notre Dame des Ondes, 24 rue Paul Sisley, 69003 Lyon – **Strasbourg** 1278kHz (Rlg) Sun 0800-1100. First Sun 1207-1300 prgr in cooperation with SWR (Freiburg), Studio Karlsruhe and Radio DRS (Basel). Prgr in Alsatian language 0600-1100 + 1340-1530 ✉ See under F.B. Alsace

RADIO FRANCE INTERNATIONALE (Pub)
✉ 116 av. du Président Kennedy, 75016 Paris ☎ +33 1 56401212 **W:** www.rfi.fr **LP:** ?
RFI1 (French service): Paris **FM** 89MHz 10kW (stereo).

EXTERNAL SERVICE see International Broadcasting section.

PRIVATE MW STATIONS
Radio Orient ✉ see entry under FM – **Nice** 1350kHz 10 kW, **Nîmes** 1602kHz 1 kW

PRIVATE FM STATIONS:

FM	Station	MHz	kW	FM	Station	MHz	kW
25)	Auxerre	87.6	1	17)	Angers	88.1	1
23)	Bayonne	87.6	3	3)	Avignon	88.1	1
20)	Bernay	87.6	1	6)	Brive la Gaillarde	88.1	1
17)	Besançon	87.6	1	18)	Châtellerault	88.1	1
23)	Castres	87.6	1	23)	Dole	88.1	1
26)	Laval	87.6	1	6)	Nice	88.1	5
20)	Le Havre	87.6	1	17)	Rouen	88.1	1
26)	Le Mans	87.6	1	9)	Soissons	88.1	1
22)	Niort	87.6	1	3)	Fontenay le Comte	88.2	1
7)	Orléans	87.6	2	4)	Laval	88.2	1
17)	Romilly sur Seine	87.6	1	17)	Le Havre	88.2	1
22)	Vannes	87.6	1	10)	Metz	88.2	1
8)	Yssingeaux	87.6	1	6)	Nancy	88.2	1
23)	Bourges	87.7	1	6)	Saint Quentin	88.2	1
13)	Clermont Fd	87.7	1	9)	Strasbourg	88.2	4
7)	Corte	87.7	1	22)	Tours	88.2	2
5)	Figeac	87.7	1	13)	Bonifacio	88.3	1
19)	Nice	87.7	2	13)	Brioude	88.3	1
21)	Saint Omer	87.7	1	17)	Dijon	88.3	1
9)	Tours	87.7	2	9)	L'Ile Rousse	88.3	1
19)	La Flèche	87.8	1	6)	Lorient	88.3	1
7)	Le Blanc	87.8	1	9)	Moulins	88.3	1
19)	Mayenne	87.8	1	17)	Roanne	88.3	1
23)	Mazamet	87.8	1	17)	Saint Flour	88.3	1
7)	Montluçon	87.8	1	14)	Amiens	88.4	1
7)	Verdun	87.8	1	5)	Laon	88.4	1
6)	Dijon	87.8	1	9)	Luxeuil les Bains	88.4	1
21)	Menton	87.9	1	17)	Lyon	88.4	4
6)	Montreuil	87.9	1	6)	Mont de Marsan	88.4	1
17)	Reims	87.9	2	19)	Nantes	88.4	2
5)	Saint Raphaël	87.9	1	21)	Sarrebourg	88.4	1
2)	Toulon	87.9	1	21)	Sarreguemines	88.4	1
9)	Yvetot	87.9	1	3)	Thouars	88.4	1
17)	Aubusson	88.0	1	5)	Tonnerre	88.4	1
10)	Calais	88.0	1	8)	Bordeaux	88.5	4
17)	Châteauroux	88.0	1	10)	Compiègne	88.5	1
23)	Colmar	88.0	1	6)	Nogent le Rotrou	88.5	1
17)	St Gilles Croix de Vie	88.0	1	20)	Quimper	88.5	1
17)	Vesoul	88.0	1	17)	Annecy	88.6	1
3)	Villefranche sur Saône	88.0	1	17)	Châlons en Champ.	88.6	1
9)	Vitry le François	88.0	1	6)	Châteaubriant	88.6	1

FM	Station	MHz	kW	FM	Station	MHz	kW
8)	Chaumont	88.6	1	21)	Roanne	89.8	1
19)	Confolens	88.6	1	6)	Sablé sur Sarthe	89.8	1
16)	Paris	88.6	4	18)	Toulon	89.8	4
23)	Porto Vecchio	88.6	1	18)	Alès	89.9	1
18)	Vichy	88.6	1	17)	Cognac	89.9	1
10)	Alençon	88.7	1	18)	Douai	89.9	1
7)	Avallon	88.7	1	20)	Epinal	89.9	1
25)	Bastia	88.7	1	19)	Montpellier	89.9	3
8)	Caen	88.7	2	20)	Nancy	89.9	1
19)	Chartres	88.7	1	28)	Paris	89.9	10
18)	Châteauroux	88.7	1	3)	Périgueux	89.9	1
18)	Etampes	88.7	1	18)	Saint Dizier	89.9	1
25)	Ghisonaccia	88.7	4	20)	Saint Girons	89.9	1
3)	Gray	88.7	1	18)	Saint Raphaël	89.9	1
18)	Saint Flour	88.7	1	20)	Bagnères de Bigorre	90.0	1
13)	Saintes	88.7	1	17)	Bayeux	90.0	1
22)	Toulouse	88.7	5	22)	Brest	90.0	3
6)	Bonnières sur Seine	88.8	2	13)	Cosne Cours s. Loire	90.0	1
12)	Clermont Ferrand	88.8	1	23)	Marseille	90.0	10
8)	Nantes	88.8	3	21)	Quimperlé	90.0	1
8)	Reims	88.8	2	9)	Royan	90.0	1
17)	Saint Dizier	88.8	1	3)	Vichy	90.0	1
4)	Bagnères de Bigorre	88.9	1	6)	Béthune	90.1	1
17)	Bordeaux	88.9	1	22)	Evreux	90.1	1
13)	Montluçon	88.9	1	18)	Nantes	90.1	3
23)	Rennes	88.9	1	9)	Neufchâteau	90.1	1
6)	Aurillac	89.0	1	19)	Perpignan	90.1	3
6)	Avignon	89.0	1	5)	Poligny	90.1	1
6)	Avranches	89.0	1	9)	Toul	90.1	1
17)	Brest	89.0	3	3)	Angoulême	90.2	1
17)	Clamecy	89.0	1	23)	Bar le Duc	90.2	1
13)	Moulins	89.0	1	3)	Bergerac	90.2	1
23)	Bernay	89.1	1	9)	La Ferté s. Jouarre	90.2	1
1)	Bourges	89.1	1	13)	Melun	90.2	1
5)	Gien	89.1	1	18)	Mimizan	90.2	1
18)	Perpignan	89.1	3	28)	Nevers	90.2	1
8)	Saint Nazaire	89.1	1	2)	Pau	90.2	1
22)	Saint Quentin	89.1	1	20)	Porto Vecchio	90.2	1
22)	Valenciennes	89.1	1	9)	Thionville	90.2	1
19)	Brive la Gaillarde	89.2	1	17)	Vannes	90.2	2
23)	Châteaubriant	89.2	1	5)	Bastia	90.3	4
9)	Châtellerault	89.2	1	13)	Compiègne	90.3	1
6)	Decazeville	89.2	1	18)	Decazeville	90.3	1
22)	Lille	89.2	2	17)	Montargis	90.3	1
18)	Marseille	89.2	10	4)	Montmorillon	90.3	1
13)	Montbard	89.2	1	24)	Pamiers	90.3	1
17)	Nevers	89.2	1	3)	Saumur	90.3	1
23)	Ussel	89.2	1	19)	Valence	90.3	2
17)	Vichy	89.2	1	17)	Abbeville	90.4	1
17)	Castres	89.3	1	18)	Auch	90.4	1
17)	Cholet	89.3	1	6)	Bourg en Bresse	90.4	1
13)	Longwy	89.3	1	10)	Caen	90.4	2
4)	Niort	89.3	1	5)	Calvi	90.4	1
9)	Nogaro	89.3	1	13)	Châteaudun	90.4	1
23)	Rouen	89.3	2	9)	Dinan	90.4	1
25)	Arras	89.4	1	21)	Longwy	90.4	1
17)	Aurillac	89.4	1	28)	Paris	90.4	10
18)	Bayeux	89.4	1	23)	Sablé sur Sarthe	90.4	1
18)	Bayonne	89.4	2	3)	Alès	90.5	1
6)	Chambéry	89.4	1	6)	Bourges	90.5	1
23)	Marmande	89.4	1	26)	Brest	90.5	1
6)	Roanne	89.4	1	13)	Chartres	90.5	1
8)	Saint Dizier	89.4	1	23)	Le Mans	90.5	2
15)	Toulon	89.4	2	24)	Limoges	90.5	1
5)	Saintes	89.4	1	9)	Mont de Marsan	90.5	1
23)	Chaumont	89.5	1	6)	Narbonne	90.5	1
6)	Strasbourg	89.5	4	19)	Rodez	90.5	1
18)	Ajaccio	89.6	8	23)	Tours	90.5	2
14)	Angers	89.6	1	4)	Lourdes	90.6	3
6)	Auch	89.6	1	9)	Maubeuge	90.6	1
6)	Clermont Fd.	89.6	2	20)	Melun	90.6	1
10)	La Rochelle	89.6	1	8)	Millau	90.6	1
17)	Le Havre	89.6	1	26)	Creil	90.7	2
4)	Marseille	89.6	4	7)	Dijon	90.7	1
21)	Mende	89.6	1	18)	Figeac	90.7	1
6)	Vierzon	89.6	1	4)	Laon	90.7	1
5)	Aubusson	89.7	1	3)	Laval	90.7	1
23)	Bastia	89.7	1	21)	Périgueux	90.7	1
13)	Nevers	89.7	1	6)	Soustons	90.7	1
10)	Nîmes	89.7	1	13)	Troyes	90.7	1
23)	Perpignan	89.7	3	6)	Avallon	90.8	1
18)	Saint Nazaire	89.7	1	1)	Bastia	90.8	1
2)	Tours	89.7	2	3)	Château Thierry	90.8	1
13)	Troyes	89.7	1	5)	La Flèche	90.8	1
6)	Agen	89.8	1	3)	Vannes	90.8	1
6)	Brioude	89.8	1	23)	Vesoul	90.8	1
23)	Corte	89.8	1	17)	Annonay	90.9	1
23)	Gray	89.8	1	19)	Brest	90.9	3
18)	Quimper	89.8	1	9)	Brive la Gaillarde	90.9	1

FM	Station	MHz	kW	FM	Station	MHz	kW	FM	Station	MHz	kW	FM	Station	MHz	kW
13)	Montreuil	90.9	1	13)	Pamiers	92.0	1	13)	La Tour du Pin	93.1	1	25)	Chartres	94.1	1
14)	Poitiers	90.9	1	8)	Saint Affrique	92.0	1	20)	Mulhouse	93.1	1	19)	Decazeville	94.1	1
17)	Segré	90.9	1	7)	Saint Brieuc	92.0	1	23)	Royan	93.1	1	12)	Dijon	94.1	1
7)	Villefrnch s. Saône	90.9	1	10)	Saintes	92.0	1	13)	Saint Etienne	93.1	2	18)	Grenoble	94.1	1
5)	Ajaccio	91.0	8	19)	Soissons	92.0	1	7)	Toulon	93.1	4	6)	Mayenne	94.1	1
19)	Besançon	91.0	1	3)	Brive la Gaillarde	92.1	1	19)	Avallon	93.2	1	24)	Mont de Marsan	94.1	1
17)	Bourges	91.0	1	21)	Cambrai	92.1	1	6)	Bergerac	93.2	1	13)	Montmorillon	94.1	1
10)	Chambéry	91.0	1	6)	Menton	92.1	1	9)	Commercy	93.2	1	5)	Narbonne	94.1	1
9)	Colmar	91.0	1	18)	Nontron	92.1	1	5)	Evreux	93.2	1	4)	Saint Gaudens	94.1	1
13)	Fleurance	91.0	1	19)	Troyes	92.1	1	8)	Guéret	93.2	1	13)	Soissons	94.1	1
24)	Le Puy en Velay	91.0	1	13)	Amiens	92.2	1	23)	Nevers	93.2	1	13)	Châlons en Champ.	94.2	1
15)	Limoges	91.0	2	22)	Béthune	92.2	1	21)	Provins	93.2	1	3)	Chaumont	94.2	1
4)	Sarrebourg	91.0	1	10)	Bordeaux	92.2	1	21)	Romilly sur Seine	93.2	1	13)	Reims	94.2	1
7)	Sens	91.0	1	7)	Colmar	92.2	1	22)	Saint Tropez	93.2	1	5)	Saint Omer	94.2	1
10)	Vichy	91.0	1	7)	Dunkerque	92.2	1	5)	Ussel	93.2	1	23)	Tarbes	94.2	1
25)	Boulogne sur Mer	91.1	1	4)	Lannemezan	92.2	1	13)	Arras	93.3	1	6)	Bordeaux	94.3	5
23)	Dunkerque	91.1	1	9)	Laon	92.2	1	5)	Dreux	93.3	1	18)	La Côte St. André	94.3	1
8)	Metz	91.1	1	7)	Limoges	92.2	2.2	13)	Grenoble	93.3	1	18)	Le Mans	94.3	2
19)	Montélimar	91.1	1	22)	Metz	92.2	1	7)	Lyon	93.3	1	23)	Lille	94.3	1
8)	Nancy	91.1	1	22)	Mont de Marsan	92.2	1	6)	Marmande	93.3	1	12)	Lorient	94.3	1
19)	Orange	91.1	1	5)	Montélimar	92.2	1	23)	Meaux	93.3	3	15)	Paris	94.3	4
23)	Pau	91.1	1	7)	Mulhouse	92.2	1	4)	Montauban	93.3	1	23)	Saint Dizier	94.3	1
3)	Villeneuve sur Lot	91.1	1	18)	Carcassonne	92.3	1	8)	Montluçon	93.3	1	1)	Saint Etienne	94.3	2
7)	Aubusson	91.2	1	7)	Mimizan	92.3	1	18)	Orléans	93.3	2	10)	Saint Raphaël	94.3	1
8)	Épinal	91.2	1	18)	Rennes	92.3	1	5)	Pamiers	93.3	1	21)	Sens	94.3	1
9)	Grenoble	91.2	1	13)	Vitry le François	92.3	1	3)	Poitiers	93.3	1	8)	Clermont Ferrand	94.4	1
6)	Laval	91.2	1	23)	Albi	92.4	1	17)	Argentan	93.4	1	5)	Le Puy en Velay	94.4	1
22)	Mulhouse	91.2	1	20)	Brest	92.4	1	25)	Bourges	93.4	1	22)	Loches	94.4	1
17)	Orléans	91.2	2	14)	Montpellier	92.4	3	21)	Epernay	93.4	1	19)	Orléans	94.4	1
6)	Saint Tropez	91.2	1	22)	Romilly sur Seine	92.4	1	6)	Le Chambon s Lignon	93.4	1	4)	Parthenay	94.4	1
19)	Agen	91.3	1	5)	Saint Quentin	92.4	1	13)	Lille	93.4	1	18)	Pau	94.4	1
19)	Cahors	91.3	1	6)	Vannes	92.4	1	8)	Marseille	93.4	4	6)	St Gilles Croix de Vie	94.4	1
9)	Cambrai	91.3	1	23)	Avignon	92.5	1	7)	Moulins	93.4	1	9)	Saintes	94.4	1
9)	Dinan	91.3	1	4)	Brive la Gaillarde	92.5	1	10)	Narbonne	93.4	1	19)	Toulouse	94.4	1
3)	Paris	91.3	10	4)	Cahors	92.5	1	23)	Quimper	93.4	1	8)	Creil	94.5	2
27)	Reims	91.3	1	17)	Fontenay le Comte	92.5	1	6)	Vic Fezensac	93.4	1	5)	Gournay en Bray	94.5	1
9)	Valonco	91.3	1	17)	Issoudun	92.5	1	22)	Ajaccio	93.5	8	7)	La Rochelle	94.5	1
19)	Amiens	91.4	1	9)	Le Havre	92.5	1	13)	Béthune	93.5	1	9)	Laval	94.5	1
13)	Bastia	91.4	4	5)	Lille	92.5	1	18)	Dax	93.5	1	9)	Montmorillon	94.5	1
10)	Béziers	91.4	1	7)	Lourdes	92.5	3	14)	Metz	93.5	1	9)	Nevers	94.5	1
17)	Brive la Gaillarde	91.4	1	19)	Rodez	92.5	1	20)	Neufchâteau	93.5	1	7)	Rennes	94.5	2
18)	Jonzac	91.4	1	1)	Aix en Provence	92.6	1	13)	Amiens	93.6	1	17)	Arcachon	94.6	1
21)	Morlaix	91.4	1	3)	Calvi	92.6	1	10)	Angers	93.6	1	13)	Chambéry	94.6	1
3)	Beaune	91.5	1	3)	Charolles	92.6	1	6)	Brest	93.6	1	5)	Colmar	94.6	1
3)	Blois	91.5	1	10)	Clermont Fd.	92.6	1	4)	Calvi	93.6	1	18)	Lannemezan	94.6	1
6)	Boulogne sur Mer	91.5	1	3)	Corte	92.6	1	18)	Evreux	93.6	1	22)	Perpignan	94.6	3
22)	Le Puy en Velay	91.5	1	3)	Nîmes	92.6	1	19)	La Roche sur Yon	93.6	1	13)	Pouzauges	94.6	1
26)	Roanne	91.5	1	17)	Quimper	92.6	1	19)	Laon	93.6	1	12)	Reims	94.6	1
7)	Clermont Fd.	91.6	1	7)	Saint Raphaël	92.6	1	17)	Mazamet	93.6	1	23)	Romilly sur Seine	94.6	1
9)	Corte	91.6	1	3)	Bastia	92.7	4	6)	Montbard	93.6	1	7)	Saint Lô	94.6	1
5)	Dunkerque	91.6	1	23)	Boulogne sur Mer	92.7	1	6)	Pau	93.6	1	5)	Béziers	94.7	1
6)	Épernay	91.6	1	1)	Dreux	92.7	1	22)	Saint Gaudens	93.6	1	18)	Fougères	94.7	1
17)	La Châtre	91.6	1	6)	Lorient	92.7	1	23)	Grenoble	93.7	1	18)	La Ferté Macé	94.7	1
6)	Lens	91.6	1	13)	Montélimar	92.7	1	10)	Le Havre	93.7	1	13)	Le Havre	94.7	1
5)	Perpignan	91.6	3	22)	Rennes	92.7	1	8)	Lyon	93.7	1	2)	Limoges	94.7	2
13)	Royan	91.6	1	9)	Béthune	92.8	1	17)	Nancy	93.7	1	7)	Mende	94.7	1
7)	Tours	91.6	2	10)	Blois	92.8	1	10)	Orléans	93.7	2	5)	Nantes	94.7	3
10)	Agen	91.7	1	22)	Castres	92.8	1	20)	Saint Nazaire	93.7	1	4)	Poitiers	94.7	1
8)	Bourgoin Jallieu	91.7	1	8)	Châteauroux	92.8	1	6)	Saintes	93.7	1	8)	Quimper	94.7	1
23)	Cholet	91.7	1	25)	Marseille	92.8	4	13)	Toulon	93.7	4	17)	Saint Etienne	94.7	2
17)	Mrtgne au Perche	91.7	1	22)	Nice	92.8	5	17)	Alençon	93.8	1	22)	Sarrebourg	94.7	1
14)	Saint Etienne	91.7	1	23)	Vannes	92.8	1	27)	Marseille	93.8	4	5)	Vesoul	94.7	1
17)	Villefrnch s. Saône	91.7	1	3)	Cambrai	92.9	1	18)	Montauban	93.8	3	4)	Angers	94.8	2
7)	Amiens	91.8	1	20)	Château Gontier	92.9	1	7)	Orange	93.8	1	23)	Annecy	94.8	1
7)	Bordeaux	91.8	5	26)	Colmar	92.9	1	21)	Avallon	93.9	1	20)	Chalon sur Saône	94.8	1
8)	Brioude	91.8	1	13)	Lyon	92.9	10	7)	Bar le Duc	93.9	1	3)	Chaumont	94.8	1
3)	Castres	91.8	1	22)	Menton	92.9	1	17)	Bourg en Bresse	93.9	1	22)	Forbach	94.8	1
18)	La Rochelle	91.8	1	7)	Montauban	92.9	3	19)	Bourges	93.9	1	6)	Longwy	94.8	1
21)	Montélimar	91.8	1	10)	Orléans	92.9	2	7)	Carcassonne	93.9	1	5)	Mulhouse	94.8	1
7)	Montpellier	91.8	3	7)	Rochefort	92.9	1	13)	Château Gontier	93.9	1	22)	Nancy	94.8	1
7)	Saint Dizier	91.8	1	5)	St Amand Montrond	92.9	1	20)	Condom	93.9	1	6)	Nîmes	94.8	1
7)	Saint Malo	91.8	1	13)	Ajaccio	93.0	8	5)	Epernay	93.9	1	20)	Riscle	94.8	1
7)	Saint Quentin	91.8	1	22)	Bonifacio	93.0	1	20)	Guéret	93.9	1	5)	Avignon	94.9	1
7)	Vichy	91.8	1	18)	Courtenay	93.0	1	13)	Lille	93.9	1	12)	Bastia	94.9	1
7)	Bressuire	91.9	1	18)	Hirson	93.0	1	25)	Nogent le Rotrou	93.9	1	14)	Bordeaux	94.9	1
7)	Chalon sur Saône	91.9	1	21)	Lille	93.0	2	13)	Saint Brieuc	93.9	1	17)	Caen	94.9	1
19)	Chaumont	91.9	1	13)	Lourdes	93.0	3	20)	Vannes	93.9	1	13)	Hirson	94.9	1
4)	Civray	91.9	1	22)	Saint Raphaël	93.0	1	7)	Verdun	93.9	1	19)	La Roche sur Yon	94.9	1
7)	Epinal	91.9	1	17)	Verdun	93.0	1	7)	Avignon	94.0	1	13)	Le Puy en Velay	94.9	1
7)	Le Puy en Velay	91.9	1	13)	Annecy	93.1	1	6)	Pau	94.0	1	19)	Lyon	94.9	1
7)	Lessay	91.9	1	13)	Arcachon	93.1	1	9)	Rochefort	94.0	1	5)	Montpellier	94.9	3
7)	Porto Vecchio	91.9	1	7)	Bayeux	93.1	1	22)	Saint Flour	94.0	1	8)	Rennes	94.9	1
8)	Salon de Provence	91.9	1	21)	Châlons en Champ.	93.1	1	4)	Thionville	94.0	1	24)	Alès	95.0	1
8)	Aix en Provence	92.0	1	20)	Châteaudun	93.1	1	1)	Troyes	94.0	1	21)	Autun	95.0	1
8)	Albi	92.0	1	7)	Coutances	93.1	1	21)	Ussel	94.0	1	7)	Chambéry	95.0	1
7)	Arcachon	92.0	1	13)	Dole	93.1	1	6)	Arcachon	94.1	1	5)	Cholet	95.0	1
7)	Auxerre	92.0	1	8)	Ernée	93.1	1					19)	Clermont Ferrand	95.0	1
6)	Lille	92.0	2	23)	Fontenay le Comte	93.1	1					8)	Dinan	95.0	1
23)	Montargis	92.0	1												

FM	Station	MHz	kW
19)	Grenoble	95.0	1
10)	Lorient	95.0	1
13)	Mimizan	95.0	1
9)	Montauban	95.0	3
7)	Nice	95.0	5
13)	Niort	95.0	1
13)	Porto Vecchio	95.0	1
3)	Aubusson	95.1	1
17)	Douai	95.1	1
23)	Épinal	95.1	1
17)	Mâcon	95.1	1
24)	Marseille	95.1	4
17)	Pithiviers	95.1	1
10)	Saint Étienne	95.1	2
9)	Saint Raphaël	95.1	1
3)	Ussel	95.1	1
3)	Béziers	95.2	1
21)	Dunkerque	95.2	1
21)	Fontenay le Comte	95.2	1
5)	Jussey	95.2	1
9)	Périgueux	95.2	1
24)	Tarascon	95.2	1
21)	Argentan	95.3	1
3)	Bordeaux	95.3	5
20)	Chartres	95.3	1
20)	Château Thierry	95.3	1
7)	Dax	95.3	1
3)	Evreux	95.3	1
10)	Le Puy en Velay	95.3	1
21)	Lisieux	95.3	1
3)	Lyon	95.3	10
3)	Mirande	95.3	1
3)	Montélimar	95.3	1
13)	Nancy	95.3	1
3)	Tarbes	95.3	1
3)	Toulon	95.3	4
18)	Cahors	95.4	1
18)	Chambéry	95.4	1
13)	Commercy	95.4	1
19)	Le Mans	95.4	2
23)	Orléans	95.4	2
17)	Pouzauges	95.4	1
17)	Ruffec	95.4	1
8)	Angers	95.5	1
3)	Annonay	95.5	1
24)	Bergerac	95.5	1
23)	Besançon	95.5	1
13)	Calvi	95.5	1
5)	Corte	95.5	1
17)	La Rochelle	95.5	1
6)	Mâcon	95.5	1
19)	Marseille	95.5	10
9)	Millau	95.5	1
6)	Nogent le Rotrou	95.5	1
6)	Niort	95.6	1
11)	Paris	95.6	4
9)	Saint Tropez	95.6	1
19)	Vannes	95.6	1
23)	Le Puy en Velay	95.7	1
19)	Lorient	95.7	1
22)	Lyon	95.7	4
23)	Metz	95.7	1
23)	Nancy	95.7	1
6)	Perpignan	95.7	3
17)	St Amand Montrond	95.7	1
13)	Angoulême	95.8	1
22)	Chambéry	95.8	1
6)	Montpellier	95.8	3
3)	Nice	95.8	5
21)	Saint Brieuc	95.8	1
23)	Thionville	95.8	1
6)	Toulon	95.8	4
23)	Beauvais	95.9	1
18)	Béthune	95.9	1
10)	Bourges	95.9	1
13)	Brioude	95.9	1
18)	Cavaillon	95.9	1
18)	Commercy	95.9	1
3)	La Tour du Pin	95.9	1
10)	Limoges	95.9	2
22)	Mazamet	95.9	1
23)	Montélimar	95.9	1
3)	Saint Étienne	95.9	2
3)	Annecy	96.0	1
9)	Brignoles	96.0	1
3)	Châteaudun	96.0	1
13)	Châtillon sur Seine	96.0	1
3)	Cognac	96.0	1
23)	Grenoble	96.0	1
18)	Lille	96.0	2
6)	Lisieux	96.0	1
13)	Marseille	96.0	4
23)	Paris	96.0	10
23)	Valence	96.0	2
22)	Auxerre	96.1	1
22)	Béziers	96.1	2
23)	Chartres	96.1	1
8)	Decazeville	96.1	1
6)	Le Puy en Velay	96.1	1
23)	Lyon	96.1	4
23)	Montauban	96.1	3
23)	Moulins	96.1	1
6)	Nancy	96.1	1
13)	Saint Dizier	96.1	1
13)	Tours	96.1	2
17)	Vire	96.1	1
25)	Aix en Provence	96.2	1
19)	Alençon	96.2	1
13)	Bar le Duc	96.2	1
18)	Brive la Gaillarde	96.2	1
22)	Châteauroux	96.2	1
23)	Clermont Ferrand	96.2	1
23)	Compiègne	96.2	1
23)	Douai	96.2	1
6)	Dunkerque	96.2	1
23)	Montbard	96.2	1
6)	Saint Brieuc	96.2	1
13)	Sedan	96.2	1
12)	Amiens	96.3	1
23)	Annonay	96.3	1
6)	Bourg en Bresse	96.3	1
7)	Caen	96.3	2
7)	L'Aigle	96.3	1
9)	Montluçon	96.3	1
6)	Morlaix	96.3	1
7)	Nogent le Rotrou	96.3	1
17)	Rennes	96.3	1
9)	Rodez	96.3	1
7)	Saint Étienne	96.3	2
22)	Bastia	96.4	1
22)	Calvi	96.4	1.3
20)	Cosne Cours s. Loire	96.4	1
7)	Épernay	96.4	1
13)	Granville	96.4	1
2)	Lille	96.4	2
6)	Lorient	96.4	1
13)	Mont de Marsan	96.4	1
2)	Paris	96.4	4
3)	Saint Quentin	96.4	4
19)	Sarrebourg	96.4	1
20)	Bourges	96.5	1
6)	Brest	96.5	3
10)	Lyon	96.5	4
20)	Marmande	96.5	1
23)	Saint Flour	96.5	1
23)	Saint Nazaire	96.5	1
23)	Saint Omer	96.5	1
5)	Auxerre	96.6	1
22)	Châteauroux	96.6	1
7)	Clermont Ferrand	96.6	2
17)	Nice	96.6	1
9)	Nîmes	96.6	1
9)	Toulon	96.6	4
6)	Yssingeaux	96.6	1
23)	Abbeville	96.7	1
23)	Limoges	96.7	1
22)	Montargis	96.7	1
17)	Saint Lô	96.7	1
22)	Thionville	96.7	1
4)	Angoulême	96.8	1
23)	Brive la Gaillarde	96.8	1
6)	Caen	96.8	2
6)	Cahors	96.8	1
17)	Cannes	96.8	1
20)	Châtellerault	96.8	1
14)	Dreux	96.8	1
3)	Lille	96.8	1
18)	Mont de Marsan	96.8	1
13)	Nantes	96.8	3
13)	Redon	96.8	1
13)	Roanne	96.8	1
13)	Rochefort	96.8	1
13)	Valence	96.8	1
23)	Arras	96.9	1
13)	Guéret	96.9	1
7)	Montbard	96.9	1
3)	Montpellier	96.9	3
17)	Moulins	96.9	1
18)	Rennes	96.9	1
1)	Toulouse	96.9	1
25)	Calvi	97.0	1
21)	Chambéry	97.0	1
9)	Condom	97.0	1
23)	Mazamet	97.0	1
13)	Albi	97.1	1
9)	Bar le Duc	97.1	1
21)	La Ferté s. Jouarre	97.1	1
26)	Montélimar	97.1	1
6)	Montluçon	97.1	1
6)	Pouzauges	97.1	1
7)	Bagnères de Bigorre	97.2	1
10)	Bourg en Bresse	97.2	1
22)	Chaumont	97.2	1
19)	Épinal	97.2	1
7)	Pithiviers	97.2	1
23)	Propriano	97.2	1
18)	Saint Omer	97.2	1
20)	Alençon	97.3	1
7)	Auch	97.3	1
13)	Bordeaux	97.3	5
22)	Le Havre	97.3	1
25)	Lyon	97.3	1
9)	Poitiers	97.3	1
8)	Rodez	97.3	1
6)	Vire	97.3	1
21)	Agen	97.4	1
22)	Bayeux	97.4	1
13)	Brest	97.4	1
23)	Mont de Marsan	97.4	1
4)	Morhange	97.4	1
21)	Nice	97.4	5
9)	Paris	97.4	4
18)	Saint Malo	97.4	1
3)	Toulouse	97.4	1
23)	Argentan	97.5	1
18)	Béziers	97.5	1
23)	Carmaux	97.5	1
13)	Corte	97.5	1
13)	Dijon	97.5	1
7)	Mayenne	97.5	1
7)	Neufchâteau	97.5	1
3)	Nogent le Rotrou	97.5	1
3)	Rouen	97.5	2
3)	Alès	97.6	1
18)	Avallon	97.6	1
23)	Caen	97.6	2
5)	Chambéry	97.6	2
22)	Fontenay le Comte	97.6	1
3)	Le Mans	97.6	2
7)	L'Île Rousse	97.6	1
18)	Menton	97.6	1
7)	Metz	97.6	1
13)	Montauban	97.6	3
7)	Pamiers	97.6	1
3)	Perpignan	97.6	1
13)	Rennes	97.6	3
6)	Bayonne	97.7	5
9)	Castres	97.7	1
7)	Compiègne	97.7	1
4)	Dreux	97.7	1
7)	Figeac	97.7	1
28)	Laval	97.7	1
7)	Maubeuge	97.7	1
9)	Montargis	97.7	1
22)	Nantes	97.7	3
8)	Ussel	97.7	1
15)	Vienne	97.7	1
24)	Brive la Gaillarde	97.8	1
6)	Chalon sur Saône	97.8	1
1)	Grenoble	97.8	1
17)	Porto Vecchio	97.8	1
3)	Reims	97.8	2
6)	Saint Étienne	97.8	2
4)	Bastia	97.9	1
13)	Parthenay	97.9	1
4)	Toulouse	97.9	5
3)	Angers	98.0	2
8)	Montélimar	98.0	1
23)	Montluçon	98.0	1
23)	Moulins	98.0	1
9)	Vannes	98.0	1
23)	Ajaccio	98.1	8
18)	Besançon	98.1	1
6)	Dax	98.1	1
28)	Nice	98.1	5
5)	Périgueux	98.1	1
9)	Saint Flour	98.1	2
20)	Saintes	98.1	1
13)	Samatan	98.1	1
13)	Sens	98.1	1
12)	Strasbourg	98.1	1
13)	Annonay	98.2	1
13)	Auxerre	98.2	1
7)	Avignon	98.2	1
22)	Bernay	98.2	1
19)	Bordeaux	98.2	1
22)	Bourges	98.2	1
12)	Compiègne	98.2	1
19)	Limoges	98.2	2
9)	Lourdes	98.2	3
13)	Mâcon	98.2	1
17)	Narbonne	98.2	1
22)	Nevers	98.2	1
13)	Niort	98.2	1
12)	Paris	98.2	4
8)	Quimperlé	98.2	1
1)	Sablé sur Sarthe	98.2	1
1)	Toulon	98.2	1
14)	Tours	98.2	2
13)	Aix en Provence	98.3	1
18)	Bar le Duc	98.3	1
9)	Gien	98.3	1
17)	Montpellier	98.3	3
21)	Rouen	98.3	2
21)	Saint Affrique	98.3	1
23)	Saint Quentin	98.3	1
23)	Sarrebourg	98.3	1
23)	Amiens	98.4	1
13)	Chaumont	98.4	1
3)	La Flèche	98.4	1
18)	Mazamet	98.4	1
5)	Mirande	98.4	1
3)	Royan	98.4	1
18)	Agen	98.5	1
3)	Alençon	98.5	1
18)	Bastia	98.5	1
3)	Beauvais	98.5	1
17)	Béziers	98.5	1
3)	Bourg en Bresse	98.5	1
21)	Hirson	98.5	1
3)	Laval	98.5	1
3)	Albi	98.6	1
22)	Bergerac	98.6	1
9)	Cognac	98.6	1
20)	Dax	98.6	1
18)	La Roche sur Yon	98.6	1
18)	Vannes	98.6	1
7)	Auch	98.7	1
21)	Brioude	98.7	1
12)	Caen	98.7	1
10)	Chartres	98.7	1
13)	La Rochelle	98.7	1
9)	Le Puy en Velay	98.7	1
6)	Niederbronn l. Bains	98.7	1
3)	Argentan	98.8	1
20)	Cannes	98.8	1
21)	Castres	98.8	1
7)	Grenoble	98.8	1
20)	Lorient	98.8	1
20)	Nice	98.8	1
19)	Toulon	98.8	4
7)	Valence	98.8	1
3)	Arcachon	98.9	1
6)	Auxerre	98.9	1
7)	Brest	98.9	3
6)	Le Creusot	98.9	1
3)	Lyon	98.9	1
3)	Mende	98.9	1
3)	Montauban	98.9	3
3)	Sens	98.9	1
3)	Vierzon	98.9	1
2)	Amiens	99.0	1
22)	Bayonne	99.0	2
10)	Boulogne sur Mer	99.0	1
9)	Carcassonne	99.0	1
3)	La Ferté Macé	99.0	1
18)	Metz	99.0	1
22)	Poitiers	99.0	1
3)	Royan	99.0	1
17)	Saint Raphaël	99.0	1
6)	Ussel	99.0	1
3)	Aurillac	99.1	1
9)	Cervione	99.1	2
7)	Châteauroux	99.1	1

FM	Station	MHz	kW
5)	Châtillon sur Seine	99.1	1
9)	Limoges	99.1	2
20)	Provins	99.1	1
18)	Toulouse	99.1	5
3)	Abbeville	99.2	1
25)	Alençon	99.2	1
23)	Aubusson	99.2	1
7)	Bourges	99.2	1
13)	Brive la Gaillarde	99.2	1
22)	Calais	99.2	1
4)	Châtellerault	99.2	1
7)	Condom	99.2	1
7)	Mont de Marsan	99.2	1
20)	Narbonne	99.2	1
9)	Nice	99.2	5
25)	Saint Lô	99.2	1
23)	Vichy	99.2	1
13)	Argentan	99.3	1
22)	Cambrai	99.3	1
13)	L'Aigle	99.3	1
14)	Laval	99.3	1
18)	Montpellier	99.3	3
6)	Saint Nazaire	99.3	1
10)	Avignon	99.4	1
7)	Bastia	99.4	4
7)	Calvi	99.4	1
5)	Charolles	99.4	1
25)	Clermont Ferrand	99.4	1
5)	Fontainebleau	99.4	2
3)	Mâcon	99.4	1
7)	Mazamet	99.4	1
27)	Metz	99.4	1
13)	Mulhouse	99.4	1
5)	Saint Malo	99.4	1
3)	Châteaudun	99.5	1
13)	Eauze	99.5	1
13)	Toulouse	99.5	1
6)	Abbeville	99.6	1
25)	Aurillac	99.6	1
18)	Bordeaux	99.6	5
6)	Bourges	99.6	1
3)	Carcassonne	99.6	1
17)	Carmaux	99.6	1
22)	Cholet	99.6	1
18)	Dijon	99.6	1
5)	Ile de Ré	99.6	1
17)	Limoges	99.6	2
5)	Porto Vecchio	99.6	1
17)	Quimperlé	99.6	1
7)	Salon de Provence	99.6	1
9)	Vichy	99.6	1
6)	Bagnères de Bigorre	99.7	1
3)	Brest	99.7	3
13)	La Flèche	99.7	1
7)	Marseille	99.7	4
22)	Montauban	99.7	3
6)	Nevers	99.7	1
2)	Orléans	99.7	1
3)	Troyes	99.7	1
6)	Ajaccio	99.8	8
21)	Chartres	99.8	1
9)	Guéret	99.8	1
17)	Lavaur	99.8	1
9)	Menton	99.8	1
18)	Montargis	99.8	1
6)	Mulhouse	99.8	1
21)	Noyon	99.8	1
21)	Parthenay	99.8	1
19)	Argentan	99.9	1
17)	Chaumont	99.9	1
9)	Mimizan	99.9	1
7)	Nîmes	99.9	1
24)	Paris	99.9	4
9)	Quimper	99.9	1
7)	Belfort	100.0	1
23)	Béziers	100.0	1
9)	Fontenay le Comte	100.0	1
2)	Laval	100.0	1
3)	L'Ile Rousse	100.0	1
13)	Limoges	100.0	2
9)	Montélimar	100.0	1
9)	Pithiviers	100.0	1
9)	Poitiers	100.0	1
22)	Porto Vecchio	100.0	1
3)	Rodez	100.0	1
13)	Romilly sur Seine	100.0	1
23)	Toulouse	100.0	1
18)	Angers	100.1	1
9)	Bagnères de Bigorre	100.1	1
3)	Bayonne	100.1	3
19)	Carcassonne	100.1	1
13)	Châteauroux	100.1	1
3)	Marseille	100.1	4
9)	Meaux	100.1	3
9)	Melun	100.1	1
22)	Reims	100.1	2
20)	Saint Brieuc	100.1	1
9)	Sens	100.1	1
23)	Alès	100.2	1
14)	Brest	100.2	1
7)	Chinon	100.2	1
5)	Coutances	100.2	1
13)	Gien	100.2	1
6)	Guéret	100.2	1
9)	La Rochelle	100.2	1
23)	Montpellier	100.2	3
3)	Orthez	100.2	1
9)	Troyes	100.2	1
9)	Valence	100.2	2
14)	Agen	100.3	1
6)	Angoulême	100.3	1
7)	Le Mans	100.3	2
6)	Lyon	100.3	4
13)	Mende	100.3	1
3)	Mont de Marsan	100.3	1
9)	Narbonne	100.3	1
9)	Paris	100.3	10
19)	St Gilles Croix de Vie	100.3	1
9)	Soissons	100.3	1
24)	Arcachon	100.4	1
6)	Besançon	100.4	1
21)	Bourges	100.4	1
9)	Chartres	100.4	1
22)	Chaumont	100.4	1
4)	Corte	100.4	1
13)	Lens	100.4	1
6)	Limoges	100.4	2.2
9)	Niort	100.4	1
9)	Orléans	100.4	2
22)	Royan	100.4	1
21)	Toulon	100.4	4
9)	Toulouse	100.4	5
17)	Tours	100.4	2
9)	Alençon	100.5	1
6)	Annecy	100.5	1
9)	Argentan	100.5	1
21)	Brive la Gaillarde	100.5	1
9)	Château Gontier	100.5	1
6)	Compiègne	100.5	1
3)	La Tour du Pin	100.5	1
12)	Marseille	100.5	2
23)	Mulhouse	100.5	1
9)	Nogent le Rotrou	100.5	1
18)	Rodez	100.5	1
9)	Rouen	100.5	2
18)	Ruffec	100.5	1
22)	Saint Étienne	100.5	2
9)	Saint Nazaire	100.5	1
9)	Albi	100.6	1
9)	Avallon	100.6	1
7)	Blois	100.6	1
3)	Bourg en Bresse	100.6	1
3)	Brioude	100.6	1
9)	Carcassonne	100.6	1
9)	Dijon	100.6	1
3)	Douarnenez	100.6	1
9)	Ghisonaccia	100.6	4
5)	Parthenay	100.6	1
9)	Reims	100.6	2
17)	Saint Brieuc	100.6	1
20)	Villeneuve sur Lot	100.6	1
13)	Béziers	100.7	1
6)	Decazeville	100.7	1
13)	Laon	100.7	1
13)	Laval	100.7	1
13)	Le Mans	100.7	2
3)	Le Puy en Velay	100.7	1
4)	Paris	100.7	10
9)	Bastia	100.8	4
9)	Calvi	100.8	1
20)	Castres	100.8	1
23)	Chambéry	100.8	1
3)	Clermont Fd.	100.8	1
2)	Grenoble	100.8	1
5)	Lisieux	100.8	1
4)	Nîmes	100.8	1
12)	Perpignan	100.8	1
7)	Saint Gaudens	100.8	1
8)	Thouars	100.8	1
20)	Vire	100.8	1
6)	Alençon	100.9	1
9)	Bayonne	100.9	5
9)	Besançon	100.9	1
10)	Marseille	100.9	10
3)	Nancy	100.9	1
22)	Rodez	100.9	1
3)	Amiens	101.0	1
24)	Aurillac	101.0	1
14)	Avignon	101.0	1
23)	Bergerac	101.0	1
13)	Château Thierry	101.0	1
9)	L'Aigle	101.0	1
5)	Lourdes	101.0	3
6)	Quimper	101.0	1
9)	Agen	101.1	1
9)	Aubusson	101.1	1
17)	Bar le Duc	101.1	1
10)	Beauvais	101.1	1
9)	Châteauroux	101.1	1
4)	Ghisonaccia	101.1	1
6)	La Roche sur Yon	101.1	1
10)	Laval	101.1	1
11)	Le Havre	101.1	1
13)	Metz	101.1	1
10)	Paris	101.1	10
23)	Poitiers	101.1	1
9)	Saint Malo	101.1	1
9)	Ajaccio	101.2	8
24)	Albi	101.2	1
9)	Arras	101.2	1
13)	Blois	101.2	1
21)	Chaumont	101.2	1
9)	Clermont Ferrand	101.2	1
7)	Épinal	101.2	1
3)	Chambéry	101.3	1
21)	Châtellerault	101.3	1
22)	Dreux	101.3	1
9)	Dunkerque	101.3	1
4)	Forbach	101.3	1
6)	Jonzac	101.3	1
22)	La Rochelle	101.3	1
7)	La Tour du Pin	101.3	1
21)	Le Blanc	101.3	1
9)	Lille	101.3	1
20)	Orange	101.3	1
19)	Saint Étienne	101.3	2
9)	Sarlat la Canéda	101.3	1
10)	Amiens	101.4	1
9)	Caen	101.4	2
17)	Longwy	101.4	1
21)	Marseille	101.4	10
5)	Nice	101.4	5
21)	St Gilles Croix de Vie	101.4	1
24)	Toulouse	101.4	1
5)	Vic Fezensac	101.4	1
18)	Alès	101.5	1
9)	Cahors	101.5	1
14)	Évreux	101.5	1
5)	Montbard	101.5	1
18)	Nevers	101.5	1
14)	Paris	101.5	10
13)	Poitiers	101.5	1
21)	Redon	101.5	1
21)	Rodez	101.5	1
17)	Valence	101.5	1
19)	Vendôme	101.5	1
18)	Cambrai	101.6	1
5)	Chaumont	101.6	1
18)	Issoudun	101.6	1
10)	Le Mans	101.6	2
5)	Mâcon	101.6	1
20)	Montargis	101.6	1
23)	Périgueux	101.6	1
10)	Quimper	101.6	1
21)	Saint Malo	101.6	1
13)	Valence	101.6	1
21)	Albi	101.7	1
6)	Bayeux	101.7	1
5)	Bayonne	101.7	5
18)	Compiègne	101.7	1
6)	Cosne Crs s. Loire	101.7	1
17)	Le Puy en Velay	101.7	1
22)	Limoges	101.7	2.2
21)	Mazamet	101.7	1
18)	Montluçon	101.7	1
22)	Montpellier	101.7	1
23)	Morlaix	101.7	1
9)	Provins	101.7	1
7)	Reims	101.7	2
9)	Romilly sur Seine	101.7	1
22)	Tarascon	101.7	1
6)	Aubusson	101.8	1
9)	Auxerre	101.8	1
9)	Bergerac	101.8	1
23)	Brest	101.8	3
7)	Laon	101.8	1
6)	Le Havre	101.8	1
4)	Aix en Provence	101.9	1
3)	Cahors	101.9	1
9)	Châtillon s. Seine	101.9	1
6)	Cognac	101.9	1
9)	Coutances	101.9	1
7)	Évreux	101.9	1
4)	Martigues	101.9	1
9)	Mayenne	101.9	1
18)	Moulins	101.9	1
7)	Paris	101.9	10
9)	Tonnerre	101.9	1
7)	Abbeville	102.0	1
6)	Bar le Duc	102.0	1
17)	Beaune	102.0	1
5)	Épinal	102.0	1
6)	Falaise	102.0	1
23)	La Rochelle	102.0	1
4)	Metz	102.0	1
5)	Neufchâteau	102.0	1
22)	Quimper	102.0	1
6)	Rennes	102.0	3
21)	Saint Quentin	102.0	1
24)	Toulouse	102.0	60
7)	Annecy	102.1	1
20)	Avallon	102.1	1
20)	Calvi	102.1	1
9)	Charolles	102.1	1
18)	Limoges	102.1	2.2
26)	Melun	102.1	1
9)	Mulhouse	102.1	1
6)	Nîmes	102.1	1
7)	St Amand Mntrnd	102.1	1
18)	Strasbourg	102.1	4
9)	Arcachon	102.2	1
9)	Blois	102.2	1
21)	Dole	102.2	1
17)	La Ferté Macé	102.2	1
7)	Montargis	102.2	1
9)	Thouars	102.2	1
7)	Troyes	102.2	1
9)	Avranches	102.3	1
13)	Cahors	102.3	1
17)	Chambéry	102.3	1
6)	Forbach	102.3	1
21)	Le Puy en Velay	102.3	1
6)	Marseille	102.3	10
9)	Montbard	102.3	1
18)	Nancy	102.3	1
21)	Nevers	102.3	1
26)	Paris	102.3	4
3)	Quimperlé	102.3	1
9)	Saint Brieuc	102.3	1
9)	Saint Omer	102.3	1
10)	Tours	102.3	2
7)	Auxerre	102.4	1
9)	Bordeaux	102.4	5
9)	Brest	102.4	1
6)	Castres	102.4	1
3)	Chalon sur Saône	102.4	1
20)	Chaumont	102.4	1
3)	Decazeville	102.4	1
10)	Grenoble	102.4	1
6)	Haguenau	102.4	1
5)	Montmorillon	102.4	1
9)	Nantes	102.4	3
7)	Perpignan	102.4	3
2)	Rennes	102.4	1
9)	Romorantin Lnthny	102.4	1
5)	Thionville	102.4	1
6)	Toulouse	102.4	5
3)	Vienne	102.4	1
22)	Angers	102.5	1
18)	Calais	102.5	1
24)	Carmaux	102.5	1
5)	Chartres	102.5	1
6)	Commercy	102.5	1
3)	Dijon	102.5	1
18)	Gourdon	102.5	1
7)	Melun	102.5	1

FM	Station	MHz	kW	FM	Station	MHz	kW	FM	Station	MHz	kW	FM	Station	MHz	kW
8)	Niort	102.5	1	20)	Orthez	103.3	1	20)	Bordeaux	104.2	5	5)	Beauvais	104.7	1
18)	Angoulême	102.6	1	19)	Rouen	103.3	1	21)	Dijon	104.2	1	5)	Brest	104.7	3
13)	Bergerac	102.6	1	20)	Sarlat la Canéda	103.3	1	20)	Grenoble	104.2	1	24)	Carcassonne	104.7	80
21)	Carcassonne	102.6	1	20)	Strasbourg	103.3	4	20)	Lyon	104.2	4	5)	Cholet	104.7	1
21)	Montauban	102.6	3	10)	Toulon	103.3	1	20)	Mende	104.2	1	5)	Clermont Fd.	104.7	2
27)	Orléans	102.6	1	7)	Vichy	103.3	1	4)	Mirande	104.2	1	5)	Dijon	104.7	1
3)	Quimper	102.6	1	2)	Bastia	103.4	1	21)	Nogent le Rotrou	104.2	1	22)	Ghisonaccia	104.7	3
9)	Saint Gaudens	102.6	1	25)	Cahors	103.4	1	21)	Troyes	104.2	1	5)	La Rochelle	104.7	1
20)	Troyes	102.6	1	13)	Carcassonne	103.4	1	20)	Ajaccio	104.3	8	5)	Le Mans	104.7	2
9)	Abbeville	102.7	1	7)	Metz	103.4	1	21)	Amiens	104.3	1	5)	Limoges	104.7	2.2
22)	Avallon	102.7	1	7)	Nantes	103.4	3	21)	Angers	104.3	1	5)	Lorient	104.7	1
3)	Limoges	102.7	2	12)	Orléans	103.4	1	20)	Arles	104.3	1	24)	Montpellier	104.7	1
5)	Morlaix	102.7	1	20)	Rodez	103.4	1	20)	Bastia	104.3	4	5)	Nantes	104.7	3
9)	Nérac	102.7	1	25)	Tours	103.4	2	20)	Bayonne	104.3	5	5)	Orléans	104.7	2
8)	Paris	102.7	10	6)	Beauvais	103.5	1	20)	Béziers	104.3	1	5)	Paris	104.7	10
20)	Rochefort	102.7	1	7)	Dinan	103.5	1	20)	Bonifacio	104.3	1	5)	Poitiers	104.7	1
9)	Saint Dizier	102.7	1	6)	Épinal	103.5	1	21)	Brest	104.3	3	5)	Quimper	104.7	1
5)	Saint Flour	102.7	1	19)	Le Havre	103.5	1	21)	Clermont Ferrand	104.3	2	5)	Rennes	104.7	2
18)	Valence	102.7	1	9)	Le Mans	103.5	1	13)	Épinal	104.3	1	5)	Saint Nazaire	104.7	1
13)	Alès	102.8	1	9)	Morlaix	103.5	1	21)	La Ferté Macé	104.3	1	5)	Soissons	104.7	1
9)	Annecy	102.8	1	4)	Paris	103.5	10	21)	La Rochelle	104.3	1	5)	Toulon	104.7	4
18)	Annonay	102.8	1	9)	Saint Affrique	103.5	1	21)	Le Havre	104.3	1	5)	Troyes	104.7	1
13)	Avignon	102.8	1	23)	Angers	103.6	2	21)	Le Mans	104.3	2	5)	Vannes	104.7	1
23)	Bordeaux	102.8	5	21)	Blois	103.6	1	21)	Limoges	104.3	2.2	5)	Annecy	104.8	1
9)	Bourg en Bresse	102.8	1	7)	Longwy	103.6	1	21)	Lorient	104.3	1	5)	Arcachon	104.8	1
22)	Brive la Gaillarde	102.8	1	5)	Montluçon	103.6	1	20)	Marseille	104.3	10	3)	Argentan	104.8	1
21)	Dax	102.8	1	20)	Saint Gaudens	103.6	1	17)	Montbard	104.3	1	20)	Aubusson	104.8	1
17)	Lorient	102.8	1	7)	Saint Nazaire	103.6	1	20)	Montpellier	104.3	3	5)	Auxerre	104.8	1
20)	Parthenay	102.8	1	23)	Alençon	103.7	1	21)	Nantes	104.3	3	5)	Bernay	104.8	1
9)	Saint Étienne	102.8	2	6)	Creil	103.7	2	13)	Neufchâteau	104.3	1	5)	Cambrai	104.8	1
2)	Saint Raphaël	102.8	3	6)	Fontainebleau	103.7	2	20)	Nîmes	104.3	1	5)	Châlons en Chmpgn	104.8	1
7)	Tours	102.8	2	17)	Grenoble	103.7	1	21)	Orléans	104.3	2	4)	Gourdon	104.8	1
9)	Vitré	102.8	1	23)	Laval	103.7	1	21)	Paris	104.3	10	5)	La Tour du Pin	104.8	1
13)	Charolles	102.9	1	6)	Meaux	103.7	3	21)	Pau	104.3	1	5)	Marseille	104.8	10
14)	Clermont Ferrand	102.9	1	20)	Mirande	103.7	1	20)	Péronne	104.3	1	21)	Metz	104.8	1
21)	Confolens	102.9	1	18)	Niort	103.7	1	20)	Perpignan	104.3	3	18)	Neufchâteau	104.8	1
5)	Guéret	102.9	1	21)	Bastia	103.8	4	21)	Poitiers	104.3	1	13)	St Amand Mntrnd	104.8	1
1)	Le Mans	102.9	2	21)	Bergerac	103.8	1	21)	Quimper	104.3	1	5)	Saint Étienne	104.8	2
21)	Lourdes	102.9	3	17)	Chinon	103.8	1	20)	Rennes	104.3	3	18)	Saint Lô	104.8	1
9)	Lunéville	102.9	1	24)	Figeac	103.8	1	20)	Saint Affrique	104.3	1	5)	Valence	104.8	1
23)	Nantes	102.9	3	22)	Lorient	103.8	1	21)	St Amand Mntrnd	104.3	1	5)	Abbeville	104.9	1
9)	Saint Lô	102.9	1	20)	Lourdes	103.8	3	21)	Saint Nazaire	104.3	1	5)	Agen	104.9	1
24)	Villeneuve sur Lot	102.9	1	4)	Nantes	103.8	2	21)	Soissons	104.3	1	5)	Besançon	104.9	1
17)	Carcassonne	103.0	1	5)	Saint Brieuc	103.8	2	20)	Toulon	104.3	4	7)	Chartres	104.9	1
9)	Chambéry	103.0	1	18)	Troyes	103.8	1	20)	Toulouse	104.3	5	5)	Compiègne	104.9	1
9)	Châteaudun	103.0	1	9)	Ussel	103.8	1	20)	Valence	104.3	1	7)	La Roche sur Yon	104.9	1
13)	Colmar	103.0	1	24)	Bayonne	103.9	5	21)	Vannes	104.3	1	22)	Laval	104.9	1
6)	Condom	103.0	1	18)	Beauvais	103.9	1	21)	Aubusson	104.4	1	5)	Mont de Marsan	104.9	1
18)	Le Puy en Velay	103.0	1	21)	Calvi	103.9	1	21)	Auxerre	104.4	1	7)	Montereau Fault Y.	104.9	1
9)	Lyon	103.0	10	18)	Épinal	103.9	1	7)	Bourg en Bresse	104.4	1	7)	Moulins	104.9	1
3)	Metz	103.0	1	18)	Le Havre	103.9	1	21)	Jonzac	104.4	1	7)	Parthenay	104.9	1
21)	Moulins	103.0	1	20)	Le Mans	103.9	2	20)	Le Puy en Velay	104.4	1	24)	Périgueux	104.9	1
17)	Neufchâtel en Bray	103.0	1	13)	Montpellier	103.9	2	19)	Montargis	104.4	1	5)	Rouen	104.9	2
12)	Poitiers	103.0	1	18)	Paris	103.9	10	7)	Nice	104.4	5	21)	Royan	104.9	1
7)	Tonnerre	103.0	1	9)	Rennes	103.9	1	21)	Reims	104.4	2	21)	Angoulême	105.0	1
23)	Angoulême	103.1	1	21)	Saint Dizier	103.9	1	24)	Rodez	104.4	1	20)	Auch	105.0	1
21)	Arcachon	103.1	1	19)	Saint Flour	103.9	1	18)	Romorantin Lnthny	104.4	1	21)	Bar le Duc	105.0	1
3)	Bar le Duc	103.1	1	5)	Saint Lô	103.9	1	13)	Ruffec	104.4	1	21)	Caen	105.0	2
20)	Bergerac	103.1	1	3)	Saint Quentin	103.9	1	21)	Saint Étienne	104.4	1	24)	Cahors	105.0	1
17)	Charensat	103.1	1	21)	Toulouse	103.9	5	20)	Agen	104.5	1	5)	L'Aigle	105.0	1
2)	Marseille	103.1	4	21)	Vierzon	103.9	1	20)	Alençon	104.5	1	13)	Luxeuil les Bains	105.0	1
20)	Mont de Marsan	103.1	1	20)	Arcachon	104.0	1	20)	Avignon	104.5	1	21)	Lyon	105.0	4
20)	Paris	103.1	10	21)	Besançon	104.0	1	7)	Baccarat	104.5	1	5)	Morlaix	105.0	1
5)	Roanne	103.1	1	3)	Cervione	104.0	2	20)	Chambéry	104.5	1	23)	Reims	105.0	1
24)	Saint Affrique	103.1	1	3)	Mauriac	104.0	1	11)	Chartres	104.5	1	20)	Alençon	105.1	1
3)	Saint Dizier	103.1	1	2)	Metz	104.0	1	21)	Compiègne	104.5	1	3)	Angers	105.1	2
3)	Saint Flour	103.1	1	18)	Millau	104.0	1	19)	Forbach	104.5	1	21)	Bayonne	105.1	5
10)	Toulouse	103.1	5	21)	Romorantin Lanth.	104.0	1	19)	Gien	104.5	1	21)	Bonifacio	105.1	5
22)	Amiens	103.2	1	18)	St Gilles Crx de Vie	104.0	1	17)	La Roche sur Yon	104.5	1	21)	Charolles	105.1	1
21)	Belfort	103.2	1	21)	Tours	104.0	2	5)	Laval	104.5	1	20)	Clermont Ferrand	105.1	2
21)	Cervione	103.2	1	24)	Villefr. de Rouergue	104.0	1	5)	Le Creusot	104.5	1	5)	Dinan	105.1	1
17)	Dole	103.2	1	21)	Abbeville	104.1	1	20)	Melun	104.5	1	25)	Le Puy en Velay	105.1	1
6)	Douarnenez	103.2	1	21)	Alençon	104.1	1	17)	Redon	104.5	1	20)	Limoges	105.1	2
3)	Grenoble	103.2	1	9)	Bressuire	104.1	1	21)	Rouen	104.5	2	21)	Nancy	105.1	1
9)	Mirande	103.2	1	18)	Chartres	104.1	1	5)	Tours	104.5	2	20)	Niort	105.1	1
20)	Montmorillon	103.2	1	20)	Compiègne	104.1	1	1)	Alès	104.6	1	17)	Toulon	105.1	4
9)	Niort	103.2	1	17)	Confolens	104.1	1	3)	Avallon	104.6	1	7)	Ajaccio	105.2	8
20)	Nogent le Rotrou	103.2	1	21)	Laval	104.1	1	20)	Bayeux	104.6	1	20)	Brive la Gaillarde	105.2	1
24)	Perpignan	103.2	10	20)	Mâcon	104.1	1	5)	Bordeaux	104.6	5	13)	Épinal	105.2	1
20)	Albi	103.3	1	24)	Mazamet	104.1	1	20)	Grenoble	104.6	1	9)	Issoudun	105.2	1
18)	Aurillac	103.3	1	21)	Melun	104.1	1	5)	L'Aigle	104.6	1	3)	Lons le Saunier	105.2	1
21)	Avesnes sur Helpe	103.3	1	8)	Menton	104.1	1	5)	Lyon	104.6	4	5)	Montauban	105.2	3
6)	Carpentras	103.3	1	20)	Montauban	104.1	3	20)	Nevers	104.6	1	5)	Saint Étienne	105.2	2
9)	Chartres	103.3	1	20)	Montélimar	104.1	1	20)	Nogent le Rotrou	104.6	1	13)	Saint Lô	105.2	1
9)	Compiègne	103.3	1	21)	Montluçon	104.1	2	20)	Saint Flour	104.6	1	21)	Vitré	105.2	1
20)	La Rochelle	103.3	1	2)	Nancy	104.1	1	21)	Saint Raphaël	104.6	1	3)	Chartres	105.3	1
20)	Lille	103.3	2	6)	Rouen	104.1	2	22)	Zonza	104.6	1	19)	Cholet	105.3	1
7)	Nancy	103.3	1	20)	Annecy	104.2	1	5)	Amiens	104.7	1	5)	Metz	105.3	1
7)	Nérac	103.3	1					5)	Angers	104.7	1				

FM	Station	MHz	kW
13)	Rouen	105.3	2
22)	Sens	105.3	1
13)	Strasbourg	105.3	4
18)	Dole	105.4	1
5)	Nancy	105.5	1
5)	Béziers	105.7	1
23)	Bonifacio	105.7	1
7)	Lannemezan	105.7	1
21)	Le Creusot	105.7	1
20)	Lesparre Médoc	105.7	1
21)	Loches	105.7	1
14)	Marseille	105.7	1
7)	Neufchâteau	105.7	1
5)	Redon	105.7	1
3)	Saint Flour	105.7	2
7)	Sancerre	105.7	1
21)	Strasbourg	105.7	4
13)	Vesoul	105.7	1
17)	Argenton s. Creuse	105.8	1
5)	Carcassonne	105.8	1
5)	Dijon	105.8	1
3)	Grenoble	105.8	1
9)	Nîmes	105.8	1
23)	Segré	105.8	1
8)	Bourges	105.9	1
18)	Brest	105.9	3
5)	Caen	105.9	1
22)	Clermont Ferrand	105.9	1
21)	Corte	105.9	1
20)	Ghisonaccia	105.9	2
9)	Le Mans	105.9	2
18)	Mende	105.9	1
22)	Paris	105.9	10
5)	Pau	105.9	1
20)	Périgueux	105.9	1
9)	Perpignan	105.9	1
13)	Saint Nazaire	105.9	1
21)	Saintes	105.9	1
7)	Toulouse	105.9	5
23)	Troyes	105.9	1
21)	Valence	105.9	1
21)	Ajaccio	106.0	8
22)	Besançon	106.0	1
22)	Blois	106.0	1
24)	Bordeaux	106.0	5
7)	Cahors	106.0	1
7)	Forbach	106.0	1
17)	L'Aigle	106.0	1
9)	Limoges	106.0	2
9)	Lorient	106.0	1
9)	Marseille	106.0	1
20)	Mauriac	106.0	1
21)	Mayenne	106.0	1
21)	Montargis	106.0	1
21)	Niort	106.0	1
9)	Rennes	106.0	3
8)	Roanne	106.0	1
13)	St Gilles Crx de Vie	106.0	1
23)	Agen	106.1	1
3)	Albi	106.1	1
27)	Amiens	106.1	1
9)	Angers	106.1	2
8)	Aubusson	106.1	1
5)	Bastia	106.1	4
5)	Brive la Gaillarde	106.1	1
19)	Calvi	106.1	1
21)	Chartres	106.1	1
5)	Commercy	106.1	1
5)	Melun	106.1	1
9)	Montpellier	106.1	3
10)	Rouen	106.1	1
5)	Saint Dizier	106.1	1
5)	Sarrebourg	106.1	1
13)	Tarbes	106.1	1
21)	Angoulême	106.2	1
7)	Argentan	106.2	1
7)	Avignon	106.2	1
5)	Bergerac	106.2	1
5)	Etampes	106.2	1
20)	Laval	106.2	1
13)	Morlaix	106.2	1
9)	Nantes	106.2	2
6)	Neufchâteau	106.2	1
22)	Tonnerre	106.2	1
22)	Toulon	106.2	1
21)	Vendôme	106.2	1
21)	Arras	106.3	1
13)	Bourges	106.3	1
5)	Castres	106.3	1
5)	Ghisonaccia	106.3	1
6)	Laon	106.3	1
20)	Moulins	106.3	1
21)	Pau	106.3	1
13)	Quimper	106.3	1
22)	Saint Brieuc	106.3	1
5)	Sarlat la Canéda	106.3	1
5)	Toulouse	106.3	5
13)	Tours	106.3	1
8)	Vannes	106.3	1
5)	Avallon	106.4	1
15)	Bordeaux	106.4	5
13)	Caen	106.4	2
8)	Chambéry	106.4	1
18)	Clermont Ferrand	106.4	1
9)	Marseille	106.4	10
5)	Montargis	106.4	1
10)	Troyes	106.4	1
10)	Valence	106.4	1
7)	Agen	106.5	1
5)	Aurillac	106.5	1
5)	Blois	106.5	1
5)	Châteauroux	106.5	1
15)	Évreux	106.5	1
9)	Fougères	106.5	1
5)	Lons le Saunier	106.5	1
22)	Lourdes	106.5	1
13)	Nogent le Rotrou	106.5	1
22)	Périgueux	106.5	1
5)	Reims	106.5	2
23)	Saint Étienne	106.5	2
17)	Yvetot	106.5	1
22)	Albi	106.6	1
10)	Brest	106.6	3
20)	Cahors	106.6	1
5)	Châtellerault	106.6	1
17)	Châtillon s. Seine	106.6	1
21)	Commercy	106.6	1
15)	Dreux	106.6	1
9)	Gournay en Bray	106.6	1
9)	La Flèche	106.6	1
6)	La Rochelle	106.6	1
5)	Le Puy en Velay	106.6	1
25)	Montélimar	106.6	1
20)	Montluçon	106.6	1
23)	Quimperlé	106.6	1
13)	Saint Malo	106.6	1
8)	Toulon	106.6	1
9)	Vire	106.6	1
18)	Alençon	106.7	1
9)	Angoulême	106.7	1
18)	Bourges	106.7	1
6)	Calvi	106.7	1
10)	Carcassonne	106.7	1
5)	Chalon sur Saône	106.7	1
5)	Condom	106.7	1
18)	Laval	106.7	1
25)	Lisieux	106.7	1
15)	Lyon	106.7	1
5)	Mende	106.7	1
10)	Nantes	106.7	4
1)	Paris	106.7	4
3)	Roanne	106.7	1
5)	Royan	106.7	1
5)	Saint Gaudens	106.7	1
20)	Ussel	106.7	1
6)	Vitry le François	106.7	1
4)	Alès	106.8	1
5)	Avallon	106.8	1
22)	Bordeaux	106.8	5
20)	Brioude	106.8	1
4)	Chartres	106.8	1
13)	Château Renault	106.8	1
20)	Grasse	106.8	1
5)	Marseille	106.8	4
22)	Niort	106.8	1
5)	Pau	106.8	1
13)	Perpignan	106.8	1
3)	Rennes	106.8	3
22)	Rethel	106.8	1
18)	Saint Affrique	106.8	1
23)	Béthune	106.9	1
21)	Bourg en Bresse	106.9	1
19)	Châteauroux	106.9	1
22)	Compiègne	106.9	1
8)	Grenoble	106.9	1
8)	La Roche sur Yon	106.9	1
7)	Le Havre	106.9	1
8)	Le Mans	106.9	1
7)	Lorient	106.9	1
9)	Mantes la Jolie	106.9	2
5)	Mazamet	106.9	1
23)	Melun	106.9	1
3)	Mers les Bains	106.9	1
21)	Montpellier	106.9	3
8)	Périgueux	106.9	1
18)	Poligny	106.9	1
20)	Propriano	106.9	1
5)	Provins	106.9	1
5)	Romilly sur Seine	106.9	1.2
26)	Saint Lô	106.9	1
2)	Strasbourg	106.9	1
5)	Bar le Duc	107.0	1
8)	Bressuire	107.0	1
8)	Cahors	107.0	1
7)	Château Thierry	107.0	1
2)	Clermont Ferrand	107.0	1
23)	La Ferté Macé	107.0	1
8)	L'Aigle	107.0	1
19)	Le Puy en Velay	107.0	1
21)	Mont de Marsan	107.0	1
8)	Montauban	107.0	1
17)	Montluçon	107.0	1
23)	Nice	107.0	5
21)	Nîmes	107.0	1
18)	Porto Vecchio	107.0	1
7)	Rouen	107.0	1
18)	Saint Quentin	107.0	1
1)	Valence	107.0	1
19)	Abbeville	107.1	1
10)	Arcachon	107.1	1
5)	Bourges	107.1	1
2)	Caen	107.1	2
21)	Carmaux	107.1	1
23)	Dijon	107.1	1
8)	Laval	107.1	1
21)	Mulhouse	107.1	1
9)	Nancy	107.1	1
10)	Poitiers	107.1	1
7)	Quimper	107.1	1
18)	Saint Étienne	107.1	2
21)	Saint Flour	107.1	1
5)	St Méen le Grand	107.1	1
21)	Alès	107.2	1
2)	Angers	107.2	1
21)	Avignon	107.2	1
21)	Bastia	107.2	1
20)	Blois	107.2	1
21)	Figeac	107.2	2
14)	Limoges	107.2	2
19)	Mâcon	107.2	1
2)	Nantes	107.2	3
10)	Pau	107.2	1
8)	Rochefort	107.2	1
7)	Soissons	107.2	1
2)	Toulouse	107.2	1
20)	Tours	107.2	2
24)	Ussel	107.2	1
7)	Arnay le Duc	107.3	1
3)	Arras	107.3	1
10)	Auxerre	107.3	1
2)	Bordeaux	107.3	1
2)	Brest	107.3	3.2
10)	Brive la Gaillarde	107.3	1
1)	Carcassonne	107.3	1
10)	Chantilly	107.3	4
3)	Châteauroux	107.3	1
21)	Colmar	107.3	1
8)	Dax	107.3	1
23)	Évreux	107.3	1
3)	Lens	107.3	1
18)	Lorient	107.3	1
10)	Lyon	107.3	2
6)	Mazamet	107.3	1
2)	Menton	107.3	1
3)	Metz	107.3	1
5)	Millau	107.3	1
10)	Montpellier	107.3	3
20)	Orléans	107.3	1
9)	Parthenay	107.3	1
21)	Perpignan	107.3	3
23)	Saint Brieuc	107.3	1
23)	Saint Raphaël	107.3	1
9)	Verdun	107.3	1
23)	Dreux	107.4	1
5)	Granville	107.4	1
7)	Lisieux	107.4	1
8)	Nevers	107.4	1
18)	Provins	107.4	1
4)	Château Gontier	107.5	1
20)	Châteaudun	107.5	1
21)	Cherbourg Octeville	107.5	1
20)	Saint Dizier	107.5	1
20)	La Ferté Macé	107.9	1
20)	L'Aigle	107.9	1

NB: Stns under 1kW not mentioned.

As of August 2012, 4900 licenses (txs) were allocated to private commercial and non-commercial FM stns. Approx. 3370 stns are affiliated to one of the following private commercial national networks.
Addresses:
1) Beur FM 2 rue du Nouveau Bercy, 94220 Charenton le Pont +33 1 53481056 **W:** www.beurfm.net. + 4 tx less than 1kW – **2) BFM Business** 12 rue d'Oradour sur Glane, 75740 Paris Cedex 15 +33 1 71191181 **W:** www.bfmtv.com/economie + 3 txs less than 1kW – **3) Chérie FM** 22 rue Boileau, 75016 Paris +33 1 40714000 +33 1 40714040 **W:** www.cheriefm.fr+ 57 txs less than 1kW – **4) COFRAC** 6 bd Edgard Quinet, 75014 Paris +33 1 56564444 **W:** www.cofrac-media.com + 17 txs less than 1kW – **5) Europe 1** 26 bis rue François 1er, 75008 Paris +33 1 44319000 +33 1 47231900 **W:** www.europe1.fr **LW:** 183kHz 2000kW see Germany. + 134 txs less than 1kW – **6) Virgin Radio** 26 bis rue François 1er, 75008 Paris +33 1 47231000. **W:** www.virginradio.fr + 95 txs less than 1kW – **7) Fun Radio** 20 rue Bayard, 75008 Paris +33 1 40704848. +33 1 40704800 **W:** www.funradio.fr + 97 txs less than 1kW – **8) MFM Radio** 104 avenue du Président Kennedy, 75016 Paris +33 1 55745570 +33 1 55745588 **W:** www.mfmradio.fr + 34 txs less than 1kW – **9) NRJ** 22 rue Boileau, 75016 Paris +33 1 40714000 +33 1 40714040 **W:** www.nrj.fr + 140 txs less than 1kW – **10) Radio Classique** 12 bis place Henri Bergson, 75382 Paris. Cedex 08 +33 1 40085000 +33 1 40085080 **W:** www.radioclassique.fr + 24 txs less than 1kW – **12) Radio Courtoisie** 61 bd Murat 75016 Paris +33 1 46510085 +33 1 46512182 **W:** www.radiocourtoisie.fr + 3 txs less than 1kW – **12) Radio FG** 51 rue de Rivoli, 75001 Paris +33 1 40138800 +33 1 40138801 **W:** www.radiofg.com. + 5 txs less than 1kW – **13) Nostalgie** 22 rue Boileau, 75016 Paris +33 1 40714000. +33 1 40714040 **W:** www.nostalgie.fr + 107 txs less than 1kW – **14) Radio Nova** 127 avenue Ledru Rollin, 75011 Paris +33 1 53333300 **W:** www.novaplanet.com + 4 txs less than 1kW – **15) Radio Orient** 98 bd Victor Hugo, 92110 Clichy +33 1 41061600 +33 1 41061619 **W:** www.radioorient.com + 9 txs less than 1kW

– 16) Radio Soleil ✇ 57 rue Avron, 75020 Paris ☎ +33 1 43488974 🖃 +33 1 43485558 **W:** www.radio-soleil.com + 2 txs less than 1kW **– 17) RCF** ✇ 7 place Saint Irénée, 69321 Lyon Cedex 05 ☎ +33 4 72382022. 🖃 +33 4 72382057 **W:** www.rcf.fr + 117 txs less than 1kW **– 18) RFM** ✇ 28 rue François 1er, 75008 Paris ☎ +33 1 42322000 🖃 +33 1 47232466 **W:** www.rfm.fr + 84 txs less than 1kW **– 19) Rire et Chansons** ✇ 22 rue Boileau, 75016 Paris ☎ +33 1 40714000 🖃 +33 1 40714040 **W:** www.rireetchansons.fr + 42 txs less than 1kW **– 20) RMC** ✇ 12 rue d'Oradour sur Glane, 75740 Paris Cedex 15 ☎ +33 1 71191191 🖃 +33 01 71191190 **W:** www.rmc.fr **LW:** Roumoules 216kHz 1400kW See Monaco. + 117 txs less than 1kW **– 21) RTL** ✇ 22 rue Bayard, 75008 Paris. ☎ +33 1 40704070 🖃 +33 1 40704450 **W:** www. rtl.fr **LW:** 234kHz 2000kW see Luxembourg. + 104 txs less than 1kW **– 22) RTL 2** ✇ 22 rue Bayard, 75008 Paris ☎ +33 1 40704000 🖃 +33 1 40704800 **W:** www.rtl2.fr + 63 txs less than 1kW **– 23) Skyrock** ✇ 37 bis rue Greneta, 75002 Paris ☎ +33 1 44888200 **W:** www.skyrock. fm + 92 txs less than 1kW **– 24) Sud Radio** ✇ Im. Les Allées du Lac, bât B, rue du Lac, 31681 Labège Cedex ☎ +33 5 61632020 **W:** www. sudradio.fr + 29 txs less than 1KW **– 25) Jazz Radio** ✇ 40 quai Rambaud, 69002 Lyon ☎ +33 4 72101535 **W:** www.jazzradio.fr + 14 txs less than 1 kW **– 26) Ouï FM** ✇ 2 rue de la Roquette, 75011 Paris ☎ +33 1 55281414 **W:** www.ouifm.fr + 11 txs less than 1 kW **– 27) France Maghreb 2** ✇ 84 rue des Couronnes, 75020 Paris ☎ +33 1 40339081 **W:** www.francemaghreb2.fr + 3 txs less than 1kW **– 28) TSF Jazz** ✇ 127 avenue Ledru Rollin, 75011 Paris ☎ +33 1 53332280 **W:** www.tsfjazz.com + 4 txs less than 1kW.

DMB: New licences to be granted on VHF band III using T-DMB technology were postponed to 2013. Tests in Lyon 6D and Nantes 9A

FRENCH GUIANA

L.T: UTC -3h — **Pop:** 210,000 — **Pr.L:** French — **E.C:** 50Hz, 127/220V — **ITU:** GUF — **Int. dialling code:** +594

Guyane Première
✇ B.P. 7013, 97305 Cayenne ☎ 594 301500 🖃 594 302649 **W:** http//guyane.la1ere.fr **Dir:** Anastasie Bourquin. **Dir. Tec:** Serge Sulpice-Timothe. **PD:** Jean-Pierre Karam
FM: Cacao, Ouanary 90.0MHz – Sinnamary Corossony, Saint Lauren, Grand Saint, Maripasoula 91.0MHz – Cayenne, Iracubo 92.0MHz – Mana, Kourou, Saint-Georges, Apatou, Kourou 94.0MHz – Papaichton, Camopi - 95.0MHz **D.Prgr:** 24h **Ann:** "Ici Cayenne, RFO Guyane" **IS:** "Nos richesses" on guitar. **V.** by QSL-folder. Rec. acc.

Other stations in Cayenne: R. Mosaique 88.1MHz – Ouest FM 89.4MHz – R. Metis 90.6MHz – R. Jam 96.2MHz – R. 2000 96.9MHz – NRJ, 97.3MHz – RVLD 98.3MHz – Nostalgie Guyane 99.6MHz – Vinyl R. 102.9MHz – RTM 103.3MHz – Trace 104.3MHz – Chéri 104.7MHz – R. RMP 105.9MHz

RADIO FRANCE INTERNATIONALE RELAY STATION
✇ TDF Montsinery, B.P. 97307, Cayenne Cedex
FM: Cayenne 98.7MHz, 102.0MHz. Sinnamary 104.0MHz

FRENCH POLYNESIA

L.T: Tahiti: UTC-10h, **Marquesas Is:** -9½h **Gambier Is:** -9h — **Pop:** 294,935 — **Pr.L:** French, Tahitian — **E.C:** 60Hz, 220V — **ITU:** OCE

CONSEIL SUPERIOR DE L'AUDIOVISUEL
Comite territorial de l'audiovisuel de Polynesie francaise
✇ Immeuble Charles Levy, B.P. 20659, boulevard Pomare, 98713, Papeete-Tahiti ☎+689 548888 **W:** www.csa.fr **E:** cta-papeete.csa@mail.pf
Regulator of broadcasting for French Polynesia.

POLYNESIE LA PREMIÈRE (Gov)
✇ Centre Pamatai, FAAA BP 60125-98702, Papeete-Tahiti ☎ +689 689861616 🖃 +689 689861611 **W:** www.polynesie.la1ere.fr **Prgr:** 24h

MW	kHz	kW
Mahina,Tahiti	738	20

FM	MHz	FM	MHz
Atuona, Hiva Oa	88.2	Punauaia, Tahiti	89.6
Mahatea,Moorea	89.0	Rairua, Raivavae	89.6
Mont Muake, Nuku Hiva	89.0	Rautini, Arutua	90.5
Papeete, Tahiti	*89.0	Taiohae, Nuku Hiva	90.5
Tapeata, Hiva Oa	89.5	Tiarei, Tahiti	90.5
Moerai, Rurutu	89.6	Vaipaee, Ua Huka	91.0
Papetoai, Moorea	89.6	Hakahau, Ua Pou	91.5

FM	MHz	FM	MHz
Mont Marau, Tahiti	*91.8	Turipaoa, Manihi	94.4
Arutua, Raitahiti	93.6	Fakamaru, Tureia	94.8
Pahua, Mataiva	93.6	Fakatopatere, Takapoto	94.8
Raitahiti, Kaukura	93.6	Teana, Fangatau	94.8
Teavarao, Takaroa	93.6	Tuherahera, Tikehau	94.8
Tepukamaruia, Napuka	93.6	Tukuhora, Anaa	94.8
Aeroport, Rangiroa	94.0	Tumukuru, Tatakoto	94.8
Hitianau, Faaite	94.0	Mahaena, Tahiti	95.2
Manihi, Tuamotu	94.0	Marautangaroa, Pukarua	95.2
Pouheva, Makemo	94.0	Niutahi, Apataki	95.2
Pukapuka, Tuamotu	94.0	Papara, Tahiti	*95.2
Tavana, Nukutavake	94.0	Apataki, Tuamotu	95.5
Uturoa, Raiatea	94.0	Vaitape, Bora Bora	96.6
Otepa, Hao	94.4	Mahina, Tahiti	99.0
Pouheva, Tuamotu	94.4	Taravao, Tahiti	99.0
Rapuarava, Reao	94.4	Ahurei, Rapa	99.4
Rikitea, Gambier Islands	94.4	Amaru, Rimatara	99.4
Rotoava, Fakarava	94.4	Mataura, Tubuai	99.4
Tarione, Fakahina	94.4		

* = 24h satellite relay of **Radio Ô** (Pub) from Paris **W:** www.radioo.fr

Other Stations

FM	Location	MHz	kW	Station
1)	Taravao, Tahiti	87.6	1	R.Maria No Te Hau
5)	Taputapuatea, Raitea	88.0	0.5	R.Paofai
3)	Mont Marau, Tahiti	88.2	3	R.Maohi
4)	Maiao, Moorea	88.6	4	NRJ
4)	Faaa, Tahiti	88.6	3	NRJ
3)	Tiarei, Tahiti	88.7	0.3	R.Maohi
6)	Uturoa, Raiatea	88.8	0.2	R.Bora Bora
8)	Mahina, Tahiti	89.4	0.3	R.Te Reo o Tefana
5)	Papeete, Tahiti	89.9	0.2	R.Paofai
8)	Uturoa, Raiatea	90.0	0.5	R.Te Reo o Tefana
4)	Taiarapu, Tahiti	90.1	0.5	NRJ
5)	Tahaa	90.8	0.5	R.Paofai
9)	Taiarapu, Tahiti	90.9	1	Radio 1
10)	Mont Marau, Tahiti	91.4	3	R.Te Vevo o Te Tiaturiraa
11)	Atuona, Hiva Oa	92.0	6	R.Te Oko Nui
14)	Moerai, Rurutu	92.0	0.05	R.Rurutu
3)	Maatea, Moorea	92.3	3.6	R.Maohi
11)	Taiohae, Nuku Hiva	92.5	0.3	R.Te Oko Nui
1)	Uturoa, Raiatea	92.6	0.3	R.Maria No Te Hau
8)	Mont Marau, Tahiti	92.8	0.5	R.Te Reo o Tefana
12)	Taiohae, Nuku Hiva	93.5	3	R.Te Vevo Te Tiaturiraa
10)	Taravao, Tahiti	93.5	0.5	R.Te Vevo o Te Tiaturiraa
1)	Papeete, Tahiti	93.8	0.2	R.Maria No Te Hau
5)	Taiarapu, Tahiti	93.9	0.5	R.Paofai
11)	Mont Muake, Nuku Hiva	94.5	6	R.Te Oko Nui
13)	Uturoa, Raiatea	94.5	0.5	R.La Voix de l'Esperance
3)	Taravao, Tahiti	94.8	1	R.Maohi
14)	Manureva, Rurutu	95.0	0.5	R.Rurutu
9)	Uturoa, Raiatea	95.0	0.5	R.Tiare
6)	Vaitape, Bora Bora	95.4	0.2	R.Bora Bora
13)	Mont Marau, Tahiti	95.6	3	R.La Voix de l'Esperance
19)	Moorea	95.8		Taui FM
15)	Ahurei, Rapa	96.0	0.3	R.Kotokoto
16)	Marutea Sud	96.0	1	R.Marutea Sud
13)	Vaitape, Bora Bora	96.2	0.2	R.La Voix de l'Esperance
1)	Mont Marau, Tahiti	96.4	3	R.Maria No Te Hau
3)	Papeete, Tahiti	96.8	0.6	R.Maohi
17)	Mataura, Tubuai	97.0	0.2	R.Te Reo No Tubuai
10)	Uturoa, Raiatea	97.2	0.5	R.Te Vevo o Te Tiaturiraa
8)	Afareaitu, Moorea	97.4	3	R.Te Reo o Tefana
8)	Maatea, Moorea	97.4	4.25	R.Te Reo o Tefana
8)	Niau, Tuamotu	97.4	0.1	R.Te Reo o Tefana
19)	Maatea, Moorea	97.8	12	Taui FM
1)	Aeroport, Rangiroa	98.0	1	R.Maria No Te Hau
18)	Papeete, Tahiti	98.0	0.3	R.Poroi
9)	Taravao, Tahiti	98.3	1	R.Tiare
19)	Uturoa, Raiatea	98.4	0.4	Taui FM
20)	Otepa, Hao	98.5	0.1	R.Hao
21)	Pouheva, Makemo	98.5	0.2	R.Tanginui
22)	Punauaia, Tahiti	‡98.5	0.3	R.Nono
9)	Papeete, Tahiti	98.8	0.2	R. 1
13)	Maatea, Moorea	99.5	3	R.La Voix de l'Esperance
9)	Nunue, Bora Bora	99.7	0.5	R.Maohi
1)	Faaone	99.8	0.5	R.Maria No Te Hau
9)	Afareaitu, Moorea	100.0	3	Radio 1
1)	Mangareva	100.0	0.7	R.Maria No Te Hau
23)	Taugaraufara, Manihi	100.0	0.1	R.Poe Rava
5)	Taiarapu, Tahiti	100.3	0.5	R.Paofai
24)	Papeete, Tahiti	100.5	0.8	R.Fara
9)	Uturoa, Raiatea	100.9	0.5	Radio 1
25)	Aeroport, Rangiroa	101.0	1	R.Te Reo Tuamotu

FM	Location	MHz	kW	Station
26)	Muake, Nuku Hiva	101.3	0.3	R.Marquises
27)	Taiarapu, Tahiti	101.3	0.5	R.Taiarapu
1)	Afareaitu, Moorea	101.5	2	R.Maria No Te Hau
3)	Uturoa, Raiatea	101.7	0.5	R.Maohi
10)	Aeroport, Rangiroa	102.0	1	R.Te Vevo Te Tiaturiraa
32)	Papara, Tahiti	102.2	0.3	R.Te Vevo No Papara
30)	Papeete, Tahiti	102.2	1	R.Tahiti Nui FM
9)	Nunue, Bora Bora	102.4	0.3	Radio 1
4)	Mont Marau, Tahiti	103.0	3	NRJ
26)	Taiohae, Nuku Hiva	103.3	0.05	R.Marquises
9)	Papeete, Tahiti	103.4	0.2	R.Tiare
9)	Mont Marau, Tahiti	103.8	3	Radio 1
9)	Mont Marau, Tahiti	104.2	3	R.Tiare
31)	Nuku Hiva	104.5	0.05	R.Te Tau Vae'ia
5)	Afareaitu, Moorea	104.7	2	R.Paofai
13)	Taravao, Tahiti	105.1	0.8	R.La Voix de l'Esperance
1)	Uturoa, Raiatea	105.4	1	R.Maria No Te Hau
9)	Maatea, Moorea	105.5	3	R.Tiare
19)	Taravao, Tahiti	105.8	0.4	Taui FM
9)	Papeete, Tahiti	106.0	0.5	R.Tiare
2)	Maiao, Moorea	106.4	4.25	Pacifique FM
27)	Vairau, Tahiti	106.6	0.5	R.Taiarapu
8)	Taravao, Tahiti	107.0	0.4	R.Te Reo o Tefana
19)	Faaa, Tahiti	107.3	1	Taui FM

NB: Under Review. New applications have been called [July 2012] for operation of social, local and regional independent stns on 29 FM frequencies throughout the territory. ‡ = inactive

Addresses and other information
1) BP 94-98713 Papeete. Dir: Mme Irene Paofai ☎ +689 689420011 ☎ +689 689420635 **E:** contactmnth@radiomarianotehau.pf **W:** www.radiomarianotehau.com – **2)** BP 14150-98701, Arue. Dir: Thierry Demary ☎ +689 689583747 ☎ +689 689429164 **E:** pacificfm@caramail.com – **3)** Maison des Jeunes, BP 5038 Pirae ☎ +689 689501616 **W:** www.radiomaohi.pf **E:** courier@radiomaohi.pf – **4)** BP 50-98713 Papeete ☎ +689 689421042 ☎ +689 689464346 **W:** www.nrj.pf **E:** nrj@mail.pf **LP:** GM: Nadine Richardson – **5)** BP 113-98713 Papeete, Dir: Maea Tematua Tech: Maurice Tupea Sec: Iteata Tevaarauhara ☎ +689 689460624/689460606 ☎ +689 689419357 **E:** radiopaofai@epm. pf **W:** www.radio.radiopaofai.org – **6)** Vaitape, Bora Bora, Dir: Jean Claude. ☎ +689 689605873/689605888 ☎ BP 6295 Faaa, Papeete ☎ +689 689819797 ☎ +689 689825493 **E:** toroo@mail.pf. **LP:** GM: Terimateatea Mana – **9)** BP 3601-98713 Papeete. Dir: Mme Sonia Aline ☎ +689 689434100/689436100 ☎ +689 689422421/689423406 (Radio 1/R. Tiare) **E:** radio1@aline.pf **W:** Radio 1: www.radio1.pf R. Tiare: www.tiare.pf and www.facebook.com/pages/tiarefm – **10)** BP 1817-98713 Papeete, 51, rue Dumont D'Urville, Orovini, Papeete. Dir: Christian Bradai ☎ +689 689412341 ☎ +689 689412322 **E:** contacts@ mail.pf – **11)** Mission Catholique, Taiohae, Nuku Hiva – **12)** BP 1817 Papeete ☎ +689 689412341 ☎ +689 689412322. **E:** contacts@mail.pf – **13)** BP 95-97813 Papeete, Dir: Hubert Terorotua ☎ +689 689508259 ☎ +689 689451427 – **14)** Moerai, Rurutu ☎ +689 689940468 – **15)** ☎ +689 689957272 – **16)** ☎ +689 68946151 – **17)** ☎ +689 689950821 – **18)** Catholic Mission, Papeete – **19)** BP 60076 Faa'a-Centre, Papeete ☎ +689 689854747 ☎ +689 689412155 **W:** www.taui-fm.com **E:** tauifm@mail.pf – **20)** Association Jeunesse et Developpement de Hao [reported inactive] – **21)** Makemo, iles Tuamotu-Gambier – **22)** Association Pacifique Sound, Punaauia, Tahiti – **23)** Manihi, iles Tuamotu-Gambier – **24)** Servitude Graffe, Taumoa, Dir: Mme Roti Make ☎ +689 689419125 – **25)** Cultural Association Iva Manu-Manu Arii, Avatoru, Rangiroa, Tuamotu-Gambier [reported silent] – **26)** BP 338,Taiohae, Nuku Hiva 98742 ☎ +689 689920790 ☎ +689 689920729 **W:** www.facebook.com/pages/radio-marquises **E:** radiomarquises@ mail.pf – **27)** "Le Rythme de la Presque'ile", Vairao-Taiarapu, Tahiti ☎ +689 689575208 **L.P:** Denis Tariou – **30)** SARL Tahiti CD-Tahiti Pub, Papeete, Tahiti [inactive] – **31)** College de Taiohae, Taiohae, Nuku Hiva 98742 **E:** direction@clgtaio.ensec.edu.pf – **32)** Mairie de Papara, pk 34,800, Papara 98712, Tahiti ☎ +689 689279574

FRENCH SOUTHERN & ANTARCTIC LANDS

L.T: UTC+5h — **Pop:** 150 (wi), 310 (su) — **Pr.L:** French — **E.C:** 50Hz, 220V — **ITU:** none (**WRTH:** FSA); Isles Kerguelen: ITU: KER

FM	MHz	Station	FM	MHz	Station
1)	98.0	Radio Ker	3)	100.0	RTL
2)	100.0	France Inter			

Addresses & other information:
1) Port-aux-Francais, District de Kerguelen, Terres Australes & Antarctiques Francaises [via Reunion, Indian Ocean]. 24h community

station. – **2)** 24h satellite relay from Paris, Mon-Fri. – **3)** 24h satellite relay from Paris, weekends

GABON

L.T: UTC +1h — **Pop:** 1.5 million — **Pr.L:** French, Fang, Bopounou, Obamba, Djebi — **E.C:** 50Hz, 220V — **ITU:** GAB

CONCEIL NATIONAL DE LA COMMUNICATION(CNC)
✉ B.P. 6437, Libreville ☎+241 762796 **L.P:** Pres: Pierre-Marie Dong

RADIODIFFUSION-TÉLÉVISION GABONAISE(RTG,Gov.)
✉ B.P. 10150, Libreville ☎+241 732459 ☎ +241 739775
L.P: DG RTG-1: Willy Kombény. DG RTG-2: Jules Legnongo. Asst. DGs: Radio: Gilles Terence Nzoghe. Tech: Claude Nganga. Provincial Stns: Robert Aloli.

MW	kHz	kW	N	Times
Oyem	549	20	2	0430-0630, 1030-1430, 1600-2230

SW relays via Moyabi on 4777/7270kHz not heard recently., irr.
FM(MHz): Libreville 87.7/96.54 (**1**), 92.5 (2), Franceville 87.86 (**2**), Makokou 100.5 (**2**), Oyem 87.94 (**2**), Pt. Gentil 88.03 (**2**), Tchibanga 91.04 (2).
1 = **RTG Chaîne 1** in French **2** = **RTG Chaîne 2** (provincial netw.) in French & cthnic languages. **Pr.L:** 0500-2305 on FM only.
Ann: 1: "Ici Libreville, vouz écoutez Radio Gabon, chaîne 1".
IS: Indigenous instruments. Opens and closes with National Anthem.

AFRICA No. 1 (Comm.)
✉ B.P. 1, Libreville ☎+241 760001 ☎+241 742133 ✉ **in France:** 33 Rue du Faubourg Saint Antoine, F-75011 Paris +33 1 55075801 ☎ +33 1 55079748 **W:** www.africa1.com **L.P:** MD: Bachir Aboubakeur.
FM: Libreville 94.5MHz + rel. in other countries.
Africa Plus Gabon 99.5MHz. **SW:** see International section.

Other stations:
R. Émergence, B.P. 06, Libreville: 91.6MHz 30W **W:** f-i-a.org/emergence – **R. Génération Nouvelle**, B.P. 727, Libreville: 97.4MHz – **R. Mandarine**, B.P. 511, Libreville: 106.6MHz – **R. Nostalgie**, B.P. 13050, Libreville: 93.0MHz – **R. Notre-Dame de Sainte-Marie**, B.P 20348, Libreville: 99MHz – **R. Soleil FM**, B.P. 5420, Libreville: 107.7MHz – **Top FM**, B.P. 6554, Libreville: 105.5MHz (also rel. VOA) – **R. Unité**, B.P. 2676, Libreville: 100.5MHz.
RFI Afrique in Franceville, Libreville & Port-Gentil on 104MHz

GALAPAGOS ISLANDS (Ecuador)

L.T: UTC -6h — **Pop:** 19,000 — **Pr.L:** Spanish — **E.C:** 60Hz 110/220V — **ITU:** EQA (**WRTH:** GAL)

LA VOZ DE GALAPAGOS (Rlg)
Prefectura Apostólica de Galápagos, Puerto Baquerizo Moreno ☎ +593 5 459435
MW: La Voz de Galápagos 530kHz 5kW (inactive)
FM: Galápagos Stereo 97.1MHz **V.** by QSL card
FM in Pto Baquerizo Moreno (MHz): 91.1 R. Pública/Nacional del Ecuador – 94.7 R. Mar – 97.1 LV de Galápagos FM – 100.7 R. María – 101.9 Encantada FM – 104.3 Telegalápagos FM
FM in Pto Ayora (MHz): 88.7 R. Santa Cruz – 89.9 Caravana AM – 93.5 Pacífica 94 – 94.7 R. Mar – 95.9 Antena 9 FM – 98.3 Stereo Zaracay – 101.9 Encantada FM

GAMBIA

L.T: UTC — **Pop:** 1.8 million — **Pr.L:** English, Mandinka, Fula, Wolof, Jola, Serahuleh, Manjago, Aku — **E.C:** 50Hz, 230V — **ITU:** GMB

MINISTRY OF COMMUNICATIONS, INFORMATION & INFORMATION TECHNOLOGY (MOCIIT)
✉ New GRTS Building, MDI Road, Kanifing +220 4378000 ☎ +220 4378029 **W:** doscit.gm **E:** doscit@gamtel.gm
L.P: Perm. Sec.: S.S. Jallou

GAMBIA RADIO AND TELEVISION SERVICE (GRTS)
✉ Mile 7 Studios, P.O. Box 387, Banjul ☎+220 4495101/4497419 ☎ +220 4495102 **W:** grts.gm
L.P: DG: Mr. Modou Sanyang. Deputy DG: Mr. Alhaji Modou Joof.
MW: Bonto 648kHz 50kW (inactive), Basse 747kHz 10kW.
FM: Serrekunda 96.0MHz, Banjul 98.6MHz, Bonto 102.6MHz.
D.Prgr: in E/local langs: 0600-2400. N. in E: 0700, 1300, 1800, 2200.
Ann: "GRTS Radio". **IS:** Cora (harp).

Other stations (all MHz):
City Limits R., Serrekunda: 93.6 0.25kW – **Hill Top R.,** Serrekunda: 104.7 100kW – **Paradise FM,** Farafenni/Serrekunda: 105.5 1kW. **W:** paradisefm.gm – **R. KWT** (Kids With Talent), Banjul: 107.6 – **Unique FM,** Banjul/Basse: 101.7 **W:** uniquefm.gm – **West Coast R.,** Serrekunda: 92.1. **W:** westcoast.gm . Also rel. BBC.
RFI Afrique: Banjul 89.0MHz

GEORGIA

L.T: UTC +4h — **Pop:** 4.5 million — **Pr.L:** Georgian, Abkhaz, Ossetic — **E.C:** 50Hz, 220V — **ITU:** GEO

GEORGIAN NATIONAL COMMUNICATIONS COMMISSION (GNCC)
Ave. Ketevan Tsamebuli/Bochorma St. 50/18, Tbilisi 0144 ☎ +995 32 22921667 ▤ +995 32 22921625 **E:** post@gncc.ge **W:** www.gncc.ge
L.P: Chmn: Irakli Chikovani
NB: GNCC is the regulatory authority for broadcasting.

SAKARTVELOS SAZOGADOEBRIVI MAUTS'Q'EBELI
(Georgian Public Broadcaster)
M.Kostava St. 68, Tbilisi 0171 ☎ +995 32 22409477 ▤ +995 32 22409477 **E:** info@gpb.ge **W:** www.gpb.ge
L.P: Chmn: Levan Gakheladze

FM (MHz)	R.1	R.2	kW		R.1	R.2	kW
Akhaltsikhe	102.4	-	1	Lentekhi	102.4	-	0.2
Ambrolauri	102.9	-	0.25	Mestia	102.4	-	0.2
Batumi	102.4	-	1	Sachhkere	102.4	-	0.2
Chiatura	102.4	-	0.25	Tbilisi	102.4	100.9	2
Gori	100.6	-	0.5	Telavi	100.6	-	0.05
Kutaisi	100.3	-	2	Zugdidi	101.3	-	1

D.Prgr: Radio 1: 24h. – **Radio 2:** 0400-2200.

OTHER STATIONS

FM	MHz	kW	Location	Station
14)	93.9	1	Tbilisi	5 Lines
15)	94.4	1	Tbilisi	R. GIPA
22)	94.7	1	Tbilisi	R. Natsnobi
23)	95.1	1	Tbilisi	Avtoradio
3)	95.5	1	Tbilisi	R. Komersant
6)	95.9	1	Tbilisi	R. Muza
17)	96.3	5	Tbilisi	R. Jako
5C)	96.7	1	Tbilisi	R. Ar Daidardo
18)	97.1	1	Tbilisi	R. Akhali talga
10)	98.0	1	Tbilisi	R. Utsnobi
21)	98.8	1	Gori	Abhkazesis khma
21)	98.8	1	Qutaisi	Abhkazesis khma
21)	98.9	1	Tbilisi	Abhkazesis khma
25)	99.3	1	Tbilisi	Folk FM
5D)	99.7	1	Tbilisi	Guru FM
9)	100.0	1	Gori	R. Imedi
9)	100.1	1	Batumi	R. Imedi
7)	100.3	1	Tbilisi	Beat FM
9)	100.9	5	Qutaisi	R. Imedi
2)	101.4	5	Tbilisi	R. Monte-Karlo
12)	101.5	1	Gori	R. Mtsvane talga
19)	101.9	1	Tbilisi	R. Kalaki
5C)	102.7	2.5	Qutaisi	R. Ar Daidardo
5B)	103.4	1	Tbilisi	R. Fortuna+
5B)	103.4	5	Gori	R. Fortuna+
5B)	103.4	5	Batumi	R. Fortuna+
5B)	103.4	1	Qutaisi	R. Fortuna+
12)	103.6	1	Zugdidi	R. Mtsvane talga
24)	103.9	1	Tbilisi	R. Palitra
9)	104.2	1	Zugdidi	R. Imedi
4)	104.3	1	Tbilisi	R. Sindikat
6)	104.6	2	Zugdidi	R. Muza
16)	104.8	1	Gori	R. Trialeti
20)	105.0	1	Qutaisi	White FM
8)	105.0	1	Tbilisi	R. 105
1)	105.4	5	Batumi	R. Iveria
1)	105.4	1	Qutaisi	R. Iveria
1)	105.4	1	Tbilisi	R. Iveria
9)	105.9	1	Tbilisi	R. Imedi
11)	106.4	10	Tbilisi	Pirveli R.
11)	106.4	1	Gori	Pirveli R.
5A)	106.9	1	Tbilisi	R. Fortuna
5A)	106.9	1	Gori	R. Fortuna
5A)	106.9	1	Batumi	R. Fortuna
21)	107.2	1	Zugdidi	Abhkazesis khma

FM	MHz	kW	Location	Station
12)	107.4	10	Tbilisi	R. Mtsvane talga
12)	107.5	2	Qutaisi	R. Mtsvane talga
13)	107.9	1	Tbilisi	R. Saqartvelos khma

NB: Txs below 1kW not listed.

Addresses & other information:
1) Erekle II square 1, Tbilisi 0105. **E:** iveria105.4@yahoo.com – **2)** M.Kostava St. 14, Tbilisi 0169. In Russian. – **3)** Nadiradze St. 8, Tbilisi 0102. **E:** info@commersant.ge – **4)** Ateni St. 18a, Tbilisi 0179. **E:** syndicate@radiosyndicate.ge. In Georgian & English. – **5A,B,C,D)** Marshal Gelovani St. 2, Tbilisi 0179. **E:** 5A,B) thc@radio.fm; 5C) tamara@fortuna.ge – **6)** Zandukeli St. 12, Tbilisi 0108. **E:** info@radiomuza.ge In Georgian & English. – **7)** Tsinamdzgvrishvili 95, Tbilisi 0102. **E:** info@beatfm.ge – **8)** Agladze St. 31, Tbilisi 0119. **E:** n1001@geo.net.ge – **9)** Lubliana St. 5, Tbilisi 0159. **E:** info@radio-imedi.ge – **10)** M.Kostava St. 68, Tbilisi 0171. **E:** radio@ucnobifm.ge – **11)** Aleksidze St. 1, Tbilisi 0193. **E:** 106.4@radioone.ge – **12)** Vazha-Pshavela Ave. 45, Tbilisi 0177. **E:** gwave@greenwave.ge – **13)** Tashkenti St. 51, Tbilisi 0160. – **14)** Amaghleba St. 11, Tbilisi 0105. **E:** 5lines@5linesradio.ge – **15)** Marie Brosset St. 2, Tbilisi 0108. – **16)** Chavchavadze St. 45, Gori 1400. **E:** contact@trialeti.ge – **17)** Tbilisi. – **18)** Tbilisi. – **19)** M.Kostava St. 68, Tbilisi 0171. **E:** info@radiokalaki.ge – **20)** Tamar Mepe Ave. 56, Qutaisi 4600. – **21)** Vazha-Pshavela Ave. 76b, Tbilisi 0186. **E:** info@amc.ge – **22)** M.Kostava St. 68, Tbilisi 0171 – **23)** Tbilisi. – **24)** M.Kostava St. 77, Tbilisi 0161. **E:** info@radiopalitra.ge – **25)** Tbilisi.

ABKHAZIA

APSNYTWI AXWYNTKARRATW TELERADIOEILAXWYRA (Abkhaz State Radio & TV Co.)
Lasuria St. 16, Sokhumi ☎ +7 840 2264867 ▤ +7 840 2266144 **W:** www.apsua.tv
L.P: Dir: Zurab Argun

MW	kHz	kW			
Sokhumi	1350	30			

SW	kHz	kW	SW	kHz	kW
Sokhumi	9495v	5	Sokhumi	9535v	5

FM: Sokhumi 68.80MHz
D.Prgr: Apsua R. with own prgrs in Abkhaz, Russian: 0200-0500, 0700-0830, 1100-1130, 1400-1430, 1700-1730 on FM. Outside of own prgrs, various other stns may be relayed: R. Rossii from Russia (incl. reg. prgrs of GTRK "Kuban", Krasnodar & GTRK "Sochi", Sochi), or commercial stns. On MW/SW: limited schedule, changing frequently.

OTHER STATIONS

FM	MHz	kW	Location	Station
1)	91.2	-	Ochamchire	R. Soma
A)	100.7	-	Ochamchire	Golos Rossii relay
3)	101.1	-	Sukhumi	R. Xara Xradno
3)	101.7	-	Gagra	R. Xara Xradno
4)	101.9	-	Sukhumi	R. Rio Rita
A)	104.4	-	Sukhumi	Golos Rossii relay
7)	104.8	-	Gagra	Pervoye R.
5)	105.1	-	Sukhumi	Serebryanyy dozhd
6)	105.6	-	Sukhumi	R. Shanson
1)	106.1	-	Tkvarcheli	R. Soma
2)	107.1	-	Gagra	Avtoradio
1)	107.9	1.5	Sokhumi	R. Soma

Addresses & other information:
1) Zvanba St. 9, Sokhumi. **E:** info@radiosoma.com Incl. rel. Golos Rossii (Russia) – **2)** Sokhumi. Rel. Avtoradio (Russia) – **3)** Sokhumi. – **4)** Sokhumi. Rel. Serebryanyy dozhd (Russia) – **5)** Sokhumi. Rel. R. Shanson (Russia) – **7)** Sokhumi. – **A)** Rel. Golos Rossii (Russia).

SOUTH OSSETIA

PTRK "IR" (State Radio & TV Co. "Ir")
Geroev St. 48, Tskhinvali ☎ +7 9974 451218 **E:** radio-ir@yandex.ru
L.P: Dir: Robert Kulumbegov
FM: Tskhinvali 102.3MHz.
D.Prgr: Ir FM in Russian, Ossetic: 24h.

OTHER STATIONS

FM	MHz	kW	Location	Station
3)	104.1	-	Tskhinvali	R. City
A)	104.5	-	Kvaysa	Vesti FM relay
1)	105.9	-	Tskhinvali	Volna FM
B)	106.3	-	Tskhinvali	R. Mayak relay
2)	107.3	-	Tskhinvali	R. Yuzhnyy gorod

Addresses & other information:
1) Tskhinvali. – **2)** Tskhinvali. **E:** info@yugfm.ru – **2)** Tskhinvali. Incl. rel. Golos Rossii (Russia) – **A)** Rel. Vesti FM (Russia) – **B)** Rel. R. Mayak (Russia)

GERMANY

L.T: UTC +1h (31 Mar-27 Oct: UTC +2h) — **Pop:** 82 million— **Pr.L:** German — **E.C:** 50Hz, 230V — **ITU:** D

BUNDESNETZAGENTUR
Authority responsible for frequency allocation matters.
✉ Postfach 8001, 53105 Bonn (office location: Tulpenfeld 4) ☎ +49 (228) 14 0 🖷 + 49 228 14 8872 **W:** bnetza.de

NB: Due to the complexity of the broadcasting system in Germany, AM-transmitters (public service, commercial and military) are listed in a combined frequency table below. FM stations and other info can be found under the respective public radio station (section I), federal state (section II) or military station (section III).

LW/MW

Stn	kHz	kW	Site	Prgr
A)	153	500/250°	Donebach (Mudau)	DLF (1)
A)	177	500	Zehlendorf (Oranienbg.)	DK (1)
U)	183	2000°	Felsberg (Saarlouis)	Europe 1 (2)
A)	207	500/250°	Aholming (Deggendorf)	DLF (1)
A)	549	100	Nordkirchen	DLF (1)
A)	549	100	Thurnau-Tannfeld	DLF (1)
M)	603	20	Zehlendorf (Oranienbg.)	(F.Pl.) (3)
R)	630	100/16	Scheppau (Braunschw.)	Voice of Russia (4)
M)	693	250	Zehlendorf (Oranienbg.)	Voice of Russia (4)
E)	702	5	Flensburg	NDR Info Spezial
J)	720	85	Langenberg	WDR Event
B)	729	0.2	Hof	Bayern Plus
B)	729	1	Würzburg	Bayern Plus
J)	774	5	Bonn	WDR Event
A)	756	200/200°	Scheppau (Braunschw.)	DLF (1)
A)	756	100	Ravensburg	DLF (1)
D)	783	100	Wiederau (Leipzig)	MDR Info (5)
E)	792	5	Lingen	NDR Info Spezial
B)	801	100	Ismaning (München)	Bayern Plus
B)	801	10	Dillberg (Nürnberg)	Bayern Plus
E)	828	20/5	Hemmingen (Hannover)	NDR Info Spezial
	873	150°	Weißkirchen (Oberursel)	AFN Power Netw.
E)	972	100	Hamburg-Billwerder	NDR Info Spezial
A)	990	100	Berlin-Britz	DK (1)
D)	1044	20	Wilsdruff (Dresden)	MDR Info (5)
	1107	10	Kaiserslautern	AFN Power Netw.
	1107	10	Vilseck	AFN Power Netw.
	1143	10	Stuttgart-Hirschlanden	AFN Power Netw.
	1143	1	Mönchengladbach	AFN Benelux
	1143	1	Spangdahlem/Bitburg	AFN Power Netw.
	1143	1	Heidelberg	AFN Power Netw.
	1143	0.3	Bamberg	AFN Bavaria
	1143	0.01	Schweinfurt	AFN Bavaria
H)	1179	10	Heusweiler	SR Antenne Saar
D)	1188	3	Reichenbach (Görlitz)	MDR Info (5)
A)	1269	300°	Arpsdorf (Neumünster)	DLF (1)
X)	1323	1000°/150°	Wachenbrunn (Themar)	Voice of Russia (4)
A)	1422	400	Heusweiler	DLF (1)
V)	1431	250/150	Wilsdruff (Dresden)	Voice of Russia (4)
	1485	0.3	Ansbach	AFN Power Netw.
	1485	0.3	Hohenfels	AFN Bavaria
	1485	0.3	Garmisch-Partenkirchen	AFN Power Netw.
	1593	max. 10	Kall-Krekel (Euskirchen)	(tests) (6)

Powers day/night (usually 0500-1800/1800-0500). ° = directional.
N.B Remaining SW txs in Germany see Int. Broadcasting section.
Stn: Public stations **A-J** see section I. – Commercial and other stations see section II, chapters **M-X**, Voice of Russia schedules and contact details see under Russia in International Broadcasting Section – **AFN** see section III. Txs on air 24h unless otherwise stated.
Notes: 1) 153/177/990 kHz also Dokumente&Debatten. 855/6190 kHz txs closed in 2012, Berlin-Britz site slated for complete closure. At a later point 1422kHz operated by Saarländischer Rundfunk. Other txs operated by Media Broadcast, contracts in place until 2016 – **2)** 0300-2400. Operating on aux antenna after main antenna failed in 2012 – **3)** Provided for China Radio International, allocation procedures under way at time of editing – **4)** 0500-2300. 1323kHz: Beam 310° 0300-1600, 220° 1600-2400. Txs operated by Media Broadcast – **5)** 1044kHz also Dresden parliament coverage. Txs operated by Media Broadcast – **6)** Engineering tests by Radio 700, see International Broadcasting section. Langenberg tx on 1593kHz closed down.

I. PUBLIC STATIONS

A) DEUTSCHLANDRADIO
Operates on behalf of all German states for nationwide coverage.

Cologne seat: ✉ Raderberggürtel 40, 50968 Köln ☎ +49 221 345 0 🖷 +49 221 345 4803
Berlin seat: ✉ Hans-Rosenthal-Platz, 10825 Berlin ☎ +49 30 8503 0 🖷 +49 30 8503 6168 **W:** dradio.de

FM (MHz)	DLF	DK	kW	FM (MHz)	DLF	DK	kW
Baden-Württemberg				Bad Camberg	99.8	-	0.2
Baden-Baden	-	107.9	0.1	Bad Hersfeld	102.9	-	0.3
Biberach	100.5	-	0.5	Darmstadt	102.0	98.2	0.3
Blauen	105.1	-	10	Eschwege	100.6	-	0.5
Esslingen	96.7	-	0.1	Frankfurt/M.	97.6	91.2	0.3
Freiburg	(F.Pl.)	90.6	0.2	Friedberg	89.9	-	0.3
Geislingen	-	87.7	0.2	Fritzlar	-	96.0	0.1
Göppingen	99.8	-	0.1	Fulda	-	90.7	0.3
Heidelberg	106.5	(F.Pl.)	0.4	Gelnhausen	93.9	-	0.2
Heidenheim	94.0	100.8	0.1	Gießen	103.1	107.5	0.6/0.3
Heilbronn	91.3	93.3	0.1	Hanau	92.4	107.7	0.3
Hornisgrinde	106.3	-	80	Heusenstamm	-	99.8	0.2
Kirchheim	91.3	-	0.1	Hofgeismar	106.9	-	0.3
Konstanz	-	94.5	0.2	Kassel	92.7	-	0.1
Lörrach	-	95.0	0.1	Korbach	92.8	-	0.1
Ludwigsburg	94.1	97.3	0.5/0.1	Limburg	103.3	105.1	0.3
Pforzheim	89.2	95.2	0.1/0.5	Mainz-Kastel	-	107.2	0.4
Rottweil	106.0	-	0.1	Marburg	103.5	93.3	0.5/0.1
Schwäb. Hall	95.8	-	0.1	Michelstadt	100.5	107.2	0.2
Schw. Gmünd	-	95.9	0.2	Oberursel	103.5	101.8	0.1
Stuttgart	96.0	87.9	0.5/1	Rimberg	91.3	-	50
Tübingen	93.9	99.4	0.5/1	Wetzlar	103.7	97.3	0.5/0.3
Ulm	103.5	91.5	0.5/1	Wiesbaden	103.7	-	0.5
Witthoh	100.6	-	40	**Mecklenburg-Vorpommern**			
Wörth	-	96.6	0.2	Anklam	107.4	-	1
Bayern				Barth	100.3	-	0.1
Amberg	-	107.9	0.1	Dargun	89.8	-	0.5
Ansbach	92.7	102.7	0.2	Greifswald	104.3	106.8	0.2
Aschaffenbg.	-	94.8	0.1	Güstrow	106.0	-	0.8
Augsburg	97.8	100.0	0.3/15	Helpterberg	96.5	97.1	10/30
B. Reichenhall	-	92.6	0.1	Heringsdorf	98.4	107.1	0.5
Bad Tölz	87.8	93.2	0.1	Marlow	-	96.7	30
Berchtesgd.	91.6	103.4	0.1	Neukloster	90.6	-	0.3
Brotjacklrieg.	100.1	-	100	Neustrelitz	97.9	-	1
Burgbernhm.	106.3	94.3	0.2/0.3	Ribn.-Damg.	102.1	-	0.2
Burglengenf.	-	107.3	0.1	Röbel	102.4	90.0	3
Cham	-	101.4	0.1	Rostock	106.5	-	1
Freilassing	100.3	-	15	Sassnitz	104.0	101.4	8
Füssen	87.6	103.4	0.1	Schwerin	106.3	95.3	2/100
Hof Waldst.	-	89.3	20	Stralsund	89.3	-	0.3
Hohe Linie	-	101.3	0.2	Waren/Mü.	91.3	-	0.2
Hohenpeißbg.	94.7	-	0.1	**Niedersachsen**			
Ingolstadt	107.0	88.6	0.5	Aurich	101.8	106.9	100/1
Kaufbeuren	-	107.3	0.1	Cloppenbg.	-	95.5	0.1
Kempten	89.3	89.8	0.1	Cuxhaven	101.6	107.7	2/20
Landsberg	90.3	107.9	0.1	Damme	95.4	97.5	0.3
Landshut	95.9	100.5	0.2	Emden	-	93.4	1
Mittenwald	91.9	105.2	0.1	Göttingen	101.0	-	0.1
München	101.7	96.8	0.3	Hannover	94.0	-	0.1
Nürnberg	90.1	105.6	0.1	Hann. Münd.	98.5	-	0.5
Oberstdorf	92.0	96.5	0.1	Höhbeck	102.2	-	100
Ochsenkopf	100.3	-	100	Jever	-	89.0	0.5
Passau	-	97.7	0.5	Leer	-	91.5	0.5
Pfronten	96.5	-	0.02	Lingen	102.0	-	25
Regensburg	95.5	101.3	0.2		-	91.6*	0.4
Rhön	103.3	-	100		-	102.9*	0.3
Rosenheim	92.7	96.2	0.1	Lübbecke	-	97.7	0.2
Rosenh.-D'bg.	97.7	-	0.1	Meppen	-	100.7	0.3
Starnberg	87.9	94.7	0.1	Norden	-	105.3	0.3
Straubing	-	88.7	0.4	Nordhorn	-	97.1	0.2
Traunstein	-	88.3	0.1	Oldenburg	-	102.8	1
Weiden	-	103.7	0.1	Osnabrück	101.8	-	0.5
Weilheim	94.7	-	0.05	Seesen	88.0	-	0.1
Würzburg	100.3	101.3	0.1	Soltau	89.3	-	0.1
Berlin & Brandenburg				Stadthagen	106.1	-	1
Berlin A'platz	97.7	-	100	Tecklenburg	-	101.1	0.5
Berlin-Britz	-	89.6	100	Torfh./Harz	103.5	-	100
Calau	-	90.8	20	Uelzen	107.5	-	0.5
Casekow	105.2	-	6	Visselhövede	-	88.8	1
Cottbus	88.6	-	3	Warendorf	107.2	-	1
Eisenhütt.st.	102.2	-	1	**Nordrhein-Westfalen**			
Frankfurt (Bo.)	97.3	92.7	0.5/5	Aachen	102.7	-	0.5
Herzberg/Els.	94.5	-	0.3	B. Oeynhsn.	93.9	-	0.1
Rhinow	-	103.7	0.2	Beckum	91.5	-	0.2
Bremen				Bielefeld	95.5	106.2	0.1
Bremen	107.1	100.3	100/1	Bonn	89.1	98.9	5/0.1
Bremerhaven	103.4	106.2	0.5/5	Eifel-Bärbelk.	-	106.1	20
Hamburg				Gronau	-	94.6	0.2
Hamburg	88.7	89.1	3/0.1	Kleve	-	90.1	1
Hessen				Köln	91.3	-	0.1
Alsfeld	104.0	-	0.1	Langenberg	-	96.5	35

FM (MHz)	DLF	DK	kW
Lemgo	92.2	88.9	0.3
Lennestadt	-	96.9	0.1
Lübbecke	-	97.7	0.2
Münster	104.5	97.5	0.3/0.1
Nordhelle	102.7	-	20
Olpe	-	96.3	0.1
Olsberg	-	106.1	10
Paderborn	94.5	-	0.2
Schwerte	104.4	-	0.2
Siegen	94.2	100.2	0.1
Stadthagen	106.1	-	1
Steinfurt	-	91.0	0.2
Tecklenburg	-	101.1	0.5
Warendorf	107.2	-	1
Warburg	106.6	-	0.2
Wesel	102.8	-	50
Wuppertal	91.0	-	0.3
Rheinland-Pfalz			
B. Kreuznach	106.5	-	0.1
Bingen	-	106.3	0.2
Bitburg	-	95.3	0.1
Boppard	90.5	88.9	0.1
Idar-Oberst.	89.5	94.7	0.2
Kaiserslaut.	105.1	98.1	0.2
Koblenz	99.8	105.3	0.5
Limburg	103.3	105.1	0.3
Linz	-	98.3	0.1
Lorch	88.1	-	0.1
Ludwigshafen	-	97.3	0.1
Mayen	100.8	-	0.2
Pirmasens	106.1	94.4	0.4
Prüm	95.4	-	0.1
Saarburg	104.6	105.3	20/0.1
Traben-Trarb.	88.7	106.2	0.3
Trier	-	94.3	0.2
Wörth	-	96.6	0.2
Saarland			
Lebach	-	107.9	0.1
Neunkirchen	-	105.0	5
Oberperl	-	106.2	5
Saarbrücken	90.1	107.5	1/0.4
Saarlouis	-	96.3	0.1
Völklingen	-	88.6	0.1
Sachsen			
Bad Düben	-	99.4	0.2
Bärenstein	-	104.3	1
Belgern	-	101.1	1
Chemnitz	-	106.3	0.5
Collmberg	-	96.1	0.3
Döbeln	-	101.3	1
Dresden	97.3	93.2	100/1
Eilenburg	-	92.0	0.2
Freiberg	-	101.3	1

FM (MHz)	DLF	DK	kW
Geyer (Erzg.)	97.0	-	100
Grimma	-	91.6	0.1
Hoyerswerda	-	89.7	0.5
Leipzig-Holzh.	-	100.4	2
Löbau	99.5	103.0	5/2
Pulsnitz	-	106.7	0.5
Schöneck	94.5	-	3
Weißwasser	-	97.7	2
Wiederau	96.6	-	100
Zwickau	-	104.6	0.2
Sachsen-Anhalt			
Brocken/Harz	-	97.4	100
Dessau	107.1	-	0.3
Dequede	-	96.9	7
Eisleben	103.8	-	0.5
Schönebeck	102.0	-	20
Wittenberg	89.3	107.7	1/0.5
Zeitz	-	91.8	0.5
Schleswig-Holstein			
Bungsberg	101.9	103.1	95/0.2
Flensburg	103.3	92.1	20/0.2
Garding	102.3	101.7	0.5
Güby	-	105.0	0.2
Heide	104.4	92.2	1/0.1
Helgoland	107.4	103.0	0.1
Husum	-	101.0	0.1
Itzehoe	102.2	97.5	0.4/0.1
Kaltenkirchen	-	105.5	0.1
Kiel	-	104.7	0.3
Lauenburg	-	95.8	0.1
Neumünster	-	107.8	0.5
Niebüll	-	104.2	0.3
Rendsburg	-	95.2	0.3
Schleswig	-	105.0	0.2
Sylt	90.3	103.9	0.2
Thüringen			
Altenburg	-	97.3	0.4
Bleßberg	-	94.2	100
Eisenach	106.5	-	0.5
Erfurt	103.1	-	2
Gera	94.3	93.6	0.3
Gotha	94.0	-	0.1
Ilmenau	99.9	-	0.1
Inselsberg	-	97.2	100
Jena	104.5	98.2	0.3
Mühlhausen	107.0	-	1
Nordhausen	96.4	-	0.1
Pößneck	89.2	-	0.1
Saalfeld	98.7	-	0.1
Sondershaus.	101.9	-	0.1
Suhl	98.8	-	0.1
Weimar	89.7	-	0.5

*) Directional with different beams
DAB: See section II.
Satellite: Astra 2C, 11.954GHz h.
Deutschlandfunk: From Köln studios, emphasis on current affairs.
Deutschlandradio Kultur: From Berlin studios, emphasis on culture.
DRadio Wissen: From Köln studios, for young audiences, via digital distribution platforms only.
Dokumente&Debatten: Parliament coverage, audio of TV talkshows and other special prgrs. Sea weather forecasts and nautical warnings: 0005, 0540, 1005, 2005 on 177/1269kHz.

ARBEITSGEMEINSCHAFT DER ÖFFENTLICH-RECHTLICHEN RUNDFUNKANSTALTEN DEUTSCHLANDS (ARD)

Umbrella organization of the public broadcasting institutions

Arnulfstraße 42, 80335 München ☎ +49 89 5900 3344 **W:** ard.de
Overnight programming: ARD-Hitnacht (oldies), produced by SR 3; ARD-Popnacht (AC), produced by SWR 3; ARD-Nachtkonzert (classical), produced by BR Klassik; ARD-Infonacht (news, with local opt-outs), produced by MDR Info.
Satellite: Astra 1M, 12.266 GHz; carrying almost all ARD radio stns.
DAB: See section II.

B) BAYERISCHER RUNDFUNK (BR)

Public broadcasting institution of Bavaria.

Bayerischer Rundfunk, 80300 München (headquarters: Rundfunkplatz 1) ☎ +49 89 5900 01 ▤ +49 89 5900 2375 **W:** br-online.de

FM (MHz)	B1	B2	B3	BR K	B5	kW
Augsburg	–	–	–	–	105.3	0.5
Bad Reichenhall	91.8	89.9	96.7	98.3	105.0	0.3

FM (MHz)	B1	B2	B3	BR K	B5	kW
Bamberg	94.8N	98.6	99.8	102.9	97.4	25/5
Berchtesgaden	90.4	99.6	96.9	94.2	106.4	0.3/0.1
Brotjacklriegel	92.1R	96.5	94.4	100.9	106.9	100/50
Büttelberg	91.4N	88.2	99.3	95.5	104.0	25/10
Coburg	93.5N	88.3	99.2	97.7	92.8	5/0.3
Dillberg	88.9N	92.3	97.9	87.6	102.0	25
	104.5R					5
Eichstätt	101.6	90.5	97.6	89.0	106.1	25/10
Garmisch-Partenk.	89.2	93.5	97.7	95.9	104.9	0.1
Grünten (Allgäu)	90.7U	88.7	95.8	101.0	106.9	50/100
Herzogstand	88.1	97.0	91.0	–	106.7	0.1
Hochberg-Traunst.	98.0	91.5	95.9	97.0	107.1	5/0.5
Hohenpeißenberg	92.8	94.2	99.2	100.4	–	25
Hoher Bogen	96.8R	91.6	94.7	88.3	104.4	50/5
Hühnerberg	91.9U	96.1	99.5	93.1	107.6	25/11
Kreuzberg (Rhön)	98.3W	93.1	96.3	107.9	105.3	100/50
Landshut	90.2R	97.8	95.3	93.2	106.6	0.1
Lindau	88.1U	92.0	94.0	87.6	100.4	0.5/0.1
München-Ismaning	91.3	88.4	97.3	103.2	90.0	25
Ochsenkopf	90.7N	96.0	99.4	102.3	107.1	100/50
	91.2R					20
Passau	87.7R	93.2	90.4	95.6	105.9	0.5/0.3
Pfaffenberg	95.6W	88.4	93.4	98.0	106.4	25/1
Regensburg	95.0R	93.0	99.6	97.0	105.0	25/5
Untersb. Geiereck*)	87.8	92.9	96.1	100.7	–	0.1
Wallberg	94.0	87.7	99.7	97.9	101.8	0.1
Wendelstein	93.7	89.5	98.5	102.3	105.7	100
Würzburg	90.9W	90.0	97.6	89.0	105.7	5/0.2

*) Site in Austria.

Bayern 1: Oldies, at night rel. ARD-Hitnacht, Mon-Fri 1105-1200 and 1805-1855 regional prgr. from Nürnberg (N), Regensburg (R), Würzburg (W) and Ulm (U) – **Bayern 2:** Various prgr., at night rel. ARD-Nachtkonzert – **Bayern 3:** AC, 24 hours – **BR Klassik:** Classical music, 24 hours – **B5 aktuell:** News, mono signal, at night rel. ARD-Infonacht – **Bayern Plus:** On 729/801kHz, satellite and DAB, German light and folk music, 24 hours – **on3radio:** On satellite and DAB, alternative youth format, 24 hours – **Bayern5plus:** On satellite and DAB, coverage of parliament, sports and other events – **Bayern2plus, BR Verkehr:** On DAB only.

C) HESSISCHER RUNDFUNK (HR)

Public broadcasting institution of Hessen.

✉ 60222 Frankfurt am Main (headquarter location: Bertramstraße 8)
☎ +49 69 155 1 ▤ +49 69 155 2900 **W:** hr-online.de

FM (MHz)	hr1	hr2	hr3	hr4	kW
Alsfeld-Homberg	–	–	105.6	–	0.1
Bad Hersfeld	88.9	–	102.9	–	0.3
Biedenkopf	91.0	99.6	87.6	104.3M	100
Bingen	–	–	91.1	–	0.3
Feldberg (Taunus)	94.4	96.7	89.3	102.5R	100
Frankfurt (HR headq.)	–	87.9	–	–	0.1
Fulda	–	106.6	88.5	103.9N	0.3
Habichtswald	–	–	101.2	103.2N	20
Hardberg (Odenw.)	90.6	95.3	92.7	101.6R	50
Heidelstein (Rhön)	104.8	–	106.2	107.3N	50
Hoher Meißner	99.0	95.5	89.5	101.7N	100
Kassel	94.3	93.7	–	–	0.5
Limburg	–	100.8	–	97.1M	0.3/0.2
Marburg	–	–	–	102.8M	1
Rimberg	–	95.0	–	91.9N	50/20
Rotenburg	–	–	105.7	–	0.3
Schlüchtern	–	–	88.9	–	0.3
Weilburg	–	–	–	97.9M	0.1
Wetzlar	–	–	–	90.5M	0.3
Wiesbaden	98.3	93.1	–	–	0.1
Würzburg (Odenw.)	88.1	97.4	89.7	103.8R	5

FM (MHz)	You FM	hr-info	kW
Alsfeld-Homberg	–	104.0	0.1
Bad Hersfeld	–	106.9	0.3
Badd Orb	–	89.8	0.3
Bensheim	90.2	91.2	0.2/0.1
Biedenkopf	–	102.3	10
Bingen	92.3	–	0.3
Darmstadt	104.3	107.0	0.8/5
Eltville	96.2	–	0.5
Eschwege	106.6	–	0.1
Frankfurt/Main	90.4	103.9	0.5
Friedberg	94.0	92.1	0.3
Fritzlar	–	106.6	0.1
Fulda	93.6	89.7	0.3/0.2
Gelnhausen	99.4	–	0.3
Gießen	97.9	99.2	0.5/0.3
Kassel-Wilhelmsh.	100.1	107.5	0.5/1
Korbach	–	102.6	0.1

FM (MHz)	You FM	hr-info	kW
Limburg	90.7	99.2	0.2/0.3
Marburg	93.9	98.5	1/0.3
Michelstadt	91.0	–	0.2
Reinhardshain	–	92.9	0.2
Rimberg	97.7	–	50
Rotenburg	–	96.8	0.3
Schlüchtern	88.2	91.5	0.3
Seeheim	–	88.2	0.1
Sontra	–	90.8	0.1
Wetzlar	105.5	–	0.3
Wiesbaden	99.7	97.2	0.2/0.1
Witzenhausen	91.1	–	0.3

hr1: Oldies, at night rel. ARD-Popnacht – **hr2**: Culture and classical music, at night rel. ARD-Nachtkonzert – **hr3**: AC, at night rel. ARD-Popnacht – **hr4**: Produced at Kassel (Wilhelmshöher Allee 347, 34131 Kassel), light music format, at night rel. ARD-Hitnacht, regional news Nordhessen (N; Kassel/Fulda), Mittelhessen (M; Gießen) and Rhein-Main (R; Frankfurt/Darmstadt) – **You FM**: CHR, 24 hours – **hr-info**: News, at night rel. ARD-Infonacht.

D) MITTELDEUTSCHER RUNDFUNK (MDR)

Public broadcasting institution of Sachsen, Sachsen-Anhalt and Thüringen.

✉ Kantstraße 71-73, 04360 Leipzig (TV and administration) **W:** mdr.de

✉ Gerberstraße 2, 06110 Halle/Saale ☎ +49 345 300 0 🖷 +49 345 300 5544. (radio, except MDR 1 stns, see below)

FM (MHz)	MDR 1	JumpFigaro	Info	Sputnik	kW
Txs in Sachsen:					
Altenburg	–	–	101.5	–	1
Annaberg-Buchholz	–	–	91.2	–	0.2
Aue	–	–	95.1	–	1
Auerbach	–	–	101.7	–	0.4
Bautzen	–	98.8	87.9	–	0.2/0.1
Chemnitz-Reichenh.	–	–	94.7	–	0.5
Collmberg	101.8L	103.7	98.9	105.9	2x5/0.5/30
Döbeln-Mockritz	–	–	99.6	–	0.1
Dresden-Wachwitz	92.2	90.1	95.4	106.1	3x100/0.5
Eilenburg	–	–	92.4	–	0.2
Freiberg	99.1C	–	93.7	–	1/0.2
Freital	–	–	95.9	–	0.2
Geyer (Erzgebirge)	92.8C	89.8	87.7	–	100
Grimma-Hohnstädt	–	–	100.6	–	0.2
Görlitz	–	–	106.9	–	1
Hoyerswerda	93.0B	89.0	94.7	94.2	1/0.5/1/1
	100.4				30
Klingenthal	93.7C	–	98.4	–	0.2
Leipzig city	–	–	95.6	–	0.5
Löbau	98.2B	91.8	96.2	–	5
Markneukirchen	104.8C	–	106.4	–	0.5
Meißen-Korbitz	–	–	94.9	–	1
Neustadt	–	–	89.6	–	0.2
Plauen	–	–	102.0	–	1
Raschau	–	–	91.6	–	0.2
Seifhennersdorf	94.5B	96.9	103.4	–	0.25/0.3
Schöneck	88.7C	101.2	98.7	–	3/30/3
Stollberg	–	–	89.3	–	0.1
Torgau	88.9L	–	93.0	–	0.5/0.2
Weißwasser	–	–	90.5	–	1
Wiederau (Leipzig)	93.9L	90.4	88.4	–	100
	106.5H				*30
Zittau	87.7B	107.1	95.4	106.4	0.2/0.5
Zschopau	–	–	99.5	–	0.2
Zwickau	–	–	91.4	–	1
Txs in Sachsen-Anhalt:					
Aschersleben	–	–	102.8	–	1
Brocken	94.6	91.5	107.8	–	60/100/10
Burg	–	–	89.6	–	1
Dequede	94.9St	98.9	89.4	–	10
Dessau-Mildensee	–	–	90.0	–	0.3
Fleetmark	–	–	90.1	105.0	2/1
Gernrode	–	–	91.0	–	0.1
Haidberg	–	–	100.7	–	5
Haldensleben	–	–	99.1	–	1
Halle Petersberg	100.8H	–	95.3	104.4	5/2/10
Halle city	–	89.6	107.3	–	0.1
Hergisdorf	92.9H	–	–	–	1
Jerichow	–	–	–	90.5	1
Jessen	–	–	87.6	–	1
Klötze	–	–	–	100.7	5
Köthen	–	–	106.4	–	0.3
Magdeburg	96.1	–	107.4	–	10/30
Naumburg	92.3H	–	–	93.1	1/0.5
Sangerhausen	101.1H	–	99.9	–	0.1/1
Schneidlingen	–	–	106.7	–	0.5

FM (MHz)	MDR 1	JumpFigaro	Info	Sputnik	kW
Schönebeck	–	–	91.1	105.2	2/1.5
Stendal-Borstel	–	–	87.8	104.8	1
Weißenfels	–	–	88.8	–	1
Wernigerode	–	–	98.6	–	1
Wittenberg	88.1D	101.6	104.0	–	30/2x55
Zeitz-Hainichen	–	–	–	89.4	0.5
Txs in Thüringen:					
Apolda	–	–	91.2	–	1
Arnstadt	–	–	106.1	–	0.5
Bad Salzungen	–	–	94.0	–	0.1
Bleßberg	91.7S	96.9	–	–	100/20
Eisenach	–	–	100.0	–	0.2
Erfurt	94.4	–	97.8	–	2/1
Gera	–	–	91.1	–	1
Gotha	–	–	88.8	–	0.5
Greiz	–	–	93.3	–	0.2
Heiligenstadt	93.6He	–	90.5	–	0.1
Ilmenau	–	–	93.0	–	0.1
Inselsberg	92.5	90.2	87.9	–	100/100/60
Jena-Oßmaritz	88.2G	101.9	96.4	89.5	1/0.2
Keula	98.5He	–	–	–	20
Lobenstein	95.5G	–	101.8	–	2/0.5
Magdala	92.9	–	99.2	–	0.01/0.05
Meiningen	–	–	94.7	–	0.2
Mühlhausen	–	–	105.8	–	0.1
Nordhausen	88.3He	–	93.7	–	0.1
Pößneck	–	–	101.6	–	0.2
Remda	103.6	105.6	100.7	–	60
Ronneburg	97.8G	100.9	103.9	–	10/30/30
Saalfeld	–	–	104.6	–	0.1
Schleiz	–	–	105.1	–	0.2
Schmalkalden	–	–	100.0	–	0.1
Schmölln	–	–	107.9	–	0.2
Sondershausen	100.1He	–	95.1	–	0.05/0.1
Sonneberg	–	–	105.8	–	0.1
Suhl Erleshügel	93.7S	91.1	89.8	97.5	– 1/0.1/0.2/5
Weimar Ettersberg	93.3	–	–	–	5
Weimar Belvedere	–	–	102.6	–	2

*) Directional, to north and west only

MDR 1 Radio Sachsen: Königsbrücker Str. 88, 01099 Dresden, regional prgr. from studios Bautzen (freq. marked B), Chemnitz (C) and Leipzig (L); **MDR Sachsen-Anhalt:** Stadtparkstr. 8, 39114 Magdeburg, regional prgr. Dessau (D), Halle (H) and Stendal (St); **MDR Thüringen:** Gothaer Str. 36, 99094 Erfurt; regional prgr. Gera (G), Heiligenstadt (He) and Suhl (S). 2200-0400 on all MDR 1 stn's common prgr. – **MDR Jump:** CHR, 24 hours – **MDR Figaro:** Culture, at night rel. ARD-Nachtkonzert – **MDR Info:** News, 24 hours, also on 783/1044/1188kHz – **MDR Sputnik:** CHR, 24 hours – **MDR Klassik:** On satellite and DAB only, classical music, at times rel. MDR Figaro – **Serbske Rozhlas:** MDR, Studio Bautzen, Am Postplatz 2, 02607 Bautzen. Prgr. in Upper Sorbian on 100.4MHz Mon-Fri 0405-0700, Sat 0505-0800, Sun 1000-1130. "Radio Satkula" for young listeners Mon 1900-2100. Also rel. Bramborske Serbske Radio, see G).

E) NORDDEUTSCHER RUNDFUNK (NDR)

Public broadcasting institution of Hamburg, Mecklenburg-Vorpommern, Niedersachsen and Schleswig-Holstein.

✉ Rothenbaumchaussee 132, 20149 Hamburg ☎ +49 40 4156 0 🖷 +49 40 447 602 **W:** ndr.de **N.B** Addresses for regional NDR 1 services see below.

FM (MHz)	NDR 1	NDR 2	NDR-K	Info	N-Joy	kW
Txs in Hamburg:						
Moorfleet	90.3	87.6	99.2	92.3	94.2	80/5/1
	89.5No					10
Txs in Mecklenburg-Vorpommern:						
Anklam	94.6Gr	–	–	103.0		6.3/1.25
Bad Doberan	94.3R	–	–	103.7		0.2/5
Barth	87.6Gr	–	–	95.0		0.4/0.3
Dömitz	88.3	–	–	–		1
Garz/Rügen	102.5Gr	99.8	91.5	88.6	95.5	50/10
Greifswald	101.0Gr	–	–	–		0.16
Grevesmühlen	100.7W	–	–	103.4		0.5/5
Güstrow-Strentz	92.5R	–	–	104.4		1.25/0.63
Helpterberg	90.5N	99.1	96.0	101.8	103.2	100/1.25
	94.2Gr					6.3
Heringsdorf	97.6Gr	94.0	102.7	100.5	92.3	1
Marlow	91.0R	93.5	88.2	102.8	–	100/30/100
Malchin	–	–	–	103.5	94.4	1
Neubrandenburg	–	–	–	–	89.5	1
Pasewalk	93.7Gr	–	–	94.8	–	2.5/1.25
Ribnitz-Damgarten	–	–	–	–	99.4	0.3
Röbel	88.5N	107.0	94.7	100.4	97.4	10/60/4
Rostock	95.8R	–	–	–	88.9	0.16/2
Schwerin	92.8	98.5	89.2	105.3	99.5	30/100/2

FM (MHz)	NDR 1	NDR 2	NDR-K	Info	N-Joy	kW
Stralsund	92.1Gr	–	–	–	–	0.4
Ueckermünde	90.1Gr	–	–	–	104.1	4/1.5
Wismar	96.2W	–	–	–	–	0.2
Wolgast-Moeckow	89.0Gr	–	–	–	93.2	0.4/0.3

Txs in and for Niedersachsen:

FM (MHz)	NDR 1	NDR 2	NDR-K	Info	N-Joy	kW
Alfeld	87.8B	93.6	96.5	91.1	92.9	0.05
Aurich-Popens	95.8Ol	98.1	90.0	96.4	92.7	25/10/1
Bad Pyrmont	88.6	92.6	95.7	98.5	–	0.05
Bad Rothenfelde	–	–	–	97.9	91.2	0.2/0.1
Braunlage	–	–	–	–	96.1	0.02
Braunschweig	–	–	–	–	100.3	15
Bremen-Walle	–	–	–	95.0	–	1
Bremerhaven	–	–	–	98.9	92.8	0.5/0.05
Cloppenburg	–	–	–	103.7	93.5	1
Cuxhaven	105.4Ol	97.9	94.6	93.1	91.6	20/10/1/10
	98.4					1
Damme	–	–	–	106.5	105.0	0.5/1
Dannenberg	91.2L	96.4	93.3	90.7	94.0	25/10/3/1
Goslar	88.2B	93.7	95.1	96.0	96.5	0.1
Göttingen	88.5B	94.1	96.8	99.9	95.9	5/0.5/5/0.5
Hann. Münden	88.2B	96.1	90.8	92.9	94.8	0.05
Hannover-Hemm.	90.9	96.2	98.7	88.6	92.6	15/5/15/0.5/25
Hildesheim	–	–	–	–	95.7	0.5
Holzminden	92.7B	96.0	98.4	88.6	99.7	0.5/0.1
Jever	–	–	–	–	97.3	0.3
Königslutter-Elm	–	–	–	88.7	–	0.2
Lingen	92.8O	97.8	90.2	88.9	96.6	15/0.2/0.5
Meppen	–	–	–	–	93.3	0.05
Osnabrück	92.4O	89.2	98.8	87.6	96.4	8/2x0.2
Rinteln	–	–	–	95.3	105.2	0.1/0.04
Rosengarten	103.2L	–	–	–	91.4	20/0.3
Seesen	–	–	–	90.4	96.6	0.2/0.05
Stadthagen	100.8	102.6	104.4	98.2	91.3	25/1
Steinkimmen	91.1Ol	99.8	94.4	98.6	92.9	100/3/1
Torfhaus	98.0B	92.1	89.9	99.5	–	100/50
Visselhövede	91.8L	95.9	87.8	98.4	97.6	5/2/5/1/30
Wedel	–	–	–	–	95.6	0.2
Wolfsburg	–	–	–	88.2	–	0.1

Txs in Schleswig-Holstein:

FM (MHz)	NDR 1	NDR 2	NDR-K	Info	N-Joy	kW
Bungsberg	97.8Lb	91.9	89.9	96.6	99.0	50/1/0.5
Flensburg	89.6F	93.2	96.1	87.7	91.0	25/10/0.5
Garding-Katingsiel	–	–	–	–	88.8	0.5
Heide-Welmbüttel	90.5H	96.3	99.4	87.9	94.9	15/0.5
Helgoland island	88.9H	93.4	97.0	92.5	91.5	0.01
Husum	–	–	–	–	93.7	0.05
Kiel-Kronshagen	91.3	98.3	95.7	99.7	94.5	15/1/0.4/15
Lauenburg	94.7Lb	–	–	96.8	99.8	0.3
Lübeck	93.1Lb	90.7	88.0	95.9	94.0	0.5/0.1/0.5
Mölln	104.5Lb	–	–	–	90.9	0.05
Neumünster	106.4No	–	–	90.8	98.7	20/1/0.5
Niebüll-Süderlügum	–	–	–	–	91.5	0.2
Sylt	90.9F	98.7	94.3	92.7	95.6	5
Wedel	–	–	–	–	95.6	0.2

NDR 90,3: from Hamburg studios, on 90.3/98.4MHz; **NDR 1 Radio MV:** Schloßgartenallee 61, 19061 Schwerin; via txs in Mecklenburg-Vorpommern, regional prgr. Greifswald (Gr), Neubrandenburg (N), Rostock (R) and Wismar (W, from Schwerin studios); **NDR 1 Niedersachsen:** Rudolf-von-Bennigsen-Ufer 22, 30169 Hannover; via txs in Niedersachsen, regional prgr. Braunschweig (B), Göttingen (G), Lüneburg area (L, from Hannover studios), Oldenburg (Ol) and Osnabrück (O); **NDR 1 Welle Nord:** Postfach 34 80, 24033 Kiel (studio location: Eggerstr. 16); via txs in Schleswig-Holstein and 89.5MHz; regional prgr. Flensburg (F), Heide (H), Lübeck (Lb) and Norderstedt (No). 2110-0430 common prgr. on all NDR 1 stns – **NDR 2:** AC, 24 hours – **NDR Kultur:** Classical music, at night rel. ARD-Nachtkonzert – **NDR Info:** Mon-Fri 0500-1850 and Sat 0500-1700 news format, other times diverse prgrs. – **NDR Info Spezial:** On 702/792/828/972kHz, rel. Mon-Fri 1500-2000 Funkhaus Europa (see J), Sun 0500-0700 NDR 90,3 (for Hamburger Hafenkonzert prgr., broadcast since 1929). Only on 702/972kHz and satellite: Sea weather forecasts at 2305 (also via NDR Info FM txs in Mecklenburg-Vorpommern), 0730 and 2105. – **N-Joy:** CHR, 24 hours.

F) RADIO BREMEN (RB)

Public broadcasting institution of Bremen

✉ Diepenau 10, 28195 Bremen ☎ +49 421 246 0 🖷 +49 421 246 1010 **W:** radiobremen.de

FM (MHz)	Eins	NWRadio	Vier	Europa	kW
Bremen-Walle	93.8	88.3	101.2	96.7	100/50
Bremerhaven	89.3	95.4	100.8	92.1	25

Bremen Eins: Oldies, rel. 2305-0400 (Sun to 0500) SWR1 – **Nordwestradio:** Culture, in cooperation with NDR. Rel. 2305-0500 ARD-Nachtkonzert – **Bremen Vier:** AC, at night rel. ARD-Popnacht – **Funkhaus Europa:** See J).

G) RUNDFUNK BERLIN-BRANDENBURG (RBB)

Public broadcasting institution of Berlin and Brandenburg, operating from two main seats:

Potsdam: ✉ Marlene-Dietrich-Allee 20, 14482 Potsdam-Babelsberg ☎ +49 331 731 0 🖷 +49 331 731 3571

Berlin: ✉ 14046 Berlin (studio/office location: Masurenallee 8-14) ☎ +49 30 3031 0 🖷 +49 30)3015 062 **W:** rbb-online.de

Txs in Berlin:

MHz	kW	Site	Program
88.8	80	Scholzplatz	Radio Berlin
92.4	80	Scholzplatz	Kulturradio
93.1	25	Scholzplatz	Inforadio
95.8	100	Alexanderplatz	radioeins
96.3	80	Scholzplatz	Funkhaus Europa
99.7	100	Alexanderplatz	Antenne Brandenburg
102.6	20	Alexanderplatz	Fritz

Txs in Brandenburg:

FM (MHz)	Ant.B.	Eins	Fritz	Kultur	Info	kW
Belzig-Lütte	106.2	99.3	91.9	100.2	–	100/10
Booßen	87.6F	89.1F	101.5	96.8	102.0	5/30/1.5
Calau	98.6C	95.1C	103.2	104.4	93.4+	100/30
Casekow	91.1Pr	106.1	100.1	104.4	–	60/10
Cottbus	–	–	–	–	99.9	1
Guben	100.9C	–	–	–	–	6
Lübben	–	–	–	–	92.4	0.4
Perleberg	–	–	–	–	92.3	1
Prenzlau	99.4Pr	–	–	–	98.6	0.5
Pritzwalk	106.6Pe	99.9	103.1	91.7	–	100/10
Wittstock	–	–	–	–	97.7	1.3
Zehlendorf	90.8F	–	–	–	–	1.3

From Berlin studios: Radio Berlin, Berlin city prgr., at night rel. ARD-Popnacht – **Inforadio**, news, at night rel. ARD-Infonacht – **Kulturradio**, classical music, at night rel. ARD-Nachtkonzert. **From Potsdam studios: Antenne Brandenburg**, light music, regional prgr. from studios Perleberg (Pe), Prenzlau (Pr), Frankfurt/Oder (F) and Cottbus (C), 2100-2305 common prgr. with Radio Berlin, 2305-0400 rel. ARD-Nachtexpress – **radioeins**, progressive-style rock/pop and information, 24 hours, regional prgr. from Frankfurt/Oder and Cottbus – **Fritz**, youth, 24 hours. **Funkhaus Europa:** See J).

+) **Bramborske Serbske Radio**: RBB, Studio Cottbus, Berliner Straße 155, 03046 Cottbus. Prgr. in Lower Sorbian Mon-Fri 1100-1200 and repeat at 1800-1900, Sundays and holidays 1130-1300, otherwise rel. Inforadio and Serbske Rozhlas (see D).

H) SAARLÄNDISCHER RUNDFUNK (SR)

Public broadcasting institution of the state of Saarland.

✉ Funkhaus Halberg, 66100 Saarbrücken ☎ +49 681 602 0 🖷 +49 681 602 3874 **W:** sr-online.de

FM (MHz)	SR 1	SR 2	SR 3	UnserDing	kW
Bliestal-Webenheim	92.3	98.0	89.1	–	5
Göttelborner Höhe	88.0	91.3	95.5	–	100
Homburg	–	–	–	98.6	0.2
Merzig-Hilbringen	89.3	92.1	98.0	–	0.1
Neunkirchen	–	–	–	–	5
Oberperl	91.9	88.6	96.1	–	5
Saarbr. Schocksberg	–	–	–	103.7	100
Sankt Wendel	–	–	–	90.3	0.1

SR 1 Europawelle Saar: AC, at night rel. ARD-Popnacht – **SR 2 KulturRadio:** Culture, at night rel. ARD-Nachtkonzert – **SR 3 Saarlandwelle:** Light music, 24 hours, news in French at 0805 – **Unser Ding:** Prgr. for teenagers, at times rel. Das Ding (SWR) – **SR Antenne Saar:** On 1179kHz and DAB, rel. of SR 2, SWR cont.ra and Radio France Internationale.

I) SÜDWESTRUNDFUNK (SWR)

Public broadc.institution of Baden-Württemberg and Rheinland-Pfalz

✉ 76522 Baden-Baden (Location: Hans-Bredow-Straße) ☎ +49 7221 929 0 🖷 +49 7221 929 2010

Broadcasting house Mainz: ✉ Postfach 3740, 55122 Mainz (Location: Am Fort Gonsenheim 39) ☎ +49 6131 929 0

Broadcasting house Stuttgart: ✉ Postfach 106040, 70049 Stuttgart (Location: Neckarstraße 230) ☎ +49 711 929 0 **W:** swr.de

FM (MHz)	SWR1	SWR2	SWR3	SWR4	DasDing	kW

Txs in and for Baden-Württemberg:

FM (MHz)	SWR1	SWR2	SWR3	SWR4	DasDing	kW
Aalen Braunenberg	95.1	91.1	98.1	96.9U	–	50/5
Albstadt-Mahlesfeld	–	–	99.5Tu	89.1	87.8	0.1/0.3
Bad Bellingen	–	–	96.6F	–	–	0.1
Bad Mergentheim	87.8	93.2	99.7	105.5H	100.5	10/0.1
Baden-Baden	90.9	98.9	99.6	88.5Ka	91.7	0.8/0.4
Baiersbronn	–	–	–	87.9O	–	0.1
Basel St. Crischona*)87.9		92.0	98.3	89.5L	–	5

FM (MHz)	SWR1	SWR2	SWR3	SWR4	DasDing	kW
Blauen-Hochblauen	89.2	92.6	97.0	–	–	8.4
Buchen	91.9	97.1	94.1	107.5M	100.6	0.1/25
Elzach Hörnleberg	–	–	–	101.8F	–	0.1
Feldberg	89.8	97.9	93.8	104.0F	–	5
Freiburg-Lehen	107.0	91.1	99.2	100.7F	–	0.1/1
Freudenberg	90.3	97.2	94.9	91.6H	–	0.01
Geislingen	93.0	88.5	95.5	107.9	–	0.5/0.1
Grünten*	98.7	–	103.0	–	–	30
Hausach Brandenkopf	95.4	–	99.7	97.6O	–	0.5/0.1
Heidelberg Königstuhl	97.8	88.8	99.9	104.1M	–	100
Heilbronn	–	–	–	99.5H	–	2
Hornisgrinde	93.5	96.2	98.4	94.0O	–	80/5
Karlsruhe-Ettlingen	–	–	–	97.0Ka	–	20
Klettgau	95.1	92.8	98.5	87.7Lö	–	2.6
Lichtenstein	99.1	–	–	89.0Tü	–	0.1
Mannheim	–	–	–	–	91.5	4
Mötzingen	–	–	97.2	87.6Tü	90.5	1
Mühlacker	–	–	–	95.7B	–	2
Pforzheim	92.9	88.1	99.3	87.6Ka	–	5/0.2/0.5
Raichberg	88.3	91.8	94.3	107.3Tü	–	40/25
Ravensburg	99.0	–	87.9	–	107.2	0.1
Reutlingen	–	–	–	–	97.7	2
Schiltach-Simonsberg	90.8	–	94.5	99.2O	–	0.1
Schwäbisch Gmünd	–	–	–	100.9U	–	0.1
Sigmaringen	–	–	–	101.2Fr	–	0.1
Strasbourg*	–	–	–	88.9O	–	1
Stuttgart-Degerloch	94.7	105.7	92.2	90.1	90.8	100/2
Stuttgart (town)	99.6	93.1	–	–	–	0.5/0.2
					†91.5	0.3
Tübingen	–	–	–	–	97.3	2
Ulm Kuhberg	92.6	89.2	97.4	94.5U	98.9	10/1
Vaihingen	–	98.6	–	–	–	0.1
Villingen-Schwenningen	–	–	–	91.1F	–	1
Waldenburg	98.8	93.8	96.5	106.6H	–	100/50
Waldburg	–	94.9	–	99.5I	–	60
				91.2Fr	–	25
Weinheim	97.1	–	99.5	100.7M	–	0.04/0.1
Wertheim	96.9	91.8	94.6	101.2H	–	0.1
Witthoh	92.4	90.4	97.1	89.0Fr	–	40/5
Zell Hohe Möhr	87.6	–	96.8	100.2F	–	0.1
Zwiefalten	93.7	–	92.8	87.6Fr	–	0.1

†) SWR Info. *Basel site in Switzerland, Strasbourg site in France, Grünten site in Bayern.

Txs in and for Rheinland-Pfalz:

Bad Kreuznach	–	–	–	–	90.9	0.1
Bleialf-Buchet	88.3	99.7	98.9	94.6T	–	0.1
Daun	91.1	–	98.5	93.6T	–	8
Diez-Geisenberg	88.4	93.4	98.2	87.9K	–	0.01/0.1
Donnersberg	99.1	92.0	101.1	105.6KI	–	60
Haardtkopf	97.7	93.0	90.0	107.1T	–	50/25
Hohe Wurzel	–	–	–	107.9M	–	6.2
Idar-Oberstein	88.5	95.1	98.1	106.4T	–	0.01/1
Kaisersl. Bornberg	90.8	93.9	97.5	99.6KI	92.5	25/0.3
Koblenz-Waldesch	96.1	94.0	91.6	107.4K	99.4	10/40/0.2
Kreuzweiler	–	–	–	97.3T	–	0.1
Linz	92.4	–	94.8	97.4K	–	50
Mainz-Kastel*	87.7	103.2	93.7	91.4M	105.2	1
Mainz-Wolfsheim	–	–	–	94.9M	–	5
Marienberger Höhe	89.8	95.4	92.8	106.3K	91.3	25/0.1
Nierstein-Oppenheim*	–	–	–	92.9M	98.4	0.1/0.3
Pirmasens Kettrichhof	100.8	–	107.2	104.2KI	–	5
Rüdesheim*	–	99.4	93.3	98.6M	–	0.1/0.5
Saarburg	99.2	93.8	90.6	101.2T	–	5
Trier	94.9	89.4	98.2	98.8T	91.7	0.1/0.3
Tübingen Herrenberg	–	–	97.2	87.6Tü	90.5	1
Weinbiet	89.9	102.2	–	95.9L	–	25
Zweibrücken	–	–	–	90.5KI	–	0.2

*) Site in Hessen. +20 stns below 0.1kW

From Stuttgart studios, via txs in Baden-Württemberg: **SWR1 Baden-Württemberg**, oldies, at night common SWR1 prgrs from Baden-Baden; **SWR4 Baden-Württemberg**, light music, Mon-Sat 0500-0700, 0900-1000, 1130-1300, 1530-1700, Sun 1200-1300, 1600-1700 local prgr. from Freiburg (F), Friedrichshafen (F), Heilbronn (H), Karlsruhe (Ka), Lörrach (Lö), Mannheim (M), Offenburg (O), Tübingen (T) and Ulm (U), at night rel. ARD-Hitnacht.
From Mainz studios, via txs in Rheinland-Pfalz: **SWR1 Rheinland-Pfalz**, oldies, at night common SWR1 prgrs from Baden-Baden; **SWR4 Rheinland-Pfalz**, light music, Mon-Sat 1100-1200 local prgrs from Kaiserslautern (KI), Koblenz (K), Ludwigshafen (L) and Trier (T), at night rel. ARD-Hitnacht.
From Baden-Baden studios: SWR2, culture, 1740-1800 prgr. from Mainz/Stuttgart, at night rel. ARD-Nachtkonzert; **SWR3**, AC, 24 h; **Das Ding**, youth, 24 h; **SWR Info**, news, at night rel. ARD-Infonacht.

J) WESTDEUTSCHER RUNDFUNK (WDR)
Public broadcasting institution of Nordrhein-Westfalen
✉ 50600 Köln (Location: Appellhofplatz 1) ☎ +49 221 220 1 🖷 +49 221 220 4800 **W:** wdr.de

FM (MHz)	ELive	WDR 2	WDR 3	WDR4	WDR5	kW
Aachen-Stolberg	106.4	100.8A	95.9	93.9	101.9	20
Arnsberg	96.0	99.4S	97.5	91.7	88.5	0.1
Bad Oeynhausen	107.7	99.1B	92.7	90.1	87.7	0.1
Bergheim	–	88.4K	–	–	–	0.5
Bonn Venusberg	102.4	100.4K	93.1	90.7	88.0	50
Dortmund	–	87.8D	–	–	–	2
Ederkopf	107.2	101.8S	–	100.7	95.8	15/20
Eifel-Bärbelkreuz	105.5	101.0	96.3	104.4	89.6	20/10/20/10
Gummersbach	–	91.8W	–	–	–	10
Hallenberg	105.7	–	–	96.1	88.3	0.1
Höxter Hasselberg	107.3	96.4B	95.2	87.8	93.9	0.5
Ibbenbüren	102.5	96.0M	97.3	99.5	88.5	0.5
Klever Berg	103.7	93.3Dü	97.3	101.7	99.7	2
Köln	87.6	98.6K	–	–	–	0.3/0.5
Langenberg	106.7	99.2Dü	95.1	101.3	88.8	100
					*103.3	100
Lübbecke	93.6	96.0B	91.7	99.6	88.6	0.1
Münster-Baumberge	107.9	94.1M	89.7	100.0	92.0	25
Nordhelle	104.7	93.5S	98.1	103.8	90.3	35
Olsberg	107.0	102.1S	–	104.1	98.6	10
Remscheid	–	95.7W	–	–	–	1
Schmallenberg	100.1	93.8S	97.8	101.1	90.0	0.1
Siegen	107.5	97.1S	98.4	101.2	97.6	0.5/1/0.5/1
Teutoburger Wald	105.5	93.2B	97.0	100.5	90.6	100
Warburg	98.2	91.8B	94.3	104.5	88.4	0.5
Wittgenstein	–	92.3S	88.7	–	–	15
Wuppertal	–	99.8W	–	–	–	1

*Funkhaus Europa.

1 Live: CHR, 24 hours – **WDR 2:** AC, 24 h, incl. local news from Aachen (A), Bielefeld (B), Köln (K), Dortmund (D), Düsseldorf (Dü), Münster (M), Siegen (S), Wuppertal (W) – **WDR 3:** Culture, at night rel. ARD-Nachtkonzert – **WDR 4:** Light music, at night rel. ARD-Hitnacht – **WDR 5:** Information, 24 h with repeats overnight – **Funkhaus Europa:** Multicultural, from Bremen and RB txs (see F/G) and with some prgrs from their Bremen/Berlin studios – **VERA:** Continuous traffic jam information, 24 h on satellite and DAB, at peak times also on 720/774kHz – **WDR Event:** On 720/774kHz, satellite and DAB, live coverage of various events. MW txs otherwise rel. WDR 2 / VLHA – **1 Live Diggi:** Via satellite and DAB, continuous CHR music – **Kiraka:** Via satellite and DAB, repeats of childrens prgrs from other WDR networks.

II. COMMERCIAL AND OTHER STATIONS
NB: In Germany supervision and frequency allocation for commercial broadcasting services is the responsibility of the federal states. Each state (listed below) has its own media institution, with the exceptions of Berlin and Brandenburg as well as Hamburg and Schleswig-Holstein, respectively, who have common institutions. As a result of this situation most commercial stations broadcast on the territory of one state only.

K) BADEN-WÜRTTEMBERG
Media institution: Landesanstalt für Kommunikation (LfK) ✉ Postfach 102927, 70025 Stuttgart (office location: Reinsburgstraße 27 ☎ +49 711 669910 🖷 +49 711 6699111 **W:** lfk.de
Commercial stations:

FM	MHz	kW	Site	Station
2)	87.8	1	Mannheim	big FM
6)	88.6	2	Langenburg	R. Ton
3)	89.1	0.5	Heilbronn	Hit-R. Antenne 1
3)	89.3	0.1	Bad Urach	Hit-R. Antenne 1
2)	89.5	10	Stuttgart Frauenkopf	big FM
3)	89.5	0.1	Wertheim	Hit-R. Antenne 1
2)	89.7	1	Tübingen	big FM
10)	90.4	2	Karlsruhe	Klassik R.
9)	90.5	2	Achern	Hitradio Ohr
2)	90.5	0.1	Heidelberg city	big FM
15)	91.4	3	Lützenhardt	R. TV R.
7)	91.4	0.5	Pforzheim	die neue welle
18)	92.4	1	Hockenheimring	Rennradio
2)	92.7	1	Horb	big FM
9)	93.0	0.1	Haslach	Schwarzwald R.
16)	93.1	1	Rottweil-Zimmern	R. Neckarburg
15)	94.7	0.5	Freiburg-Lehen	baden.fm
17)	95.4	0.5	Stuttgart SWR bldg.	Metropol FM
6)	95.6	1	Balingen	R. Ton
6)	96.0	0.1	Künzelsau	R. Ton
10)	96.4	1	Überlingen	R. Seefunk
6)	96.8	0.3	Eppingen	R. Ton
4)	96.9	0.1	Schussental	R. 7
12)	97.2	1	Stuttgart-Münster	Flux FM

FM	MHz	kW	Site	Station
2)	97.2	0.5	Sinsheim-Dühren	big FM
13)	97.5	0.5	Esslingen	Die Neue 107.7
8)	97.6	0.3	Rudersberg	Energy Stuttgart
2)	99.0	0.5	Rottweil	big FM
6)	99.0	0.1	Bad Urach	R. Ton
15)	99.2	0.2	Herrenberg	R. TV R.
9)	99.2	0.1	Oberkirch	Hitradio Ohr
10)	99.3	5	Friedrichshafen	R. Seefunk
2)	99.7	1	Ulm	big FM
3)	100.1	50	Schwäbisch Hall	Hit-R. Antenne 1
6)	100.1	0.1	Hechingen	R. Ton
2)	100.3	5	Geislingen	big FM
1)	100.4	80	Hornisgrinde	R. Regenbogen
8)	100.7	20	Güglingen	Energy Stuttgart
6)	100.9	1	Tübingen	R. Ton
7)	100.9	0.8	Baden-Baden	die neue welle
1)	101.1	8.4	Blauen-Müllheim	R. Regenbogen
4)	101.2	0.1	Villingen-Schwenningen	R. 7
3)	101.3	75	Stuttgart Frauenkopf	Hit-R. Antenne 1
9)	101.6	0.5	Brandenkopf	Hit-R. Ohr
7)	101.8	25	Karlsruhe	die neue welle
4)	101.8	10	Ulm-Ermingen	R. 7
10)	101.8	10	Konstanz	R. Seefunk
8)	101.8	1	Backnang	Energy Stuttgart
10)	101.9	0.1	Schopfheim	R. Seefunk
16)	102.0	3	Villingen-Schwenningen	R. Neckarburg
5)	102.1	25	Mudau	sunshine live
4)	102.2	0.2	Laufenburg [Switzerl.]	R. Seefunk
4)	102.5	40	Witthoh-Tuttlingen	R. 7
6)	102.6	0.5	Schwäbisch Hall	R. Ton
10)	102.6	0.3	Ravensburg	R. Seefunk
8)	102.6	0.1	Bad Wildbad	Energy Stuttgart
8)	102.7	0.1	Nagold	Energy Stuttgart
1)	102.8	50	Heidelberg.Königstuhl	R. Regenbogen
2)	102.8	0.5	Freiburg	big FM
11)	103.0	1	Göppingen	Klassik R.
8)	103.0	0.3	Calw	Energy Stuttgart
10)	103.1	5	Rheinfelden	R. Seefunk
3)	103.1	0.1	Reutlingen	Hit-R. Antenne 1
6)	103.2	25	Heilbronn	R. Ton
3)	103.4	50	Raichberg	Hit-R. Antenne 1
6)	103.5	20	Bad Mergentheim	R. Ton
4)	103.7	50	Aalen	R. 7
16)	103.7	0.1	Schramberg	R. Neckarburg
2)	103.8	2	Baden-Baden	big FM
10)	103.9	10	Iberger Kugel	R. Seefunk
11)	103.9	2	Stuttgart-Münster	Klassik R.
10)	104.2	1	Sigmaringen	R. Seefunk
6)	104.2	0.1	Heidenheim	R. Ton
8)	104.3	2	Sindelfingen	Energy Stuttgart
10)	104.3	0.1	Lörrach	R. Seefunk
8)	104.5	2	Waiblingen	Energy Stuttgart
8)	104.5	0.1	Winnenden	Energy Stuttgart
16)	104.6	1	Oberndorf	R. Neckarburg
14)	104.6	0.3	Biberach	Donau 3 FM
1)	104.6	0.1	Buchen	R. Regenbogen
2)	104.7	0.2	Heilbronn	big FM
2)	104.7	0.1	Wertheim	R. Ton
13)	104.7	0.1	Geislingen	Die Neue 107.7
6)	104.8	1	Reutlingen	R. Ton
9)	104.9	5	Offenburg-Ohlsbach	Hit-R. Ohr
5)	104.9	1	Stuttgart-Münster	sunshine live
4)	105.0	50	Grünenbach	R. 7
2)	105.1	0.2	Aalen	big FM
2)	105.2	20	Pforzheim	big FM
10)	105.3	0.5	Singen	R. Seefunk
3)	105.4	1	Geislingen	Hit-R. Antenne 1
3)	105.4	0.3	Balingen	Hit-R. Antenne 1
10)	105.4	0.1	Waldshut-Tiengen	R. Seefunk
9)	105.5	0.5	Bühl	Hit-R. Ohr
14)	105.9	5	Ulm-Ermingen	Donau 3 FM
15)	106.0	8.4	Blauen-Müllheim	baden.fm
3)	106.0	0.1	Bad Mergentheim	Hit-R. Antenne 1
5)	106.1	1	Heidelberg-Königstuhl	sunshine live
13)	106.1	1	Göppingen	Die Neue 107.7
14)	106.2	0.5	Riedlingen	Donau 3 FM
13)	106.5	0.1	Kirchheim	Die Neue 107.7
15)	106.6	0.1	Titisee-Neustadt	baden.fm
13)	106.8	1	Nürtingen	Die Neue 107.7
3)	106.9	0.1	Leonberg	Hit-R. Antenne 1
10)	107.0	5	Wannenberg-Klettgau	R. Seefunk
3)	107.0	1	Pforzheim	Hit-R. Antenne 1
6)	107.1	20	Aalen	R. Ton
5)	107.1	0.1	Wiesloch	sunshine live
7)	107.3	0.1	Bruchsal	die neue welle
9)	107.4	5	Lahr	Hit-R. Ohr
13)	107.4	0.1	Gosbach	Die Neue 107.7
13)	107.7	4	Stuttgart Frauenkopf	Die Neue 107.7
15)	107.7	0.5	Freiburg-Littenweiler	baden.fm
5)	107.7	0.1	Weinheim	sunshine live
6)	107.9	1	Sickingen	R. Ton
5)	107.9	0.1	Mosbach	sunshine live
7)	107.9	0.1	Bretten	die neue welle

Addresses and other information:

1) P.O.-Box 10 26 55, 68026 Mannheim (studio location: Dudenstr. 12-26); W: regenbogenweb.de AC – 2) Kronenstr. 24, 70173 Stuttgart; W: bigfm.de CHR, further txs see T), U) – 3) Plieningerstr. 150, 70567 Stuttgart; W: antenne1.de AC – 4) Gaisenbergstr. 29, 89073 Ulm; W: radio7.de AC – 5) Hafenstr. 68-72, 68159 Mannheim; W: sunshine-live.de Techno, also via Astra 2C, 12.148GHz – 6) Allee 2, 74072 Heilbronn; W: radio-ton.de AC – 7) Albert-Nestler-Str. 26, 76131 Karlsruhe; W: meine-neue-welle.de AC – 8) Anton-Schmidt-Str. 36, 71332 Waiblingen; W: energy-stuttgart.de CHR – 9) Postfach 20 80, 77610 Offenburg (studio location: Hauptstr. 83a); W: hitradio-ohr.de schwarzwaldradio.com AC – 10) Konzlstr. 1, 78462 Konstanz; W: radio-seefunk.de AC – 11) see O) – 12) see M), stn. 4 – 13) Königstr. 2, 70173 Stuttgart; W: dieneue1077.de Rock – 14) Basteistr. 37, 89073 Ulm; W: donau3fm.de AC – 15) Munzingerstr. 1, 79111 Freiburg; W: baden.fm AC – 16) August-Schuhmacher-Str. 10, 78664 Eschbronn-Mariazell; W: radio-neckarburg.de – 17) see M), stn. 15 – 18) during Hockenheimring races only.

Non-commercial stations:

FM	MHz	kW	Site	Station
10)	88.4	0.3	Freiburg university	echo-fm
6)	88.6	1	Stuttgart-Münster	Hochschulr. Stuttg.
9)	89.2	0.1	Horb	Freies R. Freudens.
1)	89.6	0.1	Mannheim	bermuda.funk
4)	91.2	0.1	Bruchsal	LernR.
8)	96.6	1	Tübingen	Wüste Welle
2)	97.5	0.1	Schwäbisch Hall	R. StHörfunk
9)	99.2	0.3	Stuttgart-Münster	Freies R. f. Stuttg.
9)	100.0	0.5	Freudenstadt	Freies R. Freudens.
10)	102.3	1	Freiburg Vogtsbg.	R. Dreyeckland
7)	102.6	1	Ulm-Ermingen	R. FreeFM
9)	104.1	0.1	Baiersbronn	Freies R. Freudens.
12)	104.5	0.5	Hohe Möhr	R. Kanal Ratte
3)	104.8	1	Karlsruhe	Querfunk
2)	104.8	0.1	Crailsheim	R. StHörfunk
1)	105.4	0.1	Heidelberg Königstuhl	bermuda.funk

Addresses and other information:

1) Brückenstr. 2-4, 68167 Mannheim; W: bermudafunk.org. Also rel. R. Aktiv (Universität Mannheim, Postfach 144, 68131 Mannheim); W: radio-aktiv-online.de; Mon-Wed 0600-1000 and 1700-1900, Thu-Fri 2300-1000 and 1700-1900, Sun 1900-2100 – 2) Haalstr. 9, 74523 Schwäbisch Hall; W: sthoerfunk.de – 3) Steinstr. 23, 76133 Karlsruhe; W: querfunk.de, rel. Mon-Fri 0600-1100 and Mon-Thu 1600-2100 stn. 4) – 4) Hochschule für Musik, Postfach 6040, 76040 Karlsruhe (studio location: Wolfartsweierer Str. 7a); W: lernradio.de – 5) Freies R. für Stuttgart, Rieckestr. 24, 70190 Stuttgart; W: freies-radio.de – 6) Hochschulradio Stuttgart, Nobelstr. 10, 70569 Stuttgart; W: horads.de – 7) Schützenstr. 206, 89077 Ulm; W: freefm.de – 8) Hechinger Str. 203, 72072 Tübingen; W: wueste-welle.de Rel. Sun 0900-1300 Tübingen university prgr. and Tue-Thu 0700-0800 Helle Welle (religious). – 9) Freies R. Freudenstadt, Forststr. 23, 72250 Freudenstadt; W: radio-fds.de – 10) Adlerstr. 12, 79098 Freiburg; W: rdl.de – 11) Georges-Köhler-Allee Geb. 076, 79110 Freiburg; W: echo-fm.uni-freiburg.de – 12) Bahnhofstr. 3, 79650 Schopfheim; W: kanalrattefm.de

DAB: 7 txs on 178MHz (ch. 5C) DLF (L2 128k), DK (L2 128k), DRadio Wissen (AAC 56k), Dokumente&Debatten (AAC 40k), ERF Plus (AAC 72k), Klassik R. (AAC 72k), Absolut R. (AAC 72k), Lounge FM (AAC 72k), Energy (AAC 72k), 90elf (AAC 72k, during Bundesliga football matches split in up to five channels), BOB (AAC 72k), Kiss FM (AAC 64k), R. Horeb (AAC 48k) – 5 txs on 201MHz (ch. 8D) and 3 txs on 208MHz (ch. 9D) SWR1 BW (L2 192k), SWR2 (AAC 120k), SWR3 (AAC 120k), SWR4 BW (AAC 120k), DasDing (AAC 120k), SWR Info (L2 192k) – 11 txs on 219MHz (ch. 11B) SWR1 BW (L2 160k), SWR2 (AAC 120k), SWR3 (AAC 120k), SWR4 BW (AAC 120k), DasDing (AAC 120k), SWR Info (L2 128k), BigFM World Beats (AAC 72k), Live R. (AAC 72k), Schwarzwaldradio (AAC 72k).

L) BAYERN

Media institution: Bayerische Landeszentrale für Neue Medien (BLM) ✉ Heinrich-Lübke-Straße 27, 81737 München ☎ +49 89 638 080 🖷 +49 89 63808140; W: blm.de

FM networks:

Location	Ant.B.	Rock.	Klass	egoFM	Galaxy	kW
Amberg	–	–	–	–	105.5	0.1
Ansbach	–	–	–	–	105.8	0.1

Location	Ant.B.	Rock.	Klass	egoFM	Galaxy	kW
Aschaffenburg	103.0	–	–	–	91.6	25/0.1
Augsburg	104.2	87.9	92.2	94.8	–	0.1/0.3
Bad Reichenhall	103.7	–	–	–	–	0.3
Bamberg	101.1	–	–	–	104.7	25/0.5
Bayreuth	–	–	–	–	92.7	0.1
Bayrischzell	106.7	–	–	–	–	0.1
Berchtesgaden	107.9	–	–	–	–	0.3
Breithart	101.5	–	–	–	–	25
Brotjacklriegel	103.5	–	–	–	–	100
Coburg	103.8	–	–	–	90.4	5/0.2
Dillberg	100.6	–	–	–	–	25
Eichstätt	100.2	–	–	–	–	25
Enterbach	101.1	–	–	–	–	0.5
Grünten	104.4	–	–	–	–	50
Heidelstein	101.9	–	–	–	–	100
Herzogstand	102.0	–	–	–	–	0.1
Hochries	107.7	–	–	–	–	50
Hof	–	–	–	–	94.0	0.2
Högl-Freilassing	105.3	–	–	–	–	1
Hohenpeißenb.	103.8	–	–	–	–	25
Hoher Bogen	101.9	–	–	–	–	50
Ingolstadt	–	–	–	–	107.9	0.1
Kempten	–	–	–	–	88.1	0.3
Konradsreuth	–	–	–	–	98.1	0.1
Landshut	99.3	–	–	–	99.8	0.2
Lindau	99.0	–	–	–	–	0.5
Münchberg	–	–	–	–	98.1	0.1
München	101.3	–	107.2	100.8	–	0.3/1/0.3
Naila	–	–	–	–	96.5	0.1
Nördlingen	103.3	–	–	–	–	25
Nürnberg	–	–	105.1	103.6	–	0.5/0.3
Oberaudorf	94.6	–	–	–	–	0.1
Ochsenkopf	103.2	–	–	–	–	100
Passau	102.1	–	–	–	91.7	1/0.2
Pfaffenhofen	92.6	–	–	–	–	0.5
Regensburg	103.0	–	91.1	107.5	–	25/0.3/0.3
Reit im Winkel	101.6	–	–	–	–	0.1
Rosenheim	–	–	–	–	106.6	0.1
Selb	–	–	–	–	93.4	0.1
Sonthofen	93.6	–	–	–	–	0.1
Traunstein	103.7	–	–	–	–	5
Ulm	104.8	–	–	–	–	0.1
Weiden	–	–	–	–	89.8	0.1
Weiler Simm.	106.0	–	–	–	–	0.1
Wunsiedel	–	–	–	–	97.3	0.2
Würzburg	104.4	–	92.1	95.8	–	5/0.3
Zugspitze	102.7	–	–	–	–	2

Addresses and other information:
Antenne Bayern (AC), **Rockantenne (rock):** Münchener Straße 101c, 85737 Ismaning; also via Astra 2C, 12.148GHz h; **W:** antenne.de rock-antenne.de – **Klassik R.:** see O) – **egoFM:** Leopoldstraße 254, 80807 München; also via Astra 1M, 12.460GHz; **W:** egofm.de Alternative – **R. Galaxy:** Lilienthalstraße 3c, 93049 Regensburg, **W:** radiogalaxy. de CHR. Mon-Fri 1400-1800 local prgr., produced by stns 17), 26), 29), 30/31), 32), 33), 35) (R. Euroherz), 36), 41), 42), 43) and 48) listed below.

Local stations:

FM	MHz	kW	Site	Station
39)	87.9	0.3	Straubing Bogenberg	R. AWN
44)	87.9	0.1	Erding	Hitwelle Erding
35)	88.0	5	Großer Waldstein	extra~rad. / Euroherz
19)	88.1	0.1	Krumbach-Kirchberg	R. Prima 1
18)	88.2	0.2	Kaufbeuren	R. Ostallgäu
51)	88.2	0.1	Bad Reichenhall	R. Untersberg
32)	88.5	0.5	Bamberg Rothof	R. Bamberg
36)	88.5	0.1	Tirschenreuth	R. Ramasuri
27)	88.6	0.1	Karlstadt	R. Charivari
5)	89.0	0.3	München Olympiaturm	2DAY/Neues Europa
42)	89.0	0.1	Dingolfing	R. Trausnitz
51)	89.0	0.1	Högl-Freilassing	R. Untersberg
26)	89.1	0.1	Wassertrüdingen	R. 8
31)	89.2	0.5	Coburg Eckardtsberg	R. EINS
17)	89.3	0.1	Oberstdorf-Steinach	RSA R.
40)	89.3	0.2	Regen Geiskopf	Unser R. Deggendorf
26)	89.4	0.5	Ansbach Ludwigshöhe	R. 8
24)	89.7	0.1	Dillingen	RT.1 Nordschwaben
38)	89.7	0.3	Regensburg Ziegetsberg	gong fm
41)	89.7	0.3	Bad Griesbach	Unser R. Passau
26)	89.8	0.1	Dinkelsbühl	R. 8
45)	89.8	0.1	Landsberg-Stoffen	R. 106.4
31)	90.0	0.1	Kronach-Neuses	R. EINS
19)	90.2	0.32	Bad Grönenbach	R. Prima 1
26)	90.2	0.1	Gunzenhausen	R. 8
47)	90.2	0.1	Miesbach-Bergham	R. Alpenwelle
21)	90.3	0.1	Günzburg	Hitradio X

FM	MHz	kW	Site	Station
26)	90.4	0.2	Neuastadt / Aisch	R. 8
27)	90.4	0.1	Gemünden / Lohr	R. Charivari
49)	90.4	0.1	Mühldorf	Inn-Salzach-Welle
30)	90.5	0.1	Bad Kissingen	R. PrimaTon
29)	90.8	0.2	Alzenau	R. Primavera
15)	91.0	0.2	Fürth	Vil R.
47)	91.7	0.1	Holzkirchen Jasberg	R. Alpenwelle
42)	91.8	0.2	Pfeffenhausen-Stollnried	R. Trausnitz
47)	92.0	0.1	Wolfratshausen	R. Alpenwelle
6)	92.4	0.3	München Olympiaturm	(shared freq.)
16)	92.7	0.1	Weiler Simmerberg	Welle Bodensee
37)	92.7	0.4	Hoher Bogen	Charivari Regensbg.
49)	92.7	0.3	Reichertsheim	Inn-Salzach-Welle
13)	92.9	0.3	Nürnberg	Hi R. N1
17)	93.0	0.1	Immenstadt	RSA R.
49)	93.1	0.1	Burgkirchen-Gendorf	Inn-Salzach-Welle
2)	93.3	0.3	München Olympiaturm	Energy 93.3
33)	93.3	0.1	Pegnitz	R. Mainwelle
23)	93.4	0.3	Augsburg	R. Fantasy
9)	93.6	0.3	Erlangen	Energy Nürnberg
36)	93.6	0.1	Waidhaus Fischerberg	R. Ramasuri
19)	93.9	0.3	Mindelheim-Altensteig	R. Prima 1
41)	93.9	0.3	Vilshofen-Otterkirchen	Unser R. Passau
30)	94.0	0.1	Bad Brückenau	R. PrimaTon
37)	94.0	1	Seubersdorf Göschberg	Charivari Regensbg.
7)	94.5	0.1	München Blutenburgstr.	M 94,5
11)	94.5	0.3	Nürnberg	R. F / Jazztime
43)	94.6	0.1	Schrobenhausen	R. IN / R. ND1
47)	95.0	0.2	Bad Tölz	R. Alpenwelle
35)	95.1	0.1	Marktredwitz	extra~r. / Euroherz
36)	95.3	1	Hirschberg Rothbühl	R. Ramasuri
31)	95.4	0.3	Lichtenfels	R. EINS
43)	95.4	0.1	Ingolstadt	R. IN
3)	95.5	0.3	München Olympiaturm	Charivari 95.5
24)	95.6	1	Harburg Hühnerberg	RT.1 Nordschwaben
30)	95.7	0.1	Haßfurt/Main	R. PrimaTon
39)	95.7	0.1	Mallersdorf-Hofkirchen	R. AWN
14)	95.8	0.3	Nürnberg	R. Z
4)	96.3	0.3	München Olympiaturm	R. Gong 96,3
38)	96.3	0.32	Burglengenfeld	gong fm
32)	96.6	0.1	Forchheim Pinzberg	R. Bamberg
45)	96.6	0.1	Starnberg	R. 106.4
17)	96.7	0.1	Kempten town	RSA R.
22)	96.7	0.3	Augsburg	Kit R. RT.1
48)	96.7	0.3	Flintsbach Dandlberg	Charivari Rosenheim
12)	97.1	0.3	Nürnberg	Gong 97.1
24)	97.1	0.1	Donauwörth	RT.1 Nordschwaben
41)	97.2	0.1	Grafenau Liebersberg	Unser R. Passau
26)	97.3	0.3	Feuchtwangen	R. 8
38)	97.3	0.1	Schwandorf Weinberg	gong fm
46)	97.5	0.1	Weilheim	R. Oberland
17)	97.6	1	Kempten Blender	RSA R.
48)	98.0	0.1	Füssen	R. Ostallgäu
51)	98.1	0.1	Berchtesgaden	R. Untersberg
37)	98.2	0.3	Regensburg Ziegetsberg	Charivari Regensb.
41)	98.3	0.2	Passau-Haidenhof	Unser R. Passau
10)	98.6	0.3	Nürnberg	Charivari 98.6
40)	98.7	0.1	Deggendorf-Hochobernd.	Unser R. Deggendorf
37)	98.8	0.5	Burglengenfeld	Charivari Regensbg.
34)	98.9	0.1	Stadtsteinach	R. Plassenburg
25)	99.0	0.2	Lauf Moritzberg	star fm
27)	99.0	0.1	Marktheidenfeld	R. Charivari
43)	99.1	0.1	Eichstätt-Seuversholz	R. IN
50)	99.4	0.3	Haslach-Einham	R. Chiemgau
36)	99.9	0.2	Weiden Fischerberg	R. Ramasuri
47)	99.9	0.1	Herzogstand	R. Alpenwelle
29)	100.4	1	Aschaffenburg	R. Primavera
30)	100.5	0.5	Schweinfurth	R. PrimaTon
26)	100.8	0.1	Burgbernheim	R. 8
43)	101.2	0.2	Neuburg/Donau	R. IN / R. ND1
46)	101.2	0.1	Oberammergau	R. Oberland
46)	101.4	0.3	Sindelsdorf	R. Oberland
30)	101.5	1	Bad Neustadt-Unsleben	R. PrimaTon
41)	101.5	0.1	Freyung Geyersberg	Unser R. Passau
50)	101.5	0.3	Trostberg	R. Chiemgau
34)	101.6	5	Kulmbach Rehberg	R. Plassenburg
27)	102.4	0.3	Würzburg	R. Charivari
37)	102.6	0.32	Waldmünchen Perlhütte	Charivari Regensbg.
16)	103.6	0.5	Lindau Hoyerberg	Welle Bodensee
36)	103.9	0.1	Amberg Eisberg	R. Ramasuri
37)	103.9	0.5	Kelheim Leitenberg	Charivari Regensbg.
1)	104.0	0.1	München Blutenburgstr.	R. Arabella
42)	104.1	1	Landshut	R. Trausnitz
48)	104.2	0.3	Oberaudorf-Hölzelau	Charivari Rosenheim
33)	104.3	10	Oschenberg	R. Mainwelle

FM	MHz	kW	Site	Station
47)	104.3	0.5	Enterbach-Ringberg	R. Alpenwelle
46)	104.6	0.1	Herzogstand	R. Oberland
43)	104.8	0.2	Pfaffenhofen Wolfsberg	R. IN
36)	105.1	0.5	Wiesau-Fuchsmühle	R. Ramasuri
1)	105.2	25	München-Isen	R. Arabella
18)	105.2	0.1	Obergünzburg	R. Ostallgäu
43)	105.4	0.1	Beilngries	R. IN
37)	105.5	0.3	Lam-Koppenhof	Charivari Regensbg.
42)	105.5	0.32	Landau	R. Trausnitz
20)	105.9	5	Ulm-Ermingen	R. Donau 1
37)	105.9	0.32	Nabburg Galgenberg	Charivari Regensbg.
32)	106.1	0.1	Burglesau Reisberg	R. Bamberg
8)	106.2	0.2	Erlangen	afk max
46)	106.2	0.3	Garmisch-Partenkirchen	R. Oberland
47)	106.2	0.1	Schliersbergalm	R. Alpenwelle
18)	106.3	0.5	Eisenberg Schloßberg	R. Ostallgäu
36)	106.4	0.1	Königstein Gr. Ossinger	R. Ramasuri
45)	106.4	2	Fürstenfeldbruck	R. 106.4
49)	106.4	0.3	Lohkirchen	Inn-Salzach-Welle
8)	106.5	0.1	Nürnberg	afk max
28)	106.9	5	Würzburg	R. Gong 106,9
9)	106.9	0.3	Nürnberg	Energy Nürnberg
42)	107.4	1	Pfarrkirchen-Postm.	R. Trausnitz
25)	107.8	0.2	Schwabach Heidenberg	star fm
40)	107.9	0.2	Brotjacklriegel	Unser R. Deggendorf

+ 28 txs less than 0.1kW

Adresses and other information:
Dienstleistungsgesellschaft für Bayerische Lokal-Radioprogramme (BLR) ✉ Rosenheimer Straße 145c, 81671 München **W:** blr.de and radiodienst.de Program supplier for many of the above listed stns. Nationwide content delivery under the brand RadioDienst.
1) Paul-Heyse-Str. 2-4, 80336 München, **W:** radioarabella.de – **2)** Pestalozzistr. 15-19, 80469 München, **W:** energy.de/muenchen – **3)** Postfach 20 16 09, 80016 München (studio location as stn. 1), **W:** charivari.de – **4)** Franz-Joseph-Str. 14, 80801 München, **W:** radiogong.de – **5)** Schneemanstr. 25, 81369 München, **W:** radio2-day.de Rel. Sat 2300-Mon 0500 R. Neues Europa: Konviktstr. 1, 85049 Ingolstadt – **6) Radio Horeb**, Postfach 1165, 87501 Immenstadt; **W:** radiohoreb.de Religious. Also via Astra 1L, 12.604GHz h. On 92.4MHz Mon-Fri 2300-1500, Sat/Sun 2300-0500, Sun 0900-1200 and 1300-2000. **Christliches Radio München**, Postfach 310201, 80102 München; **W:** christlichesradiomuenchen.de Religious, Mon-Fri 1500-1600, Sun 0800-0900 and 1200-1300. **Lora München**, Gravelottestr. 6, 81667 München, **W:** lora924.de Non-commercial. Mon-Fri 1600-2300. **Feierwerk München**, Hansastr. 39, 81373 München; **W:** feierwerk.de Non-commercial. Sat 0500-2300, Sun 0600-0800 and 2000-2200 – **7)** Schwere-Reiter-Str. 35, 80797 München, 80538 München, **W:** m945.de/de Journalist training stn. – **8)** Fürther Str. 212, 90429 Nürnberg, **W:** afkmax.de Journalist training stn. – **9)** Ostendstr. 100, 90482 Nürnberg, **W:** energy.de/nuernberg – **10),11),12),13)** Funkhaus Nürnberg, Senefelder Str. 7, 90409 Nürnberg, **W:** funkhaus.de 92,0MHz also rel. Camillo 92.9 (Mon, Tue, Sun 2000-2200), R. AREF (Sun 0900-1100), Pray 92.9 (Sun 1100-1200), R. Meilensteine (Sun 0800-0900), 94.5MHz also rel. Jazztime Nürnberg (Mon 2100-2200, Thu 2000-2100). – **14)** Kopernikusplatz 12, 90459 Nürnberg, **W:** radio-z.net 1300-0100 only, other times rel. stn. 25) – **15)** Platnersgasse 1, 90403 Nürnberg, **W:** vilradio.de – **16) W:** welle-bodensee.de – **17)** Rottachstr. 17, 87439 Kempten, **W:** allgaeuseite.de/rsa_radio – **18)** roal.de – **19)** Hirschgasse 1, 87700 Memmingen, **W:** prima1.de – **20)** Leipzigstr. 26, 88400 Biberach, **W:** radiodonau1.de – **21)** Augsburger Str. 112, 89312 Günzburg, **W:** hitradiox.de – **22)** Curt-Frenzel-Str. 4, 86167 Augsburg, **W:** radio-rt1.de – **23)** Ludwigstr. 1, 86150 Augsburg, **W:** fantasy.de Rel. Mon 2100-2400 Kanal C (university stn.): Eichleitnerstr. 30, 86159 Augsburg, **W:** kanal-c.de – **24)** Artur-Proeller-Str. 4, 86609 Donauwörth, **W:** rt1-nordschwaben.de – **25)** O'Brien Str. 2, 91126 Schwabach; **W:** rocksender.de/rocksender_nuernberg/ – **26)** Postfach 8, 91510 Ansbach (studio location: Schalkhäuser Landstr. 5); **W:** radio8.de – **27), 28)** Semmelstr. 15, 97070 Würzburg, **W:** charivari.fm and gong.fm Also rel. Radio Opera – **29)** Am Funkhaus 1, 63743 Aschaffenburg, **W:** radio-primavera.de – **30),31)** Seifartshofstr. 21, 96450 Coburg, **W:** radioeins.com – **32)** Gutenbergstr. 5, 96050 Bamberg, **W:** radio-bamberg.de – **33)** Postfach 10 11 60, 95411 Bayreuth (studio location: Richard-Wagner-Str. 33), **W:** mainwelle.de – **34)** E.C.-Baumann-Str. 5, 95326 Kulmbach, **W:** radio-plassenburg.de – **35)** 0900-1000, 1200-1300 and 1800-2000 **extra~radio**, Postfach 1745, 95016 Hof (studio location: Kreuzsteinstr. 2-6); **W:** extra-radio.de; otherwise: **R. Euroherz**, Pfarr 1, 95028 Hof, **W:** euroherz.de – **36)** Unterer Markt 35, 92637 Weiden, **W:** ramasuri.de – **37),38)** Lilienthalstr. 3c, 93049 Regensburg, **W:** charivari.de and www.gongfm.de – **39),40)** Bahnhofstr. 28, 94469 Deggendorf, **W:** unser-radio.de – **41)** Medienstr. 5, 94036 Passau, **W:** as stn. 40) – **42)** Altstadt 361, 84028 Landshut, **W:** radio-trausnitz.de – **43)** Donaustr. 11, 85049

Ingolstadt, **W:** radio-in.de, rel. 0500-0900 on 94.6/101.2MHz R. ND1 – **44)** Postfach 1155, 84420 Isen, **W:** hitwelle.de – **45)** Schöngeisingerstr. 11, 82256 Fürstenfeldbruck, **W:** radio1064.de – **46)** Postfach 1752, 82467 Garmisch-Partenkirchen (studio location: Marienplatz 17), **W:** radio-oberland.de – **47)** W: radio-alpenwelle.de – **48)** Hafnerstr. 5-7, 83022 Rosenheim, **W:** radio-charivari.de – **49)** Mozartstr. 3a, 84508 Burgkirchen/Alz, **W:** inn-salzach-welle.de – **50)** Rupertistr. 40-42, 83278 Traunstein, **W:** radio-chiemgau.de – **51)** untersberg.de **N.B** stns 49), 50), 51) also rel. prgr. of independent producers.
DAB: 6 txs on 178MHz (ch. 5C), mux details see K) – Augsburg tx on 206.4MHz (ch. 9C) RT1 (AAC 80k), Fantasy (AAC 80k), Fantasy Aktuell (AAC 72k), R. Augsburg (AAC 88k), Smart R. (AAC 88k), Magic Star (AAC 72k) – Nürnberg txs on 213MHz (ch. 10C) Energy Nürnbg. (AAC 80k), Pirate Gong (AAC 80k), Vil R. (AAC 80k), Magic Star (AAC 72k) – Ingolstadt txs on 217MHz (ch. 11A) R. IN (L2 160k), Cool R. Jazz (L2 160k), Magic Star (AAC 72k) – München txs on 220MHz (ch. 11C) R. Gong (AAC 80k), Gong Mobil (AAC 80k), Digital Classix (AAC 80k), 2Day (AAC 80k), Magic Star (AAC 72k) – 11 txs on 222MHz (ch. 11D) Bayern 1 (L2 160k), Bayern 1 local versions (4 x AAC 80k each), Bayern 2 (L2 160k), Bayern 3 (L2 160k), B5 aktuell (AAC 80k), Bayern2plus (AAC 80k), BR Verkehr (L2 mono) – 39 txs on 229MHz (ch. 12D) BR Klassik (L2 192k), on3radio (L2 128k), Bayern plus (L2 128k), B5 plus (L2 mono), Rockantenne (AAC 80k), Radio Galaxy (AAC 80k), Antenne Info (AAC 40k), Antenne Top40 (AAC 72k), Megaradio Bayern (AAC 72k), RT1 in the mix (AAC 72k), Absolut Relax (AAC 72k).

M) BERLIN & BRANDENBURG
Media institution: Medienanstalt Berlin-Brandenburg (MABB) ✉ Kleine Präsidentenstraße 1, 10178 Berlin ☎ +49 30 264 9670 🖷 +49 30 264 96730 **W:** mabb.de

Berlin sites:

FM	MHz	kW	Site	Station
14)	87.9	1	Alexanderplatz	Star FM
16)	88.4	0.5	Hallesches Ufer	88vier
19)	90.2	16	Alexanderplatz	R. Teddy
16)	90.7	0.1	Schäferberg	88vier
2)	91.4	100	Alexanderplatz	Berliner Rundfunk
10)	93.6	3	Alexanderplatz	JAM FM
3)	94.3	20	Alexanderplatz	rs2
12)	94.8	4	Schäferberg	BBC WS
17)	96.7	0.5	Hallesches Ufer	RFI
13)	97.2	0.1	Hallesches Ufer	R. Russkij
9)	98.2	8	Scholzplatz	R. Paradiso
11)	98.8	1	Alexanderplatz	KISS FM
4)	100.6	13	Alexanderplatz	Flux FM
8)	101.3	5	Alexanderplatz	Klassik R.
15)	101.9	0.5	Alexanderplatz	Metropol FM
5)	103.4	10	Alexanderplatz	Energy Berlin
18)	104.1	0.2	Hallesches Ufer	NPR FM Berlin
6)	104.6	10	Alexanderplatz	104.6 RTL
7)	105.5	5	Alexanderplatz	Spreeradio
21)	106.0	1	Alexanderplatz	R. B2
12)	106.8	2	Scholzplatz	Jazz R.
1)	107.5	13	Schäferberg	BB R.

Brandenburg sites:

FM	MHz	kW	Site	Station
8)	87.6	0.4	Brandenburg/Havel	Klassik R.
5)	87.6	0.2	Prenzlau	Energy Berlin
6)	88.0	1	Crinitz	104.6 RTL
20)	88.3	0.5	Neuruppin	Power R.
6)	89.5	0.5	Elsterwerda-Hohenl.	104.6 RTL
23)	90.3	0.5	Spremberg	R. Cottbus
9)	90.4	0.2	Guben-Reichenbach	R. Paradiso
1)	90.9	0.8	Rhinow	BB R.
8)	91.0	0.5	Booßen (Frankf./O.)	Klassik R.
3)	91.3	1	Lauchhammer West	rs2
5)	91.6	1.3	Casekow	Energy Berlin
21)	91.6	0.5	Cottbus-Klein Oßnig	R. B2
5)	91.7	0.1	Herzberg/Elster	Energy Berlin
20)	91.8	1.3	Zehlendorf	Power R.
23)	92.1	1	Guben-Reichenbach	R. Cottbus
20)	93.3	0.5	Schwedt	Power R.
22)	93.9	3	Fürstenwalde	Sender KW
20)	94.4	1.3	Perleberg	Power R.
23)	94.5	0.3	Cottbus-Madlow	R. Cottbus
3)	94.7	3	Booßen (Frankf./O.)	rs2
25)	94.9	–	Templin	(closed down)
20)	95.2	0.4	Belzig-Lütte	Power R.
20)	95.3	0.1	Fürstenwalde	Power R.
1)	95.4	1.3	Zehlendorf	BB R.
9)	95.5	0.3	Eisenhüttenstadt	R. Paradiso
3)	95.6	1.3	Cottbus-Klein Oßnig	rs2
5)	96.6	0.5	Wittstock	Energy Berlin
3)	96.7	1	Crinitz	rs2

FM	MHz	kW	Site	Station
20)	97.0	0.3	Erkner	Power R.
22)	99.1	0.2	Lübben	Sender KW
23)	99.3	0.8	Booßen (Frankf./O.)	R. Frankfurt/O.
3)	100.1	3	Lübben	rs2
2)	100.9	5	Casekow	Berliner Rundfunk
1)	102.1	20	Casekow	BB-R.
2)	102.2	3	Cottbus-Klein Oßnig	Berliner Rundfunk
23)	102.7	0.5	Forst	R. Cottbus
1)	103.7	0.6	Eisenhüttenstadt	BB R.
24)	103.8	1.5	Großräschen	Elsterwelle
3)	103.9	6	Forst	rs2
2)	104.2	20	Booßen (Frankf./O.)	Berliner Rundfunk
1)	104.3	100	Pritzwalk-Buchholz	BB R.
21)	104.9	1.3	Zehlendorf	R. B2
1)	105.0	3	Brandenburg-Krahne	BB R.
22)	105.1	0.8	Königs Wusterh.	Sender KW
9)	105.9	1.6	Booßen (Frankf./O.)	R. Paradiso
3)	106.3	4	Spremberg	rs2
1)	107.2	100	Calau	BB R.
3)	107.3	12	Casekow	rs2
3)	107.8	30	Booßen (Frankf./O.)	BB R.
1)	107.9	5	Zehlendorf	BB R.

Addresses and other information:
1) Großbeerenstr. 185, 14482 Potsdam; **W:** bbradio.de. AC, with short local insertions (different ones on both Zehlendorf freq.) – **2)** Grunewaldstr. 3, 12165 Berlin; **W:** berliner-rundfunk.de Oldies – **3)** as stn. 2); **W:** rs2.de. AC – **4)** Pfuelstr. 5, 10997 Berlin; **W:** fluxfm. de. Alternative. Further txs see N), K) – **5)** Hardenbergstr. 4-5, 10623 Berlin; **W:** energy.de/berlin. CHR – **6), 7)** Kurfürstendamm 207-208, 10719 Berlin; **W:** 104.6rtl.com (CHR), spreeradio.de (oldies) – **8)** see O) – **9)** Am Kleinen Wannsee 5, 14109 Berlin; **W:** paradiso.de. Soft AC. Run by Protestant church – **10)** as stn. 9); **W:** kissfm.de. CHR – **12)** See International Broadcasting section under UK – **13)** Kochstr. 54, 10969 Berlin; **W:** radio-rb.de. In Russian – **14)** Dircksenstr. 48, 10178 Berlin; **W:** starfm.de. Rock – **15)** Markgrafenstr. 11, 10969 Berlin; **W:** metropolfm.de; prgr. in Turkish. Further txs see K) and T) – **16)** c/o ALEX, Voltastr. 5, 13355 Berlin; **W:** alex-berlin.de. Run by MABB, citizen radio and prgr. from various small ventures, on 88.4MHz in mono – **17)** See International Broadcasting section under France – **18)** See National Public Radio under USA; **W:** nprberlin.de – **19)** August-Bebel-Str. 26-53, 14482 Potsdam; **W:** radioteddy.de; childrens prgr., also via Astra 2C, 12.148GHz h. Further txs see P), Q), T) – **20)** Potsdamer Str. 131, 10783 Berlin; **W:** powerradio918.de. Oldies – **21)** Pfalzburger Str. 43-44, 10717 Berlin; **W:** radiob2.de Use of 106MHz subject of legal action – **22)** Am Funkerberg, Senderhaus 1, 15711 Königs Wusterhausen; **W:** senderkw.de – **23)** Schloßkirchplatz 3, 03046 Cottbus; **W:** radiocottbus. de and radiofrankfurt.de. AC – **24)** see V), stn. 8).
MW: On 693kHz Voice of Russia. **F.PI.:** China R. Int. on 603kHz.
DVB-T: Alexanderplatz and Schäferberg txs on 615MHz (ch. 39) 104.6RTL, Spreeradio, The Wave, Sunshine Live.
DAB: Alexanderplatz and Scholzplatz txs on 178MHz (ch. 5C), mux details see K) – Alexanderplatz tx on 191MHz (ch. 7B) R. Paradiso (AAC 72k), R. B2 (AAC 72k), R. Paloma (AAC 72k), Bayern Plus (AAC 96k), SWR Info (AAC 72k) – Alexanderplatz and Scholzplatz txs on 194MHz (ch. 7D) R. Berlin (AAC 96k), Antenne Brandenburg (AAC 88k), radioeins (AAC 96k), Fritz (AAC 88k), Kultur+ (AAC 112k), Infor. (AAC 64k), Funkhaus Europa (AAC 96k), WDR 2 (L2 128k), Bayern 2 (AAC 96k), BR Klassik (AAC 96k), SWR3 (AAC 88k), MDR Jump (AAC 88k).

N) BREMEN
Media institution: Bremische Landesmedienanstalt (Brema) ▣ Grünenweg 26, 28215 Bremen ☎ +49 421 334940 ▤ +49 421 323533 **W:** bremische-landesmedienanstalt.de

FM	MHz	kW	Site	Station
1)	89.8	1	Bremen-Walle	Energy Bremen
4)	90.7	0.2	Bremerhaven	R. Weser TV
4)	92.5	0.2	Bremen Neuenstr.	R. Weser TV
3)	97.2	0.5	Bremen-Walle	Flux FM
1)	104.3	8	Bremerhaven	Energy Bremen
2)	104.8	0.1	Bremen-Walle	Hit-R. Antenne
5)	107.6	0.2	Bremen-Walle	R. 21
2)	107.9	0.3	Bremerhaven	Hit-R. Antenne

Addresses and other information:
1) Erste Schlachtpforte, 28195 Bremen; **W:** energy.de/bremen CHR – **2)** see M) – **3)** see M), stn. 4) – **4)** Richtweg 14, 28195 Bremen; **W:** radioweser.tv Citizen radio – **5)** see R).
DAB: Bremen-Walle tx on 178.4MHz (ch. 5C), mux details see K).

O) HAMBURG & SCHLESWIG-HOLSTEIN
Media institution: Medienanstalt Hamburg / Schleswig-Holstein (MA HSH) ▣ Rathausallee 72-76, 22846 Norderstedt ☎ +49 40

3690050 ▤ +49 40 36900555 **W:** ma-hsh.de

FM	R.SH	delta	Nora	Klass.	kW
Ahrensburg	–	96.5	–	–	2
Bredstedt	–	–	98.1	–	0.1
Bungsberg (Eutin)	100.2	104.1	106.2	97.2	2x50/0.2
Flensburg-Freienwill	101.4	105.6	–	–	20
Flensburg-Harrislee	–	–	88.5	106.5	0.5
Garding	–	–	94.1	91.7	0.5
Hamburg-Bergedorf	102.0	107.7	93.7*	–	0.1
Hamburg Hertz-T.	100.0	93.4	–	98.1	2x2/0.1
Heide-Welmbüttel	103.8	100.4	–	–	15
Heide (town)	–	–	96.9	–	0.3
Helgoland (island)	100.0	103.5	101.6	89.8	0.1
Husum	–	–	92.0	–	0.1
Itzehoe	–	–	104.9	92.7	1/0.5
Kaltenkirchen	102.9	107.4	101.1	–	20
Kiel	102.4	105.9	97.0	97.4	2x15/0.3
Lauenburg	102.5	105.6	97.4	–	1/1/0.3
Lübeck	–	–	91.5	–	0.3
Mölln-Berkenthin	101.5	107.9	91.5	93.6	2x20/0.3
Neumünster	–	–	88.9	–	0.5
Niebüll	–	–	107.2	94.7	0.2
Rendsburg	–	–	93.6	92.9	0.5
Schleswig (town)	–	–	92.4	100.8	1/0.5
Schleswig-Borgwedel	–	–	–	93.9	0.5
Westerland (Sylt)	102.8	104.8	89.1	89.8	5/5/1/0.5

*) Not on air yet at time of editing.
Addresses and other information:
R.SH (AC), **delta radio** (CHR), **R. Nora** (oldies): Wittland 3, 24109 Kiel; **W:** rsh.de deltaradio.de radionora.de – **Klassik R.**: Postfach 57 03 60, 22772 Hamburg (studio location: Planckstr. 15); **W:** klassikradio. de Classical music. Further txs see K), L), M), P), R), X). Also via Astra 1M, 12.460GHz.

Hamburg area only:

FM	MHz	kW	Site	Station
1)	88.1	0.1	Bergedorf	Oldie 95
1)	88.5	2	Otterndorf*)	R. Hamburg
2)	91.7	0.1	H.-Hertz-Turm	917xfm
2)	93.6	2	Otterndorf*)	Alsterradio
1)	95.0	0.1	H.-Hertz-Turm	Oldie 95
3)	97.1	0.1	H.-Hertz-Turm	Energy Hamburg
1)	100.9	0.1	Bergedorf	Energy Hamburg
3)	101.6	0.1	Wedel	Energy Hamburg
1)	103.6	80	Moorfleet	R. Hamburg
1)	104.0	0.2	H.-Hertz-Turm	R. Hamburg
1)	105.8	0.5	Ahrensburg	Oldie 95
2)	106.8	40	Rahlstedt	106!8 rock'n pop

*) Tx in Niedersachsen, serving Neuwerk and Scharhörn islands (belonging to Hamburg).
Addresses and other information:
1) Postfach 10 01 23, 20001 Hamburg (studio location: Spitalerstraße 10); **W:** radiohamburg.de (AC), oldie95.de (oldies) – **2)** Messberg 4, 20095 Hamburg; **W:** 106acht.de (AC), 917xfm.de (alternative) – **3)** Winterhuder Marktplatz 6, 22299 Hamburg; **W:** energy.de/hamburg CHR

Non-commercial stations:

FM	MHz	kW	Site	Station
1)	93.0	0.1	Hamburg Hertz-Turm	Freies Sender Kombinat
2)	96.0	0.1	Hamburg Hertz-Turm	TIDE 96.0 / HLR
4)	97.6	0.5	Garding	OK Westküste
5)	98.8	0.5	Lübeck-Stockelsdorf	OK Lübeck
4)	98.8	0.1	Husum	OK Westküste
3)	101.2	0.1	Kiel	Kiel FM
5)	105.2	0.1	Heide	OK Westküste

Addresses and other information:
1) Schulterblatt 23c, 20357 Hamburg; **W:** fsk-hh.org – **2)** TIDE 96.0, Uferstraße 2, 22081 Hamburg; **W:** tidenet.de Run by Hamburg Media School. Mon 0500-2300 and thorough Tue 0500 til Sun 0500. **Hamburger Lokalradio**, Kulturzentrum LOLA, Lohbrügger Landstraße 8, 21031 Hamburg; **W:** hhlr.de On 96.0MHz Sun 0500 til Mon 0500 and night Mon/Tue 2300-0500. SW freq. see International Broadcasting section – **3)** Hamburger Chaussee 36, 24113 Kiel; **W:** kielfm.de – **4)** Landvogt-Johannsen-Str. 11, 25746 Heide; **W:** okwestkueste.de – **5)** Kanalstr. 42-48, 23554 Lübeck; **W:** ok-luebeck.de
DAB: Hamburg and Kiel txs on 178MHz (ch. 5C), mux details see K) – Hamburg txs on 189MHz (ch. 7A) NDR 90,3, NDR 2, NDR Kultur, NDR Info, NDR Info Spezial, N-Joy, NDR Musik Plus, NDR Traffic (AAC 48k, others AAC 96k) – Kiel tx on 206MHz (ch. 9C) NDR 1 Welle Nord (AAC 96k), otherwise as Hamburg txs.

P) HESSEN
Media institution: Hessische Landesanstalt für Privaten Rundfunk (LPR) ▣ Wilhelmshöher Allee 262, 34131 Kassel ☎ +49 561 935860 ▤ +49 561 9358630; **W:** lpr-hessen.de

FM	FFH	plan.	Kla.	Bob	Ener	harm	kW
Alsfeld	88.1	–	–	101.5	–	94.1	4/0.1
Bad Camberg	–	–	–	–	–	105.4	0.2
Bad Hersfeld	95.9	–	93.8	99.8	–	88.4	0.1/0.3
Bad Nauheim	–	104.6	–	106.6	–	100.4	0.5/1
Bensheim	–	–	–	103.3	–	107.5	0.2
Bingen	106.9	–	103.4	–	–	101.8	0.2/0.3
Butzbach	–	–	96.0	–	–	–	0.1
Darmstadt	–	–	–	92.4	100.8	–	0.2/0.5
Dieburg	–	90.1	–	99.5	–	104.7	1/0.2
Dillenburg	100.0	–	–	–	–	–	30
Driedorf	106.8	–	–	–	–	–	30
Eisenberg	–	100.3	–	–	–	–	50
Eltville	90.3	–	–	–	–	–	0.2
Eschwege	–	104.6	–	103.0	–	88.3	0.5/0.3
Feldberg	105.9	–	–	–	–	–	100
Frankfurt	–	100.2	107.5	101.4	95.1	105.4	1/0.1
						97.1	0.2
Fritzlar	–	–	–	88.4	–	–	0.1
Fulda	–	99.9	102.8	105.7	–	95.7	0.2/0.3
Gießen	–	93.7	88.0	92.6	105.2	102.0	0.5/0.1
Glashütten	–	–	–	–	–	93.2	0.5
Habichtsw.	103.7	–	–	–	–	–	20
Hanau	–	–	–	–	97.3	106.8	0.5
Heidelstein*	100.9	–	–	–	–	–	50
Hofgeismar	–	–	–	88.8	–	–	0.1
Hoherodskopf	–	–	–	94.7	–	–	0.1
Homberg	–	–	–	99.3	–	–	0.1
H. Meißner	105.1	–	–	–	–	–	100
Idstein	–	–	–	–	–	93.2	0.5
Kassel	–	104.6	104.1	99.4	–	96.6	0.5/0.2
Krehberg	105.0	–	–	–	–	–	20
Korbach	107.7	94.0	–	96.5	–	107.4	20/0.2
Limburg	–	97.6	102.0	90.2	–	92.1	0.5/0.2
Marburg	–	101.0	104.9	103.9	–	96.2	0.3/0.1
Michelstadt	96.1	–	–	98.5	–	104.6	0.1/1
Offenbach	–	–	–	–	–	99.3	0.3
Rimberg	–	–	–	90.5	–	–	0.1
Rotenburg	–	–	–	93.5	–	104.5	0.1
Schlüchtern	–	–	–	101.3	–	–	0.2
Schotten	–	–	–	94.7	–	–	0.1
Vogelsberg	–	–	–	94.7	–	–	0.1
Wetzlar	–	–	100.5	88.2	105.0	101.3	0.3/0.5
Wiesbaden	102.0	90.1	–	101.4	95.1	88.2	0.1/0.5

Addresses and other information:
Hit-R. **FFH** (AC), **Planet R.** (black/CHR), **harmony.fm** (oldies)**:** FFH-Platz 1, 61111 Bad Vilbel; **W:** ffh.de, planet-radio.de, harmonyfm.de; also via Astra 1L, 12.633GHz (harmony.fm using two freq. at Frankfurt due to interference situation) – **Klassik R.** see O) – **R. Bob**, Friedrich-Ebert-Str. 2, 34117 Kassel; **W:** radiobob.de. Rock – **Energy Rhein-Main**, Rüsselsheimer Str. 22, 60326 Frankfurt am Main; **W:** energy.de/rhein-main. CHR

Other stations:

FM	MHz	kW	Site	Station
5)	90.1	0.1	Marburg-Lahnberge	R. Unerhört
3)	90.9	0.3	Rüsselsheim	R. Rüsselsheim
8)	91.7	0.2	Kassel Tannenwäldchen	R. Teddy
1)	91.8	0.1	Frankfurt-Ginnheim	R. X
2)	92.5	0.1	Wiesbaden	R. RheinWelle 92,5
7)	96.5	0.3	Witzenhausen	RundFunk Meißner
9)	99.2	0.3	Fulda	Domradio
7)	99.4	0.1	Sontra	RundFunk Meißner
7)	99.7	0.5	Eschwege	RundFunk Meißner
7)	102.6	0.3	Hessisch Lichtenau	RundFunk Meißner
4)	103.4	0.3	Darmstadt	R. Darmstadt
6)	105.8	0.5	Kassel Tannenwäldchen	Freies R. Kassel

Addresses and other information:
1) Schützenstr. 12, 60311 Frankfurt; **W:** radiox.de – **2)** Postfach 49 20, 65039 Wiesbaden; **W:** rheinwelle.de – **3)** Ludwigstr. 13-15, 65428 Rüsselsheim; **W:** radiok2r.de – **4)** Steubenplatz 12, 64293 Darmstadt; **W:** radiodarmstadt.de – **5)** Rudolf-Bultmann-Str. 2b, 35039 Marburg; **W:** radio-rum.de – **6), 7)** Niederhoner Str. 1, 37269 Eschwege; **W:** eschwege.de/rfm – **8)** see M) – **9)** see S)
DAB: 6 txs on 178MHz (ch. 5C), mux details see K) – 4 txs on 191MHz (ch. 7B) hr1 (AAC 120k), hr2 (AAC 144k), hr3 (AAC 120k), hr4 (AAC 112k), You FM (AAC 112k), hr-info (AAC 88k) – Feldberg and Frankfurt txs on 220MHz (ch. 11C) FFH (AAC 72k), Planet R. (AAC 72k), Harmony (AAC 72k), R. Teddy (AAC 72k), Absolut Relax (AAC 72k), Antenne 50plus (AAC 48k).

Q) MECKLENBURG-VORPOMMERN

Media institution: Landesrundfunkzentrale Mecklenburg-Vorpommern, ✉ Bleicheufer 1, 19053 Schwerin ☎ +49 385 5588 10 📠 +49 385 5588 130 **W:** lrz-mv.de

Commercial stations:

Location	A.MV	Osts	103.3	Klass	Tedd	kW
Ahrenshoop	–	–	103.3	–	–	0.3
Garz (Rügen)	105.1	107.6	–	–	–	50
Grevesmühlen	105.8	94.7	–	–	–	0.2/0.1
Güstrow	107.7	98.0	–	–	–	1/0.4
Helpterberg	103.8	105.8	–	–	–	100
Heringsdorf	105.4	103.3	–	–	–	10/2
Marlow	100.8	104.8	–	–	–	100
Röbel	93.8	92.2	–	–	–	50/0.1
Rostock	97.3	105.6	–	–	–	2
Schwerin	101.3	107.3	–	90.1	102.9	100/0.2
Stralsund	–	–	–	98.9	–	0.4
Waren	98.3	93.0	–	–	–	0.2/0.1
Wismar	88.7	93.7	–	97.0	–	0.2/0.1
Wolgast	–	–	–	–	–	0.5

Addresses and other information:
Antenne MV, 19086 Plate; **W:** antennemv.de. AC – **Ostseewelle**, Warnowufer 59a, 18057 Rostock; **W:** ostseewelle.de. CHR – **103.3 Ihr Lokalradio**, Cubanzestr. 19b, 18211 Kühlungsborn (office; studio in Wieck); **W:** radio1033.de. Oldies – **Klassik R.** see O) – **Radio Teddy** see M), stn. 19)

Non-commercial stations:

FM	MHz	kW	Site	Station
1)	88.0	0.8	Neubrandenburg	NB-Radiotreff
3)	90.2	0.1	Rostock-Stadtweide	LOHRO
2)	98.1	0.2	Greifswald	R. 98eins
1)	98.7	0.1	Malchin	NB-Radiotreff

Addresses and other information:
1) Treptower Str. 9, 17033 Neubrandenburg; **W:** nb-radiotreff.de; run by Landesrundfunkzentrale, also prgr. from Malchin studio – **2)** Domstr. 12, 17489 Greifswald; **W:** 98eins.de; run by university, Mon-Fri 1800-2200 only, otherwise rel. stn. 1) – **3)** Margaretenstr. 43, 18057 Rostock; **W:** lohro.de
DAB: Schwerin tx on on 178MHz (ch. 5C) with K) mux, on 226MHz (ch. 12B) NDR 1 R. MV, NDR 2, NDR Kultur, NDR Info, NDR Info Spezial, N-Joy, NDR Musik Plus, NDR Traffic (AAC 48k, others AAC 96k).

R) NIEDERSACHSEN

Media institution: Niedersächsische Landesmedienanstalt für privaten Rundfunk (NLM), ✉ Seelhorststraße 18, 30175 Hannover ☎ +49 511 28477 0 📠 +49 511 28477 36 **W:** nlm.de

FM	ffn	Ant.	R. 21	Klass	kW
Aurich	103.1	104.9	100.6	–	2x25/1
Bad Rehburg	–	–	89.4	–	0.5
Barsinghausen	101.9	103.8	–	–	25
Braunschw.-Broitzem	103.1	106.9	104.1	–	15/13/1
Celle	–	–	93.5	–	0.2
Cuxhaven-Otterndorf	102.6	104.6	–	–	20
Dannenberg-Zernien	102.7	106.1	–	–	25
Delmenhorst	–	–	107.6	–	0.1
Goslar	–	–	87.7	–	0.5
Göttingen	102.8	106.0	93.4	–	2x5/1
Hannoversch Münden	100.7	106.7	–	–	0.5
Hannover	–	–	104.9	107.4	0.5/0.2
Helmstedt	–	–	94.1	–	0.5
Hildesheim	–	–	105.8	–	1
Holzminden	102.2	105.7	–	–	0.5
Leer-Nüttermoor	–	–	104.5	–	0.3
Lingen-Damaschke	101.5	104.3	106.9	–	2x15/0.5
Oldenburg	–	–	104.1	–	0.2
Osnabrück	103.4	105.9	95.3	–	2x10/0.1
Rosengarten	100.6	105.1	–	–	20
Seesen	–	100.9	–	–	0.1
Steinkimmen	102.3	105.7	–	–	100
Torfhaus (Harz)	102.4	106.3	–	–	100
Visselhövede	101.7	104.2	101.0	–	2x10/1
Wilhelmshaven	–	99.1	–	–	0.3
Wolfsburg	–	95.1	–	–	0.1

N.B R. Hamburg / 106!8 rock'n pop txs at Cuxhaven see O).
Addresses and other information:
R. ffn, Stiftstraße 8, 30159 Hannover; **W:** ffn.de AC – **Hit-R. Antenne**, Goseriede 9, 30159 Hannover; **W:** antenne.com. AC – **R. 21**, An der Feuerwache 3-5, 30823 Garbsen; **W:** radio21.de Rock, cooperates with Rockland Radio, see T). Bremen tx see N). F – **Klassik R.** see O). **F.P.I.:** More FM txs for R. 21.

Local stations:

FM	MHz	kW	Site	Station
4)	87.7	0.2	Emden	R. Ostfriesland
3)	87.8	1	Wilhelmshaven	R. Jade
1)	88.0	1	Uelzen	R. ZuSa
5)	89.7	0.5	Dannenberg-Zernien	R. ZuSa
4)	94.0	1	Aurich-Haxtum	R. Ostfriesland
8)	94.8	0.1	Bad Pyrmont	R. Aktiv

FM	MHz	kW	Site	Station
2)	95.2	0.2	Nordhorn	Ems-Vechte-Welle
1)	95.5	1	Lüneburg	R. ZuSa
5)	95.6	1	Lingen-Schepsdorf	Ems-Vechte-Welle
5)	99.3	1	Molbergen-Cloppenburg	Ems-Vechte-Welle
8)	100.0	0.3	Hameln	R. Aktiv
12)	100.0	0.1	Hannover Bettfedernf.	R. Flora
4)	103.9	0.2	Leer	R. Ostfriesland
10)	104.6	0.5	Braunschweig-Broitzem	R. Okerwelle
6)	104.8	1	Osnabrück	OS R. 104,8
11)	105.3	1	Hildesheim	R. Tonkuhle
2)	106.5	1	Oldenburg-Wahnbek	Oldenburg Eins
7)	106.5	0.3	Hannover Telemaxx tower	Leinehertz
9)	107.1	1	Göttingen	StadtR. Gött.

Adresses and other information:
1) Ilmenauufer 47, 29525 Uelzen and Scharnhorststr. 1, 21335 Lüneburg; **W:** zusa.de – **2)** Bahnhofstr. 11, 26122 Oldenburg; **W:** uni-oldenburg.de/ok_ ol/ – **3)** Kieler Str. 31, 26382 Wilhelmshaven; **W:** radio-jade.de – **4)** VHS Emden, An der Berufsschule 3, 26721 Emden; **W:** radio-ostfriesland.net – **5)** Halle IV, Kaiserstr. 10a, 49809 Lingen; **W:** emsvechtewelle.de – **6)** Lohstr. 45a, 49074 Osnabrück; **W:** os-radio.de – **7)** Hildesheimer Str. 29, 30169 Hannover; **W:** leinehertz.de – **8)** Hefehof 23, 31785 Hameln; **W:** radio-aktiv.de – **9)** Groner Str. 2, 37073 Göttingen; **W:** stadtradio-goettingen.de – **10)** Rebenring 18, 38106 Braunschweig; **W:** okerwelle. dc **11)** Andreas-Passage 1, 31134 Hildesheim; **W:** tonkuhle.de – **12)** Zur Bettfedernfabrik 3, 30451 Hannover; **W:** radioflora.de; on 100.0MHz during special events, otherwise via webstream only.
F.P.I.: New stns R. Hannover, R. 38 (Braunschweig) and Teutoradio (Osnabrück), freq. not determined yet at time of editing.
Permanent special stns: R. SWS (**W:** radio-sws.de), Norderney 104.0MHz; **R. S.A.S.** (**W:** radio-sas.de), Stadthagen 94.5MHz; **Lamberti-Kirchenfunk** (**W:** soerenkoenig.com/Radlam) Aurich 106.0MHz; **Kirchenfunk Esterwegen**, 106.6MHz; **Kirchenfunk Lorup**, 107.6MHz; **Kirchenfunk Herzlake**, 106.1MHz; **Pfarrfunk Breitenberg**, 98.4MHz; **Kirchenfunk Meppen**, 95.0MHz; **Pfarrradio Warsingsfehn**, Moormerland 95.2MHz.
MW: On 630kHz Voice of Russia
DAB: Hannover/Osnabrück/Braunschweig txs on 178MHz (ch. 5C), mux details see K) – Visselhövede tx on 182MHz (ch. 6A), Hannover tx on 187MHz (ch. 6D), Steinkimmen tx on 224MHz (ch. 12A) NDR 1 Niedersachsen, NDR 2, NDR Kultur, NDR Info, NDR Info Spezial, N-Joy, NDR Musik Plus, NDR Traffic (AAC 48k, others AAC 96k).

S) NORDRHEIN-WESTFALEN
Media institution: Landesanstalt für Medien Nordrhein-Westhalen (LfM) ⊠ Postfach 10 34 43, 40025 Düsseldorf (office location. Zollhof 2) ☎ +49 211 77 007 0 🗏 +49 211 727 170 **W:** lfm-nrw.de
R. NRW, Essener Str. 55, 46047 Oberhausen; **W:** radionrw.de The following stns are affiliates with some hours of own prgrs per day, other times rel. R. NRW with local IDs inserted automatically.

FM	MHz	kW	Site	Station
5)	87.7	0.2	Krefeld-Oppum	Welle Niederrhein
26)	88.1	4	Eggegebirge	R. Hochstift
19)	88.2	0.5	Lüdinghausen	R. Kiepenkerl
37)	88.2	0.5	Siegen	R. Siegen
35)	88.3	0.1	Meinerzhagen	R. MK
16)	88.4	1	Bocholt	Westmünsterlandw.
36)	89.1	0.2	Schmallenberg	R. Sauerland
7)	89.4	1	Düsseldorf Rheinturm	NE-WS 89.4
6)	90.1	0.3	Mönchengladbach	R. 90,1
31)	90.8	0.1	Herne	Herne 90acht
30)	91.2	0.2	Dortmund	R. 91.2
39)	91.2	0.2	Siegburg	R. Bonn/Rhein-Sieg
42)	91.4	0.1	Bergheim	R. Erft
35)	91.5	0.1	Altena	R. MK
33)	91.5	0.1	Hattingen-Schierken	R. en
3)	91.7	0.1	Moers-Meerbeck	R. K.W.
23)	91.7	0.1	Vlotho	R. Herford
4)	92.2	0.1	Duisburg	R. Duisburg
35)	92.5	0.3	Iserlohn	R. MK
20)	92.6	1	Sendenhorst	R. WAF
43)	92.7	0.5	Düren-Hürtgenwald	R. Rur
13)	92.9	0.5	Mülheim-Saarn	R. Mülheim
29)	92.9	0.1	Selm	antenne unna
16)	93.0	0.5	Ahaus	Westmünsterlandw.
26)	93.7	0.1	Paderborn	R. Hochstift
39)	94.2	0.1	Much-Wersch	R.Bonn/Rhein-Sieg
9)	94.3	0.2	Solingen	R. RSG
15)	94.6	0.1	Recklinghausen	Hit R. Vest
20)	94.7	0.2	Warendorf	R. WAF
36)	94.8	0.1	Marsberg	R. Sauerland
23)	94.9	0.5	Herford	R. Herford
24)	95.1	0.1	Rahden	R. Westfalica

FM	MHz	kW	Site	Station
18)	95.4	0.2	Münster	Antenne Münster
15)	95.6	0.1	Berghaltern	Hit R. Vest
24)	95.7	0.5	Minden Jakobsberg	R. Westfalica
20)	95.7	0.3	Beckum	R. WAF
14)	96.1	0.1	Gelsenkirchen	REL
36)	96.2	0.4	Olsberg-Antfeld	R. Sauerland
20)	96.3	0.3	Oelde	R. WAF
38)	96.9	0.5	Leverkusen-Opladen	R. Berg
1)	97.2	0.1	Simmerath	Antenne AC
35)	97.2	0.1	Werdohl	R. MK
37)	97.3	0.1	Bad Laasphe	R. Siegen
29)	97.4	0.5	Lünen	Antenne Unna
11)	97.6	4	Langenberg	R. Neandertal
16)	97.6	1	Borken	Westmünsterlandw.
22)	97.6	0.4	Friedrichsdorf	R. Bielefeld
39)	97.8	0.5	Bonn Venusberg	R.Bonn/Rhein-Sieg
2)	98.0	1	Kleve	Antenne Niederrhein
22)	98.3	0.1	Bielefeld	R. Bielefeld
32)	98.5	0.5	Bochum	R. 98.5
14)	98.7	0.5	Bottrop	REL
37)	98.9	0.1	Neunkirchen	R. Siegen
35)	99.5	0.1	Plettenberg	R. MK
44)	99.7	0.5	Euskirchen	R. Euskirchen
38)	99.7	0.5	Gremberg	R. Berg
39)	99.9	0.5	Bonn-Königswinter	R.Bonn/Rhein-Sieg
1)	100.1	0.4	Aachen Karlshöhe	Antenne AC
35)	100.2	0.5	Lüdenscheid	R. MK
5)	100.6	1	Viersen	Welle Niederrhein
27)	100.9	1	Soest-Möhnesee	Hellweg R.
25)	101.0	0.5	Schieder-Schwalenbg.	R. Lippe
7)	102.1	0.3	Grevenbroich	NE-WS 89.4
12)	102.2	0.3	Essen-Werden	R. Essen
29)	102.3	1	Schwerte Sommerberg	Antenne Unna
5)	102.5	0.3	Viersen Süchtelner Höhe	Welle Niederrhein
16)	103.6	0.1	Gronau	Westmünsterlandw.
27)	103.6	0.1	Lippstadt	Hellweg R.
17)	104.0	1	Tecklenburg	R. RST
8)	104.2	1	Düsseldorf	Antenne Düsseldorf
33)	104.2	0.1	Witten-Stockum	R. en
26)	104.8	0.5	Neuhaus-Hasselberg	R. Hochstift
26)	104.8	0.1	Büren	R. Hochstift
36)	104.9	0.1	Meschede	R. Sauerland
1)	105.0	0.1	Monschau	Antenne AC
12)	105.0	0.1	Essen-Holsterhausen	R. Essen
28)	105.0	0.1	Hamm	R. Lippewelle
38)	105.2	4	Lindlar	R. Berg
37)	105.2	4	Schöppingen	R. RST
15)	105.2	0.1	Dorsten	Hit Radio Vest
37)	105.4	4	Aue-Kirchhundem	R. Siegen
38)	105.7	1	Waldbröl	R. Berg
2)	105.7	0.5	Geldern	Antenne Niederrhein
33)	105.7	0.1	Gevelsberg	R. en
42)	105.8	1	Köln-Ehrenfeld	R. Erft
13)	106.2	0.1	Oberhausen	R. Oberhausen
19)	106.3	0.2	Dülmen	R. Kiepenkerl
36)	106.5	0.5	Hallenberg	R. Sauerland
36)	106.5	0.3	Arnsberg	R. Sauerland
25)	106.6	1	Lemgo	R. Lippe
24)	106.6	0.1	Lübbecke	R. Westfalica
21)	106.8	0.4	Borgholzhausen	R. Gütersloh
45)	106.9	4	Schleiden (Eifel)	R. Euskirchen
41)	107.1	0.5	Köln Neumarkt	R. Köln
33)	107.2	0.1	Herdecke	R. en
27)	107.3	0.2	Wickede	Hellweg R.
19)	107.4	1	Coesfeld	R. Kiepenkerl
25)	107.4	1	Linderhofe-Dörenberg	R. Lippe
10)	107.4	0.5	Wuppertal	R. Wuppertal
44)	107.4	0.1	Bad Münstereifel	R. Euskirchen
21)	107.5	1	Oelde	R. Gütersloh
43)	107.5	0.1	Linnich	R. Rur
36)	107.6	0.5	Sundern	R. Sauerland
3)	107.6	0.2	Wesel-Büderich	R. K.W.
40)	107.6	0.1	Leverkusen-Wiesdorf	R. Leverkusen
27)	107.7	0.2	Belecke-Sennhöfe	Hellweg R.
34)	107.7	0.1	Hagen	R. Hagen
1)	107.8	0.4	Aachen Stolberg	Antenne AC
39)	107.9	0.1	Herchen-Rosbach	R.Bonn/Rhein-Sieg
9)	107.9	0.1	Remscheid	R. RSG

Adresses and other information:
1) Merzbrück 214, 52146 Würselen, **W:** antenne-ac.de – **2)** Stechbahn 2-8, 47533 Kleve, **W:** antenneniederrhein.de – **3)** Rheinstr. 24-26, 47495 Rheinberg, **W:** radiokw.de – **4)** Ruhrorter Str. 187, 47119 Duisburg, **W:** medien.freepage.de/guidojansen – **5)** Uerdinger Str. 543, 47800

Krefeld, **W:** welleniederrhein.de − **6)** Lüpertzender Str. 159, 41061 Mönchengladbach, **W:** radio901.de − **7)** Moselstr. 16, 41464 Neuss, **W:** news894.de − **8)** Kaistr. 7, 40221 Düsseldorf, **W:** antenneduesseldorf.de − **9)** Postfach, 42601 Solingen (studio location: Alleestr. 1) **W:** radiosg. de − **10)** Friedrich-Engels-Allee 426, 42283 Wuppertal, **W:** radiowuppertal.de − **11)** Elberfelder Str. 81, 40804 Remscheid, **W:** radioneandertal. de − **12)** Sachsenstr. 36, 45128 Essen **W:** radio-essen.de − **13)** Essener Str. 99, 46047 Oberhausen **W:** 106.2.radiooberhausen.de and 92.9.radiomülheim.de − **14)** Hochstr. 68, 45894 Gelsenkirchen, **W:** radioemscher-lippe.de − **15)** Schaumburgstr. 14, 45657 Recklinghausen, **W:** hitradiovest.de − **16)** Heinrich-Hertz-Str. 6, 46325 Borken **W:** radiowmw. de − **17)** Postnstr. 3, 48431 Rheine, **W:** radiorst.de − **18)** Nevinghoff 14/16, 48147 Münster, **W:** antennemuenster.de − **19)** Tiberstr. 21, 48249 Dülmen, **W:** radio-kiepenkerl.de − **20)** Am Schweinemarkt 3, 48231 Warendorf, **W:** radiowaf.de − **21)** Feldstr. 14, 33330 Gütersloh **W:** radioguetersloh.de − **22)** Niedernstr. 21-27, 33602 Bielefeld **W:** radiobielefeld.de − **23)** Berliner Str. 30, 32052 Herford **W:** radioherford. de − **24)** Johanniskirchhof 2, 32423 Minden **W:** radiowestfalica.de − **25)** Lagesche Str. 17, 32756 Detmold **W:** radiolippe.de − **26)** Frankfurter Weg 22, 33106 Paderborn **W:** radiohochstift.de − **27)** Jakobistr. 46, 59494 Soest **W:** hellwegradio.de − **28)** Königstr. 39, 59065 Hamm **W:** lippewelle.de − **30)** Karl-Zahn-Str. 11, 44141 Dortmund **W:** radio912.de − **31)** Bahnhofstr. 45, 44623 Herne **W:** radio-herne.de − **32)** Westring 26, 44787 Bochum, **W:** ruhrwelle-bochum.de − **33)** Mühlenstr. 25, 58285 Gevelsberg **W:** radio-en.de − **34)** Rathausstr. 23, 58095 Hagen, **W:** radiohagen.de − **35)** Vinckestr. 9-13, 58636 Iserlohn, **W:** radio-mk.de − **36)** Steinstr. 32, 59872 Meschede, **W:** radio-sauerland.de − **37)** Postfach 10 02 42, 57002 Siegen (studio location: Obergraben 33), **W:** radio-siegen. de − **38)** Friedrich-Ebert-Str., 51429 Bergisch Gladbach, **W:** radioberg.de − **39)** Kennedybrücke 4, 53225 Bonn, **W:** radiobonn.de − **40)** Bismarckstr. 71, 51373 Leverkusen, **W:** radioleverkusen.de − **41)** Stolberger Str. 374, 50933 Köln, **W:** radiokoeln.de − **42)** Hürth Park, 50354 Hürth, **W:** radioerft.de − **45)** August-Klotz-Str. 21, 52349 Düren, **W:** radiodur.de − **45)** Rheinstr. 55, 53881 Euskirchen, **W:** radioeuskirchen.de

Stn's not affiliated to Radio NRW:

FM	MHz	kW	Site	Station
12)	87.9	0.05	Bielefeld	Hertz 87.9
13)	89.4	0.03	Paderborn	L'Unico
9)	90.0	0.3	Bochum	CT das radio
11)	90.9	0.05	Münster university	R. Q
1)	92.0	0.05	Pulheim	Domradio
2)	92.1	0.03	Siegen university	Radius 92,1
8)	93.0	0.05	Dortmund university	Eldoradio
3)	94.3	0.05	Bielefeld-Bethel	Antenne Bethel
14)	94.7	0.05	Meschede	R. FH
7)	96.8	0.5	Bonn	(shared freq.)
6)	97.1	0.04	Düsseldorf-Bilk	Hochschulr. Düssel.
15)	89.4	0.03	Paderborn university	L'Unico FM
4)	99.1	0.1	Aachen	Hochschulr. Aachen
5)	100.0	0.1	Köln Sternengasse	Kölncampus
1)	101.7	0.03	Köln Sternengasse	Domradio
11)	103.9	0.5	Steinfurt college	R. Q
10)	104.5	0.2	Essen university	Campus FM
10)	105.6	0.05	Essen university	Campus FM

Adresses and other information:
1) Domkloster 3, 50667 Köln; **W:** domradio.de; further txs see P) and T), also via Astra 1L, 12.460GHz h. Run by Catholic church − **2)** Hölderlinstr. 3, 57068 Siegen; **W:** radius921.de − **3)** Quellenhofweg 25, 33617 Bielefeld-Bethel; **W:** antenne-bethel.de Run by diacony − **4)** Wüllnerstr. 5, 52056 Aachen; **W:** hochschulradio-aachen.de − **5)** Albertus-Magnus-Platz, 50923 Köln; **W:** koelncampus.de − **6)** Universitätsstr. 1, 40225 Düsseldorf; **W:** hochschulradio.uni-duesseldorf.de − **7)** shared by six groups − **8)** Vogelpothsweg 74, 44227 Dortmund; **W:** eldoradio.de − **9)** 44780 Bochum (studio location: Ruhr university, room 04/452); **W:** radioct.de − **10)** Universitätsstr. 2, 45141 Essen; **W:** campusfm.info − **11)** Bismarckallee 3, 48151 Münster; **W:** radioq.de − **12)** Universitätsstr. 25, 33615 Bielefeld; **W:** radiohertz.de − **13)** Warburger Str. 100, 33098 Paderborn; **W:** l-unico.de − **14)** Jahnstr. 23, 59872 Meschede; **W:** radiofh.de − **15)** Warburger Str. 100, 33098 Paderborn; **W:** l-unico.de − **16)** Radio Triquency, Liebigstr. 87, 32657 Lemgo; **W:** triquency.de Via lp. txs on 95.9/96.1/99.4MHz **N.B** Stn's 2) and 4)-16) university/college.

DAB: 6 txs on 178MHz (ch. 5C), mux details see K) − 24 txs on 229MHz (ch. 12D) Eins Live (AAC 128k), WDR 2 (L2 128k), Funkhaus Europa (AAC 112k), Eins Live diggi (AAC 128k), Kiraka (AAC 112k), WDR Event (takes capacity from others when on air), Vera (L2 mono), Domradio (L2 mono).

T) RHEINLAND-PFALZ
Media institution: Landesanstalt für Medien und Kommunikation (LMK) ✉ Postfach 21 73 63, 67072 Ludwigshafen (office location: Turmstraße 8) ☎ +49 621 5252 0 📠 +49 621 5252 152 **W:** lmk-online.de

FM	RPR 1	bigFM	Rockl.	Metrop	kW
Bad Bergzabern	103.3	–	–	–	0.3
Bad Dürkheim	98.1	96.4	–	–	0.1
Bad Kreuznach	89.7	104.8	–	–	0.1/0.2
Bad Marienberg	102.9	–	–	–	25
Bernkastel-Kues	–	100.5	–	–	0.1
Betzdorf	–	107.7	–	–	0.5
Bitburg	–	–	107.9	–	0.1
Bornberg-Eßweiler	103.1	107.6	–	–	25
Daun (Eifel)	102.1	106.6	–	–	20
Diezer Hain	101.2	100.4	–	–	0.1
Grünstadt/Mertesh.	103.3	–	–	–	0.1
Haardtkopf	100.1	–	–	–	50
Heckenbach	103.5	104.9	–	–	30
Hohe Wurzel	–	–	107.9	–	6
Idar-Oberstein	100.3	101.9	–	–	1
Kalmit	103.6	106.7	–	–	25
Kirchheimbolanden	–	–	97.1	–	0.2
Kleinkarlbach	91.1	–	–	–	0.1
Koblenz Kühkopf	101.5	104.0	–	–	40
Koblenz-Bendorf	–	–	88.3	107.8	0.3
Linz	–	–	96.9	–	0.2
Ludwigshafen	–	–	–	88.4	0.1
Mainz Ober-Olm	100.6	104.5	–	–	20
Mainz (city)	98.1	106.6	–	96.0	0.2/0.4
Mannheim	–	–	93.2	–	1
Pirmas. Kettrichhof	104.7	–	–	–	5
Pirmasens (town)	–	96.7	–	–	0.4
Rivenich	–	95.8	–	–	0.2
Saarburg	102.6	96.5	–	–	0.1
Trier Petrisberg	102.9	106.4	105.8	–	0.1/0.5
Zweibrücken	103.3	106.6	–	–	2/0.1

Addresses and other information:
RPR 1, Turmstr. 8, 67059 Ludwigshafen; **W:** rpr1.de − **bigFM:** see K), stn.2); rel. of adopted version in responsibility of RPR − **Rockland R.**, Wallstr. 1-5, 55122 Mainz; **W:** rockland.de; cooperates with R. 21, see R) − **Metropol FM** see M), stn. 15

Local stations:

FM	MHz	kW	Site	Station
3)	87.6	0.2	Idar-Oberstein	R. Idar-Oberstein
7)	87.8	0.1	Welschbillig	Cityradio Trier
10)	87.9	0.1	Bretzenheim (church)	Studio Nahe
2)	88.3	0.1	Bad Kreuznach	Antenne Bad Kreuznach
7)	88.4	0.5	Trier Petrisberg	Cityradio Trier
6)	88.4	0.3	Pirmasens	R. Pirmasens
8)	94.1	0.3	Mommenhein	Antenne Mainz
5)	94.2	1	Neustadt/Weinstr.	Antenne Pfalz
9)	94.7	0.2	Wittlich	R. Wittlich
7)	94.7	0.1	Trierweiler	Cityradio Trier
5)	94.8	0.1	Landau	Antenne Landau
4)	96.9	0.5	Kaiserslautern	Antenne Kaiserslautern
8)	97.1	0.1	Bodenheim	Antenne Mainz
11)	87.8	0.1	Koblenz	R. Tedy
1)	98.0	1	Koblenz Moselw. Str.	Antenne Koblenz
1)	98.0	1	Neuwied	Antenne Koblenz
1)	98.9	1	Koblenz-Bendorf	Antenne Koblenz
8)	106.6	0.1	Mainz	Antenne Mainz

Addresses and other information:
1) Friedrich-Ebert-Ring 54, 56068 Koblenz; **W:** akoblenz.de − **2)** Kreuzstr. 31-33, 55543 Bad Kreuznach; **W:** antenne-kh.de − **3)** Auf der Idar 2a, 55743 Idar-Oberstein; **W:** radio-io.de − **4)** Am Altenhof 11-13, 67655 Kaiserslautern; **W:** antenne-kl.de − **5)** Europastr. 3, 67433 Neustadt/ Wstr.; **W:** antenne-landau.de antenne-pfalz.de − **6)** Schloßstr. 44, 66953 Pirmasens; **W:** radio-pirmasens.de − **7)** Paulinstr. 1, 54292 Trier; **W:** cityradio-trier.de − **8)** Hechtsheimer Str. 35, 55131 Mainz; **W:** antenne-mainz. de − **9)** Schloßstr. 7a, 54516 Wittlich; **W:** radio-wittlich.de − **10)** Obere Grabenstr. 29, 55450 Langenlonsheim; **W:** studio-nahe.de Run by Catholic church, mostly rel. Domradio, see S) − **11)** See M), stn. 19).
DAB: 8 txs on 217MHz (ch. 11A) SWR1 RP (L2 160k), SWR2 (AAC 120k), SWR3 (AAC 120k), SWR4 RP (AAC 160k), DasDing (AAC 120k), SWR Info (L2 128k), Big FM World Beats (AAC 72k) − Scharteberg tx on 224MHz (ch. 12A), rel. 178MHz mux, see K).

U) SAARLAND
Media institution: Landesmedienanstalt Saar (LMS) ✉ Postfach 11 01 64, 66010 Saarbrücken (office location: Nell-Breuning-Allee 4) ☎ +49 681 389880; 📠 +49 681 3898820; **W:** lmsaar.de

FM networks:

Location	Salü	C.Ro.	bigFM	Saar.	kW
Homburg	–	–	–	89.6	1
Merzig	103.0	–	92.6	105.1	0.1/0.5
Mettlach	104.2	–	–	105.1	0.3
Neunkirchen	–	99.3	–	94.6	1/0.6
Oberperl	100.3	–	–	–	5

Location	Salü	C.Ro.	bigFM	Saar.	kW
Saarbr. Schoksbg.	101.7	–	–	–	100
Saarbr. Halberg	–	–	94.2	–	1
Saarbr. Winterberg	–	92.9	–	–	1
Saarbr. Schwarzenbg.	–	–	–	99.6	0.1
Saarlouis	–	102.8	–	–	1
St. Ingbert	–	100.6	–	–	0.1
Sulzbach	–	–	96.8	–	0.1
Webenheim	100.0	–	–	–	5

Addresses and other information:
R. Salü, Classic Rock R.: Postfach 10 08 44, 66008 Saarbrücken (studio location: Richard-Wagner-Str. 58-60); **W:** salue.de, classic-rock-radio.de – **bigFM Saarland:** Gutenbergstr. 11-23, 66103 Saarbrücken; **W:** bigfm-saarland.de; mostly rel. Stuttgart prgr. (see K), stn. 2) – **R. Saarbrücken, R. Merzig, R. Neunkirchen, R. Homburg:** Nell-Breuning-Allee 6, 66115 Saarbrücken; **W:** radio-sb.de, radiomerzig.de, antenneneunkirchen.de, radio-homburg.de
LW: On 183kHz Europe 1, see France. Tx in responsibility of Groupe Lagardère Saarbrücken branch, also operating R. Salü / Classic Rock R.
DAB: Saarbrücken tx on 178MHz (ch. 5C), mux details see K) – 5 txs on 203MHz (ch. 9A) SR 1 (L2 192k), SR 2 (L2 192k), SR 3 (L2 192k), Unser Ding (AAC 96k), Antenne Saar (AAC 96k), Radio Salü (AAC 72k).

V) SACHSEN

Media institution: Sächsische Landesanstalt für privaten Rundfunk und neue Medien (SLM) ✉ Postfach 10 16 62, 04016 Leipzig ☎ +49 341 22 59 0 ▤ +49 341 22 59 199; **W:** slm-online.de; office location: Ferdinand-Lassalle-Straße 21.

FM	PSR	R.SA	RTL	Radio	Energ.	kW
Annaberg-Buchholz	–	104.8	–	–	–	0.5
Auerbach	–	107.9	–	–	–	0.1
Bärenstein	–	–	–	107.2E	–	0.2
Beilrode	–	99.6	–	–	–	1
Borna	–	–	–	99.5L	–	0.1
Chemnitz-Reichenh.	–	91.0	–	102.1C	97.5	3
Collmberg	98.0	–	104.7	–	–	5/10
Döbeln	–	107.9	–	–	98.3	1/0.2
Dresden-Gompitz	–	–	–	91.1D	–	1
Dresden-Wachwitz	102.4	89.2	105.2	103.5D	100.2	100/2
Ebersbach	–	106.1	–	–	–	0.5
Elsterberg	–	99.7	–	–	–	0.2
Flöha	–	98.4	–	99.0C	–	0.1
Freiberg	–	90.0	–	104.2D	98.4	0.2/0.5
Freital	–	88.3	–	107.0D	–	0.2
Geyer (Erzgebirge)	100.0	–	105.4	–	–	100
Görlitz	–	105.1	–	–	–	1
Grimma	–	107.4	–	90.9I	93.3	2/0.3
Hoyerswerda-Zeißig	–	96.9	–	–	87.6	0.2/0.3
Leipzig-Holzhausen	–	–	–	91.3L	99.8	4
Leipzig-Reudnitz	–	98.2	–	–	–	1
Leisnig	–	100.5	–	–	–	0.2
Limbach-Oberfrohna	–	–	–	107.3C	–	0.1
Löbau Schafberg	101.0	–	105.6	107.6G	–	30
Löbau town	–	87.6	–	–	–	0.5
Markneukirchen	–	89.6	–	–	–	1
Meerane	–	–	–	89.2Z	–	0.1
Meißen-Korbitz	–	–	–	107.5D	–	0.2
Mittelherwigsdorf	–	100.0	–	94.3G	–	0.5/0.3
Mügeln	–	91.2	–	–	–	0.5
Neukirchen	–	–	–	95.8C	–	1
Niederschöna	–	94.4	–	–	–	0.5
Nossen	–	91.4	–	–	–	0.2
Oelsnitz (Vogtland)	–	91.5	–	–	–	0.1
Olbernhau	–	101.0	–	–	–	0.5
Oschatz	–	89.1	–	–	–	0.3
Pirna	–	–	–	96.4D	–	0.1
Plauen	–	93.5	–	–	–	1
Reichenbach/Vogtl.	–	92.4	–	–	–	0.2
Riesa	–	106.4	–	–	91.7	2/1
Rothenburg	–	100.0	–	–	–	0.2
Schöneck	92.0	–	106.0	–	–	10/30
Sohland	–	107.0	–	–	–	1
Stollberg	–	93.4	–	–	–	1
Torgau	–	91.1	–	–	–	0.2
Werdau	–	–	–	90.9Z	–	0.3
Wiederau (Leipzig)	102.9	–	106.9	–	–	100
Wilkau-Haßlau	–	92.3	–	103.4Z	–	0.5
Wilthen	–	106.5	–	–	104.9	1/0.5
Wurzen	–	95.0	–	–	–	0.4
Zschopau	–	–	–	91.7C	–	0.3
Zwickau-Ebersbrunn	–	–	–	96.2Z	98.2	0.5/0.3

Addresses and other information:
R. PSR (AC), **R.SA** (oldie-based AC), **Energy Sachsen** (CHR): Thomasgasse 2, 04102 Leipzig; **W:** radiopsr.de rsa-sachsen.de nrj.de – **Hitradio RTL** (AC), **R. Chemnitz / Dresden / Erzgebirge /**

Lausitz / Leipzig / Zwickau (AC, on freq. marked C, D, E, G, L, Z, with some content from local studios): Ammonstr. 35, 01067 Dresden; **W:** bcs-sachsen.de

Other stations:

	FM	MHz	kW	Site	Station
7)		88.2	0.4	Auerbach	Vogtland R.
9)		88.2	1	Weißig (Bernsdorf)	Elsterwelle
1)		88.9	1	Chemnitz-Reichenhain	Apollo R.
10)		89.2	1	Weißwasser	R. WSW
2)		89.2	0.1	Leipzig-Reudnitz	R. Blau
2)		94.4	0.3	Leipzig-Stahmeln	R. Blau
10)		94.9	0.2	Wilthen	R. WSW
2)		95.4	2	Plauen	Vogtland R.
5)		97.6	4	Leipzig-Holzhausen	mephisto 97.6
3)		98.4	0.1	Dresden-Gompitz	coloRadio
2)		99.2	0.5	Leipzig-Connewitz	R. Blau
3)		99.3	0.1	Freital (Dresden)	coloRadio
6)		99.3	0.1	Mittweida	R. Mittweida
7)		100.5	1	Reichenbach/Vogtland	Vogtland R.
4)		102.7	1	Chemnitz-Reichenhain	R. T
9)		102.8	0.5	Hoyerswerda-Zeißig	Elsterwelle
7)		103.8	0.5	Markneukirchen	Vogtland R.
8)		107.7	2	Fichtelberg	R. Erzgebirge

Adresses and other information:
1) As Hitradio RTL; **W:** apolloradio.de; classical music and jazz, also Mon-Fri 2200-1700, Sat-Sun 2300-1100 via txs of stn's 2), 3), 4) – **2)** Paul-Gruner-Str. 62, 04107 Leipzig; **W:** radioblau.de – **3)** Jordanstr. 5, 01099 Dresden; **W:** coloradio.org – **4)** Karl-Liebknecht-Str. 19, 09111 Chemnitz; **W:** radiot.de; rel. 1700-1800 Chemnitz university prgr. – **5)** Ritterstr. 9-13, 04109 Leipzig; **W:** mephisto976.uni-leipzig.de, run by Leipzig university; Mon-Fri 0900-1100 and 1700-1900, other times rel. R.SA – **6)** Leisniger Str. 9, 09648 Mittweida; **W:** radio-mittweida.de, run by Mittweida college – **7)** Haselbrunner Str. 114, 08225 Plauen; **W:** vogtlandradio.de – **8)** Vierenstr. 11, 09484 Oberwiesenthal; **W:** radioerzgebirge-online.de – **9)** Walther-Rathenau-Str. 27, 02977 Hoyerswerda; **W:** elsterwelle.de, 103.8MHz tx see M) – **10)** Werner-Seelenbinder-Str. 54a, 02943 Weißwasser; **W:** radiowsw.de
MW: On 1431kHz Voice of Russia.
DAB: Dresden and Leipzig txs on 178MHz (ch. 5C), mux details see K) – Leipzig tx on 185MHz (ch. 6C) and Dresden tx on 206MHz (ch. 9C) MDR 1 R. Sachsen (AAC 88k), MDR 1 R. Sachsen Leipzig (AAC 88k), MDR Jump (AAC 88k), MDR Figaro (AAC 88k), MDR Sputnik (AAC 88k), MDR Info (AAC 72k), MDR Klassik (AAC 96k) – 5 txs on 224MHz (ch. 12A) DLF (L2 128k), DK (L2 128k), DRadio Wissen (AAC 64k), Dokumente&Debatten (AAC 48k), ERF Plus (AAC 72k) plus MDR prgr. as on 185/206MHz.

W) SACHSEN-ANHALT

Media institution: Medienanstalt Sachsen-Anhalt (MSA) ✉ Reichardtstraße 9, 06114 Halle/Saale ☎ +49 345 52550 ▤ +49 345 5255 121 **W:** msa-online.de

FM	R Bro	RTL	SAW	Rock	kW
Bernburg	–	–	–	95.0	1
Blankenburg	99.9	–	95.7	–	0.3/0.1
Brocken	–	89.0	101.4	–	60/100
Dequede	101.0	–	95.6	–	60/1
Dessau-Mildensee	90.6	–	92.6	94.1	0.8/2/0.3
Eisleben	93.7	–	–	–	1
Fleetmark-Lüge	–	–	103.9	–	5
Halle Petersberg	93.5	–	103.3	–	5
Halle city	–	–	–	98.3	0.5
Hergisdorf-Wolferode	93.7	–	–	–	1
Köthen	–	–	–	97.1	1
Magdeburg-Buckau	–	–	–	98.7	0.2
Naumburg	98.8	–	95.1	99.6	10/0.5/1
Sangerhausen	107.1	–	99.4	–	0.1
Schneidlingen	–	–	–	107.2	2.5
Schönebeck	105.7	–	100.1	–	15/20
Stendal Tucholsky-Str.	–	–	100.5	–	0.5
Weißenfels	–	–	–	88.0	1
Wernigerode	105.4	–	90.8	–	0.5/1
Wiederau (Leipzig)	–	–	104.9	–	*90
Wittenberg-Gallun	102.3	–	98.4	–	4/5
Zeitz-Hainichen	99.1	–	–	–	0.5
Ziesar	–	–	102.8	–	2

*) Tx in Sachsen, sharply directional towards Sachsen-Anhalt.

Addresses and other information:
R. Brocken (oldie-based AC), **89.0 RTL** (CHR): Große Ulrichstr. 60D, 06108 Halle; **W:** brocken.de, 89.0rtl.de – **R. SAW** (AC), **Rockland Sachsen-Anhalt:** Hansapark 1, 39116 Magdeburg; **W:** radiosaw.de rockland-digital.de

Non-commercial stations:

	FM	MHz	kW	Site		Station
2)		92.5	1	Aschersleben		R. hbw
1)		95.9	0.6	Halle Petersberg		R. Corax

Adresses and other information:
1) Unterberg 11, 06108 Halle; **W:** radiocorax.de – **2)** Herrenbreite 9, 06449 Aschersleben; **W:** radio-hbw.de
DAB: Petersberg tx on 178MHz (ch. 5C) with K) mux, on 220MHz (ch. 11C) MDR Sachsen-Anhalt (AAC 88k), MDR Sachsen-Anhalt Halle (AAC 88k), MDR Jump (AAC 88k), MDR Figaro (AAC 88k), MDR Sputnik (AAC 88k), MDR Info (AAC 72k), MDR Klassik (AAC 96k), R. SAW (AAC 88k), Rockland (AAC 88k), 89.0 RTL (AAC 72k), R. Brocken (AAC 72k) – 6 txs on 227MHz (ch. 12C) DLF (L2 80k), DK (L2 96k), DRadio Wissen (AAC 64k), MDR 1 Sachsen-Anhalt (AAC 72k), MDR Jump (AAC 72k), MDR Figaro (AAC 80k), MDR Sputnik (AAC 72k), MDR Info (AAC 64k), MDR Klassik (AAC 96k), R. SAW (AAC 88k), Rockland (AAC 88k), 89.0 RTL (AAC 72k), R. Brocken (AAC 72k).

X) THÜRINGEN

Media institution: Thüringer Landesmedienanstalt (TLM) ✉ P.O.-Box 90 03 61 (office location: Steigerstraße 10), 99096 Erfurt
☎ +49 361 211770 🖷 +49 361 2117755 **W:** tlm.de

FM	Ant.T	LW	Top 40	Klass	kW
Altenburg	–	–	98.4	107.5	0.5
Bleßberg	102.7	106.7	–	–	60
Dingelstädt	103.9	–	–	–	5
Eisenach	–	–	93.5	90.9	0.2
Erfurt-Windischh.	100.2	99.7	–	–	3/0.5
Erfurt-Hochheim	–	–	88.6	–	0.5
Gera	98.3	105.8	95.3	104.5	0.2/1
Gotha	–	–	90.8	99.3	0.1/0.2
Heiligenstadt	–	88.7	–	–	0.1
Ilmenau	–	–	94.8	–	0.1
Inselsberg	102.2	104.2	–	–	100
Jena-Oßmaritz	90.9	106.1	–	–	1
Jena Kernberge	–	–	94.8	–	0.2
Keula	–	104.5	–	–	10
Kulpenberg	104.7	96.8	–	–	3
Lobenstein	93.2	98.5	–	–	1/2
Meiningen	–	–	99.5	–	0.2
Mühlhausen	–	–	93.8	–	0.2
Nordhausen	106.8	105.8	103.0	–	0.1
Pößneck	–	–	98.9	–	0.2
Remda Kalmberg	107.6	95.7	–	–	60/10
Ronneburg	102.5	94.9	–	–	30/3
Saalfeld	–	–	97.6	–	0.1
Sömmerda	–	–	91.0	–	0.1
Sondershausen	–	–	90.7	–	0.2
Sonneberg	–	–	88.8	–	0.1
Suhl	101.3	88.6	92.1	–	2x1/0.1
Weimar Ettersberg	107.2	89.2	–	–	0.25
Weimar Belvedere	–	–	97.9	88.7	0.1

Addresses and other information:
Antenne Thüringen (AC), **Top 40** (rock): Belvederer Allee 25, 99425 Weimar; **W:** antennethueringen.de radiotop40.de; Top 40 also via Astra 1H, 12.633GHz – **LandesWelle Thüringen** (AC): Mehringstr. 5, 99086 Erfurt; **W:** landeswelle.de – **Klassik R.** see O); further freq. licensed but not in use.
Non-commercial and other stations:

FM	MHz	kW	Site	Station
1)	96.2	0.6	Erfurt-Hochheim	Funkwerk, F.R.E.I.
4)	96.5	0.2	Eisenach	Wartburg-R.
3)	98.1	0.1	Ilmenau	hsf Studentenradio
6)	100.4	0.1	Nordhausen	Offener Kanal Nordh.
7)	101.4	0.1	Saalfeld	SRB
5)	103.4	0.3	Jena-Oßmaritz	R. OKJ
2)	106.6	2	Weimar Belvedere	Funkwerk, Lotte, b11

Addresses and other information:
1) Funkwerk, Juri-Gagarin-Ring 96, 99084 Erfurt; **W:** funkwerk.de Mon-Fri 1200-2000, Fri 2300- Sat 2300. **F.R.E.I.**, Gotthardstr. 21, 99084 Erfurt; **W:** radio-frei.de Mon-Thu 0600-1200 and 2000-2400, Fri 0600-1200 and 2000-2300, Sat 2300- Sun 2400 – **2) R. Lotte**, Herderplatz 14, 99423 Weimar; **W:** radiolotte.de Mon 0600-1200 and 2300-2400, Tue-Thu 0600-1200 and 2000-2400, Fri 0600-1200 and 2000-2300, Sat 2300- Sun 2400. **studio b11**, Bauhaus-Universität, Bauhausstr. 11, 99421 Weimar; **W:** radiostudio.org. Mon 1900-2300 only. Also rel. Funkwerk from Erfurt – **3)** Postfach 100 565, 98684 Ilmenau; **W:** hsf.tu-ilmenau.de – **4)** Georgenstr. 43, 99817 Eisenach; **W:** wartburgradio.com – **5)** Helmboldstr. 1, 07749 Jena; **W:** radio-okj.de – **6)** August-Bebel-Platz 6, 99734 Nordhausen; **W:** ok-nordhausen.de – **7)** Tiefer Weg 7, 07318 Saalfeld; **W:** srb.fm.
MW: On 1323kHz Voice of Russia.
DAB: Weimar tx on 178MHz (ch. 5C) with K) mux, on 206MHz (ch. 9C) MDR Thüringen (AAC 88k), MDR Thüringen Gera (AAC 88k), MDR Jump (AAC 88k) MDR Figaro (AAC 88k), MDR Sputnik (AAC 88k), MDR Info

(AAC 72k), MDR Klassik (AAC 96k) – 6 txs on 226MHz (ch. 12B) DLF (L2 128k), DK (L2 128k), DRadio Wissen (AAC 64k), Dokumente&Debatten (AAC 48k), ERF Plus (AAC 72k) plus MDR prgr. as on Weimar tx.

III. ARMED FORCES STATIONS

FM	MHz	kW	Site	Station
Baden-Württemberg				
2)	102.3	100	Stuttgart Frauenkopf	AFN Stuttgart
2)	104.6	0.4	Heidelberg-Wieblingen	AFN Kaiserslautern
	107.3	–	Mannheim-Käfertal	(closed down)
Bayern				
3)	87.7	0.1	Schweinfurt	AFN Bavaria
1)	89.4	0.2	Hohenfels	AFN Power Network
1)	90.0	0.2	Amberg	AFN Power Network
3)	90.3	0.1	Garmisch-Partenk.	AFN Bavaria
3)	98.5	0.1	Grafenwöhr	AFN Bavaria
3)	98.9	0.1	Bamberg	AFN Bavaria
1)	101.4	0.2	Grafenwöhr	AFN Power Network
3)	104.9	0.4	Illesheim	AFN Bavaria
3)	107.3	1	Ansbach-Katterbach	AFN Bavaria
1)	107.6	0.2	Vilseck	AFN Power Network
Hessen				
4)	98.7	50	Feldberg (Taunus)	AFN Wiesbaden
Niedersachsen				
7)	93.0	40	Braunschweig	BFBS Germany
7)	95.2	0.1	Bad Fallingbostel	BFBS R. 2
7)	95.4	0.2	Celle	BFBS R. 2
7)	99.3	0.1	Hameln	BFBS Germany
7)	100.1	0.1	Bad Fallingbostel	BFBS R. 2
7)	104.7	0.2	Bergen-Hohne	BFBS Germany
7)	106.7	0.2	Bergen-Hohne	BFBS Germany
7)	106.8	0.1	Hameln	BFBS R. 2
Nordrhein-Westfalen				
7)	91.3	0.1	Rheindahlen	BFBS Germany
7)	91.7	0.3	Gütersloh	BFBS R. 2
7)	92.5	0.8	Dülmen	BFBS Germany
7)	101.6	0.3	Bielefeld	BFBS R. 2
7)	101.9	7	Wulfen	BFBS Germany
7)	102.2	0.3	Münster	BFBS R. 2
7)	103.0	70	Bielefeld Hünenburg	BFBS Germany
7)	104.0	2.4	Niederkrüchten	BFBS Germany
7)	104.3	0.3	Rheindahlen	BFBS R. 2
7)	105.0	0.3	Paderborn	BFBS R. 2
7)	105.1	0.5	Rheinberg	BFBS Germany
7)	106.0	3	Dortmund	BFBS Germany
Rheinland-Pfalz				
5)	100.2	1	Kaiserslautern	AFN Kaiserslautern
8)	101.9	0.1	Ramstein	CFN/RFC Brunssum
5)	103.0	0.4	Pirmasens	AFN Kaiserslautern
6)	105.1	1	Spangdahlem	AFN Spangdahlem
5)	106.1	0.1	Baumholder	AFN Kaiserslautern
Schleswig-Holstein				
7)	88.4	0.1	Kiel-Holtenau	BFBS Germany

N.B Geilenkirchen airbase served by AFN, BFBS and CFN txs at Brunssum, see under Netherlands.
Addresses and other information:
1) AFN Europe, Coleman Barracks, 68307 Mannheim-Sandhofen; 🖷 +49 (621) 46085 335; **W:** afneurope.net. Produces AFN Power Network (talk format, includes rel. of NPR and commercial US stns) and The Eagle (AC format) for distribution by affiliates 2)...6), AFN Benelux (see under Belgium, also rel. by Mönchengladbach tx on 1143kHz) and AFN South stn's (see under Italy). To move out of Mannheim in 2013, reconsideration of future location (planned: Sembach Kaserne, 09142 Sembach) under discussion at time of editing – **2) AFN Stuttgart**, Robinson Barracks, 70376 Stuttgart; **W:** stuttgart.afneurope.net Own prgr. Mon-Fri 0400-0800 and 1400-1700 – **3) AFN Bavaria**, Rose Barracks, 92249 Vilseck; **W:** bavaria.afneurope.net Own prgr. Mon-Fri 0500-0800 and 1400-1700 – **4) AFN Wiesbaden**, Würgelstr. 1217, Flugplatz Erbenheim, 65205 Wiesbaden; **W:** wiesbaden.afneurope.net Own prgr. Mon-Fri 0500-0900 and 1300-1700 – **5) AFN Kaiserslautern**, Vogelweh, Bldg. 2058, 67661 Kaiserslautern; **W:** kaiserslautern.afneurope.net Own prgr. Mon-Fri 0500-1700, Sat 0700-1100. 103.0MHz rel. Sat 1100-Mon 0500 Power Network instead. Closure of Heidelberg txs to be expected in 2013 – **6) AFN Spandahlem**, Spangdahlem Air Base, 54529 Spangdahlem; **W:** spangdahlem.afneurope.net Own prgr. Mon-Fri 0500-0900 and 1300-1600, Sat 0800-1100 – **7) BFBS Germany**, Bergen-Hohne Garrison, Lager Hohne, 29303 Lohheide; **W:** bfbs-radio.com. Also via Eutelsat 10A, 11.221GHz v. Closure of 93.0/95.4MHz txs to be expected. 97.6MHz now used by NDR, see E) – **8)** See under Netherlands.

R. Andernach (German forces broadcasting sce.): Bundeswehr, Zentrum

Operative Information, Kürrenberger Steig 34, 56727 Mayen; **W:** radio-andernach.de At present on air in Bosnia (Rajlovac 97.7MHz), Serbia (Suva Reka 89.9MHz, Prizren 106.9MHz) and Afghanistan (Kabul 107.5MHz), carrying satellite feeds from Mayen and local shows.

GHANA

L.T: UTC — **Pop:** 23 million — **Pr.L:** English, Akan, Dagbani, Ga, Ewe, Hausa, Nzema, others — **E.C:** 50Hz, 230V — **ITU:** GHA

NATIONAL COMMUNICATIONS AUTHORITY (NCA)
✉ P.O. Box CT 1568, 1st Rangoon Close, Switchback Rd, Cantonments, Accra ☎ +233 30 2776621 🖷 +233 30 2763449 **W:** nca.org.gh **E:** info@nca.org.gh **L.P:** Acting DG: Major J. R. K. Tandoh.

GHANA BROADCASTING CORPORATION (GBC, Pub.)
✉ P.O. Box 1633, Broadcasting House, Ring Road Central, Kanda, Accra ☎ +233 30 2786567 🖷 +233 30 2773247
W: www.gbcghana.com **E:** info@gbcghana.com **L.P:** DG: Mr. Kwabena Sarpong-Anane. Dir. Radio: Theo Agbam. Dir. Eng: Mrs. Sarah Boye.
Network N. in E (rel. by all GBC stations): 0600, 0700, 0900, 1100SS, 1300, 1400, 1800, 2000, 2200, 2345.

GBC Regional & partnership stations:

FM	MHz	Name	Web/Addr./Area
Bolgatanga	89.5	URA R.	Upper East
Han	90.1	Upper West R.	Upper West
Tamale	91.2	R.Savannah	North
Ho	91.5	Volta Star R.	Volta
Kumasi	92.1	Garden City R.	Ashanti
Cape Coast	92.5	R.Central	Central
Accra	93.7	R. Ada	P.O. Box 9482, K.I.A
Wa	93.9	Upper West R.	Upper West
Sunyani	94.7	R. Bar	Brong Ahafo
Sekondi-Takoradi	94.7	Twin City R.	West
Dormaa-Ahenkro	94.9	R. Dormaa	Brong Ahafo
Accra	95.7	Uniiq FM	Greater Accra
Accra	96.5	Obonu FM	Greater Accra
Apam	96.5	Apam R.	Central
Swedru	98.6	Swedru R.	Central
Kumasi	99.5	Luv FM	P.O. Box 17207. Accra
Accra	99.7	Joy FM	www.myjoyonline.com
Koforidua	106.7	Sunrise FM	East

Other FM stations in Accra:
Asempa FM, P.O. Box 17013, Accra-North: 94.7MHz — **Atlantis R,** P.O. Box 14629, Accra: 87.9MHz 5kW — **Channel R,** P.O. Box AN 8135, Accra-North: 92.7MHz — **Choice FM,** Accra: 102.3MHz. **W:** www.choice-fmghana.com — **Citi FM,** P.O. Box 30211, K.I.A, Accra: 97.3MHz — **Happy FM,** P.O. Box 1538, Dansoman, Accra: 98.9MHz — **Hot FM,** P.O. Box KD594, Kanda, Accra: 93.9MHz — **Peace FM,** Accra: 104.3MHz 5kW. **W:** www.peacefmonline.com — **R. Gold FM,** P.O. Box 17298, Accra: 90.5MHz – **R. Hit,** P.O. Box 17013, Accra-North: 103.7MHz – **R. Universe,** P.O. Box 25, Legon: 105.7MHz – **Sunny FM,** Box CT 3850, Cantonments, Accra: 88.7MHz – **Top R,** P.O. Box CT 4748, Cantonments, Accra: 103.1MHz – **Vibe FM,** Priv. Mailbag CT 183, Accra 91.9MHz.
+ 75 more stations elsewhere.
BBC World Sce: Accra 101.3MHz, Sekondi-Takoradi 104.7MHz.
RFI Afrique: Accra 89.5MHz, Kumasi 92.9Mhz in French/English.
VOA Africa: Accra 98.1MHz

GIBRALTAR (UK)

L.T: UTC +1h (31 Mar-27 Oct: +2h) — **Pop:** 29,000 — **Pr.L:** English, Spanish — **E.C:** 50Hz, 240V — **ITU:** GIB

GIBRALTAR BROADCASTING CORP.
✉ Broadcasting House, 18 South Barrack Rd, Gibraltar ☎ +350 200 79760 🖷 +350 20078673 **W:** www.gbc.gi **E:** radiogibraltar@gbc.gi
L.P: CEO: Allan King, Head of Radio: James Neish, Head of Engineering: John Tewkesbury
MW: 1458kHz 2kW
FM: 91.3MHz 0.2kW, 92.6MHz 1.0kW, 100.5MHz 0.2kW
D. Prgr: 24h. Spanish M-F 1300-1500 **Ann:** "Radio Gibraltar"

BRITISH FORCES BROADC. SCE. GIBRALTAR
✉ BFBS Gibraltar, BFPO 52 ☎ +350 20055389 🖷 +350 20055528 **W:** http://bfbs.com/radio **E:** gib@bfbs.com
L.P: Mng Ed: Mario Chrisostomou
FM: BFBS Radio 1: North Mole 93.5MHz; O'Hara's Battery 97.8MHz 1kW BFBS Radio 2: North Mole 89.4MHz; O'Hara's Battery 99.5MHz 0.25kW
D. Prgr: 24h **Ann:** "BFBS Community Radio on the Rock, BFBS 1/2 FM"

GREECE

L.T: UTC +2h (31 Mar-27 Oct: +3h) — **Pop:** 11 million — **Pr.L:** Greek — **E.C:** 50Hz, 220V — **ITU:** GRC

ETHNIKO SIMVOULIO RADIOTILEORASIS (ESR, National Council for Radio & Television)
✉ Panepistimiou & Amerikis 5, 10564 Athina ☎ +30 210 3354500 🖷 +30 210 3319881 **W:** esr.gr **E:** ncrtv@otenet.gr
L.P: President: Ioannis Laskaridis.

ELLINIKI RADIOFONIA (ERA, Greek Public Radio)
✉ Leof. Mesogeion 432, 15342 Agia Paraskevi, Athina ☎ +30 210 6066000. 🖷 +30 210 7292826 **W:** tvradio.ert.gr/radio **E:** ntheleriti@ert.gr **L.P:** DG: Antonis Andrikakis. Dir. Network Op: Mihalis Tzouvelekis. Dir. Int. Rel: Evi Demiri. Head of Eng. : Kostantinidis Tsiakalos

MW	kHz	kW	Prgr.		MW	kHz	kW	Prgr.
Athina	666	100	F	7)	Thessaloniki2	1179	50	M2,4
Athina 1	729	100	1	9)	Florina	1278	10	R
5) Thessaloniki	792	100	4	10)	Tripolis	1314	10	R
3) Zakynthos	927	50	1,2,4	12)	Komotini	1404	100	R
Athina 4	981	200	4	15)	Rhodes	1494	100	R
6) Kerkyra	1008	100	R	16)	Chania	1512	100	R

FM(MHz)	NET	ERA2	ERA3	ERASp	Reg.	kW
17) Agios Ioannis					96.4	1
5) Ahentrias	94.4	96.4			105.6	3/10
3) Ainos	96.9	98.9	104.2	106.8	93.2	10
2) Akarnanika	88.9	91.3	102.5	97.3	100.3	10/5
Amfissa		107.0				1
9) Assea	88.3	103.5	90.3	95.3	101.5	10/3
Borsa	106.6	90.5				3
1) Bournias		104.8		106.8	89.7	10/2
Didima	101.2	99.4		103.2		3
8) Dovroutsi					98.3	2
12) Erateini		96.5		94.5	89.9	10/2
10) Frangopidima					102.4	10
Geraneia	97.9	99.9		105.0		3
Hamezi	89.9	89.0				1
Hlomo		101.5		107.4		2
Hortiatis	88.0	90.0	92.0	93.9		5
1) Ikarla					89.1	1
Imittos	105.8	103.7	90.9	101.8		100
12) Kalavrita					93.9	10
19) Kastania		103.6	88.2	105.6	100.2	10
17) Kefalohori					101.5	3
Lefkes		98.9		102.7		10
2) Ligiades	97.8	99.8	102.1	88.2	106.1	10/3
Lihada	104.2	88.8				3
Makrovouni		99.4		97.4		10
15) Malaxa					100.6	1/3
2) Manoliassas					102.1	10
1) Merovigli			102.1	100.1	1
14) Monte Smith					93.1	1
1) Olympos	92.3	94.3	106.4		104.4	3/10
18) Paggaio	89.2	91.2	97.5	107.3	96.3	2
12) Panahaiko		102.3	104.3	87.9	92.5	3/10
6) Pantokratoras	91.8	93.8	89.8	101.1	99.3	10/3
Parnitha	91.6	102.9	95.6	100.9		100
16) Petalidi	92.2	94.2	89.3	100.4	105.4	3
13) Pilio	92.8	94.8	96.8	107.1	101.2	10
7) Pithion	98.9	93.8	88.1	89.4	101.0	2
1) Platanos		87.7			91.7	1
11) Plaka		90.6			98.1	4 / 2
7) Plaka					103.5	2
14) Prof. Ilias (R)	88.4	90.4	103.4	101.4	92.7	10/3
Reihea	96.2	91.0	93.0	104.8		3
5) Rogdia	104.8	99.2	91.3	93.9	97.5	3
15) Skloka	92.9	94.9	106.0	90.1	104.0	3/10
3) Skopos					95.2	2
10) Smerna					103.7	10
13) Soros					100.7	2
3) Stavros					105.3	1
14) Sympetro	107.9	100.3		96.1	98.4	1
1) Thanos					96.5	1
18) Thasos Isl.		95.1		104.7	106.7	10
1) Tholo Potami					95.2	2
1) Vathi					89.7	1
8) Vitsi	88.6	90.6	103.1	106.1	96.6	3/10
Xanthi (Pilima)		101.4		101.1		10

+15 stations under 1 kW.
Prgrs: 1=ERA NET, 4=ERA Spor, 5=Voice of Greece, M1=Macedonia,

M2=Macedonia 2, R=Regional prgrs & rel. ERA 1,2 & 4. F= Filia Radio (mainly foreign language programmes).

Other ERT Stations:

Athina: Kosmos Radio. Parnitha 93.6, Imittos 107.0 100kW.

Athina: Filia Radio 666kHz & 106.7 MHz (Parnitha), rel. VO Greece Mon-Thu 0500-0600, Fri 0500-0600 and 1700-2200, SS 2000-2300, rel. Kosmos MF 2200-0500, Sat 2300-0700, Sun 1800-0500).

D.Prgr: All 24h. **ERA (1) (NET):** News, talk, current affairs. **N:** every hr. 0400-2300 except 0700 & 1600, common prgr. with ERA 2 0300-0400. **ERA 2:** Mainly music. **N:** every h, common prgr. with NET 0300-0400. **ERA 3:** Classical music, arts & drama. **ERA (4) Spor: N:** every half hour, Sport N: every hour, common prgr. with ERA 2, 0100-0400. **Regional programmes:** typically MF 0500-1200, 1400-1700 + sometimes SS. At other times rel. NET, ERA 2, ERA Spor.

Regional station addresses:

1) Northern Aegean: E. Bostani 69, GR-81100 Mitilini **2) Ioannina:** N. Papadopulou 2, GR-45444 Ioannina **3) Zakynthos:** Ampelokipoi, GR-201 00 Zakynthos **4) Larissa:** Iroon Politehniou 1, 1h Stratia, GR-412 22 Larissa **5) Heraklion:** Maxis Kritis 161, GR-71303 Iraklio **6) Kerkira:** Ethniki Lefkimis, GR-49100 Kerkira **7) Orestiada:** Euripidou 15, GR-68200 Orestiada **8) Florina:** Megarovou 20, GR-53100 Florina **9) Tripoli:** Erithrou Staurou 1, 221 00 Tripoli **10) Pirgos:** Olympion 70, GR-27100 Pirgos **11) Komotini:** P.O. Box 5, Kosmiou Terma, GR-69100 Komotini **12) Patra:** Riga Feraiou 104, GR-26221 Patra **13) Volos:** Pl. Agiou Konstantinou, GR-32222 Volos **14) Southern Aegean:** 30 km. Leof. Kallitheas, GR-85100 Rhodes **15) Chania:** Ellis 40, GR-73200 Chania **16) Kalamata:** Anataliko Kentro 10-11, GR-24100 Kalamata **17) Serres:** P.O. Box 91, Stratopedou Kolokotroni, GR-62100 Serres **18) Kavala:** Sof. Venizelou & Iokastis, Ag. Paraskevi, GR-65100 Kavala **19) Kozani:** I. Tranta 19, GR-50100 Kozani.

IS: The opening notes of the Greek folk song "Tsopanakos Imouna" (Once I Was A Shepherd Boy) played on flute and sheep bells.

EXTERNAL SERVICES: The Voice of Greece (ERA 5th Prgr.): see International Radio section.

RADIOFONIKOS STATHMOS MAKEDONIAS (Gov.)

✉ Angelaki 2, 546 36 Thessaloniki ☎+30 2310 299400 🖷 +30 2310 299451 **W:** ert3.gr **E:** pr@ert3.gr **LP:** Dir.: Klearhos Tsaousidis, Head of Int. Rel.: Lefty Kongalides, Tech. Dir.: Papagiannis Vouras.

Makedonia 1: MW: 1044kHz, **FM:** Hortiatis 102.0MHz 10kW, 24h., Agios Ioannis (Serres) 89.6MHz 2kW, Metaxas (Kozani) 89.1MHz 2kW, Poligiros 102.0MHz, Thasos 100.8MHz 10kW Vitsi (Kastoria) 100.6MHz 10kW.

Makedonia 2: MW: 1179kHz, **FM:** Hortiatis 95.8MHz 10kW, Poligiros 95.8MHz, 24h.

Relays on shortwave: see International Radio section.

ANN: "Elliniki Radiophonia, Radiofonikos Stathmos Makedonias"

RADIOFONIKOS STATHMOS AMALIADAS (Comm.)

✉ Ag. Trifonos 5, 27200 Amaliada. **W:** rsafm.gr **D.Prgr:** 24h.
MW: Kastro 1584kHz 1kW. **FM:** Frangapidima 92.7MHz 2kW.

1431 AM (Educ.)

✉ Aristotle University of Thessaloniki. 1os Orofos Ptergas THMMHY, Politehniki Sholi, 54124 Thessaloniki. **W:** 1431am.gr **D.Prgr:** 24h.
MW: Thessaloniki 1431kHz 350W.

PRIVATE FM STATIONS in Athina and Thessaloniki
Athina

FM	MHz	Station	kW	FM	MHz	Station	kW
1)	87.5	Kriti FM	2	21)	94.6	NovaSpor FM	10
2)	87.7	En Lefko	10	22)	94.9	Rythmos 949	10
3)	88.0	Oasis 88	10	23)	95.2	Athens DJ	10
4)	88.3	VFM 88,3	17	24)	96.0	Flash 96	10
5)	88.6	NRJ	10	25)	96.3	Red 96,3	10
6)	88.9	Play 88,9	14	26)	96.6	Pepper 96,6	10
7)	89.2	Music 89,2	10	27)	96.9	Rock 969	10
8)	89.5	Ekklesia Ell.	19	28)	97.2	Easy 97,2	10
9)	89.8	Dromos 89,8	10	29)	97.5	Love R.	10
10)	90.1	902 Aristera	10	30)	97.8	Real FM	10
11)	90.4	Kanali 1	10	31)	98.0	Free FM	5
12)	90.6	Art FM	5	32)	98.3	Athena 9,84	10
13)	91.2	Peiraiki Ekkl.	10	33)	98.6	Derti 98,6	10
14)	91.4	Kritiki Radiof.	5	34)	98.9	Alpha 989	10
15)	92.0	Galaxy 92	10	35)	99.2	Melodia FM	10
16)	92.3	Lampsi 92,3	10	36)	99.5	Vima FM	10
17)	92.6	Best 92,6	10	37)	99.8	99,8 FM	10
18)	92.9	Kiss FM	17	38)	100.3	Skai 100,3	12
19)	93.2	Orange	10	39)	101.3	Diesi 101,3	10
20)	94.0	Epikinonia	5	40)	102.2	Sfera 102,2	10

FM	MHz	Station	kW	FM	MHz	Station	kW
41)	102.5	Nitro R.	10	49)	105.2	Atlantis FM	10
42)	102.8	Top FM	2	50)	105.5	Sto Kokkino	10
43)	103.1	R. Blackman	5	51)	106.2	Mad R.	10
44)	103.3	Sentra FM	10	52)	106.4	R. Argosanic	5
45)	104.0	Parea FM	10	53)	107.2	Bad R.	10
46)	104.3	Minore FM	10	54)	107.4	New R.	5
47)	104.6	Paradise R.	5	55)	107.7	Star FM	5
48)	104.8	Styl FM	10	56)	108.0	Ihorama FM	5

Thessaloniki

FM	MHz	Station	kW	FM	MHz	Station	kW
57)	87.6	Laikos FM	5	84)		98.7	Athlitika Nea	5
58)	88.6	Music R.	5	85)	99.0	R. Ena	20
59)	89.0	89 Rainbow	15	86)	99.4	Flash 99,4	15
60)	89.4	Thes. Deejay	10	87)	99.8	Radio Ekrixi	5
61)	89.7	Imagine 89,7	3	88)	100.0	FM 100	20
62)	90.4	904 Aristera	30	89)	100.3	Republic 100,3	15
63)	90.8	Zoo R.	5	90)	100.6	FM 100,6	20
64)	91.1	Venus 91,1	5	91)	101.0	FM 101	20
65)	91.4	Ola FM	15	92)	101.3	POPS 101,3	5
66)	91.7	RSO 91,7	5	93)	101.7	Kalamaria FM	25
67)	92.4	Radio Ekfrasi	5	94)	102.3	R. Akrites	10
68)	‡92.8	Aris FM	15	95)	102.6	Plus R.	10
69)	93.1	Heart FM	5	96)	103.0	Sport 103	5
70)	93.4	Mythos FM	3	97)	103.6	Studio 3	5
71)	93.7	R. Gnomi	2	98)	104.0	Rythmos 104	20
72)	94.2	R. Lydia	18	99)	104.4	Radiokymata	5
73)	94.5	R. Thessaloniki	5	100)	104.7	Rock R.	10
74)	94.8	Eroticos FM	5	101)	104.9	R. TIF	15
75)	95.1	Cosmoradio	20	102)	105.2	Live 105,2	5
76)	95.5	Metropolis FM	5	103)	105.5	1055 Rock	5
77)	96.1	Mylos 96,1	10	104)	105.8	Mou. Galaxias	2
78)	96.5	Palmos 96,5	5	105)	106.1	City Int'l	2
79)	96.8	Velvet 96,8	5	106)	106.5	1055 Rockxtreme	5
80)	‡97.1	Star FM	30	107)	106.8	Iera Mt. Langada	2
81)	97.5	Antenna 97,5	25	108)	107.1	Real FM	3
82)	98.0	R. North	20	109)	107.4	Libero 107,4	5
83)	98.4	Panorama 9,84	20	110)	107.7	Sunshine FM	5

‡ inactive

Patra FM (MHz): Entexnos FM 87.5 – Relax by MTV 88.2 – Iera Mitropoli Patras 88.5 – Melody FM 88.8 – Politia FM 89.1 – Skai Patras 89.4 – Oasis FM 89.7 – Omega R. 90.0 – Imera FM 90.4 – Mythos FM 90.6 – Yes R. 91.2 – Radio 91,5 91.5 – Heaps R. 91.7 – Kiss FM 92.2 – Top FM 93.0 – Max FM 93.4 – R. Gamma 94.0 – Alpha Patras 94.4 – Studio Patras 94.9 – Oxygen 95.3 – Spor FM Patras 96.3 – Sfera Patras 96.6 – Wave R. 97.4 – R. Messatida 98.0 – R. Blackman 98.5 – Flash Patras 98.7 – R. Aigio 99.2 – Fasma FM 99.7 – You FM 100.1 – Melodia Patras 100.4 – Smart FM 100.7 – Studio 20 101.1 – Hroma FM 102.1 – M FM 102.7 – R. Seven 103.0 – Mousiki Lampsi 103.3 – Dytikos FM 103.7 – Palmos FM 104.1 – Mythos FM 104.8 – Peiraiki Ekkl. 105.0 – Antenna Patras 105.3 – Derti 105.7 – Galaxy FM 106.1 – R. Patra 106.5 – Hristianismos FM 107.2 – Mojo R. 107.7. Powers 1–5kW.

+ approx 1100 additional private stns nationwide.

NB: no official information available about powers of Athina stations and Thessaloniki powers are mostly based on estimates.

Addresses & other information:

1) Peloponissou 42, 18121 Koridallos **W:** 875.gr – 2) Fragkoklisias 8, 15125 Maroussi **W:** enlefko.fm – 3) Mesogeion 174, 15125 Maroussi **W:** oasis88.gr – 4) I. Metaxa 80, Karellas, 19400 Koropi **W:** vfm883. gr – 5) Mesogeion 174, 15125 Maroussi **W:** nrjradio.gr – 6) Eth. Makariou & Delta Falireos 2, 18547 Neo Faliro **W:** play889.gr – 7) Apostolou Pavlou 7, 15125 Maroussi **W:** music892.gr – 8) Iasiou 1, 11526 Athina **W:** ecclesia.gr – 9) Viltanioti 36, 14564 Kato Kifisia **W:** dromosfm.gr – 10) Leof. Irakliou 145, 14231 Nea Ionia **W:** 902.gr – 11) Evripidou 79, 18532 Piraeus **W:** kanaliena.gr – 12) Praxitelous 58, 17674 Kallithea **W:** stylegr.com/radio.html – 13) Deligiorgi 47, 18535 Piraeus **W:** pe912fm.com – 14) Athina **W:** radiocreta.gr – 15) Pirronos 12, 16346 Ilioupoli **W:** galaxy92.gr – 16) Viltanioti 36, 14564 Kato Kifisia **W:** lampsifm.com – 17) I. Metaxa 80, Karellas, 19400 Koropi **W:** bestradio.gr – 18) Vas. Sofias 85, 15124 Marouss **W:** kiss.gr – 19) Dimitros 31, 17778 Tavros **W:** orange932.gr – 20) S. Karagiorgi 2 & M. Antypa, 14121 Iraklio **W:** 94fm.gr – 21) Davaki 50, 17672 Kallithea **W:** sport-fm.gr – 22) Theotokopoulou 4 & Astronafton, 15124 Maroussi **W:** rythmosfm.gr – 23) Leof. Kifisias 215, 15124 Maroussi **W:** athensdeejay.gr – 24) Leof. Kifisias 64, 15125 Maroussi **W:** flash.gr – 25) Eth. Makariou/Delta Falireos 2, 18547 Neo Faliro **W:** redfm.gr – 26) Mesogeion 174, 15125 Maroussi **W:** pepper966.gr – 27) Viltanioti 36, 14564 Kato Kifisia **W:** rockfm.gr – 28) Leof. Kifisias 10-12, 15125 Maroussi **W:** easy972.gr – 29) Dimitros 31, 17778 Tavros **W:** loveradio. gr – 30) Leof. Kifisias 197, 15124 Maroussi **W:** realfm.gr – 31) Athina – 32) Leof. Peiraios 100, 11854 Athina **W:** athina984.gr – 33) N.

Plastira 172, 13561 Ag. Anargiroi **W:** derti.gr – **34)** 40o km. Attikis Odou, SEA Mesogeion, Ktirio 6, 19002 Paiania **W:** alpha989.com – **35)** Eth. Makariou/Delta Falireos 2, 18547 Neo Faliro **W:** melodia.gr – **36)** Mihalakopoulou 80, 11528 Athina **W:** vimafm995.gr – **37)** Athina **W:** 998fm.gr – **38)** Eth. Makariou/Delta Falireos 2, 18547 Neo Faliro **W:** skai.gr/1003/ – **39)** Leof. Mesogeion 411, 15343 Agia Paraskevi **W:** diesi.gr – **40)** M. Antypa 41-45, 14121 Neo Iraklio **W:** sfera.gr – **41)** M. Antypa 41-45, 14121 Neo Iraklio **W:** nitroradio.gr – **42)** Athina – **43)** Papanastasiou 25, 18755 Keratsini **W:** mariosblackman.gr – **44)** Benaki 5, 15238 Metamorfosi Halandriou **W:** sentrafm.gr – **45)** Thiseos 218, 17675 Kallithea **W:** pareafm.gr – **46)** Athina **W:** minorefm.gr – **47)** Emporiko Kentro Porou, 18020 Poros **W:** paradiseradio.gr – **48)** Athina **W:** stylfm.gr – **49)** Ag. Konstantinou 11, 18544 Piraeus. **W:** atlantisfm.gr – **50)** Sarri 19, 10554 Athina **W:** stokokkino.gr – **51)** Eth. Antistaseos 253 & E. Kostopoulou, 15351 Pallini **W:** madradio.gr – **52)** Dritseika Methanon, 18030 Methana **W:** radioargosaronikos.gr – **53)** Athina – **54)** Athina – **55)** Athina **W:** star-radio-athens.com – **56)** Athina **W:** hxorama.gr – **57)** G. Kranidioti 2, 57001 Pylaia Thessaloniki. **W:** laikos.gr – **58)** 4hs Avgoustou 6, 57003 Agios Athanasios Thessaloniki – **59)** Leof. Karamanli 62, 54642 Thessaloniki **W:** 89rainbow.gr – **60)** Orfanidou 2, 54626 Thessaloniki **W:** athensdeejay.gr – **61)** Adrianoupoleos 20A, 55133 Kalamaria Thessaloniki **W:** imagine897.gr – **62)** Egnatias 69, 54631 Thessaloniki – **63)** Aristotelous 3, 54624 Thessaloniki **W:** zooradio.gr – **64)** Vas. Irakliou 30, 54624 Thessaloniki **W:** 911.gr – **65)** 1o km. Filiro-Langada, 57010 Filiro Thessaloniki **W:** olafm.gr – **66)** 1o km. Filiro-Langada, 57010 Filiro Thessaloniki **W:** rso.gr – **67)** I. Korovagou 3, 4os Orofos, 54627 Thessaloniki **W:** fm-ekfrasi.gr – **68)** Aristotelous 3, 54624 Thessaloniki **W:** arisfm.gr – **69)** Aristotelous 5, 54624 Thessaloniki **W:** heartfm.gr – **70)** Leof. Karamanli 84, 54644 Faliro Thessaloniki **W:** mythosradio.gr – **71)** Ag. Sofias 43, 54623 Thessaloniki **W:** gnominet.gr – **72)** Eleftherias 15, 56123 Ambelokipi Thessaloniki **W:** radiolydia.gr – **73)** 17o km. Moudianon, Kombos Risiou, 57001 Thermi Thessaloniki **W:** rthess.gr – **74)** 170 km. Moudianon, Kombos Risiou, 57001 Thermi Thessaloniki **W:** eroticos.gr – **75)** Tsimiski 51, 6os Orofos, 54623 Thessaloniki **W:** cosmoradio.gr – **76)** K. Palama 6A, 54352 Thessaloniki **W:** metropolisradio.gr – **77)** An. Georgiou 56, 54627 Thessaloniki **W:** mylosfm.gr – **78)** K. Kristalli 30, 54630 Thessaloniki **W:** palmos965.gr – **79)** K. Palama 16G, 54630 Thessaloniki **W:** velvet968.gr – **80)** Aristotelous 3, 54624 Thessaloniki **W:** starfm.gr – **81)** 26hs Oktovriou 90, 54627 Thessaloniki **W:** ant1fm.gr – **82)** Loof. Karamanli 60, 54623 Thessaloniki. **W:** radionorth.gr – **83)** Mitropoleos 34, 54623 Thessaloniki **W:** panorama984.com – **84)** Mitropoleos 61, 54623 Thessaloniki **W:** athlitikanea.gr – **85)** K. Karamanli 175, 54249 Thessaloniki **W:** 99fm.gr – **86)** P.O. Box 680, 57001 Neo Risio Thessaloniki **W:** flash.gr – **87)** Melenikou 31A, 56224 Evosmos Thessaloniki **W:** ekrixifm.gr – **88)** N. Germanou 1, 54645 Thessaloniki. **W:** fm100.gr – **89)** Tsimiski 60, 54622 Thessaloniki **W:** republicradio.gr – **90)** N. Germanou 1, 54645 Thessaloniki **W:** fm100.gr – **91)** N. Germanou 1, 54645 Thessaloniki **W:** fm100.gr – **92)** Isminis 46, 54633 Thessaloniki – **93)** Andrianoupoleos 8 & Epanomis 26, 55133 Kalamaria Thessaloniki **W:** kalamariafm.gr – **94)** Vas. Othonos 12, 54629 Stavroupoli Thessaloniki **W:** akritestoupontou.gr – **95)** Aristotelous 7, 54624 Thessaloniki **W:** plusradio.gr – **96)** Monastiriou 85, 54627 Thessaloniki **W:** sport103.gr – **97)** Palamidou 4, Ano Poli, 54633 Thessaloniki **W:** studio3.gr – **98)** 26hs Oktovriou 90, 54627 Thessaloniki **W:** rythmosfm.gr – **99)** A. Papandreou 27, 56334 Kordelio Thessaloniki **W:** radiokymata.gr – **100)** Kouskoura 5, 54625 Thessaloniki **W:** rockradio.gr – **101)** Egnatias 154, 54636 Thessaloniki **W:** radio1049.gr – **102)** Thessaloniki – **103)** Aggelaki 31, 54621 Thessaloniki **W:** 1055rock.gr – **104)** Kromnis 10, 54453 Toumpa Thessaloniki **W:** g-radio.gr – **105)** Karatassou 31, 55132 Kalamaria Thessaloniki **W:** cityinternational.gr – **106)** Aggelaki 31, 54621 Thessaloniki **W:** 1055rock.gr – **107)** 57200 Langadas Thessaloniki **W:** imlagada.gr – **108)** Navmahias Ellis 4, Thessaloniki **W:** realfm.gr – **109)** Aristotelous 10, 54624 Thessaloniki **W:** libero.gr – **110)** Aristotelous 4, 3os Orofos, 54624 Thessaloniki. **W:** sunshinefm.gr

AMERICAN FORCES RADIO & TV SERVICE (Mil.)
W: myafn.dodmedia.osd.mil **FM:** "107.3 The Odyssey": Souda Bay 107.3MHz 0.5kW

GREENLAND (Denmark)

L.T: UTC -3h (DST*: -2h). Qaanaaq & Thule Air Base: UTC -4h (DST*: -3h; not Thule AB), Ittoqqortoormiit: UTC -1h (DST*: UTC), Danmarkshavn. UTC. *) 31 Mar-27 Oct — **Pop:** 58,000 — **Pr.L:** Greenlandic, Danish — **E.C:** 50Hz, 220V — **ITU:** GRL

KALAALIT NUNAATA RADIOA – KNR (Pub. Comm.)
✉ Kissarneqqortuunnguaq 15, PO Box 1007, DK-3900 Nuuk ☎ +299 361500 🖷 +299 361502 **W:** www.knr.gl **E:** info@knr.gl

L.P: Chrmn: Hans Peter Poulsen. MD: Ivalo Egede. Hd of R: Henriette Rasmussen. CE: Nathan Biilmann

FM	MHz	kW	FM	MHz	kW
Nuuk*	90.5	0.05	Aasiaat	95.5	0.1
Sisimiut	95.0	0.1	Ilulissat	96.0	0.05
Kangerlussuaq	96.0	0.01	Tasillaq	96.0	0.05
Uummannaq	95.0	0.05	Sanderson Hope	96.0	0.1

+ 60 additional stns 0.05kW or less. *) = stereo
D.Prgr: 24h N: Greenlandic: 1515, 2130. Danish: 1530, 2200
Ann: "Kallaallit-Nunaata Radioa", "Grønlands Radio" **IS:** "Sunnia Kalippoq" (The Whaleboat "Sonja" drags whale) played on celeste.

DR P1, Denmark. Satellite relay 24h: Nuuk 98.0MHz 0.1kW
RÚV Rás 2, Iceland. Satellite relay 24h: Narsaq 106.0MHz

INUUNERUP NIPAA (Rlg)
✉ Ilivinnguaq 1, PO Box 67, DK-3900 Nuuk ☎ +299 321382 🖷 +299 321226 **W:** www.ino.gl/content/dk/missioner/lokal_radio **E:** ino.nuuk@greennet.gl
L.P: Chrmn: John Østergaard Nielsen. Hd of Prgr: Jan Berthelsen

FM	MHz	kW	FM	MHz	kW
Nuuk	88.5	0.05	Qaqortoq	88.5	0.05
Aasiaat	88.5	0.05	Maniitsoq	88.5	0.05
Sisimiut	88.5	0.05	Tasiilaq	88.5	0.05
Qaanaaq	88.5	0.05			

D.Prgr: 1030-1430, 1700-1030 & 2200-0030. Most prgrs in Greenlandic
F.pl.: Txs in Kullorsuaq, Upernavik, Uummannaq, Ilulissat & Nanortalik

PRIVATE STATIONS (local radio):
Akisuasoq Radio, Box 29, 3912 Maniitsoq: 90.5MHz (0.3kW), 93.0MHz (0.1kW), 99.0MHz (0 1kW) **W:** www.akisuasoq.gl/radio.html – **Kangaatsiap Tusaataa**, Box 62, 3955 Kangaatsiaq: 103.0MHz – **Kap York Radio**, Box 157, 3971 Qaanaaq: 93.5MHz – **Kassak Radio**, Box 516, 3952 Ilulissat: Aasiaat 103.0MHz, Ilulissat: 103.0MHz, Kangaatsiaq: 90.0MHz, Qasigiannguit: 90.0MHz, Qeqertarsuaq: 103.0MHz, Uummannaq: 103.0MHz – **Lokal Radio Ilulissat**, Box 1004, 3952 Ilulissat: 99.0MHz – **Nanortalik Lokalradio**, Box 120, 3922 Nanortalik: FM 90.0MHz – **Nuuk FM**, Nuukullak 32-B, Box 1462, 3900 Nuuk: 93.0MHz (0.1kW) – **Paamiut Tusaataat**, Box 229, 3940 Paamiut: 93.0MHz – **Qasigiannguit Tusaataat**, B20, 3951 Qasigiannguit. 103.0MHz – **Radio 50Z20**, Den Danske Radio, SPE, Box 139, Thule Air Base, 3970 Pituffik: 97.1MHz (0.1kW) – **Radio Narsaq FM**, Josifip aqq. 543, Box 74, 3962 Upernavik. 93.0MHz (0.025kW) **W:** www.radionarsaq.gl – **Radio Upernavik**, Box 244, 3962 Upernavik: 93.0MHz – **Seekon Radio**, Box 361, 3920 Qaqortoq: 93.0MHz – **Sisimiut Tusaataa**, Box 312, 3911 Sisimiut: Sarfannguit 91.0MHz (0.02kW), Sisimiut 93.0MHz (0.05kW), Kangerlussuaq 93.0MHz (0.02kW), Sarfannguit 98.0MHz (0.02kW) – **Tusaat TV Aasiaat**, Box 20, 3950 Aasiaat: 93.0MHz (0.1kW) – **Uummannap Tusaataa**, Atuarfiup Aqq. B-8, 3961 Uummannaq: 103.0MHz (0.075kW)

GRENADA

L.T: UTC -4h — **Pop:** 109,000 — **Pr.L:** English — **E.C:** 50Hz, 230/400V — **ITU:** GRD

GRENADA BROADCASTING NETWORK – G.B.N. Radio (Gov, Comm.)
✉ Observatory Road, P.O. Box 535, St. George's ☎ +1 473 444 5522 🖷 +1 473 444 4180 **W:** www.klassicgrenada.com
E: gbn@spiceisle.com **L.P:** GM: Ruel Edwards. Op.Mgr.: Clarence Cosmos Baker. CEN: Kennedy Bowen
MW: Klassic AM: 540kHz 10kW: 0900-0200. Rel. BBC 0200-0900
FM: HOTT FM: 98.5/98.7MHz 1000-0300 — **CSS CARIBBEAN SUPERSTATION:** 105.5(South) /105.9(North)MHz (Relay Trinidad)

HARBOUR LIGHT OF THE WINDWARDS (Rlg.)
✉ Carriacou ☎ +1 473 443 7628 🖷 +1 473 443 7628 **W:** www.harbourlightradio.org & www.lastchanceministries.com/harbourlight.htm **E:** harbourlight@spiceisle.com **L.P:** SM: Randy Cornelius
MW: 1400kHz 5kW **FM:** 92.3MHz 0.25kW, 94.5MHz 0.25kW
D.Prgr: MW: 0953-0245. FM: 24h. **N:** rel. BBC & VOA
Ann: "This is the Harbour Light of the Windwards broadcasting from beautiful and friendly Carriacou"

PRIVATE STATIONS:
Boss FM, Sauteurs, St Patricks ☎+1 473 442 1177 **W:** www.bossfmgrenada.com – **City Sound**, River Road, St George's ☎+1 473 440 9616 🖷+1 473 440 7838 **W:** www.citysoundfm.com **L.P:** Mgr Alphonses Strachan. **FM:** 97.5MHz – **CRFM Community Radio:** Morne Jaloux, St George's ☎+1 473 440 4848 🖷 +1 473 440

4991 L.P: Mgr Rawl Ghatts. **FM:** 89.5MHz – **Funcity FM,** Central Depradive St., Gouyare, St John's ☎+1 473 417 0433. **W:** www.funcity909.webs.com **FM:** 90.9MHz – **GFN – Grenada Family Network,** PO Box 2747, St George's ☎+1 473 435 4297. **W:** www.globalfamilynetwork.net L.P.: Pres. David Gates. **FM:** 91.3/100.3MHz. Format: Rlg. (Adventist) – **GNCN - Good News Catholic Radio,** Church St., Box 224, St George's ☎+1 473 435 0143 **W:** www.stgdiocese.org/diocese/gncnradio L.P.: Cyril Hopkin. **FM:** 99.5MHz. Format: Rlg – **GTC Radio,** Grenada Trace Center, Grand Anse, St George's ☎+1 473 439 9700. **W:** www.gtcradio.caster.fm. **FM:** 89.9/90.3MHz – **Kyak 106 FM,** Church Street, Hillsborough, Carriacou ☎+1 473 443 6262 **W:** www.kyak106.com **FM:** 106.3MHz – **Real FM Grenada,** High Street, St. Patrick. ☎+1 473 442 0975. **W:** realfmgrenada.com. **FM:** 91.5/91.9MHz – **SGU 107.5,** Office of University Communications, 2nd floor, Chancellery, St George's University, St George's ☎+1 473 444 4175 ext. 2191 🖷+1 473 444 3153 **W:** www.sgu.edu **FM:** 107.5MHz. Format: Non-commercial community radio – **Sister Isle Radio,** Fort Hill, Hillsborough, Carriacou ☎+1 473 443 8141/8142. **W:** www.sisterisleradio.com **FM:** 92.9MHz – **Spice Capital Radio,** Rpss Point, PO Box 90, St George's ☎/🖷+1 473 435 3563 **W:** www.spicecapitalradio.com L.P.: Mgr Paul Roberts. **FM:** 90.1MHz – **VOG FM - Voice of Grenada,** Moving Target Co., Lagoon Road, St George's ☎+1 473 440 8171 🖷 +1 473 440 8505 **W:** www.vogfm.com **FM:** 88.9/95.7/103.3MHz – **Wee FM,** Grenada Wireless Comm Network, Cross St, PO Box 555, Gouyave, St John's ☎+1 473 440 4933 🖷+1 473 440 8724 **W:** www.weefmgrenada.com L.P.: GM: Alvin Dabreo. **FM:** 93.3/93.9MHz

GUADELOUPE (France)

L.T: UTC -4h — **Pop:** 394,000 — **Pr.L:** French, Créole Patois — **E.C:** 50Hz, 230V — **ITU:** GLP

GUADELOUPE PREMIÈRE (Pub)

🖳 Morne Bernard-Destrellan, B.P. 180, F-97122 Baie-Mahault. ☎+590 590939696. 🖷+590 590939682 **W:** guadeloupe.la1ere.fr **L.P:** Dir: R.Surjus. Editor-in-Chief: Philippe Goudé. PD: L.Francil. Head Comms Dept: Sonia Gémieux

MW: Point-à-Pitre 640kHz 40kW

FM: Point-à-Pitre 88.9MHz 1kW, Haut du Morne des Pères 89.1MHz 1kW, Deshaies 96.8MHz 0.1kW, Basse-Terre 97.0MHz 3kW, Pointe-Noire 97.4MHz 16kW

D.Prgr: 24h. **N:** 1100, 1700, 2230, plus relays of France-Inter.

Ann: "Ici Point-à-Pitre, La Première Guadeloupe".

IS: "Biguin" (guitar) **V.** by QSL-card. Rp.

RADIO CARAÏBES INTERNATIONAL (Comm.)

🖳 **RCI Guadeloupe,** B.P. 1309, F-97187 Point-à-Pitre Cédex. ☎ +590 590839696 🖷 +590 590839697

FM: Basse-Terre 98.6MHz 1kW, Deshaies 98.6MHz 0.3kW, Morne-à-Louis 100.2MHz 2kW, Point-à-Pitre 106.6MHz 1kW, Haut du Morne 106.6MHz 0.05kW. **D.Prgr:** 24h.

RADIO BASSES INTERNATIONALE (Comm)

🖳 Stations de radio, Lieu-dit les Basses, 97112 Grand Bourg ☎ +590 590977088 🖷 +590 590978062

FM: Haut du Morne des Pères 88.7MHz 1kW, Grand-Bourg 90.4MHz 1kW, Morne-à-Louis 98.2MHz 2kW, Basse-Terre 102.2MHz 1kW

RADIO MASSABIELLE (RCF) (Rlg)

🖳 B.P. 607, 97168 Point-à-Pitre ☎+590 590 832521 🖷 +590 590 834861. **L.P:** Pres: José Colat-Jolivière, Dir: Père Silvère Numa **W:** www.radiomassabielle.fr **E:** contact@radiomassabielle.fr **FM:** Point-à-Pitre 97.8MHz 0.6kW, Pointe-Noire 101.8MHz 1kW

RADIO SAPHIR FM

🖳 rue Bel Air Bourg, 97170 Petit-Bourg ☎+590 690 352274 **E:** saphirfm@live.fr **W:** www.radiosaphirfm.com **FM:** Point-à-Pitre 89.4MHz 1kW

Other stations (all MHz):
France Inter, Pointe-à-Pitre 91.2 1kW, Haut du Morne des Pères 91.7 1kW, Morne-à-Louis 95.0 16kW, Basse-Terre 95.4 3kW – **NRJ Guadeloupe,** Pointe-à-Pitre, 100.6 1kW, Basse-Terre 102.6 1kW, Morne-à-Louis 107.2 2kW – **Antilles Infos,** 105.8 2kW, 106.5 1kW – **Bel'Radio,** 96.3 1kW, 106.9 1kW – **Fréquence Alizée,** 96.6 1kW, 103.4 2kW – **R. Éclair,** 96.0 1kW, 101.0 2kW – **R. Gaïac FM,** 99.8 1kW, 104.7 1kW – **R. Haute Tensi,** 89.8 1kW, 90.8 1kW – **R. Karata,** 90.6 1kW, 106.5 1kW – **Radio Madras FM,** 92.5 2kW, 92.9 1kW – **Radio Nostalgie,** 105.4 1kW, 107.6 2kW – **Trace FM,** 92.1 2kW, 94.1 1kW. **NB:** +11 other stations

GUAM (USA)

L.T: UTC +10h — **Pop:** 178,430 — **Pr.L:** English, Chamorro, Filipino — **E.C:** 60Hz, 110/220V — **ITU:** GUM

FEDERAL COMMUNICATIONS COMMISSION (FCC)
see USA for details

MW		kHz	kW		MW	kHz	kW
1)	KGUM	567	10	13)	KUSG	1350	0.25
2)	KUAM	630	10	14)	KVOG	1530	0.25
3)	KTWG	801	10				
FM		**MHz**	**kW**		**FM**	**MHz**	**kW**
4)	KHMG	88.1	8	1)	KZGZ	97.5	40
5)	KPRG	89.3	9.2	9)	KOKU	100.3	50
16)	—	‡90.1	4	12)	KNUT	101.1	8
6)	KOLG	90.9	5.7	10)	KTKB-FM	101.9	46
7)	KSDA-FM	91.9	3.8	8)	KISH	102.9	25
3)	KMOY	92.7	42	11)	KIJI	104.3	12.5
13)	KUSG-FM	92.9	0.01	1)	KGUM-FM	105.1	12
2)	KUAM-FM	93.9	5.2	15)	KGCA-LP	106.9	0.07
8)	KSTO	95.5	2	15)	KGCA-LP	107.9	0.023

‡ currently inactive

Addresses and other information

1) 111 Chalan Santa Papa, Suite 800; Hagatna, GU 96910-5193 ☎+1 671 477-5700, +1 808 524-6495, 🖷+1 671 477-3982 **Brands:** KGUM-AM Talk, news **W:** www.k57.com; KZGZ Power98 CHR **W:** www.power-98guam.com – **2)** 600 Harmon Loop Road, Suite 102; Dededo, GU 96929-6536 ☎+1 671 637-KUAM (637-5826) 🖷+1 671 637-9865 **W:** www.kuam.com **Brands:** Isla63 'Island Pride' contemporary island music; i94 Champion Radio CHR – **3)** Cornerstone 800AM, 1868 Halsey Drive; Asan, GU 96910-1505 ☎+1 671 477-5894 🖷+1 671 477-6411 **W:** www.ktwg.com **E:** am800guam@gmail.com Format: Protestant Christian talk and instruction, gospel music **NB:** Korean Mon & Fri 0800-0830, Tagalog Wed 0800-0830, Chamorro Thu 0800-0815 & Sun 0700-0730, Japanese Thu 0815-0830 – **4)** Harvest Family Radio, PO Box 23189 Barrigada, GU 96921 ☎+1 671 477 6341🖷+1 671 477 7136 **W:** www.hbcguam.net **E:** khmg@hbcguam.net **L.P:** GM: John Collier **Prgr:** 24h religious– **5)** c/o University of Guam, 303 University Drive; UOG Station; Mangilao, GU 96923-1871 **NB:** BBCWS Daily 0700-0800, Sun 1900-2100, Mon 1900-2000, Tue 1400-2000, Wed & Thu 1400-1800 & 1900-2000, Fri 1400-1800, Sat 1700-2000 **W:** www.kprgfm.com – **6)** Catholic Educational Radio, Chalan Santo Papa; P.O. 23006, Guam Mail Facility, Barrigada, GU 96921-3006 **W:** www.kolg.com **L.P:** GM: Deacon Frank Tenorio, Dir.Prgr: Chuck White **Prgr:** 24h relig – **7)** Good News Broadcasting Corp, Joy FM, 290 Chalan Palasyo, Hagatna Heights, GU 96910-6405 ☎ +1 671 472 1111, 🖷 +1 671 477 4678 **W:** www.joyfmguam.com **Prgr:** 24h religious **Languages:** English, Chinese, Chuukese, Japanese, Korean, Tagalog – **8)** Nimitz Hill, 1868 Halsey Drive, Piti, GU 96910-1505 – **9)** Guam Hit Radio 100, 107 Julale Center, 424 West O'Brien Drive, Hagatna, GU 96910-5078 **W:** www.hitradio100.com **E:** marketing@hitradio100.com **KOKU:** "Guam's #1 Hit Music Station" Format: CHR **KMOY – 10)**177-B Ilipog Drive, Suite 203; Tamuning, GU 96913-4107 **E:** rolly@ktkb.com **W:** www.ktkb.com **Brand:** Megamixx 101.9 **Format:** OPM Origil Pilipino Music **Prgr** Language: Tagalog – **11)** 543A N Marine Dr, Tamuning, GU 96913-4217 **L.P:** SM: Rich de Vera ☎+1 671 478-0104 🖷+1 671 647-7480 **W:** www.kijifm104.com **E:** rich@kijifm104.com – **12)** Choice Broadcasting Co. LLC, 453A N Marine Corps Drive, Tamuning GU 96913 ☎ +1 671 4780104 🖷 +1 671 6477480 **Format:** Islands Music – **13)** Management Advisory Services Inc, 125 Tun Jesus, Crisotomo Street #308, Tamuning GU 96913 ☎+1 671 648-4262 – **14)** Guam Power II Inc, 1100 Alakea #1800, Honolulu HI 96813-2839 ☎+1 808 521-4711 – **15)** Pioneer Inspirational Radio, Melodies of Prayer Inc, 154 Calachucha Ave, Barrigada GU 96913 ☎+1 671 637 5975 **W:** www.melodiesofprayer.com **E:** mail@melodiesofprayer.com **L.P:** Chair: Edwin Supit **Prgr:** 24h religious – **16)** Hurao Inc, 264 Calle de los Marteres St, Agat GU 96935 ☎ +1 671 482-4630

ADVENTIST WORLD RADIO - ASIA (Rlg.) and TRANS WORLD RADIO - ASIA (Rlg.): See International Radio section

GUATEMALA

L.T: UTC -6h — **Pop:** 13 million — **Pr.L:** Spanish — **E.C:** 60Hz, 120V — **ITU:** GTM

SUPERINTENDENCIA DE TELECOMUNICACIONES

🖳 4a Avenida N° 15-51, Z-10, Guatemala ☎+502 2321100 ext. 101 **W:** www.sit.gob.gt

CAMARA DE RADIODIFUSION DE GUATEMALA

🖳12 Calle 1-25, Zona 10, Edificio Geminis 10, Torre Norte, Of. 812,

Guatemala ☎+502 23353077 **W**: camaraderadiodifusiongt.com

MW Call	kHz	kW	Station, location, h. of tr.
AV01)	‡540		R. Cobán, Cobán
SO03)	540	0.02	R. Amistad, San Pedro de Laguna
GU01) RV	‡560	10	R. 560, Guatemala
SM01)	560	1	R. Quetzal, Malacatán
ES01) PA	570	1	R. Palmeras, Escuintla
GU02) Y	580	5	R. Progreso, Guatemala: 1200-0300
QU01) RQ	590	5	R. Quiché, Sta Cruz del Quiché: 1100-0400
ES02) RC	‡600	1	R. Campesina, Escuintla
GU03) GA	610	5	R. Alianza, Guatemala: 1000-0300
TO01) PQ	620	5	R. 6-20, San Cristóbal: 1200-0400
PE01) EL	630		R. Cultural Porvenir, Sta Elena: (r. 730)
QE01) Q	660	3	LV de Quetzaltenango: 1100-0400
AV02) VP	680	10	R. Norte, Cobán: 1000-0500
JU01) VB	690	1	R. Tamazulapa, Jutiapa
ES03) AJ	700	1	R. Inspiración, Escuintla
GU06) HR	700	15	R. Mundial, Guatemala
QE02) XL	710	1	R. Tecún Umán, Quetzaltenango (r. 730)
IZ01) RO	‡720	1	R. Corona, Morales
GU07) N	730	10	R. Cultural, Guatemala
GU08) HB	‡760	5	Nueva R. Super, Guatemala: 1000-0500
QE03) BX	‡770	1	R. Nueva Fraternidad, Quetzaltenango: 1000-0600
ZA01) CK	780	1	Sultana La Cristiana, Zacapa
GU09) O	‡790	3	R. Festival, Guatemala: 1100-0400
SR01) YZ	‡800	1	R. Rosa, Chiquimulilla
PE02)	810		R. Moapán, Sta Elena
SA01)	810		R. Circuito San Juan, San Juan
SM06) END	810		R. Constelación, San Marcos: 1200-2400
GU10) TO	820	10	R. Kyrios/R. Internacional, Guatemala:1000-0600
SU01) AV	830	5	R. Satélite, Mazatenango: 1100-0400
AV06)	840	2.5	R. Luz, San Pedro Carchá
JU04)	840		R. Idea 840, Jutiapa
GI11) X	‡850	10	R. Ciro, Guatemala
SU02) L	870	0.5	R. Victoria, Mazatenango
GU12) J	‡880	10	R. Nuevo Mundo, Guatemala: 1030-0500
ES04) HU	890	1	R. Escuintla, Escuintla
IZ02) MA	900	1	R. Amatique, Puerto Barrios
GU30) KL	910	10	R. Fe y Esperanza, Guatemala: 1130-0600
ES05) RS	920	0.2	R. Cultural, Escuintla (r. 730)
GU13) TL	940	10	Eventos Católicos R., San Pedro Sacatepéquez, Guatemala: 1200-0500
SU03) AF	950	1	R. Indiana, Mazatenango
GU14) AX	970	5	R. Continental, Guatemala: 1200-0430
SM04) MQ	‡980	1	R. Retama, San Marcos: 1200-0500
CH01) AL	990	1	R. Perla de Oriente, Chiquimula
CM02)	1000		R. Cultural y Educativa, Patzún
GU32)	1000		R. Revelación y Verdad, Guatemala: 1055-0500
IZ06)	1010	1	R. Caribe, Izabal
QU03) XI	1010	1	R. Ixil, Nebaj: 1100-0200
SM05) CM	1020	5	R. Frontera, Pajapita: 1100-0400
GU15) UX	1030	10	R. Panamericana, Guatemala: 1200-0200
JA01) JP	1040	1	R. Revelación, Jalapa
HU01) SL	1050	5/1	LV de los Cuchumatanes, Huehuetenango:1100-0600
GU16)	‡1060	10	R. Favorita, Guatemala: 1100-0600
QE04) D	1070	3/2	LV de Occidente, Quetzaltenango: 1200-0400
ZA02) LU	1080	1	R. Novedad, Zacapa
QE05) SR	1100	1	R. Superior, Coatepeque
AV04) MK	1110	1	R. Verapaz, Cobán
GU17) C	1120	0.5	R. Poderosa "La Voz de la Liberación", Guatemala: 1100-0600
RE01) VR	1130	1	Em. Unidas LV de la Costa Sur, Retalhuleu
GU17) T	1150	10	R. Sonora, Guatemala: 1100-0600
IZ03) RI	1160	1	R. Izabal, Morales (r. 730): 1300-0300
QE06) RL	1170	5	R. Cadena Landívar, Quetzaltenango: 0900-0300
GU33)	1180		R. 10, Guatemala
JU02) RJ	1200	12	R. Unción, Jutiapa
GU19) MX	1210	10/5	R. Miel, Guatemala
IZ04) AT	1230	1	R. Atlántida, Puerto Barrios: 1130-0500
SU04)	1230		R. América, Cuyotenango
GU20) K	1240	5	R. Luz, Guatemala
CH02) PY	1250	1	R. Payakí, Esquipulas: 1100-0300
TO04)	1250	1	LV Cristiana, Totonicapán
GU21) CQ	1270	2.5	R. Exclusiva, Guatemala
BV01) VY	‡1280	2.5	R. Zamaneb "LV del Urram", Salamá: 1100-0200
ZA03)	1290		R. Miramundo "LV del Ejercito", Zacapa
QE07) AN	1310	1	R. LV de los Altos, Quetzaltenango: 1100-0700
JU03) ME	1320	0.5	R. Quezada, Jutiapa
GU22) MU	1330	5	Unión R., Guatemala: 1100-2330
AV05) MC	1350	1	R. Monja Blanca, Cobán
GU15) LK	1360	10	R. Tic Tac "LV del Evangelio", Guatemala

MW Call	kHz	kW	Station, location, h. of tr.
QE09) AC	1370	1	LV de Colomba, Colomba
TO03) EB	1380	0.5	R. Momostenango Educativa, Momost.:1100-0300
IZ05) RB	‡1400	1	R. Porteña, Puerto Barrios
QE10) GH	1410	5	Nueva R. Xelajú, Quetzaltenango: 1200-0600
GU24) RP	‡1420	1	R. Capital, Guatemala: 1130-0600
HU02) AG	1430	1.2	LV de Huehuetenango: 1100-0400
SU05) MS	1440	0.5	R. Nacional, Mazatenango: 0000-0400
GU06) LG	1450	1	R. Hosanna, Guatemala: 1000-0600
PE04) RN	1460	2.5	R. Petén, Flores: 1100-0500
GU25) HB	1480	5	R. Horizontes, Guatemala: 1030-0200
RE02) RE	1490	1	R. Modelo, Retalhuleu
GU32) DX	‡1510	5	R. Centroamericana del Amor, Guatemala: 1055-0500
PE05)	1520		R. Taysal, Sta Elena de la Cruz
QE11) RS	‡1520	1	R. Superior, Coatepeque
GU29)	‡1540	1	R. Cultura y Deportes, Guatemala
QE12)	1560		R. Inspiración, Quetzaltenango
GU27) VE	1570	10	VEA-Voz Evangélica de América, Guatemala: 1030-0600
CM01) XC	1590	1	R. Triunfadora, Chimaltenango

SW Call	kHz	kW	Station, location & h. of tr
CH04)	AV	4055	0.5	R. Verdad, Chiquimula: 0910-0600

Call TG—, ‡ = inactive, (r) = repeater, ± = varying fq.

State abbreviations: (Departamentos) AV = Alta Verapaz, BV = Baja Verapaz, CH = Chiquimula, CM = Chimaltenango, ES = Escuintla, GU = Guatemala, HU = Huehuetenango, IZ = Izabal, JA = Jalapa, JU = Jutiapa, PE = Petén, QE = Quetzaltenango, QU = Quiché, RE = Retalhuleu, SA = Sacatepéquez, SR = Santa Rosa, SM = San Marcos, SO = Sololá, SU = Suchitepéquez, TO = Totonicapán, ZA = Zacapa.
N.B: These abbreviations are not recognized by the Post Office. Letters should therefore carry the full name.

Addresses and other information:
AV00) ALTA VERAPAZ
AV01) 5 Calle 1-06, Z-3, 16001 Cobán – **AV02)** 2 Calle 5-57, Z-3, 16001 Cobán – **AV04)** 2 Calle 5-57, Z-3, 16001 Cobán – **AV05)** Edif Municipalidad, 5a Calle 1-06, 16001 Cobán – **AV06)** 11 Av Zona 1, Colonia Cuatro Caminos, San Pedro Carchá (or Apartado Postal 14, 16001 Cobán) - 1100-0400.
BV00) BAJA VERAPAZ
BV01) Inst de Educación Básica, Barrio Abajo San Jerónimo, 15001 Salamá. Prgrs. in Spanish, Achi and Q'eqchí
CH00) CHIQUIMULA
CH01) 7 Calle Av 4-00, Z-1, 20001 Chiquimula (or: 6 Av 0-60, Z-4, Torre Prof II, Of 904, 01004 Guatemala) – **CH02)** 5 Av 6-37, Z-1, 20007 Esquipulas - **FM:** 91.5MHz – **CH04)** Estación Educativa Evangélica, Ap. 5, 20901 Chiquimula. **W:** radioverdad.org – FM: 102.7MHz
CM00) CHIMALTENANGO
CM01) 2 Calle 3-33, Z-3, 04001 Chimaltenango – **CM02)** 6ta Calle 3-88, Zona 5, Patzún 050, Chimaltenango.
ES00) ESCUINTLA
ES01) 15 Calle 2-48, Z-3, 5001 Escuintla – **ES02)** Col 15 de Junio, Z-3, Tiquisate, 05001 Escuintla - FM: 92.3MHz – **ES03)** 4 Av 12-27, Z-1, 05001 Escuintla. E: radioinspiracion@gmail.com – **ES04)** 4 Av 11-38, Z-1, 05001 Escuintla – **ES05)** Central American Benevolent Association, 05001 Escuintla – **FM:** 96.3MHz
GU00) GUATEMALA
GU01) 8 Calle 1-11, Z-1, 01001Guatemala – **GU02)** 9 Av 0-32, Z-2, 01002 Guatemala. **W:** radioprogresoguatemala.com – **GU03)** 34 Av "A" 7-60 Tikal 2, Z-7, 01007 Guatemala – **GU04)** 18 Calle 6-72, Z-1, 01001 Guatemala – **GU06)** 8 C 10-54, Zona 11, Col. Roosevelt, 01011 Guatemala. **W:** radiomundial.com.gt – **GU07)** Ap 601 (or: 4 Av 30-09, Z-3), 01901 Guatemala - **English:** 0300-0430 on 730 kHz. **W:** radiocultural.net – **GU08)** 30 Av 3-86, Z-11, Utatlán II, 01011 Guatemala – **GU09)** 11 Calle 2-43, Z-1, 01001 Guatemala – **GU10)** 25 Calle 4-91, Zona 12, Barrio La Reformita, 01012 Guatemala. **W:** radiokyrios.org.gt – **GU11)** Calzada San Juan 7-90, Edif.Acuario, Z-7, 01007 Guatemala – **GU12)** 6a Av 0-60, Zona 4, Torre Profesional 1, Niv. 9, Of. 911, 01004 Guatemala – **GU13)** 10a Avenida "A" 2-43 Zona 1, 01001 Guatemala **W:** www.eventoscatolicos.com.gt – **GU14)** 15 Calle 3-45, Z-1, 01001 Guatemala – **GU15)** 1 Av 35-48, Z-7, Col Toledo, 01007 Guatemala. **W:** radiotictaclavozdelevangelio.blogspot.com – **GU16)** 1 Calle 5-20, Z-1, 01001 Guatemala – **GU17)** 2 Calle 18-07, Zona 15, Vista Hermosa I, 01015 Guatemala. **W:** sonora.com.gt – **GU19)** 4 Av 1-14, Z-1, 01001 Guatemala. **W:** centralpalabramiel.org – **GU20)** Ap 281, 01901 Guatemala – **GU21)** 7 Av. 15-13, Zona 1, Edificio Ejecutivo, Niv. 8, 01001 Guatemala. **W:** radioexclusiva.org – **GU22)** Ap 51-C, 01015 Guatemala. **W:** unionradiogt.com – **GU24)** 4 Av 0-60, Z-4, 01004 Guatemala. **W:** radiocapital1420am.com.gt – **GU25)** 17 Av.21, Cnt. Com Las Pergolas, Z-11, 01011 Guatemala – **GU27)** Ap 1213, (or: 30

Av "A" 7-33, Z-7, Col Tikal, 01007 Guatemala), 01901 Guatemala. **W:** radiovea.org – **GU29)** Guatemala – **GU30)** 10a Avenida 0-61, Z-19, Colonia La Florida, 01019 Guatemala – **GU32)** 17 Av. 5-47, Zona 11, Col. Miraflores, 01011 Guatemala – **GU33)** 6a Avenida 11-77, Zona 10, Pent House, Guatemala

HU00) HUEHUETENANGO
HU01) 2 Calle 4-42, Z-1, 13001 Huehuetenango – **HU02)** Ap 13, 13901 Huehuetenango **W:** lavozdehuehue.comlu.com – **HU04)** 13025 San Sebastián Coatán Programming in Spanish & Chuj Coatán. FM: 92.5MHz –**HU05)** 13020 San Sebastián H, Huehuetenango. **W:** tgmi-radiobuenasnuevas.com

IZ00) IZABAL
IZ01) Calle Principal, Morales – **IZ02)** Ruta Atlántico km 291, 18001 Puerto Barrios – **IZ03)** Barrio El Carrizal, Morales – **IZ04)** Ap 425, 18901Puerto Barrios – **IZ05)** 8 Av 15 y 16 Calle, 18001 Puerto Barrios – **IZ06)** Izabal

JA00) JALAPA
JA01) San Carlos Alzatate, 21001 Jalapa. **W:** revelacion2.byethost6.com

JU00) JUTIAPA
JU01) 4 Avenida 4-79, Zona 1, Colonia El Latino, 22001 Jutiapa – **JU02)** Carr Interamericana km 117, 22001 Jutiapa. **W:** radiouncio-njutiapa.com – **JU03)** Quezada – **JU04)** 6ta Calle 5-00, Zona 3, a un costado del puente del Incienso, 22001 Jutiapa

PE00) PETÉN
PE01) Sta Elena de la Cruz **FM:** 96.9MHz – **PE02)** Sta Elena de la Cruz – **PE04)** Isleta Sta Bárbara, 17001 Flores (or: 1 Av 1-22, Z-1, Guatemala) **W:** radiopeten.com.gt - FM: 105.3MHz– **PE05)** Ministerio de la Defensa Nacional, Sta Elena de la Cruz

QE00) QUETZALTENANGO
QE01) Ap 113 (or 13 Av 8-19, Z-1), 09901 Quetzaltenango – **QE02)** 6 Av 6-41, Z-1, 09001 Quetzaltenango – **QE03)** 5 C 13-56, Zona 3, Xelajú (Ap 90), 09901 Quetzaltenango - FM: 99.1MHz– **QE04)** 7 Av 0-26, Z-2, 09002 Quetzaltenango. **W:** radiotgd.com – **QE05)** 3 Calle 3-38, Z-1, Coatepeque – **QE06)** 14 Av "A" 0-78, Z-1, 09002 Quetzaltenango – **QE07)** Ap 107, 09901 Quetzaltenango – **QE09)** Calle Principal, Z-2, Colomba. - FM: 99.1MHz– **QE10)** 4 Calle 15A-62, Z-1, 09002 Quetzaltenango. **W:** www.nuevaradioxelaju.com – **QE11)** 3 Calle 3-38, Z-1, Coatepeque, Retalhuleu – **QE12)** Km 211, Aldea Duraznales, Concepción, Chiquirichapa, Quetzaltenango.

QU00) QUICHÉ
QU01) 7 Calle 3-67, Z-5, 14001 Sta Cruz del Quiché **W:** radioscatoli-casdequiche.com - FM: 90.7 MHz – **QU03)** 5 Av 1-32, Canton Batzbaca, 14013 Nebaj

RE00) RETALHULEU
RE01) Ap 84, 11901Retalhuleu – **RE02)** 7 Av 6-72, 11001 Retalhuleu (or: Ap 183-A, Guatemala): 0900-0300

SA00) SACATEPÉQUEZ
SA01) San Juan Sacatepéquez. **W:** radiocircuitosanjuan.com

SR00) SANTA ROSA
SR01) Edif Municipal, Chiquimulilla.

SM00) SAN MARCOS
SM01) 4 Avenida 4-32, Z-1, Malacatán – **SM04)** 5 Calle 8-21, Z-1, San Pedro – **SM05)** Pajapita, 12001 San Marcos – **SM06)** 12001 San Marcos

SO00) SOLOLA
SO03) Iglesia Bautista Getsemani, San Pedro La Laguna (or: International Mission Board, SBC, Ap 25, Bulevares, MX 53140, México) - **FM:** 97.6MHz

SU00) SUCHITEPEQUEZ
SU01) 1000 Mazatenango - 1100-0400 – **SU02)** La Libertad 9-91, Z-1, 10001 Mazatenango – **SU03)** 6 Av 10-54, Z-1, 10001 Mazatenango – **SU04)** 13 Av 23-60, Z-12, 10012 Coyotenango – **SU05)** Calle 30 de Junio 1a y 2a, Z-5, 10001 Mazatenango

TO00) TOTONICAPAN
TO01) Barrio La Cienaga, 08002 San Cristóbal Totonicapán – **TO03)** Momostenango, 08001 Totonicapán – **TO04)** Totonicapán

ZA00) ZACAPA
ZA01) 4 Calle 12-54, Z-1, 19001 Zacapa – **ZA02)** 4 Calle 10-34, Z-1, 19001 Zacapa – **ZA03)** Zona Militar N° 7, 19001 Zacapa

FM in Guatemala City (MHz): 88.1 Fabuestereo - 88.5 Galaxia La Picosa – 88.9 Fabulosa 88.9 – 89.3 Estrella – 89.7 Em.Unidas – 90.1 Yo Sí Sideral – 90.5 Punto – 90.9 Exitos – 91.3 Furia Musical – 91.7 Fiesta – 92.1 Universidad – 92.5 40 Principales – 92.9 Disney – 93.3 FM Joya – 93.7 Mía – 94.1 94 FM – 94.5 La Sabrosita – 94.9 Nueve Cuatro Nueve – 95.3 Kyrios – 95.7 Ranchero – 96.1 Nuevo Mundo – 96.5 Atmósfera – 96.9 Sonora – 97.3 Alfa – 97.7 Kiss FM – 98.1 Doble S – 98.9 Globo – 99.3 La Grande – 99.7 Conga – 100.1 Infinita – 100.5 Cultural – 100.9 La Hit FM – 101.3 R. Extrema – 101.7 R. Activa – 102.1 Stereo 102 – 102.5 FM Fama – 102.9 Caliente – 103.3 R. María

– 103.7 R. Fiesta – 104.1 Stereo Visión – 104.5 TGRF R. Faro Cultural – 104.9 Tropicálida – 105.3 Celebra FM – 105.7 Union – 106.1 Red Deportiva – 106.5 Clásica – 106.9 ¡UyUyUy! – GU04) 107.3 TGW LV de Guatemala – 107.7 Mega

FM in Quetzaltenango (MHz): 88.1 Dinámica – 88.5 La Consentida – 89.5 Emisoras Unidas – 89.9 Prisima FM – 90.3 Tropicálida – 90.7 María – 91.1 La Nueva Mega – 91.7 La Rubia – 92.3 R. Cadena Sonora – 92.7 Cadena Caliente – 93.1 Nahual Estereo – 93.7 Fiesta – 94.3 Diamante – 94.7 Punto – 95.1 Ke Buena – 95.5 Evolución – 95.9 FM Globo – 96.3 FM Intima – 97.1 Exa FM – 97.5 Gaviota FM – 98.3 La Grande – 98.7 Yo Sí Sideral – 99.1 RTVA Arqueocesana – 99.5 Génesis – 99.9 Galaxia – La Picosa – 100.3 Stereo Cien – 100.7 R. Culturas – 101.1 R. Estéreo Tulán – 101.5 Estéreo Alegre – 102.3 Precencias R. – 102.9 Cristal – 103.3 La Voz de Dios – 104.3 Emisoras Unidas – 104.7 Razón – 105.3 La Voz del Evangelio – 105.9 FM Luna – 106.3 La Visión F – 106.7 Alfa – 107.1 R. Exitos – 107.5 TGQ La Voz de Quetzaltenango – 107.9 R. Estéreo Vida

GUINEA

L.T: UTC — **Pop:** 10 million — **Pr.L:** French, Fulah, Maninké, Soussou — **E.C:** 50Hz, 220V — **ITU:** GUI

CONSEIL NATIONAL DE LA COMMUNICATION (CNC)
▢ Conakry **W:** www.guinee.gov.gn **L.P:** Chmn: Mounir Camar.

RADIO TÉLÉVISION GUINÉE (RTG, Gov.)
▢ B. P. 391, Conakry ☎+224 30 41 55 19. **W:** www.rtg- conakry.com **L.P:** DG: Alpha Kabinet Keita. Dir. Tech: Aladji Touré.
SW: Conakry (Sonfonia): 7125kHz 50kW (irreg.).
FM: Conakry 88.55/91.7MHz.
D.Prgr. in French/Others: W 0555-2400, Sun 0800-2400. **N: French:** 0645, 0915Sun, 1200Sun, 1245W, 1300Sun, 1615W, 1945W, 2000Sun, 2200, 2350. **English:** 1845 (irr.).
Ann: F: "R. Conakry", "R. Guineé". **IS:** Guitar.

RADIO RURALE (RTG rural stations)
R. Rurale de la Moyenne Guinée, Labé: 87.6MHz – **R. Rurale de la Haute Guinée:** Mandiana 88.2MHz, Kankan 92.1MHz, Dabadou 93MHz, Siguiri 97MHz, Douabou 99MHz – **R. Rurale de Kindia:** 88.3MHz, Kakoulima 98.7MHz, Koliadi 99.9MHz – **R. Rurale de N´Zerekore:** 89MHz.

RADIO RENAISSANCE (Rlg, operated by Actualité Féminine en Guinée, former Familia FM)
▢ Conakry **L.P:** DG: Mrs. Colette Baudais.
SW: Timbi-Madina 4900kHz 1kW. (currently off the air, waiting for licence renewal.)**FM:** Conakry 95.9MHz **D.Prgr.** in French/Susu/Kpèlè/Pular/Maninka: FM: 0600-2400.

Private stations:
R. Djiguii, Conakry: 105.7/107.7MHz. **W:** djiguii.com – **R. FM Liberté:** Conakry 101.3MHz – **R. Nostalgie Guinée:** Conakry: 98.2MHz – **Sabari FM,** Conakry: 97.3MHz. **W:** sabarifm.com – **Soleil FM:** Conakry 101.7MHz.
R. France Int: Conakry/Labé 89.9MHz

GUINEA-BISSAU

L.T: UTC — **Pop:** 1.5 million — **Pr.L:** Portuguese, Crioulo, others — **E.C:** 50Hz, 220V — **ITU:** GNB

INSTITUTO DAS COMUNICAÇÕES DA GUINÉ-BISSAU(ICGB)
▢ Av. Domingos Ramos 53, C.P. 1372, Bissau ☎+245 3204873/74 ▢ +245 3204876 **E:** icgb@mail.bissau.net

RADIODIFUSÃO NACIONAL (RDN, Gov.)
▢ C.P. 191, Bissau ☎+245 3212426 **L.P:** DG: Hipolito José Mendes.
FM: 88/91.5/93.7/98MHz. **D.Prgr:** 0600-1330, 1530-2400.
Ann: "Escutam a Radiodifusão Nacional da República da Guiné-Bissau"

Other stations:
R. Bombolom, Bissau: 106.2MHz. Also rel. BBC & DW – **R. Mavegro,** Bissau: 100.0MHz. Also rel. BBC – **R. Nossa** (Rlg.), Bissau: 98.9MHz – **R. Pindjiguiti,** Bissau: 95.0MHz. Also rel. VOA – **R. Sol Mansi** (Rlg.) Mansoa: 90.0MHz 4kW, Bissau/Bafatá 101.8MHz 1kW. 0630-2300. Also rel. Vatican R. and UN prgrs.
RFI Afrique: Bissau 94.7MHz in French/Portuguese.
RDP África: Nhacra 88.4MHz 25kW, Gabú 100MHz 1kW +1tx under 1kW. +20 community radio stations

GUYANA

LT: UTC -4h — **Pop:** 772,000 — **Pr.L:** Creole, English, Hindi, Urdu, Amerindian dialects — **E.C:** 50Hz, 240V — **ITU:** GUY

PUBLIC UTILITIES COMMISSION
⌨ Parliament Buildings, Brickdam, Georgetown ☎ +592 227 3293
🖷 +592 227 3534

NATIONAL COMMUNICATIONS NETWORK INC.
(ex. GUYANA BROADCASTING CORP)
⌨ Broadcasting House, P.O. Box 10760, Georgetown ☎+592 223 6049, +592 223 1566/1577 🖷+592 226 2253 **W:** www.ncnguyana.com
E: feedback@ncnguyana.com
LP: SEO: Mohammed Sattaur GM: Mazrul Bacchus Prod. Mgr: Martin Goolsarran
MW: Georgetown 560/‡760kHz 10kW, Linden 700kHz 1kW
NB: 760kHz is inactive
SW: Georgetown: 3290/5950kHz 10kW
FM: Georgetown 100.1/102.5MHz, Linden 106.5MHz
R. Roraima: 0800-0200 on (760kHz‡) + 100.1MHz. **N:** 0900, 1000, 1100, 1330, 1500, 1900, 2100, 2230 (Sun), 2300 (W), 0100.
Voice of Guyana: 24h on 560kHz 2200-0900 on 3290kHz **N:** as R. Roraima. **V.** by letter.
Other stations: Megajams, Georgetown 87.7MHz – R.Guyana, Georgetown 98.1MHz

HAITI

LT: UTC -5h; DST (10 Mar-3 Nov: -4h) subject to confirmation — **Pop:** 8.9 million — **Pr.L:** Créole, French — **E.C:** 50+60Hz, 110V — **ITU:** HTI

CONSEIL NATIONAL DES TELECOMUNICATIONS (CONATEL)
⌨ B.P.2002 (or: Cité de l'Exposition 16), Port-au-Prince ☎ +509 25163325 🖷+509 22239229
W: www.conatel.gouv.ht **E:** info@conatel.gouv.ht

MW	kHz	kW	Station, location
4)	630	1	Rdif. Jérémienne, Jérémie
6)	660	5	R. Lumiere, P-au-P
6)	720	1	R. Lumière, Petite Riv.
6)	740	1	R. Lumière, Pignon
6)	760	2	R. Lumière, Cayes
8)	780	0.5	R. Lumrie, Jérémie
8)	780	10	Eben-Ezer, Mirebalais
9)	810	0.05	R. Atlantique, Gonaives
11)	840	10	R. 4VEH, Cap Haitien
13)	860	3	R. Men Kontre, Cayes
14)	870	1	R. Express, Jacmel
15)	880	0.3	R. Independance, Gonaives
16)	890	0.5	R. Trans Artibonite, Gonaives
17)	890	1	Voix du Nord'est, Forte Liberte
20)	930	5	R. Cap Haitien, Cap Haitien
21)	930	0.1	R. Echo 2000, Val. de Jacmel
22)	940	0.25	R. St Marc, St marc
23)	940	0.2	Rdif. Jacmelienne, Jacmel
66)	1030		R. Ginen, P-au-P
27)	1080	20	R. Nationale, P-au-P
30)	1170		R. Tropicale Internationale, Jérémie
31)	1190	0.3	R. Grand Anse, Jérémie
32)	1200		Voix de la Paix, Port de Paix
33)	1220	1	Voix du Plateau Central, Hinche
34)	1230	1	Voix de L'ave Maria, Cap Haitien
36)	1280		R. Transcaribbean International, Jean Rabel
37)	1330	10	R. Haiti Inter, P-au-P
38)	1350	0.25	R. Dame Marie, Dame Marie
40)	1370	0.5	R. Citadelle, Cap Haitien
41)	1370	1	Rdif. Cayenne, Cayes
43)	1410	3	Voix de Nord-ouest, Port de Paix
44)	1420	0.5	R. Messie Continental, Dessalines
46)	1460	0.2	Voix du Nord, Cap Haitien

Abbreviations: P-au-P = Port-au-Prince.
NB: only R. 4VEH 840 kHz has been reported active lately.
Addresses and other information:
4) 82, Rue Eugene Magron, Jérémie – **6)** Côte Plage 16, Carrefour, P-au-P (or BP 1050) **H of tr:** 1000-0200 **W:** www.radiolumiere.org – **8)** 27, Rue Clair Heureuse, Mirebalais – **9)** Rlle Laporte, Gonaive – **11)** Box 1, Cap-Haitien (or: Radio 4VEH, P.O.Box 24638, West Palm Beach, FL 33416, USA) ☎ +509 454 1334 **W:** www.radio4veh.org **E:** contact@radio4veh.org – **13)** 137, Rue Simon, Cayes – **14)** 31, Rue Stenio Vincent, Jacmel – **15)** Rue Egalite, Gonaives – **16)** Rue du Quai,

Gonaives – **17)** Rue Bourbons, Forte Liberte – **20)** 30 Rue 10A, Cap Haitien – **21)** 15, rue Alcius Charmant, Jacmel – **22)** 20 Rue A Thoby, St Marc – **23)** 32, Rue D'Orleans, Jacmel – **26)** Vaudreuil, Cap Haitien – **27)** Rue du Magasin d'État (or B.P 1143), P-au-P – **30)** Jérémie – **31)** 54, Rue Eugene Magron, Jérémie – **32)** Eveché de P.de.P, Rue L'Hôpital, Port de Paix – **33)** 657, Rue Toussaint L'Ouverture, Hinche – **34)** Rue 19H, Cap Haitien **E:** radiovoixavemaria@hotmail.com – **36)** 28, Cité James, Coicou, Jean Rabel – **37)** Delmas 66A, P-au-P – **38)** 252, Rue Frere Portier, Dame Marie – **40)** Rue 10-11-E, Cap Haitien – **41)** 77, Rue Duvivier-Hall, Cayes – **43)** 84, Rue Christophe, Port de Paix – **44)** 15, Rue Jacques 1er, Marchands Dessalines, Dessalines – **46)** Rue 20-A-B, Cap Haitien – **66)** 9 Bis, Delmas 31, P-au-P
FM in Port au Prince (MHz): 88.1 R. Visa FM – 88.5 R. Kyskeya – 88.9 R. Indigène – 89.3 RFI – 89.7 LV de l'Espérance – 90.1 R. One – 90.5 R. Signal FM – 90.9 R. Ti Moun – 91.3 Tropic FM – 91.7 R. Etoile – 92.1 R. Lumière – 92.5 R. Commerciale – 92.9 R. Ginen – 93.3 Antilles Internationales – 93.7 R. Vasco – 94.1 R. Nouvelle Génération – 94.5 Caraïbes FM Stéréo – 94.9 R. MBC – 95.3 LV de l'Evangile – 95.7 R. Horizon 2000 – 96.1 R. Communauté Haïtienne 2000 – 96.5 R. Sky FM – 96.9 R. Antilles Internationales – 97.3 R. Mega Star – 97.7 R. Lumière – 98.1 R. Maxima FM – 98.5 R. Ibo – 98.9 R. Maximum Power – 99.3 R. Vision 2000 – 99.7 Sweet FM – 100.1 R. Métropole – 100.5 R. Eclair – 100.9 R. Magik 9 – 101.3 R. Univers FM – 101.7 Energie FM – 102.1 R. Nationale – 102.5 Zenith FM – 102.9 R. Super Star – 103.3 R. Mélodie FM – 103.7 R. Lakensyèl – 104.1 R. SODEC Service – 104.5 R. Galaxie – 104.9 R. RFM – 105.3 R. Nationale – 105.5 R. Soleil – 106.1 R. Haïti Inter – 106.5 R. Planet Kreyol – 106.9 R. Kadans – 107.3 R. Solidarité – 107.7 R. Vertières

RADIO FRANCE INTERNATIONALE
FM: Port-au-Prince 89.3MHz, Cap Haïtien 100.5MHz

HAWAII (USA)

LT: UTC -10h — **Pop:** 1.28 million — **Pr.L:** English, Japanese, Filipino — **E.C:** 60Hz, 120V — **ITU:** HWA

FEDERAL COMMUNICATIONS COMMISSION (FCC)
see USA for details

THE HAWAII ASSOCIATION OF BROADCASTERS, INC.
⌨ P.O. Box 61562, Honolulu HI 96839 **W:** www.hawaiibroadcasters com **E:** jamie.hartnett@gmail.com **LP:** Pres: Susii Hearst, Exec. Dir: Jamie Hartnett

MW	kHz	kW	Call	Location
1)	550	5	KMVI	Wailuku, Maui
37)	570	1	KQNG	Lihue, Kauai
3)	590	7.5	KSSK	Honolulu, Oahu
4)	620	5	KHNU	Hilo, Hawaii
4)	620	10	KHNU	Kalaoa, Hawaii
4)	620	5	KHNU	Naalehu, Hawaii
5)	650	10	KRTR	Honolulu, Oahu
6)	670	5	KPUA	Hilo, Hawaii
7)	690	10	KHNR	Honolulu, Oahu
37)	720	5	KUAI	Eleele, Kauai
35)	740	5	-	Kihei, Maui (CP)
7)	760	5	KGU	Honolulu, Oahu
1)	790	5	KKON	Kealakekua, Hawaii
3)	830	10	KHVH	Honolulu, Oahu
1)	850	5	KHLO	Hilo, Hawaii
7)	880	2	KHCM	Honolulu, Oahu
1)	900	5	KNUI	Kahului, Maui
5)	940	10	KKNE	Honolulu, Oahu
3)	990	5	KIKI	Honolulu, Oahu
9)	1040	5	KLHT	Honolulu, Oahu
30)	1060	5	KIPA	Hilo, Hawaii*
11)	1080	5	KWAI	Honolulu, Oahu
2)	1110	5	KAOI	Kihei, Maui
12)	1130	1	KPHI	Honolulu, Oahu
36)	1180	1	KORL	Honolulu, Oahu*
13)	1210	1	KZOO	Honolulu, Oahu
12)	1250	5/0.21	-	Kahului, Maui (CP)
8)	1260	5/1	-	Keaau, Hawaii (CP)
14)	1270	5	KNDI	Honolulu, Oahu
16)	1370	6.2	KUPA	Pearl City, Oahu
41)	1400	2.5	-	Paukaa, Hawaii (CP)
17)	1420	5	KKEA	Honolulu, Oahu
42)	1450	5	KMCA	Hilo, Hawaii (CP)
17)	1460	5	KHRA	Honolulu, Oahu
17)	1500	10	KHKA	Honolulu, Oahu
19)	1540	5	KREA	Honolulu, Oahu
20)	1570	15	KUAU	Haiku, Maui

FM	MHz	kW	Call	Location
21)	88.1	39	KHPR	Honolulu, Oahu
21)	88.1	1	KHPR-FM1	Makaha, Hawaii
21)	88.1	3	KHPR-FM3	Kailua, Hawaii
21)	88.7	6.5	KHPH	Kailua, Hawaii
9)	88.9	21	KHJC	Lihue, Kauai
21)	89.3	38.5	KIPO-FM	Honolulu, Oahu
21)	89.3	1	KIPO-FM1	Makaha, Hawaii
21)	89.3	3	KIPO-FM2	Kailua, Hawaii (CP)
21)	89.7	62	KIPM	Hana, Maui
22)	90.1	3	KTUH	Honolulu, Oahu
38)	90.1	4	-	Lihue, Kauai (CP)
22)	90.3	3	KTUH	Honolulu, Oahu
23)	90.3	5	KCIF	Hilo, Hawaii
25)	90.5	2.2	-	Hauula, Oahu (CP)
24)	90.5	9	KPHL	Ocean View, Hawaii*
21)	90.7	56	KKUA	Wailuku, Maui
26)	90.9	0.9	KKCR	Hanalei, Kauai
21)	91.1	30	KANO	Hilo, Hawaii
15)	91.3	28.5	KLEI-FM	Kailua-Kona, Hawaii (CP)
27)	91.7	1.8	KAHU	Pahala, Hawaii
26)	91.9	6	KAQA	Kilauea, Kauai
30)	92.1	4.5	KHWI	Holualea, Hawaii
3)	92.3	100	KSSK-FM	Waipahu, Oahu
1)	92.5	1.7	KLHI-FM	Kahului, Maui
30)	92.7	7.5	KHBC	Hilo, Hawaii*
37)	93.1	100	KQMQ-FM	Honolulu, Oahu
6)	93.1	10	KMWB	Captain Cook, Hawaii
1)	93.5	72	KPOA	Lahaina, Maui
37)	93.5	51	KQNG-FM	Lihue, Kauai
3)	93.9	100	KHJZ	Honolulu, Oahu
1)	93.9	7.3	KLUA	Kailua-Kona, Hawaii
2)	94.3	2	KDLX	Makawao, Maui
39)	94.3	100	-	Hanapepe, Kauai (CP)
37)	94.7	100	KUMU-FM	Honolulu, Oahu
6)	94.7	51	KWXX-FM	Hilo, Hawaii
1)	95.1	3.5	KAOI-FM	Wailuku, Maui
7)	95.5	100	KAIM-FM	Honolulu, Oahu
5)	95.9	39	KPVS	Hilo, Hawaii
37)	95.9	51	KSRF	Poipu, Kauai
5)	96.3	75	KRTR-FM	Kailua, Oahu
29)	96.9	100	KFMN	Lihue, Kauai
28)	97.1	38	KNWB	Hilo, Hawaii
12)	97.3	1.5	KRKH	Wailea-Makena, Maui
7)	97.5	80	KHCM-FM	Honolulu, Oahu
1)	97.9	51	KKBG	Hilo, Hawaii
12)	98.1	51	KJMQ	Lihue, Kauai
12)	98.3	9.4	KJMD	Pukalani, Maui
3)	98.5	51	KDNN	Honolulu, Oahu
12)	98.9	51	KITH	Kapaa, Kauai
1)	99.1	7.3	KAGB	Waimea-Kamuela, Hawaii
7)	99.5	100	KGU-FM	Honolulu, Oahu
12)	99.9	72	KJKS	Kahului, Maui
12)	99.9	51	KTOH	Kalaheo, Kauai
1)	100.3	35	KAPA	Hilo, Hawaii
1)	100.3	7.3	KAPA-FM1	Puueo, Hawaii
5)	100.3	50	KCCN-FM	Honolulu, Oahu
40)	100.7	2.2	KKHI	Kihei, Maui
12)	101.1	100	KORL-FM	Waianae, Oahu
12)	101.1	0.98	KORL-FM	Lahaina, Maui
6)	101.1	6.5	KAOY	Kealakekua, Hawaii
3)	101.9	100	KUCD	Pearl City, Oahu
37)	102.1	50	KTBH-FM	Kurtistown, Hawaii
2)	102.3	1.9	KMKK-FM	Kaunakakai, Molokai
37)	102.7	61	KDDB	Waipahu, Oahu
30)	102.9	1.5	KLZY	Paia, Maui*
2)	103.3	51	KSHK	Kekaha, Kauai
31)	103.5	2.2	KHAI	Wahiawa, Oahu
2)	103.7	100	KNUQ	Paauilo, Maui
5)	104.3	75	KPHW	Kaneohe, Oahu
12)	104.7	72	KONI	Lanai City, Maui
5)	105.1	100	KINE-FM	Honolulu, Oahu
4)	105.3	28	KBGX	Keaau, Hawaii
4)	105.3	1	KBGX-FM5	Naalehu, Hawaii
32)	105.5	9	KPMW	Haliimaile, Maui
37)	105.9	100	KPOI-FM	Honolulu, Oahu
1)	106.1	7.3	KLEO	Kahaluu-Kona, Hawaii
12)	106.5	72	KRYL	Haiku, Maui
33)	106.7	25	KNAN	Nanakali, Oahu*
34)	106.9	5.5	KWYI	Kawaihae, Hawaii
4)	107.7	28	KKOA	Volcano, Hawaii
4)	107.7	1	KKOA-FM5	Naalehu, Hawaii
7)	107.9	100	KKOL	Aiea, Oahu

Txs on air or CP less than 1kW not mentioned. *) currently silent

Addresses and other information:

Addresses: Add state abbreviation HI between location and zip code as appropriate. **Prgr:** All stns 24h unless otherwise stated

1) Pacific Radio Group, Maui: KMVI **W:** www.espn550.com KNUI **W:** www.foxnews900.com KLHI-FM **W:** www.x925.fm KPOA **W:** www.kpoa.com KJMD **W:** www.dajam983.com KJKS **W:** www.kiss99fm.com ✉ 311 Ano Street, Kahului, 96732-1304; **Hawaii:** KKON **W:** www.espnhawaii.com KHLO **W:** www.espnhawaii.com KLUA KPVS KKBG **W:** www.kbigfm.com KAGB **W:** www.kaparadio.com KAPA **W:** www.kaparadio.com KLEO **W:** www.kbigfm.com ✉ 913 Kanoelehua Ave, Hilo 96720-5116 – **2) Visionary Related Entertainment LLC, Molokai:** KMKK-FM **W:** www.vremaui.com/kmkk ✉ 130 Kamehameha V Highway, Kaunakaka 96748; **Maui:** KAOI **W:** www.kaoi1110.com KAOI-FM **W:** www.kaoifm.com KNUQ **W:** www.q103maui.com KDLX ✉ 1900 Main Street, Wailuku 96793-1900 – **3) Capstar TX Ltd Partnership, Oahu:** KSSK **W:** www.ksskradio.com KHVH **W:** www.khvhradio.com KHBZ **W:** www.khbz.com KSSK-FM KHJZ **W:** www.939jamz.com KDNN **W:** www.island985.com KUCD **W:** www.star1019.com ✉ 650 Iwilei Rd #400, Honolulu 96817-5319 – **4) Mahalo Broadcasting LLC, Hawaii:** KHNU KBGX **W:** www.lava1053.com KKOA ✉ 74-5605 Luhia St #B-7, Kailua-Kona 96740-1678 – **5) Cox Radio Inc, Oahu:** KRTR **W:** www.650amhawaii.com KKNE **W:** www.am940hawaii.com KRTR-FM **W:** www.krater96.com KCCN-FM **W:** www.kccnfm100.com KPHW **W:** www.power1043.com KINE **W:** www.hawaiian105.com F.PL 50kW ✉ 900 Fort St Mall #700, Honolulu 96813-3797 – **6) New West Broadcasting Corporation, Hawaii:** KPUA **W:** www.kpua.net KWXX-FM **W:** www.kwxx.com KNWB **W:** www.b97hawaii.com KMWB **W:** www.b97hawaii.com KAOY **W:** www.kwxx.com ✉ 1145 Kilauea Ave, Hilo 96720-4203 – **7) Salem Media of Hawaii Inc, Oahu:** KHNR **W:** www.khnrtownhall.com KGU **W:** www.kguradio.com KGU-FM **W:** www.995kgufm.com KHCM **Prgr:** 24h. China R. International relay in English, Chinese, Korean & Japanese KAIM-FM **W:** www.thefishhawaii.com KHCM-FM **W:** www.975countrykhcm.com KKOL **W:** www.oldies1079honolulu.com ✉ 1160 N King St #200, Honolulu 96817-330 – **8) Wagenvoord Advertising Group Inc,** 2360 NE Coachman Road, Clearwater FL 33765-2216 **Hawaii:** K**** [1260] – **9) Calvary Chapel of Honolulu Inc, Oahu:** KLHT **W:** www.klight.org ✉: 98-106 Komo Mai Drive, Aiea 96701-1901; **Kauai:** KHJC: ✉ 2970 Kele St #117, Lihue 96766-1803 – **11) Radio Hawaii Inc, Oahu:** KWAI **W:** www.kwai1080am.com ✉ 100 N Beretania St #401, Honolulu 968174724 – **12) Hochman-McCann Hawaii Inc, Oahu:** KPHI KORL-FM ✉ 900 Fort St Mall #450, Honolulu 96813-3713; **Maui:** K**** [1250] KRKH KONI KRYL ✉ 300 Ohukai Road #C-318, Kihei 96753-7050; **Kauai:** KJMQ KITH KTOH ✉ 4334 Rice St #204-B, Lihue 96766-1801 **W:** www.hhawaiimedia.net – **13) Polynesian Broadcasting Inc, Oahu:** KZOO **W:** www.kzoohawaii.com **Prgr:** Japanese. ✉ 2752 Woodlawn Drive #5-204, Honolulu 96822-1855 – **14) Broadcast House of the Pacific Inc, Oahu:** KNDI **W:** www.kndi.com **Prgr:** multicultural, religious. ✉ 1734 S King St, Honolulu 96826-2042 – **15) Aina'E Co, Ltd: Hawaii:** KLEI-FM 875 Waimanu St #640, Honolulu 96813 – **16) Broadcasting Corporation of America, Oahu:** KUPA: 4766 Holladay Blvd, Holladay UT 84117 – **17) Blow Up LLC, Oahu:** KKEA **W:** www.sportsradio1420.com ✉ 1088 Bishop St #112, Honolulu 96813-3113 – **18) RK Media Group, Oahu:** KHRA **Prgr:** Korean. ✉ 1311 Kapiolani Blvd #204, Honolulu 96814-4513 – **19) JMK Communications Inc, Oahu:** KREA **Prgr:** Korean. ✉ 1839 S King St #203, Honolulu 96814-2147 – **20) First Assembly King's Cathedral & Chapel, Maui:** KUAU **W:** www.kingscathedral.com ✉ 777 Mokulele Hwy, Kahului 96732 – **21) Hawaii Public Radio Inc, Oahu:** KHPR **W:** www.hawaiipublicradio.org] KIPO [includes BBC relay] ✉ 738 Kaheka St #101, Honolulu 96814-3726; **Simulcast: Maui:** KKUA **F.PL:** KIPM [KIPO relay] **Hawaii:** KANO **F.PL:** KIPH (KIPO relay) – **22) The University of Hawaii, Oahu:** KTUH **F.PL:** 6kW **W:** www.ktuh.org ✉ 202 Hemenway Hall, University of Hawaii, 2445 Campus Road, Honolulu 96822-2216 – **23) Hilo Christian Broadcasting Corporation, Hawaii:** KCIF **W:** www.kcifhawaii.org ✉ 180 Kinoole St, Hilo 96720-2827 – **24) Vineyard Christian Fellowship of Honolulu Inc, Hawaii:** KPHL ✉ 250 Kawaihea St #15E, Honolulu 96825 – **25) Halau Lokahi Public Charter School, Oahu:** K*** [90.5]: 401 Waikakamilo Road #1A, Honolulu 96817 – **26) Kekahu Foundation Inc, Kauai:** KKCR **W:** www.kkcr.org KAQA **W:** www.kkcr.com **F.PL:** 6kW] ✉ 4520-D Hanalei Plantation Road, PO Box 825, Hanalei 96714-0825 – **27) Haola Inc, Hawaii:** KAHU **F.PL:** 1.8kW: PO Box 5024, Hilo 96720-1054 – **28) Captain Cook Broadcasting Inc, Hawaii** KMWB [see #6] 8215 Birch St, New Orleans LA 70118 – **29) FM97 Associates, Kauai:** KFMN **W:** www.kfmn97.com ✉ 1860 Leleiona Road, Lihue 96766-9000 – **30) Chaparral Broadcasting Inc, Hawaii** KIPA KHBC KHWI **Maui:** KLZY: c/o Jerrold T Lundquist, 14 Cockenoe Drive, Westport CT 06880-6908 – **31) Educational Media Foundation, Oahu:** KHAI: 5700 W Oaks Blvd, Rocklin CA 96765 [**F.PL:** 53kW] – **32) Rey-Cel**

Broadcasting Inc, Maui: KPMW **W:** www.myspace.com/wild105 ✉ 230 Hana Hwy, Kahului 96732 – **33) Big D Consulting Ltd, Oahu:** KNAN: 3800 Howard Hughes Parkway 17th Floor, Las Vegas NV 89109 – **34) Colin H Naito, Hawaii:** KWYI ✉ 64-1040 Mamalahoa Hwy #4, Kamuela 96743-6540 – **35) IHR Educational Broadcasters, Maui:** K**** PO Box 180, Tahoma CA 96142 – **36) James L. Primm, Oahu:** KORL 41-625 Eclectic #J1, Palm Desert CA 92260 – **37) Ohana Broadcast Company LLC, Kauai:** KQNG KQNG-FM **W:** www. kongradio.com KUAI KSRF **W:** www.surf959fm.com KSHK **W:** www. shaka103.com 4271 Halenani St, Lihue 96766-1312 **Oahu:** KQMQ-FM **W:** www.931thezone.net KUMU-FM **W:** www.kumu.com KDDB KPOI-FM **W:** www.kpoifm.com 765 Amana St #206, Honolulu 96814-3248 **Hawaii:** KTBH F.P.L move to 102.5 with 21kW – **38) Calvary Chapel Kauai, Kauai:** K*** [90.1] PO Box 1062, Kapa'a 96746 – **39) Virtues Communications Network, LLC: Kauai:** K*** [94.3] PO Box 215, Kings Park NY 11754 – **40) Future Modulation Broadcasting, LLC: Maui:** KKHI 4700 Allan Road, Cheyenne WY 82009 – **41) Murphy Broadcasting System,** 101 Turtle Point Court, St Simons Island, GA 31522 **Hawaii:** K**** [1400] – **42) Mark C Allen,** 4575 Nantucket Dr, Redding CA 96001 **Maui** KMCA

HONDURAS

L.T: UTC -6h — **Pop:** 7.6 million — **Pr.L:** Spanish — **E.C:** 60Hz, 110V — **ITU:** HND

COMISION NACIONAL DE TELECOMUNICACIONES (CONATEL)
✉ Ap. 15012 (or Edificio CONATEL, Colonia Modelo, Sexta Avenida Suroeste Contigua a Hondutel), Tegucigalpa ☎ +504 2234 8600 🖷 +504 2236 8611 **W:** www.conatel.hn **E:** conatel@conatel.gob.hn

ASOCIACION NACIONAL DE RADIODIFUSORES DE HONDURAS (ANARH)
✉ Ap. 4039, Tegucigalpa

Hrs of tr 24h unless otherwise stated. Call HR–

MW	Call	kHz	kW	Station, location
155)	XT	550	1	R. X, Tegucigalpa
2)	XD	550	0.5	R. Manantial, Sta Rosa de Copán: 1115-0300
70)	VF	560	1	R. Valladolid, Comayagua
3)	RZ	560	5	VRZ R. Juticalpa, Juticalpa: 1100-0400
4)	KL	560	1	R. Reloj, San Pedro Sula
157)	UX	570	1	R. El Triunfo, Choluteca
5)	LP	570	1	R. América, Tela (r: 610)
6)	ZQ	580	3	R. Notícias STC, Tegucigalpa
112)	EO	580		Super Estrella de Occidente, Sta Rosa de Copán
5)	LP3	590	1	R. América, San Pedro Sula
227)	RE	590	1	R. Renacer, Catacamas
209)	EK	600	1	R. Orion, La Ceiba
5)	LD	610	10	R. América, Tegucigalpa: 1030-0400
5)	LP	610	10	R. América, Sta Rosa de Copán (r:610)
5)	LP5	620	1	R. América, Comayagua (r:610)
5)	LP	620	1	R. América, Juticalpa (r:610)
28)	LP17	620	1	R. Continental, San Pedro Sula
218)	LO	620	1	R. Litoral, Tocoa
5)	LP	630	1	R. América, Choluteca (r:610)
5)	LP7	630	1	R. América, La Ceiba (r:610)
8)	UP	640	1	R. Centro, Tegucigalpa: 1045-0500
185)	JT	640		R. Jerusalen, Sta Bárbara
241)	VS	650	25	Nuestra Señora de La Esperanza, San Pedro Sula
5)	LP	650	15	R. América, Danlí (r:610)
182)	TA	650	1	R. Turquesa, Siguatepeque
198)	VS	650	1	R. Católica Olancho, Olanchito
8)	NN18	660	3	LV de Honduras, La Ceiba (r:670)
239)	KV	ǂ660		R. Betania, Choluteca
8)	N	670	10	LV de Honduras, Tegucigalpa
8)	NN20	670	1	LV de Honduras, Sta Rosa de Copán (r:670)
8)	NN8	680	10	LV de Honduras, San Pedro Sula (r:670)
8)	NN11	680	10	LV de Honduras, Tocoa (r:670)
8)	NN2	680	10	LV de Honduras, Siguatepeque (r:670)
8)	NN7	680	1	LV de Honduras, Danlí (r:670)
8)	NN10	680	1	LV de Honduras, Juticalpa (r:670)
8)	NN9	680	1	LV de Honduras, Tela (r: 670)
8)	NN3	690	1	LV de Honduras, Choluteca (r:670)
203)	KL	700	5	R. Reloj, Tegucigalpa
8)		700		LV de Honduras, Olanchito (r: 670)
9)	RH	710	3	LV de Occidente, Sta Rosa de Copán
14)	UP3	710	1	R. Rock 'n Pop, San Pedro Sula
10)	LK	710	2	R. Comayagua/LV Católica, Comayagua
11)	KN	710	2.5	LV de Olancho, Catacamas
8)	NN13	710	1	LV de Honduras, Yoro (r:670)

MW	Call	kHz	kW	Station, location
79)	NN3	720	1	R. Caribe, La Ceiba
238)	ZN	720	1	R. San Lorenzo, San Lorenzo
8)	NN4	730	1	R. Exitos, Tegucigalpa
162)	XG	730	0.25	R. Cadena Dial, Sta Bárbara
12)	QQ	740	1	R. Intibuca, La Esperanza: 1100-0100
13)	IH	740	1	7-40 La Super Grande, Juticalpa: 1200-0400
14)	TG2	740	1	R. Satélite, San Pedro Sula: 1100-0600
90)	VC	740		LV Evangélica, Olanchito (r: 1390)
18)	XW	760	2.5	R. Comayagüela/Stereo Azul, Comayagüela
231)	IJ	760	1	R. Jicatuyo, San José de Colinas
14)	NN21	770	10	R. Norte, San Pedro Sula
19)	MV	770	0.5	R. Aguán, Olanchito
30)	PI	770	1	R. Sui Generis, Comayagua
135)	RD	770	1	R. Majestad "LV del Guayape", Juticalpa
5)	QN	780	1	R. Sonora, La Ceiba
163)	SE	780	1	Alabanza Estéreo, Choluteca
20)	FI	790	1	R. Feliz, Sta Bárbara
8)	TG	790	3	R. Satélite, Tegucigalpa
21)	DL	±800	1	R. Corporación, Comayagua: 1100-0400
22)	QN	800	1	R. Sonora, Danlí
217)	MD	800		R. Yoro, Jocon
170)	GW	800		R. Patria, Catacamas
17)	MA	800	3	R. Moderna, San Pedro Sula
90)	VC	810	6	LV Evangélica, La Ceiba (r:1390)
25)	LP24	810	3	R. Valle, Choluteca: 1000-0400
5)	LP16	820	5	R. Moderna, Tegucigalpa
84)	KW	820	7/3	R. Sultana, Sta Rosa de Copán: 1100-0400
24)	RU	830	1	R. Uno, San Pedro Sula
26)	JB	830	1	Cadena Radial Impacto, Comayagua
27)	VQ	830	1	R. Excelsior, Juticalpa: 1100-0400
216)	TB	830		R. Colón, Tocoa
18)	CR	840	1	Dif. Cristiana de R. "DCR", Choluteca: 1200-0400
90)		840		LV Evangélica, Tela (r. 1390)
8)	UP	850	10	R. Televisión, Tegucigalpa
165)	IF	850	0.5	R. Inspiración, La Entrada: 1100-0300
28)	BS	860	10	R. San Pedro, San Pedro Sula
110)	LS	860	0.5	R. Dinorama, La Paz
215)	NZ	860		La Respuesta es la Cruz, Olanchito
225)	BV	860		R. Piedra Blanca-LV de Nuestra Gente, Catacamas
1)	H9	870	5	R. Nacional de Honduras, La Ceiba (r:880)
1)	H10	870	5	R. Nacional de Honduras, Puerto Lempira (r:880)
1)	H4	870	3	R. Nacional de Honduras, Nacaome (r:880)
1)	H	880	10	R. Nacional de Honduras, Tegucigalpa
1)	H5	880	5	R. Nacional de Honduras, Sta Rosa de Copán
1)	H3	890	10	R. Nal de Honduras, San Pedro Sula (r:880)
1)	H7	890	3	R. Nacional de Honduras, Juticalpa (r:880)
1)	H9	890	10	R. Nacional de Honduras, Siguatepeque (r:880)
1)	H2	890	1	R. Nacional de Honduras, Comayagua (r:880)
1)	H6	890	1	R. Nacional de Honduras, El Paraíso (r:880)
1)	H8	890	5	R. Nacional de Honduras, Olanchito (r:880)
1)	H	890	1	R. Nacional de Honduras, Danlí (r: 880)
8)	UP6	900	1	R. Satélite, La Ceiba
8)	UP	900	1	R. Centro, Choluteca
29)	VS	910	10	R. Católica "LV de Suyapa", Tegucigalpa
151)	NM	910	2.5	R. Comunidad, Ocotepeque: 1100-0300
21)	RM	920	1	R. Sistema, Comayagua
31)	ZV	920	1	Una Voz que clama en el desierto, San Pedro Sula
32)	SK	920	5	R. Catacamas, Catacamas: 1200-0400
1)	H11	920	1	R. Nacional de Honduras, Danlí (r:880)
214)	VS	920		R. Católica, Tocoa
208)	CQ	930		Cadena R. Samaritano, La Ceiba
237)	LD	930		R. Estéreo Leed, Nacaome
18)	CR	940	1	R. Dif. Cristiana de R. "DCR", Tegucigalpa
15)	BO	940	1	R. Cadena Occidental, La Entrada
34)	QL	950	1	Centro Radial Hondureño, Siguatepeque: 1100-0300
35)	ZE	±950	1.5	R. Cortés AM, Puerto Cortés: 1200-0300
213)	XI	950		R. El Camino, Olanchito
224)	QJ	950		R. Agalta, San Esteban
246)		950	6	R. Choloma, Choloma
36)	YF	960	1	R. Fergusón, Choluteca
203)	XB	960		R. Bautista Buenas Nuevas, Puerto Lempira
38)	LY	970	2	R. Milenium, Tegucigalpa
230)	KI	970		La Picosa, N. Ocotepeque
41)	AO	980	1	R. Tocoa, Tocoa
39)	ZC	980	2	R. Monumental, San Pedro Sula: 1200-0600
90)	VC	980		LV Evangélica, Siguatepeque (r:1390)
223)	UI	ǂ980		Super 10, Catacamas
140)	PR	990	3.5	R. Paz, Choluteca: 1000-0400
207)	OJ	990	1	R. La Voz de Jesús, La Ceiba
44)	XZ	1000	1	R. Alfa, Tegucigalpa: 1000-0600
256)		1000	6	R. Río de Piedras, Lempira
5)	QN	1010	1	R. Sonora, San Pedro Sula

MW	Call	kHz	kW	Station, location
89)	CD	1010	1	R. Constelación. Juticalpa
228)	AE	1010		R. Apaguiz, Danlí
255)		1010		R. Visión Cristiana, Tocoa
236)	PN	1020		R. Visión Cristiana Roca de Salvación, Marcovia
152)	RJ	1030	1	R. Ticante, Ocotepeque: 1200-0400
8)	UP3	1030	1	R. Rock 'n Pop, Tegucigalpa
14)	NNY	1040	3	Exitos, San Pedro Sula
33)	MJ	1040	1	R. Renovación, Comayagua
90)	VC	1040		LV Evangélica, Juticalpa (r:1390)
90)	VC	1040		LV Evangélica, Danlí (r: 1390)
206)	OK	1050		R. Roatán, Roatán
7)	KT	1060	2	La Catracha, Tegucigalpa
50)	FA	1060	0.5	R. Peña Blanca, Sta Barbara
52)	GR	1070	3	Cadena Guaymuras, El Paraíso: 1100-0400
53)	LE	1070	1	R. Unica AM, San Pedro Sula
54)	QN	1070	2.5	R. Sonora, Siguatepeque
180)	BB	1070		R. Unidad Evangélica, Catacamas
56)	ID	1080	1	R. Miramar, Tela: 1200-0400
235)	IE	1080		R. Evangélica Senda de Vida, Nacaome
8)	LB	1090	1	R. La Mejor, Sta Rosa de Copán
90)	CQ	1090	1	Cad. Radial Samaritano, Tegucigalpa
58)	ND	1100	1	R. Esperanza, La Esperanza: 1100-0300
59)	VA	1100	1	R. Tiempo/R. Fama, San Pedro Sula
60)	FQ	1100	1	R. Máxima, Olanchito
222)	AJ	1100		R. Antena 5, Catacamas
5)	QN	1110		R. Sonora, Choluteca
38)	TL	1120	2	R. Fiesta, Sabanagrande
196)	VR	1120		R. Marchala, Ocotepeque
61)	PL	1130	5	R. Progreso, El Progreso
63)	BT	1130	1	R. San Francisco, San Francisco de la Paz 1100-0200
99)	HP	1130	1	R. Pinares, Siguatepeque
249)		1130		R. Pirata, Sonaguera
65)	UL	1140	1	R. Pico Bonito1140 AM, La Ceiba
90)	VC	1140		LV Evangélica, Choluteca (r: 1390)
5)	LP12	1150	1	R. Universal, Tegucigalpa
66)	AV	1150	5	Ondas del Ulúa, Sta Bárbara: 0900-0400
68)	GF	±1160	0.5	R. El Paraíso, El Paraíso
34)	VZ	1160	1	R. Juan Pablo II, Siguatepeque
204)	FJ	1160		R. País "LV del Valle de Sula", Progreso
212)	HZ	1160		R. Liberación, Tocoa
221)	BJ	1160		R. Nueva Palestina, Nueva Palestina
45)	AF	1170	2	R. Campeonísima, Choluteca
149)	VS	1180	1/0.8	R. Congolon, Gracias: 1100-0500
188)	AZ	1180	1	R. La Tigre, Tegucigalpa
134)	GK	1190	1	R. Brassabola, Minas de Oro
240)	ZQ	1190	1	R. Notícias STC, El Progreso
259)		1190		R. Ecológica de Olancho, Catacamas
72)	SI	1200	1	R. Impacto, Tela: 1200-0400
73)	RO	1210	1	R. Capital, Comayagüela
114)	MY	1210	1	LV Evangélica, La Entrada (r: 1390)
74)	OP	1220	1	R. Costeña Ebenezer, San Pedro Sula: 1100-0600
75)	YS	1220	1	R. Suari, Marcala
148)	SD	1220	3	R. Destellos de Luz, Sabá
260)		1220		R. Sintonía, Juticalpa
56)	QW	1230	10	R. Tela, Tela
171)	CQ	1230	0.25	R. Samaritano, San Marcos de Colón
133)	ZC	1240	1	R. Vanguardial, Tegucigalpa
172)	VN	1240	1	R. Venus, Sta Bárbara
51)	YF	1250	1	R. Renacimiento, Comayagua
115)	DG	1250	1	R. Oriental, Danlí
200)	YL	1250		R. Sonaguera, Sonaguera
253)		1250		Super R., San Pedro Sula
77)	FP	1260	1	R. Amistad, San Marcos de Colón
5)	QN	1270	1	R. Sonora, Tegucigalpa
117)	OF	1270	1	Ecos del Celaque, Gracias
78)	AM	1280	1	R. Unción AM, Olanchito
136)	RF	1280	1	R. Cadena de Notícias, San Pedro Sula
107)	BN	1280	1	R. San Miguel, Marcala: 1000-0400
251)		1280		R. Armonía, Juticalpa
81)	NN26	1290	1	R. Choluteca, Choluteca: 1050-0400
118)	GS	1290	1	R. HRGS/Bay Island Christian Network, Utila
82)	LR	1300	5	R. Sta Rosa, Sta Rosa de Copán
83)	IV	1300	1	R. C.C.I., Tegucigalpa
90)	VC	1310	2.5	LV Evangélica, San Pedro Sula (r:1390)
103)	RL	1310	1	R. Libertad, Marcala, La Paz: 1200-0500
258)	CM	1310	5	R. Universidad de Agricultura, Catacamas
119)	MG	1320	1	R. Bahía "La Super Grande", La Ceiba
173)	FL	1330	1	R. Florida, La Entrada
262)		1330		R. Emisora Evangélica, Tegucigalpa
153)	TQ	1340	10	R. 1430/R. El Mundo, San Pedro Sula
120)	CQ	1340	1	Cadena Radial Samaritano, Comayagua
245)		1340		Telecolor R., Catacamas
143)	JV	1350	1	R. Henecan, San Lorenzo
193)	EL	1350		R. Estelar, La Ceiba
28)	BS	1360	1	R. San Pedro, Tegucigalpa (r:860)
197)	BH	1360	5	R. Sta Bárbara, Sta Bárbara: 1200-0400
175)	SQ	1370	1	R. El Shaddai R., Siguatepeque
88)	ST	1370	1	R. Fraternidad, San Pedro Sula
220)	ZG	‡1370		R. Guayapeña, Catacamas
263)		1370		R. Regional, Tocoa
127)	AH	1380	0.5	R. Redención, Jutiapa: 1200-0600
176)	EJ	1380	1	R. Monjaras, Choluteca
90)	VC	1390	10/5	LV Evangélica, Tegucigalpa
90)	VC	1390	1	LV Evangélica, Sta Rosa de Copán (r:1390)
80)	YT	1400	1	R. Estrella de Oro, San Pedro Sula 1100-0200
177)	AU	1400	1	R. Alegre, Sava Colón
187)	BO	1400		R. Punto, Comayagua
219)	UV	1400		R. Universitaria, Catacamas
94)	SL	1420	1	R. Stereo Actualidad, Trinidad
244)	GB	1420		R. Sabanagrande, Sabanagrande
90)	FO	1430	1	LV Evangélica, Puerto Cortés (r. 1390)
97)	VM	1430	1	R. Maranatha, La Paz
211)	QV	1430		La Nueva Potencia, Olanchito
250)		1430		Ministerios Cristianos Fuente de Vida, Juticalpa
98)	RD	1440	5	R. Belén, La Ceiba
121)	RY	1440	0.5	R. Ekklesia Int./R. Mía, San Marcos de Colón
144)	BR	1450	1	R. Cultural, La Entrada
244)	GB	1450		R. Sabanagrande, Tegucigalpa
202)	GC	1460	2.5	R. Reino, San Pedro Sula
122)	CX	1460	0.5	LV de Patuca, Catacamas: 1000-0400
113)	KS	1460	0.5	R. Ministerio Bautista, Yoro
242)	FR	1460		R. Firmamento, La Paz
234)	XH	1470		R. Globo Grupera/R. Nacaome, Nacaome
145)	WP	1480	1	R. Soberanía, San Marcos, Ocotepeque
102)	EZ	°1480	1	LV de Misiones "R. MI", Comayagüela
35)	GO	1490	1.2	R. Porteña, Puerto Cortés
104)	OM	1490	1	R. Omega "Sonido Internacional", La Esperanza: 1100-0400
210)	OE	1490		R. Pijol, Morazán
264)		1490		R. Así se informa, La Unión
105)	TX	1500	1	R. Victoria, Choluteca
109)	VP	1500		R. Sion, La Ceiba
261)		1500		R. MI-EL, Sabá
124)	PG	1510	1	R. Gualcho, Tegucigalpa
106)	EM	1510	1	R. Emanuel, Ocotepeque
108)	CR	1520	1	Dif. Cristiana de Radio "DCR", San Pedro Sula: 1200-0400
131)	HJ	1520	1	R. Santiago, Yoro
183)	DF	1520		R. Rios de Agua Viva, Siguatepeque
192)	MQ	1520	1	R. Manantial de Vida Eterna, Juticalpa
247)		1530		La Guarachera, Choluteca
194)	VK	1540	1	R. Nuevo Mundo "Cadena Radial Reloj", Tegucigalpa
132)	JX	1550	1	R. Cristiana Nueva Vida, San Pedro Sula 1000-0200
101)	JO	1550	1	R. Campeona, Comayagua
248)		1550		R. Wuampu, Dulce Nombre de Culmi
233)	FD	1560		R. Mi Preferida, Choluteca
57)	RF	1570	2.5	R. Cad Nal de Noticias "RCN", Tegucigalpa
229)	TF	1570		Difusora Cristiana Torre Fuerte, Gracias
252)		1580		R. La Voz Lenca, La Esperanza
181)	BX	1580		R. Perla, El Progreso
232)	ZL	1590		R. Zol, Choluteca
111)	PC	°1600	1	R. Luz y Vida, San Luís: 1200-0300
243)	PQ	1600		R. Poderosa, Tegucigalpa

SW	Call	kHz	kW	Name and h of tr
111)	PC	±3250	1	R. Luz y Vida, San Luís: 1100-1600, 2200-0400
102)	EZ	3340		R. Misiones Int. "R.MI", Comayagüela
102)	EZ	‡5010	1	R. Misiones Int., Comayagüela: 1200-0500

° = also on SW, ‡ = inactive, (r) = repeater, ± = varying fq.
Stns with a (*) are reported to be inactive, but may occasionally be reactivated for variable periods of time.

Addresses and other information:
1) Ap 403 (or Avenida Miguel de Cervantes, Ed Lucía, frente a la Iglesia Menonita, Colonia: Av La Paz), Tegucigalpa W: www.rnh.hn – 2) 1a Av 439, Barrio San Martín, Sta Rosa de Copán ☎ +504 2662 0318 – 3) Ap 3, Juticalpa - FM: 97.9MHz – 4) Ap 24, San Pedro Sula – 5) Edif Audio Video, Ap 259, Tegucigalpa W: www.radioamerica.hn ☎+504 2290 4950 +504 2232 2923 – 6) Blvd Morazán, Edificio Classic, 2ndo piso, Frente a Banco Ficohsa, Tegucigalpa W: www.radiocadenavoces.com – 8) Emisoras Unidas, Col Florencia, Blv Suyapa (or: Ap 642), Tegucigalpa W: www.radiohrn.hn E: noticias@radiohrn.hn – 9) Ap 206, Sta Rosa de Copán - FM: 92.1MHz – 10) Ap 347, Comayagua - FM:

90.3MHz – **12)** Barrio El Way, Calle Principal, La Esperanza, Intibucá ☎ +504 2783 0171 – **13)** Ap 9, Juticalpa – **14)** Emisoras Unidas, Ap 163, San Pedro Sula – **15)** Atras de Gasolinera Shell, La Entrada, Copán ☎ +504 2661 2425 – **17)** Av New Orleans 20C, San Pedro Sula – **18)** Ap 3448 (or: Iglesia Amor Viviente, Col Godoy frente a F.H.I.S.), Tegucigalpa – **19)** Coyoles Central, Olanchito, Yoro – **20)** Ap 26, Sta Bárbara - **FM:** 90.9MHz – **21)** Barrio San Francisco, Fte Parque, Comayagua - **FM:** 99.9MHz – **22)** Danlí, El Paraíso – **24)** Edif.Maranata, Calle 8 y 9, San Pedro Sula ☎ +504 2350 4614 – **25)** Ap 29, Choluteca – **26)** Ap 33, Comayagua – **27)** Ap 28, Juticalpa ☎ +504 2885 1277 – **28)** Ap 364 (or Av.New Orleans), San Pedro Sula – **29)** Ap 480 (or: Edif Radio Católica, Av Paz Barahona), Tegucigalpa **E:** rcatolica@unete.com ☎+504 2237 2848 🖳+504 2237 2017 – **30)** Comayagua – **31)** Ap 2918 (or: 5 Calle, 10 y 11 Av S.O 91), San Pedro Sula **E:** radiofabulosa@sigmanet.hn - **FM:** 102.1MHz Radio Fabulosa ☎ +504 2553 1228 – **32)** Ap 50, Catacamas - **FM:** 104.5MHz ☎ +504 2899 4891 – **33)** Ap 10, 12101 Comayagua 1100-2400 ☎ +504 2772 6581 🖳+504 2772 1926 - **FM:** 89.1MHz R. Vida – **34)** Barrio Abajo, 2da Ave, 2 y 3 Calle, Siguatepeque - **FM:** 95.7MHz ☎ +504 2773 1632 – **35)** 3 Av entre 7 y 8 Calles N° 772, Puerto Cortés ☎ +504 2665 2810 **E:** radiocortes@lemaco.hn - **FM:** 88.9MHz +105.7MHz – **36)** Calle Vicente Williams, Edif Fergusón, Choluteca **W:** http://hometown.com/djrubbik/stereoF.html - **FM:** 103.3MHz–**38)** Ap 2821, Tegucigalpa ☎ +504 2237 7927 – **39)** Ap 996 (or: 9 Calle, S.O 44, Entre 8 y 9 Av), San Pedro Sula - **FM:** 98.5MHz Estéreo Mass – **41)** Tocoa, Colón- **44)** Ap 614 (or: Barrio Abajo, 6 Calle), Tegucigalpa – **45)** Ap 78, Choluteca ☎+504 2990 3796 - **FM:** 97.3MHz – **50)** Peña Blanca, 10 km al norte de Las Vegas, Sta Bárbara – **51)** Barrio Costado Norte Cine Valladolid, Comayagua – **52)** Barrio Sta Clara, El Paraíso – **53)** 9 Av 4 Calle, Edif Las Fuentes, San Pedro Sula - **FM:** 88.3MHz – **54)** Barrio Fatima, Edif Audiovideo, Siguatepeque 1055 – **56)** Av Panamá, Edif Canales N° 861, Tela, Atlántida - **FM:** 104.7MHz ☎ +504 2448 2957 – **57)** Ap 2250, Tegucigalpa – **58)** Ap 25, La Esperanza, Intibucá ☎+504 2783 0025 🖳+504 2783 0644 – **59)** Ap 906, San Pedro Sula - **FM:** 97.9MHz – **60)** Calle El Calvario Frente Al Parque. Edif Plaza, Olanchito, Yoro - **FM:** 88.7MHz – **61)** Ap 20, El Progreso, Yoro - **FM:** 103.3MHz Stereo Alegría – **63)** San Francisco de la Paz, Olancho – **65)** Barrio La Isla, La Ceiba – **66)** Ap 004, Sta Bárbara ☎+504 2643 2406 🖳+504 2643 2940 - **FM:** 97.5MHz – **68)** Barrio San Isidro, El Paraíso - **FM:** 93.3MHz – **72)** Calle José Trinidad Cabañas, Edif Hotel Presidente, Tela - **FM:** 88.9 – **73)** Col El Prado 1C-107A, Comayagüela ☎ +504 2239 2228 – **74)** Iglesia de Cristo, Ministerio Ebenezer, 1ª Calle A, Costado Sur de Wendy's Circunvalación (or: Ap 34-76), San Pedro Sula – **W:** www.ebenezer.hn - **FM:** 91.9MHz +93.7MHz – **75)** Calle Principal, Marcala, La Paz – **76)** Barrio Abajo, Comayagua – **77)** San Marcos de Colón, Choluteca – **78)** Olanchito, Yoro – **79)** Emisoras Unidas, Solares Nuevos, Av República, La Ceiba – **80)** Ap 303, San Pedro Sula **E:** efmhonduras@globalnet.hn - **FM:** 97.3MHz – **81)** Barrio Campo Luna, Choluteca – **82)** Ap 203, Sta Rosa de Copán - **FM:** 94.5MHz – **83)** Ap 955, Tegucigalpa – **84)** Ap 204, Sta Rosa de Copán - **FM:** 90.3MHz Rosa de Copán – **88)** Colonia Fesitran, San Pedro Sula – **89)** Juticalpa **1200-0400** – **90)** Ap 3252, Tegucigalpa – (Owned and operated by Conservative Baptist Home Mission Society, Box 828, Wheaton, IL 60187, USA) ☎ +504 2234 6640 **W:** www.hrvc.org - **E:** gerencia @hrvc.org – **94)** Barrio El Centro, 22115 Trinidad, Sta Bárbara ☎+504 2664 1706 🖳+504 2664 1663 - **FM:** 105.3MHz – **95)** 12 Calle 2a Ave 206, Barrio La Curva, Puerto Cortés – **97)** Santiago de la Paz, La Paz (or: Col.21 de Octubre, Sector 3, Bloque 2, Casa 5, Tegucigalpa) – **98)** Av San Isidro, Entre Calles 9 y 10, La Ceiba – **99)** Casa 269, Barrio Abajo, Siguatepeque 1155- - **FM:** 91.5MHz – **101)** Barrio Abajo 229, Comayagua – **102)** Ap 20583, Comayagüela (or: IMF World Misiones, PO Box 6321, San Bernardino, CA 92412, USA) - 1100-0300 – **103)** Barrio San Miguel, Calle Principal, Marcala, La Paz ☎ +504 2764 5377 – **104)** Av España, La Esperanza, Intibucá ☎ +504 2898 2063 – **105)** Barrio La Cruz, Calle Chorotega, Choluteca - **FM:** 96.2 – **106)** Barrio San Andrés, Ocotepeque – **107)** Barrio Concepción, Marcala, La Paz (or: Palacio Arzobispal, Av.Cervantes, Barrio El Centro, Tegucigalpa) – **108)** Ap 2017, San Pedro Sula – **109)** La Cruzada del Evangélico de Honduras, La Ceiba – **110)** Parque Central, La Paz – **111)** Barrio Luz y Vida, San Luis, Sta Bárbara (or: Ap 303, San Pedro Sula) **English:** Sat 0300-0400, Sun 0230-0400 **E:** efmhonduras@globalnet.hn – **112)** Sta Rosa de Copán – **113)** Ap.23301, Olanchito, Yoro – **114)** Barrio El Progreso, 2da y 3ra Calle, Av.La Entrada, La Entrada, Copán ☎ +504 2661 2049 – **117)** 2a Av 9C N° 9, Barrio Rosario No 9, Gracias, Lempira ☎ +504 2686 1087 – **118)** Col de Jerico, Utila **W:** www.ibnet.org – **119)** Barrio La Bara, Calle Pavimentada, Casa 1185, La Ceiba ☎ +504 443 2481 – **120)** Calle del Comercio 12A, Comayagua – **121)** San Marcos de Colón, Choluteca – **122)** Barrio La Mora, Catacamas, Olancho - **FM:** 99.1MHz – **124)** Col 21 de Octubre, Sector 3, Bl 1, Casa 4, Tegucigalpa – **127)** 1 Av Calle Principal, Jutiapa, Atlántida - **FM:** 95.7 ☎ +504 2898 4918 – **128)** Radio Ensenanzas Evangelicas, Puerto Lempira – **131)** Yoro. Dir: Jamil N Hawit Castro – **132)** Ap 2424, San Pedro Sula – **133)** Ap 914, Tegucigalpa – **134)** Barrio La Manzana, Minas de Oro, Comayagua – **135)** Ap 15, 16101 Juticalpa - **FM:** 106.3MHz Prgrs in Sp and E – **136)** Col Río Piedras, 5 Calle 26 Av., San Pedro Sula – **140)** Ap 40, Choluteca - **FM:** 95 5MHz – **143)** San Lorenzo – **144)** La Entrada, Copán – **145)** Barrio San Sebastián 2 Calle, San Marcos, Ocotepeque – **147)** Ap 888, (or: Centro Comercial San José), La Ceiba ☎+504 2441 5973 **W:** www.applegatefellowship.org/missions/honduras.asp **E:** radiolitoral@psinet.hn **English:** Weekends 0400-0500 – **148)** Barrio La Pava, Sabá, Colón ☎ +504 2424 8249 – **149)** Frente al Parque "Lempira", Gracias, Lempira (or: Ap.1579, Tegucigalpa) - **FM:** 95.1MHz R Galaxia 21 FM Stereo ☎ +504 2656 1068 – **151)** Ocotepeque, Ocotepeque **W:** www.cauaguanca.com/radiocomunidad **E:** radiocomunidad910@yahoo.es ☎ +504 2653 3994 – **152)** Media Cuadra Al Norte del ParWque, B:o El Centro, Ocotepeque - **FM:** 92.1MHz – **153)** Ap 210 (or: 5 Calle, 10 y 11 Av S.O., Barrio Beuque), San Pedro Sula - **FM:** 90.7MHz – **155)** Col Miraflores, Tegucigalpa ☎+504 2661 2327 – **157)** Calle Vicente Williams 345, Choluteca – **162)** 2 Av Calle 38, Trinidad, Sta Bárbara ☎ +504 2664 1681 – **163)** Barrio La Esperanza 4A N° 142, Choluteca - **FM:** 98.5MHz – **165)** Barrio El Banco, La Entrada ☎+504 2661 2327 - **FM:** 103.5MHz – **170)** Calle del Estadio, Barrio El Campo, Catacamas – **171)** San Marcos de Colón, Choluteca – **172)** Av Independencia, Sta Bárbara - **FM:** 89.7MHz – **173)** Barrio Miraflores, La Entrada – **175)** Barrio El Centro, Siguatepeque   **176)** Barrio Guadalupe, Choluteca - **FM:** 100.9MHz – **177)** Barrio El Coyol, Sava Colón – **180)** Barrio La Cruz, Contiguo a la Iglesia el Encuentro, Catacamas, Olancho ☎ +504 2899 4329 – **181)** 4 y 5 Ave, 3 Calle 442, Barrio Las Delicias, El Progreso, Yoro ☎ +504 898 4803 – **182)** Barrio El Campo, Frente a la Ferreteria San António, Sigiatepeque – **183)** Barrio El Centro, Valle del Boulevard, Contiguo a la Iglesia Adventista, Siguatepeque – **185)** Barrio El Centro, Contiguo al Banco Atlántida, Las Vegas, Sta Bárbara ☎ +504 2659 3156 – **187)** Balneareo Pasada del Sol, Barrio Arriba, Comayagua ☎ +504 772 0565 – **188)** Tegucigalpa – **192)** Barrio de Jesús, Casa 7, Calle Principal, Juticalpa – **193)** Col.Irias, Primera Calle, 5 Casas a Mano Izquierda, La Ceiba ☎ +504 2441 0238 – **194)** Radio Industrias de Honduras, Tegucigalpa – **196)** Barrio San José, Juticalpa ☎ +504 2443 0435 – **197)** Apartado 004, Sta Bárbara – **198)** Olanchito, Yoro – **200)** Sonaguera, Colón – **202)** Misión Cristiana Internacional El Shaddai, San Pedro Sula – **203)** Puerto Lempira – **204)** Progreso, Yoro ☎ 504 2647 1717 - **205)** Puerto Lempira, Gracias a Dios – **206)** Roatán, Islas de la Bahía – **207)** La Ceiba, Atlántida – **208)** La Ceiba, Atlántida – **209)** La Ceiba, Atlántida – **210)** Morazán, Yoro – **211)** Olanchito, Yoro – **212)** Tocoa, Colón – **213)** Olanchito, Yoro – **214)** Tocoa, Colón – **215)** Olanchito, Yoro – **216)** Tocoa Colón – **217)** Jocón, Yoro – **218)** Tocoa, Colón – **219)** Catacamas, Olancho – **220)** Catacamas, Olancho – **221)** Nueva Palestina, Olancho – **222)** Catacamas, Olancho – **223)** Catacamas, Olancho – **224)** San Esteban, Olancho – **225)** Catacamas, Olancho – **227)** Catacamas, Olancho – **228)** Danlí, El Paraíso – **229)** Lempira, Gracias a Dios – **230)** Nueva Ocotepeque, Ocotepeque – **231)** San José de Colinas, Santa Bárbara – **232)** Choluteca – **233)** Choluteca – **234)** Nacaome, Valle – **235)** Nacaome, Choluteca – **236)** Marcovia, Choluteca – **237)** Nacaome, Valle – **238)** San Lorenzo, Valle – **239)** Choluteca, Choluteca – **240)** El Progreso, Yoro – **241)** San Pedro Sula – **242)** La Paz, La Paz – **243)** Tegucigalpa – **244)** Sabanagrande, Francisco Morazán – **245)** Catacamas, Olancho – **246)** Choloma, Cortés – **247)** Choluteca – **248)** Dulce Nombre de Culmi, Olancho – **249)** Intibucá – **250)** Juticalpa, Olancho – **251)** Juticalpa, Olancho ☎ +504 2785 2609 **E:** manantial1520@yahoo.com – **252)** Copinh, La Esperanza, Intibucá – **253)** San Pedro Sula – **254)** Sonaguera, Colón – **255)** Tocoa, Colón ☎ +504 2444 3972 – **256)** Lempira – **257)** Puerto Cortés, Cortés – **258)** Universidad Nacional de Agricultura, Catacamas, Olancho – **259)** Barrio El Centro, Esquina opuesta a Edificio Villatoro, Catacamas, Olancho – **260)** Juticalpa, Olancho – **261)** Iglesia de Cristo Elim, Sabá, Colón – **262)** Asociación de Iglesias Evangélicas Centroamericanas, Tegucigalpa – **263)** Tocoa, Colón – **264)** La Unión, Olancho

FM in Tegucigalpa (MHz): 88.1 Ke Buena – 88.7 Globo Grupera – 89.3 Power – 89.9 R. Red de Radiodifusión Bíblica – 90.5 R. Corazón 90.5 – 91.1 R. Kairos FM – 91.7 R. Buenísima – 92.3 Rock & Pop – 92.9 La Voz de Honduras – 93.3 Estéreo Fantasía – 93.5 R. Notícias STC – 94.1 FM 94 – 94.7 América – 95.3 Digital – 95.9 R. Panamericana – 96.5 R. Estéreo Fiel – 97.1 EstéreoTic Tac – 97.7 Azul – 98.3 Estéreo Concierto – 98.9 Estéreo Fe – 99.5 Suprema – 100.1 Super 100 – 100.7 R. Exa FM – 101.3 R. Nacional de Honduras – 101.9 Vox – 102.5 Suave – 103.1 FM 103.1 – 103.7 Luz – 104.3 Momentos FM – 104.9 Estéreo Amor – 105.5 Musiquera – 106.1 Romántica – 106.7 Stereo Rumba – 107.3 W107 Energía Estéreo – 107.9 Top Music con La Onda del Nuevo Mundo.

AFRTS (Air Force)
🖳 JTF-B, APO AA 34042, USA **E:** PAO@jtfb-emh1.army.mil
FM: 106.5MHz Soto Cano Air Base, 0.25kW **D.Prgr:** 24h

HONG KONG (China, SAR)

L.T: UTC +8h — **Pop:** 7.2 million — **Pr.L:** Cantonese, English — **E.C** 50Hz, 200/220V — **ITU:** HKG

RADIO TELEVISION HONG KONG (Gov.)
Broadcasting House, 30 Broadcast Drive, Kowloon, Hong Kong ☎ +852 2272 0000 🖷 +852 2336 9314 **E:** ccu@rthk.org.hk **W:** www.rthk.org.hk **L.P:** Dir. of Broadc: Franklin Wong War-kay, Asst. Dir. of Broadc. (Radio): Tai Keen-man

MW (kHz)	Network	Location	kW
567	Radio 3	Golden Hill	20
621	P. Ch	Golden Hill	20
675	Radio 6	Peng Chau	10
783	Radio 5	Golden Hill	20
1584	Radio 3	Chung Hom Kok	0.1

P. Ch = Putonghua Channel

FM(MHz)	Network	kW	Tx Location	Target Div.
92.3	Radio 5	0.038	Tin Shui Wai	
92.6	Radio 1	3	Mt. Gough	Kowloon
92.9	Radio 1	0.1	Golden Hill	Tsuen Wan
93.2	Radio 1	0.5	Cloudy Hill	Fan Ling
93.4	Radio 1	0.7	Castle Peak	Tuen Mun
93.5	Radio 1	0.15	Beacon Hill	Sha Tin
93.6	Radio 1	0.5	Lamma Island	HK Island south
94.4	Radio 1	1	Kowloon Peak	HK Island north, Sai Kung
94.8	Radio 2	3	Mt. Gough	Kowloon
95.2	Radio 5	0.02	Mt. Nicholson	Jardine's Lookout
95.3	Radio 2	0.5	Cloudy Hill	Fan Ling
95.6	Radio 2	0.1	Golden Hill	Tsuen Wan
96.0	Radio 2	0.5	Lamma Island	HK Island south
96.3	Radio 2	0.15	Beacon Hill	Sha Tin
96.4	Radio 2	0.7	Castle Peak	Tuen Mun
96.9	Radio 2	1	Kowloon Peak	HK Island north, Sai Kung
97.6	Radio 4	3	Mt. Gough	Kowloon
97.8	Radio 4	0.5	Cloudy Hill	Fan Ling
97.9	Radio 3	0.02	Mt. Nicholson	Jardine's Lookout
98.1	Radio 4	0.15	Beacon Hill	Sha Tin
98.2	Radio 4	0.5	Lamma Island	HK Island south
98.4	Radio 4	0.1	Golden Hill	Tsuen Wan
98.7	Radio 4	0.7	Castle Peak	Tuen Mun
98.9	Radio 4	1	Kowloon Peak	HK Island north, Sai Kung
99.4	Radio 5	0.015	Tseung Kwan O	Jank Bay
100.9	P. Ch	0.005	Tai Hang Road	
100.9	P. Ch	0.003	Castle Peak	Tuen Mun
103.3	P. Ch	0.015	Tseung Kwan O	Jank Bay
103.3	P. Ch	0.038	Tin Shui Wai	
106.8	Radio 5	0.01	Castle Peak	Tuen Mun
106.8	Radio 3	0.06	Chung Hom Kok	HK Island south
107.8	Radio 3	0.015	Tseung Kwan O	Jank Bay
107.8	Radio 3	0.038	Tin Shui Wai	

RTHK Radio 1 in Cantonese/Chinese: 24h – **RTHK Radio 2** in Cantonese: 24h – **RTHK Radio 3** in English: 24h – **RTHK Radio 4** in English/Cantonese: 24h – **RTHK Radio 5** in Cantonese/Chinese: 24h – **RTHK Radio 6** Relay BBCWS English: 24h – **RTHK Putonghua Channel** in Chinese: 24h
Ann: Cantonese: "Hoenggong dintoi dai (number) toi".

HONG KONG COMMERCIAL BROADC. CO. LTD
3 Broadcast Drive, Kowloon, Hong Kong ☎ +852 2336 5111 🖷+852 2338 0021 **E:** cs@881903.com **W:** www.881903.com

MW (kHz)		kW	Location	Prgr.
864		10	Peng Chau	Quote AM
FM(MHz)	Network	kW	Tx Location	Target Div.
88.1	CR1	3	Mt.Gough	Kowloon
88.3	CR1	0.5	Cloudy Hill	Fan Ling
88.6	CR1	0.7	Castle Peak	Tuen Mun
88.9	CR1	0.1	Golden Hill	Tsuen Wan
89.1	CR1	0.5	Lamma Island	HK Island south
89.2	CR1	0.15	Beacon Hill	Sha Tin
89.5	CR1	1	Kowloon Peak	HK Island north, Sai Kung
90.3	CR2	3	Mt.Gough	Kowloon
90.7	CR2	0.5	Cloudy Hill	Fan Ling
90.9	CR2	0.1	Golden Hill	Tsuen Wan
91.1	CR2	0.15	Beacon Hill	Sha Tin
91.2	CR2	0.7	Castle Peak	Tuen Mun
91.6	CR2	0.5	Lamma Island	HK Island south
92.1	CR2	1	Kowloon Peak	HK Island north, Sai Kung

HKCR CR1 (Supercharged 881) in Cantonese. 24h **N:** half-hourly.
HKCR CR2 (Ultimate 903) in Cantonese. 24h **N:** hourly. **Ann:** "Cikzak gaulingsaam".
HKCR AM864 in English, partly Filipino on Fri and Sat 1300-1500. 24h **N:** On the h from 2300-1600.

METRO BROADCAST CORPORATION LTD.
Basement 2, Site 6, Whampoa Gardens Hunghom, Kowloon, Hong Kong ☎ +852 3698 8000 🖷+852 2123 9889 **E:** prenquiry@metroradio.com.hk **W:** www.metroradio.com.hk

MW (kHz)	Network	kW	Location	
1044	Metro Plus	10	Peng Chau	
FM(MHz)	Network	kW	Tx Location	Target Div.
99.7	Metro Info	3	Mt.Gough	Kowloon
100.0	Metro info	0.5	Cloudy Hill	Fan Ling
100.4	Metro info	0.7	Castle Peak	Tuen Mun
100.5	Metro Info	0.15	Beacon Hill	Sha Tin
101.0	Metro Info	0.01	Stanley	
101.6	Metro Info	0.1	Golden Hill	Tsuen Wan
101.8	Metro Info	1	Kowloon Peak	HK Island north
102.1	Metro Info	0.5	Lamma Island	HK Island south
102.4	Metro Finance	0.15	Beacon Hill	Sha Tin
102.5	Metro Finance	0.7	Castle Peak	Tuen Mun
102.6	Metro Finance	0.01	Stanley	
104.0	Metro Finance	3	Mt.Gough	Kowloon
104.5	Metro Finance	0.5	Lamma Island	HK Island south
104.7	Metro Finance	0.5	Cloudy Hill	Fan Ling
105.5	Metro Finance	0.1	Golden Hill	Tsuen Wan
106.3	Metro Finance	1	Kowloon Peak	HK Island north

Metro Plus in English (Partly Cantonese, Mandarin, Filipino and Indonesian). 24h music, news and information. **Metro Info** in Cantonese. 24h. **Ann:** "Sanseng dintoi zisoen toi". **Metro Finance** in Cantonese. 24h

DIGITAL RADIO (DAB)
Three broadcasters share 18 channels of one frequency – DAB+ Ch 11C (220.352MHz): 7 channels by Radio Television Hong Kong, 3 channels by Metro Broadcast Corporaion Ltd., 5 channels by Digital Broadcasting Corporation Hongkong Ltd. Unit 302, Level 3, IT Street, Cyberport 3, 100 Cyberport Road, Hong Kong **W:** www.dbc.hk, 3 channels by Phoenix U Radio Ltd. No. 2-6 Dai King Street, Tai Po Industrial Estate, Tai Po, N.T., Hong Kong **W:** www.uradiohk.com

HUNGARY

L.T: UTC +1h (31 Mar-27 Oct: UTC +2h) — **Pop** 9.941 million — **Pr.L:** Hungarian — **E.C:** 50Hz, 230V — **ITU:** HNG

MAGYAR RÁDIÓ
Bródy Sándor u. 5-7, H-1088 Budapest ☎ +36 1 3287000 🖷 36 1 3287332 **W:** www.radio.hu **L.P:** CEO: István Jónás
MR1 Kossuth Rádió ☎ +36 1 3287945 **E:** info@radio.hu **MR2** Petöfi Rádió ☎ +36 1 3288555 **E:** mr2@mr2.hu
MR3 Bartók Rádió ☎ +36 1 3288772 **E:** mr3@radio.hu

MW	kHz	kW	Prg	MW	kHz	kW	Prg
Solt	540	2000	1	Marcali	1188	300	4
Lakihegy	873	20	4	Szolnok	1188	100	4
Pécs	873	20	4	Szombathely	1251	25	6c
Miskolc	1116	15	6b	Nyíregyháza	1251	25	6a
Mosonmagyaróvár	1116	5	6c	Györ	1350	5	6c

FM (MHz):	MR1	MR2	MR3	MR6+7	kW
Aggtelek	94.6				3
Balassagyarm	93.7				2.5
Békéscsaba	97.3				1
Budapest	107.8	94.8	105.3		83/77/81
Cegléd	93.0				1
Csávoly		89.4			6
Debrecen	99.7	89.0	106.6	91.4a	1.4/1/1/1.2
Fehérgyarm	105.9				5
Gerecse	105.6				10
Györ	106.4	93.1	106.8		1/7.5/7.4
Kabhegy	102.3	93.9	105.0		3/65/69
Kaposvár	96.7				3
Karcag	97.9				10
Kecskemét	104.9				1
Kékestetö	99.8	102.7	90.7		0.3/30/28
Kiskörös		95.1	105.9		1.7/3
Komádi	89.9	96.7	105.1		5/37/30
Miskolc	103.8	102.3*	107.5	102.3b	5/1.4/1.4
Mosonm.óvár	95.0				1
Nagykanizsa	100.7	94.3	104.3		5/12/20
Pécs	104.6	103.7	107.6	101.7e	5/49/10/2
Rábaszentand	105.2				5.2
Sátoraljaújh	91.9				1
Siófok	93.6				3
Sopron	101.6	99.5	107.6		0.5/9/7
Szeged	101.9	104.6	105.7	93.1d	2/5/2/0.7
Szentes	91.6	98.8	107.3		1/32/34
Szolnok	94.3			101.2d	6.3/2

FM (MHz):	MR1	MR2	MR3	MR6+7	kW
Telkibánya	90.2				3
Tokaj	88.3	92.7	105.5		5/50/50
Úzd		90.3	106.9		3/3
Vasvár	103.6	98.2	106.9		5/7.5/3

* 0500-1700 MR6; 1700-0500 MR2. + 20 MR1 txs below 1kW

Prgrs: 1= **MR1 Kossuth** (news-talk) 2=**MR2 Petöfi** (pop) 3=**MR3 Bartók** (classical) 4=**MR4 Nemzetiségi** (Ethnic), **MR5 Parlament** (internet/satellite only), 6a-e=**MR6** (regional) 7=**MR7** (folk+operetta) **D.Prgr:** 24h exc **MR1+MR6** MW: Mo-Fr 0325-2005, Sa-Su: 0355-2005 (**NB:** tr. is cut on MR1/MR6 MW, continues on FM); **MR4** MW: 0700-1900 **ANN: MR1:** "Kossuth Rádió, a szavak ereje" **MR2:** "Petöfi Rádió, nagyon zene", **MR3:** "Bartók Rádió, a klasszikus zene rádiója" **MR6:** "Itt a Régió Rádió Debrecen/Miskolc/Györ/Szeged/Pécs." **MR7:** "Itt az MR7 a dalok és dallamok rádiója". **S/on:** Rákóczi March (MR1 MW), **S/off** 2005 MR1 MW and 2300 MR2: Nat. Anthem, 2258 on MR3: "Szózat"; 1100 MR1, MR2, MR4, MR6: midday church bell toll **MR4 Nemzetiségi Ethnic Prgrs:** ☎ +36 (1) 328-8672 ▤ +36 (1) 328-8682. **W:** http://mr4.radio.hu/ **Daily:** Croatian: 0700-0900, German: 0900-1100, Serbian: 1300-1500, Romanian: 1500-1700, Slovak: 1700-1900; **Mo-Fr:** Roma/Gipsy: 1103-1200; Minority music: 1230-1300; **Weekly at 1200-1230:** Mo: Slovenian, Tu: Rusyn /Ruthenian, We: Greek, Th: Bulgarian, Fr: Ukranian, Sa: Armenian; Sa: Polish 1230-1300; Su: Hungarian "In One Home" 1100-1300.

MR6 Regional Network: **W:** www.mr6.hu **a) MR6 Debrecen** ▤ 4024 Debrecen, Piac u. 28/c ☎ +36 52 525-325 ▤ 36 52 525-333 **E:** MR6debrecen@radio.hu **b) MR6 Miskolc** ▤ 3527 Miskolc, Bajcsy-Zsilinszky u. 15 ☎ +36 46 502-719 ▤ 36 46 502-728 **E:** MR6miskolc.hu **c) MR6 Györ** ▤ 9027 Györ, Nagy Imre u. 28 ☎ +36 96 514-222 ▤ 36 96 514-224 **E:** MR6gyor@radio.hu **d) MR6 Szeged** ▤ 6720 Szeged, Stefánia 7 ☎+36 62 554-814 ▤ 36 62 554-804 **E:** MR6szeged@radio.hu **e) MR6 Pécs** ▤ 7621 Pécs, Szent Mór u. 1 ☎ +36 72 518-313 ▤ 36 72 518-320 **E:** MR6pecs@radio.hu **Local Prgr:** 0500-1630. rel MR7 (see MR7), other times on AM rel MR1, Miskolc on FM rel MR2 **MR7: W:** mr7.hu 24h online, AM/FM 0400-0500, 1700-2005, FM only 2005-0400 on the MR6 network

National Media and Communications Authority (NMHH)
▤ 1015 Budapest, Ostrom utca 23-25 ☎ +36 1 4577100 ▤ +36 1 3565520 **W:** http://nmhh.hu **E:** info@nmhh.hu

Media Council
▤ 1088 Budapest, Reviczky u. 5 ☎ +36 1 4298600, 2672590 ▤ +36 1 2672612 **W:** http://mediatanacs.hu **E:** mediatudomanyiintezet@mtmi.hu

Antenna Hungária Broadc. & Radiocommunications Ltd (AH Zrt.)
▤ 1119 Budapest, Petzvál József u. 31-33 ☎ +36 1 4642464 ▤ +36 1 4642525 **W:** http://ahrt.hu **E:** antennah@ahrt.hu

Hungarian Federation of Free Radios (SZARÁMASZER)
▤ 1077 Budapest Rózsa utca 34 fsz 9 ☎/▤ +36 1 3111855 **W:** www.szabadradio.hu **E:** iroda@szabadradio.hu

National Association of Local Radios (HEROE)
▤ 8000 Székesfehérvár, Donát u. 92 ☎ +36 22 505310 ▤ +36 22 505 312 **W:** http://heroe.firtos.hu **E:** heroe@fehervarradio.hu **DX data:** www.radiosite.hu, www.frekvencia.hu, www.helyiradiok.hu

National stations and networks
CLASS FM (National, Comm.)
▤ 1089 Budapest, Üllöi út 102 ☎ +36 1 8153000 **W:** http://classfm.hu **E:** classfm@classfm.hu

NEO FM (National, Comm.)
▤ 1025 Budapest, Csévi u. 7/B ☎ +36 1 5551000 **W:** http://neofm.hu **E:** info@neofm.hu

FM	CLA	NEO	kW	FM	CLA	NEO	kW
Budapest	103.3	100.8	81/79	Nagykanizsa		90.2	8
Csávoly		96.7	6.3	Pécs	105.5	95.9	50/25
Debrecen	101.1		1	Sopron	102	96.8	22/9
Györ	101.4	87.6	7.6	Szeged	94.9	90.3	0.6
Kabhegy	100.5	107.2	67/71	Szentes		100.4	34
Kékes	104.7	95.5	27/20	Tokaj	103.5	97.5	50
Kiskörös		88.4	2	Uzd		101.5	3
Komádi	101.6	103.0	22/39	Vasvár		91.6	6.8
Miskolc	98.3	97.1	5.6				

Other Stations
MW	kHz	kW	Location	Station
19)	1485	0.2	Mohács	Régió Rádió (0455-1900)

FM	MHz	kW	Location	Station
20)	87.9	1	Szeged	Európa R.
9)	88.1	1	Budapest	Info R. (news)
2)	88.3	1	Komárom	Mária R. (rlg)
1)	89.5	77	Budapest	Music FM
5)	90.3	0.4	Budapest	Tilos R. (community)

FM	MHz	kW	Location	Station
7)	90.6	1	Sátoraljaú.h.	Szent István R. (rlg)
26)	90.9	2	Budapest	Jazzy (smooth jazz)
6)	91.5	1	Györ	Kék Duna R.
11)	91.6	1	Cece	Fortuna R.
2)	91.7	1.2	Kiskörös	Mária R. (rlg)
7)	91.8	0.46	Eger	Szent István R. (rlg)
28)	92.1	2.2	Budapest	Klasszik R. (classical)
23)	93.4	1	Dabas	Dabas R.
24)	93.5	1	Debrecen	Klubrádió (mono, talk)
2)	94.2	1	Budapest	Mária R. (rlg)
20)	94.4	1	Debrecen	Európa R.
7)	95.1	1	Miskolc	Szent István R. (rlg)
29)	95.1	1	Zalaegerszeg	Rádió 1 (CHR)
24)	95.3	1	Budapest	Klubrádió (talk)
18)	95.7	1	Balassagyarmat	Gazdasági R.
14)	96.1	0.1	Székesfehérv.	Magyar Katolikus R. (rlg)
25)	96.5	2	Kecskemét	Gong R.
15)	96.8	1	Budapest	Rádió 17
33)	97.4	1	Dunaföldvár	EL-DO R.
24)	97.7	1	Kecskemét	Klubrádió (mono, talk)
32)	97.7	1	Szombathely	Frisss FM
12)	98.0	0.14	Budapest	Civil R. (community)
30)	98.9	1	Szigetvár	N-Joy R.
13)	99.5	3	Budapest	R. Q
27)	99.9	2.2	Kaposvár	Kapos R.
10)	100.0	1	Sátoraljaú.h.	R. Aktív
20)	100.5	1	Nyíregyháza	Európa Rádió
21)	100.7	1	Eger	Gazdasági R. (financ. talk)
16)	100.3	1	Budapest	Lánchíd R. (newstalk)
2)	100.6	3	Telkibánya	Mária Rádió (rlg)
8)	101.3	1	Eger	Rádió Eger
21)	101.6	1	Miskolc	Rádió M (CHR)
4)	101.8	2	Székesfehérvár	R. 1 (CHR)
31)	101.9	1	Tamási	Tamási R.
14)	102.1	0.74	Budapest	Magyar Katolikus R. (rlg)
22)	103.9	1	Nyíregyháza	Retro R.
3)	103.9	0.82	Budapest	Juventus R. (AC)
17)	104.0	1	Békéscsaba	Csaba R.
18)	105.9	3	Budapest	Gazdasági R (financ. talk)
14)	107.4	0.5	Szombathely	Magyar Katolikus R. (rlg)

+ approximately 200 additional FM txs below 1kW

Addresses and other information
1) ▤ 1138 Budapest, Népfürdö utca 22. B torony V. em ☎ +36 1 7998895 **W:** musicfm.hu **E:** info@musicfm.hu – **2)** ▤ 1142 Budapest, Szönyi út 16 ☎ +36 1 3730701 **W:** www.mariaradio.hu **E:** info@mariaradio.hu **NB:** total 21 txs – **3)** ▤ 1134 Budapest, Róbert Károly körút 82/84 ☎+36 1 2375300 **W:** juventus.hu **E:** musicradio@juventus.hu – **4)** ▤ 8000 Székesfehérvár, Berényi út 72-100 ☎ +36 22 501094 **NB:** total 13 local studios & 18 txs in Rádió 1 Network **W:** www.radio1.hu **E:** radio1@radio1.hu – **5)** ▤ 1092 Budapest, Kinizsi u. 28 ☎ +36 1 4768491 **W:** tilos.hu **E:** radio@tilos.hu **NB:** Some English px – **6)** ▤ 9021 Györ, Szent István út 10/a ☎ +36 96 524444 **W:** www.kekduna.hu **E:** gyor@kekduna.hu **NB:** total 6 txs – **7)** ▤ 3301 Eger, Pf 86 ☎ +36 36 510-610 **W:** www.mkr.hu **E:** info@szentistvanradio.hu **NB:** total 6 txs – **8)** ▤ 3300 Eger, Trinitárius út 1 ☎ +36 36 410450 **W:** www.radioeger.hu **E:** info@radioeger.hu – **9)** ▤ 1033 Budapest, Polgár u. 8-10 ☎ +36 1 4832950 **W:** http://inforadio.hu **E:** info@inforadio.hu – **10)** ▤ 3980 Sátoraljaújhely, Jókai u. 56 ☎ +36 21 2024147 **W:** www.radioaktiv-fm100.hu/ **E:** mail@radioaktiv-fm100.hu – **11)** ▤ 7030 Paks, Dózsa György út 98 ☎ +36 75 411411 **W:** www.fortunaradio.hu **E:** info@fortunaradio.hu **NB:** total 3 txs – **12)** ▤ 1116 Budapest, Sztregova utca 3 ☎ +36 1 489-0997 **W:** www.civilradio.hu **E:** civilradio@civilradio.hu – **13)** ▤ 1119 Budapest, Keveháza u. 1-3 ☎ +36 1 3539453 **W:** www.radioq.hu **E:** bognar.eva@radioq.hu – **14)** ▤ 1062 Budapest, Délibáb u. 15-17 ☎ +36 1 255-3366 **W:** www.katolikusradio.hu **E:** info@katradio.hu – **15)** ▤ 1103 Budapest, Köér u. 5 ☎ +36 1 2540968 **W:** www.radio17.hu **E:** info@radio17.hu – **16)** ▤ 1089 Budapest, Üllöi út 102 ☎ +36 1 8148730 **W:** http://mno.hu/lanchidradio **E:** info@lanchidradio.hu **NB:** total 7 txs – **17)** ▤ 5600 Békéscsaba, Bartók Béla út 7 ☎ +36 66 441111 ▤ +36 66 441112 **W:** www.csabaradio.hu **E:** info@csabaradio.hu – **18)** ▤ 1133 Budapest, Váci út 78/B ☎ +36 1 8881500 **W:** www.gazdasagiradio.hu **E:** info@gazdasagiradio.hu – **19)** ▤ 7700 Mohács, Bakasza, u. 5. ☎ +36 69 511555 – **20)** ▤ 3530 Miskolc, Toronyalja utca 13. ☎ +36 46 509904 **W:** www.refradio.eu/radio/euradio **E:** euradio@euradio.hu, euradiodebrecen@gmail.com, nyiregyhaza@euradio.hu **NB:** total 7 txs – **21)** ▤ 3525 Miskolc, Széchenyi István út 46. I. em. 5 ☎ +36 46 320075 **W:** www.fmradiom.com **E:** hir@fmradiom.hu – **22)** ▤ 4400 Nyíregyháza, Eötvös utca 9/A ☎ +36 42 401035 **W:** www.retrofm.hu **E:** info@retrofm.hu – **23)** ▤ 2370 Dabas, Szent István tér 1/b ☎ +36 29 562562 **W:** www.radiodabas.hu **E:** info@radiodabas.hu – **24)** ▤ 1037 Budapest, Bokor u 1-3-5 ☎ +36 1 2406953 **W:** www.klubradio.hu

E: info@klubradio.hu **NB:** total 6 txs – **25)** ☐ 6000 Kecskemét, Petöfi Sándor u 1/b ☎ +36 76 414020 **W:** www.gongradio.hu **E:** gongradio@gongradio.hu **NB:** total 7 txs – **26)** ☐ 1022 Budapest Detrekö u. 12 ☎ +36 1 7876992 **W:** www.jazzy.hu **E:** jazzy@jazzy.hu – **27)** ☐ 7400 Kaposvár, Dózsa György u. 18 ☎ +36 82 555995 **W:** www.kaposradio.net/main.cgi **E:** info@kaposradio.net – **28)** ☐ 1022 Budapest, Detrekö u. 12 ☎ +36 1 7866464 **W:** www.klasszikradio.hu **E:** info@klasszikradio.hu – **29)** ☐ 8900 Zalaegerszeg, Tompa utca 1-3 ☎ +36 92 707951 ☐ +36 1 4732610 **W:** www.radio1.hu **NB:** total 13 local studios & 18 txs in Rádió 1 Network – **30)** ☐ 7400 Kaposvár, Arany János u. 97 ☎ +36 82 814700 **W:** www.n-joyradio.hu **E:** enjoyradio@enjoyradio.hu **NB:** total 7 txs – **31)** ☐ 7090 Tamási, Szabadság utca 54 ☎ +36 74 570260 **W:** tamasiradio.tamasinet.hu **E:** tamasiradio@tamasinet.hu – **32)** ☐ 9700 Szombathely, Mártírok tere 5/B ☎ +36 94 506977 **W:** www.frisss.hu **E:** info@frisss.hu **33)** ☐ 2401 Dunaújváros, PF 375 ☎ +36 25 407727 **W:** www.eldoradio.hu **E:** reklam@eldoradio.hu

Kisközösségi rádió (lowpower community radio)
69 non-profit low-power stns (0.1–10W) had been granted licences in cities and country villages. Info: **W:** www.szabadradio.hu Low power txs in Budapest **FM**(MHz): 87.6, 93.5, 93.7, 97.0, 101.4, 107.3. Cities with most LP stations: Miskolc (8 tx), Székesfehérvár (4 tx), Nyíregyháza (3 tx).

DAB+: Budapest – Hármashatár-hegy, Budapest – Széchenyi-hegy, Budapest – Száva utca, MuxA: "Commercial": Neo FM; "Test": MR1-3, Magyar Katolikus R, InfoRádió, Klubbrádió, Lánchíd R. on 222.064 MHz (ch 11D) 3 x 250W.

ICELAND

L.T: UTC — **Pop:** 320,000 — **Pr.L:** Icelandic — **E.C:** 50Hz, 230V — **ITU:** ISL

FJÖLMIÐLANEFND (Mass Media Council)
☐ Borgartún 21, 105 Reykjavik ☎ +354 4150415 ☐ +354 4150410 **E:** postur@fjolmidlanefnd.is **W:** www.fjolmidlanefnd.is
L.P: Dir: Elfa Ýr Gylfadóttir
NB. Fjölmiðlanefnd issues broadcasting licenses.

RÍKISÚTVARPIÐ (RÚV) (Pub)
☐ Efstaleiti 1, 150 Reykjavik ☎ +354 5153000 ☐ +354 5153010 **E:** frettir@ruv.is **W:** www.ruv.is **L.P:** Dir (Radio): Páll Magnússon

LW	kHz	kW	Prgr	LW	kHz	kW	Prgr
Gufuskálar	189	300	Rás 1/2	Eiðar	207	100	Rás 1/2

FM (MHz)	Rás 1	Rás 2	Rondó	kW
Almannaskarð	90.3	104.8	-	1
Auðsholt	91.3	95.3	-	2.5
Borgarland	88.0	96.3	-	3/3.5
Gagnheiði	98.8	87.7	-	5
Girðisholt	92.9	-	-	3.5
Háfell	93.8	98.7	-	14/34
Hegranes	90.6	98.8	-	3.1/5
Hnjúkar	89.1	95.5	-	6/6.2
Skálafell	92.4	99.9	-	24
Vaðlaheiði	91.6	96.5	-	9.3
Vatnsendi	93.5	90.1	87.7	3.4/2/2
Vestmannaeyar	97.1	88.1	-	17/24
Viðarfjall	88.1	96.1	-	3.3

NB: Sites with only txs below 1kW not listed.
D.Prgr: Rás 1: 24h. – **Rás 2:** 24h. – **Rondó:** 24h.
On LW: 0000-0700 Rás 1, 0700-0900 Rás 2, 0900-1400 Rás 1, 1400-1600 Rás 2, 1600-1615 Rás 1, 1615-1930 Rás 2, 1930-1945 Rás 1, 1945-2200 Rás 2, 2200-2400 Rás 1. SS: 0000-1615 Rás 1, 1615-1930 Rás 2, 1930-1945 Rás 1, 1945-2200 Rás 2, 2200-2400 Rás 1.

OTHER STATIONS

FM	MHz	kW	Location	Station
5)	88.5	1	Reykjavík	XA Radíó
1E)	90.4	2	Vestmannaeyjar	Xið
1C)	90.9	2	Mosfellsbær	GullBylgjan
1A)	92.7	2	Vaðlaheiði	Bylgjan
A)	94.3	2	Mosfellsbær	BBCWS relay
1A)	94.5	2	Háfell	Bylgjan
1B)	94.7	1	Egilsstaðir	FM957
1B)	95.1	1	Hegranes	FM957
1B)	95.7	2	Reykjavík	FM957
7)	96.3	1	Selfoss	Suðurland FM
1D)	96.7	2	Mosfellsbær	LéttBylgjan
6)	97.2	2	Reykjavík	Útvarp Flensborg
1E)	97.7	2	Mosfellsbær	Xið
1A)	97.9	1	Hegranes	Bylgjan

FM	MHz	kW	Location	Station
4)	98.7	1	Vaðlaheiði	Voice 987
1A)	98.9	2	Vatnsendi	Bylgjan
1A)	98.9	2	Hnjúkar	Bylgjan
3)	100.5	1	Bláfjöll	Kaninn
1A)	100.9	2	Vestmannaeyjar	Bylgjan
1B)	101.7	2	Vestmannaeyjar	FM957
1F)	102.2	2	Vatnsendi	Barnaútvarpið
1B)	102.5	1	Skáneyjarbunga	FM957
2)	102.9	2	Reykjavík	Lindin
1B)	103.2	1	Selfoss	FM957
1A)	103.3	1	Skáneyjarbunga	Bylgjan

NB: Txs below 1kW not listed.
Addresses & other information:
1A-1F) Skaftahlíð 24, 105 Reykjavík. **E:** 1A) bylgjan@bylgjan.is, 1B) fm957@fm957.is, 1C) gull@bylgjan.is, 1D) lettbylgjan@lettbylgjan.is – **2)** Krókhálsi 4a, 110 Reykjavík. **E:** lindin@lindin.is – **3)** Grænásbraut 619, 235 Reykjanesbæ. **E:** kaninn@kaninn.is – **4)** Ráðhústorg 7, 2 hæð, 600 Akureyri. **E:** voice@voice.is – **5)** Brávallagötu 18, 101 Reykjavík. Mainly in English. – **6)** Pósthólf 240, 222 Hafnarfjörður. – **7)** Hrísmýri 6, 800 Selfoss. **E:** 963@963.is – **A)** Lynghálsi 5, 110 Reykjavík. Rel. BBCWS (UK).

DAB (Trial): Reykjavík ch11C (220.352MHz). **Operator:** RÚV

INDIA

L.T: UTC +5½h — **Pop:** 1,166 million — **Pr.L:** Assamese, Bangla, Bodo, Dogri, English, Gujarati, Hindi, Kannada, Kashmiri, Maithili, Marathi, Malayalam, Nepali, Odia, Punjabi, Santhali, Sindhi, Tamil, Telugu & Urdu — **E.C:** 50Hz 220/400V — **ITU:** IND

MINISTRY OF INFORMATION & BROADCASTING
Main Secretariat: ☐ A-Wing, Shastri Bhawan, New Delhi-110001 **W:**www.mib.nic.in
LP: Minister of Info. & Broadcasting: Ms Ambika Soni

PRASAR BHARATI (BROADCASTING CORPORATION OF INDIA) (Public Corporation)
☐ 2nd Floor, PTI Building, Parliament Street, New Delhi-110001 ☎ +91 11 23382094/5/7/8/9 ☐ +91 11 23386507 **LP:** Chairperson: Ms Mrinal Pande ☎ 91 11 23753687 ☐ 91 11 23737589, CEO: Jawhar Sircar ☎ 91 11 23737603, 23352558 ☐ 91 11 23352549 **E:** ceobci@yahoo.com

AKASHVANI – ALL INDIA RADIO
Administration/Engineering: ☐ Directorate General, All India Radio, Akashvani Bhawan, Parliament Street, New Delhi-110001
☎ +91 11 23421006, 23715413 ☐ +91 11 23711956
E: airlive@air.org.in **W:** www.allindiaradio.gov.in
LP: DG: Leeladhar Mandloi ☎ +91 11 23710300 ☐ 91 11 23421956
E: dgair@air.org.in Engineer in Chief: R.K.Jain ☎+91 11 23421058 ☐ +91 11 23421459 **E:** einc@air.org.in
Spectrum Management & Synergy: Room No.204, All India Radio, Akashvani Bhavan, Parliament Street, New Delhi-110001 **LP:** Dir. M.S.Ansari, Dir (Engg) B.K. Oberoi ☎ +91 11 23421062, 23421145 **E:** spectrum-manager@air.org.in
Programming: ☐ New Broadcasting House, 27 Mahadev Road, New Delhi-110 001 ☎ +91 (11) 23421218
☐ Akashvani Bhawan, Parliament Street, New Delhi-110001 ☎ +91 11 23715411
News Services Division: ☐ New Broadcasting House, 27 Mahadev Road, New Delhi-110 001. Newsroom ☎ +91 11 23421100 ☐+91 11 23421219 **E:** nbhnews@air.org.in **W:** www.newsonair.nic.in **LP.** Dir. Gen. (News): G.Mohanty **E:** dgn@air.org.in News on phone: English ☎ +91 11 2332-4343/1259, Hindi +91 11 2332-4242/1258
Commercial Service (Vividh Bharati): All India Radio, ☐ Gorai Road, Borivli West, Mumbai-400 091, Maharashtra ☎ +91 22 28692698 **E:** vbsmumbai@gmail.com
National Channel: ☐ All India Radio, Todapur, New Delhi 110012 ☎ +91 11 25843207 **E:** senchair@yahoo.com
Research & Development: ☐ Office of the Chief Eng R & D, All India Radio, 14-B, Indra Prashta Estate, Ring Road, New Delhi-110002 ☎ +91 11 23378211, 23378212 **E:** researchdelhi@yahoo.co.in
Monitoring: ☐ International Monitoring Stn., All India Radio, Dr. K.S. Krishnan Rd, Todapur, New Delhi-110012 ☎ +91 11 25842939 ☐ Central Monitoring Stn, All India Radio, Ayanagar, New Delhi-110047.
Audience Research: ☐ Audience Research Unit, AIR, Akashwani Bhavan, Parliament Street, New Delhi 110001 ☎ +91 11 23421022

Regional Headquarters: (Office of the Chief Engineer)
North Zone: AIR, Jamnagar House, Shahjahan Road, New Delhi-110011 ☎ +91 11 23389000

East Zone: AIR, 4th Floor, Akashvani Bhawan, Eden Garden, Kolkata-700001 ☎ +91 33 22489131
North-East Zone: AIR, Dr P Kakati's Building, G.S. Road, Guwahati-781006, Assam ☎ +91 361 2230338
West Zone: AIR, 101 M.K.Road, Mumbai-400020, Maharashtra ☎ +91 22 22031351
South Zone: AIR, Swami Sivananda Salai, Chepauk, Chennai-600005 ☎ +91 44 25360400

NB: Thiruvananthapuram is given in all cases as Trivandrum.

MW: c) Vividh Bharati, e) ext.sce., n) national channel, r) relay stn *) off air due to installation of new transmitter

KHz	Station	kW	reg	KHz	Station	kW	reg
531	Jodhpur A	300	N	1116	Srinagar A	300	N
540	Aizawl	20	NE	1125	Tezpur	20	NE
549	Ranchi A	100	E	1125	Udaipur	20	N
558	Mumbai B	100	W	1134	Chinsurah*	1000	E, ner
567	Dibrugarh	300	NE	1143	Ratnagiri	20	W
576	Alappuzha	200	S, r	1143	Rohtak	20	N
585	Nagpur A	300	W	1161	Trivandrum	20	S
594	Chinsurah*	1000	E, er	1170	Hyderabad (St'by)	1	S
603	Ajmer	200	N, r	1179	Rewa	20	W
612	Bengaluru A	200	S	1188	Mumbai C	50	W,c
621	Patna A	100	E	1197	Shillong (St'by)	1	NE
630	Thrissur	100	S	1197	Tirunelveli	20	S
639	Kohima	100	NE	1206	Bhawanipatna	200	E
648	Indore A	200	W	1215	New Delhi	20	N, n
657	Kolkata A	200	E	1215	Puducherri	20	S
666	New Delhi B	100	N	1224	Srinagar C	10	N
675	Bhadravathi	20	S	1233	Tura	20	NE
675	Chhatarpur	20	W	1242	Varanasi	100	N
675	Itanagar	100	NE	1251	Sangli	20	W
684	KozhikodeA	100	S	1260	Ambikapur	20	W
684	Port Blair	100	S	1269	Agartala	20	NE
684	Kargil A	200	N	1269	Madurai	20	S
702	Jalandhar A	200	N, e	1278	Lucknow C	10	N, c
711	Siliguri	200	E	1287	Panaji A	100	W
720	Chennai A	200	S	1296	Darbhanga	10	E
729	Guwahati A	100	NE	1305	Parbhani	20	W
738	Hyderabad A	200	S	1314	Bhuj	20	W
747	Lucknow A	300	N	1314	Cuttack B	1	F, c
756	Jagdalpur	100	W	1323	Kolkata C	20	E, c
765	Dharwad A	200	S	1332	Tezu	10	NE
774	Shimla	100	N	1341	Kohima	1	NE
783	Chennai C	20	S, c	1350	Jalandhar C	1	N, c
792	Pune A	100	W	1350	Kupwara	20	N, r
801	Jabalpur	200	W	1368	New Delhi C	20	S, c
810	Rajkot A	300	W	1377	Hyderabad B	20	S
819	New Delhi A	200	N	1386	Gwalior	20	W
828	Panaji A	20	W, c	1395	Bikaner	20	W
828	Silchar	20	NE	1404	Gangtok	20	NE
837	Vijayawada A	100	S	1413	Kota	20	N
846	Ahmedabad A	200	W	1440	Kurseong	1	E
864	Shillong	100	NE	1449	Kanpur	1	N, c
873	Jalandhar B	300	N	1458	Barmer	20	N
882	Imphal	300	NE	1458	Bhagalpur	20	E
891	Rampur	20	N	1467	Jeypore	100	E
900	Kadapa	100	S	1476	Jaipur A	1	W
909	Gorakhpur	100	N	1485	Adilabad	1	S
918	Suratgarh	300	N	1485	Ahwa	1	W
927	Visakhapatnam	100	S	1485	Chamoli	1	N
936	Tiruchirapalli A	100	S	1485	Drass	1	N, cr
945	Sambalpur	100	E	1485	Joranda	1	E
954	Najibabad	200	N	1485	Khaltsi	1	N, cr
963	Jalgaon	20	W	1485	Nongstoin	1	NE
972	Cuttack A	300	E	1485	Nyoma	1	N, r
981	Raipur	100	W	1485	Pithoragarh	1	N, r
990	Jammu A	300	N	1485	Soro	1	E
999	Almora	1	N	1503	Vijayawada B	1	S, c
999	Coimbatore	20	S	1512	Kokrajhar	20	NE
1008	Kolkata B	100	E	1521	Tawang	10	NE
1017	Chennai B	20	S	1530	Agra	20	N
1017	New Delhi	10	N	1566	Nagpur	1000	W, nr
1026	Allahabad A	20	N	1584	Diphu	1	NE
1035	Guwahati B	10	NE	1584	Himmat Nagar	1	W
1044	Mumbai A	100	W	1584	Jamshedpur	1	E
1053	Leh	20	N	1584	Kalpa	1	N, r
1053	Tuticorin	200	S, e	1584	Kargil B	1	N
1062	Pasighat	10	NE	1584	Kavaratti	1	S
1071	Rajkot	870	W, e	1584	Keonjhar	1	E
1080	DRM			1584	Mathura	1	
1089	Udipi	20	S, r	1584	Mon	1	NE
1089	Naushera	20	N, r	1584	Padam	1	N,c
1107	Gulbarga	20	S	1593	Bhopal A	10	W

KHz	Station	kW	reg	KHz	Station	kW	reg
1602	Diskit	1	N cr	1602	Udagamangalam	1	S
1602	Pauri	1	N	1602	Uttarkashi	1	N, r
1602	Saiha	1	NE	1602	Varanasi B	1	N, c
1602	Solapur	1	W	1602	William Nagar	1	NE
1602	Tiesuru	1	N,cr	1602	Ziro	1	NE
1602	Tuensang	1	NE				

D.Prgr: Varies from stn to stn. Most stns have 3 trs daily ie Morning/Noon/Evening. Some smaller stns have only 1 or 2 trs. Extended coverage during sports or special events.
National Ch.: 1325-0043 on 1215, 1566, 9425, 9470 kHz
F.PI: DRM at 73 MW stations. **New:** 1kW at Dharmanagar, Dungarpur (1485 kHz). **Current: stns:** 1000kW Chinsurah, Replacement of 1kW MW to 10kW FM: Adilabad, Jaipur, Cuttack, Keonjhar, Kurseong, Solapur. 1 kW to 10 KW: Kavaratti. 10 kW to 20 kW Guwhati B, Tawang. 10 kW to 100 kW Passighat, 100 kW to 200 kW Itanagar

Addresses of MW stations (See also SW stn addresses):
1000kW MW stations:
1) Super Power Transmitter, Chinsurah-712102, Paschim Banga – **2)** National Channel, Seminary Hills, Nagpur-440006, Maharashtra – **3)** Super Power Transmitter, R. Colony, Jamnagar Road, Rajkot -360006, Gujarat

Other MW stations:
Adilabad-504002, Andhra Pradesh – Palace Compound, North Gate – **Agarthala**-799001, Tripura – Vivbhav Nagar, **Agra**-282001, Uttar Pradesh – Ashram Rd, Navarangpura, **Ahmedabad**-380009, Gujarat – **Ahwa**-394710, Dangs Dist., Gujarat – 21/10 Vaishali Nagar, **Ajmer**-305001, Rajasthan – Pathirapally, **Alappuzha**-688521, Kerala – Z-9 Dayanand Marg, **Allahabad**-211001, Uttar Pradesh – **Almora**-263601, Kumaon Dist., Uttarakhand – Kumar Palace, **Ambikapur**-497001, Surguja Dist., Chhatisgarh –Raj Bhavan Rd, **Bengaluru**-560001, Karnataka – Laxmi Nagar, **Barmer**-344001, Rajasthan –J.P.S.Colony, Paper Tower, **Bhadravati**-577302, Karnataka – Port Campus, **Bhagalpur**-812001, Bihar – **Bhawanipatna**-766001, Nektiguda, Kalahandi Dist., Odisha – **Bhuj**-370001, Kutch Dist., Gujarat – **Bikaner**-334001, Rajasthan – **Chamoli**-246424, Gopeshwar, Uttarakhand – 7, Kamarajar Salai, Mylapore, **Chennai**-600004. Tamilnadu – **Chhatarpur**-471001, Madhya Pradesh – Trichy Rd, Ramanathapuram, **Coimbatore**-641045, Tamilnadu – Madhupur House, Bakshi Bazar, Cantonment Rd, **Cuttack**-753001, Odisha – **Darbhanga**-846004, Bihar – Saptapur, **Dharwad**-580008, Karnataka – Malakhubasa, **Dibrugarh**-786001, Assam – **Diphu**-782460, Kabri Anglong Dist., Assam – **Diskit**-194401, Leh Dist., Jammu & Kashmir– **Drass**-194102, Kargil, Jammu & Kashmir – Aiwan-e-Shahi, Municipal Garden, **Gulbarga**-585103, Karnataka – Gandhi Rd, **Gwalior**-474002, Madhya Pradesh – **Himmat Nagar** – 383001, Gujarat – Malwa House, Residency Area, **Indore**-452001, Madhya Pradesh – 373 Napier Town, **Jabalpur**-482001, Madhya Pradesh – Collectorate Rd, **Jagdalpur**-494 001, Bastar Dist., Chhattisgarh – **Jalandhar**-144001, Punjab – Jilhapet, **Jalgaon**-425001, Maharashtra – Adityapur, Gamharia Rd, **Jamshedpur**-831013, Jharkhand – Paoata 'C' Road, **Jodhpur**-342006, Rajasthan – **Joranda**-759014, Dhenkanal Dist., Odisha – Cooperative Colony, **Kadapa**-516001, Andhra Pradesh – **Kalpa**-172108, Kinnaur Dist., Himachal Pradesh – **Kanpur**-208001, Uttar Pradesh – **Kargil**-194103, Jammu & Kashmir – **Kavaratti**-682555, Lakshadeep – **Keonjhar**-758001, Odisha – **Khaltsi**-194106, Leh, Jammu & Kashmir –**Kokrajhar**-783370, Assam – Jawahar Rd, **Kota**-324001, Rajasthan – Beach Rd, **Kozhikode**-673001, Kerala – **Kupwara**- 193222, Jammu & Kashmir –Lady Doak College Rd, Chokkikulam, **Madurai**-625002, Tamilnadu –Vrindavan Rd, Gayatri Tapobhumi, **Mathura**-281003, Uttar Pradesh – **Mon**-798621, Nagaland – Broadcasting House, Backbay Reclamation, Mumbai-400001, Maharashtra – Civil Lines, Palam Rd, **Nagpur**-440001, Maharashtra – Kotwali Rd, **Najibabad**-246763, Bijnor Dist., Uttar Pradesh – **Naushera**-193125, Jammu & Kashmir – **Nongstoin**-793119, West Khasi Hills, Meghalaya – **Nyoma**-194101, Leh Dist, Jammu & Kashmir – **Obra**-231219, Uttar Pradesh – **Padam**, Jammu & Kashmir - Altinho, **Panaji**-403001, Goa – Jamakar Colony, Nawa Mondha, **Parbhani**-431401, Maharashtra – **Pasighat**-791102, East Siang Dist., Arunachal Pradesh – Frazer Road, Chhaju Bagh, **Patna**-800001, Bihar – **Pauri**-246001, Uttarakhand – **Pithorgarh**-262501, Uttarakhand – Indira Nagar, Gorimedu, **Puducherri**-605006 – University Rd, Shivaji Nagar, **Pune**-411005, Maharashtra – Sitaram Pandit Marg, **Rajkot**-360001, Gujarat – **Rampur**-244901, Uttar Pradesh – Thiba Palace Rd, **Ratnagiri**-415612, Maharashtra – 6 Civil Lines, **Rewa**-486001, Madhya Pradesh – Subhash Rd, **Rohtak**-124001, Haryana – **Saiha**-796901, Chhimtuipui Dist., Mizoram – 3, Kuchery Rd, **Sambalpur**-768001, Odisha – Market Yard, Kolhapur Rd, **Sangli**-416416, Maharashtra – **Silchar**-788001, Cachar Dist.,

Assam – 2 Mile Sevoke Rd, **Siliguri**-734401, Darjeeling Dist., Paschim Banga – **Solapur**-413006, Maharashtra – **Soro**-756045 , Balasore Dist, Odisha – **Suratgarh**-335804, Sriganganagar Dist., Rajasthan – **Tawang**-790104, Arunachal Pradesh – **Tezpur**-784001, Sonitpur Dist., Assam – **Tezu**-792001, Lohit Dist., Arunachal Pradesh – Ramavarmapuram, **Thrissur**-680631, Kerala – **Tiesuru**, Jammu & Kashmir, 28-3 Promenade Rd, **Tiruchirapalli**-620001, Tamilnadu – Sarojini Park, Palayamkottai, **Tirunelveli**-627006, Tamilnadu – **Tuensang**-798612, Nagaland – Lower Chandmari, **Tura**-794001, Meghalaya – Millerpuram, Playamkottai Road, **Tuticorin**-628008, Tamilnadu – Chetak Circle, **Udagamangalam**-643001, Nilgris, Tamilnadu – **Udaipur**-313001, Rajasthan – Brahmavar, **Udipi**-576213, Dakshina Kanara Dist., Karnataka – **Uttar Kashi**-249193, Uttarakhand –Mahmoorganj, **Varanasi**-221010, Uttar Pradesh – Bandar Rd, Punnammathota, **Vijayawada**-520010, Andhra Pradesh – Siripuram, **Visakhapatnam**-530003, Andhra Pradesh – **William Nagar**, Meghalaya – **Ziro**-791120, Lower Subansiri Dist., Arunachal Pradesh.

Regional Domestic SW stations:

kHz	kW	Station	H. of tr.
3945#	50	Gorakhpur	0230-0300
4760	10	Leh	s0128/w0213-0430, 1130-1630
4760	8.5	Port Blair	2355-0300, 1030-1700(Sat, Sun -1730)
4775	50	Imphal	s0000/w0030-0215, 1030-1700/1730
4800	50	Hyderabad	0020-0215, 1130-1742
4810	50	Bhopal	0025-0215 1130-1742
4820	50	Kolkata	0025-0410 1130-1843
4830†	50	Jammu	0025-0445(Sun –0450), 1030-1741
4835	10	Gangtok	0100-0500 1030-1600
4840	50	Mumbai	2355-0400 1230-1730
4850	50	Kohima	0000-0415 1000-1600/1630/1700
4860	50	Shimla	0025-0200 1235v-1730(SS -1741)
4870#	100	Delhi (Kingsway)	0230-0330 1430-1530 (R. Sadaye Kashmir)
4880	50	Lucknow	0025-0430 (Sun 0415), 1215-1741
4895	50	Kurseong	0055-0400 1130-1700(Sat, Sun 1741)
4910	50	Jaipur	0025-0430 (Sun 0530) 1130-1741
4920	50	Chennai	0015-0245 1200-1739
4940	50	Guwahati	s0000/w0025-0415, 1135v-1700(Sat -1741)
4950	50	Srinagar	s0030/w0120-0215 1120-1739 (2145v-2245v during Ramadan)
4960†	50	Ranchi	0025-0445 1100 (Sun 1130) -1741
4970	50	Shillong	0025-0400 1056-1630
4990	50	Itanagar	0020-0400 1000-1630
5010	50	Trivandrum	0025-0215 1130 (Sun 1100)-1740
5040	50	Jeypore	0025-0435(Sun –0445), 1115-1741
5050	10	Aizawl	0025-0400 1130-1630
5965†	50	Jammu	0630-0930
5985†	50	Ranchi	0630-1000
6000	10	Leh	0700 (Sun 0630)-0930
6020	50	Shimla	0215-0410, 0700-0930 (Sun 0415-1000), 1130-1230
6030	100	Delhi (Kingsway)	0200-0310
6030	250	Delhi (Khampur)	1215-1430
6040	50	Jeypore	0700-1000
6065†	50	Kohima	0430-0510 0700-0900
6085	10	Gangtok	For special broadcasts in day time
6100	250	Delhi (Khampur)	0730-0830 (Radio Sadaye Kashmir)
6100	50	Delhi (Khampur)	0900-1200 (Vividh Bharati, DRM)
6110	50	Srinagar	0225-0509 (Sun 1115), 0600-1115
6150	50	Itanagar	0700-0900
7210	50	Kolkata	0730-1001
7230	50	Kurseong	0620-1030
7240	50	Mumbai	0430-1035
7250#	50	Gorakhpur	1130-1140
7270#	100	Chennai	0130-0430
7280	50	Guwahati	0600-0930 0945-1130 (Sun 0530-1145)
7290	50	Trivandrum	0230-0430 (Sat , Sun 1030), 0630-1000
7295	10	Aizawl	0700-1000
7315	50	Shillong	0656-0931
7325	50	Jaipur	0630-0931
7335	50	Imphal	0225-0400 (Sun 0430), 0630(Sun 0600)-1000
7340#	100	Mumbai	1130-1140
7380	50	Chennai	0300-0430 (Sun 0500), 0610-0930 (Sun 1130)
7390	8.5	Port Blair	0315-0400(SS -0500), 0700-0931(Sun -1000)
7420	50	Hyderabad	0225-0400(Sat 0500, Sun 0430), 0545/0600/0610-0930 (Sun 0530-1030)
7420#	50	Guwahati	0230-0300,1515-1600,1730-1740
7430	50	Bhopal	0225-0447(SS 0531), 0630/0700-0931/1001/1031
7440	50	Lucknow	0700(Sun 0430)-1000, 1005-1006
9425	250	Delhi	1320-0043 (National Channel)
9470	250	Aligarh	1320-0043 (National Channel)
9870	500	Benguluru	0025-0435, 0900-1200, 1245-1740 (Vividh Bharati)
11620#	250	Delhi (Khampur)	1130-1140

s = summer, w = winter, v = timing/frequency varies. † = irregular/off air, #= Frequency also used by External Services at other times

N in English originating in New Delhi and relayed by most stns: 0035-0040, 0245-0300, 0335-0340, 0435-0440, 0630-0635, 0730-0735, 0830-0900, 0935-0940, 1030-1035, 1135-1140, 1230-1235, 1430-1435, 1435-1440(Sports), 1530-1545, 1730-1735. Extended broadc. for special events, important Parliament sessions, sports and on January 26 (Republic Day) and August 15 (Independence Day)

V. by QSL-card. Reception Reports for SW stations only to: ✉ Director (Spectrum Management & Synergy), All India Radio, Room No.204, Akashvani Bhavan, New Delhi-110001 ▤91-11-23421062, 23421145 **E:** spectrum-manager@air.org.in In charge of processing reception reports: Director: M.S.Ansari. Local stns also verify directly in many cases by letter or email. No return postage is necessary.

F.PI.: Replacement of SW transmitters by DRM 2x250 kW Aligarh, 1x500 kW Bengaluru, 2x 250 kW & 2 x100 kW New Delhi

Addresses of SW stations: (Reception reports may be addressed to the Station Engineer)

1) Aizawl: R. Tila, Tuikhuahtlang, Box 13, Aizawl-796001 ☎+91 389 2322415 **E:** airaizawl@gmail.com– **2) Aligarh**: Anoopshahar Road, Aligarh-202001, Uttar Pradesh ☎+91 571 2700972 **E:** airaligarh@ rediffmail.com – **3) Bengaluru**: Super Power Transmitters, Yelahanka New Town, Bengaluru-560064, Karnataka ☎+91 80 27601149 **E:** sptairynk@rediffmail.com– **4) Bhopal**: Shyamla Hills, Bhopal-462002, Madhya Pradesh ☎+91 755 2660088 **E:** se_airbpl@dataone.in – **5) Chennai**: S.M.Nagar PO, Avadi, Chennai-600062, Tamilnadu. Tel. 91 44 26383204. email : airavadi@rediffmail.com – **6) Gangtok**: Old MLA Hostel, Gangtok-737101, Sikkim ☎+91 3592 202636 **E:** seairgtk@yahoo.co.in – **7) Gorakhpur**:Town Hall, Gorakhpur-273001, Uttar Pradesh ☎+91 551 2337401 **E:** seairgkp@rediffmail.com – **8) Guwahati**: Chandmari, Guwahati-781003 Assam ☎+91 361 2660378 **W:** airguwahati.gov.in **E:** en@ airguwahati.gov.in – **9) Hyderabad**: Rocklands, Saifabad, Hyderabad-500004, Andhra Pradesh ☎+91 40 23234904. **E:** airhyderabad@rediffmail.com – **10) Imphal**: Palace Compound Imphal-795001, Manipur ☎+91 385 2450534. **W:** http:// cicmanipur.nic.in/html/air_imp.htm **E:** airimfal@sancharnet.in – **11) Itanagar**: 'C' Sector, Itanagar-791111, Arunachal Pradesh ☎+91 360 2213007 **E:** air-ita@rediffmail.com – **12) Jaipur**: 5 Park House, Mirza Ismail Road, Jaipur-302001, Rajasthan ☎91 141 2366263. **E:** jaipur@ air.org.in – **13) Jammu**: R. Kashmir, Begum Haveli, Old Palace Road, Jammu-180001, Jammu & Kashmir ☎+91 191 2544411. **E:** jammu@ air.org.in – **14) Jeypore**:764005, Odisha ☎+91 6854 232524 **E:** air-jeypore@rediffmail.com – **15) Kohima**:797001, Nagaland ☎+91 370 2245556 **E:** kohima@air.org.in – **16) Kolkata**: Eden Gardens, Kolkata-700001, Paschim Banga ☎+91 33 22481705 **E:** sgeairkolkata@ rediffmail.com – **17) Kurseong**: Mehta Club Bldg, Kurseong-734203, Darjeeling Dist., Paschim Banga ☎+91 354 2344350 **E:** kurseong@air. org.in – **18) Leh**: Leh-194101, Ladakh Dist., Jammu & Kashmir ☎+91 1982 252063 **E:** seairleh@rediffmail.com – **19) Lucknow**:18 Vidhan Sabha Marg, Lucknow-226001, Uttar Pradesh ☎+91 522 2237476 **E:** lucknow@air.org.in – **20) Mumbai**: Marve Road, Malwani, Malad West, Mumbai 400095, Maharashtra. Tel. 91 22 28882867. **W:** www. hptmald.org.in **E:** hptmalad@yahoo.co.in – **21A) New Delhi**: High Power Transmitters, Khampur, New Delhi -110036 ☎+91 11 27831474 **E:** hptkhampur@yahoo.co.in **W:** www.wix.com/hptkhampur/airkham-pur – **21B)** High Power Transmitters, Kingsway, New Delhi-110009 ☎+91 11 27606661 **E:** hptkingsway@yahoo.com – **22) Panaji**: Goa University PO, Panaji-403206 ☎+91 832 2459096 **E:** airtrgoa@san-charnet.in – **23) Port Blair**: Haddo Post, Dilanipur, Port Blair-744102, Andaman & Nicobar Islands ☎+91 3192 230682 **E:** airportblair@ rediffmail.com – **24) Ranchi**: 6 Ratu Rd, Ranchi-834001, Jharkhand ☎+91 651 2283310 **E:** ranchi@air.org.in – **25) Shillong**: North Eastern Service, Pomdngiem, Opposite GPO, Shillong-793001, Meghalaya **W:** www.airshillong.org ☎+ 91 364 2224443 **W:** www.airshillong.org **E:** airneshill@gmail.com **26) Shimla**: Choura Maidan, Shimla-171004, Himachal Pradesh ☎+91 177 2811355 **W:** www.airshimla.com **E:** shimla@air.org.in – **27) Srinagar**: R. Kashmir, Sherwani Rd, Srinagar-190001, Jammu & Kashmir ☎+91 194 2452100 **E:** stationdirector@ yahoo.co.in – **28) Thiruvanathapuram** : Bhakti Vilas, Vazuthacaud, Thiruvanathapuram-695014, Kerala ☎+91 471 2325009 **W:** www. airtvm.com **E:** se_airtvm@rediffmail.com

FM: b) FM Rainbow c) Vividh Bharati g) FM Gold r) relay stn

MHz	location	kW	reg	MHz	location	kW	reg
93.9	Vadodara	10	W, c	100.1	Kothagudem	6	S
96.7	Ahmedabad	10	W, c	100.1	New Delhi	5	N
100.1	Ahmednagar	6	W	100.2	Darjeeling	5	E
100.1	Bengaluru	3	S	100.2	Haflong	6	NE
100.1	Gangtok	10	NE	100.2	Kolkata	20	E, g
100.1	Gorakhpur	10	N, c	100.2	Patiala	6	N

MHz	location	kW	reg	MHz	location	kW	reg
100.2	Shivpuri	6	W	102.3	Hissar	6	N
100.3	Allahabad	10	N, c	102.3	Karimnagar	5	S
100.3	Asansol	6	E, r	102.3	Karwar	3	S
100.3	Jaipur B	6	N, c	102.3	Kochi A	10	S
100.3	Jammu A	3	N	102.3	Kurseong	5	E, b
100.3	Karaikal	6	S	102.3	Purnea	6	E
100.3	Mangalore	10	S	102.4	Akola	6	W
100.4	Bareilly	6	N	102.4	Kurnool	6	S
100.4	Mandla	1	W, c	102.4	Rajkot	10	W, c
100.5	Dhule	6	W	102.5	Dharmapuri	10	S
100.5	Hospet	6	S	102.5	Kullu	6	N, r
100.5	Kodaikanal	10	S, b	102.5	Patna	10	E, c
100.6	Berhampur	6	E	102.6	Chitradurga	6	S
100.6	Mysore	10	S	102.6	New Delhi	20	N, b
100.6	Nagpur	10	W, c	102.6	Rourkela	6	E
100.6	Varanasi	10	N,c	102.6	Sagar	5	W
100.7	Aizawl	6	NE	102.6	Srinagar	10	N, c
100.7	Churu	6	N	102.6	Tirunelveli	10	S
100.7	Lucknow	10	N, b	102.7	Jalandhar	10	N,b
100.7	Mumbai	20	W, g	102.7	Kolhapur	6	W
100.7	Poonch	6	N	102.7	Manjeri	10	S, b
100.7	Raigarh	6	W, c	102.7	Nagaon	6	NE
100.7	Rajgarh	3	W	102.7	Obra	6	N
100.8	Guwahati	10	NE, c	102.7	Yavatmal	6	W
100.8	Jamshedpur	6	E, c	102.8	Hyderabad	10	S, c
100.9	Mokokchung	6	NE	102.8	Puducherry	10	S,b
100.9	Port Blair	10	S, c	102.8	Saraipalli	1	W, c
101.0	Bhaderwah	6	N	102.9	Baripada	6	E
101.0	Nagercoil	10	S	102.9	Beed	6	W
101.0	Pune	10	W, c	102.9	Bengaluru	10	S
101.0	Suryapet	1	S, r	102.9	Chittorgarh	6	N
101.1	Bathinda	6	N	102.9	Jabalpur	10	W, c
101.1	Jowai	6	NE	102.9	Rampur	1	N
101.1	Nanded	6	W	103.0	Chandrapur	6	W
101.1	Surat	10	W, c	103.0	Coimbatore	10	S, b,c
101.2	Khandwa	6	W	103.0	Daltonganj	6	E
101.3	Aligarh	6	N, br	103.0	Dharwad	6	S, c
101.3	Balaghat	6	W	103.0	Jhansi	6	N
101.3	Banswara	10	N	103.0	Kohima	10	NE
101.3	Bengaluru	10	S, b	103.1	Alwar	10	N
101.3	Cuttack	6	E, b	103.1	Betul	6	W
101.3	Osmanabad	6	W	103.1	Chandigarh	6	N, c
101.4	Chennai	20	S	103.1	Itanagar	10	NE
101.4	Churachandpur	6	NE	103.1	Macherla	3	S
101.4	Devikulam	6	S	103.1	Madikeri	6	S
101.4	Kurukshetra	6	N	103.1	Satara	6	W
101.4	Nashik	6	W	103.1	Shanthi Nikethan	3	E
101.4	Siliguri	10	E, c	103.2	Bilaspur	6	E
101.5	Amravati	10	W,cr	103.2	Jhalawar	6	N
101.5	Kannur	6	S	103.2	Kailashahar	6	NE
101.5	Markapur	6	S	103.2	Nizamabad	6	S
101.5	Sawai Madhopur	6	N	103.2	Tirupati-I	6	S
101.6	Agartala	10	NE, c	103.3	Bellary	10	S
101.6	Indore	6	W, c	103.3	Dhubri	6	NE, r
101.6	Raipur	10	W	103.3	Madurai	10	S
101.7	Anantapur	6	S	103.3	Ranchi	6	E, c
101.7	Aurangabad	10	W, c	103.4	Dharamsala	6	N
101.7	Chaibasa	6	E	103.4	Jorhat	10	NE
101.7	Udaipur	6	N, c	103.4	Puri	6	E
101.8	Bijapur	6	S	103.4	Sasaram	6	E
101.8	Hamirpur	6	N	103.5	Bhopal	6	W, c
101.8	Jaisalmer	10	N	103.5	Imphal	6	NE c
101.9	Bolangir	6	E	103.5	Mount Abu	6	N
101.9	Faizabad	6	N	103.5	Rohtak	10	N, c
101.9	Hyderabad	10	S, b	103.5	Srinagar	6	N, c
101.9	Lungleh	6	NE	103.5	Warangal	6	S
101.9	Rajouri	10	N, r	103.6	Kozhikode	10	S
101.9	Trivandrum	10	S, c	103.6	Oros	5	W
102.0	Shahdol	6	W	103.6	Shillong	10	NE, b
102.0	Visakhapatnam	10	S, b	103.7	Belonia	6	NE
102.1	Hazaribagh	6	E	103.7	Gulbarga	10	S,c
102.1	Jodhpur	6	N, c	103.7	Kanpur	10	N
102.1	Mussoorie	10	N, br	103.7	Nagaur	6	N
102.1	Raichur	6	S	103.7	Shimla	6	N, c
102.1	Tiruchirapalli	10	S, b,c	104.5	Jammu B	6	N
102.2	Chindwara	6	W	105.4	Panaji	6	W, b
102.2	Godhra	6	W	106.4	New Delhi	20	N, g
102.2	Hassan	6	S	106.6	Bikaner	6	N
102.2	Kathua	10	N	107.0	Kolkata	20	E, b
102.2	Murshidabad	6	E	107.1	Mumbai	20	W, b
102.2	Vijayawada	10	S, b	107.1	Kasauli	6	N, bcr
102.3	Chennai	20	S, g	107.5	Puri	10	S, bc
102.3	Daman	3	W	107.5	Tirupati -II	3	S
102.3	Guna	6	W	+ about 100 relay stns of 100W			

UTC daily. TWR in Hindi / English at 1631 -1645 UTC Fridays. FEBA, R. Atmeeya Yatra etc. also broadcasting via AIR stns on MW, SW & FM.

F.PI: DRM at many stns. **100W:** relay stns in about 100 locations. **1kW:** Anini, Bhadravati, Bomdila, Champawat, Changlang, Cherapunjee, Chempai, Cuddapah, Daporijo, Dibrugarh, Gairsen, Goalpara, Jeypore, Karimganj, Khonsa, Kolasib, Kota, Lumding, New Tehri, Nutan Bazar, Parbhani, Phek, Rairangpur, Rampur, Ratnagiri, Sangli, Srikakulam, Tamenglong, Tezpur, Thrissur, Tuipang, Tuticorin, Udaipur(Tripura), Ukhrul, Wokha, Zunheboto. **5kW:** Agra, Ajmer, Almora, Ambikapur, Bageshwar, Bhawanipatna, Bhuj, Chhatarpur, Gwalior, Jalgaon, Kurseong, Longtherai, Oras, Sambalpur, Silchar, Tura, Ujjain. **10kW:** Balurghat, Banda, Bardhaman, Chandigarh(Kasauli), Coochbehar, Darjeeling, Dehradun(Mussoorie), Dhanbad, Green Ridge, Haldwani, Himbotingla, Junagadh, Kochi, Lakhimpur Kheri, Maunath Bhanjan, Mehaboobnagar, Natha Top, Naushera, Srinagar, Suryapet. **20kW:** Amristsar, Chautan Hill, Fazilka, Rai Bareilly. **Change of 1kW MW to 10kW FM:** Adilabad, Jaipur, Cuttack, Keonjhar, Kurseong, Solapur.

Addresses of FM stations (See also SW & MW stn addresses):
Ahmednagar-414001, Maharashtra – **Akola**-444001, Maharashtra – Scheme No 6, Mangal Vihar, **Alwar**-301001, Rajasthan – Near Tapovan Gate, Camp, **Amravati**-444602, Maharashtra – Near Collectorate, **Anantapur**-515001, Andhra Pradesh – **Asansol**-713301, Burdwan Dist., Paschim Banga – Jalna Rd, **Aurangabad**-431005, Maharashtra – **Aurangabad**-842101, Bihar – **Balaghat**-481001, Madhya Pradesh – **Banswara**-327001, Rajasthan – No 15, Lal Phatak, Badaun Road, **Bareilly**-243004, Uttar Pradesh – **Baripada**-757001, Mayurbhanj Dist., Odisha – Khandeshwari Road, **Beed**-431122, Maharashtra – **Bellary**-583101, Karnataka – **Belonia**-799155, Tripura – **Berhampur**-760001, Ganjam Dist., Odisha – **Betul**-460001, Madhya Pradesh – **Bathinda**-151005, Punjab – **Bhaderwah**-182222, Doda Dist., Jammu & Kashmir – **Bijapur**-586101, Karnataka – Nutan Colony, **Bilaspur**-495001, Chhattisgarh – **Bolangir**-767001, Odisha – Tungri Maidan, **Chaibasa**-833201, Singhbhum Dist., Jharkhand – **Chandrapur**-442401, Maharashtra – Sector-19B, **Chandigarh**-160019 – **Chindwara**-480001, Madhya Pradesh – **Chitradurga**-577501, Karnataka – Sector 4, Gandhi Nagar, **Chittorgarh**-312001, Rajasthan – **Churu**-331001, Rajasthan – **Churachandpur**- 795128, Manipur – **Daltonganj**-822101, Jharkhand – Opp. Varkunt, Mota Fliya, **Daman**-396210, Daman & Diu – **Darjeeling**-734101, Paschim Banga – **Devikulam**-685613, Idukki Dist., Kerala – **Dharmapuri**-636701, Tamilnadu – **Dharmasala**-176215, Kangra Dist., Himachal Pradesh – **Dhubri**-783301, Assam – **Dhule**-424001, Maharashtra – Begumganj Garahiya, **Faizabad**-224001, Uttar Pradesh – **Godhra**-389001, Gujarat – **Guna**-473001, Madhya Pradesh – **Haflong**-788819, Assam – **Hamirpur**-177001, Himachal Pradesh – Salagame Road, **Hassan**-573201, Karnataka – Jail Road, **Hazaribagh**-825301, Jharkhand – **Hissar**-125001, Haryana – **Hospet**-583201, Karnataka – Vyas Colony, **Jaisalmer**-345001, Rajasthan – Jungle Road, **Jhalawar**-326001, Rajasthan – Kanpur Road, **Jhansi**-284128, Uttar Pradesh – **Jorhat**-785001, Assam – **Jowai**-793150, Jaintia Hills, Meghalaya – **Kailashahar**-799277, Tripura – **Kannur**-670001, Kerala – Radio Avenue, Nehru Ngr., **Karaikal**-609606, Puducherri – **Karimnagar**-505001, Andhra Pradesh – **Karwar**-581301, Karnataka – **Kasauli**-173204, Solan Dist., Himachal Pradesh – **Kathua**-184104, Jammu & Kashmir – **Khandwa**-450001, Nimar Dist., Madhya Pradesh – BMC PO, **Kochi**-682021, Ernakulam Dist., Kerala – Anandagiri, **Kodaikanal**-624101, Tamilnadu – Sardar Cly, Taravai Park, **Kolhapur**-416003, Maharashtra – Ramavaram, **Kothagudem**-507118, Khammam Dist., Andhra Pradesh – **Kulu**-175101, Himachal Pradesh – Bellary Road, **Kurnool**-518003, Andhra Pradesh – **Kurushetra**-132118, Haryana – **Lungleh**-796701, Mizoram – **Macherla**-522426, Guntur Dist., Andhra Pradesh – **Madikeri**-571201, Kodagu Dist., Karnataka – Kadri Hills, **Mangalore**-575004, Dakshin Kanara Dist., Karnataka – **Manjeri**-676121, Kerala – **Mandla**-481661, Madhya Pradesh - **Markapur**-523316, Prakasam Dist., Andhra Pradesh – **Mokokchung**-798601, Nagaland – **Mount Abu** -307501, Sirohi Dist., Rajasthan – **Murshidabad**-742101, Paschim Banga – **Mussoorie**-248179, Dehradun Dist., Uttarakhand – Yadavagiri, **Mysore**-570020, Karnataka – **Nagaon**-782002, Assam – Basni Rd, **Nagaur**-341001, Rajasthan – Konam, **Nagercoil**-629004, Kanya Kumari Dist., Tamilnadu – Vasrania, **Nanded**-431601, Maharashtra – **Nashik**-422001, Maharashtra – **Nizamabad**-503012, Andhra Pradesh – Tambri Vibhag, **Oros**-416812, Sindhudurg Dist, Maharashtra – **Osmanabad**-413501, Maharashtra – Phase-I, Urban Estate, Rajpura Rd, **Patiala**-147002, Punjab – **Poonch**-185101, Jammu & Kashmir – **Puri**-751001, Odisha – **Purnea**-854302, Bihar – **Raichur**-584101, Karnataka – Chote Atarmude, **Raigarh**-496001, Chhattisgarh – Kamla Nehru Marg, Civil Lines, **Raipur**-492001, Chhattisgarh – **Rajgarh** -465661, Madhya Pradesh – **Rajouri**-185131, Jammu & Kashmir – **Rourkela**-769001,

NB: Broadcasts via AIR FM Rainbow : R. Japan in Hindi at 1600-1630

Odisha – **Sagar**-470001, Madhya Pradesh – **Saraipalli**-493558, Raipur, Chhatisgarh – **Sasaram**-821115, Rohtas Dist., Bihar – **Satara**-415001, Maharashtra – Pali Road, **Shahdol**-484001, Madhya Pradesh – **Shanthi Nikethan**, Paschim Banga – Physical College, **Shivpuri**-473551, Madhya Pradesh – **Surat**-395001, Gujarat – **Suryapet**-508213, Nalgonda Dist., Andhra Pradesh – **Swai Madhopur**-322001, Rajasthan – **Tirupati**-517501, Andhra Pradesh – Makarpura Rd, **Vadadora**-390009, Gujarat – **Warangal**-506002, Andhra Pradesh – **Yavatmal**-445001, Maharashtra

EXTERNAL SERVICES: All India Radio
see International Broadcasting section

Private FM Stations:

Location	MHz	Station	Location	MHz	Station
Agartala	91.9	R.Ooo La La	Hissar	91.9	R. Mantra
Agra	91.9	R. Mantra	Hissar	92.7	Big 92.7 FM
Agra	92.7	Big 92.7 FM	Hissar	104.0	R. Tarang
Ahmedabad	91.1	R. City	Hissar	106.4	Dhamaal 24
Ahmedabad	93.5	Red FM	Hyderabad	91.1	R. City
Ahmedabad	94.3	My FM	Hyderabad	92.7	Big 92.7 FM
Ahmedabad	98.3	R.Mirchi	Hyderabad	93.5	Red FM
Ahmedabad	95.0	R. One	Hyderabad	98.3	R. Mirchi
Ahmednagar	91.1	R. City	Indore	92.7	Big 92.7 FM
Ahmednagar	106.4	Dhamaal 24	Indore	93.5	Red FM
Ajmer	91.1	R. City	Indore	94.3	My FM
Ajmer	92.7	Big 92.7 FM	Indore	98.3	R. Mirchi
Ajmer	94.3	My FM	Itanagar	91.9	R. Ooo La La
Akola	91.1	R. City	Jabalpur	93.5	Red FM
Aligarh	92.7	Big 92.7 FM	Jabalpur	94.3	My FM
Allahabad	92.7	Big 92.7 FM	Jabalpur	98.3	R. Mirchi
Allahabad	93.5	Red FM	Jabalpur	106.4	Dhamaal 24
Amritsar	92.7	Big 92.7 FM	Jaipur	91.1	R. City
Amritsar	94.3	My FM	Jaipur	93.5	Red FM
Amritsar	104.8	Oye FM	Jaipur	94.3	My FM
Asansol	92.7	Big 92.7 FM	Jaipur	95.0	Tadka 95 FM
Asansol	93.5	Red FM	Jaipur	98.3	R. Mirchi
Aurangabad	93.5	Red FM	Jalandhar	91.9	R. Mantra
Aurangabad	98.3	R. Mirchi	Jalandhar	92.7	Big 92.7 FM
Bareilly	91.9	R. Mantra	Jalandhar	94.3	My FM
Bareilly	92.7	Big 92.7 FM	Jalandhar	98.3	R. Mirchi
Bengaluru	91.1	R. City	Jalgaon	91.1	R. City
Bengaluru	91.9	R. Indigo	Jalgaon	106.4	Dhamaal 24
Bengaluru	92.7	Big 92.7 FM	Jammu	92.7	Big 92.7 FM
Bengaluru	93.5	Red FM	Jamshedpur	92.7	Big 92.7 FM
Bengaluru	94.3	R. One	Jamshedpur	93.5	Red FM
Bengaluru	98.3	R. Mirchi	Jamshedpur	104.8	R. Dhoom
Bengaluru	104.0	Fever FM	Jhansi	92.7	Big 92.7 FM
Bhopal	92.7	Big 92.7 FM	Jodhpur	92.7	Big 92.7 FM
Bhopal	93.5	Red FM	Jodhpur	94.3	My FM
Bhopal	94.3	My FM	Jodhpur	104.8	Oye FM
Bhopal	98.3	R. Mirchi	Kannur	91.9	R. Mango
Bikaner	92.7	Big 92.7 FM	Kannur	93.5	Red FM
Bilaspur	94.3	My FM	Kannur	94.3	Club FM
Chandigarh	92.7	Big 92.7 FM	Kanpur	95.0	Best FM 95
Chandigarh	94.3	My FM	Kanpur	92.7	Big 92.7 FM
Chennai	91.1	R. City	Kanpur	93.5	Red FM
Chennai	91.9	Aahaa FM	Kanpur	98.3	R. Mirchi
Chennai	92.7	Big 92.7 FM	Karnal	91.9	R. Mantra
Chennai	93.5	Suryan FM	Karnal	106.4	Dhamaal 24
Chennai	94.3	R. One	Kochi	91.9	R. Mango
Chennai	98.3	R. Mirchi	Kochi	93.5	Red FM
Chennai	104.8	Chennai Live	Kochi	94.3	Club FM
Chennai	106.4	R.Hello 106.4 FM	Kolhapur	94.3	Tomato FM
Coimbatore	91.1	R. City	Kolhapur	98.3	R. Mirchi
Coimbatore	93.5	Suryan FM	Kolkata	91.9	Friends FM
Coimbatore	98.3	R. Mirchi	Kolkata	92.7	Big 92.7 FM
Coimbatore	106.4	R.Hello 106.4 FM	Kolkata	93.5	Red FM
Cuttack	92.7	Big 92.7 FM	Kolkata	94.3	R. One
Cuttack	93.5	Red FM	Kolkata	98.3	R. Mirchi
Cuttack	104.0	R. Choklate	Kolkata	104.0	Fever FM
Dhule	106.4	Dhamaal 24	Kolkata	104.8	Oye FM
Gangtok	91.9	Nine FM	Kolkata	106.2	Amar FM
Gangtok	93.5	Red FM	Kolkata	107.8	Power FM
Gangtok	95.0	R. Misty	Kota	92.7	Big 92.7 FM
Gorakhpur	91.9	R. Mantra	Kota	94.3	My FM
Gulbarga	93.5	Red FM	Kota	95.0	Tadka 95 FM
Guwahati	91.9	R. Ooo La La	Kozhikode	91.9	R. Mango
Guwahati	92.7	Big 92.7 FM	Kozhikode	93.5	Red FM
Guwahati	93.5	Red FM	Lucknow	91.1	R. City
Guwahati	94.3	Gup Shup	Lucknow	92.7	Big 92.7 FM
Gwalior	91.9	Suno Lemon	Lucknow	93.5	Red FM
Gwalior	92.7	Big 92.7 FM	Lucknow	98.3	R. Mirchi
Gwalior	94.3	My FM	Madurai	93.5	Suryan FM
Gwalior	95.0	Tadka 95 FM	Madurai	98.3	R. Mirchi

Location	MHz	Station	Location	MHz	Station
Madurai	106.4	R.Hello 106.4 FM	Ranchi	104.8	R. Dhoom
Mangalore	92.7	Big 92.7 FM	Ranchi	106.4	Dhamaal 24
Mangalore	93.5	Red FM	Rourkela	92.7	Big 92.7 FM
Mangalore	98.3	R. Mirchi	Rourkela	104.0	R. Choklate
Mumbai	91.1	R. City	Sangli	91.1	R. City
Mumbai	92.7	Big 92.7 FM	Shillong	91.9	R. Ooo La La
Mumbai	93.5	Red FM	Shillong	93.5	Red FM
Mumbai	94.3	R. One	Shimla	91.9	Big FM
Mumbai	98.3	R. Mirchi	Shimla	104.8	Oye FM
Mumbai	104.0	Fever FM	Shimla	106.4	Dhamaal 24
Mumbai	104.8	Oye FM	Siliguri	91.9	Nine FM
Muzzafarpur	106.4	Dhamaal 24	Siliguri	92.7	High 92.7 FM
Mysore	92.7	Big 92.7 FM	Siliguri	93.5	Red FM
Mysore	93.5	Red FM	Siliguri	94.3	R. Misty
Nagpur	91.1	R. City	Solapur	91.1	R. City
Nagpur	93.5	Red FM	Solapur	92.7	Big 92.7 FM
Nagpur	94.3	My FM	Srinagar	92.7	Big 92.7 FM
Nagpur	98.3	R. Mirchi	Surat	91.1	R. City
Nanded	91.1	R. City	Surat	92.7	Big 92.7 FM
Nashik	93.5	Red FM	Surat	94.3	My FM
Nashik	98.3	R. Mirchi	Surat	98.3	R. Mirchi
New Delhi	91.1	R. City	Trivandrum	92.7	Big 92.7 FM
New Delhi	92.7	Big 92.7 FM	Trivandrum	93.5	Red FM
New Delhi	93.5	Red FM	Trivandrum	94.3	Club FM
New Delhi	94.3	R. One	Trivandrum	98.3	R. Mirchi
New Delhi	95.0	Hit FM	Thrissur	91.1	Red FM
New Delhi	98.3	R. Mirchi	Thrissur	91.9	R. Mango
New Delhi	104.0	Fever FM	Thrissur	95.0	Best FM 95
New Delhi	104.8	Oye FM	Thrissur	104.8	Club FM
Panaji	91.9	R. Indigo	Tiruchirapalli	93.5	Suryan FM
Panaji	92.7	Big 92.7 FM	Tiruchirapalli	106.4	R.Hello 106.4 FM
Panaji	98.3	R. Mirchi	Tirunelveli	93.5	Suryan FM
Patiala	92.7	Big 92.7 FM	Tirunelveli	106.4	R.Hello 106.4 FM
Patiala	104.8	Oye FM	Tirupati	92.7	Big 92.7 FM
Patiala	106.4	Dhamaal 24	Tirupati	93.5	Red FM
Patna	98.3	R. Mirchi	Tuticorin	93.5	Suryan FM
Puducherry	92.7	Big 92.7 FM	Tuticorin	106.4	R.Hello 106.4 FM
Puducherry	93.5	Suryan FM	Udaipur	92.7	Big 92.7 FM
Puducherry	106.4	R.Hello 106.4 FM	Udaipur	94.3	My FM
Pune	91.1	R. City	Udaipur	95.0	Tadka 95 FM
Pune	93.5	Red FM	Vadodara	91.1	R. City
Pune	94.3	R. One	Vadodara	92.7	Big 92.7 FM
Pune	98.3	R. Mirchi	Vadodara	93.5	Red FM
Raipur	94.3	My FM	Vadodara	98.3	R. Mirchi
Raipur	95.0	Tadka 95 FM	Varanasi	91.9	R. Mantra
Raipur	98.3	R. Mirchi	Varanasi	93.5	Red FM
Raipur	104.8	Rangila FM	Varanasi	98.3	R. Mirchi
Rajahmundry	93.5	Red FM	Vijayawada	93.5	Red FM
Rajkot	92.7	Big 92.7 FM	Vijayawada	98.3	R. Mirchi
Rajkot	93.5	Red FM	Visakhapatnam	91.1	R. City
Rajkot	98.3	R. Mirchi	Visakhapatnam	92.7	Big 92.7 FM
Ranchi	91.9	R. Mantra	Visakhapatnam	93.5	Red FM
Ranchi	92.7	Big 92.7 FM	Visakhapatnam	98.3	R. Mirchi
Ranchi	104.0	R. Tarang	Warangal	93.5	Red FM

F.PI: 839 New stns in 290 cities

Web addresses: Aahaa FM: www.aahaafm.com **Big FM:** www.big927fm.com **Chennai Live:** www.chennailive.fm **Club FM:** http://www.clubfm.in **Dhamaal 24:** http://dhamaal24.com **Fever FM:** www.fever.fm **Friends FM:** http://www.abp.in/30002.html **Hello 106.4 FM:** www.hello.fm **My FM:** www.myfmindia.com **Oye FM:** http://oyefm.in **Power FM:** http://power1078fm.com **R. Chaska:** http://www.radiochaska.com **R. Choklate:** www.radiochoklate.com **R. Indigo:** www.radioindigo.fm **R. Mango:** www.radiomango.co.in **R. Mirchi:** www.radiomirchi.com **R. One:** www.radioone.in **Red FM:** www.sunnetwork.org/redfm/Index.htm **Suryan FM:** www.sunnetwork.org/suryanfm

Gyan Vani (Educational FM Channel)
Electronic Media Production Centre, Sanchar Kendra, Indira Gandhi National Open University (IGNOU), Maidan Garhi, New Delhi-110068 ☎ 91-11-29533079 ▤ 91-11-29534299 **E:** gyandarshan@ignou.ac.in **W:** www.ignou.ac.in/ignou/aboutignou/broadcast/schedule/schedule

Location	MHz	kW	Location	MHz	kW
Agra	105.6	10	Coimbatore	91.9	10
Ahmedabad	105.6	6	Cuttack	105.6	10
Allahabad	107.4	10	Hyderabad	105.6	10
Aurangabad	105.6	10	Indore	105.6	10
Bengaluru	106.4	10	Guwahati	107.8	10
Bhopal	105.0	10	Jabalpur	105.6	10
Chandigarh	105.6	10	Jaipur	105.6	10
Chennai	105.6	10	Jalandhar	105.6	10

Location	MHz	kW	Location	MHz	kW
Kanpur	105.6	10	Pune	105.6	10
Kochi	105.6	10	Raipur	105.6	10
Kolkata	105.4	10	Rajkot	105.6	10
Lucknow	105.6	10	Shillong	103.6	10
Madurai	105.6	10	Srinagar	107.8	10
Mumbai	105.6	10	Trivandrum	105.6	10
Mysore	105.6	10	Tiruchirapalli	104.8	10
Nagpur	105.6	10	Tirunelveli	105.6	10
New Delhi	105.6	10	Varanasi	105.6	10
Panaji	107.8	10	Visakhapatnam	106.4	10
Patna	105.6	10			

NB: Txs located at and maintained by AIR.

Community FM Radio Stations: Over 151 stns run by Educational Institutions, NGOs and others with 50W on FM 90.4MHz, 90.8MHz, 91.2MHz, 96.9MHz, 106.8MHz, 107.2MHz, 107.4MHz and 107.8MHz. **F.PI.** More community stns by different institutions.

INDONESIA

L.T: We. Indonesia (Java, Sumatra, We. & Ce. Kalimantan): UTC +7h; Ce. Indonesia (So. & Ea. Kalimantan, Sulawesi, Bali, Nusa Tenggara): UTC +8h; Ea. Indonesia (Maluku, Papua): UTC +9h — **Pr.L**: Bahasa Indonesia (Indonesian) — **Pop**: 245 million — **E.C**: 50 H∠, 230V — **ITU**: INS

DIRECTORATE GENERAL OF POSTS & TELECOMMUNICATIONS (Direktorat Jenderal Pos dan Telekomunikasi)
Gedung Sapta Pesona, Medan Merdeka Barat 17, Jakarta 10110
☎ +62 21 3835955 ▤ +62 21 3860754 **W:** www.postel.go.id **E:** admin@postel.go.id

INDONESIAN BROADCASTING COMMISSION (Komisi Penyiaran Indonesia, KPI)
Gedung Sekretariat Negara Lt VI, Jl. Gajah Mada 8, Jakarta 10120
☎ +62 21 6340713 ▤ +62 21 6340667 **W:** www.kpi.go.id
LP: Head: Mr Mochamad Riyanto. Deputy Head: Ms Ezki Tri Rezeki Widianti.

RADIO REPUBLIK INDONESIA (RRI) (Gov.)
National Station: RRI, Jakarta ▤ Jl. Medan Merdeka Barat 4-5, Jakarta 10110, or Tromolpos 1157 (or Kotak Pos 356), Jakarta 10001 ☎ +62 21 3842083 ▤ +62 21 3457132 **W:** www.rri.co.id **E:** info@rri.co.id
Pro 1 (Prosatu): Information and entertainment on 91.2MHz **Pro 2 (Produa):** Prgrs for young people on 105.0MHz **Pro 3 (Protiga):** National news network on 999kHz, 88.8MHz 24h, also relayed in full on FM by most regional stns. N: on the h. Sports N. (Berita Olahraga): 0400, 0800. **Pro 4 (Proempat):** Educational and cultural prgrs on 1332 & 9680kHz, 92.8MHz 24h Relays Pro 3 1700-2200.
Local Stations: Transmit up to four services. Pro 1 (music and information), Pro 2 (for young people), Pro 3 (relay of Pro 3 Jakarta), Pro 4 (education and culture). MW and SW freqs below carry the local Pro 1 sce except where marked "3" or "4". **H of tr:** Pro 3 24h, others usually 0430/0500-2400 local time.

MW	kHz	kW	Station	MW	kHz	kW	Station
JB01	540	2/10	Bandung 4	GO01	1008		Gorontalo
JT01	585	50	Surabaya 4	JT04	1008	10	Madiun
SL01	630	50	Makassar	PA03	1026	5	Serui
PB01	702	2/10	Manokwari	LA01	1035	1/5	Bandar Lampung
MA01	720	10	Ambon	SH01	1035		Palu
PA06	729		Nabire	PA04	1044	2	Biak
BE01	747	10	Bengkulu	ST02	1044	10	Tahuna
JH03	756	2/10	Purwokerto	SU02	1044	10	Sibolga
MA02	765	1	Tual	PA01	1053	10	Jayapura
PB02	774		Fak-Fak	BA02	1080	2/10	Singaraja
NT02	783	2/10	Ende	JA01	1098	2/10	Jambi
JH01	801	10	Semarang	JT05	1098	2/10	Sumenep
SU01	801	1/50	Medan 4	NT01	1107	1	Kupang
PA02	810	7.5	Merauke	YG01	1107	1/10	Yogyakarta 4
NB01	855	2/10	Mataram	KS01	1134	1/25	Banjarmasin 4
JB03	864	2/10	Cirebon	SB01	1179	2/10	Padang
JT02	891	10	Malang	ST01	1188	10	Manado 4
MU01	891	10	Ternate	KH01	1197	10	Palangkaraya
PB03	909	5/10	Sorong	JB01	1215		Bandung 3
RI01	927	25	Pekanbaru 4	KT01	1215	0.5/10	Samarinda
SG01	954	10	Kendari	KB01	1233	02/1/5	Pontianak
JT03	963	2/10	Jember	JB02	1242	10	Bogor
JH02	972	50	Surakarta	AC01	1251	10	Banda Aceh
JK01	999	1/150	Jakarta 3	JK01	1332	10	Jakarta 4

MW	kHz	kW	Station	MW	kHz	kW	Station
KR01	1341	1/5	Tanjung Pinang	PA05	1395	1	Wamena
KT02	1350	10	Tarakan	BB01	1413	5	Sungai Liat
SH02	1377	10	Tolitoli	SB02	1512	10	Bukittinggi

SW	kHz	kW	Station, h. of tr.
KH01	3325	10	Palangkaraya: 2200-0100, 0900-1610
MU01	3345	10	Ternate*
SH01	v3960		Palu: 2000-2400, 0900-1600 irr.
SG01	3995	5	Kendari*
SL01	4750	20	Makassar: 2100-0000, 0745-1600 irr.
PB02	4790		Fak-Fak*
PA05	4870		Wamena: 2000-2315, 0800-1500
PA04	4920		Biak*
PA06	7290		Nabire: 2200-2300, 0500-0815v
JK01	9680	250	Jakarta (Cimanggis): 2200-1500v

NB: During the Muslim fasting month of Ramadan several stns begin morning transmissions as early as 1800.

Addresses (JI = Jalan). All **FM:** in MHz. FM freqs are listed in order of prgr (Pro 1, Pro 2, Pro 3, Pro4) exc. where noted. Local FM relays are marked after + and generally carry Pro-1.
AC01) Jl Sultan Iskandar Muda 13, P.O Box 112, Banda Aceh 23423, Nanggroe Aceh Darussalam **E:** sekretariat@rribandaaceh.net - **FM:** 97.7/88.6/92.6 + 90.5 (Tapaktuan), 91.9 (Langsa), 92.0 (Sinabang), 92.3 (Kutacane), 93.0 (Subulussalam), 95.1 (Lamno), 97.3 (Jantho), 97.5 (Calang), 99.7 (Beuneureuen) – **AC02)** Jl Peutua Ibrahim 75, Teumpok Teungoh, Lhokseumawe 24352, Nanggroe Aceh Darussalam - **FM:** 89.3/100.9/95.2 – **AC03)** RRI Sabang, Jl Yos Sudarso 65, Cot Bak U, Kecamatan Sukajaya, Sabang, Nanggroe Aceh Darussalam **E:** rrisabang@gmail.com - **FM:** 94.0 – **AC04)** RRI Takengon, Jl Lembaga Kemili, Takengon, Aceh Tengah, Nanggroe Aceh Darussalam - **FM:** 93.0 – **AC05)** RRI Meulaboh, Meulaboh, Nanggroe Aceh Darussalam - **FM:** 97.0 (Pro 1)/88.7 (Pro 3) – **AC06)** RRI Singkil, Singkil, Nanggroe Aceh Darussalam – **FM:** 92.2
BA01) Jl Hayam Wuruk 70, Keladis, Denpasar 80233 (Kotak Pos 31, Denpasar 80001), Bali - **FM:** 88.6/100.9/93.0/95.3 – **BA02)** Jl Gajah Mada 144, Tromolpos 153, Singaraja 81113, Bali **E:** rri.singaraja@ yahoo.com - **FM:** 97.9/103.7/102.0 + 99.5 (Bukit Kutul)
BB01) Jl Jend Ahmad Yani, Sungai Liat 33211, Bangka, Bangka Belitung - **FM:** 96.4/101.4/97.2 + 90.4 (Toboali), 95.4 (Mentok), 95.5 (Tanjung Pandan), 99.8 (Pangkalpinang)
BE01) Jl Let Jend S Parman 25, Kotak Pos 13, Bengkulu 38227, Bengkulu - **FM:** 92.5/105.1/90.9 + 95.4 (Muko-Muko), 97.0 (Bintuhan), 98.0 (Curup), 101.3 (Ipuh)
GO01) Jl Jenderal Sudirman 30, Gorontalo 96128, Gorontalo **E:** layanan@rrigorontalo.com - **FM:** 101.8/92.4/96.7 + 92.5 (Baroko), 94.9 (Paguyaman), 97.0 (Marisa)
JA01) Jl Jendral A Yani 5, Telanaipura, Jambi 36122, Jambi **E:** rrijambi@rri.co.id - **FM:** 88.5/90.9/94.4 + 95.8 (Bangko), 99.0 (Kualatungkal), 99.0 (Sarolangun), 99.8/101.0 (Sungai Penuh), 99.8 (Tungkal Ilir), 101.0 (Muara Bungo)
JB01) Jl Diponegoro 61, Bandung 40122 (Kotak Pos 1055, Bandung 40001), Jawa Barat - **FM:** 97.6/96.0 + 95.0 (Gunung Malang), 97.0 (Purwakarta/Subang), 97.8 (Tasikmalaya), 98.0 (Bayah), 98.2 (Puncak Surangga), 98.9 (Saketi), 102.5 (Cikuray), 103.3 (Garut) – **JB02)** Jl Pangrango 30, P.O Box 232, Bogor 16161, Jawa Barat - **FM:** 93.7/106.8 – **JB03)** Jl Brigjen Dharsono/By Pass, Cirebon 45132, Jawa Barat **E:** rricirebon@rricirebon.info - **FM:** 93.7/94.8/97.5
JH01) Jl Ahmad Yani 144-146, Kotak Pos 1307, Semarang 50241, Jawa Tengah - **FM:** 89.0/95.3/88.2/91.4 + 94.2 (Colo), 96.7 (Batang), 97.7 (Gunung Gantungan), 99.4 (Gunung Depok), 99.5 (Gunung Periksa) – **JH02)** Jl Abdul Rahman Saleh 51, Kotak Pos 40, Surakarta 57133, Jawa Tengah - **FM:** 105.5/97.0/95.1 + 96.3/102.0 (Tawangmangu) – **JH03)** Jl Jendral Sudirman 427, Kotak Pos 5, Purwokerto 53116, Jawa Tengah - **FM:** 93.1/99.0/107.3
JK01) Jl Medan Merdeka Barat 4-5, Jakarta 10110 (Tromolpos 1157, Jakarta 10001).
JT01) Jl Pemuda 82-90, Kotak Pos 239, Surabaya 60271, Jawa Timur - **FM:** 99.2/95.2/106.3 + 91.1 (Cemoro Lawang), 97.9 (Pacitan), 99.2 (Alas Malang), 99.2 (Pare),102.3 (Pulau Bawean) – **JT02)** Jl Candi Panggung 58, Kotak Pos 78, Mojolangu, Malang 65142, Jawa Timur - **FM:** 94.6/99.4/105.3/91.9 – **JT03)** Jl D.I Panjaitan 61, Jember 68110 (Kotak Pos 166, Jember 68101), Jawa Timur - **FM:** 95.4/89.5/87.9 – **JT04)** Jl Imam Bonjol 12, Madiun 63133, Jawa Timur **E:** info@rrimadiun.net - **FM:** 99.7/97.7/104.0 + 96.3 (Kemiri) – **JT05)** Jl Urip Sumoharjo 26, Sumenep 69411, Madura, Jawa Timur - **FM:** 98.5/101.3/103.0 – **JT06)** RRI Sampang, Jl Peliang Km 2, Torjun, Sampang, Madura, Jawa Timur - **FM:** 93.1
KB01) Jl Jendral Sudirman 7, Kotak Pos 6, Pontianak 78111, Kalimantan Barat - **FM:** 104.2/101.8/90.3 + 95.0 (Nangamerakai), 96.8 (Ketapang),

97.0 (Sanggau), 97.7 (Sambas), 97.7 (Singkawang), 98.0 (Kendawangan), 98.2 (Semitau), 99.3 (Sanggau Ledo), 100.2 (Balaikarangan) – **KB02)** RRI Sintang, Jl Oevang Oeraya, Baning, Sintang, Kalimantan Barat - **FM**: 96.6/90.7/102.5 – **KB03)** RRI Entikong, Jl Lintas Negara Indonesia-Malaysia, Entikong – Sanggau, Kalimantan Barat - **FM**: 100.2

KH01) Jl M Husni Thamrin 1, Palangkaraya 73112, Kalimantan Tengah - **FM**: 89.2/92.4/95.9 + 93.6 (Kuala Kapuas), 93.6 (Sampit), 96.0 (Muara Teweh), 97.1 (Pulang Pisau), 97.3 (Buntok), 99.2 (Pangkalan Bun)

KR01) Jl Ahmad Yani Km 4, Kotak Pos 8, Tanjung Pinang 29133, Bintan, Kepulauan Riau - **E:** pro3tanjungpinang@gmail.com - **FM:** 98.3/92.2/101.3 + 90.9 (Batam), 96.6 (Karimun), 99.6 (Tarempa) – **KR02)** RRI Ranai, Jl Sepempang, Ranai, Pulau Natuna Besar 29183, Kepulauan Riau - **FM:** 90.0/105.9/104.0 – **KR03)** RRI Batam, Jl. Park Way, Gedung Sumatra Expo Lantai III Batam Centre, Batam, Kepulauan Riau E: rri.batam@yahoo.co.id - **FM:** 105.1/105.5 (Pro 3)

KS01) Jl Jenderal A. Yani Km 3.5 No 234, Kotak Pos 117, Banjarmasin 70234, Kalimantan Selatan - **FM:** 97.6/95.2/92.5/87.7 + 89.4 (Batu Licin), 90.2 (Kotabaru), 94.0 (Amuntai), 105.7 (Kandangan)

KT01) Jl Moh Yamin 8, P.O Box 45, Samarinda 75110, Kalimantan Timur **E:** layananusaha@gmail.com - **FM:** 97.6/88.5/98.4 + 95.5 (Pulau Sebatik), 96.0 (Penajam), 96.7 (Berau), 96.8 (Tanah Grogot), 97.0 (Balikpapan), 97.4 (Melak), 97.4 (Bontang/Sangata), 99.0 (Tenggarong) – **KT02)** Jl Sungai Mahakam 10, Kampung Empat, Tarakan Timur 77125, Kalimantan Timur - **FM:** 97.9/101.9/88.8 – **KT03)** RRI Malinau, Jl Pelajar Perumda II, Malinau, Kalimantan Timur - **FM:** 95.5 – **KT04)** RRI Nunukan, Jl TVRI 77, Nunukan, Kalimantan Timur - **FM:** 97.1 – **KT05)** RRI Sendawar, Jl D.I. Panjaitan 61, Dusun Busur, Kampung Barong Tongkok, Sendawar, Kalimantan Timur - **FM:** 103.3

LA01) Jl Gatot Subroto 26, Kotak Pos 24, Pahoman, Bandar Lampung 35213, Lampung **E:** rri_bdl@yahoo.com - **FM:** 90.9/92.5/87.7 + 95.8 (Kotabumi), 97.0 (Kota Agung), 99.0 (Simpang Pematang), 99.4 (Liwa), 99.7 (Padang Cermin), 100.2 (Tulungbawang).

MA01) Jl Jendral Akhmad Yani 1, Ambon 97124, Maluku - **FM:** 95.4/98.4/102.0 + 92.0 (Amahai/Masohi), 94.3 (Saumlaki) – **MA02)** Jl Sukarno-Hatta, Kec Wat Deh, Tual 97661, Pulau Kai, Maluku - **FM:** 93.2/97.6/103.6

MU01) Jl Sultan Khairun 2, Kedaton, Ternate 97720, Maluku Utara **E:** multimedia45@yahoo.com - **FM:** 101.8/96.7/104.1 + 92.8 (Pulau Morotai), 93.7 (Soasiu)

NB01) Komplek Perumahan RRI Mataram, Jl Majapahit, P.O Box 2, Mataram, Lombok, Nusa Tenggara Barat **E:** pro1mataram@gmail. com - **FM:** 89.2/104.2/93.4 + 89.1 (Dompu), 89.3 (Sumbawa Besar), 91.4 (Bima), 92.4 (Lombok Utara), 96.3 (Lombok Tengah), 97.9 (Lombok Timur)

NT01) Jl Tompello 8, Kupang 85225, Timor, Nusa Tenggara Timur - FM: 94.4/90.0/101.9 + 88.8 (Soe), 90.7 (Kefamenanu) – **NT02)** Jl Durian, Ende 86317, Flores, Nusa Tenggara Timur - **FM:** 100.5/104.8/92.2 – **NT03)** RRI Rote Ndao, Baa, Rote 85371, Nusa Tenggara Timur **E:** rripro3rotendao@gmail.com - **FM:** 93.3 – **NT04)** RRI Atambua, Komplek Kantor Bupati Belu, Jl Eltari 1, Atambua, Timor, Nusa Tenggara Timur - **FM:** 91.5

PA01) Jl Tasangkapura 23, Kotak Pos 1077, Jayapura 99200, Papua - **FM:** 96.0/90.1/105.9/89.3 + 93.5 (Sentani), 94.5 (Timika), 96.5 (Sarmi), 96.7 (Sorendiweri), 100.0 (Genyem) – **PA02)** Jl Jendral Ahmad Yani 11, Mopa Baru, Merauke 99611 (Kotak Pos 111, Merauke 99601), Papua **E:** rrimerauke@gmail.com - **FM:** 90.0&95.4 (Pro-1)/98.1/105.0 – **PA03)** Jl Pattimura, Serui 98213, Papua - **FM:** 96.4/101.5/94.5 – **PA04)** Jl Majapahit, Kotak Pos 505, Biak 98117, Papua - **FM:** 96.9/95.3/95.8 + 96.3/97.6 (Numfor) – **PA05)** Jl Jendral A Yani 64, Wamena 99511 (Kotak Pos 10, Wamena 99501), Papua - **FM:** 97.1/96.3/94.7 – **PA06)** Jl Merdeka 74, Nabire 98811 (Kotak Pos 110, Nabire 98801), Papua - **FM:** 97.6/90.1/94.4 – **PA07)** RRI Boven Digul, Jl Trans Papua 17, Tanah Merah, Papua – **E:** rribovendigoel@yahoo.com - **FM:** 93.6 – **PA08)** RRI Oksibil, Jl. Perbukitan Okpol, Oksibil, Papua - **FM:** 90.0 – **PA09)** RRI Skow, Jl RRI Stasiun Perbatasan, Skow, Papua - **FM:** 98.3

PB01) Jl Merdeka 68, Manokwari 98311, Papua Barat - **FM:** 94.3/97.8/95.1 – **PB02)** Jl Kapt P Tendean, Kotak Pos 154, Fak-Fak 98612, Papua Barat **E:** rrifakfak@rri.co.id - **FM:** 97.2/99.0/93.15 + 98.1 (Kokas) – **PB03)** Jl Sam Ratulangi 4, Kotak Pos 146, Sorong 98414, Papua Barat - **FM:** 102.6/95.9/95.1 + 95.9 (Bintuni), 96.3 (Teminabuan) – **PB04)** RRI Kaimana, Jl Air Merah, Kaimana, Papua Barat - **FM:** 96.3

RI01) Jl Jend Sudirman 440, Kotak Pos 51, Pekanbaru 28115, Riau **E:** admin@rripekanbaru.com - **FM:** 99.1/88.4/91.2/93.9 + 92.6 (Pasir Pangaraian), 93.0 (Dumai), 94.7 (Selat Panjang), 96.5 (Sei Pakning), 98.5 (Baserah), 99.3 (Tembilahan), 99.9 (Siak)

SB01) Jl Jendral Sudirman 12, Kotak Pos 77, Padang 25124, Sumatera Barat **E:** rripadang@rri.co.id - **FM:** 97.5/90.8/88.4 + 88.4 (Pandai Sikek Padang Pariaman), 89.5 (Bukit Gompong Solok), 92.0 (Bungkit Palakat), 96.0 (Lubuk Sikaping), 96.8 (Pasaman Barat), 97.9 (Bukit Langkisau Painan), 97.9 (Dharma Seraya), 98.5 (Mentawai) – **SB02)** Jl.Prof Muhammad Yamin 199, Kotak Pos 3, Aurkuning, Bukittinggi

26131, Sumatera Barat - **FM:** 94.8/97.2/90.5 – **SB03)** RRI Pariaman, Jl Diponegoro 48, Pariaman, Sumatera Barat - **FM:** 97.1

SG01) Jl Laute Mandonga 44, Kotak Pos 7, Kendari 93111, Sulawesi Tenggara **E:** rrikdi@gmail.com - **FM:** 96.7/90.8/91.6 + 93.5 (Boepinang), 97.0 (Raha), 99.4 (Bau-Bau), 99.5 (Lasolo)

SH01) Jl R.A Kartini 39, Palu 94112, Sulawesi Tengah - **FM:** 90.8/105.0/92.4 + 95.4 (Ampana), 95.5 (Tanjung Santigi), 96.0 (Banggai), 96.2 (Poso), 97.1 (Toboli), 99.2 (Luwuk) – **SH02)** Jl Jenderal Sudirman, Tolitoli 94514, Sulawesi Tengah - **FM:** 102.0/90.2/94.5 – **SH03)** RRI Ampana, Jl Tanjungulu Tojo Una-Una, Ampana, Sulawesi Tengah - **FM:** 93.0

SL01) Jl Riburane 3, Kotak Pos 103, Makassar 90111, Sulawesi Selatan.- **FM:** 94.4/96.8/106.3/92.9 + 90.6 (Bontu Tabang), 94.0 (Baraka), 96.0 (Mamuju), 99.0 (Parepare), 99.0 (Bantaeng)

SS01) Jl Radio 2 Km 4, Palembang 30128, Sumatera Selatan **E:** rripalembang@yahoo.co.id - **FM:** 92.4/91.6/91.7/88.4 + 90.3 (Sekayu), 90.5 (Baturaja), 90.5 (Pagar Alam), 95.1 (Lubuklinggau), 97.7 (Prabumulih), 99.9 (Muara Enim)

ST01) Jl Radio 1, Kotak Pos 1110, Tikala Ares, Manado 95124, Sulawesi Utara - **FM:** 94.5/97.7/104.4/99.9 + 92.0 (Lirung), 92.5 (Buroko), 98.1 (Tondano), 99.5 (Melonguane Pro-3) – **ST02)** Jl Tona, Tahuna, Sangihe, Sulawesi Utara - **FM:** 98.7/92.0/105.4

SU01) Jl Jend Gatot Subroto Km 5.6, Medan 20123, Sumatera Utara - **FM:** 94.3/92.4/88.8 + 90.0 (Natal), 90.3 (Teluk Dalam), 90.6 (Rantau Prapat), 91.9 (Kotanopan), 92.0 (Prapat), 92.0 (Sidikalang), 94.5 (Simar Jarunjung), 96.1 (Pematang Siantar), 96.3 (Tarutung), 99.1 (Sibuhan), 99.3 (Pulau Raja) – **SU02)** Jl Ade Irma Suryani Nasution 11, Sibolga 22513, Sumatera Utara - **FM:** 97.2/94.8/103.1 + 99.9 (Padangsidempuan) – **SU03)** RRI Gunungsitoli, Desa Iraonogeba, Gunungsitoli, Nias, Sumatera Utara - **FM:** 96.2/101.3/90.3

YG01) Jl Ahmad Jazuli 4, Tromolpos 18, Kotabaru, Yogyakarta 55224, Daerah Istimewa Yogyakarta - **FM:** 91.1/102.5/102.9

FEDERATION OF INDONESIAN NATIONAL COMMERCIAL BROADCASTERS (Persatuan Radio Siaran Swasta Nasional Indonesia)

✆ Pengurus Pusat, Persatuan Radio Siaran Swasta Nasional Indonesia, Jl. Raya Pondok Gede 96, Jakarta 13810 ☎ +62 21 8414311 🖷 +62 21 8414314 **W:** www.radioprssni.com **E:** radioprssni@ radioprssni.com or ppjkt @indosat.net.id **LP:** Chmn: Shidki Wahab. **PRSSNI** has 758 members. Commercial station permitted power: 1kW (MW) and 10kW (FM).

LOCAL PUBLIC BROADCASTING STATIONS (Lembaga Penyiaran Publik Lokal)

Local government stations have made the transition to local government owned but autonomous public broadcasters. As a result, the names of former local government radio stations (Radio Siaran Pemerintah Daerah) have been changed. Where occasionally still referred to, these station headings apply: **RKIP:** Radio Khusus Informasi Pertanian – **RKPD:** Radio Khusus Pemerintah Daerah – **RPD:** Radio Pemerintah Daerah – **RPD Kotamadya:** Radio Pemerintah Daerah Kotamadya (only intended for particular cities) – **RPK:** Radio Pemerintah Kabupaten – **RSPD:** Radio Siaran Pemerintah Daerah – **RSPK:** Radio Siaran Pemerintah Kabupaten.

INDONESIAN COMMUNITY RADIO NETWORK (Jaringan Radio Komunitas Indonesia)

✆ Sekretariat, Jaringan Radio Komunitas Indonesia, Jl Dwi Sri 10, Bandung, Jawa Barat ☎ +62 22 5224205 **W:** http://jrki.wordpress. com **E:** suara.jrki@gmail.com or jrk_kongres04@yahoo.com **LP:** Chmn: Bowo Usodo.
The majority of community stns operate from 107.7 to 108.0 MHz. Maximum power is 50 Watts.

MW	kHz	kW	Station, location
BN01)	531		R. Palanta, Tangerang
JB04)	549		Inyong R., Depok
JH04)	558	0.5	R. Diantara Vita Kharisma (D.V.K.), Kebumen
BN07)	v576		R. Hutama Buana Suara (HBS), Ciledug
JK03)	v594		R. Sekuntum Bunga Yonina (SBY), Jakarta
NB02)	612		R. Yayasan Attohiriyah Alfadiliyah (R. Yatofa), Bodak-Praya
SS02)	612		R. Swara Betung Indah, Betung-Musi Banyuasin
KB04)	621		R. Kijang Berantai (Kiber) Perkasa, Sambas
JK04)	630	1	R. Samhan, Jakarta
JH05)	648		R. Santo Bernadus D.S., Pekalongan
JH06)	648		R. Roro Djonggrang B.S., Prambanan*
JH07)	‡648		R. Aji Satria, Ajibarang
JK05)	648		R. Rahmat Emmanuel Ministries (REM), Jakarta
JH08)	666	0.25	R. Ramakusala (R. Rama Solo), Surakarta

MW	kHz	kW	Station, location
JH09)	666		R. Tunggul Suara Dirgantara, Purbalingga
JK06)	684		Charismatic R. (C R.), Jakarta
JT07)	±693		R. Canda Bhirawa (R. CB, RSPD Kediri), Kediri
JB05)	‡702		R. Bravo, Bandung
JK07)	702		R. Tona, Jakarta
PA10)	702		R. Suara Kasih Agung, Jayapura
YG02)	702		R. Suara Konco Tani, Sidokarto
JB06)	720		R. Silaturahim, Cibubur
JH10)	720	0.25	R. Lusiana Namberwan (R. Silaturahim), Semarang
JH11)	720		R. Gagah Sehat Berbobot (Gasebo), Majenang
NT05)	720		RSPD Sumba Timur, Waingapu
NB03)	‡729		R.Dewi Anjani, Selong
BN02)	738		R. Bharata Bhakti Nusa, Tangerang
JT08)	738		R. Suara Pamekasan Indah, Pamekasan
KB05)	738		R. Swara Pinohperkasa, Sintang
NT06)	738		RSPD Timor Tengah Selatan, Soe
SL02)	738		R. Rina Bestari, Rantepao
JA02)	740		RSPD Batanghari, Muarabulian
NT07)	743	0.3	RPD Sumba Barat, Waikabubak
JB07)	756		R. Rodja, Cileungsi - Bogor
BN03)	774		R. Klasik Galih Lestari (Gless R.), Tangerang
JH12)	‡774	0.2	R. Leonardus Buana Suara, Salatiga
JT09)	774		R. Pesona 2000, Sumenep
JT010)	774		R. Suara Al Iman, Surabaya
SB04)	774	0.35	RSPD Kotamadya Payakumbuh
SL03)	774		R. Suara Adyafiri, Watansoppeng
YG03)	774		R. Swara Kenanga, Yogyakarta
KS02)	±783		R. Dakwah Masjid Raya Sabilal Muhtadin, Banjarmasin
JT11)	±790	0.5	R. Suara Jombang (RKPD Jombang), Jombang
JB08)	792		R. Swara Citra Cianjur Mandiri, Cianjur
JH13)	792		R. Bayu Sakti, Kroya
JK08)	792	1	R. As Syati'iyah, Jakarta
NB04)	792		R. Mitra Idola Kita, Pancor
SS03)	792		R. Suara Ria Jaya Sentosa (S.R.J.S.), Baturaja
JB09)	810		RSPD Kabupaten Bandung (R. Kandaga)
JH14)	810		R. Suara Maung Sakti, Banjarnegara
JK09)	‡810		R. Universitas Mercu Buana, Jakarta
SL04)	810		R. Megapesona, Enrekang
JH15)	819		R. Pancabayu Madugondo (Suara R.P.M.), Sukoharjo
BA03)	828		R. Suara Yudha, Denpasar
JB10)	828	0.25	R. Leidya Swara Utama (R. Kharisma), Bandung
JB11)	828		R. Adhika Pariwara, Pelabuhanratu
JK10)	828		R. Berita Klasik (RBK), Jakarta
KB06)	828		R. Mahkota Ngabang Gemaswara, Ngabang
SL05)	828		R. Swara Christy Ria, Makassar
YG04)	828		R. Suara Parangtritis, Parangtritis
JA03)	837		R. Kelapa Indah (R. KIN), Tanjung Jabung Barat
JK11)	837		R. Muslim Jakarta, Jakarta
JH16)	846		R. Swara Anggada Senatama, Purbalingga
JH17)	846		R. Suara Tegal Agung Raya (Star), Tegal
JT12)	846	0.5	RKPD Ponorogo (R. Suara Ponorogo)
JT13)	846		R. Miniwatt Pesona Indah, Surabaya
JK12)	864		R. Hana Citra Swara Jakarta (Suara Jakarta), Jakarta
SL06)	864		Suara AsAdiyah, Sengkang
YG05)	864		R. Gemma Satunama, Gunung Kidul
JH18)	873	0.5	R. Buana Asri (R. Publik Kabupaten Sragen), Sragen
JB12)	882		R. Suara Anggada Senatama (S.A.S.), Banjarsari
JK13)	882		R. Pelangi Nusantara, Jakarta
JH19)	882		R. Swara Kranggan Persada, Temanggung
SL07)	882	0.5	R. Bambapuang, Pangkajene
SR01)	882		RPK Majene
AC07)	900		R. Siaran Cempaka Nadacitra, Desa Tonjong
JA04)	900	0.25	R. Gema Nugraha, Sungai Penuh
JH20)	900		R. Bintoro Karya, Demak
JH21)	900		R. Suara Sendang Mas, Banyumas
JK14)	±900		R. Sindajaya, Jakarta
KB07)	900		R. Aries Sanggau Perkasa, Sanggau
SB05)	900		R. Elkartika Angkasa Niaga, Padang*
SU06)	±900		R. Aksi Bethany, Medan
JH22)	909		R. Blora Sakti (R.B.S.), Cepu - Blora
JB13)	918		R. Gema Nury (El Nury), Bogor
JB14)	‡918	1.5	R. Citra Wahana Indonesia (R. Debora), Bandung
JH23)	918		R. Suara Selomanik (R.S.S.), Banjarnegara
JH24)	936		R. Kelana Sumbangsihku (Kasihku), Bumiayu
JK15)	936	0.25	R. Puspa Dwi Swara Cipta (P2SC), Jakarta
JH25)	945		R. Swara Buana Asri, Wonosobo
SB06)	945		R. Galundi Pradana, Gando Sulit Air
SU07)	945		R. Tuah Swara Murni, Lubukpakam
BN08)	±954		R. Benda Baru (RBB), Pamulang, Tangerang
JT14)	954	0.25	R. El Bayu, Gresik
SS04)	954	0.15	R. Garuda Kenten Jaya (Bazz R., Islamic R. Palembang), Palembang
BN04)	972		R. Pusako Minangkabau, Tangerang
JT15)	‡972		R. Suara Harmoni, Situbondo
JB15)	990		R. Samhan Mulya, Sumedang
JH26)	990		R. Gita Lestari, Brebes
JH27)	990		R. Pesona Bahari, Weleri
KS03)	990		R. Bahana Al-Mursyidul Amin, Martapura
SR02)	990		R. Suara Sawerigading, Wonomulyo
KB08)	1008		R. Suara Pemangkat, Pemangkat
BA04)	1023		R. Diva, Denpasar
NT08)	1024	0.25	RPD Belu, Atambua
AC08)	1026		R. Gema Cakrawala Utama, Kuala Simpang
JK16)	‡1026		Suara Multazam, Jakarta Utara
SS05)	1026		R. Suara Enim Jaya Perkasa (En-J), Muara Enim
JB16)	1029	0.5	RPK Ciamis
NT09)	1034		RSPK Ngada, Bajawa
JB17)	1044		R. Duta Angkasa, Pangandaran
JB18)	‡1044		R. Iima Swara Mandiri (Purnayudha), Bekasi
KB09)	‡1044		R. Ramagentara, Sungai Pinyuh
AC09)	1050		RPD Aceh Timur, Langsa
JH28)	1062		R. P.T.D.I. Unisa 205, Semarang
JK17)	±1062	0.25	R. Cendrawasih Pusat, Jakarta
JT16)	1062	1	R. Sangkakala, Surabaya
PA11)	±1062		R. Swara Lembah Baliem, Wamena
SS06)	1062		R. Suara PGRI, Palembang
SU08)	1062		R. Tembang Perbaungan Indah, Perbaungan
JT17)	1071		RKPD Pacitan (Suara Pacitan)
JK18)	1080		R. JIC (Islamic R.) Jakarta
KH02)	1080		R. Bahana Nusantara, Ampah
KH03)	1080		R. Citra Barito, Muarateweh
SG02)	1080		R. Gema Gersamata, Kolaka
SL08)	1080		R. Suara Viktori, Makassar
JK19)	1098		R. Media Mahasiswa Tarumanegara, Jakarta*
BN05)	1107		R. Swara Mitra, Tangerang
JB19)	±1116		R. Adhika Swara (R. Alawiyah), Bekasi
JB20)	1116	1	R. Barani, Bandung
SL09)	1116		R. Mitra Bayu Suara Utari, Bantaeng
SS07)	1116		R. Dian Bahagia Sentosa, Prabumulih Barat
JT18)	±1117	0.25	R. Carolina Arjuno, Surabaya
SL10)	1125	0.25	RPD Luwu, Palopo
JK20)	1134		R. Swara Mega Asri (R. Safari), Jakarta
JH29)	±1143		R. Swara Delanggu (Swadesi), Delanggu
JB21)	1152		R. Rama Sutra, Sukamandi-Subang
JK21)	1152		R. Musik Asik Nusantara (R. Muara), Jakarta
JT19)	1152		R. Yasmara, Surabaya
YG07)	1152		R. Suara Istana, Yogyakarta
BE02)	1160		R. Ratu Anda Swara, Argamakmur
AC10)	1170		R. Kazuma Bawana Swara, Lhokseumawe
JB22)	±1170		R. Dios (R. Paksi), Bandung
JT20)	‡1170		R. Rajawali, Surabaya
PA12)	1170		R. Suara Nusa Bahagia, Jayapura
SR03)	±1170		R. Lariang Indah, Mamuju
JH30)	±1180	0.5	RSPD Wonogiri
JB23)	1188		R. Duta Swara Parahyangan (DSP), Bekasi
JH31)	1188		R. Suara Ayukarya Banjaran Adiwerna (RSA-Abadi), Tegal
JT21)	1188		R. Swara Perak Jaya P.T.D.I., Surabaya
AC11)	1206		R. Geunta Suara, Geudong
SB07)	1206		R. Suara Dikara Bawana (Dirgan Bravo), Padang
JH32)	±1213	0.25	R. Suara Perwira (RSPK Purbalingga), Purbalingga
JH33)	1224		R. Angkasa Bahana Citra (A.B.C.), Purbalingga
JH34)	1224		R. Suara Sendang Mas (RSPD Banyumas), Purwokerto
SL11)	±1242		R. Suara Bulusaraung, Pangkep
YG06)	1251		R. Edukasi, Yogyakarta
JB24)	1260		R. Suara Pekerja (SP), Bekasi
JH35)	1260		R. P.T.D.I. Suara Kaliwungu Dirgantara, Kaliwungu
SB08)	1260		R. Gitamitra Suara Perdana, Lubuk Basung
SL12)	1260		R. Molina Indah Pesona, Sinjai
JT22)	1278		R. Antariksa Radang IV, Surabaya
PA13)	1278		R. Pikonane, Yahukimo
SU09)	‡1278		R. Cempaka Selaras Silindung, Tarutung
JH36)	1287		Java Radio Station, Semarang
KH04)	1296		R. Merak Jaya, Muarateweh
NB05)	‡1296	0.5	R. Duta Gita Bhyomantara Sinta Rama, Cakranegara

MW	kHz	kW	Station, location
JT23)	1304	0.5	RKPD Nganjuk
JB25)	1314		R. Mutiara, Bandung
JH37)	1314		Suara Sion Perdana, Karanganyar
JH38)	1314		R. Gema Sritanjung Mediatama (G.S.M.), Jatibarang
JT24)	1332		RKPD Ngawi (Suara Ngawi)
SG03)	‡1332		R. Suara Bhakti Nusantara, Bau-Bau
SH04)	1341		R. Bittara Indah, Tolitoli
JT25)	1350		R. Gelora Surabaya (RGS)
SS08)	1350		R. Baturaja Mutiara Wahana (B.M.W.), Baturaja
JB26)	‡1368		R. Suara Citra Aditama, Bekasi
SH05)	1386		R. Swara Maya Prastha, Poso
SS09)	1404		R. Puspa Irama, Belitang Oku
JT26)	1422		R. Perkasa Muda Agung (P.M.A.), Kraksaan
SU10)	‡1431		R. Buana Serdang, Dolok Masihul
BN06)	±1440		R. Edukasi, Tangerang
SH06)	1440		R. Setia Nada, Luwuk
JT27)	±1449	0.7	R. Pertanian Wonocolo, Surabaya
JB27)	1458		R. Fajri, Bandung
SH07)	1458	1	R. Kareme Nuvula (RPK Parigi Moutong), Parigi
JB28)	1475		RKDT Karawang (Studio Radio Daerah Pangkal Perjuangan)
JB29)	1476		R. Rodja Bandung, Bandung
PA14)	1476		R. Wagadei, Paniai
JK22)	±1490		R. Karya Bersama, Jakarta
ST03)	1494		R. Swara Kasih, Tahuna
SU11)	1494		R. Al Rona Bahana, Padangsidempuan*
KT06)	1512	0.25	R. Swara Mitra Dirgantara (Rasmira), Balikpapan
SS10)	1521		R. Suara Musijaya Pratama, Sekayu
JB30)	±1523		R. Swara Primadona Mahardika, Cikampek
JK23)	1530		R. Islam Sabili (R.I.S., Radio Dakta), Jakarta
JK24)	1584		R. Suara Kemang, Jakarta
KS04)	1584		Swara Al Karomah Pratama, Martapura

NB: ‡ = r. inactive or moved to FM ± = variable

EXTERNAL SERVICES: The Voice of Indonesia
see International Broadcasting section.

Addresses (Jl = Jalan)
AC00) NANGGROE ACEH DARUSSALAM (State of Aceh)
AC07) Jl Teuku Umar Km 10, Desa Tonjong, Lho'nga Leupeung 23353 – **AC08)** Jl Mayjen Sutomo 31, Kuala Simpang 24475 – **AC09)** Langsa – **AC10)** Jl Rel Kereta Api 14, Lhokseumawe 24310 – **AC11)** Jl Kreung Pase 12, Geudong, Lhokseumawe 24374.-
BA00) BALI
BA03) Jl Gunung Catur II Blok E/6, Denpasar 80117 – **BA04)** Jl Imam Bonjol, Gang Gunung Sabha 6, Banjar Abian Timbul, Denpasar 80119.
BE00) BENGKULU
BE02) Argamakmur, Bengkulu Utara.
BN00) BANTEN
BN01) Jl Gatot Subroto Km 8, Jatake, Tangerang – **BN02)** Jl Radeh Fatah, Perum Lembang Baru I/3, Ciledug, Tangerang 15151 – **BN03)** Jl Utama Ujung 334-350, Komplek P&K, RT005/05, Tangerang 15148 – **BN04)** Cipondoh, Tangerang – **BN05)** Tangerang – **BN06)** Pusat Teknologi Informasi dan Komunikasi (PUSTEKKOM), Departemen Pendidikan Nasional (DEPDIKNAS), Ciputat, Tangerang – **BN07)** Jl Raden Fatah, Perum. Lembang Baru I/3 , Ciledug, Tangerang 15151 – **BN08)** Benda Baru, Pamulang, Tangerang.
JA00) JAMBI
JA02) Jl.Gajah Mada, Muarabulian 36610 – **JA03)** Jl Panglima H Saman 297B, Kuala Tungkal, Tanjung Jabung Barat 36513 – **JA04)** Jl Yos Sudarso 55, Sungai Penuh, Kerinci.
JB00) JAWA BARAT (West Java)
JB04) Jl Perintis I, Kalimulya, Depok – **JB05)** Jl. Raya Batujajar 288, Bandung Barat 40561 – **JB06)** Jl Masjid Silaturahim 36, Kalimanggis, Cibubur, Bekasi – **JB07)** Masjid Al Barkah, Jl Pahlawan kp Tengah, Cileungsi - Bogor – **JB08)** Cianjur – **JB09)** Jl Adikusumah, Bale Endah, Dayeuh Kolot, Bandung – **JB10)** Jl Siliwangi 5, Bandung 40132 – **JB11)** Jl Siliwangi 103, Pelabuhanratu, Sukabumi 43164 – **JB12)** Jl Raya Barat 98, Banjarsari, Ciamis 46383 – **JB13)** Jl Raya Kedung Halang 2, Waru Jambu, Bogor 16710 – **JB14)** Jl Soekarno-Hatta 613B, Bandung 40257 – **JB15)** Jalan Raya Jatinagor 138, Sumedang 45363 – **JB16)** Jl Ir H Juanda 128, Ciamis 46211 – **JB17)** Jl Pramuka 653, Pangandaran, Ciamis – **JB18)** Jl Cendana 70, Bekasi 17100 – **JB19)** Jl Raya Jatiwaringin 50, Bekasi 17411– **JB20)** Jl Raya Cinunuk 84, Cileunyi, Bandung 40393 – **JB21)** Jl A Yani 56, Ciasem, Sukamandi-Subang – **JB22)** ITC Kosambi Blok G-16 Lt I, Jl Baranangsiang, Bandung 40112 – **JB23)** Bekasi – **JB24)** Jl Ahmad Yani 1, Bekasi – **JB25)** Jl Cikamiri 7, Cisadea, Bandung – **JB26)** Tambun Selatan, Bekasi – **JB27)** Jl Sukajadi Atas (Belakang) 227, Bandung – **JB28)** Jl Siswa 56, Cikampek, Karawang 41373 – **JB29)** Masjid Umar Ibnul

Khatab, Desa Selacau RT 02/05, Lembur Tengah, Batujajar, Bandung Barat 40561 – **JB30)** Jalan Brigpol Nasuha 2, Karawang.
JH00) JAWA TENGAH (Central Java)
JH04) Jl Kutoarjo 60, Kebumen 54312 – **JH05)** Jl Barito 4, Pekalongan 51116 – **JH06)** Jl Pamukti Baru 9, Prambanan, Klaten 57454 – **JH07)** Jl Pancurendang 26, Ajibarang, Banyumas 53163 – **JH08)** Jl Purworejo VI/10, Surakarta – **JH09)** Jl Mayjen Sungkono 89, Purbalingga – **JH10)** Jl Raung 7, Candi Baru, Semarang – **JH11)** Jl Pang Diponegoro 18, Majenang, Cilacap 53257 – **JH12)** Jl Kemuning 30, P.O Box 48, Salatiga 50724 – **JH13)** Jl Kendeng (Pesayangan) 55, Kroya, Cilacap – **JH14)** Jl Letjend S Parman 28, Banjarnegara – **JH15)** Jl Madugondo 15, Grogol, Sukoharjo 57552 – **JH16)** Jl Raya Barat 99, Banjarsari, Purbalingga – **JH17)** Jl Raya Kramat Km 7, Tegal 52181 – **JH18)** Jl Veteran 21, Sragen 57211 – **JH19)** Jl Kanjengen C-308, Kranggan, Temanggung 56271 – **JH20)** Jl Kyai Jebat 1, Demak – **JH21)** Jl Kompleks Kawedanan Lama 296, Banyumas 53192 – **JH22)** Jl Pemuda 55, Cepu, Blora 58312 – **JH23)** Jl D.I Panjaitan 3, Banjarnegara 53415 – **JH24)** Jl Pasar Hewan 75, Bumiayu 52273 – **JH25)** Jl Raya Kertek-Kalikajar 33, Wonosobo 56311 – **JH26)** Jl Pesantren 19, Ketanggungan, Brebes 52263 – **JH27)** Jl Bahari 325, Weleri, Kendal 51355 – **JH28)** Yayasan Badan Wakaf Sultan Agung (YBWSA), Universitas Islam Sultan Agung, Jl Raya Kaligawe Km 4, Semarang 50012 – **JH29)** Jl Raya Delanggu Utara 53, Delanggu, Klaten 57471 – **JH30)** Komplek Perluasan Kota, Jl Plongkowati, Wonogiri – **JH31)** Jl Raya Banjaran 34B, Adiwerna, Tegal 52194 – **JH32)** Jl Jend. Sudirman 131, Purbalingga – **JH33)** Jl Kapt Mulyadi 117, Surakarta 57113 – **JH34)** Jl Komplek Kewedanan Lama 296, Purwokerto 53192 – **JH35)** Jl Raya Kramat 1, Kaliwungu, Kendal 51372 – **JH36)** Semarang – **JH37)** Jl Dr Muwardi 47, Badranasri, Karanganyar 5771 – **JH38)** Jl Syah Alibahayar Salamah 2, Jatibarang, Brebes 52261.
JK00) JAKARTA
JK03) Jl Matraman 39, Jakarta – **JK04)** Jl Swadaya Raya 26/143, Raden Inten, Jakarta – **JK05)** Apartemen Robinson Lt 6, Jembatan Dua Raya 2, Jakarta – **JK06)** Jl Kwinii 1/B8, Senen Raya, Jakarta – **JK07)** Jl Bintaro Rosali IV/10, Bumi Pintaro Permai, Jakarta – **JK08)** Jl Masjid Al Barkah 17, Tebet, Jakarta Selatan – **JK09)** Universitas Mercu Buana, Meruya Selatan, Jakarta Barat – **JK10)** Jl Danau Agung II/5-7, Sunter Agung, Podomoro, Jakarta Utara 14350 – **JK11)** Jl. Sadar Raya 1, Jagakarsa, Ciganjur, Jakarta Selatan – **JK12)** Gedung AKA, Jl Bangka Raya 2, Kebayoran Baru, Jakarta Selatan 12720 – **JK13)** Gedung Sasana Kriya TMII Lantai 2, Jl Pondok Gede Arena Taman Mini Indonesia Indah, Jakarta Timur – **JK14)** Kampung Beting, Jakarta Utara – **JK15)** Jl Dakota V/1, Kemayoran, Jakarta 10630 – **JK16)** Gedung Auditorium (GLJU) Lantai 2, Jl Yos Sudarso 25-26, Kebon Bawang, Jakarta Utara 14320 – **JK17)** Jl Batu Ceper V/52, Jakarta Pusat 10120 – **JK18)** Jakarta Islamic Centre, Jl Kramat, Kroya, Jakarta 14260 – **JK19)** Jl Letjen S Parman 1, Jakarta Barat – **JK20)** Jl Bangka Raya 2, Kebayoran Baru, Jakarta Selatan 12720 – **JK21)** Jl Cipinang Timur 15, Rawamangun, Jakarta 13240 – **JK22)** Kemang, Jakarta – **JK23)** Graha Sabili, Jl Cipinang Cempedak II/11A, Polonia, Jakarta – **JK24)** Bungur, Kemang, Jakarta.
JT00) JAWA TIMUR (East Java)
JT07) Jl Panglima Besar Sudirman 141, Kediri – **JT08)** Jl P. Trunojoyo 222, Barurambat, Pamekasan 69313, Madura – **JT09)** Jl Yos Sudarso 173, Sumenep – **JT10)** Komplek STAI Ali Bin Abi Thalib, Jl Sitopo Kidul 51, Surabaya – **JT11)** Jl K.H. Wakhid Hasyim 133, Jombang 61419 – **JT12)** Jl Alun-Alun Utara 3, Ponorogo 63413 – **JT13)** Jl Dharmhusada Indah Blok A75, Surabaya 60285 – **JT14)** Jl Aipda Karel Sasuit Tubun 15, Gresik 61114 – **JT15)** Perum Panorama Indah I/3-9, Situbondo – **JT16)** Kompleks Manyar Indah Plaza, Jl Ngagel Jaya Selatan, Surabaya – **JT17)** Jl Jaksa Agung Suprapto 8, Pacitan 63512 – **JT18)** Jl Ngagel Jaya Utara IV/21, Surabaya 60283 – **JT19)** Jl Amir Hamzah 18, Surabaya 60241 – **JT20)** Jl Panglima Sudirman 72, Surabaya 60242 – **JT21)** Jl Teluk Aru 68, Surabaya 60165 – **JT22)** Jl Kusuma Bangsa 4, Surabaya 60241 – **JT23)** Jl Dr Sutomo 60, Nganjuk – **JT24)** Jl Teuku Umar 12, Ngawi – **JT25)** Humas Gelora 10 Nopember, Jl Tambaksari, Surabaya 60136 – **JT26)** Jl P Sudirman 62, Kraksaan, Probolinggo 67282 – **JT27)** Jl Ahmad Yani 112, Wonokromo, Surabaya.
KB00) KALIMANTAN BARAT (West Kalimantan)
KB04) Jl Raya Sambas Bukitluwing 1, Sambas 79162 – **KB05)** Jl Kelam Akcaya I/18, Sintang 78611 – **KB06)** Jl Raya Ngabang 72, Ngabang, Pontianak – **KB07)** Jl Kom Yos Sudarso 9, Sanggau 78582 – **KB08)** Jl Pembangunan RT 003/XIV, Desa Harapan, Pemangkat 79153 – **KB09)** Jl Pendidikan II, Sungai Pinyuh 78353.
KH00) KALIMANTAN TENGAH (Central Kalimantan)
KH02) Jl Pongsongteleng 47, Ampah 73652 – **KH03)** Jl Bangau 23, Muarateweh – **KH04)** Jl Merak 34, Muarateweh 73810.
KS00) KALIMANTAN SELATAN (South Kalimantan)
KS02) Jl Jend. Sudirman 1, Banjarmasin 70114 – **KS03)** Jl Barintik 35, P.O Box 48, Martapura 70613 – **KS04)** Jl Jend A Yani, Pesayangan Utara, Martapura 70619.

KT00) KALIMANTAN TIMUR (East Kalimantan)
KT06) Jl A Yani 50, Balikpapan 76123.-
NB00) NUSA TENGGARA BARAT (West Nusa Tenggara)
NB02) Bodak, Praya, Lombok – **NB03)** Jl Raya Labuhan Lombok, Kelayu, Selong 83613, Lombok – **NB04)** Jl Jend Sudirman 10, Pancor, Selong 83611, Lombok – **NB05)** Jl Miru 72, Cakranegara, Mataram 83511, Lombok.
NT00) NUSA TENGGARA TIMUR (East Nusa Tenggara)
NT05) Waingapu, Sumba – **NT06)** Soe, Timor – **NT07)** Waikabubak, Sumba – **NT08)** Jl Basuki Rahmat 2, Atambua 85711, Timor – **NT09)** Jl Sukarno-Hatta, Bajawa, Flores.
PA00) PAPUA (formerly Irian Jaya)
PA10) Jl Trikora 30 Lantai 2, Dok V, Jayapura – **PA11)** Jl Bhayangkara, Wamena – **PA12)** Jl Skyline, Jayapura – **PA13)** Anyelma, Kurima, Yahukimo – **PA14)** Enarotali, Paniai.
SB00) SUMATERA BARAT (West Sumatra)
SB04) Jl Jend Sudirman 18, Payakumbuh 26211 – **SB05)** Jl Sisingamangaraja 1, Padang 25122 – **SB06)** Jl Limo Singke Baringin, Gando Sulit Air, Solok – **SB07)** Jl W.R Mongonsidi 4B, Lantai 2, Padang – **SB08)** Lubuk Basung, Agam
SG00) SULAWESI TENGGARA (South-East Celebes)
SG02) Kompleks Baledante Indah Blok 19/16, Kolaka – **SG03)** Bau-Bau, Buton.
SH00) SULAWESI TENGAH (Central Celebes)
SH04) Jl Magamu 33, Tolitoli 94514 – **SH05)** Jl Pulau Kalimantan 45, Poso 94610 – **SH06)** Jl Jenderal Sudirman 128, Luwuk 94715, Banggai – **SH07)** Jl Toraraga 234, Parigi 94371.
SL00) SULAWESI SELATAN (South Celebes)
SL02) Jl Ratulangi 17, Rantepao 91831 – **SL03)** Jl Poros Cabenge 1, Watansoppeng – **SL04)** Jl Abubakar Lambogo 11, Enrekang 91711 – **SL05)** Jl Manggis 16, Makassar 90112 – **SL06)** Jl Mesjid Raya 100, Sengkang, Wayo 90914 – **SL07)** Jl Andi Naboang 1, Pangkajene – **SL08)** Kompleks Ruko Somba Opu Blok B/19, Tanjung Bunga - Makassar – **SL09)** Jl Gelatik 2, Kel Pallanting, Bantaeng 92411 – **SL10)** Jl Mangga 1, Palopo 91921 – **SL11)** Jl Sultan Hasanuddin 94, Pangkep – **SL12)** Jl K.H. Agus Salim 36, Sinjai 92612.
SR00) SULAWESI BARAT (West Celebes)
SR01) Jl Gatot Subroto 59, Majene – **SR02)** Jl. Brawijaya 7, Wonomulyo – **SR03)** Jl Pasar Sentral 48, Mamuju.
SS00) SUMATERA SELATAN (South Sumatra)
SS02) Jl Raya Betung 281, Betung, Musi Banyuasin – **SS03)** Jl Cut Nyak Din 3, Baturaja, OKU 32111 – **SS04)** Jl Dr M Isa 38, 8 Ilir, Palembang 30114 – **SS05)** Jl Pramuka I/15, Muara Enim – **SS06)** Universitas PGRI, Palembang –**SS07)** Jl Jend Sudirman 182/IV, Prabumulih Barat 31123 – **SS08)** Jl Mayor Iskandar 427, Baturaja – **SS09)** Jl Sakura 103, RT 04, Bedilan, Belitang 32182 – **SS10)** Jl Kol Wahid Udin 565, Lingkungan 7, Sekayu, Musi Banyuasin.
ST00) SULAWESI UTARA (North Celebes)
ST03) Manente, Tahuna, Kepulauan Sangihe.
SU00) SUMATERA UTARA (North Sumatra)
SU06) Jl Pabrik Tenun 102, Medan – **SU07)** Jl Galang 9, Lubukpakam 20510 –**SU08)** Jl Deli Gg Kereta Api 6, Perbaungan, Deli Serdang 20586 – **SU09)** Jl Kol Liberti Malau, Pasar Baru, Tarutung – **SU10)** Jl Besar 159, Dolok Masihul, Serdang Bedagai – **SU11)** Jl Kamboja 1, Padangsidempuan 22730.
YG00) DAERAH ISTIMEWA YOGYAKARTA (Yogyakarta Special Reg.)
YG02) Jl Godean Km 9, Dukuh Sidokarto Godean, Sleman – **YG03)** Jl Panti Wreda 5, Giwangan, Umbulharjo, Yogyakarta 55163 – **YG04)** Jl Parangtritis 22, Tegalsari RT46, Donotirto Kretek, Parangtritis 55772, Bantul – **YG05)** USC Satunama, Wiladeg, Gunung Kidul – **YG06)** Balai Pengembangan Media Radio, Pusat Teknologi Informasi dan Komunikasi Pendidikan, Departemen Pendidikan Nasional, Jl Sorowajan Baru 367, Banguntapan, Yogyakarta 55198 –**YG07)** Jl Puro Pakualaman, Yogyakarta 55122.

FM: A large number of FM stns operate throughout the country. See RRI address list for RRI FM freqs.
Jakarta area FM (MHz): 87.6 Antarnusa Jaya (Hard Rock) – 87.8 Bogor Swaratama (Sheba), Bogor – 88.0 Mustang Utama – 88.2 M2, Bekasi – 88.4 Arief Rahman Hakim (ARH/Global R.) – 88.6 Prestasi – 89.2 Metro Jaya Kartika (R. 68H/Green R.) – 89.4 Sipatahunan (RSPK Bogor), Bogor – 89.6 Mustika Abadi (I R.) – 90.0 Elshinta – 90.4 Muara Abdi Nusa (Cosmopolitan) – 90.6 Orentz, Bogor – 90.8 Suara Gema Pembangunan Utama (Oz R. Jakarta) – 91.6 Indika Millenia – 92.0 Sonora – 92.2 77 Radio Bogor – 92.4 Primaswara Adi Spirit Semesta (PAS/R. Bisnis Jakarta) – 93.0 Teman, Bogor – 93.2 Merpati Dharmawangsa (MD R.) – 93.4 Kancah Irama Suara Indonesia (KISI), Bogor – 93.6 Gema Wargakarya Satnawa (Gaya), Bekasi – 93.9 Swara Mersidiona (Mersi), Tangerang – 94.3 Gardia Asia Bumi (Woman) – 94.7 Agustina Yunior (U) – 94.9 DOS-Q, Bogor – 95.1 Kirana Indah Suara (KIS) – 95.3 Pertanian Ciawi, Bogor – 95.5 Siaran Alaikassalam Sejahtera (RAS) – 95.9 Smart Media Utama – 96.3 Pelita Kasih (RPK) – 96.7 Swara Rhadana Dunia (Rhadio A) – 97.1 Suara Monalisa (Dangdut Indonesia) – 97.5 Safari Bina Budaya (Motion) – 97.9 Bahana Sanada Dunia (Female), Tangerang – 98.1 One Center, Bekasi – 98.3 Cakrawala Gita Swara – 98.5 Islamic Centre Dakwah Al-Awwabin (Rida) , Depok– 98.7 Attahiriyah (Gen) – 99.1 Delta Insani – 99.3 Fajri, Bogor – 99.5 Kayumanis – 99.7 Nagaswara, Bogor – 99.9 Draba (Ninetyniners) – 100.1 Lesmana, Bogor – 100.3 Elgangga, Bekasi – 100.6 Jati Yaski Mandiri (Heartline), Tangerang – 100.8 Megaswara, Bogor – 101.0 Suara Irama Indah (Jak) – 101.4 Suara Kejayaan (Trax) – 101.8 Terik Matahari Bahana Pembangunan –102.0 Bahana Suara Alam (WADI), Bogor – 102.2 Prambors – 102.4 Media Akbar Zhapin (ZFM), Depok – 102.6 Camajaya Surya Nada – 102.8 Gema Annisa Persada, Cikarang-Bekasi – 103.0 Irnusa Ria, Depok – 103.2 Duta Swara Parahyangan, Bekasi – 103.4 Taman Mini (DFM) – 103.6 Swara Irama Kusuma Sena (Elpas), Bogor – 103.8 Pesona Gita Anindita (Brava) – 104.0 Forum 77 (8EH), Bekasi – 104.2 Media Suara Trisakti (MS-Tri) – 104.4 Swara Widya Sari (Puncak), Bogor – 104.6 Trijaya Sakti (Sindo R.) – 105.2 Mazmur – 105.4 Niaga Chakti Bhudi Bhakti (CBB) – 105.6 Suara Pendidikan Al-Ihya dan Insan Kamil, Bogor – 105.8 Ramako Jaya Raya (Lite) – 106.0 Bogor Madinatur (Mars), Bogor – 106.2 Bergaya Nyanyian Irama Sejati, Tangerang (Bens) – 106.4 R. Attaqwa FM, Bekasi – 106.6 Sabda Sosok Sohor (V Radio) – 107.0 Nada Komunikasi Utama (Dakta), Bekasi – 107.2 Cemerlang, Depok – 107.3 Suara Tunggal Angkasa Raya (Star), Tangerang – 107.5 Mitra Carita Enambelas, Depok (Music City / MC) – 107.7 Islamic R. – 107.7 UG, Depok – 107.7 Komunitas Institut Pertanian Bogor (Agri), Bogor – 107.9 Suara Sorak Kemenangan – 107.9 Telekomunikasi Cipta (UI FM), Depok – 107.9 Jalesviva Jayamahe (Suara Samudera).

Bandung FM (MHz): 87.7 Ekacita Swara Buana (Hard Rock FM) – 88.1 Swara Emas (SE) – 88.5 Mora Purna Karsa – 88.9 Hasil Era Reformasi (Auto Radio) – 89.3 Cipta Swara Global (Elshinta) – 89.7 Media Wisata Sariasih (Global R.) – 90.1 Karang Tumaritis (Zora) – 90.9 Lita Sari – 91.3 Manca Suara (Sindo R.) – 91.7 Citra Bahana Limbangan (CBL) – 92.1 Bandung Suara Indah (Mei Sheng) – 92.5 Madah Ekaristi Swaratronika (Maestro) – 92.9 Aruc Rizki (ARFM), Cimahi– 93.3 Ganesha Nada (Walagri) – 93.7 Paramuda – 94.1 Sanndy Qyu, Soreang – 94.4 Bandung Cipta Perdana (Delta FM) – 94.8 Galang Wahana Raya (Radio ON) – 95.2 Swara Pandawa Lima Shakti (Bandung R.) – 95.6 Suara Buriinyay (B Radio) – 96.4 Swaratama Cicalengka (Bobotoh) – 96.8 Nada Kencana Agung – 97.2 Shinta Buana – 98.0 Maya Nada – 98.4 Suara Sembilan Delapan Lima (Prambors) – 98.8 Candrika Widya Swara (Sonora) – 99.2 Manggala Gemini Bandung (Kids FM) – 99.6 Utamanda Suarakota (Dangdut Indonesia) – 100.0 Swara Milliard Artha (Ninety-Niners) – 100.4 Ilnafir Karanglayung Citra Budaya Suara (KLCBS) – 101.1 Swakarsa Megantara (MGT) – 101.5 Dahlia Flora – 101.9 Putramas Mulia Rahayu (Cosmo) – 102.3 Tiara Rase Perdana – 102.7 Madinatussalam Bandung (MQ) – 103.1 Mitragamma Swara (Oz FM) – 103.5 Citrahutama Eltravidya (Chevy) – 103.9 Antassalam Bagja – 104.3 Generasi Muda (U FM) – 104.7 Salam Rama Dwihasta – 105.1 Gema Dwipa – 105.5 Garuda Tunggal Angkasa – 105.9 Ardan Swaratama – 106.3 Bhakti Musik Wastukencana (Urban R) – 106.7 Mara Ghita – 107.1 Lintas Kontinental (K-Lite) – 107.5 Mustika Parahyangan (PR FM)

Batam FM (MHz): 87.6 Discovery Minang – 91.7 Aljabar Serumpun – 100.7 Ramako Batam (Batam FM) – 101.6 Matram Komersial Batam (Zoo FM) – 102.3 Kencana Ria Indah Suara (Kei FM) – 103.2 R. Juan FM – 104.3 Lintas Sei Ladi (Seila) – 104.7 Batam Indah Gelora Suara (BiGSFM) – 106.0 Hang FM – 106.5 Suara Marga Semesta (Sing FM) – 107.0 Be FM – 107.7 R. Alfa Omega – 107.9 R. Komunitas Hang Tuah FM

Denpasar (Bali) FM (MHz): 87.8 Baturiti Menara Swara (Hard Rock) – 89.4 Gema Sunari Indah – 89.8 Organik Lestari Sejahtera (Pak Oles), Tabanan – 90.2 Swara Sanathana Dharma* – 90.6 Gema Megantara Pratama (Megantara Bali), Tabanan – 91.0 Gita Bakti Persada (Phoenix) – 91.8 Flamboyant Bali Indah (FBI) – 92.2 Gema Megantara Pesona (Heartline) – 92.6 RPKD Denpasar – 93.0 Gita Semara Persada (GSP), Semarapura – 93.8 Suara Cakrawy, Semarapura – 94.5 Citra Dharma Bali Satya (CDBS) – 94.9 Click Gita Saraswati, Bangli – 96.1 Genta Suara Bali – 96.5 Swara Kinijani (Global), Tabanan – 96.9 Elang Kosa Gagana (Elkoga) – 97.3 Sonata Indah (Soni) – 97.7 Gema Merdeka – 98.1 Gia, Gianyar – 98.5 Plus, Sanur – 98.9 Bali Perkasa (Bali FM), Gianyar – 99.3 Duta Dewata (Duta Female) – 101.2 Bali Swara Mitragama (Oz), Kuta – 102.0 Suara Denpasar Chakti (Cassanova) – 102.4 Balina Citra (B), Bangli – 102.8 Menara – 103.2 Mega Nada, Tabanan – 103.6 Pinguin – 104.4 Aneka Rama (AR) – 104.8 R. Jegeg Bali, Gianyar – 105.2 Surya Permai (Storm FM) – 105.6 Bali Mandala

Perkasa, Gianyar – 106.0 Swara Kreasi Utama (Kuta R.), Kuta – 106.4 Gelora Gianyar (RPK Gianyar), Gianyar – 107.5 Suara Udayana – 107.5 YPG, Gianyar – 107.7 Komunitas Dwijendra – 107.9 Triatma, Kuta – 108.0 R. 108 MHz.

Surabaya FM (MHz): 87.7 R. Zodiac (Colors) – 88.1 Kota Buaya Mandiri – 88.5 Metro Gema Mega – 88.9 JT-FM (Smart FM)– 89.3 Surabaya Pesona Femina (Prambors) – 89.7 Hafini Jaya Mandiri (Hard Rock FM.) – 90.1 Media Caraka Angkasa – 90.5 Ampel Denta – 90.9 Global Nada Prima – 91.3 Suzana Suara Bhakti – 91.7 Suara Mitra – 92.5 Kreasi Indah Dunia Swara (Kosmonita) – 92.9 BFM – 93.3 Eka Laras Vicaksana Torya (El Victor) – 93.8 Shamsindo Indonusa (Sham FM) – 94.4 Suara Digital Indonesia(My Radio) – 94.8 Devina Jelita (DJ FM) – 96.0 Mercury Masa Depan Sukses – 96.4 Bahtera Yudha – 96.8 Delta FM – 97.2 Media Assalam Surabaya (SAS FM) – 97.6 Shinta Warga Gemilang (Elshinta) – 98.0 Salvatore Surabaya (Sonora) – 98.8 Kartika Bahari Dirgantara (M R.) – 99.6 Gitaya Gegana (She R.) – 100.0 Fiskaria Jaya Suara Surabaya – 100.4 Suara Masa Depan Cerah (MDC) – 101.1 Laras Pancar Istana Suara (Istara) – 101.5 Cakrawala Bhakti – 101.9 Stratosfir (Strato) – 102.7 Suara Mahasiswa Turun Bekerja (MTB) – 103.1Camar (Gen FM) – 103.5 Wijaya – 104.3 Bisnis Surabaya (PAS FM) – 104.7 Cakra Awigra (Sindo R.) – 105.1 Wahana Informasi Gemilang (JJ FM) – 105.9 Era Bimasakti Selaras (EBS) – 106.7 Merdeka Lokatama – 107.1 Nafiri – 107.5 Oxcy – 107.7 TOC FM (R. Spirit) – 107.9 Suara An-Nida

IRAN

L.T: UTC +3½h (22 Mar–21 Sept: +4½h) — **Pop:** 66 million — **Pr.L:** Farsi (Persian) — **E.C:** 50Hz, 230V — **ITU:** IRN

ISLAMIC REPUBLIC OF IRAN BROADCASTING (Gov.)
P O. Box 19395-333, Tehran. (Int. Tech. Affairs: P.O. Box 15875-4344, Tehran) ☎+98 21 2204 1093 ▤ +98 21 2222 1508
W: radio.ir **E:** radio@irib.ir
LP: President: Ezatollah Zarghami. DG: Gholamali Ramezani.

MW:

Prov & Location	kHz	kW	N	Prov & Location	kHz	kW	N
3 Azarshahr	531	500	I	32 Mahabad	882	60	R
24 Iranshahr	531	600	I	16 Yasuj/Dehdasht	891	50	R
29 Mashhad	540	200	I	25 Tehran	900	600	I
13 Sirjan	549	400	I	7 Lar	909	50	R
21 Gheslagh	558	1000	F	13 Jiroft	918	50	I
15 Mahshahr	576	750	R/E	18 Dorud	927	50	I
25 Tehran	585	600	Q	2 Urumiyeh	936	100	R
7 Shiraz (Dehnow)	594	400	R	17 Dehgolan	945	100	I
24 Zahedan	603	50	I	30 Birjand	963	50	I
29 Unknown loc.	603		R	12 Ilam	972	100	R
14 Qasr-e-Shirin	612	600	R	10 Hamadan	981	100	I
11 Bandar Abbas	621	50	R	7 Shiraz (Dehnow)	990	400	I
30 Birjand	621	200	R	17 Bam	999	50	R
3 Bonab	639	400	E	23 Semnan	1008	100	R
5 Shahr-e-Kord	648	50	I	11 Bandar Abbas	1017	50	I
8 Kiashahr	657	100	I	24 Zahedan	1017	50	I
24 Zahedan	657	100	I	3 Tabriz	1026	100	R
5 Shushtar	666	50	I	26 Yazd	1035	50	R
10 Hamadan	675	50	I	12 Dehloran	1044	50	I
29 Mashhad	684	100	R	18 Khorramabad	1053	100	I
11 Bandar Lengeh	693	100	R	24 Saravan	1053	25	I
4 Bushehr	702	100	I	13 Kerman	1062	200	I
8 Kiashahr	702	500	E	22 Qom	1071	100	M
15 Ahwaz	711	200	R	15 Mahshahr	1080	750	E
14 Mahidasht	720	750	R/E	23 Biarjmand	1089	50	R
29 Tayebad	720	400	R/E	24 Zabol	1098	200	E/I
4 Dayyer	738	50	R	29 Sabzevar	1107	50	R
9 Gonbad	747	150	I	26 Ardekan	1116	200	I
13 Kerman	747	100	R	21 Qazvin	1125	50	I
24 Chabahar	765	1000	E	3 Kalibar	1134	10	I
18 Sepid Dasht	765	200	R	7 unk. location	1134	50	R
19 Arak	774	100	R	28 Bojnurd	1134	50	I
24 Iranshahr	783	150	R	16 Yasuj	1143	50	I
27 Sohravard (Zanjan)	792	50	R	14 Qasr-e-Shirin	1161	600	E
29 Kashmar	801	50	R	22 Eshtehard	1170	400	I
5 Shahr-e-Kord	810	50	R	23 Damghan	1170	50	I
18 Khorramabad	810	100	R	9 Gonbad	1179	50	I
20 Sari	819	30	R	24 Chabahar	1179	50	I
26 Tabas	828	50	R	25 Tehran	1188	300	P
6 Habibabad	837	300	R	1 Moghan	1197	50	I
3 Mianeh	846	10	I	7 Dasht	1197	50	R
14 Qasr-e-Shirin	864	50	R	30 Unknown loc.	1206	50	I
20 Sari	873	100	R	20 Chalus	1215	50	R
28 Bojnurd	873	50	R	Unknown loc.	1224		I

Prov & Location	kHz	kW	N	Prov & Location	kHz	kW	N
13 Kerman	1224	400	E	17 Marivan	±1476	20	R
7 Abadeh	1233	50	I	2 Khoy	1485	10	R
27 Zanjan	1242	50	I	7 Jahrom	1485	10	R
8 Kiashahr	1251	100	I	15 Abadan	1485	10	R
6 Khur	1260	10	I	23 Damghan	1485	1	I
1 Khalkhal	1269	50	I	29 unknown loc.	1494		R
14 Kermanshah	1278	100	R	4 Bushehr	1503	200	I
7 Lar	1287	100	R	1 Ardabil	1512	50	I
24 Zabol	1296	50	R	26 Yazd	1530	50	I
4 Bushehr	1305	50	R	9 Gorgan	1539	50	R
1 Ardabil	1314	50	I	16 Gachsaran	1548	10	R
3 Jolfa	1323	50	R	17 Sanandaj	1548	10	I
25 Tehran	1332	300	T	20 Larijan	1548	10	R
13 Bam	1341	20	I	22 Eshtehard	1548	50	I
7 Darab	1359	50	I	30 Ferdows	1548	10	I
9 Gorgan	1368	100	R	24 Zabol	1557	50	I
24 Chabahar	1377	50	R	11 Bandar Abbas	1566	100	I
14 Paveh	1377	50	R	15 Abadan	1575	800	I
11 Hajiabad	1395	50	I	2 Maku	1584	10	I
7 Dasht	1404	10	I	23 Semnan	1584	–	R
7 Estahban	1413	10	I	15 Dezful	1602	1	R
6 Habibabad	1431	200	I	7 Estahban	1602	1	I
7 Lamerd	1431	50	R	7 Kazerun	1602	1	I
9 Bandar-e-Torkamen	1449	400	E	26 Bahabad	1602	1	I
30 Birjand	1458	50	R	23 Semnan	1602	10	R
22 Alborz	1467	100	R	± variable *inactive			

FM:

Pr. Location	I	R	Q	P	M	J	F	V/Tj
1 Ardabil	88.8	101.6	94.8	100.9	98.3	102.4	89.3	105.2
1 Khalkhal		94.4	99.2	90.1		103.9	95.8	94.0
2 Parsabad		92.4	92.8	106.5	98.0		99.3	
2 Khoy		95.0	93.8	98.2		101.8		
2 Maku	100.0	102.6		92.2	104.9			
2 Urumiyeh	106.5	91.1	106.1	95.8		92.6	102.6	99.1
2 Maragheh		94.7	95.3	101.5		98.0		
3 Tabriz	98.7	96.3	90.7	102.9	96.1	93.9	94.2	99.4
4 Bushehr	94.2	92.2	99.0	104.4	96.2		94.2	106.6
5 Ardal		106.9	99.8	93.2	90.2	96.5	103.2	
5 Ben			94.4	97.7	91.2			
5 Borujen		92.0	106.7	96.2	103.1	99.6	93.1	90.0
5 Farsan		99.5	94.5	98.5	100.5	106.5		92.5
5 Lordegan	90.8		100.0	95.8	102.6	91.2		95.8
5 Saman		98.8		89.3	95.5	92.3	102.3	105.9
5 Shahr-e-Kord	97.1	90.0	96.0	104.3	93.6	98.0	87.6	
5 Shalamzar		88.2		97.8	101.3	94.5	91.3	104.9
6 Fereydunshahr	101.8	108.0			96.6		93.3	103.3
6 Golpayegan	106.0			93.8			97.0	107.2
6 Isfahan		88.1	96.8	107.2	88.5	96.8		98.6
6 Kashan	98.0	101.1	102.8		105.5			96.8
6 Khonsar			99.3	107.3	102.8		106.0	
6 Nain	98.1			93.3	92.8		91.1	
6 Semirom	99.0	105.6		90.8	102.0		93.8	
7 Marvdasht			96.2		93.0		99.5	107.3
8 Shiraz	88.3	94.7	95.6	93.7	107.3	96.0	91.6	96.5
8 Rasht	98.5	92.5	101.3	104.9	104.1	91.3	106.0	107.7
8 Rudbar	91.8		97.6	108.0	91.8			
9 Gorgan		97.5	96.8	91.0	101.0	103.6	97.5	94.2
10 Hamadan	96.0	101.4	91.4	97.8	103.7	90.0	106.1	88.4
10 Malayer		96.1	96.3	93.1				96.0
10 Nahavand		94.2	94.7	101.0		101.7		
11 Band Jask		105.0	100.7		94.6	88.3	91.4	97.9
11 Bandar Abbas	93.4	97.0	90.1	99.7	95.2	94.2	104.6	105.6
11 Hajiabad		98.0	101.5	105.1	94.7	88.4	91.5	
11 Kish Island	103.9			89.9			107.1	
11 Parsian		96.3	104.6	107.8	94.3			
12 Dehloran	100.7	102.9			94.7		101.4	
12 Ilam	92.1	106.1	105.0	95.3	100.0	93.5	98.6	102.1
12 Malekshahy	98.6	104.3	95.7	96.8	92.5			
13 Jiroft			103.2	96.4	99.7		94.5	
13 Kerman	92.8	90.2	96.3	96.5	93.9	93.9	95.1	99.8
13 Sirjan			90.7	100.7	104.3		97.2	
13 Zarand			103.5	93.3	93.5		101.1	
14 Kermanshah			106.9	93.3	90.2	93.0	99.8	103.3
15 Abadan	89.7	98.8	107.6	87.6	104.5		106.4	93.8
15 Ahwaz	106.0	93.3	103.0	93.7	99.9	90.0	99.6	107.4
15 Dezful			104.2	103.0	107.3		93.7	
15 Masjed Soleiman			105.4	97.5	104.5		99.3	
16 Yasuj	97.7	100.0	106.5	96.1	89.8	99.4	92.9	102.9
17 Baneh	107.0		93.2	99.7		96.4	103.2	
17 Bijar			100.2	90.6	103.7	96.9	107.3	93.7
17 Dehgolan		95.2			100.0	102.0	98.5	
17 Divandareh	90.0		93.5	103.5		96.7	100.0	
17 Kamyaran	87.5		93.0	99.5		96.2	103.0	

Pr.	Location	I	R	Q	P	M	J	F	V/Tj
17	Marivan	93.5		95.7	102.5		99.0		92.5
17	Qorveh			102.8		96.0	92.8	99.3	
17	Sanandaj	89.4	97.1	95.7	92.5		102.5	99.0	106.1
17	Saqez	106.1		92.5	99.2		95.7	102.5	
18	Sarvabad			92.9	106.5		100.2	99.4	89.8
18	Borujerd	89.3	92.9	94.9	89.0	98.2		93.6	
18	Khorramabad			93.2	91.0	101.0	100.1	94.2	
18	Kuhdasht			106.2	94.6	102.6		92.4	
19	Arak	90.1	88.5	99.7	105.8	93.2		106.8	96.4
19	Ashtian	101.0		97.5	87.9	91.0	94.2	97.3	104.6
19	Delijan	95.7	96.0	102.5	92.5	99.0	89.4	100.6	106.1
19	Komejan	91.0		94.2	97.5	104.6	101.0		87.9
19	Khomein	87.7		97.3	94.0	90.8	103.8	100.8	104.4
19	Khondab	106.6		91.4	97.8	102.0	104.0	101.4	103.0
19	Mahallat	94.9		88.6	101.7	91.7	98.2	107.6	105.3
19	Saveh	90.7		101.2	94.4	97.2	107.0	87.8	103.4
19	Shazand	93.6		90.5	96.8	100.1	103.6	107.2	89.4
19	Tafresh	91.0	89.1	101.0	100.0	97.5	92.2	103.2	94.2
20	Behshahr			96.8	87.7	96.2		93.0	
20	Chalus	97.5		98.2		88.6		91.7	
20	Sari	101.1	96.5	94.2	98.6	96.2	105.7	102.1	92.1
21	Abgarm				90.9	87.8	94.1	100.9	97.4
21	Moallem Kalayeh		92.0	102.0	95.2	88.9	98.5		105.6
21	Ghazvin	94.3	100.1	107.2	103.7	93.6	96.8	91.1	97.6
22	Qom				96.6	93.4			
23	Biarjmand			95.9	98.5	98.5		88.9	
23	Semnan	92.7	94.5	94.0	89.6	102.7		101.5	99.2
23	Shahrud	90.8		97.3	100.8		104.4	90.8	94.0
24	Saravan	95.5	92.2	95.4		92.2			
24	Zabol	92.0	96.0	87.9	97.5	91.0		94.2	
24	Zahedan	93.7	90.5	93.7	90.5	100.1	100.1	103.7	107.3
25	Tehran			91.3	104.7	99.6	88.1	106.7	102.5
26	Ardakan	100.0		99.4	92.2	102.9	101.5	92.9	92.7
26	Bafgh			90.8	95.7	99.0		92.5	
26	Tabas	101.0	100.0		102.7	102.4		98.9	
26	Yazd	101.5	97.1	99.6	94.4	96.3	94.7	93.1	103.1
27	Mahnshan	92.3			102.0	94.1			99.8
27	Zanjan	99.7	93.2	105.4	96.4	103.2	90.1	93.2	106.8
28	Bojnurd	88.1	101.0	103.0		93.5	90.1	95.0	
29	Dorud	94.5		104.8	102.9	101.2		98.6	
29	Ferdows	89.0			94.3	96.0	96.7		93.6
29	Torbat	94.0	100.9	92.6				98.0	
29	Mashhad	94.8	98.1	95.2	101.6	105.8	98.7	102.2	91.6
29	Sabzevar	92.9			96.0	96.4		91.1	
30	Birjand	102.3	96.0	91.2	105.6	94.5	101.3	98.2	
32	Mahabad	91.1		97.0	92.2				93.4

NB: Iran has not provided comprehensive update information regarding their transmitter network in recent years and all information is based on various web sources and monitoring observations.

Provinces: 1) Ardabil **2)** West Azerbayjan E: 162-waz@irib.ir **3)** East Azerbayjan E: tabriz@irib.ir **4)** Bushehr E: prbushehr@irib.ir **5)** Chaharmahal & Bakhtiari **6)** Isfahan E: isfahan@irib.ir **7)** Fars E: fars162@irib.ir **8)** Gilan E: gilan@irib.ir **9)** Golestan **10)** Hamadan **11)** Hormozgan E: modirkol-klf@irib.ir, kish@irib.ir **12)** Ilam **13)** Kerman **14)** Kermanshah **15)** Khozestan E: abadan@irib.ir **16)** Kohgiluyeh & Boyerahmad **17)** Kurdistan **18)** Lorestan **19)** Markazi **20)** Mazandaran E: 162-mzn@irib.ir **21)** Qazvin **22)** Qom E: khoshi@irib.ir **23)** Semnan E: semnan@irib.ir **24)** Systan & Baluchestan E: zahedan@irib.ir **25)** Tehran **26)** Yazd **27)** Zanjan **28)** North Khorasan E: kh-shomali@irib.ir **29)** Razavi Khorasan E: infoplanning-ksnr@irib.ir **30)** South Khorasan E: birjand@irib.ir **31)** Alborz **32)** Mahabad.

Networks:
I=Radio Iran: 24h, but hrs. of operation vary by station. Frequencies for R. Iran and provincial prgrs at the same site can often be swapped. **N:** on the half hour – **R=Regional (Provincial) network.** Studios in 32 centres producing prgrs in Farsi and local langs, including some locally produced Ext. Sce. prgrs. Regional prgrs are usually between 0230-1630, in some cases 24h, and they may r. R. Iran network 1630-2030 or overnight – **Q=R. Quran**(rlg.): 24h on MW 585kHz and FM – **P=R. Payam** ("Message", actualities): 24h on MW 1188kHz + FM. **M=R. Ma'aref** ("Presentation", rlg.): 24h on MW 1071kHz & FM **English: Call of Islam R.** on satellite and Internet: mms://62.220.122.10/maarefeng – **J=R. Javan** (Youth): 24h on MW 1206kHz and FM – **F=R. Farhang** (cultural): 24h on MW 558kHz & FM – **V=R. Varzesh** (sports) and **Tj=R. Tejarat** (R. Trade) on FM. Partly sharing their frequencies – **T=Tehran City Prgr.** 24h on MW 1332kHz & FM 95.0MHz – **R. Salamat** (Health R): 0230-1430 in Tehran on 103.9MHz – **R Ava/Nava,** Tehran: 24h on 107.2MHz. – **R. Goftegoo,** Tehran: 0230-2030 on 103.9MHz.
Foreign Language prgrs in Tehran: 100.7MHz: various 24h. On 106.7MHz: **English:** 2130-2230, 2030-2130. **Russian:** 1930-2030.

Ann: S: "Inja Tehran ast, Sedaye Jomhuriye Islamiye Iran, Radyoe Iran". Farhang: "Inja Tehran ast, Sedaye Jomhuriye Islamiye Iran, shabakeye Farhang". **M:** "Inja Qom ast, shabakeye Ma'aref, Sedaye Jomhuriye Islamiye Iran". **Q:** "Radyoe Qur'an". **R:** "Inja (capital) ast, Sedaye Jomhuriye Islamiye Iran, shabakeye/markazye (province)."

EXTERNAL SERVICE: Voice of the Islamic Republic of Iran; see International Radio section

IRAQ

L.T: UTC +3h — **Pop:** 28 million — **Pr.L:** Arabic, Kurdish, Assyrian, Turkoman — **E.C:** 50Hz, 230V — **ITU:** IRQ

COMMUNICATIONS AND MEDIA COMMISSION (CMC)
P.O. Box 2044, District 929, Street 32, Building 18 , Jadreiah, Baghdad ☎+964 1 7180009 ✆ +964 1 719 5839 **W:** nmc.rq **E:** enquiries@cmc.iq **L.P:** Deputy Dir: Ali Nasir.

IRAQI MEDIA NET - REPUBLIC OF IRAQ RADIO (Gov)
near Al-Mansoor Melia Hotel, Salihiya, Baghdad **W:** imn.iq **E:** info@imn.iq **L.P:** DG: Hassan Al-Musawi. Dir. Eng: Emad Aziz.

MW	kHz	kW	Prgr.
Mosul	603	20	R. Nineva/Main
Kirkuk	657	1	Main
Baghdad	675	1	Main
Nasiriya	846	20	Main
Ramadi	864	10	Main
Basra	909	25	Provincial
Hilla	1071	20	R. Babil
Tikrit	1215	10	Main

N.B: Most MW transmitters reported inactive.

FM	MHz	kW	Prgr.
Diwaniya	88.1		Provincial
Karbala	88.4	1	Main
Nasiriya	88.8		Main
Hilla	92.2		Main
Sinjar	90.5		Main
Karbala	91.2		Provincial
Diwaniya	92.2	10	Main
Samawa	92.2/92.7		Main
Babylon	93.7		Provincial
Shumali	94.2	10	Main
Baquba	94.8	10	R. Diyala
Basra	96.0	1	Quran
Tikrit	90.0/97.9/98.2		Main
Najaf	96.5	5	Quran
Basra	98.1	1	Main
Baghdad	98.3	1	Main
Nasiriya	99.0		Quran
Faluja	99.9	1	Main
Basra	100.0	5	Main
Kut	100.5	1	Main
Mosul	88.7/103.4		Main
Najaf	101.0	5	Provincial
Baghdad	103.3		Main
Amara	104.1		Quran
Baghdad	105.0		Al Jel
Amara	106.0		Main

Main Prgr (Republic of Iraq R.): 24h in Arabic on on MW and FM except for Provincial programmes on some transmitters during the day. **Quran prgr:** 24h. **R. Al Jel** (for youth). **R. Nineva:** daytime on Mosul trs. **R. Babil:** on 1071kHz and FM. **Ann:** Main prgr: "Idha'at Jumhuriyah al-Iraq min Baghdad".

Other stations:

	MW	kHz	kW	Location	Station	H of tr
10)		756	3	Basra	R. Dar as-Salam	0400-2100
8)		810	5/3	Baghdad	R. Om Al-Qura	0400-1830
3)		819	10	Basra	R. Al-Amal	0400-1830
10)		882	5	Mosul	R. Dar as-Salam	0400-2100
18)		936	20	Basra	R. as-Safir	
5)		999	20	Baghdad	R. Bilad	0400-1700
6)		1008	20	Najaf	Sowt al-Fadhila	
		1017	10	Karbala	R. Karbala	
7)		1053	3	Baghdad	R. As-Salam	0700-1700
10)		1116	20	Baghdad	R. Dar as-Salam	0400-2100
11)		1179	30	Baghdad	R. Voice of Iraq	0400-1800
10)		1197	1	Kirkuk	R. Dar as-Salam	0400-2100
4)		1404		Maysan	R. Kull al-Iraq	

	FM	MHz	kW	Location	Station	H of tr
14)		87.5		Penjwin	R. Garmiyan (Yekgirtu R.)	
48)		87.5		Kirkuk	R. Vision	
21)		87.7	1	Baghdad	Monte-Carlo Doualiya	24h

FM	MHz	kW	Location	Station	H of tr
9)	87.8		Kirkuk	Vo Kurdistan	0300-2000
10)	88.0		Kirkuk	R. Dar as-Salam	0400-2100
19)	88.0	2	Basra	BBC English	24h
20)	88.0		Sulaimaniya	R. Sawa	24h
21)	88.1	1	Mosul	Monte-Carlo Doualiya	24h
43)	88.2		Baghdad	R. Dijla	0500-0100
43)	88.4		Basra	R. Dijla	0500-0100
22)	88.4	1	Sulaimaniya	R. Free Iraq/VOA	24h
46)	88.5		Mosul	R. Nawa (Arabic)	
23)	88.6	1	Baghdad	Panorama FM	24h
38)	88.6	1	Halabja	R. Dênge Nwe	0500-1700
47)	88.9		Erbil	R. Duhok	0400-2300
19)	89.0	2	Baghdad +2 stns	BBC Arabic	24h
39)	89.0		Kirkuk	R. Ashur	
47)	89.0		Amediye	R. Duhok	0400-2300
46)	89.1		Penjwin	R. Nawa (Kurdish)	
14)	89.1		Kalar	R. Garmiyan (Yekgirtu R.)	
3)	89.1		Basra	R. Al-Amal	
46)	89.3		Saidsadeq	R. Nawa (Kurdish)	
45)	89.3		Amara	Al-Mirbad R.	24h
46)	89.3		Halabja	R. Nawa (Kurdish)	
10)	89.4		Mosul	R. Dar as-Salam	0500-2100
18)	89.4		Basra	R. As-Safir	
	89.4			R. Melbend	
46)	89.5		Kirkuk	R. Nawa (Kurdish)	
47)	89.5		Duhok	R. Duhok	0400-2300
	89.6			VO Islam (Kurdish)	
31)	89.7		Karbala	Al-Huda Islamic R.	24h
46)	89.9		Baghdad	R. Nawa (Kurdish)	
19)	90.0	1	Basra/Shumali	BBC Arabic	24h
24)	90.0		Kirkuk	Turkoman FM	0510-2200
39)	90.0		Mosul	R, Ashur	
27)	90.3		Baghdad	R. Al-Noor	(inactive)
20)	90.4	1	Hillah	R. Sawa	24h
26)	90.4		Baghdad	R. Al-Yauwm	-1500
4)	90.6	0.2	Basra	R. Shanasheel	0400-2300
17)	90.6	0.1	Kirkuk	R. Lawani Kurdistan	
46)	90.6		Sulaimaniya	R. Nawa (Arabic)	
10)	91.0	1	Baghdad/Tikrit	R. Dar as-Salam	0500-2100
39)	91.1		Nineva	R. Ashur	
3)	91.3		Najaf	R. Al-Amal	
9)	91.4		Salah al Din	Vo Kurdistan	0300-2000
28)	91.5	5	Baghdad/Basra	Al-Rasheed R.	0300-2300
9)	91.5		Erbil	VO Kurdistan	0300-2000
47)	91.5		Zakho	R. Duhok	0400-2300
34)	91.7		Sulaimaniya	Zed R.	
40)	91.8		Basra	Sumer FM	24h
7)	92.0	0.3	Baghdad	R. As-Salam	0700-1700
21)	92.0		Basra	Monte-Carlo Doualiya	24h
28)	92.0		Kirkuk	Al-Rasheed R.	0300-2300
17)	92.0	0.1	Ranye	R. Lawani Kurdistan	
46)	92.0		5 locations	R. Nawa (Kurdish)	
46)	92.0		Basra	R. Nawa (Arabic)	
34)	92.3		Erbil/Duhok	Zed R.	
34)	92.5		Kirkuk	Zed R.	
46)	92.6		Erbil	R. Nawa (Arabic)	
46)	92.7		Duhok	R. Nawa (Arabic)	
19)	92.8	2	Kirkuk	BBC Arabic	24h
32)	92.8	0.6	Basra	Al-Nakhil R.	0300-2100
40)	92.8		Sulaimaniya	Sumer FM	24h
43)	93.0		Sulaimaniya	R. Dijla	0500-0100
45)	93.3		Basra	Al-Mirbad R.	24h
9)	93.3		Dohuk	Vo Kurdistan	0300-2000
43)	94.0		Mosul	R. Dijla	0500-0100
8)	94.5	5	Baghdad	R. Om Al-Qura	0400-1830
46)	94.6		Kirkuk	R. Nawa (Arabic)	
4)	94.6		Basra	R. Nahrain	
28)	95.5		Mosul	Al-Rasheed R	0300-2300
12)	95.5		Kirkuk	VO People Kurdistan	0500-2100
20)	95.7	10	So. Iraq	R. Sawa	24h
19)	96.0	2	Erbil/Mosul	BBC Arabic	24h
20)	96.0	1	Tikrit	R. Sawa	24h
	96.1		Najaf	Al-Ghadeer R.	
30)	96.1		Babylon	R. Al-Hilla	
33)	96.1	5	Baghdad	R. Al-Mahaba	
35)	96.3		No. Iraq	Guven R.	
46)	96.5		Koya/Qaladezi	R. Nawa (Kurdish)	
1)	96.6	5	Baghdad	R. Al-Nas	0400-1500
22)	96.8	1	Kirkuk	R. Free Iraq	24h
19)	96.9	2	Baghdad	BBC English	24h
46)	97.1		Ranya/Sara	R. Nawa (Kurdish)	
37)	97.3		Baghdad	Sowt al-Jam'ah	
46)	97.5		Darbandekhan	R. Nawa (Kurdish)	
12)	97.9		Baghdad	Al-Hurriyah R.	0500-2100
24)	98.0	0.1	Erbil	Turkoman FM	0510-2200
46)	98.0		Zakho	R. Nawa (Kurdish)	
40)	98.2		Erbil	Sumer FM	24h
46)	98.5		Zakho	R. Nawa (Arabic)	
43)	98.8		Erbil	R. Dijla	0500-0100
36)	98.8	5	Baghdad	Ur FM	24h
20)	98.8	1	Kirkuk	R. Sawa	24h
	98.8		Babylon	University R.	
25)	99.1		Karbala	Karbala FM	0300-1500
15)	99.3	3	Bahrez	Ind. RTV Netw.	0500-2100
39)	99.4		Baghdad	R. Ashur	0600-1700
40)	99.9	5	Baghdad	Sumer FM	24h
40)	99.9		Dohuk	Sumer FM	24h
19)	100.0	2	Nasiriya	BBC Arabic	24h
14)	100.2		Tawella	R. Garmiyan (Yekgirtu R.)	
20)	100.4	10	Baghdad	R. Sawa	24h
4)	100.4		Basra	R. Nahrain	
42)	101.0		Baghdad	R. Al-Ahd	
45)	101.1		Nasiriya	Al-Mirbad R.	24h
17)	101.5		Baghdad	VO Iraqi National Congress	
41)	102.0	3	Baghdad	R. Shafaq	0300-2300
22)	102.4	10	Baghdad	R. Free Iraq/VOA	24h
21)	103.0		Erbil	Monte-Carlo Doualiya	24h
20)	103.2	1	Erbil	R. Sawa	24h
49)	103.3		Kirkuk	R. Justice	
14)	103.4		Kifri	R. Garmiyan (Yekgirtu R.)	
12)	104.0		Kirkuk	R. Kirkuk	
22)	104.5	1	Erbil	R. Free Iraq/VOA	24h
22)	104.6	5	Mosul	R. Free Iraq/VOA	24h
22)	105.0	10	Basra	R. Free Iraq/VOA	24h
14)	105.4		Darbandikhan	R. Garmiyan (Yekgirtu R.)	
20)	105.8	1	Sulaimaniya	R. Sawa	24h
40)	105.8		Diwaniya	Sumer FM	24h
21)	106.3		Tikrit	Monte-Carlo Doualiya	24h
44)	106.0	1	Baghdad	As-Salam 106 FM	24h
20)	106.6	5	Mosul	R. Sawa	24h
20)	107.0	10	Basra	R. Sawa	24h
	107.7		Zakho	R. Hizal	

Addresses and other information:

3) ("Hope"). **W:** alamel.org – 4) R. Kull al-Iraq ("All of Iraq"), Maysan – 5) R. Bilad ("Lands"). Operated by the Islamic Virtue Party. **W:** albilad.org Email: albilad@albilad.org – 6) Sowt al- Fadhila ("Voice of Virtue"), Najaf – 7) R. As-Salam ("Peace")Email: safa565@hotmail. com Alt. freq. 1030/1035kHz – 8) **W:** heyetnet.org – 9) Operated by the Kurdistan Democratic Party **W:** kurdistanradio.net Email: info@kurdis-tanradio.net Prgrs in Sorani Kurdish/Arabic – 10) R. Dar As-Salam ("Haven of Peace"), The Voice of the Iraqi Islamic Party. **W:** darusalam. net – 11) Operated by Imam Al-Shirazi International Association. **W:** www.voiraq.com Email: voiceiraq@yahoo.com Prgrs in Arabic/English/ Turkmen – 12) Operated by the Patriotic Union of Kurdistan **W:** hurriya. net Email: hurriyanet@yahoo.com . In Sorani Kurdish/Arabic – 13) Operated by the Kurdistan Islamic Group. **W:** komalnews.net . Prgrs in Arabic/Kurdish/Turkish – 14) **W:** radiogarmyan.net – 15) Email: kahoofy2005@yahoo.com – 17) Kurdistan Youth R. **W:** www.mosy-krg. org – 18) Basra. **W:** aliraqnews.com – 19) BBC Arabic Service Email: arabicservice@bbc.co.uk – 20) R. Sawa ("Together"). Also on MW via Kuwait 1548kHz 600kW 24h. For more details see International Radio section (USA) – 21) R. France Internationale & Monte-Carlo Doualiya. prgrs in Arabic/French. For details see International radio section (France). 22) Iraqi Sce. of R. Free Europe/R. Liberty. Also on MW via Kuwait 1593kHz 150kW 1400-0700. In Arabic incl. VOA in Kurdish/English. For more details see International Radio section (USA) – 23) See MBC entry under UAE – 24) **W:** www.kerkuk.net Prgrs in Turkmen/Arabic – 25) ✉ Shammasyia St. 29, Quarter 318, Line 55, House 31, Adhadmyia, Baghdad – 26) R. Al-Yauwm ("Today Radio") – 27) R. Al-Noor ("Light"). Email: alnoor903fm@yahoo.com – 28) **W:** alrasheedmedia.com Email: alrasheedfm@yahoo.com . Different prgr. to each region – 31) **W:** al-hodaonline.com/radio Email: alhod-aonline@gmail.com – 32) Operated by the Islamic Supreme Council of Iraq. **W:** www.almejlis.org Email: info@almejlis.org – 33) R. Al-Mahaba ("Friendship"), Voice of Iraqi Women. Supported by the United Nations Development Fund for Women (UNIFEM). **W:** www.okiinc. org/vow_radio.html – 34) **W:** www.zagrostv.com – 35) Operated by the Turkish army – 36) **W:** radiourfm.com Email: info@radiourfm.com – 37) Sawt al-Jam'ah ("Voice of the University") – 38) R. Dênge Nwe ("New Voice"). **W:** halabja.info/Radio halabja.htm E: dangynwe@yahoo.com – 39) Operated by the Assyrian Democratic Movement (ADM/ZOWAA) **W:** www.zowaa.org Email: info@zowaa.org .In Assyrian/Arabic – 40) **W:** sumerfm.com – 41) R. Shafaq ("Twilight"). **W:** shafaaq.com . In Kurdish/Arabic – 42) R. Al-Ahd (Oath), Baghdad – 43) R. Dijla (Tigris). **W:** radiodijla.com – 44) As-Salam (Peace) 106 FM. **W:** peace106fm. com E-mail: peace106fm@yahoo.com – 45) **W:** almirbad.com Email:

info@almirbad.com – **46) W:** radionawa.com Email: info@radionawa.
com – **47) W:** duhokradio.org – **48)** Operated by the Iraqi Turkmen
Brotherhood Party – **49)** Operated by the Iraqi Turkmen Justice Party
– **50) W:** uobabylon.edu.iq

IRELAND

L.T: UTC (31 Mar-27 Oct: +1h) — **Pop:** 4.5 million — **Pr.L:** Irish Gaelic,
English — **E.C:** 50Hz, 230V — **ITU:** IRL

RAIDIÓ TEILIFÍS EIREANN (Statutory Corporation)
🖳 Donnybrook, Dublin 4 ☎ +353 1 208 3111 🖷 +353 1 208 3080 **E:**
info@rte.ie **W:** www.rte.ie
L.P: DG: Noel Curran; Ch. Fin. Offr.: Conor Hayes. MD TV: Glen Killane.
MD Radio: Clare Duignan; Dir Corp.Dev.: Brian Dalton, Ch. Tech. Offr:
Richard Watson.
Raidió Na Gaeltachta: Casla, Conamara, Co Galway ☎ +353 91
506677 🖷 +353 91 506666 **E:** rnag@rte.ie **W:** www.rte.ie/rnag
Lyric FM: Cornmarket Square, Limerick ☎ +353 61 207300 🖷 +353
61 207390 **E:** lyric@rte.ie **W:** www.rte.ie/lyricfm **Pub.:** RTE Guide
Networks:1=R1, 2=2FM, 3=Raidió Na Gaeltachta, 4=Lyric FM

LW	kHz	kW	N		
Summerhill	252	300	1		
FM (MHz)	**1**	**2**	**3**	**4**	**kW**
Achill	89.9	92.1	94.3	99.5	3
Aranmore	89.6	91.8	94.0	99.2	3
Ballybofey	89.7	91.9	94.1	99.3	0.5
Bantry	88.7	90.9	93.1	98.3	1
Cahirciveen	89.5	91.7	93.9	99.1	3
Cairn Hl (Longford)	89.8	-	-	-	20
Casla	88.4	90.6	92.8	98.0	2
Castlebar	89.3	91.5	93.7	98.9	3
Castletownbere	88.3	90.5	92.7	97.9	3
Clermont Carn	87.8	97.0	102.7	95.2	40
Clifden	89.5	91.7	93.9	99.1	3
Clonmel	89.3	90.5	92.7	97.9	1
Cnoc an Oir	89.2	91.4	93.6	98.7	1
Cork (Spur Hill)	89.2	91.4	93.6	98.8	5
Crosshaven	88.2	90.4	92.6	97.8	3
Dungarvan	88.5	90.7	92.9	98.1	3
Fanad	89.8	92.0	94.2	99.4	4
Greystones	89.5	91.7	93.9	99.1	1
Holywell Hill	89.2	91.4	93.6	98.8	6
Kilduff	90.2	-	-	-	3
Kippure	89.1	91.3	93.5	98.7	50
Knockmoyle	88.4	90.6	92.8	98.0	1
Limerick City	89.4	91.6	93.8	99.0	2.5
Maghera	88.8	91.0	93.2	98.4	160
Malin	89.9	91.1	93.3	98.5	2
Monaghan	88.9	91.1	93.3	98.5	2.5
Moville	88.3	90.5	92.7	97.9	1
Mt. Leinster	89.6	91.8	94.0	99.2	200
Mullaghanish	90.0	92.2	94.4	99.6	160
Suir Valley	89.0	91.2	93.4	98.6	3
Three Rock	88.5	90.7	92.9	96.7	10
Truskmore	88.2	90.4	92.6	97.8	120

+ 10 relays below 0.5kW

1) RTE R. 1: 24h in English & Irish on LW, FM, satellite and internet.
N. in English: on the h **N. in Irish Gaelic:** 2150 – **2) 2FM:** 24h in
English on FM, satellite and internet. – **3) Raidió Na Gaeltachta:**
24h in Irish Gaelic on FM, satellite and internet – **4) Lyric FM:** 24h on
FM, satellite and internet.

EXTERNAL SERVICE (RTE Radio Worldwide): see Int. section

DIGITAL RADIO (DAB): DAB trs are on Band 3. **RTE national multiplex** Block 12C 227.360 MHz trs. in Dublin, NE Ireland, Cork, Limerick
carrying 11 RTE services (R1, 2FM, Lyric FM, R Na Gaeltachta, 2XM,
Chill, Choice, Junior, Gold, R1 Extra, Pulse).
Independent test multiplexes: DB Digital Broadcasting Block
12A 223.936 MHz trs, in Dublin, Cork, Limerick carrying All R. 80s, All
R. 80s+, R. Ri-Ra, R. Ri-Ra+, UCB R., UCB+. **Total Broadcast** Block 9B
204.640 MHz trs Blackstairs Mountain, Waterford carrying simulcast
of several commercial stns. Further information: **W:** www.dbdb.ie,
www.totalbroadcast.net

BROADCASTING AUTHORITY OF IRELAND (BAI)
🖳 2-5 Warrington Place, Dublin 2 ☎ +353 1 644 1200 🖷 +353 1
644 1299 **E:** info@bai.ie **W:** www.bai.ie **L.P:** Chief Exec: Michael
O'Keeffe.
Responsible for regulation of commercial broadcasting in the Irish
Republic. Full list of licensed stns can be found on BCI website

TODAY FM (Comm.)
🖳 Marconi House, Digges Lane, Dublin 2 ☎ +353 1 804 9000 **W:**
www.todayfm.com

FM	MHz	kW	FM	MHz	kW
Crosshaven	100.0	6	Knockanore	101.0	2
Truskmore	100.0	250	Castlebar	101.1	6
Moville	100.1	2	Woodcock Hill	101.2	5
Clonmel	100.1	2	Greystones	101.3	1
Knockmoyle	100.2	2	Clifden	101.3	6
Dungarvan	100.3	6	Kilkeaveragh	101.3	6
Maghera	100.6	320	Mt. Leinster	101.4	400
Monaghan	100.7	5	Fanad	101.6	8
Suir Valley	100.8	6	Achil	101.7	6
Kippure	100.9	100	Mullaghanish	101.8	320
Holywell Hill	101.0	12	Three Rock	101.8	2
Spur Hill, Cork	101.0	10	Clermont Carn	105.5	80

+ 5 trs.under 1kW
D.Prgr: 24h **N:** on the h, also on the half h at peak times.

NEWSTALK (Comm.)
🖳 Marconi House, Digges Lane, Dublin 2 ☎ + 353 1 644 5100 🖷 +
353 1 644 5101 **W:** www.newstalk.ie **E:** info@newstalk.ie
L.P: CE Frank Cronin

FM	MHz	kW	FM	MHz	kW
Monaghan	103.3	2.5	Mullaghanish	107.4	80
Capard	105.8	4	Truskmore	107.4	80
Three Rock	106.0	10	Mohercrom	107.4	10
Holywell Hill	106.9	12	Waterford	107.4	2
Longford	106.9	5	Maghera	107.6	32
Limerick City	107.0	2	Saggart	107.6	2
Nagles	107.0	0.5	Dungarvan	107.6	5
Ballyguile	107.0	2	Cork City	107.8	10
Kilitimagh	107.2	6	Kilduff	107.8	2
Mt Leinster	107.2	2	Gorey	107.8	1
Knockmoyle	107.2	4			

+6 trs. under 1 kW

SPIRIT RADIO (Rlg.)
🖳 PO Box 11993, Ballsbridge, Dublin 4 ☎ + 353 1 614 4839 **W:** www.
spiritradio.ie

MW	kHz	kW			
Carrickroo	549	25			
FM	**MHz**	**kW**	**FM**	**MHz**	**kW**
Limerick	89.8	0.4	Cork	90.9	0.5
Dublin	89.9	0.8	Galway	91.7	0.4
Waterford	90.1	0.2			

D.Prgr: 24h

Local Stations:

FM	MHz	kW	Station, tx location
31)	87.8	1	Connemara Community R
35)	94.6	1	Classic Hits 4FM, Saggart
32)	94.7	5	Spin South West, Clifden
18)	94.8	4	Northern Sound, Slieve Glah
35)	94.8	3	Classic Hits 4FM, Churchfield (Mallow)
1)	94.9	9	East Coast FM, Avoca
35)	94.9	3	Classic Hits 4FM, Three Rock
2)	95.0	10	Limerick's Live 95 FM, Woodcock Hill
16)	95.1	10	WLR FM, Faha, Dungarvan
10)	95.2	2	Highland R, Aran Mor
35)	95.4	9	Classic Hits 4FM, Nowen Hill
7)	95.5	2	Clare FM, Kilrush
17)	95.6	1	Cork's 96 FM, Kilworth,NE Cork
3)	95.6	4	South East R, Mt.Leinster
4)	95.8	10	LM FM, Mt. Oriel
17)	95.8	10	Cork's 96 FM, Nowen Hill
7)	95.9	2	Clare FM, Woodcock Hill
8)	96.0	1	KCLR, Corbally Wood
5)	96.1	10	MWR FM, Kiltimagh
17)	96.1	1	Cork's 96 FM, Mount Hillary
20)	96.2	6	R. Kerry, Cahirciveen
1)	96.2	10	East Coast FM, Bray
18)	96.3	10	Northern Sound, Monaghan
7)	96.4	10	Clare FM, Maghera
17)	96.4	2	Cork's 96 FM, Holly Hill
8)	96.6	10	KCLR , Johns Well
9)	96.8	10	Galway Bay FM, Knockroe
8)	96.9	4	KCLR, Rossmore
34)	96.9	9	iRadio, Scalp Mountain
20)	97.0	40	R. Kerry, Mullaghanish
11)	97.1	10	Tipp FM, Scrouthea
5)	97.1	3	MWR FM, Achill
12)	97.3	5	KFM, Rossmore
35)	97.4	4	Classic Hits 4FM, Bweeng Mountain

FM	MHz	kW	Station, tx location
9)	97.4	2	Galway Bay FM, Redmount Hl
16)	97.5	10	WLR FM, East Waterford
20)	97.6	2	R. Kerry, Knockanore
12)	97.6	4	KFM, Slieve Thuile
13)	98.1	9	98 FM, Three Rock
1)	99.9	9	East Coast FM, Saggart Hill
33)	100.3	12	R. Nova, Three Rock
24)	102.0	13	Beat 102-103 FM, Mount Leinster
34)	102.1	9	iRadio, South Galway
10)	102.1	1.3	Highland R., Feirn Hill
24)	102.2	6	Beat 102-103 FM, West Waterford
26)	102.2	5	Q 102, Three Rock
32)	102.3	1	Spin South West, Ennistynmon
24)	102.4	10	Beat 102-103 FM, Clonmel
21)	102.5	4	Ocean FM, Truskmore
32	102.5	5	Spin South West, Knockmoyle
17a)	102.6	2	C103, Cork City
32)	102.7	9	Spin South West, Maghera
24)	102.8	10	Beat 102-103 FM, East Waterford
1)	102.9	16	East Coast FM, Ballyguille
1)	102.9	2	East Coast FM, Baltinglass
17)	102.9	1	C103, NE Cork
32)	102.9	9	Spin South West, Cahirciveen
32)	103.0	2.5	Spin South West, Woodcock Hill
34)	103.1	9	i Radio, Longford
34)	103.1	3	i102-104, Achill
34)	103.1	1	i Radio, Senafaistin
22)	103.2	0.5	Dublin City FM, Three Rock
10)	103.3	10	Highland R, Scalp Mountain
17a)	103.3	10	C103, Nowen Hill
34)	103.3	4	i Radio, Clifden
6)	103.5	2.5	Midlands 103, Sliabh Bloom
32)	103.5	1	Spin South West, Knockmoyle
17a)	103.7	5	C103, Mt. Hillary
34)	103.7	9	i Radio, Castlebar
25)	103.8	5	Spin 103.8, Three Rock
11)	103.9	3.2	Tipp FM, Kilduff
34)	104.0	2	i Radio, Aranmore
14)	104.1	5	Shannonside 104FM, Sliabh Bawn
35)	104.2	9	Classic Hits 4FM, Limerick
15)	104.4	10	FM 104, Three Rock
34)	104.4	9	i Radio, Sligo (Truskmore)
28)	104.5	10	Red FM, W. Cork (Nowen Hill)
10)	104.5	2	Highland R, Back Mountain
35)	104.6	9	Classic Hits 4FM, Maghera,Co Clare
34)	104.7	1	i Radio, Saggart
19)	104.8	10	Tipperary Mid-West R, Dangandargan
34)	104.8	2.5	i Radio, Cavan (Sliabh Giah)
35)	104.9	9	Classic Hits 4FM, Galway City
21)	105.0	10	Ocean FM, Mt.Charles
34)	105.0	5	i Radio, Mt Oriel (Louth)
30)	105.0	4	Inishowen Community R, Malin
28)	105.0	1	Red FM, Newmarket
29)	105.2	4	Phantom FM, Three Rock
28)	105.7	5	Red FM, North Cork (Nagles)
28)	106.1	2	Red FM, Churchfield, Cork
34)	106.2	5	i Radio, Capard
23)	106.4	2	Raidió Na Life, Three Rock
34)	106.7	10	i Radio, Monaghan
27)	106.8	4	Sunshine 106.8, Three Rock

+ approx 110 additional txs of less than 1kW

Addresses and other information:
1) Radio Centre, Killarney Rd, Bray, Co Wicklow **E:** reception@eastcoast.fm — **W:** www.eastcoast.fm — **2)** Unit 5-6 Richard Court, , Dock Rd, Limerick **E:** mail@live95fm.ie **W:** www.live95fm.ie — **3)** Custom House Quay, Wexford Town **E:** info@southeastradio.ie **W:** www.southeastradio.ie — **4)** Broadcasting House, Rathmullen Rd, Drogheda, Co Louth **E:** info@lmfm.ie **W:** www.lmfm.ie — **5)** Clare Str, Ballyhaunis, Co Mayo **W:** www.midwestradio.ie — **6)** Tindle House, Axis Business Park, Tullamore, Co Offaly **E:** info@midlandsradio.fm **W:** www.midlandsradio.fm — **7)** Abbeyfield Centre, Francis Str, Ennis, Co Clare **W:** www.clare.fm — **8)** Leggetsrath Business Park, Dublin Rd, Kilkenny **W:** www.kclr96fm.com — **9)** Unit 13, Sandy Rd, Galway **E:** info@galwaynews.ie **W:** www.galwaynews.ie — **10)** Pine Hill, Letterkenny, Co Donegal **E:** enquries@highlandradio.com **W:** www.highlandradio.com — **11)** Broadcast Centre, 4A Gurtnafleur Business Park, Clonmel, Co Tipperary **E:** sales@tippfm.com **W:** www.tippfm.com — **12)** KFM Broadcast Centre, M7 Business Park, Newhall, Naas, Co Kildare **E:** info@kfmradio.com **W:** www.kfmradio.com — **13)** South Block, The Malt House, Grand Canal Quay, Dublin 2 **E:** website@98fm.com **W:** www.98fm.com — **14)** Unit 1E Master Tech Business Park, Athlone Rd, Longford **W:** www.shannonside.ie — **15)** Macken House, Mayor Str Upper, Dublin 1 **E:** sales@fm104.ie **W:** www.

fm104.ie – **16)** Broadcast Centre, Ardkeen, Dunmore Rd, Waterford **E:** reception@wlrfm.com **W:** www.wlrfm.com – **17)** Broadcasting House, Patrick's Place, Cork **E:** info@96fm.ie **W:** www.96fm.ie – **17a)** Weir Str., Bandon, Co. Cork **E::** info@c103.ie **W:** www.c103.ie - **18)** Unit 3 Milltown Business Park, Monaghan & Thomas Ashe St.,Cavan **E:** info@norththernsound.ie **W:** www.northernsound.ie – **19)** St Michael Str, Tipperary **W:** www.tippmidwestradio.com – **20)** Maine St, Tralee, Co Kerry **E:** info@radiokerry.ie **W:** www.radiokerry.ie – **21)** Ocean FM Broadcasting Centre, North West Business Park, Collooney, Co Sligo **E:** sales@oceanfm.ie **W:** www.oceanfm.ie – **22)** Docklands Innovation Park, Unit 6, 128-130 Eastwall Rd, Dublin 3 **E:** info@dublincityfm.ie **W:** www.dublincityfm.ie – **23)** 7 Merrion Square, Dublin 2 **E:** eolas@raidi-onalife.ie **W:** www.raidionalife.ie (Irish language stn) – **24)** Broadcast Centre, Ardkeen, Dunmore Rd, Waterford **E:** info@beat102103.com **W:** www.beat102103.com – **25)** Level 3, South Block, Malt House, Grand Canal Quay, Dublin 2 **E:** info@spin1038.com **W:** www.spin1038.com – **26)** Macken House, 39-40 Upper Mayor Str, Dublin 1 **E:** info@q102..ie **W:** www.q102.ie – **27)** Radio Centre, Killarney Rd, Bray, Co Wicklow **E:** mail@sunshineradio.ie **W:** sunshineradio.ie – **28)** 1 University Technology Centre, Bishopstown, Cork **E:** info@redfm.ie **W:** www.redfm.ie – **29)** Marconi House, Digges Lane, Dublin 2 **E:** info@phantom.ie **W:** www.phantomfm.ie – **30)** Pound Str., Carndonagh, Inishowen, Co Donegal **E:** studio@icrfm.ie **W:** www.icrfm.ie – **31)** Connemara West Centre, Letterfrack, Co Galway **E:** info@connemarafm.com **W:** www.connemarafm.com – **32)** 2nd Floor Landmark Building, Raheen, Limerick **E:** info@spinsouthwest.com **W:** www.spinsouthwest.com – **33)** 1st Floor, Castleforbes House, Castleforbes Rd, Dublin 1 **E:** info@nova.ie **W:** www.nova.ie. – **34)** iRadio, Level 3, Unit C, Monksland Business Park, Athlone. **E:** info@iradio.ie **W:** www.iradio.ie – **35)** Ground Floor, Castleforbes House, Castleforbes Rd, Dublin 1. **E:** info@4fm.ie **W:** www.classichits.ie

Unofficial MW stations:

kHz	kW	Station, tx location
846	1	R. North, Redcastle, Co Donegal
981	1	R. Star Country, Emyvale, Co Monaghan
1395	0.4	Energy, Dublin: (Weekends - irreg)
1512	0.2	Tyrone Community R., Lifford, Co Donegal

Community/special interest stns: 29 stns in operation at October 2012. **Hospital/Institutions:** 5 stns. **Temporary/Special Event services:** see BAI **W:** www.bai.ie. **Wireless Public Address System (WPAS):** religious and other sces broadc. to housebound via CB radio 26.7–27.99MHz

ISRAEL

L.T: UTC +2h (29 Mar - 6 Oct: +3h) — **Pop:** 7.7 million — **Pr.L:** Hebrew, Arabic — **E.C:** 50Hz, 230V — **ITU:** ISR

ISRAEL BROADCASTING AUTHORITY (IBA)
161 Jaffa Road, P.O. Box 28080, Jerusalem 91280 ☎ +972 2 5015555 📠 +972 2 5015504 **W:** iba.org.il **E:** webmaster@iba.org.il **L.P:** Chairman: Amir Gilat. DG: Moti Sklar (pending replacement). Transmission Mgr: David Gombosh.

KOL ISRAEL (Pub.)
Heleni Hamalka 21, P.O. Box 1082, Jerusalem 91010 ☎ +972 3 6944777 & inside Israel 1599 509510 **W:** iba.org.il/world **E:** reception@iba.org.il **L.P:** Dir. & PD (Radio): Michael Miro. Dir. of Eng: Efraim Porat. Dir. Liaison & Coordination: Raphael Kochanowski.

MW	kHz	kW	Prgr.	MW	kHz	kW	Prgr.
Yavne	531	50	A	Akko (Acre)	738	10	D
Yavne	657	100	B	She'ar Yashuv	882	10	D
Yavne	1080	50	D	She'ar Yashuv	1458	10	A
Acre	1206	50	A	Eilat	1458	10	A

FM (MHz)	A	B	C	D	M	X	R	kW
Akko (Acre)							101.3	40
Atara	105.3	95.2	97.5	93.7				40/20
Beersheba	96.4	94.4	105.5	92.4	98.4	88.5	101.8	80/4
Eilat			90.7	100.5		97.0		2
Ein Yahav			95.2	97.5				4
Eitanim	105.1	95.5	97.8	88.8	91.3	87.6	100.3	160/100
Grofit			95.0	97.8		91.3		2
Haifa	104.8	94.4	105.5	92.4	100.2	88.0		80/4
		95.0		88.8				2
Heletz	104.8							20
Jerusalem	104.8	95.0	89.7	99.3		88.0	101.3	8/2
Kalya		95.5	97.8	88.8	91.3			0.5
Katzir		95.2		93.7				40
Kohav Hayarden		95.0	88.9		97.2		100.7	40/10
Menara	104.8	95.0	89.7		97.2		101.3	2

FM (MHz)	A	B	C	D	M	X	R	kW
Mitzpe Ramon		95.5	89.7		97.2			20/4
Netanya							100.5	4
Safed	105.1	95.5	97.8	88.8	98.5	87.6	100.3	40/8
Sha'ar HaNegev		95.0		99.3				4/1
Tel Aviv	104.8	95.0	89.7		97.2	88.0	101.3	10/4

Prgrs (in Hebrew if not mentioned otherwise):
A: "Reshet Alef": Talk & cultural programming 24h excl. times listed in Reshet Moreshet below. **N.** in Hebrew: rel. Prgr. B. – **B: "Reshet Bet":** 24h. News, current affairs & sports. **N:** on the h. – **C: "Reshet Gimel":** 24h Israeli popular music. **N:** rel. Prgr. B. – **D: "Reshet Dalet"** (Arabic). 24h. Ann: "Sowt Israel" – **X: "88 FM":** 24h. **N:** rel. Prgr. B. Light music, traffic reports – **R: REQA** (Reshet Qlitat Aliya): immigrants network, 24h in Russian, Amharic, French, Yiddish, Ladino, Romanian, Spanish, Moghrabi, Bukharian, Georgian, Hungarian and English 0430-0445, 1030-1045 & 1830-1845 – **M: "Kol Ha Musica"** (VO Music): 24h, classical music and drama. – **"Reshet Moreshet"** (Heritage Network). Religious programming on Reshet Alef. Sun-Thurs 1400-2200, Fri 0600-1500, Sat 1900-2200.

EXTERNAL SERVICE: see International Radio section.

GALEI TZAHAL (Israel Defence Forces R, Mil.)
✉ Military Post Office Box 01005, 23 Yehuda Hayamit, Jaffa ☎+972 3 5126666 **W:** www.glz.co.il **E:** glz@galatz.co.il
L.P: Commander: Yaron Dekel.

MW	kHz	kW	MW	kHz	kW
Yavne	945	100	Rosh-Pina	1305	50
Beersheba	1224	20	Shivta	1368	20

FM (MHz)	Main	kW	GalGalatz	kW
Beersheba	102.3	100	99.8	100
Bet Shean	99.8	10	-	-
Eilat	104.0	1	106.4	5
Haifa	102.3	100	107.0	100
Jerusalem	96.6	40	93.9	1
Kalya	96.9	1	93.6	1
Kiryat Shmona	-	-	104.0	1
Mitzpe Ramon	104.0	1	106.4	1
Nebi Yesha	93.9	5	-	-
Tel Aviv	104.0	4	91.8	20

Main Prgr on MW&FM: 24h. (news, talk show, music). **N:** on the h.
GalGalatz on FM(traffic reports and music): 24h.
Ann: Main Prgr: "Galei Tzahal, Shidure Tsva Hagana Le'Yisrael".
Relays on shortwave for Europe: see International Radio section.

Regional commercial FM radio (All in Hebrew except as noted):
ECO99fm, Hertzliyah: 99.0MHz **W:** echo99.fm – **Galey Israel:** Benjamin area 89.3MHz, Central Israel 94.0MHz, South 102.5MHz, Dan area 106.5 MHz, . **W:** srugim.co.il/galeyisrael – **Pervoye R**, Rishon Le'Zion. In Russian: Ashdod 89.1MHz. **W:** www.891fm.co.il – **R. A'shams** (The Sun) in Arabic at Nazareth-Ein Hahoresh area. 98.1 & 101.1MHz. **W:** ashams.com – **R. Darom** (Southern R.): Beersheba 97.0MHz, Kiryat Gat, Ashkelon. Arava & Dead Sea settlements: 95.8MHz. **W:** dromi.co.il/radio/index.asp **R. Darom** (Southern R.) :101.5MHz. **W:** dromi.co.il/1015/index.asp – **R. Haifa**, Haifa: 99.5, 107.5MHz. **W:** radiohaifa.mediacast.co.il – **R. Jerusalem:** Jerusalem 101.0MHz, Bet Shemesh 89.5MHz. **W:** www.tapuz.co.il/minisites/radiojerusalem – **R. Kol Barama**, Tel Aviv 92.1MHz, Beersheva 104.3MHz, Jerusalem 105.7MHz. **W:** kol-barama.co.il – **R. Kol Chai**: Bene Brak 92.8, Jerusalem 93.0MHz. **W:** www.93fm.co.il – **R. Kol Rega**: Galilee 96.0MHz, Tiberias 91.5MHz. **W:** 96fm.co.il – **R. Lev Ha Medina**: Shfela 91.0MHz, Beersheba 93.3MHz. **W:** 91fm.co.il – **Kol Ha Yam Ha Adom** (VO the Red Sea): 101.1, 102.0MHz IW. **W:** fm102.co.il – **R. L'Lo Hafsaka** (Nonstop): Upper Galilee 101.5MHz, Ramat Gan 103.0MHz, Lower Galilee 104.5MHz. **W:** 103.fm – **R. Tel Aviv**: 102.0MHz. **W:** www.tapuz.co.il/minisites/102fm – **R. Tishim**, (90), Tel Aviv: 90.0, 94.7MHz. **W:** 90fm.co.il – **Radius 100 FM**, Tel Aviv: 100.0MHz. **W:** 100fm.co.il

WEST BANK & GAZA STRIP (Palestinian territories)
L.T: UTC +2h (29 Mar-7 Oct: +3h; suspended during month of Ramadan), dates subject to change — **Pop:** 4 million — **Pr.L:** Arabic — **E.C:** 50Hz, 230V — **ITU:** XWB (West Bank), XGZ (Gaza Strip)

PALESTINIAN BROADCASTING CORPORATION (Gov)
✉ P.O. Box 984, Al-Bireh, Ramallah, West Bank ☎+970 2 2988888
📠 +970 2 2959891 **W:** www.pbc.gov.ps **E:** pbcinfo@pbc.gov.ps
L.P: Chmn: Radwan Abu Ayyash.
FM: Ramallah 90.7MHz, Gaza 99.4MHz, Jenin 102.2MHz.
D.Prgr. in Arabic: 0400-2300 **Ann:** "Sawt Filastin".

Private FM stations:
Al-Balad FM, Jenin: 104.8/105.8MHz. **W:** albaladfm.com – **Al-Manar R,** Gaza: 92.0MHz. **W:** manarfm.com – **Al-Qamar R,** Jericho: 89.4MHz. **W:** maannet.org – **Ajyal R:** Ramallah 103.4MHz, Hebron 107.1MHz. **W:** arn.ps – **Amwaj R.,** Ramallah 91.5MHz, south 99.4MHz, north 104.8MHz. **W:** amwaj.ps – **Angham R.,** Ramallah: 92.3MHz. **W:** radioangham.com – **Cool FM:** 104.0MHz, all English. **W:** coolfm.ps – **Gaza FM:** 100.9MHz. **W:** gazafm.net – **Hala FM:** 94.3MHz. See main entry under Jordan – **Hebron R:** 90.4MHz. **W:** hebronradio.com – **Holy Qur'an R,** Jerusalem 88.4MHz, Nablus 96.9MHz. **W:** quran-radio.com – **Iman R,** Gaza: 96.2MHz **W:** imanradio.com – **Kul Al-Nas R**, Tulkarem: 107.3MHz – **Najah FM,** Nablus: 92.3MHz. **W:** najah.edu/fm – **Quds R,** Gaza: 102.7MHz. **W:** www.qudsradio.ps – **R. Al-Shamal,** Qalqiliya: 96.6MHz. **W:** alshamal.net – **R. All for Peace,** Ramallah: 107.2MHz (Hebrew), 89.8MHz (Arabic). **W:** allforpeace.org Also rel. VOR R. Japan and Polish R. – **R. Bethlehem 2000,** Bethlehem: 89.6/106.4MHz 5kW. **W:** www.radiobethlehem2000.net Also rel. BBC&DW – **R. Isis,** Bethlehem: 87.5MHz. **W:** radioisis.net – **R. Manbar Al-Hurriya,** Hebron: 92.7MHz – **R. Marah,** Hebron: 100.4MHz. **W:** marah-fm.ps – **R. Mawwal,** Bethlehem 101.7MHz. **W:** mawwal.ps – **R. Nagham,** Qalqiliya: 99.6MHz. **W:** radionagham.com – **R. Nisaa,** Ramallah: 96.0MHz, Gaza 96.2MHz. **W:** radionisaa.net – **R. Tariq al-Mahabeh,** Nablus: 97.7/108.0MHz. **W:** tmfm.net – **Sawt al-Aqsa,** Gaza: 107.6MHz **W:** alaqsavoice.ps– **Sawt al-Asra,** Gaza: 107.9MHz. **W:** asravoice.ps – **Sirajj R.** Hebron: 105.7MHz **W:** sirajfm.com – **VO Love and Peace,** Ramallah: freq. not known **W:** www.volpfm.com – **Monte-Carlo Doualiya:** Ramallah 94.6MHz, Nablus 97.3MHz, Hebron 99.7MHz – **R. Sawa:** Bethlehem: 94.2MHz

ITALY

L.T: UTC +1h (31 Mar-27 Oct: +2h) — **Pop:** 58 million — **Pr.L:** Italian — **E.C:** 50Hz, 220V — **ITU:** I

RAI-RADIOTELEVISIONE ITALIANA (Pub.)
✉ Viale Mazzini 14, 00195 Roma ☎ +39 06 38781 📠 +39 06 3622621
✉ (Listeners) Centro Corrispondenza, C.P. 320, 00100 Roma ☎ +39 06 3317 2591 📠 +39 06 3317 1895 **E:** service@rai.it **W:** www.rai.it Tech. Dept: Rai Teche: Via Cernaia 33, 10121 Torino, Dir.Barbara Scaramucci **W:** www.teche.rai.it **E:** teche@rai.it Rai Way:Centro Ascolto e Qualità Controllo Servizio RAI Monza, Via Parco Mirabellino 1, 20052 Monza. **L.P:** Pres.: Francesco di Domenico **W:** www.raiway.rai.it **E:** raiway@rai.it **V:** QSL-card. No Rp. Sedi Regionali: **W:** www.sediregionali.rai.it **E:** sedi.regionali@rai.it
L.P: Pres.: Anna Maria Tarantola, GM: Luigi Gubitosi, Dir.Reg.Radio: Alberto Maccari, Dir.Rai Italia: Daniele Renzoni.
Regional Centres: 🖳 **1** Abruzzo: Viale de Amicis 27, 65123 Pescara – **2** Alto Adige: Piazza Mazzini 23, 39100 Bolzano/Bozen – **3** Basilicata: Via dell'Edilizia 2, 85100 Potenza – **4** Calabria: Viale G. Marconi 1, 87100 Cosenza – **5** Campania: Via Marconi 11,80125 Napoli – **6** Emilia-Romagna: Viale della Fiera 13, 40127 Bologna – **7** Friuli-Venezia-Giulia: Via Fabio Severo 7, 34133 Trieste – **8** Lazio: Largo Willy de Luca 4, 00188 Roma – **9** Liguria: Corso Europa 125, 16132 Genova – **10** Lombardia: Corso Sempione 27, 20145 Milano – **11** Marche: Piazza della Repubblica 1, 60121 Ancona – **12** Molise: Viale Principe di Piemonte 59, 86100 Campobasso – **13** Piemonte: Via G.Verdi 16, 10121 Torino – **14** Puglia: Via Dalmazia 104, 70121 Bari – **15** Sardegna: Via Barone Rossi 27, 09125 Cagliari – **16** Sicilia: Viale Strasburgo 19, 90146 Palermo – **17** Toscana: Largo Alcide de Gasperi 1, 50136 Firenze – **18** Trentino: Via Fratelli Perini 141, 38100 Trento – **19** Umbria: Via L. Masi 2, 06121 Perugia – **20** Valle d'Aosta: Loc.Grande Charriere 70, 11020 Saint Cristophe – **21** Veneto: Palazzo Labia, Campo S. Geremia,Sestiere Cannaregio 275, 30121 Venezia.

MW Station		kHz	kW	Prg
16)	Caltanissetta (St.Anna)	567	20	R1 (b) closed in 2013
2)	Bolzano (Monticolo)	657	25	R1 (e)
17)	Pisa (Coltano)	657	55	R1
3)	Potenza	693	20	R
7)	Trieste (Monte Radio)	819	20	R1
14)	Taranto	873	1	R1
10)	Milano (Siziano)	900	600	R1
16)	Trapani	936	10	R1
21)	Venezia (Campalto)	936	20	R1 (+a)
7)	Trieste(Monte Radio)	981	10	S
4)	Vibo Valentia(CapoVatic)	999	2	R1
19)	Perugia(Torgiano)	999	20	R1
6)	Rimini (Viserba)	999	10	R1
13)	Torino (Volpiano)	999	10	R1
1)	Pescara (SanSilvestro)	1035	10	R1
14)	Lecce(SalentoSpecchia)	1035	2	R1
11)	Ancona (Montagnolo)	1062	10	R1

MW Station		kHz	kW	Prg
15)	Cagliari (Sestu)	1062	25	R1 (d)
16)	Catania (Barriera del B)	1062	2	R1 (c)
18)	Trento (Villazzano)	1062	2	R1
8)	Roma (Monte Ciocci)	1107	10	R1
20)	Aosta (Gerdaz)	1116	2	R1 (f)
13)	Cuneo (Tetti Pesio)	1116	20	R1
16)	Palermo(MtePellegrino)	1116	10	R1 (c)
3)	Matera	1314	2	R1
14)	Foggia	1431	2	R1
13)	Biella (S.Paolo)	1449	2	R1
2)	Bolzano (Bressanone)	1449	2	R1 (e)
2)	Bolzano (Brunico)	1449	2	R1 (e)
10)	Sondrio	1449	2	R1
12)	Campobasso	1575	2	R1
9)	Genova (Portofino)	1575	50	R1
7)	Gorizia (Piuma)	1575	2	R1 (a)
16)	Nuoro (S.Onofrio)	1575	1	R1 (d)
19)	Terni (S.Lorenzo)	1584	2	R1

FM (MHz)		R1	R2	R3	R4	GRP	kW
6)	Bertinoro	90.8	93.4	99.6		89.7	30
6)	Bologna	89.5	91.7	93.9		93.6	60
2)	Bolzano	91.5	93.7	97.1	99.6	95.1	14
6)	Ca' del Vento	92.1	96.5	98.5		90.6	40
4)	Canepina-PNibbio	93.7	99.4				12
4)	Capo Spartivento	95.6	97.6	99.7		104.2	10
21)	Col Visentin	91.1	93.1	95.5			30
4)	Crotone	94.9	97.9	99.9		97.4	10
17)	Firenze	87.8	91.1	98.4		88.0	10
7)	Friscano	88.4	90.5	94.1			10
4)	Gambarie	95.3	97.3	99.3			40
			103.9				40
9)	Genova	89.5	91.9	95.1		104.5	30
5)	Golfo di Policastro	88.5	90.5	92.5			10
5)	Golfo di Salerno	95.1	97.1	99.1			20
7)	Gorizia	89.5	92.3	98.3	106.8		10
14)	Martina Franca	89.1	91.1	93.1		90.3	100
10)	Milano	90.6	93.7	99.4	102.2	88.3	60
17)	Monte Argentario	90.1	92.1	94.3		99.6	70
			89.0				16
9)	Monte Beigua	91.5	94.6	98.9		100.5	40
14)	Monte Caccia	94.6	96.7	99.2		98.2	100
16)	Monte Cammarata	91.1	95.9	99.9		98.3	100
6)	Monte Canate			95.9			24
8)	Monte Cavo	87.6	91.2	98.4		99.3	80
11)	Monte Conero	88.3	90.3	92.3		105.2	100
5	Monte Faito	94.1	96.1	98.1		91.0	100
16)	Monte Lauro	94.7	96.7	98.7		89.0	100
15)	Monte Limbara	88.9	95.3	99.3			60
17)	Monte Luco	88.1	92.5	96.2		103.2	30
11)	Monte Nerone	94.7	96.6	98.7		88.1	100
19)	Monte Miranda	95.7	97.7	99.7		102.1	60
				88.3			30
10)	Monte Penice	94.2	97.4	99.9		88.2	120
			103.0				120
3)	Monte Pierfaone	88.1	90.1	92.1		91.2	45
19)	Monte Sambuco	88.6	90.7	93.5			100
			100.7				100
4)	Monte Scuro	88.5	90.5	92.5		98.4	30
15)	Monte Serpeddi	90.7	92.7	96.3		106.5	70
17)	Monte Serra	88.5	90.5	92.9		88.2	70
16)	Monte Soro	88.7	91.9	93.9		104.2	30
19)	Monte Subasio	89.3	91.4	93.5		104.6	30
21)	Monte Venda	88.1	89.0	89.9			160
5)	Monte Vergine (AV)	87.9	90.3	92.3		93.0	20
5)	Napoli Camaldoli	89.3	91.3	93.3	103.9	101.0	12
3)	Nova Sisi			89.5			10
16)	PalermoMtePellegri	94.9	96.9	98.9		90.3	40
1)	Pescara S. Silvestro	89.2	94.3	96.4		102.0	70
3)	Pomarico	88.7	92.7	95.7			10
15)	Punta Badde Urbara	91.3	93.3	97.3			70
8)	Roma M. Mario	89.7	91.7	93.7		100.3	100
8)	Roseto Capo Spulico	94.4	96.5	98.5			10
14)	Salento Turrisi	90.7	95.5	97.5		91.0	60
17)	San Cerbone	95.3	97.3	99.3			12
21)	SanZenodiMontagna	93.2	96.5	98.5		89.5	10
10)	Selva Piana	88.4	90.3	92.4			20
13)	Torino Eremo	92.1	95.6	98.2	101.8	88.2	100
16)	Trapani Erice	88.4	90.5	92.5		90.8	60
7)	TriesteMteBelvedere	91.5	93.6	95.8	103.9	106.7	30
9)	Udine	94.9	97.2	99.8			60
8)	Velletri	88.7	90.7	92.7			15

+ over 6000 stns below 1kW not mentioned.
D.Prgr: All stns transmit from 0500 to 2300, except for Milano 900kHz,

---

Roma 1107kHz 24h **R1**=Radiouno, **R2FM**=Radiodue, **R3FM**=Radiotre, **S**=Special Prgrs.

Regional Prgrs: 0620-0628 Mon/Sat RAI1; 1110-1127 Mon/Sun. **(a) Friuli:** 0620-0657 Mon-Sat RAI1, 1003-1157 Mon-Sat RAI1, 1130-1157 Sun RAI 1,1300-1415 Mon-Fri RAI1, 1330-1400 Sat RAI1, 1730-1756 Mon/Fri RAI1, 1715-1756 Sat RAI1, 0740-0910, 1108-1157, 1730-1756 Sun sport RAI1; (+a): "L'ora della Venezia Giulia" 1445-1545 Mon/Sat RAI1, 1330-1400 Sun RAI1. – **(b) Sicilia:** 1230-1245, Mon/Sat RAI1 Arabic sce only on FM stns. – **(c) Sicilia:** 0630-0657,1110-1127,1315-1400, 1730-1756 Mon/Sat; RAI1 1140-1157,1730-1756 Sun sport RAI1. – **(d) Sardegna:** 0630-0657,1315-1400, 1730-1756 Mon/Sat RAI1; 1730-1756 Sun sport RAI1. – **(f) Valle D'Aosta:** 1315-1400 Mo/Sat, 1730-1756 Sun sport RAI1(Bilingual). – **(e) Alto Adige** 0630-0657, 1315-1400, 1730-1756 Mon/Sat; 1730-1756 Sun sport RAI1. **NB:** All 1h earlier in Summertime.

SPECIAL PRGRS

ISO Radio: 24h sce for motorway users on 103.3MHz FM (220 txs of 5kW or less);103.2MHz Milano,Como,Lecco area; 103.5MHz, Rome area **W:** www.isoradio.it

GR Parlamento: 24h sce. Italian Parliament channel. 2000-0455. FM (150 txs of 5kW or less) **W:** www.radio.rai.it/grparlamento

Sender Bozen (Bolzano): Prgrs in German on FM (46 txs of 1kW or less) DPrgr: 0500 (Sun 0600)-2300. N. 0615 (W), 0800 (Sun), 1000 (W), 1100, 1200, 1300, 1700 (W), 1930. **W:** www.senderbozen.rai.it

Regional Prgr. in Slovene: Trieste 981kHz 10kW + 103.9MHz 20kW (and 22 additional FM-txs). **D. Prgr:** 0500 (Sun 0600)-2300. **N:** W 0500, 0700, 0900, 1200, 1300, 1600, 1800; Sun 0700, 1200, 1300, 1800. **N.** in German: 0900 (W). Night : Relay V channel Filodiffusione or Notturno Italiano 1900-0500

Ann: Home Sce: "RAI Radiouno", "RAI Radiodue", "RAI Radiotre" as appropriate. Night Prgr: "RAI-Radiotelevisione Italiana stazioni a onda media di Milano kHz 900, di Roma kHz 1107, Notturno Italiano".

Notturno Italiano: musical and cultural prgr with I/E/F/ news. irr. schedule

R.A.S.

✉ Europaallee 164/A, 39100 Bozen ☎ +39 0471 546666 🖷 +39 0471 200378 W: www.ras.bz.it E: info@ras.bz.it
L.P: Pres: . Rudi Gamper MD: Georg Plattner . Dir. Tec: Dr .Johann Silbernagl RAS is a public body of the autonomous Region of Southern Tyrol whose purpose is to relay TV and radio from Germany, Austria and Switzerland to the German-speaking population.

FM (MHz)	RAS 1	RAS 2	RAS 3	kW
Kronplatz	100.7	103.0	104.7	2
Meransen	101.3	103.9	107.3	1
Obervinschgau	100.5	103.0	106.1	0.6
Penegal	103.3	100.3	104.7	2
Perdonig	101.8	104.0	106.0	1
Plose	99.8	102.0	105.6	1
Vinschgau	101.1	102.9	105.0	2

+ 880 low power stns

RAS 1: rel. OE-3 (Austria) - **RAS-2:** rel. OE-R (Austria) - **RAS-3:** rel. OE-1 (Austria)

DAB: RAI & RAS on Blocks 12A-12DA, 223.936MHz - 229.072MHz Consorzio DAB Italia on block 9D. 208.064MHz **W:** www.dab.it

PRIVATE STATIONS

Only stns with MW/SW broadcasts and FM networks are listed. A number of other stns are heard irr. There are approx. 600 FM stns

MW	kHz	kW	Station, location and h of tr.
1)	1368	10	Challenger R., Villa Estense: prgrs Studio Dx, IRRS-Nexus
2)	1503	0.5	Onda Media Broadcast, San Pietro in Casale: 24h irr.prgrs La Voce di Russia
2)	1512	0.5	Onda Media Broadcast, San Pietro in Casale: 0500-2130 irr prgrs RTSI Svizzera Italiana
1)	1566	1	Challenger Radio, Roma: 24h prgrs: Studio Dx, IRRS.Nexus
3)	1566	0.1	R. Kolbe Sat, Schio: 24h irr.
4)	1584	12	R. Studio X, Momigno: 24h

Addresses and other information:
1) Via Legnaro 6, 35040 Villa Estense (PD) 🖷 +39 0429 662280 **W:** www. challenger.it **E:** challenger@challenger.it **V.** by letter Rp. SM: Maurizio Anselmo – **2) E:** ondamediabroadcast@gmail.com SM: Roberto Furlan ☎ +39 3927558283 – **3)** R. Kolbe Sat , Via Ischia 9, 36015 Schio (VI) ☎ +39 0445 505035 **W:** www.radiokolbe.it **E:** segreteria@radiokolbe.net SM: Alberto De Petto – **4)** Via Mammianese 687, 51100 Momigno (PT) **W:** www.radiostudiox.it **E:** info@radiostudiox.it SM: Luca Betti.i- FM: 87,30MHz 5kW **V.** by letter Rp

FM NETWORKS IN MAJOR CITIES (MHz):

	Network	To	Mi	Ve	Bo	Ge
1)	Circuito Margherita	91.8	89.5	-	-	90.1
2)	Kiss Kiss	92.4	97.6	-	101.8	104.9
3)	InBlu R.	89.0	95.3	94.6	92.3	88.8
4)	Latte Miele	88.5	92.2	106.2	105.0	-
5)	m2o	93.0	93.1	87.8	89.0	88.6
6)	Popolare Network	97.6	107.6	97.3	96.2	-
7)	R. Capital	90.3	90.1	98.5	99.4	93.9
8)	R. 105	99.6	99.1	98.9	103.5	99.5
9)	R. 101	101.0	100.9	107.3	96.0	105.2
10)	R. Classica	98.7	94.0	-	-	-101.1
11)	R. Cuore	92.7	92.4	-	-	-
12)	R. Deejay	106.9	99.7	94.8	99.7	96.9
13)	R. RDS	96.4	94.4	99.8	104.2	95.7
14)	R. Italia Anni 60	103.7	106.3	101.7	102.1	91.3
15)	R. Italia S.M.I	106.6	98.4	101.5	100.6	106.3
16)	R. Maria	107.5	89.0	106.5	90.5	106.6
17)	R. Mater	105.7	95.3	100.1	100.2	102.0
19)	R. Padania Libera	106.0	103.5	93.8	106.2	96.0
20)	R. Radicale	102.8	87.9	104.7	92.0	95.4
21)	R. RMC1	105.5	105.3	100.4	101.3	104.2
23)	R. 24	105.0	104.8	106.8	107.0	97.2
24)	RTL 102.5	102.5	102.5	102.5	101.6	102.4
25)	Virgin R.	90.9	104.5	93.1	106.5	105.5
26)	R. Sportiva	101.5	95.9	-	88.4	105.8

	Network	Fi	Rm	Na	Ba	Pa
1)	Circuito Margherita	96.7	-	100.7	95.2	95.2
2)	Kiss Kiss	92.8	97.9	89.0	100.8	103.0
3)	InBlu R.	93.9	96.3	93,45	100.0	88.0
4)	Latte Miele	91.4	93.1	101.2	93.5	94.6
5)	m2o	105.8	97.0	98.3	88.5	107.8
6)	Popolare Network	93.6	103.3	-	97.3	-
7)	R. Capital	97.6	95.5	104.6	99.5	92.9
8)	R. 105	105.0	96.1	99.7	87.9	105.1
9)	R. 101	94.9	92.0	93.0	100.0	97.2
10)	R. Classica	99.4	89.5	-	-105.0	99.5
11)	R. Cuore	100.2	-	-	105.3	89.1
12)	R. Deejay	100.6	101.0	92.3	93.2	107.5
13)	R. RDS	88.3	103.0	107.5	89.1	106.6
14)	R. Italia Anni 60	96.2	-	104.1	89.6	95.8
15)	R. Italia S.M.I	107.6	104.2	96.8	103.5	104.8
16)	R. Maria	88.8	95.1	98.8	102.0	89.4
17)	R. Mater	93.9	93.5	-	95.4	-
18)	R. Norba	-	-	92.7	105.5	-
19)	R. Padania Libera	-	-	-	-	104.0
20)	R. Radicale	97.0	88.6	101.6	89.3	92.0
21)	R. RMC1	106.6	106.3	91.6	92.0	90.0
22)	R. Subasio	94.5	94.5	106.5	-	-
23)	R. 24	103.8	107.9	103.5	88.2	104.5
24)	RTL 102.5	100.9	102.1	102.6	102.5	102.3
25)	Virgin R.	107.2	98.7	93.5	106.6	93.2
26)	R. Sportiva	94.2	-	107.0	100.2	100.5

To=Torino Mi=Milano Ve=Venezia Bo=Bologna Ge=Genova Fi=Firenze Rm=Roma Na=Napoli Ba=Bari Pa=Palermo
Reference to Italian frequency on **W:** www.fmdx.altervista.org

Addresses and other information
1) Via Marchese di Villabianca 82, 90143 Palermo (PA) ☎ +39 091 302712 ▤ +39 091 8724835 **W:** www.radiomargherita.com **E:** info@radiomargherita.com SM: Giuseppe Orobello **V.** by letter. Rp. – **2)** Via Sgambati 61, 80131 Napoli (NA) ☎ +39 081 5461212 ▤ +39 081 5467789 **W:** www.kisskiss.it, ufficiotecnico@kisskiss.it SM: Antonio Niespolo TM: Ugo Lombardi **V.** by letter. Rp. – **3)** Via Aurelia 796, 00165 Roma (RM) ☎ +39 06 6650851 ▤+39 06 66508516 **W:** www.radioinblu.it **E:** info@radioinblu.it TM: Marco Giubileo. **V.** by letter. Rp – **4)** Via Andrea Costa 10, 40013 Castelmaggiore (BO) ☎ +39 051 70928 ▤ +39 051 6325710 **W:** www.lattemiele.com **E:** info@lattemiele.com SM: Franco Magnani – **5)** Piazza della Repubblica 23/c, 00185 Roma (RM) ☎ +39 06 492311 ▤ +39 06 4453758 **W:** www.m2o.it **E:** contatti@m2o.it PM: Fabrizio Tamburini **V.** by letter. Rp. – **6)** Via U.Olleare 5, 20155 Milano (MI) ☎ +39 02 392411 ▤ +39 02 39273125 **W:** www.radiopopolare.it **E:** Radiopop@radiopopolare.it SM: Stefano Di Blasio **V.** by QSL-card. Rp – **7)** Via C. Colombo 90, 00147 Roma (RM) ☎ +39 06 494321 ▤ +39 06 44702290 **W:** www.capital.it **E:** infoline@capital.it SM: Vittorio Zucconi. **V.** by QSL-card. Rp – **8)** Largo G. Donegani 1, 20121 Milano (MI) ☎ +39 02 6596116 ▤ +39 02 6592272 **W:** www.105.net **E:** diretta@105.net, altafrequenza@radioengineering.net SM: Alberto Hazan **V.** QSL-Card. Rp. – **9)** Via Giovanni Ventura 3, 20134 , Milano (MI) ☎ +39 02 210831 ▤ +39 02 21083210 **W:** www.r101.it **E:** infor101@r101.it SM: Guido Monti **V.** by QSL-card. Rp. – **10)** Via M.Burigozzo 5, 20122 Milano (MI) ☎+39 02 58219600 ▤ +39 02 58219407 **W:** www.radioclassica.fm **E:** radioclassica@class.it SM: Carla Signorile

V. by letter. Rp. – **11)** Via Giovanni da Verrazzano 16, Localita Le Melorie, 56038 Ponsacco (PI) ☎ +39 0587 2861 ▤ +39 0587 733861 **W:** www.mediahit.it/ **E:** info@mediahit.it SM: Italo Bessi **V.** by letter. Rp – **12)** Via Massena 2, 20154 Milano (MI) ☎ +39 02 342522 ▤ +39 02 342888 **W:** www.deejay.it **E:** segnalazioni@deejay.it SM: Linus **V.** by QSL-card. Rp.– **13)** Via G.Mazzini 119, 00195 Roma (RM) ☎ +39 06 377051 ▤ +39 06 3725336 **W:** www.rds.it **E:** ufficiotecnico@rds.it SM: Stefano Montefusco **V.** by letter. Rp. – **14)** Via Zambra 11, 38121 Trento (TN) ☎ +39 0461 828990 ▤ +39 0461 428960 **W:** www.radioitaliaanni60.it **E:** info@radioitaliaanni60.it SM: Franco Nisi **V.** by letter. Rp. – **15)** Viale Europa 49, 20093 Cologno Monzese (MI) ☎ +39 02 25441 ▤ +39 02 25444220 **W:** www.radioitalia.it **E:** info@radioitalia.it SM: Mario Volanti **V.** by letter. Rp. – **16)** Via F.Turati 7, 22036 Erba (CO) ☎ +39 031 610600 ▤ +39 031 611288 **W:** www.radiomaria.it **E:** info.ita@radiomaria.org SM: Don Livio Fanzaga **V.** by QSL-card. Rp. – **17)** Via G.Marconi 85, 22036 Arcellasco d'Erba (CO) ☎ +39 031 645214 ▤ +39 031 6490527 **W:** www.radiomater.com **E:** info@radiomater.com SM: Don Mario Galbiati **V.** by letter. Rp. – **18)** Via Foggia 29, 70014 Conversano (BA) ☎ +39 80 4951229 ▤ +39 80 4953079 **W:** www.radionorba.it **E:** radionorba@radionorba.it SM: Annamaria Fantasia **V.** by letter. Rp. – **19)** Via C.Bellerio 41, 20161 Milano (MI) ☎ +39 02 66203529 ▤ +39 02 66220964 **W:** www.radiopadania.net **E:** direzione@radiopadania.net SM: Cesare Bosetti **V.** by letter. Rp. – **20)** Centro di Produzione, Via Principe Amedeo 2, 00185 Roma (RM) ☎ +39 06 488781 ▤ +39 06 4880196 **W:** www.radioradicale.it **E:** staff@radioradicale.it SM: Paolo Martini **V.** by letter. Rp. – **21)** Via Principe Amedeo 2, 20121 Milano (MI) ☎ +39 02 29001636 ▤ +39 02 6551451 **W:** www.radiomontecarlo.net **E:** rmc@radiomontecarlo.net, altafrequenza@radioengineering.net SM: Paolo Del Forno **V.** by QSL-card.Rp. – **22)** Localita Colle de Bensi, 06081 Assisi (PG) ☎ +39 075 8060 ▤ +39 075 8065419 **W:** www.radiosubasio.it **E:** subasio@radiosubasio.it SM: Rita Settimi **V.** by letter. Rp – **23)** Via Monte Rosa 91, 20149 Milano (MI) ☎ +39 02 30221 ▤ +039 02 30224462 **W:** www.radio24.it **E:** info@radio24.it SM: Elia Zamboni **V.** by letter. Rp – **24)** Viale Piemonte 61/63, 20093 Cologno Monzese (MI) ☎ +39 02 251515 ▤ +39 02 25096201 **W:** www.rtl.it **E:** qualita@rtl.it SM: Luigi Tornari **V.** QSL-card. Rp. – **25)** Largo Donegani 1, 20121 Milano (MI) ☎ +39 02 6596116 ▤ +39 02 62537460 **W:** www.virginradioitaly.it **E:** guastivirgin@virginradio.it altafrequenza@radioengineering.net SM: Francesco Migliozzi **V.** QSL-Card. Rp. – **26)** Via Giovanni da Verrazzano 16, Localita Le Melorie, 56038 Ponsacco (PI) ☎ +39 0587 2861 ▤ +39 0587 733861 **W:** www.radiosportiva.com **E:** info@mediahit.it SM: Italo Bessi **V.** by letter. Rp

EXTERNAL SERVICES:
NEXUS - INTERNATIONAL BROADCASTING ASSOCIATION
See International Broadcasting section

AMERICAN FORCES NETWORK EUROPE (U.S. Mil.)
W: www.afneurope.net **E:** harringtonj@afns.vicenza.army.mil
1st Prgr. The Eagle on 106.0MHz Key stns: Vicenza (10kW) AFN,C/o Caserma Ederle, Via della Pace 100, 36100 Vicenza (VI) **E:** vicenza.afneurope.net ☎+039 0444 397111 **V.** by letter. No Rp. Livorno (10kW) AFN Livorno,UNIT 31301,Box 64,APO AE,09613,USA. Local prgr 0500-0800, 1000-1200, 1400-1700, 2000-2200 Mon-Fr **W:** livorno.afneurope.net Other stns:, Napoli "LAVA 106" (10kW), PSC 817,Box 31,FPO AE 09622,USA **E:** naples.afneurope.net **E:** ask.nsa@nsa.naples.navy.mil **2nd Prgr.** Power Network on 107.0MHz Key Station: Vicenza (10kW) AFN,C/o Caserma Ederle, Via della Pace 100, 36100 Vicenza (VI) **W:** vicenza.afneurope.net ☎+039 0444 397111 **V.** by let-

ter. No Rp. **Other stns**: Livorno/Sigonella (all 5kW) **E:** jeffrey.wells@afn.sicily.army.mil Napoli (10kW), San Vito (0.5kW)

IVORY COAST

L.T: UTC — **Pop:** 21 million — **Pr.L:** French, Diola, 12 ethnic — **E.C:** 50Hz, 220V — **ITU:** CTI

CONSEIL NATIONAL DE LA COMMUNICATION AUDIOVISUELLE (CNCA)
✉ Place de la République, B.P. V 56, Abidjan ☎+225 20 311580 **W:** lecnca.net **E:** infos@lecnca.net **L.P:** Gen. Secr: Franck Anderson Kouassi. Chmn: Jerome Diegou Bailly

RADIODIFFUSION-TÉLÉVISION IVOIRIENNE(RTI, Gov.)
✉ B.P. 191, Abidjan ☎+225 20 214800 ▤ +225 20 215038
W: www.rti.ci **L.P:** Interim DG: Pascal Aka Brou. Deputy DG for Tech: Issa Yéresso Sangaré. Dir. Broadc: Robert Kissi N'Da.

FM (MHz)	1	2	kW	FM (MHz)	1	2	kW
Abobo-Abidjan	90.0	92.0	5	Man	96.9	100.2	-
Bouaflé	99.0	102.6	-	Naingbo	93.0	103.0	-
Dabakala	91.0	101.0	-	Niangue	93.0	95.9	-
Dimbokro	99.0	102.9	-	Séguéla	89.0	95.0	-
Divo	88.0	90.8	10	Tengréla	96.3	99.6	-
Grabo	88.0	91.0	0.5	Tiémé	88.0	91.0	5
Kouakoussikro	89.3	92.4	-	Touba	94.7	101.5	-
Koun Fao	94.2	101.0	-				

R. Côte d'Ivoire (1): 0500-2400. **Fréquence Deux (2):** 24h.
Ann: "R. Côte d'Ivoire" or "Fréquence Deux". **IS:** s/on with clock chimes.

Other stations:
City FM, Abidjan: 106.1MHz — **Cocody FM,** Abidjan: 98.5MHz 1kW. W: radiococodyfm.com — **Fréquence Vie,** Abidjan: 89.4MHz 1kW. W: frequencevie.en-fete.org — **La Voix de l'Évangile,** Abidjan: 102.5MHz — **N'Gowa FM,** Abidjan: 89.7MHz — **R. Al Bayane,** Abidjan: 95.7MHz. W: radio-albayane.com — **R. Arc-en-ciel,** Abidjan: 102.0MHz — **R. Espoir,** Abidjan: 102.8MHz. W: radioespoir.ci — **R. Jam:** Yamoussokro 88.1MHz 1kW, Abidjan 99.3MHz 3kW. W: radiojam.ci — **R. Nostalgie,** Abidjan: 101.1MHz. W: nostalgie.ci — **Zenith FM,** Abidjan: 92.8MHz **Africa No 1:** Abidjan 91.1MHz (see main entry under Gabon).
BBC African Sce: Abidjan 94.3MHz.
RFI Afrique: Abidjan/Bouaké/Korogho on 97.6MHz.
Voice of America, Abidjan: 99.0MHz

JAMAICA

L.T: UTC -5h — **Pop:** 2.9 million — **Pr.L:** English — **E.C:** 50Hz, 110/220V — **ITU:** JMC

RJR COMMUNICATIONS GROUP
RADIO JAMAICA LTD (Comm.)
✉ 32 Lyndhurst Road, P.O. Box 23, Kingston 5 ☎ +1 876 926 1100 ▤ +1 876 929 7467 **E:** webmaster@radiojamaica.com
W: www.radiojamaica.com
L.P: Chmn. J.A. Lester Spaulding. MD: Gary Allen
FM (MHz): RJR94: 94.1/94.3/94.5/94.7/94.9 — **Fame95:** 95.1/95.3/95.5/95.7/95.9 — **Hitz92:** 92.1/92.3/92.5/92.2/92.9

Other Stations:
BBC 104 FM. FM: 104.1/104.3/104.5/104.7/104.9MHz D.Prgr: 24h relay of the BBC World Service — **Bess FM,** 4 East Bloomsbury Rd, Kingston 10 ☎ +1 876 754 1898 ▤ +1 876 920 4749 **W:** www.bessfm.com **FM:** 100.1/100.3/100.5MHz — **Free FM,** General Penitentiary, South Camp Rd, Kingston. **FM:** Kingston 88.9MHz. Prison Community Radio — **Gospel JA,** 7 Brettford Ave, Molynes Rd, Kingston 10 ☎ +1 876 816 3468 **W:** www.gospelja.com **FM** 91.7/91.9MHz — **Hot 102FM,** 37 St. James St., Montego Bay ☎ +1 876 952 3056 **W:** www.hot102.fm. **L.P:** GM: Ken Williams. **FM:** 94.1/102.3/102.5/102.7/102.9MHz. Format: Talk & hit radio — **Irie FM,** P.O Box 282, Coconut Grove, Ocho Rios ☎ +1 876 974 5051/968 5023 ▤ +1 876 974 5943 **E:** info@iriefm.net **W:** www.iriefm.net. **L.P:** MD Chad Young **FM:** 107.1/107.3/107.5/107.7/107.9MHz. Format: Reggae — **JA105FM,** 40-40 Beechwood Ave, Kingston 5 ☎ +1 876 501 5728 ▤ +1 876 929 6173 **L.P:** CEP Danville Walker **FM:** 105.3/105.5/105.7MHz — **Jet FM,** Hills of St Mary. FM: 88.9. Format: Community radio operated by Jeffrey Town Farmers Association Ltd. — **Klas FM,** 17 Haining Rd, Kingston 5 ☎ +1 876 929 1344 ▤ +1 876 906 0572 **W:** www.klassportsradio.com **FM:** 89.1/89.3/89.5/89.9MHz Format: Sport — **Kool 97 FM,** 1 Braemar Ave, Kingston 10 ☎ +1 876 978 4037 ▤ +1 876 978 6080 **W:** www.kool97fm.com **L.P:** GM Delroy Brown. **FM:** 97.1/97.3/97.5/97.7/97.9M Hz — **Love 101,** 81 Hagley Pk Rd, Kingston 11 ☎ +1 876 968 9596 ▤

+1 876 968 7545 **W:** www.love101.org **L.P:** GM: Moya Thomas. **FM:** 10 1.1/101.3/101.5/101.7/101.9MHz. Format: Rlg. — **Linkz FM,** 8 Beckford St., Savanna-la-mar ☎ +1 876 955 9523 ▤ +1 876 955 9523. **W:** www.linkzfm.com. **L.P:** CEO Roger Allen. **FM:** 96.5/96.9MHz — **Mega Jamz,** 20 Ballater Av., Kingston 10 ☎ +1 876 631 5269 ▤ +1 876 929 9566 **W:** www.megajamz98fm.com **L.P:** MD Lorraine Vonstrolley. **FM:** 98.1/98.3/98.5/98.7/98.9MHz. Format: Oldies — **Mello FM,** 63 Barnett St, Montego Bay ☎ +1 876 971 4163 **W:** www.mellofmjamaica.com. **L.P:** CEO Al Robinson. Ops Mgr Edwin George. **FM:** 88.1/88.3/88.5MHz — **Music 99,** 6 Bradley Av, Kingston 10 ☎ +1 876 968 4880 ▤ +1 876 968 9165 **L.P:** MD Newton James. **FM:** 99.1/99.3/99.5/99.7/99.9MHz — **Nationwide Radio,** 27 Mannings Hill Rd, Kingston 8 ☎ +1 876 755 6397 ▤ +1 876 924 5375 **W:** www.nationwideradiojm.com **L.P:** CEO: Chris Hughes. Op.Mgr Lennie Gordon. **FM:** 90.3/90.5/90.7MHz — **NCU 91 FM,** Northern Caribbean University, East Campus, Manchester Rd, Mandeville ☎ +1 876 963 7711. **W:** www.ncumediagroup.com/ncufm.htm **FM:** 91.1/91.3/91.5MHz. Format: Rlg. (Adventist) — **Newstalk 93FM,** Universal Media Company, 18 Ring Rd., Mona, Kingston 7 ☎ +1 876 970 2345 ▤ +1 876 970 2472 **W:** www.newstalk.com.jm. **L.P:** GM Jennifer Cheesman. **FM:** 93.1/93.3/93.5/93.7/93.9MHz — **Power 106 FM,** 6 Bradley Av., Kingston 10 ☎ +1 876 968 4880 ▤ +1 876 968 9165 **E:** power106@cwjamaica.com **W:** www.go-jamaica.com/power **L.P:** MD Newton James. **FM:** 106.1/106.3/106.5/106.7/ 106.9MHz — **Roots FM,** 1 Mahoe Drive, Kingston 11 ☎ +1 876 923 6488 ▤ +1 876 923 6000 **W:** www.rootsfmjamaica.com **FM:** Kingston 96.1MHz — **Stylz FM,** 4 Boundbrooke Ave, Port Antonio PO, Portland ☎ +1 876 453 1444. **W:** www.stylzfm.com. **FM:** 96.1/96.3/96.7MHz — **Sun City Radio,** Mother In Crisis, Lot 12, 2nd Dolphon Way, Braeton, Phase 1, St. Catherine ☎ +1 876 938 8132. **W:** suncityradio.fm. **L.P:** CEO Doreen Billings. **FM:** 104.9MHz — **TBC FM (The Breath of Change),** 51 Molynes Rd, Kingston 10 ☎ +1 876 754 5120 ▤ +1 876 968 9159 **W:** www.tbcradio.org. **L.P:** Joy Hall. **FM:** Kingston 88.5MHz. Format: Rlg (Baptist). — **Vybz FM,** 98 Great George Street, Savanna-la-Mar, Westmoreland ☎ +1 876 918 2521 ▤ +1 876 918 2394 **FM:** Westmoreland 96.3MHz — **Zip 103,** 1B Derrymore Road, Kingston ☎ +1 876 929-2748/6233 ▤ +1 876 960 0523 **W:** www.zipfm.net. **L.P:** MD Chad Young. **FM:** 103.1/103.3/103.5/103.7/103.9MHz. Format: Techo/dance/alternative.
RADIO FRANCE INTERNATIONALE, FM: 96.5MHz

JAPAN

L.T: UTC +9h — **Pop:** 127.5 million — **Pr.L:** Japanese — **EC:** 50 & 60Hz, 100V — **ITU:** J

INFORMATION AND COMMUNICATIONS POLICY BUREAU, MINISTRY OF INTERNAL AFFAIRS AND COMMUNICATIONS (SOUMU SHO)
✉ 1-2, Kasumigaseki 2-chome, Chiyoda-ku, Tokyo 100-8926 ☎ +81 3 5253 5111 **W:** www.soumu.go.jp **L.P:** Minister: T.Kawabata

NIPPON HOSO KYOKAI (NHK)
(The Japan Broadcasting Corporation)
✉ 2-1, Jinnan 2-chome, Shibuya-ku, Tokyo 150-8001 ☎ +81 3 3465 1111 **W:** www.nhk.or.jp
L.P: Chmn. (Board of Governors): K.Hamada. Pres: M.Matsumoto. Exec. Vice-Pres: N.Ono. Gen. MD's: H.Tsukada, K.Yoshikuni. MD & Exec. Dir. Gen: K.Kubota. MD's: Y.Shimizu, K.Shinyama, K.Ishida, Y.Kida, Y.Itano, K.Uwataki, T.Fukui. **Pub:** NHK Nenkan (Japanese), NHK Update (English)

MW Loc. & Prgr	Call	kHz	kW	MW Loc. & Prgr	Call	kHz	kW
F2) Morioka 1	QG	531	10	E6) Oita 1	IP	639	5
E2) Nago 1		531	1	C3) Shizuoka 2	PB	639	10
F3) Yamagata 1	JG	540	5	C4) Toyama 1	IG	648	5
E3) Miyazaki 1	MG	540	5	B1) Osaka 1	BK	666	100
E4) Kitakyushu 1	SK	540	1	G5) Hakodate 1	VK	675	5
A2) Matsumoto 1		540	1	D3) Yamaguchi 1	UG	675	5
C2) Nanao 1		540	1	E7) Nagasaki 1	AG	684	5
E2) Ishigaki 1		540	1	A1) Tokyo 2	AB	693	500
E2) Okinawa 1	AP	549	10	G6) Kitami 2	KD	702	10
G1) Sapporo 1	IK	567	100	D1) Hiroshima 2	FB	702	10
E5) Kagoshima 1	HG	576	5	C1) Nagoya 1	CK	729	50
C3) Hamamatsu 1	DG	576	1	G1) Sapporo 2	IB	747	500
G2) Kushiro 1	PG	585	10	E8) Kumamoto 1	GK	756	10
A1) Tokyo 1	AK	594	300	F4) Akita 2	UB	774	500
D2) Okayama 1	KK	603	5	C5) Takayama 1		792	1
G3) Obihiro 1	OG	603	5	G4) Enbetsu 1		792	1
E1) Fukuoka 1	LK	612	100	A3) Takada 1		792	1
G4) Asahikawa 1	CG	621	3	E5) Naze 1		792	1
B2) Kyoto 1	OK	621	1	A2) Nagano 1	NK	819	5
A2) Iida 1		621	1	B1) Osaka 2	BB	828	300
E3) Nobeoka 1		621	1	A3) Niigata 1	QK	837	10

MW Loc. & Prgr	Call	kHz	kW		MW Loc. & Prgr	Call	kHz	kW
G4) Nayoro 1		837	1		F5) Fukushima 1 FP		1323	1
F5) Koriyama 1		846	5		F2) Yamada 1		1323	1
H1) Uwajima 1		846	1		E8) Minamata 1		1341	1
E8) Hitoyoshi 1		846	1		F5) Iwaki 1		1341	1
E8) Kumamoto 2 GB		873	500		H4) Takamatsu 1 HP		1368	5
C3) Shizuoka 1 PK		882	10		D4) Tottori 1 LG		1368	1
F1) Sendai 1 HK		891	10		F3) Tsuruoka 1		1368	1
C1) Nagoya 2 CB		909	10		D3) Yamaguchi 2 UC		1377	5
A4) Kofu 1 KG		927	5		E7) Nagasaki 2 AC		1377	1
C6) Fukui 1 FG		927	5		F6) Hachinohe 2		1377	1
G4) Wakkanai 1		927	1		F2) Morioka 2 QC		1386	10
D2) Tsuyama 1		927	1		C2) Kanazawa 2 JB		1386	10
H2) Tokushima 1 XK		945	5		E5) Kagoshima 2 HC		1386	10
G7) Muroran 1 IQ		945	3		D2) Okayama 2 KB		1386	5
B3) Hikone 1 QP		945	1*		G5) Hakodate 2 VB		1467	1
E7) Fukue 1		945	1		A2) Nagano 2 NB		1467	1
E9) Saga 1 SP		963	1		E6) Oita 2 ID		1467	1
D4) Yonago 1		963	1		E3) Miyazaki 2 MC		1467	1
D3) Hagi 1		963	1		G4) Wakkanai 2		1467	1
F6) Aomori 1 TG		963	5		A2) Iida 2		1476	1
H1) Matsuyama 1 ZK		963	1		F4) Akita 1 UK		1503	10
A2) Kisofukushima 1		963	1		E8) Aso 1		1503	1
E7) Sasebo 1		981	1		H1) Matsuyama 2 ZB		1512	5
H3) Kochi 1 RK		990	10		F5) Koriyama 2		1512	1
F6) Hachinohe 1		999	1		A2) Matsumoto 2		1512	1
D1) Fukuyama 1		999	1		F3) Yamagata 2 JC		1521	1
H3) Nakamura 1		999	1		F6) Aomori 2 TC		1521	1
E1) Fukuoka 1 LB		1017	50		C3) Hamamatsu 2 DZ		1521	1
C4) Toyama 2 IC		1035	1		C6) Fukui 2 FC		1521	1
H4) Takamatsu 2 HD		1035	1		D4) Yonago 2		1521	1
F3) Tsuruoka 2		1035	1		H3) Nakamura 2		1521	1
D1) Hiroshima 1 FK		1071	20		E2) Ishigaki 2		1521	1
F1) Sendai 2 HB		1089	10		A3) Niigata 2 QB		1593	10
E2) Okinawa 2 AD		1125	10		D5) Matsue 2 TB		1593	10
G3) Obihiro 2 OC		1125	1		A4) Kofu 2 KC		1602	1
G7) Muroran 2 IZ		1125	1		E4) Kitakyushu 2 SB		1602	1
D4) Tottori 2 LC		1125	1		F5) Fukushima 2		1602	1
G4) Nayoro 2		1125	1		D1) Fukuyama 2		1602	1
D3) Hagi 2		1125	1		G4) Enbetsu 2		1602	1
C5) Takayama 2		1125	1		G4) Asahikawa 2 CC		1602	1
G2) Kushiro 2 PC		1152	10		H1) Uwajima 2		1602	1
H3) Kochi 2 RB		1152	10		E8) Hitoyoshi 2		1602	1
G6) Kitami 1 KP		1188	10		E3) Nobeoka 2		1602	1
C2) Kanazawa 1 JK		1224	10		E5) Naze 2		1602	1
D5) Matsue 1 TK		1296	10					

+ approx 240 stns below 1kW
1: NHK Radio One, **2:** NHK Radio Two. **Call: JO(call).** *stn announces its callsign as "JOBK".

FM Location	Call	MHz	kW		FM Location	Call	MHz	kW
A5) Utsunomiya BP		80.3	5		E1) Fukuoka LK		84.8	3
A6) Chiba MP		80.7	5		E2) Miyakojima		85.0	1
C4) Toyama IG		81.5	1		A10) Saitama LP		85.1	5
A7) Maebashi TP		81.6	1		G1) Sapporo IK		85.2	5
C7) Tsu NP		81.8	3		F5) Fukushima FP		85.3	1
A8) Yokohama GP		81.9	5		E8) Kumamoto GK		85.4	1
F3) Yamagata JG		82.1	1		A4) Kofu KG		85.6	1
C2) Kanazawa JK		82.2	1		E5) Kagoshima HG		85.6	1
A3) Niigata QK		82.3	1		D5) Hamada		85.8	1
A1) Tokyo AK		82.5	10		F6) Aomori TG		86.0	3
C1) Nagoya CK		82.5	10		H4) Takamatsu HP		86.0	1
F1) Sendai HK		82.5	5		F4) Akita UK		86.7	3
B2) Kyoto OK		82.8	1		H1) Matsuyama ZK		87.7	1
F2) Morioka QG		83.1	1		B1) Osaka BK		88.1	10
A9) Mito EP		83.2	1		E2) Okinawa AP		88.1	1
C6) Fukui FG		83.4	1		G4) Nayoro		88.2	1
H2) Tokushima XK		83.4	1		D1) Hiroshima FK		88.3	1
A3) Yamato		83.5	1		D2) Okayama KK		88.7	1
C5) Gifu OP		83.6	1		C3) Shizuoka PK		88.8	1
B3) Otsu QP		84.0	1		E6) Oita IP		88.9	1
B4) Himeji		84.2	1		G4) Chitose		89.1	1
E5) Tanegashima		84.4	1		G2) Nakashibetsu		89.9	1

+ approx 481 stns below 1kW **Call: JO(call)-FM**

Addresses of regional HQs:
A) Kanto-Koshinetsu area = Tokyo A1): same as NHK general HQ address. **B)** Kinki area = Osaka B1): 1-20, Otemae 4-chome, Chuo-ku, Osaka 540-8501. **C)** Tokai-Hokuriku area = Nagoya C1): 13-3, Higashisakura 1-chome, Higashi-ku, Nagoya 461-8725. **D)** Chugoku area = Hiroshima D1): 11-10, Otemachi 2-chome, Naka-ku, Hiroshima 730-8672. **E)** Kyushu area = Fukuoka E1): 1-10, Ropponmatsu 1-chome, Chuo-ku, Fukuoka 810-8577. **F)** Tohoku area = Sendai F1): 11-1, Nishiki-machi 1-chome, Aoba-ku, Sendai 980-8435. **G)** Hokkaido area = Sapporo G1): 1, Odori Nishi 1-chome, Chuo-ku, Sapporo 060-8703 **H)**

Shikoku area = Matsuyama H1): 5, Horinouchi, Matsuyama 790-8501.

NHK R. One (General prgr): 24h **N:** every h(exc Sun 0000). Also at 2030(exc Sat), 2140(exc Sat), 2230(exc Fri&Sat), 2330(exc Sat), 0030(exc Sat&Sun), 0130(exc Sat&Sun), 0230(exc Sat&Sun), 0430(exc Sat&Sun), 0535(exc Sat&Sun), 0630(exc Sat&Sun), 0730(exc Sat&Sun), 1130(exc Sat&Sun). **Regional and local prgrs** (the amount of local prgrs varies between stns) 2055wrp, 2125N/wrp/inf, 2155 wrp/inf, 2215(Fri&Sat 2210)N/wrp, 2240(Fri&Sat 2255)N/wrp/inf, 2355N/wrp/inf, 0055(exc Sun)N/wrp/inf, 0155N/wrp/inf, 0250wrp/inf, 0315(Sat & Sun 0310)N/wrp, 0355(exc Sun)N/wrp/inf, 0455N/wrp/inf, 0555N/wrp/inf, 0655N/wrp/inf, 0755N/wrp/inf, 0855N/wrp/inf, 0950N/wrp/inf, 1015(Sat & Sun)N/wrp, 1045(exc. Sat &Sun)N/wrp, 1055(Sat)wrp/inf, 1155(exc. Sat &Sun)N/wrp/inf, 1255N/wrp/inf, 1410(Sat & Sun 1405)N/wrp. **IS:** Original music played by Celesta. **Ann:** "JO(call), NHK (location) Daiichi Hoso desu". Local ID's with call letters, network & location given by studio stns just before: 2000, 0300, 1000.
NHK R. Two (Educational prgr): 2100-1540(variable). No regular regional and local prgrs. **Foreign language N** (rel. NHK World - R. Japan): **Chinese:** 0900-0915(Sat&Sun 0910). **Korean:** 0915-0930(Sat&Sun 0910-0920). **English:** 0500- 0530(Sat&Sun 0510). **Portuguese:** 0930-0945(Sat&Sun 0920-0930). **Spanish:** 0400-0415(Sat&Sun 0410). Weather map: 0010, 0700, 1300 (all 20 mins.) **IS:** Original music played by Celesta. Nat. Anthem at s/on on national holidays & s/off. **Ann:** "JO(call), NHK (location) Daini Hoso desu". Local IDs on certain stns (as 1st Netw) just before 2100, 0030, 0720, 1320 and sign off.
NHK FM Netw: 24h. 1600-2000 relays R. One, **N:** 2200, 0300, 0950(local), 1000. **Ann:** "JO(call)-FM, NHK (location) FM Hoso desu". Local IDs just before 2000, 0300, 1000.
V: NHK officially has no organised QSL sce. However, many local stns verify by QSL card or letter for DX reports.

EXTERNAL SERVICES:
RADIO JAPAN, NHK WORLD NETWORK
See International Broadcasting section

THE JAPAN COMMERCIAL BROADCASTERS ASSOCIATION (NIPPON MINKAN HOSO RENMEI)
✉ 3-23, Kioi-cho, Chiyoda-ku, Tokyo 102-8577 ☎ +81 3 5213 7711 🖷 +81 3 5213 7703 **W:** www.j-ba.or.jp
LP: Pres: H.Inoue. Vice-Presidents: T.Ishihara, Y.Okubo, H. Hayakawa, K. Toyoda, M.Shimada, T.Araki, N.Mochizuki, K.Terasaki. Exec. Dir: S.Kimura. **Pub:** Nippon Minkan Hoso Nenkan, Gekkan Minpo, Minkan Hoso (all Japanese) and NAB Handbook (English) etc.

MW	Call	kHz	kW	ID	Station, location & h of tr
1)	CR	558	20	CRK	R. Kansai, Kobe
2)	WN	639	5	STV	STV Radio, Hakodate
3)	DF	684	5	IBC	Iwate Hoso, Morioka
3)	LO	684	1	IBC	Iwate Hoso, Ofunato
4)	IL	720	5	KBC	Kyushu Asahi Hoso, Kitakyushu
5)	LR	738	5	KNB	Kita Nihon Hoso, Toyama
5)		738	1	KNB	Kita Nihon Hoso, Takaoka
6)	RR	738	10	RBC	Ryukyu Hoso, Naha
7)	JF	765	5	YBS	Yamanashi Hoso, Kofu
8)	PF	765	5	KRY	Yamaguchi Hoso, Shunan
9)	XR	864	10	ROK	R. Okinawa, Naha: 2000-1900(Sat -1800, Sun -1600)
10)	SO	864	1	SBC	Shin'etsu Hoso, Matsumoto
11)	HE	864	3	HBC	Hokkaido Hoso, Asahikawa
11)	QF	864	1	HBC	Hokkaido Hoso, Muroran
11)		864	1	HBC	Hokkaido Hoso, Enbetsu
12)	PR	864	5	FBC	Fukui Hoso, Fukui
13)	XN	864	1	CRT	Tochigi Hoso, Nasu
2)	WS	882	5	STV	STV Radio, Kushiro
2)		882	1	STV	STV Radio, Esashi
11)	HO	900	5	HBC	Hokkaido Hoso, Hakodate
14)	HF	900	5	BSS	San'in Hoso, Yonago: (off air Sat1800-1855, Sun1500-1855)
15)	ZR	900	5	RKC	Kochi Hoso, Kochi
2)	VX	909	5	STV	STV Radio, Abashiri
16)	EF	918	5	YBC	Yamagata Hoso, Yamagata
16)		918	1	YBC	Yamagata Hoso, Tsuruoka
16)		918	1	YBC	Yamagata Hoso, Yonezawa
16)		918	1	YBC	Yamagata Hoso, Shinjo
8)	PM	918	1	KRY	Yamaguchi Hoso, Shimonoseki
8)	PN	918	1	KRY	Yamaguchi Hoso, Iwakuni
17)	TR	936	5	ABS	Akita Hoso, Akita
18)	NF	936	5	MRT	Miyazaki Hoso, Miyazaki
18)		936	1	MRT	Miyazaki Hoso, Nobeoka
18)		936	1	MRT	Miyazaki Hoso, Nichinan
18)		936	1	MRT	Miyazaki Hoso, Kobayashi
18)		936	1	MRT	Miyazaki Hoso, Takachiho

MW	Call	kHz	kW	ID	Station, location & h of tr
19)	KR	954	100	TBS	TBS Radio, Tokyo
20)	NR	1008	50	ABC	Asahi Hoso, Osaka
21)	AR	1053	50	CBC	Chubu Nippon Hoso, Nagoya: (S)
2)	WM	1071	5	STV	STV Radio, Obihiro
10)	SR	1098	5	SBC	Shin'etsu Hoso, Nagano
10)	SW	1098	1	SBC	Shin'etsu Hoso, Iida
22)	MF	1098	1	NBC	Nagasaki Hoso, Sasebo
23)	GF	1098	5	OBS	Oita Hoso, Oita
24)	WO	1098	5	RFC	R. Fukushima, Koriyama
25)	CF	1107	20	MBC	Minami Nihon Hoso, Kagoshima
25)		1107	1	MBC	Minami Nihon Hoso, Akune
25)		1107	1	MBC	Minami Nihon Hoso, Oguchi
25)		1107	1	MBC	Minami Nihon Hoso, Sendai
26)	MR	1107	5	MRO	Hokuriku Hoso, Kanazawa
26)		1107	1	MRO	Hokuriku Hoso, Nanao
27)	AF	1116	5	RNB	Nankai Hoso, Matsuyama
27)	AL	1116	1	RNB	Nankai Hoso, Niihama
27)	AM	1116	1	RNB	Nankai Hoso, Uwajima
28)	DR	1116	5	BSN	Niigata Hoso, Niigata
29)	QR	1134	100	NCB	Bunka Hoso, Tokyo
30)	BR	1143	20	KBS	KBS Kyoto, Kyoto
31)	OR	1179	50	MBS	Mainichi Hoso, Osaka
15)		1197	1	RKC	Kochi Hoso, Nakamura
32)	FO	1197	1	RKB	RKB Mainichi Hoso, Kitakyushu
33)	BF	1197	10	RKK	Kumamoto Hoso, Kumamoto
33)		1197	1	RKK	Kumamoto Hoso, Hitoyoshi
33)		1197	1	RKK	Kumamoto Hoso, Aso
33)		1197	1	RKK	Kumamoto hoso, Goshoura
34)	YF	1197	1	IBS	Ibaraki Hoso, Mito: 2040 (Fri 2045)-2000 (Sat 2100-Sun 1530)
2)	WL	1197	3	STV	STV R., Asahikawa
2)		1197	1	STV	STV R., Wakkanai
2)		1197	1	STV	STV R., Nayoro
2)		1197	1	STV	STV R., Enbetsu
30)	BO	1215	2	KBS	KBS Kyoto, Maizuru
30a)	BW	1215	1	KBS	KBS Shiga, Hikone
22)	UR	1233	5	NBC	Nagasaki Hoso, Nagasaki
35)	GR	1233	5	RAB	Aomori Hoso, Aomori
36)	LF	1242	100	NBS	Nippon Hoso, Tokyo: (S)
37)	IR	1260	20	TBC	Tohoku Hoso, Sendai
11)	HW	1269	5	HBC	Hokkaido Hoso, Obihiro
11)	FM	1269	1	HBC	Hokkaido Hoso, Esashi
38)	JR	1269	5	JRT	Shikoku Hoso, Tokushima
38)		1269	1	JRT	Shikoku Hoso, Ikeda
32)	FR	1278	50	RKB	RKB Mainichi Hoso, Fukuoka
11)	HR	1287	50	HBC	Hokkaido Hoso, Sapporo
39)	UF	1314	50	OBC	R. Osaka, Osaka: (S)
40)	SF	1332	50	Tokai	R. Hoso, Nagoya
41)	ER	1350	20	RCC	Chugoku Hoso, Hiroshima
11)	TS	1368	1	HBC	Hokkaido Hoso, Wakkanai
1)	CE	1395	1	CRK	R. Kansai, Toyooka
24)	WE	1395	1	RFC	R. Fukushima, Wakamatsu
11)	QL	1404	5	HBC	Hokkaido Hoso, Kushiro
42)	VR	1404	10	SBS	Shizuoka Hoso, Shizuoka
42)	VO	1404	1	SBS	Shizuoka Hoso, Hamamatsu
4)	IF	1413	50	KBC	Kyushu Asahi Hoso, Fukuoka
43)	RF	1422	50	RF	RF R. Nippon, Yokohama
14)	HL	1431	1	BSS	San'in Hoso, Tottori: (as 900kHz)
14)		1431	1	BSS	San'in Hoso, Izumo: (as 900kHz)
22)		1431	1	NBC	Nagasaki Hoso, Fukue
24)	WW	1431	1	RFC	R. Fukushima, Iwaki
44)	VF	1431	5	WBS	Wakayama Hoso, Wakayama: (S)
45)	ZF	1431	1	GBS	Gifu Hoso, Gifu: 2030-1600.
2)	WF	1440	50	STV	STV Radio, Sapporo
2)		1440	3	STV	STV Radio, Muroran
2)		1440	1	STV	STV Radio, Tomakomai
11)	QM	1449	5	HBC	Hokkaido Hoso, Abashiri
46)	KF	1449	5	RNC	Nishi Nippon Hoso, Takamatsu
46)		1449	1	RNC	Nishi Nippon Hoso, Marugame
22a)	UO	1458	1	NBC	Nagasaki Hoso, Saga
24)	WR	1458	1	RFC	R. Fukushima, Fukushima
34)	YL	1458	1	IBS	Ibaraki Hoso, Tsuchiura
34)		1458	1	IBS	Ibaraki Hoso, Sekijo
41)		1458	1	RCC	Chugoku Hoso, Shobara
8)	PL	1485	1	KRY	Yamaguchi Hoso, Hagi
35)	GO	1485	1	RAB	Aomori Hoso, Hachinohe
11)	TL	1494	1	HBC	Hokkaido Hoso, Nayoro
47)	YR	1494	10	RSK	Sanyo Hoso, Okayama
47)		1494	1	RSK	Sanyo Hoso, Takahashi
47)		1494	1	RSK	Sanyo Hoso, Tsuyama
47)		1494	1	RSK	Sanyo Hoso, Niimi
47)		1494	1	RSK	Sanyo Hoso, Bizen
47)		1494	1	RSK	Sanyo Hoso, Ochiai
28)	DO	1530	1	BSN	Niigata Hoso, Joetsu
13)	XF	1530	5	CRT	Tochigi Hoso, Utsunomiya
41)	EO	1530	1	RCC	Chugoku Hoso, Fukuyama
41)		1530	1	RCC	Chugoku Hoso, Mihara

Relay stns below 1kW (approx 125 stns) not included.

Call: JO(call). **(S):** AM Stereo (C-QUAM System). **Schedule:** 24h unless otherwise indicated above. Most 24h stns are off the air for 1 to 5 hours until 1900 or 2000 on Sun unless mentioned. All other days a network prgr is aired 1600 or 1800 to 2000 on most stns. Network prgrs may also be broadcast at other times of day. **ID:** Company initials are usually used as stn identification.

Addresses and other information:

1) R Kansai Co., Ltd., 5-7, Higashi Kawasaki-cho 1-chome, Chuo-ku, Kobe 650-8580 **W:** http://jocr.jp — **2)** The STVradio Broadcasting Co., Ltd, 1-1, Nishi 8-chome, Kita 1-jo, Chuo-ku, Sapporo 060-8705 **W:** www.stv.ne.jp — **3)** Iwate Broadc Co., Ltd., 6-1, Shike-cho, Morioka 020-8566 **W:** www.ibc.co.jp — **4)** Kyushu Asahi Broadc Co., Ltd, 1-1, Nagahama 1-chome, Chuo-ku, Fukuoka 810-8571 **W:** www.kbc.co.jp — **5)** Kita-nihon Broadc Co., Ltd.,10-18, Ushijima-machi, Toyama 930-8585 **W:** www.knb.ne.jp — **6)** Ryukyu Broadc Co., Ltd., 3-1, Kumoji 2-chome, Naha 900-8711 **W:** www.rbc.co.jp — **7)** Yamanashi Broadc System, Inc., 6-10, Kitaguchi 2-chome, Kofu 400-8525 **W:** www.ybs.jp — **8)** Yamaguchi Broadc Co., Ltd., Koen-ku, Shunan 745-8686 **W:** http://kry.co.jp — **9)** R Okinawa Corp., 4-8, Nishi 1-chome, Naha 900-8604 **W:** www.rokinawa.co.jp — **10)** Shin-etsu Broadc Co., Ltd., 1200, Toigoshomachi, Nagano 380-8521 **W:** http://sbc21.co.jp — **11)** Hokkaido Broadc Co., Ltd., 2, Nishi 5-chome, kita 1-jo, Chuo-ku, Sapporo 060-8501 **W:** www.hbc.jp — **12)** Fukui Broadc Corp., 37-1-1, Owada-cho, Fukui 910-8588 **W:** www.fbc.jp –**13)** Tochigi Broadc Co., Ltd., 12-11, Honcho, Utsunomiya 320-8601 **W:** www.crt-radio.co.jp — **14)** Broadc System of San-in, 1-71, Nishi-Fukubara 1-chome, Yonago 683-8670 **W:** http://bss.jp — **15)** Kochi Broadc Co., Ltd., 2-15, Hon-machi 3-chome, Kochi 780-8550 **W:** www.rkc-kochi.co.jp — **16)** Yamagata Broadc Co., Ltd., 5-12, Hatago-machi 2-chome, Yamagata 990-8555 **W:** www.ybc.co.jp — **17)** Akita Broadc System, 9-42, Sanno 7-chome, Akita 010-8611 **W:** www.akita-abs.co.jp –**18)** Miyazaki Broadc Co., Ltd., 6-7, Tachibanadori-nishi 4-chome, Miyazaki 880-8639 **W:** www.mrt.jp — **19)** TBS Radio & Communications, Inc., 3-6, Akasaka 5-chome, Minato-ku, Tokyo 107-8006 **W:** www.tbs.co.jp/radio — **20)** Asahi Broadc Corp., 1-30, Fukushima 1-chome, Fukushima-ku, Osaka 553-8503 **W:** http://asahi.co.jp — **21)** Chubu-Nippon Broadc Co., Ltd., 2-8, Shinsakae 1-chome, Naka-ku, Nagoya 460-8405 **W:** http://hicbc.com — **22)** Nagasaki Broadc Co., Ltd., 1-35, Uwa-machi, Nagasaki 850-8650 **W:** www.nbc-nagasaki.co.jp — **22a)** Nagasaki Broadc Co., Ltd Saga station, 1249, Honjo-machi, Saga 840-0027 **W:** www.nbc-saga.co.jp — **23)** Oita Broadc System, 1-1, Imazuru 3-chome, Oita 870-8620 **W:** www.e-obs.com — **24)** R Fukushima Broadc Co., Ltd., 8, Shimoarako, Fukushima 960-8655 **W:** www.rfc.co.jp — **25)** Minaminihon Broadc Co., Ltd., 5-25, Korai-cho, Kagoshima 890-8570 **W:** www.mbc.co.jp — **26)** Hokuriku Broadc Co., Ltd., 2-1, Honda-machi 3-chome, Kanazawa 920-8560 **W:** www.mro.co.jp — **27)** Nankai Broadc Co., Ltd., 1-1, Honmachi 1-chome, Matsuyama 790-8510 **W:** www.rnb.co.jp — **28)** Broadc System of Niigata, Inc., 18, Kawagishi-cho 3-chome, Chuo-ku, Niigata 951-8655 **W:** www.ohbsn.com — **29)** Nippon Cultural Broadc., Inc.,31, Hamamatsu-cho 1-chome, Minato-ku, Tokyo 105-8002 **W:** www.joqr.co.jp — **30)** Kyoto Broadc System Co., Ltd., Kamichojamachi, Karasumadori, Kamigyo-ku, Kyoto 602-8588 **W:** www.kbs-kyoto.co.jp — **30a)** KBS Shiga Station, 13-1, Daito-cho, Hikone 522-0074 – **31)** Mainichi Broadc System, Inc., 17-1, Chayamachi, Kita-ku, Osaka 530-8304 **W:** www.mbs.jp — **32)** RKB Mainichi Broadc Corp., 3-8, Momochihama 2-chome, Sawara-ku, Fukuoka 814-8585 **W:** http://rkb.jp — **33)** Kumamoto Broadc Co., Ltd., 30, Yamasaki-machi, Kumamoto 860-8611 **W:** www.rkk.co.jp — **34)** Ibaraki Broadc System, 2084-2, Senba-cho, Mito 310-8505 **W:** www.ibs-radio.com — **35)** Aomori Broadc Corp., 8-1, Matsumori 1-chome, Aomori 030-8655 **W:** www.rab.co.jp — **36)** Nippon Broadc System, Inc., 9-3, Yurakucho 1-chome, Chiyoda-ku, Tokyo 100-8439 **W:** www.jolf.co.jp — **37)** Tohoku Broadc Co., Ltd., 26-1, Kasumi-cho, Yagiyama, Taihaku-ku, Sendai 982-8668 **W:** www.tbc-sendai.co.jp — **38)** Shikoku Broadc Co., Ltd., 5-2, Nakatokushima-cho 2-chome, Tokushima 770-8573 **W:** www.jrt.co.jp — **39)** Osaka Broadc Corp., 2-4, Benten 1-chome, Minato-ku, Osaka 552-8501 **W:** www.obc1314.co.jp — **40)** Tokai Radio Broadc Co., Ltd., 14-27, Higashisakura 1-chome, Higashi-ku, Nagoya 461-8503 **W:** www.tokairadio.co.jp — **41)** RCC Broadc Co., Ltd., 21-3, Moto-machi, Naka-ku, Hiroshima 730-8504 **W:** www.rcc.net — **42)** Shizuoka Broadc System, 1-1, Toro 3-chome, Suruga-ku, Shizuoka 422-8680 **W:** www.at-s.com — **43)** RF Radio Nippon Co., Ltd., 85, Choja-machi 5-chome, Naka-ku, Yokohama 231-8611 **W:** www.jorf.co.jp — **44)** Wakayama Broadc System, 3, Minato-honmachi 3-chome, Wakayama 640-8577 **W:** www.wbs.co.jp — **45)** Gifu Broadc System, 52, Hashimotocho 2-chome, Gifu 500-8588 **W:** www.zf-web.com — **46)**

Nishi-nippon Broadc Co., Ltd., 8-15, Marunouchi, Takamatsu 760-8575 **W:** www.rnc.co.jp – **47)** Sanyo Broadc Co., Ltd., 1-3, Marunouchi 2-chome, Okayama 700-8580 **W:** www.rsk.co.jp.
V: Most stns verify by QSL-card. Rec acc. Rp.

NIKKEI RADIO BROADCASTING CORPORATION (RADIO NIKKEI)

✉ 9-15, Akasaka 1-chome, Minato-ku, Tokyo 107-8373 ☎ +81 3 3583 8151 🖷 +81 3 3583 7441 **W:** www.radionikkei.jp

SW	kHz	kW	Prgr	SW	kHz	kW	Prgr
JOZ	3925	50	1	JOZ6	6115	50	2
JOZ4	*3925	10	1	JOZ3	9595	50	1
JOZ5	3945	10	2	JOZ7	9760	50	2
JOZ2	6055	50	1				

*) Nemuro; others Nagara (Chiba)
1st Prgr: 2155-1500 on 3925/ 6055/9595kHz; as above except 2300-0750 on 3925kHz (Nemuro).
2nd Prgr: Sun-Thu 2300-0605, Fri & Sat 2300- 0900 (9760kHz: 0800)
IS: Slow tempo chime with Japanese instrument "Koto" at sign on and sign off - **V.** by QSL card. Rp.

COMMERCIAL FM STATIONS:

FM	Call	MHz	kW	Station, location & h of tr
1)	QU	76.1	1	FM Iwate, Morioka
2)	LU	76.1	1	FM Fukui, Fukui
3)	DW	76.1	10	Inter FM, Tokyo
4)	FW	76.1	1	Love FM, Fukuoka
5)	SV	76.4	1	R. Berry, Utsunomiya
6)	AW	76.5	10	FM COCOLO, Osaka
7)	VV	76.8	1	FM Okayama, Okayama
8)	UV	77.0	1	E-Radio, Otsu
9)	JU	77.1	5	Date FM, Sendai
10)	SU	77.4	1	FM Kumamoto, Kumamoto
11)	VU	77.4	0.5	V-air, Matsue
12)	XU	77.5	1	FM Niigata, Niigata
13)		77.6	1	Kiss-FM, Himeji
14)	QV	77.8	10	ZIP FM, Nagoya
15)	NV	77.9	0.5	FM Saga, Saga
16)	GV	78.0	5	bayfm, Chiba
17)	GU	78.2	1	Hiroshima FM, Hiroshima
18)	YU	78.6	1	FM Kagawa, Takamatsuh
19)	RV	78.7	3	CROSS FM, Kitakyushu (Fukuoka)
20)	NU	78.9	3	Radio Cube, Tsu
21)	WV	79.0	1	FM Port, Niigata: (off air SS 1600-2100)
22)	KU	79.2	1	K-MIX, Hamamatsu (Shizuoka)
23)	UU	79.2	1	FM Yamaguchi, Yamaguchi
24)	HU	79.5	1	FM Nagasaki, Nagasaki
25)	DV	79.5	5	NACK 5, Saitama
26)	EU	79.7	1	FM Ehime, Matsuyama: 2057-1803 (Fri -2003, Sat -1703, Sun -1603)
27)	ZU	79.7	1	FM Nagano, Matsumoto (Nagano)
28)	OV	79.8	1	μ FM, Kagoshima
29)	WU	80.0	1	FM Aomori, Aomori
30)	AU	80.0	10	Tokyo FM, Tokyo
31)	XV	80.0	1	Radio 80, Ogaki (Gifu)
32)	FV	80.2	10	FM 802, Osaka
33)	FU	80.4	5	AIR-G', Sapporo
34)	EV	80.4	1	Rhythm Station, Yamagata
35)	HV	80.5	1	FM Ishikawa, Kanazawa
36)	CU	80.7	10	FM Aichi, Nagoya
37)	MV	80.7	1	FM Tokushima, Tokushima
38)	DU	80.7	3	FM Fukuoka, Fukuoka
39)	AV	81.3	7	J-WAVE, Tokyo
40)	LV	81.6	0.5	Hi-six, Kochi
41)	TV	81.8	1	Fukushima FM, Koriyama(Fukushima)
42)	PV	82.5	5	FM North Wave, Sapporo
43)	OU	82.7	1	FM Toyama, Toyama
44)	PU	82.8	3	FM Akita, Akita
45)	CV	83.0	1	FM Fuji, Kofu: 1950-1715 (Wed -1745, Thu -1800, Fri-1815),(Fri1930-Sat1900, Sat2000-Sun1530)
46)	MU	83.2	1	Joy FM, Miyazaki
47)	TU	84.7	5	FM Yokohama, Yokohama
48)	BU	85.1	10	FM Osaka, Osaka
49)	RU	86.3	1	FM Gunma, Maebashi
12)		86.5	1	FM Niigata, Yamato
11)		86.6	1	V-air, Hamada
50)	IU	87.3	1	FM Okinawa, Naha
51)	JV	88.0	1	FM Oita, Oita
52)	KV	89.4	3	Alpha-Station, Kyoto
13)	IV	89.9	1	Kiss-FM, Kobe

NB: Relay stns below 1kW and community stns are not included.
Call: JO(call)-FM. **Schedule:** 24h unless otherwise indicated above. Most 24h stns are off the air for 2 to 5 hours until 1900, 2000 or 2100 on Sun.

Addresses and other information:

1) FM Iwate Broadc Co., 2-10, Uchimaru, Morioka 020-8512 **W:** www.fmii.co.jp – **2)** Fukui FM Broadc Co., Ltd., 1-1, Miyuki 1-chome, Fukui 910-8553 **W:** www.fmfukui.co.jp – **3)** FM Inter-wave Inc., 3-3, Higashi-shinagawa 1-chome, Shinagawa-ku, Tokyo 140-0002 - Prgr in English & foreign languages **W:** www.interfm.co.jp – **4)** LOVE FM International Broadc Co., Ltd., 1F, Soralia Plaza, 2-43, Tenjin 2-chome, Chuo-ku, Fukuoka 810-0001 Prgr in English, Chinese and Korean etc **W:** http://lovefm.co.jp – **5)** FM Tochigi Brordc co.,ltd., 2-1, Chuo 1-chome, Utsunomiya 320-8550 **W:** www.berry.co.jp – **6)** FM 802 Co., Ltd., See 32). Foreign language prgr in English, Chinese, Korean, etc. Since April 2012, the business has been transfered from Kansai Intermedia Corp. to FM 802 Co. Ltd. **W:** http://cocolo.jp – **7)** Okayama FM Broadc Co., Ltd., 1-8-45, Nakasange, Okayama 700-0821 **W:** www.fm-okayama.co.jp – **8)** FM Shiga Co., Ltd., 19-10, Nishinosho, Otsu 520-0818 **W:** www.e-radio.co.jp – **9)** Sendai FM Broadc., Inc., 10-28, Honcho 2-chome, Aoba-ku, Sendai 980-8420 **W:** www.datefm.co.jp – **10)** FM Kumamoto Broadc Co., Ltd., 5-50, Chibajomachi, Kumamoto 860-0001 **W:** http://fmk.fm – **11)** FM San-in Co., Ltd., 383, Tono-machi, Matsue 690-8508 **W:** www.fm-sanin.co.jp – **12)** FM Radio Niigata Co., Ltd., 3-5, Saiwainishi 4-chome, Chuo-ku, Niigata 950-8581 **W:** www.fmniigata.com – **13)** Kiss-FM KOBE Inc., 5-4 Hatoba-cho, Chuo-ku, Kobe 650-8589 **W:** www.kiss-fm.co.jp – **14)** ZIP-FM Inc., 20-17, Marunouchi 3-chome, Naka-ku, Nagoya 460-8578 **W:** http://zip-fm.co.jp – **15)** FM Saga Co., Ltd., 286-5, Fukuro, Honjo-machi, Saga 840-0023 **W:** www.fmsaga.co.jp – **16)** bayfm78 Co., Ltd., 6-1, Nakase 2-chome, Mihama-ku, Chiba 261-7127 **W:** www.bayfm.co.jp – **17)** Hiroshima FM Broadc Co., Ltd., 8-2, Minamimachi 1-chome, Minami-ku, Hiroshima 734-8511 **W:** www.hfmweb.jp – **18)** FM Kagawa Broadc Co., Ltd., 4-23, Saiho-cho 1-chome, Takamatsu 760-8584 **W:** www.fmkagawa.co.jp – **19)** Cross FM Co., Ltd. 1-1, Kyomachi 3-chome, Kokurakita-ku, Kitakyushu 802-8570 **W:** www.crossfm.co.jp – **20)** Mie FM Broadc co., Ltd., 1043-1, Kannonji-cho, Tsu 514-8505 **W:** www.fmmie.jp – **21)** Niigata Kenmin FM Broadc Co., Ltd., 1-1, Bandai 2-chome, Chuo ku, Niigata 950-8579 **W:** www.fmport.com – **22)** Shizuoka FM Broadc Co., Ltd, 133-24, Tokiwa-cho, Naka-ku, Hamamatsu 430-8575 **W:** www.k-mix.co.jp – **23)** FM Yamaguchi Co., Ltd., 3-31, Midori-cho, Yamaguchi 753-8521 **W:** www.fmy.co.jp – **24)** FM Nagasaki Co., Ltd., 5-5, Sakae-machi, Nagasaki 850-8550 **W:** www.fmnagasaki.co.jp – **25)** FM Nack 5 Co Ltd., 682-2, Nishiki-cho, Omiya-ku, Saitama 330-8579 **W:** www.nack5.co.jp – **26)** FM Ehime Broadc Co., 10-7, Takewara-machi 1-chome, Matsuyama 790-8565 **W:** www.joeufm.co.jp – **27)** Nagano FM Broadc Co., Ltd 13-5, Honjo 1-chome, Matsumoto 390-8520 **W:** www.fmnagano.co.jp – **28)** FM Kagoshima Co., Ltd., 1-38, Higashisengoku-cho, Kagoshima 892-8579 **W:** www.myufm.jp – **29)** Aomori FM Broadc Co., Ltd., 7-19, Tsutsumi-machi 1-chome, Aomori 030-0812 **W:** www.afb.co.jp – **30)** Tokyo FM Broadc Co., Ltd., 7, Kojimachi 1-chome, Chiyoda-ku, Tokyo 102-8080 **W:** www.tfm.co.jp – **31)** Gifu FM Broadc Co., Ltd., 35-10, Kono 4-chome, Ogaki 503-8580 **W:** www.radio-80.com – **32)** FM 802 Co., Ltd., Kita 2-6, Tenjinbashi 2-chome, Kita-ku, Osaka 530-8580 **W:** www.funky802.com – **33)** FM Hokkaido Broadc Co., Ltd., 1, Nishi 2-chome, kita 1-jo, Chuo-ku, Sapporo 060-8532 **W:** www.air-g.co.jp – **34)** FM Yamagata Co., Ltd., 14-69, Matsuyama 3-chome, Yamagata 990-9543 **W:** www.rfm.co.jp – **35)** FM Ishikawa Broadc Co., Ltd., 1-45, Hikoso-machi 2-chome, Kanazawa 920-8605 **W:** http://hel-lofive.jp – **36)** FM Aichi Broadc Co., Ltd., 15-18, Chiyoda 2-chome, Naka-ku, Nagoya 460-8388 **W:** www.fma.co.jp – **37)** FM Tokushima Broadc Co., 6, Saiwai-cho 1-chome, Tokushima 770-8567 **W:** www.fm807.jp – **38)** Fukuoka FM Broadc Co., Ltd., 9-19, Kiyokawa 1-chome, Chuo-ku, Fukuoka, 810-8575 **W:** http://fmfukuoka.co.jp – **39)** J-WAVE Inc., Roppongi Hills Mori Tower 33F, 10-1, Roppongi 6-chome,, Minato-ku, Tokyo 106-6188 **W:** www.j-wave.co.jp – **40)** FM Kochi Broadc Co., Ltd., 1-5, Takashocho 2-chome, Kochi 780-8532 **W:** www.fmkochi.com – **41)** FM Fukushima Inc., 4-4 Shinmei-cho, Koriyama, 960-8013 **W:** www.fmf.co.jp – **42)** FM North Wave Co., Ltd., 3-1, Nishi 4-chome, Kita 2-jo, Kita-ku, Sapporo 060-8557 **W:** http://825.fm/northwave – **43)** Toyama FM Broadc Co., Ltd., 2-11, Okuda-machi, Toyama 930-8567 **W:** www.fmtoyama.co.jp – **44)** FM Akita Broadc Co.,Ltd., 7-10, Yabase-Honcho 3-chome, Akita 010-9979 **W:** www.fm-akita.co.jp – **45)** FM Fuji Co Ltd., Aria 105, Kawadamachi, Kofu 400-8550 **W:** www.fmfuji.co.jp – **46)** Miyazaki FM Broadc Co., Ltd., 78, Gion 2-chome, Miyazaki 880-8583 **W:** www.joyfm.co.jp – **47)** Yokohama FM Broadc Co., Ltd., 2-1, Minato-Mirai 2-chome, Nishi-ku, Yokohama 220-8110 **W:** www.fmyokohama.co.jp – **48)** FM Osaka Co., Ltd., 3-1, Minatomachi 1-chome, Naniwa-ku, Osaka 556-8510 **W:** http://fmosaka.net – **49)** FM Gunma Broadc Co., Ltd., 4-8, Wakamiyacho 1-chome, Maebashi 371-8533 **W:** www.fmgunma.com – **50)** FM Okinawa Broadc Corp., 40, Kowan, Urasoe, Okinawa 901-2525 **W:** www.fmokinawa.co.jp – **51)** FM Oita Broadc., Co., Ltd., 17-19, Higashikasuga-machi, Oita 870-8558 **W:** www.fmoita.co.jp – **52)** FM Kyoto, Inc., CoCon Karasuma 8F, 620, Suginya-cho, Karasuma-dori Shijo-sagaru, Shimogyo-ku, Kyoto 600-

8566 **W:** http://fm-kyoto.jp
V. Most stns verify by QSL card. Rec acc. Rp.

THE OPEN UNIVERSITY OF JAPAN (HOSO DAIGAKU)

⌨ Hoso Daigaku, 2-11, Wakaba, Mihama-ku, Chiba 261-8586 ☎ +81 43 276 5111 **W:** www.ouj.ac.jp
FM: JOUD-FM 77.1MHz 10kW, Tokyo. 78.8MHz 1kW, Maebashi **D. Prgr:** 2100-1500 **V.** by QSL card. Rp.

AMERICAN FORCES NETWORK (AFN) (U.S. Mil.)

The network serves the members of the US forces. The stns in Japan broadcast by authority of Commander, US Forces, Japan, in cooperation with the Information and Communications Policy Bureau in Japan. Stns are linked by land line and microwave.

⌨ **AFN Tokyo,** Det 10, Unit 5091 Bldg 3266, Yokota Air Base, Fussa, Tokyo 197-0001 or Det 10, Unit 5091 Bldg 3266, APO/AP 96328-5091 ☎ +81 42 552 2511 ext 52374 ▤ +81 42 552 2511 ext 52386 **E:** AFN.Eagle810@yokota.af.mil **W:** http://www.facebook.com/pages/Eagle810/168492266529725
Other stns AFN Okinawa: Okinawa **E:** AFNRadio@us.kadena.af.mil **W:** http://kadenaforcesupport.com/AFN/index.html – **AFN Misawa:** Misawa, Aomori **E:** afn@misawa.af.mil **W:** www.facebook.com/AFNMisawa **AFN Iwakuni:** Iwakuni, Yamaguchi **W:** www.facebook.com/AFNIwakuni – **AFN Sasebo:** Sasebo, Nagasaki **W:** www.cnic.navy.mil/Sasebo/NewsAndCurrentInfo/AmericanForcesNetwork

MW	kHz	kW	MW	kHz	kW
Okinawa	648	10	Misawa	1575	0.6
Tokyo	810	50	Sasebo	1575	0.25
Iwakuni	1575	1			

FM: Okinawa 89.1MHz 20kW.
D. Prgr: 24h **N:** on the h. **Ann:** "This is the American Forces Network" **V.** by QSL card or letter

JORDAN

L.T: UTC +2h (Mar-Oct: +3h); currently on continuous DST — **Pop:** 6.4 million — **Pr.L:** Arabic — **E.C:** 50Hz, 230V — **ITU:** JOR

AUDIOVISUAL COMMISSION (AVC)

⌨ P.O.Box 142515, Amman 11814 ☎+ 962 6 5549720 ▤ + 962 6 5535093 **W:** www.avc.gov.jo **L.P:** Dir: Hussein Bani Bani.

JORDAN RADIO & TELEVISION CORP. (JRTV, Gov.)

⌨ Al-Shara Al-Musharrafah St, P.O.Box 1041, JO-11118 Amman ☎+962 6 4773111 ▤+962 6 4778 578 **W:** jrtv.gov.jo **E:** rj@jrtv.gov.jo
L.P: CEO: Adnan El-Zobe. Dir. Radio: Mazen Majali. Dir. Eng: Sufian Nabulsi. Dir. Int. Rel: Mrs. Jihan Al-Haeyk.

MW	kHz	kW	Prgr.	Times
Shobak	612	200	Main	0330-0015
Ajlun	801	10	Main	0330-0015
Amman	855	10	Quran	0430-2000
Amman	1035	20	Main	0430-2000

FM	Main Amman FM	English	Quran	Hadaf	kW
Ajlun	95.8	90.9	98.7	88.0	10/5
Amman 90.0/106.7	99.0	96.3	93.1		5/10
Aqaba	101.5	105.6	99.7	91.5	5/1
Irbid	103.6		98.7		1
Kerak	103.6		98.7		1
Salt		105.0			1
Tafeleh	90.8				1
Zarqa	100.6				1

Main Arabic sce: 24h. **N:** on the h. (not 0400, 1100 Fri, 1300, 1700). Jordan Armed Forces R: 1400-1600. Also relayed on SW. **Amman FM,** in Arabic: 0430-2000 (Irbid with some local prgr). **English prgr:** 0300-2400. **French:** 1400-1600 on English prgr fqs. **Quran Prgr:** 0500-2200 on FM & MW 855kHz. **Hadaf** (sports prgr.): 24h.
Ann: Arabic: "Huna Amman, Idha'atu-l-Mamlaka al-Urdoniya al-Hashemiya". Armed forces R: "Idha'at Al-Quwwat Al-Musala al-Urdoniya, al-Gayish al-Arabi". E: "This is R. Jordan broadcasting from Amman".

EXTERNAL SERVICE: see International Radio section.

Other stations (FM MHz):
Amen FM: Amman/Aqaba 89.5, Irbid 89.7. **W:** amenfm.jo – **Ayyam FM:** Amman 91.5, Irbid 91.9, Petra 92.1. **W:**ayyamfm.jo – **Beat FM,** Amman: 102.5. English. **W:** www.mybeat.fm – **Energy FM,** Amman: 97.7. English. **W:** energyradio.jo– **Hala FM:** Aqaba 91.1, Irbid/Ruweished 91.3, Al-Karak 94.3, Al-Salt/Tafilaq 94.7, Ajlun 94.3, Amman 102.1, Petra 105.4. **W:** hala.jo – **Hawa FM,** Amman: 105.9MHz. **W:** ammancity.gov.jo – **Hayat FM:** Irbid 94.7, Amman

104.7, Azraq 105.4. **W:** www.hayat.fm – **Mazaj FM:** Amman 95.3, Irbid 101.7. **W:** mazajfm.com – **Melody FM:** Amman 91.1, Zarqa 105.5. – **Mood FM,** Amman: 92.0. English. **W:** mood.fm – **Play FM:** Amman 99.6, Irbid 105.3. English. **W:** play.jo – **R. Al-Balad,** Amman: 92.4 **W:** ammannet.net – **R. Fann:** Aqaba 91.1, Irbid/Ruweished 91.3, Ajlun/Karak 94.3, Salt/Tafileh 94.7, Amman 102.1/104.2, Petra/Azraq 105.4. **W:** radiofann.com – **R. Farah Al-Nas,** Amman: 98.5. **W:** farahalnas.jo – **Rotana R:** Irbid 90.5, Amman 99.9. **W:** rotana.net – **Sawt Al-Janoub,** Ma'an: 90.5 – **Sawt al-Madina:** Amman: 88.7. **W:** sawtalmadenah.net – **Sawt el-Ghad:** Amman 101.5. **W:** sawtelghad.com – **Spin Jordan:** Irbid 88.3, Ma'an 88.5, Amman 94.1, Aqaba 103.5. English. **W:** spin.jo – **Sunny,** Amman: 105.1. English. **W:** sunny.jo – **Virgin R. Jordan,** Amman: 93.7. **W:** virginradiojordan.com – **Yarmouk FM,** Irbid: 105.7. **W:** www.yu.edu.jo
BBC Arabic Sce: Amman 103.1 5kW, Ajlun 89.1 10kW.
Monte Carlo Doualiya/DW: Amman 97.4, Ajlun 106.2.
R. Sawa: Amman 98.1 10kW, Ajlun 107.4

KAZAKHSTAN

L.T: UTC +6h (West Kazakhstan: +5h) — **Pop:** 16.6 million — **Pr.L:** Kazakh, Russian — **E.C:** 50Hz, 220V — **ITU:** KAZ

MÄDENÏET JÄNE AQPARAT MÏNÏSTRLIGI (Ministry of Culture and Information)

⌨ House of Ministries, 010000 Astana ☎ +7 7172 740251
W: www.mk.gov.kz
L.P: Minister: Darxan Miñbay
NB. The ministry issues broadcasting licenses.

"QAZAQSTAN" RESPWBLÏKALIQ TELERADÏO-KORPORACÏYASI ("QAZAQSTAN" RTRK) (Gov) (Republican Broadcasting Corp. "Qazaqstan")

⌨ Almati broadcasting house: Jeltoqsan kös. 175a, 050013 Almati ☎ +7 727 2721360 ▤ +7 727 2613777 ⌨ Astana broadcasting house: Moskovskaya kös. 55a, 010032 Astana ☎ +7 7172 394969 ▤ +7 7172 393159 **W:** www.kaztrk.kz
L.P: Chair ("Qazaqstan" RTRK): Nurjan Nuxamedjanova

MW	kHz	kW	Prgr
Aqtaw	1341	25	QR

FM (MHz)	QR	SR	FM	QR	SR
Almati	101.0	106.5	Petropavl	106.8	-
Aqtaw	100.1	102.1	Qaragandi	103.4	102.3
Aqtöbe	102.2	105.7	Qizilorda	102.0	101.0
Astana	106.8	100.4	Qostanay	105.4	107.4
Atiraw	100.1	102.8	Semey	100.1	104.4
Köksetaw	101.0	-	Simkent	100.0	102.7
Oral	101.2	103.2	Taraz	100.8	102.6
Öskemen	104.0	105.6	Türkistan	101.0	-
Pavlodar	101.0	-	Ülken Sagan	101.0	-
+ translators					

D.Prgrs: Qazaq radïosi (QR) in Kazakh, Russian: 24h. For ethnic minorities ("Dostiq"): Mon-Sat 1105-1125 (Mon German, Tue Uighur, Wed Korean, Thur Turkish, Fri Tatar, Sat Azeri) – **Salqar radïosi (SR)** in Kazakh: 0000-1800. – **Local station: Astana radïosi** on Astana 101.4 in Kazakh, Russian: 24h.

"QAZAQSTAN" RTRK Regional Services

The regional branches (oblistiq fïlïali) of "Qazaqstan" RTRK are broadcasting on own FM frequencies at various times in Kazakh and languages of ethnic minorities.
a) **Aqmola oblistiq fïlïali:** Awezov kös. 230, 020000 Köksetaw. **E:** akmol_tv@mail.ru – b) **Aqtöbe oblistiq fïlïali:** Axtanov kös. 54, 030000 Aqtöbe. **E:** atrk@aktobe.kz – c) **Atiraw oblistiq fïlïali:** Moldagalïev kös. 29, 060005 Atiraw. **E:** bayan-baha@mail.ru – d) **Batis Qazaqstan oblistiq fïlïali:** Amanjolov kös. 104, 090000 Oral. **E:** zapad_tv@mail.kz – e) **Jambil oblistiq fïlïali:** Swleymenov kös. 6, 080000 Taraz. **E:** otrk@taraz.kz – f) **Mañgistaw oblistiq fïlïali:** 24 iqsam awdani, 130000 Aqtaw. **E:** gulek.aktau@mail.ru – g) **Pavlodar oblistiq fïlïali:** Derïbas kös. 21, 140000 Pavlodar. **E:** oblradio@nursat. kz . On Pavlodar 100.5 + translators. – h) **Qaragandi oblistiq fïlïali:** Jaw-ïnternacïonal'istov kös. 14, 100000 Qaragandi. **E:** obltrk@nursat. kz – i) **Qostanay oblistiq fïlïali:** Puskïn kös. 54, 110000 Qostanay. **E:** office@otrk.kst.kz – j) **Qizilorda oblistiq fïlïali:** Jeltoqsan kös. 11, 120014 Qizilorda. **E:** o14@kazakstan.kz – k) **Semey oblistiq fïlïali:** Sugaev kös. 157, 071403 Semey. On Semey 106.9 (R.7). **E:** semey-tv@ kazakstan.kz – l) **Soltüstik Qazaqstan oblistiq fïlïali:** Brwsïlovskïy kös. 1, 150000 Petropavl. **E:** otrk@inbox.ru – m) **Sigiz Qazaqstan oblistiq fïlïali:** Staxanov kös. 70, 070020 Öskemen. **E:** vktrk@ukg.kz – n) **Öñtüstik Qazaqstan oblistiq fïlïali:** Qazibek bi kös. 20, 160000 Simkent. **E:** uktv_aha@mail.ru.

OTHER STATIONS:

MW	kHz	kW	Location	Station
B)	1098	-	Almati	BBCWS relay*
B)	1188	-	Abay	BBCWS relay*
B)	1197	10	Astana	BBCWS relay*
A)	1341	30	Almaty	RFE-RL relay
B)	1440	-	Qizilorda	BBCWS relay*

FM	MHz	kW	Location	Station
3)	101.2	1	Simkent	Love R.
4)	101.4	1	Aqtaw	Tengri FM
4)	101.4	1	Semey	Tengri FM
4)	102.7	1	Aqtöbe	Tengri FM
2)	102.8	1	Almati	R. Classic
5)	103.2	1	Astana	Delovaya volna
3)	103.5	2	Almati	Love R.
4)	103.5	1	Öskemen	Tengri FM
1)	104.0	1	Qaragandi	Retro FM
4)	104.5	1	Astana	Tengri FM
4)	104.7	1	Simkent	Tengri FM
1)	105.0	1	Astana	Retro FM
4)	105.8	1	Oral	Tengri FM
1)	107.0	1	Almati	Retro FM
4)	106.7	1	Sagan	Tengri FM
4)	107.5	1	Almati	Tengri FM
4)	107.6	1	Köksetaw	Tengri FM
4)	107.7	1	Taraz	Tengri FM

NB: Txs below 1kW not listed. *) lease by BBC in 2013 subject to confirmation. Txs may carry Qazaq radïosi as filler.

Addresses & other information:
1) Respwblik alana 13, 050013 Almati. **E:** radio@retrofm.kz – **2)** Jeltoqsan kös. 185, 050013 Almati. **E:** radio@khabar.kz – **3)** Minbaev kös. 53, 050057 Almati. **E:** radio@loveradio.kz – **4)** Begalïn kös. 148, 050051 Almati. – **5)** Jeltoqsan kös 49, 010000 Astana. **E:** radio@astv.kz – **A)** Rel. RFE-RL (USA) – **B)** Rel BBCWS (UK).

KENYA

L.T: UTC +3h — **Pop:** 38 million — **Pr.L:** English, Swahili, Kikuyu, Luhya, Luo, Kalenjin, Somali, others — **E.C:** 50Hz, 240V — **ITU:** KEN

COMMUNICATIONS COMMISSION OF KENYA (CCK)
+ P.O. Box 14448, Nairobi 00800 ☎+254 20 4242000 🖷 +254 20 4451866 **W:** www.cck.go.ke **E:** info@cck.go.ke

KENYA BROADCASTING CORPORATION (KBC, Pub.)
🖳 P.O. Box 30456, Nairobi 00100 ☎+254 20 2766000 🖷 +254 20 2220675 **W:** www.kbc.co.ke **E:** md@kbc.co.ke **L.P:** Chmn: Charles Musyoki Muoki. MD: Waithaka Waihenya.

MW	kHz	kW	Netw.	MW	kHz	kW	Netw.
Voi	‡540	100	S	Malindi	‡927	100	S
Kapsimotwa#	‡558	25	W	Nyamninia#	‡954	100	E
Garissa	567	50	S	Voi	‡981	100	E
Ngong§	612	100	S	Malindi	‡1044	100	S
Garissa	‡639	50	E/N	Maralal	1107	100	S
Marsabit	675	50	S	Kitale	1134	50	E
Marania+++	‡702	100	S	Wajir	1152	50	S
Ngong§	747	100	E/C	Marsabit	1233	50	E
Nyamninia#	‡846	100	S	Wajir	1305	50	E/N
Kitale	‡882	50	S	Maralal	1386	100	E
Marania§§	‡900	100	E				

#) near Kisumu, §) near Nairobi, §§) near Meru. ‡=inactive.

FM	S	E	V	Co	Pw	Mi	Ki	Ma
Limuru*	92.9	95.6	101.9	99.5	-	-	-	-
Malindi	-	93.3	90.1	-	93.7	-	-	-
Meru**	90.4	103.5	97.5	103.0	-	-	-	-
Nyeri	87.6	100.7	97.0	102.3	-	-	-	-
Mombasa	100.7	103.1	89.1	-	104.7	-	-	-
Timboroa	88.6	91.5	-	-	-	-	-	-
Nakuru	104.1	96.5	94.5	-	-	-	-	-
Eldoret	-	-	97.9	-	-	-	92.9	-
Kapsimotwa	-	-	100.9	-	-	-	-	-
Kisumu	104.5	-	87.7	-	-	-	-	93.5
Kisii	103.3	-	-	-	-	101.7	-	-
Nyadundo	-	-	-	99.7	-	-	-	-

*Limuru txs serve Greater Nairobi. **) also called Nyambene.

Networks (from Nairobi studios unless stated):
S=Swahili Sce ("KBC Radio Taifa"): 0200-2110. Also rel. China R. Int. – **E=English Sce:** 0200-2105 (on FM non-stop music 2105-0200). Includes schools prgrs & relays of China R. Int. Some MW freqs carry N & C sces at times – **N=(North) Eastern Sce.** in local langs: MF variable between 0900-1905 – **C=Central Sce.** in local langs: Mon-Sat variable times between 0200-2010 – **W=Western Sce.** from Kisumu studios in local langs pm 558kHz & 100.2MHz – **V=Venus FM** (ex Metro FM) ("House of Reggae") in English/Swahili – **Co=Coro FM** in Kikuyu –

Pw=Pwani FM from Mombasa studios – **Mi=Minto FM** (from Keroka studios in Kisii) – **Ki=Kitwek FM** in Kalenjin – **Ma=Mayienga FM** (from Kisumu studios in Luo) – **Nosim FM:** Narok 90.5MHz in Masai. **Ann:** E: "This is KBC English Service". **IS:** Flute & drum melody in some services.

ROYAL MEDIA SERVICES LTD. (RMS)
🖳 P.O. Box 7468, Nairobi 00300 ☎+254 20 2721415/6 🖷 +254 20 2724211 **W:** royalmediaservices.co.ke Email: info@royalmedia.co.ke **L.P:** Owner: Samuel K. Macharia. MD: Wachira Waruru.
FM(MHz): R. Citizen in Swahili/Eng: Eldoret 90.4, Voi 91.8, Chuka 93.1, Machakos 94.2, Meru 94.3, Kibwezi 95.4, Narok 95.5, Garissa 95.7, Maralal 95.9, Kapenguria 96.1, Kanyenyeini 96.5, Wajir 97.0, Mombasa 97.3, Malindi 97.4, Kisumu 97.6, Marsabit 98.0, Kitui 98.6, Nakuru 100.5, Nyadundo 103.6, Nyeri 104.3, Homa Bay 105.2, Nairobi/Namanga 106.7, Kisii not known. – **Hot 96 FM** in Eng/Sheng/Swahili: Nairobi 96.0, Eldoret 87.6, Kisumu 103.1, Mombasa 90.4, Nakuru 102.5, Nyeri 88.6.
RMS also operates the following stns for specific lang. communities: **FM (MHz): Bahari FM** (in Swahili & coastal langs): Mombasa 94.2 – **Chamgei FM** (in Kalenjin): 90.4, Nakuru 95.0, Eldoret 97.5 – **Egesa FM** (in Kisii): Kisii 94.6, Nairobi 103.2 – **Inooro FM** (in Kikuyu): Nyadundo 88.9, Nakuru 88.8, Meru 95.1, Muranga 96.9, Nyeri 97.8, Nairobi 98.9, Mombasa 99.2, Chuka 102.0, Eldoret 107.0 – **Mulembe FM** (in Luhya): Webuye 89.6, Rift Valley 94.0, Eldoret 95.8, Nairobi 97.9 – **Musyi FM** (in Kamba): Nairobi 102.2, Kitui 103.6 – **Muuga FM** (in Meru): Meru 88.9 – **Ramogi FM** (in Luo): Nakuru 96.4, Mombasa 96.0, Homa Bay 97.0, Siaya 98.4, Nairobi 107.1, Kisumu 107.6 – **Wimwaro FM** (in Embu): Embu 93.0.

RADIO AFRICA LTD.
🖳 P.O. Box 74497, Nairobi ☎+254 20 4244000 🖷 +254 20 4447410 **W:** kissfm.co.ke **E:** info@kissfm.co.ke **L.P:** MD: Patrick Quarcoo.
FM(MHz): Kiss 100 in Eng/Swahili: Nairobi 100.3, Eldoret 89.1, Kisumu 92.5, Meru 93.5 , Mombasa 88.7, Nakuru 98.1, Nyeri 100.1, Webuye 104.7 – **Classic 105 FM** in Eng/Swahili: Nakuru 95.7, Nairobi 105.2, Mombasa 107.5 – **East FM** (Asian): Nairobi 106.3, Mombasa 89.5 – **Jambo FM** (sports): Kisii 89.3, Mombasa 92.3, Meru 92.7, Webuye 95.3, Nakuru 96.9, Maralal/Narok/Nyahururu 97.3, Nairobi 97.5, Malindi 98.1, Nyeri 99.3, Eldoret 99.5, Kapenguria 99.7, Kisumu 100.1, Garissa 104.3, Kibwezi/Lamu 104.7, Kitui 104.9, Voi 105.7 – **X FM** (rock music): Nairobi 105.5 – **Relax FM** (R&B music): Nairobi 103.5.

NATION MEDIA GROUP LTD.
🖳 P.O. Box 49010, Nairobi 00100 ☎+254 20 3200000 **W:** www.nationmedia.com **L.P:** Chmn: Wilfred Kiboro. CEO: Linus Gitahi. Managing Ed. Broadc. Div: Linus Kaikaı.
FM(MHz): Easy FM in Eng/Swahili: Nairobi 96.3, Eldoret 102.7, Kisumu 102.1, Meru 93.9, Mombasa 101.5, Nakuru 97.7, Nyeri 104.9 – **QFM** in Swahili: Nairobi 94.4, Eldoret 96.7, Meru 107.1, Mombasa 87.9, Nakuru 103.3, Nyeri 90.9.

OTHER FM STNS IN NAIROBI (including relays elsewhere; freqs are in Nairobi unless stated, & in MHz): **1 FM** (ex Countryside FM): 97.1, Meru 99.1, Nyeri 106.1, Nakuru 106.5, Mombasa 107.3 – **Biblia Husema Broadcasting** (Christian): 90.7, Eldoret 96.3, Lokichokio 102.5, Nakuru 102.9, Machakos 96.7, Timboroa 101.5 – **Capital FM** (in Eng): 98.4, Garissa 102.7, Kitui 106.5, Malindi 104.5, Meru 103.9, Mombasa 98.4, Nakuru 98.5, Nyeri 98.5, Timboroa 93.0, Voi 104.9 – **East Africa R.** (in Eng/Swahili - relay of Tanzanian stn): 94.7 – **ECN FM** (Kenya Institute of Mass Communication): 104.7 – **R. 316** (Christian, formerly Family FM): 103.9, Kisumu 96.5, Mombasa 97.9, Nakuru 102.1 – **Frontier FM** (in Somali, also known as Garissa FM): 88.7, Garissa 107.5, Wajir 88.9. Also rel. VOA – **Ghetto R.** (in Sheng): 89.5 – **Homeboyz R.:** 103.5 – **Hope FM** (Pentecostal Church): 93.3, Mombasa 101.9, Timboroa 93.9 – **Iqra FM** (Islamic): 95.1 – **Kameme FM** (mainly in Kikuyu): 101.1, Eldoret 101.9, Nakuru 99.3, Nyeri 92.3, Meru 88.3. Also rel. BBC – **Kass FM** (in Kalenjin): 89.1, Eldoret 90.0, Kisumu 91.0, Nakuru 99.3, Mombasa 102.7 – **Milele FM** (in Swahili): 93.6, Kapenguria 88.3, Taita-Taveta (Voi) 89.7, Nakuru/Nyahururu 90.2, Kitui/Lamu 91.3, Nyeri 91.7, Webuye 92.7, Kisii 95.1, Mombasa 96.7, Maralal/Narok 98.7, Kisumu 97.9, Garissa 99.9, Malindi 101.3, Meru 101.5, Eldoret 103.1, Kibwezi 104.3 – **R. Maisha** 102.7, Nakuru 104.5, Mombasa/Meru 105.1, Kisumu 105.3, Nyeri 105.7 – **Sound Asia:** 88.0, Mombasa 89.9 – **Star FM** (in Somali/Swahili/Eng): 105.9, Dadaab/Garissa 97.1, Wajir 97.3, Mandera 97.5. Also rel. BBC. **W:** starfm.co.ke – **R. Umoja:** 101.5, Kisumu 97.3, Mombasa 94.7, Nakuru 104.9 – **Uptown Radio:** 91.1 – **R. Waumini:** 88.3. **W:** catholicchurch.or.ke
NB: 99.9MHz is assigned for use in Nairobi by several very low-powered community stns. There are many private FM stns outside

Nairobi. A full list of allocations is at: cck.go.ke/licensing/broadcasting/register.html
Relays of International Stations (FM MHz): BBC WS (E/Swahili): Nairobi 93.9, Mombasa 93.9, Kisumu 88.1 – **VOA** (E/Swahili): Nairobi 107.5 – **RFI Afrique** (F/E/Swahili): Nairobi 89.9, Mombasa 105.5 – **China R. Int.** (E/Swahili/Chinese): Nairobi 91.9

KIRIBATI

L.T: UTC +12h — **Pop:** 100,743 — **Pr.L:** I-Kiribati, English, Gilbertese — **E.C:** 50Hz, 240V — **ITU:** KIR

BROADCASTING & PUBLICATIONS AUTHORITY RADIO KIRIBATI
PO Box 78, Bairiki, Tarawa **LP:** Mgr Betarim Rimon C.E: Rubeiariki Kautabuki ☎ +686 21187 🖷 +686 21096. **W:** www.bpa.org.ki
MW: Bairiki 1440kHz 10kW **FM:** 88.0MHz 0.1kW
D.Prgr: I-Kiribati (90%) English (10%): 1800-2000, 0000-0130, 0530-0930 **N. in English:** 0600 (rel.BBC, Radio Australia) followed by local news bulletin.
Ann: "This is Radio Kiribati, the national broadcasting service of Kiribati in the Central Pacific" "Aio bwanaan Kiribati te botaki ni kanako bwanaa I bukin Kiribati I nukan te Betebeke."

RADIO KIRIBATI CHRISTMAS FM
Ronton, Kiritimati Island, Kiribati, Central Pacific **FM:** Ronton (London) 93.5MHz 0.5kW **Prgr:** Satellite feed from R. Kiribati 88.0 FM and local prgrs for Kiritimati (Christmas), Fanning and Washington islands in the Line Islands.

Other Stations

FM	Location	MHz	Station
3)	Ambo, Betio	89.0	Newair FM89
1)	Bairiki	90.0	Radio Australia
2)	Bairiki	95.0	BBC
2)	Tarawa	100.0	BBC
3)	Bairiki	101.0	Newair FM101

1) 24h English for the Pacific satellite relay – **2)** 24h Pacific stream satellite relay – **3)** PO Box 204, Bairiki, Tarawa. **LP:** Sir Ieremia Tabai. **D.Prgr:** Local commercial prgrs in English & I-Kiribati ☎ +686 21671 **E:** newairfm89kiribati@gmail.com

KOREA (North, DPR)

L.T: UTC +9h — **Pop:** 26 million — **Pr.L:** Korean — **E.C:** 60Hz, 100/200/220V — **ITU:** KRE

THE RADIO AND TELEVISION BROADCASTING COMMITEE OF THE DEMOCRATIC PEOPLE'S REPUBLIC OF KOREA
Jonsung-dong, Moranbong District, Pyongyang ☎ +850 2 816035.

KOREAN CENTRAL BROADCASTING STATION (Joson Jung-ang Pangsong)
Jonsung-dong, Moranbong District, Pyongyang ☎ +850 2 812301

MW	kHz	kW	Prgr	MW	kHz	kW	Prgr
Chongjin	702	50	C/R	Wonsan	882	250	C/R
Wiwon*	720	500	C/R	Hwangju+	927	50	C/R
Hyesan	765	50	C/R	Hamhung	999	250	C/R
Kaesong	810	50	C/R	Haeju	1080	1500	C/R
Pyongyang	819	500	C	Pyongyang	1368	2	E
Sinuiju	873	250	C/R				

SW	kHz	Prgr	SW	kHz	Prgr
Sariwon	2350	C/R	Wonsan	3970	C/R
Pyongyang	2850	C	Chongjin	3980	C/R
Hamhung	3220	C/R	Kanggye	6100	C
Pyongsong	3350	C/R	Pyongyang	9665	C
Hyesan	3920	C/R	Kanggye	11680	C
Kanggye	3960	C/R			

*= Kanggye, += Sariwon, C = Central Broadcast from Pyongyang, R = Regional Sce, E = rel. Ext. Sce.
NB: all freqs variable **FM:** Kaesong 102.3MHz
D.Prgr in Korean: 2000-1800 on all freqs exc. 6100 (2000-0630 & 1330-1800). **N:** 2100, 2200, 0100, 0300, 0600, 0800, 1100, 1200, 1300. Regional Prgrs: W0500-0600. Rel. Pyongyang Broadc. St: 1500-1800 on 702/720/864kHz 1500-2000 on 102.3MHz 1800-2000 on 3220/3940/3970kHz
Ann: "Joson Jung-ang Pangsong-imnida". Reg. Prgrs: "(location) Pangsong-imnida". **IS:** Song of General Kim Il Sung. Opening & closing music: Nat. Anthem. **V:** not verified.

EXTERNAL SERVICES: Voice of Korea, Pyongyang Broadcasting Station, Pyongyang Branch of the Anti-Imperialist National Democratic Front – See International Broadcasting section

PYONGYANG FM BROADCASTING STATION (Pyongyang FM Pangsong)

FM	MHz	kW	FM	MHz	kW
Pyongsong	90.1	2	Komdok	102.1	1
Kaesong	92.5	2	Sariwon	103.0	2
Kanggye	93.3	5	Haeju	103.7	10
Hyesan	93.8	2	Pyongyang	105.2	20
Wonsan	95.1	5	Chongjin	105.5	10
Heaju	97.8	10	Hamhung	106.1	20
Sinuiju	101.3	5	Nampo	107.2	2

D.Prgr: 0700-2000, 2100-2400 (National holidays: 2100-2030) (music, drama and novel).
Ann: "Pyongyang FM Pangsong-imnida". **IS:** Song of General Kim Jong Il. Opening music: Pyongyang Is My Heart

FRONTLINE SOLDIERS RADIO (Jonyon Chobyongdurul Wihan Pangsong)
MW: ±1613kHz (irr.), **SW:** 3025kHz (irr.) **D.Prgr in Korean:** 2030-2230 and 0730-0930. Almost relay of Korean Central Broadcasting Station. Times and freqs are variable.
Ann: "Jonyon Chobyongdurul Wihan Pangsong-imnida"

KOREAN PEOPLE'S ARMY FM BROADCASTING STATION (Josong Inmingun FM Pangsong)
FM: 95.5MHz **Ann:** "Josong Inmingun FM Pangsong-imnida"

KOREA (South, Rep.)

L.T: UTC +9h — **Pop:** 47 million — **Pr.L:** Korean — **E.C:** 60Hz, 110/220V — **ITU:** KOR

KOREAN BROADCASTING SYSTEM (KBS) (Hanguk Bangsong Gongsa) (Public Corporation)
13, Yeouigongwon-ro, Yeongdeungpo-gu, Seoul 150-790 ☎ +82 2 781 1000 🖷 +82 2 761 2499 **W:** www.kbs.co.kr
LP: Pres & CEO: Kim In-Kyu. Auditor General: Lee Gil-Yung. Exec. Vice Pres:Gil Hwan-Young, Exec. Man. Dirs: Park Kab-Jin(Audience Relations), Lee Hwa-Seob(N & Sports), Chun Yong-Kil(Content), Kim Seon-Kwon (New Media & Tech), Lee Jun-Sam (Policy Planning). Dir. Int. Rel. Div:Min Eun-Gyung.

MW	Location	Call	kHz	kW	MW	Location	Call	kHz	kW
9)	Jangsu	-	540	1	4)	Taebaek	-	621	10
13)	Jeomchon	-	540	1	19)	Seogwipo	-	621	10
8)	Hongseong	-	540	10	6)	Yeongdong	-	621	1
10)	Jangheung	-	540	1	3)	Inje	-	630	5
13)	Daegu+2	QH	558	250	12)	Yeosu	-	630	10
3)	Jeonju+	KF	567	100	10)	Boseong	-	648	1
12)	Suncheon 3		576	1	3)	Chuncheon+	KM	657	50
14)	Yeongju	-	594	10	9)	Jeonju 3	-	675	10
N2)	Namyang*	SA	603	500	N1)	Sorae*	KA	711	500
13)	Daegu+	KG	738	100	5)	Wonju+	CW	1152	10
10)	Gwangju+	KH	747	100	K2E)	Gimje*	SR	1170	500
N1)	Yeoju*	-	756	100	5)	Jeongseon	-	1206	1
5)	Yeongwol	-	783	10	14)	Cheongsong	-	1206	1
3)	Yanggu	-	846	5	10)	Gwangju 3	-	1224	20
4)	Gangneung+	KR	864	100	5)	Pyeongchang	-	1233	1
8)	Daejeon+	KI	882	20	9)	Namwon	-	1260	10
6)	Busan+	KB	891	250	N1)	Yangju	-	1269	10
13)	Gumi	-	909	10	9)	Gurye	-	1269	1
N1)	Yeoncheon*	-	918	50	16)	Hapcheon	-	1278	1
18)	Buyeo	-	927	10	15)	Uljin	-	1305	10
5)	Hadong	-	927	1	10)	Yeonggwang	-	1323	1
5)	Hongcheon	-	927	1	15)	Ulleung	-	1323	1
16)	Changwon 3	-	936	10	9)	Muju	-	1368	1
6)	Boeun	-	945	10	N1)	Cheorwon*	-	1395	10
19)	Jeju+	KS	963	10	17)	Ulsan+	QB	1449	10
14)	Andong+	CR	963	10	18)	Hamyang	-	1458	1
K1)	Dangjin*	CA	972	1500	14)	Bonghwa	-	1458	1
4)	Gangneung 3	-	1008	50	11)	Mokpo+	KN	1467	50
3)	Hwacheon	-	1026	1	12)	Goheung	-	1485	1
18)	Geochang	-	1026	1	8)	Gongju	-	1485	1
15)	Pohang+	CP	1035	10	13)	Gimcheon	-	1503	1
4)	Samcheok	-	1044	10	19)	Gosan	-	1539	1
7)	Jecheon	-	1044	10	7)	Danyang	-	1584	1
6)	Cheongju+	KQ	1062	10	18)	Sancheong	-	1584	1
7)	Chungju+	CH	1089	10	8)	Geumsan	-	1584	1
18)	Jinju+	CJ	1098	20	5)	Sabuk	-	1602	1
N3)	Hwaseong*	KC	1134	500					

MW: N1 = KBS R. One, N2 = KBS R. Two, N3 = KBS R. Three, K1 = Global Korean Network 1, K2 = Global Korean Network 2, E = also used for Ext. sce., KBS WORLD R, N = Netw. or local stn. area, *) Key stn, +) = Regional key St, 2 = rel N2 exc. for local prgrs, 3 = rel N3 (other local st take N1), Call: HL(call).

NB: Global Korean Network stns and FM-stns do not use call letters (even if assigned). Other stns without call letters use the calls from their regional key stns.

FM	Location	I	II	III	kW
1)	Namsan		93.1	89.1a	-/10/10
1)	Gwanaksan	97.3*		106.1b	10/-/10
1)	Gwanaksan			104.9c	-/-/2
1)	Yongmunsan	90.3*			1
2)	Yeongdo	103.7	92.7	97.1b	3/5/3
3)	Hwaaksan	99.5*	91.1	98.7b	5/5/3
4)	Gwaebangsan	98.9*	89.1	102.1b	1/5/5
5)	Baegunsan	97.1	89.5		1/3
5)	Taegisan	95.5*			1
4)	Hambaeksan	93.7*	97.3		1/3
6)	Sikchangsan		102.1		-/3
6)	Sikchangsan			100.9b	-/-/3
6)	Heukseongsan	89.9*			1
6)	Uamsan	89.3	94.1		1/1
6)	Gayeopsan			90.9b	-/-/3
7)	Gayeopsan	92.1*	100.3		1/3
8)	Gyeryongsan	94.7*	98.5		1/5
9)	Moaksan	96.9*	100.7	92.9b	5/5/?
9)	Nogodan	88.3*	104.5		1/3
10)	Mudeungsan	90.5*	92.3	95.5b	5/5/3
11)	Yangulsan		98.3		-/1
11)	Daedunsan	105.9			1
12)	Suncheon			102.7b	-/-/3
12)	Mangunsan	95.7*	94.5		1/3
13)	Palgongsan	101.3*	89.7	102.3b	5/5/3
14)	Ilwolsan	90.5*			1
14)	Hakkasan		88.1		-/3
15)	Johangsan	95.9*	93.5		1/3
16)	Bulmosan	91.7*	93.9	106.1b	1/1/3
17)	Muryongsan	90.7*	101.9		1/3
18)	Gamaksan		92.1		-/3
18)	Mangjinsan	90.3	89.3		1/1
19)	Gyeonwolak	99.1*	96.3	91.9b	5/3/3
19)	Sammaebong		99.9	89.7b	-/3/1

+ low power relay stn

Reg = region in MW section. I-Standard FM (R. One); II-KBS FM One; III a = KBS FM Two, b = R. Two, c=R. Three. *) also SCA (R. Three).

KBS R. One (KBS Je-il Radio, HLKA): 24h Non-commercial nationwide news sce. Key freqs 711/756kHz, 90.3/97.3MHz. Also rel. by Standard FM stns and most reg. stns. Reg. stns may broadcast local prgrs at designated times. **N:** hourly 2000-1600 except 1100(W). Local N: 2205(Sun), 2210(W), 0000(Sun), 0005(w), 0310(Sun), 0315(W), 0605, 0805(Mon-Fri), 0900(Sun), 0905(W).

KBS R. Two (KBS Je-i Radio, Happy FM, HLSA): 2000-1800 (558kHz to 1500). Commercial. Key freq's 603kHz/106.1MHz. Reg. stns may broadcast local prgrs at designated times. **N:** hourly 0900-1200. Local N: 2300, 0400, 0700, 1200. Global Korean Network prgr 1700-1800.

KBS R. Three (KBS Je-sam Radio, Sarang-ui Sori Bangsong, HLKC): 1200-1800. Non-comm. sce. **N:** 0000(W), 0100(W), 0300(W), 0800(Mon-Fri).

KBS FM One (KBS Je-il FM Bangsong, Classic FM, HLKA-FM): 24h. Mainly Korean traditional and western classical music.

KBS FM Two (KBS Je-i FM Bangsong. Cool FM, HLKC-FM): 24h. Mainly Korean and western popular and light classical music.
NB: Regional FM One stns relay FM Two 2100-2200.

KBS Global Korean Network (Hanminjok Bangsong)
See International Broadcasting section

Ann: N1: "AM Chilbaek-sib-il(711)kHz, FM Gusib-chil-jeom-sam(97.3)MHz, Je-il Radiomnida. HLKA". N2: "KBS Je-i Radiomnida". N3: "KBS Je-sam Radio, Sarang-ui Sori Bangsong-imnida. HLKC". Global Korean Network 1:"Jungpa Gubaek-chilsib-i(972)kHz, Hanminjok Neteuwokeu Chaeneol, KBS Hanminjok Je-il Bangsong-imnida". Global Korean Network 2:"Jungpa Cheonbaek-chilsip(1170)kHz, Daehan Mingook Seoureseo Bonae Deurineun Hanminjok Neteuwokeu Chaeneol, KBS Hanminjok Je-il Bangsong-imnida".

Addresses of regional key stations:
2) 429, Suyeong-ro, Suyeong-gu, Busan 608-790 – **3)** 109, Bangsong-gil, Chuncheon-si, Gangwon-do 200-100 – **4)** 13, Imyeong-ro 131beon-gil, Gangneung-si, Gangwon-do 210-070 – **5)** 37, Wonil-ro, Wonju-si, Gangwon-do 220-060 – **6)** 41428, Seobu-ro, Heungdeok-gu, Cheongju-si, Chungcheongbuk-do 361-790 – **7)** 3448, Jungwon-daero, Chungju-si, Chungcheongbuk-do 380-790 – **8)** 128, Dunsan-daero 117beon-gil, Seo-

gu, Daejeon 302-790 – **9)** 186, Gwonsandeuk-ro, Deokchin-gu, Jeonju-si, Jeollabuk-do 560-790 –**10)**287, Uncheon-ro, Seo-gu, Gwangju 502-270 – **11)** 221, Yangeul-ro, Mokpo-si, Jeollanam-do 530-360 – **12)** 412, Jungang-ro, Suncheon-si, Jeollanam-do 540-100 – **13)** 30, Dalgubeol-daero 496-gil, Suseong-gu, Daegu 706-790 – **14)** 27, Gamnamu 3-gil, Andong-si, Gyeongsangbuk-do 760-790 – **15)** 72, Jungseom-ro, Nam-gu, Pohang-si, Gyeongsangbuk-do 790-790 – **16)** 97-1, Sinwol-dong, Changwon-si, Gyeongsangnam-do 641-790 – **17)** 212, Beonyeong-ro, Nam-gu, Ulsan 680-790 – **18)** 85, Sinan-ro, Jinju-si, Gyeongsangnam-do 660-790 – **19)** 104, Sin-daero, Jeju-si, Jeju 690-170.

Local identifications: Within local prgrs. **N1:** just before the h. at 2000, 2200(Sun), 2300, 0000(W), 0200, 0300, 0500, 0700(Mon-Fri), 0800, 0900(Sun), 1000(W), 1100(Sun), 1300, 1400, 1500(Sun), 1600. **N2:** just before the h. 2000-1700. **N3:** just before the h. 2100-1700. **FM One:** just before the h. at 2000-2200, 0000, 0200, 0300, 0500, 0700-0900, 1100, 1300, 1500, 1600, 1800. **FM Two:** just before the h.

EXTERNAL SERVICES: KBS WORLD RADIO
See International Broadcasting section

KOREA EDUCATIONAL BROADCASTING SYSTEM (EBS) (Gyoyuk Bangsong) (Pub.)
✉35, Baumoe-ro 1-gil, Seocho-gu, Seoul 137-900 ☎ +82 2 526 2000 📠 +82 2 526 2419 **W:** www.ebs.co.kr
Call letters HLQL used for all the stns.

FM	Tx location	MHz	kW
Chungju	Gayeopsan	104.1	5
Changwon	Bulmosan	104.3	5
Seoul	Gwanaksan	104.5	5
Jinju	Gamaksan	104.7	3
Gangneung	Gwaebangsan	104.9	3
Wonju	Baegunsan	104.9	3
Seogwipo	Sammaebang	104.9	3
Daegu	Palgongsan	105.1	5
Gwangju	Mudeungsan	105.3	5
Daejeon	Gyeryongsan	105.7	5
Ulsan	Muryongsan	105.9	3
Yeosu	Mangunsan	106.3	1
Chuncheon	Hwaaksan	106.5	5
Pohang	Johangsan	106.7	3
Jeonju	Moaksan	106.9	5
Taebaek	Hambaeksan	107.1	3
Jeju	Gyeonwolak	107.3	3
Namwom	Nogodan	107.5	3
Andong	Hakkasan	107.7	3
Busan	Yeongdo	107.7	3
Cheongju	Sikjangsan	107.9	3

+ low power relay stns
D.Prgr: 2000-1700 **Ann:** "EBS, Gyoyuk Bangsong-imnida".

GUGAK FM BROADCASTING SYSTEM (Gugak Bangsong) (Pub.)
✉ DMS Bldg., 260-16, Sang-am-dong-gil, Mapo-gu, Seoul 120-803 ☎ +82 2 300 9990 📠 +82 2 300 9959
W: www.gugakfm.co.kr
Stations: Seoul HLQA-FM 99.1MHz 5kW: 24h, Namwon 95.9MHz 1kW: 24h, Namdo 94.7MHz 0.5kW, Gyeongju/Pohang 107.9MHz 3kW: 24h, Jeonju 95.3MHz 1kW: 24h, Busan 98.5MHz 1kW: 24h.
Ann: "Gugak Bangsong-imnida."

MUNHWA BROADCASTING CORP. (MBC) (Munhwa Bangsong) Nationwide comm. netw.
✉ 96, Yeouinaru-ro, Yeongdeungpo-gu, Seoul 150-728 ☎ +82 2 784 2000 **W:** www.imbc.com

MW	Call	kHz	kW	Station	MW	Call	kHz	kW	Station
1)	CQ	765	10	Daejeon MBC	11)	AT	1080	10	Yeosu MBC
2)	AJ	774	10	Jeju MBC	12)	AV	1107	10	Pohang MBC
3)	AN	774	10	Chuncheon MBC	13)	KU	1161	20	Busan MBC
4)	CT	810	20	Daegu MBC	14)	AK	1215	10	Jinju MBC
5)	CN	819	20	Gwangju MBC	15)	SB	1242	10	Wonju MBC
6)	AU	846	10	Ulsan MBC	16)	AF	1287	10	Gangneung MBC
7)	CX	855	10	Jeonju MBC	17)	AX	1287	10	Cheongju MBC
8)	KV	900	50	Seoul MBC	18)	AQ	1332	10	Chungju MBC
9)	AP	990	10	Changwon MBC	19)	AG	1350	10	Samcheok MBC
10)	AW	1017	10	Andong MBC	20)	AM	1386	10	Mokpo MBC

D.Prgr: All 24h

		Music FM		Standard FM	
FM	Location	MHz	kW	MHz	kW
8)	Seoul	91.9	10	95.9	10
13)	Busan	88.9	5	95.9	3
4)	Daegu	95.3	5	96.5	5
5)	Gwangju	91.5	5	93.9	5

FM	Location	Music FM MHz	kW	Standard FM MHz	kW
	Gwangju	95.1	3	-	-
1)	Daejeon	97.5	5	92.5	3
7)	Jeonju	99.1	5	94.3	2
	Jeonju (Namwon)	-	-	101.7	3
9)	Changwon	100.5	1	98.9	3
3)	Chuncheon	94.5	3	92.3	3
17)	Cheongju	99.7	1	107.1	1
2)	Jeju	90.1	3	97.9	1
	Jeju(Seogwipo)	102.9	3	97.1	1
6)	Ulsan	98.7	3	97.5	1
16)	Gangneung	94.3	5	96.3	3
14)	Jinju	97.7	1	91.1	3
	Jinju	96.1	3	93.5	1
20)	Mokpo	102.3	1	89.1	2
11)	Yeosu	98.3	2	100.3	1
10)	Andong	91.3	3	100.1	3
15)	Wonju	98.9	3	92.7	1
	Wonju	-	-	102.5	1
18)	Chungju	88.7	3	96.1	1
19)	Samcheok	98.1	3	101.5	1
	Samcheok	99.9	1	93.1	3
12)	Pohang	97.9	3	100.7	3
	Pohang(Uljin)	94.9	1	102.7	1

+low power rel. stns

NB: Standard FM stns simulcast with the MW stn in the same city. A separate sce. is provided to the Music FM stns. All regional stns broadcast a combination of a feed from Seoul and their own local prgrs. Standard FM stns follow the same schedule as their corresponding MW outlet. Music FM of Seoul MBC sched: 24h.

Ann: "(freq. and location)Munhwa Bangsong-imnida. (Call)" or "Munhwa Bangsong-imnida" or "MBC". Seoul: "Jungpa Gubaek (900)kHz, Pyojun FM Gushib-o-jeom-gu 95.9MHz Munhwa Bangsong-imnida"

Addresses and other information
NB: Add "(location) Munhwa Broadc. Corp." to addr.
1) 161, EXPO-ro, Yuseong-gu, Daejeon 305-740 **W:** www.tjmbc.co.kr – **2)** 35, Munyeon-ro, Jeju-si, Jeju Special Self-do 690-170 **W:** www.jejumbc.co.kr – **3)** 54, Subyengongwon-gil, Chuncheon-si, Gangwon-do 200-200 **W:** www.chmbc.co.kr – **4)** 33, Dongdaegu-ro, Suseong-gu, Daegu 706-728 **W:** www.tgmbc.co.kr – **5)** 17, Wolsan-ro 116byeon-gil, Nam-gu, Gwangju 503-728 **W:** www.kjmbc.co.kr – **6)** 12, Cheongsan 2-gil, Jung-gu, Ulsan 681-728 **W:** www.ulsanmbc.co.kr – **7)** 50, Sanneomeo 1-gil, Wansan-gu, Jeonju-si, Jeollabuk-do 560-728 **W:** www.jmbc.co.kr – **8)** National addr. – **9)** 11-11, Yangdeokseo 9-gil, Masan Hoewon-gu, Changwon-si, Gyeongsangnam-do 630-713 **W:** www.changwonmbc.co.kr – **10)** 709-1, Taehwa-dong, Andong-si, Gyeongsangbuk-do 760-290 **W:** www.andongmbc.co.kr – **11)** 50-15, Yeomun-ro, Yeosu-si, Jeollanam-do 550-728 **W:** www.ysmbc.co.kr – **12)** 421, Saecheingnyeng-ro, Pohang-si, Gyeongsangbuk-do 790-728 **W:** www.phmbc.co.kr – **13)** 69, Gamporo 8beon-gil, Suyeong-gu. Busan 613-728 **W:** www.busanmbc.co.kr – **14)** 13, Gaho-ro, Jinju-si, Gyeongsangnam-do 660-728 **W:** www.jinjumbc.co.kr – **15)** 12, Cheongsan 2-gil, Wonju-si, Gangwon-do 220-031 **W:** www.wjmbc.co.kr – **16)** 126, Gajak-ro, Gangneung-si, Gangwon-do 210-112 **W:** www.gnmbc.co.kr – **17)** 1322, 2 Sunhwan-ro, Heungdeok-gu, Cheongju-si, Chungcheongbuk-do 361-855 **W:** www.mbccj.co.kr – **18)** 3250, Jungwon-daero, Chungju-si, Chungcheongbuk-do 380-130 **W:** www.cjmbc.co.kr – **19)** 629-59, Saecheongnyeon-doro, Samcheok-si, Gangwon-do 245-090 **W:** www.scmbc.co.kr – **20)** 334, Yeongsan-ro, Mokpo-si, Jeollanam-do 530-728 **W:** www.mokpombc.co.kr

CHRISTIAN BROADCASTING SYSTEM (CBS)
(Gidokkyo Bangsong)

	MW Call	kHz	kW	Station and h.of tr.
1)	KY	837	50	CBS Seoul: 24h
2)	CL	999	10	CBS Gwangju: 2000-1600
4)	KT	1251	10	CBS Daegu: 2000-1600
5)	CM	1314	10	CBS Jeonbuk: 2000-1600
6)	KP	1404	10	CBS Busan: 2000-1600

CBS FM	Call	MHz	kW	h. of tr.
1) CBS-FM Seoul	HLKY-FM	93.9	7	24h (Music FM)
1) CBS Seoul	HLKY-SFM	98.1	10	24h
2) CBS Gwangju	HLCL-SFM	103.1	3	2000-1600
3) CBS Jeonnam	HLCL-FM	102.1	2	2000-1600
4) CBS Daeju	HLKT-SFM	103.1	5	2000-1600
5) CBS Jeonbuk	HLCM-SFM	103.7	5	2000-1600
6) CBS Busan	HLKP-SFM	102.9	5	2000-1600
6) CBS-FM Busan	HLKP-FM	102.1	1	24h
7) CBS Cheongju	HLAC-FM	91.5	3	2000-1600
8) CBS Chuncheon	HLDC-FM	93.7	3	2000-1600
9) CBS Daejeon	HLDX-FM	91.7	5	2000-1600

CBS FM	Call	MHz	kW	h. of tr.
10) CBS Pohang	HLCB-FM	91.5	3	2000-1600
11) CBS Gyeongnam	HLCC-FM	106.9	5	2000-1600
12) CBS Jeju	HLKO-FM	93.3	3	2000-1600
12) CBS Jeju	(S)	90.9	1	2000-1600
13) CBS Yeongdong	HLCO-FM	91.5	3	2000-1600
14) CBS Ulsan	HLKP-FM	100.3	1	2000-1600

+low power relay stns (S)= Seogwipo relay st

Addresses and other information:
1) 159-1, Mokdongseo-ro, Yangcheon-gu, Seoul 158-701 ☎ +82 2 2650 7000 W: www.cbs.co.kr **Ann:** "Jeongjikhan Sesang-eul Gakkuneun AM Palbaek-samsip-chil(837)kHz, Pyojun FM Gusip-pal-jeom-il(98.1)MHz, CBS-mnida. HLKY." – **2)** 89, Uncheon-ro, Seo-gu, Gwangju 506-154 ☎ +82 62 376 8500 – **3)** 117-5, Maegok-dong, Suncheon-si, Jeollanam-do 540-947 ☎ +82 61 902 1000 – **4)** 3-7, Chimsan 2-dong, Buk-ku, Daegu 702-703 ☎ +82 53 426 8001 – **5)** 114-8, Daga-dong, Wansan-gu, Jeollabuk-do 560-053 ☎ +82 63 281 0430 – **6)** 1155-2, Beomchon 4-dong, Busanjin-gu, Busan 614-024 ☎ +82 51 636 0050 – **7)** 1010, Sugok-dong, Heungdeok-gu, Cheongju-si, Chungcheongbuk-do 361-150 ☎ +82 43 292 4100 – **8)** 174-3, Ungyo-dong, Chuncheon-si, Gangwon-do 200-080 ☎ +82 33 255 2001 – **9)** 1-13, Munhwa-dong, Jung-gu, Daejeon 301-130 ☎ +82 42 259 8888 – **10)** 640-7, Daedo-dong, Nam-gu, Pohang-si, Gyeongsangbuk-do 790-824 ☎ +82 54 277 5500 – **11)** 323-3, Sanho-dong, Masan Happo-gu, Changwon-si, Gyeongsangnam-do 630-811 ☎ +82 55 224 5600 – **12)** 271, Yeon-dong, Jeju-si, Jeju Teukbyeol Jachido 690-813 ☎ +82 64 744 0933 – **13)** 935-1, Gyo 1-dong, Gangneung-si, Gangwon-do 210-923 ☎ +82 33 642 9131 - **14)** 186-11, Sinjeong 3-dong, Nam-gu, Ulsan 680-822 ☎ +82 52 256 3333 **Ann:** stns 2)-8): "Jeongjikhan Sesang-eul Kakkuneun (freq.), CBS (location) Bangsong-imnida. (call)" or "Maeumgwa Maeumi Mannaneun Bangsong, (freq.), CBS (location) Bangsong-imnida. (call)"
F.PI: Relay stns in Chungju, Wonju, Jinju, Gongju, Seosan. Music FM in Daejeon, Gwangju, Jeju, Ulsan, Jeonbuk (Jeonju), Gyeongnam (Changwon), Busan, Daegu.

SEOUL BROADCASTING SYSTEM (SBS)
🖳 920 Mok-dong, Yangcheon-gu, Seoul 158-725 ☎ +82 2 2061 0006 📠 +82 2 2113 3169 **W:** www.sbs.co.kr
MW: HLSQ Goyang (near Seoul) 792kHz 50kW **D.Prgr:** 24h
Standard FM (Love FM): 103.5MHz HLSQ-SFM 10kW: 24h
Music FM (Power FM): 107.7MHz HLSQ-FM 10kW: 24h
Ann: "AM Chilbaek-gusib-I 792kHz, FM Baek-sam-jeom-o 103.5MHz, SBS Love FM-imnida. HLSQ", "FM Baek-chil-jeom-chil 107.7MHz, Yeoreobune SBS Power FM-imnida. HLSQ"

FAR EAST BROADCASTING CO., KOREA (Rlg.)

MW	kHz	kW	Station, location
1)	1188	100	HLKX, Seoul
2)	1566	250	HLAZ, Jeju

FM	MHz	kW	Station, location
1)	106.9	5	HLKX-SFM, Seoul
3)	93.3	5	HLAD-FM, Daejeon
4)	98.1	5	HLDD-FM, Changwon
5)	90.1	3	HLDY-FM, Yeongdong
6)	100.5	1	HLKW-FM, Mokpo
7)	90.3	3	HLDZ-FM, Pohang
8)	107.3	3	HLQR-FM, Ulsan
9)	93.3	1	HLQQ-FM, Busan
10)	91.9	1	HLCU-FM, Daegu
11)	93.1	1	HLED-FM

+ low power relay stns

Addresses and other information
1) Far East Broadc. Co.(Geukdong Bangsong), 89, Sangsu-dong, Mapo-gu, Seoul 121-707 ☎ +82 2 320 0114 📠 +82 2 320 0229 **W:** www.febc.net **D.Prgr:** 1900-1700. Korean: 1900-1100, 1600-1700(Stangdard FM: 1900-1700) **English:** 1100-1200(1188kHz) **Chinese:** 1500-1600(1188kHz). **VOA Relay in Korean:** 1200-1500(1188kHz). **Ann:** Korean "Jungpa Cheonbaek-palsip-pal(1188)kHz, Pyojun FM Paeng-nyuk-jeom-gu(106.9)MHz, Areumdaun Chanyanggwa Gibbeun Sosigeul Jeonhaneun Geukdong Bangsong-imnida.". English: "This is HLKX Radio broadcasting with 100,000 watts of power on 1188kHz" **FI:** by contributions & free will offerings – **2)** Jeju Geukdong Bangsong, 2761, Hagwi-ri, Aewol-up, Bukjeju-gun, eju Teukbyel Jachido 695-750 ☎ +82 64 799 8100 **D.Prgr:** 24h. **Korean:** 1900-1100. **Chinese:** 1100-1230, 1345-1730, 1730-1835. **Japanese:** 1230-1345. **Russian:** 1830-1900 – **3)** Daejeon Geukdong Bangsong, 233-15, Chijok-dong, Yuseong-gu, Daejeon 305-711 ☎ +82 42 828 9330. **D.Prgr:** 24h – **4)** Changwon Geukdong Bangsong, 117, Jungang-dong, Changwon-si, Gyeongsang-nam-do 641-030 ☎ +82 55 269 9810 **D.Prgr:** 24h – **5)** Yeongdong Geukdong Bangsong, 500-1, Jangsa-dong, Sokcho-si, Sokcho-si, Gangwon-do 217-130 ☎ +82 33 638 9000 **D.Prgr:** 1900-

1700 – **6)** 878-9, Sang-dong, Mokpo-si, Jeollanam-do 530-822 ☎ +82 61 284 9000 **D.Prgr:** 1900-1700 – **7)** 122-4, Deoksan-dong, Buk-gu, Pohang-si, Gyeongsangnam-do 791-020 ☎ +82 54 256 3000 **D.Prgr:** 24h – **8)** 589-3, Dal-dong, Nam-gu, Ulsan-si 680-080 ☎ +82 52 256 2000 **D.Prgr:** 24h – **9)** 4th Floor, Centum Venture Town, 1475, U-dong, Haeundae-gu, Busan 612-020 ☎ +82 51 759 6000 **D.Prgr:** 24h – **10)** 1326-3, Manchon 1-dong, Suseong-gu, Daegu ☎ +82 53 770 3000 **D.Prgr:** 24h – **11)** 1209-2, Chipyeong-dong, Seo-gu, Gwangju ☎ +82 62 373 1000 **D.Prgr:** 24h. **F.PI:** Regional stns in Yeosu. Standard FM in Jeju. Relay stn in Taebaek.

PYEONGHWA BROADCASTING CORP. (PBC)
(Pyeonghwa Bangsong) Endowment by the Catholic Church.
Stations:
1) Seoul HLQP-FM 105.3MHz 5kW: 1957-1702 – **2)** Gwangju HLDL-FM 99.9MHz 5kW, 99.5MHz 1kW(rel. stn in Yeosu): 1957-1702 – **3)** Deagu HLDK-FM 93.1MHz 3kW, 96.9MHz 0.5kW(rel. st. in Pohang), 100.7MHz (rel. stn in Andong): 1957-1702 – **4)** Busan HLDW-FM 101.1MHz 3kW, 94.3MHz 0.5kW(rel. st in Ulsan), 105.5MHz(rel. st. in Changwon): 1957-1702 – **5)** Daejeon HLQO-FM 106.3MHz 3kW: 1957-1702.
Addresses:
1) 2-3, Jeo-dong 1-ga, Jung-gu, Seoul 100-031 ☎ +82 2 2270 2114 🖹 +82 2 2270 2210 **W:** www.pbc.co.kr **Ann:** "Saengmyeong Sarang, FM Baeg-o-jeom-sam(105.3)MHz, Gibbeun Sosik. Balgeun Sesang, PBC Pyeonghwa Bangsong-imnida. HLQP." – **2)** 3-5, Geumnam-ro 3-ga, Dong-gu, Gwangju 501-023 – **3)** 71, Gyesan-dong 2-ga, Jung-gu, Daegu 700-082 – **4)** 81-1, Daecheong-dong 4-ga, Jung-gu, Busan 600-094 – **5)** 189, Daeheung-dong, Jung-gu, Daejeon 301-802 ☎ +82 42 250 3200.

BUDDHIST BROADCASTING SYSTEM (BBS)
(Bulgyo Bangsong) Owned and operated by the Buddhistns.
Stations:
1) Seoul HLSG-FM 101.9MHz 5kW: 2000-1700 – **2)** Gwangju HLDB-FM 89.7MHz 3kW: 2000-1700 – **3)** Busan HLDA-FM 89.9MHz 5kW, 89.5MHz 0.5kW (rel. stn in Changwon): 2000-1700 – **4)** Daegu HLDI-FM 94.5MHz 3kW, 105.5MHz 0.5kW (rel. stn in Pohang), 97.7MHz 0.5kW (rel. stn in Andong) – **5)** Cheongju HLDJ-FM 96.7MHz 3kW: 2000-1700 – **6)** Chuncheon HLQM-FM 100.1MHz 3kW: 2000-1700 – **7)** Ulsan HLQU-FM 105.3MHz 1kW: 2000-1700.
Addresses:
1) Dabo Building; 140, Mapo-dong, Mapo-gu, Seoul 121-050 ☎ +82 2 705 5114 🖹 +82 2 705 5229 **W:** www.bbsfm.co.kr – **2)** Daesaeng Bldg, 78-2, Im-dong, Buk-gu, Gwangju 500-010 ☎ +82 62 520 1114 – **3)** Bosaeng Bldg, 833-13, Beomil 2-dong, Dong-gu, Busan 601-060 ☎ +82 51 520 5114 – **4)** Jingak Hoegwan, 156-1, Daebong-dong, Jung-gu, Daegu 700-430 ☎ +82 53 427 5114 – **5)** 1646, Yongam-dong, Sangdang-gu, Cheongju-si, Chungcheongbuk-do 360-181 ☎ +82 43 294 5114 – **6)** 4-1, Yoseon-dong, Chuncheon-si, Gangwon-do 200-030 ☎ +82 33 250 2114 – **7)** 1359-11, Dal-dong, Nam-gu, Ulsan ☎ +82 52 279 8114.
Ann: 1) "FM Baeg-il-jeom-gu (101.9)MHz, BBS Bulgyo Bangsong-imnida. HLSG." **F.PI:** Relay stn in Gangneung

SEOUL TRAFFIC BROADCASTING SYSTEM (TBS)
(Gyotong Bangsong)
Municipal Station. This stn is operated by the Seoul Municipal Traffic Broadcast Headquarters to provide traffic information and education to the citizens of Seoul and surroundings.
🖳 3-8, Yejang-dong, Jung-gu, Seoul 100-250 ☎ +82 2 311 5114 🖹 +82 2 311 5219 **W:** www.tbs.seoul.kr
Station: HLST-FM(Live FM) 95.1MHz 5kW: 24h in Korean. HLSW-FM(Soul FM) 101.3MHz 1kW: 2000-1700 in English.
Ann: "FM Gusib-o-jeom-il(95.1)MHz, TBS Gyotong Bangsong-imnida","You're listening to 101.3 tbs-eFM"

TRAFFIC BROADCASTING NETWORK (TBN)
(Hanguk Gyotong Bangsong)
🖳 171, Sindang-dong, Jung-gu, Seoul 100-789 ☎ +82 2 2230 6114 🖹 +82 2 2230 6269 **W:** www.tbn.or.kr
Stations:
1) Busan 94.9MHz HLDN-FM 3kW, 100.1MHz 1kW(rel. st. in Jinju): 24h – **2)** Gwangju 97.3MHz HLDM-FM 3kW, 103.5MHz 1kW (rel. st. in Gwangyang): 24h – **3)** Daejeon 102.9MHz HLDT-FM 3kW: 24h – **4)** Daegu 103.9MHz HLDU-FM 3kW – **5)** Incheon 100.5MHz HLSU-FM 1kW – **6)** Gangwon(Wonju) 105.9MHz HLSV-FM 3kW: 24h, Gangwon(Chuncheon) 103.7MHz 3kW: 24h , Gangwon(Gangneung) 105.5MHz 1kW: 24h – **7)** Jeonju 102.5MHz HLCM-FM 3kW: 24h – **8)** Ulsan 104.1MHz HLCV-FM 1kW: 24h
+ low power relay stns
Addresses and other information
1) 580-8, Daeyeon 3-dong, Nam-gu, Busan 608-023 ☎ +82 51

6105 114 **Ann:** "FM Gusib-sa-jeom-gu(94.9)MHz, Busan Gyotong Bangsong-imnida. HLDN-FM" – **2)** 665-2, Ssangam-dong, Gwangsan-gu, Gwangju 506-303 ☎ +82 62 9701 114 **Ann:** "FM Gusib-chil-jeom-sam(97.3)MHz, Gwangju Gyotong Bangsong-imnida. HLDM" – **3)** 152-7, Nae-dong, Seo-gu, Daejeon 302-181 ☎ +82 42 6001 114 **Ann:** "FM Baeg-i-jeom-gu(102.9)MHz, Dallineun Radio Daejeon Gyotong Bangsong-imnida." – **4)** 1679-2, Daemyeong-dong, Nam-gu, Daegu 705-031 ☎ +82 53 6060 114 **Ann:** "FM Baek-sam-jeom-gu(103.9)MHz, Daegu Gyotong Bangsong-imnida. HLDU-FM" – **5)** 401-74, Hagik-dong, Nam-gu, Incheon 402-865 ☎ +82 32 4531 114 **Ann:** "FM Baek-jeom-o(100.5)MHz, TBN Incheon Gyotong Bangsong-imnida. HLSU" – **6)** 1400, Bangok-dong, Wonju-si, Gangwon-do ☎ +82 33 7490 114 **Ann:** "Haengbogui Giljabi, Ggumi Inneun Bangsong, FM Baeg-o-jeom(105.9)MHz, Gangwon Gyotong Bangsong-imnida." – **7)** 410-1, Jinbuk-dong, Deokjin-ga, Jeonju 561-162. ☎ +82 63 2593 114 **Ann:** "FM Baeg-i-jeom-chil(102.7)MHz, TBN Jeonju Gyotong Bangsong-imnida. HLCM" – **8)** 828-1, Seongan-dong, Jung-gu, Ulsan
F.PI: Regional stns in Jeju, Changwon.

KOREA NEW NETWORK CORP. (KNN)
🖳 603-8, Yeonsan-4-dong, Yeonje-gu, Busan 611-084 ☎ +82 1 850 9000 **W:** www.knn.co.kr **Station:** HLDG-FM 99.9MHz 3kW: 24h **Ann:** "Guship-gu-jeom-gu (99.9), KNN Radiomnida.HLDG"

TAEGU BROADCASTING CORPORATION (TBC)
(Daegu Bangsong)
🖳 201-9, Tusan-dong, Susong-gu, Daegu 760-080 ☎ +82 53 760 1900 **W:** www.tbc.co.kr
Station: HLDE-FM(Dream FM) 99.3MHz 5kW: 24h. Relay stn: Pohang 99.7MHz. **Ann:** "HLDE-FM TBC Dream FM-imnida."

KWANGJU BROADCASTING CO., LTD. (KBC) (Gwangju Bangsong)
🖳 111-14, So-dong, Nam-gu, Gwangju 503-010 ☎ +82 62 650 3114 **W:** www.ikbc.co.kr **Station:** HLDH-FM(MY FM) 101.1MHz 5kW: 24h. Relay stn: Yeosu 96.7MHz. **Ann:** "HLDH, FM 101.1MHz, 96.7MHz, Yeollin Sesang, Joheun Chingu, KBC MY FM."

TAEJON BROADCASTING CO., LTD. (TJB)
(Daejeon Bangsong)
🖳 122-1, Hyo-dong, Tong-gu, Daejeon 300-722 ☎ +82 42 281 1101 **W:** www.tjb.co.kr
Station: HLDF-FM(Power FM) 95.7MHz 5kW: 24h Relay stn: Seosan 96.5MHz **Ann:** "Gusib-o-jeom-chil(95.7), Gusim-nyuk-jeom-o(96.5)MHz, TJB Power FM-imnida. HLDF"

JEONJU TELEVISION CORPORATION (JTV)
(Jeonju Bangsong)
🖳 656-3, Seonosong-dong, Deokjin-gu, Jeonju-si, Jeollabuk-do 561-090 ☎ +82 63 250 5200 **W:** www.jtv.co.kr
Station: HLDQ-FM(Magic FM) 90.1MHz 5kW: 24h
Ann: "FM Gusib-jeom-il(90.1)MHz, JTV Magic FM-imnida. HLDQ"

CHEONGJU BROADCASTING CORPORATION (CJB)
(Cheongju Bangsong)
🖳 12-16, Sajik 2-dong, Hongdeok-gu, Cheongju-si, Chungcheongbuk-do 361-102 ☎ +82 43 265 7000 **W:** www.cjb.co.kr
Station: HLDI-FM(Joy FM) 101.5MHz 5kW: 24h
Ann: "FM Baeg-il-jeom-o(101.5)MHz, CJB Joy FM-imnida. HLDI"

ULSAN BROADCASTING CORPORATION (UBC)
(Jeonju Bangsong)
🖳 1521-1, Samsan-dong, Nam-gu, Ulsan 680-732 ☎ +82 52 228 6000 **W:** www.ubc.co.kr
Station: HLDP-FM(Green FM) 92.3MHz 5kW: 24h
Ann: "Gusib-i-jeom-sam(92.3)MHz, UBC Green FM Bangsong-imnida. HLDP"

JEJU FREE INTERNATIONAL CITY BROADCASTING SYSTEM (JIBS) (Jeju Gukje Jayu Dosi Bangsong)
🖳 2750, Ora 3-dong, Jeju-si, Jeju Teukbyeol Jachido 690-163 ☎ +82 64 740 7800 **W:** www.jibstv.com
Station: HLQC-FM(Power FM) 101.5MHz 3kW: 24h. Relay stn: Seogwipo 98.5MHz
Ann: "JIBS New Power FM Bangsong-imnida."

GANGWON TELEVISION BROADCASTING CO., LTD (GTB)
(Gangwon Minbang)
🖳 635, Janghak-ri, Dong-myeon, Chuncheon-si, Gangwon-do 200-853 ☎ +82 33 248 5000 **W:** www.igtb.co.kr
Station: HLCG-FM(Fresh FM) 105.1MHz 3kW: 24h. Relay stn: Gangneung 106.1MHz 3kW, Wongju 103.1MHz 1kW.

Ann: "Chuncheon Baeg-o-jeom-il(105.1)MHz, Gangneung Baeng-ryuk-jeom-il(106.1)MHz, GTB Fresh FM, HLCG"

KYONGGI BROADCASTING CO. (KFM) (Gyeonggi Bangsong)
961-17, Yeongtong-dong, Yeongtong-gu, Suwon-si, Gyeonggi-do 443-810 ☎ +82 31 210 0999 **W:** www.kfm.co.kr
Station: HLDS-FM 99.9MHz 5kW: 24h
Ann: "FM Gusib-gu-jeom-gu(99.9)MHz, Gyeonggi Bangsong-imnida. HLDS"

Kyung-In Broadcasting SUNNY FM
1, Aam 5-gil, Nam-gu, Incheon 402-773 ☎ +82 32 830 1000 **W:** www.sunnyfm.co.kr
Station: HLDO-FM 90.7MHz 1kW: 24h **Ann:** "Gusib-jeom-chil(90.7)MHz, Gyeong-In Bangsong, Sunny FM-imnida"

YTN RADIO(YTN FM)
YTN Tower, 6-1, Namdaemun-ro 5-ga, Jung-gu, Seoul 100-800 ☎ +82 2 398 8000 **W:** www.ytnfm.co.kr
Station: HLQV-FM 94.5MHz 3kW: 24h **Ann:** "FM Gusib-sa-jeom-o(94.5)MHz, YTN FM-imnida. HLQV"

WON-BUDDHISM BROADCASTING SYSTEM (WBS) (Woneum Bangsong)
1) 1-3, Heukseok 1-dong, Dongjak-gu, Seoul 156-856 ☎ +82 2 2102 7700 **W:** www.wbsfm.com - **2)** 38-6, Sinchang-dong 1-ga, Jung-gu, Busan 600-061 ☎ +82 51 247 3844 - **3)** 344-2, Sinyongdong, Iksan-si, Jeollabuk-do 570-754 ☎ +82 63 837 0979- **4)** 1286, Ssangchon-dong, Seo-gu, Gwanju
Stations:
1) Seoul HLQK-FM 89.7MHz 1kW: 24h – **2)** Busan HLQJ-FM 104.9MHz 3kW: 24h – **3)** Jeonbuk(Iksan) HLDV-FM 97.9MHz 3kW: 24h.
Ann: 1) FM Palsib-gu-jeom-chil(89.7)MHz, WBS Woneum Bangsong-imnida. HLQK – **2)** "FM Baeg-sa-jeom-gu(104.9)MHz, WBS Busan Woneum Bangsong-imnida. HLQJ – **3)** "FM Gusib-chil-jeom-gu(97.9)MHz, WBS Jeonbuk Woneum Bangsong-imnida. HLDV" – **4)** "FM Baek-chil-jeom-gu(107.9)MHz, WBS Gwangju Woneum Bangsong-imnida. HLQN"
F.PI: Regional stns in Daegu on 98.3MHz

KOREA INTERNATIONAL BROADCASTING FOUNDATION (Arirang Radio)
Arirang Tower, 1467-80, Seocho-dong, Seocho-gu, Seoul 137-878 ☎ +82 2 3475 5000 **W:** www.arirang.co.kr
Station: Jeju HLQE-FM 88.7MHz: 24h in English. Relay stn: Seogwipo 88.1MHz. **Ann:** "You're listening to Arirang Radio"

GFN Foundation
177-39, Sa-dong, Nam-gu, Gwangju 503-030 ☎ +82 62 460 0987 **W:** www.gfn.or.kr
Station: HLSY-FM 98.7MHz 1kW: 2000-1700 in English. **Ann:** "Listen more Feel more! GFN 98.7 FM"

Busan e-FM
15, Jeongbo Town 5-ro, Yeonje-gu, Busan 611-711 ☎ +82 51 861 8601 **W:** www.befm.or.kr
Station: HLSX-FM 90.5MHz 1kW: 2000-1700 in English. **Ann:** "Now you're listening to Busan e-FM 90.5"

KOREAN FORCES NETWORK (Friends FM) (Gukkun Bangsong)
San 2, Yongsan-dong 2-ga, Yongsan-gu, Seoul 140-022 **W:** www.dema.mil.kr/web/fm.do
Stations: FM (operated by KBS): Hwaaksan HLSE-FM 96.7MHz 5kW, Namsan 96.7MHz 2kW, Yongmunsan 101.1MHz 3kW, Gwaebangsan 92.5MHz 3kW + 5 lp stns
D.Prgr: 24h. Own prgrs 2100-1400, other times relay KBS R. One (HLKA). prgrs for soldiers located near the demilitarized zone. Also 0805-0900(Sun) via KBS R. One network.
Ann: "Hamggehaeyo Seonjin Ganggun, Silcheonhaeyo Noksaek Seongjang, Friends FM Gukkun Bangsong Radio""

AMERICAN FORCES NETWORK KOREA (AFN)
As below ☎ +82 2 7914 6495/6 **W:** afnkorea.com

MW & FM Stations		kHz	kW	MHz	kW
1)	Seoul/Yongsan	1530	5	102.7	5
2)	Munsan/Western Corridor	576	5	88.5	0.05
3)	Daegu/Camp Walker	1080	5	88.5	1
4)	Busan/Camp Hialeah	+1260	5	88.1	0.25
	Chuncheon/Camp Page	1044	1	88.5	0.1
	Uijeongbu/Camp Red Cloud	1161	0.25	88.5	0.1
5)	Dongducheon/Camp Casey	+1197	1	88.3	0.25
	Chuncheon/Camp Page (F.PI)	1260	1	88.5	0.1
6)	Songtan/Osan Air Base	*1359	1	88.5	0.05
7)	Pyeongtaek/Camp Humphroys	+1440	1	88.3	0.05

MW & FM Stations		kHz	kW	MHz	kW
8)	Gunsan/Gunsan Air Base	1440	1	88.5	0.25
	Wonju/Camp Long	1440	0.25	88.3	0.05
	Waegwan/Camp Carrol	1440	0.25		
2)	Munsan/Western Corridor (F.PI)	1440	5	88.5	0.05
	Pohang/Camp Libby	1512	0.25		
	Jinhae/Naval St.	1512	0.25	88.5	0.05
	Kotar Range	1512			

Lp: 1512kHz (Sangdong, Jeju Teukbyel Jachido); 88.5MHz Gwangju Air Base. += local prgrs 2005-0000 Mon-Fri; otherwise rel.1).
*= local prgrs 2005-0000 & 0605-0900 Mon-Fri; otherwise rel.1).
D.Prgr: 24h (MW/FM sep. prgrs). N. on the h. Formal sign on at 1505.
Ann: AM: "American Forces Network Korea", FM (Seoul): "This is Eagle FM"
Addresses
1) Headquarters, American Forces Network Korea, Unit #15324, APO AP 96205-0097, USA (+82(2) 7914 6495. Commanding Officer: LTC Chad C. Starr – **2)** Unit #15325, APO AP 96251-0098, USA – **3)** Unit #15029, APO AP 96218-0186, USA – **4)** Unit #15184. APO AP 96259-0274, USA – **5)** Unit #15116, APO AP 96224-0380, USA – **6)** Unit #2034. APO AP 96278-5000, USA – **7)** Unit #15473. APO AP 96271-0543, USA – **8)** Unit #2011, APO AP 96264-5000, USA

KOSOVO

L.T: UTC +1h (31 Mar-27 Oct: +2h) — **Pop:** 1.7 million — **Pr.L:** Albanian, Serbian — **E.C:** 50Hz, 220V — **ITU:** pending (**WRTH:** RKS)

KOMISIONI I PAVARUR PËR MEDIA (KPM) (Independent Media Commission)
Rr. "Gazmend Zajmi" nr. 1, 10000 Prishtinë ☎ +381 38 245031 🖷 +381 38 245034 **E:** info@kpm-ks.org **W:** www.kpm-ks.org
L.P: Chair: Filloreta Bytyçi
NB. KPM is the licensing body for broadcasting.

RADIO TELEVIZIONE KOSOVËS (RTK) (Pub)
Rr. "Xhemail Prishtina" nr. 12, 10000 Prishtinë ☎+381 38 230102 🖷 +381 38 230103 **E:** post@rtklive.com **W:** www.rtklive.com
L.P: Pres: Rrahman Paçarizi
R.Kosova/R.Blue Sky: Rr. "Nëna Tereze" pa numër, 10000 Prishtinë ☎ +381 38 249077 (R.Kosova); +381 38 226553 (R.Blue Sky) **E:** radiokosova@rtklive.com; radiobluesky@rtklive.com.

MW	kHz	kW	Prgr
Prishtinë	549	10	1

FM (MHz)	Prgr 1	Prgr 2	kW	FM	Prgr 1	Prgr 2	kW
Cërnusha	87.6	91.5	0.5	Prishtinë	91.9	93.3	0.5
Maja e Gjelbërt	88.5	90.5	0.5	Zatriqi	88.9	92.4	0.5
Goleshi	95.7	97.7	5				

D.Prgr: Prgr 1 (R. Kosova): 24h in Albanian. – **Prgr 2 (R. Blue Sky):** 0600-2400 in Albanian; exc. 1300-1500 Serbian, 1500-1600 Turkish.

OTHER STATIONS

FM	MHz	kW	Location	Station
C)	89.6	1	Mitrovicë	RFI relay
2)	92.7	1	Maja e Gjelbërt	R. Dukagjini
2)	94.5	1	Zatriqi	R. Dukagjini
1)	94.8	1	Maja e Gjelbërt	R. 21
A)	96.2	1	Prishtinë	RFE-RL/VOA relay
B)	98.6	5	Goleshi	BBC relay
2)	99.7	1	Goleshi	R. Dukagjini
C)	101.0	1	Prishtinë	RFI relay
1)	102.8	1	Goleshi	R. 21
1)	103.9	1	Zatriqi	R. 21

NB: Txs below 1kW not listed.
Addresses & other information:
1) Pallati i mediave, aneks II, 10000 Prishtinë. **E:** radio21@rtv21.tv – **2)** Rr. "Ismail Qemajli" nr. 7, 30000 Pejë. **E:** info@dukagjini.com – **A)** Rel. RFE-RL & VOA (USA) – **B)** Rel. BBCWS (UK) – **C)** Rel. RFI (France)

KUWAIT

L.T: UTC +3h — **Pop:** 2.7 million — **Pr.L:** Arabic — **E.C:** 50Hz, 240V — **ITU:** KWT

MINISTRY OF INFORMATION
P.O. Box 193, 13002 Safat ☎+965 22415301 🖷 +965 22434511

RADIO OF THE STATE OF KUWAIT
P.O. Box 967, 13010 Safat ☎+965 22436193 🖷 +965 22417830 **W:** media.gov.kw **E:** kwtfreq@media.gov.kw
L.P: Mr. Hani Al-Naqi, Dir. Freq. Mgmt.

MW(kHz)	kW	Prgr.	Times
540	600	Main Arabic	24h
630	10	Quran prgr.	24h
963	20	Main Arabic	1200-1600, 2100-0500
		Multilingual	0500-1200, 1600-2100
1134	100	Main Arabic &Sports	24h
1269	100	Classical Arab Music	24h
1341	100	Quran prgr.	2100-0700
		2nd Arabic	0700-2100

FM(MHz)	kW	Prgr.	Times
87.9	20	Classical Arab Music	24h
89.5	20	Main Arabic	24h
92.5	5	Easy FM	24h
93.3	20	Multilingual	24h (also Nat.Assembly)
94.9	20	Folklore prgr.	24h
96.3	20	Easy FM	24h
97.5	20	Quran prgr.	2100-0700
		2nd Arabic	0700-2100
98.9	20	Quran prgr.	24h
99.7	20	Super Station	24h
100.5	3	TV sound (Prgr. 1)	24h
103.7	20	Modern Arab Music	24h

Main Arabic prgr: 24h. **N:** 0300, 0500, 1000, 1700, 2100 – **2nd Arabic prgr:** 0700-1700 – **Classical Arab Music prgr:** 24h – **Modern Arab Music prgr:** 24h – **Multilingual prgr:** English 0500-0800, 1800-2100, Persian 0800-1000, Filipino 1000-1200, Urdu 1600-1800 – **Quran prgr:** 24h – **"Easy FM" in English:** 24h – **"FM Super Station"** in English: 24h. **N:** on the hour.
Ann: "Idha'at al-Dawlat Al Kuwait".
External service on shortwave: see International Radio section.

Other Stations:
Marina FM, 88.8MHz. **W:** www.marinafm.com
Mix FM, 98.4MHz. **W:** www.mix984.com
AFN: Al-Jabber/Camp Doha 101.5/107.9MHz 50W/5kW.
BBC World Sce, Kuwait City: Arabic 90.1MHz, English 100.1MHz.
Panorama FM: 91.4MHz. See main entry under UAE.
Monte Carlo Doualiya: 107.4MHz 1kW. **RFI:** 106.3/106.6MHz.
R. Sawa: 1548kHz 300/600kW, 95.7MHz 5kW, both 24h.
VOA: 96.9MHz 1kW. **VOA/RFERL** MW: 1593kHz 150kW 1400-0700

KYRGYZSTAN

L.T: UTC +6h — **Pop:** 5.5 million — **Pr.L:** Kyrgyz, Russian, Uzbek — **E.C:** 50Hz, 220V — **ITU:** KGZ

MADANIYAT ZHANA TURIZM MINISTRILIGI
(Ministry of Culture and Tourism)
✉ Pushkin St. 78, 720040 Bishkek ☎ +996 312 620482 **E:** mincultkr@mail.ru **L.P:** Minister: Ibragim Junusov
NB. The Ministry is responsible for issuing broadcasting licenses.

KOOMDUK TELERADIO BERÜÜ KORPORATSIYASY (KTRK) (Public Broadcasting Corp.)
✉ Jash Gvardiya blvd. 59, 720010 Bishkek ☎ +996 312 392059 **E:** ktrk@ktrk.kg **W:** www.ktrk.kg **L.P:** DG: Kubat Otorbaev

MW	kHz	kW	Prgr	MW	kHz	kW	Prgr
Bishkek (a)	612	150	KGR2	Haidarkan	1404	7	KGR1
Bishkek (a)	1287	150	KGR1	Jojomel	1404	20	KGR1
Naryn	1404	7	KGR1	Orgochor	1404	-	KGR1
Cholpon-Ata	1404	1	KGR1	Jalal-Abad	1431	40	KGR1
SW	kHz	kW	Prgr	SW	kHz	kW	Prgr
Bishkek (a)	4010	100	KGR1	Bishkek (a)	4795	15	KGR1
FM (MHz)	KGR1	KGR2	kW	FM	KGR1	KGR2	kW
Batken	104.2	-	-	Kara-Kul	102.4	106.0	-
Bishkek	104.1	106.9	1	Naryn	100.5	103.2	-
Chuy	104.1	-	-	Osh	100.7	-	-
Jalal-Abad	104.7	105.9	-	Talas	102.0	107.6	-

(a) Krasnaya Rechka
D.Prgr: KGR1 (Birinchi radio): 0000-1800 in Kyrgyz, Russian. – **KGR2 (Kyrgyz radiosu):** 0000-1800 in Kyrgyz. – **Local Station "Ming kyyal FM":** on Bishkek 103.7MHz (1kW) 24h.

OTHER STATIONS

MW	kHz	kW	Location	Station
A)	882	-	Bishkek (a)	R. Rossii relay
C)	1467	150	Bishkek (a)	TWR relay
A)	4050	100	Bishkek (a)	R. Rossii relay
FM	MHz	kW	Location	Station
A)	66.26	17	Karakol	R. Rossii relay
A)	67.94	17	Bishkek	R. Rossii relay
A)	68.66	17	Kara-Kul	R. Rossii relay
A)	69.92	17	Osh	R. Rossii relay

(a) Krasnaya Rechka

FM	MHz	kW	Location	Station
A)	69.95	17	Kazarman	R. Rossii relay
A)	70.07	17	Arstanbap	R. Rossii relay
A)	70.40	17	Suluktu	R. Rossii relay
A)	70.82	17	Narin	R. Rossii relay
A)	72.20	17	Jalal-Abad	R. Rossii relay
A)	72.44	17	Suluktu	R. Rossii relay
6)	87.5	1	Bishkek	R. Mir
B)	88.0	1	Bishkek	R. Mayak relay
4)	89.0	1	Bishkek	Love R.
9)	101.4	1	Cholpon-Ata	Hit FM
7A)	101.7	1	Bishkek	Evropa Plus
5)	102.9	1	Bishkek	R. Manas FM
1)	103.2	1	Cholpon-Ata	Russkoye R.
7B)	104.5	1	Bishkek	Russkaya volna
3)	105.0	1	Bishkek	Russkoye R.
8)	106.3	1	Kara-Balta	R. Tatina

NB: Txs below 1kW not listed. (a) Krasnaya Rechka
Addresses & other information:
1) Almaty St. 4b, 720082 Bishkek. **E:** rusradio@europa.kg – **2)** Bishkek. **3)** Jantoshev St. 70, 720005 Bishkek. **E:** pyramid@mail.elcat.kg – **4)** Ibraimov St. 24, 720031 Bishkek. **E:** office@loveradio.kg – **5)** Mir pr. 56, 720044 Bishkek. **E:** manasfm@manas.kg – **6)** Bishkek. – **7A,B)** Bishkek – **8)** Gvardeyskaya St. 18, 722030 Kara-Balta. **E:** tatina@infotel.kg – **9)** Bishkek. – **A)** Rel. R. Rossii (Russia) – **A)** Rcl. R. Mayak (Russia) – **C)** Rel. TWR (USA)

LAOS

L.T: UTC +7h — **Pop:** 6.5 million — **Pr.L:** Lao (Lao Soung, Lao Theung dialects), Hmong, Khmu — **E.C:** 50Hz, 230V — **ITU:** LAO

LAO NATIONAL RADIO – LNR (Gov.)
✉ PO Box 310, Vientiane; Phaynam Rd, Ban Sisakhet, Chantabouly District, Vientiane ☎ +856 21 243250 ≡ +856 21 212430 **W:** www.laonationalradio.com **L.P:** DG: Mr Sipha Nonglath.
City and Provincial sces: These are operated by the local governments ✉ Sisavangvong Rd, Ban Pakhame, Luang Prabang – Km 2 Route 13 South, Oudomsavane Village, Pakse, Champassak Province - Manthatulat Road, Vientiane – Houamouangtai Village, Savannakhet, Khantabouly – Nongbouakham Village, Tha Khek, Khammouane

MW	kHz	kW	S	H of tr
Vientiane*	567	200	N	2200-0800, 0900-1600
Khantabouly, Sa	585	20	P	2230-1300
Luang Prabang	705	10	P	2200-0800, 1025-1500
Tha Khek, Kh	765	10	P	r. inactive
SW	kHz	kW	S	H of tr
Sam Neua, HP	‡4413	1	P	2300-0130, 0925-1230
Vientiane	6130	50	N	2200-0800, 0900-1600

S=Sce., **N**=National, **P**=Provincial
*) Transmitter loc.: Kilometre 49 (GC: 18N20 102E27); alt. freq: 580kHz
‡) Currently inactive.
HP=Houa Phan prov., Kh=Khammouane prov., Sa=Savannakhet prov.
Reg. stns generally rel. national news at 0000, 0500, 1200
National Sce in Lao: 2300-0600, 0900-1400; **Hmong:** 2200-2230, 0600-0700; **Khmu:** 2230-2300, 0700-0800; **English:** 1400-1430; **French:** 1430-1500; **Vietnamese:** 1500-1530; **Khmer:** 1530-1600. **N:** 2300, 0000, 0500, 0800, 1200.
Ann: LNR: "Thini Sathani Vitthayou Krachaisiang Hengsat". Sam Neua: "Thini Vitthayou Krachaisiang Houa Phan, krachaisiang chak Muang Sam Neua".
IS: Music on Khéne (mouth organ) & Solo (bamboo instrument).

LNR FM (MHz): Vientiane FM 103.7 20kW: 2300-1600 – VIP Radio 97.2 20kW: 2200-1700 – Phoenix Radio 95.0: 2230-1700.
Vientiane City FM (MHz): Vientiane 105.5: 2330-1700 – Vientiane 98.8: operated by Butterfly Media Co. Ltd.
Provincial FM (MHz): Attapeu: 102.7 100W, (r. inactive) – Bolikhamsay prov: 101.5 5kW – Houai Xay, Bokeo prov: 102.75 1kW – Khantabouly, S: 100.75 1kW Luang – Namtha prov:. 98.0 1kW Luang Prabang: 103.5MHz 10kW. Muang Hay, O: 100MHz 100W – Muang Khong, C: 97.2 – Pakse, Champassak prov: 103.7 1kW – Phonsavan, XK: 97.5 5kW – Phongsali prov: 102 100W – Sam Neua, HP: 102.75 100W (ann. freq.): as 4640kHz – Saravane: 101.2 300W – Saiyabouly: 96.5 5kW – Saysomboun Special Reg.: 100 5kW – Sekong: 102.7 100W – Tha Khek, Kh: 95.5 100W.

EXTERNAL SERVICES: see International Broadcasting section.

OTHER STATIONS:
China R. International: Vientiane 93.0MHz 10kW **D.Prgr:** 0300-

1530 rel. CRI from Beijing in Chinese, English & Lao.
R. Australia: Vientiane 96.0 MHz **D.Prgr:** 24h in English.
R. France Internationale: Vientiane 100.5 MHz **D.Prgr:** 24h rel. RFI from Paris in French

LATVIA

L.T: UTC +2h (31 Mar-27 Oct: +3h) — **Pop:** 2.2 million — **Pr.L:** Latvian, Russian — **E.C:** 50Hz, 220V — **ITU:** LVA

NACIONALA ELEKTRONISKO PLAŠSAZINAS LIDZEKLU PADOME (NEPLP)
(National Council for Electronic Media)
✉ Smilšu iela 1/3, LV-1939 Riga ☎ +371 67221848 📠 +371 67220448 **E:** neplpadome@neplpadome.lv **W:** www.neplpadome.lv
L.P: Chmn: Ainars Dimants
NB: NEPLP is the licensing body for broadcasting.

LATVIJAS RADIO (Pub)
✉ Doma laukums 8, LV-1505 Riga ☎ +371 67206722 📠 +371 67206709 **E:** radio@latvijasradio.lv **W:** www.latvijasradio.lv
L.P: DG: Janis Siksnis

FM (MHz)	LR1	LR2	LR3*	LR4	kW
Aluksne	106.8	104.3	-	-	3.5
Auce	99.6	-	-	-	1
Cesvaine	102.5	105.0	103.5	107.9	2x20/2x5
Dagda	102.6	-	-	-	1.7
Daugavpils	106.1	100.7	90.6	104.0	6.5/10/3.2
Dundaga	91.1	106.7	-	-	4
Kuldiga	95.9	101.3	92.0	-	10/16.6/3.3
Liepaja	107.1	101.0	104.6	97.9	2x10/1/5
Rezekne	104.2	101.0	101.8	107.5	3x20/5
Riga	90.7	91.5	103.7	107.7	15/3.5/5/6.3
Valmiera	104.0	101.5	87.6	-	18
Ventspils	99.2	103.0	89.8	95.3	3x0.3/1
Viesite	107.6	104.7	102.2	-	5
Vitrupe	105.5	-	-	-	1.6
Zilupe	-	-	-	100.1	1.7

*) time-shared with LR5 (exc. Riga 103.7)
D.Prgr: LR1 (Latvijas R. Viens): 24h. – **LR2 (Latvijas R. Divi):** 24h. **LR3 (Klasika)** 24h. – **LR4 (Doma laukums/Domskaya ploshchad):** 24h, mainly in Russian. For other ethnic minorities: Mon-Wed 1705-1800. – **LR5 (R. NABA/Saemas kanals):** 24h. On Riga 93.1 (5kW) & parttime via LR3 network. ✉**R. NABA:** Aspazijas bulv. 5, LV-1050 Riga. **E:** naba@radionaba.lv.

OTHER STATIONS

MW	kHz	kW	Location	Station
22)	1485	1.25	Riga	R. Merkurs

FM	MHz	kW	Location	Station
3B)	87.7	1.6	Liepaja	Krievu Hitu R.
2)	87.9	2.5	Madona	Star FM
2)	88.1	2.5	Selpils	Star FM
3B)	88.4	1	Gulbene	European Hit R.
9)	88.4	2.2	Liepaja	Kurzemes R.
4C)	88.6	1	Riga	Jumor FM
1C)	89.2	4	Riga	R. SWH Rock
1A)	89.3	1	Dundaga	R. SWH
3A)	90.3	1	Matisi	Super FM
5)	90.8	1	Ventspils	Kristigais R.
3A)	90.9	3	Madona	Super FM
2)	91.0	1.9	Liepaja	Star FM
12)	91.6	1	Preili	R. 1
8)	91.9	2	Iecava	Top R.
2)	91.9	1.5	Rezekne	Star FM
2)	92.0	1	Limbazi	Star FM
17)	92.3	1	Liepaja	City R.
9)	92.4	1.3	Tukums	Kurzemes R.
6B)	92.8	1	Limbazi	R. Skonto Vidzeme
16)	93.5	2.2	Liepaja	R. 101
4D)	93.9	2.8	Riga	R. Baltkom
3A)	94.3	1.6	Talsi	Super FM
6B)	94.6	1	Valka	R. Skonto Vidzeme
1A)	94.7	1.4	Saldus	R. SWH
7)	94.9	1	Riga	Capital FM
3A)	95.2	1.6	Liepaja	Super FM
20)	95.2	6.3	Daugavpils	Latgolys Radeja
8)	95.4	1	Riteri	Top R.
20)	95.8	1	Jekabpils	Latgolys Radeja
7)	95.9	1	Valmiera	Capital FM
21)	96.1	2.1	Kraslava	Autoradio
3B)	96.1	1.6	Liepaja	European Hit R.
3B)	96.2	2	Riga	Krievu Hitu R.
3A)	96.8	1	Riga	Super FM

FM	MHz	kW	Location	Station
6B)	97.0	1	Valmiera	R. Skonto Vidzeme
10)	97.3	2.6	Riga	Retro FM
6A)	97.5	3	Liepaja	R. Skonto Kurzeme
8)	97.7	1	Livani	Top R.
2)	97.7	1.1	Pure	Star FM
18)	98.1	1	Valmiera	R. Valmiera
8)	98.3	1.6	Riga	Top R.
5)	98.5	3.3	Kuldiga	Kristigais R.
13)	99.0	2	Jurmala	R. Jurmala
21)	99.4	1.6	Daugavpils	Autoradio
20)	99.5	2	Balvi	Latgolys Radeja
4B)	99.5	2.8	Riga	R.99.5 FM
6B)	99.8	2	Cesvaine	R. Skonto Vidzeme
5)	99.9	2	Daugavpils	Kristigais R.
15)	100.0	2.5	Riga	R. PIK
5)	100.1	1	Valmiera	Kristigais R.
1A)	100.3	5	Cesvaine	R. SWH
A)	100.5	1.3	Riga	BBCWS relay
6A)	100.5	1	Ventspils	R. Skonto Kurzeme
5)	100.6	1.6	Liepaja	Kristigais R.
3B)	100.8	1	Talsi	European Hit R.
16)	101.0	2.6	Riga	R. 101
1A)	101.2	2.5	Jekabpils	R. SWH
5)	101.3	1.1	Kraslava	Kristigais R.
14)	101.6	3	Daugavpils	Alise Plus
5)	101.8	5.6	Riga	Kristigais R.
3B)	101.9	1	Ventspils	European Hit R.
2)	102.0	2	Saldus	Star FM
1A)	102.2	4	Talsi	R. SWH
4A)	102.7	2.8	Riga	Mix FM
5)	102.8	1	Jekabpils	Kristigais R.
20)	103.0	1.8	Rezekne	Latgolys Radeja
3A)	103.2	1	Kuldiga	Super FM
2)	103.2	5	Svente	Star FM
2)	103.8	1.3	Daugavpils	Star FM
3B)	104.3	4.8	Riga	European Hit R.
16)	104.7	1.1	Cesis	R. 101
2)	105.0	1.6	Pope	Star FM
5)	105.1	5	Liepaja	R. SWH
3B)	105.1	1.3	Rezekne	Krievu Hitu R.
1A)	105.2	2.2	Daugavpils	R. SWH
1A)	105.2	13.2	Riga	R. SWH
1A)	105.4	1	Ventspils	R. SWH
21)	105.5	2	Rezekne	Autoradio
1B)	105.7	4.1	Riga	R. SWH+
11)	105.8	1	Liepaja	Rietumu R.
5)	105.9	3.5	Cesvaine	Kristigais R.
2)	106.2	6.3	Riga	Star FM
9)	106.4	11.5	Kuldiga	Kurzemes R.
1A)	106.5	4	Rezekne	R. SWH
1A)	106.5	2	Valmiera	R. SWH
2)	106.6	1	Bauska	Star FM
12)	107.0	0.9	Jekabpils	R. 1
1B)	107.2	3.2	Daugavpils	R. SWH+
6)	107.2	4	Riga	R. Skonto
3B)	107.4	1.3	Kuldiga	European Hit R.
2)	107.4	2	Valmiera	Star FM
19)	107.6	1.6	Liepaja	R. Liepaja (+ Top R.)
9)	107.9	1	Ventspils	Kurzemes R.

NB: Txs below 1kW not listed.
Addresses & other information:
1A-C) Skanstes iela 50, LV-1013 Riga. 1B) in Russian. **E:** 1A) radio@radiosh.lv, 1B) plus@radioswh.lv, 1C) rock@radioswh.lv – **2)** Dzelzavas iela 120G, LV-1021 Riga. **E:** info@starfm.lv – **3A-C)** Elijas iela 17, LV-1050 Riga. 3C) In Russian. **E:** 3A) birojs@superfm.lv, 3B) radio@europeanhitradio.com, 3C) radio@hitirossii.lv – **4A-D)** Kr.Valdemara iela 8, LV-1010 Riga. In Russian, incl. rebroadcasts of prgrs from Russia*: 4B) Europa+, 4C) Yumor FM, 4D) Ekho Moskvy. **E:** 4A) mixfm.lv, 4C) radio@jumorfm.lv, 4D) radio@radiobaltkom.lv – **5)** Lacpleša iela 37, LV-1011 Riga. In Latvian & Russian. **E:** lkr@lkr.lv – **6)** Kr.Valdemara iela 100, LV-1013 Riga. **E:** studija@radioskonto.lv. Reg. stns: **6A)** Zivju iela 3-216, LV-3401 Liepaja. **E:** kurzeme@radioskonto.lv; **6B)** Rigas iela 13, LV-4201 Valmiera. **E:** vidzeme@radioskonto.lv – **7)** L.Nometnu iela 62, LV-1002 Riga. **E:** info@capitalfm.lv – **8)** Terbatas iela 83B, LV-1001 Riga. In Russian. **E:** topradio@inbox.lv – **9)** Pilsetas laukums 4, LV-3301 Kuldiga. **E:** studija@kurzemesradio.lv – **10)** Lielirbes iela 17A, LV-1047 Riga. In Russian. Incl. rebroadcasts of Retro FM (Russia)* – **11)** Zivju iela 4, LV-3401 Liepaja. **E:** info@rietumuradio.lv – **12)** Brivibas iela 116, LV-5201 Jekabpils. **E:** info@radio1.lv – **13)** Brivibas bulv. 30, LV-1050 Riga. **E:** reinholds.pelse@jpd.gov.lv – **14)** Raina iela 28, LV-5401 Daugavpils. In Russian. **E:** radio@aliseplus.lv – **15)** Brivibas bulv. 30, LV-1050 Riga. In Russian, incl. Golos Rossii (Russia)*. **E:** info@pik.lv – **16)** Elizabetes iela 55, LV-1050 Riga. **E:** birojs@radio101.lv – **17)**

Zivju iela 3, LV-3401 Liepaja. **E:** radio@cityradio.lv – **18)** Rigas iela 13, LV-4201 Valmiera. **E:** info@radiovalmiera.lv – **19)** Klaipedas iela 19/21-407, LV-3401 Liepaja. In Russian, incl. rel. Top R. (Riga). **E:** radio-liepaja@ostkom.lv – **20)** Atbrivošanas aleja 81/5, LV-4601 Rezekne. In Latgalian. **E:** radeja@lr.lv – **21)** Zakusalas krastmala 5, LV-1509 Riga. In Russian, incl. rebroadcasts of prgrs from Russia*: Avtoradio (daytime), Golos Rossii (nighttime). **E:** info@avtoradio.lv – **22)** P.O.Box 371, LV-1010 Riga. **E:** rni@apollo.lv – **A)** Rel. BBCWS (UK). *) Pre-recorded

LEBANON

L.T: UTC +2h (31 Mar–27 Oct: +3h) — **Pop:** 4 million — **Pr.L:** Arabic, French, English, Armenian — **E.C:** 50Hz, 110/220V — **ITU:** LBN

MINISTRY OF INFORMATION
Hamra, Beirut ☎+961 1 754400 **W:** www.ministryinfo.gov.lb

RADIO LEBANON (Gov.)
Rue Lyon, Sanayeh, P.O. Box 4848, Beirut ☎+961 1 743531 **W:** www.96-2.com **E:** mykee@cyberia.net.lb
L.P: Dir: Fuad Hamdan. Tech. Dir: Nazih Chahine. Chief, Prgr. Dept: Waheed Jalal. Chief, Public Rel: Faouzi Fehmy.
1st Prgr. in Arabic: 0330-2330 on 98.1/98.5MHz. **2nd Prgr. in French/ English/Armenian:** 24h on 96.2Ml lz. **Rel. R. France Int:** 13h daily. **Ann:** A: "Iza'at Loubnan min Beirut". F: "Ici Radio Liban émettant de Beyrouth" **IS:** Opening notes from the Lebanese National anthem played on guitar.

OTHER STATIONS:

FM	MHz	Name	FM	MHz	Name
14)	87.5	VO Charity	12)	97.4	Voice of Faith
32)	87.7	R. Sawa	26)	97.7	R. Strike
20)	87.8	R. Nostalgie	32)	98.7	R. Sawa, Akkar
4)	88.5	R. Orient	5)	99.0	NRJ
13)	89.1	Holy Quran R.	12)	99.3	Voice of Faith, Beit Meri
7)	89.4	Risala R.	15)	99.7	Fame FM
16)	89.9	Cedars R - VOL Plus	24)	100.0	R. Scope, Zahle
13)	90.1	Holy Quran R.	1)	100.4	Voice of Lebanon
12)	90.3	Voice of Faith	25)	101.1	R. Scope
17)	90.6	R. Light FM	31)	101.4	R. Sevan
31)	90.9	R. Sevan	22)	102.0	R. Delta
8)	91.3	Nidaa al-Maarifa	9)	102.5	R. Free Lebanon
3)	92.0	R. Al-Nour	21)	103.0	Pax R.
28)	92.7	Sawt el-Mada	29)	103.3	Monte-Carlo Doualiya
23)	93.3	Voice of Lebanon	2)	103.9	Voice of the People
6)	94.0	Radio One	19)	104.6	Mix FM, Achrafieh
13)	94.1	Holy Quran R	6)	105.3	Radio One
6)	94.5	Radio One	14)	106.0	Voice of Charity
10)	94.8	Voice of Van	27)	106.7	Sound of Music
5)	95.1	NRJ, Farya Mzaar	18)	107.4	Master Broadc. Station
12)	95.5	Voice of Faith	14)	107.7	Voice of Charity
30)	95.9	Sawt el-Noujoum	30)	107.8	Sawt el-Noujoum
11)	96.9	Sawt el-Ghad			

NB: the stns have been allocated 400kHz frequency range, of which the centre freq. is listed above. In many cases the trs from various sites are placed on both upper and lower limits of this range.
Addresses & other information:
1) P.O. Box 165271, Ashrafieh, Bachir el Gemayel Ave, Beirut. **W:** sawtlebnan.com – **2)** Jabal el Arab St, Wata el Mousaitbeh, P.O.Box 14/5425, Beirut. 0400-2300 – **3)** Al-Nour Bldg, Abdel Nour St, Haret Hreïk, P.O.Box 25-197, Ghbeiry, Beirut. **W:** www.alnour.com.lb . Also relayed via Tartus, Syria on 1071 kHz – **4)** Annajah Centre, Mar Elias St, Karakol Druz, P.O. Box 11-6362, Beirut. **W:** www.radioorient.com.lb – **5)** Studiovision Bldg,Naccache, Metn, Beirut. **W:** nrjlebanon.com 24h in English – **6)** Zakhem Bldg, Beit Meri El Metn. **W:** radiooneglobal.com . 0400-2300 in English – **7)** Fraiha Bld. 3rd Floor, Barbour Beirut. **W:** risalaradio.com – **8)** Shaykh Ahmad Iskandarani Centre, Bourj Abi Haidar, Beirut. **W:** nidaa.fm – **9)** Kebbe Bldg, Adonis, Zouk Mosbeh, P.O.Box 110, Zouk Mekhael, Jounieh. **W:** www.rll.com.lb 0340-2300 – **10)** 2nd floor, Disco Samir Bldg, Zalka Rd, El Metn. P.O. Box 80-860, Beirut. **W:** www.voiceofvan.net 24h in Armenian & Arabic – **11)** 2nd floor, Disco Samir Bldg, Zalka Rd, El Metn. **W:** www.sawtelghad.com – **12)** Near Riyad el Solh Palace, Bir Hassan, P.O. Box 83/25, Ghbeiri, Beirut – **13)** Dar al Fatwa, P.O. Box 14-5380, Al Mazraa-Beirut. **W:** www.darelfatwa.gov.lb – **14)** Couvent St. Jean, Fouad Chehab St, P.O. Box 850, Jounieh. **W:** www.radiocharity.org 24h in Arabic/French/others. Also rel. by Vatican R. (wi: 0530-0555 9645. su: 0430-0455 11715) – **15)** 3rd floor, La Perla Centre, Sabra Highway, Jounieh. **W:** www. famefm.com – **16)** Achrafieh, Kobayate St, Tutunji Center 7th floor, Beirut 1100 **W:** cedarsradio.com – **17)** 8th floor, Mansour Bldg, Independence St, Sassine Square, Achrafieh, Beirut. **W:** www.radio-lightfm.com 0500-2200 in English/French – **18)** St. Paul bldg, facing La Cite, Jounieh – **19)** Alfred Naccache Ave, P.O. Box 166-815, Achrafieh, Beirut. **W:** www.mixfm.com.lb 24h in English – **20)** Mont Liban Bldg, Ave. Fouad Chehab, Fassouh, P.O.Box 16-6000, Achrafieh, Beirut. **W:** www.nostalgie.com.lb 24h in French – **21)** P.O. Box 116-5104, Beirut. 24h in English. **W:** paxradio.page.tl – **22)** Kahalé Bldg, Old St, P.O.Box 1306, Beit Meri el Metn. **W:** www.4com.net.lb/delta – **23)** c/o Modern Media Company, Dbayeh, Beirut. **W:** vdl.com.lb – **24)** facing Tal-Shiha Hospital, Tal-Shiha, Zahlé. 0400-2200 in Arabic – **25)** 4th Floor, Hawa Chicken Building, Damascus Highway, Hazmiyé – **26)** 2nd floor, Abi Jaber Bldg, Al Saideh St, Sin El-Fil, Beirut. **W:** www.radiostrike.com 0600-2200 in Arabic – **27)** Centre Nasrallah, Rue Al-Anwar, Jdeideh, P.O. Box 90-1119, Beirut. **W:** www.sawtelmousika.com 0430-2400 in Arabic – **28)** Mirna el Chalouhi Centre 2nd floor, Sin el-Fil, Beirut. **W:** sawtlemada.com – **29)** txs in Beirut/Tripoli/Tyros/Sidon. For details see IntRad under France – **30)** Kreshet Bldg. 7th floor, Suyoufi St, Algazlep, Achrafieh, Beirut. **W:** sawtelnoujuom.com – **31)** Khatchadurian Street, Khederlarian Building, Ground Floor, Beirut. **W:** radiosevan.com – **32)** 87.7: Beirut/Bekaa/Sidon/Tripoli/Zahle (see Int. section under USA)

LESOTHO

L.T: UTC +2h — **Pop:** 2.2 million — **Pr.L:** Sesotho, English — **E.C:** 50Hz, 220V — **ITU:** LSO

LESOTHO COMMUNICATIONS AUTHORITY (LCA)
P.O. Box 15896, 6th Floor, Moposo House, Kingsway Road, Maseru ☎+266 22224300 ◧ +266 22310984 **W:** lca.org.ls **E:** lca@lca.org.ls

LESOTHO NATIONAL BROADCASTING SERVICE (LNBS, Pub.) - Radio Lesotho
P. O. Box 552, Lerotholi St, Opposite Royal Palace, Maseru 100 ☎+266 22321460 ◧ +266 22313980 **W:** www.gov.ls **L.P:** Dir. of Broadc: Mr. Lebohang Dada Mokasa. CE: Mr. Motlatsi Monyane. Principal Tech. Officer: Masekoala Ratia.
MW: Maseru (Lancer's Gap): 639kHz 100kW, 891kHz 50kW.

FM	MHz	kW	FM	MHz	kW
Mokhele	90.5	1	Likhoele	97.2	1
Maseru (Berea)	93.3	1	Thaba-Ntso	98.9	0.25
Chafo	96.0	1	Sheep Stud Hill	102.4	1
Maseru (Ponnare)	96.2		Popa	103.6	0.25
Matshoana	96.8	1	Souru	105.4	

D.Prgr in Sesotho/English: 24h. **F.PI:** four new FM trs.
Ultimate FM in English: Lancer's Gap 891kHz & 99.8MHz, 24h.
Ann: E: "This is Radio Lesotho" or "This is the Lesotho National Broadcasting Service, Maseru". Sesotho: "Se-ea-le-moea sa Lesotho, Maseru". **IS:** native horn instruments.

OTHER STATIONS:
Catholic R. FM: Qoatsaneng, Maseru 103.3MHz – **Dope FM,** Maseru: 103.6 MHz – **Fill the Gap (Jesu ke Karabo):** Mafeteng 87.6MHz, Leribe 102.8MHz, Lancer's Gap 105.3MHz – **Harvest FM:** Lancer's Gap, Maseru 98.9MHz – **Joy FM**, Private Bag A68, Maseru 100: 106.9MHz via FM **W:** www.joyfm.co.ls Also rel. VOA. F.PI: trs in Mafeteng and Maputsoe – **Lesotho Evangelical Church R,** Lancer's Gap, Maseru: 102.4MHz – **MoAfrika FM:** Leribe 89.7MHz, Mafeteng 90.7MHz, Lancer's Gap 99.3MHz. **W:** www.moafrika.co.ls – **People's Choice FM,** Development House, Block D, Floor 9, Kingsway Str, Maseru: 95.6MHz. **W:** www.pcfm.co.ls – **Thaha-Khube FM,** Ha Ts'osane, Maseru: 97.6MHz.
Family R, Maseru. **MW:** 1197kHz 100kW. **D.Prgr:** English 0300-0500, 1600-1900, 2000-2300, Portuguese 1900-2000. For further details see International Radio section (USA).
BBC African Sce: Lancer's Gap, Maseru 90.2MHz.
RFI Afrique: Lancer's Gap, Maseru 96.5MHz in French/English

LIBERIA

L.T: UTC — **Pop:** 3.5 million — **Pr.L:** English, 18 ethnic — **E.C:** 60Hz, 120V — **ITU:** LBR

LIBERIA TELECOMMUNICATIONS AUTHORITY (LTA)
National Investment Commission Annex, 12th Street, Sinkor, Tubman Boulevard, Monrovia ☎+231 770 54054 ◧ +231 770 00825 **W:** www.lta.gov.lr **E:** info@lta.gov.lr

LIBERIA BROADCASTING SYSTEM (LBS, Pub.)
P.O. Box 594, Paynesville **W:** liberiabroadcastingsystem.net **E:** info@liberiabroadcastingsystem.com **L.P:** Dir: Charles Snetter.
FM: R. Liberia: 99.9MHz 1kW.
D.Prgr: FM 0455-1005 & 1200-2400, Sat 0450-2400, Sun 0650-2400.

RADIO ELWA (Rlg.)
✉ P.O. Box 192, Monrovia **W:** www.elwaministries.org **E:** elwaradio@yahoo.com **LP:** GM: Moses T. Nyantee.
SW: Monrovia 4760kHz 1kW, 6070kHz 2kW (both inactive).
FM: Monrovia 94.5MHz 0.25kW.
D.Prgr in English/local lang's: 0600-1000, 1730-2300 (SS -2230).

STAR RADIO (Priv.)
✉ 12 Broad St, Snapper Hill, Monrovia ☎+231 77104411
SW: 3960kHz 2.5kW (inactive). **FM:** Monrovia: 104.0MHz 1kW (status uncertain). **D.Prgr** in English/Local languages: 0500-0905, 1700-2105.

UNMIL RADIO (United Nations Mission in Liberia)
✉ UNMIL Force HQ, Star Building, Monrovia **W:** unmilradio.org **E:** webmaster@unmil.org **LP:** Dir: Joseph Roberts-Mensah.
FM: Gbarnga 90.5MHz, Harper/Monrovia/Zwedru 91.5MHz, Sanniquellie 95.1MHz. Greenville/Voinjama 97.1MHz (Harper/Sanniquelle 1kW, others 5kW). **D.Prgr:** 24h in English/local langs

NB: Radio Vertitas closed in 2012 but may return after restructuring

Other stations:
ABCU R, Yekepa: 95.7MHz 0.6kW. **W:** africanbiblecolleges.org/abcu_liberia.php — **City FM,** Monrovia: 90.2MHz — **Crystal FM,** Monrovia 95.5MHz — **DC 101.1 FM,** Monrovia: 101.1MHz. Also rel. BBC African Sce. — **King's FM,** Monrovia: 88.5MHz. Also rel. VOA. — **Liberian Christian Broadcasting Network,** Monrovia: 102.3MHz — **Love FM,** Monrovia: 105.5MHz — **Power FM,** Monrovia 93.3MHz — **Magic FM,** Monrovia: 99.2MHz — **R. Monrovia:** 92.1MHz. **W:** radiomonrovia247.com — **Sky FM,** Monrovia: 107.0MHz. Email: skyliberia@yahoo.com — **Truth FM,** Monrovia 96.1MHz. **W:** truthfm.com.lr — **United Metodist Church R,** Monrovia: 98.7MHz 0.3kW.
BBC African Sce, Monrovia: 103.0MHz
RFI Afrique: Monrovia 106.0MHz in French/English.
About 35 community radio stations are in operation

LIBYA

L.T: UTC +2h — **Pop:** 6.5 million — **Pr.L:** Arabic — **E.C:** 50Hz, 127/230V — **ITU:** LBY

LIBYAN RADIO & TELEVISION NETWORK (Gov)
✉ El Fath Rd, P.O. Box 80237, Tripoli ☎+218 21 4442252 ▤ +218 21 3403458.

MW	kHz	kW	Prgr.
Benghazi	675	100	R. Free Libya
Tripoli	1053	100	VO Homeland
El Beida	1125	500	R. Free Libya
Misrata	1449	500	R. Misrata

FM: El Beida 87.9MHz, Benghazi 88.5MHz, Tripoli 96.6MHz, El Beida 98.1MHz, Al-Zawiyah 101.3MHz.
Ann: M: "Shabakat Radio wa Television Libya: Radio Libya min Tarablus al-assema".

EXTERNAL SERVICE: R. Libya: see International Radio section.

Other stations:

FM	MHz	Station, Prgr & other info:
Benghazi	88.1	R. Sawa
Tripoli	88.8	Al-Shababiya: (Youth R. of 17th February)
Derna	89.3	R. Free Derna
Benghazi	91.5	BBC WS: (in Arabic/English)
MIsrata	91.5	BBC WS: (in Arabic/English)
Ajdabiya	92.4	Al Jazeera: (Arabic sceTV sound relay)
Benghazi	92.4	Tribute FM: (**W:** tributefm.com, in English)
Nalut	98.2	R. Free Nalut: (in Tamazight)
Benghazi	99.9	Al Jazeera: (Arabic sce TV sound relay)
Benghazi	101.1	Libyana FM: (**W:** libyana.fm)
Ajdabiya	103.0	Libya Free TV sound. (**W:** libya.tv)
Tripoli	106.6	R. Sawa: 2kW

F.PI. Al-Assema R. on FM in Tripoli. **W:** alassema.net

LIECHTENSTEIN

L.T: UTC +1h (31 Mar-27 Oct: +2h) — **Pop:** 36,000 — **Pr.L:** German, Alemannic — **E.C:** 50Hz, 230V — **ITU:** LIE

LIECHTENSTEINISCHER RUNDFUNK (Pub)
✉ Dorfstr. 24, 9495 Triesen, Fürstentum Liechtenstein ☎+423 3991313 ▤ +423 3991366 **E:** admin@radio.li **W:** www.radio.li
L.P: CEO: Alois Ospelt

FM (MHz): Radio L: Buchs 89.2 (0.5kW), Trübbach 95.0 (0.02kW), Steg 96.6 (0.25kW), Vaduz 96.9 (0.1kW), Nendeln I 100.2 (0.05kW), Vilters-Targön 103.4 (0.1kW), Nendeln II 103.7 (0.1kW), Rüthi 106.1 (1kW). **D.Prgr:** 24h

LITHUANIA

L.T: UTC +2h (31 Mar-27 Oct: +3h) — **Pop:** 3 million — **Pr.L:** Lithuanian, Polish, Russian — **E.C:** 50Hz, 220V — **ITU:** LTU

LIETUVOS RADIJO IR TELEVIZIJOS KOMISIJA (LRTK)
✉ Vytenio g. 6, 03113 Vilnius ☎ +370 5 2330660 ▤ +370 5 2647125 **E:** lrtk@rtk.lt **W:** www.rtk.lt **LP:** Chmn: Paulius Subacius
NB. LRTK is the regulatory authority for broadcasting.

LIETUVOS NACIONALINIS RADIJAS IR TELEVIZIJA (LRT) (Pub)
✉ S.Konarskio g. 49, 03123 Vilnius ☎ +370 5 2363209 ▤ +370 5 2363208 **E:** lrt@lrt.lt **W:** www.lrt.lt
L.P: DG (LRT): Audrius Siaurusevicius

FM (MHz)	Prgr 1	Prgr 2	Prgr 3	kW
Anykščiai	101.9	104.4	106.5	17.4/4/0.5
Birzai	100.8	87.5	-	10/5
Bubiai	100.9	103.4	90.5	1.3/10/0.5
Druskininkai	102.3	103.7	-	5
Ignalina	92.3	99.6	-	1/2
Juragiai	102.1	96.2	98.0	20/10/1
Kalvarija	104.8	-	-	2
Klaipeda	102.8	105.3	91.9	2x17/0.5
Mazeikiai	93.3	101.8	-	5/0.5
Pazagieniai	107.5	105.3	93.7	2x1.5/1
Plunge	88.0	105.0	-	1/2
Skuodas	99.3	103.5	-	0.7/4
Taurage	98.8	107.4	104.2	4/1/0.5
Vilnius	102.6	105.1	-	5
Visaginas	102.9	100.8	98.3	2x11/0.5

NB. Sites with only txs below 1kW not listed.
D.Prgr: Prgr 1 (LRT radijas): 24h. Russian: 1430-1500. – **Prgr 2 (LRT Klasika):** 0400-2200. For ethnic minorities: 1300-1330 Belarusian (Tue/Sat), Russian (Wed/Thu/Sun), Ukrainian (Fri); 1330-1400 Polish. – **Prgr 3 (LRT Opus):** 24h.

OTHER STATIONS:

MW	kHz	kW	Location	Station
24A)	612	100	Vilnius	R. Baltic Waves (rel.)
24B)	1386	500	Sitkunai	R. Baltic Waves Int (rel.)

FM	MHz	kW	Location	Station
24B)	68.24	6.3	Visaginas	R. Baltic Waves Int (rel.)
3A)	70.22	1	Kaunas	Pukas
2B)	88.2	3.2	Bubiai	ZIP FM
14)	88.7	1.6	Palanga	Hot FM
3B)	90.1	2	Girulai	Pukas 2
2C)	90.6	2.3	Girulai	Russkoje R. Baltija
2A)	91.2	4	Tryškiai	Radiocentras
2B)	91.6	2	Skuodas	ZIP FM
7)	91.8	2	Siauliai	Marijos radijas
2A)	92.2	3.5	Bubiai	Radiocentras
4)	92.3	1	Utena	Ziniu radijas
3B)	92.4	3.2	Kaunas	Pukas 2
2B)	92.5	4.5	Klaipeda	ZIP FM
2B)	92.7	2.1	Mazeikiai	ZIP FM
1A)	92.8	11.7	Krakes	M-1
4)	93.4	2.5	Marijampole	Ziniu radijas
3A)	94.0	2.5	Alytus	Pukas
3A)	94.2	4.8	Raseiniai	Pukas
3A)	94.6	2	Ukmerge	Pukas
3A)	94.2	2.5	Marijampole	Pukas
15A)	94.9	3.2	Girulai	Laluna
7)	95.0	4	Viešintos	Marijos radijas
2A)	95.2	1	Krakes	Radiocentras
19)	95.4	4	Telšiai	Zemaitijos radijas
A)	95.5	3.2	Vilnius	BBC relay
3A)	95.7	2	Siauliai	Pukas
9)	95.9	2	Vilnius	Power Hit R.
4)	96.4	1.8	Mazeikiai	Ziniu radijas
11)	96.4	1.4	Vilnius	A2
10)	96.6	1	Panevezys	Pulsas
9)	96.7	2.3	Girulai	Power Hit R.
3B)	97.4	1	Siauliai	Pukas 2
1B)	97.6	4	Juragiai	M-1 Plius
21)	97.8	1.6	Siauliai	Antroji radijo stotis
1B)	98.3	3.4	Girulai	M-1 Plius
1B)	98.7	1.6	Utena	M-1 Plius
12)	99.0	3.2	Alytus	FM 99

FM	MHz	kW	Location	Station
13)	99.7	1	Vilnius	European Hit R.
6)	99.8	2	Girulai	Kelyje
2A)	99.9	2	Raseiniai	Radiocentras
2B)	100.1	4	Vilnius	ZIP FM
1B)	100.2	5	Pazagieniai	M-1 Plius
23)	100.2	1	Klaipeda	Extra FM
8)	100.4	4	Mazeikiai	Mazeikiu aidas
2C)	100.4	2.4	Kaunas	Russkoje R. Baltija
1B)	100.5	3	Bubiai	M-1 Plius
15B)	100.8	1.3	Klaipeda	Raduga
3B)	100.9	1.1	Vilnius	Pukas 2
2A)	101.0	2	Utena	Radiocentras
2A)	101.1	1.4	Alytus	Radiocentras
2A)	101.4	3.8	Pazagieniai	Radiocentras
2A)	101.5	2	Girulai	Radiocentras
3A)	101.6	1.7	Taurage	Pukas
2A)	101.6	1.9	Druskininkai	Radiocentras
16)	101.7	1.6	Bubiai	Relax FM
2A)	101.8	2	Marijampole	Radiocentras
3A)	102.0	1	Visaginas	Pukas
4)	102.2	1.6	Girulai	Ziniu radijas
17)	102.5	3.4	Bubiai	Saules radijas
3A)	102.6	1	Skuodas	Pukas
2A)	102.7	1.5	Taurage	Radiocentras
18)	102.9	4	Juragiai	Tau
1C)	103.0	2.2	Pazagieniai	Lietus
1C)	103.0	1.1	Tryškiai	Lietus
1C)	103.1	2.5	Vilnius	Lietus
1C)	103.1	1.7	Taurage	Lietus
1C)	103.3	1	Birzai	Lietus
1C)	103.4	1.1	Utena	Lietus
1C)	103.5	4.2	Juragiai	Lietus
1C)	103.7	1.6	Girulai	Lietus
4)	103.7	1.1	Visaginas	Ziniu radijas
20)	103.8	1.8	Vilnius	Znad Wilii
1C)	103.9	3.7	Bubiai	Lietus
5)	104.1	4	Girulai	Laisvoji banga
2B)	104.1	20	Juragiai	ZIP FM
1B)	104.3	2	Marijampole	M-1 Plius
5)	104.3	1.2	Bubiai	Laisvoji banga
5)	104.5	4	Juragiai	Laisvoji banga
5)	104.7	1	Vilnius	Laisvoji banga
5)	104.8	1.2	Pazagieniai	Laisvoji banga
4)	104.8	2.2	Taurage	Ziniu radijas
4)	104.9	1	Juragiai	Ziniu radijas
2B)	105.0	1	Utena	ZIP FM
2B)	105.2	1.3	Raseiniai	ZIP FM
22)	105.4	3.9	Kaunas	Kauno Fonas
2B)	105.4	10	Visaginas	ZIP FM
2A)	105.5	1.7	Birzai	Radiocentras
2C)	105.6	2.2	Vilnius	Russkoje R. Baltija
2B)	105.7	2	Taurage	ZIP FM
2C)	105.8	4.2	Bubiai	Russkoje R. Baltija
1A)	105.9	3.2	Ignalina	M-1
6)	105.9	1	Kaunas	Kelyje
1A)	106.0	2.2	Pazagieniai	M-1
1A)	106.0	2	Tryškiai	M-1
1A)	106.2	1.5	Taurage	M-1
1B)	106.2	4	Vilnius	M-1 Plius
1A)	106.3	3.9	Marijampole	M-1
1A)	106.3	2.5	Bubiai	M-1
1A)	106.3	2	Utena	M-1
1A)	106.4	2	Raseiniai	M-1
1A)	106.5	3	Giruliai	M-1
1A)	106.6	4	Juragiai	M-1
2B)	106.7	2	Laukuva	ZIP FM
1A)	106.8	1	Vilnius	M-1
2A)	107.1	3.9	Juragiai	Radiocentras
3A)	107.3	2	Vilnius	Pukas
10)	107.3	3.2	Birzai	Pulsas
3A)	107.6	3.7	Kaunas	Pukas
3A)	107.8	4.5	Girulai	Pukas
4)	107.9	1	Pazagieniai	Ziniu radijas

NB: Txs below 1kW not listed.

Addresses & other information:
1A-C) Laisves pr. 60, 05120 Vilnius. **E:** 1A) m-1@m-1.fm, 1B) pliusas@pliusas.fm, 1C) lietus@lietus.fm – **2A-C)** Laisves pr. 60, 05120 Vilnius. 2C) in Russian. **E:** 2A) programa@rc.lt; 2B) info@zipfm.lt; 2C) rusradio@rc.lt – **3A,B)** Šaldytuvu g. 25, 45123 Kaunas. **E:** radio@pukas.lt – **4)** Laisves pr. 60, 05120 Vilnius. **E:** biuras@ziniur.lt – **5)** Gedimino pr. 50/2, 01110 Vilnius. **E:** info@laisvojibanga.lt – **6)** Savanoriu pr. 151, 50174 Kaunas. **E:** kelyje@takas.lt – **7)** M.Daukšos g. 21, 44282 Kaunas. **E:** direktorius@marijosradijas.lt – **8)** Sodu g. 13-93, 89116 Mazeikiai. **E:** info@mazeikiuaidas.lt – **9)** Kalvariju g. 143, 08221 Vilnius. **E:** info@powerhitradio.lt – **10)** Respublikos g. 28, 35174 Panevezys. **E:** pulsas@

elektra.lt – **11)** Laisves pr. 3, 04215 Vilnius. **E:** a2@a2.lt – **12)** Rotušes a. 2a, 62141 Alytus. **E:** fm99@fm99.lt – **13)** Jasinskio g. 16g, 01112 Vilnius. **E:** info@ehr.lt – **14)** Virbališkes takas 3, 00127 Palanga. **E:** info@hotfm.lt – **15A,B)** Taikos pr. 81, 94114 Klaipeda. 15B) in Russian. **E:** 15A) laluna@laluna.lt; 15B) info@raduga.lt – **16)** Laisves pr. 60, 05120 Vilnius. **E:** info@relaxfm.lt – **17)** Aušros al. 64, 76240 Šiauliai. **E:** info@saulesradijas.lt – **18)** Draugystes g. 19, 51230 Kaunas. **E:** info@tau.lt – **19)** Mazeikiu g. 18, 87101 Telšiai. **E:** zemaitijos@radijas. lt – **20)** Laisves pr. 60, 05120 Vilnius. **E:** radio@znadwilii.lt. In Polish. – **21)** Varpo g. 22, 76297 Šiauliai. **E:** admin@2ra.lt – **22)** Savanoriu pr. 192-802, 44151 Kaunas. **E:** info@kf.lt – **23)** Konstitucijos pr. 7, 09308 Vilnius. **E:** info@extrafm.lt – **24A,B)** Švitrigailos g. 11a-211, 03228 Vilnius. **E:** radio@balticwaves.cjb.net. Rel. on 612/1386kHz: see Int. R. section. Rel. on 68.24MHz: Euroradio (Poland) in Belarusian: 24h. – **A)** Rel. BBC (UK)

DAB (Trial): Vilnius ch13A (230.784MHz) 0.5kW. **Operator:** LRTC

LORD HOWE ISLAND (Australia)

L.T: UTC +10½ (7 Oct 12-7 Apr 13, 6 Oct 13-6 Apr 14: +11h) — **Pop:** 347 — **Pr.L:** English — **E.C:** 50Hz, 240V. — **ITU:** AUS (**WRTH:** LHW)

AUSTRALIAN BROADCASTING CORP. (ABC)
See Australia. 24h satellite relay.

FM	MHz	Call	kW	Station
	104.1	2ABCFM	0.02	ABC Classic FM
	105.3	2JJJ	0.02	Triple J
	106.1	2ABCFM	0.02	ABC Classic FM

Other Stations

FM	MHz	Call	kW	
1)	100.1	-	0.02	Lord Howe Island R.
2)	106.5	8SAT	0.02	Flow FM

Addresses & other information
1) The Shack, New Jetty Complex, Lagoon Road (PO Box 52), Lord Howe Island NSW 2898 ☎ +61 2 6563 2123 📠 +61 2 6563 2127 **Prgr:** Thu night only, irregular at other times. Local community stn. **2)** 24h satellite relay from Flow FM, Kapunda SA **W:** www.flowfm.com.au

LUXEMBOURG

L.T: UTC +1h (31 Mar-27 Oct: +2h) — **Pop:** 511,840 — **Pr.L:** Luxembourgish, French, German — **E.C:** 50Hz, 110/220V — **ITU:** LUX

RTL (Comm.)
📧 45 blvd. Pierre Frieden, L-1543 Luxembourg ☎ +352 4214 22175 📠 +352 4214 22756 **W:** http://radio.rtl.lu **L.P:** Pres: Jacques Santer.
Luxembourg Sce: RTL Radio Lëtzebuerg: ☎ +352 4214 23 📠 +352 4214 22737 **W:** www.rtl.lu
German Sce: RTL Radio – die Grössten Oldies: ☎ +352 4214 23500 📠 +352 4214 22738 **W:** www.rtlradio.de **L.P:** PD: Holger Richter
LW/SW: See International Broadcasting section

FM (MHz)	Station	Location	kW
88.9	R. Lëtzebuerg	Dudelange	100
92.5	R. Lëtzebuerg	Hosingen	50
93.3	R. – die Grössten Oldies	Dudelange	100
97.0	R. – die Grössten Oldies	Hosingen	100
100.7	R. Socioculturelle	Dudelange	100

Also FM relays in France & Germany.
RTL Radio Lëtzebuerg in English/German/Luxembourgish: 24h on 92.5MHz (2000-0500 rel. German Sce.)

OTHER STATIONS (all MHz)
R. City FM - **FM:** 100.2 – **R. Honnert.7**, b.p. 1833, 1018 Luxembourg **W:** www.100komma7.lu - **FM:** 100.7 – **Den Neie R.**, P.O. Box 1522, 1015 Luxembourg **W:** www.dnr.lu - **FM:** 102.9/104.2/107.7 – **R. Latina**, 2 rue Astrid, 1143 Luxembourg **W:** www.radiolatina.lu **FM:** 101.2/103.1 – **R. Ara**, 2 rue de la Boucherie, 1247 Luxembourg **W:** www.ara.lu - **FM:** 103.3/105.2 – **R. Eldoradio**, B.P. 1344, 1013 Luxembourg **W:** eldoradio.lu - **FM:** 105.0/107.2 – **R. Challenger** - **FM:** 102.2 – **R. Lora**, 32 Av. de la Gare, 9233 Diekirch - **FM:** 102.2 – **R. LNW**, 27, rue Général Patton, 9551 Wiltz **W:** www.radiolnw.eu - **FM:** 102.2 – **R. Diddeleng**, Place de l'hôtel de ville, 3590 Dudelange **W:** www.dudelangefm.lu - **FM:** 103.6 – **R. LRB**, B.P. 8, 3201 Bettembourg **W:** www.lrb.lu - **FM:** 103.9/105.7 – **R. Interculturelle**, 4 rue principale, 9370 Gilsdorf; **FM:** 103.9 – **R. Gudd Laun**, B.P.24, 4001 Elsh/Alzette **W:** www.rgl.lu - **FM:** 106.1 – **R. Amizade**, 10 Rue du Parc, 3872 Schifflange - **FM:** 106.1 – **R. Classique vu Bergem** - **FM:** 106.1 – **R. Aktiv**, Rue du pont, 6471 Echternach **W:** www.radioaktiv106-5.org – **FM:** 106.5 – **R. Sympa**, 15 Rue René de Geysen, 4971 Dippach - **FM:** 106.5 – **ROM - Lokalradio vu Miedernach**, 28 rue

Savelborn, 7660 Medernach **W:** www.rom.lu - **FM:** 106.5 – **R. Belle Vallée**, 312 Route d'Esch, 4451 Belvaux - **FM:** 107.0

MACAU (China, SAR)

L.T: UTC +8h — **Pop:**568,700 — **Pr.L:** Portuguese, Cantonese — **E.C:** 50Hz, 220V — **ITU:** MAC

TELEDIFUSÃO DE MACAU, SARL (Priv. Comm.)
⌨ Avenida Dr. Rodrigo Rodrigues, No. 223-225, Edif. "Nam Kwong" 7 Andar, Macau ☎ +853 28713025 🖷 +853 28717194 **E:** rmacau@tdm. com.mo **W:** www.tdm.com.mo
FM: 98.0MHz 2.5kW **D.Prgr:** Portuguese 24h except Indonesian at 1200-1300 on Sunday, 100.7MHz 2.5kW **D.Prgr:** Cantonese and Chinese 24h:

RÁDIO VILAVERDE LDA (Priv. Comm.)
⌨ Hipódromo da Taipa, Macau ☎ +853 28820338 🖷 +853 28820337 **E:** am738@am738.com **W:** www.am738.com
MW: 738kHz 10kW **D.Prgr:** Cantonese 24h:

MACEDONIA

L.T: UTC +1h (31 Mar-27 Oct: +2h) — **Pop:** 2.1 million — **Pr.L:** Macedonian, Albanian — **E.C:** 50Hz, 220V — **ITU:** MKD

SOVET ZA RADIODIFUZIJA NA REPUBLIKA MAKEDONIJA (SRD) (Broadc. Council of Rep. of Macedonia)
⌨ bul. VMRO 3, 1000 Skopje ☎ +389 2 3103400 🖷 +389 2 3103401 **E:** sovet@srd.org.mk **W:** www.srd.org.mk
L.P: Pres: Zoran Trajcevski
NB. SRD is the regulatory authority for broadcasting.

MAKEDONSKO RADIO (MR) (Pub)
⌨ bul. Goce Delcev bb, 1000 Skopje ☎ +389 2 3112200 🖷 +389 2 3112200 **E:** deskvesti@mtv.com.mk **W:** www.mtv.com.mk
L.P: Dir (Radio): Ajten Mehmeti

MW	kHz	kW	Prgr
Sveti Nikole	810	1200	MR1, External Service

FM (MHz)	MR1	*MR2	MR3	kW
Belasica	91.5	97.8	106.8	10
Boskija	95.3	98.1	105.4	10
Bukovic	89.2	95.9	104.3	1
Cocon	88.8	93.8	98.1	1
Crn Vrv	97.3	94.1	101.3	100
Gevgelija	99.2	102.4	96.5	10
Golak	94.5	97.0	107.7	10
Mali Vlaj	93.3	97.7	91.0	10
Pelister	92.3	96.1	102.6	20
Popova Šapka	88.8	96.3	98.3	5
Stogovo	95.3	101.0	91.3	3
Tepavci	94.9	103.4	91.5	1
Turtel	93.3	90.5	99.7	50
Vodno	98.9	92.4	87.8	10

NB: Txs below 1kW not listed. *) Txs relay MR3 2100-0100, Kanal 103 0100-0500.
D.Prgr: MR1 (R. Skopje): 24h. – MR2 (R. 2): 0500-2100. – MR3 (Treta programa): 24h in Albanian & other minority langs. – **Local Station "Kanal 103":** 24h on Vodno (Skopje) 103.0MHz (0.5kW).

External Service (R. Makedonija): see Int. Radio section.

OTHER STATIONS

MW	kHz	kW	Location	Station
4)	639	1	Štip	R. Štip

FM	MHz	kW	Location	Station
2)	89.7	1	Vodno	Kanal 77
3)	89.8	3	Pelister	R. Bitola
A)	91.3	1	Skopje	RFI relay
1)	92.9	1	Pelister	Antena 5
1)	95.5	1	Vodno	Antena 5
5)	96.6	1	Štip	R. Štip
4)	98.8	1	Ohrid	R. Ohrid
1)	104.8	1	Turtel	Antena 5
1)	106.3	1	Boskija	Antena 5

NB: Txs below 1kW not listed.
Addresses & other information:
1) ul. Tetovska 35, 1000 Skopje. **E:** mail@antenna5.com.mk – **2)** ul. 5ta Partiska Konferencija b.b., 2000 Štip. **E:** web@kanal77.com.mk – **3)** ul. Tomaki Dimitrovski 7, 7000 Bitola. **E:** radiobt@freemail.com.mk – **4)** ul. Sv. Klement Ohridski 2, 6000 Ohrid. **E:** radiooh@sonet.com.mk – **5)** ul. Vanco Prke bb, 2000 Štip. **E:** radiostip@mt.net.mk – **A)** Rel. RFI (France)

MADAGASCAR

L.T: UTC +3h — **Pop:** 21 million — **Pr.L:** Malagasy, French — **E.C:** 50Hz, 220V — **ITU:** MDG

RADIO MADAGASIKARA - RADIO NATIONALE MALAGASY (RNM, Pub.)
⌨ BP 4422, Anosy, 101 Antananarivo ☎+261 20 2221745 🖷 +261 20 2232715 **L.P:** Dir: Johary Ravoajanarahy.

MW	kHz	kW	H of tr
Fenoarivo	630	75	0300-1900

SW	kHz	kW	H of tr
Ambohidrano	5010	100	0300-0500, 1500-1900
Ambohidrano	6135	30	0500-1500
Ambohidrano	7245	20	0500-1500

All transmitters reported irregular.
FM: Antananarivo 99.2MHz (0.5kW) & relay txs.
D.Prgr: 0300-1900 (SS 2200) in Malagasy & French.
Ann: Malagasy: "R. Madagasikara"; F: "R. Nationale Malagasy".

OTHER STATIONS

SW	kHz	kW	Location		Station
1)	6155	50	Talata-Volonondry		R. Feon'ny Filazantsara
FM	MHz	kW	Location		Station
2)	88.6		Antananarivo		R. Fahazavana
	89.2		Antananarivo		BBCWS relay
3)	92.0		Antananarivo		Alliance FM (also r. RFI)
4)	93.4		Antananarivo		R. Don Bosco
5A)	94.4		Antananarivo		R. Tana
	96.0				RFI
6)	96.6		Antananarivo		R. Des Jeunes
7)	97.6		Antananarivo		R. Antsiva
8)	98.2		Toamasina		R. Voanio
5B)	102.0		Antananarivo		R. 102
9)	105.2		Antananarivo		Ma FM
10)	106.0		Antananarivo		R. Lazan Iarivo
11)	107.4		Antananarivo		R. FMFOI

NB: Unlicensed stns are operating in many parts of the country.
Addresses & other information:
1) BP 95, 110 Antsirabe. **E:** flm@wanadoo.mg. In Malagasy: 1630-1700. Tr. is relayed by RNW – **2)** BP 623, Lot II J 11, Faravohitra, Rue Joël Rakotomalala, 101 Antananarivo. **W:** radiofahazavana. agilityhoster.com – **3)** Enceinte Maison Laborde, Andohalo, 101 Antananarivo. **W:** alliancefr.mg/institution/part_dg.htm#alliance92 – **4)** BP 60, Maison Don Bosco, Ivato Airport, 105 Antananarivo. **W:** radiodonbosco.mg – **5A-B)** Enceinte Sitram, Ankorondrano, 101 Antananarivo. **W:** www.rta.mg . A) in Malagasy, B) in French –**6)** BP 4370, Immeuble Vitasoa, Analakely, 101 Antananarivo. **W:** rdeejay. net – **7)** BP 12170, Zone Zital Ankorondrano, Enceinte RTA, 101 Antananarivo. **W:** www.antsiva.mg –**8)** BP 489, 11 Rue Grandidier, 501 Toamasina. **W:** voanio.com – **9)** BP 1414, Ankorondrano, 101 Antananarivo. **W:** matv.mg **–10)** BP 6319, V.A 49 Andafiavaratra, 101 Antananarivo. **W:** rli106fm.com – **11)** Rue Docteur Ralarosy V W01, Ambohipotsy, 101 Antananarivo. **W:** fmfoi.ifrance.com

MADEIRA (Portugal)

L.T: UTC (31 Mar-27 Oct: +1h) — **Pop:** 300,000 — **Pr.L:** Portuguese — **E.C:** 50Hz, 220/380V — **ITU:** MDR

ANACOM-Autoridade Nacional de Comunicações, Delegação da Madeira
⌨Rua do Vale das Neves, 19, São Gonçalo, 9050-332 Funchal ☎ +351 291 79 02 00 🖷+351 291 79 02 01

RADIODIFUSÃO PORTUGUESA, S.A. Centro Regional da RDP-Madeira
⌨ Rua Tenente Coronel Sarmento, 15, 9000-020 Funchal ☎ +351 291 20 20 00 🖷 +351 291 23 07 53 **W:** www.rtp.pt **E:** rdpmadeira@rtp.pt
L.P: Dir: Tito de Freitas
MW (Antena 1 Madeira): RDP halted MW broadcasts in Madeira & Porto Santo. There are no current plans to reactivate the network.

FM (MHz)	Ant. 1	Ant.2	Ant. 3	kW
Achada da Cruz	104.3		105.0	0.8
Cabo Girão	96.7	99.4	94.8	1/3/1
Calheta	105.4		107.5	0.1
Caniço	101.6	99.0	89.3	0.5
Encumeada	93.1		90.8	0.06
Gaula	98.5	106.3	91.3	1/0.7/1
Maçapez	92.0		95.7	0.1
Monte	104.6	102.4	89.8	1/1/0.7
Paúl da Serra	101.9		93.3	1

FM (MHz)	Ant. 1	Ant.2	Ant. 3	kW
Pico do Areeiro	95.5		94.1	13/15
Pico do Facho	93.1		90.8	0.03
Ponta do Pargo	90.2		94.6	1
Porto Santo	100.5	103.3	96.5	10
Ribeira Brava	105.6		103.1	1
Santa Clara	104.6	102.4	89.8	

DAB: RDP halted T-DAB broadcasts in June 2011. There are no current plans to reactivate this service, which does not mean that it will not be restored in future.
D.Prgr: all networks 24h. Antena 1 of RDP Madeira provides regional prgrs M-F 0700-2000, Sat 0700-1800, Sun 0900-1800 LT; Antena 2 relays Lisboa 24h; Antena 3 Madeira carries own prgrs. M-F 0700-2400, Sat 0000-0300 & 0600-2400, Sun 0800-2400 LT. Technical info may be obtained for **W:** gabinete.tecnologias@rtp.pt
V. by QSL-card via RDP Lisboa.

RÁDIO RENASCENÇA – Em. Católica Portuguesa (Rlg/Comm)
☞ (see Portugal) - **FM:** Pico do Silva 88.0MHz 44kW (RR), 93.6MHz 44kW (RFM)

PEF – Posto Emissor de Radiodifusão do Funchal (Priv., comm.)
☞Rua Ponte de São Lázaro 3, 9000-027 Funchal ☎ +351 291 23 03 93 🖷 +351 291 22 1/ 97 **E:** pef@netmadeira.com **W:** www.pef.pt
MW: Funchal 1530kHz 3kW (nominal power: 10kW),
FM: 92.0MHz 2kW **D.Prgr:** 24h Relays R. Renascença, Lisboa, at certain times **Ann:** "PEF – a sua rádio regional"

Local FM stations:

FM	Island	Station & location	MHz	kW
4)	Madeira	R. Jornal da Madeira, Funchal	88.8	1
13)	Madeira	R. São Vicente, São Vicente	89.2	0.5
6)	Madeira	R. Zarco, Machico	89.6	1
9)	Pto Santo	R. Praia, Porto Santo	91.6	0.5
12)	Madeira	Santana FM, Santana	92.5	0.5
11)	Madeira	R. Palmeira, Santa Cruz	96.1	0.5
10)	Madeira	Girão FM, Ribeira Brava	98.4	0.5
1)	Madeira	R. Calheta, Calheta	98.8	0.5
5)	Madeira	R. Notícias/TSF, Funchal	100.0	2
2)	Madeira	R. Popular da Madeira, Câm. de Lobos	101.0	2
8)	Madeira	R. Porto Moniz, Porto Moniz	102.9	0.5
7)	Madeira	R. Sol, Ponta do Sol	103.7	0.5
3)	Madeira	R.Clube da Madeira, Funchal	106.8	0.4

+ five 50W repeaters used by three stns
Addresses and other information (add +351 to tel/fax nos)**:**
1) Edifício Ondaparque, Av.ª D. Manuel I, 9370-133 Calheta ☎ 291 82 01 32/6, 🖷 291 82 01 38 **E:** radiocalheta@gmail.com **W:** www.radiocalheta.pt – **2)** Rua Estados Unidos da América 147 a 150 - 9000-090 Funchal ☎ 291 703 478 & 291 764 124 🖷 291 20 23 86 **E:** radio-popular101@hotmail.com – **3)** Rua dos Estados Unidos da América, 146-150, 9000-090 Funchal ☎ 291 703 471 **E:** 106.8@radioclube.pt, ssfranco@radioclube.pt **W:** www.radioclube.pt – **4)** Rua Dr. Fernão de Ornelas, 35-r/c, 9054-528 Funchal ☎ 291 202 385 🖷291 231 028 **E:** radio@jornaldamadeira.pt **W:** radio.jornaldamadeira.pt – **5)** Rua Fernão de Ornelas, 56-3º, 9050-021 Funchal ☎ 291 20 23 94/5/6 🖷 291 20 23 87; relays TSF Lisboa **E:** rmoliveira@dnoticias.pt **W:** www.dnoticias.pt/tsfmadeira – **6)** Conjunto Habitacional da Bemposta Ap-A1/A2 - Água Pena 9200-000 Machico ☎ 291 526 896 –**7)** Rua dos Netos, 23 9000-084 Funchal☎ 291 764 124🖷 291 202 386 – **8)** 9240 São Vicente ☎ 291 84 21 35 🖷291-84 26 66 – **9)** Hotel Praia Dourada, Rua Dr. Estêvão Alencastre ☎ 291 98 01 30 🖷 291 982 487 **E:** radiopraia91.6fm@gmail.com **W:** www.radiopraia.com – **10)** (see 7) – **11)** (see 6) – **12)** Rua da Igreja, 8-3º, 9325-031 Estreito de Câmara de Lobos ☎ 291 573 830 🖷 291 573 833 **E:** santanafm@gmail.com, noticiasradios@gmail.com **W:** www.santanafm.com.pt – **13)** Bombeiros Voluntários de São Vicente e Porto Moniz, Vila de São Vicente, 9240 São Vicente ☎ 291 84 26 94 & 291 84 26 44 🖷 291 84 23 93

MALAWI

L.T: UTC +2h — **Pop:** 14 million — **Pr.L:** English, Chichewa, Tumbuka, Lomwe, Sena, Yao, Nkhonde, Tonga — **E.C:** 50Hz, 230V — **ITU:** MWI

MALAWI COMMUNICATIONS REGULATORY AUTHORITY (MACRA)
☞ Salmon Amour Rd, Private Bag 261, Blantyre ☎+265 1 623611 🖷 +265 1 623890 **L.P:** DG: Allexon Chiwaya. Dir of Broadc: Fegus Lipenga. **W:** www.macra.org.mw **E:** info@macra.org.mw

MALAWI BROADCASTING CORPORATION (MBC, Pub.)
☞ P.O. Box 30133, Chichiri, Blantyre 3 ☎+ 265 1 871461 **E:** dgmbc@

malawi.net **L.P:** DG: Dr. Benson Tembo. Ag. Dir. Prgr. & News: Hamilton Chimala. Dir. of Eng: Joseph Chikagwa.

MW	kHz	kW	MW	kHz	kW
Mangochi	540	10	Blantyre	756	10
Karonga	558	10	Bangula	810	10
Lilongwe	594	30	Chitipa	1404	10
Ekwendeni	675	50	Matiya	1422	10

FM	R1	R2FM	FM	R1	R2FM
Blantyre	95.4	92.2	Lilongwe	94.7	91.5
Chikangawa	105.9	103.0	Livingstonia	90.1	104.5
Chitipa	90.7	100.5	Mzuzu	97.8	91.3
Dedza	90.1	104.5	Nkhotakota	95.6	
Dwangwa	93.6	103.6	Ntchisi	100.5	92.4
Karonga	95.5	98.7	Zomba	94.1	96.8
Kasungu	94.5	96.2			

Radio 1 in English/Chichewa/Others on MW/FM: 24h.
Radio 2FM in English/Chichewa on FM: 24h.
Ann: E: R1: "Radio 1", R2: "Radio 2FM". Chichewa: "Kuno ndi ku Radio ya MBC". **IS:** 0253 Cock crow and rapid drum beat.

Other stations (FM MHz):
R. Alinafe, Lilongwe: 97.1. **E:** radioalinafe@sdnp.org.mw – **Calvary Family Church R,** Blantyre 3: 105.8 0.25kW. E: calvaryministries@hotmail.com – **Capital R:** Blantyre/Mzuzu 102.5, Dedza 105.2, Lilongwe 102.8m Zomba 96.1. **W:** www.capitalradiomalawi.com – **Channel For All Nations,** Lilongwe: 101.5 – **FM 101 Power:** (all txs 0.5/1kW): Ntcheu 88.1, Livingstonia 93.2, Chintheche 98.6, Mzuzu 99.0, Nkhoma 100.3, Blantyre/Lilongwe/Nkhota-kota 101, Dedza 103.9, Ntchisi 104, Dwangwa 107.2. **W:** www.fm101.malawi.net – **Joy R,** Blantyre: 89.6 – **MIJ R,** Blantyre 3: 90.3 **W:** www.mijmw.net/radio.htm – **R. Islam:** Blantyre 97.6, Dedza 105.7, Dowa 89.7, Karonga 97.7, Lilongwe 97.6, Mtengo Wa Ung'ono 99.7, Mangochi 101.8, Mzuzu 97.0, Namwera 97.4, Zomba 102.9, all 1kW. **W:** radioislam.org.mw – **R. Maria Malawi:** Mangochi 88.5 1kW, Dowa 94.0 1kW, Blantyre 99.2 1kW, Zomba 99.4 2kW, Dedza 99.7 2kW. **W:** www.radiomaria.mw – **Star FM,** Blantyre: 89.0 – **Trans World Radio Malawi:** Blantyre 89.1, Ntchis 90.7, Mvera 91.1, Dedza 96.4, Yawo 106.2, Chikangawa/Zomba 106.4, Lilongwe 106.5, Thyolo 107.1, all 2kW. **W:** twrmalawi.word-press.com – **Zodiak BS:** Chitipa 89.5, Dedza 89.0, Dowa 92.9, Karonga 93.7, Lilongwe 95.1, Livingstonia 95.0, Mpingwe 97.0, Mzuzu 95.1, Namwera 103.3, Zomba 89.3. **W:** zbsmw.com
BBC African Sce: Mzuzu 87.9, Lilongwe 98.0, Blantyre 98.1

MALAYSIA

L.T: UTC +8h — **Pop:** 28 million — **Pr.L:** Bahasa Malaysia (Malay), English, Chinese. In West Malaysia also Tamil and various Orang Asli languages, East Malaysia also 12 local languages or dialects — **E.C:** 50Hz, 240V — **ITU:** MLA

MALAYSIAN COMMUNICATIONS AND MULTIMEDIA COMMISSION (MCMC) (Suruhan Komunikasi dan Multimedia Malaysia, SKMM)
Regulatory body for the communications & multimedia industries.
☞ 63000 Cyberjaya, Selangor ☎ +60 3 8688 8000 🖷 +60 3 8688 1000 **W:** www.skmm.gov.my **L.P:** Chairman: Yg Bhg Tan Sri Khalid Bin Ramli

JABATAN PENYIARAN MALAYSIA (Dept of Broadcasting of Malaysia) (Gov.)
Parent body of RTM ☞ Angkasapuri, 50614 Kuala Lumpur ☎ +60 322825333 🖷 +60 2282 5103

RADIO TELEVISION MALAYSIA - RTM (Gov.)
☞ Dept. of Broadcasting, Angkasapuri, Bukit Putra, 50614 Kuala Lumpur ☎ +60 322825333 🖷 +60 322824735 **W:** www.rtm.gov.my **E:** teknikalradio@rtm.net.my
L.P: DG: Datuk Norhyati Ismail. Prgr Dir (Radio): Haji Mohammad Bin Mat Hussin. Dir. Tech. Sces: Hj Ab. Wahid Bin Ab. Hamid.

SW: Kajang:

kHz	kW	Sce.	H of tr	kHz	kW	Sce.	H of tr
5965±	100	1	24h	7295	100	4	24h
6050±	50	†	24h				

† = Rel. Asyik FM 0000-1500, rel. Salam FM 1500-2400. ±) variable

FM (MHz)	Site	1	2	4	5	6	kW
Alor Setar	a	94.9	100.5	98.7	101.3	96.7	5
Balik Pulau		99.5	93.9	90.1	92.1	98.9	0.1
Baling	c	88.7	89.7	91.7	92.5	93.3	1
Besut	d	94.3	98.8	97.0	97.8	95.3	0.1

FM (MHz)	Site	1	2	4	5	6	kW
Cameron	e	89.1	93.1	101.1	103.5	104.3	0.1
Dungun	f	95.9	96.9	98.9	99.7	100.7	1
Gerik	g	97.8	95.4	98.4	100.8	100.0	0.1
Ipoh	h	88.3	90.9	90.1	92.1	98.9	1
Jeli		88.4	89.2	90.8	91.6	92.4	0.1
Jerantut		88.1	93.5	89.9	90.7	91.9	0.1
Johor Bahru	k	106.7	105.7	102.9	104.9	101.1	5
Kota Bharu	l	101.1	101.9	104.7	105.7	106.7	1
Kuala Lumpur	m	87.7	88.5	90.3	89.3	92.3	1
KL2		93.8	95.3	100.1	106.7	96.3	1
KT	o	92.5	91.7	89.7	90.5	87.9	1
Kuantan	p	107.9	107.1	105.3	106.1	103.3	1
Machang	q	95.5	96.5	98.5	99.3	100.9	2
Melaka	r	93.6	96.6	97.4	100.4	103.3	0.5
Mersing	s	90.1	90.9	92.9	89.1	88.3	1
Seremban	t	87.9	91.7	88.7	89.7	90.5	0.1
Sik	v	95.5	102.7	105.9	106.7	107.5	1
Taiping	w	103.3	107.1	105.3	106.1	107.9	0.1
U. Tembeling	x	90.1	88.5	-	87.5	-	0.1

National networks 1-6: see below. KL2=KL/Selangor/Pahang (West). KT=Kuala Terengganu.

Sites: a) Gunung Jerai, b) Bukit Genting (Penang) c) Bukit Palong, d) Bukit Bintang, e) Gunung Berinchang, f) Bukit Bauk, g) RTM Gerik h) Bukit Keledang, i) Bukit Tangki Air, j) Bukit Istana, k) Gunung Pulai, l) Telipot, m) Menara KL (Bukit Nanas), n) Gunung Ulu Kali, o) Bukit Besar, p) Bukit Pelindung, q) Bukit Bakar, r) Gunung Ledang (Mt Ophir), s) Bukit Tinggi, t) Bukit Telapa Burok, u) RTM Seremban, v) Bukit Dedap, w) Bukit Larut (Maxwell Hill) x) Kampung Bantal, Ulu Tembeling.

Asyik FM/Salam FM: Cameron Highlands 105.1MHz, Gunung Ledang 95.6MHz, Gunung Ulu Kali 102.5MHz, Kuala Lumpur 91.1MHz, Ulu Tembeling 89.3MHz.

FM: All powers throughout are TRP.

RTM national services
(1) Klasik Nasional FM: 24h news, information & Malay oldies presented in Malay. **(2) Nasional FM:** 24h General sce presented in Malay. **(4) Traxx FM:** 24h News, music and travel sce in English. **(5) Ai FM:** 24h General Sce in Chinese (Mandarin exc. news at 0200 in Hakka, 0500 Cantonese, 0700 Hakka & 1300 Chaozhou). **(6) Minnal FM:** 24h General sce in Tamil. **Asyik FM:** 0000-1500 for Orang Asli in Jakun, Malay, Semai, Temiar & Temuan. **Salam FM:** Rlg. prgrs in Malay from Jabatan Kemajuan Islam Malaysia 1500-2400 **V.** occasionally by letter or Email. **Ann:** names of networks and regional sces are sometimes preceded by the words "Radio Malaysia".

RTM regional services in West Malaysia:
Most sces. operate 24h in Malay (exceptions include Langkawi, which carries local & tourist information in English and Malay. Some sces relay RTM Klasik Nasional overnight. Refer to above lists for tx sites and powers for frequencies marked a-w.
Johor: Johor FM (JFM), Karung Berkunci 716, 80990 Johor Bahru, Johor **W:** johor.dapat.fm **E:** rmjb@rtmjb.net.my On 92.1MHz s, 101.9MHz k, 105.3MHz r — **Kedah:** Kedah FM, Kompleks Penerangan dan Penyiaran Sultan Abdul Halim, KM 3, Jalan Kuala Kedah, 05400 Alor Setar, Kedah **W:** www.kedahfm.gov.my **E:** rtmas@rtm.net.my On 88.5MHz Selama-Bandar Baharu (site Bukit Sungai Kecil Hilir) 0.25kW, 90.5MHz b, 97.5MHz a, 105.1MHz v, 105.7MHz Gunung Raya 1kW, 107.0MHz Kuah — **Kelantan:** Kelantan FM, Peti Surat 143, 15720 Kota Bharu, Kelantan **E:** rtmkb@rtm.net.my On 88.1MHz FELDA Paloh 1kW, 97.3MHz q 102.9MHz l, 89.1MHz Gua Musang 0.1kW, 92.0MHz j, 88.9MHz Taman Wangi 0.1kW, 107.1MHz d — **Kuala Lumpur:** KL.fm On 97.2MHz m **W:** www.kl.fm — **Langkawi (Kedah):** Langkawi FM, Tingkat 2, Bangunan Tabung Haji, Jalan Padang Mat Sirat, 07000 Kuah, Langkawi **W:** www.langkawifm.gov.my On 87.5MHz Kuah 0.1kW, 104.8MHz Gunung Raya 1kW **English:** 0100-0400, 0700-1000 Malay/English 1300-1600 — **Melaka:** Melaka FM (MFM), Jalan Taming Sari, 75614 Melaka **W:** www.melakafm.webs.com **E:** rtmmlk@rtm.net.my On 102.3MHz r — **Negeri Sembilan:** Negeri FM, Jalan Raja Ali, 71000 Seremban, Negeri Sembilan **W:** www.negeri.fm On 92.5MHz t, 95.7MHz Gunung Tampin 0.1kW, 107.7MHz r — **Pahang:** Pahang FM, Peti Surat 152, 25710 Kuantan, Pahang **W:** www.pahangfm.gov.my **E:** rtmktn@rtm.net.my On 104.1MHz p, 107.5MHz n 100.3MHz e, 92.7MHz j, 92.0MHz Maran (Bukit Senggora) 0.25kW, 91.9MHz Rompin 0.25kW — **Perak:** Perak FM, Jalan Dairy, 31400 Ipoh, Perak **W:** www.perakfm.my **E:** rtmipoh@rtm.net.my On 657kHz, 89.6MHz Bukit Asa, 94.2MHz Lenggong (Bukit Ladang Teh) 0.025kW, 94.7MHz e, 95.6MHz g, 96.1MHz h, 97.3MHz Changkat Rembian 0.5kW, 104.1MHz w — **Perlis:** Perlis FM, Tingkat 6, Bangunan WSP, Jalan Bukit Lagi, 01000 Kangar, Perlis **E:** rtmkgr@rtm.net.my On 102.9MHz Pauh 2kW — **Pulau Pinang (Penang):**

Mutiara FM, Jalan Burmah, Peti Surat 433, 10350 Pulau Pinang **W:** www.mutiarafm.gov.my **E:** rtmpp@rtm.net.my On 90.9MHz b, 93.9MHz a, 95.7MHz Bukit Penara 1kW — **Selangor:** Selangor FM Bangunan Sultan Salehudin Abdul Aziz Shah, 40000 Shah Alam, Selangor **W:** rms.mmu.edu.my On 100.9MHz r — **Terengganu:** Terengganu FM, Peti Surat 63, 20914 Kuala Terengganu, Terengganu **W:** tfm.gov.my **E:** rtmkt @rtm.net.my On 88.7MHz o, 96.2MHz c, 97.7MHz f.

RADIO TELEVISION MALAYSIA SABAH (Gov)
2.4km, Tuaran Road, Beg Berkunci 2022, 88614 Kota Kinabalu ☎ +60 88213444 🖃 +60 88223493 **W:** www.rtmsabah.gov.my
Addresses of local stns: Tingkat 6, Wisma Persekutuan, W.D.T. 52, 90500 Sandakan - Peti Surat 606, 91008 Tawau.
L.P: Dir. Broadcasting: Encik Zubad Jamrin. Dir. Tech. (Radio): Abdul Jalani bin Mahmud. Dep. Dir. (Radio Prgr): Tuan Haji Hashim Jaffrey.

RADIO TELEVISION MALAYSIA LABUAN (Gov)
5004 Tanjung Taras, Peti Surat 299, 87008 WP Labuan ☎ +60 87415677 🖃 +60 87416658 **W:** www.labuanfm.gov.my **E:** kejuruteraan@labuanfm.net.my

MW	kHz	kW	Netw.	H of tr
Tenom	565	10	SF	1000-1500
Kudat	801	10	SF	2130-0800
Kudat	±1197	10	SV	2030-0800
Tuaran	d1475	700	SM	1100-1330

FM (MHz)	Tx	SF	SV	1	2	4	5	kW
FELDA S	a	104.1	106.7	99.9	102.9	104.9	105.7	0.1
Gadong	b	89.3	92.6	88.0	88.9	90.7	91.6	0.1
Kota Belud	c	101.5	104.1	99.9	100.7	102.5	103.3	0.1
K. Kinabalu	d	89.9	92.7	88.1	88.9	90.7	91.9	1
Kudat	e	95.9	98.9	94.1	94.9	96.7	98.1	1
Labuan	f		93.3	87.6	88.5	90.3	92.3	0.1
Lahad Datu	g	89.7	92.6	87.9	88.7	90.5	91.7	1
Langkon		97.1	91.1	101.6	90.1	89.0	87.7	0.1
Layang-L.	h	104.5	107.1	99.5	100.3	105.3	106.3	1
Luasong				87.7	88.5	89.3	90.1	0.1
Sandakan	j	92.9	96.1	91.1	92.1	94.3	95.1	1
Sipitang	k	97.9	102.9	95.5	96.5	99.1	99.9	1
Tawau	l	95.7	99.3	93.9	94.7	97.1	98.1	1
Tenom	m	90.3	93.3	85.9	88.3	89.3	91.7	92.3	1

Sites: , a) FELDA Sahabat, b) Bukit Gadong, c) Bukit Pompoda d) Kota Kinabalu (Bukit Lawa Mandau) e) Bukit Kelapa, f) Bukit Timbalai, g) Gunung Silam, h) Layang-Layang (Mount Kinabalu) j) Bukit Trig, k) Bukit Tampulagus, l) Gunung Andrassy, m) Bukit Sigapon.
National networks: 1-5: see RTM national sces above.
State networks: SF= Sabah FM in Malay 24h. **Reg. N:** 2200, 2330, 0400, 0530, 0830, 1400. **SV**= Sabah V FM in English 0300-0700 & 1500-1800, Mandarin 0030-0300 inc. news in Hakka at 0110, Bajau 1800-2000 & 0830-1100, Dusun 2300-0030, 1300-1500, Kadazan 2100-2300 & 0600-0830, Murut 2000-2100 & 1100-1300. **N.** (English): 0500, 1500. **SM**=Suara Malaysia (Overseas Sce) in Tagalog to the Philippines 1100-1330 from studios in Kota Kinabalu, also on 94.7MHz (studio link to MW tx).
Local Sces: Labuan FM on 89.4MHz 0.1kW (Bukit Timbalai) & 103.7MHz 0.1kW (RTM Labuan): 2145-1200 incl. English 0100-0300 – Tawau FM on 100.1MHz 1kW (Gunung Andrassy): 2145-1100 – Sandakan FM on 90.1MHz 1kW (Bukit Trig): 2150-1000 – Keningau FM on 89.4MHz: 2300-0900 in Malay, Dusun and Murut.

RADIO TELEVISION MALAYSIA SARAWAK (Gov.)
Broadcasting House, Jalan P. Ramlee, 93614 Kuching ☎ +60 82 248422 🖃 +60 82 246523 **W:** www.rtmsarawak.gov.my **E:** rtmsar@rtm.gov.my **L.P:** Dir. Broadcasting:Tuan Haji Monshi Abdullah.
Addresses of local stns: Bangunan Penyiaran, 98700 Limbang – Bangunan Penyiaran, Jalan Brighton, 98000 Miri – Bangunan Penyiaran, 96009 Sibu – Bangunan Penyiaran, 95000 Sri Aman– Bangunan Penyiaran, Jalan Sommerville, Bintulu

Stations: Kajang (near Kuala Lumpur).

SW	kHz	kW	Netw.	SW	kHz	kW	Netw.
Kajang	9835	100	SF	Kajang	11665	100	W

FM (MHz)	Tx	SF	Red	1	2	4	5	kW
Belaga		105.4	107.8	103.8	104.6	106.2	107.0	0.1
Betong	a	94.4	97.8	92.8	93.6	95.2	96.0	0.1
Bintulu	b	93.7	100.5	87.9	90.3	98.5	99.3	1
Bintulu	c	94.7	96.7					1
Dalat			96.9					1
Kapit	d	92.7	89.9	90.7	91.9	88.1	88.9	0.1
Kuching	e	88.9	91.9	92.9	88.1	89.9	90.7	10
Lambir Hills	f	88.1	90.7	91.9	92.7	88.9	89.9	1
Lawas	g	97.5	100.5	94.7	96.7	98.5	99.3	1
Limbang	h	101.5	104.1	90.3	98.1	102.3	103.3	1

FM (MHz) Tx		SF	Red	1	2	4	5	kW
Limbang	j	100.0	107.7	95.3	99.2	106.0	106.8	0.1
Marudi	k	-	-	102.9	-	-	-	0.1
Miri	l	100.3	106.3	107.1	99.3	104.5	105.3	0.1
Mukah		89.9	92.3	88.3	89.1	90.7	91.5	0.5
Sarikei	m	91.5	89.2	87.9	90.3	92.3	93.6	10
Serian	n	94.8	97.2	98.0	94.0	95.6	96.4	0.5
Sibu	o	101.5	104.1	95.5	98.5	102.5	103.3	0.1
Song		95.7	99.0	-	-	-	-	
Sri Aman	q	100.3	106.3	107.3	98.9	92.3	105.3	1
Stapong	r	95.1	101.1	93.3	94.1	95.9	97.1	1

SF=Sarawak FM, Sd=Sada FM, W=Wai FM, Red=Red FM L=Limbang FM S=Sibu **National networks:** 1, 2, 4, 5: see RTM national sces

SW: 9835kHz: 2200-1600 (rel. Sarawak FM). 11630kHz (irreg.) & 11665kHz: 2200-1600 (rel. Wai FM).

FM: Additional local sce. freqs: Gunung Serapi (Kuching) 101.3MHz 10kW (Sada FM) & 106.1MHz (Wai FM), Bukit Ampangan 106.9MHz 0.5kW (Wai FM), Bukit Lima 87.6MHz 0.1kW (Sibu FM), Bukit Kayu Malam 94.6MHz 1kW (Sibu FM), Bukit Song 99.8MHz (Sibu FM), Bukit Kapit 94.3MHz 0.1kW (Sibu FM), Belaga 103.0MHz 0.1kW (Sibu FM), Bukit Singgalang 102.1MHz 1kW (Sibu FM), Mukah 98.7MHz 0.5kW (Sibu FM), Bukit Nyabau (Bintulu) 97.5MHz 1 kW (Bintulu FM), Lambir Hills 95.7MHz 1kW (Miri FM), Miri (RTM Miri) 98.0MHz 0.1kW (Miri FM), Bukit Temunduk 89.5MHz 1kW (RaSa FM), Bukit Mas 104 9MHz 1kW (Limbang FM).

Sites: a) Off. Spaoh b) Bukit Setiam c) Bukit Nyabau d) Bukit Kapit e) Gunung Serapi f) Bukit Lambir g) Bukit Tiong h) Bukit Mas j) Bukit Sagan Rudang, k) Bukit Kayu Malam, l) RTM Miri, m) Bukit Dabei, n) Bukit Ampangan o) Bukit Lima p) Bukit Song q) Bukit Temunduk r) Bukit Singgalang.

State networks: Sarawak FM in Malay 24h. **N.** (Kuching): 2200, 0400, 1000, 1400. **Red FM** 2200-1600, in Chinese: 2200-0200, 0700-1300; English: 0200-0700, 1300-1600. Educational prgs during school terms: MF 0100-0300. **N.** (Kuching): English 0400, 0700, 1300; Chinese 0000, 0801, 1000, 1245; Hakka 1030; Hokkien 1045. **Sada FM:** 2200-1600 in Iban. Relays Limbang FM Mon/Thurs 1300-1400. **Wai FM:** 2200-1600, in Bidayuh: 2200-0400 & 1000-1600; Kayan/Kenyah: 0400-1000. FM txs of all state networks relay Sarawak FM 1600-2200.

Local sces: Bintulu FM: 0100-1100 in Malay and Iban. **Limbang FM:** in Malay 0100-0400, 1000-1300; Lun Bawang (Murut) 0400-0700, also relayed via Kuching 7270kHz; Bisaya 0700-1000; Iban 1300-1400 also relayed by Sada FM Mon/Thurs. **Miri FM**: in Malay 0100-0400, 1000-1300, Chinese 0700-1000 (Tues/Thurs 0900), Iban 0400-0700, Tues/Thurs 0900-1000. **Sibu FM:** in Malay 0100-0400, 1000-1300, Chinese 0700-1000, Iban 0400-0700. **Sri Aman** (RaSa FM): in Malay, Iban. Local sces relay Sada FM in Iban 2200-0100 and from close of local prgrs until 1600, and relay Sarawak FM 1600-2200.

IS: A musical phrase (played on a native instrument, the Sape), alternating between A and F.

EXTERNAL SERVICE: RTM Overseas Sce
see International Broadcasting section.

AMP RADIO NETWORKS SDN. BHD. (ASTRO) (Comm.)
✉ All Asia Broadcast Centre, Technology Park Malaysia, Bukit Jalil, 57000 Kuala Lumpur **W:** www.ampradio.net
L.P: Exec. Dir: Datuk Borhanuddin Osman.

FM(MHz)	Tx	MY	ERA	Lite	Mix	Hitz	Sin	Mel
Alor Setar	a	99.7	103.6	104.4	91.0	92.8	97.1	106.5
Ipoh	b	100.6	103.7	101.5	94.3	92.7	96.9	98.5
Johor Bahru	c	95.4	104.5	94.6	99.1	97.6	87.8	98.4
Johor Bahru	d	-	-	-	-	-	-	103.3
Kota Bharu	e	102.3	103.3	104.3	94.6	92.8	93.8	99.8
KK	f	104.0	102.4	103.2	101.6	100.8	104.9	98.6
KT	g	101.2	102.8	105.9	98.3	94.8	97.5	104.0
KL/Selangor	h	101.8	103.3	105.7	94.5	92.9	96.7	103.0
Kuantan		101.1	98.0	104.7	94.1	93.2	97.2	100.0
Kuching	j	96.9	96.1	100.1	97.7	95.3	102.1	103.7
Langkawi	k	100.1	90.7	-	-	92.4	100.9	-
Melaka	l	106.4	90.3	92.2	91.1	93.0	96.0	107.3
Miri	m	103.2	101.3	-	102.4	105.8	87.7	-
Seremban	n	100.6	103.6	104.6	94.2	95.0	96.9	97.9
Taiping	o	100.2	95.2	89.3	91.3	93.6	96.4	104.9
Tapah	p	-	102.0	-	-	-	-	-

Prgrs: MY FM: Music channel in Mandarin & Cantonese. **ERA:** Contemporary Malaysian music channel in Malay. **Lite FM:** Easy listening music in English. **Mix FM:** Music and variety in English. **Hitz. fm:** Top 40 presented in English. **Sinar FM:** Malay oldies. **Melody FM:** Programming in Chinese (on test at editorial deadline). **THR.fm:** see Radio Lebuhraya Sdn Bhd below.

Sites: a) Gunung Jerai b) Bukit Keledang c) Gunung Pulai d) Metropolis Tower, JB e) Bukit Panau f) Kota Kinabalu (Bukit Kokol) g) Kuala

Terangganu (Bukit Jerung) h) Ulu Kali i) Bukit Pelindong j) Muara Tabuan k) Gunung Raya l) Gunung Ledang m) Tanjong Lobang n) Telapa Barok o) Bukit Larut p) Changkat Rembian. **TRP:** generally 2kW, exc. Sinar FM at sites e, f, j, k and l: 0.25kW.

BFM MEDIA (Comm.)
✉ 5.01 Wisma BU8, 11 Lebuh Bandar Utama, 47800 Petaling Jaya
☎ +60 3 7629 7112 **W:** www.bfm.my **L.P:** Exec. Dir: Malek Ali
BFM: Kuala Lumpur/Klang Valley (Gunung Ulu Kali) 89.9MHz, 24h business prgrs and music in English and Malay.

DIGITAL MEDIA BROADCASTING SDN. BHD. (Bernama News Agency) (Gov.)
✉ 15th Fl, Wisma Bernama, 28 Jalan 1/65A, off Jalan Tun Razak, 53300 Kuala Lumpur **W:** www.radio24.com.my
Bernama Radio24: Kuala Lumpur/Klang Valley (Bukit Nanas), 93.9MHz 1kW & Johor Bahru 107.5MHz 1kW, 24h in E and Malay.

HUSA NETWORK SDN. BHD. (Comm.)
✉ 4213C Tingkat 2, Lot 51 & 52, Seksyen 27, Jalan Kebun Sultan, 15350 Kota Bharu, Kelantan ☎ +60 97436661 🖷 +60 97436664
W: www.manis.fm
Manis FM: Kota Bharu (Bangunan Billion) 90.6MHz, Kuantan (Bukit Pelindong) 95.1MHz, Kuala Tcrengganu (Bukit Jerung) 102.0MHz. Prgrs in Malay. **TRP:** all sites 2kW.

INSTITUT KEFAHAMAN ISLAM MALAYSIA (Institute of Islamic Understanding) (Gov., Rlg.)
✉ No 2, Langgak Tunku, Off Jalan Duta, 50480 Kuala Lumpur
☎+60 362046273 🖷 +60 3620462779 **W:** www.ikim.gov.my/ikim.fm/
L.P: Dir. of Radio: Nik Roskiman bin Abdul Samad.

FM	Tx	MHz	FM	Tx	MHz
Alor Setar	a	89.0	Kuantan	g	89.5
Ipoh	b	102.7	Kuching	h	93.6
Johor Bahru	c	106.2	Klang Valley (KL)	i	91.5
Kota Bharu	d	89.9	Melaka	j	89.5
Kota Kinabalu	e	93.9	Negeri Sembilan	k	102.7
Kuala Terengganu	f	100.2			

Radio Ikim (IKIM.FM): 24h in Malay with limited Arabic and English. **Sites:** a) Gunung Jerai, b) Bukit Keledang, c) Gunung Pulai, d) Bukit Panau, e) Bukit Kokol, f) Bukit Besar, g) Bukit Pelindong 2, h) Pending, i) Bukit Cincin, j) Gunung Ledang, k) Bukit Telapa Burok. **TRP:** all sites 2kW.

KRISTAL HARTA SDN. BHD. (CATS RADIO) (Comm.)
✉ Lot 287, Jalan Bako, Petra Jaya, 93050 Kuching, Sarawak ☎ +60 82 311799 🖷 +60 82 254993 **W:** www.catsfm.my **L.P:** Chmn: Tan Sri Datuk Amar Haji Bujang Mohd Nor. GM: Haji Mohd Iskandar Hajni Mohd Nawawi.

FM	Tx location	MHz	FM	Tx location	MHz
Bintulu	Bukit Setiam	88.3	Sarikei	Bt. K. Malam	96.7
Kuching	Gunung Serapi	99.3	Sibu	Bukit Lima	88.4
Limbang	Bukit Mas	88.7	Sibu	Bt. Singgalang	99.9
Miri	Lambir Hills	93.3	Sri Aman	Bt. Temudok	88.7
Mukah	Mukah	97.9			

Prgr.: 24h in Malay, English and Iban. **TRP:** all sites 1kW.

MEDIA PRIMA BHD. (Comm.)
✉ Tingkat 2, South Wing, Sri Pentas, Persiaran Bandar Utama, 47800 Petaling Jaya, Selangor Darul Ehsan ☎ +60 3 77105022 🖷 +60 3 77107098 **W:** www.hotfm.com.my or www.flyfm.com.my or www. onefm.com.my
L.P: Head of Radio Ntwks: Ahmad Izham Omar

FM(MHz)	Tx	Hot	Fly	One	FM(MHz)	Tx	Hot	Fly	One
Alor Setar	a	88.2	99.1	87.8	Kuantan	h	92.4	87.6	100.4
Ipoh	b	104.5	87.9	87.6	Kuching		94.3	-	98.3
Johor Bahru	c	90.1	102.5	105.3	Melaka	j	104.3	94.0	88.1
Kota Bharu	d	105.1	107.4	-	Penang	k	-	89.9	-
Kota Kinabalu	e	87.7	-	95.7	Seremban	l	99.5	98.6	88.3
KL/Selangor	f	97.6	95.8	88.1	Taiping	m	90.5	-	-
KT	g	105.0	107.5	-					

Hot FM: 24h in Malay. Hot FM freqs are licensed to Synchrosound Studios Sdn Bhd. **Fly FM:** 24h in English/Malay. FlyFM freqs are licensed to Malaysian Airports (Sepang) Sdn Bhd. **One FM:** 24h in Mandarin and Cantonese.
Sites: a) Gunung Jerai exc. 99.1MHz: Wisma PKNK, Alor Setar b) Bukit Keledang c) Gunung Pulai exc. 105.3MHz: Taman Sentosa, JB (testing) d) Peringat e) Bukit Kokol f) Bukit Cincin exc. Hot FM: Ulu Kali g) Kuala Terengganu h) Bukit Pelindong i) Muara Tabuan j) Gunung Ledang k) Bukit Penara l) Bukit Telapa Burok m) Bukit Larut. **TRP:** Fly FM 0.25kW exc. Bukit Cincin: 2kW

RADIO LEBUHRAYA SDN. BHD. (THR.FM) (Comm.)
✉ 20th Flr, Plaza Berjaya, 12 Jalan Imbi, 55100 Kuala Lumpur
☎ +60 (3) 2433088 **W:** www.thr.fm Operated by AMP R. Networks.

FM Area	Tx	MHz	FM Area	Tx	MHz
Kota Bharu+	a	88.1	Negeri Sembilan	g	101.5
Kuantan+	b	88.8	No. Perak (Taiping)	h	102.1
Ce. Perak (Ipoh)	c	97.9	Kedah (Alor Setar)	i	102.4
KL/Selangor	d	99.3	Johor Bahru	j	103.7
So. Penang	e	99.3	KualaTerengganu	k	+106.8
Melaka	f	99.7			

D.Prgr: THR Raaga: Music and traffic information presented in Tamil: 24h.**'+'** = **THR Gegar**: Separate prgrs in Malay for East Coast
Sites: a) Bukit Panau b) Bukit Pelindong c) Upper Keledang 0.5kW d) Gunung Ulu Kali e) Bukit Penara 0.5kW f) Gunung Ledang g) Bukit Telapa Burok h) Bukit Larut 0.5kW i) Gunung Jerai j) Gunung Pulai k) Bukit Jerung. Affiliated with AMP Radio Networks (see above). **TRP:** 1kW, exc. where indicated under sites.

RIMAKMUR SDN. BHD. (Comm.)
✉ Tropicana City Office Towers, Level 2.01, No. 3, Jalan SS 20/27, 47400 Petaling Jaya, Selangor Darul Ehsan ☎ +60 3 78851188 🖷 +60 3 78851099 **W:** www.suriafm.com.my **L.P:** COO: Engku Emran Engku Zainal Abidin

FM	Tx	MHz	FM	Tx	MHz
Alor Setar	a	106.9	Kuala Terengganu	g	102.4
Ipoh	b	96	Kuantan	h	96.1
Johor Bahru	c	101.4	Melaka	i	88.5
Klang Valley (KL)	d	105.3	Seremban	j	107
Kota Bharu	e	106.1	Taiping	k	91.7
Kota Kinabalu	f	105.9			

Suria FM: 24h in Malay. **Sites:** a) Gunung Jerai b) Bukit Keledang c) Gunung Pulai d) Bukit Cincin 2kW e) Bukit Panau f) Bukit Kokol g) Bukit Besar h) Bukit Pelindong 2 i) Gunung Ledang j) Gunung Telapa Burok k) Bukit Larut. Kota Kinabalu 105.9MHz carries local prgrs at times.

STAR MEDIA GROUP (Comm.)
✉ Concorde Hotel, Jalan Sultan Ismail, Kuala Lumpur **W:** www.capitalfm.com.my
Capital FM: Kuala Lumpur/Klang Valley (Gunung Ulu Kali) 88.9MHz, 24h in English and Malay.

STAR RFM SDN. BHD. (Comm.)
✉ Tropicana City Office Towers Level 2.01 No 3, Jalan SS20/27, 47400 Petaling Jaya, Selangor Darul Ehsan ☎ +60 378851188 🖷 +60 378851099 **W:** www.988.com.my or www.red.fm **E:** info@starrfm.com.my or rfm988@silicon.net.my

FM(MHz)	Tx	Red	988	FM(MHz)	Tx	Red	988
Alor Setar	a	98.1	96.1	Kuantan	e	91.6	90.4
Ipoh	b	106.4	99.8	Melaka	f	98.9	98.2
Johor Bahru	c	92.8	99.9	Penang	g	107.6	94.5
KL/Selangor	d	104.9	98.8	Seremban	h		93.3

Red FM: 24h in English & Malay. **988** (jiu ba ba): 24h in Mandarin & Chinese dialects. **Sites:** a) Gunung Jerai b) Gunung Keledang c) Gunung Pulai d) Gunung Ulu Kali e) Bukit Pelindong f) Gunung Ledang g) Bukit Penara h) Bkt Telapa Burok i) Bukit Larut

SUARA JOHOR (Comm.)
✉ Bukit Pelangi, Jalan Pasir Pelangi, 80050 Johor Bahru, Johor ☎ +60 7 3314104 🖷 +60 7 3351104 **L.P:** CEO: Haji Bakhtiar Haji Arshad
BEST 104: Melaka & Segamat (Gunung Ledang) 94.8MHz, Johor Bahru (Gunung Pulai) 104.1MHz 10kW TRP, Kuala Lumpur/Selangor (Gunung Ulu Kali) 104.1MHz, Mersing (Bukit Tinggi) 102.5MHz.
D.Prgr: 24h (Malay & English music).

University stations:
Putra FM, ✉ Tingkat 2 Jabatan Komunikasi, Fakulti Bahasa Moden dan Komunikasi, Universiti Putra Malaysia, 43400 UPM Serdang, Selangor **W:** www.putrafm.upm.edu.my
Station: 90.7MHz 1kW: Mon-Fri 0200-1600 in Malay & English.
Radio UiTM (UFM), ✉ Level 13, Menara Ilmu Universiti Teknologi MARA, 40450 Bandaraya Shah Alam, Selangor **W:** www.uitm.edu.my/ufm **Station:** 93.6MHz 1kW

L.T: UTC +5h — **Pop:** 400,000 — **Pr.L:** Dhivehi (Maldivian) — **E.C:** 50Hz, 230V — **ITU:** MLD

MALDIVES BROADCASTING CORPORATION (MBC, Pub.)
✉ M Radio Bldg, Buruzu, Magu, Male ☎+960 3000200 🖷 +960

3317273 **W:** mbc.mv **E:** info@mbc.mv **L.P:** MD: Ibrahim Khaleel. Asst. Eng: Mohammed Hashim.
MW: 1449kHz 10kW. **"Dhivehi Raajjeyge Adu"** (VO Maldives) 1449kHz in Dhivehi: 24h. English: 1300-1315.
FM: Male 91.0MHz 1kW, 103.8MHz 20W, Addu 90.0MHz 500W, Foahmula 89.0MHz 0.5kW. **"Rajjee FM"** (music channel) on 91.0MHz.
R. Eke (music, sports & entertainment) on 103.8MHz: 1745-0020.
Ann: MW: "Mee Dhivehi Raajjeyge Adu".

Other stations:
Capital R, Male: 95.6MHz 1 kW – **Dhi FM,** Male: 95.2MHz. **W:** dhifm.mv – **Faraway FM,** Male: 96.9MHz – **H FM,** Male: 92.6MHz. **W:** hfm.com.mv

L.T: UTC — **Pop:** 13 million — **Pr.L:** French, Bambara, Peuls, Sonrhai, Sarakolé, Bobo, others — **E.C:** 50Hz, 220V — **ITU:** MLI

CONSEIL SUPÉRIEUR DE LA COMMUNICATION (CSC)
✉ B.P. 116, Bamako ☎+223 20232101

OFFICE DE RADIODIFUSION TÉLÉVISION DU MALI (ORTM, Gov.)
✉ B.P. 171, Rue del Marne 287, Bamako ☎+223 20212019 🖷 +223 20214205 **W:** www.ortm.ml **Email:** ortm@ortm.ml
L.P: DG: Sidiki Konate. DG Adj: Nouhoum Traore. Dir. Radio: Seydou Baba Traore. Dir. Rural Radio: Mme Gnouma Keita. Dir. Research & New Tech.: Gaoussou Singare.
SW: Bamako (Kati) 50/100kW

kHz	Times	kHz	Times
5995	0555-0800, 1800-2400	9635	0800-1800

FM:
National R. Bamako: 92.0MHz 1 kW + 47 txs of 0.5/0.25kW
Regional R. (Channel 2)

Location	MHz	kW	Location	MHz	kW
Mopti	94.4	10	Ségou	96.8	1
Bamako	95.2	1	Sikasso	98.3	1
Kayes	95.4	10			

National R. (Radio Mali) in French/Arabic/English/Bambara/others: SW & FM. **D.Prgr:** 0555-2400. **N. in English:** Sat 1905-1920.
Regional R. (Channel 2) on FM only: **D.Prgr:** 0800-1945.
Ann: "Vous écoutez l'office de Radiodiffusion-Télévision Malienne émettant de Bamako". **E:** "This is Bamako, Mali Radio Telecommunications". **IS:** Guitar.
R. Rurale on FM in Kayes 89.1MHz, Kolondieba 93.7MHz, Koutiala and Macina.

Other stations in Bamako:
R. Patriote FM 88.1MHz – **R. Canal 2000:** 90.7MHz. **W:** membres.lycos.fr/canal2000 – **R. Mirador** 91.1MHz – **La Voix de la Verité** 91.5MHz – **Fréquence 3** 93.8MHz – **R. Tabalé** 94.3MHz – **R. Guintan** 94.7MHz – **R. Benkan** 97.1MHz – **R.Liberté** 97.7MHz. **W:** www.comfm.com/live/radio/radioliberte **E:** liberte@mtelecom-mali.net – **R. Bamankan** 100.3MHz – **R. Klédu** FM 101.2MHz – **R Jakafo** 100.7MHz – **R. Kayira** FM 104.4MHz – **R. Voix de l'Islam** 107.4MHz.
RFI Afrique: Bamako 98.5MHz. Gao 92.1MHz, Kayes 102.2MHz, Mopti 97.7MHz, Segou 93.6MHz, Sikasso 95.0MHz.
Africa No. 1: Bamako 102MHz (see main entry under Gabon).
BBC African Service: Bamako 88.9MHz.
China R. Int relay station: see International Radio section

L.T: UTC +1h (31 Mar-27 Oct: +2h) — **Pop:** 405,000 — **Pr.L:** English, Maltese — **E.C:** 50Hz, 240V — **ITU:** MLT

MALTA BROADCASTING AUTHORITY (Regulatory Authority)
✉ 7 Mile-end Rd, Hamrun HMR1719 ☎ +356 21221281, 21247908 🖷 +356 21240855 **E:** info@ba-malta.org **W:** www.ba-malta.org **L.P:** Chairman: Mr. Anthony J. Tabone, Chief Exec: Dr. Pierre Cassar

PUBLIC BROADCASTING SERVICES LTD
✉ 75, St. Luke's Road, Gwardamangia MSD 09 ☎ +356 21225051 🖷 +356 21244601 **E:** info@tvm.com.mt **W:** www.tvm.com.mt/radio
L.P: Head of News: Natalino Fenech. Chief Executive: Anton Attard, Executive Engineer: Costantino Abela
RADIO MALTA
MW: Bizbizja 999kHz 5kW

FM: Bizbizja 93.7MHz 8kW, 107.5MHz 0.025kW
D.Prgr: 24h. **N:** 0600, 0700, 0900, 1100, 1400, 1700, 2130 (BBC WS night relay). BBC News Mon-Fr 0600-0640, 0900, 1100, 1500 - Sat 0600-0640, 0900, 1500 - Sun 0600-0640, 1500
MAGIC 91.7: FM: 91.7MHz 8kW, 24h.
MALTIN BISS: FM: 106.6MHz 8kW, 24h (live coverage of debates in the Maltese Parliament and maltese music)

DIGI B NETWORK LTD.
136, Alwetta Street, Mosta MST4508 ☎ +356 27420570 **E:** info@digibnetwork.com **W:** http://www.dab.com.mt **LP:** Managing director: Sergio D'Amico. **DAB+:** 6A, 6C, 12A, LP. Bouquet includes local, gov., and international stations

COMMERCIAL STATIONS:
89.7 BAY, Eden Place, St. George's Bay STJ3310 ☎ +356 23710800 +356 23710845 **E:** 897@bay.com.mt **W:** www.bay.com.mt. - **FM:** 89.7MHz 8kW. **LP:** Station Manager: Kevin DeCesare Jnr - Sales Manager: Simon Baldacchino Barthet – **CAMPUS FM,** University Broadcasting Services, Old Humanities Building, University of Malta, Tal-Qroqq Msida MSD 06 ☎ +356 21333313 +356 21314485. **E:** campusfm@um.edu.mt **W:** http://campusfm.um.edu.mt - **FM:** 103.7MHz 8kW. **LP:** Station Manager: Rev. Joseph Borg. Also relay of BBC WS. – **CALYPSO 101.8,** 28 New Street in Valletta Road, Luqa ☎ +356 21578022 +356 21578026 **E:** info@calypsoradio **W:** www.calypsoradio.com - **FM:** 101.8MHz 8kW. **LP:** Director: Frank Camilleri – **R. 101,** 2 Triq Herbert Ganado, Pieta' PTA1450 ☎ +356 25965407 +356 21240261 **E:** news@media.link.com.mt. **W:** www.radio101.com.mt - **FM:** 101.0MHz 8kW, 95.5MHz 300W. (Operated by Maltese Nationalist Party's) – **R. MARIJA,** Kunvent Patrijiet Dumnikani, Misrah San Duminku, Rabat RBT 06 ☎ +356 21453105, 21453106 +356 21453103. **E:** info.mal@radiomaria.org **W:** http://www.radjumarija.org - **FM:** 102.3MHz 8kW, 107.8MHz 200W. **LP:** Director: Fr. Charles Fenech – **RTK, MEDIA CENTRE,** Archdiocese of Malta and Diocese of Ghawdex, Triq Nazzjonali, Blata-Badja HMR02 ☎ +356 2569 9100, +356 2569 9158 +356 2569 9151, +356 2569 9160 **E:** info@rtk.org.mt **W:** www.rtk.org.mt - **FM:** 103.0MHz 8kW, Ghawdex 97.8MHz 400W, Malta 97.6MHz 250W. **LP:** Chairman: Franco Azzopardi (fazzopardi@mediacentre.org.mt). General Manager: Michael Francalanza (mfrancalanza@mediacentre.org.mt). Mktg mngr: Sylvana Magro. Format: news, educational, entertainment – **SMASH R.,** 4 Thistle Lane, Paola PLA 19 ☎ +356 21667777 +356 21697830 **E:** smash@vol.net.mt **W:** www.smashmalta.com - **FM:** 104.6MHz 8kW. **LP:** Head: Jesmond Saliba. – **SUPER 1,** A28B, Industrial Estate, Marsa, LQA 06 ☎ +35625682568 +35621248249 **E:** radio@super1.com **W:** www.one.com.mt - **FM:** 92.7MHz 8kW, 88.2MHz 200W, 88.0MHz 25W. **LP:** Managing Director: Dr. Michael Vella-Haber, Senior Manager Broadcasting: Ms. Ruth Vella, Senior Manager Radio: Mr. Ray Azzopardi. (Operated by Maltese Labour Party) – **VIBE FM,** Triq Tas-Sliema, Kappara, San Gwann ☎ +356 21385887 +356 21383826 **E:** info@vibefm.com.mt **W:** www.vibefm.com.mt. - **FM:** 88.7MHz 8kW. **LP:** Head: Justin Chircop – **XFM 100.2,** 111, Annunciation Street, St. Venera, SVR 1021 ☎ +356 21230228 +356 21378167 **E:** news@xfmmalta.com **W:** www.xfmmalta.com - **FM:** 100.2MHz 8kW. **LP:** Station manager: Donny Hughes. Marketing Manager: Antonella Vassallo

Established Community Stations (all MHz):
96.1 Vilhena FM: 96.1, Bastjanizi FM: 95.0, Big FM: 107.1, BKR Radio: 94.5, Christian Light Radio: 105.4, Deejays Radio: 95.6, Energy FM: 96.4, Fantasy Radio: 104.1, Kiss FM: 89.3, La Salle Radio: 99.4, Lehen il-Belt Gorgjana: 105.6, Lehen il-Belt Victoria: 104.0, Power FM: 90.4, Radio Sacro Cuor: 105.2, Radju Bambina: 98.3, Radio City Valletta: 107.6, Radio Galaxy: 105.0, Radju Hal Tarxien: 99.0, Radju Hompesch: 90.0, Radju Katidral: 90.9, Radju Kottoner: 98.0, Radju Lehen il-Guzeppini: 89.1, Radju Lehen il-Qala: 106.3, Radju Luminaria: 106.9, Radju Prekursur: 99.3, Radju Santa Katerina: 90.6, Radju Sokkors: 95.1, Radju St Vincent de Paule: 92.2, Radju Vilhena: 106.0, Radju Xeb-er-ras: 90.8, South End Radio: 91.0, Three Cities Radio: 99.4

Temporary Community Stations (all MHz):
Temporary licences for up to 2 years and powers of 0.25-1W: Banda Fgura FM: 93.1, District Convention of Jehovah's Witnesses: 108.0, Elenjani FM: 95.8, Kottoner 98 FM: 98.0, Lehen il-Karmelitani: 101.4, MMG FM: 97.5, Pure-Gold Christian Radio: 97.8, Radju 12th May: 96.5, Radju 15 t'Awwissu: 98.3, Radju Bartilmew: 103.3, Radju Belt Rebbieha: 97.0, Radju Elenjani: 95.8, Radju Festa: 99.2, Radju Gilju Rebbieh: 105.5, Radju Kazin Banda San Filep: 106.3, Radju Lauretana: 96.5, Radju Lehen il-Guzeppini: 89.1, Radju Leonardo: 105.2, Radju Margerita: 96.1, Radju Marija Assunta: 98.9, Radju Maria Bambina: 90.2, Radju MMG: FM 97.5, Radju Pawlin: 97.2, Radju San Gwann: 96.9, Radju Sant'Andrija: 88.4, Radju Santa Venera: 91.2, Radju Vizitazzjoni: 92.4, Tal-Gilju FM:

95.4, Trinitarji FM: 89.3, VSB FM 103.40: 103.4

MARSHALL IS (USA associated)

L.T: UTC +12h — **Pop:** 64,522 — **Pr.L:** English, Kajin Majol— **E.C:** 60Hz, 110/220V — **ITU:** MHL

RADIO MARSHALLS (Gov/Comm)
PO Box 19, Majuro 96960 ☎+692 625 8413. Studio ☎ + 692 625 8411 **E:** v7ab@ntamar.net
L.P: GM: Antari Elbon, PD: Nixon Elisha, CE: Jambre Ralpho
MW: V7AB 1098kHz 25kW **FM:** 97.9MHz **D.Prgr:** 1900 (Sun 2000)-1130 **News:** Local bulletins and BBC hourly.

Other Stations:

MW	kHz	kW	Station			
1) Kwajalein	1224	1	AFN			

FM	MHz	kW	Station	FM	MHz	kW	Station
2) Majuro	95.5		V7MI	1) Kwajalein	101.1	1	AFN
6) Majuro	96.5	0.03	WSO-FM	1) Kwajalein	102.1	1	AFN
9) Roi-Namur	97.9	0.01	KVZI-FM	4) Majuro	102.5		V7DJ
5) Majuro	98.5	0.25	R. Australia	3) Majuro	104.1		V7AA
1) Kwajalein	99.9	1	AFN	8) Majuro	105.0		V7WU
7) Majuro	99.9		V7BNJ				

Addresses and other information:
1) Armed Forces Network, Box 23 APO San Francisco CA 96555 **MW:** National Public Radio via satellite from Washington DC **FM:** Country Music (99.9), Active Rock Music (101.1) Hot AC Music (102.1) via satellite from AFRS. **D.Prgr:** 24h Local studio facilities are available, local breakfast show on 101.1 FM – **2)** Pacific Media Services, Majuro 96960 ☎+692 625 2911 **E:** v7emon@ntamar.net **L.P:** Mgr: Fred Pedro, CE: Benitito Kom **ID:** "V7Emon" [= 'V7Good'] – **3)** Majuro Independent Baptist Church, PO Drawer H, Majuro 96960-1008 ☎+692 625 3141 +692 625 3141 **E:** v7aafm@ntamar.net **ID:** "The Change 104.1 FM" – **4)** Ace Broadcasting, Majuro 96960 **LP:** Mgr: Harry Doulatram ☎+692 247 8735 – **5)** 24h English for the Pacific stream satellite rel. from Melbourne – **6)** National Weather Radio, Majuro 96960. Live and recorded local weather and emergency information for the Majuro atoll area, 24h – **7)** Bukot Non Jesus Church [Assembly of God Part Two], Majuro 96960 ☎+692 625 7914 **E:** eagle1@ntamar.net **LP:** Pastor Paul & Laura Hensene **ID:** 'V7Eagle' – **8)** WUTMI-FM, Women United Together Marshall Islands, PO Box 105, Majuro 96960 **W:** www.wutmirmi.com **Prgr:** women's prgrs 10.5 hours daily **FPL:** AM coverage beyond Majuro – **9)** P.O. Box 8199, Roi Namur RMI, APO AP 96557 **E:** roiradio@hotmail.com

MARTINIQUE (France)

L.T: UTC -4h — **Pop:** 409,000 — **Pr.L:** French, Creole — **E.C:** 50Hz, 220V — **ITU:** MRT

MARTINIQUE PREMIÈRE (groupe France Télévision)
La Clairière, BP 662, 97263 Fort-de-France Cédex ☎+596 596595200 +596 596595280 **W:** martinique.la1ere.fr/radio
L.P: Dir. Régional: Jean-Philippe Pascal, CE: Charles Diony
MW: Lamentin 1310kHz 5kW
FM: 92.0/93.0/93.2/94.5/100.9MHz
D.Prgr: 24h. **Main N:** 1000, 1100, 1200, 1700, 2000. Rel. France-Inter & France Info

RADIO CARAÏBES INTERNATIONAL MARTINIQUE (Comm)
2 Boulevard de la Marne, 97200 Fort-de-France ☎+596 596639870 +596 596632659 **W:** www.rcimartinique.fm **LP:** Dir: José Anelka. Editor-in-Chief: Jean Philippe Ludon CE: Guy Lenormand
FM: 91.2/92.6/98.7/103.0/104.6MHz
D.Prgr: 24h. **N:** on the h. (rel. Europe 1). **Ann.:** RCI

Other FM stations in Fort-de-France (in MHz):
88.1 Radio Liberté – 88.9 FM Plus – 89.3 Radio Sud Est – 90.1 Radio Inter Tropical – 90.9 France Inter – 91.6 Radio Esperance – 92.4 Radio Transat – 92.8 Radio Actif – 93.6 RFA Radio Frequence Atlantique – 94.0 Radio Bel'Age – 94.9 Radio APAL – 95.3 Radio Fusion – 95.8 France Inter – 96.2 Radio Imagine – 96.7 Nostalgie – 97.1 Trace FM – 97.5 RLDM Radio Lévé Doubout Matinik – 98.1 Super Radio – 99.1 REM Radio Evangile Martinique – 99.5 Radio Saint Louis – 100.6 Radio Canal Antilles & Radio France Internationale – 101.6 Chérie FM – 102.0 Ekla FM – 103.4 RBR Radio Banlieue Relax – 103.9 Radio Liberté – 104.4 NRJ – 104.8 Radio Mouv' Martinique – 105.5 Campus FM – 105.7 Super Radio – 106.2 Radio AS & Radio France Internationale – 107.3 Radio Maxxi – 107.6 Nostalgie

MAURITANIA

L.T: UTC — **Pop:** 3.3 million — **Pr.L:** Arabic, French, Poular, Soninké, Wolof — **E.C:** 50Hz, 220V — **ITU:** MTN

HAUTE AUTORITÉ DE LA PRESSE ET DE L'AUDIOVISUEL (HAPA)
✉ BP 3192, Ilot C Lot 406, Tevragh Zeina, Nouakchott ☎+222 45241088 🖷 +222 45241051 **W:** hapa.mr **L.P:** Dir: M. Imam Cheikh Ould Ely.

RADIO MAURITANIE (RM, Gov.)
✉ Av. Gamal Abdel Nasser 387, BP 5522 , Nouakchott ☎+222 45253 266 🖷 +222 4525 4069 **E:** rm@mauritania.mr **L.P:** DG: Yeslem Ben Abdem.
MW: Nouakchott 783kHz 50kW.
SW: Nouakchott 7245kHz 100kW (inactive).
FM (MHz): Nouakchott 93.3 2kW, Nouadhibou 94.7 + 98.0 (local st.), Néma 98.5, Aïoun 94.7, Kiffa 96.7, Akjoujt 98.7, Aleg 96.1 1kW + 90.8 1kW (local stn), Atar 98.5, Kaedi 98.3, Rosso 96.7 + 98.0 (local st.), Sélibabi 97.7, Tidjikja 98.5, Zouérate 96.7, Barkéol 100. Where no power level is shown, stns are 0.1kW.
Youth R: Nouakchott 98.0MHz. **F.PI:** Quran prgr.
D.Prgr. in Arabic/French/others: 24h. N: Arabic: 0700, 1100(not Fri), 1200, 1300, 1500(not Fri), 1600(Fri), 2200, 2400. French: 0731, 1430, 1800v. **Ann:** A: "Huna Nouakchott, Idha'at al-Gumhuriyati al-Islamiyya al-Mauritaniya". F: "Ici Nouackchott, R. Mauritanie". **IS:** Mauritanian guitar.

Other Stations:
MFM: Nouadhibou 101.1MHz.
BBC Arabic Sce: Nouakchott 106.9MHz, Nouadhibou 102.4MHz.
China R. Int: Nouakchott 95.7MHz.
DW/Monte-Carlo Doualiya, Nouakchott: 90.2MHz 1kW.
RFI Afrique: Nouakchott 88.0MHz
Monte-Carlo Doualiya: Nouakchott 90.2MHz

MAURITIUS

L.T: UTC +4h — **Pop:** 1.3 million — **Pr.L:** English, French, 6 Indian langs, Chinese — **E.C:** 50Hz, 240V — **ITU:** MAU (Rodrigues: ROD)

INDEPENDENT BROADCASTING AUTHORITY
✉ 5 De Courson Str, Curepipe Rd, Forest Side **W:** iba.gov.mu **E:** iba@intnet.mu

MAURITIUS BROADCASTING CORPORATION (MBC, Pub)
✉ 1 Louis Pasteur Str, Forest Side ☎+230 6021200 🖷 +230 6757332 **W:** mbc.intnet.mu **E:** mbc@mbc.intnet.mu **L.P:** DG: Dhanjay Callikan. Ag. CE: Cyril Nankoo.
MW: RM1, R.Maurice, Malherbes: 684kHz 10kW **D.Prgr:** 24h in French. Relay of KOOL FM during daytime and VOA English during local nighttime. **N** on the h. **English:** 0500-0515.
RM2, R.Mauritius, Malherbes: 819kHz 10kW **D.Prgr:** 24h in Indian languages.
R. Rodrigues, Citronelle: 1206kHz 1kW **Prgr:** Relay of RM1. Local prgr. 1400-1415. **FM**(MHz): 97.3 0.5kW 24h.

MBC FM	Location	MHz	kW
Kool FM	Signal Mt.	91.7	0.5
Kool FM	Plaine Wilhelms	97.3	1.0
Kool FM	Jurançon	89.3	0.5
Taal FM	Signal Mt.	98.2	0.5
Taal FM	Plaine Wilhelms	94.0	1
Taal FM	Jurançon	95.6	0.5
One World FM	Signal Mt.	94.9	0.5
One World FM	Plaine Wilhelms	90.8	1
One World FM	Jurançon	92.4	0.5

Other stations:
R. Plus, Labourdonnais Str, Port Louis. **FM**(MHz): Centre 87.7, North 88.6, South 98.9 – **R. One,** Brown Sequard Str, Port Louis. **FM**(MHz): Centre 100.8, North 101.7, South 102.4 – **Top FM Skywave: FM**(MHz): Centre 104.4, North 105.7, South 106.0.
BBC World Sce: Bigara 1575kHz 2kW. 24h.
RFI Afrique: Port-Louis 100.8MHz, Rodrigues 93.2MHz

MAYOTTE (France)

L.T: UTC +3h — **Pop:** 200,000 — **Pr.L:** French, Mahorian — **E.C:** 50Hz, 220V — **ITU:** MYT

MAYOTTE LA PREMIÈRE
✉ B.P. 103, Rue de jardins, 97610 Dzaoudzi ☎+262 269601017 🖷 +262 269601852 **W:** mayotte.la1ere.fr **L.P:** DG: Georges Chow-Toun.
MW: Pamandzi 1458kHz 5kW
FM: Dzaoudzi 91.0MHz 0.1kW, M'lima Combani 92.0MHz 0.5kW, Kanikeli-Choungui 101.3MHz 0.5kW, Mtsanboro-Madjabalini 103.2MHz 0.5kW.
D.Prgr in French/Mahorian: Local prgr. Mon-Sat 0000-1900, Sun 0145-1830. Relays RFI overnight.
Ann: "Vous êtes à l'écoute de Mayotte Première".
IS: Melody on guitar.

Europe 2: Boueni 90.2MHz, Mamoudzou 99.1MHz, Pamandzi 97.7MHz
France-Inter: Dzaoudzi 101.0MHz 24h

MEXICO

L.T: UTC -6h (DST*: -5h). BS, CH, NA, SN, SO: UTC -7h (DST* exc. SO: -6h); BC: UTC -8h (DST**: -7h) *) 7 Apr-27 Oct **) 10 Mar-3 Nov (**NB:** the latter DST period also applies to QR, and certain towns/areas along the border with the USA) — **Pop:** 110 million — **Pr.L:** Spanish — **E.C:** 60Hz, 127V — **ITU:** MEX — **Intl. dialling code:** 52

COMISION FEDERAL DE TELECOMUNICACIONES (COFETEL)
Unidad de Sistemas de Radio y Televisión
✉ Bosque de Radiatas # 44, Col. Bosques de las Lomas, 05120 Del. Cuajimalpa, México, D.F ☎ +52 55 5015 4000

DIRECCION DE RADIO
Departamento de Asignación de Frecuencias
✉ Eugenia 197, Col.Narvarte, 03020 Delg. Benito Juárez México, D.F ☎ +52 55 5015 4785

Call XE–,° = also on SW, * = inactive, (r) = repeater, v = varying fq, d = daytime operation. The letters preceding the stn number indicate the state. Addresses are listed by state in alphabetical order. Hrs of tr usually 24h – see address section for variations.

MW Call	kHz	kW	Station, location
BC19) SURF	540	0.1	R. Zion, Tijuana
CH15) TX	540	5	La TX/La Ranchera de Paquime, Nuevo Casas Grandes
CS22) MIT	540	5/1	LV de BalúnCanán, Comitán
ME09) WF	540	20/2.5	La Poderosa, Ixtapaluca
NL01) WA	540	1	W R., Monterrey: (r. XEW 900kHz)
SL10) WA	540	150	W R., San Luis Potosí: (r. XEW 900kHz)
SN13) HS	540	5/2.5	La Mejor, Los Mochis: (r. XHHS 90.9)
CH01) PL	550	5/0.15	La Super Estación, Cd. Cuauhtémoc
GR01) ACD	550	1	Los 40 Principales, Acapulco
JL23) ZK	550	2.5/1	Poder 55, Tepatitlán
NA14) TNC	550	25/0.15	R. Nayarit, Tepic
OX01) HLL	550	1.5/0.25	Los 40 Principales, Salina Cruz: (r. XHHLL 97.1)
VE01) KL	550	5/0.25	W Radio, Xalapa: (rel. XHKL 93.7)
YU01) QW	550	2/0.35	Mexicanísima, Mérida
CO07) GIK	550	1.4/0.25	La Acerera, Monclova
CS06) IN	560	2/0.25	LV del Valle, Cintalapa
DF01) OC	560	0.75/0.5	R. Chapultepec, México
DG05) SRD	560	10/0.1	La Tremenda, Santiago Papasquiaro
JL33) MZA	560	10/1	Fórmula Melódica del Pacífico, Manzanillo
QR13) QAA	560	5/1	La Poderosa, Chetumal
SO37) YO	560	1/0.5	R. Lobo, Huatabampo
ZC12) XZ	560	5/1	Ke Buena, Zacatecas
CO01) TJ	570	1	Estereo Vida, Torreón
MI01) LQ	570	2/1.7	R. 5-70, Morelia
NA10) TD	570	5/1	R. Red, Tecuala
NL02) BJB	570	5/0.5	R. 570, Monterrey
OX02) OA	570	2/2.5	O-A R. Mexicana, Oaxaca
PU13) VJP	570	0.5	R. Xicotepec, Xicotepec de Juárez
SO26) UA	570	0.5/0.25	Tu Expresión, Caborca
TB01) VX	570	10/2.5	La Grande de Tabasco, Villahermosa
YU09) ME	570	2.5	La Poderosa del Oriente, Valladolid: (rel. XHME 91.9)
CH08) FI	580	5/0.7	R. Mexicana, Chihuahua
CO02) MU	580	5/0.5	La Rancherita del Aire, Piedras Negras
CS01) UE	580	1/0.25	La Más Perrona, Tuxtla Gutiérrez: (r. XHUE 99.3)
JL02) AV	580	10/1	Canal 58, Guadalajara
QE08) UAQ	580	0.25	R. Universidad, Querétaro: (r. XHUAQ 89.5)
QR01) YI	580	1/0.25	Mix FM, Cancún: (rel. XHYI 93.1)
SO06) HO	580	1/0.25	La Fuerza de la Palabra, Cd.Obregón
TM01) HP	580	1	La Más Prendida, Cd.Victoria
VE02) DZ	580	1/0.5	Imagen R, Córdoba
CS02) ZZZ	590	5/1	Triple Z, Tapachula
DF02) PH	590	25/10	Sabrosita 590, México

MW Call	kHz	kW	Station, location
DG01) E	590	1	R. Fórmula, Primera Cad., Durango: (r. XHE 105.3)
GJ10) GTO	590	10/0.25	Tu Recuerdo, León: (r XHGTO 95.9)
JL31) CJU	590	10/1	La Explosiva 590, Puerto Vallarta
SO01) BH	590	1	La Mejor, Hermosillo: (r. XHBH 98.5)
TM02) FD	590	5/0.5	La Mejor, Reynosa
VE17) OM	590	1	R. Fórmula, Coatzacoalcos
CO01) DN	600	1	La Mexicana, Torreón
CS24) OCH	600	10/1	K'in Radio, Ococingo
GR03) BB	600	5/1	La Comadre, Puros Éxitos, Acapulco: (r. ZHBB 101.5)
JL36) LAZ	600	2.5	La Mejor, Cd.Guzmán
MI02) TA	600	1	600 Solo Hits, Zitácuaro
NL03) MN	600	1/0.5	La Regiomontaña, Monterrey
SL16) CV	600	5/1	La Gran Compañía, Cd.Valles
SN20) HW	600	5/1	La Kañona, Rosario
YU02) Z	600	20/1	R. Fórmula, Segunda Cad., Mérida: (r. XHZ 105.1)
CO03) BX	610	5/0.5	La Primera, Sabinas
CO26) SAC	610	1	R. Lobo, Saltillo
MI03) UF	610	5/1	Variadísima, Uruapan: (r XHUF 100.5)
OX03) KZ	610	5/1	La Poderosa, Tehuantepec
SN02) GS	610	1/0.5	La GS/La Ley, Guasave
VE01) JA	610	0.1	Ke Buena, Xalapa
ZC01) EL	610	5/0.1	El Super Canal 610, Fresnillo
YU04) UM	610	10	Candela FM, Valladolid: (r. XHUM 92.7)
BC09) SS	620	5	ESPN Deportes, Ensenada
CH36) BU	620	5/1	La Norteñita, Chihuahua
DF03) NK	620	50/5	R. 6-20, México (Ecatepec ME)
DG02) CK	620	1/0.5	R. 6-20, Durango
NA01) OO	620	5/1	W Radio, Tepic
SL14) WZ	620	2.5/0.5	R. Novedades, San Luis Potosí
TB13) HGR	620	2.5/1	R. Fórmula 620, Villahermosa
TM30) GH	620	1/0.25	La Lupe, Reynosa: (r. XHCAO 89.1)
GR27) JR	630	5	Coral 630, Zihuatanejo
JL34) JB	630	10/0.5	Jalisco R., Guadalajara
NL03) FB	830	10	F-B La - "Estación que da las noticias", Monterrey
QR08) CCQ	630	0.5	Frecuencia Turquesa, Cancún: (r. XHCCQ 91.5)
SN03) OPE	630	5/1	Exa, Mazatlán: (r. XHOPE 89.7)
SO02) FX	630	1/0.25	Doble X, Guaymas
TM27) ERO	630	1/0.15	R. Tamaulipas, Altamira
VE03) FU	630	10/0.75	La Nueva Voz, Cosamaloapan: (r. XHFU 103.3)
CH27) JUA	640	5	Milenio TV, Cd.Juárez
CH29) HHI	640	10/1	R. Uno/La Número Uno, Hidalgo del Parral
CS03) WM	640	5/1	Suprema 64, San Cristóbal de las Casas
HG04) NQ	640	10	N-Q La Superestación, Tulancingo: (r. XHNQ 90.1)
OX26) HDI	640	5/1	Aro-AM, Huajuapán de León
TM19) TAM	640	1/0.25	Ke Buena, Cd.Victoria: (r. XHTAM 96.1)
ZC09) YQ	640	5/1	La Tremenda, Fresnillo: (r. XHYQ 98.5)
CO13) RCG	650	5	R. Vida, Cd. Acuña
GR21) CHH	650	5/1	Capital Máxima, Chilpancingo: (r. XHCHH 97.1)
JL03) EJ	650	10/2.5	La Z, Puerto Vallarta
MI04) ZM	650	5/1	La Zamorana, Zamora
OX12) PX	650	5/0.2	LV de Ángel/R. Fórmula, Puerto Ángel
SL04) IY	650	1	Espectacular, Río Verde
SN04) TNT	650	5/1	W R., R. 65, Los Mochis
SO32) VSS	650	1/0.25	R. 13, Hermosillo
TB15) VILL	650	1/0.1	650 Notícias, Villahermosa
YU13) VG	650	1	R. Fórmula, Primera Cad, Mérida: (r. XHVG 94.5)
AG01) EY	660	50/10	6-60 La Consentida, Aguascalientes
BS06) SJC	660	0.25	KVOZ, San José del Cabo
CH04) ACB	660	5	R. 6-60/La Tremenda N:o Uno, Cd. Delicias
DF04) DTL	660	50	R. Ciudadana, México
DG01) WX	660	1/0.5	R. Mexicana, Durango: (r. XHWX 98.1)
NL02) FZ	660	10/1	ABC R., Monterrey
OX04) YG	660	1/0.5	R. 660/R. Fiesta Mexicana, Matías Romero
QR09) CPR	660	1	R. Chan Santa Cruz - "LV de los Mayas", Felipe Carillo Puerto
TM20) AR	660	5	La Mexicana, Reynosa: (r. XHAR 101.7)
CO04) TOR	670	5/0.5	R. Ranchito, Torreón
CS10) OB	670	5/0.5	La Máquina Musical, Pichucalco
JL01) IS	670	5/1	La Rancherita Consentida, Cd.Guzmán
NA08) LH	670	5/0.1	La Zeta 670, Acaponeta
QE01) OG	670	1/0.1	ABC R. 670, Querétaro
VE38) SIC	670	1/0.1	Tu Recuerdo, Córdoba: (r. XHSIC 96.1)
CH08) FO	680	1/0.25	Extasis Digital, Chihuahua
CS04) KQ	680	5/3	La Mexicana, Tapachula
GJ25) LG	680	10/3	LG, La Grande, León
GR15) CHG	680	5/2.5	Ke Buena, Chilpancingo: (r. XHCHG 107.1)
OX27) OAX	680	5	Aro AM "la radio que une a Oaxaca", Oaxaca
PU01) FJ	680	1/0.1	La Consentida, Tezīutlán: (r. 95.1 XHFJ)
SN05) ORO	680	1/0.5	La Mera Jefa, Guasave
SO35) SON	680	1	Éxtasis, Hermosillo
YU03) PY	680	2.5/1	Retro 103 FM, Mérida: (r. XHPY 103.5)
BC01) WW	690	78/50	W R. América, LV del Pueblo, Tijuana
CL03) CS	690	5/1	La Mejor, Manzanillo
DF08) N	690	50/5	La 69, México
MI10) XL	690	2.5	La Ley, Pátzcuaro
NL04) RG	690	10/1	La Deportiva 6-90/La R-G, Monterrey
SN19) ST	690	2/0.25	La Invasora, Mazatlán
VE07) AFA	690	2.5	Ke Buena, Coatzacoalcos: (r. XHAFA 99.3)
ZC03) MA	690	50/2	M-A/La Madre de Todas, Fresnillo
CA09) XPUJ	700	5	LV del Corazón de la Selva, X'pujil
CH25) GD	700	5/0.25	La Poderosa, Hidalgo del Parral
JL12) DKR	700	1	R. Red, Guadalajara
MI02) LX	700	5	La Ke Buena, Zitácuaro
SO44) ETCH	700	5d	LV de los Tres Ríos, Etchojoa
TB12) RV	700	2.5/0.5	Yo FM, Villahermosa: (r. XHRVI 106.3)
VE14) VC	700	2.5/0.1	La Más Buena, Córdoba: (r. XHEVC 104.5)
CH05) DP	710	7/0.1	La Ranchera de Cuauhtémoc, Cd.Cuauhtémoc
CL01) RL	710	1	La R-L de Colima, Colima: (r. XHRL 98.9)
CO04) LZ	710	5/0.25	La Reina, Torreón: (r. XHLZ 103.5)
CS05) ON	710	4.5/1	R. Mexicana, Tuxtla Gutiérrez
DF04) MP	710	10	Interferencia 7 Diez, Mexico
GR03) MAR	710	1	Amor, Acapulco: (r. XHMAR 98.5)
NA02) RK	710	1	R. Korita, Tepic
OX05) RPO	710	5/0.5	La Ley 710, Oaxaca
SL19) SMR	710	1/0.25	R. Fórmula, San Luis Potosí
SN01) BL	710	5/0.25	La Ke Buena, Culiacán: (r. XHBL 91.9)
SO03) PS	710	1/0.25	La Super Grupera, Guaymas
TM10) OLA	710	1	Huasteca, Tampico: (r. XHOLA 107.9)
YU14) YK	710	5/0.25	La Z, Mérida
CH30) JCC	720	1	Extremo 7-20, Cd. Juárez
CO19) DE	720	8/0.25	La Kaliente, Saltillo
JL05) QZ	720	1/0.25	Ritmo 720/La Máquina Musical, San Juan de los Lagos
QR05) CPQ	720	2d	La Estrella Maya Que Habla, Felipe Carillo Puerto
SN19) VU	720	1/0.5	Magia. Mazatlán: (r XFHVU 97.1)
VE49) AVR	720	10/0.25	R. Fórmula, Primera Cadena, Veracruz
BC21) EBC	730	1/0.25	Ke Buena, Ensenada: (r. XHEBC 97.3)
BS07) LBC	730	10/1	R. La Giganta 730 AM, Loreto: (r. XHLBC 95.7)
CH07) HB	730	50/1	Ke Buena, Hidalgo del Parral
CO05) PQ	730	5/0.1	La 73/La Sabrosita, Cd.Muzquiz
CS14) VF	730	10/5	R. Villaflores, Villaflores
DF06) X	730	100	TDW Radio, México
JL30) GDL	730	5/1	La Explosiva, Guadalajara
SO39) SOS	730	10	R. Uno, Agua Prieta
YU10) PET	730	10d	LV de los Mayas, Peto
AG05) LTZ	740	1	FM Globo, Aguascalientes: (r. XHLTZ 106.1)
CO28) QN	740	10/1	R. Fórmula, Primera Cadena, Torreón: (r. XERFR 970kHz)
GJ04) OF	740	5/1	Hit FM, Celaya: (r. XHEOF 101.9)
JL25) VAY	740	1	Amor, Puerto Vallarta: (r. XHVAY 92.7)
OX19) POR	740	5/1	La Explosiva/R. Fórmula, Putla de Guerrero
QR11) CAQ	740	20/10	R. Fórmula QR Cancún, Cancún: (r. XHCAQ 92.3)
SN18) CW	740	10/1	R. Variedades, Los Mochis
TB14) KV	740	10/1	Exa FM, Villahermosa: (r. XHKV 88.5)
VE29) GF	740	2/0.25	La Ley, Gutiérrez Zamora: (r. XHGF 97.3)
CH21) OH	750	1/0.75	La Pantera, Camargo
CS11) MG	750	1/0.25	La Ke Buena, Arriaga
GR01) KOK	750	5/0.25	Extasis Digital, Acapulco: (r. XHKOK 107.5)
MI29) URM	750	10/1	Los 40 Principales, Uruapán
NA09) JMN	750	10d	LV de los Cuatro Pueblos, Jesús María
OX06) CON	750	1/0.1	Ke Buena, Loma Bonita
SL17) RASA	750	1/0.1	Candela 750/Candela Pasión Grupera, San Luis Potosí: (r. XHRASA 94.1)
SN23) CSI	750	1/0.25	Vida 750, Culiacán: (r. XHCSI 89.5)
VE31) TI	750	10/0.25	La Huasteca, Tempoal: (r. XHTI 90.5)
CH03) ES	760	10	Antena Musical 7-60, Chihuahua
CS07) RA	760	5/0.5	R. Uno, San Cristóbal las Casas
DF07) ABC	760	70/10	ABC Radio, México (La Paz ME)
DG03) DGO	760	50/5	La Mejor, Durango: (r. XEDGO 103.7)
JL15) ZZ	760	5/1	R. Gallito, Guadalajara
SO07) EB	760	5/1	Preciosa, Cd.Obregón
SO17) NY	760	5/0.1	R. Geny, Nogales
YU01) YW	760	2.5/0.5	R. María, Mérida
GR20) SUR	770	5/1	Tu Ritmo Musical, Chilapa
MI05) ML	770	5/1.5	La Ranchera, Apatzingán
NL07) ACH	770	25/1	R. Fórmula Primera Cadena, Monterrey
OX28) MPO	770	1	Aro-AM, Matías Romero
OX29) HUA	770	1	Aro-AM, Sta Cruz Huatulco
SL13) ANT	770	10	LV de las Huastecas, Tancanhuitz de los Santos
SN04) REV	770	1/0.1	Los 40 Principales, Los Mochis: (r. XHREV 104.3)
VE53) QRV	770	5/0.5	Ultra, Veracruz: (r. XHQRV 92.5)
ZC01) IH	770	10/1	La Unica, Fresnillo
CO31) WGR	780	10/0.25	Exa FM, Monclova: (r. XHWGR 101.1)
CS02) TS	780	5/1	Ke Buena, Tapachula: (r. XHETS 94.7)

MW Call	kHz	kW	Station, location
GJ04) ZN	780	5/1	EXA FM, Celaya: (r. XHZN 104.5)
GR04) XY	780	2.5/1	LV del Balsas, Cd.Altamirano
JL07) LD	780	5/0.5	R. Costa, Autlán: (r. XHLD 103.9)
OX15) GLO	780	10	LV de la Sierra Juárez, Guelato de Juárez:
TM32)MTS	780	2.3/0.25	R. Fórmula, Tampico
TM25)SFT	780	5/1	La Triple T/La Caliente, San Fernando
AG03) BI	790	10/5	R. B-I, La Estación que da las Notícias, Aguascalientes: (r. XHBI 88.7)
BC06) SU	790	1/0.25	R. 790/La Dinámica, Mexicali: (r. XHSU 105.9)
BS01) NT	790	5/0.75	La Paz/R. Fórmula, La Paz
CH02) RPC	790	5/0.4	R. Ranchito, Chihuahua
CO01) GZ	790	1	Colorín Colorradio, Torreón
DF08) RC	790	50/1	Formato 21, México
JL28) GAJ	790	0.25	R. Fórmula, Primera Cadena, Guadalajara
TB03) VA	790	25/5	R. Tabasco, La Em. del Hogar, Villahermosa (r. XHVA 91.7)
TM03)FE	790	1/0.5	La Fiesta, Nuevo Laredo
VE11) COV	790	1/0.5	R. Lobo, Poza Rica: (r. XHCOV 105.9)
YU06) UP	790	2.5/1	Candela, Tizimín: (r. XHUP 96.3)
BC03) SPN	800	0.5/0.25	Notícias 800 Con Imagen, Tijuana
CH12) ROK	800	50	R. Cañon, Cd.Juárez
CO29) ZR	800	2/0.25	La Traviesa de Coahuila, Zaragoza
CS13) UI	800	5/1	R. Comitán, Comitán
GJ19) GX	800	5/1	Fiesta Mexicana , San Luis de la Paz
GR09) ZV	800	5d	LV de la Montaña, Tlapa de Comonfort
JL27) AN	800	1/0.1	R. Alegría, Ocotlán
NL10) DD	800	10/2.5	La Tremenda, Montemorelos
VE09) QT	800	1	La Poderosa, Veracruz: (r. XHQT 106.9)
CA12) IC	810	0.1	R. I-C, Campeche
CH07) SB	810	1	R. Mexicana/La S B, Santa Bárbara
CL05) MAX	810	3/0.25	Radiomax, Tecomán: (r. XHMAX 106.1)
CO06) IM	810	1/0.5	Fiesta Mexicana, Saltillo
CS04) OE	810	2.5/1.5	Romántica, Tapachula: (r. XHOE 96.3)
GJ12) EMM	810	1/0.5	La Salmantina, Salamanca
GR01) AGR	810	7/0.6	R. Fórmula, Primera Cad., Acapulco: (r. XHAGR 105.5)
NA03) UX	810	10/0.25	La Legendaria, Tepic
QR04) RB	810	2.5/0.25	Sol Estéreo, Cozumel: (r. XHRB 89.9)
S004) RSV	810	5d	Tribuna R.I., Cd. Obregón
TM04)RI	810	10/0.1	R. Rey, Reynosa
TM05)FW	810	50/1	R. Estrella, Tampico
TX01) HT	810	10	R. Huamantla, Huamantla
YU03) MQ	810	2/0.25	W R., Mérida: (r. XHMQ 90.9)
ZC05) CZ	810	5/1	R. Felicidad, Río Grande
BC07) ABCA	820	3.5/0.5	R. Frontera, Mexicali
CA01) ESC	820	0.75d	R. Escárcega, Escárcega
DG01) DRD	820	10/0.5	W R., Durango
GR17) GRC	820	1d	Soy Guerrero, Coyuca de Catalán
JL15) BA	820	10/1	La Consentida, Guadalajara
OX23) YN	820	10/5	Los 40 Principales, Oaxaca
SL19) BM	820	10/1	La Mera Mera, San Luis Potosí: (r. XHBM 105.7)
SN14) UDO	820	1/0.25	R. Cultural, Los Mochis
VE14) KG	820	2.5/0.1	La Dorada, Córdoba: (r. XHKG 107.5)
CO15) IK	830	5	La Norteñita 8-30AM/R. Fórmula, Piedras Negras
DF19) ITE	830	10/5	R. Capital, México
MI06) PUR	830	8d	LV de los P'urhepechas, Cheran
NL13) LN	830	3/0.25	La Caliente 830 AM, Linares: (r. XHLRS 95.3)
OX20) TLX	830	6	La Poderosa/R. Tlaxiaco, Tlaxiaco
SN12) VQ	830	5/1	La Superestación - "La Grande de Sinaloa", Culiacán
S003) DR	830	5	Digital 99, Guaymas: (r. XHDR 99.5)
TB09) DQ	830	5/1	R. Futurama, Villahermosa
VE26) DQ	830	1	R. Alegría, San Andrés Tuxtla
ZC12) LK	830	10/0.5	Digital, Zacatecas: (r. XHLK 106.5)
CS01) IO	840	10/2.5	La Más Picuda, Tuxtla Gutiérrez: (r. XHIO 90.3)
GJ04) FG	840	5/0.5	La Pachanga, Celaya: (r. XHEFG 89.1)
JL16) XXX	840	5/1	Fiesta Mexicana/Fiesta Digital, Tamazula
NA02) TEY	840	1/0.25	R. Sensación, Tepic: (r. XHTEY 93.7)
TM18)MY	840	1d	La Jefa, Cd.Mante
VE11) PV	840	2.5/0.1	La Fiera Grupera, Papantla: (r. XHPV 97.3)
BC04) ZF	850	0.25d	Éxtasis Digital, Mexicali
CH03) M	850	5/1	Renacimiento 850 , Chihuahua
JL08) MIA	850	3/1	Mundo de Ofertas, Guadalajara
MI14) ZI	850	1d	Maxistar, Zacapu
QE02) JAQ	850	1	R. Joya, Jalpan
S005) US	850	1/0.2	R. Univ. de Sonora, Hermosillo: (r. XHUSH 107.5)
TB07) RTM	850	5/0.5	R. Variedades, Macuspana
VE04) TQ	850	10/1	Romántica, Orizaba: (r. XHTQ 101.3)
AG05) PLA	860	2.5	La Mexicana, Aguascalientes
BC05) MO	860	10/7.5	La Poderosa 860, Tijuana
CH33) ZOL	860	5/1	R. Noticias 860, Cd.Juárez
CL02) AL	860	5/0.1	R. Mundo/R. Fórmula, Manzanillo
CS08) DB	860	5/0.25	La Máquina Musical, Tonalá
DF10) UN	860	45/10	R. UNAM, México
DG03) DU	860	1/0.5	D-U la que le gusta a Usted, Durango
MI12) IW	860	1	R. 860, Uruapan
NL04) NL	860	5/2	R. Recuerdo, Monterrey
QR06) CTL	860	5/1	R. Chetumal, Presencia Mexicana en el Caribe, Chetumal
QR07) CCN	860	5	R. Caribe, Cancún: (r. XHCBJ 106.7)
SN07) NW	860	1/0.25	Máxima 103.3, Culiacán: (r. XHNW 103.3)
S040) HX	860	5/0.25	La Mia, Ciudad Obregón
TB04) ZX	860	1/0.15	LV de Usumacinta, Tenosique
TM05)TW	860	1/0.25	R. Fiesta, Tampico
YU14) RRF	860	5/0.5	860 AM, Mérida
CH18) TAR	870	10d	LV de la Sierra Tarahumara, Guachochi
GJ05) AMO	870	1/0.5	AMO 870, Irapuato
GR14) GRO	870	1	Soy Guerrero, Chilpancingo: (r. XHGRC 97.7)
MI01) LY	870	1/0.1	Candela, Morelia: (r. XHLY 92.3)
OX07) ACC	870	5/0.25	R. Fórmula/LV del Puerto, Puerto Escondido
PU06) NG	870	1/0.1	Canal 87, Huauchinango
SN19) FIL	870	1/0.25	R. Notícias, Mazatlán
CH14) V	880	5/0.25	R. Fórmula, Primera Cadena Nacional, Chihuahua: (r. XERFR 970kHz)
CO16) TC	880	10/1	880 AM/Estéreo Mayran, Torreón
GR10) IG	880	2.5/1	Los 40 Principales, Iguala
JL09) AAA	880	20/1	R. 880/La Triple A, Guadalajara
PU12) RTP	880	1	La Poderosa, S. M. Texmelucan: (r. XHRTP 90.7)
SL04) EM	880	5/1	La M Mexicana, Río Verde
SN18) PNK	880	10/2	Canal 88/Superestación, Los Mochis
TB10) QQQ	880	10/1	Ke Buena, Villahermosa: (r. XHQQQ 89.3)
VE19) YV	880	10/1	El Patrón, Córdoba: (r. XHYV 94.5)
CS18) FRT	890	10/1	R. Frontera, Comitán
GJ11) AK	890	5/0.5	R. Consentida, Acámbaro
NA02) PNA	890	1/0.25	R. Joya/R. Fórmula, Tepic
SN01) NZ	890	5/1	La Sinaloense, Culiacán: (r. XHENZ 92.9)
VE24) BY	890	1/0.3	Extasis Digital, Tuxpan: (r. XHBY 96.7)
ZC06) PC	890	5/1	Sonido Estrella, Zacatecas
CH31) DT	900	5/1	Hits FM, Cuahtémoc: (r. 98.3)
CS04) TAK	900	1/0.75	Extasis, Tapachula: (r. XHTAK 103.5)
DF06) W	900	250	W R., México: (r:. XEW 96.9)
JL21) ED	900	1	La Líder 900 AM, Arneca
VE05) WB	900	50/10	Los 40 Principales, Veracruz :(r. XHBW 98.9)
NL05) OK	900	10/2.5	OK Notícias/R. Tráfico, Monterrey
BC06) AO	910	0.25	R. Mexicana, Mexicali
GJ06) ACN	910	5/0.1	R. Metrópoli, León
NA01) NAY	910	10/1	W R., Puerto Vallarta
PU02) OL	910	10/2.5	R. Impacto, Teziutlán
TB06) ACM	910	5/1	R. Exitos, Cárdenas
CA11) TEB	920	1.5/0.5	Voces, Campeche
CH36) QD	920	1/0.25	R. Noticias 920, Chihuahua
CO04) RCA	920	5/0.2	Planeta, Torreón: (r. XHRCA 102.7)
CO08) MJ	920	1/0.25	La Más Jóven, Piedras Negras
CS05) VV	920	10/0.5	La Mejor, Tuxtla Gutiérrez: (r. XHVV 101.7)
GJ07) RE	920	5/1	La Comadre, Puros Éxitos, Celaya: (r. XHRE 88.1)
JL15) LT	920	10	R. María, Tlaquepaque
MI27) LCM	920	5/2.5	R. La Mexicana, Cd.Lázaro Cárdenas
OX24) PNX	920	1/0.15	R. Costa/Ke Buena, Santiago Pinotepa Nal
PU5) ZAR	920	1	La Z, Puebla
SN08) CQ	920	5/0.5	La Nueva Ranchera, Culiacán: (r. XHECQ 104.1)
S001) HQ	920	5/1	R. Capital, Hermosillo
TM32)LE	920	10	La Preferida, Tampico
CL01) TTT	930	1	Magia, Colima: (r. XHTTT 104.5)
CO17) SHT	930	1/0.25	La Poderosa, Saltillo
CS12) MK	930	5/2.5	M-K R. Mexicana, Huixtla
HG02) CY	930	2/1	R. Diversión, Huejutla
MI16) ZU	930	1	La Explosiva, Zacapu
OX17) TLA	930	5d	LV de la Mixteca, Tlaxiaco
VE06) U	930	10/1	La U de Veracruz, Veracruz: (r. XHU 98.1)
YU03) UL	930	2.5/0.2	Átomo, Mérida: (r. XHUL 96.9)
ZC03) QS	930	10/3	Romance en Radio/R. Fórmula, Fresnillo
BC07) MMM	940	1/0.1	940 AM Oldies/R. Fórmula, Mexicali
BS08) RLA	940	10/1	R. Santa Rosalía, Santa Rosalía
CO09) YJ	940	15/0.5	La YJ Mexicana, Sabinas
DF06) Q	940	50	Bésame 9-40, México
JL20) HE	940	1d	La Melódica, Atotonilco
TB18) REC	940	1/0.25	Romántica, Villahermosa
TM07)RKS	940	1d	La Poderosa, Reynosa
AG05) CAA	940	1	Life FM, Aguascalientes: (r. XHCAA 100.9)
BC08) KAM	950	20/5	R. Fórmula Californías, Tijuana
CA02) MAB	950	3/0.9	La Poderosa, Cad. del Carmen: (r. XHMAB 101.7)
CH02) FA	950	1/0.5	La Poderosa, Chihuahua: (r. XHFA 89.5)
CS01) TUG	950	1/0.25	Éxtasis, Tuxtla Gutiérrez: (r. XETUG 103.5)
GJ24) CEL	950	10/1	R. Lobo Bajío, Celaya
GR02) ACA	950	5/1	R. Fórmula, Segunda Cadena, Acapulco
JL22) MEX	950	5/0.5	La Mexicana, Cd.Guzmán: (r. XHMEX 104.9)
NA07) ZE	950	2.5/1	La Poderosa, Santiago Ixcuintla
NL06) RN	950	5/1	R. Naranjera, Monterrey
OX16) OJN	950	10d	LV de la Chinantla, San Lúcas Ojitlán

MW Call	kHz	kW	Station, location
SN18) ORF	950	5/0.5	R. Exitos, Los Mochis
SO12) PB	950	10/0.1	La Grande/R. Amor, Hermosillo
TM20) TO	950	5/2	Romántica, Tampico
CH11) FAMA	960	10/1	R. Fama, Cd.Camargo
CO10) KS	960	0.5/0.1	XEKS 960/LV del Tiempo, Saltillo
CS04) TAP	960	5/1	La Poderosa, Tapachula: (r. XHTAP 98.7)
GR05) UQ	960	1/0.5	R. Variedades, Zihuatanejo
GR12) XC	960	1	ABC R. 960, Taxco
JL10) HK	960	10/2.5	LV de Guadalajara, Guadalajara
MI07) MM	960	1	960 Notícias, Morelia
QR02) ROO	960	5/0.5	La Guadalupana, Chetumal
SL03) CZ	960	1	ABC R., San Luis Potosí
SO07) IQ	960	1/0.5	Éxtasis, Cd.Obregón
TM08) K	960	5/1	La Radio 9-60/La Estación Grande, Laredo
VE07) GB	960	1/0.5	Stereo Vida, Coatzacoalcos(r. XHGB 103.5)
VE08) OZ	960	1/0.5	Amor, Xalapa: (r. XHOZ 91.7)
CH22) SW	970	1/0.5	R. Madera/La Mera Mera, Cd. Madera
CH30) J	970	10/5	La J Mexicana, Cd.Juárez
CO31) MF	970	1	La Mejor, Monclova
DF11) RFR	970	50/4	R. Fórmula, Primera Cadena, México
GJ08) UG	970	1	R. Universidad de Guanajuato, Guanajuato
MI08) CJ	970	1/0.25	R. Apatzingán, Apatzingán: (r. XHCJ 94.3)
SN10) VOX	970	10/1	Fiesta Mexicana, Mazatlán
SO08) EZ	970	5/0.5	La Mejor, Caborca
TB05) VT	970	10/5	VT, Villahermosa: (r. XHVT 104.1)
TM01) BJ	970	1	Imagen, Cd. Victoria
TM09) O	970	1	NotiGape 970 AM, Matamoros
YU03) MH	970	5/0.5	Candela FM, Mérida: (r. XHMH 95.3)
ZC12) ZAZ	970	1/0.5	De Mil Amores 9-70, Zacatecas
CH24) JK	980	1	La Poderosa, Cd.Delicias
CO12) NR	980	5/0.5	R. 980, Nueva Rosita
MI09) LC	980	5/0.2	Dual Stereo, La Piedad (r. XELC FM 92.7)
NA04) XT	980	1	R. Capital/Capital Máxima, Iepic
PU09) RS	980	5	R. Matamoros, Izúcar de Matamoros
SO09) FQ	980	2.5/0.5	LV de la Ciudad del Cobre, Cananea
SO10) KE	980	5	KE-98, Solo para ti, Navojoa
TM10) TU	980	5	Estéreo Vida, Tampico: (r. XHTU 99.3)
VE03) QO	980	5/1	R. Romance, Cosamaloapan: (r. XHQO 90.7)
BC04) CL	990	1.4/3	Rockola 990, Mexicali
BS02) HZ	990	5/0.25	HZ La Pura Sabrosura, La Paz
CH13) ER	990	5/0.25	R. Lobo, Cd.Cuauhtémoc
CS09) TG	990	20/1	La Grande del Sureste, Tuxtla Gutiérrez
GR28) PI	990	20/5	W R., Chilpancingo
JL01) BC	990	1/0.1	La Buena Onda, Cd.Guzmán (r. XHBC 95.1)
MI28) ATM	990	1	R. Fórmula, Morelia
NL04) T	990	50	La T Grande, Monterrey
OX08) IU	990	1	Amor, Oaxaca: (r. XHIU 105.7)
VE15) ID	990	1/0.25	R. K-ñon, Álamo
ZC10) FP	990	10/3	R. Alegría, Xalpa
CH33) FV	1000	1	La Rancherita, Cd.Juárez
CH29) HPC	1000	1	R. Mil/R. Fórmula, Hidalgo del Parral
CS02) TAC	1000	10/1	Exa FM, Tapachula: (r. XHTAC 91.5)
DF02) OY	°1000	50/20	R. Mil, México
GJ23) RZ	1000	1	W R., León: (r. XHRZ 93.1)
SN11) MIL	1000	1/0.25	Planeta Mil, Los Mochis
SN24) MMS	1000	1	Ke Buena, Mazatlán
TM24) NLT	1000	1/0.1	R. Fórmula/Laredo R., Nuevo Laredo
VE30) CSV	1000	1	Máxima FM, Coatzacoalles: (r. XHCSV 93.1)
YU01) MYL	1000	5/0.25	Los 40 Principales, Mérida: (r. XHMYL 92.1)
BC22) DX	1010	2/0.5	Cadena 1010 AM, Ensenada
CH14) LO	1010	5/1	La X/Lobo Latino, Chihuahua
CO01) VK	1010	5/1	La Poderosa 10-10 AM, Torreón
CO13) KD	1010	0.5/0.25	La Mejor, Cd.Acuña
HG11) HGO	1010	1d	R. Hidalgo, Huejutla
JL15) HL	1010	50/5	Estadio W, Guadalajara
MI32) TUMI	1010	5d	LV Mazahua Otomi/LV de la Sierra Oriente, Tuxpan
PU19) PA	1010	20/2	Punto 10 R, Puebla
SN12) WS	1010	5/1	Romántica, Culiacán: (r. XHWS 102.5)
SO11) XN	1010	0.5/0.2	R. Ures, Ures
VE09) FM	1010	5/0.5	La Máquina Tropical, Veracruz
CL09) VE	1020	1	W R., Colima
NA02) PIC	1020	1	R. Hits, Tepic
OX14) OU	1020	5/1	La Primera, Huajuapan de León
QE06) KH	1020	1	Top Music 91.7, Querétaro: (r. XHKH 91.7)
QR03) WO	1020	1/0.1	97.7, Chetumal: (r. XHWO 97.7)
VE11) PR	1020	5/0.5	Los 40 Principales, Poza Rica: (r. XEPR 102.7)
BC09) SSD	1030	10	La Tremenda, Ensenada
CA05) BCC	1030	1/0.25	Los 40 Principales, Cad. del Carmen: (r. XHBCC 100.5)
CH32) YC	1030	5/0.5	R. Fórmula, Cd.Juárez
CS15) VFS	1030	10/0.25	LV de la Frontera Sur, Las Margaritas
DF08) QR	1030	5/1	R. Centro, México
GR01) VP	1030	1/0.5	W R., Acapulco
JL11) LJ	1030	20/2	Ke Buena, Lagos de Moreno: (r. XHLJ 105.7)
OX11) TEKA	1030	1/0.5	R. T-K, Juchitán
QR12) NKA	1030	5d	LV del Gran Pueblo, Felipe Carillo Puerto
SL07) IE	1030	5/1	R. Alegría, Matehuala
SN13) MPM	1030	10/1	Exa FM, Los Mochis: (r. XHMPM 98.9)
TM10) PAV	1030	1/0.5	La Picosita, Tampico
CH08) HES	1040	5/0.25	Éxtasis Digital, Chihuahua
CS27) PLE	1040	5/0.5	R. Palanque, Palenque
GJ26) SAG	1040	1/0.25	R. Lobo, Irapuato
JL09) BBB	1040	10/1	R. Mujer, Guadalajara: (occ. r. XHRX La Tapatía 103.5)
ME05) CH	1040	5/0.75	R. Capital, Toluca
SO42) GYS	1040	5/0.25	La Primera/La Número Uno, Guaymas (r. XHGYS 90.1)
VE01) GR	1040	2.5/1	OK Radio, Xalapa (rel XHGR 104.1)
AG06) DC	1050	1	Amor, Aguascalientes (r. XHDC 104.5)
BC06) D	1050	10	Radiorama Siglo 21/W R., Mexicali
BS05) BCS	1050	10/1	R. Cultura Surcalifornia, La Paz
GR29) ZUM	1050	15	ABC R., Chilpancingo
MI29) IP	1050	1/0.5	La Poderosa, Uruapán (r. XHIP 89.7)
NA12) RIO	1050	5	La Poderosa, Ixtlán del Río
NL08) G	1050	100	La Ranchera 1050, Monterrey
QR10) OOO	‡1050	35/2.5	R. Imagen, Cancún: (r. XHQOO 90.7)
TB03) TAB	1050	10/5	¡Ya! FM, Villahermosa: (r. XHTAB 95.7)
VE25) JF	1050	5d	R. Max, Tierra Blanca
DF12) EP	°1060	100/20	R. Educación, México
CA02) IT	1070	1/0.25	Exa FM, Cad. del Carmen: (r. XHIT 99.7)
CS01) RPR	1070	2.5	Oye, Siempre Hits, Tuxtla Gutiérrez: (r. XHRPR 104.3)
GR03) AGS	1070	1/0.2	Digital 101.3,/Solo Exitos Acapulco: (r. XHAGS 101.3)
JL12) SP	1070	10/1	10-70 R. Notícias, Guadalajara
PU03) GY	1070	1/0.25	La Mejor, Tehuacán
SL02) EI	1070	5/0.25	Antena, San Luis Potosí: (r. XHEI 93.1)
SO18) OBS	1070	1/0.25	R. Fórmula, Cd.Obregón
VE10) MI	1070	0.5/0.1	La Poderosa, Minatitlán: (r. XHEMI 105.7)
BS09) PAB	1080	0.5/0.25	R. Celebridad, La Paz
CL04) UU	1080	1/0.5	La Mejor, Colima: (r. XEUU 92.5)
GJ05) CN	1080	1/0.5	Los 40 Principales, Irapuato
JL32) JLV	1080	5d	Sistema Jalisciense, Puerto Vallarta
ME07) TUL	1080	1/0.5	R. Mexiquense Valle de México, Tultitlán
OX09) AX	1080	5/0.5	R. Fórmula Oaxaca, Oaxaca: (r. XHAX 93.7)
SO31) DY	1080	1/0.25	R. Gallo, San LuisRíoColorado
VE20) XK	1080	10/0.25	R. Fórmula, Poza Rica
BC11) PRS	1090	50	XX 1090 AM, Rosarito
JL13) LB	1090	5/1	La Buenísima, La Barca
NL04) AU	1090	5/0.5	Milenio TV, Monterrey
PU16) HR	1090	1	La HR, Puebla
QE07) XE	1090	2.5/1	R. Grupo Fórmula Querétaro, Querétaro: (r. XHXE 92.7)
TM08) WL	1090	1	La Romántica, Nuevo Laredo
VE50) MCA	1090	10	La Grande de las Huastecas, Pánuco
VE13) IL	1090	1/0.5	La Nueva Mix, Veracruz: (r. XHIL 88.5)
YU01) HFC	1090	10/0.25	Super Stereo, Mérida: (r. XHFC 105.9)
BS10) BAC	1100	1	R. Asunción/R. Sur California, Bahía Asunción
GJ09) BV	1100	5	R. Alegría, Moroleón
GR24) GRM	1100	1d	Soy Geurrero, Ometepec
QR15) CAN	1100	4	R. Mundo Maya Turquesa, Cancún
SL19) PO	1100	1/0.25	Imagen, San Luis Potosí: (r. XHEPO 103.1)
SO43) NAS	1100	1/0.5	Unica 1100 AM, Navojoa
VE55) HTY	1100	1/0.1	La Mejor, Tlapacoyan: (r. XHHTY 107.1)
ZC11) TGO	1100	5/0.5	R. Cañón, Tlaltenango
CH33) WR	1110	1/0.5	R. Guadalupana, Cd.Juárez
CO33) PU	1110	0.25	Patronato Cultural Monclova, Monclova
DF08) RED	1110	100	R. Red, México (Tlalnepantla ME)
GJ25) LEO	1110	5/1	La Rancherita, León
JL35) PVJ	1110	1/0.2	Ke Buena, Puerto Vallarta: (r. XHPVJ 94.3)
OX22) TEO	1110	0.4	ARO AM, Teotitlán de Flores Magon
OX30) TUX	1110	0.5	ARO AM, Tuxtepec
SO32) VS	1110	1/0.25	Maxima YN, Hermosillo: (r. XHVU 96.3)
TM02) OQ	1110	1	Notigape 11-10/R. Fórmula, Reynosa
VE51) HTY	1110	10	La Mejor, Tlapacayan: (r. XHHTY 107.1)
BC07) MX	1120	0.4/0.1	MIC R., Mexicali
JL14) UNO	1120	0.5	R. Uno La Popular , Guadalajara
OX09) ZB	1120	2/0.25	R. Oro/La Tremenda, Oaxaca
PU16) POP	1120	5	Fórmula 11-20 AM, Puebla
QE04) GV	1120	1/0.5	11-20 Notícias, Querétaro
SL05) TR	1120	1	R. Panorámica, Cd.Valles
TB17) TQE	1120	5/0.5	La Morena 1230 AM, La Más Choca de Todas, Tenosique: (r. XETVH 1230kHz)
YU08) RUY	1120	1	R. Universidad, Mérida: (r. XHRUY 103.9)
AG03) YZ	1130	10/2.5	La Poderosa, Aguascalientes: (r. XHYZ 107.7)
ME10) TOL	1130	10/5	11-30 Notícias, Toluca
MI11) FN	1130	1/0.1	R. Moderna, Uruapan: (r. XHFN 91.1)
NA05) LUP	1130	1	R. Lupita, Las Varas
SN27) MOS	1130	1/0.25	La Invasora, Los Mochis

MW Call	kHz	kW	Station, location
SO36) HN	1130	1	Ke Buena/Mariachi Estéreo, Nogales
VE08) ZL	1130	10/1	Yo FM, Xalapa: (r. XHZL 103.3)
CS28) TEC	1140	1/0.5	R. Tecpatán, Tecpatán
GJ23) XF	1140	5/1	R. Felicidad, León
HG12) PEC	1140		Hidalgo R., San Bartolo Tutotepec
MI22) LIA	1140	5/0.5	La Tremenda, Morelia
NL02) MR	1140	50	R. Esperanza, Monterrey
PU04) TE	1140	5	1140 Punto Digital, Tehuacán
BC06) RM	1140	1	R. Fórmula, Mexicali
CH16) JS	1150	1/0.5	R. Exitos/JS Digital, Hidalgo del Parral
CO14) BF	1150	2.5/1	R. Extremo, San Pedro
DF08) JP	1150	50/10	El Fonógrafo, México
JL06) AD	1150	50/1	R. Metrópoli, Guadalajara
OX10) XP	1150	10/1	La Mejor, Tuxtepec
SN16) UAS	1150	10/0.15	R. Universidad/ R. UA Sinaloa, Culiacán: (r. XHUAS 96.1)
SO18) SO	1150	5/0.3	La Poderosa, Cd.Obregón
VE24) TVR	1150	1.5/0.5	La Nueva Azul, Tuxpán: (r. XETVR 106.9)
ZC08) XM	1150	5/1	R. Jerez, Jerez de García Salinas
BC20) QIN	1160	10	LV del Valle, San Quintín
GJ11) VW	1160	2.5/0.5	R. Sensación, Acámbaro
MI33) IW	1160	2.5	Canal Stereo Juvenil, Aruapan
SL12) GI	1160	1/0.1	R. Reyna - "La Gigante del Cuadrante", Tamazunchale
VE16) BE	1160	5/0.1	Que tal R, Perote: (r. XHBE 88.9)
AG03) UVA	1170	10/2.5	UVA, Aguascalientes: (r. XHUVA 90.5)
CO11) MDA	1170	1/0.5	La Ley 11-70, Monclova
JL19) JTF	1170	1/0.1	Prisma La Poderosa/Prisma Musical, Zacoalco de Torres
ME01) RLK	1170	1/0.25	Super Stereo Miled, Atlacomulco: (r. XHRLK 104.1)
PU05) CD	1170	10/2.5	R. Oro, Puebla
SO33) IB	1170	1	La Primera/La Número Uno, Caborca
SO35) FEM	1170	5/0.1	R. Manantial, Hermosillo
TM07) RT	1170	5	Ke Buena, Reynosa
VE46) ZS	1170	2.5/1	R. Hits, Coatzacoalcos: (r. XHZS 92.3)
BS05) UBS	1180	10	R. Universidad Autonoma de Baja California Sur, La Paz
CH35) DCH	1180	5/1.5	Ke Buena, Cd. Delicias
DF14) FR	1180	10/5	R. Felicidad, México
GJ05) YA	1180	1/0.8	La Picosa, Irapuato
OX11) AH	1180	0.5	Hits, Juchitán
VE34) GN	1180	10/1	La Gigante, Piedras Negras
BC07) MBC	1190	0.25/0.1	Canal 1190 AM, Mexicali
CH30) PZ	1190	5/0.1	R. Norteña, Cd.Juárez
JL15) WK	1190	50/10	W R./W Guadalajara, Guadalajara
MI13) SOL	1190	5/1	R. Sol, la pura ley, Cd.Hidalgo
M001) JPA	1190	5	La Poderosa, Cuernavaca: (r. XHJPA 90.3)
NL08) CT	1190	10/0.1	Contacto 11-90, Monterrey
SL08) XQ	1190	25/1	R. Universidad, San Luís Potosí
TM33) TOT	1190	10/2.5	ABC R., Tampico
VE32) PP	1190	5	La Comadre, Orizaba: (r. XHPP 100.3)
AG05) AGA	1200	1	La Bonita, Aguascalientes
BS11) PAS	1200	1	R. Punta Abreojos, Punta Abreojos
ME02) QY	1200	2.5	La Mexicana, Toluca
QE10) QJAL	1200	5	R. Querétaro, Jalpán
SN06) WT	1200	1/0.25	W R., Culiacán: (r. XHWT 97.7)
SO29) YF	1200	1/0.25	R. Fórmula Hermosillo, Hermosillo: (r. XERFR 970kHz)
VE11) PW	1200	1/0.3	W R., Poza Rica: (r. XHPW 94.7)
CS26) COPA	1210	5d	LV de los Vientos, Copainalá
GJ27) ITC	1210	1	R. Tecnológico, Celaya
PU16) PUE	1210	1	Méxicana, Puebla
VE27) BD	1210	10/0.25	El Patrón, Xalapa: (r. XHBD 104.9)
VE33) VZ	1210	5/1	Ke Buena, Acayucan: (r. XHVZ 93.9)
CO32) SAL	1220	2.5d	R. Universidad Agraria, Saltillo
DF04) B	1220	100	La B Grande, México
JL28) DKN	1230	1/0.25	R. Fórmula, Segunda Cadena, Guadalajara
MI30) LP	1230	1	R. Pía, La Piedad
NL07) IZ	1230	1	R. Fórmula Cadena 3, Monterrey
PU20) TCP	1230	1	W R. La Romántica, Tehuacán
SN12) EX	1230	10/2	R. Fórmula, Culiacán
TB11) TVH	1230	20/1	La Morena 1230, La Más Choca de Todas, Villahermosa
AG03) RO	1240	10/2.5	La Invasora, Aguascalientes: (r. XHERO 98.9)
CH12) WG	1240	1	Cambio 1240, Cd.Juárez
CH17) BN	1240	1	Radiola, Cd.Delicias
CO15) VM	1240	1	Amor 107, Piedras Negras: (r. XHPNS 107.1)
CS01) LM	1240	2.5	Romántica 12-40, Tuxtla Gutiérrez
HG08) RD	1240	3	La Comadre, Pachuca: (r. XHRD 104.5)
MI15) RPA	1240	25/2	R. Ranchito, Morelia
NA06) SI	1240	1	R. Positiva, Santiago Ixcuintla
OX25) CE	1240	2.5/1	Ke Buena, Oaxaca: (r. XHCE 97.7)
SO36) CG	1240	1	Romántica, Nogales
SO14) BQ	1240	1	FM 105, Guaymas (r. XHBQ 105.3)
TM10) S	1240	1/0.25	W R., Tampico
VE04) OV	1240	2.5/0.5	La Picosa, Orizaba: (r. XHOV 97.3)
CH19) AT	1250	5/0.25	R. Imagen/Nueva Imagen, Hidalgo del Parral
CO03) SC	1250	1/0.5	La Pantera R. 1250, Sabinas
CO30) SJ	1250	5/0.5	La Sarapera, Saltillo: (r. XHSJ 103.3)
JL26) DK	1250	10/1	DK 12-50, Guadalajara
ME07) TEJ	1250	5/0.5	R. Mexiquense, Tejupilco
PU17) ZT	1250	5/0.5	La Mejor, Puebla
QE07) JX	1250	5/1	Cadena R. Uno, Grupo Fórmula, Querétaro (r. XEDF 1500kHz)
SO32) DL	1250	1/0.5	R. 13/DL/Fuerza de la Palabra, Hermosillo (r. XEDA 1290kHz)
VE49) TF	1250	10	R. Fórmula Segunda Cadena, Veracruz
CH20) OG	1260	5/0.5	R. Ranchito, Ojinaga
DF14) L	1260	20/10	La 12-60, México (La Paz ME)
GJ13) ZH	1260	1/0.25	La Estación que se Escuche, Salamanca
JL24) JY	1260	5/1	La Mejor, Autlán: (r. XHJY 101.5)
MI04) QL	1260	1	Catedral de la Música, Zamora
NL13) R	1260	1/0.25	Hits 12-60, Linares
OX18) JAM	1260	10d	LV de la Costa Chica, Santiago Jamiltepec
SL16) XR	1260	5/1	R. Mensajera, Cd.Valles
SN26) SA	1260	5/0.5	La Mexicana, Culiacán: (r. XHESA 101.7)
SO15) MW	1260	5/0.5	R. San Luis/Sonido Z, San Luis Río Colorado
VE22) MTV	1260	1	R. Lobo de Mina, Minatitlán: (r. XHMTV 100.9)
VE48) TBV	1260	1	Ke Buena, Tierra Blanca: (r. XHTBV 100.9)
BC12) AZ	1270	0.5	Canal 1270, Zeta 13, Tijuana
CO04) WN	1270	05/0.15	El Fonógrafo del Recuerdo, Torreón
DG04) HD	1270	1.5/0.5	R. Universidad, Durango
GJ01) RPL	1270	10/0.15	La Poderosa RPL, León: (r. XHRPL 93.9)
HG05) QH	1270	3	Milenium R., Ixmiquilpán
SO16) GL	1270	5/0.5	Digital 12-70, Navojoa
TB18) VHT	1270	1	W R., Villahermosa
TM10) RRT	1270	2/0.5	Sport R., Cd.Madero
VE11) RRR	1270	1/0.25	Romántica, Papantla
CA03) CAM	1280	2.5/1	Kiss FM, Campeche: (r. XHCAM 101.9)
CH36) BW	1280	1/0.1	Palabra Viva, Chihuahua
CS12) KY	1280	1/0.1	Oye 1280, Siempre Hits, Huixtla
GJ14) SQ	1280	2.5/1.15	R. San Miguel. San Miguel de Allende
JL28) BON	1280	0.5/0.25	R. Fórmula, Tercera Cadena, Guadalajara
NL04) AW	1280	10/1	Teleradio A-W, Monterrey
PU18) EG	1280	1/0.5	ABC Radio, Puebla
TM12) TUT	1280	1	R. Tamaulipas, Tula
VE18) AG	1280	2/1	La Mejor, Córdoba: (r. XHAG 102.1)
CA04) TH	1290	25.0d	R. Palizada, Palizada
DF09) DA	1290	20/5	R. Trece, México
GJ03) FAC	1290	5/0.25	La Mera Mera, Salvatierra
MI17) IX	1290	1/0.5	Enlace Digital 12-90/La Pantera, Sahuayo
SN10) NX	1290	10/1	R. Mujer, Mazatlán
SO18) AP	1290	1/0.25	Romántica 1290, Cd.Obregón
CH30) P	1300	50	R. 13/R. Centro, Cd.Juárez
GJ15) XV	1300	10/0.75	La Z, León: (r. XHXV 88.9)
HG13) AWL	1300	1/0.3	R. Jacala/Hidalgo R.,Jacala
MI07) KW	1300	1	La Guadalupana, Morelia
SN15) JL	1300	1/0.1	La 130, La Ley, Guamuchil
SO13) XW	1300	1/0.1	W R., Nogales
HU	1300	1	La Que Manda, Martinez de la Torre
BC13) C	1300	1	R. Enciso, Tijuana
BS12) BTS	1310	1d	R. Bahía de Tortugas, Bahía de Tortugas
BS13) LPZ	1310	1	R. La Paz, La Paz
CH23) RU	1310	1/0.25	R. Universidad, Chihuahua: (r. XHRU 105.3)
GR23) GRT	1310	1d	Soy Guerrero, Taxco
JL06) TIA	1310	10/1	R. Vital, Guadalajara
NL02) VB	1310	1	R. Mujer, Monterrey
PU14) HIT	1310	5/1	R. Felícidad, Puebla
QE06) HY	1310	5	Mia 93.9, Querétaro: (r. XHHY 93.9)
SO19) FH	1310	1/0.1	R. Plan de Agua Prieta, Agua Prieta
TM14) AM	1310	5/0.25	La M Grande, Matamoros
VE06) HV	1310	2.5/1	La Fiera, Veracruz: (r. XHHV 94.1)
AG07) NM	1320	1	R. 1320, Estación sin fronteras, Aguascalientes
BS03) SR	1320	0.5/0.25	R. Cachanía, Santa Rosalia
CH06) JZ	1320	2.5/0.25	La Campera/R. Fórmula, Cd.Jimenez:
CO25) CPN	1320	10/0.1	La Poderosa, Piedras Negras
MI18) NI	1320	1	Stereo Vida, Uruapán
OX10) UH	1320	10/2	X R., Tuxtepec
SN03) RJ	1320	10/2	La Nueva Ranchera, Mazatlán: (r. XHRJ 107.5)
TB19) PAR	1320	2.5/1	Los 40 Principales, Villahermosa (r. XHEPAR 101.5)
CL08) MAC	1330	1	Ke Buena, Manzanillo
CO18) WQ	1330	4/0.25	R. Triunfadora, Monclova
CO27) AJ	1330	5/0.9	La Explosiva, Saltillo
GJ16) BO	1330	5/1	R. Variedades, Irapuato
PU07) EV	1330	0.5d	R. Festival, Izúcar de Matamoros
TM10) RP	1330	1/0.1	La Tremenda, Cd.Madero
BC24) AA	1340	1	13-40 AM, Mexicali

MW Call	kHz	kW	Station, location
CH20) RCH	1340	1/0.5	R. Exitos, Ojinaga
CO13) DH	1340	1	R. Amistad, Cd.Acuña
GR03) CI	1340	1	Romántica 13-40, Acapulco
HG03) QB	1340	1	La Divertida/R. Fórmula, Tulancingo
JL26) DKT	1340	5/1	R. Ranchito, Guadalajara
MI05) APM	1340	1	Candela, Apatzingán (r. XHAPM 95.1)
MI19) CR	1340	1	La Zeta, Morelia: (r. XHCR 96.3)
MO01) ASM	1340	5	Romántica 107.7, Cuernavaca: (r.XHASM 107.7)
NL02) NV	1340	1	91X La Experiencia, Monterrey: (r. XHXL 91.7)
PU08) LU	1340	10/5	Ke Buena Puebla, Cd. Serdán: (r. XHLU 93.5)
SL02) SL	1340	2	Ke Buena, San Luis Potosí: (r. XHESL 102.1)
SN17) QE	1340	1d	La Kañona, Escuinapa
SO40) OS	1340	1	R. Mujer, Cd.Obregón
TM01)RPV	1340	1	La Cotorra, Cd.Victoria: (r. XHVIR 101.7)
TM14)MT	1340	1	Mi Radio 13-40 - Nostalgia, Matamoros
TM15)BK	1340	1	Mega ¡Sí pega!, Nuevo Laredo: (r.XHBK 95.7)
CO04) TB	1350	5/0.5	R. Laguna, Torreón
CS16) CAH	1350	5/1	La Popular 13-50/La Voz de Soconusco, Cacahoatán
DF04) QK	1350	5/1	Tropicalísima 13-50, México
PU15) CTZ	1350	10d	LV de la Sierra Norte, Cuetzalán
SO15) LBL	1350	8	R. Centro, San Luis Río Colorado
TM16)ZD	1350	1/0.25	Mi Radio 1350, La Preferida, Camargo
CH02) DI	1360	1/0.4	La Nueva, Chihuahua: (r. XHDI 88.5)
CS09) UD	1360	5/0.5	Ke Buena, Tuxtla Gutiérrez: (r. XHUD 100.1)
GJ07) Y	1360	1/0.25	R. Fiesta Retro, Celaya
GR08) KF	1360	1	La Z, Iguala
VE42) ZON	1360	10d	LV de la Sierra, Zongolica
BC06) HG	1360	0.5	Romántica, Mexicali
CA06) A	1370	1	Ke Buena, Campeche
DG07) RPU	1370	1/0.25	La Z, Durango: (r. XERPU 102.9)
GJ17) JE	1370	5/1.5	R. Reyna, Dolores Hidalgo
JL08) PJ	1370	10/1	Frecuencia Deportiva, Guadalajara
MI20) SV	1370	1/0.5	R. Nicolaita, Morelia
NL07) MON	1370	10	R. Fórmula, Segunda Cadena, Monterrey
SO36) HF	1370	5	R. Fórmula, Nogales
TM31)GNK	1370	5/0.5	Mariachi Estéreo, Nuevo Laredo
CO01) RS	1380	1/0.5	R. Señal, Torreón
CO20) VO	1380	1/0.1	R. Sensación, Allende
DF13) CO	1380	50/5	Romántica AM Digital, México
TM01)GW	1380	5/1	Mazz W, Cd.Victoria
VE27) TP	1380	10/1	Sensación FM, Xalapa: (r. XHTP 95.5)
BC14) KT	1380	5/0.1	La Súper Estación, Tecate
CL06) TY	1390	10/2.5	Los 40 Principales, Tecomán: (r. XHTY 91.3)
GJ06) RW	1390	10/0.25	Alma de México, León
HG06) ZG	1390	0.5d	R. Mezquital y Huasteca Hidalguense, Ixmiquilpán
MO03) CTA	1390	1	Retro FM, Cuautla: (r. XHYTE 90.9)
SO21) QC	1390	1/0.15	LV de Pto Peñasco/La Reyna del Mar, Pto Peñasco
TM18)XO	1390	5/1	La Super Buena, Cd.Mante
TM02)OR	1390	1	NotiGape 1390 AM, Reynosa
VE54) TL	1390	5/1	R. Ola, Tuxpan: (r. XHTL 91.5)
AG02) AC	1400	1	Ke Buena, Aguascalientes: (r. XHAC 106.9)
BC15) PF	1400	1	La Efectiva/La Rancherita, Ensenada
GR01) KJ	1400	1	Mariachi Stereo, Acapulco
ME03)XI	1400	2.5/1	La "I" de Ixtapan, Ixtapan de la Sal
MI21) OJ	1400	5/1	R. Horizonte/R. Fórmula, Cd.Lázaro Cárdenas
MI22) I	1400	5	R. Trece, Morelia
NL09) SH	1400	51	R. Sabinas, Cd.Sabinas
OX21) UBJ	1400	1	R. Universidad Benito Juárez, Oaxaca
QE03) VI	1400	1	EXA FM 99.1, San Juan del Río: (r. XHVI 99.1)
SL06) WU	1400	0.25	La Poderosa, Matehuala
SO23) AB	1400	0.25	R. Santa Ana, Santa Ana
CA13) CUA	1410	1/0.25	R. Universidad, Campeche
CO01) YD	1410	1/0.1	La Grande de Madero, Torreón
DF02) BS	1410	25/1	La Más Perrona, México
GR25) ZHO	1410	2/1	Aquamarina R., Zihuatanejo
JL17) KB	1410	25/10	Canal 14-10, Guadalajara
SL11) IR	1410	5/0.5	XEIR, La Señal Perfecta, Cd.Valles
SN13) CF	1410	10/0.5	La Mexicana, Los Mochis: (r. XHCF 93.3)
TM08)AS	1410	1	Ke Buena, Nuevo Laredo: (r. XHAS 101.5)
BC16) XX	1420	2	R. Mexicana/R. Fórmula 1420, Tijuana
CH33) F	1420	5/0.5	Tu Recuerdo, Cd.Juárez
GJ05) WE	1420	10/1	La Estación Familiar, Irapuato
HG08) PK	1420	1	R. Felicidad 14-20, Pachuca
JL18) KMX	‡1420	1d	La Super X, Sayula
NL03) H	1420	5/1	La H, Antología Vallenata, Monterrey
PU03) WJ	1420	2.5	Exa FM, Tehuacán: (r. XHWJ 102.9)
TM21)EW	1420	1	W1420/LV del Bajo Bravo, Matamoros
VE10) AFQ	1420	1	Romántica, Minatitlan: (r. XHAFQ 88.5)
CA06) RAC	1430	0.25	La Número Uno en Campeche/R. Fórmula, Campeche
CL09) COC	1430	1	Inolvidable, Colima
SO24) OX	1430	5/0.5	Exa FM 106.5, Cd.Obregón: (r. XHOX 106.5)
TM22)WD	1430	5/0.15	La Grande de Ciudad Miguel Alemán, Cd. Miguel Alemán
TX02) TT	1430	5/1	R. Tlaxcala, Tlaxcala: (r. XHLL 90.1)
VE06) LL	1430	5/1	Latido, Veracruz: (r. XHLL 90.1)
BS04) VSD	1440	1/0.15	La Señal del Progreso, Cd. Constitución
DF16) EST	1440	25/5	Quiéreme 14-40, México
JL02) ABCJ	1440	10/1	ABC Radio/Corazón , Guadalajara (r. XEABC 760kHz)
CH26) ARE	1450	1/0.25	R. Pegüis/R. Lobo, Ojinaga
CO01) BP	1450	1	Bonita, Torreón
GR11) RY	1450	2/1	La Poderosa V del Sur, Arcelia
MI17) RNB	1450	1	R. Impacto, Sahuayo y Jiquilpan
NL04) JM	1450	5/1	La Caliente, Monterrey: (r. XET 94.1)
OX32) PNO	1450	0.4	ARO AM, Santiago Pinotepa Nal
QE05) NA	1450	5/1	Yo FM, Querétaro: (r. XHNAQ 104.9)
SN18) CU	1450	10/1	La Rancherita, Los Mochis
SO25) DJ	1450	0.5	R. Clave, Magdalena
TM18)CM	1450	1	Bonita, Cd.Mante
TM34)RDO	1450	5/1	La Radio 14-50, Reynosa
VE11) JD	1450	1	R. Mundo, Poza Rica: (r. XHEJD 100.9)
VE22) KM	1450	1	KM-FM/R. Mina, Minatitlán: (r. XHKM 95.3)
OX05) KC	1460	5/0.5	Estéreo Exitos, Oaxaca: (r. XHKC 100.9)
SO15) CB	1460	10/1	R. Ranchito, San Luis Río Colorado
VE52) JH	1460	1/0.1	ABC R., Xalapa: (r. XEABC 760)
BC05) RCN	1470	10/5	R. Hispana 14-70 San Diego y Tijuana, Tijuana (Relays of CRI 12h)
CA08) BAL	1470	2.5/0.5	R. Voz Maya de México, Bécal
DF11) AI	1470	50/5	Fórmula Femenina, México
DG03) CAV	1470	5/1	Play 14-70, Tocando Tu Memoria, Durango
GJ26) IRG	1470	1	La Campirana, Irapuato
HG07) IND	1470	1/0.5	LV Sierra Hidalguense, Tlanchinol: (occ. r. XHBCD 98.1 Hidalgo R.)
SN21) ACE	1470	1/0.1	R. Fórmula Mazatlán, Mazatlán: (r. XHACE 91.3)
TM04)NH	1470	10/0.25	Mi Radio 1470, Puro Cañonazo, Ciudad Miguel Alemán
CO21) XU	1480	1/0.1	La Poderosa, Monclova
CH28) HM	1480	1/0.5	H-M Radio, Cd.Delicias
HG10) CARH	1480	2.5	LV del Pueblo Hña-hñu, Cárdonal
JL10) ZJ	1480	2/1	Ciudad 1480, Guadalajara
NL04) TKR	1480	10/1	TKR Rancherita y Regional, Monterrey
SO10) NS	1480	5/0.25	Z14, Solo Exitos, Navojoa
TM28)VIC	1480	5/0.15	R. Tamaulipas, Cd.Victoria
CH10) CJC	1490	1	R. Net, Cd.Juárez
MI04) GT	1490	5/1	W R., Zamora: (r. XHGT 94.1)
MI23) KN	1490	1	R. Variedades, Huetamo
NA11) SK	1490	1/0.25	La Super K/La Costeñita, Cd.Ruiz
SL06) FF	1490	1/0.25	R. Norteña, Matehuala
SO27) AQ	1490	1	La Caliente, Agua Prieta
TM29)MS	1490	1	R. Mexicana, Matamoros
VE28) YT	1490	1	R. Teocelo, Teocelo
CO22) JQ	1500	0.4	La Explosiva, Parras
DF11) DF	1500	50	R. Fórmula 1500, Segunda Cadena, México
GJ20) FL	1500	1/0.5	R. Santa Fe, Guanajuato: (r. XHFL 90.7)
HG09) HUI	1510	0.25	R. Huichapán, Huichapán: (occ. r. XHBCD 98.1 Hidalgo R.)
NL11) QI	1510	10	La Nueva Radio, Monterrey
CO23) VUC	1520	1	La Norteñita, Allende
ME07)ATL	1520	1/0.25	R. Mexiquense, Atlacomulco
MO02)ART	1520	2	Señal 152, Jojutla: (r. XHART 89.3)
SO15) EH	1520	1	R. Exitos, San Luis Río Colorado
TM18)YP	1520	1/0.5	Imagen, Cd. Mante
VE35) VO	1520	1d	La Furia, San Rafael
DF13) UR	1530	50/1	R. Fiesta 15-30, México
GJ21) SD	1530	10/0.1	Los 40 Principales, Silao: (r. XESD-FM 99.3)
MI24) GQ	1530	1	La Reyna de los Reyes, Los Reyes
GJ28) NC	1540	1/0.25	La Auténtica 15-40, Celaya
NL04) STN	1540	0.5	R. Red, Monterrey: (r. XERED 1110kHz)
SO29) HOS	1540	5	La Poderosa, Hermosillo
BC03) BG	1550	1	Cadena 1550 AM, Tijuana
MI26) REL	1550	1	R. Michoacán, Morelia: (r. XHREL 106.9)
TM31)NU	1550	5/0.25	La Rancherita, Nuevo Laredo
VE36) RUV	1550	10	R. Universidad Veracruzana, Xalapa
CA07) SE	1560	0.25	LV de Campeche, Champotón
CH33) JPV	1560	1	R. Viva, Cd. Juárez
CS29) CHZ	1560	20/0.15	R. Lagarto/LV Viva de Chiapas, Chiapa de Corzo
DF08) INFO	1560	50/10	15-60 AM, México (Tlalnepantla ME)
GJ12) MAS	1560	1/0.25	Ke Buena, Salamanca
MI25) LAC	1560	5/1	R. Azul/LV del Balsas, Cd.Lázaro Cárdenas
CO24) RF	1570	100	La Poderosa, Cd.Acuña
GJ28) AF	1580	1/0.5	La Temeraria 15-80, Celaya
GR13) LI	1580	1/0.25	Super 94.7, Chilpancingo: (r. XELI 94.7)
ME06)VAB	1580	20	Super Stereo Miled, Valle del Bravo
SO35) DM	1580	10	DM Noticias, Hermosillo
BC10) HC	1590	1	R. Bahía, Ensenada
CH24) BZ	1590	1/0.25	Extasis Digital, Cd.Delicias

MW	Call	kHz	kW	Station, location
DF13	VOZ	1590	20/10	R. Mexicana, México (La Paz ME)
VE39	PT	1590	1/0.1	La Nueva Misantla R, Misantla
GR26	TPA	‡1600	1	Soy Guerrero, Tlapa de Comonfort
ME07	GEM	1600	5	R. Mexiquense, Metepec
ME08	UACH	1610	0.25	R. Chapingo, Chapingo
BC25	UT	1630	10/1	R. Universidad UABC, Mexicali
DF21	ARZ	1650	5	ZER R. 16-50, México
ME11	ANAH	1670	1	R. Anáhuac, Huixquilucan
BC02	PE	1700	10	ESPN R., Tecate

SW	Call	kHz	kW	Station, location & h of tr
DF18	RTA	‡4800	1/0.4	XERTA R. Transcontinental de América, México
DF02	OI	‡6010	1	R. Mil, México
SL08	XQ	‡6045	1	R. Universidad, San Luis Potosí: 1300-0500
YU03	QM	‡6105	0.25	RASA, Mérida (rel. different Mérida stns)
DF12	PPM	6185	10	R. Educación, México: 1400-0500

Stns with (‡) are reported to be inactive.

State abbreviations: AG = Aguascalientes; BC = Baja California; BS = Baja California Sur; CA = Campeche; CH = Chihuahua; CL = Colima; CO = Coahuila; CS = Chiapas; DF = Distrito Federal; DG = Durango; GJ = Guanajuato; GR = Guerrero; HG = Hidalgo; ME = Estado de México; MI = Michoacán; MO = Morelos; NA = Nayarit; NL = Nuevo León; OX = Oaxaca; PU = Puebla; QE = Querétaro; QR = Quintana Roo; SL = San Luis Potosí; SN = Sinaloa; SO = Sonora; TB = Tabasco; TM = Tamaulipas; TX = Tlaxcala; VE = Veracruz: YU = Yucatán; ZC = Zacatecas.

N.B: These abbreviations are not officially recognized by the Mexican Post Office. Letters should therefore carry the abbreviations in brackets or full state name.

Addresses and other information:
AG00) AGUASCALIENTES (Ags.)
AG01) Av Universidad N° 1001, Desp 614, Edif.Torre Plaza Bosques, 20127 Aguascalientes – **AG02)** Bahía No 201, Fracc.La Fuente, 20239 Aguascalientes – **AG03)** Morelos 222, Col Centro, 20000 Aguascalientes **W:** www.radiogrupo.com.mx – **AG05)** Madero 333, 1er piso, Col.Centro, 20000 Aguascalientes - 1200-0600 – **AG06)** San Miguel 117-A, Col.Salud, 20240 Aguascalientes ☎ (449) 9182370 ▤ (449) 9182371 – **AG07)** Av.28 de Agosto s/n, 2020259 Aguascalientes - 1200-0600 ☎+52 449 994 6470 **W:** www.aguascalientes.gob.mx/ryta/default.aspx **E:** ryta@aguascalientes.gob.mx
BC00) BAJA CALIFORNIA (B.C.)
BC01) Ap.100, 22000 Tijuana (or: c/o Noble Broadcasting of San Diego, 4891 Pacific Highway, San Diego, CA 92110, USA) **W:** xtrasports.com – **BC02)** 3655 Nobel Drive, Suite 470, San Diego, CA 92122-1005, USA **W:** http://sandiego1700am.com – **BC03)** Av.de los Olivos 3401, Fracc. Cubillas, 22410 Tijuana – **BC04)** Pasaje Vallarta 1128 Altos, Centro Cívico, 21010 Mexicali (or: Box 1014, Calexico, CA 92231, USA) - 1300-0100 – **BC05)** Gral.Manuel Márquez de León 950, Zona Río, 22320 Tijuana (or: 713 Broadway, Suite "F", Chula Vista, CA 91910, USA) - 1300-0800 – **BC06)** Av.Calafia 519, Centro Cívico, 21000 Mexicali - 1400-0300 – **BC07)** Francisco L.Montejano 2200, Fracc.Fovisste, 21030 Mexicali (or: P.O.Box 872125, Calexico, CA 92232, USA) - 1400-0800 ☎ 6556 0600 ▤ 6556 0662 **W:** www.mvs.com.mx – **BC08)** Carr Escenica Tijuana-Ensenada km 22.5, 22440 Tijuana – **BC09)** Calle 3a N° 1323-15, Plaza Elva, 22800 Ensenada - 1400-0800 – **BC10)** Ap.777, 22800 Ensenada - 1400-0700 – **BC11)** Blvd.Agua Caliente 10535-506, Fracc.Chapultepec 22420 Tijuana (or: 3655 Nobel Drive, Suite 470, San Diego, CA 92122-1005, USA) – **BC12)** Baja California 1310, Zona Norte, 22100 Tijuana (or: Box 430233, San Ysidro, CA 92073, USA) – **BC13)** Ap.23, 22000 Tijuana – **BC14)** Ap.19, 21400 Tecate – **BC15)** Ap.123, 22800 Ensenada – **BC16)** Carlos Robirosa 3110, Fracc.Aviación, 22240 Tijuana – **BC19)** Blvd.Lázaro Cárdenas 10183, Desp.201, 22450 Tijuana – **BC20)** Calle Octava n° 139, Fracc Cd San Quintín, 22930 San Quintín - 1200-0200 (Sun – 2200) ☎ 6165 2023 Prgrs in Sp., Mixteco, Triqui and Zapateco – **BC21)** Calle 16, N° 159, Centro, 22800 Ensenada – **BC22)** Ap.526, 22800 Ensenada - 1400-0800 **W:** www.bajanet.com.mx/cbc – **BC23)** Lázaro Cárdenas, Esq.Colegio Militar, Centro Comercio, Villa Fontana, Loc 33 y 34, 21180 Mexicali – **BC24)** Boulevard Benito Juárez No 1990, Local 12, Plaza Fimbres, Col Jardines del Valle, 21270 Mexicali – **BC25)** Edif.Rectoria, Av.Alvaro Obregón y Calle Julián Carillo s/n, Col.Nueva, 21100 Mexicali (or: UABC Radio, 233 Paulin Avenue, P O Box MSC 5163, Calexico, CA 92231-2646, USA) - 1400-0800 **W:** www.uabc.mx/RadioU/radio.htm – **FM** 104.1MHz
BS00) BAJA CALIFORNIA SUR (B.C.S.)
BS01) Ap.105, 23010 La Paz - 1300-0700 – **BS02)** Hidalgo 314-B, Centro, 23000 La Paz – **BS03)** Av.Las Flores 1, 23920 Santa Rosalía - 1200-0600 – **BS04)** Ap.279, 23600 Cd.Constitución - 1300-0700 – **BS05)** Ap.19-B, 23010 La Paz - 1300-0500 – **BS06)** Blvd.Mauricio Castro, Dorada's Plaza 4, 23400 San José del Cabo - 1200-0700 – **BS07)** 23880 Loreto – **BS08)** Av de Las Flores 1, 23920 Santa Rosalía – **BS09)** 23010 La Paz – **BS10)** 23960 Bahía Asunción – **BS11)** 23970 Punta Abreojos – **BS12)** 23950 Bahía de Tortugas – **BS13)** 23010 La Paz.

CA00) CAMPECHE (Camp.)
CA01) Calle 44 y 21 s/n, 24350 Escárcega1200-2400 – **CA02)** Calle 22 N° 131, 24100 Cd.del Carmen - 1200-0400 – **CA03)** Av.Luis Álvarez Barret 11, 24000 Campeche 1155-0500 – **CA04)** Ap.22, 24200 Palizada - 1200-2400 – **CA05)** Calle 32 N° 23-2 P.B., Centro, 24100 Cd.del Carmen - 1200-0500 – **CA06)** Tamaulipas 15, Col.Santa Ana, 24050 Campeche - 1200-0600 – **CA07)** Tamaulipas 15, Col Santa Ana, 24050 Campeche - 1200-2400 – **CA08)** Ap.1, 24930 Bécal - 1200-0600 – **CA09)** Domicilio Conocido, 24640 X'pujil - 1100-1600, 2000-0600 - Prgrs in Sp., Maya and Chol – **CA10)** 24000 Campeche – **CA11)** Prol. Calle 53, Esq.Av.16 de Septiembre s/n, 24000 Campeche - 1200-0600 – **CA12)** Instituto Campechano, 24000 Campeche – **CA13)** Universidad Autónoma de Campeche, Orquidea y Narcisos s/n, Col Jardines, 24000 Campeche - 1200-0200.
CH00) CHIHUAHUA (Chih.)
CH01) Calle Agustín Melgar 473, 31500 Cd.Cuauhtémoc – **CH02)** Julián Carrillo No 701, 31000 Chihuahua – **CH03)** Boulevard Ortíz Mena No 3406, Col Lomas del Santuario 2ª Etapa, 31240 Chihuahua - 1300-0500 – **CH04)** Calle 4a Poniente 606, 33000 Cd.Delicias - 1200-0600 – **CH05)** Calle 2A N° 437 (or: Ap.271), 31500 Cd.Cuauhtémoc - 2300-0700 – **CH06)** Allende 613, 33980 Cd.Jiménez - 1300-0200 – **CH07)** Boulevard Ortíz Mena No 54, Centro, 33800 Hidalgo del Parral – **CH08)** Julián Carrillo 705-A, 31000 Chihuahua - 1200-0200 – **CH09)** Coronado 71, 33580 Santa Bárbara – **CH10)** José Borunda 1178 Oriente, 32030 Cd.Juárez **W:** www.radionet1490.com – **CH11)** Gonzáles Ortega 1130, Centro, 33700 Cd.Camargo ☎+52 648 462 0527 ▤ +52 648 462 3333 – **CH12)** Av.Insurgentes 2127, Col.Ex-Hipódromo, 32330 Cd Juárez **E:** radiocanon800@latinmart.com – **CH13)** Ap.1771, 31500 Cd.Cuauhtémoc - 1300-0600 – **CH14)** Cuauhtémoc 2000, Col.Centro, 31020 Chihuahua - 1200-0600 – **CH15)** Jesús Urueta 504, 31700 Nuevo Casas Grandes - 1200-0400 ☎ +52 636 694 0083 – **CH16)** Ap.125, 33800 Hidalgo del Parral - 1245-0500 – **CH17)** Ap.222, 33000 Cd.Delicias - 1300-0400 – **CH18)** Francisco M Blancarte y Felipe Angeles, Colonia El Salto, 33180 Guachochi - 1200-0100 ☎/▤ 1543 0168 –Prgrs in Sp., Tarahumara, Tepehuáno and Guarijío – **CH19)** Ap.122, 33800 Hidalgo del Parral - 1200-0500 – **CH20)** Calle de la Paz 602, 32880 Ojinaga - 1200-0400 – **CH21)** Av.Mariano Negrete 8, Fracc Los Pinos, 33700 Cd.Camargo ☎ +52 648 462 1316 – **CH22)** Calle 3a N° 1204, 31940 Cd.Madero - 1300-0400 – **CH23)** Universidad de Chihuahua, 31000 Chihuahua – **CH24)** Ap.250, 33000 Cd.Delicias - 1300-0500 – **CH25)** Ap.190, 33800 Hidalgo del Parral - 1200-0600 – **CH26)** Juárez y 2a 201, 32881 Ojinaga (or: Box 276, Presido, TX 79845, USA) - 1200-0500 – **CH27)** Avenida Tecnológico 1770, Colonia Fuentes del Valle, Galería C, Local D-07, 32000 Cd.Juárez - 1200-0700 – **CH28)** Av.del Parque Sur 6, 33000 Cd.Delicias - 1300-0300 – **CH29)** Blvd.Ortíz Mena 54, P3, 33800 Hidalgo del Parral – **CH30)** Av Vicente Guerrero 2329, Col. Partido Romero, 32280 Cd.Juárez - 1200-0500 – **CH31)** Agustín Melgar 602, Niños Heroes, 31500 Cuauhtémoc. **W:** www.mmradio.com/hitsfm – **CH32)** José Borunda 1178, Col.Partido Romero, 32030 Cd.Juárez – **CH33)** Chapultepec 316, Col Cauahtémoc, Edificio NAFTA Center, 32000 Cd.Juárez - 1200-0200 **W:** http://radioguadelupana.org (or: Box 17718, El Paso, TX 79917-7718, USA) ☎ +52 656 614 2869 – **CH35)** Calle 2a Norte N° 309, Interior 107, Col.Centro, 33000 Cd.Delicias - 1200-0600 – **CH36)** Ignacio Allende No 2211, Colonia Zarco, 31020 Chihuahua - 1200-0700.
CL00 COLIMA (Col.)
CL01) Calzada la Armonía 270, 28020 Colima - 1100-0600 ☎ (3) 313 1940 ▤ (3) 313 1500 **W:** www.radiolevy.com/xetttinfo.htm **E:** grlevy@col1.telmex.net.mx – **CL02)** Boulevard Costera Miguel de la Madrid No 801-3, Crucero Las Brisas, 28200 Manzanillo - 1100-0700 – **CL03)** Carretera Manzanillo-Minatitlán, km 0.2, 28200 Manzanillo – **CL04)** Ignacio Sandoval 13, 28000 Colima - 1200-0600 – **CL05)** Allende 408-102, 28100 Tecomán - 1100-0400 ☎ (3) 324 1950 ▤ (3) 324 1616 **W:** radiolevy.com/xemaxinfo.htm **E:** grlevy@prodigy net.mx – **CL06)** Av.Antonio Leaño del Castillo 663, 28160Tecomán - 1100-0300 – **CL07)** Ap.2-1690, Suc.A, 28950 Colima – **CL08)** Lote 4, Manzana B, Parque Industrial Fondeport, 28200 Manzanillo - 1100-0600 – **CL09)** Av.Félipe Sevilla del Río 585, Col.Jardines Cista Hermosa, 28017 Colima - 1200-0400.
CO00) COAHUILA (Coah.)
CO01) Blvd.González de la Vega 195, 27000 Torreón – **CO02)** Ap.3, 26000 Piedras Negras (or: Box 196, Eagle Pass, TX 78853-0196, USA) **W:** www.larancherita.com.mx - **E:** xemu@larancherita.com mx – **CO03)** Ap.60, 26700 Sabinas - 1100-0600 – **CO04)** Priv.Eulogio Ortiz y Pamanes, Col.Ampl.Los Angeles, 27140 Torreón - 1200-0600 – **CO05)** Ap.71, 26340 Cd.Múzquiz - 1200-0400 – **CO06)** Piedras Negras 1812, 25280 Saltillo - 1200-0600 – **CO07)** De la Fuente 223 Pte, 25700 Monclova – **CO08)** Rassini 617, Col.Bravo, 26000 Piedras Negras - 1200-0600 – **CO09)** Zaragoza Pte 1270, Del Valle, 26788 Sabinas ☎ (861) 614 - 1200 – **CO10)** Gral.Manuel Pérez Trevino 839, Pte Interior, Centro, 25000 Saltillo - 1100-0600 ☎ +52 018 414 8149

W: xeksradio.com.mx/set-b01.html **E:** xeks@infosel.com – **CO11)** Venustiano Carranza 612-2 Ote, 25700 Monclova - 1300-0600 – **CO12)** Pte Carranza 1000, Col.Comercial, 26850 Nueva Rosita - 1155-0600 – **CO13)** Madero 274 Pte. (Ap.10), 26200 Cd.Acuña - 1200-0600 ☎ 877 772 51 21 – **CO14)** Pedro G Garza s/n, Col Magisterial, 35000 San Pedro – **CO15)** Av Carranza 1104, Col.Roma, 26000 Piedras Negras (or: Box 1261, Eagle Pass, TX 78852, USA) - 1100-0600 – **CO16)** Acuña 276 Sur, P2, 27000 Torreón – **CO17)** América Latina y Alaska s/n, Col.Virreyes, 25230 Saltillo – **CO18)** De la Fuente 304 Ote, 25700 Monclova – **CO19)** Av.Universidad No 1035, Col Universidad, 25260 Saltillo – **CO20)** Juárez - 1400 Sur, 26530 Allende - 1200-0400 – **CO21)** Pte Carranza Carr 4 Ciénegas, 25700 Monclova - 1200-0600 – **CO22)** Fco.I.Madero 501 Pte, 27980 Parras - 1100-0100 – **CO23)** Boulevard Leonides Guadarrama No 890 Norte, Centro, 26170 Nava - 1200-0200 – **CO24)** Madero # 600, 26200 Cd.Acuña **W:** www.lapoderosa.imer.com.mx **E:** lapoderosa1570@imer.com.mx – **CO25)** Lerdo 1612, Col.Nísperos, 26020 Piedras Negras – **CO26)** Chihuahua 151, P1, Col.Reública, 25280 Saltillo - 1200-0600 – **CO27)** Av Universidad 1035, Col.Universidad, 25260 Saltillo ☎ (844) 438 8108 **E:** 1330radio@mail.com – **CO28)** Av.Morelos 1320-204, Edif.Monterrey, 27000 Torreón – **CO29)** 505 Sur Alto, Ap 26850, 26450 Zaragoza - 1200-0400 – **CO30)** América Latina y Alaska, Col. Virreyes Residencial, (Ap.27), 25230 Saltillo – **CO31)** Cipres 321, Col. Guadalupe, 25750 Monclova – **CO32)** Universidad Autónoma Agraria, "Antonio Narro", Buenavista, 25315 Saltillo

CS00 CHIAPAS (Chis.)
CS01) Ap.59, 29000 Tuxtla Gutiérrez - 1100-0600 – **CS02)** 2ª Calle Poniente No 4, Centro, 30700 Tapachula - 1100-0500 **W:** www.radio-nucleo.com – **CS03)** Ap.74, 29250 San Cristóbal de las Casas - 1200-0600 – **CS04)** Ap.76 (or: 1a Av.Sur N° 2), 30700 Tapachula - 1100-0400 – **CS05)** Av.Central Pte 554-4, 29000 Tuxtla Gutiérrez - 1200-0600 – **CS06)** Ap.60, 30400 Cintalapa - 1100-0500 – **CS07)** Avenida Benito Juárez No 48, Interior Altos, 29200 San Cristóbal las Casas – **CS08)** CrR Tonalá-Arriaga 1500, 30500 Tonalá - 1100-0500 – **CS09)** Blvd. Belisario Domínguez 4820, 29000 Tuxtla Gutiérrez - 1100-0700 – **CS10)** Aurora No 31 Centro, 29520 Pichucalco - 1100-0500 – **CS11)** Ap.28, 30450 Arriaga - 1200-0400 – **CS12)** Av.Central Norte 8, 30640 Huixtla - 1100-0300 – **CS13)** 2a Norte N° 2, 30000 Comitán - 1200-0400 – **CS14)** 1a Av.Norte Pte N° 53, 30470 Villaflores - 1200-0400 – **CS15)** 14 Sur-Poniente s/n, Barrio San Sebastián, 30180 Las Margaritas - 1200-0300 (SS – 2400) Prgrs in Sp., Tojobal, Mame, Tzeltal and Tzotzil – **CS16)** Km 1.5 Carr Cacahoatán-Unión Juárez, Ejido Rosario Ixtal, 30890 Cacahoatán - 1100-0700 – **CS17)** Carr Boca del Limókm 2.5, 29500 Reforma – **CS18)** Primera Calle Norte Pte 7, 30000 Comitán - 1100-0500 – **CS22)** Av.Chichima 405, 30000 Comitán - 1100-0700 – **CS24)** Gobierno del Estado de Chiapas, 29950 Ococingo – **CS26)** Primera Oriente s/n, Barrio Siete Hescos, 29650 Copainalá 1230-2230 Prg in Sp., Zoque and Tzotzil – **CS27)** 29960 Palenque 1000-0400 (belongs to Gobierno del Estado de Chiapas) – **CS28)** 2ª Sur y 1ª s/n, 29610 Tecpatan (belongs to Gobierno del Estado de Chiapas) –**CS29)** Km 14 Libramiento Norte, 29160 Chiapa de Corzo.

DF00) DISTRITO FEDERAL (D.F.)
DF01) Av.Chapultepec 473, P7, Col.Juárez, 06600 México.1100-0700. **W:** www.lamejor560.com – **DF02)** NRM Comunicaciónes, Prolongación Paseo de la Reforma 115, Col.Paseo de las Lomas, 01330 México. **W:** www.nrm.com.mx – R. Mil: Ap.21-1000, 04021 México **W:** radiomil.com.mx – **DF03)** Radiodifusoras Asociadas, Durango 341, Planta Baja, Col.Roma, 06700 México **W:** www.rasa.com.mx – **DF04)** Instituto Mexicano de la Radio, Real de Mayorazgo 83, Barrio Xoco, 03330 México. **W:** imer.gob.mx – **DF05)** Universidad Autónoma Metropolitana, Prol. Canal de Miramontes 3855, Col. Ex-Hacienda de San Juan de Dios, 14387 México. **W:** www.uamradio.uam.mx – **DF06)** Televisa Radio, Calzada de Tlalpan 3000, Col. Espartaco, 04870 México. **W:** televisa.com wradio.com.mx los40.com.mx kebuena.com.mx besame.com.mx televisadeportes.esmas.com/tdn – **DF07)** México Radio, Basilio Vadillo 29, Col Tabacalera, 06030 México. **W:** www.oem.com.mx/abcradio www.760.com.mx – **DF08)** Grupo R. Centro, Av. Constituyentes 1154, Col. Lomas Altas, 11950 México. **W:** radiocentro.com.mx – **DF09)** Radio S.A., Rodolfo Emerson 412, Col.Chapultepec Morales, 11570 México. **W:** www.radio13.com.mx – **DF10)** Universidad Nacional Autónoma de México, Adolfo Prieto 133, Col. del Valle, 03100 México. **W:** www.radiounam.unam.mx – **DF11)** Grupo R. Fórmula, Av. Universidad 1273, Col. del Valle, 03100 México. **W:** www.radioformula.com.mx – **DF12)** Radio Educación, Ángel Urraza 622, Col.del Valle, 03100 México. **W:** www.radioeducacion.edu.mx – **DF13)** Radiorama, Paseo de la Reforma 56, P1, Col.Juárez, 06600 México. **W:** www.radiorama.com.mx – **DF14)** Instituto Politécnico Nacional, Av.Santa Ana 1000, San Fco. Culhuacán, 04430, México. **W:** radio.ipn.mx – **DF15)** Imagen Telecomunicaciones, Av. Prol. Prado Sur 150, Col. Lomas de Chapultepec, 11000 México. **W:** imagen.com.mx reporte.com.mx – **DF16)** Grupo 7 División Radio, Montecito 59, Col.Nápoles, 03810 México. **W:** www.gruposiete.com.mx – **DF17)** MVS Radio, Mariano Escobedo 532, Col. Anzures, 11300

México. **W:** mvsradio.com – **DF18)** Radio Transcontinental de América S.A de C.V., Gabriel Guerra 13, Col Zona Escolar Oriente, 07230 México. **W:** radioxerta.com.mx – **DF19)** Grupo Radiodifusoras Capital, Montes Urales 425, Col. Lomas de Chapultepec, 11000 México. **W:** gruporadiocapital.com.mx – **DF20)** Universidad Iberoamericana, Av. Prol. Paseo de la Reforma 880, Lomas de Santa Fe, 01219 México. **W:** ibero909.fm – **DF21)** **W:** facebook.com/GrupoRadiofonicoZer

DG00) DURANGO (Dgo.)
DG01) Manuel Rangel 100, P3, 34270 Durango - 1200-0600 – **DG02)** Av.20 de Noviembre 1918 Ote, Col.Guillermina, 34270 Durango - 1200-0600 – **DG03)** Negrete 405-B Oriente, 34270 Durango - 1100-0500 – **DG04)** Universidad Juárez del Estado de Durango, 34270 Durango – **DG05)** Fco.I.Madero y Heroico Colegio Militar s/n, 34600 Santiago Papasquiaro - 1200-0400 – **DG07)** Capitán de Ibarra 1203, Farcc.del Lago, 34080 Durango – **DG08)** Blvd.González de la Vega 195, Sur Zona Industrial, 35000 Gómez Palacio.

GJ00) GUANAJUATO (Gto.)
GJ01) Cañada 310, Esq.Roca, Col Jardines de Moral, 37160 León **W:** www.radioramabajio.com ☎ +052 477 773 3606 🖹 +52 477 773 2470 – **GJ02)** Ap.301, 37160 León – **GJ03)** Morelos 704, Centro, 38900 Salvatierra - 1230-0130 ☎ +52 466 663 0365 – **GJ04)** Blvd. López Mateos Ote 1117, 38070 Celaya - 1200-0600 **E:** telradio@mail.mindvox.ciateg.mx ☎ +52 461 613 4400 🖹 +52 461 612 1164 – **GJ05)** Morelos 110, 36500 Irapuato - 1200-0600 **W:** www.intercon.net.mx/radio **E:** radiogpo@intercon.net.mx ☎ +52 462 626 - 1200 – **GJ06)** Blvd.Mariano Escobedo Pte 4206, Col.Flores Magón, 37350 León ☎+52 477 7777 1943 – **GJ07)** Corporación ACIR Celaya, Guanajuato 106, Col Alameda, 38090 Celaya - 1300-0600 ☎ +52 461 612 4710 – **GJ08)** Palacio Federal, Casa de Moneda, Sopeña 1m, P2, 36000 Guanajuato - 1300-0500 **W:** http://radioug.ugto.mx ☎ +52 473 732 1684 – **GJ09)** Elodia Ledezma 658, 38890 Morolcón - 1200-0600 – **GJ10)** Av Roma 910, Col Andrade, 37370 León ☎ +52 477 714 0002 **FM:** 95.9 – **GJ11)** Allende 17, 38600 Acámbaro - 1200-0400 ☎ +52 417 172 1960 – **GJ12)** Ap.300, 36700 Salamanca - 1300-0600 ☎ +52 464 648 9200 – **GJ13)** Ap.24, 36700 Salamanca - 1300-0500 ☎ +52 464 648 0227 – **GJ14)** Calle Solano 4, 37700 San Miguel de Allende - 1200-0400 ☎ +52 415 152 0227 – **GJ15)** Ap.13, 37000 León - 1200-2400 ☎/🖹 +52 477 770 0468 – **GJ16)** Ap.72, 36500 Irapuato 1030-0600 ☎+52 462 626 3733 – **GJ17)** Ap.43, 37800 Dolores Hidalgo - 1200-0600 ☎ +52 418 182 0413 – **GJ19)** Ap.67, 37900 San Luis de la Paz - 1300-0300 ☎ +52 468 688 2849 – **GJ20)** Municipio Libre 8, 36080 Guanajuato - 1300-0300 ☎ +52 473 732 9909 – **GJ21)** Ap.60, 36100 Silao ☎+52 472 722 0302 – **GJ22)** Ap.528, 38000 Celaya – **GJ23)** Ap.311, 37530 León - 1200-0600 **E:** acir_leon@infosel.net.mx ☎ +52 477 711 7388 🖹 +52 477 711 7374 – **GJ24)** Corporación Celaya Radio, Privada Venustiano Carranza 119, P1, 38000 Celaya - ☎+52 461 613 0977 🖹 +52 461 613 9410 – **GJ25)** Ap.642, 37160 León - 1300-0100 ☎ +52 477 712 2000 – **GJ26)** Av.Guerrero y Francisco Sarabia, Centro Plaza Magna, Local 3-B, 36500 Irapuato - 1300-0100 **W:** www.radioramabajio.com ☎ +52 462 624 4665 – **GJ27)** Av Tecnológico y García Cubas s/n, 38110 Celaya - 1200-0600 **E:** xeite@ite.mx ☎ +52 461 611 8040 – **GJ28)** Grupo Radiocomunicación Trébol, Privada Ronavicienovación 135, Floresta del Sur, 38090 Celaya - 1200-0800 ☎ +52 461 613 1580.

GR00) GUERRERO (Gro.)
GR01) Calle de la Paz 190, P2, Edif.Nick, 39300 Acapulco – **GR02)** Ap.60, 39390 Acapulco – **GR03)** Av. La Suiza 19, Fracc.Las Playas, 39390 Acapulco - 1200-0600 – **GR04)** Fray Bautista Moya 410, Centro, 40660 Cd.Altamirano - 1200-0430 – **GR05)** Paseo de Zihuatanejo Pte No 143, Col.Limón, 40880 Zihuatanejo - 1200-0300 – **GR06)** Avenida Insurgentes No 125, 39170 Tixtla de Guerrera – **GR08)** Juan N.Álvarez 3 Altos, 40000 Iguala 1155-0500 – **GR09)** Av Heroico Colegio Militar No 234, Col Aviación, 41304 Tlapa de Comonfort - 1200-0100 (SS -2000) ☎ +52 755 476 0156 Prgrs in Sp., Náhuatl, Mixteco and Tlapaneco – **GR10)** Av Bandera Nacional 51-A, P1, (or: Ap.52) 40000 Iguala - 1200-0600 – **GR11)** Avenida Lázaro Cárdenas No 54, Col Héroes Surianos, 40500 Arcelia - 1200-0300 – **GR12)** Cerro de la Bermeja s/n, Taxco de Juan Ruíz de Akarcón, 40200 Taxco - 1200-0300 – **GR13)** Ap.40, 39000 Chilpancingo – **GR14)** Palacio de la Cultura "Ignacio Manuel Altamirano", tercer piso, Plaza Cívica 1er Congreso de Anahuac, Col Centro, 39000 Chilpancingo - 1200-0700 – **GR17)** Av Revolución 6, 40700 Coyuca de Catalán – **GR19)** Morelos 6-3, 39000 Chilpancingo - 1200-0400 – **GR20)** Calle 5 Sur 305, 41100 Chilapa - 1200-0200 – **GR21)** Av.Guerrero 10-B, P1, Desp.2, Centro, 39000 Chilpancingo - 1200-0400 **W:** www.pmp.com.mx/radio.html – **GR23)** Hacienda del Cernillo, Casa Gallos s/n, 40200 Taxco - 1200-0400 – **GR24)** Benito Juárez 19-A, Barrio del Carmen, 41700 Omotepec (belongs to Gobierno del Estado de Guerrero) – **GR25)** Avenida Benito Juárez No 21-A, Col Centro, 40880 Zihuatanejo – **GR26)** 41300 Tlapa de Comonfort (belongs to Gobierno del Estado de Guerrero) – **GR27)** Paseo de la Boquita No 53, Col Centro, 40880 Zihuatanejo ☎ +52 755 554 9520 – **GR28)** Eje Central

No 3, entre Avenida Rufo Figueroa y Circuito Poniente, Col Burócratia, 39090 Chilpancingo – **GR29)** Zapata 28, 2do piso, Col. Centro, 39000 Chilpancingo - 1200-0400

HG00 HIDALGO (Hgo.)
HG01) Ap.123, 42000 Pachuca – **HG02)** Ap.35, 43000 Huejutla - 1100-0200 – **HG03)** Hidalgo Ote.209, 43600 Tulancingo - 1200-0600 – **HG04)** Plaza Constitución y Manuel F Soto (or: Ap.96), 43600 Tulancingo – **HG05)** Carr a Cardonal km 2.689, Barrio San Nicolás, 42300 Ixmiquilpán - 1200-0500 – **HG06)** Félipe Ángeles s/n, 42300 Ixmiquilpán - 1300-0100 – **HG07)** 43150 Tlanchinol - 1200-0200 – **HG08)** Plaza Juárez 103 (or: Ap.123), 42000 Pachuca - 1200-0600 **E:** acirpachuca@netpac.net.mx – **HG09)** Chávez Macotela 8, 42400 Huichapan – **HG10)** Domicilio Conocido, Col Buenos Aires, 42370 Cárdonal - 1300-2300 Prgrs in Sp., Otomí and Náhuatl – **HG11)** Radio y Televisión de Hidalgo, 43000 Huejutla - 1100-0300 – **HG12)** Radio y Televisión de Hidalgo, 43440 San Bartolo Tutotepec - 1200-0100 – **HG13)** Radio y Televisión de Hidalgo, 42200 Jacala - 1200-0300.

JL00) JALISCO (Jal.)
JL01) Hidalgo 158, Centro, 49000 Cd.Guzmán - 1200-0600 – **JL02)** c/o El Periodico el Occidental, Calzada Independencia Sur 324, Col Centro, 44100 Guadalajara – **JL03)** Paseo de las Gaviotas 198, Fracc. Las Gaviotas, 48328 Puerto Vallarta – **JL05)** Carr Tampico-Barra de Navidad km 695, 47000 San Juan de los Lagos - 1300-0300 – **JL06)** Av.México 3150, Activa de Centro SA de CV, 44670 Guadalajara – **JL07)** Avenida Hidalgo 111-C, 48900 Autlán – **JL08)** Av.Lázaro Cárdenas 2820, Jardines del Bosque, 44520 Guadalajara - 1200-0600 – **JL09)** Av.Mariano Otero 3405, Fracc.Verde Valle, 45060 Guadalajara – **JL10)** Vidrio 2056, 44100 Guadalajara **W:** http://ciudad1480.com – **JL11)** Constituyentes 262, 47040 Lagos de Moreno – **JL12)** Pablo Casal 567, Prados Providencia, 44670 Guadalajara – **JL13)** Km 6.5 Carr La Barca-Guadalajara, 47910 La Barca - 1200-0400 – **JL14)** Hidalgo 2055 Esq Tomas de Gómez, Col Arcos Sur, 44500 Guadalajara **E:** xkguad@mail.udg – **JL15)** Televisa Radio, Rubén Dario 158, Circunvalación vallarta, 44680 Guadalajara Radio María México-address: Av Cruz del Sur 3195, P3, Lomas de Victória, 44580 Tlaquepaque, Jalisco - 1230-0600 – **JL16)** Portal Hidalgo 13, Int.10, Centro, 49650 Tamazula - 1200-0600 – **JL17)** Av Francia 1783, Col.Moderna, Sector Juárez, 44190 Guadalajara - 1200-0600 – **JL18)** Ap.36, 49300 Sayula - 1200-2400 – **JL19)** Fco. I.Madero 77, 45750 Zacoalco de Torres - 1300-0100 **JL20)** Centro Comercial del Valle de Atotonilco, Local 17, Centro, 47750 Atotonilco - 1300-0100 **☎** (391) 917 1358 – **JL21)** Ap.16, 46600 Ameca - 1200-0400 – **JL22)** Primero de Mayo 126-8, 49000 Cd.Guzmán - 1200-0600 – **JL23)** Lerdo de Tejada 184, 47600 Tepatitlán - 1200-0300 – **JL24)** 18 de Marzo No 45, Centro, 48740 El Grullo - 1200-0300 – **JL25)** Paseo de las Gaviotas, 48328 Puerto Vallarta - 1200-0600 – **JL26)** Studios: Av.Lázaro Cárdenas 3126, Col.Chapalita, 45040 Guadalajara Commercial sve: Av.de los Niños Heroes 1555, P6, Ofc 602, Plaza Tolsa, Col Moderna, 44100 Guadalajara – **JL27)** Monterrey 190, Fracc. Camino Real, 47820 Ocotlán - 1200-0400 – **JL28)** Av.México 3370, Plaza Bonita, Local Subanda P, 45120 Guadalajara - 1300-0700 – **JL29)** Montezuma 68, 49000 Cd.Guzmán – **JL30)** Avenida Enrique Díaz de León No 285-2, Col Jesús, 44200 Guadalajara - 1300-0100 – **JL31)** Blvd.Francisco Medina Asencio km 7.5, Plaza Marina Local 101, Col. Marina Vallarta, 48300 Puerto Vallarta – **JL32)** Oceano Pacífico 201, Palmar de Aramara, 48300 Puerto Vallarta – **JL33)** Av.México 3150, 44670 Guadalajara - 1200-0500 **W:** www.unidifusion.com.mx – **JL34)** Av Constituyentes 21, Nucleo Agua Azul, 44190 Guadalajara - 1300-0700 – **JL35)** Honduras 309 Int 161, Hotel Paloma del Mar, Col.5 de Diciembre, 48350 Puerto Vallarta – **JL36)** Moctezuma 68, Centro, 49000 Cd.Guzmán - 1200-0600 **☎** (341) 412 5710

ME00) ESTADO DE MÉXICO (Edo.Méx.)
ME01) Grupo Corporativo Miled México, Carretera Panamericana km 24, 50450 Atlacomulco. **W:** miled.com/superstereomiled – **ME02)** Grupo Radiorama, Paseo Tollocan 613, Oriente, Col. Valle Verde, 50130 Toluca. **W:** radiorama.com.mx – **ME03)** José María Morelos 948, Esq. Carretera a Tonatico, 51900 Ixtapan de la Sal. **W:** radioixtapan.net 1200-0600 – **ME04)** Independencia 19, 50600 El Oro – **ME05)** Grupo Rdif. Capital, Ernesto Monroy, Lote 7, Manzana 3, Parque Industrial Exportec II, 50200 Toluca. **W:** gruporadiocapital.mx 1100-0600 – **ME06)** Grupo Corporativo Miled México, Independencia 506, 51200 Valle del Bravo. **W:** miled.com/superstereomiled 1300-0400 – **ME07)** Sistema de R. y TV Mexiquense, Av. Estado de México km 1, Col. La Virgen, 52140 Metepec. **W:** edomexico.gob.mx/tvmex/tvmex.html 1200-0600 – **ME08)** Universidad Autónoma de Chapingo, Carr. México-Texcoco km 38.5, 56235 Chapingo. **W:** chapingo.mx 1800-0200 – **ME09)** Radiorama del Valle de México, Av. Cuauhtémoc 3, Col. Santa Bárbara, Oficinas en Galerías Ixtapaluca, local G5, 56530 Ixtapaluca. **W:** radiorama.com.mx 1200-0600 – **ME10)** Grupo ACIR Toluca, Paseo Tollocan Poniente 300, Col. Univerisdad, 50130 Toluca. – **ME11)** Cabina 5, Edificio CAD, Escuela de Comunicación, Av. Universidad Anáhuac 46, Col. Lomas Anahuac, Huixquilucan. **W:** anahuac.mx/radio

MI00) MICHOACÁN (Mich.)
MI01) Aqua 78, Col.Prados del Campestre, 58297 Morelia - 1200-0300 **☎**+52 443 315 1810 – **MI02)** Av Revolución Sur 66 (or: Ap.50), 61500 Zitácuaro - 1200-0600 (SS -0400) – **MI03)** Ap.61, 60100 Uruapan – **MI04)** Av.5 de Mayo 501 Sur, Jardines de Catedral, 59670 Zamora - 1200-0600 – **MI05)** Av.Constitución de 1814 Norte 10 Altos, 60600 Apatzingán - 1200-0500 – **MI06)** Domicilio Conocido, Predio INI, 60270 Cheran - 1300-0020 Prgrs in Sp and Purépecha – **MI07)** Laguna de Parras 630, Col.Ventura Puente, 58020 Morelia **☎**+52 443 314 3518 – **MI08)** Av.Constitución de 1814 Norte 2 Altos, 60600 Apatzingán - 1200-0400 – **MI09)** Ap.10, 59300 La Piedad - 1230-0500 – **MI10)** Ap.244, 61600 Pátzcuaro - 1200-0600 **MI11)** Ap.132, 60000 Uruapan **E:** moderna@mail.compuscp.com – **MI12)** Mazatlán 30, 60050 Uruapan - 1300-0400 – **MI13)** Altos Mercado Emiliano Zapata, 61100 Cd.Hidalgo - 1200-0400 **☎**+52 715 154 0212 – **MI14)** Avenida Morelos No 529, Plaza Ruíz, Centro, (Ap.65), 58600 Zacapu - 1200-0200 – **MI15)** Av.Madero Pte 644, 58000 Morelia - 1200-0300 **☎**+52 443 317 2158 – **MI16)** Ap.50, 58600 Zacapu – **MI17)** Av. Díaz Ordaz #225A (Ap.60), 59000 Sahuayo - 1300-0400 – **MI18)** Venezuela 116, Col. Ángeles, 60160 Uruapan – **MI19)** Aquiles Serdán 548 , 58020 Morelia **☎**+52 443 312 3214 – **MI20)** Universidad Michoacana de San Nicolás de Hidalgo, Cd Universitaria,, 58000 Morelia - 1200-0600 – **MI21)** Av.Río Balsas 7, 60950 Cd.Lázaro Cárdenas - 1200-0400 – **MI22)** 20 de Noviembre 358, 58000 Morelia - 1200-0400 **☎**+52 443 312 0903 – **MI23)** Madero Norte 15, 61940 Huetamo – **MI24)** Mariano Jiménez Norte 8-1, Centro, 60300 Los Reyes - 1200-0200 – **MI25)** Ap.430, 60950 Cd.Lázaro Cárdenas - 1100-0600 – **MI26)** Camino de los Gatos 200, 58000 Morelia **W:** www.smrtv.michoacan.gob.mx – **MI27)** Carr Lázaro Cárdenas-La Mira, 5 de Mayo, 60990 Lázaro Cárdenas – **MI28)** Dulcaramara s/n, 58254 Morelia - 1200-0900 – **MI29)** Macarena 32, Inhuambo, 60130 Uruapan – **MI30)** Ap.73, 59300 La Piedad - 1300-0300 – **MI32)** Carretera Federal N° 15 Morelia-Zitácuaro km 125.6, 61420 Tuxpán - 1200-2330 Prgrs in Sp., Mazahua, Otomí and Matlatzinca – **MI33)** Mazatlán # 30, Col. La Magdalena, 60080 Uruapan

MO00) MORELOS (MoR)
MO01) Av.Morelos 309, Col.Centro, 62000 Cuernavaca - 1200-0600 **☎**+52 777 312 8872 ▤ +52 777 312 4388 **W:** www.radioramamorelos.com.mx – **MO02)** Plaza Yuliana, P2, 62900 Jojutla - 1200-0100 **☎** +52 734 342 1778 ▤ +52 734 342 1777 – **MO03)** 62746 Cuautla (alt.address: Hidalgo 105, 62220 Ocotepec, Cuernavaca) **☎**+52 777 313 6123.

NA00) NAYARIT (Nay.)
NA01) Puebla 64, Sur Centro, 63060 Tepic – **NA02)** Insurgentes 1046 Pte, Col.El Rodeo, 63000 Tepic - 1200-0600 – **NA03)** Av.Juarez N° 160 Ote, Col.Centro, 63000 Tepic **E:** XEUXAM@yahoo.com.mx – **NA04)** Calle María Curie No 67, entre Madero y Sócrates, Colonia Burócrata, 63180 Tepic - 1300-0700 – **NA05)** López Mateos 61, 63715 Las Varas - 1300-0100 – **NA06)** P Sánchez 87 (or: Ap.22), 63310 Santiago Ixcuintla - 1300-0500 – **NA07)** Amado Nervo 106-B Ote, (or: Ap.4), 63310 Santiago Ixcuintla - 1200-0600 – **NA08)** Morelos No 54 Poniente, Planta Alta, Depto 1, 63440 Acaponeta - 1300-0100 – **NA09)** Domicilio Conocido, 63530 Jesús María - 1200-2000 Prgrs in Sp., Cora, Huichol, Tepehuáno and Náhuatl – **NA10)** Ap.7, 63440 Tecuala - 1200-2400 – **NA11)** Puebla 3, 63600 Cd.Ruíz - 1200-0600 – **NA12)** Justo Barajas No 50 Norte, Centro, 63940 Ixtlán del Río - 1300-0100.

NL00) NUEVO LEÓN (N.L.)
NL01) Carr a Verde km 6.5, Col.Juárez, 78000 San Luis Potosí, S.L.P – **NL02)** Avenida Madero Oriente No 1110, 64000 Monterrey. **W:** gruporadioalegria.com – **NL03)** Juan Ignacio Ramón 506 Oriente, P20, Edif Latino, 64000 Monterrey – **NL04)** Paricutín Sur 316, Col.Roma, (or: Ap.203) 64700 Monterrey - 1200-0700 – **NL05)** Calle Monterrey 698, Esq.Cerralvo, Col.Libertad, 64130 Cd Guadalupe – **NL06)** Privada Rhin 647, 64000 Monterrey – **NL07)** Av Paseo de los Leones No 2935, Local C, Col Cumbres, 64000 Monterrey - 1200-0000 – **NL08)** Ap.118, 64000 Monterrey – **NL09)** Calle Reforma s/n, Col Lozano, 65290 Cd.Sabinas Hidalgo - 1200-0600 – **NL10)** Capitán Alonso de León s/n o Antigua Carretera Nacional km 904, Barrio Zaragoza, (Ap.45), 67500 Montemorelos – **NL11)** Av San Francisco y Loma Grande, Col.Loma Grande, 64000 Monterrey **☎** (81) 8347 6573 – **NL12)** Ap.62, 67701 Linares – **NL13)** Ap.81, 67701 Linares - 1200-0600

OX00) OAXACA (Oax.)
OX01) M.Ávila Camacho 514, P3, 70600 Salina Cruz - 1200-0500 – **OX02)** Ap.175, 68000 Oaxaca – **OX03)** Ap.21, 70760 Tehuantepec - 1200-0600 – **OX04)** Aquiles Serdán y Mina, 70301 Matías Romero - 1200-0100 – **OX05)** Netzahualcóyotl 216, Col Reforma, 68050 Oaxaca - 1200-0600 – **OX06)** Carr Cd.Alemán a Sayula km 27, 68400 Loma Bonita - 1200-0400 – **OX07)** Carr Puerto Escondido-Pochutla km 143, 71980 Puerto Escondido - 1300-0600 – **OX08)** Jazmines 907, 68000 Oaxaca - 1200-0600 **☎** 9513 4344 – **OX09)** Gómez Farias 113, 68000 Oaxaca - 1200-0400 – **OX10)** Abasolo 37, Centro, 68300 Tuxtepec - 1200-0100 – **OX11)** Carr Cristóbal Colón km 819.5, 70030 Juchitán 1130-0630 **☎** 9711 1233 (Ap.60), 70030 Juchitán - 1200-0200 – **OX12)**

Ap.35, 70900 Puerto Angel - 1200-0200 – **OX14)** Venustiano Carranza 74-A, Col Altavista de Juárez, (Apartado 48), 69005 Huajuapan de León - 1300-0100 ☎ +52 953 532 2004 **W:** www.xeouradio.com – **OX15)** Lázaro Cardenas s/n, 68770 Guelato de Juárez - 1200-0130 Prgrs in Sp., Zapoteco, Mixe and Chinanteco – **OX16)** Domicilio Conocido, 68470 San Lúcas Ojitlán - 1400-2200 Prgrs in Sp., Mazateco, Cuicateco and Chinanteco – **OX17)** Carr Yucudaa km 54.5, 69899 Tlaxiaco - 1200-2400 Prgrs in Sp., Mixteco and Triqui – **OX18)** Plaza de la Constitución y Negrete s/n, 71700 Santiago Jamiltepec Prgrs in Sp., Mixteco, Amuzgo and Chatino - 1200-2400 – **OX19)** Morelos 6-2, 71000 Putla de Guerrero - 1200-0130 ☎/🖷 +52 (953) 533 0000 – **OX20)** José Inés Dávila 2, Centro, 69800 Tlaxiaco - 1200-0500 – **OX21)** Universidad AutónomaBenito Juárez, 68000 Oaxaca – **OX23)** Macedonio Alcala 915, 68000 Oaxaca – **OX24)** Av.Alfonso Perez Gasca 504, 71600 Pinotepa Nacional - 1200-0600 – **OX25)** Valerio Trujano 708, 68000 Oaxaca - 1130-0600 – **OX26)** 69000 Huajuapán de León (belongs to Gobierno del Estado de Oaxaca) – **OX27)** Corporación Oaxaqueña de Radio y Televisión, Madero s/n, Centro Cultural, 68000 Oaxaca – **OX28)** 70300 Matías Romero (belongs to Gobierno del Estado de Oaxaca) – **OX29)** 70989 Sta Cruz Huatulco (belongs to Gobierno del Estado de Oaxaca) – **OX30)** 68300 Tuxtepec (belongs to Gobierno del Estado de Oaxaca) – **OX31)** 68500 Huautla de Jiménez – **OX32)** 71600 Santiago Pinotepa Nacional – **OX33)** Carr Ixtepec-Juchitán km 2, 70110 Ixtepec

PU00) PUEBLA (Pue.)
PU01) Allende 501, Col. Centro, 73800 Teziutlán **W:** xefj.com.mx 1200-0400 – **PU02)** Av. Juárez 1002, Col. Centro, 73800 Teziutlán. **W:** xeol.com.mx – **PU03)** Uno Sur 112, Mezzanine (or: Ap.84), 75700 Tehuacán. **W:** mvsradio.com 1200-0700 – **PU04)** Primera Norte 101-103, Desp.6, 75700 Tehuacán **W:** cincoradio.com.mx 1300-0100 – **PU05)** Teziutlán Sur 17, Col. La Paz, 72160 Puebla **W:** radiooro. mx – **PU06)** Matamoros No. 29-C, Col. Centro, 73160 Huauchinango . **W:** xengradio.com – **PU07)** Prof. Emilio Carranza 122, Barrio Santiago Mihuacán, 74420 Izúcar de Matamoros - 1200-0600 – **PU08)** Esmeralda Comunicaciones, Prol. Manuel M. Flores s/n, 75520 Cd. Serdán. **W:** www.kebuenapuebla.com 1300-0100 – **PU09)** Zaragoza 31-A, Centro, 74400 Izucár de Matamoros – **PU12)** Edificio Impacto, Tlaxcala 3, Col. La Santísima, (Ap.4), 74000 San Martín Texmelucan - 1200-0600 – **PU13)** Plaza de la Constitución 102, altos 1, 73080 Xicotepec de Juárez. **W:** radioxicotepec570am.com – **PU14)** Av. 15 Pte. 1306, Col.Santiago, 72000 Puebla **W:** grupoacir. com.mx – **PU15)** Priv. Miguel Alvarado s/n, 73560 Cuetzalán. **W:** cdi.gob.mx 1200-0100 prgrs in Sp, Náhuatl and Totonaco – **PU16)** Av. 15 de Mayo 2939, Col. Las Hadas, 72070 Puebla **W:** cincoradio. com.mx – **PU17)** Calle Matamoros 77, esq. San Martin Texmelucan, Col. La Paz, Puebla. **W:** tribunacomunicacion.com – **PU18)** Marconi Comunicaciones, San Martín Texmelucan 57, Col. La Paz, 72160 Puebla W. abcradiopuebla.com.mx – **PU19)** Blvd. Atlixco 37, Local 218, Plaza JV San José, 72170 Puebla. **W:** punto10.mx – **PU20)** 1 Sur 108, Desp. 307, Col. Centro, 75700 Tehuacan. **W:** radiorama.com.mx

QE00) QUERÉTARO (Qro.)
QE01) Avenida Constituyentes Oriente No 122, Colonia Los Arquitos, 76048 Querétaro – **QE02)** Carr San Juan del Rio-Xilitla km 181, Col. San José, 76340 Jalpan - 1200-0600 – **QE03)** Av.Juárez 38 Pte, 76800 San Juan del Río - 1200-0400 **W:** exafm.com – **QE04)** Paseo del Prado 102, Desp 401, Fracc.del Prado, 76030 Querétaro – **QE05)** Ing José Antonio Septién 28, Col Alameda, 76000 Querétaro - 1200-0600 – **QE06)** Av.Carrizal 28-F2, Fracc.Ampliación Carrizal, 76030 Querétaro - 1200-0600 **W:** topmusic.mx – **QE07)** Av.Tecnológico Sur 2, Local 106, Col.Niños Héroes, 76010 Querétaro – **QE08)** Centro Universitario, 76010 Querétaro - 1200-0600 **W:** uaq.mx – **QE09)** Av.Tecnológico 100, Desp.306-307, Edif.Tec 100, 76000 Querétaro – **QE10)** Camino de Piedras Anchas No. 100, Cabecera Municipal de Jalpán de Serra, 76000 Jalpán.

QR00) QUINTANA ROO (Q.Roo.)
QR01) Calle 63, Super Manazana 61, Mzna 7, Lote 1, 77500 Cancún - 1100-0600 ☎ +52 (988) 9884 1068 – **QR02)** Avenida Quinana Roo No 221, Col Venustiano Carranza, 77012 Chetumal - 1200-0500 – **QR03)** Prol.Av.Heroes 680, 77000 Chetumal - 1200-0400 – **QR04)** Ap.299, 77600 Cozumel ☎ +52 (987) 9872 0948 – **QR05)** Ap.13, 77200 Félipe Carillo Puerto - 1300-0100 – **QR06)** Av.Miguel Hidalgo 201, 77000 Chetumal - 1100-0700 – **QR07)** Av.Uxmal s/n, 77500 Cancún - 1100-0500 – **QR08)** Región 92, Manzana 62, Lotes 21-23, Z-7, 77500 Cancún - 1200-0300 – **QR09)** Av.Lázaro Cárdenas 46, 77200 Félipe Carillo Puerto – **QR10)** Av.Náder 25, SM2 Mzna 13, Desp.401, 77500 Cancún ☎ +52 (988) 9887 4550 **W:** www.radiopirata. com – **QR11)** Nader 27, Desp.1043, 77500 Cancún ☎ +52 (988) 9887 6660 – **QR12)** Carr Carillo Puerto-Cancún km 1, Col Emiliano Zapata, 77229 Félipe Carillo Puerto - 1200-1700 Prgrs in Sp and Maya – **QR13)** André Quintana Roo No 221, Esq Primo de Verdad, 77000 Chetumal – **QR15)** 77500 Cancún.

SL00) SAN LUIS POTOSÍ (S.L.P.)
SL01) Carr a Verde km 6.5, Col.Juárez, 78000 San Luis Potosí – **SL02)** Capitan Caldera 315, Col.Tequisquiapan, 78250 San Luis Potosí - 1200-0600 – **SL03)** Los Bravo 445 Altos, 78000 San Luis Potosí – **SL04)** Hidalgo 7-A, 79600 Río Verde - 1300-0100 – **SL05)** Avenida México Laredo No 29, Sur, 79050 Cd.Valles – **SL06)** Ap.80, 78700 Matehuala - 1200-0400 – **SL07)** Betancourt No 401, 78700 Matehuala 1155-0405 – **SL08)** General Mariano Arista 245, Centro Histórico, 78000 San Luis Potosí ☎ (444) 4826-13-48 **W:** www.uaslp.mx – **SL10)** Saturnino Cedillo No 200, Col Benito Juárez, 78437 San Luis Potosí – **SL11)** Carretera México-Laredo Sur s/n, Lomas Poniente, 79099 Cd.Valles – **SL12)** Privada Pemex 3 Barrio San Rafael, 79960 Tamazunchale - 1200-0800 – **SL13)** Josefa Oríz de Domínguez s/n, 79800 Tancanhuitz de Santos - 1200-0700. Prgrs in Sp., Náhuatl, Pame and Huasteco – **SL14)** Fausto Nieto 220, 78000 San Luis Potosí - 1200-0400 – **SL15)** Venustiano Carranza 460, 78000 San Luis Potosí - 1200-0100 – **SL16)** Londres y atenas s/n, Fracc.Lomas, 79090 Cd.Valles - 1200-0500 – **SL17)** Carranza 1408-interior, 78250 San Luis Potosí – **SL19)** Av Dr Salvador Nava Martínez No 278, Col El Paseo, 78320 San Luis Potosí.

SN00) SINALOA (Sin.)
SN01) Av.Lazaro Cardenas 750 sur altos, Local I-1, Plaza Palacio, 80129 Culiacán – **SN02)** Ap.61, 81000 Guasave - 1230-0800 – **SN03)** Av.Juan Carrasco y Pequeira, Local 5-D, Plaza Las Américas, 82010 Mazatlán – **SN04)** Sinaloa 442 Pte, 81200 Los Mochis ☎ 6812 7879 **W:** www. promored.com.mx – **SN05)** Ap.68, 81000 Guasave - 1200-0600 – **SN06)** Av.Álvaro Obregón 24 Sur, L-50, Centro, 80000 Culiacán – **SN07)** Paseo Niños Héroes No 802 Poniente, Centro, 80000 Culiacán - 1300-0600 – **SN08)** Ap.233, 80000 Culiacán – **SN10)** Av Miguel Alemán No 312, Centro (Ap.148), 82006 Mazatlán – **SN11)** Antonio Rosales 223 Norte, 81200 Los Mochis - 1200-0700 – **SN12)** Av.Álvaro Obregón 650-1 Norte, 80000 Culiacán - 1300-0200 – **SN13)** Aquiles Serdán 860 Pte, 81200 Los Mochis - 1300-0700 – **SN14)** Universidad de Occidente, Blvd. Macario Gaxiola y Carr Internacional, 81200 Los Mochis - 1300-0500 – **SN15)** Blvd Antonio Rosales 509 Ote, Col.Morelos, 81460 Guamuchil - 1200-0800 – **SN16)** Universidad de Sinaloa, Rosales 284 Pte, 80000 Culiacán - 1300-0200 – **SN17)** Hidalgo 408, 82400 Escuinapa - 1200-0200 – **SN18)** Hidalgo 755 Pte, 81200 Los Mochis - 1200-0400 **W:** oir-mochis.com.mx/ – **SN19)** Av.Miguel Aleman 619 Ote, 82000 Mazatlán - 1300-0700 – **SN20)** Ap.35, 82800 Rosario - 1200-0700 – **SN21)** Av.Del Mar 548, 82000 Mazatlán – **SN23)** Insurgentes 334 Sur, Centro Sinaloa, 80129 Culiacán – **SN24)** Av.del Mar 80, 82010 Mazatlán - 1300-0700 – **SN26)** Insurgentes Sur No 346, 2° Piso, Centro (Ap.113), 80129 Culiacán – **SN27)** Sinaloa 442 Pte, Col.Centro, 81200 Los Mochis.

SO00) SONORA (Son.)
SO01) Yáñez 5, entre Zacatecas y San Luis Potosí, 83000 Hermosillo - 1200-0700 ☎ (6) 215 1522 – **SO02)** Ap.630, 85480 Guaymas – **SO03)** Calle 19 N° 81, entre 15 y 16, Centro, 85400 Guaymas (tx-site Empalme) - 1300-0700 – **SO04)** Durango 901 Sur Altos, 85160 Cd.Obregón - 1300-0200 ☎ 6416 3878 – **SO05)** Ap.1817, 83000 Hermosillo - 1200-0620 – **SO06)** Blvd.Rodolfo Elias Calles 252 Ote, 85000 Cd.Obregón – **SO07)** Sinaloa Sur N° 408, 85000 Cd.Obregón – **SO08)** Obregón Este 184, Col. Centro, 83600 Caborca - 1400-0600 – **SO09)** Av.Juárez y 11ª Este 226, 84620 Cananea - 1200-0700 – **SO10)** Ap.226, 85800 Navojoa - 1200-0700 – **SO11)** Ap.6, 84900 Ures - 1300-0500 – **SO12)** Heriberto Aja 96, 83000 Hermosillo - 1300-0800 – **SO13)** Vasquez 127, P.PA, Local 1, Col. Fundo Legal, 84000 Nogales ☎ +52 (631) 312 0960 – **SO14)** Ap.371, 85400 Guaymas – **SO15)** Ave. Francisco Eusebio Kino y Calle 5 No 470, Barrio Comercial (Ap.44), 83449 San Luis Río Colorado - 1300-0100 ☎ 6534 1901 – **SO16)** Av.Morelos y Ramón Corona s/n, Col.Constitución, 85830 Navojoa - 1200-0700 – **SO17)** Ap.256, 84000 Nogales (or: Box 1472, Nogales, AZ 85628, USA) – **SO18)** Guerrero y California, Plaza Tutuli, Local E17, 85000 Cd.Obregón - 1200-0800 – **SO19)** Ap.28, 84200 Agua Prieta - 1400-0300 – **SO21)** Ap.66, 83550 Pto Peñasco - 1200-0100 – **SO22)** Allende 914 Oriente, Esq.con Sinaloa, 85000 Cd Obregón ☎ +52 (644) 413 0067 – **SO23)** Ap.44, 84600 Santa Ana - 1400-0500 – **SO24)** Ap.158, 85000 Cd.Obregón – **SO25)** Ap.63, 84160 Magdalena - 1300-0300 – **SO26)** Morelos y Calle Obregón, 83600 Caborca – **SO27)** Ap.28, 84200 Agua Prieta 1500-0600 – **SO29)** Blvd Navarrete 38, Local 2, Col.Valle Hermoso, 83209 Hermosillo ☎ +52 (662) 215 4900 🖷 – **SO30)** Ap.53, 85000 Guaymas ☎ +52 (662) 215 4940 – **SO31)** Ap.148, 21960 Cd Morelos, BC - 1200-0700 - (transmitter site: San Luís Colorado, Sonora) – **SO32)** Heriberto Aja 96 y Nayarit, 83000 Hermosillo – **SO33)** Av.13 de Julio 5, 83600 Caborca – **SO35)** Ap.285, 83000 Hermosillo - 1300-0700 – **SO36)** Padre Nacho No 712, Col Fondo Legal, 84030 Nogales - 1200-0200 – **SO37)** Juarez 33 Ote, 85900 Huatabampo - 1300-0700 – **SO39)** Calle Internacional y Av.5 Int 8-C, 84200 Agua Prieta ☎ 6338 2017 – **SO40)** Veracruz 230 Sur Altos, 85000 Cd.Obregón – **SO42)** Edif.Leo, Abelardo Rodríguez 180, Desp.45, Col.Centro, 85400 Guaymas – **SO43)** Blvd Álvaro Obregón No 216-1, Col Reforma, 85830 Navojoa ☎ +52 (6) 422 2999 – **SO44)** Carr a Novojoa km 27, 85280 Etchojoa - 1300-0100. Prgrs in Sp., Mayo, Yaqui and Guarijío.

TB00) TABASCO (Tab.)
TB01) Paseo de la Ceiba 102, P1, Col.3 de Mayo, 86190 Villahermosa - 1000-0600 – **TB02)** J.Alvarez 301, 86000 Villahermosa – **TB03)** Paseo Usumacinta y Ayuntamiento, 86100 Villahermosa - 1000-0600 – **TB04)** Calle 28 N° 117, 86900 Tenosique - 1200-0200 – **TB05)** Rosendo Taracena s/n, Local 97, 86030 Villahermosa – **TB06)** Leandro Adriano y Rogelio Ruiz Rojas, 86500 Cárdenas - 1200-0600 – **TB07)** Santa María No 214, 9, Esquina Vicente Guerrero, Local 3, Centro, 86700 Macuspana - 1200-0600 ☎ 9302 2644 – **TB08)** José Julián Dueñas 201, Parque Hidalgo, 86800 Teapa – **TB09)** Av.Méndez 1407, P1, Col.Nueva Villahermosa, 86070 Villahermosa - 1200-0300 – **TB10)** José Martí 101-107, 86000 Villahermosa - 1100-0500 – **TB11)** Prolongación 27 de Febrero 1001, Col.F.Galaxias, 86035 Villahermosa - 0620 ☎ +52 993 316 3317 – **TB12)** Sánchez Mármol 408, 86000 Villahermosa - 1100-0500 – **TB13)** José Pagés Ilergo No 116, Col Fracc Nueva Villahermosa, 86070 Villahermosa - 1200-0600 – **TB14)** Av Ruíz Cortines No 1228, Fracc Oropeza, 86030 Villahermosa – **TB15)** Calle de la Ceiba 102-3, Primero de Mayo, 86190 Villahermosa – **TB16)** Constitución 1011, Centro, 86000 Villahermosa – **TB17)** 86900 Tenosique (belongs to Gobierno del Estado de Tabasco) – **TB18)** Antonio Rullán Ferrer No 201, Col Mayito, 86090 Villahermosa – **TB19)** Av Rullán Ferrer No 201, Esquina Arista, Zona Centro, 86000 Villahermosa - 1200-0100.

TM00) TAMAULIPAS (Tamps.)
TM01) Gaspar de la Garza 170 Sur, 87000 Cd.Victoria - 1200-0600 – **TM02)** Ap.134, 88500 Reynosa - 1300-0100 – **TM03)** Ap.4, 88000 Nuevo Laredo 1230-0600 – **TM04)** Séptima No 233, Altos Centro, 88300 Ciudad Miguel Alemán - 1155-0500 – **TM05)** Ap.797, 89160 Tampico - 1200-0600 – **TM06)** Ap.79, 89901 Cd.Mante – **TM07)** Tiburcio Garza Zamora No 1245, Col Beatty, 88630 Reynosa - 1200-0400 – **TM08)** Paseo Colón No 3822, Plaza Cristal, Local 20, Col Jardin, 88260 Nuevo Laredo - 1200-0200 – **TM09)** Calle 14 y Abasolo Esq No 76, 87300 Matamoros - 1200-0600 – **TM10)** Valentín Gómez Farías, 89150 Tampico - 1200-0600 – **TM11)** Gonzales y Mendoza 747, Col. Centro, 88000 Nuevo Laredo (or: 1510 Calle del Norte, Suite 2, Laredo, TX 78041, USA) **E:** xe2xpk@nld.bravo.net – **TM12)** Diego Acuña, 87900 Cd.Tula - 1200-0400 – **TM13)** Aquiles Seldan 119 Sur, 89000 Tampico – **TM14)** Ap.540, 87300 Matamoros - 1200-0700 – **TM15)** Ap.232, 88000 Nuevo Laredo - 1155-0600 (Sat –0800, Sun -0200) – **TM16)** Carretera Ribereña KM 62, 88440 Cd.Camargo - 1200-0400 – **TM18)** Av.Juárez 703 Ote, 89800 Cd.Mante - 1200-0100 – **TM19)** Carretera Victoria-Mante Km 2 s/n, Col Las Brisas, 87180 Cd.Victoria – **TM20)** Benito Juárez 506-A, Col.Tolteca, 89160 Tampico **W:** radioramatampico.com **TM21)** Av.Cuauhtémoc y Calle 12, Col.San Francisco, 87350 Matamoros - 1155-0600 ☎ 8812 0202 – **TM22)** Ap.13, 83000 Cd.Miguel Alemán 1155-0400 – **TM23)** Ap.1, 83000 Cd.Miguel Alemán – **TM24)** Morelos 2513, Juarez, 88209 Nuevo Laredo - 1200-0600 – **TM25)** Zaragoza 85, 87600 San Fernando - 1200-0600 – **TM27)** Altamira Calle Principal de Estereos, Carr Tampico-Gonzalez, 89600 Altamira - 1200-0400 – **TM28)** Calle 8 y Cuauthémoc 125, Col.Pedro Sosa, 87120 Cd Victoria - 1200-0800 – **TM29)** Sexta y Fuerza Aérea, Edif María Rebeca , 87300 Matamoros – **TM30)** Lázaro Cárdenas 210, Local 19,20 y 21, Col.Centro, 88500 Reynosa – **TM31)** González y Mendoza No 3848, Centro, 88000 Nuevo Laredo - 1200-0200 – **TM32)** – Boulevard Adolfo López Mateos No 3205, Local 9 y 10, Santo Niño, 89160 Tampico - 1200-0600 – **TM33)** Altamira No 311, Poniente, Zona Centro, 89000 Tampico – **TM34)** Carretera Monterrey-Reynosa No 210, Conjunto Inlosa, Planta Alta, Local 16, Col Portal de S Miguel, 88500 Reynosa - 1200-0600.

TX00) TLAXCALA (Tlax.)
TX01) Av.Juárez Norte 203, 90500 Huamantla - 1200-0600 – **TX02)** Calle Uno 420, 90070 Tlaxcala - 1200-0600.

VE00) VERACRUZ (VeR)
VE01) Plaza Crystal, Local 26, 91150 Xalapa. **W:** avanradio.com.mx – **VE02)** Av. Tres 425, 94500 Córdoba **W:** www.imagen.com.mx 1230-0430 – **VE03)** Ruíz Cortines 303, Col. Centro, 95400 Cosamaloapan. **W:** xefuradio.com.mx – **VE04)** Av.Oriente 6 No 261-210, 94300 Orizaba. **W:** rogsa.com 1200-0600 – **VE05)** Playa Aventura s/n, Col. Playa Linda, 91810 Veracruz **W:** los40.com.mx – **VE06)** Corporativo Pazos, Melchor Ocampo 119, piso 7, Edif. Pazos, 91700 Veracruz. **W:** gpazos.com – **VE07)** Av. Hidalgo 1117-A Altos, 96400 Coatzacoalcos **W:** radiorama.com.mx – **VE08)** Moctezuma 77, Bis Col. Centro, 91000 Xalapa. **W:** gruporadiocapital.mx/xezl – **VE09)** Benjamín Franklin 4, Col. Centro, 91700 Veracruz. **W:** avanradio-radiorama.com – **VE10)** Av. Benito Juárez 100, Col. Centro, 96700 Minatitlán - **W:** mix885.mx – **VE12)** Ignacio de la Llave 38, 92000 Pánuco – **VE13)** Av.Salvador Díaz Mirón 2625, Esq. Heroico, Col. Militar, 91700 Veracruz. **W:** mix885.mx – **VE14)** Calle 9 y Ave 5 No. 311, Col. Centro, 94500 Cordoba – **VE15)** Esq.Comunicación, Gabino Gonzales, 92730 Álamo. **W:** radioxeid990. mx 1200-0400 – **VE16)** Humboldt Sur 36, 91270 Perote . **W:** – **VE17)** Zaragoza 300, Local AI14, Centro, 96400 Coatzacoalcos **W:** radioformula.com – **VE18)** Grupo R. Digital, Quinta Los Ángeles km 335, Carretera Córdoba-Fortín, Córdoba. **W:** lamejor.com.mx/cordoba – **VE19)** Oliva R, Av. Una 211, entre Calles 2 y 4, Col. Centro, 94500 Córdoba. **W:** elpatronfm.com.mx – **VE20)** Ave. 20 de Noviembre 1005, Col. Cazones, 93230 Poza Rica **W:** ramsa.radioformula.com – **VE21)** Bravo 1103 N° 201, 91700 Veracruz **W:** radioramapozarica.com.mx – **VE22)** Eulalio Vela 15, Col. Obrera, 96700 Minatitlán. **W:** gruporadiomina.com – **VE23)** Ferrer No. 300, 93600 Martínez de la Torre – **VE24)** Morelos No. 37 Altos 3er. Piso Frente al Parque Reforma, Col. Centro, 92800 Tuxpan. **W:** radiorama.com.mx – **VE25)** Libertad y Morelos 301, 96100 Tierra Blanca - 1200-0200 – **VE26)** Francisco González Bocanegra No 10-B, Centro, 95700 San Andrés Tuxtla. **W:** grupoacir.com – **VE27)** Plaza Crystal, Local 20, 91150 Xalapa. **W:** olivanoticias.com 1200-0600 – **VE28)** Bernarda Soto Mercado 2, 91615 Teocelo. **W:** radioteocelo. org 1100-0200 – **VE29)** Av.Manuel Avila Camacho 11, Col. Centro, 93550 Gutiérrez Zamora – **VE30)** R. Mil de Veracruz, Ignacio Zaragoza 519, 96400 Coatzacoales **W:** maxima931.com.mx – **VE31)** Calle Bella Vista 65, Col. Cerro de la Cruz, 92123 Tantoyuca. **W:** radioramatampico.com – **VE32)** Sur 31 N° 336, 94300 Orizaba. **W:** grupoacir. com.mx 1200-0600 – **VE33)** Col. Centro, Ap. 26, 96000 Acayucan. **W:** kebuenaacayucan.com.mx 1200-0600 – **VE34)** Av.Libertad 201, 95220 Piedras Negras – **VE35)** Cra. Nacional 38, 93620 San Rafel - 1300-0100 – **VE36)** Universidad Veracruzana, Francisco de Clavijero 24, 91000 Xalapa. **W:** uv.mx/radio 1300-0700 – **VE37)** Zamora 364-Altos, 91700 Veracruz – **VE38)** Radiorama Córdoba, Calle Ocho 119, Entre Av 1 y 3, 94500 Córdoba **W:** radiorama.com.mx – **VE39)** 5 de Mayo 212, 93820 Misantla – **VE41)** Fernando Silíceo 801, 91970 Veracruz – **VE42)** Azueta No. 8, Col. Centro, 95000 Zongolica – **VE43)** Banderas 4, 92800 Tuxpam – **VE46)** Av. Guerrero 202 Sur, Zona Centro, 96400 Coatzacoalcos **W:** radiohit.com.mx – **VE48)** Libertad No 315, Altos, entre Juárez y Madero, Centro, 95100 Tierra Blanca. **W:** radiorama.com.mx – **VE49)** 16 de Septiembre 341, 2° Piso esq. Canal, Plaza Faros, 91700 Veracruz. **W:** www.radioformula.com.mx – **VE50)** Ignacio de la Llave 36, Centro, 93990 Pánuco. **W:** grupomiradio.mx/portal/ estaciones/panuco – **VE51)** W: lamejor.com.mx/tlapacoyan – **VE52)** Carretera Xalapa-Veracruz 200; 91190 Xalapa. **W:** www.abcradio.com. mx – **VE53)** Ave. Jiménez Sur 4286, Col. Pascual Ortíz Rubio, 91750 Veracruz. **W:** ultra.com.mx – **VE54)** Garizuriata 25, Zona Centro, 92800 Tuxpan. **W:** radioola.com.mx – **VE55)** Pedro Belli 229, Col. Centro, 93600 Martínez de la Torre. **W:** lamejor.com.mx/tlapacoyan

YU00) YUCATÁN (Yuc.)
YU01) Calle 62 N° 465, Entre 53 y 55, 97000 Mérida - 1130-0100 – **YU02)** Ap.152, 97001 Mérida – **YU03)** Edificio Publicentro, Calle 62, No 508 Altos, (Ap.217), 97001 Mérida - 1200-0600 (XEQM-6105 rel XHMH 95.3 "Candela FM" and also XEMH 970kHz) – **YU04)** Km 1 Carr Valladolid-Carillo Puerto, 97780 Valladolid - 1100-0500 ☎ 985 9856 2101 – **YU05)** Calle 56 N° 447, 97000 Mérida – **YU06)** Ap.5, 97700 Tizimín - 1200-0500 – **YU07)** Ap.78, 97320 Progreso – **YU08)** Universidad Autonoma de Yucatán, Ap.63-B, 97000 Mérida - 1200-0600 – **YU09)** Calle 60 N° 194-A, Entre 35 y 37, 97000 Valladolid - 1200-0400 – **YU10)** Domicilio Conocido, 97930 Peto - 1100-0100 (Sun - 1300-2200) Prgrs in Sp And Maya – **YU11)** Calle 60 N° 451, Entre 49 y 51, 97000 Mérida – **YU12)** 97780 Valladolid – **YU13)** Calle 33-B, No 513 x 6, Col García Ginerés, 97000 Mérida – **YU14)** Calle 7, No 91 x 20 y 22, Col San Antonio Cinta, 97139 Mérida - 1200-0400.

ZC00) ZACATECAS (Zac.)
ZC01) Carr Panamericana km 724.6, 99030 Fresnillo - 1200-0600 **E:** xeelxeih@logicnet.com.mx – **ZC03)** Av.Hidalgo 316, P1, Centro, 99000 Fresnillo **E:** gpb15@gauss.logicnet.com.mx – **ZC05)** DR Gilberto Delgadillo 18-3, 98400 Río Grande - 1200-0500 – **ZC06)** Radio S.A.Julián Aguirre 110, Col.Lomas de la Soledad, 98040 Zacatecas – **ZC08)** Ramón López Velarde No 43, Colonia Centro, 99300 Jerez de García Salinas - 1200-0400 – **ZC09)** Ap.324, 99000 Fresnillo - 1200-0700 – **ZC10)** Ocampo No 622, Colonia Sagrado Corazón, 99601 Xalpa – **ZC11)** Joseph Ortiz de Dominguez 51, P3, 99700 Tlaltenango - 1200-0600 – **ZC12)** Juan de Tolosa 402, Col.Sierra de Alica, 98000 Zacatecas - 1100-0800

FM in México City (MHz): DF08) 88.1 R. Red FM – DF14) 88.9 Noticias – DF02) 89.7 Oye 89.7 – DF15) 90.5 R. Imagen – DF20) 90.9 Ibero – DF08) 91.3 Alfa – DF08) 92.1 Universal – DF06) 92.9 La Ke Buena – DF08) 93.7 Stereo Joya – DF05) 94.1 UAM R. – DF14) 94.5 Opus 94 – DF14) 95.3 La Nueva Amor – DF14) 95.7 El Politécnico en Radio – DF10) 96.1 UNAM – DF06) 96.9 W Radio – DF08) 97.7 Stereo 97-7 – DF15) Reporte 98.5 – DF14) 99.3 Digital 99 – DF02) 100.1 Stereo Cien – DF02) 100.9 Beat – DF06) 101.7 Los 40 Principales – DF17) 102.5 MVS R. – DF11) 103.3 R. Fórmula Primera Cadena – DF11) 104.1 R. Fórmula Segunda Cadena – DF17) 104.9 Exa FM – DF04) 105.7 (HD Radio: ch1: Reactor 105, ch2: RMI, ch3: XEB) – DF14) 106.5 Mix 106 – DF08) 107.3 La Z – DF04) 107.9 Horizonte 108

MICRONESIA (USA associated)

L.T: Chuuk, Yap: UTC +10h; Kosrae, Pohnpei: UTC +11h — **Pop:** 106,836 — **Pr.L:** Yapese, Trukese, Ponapean, Kosraean, English — **E.C:** 60Hz, 110/220V — **ITU:** FSM

FEDERATED STATES OF MICRONESIA BROADCASTING SERVICE (Gov.)

Public Information Office, P.O. Box 34, Palikir Station, Pohnpei State FSM 96941 **L.P:** Chairman, Board of Directors: Shelten G Neth **E:** chairman@mail.fm ☎ +691 320 2548 ▤ +691 320 4356

CHUUK STATE

MW Call	kHz	kW		MW Call	kHz	kW
1) V6A	1350	1	2)	V6AK	1593	5
FM Call	MHz	kW		FM Call	MHz	kW
3) V6BC	88.1	0.1	4)	V6CWS	89.5	
5)	89.1	0.2	4)	V6CWS	98.5	
2) BWXX	89.5					

Addresses and other information
1) Baptist Mid-Missions P.O. Box 819, Weno, Chuuk State FSM 96942 **L.P:** Pastor Jody J Colson ☎ +691 330 3453 **E:** jtcolson@mail.fm – **2)** FSMBS R. Chuuk, PO Box 189, Weno, Chuuk State FSM 96942 **L.P:** Mgr Ennis Timothy ☎+691 3302374 ▤ +691 3302593 **W:** www.fm/chuuk/radio **ID:** "Ach nenien appio V6AK ion Chuuk' **D.Prgr:** 1900-2300 daily restricted service because of power disruptions and lack of fuel for generator. BWXX-FM repeater [currently inactive] – **3)** Baptist Church, Weno, Chuuk State FSM 96942 **L.P:** Rev.Tom Phillips **Prgr:** conservative religious music and supplied paid prgrs – **4)** National Weather R. [WSO FM], PO Box A, Weno, Chuuk State, FSM 96942. Live and recorded local weather and emergency information for Chuuk Lagoon area 24h – **5)** New Shine R., New Shine Church, Weno, Chuuk State FSM 96942 [currently inactive]

KOSRAE STATE

MW	Call	kHz	kW
1)	V6AJ	1503	1

Addresses and other information
1) FSMBS R. Kosrae, PO Box 147, Tofol, Kosrae State FSM 96944 **L.P:** Mgr Keitson Jonas ☎ +691 370 3040 ▤ +691 370 3880 **W:** www.fm/kosrae/radio **E:** v6aj@mail.fm **ID:** "Painge station V6AJ, fwin an Kosrae" **D.Prgr:** 2000-1400, 24h during adverse weather.

POHNPEI STATE

SW	Station	kHz	kW				
4)	V6MP	4755	1				
MW	Station	kHz	kW	MW	Station	kHz	kW
1)	V6AF	999	1	2)	V6AH	1449	10
FM	Station	MHz	kW	FM	Station	MHz	kW
9)	R. Australia	88.1	0.2	7)	Magic FM	100.3	
4)	V6MA	88.5	0.3	8)	V6AV	101.0	
5)	V6CR	88.9		1)	V6AF	104.1	
6)	V6W1	89.5					

Addresses and other information
1) Baptist R. Pohnpei, PO Box H, Kolonia, Pohnpei State FSM 96941. **L.P:** Dave Arthurs ☎+691 3202475 **E:** arthurs@wwntbm.com **D.Prgr:** 24h – **2)** FSMBS R. Pohnpei, PO Box 1086, Kolonia, Pohnpei State FSM 96941 **L.P:** Commissioner Shelten G Neth ☎+691 320 2296 ▤+691 320 5212 **W:** www.fm/pohnpei/radio **E:** v6ah_radio@mail.fm **ID:** "Met Station V6AH nan Pohnpei" **D.Prgr:** 2000-1400, 24h during adverse weather – **3)** Bernard's Enterprises, Kolonia, Pohnpei State FSM 96941 ☎+691 320 2441 ▤+691 320 2444 – **4)** the Cross, Pacific Missionary Aviation, Radio Station, PO Box 517, Kolonia, Pohnpei State FSM 96941 ☎ +691 320 1122/2496 **W:** www.pmapacific.org **E:** radio@pmapacific.org **SW:** Ninseitamw, Kolonia, simulcast of 88.5MHz – **5)** College of Micronesia, Media Studies Program, PO Box 159, Kolonia, Pohnpei State FSM 96941 ☎ +691 320 2480 ▤ +691 320 2479 **E:** national@comfsm.fm – **6)** R. Paradiise, Paradise Media, PO Box 1748, Kolonia, Pohnpei State FSM 96941 **W:** www.paradisemediapni.com **E:** paradiseradiopni@gmail.com **L.P:** GM: William Hoffman – **7)** Kolonia, Pohnpei State FSM 96941, joint ownership with KWAW Saipan CNM – **8)** 24h BBC Pacific stream satellite rel from London – **9)** 24h English for the Pacific stream satellite relay from Melbourne.

YAP STATE

MW	Station	kHz	kW				
1)	V6AI	1494	5				
FM	Station	MHz	kW	FM	Station	MHz	kW
1)	KUTE FM	88.1		3)	V6AA	89.7	
2)	V6JY	88.9	0.25	4)	YEC-FM	101.1	0.25

Addresses and other information
1) FSMBS R. Yap, PO Box 117, Colonia, Yap State FSM 96943 **L.P:** Mgr Sebastian Tamagken ☎ +691 350 2174 ▤ +691 350 2160 **W:** www.fm/yap/radio **E:** s_tamagken@yahoo.com **ID:** "Pary e radio station V6AI nu Waab" **D.Prgr:** 2000-1400, 24h during adverse weather. KUTE-FM is repeater – **2)** Joy Family R., Colonia, Yap State FSM 96943 ☎ +691 350 8483 **D.Prgr:** 24h religious – **3)** Voice of Hope, Colonia, Yap State FSM 96943 **Prgr:** religious – **4)** Yap Evangelical Church, Colonia, Yap State FSM 96943 ☎ +691 350 6101 **Prgr:** religious

MOLDOVA

L.T: UTC +2h (31 Mar-27 Oct: +3h) — **Pop:** 3.5 million — **Pr.L:** Moldovan (Romanian), Ukrainian, Russian, Gagauz — **E.C:** 50Hz, 220V — **ITU:** MDA

CONSILIUL COORDONATOR AL AUDIOVIZUALULUI (CCA) (Coordinating Audio-Visual Council)

str. Vlaicu Parcalab 46, 2012 Chisinau ☎ +373 22 277551 ▤ +373 22 277471 **E:** office@cca.md **W:** www.cca.md
L.P: Pres: Marian Pocaznoi
NB: CCA is the licensing authority for broadcasting.

TELERADIO MOLDOVA (Pub)

str. Miorita 1, 2028 Chisinau ☎ +373 22 721388 ▤ +373 22 723537 **E:** info@trm.md **W:** www.trm.md
L.P: Dir (Radio): Alexandru Dorogan

MW	kHz	kW	Prgr	MW	kHz	kW	Prgr
Chisinau (a)	873	75	1	Edinet	1494	20	1
Cahul	1494	30	1	(a) Codru			
FM (MHz)	1	2	kW	FM	1	2	kW
Balti	-	99.4	1	Mindrestii Noi	104.9	-	2
Cahul	100.7	-	4	Straseni	100.5	-	5
Causeni	106.8	103.6	4/0.3	Trifesti	103.3	-	4
Cimislia	103.5	-	2	Ungheni	102.0	-	4
Edinet	101.3	-	4	**NB:** Txs below 1kW not listed.			

D.Prgr: Prgr 1 (R. Moldova Actualitati) 24h. – **Prgr 2 (R. Moldova Tineret):** 24h. – **Prgr 3 (R. Moldova Muzical):** 24h on the Internet.

OTHER STATIONS

FM	MHz	kW	Location	Station
B)	68.48	17	Straseni	RFE-RL relay
B)	69.53	17	Ungheni	RFE-RL relay
B)	70.31	17	Edinet	RFE-RL relay
10)	71.57	2.5	Chisinau	Vocea Basarabiei
3)	87.6	1	Chisinau	R. Stil
2)	88.0	1	Chisinau	Prime FM
20)	88.7	4	Edinet	Maestro FM
14)	89.1	2	Chisinau	Retro FM
2)	89.5	4	Edinet	Prime FM
17)	89.6	1	Chisinau	R. Chisinau
15)	90.4	1.8	Chisinau	Pro FM Chisinau
2)	90.5	2	Balti	Prime FM
21)	90.7	3.2	Chisinau	Aquarelle FM
9)	90.9	2.8	Causeni	Serebryanyy dozhd
20)	91.0	3.2	Balti	Maestro FM
10)	91.9	2	Causeni	Vocea Basarabiei
2)	92.3	1.25	Ungheni	Prime FM
2)	92.6	2	Cahul	Prime FM
2)	94.7	1	Varnita	Prime FM
16)	96.7	2	Chisinau	R. Alla
23)	97.2	3.1	Chisinau	R. Plai
23)	98.8	2.5	Cimislia	R. Plai
6)	99.7	1.4	Chisinau	R. Noroc
6)	99.9	3.2	Causeni	R. Noroc
18)	99.9	3.2	Glodeni	R. Prim
8)	100.1	3.2	Chisinau	Jurnal FM
10)	100.3	1	Glodeni	Vocea Basarabiei
5)	100.7	1.3	Mindrestii Noi	Micul Samaritean
12)	100.9	2	Chisinau	Kiss FM
6)	100.9	1.6	Iargara	R. Noroc
1)	101.1	1.25	Proteagailovca	Hit FM
22)	101.3	2	Chisinau	R. Sport
19)	101.4	1	Cahul	Univers FM
23)	101.5	16	Causeni	R. Plai
1)	101.7	1	Chisinau	Hit FM
10)	101.9	5	Taraclia	Vocea Basarabiei
5)	102.0	1	Causeni	Micul Samaritean
10)	102.3	10	Straseni	Vocea Basarabiei
13)	102.7	1	Chisinau	R. 21
4)	103.0	3.2	Causeni	Russkoye R.
3)	103.5	1.6	Balti	R. Stil
4)	103.7	1.6	Chisinau	Russkoye R.

FM	MHz	kW	Location	Station
5)	103.8	10	Edinet	Micul Samaritean
5)	104.2	1	Chisinau	Micul Samaritean
6)	104.3	5	Floresti	R. Noroc
1)	104.5	20	Ungheni	Hit FM
1)	105.2	20	Cahul	Hit FM
5)	105.4	10	Trifesti	Micul Samaritean
11)	105.6	1.6	Balti	Megapolis FM
10)	105.7	5	Nisporeni	Vocea Basarabiei
7)	105.9	5	Chisinau	Fresh FM
17)	106.1	2.5	Proteagailovca	R. Chisinau
5)	107.0	20	Ungheni	Micul Samaritean
A)	107.3	10	Straseni	RFI relay
1)	107.6	20	Mîndrestii Noi	Hit FM
5)	107.7	20	Cahul	Micul Samaritean
9)	107.9	1	Chisinau	Serebryanyy dozhd
8)	107.9	10	Edinet	Jurnal FM

NB: Txs below 1kW not listed.

Addresses & other information:
1) str. Bucuresti 68, 2012 Chisinau. Rel. Hit FM (Russia) – **2)** str. Veronica Micle 10, 2012 Chisinau – **3)** str. Sciusev 93, 2012 Chisinau. Rel. R. Shanson (Ukraine) – **4)** sos. Hîncesti 59/1, 2028 Chisinau – **5)** str. Bucuresti 68, 2012 Chisinau – **6)** bd. Negruzzi 6, 2001 Chisinau – **7)** str. Bucuresti 68, 2012 Chisinau – **8)** str. Mihai Vitezul 1, 2004 Chisinau – **9)** sos. Hîncesti 59/1, 2028 Chisinau. Rel. Serebryanyy dozhd (Russia) – **10)** str. A.Puskin 20a, 2012 Chisinau – **11)** str. Alba Iulia 75, 2028 Chisinau – **12)** str. Ismail 33, 2011 Chisinau. Rel. Kiss FM (Romania) – **13)** str. Alecu Russo 1, 2068 Chisinau. Rel. R. 21 (Romania) – **14)** str. Frumusica 1, 2002 Chisinau. Rel. Retro FM (Russia) – **15)** str. Maior Petru 7, 2001 Chisinau. Rel. Pro FM (Romania) – **16)** str. Bucuresti 68, 2012 Chisinau. Rel. R. Alla (Russia) – **17)** str. Bucuresti 42A, ap. 3, 2012 Chisinau. Own prgrs & rel. R.România Actualitati (Romania) – **18)** str. Suveranitati 5, 2901 Glodeni – **19)** str. I.Spirin 106, 3909 Cahul – **20)** bd. Moscovei 21, 2068 Chisinau – **21)** str. Puskin 47/1C, 2012 Chisinau – **22)** str. Gradinilor 25-13, 2001 Chisinau – **23)** str. Inculet Ion 105, 2025 Chisinau – **A)** Rel. RFI (France) – **B)** Rel. RFE-RL (USA).

GAGAUZIA

GAGAUZIYA RADIO TELEVISIONU KULESI (GRT) (Pub)
✉ str. Lenin 164, 3805 Comrat ☎ +373 298 23086 🖷 +373 298 26934
E: gagauztv@gagauztv.md **W:** www.gagauztv.md
L.P: Chair: Ecaterina Jekova

FM	MHz	kW	FM	MHz	kW
Comrat	102.1	5	Baurci	104.6	1.25
Vulcanesti	103.6	0.2			

D.Prgr: GRT FM in Gagauz, Russian: 0500-2200.

OTHER STATIONS

FM	MHz	kW	Location	Station
20)	98.0	2.5	Comrat	Maestro FM
6)	99.5	2.5	Comrat	R. Noroc
23)	100.3	1	Comrat	PRO 100 R.
5)	103.2	1	Ciadîr-Lunga	Micul Samaritean
1)	106.6	5	Comrat	Hit FM
2)	107.5	1	Baurci	Prime FM

NB: Txs below 1kW not listed.
Addresses & other information: see main table. **23)** str. Novaia 23, 3801 Comrat.

TRANSNISTRIA

RADIO PMR (Gov)
✉ ul. Pravdy 31, 3300 Tiraspol, Transnistria ☎ +373 533 60701 🖷 +373 533 77758 **E:** radiopmr@inbox.ru **W:** www.radiopmr.org
L.P: Dir: Anatoliy A. Kirsa

MW	kHz	kW			
Maiac	621	150			

FM	MHz	kW	Location	MHz	kW
Slobozia	74.00	0.1	Camenca	104.0	-
Valea Adinca	100.1	-	Maiac	105.0	-
Dnestrovsc	100.3	-	Voroncovo	106.0	1
Slobodzia	100.7	1.5	Camenca	106.4	-
Pervomaisc	103.4	-	Maiac	106.5	0.2
Tiraspol	104.0	0.2			

D.Prgr: R. Pridnestrovya in Russian, Ukrainian, Moldovan: 0400-2200 on FM. Own prgrs and rel. Golos Rossii (Russia). Limited schedule on MW.
External Service (R. PMR): see International Radio section.

OTHER STATIONS

FM	MHz	kW	Location	Station
4)	88.3	-	Tiraspol	Tiraspol FM
3)	88.8	3	Tiraspol[1]	R. Shanson

FM	MHz	kW	Location	Station
6)	89.3	-	Varnita	R. Novaya volna
5)	89.6	-	Slobozia	Hit FM
7)	90.1	-	Tiraspol	Retro FM
14)	90.5	-	Tiraspol	Love R.
17)	91.2	-	Tiraspol	Klevoye R.
9)	91.5	-	Slobozia	Yumor FM
18)	91.7	-	Dubasari	Dubasari FM
15)	92.5	-	Tiraspol	R. Tochka
)	93.7	-	Bender	R. Dacha
13)	98.7	1	Rîbnita	R. Zhelannoye
)	100.1	-	Slobozia	R. Gardarika
5)	100.9	-	Voroncovo	Dorozhnoye R.
10)	100.3	0.03	Dubasari	Dubossarskoye R.
A)	104.6	-	Ribnita	R. Rossii relay
11)	104.6	0.1	Slobozia	Ekho Moskvy
5)	105.4	2	Bender	Dorozhnoye R.
12)	106.3	-	Tiraspol[1]	R. Rekord
9)	106.7	-	Ribnita	Yumor FM
16)	107.1	-	Slobozia	Avtoradio
5)	107.7	1	Tiraspol[1]	R. Inter FM

[1] Synchro-network with txs in several towns

Addresses & other information:
1) ul. K.Libnikhta 1/2, 3300 Tiraspol **E:** reklama@inter-fm.idknet.com – **2)** Rel. Hit FM* – **3)** ul. K.Libnikhta 1/2, 3300 Tiraspol. Rel. R. Shanson* – **4)** Tiraspol – **5)** Tiraspol. Rel. Dorozhnoye R.* – **6)** ul. Internatsionalistov 13, Bender. **E:** nv893@mail.ru Rel. Love R.* – **7)** Rel. Retro FM* – **8)** Rel. R. 7*. – **9)** Rel. Yumor FM* – **10)** ul. Dzerzhinskogo 4, 4501 Dubasari. Rel. Dorozhnoye R.* – **11)** Rel. Ekho Moskvy* – **12)** Rel. R. Rekord* – **13)** ul. Kirova 130a, 5500 Rîbnita. **E:** radio987@lan-rybnitsa.com – **14)** Rel. Love R.* – **15)** Tiraspol – **16)** Rel. Avtoradio* – **17)** ul. Yunosti 1, 3300 Tiraspol – **16)** Dubasari – **A)** Rel. R. Rossii* (*= Relays from Russia)

Int rel. on MW: (operated by Pridnestrovskiy radioteletsentr) Grigoriopol (Maiac) 621kHz 150kW, 999/1413/1548kHz 1000kW. See Int. Radio section.

MONACO

L.T: UTC +1h (31 Mar-27 Oct: +2h) — **Pop:** 33,000 — **Pr.L:** French — **E.C: 50Hz, 220V** — **ITU:** MCO

MONTE CARLO RADIODIFFUSION (Comm.)
✉ 10 Quai Antoine 1er, MC-98000 Monaco ☎ +377 97974799 🖷 +377 97974707 **W:** www.mcr.mc **E:** mcradiodiffusion@mcr.mc
L.P: Patrick Jean.

MW	kHz	kW	Prgr.
Col de la Madone (France)	702	200	R.Chine Int. (0800-2300)*
Roumoules (France)	1467	1000	TWR relay (1915-2245) **
Col de la Madone (France)	1467	40	R. Maria France (0500-1900)***

*in French & Italian, **mainly Arab & Eng. Prgs, ***R. Marie France, BP 50048, F-83180 Six-Fours-Les-Plages Cedex, France **W:** www.radiomaria.fr **E:** info@radiomaria.fr **V.** by Letter Rp.

RMC INFOS (Comm.)
✉ HQ: 12 Rue d'Oradour sur Glane, F-75740 Paris Cedex 15, France ☎ +33 1 71191191 🖷 +331 71191190 **W:** www.rmc.fr **E:** technique@rmc.fr **L.P:** Pres: Alain Weill, GD: Franck Lanoux
LW: Roumoules (France) 216kHz 1400kW (reduced to 900kW), RMC INFOS 0330-2305 (Id as "RMC" only)
FM: Mont Agel 98.5MHz 50kW; Monaco Jardin Exotique 98.8MHz 1kW 24h **V.** by QSL-card. Rp.

RADIO MONACO (Comm.)
✉ HQ: 7 Rue du Gabian, Gildo Pastor Centre, MC-98000 Monaco ☎ +377 97700700 🖷 +377 97700701 **W:** www.radio-monaco.com
FM: Monaco Mont Agel 98.2MHz 1kW; Mont Agel 95.4MHz 40kW, Grasse (France) 103.2MHz 0.5kW **E:** info@radio-monaco.com

EXTERNAL SERVICE: see International Radio section for details

RADIO MONTE CARLO ITALIE (Comm.)
✉ 8 Quai Antoine 1er, MC-98000 Monaco ☎ +377 97976666 🖷 +377 97708661 **W:** www.radiomontecarlo.net **E:** rmc@radiomontercarlo.net
FM: RMC1 Monaco Mont Agel 106.8MHz 1kW; Monaco Jardin Exotique 107.4MHz 1kW; RMC2 : RMC2 Monaco Jardin Exotique 92.7MHz 1kW; Col de la Madone 101.6MHz 10kW **V.** by QSL-card. Rp.

RIVIERA RADIO (Comm)
✉ 10 Quai Antoine 1er, MC-98000 Monaco ☎ +377 97979494 🖷 +377 97979495 **W:** www.rivieraradio.mc **E:** info@rivieraradio.mc

LP: MD: Paul Kavanagh. Tech. Manager: Peter Miller
FM: Monaco Jardin Exotique 106.3MHz 1kW; Mont Agel 106.5MHz 10kW **D.Prgr**. in English: 24h Rel. BBCWS N every h

Other FM stations (all sces. 24h):

FM	MHz	kW	Station, location
-)	88.2	0.1	R. 105, Monaco Jardin Exotique
-)	90.3	50	MFM, Mont Agel
1)	91.4	0.1	Chik R. Monaco Jardin Exotique
-)	93.5	50	R. Nostalgie, Col de la Madone
-)	93.8	1	R. Nostalgie, Mont Agel
3)	94.5	0.1	Hit R. Morocco, Monaco Port
-)	95.7	0.1	Jazz R., Monaco Port
-)	96.0	0.1	R. Chine Int., Monaco Jardin Exotique
-)	96.4	0.1	FG R., Monaco Jardin Exotique
-)	99.4	0.1	R. 105 Italia, Monaco Jardin Exotique
-)	100.9	50	Music 100.9, Mont Agel
-)	101.1	0.1	Virgin R. Italia, Monaco Jardin Exotique
-)	102.1	0.1	RTL 2, Monaco Jardin Exotique
2)	102.4	1	R. Rire & Chansons, Monaco Jardin Exotique
-)	102.7	50	R. Classique, Mont Agel
-)	103.0	1.5	RFM, Mont Agel
-)	103.3	0.4	RDS Italia,Monaco Jardin Exotique
-)	104.5	0.1	Cherie FM, Monaco Jardin Exotique

Addresses:
1) in Russian, **E:** contact@chikradio.com **W:** www.radiochik.com - **2)** in Italian, French, English, German **E:** info@music1009.com **W:** www.music1009.com - **3) W:** www.hitradio.ma

MONGOLIA

L.T: UTC +8h — **Pop:** 2.8 million — **Pr.L:** Mongolian — **E.C:** 50Hz, 220V — **ITU:** MNG

HUUL EÜY DOTOOD HERGIYN YAM
(Ministry of Justice and Home Affairs)
Hudaldaanï gudamj 6/1, Ulaanbaatar 210646 ☎ +976 11 267014 +976 11 325225 **LP:** Minister: Tsendïn Nyamdorj
NB. The Ministry of Justice and Home Affairs is issuing broadcasting licenses.

MONGOLÏN ÜNDESNIY OLON NIYTIYN RADIO, TELEVIZ (MÜONRT) (Mongolian National Broadcaster)
Huvsgalïn zam 3, Ulaanbaatar 210524 ☎ +976 11 328334 +976 11 328334 **E:** mr@mongol.net **W:** www.mnb.mn
LP: DG: Naranbaatar Myanganbuu

LW	kHz	kW	Prgr	LW/MW	kHz	kW	Prgr
Ulaanbaatar (a)	164	500	1	Altay	227	75	1
Choybalsan	209	75	1	Mörön	882	75	1
Dalanzadgad	209	75	1	Ulaanbaatar (a)	990	500	F
Ölgiy	209	30	1				

(a) Honhor; F=External Service

SW	kHz	kW	Prgr	SW	kHz	kW	Prgr
Altay	4830	10	2	Ulaanbaatar (a)	7260	°50	2
Mörön	4895	10	2				

(a) Honhor; °) 0500-1500: 250kW

FM (MHz)	MR1	MR2	kW	FM (MHz)	MR1	MR2	MR3	kW
Altay	107.0	-	-	Ölgiy	107.0	-	-	-
Choybalsan	-	101.5	-	Saynshand	100.9	104.5	-	-
Dalanzadgad	-	107.5	-	Ulaanbaatar	106.0	-	100.9	1
Mörön	-	103.0	-					

+ translators
D.Prgr: MR1 (Mongolïn R.): 2200-1500. – **MR2 (Höh tenger):** 2300-1500. – **MR3 (R3):** 2300-1500.
External Service (Voice of Mongolia): See Int. Radio section.

OTHER STATIONS

FM	MHz	kW	Location	Station
11)	93.0	0.05	Erdenet	Avtoradio
24)	96.3	-	Ulaanbaatar	Avto FM
27)	98.1	-	Ulaanbaatar	Formula
25)	98.5	-	Ulaanbaatar	Best R.
26)	98.9	-	Ulaanbaatar	Hifi R.
13)	99.3	1	Ulaanbaatar	Ineemselgel R.
28)	99.7	-	Ulaanbaatar	Ih Mongol
8)	100.1	-	Ulaanbaatar	R. Elgen Nutag
12)	100.4	0.05	Erdenet	Nomïn FM
9)	100.5	1	Ulaanbaatar	R. Miniy Mongol
30)	101.5	-	Saynshand	Miniy nutag
10)	101.7	-	Ulaanbaatar	R. Höh Mongol
14)	102.1	-	Ulaanbaatar	Eh Oron R.

FM	MHz	kW	Location	Station
2)	102.5	-	Ulaanbaatar	Ulaanbaatar R.
15)	102.5	-	Baruun-Urt	Talïn Tsurai
A)	103.1	-	Ulaanbaatar	BBC Relay
29)	103.5	-	Baruun-Urt	Kiss You
16)	103.6	-	Ulaanbaatar	TV FM
17)	103.6	-	Dalanzadgad	Govïn Dolgion
18)	103.7	-	Darhan	Darhan FM
3)	104.0	-	Ulaanbaatar	Life FM
19)	104.0	-	Sühbaatar	Ögrön Selenge
7)	104.5	-	Ulaanbaatar	Ger Büülïn R.
31)	104.5	-	Saynshand	Songodog FM
4)	105.0	-	Ulaanbaatar	Tany Degred
1)	105.5	-	Ulaanbaatar	Hotïn Högjim
20)	106.0	-	Darhan	Orhon R.
21)	106.2	-	Önderhaan	Dölgöön Herlen
22)	106.4	-	Choybalsan	Züün Büsïn Olon Hiytiyn
23)	106.5	-	Mörön	Möröngïn Dolgion
B)	106.6	1	Ulaanbaatar	VOA relay
6)	107.0	-	Ulaanbaatar	Shine Zuuny R.
5)	107.5	-	Ulaanbaatar	Shine Dolgion R.
32)	107.5	-	Baruun-Urt	Ertöntsiyn ayalguu
33)	107.5	-	Saynshand	Saynshand FM

Other information:
11) Rel. Avtoradio (Russia) – **A)** Rel. BBC (UK) – **B)** Rel. VOA (USA)

MONTENEGRO

L.T: UTC+1h (31 Mar-27 Oct: +2h) — **Pop:** 672,180 — **Pr.L:** Serbian — **E.C:** 50Hz, 220V — **ITU:** MNE

RADIO TELEVIZIJA CRNE GORE
Bul. Revolucije 19, 81000 Podgorica ☎ +382 20 245595 **W:** www.rtcg.me **E:** marketing@rtcg.org **LP:** DG: S. Sestic

MW	kHz	kW	Station, h. of tr.
Podgorica	882	5	R. Podgorica 1, 24h

FM (MHz)	RCG 1	R. 98	kW	FM (MHz)	RCG 1	R. 98	kW
Bjelasica	92.1	99.3	54	Podgorica	96.5	89.3	10
Durmitor	96.1	91.3	10	Sudj. Glava	88.0	88.0	10
Lovcen	94.9	98.0	54	Velji Grad	99.8	89.6	10
Mozura	97.3	93.4	10				

+ 11 txs.less than 1kW

Local/private stations
R. Antena M, Podgorica 87.6MHz + 5 relays – **R. Cetinje** 94.5MHz + 1 relay – **R. Elmag**, Podgorica 96.0MHz + 7 relays – **R. Bar** 91.8MHz + 1 relay – **R. Berane** 88.2MHz +1 relay – **R Bijelo**, Polje 101.1MHz + 1 relay – **R. Budva** 98.7MHz + 1 relay – **R. Corona**, Bar 88.9MHz +1 relay – **R. D**, Podgorica 88.6MHz + 2 relays – **R. Danilovgrad** 92.9MHz – **R. Fokus**, Bijelo Polje 93.9MHz – **R. Free Montenegro**, Podgorica 103.0.MHz – **R. Glas** Plava, Plav 102.9MHz – **R. Gorica**, Podgorica 93.3MHz +1 relay – **R. Herceg** Novi 90.0MHz +1 relay – **R. Jupok**, Rozaje 98.7MHz +1 relay – **R. Kotor** 95.3MHz + 1 relay – **R. Max**, Danilovgrad 107.5MHz + 1 relay – **R. Mir**, Tuzi 106.1MHz + 1 relay – **R. Mojkovac** 92.8MHz – **R. Montena**, Podgorica 105.7MHz + 5 relays – **R. Niksic** 89.8MHz + 2 relays – **R. Ozon**, Kolasin 97.6MHz – **R. Panorama**, Pljevlja 89.2MHz – **R. Pljevlja** 94.8MHz – **R. Rozaje** 104.4MHz – **R. Svetigora**, Cetinje 101.0.MHz – **R. Tivat** 88.5.MHz – **R. Ulcinj** 91.3MHz + 1 relay – **R. Zeta**, Podgorica 93.8.MHz – **R. City**, Podgorica 107.3MHz

MONTSERRAT (UK)

L.T: UTC -4h — **Pop:** 5,000 — **Pr.L:** English — **E.C:** 60Hz, 220V — **ITU:** MSR

RADIO MONTSERRAT (Gov. Comm.)
PO Box 51, Sweeneys ☎ +1 664 491 2885 +1 664 491 9250 **W:** www.zjb.gov.ms **E:** zjb@gov.ms **LP:** SM: Herman Sargeant. Technician: Ivor Greenaway
FM: 88.3MHz, 0.1kW (Isles Bay Hill), 95.5MHz, 5kW (Silver Hills)
D.Prgr: 24h BBC relay at night 0400-0930
Ann: "ZJB Radio Montserrat, the Voice of Montserrat"

Other stations:
ETERNAL LIFE RADIO Cavalla Hill ☎ +1 664 496 6982.**W:** www.eternal-liferadio.com - **FM:** 106.1MHz – **CSS CARIBBEAN SUPER STATION - FM:** 93.9MHz (relay Trinidad) – **VIBZ FM - Family Radio Network** P.O. Box 350, Baker Hill ☎ +1 664 491 7331 **W:** www.vibzfm.com - **FM:** 89.9/90.9MHz (relay Antigua)

MOROCCO

L.T: UTC; DST (28 Apr-29 Sep: +1h; suspended during month of Ramadan) subject to confirmation — **Pop:** 35 million — **Pr.L:** Arabic, French, Spanish, English, Berber languages, Hassania — **E.C:** 50Hz, 127/220V — **ITU:** MRC

HAUTE AUTORITÉ DE LA COMMUNICATION AUDIOVISUELLE (HACA)

✉ Espace les Palmiers, Lot 26,Angle Avenues Anakhil et Mehdi Ben Barka, B.P. 20590, Rabat Ryad ☎+212 53 7579600 🖷 +212 53 7714274 **W:** www.haca.ma **E:** info@haca.ma **L.P:** DG: Ahmed Akhchichine.

SOCIÉTÉ NATIONALE DE RADIODIFFUSION ET DE TÉLÉVISION (SNRT) - RADIO MAROCAINE (Pub.)

✉ 1, Rue El Brihi, B.P. 1042, MA-10000 Rabat ☎+212 53 7700 319 🖷 +212 53 772 2047 **W:** www.snrt.ma **Reg.** ✉ B.P. 459, Laayoune. **L.P:** DG: Mohamed Ayad. Dir. Tech: Allal Kacimi.

LW/MW	kHz	kW	N	LW/MW	kHz	kW	N
Azilal	207	400	A	Laâyoune	711	300	R
Sidi Bennour	540	600	A/R	Agadir	936	100	C/R
Oujda	*594	50	A/R	Sebaa-Aioun	1044	300	C
Sebaa-Aioun	612	300	A	*alt. fq 595 kHz.			

FM (MHz)	A	B	C	Q&R	kW
Agadir	91.0	94.2	97.5	87.9	
Beni Mellal	89.8	92.9	96.1		10
Casablanca	96.0	90.0	95.3	98.6	
Dakhla	93.5	91.8		91.8	
El Houceima	105.7	92.1	95.3		8
El Jadida	90.4				
Errachidia	91.3	97.8	94.5		
Essaouira	97.9	91.4			
Fès	88.8	95.1	101.9	98.4	
Figuig	91.9	95.1	98.4		
Ifrane	90.5	93.6	96.8		
Khenifra	91.6	87.9	104.6	94.2	10
Lâayoune	93.9	97.9	91.1	94.2	10
Marrakech	94.9	98.8		91.0	30
Meknès	88.8	95.1	101.9	92.5	10
Nador	86.7	93.9	97.2		
Ouarzazate	90.3	93.4	96.6		
Oujda	89.9	99.4		96.1	10
Oum Dreiga	97.9				
Rabat	91.0	87.9	104.6	94.2	40
Safi	90.9		94.1		
Settat	92.1	89.0			
Tanger	88.7	91.8	95.0	88.7/104.0	
Tantan	90.3				
Taza	91.7	94.9			10
Tétouan	90.6	100.2		93.7	12

A: National Network in Arabic: 0500-0100. **N:** on the h. – **Netw. B, Chaîne Inter:** 0600-0100. **English:** W 1000-1200, Sun 1400-1500v. **Spanish:** 0900-1000. Other times in French. – **Netw. C in Berber/Arabic dialects:** 1200-2400 (incl. rel. Netw. A 0600-1200). **Netw. Q: Quran R. "Mohammed VI":** 24h, MW 1800-0600. **Regional Prgrs** (FM on Q network). **MW: Agadir:** Avenue Hassan II, Agadir: on 936kHz. **Casablanca,** Ain Chock, Casablanca: **Laâyoune/ Dakhla:** on 711kHz. **Marrakech:** 40 Ave. Yugoslavie, Marrakech: on 540kHz. **Fès & Meknès:** on 612kHz (Fès 0600-1200, Meknès 1200-1800). **Oujda,** Avenue Omar Errifi, Oujda: on 594kHz. **Tangier:** 33, Avenue Amir Moulay Abdallah, Tangr: on 540kHz. **Tetouan,** 30, Avenue Mohammed V, Tetouan.
Ann: Arabic: "Huna Ribat, Idha'atu-l-Mamlaka al Maghribiyya" or "Idha'at al-Wataniya". French: "Ici Rabat, Radiodiffusion Télévision Marocaine". Berber: "Dahab Rbad Lidaa Attalfaza Li Mamlaka L'Maghrib"

EXTERNAL SERVICE: R. Marocaine, see International Radio section.

RADIO MEDITERRANÉE INTERNATIONALE - MEDI 1 RADIO (Comm, Semi-Gov.)

✉ B.P. 2055, 3/5 rue Emsallah, 90000 Tanger ☎&🖷 +212 539936363 **W:** medi1.com **E:** medi1@medi1.com
LW/SW: Nador 171kHz 1600kW & 9575kHz 250kW: see International Radio section.
FM (MHz):Agadir 104.6 20kW, Al Hoceima/El Jadida 96.7, Beni Mellal 102.9, Casablanca 99.6 9kW, Dakhla 96.4, Enjil 97.0, Essaouira 94.6 12kW, Fès 101.4 2kW, Laâyoune 101.0 10kW, Marrakech 105.3 1kW, Meknès 105.5 10kW, Merchiche 87.6, Nador 105.3 10kW, Ouarzazate/ Zaio 99.9, Oujda 102.9 12kW, Rabat 97.5 20kW, Safi 97.0, Slokia

95.3, Taliouine 92.2, Tanger 101.0 1kW, Tantan 93.4, Taroudante 95.4, Tetouan 103.7 12kW, Zagora 97.0.
D.Prgr. in Arabic/French: 24h. **N. in Arabic:** 0600, 0700, 0800, 1200, 2000, 2300. **N. in French:** 0630, 0730, 0830, 1230, 1700, 1930, 2200.**Ann:** "Médi 1".

Other stations:

FM	1)	2)	3)	4)	5)	6)	7)	8)	9)	10)
Agadir	100.4	93.1	96.5		95.6		89.3	103.7		
Al Hoceima	97.7	93.3		102.1					94.4	
Béni Mellal	94.0				98.1		94.7	91.6	105.1	
Boujdour						88.9				
Casablanca	104.3	93.1	88.7		100.3	92.5	88.2	100.8	91.2	102.1
Dakhla	89.7				99.7		88.7	88.0		
El Jadida	95.1	93.1			94.5	97.3	89.3	96.2	91.5	101.3
Errachidia	102.5					104.1		100.5	105.6	
Essaouira	92.8	93.3	99.9		96.1		89.8			
Fès	103.9				94.1	98.8			89.4	103.2
Figuig		93.1	105.5							
Gharb	99.3									
Guelmim					98.5					
Goulmima		93.1				91.0				
Ifrane	103.6									103.2
Khenifra	102.4									
Laâyoune	104.6		107.1		91.6		89.4	98.6		
Larache					92.8					
Marrakech	100.6	93.8	97.7		94.4	90.5	98.6	98.5		
Meknès	99.9	93.7	102.5			97.2			90.7	92.9
Nador	104.3		101.0	90.7					100.7	101.4
Oujda	102.0			92.9	98.5		106.5	97.7	87.8	
Ouarzazate	91.2				92.0		88.9	103.4		
Rabat	95.7	93.5			99.8	106.9	90.2	103.7	96.5	97.0
Safi	103.6						90.3			
Sarsar										90.1
Settat	103.8				99.8	106.4	93.4	97.9	94.7	96.4
Skhour	102.2		102.6		95.8		88.0			
Smara							91.8			
Tafraoute			99.2							
Tamanar			98.4							
Tantan		93.1	99.9				101.3			
Tanger	102.3	93.3		105.4	96.4	103.3			92.3	91.1
Tarfaya						89.6				
Targuist			95.8							
Taroudante	101.3						88.1			
Taza	95.8				98.6		97.8			101.7
Tétouan	105.9	93.9		104.5	97.8					93.0
Tiznit			104.2		91.5		88.4			
Zagora							105.9			

1) Aswat FM: Ghandi Mall, Imm 9, Bd. Ghandi, Casablanca. **W:** aswat. ma – **2) Radio 2M** (Semi-Gov.): Km 7300 route de Rabat Ain Seeba, Casablanca. **W:** www.2m.tv/radio2M – **3) MFM Atlas/Oriental/ Sahara/Saïss/Souss & Casa FM**: Groupe New Publicity, 58 Av. des FAR, Tour des Habous, 18ème étage, Casablanca. **W:** radiocasafm.ma – **4) Cap Radio**: Zone industrielle, Route de Tétouan, Allée principale lot n°123, Tanger. **W:** capradio.ma – **5) Hit Radio**: 3 rue Assouhaili, Agdal, Rabat. **W:** hitradio.ma – **6) R. Atlantic**: Eco-Médias, 70 Bd. Massira Khadra, Casablanca. **W:** atlanticradio.ma – **7) Med Radio**: 55, intersection Blvd Zerktouni et rue Sebta, 5ème étage n° 20, Casablanca. **W:** medradio.ma – **8) R. Chada FM**: Société R. Kolinass, 42 Bd. Idriss 1er quartier des Hôpitaux, Casablanca. **W:** chadafm.net – **9) R. Mars**: 30 Ave. des Far 13ème étage, Casablanca 20000. **W:** radiomars.ma – **10) Medina FM:** Rue Oued ziz imm 51 appt 4 agdal, Rabat. **W:** medinafm.net
R. Sawa: Rabat & Agadir 101.0MHz 20kW, Casablanca 101.5MHz 10kW, Marrakech 101.7MHz 12kW, Meknès 91.9MHz, Fès 97.9MHz 2kW, Tetouan 92.1/101.8MHz 20kW.

CEUTA (Spain)
L.T: see Spain — **Pop:** 80,000 — **Pr.L:** Spanish

R. Nacional de España, Real 90, E-51001 Ceuta. FM: RNE-1 97.2MHz, R. Clásica 100.8MHz, RNE5TN 101.9MHz, RNE-3 106.6MHz, all 1kW.
SER Radiolé - R. Ceuta, Poblado Marinero, Local 32, E-51001 Ceuta. **MW:** 1584kHz 5kW 24h rel. of Radiolé netw. FM: 96.2MHz R. Ceuta
COPE, Sargento Mena 8,1°izq, E-11701Ceuta. FM: 89.8MHz COPE Ceuta/Cadena 100.
Onda Cero R, Grupos Alfa 4,3°nz, E-11701Ceuta. FM: 101.4MHz Onda Cero R. 3kW.
RTV Ceuta: 99.0MHz. **W:** rtvce.es

MELILLA (Spain)
L.T: see Spain — **Pop:** 70,000 — **Pr.L:** Spanish

R. Nacional de España, Altos de la Vía 3, E-52004 Melilla. **MW:**

RNE1 972kHz 5kW. **FM:** (0.3kW): 97.7MHz (R1), 100.1MHz (RNE5TN) ,105.3MHz (R3), 107.6MHz (R. Clásica).
SER R. Melilla, Muelle Ribera s/n, E-52005 Melilla. Email: radiome-lilla@unionradio.es .**MW:** 1485kHz 1kW 24h. **FM:** (MHz): 96.3 Cadena 40 Melilla, 101.1 Dial Melilla.
COPE, C/ Pablo Vallescá 6 "Edificio Ánfora"2º - 1, E-52001 Melilla. **FM:** 91.3MHz Cadena 100, 98.4MHz COPE Melilla.
Onda Cero R, General Mola 26 E-29804 Melilla. **FM:** (MHz): 89.6 Onda Cero R, 98.4 Europa FM.
esRadio, Melilla: 92.2MHz

MOZAMBIQUE

L.T: UTC +2h — **Pop:** 22 million — **Pr.L:** Portuguese, 20 ethnic lan-guages — **E.C:** 50Hz, 220V — **ITU:** MOZ

INSTITUTO NACIONAL DAS COMUNICAÇÕES (INCM)
✉ Av. Eduardo Mondlane, 123/127, PO Box 848, Maputo ☎+258 21 490131 🖷 +258 21 494435. **W:** www.incm.gov.mz **E:** info@incm.gov.mz
RÁDIO MOÇAMBIQUE (Pub.)
✉ Rua da Rádio n.º 2, C.P. 2000, Maputo ☎+258 21 431687 🖷 +258 21 321816 **W:** www.rm.co.mz **E:** caprimoe@zebra.uem.mz
L.P: Chmn/CEO: Ricardo Malate. TD: Mr Hermenegildo Basílio Mula. Int. Rel. Dir. Ms. Maria Cremilda Massingue. Fin. Dir: Arlindo Piedade de Sousa.

MW	kHz	kW	N	MW	kHz	kW	N
1) Maputo	738	50	N	4) Chimoio	1026	50	EP
3) Nampula	765	50	EP	7) Quelimane	1179	50	EP
10) Xai-Xai	810	50	EP	5) Inhambane	1206	50	EP
2) Beira	873	50	EP	8) Pemba	1224	50	EP
9) Tete	963	50	EP	6) Lichinga	1260	50	EP
1) Maputo	1008	50	EP				

FM	MHz	kW	N	FM	MHz	kW	N
10) Xai-Xai	87.8	-	N	1) Maputo	97.9	5	C
5) Massinga	89.9	0.12	N	9) Tete	100.7	-	EP
9) Tete	90.7	-	N	5) Inhambane	101.6	-	N
10) Xai-Xai	90.9	-	N	6) Lichinga	101.7	-	N
2) Beira	91.6	-	N	1) Maputo	102.3	-	M
7) Quelimane	92.1	10	N	4) Chimoio	102.5	-	EP
1) Maputo	92.3	10	N	5) Inhambane	105.1	-	EP
1) Maputo	93.1	-	D	2) Beira	105.2	-	C
3) Nampula	95.1	-	N	3) Nampula	105.5	0.25	EP
8) Pemba	95.3	-	N	1) Maputo	105.9	-	E

Antena Nacional (N) in Portuguese: 24h.
Cidade FM (C) in Portuguese: 24h. Also rel. BBC.
RM Desporto (D) in Portuguese: 0300-2200.
Maputo Corridor R. (E) in English: 1000-2200. Also rel. BBC.
Emissão Provincial (EP) in Portuguese/ethnic: Provincial prgrs (between 0240-2100) and rel. of Antena Nacional on MW/FM: 24h.
1) EP de Maputo – **2)** EP de Sofala, C.P. 1942, Beira – **3)** EP de Nampula, C.P. 93, Nampula – **4)** EP de Manica, C.P. 390, Chimoio – **5)** EP de Inhambane, C.P. 196, Imhambane – **6)** EP do Niassa, C.P. 171, Lichinga – **7)** EP de Zambézia, C.P. 333, Quelimane – **8)** EP de Cabo Delgado, C.P. 45, Pemba – **9)** EP de Tete, C.P. 384, Tete – **10)** EP de Gaza, C.P. 130, Xai-Xai.
Ann: "Rádio Moçambique, Antena Nacional", EP: "Rádio Moçambique, (province)". **IS:** Mbira (indigenous xylophone). Opens and closes with National Anthem.

LM RÁDIO (Comm.)
✉ Hotel Cardoso, Av Martires de Mueda, Maputo. Operating Company: T & W Management Pty Ltd, P.O.Box 2722, Lonehill, 2062, South Africa ☎+27 76 372 1847/+258 82 279 6842 **W:** lmradio.net **E:** feedback@lmradio.net **L.P:** CEO: Chris Turner. PD:.Peter de Nobrega.
MW: via Lancer's Gap, Lesotho 1197kHz 50k**W:** 0500-1500.
FM: Maputo 87.8MHz 1kW 24h.
D.Prgr: 24h in English and occ. Portuguese & Afrikaans.

Other Stations (all MHz):
R. A Voz do Islão, Maputo: 96.3 – **R. Capital,** Maputo: 90.7 (also rel. TWR) – **R. Haq,** Nampula: 104.4 – **R. Maria Moçambique:** Maputo 103.1, Villankulo/Xai Xai 102, Chokwe 101.4, Govure 102.5, Quissico 106.4, Maxixe 104.2, Nova Mambone 104 **W:** www.radiomaria.org. mz – **R. Miramar,** Maputo :101.4 – **R. N'tyana,** Maputo: 93.5 – **R. SFM,** Maputo: 94.6 – **R. 99,** Maputo: 99.3 – **RTV Klint,** Maputo: 88.3 – **R. Terra Verde,** Maputo: 98.6 – **R. TGV 9FM,** Maputo: 99.3 **W:**www.99fm.co.mz – **R. Viva,** Maputo: 99.6 1kW. **W:** radioviva.fm – **Top R,** Maputo: 104.2
BBC African Service: Tete 87.8, Nampula 88.3, Bejra 88.5, Quelimane 95.3, Maputo 95.5 1kW, Xai-Xai 100.9 – **RDP África:** Beira 94.8, Maputo 89.2, Nampula 91.9, Quelimane 89.0 (all 50kW) – **RFI Afrique:**

Maputo 105.0 1kW in French/English/ Portuguese.
In addition about 100 community radio stations are in operation

MYANMAR

L.T: UTC + 6½h — **Pop:** 54 million — **Pr.L:** Burmese (Bamar), English. Major minority languages: Kachin, Kayah, Kayin (Po & Sakaw), Chin, Mon, Rakhine, Shan — **E.C:** 50Hz, 230V — **ITU:** BRM

MINISTRY OF INFORMATION
✉ Yaza Thingaha Rd, Zeya Theiddhi Ward, Nay Pyi Taw ☎ +95 67 412323

MYANMA RADIO AND TELEVISION DEPT, MRTV (Gov.)
MYANMA RADIO
✉ Tatkon Township, Nay Pyi Taw ☎ +95 67 79483 🖷 +95 67 79403
Yangon centre: Pyay Rd, Kamayut-11041, Yangon ☎ +95 1 527119 🖷 +95 1 534211 **E:** mrtv@mptmail.net.mm **L.P:** DG: U Khin Maung Htay, Dir. Radio: U Win Kyi. CE: U Tin Wan, Dir TV: U Myo Myint Aung, CEng: U Tin Wan.

MW (kHz)	kW	Loc	Pr	H. of tr.
576	200	Y	P	2300-0010v
			N	0030-0730, 0930-1630
594	200	N	N	0030-0730, 0930-1630
711	400	N	P	2300-0130, 0730-1000, 1130-1530
729	100	Y	N	2330-0530, 0730-1330
			E	1330-1500

SW (kHz)	kW	Loc	Pr	H. of tr.
5915	50	N	Mi	2330-0730, 0930-1330
			E	1330-1500
5985+	50	Y	P	2300-0130
			N	0930-1630
7200±	50	Y	Y	2330-0130v,1010v-1330v
9731±	50	Y	N	0215v-0730
			P	0730-1000

FM: Yangon area 98.0MHz (N prgr), 100.0MHz (P prgr). Other FM freqs may be in operation, details not available. ±) variable
Loc=Location: N=Nay Pyi Taw. Y=Yangon. **Pr=Prgr:** N=National prgr in Burmese, English. M=minorities prgrs in Kachin, Shan, Phalan Chin, Mindat Chin, Rakhine, Wa and Kokang. Y=Yangon prgr in Sakaw Kayin, Po Kayin, Mon, Kayah, Gekho and Gebo. E=Educational prgr in Burmese and English. P="Padauk Myay" music prgr in Burmese.
English (in N Prgr): 0230-0330, 0700-0730, 1530-1630. **N:** Generally 30 mins past the UTC h on N and P prgrs; in English on N prgr at 0230, 0700, 1530.
Ann: E: "This is Myanma R" **IS:** Myanma Orchestral Music.

THAZIN RADIO (Mil.)
✉ Pyin U Lwin. Operated by the Directorate of Public Relations and Psychological Warfare, Ministry of Defence.

MW (kHz)	Pr	H. of tr.			
639	M	2330-0200, 0430-0630, 1030-1500			

SW (kHz)	Pr	H. of tr.	SW (kHz)	Pr	H. of tr.
6030	M	2330-0200	7345	Mi	1030-1330
7110	Mi	2330-0130	9460	M	0430-0630
7110	M	1030-1500	9590	Mi	0130-0330, 0430-0830

Pr=Prgr: M=Main prgr in Burmese, exc.English 0130-0200, 0430-0630, 1430-1500. Mi=minorities prgr in Chin, Kachin, La, Po, Geba, Kokang, Karen, Shan, Kayah, Gekho and Mon.

Other Stations:
Cherry FM (Comm.) Operated by Zaykabar Co. ✉ Taunggyi. Yangon office: 1 No 3, Main Rd, Mingalardon Garden City, Yangon. **FM:** Taunggyi 89.8MHz, Shan State (east) 88.0/88.6/91.3MHz – **City FM (FM-89) (Gov.)** ✉ Yangon City Development Committee, City Hall, Mahabandoola St corner Sule Pagoda Rd, Yangon. **FM:** Yangon 89.0MHz – **FM Bagan (Comm.)** Operated by Htoo Co. **FM:** 89.8MHz (may not yet be operating) – **Mandalay FM (Gov.)** ✉ Mandalay. Yangon office: Rm 1402-3, Olympic Twr, Bo Aung Kyaw St, Yangon. Joint venture of Forever Group and Mandalay City Development Committee (MCDC). **FM:** Mandalay (Sagaing Hill)/Taungoo/Yangon 87.9MHz, unk. loc. 88.3MHz – **Padamyar FM (Comm.) (Ruby FM.)** ✉ Sagaing. **FM:** Monywa 88.6MHz, Myitkyina/Sagaing 88.9MHz, unk. locs. 91.0/103.0MHz – **Pyinsawaddy FM (Comm.)** Operated by Forever Group. ✉ Sittwe, Rakhine State. **FM:** Sittwe 88.9MHz – **Shwe FM (Comm.)** Operated by Shwe Thanlwin Co. ✉ Bago. **FM:** Bilin/Nyaunglaybin 89.5MHz, Bago/Kyaikto/Mon State 89.8MHz, Yangon 90.0MHz – **Defence Forces Broadcasting Unit (Mil.)** ✉ Taunggyi, Shan State **SW:** 5770kHz 10kW **D.Prgr.** in Burmese and minority langs: 0030-0430, 0830-0930, 1130-1530 (r. inactive at editorial deadline)

NAMIBIA

L.T: UTC +1h (2 Sep 12-7 Apr 13, 1 Sep 13-6 Apr 14: +2h) — **Pop:** 2.1 million — **Pr.L:** English, Afrikaans, German, local languages — **E.C:** 50Hz, 220V — **ITU:** NMB

COMMUNICATIONS REGULATORY AUTHORITY OF NAMIBIA (CRAN)
☞ Private Bag 13309, Communication House, 56 Robert Mugabe Ave, Windhoek ☎+264 61 222666 📠 + 264 61 238646 **W:** www.ncc.org.na **E:** info@cran.na **LP:** CEO: Stanley Shanapinda. Head Eng.: Ronel le Grange.

NAMIBIAN BROADCASTING CORPORATION (Pub)
☞ P.O. Box 321, Pettenkofer Str, Windhoek West 9000 ☎+264 61 291 9111 📠 + 264 612 913325 **W:** nbc.na **E:** pr@nbc.com.na **LP:** Chmn: Mr. Ponhele Ya France. DG: Albertus Aochamub. Tech. Mgr: Ruben Prinz.

FM (MHz)	Afr.	Nat.	Ger.	Ova.	Her.	D/N.	Kav.Lozi	Tsw.	San.
Aminuis	88.9	92.0			95.2			98.5	
Andara		92.5		95.7			106.1102.5		
Arendsnes	88.7	90.1	91.8	96.4	99.7	106.8	93.2 95.0	98.3	103.2
Aroab	87.9	94.2			104.6				
Aus	92.5		95.8	102.6		160.2			
Aussenkjer	92.5	95.7		98.7		102.5			
Bethanien	88.1	91.2	94.4	97.7	101.2	104.8			
Brukkaros	90.2	96.5			106.9				
Buitepos		95.0		98.3	101.8			105.4	
Ekuli		91.5		88.4			94.7 98.0		
Epukiro	91.6	98.1		101.6				105.2	
Erongo	90.6	93.7	96.9	100.2	103.7	107.3			
Gam		92.6		102.6	99.1				95.8
Gibeon					100.7				
Gobabis	87.6	90.7	93.9	102.9	100.7	104.3	106.5 92.9	97.2	
Gross-Herzog	88.6	91.7	94.9	98.2	101.7	105.3			
Kamanjab	89.7				106.4				
Katima Mulilo	89.5	92.6	90.9	99.1	94.1	106.2	100.9 95.8	87.8	
Keetmanshoop	87.6	90.7	93.9	97.2	89.3	104.3			
KL. Waterberg	89.6	92.7	95.9	99.2	102.7	106.3			
Koës	88.8	95.1			105.5				
Kongola		88.3		91.4			94.6 97.9		
Lüderitz	89.7	92.8	96.0	99.3	100.2	103.7			
Maltahöhe	88.5		94.8		105.2				
Mariental	87.7	90.8	94.0	101.8	105.4	104.4			
Nakop	90.6	93.7		100.2		103.7			
Nkurenkuru		90.7		87.6	97.2		105.1 93.9		
Noordoewer	87.7	90.8		97.3		100.8			
Okongo		89.0		92.1		95.3	98.6		
Omega		89.4		92.5			95.7 99.0		
Omuthiya		89.2		98.8	102.3	103.6			
Opuwo		91.1		97.6	101.1				
Oranjemund	90.0	93.1		99.6		106.7			
Oshakati	89.2	87.8	96.4	97.4	98.8	105.9	92.3 90.9	99.7	
Otjimbingwe					102.3	105.9			
Otjinene	90.2	93.5			96.7			103.5	
Paresis	88.7	91.8	95.0	98.3	101.8	105.4			
Renosterkop	87.9	91.0			101.0	104.6			
Rietfontein		92.2		89.1	95.4			98.7	
Rosh Pinah	90.3	93.4		96.0		99.9			
Rössing	89.7	92.8	96.0	99.3	101.1	106.4			
Rundu		89.6					95.9		
Sesfontein		91.6		98.1	101.6	105.2			
Shamvura		91.3		97.8			94.5104.9		
Signalberg	87.7	90.8	94.0	97.3	100.8	104.4			
Stampriet	89.7	92.8	96.0			106.4			
Terrace Bay		104.3							
Tsumeb	88.6	91.7	94.9	98.2		105.3			
Tsumkwe		90.4		100.0	93.5				103.5
Ur	89.8	92.9	96.1	99.4	102.9	106.5			
Windhoek	89.5	92.6	95.8				107.1 93.5	90.4	

Afrikaans Sce: MF 0900-1600 & 1700-2000, SS 0600-2000. Relayed on other services overnight. – **National R. in English:** 24hrs – **German Sce:** 24h –**Oshiwambo Sce in Ovambo/Kwanyama:** 0900 (SS 0500)-2200 – **Otjiherero Sce in Herero/Setswana:** MF 0900-1600 & 1700-2000, SS 0500-2000 – **Damara/Nama Sce:** MF 0900-1600 & 1700-2000, SS 0500-2000 – **Rukavango Sce in Kwangali:** 0900 (Sat/Sun 0500)-2000 – **Lozi Sce** – **Tirelo ya Setswana Sce.**
Ann: National Sce: "National Radio". On all NBC trs overnight: "Here is the National Sce of the NBC Nationwide". G: "Hier ist das Deutsche Hörfunkprogramm der NBC". Damara/Nam: "Nes ge Damara/Nama Gowab loabas NBC's disa". A: "Dit is die Afrikaanse

diens van die NBC". Otjiherero: "Indji oradio ja Namibia morupa rueraka Otjiherero".
IS: at s/on: National Anthem with choir/orchestra.

Other Stations (FM MHz):
Base FM, P.O. Box 70448, 17 Clemence Kapuuo Str, Khomasdal. **W:** www.basefm.com.na . Katatura 106.2 – **E FM,** P.O. Box 11525, 17 Jan Jonker Str, Klein Windhoek. **W:** efm913.blogspot.com . Klein Windhoek 91.3 0.25kW – **Fresh FM,** P.O. Box 40775, 158 Jan Jonker Str, Klein Windhoek. **W:** www.freshfm.com.na . Windhoek 102.9 – **Hitradio Namibia,** P.O. Box 30765, Windhoek. **W:** hitradio.com.na . In German. Swakopmund 97.5 1kW, Windhoek 99.5 1kW – **Kanaal 7,** Box 20500, Ara Str, Dorado Park, Windhoek: 102.3 + 18 FM fq's. **W:** www.k7.com.na – **Kosmos,** P.O. Box 9639, 17 Eros, Windhoek. **W:** kosmos.com.na . Klein Windhoek 94.1 – **Kudu FM,** P.O. Box 5369, 158 Jan Jonker Str, Windhoek. **W:** kudufm.com . In English. Otjiwarongo 90.9 0.1kW, Tsumeb 92.6 0.1kW, Rundu 92.7 0.1kW, Oranjemund 94.0, Swakopmund 94.3 0.5kW, Karibib/Omaruru/Usakos 94.6 0.1kW, Lüderitz 94.7 0.1kW, Walvis Bay 95.1 0.1kW, Grootfontein/Ondangwa/Ongwediva/Oshakati 95.5 1kW, Gobabis/Keetmanshoop 95.6 0.1kW, Mariental 97.3 0.1kW, Rosh Pinah 103.4 0.1kW, Okahandja/Rehoboth/Windhoek 103.5 1kW, Katima Mulilo 107.4 0.1kW – **Live FM,** P.O. Box 3363, 253 Bahnhof Str, Rehoboth. **E:** livefm@iway.na . Rehoboth 90.3 – **R. 99,** P.O. Box 11849, 14 General Muratala Muhammed Ave, Eros, Windhoek. **W:** 99fm.com.na. Walvis Bay & Swakopmund 96.5, Windhoek 99.0, Otjiwarango 99.9, Tsumeb 101.7, Oshakati & Ondangwa 104.5 – **R. Energy,** P.O. Box 676, 17 Bismarck Str, Windhoek West 9000. **W:** www.energy100fm.com . Walvis Bay 88.8 0.5kW, Klein Windhoek 100.0 0.5kW, Oshakati 100.9 2kW – **Omulunga R,** P.O. Box 40789, 158 Jan Jonker Str, Windhoek. Prgrs in Oshiwambo. **W:** omulunga.com. Otjiwarongo 87.8 0.1kW, Grootfontein 92 0.1kW, Mariental 95.0 0.1kW, Rundu 99.2 0.1kW, Rehoboth/Windhoek 100.9 1kW, Ongwediva/Oshakati 102.3 1kW, Swakopmund/Walvis Bay 105.5 0.1kW, Keetmanshoop 106 0.1kW, Lüderitz 106,4 0.1kW, Gobabis 107.5 0.1kW – **R. Wave,** P.O. Box 9953, 19 Michael Scott Str, Windhoek. **W:** www.radiowave.com.na . Otjimbingwe 87.8 1.5kW, Grootfontein 88.9 0.1kW, Lüderitz 90.6 0.1kW, Rossing 91.1 0.25kW, Walvis Bay 91.9 0.1kW, Usakos 92.2, Keetmanshoop 92.4 0.1kW, Tsumeb 95.8 0.1kW, Klein Windhoek 96.7 1.5kW, Otjiwarongo 100.9 0.1kW, Katima Mulilo 104.5 0.35kW, Rundu 105.4 0.35kW, Oshakati 106.8 0.35kW– **UNAM R,** Private Box 13301, Windhoek. **W:** unam.na/unam radio/index_unam_radio.html . Windhoek 97.4 0.1kW – **West Coast FM,** P.O. Box 4420, Swakopmund. **W:** westcoastfmnamibia.com. In Afrikaans/E. Swakopmund 107.7 0.25kW.
R. France Int, Windhoek: 107.9

NAURU

L.T: UTC +12h — **Pop:** 9,322 — **Pr.L:** English, Nauruan — **E.C:** 50Hz, 110/240V — **ITU:** NRU

NAURU BROADCASTING SERVICE (Gov)
☞ P O Box 429, Rep. of Nauru, Ce. Pacific ☎ +674 555 6066 📠 +674 4443195 **E:** radionaurufm@hotmail.com **LP:** SM: Dominic Appi, Tech. Mgr: Max Gadaloa
FM: 105.1MHz **D.Prgr:** 1900-1130 now includes local health, sports and education prgrs. Other times carries **Radio Australia** English for the Pacific satellite relay 1130-1900 **N:** hourly from R. Australia.

RADIO PASIFIK NAURU Triple 9 FM (Edu)
☞ University of the South Pacific Campus, Private Bag, Nauru PO, Nauru 00674 ☎ +674 4443774 **FM:** 99.9MHz 0.03kW **LP:** Dir: Alamanda Lauti. **D.Prgr:** Mon-Sat 3 hrs daily [6-9pm] includes local prgrs and lectures & tutorials supplied digitally from USP Suva, Fiji.

NEPAL

L.T: UTC +5¾h — **Pop:** 25.3 million — **Pr.L:** Nepali, English — **E.C:** 50Hz, 220V — **ITU:** NPL

RADIO NEPAL (Semi-Gov, Comm.)
☞ Radio Broadcasting Service, G.P.O. Box 634, Singha Durbar, Kathmandu ☎+977 1 4231804 📠+977 (1) 4221952 **W:** www.radi-onepal.org **E:** radio@rne.wlink.com.np (Eng. div: +977 1 4241923 **E:** radio#engg.wlink.com.np)
LP: Exec. Dir: Er. R.S. Karki. Dep. Exec. Dirs: Mr Rajendra Prasad Sharma & Mr Sushil Koirala. Chief Eng.: Er. Ramesh Jung Karkee.

MW	kHz	kW	MW	kHz	kW
Surkhet	576	100	Kathmandu	792	100
Dhankuta	648	100	Dipayal	810	10
Pokhara	684	100	Bardibas	1143	10

SW: Khumaltar 5005kHz 100kW/5kW (irreg.)
D.Prgr on MW/SW: 2315-1715 (SW except 0515-0715 m-f). **N.** in
Nepali at 0015,0115, 0315, 0515, 0715, 0915, 1315, 1515, 1715**;** in
English: 0215, 0815, 1415 & Brief **N** at other times on the hour; in
Hindi: 1615; in **Sanskrit** 0010; in **Newari** 0325; in **Maithili** 1215
Variation at Regional Centres: 0400-0415 & 1145-1200,
Ann: Nepali: "Yo Radio Nepal Ho"; English: "This is Radio Nepal"
IS: Instruments used are conch shell, violin, piano and jal tarang.
V. by QSL-card.

FM STATIONS:

FM	MHz	Station	FM	MHz	Station
Achhaam	88.2	R. Vaijnath FM	Dhading	105.6	R. Trishuli
Achhaam	92.0	R. Ramaroshan†	Dhading	106.0	R. Dhading†
Arghakhanchi	101.0	R. Deurali†	Dhankuta	87.6	Heart FM
Arghakhanchi	105.8	R. Argakhanchi†	Dhankuta	92.2	R. Makalu†
Baglung	91.6	Sayapatri FM†	Dhankuta	96.1	R. Kantipur
Baglung	96.4	Baglung FM†	Dhankuta	96.8	Youth FM
Baglung	98.6	Dhawalagiri FM†	Dhankuta	97.9	Image FM
Baglung	104.1	R. Dhorpatan	Dhankuta	105.2	R. Laliguransh
Baglung	107.4	Sarathi FM	Dhankuta	106.2	R. Dhankuta†
Baitadi	103.6	Saugat FM	Dhanusha	91.0	R. Today†
Baitadi	106.6	R. Sansher	Dhanusha	97.0	R. Janakpur†
Bajhang	93.6	Seti FM	Dhanusha	99.4	Mithilanchal FM
Bajhang	98.0	R. Nepal	Dhanusha	100.8	R. Mithila‡
Bajhang	100.6	Saipal R.†	Dhanusha	101.8	Janakpur FM‡
Bajura	104.0	R. Bajura	Dhanusha	105.0	Mithilanchal FM
Banke	88.4	R. Xpress FM	Dhanusha	106.0	Janaki FM†
Banke	94.0	R. Krishnasar †	Dolakha	103.4	Hamro R. †
Banke	94.6	R. Bageshwari†	Dolakha	104.0	R. Sailung†
Banke	95.6	R. Bheri Aawaj†	Dolakha	106.4	Kalinchowk FM R.†
Banke	96.8	Youth FM	Dolpa	100.0	R. Nepal
Banke	97.3	R. Jana Awaj	Doti	94.4	Triveni FM
Banke	97.9	Image FM	Doti	105.9	R. Shaileshwari FM
Banke	101.2	R. Kohalpur†	Gorkha	92.8	R. Gorkha†
Banke	101.0	Kantipur FM	Gorkha	102.4	R. Manakamana
Banke	102.4	R. Pratibodh	Gorkha	103.6	Gorakhkali FM
Banke	104.2	R.Janawaj†	Gorkha	103.9	R. Manaslu†
Banke	104.5	R. Rubaru†	Gorkha	105.4	R. Harmi
Banke	104.8	Nepalgunj FM	Gorkha	107.2	Mero Saathi
Banke	105.4	Bheri FM†	Gulmi	88.4	R. Sky FM
Bara	88.8	Sanskar FM	Gulmi	91.2	R. Gulmi
Bara	106.0	R. Simara	Gulmi	94.8	Ruru FM
Bardiya	100.6	Fulbari FM	Gulmi	100.0	R. Nepal
Bardiya	106.0	R. Babai	Gulmi	106.2	R. Resunga
Bardiya	106.4	R. Gurubaba†	Humla	100.0	R. Nepal
Bhaktapur	88.8	Nepali Ko R.	Humla	103.4	R. Kailash†
Bhaktapur	105.4	Bhaktapur FM	Ilam	90.6	R. Fikkal
Bhojpur	98.6	R. Chomolungma	Ilam	93.0	Ilam FM†
Chitawan	89.8	Samudayik	Ilam	94.9	R. Nepalvani†
Chitawan	91.0	Kalika FM	Ilam	100.0	R. Nepal
Chitawan	91.6	Synergy FM	Ilam	104.0	Sandakpur FM
Chitawan	94.0	Hamro FM	Jajarkot	107.6	Khalanga FM
Chitawan	94.6	R. Chitawan†	Jhapa	88.8	R. Saragam
Chitawan	95.2	Kalika FM†	Jhapa	89.1	Hamro Sanchar
Chitawan	96.1	Kantipur FM	Jhapa	92.6	Kanchanjungha FM
Chitawan	96.8	Youth FM	Jhapa	93.6	Pathivara FM†
Chitawan	97.9	Image FM	Jhapa	96.8	FM Mechi Tunes
Chitawan	100.6	R. Triveni	Jhapa	101.6	Saptarangi FM‡
Chitawan	103.0	R. Nepal	Jhapa	103.9	R. Sandesh
Chitawan	104.5	R. Arpan	Jhapa	105.0	Birta FM
Chitawan	105.2	R. Narayani†	Jhapa	105.9	R. Sunrise
Chitawan	107.6	R. Madi	Jhapa	106.9	Seemana FM
Dadeldhura	95.0	R. Sudur Aawaj	Jhapa	107.5	Nagarik FM
Dadeldhura	104.8	Aafno FM†	Jumla	100.0	R. Nepal
Dailekh	89.8	R. Dhurbatara	Jumla	100.6	Hamro Aawaj H S
Dailekh	104.0	R. Panchakoshi†	Jumla	105.2	R. Karnali
Dang	88.0	R. Jharana	Kailali	87.9	Godavari FM
Dang	89.0	R. Hamro Pahuch	Kailali	88.8	Paschim Today FM
Dang	91.4	R. Madhyapaschim†	Kailali	89.4	R. Jana Aawaj
Dang	92.4	Indreni FM	Kailali	91.4	Ghodaghodi FM
Dang	93.4	R. Prakriti	Kailali	93.2	Fulbari FM†
Dang	95.1	R. Ganatantra Rapti	Kailali	93.8	Dinesh FM‡
Dang	98.0	R. Nepal	Kailali	98.2	Khaptad FM
Dang	100.2	R. Tulsipur†	Kailali	101.0	Tikapur FM†
Dang	102.8	R. Swargadwari†	Kailali	101.8	Kantiur FM
Dang	103.5	R. Highway	Kailali	103.0	R. Nepal
Dang	104.0	R. Saryu Ganga	Kailali	103.7	R. Kailali FM
Dang	106.4	Super FM	Kailali	107.0	Hamra Malika FM
Dang	107.0	Dang FM†	Kailali	107.3	Hamro Fulbari FM
Dang	107.3	R. Naya Yug	Kalikot	100.0	R. Nepal
Darchula	98.0	R. Nepal	Kalikot	101.2	R. Bhek Aawaj†
Darchula	102.2	R. Kalapani†	Kalikot	101.8	R. Chulimalika†
Darchula	104.5	R. Naya Nepal	Kalikot	102.8	R. Naya Karnali†
Dhading	89.4	R. Loktantra†	Kanchanpur	96.2	R. Mahakali†
Dhading	105.0	Krishi R.†	Kanchanpur	99.4	Shuklafanta FM‡

FM	MHz	Station	FM	MHz	Station
Kanchanpur	104.3	Angel FM	Makwanpur	101.3	R. Makwanpur
Kapilvastu	89.6	R. Buddha Aawaj	Makwanpur	103.4	R. Shakti
Kapilvastu	104.2	R. Kapilvastu†	Makwanpur	106.6	R. Asmita
Kapilvastu	105.4	R. Samanata	Makwanpur	107.2	R. Palung†
Kapilvastu	107.6	Tilarakot R.	Morang	87.9	Jagriti FM
Kaski	87.9	R. Chhunumunu	Morang	91.2	B FM†
Kaski	90.2	R. Gandaki†	Morang	94.3	Koshi FM
Kaski	91.0	Madhhapuchhre FM	Morang	101.0	R. Chamatkar
Kaski	92.2	Himchuli FM†	Morang	102.1	R. Makalu
Kaski	93.4	R. Annapurna†	Morang	102.6	R. Sunakhari
Kaski	95.8	Pokhara FM	Morang	104.4	R. Purbanchal†
Kaski	96.8	Youth FM	Morang	104.8	Sajha R.
Kaski	97.9	Image FM	Morang	105.6	Saptakoshi FM
Kaski	99.2	R. Barahi	Morang	106.3	R. Suseli FM
Kaski	99.6	Annapurna Music FM	Morang	106.6	Sky FM
Kaski	101.2	Big FM	Mugu	100.0	R. Nepal
Kaski	101.8	Kantipur FM	Mugu	106.6	R.Mugali
Kaski	102.2	Sunaulo FM	Mugu	107.0	R. Rara
Kaski	103.4	R. Safalta	Mugu	107.4	R. Mugu
Kaski	104.6	R. Sarangkot†	Mustang	103.0	R. Nepal
Kaski	106.0	Gorkhali R.	Myagdi	88.2	Myagdikali FM
Kaski	106.6	R. Lekhnath	Myagdi	104.4	R. Myagdi†
Kaski	107.6	Tarang Pvt. Ltd	Nawalparasi	90.2	R. Parasi†
Kathmandu	87.6	R. Upatyaka†	Nawalparasi	100.0	R. Nepal
Kathmandu	88.2	Jana Sandesh	Nawalparasi	101.0	R. Madhyavindu FM†
Kathmandu	89.4	R. Mirmire	Nawalparasi	101.6	Vijaya FM†
Kathmandu	90.6	Times FM	Nawalparasi	103.4	Daunne FM
Kathmandu	91.2	Htis FM	Nuwakot	88.4	R. Aviyan
Kathmandu	91.8	Nepal FM	Nuwakot	104.5	R. Jalapa
Kathmandu	92.4	Capital FM	Nuwakot	106.8	Nuwakot FM
Kathmandu	93.0	Gorkha FM	Okhaldhunga	100.6	Ramailo Comun.R.
Kathmandu	93.5	Mero FM†	Okhaldhunga	104.8	Afno FM†
Kathmandu	94.0	Citizen FM	Okhaldhunga	105.6	R. Okhaldhunga
Kathmandu	94.6	Metro FM	Palpa	90.8	Muktinath FM†
Kathmandu	95.2	Star FM	Palpa	93.2	Shrinagar FM
Kathmandu	96.8	Youth FM	Palpa	99.4	R. Pacchimanchal
Kathmandu	97.9	Image FM	Palpa	103.6	R. Rampur
Kathmandu	98.3	Keeps Media	Palpa	103.9	R. Palpa
Kathmandu	98.8	R. City FM	Palpa	106.9	R. Madan Pokhara†
Kathmandu	99.4	Maitri FM	Panchthar	97.3	Simhalila FM
Kathmandu	100.0	R.Nepal	Panchthar	99.2	Eagle FM
Kathmandu	100.6	Rajdhani FM	Panchthar	104.2	Sumhatlung FM†
Kathmandu	101.8	Gopikrishna FM R.	Parbat	95.2	R. Didi Bahini†
Kathmandu	103.0	R.Nepal BBC rel#	Parbat	100.6	R. Shaligram†
Kathmandu	103.6	R. Bagmati	Parbat	103.6	R. Parbat†
Kathmandu	104.8	FM Adhyatmajyoti	Parsa	91.4	Gadimai FM†
Kathmandu	105.1	Good News FM	Parsa	92.8	Bhojpuriya FM
Kathmandu	106.0	CJMC FM	Parsa	96.1	R. Kantipur
Kathmandu	106.3	R. Audio	Parsa	96.8	Youth FM
Kathmandu	107.0	TU FM	Parsa	97.6	Indreni FM
Kavre	87.9	R. Masti	Parsa	97.9	Image FM
Kavre	88.4	R. Shepherd	Parsa	99.0	R. Birgunj‡
Kavre	89.8	R. ABC†	Parsa	100.0	R. Nepal
Kavre	104.0	Madhyapurva FM†	Parsa	101.9	Aakas FM
Kavre	104.5	R. Naya Sandesh	Parsa	103.8	Narayani FM†
Kavre	106.7	R. Namobuddha†	Parsa	105.8	Birgunj Musical FM
Kavre	107.3	R. Janasanchar	Parsa	107.0	R. Tarang
Kavre	107.6	Grace FM	Pyuthan	90.0	R. Mahila Aawaj
Khotang	102.4	Haleshi FM†	Pyuthan	92.0	R. Pyuthan†
Khotang	105.0	Rupakot R.†	Pyuthan	97.0	R. Mandavi†
Kirtipur	106.6	Newa FM	Pyuthan	103.6	R. Lishne Aawaj
Lalitpur	90.0	Ujyalo 90 Netw.	Ramechhap	88.6	R. Tinlal
Lalitpur	96.1	R. Kantipur	Ramechhap	102.1	Hajurko R.
Lalitpur	97.2	Headlines &	Rasuwa	100.9	Durgam FM
		Music FM	Rasuwa	102.1	Rasuwa FM
Lalitpur	100.0	R. Nepal	Rautahat	89.6	R. Madhes
Lalitpur	100.9	R. Lalipur	Rautahat	90.4	R. Jivan Jyoti
Lalitpur	101.2	Classic FM	Rautahat	90.8	Rautahat FM †
Lalitpur	102.4	R. Sagarmatha†	Rautahat	93.2	Rajdevi FM†
Lalitpur	104.2	Paryawaran	Rautahat	98.2	R. Sanskriti
		Chakra R.†	Rautahat	98.6	Madhesh Jana
Lalitpur	105.7	BFBS			Aawaj
Lamjung	88.4	R. Lamjung	Rautahat	102.6	R. Nunthar FM
Lamjung	95.0	R. Marsyangdi†	Rolpa	93.8	R. Rolpat
Mahottari	88.4	R. Darpan†	Rolpa	104.5	R. Jaljala
Mahottari	90.4	Jaleshwamath FM†	Rukum	89.2	R. Sani Bheri
Mahottari	94.4	R. Appan Mithila†	Rukum	92.8	R. Sisnet
Mahottari	103.4	R. Rudraksha	Rukum	100.8	R. Sanobheri
Mahottari	103.7	R. Gunjan	Rupandehi	88.2	R. Republic
Mahottari	107.0	R. Sungava FM †	Rupandehi	88.6	R. Malmala
Makwanpur	88.0	R.Hetauda	Rupandehi	89.6	R. Namaste
Makwanpur	88.5	R. Aakash Ganga	Rupandehi	93.6	R. Jagaran†
Makwanpur	96.6	Hetauda FM†	Rupandehi	94.4	Butwal FM†
Makwanpur	97.0	R. Pratidhwani	Rupandehi	95.5	R. Mukti†
Makwanpur	98.0	R. Nepal	Rupandehi	96.1	R. Kantipur
Makwanpur	99.6	R. Thaha Sansar	Rupandehi	96.8	R. Lumbini†

FM	MHz Station	FM	MHz Station
Rupandehi	97.6 Image FM	Sunsari	89.4 R. Parivartan
Rupandehi	98.2 Tinau FM‡	Sunsari	90.0 Saptakoshi FM†
Rupandehi	98.8 Siddhartha FM	Sunsari	95.1 Ganatantra FM †
Rupandehi	102.0 Rupandehi FM†	Sunsari	95.6 Star FM
Rupandehi	105.0 R. Samabesi	Sunsari	96.1 R. Kantipur
Rupandehi	106.6 R. Devdaha	Sunsari	98.8 Vijaypur FM
Rupandehi	107.2 Aasha ko Sandesh	Sunsari	99.5 Popular FM†
Salyan	99.2 R. Sharada†	Sunsari	105.8 Saptakoshi FM†
Salyan	101.0 R. Salyan†	Sunsari	107.2 Namaste FM
Salyan	104.8 Rapti FM †	Surkhet	90.2 R. Surkhet†
Salyan	106.1 R. Kapurkot	Surkhet	90.8 Jagaran FM†
Sankhuwa.	100.8 R. Arun Sandesh	Surkhet	92.6 R. Himal
Sankhuwa.	105.8 Khandbari FM†	Surkhet	98.6 R. Bheri FM†
Sankhuwa.	107.5 Gurans FM	Surkhet	102.7 R. Bheri FM†
Saptari	92.8 Bhorukawa	Surkhet	103.4 Bulbule FM†
Saptari	101.4 R. Chhinnamasta	Surkhet	106.7 Himal FM
Saptari	104.6 Appan FM	Syangja	89.2 R. Waling
Sarlahi	89.3 R. Madhes†	Syangja	89.6 R. Syangja†
Sarlahi	94.6 R. Ekata	Syangja	105.4 R. Aandhi Khola†
Sarlahi	105.6 R. Sarlahi†	Tanahu	88.2 Dhorbarahi FM
Sarlahi	107.4 Mai FM†	Tanahu	88.8 R. Bandipur†
Sindhuli	92.0 R. Sindhuligadi†	Tanahu	94.2 Damauli FM†
Sindhuli	104.2 R. Sahara	Tanahu	97.2 R. Tanahun†
Sindhup.	89.1 R. Avarv	Tanahu	102.6 R. Devghat
Sindhup.	96.8 Youth FM	Tanahu	104.2 R. Bhanubhakta†
Sindhup.	102.8 Sindhu FM	Tanahu	105.8 Madi Seti FM†
Sindhup.	105.0 R. Sindhu†	Taplejung	94.0 R. Taplejung
Siraha	88.1 R. Saugat	Taplejung	102.0 R. Tamort
Siraha	88.8 R. Salhesh†	Tehrathum	102.6 R. Menchhyayam†
Siraha	102.6 Samad FM†	Udaypur	91.6 Amurta FM†
Siraha	105.4 Fulbari Comu R.	Udaypur	102.4 R. Udayapur†
Siraha	107.8 R. Samagra	Udaypur	104.0 R. Triyuga
Solukhumbu	94.6 R. Dudhkoshi	Udaypur	106.8 UK FM
Solukhumbu	101.2 Solu FM		
Solukhumbu	105.3 R. Everest	**NB:** Sankhuwa.=Sankhuwasabha,	
Sunsari	88.5 Dantakali FM	Sindhup.= Sindhupalchok	

BBCWS daily MW relay via R. Nepal Surkhet 576 kHz : 1600-1630 Hindi ; 1630-1730 hrs. WS in English. Variation at Surkhet MW : R. Nepal's News in Hindi broadcast at 1730-1742 hrs (rec. of 1615 hrs broadcast earlier on other R. Nepal Channels).and R. Nepal's News in Nepali at 1742-1747 hrs (rec. of 1715 hrs broadcast earlier on other R. Nepal channels).

Other Stations:
Guru-Baba FM: Bansgadi, 106.4MHz 0.1kW. Prgrs in Tharu
BFBS: Gurkha Radio, Kathmandu **FM:** 92.1MHz (English), 99.6MHz (Gurkha)

NETHERLANDS

L.T: UTC +1h (31 Mar-27 Oct: +2h) — **Pop:** 16.7 million — **Pr.L:** Dutch — **E.C:** 50Hz, 230V — **ITU:** HOL

NEDERLANDSE OMROEP STICHTING (NOS)
✉ Mediapark, Sumatralaan 45, 1217 GP Hilversum; Postbus 26600, 1202 JT Hilversum ☎ +31 35 6779222 🖷 +31 35 6772649
W: www.nos.nl **E:** publieksreacties@nos.nl

NTR
✉ Mediapark, Sumatralaan 49, 1217GP Hilversum or P.O. Box 29000, 1202 MA Hilversum ☎ +31 88 100 3100 🖷 +31 88 100 3138 **W:** www.ntr.nl
Dutch national public prgrs are provided by the **NOS**, **NTR** and the following broadcasting organisations: **AVRO, BNN, EO, KRO, NCRV,TROS, VARA** and **VPRO**.

MW	kHz	kW	Prgr		
Zeewolde	747	400	R. 5/R. 5 Nostalgia (200kW night time)		
Emmaberg	1251	5	R. 5/R. 5 Nostalgia		

FM	Radio 1	Radio 2	3FM	Radio 4	kW
Amsterdam	98.6	92.3	96.5	94.5	0.03/0.03/0.03/0.03
Arnhem	98.6	92.9	96.5	92.1	0.07/0.07/0.07/0.07
Eys	-	97.2	-	-	10
Goes	104.4	94.4	99.8	95.0	40/0.1/15/15
Emmaberg	105.3	93.4	103.9	98.7	10/10/10/10
Hulst	-	107.1	-	-	0.1
Loon op Zand	-	-	-	98.2	55
IJsselstein	98.9	92.6	96.8	94.3	70/70/70/50
Jirnsum	104.3	-	-	-	0.1
Markelo	98.4	104.6	96.2	91.4	100/100/100/100
Westdorpe	-	97.8	-	-	95
Roermond	104.8	88.2	90.9	94.5	100/100/100/100
Rotterdam	98.6	92.9	97.1	94.7	0.1/0.1/0.04/13
Hoogersmilde	91.8	88.0	88.6	94.8	100/100/40/100
Wieringerwerf	95.0	92.9	97.1	101.6	15/15/15/35

Ann: "Dit is de VARA", "Dit is de VPRO" etc. R. 1: news, sport; R. 2 and 3 FM: music; R. 4: classical music; R. 5: daytime: R. 5 Nostalgia: evening and weekend: R. 5 avond en weekend music, information, service and games

Regional stations:

FM	Mhz	kW	Location	Station
2)	87.6	8	Mierlo	Omroep Brabant
4)	87.9	15	Goes	Omroep Zeeland
9)	88.9	10	Amsterdam	R. Noord-Holland
6)	89.1	5	Megen	R. Gelderland
13)	89.3	10	Rotterdam	R. 89 3 West
10)	89.4	10	Hengelo	R. Oost
12)	89.8	25	Lelystad	R. Flevoland
6)	90.4	10	Ruurlo	R. Gelderland
5)	90.8	4	Hoogersmilde	R. Drenthe
2)	91.0	15	Roosendaal	Omroep Brabant
2)	91.9	2	Loon op Zand	Omroep Brabant
3)	92.2	25	Jirnsum	Omrop Fryslân
7)	93.1	4	IJsselstein	R. M
11)	93.4	10	Rotterdam	R. Rijnmond
9)	93.9	11	Wieringerwerf	R. Noord-Holland
1)	95.3	10	Emmaberg	L1 R.
10)	95.6	5	Markelo	R. Oost
2)	95.8	5	Megen	Omroep Brabant
8)	97.5	20	Groningen	R. Noord
7)	97.9	3	Rhenen	R. M
10)	99.4	25	Zwolle	R. Oost
1)	100.3	100	Roermond	L1 R.
6)	103.5	20	Ugchelen	R. Gelderland

+5 low-power relays
Addresses:
1) Postbus 31, 6200 AA Maastricht ☎ +31 43 3467777 🖷 +31 43 3467715 **E:** redactie@L1.nl **W:** www.l1.nl – **2)** Postbus 108, 5600 AC Eindhoven ☎ +31 40 2949494 🖷 +31 40 2949320 **W:** www.omroepbrabant.nl – **3)** Postbus 7600, 8903 JP Leeuwarden ☎ +31 58 299 7799 🖷 +31 58 2997778 **E:** direksje@omropfryslan.nl **W:** www.omropfryslan.nl – **4)** Postbus 1090, 4388 ZH Oost-Souburg ☎ +31 118 499900 🖷 +31 118 499929 **W:** www.omroepzeeland.nl – **5)** Postbus 999, 9400 AZ Assen ☎ +31 592 338080 🖷 +31 592 331048 **E:** redactie@rtvdrenthe.nl – **6)** Postbus 747, 6800 AS Arnhem ☎ +31 26)3713713 🖷 +31 26 3713710 **E:** rtv@omroepgelderland.nl **W:** www.omroepgelderland.nl – **7)** Postbus 1012, 3500 BA Utrecht ☎ +31 30 8500600 🖷 +31 30 8500601 **E:** info@radiom.nl **W:** www.rtvutrecht.nl – **8)** Postbus 30101, 9700 RP Groningen ☎ +31 50 3199999 🖷 +31 50 3185147 **E:** radio@rtvnoord.nl – **9)** Postbus 9823, 1006 AM Amsterdam ☎ +31 20 8505050 🖷 +31 20 8505850. **E:** info@rtvnh.nl **W:** www.rtvnh.nl – **10)** Hazenweg 25, 7556 BM Hengelo (Ov) ☎ +31 74 2456456 🖷 +31 74 2437148 **E:** info@rtvoost.nl **W:** www.rtvoost.nl – **11)** Postbus 1515, 3000 BM Rotterdam ☎ +31 10 4400600 🖷 +31 10 4400698 **E:** info@rijnmond.nl **W:** www.rijnmond.nl – **12)** Postbus 567, 8200 AN Lelystad ☎ +31 320 285085 🖷 +31 320 285099 **E:** rtv@omroepflevoland.nl **W:** www.omroepflevoland.nl – **13)** Postbus 24025, 2490 AA Den Haag ☎ +31 70 3078888 🖷 +31 70 3078844 **E:** west@rtvwest.nl

Public local stations in major cities: FM(MHz):
Amsterdam 96.1 FUN X, 99.4 Wereld FM, 105.2 Radio Zuid Oost (RAZO), 106.8 Stads FM, 107.9 Caribbean FM – **Den Haag** 92.0 Den Haag FM, 98.4 FUN X – **Rotterdam** 91.8 FUN X, 93.9 Megastad FM – **Utrecht** 96.1 FUN X, 105.7 Bingo FM, 107.7 Bingo FM
NB: FUN X is an initiative of SALTO Omroep Amsterdam, Slor Rotterdam, Stadsomroep Den Haag and Omroep RTV Utrecht

EXTERNAL SERVICE: Radio Nederland Wereldomroep (RNW)
See International Broadcasting Section

OTHER STATIONS

MW	kHz	kW	Location	Station
50)	675	120	Lopikerkapel	R. Maria Nederland (Rlg.)
56)	828	20	Heienoord	R. 10 Gold (Comm.)
14)	891	20	Emmaberg	R. 538 (Comm.)
53)	1008	200	Zeewolde	Groot Nieuws R. (Rlg.)
49)	1116	0.5	Bloemendaal	R. Bloemendaal (Rlg.)
51)	1395	10	Harlingen	R. Seagull (Comm.)
59)	1485	1	Harlingen	R. Marina (Comm.)
60)	1557	4	Den Haag	Vahon FM/Hindustani R.
52)	1584	0.15	Utrecht	R. Paradijs (Comm.)
51)	1602	1	Pietersbierum	R. Waddenzee/R. Seagull (Comm.)

FM	MHz	kW	Location	Station
20)	87.6	1	Enschede	Arrow Classic Rock Noord
23)	88.2	1	Ugchelen	100%NL
9)	88.4	43	Roosendaal	Slam FM
3)	88.6	26	Mierlo	BNR NieuwsR.

FM	MHz	kW	Location	Station
8)	88.7	1	Apeldoorn	Hot R. Hits
57)	88.8	1	Vlissingen	Arrow Jazz FM
15)	88.9	1	Den Bosch	R. 8FM
23)	89.0	3	Lochem	100%NL
11)	89.1	2	Groningen	R. NL
20)	89.2	3	Zwolle	Arrow Classic Rock Noord
15)	89.3	3	Eindhoven	R. 8FM
23)	89.5	10	Alkmaar	100%NL
23)	89.5	5	Utrecht	100%NL
11)	89.6	2	Huissen	R. NL
3)	89.6	5	Hoogersmilde	BNR NieuwsR.
30)	89.6	1	Nieuwbergen	Maasland R.
57)	89.7	1	Breda	Arrow Jazz FM
57)	89.7	2.5	Mierlo	Arrow Jazz FM
57)	89.8	1	Nijmegen	Arrow Jazz FM
26)	89.9	1	Emmen	Waterstad FM
23)	90.0	3	Breskens	100%NL
23)	90.0	17	Loon op Zand	100%NL
23)	90.2	50	Roosendaal	100%NL
27)	90.3	4	Eindhoven	R. Hollandio
57)	90.3		Groningen	Arrow Jazz FM
57)	90.4	25	Hoorn	Arrow Jazz FM
57)	90.5	8	Rotterdam	Arrow Jazz FM
57)	90.5	15	Hoogersmilde	Arrow Jazz FM
27)	90.5	4	Helmond	R. Hollandio
57)	90.7	100	IJsselstein	Arrow Jazz FM
57)	90.7	10	Enschede	Arrow Jazz FM
57)	90.8	2	Terneuzen	Arrow Jazz FM
9)	91.0	10	Tjerkgaast	Slam FM
9)	91.0	1	Markelo	Slam FM
9)	91.1	40	Hilversum	Slam FM
48)	91.1	1	Gemert	Centraal FM
18)	91.3	1	Hoogezand	Simone FM
3)	91.3	70	Rotterdam	BNR NieuwsR.
3)	91.3	1	Tilburg	BNR NieuwsR.
3)	91.5	3	Biervliet	BNR NieuwsR.
3)	91.5	10	Eys	BNR NieuwsR.
19)	91.6	5	Amsterdam	R. Veronica
23)	92.1	10	Emmaberg	100%NL
39)	92.3	1	Rijssen	R. 350
15)	92.4	3	Westdorpe	R. Hollandio
47)	92.9	1	Wellerooi	Maasland R.
44)	93.0	1	Meppel	R. Meppel
9)	93.1	1	Emmen	Slam FM
26)	93.2	20	Jirnsum	Waterstad FM
11)	93.3	1	Enschede	R. NL
11)	93.5	9	Markelo	R. NL
29)	93.6	1	Amsterdam	Wild FM HitR.
22)	93.6	4	Eindhoven	R. Oranje Natonaal
9)	93.6	6	Zwolle	Slam FM
9)	93.7	5	Enschede	Slam FM
9)	93.7	2	Hoogezand	Slam FM
40)	93.7	1	Leiden	Sleutelstad FM
9)	93.8	17	Megen	Slam FM
15)	93.9	4	Roosendaal	R. Hollandio
19)	94.0	1	Emmen	R. Veronica
27)	94.1	1	Den Bosch	R. Hollandio
11)	94.1	1	Tjerkgaast	R. NL
23)	94.9	12	Mierlo	100%NL
23)	95.0	2	Amersfoort	100%NL
23)	95.0	2	Nijmegen	100%NL
9)	95.2	25	Alphen aan de Rijn	Slam FM
15)	95.2	1	Weert	R. 8FM
3)	95.3	20	Zwolle	BNR NieuwsR.
43)	95.3	1	Bedum	Regio FM
3)	95.4	1	Emmen	BNR NieuwsR.
3)	95.5	30	Tjerkgaast	BNR NieuwsR.
6)	95.6	1	Rijswijk	Fresh FM
6)	95.7	5	Amsterdam	Fresh FM
11)	95.7	2	Meppel	R. NL
6)	95.9	3	Alphen aan de Rijn	Fresh FM
29)	96.3	1	Alkmaar	Wild FM HitR.
19)	96.3	30	Loon op Zand	R. Veronica
19)	96.6	1	Goes	R. Veronica
11)	96.6	1	Leeuwarden	R. NL
11)	97.1	1	Hoogersmilde	R. NL
11)	97.1	1	Assen	R. NL
29)	97.3	2	Haarlem	Wild FM HitR.
23)	97.6	1	Hengelo	100%NL
11)	97.6	2	Maastricht	R. NL
36)	97.6	37	Rotterdam	R. Decibel
19)	97.7	10	Arnhem	R. Veronica
19)	97.7	6	Mierlo	R. Veronica
11)	97.7	15	Landgraaf	R. NL
19)	97.8	4	IJsselstein	R. Veronica
36)	98.0	12	Amsterdam	R. Decibel
58)	98.0	1	Hengelo,Gld	R. Continu
11)	98.1	2	Eys	R. NL
36)	98.3	5	Alkmaar	R. Decibel
20)	98.5	2	Groningen	Arrow Classic Rock Noord
11)	98.5	1	Weert	R. NL
20)	98.7	20	Hoogersmilde	Arrow Classic Rock Noord
20)	98.7	5	Jirnsum	Arrow Classic Rock Noord
23)	99.1	10	Enschede	100%NL
23)	99.1	3	Hoogezand	100%NL
23)	99.1	3	Tjerkgaast	100%NL
32)	99.1	1	Geleen	Streekomroep START
9)	99.2	26	Breskens	Slam FM
9)	99.4	30	Mierlo	Slam FM
36)	99.4	2	Den Haag	R. Decibel
9)	99.6	25	Hoorn	Slam FM
9)	99.6	6	Hoogersmilde	Slam FM
3)	99.9	1	Dedemsvaart	BNR NieuwsR.
3)	99.9	3	Ugchelen	BNR NieuwsR.
3)	99.9	27	Wormer	BNR NieuwsR.
3)	100.1	100	IJsselstein	BNR NieuwsR.
3)	100.1	4	Nijmegen	BNR NieuwsR.
3)	100.2	12	Lochem	BNR NieuwsR.
13)	100.4	25	Westdorpe	QMusic
13)	100.4	7	Roosendaal	QMusic
13)	100.4	3	Rotterdam	QMusic
13)	100.4	95	Hoogersmilde	Qmusic
13)	100.4	10	Doetinchem	QMusic
13)	100.5	1	Nijmegen	QMusic
13)	100.5	5	Wieringerwerf	QMusic
13)	100.7	30	Breskens	QMusic
13)	100.7	10	Enschede	QMusic
13)	100.7	100	IJsselstein	QMusic
13)	100.7	10	Lichtenvoorde	Qmusic
24)	101.0	75	Hoogersmilde	Sky R. 101 FM
24)	101.1	10	Nijmegen	Sky R. 101 FM
24)	101.2	13	Hengelo	Sky R. 101 FM
24)	101.2	200	Hilversum	Sky R. 101 FM
24)	101.2	2	Boxtel	Sky R. 101 FM
24)	101.3	5	Roosendaal	Sky R. 101 FM
24)	101.4	10	Deventer	Sky R. 101 FM
24)	101.5	1	Arnhem	Sky R. 101 FM
24)	101.5	7	Den Bosch	Sky R. 101 FM
24)	101.5	8	Rotterdam	Sky R. 101 FM
24)	101.6	5	Mierlo	Sky R. 101 FM
24)	101.6	3	Roermond	Sky R. 101 FM
24)	101.7	5	Breda	Sky R. 101 FM
18)	101.7	1	Emmen	Simone FM
24)	101.9	2	Tilburg	Sky R. 101 FM
24)	101.9	50	Goes	Sky R. 101 FM
58)	101.9	1	Zieuwent	R. Continu
14)	102.1	100	Hilversum	R. 538
14)	102.2	10	Hoogezand	R. 538
14)	102.2	10	Hoogersmilde	R. 538
14)	102.3	20	Alkmaar	R. 538
14)	102.3	100	De Mortel	R. 538
14)	102.3	15	Lochem	R. 538
14)	102.3	2	Roermond	R. 538
14)	102.4	1	Arnhem	R. 538
14)	102.4	20	Westdorpe	R. 538
14)	102.5	8	Tilburg	R. 538
14)	102.5	50	Tjerkgaast	R. 538
14)	102.5	1	Utrecht	R. 538
14)	102.6	5	Enschede	R. 538
14)	102.6	2	Nijmegen	R. 538
14)	102.7	10	Emmen	R. 538
14)	102.7	100	Rotterdam	R. 538
19)	103.0	40	Lelystad	R. Veronica
19)	103.1	20	De Lutte	R. Veronica
19)	103.1	5	Megen	R. Veronica
19)	103.2	40	Rotterdam	R. Veronica
19)	103.2	25	Hoogersmilde	R. Veronica
19)	103.3	6	Terneuzen	R. Veronica
19)	103.4	5	Groningen	R. Veronica
19)	103.5	2	Roosendaal	R. Veronica
15)	103.6	13	Tilburg	R. 8 FM
11)	104.2	3	Alkmaar	R. NL
23)	104.4	50	Hilversum	100%NL
26)	104.4	3	Groningen	Waterstad FM
23)	104.6	87	Rotterdam	100%NL
45)	104.8	1	Zuidwolde	De StreekR.
34)	106.7	1	Lochem	Achterhoek FM

+ 446 stns below 1kW

Addresses:
3) Prins Bernhardplein 173 1097BL Amsterdam or Postbus 651, 1000

AR Amsterdam ☎ +31 20 592 8500 🖷 +31 20 592 8800 E: operations@bnr.nl W: www.bnr.nl – 4) Postbus Vervaartlaan 6, 2288GM Rijswijk ☎ +31 20 5849999 and 070-3072520 🖷 +31 20 5849980 W: www.cityfm.nl E: info@cityfm.nl – 6) Darwinstraat 20, 2722 PX Zoetermeer ☎ +31 79 3434491 🖷 +31 79 3434492 W: www.fresh. fm – 8) Hosbekkeweg 3A, 7621AC Borne ☎ +31 74 250 90 90 🖷 +31 74 250 90 99 W: www.hotradiohits.nl E: info@hotradiohits.nl – 9) Rhoneweg 54, 1043 AH Amsterdam E: radio@id-t.com W: www. id-t.com – 11) Postbus 248, 8600AE Sneek ☎ +31 515 432360 🖷 +31 35 432986 W: www.radionl.fm E: info@radionl.fm – 12) Postbus 36, 4450 AA Heinkenszand ☎ 0900 5105100 🖷 +31 113 567670 E: info@maximaal.nl W: www.maximaal.nl – 13) Postbus 102, 1200 AC Hilversum ☎ +31 35 655 2 655 🖷 +31 35 655 2 656 E: info@q-music. nl W: www.q-music.nl – 14) Postbus 2538, 1200 CM Hilversum ☎ +31 35 5385538 🖷 +31 35 6283538 W: www.radio538.nl – 15) Postbus 8, 5201 AA Den Bosch ☎ +31 73 6312003 🖷 +31 73 6313311 W: www.radio8fm.nl E: info@radio8fm.nl – 17) Postbus 1111, 6201 BC Maastricht ☎ +31 045 2315566 🖷 +31 045 3216677 – 18) Hoogveen 2, 9501 XK Stadskanaal ☎ +31 599 312183 🖷 +31 599 312187 E: info@simone.nl W: www.radiosimone.nl – 19) Postbus 1007, 1400 BA Hilversum ☎ +31 35 5277555 🖷 +31 35 5277557 W: www. radioveronica.nl – 20) Postbus 248, 8600AE Sneek ☎ +31 515 432360 🖷 +31 515 432986 W: www.arrownoord.nl E: info@arrownoord.nl – 21) Postbus 77, 9640 AB Veendam ☎ +31 598 633055 🖷 +31 598 633308 E: info@touchradio.nl W: www.touchradio.nl – 22) Postbus 153, 8330AD Steenwijk ☎ +31 85 4010550 🖷 +31 85 4010551 E: info@radiooranjenationaal.nl W: www.radiooranjenationaal.nl – 23) Postbus 813, 1200AV Hilversum W: www.100p.nl – 26) Postbus 248, 8600 AE Sneek ☎ +31 515 432360 🖷 +31 515 432 986 E: info@ waterstadfm.nl W: www.waterstadfm.nl – 27) Postbus 8, 5201AA Den Bosch E: info@hollandio.nl W: www.radiohollandio.nl – 29) Gyroscoopweg 144, 1042 AZ Amsterdam ☎ +31 20 4470808 🖷 +31 20 4118344 W: www.wildfm.nl E: spam@wildfm.nl – 30) Raadhuisstraat 7, 5854AX Nieuwbergen ☎ +31 485 341234 🖷 +31 485 343118 W: www.maaslandradio nl E: studio@maaslandradio.nl – 32) Postbus 114, 6160AC Geleen ☎ +31 46 4747555 🖷 +31 4748493 W: www. streekomroepstart.nl E: secretariaat@streekomroepstart.nl – 34) Postbus 115, 7250AC Vorden ☎ +31 575 556560 🖷 +31 575 556564 W: www.achterhoekfm.nl – 36) Wilgenweg 16A, 1031HV Amsterdam ☎ +31 909 5008000 W: www.radiodecibel.nl E: studio@decibel.nl – 39) Postbus 234, 7460AE Rijssen ☎ +31 548 681 010 🖷 +31 548 544 117 W: www.radio350.nl E: info@radio350.nl – 40) Postbus 937, 2300AX Leiden ☎ +31 71 523 5907 🖷 +31 71 523 5908 W: www. sleutelstad937.nl E: info@sleutelstad.nl – 43) W: www.regiofm.info E: info@regiofmradio.nl ☎ +31 598 4232 00 🖷 +31 8 42298 700 – 44) Emmastraat 10, 7941HR Meppel ☎ +31 522 259319 🖷 +31 522 240694 W: www.omroepmeppel.nl E: secretariaat@omroepmeppel. nl – 45) Postbus 8, 7920AA Zuidwolde ☎ +31 528 373444 🖷 +31 528 372272 W: www.streekradio.com E: info@streekradio.com – 47) Raadhuisstraat 7, 5854AX Nieuw Bergen ☎ +31 485 341234 🖷 +31 485 343118 W: www.maaslandradio.nl E: redactie@maaslandradio.nl – 48) St. Annastraat 60, 5421KC Gemert ☎ +31 492 366833 🖷 +31 492 366822 W: www.omroepcentraal.nl E: info@omroepcentraal.nl – 49) Vijverweg 14, 2061GX Bloemendaal ☎ +31 23 5250471 E: bureau@ radiobloemendaal.nl W: www.radiobloemendaal.nl D.Prgr: Sun & Christian holidays 0800-2000 & Tues 1100-1130v. reception reports to: PA0WDG@amsat.org – 50) Waalstraat 2, 5215CK 's-Hertogenbosch or Postbus 5045, 5201GA 's-Hertogenbosch ☎ +31 73 687 2000 🖷 +31 73 687 2008 W: www.radiomaria.nl E: info@radiomaria.nl; reception reports to qsl@radiomaria.org – 51) Postbus 24, 8860 AA Harlingen ☎ +31 06 28580161 🖷 +31 58 2662204 E: info@radiowaddenzee. nl W: www.radiowaddenzee.nl D.Prgr: 1602 khz: 06.00-18.00 Radio Waddenzee for tourists. 1395 khz : Radio Seagull 0600-1800; 1602 khz Radio Seagull : 1800-0600 W: www.radioseagull.com E: office@ radioseagull.nl – 52) Postbus 11122, 3505 BC Utrecht, Dir. Ruud Poeze ☎ +31 30 244 5580 E: info@radioparadijs.nl D.Prgr: 24 hours in Dutch, music; also low power transmitters on 1244 khz (0.01 kW) and 1332 khz (0.0002 kW) – 53) Einsteinlaan 41b, 3902 HN Veenendaal, Managers: Evert ten Ham and Arjan de Heer 24h rlg pgr.☎ +31 0909- 123 1008 🖷 +31 318 584 380 W: www.grootnieuwsradio.nl E: info@ grootnieuwsradio.nl V: by letter – 56) 's-Gravelandseweg 73, 1217JE Hilversum or Postbus 1056, 1200BB Hilversum ☎ +31 35 75 05 910 🖷 +31 35 628 35 38 E: info@radio10gold.nl W: www.radio10gold.nl – 57) Postbus 63560 2502JN Den Haag W: www.arrow.nl/jazz -58) Exloërkijl Zuid 38, 9571AC Tweede Exloërmond ☎ +31 599 67 11 01 🖷 +31 599 67 11 02 W: www.radiocontinu.nl E: info@radiocontinu.nl – 59) Postbus 1100, 8300BC Emmeloord ☎ +31 527 687 321 🖷 +31 527 688 991 W: www.radiomarina.nl E: info@radiomarina.nl D.Prgr: 04.00- 22.00 in Dutch, Flemish and English - 60) Newtonstraat 25, 2562KC Den Haag ☎ +31 70 365 2247 and +31 70 362 2077 W: http://vahon. fm E: info@vahonfm.nl

Military stations

FM	MHz	kW	Location	Station
2)	87.7	0.1	Maastricht	BFBS 1
1)	89.2	1	Brunssum	AFN Power Network
1)	90.2	0.1	Brunssum	BFBS 1
3)	96.9	10	Brunssum	CFN/RFC
3)	99.7	0.5	Brunssum	CFN/RFC
1)	107.9	0.1	Zeeland	AFN Power Network

Addresses and other information:

1) E: spannb@afn.shape.army.mil W: www.benelux.afneurope.net D.Prgr: 24h relay AFN SHAPE (Belgium) – 2) D.Prgr: Relays BFBS 1 prgrs Germany W: www.bfbs.com – 3) PO Box 275 6640AG Brunssum D.Prgr: 24h ☎ +31 45 5263791 🖷 +31 45 5263792 E: mail@cfnradio. com W: www.cfnradio.com

NEW CALEDONIA (France)

L.T: UTC +11h — Pop: 256,275 — Pr.L: French, Kanak and other Melanesian-Polynesian dialects — E.C: 50Hz, 220V — ITU: NCL

CONSEIL SUPERIEUR DE L'AUDIOVISUEL
Comite territorial de l'audiovisuel de Nouvelle-Caledonie et des Iles Wallis-et-Futuna
🖃 1, rue du Contre-Amiral Joseph Bouzet-Nouville, B.P. 739-98845, Noumea ☎ +687 25 40 51 🖷 +687 25 40 85 W: www.csa.fr E: ctr. noumea.csa@lagoon.nc
Regular of broadcasting for New Caledonia & Wallis and Futuna.

NOUVELLECALEDONIE PREMIÈRE (Gov)
🖃 1 rue Marechal Leclerc, Mt Coffyn, B.P. G3 - 98848 Noumea Cedex ☎ +687 267274327 🖷 +687 687281252 W: www.nouvellecaledonie. la1ere.fr (live streaming) L.P: Reg. Dir: Benoit Saudeau D.Prgr: 24h in French (local and RFO common prgr satellite feed) and Kanak (local). MW: Noumea 666kHz 20kW, Touho 729kHz 5kW

FM	Location	kW	FM	Location	kW
88.0	Bouloupari	2.2	90.0	Noumea-Mont Koghis	5
88.0	Kaala-Gomen	1.2	90.0	Poum	0.01
88.0	Mont Dore	3	90.0	Yate	0.09
88.0	Touho	0.6	90.5	Lifou	11
88.5	Canala	0.1	90.5	Paita	0.1
88.5	Mare	0.45	90.5	Poya	0.3
89.0	Iles-des-Pins	0.04	91.0	Bourail	0.3
89.0*	Noumea-Mont Coffyn	2.2	91.0	Houailou	2
89.0	Ponerihouen	3	91.0	Koumac	4
89.0	Pouebo	0.01	91.0	Mont-Dore	0.1
89.5	Iles-des-Pins	0.1	91.0	Thio	0.01
89.5	Ouvea	0.55	91.0	Yate	0.12
90.0	Canala	0.01	91.5	Lifou	0.1
90.0	Hienghene	0.01	91.5	Noumea	2.2
90.0	Kone	3.5			

*) satellite relay of Radio Ô (Gov): W: www.radioo.fr 24h in French

RADIO FRANCE INTER (Gov): satellite relay from Paris 24h in French

FM	Location	kW	FM	Location	kW
92.0	Bouloupari	2.2	93.0	Noumea-Mont Coffyn	2.2
92.0	Mont-Dore	3	94.0	Kone	3.5
93.0	Ponerihouen	3	94.0	Noumea-Mont Koghis	5

Other FM Stations:

FM	MHz	Location	kW	FM	MHz	Location	kW
1)	93.5	Noumea-Mont Coffyn	1	4)	99.0	Bourail	0.07
2)	95.0	Dumbea [Noumea]	1	4)	99.0	Houailou	0.25
3)	96.0	Belep		4)	99.0	Koumac	1.5
3)	96.0	Bouloupari	0.8	4)	99.0	Thio	0.2
3)	96.0	Kaala-Gomen	0.3	4)	100.0	Belep	0.02
3)	96.0	Mont-Dore	2.2	4)	100.0	Mont-Dore	0.75
3)	96.0	Thio	0.4	4)	100.0	Kaala-Gomen	0.3
3)	96.5	Ouvea	0.2	4)	100.0	Mont-Dore	2.2
3)	97.0	Iles-des-Pins	0	4)	100.0	Touho	0.35
3)	97.0	Ponerihouen	0.8	4)	100.4	Noumea	1.5
3)	97.0	Pouebo	0.4	4)	101.0	Iles-des-Pins	0.01
3)	97.4	Noumea	1.5	4)	101.0	Ponerihouen	0.75
3)	97.5	Mare	0.6	4)	101.0	Pouebo	0.35
4)	98.0	Canala	0.7	4)	101.5	Mare	0.6
4)	98.0	Dumbea [Noumea]	5.3	3)	102.0	Canala	0.7
4)	98.0	Hienghene	0.05	3)	102.0	Dumbea [Noumea]	5.3
4)	98.0	Kone	1	3)	102.0	Hienghene	0.05
4)	98.0	Poum	0.01	3)	102.0	Kone	1
4)	98.0	Yate	0.01	3)	102.0	Poum	0.01
3)	98.5	Lifou	1.5	3)	102.0	Yate	0.01
4)	102.5	Lifou	1.5	3)	103.0	Koumac	1.5
3)	103.0	Bourail	0.07	3)	103.0	Thio	0.5
3)	103.0	Houailou	0.25	4)	103.5	Ouvea	0.15

Stations, addresses and other information

1) NRJ, 41/43 rue Sebastopol, B.P G5 - 98848 Noumea Cedex ☎ +687 687279446 📠 +687 687279447 **W:** www.nrj.nc (live streaming) 24h – **2) R. Oceane**, 1, avenue d'Auteuill Lotissement FSH Koutio - 98835. Dumbea ☎ +687 687410095 📠 +687 687410099 **L.P:** President, Dumbea Communications – Robert Lucas, Dir: Veronique Loisel **E:** oceane.fm@lagoon.nc **W:** www.oceanefm.net (live streaming) 24h – **3) R. Djiido**, 29, rue du Marechal Juin - 98880 Noumea ☎ +687 687253515 📠 +687 687272187 **W:** www.radiodjiido.nc (live streaming) **E:** radiodjiido@radiodjiido.nc **L.P:** Thierry Kameremoin 24h **FPL:** R. Hmelom [Kone] and R. Dynamik Sud [Bourail] newly licensed – **4) R. Rythme Bleu**, B.P 578 - 98845 Noumea Cedex ☎ +687 687254500 📠 +687 687284928 **E:** rrb@lagoon.nc. 24h **FPL:** Frequence Nord [Kone] and R. Baies des Tortues [Bourail] newly licensed.

NEW ZEALAND

L.T: UTC +12h (30 Sep 12-7 Apr 13, 29 Sep 13-6 Apr 14: +13h) — **Pop:** 4.4 million — **Pr.L:** English, Maori, Samoan — **E.C:** 50Hz, 230V — **ITU:** NZL

RADIO SPECTRUM MANAGEMENT GROUP
Ministry of Business, Innovation & Employment
📧 P.O. Box 2847, Wellington 6140 ☎ +64 4 962 2603 NZ Freephone 0508 776 463 📠 +64 4 499 0797 **W:** www.rsm.govt.nz **E:** info@rsm.govt.nz **L.P:** Mgr R. Spectrum Policy & Planning: Brian Miller; Mgr R. Spectrum Management: Sanjai Raj. **RSMG** is the statutory authority responsible for radio spectrum administration.

BROADCASTING STANDARDS AUTHORITY
📧 P.O. Box 9213, Wellington ☎ +64 4 382 9508 📠 +64 4 382 9543 **W:** www.bsa.govt.nz **E:** info@bsa.govt.nz **L.P:** CE: Susan Freeman-Greene. The **BSA** statutory authority has codes of broadc. practice, broadc. standards, ethical conduct and has a complaints procedure.

NEW ZEALAND ON AIR
📧 P.O. Box 9744, Wellington 6141 ☎ +64 4 382 9524 📠 +64 4 382 9546 **W:** www.nzonair.govt.nz **E:** info@nzonair.govt.nz **L.P:** CE: Jane Wrightson, Mgr Comm. Broadc.: Keith Collins. **NZOA** is the operational funding agency for R. New Zealand, Community Access R., R. Reading Service, National Pacific R. Trust, Samoan Capital R., [bNet] and TV and New Media.

RADIO NEW ZEALAND (Non-commercial, Pub)
📧 P.O. Box 123, Wellington 6140 ☎ +64 4 474 1999 📠 +64 4 474 1730 **W:** www.radionz.co.nz **L.P:** CE: Peter Cavanagh; Infrastructure Mgr: Matthew Finn; Trs. Mgr: Gary Fowles
Network Stations: RNZ National (**N**), RNZ Concert (**C**), RNZ AM Network (**AM**). For full FM listings see website. **Prgr:** 24h from Wellington studios except for RNZ AM Network which only broadc. when Parliament in session [rel. commercial stn Southern Star at other times]. **N:** RNZ News bulletins

Network Stations MW

MW	kHz	kW	Net	MW	kHz	kW	Net
Wellington	567	50	N	Napier-Hastings	909	5.0	AM
Napier-Hastings	630	10.0	N	New Plymouth	918	2.5	N
Alexandra	639	2.0	N	Timaru	918	2.5	N
Tauranga	657	10.0	AM	Christchurch	963	10.0	AM
Wellington	657	50.0	AM	Kaikohe	981	2.0	N
Christchurch	675	10.0	AM	Masterton	1071	2.5	N
Invercargill	720	10.0	N	Nelson	1116	2.5	N
Tokoroa	729	2.5	N	Queenstown	1134	2.0	N
Auckland	756	10.0	N	Hamilton	1143	2.5	N
Dunedin	810	10.0	N	Rotorua	1188	0.4	N
Tauranga	819	10.0	N	Gisborne	1314	2	N
Kaitaia	837	2.0	N	Invercargill	1314	5	AM
Whangarei	837	2.5	N	Palmerston North	1449	2.5	N
Auckland	882	10.0	AM	Westport	1458	2.5	N
Dunedin	900	10.0	AM	Hamilton	1494	2.5	AM

Network Stations FM
Major Radio Market

FM (MHz)	N	C	FM (MHz)	N	C
Auckland	101.4	92.6	Kapiti Coast	101.5	98.3
Christchurch	101.7	89.7/99.7	Napier-Hastings	101.5	91.1
Dunedin	101.4	92.6/99.0/99.4	Nelson	101.6	91.2
Gisborne	101.3	97.3	New Plymouth	101.2	91.6
Hamilton	101.0	91.4	Palmerston N.	101.0	89.0
Invercargill	101.2	90.0	Queenstown	101.6	98.4
Rotorua	101.5	90.3	Timaru	101.1	99.5
Taupo	101.6/104.8	98.4	Wellington	101.3/101.7	92.5/96.1
Tauranga	101.0	91.4	Whangarei	101.2/104.4	100.4/105.2

EXTERNAL SERVICE: Radio New Zealand Int.
- see International broadcasting section

COMMUNITY ACCESS RADIO
12 independent stns affiliated to the **Association of Community Access Broadcasters [ACAB] W:** www.acab.org.nz **E:** info@acab.org.nz. Each stn serves local urban communities with a variety of ethnic language, cultural and comm. group prgrs. BBC WS is carried overnight on several stns. **H. of Tr:** 24h

MW	KHz	kW	Station, location
1)	783	10	Wellington Access R., Wellington
2)	999	1.5	Manawatu Access R., Palmerston North
3)	1206	0.5	Free FM89 Hamilton
4)	1431	2	R.Kidnappers, Napier-Hastings
5)	1575	2.5	OAR 105.4FM, Dunedin

FM	MHz	kW	Station, location
3)	89.0		Free FM89, Hamilton
7)	92.7		Arrow FM, Masterton
8)	96.9	3.5	Plains FM, Christchurch
9)	96.4		R.Southland, Invercargill
12)	104.4	5	Access R. Taranaki, New Plymouth
10)	104.6		Planet FM, Auckland
4)	104.7		R.Kidnappers, Napier-Hastings
11)	104.7		Coast Access R., Kapiti Coast
6)	104.8		Fresh FM, Nelson
5)	105.4		OAR 105.4FM, Dunedin

Addresses & other information
1) P.O. Box 9073, Marion Square, Wellington 6141 ☎ +64 4 385 7210 📠 +64 4 385 7212 **W:** www.accessradio.org.nz **E:** info@accessradio.org.nz **Mgr:** Phil O'Brien – **2)** P.O. Box 4666, Manawatu Mail Centre, Palmerston North 4442 ☎+64 6 357 9340 📠 +64 6 357 9345 **W:** www.accessmanawatu.co.nz **E:** info@accessmanawatu.co.nz **Mgr:** Fraser Greig **Prgr:** BBC WS 0900-2100 overnight daily – **3)** P.O. Box 110, Waikato Mail Centre, Hamilton 3240 ☎ +64 7 834 2170 📠 +64 7 834 2174 **W:** www.freefm.org.nz **F:** info@freefm.org.nz **Mgr:** Phil Grey **Prgr:** BBC WS overnight Su-Fri– **4)** P.O. Box 680, Hastings 4156 ☎+64 6 878 8710 📠 +64 6 871 0590 **W:** www.radiokidnappers.org.nz **E:** david@radiokidnappers.org.nz **Mgr:** David Teesdale **FM:** 104.7 – **5)** 301 Moray Place, Dunedin ☎ +64 3 471 6161 📠 +64 3 471 6162 **W:** www.oar.org.nz **E:** manager@oar.org.nz **Mgr:** Lesley Paris **Prgr:** BBC WS overnight 1200-1800 daily – **6)** c/o NMIT, Private Bag 19, Nelson 7042 ☎ +64 3 546 9891 📠 +64 3 546 9892 **W:** www.freshfm.net **E:** nelson@freshfm.net **Mgr:** Mike Williams **FM Network:** 89.2 Blenheim/95.2 Takaka/104.8 Nelson City-Tasman – **7)** 92 Queen Street, Masterton ☎+64 6 378 0255 **W:** www.arrowfm.co.nz **E:** quiver@arrowfm.co.nz **Mgr:** Michael Wilson – **8)** P.O. Box 22297, Christchurch ☎ +64 3 365 7997 📠 +64 3 340 0967 **W:** www.plainsfm.org.nz **E:** info@plainsfm.org.nz **Mgr:** Nicki Reece **Prgr:** BBC WS overnight 1200-1800 daily – **9)** P.O. Box 1, Invercargill ☎+64 3 218 9891 📠 +64 3 214 1425 **W:** www.radiosouthland.org.nz **E:** darren@radiosouthland.org.nz **Mgr:** Darren Ludlow **Prgr:** BBC WS overnight 1200-1800 daily – **10)** P.O. Box 44215, Pt Chevalier, Auckland 1246 ☎ +64 9 815 8600 📠 +64 9 815 8620 **W:** www.planetaudio.org.nz **E:** info@planetaudio.org.nz **Mgr:** Terri Byrne – **11)** P.O. Box 213, Waikanae ☎/📠 +64 4 293 4838 **W:** www.coastaccessradio.org.nz **E:** accessradio.kapiti@xtra.co.nz **Mgr:** Graeme Joyes – **12)** PO Box 445, Taranaki Mail Center, New Plymouth 4340. ☎ 06 751 3720 **W:** www.accessradiotaranaki.com **E:** dk@accessradiotaranaki.com **Mgr:** Daniel Keighley

COMMUNITY RADIO
Independent unaffiliated community and/or access stns.

FM	MHz	kW	Station, location
1)	104.9	2	Compass FM, Rangiora, Christchurch
2)	106.1		Hutt Community R., Lower Hutt, Wellington

Addresses & other information
1) P.O. Box 27, Rangiora 7440 ☎ +64 3 313 7101 **W:** www.compassfm.org.nz **E:** manager@compassfm.org.nz **Mgr:** Mike Le Petit **Ann:** 'The Voices of North Canterbury' – **2)** 11 Hillary Ct, Naenae, Lower Hutt ☎ +64 4 891 0446 **W:** www.huttradio.co.nz **E:** huttradio@huttradio.co.nz **Mgr:** Eddie O'Strange **Prgr:** 24h (BBC WS overnight.)

TE MANGAI PAHO
📧 P.O. Box 10004, Wellington 6143 ☎ +64 4 915 0700 📠 +64 4 915 0701 **W:** www.tmp.govt.nz **E:** radio@tmp.govt.nz **L.P:** CEO: John Bishara, Mgr Radio Portfolio: Carl Goldsmith. **TMP** is the operational funding agency for the 21 independent commercial Maori Iwi Radio stns that operate 24h and often network prgrs overnight.

MAORI IWI RADIO (Comm.)
All Iwi stns and Maori TV are connected by PungaNet2 a broadband internet system for prgr and data sharing, monitoring and archiving. **W:** www.irirangi.net

MW	KHz	kW	Station, location
1)	585	2	R.Ngati Porou, Ruatoria
2)	603	5	R.Waatea, Auckland
3)	765	2.5	R.Kahungunu, Napier-Hastings
4)	1161	5	Te Upoko o te Ika, Wellington
5)	1440	0.2	Moana AM, Tauranga
FM	**MHz**	**kW**	**Station, location**
6)	89.0		Te Arawa FM, Rotorua
7)	89.8		Kia Ora FM, Palmerston North
8)	90.5		Tahu FM, Christchurch
9)	90.6		Raukawa FM, Tokoroa
10)	90.8		Tautoko FM, Mangamuka Bridge
11)	91.7		Turanga FM, Gisborne
12)	91.9		Maniapoto FM, Te Kuiti
13)	94.4		Te Hiku o te Ika, Kaitaia
14)	94.8		Te Korimako o, Taranaki, New Plymouth
15)	95.4		R.Tainui, Ngaruawahia
16)	96.9		Atiawa Toa FM, Lower Hutt
17)	97.6		Tuwharetoa FM, Turangi
18)	98.4		Sun FM, Whakatane
19)	99.1		Ngati Hine FM, Whangarei
20)	99.5		Nga Iwi FM, Paeroa
21)	100.0		Awa FM, Whanganui

Addresses & other information (all MHz):
1) P.O. Box 55, Ruatoria 4043 ☎ +64 6 864 8020 🖷 +64 6 864 8023 **W:** www.radiongatiporou.co.nz **E:** manager@radiongatiporou.co.nz **Mgr:** Rene Robati **FM:** 88.2/89.3/90.1/93.3/98.1 – **2)** P.O. Box 43157, Favona, Mangere, Manukau 2153 ☎ +64 9 275 9070 🖷 +64 9 275 8060 **W:** www.waatea603am.co.nz **E:** info@waatea603am.co.nz **Mgr:** Willie Jackson – **3)** P.O. Box 2406, Hastings 4153 ☎ +64 6 872 8943 🖷 +64 6 876 4157 **W:** www.radiokahungunu.co.nz **E:** pat@radio-kahungunu.co.nz **Mgr:** Patricia Te Rangi **FM:** 94.3 – **4)** P.O. Box 11812, Manners Street, Wellington 6142 ☎ +64 4 801 5002 🖷 +64 4 801 5009 **E:** wena@teupoko.co.nz **Mgr:** Wena Tait – **5)** P. O. Box 382, Seventh Avenue, Tauranga 3140 ☎ +64 7 571 0009 🖷 +64 7 571 0007 **E:** charlie@moanaradio.co.nz **Mgr:** Charlie Tawhiao **FM:** 98.2 – **6)** P.O. Box 883, Rotorua 3040 ☎ +64 7 349 2959 **E:** rodger@tearawa.com **Mgr:** Rodger Cunningham – **7)** P.O. Box 1341, Palmerston NorthCentral, Palmerston North 4440 ☎ +64 6 353 1881 🖷 +64 6 353 1880 **E:** danielle@rangitaane.co.nz **Mgr:** Danielle Harris – **8)** P.O. Box 13469, Armagh, Christchurch 8141 ☎+64 3 371 3905 🖷 +64 3 371 3901 **E:** blade_jones@ngaitahu.iwi.nz **Mgr:** Blade Jones **FM Netw:** 90.5/91.1/95.0/99.6 – **9)** P.O. Box 842, Tokoroa 3444 ☎+64 7 886 0127 🖷 +64 7 886 0947 **E:** wendy@raukawafm.com **Mgr:** Wendy Biddle **FM Netw:** 90.6/95.7 – **10)** Mangamuka Bridge RD2, Okaihau 0476 ☎+64 9 401 8991 🖷 +64 9 401 9746 **E:** cyrilchapman@clear.net.nz **Mgr:** Cyril Chapman **FM Netw:** 90.8/92.8/98.2 – **11)** P.O. Box 1224, Gisborne 4040 ☎ +64 6 868 6821 🖷 +64 6 868 1564 **W:** www.turangafm.co.nz **E:** fred@turangafm.maori.nz **Mgr:** Fred Maynard **FM Netw:** 91.7/95.5/98.0 – **12)** P.O. Box 416, Te Kuiti 3941 ☎ +64 7 878 1160 🖷 +64 7 878 3002 **W:** www.maniapotofm.co.nz **E:** info@maniapotofm.co.nz **Mgr:** Jaqui Taituha **FM Netw:** 91.9/92.7/96.5/99.6 – **13)** P.O. Box 458, Kaitaia 0441 ☎ +64 9 408 3944 🖷 +64 9 408 3944 **E:** wiremu@tehiku.co.nz **Mgr:** William Harrison – **14)** P.O. Box 4232, Taranaki Mail Centre, New Plymouth 4340 ☎+ 64 6 757 9055 🖷+64 6 757 9093 **E:** tipene@tekorimako.co.nz **Mgr:** Tipene O'Brien – **15)** P.O. Box 208, Ngaruawahia 3742 ☎ +64 7 824 5650 🖷 +64 7 824 5659 **Mgr:** Trina Koroheke **FM Netw:** 94.5/96.3/96.5 – **16)** P.O. Box 36111, Waiwhetu, Lower Hutt 5043 ☎+64 4 569 7993 🖷 + 64 4 560 3278 **E:** wluke@atiawa.co.nz **Mgr:** Wirangi Luke **FM Netw:** 94.9/96.9 – **17)** P.O. Box 198, Turangi 3353 ☎+64 7 386 0935 🖷 +64 7 386 0994 **E:** katipo@tuwharetoa.co.nz **Mgr:** Katipo Te Hiini **FM Netw:** 90.4/92.6/97.6/100.6 – **18)** P.O. Box 2090, Kopeopeo, Whakatane ☎+64 7 308 0403 🖷 +64 7 308 0150 **Mgr:** William Pryor **FM Netw:** 96.9/98.4 – **19)** P.O. Box 1127, Whangarei 0110 ☎+64 9 438 6115 🖷 +64 9 438 5767 **E:** mike@ngatihinefm.co.nz **Mgr:** Michael Kake **FM Netw:** 96.4/99.5 – **20)** P.O. Box 135, Paeroa 3640 ☎+ 64 7 862 6247 🖷 + 64 7 862 6279 **E:** nifm@ngaiwifm.co.nz **Mgr:** Caroline Kara **FM Netw:** 92.2/99.5 – **21)** P.O. Box 430, Whanganui 4540 ☎+ 64 6 347 1402 🖷+64 6 347 2339 **E:** geoff@awafm.co.nz **Mgr:** Geoff Mariu **FM Netw:** 91.0/93.5/100.0

NATIONAL PACIFIC R. TRUST (PACIFIC MEDIA NETW., Comm)
🖃 P.O. Box 99582, Newmarket, Auckland ☎ +64 9 361 6656 🖷 +64 9 361 3966 **L.P:** CEO: Tom Etuata. Independent charitable trust funded by NZ On Air and Ministry for Culture & Heritage **Netw. stn: Niu FM** "The Beat of the Pacific" 24h English & Pacific community languages **W:** www.niufm.com **E:** info@niufm.com **N:** Pacific R. News

Major Radio Market

Location	MHz	Location	MHz	Location	MHz
Whangarei	103.6	New Plymouth	103.6	Dunedin	103.8
Auckland	103.8	Palmerston N.	103.4	Christchurch	104.1

Location	MHz	Location	MHz	Location	MHz
Hamilton	103.4	Wellington	103.7	Napier-Hastings	103.9
Rotorua	103.9	Wellington	100.7	Invercargill	103.6
Taupo	104.0				

MW: 531pi, Auckland 531KHz 5kW. 24h Pacific comm. langs **W:** www.radio531pi.com **E:** info@radio531pi.com **N:** Pacific R. News

RADIO BROADCASTERS ASSOCIATION
🖃 P.O. Box 3762, Auckland ☎ +64 9 378 0788 🖷 +64 9 378 8180 **W:** www.rba.co.nz **E:** bill@rba.co.nz **L.P:** CE: Bill Francis. **RBA** represents NZ commercial radio industry and sponsors NZ Radio Awards.

MAJOR COMMERCIAL NETWORKS

RADIOWORKS, Level 2, 239 Ponsonby Road, Ponsonby, Auckland 1011. 🖃 P.O. Box 8880, Symonds Street, Auckland 1150 ☎ 64 9 928 9300 🖷 +64 9 373 4000 **W:** www.mediaworks.co.nz **L.P:** Group MD: Sussan Turner, CEO RadioWorks: Belinda Mulgrew. **Prgrs:** 24h **Owner:** Ironbridge Capital (Australia). **Netw. Stns:** P.O. Box 47560, Ponsonby, Auckland 1144 ☎ +64 9 928 9000 🖷 +64 9 361 1677 **RadioLive:** P.O. Box 8880, Symonds Street, Auckland 1150 ☎+64 9 928 9270 🖷 +64 9 360 0390. **George FM:** P.O. Box 47864, Ponsonby, Auckland 1144 **T:** +64 9 928 9310 🖷 +64 9 360 0044. **Prgr:** 24h from Auckland studios. **N:** R.Live bulletins. **Netw. Brands:** The Edge **W:** www.theedge.co.nz – Kiwi **W:** www.kiwifm.co.nz – R. Live **W:** www.radiolive.co.nz – LiveSPORT **W:** www.radiolivesport.co.nz – The Rock **W:** www.therock.co.nz – The Sound **W:** www.thesound.co.nz – George FM **W:** www.georgefm.co.nz – Mai FM **W:** www.maifm.co.nz. Full FM listings at individual netw. websites. **R. Trackside:** shares LiveSPORT freqs overnight for racing commentaries. Owned by Totaliser Agency Board, P.O. Box 38899, Wellington Mail Centre, Lower Hutt 5045 **W:** www.radiotrackside.co.nz

Radio Live

MW	kHz	kW	MW	KHz	kW
Auckland	702	10	Tauranga	1107	1
Christchurch	738	5	Wellington	1233	2
Rotorua	1107	1	Napier-Hastings	1368	1

LiveSPORT

MW	kHz	kW	MW	KHz	kW
Napier-Hastings	549	1	Dunedin	1206	2
Wellington	711	5	Invercargill	1224	2
Palmerston North	828	2	Timaru	1242	1
Tauranga	873	1	Christchurch	1260	2
Hamilton	954	2	Auckland	1476	5
Nelson	990	1	Gisborne	1485	1
Ashburton	1071	1	Rotorua	1548	0.9

FM	1	2	3	4	5	6	7	8
Whangarei	94.0	-	90.8	92.4	90.0	-	-	98.0
Auckland	94.2	102.2	100.6	-	90.2	93.8	96.6	88.6
Hamilton	97.8	-	100.2	-	93.0	93.8	-	-
Tauranga	97.8	-	100.0	-	94.2	92.6	-	96.6
Rotorua	99.9	-	95.1	-	92.7	91.1	-	105.5
Taupo	88.8	-	99.2	91.2	94.4	100.0	-	-
Gisborne	99.7	-	94.9	-	94.1	96.5	-	-
Napier-Hastings	98.3	-	-	-	95.1	91.9	-	105.5
New Plymouth	94.0	-	89.2	97.2	95.6	98.0	-	-
Palmerston North	93.0	-	93.8	-	95.4	94.6	-	97.0
Kapiti Coast	97.5	-	99.1	-	91.9	94.3	-	-
Wellington	91.7	102.1	98.9	-	96.5	97.3	-	100.5
Nelson	88.8	-	96.0	-	94.4	98.4	-	-
Christchurch	88.9	102.5	99.3	-	93.7	92.9	-	88.9
Timaru	95.5	-	89.9	-	91.5	97.1	-	-
Dunedin	91.8	-	96.6	-	93.4	90.2	-	-
Queenstown	95.2	-	91.2	93.6	100.0	97.6	96.8	-
Invercargill	97.2	-	94.0	-	90.8	98.0	-	-

1= The Edge, **2=** Kiwi, **3=** R.Live, **4=**LiveSPORT, **5=** The Rock, **6=** The Sound **7=** George **8** = Mai FM
Local Brands: The Breeze **W:** www.thebreeze.co.nz – More FM: **W:** www.morefm.co.nz – R. Dunedin **W:** www.radiodunedin.co.nz Overnight and weekends often networked from Auckland except for R. Dunedin. **Prgr:** 24h. **N:** R.Live bulletins. For full FM listings see individual local brand websites.

MW	KHz	kW	Station, location
1)	531	2	More FM, Alexandra
2)	891	5	The Breeze, Wellington
3)	1305	2.5	R. Dunedin, Dunedin
22)	1359	1	More FM, Queenstown

FM	Location	1	2	FM	Location	1	2
4)	Northland	-	91.6	16)	Wairarapa	99.8	89.3/105.5
5)	Auckland	93.4	91.8	17)	Horowhenua		
6)	Waikato	99.4	92.2	18)	Kapiti	100.7	90.3
7)	Tauranga	95.8	93.4	2)	Wellington	94.0/98.5	94.7/99.7
8)	Mercury Bay	96.6		19)	Nelson	97.6	92.8

FM	Location	1	2
9)	Rotorua	91.9	95.9
10)	Taupo	-	93.6
11)	Gisborne	-	98.9/90.1
12)	Hawkes Bay	97.5	92.7
13)	Taranaki	92.4	93.2
14)	Wanganui	-	92.8
15)	Manawatu	98.6	92.2

FM	Location	1	2
20)	Marlborough	*96.1	§92.9
21)	Christchurch	94.5	92.1
3)	Dunedin	98.2	97.4
1)	Central Otago	96.7	90.3/94.3
22)	Queenstown	99.2	92.0/99.4
23)	Southland	91.6	89.2

1= The Breeze, 2=More FM, *) also 97.3/98.5, § also 94.5/96.3

Addresses & other information

1) P.O. Box 143, Alexandra 9340 ☎ +64 3 901 6200 🖷 +64 3 448 6502 – **2)** P.O. Box 11441, Manners Street, Wellington 6142 ☎+64 4 915 1000 🖷 +64 4 915 1009 – **3)** P.O. Box 1957, Dunedin 9054 **R. Dunedin:** ☎ +64 3 477 6934 **Mgr:** Cindy Davies **E:** cdavies@radioworks.co.nz **FM** 99.8MHz **The Breeze/More FM:** ☎ +64 3 951 3600 🖷 +64 3 477 6874 – **4)** P.O. Box 100, Whangarei 0140 ☎ +64 9 986 9990 🖷 +64 9 438 2348 – **5) The Breeze/More FM:** P.O. Box 8880, Symonds Street, Auckland 1150 ☎+64 9 928 9300 🖷 +64 9 373 4000 **Mai FM:** P.O. Box 68886, Newton, Auckland ☎ +64 9 977 7800 🖷 +64 9 977 7801 – **6)** P.O. Box 19293, Hamilton 3244 ☎ +64 7 958 7050 🖷 +64 7 838 2893 – **7)** P.O. Box 13344, Tauranga 3141 ☎ +64 7 928 7300 🖷 +64 7 577 0294 – **8)** P.O. Box 14358, Whitianga **v** +64 7 866 5696 🖷 +64 7 866 2553 – **9)** P.O. Box 92, Rotorua 3040 ☎ +64 7 921 7630 🖷 +64 7 348 3830 – **10)** P.O. Box 393, Taupo 3351 ☎+64 7 906 7500 🖷 +64 7 378 2701 – **11)** P.O. Box 468, Gisborne 4040 ☎+64 6 986 3700 🖷 +64 6 869 0037 – **12)** P.O. Box 193, Hastings 4156 ☎ +64 6 974 6150 🖷 +64 6 876 5626 – **13)** P.O. Box 869, Taranaki Mail Centre, New Plymouth ☎ +64 6 968 6200 🖷 +64 6 757 5020 – **14)** P.O. Box 928, Wanganui 4540 ☎ +64 6 965 6300 🖷 +64 6 345 5592 – **15)** P.O. Box 446, Palmerston North Central, Palmerston North 4440 ☎ +64 6 952 6420 🖷 +64 6 356 1317 – **16)** P.O. Box 001, Masterton ☎ +64 6 370 2548 🖷 +64 6 378 8877 – **17)** P.O. Box 603, Levin ☎+64 6 368 2827 🖷 +64 6 368 0415 – **18)** P.O. Box 132, Paraparaumu 5254 ☎ +64 4 903 0400 🖷 +64 4 297 2999 – **19)** P.O. Box 907, Nelson 7040 ☎+64 3 546 9670 🖷 +64 3 546 9427 – **20)** P.O. Box 930, Blenheim ☎+64 3 579 0393 – **21) The Breeze:** Private Bag 4750, Christchurch 8140 ☎ +64 3 961 3102 🖷 +64 3 366 5301 **More FM:** P.O. Box 25209, Victoria Street, Christchurch 8144 ☎+64 3 961 3322 🖷 +64 3 377 1993 – **22)** P.O. Box 224, Queenstown ☎+64 3 901 0810 🖷 +64 3 442 7799 – **23)** P.O. Box 1740, Invercargill ☎ +64 3 948 3900 🖷 +64 3 218 8015

C) Associated local Radioworks stations

These stns operate as independent local brands. Overnights networked from More FM.**Prgr:** 24h. **N:** R.Live bulletins.
1) Coromandel FM, Paeroa 89.0MHz, **2)** Times FM, Auckland (Orewa) 89.9MHz, **3)** Big River R., Balclutha 92.9MHz
Addresses & Other Information
1) PO Box 962, Thames 3540 ☎+64 7 868 6063 🖷 +64 7 868 6681 **Mgr:** Warren Male **W:** www.coromandelfm.co.nz **FM Netw.:** 89.0/89.1/89.9/90.3/93.8/93.9/94.0/96.2/97.5 – **2)** PO Box 755, Orewa 0931 ☎ +64 9 928 9940 🖷 +64 9 427 0251 **GM:** Anna McGovern **E:** amcgovern@mediaworks.co.nz **W:** www.timesfm.co.nz **FM Network:** 89.9/97.8 – **3)** 1st Fl. PO John Street, Balclutha ☎+64 3 418 1969 **W:** www.bigriverradio.webs.com **FM Network:** 92.9/93.7

RHEMA BROADCASTING GROUP

🖳 **Corporate:** 53 Upper Queen Street, Auckland. 🖳 **Postal:** Private Bag 92636, Symonds Street, Auckland 1150. ☎ +64 9 307 1251 🖷 +64 9 309 6888 **W:** www.rbg.co.nz **L.P:** Chief Exec: Mike Brewer **Dir.Prgr-Radio:** Gary Hoogvliet **Other Media:** Shine TV, UCB International **Owner:** NZ charitable organization.
Netw. Stns: Prgr: 24h from Auckland studios. Southern Star also broadc. on RNZ AM Netw. txs when Parliament not in session. **N:** IRN bulletins.
Netw. Brands: Life FM **W:** www.lifefm.co.nz – NZ's Rhema **W:** www.rhema.co.nz – Southern Star **W:** www.sstar.co.nz – The Word/Bible R. **W:** www.bibleradio.co.nz. Full FM listings at individual netw. brand websites.

NZ's Rhema

MW	kHz	kW	MW	KHz	kW
Tauranga	540	5	Dunedin	621	2
New Plymouth	540	3	Gisborne	684	5
Kaitaia	549	3	Nelson	801	2
Timaru	594	5	Hamilton	855	2
Wanganui	594	2	Wellington	972	5
Christchurch	612	2	Auckland	1251	5
Whangarei	621	2	Invercargill	1404	5

Southern Star

MW	kHz	kW	MW	KHz	kW
Nelson	612	1.5	Napier-Hastings	909	5
Tauranga	657	10	Christchurch	963	10
Wellington	657	50	Timaru	981	2.5
Auckland	882	10	Invercargill	1314	5
Dunedin	900	10	Hamilton	1494	3

The Word/Bible Radio

MW	kHz	kW	MW	KHz	kW
Christchurch	540*	1.5	Hamilton	576	2.5
Invercargill	1026	2.5	Dunedin	1377	3

* Operates local daytime only

FM	1	2	3	FM	1	2	3
Whangarei	-	-	98.8	Palmerston North	91.4	-	96.2
Auckland	-	-	99.8	Kapiti Coast	-	-	96.7
Hamilton	-	-	94.6	Wellington	-	-	98.1
Tauranga	-	-	94.6	Nelson	-	-	93.6
Rotorua	93.5	-	94.6	Christchurch	-	-	106.9
Taupo	95.2	88.3	107.0	Timaru	-	-	93.9
Gisborne	-	92.5	100.5	Dunedin	-	-	94.2
Napier-Hastings	99.1	-	93.5	Queenstown	94.4	107.0	-
New Plymouth	-	-	99.6	Invercargill	-	-	100.0

1 = NZ's Rhema, 2 = Southern Star, 3 = Life FM

THE RADIO NETWORK [TRN]

🖳 **Corporate:** 54 Cook Street, Auckland. 🖳 **Postal:** Private Bag 92198, Auckland Mail Centre, Auckland 1142. ☎ +64 9 373 0000 🖷 +64 9 367 4802. **W:** www.radionetwork.co.nz **L.P:** CEO: Jane Hastings Group GM Content: David Brice Dir. Eng: Norm Collinson. **Other Media:** APN News & Media newspapers and magazines **Owner:** The Australian Radio Network [50% owned by Clear Channel USA].
A) Netw. Brands: Prgr: 24h from Auckland studios **N:** NewstalkZB bulletins. **Brands:** Coast **W:** www.thecoast.net.nz - Flava **W:** www.flava.co.nz - Radio Hauraki **W:** www.hauraki.co.nz - NewstalkZB **W:** www.newstalkzb.co.nz - Radio Sport **W:** www.radiosport.co.nz - ZM **W:** www.zmonline.com. Full FM listings at individual netw. brand websites.

Radio Sport

MW	kHz	kW	MW	KHz	kW
Nelson	549	1	Napier-Hastings	1125	1
Invercargill	558	5.0	Westport	1287	2
Dunedin	693	5.0	Auckland	1332	10
Ashburton	702	1.0	Rotorua	1350	1
Whangarei	729	3.0	Levin	1377	2
New Plymouth	774	5.0	Timaru	1494	2.5
Hamilton	792	5.0	Christchurch	1503	2.5
Christchurch	*1017	2.5	Wellington	1503	5
Wanganui	1062	1.0	Tauranga	1521	1
Palmerston North	1089	2.5			

* alternate for 1503, sometimes carries NewstalkZB

NewstalkZB

MW	kHz	kW	MW	KHz	kW
Rotorua	747	0.4	New Plymouth	1053	5
Masterton	846	2.0	Auckland	1080	10
Invercargill	864	10.0	Christchurch#	1098	5
Ashburton	873	1.0	Timaru	1152	2
Palmerston N.	927	2.0	Wanganui	1197	2
Gisborne	945	2.0	Kaikohe	1215	2
Tauranga	1008	10.0	Hawera	1323	3
Christchurch	*1017	2.5	Napier-Hastings	1278	2
Kaitaia	1026	2.0	Hamilton	1296	2.5
Whangarei	1026	2	Nelson	1341	2
Wellington#	1035	20	Oamaru	1395	2
Dunedin	1044	10	Tokoroa	1413	2

* alternate for 1098, sometimes carries R.Sport

Radio Hauraki

MW	kHz	kW
Dunedin	1125	1

Coast

MW	kHz	kW	MW	KHz	kW
Whangarei	900	2.5	Palmerston North	1548	1
Dunedin	954	1	Hawera	1557	2
New Plymouth	1359	2.5	Christchurch	1593	2.5
Napier-Hastings	1584	1			

FM	1	2	3	4	5	6
Whangarei	-	106.0	93.2	-	-	94.8
Auckland	105.4	95.8	99.0	89.4	98.2	91.0
Hamilton	105.0	-	96.2	97.0	-	89.4
Tauranga	97.4	-	91.0	90.2	99.0	89.8
Rotorua	96.7	89.5	94.3	-	-	98.3
Taupo	-	-	92.8	96.0	90.4	-
Gisborne	-	-	105.3	-	-	107.4
Napier-Hastings	-	-	99.9	90.3	96.7	95.9
New Plymouth	-	-	90.8	96.4	-	98.8
Palmerston North	-	-	105.8	100.2	-	90.6
Kapiti Coast	95.9	-	-	89.5	-	91.1
Wellington	95.7	-	93.3	89.3	93.7	90.9
Nelson	100.8	-	90.4	-	-	96.8
Christchurch	-	-	106.5	100.1	-	91.3
Timaru	-	-	-	-	-	96.3
Dunedin	-	-	106.2	-	-	95.8
Queenstown	-	-	89.6	-	-	-

FM	1	2	3	4	5	6
Invercargill	92.4	93.2		95.6		

1=Coast, 2=Flava, 3=R.Hauraki, 4=NewstalkZB, 5=R.Sport, 6=ZM

B) Local Brand: Classic Hits W: www.classichits.co.nz For full FM listings see local brand websites.

MW		kHz	kW	MW		KHz	kW
1) Takaka		1269	0.4	2) Picton		1539	0.4

FM		MHz	FM		MHz	FM		MHz
23) Dunedin		89.4	18) Greymouth		90.9	2) Blenheim		96.9
11) Hawkes Bay		89.5	18) Greymouth		91.1	3) Northland		97.2
1) Nelson		89.6	20) Ashburton		92.5	18) Greymouth		97.3
13) Wanganui		89.6	16) Kapiti		92.7	4) Auckland		97.4
12) Taranaki		90.0	18) Greymouth		93.1	7) Rotorua		97.5
15) Masterton		90.1	21) Timaru		94.7	3) Northland		97.6
17) Wellington		90.1	6) Tauranga		95.0	19) Christchurch		97.7
24) Central Otago		90.4	3) Northland		95.6	14) Manawatu		97.8
25) Southland		90.4	24) Central Otago		96.2	22) Oamaru		98.4
18) Greymouth		90.5	8) Tokoroa		96.4	5) Waikato		98.6
12) Taranaki		90.8	19) Christchurch		96.5	21) Timaru		98.7
7) Rotorua		90.8	3) Northland		96.8	25) Southland		98.8
10) Gisborne		90.9	1b) Taupo		96.8	24) Central Otago		99.9

Addresses & other information

1) P.O. Box 43, Nelson 7043 ☎ +64 3 548 1064 🖷 +64 3 546 2580 – **2)** P.O. Box 225, Blenheim ☎+64 3 579 2969 🖷 +64 3 578 0981 – **3)** P.O. Box 845, Whangarei ☎ +64 9 430 4950 🖷 +64 9 430 4968 - **4)** Private Bag 92198, Auckland ☎+64 9 373 0000 🖷 +64 9 367 4802 – **5)** P.O. Box 489, Hamilton ☎+64 7 858 0700 🖷 +64 7 858 0730 – **6)** P.O. Box 642, Tauranga ☎ +64 7 578 9139 🖷 +64 7 577 8522 – **7)** P.O. Box 1147, Rotorua ☎ +64 7 348 9089 🖷 +64 7 349 5527 – **8)** P.O. Box 272, Tokoroa ☎+64 7 668 9431 🖷 +64 7 886 8391 – **9)** P.O. Box 967, Taupo ☎ +64 7 376 0550 🖷 +64 7 378 0030 – **10)** P.O. Box 1040, Gisborne ☎+64 6 867 2139 🖷 +64 6 867 8309 – **11)** P.O. Box 241, Napier ☎ +64 6 833 8400 🖷 +64 4 833 8421– **12)** P.O. Box 141, New Plymouth ☎ +64 6 759 2460 🖷 +64 6 759 2440 - **13)** P.O. Box 632, Wanganui ☎ +64 6 348 1176 🖷 +64 6 345 6402 – **14)** P.O. Box 1045, Palmerston North ☎ +64 6 350 3550 🖷 +64 6 350 3580 – **15)** P.O. Box 220, Masterton ☎+64 6 370 5014 🖷 +64 6 370 8460 – **16)** P.O. Box 596, Paraparaumu ☎+64 4 382 6677 🖷 +64 4 385 4210 – **17)** P.O. Box 300, Wellington ☎+64 4 802 4710 🖷 +64 4 385 4210 – #NewstalkZB 1035MW/90.1FM carries local breakfast show – **18)** P.O. Box 378, Greymouth ☎+64 3 768 7068 🖷 +64 3 768 7067 – **19)** P.O. Box 1484, Christchurch ☎ +64 3 379 9600 🖷 +64 3 363 3510 – #NewstalkZB 1098MW/89.3FM carries local breakfast show – **20)** P.O. Box 465, Ashburton ☎+64 3 307 8927 🖷 +64 3 307 8930 – **21)** P.O. Box 275, Timaru ☎ +64 3 684 8152 🖷 +64 3 688 6733 – **22)** P.O. Box 426, Oamaru ☎ +64 3 433 1090 🖷 +64 3 433 1087 - **23)** P.O. Box 888, Dunedin ☎+64 3 474 8400 🖷 +64 3 474 8422 – **24)** Level 1, 11 Earl Street, Church Lane, Queenstown ☎ +64 3 441 2784 🖷 +64 3 441 2785 – **25)** P.O. Box 802, Invercargill ☎+64 3 211 1500 🖷 +64 3 211 1532

C)Associated local TRN stations

These stns operate as independent local brands. Overnights are networked from Classic Hits. **Prgr:** 24h. **N:** NewstalkZB bulletins.

1) Hokonui 94.8FM PO Box 292, Gore 9700 ☎ +64 3 208 9325 🖷 +64 3 208 9326 **W:** www.hokonui.co.nz **Prgr:** local 1800-0100, network Farming Show from Dunedin 0100-0200, local 0200-0700 then relay Classic Hits Southland. Also 95.2 Tapanui. **2) South Otago's Hokonui 91.3** The Lane, Balclutha 9230 ☎ +64 3 418 2884 **Prgr:** local 1800-2200 then relays Hokonui 94.8FM **W: www.hokonui.co.nz**

INDEPENDENT STATIONS

MW	KHz	kW	Station, location
1)	729	0.1	Burn729am, Ranfurly
2)	756	0.8	Puketapu R., Palmerston
3)	783	10	Samoan Capital R., Wellington
4)	810	2	BBC World Service NZ, Auckland
5)	936	1	New Supremo, Auckland
6)	990	1	Apna 990 Auckland
7)	1179	5	R.Ake ,Auckland
8)	1242	1	1XXOne Double X, Whakatane
9)	1368	0.8/0.1	1XT Village R., Tauranga
10)	1386	10	R.Tarana, Auckland
11)	1413	1	3XP R. Ferrymead, Christchurch
12)	‡1440	1	Goldrush R., Lawrence
69)	1530	1	The Wireless Station, Napier-Hastings
13)	1593	5	R.Samoa, Auckland
14)	1602	2.5	R.Reading Service, Levin

FM	MHz	kW	Station, location
17)	89.2		Kaitaia Community R, Kaitaia
19)	89.4		The Rhythm, Waihi Beach
21)	89.8		Ski FM, Ohakune
22)	90.3		Vision FM, Tokoroa
23)	90.3		Coast FM, Westport
8)	90.5		1XX One Double X, Whakatane

FM	MHz	kW	Station, location
24)	90.6		R.Chinese Auckland
25)	90.8		Waihi Community R, Waihi
26)	90.8		Thames Valley FM, Thames
27)	91.0		Radio 1*, Dunedin
28)	92.2		R.Wanaka, Wanaka
8)	92.9		Kiwi FM, Te Puke
8)	93.0		Bayrock, Wanaka
31)	93.1		Port FM, Timaru
32)	93.5		Central FM, Waipukurau
28)	94.6		Roy FM, Wanaka
34)	95.0		95bfm* Auckland
5)	95.8	3	Real Good Life FM, Auckland
68)	96.0		Next FM, Queenstown
36)	96.2		Big River R., Dargaville
37)	96.4		Gold FM, Waihi
8)	97.7	2	Bayrock, Whakatane
38)	98.1		Raglan Community R., Raglan
39)	98.5	1.5	RDU*, Christchurch
40)	99.1		Peak FM, Taumarunui
42)	99.8		Sea Breeze FM, Himatangi Beach
43)	100.3		Blue FM, Kaikoura
33)	100.4		Cruise FM, Tokoroa
45)	100.7	4	Bay FM, Napier-Hastings
46)	100.9	5	Voice of South Pole, Christchurch
5)	104.2	3	Radio 9, Auckland
50)	105.2	1.5	Cruize 105.2, New Plymouth
51)	105.2		Labotomy Pants FM, Hamilton
52)	105.2	4	Country R., Invercargill
10)	105.3	2	Radio Tarana, Wellington
55)	105.4	8	Bollybop FM, Tauranga
12)	‡105.6	1.25	Goldrush R., Queenstown
57)	‡105.6	5	F.PL, Nelson
59)	105.6		R.Waipu, Waipu
61)	105.8		Wellsford Country R., Wellsford
65)	106.4	2	Timeless Taupo FM, Taupo
66)	106.4		Heads FM, Mangawhai

NB: Section under review because of difficulty accessing actual transmitter powers being used. ‡) inactive

Addresses & other information

1) 3 Charlemont St East, Ranfurly 9332 – **2)** 118 Ronaldsay St, Palmerston 9430 **W:** www.puketapuradio.com **Prgr:** Day: local community radio – Night: relay UK based Planet Caroline online stream – **3)** PO Box 6647, Marion Square, Wellington 6141 **Prgr:** Samoan "Siufofaga O Le Laumua" Mon-Fri 1900-0100 – **4)** Auckland Radio Trust, PO Box 800, Shortland Street, Auckland 1001 **W:** www.worldservice.co.nz **Prgr:** BBC World Service satellite relay, RNZI Dateline Pacific and local advertising – **5)** PO Box 12743, Penrose, Auckland 1642 **W:** www.chinesevoice.co.nz **Prgr:** 936AM Mandarin [incl satellite services from China & Taiwan], 99.4 FM Cantonese [incl satellite services from Hong Kong], **104.2** FM Radio 9 – Mandarin [12h daily], China R. International English [12h daily] – **6)** Level 3, 362 Great North Rd, Henderson, Waitakere 0612 **W:** www. apna990.co.nz**Prgr:** Hindi – **7)** c/o Spoke Communications, PO Box 52148, Kingsland, Auckland 1352 **Prgr:** Contemporary Urban Maori – **8)** Radio Bay of Plenty Ltd, PO Box 383, Whakatane 3158 **Brands:** 1XX **W:** www.1xx.co.nz – Kiwi FM [146 Jellicoe St, Te Puke 3119] - Bayrock **W:** www.bayrock.co.nz **W:** 97.7/99.3MHz and 93.0MHz Wanaka – **9)** PO Box 597, Seventh Avenue, Tauranga 3140 **W:** www.villageradio. co.nz **E:** taurangavillageradio@gmail.com **LP:** SM: Bonnie Leonard **Prgr:** Nostalgia Mon-Fri 2200-0500 Sat-Sun 2000-0500 Community Access at some other times – **10)** PO Box 5956, Wellesley Street, Auckland 1141 **W:** www.tarana.co.nz **Prgr:** Hindi **FM Netw:** 105.3 Wellington – **11)** PO Box 19090, Woolston, Christchurch 8241 **W:** www.radioferrymead.co.nz **Prgr:** Fri 0300-Mon 1200 including automated prgrs, Statutory Holidays & Christmas New Year period – **12)** 24 Ross Place, Lawrence 9532 **Brands:** Goldrush 1440 **W:** www.goldrush1440.com Rush99 **W:** www.rush99. net.ms Pink FM [LPFM] **W:** www.pinkfm.net.ms Independent Network News **W:** www.nzinn.org – **13)** PO Box 200105, Papatoetoe Central, Manukau 2156 **W:** www.radiosamoa.co.nz **Prgr:** Samoan – **14)** PO Box 360, Levin 5500 **W:** www.radioreading.org.nz **Prgr:** Mon-Fri 2000-1800, Sat 1200-0500, Sun 0000-0800 – RNZ National at other times – **17)** PO Box 690, Kaitaia – **19)** 7 The Crescent, Waihi Beach 3611 – **21)** PO Box 201, Ohakune **FM Netw.:** 89.5/89.8/93.4/94.4/96.6/102.6/106.3MHz **W:** www.934skifm.co.nz – **22)** 9 Glendevon Pl, Tokoroa – **23)** PO Box 249, Westport 7866 **W:** www.westportnews.co.nz **FM Netw.:** 90.3 and others – **24)** PO Box 82343, Highland Park, Auckland **W:** www.chineseradio.co.nz **Prgr:** Chinese – **25)** PO Box 260, Waihi 3641 – **26)** 529 Pollen Street, Thames – **27)** PO Box 1436, Dunedin **W:** www.r1.co.nz – **28)** PO Box 2, Wanaka 9343 **Brands:** R.Wanaka 92.2 - Roy FM 94.6 – **31)** PO Box 635, Timaru 7940 **W:** www.portfmregional.co.nz **FM Netw incl.** 91.2/92.7/9 3.7/95.0/97.9MHz with local studios in Ashburton, Timaru and Oamaru. Commercial affiliation with RadioWorks network brands The Edge, The Sound & The Rock in the region – **32)**PO Box 81, Waipukurau 4200 **W:**

www.centralfm.co.nz **FM Netw.:** 93.5/99.4/99.6 – **33)** Level 1, 203 Leith Pl, Tokoroa **W:** www.radiocruisefm.co.nz **FM Netw.:** 100.4/104.4MHz + LPFM – **34)** PO Box 4580, Shortland Street, Auckland 1001 **W:** www.95bfm.com – **36)** PO Box 199, Dargaville 0340 **W:** www.bigriverfm.co.nz – **37)** Level 1, 25 Seddon St, Waihi **W:** www.goldfm.co.nz – **38)** 42 Norrie Ave, Raglan 3225 **W:** www.raglanradio.com – **39)** PO Box 31244, Christchurch 8444 **W:** www.rdu.org.nz – **40)** PO Box 37, Raetihi 4632 **W:** www.twitter.com/peakfm958 **FM Netw.:** 92.7/99MHz and others – **42)** 42 Muapoko St, Himatangi Beach **W:** www.seabreezefm.com**Prgr:** Fri night, Sat-Sun only – **43)** Scarborough Street, Kaikoura – **45)** Heretaunga St, West, Hastings – **46)** c/o David Moore, 12 Walters Rd, Marshland, Christchurch. **Prgr:** Chinese – **50)** 603 Devon St East, New Plymouth **W:** www.facebook.com/pages/new-plymouth/cruize-fm-1052 – **51)** PO Box 1183, Hamilton – **52)** 145 Islington St, Invercargill **W:** www.countryradio-network.com/invercargill **FM Netw.:** 105.2 and LPFM – **55)** Upstairs Suite 3/39 Springs St, Tauranga **W:** www.bollybop.co.nz **E:** sales@bollybop.co.nz **Prgr:** Hindi – **57)** Wild Tomato Media, 243 Trafalgar St, Nelson – **59)** Wave FM Ltd, 7 Finch St, Marsden Cove, One Tree Point, Ruakaka 0118 – **61)** 32 Rusty Brook Rd, Wellsford – **65)** Field & Sport Ltd, 23 Scannell Rd, Taupo – **66)** PO Box 180, Mangawhai 0540 – **68)** c/o Stuart Campbell, Neplusultra St, Cromwell 9191 – **69** The Wireless Station Ltd, PO Box 8947, Havelock North **Prgr:** automated standards & rock & roll music.
NB: + stns below 1kW
Notes: 1) Stns marked * are **bNet** student radio stns, a loose prgr and advertising sales netw. **2)** An estimated 500 or more LPFM [1w or less] stns broadcast on 87.6-88.3 and 106.7-107.7 throughout the country. An updated guide to these authorized but unlicenced stns is maintained by the Radio Heritage Foundation **W:** www.radioheritage.net

NICARAGUA

L.T: UTC -6h — **Pop:** 5.8 million — **Pr.L:** Spanish — **E.C:** 60Hz, 120V — **ITU:** NCG — **Intl. dialling code:** +505

TELCOR – INSTITUTO NICARAGÜENSE DE TELECOMUNICACIONES Y CORREOS
✉ Ave. Bolívar Esquina Diagonal a la Cancillería, Managua
☎ +505 2222 7350 **W:** www.telcor.gob.ni

ASOCIACION NICARAGUENSE DE RADIODIFUSION
(ANIR) ✉ c/o R. Ya, Frente a la Universidad Centroamericana, Managua

CAMARA NICARAGUENSE DE RADIODIFUSION
✉ c/o R. Corporación, Cd. Jardín Q-20, Av. Ponciano Lombillo, Managua

MW Call	kHz	kW	Station, location & h. of tr.
MA01) A3OW	540	25	R. Corporación, Managua: 0950-0505
CH01) A2RQ	570	5	R. Veritas 5-70, Chinandega: 1030-0250
MA02) A3LP	580	10	R. 5-80, Managua: 1030-0000 (Sat 1200-, Sun 1100-)
MA03) A3MD	600	10	La Nueva R. Ya, Managua: 1000-0600 (SS 24h)
MA04) N	620	10	R. Nicaragua, Managua: 1000-0400
MA04) A4LR	640	10	La Mera Mera , Managua
MT01) A6RS	650	5	R. Muzun, Matagalpa: 1100-0100
GR01) RD	650	10/8	R. Diriangén "La Super D", Granada: 0950-2300
MA25)	‡660	5	R. Máxima, Managua
ZE01) RC	‡670		R. Caribe, Pto Cabezas
MA05) AM	680	10/2	R. La Primerísima, Managua: 1045-0500 (SS -2400)
MT02) RH	690	10/5	R. Hermanos, Matagalpa: 1000-0400
MA27) MM	700	30	R. La Poderosa, Managua: 1100-0200, Sat 1100-2400, Sun 1200-2400
MA06) A3RC	720	25	R. Católica, Managua: 1000-0430
MA07) A3LS	740	50	R. Sandino "La S Grande", Managua: 1000-0400
MA26) A3AR	760	10	R. Magic, Managua
MA08) A3RO	800	10	R. 800, Managua: 0800-0500
MA09) FAOL	820	20	R. Ondas de Luz, Managua: 1000-0400
MA10) A3NT	840	5	R. Noticias, Managua: 1030-0200
MA26) A3CO	860	5	La Gran Cadena, Managua
CT01) CD	870	10	R. Centro, Juigalpa: 1100-0200
MA11) A3EP	880	10	R. El Pensamiento, Managua: 1100-0300
MA12) A3RT	900	5	R. Tiempo, Managua: 1050-0400
JI01)	910	5	R. Jinotega, Jinotega
MA13) W	920	10	R. Mundial, Managua: 1100-0400
RS01) ACTH	960	2.5	LV del Trópico Húmedo, San Carlos: 1000-0300
MA13) A3NO	980	1	R. Redención Internac., Managua
MA15) FF	1000	10	R. Mil, Managua: 1200-0400
NS02) FAVP	1010	5	R. LV del Pinar, Ocotal: 1100-0400
JI02) VJ	1040	2	LV de Jinotega, Jinotega
MS02) LL	1050	3	R. Masaya, Masaya
ZE03)	‡1060	1	LV del Atlántico, Bluefields
MA16) A3LC	1080	10	R. 15 de Septiembre, Managua: 1100-0400

MW Call	kHz	kW	Station, location & h. of tr.
ES01) HAAL	‡1090	5	R. Alma Latina, Estelí: 1100-0400
LE01) F2MT	‡1110	1	R. Momotombo, La Paz Centro
MA17) A3CP	1120	5	R. CEPAD "El Arco Iris del Amor", Managua: 1100-0100
NS03)	1130	0.5	Voz Evangélica de Jalapa, Jalapa
ES02) HM	‡1160	1	R. Satélite, Estelí
CH03) A6RB	1190	1	R. Bendición, Cayanlipe
MA18) A3AC	1200		1200 La Radio, Managua
MA19) A3RA	1220	1	R. América, Managua: 1200-0400
AS01) MNG	1230	5	R. Manantial, Nueva Guinea: 1000-0300
MA20) A3RR	1240	5	R. Vida Managua
ES03) CR	1250	2.5	Cad. Radial Samaritano, Condega: 1000-0400
MT03) RA	1270	3	R. Amistad, Matagalpa
MA21) A2CC	1300	1	Canal 130 AM, Managua: 1200-2330
CH02) SC	1310	10/1	R. San Cristóbal, Chinandega: 1000-0200
MT04) A6RM	1330	5	R. Matagalpa, Matagalpa: 1100-0500
MA22) OS	‡1340	1	R. Ondas Sonoras, Managua
MD01) AARS	‡1370	1	R. Fronteras, Somoto
MA23) A3VA	‡1400	10	R. María, Managua
LE02) RA	1410	3/1	La Estación de la Amistad, León: 1000-0200
ES04) AARL	1430	5	R. Liberación "La Tayacana", Estelí: 1100-0300
MA24) A3MR	1440	25	R. Maranatha, Managua: 1000-0500
BO01) RY	1470	1	R. Yarrince, Boaco
MA01) PT	‡1500	1	R. Minuto, Managua
CA02) A4TS	1530	0.5	LV de Sta Teresa, Sta Teresa: 1400-2200

Hrs of tr 24h except where shown. Call YN– ‡ = inactive, ± = varying fq

Addresses and other information:
AS00) ATLANTICO SUR
AS01) TELCOR, 1½ c este, Nueva Guinea
B000) BOACO
BO01) Casa del Finquero, 20 vrs al este, Boaco
CA00) CARAZO
CA02) Entrada II Calle, ½ c abajo, Sta Teresa
CH00) CHINANDEGA
CH01) Frente Iglesia de Guadalupe (or: Ap. 12), Chinandega – **CH02)** Club Eden, 2½ c. Al Sur, (or: Ap. 59), Chinandega – **CH03)** Cayanlipe
CT00) CHONTALES
CT01) Caracoles negros,Juigalpa **W:** http://radiocentro870.com
ES00) ESTELÍ
ES01) Esquina Norte de Hospital Adb, 2 c al norte, 3½ c este, Estelí– **ES02)** Esquina Sur-Oeste de la Escuela Nexo, 25 vrs al Río, Estelí – **ES03)** Instituto Bíblico Samaritado, Calle Principal, Condega – **ES04)** Shell, 1 c al norte, Estelí **W:** www.radioliberacion.com
GR00) GRANADA
GR01) Cuerpo de Bomberos 1c al N 1c al E No. 110, Granada ☎+505 2552 2040
JI00) JINOTEGA
JI01) Escuela Gabriela Mistral, ½ al Norte, Avenida Ernesto Rosales, Jinotega. ☎ +505 2782 2247 **W:** www.radiojinotega.hostoi.com – **JI02)** Cine Betty, 2½ c al norte, Jinotega
LE00) LEÓN
LE01) Del Pto del Mct, 1 c abajo, ½ c norte, León – **LE02)** Unan 1½ c al norte, León FM 91.9
MA00) MANAGUA
MA01 Cd. Jardín Q-20, Av. Ponciano Lombillo (Apartado Postal 2442), Managua **E:** rc540@radio-corporacion.com **W:** www.radio-corpora-cion.com – **MA02)** Reparto El Carmen,Costado Oeste del Parque, Managua ☎+505 2268 2580 **W:** http://la580.com – **MA03)** Frente a la Universidad Centroamericana, Managua **W:** www.nuevaya.com.ni **E:** info@nuevaya.com.ni – **MA04)** Villa Fontana, Contiguo a TELCOR, Managua ☎+ 505 2277 2330 **W:** www.nicaragua620.com – **MA05)** Apartado Postal 4003 (or Barrio Bolonia, de Tica bus, 100 metros al sur, 100 metros al este), Managua **W:** www.radiolaprimerisima.com **E:** info@radiolaprimerisima.com – **MA06)** Altamira D'Este 621, Managua ☎+505 2278 0836 **W:** www.radiocatolica.com – **MA07)** Paseo Tiscapa (or: Ap. 4776), Managua **W:** www.rsandino.comi – **MA08)** Semaforos de Lozelsa 1c al lago, ½ abajo, Managua **W:** http://radio800.net – **MA09)** Costado Sur del Hospital Bautista N° 945, Managua ☎+505 2222 2250 – **MA10)** Ciudad Jardín, Casa N-10, Managua ☎ – **MA11)** Distribuidora Vicky, 4C Al lago, Casa 73, Managua ☎+505 2788 1633 **W:** www.radioelpensamiento.com – **MA12)** Los Robles Gimn Atlas, 1c al E. 20 vs Al S N° 217, Managua ☎+505 2278 2540 – **MA13)** Reparto Miraflores, Rest. Munich 4c Al lago 1 c al Oe, Managua ☎+505 2266 6767 – **MA14)** Calle Edgar Lang, Managua ☎+505 2270 0096 – **MA16)** Altamira de Este contiguo Embajada de Taiwán, Managua ☎+505 2278 4040 **W:** www.radio15deseptiembre.com – **MA17)** Apartado 3091, Managua– **MA18)** Managua – **MA19)** Foto Castillo 1 c Al sur ½ c, Villa Don Bosco E-182, Managua ☎+505 2244 2068 – **MA20)** Carret. Vieja a León, km 10 ¾, 500 m al N 200 al Oe,

Managua ☎+505 2265 4919 **E**: www.vidaradio1240am.com – **MA21)** Carretera a Masaya, Km 12 ¾, 450 Metros al este, Managua ☎+505 2279 9491 – **MA22)** Bo La Cruz, Cine Blanca, 5c al N, ½ c al E, Casa 1112, Managua – **MA23)** De la Iglesia San Francisco 150 metros al este, Bolonia, Managua **W**: www.radiomaria.org/ni **E**: rmaria@cable-net.com.ni – **MA24)** Rotonda Metrocentro 1 c al sur, ½ C Abajo, Casa 41, Managua ☎+505 2278 5235 **W**: http://radiomaranatha.fm **E**: maranatha@cablenet.com.ni – **MA25)** Managua – **MA26)** RATENSA, Mansión Teodolinda, 2c al Oe, Managua – **MA27)** Managua **W**: www.radiolapoderosa700.com

MD00) MADRIZ
MD01) Somoto
MS00) MASAYA
MS01) Carr. a Managua km 24½, Masaya – **MS02)** Teatro Masaya, 1½ c al Oeste, N° 135, Masaya
MT00) MATAGALPA
MT01) Frente al Catedral, Matagalpa – **MT02)** Bo. Liberación Igl. Catedral. 1c al N 25 vs al Oe, Matagalpa ☎+505 2772 2964 FM: 92.3 **W**: www.radiohermanos.com – **MT03)** Detras de la Iglesia San José, Matagalpa – **MT04)** Rep. Brenes ½c al N, Matagalpa
NS00) NUEVA SEGOVIA
NS02) Perroquita Asunción, 1 cal norte, Ocotal **W**: www.radiolavozdel-pinar.com **FM**: 100.9MHz Stereo Mogotón, 101.7MHz R. Sí. – **NS03)** Jalapa. 102.1MHz
RS00) RIO SAN JUAN
RS01) Costado Norte de la Iglesia Católica, San Carlos
ZE00) ZELAYA
ZE01) Barrio 19 de Julio, Pto Cabezas – **ZE03)** Frente al Palacio Municipal, Barrio Beholdsen, Bluefields

FM in Managua (MHz): 89.1 Exitos – 89.5 R. Visión – 89.9 Tropicálida – 90.5 Maranatha – 90.9 La Marka – 91.3 Futura – 91.7 La Primerísima – 92.1 Estación X – 92.7 Advent Estéreo – 93.1 La Buenísima – 93.5 Alfa Radio – 93.7 La Gran Cadena – 93.9 La Tigre – 94.3 Ondas de Luz – 94.7 Mujer – 95.1 La Pachanguera – 95.5 Amor – 95.9 Estéreo Ritmo – 96.3 La Gran Cadena – 96.7 Furia Magic – 97.1 Estéreo Mía – 97.5 Corporación – 97.9 Salsa 98 – 98.3 R. Viva – 98.7 Romántica – 99.1 R. Ya – 99.5 Universidad – 99.9 María – 100.3 R. Tuani – 100.7 Disney – 101.1 Güegüense – 101.5 Juvenil – 101.9 R. Clásica – 102.3 Universidad – 102.7 Magic – 103.1 Bautista – 103.5 Maranatha – 103.9 Joya FM – 104.3 Estrella del Mar – 104.7 Hit – 105.1 Mi Preferida – 105.5 Rock FM – 105.9 Rica – 106.3 Galaxia, La Picosa – 106.7 Eco Romántico – 107.1 Sol – 107.5 Sandino – 107.9 Restauración

NIGER

LT: UTC +1h — **Pop**: 14 million — **Pr.L**: French, Hausa, Zarma, Tamashek, Fulfulde, Arabic etc. — **E.C**: 50Hz, 220V — **ITU**: NGR

CONSEIL SUPÉRIEUR DE LA COMMUNICATION (CSC)
⌨ Plateau I, Niamey ☎+227 20 722356 ☎+227 20 722667 **L.P**: Chmn: Daouda Diallo. Vice Chmn: Hamidou Kô.

LA VOIX DU SAHEL – OFFICE DE RADIODIFFUSION-TÉLÉVISION DU NIGER (ORTN, Gov.)
⌨ Maison de la Radio, B.P. 361, Niamey ☎+227 20 722272 ▤ +227 20 722548 **W**: ortn.ne **E**: ortny@ortn-niger.com **LP**: DG: Amadou Harouna Yayé. Dir. Voix du Sahel: Mahaman Chamsou Maïgary. Gen. Secr: Mrs. Diaffra Fadimou Moumouni. Tech. Dir: Maraka Laouali.
MW: Niamey (Goudel) 1125kHz 20kW.
SW: Niamey (Goudel) 9704kHz 40kW (irreg, variably on 9705kHz).
FM (MHz): Maradi 88.4, Doutchi 89.7, Niamey 91.3, Zinder 91.3 2.5kW, Diffa 92.0, B. Konni 96.2, Madaoua 97.2, Tillaberi 99.0 10kW, Dosso 99.8, Tahoua 100.0, Agadez 106.8. All 1kW if not given otherwise. In addition 16 txs under 1kW.
D.Prgr in French/ethnic: 0500-2300 (Sun -2200). Local prgrs: 0700-1130 & 1500-1700. **N. in French:** 0545, 1200, 1900. **IS:** Local flute. **Ann:** F:"Ici la Voix du Sahel", A: "Idha'at al-Jumhuriya al-Niger, Sawt as-Sahel min Niamey".

Other Stations:
R. Anfani FM: Niamey/Zinder/Maradi/Diffa 100MHz 1.5kW. Also rel. DW & VOA. **E**: anfani@intnet.ne – **Dounia FM,** Niamey: 89.0MHz 3kW. **E**: radioteledounianiger@yahoo.fr – **Espoir FM,** Niamey: 101MHz **W**: espoirfm@iniger.ne – **La Voix de l'Hemicycle,** Niamey: 95.1MHz – **Radio & Musique,** Niamey: 104.5MHz 1kW. Also rel. BBC African Sce. **E**: retm@intnet.ne – **R. Saraounia,** Niamey: 102.1MHz – **Sahara FM,** Agadez: fq. not known – **Tambara FM,** Niamey: 107MHz 0.5kW – **Ténére FM,** Niamey: 98.0MHz 1kW.
R. Rurale stations on FM in Agadez, Bankilaré, Diffa, Dosso, Gaya, Maradi, Niamey, Tahoua, Tillabéri, Zinder.

Africa No. 1, Niamey: 103.0MHz (see main entry under Gabon).
BBC African Sce, Niamey: 100.4MHz.
CRI: Niamey 106.0MHz, Agadez/Maradi/Zinder: fq not known.
RFI Afrique: Niamey/Maradi/Tahoua/Zinder 96.2MHz

NIGERIA

LT: UTC +1h — **Pop**: 150 million — **Pr.L**: English, Yoruba, Hausa, Igbo — **E.C**: 50Hz, 230V — **ITU**: NIG

NATIONAL BROADCASTING COMMISSION (NBC)
⌨ Road 14, Badagry Rd, Gwarinpa, Abuja ☎+234 1 2647867 **W**: www.nbc.gov.ng **L.P**: DG: Yomi Bolarinwa. **L.P**: DG: Engr Bolarinwa.

FEDERAL RADIO CORPORATION OF NIGERIA (Gov.)
⌨ Radio House, Herbert Macauley Way, Area 10, PMB 452, Garki, Abuja, Federal Capital Territory +234 9 2341103 ▤ +234 9 2346486 **W**: radionigeriaonline.com **LP**: DG: Barrister Yusuf Nuhu. Dir. Eng. Sces: Ibrahim Abdullahi.
1) FRCN Lagos, Broadcasting House, P.M.B. 12504, Ikoyi, Lagos, Lagos State. ☎+234 1 2690301-5. **LP**: Exec. Dir: Prince Atilade Atoyebi. R. One in English. **NB**: Nigerian N. from Lagos or Abuja at 0600, 1500 & 2100 is relayed by all FRCN stations and most state stations. Ann: "This is R. Nigeria, Lagos". Metro FM in English: 0500-2300 on 97.6MHz 20kW. Bond FM in Pidgin/English/Yoruba/Hausa/Igbo on 92.9MHz 20k**W**: 0430-2300 – **2) FRCN Abuja**, Broadcasting House, Gwangwalada, P.M.B. 71, Abuja, Federal Capital Territory ☎+234 9 8821040 **L.P**: Exec. Dir: Shuaibu Ibrahim. D.Prgr: 0530-2305 (-1200 on 7275kHz) in English/Hausa/Igbo/Yoruba and others. Local **N.** in English 0500, 1700. Ann: "This is R. Nigeria, Abuja". – **3) FRCN Enugu**, Broadcasting House, Onitsha Rd, P.M.B. 1051, Enugu, Enugu State ☎+234 42 254400 ▤ + 234 42 254173 **L.P**: Exec. Dir: Eddy Agwuegbo. 0430-2315 in English/Igbo/Tiv/Efik/Izon – **4) FRCN Ibadan**, Broadcasting House, Oba Adebimpe Rd, P.M.B. 5003, Dugbe, Ibadan, Oyo State ☎+234 2 2414093 ▤ + 234 2 2413930 **W**: radionigeriaibadan.net **E**: info@radionigeriaibadan.net **L.P**: Exec. Dir: Princess Banke Ademola. D.Prgr: 0430-2305 in English/Yoruba/Edo/Igala/Urhobo. Ann: "R. Nigeria Ibadan, Station with distinction". – **5) FRCN Kaduna**, No. 7 Yakubu Gowon Way, P.O.Box 250, Kaduna, Kaduna State ☎+234 62 235390 ▤ + 234 62 245392 **L.P**: Ag. Zonal Dir: Alhaji Muhammad Sani Suleiman. Chief Tech. Officer: Shehu A. Muhammad. Ch. 1 in Hausa: 0430-2300 on 594/6090kHz. Ch. 2 in English/Hausa/Fulfulde/Kanuri/Nupe: 0430-2300 on 1107/4770kHz. English N: 10500, 100, 1600, 1700, 2000. Ch. 3 in English: 0500-2400 on 96.1MHz. Karama FM in Hausa: 92.1MHz. Ann: "This is R. Nigeria, Kaduna".

MW		kHz	kW	MW		kHz	kW
4)	Alaho	567	50	3)	Enugu	828	100
4)	Moniya	576	25	2)	Gwagwalada	909	50
5)	Jaji	594	200	5)	Jaji	1107	25
4)	Ibadan	657	100				
SW		kHz	kW	SW		kHz	kW
5)	Kaduna	6090	50	2)	Abuja	7275	100

Both SW txs irregular.
FM (MHz): **1)** 92.9/97.6 **2)** 93.5 **3)** 92.85 **4)** 93.4 **5)** 92.1/96.1.
Further federal FM stations (MHz): Abakaliki 101.5, Abeokuta 94.5, Akure 102.5, Asaba 104.5, Awka 102.5, Bauchi 98.5, Benin 101.5, Benue (Makurdi)103.5, Bida (Minna) 104.5, Birnin-Kebbi 103.5, Maiduguri (Borno) 102.5, Calabar 99.5, Damaturu 104.5, Dutse 100.5, Ado-Ekiti 100.5, Gombe 103.5, Gusau 102.5, Kano 103.5, Kastina 104.5, Ilesha 95.5, Ilorin 103.5, Jalingo 100.5, Lafia 102.5, Lokoja 101.5, Osogbo 93.5, Owerri 100.5, Port-Harcourt 98.5, Sokoto 101.5, Umuahia103.5, Uyo 104, Yenogoa 101.5, Yola 101.5.
Aso FM: Abuja: 93.5MHz. **W**: www.asoradioonline.com

STATE RADIO AND OTHER STATIONS:

MW	N	kHz	kW	MW	N	kHz	kW
19) Akure	‡	531	50	15) Ojeowode	‡	675	25
17) Sokoto		540	50	30) Damaturu	‡	684	50
14) Tukun Tawa	‡	549	25	35) Ochaja	‡	693	10
37) Ado		549	25	31) Wukari	‡	702	25
23) Calabar	‡	558	50	13) Owerri	‡	720	50
13) Owerri		567	50	14) Jogana		729	50
40) Gusau		567		42) Kaduna		747	60
6) Abakaliki	‡	585	50	15) Ibadan		756	100
9) Maiduguri		603	50	12) Minna	‡	756	50
18) Abeokuta		603	25	9) Damagum	‡	756	50
16) Ilorin		612	50	31) Wukari	‡	774	10
28) Akwa	‡	621	50	35) Okene	‡	783	50
8) Katabu		638	50	15) Gambari	‡	792	50
7) Benin City	‡	666	50	30) Damaturu		801	20

MW		N	kHz	kW	MW		N	kHz	kW
27)	Zuru		801	10	34)	Iree		1008	10
21)	Azare	‡	846	10	33)	Dutse		1026	25
8)	Kafanchan	‡	882	25	28)	Onitsha	‡	1062	10
34)	Osu	‡	891	10	23)	Ugaga		1134	20
18)	Abeokuta	‡	900	25	12)	Bida		1143	10
43)	Yola		917	50	24)	Jos	‡	1224	50
10)	Makurdi		918	50	31)	Jalingo		1269	10
27)	Birnin Kebbi		945	10	34)	Iwo	‡	1359	10
25)	Katsina		972	25	8)	Zaria	‡	1359	50
35)	Otite		972	10	35)	Egbe	‡	1395	10
20)	Ikeja		990	10	26)	Abak	‡	1395	10
21)	Bauchi		990	50	39)	Gombe	‡	1404	10
12)	Kontagora		1008	10	11)	Yola		1440	10

NB: many transmitters are irregular or inactive, marked ‡.
FM (MHz): **6)** 96.1 **7)** 95.8 **8)** 90.8 **9)** 95.3 **10)** 95.0 **11)** 95.8 **12)** 91.2 **13)** 94.4 **14)** 89.3 **15)** 98.5 **16)** 99.0 **17)** 96.4 **18)** 91.4 **19)** 96.5 **20)** 107.5 **21)** 94.6 **22)** 99.1 **23)** 92.7 **24)** 90.5 **26)** 90.5 **28)** 88.5 **29)** 88.6/97.9 **31)** 90.6 **32)** 88.1 **34)** 89.5 **35)** 94.0 **36)** 97.1 **37)** 91.5 **38)** 97.3 **39)** 96.8 **41)** 98.1
State Radio information:
6) Enugu State Broadc. Sce (ESBS), Broadcasting House, Independence Layout, P.M.B. 01600, Enugu, Enugu State. Prgr 1 on **MW:** 0430-2300 in English/others. Prgr. 2 on FM ("Sunrise 96"): 0500-2100 – **7)** Edo State Broadc. Sce, P.M.B. 1012, Aduwawa, Benin City, Edo State. 0400-2305 in English + 12 local languages – **8)** Kaduna State Media Corp, Wurno Close, P.M.B. 2013, Kaduna, Kaduna State. 0430-2315 in English/Hausa – **9)** Borno Radio & TV Corp., P.M.B. 1020, Broadcasting House, Along Shehu Laminu Way, Maiduguri, Borno State **E:** brtvnews@yahoo.com 0400-2305 in English/Hausa/Kanuri/Marghi/Suwa/Babur-Bura – **10)** R. Benue, P.M.B. 102202, Makurdi, Benue State. Prgr. 1: 0430-2305 in English/others. Prgr. 2 on FM: 0500-2105. Ann: "This is R. Benue, Makurdi" – **11)** Adamawa Broadc. Corp. (ABC), P.M.B. 2123, Yola, Adamawa State. 0430-2300 in English/Hausa + 6 Nigerian languages. Ann: "This is GBC Yola, your No. 1 Radio Station" – **12)** Niger State Media Corp. (Crystal R.), Radio House, Ibrahim Babangida St, P.M.B. 88, Minna, Niger State **E:** radioniger@yahoo.com 0430-2130 in English/others – **13)** Imo Broadc. Corp, Ebu Rd, P.O. Box 329, Owerri, Imo State. Prgr. 1: 0425-2305 on MW. Prgr. 2: 0440-2305 on FM. English: 0430-0630, 1100-1830, 2100-2300 (Sat/Sun 0100), other times Igbo – **14)** Kano State BC, 1 Ibrahim Taiwo Rd, Gidan Bello Dandago, P.M.B. 3014, Kano, Kano State. **W:** radiokanoonline.com Prgr. 1 on MW: 0430-2320. Prgr. 2: on FM: 0550-2320 in English/Hausa. Ann: "Radio Kano" – **15)** Broadc. Corp. of Oyo State, P.M.B. 1, Akodi Post Office, Ibadan, Oyo State. Prgr 1: 0400-2200 in English/Yoruba. Prgr 2: on FM: 0700-2100. Ann: "R. O-y-o" – **16)** Kwara State Broadc. Corp, Akpata Yakuba, P.M.B. 1345, Ilorin, Kwara State. 0400-2305 in English/others – **17)** Sokoto State BC, Moliba Adamawa Rd, Tudua Wada, P.M.B. 2156, Sokoto, Sokoto State. 0430-2305 in English/Hausa. Ann: "Rima Radio" – **18)** Ogun State BC, Ibara Housing Estate, P.M.B. 2084, Abeokuta, Ogun State. OGBC1 on MW, OGBC2 on FM: 0400-2400 in English/Yoruba – **19)** Ondo State Radio Corp, Broadcasting House, Oba-Ile, P.M.B. 709, Akure, Ondo State. 0400-2300 in English/others – **20)** Lagos State Broadc. Corp, Obafemi Awolowo Way, P.M.B. 21035, Ikeja, Lagos State. 0430-0005 in English/Yoruba. Ann: "NBC" – **21)** Bauchi Radio Corp, Broadc. House, Ahmadu Bello Way, P.M.B. 0133, Bauchi, Bauchi State. Prgr 1: 0430-2300 on MW, Prgr. 2: 0500-1700 (F.PI: 24h.) or FM in English/others – **22)** Rivers State Broadc. Corp, 4 Degema St, P.M.B. 5170, Port Harcourt, Rivers State. Prgr. 1: 0450-2310 on MW, Prgr. 2: 0450-2310 on FM in English/others – **23)** Cross River State Broadc. Corp. (CRBC), No. 8 IBB Way, P.M.B. 1035, Calabar, Cross River State **E:** crbc@skannet.com 0430-2315 in English/others – **24)** Plateau Radio & TV Corp. (PRTVC), 5 Joseph Gomwalk Rd, P.M.B. 2043, Jos, Plateau State. Ch. 1 on **MW:** 0500-2300, Ch. 2 on FM: 0500-2300 in English/others. Ann: "This is Radio Plateau 1 AM", "This is Radio Plateau 2, 90.5 FM Stereo" – **25)** Katsina State Radio & TV Sces (KSRTV), Former SDP State Headquarters, Batsari Rd, P.M.B. 2163, Katsina, Katsina State. 0430-2300 in English/others. Ann: "This is Katsina State R." – **26)** Akwa Ibom Broadc. Corp, 205 Aka Rd, P.M.B. 1122, Uyo, Akwa Ibom State. 0500-2300 in English/others – **27)** R. Kebbi, km 9 Kalgo Rd, Birnin Kebbi, Kebbi State. 0500-2300 in English/others – **28)** Anambra Broadc. Sce (ABS), off Arroma Junction, P.M.B. 5070, Awka, Anambra State. 0500-2300 in English/Igbo – **29)** Delta State Broadc. Sce, Broadc. House P.M.B. 5032, Asaba, Delta State. 0500-2300 in English/others – **30)** Yobe Broadc. Corp, km 6 Gujba Rd, P.M.B. 1044, Damaturu, Yobe State. 0500-2300 in English/others – **31)** Taraba State Broadc. Sces, Broadc. House, adjacent Gen. Sani Abacha State Secretariat, P.M.B. 1038, Jalingo, Taraba State. 0500-2300 in English/others – **32)** Broadc. Corp. of Abia State (BCA), Broadc. House, Government Station Layout, B.M.P. 7276, Umuahia, Abia State. **W:** www.bcnigeria.com **E:** bcniger@bcnigeria.com 0500-2300 in English/Igbo – **33)** Jigawa Broadc. Corp, Broadc. House, Kiyawa Rd,

P.M.B. 7032, Dutse, Jigawa State. 0500-2205 – **34)** Osun State Broadc. Corp, Studio 1, Ita-Akogun St, P.M.B. 4425, Osogbo, Osun State. 0500-2300 in English/others – **35)** Kogi State Broadc. Corp, 1 Danladi Zakari Rd, P.M.B. 1095 GRA, Lokoja, Kogi State. 0500-2300 in English/others. Ann: "R. Kogi" – **36)** Nasawara Broadc. Sce (NBS), Tudun K. Nasarawauri, Makurdi Rd, P.M.B. 97, Lafia, Nasarawa State. 24h in English/others – **37)** Broadc. Sce of Ekiti State, Old Ado Ekiti Local Government Secretariat, Okeyinmi, P.M.B. 5343, Ado, Ekiti State – **38)** Bayelsa State Broadc. Corp, P.M.B. 56, Ekeki, Yenagoa, Bayelsa State. "Glory FM" in English/others – **39)** Gombe State Broadc. Sce, Buhari Estate Rd, GRA, Gombe, Gombe State. 0500-2300 English/others – **40)** Zamfara State R, Mall. Yahaya Secretariat, Off Zaria Road, P.M.B. 01007, Gusau, Zamfara State – **41)** Ebonyi Broadcasting Service (EBBS), Ministry of Information building, Government House Annex, Abakaliki, Ebonyi State – **42) Nagarta R,** Nagarta Communications Complex, Katabu, Mararraban, Jos, P.O. Box 574, Kaduna. **W:** nagartaradio.tripod.com **E:** nagartaradio@yahoo.com – **43) R. Gotel,** P.O. Box 5759, Modire (After Yola Bridge), Off Yola-Mubi Expressway, Jimeta-Yola, Adamawa State. **E:** radiogotel@yahoo.com D.Prgr: 0500-2305.

EXTERNAL SCE: Voice of Nigeria: see International Radio section

Other Stations:
Brilla FM, Fleganza 634, Adeyemo Alakija House, Victoria Island, Lagos **FM:** 88.9MHz – **Choice FM, FM:** 103.5MHz – **Cool FM,** 26/A, AIM Plaza, Etim Inyang Crescent Victoria Island Annex.P.M.B. 10096, Victoria Island, Lagos. **FM:** Port Harcourt 95.9, Abuja/Lagos 96.9MHz. **W:** www.coolfm.us – **Cosmo FM,** Plot 18, Pocket Estate, Independence Layout, Enugu **FM:** 105.5MHz – **Eko-FM,** Lagos **FM:** 89.75MHz – **Freedom R,** Plot 33, Sarki Dikko, Off Ibrahim Sani Abacha Rd, Gyadi-Gyadi, Kano **FM:** 99.5MHz – **Independent R,** Benin City **FM:** frq. unknown – **Ray Power 1, FM:** Lagos/Abuja 100.5MHz. **Ray Power 2, FM:** Lagos/Kano 106.5MHz + rel. in other towns (Incl. rel. of BBC African Sce in English/Hausa) – **Rhythm FM,** 17A Commercial Ave, Yaba, Lagos **FM:** 93.7MHz – **Rhythm 94.7,** Hilltop, Karu, Abuja **FM:** 94.7MHz – **Wazobia FM:** for addr. see Cool FM above. **FM:** Port Harcourt 94.1MHz, Lagos 95.1MHz, Abuja 99.5MHz. **W:** wazobiafm.com

NIUE

L.T: UTC -11h — **Pop:** 1,311 — **Pr.L:** Niuean, English — **E.C:** 50Hz, 230V — **ITU:** NIU

BROADCASTING CORPORATION OF NIUE (BCN)
📧 P.O. Box 68, Alofi, Niue, South Pacific. Studio: Fonuakula, Alofi ☎ +683 4026 🖷 +683 4217 **E:** gm.bcn@mail.gov.nu **L.P:** Chmn: Hunukitama. GM: Patrick Lino CE: Trevor Tiakia **FM:** 91.0MHz 0.5kW, 102.0MHz 0.1kW
D.Prgr: Mon-Sat 1730-2000, 2230-0030, 0500-0830 **N:** on the h includes RNZI bulletins **Ann:** "This is Radio Sunshine"

Other Stations
1) OkaRock FM, Alofi 107.9MHz **1)** OKA-KOA Multimedia Systems, Commercial Centre, PO Box 5, Alofi, Niue, South Pacific. **T:** +683 4379 **W:** www.niuemusic.com **E:** sales@niuemusic.com **D.Prgr:** 24/7

NORFOLK ISLAND (Australia)

L.T: UTC +11½h — **Pop:** 2,169 — **Pr.L:** English, Pitcairn Norfolk — **E.C:** 50Hz, 220V — **ITU:** NFK

AUSTRALIAN BROADCASTING CORP. (ABC)
See Australia. 24h satellite relay.

FM (MHz)	Call	kW	Station
91.9	2ABCRN	0.25	R. National
93.9	2ABCFM	0.25	ABC Classic FM
95.9	2ABCRR	0.25	ABC Local R.
98.2	2JJJ		Triple J

Other Stations			
AM	kHz	Call	kW	Station
1)	1566	VL2NI	0.1	R. Norfolk
FM	MHz	Call	kW	
1)	89.9	VL2NI	0.25	R. Norfolk
2)	102.6	-	-	R. Paradise

Addresses and other information
1) Norfolk Island Broadcasting Sce. (Local Gov.). New Cascade Road (PO Box 456), Norfolk Island 2899, Australia. ☎ +672 3 22137 🖷 +672 3 23298 **E:** news@radio.gov.nf **L.P:** George Smith **D.Prgr:** 1930-0530 M-F, 1930-0230 Sat, 1930-0130 Sun. **MW:** relay R. New Zealand National overnight **FM:** relay 4ABCRR ABC Local R. overnight – **2)**

Paradise Hotel & Resort, Queen Elizabeth Drive, Norfolk Island 2899. Micro power. Irr.

NORTHERN MARIANA ISLANDS (USA Commonwealth)

L.T: UTC +10h — **Pop:** 46,050 — **Pr.L:** English, Chamorro, Carolinian, Filipino — **E.C:** 60Hz, 110V — **ITU:** MRA

FEDERAL COMMUNICATIONS COMMISSION (FCC)
see USA for details

MW	kHz	kW	Station	MW	kHz	kW	Station
1)	1080	5	KCNM	2)	1440	1.1	KKMP
FM	**MHz**	**kW**	**Station**	**FM**	**MHz**	**kW**	**Station**
3)	88.1	1.8	KRNM	4)	97.9	6.5	KRSI
3)	89.1	0.25	KRNM	4)	99.5	6.5	KPXP
6)	89.9	1.8	KORU	5)	100.3	1.1	KWAW
3)	90.7	0.62	KCKD	1)	101.1	4.1	KNUT
3)	91.5	0.06	KMOP	1)	103.9	3.2	KZMI
2)	92.1	0.01	KKMP-FM				

Addresses and other information:
1) Choice Broadcasting Company LLC, 543A N Marine Dr, Tamuning GU 96913 ☎ +1 671 4780104 🖹 +1 671 647 7480 **Format:** KCNM: News/Talk KNUT: Islands Music KZMI: Adult Contemporary **Prgr:** 24h – **2) Blue Continent Communications Inc.** PO Box 500815, Saipan 96950 ☎ +1 670 233 1440 **W:** www.cnmiradio.com **E:** cnmiradio@gmail.com **LP:** CEO: Rosemond Santos, VP: Gary Sword **Format:** 'Strickly Island' Islands Music – **3) Marianas Educational Media Services Inc** Sunny Plaza, 125 Tun Jesus Crisostomo St #301, Tamuning GU 96913 **E:** darryl@guamtech.com **LP:** CEO: Robert F Kelly, Community Radio Mgr: Darryl Taggerty **Format:** KRNM: 88.1 [silent awaiting relocation] 89.1 24h IP relay KPRG Guam with NPR, Public Radio International and 6h daily BBC World Service KCKD: temporary 24h relay WCPE classical music KMOP: Melodies of Prayer [**W:** www.melodiesofprayer.com] 24h relig – **4) Sorensen Pacific Broadcasting Inc.** GRC Building, Middle Road #305, Garapan, Saipan MP 96910 ☎ +1 670 2357996 🖹+1 670 2357998 **LP:** SM: Tina Palacios **Format:** KRSI: 'The Kat' Soul/Rock 'n' Roll/Classic Hits KPXP: 'Power99' Top 40/Islands Music **Prgr:** 24h – **5) Magic 100FM.** 1st Fl, Naru Building, Susupe, Saipan 96950 ☎ +1 670 2345929 🖹 +1 670 2342262 **W:** www.magic100radio.com **E:** kwaw100.3@magic100radio.com **D.Prgr:** 24h – **6) Good News Broadcasting Corp.** 290 Chalan Palasyo, Agana Heights, GU 96910. **Prgr:** religious

NORWAY

L.T: UTC +1h (31 Mar-27 Oct: +2h) — **Pop: 5** million — **Pr.L:** Norwegian — **EC:** 50Hz, 230V — **ITU:** NOR

POST OG TELETILSYNET
Norwegian Post and Telecommunications Authority
🖃 PB 93, NO-4791 Lillesand ☎+47 22824600 🖹 +47 22824640
W: www.npt.no
NORKRING (Transmission provider)
🖃 Telenor Broadcast, Snarøyveien 30, NO-1331 Fornebu ☎+47 67892000 🖹 +47 67893611 **W:** www.norkring.no

NRK - NORSK RIKSKRINGKASTING AS (Pub.)
🖃 NO-0340 Oslo ☎+47 23047000 🖹 +47 23047575 **Inf.Dpt:** ☎+47 81565900 **E:** info@nrk.no **W:** www.nrk.no
L.P: DG: Hans-Tore Bjerkaas

LW/MW	kHz	R	kW	LW/MW	kHz	R	kW
Ingøy	153	b	100	Røst	675	f	20

NB: Røst will stop operation by the end of 2012

FM	P1	R	P2	P3	kW
Alta	89.7	b	94.6 Þ	91.3	3.5
Bagn	91.7	h	95.3	88.0	35
Bangsberget	90.4	h			4.1
Bergen	89.1	d	94.8	99.0	46
Bjerkreim	94.2	i	98.7	91.8	60
Bokn	93.5	i	97.3	91.1	120
Bremanger	93.6	j	98.1	91.3	46
Dikkevikfjell	87.8	b	93.4 Þ	95.0	1.4
Førde	92.8	j	88.7	97.1	12
Gamlemsvet	91.9	e	96.3	90.0	50
Gausta	89.5	m	96.4	99.7	55
	101.1	a			6.7
Greipstad	88.8	k	92.5	97.0	57.5
Grong	91.9	g	96.6	88.9	95
Gulen	88.0	j	94.5	97.6	39
Hadsel	92.4	f	99.3	94.5	30
Halden	94.8	p	89.1	101.5	72.5

FM	P1	R	P2	R	P3	kW
Hammerfest	96.6	b	87.7 Þ		93.6	24
Hasvik	90.1	b	99 Þ		94.9	2
Hemnes	88.5	f	99.8		96.1	36
Hestmannen	97.0	f	90.7		93.5	1.2
Hovdefjell	87.8	k	93.7		96.0	25
Hvitingen	91.7	o				2.76
Iskuras	88.7	b	96.1 Þ		92.0	2.2
Jetta	95.9	h	99.5		91.1	85
Kappfjell	95.5	f	99.4		93.4	1.3
Karasjok	87.9	b	94.7 Þ			1.5
Kautokeino	90.3	b	93.8 Þ		99.2	35
Kistefjell	91.8	n	95.7 Þ		99.8	44
Kongsberg	91.3	a	95.5		§97.8	60/30§
Kongsvinger	89.8	c	93.9		96.1	33
	98.9	q				11
Kopparen	88.3	l	94.5		96.0	40
Lyngdal	97.6	k	88.3		95.0	50
Lyngen	93.3	n	97.5 Þ			4.2
Lønahorgi	93.3	d	88.3		96.7	48
Melhus	92.4	l	97.2		99.1	60
Mosvik	90.9	g	98.4		93.4	33
Narvik	88.8	f	98.9 Þ		91.1	90
Nordfjordeid	89.4	j	99.3		92.3	12
Nordhue	87.6	c	§97.1		92.5	70/60§
Nordkapp	89.2	b	95.4 Þ		98.2	15
Oslo	88.7	q	100.0		93.5	90
Reinsfjell	89.1	e	95.1		90.7	24
Salten	93.3	f	95.5		89.8	48
Skien	88.2	m	92.3		100.4	80
	90.3	o				7.25
Sogndal	91.5	j	95.1		98.7	25
Sprinklerfjell	94.1	o				84
Steigen	90.3	f	97.8 Þ		93.9	102/106/107
Stord	96.0	d	99.6		92.6	60
Store Jekkir	99.9	b	97.3 Þ		90.9	1.2/1.16/1.13
Tana	92.5	b	97.0 Þ		91.1	24
Trolltind	88.2	n	94.0 Þ		90.5	50
Tron	98.3	c	88.6		94.3	24
Varanger	88.1	b	91.8 Þ		100.2	30
Vega	88.3	f	95.2		98.2	55
Andalsnes			99.9			2.2

+ more than 1800 lp txs less than 1kW Þ) carries Sámi Radio
a-q) refers to reg prgrs listed below.

FM	AN	AK	MP3	FM	AN	AK	MP3
Alta	90.8	93.4	96.3	Oslo	93.0	91.9	97.0
Bangsberget	88.4	89.3	93.2	Porsgrunn	95.8	97.4	90.8
Bergen	93.8	98.2	95.4	Stavanger	93.0	99.3	96.6
Bodø	94.8	90.9	97.2	Tromsø	89.8	94.4	96.8
Bokn	95.6	92.4	92.2	Trondheim	94.9	96.3	92.7
Fredrikstad	90.7	-	87.6	Vadsø	90.7	88.8	92.2
Kristiansand	94.0	98.6	95.7				

Transmitter powers 40W-3kW, typically 50-200W

P1:🖃 NO-7005 Trondheim ☎+47 73881400 🖹 +47 73881809 24h on FM and DAB. **N:** MF on the h. also 0530, 0630, 0730, 1130, 1530, 1630. Sat on the h. also 0630, 1130. Sun on the h. also 0430. Regional Prgrs: see below.
P2: 🖃 NO-0340 Oslo ☎+47 23047297 🖹 +47 23047480 24h cultural prgr. on FM and DAB. **N:** MF on the h 0500-0000 except 1800, 1900 2000 and 2200. Also 0530, 0630, 0730, 1130, 1630. Sat: on the h. 0500-0000 except 0900, 1200, 1800, 1900, 2000. Also 0630, 1130, 1530. Sun: on the h. 0500-2300 except 1200, 1300, 1600, 1800, 1900. Also 1530.
P3: 🖃 NO-7005 Trondheim ☎+47 73881600 🖹 +47 73881609 24h youth prgr on FM and DAB. Rly P1 2300-0500. **N:** MF on the h 0500-2300 except 1600, 1800, 2000, 2200, also 0530, 0630, 0730, 0830. Sat: on the h. except 1600, 1800, 2000, 2100, 2200. Sun: on the h. except 2200.
Sámi NRK Sámiradio (special prgrs in Lappish): 🖃 PB 183, NO-9730 Karasjok ☎+47 78469200 🖹 +47 78469223
D.Prgr: P1: Sun 2030-2100 (in Norwegian). P2: MF 1230-1300. Additional prgrs on P2 in northern Norway (marked Þ in the frequency table) plus 90.1MHz (122W) in Oslo: MF 0600-0800, 1300-1630, (Fri also1200-1230, 1630-1700), Sat/sun 1700-1800
AK: NRK Alltid Klassisk: 🖃 NO-0340 Oslo ☎+47 23047882 🖹 +47 23048575. 24h FM and DAB. Classical music channel. Some rly P2.
AN: NRK Alltid Nyheter): 🖃 NO-0340 Oslo ☎+47 23047000 🖹 +47 23045141 24h rolling news sce on FM and DAB. Rly BBC World Service most of the day Sat/Sun and 2100-0500 weekdays.
MP3: NRK MPETRE: 🖃 NO-7005 Trondheim ☎+47 73881600 🖹 +47 73881609. 24h teenager channel based on techno/dance music on FM and DAB. Some rly of P3.

NRK REGIONAL SERVICES:
On **P1**. D.Prgr: MF 0503-0530, 0533-0600, 0603-0630, 0640-0700, 0703-0720, 0727-0730, 0733-0800, 0803-0805, 0903-0905, 1003-1059, 1107-1159, 1203-1205, 1303-1305, 1403-1405, 1503-1530, 1533-1600, 1603-1630. Sat: 0705-0706, 0803-0805, 0903-0905, 1003-1006, 1103-1105
a) NRK Buskerud, PB 733 Strømsø, NO-3003 Drammen: 91.3/101.1MHz Some shared prgr with Telemark and Vestfold, as NRK Østafjells. – **b)** NRK Troms og Finnmark, PB 613, NO-9811 Vadsø: **153kHz**, 87.9/88.1/ 88.7/89.2/89.790.1//90.3/92.5/96.6/99.9MHz Some shared prgr with Troms and Nordland. – **c+h)** NRK Hedmark og Oppland, PB 174, NO-2601 Lillehammer: 90.4/91.7/ 95.9MHz and NO-2418 Elverum: 87.6/ 89.8/98.3MHz Separate news hrly, remaining prgrs shared – **d)** NRK Hordaland, PB 7777, NO-5020 Bergen: 89.1/93.3/ 96.0MHz – **e)** NRK Møre og Romsdal, NO-6025 Ålesund: 89.1/91.9MHz – **f)** NRK Nordland, NO-8038 Bodø: 675kHz, 88.5/88.8/89.3/90.3/94.9/93.5/95.5/97.0MH z Some shared prgr with Finnmark and Troms. – **g+l)** NRK Trøndelag, Tyholt, NO-7005 Trondheim: 88.3/92.4MHz and Løshalla 15, NO-7712 Steinkjer: 90.9/ 91.9MHz Some separate newsbulletins, remaining prgrs shared – **i)** NRK Rogaland, PB 614, NO-4090 Hafrsfjord: 93.5/94.2MHz – **j)** NRK Sogn og Fjordane, PB 100, NO-6801 Førde: 88.0/89.4/91.5/ 92.8/93.6MHz – **k)** NRK Sørlandet, PB 413, NO-4664 Kristiansand: 87.8/88.8/97.6MHz– **m)** NRK Telemark, PB 284, NO-3901 Porsgrunn: 88.2/89.5MHz Some shared prgr with Buskerud and Vestfold, as NRK Østafjells. – **n)** NRK Troms og Finnmark, NO-9291 Tromsø: 88.2/91.8/ 93.3MHz Some shared prgr with Finnmark and Nordland. – **o)** NRK Vestfold, PB 120, NO-3101 Tønsberg: 90.3/91.7/94.1MHz Some shared prgr with Buskerud and Telemark, as NRK Østafjells. – **p)** NRK Østfold, PB 33, NO-1629 Gamle Fredrikstad: 94.8MHz – **q)** NRK Østlandssendingen, PB 4555 Nydalen, NO-0421 Oslo: 88.7/98.9MHz
Ann: 1st Prgr: "P1". 2nd Prgr: "P2". 3rd Prgr: "Petre". Lappish: "Datlae Sáméradio, Kárássjagás"

DAB: One DAB-multiplex (12D) covering parts of Norway. Includes all NRK-channels, P4. and NRK Alltid Folkemusikk. Regional DAB-multiplex (12C) for southeastern Norway. Includes NRK Østfold, Østlandssendinga, Buskerud, Vestfold, Telemark, NRK Stortinget, NRK P1 Oslofjord and Met. Oslofjord. In addition, regional multiplex 12B Rogaland, 12C Trøndelag and 13E Troms.

OTHER STATIONS:
RADIO NORGE (Comm.)
✉ P.O.Box 144, NO-1601 Fredrikstad ☎+47 07270 🖷 +47 69707601 **W:** www.radionorge.com **LP:** MD: Bente Klemetsdal
FM:

FM	MHz	kW	FM	MHz	kW
Alta	101.0	3.5	Kopparen	102.4	8
Bagn	102.1	7	Lyngdal	102.0	10
Bergen	102.5	46	Lønahorgi	100.6	4.8
Bjerkreim	101.0	6	Melhus	101.1	2.4
Bokn	90.3	120	Narvik	101.1	9
Bremanger	103.2	9.2	Nordfjordeid	101.2	2.4
Førde	102.0	2.4	Nordhue	106.5	70
Gamlemsvet	102.8	50	Nordkapp	102.5	3
Gausta	103.1	5.5	Oslo	103.9	90
Greipstad	100.1	57.5	Reinsfjell	100.2	2.4
Grong	102.0	9.5	Salten	100.4	9.8
Gulen	101.4	7.8	Skien	105.2	80
Hadsel	101.4	6	Sogndal	103.9	2.4
Hammerfest	102.8	4.2	Steigen	102.1	7
Hemnes	104.2	7.2	Stord	101.8	6
Hovdefjell	103.6	5	Store Jekkir	103.3	1.2
Jetta	101.6	8.5	Trolltind	101.7	5
Kistefjell	103.1	4.4	Tron	102.5	4.8
Kongsberg	102.5	60	Varanger	105.8	6
Kongsvinger	107.2	6.6	Vega	102.8	5.5

D.Prgr: 24h **N:** M-F: on the h. 0500-2300, also 0630, 0730, 1430, 1530. Sat: on the h. 0800-2300. Sun: on the h.0800-2300

P4 – RADIO HELE NORGE (Comm.)
✉ PB P4, NO-2626 Lillehammer ☎+47 61248444 🖷 +47 61248445 **W:** www.p4.no **LP:** MD: Kalle Lisberg
FM Main freqs (MHz): Bjerkreim: 88.5 1kW, Kistefjell: 89.4 4kW, Steigen: 91.5 10kW, Vega: 94.1 2kW, Ski: 94.5 1kW, Nordhue: 95.0 5kW, Horta: 95.6 1.1kW, Hammerfest: 96.8 7kW, Hadsel: 97.3 5kW, Førde: 98.4 4kW, Hemnes: 98.6 5kW, Sogndal: 99.9 5kW, Varanger: 102.8 8kW, Bokn: 102.8 120kW, Mosvik: 103.8 33kW, Greipstad: 104.9 38kW, Tron: 105.8 6kW, Halden: 106.1 6kW + 102 txs below 1kW
D.Prgr: 24h on FM and DAB. **N:** M-F: on the h 0500-2300, also 0530, 0630, 0730, 1430, 1530, 1630. Sat-Sun: on the h 0700-2300

RADIO 1 HITS (Comm.)
✉ PB 1102 Sentrum, NO-0104 Oslo ☎+47 22023300
🖷 +47 22952202 **W:** www.radio1.no
FM (MHz): Oslo: 103.4, Bergen: 90.4, 97.1, 106.4, 107.1, Stavanger:

107.2, Trondheim: 96.3. All txs below 1 kW.
RADIO METRO (Comm.)
✉ Akersgata 45, NO-0158 Oslo ☎+47 21555919 **W:** www.radiometro.no
FM Main freqs (MHz): Oslo: 106.8, Lillestrøm: 107.9, Drammen: 101.8, Kongsberg: 106.5, Hønefoss: 103.5, Gjøvik: 105.8, Lillehammer: 105.0, Trondheim: 104.2/107.0. All txs below 1 kW.
NRJ NORGE (Comm.)
✉ Trondheimsveien 184, NO-0570 Oslo ☎+47 22797500
🖷 +47 22797501 **W:** www.nrj.no
FM Main freqs (MHz): Oslo: 90.5, Drammen: 95.3, Kristiansand: 93.3/106.9, Stavanger: 99.3, Bergen: 98.2, Trondheim: 105.1, Bodø: 90.9, Tromsø: 94.4.
All txs below 1 kW.

Internet: Most stns provide webstreams and/or on-demand audio sces.
Satellite: Most NRK-channels, radio and TV (incl NRK regional TV), Radio Norge and P4 are available through satellite.

LOCAL FM STATIONS
Around 300 low power FM commercial stns are in operation, some sharing freqs. Many of them organised through Lokalradioforbundet
W: www.lokalradioforbundet.no.

AFRTS (U.S. Mil.)
FM: Lifjell 101.5MHz (Stavanger). D.Prgr: 24h rly AFN Europe.

SVALBARD (SPITSBERGEN) (Norwegian Territory)
L.T: UTC +1h (31 Mar-27 Oct: UTC +2h) — **Pr.L:** Norwegian — **E.C:** 50Hz, 230V

NRK - NORSK RIKSKRINGKASTING AS (Pub.)
MW: Longyearbyen: 1485kHz 1kW
D.Prgr: 24h relay NRK P1 (incl. regional prgr NRK Troms)

FM	P1	P2	P3	kW
Isfjord Radio	89.7	93.6	97.3	0.05
Longyearbyen	88.8	94.5	98.3	0.045
Ny-Ålesund	91.3	94.8		0.12
Svea	89.1	92.0		0.025

RADIO NORGE (Comm.)
FM: Longyearbyen 104.0 0.013kHz

OMAN

L.T: UTC +4h — **Pop:** 3.4 million — **Pr.L:** Arabic — **E.C:** 50Hz, 240V — **ITU:** OMA

MINISTRY OF INFORMATION
✉ Omanet Team, Oman Electronic Network, P.O.Box 600, 113 Muscat ☎+968 24603222 🖷 +968 24693770 **W:** www.omanet.om **E:** omanet@omantel.net.om **LP:** Minister: Hamad bin Mohammed Al Rashdi

RADIO SULTANATE OF OMAN (RSO, Gov.)
✉ P.O. Box 397, 113 Muscat ☎+968 24 601538 🖷+968 24 602831 **W:** www.oman-tv.gov.om **LP:** DG Radio:Nasser Al-Sybani. DG Eng.: Mohd Salim Al Marhouby. Dir. Freq: Salim Al-Nomani. Dir. Trs: Saif Al-Rashedi

MW	kHz	kW	MW	kHz	kW
Haima	576	100	Seeb	1242	200
Salahah	738	100			

F.PI: Renovation of MW network by 2012 with stations in Bideya 558kHz 100kW, Buraimi 639kHz 100kW, Barka 1242kHz 500kW and Bahla 1278kHz 100kW.

FM	MHz	FM	MHz	FM	MHz
Sumail	87.8	Al-Ansab	89.5	Al-Badiaah	92.0
Al-Hajer	87.8	Butain	89.8	Maskan	92.0
Ja'alan Bani	88.1	Al-Hamra	89.9	Wadi Rajmaa	92.0
Al-Ghubrah	88.2	Ruwi Murtafat	90.4	Qumiraa	92.2
Riyam	88.5	Salalah	90.4	Tahwat	92.3
Nizwa Main	88.5	Wad	90.5	Al-Khafdi	92.5
Al-Ghashb	88.5	Samad	90.7	Al-Qhudhift	92.5
Sh'm	88.6	Yamit	90.8	Wadi Mahram	92.6
Al-Rustaq	88.7	Tawi al-nawa	90.9	Barkha	92.8
Fanja	88.7	Tanuf	91.2	Al-Gafat	93.0
Al-Saaidi	89.0	Dhank	91.2	Siyyah	93.1
Heibi	89.0	Wadi Dima	91.3	Al Fi	93.1
Qurum	89.0	Thumrait	91.3	Al-Shurah	93.2
Sicq	89.2	Badaa	91.5	Ibra	93.2
Hatta Mts	89.3	Hawraa Mts	91.5	Tiwi	93.5
Al-Awabi	89.3	Khasab	91.5	Bi Thaat	93.8
Quriyat	89.5	Barkah	91.7	Kumzar	94.0

FM	MHz	FM	MHz	FM	MHz
Al-Ain	94.1	Al-Buraimi	97.1	Shinas	101.5
Mazrah	94.1	Sur	97.2	Maqal	101.7
M'zara	94.2	Madha	97.4	Qantab	101.8
Bidbid	94.4	Ajran	97.5	Al-Jinah	102.2
Sabt	94.4	Sidab	97.8	Khur al-Juramah	103.3
Sital	94.5	Al-Aabla	97.8	Qadi	103.4
Sultan Qaboos	94.6	Al-Taher	99.1	Saham Main	103.7
Wadi Bani Omar	94.7	Ibri	99.1	Daba	103.8
Mazbar	95.3	Tibat	99.2	Al-Jafnen	103.9
Wadi Sahtan	95.3	Mazraa al-Hadri	99.4	Al-Wasat	104.0
Al-Hujirat	95.8	City	100.5	Rawtha Lima	104.0
Saifah	96.1	Al-Qalaat	100.5	Al-Bustan	104.2
Yakka	96.1	Wadi Dimah	100.6	Al-Filaj	105.7
Yanqul	96.4	Lima	100.6	Thouyan	107.2
Harat Mts	96.5	Amirat	101.2	Bahla	107.3
Al-Waqba	96.7	Hulm	101.2	Fl'm	107.4
Qahwi Mts	97.0				

General Arabic prgr: 24h on MW & FM. **N:** 0300, 0700 (Fri 0830), 1300, 1600, 1700, 1900, 2000. **Al-Shabab (Youth) channel** on: Muscat/Salalah/Thamrat/Taqa/Murbat/Sadah 100MHz, Al-Batina region 91.7/101.5/ 103.6MHz, A'Dakhlia region/Al-Wusta/Al A'Sharqia 98.8MHz, Dhank 91.2MHz, Dhalkot/Rakhuot 94.5MHz. **R. Oman FM in English:** 0300-1800 on Muscat/Salalah 90.4MHz, Thumrait 91.3MHz. **Quran prgr.** in Muscat 93.2MHz and Salalah 96.7MHz.
Ann: A: "Idha'atul Saltanat al-Oman min Muscat." E: "This is the English Service of Radio Sultanate of Oman from Muscat".
External service on shortwave: see International Radio section.

Other stations:
Al Wisal FM, Muscat: 96.5MHz. **W:** wisal.fm – **Hala FM,** Muscat: 102.7MHz. **W:** halafm.com – **Hi FM,** Muscat: 95.9MHz. **W:** hifmradio. com – **Merge FM,** Muscat: 104.8MHz. **W:** radiomerge.fm
BBC relay station: MW (702kHz 1500-2300 & 1413kHz 0030-0400, 1300-2100) & SW: for details see International Broadcasting section.
F.PI: station for Hindi speaking community

PAKISTAN

L.T: UTC +5h — **Pop:** 177 million — **Pr.L:** Urdu, Punjabi, Sindhi, Pushto, Balochi, English — **E.C:** 50Hz, 230V — **ITU:** PAK

PAKISTAN ELECTRONIC MEDIA REGULATORY AUTHORITY (PEMRA)
⌨ Green Trust Tower, 6th Floor F-6, Jinnah Ave, Blue Area, Islamabad **W:** pemra.gov.pk **E:** info@pemra.gov.pk **L.P:** Chairman: Mian Muhammad Javed.

PAKISTAN BROADCASTING CORPORATION (PBC, Gov.) RADIO PAKISTAN
⌨ Broadcasting House, Constitution Avenue, Islamabad 44000 ☎+92 51 9214278 🖷 +92 51 9223827 **W:** radio.gov.pk **E:** info@radio. gov.pk **L.P:** DG: Ghulam Murtaza Solangi. Dir. News: Haroon Abbassi

MW	kHz	kW	R	H of tr
Peshawar	540	300	N	0045-0405, 0600-1810
Khuzdar	567	150	B	1155-1810
Islamabad (Faqirabad)	585	500	F	0045-0605, 0800-1900
Karachi (Landhi)	612	10	S	0215-0700, 0900-1645
Lahore-I	630	100	F	0200-1900
Karachi (Landhi)	639	100	S	0045-0400, 1300-1800 NBS
Dera Ismail Khan	711	100	N	F.PI.
Quetta-I (Pishin)	756	150	B	0045-0805, 1000-1810
Karachi	828	100	S	0045-0405, 0600-1900
Turbat	981	100	B	0200-1700 (irregular)
Hyderabad-I	1008	120	S	0045-0405, 0600-1900
Multan	1035	120	P	0045-0405, 0600-1810
Lahore-III	1080	50	P	1230-1705
Hyderabad-II	1098	10	S	1230-1705
Quetta (city)	1134	100	B	0200-0400, 1300-1900 NBS
Rawalpindi	1152	100	P	0200-0400,1300-1900v NBS
Peshawar	1170	100	N	0200-0400, 1300-1900 NBS
Loralai	1251	10	B	1145-1615
Peshawar	1260	400	N	F.PI.
Lahore II	1332	100	P	0200-1900 NBS
Bahawalpur	1341	10	P	0850-1810
Zhob	1449	10	B	1155-1600
Faisalabad	1476	10	P	0045-0820
Gilgit	1512	10	N	1000-1700
Skardu	1557	10	N	1000-1700
Turbat	1584	0.25	B	1300-1810
Sibi	1584	0.25	B	0755-1108

MW	kHz	kW	R	H of tr
Chitral	1584	0.25	N	1050-1515
Abbottabad	1602	0.25	N	0845-1810

NBS: National Broadcasting Service (current affairs): 0200-1800 in Urdu & English. **N. in English:** 0300, 0800, 1100, 1300, 1600, 1700. 585/612/630/729/756/1080/1098kHz carry Voice of Quran 0200-0700.
FM93 (community channel): on 93.0MHz in Abbottabad, Bannu, Bhitshah, Chitral, Dera Ismail Khan, Faisalabad, Gilgit, Gwadar, Hyderabad, Islamabad, Karachi, Khairpur, Kohat, Lahore, Larkana, Mianwali, Mithi, Multan and Sargodha. Powers 2/3 kW. (Also in Urdu & English).
Planet FM94 (English channel): Islamabad 94.0MHz.
FM101: information and entertainment channel on 101.0MHz in Faisalabad, Hyderabad, Islamabad, Kalarkahar, Karachi, Lahore, Larkana, Multan, Muree, Peshawar, Quetta and Sialkot. Powers 2kW exc. Karachi 5kW. **W:** fm101.gov.pk
Regional prgr: Khairpur 93.3MHz, Rawalpindi 93.5MHz.
R=Region: N=No. We. Frontier Province & Northern tribal areas, F=Federal District of Islamabad, P=Punjab, S=Sindh, B=Balochistan.
D.Prgr: as above in Urdu, English and regional languages. Local IDs are usually heard at sign on/off.
Ann: "This is Radio Pakistan.", "National Broadcasting Service from Islamabad".
F.PI: MW: 1000kW to Lahore. 1000/500kW at Umarkot on 558kHz. . 150kW to Quetta. 100 kW to Chamar, Gwadar, Hyderabad, Larkana, Multan, Muzaffarabad, Paranichar. 10kW to Abbottabad. **SW:** 1x100kW to be added at Islamabad (Rewat) and Karachi. **FM93:** is being extended to Umerkot, Sukkur, Nawabshah, Jacobabad, Dadu, Badin, Mirpurkhas, Sanghar and Thatta. In total the network will have 47 stns. Prgrs will be 40% English/Urdu and 60% regional.

EXTERNAL SERVICE: See International Broadcasting section.

AZAD KASHMIR RADIO (AKR, Gov.)
⌨ Broadcasting House, Muzaffarabad (AJK) 13100, via Pakistan.
L.P: Dir: Javed Iqbal.
MW: Muzaffarabad 792kHz 150kW, Mirpur 936kHz 100kW (r. 930kHz).
SW: Islamabad (Rewat) 3975 100kW. **FM:** 93.0MHz.
NB: all transmitters reported inactive
D.Prgr: Muzaffarabad channel: 0045-0445 & 1000-1810 on 792kHz. Mirpur: 0045-0515 & 1100-1810. Rawalpindi-III channel (from Islamabad 100kW): 3975kHz: 0045-0425, 1330-1810, 7265kHz 0900-1210. Prgrs of all channels also contain R. Pakistan NBS relays.
Ann: 792kHz: "Yeh Azad Kashmir Radio Muzaffarabad Hay". 936kHz: "Mediumwave na-sau-chattis (936) kHz par. Yeh Azad Kashmir Radio hay". SW: "Yeh Azad Kashmir Radio Trarkhal Hay".
IS: "Azad Kashmir" anthem at open and close.

Other stations (FM MHz):
Apna Karachi 107: Karachi 107.0: **W:** apnakarachi107.fm – **City FM 89:** Karachi/Lahore/Islamabad/Faisalabad 89.0. **W:** www.cityfm89. com – **FM 100 Pakistan:** Islamabad/Karachi/Lahore 100.0 5kW. **W:** fm100pakistan.com – **FM Sunrise Pakistan:** Jhelum 95.0, Sardogha/ Sahiwal 96.0, Islamabad 97.0. **W:** fmsunrise.com – **Hot FM 105,** Karachi: 105.0. **W:** hotfm.com.pk – **Hum FM,** Islamabad/Karachi/ lahore/Sukkur: 106.2. **W:** hum.fm – **Josh FM,** Karachi: 99.0 – **KUST FM 99,** Kohat: 98.0. **W:** radio.kust.edu.pk – **Mast FM 103,** Faisalabad/ Karachi/Lahore/Multan: 103.0. **W:** mastfm103.com.pk – **Power FM,** Abbottabad/Islamabad: 99.0. **W:** power99.com.pk – **Punjab Univ. FM,** Lahore: 104.6 0.1kW **W:** pu.edu.pk/news/fm_schedule2007.am – **Radioactive 96,** Karachi: 96. **W:** www.radioactive96.fm – **R. Awaz:** 10 sites in Punjab on 105.0 **W:** radioawaz.com.pk – **R. Buraq:** Abbottabad/Mardan/Peshawar/Sialkot: 104.0. **W:** radio-buraq.com – **R. One,** Gwadar/Islamabad/Karachi/Lahore: 91.0. **W:** fm91.com.pk – **R. Swat,** Khyber: 96.0 – **Super FM,** Bahawalnagar: 90.0. **W:** superfmnet-work.com – **VO Kashmir,** Muzaffarabad: 105.0. **W:** www.vokfm105. com – **Zab FM,** Islamabad/Karachi/Larkana: 106.6 0.5kW **W:** zabfm.org
F.PI: Ewaz FM: Kharian/Haripur/Mandi Bahuddin 97.0/98.0. **W:** ewaz.com.pk

PALAU (USA associated)

L.T: UTC +9h — **Pop:** 20,956 — **Pr.L:** Palauan, English — **E.C:** 60Hz, 115/230V — **ITU:** PLW

T8AA BROADCASTING STATION (Gov)
⌨ Box 279, Koror State, Republic of Palau 96940 ☎ +680 4882417 🖷 +680 4881932 **L.P:** SM: Ms Eunice Akiwo **E:** ecoparadise@ palaugov.net
MW: Voice of Palau T8AA 1584kHz 5kW: 1900-1300 **N:** includes R. Australia via satellite **FM:** Eco-Paradise FM 87.9MHz

Other Stations:

FM MHz	kW	Station	FM	MHz	kW	Station
4)	88.3	0.6	PWFM	5)	91.5		R.Australia
1)	88.9		KRFM I. Rhythm	2)	98.5	0.5	KDFM Pinoy FM
2)	89.5	0.5	WWFM	3)	102.5	0.75	KRST-FM

Addresses & other information

1) Sure Save Store, PO Box 2000, Koror 96940 ☎+680 4881359 **E:** rudimch@palaunet.com **D.Prgr:** 24h – **2)** Diaz Broadcasting Co, PO Box 1327, Koror 96940 ☎+680 4884848 🖷 +688 5874420 **L.P:** GM Alfonzo Diaz, Mgr KDFM: Imelda Aban. WWFM English & Palaun, KDFM Filipino, classical, jazz, easy listening format **W:** http://www. brouhaha.net/palau/wwfm.html **E:** wwfm@palaunet.com **D.Prgr:** 24h – **3)** World Harvest R., PO Box 12, South Bend IN 46614, USA ☎ (574) 2918200 🖷 (574) 2919043 **E:** whr@lesea.com **W:** www.whr.org **Prgr:** relays English language relig prgrs from SW stn T8WH – **4)** Koror. 24h contemporary music. **L.P:** Salvador Tellames – **5)** 24h English for the Pacific satellite relay.

NB: Calls beginning with K and W are unofficial as Palau regulates its own broadc. spectrum. American-style calls are more familiar to locals.

EXTERNAL SERVICES: T8WH (Rlg.) See Int. Broadcasting section

PANAMA

L.T: UTC -5h — **Pop:** 3.3 million — **Pr.L:** Spanish — **E.C:** 60Hz, 110V — **ITU:** PNR

AUTORIDAD NACIONAL DE SERVICIOS PUBLICOS
🖃 Vía España, Edificio Office Park, Ciudad de Panamá (Apartado Postal 0816-01235, Zona 5, Panamá ☎ + 507-508 4500
W: www.asep.gob.pa

ASOCIACION PANAMEÑA DE RADIODIFUSIÓN
🖃 Ap. 55-1326, Panamá

MW	Call	kHz	kW	Station, location, hr. of tr.
PA01)	U23	540	10	R. Mía Chiriquí, David (r: 650)
PA02)	PU	540	10	R. Líder, Panamá: 1000-0400
PA03)	H2	560	3	RPC R., Colón (r: 610)
PA04)	S	570	5	R. Soberana, Panamá: 1000-0300
PA03)	H4	580	10	RPC R., David (r: 610)
PA03)	H3	590	10	RPC R., Chitré (r: 610)
PA03)	HM	610	10	RPC R., Panamá
HE01)	J35	630	2	R. Provincias, Chitré
CN01)	K22	640	2.5	R.CPR, Colón
PA14)		640	2.5	R. Panamá, La Palma
PA01)	S22	650	5	R. Mía "Cadena Nacional", Panamá
PA03)	F33	660	1	RPC R., Bocas del Toro (r: 610)
PA09)		660	5	La Nueva Exitosa, Sabana Grande (r: 930)
PA06)	LY	‡670	5	R. Hogar, Panamá
DA01)		‡680	5	Voz Sin Fronteras, Meteti: 1000-2400
PA26)	F32	680	5	Mujer AM, David
VE01)	R43	‡690	10	R. Veraguas, Santiago: 1000-0300
PA18)		690	5	R. Evangelio Vivo, Panamá
PA08)	Q51	710	10	KW R. Continente, Panamá
BT01)	B52	710	5	Ondas del Caribe, Bocas del Toro: 1000-0400
HE04)	B50	720	10	R. República, Chitré: 1100-0300
PA38)		‡730	3	Asamblea Nacional, Fort Sherman, Colón
CH03)	N26	740	5	R. Cristal, David
PA37)	R44	740	2.6	La Exitosa de Chorrera, La Chorrera
HE07)		750	5	R. La Inolvidable, Chitré: 1000-2300
PA38)		‡760	3	Asamblea Nacional, Bocas del Toro
PA10)	XO	760	5	LV del Istmo, Panamá: 1145-0300
HE05)	L83	‡770	10	R. Nacional Herrera, Chitré: 1100-0100
CH04)	B55	780	10	R. Chiriquí, David: 1100-2300
PA07)		780	5	R. Recuerdo, Panamá
PA14)		790	6	R. Panamá, Santiago
CE02)		800	5	Tropical 800, Los Santos: 1030-0300
PA11)	G	810	1	R. 10, Panamá
CH05)	F28	820	5	R. Ritmo Chiriquí, David: 1100-0400
LS01)	R56	830	5	R. Península, Macaracas: 1000-0200
PA12)	L80	840	10	R. Nacional, Panamá
PA09)	T61	850	5	La Exitosa de Chiriquí, David (r: 930)
PA09)		850	1	La Exitosa de Colón, Colón
HE03)	L55	860	10	R. Reforma, Chitré: 1030-0400
PA13)	HO	±870	5.5	R. Libre, Panamá
CN02)	B51	880	1	R. Visión Panamá, Colón
PA14)		880	2.5	R. Panamá, Bocas del Toro
PA14)		880	2.5	R. Panamá, Chiriquí
HE02)	Q62	890	5	R. Ritmo Stereo, Chitré
PA14)	HA	‡900	10	R. Panamá, Panamá
CH12)	L81	‡910	10	R. Nacional, David
CN03)	L85	‡910	3	R. Nacional, Colón

MW	Call	kHz	kW	Station, location, hr. of tr.
PA12)		‡910	10	R. Nacional, Darién
PA01)	S56	920	5	R. Mía Centrales, Los Santos (r: 650)
PA09)	R46	930	10	La Nueva Exitosa, Panamá
CH06)	K85	930	2	Mi Preferida Estéreo, Pto Armuelles: 1000- (SS 1200-) 0400
PA38)		‡940	5	Asamblea Nacional, Darien
CE04)	L84	‡950	3	R. Nacional, Penonomé
PA14)		‡950	2.5	R. Panamá, Las Mercedes, Colón
PA05)		960	1	R. Capital, Panamá
CH07)	M33	960	5	CHT Stereo Digital, David
VE02)	S97	970	3	Ondas Centrales, Santiago: W 1000-0300, SS 1300-2400
PA38)		‡990	5	Asamblea Nacional, Chiriquí
PA15)		990	5	R. Impacto, Panamá: (Prgr: Filadelfia R.)
CE01)	K36	1000	10	R. Poderosa "La Fuerte", Aguadulce: 1000-0500
BT03)	L86	‡1010	3	R. Nacional, Bocas del Toro
PA16)		1020	5	R. Ancón, Panamá: 1000-0400
LS02)	J2	1040	2.5	Ondas del Canajagua, Las Tablas
PA35)		1040	3	LV del Mamoni, Panamá
PA39)	J60	1060	3.5	R. LV de Panamá "La Auténtica", Panamá: 1100-0300
CE02)		1070	3	R. Estéreo Mi Favorita, Penonomé
LS04)		‡1070	10	R. Nacional, Los Santos
PA07)	J24	1080	5	R. Mundo Internacional, Panamá
PA12)		‡1090	10	R. Nacional, La Peña
PA08)	M92	1100	5	R. Sabrosa, Panamá
PA19)	M21	1120	5	R. Sonora, Panamá: 1030-0300
CE03)	U80	1130	2.5	R. Sensación, Aguadulce
PA20)	B49	1140	5	R. Panamericana, Panamá: 1100-0500
CH08)	C20	1160	5	Ondas Chiricanas, David
PA17)	WK	1160	10	R. Metrópolis, Panamá
VE03)	U	1180	10	AM Original, Santiago: 1100-0200
PA21)		1180	10	China Visión Panamá, Panamá
PA11)	E91	1210	1	R. Diez, Panamá
PA38)		‡1220	5	Asamblea Nacional, Veraguas
CH09)	M56	1240	3	Faro de David, David
PA17)		1240	1	Comunicación de Masas, Panamá
CE05)	LY	‡1250	5	R. Hogar, Penonomé: 0955-0300
PA22)	J22	1270	5	R. Tipy Q, Panamá
CH13)	S23	1290	3	R. Única, Chiriquí
CH13)		1290	5	R. Única, Panama
CH13)		1290	5.5	R. Única, Los Santos
CH10)	I417	1300	5	R. Baha´ís, Boca del Monte
PA24)		‡1310	12	R. María, Panamá
PA25)		1330	5	LV Poderosa, Panamá
LS05)		1340	2.5	R. Tipikal, Las Tablas
PA36)	Z38	1350	5	BBN R., Panamá
CH11)	B64	1370	1	R. Sitrachilco, Pto Armuelles: 1000-0200
PA26)		1380	10	Mujer AM, Panamá: 1130-0400
PA07)		1390	5	R. Mundo Internacional, Colón
PA27)	T40	1400	10	Digital R. Luz, La Chorrera
LS03)	H779	1410	5	R. Mensabé, Las Tablas: 1000-0300
PA28)		1430	7.5	R. Kids, Panamá
PA29)		1450	5	R. Melodía, Panamá: 1000-0330
BT02)	D42	1460	0.5	LV de Almirante, Bocas del Toro: 1400-0400
PA30)		1470	5	R. La Primerísima, Panamá
PA38)		1490	3	Asamblea Nacional, Cocle
PA31)	A95	1510	5	Hosanna R., Panamá
PA32)		1530	10	R. Avivamiento, Panamá
PA33		1560	10	R. Adventista de Panamá, Panamá: 1000-0300
PA34)		1580	1	Hosanna Oeste, Panamá

Call HO–, ‡ = inactive, (r) = repeater, ± = varying fq.
Hr of tr 24h unless otherwise stated

Province abbreviations: (Provincias) BT = Bocas del Toro, CE = Coclé, CH = Chiriquí, CN = Colón, DA = Darién, HE = Herrera, LS = Los Santos, PA = Panamá, VE = Veraguas. **N.B:** These abbreviations are not recognized by the Post Office. Letters should carry the full name.

Addresses and other information:

BT00) BOCAS DEL TORO
BT01) Finca 13, Empalme, Changuinola ☎+507 758 6087 - **FM:** 90.1MHz – **BT02)** Calle 6 y Av. N. Almirante – **BT03)** Av. Central, Bocas del Toro.

CE00) COCLÉ
CE01) Ap. 090 (or: Vía al Puerto), Aguadulce **E:** r.poderosa@cwpan-amá.net ☎ +507 997 4156 🖷 +507 997 4157 - **FM:** 99.9MHz – **CE02)** Av. Juan Demóstenes Arosemena, Galerías Aro, Penonomé **E:** darfer@cwpanama.net ☎+507 997 7167 🖷+507 997 1386 - **FM:** 91.7MHz – **CE03)** Calle Pablo Arosemena, Pueblo Nuevo, Aguadulce ☎/🖷+507 997 6280 **W:** www.plateadas.com/sensacion - **FM:** 103.7MHz– **CE04)** Villa Inter-americana, Penonomé – **CE05)** La Esperanza, Penonomé ☎+507 997 8929 🖷+507 997 7340

CH00) CHIRIQUÍ
CH03) Ap. 540 (or: Av. 8 y Calle A Norte, Barrio Bolívar), David ☎+507 774 3852 - **FM:** 98.1MHz – **CH04)** Ap. 43 (or: Calle Central), David **E:** rguerra@chiriqui.com ☎+507 775 2822 - **FM:** 107.1MHz – **CH05)** Av. D.Noreste, Medio Oeste, David ☎+507 774 3352 🖹+507 774 0512 - **FM:** 93.1MHz – **CH06)** Ap. 44 (or: Barriada San José), Puerto Armuelles ☎+507 770 7408 - **FM:** 105.3MHz – **CH07)** Calle Central, David ☎+507 774 0755 🖹+507 774 8081 - **FM:** 107.9MHz – **CH08)** Ap. 172 (or: Calle Elisandro Calvo, Doleguita), David ☎+507 775 2742 - **FM:** 100.1MHz – **CH09)** Av.Estudiante, Calle 4 final, Edif.Hermanos Pinzón, David – **CH10)** Ap. 1187, David 1045-2300 🖹+507 726 5004 – **CH11)** Principal, Barriada Santa Fe, Puerto Armuelles ☎+507 770 744 🖹+507 770 7217 – **CH12)** Av. Primera Oeste, David. **CH13)** Zahita SA, Calle 45, Bella Vista, Ed. El Conquistador, Panamá. **E:** radiometropolis@hotmail.com

CN00) COLÓN
CN01) Calle 2da detras de Panamá All Brown, Colón ☎+507 441 1300 - **FM:** 101.5MHz, 103.5MHz – **CN02)** Calle 1 Paseo Washington, Colón ☎+507 433 1035 - **FM:** 105.3MHz – **CN03)** Av. Bolívar, Calle 9, Colón

DA00) DARIÉN
DA01) Calle Principal de Metetí, Metetí. (or: Ap. 87-0871 Panamá 7) ☎/🖹+507 299 6346 **E:** vozst@cwp.net.pa - **FM:** 100.1MHz

HE00) HERRERA
HE01) Ap. 423 (or: Urb.Las Mercedes), Chitré ☎+507 996 4127 🖹+507 996 2668 **W:** www.radioprovincias630.com – **HE02)** Paseo Enrique Geenzier, Chitré. **W:** ritmostereo975.com - FM: 97.5 – **HE03)** Ap. 194, Chitré ☎+507 996 4223 - **FM:** 98.5MHz – **HE04)** Ap. 191, Chitré ☎+507 994 4627 - **FM:** 103.3MHz – **HE05)** Av. Pérez, Chitré – **HE07)** Ap. 375 (or: Calle Francisco Audia), Chitré. ☎+507 996 5302

LS00) LOS SANTOS
LS01) Calle Central, Macaracas - **FM:** 93.7MHz – **LS02)** Ap. 10 (or: Av. Belisario Porras, final), Las Tablas **E:** rocavi@cwp.net.pa ☎+507 994 6674 🖹+507 994 8133 – **LS03)** Ap. 20 (or: Av. Agustín Cano Castillero), Las Tablas ☎ +507 994 6606 🖹 +507 994 8477. – **LS04)** Los Santos. – **LS05)** Los Cerritos, Las Tablas

PA00) PANAMÁ
PA01) Ap. 5117, Panamá 5. **W:** www.radiomiapanama.com **E:** rmia@sinfo.net ☎+507 227 2700 🖹+507 227 2523 – **PA02)** Parque Lefebre, Edif.Sta Elena Torre II, Ofc.11, Panamá ☎+507 222 0500 **E:** radio540@sinfo.net **W:** www.sinfo.net/radio540 – **PA03)** Ap. 0827-00116 (or: Avenida 12 de Octubre), Panamá. ☎+507 390 6700 **W:** www.rpcradio.com **E:** rpcradio@medcom.com.pa – **PA04)** Ap. 6-2323, El Dorado (or: Calle 63B, Casa N° 2), Panamá ☎+507 236 1940 **W:** www.radiosoberana.com – **PA05)** Edif. Orion, P8, Vía España frente al PIEX, Panamá ☎+507 263 0183 – **PA06)** Ap. 102 (or: San Francisco de la Caleta, via Cincuentario y Av. José Matilde Pérez), Panamá 9-A ☎ +507 270 0141 🖹 +507 270 0145 **E:** rhogas@cableonda.net **W:** www.sinfo.net/rhogar – **PA07)** Radio Hit SA, Calle 50 y 77 San Francisco 35, (Apartado 0819-0391) Panamá **W:** http://estereobahia.com – **PA08)** Ap. 87-1324, Panamá 7 (or: Vía Argentina, Edif. Carillón, Panamá) **W:** www.kwcontinente.com **E:** kwcontinente@cableonda.net ☎+507 223 8846 🖹+507 264 6230. – **PA09)** Ap. 7462, Panamá 5 **W:** www.sinfo.net/exitosa ☎ +507 225 2052 🖹 +507 225 7252 – **PA10)** Ap. 6-1192, (or: 66 Oeste N° 641) El Dorado, Panamá. **E:** atrd@panama.c-com.net ☎ +507 229 3989 🖹 +507 261 3366. – **PA11)** La Gloria 31-B Bethania, Panamá – **PA12)** Ap. 4950 (or: Edif.Dorchester, P5), Panamá 5 ☎+507 269 6594 🖹+507 269 5910 – **PA13)** Edif. Dorchester, Vía España, Panamá 4. ☎+507 264 5239 – **PA14)** Calle 54 Obarrio, Edificio Plaza Globus, 2do piso, Panamá ☎+507 263 0121/263 0078 **W:** www.radiopanama.com.pa. – **PA15)** Río Abajo, Calle 13, Panamá ☎+507 221 0110. Filadelfia Radio: Filadelfia Eglesia, Plaza El Conquistador, Local 61, Vía Domingo Diaz, Panamá. – **PA16)** Calle Cuba y Calle 37, Panamá. 🖹+507 225 0025 – **PA17)** Vía España y Calle 45, Edif. El Conquistador PB, Panamá **W:** www.sinfo.net/radiometropolis/ **E:** radiometropolis@hotmail.com 🖹+507 212 0112– **PA18)** Condominio Dorado N° 2, Ofc. 10A, Vía Ricardo J. Alfaro, Panamá **☎** Ap. 87-1165 (or: Calle 63 Oeste N° E-21, Urb. Los Angeles), Panamá 7 ☎/🖹 +507 236 3065 – **PA20)** Ap. 6956 (or: Vía José Agustín Arango), Panamá 5 – **PA21)** Sun Tower Mall, Av. Ricardo J.Alfaro, Panamá ☎+507 236 5363 🖹+507 236 9810 – **PA22)** Calle 45, Edif. Conquistador, Bella Vista, P2, Panamá ☎+507 264 4226. – **PA24)** Ap. 6- 4509, El Dorado, (or Urb. Los Angeles, Av. Los Periodistas, Casa D-5, 0819-5581 El Dorado, Panamá) Panamá **W:** www.radiomariapanama.org **E:** info.pan@radiomaria.org ☎+507 261 0449 🖹+507 261 1535 – **PA25)** Iglesia Internacional del Evangélico Cuadrangular, Los Andes N° 2, Panamá – **PA26)** Calle 51 51 Av Manuel María Icaza, Edif. Torre Cosmos, Panamá – **PA27)** Ap. 473, La Chorrera – **PA28)** Río Abajo, Panamá **☎** Ap. 87-3541 (or: Vía Fernández de Córdoba, Jardin Cosita Buena), Panamá 7 **E:** lizbethcardenas@hotmail.com ☎+507 229 1504 🖹+507 229 4850 – **PA30)** Edif.La Marqueta, Vía Porras, Panamá **E:** rlprimerisima@latinol.com ☎ +507 226 6476. **W:** www.sinfo.net/laprimerisima – **PA31)** Ap. 6-8229 (or:

Calle Erick del Valle y Vía Argentina, Edif. Vicky 2), El Dorado, Panamá **W:** www.hosanna.pma.org/sradio.htm – **PA32)** Av. Ernesto T. Lefevre, Panamá – **PA33)** Ap. 3244, Panamá 3 (or: Carrasquilla, Calle 2da N° 39, Panamá) ☎ +507 214 6430 🖹 +507 263 4255 **W:** www.tagnet.org/radioadvpma **E:** celes@usa.com - Ids: "Radio Adventista - La Voz de la Esperanza" – **PA34)** Sky Phone S.A., Cerro Peñon, Panamá. – **PA35)** Av. José Agustin Arango N° 5013, Panamá. – **PA36)** Ap. 0860-00356, (or: Vía Cincuentenario final, a 300 metros del McDonald's de Río Abajo, después del Edificio La Reina) Panamá – **PA37)** Av. Las Américas, La Chorrera. – **PA38)** Asamblea Nacional, Panamá (txs broadc. the sessions of the National Assembly only) – **PA39)** Vía España y Calle 45, Edif. El Conquistador, PB, Panamá **E:** vozdepanama@hotmail.com

VE00) VERAGUAS
VE01) Ap. 48 (or: Calle 9 y vía Panamericana), Santiago ☎/🖹+507 958 7060 **E:** radioveraguas@cerco.net - **FM:** 102.1MHz – **VE02)** Ap. 131, Santiago. – **VE03)** Ap. 286 (or: Calle 10), Santiago ☎ +507 998 1655 🖹 +507 998 5580

FM in Panamá City (MHz): 88.1 Diez – 88.5 85.5 FM Stereo – 88.9 Sol 88.9 – 89.3 Cool FM – 89.9 Estéreo 89 – 90.5 Super Q – 90.9 RPC Radio – 91.3 Los 40 Principales – 91.7 La Nueva 91.7 – 92.1 Power – 92.5 La KY – 92.9 YXY – 93.5 Metrópolis – 93.9 R. María, Una voz cristiana en tu casa – 94.5 W Panamá – 94.9 Hosanna Capital 94.9 – 95.3 La Nueva Exitosa – 95.9 KW Continente – 96.3 Stereo Fe – 96.7 Mía – 97.1 Caliente Panamá –97.5 WAO 97½ – 97.9 Mix – 98.3 La Mega – 98.9 Ultra Estéreo – 99.3 La 99 – 99.7 Tropic Q – 100.1 Antena 8 – 100.5 Fabulosa – 101.1 Estéreo Azul – 101.5 Economía – 101.9 Nacional/SERTV – 102.1 Lo Nuestro – 102.5 FM Corazón – 103.1 Blast – 103.5 Quiubo Estéreo – 103.9 Mil – 104.3 KYS FM – 104.7 La Tipik – 105.1 Estéreo Vida – 105.7 La Nueva Bahía – 106.1 Con Sabor a Romance – 106.7 Rock & Pop – 107.5 Omega Stereo

PAPUA NEW GUINEA

L.T: UTC +10h — **Pop:** 6 million — **Pr.L:** English, Tok Pisin, Motu + 860 ethnic langs — **E.C:** 50Hz, 240V — **ITU:** PNG

NATIONAL INFORMATION & COMMUNICATIONS TECHNOLOGY AUTHORITY (Gov)
🖃 P.O. Box 8444, Boroko, NCD ☎ +675 3258633 🖹 +675 3256868, 3004829 **W:** www.nicta.gov.pg **E:** licensing@nicta.gov.pg **L.P:** CEO: Charles Punaha. Regulator of broadc. and communications (2010).

NATIONAL BROADCASTING CORPORATION (Gov)
🖃 P.O. Box 1359, Boroko NCD ☎ +675 325 5233 🖹 +675 325 6296 **E:** info@nbc.com.pg **W:** www.nbc.com.pg **L.P:** MD: Memafu Kapera, Dir.Engineering: Robin Vuvut. **Networks:** NBC National (English/Tok Pisin), **NBC Kundu** (Provincial: English/Tok Pisin & local vernaculars), **Tribe FM** [National: English/Tok Pisin).

NBC National (Voice of Papua New Guinea):

SW	KHz	kW	SW	KHz	kW
Pt. Moresby	4890	25*	Pt. Moresby	§6040	10*

§) using NBC Central 3290 tx on NBC Milne Bay 6040 frequency
* used irr. for events of national importance. **F.PL:** new 25kW txs

MW	kHz	kW
Pt Moresby	585	10

FM	MHz	kW	FM	MHz	kW
Pt Moresby	90.7	1	Rabaul	103.3	0.3

Note: FM coverage of NBC National is being expanded nationwide.
D.Prgr: 1900-1400 daily **N:** on the h 1900-1400 **Format:** National public service prgr. **V:** card or letter
NBC Kundu Network (local provincial stns often funded in partnership with provincial govs):

MW	kHz	kW	Station, slogan, location
4)	675	10	NBC Wewak, "Maus Bilong Sepi", Wewak
10)	675	10	NBC Morobe, "Maus Bilong Kund", Lae
9)	810	2	NBC Rabaul, "Maus Bilong Tavuvu", Rabaul
13)	864	10	NBC Madang, "Maus Bilong Garamut", Madang
2)	900	10	NBC Kimbe, "Singaut Bilong Tavur", Kimbe

SW	kHz	kW	Station, slogan, location
4)	‡2410	10	NBC Enga, Wabag
1)	3205	10	NBC Vanimo, "Maus Bilong Sandaun", Vanimo
10)	3220	10	NBC Morobe, "Maus Bilong Kundu", Lae
2)	‡3235	10	NBC Kimbe, "Singaut Bilong Tavur", Kimbe
7)	‡3245	10	NBC Gulf, "Voice of the Seagull", Kerema
13)	3260	10	NBC Madang, "Maus Bilong Garamut", Madang
17)	3275	10	NBC Southern Highlands, Mendii
5)	3290	10	NBC Central, "Voice of the Conch-Shell", Pt Moresby
18)	3305	10	NBC Western, "Voice of the Sunset", Daru
3)	3315	10	NBC Manus, "Maus Bilong Chauka", Lorengau
19)	3325	10	NBC Buka, "Maus Bilong Sankamap", Buka ARB

SW	kHz	kW	Station, slogan, location
14)	‡3335	10	NBC East Sepik, "Maus Bilong Sepik", Wewak
12)	3345	10	NBC Northern, "Voice of the People of Oro", Popondetta
15)	3355	10	NBC Simbu, "Karai Bilong Mumbu", Kundiawa
20)	3365	10	NBC Milne Bay, "Voice of Kula", Alotau
8)	3375	10	NBC Western Highlands, "Eagle FM", Mt Hagen
9)	3385	10	NBC East New Britain, "Maus Bilong Tavuvur", Rabaul
6)	3395	10	NBC Eastern Highlands, "Karai Bilong Kumul", Goroka
3)	3905	10	NBC New Ireland, "Singaut Bilong Drongo", Kavieng
8)*‡5985		10	NBC Western Highlands, "Eagle FM", Mt Hagen
9)*‡5985		10	NBC East New Britain, "Maus Bilong Tavuvur", Rabaul
19)*‡6020		10	NBC Buka, "Maus Bilong Sankamap", Buka ARB
20)*‡6040		10	NBC Milne Bay, "Voice of Kula", Alotau
18)*‡6080		10	NBC Western, "Voice of the Sunset", Daru
14)*‡6140		10	NBC East Sepik, "Maus Bilong Sepik", Wewak

NB: Stns may operate irr. schedules or have long periods of silence because of technical, power, funding or other issues reflecting local and provincial government resources and priorites.
‡ Currently inactive on SW but could reactivate without notice.
*‡ Licensed but inactive. May be used irr. for events of nat. importance.

FM	MHz	kW	Station, slogan, location
7)	91.1		NBC Gulf, "Voice of the Seagull", Kerema
6)	91.1		NBC Eastern Highlands, "Kam Gud FM", Kainantu
8)	91.4		NBC Western Highlands, "Eagle FM", Mt Hagen
6)	91.7	3	NBC Eastern Highlands, "Kam Gud FM", Goroka
5)	95.5		NBC Central, "Voice of the Conch Shell", Pt Moresby
19)	100.0		NBC Buka, "Maus Blong Sankamap", Buka ARB
9)	103.3		NBC East New Britain, "Maus Blong Tavuvur", Kenabot
10)	105.1	1	NBC Morobe, "Kundu FM", Morobe

D.Prgr: 2000-2200, 0800-1200v. **Format:** Non-commercial local music and health, education, public safety and sports prgrs. **N:** NBC National Network. **V:** card or letter, email; send reports direct to stn.
NBC Tribe FM: Pt Moresby. New youth netw. delivered via satellite.
NB: The NBC FM section is under review and currently includes only a small number of known licensed outlets. Most provincial NBC stns now announce and use FM frequencies and more locations are now adding satellite-delivered FM coverage of NBC National and Tribe FM.
F.PL: Review of provincial stns may result in consolidation of smaller number of NBC stns. Satellite delivery of NBC National and Tribe FM expanded via local FM txs. Local NBC studio prgrs continue on FM (and SW as necessary) giving 3 NBC prgr streams at all locations.

Addresses and other information:
Regions: ARB=Autonomous Region of Bougainville, Cen=Central, Chi=Chimbu, EHP=Eastern Highlands, ENB=East New Britain, Eng=Enga, ESP=East Sepik, Gul=Gulf, Mad=Madang, Man=Manus, MBP=Milne Bay, Mor=Morobe, NCD=National Capital District, NIP=New Ireland, Or=Oro, SHP=Southern Highlands, WHP=Western Highlands, WNB=West New Britain, WP=Western, WSP=West Sepik. **NB:** Two new regions, Hela and Jiwaka were created in 2012.
1) P.O Box 37, Vanimo, WSP ☎ +675 857 1144/1149 🖷 +675 8571305 – **2)** P.O.Box 412, Kimbe, WNB ☎ +675 983 5600/5185/5010 🖷 +675 9835600 – **3)** P.O.Box 477, Kavieng, NIP ☎ +675 9842077 🖷 +675 984 2191 – **4)** P.O.Box 300, Wabag, Eng ☎ +675 5471013 🖷 +675 5471069 – **5)** P.O Box 1359, Boroko NCD ☎ +675 3217155 🖷 +675 3217110 **FM:** 90.7 carries Karai Network including Tribe FM [youth prgr] Sa 2100-0000 local; **SW:** carries FM 95.5 'Radio Gadona' – **6)** P.O Box 311, Goroka, EHP ☎ +675 732 1618/1733/1607 🖷 +675 7321533 – **7)** P.O.Box 36, Kerema, Gul. ☎ +675 6481076 🖷 +675 6481003 – **8)** P.O.Box 311, Mount Hagen WHP ☎ +675 5421000 🖷 +675 5421001 – **9)** P.O.Box 393, Rabaul, ENB ☎ +675 982 8966/67/68/69/70 🖷 +675 9828971 – **10)** P.O.Box 1262, Lae, Mor ☎ +675 472 1311/7520/4209 🖷 +675 4726423 – **11)** P.O Box 505, Lorengau, Man ☎ +675 4709079 🖷 +675 4709079 – **12)** P.O.Box 137, Popondetta, Or ☎ +675 329 7037/38 🖷 +675 3297362 – **13)** P.O Box 2036, Jomba, Mad. ☎ +675 852 2415/2301/2360 🖷 +675 8522360 – **14)** P.O Box 65, Wewak, ESP ☎ +675 856 2316/2398 🖷 +675 8562405 – **15)** P.O.Box 228, Kundiawa, Chi ☎ +675 7351012 🖷 +675 7351012 – **17)** P.O.Box 104, Mendi SHP ☎ +675 549 1017/1020 🖷 +675 5491017 – **18)** P.O.Box 23, Daru WP ☎ +675 645 9234/9151 🖷 +675 6459319 – **19)** P.O.Box 35 Buka, ARB ☎ +675 9739911 🖷 +675 9739912 – **20)** P.O.Box 111, Alotau MBP ☎ +675 641 1028/1334 🖷 +675 6411028.

MAJOR COMMERCIAL NETWORKS:
FM 100 Kalang Advertising Ltd (Telikom PNG subsidiary)
✉ P.O. Box 1534, Boroko, NCD ☎ +675 300 4300 🖷 +675 300 4316 **L.P:** CEO: Vacant, Ops Mgr: Bonner Tito **W:** www.fm100.com.pg **E:** info@fm100.com.pg **D.Prgr:** 24h via satellite **Format:** E Contemporary **Sports Relay:** 2GB Sydney NRL Live Fri/Sat/Sun
F.PL: Continued FM expansion nationwide.
FM(MHz): 100.1 Kandrian, 100.2 Kavieng/Goroka/Tabubil, 100.3 1kW Pt Moresby/Lorengau/Kimbe/Tabubil/Finschafen/Mendi, 100.4 Mt Hagen, 100.5 Popondetta/Lae/Namatanai/Daru/Tari, 100.6 Pomio/Buka, 100.8 1kW Rabaul/Madang/Mewak, 101.1 Kundiawa, 102.0 Paga Hill, 107.1 Mt Horeatoa/Mt Kainguma, 107.3 Mt Boregoro/Mt Waterholes, 107.7 Mt Dimodimo

PNGFM
✉ P.O Box 774, Port Moresby NCD ☎ +675 323 4288 🖷 +675 323 1628 **L.P:** MD: Adrian Au, CE: Clezy Rakole **W:** www.cfl.com.fj/radio-png **E:** aau@naufm.com.pg **D.Prgr:** 24h via satellite **Netw.: Nau FM** PD: Turner Arifeae **Format:** E, urban westernized youth market **Yumi FM** PD: Rosemary Botong **Format:** Tok Pisin, local and adult contemporary music **Legend FM Bikpla 101:** E, Hits of 1970s-2000s. **F.PL:** Continued FM expansion nationwide.
FM(MHz): Nau FM: 96.1 1kW Goroka, 96.3 1kW Lae/Madang, 96.5 1kW Kimbe/Port Moresby/Lihir/Rabaul/Lorengau, 96.7 Alotau, 96.9 1kW Mt Hagen. **Yumi FM:** 93.1 1kW Pt Moresby/Lihir, 93.3 Tinputz, 93.5 Mt Hagen, 93.7 1kW Lae/Madang, 93.9 Rabaul/Goroka, 95.0 Kundiawa, 96.3 Balimo. **Legend FM:** 101.1 Port Moresby/Lae/Madang/Goroka/Mt Hagen/Rabaul/Kokopo

MAJOR NON-COMMERCIAL NETWORK:
Wantok Radio Light – PNG Bible Church
✉ Papua New Guinea Christian Broadcasting Network, P.O. Box 1273, Port Moresby NCD ☎ +675 326 2933 🖷 +675 326 1104 **L.P:** GM: Pawa Warena **W:** www.wantokradio.org **E:** admin@wantokradio.org **D.Prgr:** 24h via satellite **N:** NBC National bulletins 0700, 1900 **Format:** religious **F.PL:** Continued FM expansion nationwide via satellite **Affiliation:** HCJB/Evangelical Bible Missions through Life Radio Ministries, Griffin GA, USA.
SW: 7235kHz1kW Pt Moresby. **QSL:** r. to **E:** qsl@wantokradio.org
FM(MHz): 93.9 1kW Port Moresby, 105.9 Wewak/Kimbe/Buka/Popondetta/Lae/Kokopo/Kiunga/Goroka/Mt Hagen/Ialibu/Wabag/Alotau/Mendi/Kainantu/Madang.

OTHER STATIONS:
SW	kHZ	kW	Location	Station
8)	3915	1	Kiunga WP	R.Fly
5)	4960	1	Vanimo WSP	R. St.Gabriel
8)	5960	1	Kiunga WP	R.Fly

FM		kW	Location	Station
1)	88.1	0.3	Vunapope ENB	Voice of Blessed Peter Torot
1)	88.5	0.3	Bereina Cen	Voice of Blessed Peter Torot
2)	89.3	0.3	Moro SHP	CDI FM
3)	89.9	1	Port Moresby NCD	FM Central
4)	90.0		Hela SHP	ECPNG FM
2)	90.9	0.5	Gobe SHP	CDI FM
1)	91.3	0.5	Rabaul ENB	Voice of Blessed Peter Torot
5)	91.5	0.5	Vanimo WSP	CRN R. Maria
2)	92.3	0.5	Kikori WP	CDI FM
6)	92.5	0.5	Mt Hagen WHP	KBBN
5)	92.9	0.5	Aitape WSP	CRN R. Maria
1)	94.3	0.3	Kerema Gul	Voice of Blessed Peter Torot
7)	94.7	1	Lae Mor	FM Morobe
8)	95.3	1	Kiunga WSP	R. Fly
9)	95.3	1	Maprik ESP	FM Sepik Central
23)	95.3		Buka ARB	New Dawn FM
10)	96.0		Mosa WNB	NBPOL FM
7)	97.9	1	Port Moresby NCD	2G 97.9 FM
10)	98.0		Healla WNB	NBPOL FM
10)	98.0		Kapiura WNB	NBPOL FM
12)	98.0	0.02	Lihir NIP	FM Lihir
13)	98.1	0.3	Mt Hagen WHP	Trinity FM
14)	98.3	1	Wewak WSP	Laif FM
15)	98.5	0.02	Port Moresby NCD	Campus FM
16)	98.9	0.02	Misima Mine MBP	FM Misima
17)	99.5	0.5	Port Moresby NCD	Rait FM
18)	99.5	0.01	Bereina Cen	Waima FM
19)	99.9	0.1	WSP	99.9 FM
19)	99.9	0.1	Kompian Eng	Kom Community R. 99.9 FM
20)	102.1	0.3	Lae Mor	R. Australia
21)	103.3	0.5	Mougolu SHP	Mougolu FM
5)	103.5	0.5	Port Moresby NCD	CRN R. Maria
22)	103.7	0.3	Lae Mor	CDL-103.7
8)	103.8	0.03	Tabubil WP	R. Fly
1)	105.1	0.3	Lorengau Man	Voice of Blessed Peter Torot
20)	106.7	0.1	Port Moresby NCD	BBC
20)	106.9	0.1	Lae Mor	BBC
20)	109.9	0.3	Port Moresby NCD	R. Australia

Addresses and other information
1) PO Box 300, Boroko, NCD. **T:** +675 3410110. Individually owned and operated by several Catholic Church dioceses **L.P:** Father Mlak Zdzislaw SVD **Slogan:** "Your Daily Spiritual Companion" **W:** www.catholicpng.org.pg & www.voiceoftorot.com **E:** admin@voiceoftorot.

com – **2)** CDI Foundation Trust Fund, P.O. Box 383, Port Moresby NCD ☎ +675 325 0706/1759 **W:** www.cdi.org.pg **Prgr:** 24h – **3)** HIRAD Ltd, P.O Box 333, Port Moresby NCD ☎ +675 321 0533 – **4)** Evangelical Church of PNG – **5)** Radio Maria PNG Inc [Catholic Radio Network], P.O. Box 8719, Boroko NCD ☎ +675 325 9178 **L.P:** Fr. Martin We-en **W:** www.radiomaria.org **SW:** R.St.Gabriel, P.O. Box 205, Vanimo WSP ☎ +675 857 1305 **Prgr:** local and network prgrs **QSL:** qsl@radiomaria. org – **6)** Krai Bilong Baibel [Bible FM], Bible Broadcasting Network, P.O. Box 617, Mt Hagen WHP **L.P:** Brad & Deborah Wells **W:** www. biblefm.com **E:** bwellspng@yahoo.com **Prgr:** 24h **F.PI:** Bible FM Lae and repeater in WHP – **7)** Intouch Media, P.O. Box 3310, Lae Mor ☎ +675 479 1477 – **8)** Ok Tedi Mining Company, P.O. Box 1, Tabubil WP ☎ +675 649 3924 ▤ +675 6493023 **L.P:** Team Ldr: Michael Miise **Prgr:** 24h includes overnight automated prgr **QSL:** **E:** winnie.monouluk@ oktedi.com or kabua.momo@oktedi.com – **9)** Papindo Trading – **10)** NBPOL – **11)** Pacific Adventist University (PAU), PMB, Boroko NCD ☎ +675 328 0400 **W:** www.pau.ac.pg **E:** 2g@pau.ac.pg **ID:** "Exalting God above all the earth. Psalms 97.9" – **12)** Lihir Gold Mine – **13)** Catholic Archdiocese of Mt. Hagen, Mt Hagen WHP **Prgr:** 0600-2000 – **14)** United Christian Broadcasting [UCB Pacific Partners], P.O. Box 556, Wewak ESP ☎ +675 456 1400 **L.P:** Mgr Tony Dua **Affiliation:** UCB International, Auckland NZ – **15)** University of PNG (Physics Dept), P.O. Box 320, University, Port Moresby NCD ☎ +675 326 7191 – **16)** Misima Gold Mines Pty Ltd – **17)** CHM-Rait FM, P.O. Box 1106, Boroko, NCD ☎ +675 325 6644 ▤ +675 325 0134 **L.P:** MD Raymond Chin, Mgr-Provincial Radio Richard Francisco **W:** www.chmsupersound.com **F.PI:** prov. comm. netw. – **18)** Waima Radio Station Assoc, Bereina Cen – **19)** Baptist Union of PNG, PO Box 705, Mt Hagen WHP ☎ ▤ +675 542 3726 **W:** www.bupng.net **E:** bupng@global.net.pg **L.P:** Dir: John Kaewa **Community Radio:** KOM, Kompiam, Eng 99.9 relay 95.9 Pakau; Tekin CR, Oksaprim, Sanduan 0.1kW – **20)** TEPNG, P.O. Box 1388, Boroko NCD ☎ +675 325 6322 ▤ +675 325 0350 **L.P:** Mgr Ops Wayne Wilson **E:** wwilson@tepng.com **R. Australia:** Pacific stream from Melbourne 24h satellite service **BBC:** Pacific stream from London 24h satellite service – **21)** Mougolu SHP – **22)** Catholic Diocese of Lae, Lae Mor – **23)** Buka ARB ☎ +675 973 9319 ▤ +675 973 9285 **L.P:** Stn Mgr Aloysius Laukai **W:** www.bougainville.typepad.com/newdawn **E:** tambolema@daltron.com.pg

PARAGUAY

L.T: UTC -4h (7 Oct 12-13 Apr 13, 6 Oct 13-12 Apr 13: -3h) — **Pop:** 7 million — **Pr.L:** Spanish, Guaraní — **E.C:** 50Hz, 220V — **ITU:** PRG — **Int. dialling code:** +595

COMISIÓN NACIONAL DE TELECOMUNICACIONES (CONATEL)
Offices: Pdte. Franco N° 780, Esq. Ayolas, Asunción ☎ 21 440 020 **W:** www.conatel.gov.py **L.P:** Pres: Dr. Jorge A. Seall. Sasiain

MW	Call	kHz	kW	Station, location, h. of tr
AP1)	ZP16	550	20/12	R. Parque, Ciudad del Este: 0800-0100
AM1)	ZP15	570	1	R. LV del Amambay, Pedro Juan Caballero: 0930- (Sun 1000-) 0100
MI3)	ZP39	570	1	R. San Roque, Ayolas: 0900-0200, Sat: 0900-0000, Sun: 1000-2200
SP1)	ZP32	590	5	R. Ycuámandyyú, Villa de S. Pedro: 0900-0200
BO1)	ZP30	610	25	LV del Chaco Paraguayo, Filadelfia: 0900-0230
SP2)	ZP40	±620	5	R. Nasaindý, San Estanislao: (r. v619-616.6) 0900-0230
CG1)	ZP19	±640	15	R. Caaguazú, Coronel Oviedo (r. v640-645): 0900-0500
CA1)	ZP4	650	50	R. Uno, Asunción: 24h
AP2)	ZP26	660	5	R. Itapirú, Cd del Este: 0800-0100
CA2)	ZP11	680	50	R. Caritas, Asunción: 24h
NE1)	ZP12	700	12	R. Carlos Antonio López, Pilar: (rel. R. Nal 920): 0900-0200
PH1)	ZP17	720	25	R. Pai Puku, Teniente Irala Fernández 0900-0100 Sun; 1000-0030
CA3)	ZP7	730	30	R. Cardinal, Asunción: 24h
CA4)	ZP42	750	5	LV de la Policía Nal, Asunción: 0900-0200
CA5)	ZP70	780	30	R. Primero de Marzo, Asunción: 24h
CN1)	ZP27	800	5/3	R. Mbaracayá, Salto del Guairá: 0900-0300
GU1)	ZP6	±840	5	R. Guairá, Villarrica: (v835-840): 0900-2400
CR1)	ZP28	±860	25	LV de la Cordillera, Caacupé: 0900(SS 1000)-0400
CE1)	ZP33	±890	5/0.5	R. Tres de Febrero, Itá: (v885-890): 0900-0300
CA6)	ZP1	920	100	R. Nal. del Paraguay, Asunción: 0800-2400
CA7)	ZP9	970	80	R. 9-70 , Asunción: 0800-0400
AM2)	ZP31	980	5	R. Mburucuyá, Pedro Juan Caballero: 0900-0130
CE2)	ZP36	1000	5/0.5	R. Mil, San Antonio: 24h
CA8)	ZP14	1020	25	R. Nandutí, Asunción: 24h
MI1)	ZP43	1040	5	R. Arapisandú, San Ignacio: 0900-0200
CE3)	ZP25	1080	10	R. Monumental, Luque: 1100(Sun 0900)-2330

MW	Call	kHz	kW	Station, location, h. of tr
AM3)	ZP71	1100	5	R. Ñú Verá, Capitán Bado: 0900-0200
CE4)	ZP24	1120	10	R. Nuevo Mundo, San Lorenzo
CR1)	ZP22	1140	5/2	R. Central de Notícias, Atyrá
CA9)	ZP72	1160	10	R. Antena Dos, Asunción
CG2)	ZP52	1180	5/1	R. Coronel Oviedo – RCO-AM, Coronel Oviedo: 0900-0100
AP3)	ZP45	1190	5	LV de la Libertad, Henendarias
CE5)	ZP44	1200	10	R. Libre, Fernando de la Mora:10:30-0230, (SS 11:30)
CA10)	ZP3	1250	5	R. Asunción, Asunción: 0900-0400
GU3)	ZP34	1260	5	R. Panambi Vera, Villarrica
AP4)	ZP53	1280	1/0.25	R. LV del Este, Cd. del Este
CA11)	ZP10	1300	5	R. Fe y Alegria, Villa Hayes
CA12)	ZP13	1330	10	R. Chaco Boreal, Asunción: 24h
CO1)	ZP37	1360	1	R. Yby Ya´u, Ybu Ya´u: 0900-0300
CO2)	ZP8	1380	1	R. Concepción, «LV del Norte»: 0930-0100
MI2)	ZP35	1410	2	R. Mangore, S. Juan Bautista: 1000-0130
CO3)	ZP42	1420	5	R. Güyrá Campana, Horqueta (r. 1417)
CO4)	ZP29	1450	5	R. Vallemi, Vallemi
AM4)	ZP23	1480	1	R. Dos Fronteras, Bella Vista Norte: 1000-0100
CE6)	ZP20	1480	5	R. América, Nemby: 24h
SW	**Call**	**kHz**	**kW**	**Name, location and h of tr**
BO1)		6884	0.1	LV del Chaco Paraguayo, Filadelfia: (USB feeder): 0900-0230
PH1)		6890	0.1	R. Pa´i Puku, Tte. Irala Fernández: (USB feeder): 0900-0100, Sun 1000-0030
CA6)	ZPA1‡9735		100	R. Nal. del Paraguay, Asunción
CE7)		12000	0.025	R. Licemil, Ypané (irr.)

° = on-air stn name not confirmed, ‡ = inactive, ± = varying freq.

Addresses and other information:
AM00 (AMAMBAY)
AM1) Mcal López 336, Pedro Juan Caballero 36 72210 **W:** www. amambayfm.com **E:** administracion@amambayfm.com – **FM:** 100.5MHz – **AM2)** Villa María Victoria, Fracción San Jorge, Pedro Juan Caballero **W:** www.nanduti.com.py/mburucuya.asp – **AM3)** Estrella c/4 de Enero, Capitán Bado, Amambay ☎+595 37 262 – **AM4)** Calle Iturbe 146, Bella Vista Norte **FM:** 92.5MHz
AP00 (ALTO PARANA)
AP1) Ciudad del Este – **AP2)** Av Coronel Sánchez 3800, Cd del Este **W:** www.radioitapiru.com - **FM:** 96.1MHz – **AP3)** Juan E.O´Leary 152, 1a piso, Oficina 5, Hernandarias **E:** lavozdelalibertad@telesurf.com.py – **AP4)** Avenida San Blás No 353, Ciudad del Este ☎61 512 583 **E:** lavozam@hotmail.com
B000 (BOQUERÓN)
BO1) Av Trebol 137E, Filadelfia, Chaco (Cas 984, Asunción) **W:** www.zp30.com.py ☎ 491 32031/32330 ▤ 491 32501 Operated by Mennonite Mission. **German** (20%) & 4 ethnic langs
CA00 (CAPITAL)
CA1) Av Mariscal López 2948 c/MacArthur, Asunción ☎ 2160 3400 **W:** www.radiouno.com.py **E:** info@radiouno.com.py – **CA2)** Kubischek 661 y Azara, (Cas 1313), Asunción **W:** www.uca.edu.py/caritas **E:** caritas@caritas.com.py ☎521 213 570 ▤521 204 161 – **CA3)** Calles Comendador Nicolás Bó y Guaranies 1334, Lambaré (Cas 247, Asunción) **W:** www.cardinal.com.py - **FM:** 92.3MHz – **CA4)** Comandancia de la Policia Nacional, El Paraguayo Independiente c/Chile, Asunción ☎ 21 492 515 – **CA5)** Av Perón y Concepción Prieto Yegros (Cas 1456), Asunción ☎ 21 300 380 **W:** www.780am.com.py – **CA6)** Av Blas Garay 241e/Yegros e Iturbe, Asunción ☎21 4500776 ▤21 372 233 **W:** www.rnp920am.com **E:** info@rnp920.com – **CA7)** Av Rodriguez de Francia 34, Asunción ☎21 450 283 **W:** www.radio970am.com.py **E:** info@radio970am.com – **CA8)** Choferes del Chaco 1194, Asunción ☎21 604 308 ▤21 606074 **W:** www.nanduti.com.py **E:** publicidad@ holdingradio.com.py – **CA9)** Estados Unidos 2019, Asunción – **CA10)** Capitán Lombardo 174 y Av Artigas, Asunción ☎21 282 661 **W:** www. radioasuncion.com.py **E:** radioasuncion@cmm.com.py – **CA11)** O´Leary 1847, Asunción ☎21 390 576 ▤21 390 584 **W:** www.feyalegria.org.py **E:** oficinanacional@feyalegria.org.py – **CA12)** Alejo Garcia 2589 con Rio de la Plata, Asuncion ☎ 21 425 589 **W:** www.chacoboreal.com.py **E:** info@chacoboreal.com.py
CE00 (CENTRAL)
CE1) Av Enrique Doldán Ibieta y Presidente Franco, Itá ☎24 32543 **Guaraní:** www.1000.com.py – **CE2)** Av 25 de Mayo 1160 e/Brasil y Constitución, Central de Llamadas, Asunción ☎21 209 000 **W:** www.radio1000.com.py **E:** info@radio1000.com.py – **CE3)** Av General Aquino 9999 y José Bonifacio, Luque ☎644-330 **W:** www. monumental.com.py **E:** mensajes@monumental.com.py – **CE4)** Coronel Romero y de las Residentes, San Lorenzo (Asunción: General Díaz 488, Ofic 34.) ☎21 582424 ▤21 586258 **Guaraní:** 0900-1000, 1700-1800 – **CE5)** Av Zavalas-Cué 1615, Fernando de la Mora Zona Sur ☎21 509 087 **W:** www.radiolibre.com.py **E:** radiolibre@gmail.com Rpt. to: Dr Benjamín Fernández Bogado – **CE6)** Cas 2220, Asunción **W:** www.

radioiglesia.com **E:** radioamerica@lycos.com ☎21 960 228 ▯21 963 49 – **CE7)** Liceo Militar "Acosta Nu", Ypané

CG00 (CAAGUAZÚ)
CG1) Ruta Mcal Estigarribia Km 131, Coronel Oviedo ☎/▯521 200 370 **W:** www.radiomas.com.py - **FM:** 102.3MHz – **CG2)** Av Mariscal Estigarribia 304 casi Yrendague, Coronel Oviedo **E:** rco@radiocoroneloviedo.com.py ☎/▯ 521 202579 - **Guaraní:** 50% of prgr 0900-0100 - **FM:** 91.9MHz FM del Sol

CN00 (CANINDEYÚ)
CN1) Defensa Nal y Av Paraguay, Salto del Guairá ☎462 42 350

C000 (CONCEPCIÓN)
C01) Ruta V, Ybu Ya'u ☎39 210 250. – **C02)** Panchito López 241 entre Prof.Cabral y Screiber, (Cas 78), Concepción ☎31 42254 ▯31 40919 **E:** radioconcepcion@infonorte.com.py – Prgrs in **Spanish & Guaraní:** 0930-0100. – **C03)** José Luís Arbues c/Ruta 5, Horqueta ☎32 222 364 – **C04)** Zona Urbana, Vallemi ☎351 230 329

CR00 (CORDILLERA)
CR1) Dr Venancio Pino y 3ra Proyectada, Caacupé ☎511 42363 – **CR2)** Atyrá

GU00 (GUAIRA)
GU1) Pte Franco 788 y Alejo Garcia, Villarrica ☎/▯ 54 142130 **W:** www.fmguaira.com **E:** administracion@fmguaira.com **Guaraní:** 2100-2300.0900-2400 - **FM:** 103.5MHz – **GU3)** Angostura y Olimpio, Bo Ybarotu, Villarrica ☎541 42229 **W:** www.grupopanambi.com **E:** info@grupopanambi.com

MI00 (MISIONES)
MI1) Av Mariscal López y Capitan del Puerto, San Ignacio (Misiones) ☎82 232 374 – **MI2)** Coronel Alfredo A Ramos esq San Juan, San Juan Bautista, Misiones ☎81 212 306 – **MI3)** Mil Viivendas, Ayola ☎7222 2433 ▯7222 2324 **W:** www.radiosanroque.org **E:** ventas@radiosanroque.org

NE00 (ÑEEMBUCÚ)
NE1) Alberdi 998, Pilar ☎86 32254 **W:** rnp920am.com **E:** zp12@uninet.com.py

PH00 (PRESIDENTE HAYES)
PH1) Km 389 de la Ruta Transchaco, Teniente Irala Fernández, Chaco ☎424 270 349 **W:** www.radiopaipuku.org.py **E:** radiopaipuku@chaconet.com.py o rppuku@telesurf.com.py

SP00 (SAN PEDRO)
SP1) Ruta 11 Juana M de Lara, Villa de San Pedro **W:** www.desdeparaguay.com/ycuamandyyu – **SP2)** Mariscal López y B Caballero, San Estanislao, San Pedro ☎43 4342 2095 ▯43 4342 0292 **W:** www.radionasaindy.com.py **E:** AM620@pla.net.py

FM in Metro Asunción (MHz): 87.9 LV de San Juan María Viané – 88.3 R. Nemby – 88.9 R. Sembrador – 89.1 R. Conquistador – 90.1 FM Trinidad – 90.7 Ysapy – 91.1 La Estacion – 90.1 FM Trinidad – 90.7 Ysapy – 91.1 La Estacion – 91.5 R. Top Milenium – 92.3 Cardinal Romance – 92.7 R. Fernando da la Mora – 93.1 FM Florida – 93.3 R. Luque – 93.5 R. Rebelde – 93.9 FM Universal – 94.3 RRGS – 94.7 R. Azul y Oro – 95.5 Rock & Pop – 95.9 FM Amor – 96.5 R. Disney – **CA5:** Chaco 96.9 «R. Mariscal Estigarríbia» – **CA5:** 97.1 FM Latina – 97.9 R. Nuevo Tiempo – 98.5 Yacyretá – 99.1 R. City – 100.1 R. Canal 100 – 100.5 FM Arpa –100.9 Monte Carlo – 101.3 R. San Pablo – 101.5 R. Universitaria – 102.1 R. Obedira – 102.5 R. Tropicana – 102.7 Aspen Classic FM – 103.1 FM Popular – 103.5 FM SSP – 103.7 R. Lambaré – 104.1 R. Planeta – 105.1 R. Venus– 105.5 R. Continental – 106.1 FM Paraguay – 106.9 R. Urbana – 107.3 R. Maria – 25) 107.7 FM Concert

PERU

L.T: UTC -5h — **Pop:** 29.5 million — **Pr.L:** Spanish, Quechua, Aymara — **E.C:** 60Hz, 220V — **ITU:** PRU — **Int. dialling code:** +51

MINISTERIO DE TRANSPORTES, COMUNICACIONES, VIVIENDA Y CONSTRUCCION
Dirección General de Telecomunicaciones
▭ Av. 28 de Julio 800, Lima 1 ☎ +51 1433 7800, 1433 1212, 1433 0570 **W:** www.mtc.gob.pe **E:** dgt@mtcgob.pe
L.P: Dir. de Telecomunicaciones: Ing. Carlos A. Romero Sanjinés. Dir. Freq. Div: Ing. José Villa Gamboa

ASOCIACION DE RADIO Y TELEVISION DEL PERU (ARTV)
▭ Jr. Manuel Corpancho 208, Santa Beatriz, Lima ☎ +51 1433 3908, 1433 3953 **L.P:** Pres: Humberto Maldonado Balbín. Dir: Daniel Linares Bazan

INSTITUTO NACIONAL DE COMUNICACION SOCIAL
▭ Jr. de la Unión 264, Lima **L.P:** Hernán Valdizán C. Dir. Bc: Sra. Clarisa P. de Olivera

UNION DE RADIOEMISORAS DE PROVINCIAS DEL PERU (UNRAP)
▭ Mariano Carranza 754, Santa Beatriz, Lima 1

MW Call		kHz	kW	Station, location, H of tr.
LI01	OBX4E	540	1	R. Inca del Perú, Lima: 24h
LL01	OCX2D	540	1	R. San Antonio, Trujillo
LI02	OBZ4L	±560	2	R. Oriente, Lima
LA01	OBX1H	560		Radiomar, Chiclayo
LA02	OAU1M	570	1	R. Univ. Nal. Pedro Ruiz Gallo, Lambayeque
LL51	OCU2B	570		Huamachuco
CJ01	OAX2E	580	10	R. Marañón, Jaén: 1000-0400 (Sat: 1000-0200 Sun: 1000-1800)
LL02	OCY2L	580	1	R. El Sol, La Esperanza
LI03	OAX4M	580		R. Maria, Lima: 1100-0500
AQ02	OCX6V	590	1	R. Catedral, Miraflores, Arequipa
LL03	OBX2B	600	1	R. Star, Trujillo: 24h
LI04	OBZ4W	600	10	R. Cora, Lima: 24h
MO01	OCX6D	600		R. Cultural, Ilabaya
TA01	OAX6S	600		R. Cultura Toquepala, Ilabaya
CJ32	OCY2I	610	5	R. Santa Monica, Chota: 1100-0100
PI02	OBU1E	610	1	R. Santa Rosa, Sullana
AQ01	OCX6B	620	1	R. Maria, Arequipa
CU60	OAR7H	620		Apostol de Yanaoca, Yanaoca
LL04	OAX2M	620	0.4	R. Chepen, Chepen
LI05	OBU4B	620	10	R. Ovación, San Isidro
CJ04	OAU2R	634		R. Cajamarca, Cajamarca:(n.f.: 1420): 0800-0200 (Sun -0300)
LA03	OAU1Y	640	1	R. La Luz, José Leonardo Ortiz
LI06	OAZ4K	640	10	R. Del Pacifico, Lima: 1030-0430
PU01	OBX7B	640	10	R. Onda Azul, Puno. 0900-0300
AM11	OAU9D	650		Neiva
CJ67	OBU2P	650	3	R. Bendición Cristiana, Chota
LL05	OAX2N	650	1	R. Regional del Norte, Trujillo: 1000-0500
JU02	OCX4L	660	1	R. Chinchaycocha, Junin
LA04	OCX1U	660	5	R. J.II.C., Chiclayo: 1000-0500
LI07	OCX4R	660	10	R. La Inolvidable, Lima: 1100-0700
PU02	OAX7H	670	10	R. Nacional del Perú, Puno
CJ03	OCY2Y	680	5	R. San Luis, Jaén
IC01	OAX5E	680	5	Emisora del Pacifico, Ica: 1100-0600
LL06	OBX2L	680	0.5	R. Amauta, Chócope. 1100-0500
LI08	OBX4A	±680	20	R. Tigre, San Isidro
LA07	OCX1T	693	1.5	R. Horizonte, Chiclayo (n.f.: 770)
CU04	OBU7K	700	1	R. La Salle, Urubamba
JU01	OBU4J	700	1	R. La Luz, Huancayo
LL07	OCY2H	700	1	R. Sausal Superior, Sausal
LI09	OBZ4H	700	25	R. R. Integridad, San Miguel
PI04	OBX1U	700	10	R. Cutivalú "LV del Desierto", Castilla: 1030-0100 Sun.1100-0100
PI49	OCU1B	700		Sechura
SM15	OAU9A	710		R. Canal Catolica San Gabriel, Moyobamba
AQ04	OAU6L	710	1	R. Amor, Arequipa
IC02	OBX5Q	710	5	R. Programas del Perú, Ica: 1100-0600 (r.: 730)
MD01	OCX7I	‡710	10	R. Nacional del Peru, Puerto Maldonado
PU41		710		R. Surupana, Azángaro
CU05	OBU7D	720	1	R. Alegria, Wanchaq
JU04	OAU4E	720	10	R. Sideral, La Oroya
LL08	OAX2J	‡720	25	R. Nacional del Perú, Trujillo
LA06	OAU1Q	720	1	R. Frecuencia Oceánica, Lambayque
CJ05	OBU2Q	730	5	R. Maria, Cajamarca
LI10	OAX4G	730	50	R. Programas del Perú - RPP, San Isidro:24h
PI05	OAX1D	730	10	R. del Pacifico, Piura: 1100-0500
AQ05	OAX6C	740	10	R. Continental, Arequipa: 0900-0300
CU06	OBU7C	740	1	Red Latino, Cusco
JU46	OCU4X	740		R. Vision, Huancayo
LL09	OCX2X	740	1	R. El Puerto, Pascamayo
PA01	OCX4X	750	5	R. Altura, Cerro de Pasco: 1000-0400
LL01	OBX2K	760	0.5	R. Andino, Otuzco
LI11	OBZ4X	760	10	R. Mar Plus, Chorillos: 24h
AQ06	OBX6H	770	5	Radiomar, Uchumayo
LA31	OCX1T	770	1.5	R. Vision, Chiclayo: 24h
L001	OAX8M	‡770	5	LV de la Selva, Iquitos: 0950-0300, Sun: 1100-1700
PU03	OAU7D	770	2.5	R. LV del Allinccapac, Macusani
CJ07	OBU2N	780	1	R. Coremarca, Bambamarca
LI12	OAX4X	780	3	R. Victoria,Lima: 24h
PU04	OAZ7S	780	10	R. Nuevo Tiempo, Juliaca: 1000-0500
TU01	OAX1K	780	10	R. Nacional del Perú, Tumbes
CU07	OAX7H	790	5	R. La Luz, Cusco
LL11	OAX2I	790	10	R. Programas del Perú - RPP, Trujillo
AQ07	OBX6A	800	0.3	R. Porteña, Arequipa
CJ67		800		R. Vision, Cajamarca
IC03	OBX5B	‡800	1	R. Sur, Ica
JU05	OBU4D	800	1	R. Vida, Huancayo
LI13	OAU4H	800	0.5	R. La Luz, Huaral

MW	Call	kHz	kW	Station, location, h of tr.
PI06)	OCX1P	800	1	Telecom del Norte, Piura
AY19)	OBU5E	810		Huamanga: (2011)
CU70)	OAM7E	810	5	Cusco, Gregorio Huallapamayta Quispe
LL12)	OAU2G	810	1	R. Apocali, Trujillo
PU05)	OAX7V	810	10	R. Programas del Perú - RPP, Juliaca: 24h
CJ43)	OBX2J	820	0.5	R. Nuevo Continene, Cajamarca: (r. 1560)
PI54)	OBU1X	820		R. Vision, Piura
LI14)	OAX4O	820	20	R. Libertad, Lima: 1000-0900
CU08)	OAZ7U	830	1	R. Inti Raimi, Santiago: 24h
CJ62)	OCU2M	830		R. Ebenezer, Bambamarca
HV01)	OAX3Y	830	1	R. La Selva, Rupa-Rupa: (n.f.: 1280)
JU06)	OAU4C	830	1	CPN R., El Tambo: (rel. CPN)
LL13)	OCX2Y	830	1	CPN R., Trujillo: (rel. CPN)
TA02)	OAX6D	830	10	R. Nacional del Perú, Tacna
AN01)	OAX3S	840	1	R. Vision, Casma: 24h
AN25)		840		R. Campesina, Huari: 24h
AN26)	OAU3Q	840		Casma
AQ01)	OBX6Y	840	1	R. Azul, Arequipa: 24h
CJ08)	OAU2E	840	1	R. Nuevo Continente, San Ignacio: (r.: 1575): 1200-2300
CJ65)		840		R. Campesina, Cajamarca: 24h
CU58)	OCU7I	840		R. Santa Cruz, Kunturkanki
PI50)	OCU1C	840		R. Campesina (R.Ayabaca), Ayabaca
CJ57)		850		R. San Juan, El Tambo
LI15)	OAX4A	850	40	R. Nacional del Perú, Lima: 24h
TA11)	OAU6S	‡850		R. Nacional del Peru, Tarata: 1100-0100
PU35)	OBU7Z	850		R. Pachamama, Puno: 0845-0300(SS-2300)
AY01)	OAU5Q	860	5	R. Educativo Macedonia, Ayacucho
CJ09)	OAU2J	860		R. Nor Andina, Cajamarca: (rel. CPN)
PI08)	OCX1M	860	3	R. Nuevo Norte, Sullana
CU10)	OCX7R	870	1	R. Mundo, Wanchaq: 0900-1000
JU34)	OCX4D	870	2.5	R. Huancayo, Huancayo: 0900-0500
LA08)	OBX1F	870	10	R. Programas del Perú - RPP, Chiclayo: 24h
PU06)	OAU7O	870	5	R. Libertad, Puno
PI09)	OAU1G	870	1	R. San Pedro Chanel, Sullana
AY22)	OBU5W	880		Huamanga, Augusto Palomino Ramos
LL15)	OAX2P	880	1	R. Sintonia, Trujillo: 0900-0300
LI16)	OBZ4N	880	10	R. Union, Lima: 24h
CU56)	OCU7C	890		R. Laramani, Espinar
PU07)	OBX7S	890	1	R. Bahá'í del Lago Titicaca, Chiucuito: 0900-0200
CJ10)	OAU2N	890	1	R. Panorama, Cajamarca: 1000-0400
AQ11)	OBX6K	900	1	R. Nevada, Uchumayo: 24h
CJ11)	OAU2Q	900	1	R. Nor Oriental, Jaén
HU02)	OAX3E	900		R. Ribereña, Aucaycu: 1000-0500
LA09)	OCX1D	900	1	R. Sensacional, Ferreñafe: 1000-0300
LI17)	OBX4X	900	10	R. Felicidad, Lima: 1000-0300
PI52)	OCU1P	900	1	Huarmaca
AY02)	OAU5M	910	1	R. Estacion Wari, Ayacucho
CU40)	OAU7M	910	1	R. Regional, Sicuani
PU08)	OAU7G	910	1	R. Vision del Altiplano, Juliaca
CJ66)	OAM2G	910		R. Vision, Samangay
CU12)	OCX7H	920	1	R. Programas del Perú - RPP, Cusco: 24h
IC04)	OCX5C	920	0.1	R. Stelar, Chinca Alta
LL16)	OBX2S	920	1	R. Ollantay, Virú
PI10)	OBX1J	920	10	R. Programas del Peru - RPP, Piura: 24h
PU42)		920		R. Campesina, Juli: 0900-0300
SM01)	OAX9V	920	1	R. Marginal, Tocache
AQ12)	OAX6T	930	2.5	R. Yaravi, Arequipa: 0830-500
CU67)	OAM7J	930	1	Espinar
LA40)	OCU1U	930	3	Olmos
LL17)	OCX2V	930	1	R. Inti, Chepén
LI18)	OAX4E	930	5	R. Moderna "R. Papa", Lima: 24h
PU09)	OBU7T	930		R. Cadena Colca, Juliaca
CJ58)	OBX2G	940	1	R.Cutervo, Cutervo
CU13)	OBX7L	940	1.5	W.R., Wanchaq: 24h
JU08)	OBU4E	940	1	R. Comericial, Jauja
PI47)	OBU1Y	940	1	R. Studio Satelite, Tambo Grande
AN02)	OBX3S	950	1	R. Programas del Perú - RPP, Chimbote
AP12)	OBU5R	950	1	Cotabambas
SM02)	OBX9L	950	1	R. Estacón Láser, Rioja
AQ13)	OBX6S	‡960	12	R. Hispania, Mariano Melgar
CU14)	OBU7P	960		R. Concierto Santa Monica, Espinar
JU09)	OCY4V	960	1	R. Manantial, Huancayo
LA11)	OBX1Y	±960	3	R. WSP, Chiclayo: (r. on 958): 0900-0400
LI19)	OAX4D	960	10	R. Panamericana, Lima: 24h
LO02)	OBX8H	960	1	R. Diez, Iquitos
CJ13)	OAU2K	970	1	R. Lider del Norte, Cajamarca
CU15)	OAU7A	970	1	R. Tropicana, Wanchaq
IC05)	OBX5A	970	1	R. Comericial Sonora, Ica: 1100-0500
PI11)	OBX1V	970	1	R. La Capullana, Sullana: 1100-0100
PU11)	OBU7B	970	1	R. Qollasuyo, Juliaca
AQ14)	OAX6F	980	1	R. Universidad, Arequipa: 1000-0100
AY14)	OAX5K	980		R. LV de Huamanga, Huamanga
CJ42)	OCX2R	980	1	Andina R., Chota
JU10)	OBU4H	980	1	R. OBU4H, Huancayo
LA12)	OAU1N	980	1	R. Primavera, Chiclayo
PI51)	OBU1N	980		R. Campesina, Huancabamba
TA13)		980		R. Campesina, Tarata
AN04)	OBX3L	990		R. Peruana, Chimbote
CJ14)	OBX2M	990	0.5	R. Contumaza, Contumaza: 1000-0400
LI20)	OBX4J	990	12	R. Latina, Miraflores: 24h
PA07)	OCU4A	990		Huayllay
PI12)	OBU1C	990	1	R. OBU1C, Sechuar
TA04)	OAX6K	990	10	R. Continental, Tacna
AQ15)	OBX6R	1000	1	R. Edesa, Paucarpata
CJ41)	OAU2P	1000	2	R. Bambamarca, Bambamarca: (n.f.: 1530)
CU16)	OAZ7P	1000	2	R. Prensa al Dia, Cusco
HV01)	OBX5W	1000	1	R. Lircay, Lircay
HU03)	OBX3V	1000		R. Huanuco
LA13)	OAU1P	1000	1	R. San Jose, Lambayque
AM10)	OBX9T	1010	1	R. Ministerio Mundial, Utcubamba
AP01)	OAU5G	1010	1	R. Amistad, Abancay
CI15)	OBX2P	‡1010	1.5	R. San Francisco, Cajamarca
HU11)		1010		R. Bella, Tingo Maria
LI54)	OAX4U	1010	1	R. Cielo, Lima: 24h
PI13)	OBU1L	1010		LV de las Huaringas, Huancabamba: 1045-0200
TU02)	OBZ1C	1010	1	R. Sonora, Tumbes
AN06)	OBX3U	‡1020	1	R. Nacional, Chimbote
CJ41)	OAU2P	1020	2	R. Bambamarca, Bambamarca: 1000-0300
LA38)	OBX1G	1020	5	R. Heroica, Chiclay
CU17)	OBU7O	1020	1	R. Informes, Sicuani
JU11)	OBU4F	1020	1	R. Cristo Vive, Huancayo
PI14)	OBU1D	1020	1	R. La Luz, Piura
TA05)	OAU6J	1020	1	R. Internacional, Tacna
AQ16)	OCX6L	1030	1	R. Cumbia, Arequipa
CU18)	OCX7O	1030	1	R. HG-AM, Cusco
LL19)	OAX2U	1030	3	R. Los Andes, Huamachuco
PU12)	OAX7N	1030	1	R. LV del Altiplano, Puno: 1000-0400
PU38)		1030	1	R. Sillustani, Atuncolla
CJ16)	OBX2O	1040	1	R. Nor Oriente, Jaén
CU19)	OAU7H	1040	1	Multimedio Sistena de R., Espinar
IC06)	OBX5U	1040	1	R. La Luz, Ica
LI21)	OBX4O	1040	10	R. Metropolitana, Miraflores
PI15)	OAZ1D	1040	1	R. Vecinal, Piura
AQ17)	OBX6D	1050	1	R. Bethel, Arequipa
CJ56)		1050		R. Campesina, Cajamarca
JU12)	OBZ4J	1050	1	R. Bolognesi, Huancayo
LA43)	OCU1C	1050	3	R. Bendición Cristiana, Chiclay
LL20)	OCX2B	1050	1	R. Maria, Chepen
LO04)	OBX8F	1050	1	CPN R., Iquitos: (rel.: CPN)
PU13)	OAZ7Q	1050	1	R. San Augistín, Juliaca
TU03)	OAU1C	1058	5	CPN R., Tumbes: (rel.: CPN) (n.f.: 1060)
AN27)	OAU3S	1060	3	Angelica Julian Human Lourdes, Chimbote
CJ17)	OCY2O	±1060	5	R. Sudamerica, Cutervo: 1130-0300 (Sun: 1200-2300)
CU20)	OAU7U	1060		R. 1060, Cusco
LI22)	OCY4D	1060	1	R. Exito, Lima
MO02)	OAU6R	1060	1	R. La Luz, Ilo
PI41)	OBU1F	1060		R. 1060. Piura
TU03)	OAU1C	1060	5	CPN R., Tumbes: (rel.: CPN)(r.: 1058)
AU18)	OAU6K	1070	1	R. Trinidad, Arequipa: 1000-0200
HU13)	OAU3N	1070	1	Huánuco
IC07)	OAX5A	1070	0.2	R. San Juan, San Juan de Marcona
JU13)	OBX4G	1070	1	R. Visión, San Ramón
LA14)	OAU1J	1070	1	R. Vida, Chiclay
SM03)	OBX9J	1070	3	R. Andes, Tarapoto
CJ18)	OAU2L	1080	1	R. Nueva Vida, Cajamarca
CU21)	OAX7S	1080	2.2	R. Salkantay, Cusco: 0900-0400 (Sun: 1000-0200)
LI23)	OAU4I	1080	10	R. La Luz, Lima: 24h: //1200, 1340
MO03)	OCX6X	1080	1	R. Futura, Ilo
PI16)	OBX1O	±1080	1.5	R. San Miguel, Piura: 0900-0600
PU14)	OCU7O	1080	1	R. 1080, Puno
AQ19)	OBX6X	1090	1	R. Amistad, Arequipa
AY05)	OAU5F	1090	1	R. Inti Andina, Aucara
CJ19)	OBX2A	1090	1	R. Cajabamba, Cajabamba: 0900-0500
JU14)	OCY4G	1100	1	Sonorama R., Huancayo: 1100-0300
LA15)	OBX1L	‡1100	1	R. Star, Chiclayo
LI25)	OCX4S	1100	1	R. Imperial "LV de la Provincia", Cañete: 0900-0300
LI64)	OAZ4W	1100	1	R. Programas del Peru - RPP, Barranca
LL46)	OCU2E	1100	1	R. 1000, Julcan
PU15)	OBX7Z	1100	1	R. LTC, Juliaca
CJ20)	OCX2U	1110	1	R. Jaén, Jaén: 1030-0600
CU22)	OCX7T	1110	5	R. Comer, Cusco: 0900-0100 (Sun: 0900-1600)
LI24)	OAZ4W	1110	1	R. Feliz, Lima
MO04)	OCX6F	1110	1	R. Austral, Ilo
PI17)	OCX1R	1110	0.5	R. Centro Popular, La Union: 1000-0500
AQ20)	OCX6U	1120	1	R. Municipal, Cerro Colorado
AY06)	OAU5H	1120	1	R. Dif. Sonora Comunal - R. Quispillaccta, Ayacucho: 0900-1400. 2100-0100

MW	Call	kHz	kW	Station, location, h of tr.
CJ61)	OAM2F	1120		R. Dif. Cristiana RP, Chota
HV03)	OAU5W	1120		R. Huayllahuara
LL21)	OBX2I	1120	1.5	R. Dinamica, Trujillo :0900-2400
UC09)	OBX8R	1120		Rios Perez Zosimo, Campoverde
AP02)	OAU5A	1130	1	R. Armonia, Abancay: (r.: 1587): 1030-0300
CJ21)	OAX2V	1130	1.2	R. Los Andes (RPP), Cjamarca
CU65)	OAM7F	1130	5	Cusco
JU15)	OAZ4S	1130	1	R. Chanchamayo, Chanchamayo: 1000-0300
LI27)	OAX4N	1130	2.6	R. Bacán, Lince: 24h
MO09)	OBU6Q	1130	3	Angelica Julian Human Lourdes, Moquegua
PI53)	OCU1R	1130		Huarmaca: (Fpl)
PU16)	OAU7B	1130	1	R. San Gabriel, Juliaca
AN07)	OAX3R	1140	1	R. Bahia, Chimbote: 1000-0200(Sun -2200)
AQ21)	OAX6L	1140	1	R. Concordia, Arequipa: (rel.: CPN 1470)
IC02)	OAX5W	1140	0.5	R. Chinchaysuyo, Chinca Alta: 1100-0600
JU16)	OCY4C	1140	1	R. Programas del Perú - RPP, Pilcomayo
LA16)	OAU1T	1140		R. Fraternal, Ferreñafe
LL48)	OCU2D	1140		Chami R., Otuzco: 1000-0200
PI18)	OBX1W	1140	1.5	R. Piura, Piura
CJ22)	OCY2E	1150	0.5	R. Chasqui Llacta, San Marcos: 1030-2200
CU23)	OCX7Q	1150	2.5	R. Universal, Santa Monica: 1000-0400
LO06)	OAX8D	‡1150	10	R. Loreto, Iquitos
PA02)	OBU4K	1150	5	R. Mineria, Cerro de Pasco
PU17)	OAU7K	1150	2.5	R. Frontera, Juliaca:
PI44)		1153		R. Ayabaca , Ayabaca: (r.)
AY07)	OBX5O	1160	1	R. Huanta 2000, Huanta (r 1390): 1030-0130
CJ23)	OAU2T	1160	1	R. Siglo 21, Chota
LL22)	OAX2C	1160	0.3	R. Libertad Mundo, Trujillo: 1100-0400
LA17)	OCX1S	1160	1	Radiales Nor Oriental del Marañon, Chiclayo
LI56)	OAX4C	1160	5	R. 1160, Lima: 24h
MD02)	OCX7Z	1160	1	R. del Sur, Puerto Maldonado
MO05)	OBX6G	‡1160	1	R. Nacional del Perú, Moquegua
AN08)	OAZ3K	‡1170	1	R. Nor Peruana Chimbote
AQ22)	OBX6L	1170	10	R. Programas del Perú, Arequipa
CJ24)	OAU2M	1170	1	R. Layzon, Cajamarca
CU24)	OBU7F	1170		R. Bethel, Cusco
IC19)	OAU5V	1170		R. Horizonte La Voz del Agro, Pueblo Nuevo
JU17)	OCX4Y	1170	1	R. COSAT, Satipo: 1100-0200
LO07)	OBX8M	1170	1	R. La Luz, Iquitos
PI19)	OCX1B	1170	1	R. San Juan, Talara
PU18)	OCX7Y	1170	0.5	R. Constelación, Puno
CJ25)	OBU2E	1180	1	R. La Luz, Jaen
JU18)	OCY4Z	1180	1	R. Libertad "R.RLJ", Junin
LI62)	OCE4K	1180		NSE Radio, Lima
LL23)	OCX2A	1180	1	R. Americana, Quiruvilca
PI20)	OAZ1C	1180	1	R. Chulucanas, Chulucanas
TA14)	OBU6J	1180	1	R. Corporacion Plus & Plus, Pocoally
AN09)	OBX3D	1190	5	R. Ancash, Huaraz
AQ23)	OCX6G	1190	1.5	R. Alas Peruanas
LA18)	OAX1E	1190	10	R. Em. del Pacifico, Chiclayo
CU25)	OAX7B	1190	2	R. Tawantinsuyo, Cusco: 1000-0300
PU43)	OCU1S	1190	3	R. OCU1S. Tumbes
AP03)	OBX5X	1200	1	R. Comercial, Abancay
CJ26)	OAU2A	1200	1	Frecuencia Pedagogica, Cajamarca
JU19)	OAU4G	1200	3	R. Andes, Huancayo
LI60)	OAX4B	1200	1	Cadena R. 1200, Lima
PI45)	OAU1Q	1200	1	R. San Andres, Tambogrande
PU19)	OCX7S	1200	1	R. Cultura, Juliaca
TA06)	OAU6P	1200		R. La Luz, Tacna
UC01)	OBX8N	1200		R. La Luz, Pucallpa
CU26)	OAX7M	1210	1	R. Quillabamba, Quillabamba: 1000-0300
CU55)	OCU7B	1210		R. Santo Tomas
HU12)	OBX3X	1210		Huanuco (F.P.I.)
JU20)	OCY4T	1210	1	R. Galaxia, Satipo
LL24)	OAX2Q	1210	1	R. Universo, Trujillo: 24h
LO05)	OAX8A	1210	5	R. Nacional del Perú, Iquitos: 1100-0500
PI21)		1210	1	R. Municipalidad, Ayabaca
AQ24)	OAX6X	1220	4	R. Melodia, Arequipa: 24h
CU02)	OAU7N	1220	1	R. Univ. Nal. San Antonio Abad, Cusco
IC09)	OAU5N	1220	1	R. La Luz, Ica
IC20)	OBU5I	1220		R. Amor y Paz, Pisco
LA19)	OCX1X	1220	1	R. Libertad, Chiclayo: 0900-0400
LI63)	OCU4H	1220		R. Fe, Lima
JU21)	OBZ4Y	1230	1	R. Selecciones,Tarma: 1100-0200(Sun -1800)
LI65)	OCU4C	1230		R. La Luz, Huacho
LL25)	OAX2T	1230	1	R. Albújar, Guadalupe: 1200-0400
MD03)	OBX7J	1230	0.5	R. Madre de Dios, Puerto Maldonado: 1000(Sun 1100)-0200
PA03)	OBX4Z	‡1230	1	R. LV de Oxapampa, Oxapampa
PU20)	OAU7V	1230	1	R. Frecuencia Amistad, Juliaca
AM01)	OBX9O	1230		R. Bagua Grande
AN10)	OAU3C	1240	1	R. La Luz, Chimbote
AQ25)	OAU6D	1240	5	R. Lider, Arequipa
CU27)	OBX7M	1240		R. Pachatusán, Sicuani: 1000-0100
IC10)	OAU5U	1240		R. Eco, Ica
JU22)	OAU4V	1240	10	R. Maria, Chilca: 24h
LL26)	OAU2Y	1240	1	R. Nor Andino, Santiago de Chuco, Trujillo
PI52)	OCX1C	1240		R.Campesina, Ayaviri
CJ27)	OAU2V	1250	1	HGV, Santa Cruz
CU28)	OBX7A	1250	3	R. Solar, Cusco: 1000-0500
LI30)	OAX4L	1250	5	R. Miraflores, Miraflores: 24h
MO08)	OAU6I	1250		R. Campesina, Omate
PI23)	OBZ1B	1250	1	R.B.N.S., Talara Alta
SM07)	OAX9C	1250	1	R. Americana, Rioja
UC02)	OAX8P	1250	1	R. Pucallpa, Pucallpa: 1030-0500
UC09)	OBX8S	1250	3	Angelica Julian Human Lourdes, De Calleria
PI43)		1258		R. Centinela, Huancabamba (r.)
AN11)	OAU3G	1260	1	R. Pregonero Cristiano, Chimbote
AQ26)	OBX6D	1260	1	R. Mundial, Arequipa
AQ51)		1260	1	R. Mahanaim, Mollendo
HU04)	OAU3F	1260	1	R. La Luz, Huanuco
LA20)	OCX10	1260	1	R. Nor Puruana, Chiclayo
LA21)	OAZ1A	1260	1	R. Ferrañafe, Ferrañafe
LL49)	OBX2C	1260	1	Telesistema Peruano, Otuzco
AY08)	OBX5S	1260	0.3	R. Nacional del Perú, Ayacucho
CU30)	OAU7S	1260	2	R. Horizonte, Cusco
JU23)	OBZ4T	1270	0.4	R. La Merced, Chanchamayo: 1100-1900, 2200-0200 (Sun 1200-1900)
LL28)	OCX2Z	1270	1	R. Estacion Latina, Cepén
LI31)	OAZ4H	1270	0.4	R. Huacho, Huacho
LO08)	OAX8T	1270	1	R. Eco, Iquitos: 0900-0400
PI24)	OAU1S	1270	1	R. Nor Paita, Paita
LA22)	OAU1R	‡1276	1	R. Gotas del Oro, Urrunaga: (n.f.: 1280): 0900-0500
AN12)	OBX3C	‡1280		R. Alopesa, Chimbote
AQ27)	OBX6P	1280	0.5	R. Fénix, Camaná
AQ28)	OCX6B	1280	1	R. Trebol, Mariano Melgar: (r.) (nf. 1290)
CJ28)	OBX2F	1280	1	R. Moderna, Cajamarca: 1000-0400 (Sun: 0300)
CU29)	OAU7K	1280	1	R. Stereo Nevada, Espinar
CU61)	OCU7R	1280	1	R. Ministerio Mundial, Sicuani
HU01)	OAX3Y	1280	1	R. La Selva, Rupa-Rupa (r: 830)
LA22)	OAU1R	1280	1	R. Gotas del Oro, Urrunaga (r: 1276)
AM02)	OAX9N	‡1290	10	R. Nor Oriental, Bagua Grande
AQ28)	OCX6B	1290	1	R. Trebol, Mariano Melgar (r. 1280)
AY20)	OBU5W	1290	1	Ayacucho
CJ69)	OAM2C	1290	1	R. Esetlar, Chota
JU24)	OBU4S	1290	1	R. 1290, La Oroya
LI32)	OBU4Q	1290	1	S & RD, Hualmay
PI42)		1290		R. Satelite, La Union
PU21)	OAX7X	1290	0.3	R. Juliaca, Juliaca: 0900-0300 (nf. on 1300)
TU04)	OCX1Q	1290	1	R. Programas del Perú, Tumbes: 24h
AN13)	OAX3O	1300	0.5	R. Huascarán, Independencia: 1100-0300
CJ29)	OAU2I	1300	1	R. Paraiso, Cajabamba
CU31)	OAX7P	1300	5	R. Onda Imperial, Cusco: 1200-2130
JU25)	OAZ4B	±1300	1	R. Andina, Huancayo: 0900-1400 (Sun: 1000-0300)
LA23)	OAU1U	1300	1	R. Frecuencia Lider, Morrop
LI33)	OAX4S	1300	5	R. Comas, Comas: 1000-0500
PU21)	OAX7X	1300	0.3	R. Juliaca, Juliaca(r. 1290)
SM08)	OBX9P	‡1300		R. La Luz, Tarapoto
TA07)	OAX6P	1300	0.4	R. Comercial Latina, Tacna (rel.: RPP 730)
UC03)	OAZ8B	1300		R. Nuevo Mundo, Pucallpa
AQ50)	OUA6N	1310	6	R. Libertad, Arequipa
AY21)	OBU5X	1310	2	Ayacucho
CJ30)	OBX2D	1310	1	R. Chota, Chota: 1100-0300
LI34)	OBX4L	1310	1	R. Irvisa, Huacho
LO09)	OBX8L	1310	1	R. Vision Amazonia (R. MIVIA), Iquitos
AN14)	OAX3U	‡1320	1	R. Miramar, Chimbote
JU26)	OBU4T	1320	1	R. Corporacion, Huancayo
LA24)	OBU1S	1320	1	R. Frecuencia Popular, Olmos
LI55)	OAX4I	1320	1	R. La Cronica, Lima//R. Nacional 850
PU22)	OAU7W	1320	3	R. Peru, Juliaca: -0300
AQ30)	OVX6E	1330	1	R. Ondas del Misti, Mariano Melgar
AY09)	OAU5L	1330	0.5	R. Bethel, Huamanga
CU32)	OCX7K	1330	1	R. San Miguel, Wanchaq: 0900-0300 (Sun:1100-0200)
LA25)	OAU1A	1330	1	R. Dos Mil, Chiclayo: 1000-0400
AN15)	OAU3E	1340	1	Assn. Iglesia de Dios, Chimbote
AQ31)	OAU2S	1340	1	R. Shalom, Cajamarca
IC11)	OAX5D	1340	0.5	R. Chinca, Chinca Alta
JU27)	OAU4N	1340	1	R. Jauja, Jauja: 0900-0300
LI35)	OAQ4Q	1340	2	R. Alegria, Pucasana: //1080,1200
PU23)	OBU7V	1340	1	R. Sudamericana, Juliaca
AY17)	OBU5O	1340		Huamanga
CU33)	OBU7E	1350	1	R.Santa Beatriz, Cusco
LA31)	OAU1H	1350	1	R. Vision, Chiclayo: 24h
MO06)	OBX6F	1350	1	R. Ilo, Ilo: 24h
UC04)	OBX8D	1350	1	R. Super, Pucallpa: 1030-0500
HU05)	OAX3N	‡1352	1	R. Ondas del Huallaga, Huanuco: 0930 (Sun:1100)-0300: (n.f.: 1350)

MW	Call	kHz	kW	Station, location, h of tr.
AN16)	OAU3A	1360	0.2	R. Intercontinental, Yungay
AQ32)	OCX6T	1360	1	R. Luza, Paucarpata
CU34)	OAX7R	±1360	2.5	R. Sicuani, Sicuani: (r: v1362): 0900-0300
IC12)	OBZ5Z	1360	1	R. Cruz del Sur, Palpa: 1030-0300
JU28)	OAU4O	1360	1	R. Hecabut, Tarma
LL31)	OBX2N	1360	1	R. Super Uno, Santiago de Cao
LI58)	OAX4I	1360		R. Nueva Q-FM, Lima
PI25)	OBZ1A	1360		R. del Norte, Sullana
PU24)	OUA7L	1360	2.5	R. Continente, Juliaca
AP05)	OCX5A	1370	1	Inti R., Abanacy
CJ47)	OBU2U	1370		R. Satelite, Santa Cruz
CU35)	OAZ7J	1370	1	R. Santa Monica, Wanchaq: 0900-0300
LA27)	OAU1W	1370	1	R. Chiclayo, Chiclayo
LI37)	OAZ40	1370	0.5	R. Tres de Octubre (R.Cosmos), Huacho
MO07)	OAX6T	1370		R. Moquegua, Moquegua: 0930-0500
SM09)	OBX9A	1370		R. Palmera: 1100-0500
AQ33)	OAX6O	1380	2.5	R. San Martin, Arequipa: 1000-0130
CJ33)	OAXZW	±1380	1	R. Atahualpa, Cajamarca: 1100-0500
JU29)	OBU4L	1380	1	R. Chilca, Huancayo
LI38)	OCY4U	1380	1	R. Nuevo Tiempo, Lima
LL52)		1380		R. Fraternidad, Trujillo
PI26)	OBZ1D	1380	1	R. Bellavista, Bellavista
HU06)	OBX3I	±1382	1	R. Pilco Mozo, Huanuco: (n.f.: 1380)
AQ34)	OAU6Q	1390		Difusora Neptuno, Mollendo
AY07)	OBX5O	1390	1	R. Huanta 2000, Huanta: (n.f.:1160)
CJ70)	OBU2O	1390		Frequencia del Norte, Santa Cruz
CU36)	OAU7T	1390	1	R. Enlace, Kunturkanki: 1000-0300
CU69)	OAM7A	1390	3	Telecom Ingenieros S.A.C., Sicuani
LL32)	OAU2Z	1390	1	R. La Luz, Trujillo
LA28)	OAU1V	1390	1	R. Tropical, Morrope
LA41)	OCU1G	1390	1	R. Fe, Chiclayo
PU25)	OCX7U	1390	1	R. Cultura, Yunguyo
AQ35)	OAX6J	1400	0.5	R. Landa, Arequipa
CA34)	OAU2H	1400	1	R. OAU2H, Cajamarca
CU37)	OAX7I	1400	1	R. La Hora, Cuzco: 1000-0200 (Sun: 1100-1700)
IC13)	OCX5B	1400	1	R. Interandina, Pisco: 24h
JU30)	OBX4H	1400	1	R. Luz, Tarma
LI39)	OBX4W	1400	2.5	R. Callao Super, Lima
PI27)	OCX1A	1400	1	R. MDY, Talara Alta: 1000-0600
CJ64)	OCU2Q	1410		San Marcos
LL33)	OAX2Y	1410	1	R. Heróica, Trujillo
LA29)	OBU1G	1410	1	R. Olmos, Olomos
LI40)	OBZ4V	1410	1	R. Universal, Santa Maria
LI57)	OBZ4C	1410		R. Bethel, Huacho
PU26)	OBU7A	1410	1	R. La Luz (R.Grégor), Juliaca
TU05)	OBU1H	1410	1	R. La Luz, Tumbes
UC05)	OBX8I	1410		Dif. Comercial, Pucallpa
CJ04)	OAU2R	1420		R. Cajamarca, Cajamarca: (r. 634)
CJ38)	OBX2V	1420	5	R. Ilucan, Cutervo: (r. 1476): 1100-0300 (Sun 1030-2300)
CU38)	OBU7L	1420		R. OBU7L, Yanaoca
LI41)	OBZ4G	1420	1	R. San Isidro, Lima
LO10)	OAZ8Z	1420	1	R. Oriente, Yurimaguas: 1000-0200
PI28)	OCX1H	1426	0.2	R. San Jose, La Union: 0900-0100 (n.f. 1420)
AM03)	OBX9H	1430	1	R. Utcubamba, Bagua Grande
AN17)	OBX3E	1430	1	R. Huarmey, Huarmey
CU39)	OAZ7M	1430	1	CPN R., Cusco
JU31)	OAZ4V	1430	0.5	R. Universal, El Tambo: 1100-0500
LA39)		1430		R. Nueva Juventud, Tucumé
LL34)	OBX2T	1430	1	R. Santa Bárbara, Ascope
LI42)	OCU4L	1430		San Vicente de Cañete
PU27)	OBU7U	1430	1	R. Red, Andina
TA08)	OAU6M	1430	1	R. Lider, Tacna
AN19)	OAZ3O	1440	1	R. LV de Pomabamba, Pomabamba
AQ19)	OAX6R	1440		R. Santa Monica, Arequipa
CJ35)	OAU2O	1440	1	LV de Celendin, Celendin
CU71)	OAM7L	1440		R. Solar, Espinar
LA30)	OBX1T	1440	2	R. Cooperativa Tumán, Chiclayo: 1100-0300
LI43)	OAX4K	1440	1	R. Imperial 2, Lima
CJ59)		1450		R. Super Nueva Sencacion, Chirinos
CJ36)	OAU2W	1450	1	R. San Miguel, Cajamarca: 09000400
CU41)	OCX7W	1450	1	R. Santa Rosa, Santa Ana
JU45)	OBU4Y	1450		Rdif. E.G.C S.R.L., Huancayo
LL35)	OCX2J	1450	1.5	R. San Juan, Trujillo: 0900-0600
LI44)	OBX4K	1450	1	R. Fortaleza, Barranca
PA08)	OAM4A	1450	1	Tinyahuarco
PI29)	OAX1V	1457	1	R. Sullana "LV de Chira", Sullana: (n.f. 1460)
CJ36)	OAU2W	1458	1	R. San Miguel, San Miguel: (n.f.: 1450)
AQ37)	OBX6C	1460	1	R. Bahia, Mollendo
CJ37)	OBU2E	1460		R. Comercial, Jaén
CU42)	OBU7M	1460	1	R. OBU7M, Marcapata
IC14)	OAX5K	1460	2.5	R. Internacional, Pisco
JU32)	OCY4I	1460	0.5	R. Imperial, Junin
JU33)	OAZ4F	1460	1	R. La Oroya, La Oroya: 1000-0500
PI29)	OAX1V	1460	1	R. Sullana "LV de Chira", Sullana: (r: 1457)
PU28)	OAX7W	1460	10	R. El Sol de los Andes, Juliaca
AQ38)	OAU6E	1470	1	R. Victoria, Arequipa
JU48)	OCY4Y	1470		R. Voz Cristiana, Huancayo
LL37)	OCX2G	1470	1	R. Occidente, Quiruvilca
LI45)	OAU4B	1470	20	R. Amor, Lima
TA09)	OAX6M	1470	0.8	R. Tacna, Tacna: 0900-0500
CJ38)	OBX2V	1476	5	R. Ilucan, Cutervo: (n.f.: 1420)
CU44)	OAZ7G	1480	1	R. Espinar, Yauri
CJ44)	OBU2H	1480	0.5	R. San Lorenzo, Socota: (r. 1584)
JU35)	OAU4A	1480	1	R. Laser, Santa Rosa de Sacco: 1100-2300
LL38)	OCX2C	1480	0.6	R. Comercial, Virú
LI46)	OCX4V	1480	1	R. K´ler, Paramonga
PI30)	OCX1L	1480	1	R. Supercontinental, Chulucanas: 1100-0500
AQ39)	OAX6Q	1490.1	3	R. Minuto, Cerro Colorado
AP10)	OBU5C	1490		Radiodifusora los Chankas, Andahuaylas
CU45)	OBU7I	1490	1	R. Chaski, Maras: 1000-2300. 0000-0200
IC15)	OAX5N	1490	0.3	R. Nazca, Nazca
LA31)	OAX1L	±1490	1	R. Vision, Chiclayo: 0845-0500
PA04)	OBU4N	1490	1	R. La Luz, Cerro de Pasco
PU29)	OCX7P	1490	1	R. Emisora Frontera, Puno
CJ39)	OBU2J	1500		R. San Pablo, San Pablo
HU07)	OBX3J	1500	1	R. Luz y Sonido, Huanuco: 0900-0300
JU36)	OAU4W	1500	1	R. Wanka, Huancayo:
LL39)	OBX2X	1500	1	R. Comercial, Trujillo: 0845-0300
LI47)	OBX4I	±1500	10	R. Santa Rosa, Líma
TA10)	OAU6B	1500	1	R. Bulevar, Tacna
AQ40)	OCX6Q	±1510	1	R. Alegria, Arequipa: 24h
CJ40)	OCX2O	1510		R. Inca, Los Baños del Inca: 0900-0300 (r.: 1517)
IC16)	OAX5F	1510	1	R. LV Huamanga, Nazca:
JU37)	OCX4J	1510	1	R. Tarma, Tarma: 1000-0400
LL40)	OAU2U	1510	2.5	R. Virgin de la Alta Gracia, Huamachuco
LA32)	OBU1B	1510	1	R. Super Real, Olmos
LI66)	OAU4M	1510	3	Cerro Laguna
TU06)	OCX1V	1510	1	R. Tumbes, Tumbes
UC06)	OBX8K	1510	1	R. Centro de los Medios, Sepahua
CJ40)	OCX2O	1517	1	R. Inca, Los Baños del Inca: 0900-0300 (n.f.: 1510)
CU48)	OBU7X	1520		R. Fuentes Mollo, Espinar
LA26)	OAU1H	1520		R. Cristal, Chiclayo
PU30)	OAU7Y	1520	5	R. OAU7Y, Juliaca
SM11)	OAX9X	1520	1	R. Vision, Janjui: (r.: 1545)
AN21)	OBX3H	1530	1	CPN R., Chimbote: (rel.: CPN)
CJ06)	OBX2R	1530	3	R. Oriental, Jaén
CU49)	OAZ7F	1530	0.5	Rdif. Espinar (R. Confraternidad), Yauri
CU50)	OBU7N	1530		R. Ondas del Sur Oriente, Quillabamba
IC17)	OAU5R	1530		R. Universidad, San Juan Bautista
JU38)	OBZ4S	1530	1	R. 15-50, Huancayo: 1000-0600
LI49)	OBU4C	1530	10	R. Milenia, Lima
PI31)	OCX1Y	1530	1	R. Leomar, Bellavista
PU39)		1530		R. Capachica, Capachica
AQ41)	OAU6A	1540	1	R. Milenio Universal, Arequipa: 24h
CJ63)	OCU2X	1540	5	R.Turbomix, Cajamarca
CU51)	OCX7V	1540	1	R. Los Andes, Cusco
LL42)	OBU2A	1540	2	R. Mundial AM, Trujillo
LI50)	OBZ4U	±1540	1	R. Barranca, Barranca
PA05)	OBX4N	1540	0.3	R. Corporacion, Cerro de Pasco: 0900-0500
TU07)	OBX1B	1540	1	R. LV de la Frontera, Tumbes
SM11)	OAX9X	1545	1	R. Vision, Janjui: (n.f.: 1520)
AN22)	OAU3D	±1550	1	R. Cruz, Chimbote
AY10)	OBX5J	1550	1	R. Maria, Carmen Alto
JU38)	OBZ4S	1550	1	R. 15-50, Huancayo: 1000-0600 (n.f. 1530)
LA34)	OAX1D	1550	1	R. Superior, Monsefú: 1100-0400
LI51)	OBX4P	1550	1	R. Independencia, Lima
AQ42)	OCX6N	1560	1	R. La Luz, Arequipa
CJ43)	OBX2J	1560	0.5	R. Nuvo Continente, Cajamarca: 1000-0300 (n.f.: 820)
CU52)	OAZ7N	1560	1	R. Maria, Wanchaq
LO13)	OBX8O	1560		R. Nuevo Mundo, Iquitos: 1100-0500
JU39)	OBU4G	1560	1	R. San Sebastian, Yauyos
PU32)	OAU7Z	1560	1.5	R. Carráviz, Juliaca
CJ44)	OBU2H	1564	0.5	R. San Lorenzo, Socota: (n.f.: 1480)
AN23)	OBX3N	1570	1	R. Chasqui, Yungay
AQ43)	OCX6I	1570		R. Willy, Uraca
CJ54)	OBU2L	1570		R. Colonial, Contumaza
CU62)	OCU7L	1570	1	R. Vilcanota, Sicuani
HU08)	OBX3M	1570	1	R. San Martin, Huanuco
LI59)		1570		R. Bethel, Lima
LL47)	OCU2C	1570		Radiodifusora Julcan
PI32)	OCX1Z	1570	1	R. La Nueva Esperanza, Tambo Grande
LA36)	OAX5T	1575	3/1	R. Naylamp, Lambayeque: (n.f.: 1580)
CJ08)	OAU2E	1575	1	R. Nuevo Continente, San Ignacio: 1200-2300 (n.f.: 840)
HV02)	OAU5J	1580	1	R. Virgen del Carmen, Huancavelica: 24h
JU40)	OAU4P	1580	1	R. San Juan, Tarma: 1030-0230 (Sun: 1100-2100)
LA36)	OBX1M	1580	3/1	R. Naylamp, Lambayeque: 1000-0200 (r. 1575)

MW	Call	kHzkW	Station, location, h of tr.
SM12)		1580	1 R. Central, Bellavista: 1100-0300
CU53)	OBX7Q	1584 0.5	R. El Triunfo, Cusco: (n.f.:1580)
AP02)	OAU5A	1587	1 R. Armonia, Abancay: 1030-0300 (n.f. 1130)
AQ44)	OCX6S	1590	1 R. Mundo, Arequipa
CJ68)		1590	R. Municipal, San Marcos
LL43)	OBU2C	1590	1 Agro R., Trujillo
LI52)	OAZ4Z	1590	2 R. Agricultura "La Peruanísima", Lima
PU33)	OAU7C	1590	1 R. Huaynaroque, Juliaca
CJ45)	OCY2D	1590	1 R. Int., San Pablo: 1000-1700, 2100-0300
JU44)	OBU4R	1600	R. Nuevo Tiempo, Huancayo: 1000-0500
PI46)		1600	R. San Juan, Catacaos
AQ45)	OAU6O	1610 0.5	R. Flor de los Andes, José Luis Bustamente y Rivero: (R. El Sabor, Arequipa)
LL45)		1610	R. Carabamba, Julcán (r.)

SW	Call	kHzkW	Station, location, h of tr.
HU09)		±3173	R. Municipal, Panao: 0900-1100, 2300-0200
HU07)	OAW3A	±3235	1 R. Luz y Sonido, Huánuco
HU05)	OAX3Q	±3330	5 R. Ondas del Huallaga, Huánuco: 1030-0030±
LI61)	OAW4Y	3355	1 R. JPJ, Lima; (irr.)
AQ46)	OAW6B	3375	1 R. San Antonio, Callalli: (irr.)
HU14)		4300	R. Bella, Tingo Maria
AY07)	OAZ5B	‡4747 0.5	R. Huanta 2000, Huanta: (n.f.: 4755): 1100-0100
PI13)		‡4750	R. San Francisco Solano, Sondor: (irr)
JU37)	OCX4W	4775 0.5	R. Tarma, Tarma: 1000-0400
CU64)	OAW7I	4780	Cusco
CJ47)	OAX2L	‡4781	1 R. Satelite, Santa Cruz: 2300-0300
LA31)		4790 0.5	R. Vision, Chiclayo: 24h
CU68)	OAW7J	4800	1 Cusco
SM14)	OAW9A	4810	1 Iglesia Evangelica Central de Chazuta, Chazuta
LO01)	OAX8R	4824 10	LV de la Selva, Iquitos
CU34)	OAX7T	‡4826 0.3	R. Sicuani "LV de Canchis", Sicuani: 1030-0300 (n.f.:4835)
CJ01)	OCX2E	4835	1 R. Marañon, Jaen: 1100-0200
AY17)	OAW5E	4850	1 R. Genesis, Huanta
CU37)	OAZ7A	‡4856	1 R. La Hora, Cusco: irr
HV02)	OAX5X	4887	1 R. Virgen del Carmen, Huancavelica: (nf: 4885), irr
UC07)	OAW8A	4940	1 R. San Antonio, Villa Atalaya: 2200-0030 (irr)
MD03)	OBX7I	4950	5 R. Madre de Dios, Puerto Maldonado: 1000(Sun: 1100)-0200
AY13)	OAX5S	4955	5 R. Cultural Amauta, Huanta: 1000-1400, 2100-0100
CU32)	OAZ7B	‡4965	1 R. Santa Monica, Wanchaq
LI06)	OAZ4X	±4975	5 R. Pacifico, Lima
AN09)	OAZ3B	4992	5 R. Ancash, Huaraz: (n.f.: 4990)(irr.)
JU09)		4987	R. Voz Cristiana (R. Manantial), Huancayo
PA01)	OBZ4B	5014	1 R. Altura, Cerro de Pasco
AM04)	OBX9K	±5020	5 R. Horizonte, Chachapoyas: 1100-0200
CU26)	OAX7Q	5025	5 R. Quillabamba, Quillabamba: 1000-0200
JU18)	OCY4Y	5039	1 R. Libertad de Junin, Junín: 1100-1400
PI13)	OAW1B	5059	LV de las Huarinjas, Huancabamba
CU50)		5120	1 R. Ondas del Sur Oriente, Quillabamba: 1000-0300
LL26)		5460	R. LV Bolivar, Bolivar: 2330-0130
LA24)		5485	R. Frecuencia Popular: 2330-0200 (r)
AM06)		5487	Reina de la Selva, Chachapoyas
AQ17)	OAX6A	5921	1 R. Bethel, Arequipa: (r.): 1045-0100
AQ24)	OBX6I	±5939	1 R. Melodia, Arequipa
LI12)	OAX4Q	±6020	3 R. Victoria, Lima
LI47)	OCY4H	±6047 10	R. Santa Rosa, Lima
JU47)	OAD4D	6060	Aroma Cafe R., Pichanaki
CU23)	OAZ7Q	6088 1.5	R. Universal, Santa Monica
LI16)	OBZ4O	±6115 10	R. Union, Lima: 24h
CU25)	OAX7C	6174	1 R. Tawantinsuyo, Cusco(nf: 6175): 24h
LO10)	OAX8I	‡6188	1 R. Oriente, Yurimaguas: 1000-0300 (n.f.:6190)
LI06)		9675	5 R. Pacifico, Lima: 1400-2300
LI12)	OCX4C	±9722	1 R. Victoria, Lima

° = on-air stn name not confirmed, ‡ = inactive, ± = varying freq.

Addresses and other information:
NB: Names of *departamentos* should be added to addresses.
AM00 (AMAZONAS):
AM01) Av Circunvalacion 1336, Bagua Grande – **AM02)** Simón Bolívar 433, Bagua Grande – **AM03)** Jr F Villareal 400, Utcubamba – **FM:** 96.9MHz – **AM04)** Jr Amazonas 1717 (Ap 69), Chachapoyas ☎41 777793 📠41 757004. **E:** rhorizonte@hotmail.com – **FM:** 99.9MHz – **AM05)** Jr Huayabamba 513, San Nicolas, Prov Rodríguez de Mendoza – **AM06)** Calle Ayacucho 944, Plaza Mayor, Chachapoyas ☎41 477203 📠41 477989 **W:** www.reinadelaselva.com – **E:** joreno@terra.com.pe - **FM:** 101.5MHz – **AM07)** Jr Amazonas 315, Aramango, Prov de Bagua – **AM10)** Calle Higos Urcos 651, Bagua Grande, Utcubamba – **AM11)** Av.Gonzalo Puerta s/n, Distrito de Neiva, Prov. de Condorcanqui
AN00 (ANCASH):
AN01) Av Nepeña Mza 8-C, Lote 3, Casma ☎4371 1266 **W:** www.

visionradioperu.com - **FM:** 93.7 MHz – **AN02)** Av Francisco Pizzarro, Chimbote - **FM:** 95.5MHz – **AN04)** Urb el Trapecio 2da etapa, MZ G, Lote 18, Chimbote - **FM:** 97.5MHz – **AN05)** Manzana 8 Lote Ind Primero de Mayo, Chimbote - **FM:** 105.1MHz – **AN07)** Pasaje los Jardines 129, Chimbote ☎4332 2391 – **AN08)** Pasaje Los Jardines 129, Chimbote - **FM:** 104.3MHz – **AN09)** Jr Francisco Araos 114 Independencia, Huaraz **W:** www.radioancash.org **E:** info@radioancash.org ☎4342 1381 📠4342 29992 - **FM:** 101.3MHz – **AN10)** Av Enrique Meiggs 2013, Chimbote.- ☎43 805591 - **FM:** 89.9MHz – **AN11)** Calle Ramon Castilla MZ.J, Lote 11, Chimbote – **AN12)** Av Leoncio Prado 660, Chimbote - **FM:** 89.9MHz – **AN13)** Jr San Martin 655, Huaraz - **FM:** 104.5MHz – **AN14)** San pedro 246, Chimbote ☎4332 2279 - **FM:** 106.7MHz – **AN15)** Av Pardo 6788 ,1° de Mayo, Nuvo Chimbote **W:** www.iglesia-dios.org **E:** pastorvalle@hotmail.com – **AN16)** Casero el Rayan, Yungay – **AN17)** Av Cabo Alberto Reyes 281, Huarmey - **FM:** 89.7MHz – **AN18)** Urb San Juan ZN 5, Chimbote - **FM:** 92.3MHz – **AN19)** Zona Cushuro, Pomabamba – **AN21)** Calle Aviación 298, Chimbote - **FM:** 103.5MHz – **AN22)** Jr Alfonso Ugarte 627 4° piso, Chimbote – **AN23)** Barrio Lucmapampa, Yungay – **AN24)** Plaza de Armas S/N, Chiquian – **AN25)** Huari **W:** www.agrorural.gob.pe/radio-huari-de-ancash.html – **AN26)** Tabon Alta, Fundo El Milagro, Casma – **AN27)** Av. Jorge Chávez no 364, Distr Chimbote, Prov. de Santa
AP00 (APURIMAC):
AP01) Av Scoonc s/n, Abancay – **AP02)** Jr Cusco 319, Abancay - **FM:** 92.1MHz – **AP03)** Av Nuñez 401, Abancay – **AP05)** Av Seoane 337, Region Inca, Abancay 970 5246 **W:** www.corporacionsolar.com **E:** inti-radio@corporacionsolar.com - **FM:** 103.3 Solar FM – **AP06)** Jr Apurimac s/n, Chincheros – **AP07)** Jr Cuzco 206, Abancay - **FM:** 104.5MHz – **AP08)** Guillermo Cáceres Tresierra 381, Andahuaylas ☎83 721511 – **FM:** 94.9MHz – **AP10)** Jr.Juan Antonio Trelles 278, Andahuaylas ☎83 421208 **E:** rnnalripa@yahoo.es – **FM:** 100.3MHz – **AP11)** Tres Cruces, Ocobamba, Provincia de Chincheros – **AP12)** Av.Cristo de Los Andes, Barrio El Salvador, Challhuahuacho, Cotabamba
AQ00 (AREQUIPA):
AQ01) Calle San Juan de Dios 210, Zona Alto, Arequipa 95 9871 242 **W:** www.radioazularequipaperu.com **E:** radioazulamffm@hotmail.com - **FM:** 89.5MHz – **AQ02)** Av Goyeneche 818, Miraflores, Arequipa – **AQ03)** Lote 64-5-C Km 48 Panamericana Sur, La Joya – **AQ04)** CI Dean Valdivia 418, Of.25, Urb Cercado, Arequipa ☎5480 7362 – **AQ05)** Av Independencia 600, Arequipa ☎54 224109 - **FM:** 93.5MHz – **AQ06)** Cruce Ferroc, Puno Variante, Uchumayo – **AQ07)** Calle Alto de la Luna 334, Arequipa – **AQ09)** Calle Francia 120, Urb Satélite Chico-Paucarpata, Arequipa ☎ 54 424237 - Quechua: Sun 0830-1030 - **FM:** 103.5MHz – **AQ11)** Av Victor A Belaúnde C-8, Umacollo, Arequipa ☎54 255888 📠54 251822 - **FM:** 97.1MHz – **AQ12)** Calle Los Robles 139, Urb. Orrantia, Arequipa ☎54 289952 – Quechua: Sat.2h **W:** www.radoyaravi.org.pe **E:** prensa@radioyaravi.org.pe - **FM:** 106.3MHz – **AQ13)** Calle Consuelo 404, Depto A, Arequipa ☎54 219928 - **FM:** 98.5MHz in Majes, 102.1 in Tacna – **AQ14)** Av Independencia s/n 2° piso, Pabellón de la Cultura, Ciudad Universitaria (Cas 23), Arequipa. ☎ 54 287771 **W:** www.unsa.edu.pe **E:** radiouniversidad@unsa.edu.pe – **AQ15)** At 200 Millas La Pina, Paucarpata – **AQ16)** Av Independncia 905 - 2do piso, Arequipa ☎54 204904 **W:** santamonica.blogdiario.com - **FM:** 107.7MHz – **AQ17)** Av Union 225, Miraflores, Arequipa (Also in Lima: LI59) **W:** www.bethelradio.fm **E:** betheltradio@bethelradio.com – **AQ18)** Av. La Paz 504, Arequipa ☎54 204847 **Quechua:** 1000-1200 – **AQ19)** Av Independencia 905, Arequipa ☎54 201904 – **AQ20)** Calle Mariano Melgar 500, Cerro Colorado, Prov de Arequipa – **AQ21)** Av.La Paz 512, Arequipa ☎54 446053 - **FM:** 95.8MHz – **AQ22)** Av La Paz 511 "A", Of 312 – 3er piso, Arequipa ☎54 287821 – **AQ23)** Av La Salle 124, José Luis Bustamente y Rivero, Urb Daniel Alcides Carrión G-14 ☎54 431051 – **AQ24)** Calle San Camilo 501-A Cercado, Arequipa ☎54 205811 📠54 204200 **W:** www.radiomelodia.com - **FM:** 104.3MHz – **AQ25)** Av Independencia 1819, Arequipa ☎54 286438 **E:** lideraqp@gmail.com – **AQ26)** Calle Pierola 209, Of 205, Arequipa – **AQ27)** Esq Av Lima y Bolognesi, Camaná – **AQ28)** Parque Azángaro 150, Miraflores, Arequipa – **AQ30)** Sebastian Luna 105, Arequipa – **AQ31)** Calle Cesar Vallejo 107, Mollendo – **AQ32)** Zona Rural Huayracpampa, Paucarpata, Prov de Arequipa – **AQ33)** Calle Deán Valdivia221, Cercado, Arequipa **W:** www.radiosanmartin.pe **E:** director@radiosanmartin.pe ☎54 213301 - **FM:** 97.7MHz – **AQ34)** Calle Tupac Amaru A-18, Urb Miramar, Mollendo – **AQ35)** Sucre 409, Arequipa – **AQ37)** C.Baca Flor 410, (Cas 128), Mollendo ☎54 532521 - **FM:** 101.5MHz – **AQ38)** Dean Valdivia 418, Piso 3, Cercado, Arequipa ☎54 405480 **W:** www.radiovictoria-peru.com **E:** radiovictoria_aqp@hotmail.com – **AQ39)** Santo Domingo 113 , Galerias Gamesa Of 700, Arequipa, (Ap 2330) ☎54 214997 **E:** radiominuto@terra.com.pe - **FM:** 99.9MHz – **AQ40)** Centro Comercial Independencia, Av Independencia 403-A, Ofic 433, 4° piso, Arequipa **W:** www.radiolasvegas.pe ☎54 287211 **E:** arequipa@radiolasvegas. pe - **FM:** 95.1 MHz – **AQ41)** Calle Puente Grau 122, Arequipa ☎54 507643 **Quechua:** 2000-2100 **W:** mileniouniversal.com **E:** radiomilen-

iouniversal@hotmail.com – **AQ42)** Cl. Melgar 204, Cercado Arequipa, Arequipa ☎54 330970 **W:** www.radiolaluz.com – **AQ43)** Av Progreso 58, Corire, Uraca, Prov de Castilla - **FM:** 97.9MHz – **AQ44)** Calle Castilla 39, Urb. Municipal, Arequipa – **AQ45)** Puerte Grau 122, Cercado de Arequipaa **E:** manuel_montes30@hotmail.com – **AQ46)** Parroquia San Antonio de Padua, Plaza Principal s/n, Callalli, Prov de Caylloma **E:** rsan_antonio14@hotmail.com - **FM:** 94.5MHz – **AQ47)** Calle Puno 820, Miraflores, Arequipa – **AQ49)** Sucre 409, Arequipa (Ap 105, Serpost, Cercado, Arequipa) **W:** www.radziovosdasalvacion.100megas.com – **AQ50)** Calle Trabada No 105, VI Centenario, Arequipa ☎54 202022 **W:** www.radiolibertadaqp.com **E:** radiolibertadaqp@hotmail.com – **AQ51)** Calle Mollendo 149 ☎54 28441

AY00 (AYACUCHO):
AY01) Av Los Rosales 199, Urb Jardin, Ayacucho - **FM:** 93.3MHz – **AY02)** Calle Nazareno 108H, Ayacucho **E:** macebu90@hotmail.com - **FM:** 95.3MHz – **AY05)** Plaza Mayor Felipe Guzman Poma, Aucara, Prov de Lucanas **E:** radioia1090@hotmail.com – **AY06)** Jr Chorro 274, Huamanga, Ayacucho **E:** aba-ay@wayna.rcp.net.pe ☎64 836042 Prgr mainly in **Quechua** – **AY07)** Jr Gervasio Santillana 455, Huanta ☎66 832105 **W:** www.actidigital.net/intros/radio.php - **FM:** 92.9MHz – **AY08)** Jr Piura s/n, Ayacucho - **FM:** 97.9MHz – **AY09)** Jr Arica 105, San Juan Bautista, Huamanga **E:** ayacucho@bethelradio.net - **FM:** 93.9MHz – **AY10)** Local de Obispado, Carmen Alto, Prov de Huamanga - **FM:** 106.7MHz – **AY11)** Calle Nazareno 108, Ayacucho – **AY13)** Jr Cahuide 278, Huanta (Cas 24) ☎66 322153 **W:** www.turadioamauta.com **E:** radioamauta@turadioamauta.com - **FM:** 99.9MHz – **AY14)** Calle El Nazareno, 2do Pasaje 159, Cercado, Huamanga ☎66 318767 **W:** www.diariolavozdehuamanga.com **E:** diariolavozdehuamanga@yahoo.com.ar - **FM:** 91.1MHz – **AY16)** Calle el Nazareno - 2do Pasaje 159, Ayacucho. – **AY17)** Jr.Miguel Untiverso No. 431, Huanta. – **AY18)** Calle Manco Capac 157, Huamanga – **AY19)** Jr.Angel del Señor MZ C Lote 1A, Asociacion Los Mecanicos, Huamanga – **AY20)** Av. Mariscal Cáceres No 641, Ayacucho, Prov.. Huamanga – **AY21)** Jr. Arequipa 231, Ayacucho, Huamanga – **AY22)** Av. Mariscal Cáceres No 641, Transportes y Comunicaciones, Ayacucho, Huamanga

CJ00 (CAJAMARCA):
CJ01) Jr Francisco de Orellana 343 (Ap 50), Jaén **W:** www.radio-maranon.org.pe **E:** correo@radiomaranon.org.pe ☎76 731147 - **FM:** 96.1MHz – **CJ02)** Jr 24 de Junio 189, Huambos, Chota – **CJ03)** Km 5 Carretera Jaen-San Ignacio, Jaen - **FM:** 90.9MHz – **CJ04)** Jr Revilla Peréz 194, Cajamarca ☎76 829067 - **FM:** 105.1MHz – **CJ05)** Predio Coliga, Cajamarca – **CJ06)** Av Mesones Muro 157, Jaén – **CJ07)** Jr 28 de Julio 712-716, Bambamarca **W:** www.radiocoremarca.com.pe **E:** coremarca@radiocoremarca.com.pe ☎76 353169 - **FM:** 101.1MHz – **CJ08)** Jr Villanueva Pinillos 330, San Ignacio ☎7471 6100 - **FM:** 96.3MHz – **CJ09)** Jr.Amazonas 725, Cajamarca - **FM:** 99.3MHz – **CJ10)** Jr.San Martin Cajamarca ☎76 44826251 ▤76 830238 – **CJ11)** Calle Zurumilla 1328, Jaén - **FM:** 94.9MHz – **CJ13)** Jr Huánuco 2361, Cajamarca ☎76 969049 **E:** radiolidersac@yahoo.com or radiolider970@gmail.com - **FM:** 90.3MHz – **CJ14)** Jr David León 601, Contumazá – **CJ15)** Jr Dos de Mayo 271, Cajamarca ☎76 369915 **W:** www.radiosanfranciscoperu.com **E:** radiosanfrancisco@gmail.com - **FM:** 91.9MHz – **CJ16)** Calle Bolívar 1020, Jaén – **CJ17)** Jr Ramón Castilla 491, Cutervo ☎76 737090 - **FM:** 97.7MHz – **CJ18)** Av. Via de Evitamiento S/N, Cajamarca **W:** www.www.radionuevavidacomunicaciones.com **E:** radiotvnbc@radionuevavidacomunicaciones.com or radiotvnvc@hotmail.com – **CJ19)** Jr Lara s/n, Cajabamba **E:** radiocajabamba@hotmail.com - **FM:** 90.3MHz – **CJ20)** Jr Mariscal Castilla 439, Prov de Jaén - **FM:** 96.7MHz – **CJ21)** Av San Martin De Porres s/n, Cajamarca ☎76 828566 - **FM:** 100.7MHz – **CJ22)** Jr Leoncio Prado 330, San Marcos ☎76 858083 – **CJ23)** Av Inca Garcilazo de la Vega 473, Chota – **CJ24)** Jr. Mariano Melgar 138 , Cajamarca ☎76 36897 **W:** www.layzonradio.com **E:** radiolayzon@yahoo.com - **FM:** 90.5MHz – **CJ25)** Calle Santa Rosa 914 Pi 2, Sector Pueblo Nuevo, Jaèn ☎76 318974 - **FM:** 105.7MHz – **CJ26)** Av El Maestro 290, Cajamarca – **CJ27)** Jr Simon Bolivar 280, Santa Cruz – **CJ28)** Jr 2 de Mayo 484, Cajamarca – **CJ29)** Jr Silva 673, Cajabamba **E:** radioparaiso1300@hotmail.com – **CJ30)** Jr. Santa Rosa No 674-680 (Ap 14), Chota ☎76 351240 **W:** www.radiochota.com – **CJ31)** Jr Cajamarca s/n, Cajamarca – **CJ32)** Jr 30 de Agosto 641, Chota **W:** www.radiosantamonica.org/chota **E:** radiosantamonica@hotmail.com ☎76 841477 ▤76 841132 - **FM:** 95.7MHz – **CJ33)** Juan XXIII s/n (Plaza Bolognesi), Cajamarca **W:** www.yanaocha.com.pe/comunicandonos/myradio01.htm - **FM:** 105.1MHz – **CJ34)** Jr 5 Esquinos 563, Cajamarca ☎76 823041 – **CJ35)** Jr Arica Cuadra s/n, Celendín ☎76 555112 **W:** http//frecuenciavh.loquegustes.com **E:** frecuenciavh@hotmail.com - **FM:** 95.7MHz – **CJ36)** Jr. Alfonso Ugarte No 668, Cajamarca ☎7655 7075 **W:** www.radiosanmiguelcajamarca. **E:** sanmiguelradioradio@hotmail.com - **FM:** 101.1MHz – **CJ37)** Calle Libertad 430, Jaén – **CJ38)** Jr. Lima 290, Cutervo ☎76 737010 ▤76 737269 **E:** radioilucan@hotmail.com - **FM:** 96.1MHz – **CJ39)** Av Bolognesi 851, San Pablo – **CJ40)** Jr Pachacutec 433, Los Baños del

Inca ☎76 801408 – **CJ41)** Jr Jorge Chávez 416, Bambamarca ☎44 843260 ▤44 843078 **W:** www.radiobambamarca.com - **FM:** 101.3 MHz "Stereo Líder" – **CJ42)** Anaximandro Vega 481, Plaza de Armas, Chota ☎76 351442 ▤76 352027 **W:** www.andinaradio.net **E:** webmaster@andinradio.net– **CJ43)** Amazonas 655, Cajamarca – **CJ44)** Jr Castro Alfaro s/n, Socota, Cutervo, Prov de Cutervo – **CJ45)** Av Bolognesi 532, San Pablo, Prov de San Pablo - **FM:** 100.7MHz – **CJ47)** Jr Cutervo No 543, Santa Cruz ☎76 844068 – **CJ49)** Jr Bolognesi - 1300, Barrio La Almeda, Sector Los Delfines, Cajabamba, Prov de Cajabamba – **CJ53)** Dis de Faique – **CJ54)** Jr.Jose Galvez No 698, Contumaza – **CJ56)** Av Casanova 630, Cajamarca ☎76 364656 **W:** www.radiocampesinadecajamarca.com – **CJ57)** Juana Atalaya s/n Peru, El Tambo, Bambamarca ☎ 76 833538 ▤ 76 833550**E:** rsjfcia1@hotmail.com – **CJ58)** Calle La Merced y Calle Comercio, Cutervo **E:** leo1551@hotmail.com – **CJ59)** Chirinos - **FM:** 99.3MHz – **CJ61)** 30 de Agost, Chota – **CJ62)** Los Libertadores 250, Bambamarca, Hualgayoc – **CJ63)** Jr. Miguel Iglesia 483-489, Cajamarca ☎76 366985 **W:** www.turbomix.com.pe - **FM:** 95.5MHz – **CJ64)** Jr. Leonico Prado 550, Pedro Galvez, San Marcos – **CJ65)** Cajamarca **W:** www.agrorural.gob.pe/radio-cajamarca.html – **CJ66)** Samangay **W:** www.visionradioperu.com – **CJ67)** Cajamarca **W:** www.visionradioperu.com – **CJ67)** José Osores 331, Chota ☎97 6163606 **W:** www.corporacionrbc.com **E:** carranzamori@hotmail.com – **CJ68)** Jr.Leoncios Prado 360, San Marcos ☎76 558338 **W:** www.munisanmarcos.gob.pe/radiomunicipal.html **E:** muniprovsanmarcos@hotmail.com – **CJ69)** Jr.Anaximandro Vega 688, Chota ☎76 351789 **W:** www.radioytvestelar.com **E:** digitelssac@hotmail.com – **CJ70)** Santa Cruz **W:** www.frecuenciadelnorte.globered.com

CU00 (CUSCO):
CU02) Ciudad Universitaria de Perayoc, Sotano del Pabellón "C", Cusco – **CU03)** Av.Ejercito 164, Cusco – **CU04)** Av.Charcahuaylla s/n, Distrito Maras, Prov Urubamba **E:** itdsalle@terra.com.pe - **FM:** 91.7MHz – **CU05)** Tres Cruces de Oro 205, Cusco – **CU06)** Jr Hipolito Unanue M4, Urb Industrial, Cusco – **CU07)** Calle Puputi K-3B, Cusco ☎84 505364 – **CU08)** Calle Inca 650, Santiago, Cusco 8422 8649 **E:** aqripinaf@hotmail.com - **Quechua:** 2 hrs: - 1100, 1500 – **CU10)** Cl Daniel A Carrión 602, Cusco ☎84 224371 – **CU12)** Calle "C" 13, Urb Jardin, Cusco - 24h – **CU13)** Av Infancia 527, Wanchaq ☎84 246391 **W:** www.radiolasvegas.pe/wradio **E:** radiorw@hotmail.com - **FM:** 90.1 MHz – **CU14)** Calle Nueve de Diciembre s/n, Espinar - **FM:** 103.9MHz – **CU15)** Asoc. Pro-Vivendi el Periodista Lt B-13, Wanchaq – **CU16)** Urb. Villa el Periodista Lote E-1, Cusco – **CU17)** Calle Sucre 107, Sicuaní – **CU18)** Jr Ricardo Palma Mz.L-1, Urb Santa Monica, Cusco ☎84 246201 - **FM:** 100.7MHz – **CU19)** Calle Anta s/n, Antanampa, Espinar - **FM :** 98.9MHz – **CU20)** Jr.Juan Espinoza Medrano P-13, Urb Rosas Pata, Cusco **E:** sernaquem@hotmail.com – **CU21)** Cl. Triunfo 201, Cusco ☎84 236020 - **FM:** 92.7MHz – **CU22)** Lote E-11, Urb Bancopata, Cusco - **FM:** 100.1MHz – **CU23)** José Santos Chocano, Bloque G-11, Urb. Santa Monica, Cusco ☎84 226765 ▤84 234494 **W:** www.radiouniversalcusco.com.pe **E:** radiouniversal@speedy.com.pe - **FM:** 103.3MHz – **CU24)** Calle Meloc 417, Cusco – **CU25)** Av El Sol 830, Cusco ☎84 228411 - **FM:** 91.3MHz – **CU26)** Av Martin Pio Concha 339 Quillabamba **Quechua:** 1300-1430, 2100-0100 ☎84 281002 **W:** http://quillabambanoticias.org/radioquillabamba - **FM:** 91.1MHz – **CU27)** Av Manuel Callo Cevallos 111, Sicuani **W:** http://pachatusanradio.blogspot.com – **CU28)** Pasaje Constancia 102, Of 410, Wanchaq – **CU29)** Jr 22 de Febrero 104, Espinar ☎84 301045 – **CU30)** Jr José Olaya Mz H-9, Urb Bancopata, Cusco ☎84 252591 – **CU31)** Calle Sacsaywaman K-10, Urb. Manuel Prado, Cusco - **FM:** 104.1MHz – **CU32)** Av. Huayna Capac 146, Wanchaq ☎84 225160 – **CU33)** Calle Bélen 306, Cusco – **CU34)** Jr 2 de Mayo 206, Sicuani ☎84 351136 **W:** www.radiosicuani.org.pe **E:** direccion@radiisicuani.org.pe - **Quechua:** 0930-1100, 2300-0300 0900-0300 - **FM:** 91.1MHz – **CU35)** Urb Marcavalle, P-20, Wanchaq ☎84 225357 ▤84 226555 - **FM:** 93.9MHz – **CU36)** Plaza de Armas s/n, El Descanso, Kunturkanki Canas, Prov. de Canas **E:** cpmaldonado@caritas.org.pe – **CU37)** Conjunto Habitacional Pachacútec A-105, Cusco ☎84 211371 – Rprts to Carlos Gamarra Moscoso, Av Garcilazo 411, Wanchác **E:** adalidcusco@hotmail.com – **CU38)** Av.Tupac Amaru s/n, Yanaoca, Prov de Canas – **CU39)** Jr Matara 526, Cusco - **FM:** 106.5MHz – **CU40)** Pasaje San Pablo 142, Sicuani - **FM:** 97.7MHz – **CU41)** Jr Independencia 143 Piso 2, Quillabamba – **CU42)** Plaza de Armas s/n, Marcapata, Provincia de Quispicanchi – **CU44)** Av El Sol 230, Yauri, Prov de Espinar - **FM:** 103.1MHz – **CU45)** Alameda Pachacutec B-5, Urb Bancapata (Apt 713), Cusco ☎84 225052 – **CU47)** Av. Tupac Amaru, Urb. Progreso D3, Wanchaq ☎84 504961 **W:** www.radiolasvegas.pe **E:** cusco@radiolasvegas.pe - **FM:** 100.1MHz – **CU48)** Av Panamericana 105, Yuari, Provincia de Espinar – **CU49)** Av Cusco s/n, Yauri, Provincia de Espinar – **CU50)** Jr Ricardo Palma 516, Quillabamba - **FM:** 96.5MHz – **CU51)** Cl Choquechaca 152, Cusco ☎84 802444 – **CU52)** Calle Heladeros 220, Wanchaq - **FM:** 102.1MHz – **CU53)** Calle Siete Angelitos 715, San Blas, Cusco ☎84 233101 ▤8423 1881 - **FM :** 93.3MHz – **CU55)** Comunidad de Usañaje, Calle 28 de Junio No 507, Santo Tomas, Chumbivilcas

– **CU56)** Av.San Martin No 305, Yauri, Espinar **E:** radiolaramani@latinmail.com – **CU57)** Urb Tambillo L-5, Urcos, Prov de Quispicanchi – **CU58)** Plaza de Armas s/n, Kunturkanki, Prov de Canas **E:** radiosantacruz@peru.com - **FM:** 97.7MHz – **CU60)** Av.Arequipa s/n, Yanaoca – **CU61)** Calle Arequipa 590, Sicuani, Canchis – **CU62)** Av Arequipa s/n, Sicuani, Canchis **W:** www.radiovilcanota.org **E:** contacto@radiovilcanota.org – **CU64)** Monjaspata 745, Cusco – **CU65)** Prolongación Avenida de la Cultura 1505, San Sebastian – **CU67)** Av.San Martin 311, Espinar – **CU68)** Av.Cuzco 117, San Sebastian – **CU69)** Malecón Sicuani s/n, Sicuani, Canchis – **CU70)** Cerro Ancahuachana, Cusco – **CU71)** Av. Arequipa s/n, Espinar

HV00 (HUANCAVELICA):
HV01) Puno 110, Lircay, Prov de Angaraes – **HV02)** Plaza Bolognesi 142, Cercado,, Huancavelica **W:** www.radiovirgendelcarmen.com **E:** jlopez_alvarado@hotmail.com **☎**67 451257 - SW:irr – **FM:** 99.1MHz – **HV03)** Calle Arequipa S/N, Huayllahuara.

HU00 (HUANUCO):
HU01) Av Raymondi 432, Rupa-Rupa **☎**62 562024 – **HU02)** Malecón Huallaga 1038, Aucayacu, José Crespo y Castillo – **HU03)** Jr Damasco Beraun 832 – Segundo Piso Oficina 4, Huanuco **☎**62 503049 – **HU04)** Jr. Hermilio Valdiz 272, **☎**62 516360 **W:** www.radiolaluz.org – **HU05)** Jr Leoncio Prado 723 (Cas 343), Huánuco **☎**62 511525 **⮹**62 512428 Prgr in **Sp & Quechua** - **FM:** 88.9MHz – **HU06)** Ruben Dario 128, Zona Cerro Paucarhamvilla, Distrito Amarilis, Huánuco **☎**62 512428 – **HU07)** Jr Dos de Mayo 1286, Of 208, Huánuco **E:** luzysonido@hotmail.com **☎**62 518500 **⮹**62 511985 **Quechua:** 1000-1200, 2300-0200 - **FM:** 105.7MHz – **HU08)** Jr Aguilar 744-746, Huánuco - **FM:** 100.1MHz – **HU09)** Jr Bolognesi 175, Distrito de Panao, Provincia de Pachitea (rept to Pablo Alfredo Albornoz Rojas, Jirón Tacna 385, Panao, Pachita - **FM:** 95.3MHz – **HU11)** Jr.Monzón, Cuadra 1, Tingo Maria – **HU12)** Jr. Abtao1163, Huanuco – **HU13)** Sector San Cristóbal de Huayllabamba, Distrito de San Francisco de Cayran – **HU14)** Jirón Monzón cuadra 1, Tingo Maria

IC00 (ICA):
IC01) Conde de Nieva 125, Ica – **IC02)** Av Ayacucho Esq Grau s/n, Ica **☎**56 231956 - **FM:** 105.3MHz – **IC03)** Av Conde de Nieva, Urb Luren, Ica - **FM:** 90.7MHz – **IC04)** Av San Martín 305, 2° piso, Chincha Alta, Prov de Chinca - **FM:** 89.7MHz – **IC05)** Calle Cajamarca 195, Ica - **FM:** 103.3MHz – **IC06)** Av. Leon de Bivero 100 2do Piso, Ica **☎**56 237326 **W:** www.radiolaluz.com – **IC07)** s/n Mz A21 Urb aa.Hh Tupac Amaru, San Juan de Marcona **☎**56 525268 – **IC08)** Jr Mauytua 189 (Ap 54), Chincha Alta, Prov de Chinca – **IC09)** Av.Arenales 579, Ica **☎**56 808460 – **IC10)** Calle L 204 – San Miguel, Ica.56-219-300 – **IC11)** Camino a San Juan, Chincha Alta, Prov Chincha – **IC12)** Los Portales de Escribanos 167, Plaza de Armas, Palpa **E:** radiocruzdelsur@hotmail.com - **FM:** 99.7MHz – **IC13)** Calle San Francisco, Pisco **☎**56 533150 - **FM:** 96.5MHz "Paracas" – **IC14)** Av 8 de Septiembre s/n (Cas 24), Pisco – **IC15)** San Martín 120, Urb Pencal, Nazca – **IC16)** Av los Incas 117-119 (57), Nazca – **IC17)** MZ 1, LT 1, Urb Los Viñedos, San Juan Bautista **E:** epcc@uosjb.edu.pe – **IC19)** Jr.Los Ángeles No 296 3er Piso, Publo Nuvo, Chincha **☎**56 263278 – **IC20)** Calle San Francisco 301, San Clemente, Pisco **☎**56 312416

JU00 (JUNIN):
JU01) Jr. Los Manzanos 695, El Tambo **☎**64 789459 **W:** www.radiolaluz.com - **FM:** 101.7MHz – **JU02)** Jr.Grau 642, Junin – **JU04)** Av.Tayacaja 324, Of 202, La Oroya **JU05)** Av Jorge Chavez 851, Anexo Zaños Grande, El Tambo **E:** radiovida@hotmail.com – **JU06)** Calle Ancash 543, Of 208, Huancayo - **FM:** 103.1MHz – **JU07)** Av Las Palmeras 285,La oroya **☎**64 391595 – **JU08)** Jr Acolla 935, Jauja – **JU09)** Av Calmell del Solar 469-481, Sn Carlos Hye, Huancayo **☎**64 211312. **W:** www.somosmanantial.com **E:** manantialradio960@hotmail.com **FM:** 94.9MHz. – **JU10)** Av.Mariscal Castilla 4162, Huancayo **JU11)** Esquina Prolongación Pachitea 136 y Pasaje Andaluz 106 4° piso, Huancayo – **JU12)** Av. Mariscal Castilla 4162, Huancayo - **FM:** 92.9 – **JU13)** Calle Mercado 194, San Ramón – **JU14)** Calle Real 270, El Tambo, Huancayo **☎**64 245396 **⮹**64 253921 - **FM:** 96.7MHz "R Futura" – **JU15)** Jr Tarma 545, La Merced **☎**64 531068.**⮹**64 531304 - **FM :** 105.7MHz – **JU16)** Paseo La Breña 174 2 piso Of 202, Huancayo 64421 9990 - **FM:** 89.7MHz – **JU17)** Jr Manuel Prado 459, Satipo – **JU18)** Jr Cerro de Pasco 582, (Ap 2), Junín **☎**64 344029 **W:** www.rlibertadjunin.com **E:** radiolibertadjunin@yahoo.es (SW-irr) - **FM:** 98.9MHz – **JU19)** Av Ayacucho 7300, Huancayo - **FM:** 105.7MHz – **JU20)** Av Manuel Prado 239, Satipo – **JU21)** Jr Moquegua 648, Tarma – **JU22)** Jr Ancash 555, Chilca (Apt 245, Huancayo) **E:** radiocumbrefm@hotmail.com **☎**64 218080 **⮹**64 239189 - **FM:** 98.5MHz – **JU23)** Jr Junín 163, La Merced – **JU24)** Jr Dario Leon 198, 4° piso, La Oroya – **JU25)** Calle Real 175, Chilca, Huancayo – **JU26)** Calle Real 1453, Huancayo – **JU27)** Jr Junin , 2° piso, Jauja **☎**64 362428 **⮹**64 361850 – **JU28)** Jr Jauja 494, Tarma – **JU29)** Pasaje Andalz 175, Huancayo – **JU30)** Jr Moquegua 642, Tarma **☎**64 321864 – **JU31)** Av Jose Carlos Mariátegui 699, Urb Tambo, Huancayo **☎**6424 1941

⮹6425 2840 - **FM:** 102.5MHz – **JU32)** Jr Cerro de Pasca 582, Junin – **JU33)** Marcavelle Block "F" 191,Santa Rosa de Sacco, La Oroya **E:** radiolaoroya@speedy.com.pe **☎**64 391401 **⮹**64 391748 - **FM:** 100.1MHz – **JU34)** Calle Real 517, Of 403, Huancayo **☎**64 231831 **W:** www.ldwebstudios.com/radiohuancayo - **FM:** 104.3MHz – **JU35)** Av Arevaldo 484, Anexo Chuccus, Santa Rosa de Sacco, Prov de Yauli – **JU37)** Jr Molino del Amo 167 (Cas.167), Tarma **☎**64 321510 **⮹**6432 1167 **W:** www.radiotarma.com **E:** informacion@grupomonteverde. com - **FM:** 99.3 & 101.7MHz "R Tropicana" in La Merced – **JU38)** Av Huancavelica 430, 2° piso (Ap 230), Huancayo **☎**64 233851 **W:** www.radio1550.com **E:** radio@radio1550.com - **FM:** 88.9MHz – **JU39)** Jr Arequipa 572, Yauyos - **FM:** 98.3MHz – **JU40)** Jr Huancavelica 498, 2° piso, Tarma – **JU41)** Brasilia 200, Huancayo – **JU42)** Jr Tarma 551, La Merced **☎**64 531068 **⮹**64 531304 - **FM:** 105.7MHz – **JU43)** H.Zevallos Gomez 231, La Oroya – **JU44)** Calle Principal de Lama, Pariahuanca, Huancayo – **JU45)** Av.Huancavelica N 439, Huancyo – **JU46)** Huancayo **W:** www.visionradioperu.com – **JU47)** Distrito de Pichanaki, Provincia de Chanchamayo – **HU48)** Psje. Santa Cecilia s/n Chila, Huancayo **☎**64 201011 **W:** www.radiovozcristianaperu.com **E:** radiovozcristiana1470am@hotmail.com

LA00 (LAMBAYEQUE):
LA01) Km 4 de la Carretera Pimentel, Chiclayo - **FM:** 105.1MHz – **LA02)** Calle Juan XXXIII 391 (Ciudad Universitaria), Lambayeque **E:** universitariaradio@hotmail.com – **LA03)** Psje.Woyke Nr 179 3 piso, Edifico Angelica, Chiclayo **☎**74 237850 - **FM:** 88.5MHz – **LA04)** Juan Guglievan 984, Chiclayo – **Quechua: Sun:** 0600-1100 - **FM:** 107.7MHz – **LA06)** Alfonso Ugarte 505, Distrito San José, Prov de Lambayeque (Ap 67, Correo Central, Chiclayo) - **FM:** 103.3MHz – **LA08)** Calle San José 462, Of 207, Chiclayo - **FM:** 102.9MHz – **LA09)** Jr Nicanor Carmona 177, Ferreñafe – **LA10)** Calle Santa Cecilia s/n, Olmos, Prov Lambayeque – **LA11)** Av Pedro Ruiz 1123, 3° piso, Chiclayo - **FM:** 100.5MHz – **LA12)** Alfonso Ugarte 721, 5 piso, Chiclayo **☎**74 498762 – **LA13)** Ca Antonio Monsalve Baca 204 P.J.Santa, Lambayeque **☎**74 283562 **E:** radiosanjose@hotmail.com **F:** radiosanjose@hotmail. com - **FM:** 97.7MHz – **LA14)** Calle Arica 1247, Chiclayo **☎**74 208523 – **LA15)** Av Saenz Peña 1046, Chiclayo - **FM:** 98.3MHz – **LA16)** Av Tupac Amaru 532, Ferreñafe – **LA17)** Calle San 1084, Chiclayo – **LA18)** Calle F Villareal y A Arguedas s/n, Chiclayo - **FM:** 94.1MHz – **LA19)** Av Miguel Grau 350, Oficina **⮹**, Chiclayo **☎**74 236363 – **LA20)** Calle Las Violetas s/n, Chiclayo - **FM:** 94.9MHz – **LA21)** Calle Francisco Gonzales Burgán 717, Ferreñafe **☎**74 286351 – **LA22)** Calle 1 de Mayo 278, Urrunaga, Provincia de Chiclayo – **LA23)** Caserio Tranca Falupe, Morrope, Prov Lambayeque – **LA24)** Jr San Francisco 239, Olmos, Prov de Lambayeque – **LA25)** Nicolás de Pierola 335, Distrito de José Leonardo Ortiz, Pro de Chiclayo - **FM:** 107.7MHz – **LA26)** Empresa Capimag S.R.L., Calle Justicia 102, Urb. Túpac Amaru, Chiclayo – **LA27)** Av Balta 1144, Chiclayo **W:** http//es.geocities.com/radiochiclayofm/ – **LA28)** Av.Los Incas 946, Morrope, Prov de Lambayeque – **LA29)** Calle San José 148, Olmos, Prov de Lambayequea **E:** clori1009@yahoo.es – **LA30)** Av el Tren s/n, Chiclayo – **LA31)** Calle Juan Fanning N° 457, Urb San Juan, Chiclayo **☎**74 239889 **W:** www.visionradioperu.com **E:** informes@visionradioperu.com – **LA32)** Calle Tarata 931, Olmos, Prov de Lambayeque **W:** http://radio-super-real-realmente-joven.qapacity.com – **LA34)** Av Mariscal Castilla 859, Monsefú, Prov de Chiclayo – **LA36)** Av Andrés Avelino Cáceres 800, Lambayeque **☎**74 283353 **E:** naylamp@llampallec.rep.net.pe **☎**74 283353 - **FM:** 96.1MHz – **LA38)** Juan Guelman de Cameros, Chiclayo **E:** lorryand@hotmail.com – **LA39)** Tucumé – **LA40)** Amadeo Ruiz 320, Olmos – **LA41)** Av. Victor Raúl 293, Chiclayo **E** jesusmiguela1077@hotmail.com att.: Pastor José Huamán – **LA42)** Cal. Vicente de la Vega 873 ND, Chiclayo Pl.3, Chiclayo **☎**74 224287 – **LA43)** José Osores 331, Chota (Cajamarca) **☎**97 6163606 **W:** www.corporacionrbc.com **E:** carranzamori@hotmail.com

LI00 (LIMA):
LI01) Juan Vargas 147, Chorrillos, Lima **☎**14 388850 **W:** www.radio-inca.com.pe – **LI02)** Jr.Camana Pl6 615 of 605, Urb Cercado, Lima **☎**14 272639 **W:** www.radiooriente.com – **LI03)** Calle Mama Oclio 2058, Lince, Lima **W:** www.radiomariaperu.org **E:** info.per@radiomaria.org **☎**14 458217 **⮹**14 467161 – 15 FM repeater stations – **LI04)** Av 28 de Julio 1004, Piso 4, Cercado, Lima **☎**14 247547 **W:** http://radiocora.pe – **LI05)** Calle Miguel Dasso 144, Of 2A, San Isidro, Lima **☎**12 214107 **W:** www.ovacion.com.pe/radio/ **E:** radioovacion@ovacion.com.pe – **LI06)** Av Guzman Blanco 465, 7° piso, (Ap 4236) Lima **☎**13 307349 **W:** www.pacificoradio.com **E:** administracion@grupopacifico.com **LI07)** Justo Pastor Davila 197, Chorillos **☎**61 76600 **⮹**251 3324 **W:** www.radiolainolvidable.com.pe **E:** crpradio@crpradio.com.pe – **LI08)** Av Manco Cápac 333, La Victoria, Lima 13 – **LI09)** Av. Javier Prado Este 255, Consultorio 402, Edifica Lina, San isidro, Lima (⌧ C.P. 138, La Molina, Lima)4 14 099096 **W:** www.redradiointegridad.org **E:** info@redradiointegridad.org – **LI10)** Av Paseo de la República 3866, 2° piso, San Isidro **☎**12 150200 **W:** www.rpp.com.pe – **LI11)** Justo Pastor Dávila 197, Chorillos **☎**16 176600 **⮹**12 513324 **W:** www.radiomar.com.

pe – **LI12)** Avenida Arica 248, Breña, Lima ☎14 245187 📠13 323094 **W:** www.radiovictoria.pe – **LI13)** Av Andrés Mármol Castellanos 230, Huaral ☎13 355765 – **LI14)** Av Salaverry 1082, Jesús Maria, Lima **W:** www.radiolibertad.com.pe **E:** info@radiolibertad.com.pe ☎12 660777 📠14 715319 – **LI15)** Av Petit Thouars 447, Santa Beatriz, Lima 1. Lima **W:** www.radionacional.com.pe ☎14 338956 – **LI16)** Av José Pardo 138, Edifico Neptuno, Piso 16, Miraflores ☎14 458549 📠14 458901 **W:** www.unionlaradio.com – **LI17)** Av Paseo de la Republica 3866, San Isidro **W:** www.felicidad.com.pe – **LI18)** Av Republica de Chile 295, Of. 1104, Urb. Santa Beatriz, Lima ☎13 327779 **W:** www.modernaradio-papa.com **E:** informes@radiomoderna.com – **LI19)** Paseo Parodi 340, San Isidro **W:** www.radiopanamericana.com **E:** radio@panamericana.com.pe ☎14 226787 📠14 221223 – Satellite signal downlinked by 60 FM repeaters - **FM:** 101.1MHz – **LI20)** Radio Merino 230, Santa Cruz, Miraflores ☎1442 8810 **W:** www.radiolatina.com.pe **E:** contacto@radiolatina.com.pe – **LI21)** Julio C.Tello 152, Lince, Lima ☎14 714291 **W:** www.metropolitanaradioperuana.com **E:** metropolitanaradioperuana@gmail.com – **LI22)** Julio C.Tello 152, Lince, Lima ☎14 714291 **W:** www.radioexitoperu.com **E:** radioexitoperu@gmail.com – **LI23)** 453 Av. España, Lima. **W:** www.radiolaluz.com ☎14 334599 – **LI24)** Gerardo Unger N° 6347, San Martin de Porres ☎15 373204 **W:**www. radiofelizperu.com – **LI25)** 2 de Mayo 573, Imperial ☎1284 8052 – **LI27)** Jr.Bernardo Alcedo 375, Lince, Lima 14 **W:** www.radiobacan. com **E:** bacan@radiobacan.com ☎14 2661856 📠 1471 3908 – **LI30)** Av Manco Cápac 495, 4to Piso, Of 401, Miraflores, Lima 18 **W:** www. radiomiraflores.net ☎14 441773 📠1445 0126 – **LI31)** Jr Echenique 140, Huacho – **LI32)** Mz L, Lt 7, Urb La Esperanza, Hualmay – **LI33)** Av Estados Unidos 327, Urb Huaquillay, Comas **W:** www.radiocomas.com **E:** comasam@radiocomas.com ☎15 250094 📠15 250859 – **LI34)** Jr Atahualpa 148, 5° piso, Huacho – **LI35)** Petit Thouars 1806 ☎2 659876 – **LI37)** Av Grau 538, Huacho – **LI38)** Av Comandante Espinar N° 680, Miraflores, Lima ☎16 107760 📠1610427761 **W:** www.nuevotiempo. org.pe **E:** radio@nuevotiempo.org.pe – **LI39)** Calle Juan de Carpio 140-144 2° piso, San Isidro, Lima 27 ☎14 420482 📠14 421693 **W:** www.radiocallao.com **E:** radiocallao@gmail.com – **LI40)** Ausejo Salas 153, Huacho ☎13 231976 – **LI41)** Av Petit Thouars 1806, Lince, Lima – **LI42)** Mz C Lt 5, Asoc. Virgen de la Familia, Chilca, Cañete – **LI43)** Av Separadora Industrial s/n, Villa El Salvador ☎12 913146 – **LI44)** Alfonso Ugarte 149, Barranca ☎12 354238 – **LI45)** Aviacion 5150 (dentro de Plaza Vea. 3er piso, Surco – **LI46)** Av Recreo 317, Altos, Paramonga – **LI47)** Jr Carmaná 170, (Apt 4451 San Miguel), El Cercado, Lima **W:** www.radiosantarosa.com.pe **E:** contacto@radiosantarosa. com.pe ☎14 277488 📠14 266587 **Quechua:** 1300 **English:** 0130.– **LI49)** Av.Arnaldo Márquez 1944 Jesús Maria, Lima 11 ☎14 612222 📠14 617757 **W:** www.radiomilenia.com **E:** milenia@radiomilenia.com – **LI50)** Plaza de Armas 132, Barranca ☎12 352301 – **LI51)** Jr. Yahuar Huaca Piso 3 106, Urb. Tahuantinsuyo, Independencia ☎15 260469 **W:** www.radioindependenciadelperu.com **E:** wbaldeon@radioindependenciadelperu.com – **LI52)** Av Alfonso Ugarte 1428, Of 202, Breña (Cas.11-0625), Lima ☎1424 6677 **W:** www.laperuanisima.com **E:** laperunisima@yahoo.com – **LI54)** Av. Alfonso Ugarte 1465, Lima ☎17 178485 **W:** www.radiocielo.pe – **LI55)**Av Petit Thouars 447, Santa Beatriz, Lima 1 **W:** www.radionacional.com ☎14 331404 – **LI56)** Av. Paseo Parodi 340, San Isidro, Lima. ☎14 413050 **W:** www.radio1160.com.pe – **LI57)** Huacho.– **LI58)** CRP – Justo Pastor Davila 197, Chorrillos, Lima **W:** www.radionuevaq.com.pe – **LI59)** Av. 28 de Julio 1781, La Victoria. Lima ☎16 131701 **W:** www.bethelradio.fm **E:** betheltadio@bethelradio.fm – **LI60)** Jr. Morales Bermúdez 140 Pueblo Libre (Alt. 14 de Av. Brasil), Lima 21 ☎14 248122 **W:** www.cadena1200.com – **LI61)** Manzana D, Lote 9, Asoc. Vivienda Monte Los Olivos, Distrito de San Martin de Porres ☎48 48379 **W:** www.radiojpj.com **E:** radiojpj@hotmail.com – **LI62)** Av.Salaverry 862, Lima **W:** www.nseradio.com **E:** nselima@nseradio.com ☎47 14172 – **LI63)** Av.Gerardo Unger No 6995, Independencia, Lima ☎15 331848 **W:** www.radiofe1220.com **E:** info@albertosantana.org – **LI64)** KM 193 Panamericana Norte, Barranca – **LI65)** Urb. Lever Pacocha "D" 13 Av. San Martin 1 Piso, Huacho **W:** www.radiolaluz.com – **LI66)** Luis Alberto Lizarraga Alva, Cerro Laguna, Distrito San Vicente, Provinca de Cañete

LL00 (LA LIBERTAD):
LL01) Jr Trujillo 597, Otuzco ☎44 436007 – **LL02)** Jr Benito Juarez 1753, La Esperanza – **LL03)** Calle Opalo 298 2° piso-A, Urb Sta. Ines, Trujillo ☎44 202156 - **FM:** 98.3MHz – **LL04)** Calle Lima 599, Chepén – **LL05)** San Martín 472, Trujillo ☎44 251792 – **LL06)** Av Los Incas s/n, Anexo Facala, Chócope, Prov de Ascope - **FM:** 102.5MHz – **LL07)** Calle Junin 23, Sausal, Prov de Ascope – **LL08)** Francisco Pizarro 532, Of 205, Trujillo - **FM:** 89.7MHz – **LL09)** Jr Ayacucho 65, Pacamayo, Prov Pacasmayo – **LL10)** Jr Trujillo 597, Otuzco – **LL11)** Jr Marcelo Corne 224, Urb San Andrés, Trujillo ☎44 294050 – **W:** www. radiolibertadluz.com - **FM:** 90.9MHz – **LL12)** Av V Belaunde MZ.L lote 15, Urb Santo Dominguito, Trujillo – **LL13)** Jr Francisco Pizarro 208, Of 302,.Trujillo ☎44 242666 - **FM:** 107.5MHz –**LL15)** Av del Ejercito 717, Trujillo – **LL16)** Alfonso Ugarte 222, Virú - **FM:** 102.MHz – **LL17)** Calle Trujillo 699-A, Chepén – **LL19)** Psje. Damián Niculau 108, Huamachuco. **W:** www.radiolosandeshuamachuco.com – **LL20)** Jr Atahualpa 795, Chepen ☎44 562038 **W:** www.xaski.com/radiosan-sebastian/principal.htm - **FM:** 92.7MHz – **LL21)** Mz.B-1 2-A, Urb La Libertad, Trujillo ☎44 217885 – **LL22)** Zepita 452, Trujillo ☎44 249326 📠44 252970 **W:** www.radiolibertadmundo.com **E:** contactanos@radiolibertadmundo.com – **LL23)** Jr Progreso 121, Quiruvilca – **LL24)** Bolívar 780 (Cas 1029), Trujillo ☎44 233981 – **LL25)** Victoria 229, Guadalupe, Prov de Pacasmayo – **LL26)** Jr. Cáceres s/n, Bolívar, Prov de Bolívar ☎44 230127 – **LL28)** Jr Progreso 759, Chepén - **FM:** 98.7MHz – **LL31)** Ca Camal 13, Cartavio, Prov.de Ascope ☎44 432448 – **LL32)** Mercado La Hermelinda Puesto C 288 – seccion abarrotes, Trujillo ☎44 803207 – **LL33)** Jr Gamarra 713, Of 405, Trujillo ☎44 246211 – **LL34)** Ascope – **LL35)** Pasaje San Martin 360, Urb Alto Mochica, (Ap 352) Trujillo ☎44 263592 – **LL37)** Jr Trujillo 281, Quiruvilca – **LL38)** Jr Grau s/n, Virú – **LL39)** Sebastian Barranca 469, Urb. Chimú, Trujillo – **LL40)** Pasaje Monseñor Damián Nicolau 108, Huamachuco **E:** radiolosandes@starmedia.com - **FM:** 103.1MHz – **LL41)** Calle Bolívar 130, Otuzco – **LL42)** Jr Ayacucho s/n, 5° piso Of 901, Trujillo ☎44 257431 - **FM:** 96.9MHz – **LL43)** Av España 1210, Trujillo ☎44 295214 **W:** www.agroradio1590.es.tl **E:** elparaisodedios@speedy.com – **LL44)** Jr Zepita 450, Trujillo – **LL45)** Carabamba, Prov.Julcán – **LL46)** Calle Victor Julio Rossel 324, Julcan – **LL47)** Calle Progreso 218, Barrio Alto Coscomba, Julcan – **LL48)** Calle La Libertad 120, Otuzco 4443 6565 **W:** www.chamiradio.org.pe **E:** escribenos@chamiradio.org.pe – **LL49)** Calle San Antonio 880, 2-piso, Otuzco – **LL51)** Jr.Lara No 591, Huamachuco, Sánchez Carrión – **LL52)** Trujillo

LO00 (LORETO):
LO01) Jiron Abtao 255 (Ap 207), Iquitos ☎65 265244 📠65 265244 **W:** www.radiolvs.cnr.org.pe **E:** lavozdelaselva@claroempresa.com.pe - **FM:** 93.9MHz – **LO02)** Jr Elias Agurrie 857, Iquitos - **FM:** 104.5MHz – **LO04)** Jr Lima 821, Iquitos - **FM:** 90.1MHz – **LO05)** Av.Antonio Raymondi 331, Iquitos - **FM:** 101.3MHz – **LO06)** Arica 228, Iquitos ☎65 233302 **E:** radioloreto@yahoo.es - **FM:** 103.5MHz – **LO07)** Plaza de Armas s/n, Iquitos – **LO08)** Jr Prospéro 645 Iquitos (Cas 174) - **FM:** 105.9MHz – **LO09)** Av Abelardo Quiñones km 4.5 Carretera a Nauta, Iquitos – **LO10)** Calle Progreso 112-114, Yurimaguas, Alto Amazonas **W:** www.roriente.org **E:** oriente995@yahoo.com ☎65 351611 - **FM:** 99.5MHz – **LO12)** Av Alfredo Vargas Guerra 440, Contama, Prov de Ucayali **E:** rmdpem@terra.com.pe – **LO13)** Av Miguel Grau 1029, Iquitos ☎65 224205

MD00 (MADRE DE DIOS):
MD01) Jr Guillermo Billingurst 406 PTO, Puerto Maldonado - **FM:** 101.3MHz – **MD02)** Nueva Plaza de Armas 200, Puerto Maldonado - **FM:** 100.5MHz – **MD03)** Jr Daniel A Carrion 387, Puerto Maldonado ☎82 571050 - **FM:** 92.5MHz

MO00 (MOQUEGUA):
MO01) Edifico S-27 Barrio Azul Asiento Minero, Ilabaya, Prov de Jorge Basadre - **FM:** 101.3MHz – **MO02)** Jr Callao s/n, Ilo – **MO03** Alto Ilo, Sector Arenal G-6, Ilo - **FM:** 96.7MHz – **MO04)** PP.JJ. John F. Kennedy, Mz. E Lte. 48, Ilo – **MO05)** Jr Tarapaca 260, Moquegua – **MO06)** Jr Moquegua 123, 5° piso, Ilo ☎53 781313 - **FM:** 105.5MHz – **MO07)** Jr Ayacucho 639 (Ap 22), Moquegua ☎53 761542 - **FM:** 105.3MHz – **MO08)** Omate **W:** www.agrorural.gob.pe/radio-omate-de-moquegua. html – **MO09)** Marsical Andrés A.Cáceres No 193, Distr. Moquegua, Prov de Mariscal Nieto

PA00 (PASCO):
PA01) Plazuela Gamaniel Blanco, 127- 2°Nivel - Ninguno, Chaupimarca ☎63 422398 📠63 421600 **W:** www.radiotvaltura.com **E:** radiotvaltura@hotmail.com - **FM:** 97.7MHz – **PA02)** Jr Puno s/n, Chaupimarca - **FM:** 102.5MHz – **PA03)** Jr Mullembruck 468, Urb Cercado, Oxapampa ☎63 762689 - **FM:** 101.5MHz – **PA04)** Zona Denominada Principal, Chaupimarca – **PA05)** Jiron Huamachuco No 214, Cerro de Pasco ☎63 422124 **W:** www.radiocorporacion.com.pe – **PA06)** Jr.Huamachuco 221, Caupimarca – **PA07)** Jr. Daniel Alcids Carrion 250, Huayllay – **PA08)** Av. Tupac Amaru No 1066, Colquijirca, Tinyahuarco

PI00 (PIURA):
PI02) Calle Santa Ana 471, Urb Santa Rosa, Sullana – **PI04)** Jr San Ignacio de Loyola 300, Urb Miraflores, Piura **W:** www.radiocutivalu.org/ **E:** cutivalu@ cipca.org.pe ☎73 342802 📠73 342965 - **FM:** 100.5MHz – **PI05)** Ica 419, Of 206, Piura - 1100-0500 - **FM:** 92.1MHz – **PI06)** Santa Maria C., Piura - **FM:** 94.5MHz.– **PI08)** Ugartelne 490, Sullana - **FM:** 99.3MHz – **PI09)** Calle Santa Teresa Cdra 8 s/n, Urb Santa Rosa, Sullana **W:** www.chanel.edu.pe/serviciosl.php ☎73 504760 📠73 501382 – **PI10)** Calle Tacna 260 4 piso, (frente al banco de la nación), Piura ☎73 303369 - **FM:** 103.3MHz – **PI11)** Calle San Martin N° 1041, Sullana – ☎73 503071 **W:** //lacapullana.tripod.com.pe **E:** capullanaradio@latinmail.com - **FM:** 95.7MHz – **PI12)** Jr Cesar Pinglo 345, Sechura – **PI13)** Parroquia San Miguel, Barrio El Altillo s/n, Huancabamba Re to Correo Central, Huancabamba **E:** coylemareen@speedy.com.pe – **PI14)**

Av.Sánches Cerro 582 2do Piso, Piura ☎73 304221 **W:** www.radiolaluz.com – **FM:** 107.9MHz – **PI15)** Calle Cusco 670, Piura ☎7332 4180 – **PI16)** Zona Industrial III Mz O, lote 10, Piura – **PI17)** Calle Unión 515, La Unión ☎73 374106 – **PI18)** Zona Industrial Mz D Km 5, Carretera Piura, Sullana **E:** piuraradio@terra.com.pe – **FM:** 101.9MHz – **PI19)** Urb Aproviser A2-1, Pariñas, Prov de Talara – **FM:** 98.1MHz – **PI20)** Cl Lambayeque 1005, Chulucanas ☎73 378627 – **PI21)** Calle Salaverry No 206, Ayabaca **W:** www.muniayabaca.gob.pe ☎73 471103 – **PI22)** Calle San Martín 354, Sechura – **PI23)** Calle 8 s/n, Talara Alta, Talara – **PI24)** Mz E 8, Fonavi I Etapa, Paita ☎73 611885 – **FM:** 102.9MHz – **PI25)** Jr Leoncio Prado 425, Sullana – **PI26)** Madre de Dios 258, Sullana ☎73 505026 – **PI27)** Jr Las Azucenas Urb El Milagro, Talara Alta, Talara. ☎74 495431 – **PI28)** Calle Tumbes 641, La Unión – **PI29)** Jr Sucre 556, Sullana – **PI30)** Maria Prado del Bello 500, Chulucanas, Prov Morropón ☎7337 8740 – **PI31)** Calle Cajamarca 485, Bellavista, Prov de Sullana – **FM:** 107.5MHz – **PI32)** Av Grau Cuadra 5, Cruceta San Lorenzo, Tambo Grande, Prov de Piura – **PI34)** Calle San Miguel 207, Distrito de Sondor, Región Grau, Prov de Huancabamba - **FM:** 89.1MHz – **PI35)** Av Ramon Castilla 254, Huancabamba ☎73 473369 – **PI37)** Av Quiles Escala s/n, Barrio San Francisco, Huancabamba – **PI38)** Av San Francisco Assisi s/n, Huarmaca, Prov de Huancabamba – **PI41)** AAHH.Alm Grau MZ C, Lt 21, Sector Coscomba, Piura – **PI42)** Calle Tumbes 729, La Union – **PI43)** Calle Grau 505, Centro Huancabamba ☎73 473425 – **PI44)** Jr Lima 4ta cuadara, Tambo Grande **E:** jpaivalombardi@yahoo.com – **PI46)** Catacaos – **PI47)** Av Principal, Caserio La Peñita, Tambo Grande – **PI48)** Calle Alfonso Ugarte 118, Vice, Sechura – **PI49)** A 500m del Puente Virrila, Sechura – **PI50)** Ayabaca **W:** www.agrorural.gob.pe/radio-ayabaca-de-piura.html – **PI51)** Huancabamba **W:** www.agrorural.gob.pe/radio-huancabamba-de-piura.html – **PI52)** Huancabamba **W:** www.agrorural goh pe/radio-ayaviri-de-piura.html – **PI52)** Jr. 9 de Octubre No 110, Huarmaca, Huancabamba – **PI53)** Bolivar 114, Huarmaca – **PI54)** Piura **W:** www.visionradioperu.com

PU00 (PUNO):
PU01) Jr Conde Lemos 212, Puno ☎51 351562 **W:** www.radiondazul.com **E:** ondazul@radiondazul.com - Quechua & Aymara: 6h daily - **FM:** 95.7MHz "Stereo Azul" – **PU02)** Jr Arequipa 385, Puno – **PU03)** Plaza 28 de julio s/n, Macusani, Prov de Carabaya **E:** rvamacu@terra.com.pe - **FM:** 90.5MHz – **PU04)** Carretera a Arequipa, Km 6, Chulluaquiani (Casilla 344), Juliaca ☎51 800601 **W:** www.nuevotiempo.com **E:** nuevotiempojuliaca@hotmail.com – **PU05)** Calle San Román 116, Juliaca ☎51 325357 - **FM:** 89.5MHz – **PU06)** Simon Bolivar 442, Puno – **PU07)** Av Panamericana 940, Chucuito (299, Puno), Prov de Puno **Aymara & Quechua** 0900-1400, 1900-0100 – **PU08)** Jr.Altiplano 206,Urb La Pompilio, Juliaco ☎51 322313 **FM:** 107.9MHz – **PU09)** Jir.Ramón Castilla 861 Cercado, Juliaca ☎51 502319 – **PU11)** Hipolito Unanue 240, Juliaca - 107.9MHz – **PU12)** Jr Arequipa 845, 2do nivel, (Ap 130), Puno – **PU13)** Calle Mariano Pandía 167, 2° piso, Juliaca – **PU14)** Jr Lambayeque 520, Puno – **PU15)** Jr Unión 242, Juliaca **E:** radioltcj@latinmail.com ☎51 322452 ▤51 369450 - **FM:** 102.7MHz - **Quechua & Aymara:** 1000-1100, 1800-1900 – **PU16)** Av El Maestro 1140, Juliaca - **FM:** 88.9MHz – **PU17)** Jr Antonio (Sierra) No 178, prolongación Ramón Castilla, a dos cuadras del Cuartel Bolognesi, Juliaca ☎5257 5412 **W:** http://radiofronteraperu.com – **PU18)** Jr Piura 167, Puno ☎51 353680 - **Aymara & Quechua:** 0900-1100 – **PU19)** Jr Union 229, 3° piso, Juliaca – **PU20)** Jr Apurimac 1316, Barrio Manco Capac, Juliaca **E:** trebol34@mixmail.com – **PU21)** Ramon Castilla 949, Juliaca ☎51 321372 **W:** www.radiojuliaca.com.pe **E:** webmaster@radiojuliaca.com.pe - **FM:** 90.9MHz – **PU22)** Jr Apurimac 644, Juliaca ☎51 325733 – **PU23)** Jr 2 de Mayo 790, Juliaca – **PU24)** Jr Ricardo Palma 111, Juliaca ☎51 327208 – **PU25)** Jr San Martin 134, Yunguyo – **PU26)** Jr.Moquegua 600, Juliaca **E:** asidersicuani@yahoo.es – **PU27)** Jr Chachani 220, Juliaca – **PU28)** Jr 2 de Mayo 2578, Juliaca ☎51 336103 - 0900-0200 Aymara & Quechua: 0900-1100, 1900-2100 – **FM:** 104.5MHz "El Sol de los Andes FM" – **PU29)** Jr Tacuara 160 Int C, Puno – **PU30)** Av El Maestro 1140, Barrio Tupac Amaru, Juliaca – **PU32)** Jiron 2 de Mayo 149, Juliaca **E:** carraviz@gmail.com or carraviz@hotmail.com - Listeners correspondence to: Iván Tito Vizcarra Jiron José Galvez No 542, Barria Bellavista, Julica – **PU33)** Urbanización Rinconada Frente al Colegio, 3ra Etapa, Juliaca – **FM:** 107.3MHz – **PU34)** Jr 7 de Junio 580, Juliaca – **PU35)** Jr Acora N°222, Puno ☎51 366222 **W:** www.pachamamaradio.org **E:** relacionespublicas@pachamamaradio.org – **PU36)** Túpac Amaru Altura Coliseo Juli s/n, Juli, Prov Chucuito ☎51 854173 **W:** webs.demasiado.com/radiocampesina.htm – **PU37)** Av El Sol N° 1384, Puno ☎51 365888 – **PU38)** Distrito de Atuncolla – **PU39)** Distrito de Capachica – **PU41)** Provincia de Azángaro – **PU42)** Túpac Amaru Altura Coliseo Juli s/n, Juli ☎51 554173 **W:** www.agrorural.gob.pe/radio-juli-de-puno. **E:** radiocampesinajuli@hotmail.com - **FM:** 107.1MHz – **PU43)** Av.Mariscal Castilla No 432, Tumbes
SM00 (SAN MARTIN):

SM01) Jr San Martín 257, Tocache ☎42 551031 – **SM02)** Jr Santo Toribio 1252, Rioja – **SM03)** Av Compagñón 410, Tarapoto – **SM07)** Jr. Imperio No 764, Nueva Cajamarca, Provincia de Rioja – **SM08)** Jr Bolognesi 180 Altos, Tarapoto – **SM09)** Cl Bolognesi s/n, Bellavista ☎42 544170 ▤42 544135 - **FM:** 95.1MHz – **SM11)** Peña Meza 467, Juanjuí – **SM12)** Jr Progreso 389, Bellavista ☎42 544179 – **SM13)** Tocacha, Prov de Tocache - **FM:** 96.1MHz – **SM14)** Jr.Loreto No 300, Chazuta **W:** www.ethnicradio.org – **SM15)** Jr.Callao 650, Moyobamba
TA00 (TACNA)
TA01) Edifico S-27 Barrio Azul Asiento Minero, Ilabaya – **FM:** 89.9MHz – **TA02)** Prolong Unanue 1041 (Cas 113), Tacna – **FM:** 99.9MHz – **TA03)** Av Varela 705, Tacna – **TA04)** Jr Sir Jones s/n (Cas 281), Tacna – **TA05)** Arias y Araguez 584, Tacna – **TA06)** Calle Candarave 645, Urb Bacigalupo, Tacna – **TA07)** Urb Jorge Chavez 9 (Ap 115), Tacna - **FM:** 89.5MHz – **TA08)** Av Internacional 484, Tacna ☎52 804100 - **FM:** 106.7MHz – **TA09)** Calle Aniceto Ibarra 436 (Cas 370), Tacna ☎52 414871 ▤52 723745 **W:** www.radiotacnaladecana.com **E:** radio_tacna@hotmail.com - **FM:** 104.3MHz – **TA10)** Av San Martín de Porras 209, Natividad, Tacna **E:** radiobulevar@hotmail.com ☎52 848537 – **TA11)** Jose Olaya s/n 2° piso, Tarata – **TA12)** Calle 2 Mayo 263, Tacna – **TA13)** Tarata **W:** www.agrorural.gob.pe/radio-tarata-de-tacna.html – **TA14)** Villa Universitaria Capannique A 20, Pocoally
TU00 (TUMBES):
TU01) Pza Alipio Rosales s/n, Tumbes - **FM:** 102.1MHz – **TU02)** Calle Tarapaca 163, Tumbes – **TU03)** Av del Ejercito, cuadra 5, Tumbes - **FM:** 91.1MHz – **TU04)** Panamericana Norte Km 1321, Tumbes - **FM:** 100.5MHz – **TU05)** Calle Huáscar 502 3er Piso, Tumbes ☎72 527002 - **FM:** 107.9MHz – **TU06)** Jr Bolívar 117, Tumbes ☎72 523003 – **TU07)** Jr Piura 1010, Tumbes
UC00 (UCAYALI):
UC01) Calle Diego de Almagro s/n. Pucallpa – **UC02)** Jr Inmaculada 667, (Cas 263), Pucallpa ☎61 578615 - **FM:** 89.1 – **UC03)** Av 9 de Diciembre 646, Pucallpa - **FM:** 102.5MHz – **UC04)** Jr Coronel Portillo 448-A, Pucallpa ☎61 573876 ▤61 571540 - **FM :** 103.3MHz– **UC05)** Zona San Fernando, Callería, Pucallpa – **UC06)** Calle Padre Francisco Alvares s/n, Sephua, Prov de Atalaya - **FM:** 95.5MHz – **UC07)** Cl. Iquitos 499, Villa Atalaya, Distrito de Raymondi, Prov de Atalaya ☎64 461240 **E:** rasat@terra.com.pe - **FM:** 95.5MHz – **UC08)** Jr.Coronel Portillon No 460, Pucallpa. – **UC09)** Carretera Federico Basadre Km 37, Los Pinos, Distrito de Campoverde, Prov.de Coronel Portillo – **UC10)** Av. Tupac Amaru No 957, Distr.De Calleria, Prov. de Coronel Portillo

FM in Lima (MHz): 88.3 R. Magica – 88.9 R. Felicidad – 89.7 Emisoras Perúanos (RPP) – 90.5 La Zona – 91.1 R. San Borja – 91.9 Okey R. – 92.5 R. Studio 92 – 93.1 R. Ritmo – 93.7 La Inolvidable – 94.3 R. Mega– 94.9 La Karibeña – 95.5 R. Exitosa – 96.1 Z Rock & Pop – 96.7 R. Capital – 97.3 R. Moda – 98.1 R. Onda Cero – 99.1 Doble Nueve – 100.1 R. Oasis – 101.1 R. Panamericana – **LI33)** 102.1 R. Oxigeno – 103.3 R. Unión – 103.9 R. Nacional –104.7 Viva FM – 105.5 R. Fiesta – 106.3 R. Mar – **LI58)** 107.1 R. Nueva Q – 107.7 R. Planeta

PHILIPPINES

L.T: UTC +8h — **Pop:** 102 million — **Pr.L:** Pilipino (Tagalog), English, Cebuano, Ilocano, Hiligaynon, Bicol — **E.C:** 60Hz, 220V — **ITU:** PHL

NATIONAL TELECOMMUNICATIONS COMMISSION (NTC) (Dept. of Transportation and Communications) ▤ NTC Bldg., BIR Road, East Triangle, Diliman, Quezon City 1104 ☎ +63 9254651 or 9267722 **W:** www.ntc.gov.ph
LP: Commissioner: Gamaliel A. Cordoba. Deputy Commissioners: Delilah F. Deles, Carlo Jose A. Martinez. Chief Broadcast Sces Div: Alvin Bernard N. Blanco.

KAPISANAN NG MGA BRODKASTER NG PILIPINAS (KBP) (Assoc. of Broadcasters of the Philippines) ▤ 6th Flr, LTA Bldg, 118 Perea Str, Legaspi Village, Makati C, 1226 NCR ☎ +63 (2) 815 1990/1/2 ▤ +63 (2) 815 1993 **W:** www.kbp.org.ph
L.P: Chmn: Herman Z. Basbaño. Pres: Ruperto S. Nicdao, Jr. Most stns are KBP members

PHILIPPINE FEDERATION OF CATHOLIC BROADCASTERS (Catholic Media Network, CMN) ▤ Unit 201 Sunrise Condominium, 226 Ortigas Ave, North Greenhills, San Juan, Manila 1503 NCR ☎ +63 (2) 7249850 **W:** www.catholicmedianetwork.org **L.P:** Pres: Fr. Francis B. Lucas. Chmn: Bishop Bernardino Cortez. (28 owned and affiliated stns on MW, 20 on FM)

PHILIPPINE BROADCASTING SERVICE (PBS, "Radyo ng Bayan") (Gov.) ▤ 4/F Media Center Bldg., Visayas Ave., Del Monte, Quezon C, 1105

NCR ☎ +63 (2) 9203968 **W:** www.pbs.gov.ph **L.P:** Dir. Gen: Mr John S. Manalili. Dep. Dir. Gen: Ms Monina S. Cespedes.

Manila stns: DZRB Radyo Balita (news sce) 738 kHz, DZSR Sports Radio 918 kHz, DZRM Radyo Magasin 1278 kHz, DWBR-FM Business Radio 104.3MHz

Regional MW stns: DWBT, San Antonio, Basco, 3900 Batanes. **DWFB**, Mariano Marcos State University Campus, Laoag C, 2900 Ilocos Norte. **DWFR**, Multipurpose Bldg, Provincial Capitol Compound, Bontoc, 2616 Mountain Province. **DWLC**, Perez Park, Lucena C, 4301 Quezon Province. **DWPE**, CSU Campus, Caritan Highway, Tuguegarao, 3500 Cagayan. **DWRM**, City Hall Compound, Puerto Princesa C, 5300 Palawan. **DWRP**, City Civic Center, Taal Ave, Naga C, 4400 Camarines Sur. **DWRS**, Poblacion, Tayug, 2445 Pangasinan. **DXBN**, City Hall Compound, Brgy. Doongan, Butuan C, 8600 Agusan del Norte. **DXIM**, A. Velez Str, Cagayan de Oro C, 9000 Misamis Oriental. **DXJS**, Capitol Hills, Tandag, 8300 Surigao del Sur. **DXJT**, Brgy Maloro,Tangub C, 7214 Misamis Occidental. **DXMR**, Baliwasan Chico, Zamboanga C, 7000 Zamboanga del Sur. **DXPT**, Tubig Boh, Bongao, 7500 Tawi-Tawi. **DXRG**, Dugenio Str, Gingoog C, 9014 Misamis Oriental. **DXRP**, Door 5, PTA Complex, Magsaysay Park, 2nd District, Agdao, 8000 Davao C. **DXSM**, Camp Asturias, Jolo, 7400 Sulu. **DXSO**, Satellite Office, MSU Campus, Marawi C, 9700 Lanao del Sur. **DYES**, Capitol Compd, Borongan, 6800 Eastern Samar. **DYLL**, PNRC Youth Center Bldg, Bonifacio Drive, Iloilo C, 5000 Iloilo. **DYMP**, Govt Center, Candahug, Palo, Leyte. **DYMR**, CSCST Compound, Vicente Sotto, 6000 Cebu C. **DYOG**, Butel Building, Calbayog C, 6710 W. Samar. **DYSL**, Southern Leyte State University Compound, Sogod, 6606 Southern Leyte. **DZAG**, Don Mariano Marcos Memorial State University, Agoo, 2504 La Union. **DZEQ**, Polo Field, Pacdal Circle, Baguio C, 2600 Benguet. **DZER**, Boac, 4900 Marinduque. **DZMQ**, Tondaligan Beach, Dagupan C, 2400 Pangasinan. **DZRK**, Capitol Compound, Tabuk, 3800 Kalinga. **DZVC** Virac, State College Campus, 4800 Catanduanes.

See **PB)** entries in the MW frequency list below for frequencies and powers. Regional stns usually relay news from Manila on the h., and also carry networked prgrs at times.

NB: A number of stns are operating irr or are inactive.

MW	Call	kHz	kW	Net	MW	Call	kHz	kW	Net
67)	DXGH	531	5	dz	33)	DZCV	684	5	
118)	DYDW	531	10	cm	84)	DXBC	693	10	ag
47)	DZBR	531	5		85)	DXDX	693	1	
83)	DYRB	540	1		50)	DYKX	693	1	dz
54)	DZWT	540	10	dz	91)	DYRB	693	10	dz
PB)	DWRP	549	10		106)	DZTP	693	10	
16)	DXHM	549	5	cm	31)	DZAS	702	50	
84)	DZXL	558	50		84)	DXIC	711	5	ag
67)	DXCH	567	5	dz	58)	DXRD	711	5	ss
73)	DXMF	576	10	bo	29)	DYBR	‡711	5	
PB)	DYMR	576	10		71)	DZLW	711	5	
PB)	DZMQ	576	5		60)	DZVR	711	5	bo
17)	DZHR	576	5	dz	58)	DZYI	711	5	ss
16)	DXCP	585	5	cm	50)	DYOK	720	10	ak
PB)	DYLL	585	1	su	7)	DZJO	720	5	
16)	DXDB	594	5	cm	60)	DZSO	720	5	bo
60)	DYWR	‡594	10	bo	PB)	DWPE	729	10	
36)	DZAB	594	20	su	84)	DWNY	729	5	
10)	DZLL	603	10		70)	DXOR	729	5	
84)	DXPR	603	5		45)	DYEH	729	5	
22)	DZVV	603	5	bo	72)	DZGB	729	5	
75)	DWSP	612	5	dz	PB)	DZRB	738	60	
84)	DYHP	612	10		62)	DXND	747	5	cm
84)	DXDC	621	10	ag	84)	DYHB	747	10	
PB)	DZVC	621	1		50)	DZJC	747	10	ak
85)	DZTG	621	5		PB)	DWRS	756	10	
13)	DYAG	630	5		9)	DWHL	756	1	
2)	DZMM	630	35		42)	DWNW	756	5	
84)	DXKR	639	5		121)	DXBZ	756	10	
85)	DZRL	639	1		82)	DXJM	756	2	
67)	DWRH	648	10		83)	DXGS	765	5	
84)	DXMB	648	10		58)	DYAR	765	5	ss
84)	DXMB	648	5		68)	DYPR	765	10	
50)	DYRC	648	5	ak	58)	DZYT	765	5	ss
77)	DWRN	657	5		41)	DWWW	774	25	
130)	DXDD	657	5	cm	PB)	DXSM	774	10	
PB)	DYES	657	1		PB)	DXSO	774	10	
84)	DYVR	657	5	ag	84)	DYRI	774	10	ag
98)	DZXL	657	1		94)	DXRA	783	10	
PB)	DXRP	666	10		51)	DYME	783	5	
50)	DZRH	666	50/25		75)	DZNL	783	5	ak
42)	DWLW	675	5		95)	DWES	792	5	
103)	DXGD	675	5		38)	DWGV	792	5	
85)	DYKC	675	5		PB)	DXBN	792	10	
42)	DWGW	‡684	1		73)	DXPD	792	5	bo
43)	DWJJ	684	5		66)	DYRR	792	5	
50)	DYEZ	684	10	ak	39)	DWFA	801	5	

MW	Call	kHz	kW	Net	MW	Call	kHz	kW	Net
58)	DXBL	801	1	ss	45)	DWMI	999	5	
22)	DXES	801	5	bo	84)	DXHP	999	1	
16)	DYKA	801	5	cm	PB)	DXPT	999	1	
35)	DYWC	801	5	cm	91)	DYSS	999	5	su
60)	DZNC	801	10	bo	PB)	DZEQ	999	5	
90)	DZRJ	810	10		16)	DWBS	1008	5	cm
58)	DWAR	819	5	ss	102)	DWGO	1008	5	
114)	DWMG	819	1		85)	DXXX	1008	10	
101)	DXSC	819	1		42)	DWDC	1017	10	
53)	DXUM	819	10		PB)	DWLC	1017	10	
50)	DYVL	819	10	ak	44)	DXAM	1017	10	
39)	DWZR	828	5		138)	DXSN	1017	5	cm
84)	DXCC	828	10	ag	PB)	DYRP	‡1017	10	
46)	DYER	828	10/5		73)	DXMC	1026	5	bo
135)	DZTC	828	1		111)	DXMI	‡1026	1	
PB)	DXJS	837	5		58)	DZAR	1026	10	ss
58)	DXRE	837	5	ss	139)	DXUZ	1035	5/1	
22)	DYFM	837	10	bo	88)	DYRL	1035	10	
30)	DZXE	‡837	5		111)	DYUM	‡1035	5/2.5	
87)	DZRV	846	5	cm	22)	DZWX	1035	5	bo
67)	DXGO	855	10	ak	88)	DXCO	1044	5	
42)	DXWG	‡855	1		81)	DXLL	1044	5	uk
17)	DXZH	855	5	dz	90)	DXML	1044	1	
33)	DZGE	855	10		17)	DYMS	±1044	5	ak
58)	DWSI	864	5	ss	60)	DZNG	±1044	10	bo
128)	DYHH	864	10		85)	DXKD	1053	5	
140)	DZIP	864	10		112)	DYSA	1053	5	cm
58)	DZSP	864	5	ss	33)	DXKI	1062	5	
134)	DZWM	864	5		28)	DZEC	1062	40	
58)	DXRB	873	5		85)	DXKT	1071	5	
58)	DXRT	873	5		110)	DYXT	1071	1	
127)	DYUP	873	5		123)	DZSL	1071	1	
1)	DZPA	873	5	cm	16)	DWAM	‡1080	1	cm
33)	DZRC	873	5		72)	DWIN	1080	5	
3)	DWIZ	882	50		83)	DWRL	1080	5	
62)	DXMS	882	10	ss	85)	DXKS	1080	1	
PB)	DXRG	882	1		34)	DXRH	‡1080	5	
PB)	DYOG	882	10		67)	DYBH	1080	5	dz
12)	DWHQ	‡891	5		83)	DXCM	1089	10	uk
59)	DYSR	‡891	10		39)	DYHR	‡1089	1	
73)	DZGR	891	5		23)	DWAD	1098	10	
63)	DWNE	900	5		58)	DXCL	1098	5	ss
99)	DXIP	900	5		61)	DWDY	1107	5	
84)	DXRZ	900	5	ag	141)	DXBB	1107	5	
22)	DYOW	909	5	bo	129)	DYIN	1107	5	bo
115)	DYLA	909	5		8)	DZOM	1107	1	
91)	DYSP	909	5	su	8)	DXAS	1116	5	
16)	DZEA	909	5	cm	104)	DYTR	1116	10	
84)	DXRS	918	5	ag	113)	DZLB	1116	5	
PB)	DZSR	918	10		3)	DWAS	1125	5	
122)	DWRS	927	10		69)	DXGL	1125	10	
64)	DXMD	927	5		91)	DXGM	1125	5	su
84)	DXMD	927	5	ag	22)	DZWN	1125	10	bo
103)	DXMM	927	5	bo	26)	DWDD	1134	5	
58)	DZLG	927	5	bo	95)	DWJS	1134	5	
40)	DWIM	936	5		111)	DXMV	1134	5	uk
111)	DXON	936	5	uk	79)	DXOS	‡1134		
PB)	DXIM	936	10		PB)	DYRM	±1134	1	
84)	DYCC	936	1		77)	DWBT	1134	1	
85)	DYKW	936	1		137)	DYAF	1143	10	cm
82)	DZXT	936	1		31)	DZMR	1143	5	
PB)	DWFB	945	10		51)	DYCM	1152	5	
116)	DXDV	945	10		75)	DWCM	1161	10	
58)	DXRO	945	5	ss	111)	DXDS	1161	1	uk
4)	DYRO	‡945	5		84)	DYKR	1161	5	ag
PB)	DXJT	954	1		11)	DYRD	1161	5	
110)	DYMM	‡954	5		72)	DZMD	1161	5	
93)	DZAL	954	5		PB)	DXMR	1170	10	
20)	DZEM	954	40		PB)	DYSL	1170	5	
58)	DXYC	963	5	ss	65)	DZCA	‡1170	10	
73)	DYMF	963	10	bo	31)	DXYK	1179	5	su
136)	DZNS	963	5	cm	60)	DYCX	1179	5	
87)	DWFR	972	5		85)	DYSB	1179	5	su
45)	DWTI	972	5		86)	DZRS	1179	1	
17)	DXKH	972	5	dz	60)	DXIF	1188	10	bo
91)	DYSM	972	1	ak	82)	DXLX	1188	5	
75)	DWMT	981	5	dz	2)	DYRV	‡1188	1	
22)	DXBR	981	10	bo	82)	DZLT	1188	5	
84)	DXDR	981	5	ag	114)	DZXO	1188	5	
88)	DXOW	981	10		98)	DWBA	1197	5	
47)	DYBQ	981	5		31)	DXFE	1197	5	
58)	DZRD	981	5	ss	4)	DYRH	‡1197	5	
107)	DZQU	990	10/5		107)	DWAN	1206	10	
91)	DXBM	990	5	su	118)	DYRF	1215	10	cm
67)	DYTH	990	5	dz	50)	DWSR	1224	5	dz
67)	DZMT	990	5	dz	28)	DXED	1224	10	

MW	Call	kHz	kW	Net	MW	Call	kHz	kW	Net
PB)	DZAG	1224	10		132)	DZVT	1395	5	cm
87)	DWRV	1233		cm	58)	DXAQ	1404	-	ss
31)	DYVS	1233	5		85)	DYKB	1404	1	
32)	DWBL	1242	20		91)	DWRA	1413	5	su
105)	DXSY	1242	5		33)	DYXW	1413	5	
27)	DXZB	1242	5		109)	DWBC	‡1422	10	
50)	DXPH	‡1251	5		18)	DXMU	1422	5	
42)	DYRG	1251	1		11)	DYZD	1422	5	
72)	DZMS	1251	2.5		119)	DZOR	‡1422	1	
49)	DWMC	1260	5		89)	DYRS	1431	5	
50)	DXRF	1260	5	dz	50)	DWDH	1440	10	dz
97)	DYDD	1260	10		100)	DXSI	1440	0.01	
28)	DZEL	1260	5		52)	DXSA	1449	5	
91)	DWRC	1269	10		19)	DYAC	±1449	5	
22)	DYWB	1269	10/5	bo	31)	DWRF	‡1458	10	
60)	DZVX	1269	5	bo	97)	DYZZ	1458	10	
PB)	DZRM	1278	10		120)	DZJV	1458	10	
91)	DXRC	‡1287	5	su	87)	DWVR	1467	1	cm
50)	DZZH	1287	5	dz	131)	DXVP	1467	5	cm
4)	DWLQ	‡1296	5		92)	DWRB	1476	1	
133)	DWPR	1296	5		90)	DXRJ	1476	10	
2)	DXAB	1296	5		88)	DZYA	1476	1	
42)	DYJJ	1296	5		67)	DYDH	1485	5	dz
28)	DYFX	‡1305	10		108)	DWSS	1494	10	
25)	DWXI	1314	10		83)	DXOC	1494	5	
57)	DXAD	±1322	5		36)	DYBB	‡1503	5	su
36)	DYSI	1323	10	su	2)	DYAB	1512	10	
PB)	DZRK	1323	10		125)	DZAT	1512	10	
58)	DWAY	1332	5	ss	14)	DZME	1530	25	
85)	DZKI	1332	1		77)	DZYM	1539	5	
91)	DXRL	‡1341	10	su	36)	DZSD	1548	10	su
48)	DWUN	1350	10		16)	DYDM	1548	5	cm
36)	DXXY	‡1350	5	su	43)	DZKV	‡1548	5	
PB)	DZER	‡1350	5		5)	DXID	1566	10	
129)	DYSJ	1359	1		PB)	DYMP	‡1566	7.8	
77)	DZYR	1359	5		74)	DZIII	‡1566	10	
58)	DWTT	‡1368	5		21)	DXJR	‡1575	10	
85)	DXKO	1368	10		4)	DYAY	‡1584	10	
85)	DZBS	1368	2.5		24)	DWBR	1584	5	
15)	DZRA	1368	1		124)	DXFM	1593	10	
85)	DXKP	1377	10		113)	DZUP	1602	1	
55)	DXCR	1386	10		37)	DWGI	1638	0.6	
16)	DYVW	1386	5	cm	56)	DZBF	1674	1	
42)	DZTV	1386	25						
17)	DYCH	1395	10	dz					

‡ = r. inactive, ± = variable

SW	Call	Location	kHz	kW	H of tr
PB)			6170±		2300v-1300v
PB)	DUR2	Marulas, Valenzuela	9580±	0.25	irreg

Alt. freq for 9580: 9620kHz (r. on 9619±). Operated by PBS, Philippine Broadc. Sce, these freqs. relay various PBS AM and FM sces. 6170kHz generally relays DZRM 1278kHz.

GENERAL NOTES:
Station identifications: Generally, stn IDs are given on the h. and half h. The English alphabet is used for the call letters, while the freq. is usually expressed in Spanish- or English-language numerals. Extensive stn details are included in sign on and sign off Anns
Callsign assignments: DU = Shortwave only; DW = Luzon; DX = Mindanao and Sulu; DY = Visayas and Palawan; DZ = Luzon.
Administrative divisions: Level 1: regions, 2: provinces, cities (C.), 3: municipalities, 4: barangays (brgy.). The National Capital Region (NCR) is also known as Metropolitan Manila or Metro-Manila.
NB: Cities may be referred to with or without "City", e.g. Baguio City or Baguio. Quezon City is always referred to by its full name.

Prgr. networks: ag=R. Agong, ak=Aksyon R. bo=Bombo R., cm=Catholic Media Network (CMN, see above and entry 16) below), dz=DZRH (key: 666kHz), ss=Sonshine R. (key: 1026kHz), su=Super R., uk=Radyo Ukay.
Web URLs for broadc. networks: FEBC: www.febc.org – Bombo R. **W:** www.bomboradyo.com – R. Mindanao Netw **W:** www.rmn.com.ph – Manila Broadc. Co **W:** www.mbcradio.net – Sonshine R. **W:** www.sonshineradio.com – DZRH: dzrh.tripod.com

FM: A large number of FM stns are operating throughout the country.
Manila FM(MHz): – 88.3 DWCT-FM "Jam 88.3" (Raven Broadc. Corp.) – 89.1 DWAV "Wave 89.1" (Blockbuster Broadc. System) – 89.9 DWTM "Magic 89.9" (Quest Broadc. Inc.) – 50) 90.7 DZMB "Love R." – 91.5 DWKY "Big R." (Mabuhay Broadc. System Inc.) – 92.3 DWFM "Radyo5 92.3 News FM" (Nation Broadc. Corp.) – 93.1 DWRX "Monster R." (Audiovisual Communicators Inc.) – 84) 93.9 DWKC "iFM" – 32) 94.7 DWLL "Mellow 947" – 28) 95.5 DWDM "Pinas FM"

– 17) 96.3 DWRK "Easy Rock" – 36) 97.1 DWLS "Barangay LS" – 3) 97.9 DWQZ "97dot9 Home R." – 31) 98.7 DZFE "The Master's Touch" (FEBC) – 99.5 DWRT-FM "99.5 RT" (Real R. Network Inc.) – 90) 100.3 DZRJ "RJ 100" – 67) 101.1 DWKYS-FM "Yes! FM" – 2) 101.9 DWRR "Tambayan 101.9" – 73) 102.7 DWSM "Star FM" – 103.5 DWKX "Wow FM" (Advanced Media Broadc. Syst.) – PB) 104.3 DWBR "Business R." – 105.1 DWBM "Crossover" (Mareco Broadc. Network) – 105.9 DWLA "R. High 105.9" (All Youth Channels) – 106.7 DWET "Energy FM" (Ultrasonic Broadc. Syst. Inc.) – 141) 107.5 DWNU "Win R.":

Addresses
For each entry the organisation or company name is followed by the call letters (in alphabetical order) and addresses of the stns licensed to the organisation. When contacting a stn, use Radio Station + the call letters as stn name. In some cases the stn may be operated by a different organisation than the licensee mentioned below.
PB) See separate listing for Philippine Broadc. Sce. Above. – **1)** Abra Community Btcg. Corp. DZPA R. Totoo, Blessed Arnold Janssen Communication Center, Zamora Str corner Rizal Str, Bangued, 2800 Abra – **2)** ABS-CBN Broadc. Corp. DXAB, KM-4, Shrine Hills, Matina, 8000 Davao C. DYAB, ABS-CBN Broadc. Center, Jagobiao, Mandaue C, 6014 Cebu. DYRV, Catbalogan, 6700 Samar. DZMM, 15/F, Philcomcen Bldg, Ortigas Ave, Pasig C, NCR – **3)** Allied Broadc. Corp. DWIZ, 5th Floor, Dominga Bldg, 2113 Pasong Tamo, Makati C, 1231 NCR – **4)** Allied Broadc. Center, Inc. DWLQ, Happy Valley Str, Ibabang Dupay, Lucena C, 4301 Quezon Province. DYAY, Manuel Quezon Str, 6000 Cebu C. DYRH, JTL Bldg, North Drive, Bacolod C, 6100 Negros Occidental. DYRO. Roxas C., Capiz. DYRP R. Tagring, General Luna Str, Iloilo C, 5000 Iloilo – **5)** Association of Islamic Dev't. Cooperative. DXID, Banale Dist, Pagadian C, 7016 Zamboanga del Sur – **6)** Metropolitan Manila Development Authority (MMDA). DWAN MMDA Traffic Radio 1206, MMDA Communications and Command Center, EDSA corner Orense Str, Guadalupo Nuevo, Makati C, NCR – **7)** Dayanihan Broadc. Corp. DZJO, Infanta, 4336 Quezon Province – **8)** Ben Viduya (OMARCO). DZOM, Calapan C, 5200 Mindoro Oriental – **9)** Beta Broadc. Syst. DWHL R. Apo, 8 Kessing Str, Olongapo C, 2200 Zambales – **10)** Bicol Broadc. Syst. DZLL, BBS Bldg, Balagtas Road, Magsaysay Ave, Naga C, 4400 Camarines Sur – **11)** Bohol Chronicle Radio Corp. DYRD, Dejaresco Bldg, 56 Bernardino Inting Str, Tagbilaran C, 6300 Bohol. DYZD, Brgy Tapon, Ubay, 6315 Bohol – **12)** Caceres Broadc. Corp. DWHQ R. Oragon, Diversion Rd., Tabuco, Naga C, 4400 Camarines Sur. – **13)** Cadiz Radio & TV Netw. DYAG, Cadiz C, 6121 Negros Occidental – **14)** Capitol Broadc. Center. DZME R. Uno, 5th Floor Victory Central Mall, Victory Liner Compound, 717 Rizal Avenue Extension, Monumento, Caloocan C, NCR – **15)** Catanduanes State College. DZRA, Virac, 4800 Catanduanes – **16)** Catholic Media Network (CMN). Most MW sts ID as R. Totoo. DWAM, Basilican Site, Batangas C, 4200 Batangas. DWBS Radio Veritas, 2/F Landco Business Park, Legaspi C, 4500 Albay. DXCP, Lagao, Gen. Santos C, 9500 South Cotabato. DXDB, Communications Media Center, San Isidro Cathedral Compound, Malaybalay C, 8700 Bukidnon. DXHM, Clergy House Compound, Madang, Mati C., Davao Oriental. DYDM, SJC Extension Campus, Mambajao, Maasin C, 6600 Southern Leyte. DYKA, St Joseph Bldg, San Jose de Buenavista, 5700 Antique. DYVW, Clergy House, Baybay Blvd, Borongan, 6800 Eastern Samar. DZEA, Brgy. Nalbo, Laoag C, 2900 Ilocos Norte– **17)** Cebu Broadc. Co. DXKH, Cagayan de Oro C, 9000 Misamis Oriental. DXZH, Zamboanga C, 7000 Zamboanga del Sur. DYCH, Tanke, Talisay C, 6045 Cebu. DYMS, San Bartolome Str, Catbalogan, 6700 Samar. DYSM, Brgy. Cawayan, Catarman, 6400 Northern Samar. DZHR, Tuguegarao, 3500 Cagayan. – **18)** Central Mindanao University. DXMU, Musuan, 8710 Bukidnon – **19)** Leyte State University. VISCA Compound, Bo Pangasudan, Baybay, 6521 Leyte – **20)** Christian Era Broadc. Sce. DZEM, Maligaya Bldg 2, 887 EDSA, Quezon C – **21)** COC Broadc. Netw. DXJR, Cagayan de Oro College, Max Suniel St, Carmen, Cagayan de Oro C, 9000 Misamis Oriental – **22)** Consolidated Broadc. Syst, Inc. DXBR, Bombo R. Broadc. Center, Arujville Subd, Brgy. Libertad, Butuan C, 8600 Agusan del Norte. DXES Bombo R. Broadc. Center, Amao Rd, Brgy. Bula, Gen. Santos C, 9500 South Cotabato. DXLX, Tambo, Brgy. Hinaplon, Iligan C, 9200 Lanao del Norte. DYFM, Sky City Tower, Mapa Str, Jaro, Iloilo C, 5000 Iloilo. DYOW, Bombo R. Broadc. Center, Arnaldo Blvd, Roxas C, 5800 Capiz. DYWB, Bombo R. Broadcast Center, Lacson Str, Mandalagan, Bacolod C, 6100 Negros Occidental. DZVV, Bombo R. Broadc. Center, Brgy. Tamag, Vigan, 2700 Ilocos Sur. DZWN, Bombo R. Broadc. Center, Maramba Bankers' Village, Bonuan Catacdang, 2400 Dagupan C, Pangasinan. DZWX, Bombo R. Broadc. Center, 87 Lourdes Subdivision Rd, Baguio C, 2600 Benguet – **23)** Crusaders Broadc. Syst. DWAD, 209 E. de la Paz Str, Mandaluyong C, 1550 NCR – **24)** Dawnbreaker's Foundation. DWBR R. Baha'i, Bulac, Talavera, 3114 Nueva Ecija or P. O.Box 27, San José City 3121 – **25)** Delta Broadc. Syst. DWXI, Mathew Str, Multinational Village, Parañaque C, 1708 NCR –

26) Dept. of National Defense. DWDD, Camp Aguinaldo, EDSA, Quezon C, 1110 NCR – 27) DXZB/TV13 Cooperative, Inc. DXZB, Zamboanga C, 7000 Zamboanga del Sur – 28) Eagle Broadc. Corp. DWIN, Bo. Lucao, Dagupan C, 2400 Pangasinan. DXED, Cabiguio Ave, Agdao, 8000 Davao C. DYFX, Tanke, Talisay C., 6045 Cebu. DZEC, R Aguila, Maligaya Bldg II, 887 EDSA, Quezon C. DZEL, Bo. Mayao, Lucena C, 4301 Quezon Province – 29) East Visayan Broadc. DYBR, Sagcahan Rd, P.O. Box 80, Tacloban C, 6500 Leyte – 30) Fairwaves Broadc. Netw. DZXE R. Tirador, Mira Hills, Vigan, 2700 Ilocos Sur – 31) Far East Broadc. Co. DWAS, P.O. Box 78, Arimbay, Legaspi C, 4500 Albay. DWRF, P.O. Box 3222, Amungan, Iba, 2201 Zambales. DXAS, P.O. Box 349, Tugbungan, Zamboanga C, 7000 Zamboanga del Sur. DXFE, Circumferential Rd, Dona Vicente Village, 8000 Davao C. DKXI, P.O. Box 8004, Brgy Morales, Koronadal C, 9506 South Cotabato. DYVS, P.O. Box 393, Km. 7, Pahanocoy, Bacolod C, 6100 Negros Occidental. DZAS, 62 Karuhatan Rd, Karuhatan, Valenzuela C, 1441 NCR. DZMR Missions Radio, Maharlika Highway, Sefton Village, Santiago City, 3311 Isabela – 32) FBS Radio Netw. DWBL, Unit 908, Paragon Plaza, EDSA corner Reliance Str, Mandaluyong C, NCR – 33) Filipinas Broadc. Netw. DYXW, Baruyan, San Jose, Tacloban C, 6500 Leyte. DZCV, Ugac Norte, Tuguegarao, 3500 Cagayan. DZGE R. Numero Uno, Nordia Resort, Baras, Canaman, Naga C, 4400 Camarines Sur. DZRC, Capt. Aquendes Drive, Legaspi C, 4500 Albay – 34) First United Broadc. Corp. DXRH Radio Hermosa, Zamboanga C, 7000 Zamboanga del Sur – 35) Franciscan Broadc. Corp. DYWC R. Bandilyo, Parish Compound, St Anthony of Padua Parish, Sibulan, Dumaguete C, 6201 Negros Oriental – 36) GMA Netw, Inc. DZSD, Arellano St., Dagupan C, 2400 Pangasinan. DXXY, Dipolog C, 7100 Zamboanga del Norte. DYBB, 2nd Flr, Oscar R. Arcenas Bldg, Roxas Av, Roxas C, 5800 Capiz. DYSB, Bacolod C, 6100 Negros Occidental. DYSI, GMA Compound, MacArthur Drive, Jaro, Iloilo C, 5000 Iloilo. DZBB, GMA Netw. Center, EDSA corner Timog Ave, Diliman, 1103 Quezon C – 37) Guzman Institute of Tech. DWGI, 509 Z.P. de Guzman, Quiapo, Manila, NCR – 38) GV Broadc. Syst. DWGV R. Centro, Rizal Extension, Cut-Cut, Angeles C, 2009 Pampanga – 39) Hypersonic Broadc. Center. DWFA, Maharlika Hwy, Sorsogon C, 4700 Sorsogon. DWZR Zoom Radio, Penaranda Str, Legaspi C, 4500 Albay. DYHR, Calbayog C, 6710 W. Samar – 40) Insular Broadc. Syst. DWIM R. Mindoro, Brgy. Bayanihan, Calapan, 5200 Mindoro Oriental – 41) Interactive Broadcast Media, Inc. DWWW, 23 E. Rodriguez Sr. Blvd, Quezon C – 42) Intercontinental Broadc. Corp. R. Budyong. DWDC, A.B. Fernandez Ave, Dagupan C, 2400 Pangasinan. DWGW, Penaranda Str, Legaspi C, 4500 Albay. DWLW, Brgy. Nangalisan, Laoag C, 2900 Ilocos Norte. DWNW, Mabolo Drive, Naga C, 4400 Camarines Sur. DXWG, Iligan C, 9200 Lanao del Norte. DYBQ, Datu Puti Subdivision, ,Cubay, Jaro, Iloilo C, 5000 Iloilo. DYJJ, Roxas Ave, Roxas C, 5800 Capiz. DYRG, Roxas Ave Extension, Andagao, Kalibo, 5600 Aklan – DZTV, Quezon C., NCR – 43) Kaissar Broadc. Netw. DWJJ R.bisyon (Double J Ad Ventures), Celcor Compound, Bitas, Cabanatuan C, 3100 Nueva Ecija. DZKV, Lipa C, 4217 Batangas – 44) Kalayaan Broadc. Syst. DXAM R. Rapido, Bug-ac, Matina, 8000 Davao C – 45) Katigbak Enterprises (ConAmor Broadcasting Systems). DWMI, Calapan, 5200 Mindoro Oriental. DWTI, Broadcast Village, Ibabang Dupay, Lucena C, 4301 Quezon Province. DYEH, Puerto Princesa C, 5300 Palawan.– 46) Puerto Princesa Broadc. Co. DYER Environment Radio, Puerto Princesa C, 5300 Palawan – 47) Kumintang Broadc. Syst. DZBR R. Balisong, KBS Bldg, Capitol Hills, Batangas C, 4200 Batangas – 48) Progressive Broadcasting Corporation. DWUN UNTV Radio La Verdad, UNTV Bldg, 907 EDSA, Brgy Philam, Quezon C – 49) Magiliw Community Broadc. Co. DWMC, Tomana, Rosales, 2441 Pangasinan – 50) Manila Broadc. Co. DWDH, Lucao District, Dagupan C, 2400 Pangasinan. DWSR, Lucena C, 4301 Quezon Province. DXPH, Prosperidad, 8500 Agusan del Sur. DXRF, Matina, 8000 Davao C. DYEZ, Wilrose Building, Burgos Str, Bacolod C, 6100 Negros Occidental. DYKX, Kalibo, 5600 Aklan. DYOK, Suite 301Carlos Uy Bldg, Diversion Rd, Manurriao, Iloilo C, 5000 Iloilo. DYPH, Puerto Princesa C, 5300 Palawan. DYVL, J. Romualdez corner Real Streets, Tacloban C, 6500 Leyte. DYRC, 3rd Floor, Cinco Centrum Building, Fuente Osmeña Blvd, 6000 Cebu C. DZJC, Brgy. 29, Rizal Street, St. Joseph District, Laoag C, 2900 Ilocos Norte. DZRH, MBC Bldg, Vicente Sotto Str, CCP Complex, Pasay C, 1300 NCR. DZZH, Cabit-an, Sorsogon C, 4700 Sorsogon – 51) Masbate Community Broadc. Co. DYCM, Bogo Amusement Complex, Taytayan, Bogo, 6010 Cebu. DYME, Tugbo Str, Masbate C, 5400 Masbate – 52) Mindanao Broadc. Co, Inc. DXSA, Marawi C, 9700 Lanao del Sur – 53) Univ. of Mindanao Broadcasting Netwk. DXUM, UMBN Broadcast Center, Multi-test Bldg, Ponciano Reyes St, 8000 Davao C – 54) Mt. Province Broadc. Corp. DZWT, P.O. Box 156, Mount Beckel, La Trinidad, Baguio C, 2600 Benguet – 55) Mt. View College. DXCR Voice of Hope, MVC, Valencia, 8709 Bukidnon – 56) Municipality of Marikina. DZBF, R. Marikina, Second Floor, City Hall, Shoe Avenue, Marikina C, NCR – 57) Mindanao Dev. Multi-Purpose Coop. DXAD Radio Ranao, Marcos Blvd, Saduc, Marawi C, 9700 Lanao del Sur – 58) Swara Sug Media Corporation. DWAR, Laoag C, 2900 Ilocos Norte. DWAY, Cabanatuan C, 3100 Nueva Ecija. DWSI, North Eastern Foundation College, Santiago, 3311 Isabela. DWTT, Tarlac C, 2300 Tarlac. DXBL, Mangagoy, Bislig C, 8311 Surigao del Sur. DXAQ, Philippine-Japan Friendship Hwy, Catitipan, Davao C. DXCL, Cagayan de Oro C, 9000 Misamis Oriental. DXRB, Brgy Libertad, Butuan C, 8600 Agusan del Norte. DXRD, J.P Laurel Ave, Bajada, 8000 Davao C. DXRE, Lagao, Gen. Santos C, 9500 South Cotabato. DXRO, Don Roman Vilo Str, Cotabato C, 9600 Maguindanao. DXRT, Jolo, 7400 Sulu. DXYZ, San Jose Rd, Baliwasan, 7000 Zamboanga C. DYAR, 3rd Fl. Astron Gestus Bldg, Gorordo Ave, 6000 Cebu C. DZAR, Suite 3004, 30/F Jollibee Plaza Building, F Ortigas Jr Road, Ortigas Center, Pasig City, 1600 NCR. DZRD, Banuan Guesset, Dagupan C, 2400 Pangasinan. DZSP, San Pablo C, 4000 Laguna. DZYI, Calamagui 2nd, Ilagan, 3300 Isabela. DZYT, Cagayan Teachers College, Tuguegarao, 3500 Cagayan – 59) National Council of Churches in the Philippines. DYSR, Camp Seasite Banilad, Dumaguete C, 6200 Negros Oriental – 60) Newsounds Broadc. Netw. DXIF, Bombo R. Broadc. Center, Corrales Ave, Cagayan de Oro C, 9000 Misamis Oriental. DYCX, San Jose de Buenavista, Antique. DYWR, Bombo R. Broadc. Center, Sto. Nino cor. Imelda Ave, Tacloban C, 6500 Leyte. DZNC, Bombo R. Broadc. Center, Barrio Menante II, Cauayan, 3305 Isabela. DZNG, Bombo R. Broadc. Center, Diversion Road, Brgy. Tabuko, Naga C, 4400 Camarines Sur. DZSO, Bombo R. Broadcast Center, Pennsylvania Ave, Parian, San Fernando C, 2500 La Union. DZVR, Bombo R. Broadcast Center, 48 A, Cabungaan Airport Rd, Laoag C, 2900 Ilocos Norte. DZVX, J. Pimentel Str, Daet, 4600 Camarines Norte – 61) Northeastern Broadc. Sce. DWDY, Ground Floor, Isabela Hotel, Mirante Uno, Cauayan, 3305 Isabela – 62) Notre Dame Broadc. Corp. DXMS, Sinsuat Ave cor. Rizal Ave, Cotabato C, 9600 Maguindanao. DXND, Daang Maharlika, Kidapawan C, 9400 North Cotabato – 63) Nueva Ecija Provincial Gov. DWNE, Brgy Singalat, Palayan C, 3132 Nueva Ecija – 64) Office of the Governor, Prov. of Agusan del Sur. DXDA R. Agusan, Patin-ay, Prosperidad, 8500 Agusan del Sur – 65) Office of the Civil Defence. DZCA, Agham Rd. Science Garden, Pag-asa Planetarium, NCR – 66) Ormoc Broadc. Co. DYRR, Bantigue, Ormoc C, 6541 Leyte – 67) Pacific Broadc. Syst (subsidiary of Manila Broadc. Co.). DWRH, Santiago C, 3311 Isabela.. DXCH, Cotabato C, 9600 Maguindanao. DXGH, Purok Malakas, Lagao, Gen. Santos C, 9500 South Cotabato. DXGO, MBC Compound, Brgy. Duterte, R. Castillo Str, Agdao, 8000 Davao C. DYBH, Bacolod C, 6100 Negros Occidental. DYDH, Iloilo C, 5000 Iloilo. DYTH, Real Str, Tacloban C, 6500 Leyte. DZMT, Laoag C, 2900 Ilocos Norte – 68) Palawan Broadc. Corp. DYPR, Rey Olivar Bldg., 61 Mabini St. Puerto Princesa C, 5300 Palawan. – 69) PEC Broadc. Corp. DXGL, Butuan C, 8600 Agusan del Norte – 70) Pedro N. Roa Broadc. DXOR, Don A. Velez Str, Cagayan de Oro C, 9000 Misamis Oriental – 71) Peñafrancia Broadc. Corp. DZLW R. Isarog, Naga C, 4400 Camarines Sur – 72) People's Broadc. Netw. DZGB, Mayona Building, Imperial Court Subdivision, Legaspi C, 4500 Albay. DZMD, Vinzons Ave, Daet, 4600 Camarines Norte. DZMS, Balobo Str, Sorsogon C, 4700 Sorsogon – 73) People's Broadc. Sce. DXMC, Bombo R. Broadc. Center, Km 4 General Santos Drive, Koronadal C, 9506 South Cotabato. DXMF, Bombo R. Broadc. Center, San Pedro Str, 8000 Davao C. DXPD, Bombo R. Broadc. Center, North Diversion Road, Brgy. Banale, Pagadian C, 7016 Zamboanga del Sur. DYMF, 87-A. Borromeo Str, 6000 Cebu C. DZGR, Bombo R. Broadc. Center, Taft Str Extension, Brgy 5, Tuguegarao, 3500 Cagayan. DZLG, Bombo R. Broadc. Center, Tahao Road, Legaspi C, 4500 Albay. – 74) Philippine Air Force. DZHH, Villamor Air Base, Pasay C, 1309 NCR – 75) Philippine Broadc. Corp. DWCM, Caranglaan District, Dagupan C, 2400 Pangasinan. DWMT, Naga C, 4400 Camarines Sur. DWSP, Tuding, Itogon, nr Baguio City, Benguet. DZNL, Brgy. Pagdalagan, San Fernando C, 2500 La Union. – 77) Philippine Radio Corp. DWRN, Manipit Rd, Queborac Bagumbayan, Naga C, 4400 Camarines Sur. DYRM, Bo. Calindangan, Dumaguete C, 6200 Negros Oriental. DZYM R. Asenso, Puerto Gallenero, Pag-asa, San Jose, 5100 Mindoro Occidental. DZYR, Catbangen, San Fernando C, 2500 La Union – 79) Public Affairs Sce, Armed Forces of the Philippines. DXOS, Basilan Island, Basilan – 81) R.T. Broadc. Specialistns Philippines. DXLL, Campaner Str, Zamboanga C, 7000 Zamboanga del Sur – 82) Radio Corp. of the Philippines. DXJM, J & M Bldg, Villakananga, Butuan C, 8600 Agusan del Norte. DZLT, Bo. Ibabang Dupay, Lucena C, 4301 Quezon Province. DZXT, MacArthur H-way, Tarlac C, 2300 Tarlac – 83) DWRL Radio, Inc (subsidiary of 82 above). DWRL, Purok 5, Rawis, Legaspi C, 4500 Albay. DXGS R. Asenso, NLSA Rd, Lagao, Gen. Santos C, 9500 South Cotabato. DXOC, Manabay, Catadman, Ozamis C, 7200 Misamis Occidental. DYRB, C. Padilla St., 6000 Cebu C – 84) Radio Mindanao Netw. DXBC, Montilla Blvd, Butuan C, 8600 Agusan del Norte. DXCC, Canoy Bldg., Don Apolinar Velez Str, Cagayan de Oro C, 9000 Misamis Oriental. DXDC, San Vincente Bldg, cor. Anda & Bonifacio Stns, 8000 Davao C. DXDR, Bo. Mario Turno, Dipolog C, 7100 Zamboanga del Norte. DXHP, Flomencia Bldg. P. Castillo Mangagoy, Bislig C, 8311 Surigao del Sur. DXIC, Pafs Mejia Bldg, Roxas Str. cor Aguinaldo Str, Iligan C, 9200 Lanao del Norte. DXKR, Gen. Santos Drive,

Koronadal C, 9506 South Cotabato. DXMB, Fortich Str, Malaybalay C, 8700 Bukidnon. DXMD, Bo. Obrero National Highway, Gen. Santos C, 9500 South Cotabato. DXMY, Esteros, RH 10, Cotabato C, 9600 Maguindanao. DXPR, Mercedes Str, San Jose Dist, Pagadian C, 7016 Zamboanga del Sur. DXRS, Km. 1 Rizal Str, Surigao C, 8400 Surigao del Norte. DXRZ, Zamaveco Bldg, Pilar Str, Zamboanga C, 7000 Zamboanga del Sur. DYCC, Brgy. Obrero, Calbayog C, 6710 W. Samar. DYHB, 4th Flt, SSS Bldg. Lacson Str, Bacolod C, 6100 Negros Occidental. DYHP, 2nd Flr, Gold Palace Bldg, 168 Osmeña Blvd, 6000 Cebu C. DYKR, C. Laserna Str, Kalibo, 5600 Aklan. DYRI, St Anne Bldg, Luna Str, La Paz, Iloilo C, 5000 Iloilo. DYVR, Punta, Tabuc, Roxas C, 5800 Capiz. DZXL, 4/F, Guadelupe Commerical Complex, Guadelupe Nuevo, Makati C, 1200 NCR – 85) Radio Philippines Netw. DXDX R. Ronda, Acharon Blvd, Gen. Santos C, 9500 South Cotabato. DXKD, Gonzales corner Lopez Jaena Str, Biasong, Dipolog C, 7100 Zamboanga del Norte. DXKO R. Ronda, Gusa, National Hwy, Cagayan de Oro C, 9000 Misamis Oriental. DXKP R. Ronda, Araulio Str, Brgy Datoc, Pagadian C, 7016 Zamboanga del Sur. DXKS, Capitol Rd, Surigao C, 8400 Surigao del Norte. DXKT R. Ronda, Marfori Heights, 8000 Davao C. DXXX R. Ronda, Brgy Tugbungan, 7000 Zamboanga C. DYKB R. Ronda, Bo. Sumag, Bacolod C, 6100 Negros Occidental. DYKC, Maguikay, Mandaue C, 6014 Cebu. DYKW R. Ronda, Cagamayan, Binalbagan, 6107 Negros Occidental. DZBS R. Ronda, Agrix Supermarket cor. Magsaysay Ave. & Bakawkan, Baguio C, 2600 Benguet. DZKI R. Ronda, San Agustin, Iriga C, 4431 Camarines Sur. DZRL R. Ronda, Bo. Kawayan, Batac, 2906 Ilocos Norte. DZTG, 46 Rizal Str, Tuguegarao, 3500 Cagayan – 86) Radio Sorsogon Netw, Inc. DZRS, Don Luis Lee Bldg, Plaza Bonifacio, Sorsogon C, 4700 Sorsogon – 87) Radio Veritas Global Broadc. Syst. DWRV, Maharlika Highway, Bayombong, 3700 Nueva Vizcaya. DWVR, San Jose C, 3121 Nueva Ecija. DZRV, R. Veritas, 20/F The Centerpoint Bldg 1, 162 West Ave corner EDSA, Ortigas Center, Pasig C, 1600 NCR – 88) R. Pilipino Corp (R. Asenso). DXCO, Atco Bldg, Capistrano & Gomez Str, Cagayan de Oro C, 9000 Misamis Oriental. DXOW, Mapa, 8000 Davao C. DXYL, Camaroli Av, Lupit Subd. Bacolod C, 6100 Negros Occidental. DZYA 2/F Tanglao Bldg, Balibago, Angeles C, 2009 Pampanga. – 89) Ragde, Vicente & Sons. DYRS, Ragde Comp, Corner M. Endrinda Str and Broce Str, San Carlos C, 6127 Negros Occidental – 90) Rajah Broadc. Netw (R. Bandido). DXRJ, RJ Clubhouse, Sta. Filomena, Iligan C, 9200 Lanao del Norte. DZRJ, Ventures Bldg 1, Gen. Luna Str, Makati C, NCR – 91) Republic Broadc. Syst. (owned by GMA Network Inc.) DWRA, Baguio C, 2600 Benguet. DWRC, San Nicolas, 2901 Ilocos Norte. DXBM, Cotabato C, 9600 Maguindanao. DXGM, Shrine Hills, Matina, 8000 Davao C. DXRC, Zamboanga C, 7000 Zamboanga del Sur. DXRL, 3/F Carisma Bldg., General Santos Drive, Koronadal C, 9506 South Cotabato. DXYK, Butuan C, 8600 Agusan del Norte. DYSP, Solid Rd, Brgy San Manuel, Puerto Princesa C, 5300 Palawan. DYSS, GMA Network Center, Nivel Hills, Apas, 6000 Cebu C – 92) Ribbon Broadc. Netw. DWRB, 5/F, LCC Bldg, Lipa C, 4217 Batangas – 93) Rinconada Broadc. Corp. DZAL R. Rinconada, UNEP Compound, San Roque, Iriga C, 4431 Camarines Sur – 94) RMC Broadc. Co, Inc (Rizal Memorial Colleges). DXRA R. Arangkada, A. Pichon St., 8000 Davao C – 95) Rufin Broadc. Enterprises. DWES, Narra, 5303 Palawan. DWJS, Roxas, 5308 Palawan – 96) Rural Electrification Corp. DXML, MacArthur Hwy, Digos C, 8002 Davao del Sur – 97) Siam Broadc. Netw. Corp. (Bantay R.) DYDD, Lapu-Lapu C, 6015 Cebu. DYZZ, Guihulngan, 6214 Negros Oriental – 98) Satellite Broadc. Corp. DWBA, Bangued, 2800 Abra. DZLU, National College of Technology Campus, Barangay 1, San Fernando C, 2500 La Union – 99) Southern Broadc. Netw. DXIP Bantay R., 3/F Lachmi Shopping Mall, Bolton Street, 8000 Davao C – 100) Southern Institute of Tech. DXSI, Cagayan de Oro C, 9000 Misamis Oriental – 101) Southern Philippines Mass Comm. DXSC, Camp Navarro, Calarian, 7000 Zamboanga C – 102) Subic Broadc. Corp. DWGO Galang ng Olongapo, 1 Kasarinlan Rd, Olongapo, 2200 Zambales – 103) Sulu Tawi-Tawi Broadc. Foundation. DXGD Radio for Peace, Bongao, 7500 Tawi-Tawi. DXMM R. Totoo, Gandasuli Str, Jolo, 7400 Sulu – 104) Tagbilaran Broadc. Corp. DYTR, CAP Bldg, CPG Ave crnr Borja Str, Dampas, Tagbilaran C, 6300 Bohol – 105) Times Broadc. Corp. DXSY, Mariano Marcos, Ozamis C, 7200 Misamis Occidental – 106) Tirad Pass R/TV Broadc. Netw. DZTP R. Tirad Pass, San Nicolas, Candon, 2710 Ilocos Sur – 107) Trans-Radio Broadc. Corp. (operated by Philippine Daily Inquirer). DZIQ R. Inquirer, 2/F Media Resources Plaza, Pasong Tirad cor. Mola Str, Brgy La Paz, Makati C, NCR – 108) Supreme Broadc. Systems. DWSS, Paragon Plaza, EDSA, Mandaluyong C, NCR – 109) United Broadc. Netw. DWBC, Bo. Ugong del Norte, Quezon C, 1110 NCR – 110) Universal Broadc. Syst (owned by Radio Mindanao Network). DYMM, Sunshine Village, Esperos Str, Tacloban C, 6500 Leyte. DYXT, Luna Str, Tagbilaran C, 6300 Bohol – 111) University of Mindanao Broadc. Netwk (UMBN). DXCM, UM School Compound, Cotabato C, 9600 Maguindanao. DXDN, UM Tagum School Compound, Tagum C, 8100 Davao del Norte. DXDS, Digos C, 8002 Davao del Sur. DXMI, Iligan C, 9200 Lanao del Norte. DXMV, Mt. Kitangcad Cor.

Kanlaon Street, Valencia, 8709 Bukidnon. DYUM, Ormoc C, 6541 Leyte – 112) University of San Agustin. DYSA R. San Agustin, 2/F Univ. of S. Agustin, Gen. Luna Str, Iloilo C, 5901 Iloilo – 113) University of the Philippines. DZLB, UP Los Banos College, 4031 Laguna. DZUP, Media Center, College of Mass Comunications, UP Campus Diliman, R, Magasay Ave corner Apacible Str, Quezon C, 1104 NCR – 114) Vanguard Radio Netw (Radio Vanguard). DWMG, Solano, 3709 Nueva Vizcaya. DZXO, Ground Floor Diego Building, Maharlika Highway, Cabanatuan C, 3100 Nueva Ecija – 115) Visayas Mindanao Confederation of Trade Unions. DYLA, Alu-Vimcontu Welfare Center, Pier Area, 6000 Cebu C – 116) Vismin Radio & TV Broadc. DXDV, Baan, Butuan C, 8600 Agusan del Norte – 118) Word Broadc. Corp. DYDW Radio Diwa, Burayan, San José, Tacloban C, 6500 Leyte. DYRF R. Fuerza, Univ. of San Carlos, Pelaez Str, 6000 Cebu C – 119) Zambales Btcg. & Devt. Corp. DZOR R. Olangapo, 1683 Rizal Ave, Olongapo C, 2200 Zambales – 120) ZOE Broadc. Netw. DZJV, 140 Brgy Parian, Calamba, 4027 Laguna – 121) Baganian Broadc. Corp. DXBZ R. Bagting, Bana Str, Sta Maria District, Pagadian C, 7015 Zamboanga del Sur – 122) Solidnorth Broadcasting System. DWRS Commando Radio, Tamag, Vigan, 2700 Ilocos Sur – 123) S.O.L. Telebroadcasting Station. DZSL, Purok 2, Talisay, Camarines Norte – 124) Ranao Radio & TV Broadcast System Corp. DXFM, Pangarungan Village, Marawi C, 9700 Lanao del Sur – 125) End Time Mission (Pentecostal Missionary Church of Christ 4th Watch). DZAT, Purok Rosal, Bo. Silangan Mayao, Lucena C., 4301 Quezon Province – 127) University of the Philippines in the Visayas. DYUP UPV Radio, Miagao, Iloilo – 128) Philippine Air Force, DYHH R. ng Hukbong Himpapawid, Bogo, 6010 Cebu – 129) Inter-Island Broadc. Corp. (IBC), owned by 73) above. DYIN, Bombo R. Broadcast Center, Oyo Torong Str, cor. J. Magno. Str, Kalibo, 5600 Aklan. DYSJ, San Jose de Buenavista, Antique – 130) Dan-ag sa Dakbayan Broadc. Corp. DXDD R. Kampana. New DXDD Bldg. Rizal. Str, Ozamis C, 7200 Misamis Occidental – 131) Roman Catholic Archdiocese of Zamboanga Broadc. Network (RCA-ZBN). DXVP R. Verdadero, Sacred Heart Center, R.T. Lim Bvd, Zamboanga C, 7000 Zamboanga del Sur – 132) Apostolic Vicariate of San Jose de Mindoro. DZVT R. Totoo, Labangan Poblacion, San Jose, 5100 Mindoro Occidental – 133) Multipoint Broadc. Netwk. DWPR Power Radio, A.B. Fernandez Ave, Bolosan District, Dagupan C, 2400 Pangasinan – 134) Alaminos City Broadc. Corporation. DZWM R. Totoo, St Joseph Cathedral Compound, Alaminos, 2404 Pangasinan – 135) Government of Tarlac Province. DZTC, MacArthur Hwy, Tarlac C, 2300 Tarlac – 136) Archdiocese of Nueva Segovia. DZNS R. Totoo, Brgy Pantay Fatima, Vigan, 2700 Ilocos Sur – 137) Diocese of Bacolod. DYAF R. Veritas Bacolod, Rizal Str corner San Juan Str, Brgy. 11, Bacolod C, 6100 Negros Occidental – 138) Silangan Broadcasting Corporation. DXSN R. Magbalantay or R. Totoo, 55 Jules Chevalier Str, Surigao C, 8400 Surigao del Norte – 139)Universitad de Zamboanga. DXUZ R. Lipay, Ipil, 7001 Zamboanga Sibugay – 140) Itransmission, Inc. DZIP R. Palaweño, Dimalanta Bldg, Rizal Ave, Puerto Princesa, Palawan – 141) Sarangani Broadcasting Netwk. DXBB R. Alerto, Yumang Str, Brgy San Isidro, Gen. Santos C, 9500 South Cotabato.

EXTERNAL SERVICES: R. Pilipinas, Radio Veritas Asia, FEBC International Service, VOA/IBB
see International Broadcasting section

PITCAIRN ISLANDS (UK)

L.T: UTC -8h — **Pop:** 67 — **Pr.L:** Pitcairn English — **E.C:** 50Hz, 240V — **ITU:** PTC

Stations:

FM	MHZ	kW	Station
1)	87.5	0.0025	Pitcairn Island R.
2)	107.0	0.001	Life Talk R.

Addresses and other information
1) Adamstown, Pitcairn Island. **L.P:** Paul Warren **Prgr:** local community radio, 10h daily **Format:** Sun-Fri: country & western music, Sat: religious music – **2)** satellite relay 24h from Simi Valley CA **W:** www.lifetalk.net **Format:** religious

POLAND

L.T: UTC +1h (31 Mar-27 Oct: +2h) — **Pop:** 38.5 million — **Pr.L:** Polish — **E.C:** 50Hz, 230V — **ITU:** POL

KRAJOWA RADA RADIOFONII I TELEWIZJI (KRRiT) (National Broadcasting Council)
✉ Skwer Ksiedza Kardynala Stefana Wyszynskiego Prymasa Polski 9, 01-015 Warszawa ☎ +48 225973000 📠 +48 225973180 **E:** krrit@krrit. gov.pl **W:** www.krrit.gov.pl
L.P: Pres: Jan Dworak
NB. KRRiT is the regulatory authority for broadcasting.

POLSKIE RADIO S.A. (PR) (Pub)

✉ al. Niepleglosci 77/85, 00-977 Warszawa ☎ +48 226459212
🖷 +48 226453993 **E:** public.relations@polskieradio.pl **W:** www.polskieradio.pl; www.prsa.com.pl (corporate)
L.P: Chmn: Andrzej Siezieniewski

LW	kHz	kW	Prgr	
Solec Kujawski	225	1200*	PR1	*) 1000kW at night

FM (MHz)	PR1	PR2	PR3	PR4	kW
Bialogard (Slawoborze)	106.0	98.2	101.5	-	10/2x15
Bialystok (Cieszynska)	-	106.4	-	91.1	1/0.1
Bialystok (Krynice)	92.3	-	96.0	-	30
Bogatynia (G.Wysoka)	92.8	-	-	-	1
Bydgoszcz (Foton)	-	-	-	96.2	1
Bydgoszcz (Trzeciewiec)	106.6	97.6	102.1	-	60/2x120
Czestochowa (Bleszno)	-	-	-	98.9	2
Czestochowa (Wreczyca)	87.5	90.6	91.7	-	10/2x60
Dzierzoniów	-	103.5	-	-	1
Elblag (Jagodnik)	-	102.3	-	101.2	5/0.25
Gdansk (Chwaszczyno)	95.7	-	99.9	-	120
Gdansk	-	89.5	-	93.4	1/0.1
Gdynia (Oksywie)	-	97.2	-	-	1
Gizycko (Milki)	97.1	92.6	94.4	-	6/2x10
Gorlice (Maslana Góra)	105.4	-	-	-	10
Gorzów Wlkp. (Janice)	94.9	-	-	105.4	0.1/1
Ilawa (Kisielice)	94.8	102.7	-	104.8	2x10/5
Jelenia Góra (Sniezne Kotly)	92.5	-	94.0	-	10
Kalisz (Mikstat)	100.0	95.6	102.5	94.2	10
Katowice (Kosztowy)	97.9	105.6	99.7	-	60
Kielce (Swiety Krzyz)	92.3	-	96.2	-	60
Kielce	-	102.7	-	87.6	1/0.1
Klodzko (Czarna Góra)	97.6	-	89.2	-	10
Klodzko	-	92.4	-	-	3
Konin (Zolwieniec)	87.7	-	103.3	-	2x30
Konin	-	95.0	-	-	1
Koszalin (Gologóra)	107.9	93.8	97.4	-	60
Kraków (Choragwica)	89.4	-	99.4	-	60
Kraków (Krzemionki)	-	102.0	-	97.2	1/0.4
Krosno (Sucha Góra)	88.0	-	92.0	-	120
Krynica (G.Jaworzyna)	106.4	89.6	-	98.4	1/0.1/1
Kutno	-	96.9	-	-	1
Lebork (Skórowo Nowe)	100.5	88.2	106.3	107.5	2x10/5/10
Legnica	-	105.3	-	103.3	2/0.3
Lezajsk (Giedlarowa)	96.8	-	98.9	-	10
Lobez (Toporzyk)	-	-	-	100.6	3
Lódz	107.8	91.4	103.8	107.3	30/2x10/1.5
Lowicz	101.6	-	-	-	10
Lubaczów (Boble)	100.0	88.4	96.0	-	10
Luban (Nowa Karczma)	99.0	-	91.5	-	10/60
Lublin (Piaski)	90.8	-	104.2	-	30/90
Nowy Tomysl (Bolewice)	-	107.7	-	-	10
Olsztyn (Pieczewo)	93.0	93.7	99.1	97.9	30/2/120/0.1
Opole (Chrzelice)	88.3	94.5	90.3	-	60/10/60
Ostroleka (Lawy)	106.7	96.3	98.5	93.4	10/5/10/0.2
Pila (Staszyce)	-	102.5	-	-	10
Plock (Rachocin)	92.2	98.1	96.1	-	60/2.5/60
Poznan (Srem)	92.3	-	96.4	-	120
Przasnysz	105.9	107.1	-	-	10
Przemysl (Tatarska Góra)	87.8	94.1	99.6	91.0	5/1/5/1
Przysucha (Kozlowiec)	92.0	104.8	-	-	10
Rabka (G.Lubon Wielki)	93.4	90.4	-	-	5
Radom (Wacyn)	-	100.3	-	97.5	1/0.1
Radom	-	-	-	104.6	1
Ryki	105.1	88.7	-	-	10
Rzeszów (Baranówka)	-	105.8	-	91.5	1
Siedlce (Losice)	88.3	-	90.5	-	30
Slupsk	104.3	-	-	106.8	2.8/5
Solina (G.Jawor)	90.7	-	96.3	-	10
Stargard Szczeszinski	-	107.6	-	-	1
Suwalki (G.Krzemianucha)	105.5	92.0	96.6	-	20/2x30
Swieradów-Zdrój	-	93.2	-	90.5	10/1
Swinoujscie (Chrobrego)	107.7	-	-	-	10
Szczawnica (G.Prehyba)	88.0	-	94.7	-	10/5
Szczecin (Kolowo)	100.3	-	102.3	-	60
Szczecin (Warszewo)	-	96.3	-	88.4	1
Tarnów (G.Sw. Marcina)	-	-	-	99.9	2.5
Tarnów (Lichwin)	91.1	88.6	-	-	10
Wagrowiec (Golancz)	101.3	-	-	-	3
Walbrzych (G.Chelmiec)	-	87.9	99.8	94.3	2x5/0.5
Walcz (Rusinowo)	101.9	-	90.9	-	30
Warszawa (PKiN)	92.4	104.9	99.1	92.0	0.3/2.5/0.1/0.2
Warszawa (Raszyn)	102.4	-	98.8	-	120
Wisla (G.Skrzyczne)	91.5	-	100.8	-	10
Wloclawek (Szpetal Górny)	-	93.9	-	-	1
Wlodawa (Zolnierzy)	-	102.5	-	-	10
Wloszczowa (Dobromierz)	88.9	-	-	-	5

FM (MHz)	PR1	PR2	PR3	PR4	kW
Wroclaw (G.Sleza)	98.8	-	100.2	-	120
Wroclaw (Zórawina)	-	87.7	-	107.5	10/5
Zagan (Wichów)	91.2	104.7	87.8	-	30
Zakopane (G.Gubalówka)	92.8	90.9	98.2	-	10/0.3/10
Zamosc (Feliksówka)	105.7	-	-	95.3	10/1
Zamosc (Tarnawata)	-	87.6	91.3	-	30
Zielona Góra (Jemiolów)	105.0	89.9	94.1	-	60
Zielona Góra (Wilkanowo)	-	-	104.0		2

NB: Sites with only txs below 1kW not listed.

D.Prgr: PR1 (Jedynka): 24h. – **PR2 (Dwójka):** 24h – **PR3 (Trójka):** 24h. – **PR4 (Czwórka):** 24h. – **External Service:** see Int. Radio section.

PR Regional Services

D.Prgr: All stations broadcast 24h. **PR R.Bialystok:** ul. Swierkowa 1, 15-328 Bialystok. **E:** radiobia@radio.bialystok.pl. On 87.9 (Lomza 0.2kW), 89.4 (Bialowieza 0.1kW), 98.6 (G.Krzemianucha 30kW), 99.4 (Krynice 30kW), 104.1 (Makarki 10kW). – **PR R.Dla Ciebe (RDC):** ul. Mysliwiecka 3/5/7, 00-977 Warszawa. **E:** radio@rdc.pl. On 87.6 (Ostrów Mazowiecka 1kW), 89.1 (Wacyn 5kW), 100.8 (Ostroleka 0.25kW), 101.0 (Warszawa PKiN 10kW), 101.9 (Rachocin 60kW), 103.4 (Losice 120kW). – **PR R.Gdansk:** ul. Grunwaldzka 18, 80-006 Gdansk. **E:** poczta@radio.gdansk.pl. On 91.1 (Skórowo Nowe 10kW), 102.0 (Slupsk 1kW), 103.7 (Chwaszczyno 120kW), 106.0 (Kwidzyn 1kW), 107.0 (Bytów 10kW). – **PR R.Katowice:** ul. Ligonia 29, 40-953 Katowice. **E:** sekretariat@radio.katowice.pl. On 89.3 (Zabrze 0.5kW), 97.0 (Racibórz 1kW), 98.4 (Wreczyca 60kW), 101.2 (Bytków 1kW), 102.2 (Kosztowy 60kW), 103.0 (G.Skrzyczne 10kW). – **PR R.Kielce:** ul. Radiowa 4, 25-317 Kielce. **E:** radio@radio.kielce.com.pl. On 90.4 (Kielce 0.25kW), 101.4 (Swiety Krzyz 120kW). – **PR R.Koszalin:** ul. Pilsudskiego 43-49, 75-502 Koszalin. **E:** radio@radio.koszalin.pl. On 88.1 (Rusinowo 3kW), 89.7 (Toporzyk 0.1kW), 91.0 (Kolobrzeg 0.1kW), 92.5 (Slawoborze 15kW), 95.3 (Slupsk 2kW)*, 98.0 (G.Chelmska 0.1kW), 103.1 (Gologóra 60kW). *) incl. prgrs from Slupsk studio. – **PR R.Kraków:** ul. Slowackiego 22, 30-007 Kraków. **E:** radio@radio-krakow.pl. On 87.6 (G. Lubon Wielki 5kW), 90.0 (G.Prehyba 10kW), 97.4 (Gorlice 2kW), 98.8 (Andrychów 1kW), 100.0 (G.Gubalówka 10kW), 101.0 (G. Sw. Marcina 10kW), 101.6 (Choragwica 60kW), 102.1 (G.Jaworzyna 1kW). – **PR R.Lódz:** ul. Narutowicza 130, 90-146 Lódz. **E:** studio@radiolodz.pl. On 96.7 (Sieradz 0.5kW), 99.2 (Lódz 30kW), 104.0 (Wieruszów 1kW). – **PR R.Lublin:** ul. Obronców Pokoju 2, 20-030 Lublin. **E:** poczta@radio.lublin.pl. On 93.1 (Biala Podlaska 5kW), 102.2 (Piaski 90kW), 103.1 (Ryki 10kW), 103.2 (Feliksówka 30kW). Substation: **PR R.Freee:** **E:** redakcja@radiofreee.pl. On 89.9 (Lublin 1kW). – **PR R.Merkury:** ul. Berwinskiego 5, 60-765 Poznan. **E:** office@radio-merkury.pl. On 91.1 (Mikstat 10kW), 91.9 (Zólwieniec 30kW), 98.3 (Golancz 10kW), 100.9 (Srem 120kW), 102.4 (Bolewice 3kW), 105.6 (Rusinowo 60kW). Local substation: **PR MC Radio:** E: redakcja@mcradio.pl. On (MHz) 102.7 (Piatkowo 2kW). – **PR R.Olsztyn:** ul. Radiowa 24, 10-206 Olsztyn. **E:** radio@ro.com.pl. On 99.6 (Milki 10kW), 103.2 (Pieczewo 120kW), 103.4 (Jagodnik 0.5kW). – **PR R.Opole:** ul. Strzelców Bytomskich 8, 45-084 Opole. **E:** pro_fm@radio.opole. pl. On 88.0 (Brzeg 1kW), 89.1 (Olesno 1kW), 92.6 (Paczków 1kW), 94.8 (Glubczyce 1kW), 96.3 (Kluczbork 30kW), 101.2 (Opole 1kW), 103.2 (Chrzelice 60kW), 105.1 (Strzelce Opolskie 1kW), 107.7 (Namyslów 1kW). – **PR R.PiK:** ul. Gdanska 48-50, 85-006 Bydgoszcz. **E:** radio@radiopik.pl. On (MHz) 100.1 (Trzeciewiec 120kW), 103.0 (Wloclawek 1kW), 106.9 (Brodnica 10kW). – **PR R.Rzeszów:** ul. Zamkowa 3, 35-032 Rzeszów. **E:** radiorz@radio.rzeszow.pl. On 90.3 (Machów 1kW), 90.5 (Sucha Góra 120kW), 96.4 (Mielec 1kW), 99.2 (G.Jawor 5kW), 102.0 (Tatarska Góra 10kW), 102.9 (Giedlarowa 30kW), 103.7 (Boble 10kW), 106.7 (Magdalenka 2kW). – **PR R.Szczecin:** al. Wojska Polskiego 73, 70-481 Szczecin. **E:** sekretariat@radio.szczecin.pl. On 92.0 (Kolowo 60kW), 98.7 (Slawoborze 10kW), 103.6 (Chrobrego 10kW). Substation: **PR R.Szczecin.FM:** **E:** sekretariat@szczecin.fm. On 94.4 (Warszewo 0.5kW). – **PR R.Wroclaw:** ul. Karkonoska 8-10, 53-015 Wroclaw. **E:** sekretariatzarzadu@prw.pl. On 89.0 (G.Wysoka 1kW), 95.5 (G.Chelmiec 5kW), 96.0 (Czarna Góra 10kW), 96.7 (Sniezne Kotly 10kW), 98.0 (G.Parkowa 0.1kW), 102.3 (G.Sleza 120kW), 103.6 (Nowa Karczma 60kW). Local substation: **PR R.RAM:** **E:** ram@prw.pl. On 89.8 (Zórawina 6kW). – **PR R.Zachód:** ul. Kukulcza 1, 65-472 Zielona Góra. **E:** radio@zachod.pl. On 103.0 (Jemiolów 120kW), 106.0 (Wichów 30kW). Local substations of R.Zachód: **PR R.Zielona Góra:** E: rzg@rzg.pl. On 97.1 (Zielona Góra 1kW); **PR RMG FM:** ul. Warszawska 131, 66-400 Gorzów Wlkp. **E:** rmg@zachod.pl. On 95.9 (Janice 1kW).

OTHER STATIONS

MW	kHz	kW	Location	Station
9)	531	0.8	Zywiec	R. AM
9A)	531	0.8	Wlodawa	Twoje R. Wlodawa
9)	963	0.5	Brzesko	R. AM
9B)	963	0.1	Lipsko	Twoje R. Lipsko
9C)	963	0.8	Lubaczów	Twoje R. Lubaczów
9D)	963	0.1	Lubliniec	Twoje R. Lubliniec

MW

	kHz	kW	Location	Station
9E)	1062	0.8	Cmolas	Twoje R. Cmolas
9F)	1062	0.5	Jaroslaw	Twoje R. Jaroslaw
9)	1062	0.8	Pulawy	R. AM
9)	1062	0.8	Skarzysko	R. AM
9)	1332	0.5	Pinczów	R. AM
9G)	1404	0.8	Chojnice	R. RCH+
9)	1584	0.5	Busko-Zdrój	R. AM
9H)	1584	0.8	Andrychów	Twoje R. Andrychów
9)	1584	0.8	Slupsk	R. AM
9)	1584	0.8	Chelm	R. AM
9)	1602	0.8	Kraków	R. AM

FM

	MHz	kW	Location	Station
3)	87.7	3	Miedzyzdroje	R. Maryja
27)	87.8	2	Bialystok	R. Akadera
3)	87.8	1	Biala Podlaska	R. Maryja
1A)	87.8	1	Kraków	R. RMF Classic
17)	87.9	25	Lublin	R. eR
3)	87.9	10	Lódz	R. Maryja
2)	88.0	2	Wagrowiec	R. ZET
36)	88.1	1	Wielun	R. Fiat
1)	88.2	120	Kielce	R. RMF FM
1)	88.2	1	Polkowice	R. RMF FM
3)	88.2	1	Ostrów Wlkp.	R. Maryja
2)	88.3	60	Zielona Góra	R. ZET
3)	88.3	1	Kutno	H. Maryja
3)	88.4	10	Bielsko-Biala	R. Maryja
8)	88.4	5	Poznan	R. Zlote Przeboje 88.4FM
3)	88.5	10	Slupsk	R. Maryja
61)	88.6	1	Skierniewice	R. RSC
2)	88.7	1	Koszalin	R. ZET
3)	88.7	1	Wagrowiec	R. Maryja
5A)	88.8	1	Lomza	R. Eska Lomza
16)	88.8	2	Lodz	Studenckie Radio Zak
3)	88.9	2	Gdansk	R. Maryja
3)	88.9	120	Wroclaw	R. Maryja
4)	88.9	15	Szczecin	R. Plus Szczecin
3)	89.0	1	Warszawa	R. Maryja
39)	89.2	1	Bialystok	R. Jard
1)	89.3	60	Koszalin	R. RMF FM
1)	89.3	30	Lublin	R. RMF FM
2)	89.4	60	Luban	R. ZET
3)	89.4	2	Stargard Szczec.	R. Maryja
4)	89.5	10	Gniezno	R. Plus Gniezno
5A)	89.5	1	Sanok	R. Eska Rzeszów
4)	89.6	1	Opole	R. Plus Opole
8)	89.8	1	Szczecin	R. Zlote Przeboje 89.8FM
3)	89.8	1	Mielec	R. Maryja
30)	89.8	1	Poznan	R. Emaus
19)	90.0	1	Rybnik	R. 90
5A)	90.1	2	Lodz	R. Eska Lodz
13)	90.1	10	Zamosc	Katolickie R. Zamosc
47)	90.1	1	Koscierzyna	R. Kaszëbë
63)	90.2	1	Bielsko-Biala	R. Aniol Beskidów
43)	90.2	1	Kolobrzeg	R. Kolobrzeg
3)	90.2	10	Kamiensk	R. Maryja
3)	90.3	1	Zielona Góra	R. Maryja
8)	90.4	1	Wroclaw	R. Zlote Przeboje 90.4FM
3)	90.6	5	Kraków	R. Maryja
49)	90.6	1	Slupsk	R. FaMa Slupsk
4)	90.7	5	Radom	R. Plus Radom
5A)	90.7	2	Gdynia	R. Eska Trójmiasto
4)	90.7	2	Gryfice	R. Plus Gryfice
35)	90.8	1	Inowroclaw	R. GRA
14)	90.9	5	Walbrzych	Muzyczne R.
1)	91.0	120	Warszawa	R. RMF FM
8)	91.2	2	Katowice	R. Zlote Przeboje 91.2FM
1)	91.3	10	Lobez	R. RMF FM
38)	91.4	1	Pelplin	R. Glos
1B)	91.5	1	Slupsk	R. RMF Maxxx Pomorze
1)	91.5	15	Ostroleka	R. RMF FM
2)	91.6	10	Ryki	R. ZET
4)	91.7	1	Zielona Góra	R. Plus Zielona Góra
2)	91.8	10	Swinoujscie	R. ZET
3)	91.8	1	Ciechanów	R. Maryja
1)	91.9	30	Siedlce	R. RMF FM
2A)	92.0	1	Gdansk	R. Chilli ZET
59)	92.0	2.5	Wroclaw	R. Rodzina
8)	92.1	1	Bydgoszcz	R. Zlote Przeboje 92.1FM
2)	92.1	1	Wlodawa	R. ZET
2)	92.2	10	Opole	R. ZET
55)	92.3	1	Laziska Gorna	R. Express FM
47)	92.3	2	Gdansk	R. Kaszëbë
8)	92.5	1	Kraków	R. Zlote Przeboje 92.5FM
7)	92.6	1	Krosno	R. WAWA Rzeszów
2)	92.6	120	Lodz	R. ZET

FM (continued)

	MHz	kW	Location	Station
42)	92.6	1	Sepólno Kraj.	R. Weekend
3)	92.7	10	Lebork	R. Maryja
8)	92.8	1	Opole	R. Zlote Przeboje 92.8FM
4)	92.8	1	Torun	R. Plus Torun
49)	92.9	1	Tomaszów Maz.	R. FaMa Tomaszów
2)	92.9	10	Gryfice	R. ZET
1)	92.9	10	Wroclaw	R. RMF FM
1)	93.0	60	Katowice	R. RMF FM
5A)	93.0	10	Poznan	R. Eska Poznan
3)	93.1	1	Krynica	R. Maryja
7)	93.2	2	Szczecin	R. WAWA Szczecin
1)	93.3	120	Bydgoszcz	R. RMF FM
33)	93.3	1	Warszawa	R. VOX FM
25)	93.4	2	Gliwice	R. CCM
1)	93.5	10	Lódz	R. RMF FM
2)	93.6	120	Wroclaw	R. ZET
9)	93.7	1	Kraków	R. Planeta FM
1)	93.8	60	Luban	R. RMF FM
5A)	93.8	10	Gorzów Wlkp.	R. Eska Gorzów
3)	93.8	1	Kutno	R. Victoria
54)	93.9	1	Kedzierzyn-Kozle	R. Park FM
4)	94.0	1	Konskie	R. Plus Radom
24)	94.0	1	Warszawa	Antyradio 94 FM
5A)	94.1	1	Elblag	R. Eska Elblag
12)	94.1	1	Jaslo	VIA - Kat. R. Rzeszów
38)	94.2	1	Kartuzy	R. Glos
1)	94.3	60	Plock	R. RMF FM
3)	94.3	1	Racibórz	R. Maryja
8)	94.4	1	Zary	R. Zlote Przeboje 98.1FM
3)	94.4	1	Tarnobrzeg	R. Maryja
5A)	94.4	5	Bydgoszcz	R. Eska Bydgoszcz
23)	94.5	1	Grodzisk Maz.	R. Bogoria
3)	94.5	1	Ustrzyki Dolne	R. Maryja
1)	94.6	120	Poznan	R. RMF FM
5A)	94.6	1	Gdansk	R. Eska Trójmiasto
36)	94.7	10	Czestochowa	R. Fiat
47)	94.7	1	Rawa Maz.	R. Victoria
59)	94.8	2	Strzelin	R. Rodzina
1)	94.8	30	Zagan	R. RMF FM
4)	94.9	1	Jelenia Góra	R. Plus Legnica
31)	94.9	1	Sochaczew	R. Fama
2)	95.0	20	Lezajsk	R. ZET
3)	95.0	3	Szczecinek	R. Maryja
1)	95.1	1.6	Suwalki	R. RMF FM
64)	95.1	1	Zabrze	R. Planeta 95.1
2)	95.2	60	Szczecin	R. ZET
G)	95.2	1	Gdynia	R. TOK FM
3)	95.2	1	Swieradów-Zdrój	R. Maryja
3)	95.2	1	Sieradz	R. Maryja
56)	95.2	1	Kraków	R. Bajka
1)	95.3	60	Olsztyn	R. RMF FM
1)	95.3	60	Opole	R. RMF FM
1)	95.4	10	Tarnów	R. RMF FM
3)	95.4	5	Skierniewice	R. Maryja
3)	95.4	1	Gniezno	R. Maryja
5B)	95.5	1	Katowice	R. Eska Rock
2)	95.6	120	Bydgoszcz	R. ZET
8)	95.6	1	Lublin	R. Zlote Przeboje 95.6FM
2)	95.7	10	Wisla	R. ZET
8)	95.7	1	Rzeszów	R. Zlote Przeboje 95.7FM
5B)	95.7	1	Szczecin	R. Eska Rock
3)	95.8	1	Hrubieszów	R. Maryja
1B)	95.8	1	Warszawa	R. RMF MAXXX
37)	95.8	2	Konin	R. Konin
5A)	95.9	1	Koszalin	R. Eska Koszalin
57)	95.9	1	Olsztyn	R. UWM FM
53)	96.0	6	Lódz	R. Parada
1)	96.0	60	Kraków	R. RMF FM
1B)	96.0	1	Olesnica	R. RMF MAXXX
1)	96.1	1	Gorzów	R. RMF FM
1)	96.1	1	Legnica	R. RMF FM
4)	96.2	2	Zabrze	R. Plus Slask
1)	96.4	15	Bialogard	R. RMF FM
1B)	96.4	1	Gdansk	R. RMF MAXXX
4)	96.5	10	Warszawa	R. Plus Warszawa
3)	96.5	10	Zamosc	R. Maryja
1)	96.6	30	Walcz	R. RMF FM
2)	96.6	10	Lebork	R. ZET
8)	96.6	1	Zabrze	R. Zlote Przeboje 96.6FM
7)	96.7	3	Torun	R. WAWA Torun
1B)	96.7	2	Kraków	R. RMF MAXXX
52)	96.7	1	Skierniewice	R. Victoria
3)	96.9	7.5	Ilawa	R. Maryja
5A)	96.9	1	Szczecin	R. Eska Szczecin
2)	97.0	30	Poznan	R. ZET

FM	MHz	kW	Location	Station
3)	97.0	1	Lublin	R. Maryja
3)	97.0	2	Ciechanowiec	R. Maryja
1)	97.1	12	Wloszczowa	R. RMF FM
2)	97.2	1	Walbrzych	R. ZET
2)	97.3	60	Plock	R. ZET
5A)	97.3	1	Zamosc	R. Eska Zamosc
6)	97.4	1	Katowice	R. TOK FM
2)	97.5	30	Zagan	R. ZET
5A)	97.7	1	Kraków	R. Eska Kraków
2)	97.8	2.5	Szczawnica	R. ZET
2)	97.9	60	Walcz	R. ZET
1)	98.0	10	Kalisz	R. RMF FM
22)	98.1	60	Bialystok	R. Racja
5A)	98.1	2	Tarnów	R. Eska Tarnów
52)	98.1	1	Mszczonów	R. Victoria
34)	98.2	1	Przemysl	R. Fara
28)	98.3	1	Polkowice	R. Elka
1)	98.4	120	Gdansk	R. RMF FM
28)	98.5	1	Leszno	R. Elka
63)	98.5	1	Zywiec	R. Aniol Beskidów
51)	98.2	2	Lodz	R. Niepokalanów
2)	98.6	1	Nysa	R. ZET
2)	98.7	10	Ilawa	R. ZET
3)	98.8	10	Gorzów Wlkp.	R. Maryja
1)	98.9	30	Konin	R. RMF FM
47)	98.9	2	Reda	R. Kaszëbë
5A)	99.0	1	Szczecinek	R. Eska Szczecinek
22)	99.2	5	Biala Podlaska	R. Racja
42)	99.3	2	Chojnice	R. Weekend
64)	99.4	2.5	Poznan	R. Planeta Poznan
3)	99.5	1	Lipiany	R. Maryja
1)	99.5	1	Kluczbork	R. RMF FM
4)	99.5	1	Slupsk	R. Plus Koszalin
9)	99.6	1	Konin	R. Planeta Konin
1B)	99.7	1	Koszalin	R. RMF MAXXX Pomorze
21)	99.9	1	Zywiec	R. Bielsko
3)	100.0	5	Zielona Góra	R. Maryja
8)	100.1	1	Warszawa	R. Zlote Przeboje 100.1FM
1)	100.1	120	Krosno	R. RMF FM
66)	100.2	4	Chorzów	R. Fest
3)	100.2	1	Gizycko	R. Maryja
1)	100.2	120	Bialystok	R. RMF FM
48)	100.3	1	Racibórz	R. Vanessa
3)	100.3	1	Bogatynia	R. Maryja
3)	100.4	1	Jelenia Góra	R. Maryja
3)	100.4	10	Ostróda	R. Maryja
3)	100.4	10	Ostrów Maz.	R. Maryja
4)	100.4	5	Lódz	R. Plus Lodz
59)	100.4	2	Nowa Ruda	R. Rodzina
3)	100.4	1	Nysa	R. Maryja
41)	100.5	1	Kraków	Radiofonia
3)	100.6	10	Torun	R. Maryja
40)	100.6	60	Czestochowa	R. Jasna Góra
3)	100.6	10	Krosno	R. Maryja
3)	100.6	10	Glogów	R. Maryja
3)	100.6	5	Parczew	R. Maryja
4)	100.7	10	Gorzów Wlkp.	R. Plus Gorzów
3)	100.7	5	Rabka	R. Maryja
2)	100.7	2	Zamosc	R. ZET
1)	100.8	10	Jelenia Góra	R. RMF FM
32)	100.8	1	Kielce	FaMa Kielce
2)	100.9	10	Slupsk	R. RMF FM
3)	100.9	1	Wloclawek	R. Maryja
2A)	101.0	1	Kraków	R. Chilli ZET
5A)	101.1	2	Kalisz	R. Eska Kalisz/Ostrów
1B)	101.1	2	Radomsko	R. RMF MAXXX.
1B)	101.1	5	Walbrzych	R. RMF MAXXX
1)	101.1	30	Solina	R. RMF FM
3)	101.1	10	Zlotów	R. Maryja
1B)	101.2	1	Bytów	R. RMF MAXXX
58)	101.2	2.5	Nowy Sacz	R. RDN Malopolska
1)	101.2	10	Swinoujscie	R. RMF FM
3)	101.2	10	Zagan	R. Maryja
8)	101.3	10	Pabianice	R. Zlote Przeboje 101.3FM
24)	101.3	1	Kraków	Antyradio 101.3 FM
3)	101.3	1	Lomza	R. Maryja
3)	101.4	10	Czersk	R. Maryja
2)	101.4	30	Suwalki	R. ZET
5B)	101.5	1	Wroclaw	R. Eska Rock
3)	101.6	10	Pisz	R. Maryja
1)	101.6	10	Klodzko	R. RMF FM
3)	101.6	1	Szczecin	R. Maryja
2A)	101.6	1	Poznan	R. Chilli ZET
62)	101.7	1	Kepno	R. Sud
46)	101.7	120	Siedlce	Katolickie R. Podlasie
4)	101.7	120	Gdansk	R. Plus Gdansk
1)	101.8	60	Lezajsk	R. RMF FM
1)	101.8	10	Zakopane	R. RMF FM
3)	102.0	10	Bielsk Podl.	R. Maryja
1)	102.0	10	Gizycko	R. RMF FM
5A)	102.0	1	Leszno	R. Eska Leszno
3)	102.3	10	Lubaczów	R. Maryja
3)	102.4	1	Kartuzy	R. Maryja
1B)	102.6	1	Czestochowa	R. RMF MAXXX
4)	102.6	20	Polkowice	R. Plus Legnica
3)	102.6	10	Tarnów	R. Maryja
4)	102.6	1	Bydgoszcz	R. Plus Bydgoszcz
18)	102.6	1	Elk	R. 5 Elk
4)	102.6	1	Koszalin	R. Plus Koszalin
51)	102.7	1	Skierniewice	R. Niepokalanów
4)	102.7	5	Rabka	R. Plus Podhale
2)	102.8	10	Ostroleka	R. ZET
3)	102.8	1	Chelm	R. Maryja
3)	102.8	5	Kluczbork	R. Maryja
2)	102.8	5	Katowice	R. ZET
4)	102.8	1	Swieradów-Zdrój	R. Plus Legnica
1)	102.9	8	Walbrzych	R. RMF FM
9)	102.9	1	Slupca	R. Planeta Slupca
6)	102.9	1	Kraków	R. TOK FM
3)	102.9	10	Gryfice	R. Maryja
1B)	102.9	1	Lebork	R. RMF Maxx Pomorze
2)	102.9	12	Przysucha	R. ZET
8)	103.0	2	Gdansk	R. Zlote Przeboje 103.0i99.2
44)	103.0	3	Warszawa	R. Kolor 103 FM
2)	103.1	30	Solina	R. ZET
60)	103.1	1	Kalisz	R. Rodzina / R. Maryja
1)	103.2	10	Szczawnica	R. RMF FM
68)	103.3	1	Bialystok	R. i
2)	103.4	60	Czestochowa	R. ZET
1)	103.4	5	Lebork	R. RMF FM
1)	103.4	10	Przemysl	R. RMF FM
3)	103.5	3	Trzcinsko-Zdrój	R. Maryja
52)	103.5	5	Lowicz	R. Victoria
10)	103.5	5	Bydgoszcz	R. Roxy Bydgoszcz
58)	103.6	30	Tarnów	R. RDN Malopolska
50)	103.6	10	Lomza	R. Nadzieja
3)	103.7	3	Katowice	R. Maryja
67)	103.7	1	Wroclaw	R. PiN
2)	103.8	10	Klodzko	R. ZET
10)	103.8	1	Kraków	R. Roxy Kraków
12)	103.8	10	Rzeszów	VIA - Kat. R. Rzeszów
39)	103.9	2	Bialystok	R. Jard 2
45)	103.9	1	Ciechanów	Kat. R. Ciechanów
3)	104.0	10	Swiecie	R. Maryja
2)	104.0	10	Gizycko	R. ZET
2)	104.1	60	Kraków	R. ZET
1B)	104.1	5	Pila	R. RMF MAXXX
3)	104.2	10	Elblag	R. Maryja
3)	104.2	10	Bialogard	R. Maryja
2)	104.2	10	Jelenia Góra	R. ZET
45)	104.3	1	Plock	Kat. R. Plock
4)	104.3	1	Lipiany	R. Plus Lipiany
3)	104.4	1	Stalowa Wola	R. Maryja
2)	104.4	10	Kalisz	R. ZET
5B)	104.4	1	Gdansk	R. Eska Rock Gdansk
3)	104.5	10	Wlodawa	R. Maryja
3)	104.5	5	Wielen	R. Maryja
34)	104.5	1	Krosno	R. Fara
2)	104.6	1	Hrubieszów	R. ZET
3)	104.6	2	Opole	R. Maryja
5A)	104.7	1	Torun	R. Eska Torun
1)	104.7	120	Bialystok	R. Maryja
3)	104.7	10	Lobez	R. Maryja
15)	104.7	2	Sieradz	Nasze R.
1)	104.7	3	Rabka	R. RMF FM
5A)	104.9	60	Wroclaw	R. Eska Wroclaw
5A)	104.9	10	Krosno	R. Eska Rzeszów
11)	104.9	1	Chelm	Bon Ton R.
1)	104.9	1	Koszalin	R. RMF FM
24)	105.0	1	Bielsko-Biala	Antyradio 106.4 FM
2)	105.0	120	Gdansk	R. ZET
3)	105.1	1	Przemysl	R. Maryja
3)	105.1	30	Konin	R. Maryja
3)	105.1	10	Elk	R. Maryja
20)	105.2	1	Zakopane	R. Alex
3)	105.2	5	Wielun	R. Maryja
2)	105.3	60	Kielce	R. ZET
3)	105.3	30	Koszalin	R. Maryja
3)	105.3	1	Plonsk	R. Maryja
2)	105.4	30	Siedlce	R. ZET

FM	MHz	kW	Location	Station
10)	105.4	1	Poznan	R. Roxy Poznan
7)	105.5	1	Wroclaw	R. WAWA Wroclaw
3)	105.6	1	Kalisz	R. Maryja
5B)	105.6	1	Gdynia	R. Eska Rock
5A)	105.6	1	Pila	R. Eska Pila
5A)	105.6	3.2	Warszawa	R. Eska Warszawa
2)	105.7	20	Olsztyn	R. ZET
14)	105.8	10	Jelenia Góra	Muzyczne R.
1)	105.9	60	Czestochowa	R. RMF FM
46)	106.0	1	Zelechów	Katolickie R. Podlasie
10)	106.1	10	Wroclaw	R. Roxy Wroclaw
4)	106.1	10	Kraków	R. Plus Kraków
35)	106.1	5	Bydgoszcz	R. Gra
3)	106.2	10	Lidzbark Warm.	R. Maryja
65)	106.2	1	Warszawa	R. Warszawa
8)	106.2	1	Jelenia Góra	R. Zlote Przeboje 106.2FM
30)	106.2	1.5	Poznan	R. Emaus
69)	106.2	1	Opole	R. Planeta
3)	106.3	60	Plock	R. Maryja
3)	106.3	5	Klodzko	R. Maryja
2)	106.3	10	Zakopane	R. ZET
3)	106.3	20	Lezajsk	R. Maryja
1)	106.4	60	Zielona Góra	R. RMF FM
26)	106.4	10	Kalisz	R. Centrum Kalisz
24)	106.4	1	Zabrze	Antyradio 106,4 FM
1)	106.5	10	Elk	R. RMF FM
1B)	106.5	10	Kielce	R. RMF MaXXX
5A)	106.5	1	Lobez	R. Eska Szczecinek
10)	106.6	4	Opole	R. Roxy Opole
21)	106.7	1	Bielsko-Biala	R. Bielsko
1B)	106.7	3	Gdynia	R. RMF Maxx Trójmiasto
1)	106.7	60	Szczecin	R. RMF FM
14)	106.7	5	Swieradów-Zd.	Muzyczne R.
3)	106.8	120	Poznan	R. Maryja
5A)	106.8	1	Bochnia	R. Eska Malopolska
5A)	106.9	10	Radom	R. Eska Radom
3)	107.0	5	Czestochowa	R. Maryja
64)	107.0	1	Gizycko	R. Planeta Gizycko
5B)	107.0	1.6	Kraków	R. Eska Rock
2)	107.0	40	Lublin	R. ZET
2)	107.1	30	Konin	R. ZET
1A)	107.1	1	Gdynia	R. RMF Classic
3)	107.2	120	Kielce	R. Maryja
59)	107.2	2	Bystrzyca Klodzka	R. Rodzina
2)	107.3	120	Bialystok	R. ZET
1)	107.4	10	Ilawa	R. RMF FM
2)	107.4	30	Krosno	R. ZET
3)	107.4	2.5	Walbrzych	R. Maryja
5B)	107.4	1	Poznan	R. Eska Rock Poznan
3)	107.4	1	Koszalin	R. Maryja
2)	107.5	30	Warszawa	R. ZET
29)	107.6	60	Katowice	R. eM
1)	107.7	15	Zamosc	R. RMF FM
3)	107.7	10	Siedlce	R. Maryja
2)	107.7	20	Olsztyn	R. Maryja
2)	107.8	10	Tarnów	R. ZET
4)	107.9	1	Kielce	R. Plus Kielce
3)	107.9	20	Suwalki	R. Maryja
3)	107.9	10	Ryki	R. Maryja
4)	107.9	10	Opole	R. Plus Opole
2)	107.9	10	Przemysl	R. ZET

NB: Txs below 1kW not listed.

Addresses & other information:
1,1A,1B) al. Waszyngtona 1, 30-204 Kraków. E: redakja@rmf.fm – 2,2A) ul. Zurawia 8, 00-503 Warszawa. E: radiozet@radiozet.pl – 3) ul. Zwirki i Wigury 80, 87-100 Torun. E: radio@radiomaryja.pl – 4) ul. Zarawia 8, 00-503 Warszawa. E: – 5A) ul. Senatorska 13/15, 00-075 Warszawa. E: skrzynka@radioeska.com.pl. – 6) ul. Czerska 14, 00-732 Warszawa. E: tokfm@tokfm.com.pl – 7) ul. Senatorska 12, 00-082 Warszawa. E: radio@wawa.com.pl – 8) ul. Czerska 14, 00-732 Warszawa. – 9) ul. Fatimska 13A, 31-831 Kraków. Affiliates with own prgrs: 9A) ul. Pilsudskiego 10, 22-200 Wlodawa. E: tr_wlodawa@wp.pl. 0600-0800 (MF), 0900-1000 (SS), 1600-1700 (SS), 1500-1700 (MF). 9B) ul. Ilzecka 6a, 27-300 Lipsko. E: lipsko@radiogminne.com.pl. 0600-0800, 1600-1800. 9C) ul. M. Konopnickiej 9, 37-600 Lubaczów. E: radio.lubaczow@gmail.com. 0800-0900 (MF), 0900-1000 (Sat), 0900-1100 (Sun), 1600-1700 (MF), 1900-2000 (Wed). 9D) 42-700 Lubliniec. E: redakcja@radiolubliniec.pl 0600-0700 (MF), 1600-1700 (MF). 9E) ul. Szkolna 2, 36-105 Cmolas. E: radiocmolas@o2.pl. 0600-0800 (W), 1000-1400 (Sun), 1600-1800 (W). 9F) ul. Czarnieckiego 16, 37-500 Jaroslaw. 1500-1600 (MF). 9G) ul. Huberta Wagnera 1, 89-606 Chojnice. E: radio@chojnice24.pl. 0600-0800, 1600-1800. 9H) ul. Krakowska 74, 34-120 Andrychów. E: radio@andrychow.eu. 0700-0800, 1100-1200, 1700-1800, 2000-2100.

– 10) ul. Czerska 14, 00-732 Warszawa. – 11) ul. Wojslawicka 7, 22-100 Chelm. – 12) ul. Zamkowa 4, 35-032 Rzeszów. – 13) ul. Hetmana J. Zamoyskiego 1, 22-400 Zamosc. – 14) pl. Ks. K. Wyszynskiego 45, 58-500 Jelenia Góra. – 15) ul. Rynek 14, 98-200 Sieradz. – 16) III Dom Studenta, al. Politechniki 7, 93-590 Lódz. – 17) ul. Jana Pawla II 11, 20-535 Lublin. – 18) ul. Bulwarowa 5, 16-400 Suwalki. – 19) Os. Dabrówki 1b, 44-286 Wodzislaw Sl. – 20) ul. Smrekowa 26A, 34-500 Zakopane. – 21) ul. Olszówka 62, 43-300 Bielsko-Biala. – 22) ul. Ciepla 1/7, 15-472 Bialystok. – 23) ul. Kilinskiego 14, 05-825 Grodzisk Mazowiecki. – 24) al. Komisji Edukacji Narodowej 93, 02-777 Warszawa. 25) ul. Jana Pawla II 2, 44-100 Gliwice. – 26) ul. Lazienna 6, 62-800 Kalisz. 27) ul. Zwierzyniecka 4, 15-333 Bialystok. – 28) ul. Spóldzielcza 6, 64-100 Leszno. 29) ul. Jordana 39, 40-953 Katowice. – 30) ul. Zielona 2, 61-851 Poznan. – 31) ul. Narutowicza 1/1, 96-500 Sochaczew. – 32) ul. Piotrkowska 12/522, 25-510 Kielce. – 33) Senatorska 13/15, 00-075 Warszawa. – 34) pl. Katedralny 4, 37-700 Przemysl. – 35) ul. Chrobrego 75, 88-100 Inowroclaw. 36) al. Najswietszej Marii Panny 54, 42-200 Czestochowa. – 37) ul. Chopina 21e, 62-510 Konin. – 38) ul. Biskupa Dominika 11, 83-130 Pelplin. – 39) ul. Rzemieslnicza 4A, 15-703 Bialystok. – 40) ul. O. Augustyna Kordeckiego 2, 42-225 Czestochowa. – 41) ul. Rostafinskiego 8, 30-072 Kraków. – 42) ul. Jana Pawla II 1B, 89-804 Chojnice. 43) ul. Janusza Korczaka 2, 78-100 Kolobrzeg. – 44) ul. Narbutta 41/43, 02-536 Warszawa. – 45) ul. Tumska 3, 09-400 Plock. – 46) ul. Pilsudskiego 62, 08-110 Siedlce. – 47) ul. Zeromskiego 32, 84-120 Wladyslawowo. – 48) ul. Batorego 5, 47-400 Racibórz – 49) ul. Smugowa 1/11, 97-200 Tomaszów Mazowiecki. – 50) ul. Sadowa 3, 18-400 Lomza. – 51) ul. Zakroczymska 1, 00-225 Warszawa. – 52) ul. Seminaryjna 6A, 99-400 Lowicz. – 53) ul. Pilsudskiego 141, 92-318 Lódz. – 54) ul. Piastowska 1, 47-200 Kedzierzyn-Kozle. – 55) ul. Pilsudskiego 12, 43-100 Tychy. – 56) ul. Bokserska 1, 02-682 Warszawa. – 57) ul. Kanafojskiego 1/14, 10-724 Olsztyn. – 58) ul. Bema 14, 33-100 Tarnów. – 59) ul. Katedralna 13, 50-328 Wroclaw. – 60) ul. Widok 80/82, 62-810 Kalisz. – 61) ul. Wita Stwosza 2/4, 96-100 Skierniewice. – 62) ul. Jankowy 55, 63-600 Kepno. – 63) ul. Sw. Jana Chrzciciela 14, 43-346 Bielsko-Biala. – 64) ul. Zurawia 8, 00-503 Warszawa. – 65) ul. Floriańska 3, 03-707 Warszawa. – 66) ul. Jana Pawla II 2, 44-100 Gliwice. – 67) plac Inwalidów 10, 01-552 Warszawa. – 68) ul. Ks. A.Abramowicza 1A, 15-872 Bialystok. – 69) Pl. Teatralny 13, 45-056 Opole. NB. Networks exc. 9): addresses of local outlets not listed

PORTUGAL

L.T: UTC (31 Mar-27 Oct: +1h) — **Pop:** 10.7 million — **Pr.L:** Portuguese — **E.C:** 50Hz, 220V — **ITU:** POR

ANACOM – Autoridade Nacional de Comunicações.
HQ: Avenida José Malhoa, 12, 1099-017 Lisboa ☎+351 21 721 10 00 ᐟ +351 21 721 10 01 **W:** www.anacom.pt **E:** info@anacom.pt
Gov body responsible for licensing & monitoring radio & TV txs

APR – Associação Portuguesa de Radiodifusão (Assoc. of Portuguese Broadcasters)
Avenida Defensores de Chaves, n.º 65 - 3º 1000-113 Lisboa ☎+351 213 015 453/+351 213 015 459/ +351 213 016 999 ᐟ +351 21 301 65 36 **W:** www.apradiodifusao.pt **E:** apr@apradiodifusao.pt

RTP-Rádio e Televisão de Portugal, SGPS (Pub)
Av. Marechal Gomes da Costa, 37, 1849-030 Lisboa ☎ +351 21 382 00 00 ᐟ +351 21 382 00 98) **W:** www.rtp.pt **E:** (check www.rtp.pt)
LP: Chmn: Alberto da Ponte

Antena 1/Antena 2/Antena 3/RDP Africa/RDP Açores/RDP Madeira/RDP Internacional: ☎ +351 21 382 00 00. Antena 1 ᐟ +351-21-382 00 70 ᐟ+351-21-382 00 05, Antena 2 ☎+351-21-382 02 82 ᐟ +351-21-382 01 99, Antena 3 +351-21-382 02 02 ☎ +351-21-382 00 17, RDP África ☎+351-21-382 02 12 ᐟ +351-21 382 00 81. **News Dept:** ☎ +351-21 382 00 02 ᐟ +351-21 382 01 83 **L.P:** Chmn: bd of Dirs: Guilherme Costa, TD: Francisco Mascarenhas, Dir. of Antena 1/2/3:Rui Fernandes Pêgo, Dir. of RDP África: Jorge Oliveira Gonçalves, Reg. Dir (RDP Norte, Porto): José Alberto Lemos, Reg. Dir (RDP Centro, Coimbra): José Manuel Portugal, Reg. Dir (RDP Sul, Faro): Feliciano Estêvão, Reg. Dir. Açores & Madeira: see respective country entries, Dir. RDPI: Jorge Oliveira Gonçalves. Technical info. & support may be E: gabinete.tecnologias@rtp.pt
Ann: "Antena 1, a rádio que liga Portugal", "Antena 2, a rádio clássica"

MW Antena 1	kHz	kW	MW Antena 1	kHz	kW
Chaves	630	2	Covilhã	666	10
Miranda do Douro	630	2	Valença	666	10
Montemor-o Velho	630	10	Vila Real	666	10
Bragança	666	2	Viseu	666	10
Castanheira do Ribatejo*	666	10	Castelo Branco	720	10

MW Antena 1	kHz	kW	MW Antena 1	kHz	kW
Elvas	720	10	Mirandela	720	10
Faro	720	10	Lamego	756	2
Guarda	720	10	Portalegre	1287	2
Miramar (Porto)	720	10			

*) north of Lisbon; also known as "CEN" (Centro Emissor Nacional)

FM (MHz)	Ant. 1	Ant. 2	Ant. 3	kW
Alcoutim S	88.9	91.5	101.9	0.2
Arestal (Aveiro) C	106.7	95.2		0.5
Bornes N	92.8	91.1	102.1	10
Braga (Sameiro) N	91.3	88.0	103.0	10/2/10
Bragança N	96.4	98.2	104.2	9
Castelo Branco C	89.9	94.9	104.3	0.5
Coimbra C (a)	94.9			4
Elvas (Vª Boim)	103.8	93.2	101.6	5.4
Faro (S.Miguel) (b) S	97.6	93.4	100.7	10
Gardunha C	96.4	93.9	101.3	10
Grândola	99.2	90.6	103.6	10
Gravia C	104.5	106.8	107.9	0.1
Guarda C	94.7	88.4	100.6	6.4
Janas (Sintra)	96.9	96.0	103.8	0.2
Leiria C	98.7	104.2	106.4	1
Lisboa (Banática)	99.4	88.9		1/0.3
Lisboa (Monsanto) (c)	95.7	94.4	100.3	36/36/32
Lousã C	87.9	89.3	102.2	34/34/39
Manteigas B	104.8	91.6	100.3	0.5
Marão N	95.2	99.8	101.5	9
Marofa C	97.2	93.4	104.6	20/20/10
Mendro	87.7	91.1	102.4	20/20/44
Mértola	90.9	92.2	100.1	0.4
Minhéu N	94.9	88.0	104.7	10
Miranda do Douro N	90.3	95.7	98.9	0.05
Moledo N	102.9	88.0	92.3	0.5
Monchique (Fóia) S	88.9	91.5	101.9	25
Montargil	93.6	99.6	105.0	3
Montejunto	98.0	88.7	105.2	10
Muro N	94.9	94.6	102.0	10
Paredes de Coura N	102.9		92.3	0.1
Portalegre	97.9	92.9	102.8	10
Porto (Mte. da Virgem)N	96.7	92.5	100.4	45/44/8.8
Santarém	98.8			0.48
S. Domingos N	87.9	89.3	103.7	0.2
Serra de Ossa	88.4	95.0	102.1	2/0.5/0.5
Tróia (Setúbal)	106.7	99.7	107.9	0.07
Valença N	98.2	89.6	104.0	10
Viseu C	88.2	97.5	101.8	0.5/0.5/0.7

RDP África: a) 103.4MHz 1kW, **b)** 99.1MHz 1kW, **c)** 101.5MHz 4kW
D.Prgrs: 24h **Ant. 1**=Antena 1 (general pt rgrs, sport), **Ant. 2**=Antena 2 (serious music, culture), **Ant. 3**=Antena 3 (pop/rock music), **RDP África** (general prgrs aimed at the Portuguese-speaking African community. **C, N, S**: carry Ant. 1 reg. prgrs M-F 1300-1400 on FM only, while Ant. 1 on MW continues with a nationwide prgr

RDP Reg. Centres: N=RDP Norte: Rua Cândido dos Reis, 74, 4050-151 Porto ☎+351 22 339 99 00 📠+351 22 339 99 02. Dir. José Alberto Lemos. **C=RDP Centro:** Rua Dr. José Alberto Reis, 74, 3000-232 Coimbra ☎+351 23 979 89 00 📠+351 239 72 42 53 Dir. José Manuel Portugal **E:** rdpcentro@rdp.pt. **S=RDP Sul:** Campo Senhora da Saúde, 8001-904 Faro ☎ +351 289 89 68 69 📠+351 289 80 21 92 **E:** rdpsul@ rdp.pt. Dir. Feliciano Estêvão
RDP abroad: txs in Cape Verde, Guinea-Bissau, São Tomé e Príncipe, Mozambique, all relaying RDP África, in Timor, relaying RDPi and airing a local prgr, and in Bosnia for the Portuguese peace-keeping force: this tx received by the military (see respective country entries). **RDP África:** ✉ Av. Marechal Gomes da Costa, 37, 1849-030 Lisboa ☎ +351 21 382 00 00 📠 +351 21 382 00 81 **LP:** Dir: Jorge Oliveira Gonçalves **E:** rdpafrica@rtp.pt

Web Radio: Audio feeds at **W:** www.rtp.pt Antenas 1, 2 & 3 and RDP-África, RDP-Madeira and RDP-Açores. RTP web-only radios: 8 stns selectable in **W:** www.rtp.pt/play
SATELLITE: Europe, N. Africa & Mid. East: Hot Bird 7A (13° E), Transponder 111 (10.723GHz), Ku Band, Pol., FEC: ¾, SyR: 29.9 Ms/s, RDPi: PID 1230 (stereo), SID 4630. RDP Ant. 1: PID 1235, SID 4635, 24h. **Africa:** Intelsat 907 (27.5° W), Transponder 22/22, C Band, Right Circ. Pol., Symbol Rate 10.850 MSps (Mega Symbols per second). Freq. 3838 MHz; prgrs: RDP África: audio PID d 412, RDPi: audio PID d 413, Ant. 1: audio PID d 411.**Asia & Oceania:** Asiasat 2 (digital) (100.5°E), "European Bouquet", Transponder 10B (4GHz), C Band, Horiz. Pol. on 28.125 Ms/s, FEC ¾. RDP Int. stereo on the audio ch. 704, RDP Ant. 1 aired on the audio ch. 705 on ch. **N.America & Hawaii:** Galaxy 19 (digital) (97° W), Transponder 20, Frequency 12059.5 MHz, Ku Band, H. Pol., SyR 22.000 Ms/s, FEC ¾. RDP Int. audio PID: 4001 (stereo). **The**

Americas: Intelsat 805 (55.5° W), Transponder 16 (4080MHz), C Band, V. Pol., SyR 4340 Ms/s, FEC ¾. RDP Int.: PID 413. **S.America:** Telstar 14 / Estrela do Sul 2 (63°W), transponder 13, 11710MHz, ku Band, Vert. Pol., Sy.Rate 3200, FEC 2/3. RDP Int.: PID 268.

DAB: RDP halted T-DAB broadcasts in June 2011. There are no current plans to reactivate this service due to economic costs (which does not mean that the network cannot be restored in future).

EXTERNAL SERVICES:
RDP Internacional has suspended international broadcasting **Pro-Funk GmbH** closed down the facilities in Sines.

RÁDIO COMERCIAL, S.A. (Priv., comm.)
Owned by Media Capital Rádio – Radiofonia e Publicidade, S.A. **W:** http://mcr.clix.pt/index.asp
✉ Rua Sampaio e Pina, 24-26, 1099-044 Lisboa ☎ +351 21 382 15 00 📠 +351 21 382 15 89 **E:** info@radiocomercial.clix.pt, Northern office: Rua Tenente Valadim, 181, 4100 Porto ☎ +351 22 605 75 00 **W:** www.radiocomercial.clix.pt **LP:** Dir. Gen. MCR Rádios: Jordi Jordà

MW	kHz	kW	MW	kHz	kW
Avança	‡783	100	Cª. das Lezírias (Benavente)1035		*10

‡) currently inactive but possibly to be reactivated. *) Nominal power
D.Prgr: 24h **Ann** on MW: "Star FM"

FM	MHz	kW	FM	MHz	kW
Fóia (Monchique)	88.1	10	Grândola	96.8	10
Lamego	88.7	10	Monsanto (Lisboa)	97.4	44
Minhéu (Vila Real)	88.9	10	Monte da Virgem (Porto)	97.7	44
Esposende	89.3	0.4	Gardunha	98.2	10
Lousã	90.8	44	Sintra	98.5	0.3
Bornes (Chaves)	91.9	10	Portalegre	98.9	10
Mendro (Évora)	92.0	50	Valença	99.0	10
Bragança	93.9	10	Braga	99.2	10
Viseu	94.3	0.5	Montejunto	99.9	10
Guarda	96.1	10	Pico da Pena (Vouzela)103.1		0.2
São Miguel (Faro)	96.1	10			

D.Prgr: 24h **Ann on FM:** Rádio Comercial. **Format:** music stn
Local FM stns in the same group:
M80: (see Southern network) – **Star FM** (**W:** starfm.clix.pt): txs in Lisboa 96.6 MHz 5 kW, Valongo 105.8 1.5 kW, Cantanhede (near Coimbra) 103.0MHz 2 kW, Santarém 97.7MHz 2kW, Manteigas (near Guarda) 104.4 MHz 0.5 kW & Sabugal (near Guarda) 96.8 MHz 0.5 kW (see also R. Comercial MW) – **Best Rock FM** (**W:** www.bestrock. clix.pt): tx in Moita (near Lisboa) 101.1MHz 1.5 kW – **Cidade FM** (**W:** www.cidadefm.clix.pt): txs in Lisboa 91.6MHz 5 kW, Porto 107.2MHz 0.5 kW, Redondo (Alentejo province) 97.2MHz 0.5 kW, Alcanena (Santarém) 99.3MHz 2kW, Penacova (Coimbra) & Loulé (Algarve province), 99.7MHz 1 / 2 kW, Vale de Cambra (near Aveiro) 101.0 MHz 0.5 kW, Viseu 102.8 MHz 2 kW, Amares (Braga) 104.4MHz 1 kW, Montijo (Lisboa region) 106.2MHz 1 kW – **Smooth FM** (**W:** http://smoothfm. clix.pt): tx in Barreiro (Lisboa region) 103.0MHz 2kW, Matosinhos (near Porto) 89.5MHz 1.5 kW & Figueiró dos Vinhos (near Coimbra) 92.8MHz 1 kW – **Vodafone FM** (**W:** www.vodafone.fm): txs in Amadora (Lisboa reg.) 107.2MHz 1.5 kW, Maia (near Porto) 94.3MHz 1.5 kW – **MFM** (**W:** mfm962.com) tx in Barreiro (Lisboa reg.) 96.2MHz 2kW.

RÁDIO RENASCENÇA – Em. Católica Portuguesa (Rlg/Comm)
✉ Rua Ivens, 14, 1249-108 Lisboa ☎ +351 21 323 92 00 📠 +351 21 323 92 20 **E:** mail@rr.pt **PR: E:** rp@rr.pt **W:** www.rr.pt and www.rfm. pt and www.radiosim.pt
LP: News Dir.: Drª Graça Franco, PD (R. Renascença): Dr Nelson Ribeiro, PD (RFM): Dr. António Mendes, PD (Rádio Sim): Dina Isabel

MW: Rádio Sim	kHz	kW	MW: Rádio Sim	kHz	kW
Braga	576	10	Coimbra	981	10
Muge§	594	100	Guarda	981	1
Vila Moura	891	10	Chaves	1251	1
Évora	927	1	Valongo	1251	10
Seixal*	963	10	Castelo Branco	1251	1
Bragança	981	1	Viseu	1251	10
Vila Real	981	1			

§ usually 60-80kW; 2x10kW stand by units * 1x1kW standby unit

FM (MHz)	RR	RFM	R. Sim	kW
Aveiro	102.5	97.4		0.2
Arrábida	105.8	89.9		10/12
Bornes	89.6	101.1		10
Braga		89.7	101.1	10/1
Bragança	105.7	99.5		10
Elvas (L)			102.3	0.1
Elvas/Vª Boim (L)		107.1	99.8	1
Fóia	98.6	104.9		12
Gardunha	103.4	99.5		10
Guarda	90.2	104.0		10

FM (MHz)	RR	RFM	R. Sim	kW
Lamego	98.6	106.2		12
Leiria		107.7	95.1	1/3
Lisboa	103.4	93.2		50
Lousã	106.0	91.7		50/56
Marofa	94.2	103.0		16/10
Mendro	96.5	100.9		50
Minhéu	89.8	102.6		10
Monte da Virgem	93.7	104.1		50
Montejunto	90.2	106.8		10
Muro	103.4	90.4		10/20
Pena (Vouzela)	93.8	95.0		0.4
S. Mamede	95.3	101.1		10
São Miguel	103.8	89.6		10
Serra de Ossa	98.5	89.7		2
Sintra	105.0	106.6		0.3
Valença	100.0	95.4		10
Valongo		106.2		1
Viseu		99.4	103.6	1

L =includes local prgrs. **D.Prgr**.: 24h. **Ann:** "Renascença - música e informação dia-a-dia.", "RFM - só grandes músicas"
Stn IDs during local prgrs: Elvas "Rádio Sim de Elvas". Some prgs are simulcast on RR Canal 1 & R. Sim.
Local FM stns of the R. Renascença group: Mega Hits (W: www.mega.fm). txs in Lisboa 92.4MHz 5kW, Sintra (west of Lisboa) 88.0MHz 1 kW; Coimbra 90.0MHz 5kW, Aveiro 105.6MHz 1kW; Gondomar (Porto region) 90.6MHz 2kW and Braga 92.9 MHz 2kW.
Local FM stns relaying Rádio Sim: R. Sim Pal - Palmela (near Lisboa): 102.2 MHz 2 kW; **R. Sim Porto**- Maia (near Porto): tx in Valongo 100.8MHz 1.5kW ; **R. Sim Rio Maior** - Rio Maior (near Santarém): 92.6MHz 1kW, 99.5MHz 0.050kW ; R.Sim NoAr - Viseu: 106.4 MHz 2 kW ; **R. Sim Alentejo** – Portel (near Évora): 97.5 MHz 0.5 kW

Regional FM networks:

Northern network
RÁDIO NOTÍCIAS, PRODUÇÕES E PUBLICIDADE, S.A.
Edifício "Altejo", Rua 3 da Matinha. 3º piso, sala 301, 1900-823 Lisboa ☎ +351 21 861 25 00 🖷 +351 21 861 25 07/8 **LP:** Chmn.: Joaquim Oliveira, TD: Jaime Silva, Dir tx network: José de Sousa
TSF Northern office & Radiopress HQ: Rua Gonçal Cristóvão, 195, 4017-001 Porto ☎ +351 22 206 28 00 🖷 +351 22 206 28 03 **E:** tsf@tsf.pt **W:** www.tsf.pt
Station: TSF (priv., comm.)

FM	MHz	kW	FM	MHz	kW
Pena (Vouzela)	102.5	0.1	Guarda	106.6	10
Bornes	103.2	10	Minhéu	106.7	10
Gardunha	105.1	10	Braga	106.9	10
Valongo (Porto)	105.3	50	Bragança	107.0	10
Marofa	105.4	10	Lousã	107.4	50
Valença	105.7	10	Marão	107.6	10
Muro	106.5	10			

NB: the whole netw. relays key stn TSF 89.5MHz 5 kW Lisboa . TSF broadcasts 24 hours/ day via **R. Jovem** 105.4MHz 2kW Évora and **R. Santa Maria** 101.6MHz 2kW Faro (Algarve). TSF is also relayed most of the day via **R. Caldas** 103.1 MHz 1 kW Caldas da Rainha; in the Açores via **R. Comercial dos Açores**-TSF 99.4MHz 3kW Ponta Delgada (São Miguel isl.) and in Madeira via **R. Notícias-TSF** 100.0MHz 2kW Funchal. **Format:** mainly news. **D.Prgr.:** 24h

Southern network
LICENSEE: RÁDIO REGIONAL DE LISBOA, S.A.
(Owned by Média Capital Rádio) see R.Comercial. **W:** m80.clix.pt
Station: M80 Rádio (priv., comm.)

FM	MHz	kW	FM	MHz	kW
Porto #	90.0	5	Fafe #	103.8	1
Leiria#	93.0	2	Monsanto (Lisboa)	104.3	50
Aveiro#	94.4	2	São Miguel (Faro)	106.1	10
Penalva do Castelo#	95.6	0.5	Mendro	106.4	50
Montejunto	96.4	10	Portalegre	106.7	10
Vila Real #	97.4	1	Fóia (Monchique)	107.1	10
Coimbra #	98.4	5	Grândola	107.8	2

#) txs of associated local stns. **Format:** music oldies from 1970s-90s.
N: every h on the h. **D.Prgr:** 24h **Ann:** "M80 Rádio"

Rádio NFM (Priv., comm.)
NFM Global, Lda., Rua do Salgueiró, 69, 4585-208 Gandra PRD ☎+351 224 155 350 🖷+351 224 155 359 **E:** geral@nfm.pt **W:** radio. nfm.pt **FM:** 89.2 MHz 2 kW Amarante (near Porto), Espinho (near Porto) 88.4 MHz 1 kW, Bombarral 94.8 MHz 1 kW, Vila de Rei 103.2 MHz 0.5 kW & Ponte de Sor (near Portalegre) 96.0 MHz 2 kW + 105.6 MHz 0.050 kW. All frequencies carry also local prgrs. **D.Prgr:** 24h.

Rádio 5FM (Priv., comm.)
Avenida Visconde de Barreiros, 89, 5º, 4470-151 Maia ☎+351 229 439 380 **E:** geral@radio5.pt **W:** www.radio5.pt
FM: 89.0 MHz 2 kW Póvoa de Varzim (near Porto) **D.Prgr:** 24h
Associated local VHF-FM stns relaying Rádio 5: R. Foz do Ave (Vila do Conde): 88.6 MHz 2 kW – R. Voz de Santo Tirso (Santo Tirso): 98.4 MHz 0.4 kW Santo Tirso – R. Trofa (Trofa): 107.8 MHz 1 kW. All txs are located near Porto.

Rádio Nostalgia (Priv., comm.)
Rua Viriato nº 25 , 4º Dtº- 1050-234 Lisboa ☎+351 210 105 765 **W:** www.nostalgia.pt
FM: Lisboa 90.4 MHz 5 kW & Porto 91.0 MHz 1.5 kW **D.Prgr:** 24h

Local Stations (all priv. & comm.)
RADIO ALTITUDE
Rua Batalha Reis, 6300 Guarda +351 271 22 19 95 🖷 +351 271 22 14 92 **E:** altitude@altitude.fm **W:** www.altitude.fm **LP:** Dir: Rui Isidro
MW: ‡1584kHz 1kW 24h. (inactive, but planned to be reactivated)
FM: 90.9MHz 2kW 24h. **Ann:** "Altitude FM"

Other FM stations:

FM	MHz	kW	Station, location
57)	88.2	2	Ultra FM, Vila Franca de Xira
49)	88.6	2	R. Jornal de Setúbal, Setúbal: (effectively 0.05kW)
58)	89.1	2	R. Lezíria, Vila Franca de Xira
1)	89.7	2	R. Antena Livre, Abrantes
54)	90.5	2	R. Cidade de Tomar, Tomar
55)	90.8	2	R. Geice, Viana do Castelo
12)	91.4	2	R. Iris FM, Benavente
50)	91.8	2	Algarve FM, Silves
40)	91.8	2	R. Clube de Penafiel, Penafiel
9)	91.9	2	H. Local de Barcelos, Barcelos
15)	92.0	2	R. Beira Interior, Castelo Branco
35)	92.0	2	R. Amália, Loures
23)	92.1	2	R. Maiorca, Figueira da Foz
7)	92.7	2	ERA FM-Emissora Reg. de Amarante, Amarante
34)	92.8	2	Horizonte Tejo, Bobadela
4)		2	R. Mirasado, Alcácer do Sal
	94.0	2	R. Cidade Hoje, Vila Nova de Famalicão
29)	94.0	2	R. Douro Sul, Lamego
31)	94.0	2	R. 94 FM, Leiria
20)	94.1	2	Diana FM, Évora
19)	94.5	2	R. Despertar, Estremoz
18)	94.7	2	Voz do Sorraia, Coruche
42)	94.8	5	R. Festival, Porto
52)	94.8	2	R. Gilão, Tavira
61)	95.5	2	R. Placard, Vila Nova de Gaia
26)	95.8	2	R. Fundação, Guimarães
44)	96.1	2	R. Onda Viva, Póvoa de Varzim
8)	96.5	2	R. Aveiro FM, Aveiro
2)	96.7	2	R. Tágide, Abrantes
51)	96.9	2	R. Horizonte-Algarve, Tavira
28)	97.0	2	R. Clube de Lamego, Lamego
5)	97.8	2	RADAR, Almada
27)	98.0	2	R. Santiago, Guimarães
53)	98.0	2	R. Hertz, Tomar
14)	98.1	3	R. Marginal, Cascais
43)	98.9	5	R. Nova, Porto
48)	98.9	2	R. Azul, Setúbal: (effective power 0.25kW)
22)	99.1	2	R. Foz do Mondego, Figueira da Foz
3)	99.3	2	R. Soberania, Almada
39)	100.1	2	R. Nova Era Terra Verde 100.1, Paredes (rel 62))
41)	100.5	2	R. Portalegre, Portalegre
47)	100.6	2	R. Amália de Setúbal, Setúbal (rel R. Amália 92.0)
6)	100.8	2	R. SWtmn, Almada
30)	101.3	2	R. Liz, Leiria
37)	101.3	2	RNA-R.Nova Antena, Montemor-o-Novo
62)	101.3	2	R. Nova Era, Vila Nova de Gaia
10)	101.4	2	R. Pax, Beja
45)	101.7	2	R. Pernes, Santarém
16)	101.9	2	R. Juventude, Castelo Branco
33)	101.9	2	Estação Orbital, Loures (Sacavém)
24)	102.7	2	R. Clube de Gondomar, Gondomar (rel. 6))
46)	102.7	2	Antena Miróbriga, Santiago do Cacém
32)	103.1	2	Total FM, Loulé
21)	103.2	2	R. Telefonia do Alentejo, Évora
38)	103.7	2	R. Canção Nova, Ourém
1)	104.5	2	R. Voz da Planície, Beja
56)	104.6	2	R. Linear, Vila do Conde
59)	105.0	2	Digital FM, Vila Nova de Famalicão
63)	105.5	2	RCI-R. Club do Interior, Viseu
25)	105.8	2	R. "F", Guarda
13)	106.0	2	R. Antena Minho, Braga

FM	MHz	kW	Station, location
36)	107.1	2	R. Voz de Mangualde, Mangualde
17)	107.9	2	R. Universidade de Coimbra, Coimbra

Some stns use 0.05 kW repeaters + over 200 stns of less than 2kW

Addresses and other information:
Many stns have websites and may also have webcasting; most, if not all, have an email address.
Country code must be added to tel. & fax nos
1) Rua General Humberto Delgado, Edifício Mira Rio cv, 2200-125 Abrantes ☎ 241 360170/1 🖷 241 360179 **E:** geral@antenalivre.pt **W:** www.antenalivre.pt – **2)** Estrada Nacional 118 – nº 1010 -1º andar - Apartado 3 - 2206-906 Tramagal ☎ 241 890616/7/8 🖷 241 897169 **E:** radio.tagide@iol.pt **W:** www.radiotagide.com – **3)** Rua José Sucena, 120-3º, 3750-157 Águeda ☎ 234 602133 🖷 241-624334 **E:** radiosobera-nia@mail.telepac.pt – **4)** Rua da Fábrica, Convento dos Frades, 7580-122 Alcácer do Sal ☎ 265 622981 🖷 265 622479 **E:** mirasado@mail.telepac. pt **W:** w3.mirasado.pt – **5)** Rua Viriato, 25-6.º D, S.Sebastião da Pedreira, 1050-234 Lisboa ☎ 21 0105790 / 21 0105770 🖷 21 0105769 **E:** geral@ radarlisboa.fm **W:** www.radarlisboa.fm – **6)** Rua Viriato, 25-4º/6º, S. Sebastião da Pedreira, 1050-234 Lisboa ☎ 21 0105765 🖷 21 0105769 **E:** geral@swtmn.fm, geral@radiosw.tmn.pt **W:** www.radiosw.tmn.pt – **7)** Edifício Santa Luzia, 4600 Amarante, ☎ 255 420480/9 🖷 255 425317 **W:** www.erafm927.com **E:** erafm@iol.pt – **8)** Av. Dr. Lourenço Peixinho, 15-1º G, 3800 Aveiro ☎ 234 424601 🖷 234 428965 **E:** regional@mail. telepac.pt – **9)** Centro Comercial Bolívar, lojas 45-49, 4750-180 Barcelos ☎ 253 823530 /1 🖷 253 181265 **E:** geral@radiobarcelos.com **W:** www. radiobarcelos.com.pt – **10)** Rua de Angola, Torre C-11º, 7800 Beja ☎ 284 325 011 🖷 284 326312 **E:** radio@radiopax.com **W:** www.radiopax.com – **11)** Rua da Misericórdia, 4, 7800-285 Beja ☎ 284 311 330 🖷 284 321446 **E:** geral@vozdaplanicie.pt **W:** www.vozdaplanicie.pt – **12)** Rua dos Operários Agrícolas, 2135 Samora Correia, ☎ 263 650 730 🖷 263 650 739 **E:** director@irisfm.pt, olhonarua@irisfm.pt **W:** www.irisfm.pt – **13)** Praceta Escola do Magistério, 36, 4700-222 Braga ☎ 253 309560 🖷 253 309569 **E:** armindo.veloso@antena-minho.pt, info@antena-minho.pt **W:** www.antena-minho.pt – **14)** Rua Viriato nº 25 4ºE -105-234 Lisboa ☎ 21 0105742/63 🖷 21 0105769 **E:** geral@marginal.fm **W:** www.marginal.fm – **15)** Avª 1º de Maio, 39, 3º Dtº / Apartado 178, 6000-909 Castelo Branco ☎ 272 321 050 🖷 272 320 488 **E:** radio.interior@netvisao.pt **W:** http://radiobeirainterior.radios.pt – **16)** Rua Prof. Hugo correia Pardal, Edifício Plátano-loja "A", 6000-267 Castelo Branco ☎ 272 341758 🖷 272 347660 **E:** radio.juventude@netvisao.pt **W:** juventude.radios.pt – **17)** Apartado 1178 3001-501 Coimbra ☎ 239 410 410 & 239 410 426 🖷 239 835 446 **E:** info@ruc.pt, tecnica@ruc.pt **W:** www.ruc.pt – **18)** Rua do Couço, 29-r/c frt, 2100 Coruche ☎ 243 617436/0 🖷 243 617100 **E:** radiovozsorraia@sapo.pt – **19)** Rua Bento de Jesus Caraça Bloco C 1º Andar - Apartado 76 , 7100-104 Estremoz ☎ 268 339454 🖷 268 339456 **E:** geral@radiodespertar.net **W:** www.radiodespertar.net – **20)** MARÉ, EE08, 7000-500 Évora ☎ 266 700333 🖷 266 700555 **E:** geral@dianafm. com – **21)** Estrada de Arraiolos - Edifício Diário do Sul, 7000 Évora ☎ 266 730415 🖷 266 730411/6 **E:** telefonia@diariodosul.com.pt **W:** www. imprensaregional.com.pt/diariodosul/pagina/seccao/8/ – **22)** Rua dos Bombeiros Voluntários, 37-1.º, 3080-133 Figueira da Foz ☎ 233 040620 🖷 233 428134 **E:** fozdomondego.secretariado@gmail.com **W:** www. rcfm.web.pt – **23)** Edifício - CC Foz Center, Rua da República nº 202 l j 36, 3080-136 Figueira da Foz ☎ 233 930500 🖷 233 930499 **E:** geral@ radiomaiorcafm.com **W:** www.radiomaiorcafm.com – **24)** (see nr. 6) – **25)** Rua Soeiro Viegas, 2-B, 6300-758 Guarda ☎ 271 221468 🖷 271 221482 **E:** radiof@radiof.com **W:** www.radiof.com – **26)** Rua Arqueólogo Mário Cardozo, Ed. Guimarães Palace 411, Apartado 358, 4800-116 Guimarães ☎ 253 420520/2/5/6 🖷 253 420529 **E:** geral@radiofundacao.net **W:** www.radiofundacao.net – **27)** Rua Dr. José Sampaio, 264, Apartado 485, 4810-275 Guimarães ☎ 253 421700 🖷 253 421709 **E:** santiago@guima-raesdigital.com **W:** http://www.guimaraesdigital.com/index.php?a=p&q=rs&p=radiosantiago – **28)** Urbanização da Urtigosa, Bloco 6 - R/C, 5100-183 Lamego ☎ 254 609300/1 🖷 254 609309 **E:** geral@rclamego.pt **W:** www.rclamego.pt – **29)** Rua Fausto Guedes Teixeira, Bloco 1, Apartado 190, 5100-144 Lamego ☎ 254 611551/2 🖷 254 611550 **E:** radiodourosul@gmail.com, **W:** www.radio-dourosul.com – **30)** Urbanização Quinta do Amparo, lote 4, R/C – Esq. / Quinta da Matinha / Apartado 525, 2415-583 Leiria ☎ 244 817 707 🖷 244 813951 **E:** radio@lizfm.pt **W:** www.lizfm.pt – **31)** Av. dos Combatentes da Grande Guerra, Edifício Liz – 10º / Apartado 1113, 2400-122 Leiria, ☎ 244 860090/4 🖷 244 860098 **E:** geral@radio94fm.pt **W:** www.radio94fm.pt – **32)** Sítio do Troto, 8135-030 Almancil ☎ 289 391 031 /289 397 666 🖷 289 397110 **E:** totalfm@totalfm.pt **W:** www.totalfm. pt – **33)** Travessa do Olival, 6, 2685-086 Sacavém ☎ 21 9401019 & 21 9427750 🖷 21 9427757 **E:** orbital@orbital.pt **W:** www.orbital.pt – **34)** Rua da Boa Vista, Nº 2-B, 2685-027 Bobadela Loures ☎ 21 9559215 & 21 9553113 🖷 21 9558465 **E:** geral@horizontefm.pt **W:** www.horizonte-fm.pt – **35)** Rua Viriato, nº 25. 3º Esquerdo, 1050-234 Lisboa ☎ 21 010 57 40 🖷21 315 57 69 **E:** geral@amalia.fm **W:** www.amalia.fm – **36)** Av.

Conde D. Henrique, Bloco 4-B-r/c B, Apartado 34, 3530-112, Mangualde ☎ 232 612363 🖷 232 611490 **E:** geral@radiomangualde.com **W:** www. radiomangualde.com – **37)** Rua Francisco José Mareco, lote 28, 7050-241 Montemor-o-Novo ☎ 266 877 132 **E:** radionovaantena@gmail. com **W:** www.radionovaantena.com – **38)** Estrada da Batalha, Edifício Canção Nova/ Apartado 199, 2496-908 Fátima ☎249 530600 🖷249 530609 **E:** radiopt@cancaonova.com **W:** radio.cancaonova.pt – **39)** (see nr.62) – **40)** Rua Alfredo Pereira, 14-2º / Apartado 14, 4564-909 Penafiel ☎ 255 710040 🖷 255 710049 **E:** info.mail@radioclube-penafiel.pt **W:** www.radioclube-penafiel.pt – **41)** Av. de Santo António, 22 , Edifício Régio 1, Atelier "A" e "B", 7300-901 Portalegre ☎ 245 300550 🖷 245 331630 **E:** geral@radioportalegre.pt **W:** www.radioportalegre.pt – **42)** Rua da Alegria, 582 - 9 esqº, 4000-037 Porto ☎ 22 5370177 & 22 5101008 **E:** festival@radiofestival.pt, albertorocha@radiofestival.pt **W:** www. radiofestival.pt – **43)** Rua João de Barros, 265 - Pinhais da Foz - 4150-414 Porto ☎ 226 151000 🖷 22 6101420 **E:** nova@radionova.fm **W:** www. radionova.fm – **44)** Praça dos Combatentes, 15, 4990-439 Póvoa de Varzim ☎ 252 613686/888/878 & 252 299 570 🖷252 613898 **E:** radio-ondaviva@sapo.pt, geral@radioondaviva.pt **W:** www.radioondaviva.pt – **45)** Rua da Fé, 1, 2035 Pernes & Rua Pedro de Santarém, 10 – 3º Dto. , Apartado 511, 2001-906 Santarém ☎ 243 332922 & 243 332004 🖷 243 332 998 **E:** pernesradio@gmail.com **W:** www.radiopernes.pt – **46)** Rua Condes de Avillez, 19-21, Apartado 45, 7540-909 Santiago do Cacém ☎ 269 829920/8 **E:** antenamirobriga@antenamirobriga.pt **W:** www.antena-briga.pt – **47)** (see nr. 35) – **48)** & **49)** Rua Dr. António Rodrigues Manito, 58 - r/c "B", 2900-061 Setúbal ☎ 265 089052 & 265 573601 🖷 265 089053 & 265 573639 **E:** radioazul98.9@gmail.com, radiojornal@sapo.pt – **50)** Caixa d'água nº 5, 8300-012 Silves , ☎282 182710 **E:** algarvefm@ netvisao.pt **W:** www.algarvefm.pt – **51)** Quinta do Rosal, Sítio de São Pedro, E.N. 125 / Apartado 252 , 8800-903 Tavira ☎ 281 380 240 🖷 281 380 249 **E:** horizontealgarve@gmail.com **W:** www.algarvenoticias.com – **52)** Largo de Santana, 1, Apartado 102, 8800-902 Tavira ☎ 281 320240 🖷281 325523 **E:** radiogilao@net.vodafone.pt **W:** www.radiogi-lao.sdv.pt – **53)** Rua Centro Republicano, 135, Apartado 133, 2300-909 Tomar ☎ 249 323100/20 🖷 249 316995 **E:** radiohertz@radiohertz.pt **W:** www.radiohertz.pt – **54)** Travessa da Cascalheira, n.º 27, 2301 Tomar ☎ 249 310010 🖷 249 310016 **E:** radio@cidadetomar.pt **W:** www.radio. cidadetomar.pt – **55)** Praça 1º de Maio, 6-traseiras, 4900-534 Viana do Castelo ☎ 258 800400 🖷 258 800409 **E:** geral@radiogeice.com **W:** www.radiogeice.com – **56)** Rua das Donas, 3, 4480-910 Vila do Conde ☎ 252 642426/7/8/9 🖷 252 642303 **E:** radiolinear@gmail.com, radioli-near@clix.pt **W:** www.radiolinear.pt – **57)** Rua Fausto Nunes Dias, n.º5, 2600-145 Vila Franca de Xira ☎ 263 287590 🖷 263 287599 **E:** geral@ ultrafm.pt **W:** www.ultrafm.pt – **58)** Praça Marquês de Pombal, 2-7º,2600-222 Vila Franca de Xira ☎ 263 3286000 🖷 263 3286007 – **59)** Rua 8 de Dezembro, 214, Antas S. Tiago, Apartado 410, 4760-016 Vila Nova de Famalicão ☎ 252 308143/7 🖷 252 308144/9 **E:** comercial@ opiniaopublica.pt, jfernandes@opiniaopublica.pt **W:** www.digitalfm.pt – **60)** R. 5 de Outubro, Edifício Vilarminda, loja 204 / Apartado 218, 4764-976 Vila Nova de Famalicão ☎ 252 301781/2 🖷 252 301789 **E:** geral@ cidadehoje.pt, comercial@cidadehoje.pt **W:** www.cidadehoje.pt – **61)** Rua Raimundo de Carvalho, 242 - Sala 1, 4430-185 Vila Nova de Gaia ☎ 22 3770840/3 🖷 22 3770849 **E:** geral@radioplacard.pt **W:** www.radio-placard.pt – **62)** Rua das Camélias, 134-B, 4430-038 Vila Nova de Gaia ☎ 22 3770180 🖷 22 3759675 **E:** geral@radionovaera.pt **W:** www. radionovaera.pt – **63)** Rua do Comércio 58, 3º Andar 3500-110 Viseu ☎ 232 431 249 🖷 213 519 134 **E:** info@rci.pt **W:** www.rci.pt

Military Stations:
CINCSOUTHLANT-Commander-in-Chief South Atlantic Area/ **CINCIBERLANT**-Commander-in-Chief Iberian Atlantic Area: ✉ 2780 OEIRAS **A**. PR: +351 214 404106 - **FM** 88.4MHz 0.1kW (inactive) **D. Prgr:** AFN in English

PUERTO RICO (USA Commonwealth)

L.T: UTC -4h — **Pop:** 4 million — **Pr.L:** Spanish, English — **E.C:** 60Hz, 120V — **ITU:** PTR

FEDERAL COMMUNICATIONS COMMISSION (FCC)
see USA for details

BROADCASTERS ASSOCIATION OF PUERTO RICO
✉ Suite 212, Cobians Plaza, 1607 Ave. Ponce de León, San Juan 00926

Most stns broadcast in Sp. only °= E or mainly E. d=directional antenna ‡ = inactive Hrs of tr 24h except where indicated.

MW Call	kHz	kW	Station, location, h. of tr.
1) WPAB	550	5	WPAB 550, Ponce
2) WKAQ	580	10/5	R. KAQ, San Juan
3) WYEL	600	5	Mayagüez (r. WKAQ 580)
4) WEXS	610	1/0.25	X-AM, Patillas

MW Call	kHz	kW	Station, location, h. of tr.
5) WUNO	630	5	NotiUno, San Juan
6) WAPA	680	10	Cadena WAPA, San Juan: 0900-0400
WAPA	680	0.4	Arecibo (synchr. WAPA)
7) WKJB	710	10/0.75	KJB "Radio Isla", Mayagüez: 0915-0400
8) WIAC	740	10	Acción 740, San Juan
8) WIAC	740	0.5/0.1	Acción 740, Ponce (synchr)
9) WORA	760	5	NotiUno, Mayagüez
10) WKVM	810	50	R. Paz 810 AM, San Juan: 0900-0500
11) WXEW	840	5/1	NotiUno/R. Victoria, Yabucoa: 0830-0300
12) WABA	850	5/1	Waba "La Grande", Aguadilla
13) WQBS	870	5	La Gran Cadena QBS, San Juan: 0900-0400
14) WYKO	880	1/0.5	La Poderosa 880, Sabana Grande
15) WFAB	890	0.25	La Nave 890, Ceiba
16) WPRP	910	4.4	NotiUno, Ponce
17) WYAC	930	2.5	Acción 740, Cabo Rojo
18) WIPR	940	10	Máxima 940 AM, San Juan
19) WDNO	960	1/1.7	La Radio Que Te Bendice, Quebradillas
20) WPRA	990	0.91	La Primera, Mayagüez: 0900-0400
21) WOQI	1020	1/0.28	R. Coquí/La Señal de la Montaña, Adjuntas: 1000-0200
22) WOSO	1030	10	Total R. El Oso, San Juan: (°)
23) WZNA	1040	9/0.25	Zona 1040, Moca
24) WCGB	1060	5/0.5	La Roca, Rock R. Netw., Juana Díaz (rel. WBMJ 1190)
25) WMIA	1070	0.5/2.5	R. Arecibo del Norte, Arecibo: 0925-0400 (Sun-0200)
26) WLEY	1080	0.25	R. Isla 1080, Cayey
27) WSOL	1090	0.25/0.7	La Nueva Sol 1090, San Germán: 0930(Sun 1000-) -0400
28) WVJP	1110	2.5/0.5	R. Caguas, Caguas
29) WMSW	1120	2.6/5	R. Once, Hatillo: 1000-0200
30) WOIZ	1130	0.2/0.7	R. Antillas, Guayanilla: 0900-0200
31) WQII	1140	10	Once Q, San Juan: 1000-0400
32) WBQN	1160	5/2.5	Super Borinquén, Barceloneta-Manatí: 1100-0200
33) WLEO	1170	0.2	R. Leo, Ponce
34) WBMJ	1190	10/5	WBMJ Rock R. Netw. "La Roca", San Juan: (°)
35) WGDL	1200	0.25/1	La mejor AM, Lares
36) WHOY	1210	5	La Señal Activa de PR, Salinas: 0900-0330
37) WNIK	1230	1	Única R., Arecibo
38) WALO	1240	1	R. Oriental/Cad. R. Puerto Rico,Humacao
39) WJIT	1250	0.25/1	R. Hit, Sabana
40) WISO	1260	2.5	R. Wiso/Cadena WAPA, Ponce: 1000-0300
40) WISO	1260	2.5/0.9	R. Wiso/Cadena WAPA, Aguadilla (synchr)
40) WISO	1260	5/1.8	R. Wiso/Cadena WAPA, Mayagüez (synchr)
41) WCMN	1280	5	NotiUno 1280, Arecibo
42) WTIL	1300	1	La Voz Romántica, Mayagüez
43) WSKN	1320	5/2.3	R. Isla 1320, San Juan
44) WENA	1330	2/1.4	La Buena del Sur, Yauco
45) WWNA	1340	0.95	R. Una 1340, Aguadilla: 0900-0300
46) WEGA	1350	2.5	Nueva Victoria, Vega Baja: 1000-0200
48) WIVV	1370	5/1	WIVV Rock Radio Network "La Roca", Vieques Isl.: (rel WNMJ 1190): (°)
49) WOLA	1380	1	Prócer, Voz de la Montaña, Barranquitas: 0900-0200
50) WISA	1390	1	Acción 740, Isabela
51) WIDA	1400	1	R. Vida AM, Carolina.
52) WRSS	1410	1	R. Progreso, San Sebastián
2) WUKQ	1420	1	Ponce (r. WKAQ 580)
54) WNEL	1430	5	NotiUno/R. Tiempo, Caguas
55) WCPR	1450	1	R. Coamo, Coamo
56) WRRE	1460	0.5/0.3	Sonido Santidad, Juncos
57) WLRP	1460	0.5	R. Raíces, San Sebastián: 0900-0400
58) WKCK	1470	2.4/2.5	R. Cumbre, Orocovis: 0900-0200
59) WMDD	1480	5	El 14-80 AM, Fajardo
60) WDEP	1490	5/1	R. Isla, Ponce
61) WMNT	1500	1/0.25	R. Atenas, Manatí: 1030-0200
62) WBSG+	1510	1	R. Voz, Lajas
63) WVOZ	1520	25	R. Voz/La Voz Boricua, San Juan
64) WUPR	1530	1/0.25	Exitos 15-30, Utuado: 1000-0400
65) WIBS	1540	1d	R. Voz/R. Caribe, Guayama
66) WKFE	1550	0.25	La Isla/R. Café Dinámica Yauco
67) WRSJ	1560	5/0.75	La Bachatera del Norte, Bayamón
68) WPPC	1570	1/0.1	R. Felicidad, Peñuelas: 1300-2300
69) WEKO	1580	5/2	R. Voz 1580, Morovis
70) WXRF	1590	1	R. Voz, Guayama
71) WCMA	1600	5	Cima 1600, Bayamón: 1100-0500
72) WGIT	1660	10/1	Noticias 16-60, Canóvanas

Addresses and other information:
1) Box 7243, Ponce 00732-7243 **W:** www.wpabradio.com/index.html **E:** joselias@wpabradio.com - **FM:** WOQI 93.3MHz, WIOC 105 1MHz, WOYE 94 1MHz, Mayagüez – **2)** Box 364668, San Juan 00936-4668 **W:** wkaq580.univision.com - FM: KQ-105 La Primera 104.7MHz – **3)** Box 1370, Mayagüez 00681-1370 - **FM:** WAEL-FM 96.1MHz, Maricao – **4)** Box 640, Patillas 00723-0640 – **5)** Box 363222, San Juan 00936-

3222 **W:** www.notiuno.com - **FM:** WFID 97.7MHz, Río Piedras – **6)** Urb Baldrich, 134 Domenech Ave, Hato Rey 00918-3502 **W:** www.waparadio.com – **7)** Box 1293, Mayagüez 00709-1293 **W:** www.radioisla1320.com - **FM:** WKJB-FM 99.1MHz – **8)** Box 9023916, San Juan 00902-3916 **W:** facebook.com/Accion740 - FM: 102.5MHz – **9)** Box 43, Mayagüez 00681-0043 (or: P.O.Box 363222, San Juan, PR 00936) **W:** www.notiuno.com – **10)** Urb Roosevelt, 415 Calle Carbonell, Hato Rey 00918-2866 - **FM:** WORO 92.5MHz, Corozal – **11)** Box 100, Yabucoa 00767 **W:** www.victoria840.com – **12)** 6 Calle Munoz Rivera St., Aguadilla 00603-5154 (or: P.O.Box 188, Aguadilla, PR 00605) **W:** www.waba.850.com – **13)** Calle Bori 1508, Urb Autonsanti, San Juan 00927 – **14)** Calle Dr. Felix Tio 34, Sabana Grande, PR 00637 – **15)** P.O.Box 318, Río Blanco, PR 00744. **W:** www.radiounidadcristiana.com – **16)** Box 7771, Ponce 00732-7771 – **17)** Box 681, Cabo Rojo 00623-0681 - **FM:** WMIO 102.3MHz – **18)** Box 190909, Hato Rey 00918-0909 **W:** prnet.pr/maxima/index.htm - FM: Allegro 91.3MHz – **19)** P.O.Box 846, Aguada, PR 00602. **W:** www.zona1040am.com – **20)** Box 1293, Mayagüez 00681-1293 **W:** www.wpra990.com – **21)** Box 704, Adjuntas 00601-0704 – **22)** Box 9023940, San Juan 00902-3940 **W:** www.woso.com – **23)** Box 846, Aguada, PR 00602-0846 **W:** www.zona1040.com – **24)** Box 1414, Juana Díaz 00795-1414 (or: P.O.Box 367000, San Juan, PR 00936) – Mon-Fri 1300-1700 local programming in Spanish – **W:** www.therockradio.org – **25)** Box 1055, Arecibo 00613-1055 – **26)** Box 1186, Cayey 00737-1186 (or 100 Gran Bulevar Paseo #403A, San Juan, PR 00926) **W:** www.radioisla1320.com – **27)** Box 5000, Suite 442, San Germán 00683-0442 **W:** www.radiosol.com – **28)** Box 207, Caguas 00726-0207 - **FM:** 103.3MHz, Criolla – **29)** 550 Calle Truncado, Hatillo 00659-2712 (or P.O.Box 140961, Arecibo, PR 00614) **W:** www.radioonce.com – **30)** Box 561130, Guayanilla 00656-1130 **W:** radioantillas.4t.com – **31)** Cobian's Plaza, Santurce 00909-1820 (or: Box 193779, San Juan, PR 00919) – **32)** Box 1625 (or: Calle 16 H-6 Urb. Flamboyán), Manatí 00674 1625 **33)** Box 7213, Ponce 00732-7213 - **FM:** WZAR 101.9MHz – **34)** Box 367000, San Juan 00936-7000 (or: Av Ponce de León N° 1409, P4, Santurce 00907) (// 48)) – Mon-Fri 2300-0540 Spanish, 0540 2300 English, Sun English 24h **W:** www.therockradio.org **E:** radio@therockradio.org – **35)** Box 872, Lares, PR 00669 – **W:** www.wgdl1200am.com – **36)** Box 1148, Salinas 00751-1148 **E:** whoyam@coqui.net – **37)** Box 141526, Arecibo 00614 **W:** www.unicaradio1230.com - **FM:** 106.5MHz – **38)** Box 1240 (or: P.O.Box 9230), Humacao 00792 **W:** www.waloradio.com – **39)** Box 316, Coamo 00769-0316 (or: Box 878, Vega Alta, PR 00692) – **40)** Box 7251, Ponce 00732-7251 (or: 155 San Antonio St., Floral Park, Hato Rey, PR 00917) – **41)** Box 436, Arecibo 00613-0436 - **FM:** 107.3MHz – **42)** Box 1360, Mayagüez 00681-1360 – **43)** Box 363222, San Juan 00936-3222 **W:** www.radioisla1320.com – **44)** Box 1330, Yauco 00698-1330 **W:** www.labuena1330.com – **45)** Box 7, Moca 00676-0007 **W:** http://radiouna1340.com – **46)** Box 1488, Vega Baja 00694-1488 – **48)** HC02 Box 13903, Vieques Island, PR 00765 – Sat 1000-1300 local programming in English **W:** and **E:** as 34) – **49)** Box 669-A, Barranquitas, PR 00794 – **50)** Box 750, Isabela 00662-0750 **W:** www.wisa1390.com **E:** wisa@prtc.net - **FM:** WKSA 101.5MHz – **51)** Box 188, Carolina 00986-0188 **W:** www.cadenaradiovida.com - FM: 90.5MHz – **52)** Box 1410, San Sebastián 00685-1410 – **54)** Box 487, Caguas 00726-0487 **E:** buzoncadena@hotmail.com - **FM:** WPRM 98.5MHz, San Juan – **55)** Box 1863, Coamo 00769-1863 **W:** www.coamomall.com or coamomallradio/ – **56)** Box 1460, Las Piedras, PR 00771-1460 **W:** www.sonidosantidad.com – **57)** Box 1670, San Sebastián 00685-1670 – **58)** 10 Calle Pedro Arroyo, Orocovis 00720-2202 (or: P.O.Box 1210, Orocovis, PR 00720) **W:** www.cumbre1470.com – **59)** Box 948, Fajardo 00738-0948. **W:** www.el1480.com - FM: WDOY 96.5MHz – **60)** Box 7213, Ponce 00732-7213 **W:** www.radioisla1320.com – **61)** Box 6, Manatí 00674-0006 **W:** www.radioatenas.com **E:** info@radioatenas.com – **62)** Box 593, Lajas 00667-0593 (has requested permission to move to San Germán) – **63)** Calle Bori 1554, San Juan 00927-6113 - **FM:** 107.7MHz Carolina – **64)** Box 868, Utuado 00641-0868 **W:** www.wupr.com – **65)** Box 1540, Guayama 00785-1540 – **66)** Box 324, Yauco 00698-0324 (or: 100 Gran Bulevar Paseo #403A, San Juan, PR 00926) **W:** www.radioisla1320.com – **67)** Box 4036, Carolina 00984-4036 (or: Calle Bori 1554, San Juan, PR 00927) – **68)** Box 9064, Ponce 00732-9064 **W:** www.wppc1570am.org **E:** wppcam@prtc.net – **69)** Calle Bori 1554, San Juan, PR 00927 – **70)** Calle Bori 1554, San Juan, PR 00927 – **71)** Box 9394, Santurce 00908-9394. FM: 103.7MHz – **72)** Calle Bori 1554, San Juan, PR 00927. **W:** noticias1660am.com

FM in San Juan (MHz): 89.7 WRTU University of San Juan – 91.3 WIPR-FM – 93.7 WZNT – 98.5 WPRM-FM – 99.1 WPRM-FM – 99.9 WIOA – 102.5 WIAC-FM – 104.7 WKAQ-FM – 105.7 WCAD

AFRTS
Naval Media Center, 2713 Mitscher Road SW, Washington, DC 20373-5819, USA **W:** www.afrts.osd.mil/afnonradio
MW: AFCN 1200kHz 0.25kW, Roosevelt Roads

SW: AFCN 7507kHz USB, Roosevelt Roads
FM: AFCN 101.5MHz 1kW, Roosevelt Roads. 93.1MHz 0.25kW, Sabana Seca. 90.5MHz 0.20kW, Aguadilla. 91.1MHz 0.20kW

QATAR

L.T: UTC +3h — **Pop:** 850,000 — **Pr.L:** Arabic — **E.C:** 50Hz, 240V — **ITU:** QAT

SUPREME COUNCIL OF INFORMATION & COMMUNICATION TECHNOLOGY
P.O. Box 23264, Al Nassr Tower, Post Office Roundabout, Al Corniche St, Doha ☎+974 44 995333 ▤ +974 44 935913 **W:** ictqatar.qa **E:** info@ict.gov.qa

QATAR MEDIA CORPORATION (QMC, Gov.)
▤ P.O. Box 1414, Doha ☎+974 44 894444 ▤ +974 44 882888 **W:** qatarmedialive.com **E:** info@qatarradio.net **L.P:** Exec. Chmn: Sheikh Jabor Bin Yusuf Bin Jasim Al Thani. Dir. of Broadc: Mubarak Jaham Al-Kawari.

MW	kHz	kW	Prgr.	H. of tr.
Al Arish	675	600	A	24h
Al Arish	*954	1500	A	24h

Main Arabic Prgr. (A): 24h. On **FM:** Al-Jumailiya 90.8MHz 40kW, Umm Said 93.4MHz, Al Kohr 97.6MHz 10kW, Al-Khaisah 102.6/103.4MHz, Al Ruwais 104.0MHz.
*954kHz carries Al-Jazeera TV sound.
English/Urdu prgr: Doha 97.5MHz 10kW: English: 0300-1600, 1900-2200. Urdu 1600-1900. **Quran prgr:** freq. not known.
Oryx FM, Doha, 94.0MHz (joint QMC and RFI project in French.)
Sowt al-Khaleej (Voice of the Gulf): Doha 100.8MHz; Arabic language music sce.
Sawt Al-Rayyan: Markhiyah 102.0MHz 10kW.
Al-Jazeera English TV audio: Doha 101.7MHz.
Ann: Main Arabic prgr: "Idha'at Qatar min al-Doha".

Other stations:
Emarat FM, Doha: 104.0MHz. See UAE – **Middle East BC,** Markhiya 92.0MHz – **QF R.,** Doha: 91.7MHz English, 93.7MHz Arabic. **W:** qfradio.org.qa – **AFN,** Al Udeid Airbase: 98.9/101.3MHz – **BBC World Sce,** Doha: 107.4MHz – **Deutsche Welle,** Doha: 94.4MHz – **Monte Carlo Doualiya,** Doha: 93.4MHz 1kW – **R. Sawa,** Al-Jumailiya: 92.6MHz 20kW

RÉUNION (France)

L.T: UTC +4h — **Pop:** 800,000 — **Pr.L:** French — **E.C:** 50Hz, 220V — **ITU:** REU

RÉUNION LA PREMIÈRE
▤ 1 rue Jean-Chatel, FR-97716 St. Denis Messag Cédex 9 ☎+262 262406767 ▤ +262 262216484 **W:** reunion.la1ere.fr/radio **L.P:** Directrice Regional: Dominique Richard.
MW: St. Pierre 666kHz 20kW, St. André 1215kHz 5kW.

FM	MHz	kW	FM	MHz	kW
Petite-Ile	87.8	2	Saint-Paul	90.7	1
Saint-Denis	89.2	2	Saint-Leu	90.9	1
Le Tampon	89.6	3	Le Port	91.0	2
Plaine des Cafres	90.7	2	Saint-Benoît	106.7	2

+6 trs under 1kW.
D.Prgr: 24h. During nighttime 2300-0100 relay of RFI.
Ann: "Réunion Première". **IS:** "Séga & Maloya" (Réunion Folklore).

Other Stations:

FM (MHz)	1	2	3	4	5	6	7	8	kW
Cilaos	103.5	98.8	107.4			88.5	100.7		0.2
Etang-Salé		89.3					94.7		1
La Possession			93.4			103.0			1
Le Port	91.6	93.4	94.2	105.2	93.8		103.3		1-2
Le Tampon	99.2	97.4		98.6	104.0	105.7			1-3
Petite-Ile		91.1		105.5					1-2
Plaine des-Chafres				105.1	96.5	93.0			1-2
Plaine des-Palm.	99.2	88.2	100.1				93.6		1-3
Saint-André			94.2						1
Saint-Benoit	97.5	101.3		88.5			105.2		0.2-1
Saint-Denis	98.8	97.8	101.5	95.1	107.7	103.4	95.5	91.3	0.2-2
Sainte-Rose	99.8		87.6	107.5	89.0	93.6	102.1		0.2-1
Sainte-Suzanne	99.6	106.2		101.1		95.7			0.1-1
Saint-Joseph	107.8		98.8	98.0	107.0	90.5	103.5	88.3	0.1-1
Saint-Leu	91.5	95.0		105.3	96.7	92.8	103.1	106.8	1

FM (MHz)	1	2	3	4	5	6	7	8	kW
Saint-Paul		107.1	103.7	105.7	96.6	89.6	90.0	87.6	1-2
Saint-Philippe	101.1	91.6					102.6	96.3	0.2-1
Salazie	93.2	101.7	89.0	104.4		103.2		105.7	0.2
Saline-les-Hauts		95.2		105.5	106.6	89.4	103.3		1
Trois Bassins	91.3		107.9					95.6	1
Vincendo				101.6	105.8				1

1) France Inter W: franceinter.fr – **2) R. Freedom W:** freedom.fr – **3) Kréol FM W:** radiokreol.com – **4) RER** (Radio ést Réunion) **W:** rer.re – **5) R. Festival W:** radiofestival.re – **6) Antenne Réunion Radio W:** antennereunion.fr – **7) Fun R. W:** funradio.re – **8) R. Arc en Ciel W:** 7afm.com

ROMANIA

L.T: UTC +2h (31 Mar-27 Oct: +3h) — **Pop:** 19 million — **Pr.L:** Romanian, Hungarian, German — **E.C:** 50Hz, 230V — **ITU:** ROU

CONSILIUL NATIONAL AL AUDIOVIZUALULUI (CNA)
▤ Bd. Libertatii nr. 14, sector 5, 050706 Bucuresti ☎ +40 21 3055350 ▤ +40 21 3055354 **E:** cna@cna.ro **W:** www.cna.ro
L.P: Pres: Rasvan Popescu
NB. CNA is the regulatory authority for broadcasting.

SOCIETATEA ROMÂNA DE RADIODIFUZIUNE (SRR) (Pub)
▤ Str. Berthelot nr. 60-64, 010105 Bucuresti ☎ +40 21 3031777 ▤ +40 21 3031726 **E:** comunicare@radioromania.ro; www.srr.ro **L.P:** Pres/DG: Ovidiu Miculescu

LW/MW	kHz	kW	Prgr	MW	kHz	kW	Prgr
Brasov (Bod)	153	200	AS	Miercurea Ciuc	945	15	1
Petrosani	531	15	1	Iasi (Uricani)[2]	1053	400	R
Urziceni	531	15	AS	Cluj (Jucu)[1]	1152	400	1
Târgu Jiu[2]	558	400	1	Bacau (Galbeni)	1179	400	1
Brasov (Bod)	567	50	1	Resita (Vascau)	1179	10	1
Satu Mare	567	50	1	Brasov (Bod)[2]	1197	15	R/L/MG
Botosani	603	50	1	Constanta (d)	1314	50	AS
Bucuresti (a)	603	30	AS	Craiova	1314	15	R
Oradea	603	50	1	Timisoara	1314	25	AS/MG
Drobeta-T. Severin	603	15	R	Târgu Mures[2]	1323	15	R/MG
Timisoara (b)	630	400	R	Galati	1332	50	1
Voinesti	630	50	AS	Sighetul M.	1404	50	R/L/MG
Sighetul M.	711	50	1	Sibiu	1404	15	1
Baia Mare	720	10	1	Olanesti	1422	10	1
Nufarul	720	15	1	Constanta (d)	1458	100	1
Sinaia	720	15	1	Nufarul	1530	15	R
Lugoj (Boldur)[3]	756	400	1	Radauti	1530	15	1
Bucuresti (c)	855	400	1	Miercurea Ciuc[2]	1593	15	R/MG
Cluj (Jucu)[2]	909	200	R/MG	Ioan Corvin	1593	15	1
Timisoara	909	50	1	Oradea	1593	15	R/MG
Constanta (d)	909	25	R	Sibiu	1593	10	R/L/MG

(a) Hanestrau (b) Ortisoara (c) Tâncâbesti (d) Valul lui Traian
R=Regional prgrs, L=Local prgrs (substudios)
NB. Generally, txs are on the air 24h (except [1]=0300-2200, [2]=0400-2000, [3]=0600-2200), relaying R.Romania Actualitati at nighttime.

FM (MHz)	RR1	RR2	RR4	kW
Alexandria	91.8	89.7	-	10
Arad (Siria)	103.8	106.8	-	10
Bacau (Turn)	98.8	101.8	-	5
Baia Mare (Mogosa)	102.5	100.1	-	60
Bârlad (Popeni)	103.9	102.8	-	10
Bechet (Dabuleni)	99.1	-	-	2
Bihor (Stei)	91.0	105.8	-	60
Bistrita (Heniu)	103.9	101.3	-	4
Botosani (Sâveni)	106.0	100.8	-	10
Brasov	102.5	105.0	-	2
Bucuresti (Herastrau)	105.3	101.3	104.8	2x10/2
Buzau (Dealul Istrita)	107.0	103.7	-	14
Calafat (Plenita)	90.2	101.1	-	-
Calarasi (Baneasa)	106.6	89.1	-	30
Câmpulung M. (Rarau)	96.0	98.7	-	30
Cluj-Napoca (Feleac)	88.8	101.0	-	30
Comanesti (Laposi)	104.7	101.4	-	30
Constanta (Techirghiol)	102.7	-	-	60
Craiova	88.7	-	-	10
Deva (Magura Boiu)	103.4	105.0	-	4
Drobeta - T. Severin (Balota)	91.4	105.8	-	30
Faget	89.8	-	-	5
Focsani (Magura Odob.)	102.5	101.0	-	60
Galati (Vacareni)	106.4	101.6	-	60
Gheorgheni (Suseni)	103.4	106.8	-	60
Giurghiu	104.6	102.6	-	2

FM (MHz)	RR1	RR2	RR4	kW
Husi	101.7	-	-	2
Iasi (Pietrarie)	101.1	103.1	-	10
Lehliu Gara	106.2	-	-	1
Mahmudia	100.5	102.0	-	10
Mangalia	-	92.7	-	2
Moldova Noua	105.1	-	-	2
Negresti-Oas	89.4	-	-	2
Novaci (Cerbu)	92.9	89.5	-	100
Oradea	104.1	96.1	-	10/60
Petrosani (Parâng)	88.1	90.6	-	10
Piatra Neamt (Pietricica)	103.6	100.3	-	30
Ploesti (Costila)	102.2	104.1	97.6	100
Resita (Semenic)	102.5	-	-	100
Rm. Vâlcea (Cozia)	103.4	102.5	-	30
Sibiu (Paltinis)	101.8	103.7	-	60
Sighetul Marmatiei	106.2	-	-	2
Slobozia	96.3	-	-	2
Suceava (Mihoveni)	99.6	101.6	-	30
Sulina	100.9	-	-	2
Târgu Mures	93.6	104.9	-	10
Timisoara (Urseni)	106.4	100.7	-	10
Toplita	101.0	-	-	2
Tulcea	99.4	105.4	-	-
Tulcea (Topolog)	105.0	103.0	-	-
Turnu Magurele	105.0	-	-	30
Varatec	91.2	100.8	-	10
Vaslui	106.1	102.4	-	2
Vatra Dornei	100.7	107.7	-	2
Zalau (Mezes)	88.1	105.0	-	10

NB: Sites with only txs below 1kW not listed.

D.Prgr: RR1 (R. România Actualitati): 24h. – **RR2 (R. România Cultural):** 24h. **RR3 (R. 3 Net "Florian Pittis"):** 24h on the Internet. – **RR4 (R. România Muzical "George Enescu"):** 24h. – **Antena Satelor (AS):** 24h on FM/LW, 0400-2000 on MW. – **"Program Maghiar-German" (MG) for Hungarian & German minorities:** W 1200-1300 German & 1300-1400 Hungarian; Sun 0800-0820 Hungarian & 0820-0830 German.

External Service (R. Romania Int.): see Int. Radio section.

R. România Regional Services
⌨ **R. România Regional,** Str. Berthelot nr. 60-64, 010105 Bucuresti ☎ +40 21 3031469 🖷 +40 21 3031860 **E:** romaniaregional@ssr.ro **W:** www.romaniaregional.ro
NB: R. România Regional is the department for regional broadcasting of SHR. Some stns transmit seperate channels on FM and MW. Prgrs from substudios are produced in cooperation with local educational institutions. All reg. stns relay news from national networks at times. **ANN:** stns may identify with their individual names or "Radio România (name of studio)".

a) R. Bucuresti: Str. Berthlot nr. 60-64, 010105 Bucuresti. **E:** radiobucuresti@srr.ro. Local service "Bucuresti fm" on 98.3 (Bucuresti 10kW): 24h. – **b) R. Cluj:** Str. Donath nr. 160, 400293 Cluj-Napoca. **E:** office@radiocluj.ro. On 95.6 (Feleac 6kW): 24h; on 909 (Cluj), 1404 (*Sighetul M.), 1593 (Oradea & *Sibiu): 0400-2000 (*=except for prgrs from local substudios). Hungarian ("Kolozsvári Rádió"): 0000-0200 (MF), 0600-0800 (W), 1200-1600 (Sun), 1300-1600 (W). Local substudios with own prgrs (otherwise rel. R. Cluj): **"Antena Sibiului"** Str. Brutarilor nr. 3, 550251 Sibiu. **E:** antena.sibiului@gmail.com. On 95.4 (Sibiu), 1593 (Sibiu): 0900-1200, 1400-1700; **"R. Sighet"** Str. Plevnei nr. 8, 435500 Sighetul Marmatiei. **E:** radiosighet@yahoo.com. On 1404: 0400-0600 (W), 1200-1300 (MF), 1700-1900; incl. Hungarian ("Máramarosszigeti Rádió") 1200-1220 (MF) and Ukrainian 1800-1900 (Fri). – **c) R. Constanta:** Vila nr. 1, 900001 Mamaia. **E:** secretariat@radioconstanta.ro. Prgr 1 ("Constanta FM") on 100.1 (Techirghiol 60kW): Replaced by R. Vacanta during summer months. Prgr 2: on 909 (Valul lui Traian), 1530 (Mahmudia): 0400-2200. Incl. prgrs in Armenian, Aromanian, Greek, Russian, Tatar, Turkish. During the summer, R. Constanta produces the service **"R. Vacanta"** (for holidaymakers at the Black Sea coast, on the air last Sun in May - 3rd Sun in Sep on 100.1: 24h. N. (produced by R.Romania International) in English, French, German, Italian, Russian: 1000 & 1700 (1 Jul - 1 Sep). **E:** radio.vacanta@rdsct.ro. – **d) R. Iasi:** Str. Lascar Catargi nr. 44, 700107 Iasi. **E:** secretariat@radioiasi.ro. Prgr 1: on (MHz) 90.8 (Rarau 10kW), 96.3MHz (Pietrarie 10kW): 0400-2200; Prgr 2: on 1053kHz: 0400-2000. Incl. prgrs in Ukrainian. – **e) R. Oltenia Craiova:** Str. Stirbei Voda nr. 3, 200352 Craiova. **E:** office@radiocraiova.ro. On 603 (Drobeta-Turnu Severin), 1314 (Craiova) & 102.9 (Craiova 10kW), 105.0 (Cerbu 10kW): 0400-2200. – **f) R. Resita:** Str. Petru Maior nr. 71, 320111 Resita. **E:** secretariat@radio-resita.ro. On 105.6 (Semenic 10kW): 0400-2000. Incl. prgrs in Croatian, Hungarian, German, Romany, Serbian, Slovak, Ukrainian. – **g) R. Târgu Mures:** Bd. 1 Decembrie 1918 nr. 109, 540445

Târgu Mures. **E:** office@radiomures.ro. On 98.4 (Toplita 2kW), 98.9 (Suseni 60kW), 102.9 (Târgu Mures 10kW): 0400-2000; on 1197 (Brasov, exc. for prgrs from local substudio) 1323 (Târgu Mures), 1593 (Miercurea Ciuc: 0400-2200. Hungarian ("Marosvásárhelyi Rádió"): 0600-0900 (Sat), 0800-1600 (Sun), 0900-1600 (MF), 1200-1600 (Sat). In German ("R. Neumarkt") on MW only: 0830-0930 (Sun), 1900-2000 (W; also via Sibiu 1593). Local substudio with own prgr **"Antena Brasovului"** (otherwise rel. R.Târgu Mures): Bd. Eroilor nr. 29, 507246 Brasov. **E:** antenabv@rdsbv.ro. On 1197: 0600-0700 (MF), 0700-0800 (Sun), 0900-1100 (Sat), 1600-1700. – **h) R. Timisoara:** Str. Pestalozzi nr. 14A, 300115 Timisoara. **E:** secretariat@radiotimisoara.ro. Prgr 1 ("Timisoara FM"): on 103.8 (Faget 5kW, exc. for prgrs from substudio Arad), 105.9 (Urseni): 0400-2200; Prgr 2: on 630. For ethnic minorities: on MW only: German ("R. Temeswar"): 1100-1200 & 1800-1900; Hungarian ("Temesvári Rádió"): 1200-1300; Serbian: 1300-1400; on FM+MW on Sun: 1400-1430 Bulgarian, 1430-1500 Czech, 1500-1600 Slovak, 1600-1625 Ukrainian, 1625-1700 Romany. Local substudio with own prgr **"Arad FM"** (otherwise rel. R.Timisoara): B-dul Revolutiei nr. 77, 310130 Arad. On 103.8 (Faget 5kW): 0600-0800, 1100-1400.

OTHER STATIONS

MW	kHz	kW	Location	Station
3)	1485	1	Botosani	R. Vocea Sperantei
3)	1485	1	Medias	R. Vocea Sperantei
3)	1485	1	Oradea	R. Vocea Sperantei
3)	1584	1	Iasi	R. Vocea Sperantei
3)	1584	1	Sighetul M.	R. Vocea Sperantei
3)	1584	1	Tecuci	R. Vocea Sperantei
3)	1584	1	Vatra Dornei	R. Vocea Sperantei
3)	1602	1	Bistrita	R. Vocea Sperantei
3)	1602	1	Piatra Neamt	R. Vocea Sperantei

FM	MHz	kW	Location	Station
14)	88.0	30	Bârlad	Kiss FM
2)	88.4	10	Varatec	PRO FM
2)	88.5	100	Semenic	PRO FM
2)	88.9	10	Mahmudia	Romantic FM
4)	89.0	30	Laposi	R. Guerrilla
2)	89.1	10	Târgu Mures	PRO FM
10)	89.7	22	Suseni	R. Maria
2)	90.0	60	Magura Odobesti	PRO FM
5)	90.6	30	Topolog	Romantic FM
13)	90.7	10	Turnu Magurele	National FM
13)	90.9	10	Mahmudia	National FM
14)	91.3	30	Dealul Istrita	Kiss FM
2)	91.3	10	Urseni	PRO FM
2)	91.4	60	Suseni	PRO FM
A)	91.7	30	Feleac	RFI relay
2)	92.0	60	Vacareni	PRO FM
14)	92.0	10	Bistrita	Kiss FM
2)	92.4	60	Paltinis	PRO FM
10)	92.5	10	Mezec	R. Maria
6)	93.0	10	Mahmudia	Realiatea FM
9)	93.0	6	Suseni	Trinitas FM
13)	93.4	30	Heniu	National FM
2)	93.9	30	Baneasa	PRO FM
2)	94.3	30	Cozia	PRO FM
2)	94.9	60	Paltinis	PRO FM
9)	95.3	100	Costila	R. Trinitas
16)	95.5	10	Calafat	R. Galaxy
2)	95.7	30	Bârlad	PRO FM
2)	95.9	30	Magura Boiu	PRO FM
2)	96.2	60	Techirghiol	PRO FM
8)	96.3	5	Cozia	R. Galaxy
9)	96.5	60	Acareni	R. Trinitas
5)	96.6	60	Paltinis	Romantic FM
2)	96.7	10	Saveni	PRO FM
11)	96.9	60	Mogosa	R. Impact
4)	97.2	30	Turnu Magurele	Guerrilla FM
4)	97.8	60	Techirghiol	Guerrilla FM
2)	97.9	10	Bucuresti	PRO FM
13)	98.1	10	Varatec	National FM
2)	98.5	10	Parâng	PRO FM
2)	98.5	30	Laposi	PRO FM
12)	98.5	10	Calafat	Logos Calafat
14)	98.5	30	Baneasa	Kiss FM
5)	98.5	60	Mogosa	Romantic FM
2)	99.2	100	Pietrarie	PRO FM
14)	99.2	30	Cozia	Kiss FM
2)	99.6	100	Costila	PRO FM
2)	100.7	100	Carbu	PRO FM
13)	100.9	5	Faget	National FM
2)	101.6	10	Mezes	PRO FM
1)	102.7	5	Mezes	Europa FM
1)	103.4	9.5	Galati	Europa FM
2)	103.4	30	Mihoveni	PRO FM

FM	MHz	kW	Location	Station
14)	104.1	10	Parâng	Kiss FM
1)	104.4	5	Timisoara	Europa FM
2)	104.5	30	Feleac	PRO FM
2)	104.8	30	Rarau	PRO FM
2)	105.3	60	Siria	PRO FM
2)	105.3	60	Mogosa	PRO FM
1)	105.5	7.6	Suceava	Europa FM
2)	105.5	30	Craiova	PRO FM
1)	105.8	7.6	Focsani	Europa FM
13)	105.9	10	Parâng	National FM
1)	106.1	5.2	Constanta	Europa FM
1)	106.3	5.1	Comanesti	Europa FM
1)	106.5	5.1	Iasi	Europa FM
1)	106.6	11.7	Feleac	Europa FM
1)	106.7	23.4	Bucuresti	Europa FM
1)	107.1	5.1	Târgu Jiu	Europa FM
1)	107.4	5	Tulcea	Europa FM
1)	107.5	5	Resita	Europa FM
2)	107.6	60	Oradea	PRO FM
2)	107.8	30	Heniu	PRO FM
2)	107.9	60	Bigor (Curcubata)	PRO FM
7)	107.9	10	Tulcea	R. 21
2)	107.9	30	Balota	PRO FM

NB: Txs below 5kW not listed.
Addresses & other information:
1) Str. Horia Macelariu nr. 36-28, sector 1, 013932 Bucuresti. **E:** europafm@europafm.ro – **2)** Bd. Pache Protopopescu nr. 109, 021409 Bucuresti. **E:** profm@profm.ro – **3)** Str. Erou Iancu Nicolae nr. 38-38A, 077190 Voluntari. **E:** rvs@rvs.ro – **4)** Piata Natiunilor Unite nr. 3-5, sector 4, 040012 Bucuresti. **E:** statmajor@radioguerilla.ro – **5)** Bd. Ficusului 44A, 013975 Bucuresti. **E:** stiri@romanticfm.ro – **6)** Piata Presei Libere nr. 1, sector 1, 013701 Bucuresti. **E:** office@realitatea. net – **7)** Str. Horia Macelariu nr. 36-28, 013932 Bucuresti. **E:** radio21@radio21.ro – **8)** Bd. Carol nr. 43, 318688 Drobeta-Turnu Severin. **E:** office@radiogalaxy.ro – **9)** str. Cuza-Voda 51, 700038 Iasi. **E:** radio@trinitas.ro – **10)** Str. Barsei 18, 410423 Oradea. **E:** info.rom@ radiomaria.org – **11)** Str. Gheorghe Doja nr. 181A, 720147 Suceava. **E:** office@radioimpactfm.ro – **12)** Str. Mitropolit Firmilian nr. 3, 200381 Craiova. – **13)** str. Fabricii nr. 46B, sector 6, 060823 Bucuresti. **E:** radio@nationalfm.ro – **14)** Splaiul Independentei nr. 202A, sector 6, 060022 Bucuresti. **E:** kissfm@kissfm.ro – **A)** Rel. RFI (France).

DAB (Trial): Bucuresti ch12A (223.936MHz). **Operator:** Radiocom

RUSSIA

I.T: KA: UTC +3h; AD, AR, AS, BE, BR, CC, CV, DA, IN, IV, KB, KC, KD, KL, KO, KS, KT, KU, KV, KX, LI, MD, ME, MO, MU, NE, NN, NO, OL, PS, PZ, RO, RY, SA, SM, SO, SP, SR, ST, TA, TL, TS, TV, UD, UL, VG, VL, VN, VO, YA: +4h; BA, CB, KG, KY, OB, PR, SV, TY, YN: +6h; AK, KE, NS, OM, RA, TO: +7h; KN, RK, RT: +8h; BU: +9h; AM, IR, RS (Western), ZB: +10h; KH, PM, RS (Central), SL, YV: +11h; CK, KM*, RS (Eastern), MA: +12h — **Pop:** 143 million — **Pr.L:** Russian; additional official languages in the republics: Abaza, Adyghe, Altay, Avar, Bashkir, Buryat, Chechen, Erzya, Ingush, Kabardian, Kalmyk, Karachay-Balkar, Khakas, Komi-Zyrian, Mansi, Mari, Moksha, Nogai, Ossetic, Tatar, Tuvan, Udmurt, Yakut — **E.C:** 50Hz, 220V — **ITU:** RUS

FEDERALNAYA SLUZHBA PO NADZORU V SFERE SVYAZI, INFORMATSIONNYKH TEKHNOLOGIY I MASSOVYKH KOMMUNIKATSII (ROSKOMNADZOR)
109074 Moskva, Kitaygorodskiy proyezd 7 ☎ +7 495 9876800 +7 495 9876801 **E:** rsoc_in@rsoc.ru **W:** www.rsoc.ru
I.P: Head: Aleksandr A.Zharov
NB. Licensing body for broadcasting.

VSEROSSIYSKAYA GOSUDARSTVENNAYA TELEVIZIONNAYA I RADIOVESHCHATELNAYA KOMPANIYA (VGTRK) (Gov)
125040 Moskva, Yamskogo polya 5-ya ul. 19/21 ☎ +7 495 2514050 +7 495 2142347 **E:** vgtrk@vgtrk.com **W:** www.vgtrk.com
I.P: GD: Oleg B.Dobrodeyev
VGTRK produces the national radio networks R.Rossii, R.Mayak, R.Kultura, Yunost FM, Vesti FM, as well as regional prgrs (see Regional Services section).
RADIO ROSSII 125040 Moskva, Yamskogo polya 5-ya ul. 19/21 ☎ +7 495 9506989 +7 495 2145366. **E:** mail@radiorus.ru **W:** www.radiorus.ru – **RADIO MAYAK** 125040 Moskva, Yamskogo polya 5-ya ul. 19/21 ☎ +7 495 9558561 +7 495 9594207 **E:** pr@ radiomayak.ru **W:** www.radiomayak.ru – **YUNOST FM** 115326 Moskva, ul. Pyatnitskaya 25 ☎ +7 495 9506024 +7 495 9594198 **E:** info@radiounost.ru **W:** www.radiounost.ru – **RADIO KULTURA**

125040 Moskva, Yamskogo polya 5-ya ul. 19/21 ☎ +7 495 6335558 +7 495 633557 **E:** reklama@cultradio.ru **W:** www.cultradio.ru – **VESTI FM** 115162 Moskva, ul. Shabolovka 37 ☎ +7 495 2349768 **E:** vesti-fm@vgtrk.com **W:** radiovesti.ru.
Abbreviations: RR = R. Rossii (D-1 to D-4 refer to the timeshifted editions Dubl 1 - 4, cf. D.Prgr); RM = R. Mayak; Reg = Regional prgrs (see "VGTRK Regional Services" chapter); VFM = Vesti FM
Some txs carry timeshared prgrs not produced by VGRTK: F = External Service prgrs by Golos Rossii (GR) and/or rel. of foreign broadcasters; Rg = Region (decoding table see "VGTRK Regional Services" chapter); Geographical location: E = European part of Russia, S = Siberia, FE = Russia's Far East. **NB.** Tr times subject to change

LW/MW

Rg	Location	kHz	kW	Hrs of tr	Prgr
KH	Komsomolsk-na-A., FE	153	1200	1900-1500	RR-D2, Reg
KN	Vologochan, S	162	150	2100-1700	RR-D3, Reg
KA	Bolshakovo, E	171	150	0100-2100	RR
NS	Oyash, S	171	250	2100-1700	RR-D3, Reg
RS	Yakutsk, FE	171	150	1900-1500	RR-D2, Reg
KM	Yelizovo, FE	180	150	1700-1300	RR-D1, Reg
AM	Konstantinogradovka, FE	189	1200	1900-1500	RR-D2, Reg
MO	Kurovskaya, E	198	150	0130-2100	RM
SP	Olgino, E	198	150	0200-2100	RM
AM	Tynda, FE	209	150	2000-1500	RM
YV	Birobidzhan, FE	216	30	1900-1500	RR-D2, Reg
KN	Krasnoyarsk, S	216	150	2100-1700	RR-D3, Reg
KY	Surgut, S	225	1000	2300-1900	RR-D4, Reg
IR	Angarsk, S	234	500	2100-1700	RR-D3, Reg
MA	Arman, FE	234	500	1700-1300	RR-D1, Reg
TS	Kazan, E	252	150	0100-2100	RR, Reg
MO	Taldom, E	261	500	0100-2100	RR
BU	Selenginsk, S	279	150	2100-1700	RR-D3, Reg
SV	Yekaterinburg, S	279	150	2300-1900	RR-D4, Reg
RA	Gorno-Altaysk, S	279	50	2100-1700	RR-D3, Reg
SL	Yu-Sakhalinsk, FE	279	500	1800-1400	RR-D1, Reg
CV	Cheboksary, E	531	30	0200-2100	RM, Reg
OB	Orenburg, E	540	50	0000-1900	RM
MO	Noginsk, E	549	75	0200-2100	RM
AM	Svobodnyy, FE	549	150	2000-1500	RM
RS	Yakutsk, FE	549	50	1900-1500	RM
RO	Novocherkassk, E	549	50	0200-2100	RM
KO	Syktyvkar, E	549	150	0200-2100	RM
KA	Kaliningrad, E	549	150	0200-2100	RM
MA	Magadan, FE	549	25	1800-1500	RM
SP	Krasnyy Bor, E	549	600	0200-2100	RM
PM	Tavrichanka, FE	549	500	1800-1500	RM
VG	Volgograd, E	567	1000	0100-2100	RR, Reg
RT	Kyzyl, S	567	150	2100-1700	RR-D3, Reg
NS	Oyash, S	576	500	2300-1800	RM
KH	Khabarovsk, FE	576	150	1900-1400	RM
KM	Yelizovo, FE	576	150	1700-1200	RM
IR	Angarsk, S	576	250	2100-1600	RM
PR	Sylva, E	585	150	2300-1900	RR-D4, Reg
KY	Surgut, S	594	1000	0000-1900	RM
KN	Krasnoyarsk, S	594	150	2100-1600	RM
UD	Izhevsk, E	594	40	0000-2000	RR
AM	Skovorodino, FE	603	30	1900-1400	RM
AM	Belogorsk, FE	603	30	1900-1400	RM
KN	Vologochan, S	612	25	2100-1600	RM
KT	Pedaselga, E	612	150	0100-2000	RM
KH	Khabarovsk, FE	621	150	1900-1500	RR-D2, Reg
KO	Syktyvkar, E	621	150	0100-2100	RR, Reg
DA	Makhachkala, E	621	50	0100-2100	RR, Reg
DA	Kochubey, E	621	5	0100-2100	RR, Reg
OM	Omsk, S	639	75	2300-1900	RR-D4, Reg
ZB	Kruchina, S	657	75	2000-1500	RM
MU	Murmansk, E	657	150	0100-2100	RM
KH	Komsomolsk-na-A., FE	666	150	1900-1400	RM
KD	Sochi, E	+666	3	0200-2100	VFM
BA	Yazykovo, E	693	150	2300-1900	RR-D4
IR	Bratsk, S	702	7	2100-1600	RM
NE	Naryan-Mar, E	711	7	0100-2100	RR, Reg
KH	Nikolayevsk-na-A., FE	711	5	1900-1500	RR-D2, Reg
KM	Palana, FE	738	25	1700-1300	RR-D1, Reg
CB	Chelyabinsk, E	738	40	2300-1900	RR-D4, Reg
KT	Pedaselga, E	765	150	0100-2100	RR, Reg
VN	Voronezh, E	774	30	0200-2100	RM
SL	Aleksandrovsk, FE	792	50	1700-1300	RR-D1, Reg
RK	Abakan, S	792	25	2100-1700	RR-D3, Reg
VG	Volgograd, E	810	500	0200-2200	RM
SV	Yekaterinburg, S	810	50	0000-1900	RM
PM	Razdolnoye, FE	810	150	2100-1700	RR-D3, Reg
RT	Kyzyl, S	828	150	2200-1700	RM
KX	Elista, E	846	42	0100-2100	RR, Reg
PZ	Kamenka, E	855	50	0100-2100	RR

Rg	Location	kHz	kW	Hrs of tr	Prgr
RS	Yakutsk, S	864	25	1900-1500	Reg
MO	Lesnoy, E	873	250	0000-2000	RR
SP	Olgino, E	873	75	0000-2000	RR
SA	Samara, E	873	100	0100-2100	RR, Reg
KA	Kaliningrad, E	873	50	0200-2100	RR, Reg
ST	Stavropol, E	882	7	0200-2100	RM, Reg
TY	Tyumen, S	891	5	0000-1900	RM
ME	Sovetskiy, E	900	20	0100-2100	RM, Reg
AR	Arkhangelsk, E	918	150	0100-2100	RR, Reg
DA	Makhachkala, E	918	50	0100-2100	RR, Reg
KG	Shumikha, S	918	5	0000-1900	RM
KG	Makushino, S	918	5	0000-1900	RM
KG	Shadrinsk, S	918	7	0000-1900	RM
OB	Matveyevka, E	936	5	2300-1900	RR-D4, Reg
RO	Novocherkassk, E	945	40	0100-2100	RR, Reg
BU	Zakamensk, S	963	25	2100-1700	RR-D3
BU	Guzinoozersk, S	963	1	2100-1700	RR-D3
CB	Yuryuzan, S	990	1	0000-1900	RM
KD	Tuapse, E	1008	5	0100-2100	RR
AR	Porog, E	1026	5	0200-2100	RM
AR	Urdoma, E	1026	5	0200-2100	RM
AR	Nyandoma, E	1026	5	0200-2100	RM
KM	Ust-Kamchatsk, FE	1062	1	1700-1200	RM
AM	Zeya, FF	1071	7	2000-1500	RM
MD	Kovylkino, E	1080	100	0100-2100	RR, Reg
KM	Tilichiki, FE	1089	5	1700-1300	RR-D1, Reg
VO	Nikolsk, E	1098	5	0100-2100	RR, Reg
VO	Chagoda, E	1098	7	0100-2100	RR, Reg
KD	Sochi, E	1116	30	0100-2100	RR, Reg
MD	Kovylkino, E	1134	25	0200-2100	RM
BR	Shvedchiki, E	1134	7	0200-2100	RR, Reg
RO	Volgodonsk, E	1134	5	0100-2100	RR, Reg
RO	Salsk, E	1134	5	0100-2100	RR, Reg
MU	Murmansk, E	1134	75	0100-2100	RR, Reg
RO	Veshenskaya, E	1134	5	0100-2100	RR, Reg
IR	Tayshet, S	1143	7	2100-1600	RM
SA	Samara, E	1143	100	0200-2100	RM
KA	Bolshakovo, E	1143	150	0200-2200	RM §
KH	Komsomolsk-na-A., FE	1152	50	1900-1300	RR-D2, Reg
SR	Balakovo, E	1197	5	0100-2100	RR, Reg
SR	Balashov, E	1197	5	0100-2100	RR, Reg
SR	Yershov, E	1197	5	0100-2100	RR, Reg
ZB	Mogocha, S	1197	0.2	1900-1500	RR-D2, Reg
ZB	Ulety, S	1197	0.2	1900-1500	RR-D2, Reg
ZB	Nerchinsk, S	1197	0.2	1900-1500	RR-D2, Reg
ZB	Chernyshevsk, S	1197	0.2	1900-1500	RR-D2, Reg
AR	Plesetsk, E	1206	5	0200-2100	RM
ST	Neftekumsk, F	1251	1	0200-2100	RM
ST	Letnyaya Stavka, E	1251	5	0200-2100	RM
KC	Cherkessk, E	1251	7	0100-2100	RR, Reg
KC	Urup, E	1251	1	0100-2100	RR, Reg
BU	Bagdarin, S	1278	5	2100-1700	RR-D3, Reg
BU	Barguzin, S	1278	25	2100-1700	RR-D3, Reg
BU	Severobaykalsk, S	1278	7	2100-1700	RR-D3, Reg
CC	Groznyy	1278	50	0100-2100	RR, Reg
BU	Kyakhta, S	1287	5	2100-1700	RR-D3, Reg
SV	Serov, S	1305	7	0000-1900	RM
IR	Ust-Kut, S	1305	7	2100-1600	RM
OB	Pleshanovo, E	1314	1	2300-1900	RR-D4, Reg
RA	Ust-Kan, S	1350	5	2100-1700	RR-D1, Reg
RA	Ust-Ulagan, S	1350	5	2100-1700	RR-D1, Reg
PR	Perm, E	1359	50	0000-1900	RM
RA	Shebalino, S	1359	1	2200-1700	RM
RA	Onguday, S	1359	5	2200-1700	RM
RA	Choya, S	1359	1	2200-1700	RM
IR	Ust-Ilimsk, S	1359	7	2100-1600	RM
OB	Buguruslan, E	1395	5	2300-1900	RR-D4, Reg
RS	Sangar, FE	1413	5	1900-1500	RR-D2
ZB	Kuanda, S	1422	5	2300-1900	RR-D4
RA	Kosh-Agach, S	1440	5	2000-1600	RR-D3, Reg
RA	Ust-Koksa, S	1440	5	2000-1600	RR-D3, Reg
RA	Turachak, S	1440	5	2100-1700	RR-D3, Reg
BR	Unecha, E	1449	7	0200-2100	RM
MU	Monchegorsk, E	1449	42	0200-2100	RM
MU	Ostrovnoy, E	1449	7	0200-2100	RM
MU	Umba, E	1449	7	0200-2100	RM
MU	Kirovsk, E	1449	5	0200-2100	RM
MU	Kandalaksha, E	1449	1	0200-2100	RM
MU	Nikel, E	1449	1	0200-2100	RM
PR	Kudymkar, E	1458	7	2300-1900	RR-D4, Reg
RA	Onguday, S	1476	20	2100-1700	RR-D3, Reg
RS	Olekminsk, FE	1485	0.2	1900-1500	RR-D2
TY	Tyumen, S	1485	1	2300-1900	RR-D4, Reg
RS	Solnechnyy, FE	1485	2	2000-1500	RM
KM	Kamenskoye, FE	1485	1	1700-1100	RR-D1, Reg

Rg	Location	kHz	kW	Hrs of tr	Prgr
YN	Krasnoselkup, S	1485	1	2300-1900	RR-D4
YN	Gazsale, S	1485	1	2300-1900	RR-D4
RS	Batagay, FE	1485	1	1900-1500	RR-D2
IR	Magistralnyy, S	1503	1	2100-1700	RR-D3, Reg
YN	Salekhard, S	1503	5	0000-1900	RM
KN	Boguchany, S	1521	5	2100-1700	RR-D3
MU	Zapolyarnyy, E	1521	7	0200-2100	RM
ZB	Krasnyy Chikoy, S	1530	5	2000-1500	RM
BU	Taksimo, S	1584	1	2100-1700	RR-D3, Reg
DA	Khunzakh, E	1584	7	0100-2100	RR
KM	Klyuchi, FE	1584	1	1700-1300	RR-D1, Reg
KM	Tigil, FE	1584	1	1700-1300	RR-D1, Reg
RS	Belk.Gora, FE	1584	1	1900-1500	RR-D2
RS	Khandyra, FE	1584	0.2	1900-1500	RR-D2
BU	Novo-Ilinsk, S	1602	1	2100-1700	RR-D3, Reg
BU	Ust-Barguzin, S	1602	1	2100-1700	RR-D3, Reg
KH	Chumikan, FE	1602	0.2	1900-1500	RR-D2

SW

Rg	Location	kHz	kW	Hrs of tr	Su/Wi	Prgr
MO	Taldom, E	5905	250	1530-2100	Wi	RR
KM	Petropavlovsk-K., FE*	5930	100	1700-1300	Su	RR-D1, Reg
MU	Monchegorsk, E	5930	50	0100-2100		RR
MA	Arman, FF	5940	100	1700-1300		RR-D1, Reg
KM	Petropavlovsk-K., FE*	6010	100	1700-1300	Wi	RR-D1, Reg
KN	Krasnoyarsk, S	6085	50	2100-1700		RR-D3, Reg
RT	Kyzyl, S	6100	5	2100-1700		RR-D3, Reg
AR	Arkhangelsk, E	6160	40	0100-2100		RR, Reg
BU	Selenginsk, S	6195	50	2100-1700		RR-D3, Reg
RS	Yakutsk, E	7230	100	1900-1500		RR-D2, Reg
MO	Taldom, E	7310	250	1230-1500	Wi	RR
MA	Arman, FE	7320	100	1700-1300		RR-D1, Reg
MO	Taldom, E	7420	250	1730-2100	Su	RR
SA	Samara, E	9410	250	0610-0700	Wi	NvT
MO	Taldom, E	9410	250	1330-1700	Su	RR
SA	Samara, E	9690	250	0610-0700	Su	NvT
MO	Taldom, E	9840	250	0400-0700	Wi	RR
SA	Samara, E	11610	250	0710-0800	Wi	NvT
MO	Taldom, E	12070	250	0400-0800	Su	RR
MO	Taldom, E	12075	250	0730-1200	Wi	RR
MO	Taldom, E	13665	250	0830-1300	Su	RR
SA	Samara, E	15105	250	0410-0500	Wi	NvT
SA	Samara, E	15110	250	0410-0500	Su	NvT
SA	Samara, E	15195	250	0810-0900	Su	NvT

Keys: *) Yelizovo §) tx shared with External Service trs and/or foreign relays (see Int. Radio section); Su) summer (31 Mar-27 Oct), Wi) winter (to 30 Mar/fr 28 Oct) +) DRM; NvT=Na volne Tatarstana (see TS under "Reg.Services")

FM: All national channels are broadcast over a large network of FM txs.

D.Prgr: RR (R. Rossii): 24h. 0100-2100 via txs in European Russia, and in four time-shifted editions in other parts of the country: "Dubl 4" (RR-D4) via txs in the region between Volga and the Urals: 2300-1900, "Dubl 3" (RR-D3) for We.Siberia: 2100-1700, "Dubl 2" (RR-D2) for Ea.Siberia: 1900-1500, "Dubl 1" (RR-D1) for the Russian Far East: 1700-1300. NB: These editions are not announced on-air, and prgrs may be carried simultaneously in several editions. – **RM (R. Mayak)**, Mayak FM, R. Kultura, Vesti FM, YuFM: 24h on Internet/Satellite, limited schedule on FM/MW/LW.

VGTRK Regional Services
The regional VGTRK branches (GTRK=gosudarstvennaya teleradiokompaniya, state broadcasting company) provide reg. services in each of the regions of the Russian Federation. They are transmitted on txs shared with VGTRK's national services, usually R. Rossii (in some cases, R. Mayak or YuFM). Some GTRKs also have separate local or reg. outputs on own frequencies.

Ann: The stations typically identify with the name of their prgr (as listed below), or in the form "Radio Rossii - (name of regional capital)".

NB: Due to space limitations, schedules are listed only for regional stns that are also broadcasting on SW.

AD) Respublika Adygeya: GTRK "Adygeya", 385000 Maykop, ul. Zhukovskogo 24. **E:** trkra@radnet.ru **Reg:** On Guzeripl 68.00, Maykop 69.08, Khamyshki 70.70, Koshekhabl 71.93, Takhtamukay 73.76 in Russian, Adyghe. Also via Krasnodar 67.58 (KD). Apart from own reg. prgrs, txs relay GTRK "Kuban", Krasnodar (KD). Local channel "Adygeya+" on Maykop 67.88. **SW prgr for the Circassian minority in the Near East:** see International Radio section.

AK) Altayskiy kray: GTRK "Altay", 656045 Barnaul, Zmeinogorskiy trakt 27a. **E:** altai@gtrk.ttb.ru **Reg:** On Gorno-Altaysk (RA) 279 + Pavlovsk 66.53, Gornyak 66.59, Slavgorod 66.59, Mikhaylovka 66.59, Tselinnoye 66.74, Blagoveshchenka 66.95, Mamontovo 67.16, Ust-Kalmanka 67.85, Zmeinogorsk 68.15, B.Istok 68.27, Pankrushikha 68.36, Barnaul 68.60, Zarinsk 69.53, Rubtsovsk 69.68, Kamen-na-Obi 70.31, Shipunovo

70.35, Biysk 70.40. Local channel "Heart FM" on Barnaul 69.80/105.9.
AM) Amurskaya obl.: GTRK "Amur", 675000 Blagoveshchensk, per. Svyatitelya Innokentiya 15. **E:** gtrkamurinformrv@tsl.ru **Reg:** On Konstantinogradovka 189 + Skovorodino 67.22, Belogorsk 67.82, Zeya 68.24, Progress 68.36, Shimanovsk 68.72, Svobodnyy 69.92, Tynda 70.64, Blagoveshchensk 72.86.
AR) Arkhangelskaya obl.: GTRK "Pomorye", 163061 Arkhangelsk, ul. Popova 2. **E:** agtrk@pomorie.ru **Reg:** "R. Pomorye" on Arkhangelsk 918/6160 + Arkhangelsk 66.08, Urdoma 66.38, Nyandoma 67.31, Karpogory 67.76, Plesetsk 69.23, Vazhskiy 69.56, Pogost 69.92, Pogor 70.19 (also relayed via txs in region NE): 0310-0400 (MF), 0610-0700 (SS), 0810-0900 (SS), 0910-1000 (MF), 1410-1500 (MF).
AS) Astrakhanskaya obl.: GTRK "Lotos", 414000 Astrakhan, ul. Molodoy Gvardii 17. **E:** tvlotos@astranet.ru **Reg:** "R. Lotos" on Astrakhan 66.02, Chernyy Yar 69.98, Tambovka 70.16.
BA) Resp. Bashkortostan: GTRK "Bashkortostan", 450076 Ufa, ul. Gafuri 9/1. **E:** gtrk@bashtv.ru **Reg:** "R. Bashkortostana" on Neftekamsk 66.47, Mesyagutovo 66.86, Salavat 67.04, Baymak 67.16, Ufa 68.24, Oktyabrskiy 70.28, Belebey 70.61, Abzanovo 70.82, Burayevo 71.90, Beloretsk 72.05, Bakaly 103.7 in Bashkir, Russian. Local channel "R. Yuldash" on Ufa 105.5 & network in Bashkir, Tatar; local channel "R. Sputnik FM"on Ufa 107.0 & network in Russian.
BE) Belgorodskaya obl.: GTRK "Belgorod", 308000 Belgorod, pr. Slavy 60. **E:** trcblg@belgtts.ru **Reg:** On Stroitel 66.17, Selivanovo 66.80, Rakitnoye 68.39, Biryuch 69.29, Belgorod 70.16, Volokonovka 70.49, Ivnya 70.64, Prokhorovka 70.76, Borisovka 71.03, Staryy Oskol 71.09, Borisovka 71.30, Alexeyevka 71.78, Chernyanka 72.02, Valuyki 73.64, Krasnoye 73.67.
BR) Bryanskaya obl.: GTRK "Bryansk", 241033 Bryansk, ul. Stanke Dimitrova 77. **E:** radio@br-tvr.ru **Reg:** On Navlya 67.37, Bryansk 67.58, Shvedchiki 70.04, Unecha 70.55, Pocheb 71.54, Trubchevsk 73.94.
BU) Respublika Buryatiya: GTRK "Buryatiya", 670000 Ulan-Ude, ul. Erbanova 7. **E:** bgtrk@bgtrk.ru **Reg:** On Selenginsk 279/6195 + Severobaykalsk 66.30, Zakamensk 66.68, Ulan-Ude 69.74, Kyakhta 70.16, Sukhara & Tankhoy & Vydryno 101.0, Baykalo-Kudara 102.0, Kabansk 104.0 in Russian, Buryat: 0010-0100 (SS), 0210-0225 (MF), 0410-0500 (MF), 1010-1100 (MF), 2110-2200 (Sun-Thu), 2210-2300 (Sun-Thu).
CB) Chelyabinskaya obl.: GTRK "Yuzhnyy Ural", 454000 Chelyabinsk, ul. Ordzhonikidze 54b. **E:** radio@cheltv.ru **Reg:** "R. Yuzhnyy Ural" on Chelyabinsk 738 + Kartaly 66.65, Kyshtym 67.13, Yuryuzan 67.25, Stepnoye 68.36, Novoburino 70.82, Chelyabinsk 71.18, Zlatoust 71.69, Magnitogorsk 71.81. Local channel "Studiya 1"on Chelyabinsk 106.8.
CC) Chechenskaya respublika: GTRK "Vaynakh", 364000 Groznyy, ul. pr. Pobedy 22. **E:** gtrkvaynah@mail.ru **Reg:** On Groznyy 1287 + Goragorskiy 72.44, Naurskaya 101.2, Znamenskoye 101.7, Shelkovskaya 103.1, Groznyy 103.6, Terskoye 106.4 in Russian, Chechen.
CK) Chukotskiy avt. okrug: GTRK "Chukotka", 686710 Anadyr, ul. Lenina 18. **E:** gtrk@anadyr.ru **Reg:** On 101.6 (several txs), 102.8 (several txs), 104.7 (Anadyr & others) in Russian, Chukchi.
CV) Chuvashskaya respublika - Chuvashiya: GTRK "Chuvashiya", 428003 Cheboksary, ul. Nikolayeva 4. **E:** chradio@tvr.chtts.ru **Reg:** "R. Chuvashii" on Tsivilsk 67.04, Ibresi 70.85, Yadrin 71.12 in Russian, Chuvash. Separate prgrs in Chuvash on Cheboksary 531.
DA) Respublika Dagestan: GTRK "Dagestan", 367020 Makhachkala, ul. Amet-Khana, r-n DSK. **E:** gtrk_dagestan@mail.ru **Reg:** Radiokanal "Chirag" on Makhachkala & Kochubey 621 + Makhachkala 68.87, Kochubey 68.99, Gergebil 69.95 in Russian, Avar, Chechen, Kumyk, Lak, Nogai, Rutul, Tsakhur. On Makhachkala 918 in Russian, Aghul, Azeri, Dargwa, Lezgi, Tabassaran, Tatar.
IN) Ingushskaya respublika: GTRK "Ingushetiya", 366720 Nazran, pr. Bazorkina 72. **E:** tvi2002@mail.ru **Reg:** On Nazran 72.02 in Russian, Ingush.
IR) Irkutskaya obl.: GTRK "Irkutsk", 664003 Irkutsk, ul. Gorkogo 15. **E:** igtrk@irmail.ru **Reg:** On Angarsk 234 + Zhmurovo 66.32, Zheleznogorsk 66.56, Ulkan 66.62, Tulun 66.74, Ust-Ilimsk 66.80, Chuna 67.04, Tayshet 69.80, Nizhneudinsk 70.04, Bratsk 70.28, Irkutsk 70.31, Ust-Kut 70.64, Zima 72.14, Irkutsk 105.0, Ust-Ordynskiy 107.8.
IV) Ivanovskaya obl.: GTRK "Ivteleradio", 153647 Ivanovo, ul. Teatralnaya 31. **E:** adm@itrk.ru **Reg:** On Rodniki 70.13, Ivanovo 71.21, Furmanov 73.64.
KA) Kaliningradskaya obl.: GTRK "Kaliningrad", 236016 Kaliningrad, ul. Klinicheskaya 19. **E:** tv-rv@baltnet.ru **Reg:** "R. Yantar" on Veselovka 65.90, Kaliningrad 66.02, Bolshakovo 70.19.
KB) Kabardino-Balkarskaya respublika: GTRK "Kabardino-Balkariya", 360000 Nalchik, pr. Lenina 3. **E:** vestikbr@mail.ru **Reg:** On Samarkovo 66.62, Nalchik 70.52, Bulundu 73.70 in Russian, Kabardian, Karachay-Balkar.
KC) Karachayevo-Cherkesskaya respublika: GTRK "Karachayevo-Cherkesiya", 357100 Cherkessk, ul. Krasnoarmeyskaya 51. **E:** gtrk_kchr@rambler.ru **Reg:** On Cherkessk & Urup 1251 + Krasnogorskaya 66.98, Karachayevsk 67.34, Adyge-Khabl 68.66, Zelenchukskaya 68.81,

Kavkazkiy 68.21, Pregradnaya 69.80, Ispravnaya 69.83, Ust-Dzheguta 69.89, Teberda 69.98, Dombay 70.25, V.Mara 71.06, Storozhevaya 71.72, Kurdzhinovo 71.81, Khabez 71.84, Cherkessk 72.11, Urup 72.44 in Russian, Abaza, Karachay-Balkar, Nogai.
KD) Krasnodarskiy kray: GTRK "Kuban", 350038 Krasnodar, ul. Radio 5. **E:** owl@kubantv.ru **Reg:** "Radiostantsiya Kuban" on Sochi 1116 + Tbilisskaya 66.20, Novorossiysk 67.97, Gelendzhik 68.30, Kanevskaya 68.36, Armavir 68.57, Temryuk 70.22, Krasnyy Kut & Psebay 70.43, Tuapse 70.46, Adler 70.58, Eysk 71.15, Glubskaya 71.21, Lazarevskoye 71.54, Krasnodar 71.81, Arkhipo-Osipovka 71.93, Sochi 71.93, Apsheronsk 72.20, Belaya Glina 73.25, Kushchevskaya 73.49, Primorsko-Aktarsk 73.70 (also relayed by txs in region AD). - Territorialnoye otdeleniye GTRK "Kuban", 354000 Sochi, ul. Teatralnaya 11a. **E:** tv@sochi.ru. **Reg:** On Sochi 71.93 (tx shared with GTRK "Kuban").
KE) Kemerovskaya obl.: GTRK "Kuzbass", 650099 Kemorovo, ul. Krasnoarmeyskaya 137a. **E:** director@gtrk.kuzbass.net **Reg:** On Yurga 66.11, Novokuznetsk 66.20, Kemerovo 66.56, Klyuchevaya 67.04, Leninsk-Kuznetskiy 67.19, Tashtagol 69.80, Anzhevo-Sudzhensk 70.40, Mezhdurechensk 70.64. Local channel "Kuzbass FM" on Topki 65.93, Myski 69.38, Osinniki 68.42, Kemerovo 91.0, Klychevaya 101.2, Leninsk-Kuznetskiy 101.3, Anzhero-Sudzhensk 101.6, Mezhdurechensk 101.8, Guryevsk 102.5, Novokuznetsk 103.0, Yurga 103.6, Belovo 104.5.
KG) Kurganskaya obl.: GTRK "Kurgan", 640018 Kurgan, ul. Sovetskaya 105. **E:** headkgtrk@acmetelecom.ru **Reg:** On Shumikha 66.89, Makushino 68.48, Shadrinsk 69.23, Shatrovo 71.18, Kurgan 71.87.
KH) Khabarovskiy kray: GTRK "Dalnevostochnaya", 682632 Khabarovsk, ul. Lenina 4. **E:** main@dvtrk.khv.ru **Reg:** On Komsomolsk-na-Amure 153/1152, Khabarovsk 621, Nikoleyevsk 711 + Ayan 68.00, Chumikan 68.12, Komsomolsk 68.72, Okhotsk 69.32, Glebovo 69.47, Vyazemskiy 69.83, Bikin 69.92, Chegdomyn 70.16, Khabarovsk 72.80 (also via txs in region YV). Local channel "R. 101.8" on Khabarovsk 101.8. - GTRK "Komsomolsk-na-Amure", 681000 Komsomolsk-na-Amure, ul. Molodovargevskaya 7. **Reg:** On Komsomolsk-na-Amure 68.72 (tx shared with GTRK "Dalnevostochnaya").
KL) Kaluzhskaya obl.: GTRK "Kaluga", 248021 Kaluga, Pole Svobody 40a. **E:** gtrk@kaluga.ru **Reg:** On Kaluga 66.23, Lyudinovo 67.91, Sukhinichi 69.62, Baryatino 70.79, Mosalsk 71.39, Spassk-Demensk 72.05, Zhizda 72.92, Khvastovichi 73.07, Yukhnov 104.9.
KM) Kamchatskiy kray: GTRK "Kamchatka", 683000 Petropavlovsk-Kamchatskiy, ul. Sovetskaya 62. **E:** gtrk@kamchatka.tv **Reg:** On Yelizovo 180/5930(su)/6010(wi), Palana 738, Tilichiki 1089, Klyuchi & Tigil 1584 + Petropavlovsk 69.68: 0110-0200 (MF), 0610-0625 (MF), 0710-0800 (MF), 1800-1810 (Sun-Thu), 1930-1955 (Sun-Thu), 2200-2230 (Sun-Thu). Includes prgrs in Koryak, Itelmen, Evenki: 0610-0625 (MF), 1940-1955 (Sun-Thu), produced by the substudion (Territorialnoye otdeleniye GTRK "Kamchatka") 684620 Palana, ul. Obukhova 4. **E:** palana_tv@palana.ru. Local channel on Petropavlovsk 103.5.
KN) Krasnoyarskiy kray: GTRK "Krasnoyarsk", 660028 Krasnoyarsk, ul. Mechnikova 44a. **E:** referent@kgtrk.krsn.ru **Reg:** On Vologochan 162*, Krasnoyarsk 216/6085 + Dikson 66.13, Dudinka 66.25, Balakhta 66.32, B.Uluy 67.40, Krasnoyarsk 68.09, Solyanka 68.84, Novomikhaylovka 69.23, Uzhur 69.56, Norilsk 69.68*, Shira 70.16, Achinsk 70.52, Tyukhtet 71.42, Yeniseysk 72.74, Kansk 100.9, Nazarovo 104.8, Divnogorsk 107.9: 0110-0200 (SS), 0510-0600 (MF), 0910-1025 (MF), 2310-2400 (Sun-Thu). *) Tx also carries prgrs by substudios: a) GTRK "Norilsk", 663300 Norilsk, nab. Urvantseva 10. **E:** secr@norilsk-tv.ru **Reg:** On Norilsk 69.68; b) Territorialnoye otdeleniye GTRK "Norilsk", 647000 Dudinka, ul. Gorgogo 15. **E:** gtrktaimyr@dudinka.krasnet.ru **Reg:** On Vologochan 162 in Russian, Nenets. Territorialnoye otdeleniye GTRK "Krasnoyarsk", 663370 Tura, ul. 50 let Oktyabrya 28. **E:** heglen@tura.evenkya.ru **Reg:** On Tura 101.5 in Russian, Evenki.
KO) Resp. Komi: GTRK "Komi Gor", 167610 Syktyvkar, Oktyabrskiy pr. 164. **E:** komigor@online.ru. **Reg:** On Syktyvkar 621 + Yarashyu 65.90, Priuralsk 66.35, Ukhta 66.44, Vorkuta 66.60, Syktyvkar 66.80, Pechora 66.92, Ust-Tsilma 67.10, Sludka 67.16, Kadzherom 68.30, N.Odes 68.36, Troitsko-Pechorsk 68.60, Shoshka 68.72, Aykino 68.78, Kartayol 68.93, Shchelyabozh 68.93, Trakt 68.96, Meshchura 69.02, Mordino 69.05, Inta 69.08, Krasnobor 69.11, Okunevo 69.20, Usogorsk 69.56, Koygorodok 69.74, Myyeldino 69.83, Ust-Kulom 70.16, Petrun 70.28, Vetyu 70.40, Voyvozh 70.64, Vuktyl 71.06, Kuratovo 71.09, B.Pyssa 71.15, Usinsk 73.31, Vekshor 73.31 in Russian, Komi-Zyrian.
KS) Kostromskaya obl.: GTRK "Kostroma", 156005 Kostroma, ul. Nikitskaya 10. **E:** radio@gtrk.kmtn.ru **Reg:** On Bogovarovo 66.20, Vokhma 66.98, Kostroma 69.86, Galich 66.74, Sharya 67.10, Ostrovskoye 72.26, Pavino 73.10, Chukhloma 73.64, Pyshchug 73.88.
KT) Respublika Kareliya: GTRK "Kareliya", 185002 Petrozavodsk, ul. Pirogova 2. **E:** gtrk@petrozavodsk.rfn.ru **Reg:** On Pedaselga 765 + Nadvoitsy 66.29, Sortavala 67.13, Naystenyarvi 69.80, Loukhi 70.17, Kostomuksha 70.28, Petrozavodsk 70.52, Muyezerskiy 72.17, Medvezhyegorsk 72.47 in Russian, Finnish, Karelian, Vepsian.
KU) Kurskaya obl.: GTRK "Kursk", 305016 Kursk, ul. Sovetskaya 32. **E:**

gtrk@kursk.rfn.ru **Reg:** On Lgov 66.83, Kursk 69.71, Kshenskiy 72.41.
KV) Kirovskaya obl.: GTRK "Vyatka", 610002 Kirov, ul. Uritskogo 34. **E:** tv@gtrk-vyatka.ru **Reg:** On Vyatskiye Polyarny 66.35, Kirov 66.92, Kirs 66.86, Sovietsk 67.07, Klyuchi 67.91, Pinyug 70.55, Shmelevo 70.73, Urzhum 71.06, Omutninsk 71.33, Sanchursk 73.28.
KX) Respublika Kalmykiya: GTRK "Kalmykiya", 358000 Elista, ul. M. Gorkogo 34. **E:** kalmykiagtrk@mail.ru **Reg:** On Elista 846 + Sadovoye 66.95, Elista 67.28, Utta 68.24, Ulan-Kholl 69.59 in Russian, Kalmyk.
KY) Khanty-Mansiyskiy avt. okrug: GTRK "Yugoriya", 626200 Khanty-Mansiysk, ul. Mira 7. **E:** gtrk@wsmail.ru **Reg:** "R. Yugry" on Surgut 225 + Khanty-Mansiysk 66.08, Beloyarskiy 67.22, Langepas 67.28, Surgut 68.84, Nyagan 70.82, Beryozovo 71.42, Kogalym 71.30, Yugorsk 71.78, Nizhnevartovsk 72.56 in Russian, Khanti, Mansi. Txs also relay GTRK "Region-Tyumen", TY. (NB: KY is subordinated to region TY)
LI) Lipetskaya obl.: GTRK "Lipetsk", 398050 Lipetsk, pl. Plekhanova 1. **E:** regiontv@lipetsk.rfn.ru **Reg:** On Lipetsk 66.53, Izmalkovo 73.79, Terbuny 101.9, Dankov 102.4, Dobrinka 102.7, Ploty 102.6, Chaplygin 103.3, Lev Tolstoy 103.8, Usman 104.0, Volovo 104.4.
MA) Magadanskaya obl.: GTRK "Magadan", 685024 Magadan, ul. Kommuny 8/12. **E:** center@magtrk.ru **Reg:** On Arman 234/5940/7320 + Susuman 70.16, Evensk 100.5, Myandzha & Palatka 101.0, Ola 101.3, Omchak & Ust-Omchug 102.5: 0200-0210 (MF), 0400-0410 (MF), 1910-2000 (Sun-Thu), 2200-2210 (Sun-Thu), 2200-2300 (Fri). Local channel on Magadan 105.0.
MD) Respublika Mordoviya: GTRK "Mordoviya", 430000 Saransk, ul. Dokuchayeva 29. **E:** radiomordovii@mail.ru **Reg:** On Kovylkino 1080 + Tengushevo 66.35, Saransk 66.68, Dubenki 67.28, B.Ignatovo 67.34, Ruzayevka 67.46, Yavas 67.67, Umet 68.33, B.Berezniki 68.42, Torbeyevo 68.69, Chamzinka 68.75, Kovylkino 69.14, Ardatov 69.53, St.Shaygovo 69.65, Insar 71.03, Romodanovo 71.12, Atyuryevo 71.33 in Russian, Erzya, Moksha.
ME) Respublika Mariy El: GTRK "Mariy-El", 424014 Yoshkar-Ola, ul. Osipenko 50. **E:** tv@tv.mari.ru **Reg:** On Sovietskiy 900 + Yoshkar Ola 70.34, Sovetskiy 71.21, Kozmodemyansk 72.20, Zvenigovo 73.16 in Russian, Mari.
MO) Moskva (Federal City) & Moskovskaya obl.: no regional branch of VGTRK.
MU) Murmanskaya obl.: GTRK "Murman", 183032 Murmansk, per. Rusanova 7. **E:** radio@tvmurman.com **Reg:** On Murmansk 67.22, Kandalaksha 67.70, Revda 67.94, Alakurtti 69.50, Teriberka, Umba & Zapolyarnyy 69.74, Ostrovnoy 69.83, Kaneva & Sosnovka 70.01, Tumannyy 70.19, Kirovsk & Prirechnyy 70.34, Lovozero 70.73, Krasnoshchelye 72.38.
NE) Nenetskiy avt. okrug: Territorialnoye otdeleniye GTRK "Pomorye", 164700 Naryan-Mar, ul. Smidovicha 19. **E:** zapolyarie@mail.ru **Reg:** On Naryan-Mar 711 + 66.20 in Russian, Nenets. Apart from own reg. prgrs, txs also relay prgrs from GTRK "Pomorye", Arkhangelsk AR. (NB: NE is subordinated to region AR)
NN) Nizhegorodskaya obl.: GTRK "Nizhniy Novgorod", 603600 Nizhniy Novgorod, ul. Belinskogo 9a. **E:** radio@nnov.rfn.ru **Reg:** On Sergach 67.16, Pavlovo 67.85, N.Novgorod 67.94, Kovernino 69.53, Shakhunya 69.59, Arzamas 69.95, Lukoyanov 70.52, Krasnyye Baki 70.64, Vyksa 71.09, Kstovo 73.97.
NO) Novgorodskaya obl.: GTRK "Slaviya", 173620 Velikiy Novgorod, ul. B.Moskovskaya 10. **E:** radio@slavia.natm.ru **Reg:** "R. Slaviya" on Borovichi 69.02, Proletariy 71.39, Zaluchye 71.93, Pestovo 100.0.
NS) Novosibirskaya obl.: GTRK "Novosibirsk", 630048 Novosibirsk, ul. Rimskogo-Korsakova 9. **E:** gtrk@nsktv.ru **Reg:** On Chulym 66.35, Vengerovo 66.35, Severnoye 66.50, Ust-Tarka 66.62, Suzun 66.68, Ordynskoye 66.74, Kargat 66.89, Kyshtovka 66.98, Chistoozernoye 67.04, Dovolnoye 67.28, Proletarskiy 67.52, Novosibirsk 67.88, Bagan 68.36, Ubinskoye 68.63, Kyshovka 68.84, Karasuk 68.93, Osinovskiy 68.93, Zdvinsk 68.96, Maslyanino 69.05, Kuybyshev 69.68, Kochki 69.95, Krasnozerskoye 69.95, Cherepanovo 70.10, Moshkovo 70.22, Tatarsk 71.60, Kisilevka 71.66, Beloye 72.08 + txs below 0.1kW.
OB) Orenburgskaya obl.: GTRK "Orenburg", 460024 Orenburg, per. Televizionnyy 3. **E:** gtrc@orenburg.rfn.ru **Reg:** On Orenburg 66.02, Buzuluk 66.62, Orsk 66.92, Yasnyy 69.71, Kuvandyk 70.04, Uralskoye 101.9, Sorochinsk 102.0, Bikkulovo 102.1, Zhdanovka 102.6, Svetlyy 102.9, Pervomayskiy 103.0, Kvarkeno & Saraktash 103.1, Saraktash 103.3, Donetskoye 103.4, Izobilnoye 103.5, Ilek 103.6, Sovosergiyevka 103.9, Sol-Iletsk 104.6, Abdulino 105.1, Pleshanovo 105.2, Akbulak 105.5, Sharlyk 106.4, Alekseyevo 106.5, Tyulgan 106.6, Ponomarevka 106.9, Severnoye 107.0, Aleksandrovka 107.8 in Russian, Chuvash, Tatar.
OL) Orlovskaya obl.: GTRK "Oryol", 302028 Oryol, ul. 7 Noyabrya 43. **E:** post@ogtrk.oryol.ru **Reg:** On Livny 67.19, Oryol 70.31.
OM) Omskaya obl.: GTRK "Irtysh", 644050 Omsk, pr. Mira 2. **E:** gtrk@rtr-omsk.ru **Reg:** On Omsk 639 + Isilkul 66.50, Ust-Ishim 67.04, Nazyvayevsk 67.28, Tara 68.39, Khutora 70.43, Cherlak 71.06.
PM) Primorskiy kray: GTRK "Vladivostok", 690091 Vladivostok, ul. Uborevicha 20a. **E:** ptr@ptr-vlad.ru **Reg:** On Razdolnoye 810 + Nakhodka

66.74, Olga 67.58, Permskoye 67.79, Arsenyev 68.60, Kavalerovo 69.20, Dalnerechensk 69.32, Dalnegorsk 70.04, Novozhatkovo 70.64, Plastun & Terney 71.00, Vladivostok 71.84, Chkalovka 72.08, Kamenka & Krasnoperechenskiy & Mikhaylovka & Serafimovka 101.5, Rudnyy 101.9, Moryak Rybolov & Veselyy Yar 102.0, Agzu 103.5.
PR) Permskiy kray: GTRK "Perm", 614070 Perm, ul. Tekhnicheskaya 7. **E:** main@t7.ru **Reg:** "R. Permskogo kraya" on Sylva 584, Kudymkar 1458 + Perm 66.02, Kungur 66.65, Barda 67.10, Kudymkar 67.19*, Gayny 67.34*, Ust-Chernaya 68.84*, Ilyinskiy 68.93, Uinskoye 69.38, Karagay 69.53, Chusovoy 70.67, Krasnovishersk 71.33, Berezniki 71.87, Kosa 73.10*. – *) Also carries prgrs by the substudio (Territorialnoye otdeleniye GTRK "Perm") 617240 Kudymkar, ul. Volodarskogo 18. **E:** kudtv@mail.ru. **Reg:** in Russian, Komi-Permyak.
PS) Pskovskaya obl.: GTRK "Pskov", 180000 Pskov, ul. Nekrasova 50. **E:** oblradio@svs.ru **Reg:** On Pskov 66.05, Trutnevo 67.34, Novosokolniki 67.94, Dedovichi 69.86, Gubokoye 70.01.
PZ) Penzenskaya obl.: GTRK "Penza", ul. Lermontova 39, 440602 Penza. **E:** gtrk@penza-trv.ru **Reg:** On Pachelma 66.80, Sosnovoborsk 68.51, Meshcherskoye 66.84, Blagodatka 69.08, Penza 70.67, Narovchat 70.88, Gorodishche 100.4, Lunino 101.0, Neverkino 101.1, Issa 102.2, Nikolsk 106.1, M. Serdova 106.4.
RA) Respublika Altay: GTRK "Gornyy Altay", 659700 Gorno-Altaysk, ul. Choros-Gurkina 38. **E:** info@gtrk.gorny.ru **Reg:** On Gorno-Altaysk 279, Ust-Kan & Ust-Ulagan 1350, Kosh-Agach & Turachak & Ust-Koksa 1440, Unguday 1476 + Tashanta & Aktash 67.10, Gorno-Altaysk 67.22, Onguday 71.66, Tiyakhty 71.66 in Russian, Altai.
RK) Respublika Khakasiya: GTRK "Khakasiya", 662000 Abakan, ul. Vyatkina 12. **E:** vgtrk2003@mail.ru **Reg:** "R. Khakasiya" on Abakan 792 + Abaza 66.02, Abakan 66.89, Kopyevo 68.00, Shira 70.16, Tashtyp 71.00, Askiz 72.59, Cheremushki 73.01, Sorsk 73.19, Sonskiy 73.52, Beya 73.61 in Russian, Khakas.
RO) Rostovskaya obl.: GTRK "Don-TR", 344101 Rostov-na-Donu, ul. 1-ya Barrikadnaya 18. **E:** dontr2@dontr.ru **Reg:** On Salsk & Volgodonsk & Veshenskaya 1134 + Salsk 66.86, Morozovsk 67.07, Volgodonsk 70.13, Kamensk 70.28, Veshenskaya 70.67, Rostov-na-Donu 72.95.
RS) Respublika Sakha (Yakutiya): GTRK (NVK) "Sakha", 677007 Yakutsk, ul. Ordzhonikidze 48. **E:** gtrksakha@yandex.ru **Reg:** On Yakutsk 171/7230 + Neryungri 66.68, Aldan 69.38, Yakutsk 70.40 in Yakut, Russian: 0010-0100 (SS), 0210-0300 (SS), 0310-0355 (SS), 0810-1200 (MF), 2020-2200 (Sun-Thu), 2110-2300 (Fri/Sat), 2210-2300, 2310-2400 (Fri/Sat), Regional channel "R. Sakha" in Yakut on Yakutsk 864 + Tit-Ary 102.0, Pokrovsk 102.3, various sites 102.5, Yakutsk 107.1.
RT) Respublika Tyva: GTRK "Tyva", 66/003 Kyzyl, ul. Gornaya 31. **E:** gtrk_news@tyva.ru **Reg:** On Kyzyl 567/6100 + Kyzyl 67.10, Shagonar 70.64 in Russian, Tuvinian: 0010-0100 (MF), 0110-0200 (SS), 0410-0500 (MF), 0510-0600 (MF), 1010-1100 (MF), 1210-1300 (MF), 2210-2300 (Sun-Thu), 2310-2400 (Sun-Thu).
RY) Ryazanskaya obl.: GTRK "Oka", 390006 Ryazan, ul. Skomoroshinskaya 20. **E:** okatv@org.etr.ru **Reg:** On Kadom 68.03, Ryazan 69.32, Yermish 69.35, Mosolovo 71.66, Lesnoye-Konobeyevo 72.35.
SA) Samarskaya obl.: GTRK "Samara", 443011 Samara, ul. Sovetskoy Armii 205. **E:** gtrk7@tvsamara.ru **Reg:** On Samara 873 + Sergeyevsk 66.71, Khvorostyanka 66.98, Zhigulevsk 67.31, Chelno-Vershiny 67.43, Pokhvistnevo 69.05, Kamyshla 69.47, Samara 70.31, Yelkhovka 70.76, B. Glushitsa 71.15, Shentala 71.33, Syzran 73.10, Oktyabrsk 100.4, Kinel-Cherkassy 107.7.
SL) Sakhalinskaya obl.: GTRK "Sakhalin", ul. Komsomolskaya 209, 693000 Yuzhno-Sakhalinsk. **E:** sakhtv@gtrk.sakhalin.su **Reg:** On Vestochka 279, Aleksandrovsk-Sakhalinskiy 792 + Smirnykh 68.69, Okha 69.20, Aleksandrovsk-Sakhalinskiy 69.44, Gornozavodsk 69.50, Nogliki 69.56, Poronaysk 69.92, Tomari 70.16, Uglegorsk 70.40, Shebunino 71.63, Korsakov 72.29, Nevelsk 101.7, Dolinsk 102.0, Kholmsk 104.8, Yuzhno-Sakhalinsk 106.0, Korsakov 107.6. Incl. prgr in Korean.
SM) Smolenskaya obl.: GTRK "Smolensk", 214025 Smolensk, ul. Nakhimova 1. **E:** rukovodstvo@smolgtrk.rfn.ru **Reg:** On Smolensk 68.54, Smogiri 68.96, Vyazma 69.20, Roslavl 70.91.
SO) Respublika Severnaya Osetiya - Alaniya: GTRK "Alaniya", 362007 Vladikavkaz, Osetinskaya gorka 2. **E:** radio@osetia.ru **Reg:** On Mozdok 71.78, Vladikavkaz 72.20 in Russian, Ossetic. Local station: "R. Ir" on 103.5.
SP) Sankt Peterburg (Federal City) & Leningradskaya obl.: GTRK "Sankt-Peterburg", 197022 St.Peterburg, nab. reki Karpovki 43. **E:** info@rtr.spb.ru **Reg:** On Tikhvin 66.14, St.Peterburg 66.30, Kingisepp 67.67, Podporozhye 69.95, Yefimovskiy 72.05.
SR) Saratovskaya obl.: GTRK "Saratov", 410004 Saratov, 2-ya Sadovaya ul. 7. **E:** top@gtrk.renet.ru **Reg:** On Balakovo & Balashov & Yershov 1197 + Perelyub 66.44, Yershov 66.48, Aleksandrov Gay 69.68, Balashov 70.16, Balakovo 70.52, Saratov 71.09.
ST) Stavropolskiy kray: GTRK "Stavropolye", 355000 Stavropol, ul. Artema 35a. **E:** referent@stavropolye.tv **Reg:** "R. Stavropol" on Stavropol 882 + Ipatovo 66.77, Pyatigorsk 68.96, Stavropol 69.53,

Neftekumsk 70.01. Regional channel "R. Rus" on Stavropol 68.72/104.3, Nevinnomyssk 67.67, Ipatovo 68.39, Kurskaya 68.72, Pyatigorsk 69.74/102.5 (partly), Blagodarnyy 71.78, Neftekumsk 71.90. Local channel "Pyataya vershina" (357500 Pyatigorsk, ul. Dzershinskogo 40) on Pyatigorsk 69.74/102.5.

SV) Sverdlovskaya obl.: GTRK "Ural", 620026 Yekaterinburg, ul. Lunacharskogo 212. **E:** radio@sgtrk.ru **Reg:** "R. Urala" on Yekaterinburg 279 + Talitsa 65.93, Alapayevsk 66.50, Zaykovo 66.83, Nizhniye Sergi 67.01, Ivdel 67.76, Rezh 69.17, Bisert 69.20, Baranchinskiy 69.29, Serov 69.65, Andronovo 70.16, Afanasyevskoye & Azanka 70.43, Yekaterinburg 71.06, Pyshma 71.24, Kamyshlov 72.53.

TA) Tambovskaya obl.: GTRK "Tambov", 392720 Tambov, ul. Michurinskaya 8a. **E:** tgtrkbgt@tmb.ru **Reg:** On Tambov 71.00, Tokaryovka 103.3, Staroyuryevo 103.6.

TL) Tulskaya obl.: GTRK "Tula", 300600 Tula, Staronikitskaya ul. 1. **E:** info@tula.rfn.ru **Reg:** On Efremov 66.92, Tula 71.15, Novomoskovsk 72.35, Suvorov 102.4.

TO) Tomskaya obl.: GTRK "Tomsk", 634050 Tomsk, ul. Pushkina 19. **E:** adm@tvtomsk.ru **Reg:** "R. Tomsk" on Oyash (NS) 171 + Aleksandrovskoye 66.02, Kozhevnikovo 67.01, Tomsk 67.22, Krivosheino 67.31, Malinovka 68.39, Parabel 68.45, Kolpashevo 68.87, Strezhevoy 66.78, St.Yuvala 68.15, Strezhevoy 68.60, Teguldet 68.60, Koplashevo 68.87, Podgornoye 69.20, Belyy Yar 69.56, Bakchar 70.01, Kargasok 71.42, Asino 71.57, Molchanovo 71.84, Krasnyy Yar 72.17, Chilino 72.20, Zyryanskoye 73.01, Volodino 73.40.

TS) Respublika Tatarstan: GTRK "Tatarstan", 420015 Kazan, ul. M. Gorkogo 15. **E:** secret@trttv.ru **Reg:** "R.Tatarstan"/ "Tatarstan radiosi" on Kazan 252 + sovkhoz im. Kirova 67.28, Kazan 68.48, Naberezhnyye Chelny 67.01, Bavly 68.45, Leninogorsk 68.63, Tetyushi 69.95, Bilyarsk 70.13, Aktanysh 70.22, Nurlat 70.46, Buinsk 70.61, Cheremshan 72.14, Nizhnekamensk 72.29, A.Saplyk 72.29, Almetyevsk 103.9, Bazarnyye Mataki 107.8 in Tatar, Russian. Prgr "Na volne Tatarstana"/"Tatarstan dulkynynda" (for Tatars living in other parts of Russia): via Samara (SA) 0410-0500 on 15105(wi)/15110(su), 0610-0700* on 9410(wi)/9690(su), 0810-0900* on Kazan 252/Samara 11610(wi)/15195(su) & FM in TS (* repeats).

TV) Tverskaya oblast: GTRK "Tver", 170000 Tver, ul. Vagzhanova 9. **E:** gtrktver@tvcom.ru **Reg:** On Kashin 66.95, Andriyanovo 68.48, Selizharovo 69.68, Maksatikha 71.24, Kimry 71.48.

TY) Tyumenskaya obl.: GTRK "Region-Tyumen", 625013 Tyumen, ul. Permyakova 6. **E:** gtrk@region-tyumen.ru **Reg:** On Gagarino 66.89, Sladkovo 68.33, Masali 68.96, Yurginskoye 69.11, Uvat 71.42, Tyumen 71.66, Tobolsk 71.90, Shabanovo 72.17, Uporovo 73.19, Zavodoukovsk 104.1, Baykalovo 105.5 (also relayed via txs in region KY).

UD) Udmurtskaya respublika: GTRK "Udmurtiya", 426004 Izhevsk, ul. Komunarov 216. **E:** adm@udmtv.ru **Reg:** On Izhevsk 68.06, Balezino 70.94, Yar 72.11, Karakulino 98.4, Debyesy 101.0, Vavozh 102.7, Kambarka & Yukamenskoye 103.6, Mozhga 104.0, Valamaz 105.0, Syumsi 107.2 in Russian, Udmurt, Tatar, Mari.

UL) Ulyanovskaya obl.: GTRK "Volga", 432030 Ulyanovsk, ul. Simbirskaya 5. **E:** volga@mv.ru **Reg:** On Novospasskoye 67.07, Dimitrovgrad 67.19, Veshkayma 70.40, Ulyanovsk 71.00, Inza 73.43, Surskoye 73.58.

VG) Volgogradskaya obl.: GTRK "Volgograd-TRV", 400006 Volgograd, ul. Mira 9. **E:** trk@volgograd-trv.ru **Reg:** On Volgograd 567 + Mikhaylovka 66.83, Elton 66.95, Kamyshin 69.14, Chilekovo 69.44, Loboykovo & Uspenka 70.40, Volgograd 70.43, Yelan 70.49, Kletskiy 70.94, Surovikino 71.00.

VL) Vladimirskaya obl.: GTRK "Vladimir", 600000 Vladimir, ul. Bol. Moskovskaya 62. **E:** adm@vladtv.ru **Reg:** On Murom 66.32, Petushki 66.70, Aleksandrov 67.67, Suzdal 68.72, Gorokhovets 69.08, Sudogda 69.47, Melenki 70.25, Vyazniki 70.28, Kovrov 70.67, Sobinka 70.61, Kolchugino 73.55, Gus-Khrustalnyy 103.1.

VN) Voronezhskaya obl.: GTRK "Voronezh", 394625 Voronezh, ul. Karl Marksa 114. **E:** tv@vgtv.vrn.ru **Reg:** On Bobrov 67.04, Borisoglebsk 70.82, Boguchar 71.90, Voronezh 72.11.

VO) Vologodskaya obl.: GTRK "Vologda", 160000 Vologda, ul. Predtecheskaya 32. **E:** gtrk_vologda@pochta.ru **Reg:** On Chagoda & Nikolsk 1098 + Cherepovets 66.38, Suchob 66.77, Vitegra & Yakutino 66.86, Ozerki 66.86, Syamzha 67.88, Nyuksenitsa 68.03, Vologda 69.05, Verkhovazhye 69.08, Totma 69.71, Lipin Bor 69.65, Kurilovo 70.07, Kharovsk 102.2, Vozhega 102.5.

YA) Yaroslavskaya obl.: GTRK "Yaroslaviya", 150014 Yaroslavl, ul. Bogdanovicha 20. **E:** gtrk@nordnet.ru **Reg:** On Dubki 68.66, Volga 70.88, Lyubim 103.6, Danilov 104.3.

YN) Yamalo-Nenetskiy avt. okrug: GTRK "Yamal", 626600 Salekhard, ul. Lambinykh 3. **E:** gtrk@gtrk-yamal.ru **Reg:** On Salekhard 603 + Muzhi 68.90, Nadym 71.78, Salekhard 71.99/100.6. Txs also relay GTRK "Region-Tyumen", Tyumen TY. (NB: YN is subordinated to region TY)

YV) Yevreyskaya avt. oblast: GTRK "Bira", 679016 Birobidzhan, ul. Oktyabrskaya 15. **E:** gtrkbira@biratv.rfn.ru **Reg:** On Birobidzhan 216 + Nikolayevka 66.02, Obluchye 66.32, Smidovich 66.80, Birobidzhan 67.88, Khingansk 68.33, Birakan 68.60, Pashkovo 69.89, Bidzhan 70.07, Leninskoye 73.22, Kuldur 73.64 in Russian, Yiddish. Txs also relay GTRK "Dalnevostochnaya", Khabarovsk (KH).

ZB) Zabaykalskiy kray: GTRK "Chita", 672090 Chita, ul. Kostyushko-Grigorovicha 27. **E:** chrtv@chita.rfn.ru **Reg:** On Mogocha & Nerchinsk & Ulety & Chernyshevsk 1197 + Petrovsk-Zabaykalskiy 66.14, Chita 66.32, Khilok 68.09, Khada-Bulak 69.56, Kholbon 69.80, Orlovskiy 70.07, Krasnokamensk 70.67 in Russian, Buryat. Substudio (Territorialnoye otdeleniye GTRK "Chita"): ul. Bazara Rinchino 7, 687000 Aginskoye. **E:** abgtrk_agi@aginsk.chita.ru **Reg:** On Orlovskiy 70.07 in Russian, Buryat.

GOLOS ROSSII - RADIO KAVKAZ (Gov)

✉ 115326 Moskva, ul. Pyatnitskaya 25 **W:** www.ruvr.ru
LW/MW: Tbilisskaya 171kHz 1200kW, Groznyy 657kHz 50kW
D.Prgr: R. Kavkaz 24h via Internet (LW/MW tr times may be limited). Incl. **Chechnya Svobodnaya** in Russian/Chechen 2305-2400, 0405-0500, 1105-1200, 1905-2000. Rel. Golos Rossii outside of own prgrs.
NB. Service for listeners in Russia's Caucasus region, produced by the state broadcasting company Golos Rossii, with participation of the Ministry of Culture and Massmedia. **Also relayed at times via Gavar (Armenia) on 1395kHz (500kW):** see Int. Radio section.

RADIO ORFEY (Gov)

✉ 115326 Moskva, ul. Pyatnitskaya 25 ☎ +7 495 6335401 🖷 +7 495 690412 **E:** rgmc@muzcentrum.ru **W:** www.muzcentrum.ru
L.P: GD: Irina Gerasimova

Rg	Location	MHz	kW	Rg	Location	MHz	kW
PR	Perm	66.80	4	TL	Tula	71.93	4
SV	Yekaterinburg	69.92	4	MO	Moskva	72.14	2.5
LI	Lipetsk	70.07	1	PR	Chusovoy	73.01	4
VG	Volgograd	71.33	2	MO	Moskva	99.2	5
SP	St.Peterburg	71.66	15	KG	Kurgan	106.0	1

NB. Txs below 1kW not listed
D.Prgr: 24h via Internet, limited schedule on FM.

EXTERNAL SERVICE (Voice of Russia): see Int. Radio section.

OTHER STATIONS

MW	kHz	kW	Rg	Location	Station
1)	270	150	NS	Oyash, S	R. Slovo
15)	531	5	SL	Yuzhno-Sakhalinsk, FE	Avtoradio
	612	20	MO	Kurkino, E	Various
5)	684	10	SP	St.Peterburg, E	R. Radonezh
B)	738	5	MO	Kurkino, E	WRN relay
5)	738	50	PM	Tavrichanka, FE	R. Radonezh
7)	765	20	KH	Khabarovsk, FE°	R. Vostok Rossii
A)	810	20	MO	Kurkino, E	VOA relay
12)	810	10	KN	Krasnoyarsk, S	Avtoritetnoye R.
8)	828	10	SP	St.Peterburg, E	Radiogazeta Slovo
11)	846	150	MO	Noginsk, E	R. Podmoskovye
5)	846	150	MO	Noginsk, E	R. Radonezh
6)	1053	10	SP	St.Peterburg, E	R. Mariya
6)	1053	10	KN	Krasnoyarsk, S	R. Shanson
3)	1089	50	SP	Krasnyy Bor, E	R. Teos
3)	1134	20	MO	Kurkino, E	R. Teos
3)	1188	5	KH	Khabarovsk, FE	R. Teos
9)	1233	20	KM	Yelizovo, FE	Yumor FM
7)	1269	7	KH	Komsomolsk-na-A., FE	R. Vostok Rossii
13)	1269	5	PM	Ussuriysk, FE	R. Ussuri
10)	1440	10	SP	St.Peterburg, E	R. Zvezda
2)	1503	20	MO	Kurkino, E	R. Tsentr
16)	1584	0.1	MO	Moskva, E	MTUSI
4)	1593	0.01	SP	St.Peterburg, E	SPbGUT
14)	1602	1	IR	Zheleznogorsk-Ilimskiy, S	Ekho Moskvy

!) time-shared °) sync. netw.: additional txs on 765kHz in Ayan (1kW) and (all 5kW): Bikin, Bogorodskoye, Chegdomyn, De-Kastri, Nikoleyevsk-na-Amure, Pereyaslavka, Sovetskaya Gavan, Troitskoye, Tsimmermanskoye, Vyazemskiy, Vysokogornyy, Yagodnyy.

Addresses & other information:
1) 630011 Novosibirsk, ul. Kirova 3. **E:** rslovo@mail.ru – **2)** 109012 Moskva, ul. Nikolskaya 7. **E:** 1503am@radiocenter.net. Rel. religious prgrs. – **3)** 190000 St.Peterburg, P.O.Box 110. **E:** radio@teos.org.ru – **4)** 190068 St.Peterburg, P.O.Box 732. **E:** pr@radiomaria.ru – **5)** 113326 Moskva, ul. Pyatnitskaya 25. **E:** radonezh@radonezh.ru – **6)** 660021 Krasnoyarsk, ul. Robespyera 7. **E:** news@7fm.ru. Rel. R.Shanson (Moskva). – **7)** 680000 Khabarovsk, ul. Lenina 4. **E:** radio@erussia.khv.ru – **8)** 197022 St.Peterburg, P.O.Box 122. Also rel. Pravoslavnoye R. (St. Peterburg). – **9)** 683024 Petropavlovsk-Kamchatskiy, ul. Lukashevskogo 5. Rel. Yumor FM (Moskva). – **10)** 119160 Moskva, Kolymazhnyy per. 14. **E:** radio@tvzvezda.ru – **11)** 123007 Moskva, ul. 1-ya Magistralnaya 14. **E:** radio@rtvp.ru – **12)** 660049 Krasnoyarsk, ul. Lenina 86. **E:** info@avtoritetnoeradio.ru – **13)** 692525 Ussuriysk, ul. Kirova 28. – **14)** 665651 Zheleznogorsk-Ilimskiy, ul. Yangelya 6. Rel. Ekho Moskvy (Moskva)

– **15)** 669023 Yuzhno-Sakhalinsk, ul. Komsomolskaya 213a. **E:** office@astv.ru – **16)** c/o Moskovskiy Tekhnicheskiy Universitet Svyazi i informatiki (MTUSI), 111024 Moskva, Aviamotornaya ul. 8a.* **E:** mtuci@mtuci.ru. – **17)** c/o Sankt-Peterburgskiy gosudarstvennyy universitet telekommunikatsii (SPbGUT), 191186 St.Peterburg, nab. r. Moyki 61. * **E:** uos@sut.ru – **A)** Rel. VOA (USA). – **B)** Rel. WRN (UK). *) These stns carry various prgrs produced by students, volunteers and other non-professionals. Similar stns in other major towns are in preparation.

FM	MHz	kW	Rg	Location	Station
14)	66.08	1	AK	Barnaul	R. Shanson
1)	66.11	1	TY	Ishim	Avtoradio
27)	66.23	1	TS	Nab.Chelny	R. Dacha
19)	66.29	1	RO	Dyogtevo	Dorozhnoye R.
193)	66.32	1	PR	Barda	R. Novyy Vek
14)	66.35	4	SM	Smolensk	R. Shanson
9A)	66.41	1	AR	Plesetsk	Glavnoye R.
24)	66.68	1	BE	Belgorod	NRJ
116)	66.68	4	BA	Ufa	R. Ashkadar
57)	66.74	4	CB	Chelyabinsk	Intervolna
67)	67.04	1	TY	Tyumen	La Femme R.
202)	67.10	1	PR	Solikamsk	Soyuz FM
3)	67.46	1	SV	Yekaterinburg	Ekho Moskvy
14)	67.46	1	DA	Ufa	R. Shanson
4)	67.46	1	SL	Kholmsk	Evropa+
172)	67.52	1	NS	Bagan	R. Slovo
2)	67.58	1	BE	Valuyki	Russkoye R.
201)	67.70	1	CB	Magnitogorsk	Seven Skies
24)	67.70	1	UL	Ulyanovsk	NRJ
137)	67.79	1	TS	Nab.Chelny	R. Kunel
1)	68.00	1	MO	Moskva	Avtoradio
105)	68.03	2	ME	Yoshkar-Ola	R. 3-y Kanal
4)	68.09	1	PZ	Penza	Evropa+
9A)	68.21	1	MU	Murmansk	Glavnoye R.
5)	68.39	1	KG	Kurgan	Hit FM
61)	68.51	4	SV	Irbit	Kanal Voskreseniye
11)	68.51	1	SA	Samara	R. Maksimum
18)	68.54	1	NN	Shakhumnya	Yumor FM
151)	68.57	2	NN	N.Novgorod	R. Obraz
116)	68.60	4	BA	Mesyagutovo	R. Ashkadar
16)	68.60	1	OM	Omsk	Retro FM
61)	68.87	4	SV	N.Sergi	Kanal Voskreseniye
19)	68.90	2	KD	Sochi	Dorozhnoye R.
91)	68.90	1	CV	Cheboksary	Otkrytoye R.
3)	69.11	1	AK	Barnaul	Ekho Moskvy
9A)	69.14	2	LI	Lipetsk	Glavnoye R.
116)	69.20	4	BA	Baymak	R. Ashkadar
13)	69.26	1	MO	Moskva	R. RSN
4)	69.38	1	ME	Yoshkar-Ola	Evropa+
3)	69.44	1	RO	Rostov-na-Donu	Ekho Moskvy
3)	69.50	1	IR	Irkutsk	Ekho Moskvy
84)	69.68	4	RY	Mosolovo	Narodnoye R.
102)	69.68	1	BA	Ufa	R. 1-y Kanal
4)	69.71	1	TS	Nab.Chelny	Evropa+
7)	69.74	1	UL	Ulyanovsk	Militseyskaya volna
27)	69.80	1	TO	Tomsk	R. Dacha
5)	69.92	1	RK	Abakan	Hit FM
116)	70.04	4	BA	Burayevo	R. Ashkadar
15)	70.04	4	PR	Perm	DFM
14)	70.13	1	KH	Komsomolsk-na-A.	R. Shanson
7)	70.25	1	VN	Voronezh	Militseyskaya volna
21)	70.34	1	RY	Ryazan	R. Zvezda
136)	70.55	4	MO	Zaraysk	R. Kukuruza
8)	70.55	1	OM	Omsk	Nashe R.
117)	70.64	1	SA	Tolyatti	R. Avgust
15)	70.70	1	CB	Chelyabinsk	DFM
84)	70.73	1	LI	Lipetsk	Narodnoye R.
16)	70.85	1	KV	Kirov	Retro FM
125B)	70.88	2	NS	Novosibirsk	R. Vanya
1)	70.94	1	NS	Kuybyshev	Avtoradio
3)	71.06	1	RK	Abakan	Ekho Moskvy
60)	71.12	4	VN	Boguchar	Kanal Melodiya (Voron.)
61)	71.21	4	SV	Nizhniy Tagil	Kanal Voskreseniye
120)	71.24	15	SP	Sankt-Peterburg	R. Baltika
172)	71.27	1	NS	Novosibirsk	R. Slovo
2)	71.30	2.5	MO	Moskva	Russkoye R.
7)	71.30	1	BA	Ufa	Militseyskaya volna
60)	71.39	2	VN	Voronezh	Kanal Melodiya (Voron.)
16)	71.57	1	AK	Barnaul	Retro FM
2)	71.72	2	UD	Balezino	Russkoye R.
14)	71.72	4	KL	Kaluga	R. Shanson
1)	71.84	1	KV	Kirov	Avtoradio
22)	71.87	1	KN	Krasnoyarsk	R. KP
3)	71.93	1	KY	Surgut	Ekho Moskvy
84)	71.99	4	IV	Rodniki	Narodnoye R.

FM	MHz	kW	Rg	Location	Station
61)	72.11	4	SV	Afanasyevskoye	Kanal Voskreseniye
14)	72.11	1	KA	Kaliningrad	R. Shanson
61)	72.11	4	SV	Tavda	Kanal Voskreseniye
8)	72.14	5	SP	Sankt-Peterburg	Nashe R.
116)	72.20	4	BA	Belebey	R. Ashkadar
96)	72.29	1	ZB	Chita	Populyarnoye R.
172)	72.38	2	NS	Tatarsk	R. Slovo
60)	72.38	4	VN	Borisoglebsk	Kanal Melodiya (Voron.)
220)	72.41	4	CV	Ibresi	Nats. R. Chuvashii
1)	72.41	1	NN	N.Novgorod	Avtoradio
2)	72.41	1	ST	Stavropol	Russkoye R.
165)	72.44	1	PR	Perm	R. Sem Not
14)	72.47	4	SM	Roslavl	R. Shanson
205)	72.50	4	PZ	Kuznetsk	Svobodnaya volna
198)	72.50	1	KN	Krasnoyarsk	RU.FM
8)	72.56	4	TA	Tambov	Nashe R.
21)	72.80	1	LI	Lipetsk	R. Zvezda
61)	72.83	4	SV	Yekaterinburg	Kanal Voskreseniye
84)	72.83	1	OL	Oryol	Narodnoye R.
2)	72.83	1.5	SA	Samara	Russkoye R.
159)	72.92	1	MO	Moskva	R. Radonezh
54)	73.10	15	SP	Sankt-Peterburg	Grad Petrov
84)	73.13	1	RY	Ryazan	Narodnoye R.
13)	73.16	1	NS	Novosibirsk	R. RSN
2)	73.19	1	KV	Kirov	Russkoye R.
16)	73.25	1	KL	Kaluga	Retro FM
84)	73.25	1	KD	Krasnodar	Narodnoye R.
14)	73.28	1	AK	Biysk	R. Shanson
1)	73.37	1	KY	Nizhnevartovsk	Avtoradio
68)	73.43	1	NN	Bor	Levyy Bereg
9A)	73.43	1	VN	Borisoglebsk	Glavnoye R.
8)	73.52	1	CB	Chelyabinsk	Nashe R.
9A)	73.58	1	VN	Boguchar	Glavnoye R.
53)	73.58	1	NS	Novosibirsk	Gorodskaya volna
199)	73.61	1	SA	Samara	Samara-Maximum
17)	73.64	1	ST	Stavropol	Serebryanyy dozhd
119)	73.76	1	IR	Irkutsk	R. Avtos
10)	73.79	1	AK	Biysk	R. 7
3)	73.82	2.5	MO	Moskva	Ekho Moskvy
185)	73.88	1	MD	Saransk	R. Vaygel
16)	73.88	1	BE	St.Oskol	Retro FM
1)	73.91	1	VL	Vladimir	Avtoradio
4)	73.94	1	OM	Omsk	Evropa+
3)	73.94	1	YA	Yaroslavl	Ekho Moskvy
3)	73.97	1	CB	Chelyabinsk	Ekho Moskvy
74)	73.97	1	KV	Kirov	Mariya FM
19)	87.5	2.5	SP	Sankt-Peterburg	Dorozhnoye R.
18)	87.5	1	RO	Salsk	Yumor FM
207)	87.5	1	TS	Nab.Chelny	Tatarskoye R.
28)	87.5	1	MO	Moskva	Business FM
145)	87.6	1	KE	Kemerovo	R. Mir
23)	87.6	1	PR	Perm	Detskoye R.
6)	87.7	1	RO	Kamensk-Shakht.	Love R.
31)	87.9	5	MO	Moskva	City FM
20)	87.9	1	SR	Saratov	R. Romantika
16)	87.9	1	KH	Khabarovsk	Retro FM
42)	88.0	1	PR	Perm	Bolid FM
16)	88.0	1	SP	Sankt-Peterburg	Retro FM
2)	88.0	1	SA	Tolyatti	Russkoye R.
59)	88.0	1	KE	Kemerovo	R. Yuniton
19)	88.1	1	SM	Velizh	Dorozhnoye R.
19)	88.1	1	OM	Omsk	Dorozhnoye R.
140)	88.2	1	KE	Leninsk-Kuznetskiy	R. Leninsk
23)	88.2	1	KY	Surgut	Hit FM
7)	88.3	1	KD	Krasnodar	Militseyskaya volna
151)	88.3	1	NN	Sokolskoye	R. Obraz
18)	88.3	1	TY	Tyumen	Yumor FM
16)	88.3	5	MO	Moskva	Retro FM
15)	88.3	1	SV	Yekaterinburg	DFM
1)	88.3	2	PM	Vladivostok	Avtoradio
17)	88.3	1	TS	Kazan	Serebryanyy dozhd
23)	88.3	1	SR	Saratov	Detskoye R.
1)	88.3	1	PM	Vladivostok	Avtoradio
8)	88.4	5	SP	Sankt-Peterburg	Avtoradio
23)	88.4	1	SA	Tolyatti	Detskoye R.
1)	88.5	1	KH	Komsomolsk-na-A.	Avtoradio
1)	88.5	1	SV	Severouralsk	Avtoradio
5)	88.6	1	UL	Dimitrovgrad	Hit FM
1)	88.7	1	KH	Khabarovsk	Avtoradio
26)	88.7	1	SR	Saratov	R. Rekord
18)	88.7	5	MO	Moskva	Yumor FM
1)	88.7	1	AK	Barnaul	Militseyskaya volna
14)	88.7	1	AM	Blagoveshchensk	R. Shanson
23)	88.8	1	SV	Yekaterinburg	Detskoye R.
156)	88.8	1	TY	Tyumen	R. Pobedy

FM	MHz	kW	Rg	Location	Station
18)	88.9	5	PR	Perm	Yumor FM
18)	88.9	5	SP	Sankt-Peterburg	Yumor FM
99B)	88.9	1	SL	Yu-Sakhalinsk	Fresh FM
10)	89.0	1	BE	Shebekino	R. 7
14)	89.0	1	UL	Dimitrovgrad	R. Shanson
179)	89.1	1	PM	Ussuriysk	R. Teos
129)	89.1	1	MO	Moskva	R. Jazz
125B)	89.1	1	MU	Murmansk	R. Vanya
23)	89.2	1	SV	Yekaterinburg	Detskoye R.
23)	89.3	1	TS	Kazan	Detskoye R.
4)	89.4	1	PR	Perm	Evropa+
77)	89.5	1	MO	Moskva	Megapolis FM
24)	89.6	1	SV	Yekaterinburg	NRJ
2)	89.6	1	KH	Khabarovsk	Russkoye R.
192)	89.7	4	SP	Sankt-Peterburg	R. Zenit
24)	89.7	1	TS	Kazan	NRJ
20)	89.8	1	PR	Perm	R. Romantika
2)	89.9	1	SL	Yu-Sakhalinsk	Russkoye R.
125A)	89.9	4	SP	Vyborg	R. Dlya Dvoikh
62)	89.9	5	MO	Moskva	Keks FM
23)	90.0	1	UL	Ulyanovsk	Detskoye R.
128)	90.1	5	SP	Sankt-Peterburg	R. Ermitazh
170)	90.2	1	SV	Yekaterinburg	R. SK
1)	90.3	5	MO	Moskva	Avtoradio
16)	90.4	1	SA	Tolyatti	Retro FM
23)	90.6	1	BA	Ufa	Detskoye R.
125A)	90.6	3	SP	Sankt-Peterburg	R. Dlya Dvoikh
28)	90.6	1	SA	Samara	Business FM
24)	90.6	1	KD	Krasnodar	NRJ
69)	90.7	1	LI	Lipetsk	Lipetsk FM
2)	90.7	1	TS	Kazan	Russkoye R.
11)	90.8	1	SV	Yekaterinburg	R. Maksimum
195)	90.8	5	MO	Moskva	Relaks FM
1)	91.0	1	MO	Volokalamsk	Avtoradio
10)	91.0	1	SA	Samara	R. 7
27)	91.0	1	SR	Saratov	R. Dacha
18)	91.0	1	KH	Khabarovsk	Yumor FM
19)	91.1	1	TS	Kazan	Dorozhnoye R.
3)	91.1	1	BA	Ufa	Ekho Moskvy
17)	91.1	1	LI	Lipetsk	Serebryanyy dozhd
62)	91.1	10	SP	Sankt-Peterburg	Keks FM
3)	91.2	5	MO	Moskvy	Ekho Moskvy
3)	91.2	1	PR	Perm	Ekho Moskvy
18)	91.2	1	RO	Rostov-na-Donu	Yumor FM
4)	91.3	1	SA	Tolyatti	Evropa+
23)	91.4	1	OM	Omsk	Detskoye R.
20)	91.4	1	UL	Ulyanovsk	R. Romantika
1)	91.4	1	MO	Shatura	Avtoradio
3)	91.4	1	SV	Yekaterinburg	Ekho Moskvy
5)	91.4	1	BE	Belgorod	Hit FM
23)	91.4	1	UD	Izhevsk	Detskoye R.
193)	91.5	1	TS	Kazan	R. Novyy Vek
17)	91.5	1	KE	Kemerovo	Serebryanyy dozhd
210)	91.5	1	SA	Samara	Tok FM
3)	91.5	5	SP	Sankt-Peterburg	Ekho Moskvy
15)	91.5	1	BA	Ufa	DFM
19)	91.8	1	PR	Perm	Dorozhnoye R.
126)	91.9	1	SV	Yekaterinburg	R. Narodnaya volna
9B)	92.0	5	MO	Moskva	Govorit Moskva
136)	92.2	1	MO	Moskva	R. Kukuruza
22)	92.3	1	SV	Yekaterinburg	R. KP
20)	92.3	1	TS	Kazan	R. Romantika
27)	92.4	5	MO	Moskva	R. Dacha
1)	92.6	1	MO	Orekhovo-Zuyevo	Avtoradio
1)	92.6	1	MO	Taldom	Avtoradio
20)	92.7	1	KN	Krasnoyarsk	R. Romantika
131)	92.8	1	MO	Moskva	R. Karnaval
173)	93.2	5	MO	Moskva	R. Sport
9A)	93.6	1	KA	Kaliningrad	Glavnoye R.
63)	93.6	5	MO	Moskva	Kommersant FM
18)	94,0	1	KA	Kaliningrad	Yumor FM
93)	94.0	5	MO	Moskva	94 FM - Prosto R.
12)	94.4	5	MO	Moskva	Dobryye pesni
198)	94.8	5	MO	Moskva	RU.FM
24)	95.0	4	SP	St.Peterburg	NRJ
25)	95.2	5	MO	Moskva	Rock FM
22)	95.3	1	CB	Chelyabinsk	R. KP
16)	95.5	1	KA	Kaliningrad	Retro FM
21)	95.6	10	MO	Moskva	R. Zvezda
18)	95.6	1	NN	N.Novgorod	Yumor FM
23)	95.7	1	VG	Volgograd	Detskoye R.
95)	95.7	1	BE	Rakitnoye	R. Radio
18)	95.7	1	SA	Samara	Yumor FM
21)	95.7	1	RY	Ryazan	R. Zvezda
11)	95.8	1	KE	Belovo	R. Maksimum
23)	95.8	1	NS	Novosibirsk	Detskoye R.
141)	95.9	4	SP	St.Peterburg	Neva FM
20)	95.9	1	SV	Yekaterinburg	R. Romantika
19)	96.0	5	MO	Moskva	Dorozhnoye R.
44)	96.0	1	NN	N.Novgorod	Dinamit N.Novgorod
1)	96.0	1	SA	Tolyatti	Avtoradio
24)	96.0	1	CB	Chelyabinsk	NRJ
2)	96.2	2	NS	Novosibirsk	Russkoye R.
20)	96.2	1	UD	Izhevsk	R. Romantika
64)	96.3	1	SA	Samara	Kot FM
2)	96.3	2	KA	Kaliningrad	Russkoye R.
206)	96.4	5	MO	Moskva	Taksi FM
16)	96.4	1	CB	Chelyabinsk	Retro FM
22)	96.5	1	VG	Volgograd	R. KP
38)	96.6	1	PR	Berezniki	Beloye R.
125B)	96.7	1	SP	Lyuban	R. Vanya
176)	96.7	1	DA	Makhachkala	R. Strana gor
24)	96.8	1	NN	N.Novgorod	NRJ
23)	96.8	1	CB	Chelyabinsk	Detskoye R.
23)	96.8	5	MO	Moskva	Detskoye R.
27)	97.0	4	SP	St.Peterburg	R. Dacha
16)	97.0	2	NS	Novosibirsk	Retro FM
26)	97.2	5	MO	Moskva	R. Rekord
20)	97.4	2	NS	Novosibirsk	R. Romantika
8)	97.5	1	TV	Tver	Nashe R.
24)	97.6	1	PR	Perm	NRJ
17)	97.7	1	KA	Kaliningrad	Serebryanyy dozhd
4)	97.9	1	SA	Syzran	Evropa+
166)	98.0	10	MO	Moskva	R. Shokolad
22)	98.3	1	NS	Novosibirsk	R. KP
35)	98.4	5	MO	Moskva	Svezheye R.
104)	98.5	1	BE	Borisovka	R. 31
1)	98.6	1	MO	Zaraysk	Avtoradio
16)	98.6	1	SA	Samara	Retro FM
16)	98.7	1	KN	Krasnoyarsk	Retro FM
1)	98.7	2	NS	Novosibirsk	Avtoradio
145)	98.7	1	ST	Stavropol	R. Mir
2)	98.7	1	SA	Syzran	Russkoye R.
27)	98.7	1	CB	Chelyabinsk	R. Dacha
7)	98.7	1	PR	Berezniki	Militseyskaya volna
24)	98.8	1	VG	Volgograd	NRJ
20)	98.9	5	MO	Moskva	R. Romantika
85)	98.9	1	SV	Yekaterinburg	Nashi pesni
18)	99.0	1	MO	Taldom	Yumor FM
214)	99.0	1	KU	Zheleznogorsk	Zhelezo FM
109B)	99.0	1	BA	Kumertau	R. Kabriolet
18)	99.1	1	VN	Voronezh	Yumor FM
208)	99.1	2	KN	Krasnoyarsk	R. 99.1 FM
23)	99.1	1	NN	N.Novgorod	Detskoye R.
24)	99.1	1	NS	Novosibirsk	NRJ
3)	99.1	1	SA	Samara	Ekho Moskvy
1)	99.1	2	CB	Chelyabinsk	Avtoradio
19)	99.2	1	SR	Balakovo	Dorozhnoye R.
22)	99.3	1	TV	Tver	R. KP
18)	99.4	1	SR	Balashov	Yumor FM
107)	99.4	1	TY	Golyshmanovo	R. 7 Tyumen
28)	99.4	2	SV	Yekaterinburg	Business FM
4)	99.4	1	MO	Kolomna	Evropa+
16)	99.4	5	PR	Perm	Retro FM
19)	99.4	1	SA	Tolyatti	Dorozhnoye R.
16)	99.5	1	TY	Tobolsk	Retro FM
3)	99.5	1	CB	Chelyabinsk	Ekho Moskvy
18)	99.5	1	NS	Novosibirsk	Yumor FM
23)	99.5	1	VN	Voronezh	Detskoye R.
220)	99.5	1	NN	N.Novgorod	R. N.Novgorod
50)	99.6	10	MO	Moskva	Finam FM
19)	99.6	1	OL	Oryol	Dorozhnoye R.
22)	99.6	1	TY	Tyumen	R. KP
19)	99.6	1	SP	Lyuban	Dorozhnoye R.
136)	99.9	1	KD	Vyshestebliyevskaya	R. Kukuruza
4)	99.9	1	SA	Samara	Evropa+
19)	100.0	2	RY	Mosolovo	Dorozhnoye R.
8)	100.0	1	PR	Perm	Nashe R.
10)	100.0	1	NN	N.Novgorod	R. 7
187)	100.0	1	VG	Volgograd	R. Vedo
16)	100.0	1	SV	Yekaterinburg	Retro FM
2)	100.0	1	OL	Oryol	Russkoye R.
6)	100.1	1	SA	Tolyatti	Love R.
1)	100.1	1	PR	Berezniki	Avtoradio
82)	100.1	1	UD	Izhevsk	Moya Udmurtiya
1)	100.1	1	KA	Kaliningrad	Avtoradio
18)	100.1	1	CB	Magnitogorsk	Yumor FM
17)	100.1	5	MO	Moskva	Serebryanyy dozhd
5)	100.1	1	RO	Rostov-na-Donu	Hit FM
109A)	100.2	1	BA	Kumertau	R. Aktan

FM	MHz	kW	Rg	Location	Station
4)	100.2	1	VO	Vologda	Evropa+
4)	100.2	1	KU	Zheleznogorsk	Evropa+
4)	100.3	1	BR	Bryansk	Evropa+
4)	100.3	1	VN	Voronezh	Evropa+
14)	100.3	1	KS	Kostroma	R. Shanson
18)	100.3	5	KN	Krasnoyarsk	Yumor FM
2)	100.3	2	SA	Samara	Russkoye R.
4)	100.3	1	KO	Syktyvkar	Evropa+
4)	100.4	1	KT	Petrozavodsk	Evropa+
48)	100.4	1	OL	Oryol	Ekspress R.
135)	100.4	4	CB	Chelyabinsk	R. Kontinental
154)	100.4	5	SV	Yekaterinburg	R. Pilot
2)	100.4	1	UL	Dimitrovgrad	Russkoye R.
2)	100.4	1	NO	V.Novgorod	Russkoye R.
17)	100.4	4	NN	N.Novgorod	Serebryanyy dozhd
39)	100.5	5	MO	Moskva	Best FM
16)	100.5	1	TL	Tula	Retro FM
1)	100.5	1	TY	Tobolsk	Avtoradio
42)	100.5	1	PR	Solikamsk	Bolid FM
4)	100.5	10	SP	Sankt-Peterburg	Evropa+
167)	100.5	1	SV	Nizhniy Tagil	R. Si
14)	100.5	1	CB	Magnitogorsk	R. Shanson
7)	100.5	1	VL	Kovrov	Militseyskaya volna
207)	100.5	1	TS	Kazan	Tatarskoye R.
4)	100.5	1	TY	Ishim	Evropa+
2)	100.5	1	UD	Izhevsk	Russkoye R.
2)	100.5	1	KS	Buy	Russkoye R.
34)	100.5	4	KE	Novokuznetsk	Apeks-R.
2)	100.6	1	BA	Kumertau	Russkoye R.
135)	100.6	1	CB	Snezhinsk	R. Kontinental
15)	100.6	1	KA	Chernyakhovsk	DFM
169)	100.6	1	TY	Tyumen	R. City
2)	100.6	1	TV	Tver	Russkoye R.
4)	100.6	1	MD	Saransk	Evropa+
23)	100.6	1	AK	Barnaul	Detskoye R.
4)	100.6	1	VG	Volgograd	Evropa+
18)	100.6	1	SR	Saratov	Yumor FM
19)	100.7	1	KT	Peldozha	Dorozhnoye R.
4)	100.7	1	PM	Ussuriysk	Evropa+
4)	100.7	1	BR	Unecha	Evropa+
10)	100.7	1	ST	Stavropol	R. 7
18)	100.7	1	RY	Ryazan	Yumor FM
5)	100.7	5	PR	Perm	Hit FM
188)	100.7	3	NS	Novosibirsk	R. Yuniton
18)	100.7	1	KB	Nalchik	Yumor FM
158)	100.7	1	DA	Makhachkala	R. Priboy
27)	100.7	1	KU	Kursk	R. Dacha
26)	10U./	1	RO	Rostov-na-Donu	R. Rekord
26)	100.8	1	OB	Orenburg	R. Rekord
48)	100.8	1	OL	Livny	Ekspress R.
28)	100.8	1	CB	Chelyabinsk	Business FM
18)	100.8	1	VL	Vladimir	Yumor FM
19)	100.8	1	KN	Krasnoyarsk	Dorozhnoye R.
5)	100.8	4	KD	Tbilisskaya	Hit FM
16)	100.9	5	NN	N.Novgorod	Retro FM
136)	100.9	1	KD	Tuapse	R. Kukuruza
20)	100.9	1	OM	Tara	R. Romantika
4)	100.9	1	BA	Sterlitamak	Evropa+
94)	100.9	10	SP	Sankt-Peterburg	Piter FM
16)	100.9	1	KD	Novorossiysk	Retro FM
134)	100.9	3	MO	Moskva	R. Klassik
19)	100.9	1	LI	Lipetsk	Dorozhnoye R.
1)	100.9	1	KD	Kushchyovskaya	Avtoradio
202)	100.9	1	PR	Kudymkar	Soyuz FM
146)	100.9	1	KA	Kaliningrad	R. Monte-Karlo
10)	100.9	1	IR	Irkutsk	R. 7
104)	100.9	1	BE	Belgorod	Mir Belogorya
168)	100.9	1	ZB	Aginskoye	R. Sibir
4)	100.9	1	OL	Oryol	Evropa+
2)	101.0	2	TS	Bugulma	Russkoye R.
4)	101.0	1	MU	Murmansk	Evropa+
14)	101.0	1	TY	Tyumen	R. Shanson
14)	101.0	1	SA	Samara	R. Shanson
27)	101.0	1	OM	Omsk	R. Dacha
14)	101.0	1	SV	Nizhniy Tagil	R. Shanson
3)	101.0	1	KV	Kirov	Ekho Moskvy
19)	101.0	1	VO	Vologda	Dorozhnoye R.
118)	101.0	1	PM	Artyom	R. AVN
17)	101.0	1	CB	Magnitogorsk	Serebryanyy dozhd
34)	101.0	2	KE	Kemerovo	Apeks-R.
95)	101.1	1	AK	Kamen-na-Obi	R. Radio
4)	101.1	1	KD	Sochi	Avtoradio
10)	101.1	1	PR	Perm	R. 7
172)	101.1	2	KE	Novokuznetsk	Militseyskaya volna
4)	101.1	1	NS	Kuybyshev	R. Slovo
1)	101.1	1	KD	Yeysk	Avtoradio
3)	101.1	1	VG	Volgograd	Ekho Moskvy
203)	101.1	1	DA	Makhachkala	Star FM
16)	101.1	1	YA	Yaroslavl	Retro FM
16)	101.2	1	RO	Rostov-na-Donu	Retro FM
5)	101.2	1	KO	Pechora	Hit FM
14)	101.2	1	SA	Tolyatti	R. Shanson
19)	101.2	1	MU	Monchegorsk	Dorozhnoye R.
16)	101.2	1	KD	Krasnodar	Retro FM
2)	101.2	1	KU	Kursk	Russkoye R.
18)	101.2	1	CB	Chelyabinsk	Yumor FM
15)	101.2	10	MO	Moskva	DFM
3)	101.3	1	OB	Orenburg	Ekho Moskvy
16)	101.3	1	BA	Tuymazy	Retro FM
221)	101.3	1	TO	Tomsk	Knopka R.
6)	101.3	1	ST	Pyatigorsk	Love R.
4)	101.3	1	LI	Lipetsk	Evropa+
8)	101.3	1	KA	Kaliningrad	Nashe R.
13)	101.3	1	UD	Izhevsk	Yumor FM
16)	101.3	1	VL	Vladimir	Retro FM
2)	101.3	1	AK	Biysk	Russkoye R.
6)	101.3	2	KN	Krasnoyarsk	Love R.
19)	101.3	1	RK	Abakan	Dorozhnoye R.
2)	101.3	1	MD	Saransk	Russkoye R.
7)	101.4	1	KII	Khabarovsk	Militseyskaya volna
19)	101.4	1	ST	Stavropol	Dorozhnoye R.
1)	101.4	1	BA	Sterlitamak	Avtoradio
15)	101.4	1	SA	Syzran	DFM
1)	101.4	1	TV	Tver	Avtoradio
24)	101.4	1	TL	Tula	NRJ
49)	101.4	10	SP	Sankt-Peterburg	Eldoradio
9A)	101.4	1	KS	Kostroma	Glavnoye R.
2)	101.4	1	KD	Tuapse	Russkoye R.
193)	101.4	2	TS	Bilyarsk	R. Novyy Vek
53)	101.4	2	NS	Novosibirsk	Gorodskaya volna
11)	101.4	1	PR	Bereznlki	R. Maksimum
1)	101.4	1	VN	Rossosh	Avtoradio
5)	101.4	5	IR	Irkutsk	Hit FM
5)	101.4	1	NN	N.Novgorod	Hit FM
19)	101.4	1	TY	Omutinskiy	Dorozhnoye R.
7)	101.4	1	OL	Oryol	Militseyskaya volna
17)	101.4	1	PZ	Penza	Serebryanyy dozhd
24)	101.4	1	UL	Ulyanovsk	NRJ
16)	101.5	1	KE	Novokuznetsk	Retro FM
14)	101.5	1	SR	Saratov	R. Shanson
26)	101.5	2	SA	Samara	R. Rekord
19)	101.5	1	RY	Ryazan	Dorozhnoye R.
149)	101.5	1	PR	Perm	R. Nostalzhi
20)	101.5	1	MO	Shatura	R. Romantika
1)	101.5	1	KY	Nyagan	Avtoradio
1)	101.5	1	CV	Cheboksary	Avtoradio
1)	101.5	1	TS	Nab.Chelny	Avtoradio
27)	101.5	1	DA	Makhachkala	R. Dacha
218)	101.5	1	NO	M.Vishera	MV Diapazon
1)	101.5	1	KD	Kanevskaya	Russkoye R.
174B)	101.5	1	VG	Volgograd	Volgograd FM
1)	101.5	1	BR	Bryansk	Avtoradio
18)	101.5	3	OM	Omsk	Yumor FM
196)	101.5	2	AD	Maykop	Kazak FM
4)	101.5	1	SV	Nizhniy Tagil	Evropa+
14)	101.6	1	VG	Mikhaylovka	R. Shanson
4)	101.6	1	CB	Chelyabinsk	Evropa+
4)	101.6	2	KY	Khanty-Mansiysk	Evropa+
102)	101.6	1	BA	Ufa	R. 1-y Kanal
21)	101.6	1	OB	Saraktash	R. Zvezda
21)	101.6	1	OB	Pleshanovo	R. Zvezda
14)	101.6	1	SV	Krasnoturinsk	R. Shanson
4)	101.6	1	UL	Dimitrovgrad	Evropa+
83)	101.6	2.5	VN	Voronezh	Muz FM
1)	101.6	1	AR	Arkhangelsk	Avtoradio
2)	101.6	1	MU	Apatity	Russkoye R.
163)	101.6	1	RO	Rostov-na-Donu	R. Rostova
1)	101.7	1	AS	Astrakhan	Avtoradio
30A)	101.7	1	SP	Kingisepp	R. Gardarika
4)	101.7	1	UL	Ulyanovsk	Evropa+
90)	101.7	1	KD	Tbilisskaya	Ostrov Sochi
9A)	101.7	1	YA	Yaroslavl	Glavnoye R.
15)	101.7	1	BA	Neftekamsk	DFM
8)	101.7	10	MO	Moskva	Nashe R.
14)	101.7	1	KN	Krasnoyarsk	R. Shanson
193)	101.7	1	TS	Bugulma	R. Novyy Vek
18)	101.7	1	IR	Bratsk	Yumor FM
1)	101.7	1	VN	Borisoglebsk	Avtoradio
2)	101.7	1	YV	Birobidzhan	Russoye R.
19)	101.7	1	VO	Babayevo	Dorozhnoye R.

FM	MHz	kW	Rg	Location	Station
15)	101.7	1	RK	Abakan	DFM
186)	101.7	5	PM	Vladivostok	R. VBC
9A)	101.7	1	BE	Belgorod	Glavnoye R.
70)	101.8	1	OL	Oryol	Love Music
98)	101.8	1	PZ	Penza	R. 101.8
2)	101.8	1	ST	Stavropol	Russkoye R.
1)	101.8	1	PR	Chusovoy	Avtoradio
1)	101.8	1	KO	Syktyvkar	Avtoradio
19)	101.8	4	VL	Vladimir	Dorozhnoye R.
4)	101.8	1	TY	Tyumen	Evropa+
4)	101.8	1	TV	Tver	Evropa+
16)	101.8	4	NO	Novgorod	Retro FM
2)	101.8	1	KD	Krasnodar	Russkoye R.
16)	101.8	1	UD	Izhevsk	Retro FM
21)	101.8	1	OB	Buzuluk	R. Zvezda
1)	101.8	1	VN	Bobrov	Avtoradio
16)	101.8	1	OB	Orenburg	Retro FM
15)	101.8	1	KE	Kemerovo	DFM
4)	101.9	1	OM	Omsk	Evropa+
19)	101.9	1	KO	Ukhta	Dorozhnoye R.
5)	101.9	1	IR	Tulun	Hit FM
8)	101.9	5	TL	Tula	Nashe R.
74)	101.9	1	KV	Pinyug	Mariya FM
4)	101.9	1	KD	Novorossiysk	Evropa+
14)	101.9	1	AK	Barnaul	R. Shanson
4)	101.9	1	TS	Nab.Chelny	Evropa+
2)	101.9	1	DA	Makhachkala	Russkoye R.
26)	101.9	1	TS	Kazan	R. Rekord
1)	101.9	1	AK	Biysk	Avtoradio
1)	101.9	4	NN	N.Novgorod	Avtoradio
10)	101.9	5	KY	Surgut	R. 7
14)	102.0	1	OB	Orsk	R. Shanson
9A)	102.0	5	PR	Perm	Glavnoye R.
1)	102.0	1	SR	Pugachyov	Avtoradio
1)	102.0	1	RY	Ryazan	Avtoradio
161)	102.0	10	SP	Sankt-Peterburg	R. Roks Severo-Zapad
5)	102.0	1	MD	Saransk	Hit FM
4)	102.0	1	ZB	Chita	Evropa+
26)	102.0	1	MU	Murmansk	R. Rekord
107)	102.0	1	TY	Sladkovo	R. 7 Tyumen
4)	102.0	1	SM	Smolensk	Evropa+
14)	102.0	1	KN	Achinsk	R. Shanson
168)	102.0	1	ZB	Krasnokamensk	R. Sibir
1)	102.0	1	VN	Boguchar	Avtoradio
19)	102.0	1	BR	Bryansk	Dorozhnoye R.
19)	102.0	1	AR	Velsk	Dorozhnoye R.
4)	102.0	1	SO	Vladikavkaz	Evropa+
130)	102.0	2	VG	Volgograd	Novaya volna
18)	102.0	1	SV	Yekaterinburg	Yumor FM
1)	102.0	1	TV	Zapadnaya Dvina	Avtoradio
17)	102.0	1	MU	Kirovsk	Serebryanyy dozhd
78)	102.0	1	CV	Cheboksary	MFM
33)	102.1	1	UL	Ulyanovsk	2x2 R.
14)	102.1	2	KY	Nizhnevartovsk	R. Shanson
107)	102.1	1	TY	Yarkovo	R. 7 Tyumen
1)	102.1	1	SR	Saratov	Avtoradio
27)	102.1	1	SA	Samara	R. Dacha
4)	102.1	1	PS	Pskov	Evropa+
1)	102.1	1	LI	Lipetsk	Avtoradio
193)	102.1	2	TS	Leninogorsk	R. Novyy Vek
10)	102.1	1	KU	Kursk	R. 7
219)	102.1	1	IR	Irkutsk	MCM
14)	102.1	1	IR	Bratsk	R. Shanson
4)	102.1	1	KE	Belovo	Evropa+
146)	102.1	5	MO	Moskva	R. Monte-Karlo
1)	102.2	1	SM	Vyazma	Evropa+
17)	102.2	1	YA	Yaroslavl	Serebryanyy dozhd
1)	102.2	1	MO	Serebryanyye Prudy	Avtoradio
19)	102.2	1	RY	Sasovo	Dorozhnoye R.
4)	102.2	1	KB	Nalchik	Evropa+
17)	102.2	3	KN	Krasnoyarsk	Serebryanyy dozhd
4)	102.2	1	KD	Krasnodar	Evropa+
19)	102.2	1	AR	Kozmogorodskoye	Dorozhnoye R.
2)	102.2	1	RK	Abakan	Evropa+
167)	102.2	1	SV	Kamensk-Uralskiy	R. Si
19)	102.2	1	SP	Volkhov	Dorozhnoye R.
95)	102.2	1	AK	Blagoveshchenka	R. Radio
2)	102.2	1	BE	Belgorod	Russkoye R.
6)	102.2	2	AS	Astrakhan	Love R.
107)	102.2	1	TY	Aromashevo	R. 7 Tyumen
4)	102.2	1.5	KV	Kirov	Evropa+
16)	102.2	1	TV	Tver	Retro FM
2)	102.3	1	BA	Neftekamsk	Russkoye R.
16)	102.3	1	IR	Usolye-Sibirskoye	Retro FM
1)	102.3	1	BU	Ulan-Ude	Evropa+
6)	102.3	1	KO	Syktyvkar	Love R.
117)	102.3	1	SA	Tolyatti	R. Avgust
193)	102.3	2	TS	Shemordan	R. Novyy Vek
62)	102.3	1	VN	Voronezh	Keks FM
107)	102.3	1	TY	Uvat	R. 7 Tyumen
1)	102.3	1	KD	Armavir	Avtoradio
107)	102.3	1	TY	Armizonskoye	R. 7 Tyumen
1)	102.3	1	AM	Belogorsk	Avtoradio
125B)	102.3	1	TL	Bogoroditsk	R. Vanya
121)	102.3	1	MO	B.Karasyovo	R. Blago
180)	102.3	1	VO	V.Ustyug	R. Transmit
1)	102.3	1	PZ	Penza	Avtoradio
58)	102.4	5	IN	Nazran	ITT Veshchaniye
112)	102.4	1	VG	Mikhaylovka	R. Aprel
2)	102.4	1	KO	Ukhta	Russkoye R.
6)	102.4	1	TA	Tambov	Love R.
30B)	102.4	10	SP	Sankt-Peterburg	R. Metro
196)	102.4	5	KD	Novorossiysk	Kazak FM
4)	102.4	1	PM	Nakhodka	Evropa+
9A)	102.4	1	CB	Chelyabinsk	Glavnoye R.
16)	102.4	1	TS	Kazan	Retro FM
27)	102.4	1	UD	Izhevsk	R. Dacha
29)	102.4	1	KD	Yeysk	Pervoye R.
15)	102.4	1	VL	Vladimir	DFM
107)	102.4	1	TY	Vikulovo	R. 7 Tyumen
1)	102.4	2	BA	Belebey	Avtoradio
4)	102.4	1	DA	Makhachkala	Evropa+
19)	102.4	1	NN	N.Novgorod	Dorozhnoye R.
15)	102.4	1	AK	Barnaul	DFM
189)	102.5	1	KY	Yugorsk	R. Yurga
17)	102.5	1	RY	Ryazan	Serebryanyy dozhd
24)	102.5	5	SA	Samara	NRJ
4)	102.5	1	SL	Yu-Sakhalinsk	Evropa+
14)	102.5	1	KD	Sochi	R. Shanson
16)	102.5	1	TO	Tomsk	Retro FM
2)	102.5	1	TY	Tyumen	Russkoye R.
4)	102.5	1	CV	Cheboksary	Evropa+
196)	102.5	1	KD	Psebay	Kazak FM
16)	102.5	1	SV	Serov	Retro FM
14)	102.5	1	BA	Ufa	R. Shanson
19)	102.5	1	PS	Dedovichi	Dorozhnoye R.
27)	102.5	1	KM	Petropavlovsk-K.	R. Dacha
16)	102.5	5	KY	Surgut	Retro FM
18)	102.5	1	VN	Boguchar	Yumor FM
46)	102.5	1	SV	Yekaterinburg	Dzhem FM
2)	102.5	1	TY	Ishim	Russkoye R.
19)	102.5	1	KT	Kotkozero	Dorozhnoye R.
114)	102.5	1	BA	Kumertau	R. Aris
14)	102.5	1	PR	Lysva	R. Shanson
92)	102.5	5	MO	Moskva	Pervoye Populyarnoye R.
1)	102.5	1	MU	Murmansk	Avtoradio
2)	102.5	1	OM	Omsk	Russkoye R.
4)	102.6	1	AK	Biysk	Evropa+
10)	102.6	1	SR	Saratov	R. 7
2)	102.6	1	TY	Omutinskiy	Russkoye R.
2)	102.6	1	YA	Yaroslavl	Russkoye R.
168)	102.6	1	ZB	Chita	R. Sibir
19)	102.6	1	SP	Tikhvin	Dorozhnoye R.
1)	102.6	1	IR	Sayansk	Avtoradio
16)	102.6	1	PS	Pskov	Retro FM
18)	102.6	1	KE	Novokuznetsk	Yumor FM
193)	102.6	2	TS	Nizhnekamsk	R. Novyy Vek
1)	102.6	1	VL	Murom	Avtoradio
4)	102.6	1	KL	Kaluga	Evropa+
71)	102.6	1	PS	V.Luki	Luki FM
2)	102.6	1	BR	Bryansk	Russkoye R.
145)	102.6	1	NS	Novosibirsk	R. Mir
1)	102.6	1	KH	Sovetskaya Gavan	Avtoradio
95)	102.7	1	AK	Zaraysk	R. Radio
125B)	102.7	2	SA	Tolyatti	R. Vanya
155)	102.7	1	TV	Tver	R. Pilot
5)	102.7	1	KO	Syktyvkar	Hit FM
15)	102.7	5	PR	Perm	DFM
29)	102.7	5	KD	Krasnodar	Pervoye R.
1)	102.7	1	KU	Zheleznogorsk	Avtoradio
197)	102.7	1	VO	Vologda	ROS R.
139)	102.7	5	PM	Vladivostok	R. Lemma
4)	102.7	1	AS	Astrakhan	Evropa+
106)	102.7	1	NO	Novgorod	R. 53
4)	102.8	1	KE	Kemerovo	Evropa+
2)	102.8	1	AM	Belogorsk	Russkoye R.
4)	102.8	1	PR	Berezniki	Evropa+
104)	102.8	1	BE	Valuyki	R. 31
21)	102.8	1	SO	Vladikavkaz	R. Zvezda
14)	102.8	1	VN	Voronezh	R. Shanson

FM	MHz	kW	Rg	Location	Station
3)	102.8	1	BU	Ulan-Ude	Ekho Moskvy
80)	102.8	1	RA	Gorno-Altaysk	Molodezhnyy kanal
124)	102.8	1	PR	Chaykovskiy	R. Dixi
11)	102.8	10	SP	Sankt-Peterburg	R. Maksimum
81)	102.8	1	PZ	Penza	Most R.
4)	102.8	1	OB	Orsk	Evropa+
20)	102.8	1	TS	Nab.Chelny	R. Romantika
1)	102.8	1	NS	Kuybyshev	Avtoradio
36)	102.8	5	KN	Krasnoyarsk	Avtoritetnoye R.
40)	102.8	1	TS	Kazan	BIM-Radio
14)	102.8	1	IR	Cheremkhovo	R. Shanson
1)	102.9	1	TA	Tambov	Avtoradio
164)	102.9	1	DA	Makhachkala	R. Safinat
57)	102.9	1	CB	Chelyabinsk	Intervolna
15)	102.9	1	SA	Samara	DFM
19)	102.9	1	SP	Podporozhye	Dorozhnoye R.
2)	102.9	5	NN	N.Novgorod	Russkoye R.
1)	102.9	1	PM	Nakhodka	Avtoradio
6)	102.9	1	KA	Kaliningrad	Love R.
4)	102.9	1	VL	Vladimir	Evropa+
1)	102.9	1	IR	Bratsk	Avtoradio
18)	102.9	1	AK	Barnaul	Yumor FM
196)	102.9	4	KD	Armavir	Kazak FM
209)	102.9	1	BU	Arshan	TD FM
74)	102.9	1	KV	Kirov	Mariya FM
15)	103.0	1	CB	Magnitogorsk	DFM
162)	103.0	1	BA	Ufa	R. Roksana
2)	103.0	1	UL	Ulyanovsk	Russkoye R.
5)	103.0	1	SR	Saratov	Hit FM
1)	103.0	1	TV	Ostashkov	Avtoradio
5)	103.0	2	OB	Orenburg	Hit FM
150)	103.0	1	YN	Noyabrsk	R. Noyabrsk
19)	103.0	1	VN	Borisoglebsk	Dorozhnoye R.
1)	103.0	1	MA	Magadan	Avtoradio
21)	103.0	1	KH	Komsomolsk-na-A.	R. Zvezda
4)	103.0	1	UD	Izhevsk	Evropa+
19)	103.0	1	IV	Ivanovo	Dorozhnoye R.
107)	103.0	1	TY	Vagay	R. 7 Tyumen
14)	103.0	1	TS	Bugulma	R. Shanson
14)	103.0	10	MO	Moskva	R. Shanson
8)	103.0	1	MU	Murmansk	Nashe R.
1)	103.1	1	KT	Petrozavodsk	Avtoradio
196)	103.1	1	KD	Primorsko-Akhtarsk	Kazak FM
2)	103.1	1	KD	Sochi	Russkoye R.
16)	103.1	1	ST	Stavropol	Retro FM
4)	103.1	1	BE	St.Oskol	Evropa+
107)	103.1	1	TY	Tyumen	R. 7 Tyumen
18)	103.1	1	AK	Biysk	Yumor FM
27)	103.1	1	KH	Khabarovsk	R. Dacha
21)	103.1	1	OB	Kuvandyk	R. Zvezda
16)	103.1	1	SV	Krasnoturinsk	Retro FM
87)	103.1	1	KL	Kaluga	Nika FM
18)	103.1	3	IR	Irkutsk	Yumor FM
7)	103.1	1	MU	Apatity	Militseyskaya volna
1)	103.1	1	VG	Volgograd	Avtoradio
30A)	103.1	5	SP	Vyborg	R. Gardarika
1)	103.1	1	CB	Ozyorsk	Avtoradio
14)	103.2	1	IR	Tayshet	R. Shanson
5)	103.2	1	KG	Kurgan	Hit FM
1)	103.2	1	NO	Novgorod	Avtoradio
4)	103.2	3	NS	Novosibirsk	Evropa+
18)	103.2	1	VN	Pavlovsk	Yumor FM
11)	103.2	5	PR	Perm	R. Maksimum
4)	103.2	1	RY	Ryazan	Evropa+
1)	103.2	1	KD	Krasnodar	Avtoradio
15)	103.2	1	SA	Tolyatti	DFM
2)	103.2	1	ST	Pyatigorsk	Russkoye R.
2)	103.2	1	AS	Astrakhan	Russkoye R.
11)	103.2	1	KU	Zheleznogorsk	R. Maksimum
14)	103.2	1	SV	Yekaterinburg	R. Shanson
19)	103.2	1	SM	Vyazma	Dorozhnoye R.
14)	103.2	4	PM	Vladivostok	R. Shanson
107)	103.2	1	TY	B.Sorokino	R. 7 Tyumen
47)	103.2	1	KE	Belovo	Ekspress FM
5)	103.2	1	BE	Belgorod	Hit FM
4)	103.2	1	VL	Kovrov	Evropa+
18)	103.2	1	TS	Nab.Chelny	Yumor FM
2)	103.3	1	OB	Orsk	Russkoye R.
217)	103.3	1	BA	Salavat	M R.
2)	103.3	1	IR	Sayansk	Russkoye R.
1)	103.3	2	KY	Surgut	Avtoradio
29)	103.3	1	KD	Tbilisskaya	Pervoye R.
7)	103.3	1	TL	Tula	Militseyskaya volna
96)	103.3	1	ZB	Chita	Populyarnoye R.
136)	103.3	1	CC	Goragorskiy	R. Kukuruza

FM	MHz	kW	Rg	Location	Station
15)	103.3	1	VL	Murom	DFM
24)	103.3	2	KN	Krasnoyarsk	NRJ
27)	103.3	1	RO	Azov	R. Dacha
1)	103.3	1	TS	Kazan	Avtoradio
14)	103.3	1	KE	Kemerovo	R. Shanson
19)	103.3	1	OB	Buzuluk	Dorozhnoye R.
15)	103.3	1	PR	Berezniki	DFM
2)	103.3	1	UD	Balezino	Russkoye R.
27)	103.3	1	SR	Balakovo	R. Dacha
4)	103.3	1	OL	Livny	Evropa+
15)	103.4	5	SP	Sankt-Peterburg	DFM
4)	103.4	1	TO	Tomsk	Evropa+
1)	103.4	1	KL	Obninsk	Avtoradio
160)	103.4	1	NN	N.Novgorod	R. Randevu
1)	103.4	1	MU	Kovdor	Avtoradio
1)	103.4	1	KV	Vyatskiye Polyarny	Avtoradio
1)	103.4	1	VN	Voronezh	Avtoradio
19)	103.4	1	AR	Arkhangelsk	Dorozhnoye R.
2)	103.4	1	VL	Vladimir	Russkoye R.
1)	103.4	1	KV	Kirov	Avtoradio
29)	103.4	1	KD	Tuapse	Pervoye R.
103)	103.5	1	OM	Omsk	R. 3
1)	103.5	1	MO	Shakhovskaya	Avtoradio
1)	103.5	1	KA	Chernyakhovsk	Avtoradio
8)	103.5	1	CB	Chelyabinsk	Nashe R.
16)	103.5	1	CV	Cheboksary	Retro FM
195)	103.5	1	BA	Ufa	Relaks FM
19)	103.5	1	UL	Ulyanovsk	Dorozhnoye R.
2)	103.5	1	SM	Smolensk	Russkoye R.
16)	103.5	1	KT	Petrozavodsk	Retro FM
77)	103.5	1	KN	Norilsk	Megapolis FM
1)	103.5	1	KD	Labinsk	Avtoradio
1)	103.5	1	SO	Vladikavkaz	Avtoradio
125B)	103.5	1	OL	Oryol	R. Vanya
204)	103.5	1	BR	Bryansk	BIT Radio
4)	103.5	1	SR	Saratov	Evropa+
2)	103.6	1	TS	Nab.Chelny	Russkoye R.
143)	103.6	1	SA	Samara	R. Megapolis
85)	103.6	2	PR	Perm	Nashi pesni
4)	103.6	1	VL	Gus-Khrustalnyy	Evropa+
19)	103.6	1	VG	Volgograd	Dorozhnoye R.
4)	103.6	1	BE	Belgorod	Evropa+
4)	103.6	1	ST	Stavropol	Evropa+
5)	103.6	1	CB	Magnitogorsk	Hit FM
4)	103.7	5	NO	Novgorod	Evropa+
10)	103.7	1	TY	Tobolsk	R. 7
86)	103.7	1	KD	Sochi	Next FM
1)	103.7	1	MD	Saransk	Avtoradio
146)	103.7	1	RO	Rostov-na-Donu	R. Monte-Karlo
4)	103.7	1	OB	Orenburg	Evropa+
213)	103.7	2	KH	Khabarovsk	Vostok Rossii
11)	103.7	10	MO	Moskva	R. Maksimum
14)	103.7	1	AS	Astrakhan	R. Shanson
56)	103.7	1	OB	Orsk	Hit FM Ural
168)	103.7	1	RK	Abakan	R. Sibir
16)	103.7	1	KU	Kursk	R. Kurs
16)	103.7	1	AK	Biysk	Retro FM
167)	103.7	1	PM	Vladivostok	Retro FM
167)	103.7	5	SV	Yekaterinburg	R. Si
10)	103.7	1	KD	Krasnodar	R. 7
19)	103.7	1	KG	Kurgan	Dorozhnoye R.
2)	103.8	1	RT	Kyzyl	Russkoye R.
15)	103.8	1	TO	Tomsk	DFM
1)	103.8	1	SA	Syzran	Avtoradio
87)	103.8	1	KL	Sukhinichi	Nika FM
212)	103.8	1	KA	Sovetsk	R. Ekspress
4)	103.8	1	ST	Pyatigorsk	Evropa+
4)	103.8	1	PZ	Penza	Evropa+
16)	103.8	1	KO	Syktyvkar	Retro FM
4)	103.8	2	KN	Krasnoyarsk	Evropa+
142)	103.8	1	ME	Yoshkar-Ola	Puls R.
4)	103.8	1	IR	Irkutsk	Evropa+
8)	103.8	1	UD	Izhevsk	Nashe R.
6)	103.8	1	VN	Voronezh	Love R.
19)	103.8	1	NO	Borovichi	Dorozhnoye R.
2)	103.8	4	AR	Arkhangelsk	Russkoye R.
19)	103.8	1	YA	Yaroslavl	Dorozhnoye R.
14)	103.8	1	PR	Berezniki	R. Shanson
17)	103.8	1	TV	Tver	Serebryanyy dozhd
15)	103.9	1	PR	Chusovoy	DFM
83)	103.9	1	TA	Tambov	Muz FM
15)	103.9	2	NS	Novosibirsk	DFM
6)	103.9	1	PM	Partizansk	Love R.
168)	103.9	1	OM	Omsk	R. Sibir
16)	103.9	1	VG	Mikhaylovka	Retro FM

FM	MHz	kW	Rg	Location	Station
107)	103.9	1	TY	Isetkoye	R. 7 Tyumen
1)	103.9	1	AK	Barnaul	Avtoradio
7)	103.9	5	UL	Veshkayma	Militseyskaya volna
4)	103.9	5	NN	N.Novgorod	Evropa+
4)	104.0	1	KY	Nizhnevartovsk	Evropa+
16)	104.0	1	BA	Ufa	Retro FM
26)	104.0	1	SA	Tolyatti	R. Rekord
27)	104.0	1	ST	Svetlograd	R. Dacha
8)	104.0	10	SP	Sankt-Peterburg	Nashe R.
14)	104.0	1	KE	Novokuznetsk	R. Shanson
111)	104.0	1	IN	Nazran	R. Angusht
16)	104.0	1	MU	Murmansk	Retro FM
1)	104.0	1	SV	Kamensk-Uralskiy	Avtoradio
14)	104.0	1	TS	Kazan	R. Shanson
107)	104.0	1	TY	Ishim	R. 7 Tyumen
16)	104.0	1	VG	Volgograd	Retro FM
89)	104.0	1	KD	Novorossiysk	Novaya Rossiya
27)	104.1	1	SV	Yekaterinburg	R. Dacha
222)	104.1	1	AS	Astrakhan	Yuzhnaya volna
24)	104.1	1	RY	Ryazan	NRJ
15)	104.1	1	TS	Chistopol	DFM
2)	104.1	1	CB	Chelyabinsk	Russkoye R.
1)	104.1	2	KY	Khanty-Mansiysk	Avtoradio
5)	104.1	1	CB	Tryokhgornyy	Hit FM
18)	104.1	1	KH	Sovetskaya Gavan	Yumor FM
1)	104.1	1	AR	Plesetsk	Avtoradio
110)	104.1	5	PR	Perm	R. Alfa
6)	104.1	1	SV	Krasnoturinsk	Love R.
2)	104.1	1	IR	Bratsk	Russkoye R.
14)	104.1	1	VN	Borisoglebsk	R. Shanson
1)	104.1	1	RO	Rostov-na-Donu	Avtoradio
15)	104.1	1	OB	Orsk	DFM
6)	104.2	1	CV	Cheboksary	Love R.
2)	104.2	1	CB	Magnitogorsk	Russkoye R.
24)	104.2	10	MO	Moskva	NRJ
14)	104.2	1	KY	Surgut	R. Shanson
178)	104.2	1	KD	Temryuk	R. Temryuk
45)	104.2	1	TY	Tobolsk	Dipol FM
18)	104.2	2	TO	Tomsk	Yumor FM
10)	104.2	1	UL	Ulyanovsk	R. 7
151)	104.2	4	NN	Arzamas	R. Obraz
28)	104.2	1	KN	Krasnoyarsk	Business FM
180)	104.2	1	VO	Totma	R. Transmit
19)	104.2	1	SP	Kingisepp	Dorozhnoye R.
26)	104.2	2	IR	Irkutsk	R.Rekord
14)	104.2	1	CB	Zlatoust	R. Shanson
18)	104.2	1	SM	Vyazma	Yumor FM
4)	104.2	5	PM	Vladivostok	Evropa+
4)	104.2	1	RK	Abakan	Evropa+
180)	104.2	2	VO	Babayevo	R. Transmit
14)	104.2	1	MU	Apatity	R. Shanson
24)	104.2	1	BE	Belgorod	NRJ
5)	104.2	1	KD	Krasnodar	Hit FM
15)	104.3	5	OB	Orenburg	DFM
19)	104.3	1	KH	Khabarovsk	Dorozhnoye R.
2)	104.3	1	BA	Sterlitamak	Russkoye R.
16)	104.3	1	SR	Saratov	Retro FM
1)	104.3	1	OL	Oryol	Avtoradio
151)	104.3	4	NN	Krasnyye Baki	R. Obraz
7)	104.3	1	KE	Kemerovo	Militseyskaya volna
22)	104.3	1	VL	Vladimir	R. KP
199)	104.3	1	SA	Samara	Samara-Maximum
74)	104.4	2	TS	Shemordan	Mariya FM
6)	104.4	1	SL	Yu-Sakhalinsk	Love R.
14)	104.4	5	SP	Sankt-Peterburg	R. Shanson
2)	104.4	1	PR	Chusovoy	Russkoye R.
1)	104.4	5	TL	Tula	Avtoradio
5)	104.4	1	BA	Tuymazy	Hit FM
16)	104.4	1	TA	Tambov	Retro FM
4)	104.4	5	KD	Sochi	Evropa+
4)	104.4	1	KA	Sovetsk	Love R.
6)	104.4	1	AM	Blagoveshchensk	Love R.
16)	104.4	1	AK	Barnaul	Retro FM
180)	104.4	2	VO	Vologda	R. Transmit
10)	104.4	1	BE	Ivnya	R. 7
7)	104.4	1	VL	Murom	Militseyskaya volna
180)	104.4	1	VO	Nikolsk	R. Transmit
4)	104.4	1	KE	Novokuznetsk	Evropa+
26)	104.4	1	OM	Omsk	R. Rekord
19)	104.4	1	PS	Pushkinskiye gory	Dorozhnoye R.
2)	104.5	1	BA	Ufa	Russkoye R.
1)	104.5	1	KM	Petropavlovsk-K.	Avtoradio
14)	104.5	1	YA	Yaroslavl	R. Shanson
21)	104.5	1	OB	Sharlyk	R. Zvezda
18)	104.5	1	VG	Volgograd	Yumor FM
5)	104.5	1	KO	Ukhta	Hit FM
136)	104.5	1	BE	St.Oskol	R. Kukuruza
108)	104.5	1	UD	Izhevsk	R. Adam
27)	104.5	2	NN	N.Novgorod	R. Dacha
153)	104.5	1	CB	Chelyabinsk	R. Olimp
33)	104.5	1	UL	Dimitrovgrad	2x2 R.
4)	104.5	1	ME	Yoshkar-Ola	Evropa+
4)	104.5	1	KA	Kaliningrad	Evropa+
29)	104.5	4	KD	Kanevskaya	Pervoye R.
97)	104.5	1	MU	Murmansk	Power Hit R.
177)	104.5	1	PM	Nakhodka	R. Svob. Nakhodka
180)	104.6	1	VO	Cherepovets	R. Transmit
16)	104.6	1	IR	Irkutsk	Retro FM
168)	104.6	1	TO	Tomsk	R. Sibir
15)	104.6	1	RO	Rostov-na-Donu	DFM
6)	104.6	1.2	LI	Lipetsk	Love R.
24)	104.6	1	KU	Kursk	NRJ
65)	104.6	1	TY	Tyumen	Krasnaya Armiya
10)	104.6	1	ST	Kislovodsk	R. 7
125A)	104.6	1	SP	Volkhov	R. Dlya Dvoikh
168)	104.6	1	IR	Bratsk	R. Sibir
6)	104.6	1	PR	Berezniki	Love R.
40)	104.6	1	TS	Almetyevsk	BIM-Radio
27)	104.6	1	KN	Krasnoyarsk	R. Dacha
15)	104.7	1	TS	Kazan	DFM
26)	104.7	1	PR	Perm	R. Rekord
1)	104.7	1	KY	Nizhnevartovsk	Avtoradio
10)	104.7	5	MO	Moskva	R. 7
2)	104.7	5	KT	Petrozavodsk	Russkoye R.
4)	104.7	1	KE	Mezhdurechensk	Evropa+
8)	104.7	1	KD	Krasnodar	Nashe R.
27)	104.7	5	PM	Vladivostok	R. Dacha
18)	104.7	1	BE	Belgorod	Yumor FM
8)	104.7	1	AR	Arkhangelsk	Nashe R.
125A)	104.7	1	SP	Luga	R. Dlya Dvoikh
1)	104.7	1	CB	Magnitogorsk	Avtoradio
9A)	104.8	1	SM	Smolensk	Glavnoye R.
16)	104.8	1	BA	Sterlitamak	Retro FM
191)	104.8	1	UL	Sengiley	R. Zapad
17)	104.8	1	SR	Saratov	Serebryanyy dozhd
120)	104.8	5	SP	Sankt-Peterburg	R. Baltika
1)	104.8	1	SA	Samara	Avtoradio
2)	104.8	1	PZ	Penza	Russkoye R.
5)	104.8	1	OL	Oryol	Hit FM
24)	104.8	1	TS	Nab.Chelny	NRJ
6)	104.8	1	MU	Monchegorsk	Love R.
184)	104.8	1	DA	Makhachkala	R. Vatan
2)	104.8	1	KS	Kostroma	Russkoye R.
2)	104.8	1	KE	Kemerovo	Russkoye R.
2)	104.8	2	VN	Voronezh	Russkoye R.
1)	104.8	1	VL	Vladimir	Avtoradio
19)	104.8	1	OB	Orenburg	Dorozhnoye R.
14)	104.8	1	TV	Tver	R. Shanson
19)	104.9	1	KB	Nalchik	Dorozhnoye R.
193)	104.9	1	TS	Kutlu-Bukash	R. Novyy Vek
72)	104.9	1	CB	Chelyabinsk	L-Radio
4)	104.9	1	TL	Tula	Evropa+
14)	104.9	1	VN	Rossosh	R. Shanson
1)	104.9	1	YN	Noyabrsk	Avtoradio
7)	104.9	2	UL	Novospasskoye	Militseyskaya volna
6)	104.9	1	NN	N.Novgorod	Love R.
16)	104.9	1	KV	Kirov	Retro FM
196)	104.9	1	KD	Yeysk	Kazak FM
2)	104.9	1	VO	Vologda	Russkoye R.
148)	104.9	1	SO	Vladikavkaz	R. MSS
29)	104.9	4	KD	Novorossiysk	Pervoye R.
1)	105.0	1	KE	Novokuznetsk	Avtoradio
26)	105.0	1	KO	Ukhta	R. Rekord
7)	105.0	1	BA	Ufa	Militseyskaya volna
18)	105.0	1	BU	Ulan-Ude	Yumor FM
14)	105.0	1	KD	Tuapse	R. Shanson
183)	105.0	2	CV	Tsivilsk	Nats. R. Chuvashii
3)	105.0	1	TO	Tomsk	Ekho Moskvy
3)	105.0	1	OM	Omsk	Ekho Moskvy
16)	105.0	1	PM	Nakhodka	Retro FM
15)	105.0	1	OB	Buguruslan	DFM
18)	105.0	1	AS	Astrakhan	Yumor FM
18)	105.0	1	VN	Arkhangelskoye	Yumor FM
1)	105.0	1	KA	Sovetsk	Avtoradio
10)	105.0	1	RY	Ryazan	R. 7
1)	105.0	1	SV	Yekaterinburg	Avtoradio
7)	105.0	1	KU	Kursk	Militseyskaya volna
14)	105.1	1	PR	Perm	R. Shanson
4)	105.1	1	YA	Yaroslavl	Evropa+
16)	105.1	1	IR	Ust-Ilimsk	Retro FM

FM	MHz	kW	Rg	Location	Station
16)	105.1	1	TY	Tyumen	Retro FM
14)	105.1	1	RO	Rostov-na-Donu	R. Shanson
30A)	105.1	1	SP	Luga	R. Gardarika
9A)	105.1	1	LI	Lipetsk	Glavnoye R.
7)	105.1	1	KE	Leninsk-Kuznetskiy	Militseyskaya volna
174B)	105.1	1	VG	Volgograd	R. Sputnik
2)	105.1	1	PR	Berezniki	Russkoye R.
1)	105.1	1	ST	Stavropol	Avtoradio
138)	105.2	1	KU	Zheleznogorsk	R. Kurs
2)	105.2	2	NS	Novosibirsk	Russkoye R.
1)	105.2	1	ZB	Chita	Avtoradio
27)	105.2	1	SA	Tolyatti	R. Dacha
2)	105.2	1	KO	Syktyvkar	Russkoye R.
8)	105.2	1	KD	Sochi	Nashe R.
151)	105.2	4	NN	Sergach	R. Obraz
127)	105.2	1	PZ	Penza	R. Ekspress
86)	105.2	5	MO	Moskva	Stolitsa 24
18)	105.2	2	KY	Megion	Yumor FM
3)	105.2	1	DA	Makhachkala	Ekho Moskvy
6)	105.2	1	CB	Magnitogorsk	Love R.
1)	105.2	2	KN	Krasnoyarsk	Avtoradio
196)	105.2	5	KD	Krasnodar	Kazak FM
37)	105.2	1	KA	Kaliningrad	Baltik plus
5)	105.2	1	NS	Novosibirsk	Hit FM
151)	105.2	1	KN	Kovernino	R. Obraz
4)	105.3	1	KS	Kostroma	Evropa+
2)	105.3	1	SR	Saratov	Russkoye R.
2)	105.3	1	TL	Tula	Russkoye R.
6)	105.3	5	SP	Sankt-Peterburg	Love R.
14)	105.3	1	OB	Orenburg	R. Shanson
195)	105.3	1	TS	Kazan	Relaks FM
19)	105.3	1	UD	Izhevsk	Dorozhnoye R.
193)	105.3	1	TS	Absalyamovo	R. Novyy Vek
16)	105.3	1	VN	Voronezh	Retro FM
95)	105.3	1	IR	Usolye-Sibirskoye	R. Radio
1)	105.3	1	KE	Kemerovo	Avtoradio
16)	105.4	1	KU	Kursk	Retro FM
1)	105.4	1	TO	Tomsk	Avtoradio
20)	105.4	1	SA	Samara	R. Romantika
196)	105.4	1	KD	Pavlovskaya	Kazak FM
55)	105.4	1	CC	Groznyy	Groznenskoye R.
2)	105.4	1	AK	Barnaul	Russkoye R.
76)	105.4	1	AR	Arkhangelsk	Mega FM
29)	105.4	4	KD	Armavir	Pervoye R.
16)	105.4	1	RY	Ryazan	Retro FM
2)	105.4	1	KE	Novokuznetsk	Russkoye R.
1)	105.5	1	IR	Ust-Kut	Avtoradio
1)	105.5	1	MO	Uvarovka	Avtoradio
7)	105.5	1	KD	Tuapse	Militseyskaya volna
6)	105.5	1	TV	Tver	Love R.
2)	105.5	1	BE	St.Oskol	Russkoye R.
99A)	105.5	1	SL	Yu-Sakhalinsk	R. 105.5
15)	105.5	1	OL	Oryol	DFM
193)	105.5	2	TS	Nab.Chelny	R. Novyy Vek
2)	105.5	1	MU	Murmansk	Russkoye R.
19)	105.5	1	MA	Magadan	Dorozhnoye R.
21)	105.5	1	OB	Kvarkeno	R. Zvezda
41)	105.5	1	ME	Yoshkar-Ola	Blits FM
120)	105.5	5	SP	Vyborg	R. Baltika
180)	105.5	4	VO	Beloretsk	R. Transmit
2)	105.5	1	KB	Nalchik	Russkoye R.
95)	105.5	1	AK	Rubtsovsk	R. Radio
16)	105.5	1	UL	Ulyanovsk	Retro FM
2)	105.6	2	VG	Volgograd	Russkoye R.
4)	105.6	5	KH	Khabarovsk	Evropa+
45)	105.6	1	TY	Tyumen	Dipol FM
7)	105.6	1	MD	Saransk	Militseyskaya volna
29)	105.6	1	KD	Primorsko-Akhtarsk	Pervoye R.
21)	105.6	1	OB	Novosergiyevka	R. Zvezda
14)	105.6	5	IR	Irkutsk	R. Shanson
193)	105.6	1	TS	Bogatyye Saby	R. Novyy Vek
26)	105.6	1	TS	Almetyevsk	R. Rekord
3)	105.6	1	LI	Lipetsk	Ekho Moskvy
18)	105.7	1	SA	Tolyatti	Yumor FM
29)	105.7	1	KD	Sochi	Pervoye R.
19)	105.7	1	NO	Novgorod	Dorozhnoye R.
4)	105.7	1	RO	Rostov-na-Donu	Evropa+
1)	105.7	1	KT	Petrozavodsk	Nashe R.
28)	105.7	2	NS	Novosibirsk	Business FM
19)	105.7	1	UD	Izhevsk	Hit FM
2)	105.7	1	SV	Yekaterinburg	Russkoye R.
5)	105.7	5	VD	Vladivostok	Hit FM
19)	105.7	1	PR	Berezniki	Dorozhnoye R.
14)	105.7	1	RK	Abakan	R. Shanson
2)	105.7	10	MO	Moskva	Russkoye R.
1)	105.7	1	MU	Apatity	Avtoradio
22)	105.7	1	ST	Stavropol	R. KP
8)	105.8	1	IR	Usolye-Sibirskoye	Nashe R.
190)	105.8	1	KG	Shardinsk	R. za oblakami
6)	105.8	4	TL	Tula	Love R.
196)	105.8	5	KD	Tbilisskaya	Kazak FM
11)	105.8	1	ST	Pyatigorsk	R. Maksimum
7)	105.8	1	OB	Orenburg	Militseyskaya volna
2)	105.8	1	KN	Krasnoyarsk	Russkoye R.
1)	105.8	1	KS	Kostroma	Avtoradio
3)	105.8	1	TS	Kazan	Ekho Moskvy
10)	105.8	1	VL	Vladimir	R. 7
21)	105.8	1	OB	Buguruslan	R. Zvezda
60)	105.8	4	VN	Borisoglebsk	Kanal Melodiya (Voron.)
14)	105.9	1	BA	Neftekamsk	R. Shanson
7)	105.9	1	NN	N.Novgorod	Militseyskaya volna
14)	105.9	1	CB	Chelyabinsk	R. Shanson
2)	105.9	1	TA	Tambov	Russkoye R.
4)	105.9	1	KY	Surgut	Evropa+
1)	105.9	1	TS	Bugulma	Avtoradio
14)	105.9	1	RY	Ryazan	R. Shanson
189)	105.9	1	KY	Nizhnevartovsk	R. Yurga
132)	105.9	1	KC	Karachayevsk	R. Kavkaz Khit
19)	105.9	1	KA	Kaliningrad	Dorozhnoye R.
16)	105.9	1	SO	Vladikavkaz	Hetro FM
146)	105.9	5	SP	Sankt-Peterburg	R. Monte-Karlo
15)	106.0	1	KD	Krasnodar	DFM
182)	106.0	1	PM	Ussuriysk	R. Ussuri
4)	106.0	1	KM	Petropavlovsk-K.	Evropa+
16)	106.0	1	SV	Nizhniy Tagil	Retro FM
95)	106.0	1	IR	Nizhneudinsk	R. Radio
5)	106.0	1	TS	Nab.Chelny	Hit FM
4)	106.0	1	BA	Ufa	Evropa+
19)	106.0	1	MU	Murmansk	Dorozhnoye R.
1)	106.0	1	MO	Kolomna	Avtoradio
216)	106.0	1	IR	Irkutsk	AS FM
4)	106.0	1	SP	Vyborg	Evropa+
2)	106.0	1	SR	Balakovo	Russkoye R.
19)	106.0	1	AS	Astrakhan	Dorozhnoye R.
4)	106.0	1	CB	Magnitogorsk	Evropa+
18)	106.0	1	MA	Magadan	Yumor FM
26)	106.1	1	SP	Podporozhye	R. Rekord
1)	106.1	1	TY	Tyumen	Avtoradio
19)	106.1	2	SA	Samara	Dorozhnoye R.
1)	106.1	1	UD	Izhevsk	Avtoradio
1)	106.1	1	VO	Vologda	Avtoradio
16)	106.1	1	KE	Belovo	Retro FM
7)	106.1	1	TO	Tomsk	Militseyskaya volna
2)	106.2	1	KS	Kostroma	Dorozhnoye R.
2)	106.2	1	NS	Novosibirsk	Love R.
107)	106.2	1	TY	Tobolsk	R. 7 Tyumen
16)	106.2	1	ST	Pyatigorsk	Retro FM
2)	106.2	1	PR	Perm	Russkoye R.
16)	106.2	1	OB	Orsk	Retro FM
6)	106.2	1	UL	Ulyanovsk	Love R.
17)	106.2	1	OM	Omsk	Serebryanyy dozhd
66)	106.2	1	KE	Novokuznetsk	Kuznetskiy ekspress
6)	106.2	1	VL	Murom	Love R.
4)	106.2	10	MO	Moskva	Evropa+
19)	106.2	1	KU	Kursk	Dorozhnoye R.
125A)	106.2	5	SP	Kingisepp	R. Dlya Dvoikh
5)	106.2	4	SV	Yekaterinburg	Hit FM
21)	106.2	1	RK	Abakan	R. Zvezda
10)	106.2	1	LI	Lipetsk	R. 7
6)	106.3	1	SM	Roslavl	Love R.
17)	106.3	1	CB	Chelyabinsk	Serebryanyy dozhd
10)	106.3	1	TV	Tver	R. 7
19)	106.3	1	RO	Taganrog	Dorozhnoye R.
19)	106.3	1	SR	Saratov	Dorozhnoye R.
151)	106.3	2	NN	Shakhumnya	R. Obraz
17)	106.3	1	IV	Rodniki	Serebryanyy dozhd
2)	106.3	1	KY	Nizhnevartovsk	Russkoye R.
19)	106.3	1	TL	Yefremov	Dorozhnoye R.
19)	106.3	1	IR	Bratsk	Dorozhnoye R.
26)	106.3	5	SP	Sankt-Peterburg	R. Rekord
15)	106.3	1	MD	Saransk	DFM
16)	106.3	1	BE	Belgorod	Retro FM
11)	106.4	1	KA	Kaliningrad	R. Maksimum
11)	106.4	1	TL	Tula	R. Maksimum
19)	106.4	1	TA	Tambov	Dorozhnoye R.
16)	106.4	1	KE	Mezhdurechensk	Retro FM
119)	106.4	10	IR	Irkutsk	R. Avtos
211)	106.4	5	PM	Vladivostok	Vladivostok FM
17)	106.4	1	AK	Barnaul	Serebryanyy dozhd
9A)	106.4	1	NN	N.Novgorod	Glavnoye R.

FM	MHz	kW	Rg	Location	Station
19)	106.5	4	SP	Luga	Dorozhnoye R.
16)	106.5	1	KM	Petropavlovsk-K.	Retro FM
3)	106.5	1	YA	Yaroslavl	Ekho Moskvy
19)	106.5	1	SL	Yu-Sakhalinsk	Dorozhnoye R.
1)	106.5	1	BA	Ufa	Avtoradio
113)	106.5	1	TY	Tyumen	R. Apriori
9A)	106.5	1	MU	Murmansk	Glavnoye R.
15)	106.5	1	SR	Balakovo	DFM
16)	106.5	1	ME	Yoshkar-Ola	Retro FM
95)	106.5	5	IR	Zima	R. Radio
18)	106.5	1	BR	Bryansk	Yumor FM
4)	106.5	1	BA	Neftekamsk	Evropa+
189)	106.6	2	KY	Khanty-Mansiysk	R. Yurga
19)	106.6	1	KS	Sharya	Dorozhnoye R.
6)	106.6	3	SA	Samara	Love R.
6)	106.6	10	MO	Moskva	Love R.
133)	106.7	1	IR	Listvyanka	R. Khit Sibir
16)	106.7	1	PM	Ussuriysk	Retro FM
29)	106.7	1	KD	Temryuk	Pervoye R.
19)	106.7	1	TV	Tver	Dorozhnoye R.
215)	106.7	2	PZ	Penza	Zolotoye FM
10)	106.7	4	IV	Rodniki	R. 7
27)	106.7	1	NS	Novosibirsk	R. Dacha
181)	106.7	1	KO	Ukhta	R. Ukhta
1)	106.7	1	KD	Kropotkin	Avtoradio
1)	106.7	1	KU	Kursk	Avtoradio
19)	106.7	1	KV	Kirov	Dorozhnoye R.
14)	106.7	1	KD	Yeysk	R. Shanson
19)	106.7	5	SP	Vyborg	Dorozhnoye R.
7)	106.7	1	TS	Bugulma	Militseyskaya volna
26)	106.7	1	MU	Apatity	R. Rekord
16)	106.7	1	RK	Abakan	Retro FM
9A)	106.7	1	RY	Ryazan	Glavnoye R.
4)	106.8	2	TS	Kazan	Evropa+
88)	106.8	1	KY	Yugorsk	Nord FM
9A)	106.8	1	ST	Stavropol	Glavnoye R.
6)	106.8	1	SR	Saratov	Love R.
1)	106.8	1	OM	Omsk	Avtoradio
85)	106.8	1	SV	Nizhniy Tagil	Nashi pesni
14)	106.8	1	KD	Krasnodar	R. Shanson
19)	106.8	2	VN	Voronezh	Dorozhnoye R.
22)	106.8	1	AK	Barnaul	R. KP
4)	106.8	1	VL	Murom	Evropa+
145)	106.8	1	OB	Orenburg	R. Mir
43)	106.9	1	MU	Murmansk	Bolshoye R.
3)	106.9	1	TL	Tula	Ekho Moskvy
32)	106.9	4	SA	Tolyatti	106.9 FM
4)	106.9	1	KE	Yurga	Evropa+
10)	106.9	1	KD	Sochi	R. 7
157)	106.9	1	VO	Vologda	R. Premyer
9A)	106.9	1	VL	Vladimir	Glavnoye R.
17)	106.9	1	KA	Sovetsk	Serebryanyy dozhd
14)	106.9	1	NN	N.Novgorod	R. Shanson
196)	107.0	4	KD	Kanevskaya	Kazak FM
23)	107.0	1	YA	Yaroslavl	Detskoye R.
2)	107.0	1	CV	Cheboksary	Russkoye R.
4)	107.0	1	SL	Kholmsk	Evropa+
13)	107.0	5	MO	Moskva	R. RSN
15)	107.0	1	UD	Izhevsk	DFM
101)	107.0	1	SV	Yekaterinburg	R. 107 FM
14)	107.0	1	SR	Volsk	R. Shanson
2)	107.0	5	PM	Vladivostok	Russkoye R.
1)	107.0	1	KE	Belovo	Avtoradio
193)	107.0	1	TS	Novosheshminsk	R. Novyy Vek
18)	107.1	1	VN	Borisoglebsk	Yumor FM
6)	107.1	1	TO	Tomsk	Love R.
147)	107.1	4	IV	Rodniki	R. Most
21)	107.1	1	OB	Trotskoye	R. Zvezda
175)	107.1	1	DA	Makhachkala	R. Stolitsa
193)	107.1	2	TS	Bazarnyye Mataki	R. Novyy Vek
193)	107.1	1	TS	Aznakayevo	R. Novyy Vek
17)	107.1	1	KG	Kurgan	Serebryanyy dozhd
17)	107.1	1	KN	Krasnoyarsk	Serebryanyy dozhd
1)	107.1	1	IR	Irkutsk	Avtoradio
152)	107.2	1	RY	Ryazan	R. OK
16)	107.2	1	KO	Ukhta	Retro FM
8)	107.2	1	CB	Snezhinsk	Nashe R.
19)	107.2	1	SM	Smolensk	Dorozhnoye R.
23)	107.2	1	SA	Samara	Detskoye R.
19)	107.2	1	KT	Petrozavodsk	Dorozhnoye R.
2)	107.2	1	OB	Orenburg	Russkoye R.
122)	107.2	1	VN	Voronezh	R. Borneo
75)	107.2	1	MD	Saransk	MC Radio
193)	107.3	1	TS	Menzelinsk	R. Novyy Vek
144)	107.3	1	TS	Kazan	R. Millenium
19)	107.3	1	PS	Novosokolniki	Dorozhnoye R.
2)	107.3	1	VL	Murom	Russkoye R.
19)	107.3	1	PR	Lysva	Dorozhnoye R.
5)	107.3	1	KE	Kemerovo	Hit FM
15)	107.3	1	CB	Chelyabinsk	DFM
26)	107.3	1	SP	Luga	R. Rekord
28)	107.4	10	SP	Sankt-Peterburg	Business FM
95)	107.4	1	IR	Ust-Ilimsk	R. Radio
189)	107.4	1	TY	Tyumen	R. Yurga
9A)	107.4	1	SA	Tolyatti	Glavnoye R.
51)	107.4	2	TA	Tambov	Global FM
104)	107.4	1	BE	St.Oskol	R. 31
73)	107.4	1	KD	Sochi	Maks FM
2)	107.4	1	VN	Rossosh	Russkoye R.
21)	107.4	5	KD	Novorossiysk	R. Zvezda
115)	107.4	5	NN	N.Novgorod	R. Arsenal
5)	107.4	5	MO	Moskva	Hit FM
79)	107.4	1	VG	Mikhaylovka	Mikhaylovka FM
200)	107.4	1	KS	Kostroma	Serebryanaya ladya
194)	107.4	1	AR	Arkhangelsk	Region 29
21)	107.4	1	OB	Ilek	R. Zvezda
3)	107.5	1	PZ	Penza	Ekho Moskvy
2)	107.5	1	BU	Ulan-Ude	Russkoye R.
14)	107.5	1	TL	Tula	R. Shanson
171)	107.5	1	SV	Irbit	R. Skit
5)	107.5	1	AK	Rubtsovsk	Hit FM
28)	107.5	1	BA	Ufa	Business FM
9A)	107.5	1	KC	Karachayevsk	Glavnoye R.
19)	107.5	1	VO	Gryazovets	Dorozhnoye R.
193)	107.5	1	TS	Bavly	R. Novyy Vek
2)	107.5	1	VL	Kovrov	Russkoye R.
15)	107.5	1	TS	Nizhnekamsk	DFM
8)	107.5	1	KN	Krasnoyarsk	Nashe R.
8)	107.5	1	KG	Kurgan	Nashe R.
1)	107.6	1	NN	Arzamas	Avtoradio
123)	107.6	2	BR	Bryansk	R. Chistyye klyuchi
52)	107.6	1	SV	Yekaterinburg	Gorod FM
2)	107.6	1	KE	Leninsk-Kuznetskiy	Russkoye R.
19)	107.6	1	SP	Priozersk	Dorozhnoye R.
17)	107.6	1	KU	Kursk	Serebryanyy dozhd
22)	107.6	1	UD	Izhevsk	R. KP
16)	107.7	1	KD	Armavir	Retro FM
21)	107.7	1	OB	Yasnyy	R. Zvezda
26)	107.7	2	NS	Novosibirsk	R. Rekord
1)	107.7	1	KE	Mezhdurechensk	Avtoradio
1)	107.7	1	BE	Belgorod	Avtoradio
100)	107.7	1	KD	Krasnodar	R. 107
14)	107.7	1	NS	Novosibirsk	R. Shanson
7)	107.8	5	MO	Moskva	Militseyskaya volna
19)	107.8	1	VN	Rossosh	Dorozhnoye R.
16)	107.8	1	SR	Volsk	Retro FM
9A)	107.8	1	KD	Novorossiysk	Glavnoye R.
2)	107.8	1	SP	Sankt-Peterburg	Russkoye R.
28)	107.8	1	NN	N.Novgorod	Business FM
29)	107.8	1	KD	Kushchyovskaya	Pervoye R.
26)	107.8	1	VG	Kamyshin	R. Rekord
19)	107.8	1	TY	Ishim	Dorozhnoye R.
16)	107.8	1	PR	Berezniki	Retro FM
6)	107.8	1	TS	Kazan	Love R.
19)	107.9	1	BA	Ufa	Dorozhnoye R.
2)	107.9	1	SO	Vladikavkaz	Russkoye R.
14)	107.9	1	VL	Vladimir	R. Shanson
16)	107.9	1	KE	Kemerovo	Retro FM
2)	107.9	1	RY	Ryazan	Russkoye R.
16)	107.9	1	KD	Sochi	Retro FM
10)	107.9	1	BE	St.Oskol	R. 7
19)	107.9	1	TY	Tobolsk	Dorozhnoye R.
3)	107.9	1	SA	Tolyatti	Ekho Moskvy
1)	107.9	1	SP	Vyborg	Avtoradio

NB: Txs below 1kW not listed.

Addresses and other information:

1) 127083 Moskva, ul. 8 Marta 8. – **2)** 123298 Moskva, 3-ya Khoroshevskaya ul. 12. – **3)** 119992 Moskva, ul. Novyy Arbat 11. – **4)** 109004 Moskva, ul. Stanislavskogo 21. – **5)** 123298 Moskva, 3-ya Khoroshevskaya ul. 12. – **6)** 127299 Moskva, ul. Bolshaya Akademicheskaya 5a. – **7)** 109180 Moskva, 3-y Golutinskiy per. 8/10. – **8)** 123060 Moskva, ul. Narodnogo Opolcheniya 39. – **9A,B)** 115184 Moskva, B. Tatarskaya ul. 34. – **10)** 109004 Moskva, ul. Stanislavskogo 21. – **11)** 123298 Moskva, 3-ya Khoroshevskaya ul. 12. – **12)** 123298 Moskva, 3-ya Khoroshevskaya ul. 12. – **13)** 123298 Moskva, 3-ya Khoroshevskaya ul. 12. – **14)** 119049 Moskva, ul. Shabolovka 10. – **15)** 123298 Moskva, 3-ya Khoroshevskaya ul. 12. – **16)** 109004 Moskva, ul. Stanislavskogo 21. – **17)** 125083 Moskva, Petrovskogo-Razumovskaya aleya 12a. – **18)** 127427 Moskva, ul. Ak. Korolyova 19. – **19)** 199406

St.Peterburg, ul. Shevchenko 28. – **20)** 125040 Moskva, ul. Nizhnyaya Maslovka 9. – **21)** 119160 Moskva, Kolymazhnyy per. 14. – **22)** 127993 Moskva, Staryy Petrovsko-Razumovskiy proyezd 1/23. – **23)** 129272 Moskva, ul. Trifonovskaya 57. – **24)** 27427 Moskva, ul. Korolyova 19. – **25)** 125568 Moskva, ul. Mitinskaya 49. – **26)** 198303 St.Peterburg, pr. Stachek 105. – **27)** 127299 Moskva, ul. B. Akademicheskaya 5a. – **28)** 127287 Moskva, 2-ya Khutorskaya ul. 38a. – **29)** 350038 Krasnodar, ul. Korolenko 2/1. – **30A,B)** 192007 St.Peterburg, Ligovskiy pr. 174. – **31)** 129272 Moskva, ul. Trifonovskaya 57. – **32)** 445051 Tolyatti, Primorskiy bul. 2b. – **33)** 432030 Ulyanovsk, ul. Narimanova 75. – **34)** 650036 Novokuznetsk, pr. Metallurgov 18. – **35)** 109004 Moskva, ul. Stanislavskogo 21. – **36)** 660022 Krasnoyarsk, ul. Partizana Zheleznyaka 16d. – **37)** 236000 Kaliningrad, ul. Narva 58. – **38)** 618400 Berezniki. – **39)** 123060 Moskva, ul. Narodnogo Opolcheniya 39. – **40)** 420021 Kazan, ul. Tukaya 91. – **41)** 424000 Yoshkar-Ola, ul. Mashinostroiteley 7a. – **42)** 614007 Perm, ul. Kuybysheva 37. – **43)** 183038 Murmansk, ul. Lenina 68. – **44)** 603022 N.Novgorod, Okskiy syezd 8. – **45)** 625000 Tyumen, ul. Geologorazvedchikov 28. – **46)** 620075 Yekaterinburg, pr. Lenina 41. – **47)** 652600 Belovo, ul. Aerodromnaya 14. – **48)** 302028 Oryol, ul. 7 Noyabrya 43. – **49)** 197376 St.Peterburg, ul. Prof.Popova 47. – **50)** 115054 Moskva, B.Strochenovskiy per. 22/25. – **51)** 392020 Tambov, ul. L. Tolstoy 4. – **52)** 620014 Yekaterinburg, ul. 8 Marta 86. – **53)** 630087 Novosibirsk, ul. Nemirovicha-Danchenko 122. – **54)** 199034 St.Peterburg, nah I. Shmidta 39. – **55)** 364014 Groznyy, ul. Mayakovskogo 92. – **56)** 462419 Orsk, pr. Lenina 27. – **57)** 454091 Chelyabinsk, ul. Ordzhonikidze 81. – **58)** 386101 Nazran, ul. Moskovskaya 17. **59)** 630133 Novosibirsk, ul. Vysotskogo 9. – **60)** 394000 Voronezh, ul. K.Marksa 114v. – **61)** 620086 Yekaterinburg, ul. Repina 6a. – **62)** 109004 Moskva, ul. Stanislavskogo 21. – **63)** 125080 Moskva, ul. Vrubelya 4. – **64)** 443011 Samara, ul. Sovetskoy Armii 245e. – **65)** 625019 Tyumen, ul. Respubliki 211a. – **66)** 654007 Novokuznetsk, pr. Yermakova 9a. – **67)** 625019 Tyumen, ul. Respublika 211a. –**68)** 606440 Bor, ul. Lunacharskogo 106. – **69)** 398050 Lipetsk, ul. Plekhanova 1. – **70)** 302020 Oryol, Naugorskoye shosse 40. – **71)** 182100 Velikiye Luki, pr. Lenina 26/12. – **72)** 454091 Chelyabinsk, ul. Ordzhonikidze 41. – **73)** 354000 Sochi, ul. Severnaya 12. – **74)** 610000 Kirov, Oktyabrskiy opr. 120. – **75)** 430030 Saransk, ul. Vasenko 32. – **76)** 163040 Arkhangelsk, pr. Troitskiy 52. – **77)** 109028 Moskva, M.Trekhsvyatitelskiy per. 2/5. – **78)** 428028 Cheboksary, Traktostroiteley pr. 101. – **79)** 403302 Mikhaylovka, ul. 2-ya Krasnoznamenskaya 51. – **80)** 649220 Shebalino, ul. Sovetskaya 64. – **81)** 440026 Penza, ul. Lermontova 39. – **82)** 426069 Izhevsk, ul. Pesochnaya 9. – **83)** 392000 Tambov, ul. Derzhavinskaya 17a. – **84)** 125009 Moskva, ul. Tverskaya 7. – **85)** 620014 Yekaterinburg, pr. Lenina 41. – **86)** 103064 Moskva, ul. Kazakova 16. – **87)** 248021 Kaluga, ul. Moskovskaya 189. – **88)** 628260 Yugorsk, ul. Promyshlennaya 4. – **89)** 353900 Novorossiysk, proyezd Skoblikova 10. – **90)** 344092 Rostov-na-Donu, ul. Korolyova 7/19. – **91)** 428000 Cheboksary, pr. Lenina 35. – **92)** 123242 Moskva, Novinskiy bul. 31. – **93)** 125130 Moskva, ul. Priorova 18. – **94)** 195299 St.Peterburg, ul. Cherkasova 14. – **95)** 123001 Moskva, Vspolnyy per. 18. – **96)** 672010 Chita, ul. Amurskaya 36. – **97)** 183038 Murmansk, ul. Yegorova 14. – **98)** 440046 Penza, ul. Mira 1a. – **99A,B)** 693023 Yuzhno-Sakhalinsk, ul. Komsomolskaya 213a. – **100)** 350000 Krasnodar, ul. Gimnazicheskaya 51. – **101)** 620075 Yekaterinburg, pr. Lenina 50l. – **102)** 450043 Ufa, ul. Mushnikova 13/2. – **103)** 644010 Omsk, ul. Dekabristov 130. – **104)** 308000 Belgorod, pr. Slavy 61. – **105)** 424006 Yoshkar-Ola, 70-letiya Vooruzhennykh Sil SSSR 20. – **106)** 173020 V.Novgorod, B.Moskovskaya ul. 106. – **107)** 625000 Tyumen, ul. Sovetskaya 54. – **108)** 426069 Izhevsk, ul. Pesochnaya 11. –**109A,B)** 453300 Kumertau, PKiO im. Gagarina. – **110)** 614060 Perm, ul. Turgeneva 33a. – **111)** 386245 Troitskaya, ul. Krestyanska 4. – **112)** 403323 Mikhaylovka, ul. Kommuny 129-1. – **113)** 625013 Tyumen, ul. Tekstilnaya 1. – **114)** 453300 Kumertau, PKiO im. Gagarina. – **115)** 603057 N.Novgorod, ul. Gagarina 27. – **116)** 450076 Ufa, ul. Gafuri 9. – **117)** 445010 Tolyatti, ul. Sovetskaya 74a. – **118)** 692760 Artyom, ul. Pushkina 2. – **119)** 665831 Angarsk, 6-y mikrorayon 5. – **120)** 236000 Kaliningrad, pr. Mira 87. – **121)** 140400 Kolomna, ul. Shilova 9. – **122)** 394071 Voronezh, ul. 20-letnaya Oktyabrya 66. – **123)** 241037 Bryansk, ul. Dimitrova 70/1. – **124)** 617760 Chaykovskiy, ul. Lenina 6-3. – **125A,B)** 199406 St.Peterburg, ul. Shevchenko 28. – **126)** 620102 Yekaterinburg, ul. Volgogradskaya 193. – **127)** 440052 Penza, ul. Bogdanova 22. – **128)** 194044 St.Peterburg, per. Krapivnyy 5-206. – **129)** 125190 Moskva, Leningradski pr. 80. – **130)** 400131 Volgograd, ul. Komsomolskaya 8. – **131)** 123022 Moskva, ul. 2-ya Zvenigorodskaya 12. – **132)** 369000 Cherkessk, ul. Pervomayskaya 48. – **133)** 664047 Irkutsk, ul. Sovetskaya 3. – **134)** 125190 Moskva, Leningradskiy pr. 80. – **135)** 454080 Chelyabinsk, ul. Ordzhonikidze 58a. – **136)** 127550 Moskva, Listvennichnaya al. 12. – **137)** 423827 Nab.Chelny, bul. Yunykh Lenintsev 9. – **138)** 305004 Kursk, ul. Dimitrova 76. – **139)** 690000 Vladivostok, ul. Strelnikova 3a. – **140)** 652515 Leninsk-Kuznetskiy, ul. Pushkina 4. – **141)** 197101 St.Peterburg, ul. Mira 34a. – **142)** 424000 Yoshkar-Ola, ul. Sovetskaya 138. – **143)** 443070 Samara, ul. Aerodromnaya 13. –**144)** 420015 Kazan, ul. K.

Marksa 23/6. – **145)** 115326 Moskva, ul. Pyatnitskaya 25. – **146)** 123298 Moskva, 3-ya Khoroshevskaya ul. 12. – **147)** 153025 Ivanovo, 5-y Severniy per. 18. – **148)** 362021 Vladikavkaz, ul. Nikolayeva 84. – **149)** 614000 Perm, ul. Lenina 50. – **150)** 626726 Noyabrsk, ul. Lenina 47-412. – **151)** 603068 N.Novgorod, Yarmarochnyy proyezd 10. – **152)** 390023 Ryazan, ul. Tsilkovskogo 20. – **153)** 454090 Chelyabinsk, ul. Tsvillinga 46a. – **154)** 620102 Yekaterinburg, ul. Posadskaya 79. – **155)** 170000 Tver, ul. Mednikovskaya 55/25. – **156)** 625013 Tyumen, ul. Permyakova 3a. – **157)** 160035 Vologda, ul. Kozlenskaya 35. – **158)** 367000 Makhachkala, pr. Akushinskogo 13a. – **159)** 15326 Moskva, ul. Pyatnitskaya 25. – **160)** 603123 N.Novgorod, ul. Semashko 37. – **161)** 197376 St.Peterburg, Aptekarskiy pr. 6/4. – **162)** 450075 Ufa, ul. Blyukhera 15. – **163)** 344082 Rostov-na-Donu, Bolshaya Sadova ul. 10. – **164)** 367015 Makhachkala, ul. I Kazaka 2a. – **165)** 614000 Perm, ul. Lenina 50. – **166)** 127287 Moskva, 2-ya Khutorskaya ul. 38a. – **167)** 620014 Yekaterinburg, ul. Lenina 41. – **168)** 634003 Tomsk, per. Marinskiy 8. – **169)** 625013 Tyumen, ul. Permyakova 7. – **170)** 620109 Yekaterinburg, ul. Repina 15. – **171)** 623850 Irbit, ul. Zhukova 6a. – **172)** 630011 Novosibirsk, ul. Kirova 3. – **173)** 115184 Moskva, B. Tatarskaya ul. 35. – **174A,B)** 400117 Volgograd, bul. 30-let Pobedy 74a. – **175)** 367013 Makhachkala, pr. Gamidova 18. – **176)** 367032 Makhachkala, ul. M.Gadzhiyeva 188. – **177)** 692900 Nakhodka, ul. Sportivnaya 6. – **178)** 353500 Temryuk, ul. Volgogradskaya 2d. – **179)** 197046 St.Peterburg, ul. Michurinskaya 14/3-78. – **180)** 162610 Cherepovets, ul. Lenina 151. – **181)** 169300 Ukhta, ul. Sovetskaya 18. – **182)** 692525 Ussuriysk, ul. Kirova 28. – **183)** 428019 Cheboksary, pr. I.Ya.Yakovleva 13. – **184)** 367020 Makhachkala, ul. Nuradilova 28. – **185)** 30000 Saransk, ul. Goncharovo 39. – **186)** 690091 Vladivostok, ul. Uborevicha 20a. – **187)** 400131 Volgograd, ul. Kommunisticheskaya 6. – **188)** 630087 Novosibirsk, ul. Nemirovicha-Danchenko 122. – **189)** 625019 Tyumen, ul. Respubliki 53. – **190)** 640000 Kurgan, ul. Tobolnaya 54. – **191)** 433380 Sengiley, ul. Lenina 7. – **192)** 197101 St.Peterburg, ul. Kronverskaya 23. – **193)** 420095 Kazan, ul. Sh.Usmanova 9. – **194)** 163002 Arkhangelsk, Novgorodskiy pr. 32. – **195)** 129272 Moskva, ul. Trifonovskaya 57. – **196)** 350000 Krasnodar, ul. Levanevskogo 57. – **197)** 160035 Vologda, ul. Kozlenskaya 35. – **198)** 117218 Moskva, Krzhizhanovskogo 29. – **199)** 443010 Samara, ul. Nekrasovskaya 62. – **200)** 156961 Kostroma, pl. Konstitutsii 1. – **201)** 455026 Magnitogorsk, ul. Gagarina 35. – **202)** 614000 Perm, ul. Bolshevistskaya 84a. – **203)** 367018 Makhachkala, ul. Stepnoy Obshchezhitiye 2. – **204)** 241014 Bryansk, ul. Mariny Raskovoy 25. – **205)** 442530 Kuznetsk. – **206)** 125040 Moskva, Leningradskiy pr. 30. – **207)** 420094 Kazan, ul. Golubzatnikova 20a. – **208)** 620151 Krasnoyarsk, ul. Baumana 22. – **209)** 671023 Arshan, ul. Lermontova 52. – **210)** 443093 Samara, ul. Myagi 10a. – **211)** 690091 Vladivostok, ul. Pologaya 66. – **212)** 238753 Sovetsk, Nemanskoye shosse 2. – **213)** 680000 Khabarovsk, ul. Lenina 4. – **214)** 307170 Zheleznogorsk, ul. Lenina 60. – **215)** 440034 Penza, ul. Markina 1. – **216)** 666036 Shelekhov, 4-y mikrorayon 32b. – **217)** 453124 Sterlitamak, ul. Khudaybordina 17. – **218)** 174260 Malaya Vishera, ul. Moskovskaya 21. – **219)** 664047 Irkutsk, ul. Sovetskaya 3. – **220)** 603155 N.Novgorod, ul. B.Pecherskaya 33-1. – **221)** 634003 Tomsk, Mariiskiy per. 8. – **222)** 410000 Astrakhan.

Radio via DTT: see TV section.

Foreign Service/Int relays on MW: (txs operated by Russian TV and Radio Broadcasting Network): Angarsk, S 1080kHz 1000kW; Bolshakovo, E 1143kHz 150kW, 1215 kHz 1200kW; Chita, S (Kruchina) 801kHz 1200kW, Komsomolsk-na-Amure, FE 630kHz 500kW; Oyash, S 1026kHz 250kW; St. Peterburg, E (Krasnyy Bor) 1494kHz 600kW; Tbilisskaya, E 1089/1170kHz 1200kW; Vladivostok, FE (Ussuriysk) 648kHz 1000kW; Yuzhnyy-Sakhalinsk, FE (Vestochka) 720kHz 1000kW. See Int. Radio section.

RWANDA

L.T: UTC +2h — **Pop:** 11 million — **Pr.L:** Kinyarwanda, Swahili, French, English — **E.C:** 50Hz, 230V — **ITU:** RRW

RWANDA UTILITIES REGULATORY AGENCY (RURA)
✉ B.P. 6929, Kigali ☎ +250 252584562 🖷 +250 252584563 **W:** www.rura.gov.rw **E:** info@rura.gov.rw

RADIODIFFUSION DE LA REPUBLIQUE RWANDAISE (Gov)
✉ B.P. 83, Kigali ☎ +250 252572276 **W:** www.orinfor.gov.rw/radio **E:** radiorwanda@yahoo.com **L.P:** Dir. Broadc: Mweusi Karake. Dir. Prgrs: Paul Ndamage. Ag. Ch.Editor: Willy Rukundo. Tech. Dir: Charles Nahayo.
SW: Kigali 6055kHz 50kW. Rel. of channels I/II 0300-2100.
FM: Channel I (MHz): 89.8 Kinanira 0.5kW, 93.5 Nyarupfubire 0.5kW,

95.1 Mugogo/Rushaki 0.5kW, 97.6 Karongi 1kW, 100.7 Mt. Jali 5kW, 103.2 Byumba 0.5kW, 103.9 Butare 0.5kW + 8 trs under 0.5kW. **Channel II:** Kigali 90.7MHz 5kW (irregular). **D.Prgr** in Kinyarwanda/Swahili/French/English: 24h. N. in English: 0515, 1830. **Ann:** F: "Vous écoutez Radio Rwanda émettant de Kigali".

Other stations FM (MHz)
City R, Kigali: 88.3 1kW – **Contact FM:** Kigali 89.7 0.5kW – **Flash FM,** Kigali: 89.2 0.5kW – **KFM,** Kigali: 98.7 **W:** kfm.nationmedia.com (Cf. Kenya) – **R. Communautaire:** Cyangugu 92.9 30W, Karongi 96.5 0.5kW, Butare 100.4 0.5kW, Gisenyi 104.7 0.1kW – **R. Izuba,** Kibungo: 100.0 0.25kW – **R. Maria Rwanda:** Gitarama 88.6 1kW, Kigali 97.3 2kW, Karongi 99.8 **E:** radiomariar@yahoo.fr – **R. 10 FM:** Kigali (Mont Jari) 87.6 0.5kW **W:** www.danslevent.com/rwanda **E:** contact@danslevent.com – **R. Salus** (University R.), Butare: 97.0 1kW, Kigali ‡101.9 1kW (inactive). **W:** salus.nur.ac.rw – **R. Sana uRwanda** (Rlg.): Kigali 98.0 – **R. Umucyo,** Kigali: 102.8 0.1kW.
AWR: 106.4 0.3kW – **BBC African Sce:** Karongi 93.3, Kigali (Mont Jari) 93.9 3kW, Butare 106.1 3kW – **RFI Afrique:** Kigali 91.9 in French/Swahili – **Voice of America:** Kigali 104.3 2kW – **Deutsche Welle:** Kigali 96.0MHz 2kW.
Shortwave relay station: see International radio section

SABA (Netherlands)

L.T: UTC -4h — **Pop:** 1,400 — **Pr.L:** Dutch (official), English — **E.C:** 60Hz, 110V — **ITU:** BES

QFM, The Voice of Saba ✉ PO Box 1,The Bottom, Saba ☎ +599 4 16 3213 🖷 +599 416 3308 Owner: Max Nicholson **FM:** PJF1 93.9MHz 1kW **W:** www.mannelli.com/saba

SAMOA

L.T: UTC +13h (30 Sep 12-7 Apr 13, 29 Sep 13-6 Apr 14: +14h) — **Pop:** 193,161 — **Pr.L:** Samoan, English — **E.C:** 50Hz, 230/410V — **ITU:** SMO

OFFICE OF THE REGULATOR [Gov]
✉ Private Bag, Apia, Samoa. First Flr, G.Meredith Bldg, Tamaligi, Apia ☎ +685 30282 🖷 +685 30281 **W:** www.regulator.gov.ws **E:** admin@regulator.gov.ws **L.P:** Regulator: Donnie de Freitas. Mgr Spectrum & Tech. Scs: Untoa Auelua Fonoti

NATIONAL RADIO 2AP (Gov)
✉ Ministry of Communications and Information Technology, Government of Samoa, Level 1, CA & CT Plaza, Savalolo, Apia, Samoa ☎ +685 26177 🖷 +685 24671 **W:** www.mcit.gov.ws **E:** mcit@mcit.gov.ws ☎ 2AP Studio, Mulinu'u, Apia: +685 21422 **E:** a.ahsam@mcit.gov.ws **L.P:** CEO: Tua'imalo Asamu Ah Sam, Senior Programmer: Vaasiliega Lupati Lagaia
MW: Apia 540kHz 5kW, 747kHz 5kW
Samoan/English: 1700 (Sun 2200)-1000 on 540kHz **Edu:** brdcsts on some weekdays for Samoa and Tokelau 1930-2030 on 747kHz **World N:** 1800W, 1900W, 1930W. **Local N:** 1630W, 1730W, 1830W, 0730W **Ann:** "National Radio 2AP" or "Voice of the Nation".

OTHER STATIONS:

FM	MHz	kW	FM	MHz	kW
1) Talofa FM	88.5	0.25	5) Showers of Blessings	97.5	0.5
8) Mai FM 89.1	89.1	1	1) Magik FM	98.1	0.3
2) Aiga Fesilafa'I R.	90.5		1) Talofa FM	99.9	0.25
1) Talofa FM*	91.5	0.25	1) K-Lite FM	101.1	0.25
9) Samoa FM	93.7		6) R. Australia	102.0	
1) Star FM	96.1	0.25	9) Samoa FM*	104.1	

Location: All Apia except *Savai'i

Addresses and other information
1) R. Polynesia Ltd, P.O.Box 762, Svalalo, Apia ☎+685 25148/49/50 🖷 +685 25147 **Brands:** Magik FM - "Samoa's #1 Hit Music Station" (English) ☎ Studio +685 33981, Talofa FM "100% Local" (Samoan) Studio ☎+685 33999, K-Lite FM "Memories are Good" (English) ☎+685 33101 **N:** RNZI throughout the day, Star FM "Absolute Music Variety" (English) ☎ +685 33961 **W:** www.fmradio.ws **E:** corey@fmradio.ws **L.P:** CEO Corey Keil **D.Prgr:** 24h – **2)** Catholic Archdiocese of Samoa, P.O.Box 532, Muli'vai, Apia. L.P: Dir: Afioga Patele Fereti Tautunu T: +685 21156, 21051, 7521051 **E:** daman_auisavelio@yahoo.com **Prgr:** Samoan religious – **5)** Sogi, Apia. **Prgr:** local Samoan religious plus satellite relay – **6)** 24h English for the Pacific satellite relay from Melbourne – **8)** Samoa Quality Broadcasters, Mulinu'u, Apia ☎+685 24790/91, 21735 🖷 +685 24789 CEO: Galuemalemana Ms Faresea Matafeo **E:** ceo@

sbcl.ws **D.Prgr:** 24h (English & Samoan) Other: technical services for R. Australia 102.0FM – **9) Talamua Media & Publications Ltd,** Level 2, Nia Mall, Fugalei, Apia. PO Box 1321, Apia. ☎ +685 7777937, 7513937 **W:** www.talamua.com **E:** samoafm93.7@gmail.com **L.P:** MD: Angela Kronfeld-Polu. **ID:** "The People's Station" **D.Prgr:** 24h

SAMOA (AMERICAN) (USA)

L.T: UTC -11h — **Pop:** 67,242 — **Pr.L:** Samoan, English — **E.C:** 60Hz, 120V — **ITU:** SMA

FEDERAL COMMUNICATIONS COMMISSION (FCC)
see USA for details

MW		Call	kHz	kW			
1) Tafuna		KJAL	‡585	5			
FM		**Call**	**MHz**	**kW**	**FM**	**Call**	**MHz**	**kW**
6) Tafuna		New	‡88.1	1.5	4) Ili'Ili	KULA-LP	95.1	0.1
7) Pago Pago		New	‡88.9	0.3	4) W.District	KULA-LP	97.1	0.01
8) Nu'uuli		KMOA	‡89.7	1.5	4) C.District	KULA-LP	99.1	0.01
9) Mapusaga		KPPO	‡90.5	0.75	4) E.District	KULA-LP	‡102.5	0.02
6) Utulei		KIOE	91.3	1.5	2) Fagaitua	WVUV-FM	103.1	1.3
3) Pago Pago		KSBS-FM	92.1	15	5) Leone	KNWJ-FM	104.1	0.01
2) Pago Pago		KKHJ-FM	93.1	1.1	5) Leone	KNWJ-FM	104.7	0.3
2) Pavaiai		KKHJ-FM	93.7	0.01	‡ inactive			

Addresses and other information:
1) Asia Pacific Media Ministries, KJAL-AM, PO Box 1138, Pago Pago, American Samoa 96799. L.P: Vickie Haleck, SM. **ID:** "For You and Your Family" **NB:** uses 580kHz when on air. **F.PL:** CP 630kHz 5kW – **2)** South Seas Broadcasting Inc, PO Box 6758, Pago Pago, American Samoa 96799. L.P: Joey Cummings, GM ☎+1 684 633 4493 **W:** KKHJ-FM: www.khjradio.com **ID:** '93KHJ', **F.PL:** KKHJ CP 900kHz 5kW. **W:** WVUV-FM: www.wvuv.com **ID:** "WVUV-FM is V103 The People's Station' in Samoan/English, D.Prgr: 24h – **3)** Samoa Broadcasting System, PO Box 793, Pago Pago, American Samoa 96799-0793 ☎+1 684 633 7000 🖷+1 684 633 5727 **W:** www.ksbsfm92.com **E:** info@ksbsfm92.com L.P: Esther Prescott, GM **ID:** 'Island 92 - The Station That Belongs to You' **News:** hourly bulletins from RNZI, R. Australia, BBC, NPR, VOA. D.Prgr: 24h – **4)** Pacific Islands Bible School, PO Box 1268, Pago Pago, American Samoa 96799 – **5)** Showers of Blessings R., PO Box 997777, Pago Pago, American Samoa 96799 ☎+1 684 699 8123. 🖷+1 684 699 8126 **W:** www.fm104.org **E:** info@fm104.org – **6)** Leone Church of Christ, PO Box 5093, Pago Pago, American Samoa 96799 –**7)** Marianas Educational Media Services, 125 Tun Jesus Crisostomo St #302, Tamuning, GU 96913 – **8)** Horizon Christian Fellowship, 5331 Mt Alifan Dr, San Diego CA 91111 – **9)** Second Samoan Congregational Church of Long Beach, 655 Cedar Ave, Long Beach CA 90802-1222

SAN MARINO

L.T. UTC +1h (31 Mar- 27 Oct: +2h) — **Pop.** 30.000 — **Pr.L:** Italian — **ITU:** SMR

SAN MARINO RTV (Gov)
✉ Viale J.F.Kennedy 13, 47890 Repubblica di San Marino ☎ +378 0549 882000 🖷 +378 0549 882840 **E:** radio@sanmarinortv.sm **W:** www.smtvsanmarino.sm/radio **L.P:** Dir. Carmen Lasorella, Prgr.Dir.: Giuseppe Cesetti, T.Dir.: Fabio Pelliccioni
FM: 102.7MHz 30kW **D.Prgr:** 24h
San Marino Classic, E: classic@sanmarinortv.sm **FM:** 103.2MHz 30kW **D.Prgr:** 24h Also carries govt meetings, live service. Prgr. Dir. Stefano Coveri
F.PI. no plans to start on MW assigned freq. 711kHz
V: by QSL-card. Rpts to **E:** ufficiotecnico@sanmarinortv.sm

RADIO INTERNATIONAL SAN MARINO (Comm)
✉ Europa Radiodiffusione S.r.l. Strada Rovereta 42 RSM-47891 Falciano ☎ +378 0549 909905 🖷 +378 0549 941580 **E:** info@radiointernational.sm **W:** www.radiointernational.sm
FM: 94.25MHz 1kW **D.Prgr:** 24h

SÃO TOMÉ E PRÍNCIPE

L.T: UTC — **Pop:** 210,000 — **Pr.L:** Portuguese, Crioulo — **E.C:** 50Hz, 220V — **ITU:** STP

RÁDIO NACIONAL DE SÃO TOMÉ E PRÍNCIPE (RNSTP, Gov)
✉ Avenida Marginal 12 de Julho, C.P. 44, São Tomé ☎+239 22 22875 🖷 +239 22 23293 **E:** Rnstp04@cstome.net

L.P: Dir: Artur Meneses de Pinho. CE: Felisberto Garcia.
MW: Pinheira: 945kHz 20kW **FM:** 89.7/95.4/99.3MHz.
D.Prgr: 24h in Portuguese. **N:** 0700, 1300, 1630, 1930.
Ann: "Aqui São Tomé, Capital da República Democrática de S. Tomé e Príncipe, transmite a Rádio Nacional". **IS:** one note gong, guitar.

RDP África: São Tomé 92.8MHz 3kW, Príncipe 101.9MHz 70W.
RFI Afrique: 102.8MHz in French/Portuguese.
VOA: São José 105.5MHz 0.2kW in English/Portuguese.
VOA relay station: MW 1530kHz 600kW 0300-0630, 1600-2200 & SW. For further details see International Radio section under USA

SAUDI ARABIA

L.T: UTC +3h — **Pop:** 29 million — **Pr.L:** Arabic — **E.C:** 60Hz, 127/220V — **ITU:** ARS

MINISTRY OF CULTURE & INFORMATION (MOCI)
⌨ Nasseriya Str, Riyadh 11161 ☎+966 1 4014440 🖷 +966 1 402 3570. **W:** moci.gov.sa **L.P:** Dep. Min. of Eng. Affairs: Dr. Riyadh Najm

BROADCASTING SERVICE OF THE KINGDOM OF SAUDI ARABIA (BSKSA, Gov.)
⌨ P.O. Box 61718, Riyadh 11575 ☎+966 1 4425170 🖷 +966 1 4041692 **W:** www.saudiradio.net **E:** saudi-radio@moci.gov.sa

MW	kHz	kW	H of tr & Prgr.
Bisha	531	10	24h (Q)
Ar-Rass	549	10	0300-2300 (G)
Gizan	549	1	0300-2300 (G)
Qurayyat	549	20	24h (G)
Rafha	549	20	24h (G)
Jeddah	558	50	24h (G)
Abha	567	5	24h (Q)
Afif	567	15	24h (Q)
Gizan	576	20	24h (Q)
Riyadh	585	1200	24h (G)
Al-Hufuf	594	10	0300-2300 (G)
Duba	594	2000	0300-1500 (G)
Makkah	594	50	24h (G/P)
Al-Aflaj	612	15	24h (Q)
Hail	612	5	24h (Q)
Gizan	630	20	0300-2200 (2)
Najran	630	10	24h (Q)
Jeddah (Khumra)	648	2000	0300-2300 (G)
Rafha	657	20	24h (Q)
Abha	675	5	0300-2300 (G)
Afif	675	20	0300-2300 (G)
Jeddah	684	50	24h (2)
Riyadh	684	10	24h (2)
Bisha	702	10	24h (2)
Duba	702	40	24h (2)
Najran	747	10	0300-2300 (G)
Al-Aflaj	765	20	24h (Q)
Al-Hufuf	765	10	24h (Q)
Qurayyat	765	20	24h (Q)
Ras al-Zawr	783	100	24h (Q)
Jeddah	792	50	24h (Q)
Abha	810	20	0300-2200 (2)
Ras al-Zawr	855	100	24h (Q)
Ar-Rass	873	10	24h (Q)
Dammam	882	100	24h (Q)
Qurayyat II	900	1000	1200-0300 (G)
Al-Hufuf	927	20	24h (2)
Makkah	936	50	24h (Q)
Riyadh	936	50	24h (Q)
Hail	945	5	0300-2300 (G)
Madinah	981	20	24h (Q)
Duba	999	20	24h (Q)
Madinah	1017	20	24h (P)
Yanbu al-Bahr	1035	20	24h (2)
Bisha	1071	50	24h (G)
Najran	1080	10	0300-2200 (2)
Qurayyat	1089	20	24h (2)
Dammam	1098	100	24h (2)
Madinah	1116	20	24h (2)
Madinah	1215	20	24h (G)
Dammam	1260	500	24h (G)
Makkah	1287	5	24h (Q)
Riyadh	1422	20	24h (I)
Ras al-Zawr	1440	1600	24h (G)
Yanbu al-Bahr	1449	100	24h (G)
Hafar Al-Batin	1467	50	24h (G)
Jeddah (Khumra)	1512	1000	1500-0300 (Q)
Duba	1521	2000	1500-0300 (G)

FM (MHz)	G	2	Q	M/F
Aflaj	93.3	96.5	99.8	
Al-Baha	98.0	88.4	91.5	
Ar-Rass	96.1	102.9	99.4	
Arafat	92.2	94.0	90.8	
Arar	94.1	97.4	88.4	
Buraydah	89.3	95.6	93.2	
Dammam	92.8/93.8	94.7	90.0	103.6
Duba	89.5	95.8	92.6	
Jeddah	92.0/99.5	93.0	89.9	96.2
Jizan	95.1	88.8	91.9	
Jubail	107.7	105.6	95.3	
Kharj	93.0	96.0	90.0	
Mecca	94.7	98.0	91.5	
Medina	90.5	93.6	96.8	
Riyadh	91.2	94.4	100.0	97.7
Taif	96.5	93.3	99.8	106.9
Yanbu	97.4	93.6	90.9	

+ numerous low power stations under 10kW for local coverage.

G=General Prgr. in Arabic: 24h. **–2=Second Prgr in Arabic:** 24h, on most MW fqs 0300-2200. **– Q=Quran prgr:** 24h incl. Call of Islam 0100-0300 **– I=Call of Islam prgr:** 24h **– F=Foreign Language prgrs** (from either Riyadh or Jeddah studios): F: 0600-0800, 1000-1300, 1600-2100. F: 0800-1000, 1400-1600. **– M=Music prgr:** 24h. **– P=Pilgrimage Enlightment Radio:** 24h during two months of the "Haj" season (Dec-Feb) in Arabic/E/F/Persian/Turkish/Hausa/Indonesian/Urdu on MW and FM: 94.2/101.0MHz in Mina/Arafat/Muzdalifah.
Ann: General prgr: "Idha'at il-Mamlaka al-Arabiya as-Saudiya(, al-barnamig al-aam,) min ar-Riyadh". 2nd prgr: "Idha'at il-Mamlaka al-Arabiya as-Saudiya, al-barnamig at-thani min Jeddah". Call of Islam: "Idha'at Nidaa Al-Islam min Makka al-Mukaram". E: "This is Radio Riyadh/Jeddah".
IS: 'Ud' (oriental lute). Opens and closes with National Anthem.
F.PI: separate FM network for Call of Islam prgr.

EXTERNAL SERVICE: Saudi Radio: see International Radio section.

SAUDI ARAMCO RADIO (Serving the staff of Saudi Aramco Co.)
⌨ P.O.Box 5000, Dhahran 31311 **W:** www.saudiaramco.com **E:** webmaster@aramco.com.sa
Studio 1 (pop, rock and country music): Udhailiyah 88.8MHz, Dhahran 91.4MHz, Safaniya/Tanajib/Haradh 103.8MHz **– Studio 2** (easy listening, jazz and classical music): Udhailiyah 91.9MHz, Dhahran 101.4MHz, Safaniya/Tanajib/Haradh 107.9MHz **D.Prgr:** 24h in English.

Other stations (FM MHz):
Alif Alif FM: Riyadh 94.0, Jeddah 101.0, Dammam 107.5. **W:** alifaliffm.com **– MBC FM:** Dammam 101.9, Riyadh 102.0, Jeddah/Medina 103.0. **W:** mbc.net/mbcfm **– Mix FM:** Tabuk 93.0MHz, Riyadh & 5 sites 98.0, Jubayl 98.4, Nazran 101.0, Taif 101.4, Kharj/Skaka 103.0, Breida/Jeddah 105.5, Makkah & 3 sites 106.0, Majmaa 106.2, Baha/Rabegh 106.4. **W:** mixfm-sa.com **– Panorama FM:** Dammam 91.9, Riyadh 96, Tabuk 101.7, Jeddah 102, Madinah 102.3, Buraidah (Al Qassim) 103.3, Abha/Taif 104. See main entry under UAE **– R. Rotana:** Jeddah/Riyadh 88.0, Dammam 100.0. **W:** rotanafm.com **– uFM R.:** Riyadh 90.0, Madina 91.0, Al-Kharj/Ara'ar/Al-Dawadimi 91.5, **American Forces Network:** 93.7/100.7/103.9/107.8, Dammam 95.5, Makkah 95.8, Jeddah 97.0. **W:** ufmradio.com. New FM licenses granted to: Ghayat Al-Ibdah, Rotana, Electronic Resources and Shams R.

SENEGAL

L.T: UTC — **Pop:** 14 million — **Pr.L:** French, Wolof, Mandinga, Soninké, Pular, others — **E.C:** 50Hz, 230V — **ITU:** SEN

CONSEIL NATIONAL DE REGULATION DE L'AUDIOVISUEL (CNRA)
⌨ 15ème étage, Immeuble Fahd, Blvd Djily Mbaye, B.P. 50059, Dakar RP ☎+221 33 8499120 🖷 +221 33 8234785 **W:** cnra.sn
L.P: Chairperson: Nancy Ngom Ndiaye.

RADIODIFFUSION TÉLÉVISION SÉNÉGALAISE (Gov.)
⌨ Triangle Sud x Avenue El-Hadj Malick SY, B.P. 1765, Dakar ☎+221 33 8491212 🖷 +221 33 8223490 **W:** www.rts.sn **E:** rts@rts.sn
L.P: DG: Babacar Diagne. Dir. Radio: Oumar Seck. Dir. New Tech. & Development: Papa Abdou Diallo.

FM	N	I	R	M	kW
Bakel	95.9	107.3			5
Dakar	95.7	92.5	94.5	95.2	10
Diourbel	97.6	96.6	101.1		2
Fatick	95.7		92.8		0.5/2

FM	N	I	R	M	kW
Goudiry	106.0		91.1		0.5
Kaolack	103.0	107.0	97.9		5
Kédougou	94.6	97.7	100.0		2
Kolda	100.0	102.2	92.2		2
Koungheul	89.7		107.0		1
Linguère	92.1	89.0			5
Louga	95.0	101.8	88.7		5/2
Matam	95.6	89.1	100.6		2
Ndioum		98.4	92.7		5
Ourossogui	96.5	89.1	105.3		5/2
Podor			100.6		0.25
Richard Toll			89.6		0.1
Saint-Louis	91.9	90.1	96.3		10/5
Tambacounda	102.0	88.1	92.0		5
Thiès	96.9	94.9	100.6		5
Touba			99.2		0.25
Vélingara	99.0	89.1	92.2		2
Ziguinchor	95.2	100.2	98.9		5

N=Chaîne Nationale: 24h in French, Wolof and other national languages – **I=R. Sénégal Internationale:** 24h in French, Arabic, Portuguese and other languages – **M=RTS Mag FM:** 24h in French – **R=Chaîne Régionale:** 0600-2400, regional programming for 9 to 18 hours a day depending on station.
Ann: N: "Radiodiffusion Télévision Sénégalaise émettant de Dakar".
Int: "Radio Sénégal Internationale". **IS:** Melody on "Cora" (local harp).

Other stations (main networks):

FM	1)	2)	3)	4)	5)	6)	7)
Bakel			93.7	100.8			
Banlieue	91.7						
Bignona		91.4	88.3				
Dagana			91.7				
Dakar	98.5	94.0	88.9	101.0	103.9	98.7	97.8
Diourbel	91.1	92.4	90.9			106.0	105.5
Fatick		99.3	102.5		99.3		102.8
Joal			92.4				
Kaffrine		95.0	102.4				
Kaolack	94.6	93.9	105.0	92.7	99.7	93.1	91.9
Kébémer			91.5	101.3			
Kédogou		99.7	98.6	106.4			
Kidira			105.0				
Kolda	95.4	93.2	98.7	91.9	102.2	99.7	88.1
Linguere			102.8				
Louga		88.3	91.8		98.3	107.0	103.4
Matam	98.4	95.0		89.3	96.9	91.8	88.7
Mboro			98.6				
Mbour	106.9	95.8	102.8			104.1	
Ndioum	93.9						
Nioro		98.4					
Ourossogui			99.5				
Podor		100.0	98.7		95.4		
Richard Toll		99.0	106.0				
Saint-Louis	93.2	99.3	106.3	88.3	94.6	88.9	88.1
Sédhiou	88.0		95.3				
Tambacounda	98.5	93.2	91.0	94.0	105.6	100.5	90.3
Thiès	102.2	102.5	93.7	106.9	92.3	107.1	105.1
Toubambacké	92.8	92.4		89.1	106.2		
Velingara		96.4	102.4				
Ziguinchor	95.6	92.0	92.4			106.0	103.4

Addresses: 1) Sud FM Sen R, Immeuble Fahd, Bld. Djily Mbaye x rue Macodou Ndiaye (5ème étage), Dakar ☎+221 33 8650888 🖷 +221 33 8220250 **W:** sudfm.net – **2) R. Futurs Medias (RFM),** Rue 15x Corniche, Immeuble Elimane Ndour , B.P. 17795, Dakar ☎+221 33 8491640 **W:** futursmedias.net – **3) R. Dunyaa:** HLM 1, Rue 14 prolongée, Dakar ☎+221 33 8242424 **E:** dunyaa@sentoo.sn – **4) Express An-Nour FM,** – **5) Convergence FM,** Immeuble Lambert, Avenue Bourguiba, Dakar ☎+221 33 8253989 **W:** convergencefm.wordpress.com – **6) Océan FM** – **7) Sénégal Info**

Community radio FM (MHz):

Afia FM, Dakar: 93.0 5kW – Biyen FM, Thiès 89.5 2kW – Ferlo FM, Dahra: 94.0 2kW – Gaynaako FM, Podor 99.4 0.5kW. **W:** gaynaakofm. org – Jéeri FM, Keur Momar Sarr 97.0 0.3kW – Manoore FM, Dakar: 89.4 5kW – R. Penc Mi, Fissel: 90.6 1kW. **E:** pencmi_fm@yahoo.fr – R. Tim-Timol, Matam: 91.8 1kW.

Other Stations (MHz):

Africa No. 1: Dakar 102.0 10kW. (see main entry under Gabon).
BBC African Sce: Dakar 105.6 10kW. In French.
RFI Afrique: Ziguinchor 87.6 5kW, Tambacounda 88.9 2kW, Kaolack 91.5 5kW, Dakar 92.0 10kW, St-Louis 99.7 5kW, Thiès 100.2 5kW

SERBIA

L.T: UTC +1h (31 Mar-27 Oct: +2h) — **Pop:** 7.379.339 — **Pr.L:** Serbian — **E.C:** 50Hz, 220V — **ITU:** SRB

UDRUZENJE RADIOTELEVIZIJE SRBIJE d.O.O.
🖳 Beogradska 70, 11000 Beograd ☎ +381 11 433718, 434688 🖷 +381 11 434023, 437280 **E:** yrtcoord@eunet.rs
L.P: MD: Ms. Vjera Nikolic.
Udruzenje Radiotelevizije Srbije comprises Radio-televizija Srbije and Voice of Serbia

JP. EMISIONA TEHNIKA I VEZE/ETV (PUBLIC ENTERPRISE BROADCASTING AND COMMUNICATION)
🖳 Kneza Viseslava 88, 11030 Belgrade ☎ +381 11 3693251 🖷 +381 11 3693260, Tech.: ☎ +381 11 3211610 **W:** www.etv.rs **E:** office@etv. rs, tehnika@etv.rs, etv@etv.rs. **L.P:** Vladimir Homan

RADIO-TELEVIZIJA SRBIJE
🖳 Takovska 10, 11000 Beograd ☎ +381 11 3211000 **E:** kontaktcentar@rts.rs **W:** www.rts.rs **L.P:** DG: Aleksandar Tijanic
R. Beograd: Hilendarska 2, 11000 Beograd ☎ +381 11 3248888 **L.P:** Dir: Slobodan Divjak **W:** www.radiobeograd.co.rs

MW	kHz	kW	P	MW	kHz	kW	P
Bosilegrad	675	1	d	Novi Pazar	1062	1	a
Aleksinac	684	10	d	Vranje	1296	8	d
Negotin	693	0.5	d	Jagodina	1440	4	d
Nis	711	1	d	Crna Trava	1485	0.5	d
Medvedja	765	1	d	Tutin	1485	0.6	a
Kladovo	999	0.5	d	Beograd 202	1503	10	
Beograd 2/3	1008	0.5		Sjenica	1602	0.7	d

P: a) Beograd1+ reg. prgr d) rel. Beograd 1

FM (MHz)	I	II/III	202	kW
Avala	95.3	97.6	104.0	75/75/130
Bajina Basta	91.9	93.0	94.0	2
Beograd	88.3			2
Besna Kobila	91.7	95.3	100.1	25/25/40
Bitovik	91.7	92.9	104.3	25
Crni Vrh	89.7	99.3	101.0	25
Crveni Cot	94.5	96.5	101.8	75/75.130
Deli Jovan	87.7	94.9	98.9	25/25/40
Jastrebac	96.9	89.3	103.5	100
Kopaonik	90.9	93.7	102.1	50/50/100
Ljubovija	104.0	94.0	105.6	25
Maljen	104.5	107.9	93.4	25
Nis	99.5			3.5
Ovcar	88.1	90.1	101.6	25
Pirot	88.5	102.5	101.0	15
Subotica	88.9	101.1	98.5	50/50/0.3
Tornik	90.6	97.5	100.2	15
Trgoviste	90.1	92.3	96.9	15
Tupiznica	92.5	96.1	100.4	25
Vrsac	95.7	98.1	103.0	30

Additional low power local stns not mentioned.
R. Beograd 1: 24h. **N:** W 0303, 0330, 0400, 0430, 0500, 0540, 0700, 0800, 0900, 1000, 1100, 1200, 1300, 1400, 1600, 1700, 1830, 2100, 2200, 2300; Sun 0430, 0500, 0530, 0600, 0700, 0800, 0900, 1000, 1100, 1200, 1400, 1600, 1830, 2000, 2200, 2300. – **R. Beograd 2:** W 0400-1900 (Sun 0600-1900). **N:** W 1130, 1230, 1330, 1500, 1600, 1850. Sun 0630, 0730, 0930, 1055, 1130, 1330, 1730, 1850 – **R. Beograd 3:** 1900-2300 (Serious prgr.) – **R. Beograd 202:** 0400-2400 on 1503kHz, 104.0MHz + FM 202 (0000-0400 rel. R. Beograd 1) – **Stereorama:** 0700-1900SS on FM 202. Other times rel. Beograd 202

Local stations:

MW/FM	kHz	kW	MHz	MW/FM	kHz	kW	MHz
Arandjelovac			98.9	Novi Pazar	1062	1	90.0
Bor			91.7	Pirot			95.8
Cacak			92.8	Pozarevac			90.1
Jagodina			97.3	Priboj	1485	1	88.7
Kladovo	1458	1	89.0	Prijepolje			98.9
Kragujevac			88.9	Smed. Palanka			88.3
Kraljevo			87.6	Smederevo			96.1
Krusevac			92.2	Soko Banja			90.5
Lazarevac			89.3	Uzice			92.0
Leskovac			99.0	Valjevo			88.6
Loznica			107.4	Vranje			96.5
Majdanpek			96.7	Vrnjacka Banja			96.5
Mladenovac			97.0	Zajecar			98.1

FM stations with national coverage:

FM	MHz	FM	MHz	FM	MHz
Index	88.9	B92	92.5	R. S	94.9

FM	MHz	FM	MHz	FM	MHz
Roadstar	98.5	Fokus	101.4		

All stns have relays

Local FM stations in Beograd:

FM	MHz	FM	MHz	FM	MHz
Bumbum	89.4	TRI	95.8	Novosti	104.7
R. JAT	90.2	Centar	96.2	Nostalgie	105.2
Pingvin	90.9	Naxi FM	96.9	City	106.3
Pink	91.3	Sport FM	100.4	TOP FM	106.8
TDI	91.8	Studio B	100.8	Sl. Ljubve	107.3
MIP	93.7	MFM	102.2	Antena	107.9
R. S	94.9				

There are numerous local FM stns.

VOJVODINA (Autonomous Province)

RADIO TELEVIZIJA NOVI SAD
✉ Ignjata Pavlasa 3, 21000 Novi Sad ☎ +381 21 425588 🖷 +381 21 423348 **E:** veroslava.pop@rtv.rs **W:** www.rtv.rs

MW	kHz	kW	Notes
Orlovat	1107	50	r. Beograd 1
Srbobran	1269	3	in Serbian
Novi Sad	1485	0.5	in Serbian

FM (MHz)	I	II	III	kW
Novi Sad	87.7	90.5	100.0	50
Subotica	99.3	92.5		50
Vrsac	99.6	91.7	107.1	30

I) in Serbian, II) in Hungarian, III) prgrs for national minorities.
R. Novi Sad 1: 24h in Serbian **R. Novi Sad 2:** 0400-2305 in Hungarian.

Local stations

FM	MHz	FM	MHz	FM	MHz
Apatin	98.7	Kovin	89.5	St. Pazova	91.5
B. Palanka	95.1	Odzaci	89.7	Subotica	91.5
B. Topola	97.8	Pancevo	92.1	Temerin	93.5
B. Petrovac	91.4	Ruma	102.7	Vrbas	95.5
Beocin	97.8	Sid	89.1	Vrsac	94.0
Indjija	96.0	Sombor	97.5	Zrenjanin	103.6
Kovacica	93.2	Srbobran	102.6		

There are numerous low-power local FM stns

EXTERNAL SERVICE: International Radio Serbia
See International Broadcasting section

SEYCHELLES

L.T: UTC +4h — **Pop:** 90,000 — **Pr.L:** Creole, English, French — **E.C:** 50Hz, 240V — **ITU:** SEY

MINISTRY OF INFORMATION TECHNOLOGY & COMMUNICATION (MITC)
✉ Telecom Division, P. O. Box 1389, Oceangate House, Room 16, Victoria, Mahé ☎+248 4382039 🖷 +248 4225325 **E:** telecom@seychelles.sc **L.P:** Dir: Dr. George Ah-Thew

SEYCHELLES BROADCASTING CORPORATION (SBC, Pub.)
✉ P.O. Box 321, Hermitage, Mahé ☎+248 4289600 🖷 +248 4225641 **W:** www.sbc.sc **E:** sbcradtv@seychelles.sc
L.P: MD: Mr. Ibrahim Afif. Prgr. Mgr.(Radio): Ms. Thelma Pool. CE: Mr. Joyvani Chetty. Marketing & PR Mgr: Mrs. Jacqueline Moustache.
MW: Victoria 1368kHz 10kW (rep. inactive).
FM: Anse Soleil 93.6MHz 0.25kW, Fairyland 93MHz 0.25kW, St.Louis 93.6MHz 1kW, Praslin 100.8MHz 0.03kW.
D.Prgr: MW (spoken word): MF 0200-0930 & 1200-1800, SS 0200-1800. **N:** English: 0300, 0600, 0900, 1500. **French:** 0330, 0700, 1300, 1700. Creole: 0230, 0500, 0800, 1600.
FM: Paradise FM (musical prgr.): 24h.
Ann: E: "This is SBC Radio". F: "Ici la Radio SBC". C: "Isi Radyo SBC"
IS: Instrumental music.

RFI Afrique: St.Louis 103.8MHz 1kW, Anse Soleil 102.8MHz 0.25kW.
BBC African Sce: St.Louis 106.2MHz 0.5kW.
BBC Indian Ocean relay station: see International Radio section

SIERRA LEONE

L.T: UTC — **Pop:** 6.5 million — **Pr.L:** English, Krio, Limba, Mende, Temne, others — **E.C:** 50Hz, 230V — **ITU:** SRL

INDEPENDENT MEDIA COMMISSION (IMC)
✉ Kissy House, 54 Siaka Stevens Street, Freetown ☎+232 22

221835 **W:** www.imc-sl.org **E:** info@imc-sl.org
L.P: Chp: Mrs. Bernadette Cole.

SIERRA LEONE BROADCASTING CORPORATION (SLBC, Pub.)
✉ New England, Freetown ☎+232 22 241919 🖷 +232 22 240922
L.P: DG: Elvis Gbanabom Hallowell. Dir. Eng.: K. Koroma.
FM: Freetown 100.0MHz 4kW. Regional stations (mostly own programming): **B**o 96.5MHz 2kW, Kenema 93.5MHz 2kW, Kono 90.2MHz 1kW, Makeni 88.0MHz 1kW. In addition 4 trs under 1kW.
D.Prgr: "Power FM": 0558-2400.

COTTON TREE NEWS
FM: via R. Mount Aureol, Fourah Bay College, Freetown: 107.3MHz. Also relayed by some stations listed below.

Other stations FM (MHz):
Believers Broadcasting Network (BBN) (Rlg.), Freetown: 93.0 2kW. **W:** www.bbn-sl.org – **Capital R:** Freetown 104.9 4kW, Bo 102.3 50W. **W:** capitalradio.sl – **Eastern R:** Kenema 101.9, Kono 96.5 – **Kiss FM**, Bo: 104.0 (Also rel. VOA) – **R. Bintumani**, Kabala: 93.7 – **R. Bontico**, Bonthe: 96.9 – **R. Democracy**, Freetown: 98.1 – **R. Galaxy**, Mahera: 106.1 – **R. Gbafth**, Mile 91: 91.0 – **R. Kolenten**, Kambia: 92.4 – **R. Mankneh**, Makeni: 95.1 – **R. Moa**, Kailahun: 105.5 – **R. Modcar**, Moyamba: 94.8 – **R. Maria**, Makeni 101.1 0.5kW – **R. Numbura**, Bumbuna: 102.5 – **R. One**, Freetown: 103.7 – **R. Wanjei**, Pujehun: 101.1 – **R. Viascity**, Waterloo: 100.6 – **Skyy R**, Freetown: 106.6 – **Unity R**, Freetown: 98.4 – **Voice of Islam**, Freetown: 102.0 – **VO the Handicapped**, Freetown: 96.2 (mostly rel. BBC) – **VO the Peninsula**, Tombo: 96.0 – **VO Women**, Mattru Jong: 88.5.
BBC African Sce: Freetown 94.3 8kW, Bo 94.5 120W, Kenema 95.3 60W – **RFI Afrique:** Freetown 89.9 in French/English – **VOA**, Freetown: 102.4

SINGAPORE

L.T: UTC +8h — **Pop:** 5.2 million — **Pr.L:** English, Chinese, Malay, Tamil — **E.C:** 50Hz, 230V — **ITU:** SNG — **Int. dialling code:** +65

MEDIA DEVELOPMENT AUTHORITY OF SINGAPORE (Government statutory board)
✉ 3 Fusionopolis Way, #16-22 Symbiosis, Singapore 138633 ☎ +65 6377 3800 🖷 +65 6577 3888 **W:** www.mda.gov.sg
L.P: Chmn: Niam Chaing Meng, CEO: Aubeck Kam

MEDIACORP RADIO SINGAPORE PTE LTD (Comm.)
✉ Caldecott Broadcast Centre, Andrew Road, Singapore 299939 ☎ +65 6333 3888 🖷 +65 6359 7500 **W:** www.mediacorpr.sg
L.P: Chmn: Mr Teo Ming Kian, Dir. & CEO: Shaun Seow, MD, MediaCorp R.: Florence Lian.
Stations: FM tx centre at Bukit Batok.

	FM MHz	kW	Network	Format	Lang.
1)	89.7	6	Ria 89.7FM	CHR	Malay
2)	90.5	6	Gold 90FM	Gold	English
3)	92.4	10	Symphony 92FM	Classical	English
4)	93.3	6	Y.E.S. 93.3FM	AC	Chinese
5)	93.8	6	938LIVE	N./Info	English
6)	94.2	10	Warna 94.2FM	N./Info	Malay
7)	95.0	6	Class 95FM	AC	English
8)	95.8	10	Capital 95.8FM	*N./Info	Chinese
9)	96.3	6	Expat R. XFM	Int'l	A
10)	96.8	6	Oli 96.8FM	Full sce	Tamil
11)	97.2	6	Love 97.2FM **	Easy	Chinese
12)	98.7	6	987FM	CHR	English
13)	99.5	6	Lush 99.5FM	Urban	English

*) in Chinese: "Chengshi Pindao". **) in Chinese: "Zui'ai Pindao".
D.Prgr: all networks 24h Tr. powers shown are TRP.
A = Mon-Fri 2300-0100 "Smile Wave" in Japanese. Mon-Fri 0100-0300 rel. R. France Int. in French. Mon-Fri 0700-0900 rel. Deutsche Welle in German. Daily 0900-1200 "Masti 96.3" in Hindi. Daily 1200-1400 "K-Pop" in Korean. At other times carries music interludes.
Ownership: MediaCorp is wholly owned by Temasek Holdings, an investment company of the Government of Singapore.

SAFRA RADIO (Comm.)
Operated by the Singapore Armed Forces Reservists' Ass.
✉ Tower B #12-04, Defence Technology Towers, 5 Depot Rd, Singapore 109681 or Bukit Merah Central PO Box 1315, Singapore 911599 ☎ +65 6373 1924 🖷 +65 6278 3039 **W:** power98.com.sg or www.883jia.com.sg **L.P:** News Dir.: Lee Hui Min.
883JiaFM: 88.3MHz 5kW, 24h in Chinese
Power98FM: 98.0MHz 12kW, 24h in English

SPH UNIONWORKS PTE LTD (Comm.)
Joint venture of NTUC Media Co-operative (National Trade Unions Congress) & SPH MediaWorks (Singapore Press Holdings)
✉ 1000 Toa Payoh North, News Centre Podium Block Level 3, Singapore 318994 ☎ +65 6319 1900 🖷 +65 6319 1099 **W:** www.radio913.com or www.kiss92.sg or www.ufm1003.sg **LP:** Gen. Mgr: Goh Wee Wang. Prgr Dir R. 91.3 & 92: Jamie R. Meldrum. Prgr Dir 100.3: Carine Ang CH
HOT FM91.3: 24h in English on 91.3MHz **Kiss92 FM:** 24h in English on 92.0MHz **UFM 1003:** 24h in Chinese on 100.3MHz

BBC SINGAPORE 88.9 FM
24h rel. of BBCWS in English. The 5kW FM tx at Bukit Batok is operated by MediaCorp Technologies.

BBC FAR EASTERN RELAY STATION (Babcock Communications Ltd)
✉ 51 Turut Track, Singapore 718930 ☎ +65 6793 7511
See International Broadcasting section

SLOVAKIA

L.T: UTC +1h (31 Mar-27 Oct: +2h) — **Pop:** 5 million — **Pr.L:** Slovak — **E.C:** 50Hz, 230V — **ITU:** SVK

ROZHLAS A TELEVÍZIA SLOVENSKA (Radio and Television of Slovakia) - RTVS
SLOVENSKY ROZHLAS (SLOVAK RADIO)
✉ Mytna 1 (P.O.Box 55), 817 55 Bratislava 15 ☎ + 421 2 57273111 🖷 + 421 2 57273559 **W:** www.rozhlas.sk **E:** info@rozhlas.sk **Radio FM: W:** www.radiofm.sk **E:** info@radiofm.sk **LP:** DG: Václav Mika. PD: Lubos Machaj. Mus. Dir.: Rudolf Pepucha. CE: Robert Oravec

MW

	kHz	kW	Prgr
Kosice	702	5	S5 (daytime) + S3 (nighttime)
Nitra (Jarok)	1098	10	S5 (daytime) + S3 (nighttime)

FM (MHz)

	S1	S2	S3	S4	kW
Banská Bystrica	90.1	101.5	102.0	105.4	100/100/0.1/2
Banská Stiavnica	99.0		102.6	20/20	
Bardejov	93.5	89.3	88.8	101.7	10/1/10/10
Borsky Mikulás			95.6	102.8	1
Bratislava	96.6	99.3	104.4	89.3	100/10/10/10
Cadca				91.8	0.5
Dolny Kubin				91.7	1
Dubnica n.V.	92.2				1
Kosice	96.6	100.3			100/35
Kosice (city)			96.2	101.2	0.5/1
Lucenec	103.6	88.2		98.0	10/2/10
Martin				91.8	0.5
Modry Kamen	90.9	88.5	103.1	98.3	10
Námestovo	102.4	100.4	88.7		10
Nitra	91.2	102.2			10/10
N. Mesto n.V.	103.2	100.7	90.8		10
Nové Zámky			94.6	102.8	1
Poprad	92.2	96.9	94.2	104.3	30
Presov			106.7	101.5	0.5
Rim. Sobota		95.0			1
Roznava	97.3	88.6	90.0	105.9	1/1/1/1
Ruzomberok	103.8	100.6	104.6	102.1	5
Snina	91.2		102.2	107.6	10
Stará Lubovna	89.1	102.3	96.1		10
Sturovo	96.3	91.7	106.2	103.7	10
Trebisov		89.2	106.7	101.3	10
Trencín		95.9	97.8	101.2	10
Trnava (F.Pl.)	90.8				10
Trstená				91.9	10
Zilina	103.5	100.1	97.2	91.9	20/20/30/1
Zvolen			99.8	89.0	0.5/1

Addresses and other information:
S1 = Radio Slovensko: 24h (national prgr news). **S2** = Radio Regina: 24h (regional prgrs + prgrs for national minorities in Hungarian, Ukrainian, Ruthenian, German, Czech, Polish and Gypsy/Roma + relays of Radio Slovensko – S1). **S2 BA** = Radio Regina Bratislava, ✉ Mytna 1, 817 55 Bratislava 15. Mon-Fri 0335-2400, Sat 0500-2100, Sun 0700-2100. **S2 BB** = Radio Regina Banská Bystrica ✉ L. Sáru 1, 975 68 Banská Bystrica. Mon-Fri 0335-1730, Sat 0500-2030, Sun 0800-1930. **S2 KE** = Radio Regina Kosice ✉ Masarykova 7, 041 61 Kosice. Mon-Fri 0400-2030, Sat 0500-2030, Sun 0500-1600. **S3** = Radio Devín: 24h (cultural prgr) on FM and 1700-0500 on 702 and 1098kHz. **S4** = Radio FM: 24h (rock, pop and alternative music). N: on the h. **S5** = Radio Patria – production of prgrs for national minorities in Hungarian, Ukrainian, Ruthenian, German, Czech, Polish, Gypsy/Roma relayed on S2 and S5 txs ✉ Slovensky Rozhlas, HRNEV, Moyzesova 7, 040 01 Kosice **E:** nev@slovakradio.sk Prgrs for minorities (S5): Hungarian 0500-1700 on 702

and 1098kHz. Prgrs for national minorities (S5) on Radio Regina (S2): Mon+Wed+Fri+Sat+Sun 1700-1800, Tue+Thu 1700-1800, 1900-2000

EXTERNAL SERVICE: Radio Slovakia International
See International Broadcasting section

MAJOR PRIVATE STATIONS/NETWORKS:
ASOCIÁCIA NEZÁVISLYCH ROZHLASOVYCH STANIC (Association of Independent Radio Stations)
✉ Stúrova 9, 811 02 Bratislava ☎ +421 2 5296 2370

FUN RADIO (Comm.) ✉ Leskova 5, 815 25 Bratislava ☎ +421 2 52494601 🖷 +421 2 52495535 **W:** www.funradio.sk – **JEMNÉ MELODIE (Comm.)** ✉ Dr. Vladimíra Clementisa 10, 815 25 Bratislava ☎ +421 2 48484811 🖷 +421 2 52492701 **W:** www.jemnemelodie.sk **FM:** see list below **D.Prgr:** 24h – **RADIO VIVA (Comm.)** ✉ Salviová 1, 830 00 Bratislava ☎ +421 2 48255500 **W:** www.radioviva.sk **FM:** see list below **D.Prgr:** 24h – **RADIO EXPRES (Comm.)** ✉ Lamacská cesta 1, 841 04 Bratislava ☎ +421 2 59308900 🖷 +421 2 59308991 **W:** www.expres.sk **FM:** see list below **D.Prgr:** 24h – **EUROPA 2 (Comm.)** ✉ Seberíniho 1, 821 03 Bratislava ☎ +421 2 48224201 **W:** www.europa2.sk **FM:** see list below **D.Prgr:** 24h – **RADIO LUMEN (Relig.)** ✉ Kapitulská 2, 974 01 Banská Bystrica ☎ +421 48 4710800 🖷 +421 48 4710840 **W:** www.lumen.sk **FM:** see list below **D.Prgr:** 24h – **RADIO HEY! (Comm.)** ✉ Jelsová 11, 831 01 Bratislava ☎ +421 2 59303030 🖷 +421 2 54777777 **W:** www.radiohey.sk

Private Commercial FM Stations:

FM	MHz	kW	Station
Kosice	87.7	80	Fun R.
Banská Bystrica	87.7	10	R. Jemné melodie
Nové Mesto n.V.	88.0	8.5	R. Jemné melodie
Hlohovec	88.4	2	R. Expres
Ruzomberok	88.4	1	R. Expres
Snina	88.5	10	R. Viva
Nitra	88.8	10	R. Hey!
Trencín	89.1	10	Fun R.
Rimavská Sobota	89.3	1	R. Expres
Ruzomberok	89.7	1	R. Lumen
Nitra	89.7	1	R. Expres
Banská Bystrica	90.5	2	R. One BB
Prievidza	90.5	1	R. WOW
Trstená	90.7	1	R. Viva
Presov	90.8	2	R. Kiss
Zilina	90.8	1	R. Hit FM
Moldava nad Bodvou	91.0	1	R. Expres
Ruzomberok	91.1	1	R. Viva
Lucenec	91.6	10	Fun R.
Stropkov	92.4	1	R. Viva
Zvolen	92.6	1	R. Expres
Zilina	92.7	1	R. Viva
Zámky	92.7	1	R. Expres
Ruzomberok	92.8	1	R. Viva
Trencín	93.3	10	R. Lumen
Banská Stiavnica	93.3	2	R. Lumen
Partizánske	93.6	1	R. WOW
Bratislava	93.8	6	R. Lumen
Kosice	93.8	2	R. Best FM
Lehota p.Vtác.	93.9	1	R. Beta
Bratislava	94.3	100	Fun R.
Banská Bystrica	94.7	1	R. Rock
Kosice	94.8	1	R. Hey
Liptovsky Mikulás	95.0	1	Fun R.
Nitra	95.2	10	Europa 2
Kosice	95.2	2	R. Expres
Levoca	95.3	1	R. Expres
Bardejov	95.6	1	R. Viva
Roznava	95.7	1	R. Expres
Snina	95.9	10	R. Kiss
Lucenec	96.0	5	R. Viva
Cadca	96.1	1	R. Frontinus
Martin	96.2	1	R. Frontinus
Partizánske	96.4	1	R. Hit FM
Trstená	96.5	2	R. Expres
Zilina	96.5	1	R. Expres
Michalovce	97.0	5	R. Kiss
Banská Bystrica	97.6	100	R. Hey!
Stropkov	97.8	1	R. Kiss
Handlová	98.1	1	R. Lumen
Bardejov	98.2	1	R. Expres
Nové Mesto n.V.	98.5	8.8	Europa 2
Kosice	98.6	50	R. Jemné melodie
Nové Zámky	98.7	1	R. Max
Ruzomberok	98.8	5	R. Hey!

FM	MHz	kW	Station
Bardejov	99.1	1	R. Lumen
Zilina	99.2	20	Fun R.
Sturovo	99.4	10	R. Expres
Vychodna	99.5	1	R. Expres
Cadca	99.6	1	R. Viva
Bratislava	100.3	1	R. Hey!
Poprad	100.9	30	Europa 2
Lucenec	101.1	5	R. Expres
Roznava	101.4	1	R. Viva
Bratislava	101.8	100	R. Viva
Trencín	102.5	1	R. Expres
Poprad	102.5	1	Fun R.
Roznava	102.8	1	Fun R.
Strbské Pleso	102.9	2	R. Lumen
Kosice	102.9	1	Fun R.
Michalovce	103.3	2	R. Lumen
Presov	103.7	8	Europa 2
Banská Bystrica	104.0	100	Fun R.
Presov	104.1	1	R. Kiss
Prievidza	104.5	1	R. Hit FM
Zilina	104.6	1	R. Frontinus
Bratislava	104.8	50	Europa 2
Poprad	104.8	1	R. Viva
Martin	104.9	1	R. Viva
Banská Stiavnica	105.1	20	R. Viva
Povazská Bystrica	105.2	1	R. Expres
Trencín	105.5	10	R. Viva
Stará Lubovna	105.7	10	R. Expres
Námestovo	105.8	10	R. Lumen
Presov	105.8	2	R. Viva
Banská Bystrica	106.0	50	Europa 2
Kosice	106.2	20	R. Expres
Lucenec	106.3	3	R. Lumen
Roznava	106.3	1	R. Lumen
Modry Kamen	106.5	1	R. Expres
Bratislava	106.6	10	R.Jemné melodie
Banská Bystrica	106.6	1	R. Viva
Zilina	106.9	3	R.Jemné melodie
Dobsiná	107.0	1	R. Viva
Bardejov	107.1	10	Europa 2
Levice	107.1	4	Fun R.
Poprad	107.3	2	R. Hey!
Prievidza	107.5	1	R. Expres
Bratislava	107.6	10	R. Expres
Stará Lubovna	107.7	1	R. Jemné melodie

+ more than 60 relays of less than 1kW

SLOVENIA

L.T: UTC +1h (31 Mar-27 Oct: +2h) — **Pop:** 2 million— **Pr.L:** Slovenian — **E.C:** 50Hz, 220V — **ITU:** SVN

AGENCIJA ZA POŠTO IN ELEKTRONSKE KOMUNIKACIJE REPUBLIKE SLOVENIJE (APEK)
P.O. Box 418, 1000 Ljubljana ☎+386 1 5836300 ▤+386 1 5111101 **W:** srdf.si apek.si **E:** info.box@apek.si

RADIOTELEVIZIJA SLOVENIJA (Pub.)
Kolodvorska ulica 2, SI-1550 Ljubljana ☎+386 1 4752151 ▤ +386 1 4752150 **W:** rtvslo.si **E:** webmaster@rtvslo.si
L.P: DG (Radio): Miha Lampreht.

MW	kHz	kW	Prgr.	MW	kHz	kW	Prgr.
Beli Kriz	549	15	1/K	Domzale	918	300	1
Nemcavci	558	15	1/MMR	B. Kriz	1170	15	C/RSI

C=R. Capodistria in Italian **RSI**=R. Slovenija International, **K**=R. Koper in Slovenian, **MMR**=Muravideki Magyar R. in Hungarian

FM (MHz)	Slo 1	Slo 2	Slo 3	Reg.	kW
Beli Kriz	92.0	94.1	96.1	104.3k/97.7c	5
				102.0si	1
Blejska Dobrava				100.4si	1
Boc				90.4m	2
Golnik				89.0si	1
Koper	92.2			104.1k	1
Krim	88.0	93.5	96.5		5
Krvavec	91.8	98.9	102.0		100
Kuk	90.8	87.8	96.4	100.6k	5
Kum	94.1	99.9	103.9		30
Ljubljana-Šance				100.8si	1
Nanos	92.9	95.3	105.7	88.6k	50/50/50/25
				103.1c	100
Pec	100.1	104.0	106.0		5
Pecarovci				87.6h	5
Plešivec	90.0	92.4	101.4		10

FM (MHz)	Slo 1	Slo 2	Slo 3	Reg.	kW
Pohorje	88.5	96.9	105.3	93.1m/102.8si	5/3/2/3/8
Skalnica				100.3k	2
Tinjan	89.3	98.9	98.1	107.6k/103.6c	6/6/6/6/5
				94.6si	0.2
Trdinov Vrh	90.9	97.6	100.6		7.5/10/11
Trstelj	92.6	94.3	102.2	96.7si	5

Reg. stns: c=R. Capodistria in Italian, h=MMR in Hungarian, k=R. Koper, m=R. Maribor, si=R. Slovenija Int.
R. Slovenija 1 "Prvi program": 24h. **N. in E & German:** 2130 – **R. Slovenija 2 "Val 202":** 0500 -2300. Other times relay R. Slovenija Int.. Pop + entertainment – **R. Slovenija 3 "Program ARS":** 24h. Serious music, educational – **R. SI, R. Slovenija International**, Ilichova ulica 33, SI-2000 Maribor. **W:** radiosi.eu . Music and entertainment channel 24h on **FM** ("si") and **MW** 1170kHz 2300-0500.

RADIO KOPER – CAPODISTRIA (Pub.)
PO Box 117, SI-6000 Koper-Capodistia ☎+386 (5) 6685050 ▤ +386 (5) 6684500 (Slovenian Dept.) ☎+386 (5)6685440 (Italian Dept.) **W:** rtvslo.si/radiocapodistria **E:** radio.koper@rtvslo.si; radio.capodistria@rtvslo.si
R. Koper in Slovenian: 0500-2300 on 549kHz + FM ("k"). Other times rel. Slovenija 1 – **R. Capodistria in Italian:** 0500-2300 on 1170kHz + FM ("c"). 2300-0500 rel. R. Slovenija International.

RADIO MARIBOR (Pub.)
Ilichova ulica 33, SI-2000 Maribor ☎+386 2 4201555 **E:** radio.maribor@rtvslo **FM:** ("m"). **D.Prgr:** Mon-Sat 0405-2100, Sun 0600-2100. At other times rel. Slovenia 1.

MURAVIDEKI MAGYAR RADIO (Pub.)
Kranjceva ulica 10, SI-9220 Lendava ☎+386 2 4299700 ▤+386 2 4299712 **W:** www.rtvslo.si/mmr/ **E:** mmr.studio@rtvslo.si
MW 558kHz + **FM:** ("h"). **D.Prgr:** 0445-2300. At other times rel. Slovenia 1 on MW and R. SI on FM.

OTHER STATIONS

MW	kHz	kW	Station	Location
A)	594	0.6	Primorski Val/R. Odmev	Cerkno
B)	648	10	R. Murski Val	Nemcavci

A) Platiševa ul. 39, SI-5282 Cerkno. **E:** info@radio-odmev.net **W:** primorskival.si **D.Prgr:** 1500-1900 R. Odmev. 1900-1500 Primorski Val (a joint prgr. of Alpski Val and R. Odmev) – **B)** Ul. Arhitekta Novaka 13, SI-9000 Murska Sobota **W:** radiomurskival.si **D.Prgr:** 24h. A joint night prgr. of Koroski R., Murski val, R. Celje, R. Kranj, R. Ptuj, R. Slovenske Gorice, R. Triglav, R. Univox and R. Velenje is broadcast.

FM	MHz	kW	Station	Location
1)	87.6	1	R. Europa 05	Ljubljana-Šance
2)	87.8	1	R. Salomon	Blejska Dobrava
3)	88.3	1	R. 1 Portoroz	Malija
3)	88.4	2	R. 1 Krvavec	Krvavec
5)	89.3	1	R. Student	Ljubljana-Šance
18)	89.8	1	R. Ptuj	Majšperg
6)	90.0	2	R. Maxi	Ljutomer
3)	90.1	1	R. 1 Primorska	Nova Gorica
7)	90.2	1	R. Hit	Vrhnika
4)	90.6	1	R. 1 Orion	Krim
8)	91.7	1	R. Capris	Markovec
9)	92.6	1	R. Ljubljana	Ljubljana-Šance
25)	93.1	1	R. Zeleni Val	Polzevo
10)	93.7	2	Štajerski Val	Boc
26)	93.8	1	R. Center	Markovec
40)	94.6	5	Murski Val	Pecarovci
43)	94.6	1	R. Sraka	Trdinov Vrh
11)	94.9	1	R. Veseljak	Ljubljana-Šance
41)	95.1	2	R. Celje	Boc
7)	95.6	3	R. Hit	Dobeno
12)	95.9	1	R. MARŠ	Maribor
13)	96.0	1	R. Triglav	Ravni Valvazor
14)	97.2	1	Koroški R.	Plešivec
3)	97.3	1	R. 1 Primorska	Hrvatini
15)	97.3	1	R. Kranj	Smarjetna Gora
3)	97.4	1	R. 1 Štajerska	Ljubcina
16)	98.1	1	R. Kum	Kum
17)	98.2	1	R. 94	Postojna
18)	98.2	1	R. Ptuj	Ptuj
3)	99.1	5	R. 1 Primorska	Trstelj
20)	99.5	1	R. Robin	Nova Gorica
21)	99.5	1	R. City	Ljubljana-Šance
3)	99.6	5	R. 1 Primorska	Koper
20)	100.0	1	R. Robin	Trstelj
21)	100.2	5	R. Aktual	Krim
22)	100.2	1	Net FM	Maribor
23)	100.6	1	R. City	Maribor

FM	MHz	kW	Station	Location
23)	100.8	1	R. City	Topolšica
21)	101.2	1	R. Aktual	Ljubljana-Šance
19)	101.3	1	R. Pohorje	Maribor
2)	101.6	1	R. Salomon	Ljubljana-Šance
24)	101.8	1	R. Rogla	Konjiška Gora
3)	102.1	4	R. 1	M.Sobota/Bogojina
26)	102.4	1	R. Center	Ljubljana-Šance
21)	102.4	5	R. Aktual Obala	Hrvatini
21)	102.8	1	R. Aktual Obala	Portoroz/Šentanje
21)	103.0	5	R. Aktual Studio D	Trdinov Vrh
29)	103.2	1	R. Alfa	Rahtelov Vrh
31)	103.3	1	R. Pacient	Ljubljana-Šance
26)	103.7	1	R. Center	Maribor
42)	103.7	1	Primorski Val/R. Odmev	Javornik
17)	104.1	1	R. 94	Ilirska Bistrica
30)	104.5	100	R. Ognjišce	Krvavec
7)	104.5	5	R. Hit	Trstelj
21)	104.8	2	R. Aktual	Boc
26)	104.9	1	R. Center	Nova Gorica
3)	105.0	1	R. 1 Dolenjska	Krško
8)	105.1	5	R. Capris	Slavnik
32)	105.1	1	Primorski Val/Alpski Val	Kobariški Stol
33)	105.2	1	R. Laser	Rahtelov Vrh
34)	105.2	1	R. Antena	Ljubljana-Šance
40)	105.7	2	Murski Val	Zlatolicje
30)	105.9	5	R. Ognjišce	Kum
26)	106.4	6	R. Center	Tinjan
35)	106.4	4	R. Ekspres	Krim
36)	106.6	15	R. Krka	Trdinov Vrh
27)	106.8	1	R. Top	Maribor
37)	107.0	1	Moj R.	Topolšica
3)	107.0	1	R. Hit	Markovec
38)	107.1	1	R. 94 / R. NTR	Rovte
30)	107.3	2	R. Ognjišce	Boc
30)	107.5	2	R. Ognjišce	Skalnica
8)	107.9	1	R. Capris	Portoroz
3)	107.9	1	R. 1 Stajerska	Maribor
3)	107.9	1	R. 1 107.9	Ljubljana-Šance

NB: Txs below 1kW not mentioned.
Addresses: 1) Leskoškova 9E, 1000 Ljubljana **W:** radioeuropa05.si – **2)** Papirniški trg 17, 1260 Ljubljana-Polje. **W:** radiosalomon.si – **3)** Stegne 11B, 1000 Ljubljana **W:** radio1.si Loc.Prgr. 0100-0400 – **4)** Pozarnice 78H, Vnanje Gorice, 1351 Brezovica. **W:** r-orion.com – **5)** Cesta 27. aprila 31, 1000 Ljubljana. **W:** radiostudent.si – **6)** Prešernova ul. 3, 9240 Ljutomer. **W:** radiomaxi.si – **7)** Ljubljanska Cesta 36, 1230 Domzale. **W:** radiohit.si – **8)** ul. 15.maja 10B, 6000 Koper. **W:** radiocapris.si – **9)** Stegne 7, 1000 Ljubljana. **W:** radioljubljana.net – **10)** Drofenikova 1, 3230 Šentjur. **W:** radio-stajerski-val.si – **11)** Papirniški trg 17, 1260 Ljubljana-Polje. **W:** radioveseljak.si – **12)** Gosposvedska cesta 83, 2000 Maribor. **W:** radiomars.si – **13)** Trg Toneta Curfaja 4, 4270 Jesenice. **W:** radiotriglav.si – **14)** Meškova 21, 2380 Slovenj Gradec. **W:** koroski-radio.si – **15)** Stritarjeva 6, 4000 Kranj. **W:** radio-kranj.si – **16)** Trg Svobode 11A, 1420 Trbovlje. **W:** radio-kum.si – **17)** Kazarje 10, 6230 Postojna. **W:** radio94.si – **18)** Raiceva 6, 2250 Ptuj. **W:** radio-tednik.si – **19)** Partizanska cesta 24, 2000 Maribor. **W:** radiopohorje.si – **20)** Kromberk, Industrijska cesta 5, 5000 Nova Gorica. **W:** robin.si – **21)** Papirniški trg 17, 1260 Ljubljana-Polje. **W:** radioaktual.si – **22)** Loška ul. 13, 2000 Maribor. **W:** radionet.si – **23)** Slovenska ul. 35, 2000 Maribor. **W:** radiocity.si – **24)** Škalska 7, 3210 Slovenske Konjice. **W:** radiorogla.si – **25)** Spodna Slivnica 16, 1290 Grosuplje. **W:** zelenival.com – **26)** Zelezna cesta 14, 1000 Ljubljana. **W:** radiocenter.si – **27)** Partizanska cesta 24, 2000 Maribor. **W:** radiotop.fm – **29)** Ronkova 4, 2380 Slovenj Gradec. **W:** radio-alfa.si – **30)** Trg Brolo Št 11, 6000 Koper. **W:** radio.ognjisce.si – **31)** Savska cesta 5, 1000 Ljubljana. **W:** radiopacient.si – **32)** Poljubinj 69F, p.p.46, 5220 Tolmin **W:** primorskival.si . D.Prgr: 1500-1900 Alpski Val. 1900-1500 Primorski Val (a joint programme of Alpski Val and R. Odmev) – **33)** Legen 101A, 2380 Slovenj Gradec. **W:** laserr.si – **34)** Cesta na Brdo 27, 1000 Ljubljana. **W:** radioantena.si – **35)** Stegne 21C, 1000 Ljubljana. **W:** radioekspres.si – **36)** Ljubljanska Cesta 26, 8000 Novo Mesto. **W:** radiokrka.com – **37)** Kidriceva 2B, 3320 Velenje **W:** mojradio.com – **38)** Trzaška 148, 1370 Logatec. D.Prgr: 2300-0500, other times r. R. 94 – **40)** see B) – **41)** Prešernova 19, 3000 Celje. **W:** radiocelje.com – **42)** see A) – **43)** Valanticevo 17, 8000 Novo Mesto. **W:** radiosraka.com
DAB: Krvavec ch12B. Programmes: Slo1/Slo2/Slo3/RSI

SOLOMON ISLANDS

L.T: UTC +11h — **Pop:** 571,890 — **Pr.L:** Pidgin, English — **E.C:** 50Hz, 240V — **ITU:** SLM

SOLOMON ISLANDS BROADCASTING CORP.
(Statutory Authority, Comm.)

⌨ **Honiara**: P.O. Box 645, Honiara ☎ +677 20051 🖷 +677 23159. **Wantok FM** ☎ +677 29600 🖷 +677 29600 **Gizo**: P. O. Box 78, Gizo, Western Province ☎ +677 60160 **Lata**: P. O. Box 46, Lata, Santa Cruz ☎ +677 53047 **L.P:** GM: Cornelius Rathamana. **W:** www.sibconline.cm.sb **E:** sibcnews@solomon.com.sb

MW: R. Happy Isles [Voice of the Nation], Honiara 1035kHz 10kW (r. 6kW), R. Happy Lagoon, Gizo 945kHz [inactive] 10kW, R. Temotu, Lata 1386kHz [inactive] 5kW
SW: 5020kHz & 9545kHz 10kW. Rel. R. Happy Isles. **Schedule:** 9545 kHz Oct-Mar 2100-1800, 5020 kHz Apr-Sep 0700-0000, 1800-2200
NB: times are often approximate depending on local requirements.
FM: Wantok FM, Honiara 96.3MHz, R. Happy Lagoon, Gizo 96.3MHz.
D.Prgr: local 1900-1130, BBC 1300-1900
N. in English: 2000, 2200 (R. Australia), 0130W, 0200 (R. Australia), 0500W, 0600 (BBC), 0730, 1000 (R. Australia), 1100.
Ann: "This is the SIBC, Radio Happy Isles". **IS:** Drum and Bamboo Pipes. **V.** by QSL-card (Send rpts to Honiara address, international mail often takes more than a month to reach the station. IRC's required).

Other Stations:

FM	MHz	Station	FM	MHz	Station
8)	Gold Ridge	88.0	Gold Ridge FM	7)	Kolotubi	92.5	R. Kolotubi
1)	Honiara	88.3	Gud Nius R.	7)	Leleghia	94.3	R. Leleghia
7)	Kia	89.5	R. Kia	7)	Samasodu	94.3	R. Samasodu
7)	Tutuba	89.5	R. Tutuba	2)	Honiara	97.7	Paoa FM
6)	Tetere	89.9	R. Bosco FM	3)	Honiara	100.0	ZFM 100
7)	Buala	91.1	R. Buala	2)	Honiara	101.7	Paoa FM
7)	Susubona	91.1	R. Susubona	4)	Honiara	105.6	BBC
7)	Sigana	92.5	R. Sigana	5)	Honiara	107.0	R. Australia

Power: All 0.1kW
Addresses and other information
1) UCB Pacific Partners, P.O. Box 1415, Honiara **W:** www.pacificpartners.org **E:** solomons@pacificpartners.org **F.PI:** FM relay at Gizo. – **2)** Star FM [Paoa FM] PO Box R331, Panatina Plaza, Prince Philip Hwy, Honiara ☎ +677 38984 🖷+677 38980 **W:** www.solomonstarnews.com **E:** paoafm@solomon.com.sb **L.P:** GM Joel Lamani, News Editor: Uriel Matangani – **3)** P.O. Box 100, Honiara ☎+677 21100 🖷 +677 21100 **L.P:** Sammy 'Sharzy' Saeni. **E:** zfm@solomon.com.sb – **4)** 24h Pacific stream satellite relay – **5)** 24h English for the Pacific satellite relay – **6)** Catholic Communications Solomons, PO Box 647, Honiara ☎ +677 22125 🖷 +677 36333 **E:** ambrose@donbosco.org.sb **L.P:** Father Ambrose Pereira. **F.PI:** Pupuraka FM, Visale – **7)** Isabel Province Community FM Network, c/o Office of the Premier, PO Box 4, Buala, Isabel Province. **D.Prgr:** 0600-1100 UTC daily. **N:** SIBC local news 0730.
Note: Each stn is solar powered using 0.03kW actual power, and operates independently for each village area. Local commercial and family messages are also broadcast – **8)** Gold Ridge Mining Ltd, Guadalcanal. **L.P:** GM Jeff Alexander **D.Pgr:** 0600-2200 (local) daily

SOMALIA

L.T: UTC +3h — **Pop:** 10 million — **Pr.L:** Somali, Rahanwein (Maay), Arabic, English — **E.C:** 50Hz, 220V — **ITU:** SOM

BAR-KULAN RADIO (a joint project by Albany Associates, African Union Mission and United Nations) **W:** bar-kulan.com **E:** contactE@bar-kulan.com **L.P:** Dir: Abdirahman Omar Osman. Senior Editor: Salah Diriye. **FM:** Bosaaso 89.5MHz, Galkayo 89.5MHz, Mogadishu 92.0MHz 3.5kW, Baidoa 92.0MHz.
DALSAN RADIO: Mogadishu 91.5MHz. **W:** dalsanradio.com
GOAL RADIO, Mogadishu: 99.0MHz.
MOGADISHU CITY RADIO, Mogadishu: 102.8MHz.
MUSTAQBAL RADIO: Mogadishu 97.7MHz. **W:** mustaqbalradio.com
RADIO BANADIR: Mogadishu 103.5MHz. **W:** radiobanadir.com
RADIO DANAN: Mogadishu 94.0MHz. **W:** radiodanan.net
RADIO JUBBA: Mogadishu 99.5MHz. **W:** jubaradio.net
RADIO KULMIYE: Mogadishu 88.0MHz. **W:** kulmiyenews.com
RADIO MANTA, Mogadishu 95.5MHz.
RADIO MOGADISHU ("Voice of the Republic of Somalia", controlled by the Transitional Federal Government). Mogadishu 88.8/99.9MHz. **W:** radiomuqdisho.net
RADIO RISAALA: Mogadishu 102.2MHz. Also rel. BBC. **W:** risaala.net
RADIO SHABELLE: Marka 92.0MHz, Mogadishu 101.5MHz. Also rel. BBC. **W:** shabelle.net
RADIO SIMBA: Mogadishu 95.0MHz 1kW. **W:** simbanews.com **E:** simba@simbanews.com
STAR FM, Mogadishu: 97.0MHz. See main entry under Kenya.
STN R, Mogadishu: 98.5MHz.
VOICE OF DEMOCRACY (RADIO XAMAR): Mogadishu: 93.5MHz. **W:** xamarradio.com

XURMO RADIO: Mogadishu 96.0MHz. **W**: xurmo.net

SOMALILAND
(self-declared autonomous state in northwest Somalia)

RADIO HARGEISA

Nala soo xidhiidh, Head Quarter, Near SLNTV, Hargeisa. ☎00252-2-523094 **W**: radiohargaysa.net **E**: radiohargaysa@hotmail.com **LP**: Dir: Said Adam Ege.
Hargeisa: **MW**: 693kHz. **SW**: 7120kHz 100kW (irreg.) **FM**: 89.0MHz.
D.Prgr in Somali: 0300-2100, SW 0300-0500, 0900-1400, 1500-1830. **N**. in E: 1300, 1930.
Ann: "Halkani wa Radio Hargeysa, codka jamhuriyada Somaliland".

BBC Somali Sce: Hargeisa 89.7MHz.
Voice of America: Hargeisa 88.0MHz.

PUNTLAND
(self-declared autonomous state in northeast Somalia)

AL-XIKMA RADIO: Bacadweyn/Burtinle/Gaalkacyo/Garowe/Qardho 90.0MHz, Bosaso 92.0MHz. **W**: alxigma.piczo.com
HORSEED RADIO: Bosaso 89.2MHz 1kW. **W**: horseedmedia.net
ONE NATION RADIO: Garowe 88.8MHz, Bosaso 89.5MHz. **W**: 1nationradio.com
RADIO DALJIR: Burtinle/Garowe 88.0MHz, Bosaso/Buuhoodle/Cabudwaq/Qardho 88.8MHz, Galkacyo 89.1MHz. Also r. VOA. **W**: radiodaljir.com
RADIO GAALKACYO: Gaalkacyo 88.2MHz, Garowe 89.0MHz. **W**: radiogaalkacyo.net
RADIO GAROWE: Eyl 88.8MHz, Garowe 89.5MHz. **W**: garoweonline.com
RADIO HOBYO: Gaalkacyo 87.5MHz. **W**: hobyoradio.com
RADIO MIDNIMO: Bosaso 97.5MHz.
RADIO SBC: Garowe 88.5MHz, Qardho 88.7MHz, Bosaso 89.9MHz. **W**: allsbc.com
RADIO VOICE OF MUDUG: Gaalkacyo 89.5MHz. Relays R. Bar-Kulan. **W**: codamudug.com
RADIO VOICE OF PEACE: Gaalkacyo 88.8MHz, Bosaso 89.5MHz. Also r. BBC Somali Sce

SOUTH AFRICA

L.T: UTC +2h — **Pop**: 53 million — **Pr.L**: English, Afrikaans, isiNdebele, isiXhosa, isiZulu, Sepedi, Sesotho, Setswana, siSwati, Tshivenda, xiTsonga — **E.C**: 50Hz, 230V — **ITU**: AFS — **Int. dialling code**: +27

SOUTH AFRICAN BROADCASTING CORPORATION (SABC) (Pub)

Private Bag X1, Auckland Park 2006 ☎ +27 11 714 9111 🖷 +27 11 714 9744 **W**: www.sabc.co.za **Regional offices**: PO Box 2551, Cape Town 8000 – PO Box 1588, Durban 4000 – PO Box 563, Bloemfontein 9300 – PO Box 1040, Port Elizabeth 6000 – PO Box 395, Polokwane 0700 – PO Box 2724, Nelspruit 1200 – PO Box 1008, Kimberley 8300 – Private Bag X2158, Mafikeng 2735 – PO Box 1198, Hatfield (Pretoria) 0001. **LP**: Chmn: Dr. Ben Ngubane. Group CEO: Lulama Mokhobo. Acting COO: Hlaudi Motsoeneng. CTO: Richard Waghorn.
NB: All txs belong to SENTECH (the common carrier for broadcasting in South Africa), Private Bag X06, Honeydew 2040

MW HOME SERVICES (Comm.)

Location	Station	kHz	kW
Komga	Umhlobo Wenene FM	846	100
Welgedacht	Ligwalagwala FM	1287	2

COUNTRYWIDE FM (Comm.)

Limpopo FM (MHz)	R. Sonder Grense	SAfm	R. 2000	5 FM	R. Metro
Blouberg	102.3	105.9	-	-	-
Hoedspruit	102.0	105.6	98.5	-	-
Louis Trichardt	100.7	104.3	97.2	-	-
Modimolle	102.9	106.5	-	-	-
Mokopane	101.4	105.0	97.9	91.4	106.7
Thabazimbi	101.9	105.5	98.4	-	-
Tzaneen	102.6	106.2	107.7	-	-

NW Province FM (MHz)	R. Sonder Grense	SAfm	R. 2000	5 FM	R. Metro
Christiana	103.6	107.2	-	-	-
Groot Marico	102.3	105.9	-	-	-
Klerksdorp	101.2	104.8	97.7	-	-
Piet Plessis	102.8	106.4	-	-	-

FM (MHz)	R. Sonder Grense	SAfm	R. 2000	5 FM	R. Metro
Pomfret	101.1	104.7	-	-	-
Rustenburg	100.7	104.3	97.2	-	-
Schweizer-Reneke	103.1	106.7	99.6	-	-
Zeerust	102.6	106.2	99.1	-	-
Gauteng FM (MHz)	R. Sonder Grense	SAfm	R. 2000	5 FM	R. Metro
Heidelberg	100.8	104.4	97.3	-	-
Helderkruin	-	-	-	104.0	-
Johannesburg	101.5	105.1	99.7	98.0	96.4
Menlo Park	102.1	105.7	98.6	-	-
Pretoria	101.0	104.6	97.5	89.9	92.4
Sunnyside	-	-	-	103.6	-
Welverdiend	102.0	105.6	104.1	107.3	-
Mpumalanga FM (MHz)	R. Sonder Grense	SAfm	R. 2000	5 FM	R. Metro
Carolina	103.0	106.6	-	-	-
Davel	103.5	107.1	100.0	90.4	-
Dullstroom	100.8	104.4	-	-	-
Lydenburg	102.8	106.4	-	-	-
eMalahleni	101.8	105.4	98.3	97.0	100.3
Nelspruit	102.5	106.1	99.0	91.1	-
Piet Retief	102.1	105.7	-	-	-
Sabie	104.2	107.9	-	-	-
Volksrust	102.6	106.2	-	-	-
Northern Cape FM (MHz)	R. Sonder Grense	SAfm	R. 2000	5 FM	R. Metro
Alexander Bay	102.2#	105.8#	98.7	92.2	-
Calvinia	101.5	105.1	-	-	-
Carnavon	102.5	106.1	-	-	-
Colesberg	103.8	107.5	-	-	-
De Aar	102.0	105.6	-	-	-
Douglas	102.9	106.5	-	-	-
Faans Grove	103.0	106.6	-	-	-
Garies	100.7#	104.3#	-	-	-
Kimberley	101.0	104.6	97.5	91.0	-
Kuruman Hills	102.4	106.0	-	-	-
Pofadder	102.8	106.4	-	-	-
Prieska	100.8	104.4	-	-	-
Sringbok	101.6	105.2	-	-	-
Upington	101.7	105.3	-	-	-
Victoria West	101.1	104.7	-	-	-
Williston	103.2	-	-	-	-
Free State FM (MHz)	R. Sonder Grense	SAfm	R. 2000	5 FM	R. Metro
Bethlehem	101.9	105.5	98.4	-	-
Bloemfontein	103.0	106.8	99.5	91.6	98.1
Boesmanskop	101.2	104.8	-	-	-
Ficksburg	103.7	107.3	-	-	-
Kroonstad	103.4	107.0	99.9	93.4	-
Ladybrand	102.1	105.7	-	-	-
Petrus Steyn	102.3	105.9	98.8	-	-
Senekal	101.1	104.7	97.6	-	-
Springfontein	102.6	106.2	99.1	-	-
Theunissen	102.5	106.1	99.0	92.5	-
Witsieshoek	101.3	104.9	-	-	-
Kwazulu Natal FM (MHz)	R. Sonder Grense	SAfm	R. 2000	5 FM	R. Metro
Donnybrook	102.7	106.3	99.2	-	-
Durban	100.8	104.4	97.3	89.9	93.0
Durban North	102.5	106.1	99.0	103.8	107.9
Eshowe	103.4	107.0	99.9	-	90.3
Glencoe	103.1	106.7	99.6	-	-
Greytown	101.7	105.3	98.2	-	-
Kokstad	101.0	104.6	-	-	-
Ladysmith	101.0	104.6	97.5	-	-
Matatiele	101.5	105.1	-	-	-
Mooi River	102.2	105.8	98.7	-	-
Nongoma	102.9	106.5	99.4	-	89.8
Pietermaritzburg	101.4	105.0	97.9	100.3	-
Port Shepstone	101.3	104.9	97.8	-	-
The Bluff	102.0	105.6	98.5	107.4	-
Ubombo	102.4	106.0	98.9	-	-
Vryheid	101.2	104.8	97.7	-	-
Western Cape FM (MHz)	R. Sonder Grense	SAfm	R. 2000	5 FM	R. Metro
Beaufort West	100.7@	104.3@	-	-	-
Constantiaberg	102.1	105.7	98.6	89.0	-
Ceres	103.7	107.3	-	-	-
Franschhoek	100.7	104.3	97.2	-	-
George	101.7	105.3	98.2	91.7	-
Grabouw	101.7	105.3	-	-	-
Hermanus	100.8	104.4	-	-	-
Hex River	102.0	105.6	-	-	-
Hout Bay	100.9	104.5	97.4	87.8	-

FM (MHz)	R. Sonder Grense	SAfm	R. 2000	5 FM	R. Metro
Kleinmond	104.2	107.9	-	-	-
Knysna	102.2	105.8	98.7	92.2	-
Ladysmith	101.4	105.0	-	-	-
Matjiesfontein	102.8	106.4	-	-	-
Montagu	104.2	107.9	-	-	-
Napier	102.4	106.0	-	-	-
Oudtshoorn	102.6	106.2	99.1	92.6	-
Paarl	101.6	105.2	98.1	88.5	-
Piketberg	101.1	104.7	97.6	-	-
Plettenberg	100.8	104.4	-	-	-
Riversdale	100.9	104.5	-	-	-
Sea Point	103.5	107.1	100.0	90.4	91.7
Simonstown	100.7	104.3	97.2	87.6	-
Stellenbosch	100.9	104.5	97.4	87.8	-
Table Mountain	102.6	106.2	99.1	89.9	88.6
Tygerberg	103.0	106.6	99.5	88.2	93.0
Uniondale	103.4	107.0	-	-	-
Vanrhynsdorp	103.4	107.0	-	-	-
Villiersdorp	103.3	106.9	99.8	-	-

Eastern Cape FM (MHz)	R. Sonder Grense	SAfm	R. 2000	5 FM	R. Metro
Aliwal North	101.7	105.3	-	-	-
Andrieskraal	103.2	106.8	-	-	-
Barkly East	100.9	104.5	-	-	-
Bedford	100.8	104.4	-	-	-
Burgersdorp	103.9	107.6	-	-	-
Butterworth	101.1	104.7	97.6	-	-
Cala	103.4	107.0	-	-	-
Cradock	102.7	106.3	-	-	-
East London	101.6	105.2	98.1	88.5	107.7
Elliot	101.4	105.0	-	-	-
Graaff-Reinet	103.3	106.9	-	-	-
Grahamstown	103.5	107.1	100.0	90.4	-
Hankey	101.0	104.6	-	-	-
Kareedouw	102.9	106.5	-	-	-
King Williams Tn	103.0	106.6	-	-	-
Mount Ayliff	103.2	106.8	99.7	-	-
Noupoort	101.4	105.0	-	-	-
Patensie	101.5	105.0	-	-	-
Parsons Hill (PE)	101.0	104.6	97.5	-	87.9
Paul Sauer Dam	103.6	107.2	-	-	-
Port Elizabeth	102.3	105.9	98.8	89.2	100.5
Port St.Johns	103.7	107.3	100.2	-	-
Queenstown	102.2	105.8	98.7	-	-
Suurberg	101.8	105.4	-	-	-
Ugie	102.6	106.2	-	-	-
Umtata	102.0	105.6	98.5	-	-
Willowmore	101.2	104.8	-	-	-

mono – no RDS, @ = mono RDS

NATIONAL SW SERVICES: Meyerton (G.C: 26S35 028E08): 4 x 100kW txs + 1 standby tx

kHz	Sce.	H of tr	kHz	Sce.	H of tr
3320	RSG	1700-0500	9650	RSG	0800-1700
7285	RSG	0500-0800			

RSG=R. Sonder Grense (tr for Northern Cape region) – details below.

SABC PUBLIC BROADCASTING SERVICES (PBS) (Comm.)
Ikwekwezi FM: (isiNdebele): ✉ P.O.Box 11982, Hatfield 0028 **W:** www.ikwekwezifm.co.za ☎+27 12 431 5301 📠+27 12 431 5312 - **FM(MHz):** Middelburg 91.8/Kwamhlanga 93.8/Dullstroom 107.7/Johannesburg 106.3/Davel 94.5 + 4 rel. – **Lesedi FM:** (Sesotho): ✉ Private Bag X20707, Bloemfontein 9300 **W:** www.lesedifm.co.za ☎+27 51 503 3091 📠+27 51 503 3270 - **FM(MHz):** Bloemfontein 89.9/Johannesburg 88.4/Kroonstad 90.3MHz + 14 rel. – **Ligwalagwala FM:** (siSwati): ✉ Private Bag X11301, Nelspruit 1200 **W:** www.ligwalagwalafm.co.za ☎+27 13 759 6600 📠+27 13 755 3865 - **FM(MHz):** Nelspruit 92.5/Pretoria 89.3MHz + 10 FM rel. and on MW 1287kHz – **Lotus FM:** ✉ Private Bag X1337, Durban 4000 **W:** www.lotusfm.co.za ☎ +27 31 362 5445 📠 +27 31 362 5202 **FM(MHz):** Durban 87.7/Johannesburg 106.8/Pretoria 100.1 + 8 rel. – **Motsweding FM:** (Setswana): ✉ Private Bag X2158, Mmabatho 2735 **W:** www.motswedingfm.co.za ☎+27 18 389 7104 📠+27 18 389 7326 - **FM(MHz):** Mmabatho 88.7/Johannesburg 89.6/Pretoria 91.0/Rustenburg 87.6MHz + 24 rel. – **Munghana Lonene FM:** (xiTtsonga): ✉ PO Box 395, Polokwane 0700 **W:** www.munghanalonenefm.co.za ☎+27 15 290 0262 📠+27 15 290 0171 - **FM(MHz):** Johannesburg 103.2/Pretoria 95.6/Tzaneen 92.6/Nelspruit 89.4MHz + 4 rel. – **Phalaphala FM:** (Tshivenda): ✉ PO Box 395, Polokwane 0700 **W:** www.phalaphalafm.co.za ☎+27 15 290 0260 📠+27 15 290 0170 - **FM(MHz):** Johannesburg 107.8/Tzaneen 99.1MHz + 6 rel. – **Radio Sonder Grense** (National service in Afrikaans): ✉ PO Box 91312, Auckland Park 2006 **W:** www.

rsg.co.za ☎+27 11 714 2702 📠+27 11 714 6445 - on FM and SW as above – **Radio X-K** FM (in !Xu and Khwe languages for Khoi San communities in N.Cape): ✉ PO Box 1008, Kimberley 8300 ☎+27 53 831 8131 📠+27 53 831 8127 - **FM(MHz):** Schmidtsdrift 99.4.– **R.2000:** ✉ Private Bag X1, Auckland Park 2006 **W:** www.radio2000.co.za ☎+27 11 714 4085 📠+27 11 714 4085 - **FM:** (as above) – **SAfm** (Nat. sce in English): ✉ PO Box 91162, Auckland Park 2006 **W:** www.safm.co.za ☎ +27 11 714 4442 📠+27 11 714 4585 - **FM:** (as above) – **Thobela FM:** (Sepedi): ✉ PO Box 395, Polokwane 0700 **W:** www.thobelafm.co.za ☎+27 15 297 1848 📠+27 15 290 0172 - **FM(MHz):** Johannesburg 90.1/Pretoria 87.9/Tzaneen 89.5MHz + 10 rel. – **TruFM:** (isiXhosa & English): ✉ Private Bag X0037, Bhisho 5605 **W:** www.trufm.co.za ☎+27 40 635 0117 📠+27 40 635 0125 - **FM(MHz):** East London 104.1/Bhisho 100.3 + 2 rel. – **Ukhozi FM:** (isiZulu): ✉ PO Box 1588, Durban 4000 **W:** www.ukhozifm.co.za ☎+27 31 362 5111 📠+27 31 362 5203 - **FM(MHz):** Durban 90.8, 92.0, 92.5/Johannesburg 91.5/Pretoria 102.4MHz + 21 rel. – **Umhlobo Wenene FM:** (isiXhosa): ✉ PO Box 1040, Port Elizabeth 6000 **W:** www.uwfm.co.za ☎+27 41 391 1911 📠 +27 41 373 2702 - **FM(MHz):** Port Elizabeth 92.3/King Williams Town 93.0/Durban 96.2/Johannesburg 93.2/Cape Town 92.1MHz + 48 FM rel. and on MW 846kHz

SABC COMMERCIAL BROADCASTING SERVICES (CBS) (Comm.)
Good Hope FM: ✉ PO Box 2551, Cape Town 8000 **W:** www.goodhopefm.co.za ☎ +27 21 430 8276 📠 +27 21 434 3392 - **FM:** Cape Town 95.3MHz + 1 rel. – **R.Metro FM:** ✉ PO Box 91136, Auckland Park 2006 **W:** www.metrofm.co.za ☎ +27 11 714 2658 📠 +27 11 714 4166 - **FM:** (as above). – **5 FM:** ✉ PO Box 91555, Auckland Park 2006 **W:** www.5fm.co.za ☎ +27 11 714 2905 📠 +27 11 714 5714 - **FM:** (as above)

EXTERNAL SERVICE: Channel Africa: See Int. Broadc. section

INDEPENDENT COMMUNICATIONS AUTHORITY OF SOUTH AFRICA (ICASA)
✉ Private Bag X10002, Sandton 2146 ☎ +27 11 566 3000 📠 +27 11 566 3464 **E:** info@icasa.org.za **W:** www.icasa.org.za
The ICASA is the regulator of telecommunications and the broadcasting sectors. It issues licences for commercial and community stns.

PRIVATE STATIONS (Comm.)

MW	kHz	kW	Station	Location
1)	567	25	Cape Talk	Klipheuwel (Cape Town)

FM	MHz	kW	Station	Location
2)	89.0	-	M-Power FM	Piet Retief
2)	89.7	-	M-Power FM	Sabie
3)	89.8	-	North West FM	Rustenburg
4)	89.9	-	Capricorn FM	Thohoyandou
3)	91.8	-	North West FM	Mmabatho
3)	91.9	-	North West FM	Taung
5)	92.7	-	Talk R. 702	Johannesburg
3)	93.5	-	North West FM	Zeerust
6)	93.7	5	OFM	Sasolburg
7)	93.9	10	KFM	Beaufort West
7)	93.9	3	KFM	Garies
8)	93.9	6	R. Jacaranda	Rustenburg
8)	93.9	15	R. Jacaranda	Louis Trichardt
9)	94.0	5	Algoa FM	Bedford
8)	94.0	10	R. Jacaranda	Dullstroom
6)	94.0	9	OFM	Prieska
10)	94.0	25	East Coast R.	Durban
11)	94.0	0.1	Highveld Stereo	Heidelberg
7)	94.0	0.1	KFM	Hermanus
7)	94.1	13	KFM	Riversdale
8)	94.2	33	R. Jacaranda	Pretoria
9)	94.2	0.1	Algoa FM	Parson's Hill
10)	94.2	0.1	East Coast R.	Ladysmith
6)	94.2	-	OFM	Barkly West
6)	94.2	-	OFM	Boshof
6)	94.2	10	OFM	Kimberley
6)	94.3	-	OFM	Ventersburg
6)	94.3	12	OFM	Senekal
7)	94.3	10	KFM	Piketberg
2)	94.3	-	M-Power FM	Nelspruit
10)	94.4	10	East Coast R.	Vryheid
6)	94.4	10	OFM	Klerksdorp
10)	94.5	10	East Coast R.	Port Shepstone
7)	94.5	1.3	KFM	Tygerberg
7)	94.6	2.5	KFM	Ladismith
8)	94.6	10	R. Jacaranda	Mokopane
10)	94.6	0.3	East Coast R.	Pietermaritzburg
9)	94.6	10	Algoa FM	Noupoort

FM	MHz	kW	Station	Location
9)	94.6	-	Algoa FM	Colesberg
9)	94.6	-	Algoa FM	Middelburg
12)	94.7	-	Gagasi FM	North Coast
10)	94.7	12	East Coast R.	Matatiele
11)	94.7	38	Highveld Stereo	Johannesburg
7)	94.7	10	KFM	Calvinia
7)	94.8	17	KFM	Springbok
2)	94.8	-	M-Power FM	Carolina
8)	94.8	0.3	R. Jacaranda	Enzelberg
9)	94.8	10	Algoa FM	East London
7)	94.9	10	KFM	George
7)	94.9	-	KFM	Grabow
6)	94.9	8	OFM	Upington
10)	94.9	10	East Coast R.	Greytown
9)	94.9	10	Algoa FM	Aliwal North
9)	94.9	-	Algoa FM	Barkley East
9)	95.0	-	Algoa FM	Somerset East
9)	95.0	11	Algoa FM	Port Elizabeth
8)	95.0	11	R. Jacaranda	eMalahleni
6)	95.1	10	OFM	Bethlehem
8)	95.1	11	R. Jacaranda	Thabazimbi
8)	95.2	18	R. Jacaranda	Hoedspruit
7)	95.2	-	KFM	Hex River
11)	95.2	20	Highveld Stereo	Welverdiend
10)	95.2	0.1	East Coast R.	The Bluff
8)	95.3	9	R. Jacaranda	Piet Retief
6)	95.3	10	OFM	Ladybrand
9)	95.4	12	Algoa FM	Queenstown
10)	95.4	10	East Coast R.	Mooi River
7)	95.4	-	KFM	Alexander Bay
7)	95.4	0.2	KFM	Knysna
8)	95.5	0.1	R. Jacaranda	Groot Marico
8)	95.5	0.2	R. Jacaranda	Blouberg
6)	95.5	11	OFM	Petrus Steyn
9)	95.5	-	Algoa FM	Jeffreys Bay
9)	95.5	-	Algoa FM	Uitenhage
9)	95.5	16	Algoa FM	Port Elizabeth
10)	95.6	15	East Coast R.	Ubombo
6)	95.6	11	OFM	Kuruman Hills
7)	95.6	3	KFM	Napier
10)	95.7	6	East Coast R.	Durban North
8)	95.7	12	R. Jacaranda	Nelspruit
6)	95.7	10	OFM	Theunissen
6)	95.7	-	OFM	Welkom
7)	95.7	10	KFM	Carnavon
7)	95.8	9	KFM	Oudtshoorn
8)	95.8	10	R. Jacaranda	Volksrust
8)	95.8	11	R. Jacaranda	Zeerust
8)	95.8	12	R. Jacaranda	Tzaneen
6)	95.8	-	OFM	Colesberg
6)	95.8	-	OFM	Springfontein
10)	95.9	10	East Coast R.	Donnybrook
9)	95.9	12	Algoa FM	Cradock
13)	95.9	35	Kaya FM	Johannesburg
4)	96.0	-	Capricorn FM	Mokopane
7)	96.0	10	KFM	Matjiesfontein
7)	96.0	5	KFM	Pofadder
6)	96.1	9	OFM	Douglas
8)	96.1	0.2	R. Jacaranda	Modimolle
10)	96.1	10	East Coast R.	Nongoma
9)	96.1	-	Algoa FM	Plattenberg Bay
9)	96.1	-	Algoa FM	Cape St. Francis
9)	96.2	10	Algoa FM	King Williams Town
9)	96.2	-	Algoa FM	Bisho
6)	96.2	10	OFM	Bloemfontein
8)	96.2	9	R. Jacaranda	Carolina
10)	96.3	10	East Coast R.	Glencoe
6)	96.3	-	OFM	Warrenton
6)	96.3	-	OFM	Vryburg
6)	96.3	10	OFM	Schweitzer-Reineke
9)	96.5	-	Algoa FM	Pearson
9)	96.5	-	Algoa FM	Aberdeen
9)	96.5	10	Algoa FM	Graaf-Reinet
7)	96.5	10	KFM	Villiersdorp
7)	96.6	17	KFM	Vanrhynsdorp
10)	96.6	10	East Coast R.	Eshowe
6)	96.6	10	OFM	Kroonstad
9)	96.7	-	Algoa FM	Port Alfred
9)	96.7	10	Algoa FM	Grahamstown
8)	96.7	10	R. Jacaranda	Davel
6)	96.8	5.5	OFM	Christiana
10)	96.9	0.1	East Coast R.	Newcastle

FM	MHz	kW	Station	Location
7)	96.9	20	KFM	Ceres
6)	96.9	-	OFM	Ficksburg
3)	97.0	-	North West FM	Klerksdorp
6)	97.1	-	OFM	Potchefstroom
7)	97.1	-	KFM	Kleinmond
7)	97.1	-	KFM	Montagu
3)	97.3	-	North West FM	Schweitzer-Reineke
4)	97.6	-	Capricorn FM	Tzaneen
4)	98.0	-	Capricorn FM	Hoedspruit
12)	98.5	0.3	Gagasi FM	Pietermaritzburg
14)	99.2	35	Y-FM	Johannesburg
12)	99.5	25	Gagasi FM	Durban
12)	100.1	6	Gagasi FM	Durban North
2)	101.6	-	M-Power FM	Dullstroom
15)	102.7	0.1	Heart 104.9	Paarl
16)	102.7	35	Classic FM	Johannesburg
12)	103.5	-	Gagasi FM	Port Shepstone
15)	104.9	1.3	Heart 104.9	Tygerberg
4)	105.4	-	Capricorn FM	Makhado
2)	105.8	-	M-Power FM	Standerton
2)	106.4	-	M-Power FM	eMalahleni

Addresses and other information:

1) Private Bag X567, Vlaeberg 8018 ☎ +27 21 446 4700 🖷 +27 21 446 4800 LP: Colleen Louw W: www.capetalk.co.za E: feedback@capetalk.co.za – **2)** PO Box 361, Nelspruit, 1200 ☎ +27 13 757 9700 🖷 +27 13 757 0248 LP: Mark Schormann W: www.mpowerfm.co.za E: contact@mpowerfm.co.za – **3)** Postnet Suite 215, Private Bag X3172, Rustenburg 0300 ☎ +27 14 594 8960 🖷 +27 14 597 3345 LP: Shadrack Menyatswe W: www.northwestfm.co.za E: shadrack.menyatswe@gmail.com – **4)** Postnet Suite 93, Private Bag X9676, Polokwane, 0700 ☎ +27 15 291 0815 🖷 +27 15 291 0822 LP: Simphiwe Mdlalose W: www.capricornfm.co.za E: info@capricornfm.co.za – **5)** PO Box 5572, Rivonia 2128. ☎ +27 11 506 3702 🖷 +27 (11) 506 3663 W: www.702.co.za E: comment@702.co.za – **6)** PO Box /11/, Bloemfontein 9300 ☎ +27 51 505 0900 🖷 +27 51 505 0905 LP: Gary Stroebel W: www.ofm.co.za E: info@ofm.co.za – **7)** Private Bag X945, Cape Town, 8000 ☎ +27 21 446 4700 🖷 +27 21 446 4800 LP: Colleen Louw W: www.kfm.co.za E: comments@kfm.co.za – **8)** PO Box 11961, Centurion 0046 ☎ +27 12 673 9100 🖷 +27 12 657 0105 LP: Alan Khan W: www.jacarandafm.com E: info@jacarandafm.com – **9)** PO Box 5973, Walmer, 6065 ☎ +27 41 505 9497 🖷 +27 41 583 5555 LP: Dave Tiltmann W: www.algoafm.co.za E: dave.t@algoafm.co.za – **10)** P.O. Box 25095, Gateway, Umhlanga Rocks 4321 ☎ +27 31 570 9495 🖷 +27 86 679 4951. LP: Trish Taylor W: www.ecr.co.za E: auntyhazel@ecr.co.za – **11)** PO Box 3438, Rivonia 2128 ☎ +27 11 506 3947 🖷 +27 11 506 3393 LP: Tery Volkwyn W: www.highveld.co.za E: comments@highveld.co.za – **12)** 6 Zenith Drive, Solstice, Umhlanga New Town Centre 4319 4001 ☎ +27 31 580 5300 🖷 +27 31 566 3403 LP: Pearl Sokhulu W: www.gagasi995.co.za E: management@gagasi995.co.za – **13)** PO Box 434, Newtown, 2113 W: www.kayafm.co.za ☎ +27 11 634 9500 🖷 +27 11 634 9574 LP: Charlene Deacon E: pr@kayafm.co.za – **14)** cor.Albury Rd. & Dunkeld Cresc., South West Blocks, Dunkeld West Ext.8, Sandton 2196 ☎ +27 11 772 0800 🖷 +27 11 280 0421 LP: Kanthan Pillay W: www.yworld.co.za E: kanthan@yfm.co.za – **15)** PO Box 211, Greenpoint 8051 ☎ +27 21 406 8900 🖷 +27 21 406 8940 LP: Gavin Meiring W: www.1049.fm E: info@1049.fm – **16)** PO Box 782, Auckland Park 2006 ☎ +27 11 403 1027 🖷 +27 11 408 5451 LP: Mike Ford W: www.classicfm.co.za E: info@classicfm.co.za

COMMUNITY STATIONS
Numerous licences issued by ICASA with about 140 stns currently on the air, mainly on FM, most of them low power.

MW	kHz	kW	Station	Location
1)	576	10	R. Veritas	Meyerton
2)	657	50	R. Pulpit/R.Kansel	Meyerton
3)	1422	1	Hellenic R.	Bedfordview
4)	1485	1	R. Today	Honeydew
5)	1548	10	R. Islam	Lenasia

Addresses and other information:
1) PO Box 4599, Edenvale 1610 W: www.radioveritas.co.za ☎ +27 11 663 4700 🖷 +27 11 452 7625 LP: Emil Blaser OP, expected to come on air in 2012 – **2)** PO Box 3436, Pretoria 0001 W: www.radiokansel.co.za or www.radiopulpit.co.za ☎ +27 12 334 1200 🖷 +27 12 334 1400 Relig. prgrs in English and Afrikaans, 24h– **3)** PO Box 4077, Edenvale 1610 ☎ +27 11 453 3794 🖷 +27 11 453 3778 W: www.hellenicradio.org.za E: info@hellenicradio.org.za LP: George Zoulis, Prgrs in Greek and English 24h – **4)** PO Box 2820, Parklands 2121 W: www.1485.org.za ☎ +27 11 880 0329 🖷 +27 86 601 2950 E: info@1485.org.za Prgrs in English for over 50s 24h. – **5)** PO Box 2580, Lenasia 1820 W: www.radioislam.co.za ☎ +27 11 854 7022 🖷 +27 11 854 7024 Prgrs in English, 24h.

SOUTH SUDAN

L.T: UTC +3h — **Pop:** 9 million — **Pr.L:** Dinka, Arabic — **E.C:** 50Hz, 240V — **ITU:** SSD

MINISTRY OF INFORMATION AND BROADCASTING
✉ Juba ☎+211 922 260000 **W:** goss-online.org/magnoliaPublic/en/ministries/Information-and-Broadcasting.html **LP:** DG: Mr. Mustafa Biong Majak Koul.

SOUTH SUDAN RADIO (Gov.)
✉ P.O. Box 126, Juba ☎+211 912 452275 **LP:** DG: Mr. Arop Bagat.
MW: Bentiu 558kHz, Juba 693kHz 100kW, Malakal 909kHz 5kW, Wau 1071kHz 5kW. **NB:** MW frequencies r. irr. **FM:** Bentiu 99.0MHz.

MIRAYA FM (Joint project by UNMIS and Hirondelle Foundation)
✉ P.O. Box 69, Plot 16-17,Block 25, New Bridge St, Manshiya, Khartoum ☎+249 1 87087777 🖷 +249 1 87089465 **W:** mirayafm.org **E:** mirayasudan@mirayafm.org **LP:** Editor-in-Chief: Jean-Claude Labreque. TD: Sonam Tobgyal.
FM: Juba/Malakal/Rumbek/Wau 5kW, Torit/Yambio/Maridi/Yei/Bor 1kW, all on 101.0MHz. 24h in Arabic, Juba Arabic and English.
F.PI: txs in Khartoum and Darfur in Sudan, also on 101.0MHz.
Relays on shortwave: see International Radio section.

SUDAN RADIO SERVICE (A project by Educational Dev. Center)
✉ P.O. Box 425, Plot 48 ,Block I Korok, Juba ☎ +249 922 486 6982
W: sudanradio.org **E:** info@sudanradio.org
LP: Chief of Party: Jon Newstrom.
FM: Juba 98.6MHz 2kW.
Relays on shortwave: see International Radio section.

Other Stations (FM MHz):
Capital FM, Juba: 101.0 – **Liberty FM,** Yei: 90.0 – **R. Jonglei,** Bor: 95.9 – **R. Rumbek FM,** Rumbek: 98.0 – **Spirit FM,** Yei: freq. unk. – **Voice of Life,** Kakwa & Madi: 100.9.
Internews stations: **Mayardit FM,** Turalei 90.7 1kW – **Naath FM,** Leer/Nasir 88.0 1/2kW – **Nhomlaau FM,** Malualkon 88.0 1kW – **R. Al-Mujtama,** Kurmuk 99.0 500W – **VO Community,** Kauda: 88.0 300W.
Sudan Catholic R. Netw. (rlg.): **Bakhita R,** Juba: 91.0 – **R. Don Bosco,** Tonj: 91.0 2kW – **R. Easter,** Yei: 94.0 1kW – **R. Emmanuel,** Torit: 89.0 – **R. Good News,** Rumbek: 89.0 2.5kW – **VO Love,** Malakal: 93.6 2kW – **VO Peace,** Gidel: 107.9. **W:** sudancatholicradio.net
BBC World Sce, Juba: 88.2 (English), 90.0 (Arabic).
DW/Monte-Carlo Doualiya: Juba 90.4. **R. France Int:** Juba 90.4

SPAIN

L.T: UTC +1h (31 Mar-27 Oct: +2h) — **Pop:** 40.5 million — **Pr.L:** Castilian, Catalan, Galician, Basque — **E.C:** 50Hz, 230V — **ITU:** E

MINISTERIO DE FOMENTO
Secretaría General de Comunicaciones
✉ Paseo de la Castellana, 67, Palacio de Comunicaciones, 28071 Madrid **W:** www.fomento.gob.es **E::** fomento@fomento.es

RADIO NACIONAL DE ESPAÑA (RNE) (Pub)
✉ Casa de la Radio, Avenida de la Radio y la Televisión, 4, Prado del Rey, 28223 Pozuelo de Alarcón ☎ +34 91 581 70 00 🖷 +34 91 346 1769 **W:** www.rne.es **E::** secretaria@rtve.es
RNE1 (R. Nacional) and **RNE5** (R. 5 Todo Noticias)

MW	kHz	kW	Net	Rg	Location
AS01)	531	20	RNE5TN	AS	Oviedo °
AN02)	531	10	RNE5TN	AN	Córdoba °
GA02)	531	10	RNE5TN	GA	Pontevedra
NA01)	531	10	RNE5TN	NA	Pamplona °
VA01)	558	50	RNE5TN	VA	València °
GA01)	558	20	RNE5TN	GA	A Coruña °
EU02)	558	10	RNE5TN	EU	Donosti-San Sebastián
MU01)	567	50	RNE5TN	MU	Murcia °
CA01)	576	100	RNE5TN	CA	Barcelona °
MA01)	585	600	RNE1	MA	Madrid °
AN01)	603	50	RNE5TN	AN	Sevilla °
CL02)	603	10	RNE5TN	CL	Palencia °
CA02)	612	10	RNE1	CA	Lleida (relay)
EU01)	612	10	RNE1	EU	Vitoria-Gasteiz °
AN04)	621	10	RNE1	AN	Jaén (relay)
BA01)	621	10	RNE1	BA	Palma de Mallorca °
CL03)	621	10	RNE1	CL	Ávila (relay)
GA01)	639	300	RNE1	GA	A Coruña °
AR01)	639	10	RNE1	AR	Zaragoza °

MW	kHz	kW	Net	Rg	Location
EU03)	639	50	RNE1	EU	Bilbo-Bilbao (relay)
AN05)	639	20	RNE1	AN	Almería (relay)
CM03)	639	10	RNE1	CM	Albacete (relay)
EX02)	648	10	RNE1	EX	Badajoz (relay)
MA01)	657	50	RNE5TN	MA	Madrid °
AN01)	684	600	RNE1	AN	Sevilla °
AS01)	693	5	RNE1	AS	Boal (rel. of Oviedo)
CM01)	693	10	RNE1	CM	Toledo °
CA03)	693	10	RNE1	CA	Tortosa (rel.of Cataluñya)
AS01)	729	100	RNE1	AS	Oviedo °
AN06)	729	20	RNE1	AN	Málaga
RI01)	729	20	RNE1	RI	Logroño °
CL01)	729	10	RNE1	CL	Valladolid °
CM04)	729	10	RNE1	CM	Cuenca
VA02)	729	10	RNE1	VA	Alacant-Alicante (relay)
CA01)	738	600	RNE1	CA	Barcelona °
AN07)	747	10	RNE5TN	AN	Cádiz
VA01)	747	100	RNE1	VA	València °
EX01)	774	60	RNE1	EX	Cáceres °
EU02)	774	50	RNE1	EU	Donosti-San Sebastián
GA03)	774	10	RNE1	GA	Ourense (relay)
AN08)	774	10	RNE1	AN	Granada (relay)
AN09)	774	10	RNE1	AN	La Línea (relay)
CL04)	774	10	RNE1	CL	León (relay)
CL05)	774	10	RNE1	CL	Soria (relay)
CM05)	801	25	RNE1	CM	Ciudad Real (relay)
GA04)	801	20	RNE1	GA	Lugo (relay)
CA04)	801	10	RNE1	CA	Girona (relay)
CL06)	801	10	RNE1	CL	Burgos
CL07)	801	10	RNE1	CL	Zamora
VA03)	801	10	RNE1	VA	Castelló (relay)
MU01)	855	300	RNE1	MU	Murcia °
CT01)	855	50	RNE1	CT	Santander °
CA03)	855	20	RNE1	CA	Tarragona (relay)
GA02)	855	20	RNE1	GA	Pontevedra (relay)
AN10)	855	10	RNE1	AN	Huelva (relay)
AR02)	855	10	RNE1	AR	Teruel (relay)
CL08)	855	10	RNE1	CL	Ponferrada (relay)
CL09)	855	10	RNE1	CL	Salamanca (relay)
NA01)	855	10	RNE1	NA	Pamplona-Iruñea °
AN03)	855	5	RNE1	AN	Marbella (relay)
CM02)	864	10	RNE1	CM	Socuellamos (rel.of Toledo)
BA01)	909	5	RNE5TN	BA	Palma de Mallorca °
AR01)	936	20	RNE5TN	AR	Zaragoza °
CL01)	936	20	RNE5TN	CL	Valladolid °
VA02)	936	10	RNE5TN	VA	Alacant-Alicante
AN11)	972	5	RNE1	AN	Cabra (rel.of Sevilla)
GA05)	972	2	RNE1	GA	Monforte de Lemos (relay)
AN08)	1017	10	RNE5TN	AN	Granada
CL06)	1017	10	RNE5TN	CL	Burgos°
AN05)	1098	25	RNE5TN	AN	Almería
GA04)	1098	20	RNE5TN	GA	Lugo
CL03)	1098	10	RNE5TN	CL	Avila
AN10)	1098	5	RNE5TN	AN	Huelva
RI01)	1107	25	RNE5TN	RI	Logroño °
CT01)	1107	20	RNE5TN	CT	Santander °
EX01)	1107	20	RNE5TN	EX	Cáceres °
AR02)	1107	10	RNE5TN	AR	Teruel (rel.of zaragoza)
CL08)	1107	10	RNE5TN	CL	Ponferrada (rel.of León)
CL05)	1125	10	RNE5TN	CL	Soria
CM01)	1125	10	RNE5TN	CM	Toledo °
EU01)	1125	10	RNE5TN	EU	Vitoria-Gasteiz °
VA03)	1125	10	RNE5TN	VA	Castelló
EX02)	1125	5	RNE5TN	EX	Badajoz
AN06)	1152	20	RNE5TN	AN	Málaga
CA02)	1152	10	RNE5TN	CA	Lleida
CL07)	1152	10	RNE5TN	CL	Zamora
CM03)	1152	10	RNE5TN	CM	Albacete
MU02)	1152	10	RNE5TN	MU	Cartagena
GA03)	1305	25	RNE5TN	GA	Ourense
CM05)	1305	20	RNE5TN	CM	Ciudad Real
EU03)	1305	20	RNE5TN	EU	Bilbo-Bilbao
CL04)	1305	10	RNE5TN	CL	León
CM04)	1314	10	RNE5TN	CM	Cuenca
CA03)	1314	10	RNE5TN	CA	Tarragona
CL09)	1314	10	RNE5TN	CL	Salamanca
MA01)	1359	200	RNE1	MA	Madrid (irregular)
GA06)	1413	20	RNE5TN	GA	Vigo
AN04)	1413	10	RNE5TN	AN	Jaén
CA04)	1413	5	RNE5TN	CA	Girona
AN09)	1503	5	RNE5TN	AN	La Linea (rel.of Cádiz)
GA05)	1503	5	RNE5TN	GA	Monforte de Lemos (rel. Lugo)

° = regional key stn

FM	Location	RNE1	RNE2	RNE3	RNE4	RNE5	kW
Andalucía							
AN08)	Baza	92.6	97.3	87.8			5
AN02)	Cabra	95.1	89.5	103.8		88.0	1
AN02)	Córdoba					99.8	2
AN08)	Granada	104.2	96.4	94.4		98.5	1
AN01)	Guadalcanal		90.6				5
AN07)	Jerez	103.5	94.5	96.7		106.3	10
AN02)	Lagar de la Cruz	92.2	97.5	98.6			10
AN06)	Málaga			99.2	104.0	92.5	1
AN03)	Marbella					87.6	1
AN06)	Mijas	106.6	98.1	99.8		88.0	10
AN08)	Parapanda	103.0	91.1	93.9			5
AN05)	Pechina	100.9	92.4	94.9		106.7	5
AN10)	Punta Umbria	95.2	92.6	99.0		88.8	5
AN06)	Ronda	106.1	99.3	91.6		102.3	1
AN04)	Sierra Almadén	105.4	90.0	96.0			10
AN08)	Sierra Lújar	96.7	90.4	94.2			5
AN07)	Tajo	105.0	94.0	103.1			5
AN01)	Valencina	91.2	93.7	98.8		90.0	5
Aragon							
AR02)	Alcañiz	89.5				99.3	1
AR03)	Arguis	100.9	94.4	103.7		92.8	5
AR03)	Barbastro	89.6	97.4	105.1		100.2	1
AR01)	Caspe	90.2	99.0			103.7	1
AR01)	Ejea de los C.	94.8	98.9	106.4		91.2	
AR03)	Fraga	95.0	96.3	102.2		98.8	1
AR01)	Inogés	89.4	92.4	99.7		105.0	5
AR03)	Jaca	103.7	94.4	100.3		98.7	1
AR02)	Javalambre		90.0	93.9			1
AR01)	La Muela	94.5	90.9	96.3		103.6	10
AR02)	Montalban	90.5	92.7	96.4		105.1	
AR02)	Peracense	88.3	98.1	100.6		106.1	
AR02)	Teruel	104.7	89.2	94.5		95.6	1
Asturias							
AS01)	Avilés	100.0	87.9	95.6		102.9	1
AS01)	Boal	93.2	97.8	88.2		90.5	1
AS01)	Cangas Narcea	97.2	99.0	87.7		90.9	1
AS01)	Cangas Onis	88.8	92.5	104.0		100.3	1
AS01)	Gamoniteiro	102.5	92.2	94.4		104.4	10
AS02)	Gijón	99.2	98.5	102.0		89.9	5
AS01)	Ibias	95.8	98.7	102.9		105.1	1
AS01)	Llanes	106.1				97.3	1
AS01)	Los Oscos	89.7	104.0	105.7		96.1	1
AS01)	Luarca	96.8	93.8	100.3			1
AS01)	Mieres					101.8	1
AS01)	Oviedo	89.4	96.0	90.3		99.6	1
AS01)	Peñamelleras	93.9	96.4	100.7		104.6	
AS01)	San Martín	88.3	96.7	100.2		93.3	1
Baleares							
BA01)	Alfabia	90.1	87.9	92.3		104.5	10
BA01)	Ibiza	101.6	104.0	105.7		94.9	1
BA01)	Menorca	94.6	97.1	105.8		100.4	1
BA01)	Pollensa	93.2	95.4	97.4		99.7	1
Cantabria							
CT03)	Embalse Ebro	89.0	94.0	98.2		101.9	1
CT01)	Liérganes	96.9	93.0	102.9		105.0	10
CT02)	Torrelavega	99.5	97.9	103.4		89.4	1
Catalunya							
CA02)	Alpicat	94.6	89.2	97.8	87.9		10
CA02)	Baquéira	92.2	87.7	89.0	93.3		1
CA02)	Bossost	94.4	100.5	105.2	102.3		1
CA01)	Collserola	88.3	93.0	98.6	100.8	99.0	20
CA01)	Collsuspina	92.2	97.9	103.1	104.7		1
CA01)	Igualada	89.4	90.9	105.1	106.9		1
CA03)	Monte Caro	104.3	96.6	99.6	90.7		5
CA01)	Montserrat	94.3	99.0		103.8	98.8	2
CA03)	Musara	106.5	91.5	94.5	88.8	94.0	5
CA01)	Sant Pere Ribes	92.7	95.2	97.5	106.3	101.3	1
CA04)	Rocacorba	93.3	91.1	95.9	106.2	94.0	5
CA02)	Soriguera	99.9	103.6	106.4	90.6	97.2	1
CA03)	Ulldecona	95.0					1
CA02)	Viella	90.0	96.2	104.4	102.6		1
Castilla-León							
CL06)	Aranda Duero	90.0	92.7	101.6		106.2	1
CL03)	Arenas Pedro	102.4	90.3				1
CL03)	Avila	87.6	92.0	97.8		102.4	1
CL09)	Béjar	99.9	101.6	104.7			5
CL07)	Benavente	87.8	91.3	97.9		100.2	1
CL05)	Burgo Osma	96.1	98.4	88.7		102.8	1
CL06)	Burgos	93.6	90.3	91.2		106.6	1
CL04)	Castropodame	103.3	93.0	99.9		105.9	5
CL02)	Cervera	88.6	94.8	97.3		100.4	1
CL09)	El Cabaco	102.9	92.4	95.4			5
CL02)	Guardo	89.8	105.6			104.0	1
CL04)	León	97.1	91.1	89.3		102.2	1

FM	Location	RNE1	RNE2	RNE3	RNE4	RNE5	kW
CL02)	Palencia	91.8	101.0	97.6		88.0	1
CL06)	Pancorbo	89.7	92.0	101.7		104.5	1
CL07)	Pbla Samabria	93.6	103.5	100.3		91.9	1
CL09)	Salamanca	94.5	88.1	91.4		102.2	1
CL10)	Segovia	97.0				91.5	1
CL05)	Soria	89.7	91.5	94.3		104.7	2
CL01)	Valladolid	97.3	93.1	92.2		95.1	5
CL04)	Villablino	98.1	89.0	91.4		99.4	1
CL06)	Villadiego			102.3	103.3		1
CL04)	Villafranca	90.9	89.7	97.5		104.1	1
CL07)	Zamora	101.8	96.7	98.5		88.8	5
Castilla La Mancha							
CM03)	Almansa	91.2	98.6	95.6		94.4	1
CM03)	Chinchilla	91.8	93.6	99.0		106.3	5
CM05)	Ciudad Real	95.7	92.8	94.1		88.8	1
CM04)	Cuenca	105.6	93.0	92.0		96.1	1
CM06)	Guadalajara	103.7	93.5	96.9		102.1	1
CM05)	La Mancha	101.0	89.8	94.5		106.0	10
CM05)	Puertollano	93.1	99.1	91.8		101.8	5
CM05)	Socuéllamos	94.0					1
CM01)	Talavera	97.8	105.5	94.7		89.4	5
CM01)	Toledo	102.0	103.9	106.4		99.9	1
CM05)	Valdepeñas	92.6	95.5	97.3		102.1	
Euskadi							
EU03)	Archanda	100.7	90.6	99.2		96.3	5
EU03)	Azcoitia	88.7	104.9	106.9			1
EU02)	Beasain	100.2	98.4	94.9			1
EU02)	Eibar	92.9	98.7	95.9			1
EU02)	Jaizquibel	104.7	90.0	92.1			10
EU02)	Monte Igueldo	87.6	99.5	98.9		93.3	1
EU03)	Oiz	106.4	105.3	102.1			5
EU01)	San León					93.3	1
EU03)	Sollube	105.5	93.9	95.4			5
EU02)	Tolosa	101.9	98.8	96.0			1
EU01)	Vitoria-Gasteiz	92.5	96.9	99.5		89.4	1
Extremadura							
EX02)	Badajoz	94.9	90.1	92.2		106.0	1
EX01)	Cáceres	95.1	101.7	93.7		88.2	1
EX02)	Mérida					101.3	1
EX01)	Montánchez	105.3	99.7	99.3			5
EX01)	Plasencia	88.6		99.3		104.4	1
Galicia							
GA03)	Barco	94.7	96.4	100.3		104.6	
GA02)	Domayo	90.1	92.1	97.4			5
GA04)	Monforte					88.8	1
GA03)	Monte Meda	102.8	91.2	94.3		106.8	5
GA01)	Monte Xalo	100.4	91.6	94.5		95.8	10
GA03)	Ourense	100.6	97.2	99.4		95.1	5
GA04)	Páramo	101.7	88.2	99.6		92.8	5
GA04)	Piedrafita	89.4	92.6	105.3		95.2	
GA02)	Pontevedra		88.3				1
GA07)	Santiago	103.1	98.1	99.0		93.7	5
GA03)	Verin	90.7	98.4	106.4		94.1	1
GA06)	Vigo					96.0	5
GA04)	Xistral	89.5	93.6	104.2		106.6	1
Madrid							
MA01)	Navacerrada	104.9	98.8	95.8			30
MA01)	Torrespaña	88.2	96.5	93.2		90.3	10
Murcia							
MU01)	Carrascoy	101.7	98.2	96.0		92.1	5
MU02)	Cartagena	102.9	94.5	97.5		103.5	1
MU01)	Jumilla	89.1	93.1	100.1			1
MU01)	Yecla	88.8	93.4	103.7			1
Navarra							
NA01)	Estella	89.0	101.2	100.5		90.9	1
NA01)	Gorramendi	88.3	99.0	100.6		95.3	1
NA01)	Ibañeta	89.6	93.8	103.4		101.9	1
NA01)	Isaba	90.3	95.1	103.0		91.8	1
NA01)	Leire	88.9	101.0	99.6		90.5	1
NA01)	Lesaka	90.6	94.8	97.0		102.2	1
NA01)	Monreal	106.1	97.5	93.0		95.7	5
NA01)	Pamplona	104.8	97.1	102.3		103.7	
NA01)	San Miguel	96.7	100.0	90.3		102.7	1
NA01)	Tudela	100.9	102.2	91.3		88.3	1
La Rioja							
RI01)	Logroño	95.4	88.1	89.9		97.2	1
RI01)	Moncalvillo	102.0	88.5	94.6		103.3	40
RI01)	Monte Yerga	87.6	106.8	96.5		105.4	1
Comunitat Valenciana							
VA01)	Aitana	104.8	88.6	99.7			10
VA02)	Alcoi	95.8	92.3	91.1		105.9	1
VA02)	Alicante	105.2	99.4	97.1		103.6	
VA03)	Benicasim	89.3	90.3	92.8		95.5	5
VA02)	Benidorm	87.6	97.8	102.1			
VA02)	Elda	93.9	88.1	97.6			1

FM	Location	RNE1	RNE2	RNE3	RNE4	RNE5	kW
VA01	Monduber	97.4	99.3	100.1			5
VA01	Monte Picayo	89.8	106.6	95.1		88.2	10
VA01	Ontinyent	100.7	96.7	102.4			1
VA02	Santa Pola	92.5	100.1	94.3		104.2	5
VA02	Santa Pola					105.8	5
VA01	Utiel	98.1	96.6	89.1		87.9	1
VA02	Villena	90.7	97.1	101.1			1

RNE1 R. Nacional: (MW and FM): 24h. **N:** On the h. Regional prgrs from key stn of each region: Mon-Fri 0625-0630, 0650-0700 (//R5TN), 1208-1300, 1400-1415, 1845-1900 (only Canaries, Galicia, La Rioja, Murcia & Navarra), Sat & Sun 1230-1300 (//R5TN),– **RNE2 R.Clásica:** (FM): Classical music & cultural prgrs: 24h – **RNE3:** (FM): Young people's music prgr: 24h – **RNE4:** (FM): Regional network in Catalunya: 24h. in Catalán – **RNE5TN:** (MW and FM): 'Todo Noticias' - All news: 24h 0625-0630 (//RN), 0650-0700 (//RN), Local: 0800-0815 Mon-Fri

Addresses for RNE regional key stns:
AN Andalucia: Edif.RTVE, Parque del Alamillo, Isla de la Cartuja,41092 Sevilla – **AR Aragón**: José Luís Albareda 1-3, 50004 Zaragoza – **AS Asturias**: Calle San Esteban de las Cruces 92, 33195 Oviedo – **BA Balears**: Aragó 26, 07006 Palma de Mallorca – **CA Catalunya**: C. Roc Boronat 127, 08018 Barcelona – **CL Castilla y León**: García Morato 27-29, 47007 Valladolid – **CM Castilla La Mancha**: Plaza de San Cristóbal s/n, 45002 Toledo – **CT Cantabria**: Polígono de Raos s/n, 39609 Camargo (Santander) – **EU Euskadi**: Plaza de Simón Bolívar 13, 01003 Vitoria-Gasteiz – **EX Extremadura**: Av. Ruta de la Plata 10, 10001 Cáceres – **GA Galicia**: Paseo Méndez Nuñez 12, 15006 A Coruña – **MA Madrid**: Casa de la Radio, Prado del Rey, 28223 Pozuelo de Alarcón – **MU Murcia**: La Olma 27-29, 30005 Murcia – **NA Navarra**: Calle Aoiz, 31004 Pamplona-Iruñea – **RI La Rioja**: Vara de Rey 42, 26002 Logroño – **VA Comunitat Valenciana**: Av.Colóm 13, 46004 València.

OTHER STATIONS:
Only stns with MW broadcasts and FM networks are listed. A number of other stns are heard irr. There are approx. 2.400 FM stns

NATIONAL NETWORKS:
(ABC) ABC Punto Radio (Comm) Belongs to Grupo Vocento
C/Juan Ignacio Luca de Tena 7, 28027 Madrid ☎ +34 91-3399 600 🖷 +34 91-7417589 **W:** www.abc.es/radio **W stn list:** www.abc.es/radio/emisoras **E:** emisoras@puntoradio.com
(COPE) CADENA DE ONDAS POPULARES ESPANOLAS (Comm)
⌨ Alfonso XI N° 4, 28014 Madrid ☎ +34 91-3090000 🖷 +34 91-5317517 **W:** www.cope.es **E:** programas.madrid@cadenacope.net
Local and regional programming on AM and FM stns: Mon-Fri 0555, 0624, 0650, 0724, 1809-1859, generally at xx27 and xx57 0757-1700, 1930, 2030, 2130, 2230, 2355, 2357. Sat xx27 and xx57 0757-1400, 1557, 1657, 1810, 1840, 1910, 1940, 2040, 2257, 2330. Sun xx27 and xx57 0957-1300, xx10 and xx40 1510-1840, 2157, 2330. **Cadena 100** (music on FM only) **W:** www.cadena100.es **E:** jplane@cadena100.es **Gestiona Radio** (business prgr. on FM) **W:** www.gestionaradio.com
(D) CADENA DIAL (Comm) Belongs to Grupo Prisa
⌨ Gran Vía 32, 28013 Madrid ☎ +34 91-3470880 🖷 +34 91-5211753 **W:** www.cadenadial.com **E:** ccampillo@cadenadial.com
(EFM) EUROPA FM (Comm) Belongs to Grupo Antena 3
⌨ Fuerteventura 12, 28703 San Sebastian de los Reyes ☎+34 91-4366400 🖷+34 91-4366116 **W:** www.europafm.es
(ES) esRADIO (Comm)
⌨ C/ Juan Esplandiú 13, 28007 Madrid. **W:** www.esradio.fm ☎+34 91-4094766 🖷+34 91- 4094899
(HFM) Hit FM (Comm) Belongs to Grupo KISS Media
⌨ José Isbert 6, Ciudad de la Imagen - 28223 Pozuelo de Alarcón **W:** www.hitfm.es
(IE) INTERECONOMÍA (Comm)
⌨ Paseo de la Castellana 36-38, 20846 Madrid. **W:** www.intereconomia.com **E:** redaccion@intereconomia.com ☎+34 90-2996556 🖷+34 91- 5771314
(KFM) KISS FM (Comm)
⌨ José Isbert 6, Ciudad de la Imagen - 28223 Pozuelo de Alarcón **W:** www.kissfm.es **E:** kissfm@kissfm.es ☎+34 91-4440490 🖷+34 91-8379189
(LFM) LOCA FUN RADIO (Comm) Belongs to RTL Group France
⌨ C/ Enrique Larreta 12 bajo izq., 28036 Madrid **W:** www.locafunradio.es **E:** info@locafunfm.es ☎+34 90-2302024
(I40) Los 40 Principales (Comm) Belongs to Grupo Prisa
⌨ Gran Vía 32, 7ª planta, 28013 Madrid **W:** www.los40.es **E:** los40@los40.com ☎ +34 91-3477700 🖷 +34 91-5228693
(MFM) MAXIMA FM (Comm) Belongs to Grupo Prisa
⌨ C/ Gran Vía 32, 7ª planta, 28013 Madrid **W:** www.maxima.fm **E:** ADSanchez@prisaradio.com☎+34 91-3477624 🖷+34 91-5325808- Dir: Toni Sánchez

(M80) M-80 RADIO (Comm) Belongs to Grupo Prisa
⌨ Gran Vía 32, 7ª planta, 28013 Madrid **W:** www.m80radio.com **E:** aalvarez@m80radio.com ☎ +34 91-3477700 🖷 +34 91-5228693 Dir: Angel Alvarez
(OCR) ONDA CERO RADIO (Comm)
⌨ C/ Fuerteventura 12, 28703 San Sebastián de los Reyes, Madrid ☎ +34 91-4366400 🖷 +34 91-5386332 **W:** www.ondacero.es **E:** ondacero@ondacero.es **Prgrs: Onda Melodia**. Local and regional prgr on AM: Mon-Fri 0527, 0555, 0620, 0655, 0720, 0827, 0855, 0927, 0955, 1025, 1130, 1400, 1527, 1557, 1627, 1657, 1727, 1757, 1800, 2030, 2130, 2230, 2257, 2340, 0030. Sat-Sun 0527, 0727, 0757, 0827, 0857, 0927, 0957, 1027, 1227, 1457, 1850, 2255, 2320, 2340. Times vary.
(RA) RADIO TELEVISION AMISTAD (Rlg)
⌨ Apartado 269, 08211 Castellar del Vallés (Barcelona). 🖷+34 93-7242380 **W:** www.rtvamistad.net **E:** info@rtvamistad.tv
(RKM) RKM RADIO (Rlg)
⌨ Carretera de Ajalvir a Daganzo km 1.7, Ajalvir, 28864 Madrid. ☎ +34 91- 8844180 **W:** www.rkmradio.com **E:** madrid@rkmradio.com
(RM) RADIO MARIA (Rlg)
⌨ Paseo de Lanceros 2 (Centro Comercial), Planta 1ª, 28024 Madrid ☎+34 90-2500518 🖷 +34 91-7057727 **W:** www.radiomaria.es **E:** radiomaria@radiomaria.es
(RMA) RADIO MARCA (Comm)
⌨AvenidadeSanLuís25,28033Madrid.☎+3490- 2996111 **W:** www.marca.com **E:** radiomarca@marca.com Dir: Francisco Garcia Caridad
(RO) Radiolé (Comm) Belongs to Grupo Prisa
⌨ Gran Vía 32, , 7ª planta, 28013 Madrid ☎ +34 91-3477740 🖷 +34 91-5324769 **W:** www.radiole.com **E:** direccion@radiole.com Dir: Miguel Ángel Corral Salas
(ROCK) ROCK FM (Comm) Belongs to Grupo COPE
⌨ Alfonso XI N° 4, 28014 Madrid ☎ +34 91-5951210 🖷 +34 91-3090721 **W:** www.rockfm.fm
(SER) SOCIEDAD ESPANOLA DE RADIODIFUSION (Comm)
Belongs to Grupo Prisa
⌨ Gran Vía 32, , 7ª planta, 28013 Madrid ☎ +34 91-3477700 🖷 +34 91-3470779 **W:** www.cadenaser.com **E:** redaccion@cadenaser.com **FM** stns Local and regional prgr on AM stns: Mon-Fri 0550, 0620, 0650, 0720, 0827, 0855, 0930, 0957, 1003, 1030, 1057, 1120, 1410, 1530, 1630, 1720, 1810-1855, 1925, 2157, 2255, 2330, 0000, 0030, 0159, 0259. Sat-Sun 0750, 0855, 0955, 1055, 1105 and xx23 or xx53 in the evening. Times vary.

REGIONAL NETWORKS
(AR) ARAGON RADIO
⌨ María Zambrano 2, 50018 Zaragoza. ☎ +34 876-256500 🖷 +34 876-256519 **W:** www.aragonradio.es **E:** jmartinez@cartv.es Director de Marketing : Javier Martinez López(
(CR) CORPORACIO CATALANA DE MITJANS AUDIOVISUALS
⌨ Av. Diagonal 614-616, 08021 Barcelona ☎ +34 93-3069200 🖷 +34 93-3069201 **W:** www.catradio.cat **E:** correu@catradio.com
Prgrs: Catalunya Ràdio; Catalunya Informació; Catalunya Música
(CER) CANAL EXTREMADURA RADIO
⌨ Av. de las Américas 1, 1°, 06800 Mérida (Badajoz). ☎ +34 924-382000 **W:** http://radio.canalextremadura.es **E:** cexma@canal-extremadura.es
(CSR) CANAL SUR RADIO
⌨ Carretera Edificio Canal Sur. Avda. José Gálvez 1, 41092 Isla de la Cartuja, Sevilla ☎ +34 95-5054600 🖷 +34 95- 5054740 **W:** www.canalsur.es **E:** comunicacion@rtva.es Prgrs: Canal Fiesta: (Int. music and Spanish pop and rock music); Canal Sur Radio: (Andalucian and Spanish music, news and sports); Radio Andalucía Información.
(EI) EUSKA IRRATI TELEBISTA – RADIO TELEVISION VASCA
⌨ EiTB Donostia: Paseo Miramon 172, 20014 Donostia-San Sebastián ☎ +34 94-30116 00 🖷 +34 94-301 1995 – ⌨ EiTB Bilbao: Capuchinos de Basurto 2, 48013 Bilbo-Bilbao ☎ +34 94-6563000 🖷 +34 94-6563095 – ⌨ EiTB Vitoria: Domingo Martinez de Aragón, 5-7 bajo, 01006 Vitoria-Gasteiz ☎ +34 94-5012500 🖷 +34 94-5012695 – ⌨ EiTB Iruña: Calle Tomás Caballero 2, 31005 Pamplona-Iruña ☎ +34 94-8012200 🖷 +34 94-8153485.**Prgrs:** Euskadi Irratia (AM + FM), R. Euskadi (AM + FM), R. Vitoria (AM + FM), EiTB Músika (FM), Gaztea Irratia (FM) **W:** www.eitb.com **E:** info@eitb.com
(GR) GRUP FLAIX (Comm)
⌨ Passeig de Gràcia 55, novena planta, 08007 Barcelona. ☎ +34 93-5055555 🖷 +34 93-4880776
Prgs: Flaix FM and Flaixbac **W:** www.flaixfm.cat and www.radioflaixbac.com **E:** flaixfm@grupflaix.cat & flaixbac@grupflaix.cat
(IB3) IB3 RADIO ⌨ C/ Manuel Azaña 7-A, 07006 Palma de Mallorca. ☎ +34 971-139931 🖷 +34 971-139930 **W:** http://ib3tv.com/portada-radio **E:** info@eprtvib.com
(OC) ONA CATALANA (Comm) Belong to Grupo Prisa
⌨ C/ Casp 6, 08010 Barcelona ☎ +34 93-3441400 **W:** www.ona-

fm.cat **E** : info@onafm.cat

(OM) ONDA MADRID
Paseo del Príncipe 3, 28223 Pozuelo de Alarcón (Madrid) ☎ +34 91-5128200 ⊜ +34 91-5128300
W: www.ondamadrid.es **E:** ondamadrid@ondamadrid.es

(ORM) ONDA REGIONAL MURCIA
Avda. Libertad 6, 30009 Murcia. ☎+34 968-200000 ⊜+34 968-272665 **W:** www.orm.es **E** : info@orm.es

(RAC) RAC (Comm) Belong Grupo Godò
Av. Diagonal 477, Planta 15, 08036 Barcelona ☎+34 93-2704400 ⊜+34 93-2704464 Prgrs: RAC1 and RAC 105. **W:** www.rac1.cat and www.rac105.cat **E:** rac1@rac1.net & rac105@rac105.net

(R9) RADIO AUTONOMIA VALENCIANA
Radiotelevisió Valenciana, Polígon Accés Ademús s/n, 46100 Burjassot, València ☎ +34 96-3183000 ⊜ +34 96-3183001 **Prgrs:** Sí Radio and Radio Nou **W:** www.rtvv.es/va/radio

(RCM) RADIO CASTILLA-LA MANCHA
Edificio RTVCM, C/ Río Alberche s/n, Polígono Santa María de Benquerencia, 45007 Toledo ☎ +34 925-288600 ⊜ +34 925-288607 **W:** www.rtvsm.es **E :** comercial@rtvcm.es

(RCL) RADIO CASTILLA Y LEÓN
Edificio Promecal Burgos, Avenida Castilla y León 62-64, 09006 Burgos. ☎ +34 947-266868 ⊜ +34 947-202752 **W:** www.rtvcyl.es **E:** burgos@rtvcyl.es

(RE) RÀDIO ESTEL (Rlg)
Comtes de Bell-lloc 67-69, 08014 Barcelona ☎ +34 93-4092770 ⊜ +34 93-4092775 **W:** www.radioestel.com **E:** estudis@radioestel.com
Dir: Jaume Aymar

(RG) RADIO GALEGA – COMPAÑÍA DE RADIO TELEVISION DE GALICIA Casa da Radio, Edificio de Usos Múltiples San Marcos, 15820 Santiago de Compostela ☎ +34 981-540640 ⊜ +34 981-540949 **W:** www.crtvg.es/rg **E :** info@crtvg.es

(RP) RADIO POPULAR - HERRI IRRATIA
Alameda Mazarredo 47, 48009 Bilbo-Bilbao ☎+34 94-4239200 ⊜+34 94-4234703 **W:** www.radiopopular.com **E:** direccion@radio-popular.com

(RPA) RADIO DEL PRINCIPADO DE ASTURIAS
Camino de las Clarisas 263, 33203 Gijón ☎+34 985-185900 ⊜ +34 985-185939 **W:** www.rtpa.es/radio **E:** comunicacion@rtpa.es

(RTT) RADIO TELE TAXI (Comm)
C/ Sant Carles 40, 08922 Sta Coloma de Gramenet (Barcelona) ☎+34 93-4665656 ⊜ +34 93-4661534 **W:** www.radioteletaxi.com **E:** radioteletaxi@radioteletaxi.com

(RV) RADIO VOZ
Av. De la Prensa 84-85, Arteixo, 15142 A Coruña ☎ +34 981-180600 ⊜ +34 981-180477 **W:** www.radiovoz.com **E:** director@radiovoz.com

(XAR) La XARXA (Comm)
Travessera de les Corts 131-159, 08028 Barcelona ☎ +34 93-5080600 **W:** www.xarxaradio.cat **E:** laxarxa@laxarxa.com

MW	kHz	kW	Net	Rg	Station, location	FM (MHz)
CA07)	540	50	OCR	CA	Onda Cero Catal., Barcelona	93.5
CA08)	666	50	SER	CA	R. Barcelona, Barcelona	93.9
MU05)	711	5	COPE	MU	COPE, Murcia	89.7
EU07)	756	10	EI	EU	R. Euskadi, Bilbo-Bilbao	91.7
CA09)	783	50	COPE	CA	COPE Miramar, Barcelona	
AN15)	792	50	SER	AN	R. Sevilla, Sevilla	97.1
MA05)	810	20	SER	MA	R. Madrid, Madrid	93.9
EU08)	819	10	EI	EU	R. Euskadi, Gasteiz-Vitoria	96.5
CA13)	828	5	HFM	CA	HIT FM Catalunya, Terrassa	95.5
AN16)	837	10	COPE	AN	COPE, Sevilla	99.6
CL15)	837	10	COPE	CL	COPE, Burgos	95.5
BA05)	837	5	COPE	BA	COPE, Eivissa	89.1
GA09)	837	5	COPE	GA	COPE, El Ferrol	88.7
AR05)	873	25	SER	AR	R. Zaragoza, Zaragoza	95.3
GA10)	873	10	SER	GA	R. Galicia, Stgo de Comp.	90.6
CA10)	882	50	XAR	CA	XARXA R., Barcelona	91.0
VA07)	882	10	COPE	VA	COPE, Alacant-Alicante	95.6
AN17)	882	5	COPE	AN	COPE, Málaga	89.4
AS05)	882	5	COPE	AS	COPE, Gijón	103.6
CL16)	882	5	COPE	CL	COPE, Valladolid	88.5
EU10)	900	10	RP	EU	R. Popular, Bilbo-Bilbao	97.8
AN18)	900	5	COPE	AN	COPE, Granada	88.2
EX05)	900	5	COPE	EX	COPE Alta Extremadura, Cáceres	88.8
EX05)	900	5	COPE	EX	COPE Alta Extremadura, Plasencia (rel.)	
GA11)	900	5	COPE	GA	COPE, Vigo	87.8
MA06)	918	20	IE	MA	R. Intereconomia, Madrid	95.1
MA13)	954	50	OCR	MA	Onda Cero R., Madrid	98.0
EU09)	963	5	EI	EU	R. Euskadi, Donostia-San Sebastián	90.9
EU11)	990	10	SER	EU	R. Bilbao, Bilbo-Bilbao	89.5
AN19)	990	5	SER	AN	R. Cádiz, Cádiz	89.4
MA08)	999	50	COPE	MA	COPE, Madrid	99.5

MW	kHz	kW	Net	Rg	Station, location	FM (MHz)
CA11)	1008	10	SER	CA	R. Girona, Girona	98.5
EX06)	1008	5	SER	EX	R. Extremadura, Badajoz	96.9
VA08)	1008	5	SER	VA	R. Alacant, Alacant-Alicante	91.0
CA12)	1026	10	SER	CA	R. Reus, Reus	97.7
AS06)	1026	5	SER	AS	R. Asturias, Oviedo	97.5
GA12)	1026	5	SER	GA	R. Vigo, Vigo	99.4
AN20)	1026	5	SER	AN	R. Jaén, Jaén	96.9
AN21)	1026	5	SER	AN	R. Jerez, J. de la Frontera	97.8
CL17)	1026	5	SER	CL	R. Salamanca, Salamanca	96.9
EU12)	1044	10	SER	EU	R. San Sebastián, Donosti-S Seb.	97.2
CL18)	1044	5	SER	CL	R. Valladolid, Valladolid	90.9
AR06)	1053	25	COPE	AR	COPE, Zaragoza	88.5
VA09)	1053	5	COPE	VA	COPE, Vila-Real	91.7
AN22)	1080	10	SER	AN	R. Granada, Granada	95.4
AR07)	1080	10	SER	AR	R. Huesca, Huesca	96.9
BA06)	1080	5	SER	BA	R. Mallorca, P. de Mallorca	94.1
CM11)	1080	5	OCR	CM	Onda Cero R., Toledo	100.8
GA13)	1080	5	SER	GA	R. Coruña, A Coruña	91.0
CM12)	1116	5	SER	CM	R. Albacete, Albacete	89.6
GA14)	1116	5	SER	GA	R. Pontevedra, Pontevedra	89.1
CL19)	1134	10	COPE	CL	COPE, Salamanca	90.0
AN23)	1134	5	COPE	AN	COPE, Jerez de la Frontera	92.4
BA07)	1134	5	COPE	BA	COPE, Ciutadella	89.6
CL20)	1134	5	COPE	CL	COPE, Astorga	87.6
CM13)	1134	5	COPE	CM	COPE, Puertollano	97.5
NA05)	1134	5	COPE	NA	COPE, Pamplona-Iruñea	87.9
AN24)	1143	5	COPE	AN	COPE, Jaén	88.8
AS07)	1143	5	COPE	AS	COPE, Oviedo	92.8
CA14)	1143	5	COPE	CA	COPE, Reus	89.7
GA15)	1143	5	COPE	GA	COPE, Ourense	92.4
VA10)	1179	50	SER	VA	R. València, València	94.2
RI05)	1179	2	SER	RI	R. Rioja, Logroño	91.7
EU09)	1197	50	EI	EU	Euskadi Irratia, Vitoria-Gasteiz	95.0
AN25)	1215	5	COPE	AN	COPE, Córdoba	87.6
CL21)	1215	5	COPE	CL	COPE, León	97.7
CT05)	1215	5	COPE	CT	COPE Cantabria, Santander	88.4
MU06)	1215	5	COPE	MU	COPE, Lorca	89.2
EU13)	1224	10	COPE	EU	COPE Guipúzcoa, Donostia-S. Seb.	88.5
AN26)	1224	5	COPE	AN	COPE, Huelva	91.9
AN27)	1224	5	COPE	AN	COPE, Almería	97.1
BA08)	1224	5	COPE	BA	COPE, Palma de Mallorca	97.6
CA15)	1224	5	COPE	CA	COPE, Lleida	97.4
CM14)	1224	5	COPE	CM	COPE, Albacete	95.4
GA16)	1224	5	COPE	GA	COPE, Lugo	90.0
AN28)	1260	5	SER	AN	R. Algeciras, Algeciras	95.7
MU07)	1260	5	SER	MU	R. Murcia, Murcia	91.3
CA16)	1269	10	COPE	CA	COPE Comarques Gironines, Figueres	102.9
CM15)	1269	10	COPE	CM	COPE, Ciudad Real	93.6
CL22)	1269	5	COPE	CL	COPE, Zamora	94.9
EX07)	1269	5	COPE	EX	COPE, Badajoz	89.1
CA17)	1287	10	SER	CA	R. Lleida, Lleida	93.4
CL23)	1287	5	SER	CL	R. Castilla, Burgos	89.1
GA17)	1287	5	SER	GA	R. Lugo, Lugo	91.8
VA11)	1296	50	COPE	VA	COPE, València	99.0
AN29)	1341	10	OCR	AN	Onda Cero R., Almería	88.2
CL24)	1341	5	SER	CL	R. León, León	88.2
CM16)	1341	5	OCR	CM	Onda Cero R., Ciudad Real	92.1
EU07)	1386	50	EI	EU	Euskadi Irratia, Bilbo-Bilbao	88.9
EU08)	1476	50	EI	EU	Euskadi Irratia, Donosti-San S.	94.4
CL25)	1485	10	SER	CL	R. Zamora, Zamora	89.8
CT06)	1485	10	SER	CT	R. Santander, Santander	90.9
AN30)	1485	6	OCR	AN	Onda Cero R., Antequera	96.3
CA18)	1485	5	ABC	CA	ABC Punto R., Vilanova	
VA12)	1485	5	SER	VA	R. Alcoi, Alcoi	96.3
VA13)	1521	5	SER	VA	R. Castelló, Castelló	94.8
VA14)	1539	6	SER	VA	R. Elche - R. Elx, Elx	99.1
CA19)	1539	5	SER	CA	R. Manresa, Manresa	95.8
NA06)	1575	10	SER	NA	R. Pamplona, Pamplona	92.2
AN31)	1575	5	SER	AN	R. Córdoba, Córdoba	96.6
GA18)	1584	5	SER	GA	R. Ourense, Ourense	87.6
VA15)	1584	5	SER	VA	R. Gandia, Gandia	96.5
EU09)	1602	25	EI	EU	R. Vitoria Gasteiz Irratia, Vitoria-Gasteiz	104.1
AN32)	1602	5	SER	AN	R. Linares, Linares	94.9
CL26)	1602	5	SER	CL	R. Segovia, Segovia	93.6
MU08)	1602	5	SER	MU	R. Cartagena, Cartagena	102.3
VA16)	1602	5	SER	VA	R. Ontinyent, Ontinyent	95.3

* = inactive

FM	MHz	kW	Net	Rg	Station, location
AN41)	87.6	5	CSR	AN	Canal Sur R., Santo Pitar,Málaga
AN35)	87.7	6	HIT	AN	HIT FM, Jerez de Frontera
CA34)	87.7	20	RAC	CA	RAC1, Barcelona Collserola
AN36)	87.9	5	SER	AN	R. Morón, Morón de la Frontera ,Sevilla
CA37)	88.0	25	CR	CA	Catalunya R., La Mussara, Tarragona
EU25)	88.0	5		EU	R. Nervión, Bilbao
AN37)	88.3	5	CSR	AN	Canal Fiesta R., Algeciras

FM	MHz	kW	Net	Rg	Station, location
CA25)	88.4	5	CR	CA	Catalunya R., Montcaro, Tortosa
CA25)	88.6	20	CR	CA	Catalunya Música, Soriguera, Lleida
CA35)	88.7	10		CA	R. RM, Barcelona Collserola
AN70)	88.8	40		AN	Stereo Vision, Sevilla
CA38)	88.9	25	CR	CA	Catalunya R., Rocacorba, Girona
EU07)	88.9	20	EI	EU	Euskadi Irratia, Bilbo-Bilbao
MU17)	88.9	5	RMA	MU	R,Marca, Murcia
MA05)	89.0	20	M80	MA	M80, Madrid
CA07)	89.1	8	RMA	CA	R,Marca,, Barcelona Collserola
EU20)	89.2	5		EU	Élite FM, Barakaldo,Bilbao
EU26)	89.2	5		EU	Segura Irratia, Segura, Vitoria
GA29)	89.2	8	RMA	GA	R. Marca, A Coruña
VA21)	89.2	8	OCR	VA	Kiss FM, Alacant-Alicante
NA11)	89.3	6	OCR	NA	Kiss FM, Pamplona
GA28)	89.4	6	RA	GA	Ondas de Vida, R. Amistad, Vigo
MU14)	89.4	6	COPE	MU	COPE, Cartagena
AN42)	89.5	20	CSR	AN	Canal Fiesta R., Huelva
BA11)	89.5	8	KFM	BA	Kiss FM, Palma de Mallorca
EX11)	89.5	6	KFM	EX	Kiss FM, Cáceres
AR13)	89.7	40	ABC	AR	ABC Punto R., Zaragoza
AN43)	89.8	8	CSR	AN	R. Andalucía Informacion, Granada
CA21)	89.8	10	ABC	CA	ABC Punto R., Barcelona Collserola
AS03)	89.8	8	RPA	AS	RPA, R.Principado Asturias, Gijón
CA36)	89.9	10	ABC	CA	ABC Punto R., Rocacorba, Girona
VA08)	90.0	8	MFM	VA	Maxima FM, Alicante
AN38)	90.1	8	KFM	AN	Kiss FM, Málaga
VA30)	90.1	5		VA	Peque R., Valencia
CA25)	90.2	10	CR	CA	Catalunya R., Sant Celoni, Barcelona
AN35)	90.3	6	OCR	AN	Onda Cero R., Jerez de la Frontera
EX12)	90.4	5	OCR	EX	Onda Cero Melodía, Mérida
AN57)	90.5	70	CSR	AN	RAI R.Andalucía Informacion, Almería
CA08)	90.5	8	M80	CA	M80, Barcelona Collserola
CL31)	90.5	5	SER	CL	SER R. Miranda, Miranda de Ebro Burgos
AN39)	90.8	5	SER	AN	SER R. Puerto, El Puerto de S.M., Cadiz
AN38)	90.8	10	OCR	AN	Onda Cero R., Málaga
AN59)	90.8	64	CSR	AN	RAI R.Andalucía Informacion, Sevilla
GA29)	90.8	5	RG	GA	R. Galega Música, Vigo
EU09)	90.9	20	EI	EU	R. Euskadi, Vitoria
MA11)	91.0	100	EFM	MA	Europa FM, Madrid
AS06)	91.1	6	D	AS	Cadena Dial Asturias, Oviedo
RI02)	91.1	6	COPE	RI	COPE Rioja, Logroño
EU07)	91.2	20	EI	EU	Euskadi Gaztea, Bilbo-Bilbao
CM08)	91.3	5	RCM	CM	R. Castilla-La Mancha, Guadalajara
AR04)	91.4	40	HIT	AR	HIT FM, Zaragoza
EX13)	91.4	10	SER	EX	Los 40, Plasencia
AN40)	91.4	8	EFM	AN	Europa FM, Córdoba
CL27)	91.5	8	KFM	CL	Kiss FM, Astorga
EU21)	91.5	8	OCR	EU	Kiss FM, Donosti-San Sebastián
EX05)	91.6	6	COPE	EX	COPE, Cáceres
VA17)	91.6	10	EFM	VA	Europa FM, La Ribera València
EU07)	91.7	20	EI	EU	R. Euskadi, Bilbo-Bilbao
MA05)	91.7	100	D	MA	Cadena Dial, Madrid
CL40)	91.7	5	KFM	CL	Kiss FM, Salamanca
VA08)	91.7	8	SER	VA	SER R. Alicante, Alicante
CA25)	91.9	15	CR	CA	Catalunya Música, Alpicat, Lleida
CA34)	91.9	10	RAC	CA	RAC105, Rocacorba, Girona
CM08)	91.9	5	RCM	CM	R. Castilla-La Mancha, Toledo
CT11)	91.9	6	OCR	CT	Onda Cero R., Santander
AR05)	92.0	40	SER	AR	Máxima FM, Zaragoza
CA25)	92.0	100	CR	CA	Catalunya Informaciò, Barcelona Collserola
VA29)	92.0	10	ABC	VA	ABC Punto R., València
MA05)	92.4	14	SER	MA	Radiolé, Madrid
CA25)	92.5	100	CR	CA	Catalunya R. Barcelona Collserola
EX08)	92.6	6	SER	EX	Los 40, Cáceres
GA21)	92.6	8	RV	GA	R. Voz, A Coruña
CM21)	92.7	6	KFM	CM	Kiss FM, Albacete
AN22)	92.8	8	D	AN	Cadena Dial, Granada
VA18)	92.8	6	EFM	VA	Europa FM, Elx-Elche
CL34)	92.9	6	ABC	CL	ABC Punto R., Burgos
AN43)	93.1	5	CSR	AN	Canal Fiesta R. Baza, Granada
AN72)	93.1	8	D	AN	Cadena Dial, Málaga
EU18)	93.1	8		EU	R.Gorbea, Vitoria-Gasteiz
GA22)	93.1	5	RV	GA	R. Voz,. Pontevedra
VA11)	93.1	8	ROCK	VA	ROCK FM, València
AN73)	93.2	5	ABC	AN	ABC Punto R., Sevilla
VA08)	93.2	8		VA	Cadena Dial, Alicante
CA25)	93.3	5	CR	CA	Catalunya R., Alfabia, Palma M.
GA13)	93.4	8	SER	GA	SER R. Coruña 2, A Coruña
CA30)	93.4	5	SER	CA	SER, R. LLeida
AR05)	93.5	8	SER	AR	R. Zaragoza 2, Zaragoza
CA25)	93.5	20	OCR	CA	Onda Cero R., Collserola Barcelona
AN47)	93.8	5	EFM	AN	Europa FM, Almería
AN72)	93.8	5	RO	AN	Radiolé, Málaga
MA05)	93.9	100	SER	MA	Los 40, Madrid
CA08)	93.9	8	SER	CA	Los 40, Collserola Barcelona
AN42)	94.0	10	CSR	AN	Canal Sur R., Huelva
GA23)	94.0	6	OCR	GA	Kiss FM, Vigo
GA07)	94.1	20	RG	GA	R. Galega, Santiago de Compostela
AN12)	94.2	5	ABC	AN	ABC Punto R., Jaén
CT03)	94.2	6	RMA	CT	R. Marca, Santander
AN59)	94.3	6	CSR	AN	RAI R.Andalucía Informacion., Sevilla
AN55)	94.3	10	CSR	AN	Canal Sur R., Córdoba
CL23)	94.3	6	D	CL	Cadena Dial, Burgos
CA11)	94.4	10	MFM	CA	Maxima FM,. Girona, Rocacorba
CL39)	94.4	8	EFM	CL	Europa FM, Valladolid
EU08)	94.4	20	EI	EU	Euskadi Irratia,Donosti-S Sebastián
EX08)	94.4	6	SER	EX	SER, Cáceres
CA25)	94.5	5	CR	CA	Catalunya Informaciò, Collsuspina Barcelona
AN43)	94.6	5	CSR	AN	Canal Fiesta R., Loja,Granada
EU07)	94.7	20	EI	EU	Euskadi Gaztea, Bilbo-Bilbao
AN15)	94.8	40	M80	AN	M80, Sevilla
AN41)	94.9	60	CSR	AN	RAI R.Andalucía Informacion. Málaga
CA07)	94.9	20	EFM	CA	Europa FM, Collserola Barcelona
CM10)	95.0	6		CM	R. Surco, Albacete
EU09)	95.0	20	EI	EU	Euskadi Irratia, Vitoria-Gasteiz
AN43)	95.1	5	CSR	AN	Canal Sur R., Granada
CA11)	95.1	10	D	MA	Cadena Dial Girona, Rocacorba
MA17)	95.1	100	IE	MA	R. Intereconomia, Madrid
AS08)	95.2	6	OCR	AS	Onda Cero R., Oviedo
AR05)	95.3	13	SER	AR	Los 40, Zaragoza
CA31)	95.3	5	OCR	CA	Onda Cero R., Tarragona
AS03)	95.4	10	RPA	AS	RPA,R.Principado Asturias, Boal
AN44)	95.4	8	KFM	AN	Kiss FM, Cádiz
AN52)	95.6	8	KFM	AN	Kiss FM, Córdoba
BA02)	95.8	5		BA	Insel R., Mallorca
CA28)	95.8	20	KFM	CA	Kiss FM, Barcelona
AN45)	95.9	40	OCR	AN	Onda Cero R., Sevilla
CA32)	95.9	5	RTT	VA	R. Tele Taxi, Benicassim, Valencia
CA08)	96.0	20	RO	CA	Radiolé, Collserola Barcelona
MA02)	96.0	20	LFM	MA	Loca Fun R. Madrid
RI03)	96.0	6	KFM	RI	Kiss FM, Logroño
EU04)	96.1	20	EI	EU	Euskadi Gaztea, Zaldiaran
VA10)	96.1	10	M80	VA	M80, València
CL32)	96.2	6	OCR	CL	Europa FM, Salamanca
AN67)	96.2	6	D	AN	Cadena Dial Almería, Almería
VA22)	96.2	10	R9	VA	R. Nou, Elda
AN33)	96.3	8	OCR	AN	Onda Melodia, Malaga
MU03)	96.3	5		MU	AMC R. 5, Cartagena
CM12)	96.4	6	M80	CM	M80, Albacete
EU08)	96.5	20	EI	EU	R. euskadi, Donosti-San Sebastián
AS09)	96.5	8	SER	AS	R. Gijón, Gijón
VA22)	96.5	8	R9	VA	R. Nou, Alacant-Alicante
CL35)	96.5	5	KFM	CL	Kiss FM, León
AN43)	96.6	5	CSR	AN	Canal Sur R., Loja, Granada
GA08)	96.6	6	RG	GA	R. Galega Música, Friol
CA25)	96.7	25	CR	CA	Catalunya Música, Girona, Rocacorba
MU11)	96.7	6	KFM	MU	Kiss FM, Cartagena
AN22)	96.8	3	RO	AN	Radiolé, Granada
VA25)	96.9	20	KFM	VA	Kiss FM, València
CA08)	96.9	8	SER	CA	R. Barcelona 2, Collserola Barcelona
MA16)	96.9	20	RM	MA	R. maria España, Madrid
EX08)	97.0	6	D	EX	Cadena Dial, Cáceres
AN15)	97.1	40	SER	AN	Los 40, Sevilla
AN43)	97.1	30	CSR	AN	Canal Fiesta R., Granada
AR05)	97.1	40	D	AR	CadenaDial Zaragoza, Zaragoza
CL23)	97.1	6	SER	CL	R. Castilla, Burgos
MU04)	97.1	5		MU	Onda Mediterranea R., Cartagena
MA07)	97.2	100		MA	Top Radio Latina , Madrid
CA25)	97.3	10	CR	CA	Catalunya R., Montserrat Barcelona
EU05)	97.3	8	COPE	EU	Cadena 100, Vitoria-Gasteiz
EU06)	97.3	5		EU	Fórmula Hit, Portugalete, Gipuzcoa
VA 05)	97.3	8		VA	Onda Melodía, Altea.Alicante
CA11)	97.4	10	ONA	CA	ONA FM, Figueres, Girona
AR06)	97.5	40	COPE	AR	COPE, Zaragoza
GA13)	97.6	8	M80	GA	M80, A Coruña
MA18)	97.6	4	OCR	MA	Onda Cero R., Alcalá de Henares, Madrid
CL32)	97.6	6	OCR	CL	Onda Cero R., Salamanca
CA32)	97.7	20	RTT	CA	R. Tele Taxi, Collserola Barcelona
VA27)	97.7	20		VA	LA 97 Punto 7, València
EU10)	97.8	24	COPE	EU	COPE, Bilbo-Bilbao
AN48)	97.9	30	CSR	AN	Canal Fiesta R., Jaén
AR06)	97.9	40	COPE	AR	Cadena 100, Zaragoza
AN13)	98.0	30	COPE	AN	COPE, Alanis, . Sevilla
EU13)	98.0	8	COPE	EU	Cadena 100, Donosti-San Sebastián
EU15)	98.0	8		EU	R. Alava,Onda Vasca, Vitoria-Gasteiz
MA13)	98.0	100	OCR	MA	Onda Cero R., Madrid
AN49)	98.1	5	SER	AN	R. Nueva, Huelva
CL18)	98.1	8	MFM	CL	Maxima FM, Valladolid
EX03)	98.1	5	CER	EX	Canal Extremadura R., Zafra, Badajoz
VA07)	98.1	10	ROCK	VA	ROCK FM, València
RI04)	98.2	5	ABC	RI	ABC Punto R., Logroño
CA25)	98.3	10	CR	CA	Catalunya Informaciò, Montserrat Barcelona

FM	MHz	kW	Net	Rg	Station, location
CM25)	98.3	5	KFM	CM	Kiss FM, Toledo
NA02)	98.3	6		NA	98.3 R., Pamplona
BA06)	98.4	5	MFM	BA	Maxima FM, Alfábia, Palma M.
VA10)	98.4	20	D	VA	Cadena Dial Mediterraneo, València
CA25)	98.5	5	CR	CA	Catalunya Informació, Montcaro, Tortosa
CA40)	98.5	10	SER	CA	SER, Girona
CT11)	98.5	5	OCR	CT	Kiss FM, Santander
CM22)	98.5	5	OCR	CM	Onda Cero R., Talavera de la Reina,Toledo
AR05)	98.6	40	M80	AR	M80, Zaragoza
CL36)	98.6	8		CL	R. Arlanzón, Burgos
CM08)	98.6	5	RCM	CM	R. Castilla-La Mancha, Valdepeñas, Ciudad Real
EU11)	98.8	5	M80	EU	M80, Bilbao
MU17)	98.8	6		MU	Solo R. R, Marca, Cartagena
BA16)	98.8	5	ABC	BA	ABC Punto R., Ultima Hora., Palma de Mallorca
CA22)	98.9	10	OCR	CA	Onda Cero R., Rocacorba Girona
VA26)	98.9	5	COPE	VA	COPE, R.Sirena, Benidorm
VA11)	99.0	40	COPE	VA	Cadena 100, València
CL42)	99.1	5	KFM	CL	Kiss FM, Zamora
EU04)	99.1	5		EU	Euskadi Gaztea Vitoria-Gasteiz
MA03)	99.1	10	ES	MA	esRadio, Madrid
CL17)	99.3	6	D	CL	Cadena Dial, Salamanca
MU09)	99.3	8	KFM	MU	Kiss FM, Murcia
AN74)	99.4	30	CSR	AN	RAI R. Andalucía Informacion, Cádiz
AN55)	99.4	60	CSR	AN	RAI R. Andalucía Informacion, Córdoba
AR12)	99.4	40	OCR	AR	Onda Cero R., Zaragoza
CA08)	99.4	10	D	CA	Cadena Dial Barcelona, Barcelona
CL33)	99.4	8	KFM	CL	Kiss FM, Valladolid
AN51)	99.5	8	EFM	AN	Europa FM, Granada
MA08)	99.5	100	COPE	MA	COPE, Madrid
CA05)	99.6	10	GR	CA	Flaix FM, Girona, Rocacorba
CA25)	99.7	5	CR	CA	Catalunya R., Collsuspina, Barcelona
MA04)	99.8	10		MA	R. Sol XXI, Madrid
AN19)	99.9	8	D	AN	Cadena Dial Bahía, Cádiz
DA10)	99.9	8	RM	BA	R. Marla, Palma de Mallorca
AS03)	100.0	8	RPA	AS	R.Principado Asturias, Los Oscos
CA09)	100.0	20	COPE	CA	Cadena 100, Collserola Barcelona
CA25)	100.1	10	CR	CA	Catalunya R., Girona, Rocacorba
EU07)	100.1	20	EI	EU	EITB IrratiaMusika, Bilbo-Bilbao
CA25)	100.2	35	CR	CA	Catalunya R., La Mussara,Tarragona
GA08)	100.2	5	RG	GA	R. Galega Música, Xistral
AN58)	100.3	40	KFM	AN	Kiss FM, Sevilla
CM12)	100.3	5	SER	CM	SER Albacete
AN72)	100.4	6	SER	AN	SER, Málaga
CL18)	100.4	8	D	CL	Cadena Dial, Valladolid
EU22)	100.4	5	SER	EU	Los 40, Vitoria-Gasteiz
MA09)	100.4	5		MA	R. Círculo, Madrid
VA10)	100.4	20	SER	VA	R. Valencia 2, Valencia
AR12)	100.5	10	EFM	AR	Europa FM, Zaragoza
AS03)	100.5	20	RPA	AS	R.Principado Asturias, Gijón
CA25)	100.5	5	CR	CA	Catalunya Música, Collsuspina, Barcelona
CM08)	100.5	5	RCM	CM	R. Castilla-La Mancha, Guadalajara
CM23)	100.5	5		CM	R. Santa María, Toledo
GA12)	100.6	8	SER	GA	SER. Vigo 2, Vigo
AN48)	100.6	30	CSR	AN	Canal Sur R., Jaén
BA16)	100.6	5	GR	BA	Flaix FM, Mallorca
GA08)	100.6	5	RG	GA	R. Galega Música, Monte Páramo
CA25)	100.7	80	CR	CA	Catalunya R., Alpicat, Lleida
CA05)	100.7	10	GR	CA	Flaixbac FM, Girona, Rocacorba
MA08)	100.7	20	COPE	MA	COPE, Madrid
AN55)	100.8	5	CSR	AN	Canal Sur R., Córdoba
EX03)	100.8	5	CER	EX	Canal Extremadura R., Badajoz
VA19)	100.8	6	COPE	VA	COPE,Elche
GA24)	100.9	30	RG	GA	R. Galega, Xestiras, Pontevedra
BA11)	101.0	5	OCR	BA	Onda Melodía Mallorca
CA34)	101.0	5	RAC	CA	Catalunya R., Mont Caro, Tortosa
EU05)	101.0	8	COPE	EU	COPE, Vitoria
AN72)	101.1	10	M80	AN	M80, Málaga
CT06)	101.1	6	M80	CT	M80, Santander
VA23)	101.2	20	OCR	VA	Onda Cero R., València
AN56)	101.2	5	OCR	AN	Onda Cero R., Huelva
GA12)	101.2	6	M80	GA	M80, Vigo
VA22)	101.2	5	R9	VA	R. Nou, Benidorm
MA14)	101.3	100		MA	Onda Madrid, Madrid
AN55)	101.3	30	CSR	AN	Canal Fiesta R., Córdoba
AN43)	101.3	5	CSR	AN	R. Andalucía Informacion, Loja, Granada
AS03)	101.4	10	RPA	AS	R. Principado Asturias, Avilés
RI02)	101.4	5	COPE	RI	Cadena 100, Logroño
AN15)	101.5	40	SER	AN	Radiolé, Sevilla
CA25)	101.5	5	CR	CA	Catalunya Música, Collserola Barcelona
EU07)	101.5	24	OCR	EU	Onda Cero R., Bilbo-Bilbao
AN53)	101.6	5	EFM	AN	Europa FM Costa del Sol, Mijas, Malaga
CM08)	101.6	5	RCM	CM	R. Castilla-La Mancha, Cuenca
CA38)	101.7	25	CR	CA	Catalunya Informació, Girona, Rocacorba
AN67)	101.8	6	SER	AN	Los 40, Almería
CA06)	101.8	5	GR	CA	Flaix FM, Tarragona
AN59)	101.9	60	CSR	AN	Canal Fiesta R., Sevilla
EU04)	101.9	8	EI	EU	Euskadi Irratia, Amurrio,Alava
GA30)	101.9	6	RMA	GA	R. Marca, Vigo
AN14)	102.0	8	COPE	AN	COPE, Cádiz
CA09)	102.0	20	COPE	CA	COPE, Barcelona
CA25)	102.2	25	CR	CA	Catalunya R, Girona, Rocacorba
AN42)	102.2	30	CSR	AN	Canal Fiesta R., Huelva
VA24)	102.2	100	R9	VA	R. Nou, València
BA06)	102.3	4	M80	BA	M80 Mallorca, Palma de Mallorca
CA42)	102.3	10	LFM	CA	LOCA FUN RADIO, Barcelona
GA25)	102.3	40	RG	GA	R. Galega, Domaio
AN68)	102.4	40	D	AN	Cadena Dial Sevilla, Sevilla
CA25)	102.4	10	CR	CA	Catalunya Música, Montserrat, Barcelona
CT06)	102.4	6	SER	CT	SER, Liérganes, Santander
EU28)	102.4	6	OCR	EU	Onda Cero R., Vitoria
AN57)	102.5	70	CSR	AN	Canal Fiesta R., Almería, Pechina
CA25)	102.5	10	CR	CA	Catalunya Música, Mont Caro, Tortosa
CM08)	102.5	12	RCM	CM	R. Castilla-La Mancha, Ciudad Real
EU29)	102.5	8	OCR	EU	Onda Cero R., Donosti-San Sebastián
AN22)	102.5	8	D	AN	Cadena Dial, Granada
EX03)	102.6	60	CER	EX	Canal Extremadura R., Montánchez
EU23)	102.6	15	COPE	EU	Bizkaia Irratia, Bilbo-Bilbao
MA13)	102.7	100	KFM	MA	Kiss FM, Madrid
GA26)	102.7	8	ES	GA	esRADIO.,A Coruña
AN72)	102.8	8	SER	AN	Los 40,, Mijas, Málaga
CA25)	102.8	100	CR	CA	Catalunya R., Collserola Barcelona
CL43)	102.8	8	ABC	CL	ABC Punto R., Valladolid
BA15)	102.8	5	SER	BA	SER Ibiza, Ibiza
VA32)	102.8	90	R9	VA	Sí R., Benicassim
VA22)	103.0	120	R9	VA	R. Nou, Aitana
AN71)	103.1	5		AN	R. Pinomar, Málaga
AN15)	103.2	28	SER	AN	SER Sevilla 2, Sevilla
EU07)	103.2	20	EI	EU	R. Euskadi, Bilbo-Bilbao
MA22)	103.2	5		MA	RTC - Radio TV Cristiana, Madrid
VA23)	103.2	10	EFM	VA	Europa FM, València
AN22)	103.3	8	MFM	AN	Maxima FM, Granada
CA29)	103.4	10	RE	CA	R. Estel, Girona, Rocacorba
CL37)	103.4	5	ABC	CL	ABC Punto R., Salamanca
CM08)	103.4	5	RCM	CM	R. Castilla-La Mancha, Puertollano, Ciudad Real
EU09)	103.4	20	EI	EU	EITB Musika, Vitoria-Gasteiz
AN43)	103.5	60	CSR	AN	Canal Sur R., Sierra de Lújar, Córdoba
CA08)	103.5	20	SER	CA	Ona FM, ., Collserola Barcelona
EU08)	103.5	20	EI	EU	Euskadi Gaztea,Donosti-S. Sebastián
VA24)	103.5	10	R9	VA	R. Nou, Gandía
AN55)	103.6	5	CSR	AN	Canal Sur R., Córdoba
EU30)	103.7	24	ABC	EU	ABC Punto R., Bilbo-Bilbao
GA08)	103.7	70	RG	GA	R.Galega, Monte Páramo
VA24)	103.7	90	R9	VA	R. Nou, Castelló, Benicàssim
GA30)	103.8	6	RV	GA	R. Voz, Vigo
AN59)	103.9	30	CSR	AN	Canal Fiesta R., Sevilla, Valencina
GA25)	103.9	40	RG	GA	R. Galega, Bailadora
MA05)	103.9	30		MA	Amèrica Estereo, Madrid
MU07)	103.9	8		MU	Cadena Dial, Murcia, Murcia
CM08)	104.0	10	RCM	CM	R. Castilla-La Mancha, Chinchilla, Albacete
EX03)	104.0	5	CER	EX	Canal Extremadura R., Cáceres
AN24)	104.1	5	ROCK	MU	ROCK FM, Córdoba
AN63)	104.1	6	KFMR	AN	Kiss FM, Almería
AN43)	104.2	5	CSR	AN	Canal Sur R., Granada
AS11)	104.2	5		AS	R. Amistad, Hevia-Siero, Gijón
CA08)	104.2	37	SER	CA	Máxima FM, Collserola Barcelona
GA31)	104.2	5	RG	GA	R. Galega Música, Santiago de Compostela
MA05)	104.3	37	MFM	MA	Máxima FM, Madrid
AN42)	104.4	30	CSR	AN	Canal Sur R., Huelva
EU07)	104.4	20	EI	EU	Euskadi Irratia, Bilbo-Bilbao
CA25)	104.5	2	CR	CA	Catalunya Informació, La Mussara, Tarragona
AN41)	104.6	30	CSR	AN	Canal Sur R., Málaga
AN59)	104.6	60	CSR	AN	RAI R.Andalucía Informacion, Sevilla
MU16)	104.6	8	ORM	MU	Onda Regional Murcia, Cartagena
VA20)	104.7	5	LFM	VA	LOCA FUN RADIO, Elx
GA12)	104.7	6	MFM	GA	Máxima FM, Vigo
AN37)	104.8	30	CSR	AN	Canal Sur R., Jerez de la Frontera
AN57)	104.8	20	CSR	AN	Canal Sur R., Almería
AR14)	104.8	10	RKM	AR	RKM, Zaragoza
EU31)	104.8	5	RKM	EU	RKM, Vitoria-Gasteiz
GA25)	104.8	40	RG	GA	R. Galega, Monte Meda
AN43)	104.8	30	CSR	AN	Canal Sur R., Granada
EU23)	104.9	8	EI	EU	Euskadi Gaztea, Amurrio
CA34)	105.0	20	RAC	CA	RAC105, Collserola Barcelona
AN59)	105.1	30	CSR	AN	Canal Sur R., Sevilla
CA32)	105.1	10	RTT	CA	R. Tele Taxi, Girona, Rocacorba
MA05)	105.1	5		MA	Super Q FM , Madrid
BA18)	105.2	30	RM	BA	R. Maria, Alfabia, Palma M.
CL39)	105.2	8	OCR	CL	Onda Cero R., Valladolid

FM	MHz	kW	Net	Rg	Station, location
MU16)	105.3	60	ORM	MU	Onda Regional, Murcia
AS03)	105.4	8	RPA	AS	R.Principado Asturias, Oviedo
CA25)	105.4	20	CR	CA	Catalunya Música, La Mussara, Tarragona
MA05)	105.4	100	SER	MA	SER Madrid 2, Madrid
AN55)	105.5	6	CSR	AN	Canal Fiesta R. Cabra, Cordoba
CL38)	105.5	6	KFM	CL	Kiss FM, Burgos
VA22)	105.5	10	R9	VA	Sí R.,Sierra del Cid, Elda, Alicante
AN60)	105.6	16	CSR	AN	Canal Sur R., Algeciras
EU32)	105.6	8	ABC	EU	ABC Punto R., Vitoria-Gasteiz
CA41)	105.7	20	GR	CA	Flaix FM, Collserola Barcelona
AR12)	105.8	40	KFM	AR	Kiss FM, Zaragoza
AN41)	105.8	30	CSR	AN	Canal Fiesta R., Málaga
MA14)	106.0	30		MA	Onda Madrid R., Madrid
AN55)	106.1	6	CSR	AN	R. Andalucía Información, Cabra, Cordoba
BA06)	106.1	8	D	BA	Cadena Dial, Palma de Mallorca
CA41)	106.1	20	GR	CA	Faixbac FM, Collserola Barcelona
GA27)	106.1	8	RV	GA	R. Voz, Santiago de Compostela
EU33)	106.2	8	ABC	EU	ABC Punto R., Donosti-San Sebastián
MA26)	106.3	10	ABC	MA	ABC Punto R., Madrid
AS03)	106.4	60	RPA	AS	R.Principado Asturias, Gamoniteiro
VA28)	106.5	5	OCR	VA	Onda Cero Alicante, Alicante
CA29)	106.6	20	RE	CA	R. Estel, Collserola Barcelona
EU34)	106.7	8	KFM	EU	Kiss FM, Vitoria-Gasteiz
BA09)	106.8	100	IB3	BA	IB3, Alfábia, Palma M.
CA04)	106.8	10	EFM	CA	Europa FM, Girona, Rocacorba
AN76)	106.9	20	RMA	AN	R. Marca, Sevilla
CA43)	106.9	5		CA	RKB, R. Kanal Barcelona
MU18)	106.9	8	ABC	MU	ABC Punto R., Murcia
MA27)	107.0	2		MA	Libertad FM., Madrid
AN65)	107.1	5		AN	R. Guadalate, Bornos, Jerez de la F.
MA20)	107.2	15		MA	Fiesta FM, Madrid
CA20)	107.9	15	RA	CA	R. Amistad,Barcelona.Turó d'en Fotjà

NB: most stns less than 5kW omitted

Addresses and other information:

AN00) ANDALUCIA
AN01) Edif.RTVE, Parque del Alamillo, 41092 Sevilla. – **AN02)** Góngora 3, 14002 Córdoba – **AN03)** Av.Ricardo Soriano 11, 29600 Marbella – **AN04)** Av.de Granada 57, P1, 23001 Jaén. – **AN05)** Hermanos Machado 23, 04004 Almería – **AN06)** Av.de la Aurora 40, 29006 Málaga – **AN07)** Av.de Andalucía 67, 11007 Cádiz. – **AN08)** Plaza Carretas 5, 18009 Granada – **AN09)** Plaza de Europa s/n, 11300 La Línea de la Concepción – **AN10)** La Fuente 4, 21004 Huelva. – **AN11)** Cervantes 11, 14940 Cabra – **AN12)** C/ Bartolomé 32 bajo, 23001 Jaén. – **AN13)** C/ Triana 8, 41380 Alanis – **AN14)** C/ Algeciras 1, 2° módulo 8 "Edificio Fenicia", 11011 Cádiz – **AN15)** Rafael González Abreu 6, 41001 Sevilla E: radiosevilla@cadenaser.com – **AN16)** Rioja 4, 41001 Sevilla. E: sevilla@cadenacope.net – **AN17)** Linaje 2, 29001 Málaga E: malaga@cadenacope.net – **AN18)** Gran Vía de Colón 28, 18001 Granada E: granada@cadenacope.net – **AN19)** Paseo Marítimo 1, Edif.Reina Victoria, 11010 Cádiz E: sercadiz@cadenaser.com – **AN20)** Obispo Aguilar 1, 23001 Jaén. W: www.radiojaen.es – **AN21)** Guadalete 12, 11403 Jerez de la Frontera. W: www.radiojerez.com – **AN22)** Santa Paula 2 (or: Ap.158), 18001 Granada W: www.radiogranada.es E: radiogranada@radiogranada.es – **AN23)** San Agustín 11 (or: Ap.364), 11403 Jerez de la Frontera E: jerez@cadenacope.net – **AN24)** Federico Mendizábal 10, 23001 Jaén E: jaen@cadenacope.net – **AN25)** Plaza Cardenal Toledo 4, 14001 Córdoba E: cordoba@cadenacope.net – **AN26)** José María Amoz 2, 21001 Huelva E: huelva@cadenacope.net – **AN27)** Padre Luque 11, 04001 Almería E: almeria@cadenacope.net – **AN28)** General Castaños 2, 11201 Algeciras. E:radioalgeciras@unionradio.es – **AN29)** Av.Federico García Lorca 105, 04005 Almería – **AN30)** San Agustín 4, 29200 Antequera – **AN31)** García Lovera 3, 14002 Córdoba. W: www.radiocordoba.com – **AN32)** Plaza Ramón y Cajal 8, 23700 Linares E: radiolinares@unionradio.es – **AN33)** C/ Peregrinos 3 "Edif. Galaxia 2°" Puerta 7, 29002 Málaga **AN35)** Gaitan 10, 11402 Jerez de la Frontera. – **AN36)** Pozo Nuevo 40 bajo, 41530 Morón de la Frontera. – **AN37)** C/ Carpinteros de Ribera 3, 11007-Cádiz – **AN38)** C/ Peregrino 3 "Edif. Galaxia 2°" Puerta 7, 29002 Málaga. – **AN39)** Misericordia 10, 11500 Puerto de Santa María. – **AN40)** C/ Doctor Manuel Ruiz Maya 8,5°, 14004 Córdoba – **AN41)** Avenida Velazquez 307, 29004 Malaga – **AN42)** Carretera Huelva-San Juan del Puerto, km. 6,36. 21007 Huelva. – **AN43)** Urb. Bola de Oro, C/ Laguna de Aguas Verdes 11, 18008 Granada – **AN44)** C/ Dr. Manuel Ruíz Maya 8, 11004 Cádiz – **AN45)** Pabellón Once, Isla de Cartuja, 41092 Sevilla **AN46)** Plaza de España 15, 11006 Cádiz – **AN47)** Avenida Federico García Lorca 105, 04005 Almería. – **AN48)** Prolongación Av. De Granada s/n, Recinto Institución ferial, 23009 Jaén – **AN49)** Mendez Nuñez 15-5-6, 21001 Huelva – **AN50)** Corredera 53, 11402 Jerez de la Frontera. – **AN51)** Recogidas 37, 18005 Granada – **AN52)** Barroso 4-2, 14003 Córdoba. – **AN53)** C/ Ramón Gómez de la Serna 22 "Edificio King Edward II", 29600 Marbella. –**AN55)** Glorieta de Guadalhorce s/n, "Antigua Estación de RENFE", 14008 Córdoba – **AN56)** Arquitecto Pérez Carasa 14-16, 21001 Huelva. – **AN57)** Centro Residencial Oliveros, C/ Maestro Serrano 9, 2°-B, 04004 Almería. — **AN58)** Sevilla – **AN59)** Edificio Canal Sur, Av. José Gálvez 1, 41092 Isla de la Cartuja (Sevilla) – **AN60)** C/ Patriaca Pérez Rodríguez 36, 11201 Algeciras. – **AN61)** Placentines 2, 41004 Sevilla – **AN62)** Av.de la Borbolla 47, 41013 Sevilla. – **AN63)** Almería. – **AN65)** San Jerónimo 7, 11640 Bornos. –**AN67)** Av. Mediterráneo 159, 2° "Edificio Laura", 04007 Almería– **AN68)** Rafael Gonzáles Abreu 6, 41001 Sevilla – **AN69)** C/ San Agustín 4, 29200 Antequera. –**AN70)** Pasaje Comercial, Gran Plaza Letra F, 41005 Sevilla W: www.ministerioselshaddaisevilla.net– **AN71)** CL. Coín Parcela 1273, 29130 Alhaurín de la Torre (Málaga) – **AN72)** C/ Dr. Manuel Domínguez "Ed. Bulevar 2", 29001 Málaga – **AN73)** Edificio de Oficinas del Estadio Olímpico, Isla de la Cartuja, 41092 Sevilla – **AN74)** C/ Capinteros de Ribera 2, 11002 Cádiz.–**AN76)** Av. República Argentina 25-9°-B, 41011 Sevilla.

AR00) ARAGON
AR01) José Luís Albareda 1-3, 50004 Zaragoza. – **AR02)** Nueva 1, 44001 Teruel – **AR03)** José Gil Caves 1, 22005 Huesca **AR04)** Zaragoza W: www.hitfm.es– **AR05)** Paseo de la Constitución 21, 50001 Zaragoza E: radiozaragoza@unionradio.es – **AR06)** Paseo de Sagasta 50 (or: Ap.42), 50006 Zaragoza E: programas.zaragoza@cadenacope. net – **AR07)** Calle Alcalde Carderera 1, 22080 Huesca W: www. radiohuesca.com – **AR11)** Coso 46, 50004 Zaragoza – **AR12)** Zaragoza – **AR13)** Calle Bilbao, 2, 1ª planta, 50001 Zaragoza – **AR14)** REMAR, Av. Cataluña 225, 50003 Zaragoza.

AS00) ASTURIAS
AS01) C/ San Esteban de las Cruces 92, 33195 Oviedo. – **AS02)** Plaza del Instituto 3, 33201 Gijón. – **AS03)** Camino de las Clarisas 263, 33203 Gijón. –**AS05)** Carr.de la Costa 87 (or: Ap.235), 33205 Gijón. – **AS06)** Asturias 19, Bajo, 33004 Oviedo. W: www. radioasturias.com E: c-oviedo@copeasturias.com W: www.copeasturias.com E: c-oviedo@arrakis.es – **AS08)** C/ Cervantes 27, 5°,33003 Oviedo – **AS09)** Jovellanos 1, 33202 Gijón. – **AS11)** C/ Lugar Orial 16, 33187 Hevia-Siero

BA00) BALEARES
BA01) Aragó 26, 07006 Palma de Mallorca. – **BA02)** Paseo Marítimo 26, 07014 Palma de Mallorca – **BA03)** C/ Font i Monteros 21, 07003 Palma de Mallorca. – **BA05)** Felip II N° 26, 07800 Eivissa E: ibiza@cadenacope.net – **BA06)** Rector Bertomeu Martorell 35, Son Xigala, 07013 Palma de Mallorca E: informativos.mallorca@cadenaser.com – **BA07)** Av.Negrete 3, 07760 Ciutadela W: www.telyse.net/copemenorca E: menorca@cadenacope.net – **BA08)** Av.Jaume III N° 18, 07012 Palma de Mallorca E: mallorca@cadenacope.net – **BA09)** C/ Manuel Azaña 7-A, 07006 Palma de Mallorca. – **BA11)** Forners 7, Edif. Once, 07002 Palma de Mallorca – **BA13)** Menacor 171, 07007 Palma de Mallorca. – **BA15)** Avenida Sant Jordi s/n, 07800 Figueretes (Ibiza). – **BA16)** C/ Gremi Selleters i Basters 14, "Polígon Son Castelló", 07009 Palma de Mallorca. – **BA18)** Mallorca.

CA00) CATALUNYA
CA01) C. Roc Boronat 127, 08018 Barcelona. – **CA02)** Carrer Lluis Companys 1, 25003 Lleida – **CA03)** Rambla Nova 23, 43003 Tarragona – **CA04)** Gran Vía Jaume I N° 60, 17001 Girona. E-mail: emisora.girne@rtve.es – **CA05)** Av. Jaume I 76, 17002 Girona. – **CA06)** Plaça del Pati 2, entlo, 43800 Valls – **CA07)** Av. Diagonal 460, 3°, 08006-Barcelona W: www.radiomarcabarcelona.com E: info@radiomarcabarcelona.com – **CA08)** Casp 6, 08010 Barcelona E: radiobarcelona@unionradio.es W: www.radiobarcelona.cat – **CA09)** Diputació 238, 08013 Barcelona W: www.fm/copebarcelona E: barcelona@cadenacope.net – **CA10)** Travessera de les Corts 131-159, Recinte Martenitat, Pavello Cambo, 08028 Barcelona W: www.comradio.com – **CA11)** Placa Josep Pla 2, 17001 Girona. E: radiogirona@unionradio.es – **CA12)** Tomàs Bergadà 3, 43204 Reus E: radioreus@unionradio.es – **CA13)** Carrer de Aragón 390-394, 2a planta, 08013 Barcelona – **CA14)** Llovera 54-56, 43204 Reus E: reus@cadenacope.net – **CA15)** Acadèmia 14, 25002 Lleida. W: www.copelleida.com E: lerida@cadenacope.net – **CA16)** Sèquia 3, 17001 Girona E: girona@cadenacope.net – **CA17)** Vila Antònia 5, 25007 Lleida E: lleida@cadenaser.com – **CA18)** Relay Onda Rambla Barcelona (Local adress: Rambla Nova 69, 43003 Tarragona) – **CA19)** Calle Nou 47, 08240 Manresa E: informatius@els40.com – **CA20)** Apartado 269, 08211 Castellar del Vallès – **CA21)** Avda. Diagonal 441, 1°, 08006-Barcelona – **CA22)**Avda. Jaume 17, 3è 7a, 17001 Girona – **CA25)** El Palau Nou, Ramblas 88-94, 4ª, 08002-Barcelona **CA25)** Av Diagonal 614-616, 08021 Barcelona. E: info@catradio.cat – **W:** www.catradio.cat – **CA27)** Bulidor s/n, Polígon Industrial 1, 08960 St Just D (Barcelona) – **CA28)** Aragó 390-394, P2, 08013 Barcelona. E: onamusica@onacataluna.com – **CA29)** C/ Comtes de Bell-lloc 67-69, 08014 Barcelona E: radioestel@radioestel.com – **CA30)** Del Riu 6, 25007 Lleida. – **CA31)** Rambla Nova 38, 43004 Tarragona – **CA34)** C/ Sant Carles 40, 08922 Sta Coloma de Gramenet (Barcelona) – **CA34)** Av. Diagonal 477, 15°, 08006 Barcelona. – **CA35)** Camí Real 551, 1°, 08302 Mataró – **CA36)** Rambla de la Llibertat 6, 17004 Girona. – **CA37)** C/ Ramón y Cajal 36, 3°, 43001 Tarragona – **CA38)** Carretera

de Barcelona 33, 4º, 17001 Girona – **CA39)** Rambla d'Arago 43, 1º, 25003 Lleida.- **CA40)** Gran via de Jaume I 29-2º, 17001 Girona – **CA41)** Paseo de Gràcia 55-57, 9º, 08007 Barcelona – **CA42)** Barcelona. **W:** www.facebook.com/Locafuncatalunya **CA43)** Gran vía de les Corts Catalanes 645, 2º-1, 08007 Barcelona.

CL00) CASTILLA Y LEÓN
CL01) García Morato 27-29, 47007 Valladolid. – **CL02)** Becerro de Bengoa 9, 34002 Palencia. – **CL03)** Santa Clara 2, 05001 Avila – **CL04)** Ordoño II Nº 28, 24001 León – **CL05)** Campo 5, 42001 Soria – **CL06)** Calle Barrio Gimeno 11, 09004 Burgos – **CL07)** Av.de Requejo 21, 49012 Zamora – **CL08)** Ave María 11, (or Apartado de Correos 105, 24480 Ponferrada) 24400 Ponferrada – **CL09)** Plaza de Colón 4, 37001 Salamanca – **CL10)** Paseo Ezequiel Gonzales 24, 40002 Segovia – **CL15)** Av.del Cid 8, 09005 Burgos **E:** informativos.burgos@cadenacope.net – **CL16)** Duque de la Victoria 23, 47001 Valladolid **E:** direccion.valladolid@cadenacope.net – **CL17)** C/ Veracruz 2 bajo, 37008 Salamanca **W:** www.radiosalamanca.com – **CL18)** C/ La Estación 3, 47004 Valladolid **E:** radiovalladolid@cadenaser.com – **CL19)** Sol Oriente 11-15, 37002 Salamanca **E:** salamanca@cadenaser.net – **CL20)** Hermanos La Salle 2, 24700 Astorga **E:** astorga@cadenacope.net – **CL21)** Lope de Vega 1, 24002 León **W:** www.copeleon.com **E:** leon@cadenacope.net – **CL22)** Plaza Fernández Duró 3 (or: Ap.42), 49001 Zamora **E:** zamora@cadenacope.net – **CL23)** Plaza de España 3, 09005 Burgos **E:** radiocastilla.redaccion@unionradio.es **CL24)** Villafranca 6, 24001 León **W:** www.radioleon.com **E:** radioleon@radioleon.com – **CL25)** Calle Santa Ana 6, 49006 Zamora **E:** radioz@teleline.es – **CL26)** Plaza Cirilo Rodríguez 2, 40001 Segovia **W:** www.radiosegovia.com – **CL27)** Astorga. – **CL31)** Vitoria 24, 09200 Miranda de Ebro – **CL32)** Bermejeros 14, 37001 Salamanca. – **CL33)** Rastrojo 5, 47014 Valladolid. **CL34)** Plaza de Aragón 5, 09001 Burgos. – **CL35)** Julio del Campo 4-6, 24002 León – **CL36)** Plaza de los Vadillos 5, 09005 Burgos. **W:** www.radioarlanzon.com – **CL37)** Aliso 2 bajo, 37004 Salamanca. – **CL38)** Burgos – **CL39)** Edif.Promecal, c/los Astros s/n, 47009 Valladolid. **CL40)** Salamanca – **CL41)** Valladolid – **CL42)** Zamora – **CL43)** C/ Manuol Concsi Acevedo 1, 4706 Valladolid.

CM00) CASTILLA-LA MANCHA
CM01) Paseo de San Cristóbal s/n, 45002 Toledo. – **CM02)** Ramiro Ledesma 8, 13630 Socuéllamos – **CM03)** Nuestra. Sra. De Araceli 1, Edif.Las Torres, 02002 Albacete – **CM04)** Radio Nacional de España 2 (or: Ap.18), 16003 Cuenca – **CM05)** Ronda del Carmen s/n (or: Ap.150), 13002 Ciudad Real **E:** emisora.cr.rne@rtve.es – **CM06)** Plaza de Consejo, Centro Civico, 19001 Guadalajara – **CM07)** Ronda del Canillo 35, 45600 Talavera de la Reina. – **CM08)** Polígono Santa María de Benquerencia, C/ Río Alberche s/n, 45007 Toledo – **CM10)** C/ Gaona 8 , 4º-B, 02001 Albacete. **W:** www.radiosurco.es – **CM12)** Avenida de la Estación 5, 02001 Albacete **E:** radioalbacete@unionradio.es – **CM13)** Alejandro Prieto 2, 13500 Puertollano. **E:** puertollano@cadenacope.net – **CM14)** Tesifonte Gallego 9, 02002 Albacete **E:** albacete@cadenacope.net – **CM15)** Pasaje San Isidro 3, 13001 Ciudad Real **E:** ciudadreal@cadenacope.net – **CM21)** Av.de la Estación 5, 02001 Albacete – **CM22)** C/ Joaquina Santander 13, 1º, 45600 Talavera de la Reina. – **CM23)** Calle Trinidad 12, 45002 Toledo **W:** www.rtv.org/radio.htm **E:** rtvdiocesana@planalfa.es – **CM24)** 02001 Albacete – **CM25)** Toledo..

CT00) CANTABRIA
CT01) Polígono de Raos s/n, 39609 Camargo (Santander) – **CT02)** Av.del Besaya 1 (or: Ap.46), 39300 Torrelavega – **CT03)** C/ José María Pereda 23, 39100 Santa Cruz de Bezana. – **CT05)** Rualasal 5, 39001 Santander **E:** santander@cadenacope.net – **CT06)** Pasaje de la Peña 2, int 7, Edif.Simeon 39008 Santander **W:** www.radiosantander.com **E:** informativos@radiosantander.com – **CT11)** Fernandez de Isla 14,2º, 39008 Santander.

EU00) EUSKADI
EU01) Plaza de Simón Bolívar 13, 01003 Vitoria-Gasteiz – **EU02)** Paseo de los Fueros 2, 20006 Donosti-San Sebastián **E:** emisora.ss.rne@the.es – **EU03)** Licenciado Poza 55, 48013 Bilbo-Bilbao – C/ Poloríniviejo 4, 01003 Vitrioria-Gasteiz – **EU04)** C/ Domingo Martínez de Aragón 5-9, 01006 Vitoria-Gasteiz. **W:** www.eitb.com/eu/gaztea – **EU05)** C/ San Antonio 2 bajo, 01005 Vitoria-Gasteiz – **EU06)** C/ Alonso Allende 21, Lonja izquierda, 48920 Portugalete. – **EU07)** Capuchinos de Basurto 2, Edificio Bami, 48013 Bilbo-Bilbao **E:** radio_euskadi@eitb.com – **EU08)** Miramón 172, 20004 Donostia-San Sebastián **W:** www.eitb.com/euskara/ – **EU09)** C/ Domingo Martínez de Aragón 5-9, 01006 Vitoria-Gasteiz **W:** www.eitb.com/radiovitoria – **EU10)** Alameda Mazarredo 47, 48009 Bilbo-Bilbao **W:** www.radiopopular.com – **EU11)** C/ Epalza 8, 48007 Bilbo-Bilbao **E:** radiobilbao@unionradio.es – **EU12)** Paseo Portuetxe 51, Edificio ACB, 20018 Donostia-San Sebastián **E:** radiosansebastian@cadenaser.com – **EU13)** Miracruz 9, 20001 Donostia-San Sebastián –**EU15)** C/Portal de Gamarra, 23. Pabellón A, 01002 Vitoria-Gasteiz **W:** www.ondavasca.com – **EU17)** Vitoria-Gasteiz **EU20)** Bulevar de Beurko 4, local 2, 48902-Barakaldo **EU18)** C/ La Habana s/n, 01012 Vitoria **W:** www.radiogorbea.com

EU21) Av.de la Libertad 17, 20004 -Donosti-San Sebastián – **EU22)** General Alava 10-6 Depto 9, 01005 Vitoria-Gasteiz – **EU23)** Fontecha y Salazar 9-5, 48007 Bilbo-Bilbao – **EU24)** Eziago Poligonoa 10B, 20120 Hernani – **EU25)** C. Hurtado de Amezaga 27,17piso, 48008 Bilbo-Bilbao – **EU26)** C/ Esteban Zurbano 20, 20214 Segura (Guipúzcoa). – **EU27)** Gordóniz 44, 12º, 48002 Bilbao – **EU28)** C/ San Prudencio 8-A., 5º, 01005 Vitoria-Gasteiz. – **EU29)** Paseo Federico García Lorca 10, 4º, Puerta 1-2, 20014 Donosti-San Sebastián – **EU30)** Ribera de Elorrieta 7, 48015 Bilbo-Bilbao – **EU31)** C/ José Lejarreta 11, 01003 Vitoria-Gasteiz. – **EU32)** C/ Portal de Legutiano 6, 01002 Vitoria-Gasteiz – **EU33)** Parque Empresarial Zuazu, Ed. Ulía 8, 20018 Donosti-San Sebastián – **EU34)** Vitoria-Gasteiz.

EX00) EXTREMADURA
EX01) Av.Ruta de la Plata 10, 10001 Cáceres – **EX02)** Plaza de España 5, 06002 Badajoz. – **EX03)** Avenida de las Américas 1, 1º, 06800 Mérida. - **EX05)** C/ Comandante Sánchez Herrero 2, 1º, 10004 Cáceres **E:** caceres@cadenacope.net – **EX06)** Ramón Albarrán 2, 06002 Badajoz **E:** radioextremadura@unionradio.es – **EX07)** Menacho 12, 06001 Badajoz **E:** badajoz@cadenacope.net – **EX08)** C/ Profesor Rodríguez Moñino 1, 8º-A, 10003 Cáceres – **EX11)** Av.de España 9-6, 10004 Cáceres – **EX12)** Av.de Portugal s/n, Ctro Comercial El Foro, 06800 Mérida – **EX13)** Santa Isabel 4, 10600 Plasencia – **EX16)** Luis Alvarez Lancero 8, 10001 Cáceres.

GA00) GALICIA
GA01) Paseo Méndes Nuñez 12, (or: Ap.199), 15006 A Coruña – **GA02)** Lepanto 7, 36001 Pontevedra – **GA03)** Rua de Progreso 115 (or: Ap.268), 32003 Ourense – **GA04)** Ourense 59-63 (or: Ap.73), 27004 Lugo – **GA05)** Plaza de España 4, 27400 Monforte de Lemos – **GA06)** Av.García Barbón 36, 36201 Vigo – **GA07)** San Marcos s/n, Edif.TVE, 15780 Santiago de Compostela – **GA08)** Rúa Pascual Veiga 12-14 baixo dereita, 27002 Lugo. – **GA09)** Plaza de España 5-6, 15403 El Ferrol **E:** ferrol@cadenacope.net – **GA10)** San Pedro de Mezonzo 3 (or: Ap 469), 15701 Santiago de Compostela **E:** radiogalicia@unionradio.es – **GA11)** Principe 57, 36202 Vigo **E:** vigo@cadenacope.net – **GA12)** Areal 6-8, 36201 Vigo – **GA13)** Plaza de Ourense 3, 15004 A Coruña **W:** www.radiocoruna.com – **GA14)** Castelao 3 B, 36001 Pontevedra **E:** ser@radiopontevedra.com – **GA15)** Rua de Progreso 89, 32003 Ourense **E:** orense@cadenaser.net – **GA16)** Rua de Valiño s/n, 27002 Lugo **E:** lugo@cadenacope.net – **GA17)** Plaza de Santo Domingo 3, 27001 Lugo **W:** www.radiolugo.es – **GA18)** Rua do Paseo 30 (or: Ap.1017), 32003 Ourense **W:** www.radioourense.com **E:** cadenaser@radioourense.com – **GA21)** Ronda de Outeiro, Nº1 y 3 Bajo 15006 A Coruña– **GA22)** Salvador Moreno 30, 36001 Pontevedra **GA23)** Av.García Barbón 104, 36201 Vigo – **GA24)** Rúa Benito Corbal 14, 2º, 36001 Pontevedra – **GA25)** Casa de Campo s/n, San Marcos, 15820 Santiago de Compostela – **GA26)** . **W:** www.esradio.fm **GA27)** Salguiriños de Arriba 44, bajo, 15890 Santiago de Compostela – **GA28)** Apartado de Correos 3114, 36208 Vigo **W:** www.ondasdevida.org **GA29)** C/ Torreiro 13-15, 3º-E, 15005 A Coruña. – **GA30)** Av. García Barbón 28, 36201 Vigo – **GA31)** Rúa Costa Rica 6, 7º, 15005 A Coruña.

MA00) MADRID
MA01) Casa de la Radio, Prado del Rey, 28223 Pozuelo de Alarcón – **MA02)** C/ Enrique Larreta 12, 28036 Madrid – **MA03)** C/ Juan Esplandiú 15, 2ª, 28007 Madrid. – **MA04)** C/ San Bernardo 20, 3º, Centro, 28015 Madrid – **MA05)** Gran Vía 32, 28013 Madrid **E:** redaccion@cadenaser.com – **MA06)** Modesto Lafuente 42, 28003 Madrid **W:** www.radiointer.com **E:** radiointer@radiointer.com – **MA07)** C/ Juan Esplandiú 15, 2ª, 28007 Madrid – **MA08)** Alfonso XI Nº 4, 28014 Madrid **W:** www.cope.es **E:** programas.madrid@cadenacope.net – **MA09)** Círculo de Bellas Artes, C/ Alcalá 42, 5 planta, 28014 Madrid – **MA10)** W: www.superqfm.es **MA11)** Bueso Pineda 7, 28043 Madrid – **MA13)** José Isbert 6, Ciudad de la Imagen - 28223 Pozuelo de Alarcón **W:** www.kissfm.es **E:** kissfm@kissfm.es – **MA14)** Pso del Principe 3, Cd.de la Imagem, 28223 Pozuelo de Alarcón **W:** www.telemadrid.es – **MA16)** Av.de los Arqueros s/n, 28024 Madrid **E:** radiomaria@arsenet.com – **MA17)** Paseo de la Castellana 38-38, 28046 Madrid **W:** www.intereconomia.com – **MA18)** Sta Clara 7, 28801 Alcalá de Henares – **MA20)** C/ Juan Español 47, local bajo, 28026 Madrid. – **MA21)** C. Francisco Silvela 122 bajo, 28002 Madrid. – **MA22)** Calle de Secoya 29, Planta 3 Parte 1, 28054 Madrid – **MA24)** C/ Orense 18, piso 8, of. 9, 28020 Madrid **W:** www.rtcespana.es – **MA26)** Juan Ignacio Luca de Tena 7, 28027 Madrid – **MA27)** Paseo de la Castellana 129, 1º-C, 28046-Madrid **W:** http://radiolibertad.com

MU00) MURCIA
MU01) La Olma 27-29, 30005 Murcia **E:** emisora.mu.rne@rtve.es – **MU02)** Paseo Alfonso XIII Nº 51, 30203 Cartagena. – **MU03)** C/ Bucarest 29, 30391 Cartagena. **MU04)** C/ Carmen Conde 46, 1º, 30203 Cartagena. – **MU05)** Arco de Santo Domingo 2-3, Edif.Fontanar, 30001 Murcia **E:** murcia@cadenacope.net – **MU06)** Av.Juan Carlos I Nº 63, 30800 Lorca **E:** lorca@cadenacope.net – **MU07)** Calle Radio Murcia 4, 30001 Murcia **E:** radiomurcia@unionradio.es – **MU08)** Real 70, 30201

Cartagena **E:** informativos.cartagena@cadenaser.com – **MU09)** Murcia – **MU11)** Edif.Mediterráneo, Puerta Murcia 11, 30201 Cartagena – **MU12)** C/ Carmen 51, 1° A, 30201 Cartagena – **MU13)** Madre de Dios 15, 30004 Murcia – **MU14)** Mayor 31, 30280 Cartagena – **MU16)** Av.Libertad 6, bajo, 30009 Murcia – **MU17)** Pza de los Apóstoles 7, 30001 Murcia – **MU18)** Ed.del Periódico La Verdad, Camino Viejo de Monteagudo s/n, 30160 Murcia.

NA00) NAVARRA
NA01) Emilio Arrieta 8, P8, 31002 Pamplona-Iruñea – **NA02)** Aoiz 17, 31004 Pamplona-Iruñea – **NA03)** Ed. Ciencias Sociales, Universidad de Navarra, Campus Universitario s/n, 31080 Pamplona.-Iruñea **W:** www.unav.es/98.3 – **NA05)** Amaya 2-B, 31002 Pamplona-Iruñea **E:** pamplona@cadenacope.net – **NA06)** Polígono Plazaola, Manzana F, 2° A, 31195 Aizoain (or Apartado de Correos 71, 31080 Pamplona) **E:** informativosnavarra@cadenaser.com – **NA11)** Plaza del Castillo 43, 31001 Pamplona-Iruñea – **NA12)** Cortes de Navarra 1, 31002 Pamplona-Iruñea.

RI00) LA RIOJA
RI01) Vara de Rey 42, (or: Ap.247), 26002 Logroño – **RI02)** Residencia Universitaria Francisco Jordán, Av. Madre de Dios 17, 26001 Logroño – **RI03)** C/ Estambrera 36, 1°, 26006 Logroño. – **RI04)** C/ General Vara del Rey 74, 26002 Logroño. – **RI05)** Av.de Portugal 12 (or: Ap.149), 26001 Logroño **W:** www.radiorioja.com – **RI11)** Logroño – **RI12)** Miguel Villanueva 2, Ofc.5, 26001 Logroño.

VA00) CUMUNITAT VALENCIANA
VA01) Av Colóm 13, 46004 València – **VA02)** Angel Lozano 18, 03001 Alacant-Alicante – **VA03)** Passeig de la Ribalta 5, 12001 Castelló – **VA04)** Juan Carlos I 37, 03202 Elx. - **VA05)** Plaça dels Sports 7-8, Ed. Sabater, 03590 Altea – **VA07)** Rambla de Méndez Nuñez 45, 03002 Alacant-Alicante **E:** alicante@cadenacope.net – **VA08)** Calderón de la Barca 26, 03004 Alacant-Alicante **E:** alicante@cadenaser.com – **VA09)** Av.Francisco Tàrrega 69, 12540 Vila-Real **E:** castellon@cadenacope. net – **VA10)** Don Juan de Austria 3, 46002 València **E:** valencia@ cadenaser.com – **VA11)** Passatge Dr.Sierra 2, 46004 València **W:** www. cope.es/valencia – **VA12)** Doctor Sempere 16B y C, Bajos, 03803 Alcoi **E:** radioalcoy@radioalcoy.com – **VA13)** Moyano 5, 12002 Castelló **W:** www.radiocastellon.comdc – **VA14)** Dr.Caro 43, 03201 Elx **W:** www.radioelche.com – **VA15)** Calle Loreto 32, 46700 Gandia **E:** ser@ radiogandia.net **W:** www.radiogandia.net – **VA16)** Ereta 2A (or: Ap.84), 46870 Ontinyent **W:** www.radioontinyent.com – **VA 17)** C/ Hort dels Frares 12, 46600 Alzira. – **VA18)** C/ Doctor Caro 18 entresuelo derecha, 03201 Elx. – **VA19)** C/ La Fira 10, 03202 Elx. **VA20)** C/ Almorida 2, 4° derecha, 03201 Elx. – **VA21)** Alacant-Alicante. **E** : alicante@kissfm. es – **VA22)** C/ Segura 19, 03004 Alacant-Alicante – **VA23)** C/ San Vicente 16, entreplanta 1°, 46001 València – **VA24)** Av.Blasco Ibañez 136, 46022 València – **VA25)** València – **VA26)** Vía Emilia Ortuño 5, 3°, 03500 Benidorm **VA27)** Edificio Levante. Polígono Vara de Quart. Calle Traginers, 7 46014 València **W:** www.la977.com – **VA28)** Paseo Explanada de España 26, 03001 Alicante – **VA29)** C/ Els Gremis 1, Polígono Vara de Quart, 46014 Valencia **W:** www.abc.es/radio/valencia – **VA30)** C.C. Alfafar, Pl. Alquería de la Culla 4, Planta14, of.01, 46910 Alfafar,Valencia **W:** www.pequeradio.es – **VA32)** Av. Blasco Ibáñez 134, 46022 València – **VA33)** Av. Aragón 30, 46031 València.
For more information: **W:** www.lalistadelafm.com & www.fmlist.org

AMERICAN FORCES RADIO & TV SERVICE (Mil.)
ZFM 92.1MHz, Morón de la Frontera ✉ APO AE 09643 Moron de la Frontera (Sevilla) – **FM102 Navy** 102.5MHz, Rota. ✉ FPO AE 09645 – 0019 Base Naval, Rota (Cadiz) **D.Prgr:** All stns 24h

SRI LANKA

L.T: UTC +5½h — **Pop:** 19 million — **Pr.L:** Sinhala, Tamil, English — **E.C:** 50Hz, 230V — **ITU:** CLN

SRI LANKA BROADCASTING CORPORATION (Pub)
✉ P.O. Box 574, Independence Square, Colombo 7 ☎+94 11 2697491 📠 +94 11 2691568 **E:** ddge@slbc.lk **W:** www.slbc.lk
L.P: Chairman Hudson Samarasinghe, DG: Samantha Weliweriya, Dep. DG (Eng.) H. M. Jackson, Dep. DG (Finance): N P W Perera, Dir. News: M. I. A. Jayaranthbe, Dir. Eng. (Studios): C. N. D. Siriwardene.

FM (MHz)	A	B	C	D	E	F
Colombo	98.3	93.3	101.3	105.6	95.6	91.2
Deniyaya	99.6	89.3	104.8	92.8	90.8	102.6
Haputale	90.3	96.4	102.0	107.9	98.4	92.2
Hunasgiriya	102.0	107.3	98.8	94.2	96.4	92.2
Karagahatenna	107.6	92.7	102.4	104.5	-	95.0
Radella	97.0	106.9	103.5	105.6	100.2	94.4
Yatiyantota	90.3	107.0	94.2	104.8	96.4	92.2
Palali	-	-	-	92.2	-	-

A = Sinhala National Sce 2300-1600., **B** = Sinhala Commercial Sce 24h, **C** = Tamil National Sce 2300-1715, **D** = Tamil Commercial Sce 2300-1700, **E** = English Commercial Sce 0000-1700, **F** = City FM 24h.
Sports Sce: operates irregularly as required using freqs of Tamil National Sce and also Jaffna Palali (see reg. services below).
Vidula (Children's channel): Yatiyantota 102.6MHz, 0000-1630 in Sinhala, Tamil and English.
Regional FM services: Akkaraipattu: Haputale 102.0MHz – **Anuradhapura:** Karaghatenna 90.6MHz – **Batticaloa:** Karaghatenna 97.0MHz **Jaffna:** 102.0MHz – **Kandy:** Radella 89.7MHz, Hunasgiriya 89.3MHz – **Kurunegala:** Karaghatenna 99.6MHz – **Matara:** Haputale 105.4MHz, Deniyaya 92.8MHz 5kW. **F.PI:** Jaffna to be a nat. sce. Regional Sce operates 2300-0230 & 1000-1530.
Community Stations: Badulla 87.6MHz, Girandurukotte 95.8MHz, Mawathura 98.4MHz 0.3kW
Ann: A: "Me Sri Lanka Guwan Viduli Sansthave Welanda Sevaya". B: "Me Sri Lanka Guwan Viduli Sansthava Swadeshiya Sevaya". C: "Illangar Oliparappu Kootuthapanam Tamil Sevai". E: "This is the Sri Lanka Broadcasting Corporation"

EXTERNAL SERVICE: SLBC see International Broadcasting section

MAJOR COMMERCIAL NETWORKS (All FM MHz):
ASIA BROADCASTING CORPORATION (Pvt) Ltd.
✉ 35th Floor, East Tower, World Trade Center, Colombo 1 ☎+94 11 233 7555 📠+94 11 234 6870 **E:** md@abcradio.lk **W:** www.abcradio.lk
Stns: Gold FM: Gongala 94.7, Colombo/Hunasgiriya 99.9, Gammaduwa 102.7, Nuwara Eliya 104.2 – **Hiru FM:** Hunasgiriya/Gammaduwa 94.7, Nuwara Eliya 95.3, Colombo/Gongala 96.7, Uva 107.0 – **Sooriyan FM:** Jaffna 93.0, Gammaduwa/Hunasgiriya 97.3, Nuwara Eliya 97.9, Colombo/Gongala 103.2, Uva 103.4 – **Sun FM:** Nuwara Eliya 90.2, Magalkanda 92.8, Hunasgiriya 93.5, Colombo 98.8, Gammaduwa 103.2, Gongala 106.7
ASSET RADIO BROADCASTING (Pvt) Ltd
✉ 09C Ocean Tower Building, Station Road, Bambalapitya, Colombo 4 ☎+94 11 2507080 📠 +94 11 5342434 **E:** eng@nethfm.com **W:** nethfm.com **Stn: Neth FM** in Sinhala: Gongala 93.9, Colombo 95.0, Hunasgiriya 100.4, Laggala 105.4, Nayabedda & Magalkanda 105.9
COLOMBO COMMUNICATIONS (Pvt) Ltd
✉ 686 Galle Road, Colombo 3 ☎+94 11 5577777 📠 +94 11 2505796 **E:** info@efm.lk **W:** efm.lk **Stns: E! FM:** Hunasgiriya 93.2, Colombo 100.4, Gongala 104.5 – **RAN FM:** Nayabedda 91.5, Gongala 95.0, Gammaduwa 101.3, Colombo 102.2, Ratnapura 104.5 – **Shree FM:** Gongala/Ratnapura 93.2, Hunasgiriya 95.8, Nayabedda 98.8, Colombo 99.0, Magalkanda 99.3
INDEPENDENT TELEVISION NETWORK
✉ Wickramasinghepura, Battaramulla 10120 ☎+94 11 2774424 📠+94 11 2774591 **E:** itn@slt.lk **W:** www.itn.lk **L.P:** Chmn.: Rosmand Senarathna, Gen Mgr: W Wijesinghe. **Stns: Lakhande:** Karagahatenna 87.9, Nayabedda/Yatiyantota 88.5, Colombo/Deniyaya/ Hunasgiriya 97.6 – **Prime Radio:** Hunasgiriya 95.5, Gongala 99.0, Colombo 104.5 – **Vasantham:** Kaluthara/Magalkanda 97.3, Karagahatenna 97.6
LAKVIEW BROADCASTING (Pvt) Ltd
✉ 965 Bulugaha Junction, Wedamulla, Kelaniya, Colombo ☎+94 11 7920930 📠+94 11 7920935. **Stn: Lak FM:** Colombo/Nayabedda 92.0, Nuwara Eliya 93.3, Karagahatenna 100.1, Magalkanda 100.2
MBC NETWORKS (Pvt) Ltd
✉ PO Box 25, 36 Araliya Uyana, Depanama, Pannipitiya ☎+94 11 2851371 📠+94 11 2851373. **Stns: Shakthi FM:** ✉ 7 Braybrooke Place, Colombo. Nayabedda 91.2, Hunasgiriya/Jaffna 91.5, Nuwara Eliya 103.8, Colombo/Gammaduwa/Gongala 105.1 – **Sirasa FM:** ✉ PO Box 25, Araliya Uyana, Pannipitiya. Nuwara Eliya 88.8, Gammaduwa 101.7, Hunasgiriya/Gongala 106.2, Colombo/Nayabedda 106.5 – **Y FM:** ✉ 7 Braybrooke Place, Colombo. Kandy 91.2, Colombo 92.6, Gammaduwa 99.1, Gongala/Nayabedda 101.3– **Yes FM:** ✉ as MBC Networks. Kandy/Gangula 88.2, Colombo 89.5, Nuwara Eliya 101.0
TNL RADIO NETWORK (Telshan Networks Ltd)
✉ 7B Tower Building, 25.Station Road, Colombo.4 ☎+94 11 2706128 **L.P:** Chmn. & MD: Shan Wickremesinghe, Comm. Dir: Ms. Ishini Wickremesionghe. **Stns: Rhythm FM:** Chilaw/Kandy/Gammaduwa 87.6, Gongala 95.6, Colombo 100.7 – **Lite 89.2:** Colombo 89.2, Nuwara Eliya 90.0, Gongala 92.5, Kandy 98.2– **TNL 101.7 FM:** ✉ 52, 5th Lane, Colombo 3 ☎+94 11 7777555. Gongala 87.9, Hanthana 92.5, Colombo 101.7

Other Stations:
SLBC transmitting station Puttalam 1125kHz 50kW Available for hire by international broadcasters
Trans World Radio India MW: 882kHz 400kW Broadcasts for Sri Lanka and southern India. See International section for details.
IBB RELAY STATION see International Broadcasting section

ST BARTHÉLEMY (France)

L.T: UTC -4h — **Pop:** 7,500 — **Pr. L:** French, Creole, English — **E.C:** 50Hz, 230V — **ITU:** BLM

GUADELOUPE PREMIÈRE (Pub)
⊡ c/o Morne Bernard-Destrellan, B.P. 180, 97122 Baie-Mahault, Guadeloupe. ☎+590 590939696 ▤ +590 590939682.
FM: 88.6MHz 0.3kW

RADIO SAINT-BARTH
⊡ BP 1113, 97014 St Barthélemy. ☎+590 590 27 74 74 ▤ +590 590 27 74 10. **L.P:** Président Clemenceau Magras
FM: 98.7MHz 0.3kW, 100.7MHz 0.3kW, 103.7MHz 0.3kW.

R. France Internationale: via R. St. Barth 100.7MHz

ST EUSTATIUS (Netherlands)

L.T: UTC -4h — **Pop:** 2,500 — **Pr.L:** Dutch (official), English — **E.C:** 60Hz, 110V — **ITU:** BES

RADIO STATIA
⊡ The Mall, Korthalsweg, Oranjestad ☎ +599 3 82262
MW: Call: PJE-3, 1120kHz 1kW
FM: 92.3MHz

ST HELENA (UK)

L.T: UTC — **Pop:** 4,000 — **Pr. L:** English — **E.C:** 50Hz, 240V — **ITU:** SHN

RADIO ST HELENA
MW: 1548kHz 1kW **(closing 25 December 2012) L.P:** SM: Ralph Peters
N.B. Being replaced by **St Helena Broadcasting Corporation.** Current address: The Livery Stables, Nr The Market Clock, Jamestown, St Helena STHL 1ZZ ☎+ 290 2727 **E:** news@shbc.sh
F.PI: 3 **FM** channels, Radio St Helena, BBCWS relay, and popular music channel. No further information at editorial deadline.

SAINT FM
⊡ St Helena Media Productions Ltd, Jamestown, St Helena, So. Atlantic Ocean STHL 1ZZ. ☎+290 2660/2488 **E:** fm@cwimail.sh
W: www.saint.fm (& Webcasting) **L.P:** SM: Mike Olsson
FM (MHz): 93.1 0.25kW, 95.1 0.03kW, 106.7 0.03kW
D.Prgr: 24h. **Ann:** "Saint FM". **V.** by QSL-card, Rp. (2 IRCs). Email Rpt. accepted. Rec not returned

ST KITTS & NEVIS

L.T: UTC -4h — **Pop:** 51,000 — **Pr.L:** English — **E.C:** 60Hz, 220V — **ITU:** SCN

NATIONAL BROADCASTING CORPORATION OF ST.KITTS & NEVIS (Gov. Comm.)
⊡ PO Box 331, Springfield, Basseterre, St. Kitts ☎ +1 869 465 2621 ▤ +1 869 466 2159 **L.P:** GM: Winston McMahon **E:** info@zizonline.com **W:** www.zizonline.com
MW: Radio ZIZ ±555kHz 10kW Rel. BBC WS 0400-0800 (inactive)
FM: Radio ZIZ 95.9/96.1/96.9MHz — **Big Wave 96.7 FM** 96.7MHz

RADIO PARADISE (Rlg.)
⊡ Bath Plains, PO Box 508, Charlestown, Nevis ☎ +1 869 469 1994 ▤ +1 869 469 1642 (⊡ **in USA:** P.O. Box A, Santa Ana, CA 92711 ☎ +1 (714) 832 2950 ▤ +1 (714) 730 0661). **E:** info@radioparadiseonline.com **W:** www.radioparadiseonline.com **L.P:** Local Mgr: Andre Gilbert
MW: St. Kitts 820kHz 50kW **D.Prgr:** 24h. Local prgrs: Mon-Fri 1330-1530; sometimes later. Sun 1130-1430. Other times: relays audio feed from TBN satellite TV. **Ann:** "This is Radio Paradise, 820 on your AM dial, broadc. from St. Kitts-Nevis"

VOICE OF NEVIS (Comm.)
⊡ Bath Plains, PO Box 195, Charlestown, Nevis ☎ +1 869 469 1616/1700 ▤ +1 869 469 5329 **W:** www.vonradio.com
L.P: GM: Evered Herbert
MW: 860kHz 10kW **D.Prgr:** 24h **Ann:** "This is Von Radio on 860 AM"

Other stations:
Choice FM, Ram's, Stoney Grove, PO Box 923, Charlestown, Nevis 00109 ☎ +1 869 469 5316 ▤ +1 869 469 5306 **W:** www.choice-fm1053.com **FM:** 105.3MHz — **CSS Caribbean Superstation W:** yourcss.net **FM::** 93.1MHz (Relay Trinidad) — **Dominion Radio,** PO Box 513, Basseterre ☎ +1 869 465 1597. **W:** www.dominionradioskn.com **FM:** 91.5MHz. Format: Rlg. — **Freedom FM,** The Cable Bldg., Suite 2, Cayon St., Basseterre **W:** www.freedomskn.com. **L.P:** Clement Juni Liburd **FM:** 106.5MHz — **Goodwill Radio** P.O. Box 98, Lodge Village, St. Kitts ☎ +1 869 465 7795 ▤ +1 869 465 9556 **FM:** 103.3MHz (Nevis) & 104.5MHz (St. Kitts). Format: Rlg. — **Kyss FM - The Love FM,** 51A Stadium View, Sandy Point ☎ +1 869 466 5978 **E:** info@kyssonline.com **W:** www.kyssonline.com **FM:** 102.5MHz — **Praise FM,** Hamilton Estate, Charlestown, Nevis ☎ +1 869 667 0351. **L.P:** Steve Huggins. **FM:** 99.3MHz Format: Gospel — **RADIO ONE,** St. Kitts & Nevis Broadcasting Corp., Bakers Corner, Basseterre ☎ +1 869 466 0941 **FM:** 94.1MHz — **Radio St. Kitts Nevis,** Reef Broadcasting, #79 Castle Coakley, Christiansted, VI 99820, USA ☎ +1 401 573 1620. **FM:** 90.7MHz (relays WAXJ 103.5, US Virgin Isl.) — **Sugar City FM,** 8 Green Land's Park, Basseterre ☎ +1 869 466 1113. **W:** www.sugarcityfm.com. **FM:** 90.3MHz — **Vibz**. **FM:** 98.3MHz (reported on 97.9) (rel. Antigua) — **Winn FM,** Unit C24, Newtown Bay Rd, Basseterre, St. Kitts ☎ +1 869 466 9586. **E:** info@winnfm.com **W:** www.winnfm.com **FM:** 98.9MHz

ST LUCIA

L.T: UTC -4h — **Pop:** 162,000 — **Pr.L:** English, Creole — **E.C:** 50Hz, 220V — **ITU:** LCA

RADIO ST. LUCIA COMPANY LTD. (Gov. Comm.)
⊡ Morne Fortune, PO Box 660, Castries ☎ +1 758 452 2337 ▤ +1 758 453 1568 **E:** info@rslonline.com **W:** www.rslonline.com
L.P: MD: Vacant. CEN: Othneil Robinson. Dir. News: Kendel Burton
FM: 97.3MHz 3kW (North), 97.7MHz 0.5kW (South). **D.Prgr:** 24h **N:** 1030, 1600 & 2200

Other stations:
CARIBBEAN HARMONY, Morne Du Don, Castries ☎ +1 758 451 1079 **W:** www.caribbeanharmony.jigsy.com **FM:** 107.9MHz – **CATHOLIC TV BROADCASTING SERVICE,** Micoud Str, Castries ☎ +1 758 452 7050 **FM:** 87.75MHz (TV sound of EWTN, USA) – **CSS CARIBBEAN SUPERSTATION,** Karlione Court, Rodney Bay ☎ +1 758 451 6400. **W:** yourcss.net **FM:** 93.5(North)/94.7(South)MHz. (Relay Trinidad) – **HOT FM,** Old Victoria Rd, Morne Fortune, PO Box MF 7096, Castries ☎ +1 758 452 6040 ▤ +1 758 458 1462 **W:** www.caribbeanhotfm.com & www.caribbeankissfm.com CEO: Patrick Smith Mgr.: Sandra Recai. **Stns:** Hot FM: 96.1(South)/105.3(North)MHz, **Kiss FM:** 105.5(South)/105.9(North)MHz – **JOY FM,** PO Box MF 7149, Castries ☎ +1 758 453 6962. **FM:** 90.1(North)/96.9 (South)MHz. Format: Rlg – **LOVE-FM,** PO Box 520, Vieux-Fort ☎ +1 758 454 1111 **W:** www.lovefmstlucia.com **FM:** 103.9MHz (South). **F.pl.:** 94.9MHz (North) – **PRAYZ FM RADIO,** Sir John Compton Highway, Sans Soucis, PO Box CP6141, Castries. ☎ +1 758 452 1022/1055. **W:** www.prayzfm.org. **FM:** 92.5/98.5MHz. Format: Rlg., Adventist – **RADIO CARIBBEAN INTERNATIONAL,** 11 Mongiraud St., PO Box 121, Castries. ☎ +1 758 452 2636 ▤ +1 758 452 2637 **W:** www.rcistlucia.com. **L.P:** GM: Mr. Gibson. SM: Peter Ephraim. **FM:** 99.1 (South)/101.1 (North) MHz – **RADIO 100 HELEN FM,** Morne Fortune, PO Box 621, Castries ☎ +1 758 451 7260 ▤ +1 758 453 1737. **L.P:** PD: Valerie Albert. **FM:** 100.1/100.3/103.5MHz – **REAL 91.3 FM,** John Compton Highway, PO Box CP 6279, Castries ☎ +1 758 453 7458 **W:** realfm.mbcrealtv.com. **L.P:** Russell Lake **FM:** 91.3MHz – **RADIO FREE IYANOLA (RFI),** 22 Delieu St, Soufriere ☎ +1 758 489 1021 **W:** rfi1021slu.com. **FM:** 102.1MHz. Format: Reggae – **RHYTHM FM INC.,** Julian Charles Rd., PO Box 584, Castries ☎ +1 758 450 9494 ▤ +1 758 451 6217 **W:** www.rhythmfm.net & www.blazinfm.com. **L.P:** MD Dwayne Mendes. PD: Irvin 'Ace' Loctar. **Stns: Rhythm FM:** 95.5/99.5MHz, **Blazin FM:** 99.3MHz – **RIZZEN 102FM,** McVane Drive, Sans Soucis, Castries ☎ +1 758 451 3057 ▤ +1 758 451 3011 **W:** www.rizzen102.com. **FM:** 99.7/102.5/102.9MHz. Format: Rlg. – **SOUFRIERE FM,** Sulphur Springs Park, Soufriere. **FM:** 88.5MHz (local community stn) – **THE WAVE,** Karlione Court, Rodney Bay. PO Box CP5631, Castries ☎+1 758 451 6400 ▤+1 758 452 2633 **W:** www.thewavestlucia.com. **L.P.:** GM: Sue Monplaisir. PD: Michael Rogers **FM:** 93.7 (South) /94.5 (North) MHz – **YES FM,** Sunny Acres, PO Box 1817, Castries ☎ +1 758 451 3736 **W:** www.yesfmslu.com **FM:** 101.5(South)/101.7(North)MHz Format: Rlg.

ST MAARTEN (Netherlands)

L.T: UTC -4h — **Pop:** 33,100 — **Pr.L:** Dutch (official), English — **E.C:** 60Hz, 120V — **ITU:** SXM

BUREAU TELECOMMUNICATION AND POST
⊡ C.W.G. Buncamper Road, Harbour View Lot 3 / Unit D, P.O.Box

5054; St. Maarten ☎ +1 721 542 5557 🖷 +1 721 542 4817

MW Call	kHz	kW	Station, location
1) PJD-2	1300	1	The Voice of St. Maarten, Philipsburg

FM	MHz	kW	Station, location
4)	91.9		Island 92, Simpson Bay
5)	94.7		Mix 94.7, Philipsburg
6)	96.3		Oasis 96.3, Philipsburg
8)	98.1		Pearl FM, Philipsburg
3)	99.9		Choice FM
6)	101.1		Laser 101
1)	102.7	3.5	PJD3 VO St. Maarten/Power 102.7, Philipsburg
6)	105.5		Tropixx 105.5
2)	107.9	1	Gem R. Network, Philipsburg

Addresses and other information
1) "The Voice of St. Maarten" Back Street 187 , P.O. Box 366, Philipsburg ☎ +1 721 542 2580, 542 2764 🖷 +1 721 542 4905, 542 5531 GM/Dir: Donald R. Hughes **W**: www.pdj2radio.com – **2)** Rel. prgrs from Trinidad – **3)** W.J.A. Nisbeth Road 23, PO Box 1029, Philipsburg, St Maarten ☎ +1 721 542 2049. 🖷 +1 721 542 5791 **W**: www.sxmradio.com/choicefm.html – **4)** Federal Express Building, 2nd floor, Simpson Bay , St. Maarten ☎ +1 721 544 3377 **E**: info@island92.com **W**: www.island92.com – **5)** Lighthouse Broadcasting Network, Backstreet 59, , Philipsburg ☎+1 721 542 1133 🖷 +1 721 542 5778 – **6)** A.T. Illidge Road 106, Suite 2, Philipsburg ☎+1 721 543 2200🖷 +1 721 543 2229 **E**: marketing@philbroad.com **W**: http://oasis963.fm **W**: www.laser101.fm **W**: www.tropixx.fm – **8)** Fort Belair Road 3, Philipsburg ☎+1 721 5430 462 **E**: pearlstudio@caribserve.net **W**: www.pearlfmradio.com

ST MARTIN (France)

LT: UTC -4h — **Pop**: 36,000 — **Pr. L**: French, Creole, English, Dutch — **E.C**: 50Hz, 230V — **ITU**: MAF

RADIO GUADELOUPE PREMIÈRE
🖳 Quartier Bellevue-Marigot, 97100 Saint Martin ☎+590 590291716 **FM**: St. Martin 88.9MHz 0.3kW

RCI - RADIO CARAÏBES INTERNATIONAL (Comm.)
🖳 B.P. 173, Marigot, F-97150 Saint Martin. ☎+590 590875406 🖷 +590 590878887 **RCI FM**: 105.0MHz 0.3kW **RCI2 FM**: 102.1MHz + relays in Guadeloupe & Martinique.

RADIO SAINT MARTIN (Comm.)
🖳 Port de Marigot, 97150 Saint Martin **L.P.**: Mgr: H. Cocks. **FM**: 95.3MHz **D.Prgr**: 1000-0500(Sun 0400) in French & English exc. Spanish: 2000-2100W.

RADIO VOIX CHRETIENNES DE ST. MARTIN (Rlg.)
🖳 B.P. 103, Marigot, F-97150 Saint Martin. ☎+590 590873159 **L.P.**: Mgr: Father Cornelius Charles **FM**: 106MHz 0.25kW. **D.Prgr**: 0845-0530 in English & French.

RADIO CALYPSO
🖳 10, rue du Général de Gaule, 97150 Saint Martin ☎+590 590 522222 🖷 +590 590 52 22 23 **W**: www.radiocalypso.net **E**: calypsopub@powerantilles.com **FM**: 102.1MHz 1kW

ST PIERRE ET MIQUELON (France)

LT: UTC -3h (10 Mar-3 Nov: -2h) — **Pop**: 7,000 — **Pr.L**: French — **E.C**: 50Hz, 220V — **ITU**: SPM

RADIO ST PIERRE ET MIQUELON PREMIÈRE
🖳 B.P. 4227-97500 St. Pierre et Miquelon. ☎+508 508413824. **L.P.**: Dir: Joseph Edern. Dir. Tec: Daniel Beugin. Head of N: Jacques Barret. **FM**: St. Pierre 97.9MHz 10W, 99.9MHz 0.5kW, Miquelon 98.9MHz 50W.
D.Prgr: 0930-0230. **Rel. France-Inter**: 0230-0930. **N (local)**: 1000, 1530, 2200, (**Rel. France-Inter**) 1100, 1200, 1300, 1400, 1800, 1900 **Ann**: "Ici Radio Saint-Pierre et Miquelon Première" **IS**: La Marseillaise **V.** by QSL-card. Rec. acc.

R. Atlantique 🖳 B.P. 1282-97500 ☎+508 508412493 **W**: www.cheznoo.net/radioatlantique **FM**: 102.1MHz (also rel. R. France Int.)

ST VINCENT & THE GRENADINES

LT: UTC -4h — **Pop**: 104,000 — **Pr.L**: English — **E.C**: 50Hz, 230V — **ITU**: VCT

NATIONAL BROADCASTING CORPORATION RADIO ST. VINCENT AND THE GRENADINES – NBCSVG (Gov. Comm.)
🖳 Richmond Hill, P.O. Box 705, Kingstown ☎ +1 784 457 1111 🖷 +1 784 456 2749 **W**: www.nbcsvg.com **E**: nbcsvgadmin@vincysurf.com **L.P.**: Chmn: Kenneth Browne. GM: Corlita Ollivierre. Dep. GM: Raphael King. PM: Juanita Francois. Tech Dir: Lynford Byron. N Ed: Lesley De Bique
MW: 700kHz 10kW (inactive; emergency situations only)
FM: 89.7MHz 1kW, 90.7MHz 1kW, 107.5MHz 1kW
D.Prgr: 24h. Relays BBC 0400-0930. **N**: 1130, 1630, 2230 – Su 1230 only. **Ann**: "NBC Radio"

Other Stations (FM MHz):
BEQUIA COMMUNITY HIGH SCHOOL, PO Box 75BQ, Bequia. **FM**: 89.3 – **CROSS COUNTRY RADIO**, 50 Vigie Highway, PO Box 1000, Kingstown ☎ +1 784 458 5555 🖷 +1 784 456 4117. **W**: ccrradiosvg.com L.P.: SM Carlos Meloni **FM**: 88.5/104.3. Format: Rlg – **E-ZEE RADIO**, Dorsetshire Hill, PO Box 617, Kingstown ☎ +1 784 456 1078 **FM**: 91.1/100.5/102.7. Format: Easy listening – **GARIFUNA RADIO**, Learning Resource Center, Sandy Bay Community **FM**: 89.1 – **HITZ-FM**, St Vincent Broadcasting Corp., Dorsetshire Hill, P.O. Box 617, Kingstown ☎ +1 784 456 1078 🖷 +1 784 456 1015 **W**: www.hitz1037.com **FM**: 91.5/103.7. Format: Urban Caribbean – **HOT 97FM**, 1 Melville Street, PO Box 1716, Kingstown ☎ +1 784 452 9797 🖷 +1 784 456 2462 **W**: www.hot97svg.com **FM**: 93.1/97.1. Format: Urban Caribbean – **JEM RADIO**, Hopewell Rd, PO Box 1419, Kingstown ☎ +1 784 451 3827 **W**: www.jemradio.com **FM**: 89.1. Format: Rlg. – **NICE RADIO**, BDS Company Ltd., Dorsetshire Hill, PO Box 324, Kingstown ☎ +1 784 458 1013 🖷 +1 784 456 5556 **W**: www.niceradio.info L.P: Mgr: Douglas Defreitas. **FM**: 90.3/96.7/101.3 – **PRAISE FM**, Sion Hill, P.O.Box 443, Kingstown ☎ +1 784 456 1057 🖷 +1 784 456 1696. **W**: www.praise-fmsvg.com L.P.: PD Donny Daniel **FM**: 95.7/105.7 Format: Rlg – **STAR FM**, Murray's Rd, McKies Hill, PO Box 1651, Kingstown ☎ +1 784 453 7827 🖷 +1 784 485 7827 **W**: www.star983fm.com **FM**: 98.3/104.7 – **TOTAL FM**, 6 Mckies Hill, PO Box 360, Kingstown ☎ +1 784 457 1234 **FM**: 100.5 – **WEFM**, Windy Point, Lower Questelles, PO Box 1346, Kingstown ☎ +1 784 457 9994 🖷 +1 784 457 7123 **E**: wefm@vincysurf.com **W**: 999wefm.com L.P.: MD Julius Williams **FM**: 99.9

SUDAN

LT: UTC +3h — **Pop**: 34 million — **Pr.L**: Arabic, Nubian, Bedawi — **E.C**: 50Hz, 240V — **ITU**: SDN

MINISTRY OF INFORMATION & COMMUNICATION
W: www.sudannow.net **L.P**: Minister: Al-Zahawi Ibrahim Malek

SUDAN RADIO & TV CORPORATION - SUDAN RADIO (Gov.)
🖳 P.O. Box 1094, Mulazmin, Omdurman ☎+249 1 87572956 🖷 +249 1 87556006. **W**: sudanradio.info **E**: info@sudanradio.info
L.P: Dir: Mr. Mutasim Fadul. DG Eng. & Tech. Sces: Abbas Sidig.

MW	kHz	kW	Prgr.	MW	kHz	kW	Prgr.
Nyala	540	50	R	Wadi Halfa	873	5	R
El Obeid	639	10	R	Sennar	891	5	R
Kassala	666	10	R	Singa	891	5	R
Khartoum	747	10	G	Al-Foula	945	5	R
Port Sudan	747	5	R	Khartoum	963	100	Q/S
Omdurman	765	50	G	Al-Damazin	1026	5	R
Atbara	783	5	R	Reiba	1296	600	G
Al-Fashir	801	5	R	Al-Gadarif	1485	5	R
Dongola	819	10	R	Kosti	1584	5	R
Wad Madani	873	10	R	Kadogli	1602	5	R

SW: Khartoum (Al-Aitahab) 7200kHz 100kW 0230-1300 General prgr, 1300-2100 R. As-Salam.
FM: Khartoum: 88.6MHz (W), 90.0MHz (Q), 95.0MHz (G), 98.0MHz (E/U), 100.0MHz (N), 105.0MHz (Q). 101.0MHz (local).
Prgr. S: Khartoum 90.0MHz & Darfur: Al-Fashir/Al-Junayna 95.0MHz, Nyala 98.0MHz.
Prgrs: **G=General Prgr** (incl. **National Unity R.** 1000-1200) in Arabic: 24h. **H=Quran R**: 0200-1000. **K=Khartoum State R**: 0300-0700, 1300-1900. **N="Sudan Home Radio"**: 24h. **S=R. As-Salam** (Peace): 0530-0830, 1300-2100 on 963 & 7200kHz. **U="Nation's Memory Radio"**: 1100-1500, 1900-2300. **E=European prgr**. in English/French: 1500-1900. **W: Wadi al-Nil** (Nile Valley R.).
R=Regional stations. Not all regional stns are confirmed active and some are off air or on low power because of maintenance problems. Powers listed are the nominal ones. When on air, regional stns carry a mixture of local prgrs and relays of the General Service.
Ann: "Huna Omdurman, Idha'atu-l-Gumhuriya as-Sudan"
IS: Sudanese music.

External sce: see International radio section.

Other Stations (FM MHz):
Al-Furqan R, Khartoum 99.0 **W:** furqan.org – **Al-Kawthar R,** Khartoum 92.0 – **Al-Rabiyah FM,** Khartoum 94.0. Owned by Channel 4, UAE. **W:** alrabaafm.com – **Al-Tibbiyah FM,** Khartoum 99.3. **W:** altbya.fm – **Armed Forces R,** Khartoum 97.0 – **Capital R,** Khartoum: 91.6. **W:** facebook.com/91.6fm – **Khartoum FM,** Khartoum: 89.0. **W:** kfm89.net – **Mango FM,** Khartoum 96.0. **W:** mango96.com Also rel. BBC – **OUS R,** Khartoum: 89.5. **W:** ousmedia.com – **Police R,** Khartoum: 99.6 – **Sports FM,** Khartoum: 104.0. **W:** sportsfm104.com – **Tayba R,** Khartoum: 103.0. **W:** tayba.fm
R. Sawa, Khartoum: 97.5MHz.
UNAMID R, Darfur. **W:** unamid.unmissions.org . Relayed twice daily via R. As-Salam and Darfur stations

SURINAME

L.T: UTC -3h — **Pop:** 500,000 — **Pr.L:** Dutch, English, Sranang Tongo, Sarnami Hindi, Javanese — **E.C:** 60Hz, 110/115/127/220V — **ITU:** SUR – **Int. dialling code:** 597

TELECOMMUNICATE BEDRIJF SURINAME (TELESUR)
(Gov) ☒ P.O. Box 1839, Paramaribo ☎ 474242/473944 ▤ 404800 **W:** www.telesur.sr **E:** telesur@sr.net

STICHTING RADIO-OMROEP SURINAME (SRS)
☒ P.O. Box 271, Paramaribo ☎ 498115 ▤ 498116 **W:** www.radiosrs.com
E: adm@radiosrs.com
FM: Paramaribo 96.3MHz 1kW, Coronie, Nickerie, Moengo, Brokopando all 94.7MHz 0.1kW, Wageningen 95.6 MHz, Albina 105.7MHz 0.1kW **D.Prgr:** 0900-0700.

PRIVATE COMMERCIAL STATIONS:
SW: 8) **R. Apintie,** Paramaribo 4990kHz 1kW (irregular)
FM: 1) R. 10 88.1, 88.7 & 103.7MHz – **2) Radika** 98.3MHz – 3) R. **Garuda** 97.5, 103.4 & 105.7MHz – **4) Sky R.** 94.1 & 102.7MHz – **5) R. Katoilica** 93.1MHz – **6) R. Trishul** 90.5MHz – **7) R. Zon** 107.5 MHz – **8) R. Apintie** 97.1MHz – **9) R. Ishara** 100.7MHz – **10) R. Noer** 92.1MHz – **11) R. Paramaribo Rapar "The Hot-One"** 89.7MHz – **12) RP Acme** 91.3MHz – **13) RTV Mustika** 106.5MHz – **14) Sangeetmala R.** 99.3 & 100.1MHZ – **15) R. Shalom** 94.5MHz – **16) R. Pertjajah** 95.3MHz – **17) R. Koyeba** 104.9MHz – **18) Rasonic R.** 102.3 & 105.3MHz – **19) Kara´s Broadcasting Corp.** 101.1 & 103.1 MHz – **20) R. ABC** 101.7MHz
Addresses:
1) Stadionlaan 3 (P.O.Box 110), Paramaribo ☎ 410881 ▤ 422294 **W:** www.radio10.sr **E:** info@radio10.sr – **2)** Indira Gandhiweg 165, Paramariba ☎ 482800 – **3)** Goudstraat 20 Maretrait 4, Paramaribo 454 926 **W:** www.rtvgaruda.com – **4)** Ormosiastraat 2 (P.O.Box 1597), Paramaribo ☎ 530015 **W:** www.skyradioasuriname.com **E:** info@skyradio.sr – **5)** Paramaribo – **6)** Flocislaan 4, Boyen ☎ 439500 **W:** www.trishul.sr **E:**info@trishul.sr – **7)** Burenstraat No 60, Paramaribo ☎475261 ▤ 420233 **W:** www. radiozon.com **E:**admin@radiozon.com – **8)** verl. Gemenelandsweg 31, Paramaribo ☎ 400455 ▤ 400684 **W:** www.apintie.sr **E:** apintie@ sr.net – **9)** 109 Fredericiweg, Nickerie ☎231244 **W:** www.isharafm. com **E:** info@isharafm.com – **10)** Zwartenhovenbrugstraat 154, Paramaribo **W:** www.dbsuriname.com/radionoer.php **E:** radionoer@ gmail.com – **11) 18)** Coppenamstraat 34 (P.O. Box 975), Paramaribo ☎ 497774 Paramaribo **W:** www.dbsuriname.com/radiorpthehotone. php **E:** rpthehot1@gmail.com – **12)** Zwartenhovenbrugstraat 154, Paramaribo **W:** www.dbsuriname.com/radiorpthehotone.php – **13)** Paramaribo **W:** www.rtvmustika.net **E:** rtvmustikacontact@gmail.com – **14)** Indira Gandhiweg No 40, Wanicxa ☎ 482392 **W:** www.sgmsuri-name.com **E:** info@sgmsuriname.com – **15)** Malebatrumstraat 10-12 BV, Paramaribo ☎ 422630 ▤ 422737 **W:** www.shalomsuriname.com **E:** shalom@sr.net – **16)** Gemenlandsweg/Daneil Coutinhostraat 31, Paramaribo ☎ 401919 **W:**http://twitter.com/#!/PertjajahLuhur – **17)** van`t Hogerhuystraat 88 ☎ 403115 **W:**http://radiokoyebasuriname. com **E:** odjahh@yahoo.com – **18)** Bataviastraat 25, NW. Nickerie ☎ 231447 **W:** www.rasonictv.com – **19)** Verlengde Gemenelandsweg 177, Paramaribo ☎ 4300666 – **20)** Maystraat 57, Paramaribo ☎ 465092 **W:** www.abcsuriname.com **E:** info@abcsuriname.com

SWAZILAND

L.T: UTC +2h — **Pop:** 1.1 million — **Pr.L:** English, Siswati — **E.C:** 50Hz, 230V — **ITU:** SWZ

SWAZILAND POSTS & TELECOMMUNICATIONS CORPORATION (SPTC)
☒ Phutfumani Bldg, Warner St, P.O Box 125, Mbabane ☎+268 2405

2000 ▤ +268 24052020 **W:** www.sptc.co.sz **E:** info@sptc.co.sz
L.P: MD: Nathi Dlamini.

SWAZILAND BROADCASTING AND INFORMATION SERVICES (Gov)
☒ Corner Gwamile & Msakato Str, P.O. Box 338, Mbabane H100 ☎+268 24042761 ▤ +268 24042774 **W:** www.gov.sz/home. asp?pid=65 **E:** sbisnews@africaonline.co.sz
L.P: Dir: Percy Simelane. Asst. Principal prgrs Officer: Phesheya Dube. A/Prgr. Coordinator: Austin Dlamini. A/Tr. Engineer: Christopher Motsa.
FM: 88.5/91.6/93.6/105.2MHz 10kW + 4 low power relays.
English Sce: D.Prgr 0255-1800 on FM 91.6/93.6MHz. **N:** 0400, 0500, 1600. **Siswati Sce: D.Prgr** 0255-2100 on FM88.5/105.2MHz.
Ann: E: "This is the English sce. of Radio Swaziland". Siswati: "Lona ngu Mawakato waka Ngwane".
IS: at s/on, Cilongo (Swazi instrument). English Sce: cock crow, fan-fare, spoken ID, instrumental theme. **F.PI:** 100kW tx on 954kHz.

TRANS WORLD RADIO - VOICE OF THE CHURCH
☒ P.O. Box 4544, Corner Martin & Tenbergen St,Manzini ☎+268 25054845 ▤ +268 25054809 **L.P:** Nat. Dir: Nelson Vilakati, Adm: Tryphinah Dlamini, PM: Abel Vilakati.
FM: 95.0/97.0/101.0MHz.
MW: TWR Africa, Mpangela Ranch 1170kHz 50kW 1600-2030 & SW. For further details see International Radio section.

F.PI: private radio stations

SWEDEN

L.T: UTC +1h (31 Mar-27 Oct: +2h) — **Pop:** 9.5 million — **Pr.L:** Swedish — **E.C:** 50Hz, 230V — **ITU:** S

TERACOM AB
Responsible for distribution of prgrs produced by Sveriges Radio (Swedish Broadcasting Corporation) and by most of the commercial radio stns and community radio associations.
HQ: ☒ Box 30150, SE-10425 Sundbyberg ☎ +46 8 55542000 ▤ +46 8 55542001 **W:** www.teracom.se **E:** kundtjanst@teracom.se
L.P: MD: Christer Fritzon

PTS
PTS (Post-och telestyrelsen) is the authority that supervises activities in radio, telecom and datacom.
☒ Box 5398, SE-10249 Stockholm ☎ +46 8 6785500 **W:** www.pts.se
E: pts@pts.se **L.P:** Director General .Göran Marby

SVERIGES RADIO AB
(Swedish Broadcasting Corporation) (Pub)
☒ Radiohuset, Oxenstiernsgatan 20, Stockholm (☒SE-10510 Stockholm) ☎+ 46 8 7845000 ▤+ 46 8 7841500 **W:** www.sr.se
E: lyssnarservice@sverigesradio.se **L.P:** MD: Cilla Benkö.

FM (MHz)		1	2	3	4	kW
24)	Arvidsjaur	89.4	94.2	97.1	100.6	60
20)	Bollnäs	88.4	91.7	96.0	103.8	60
19)	Borlänge	89.4	93.0	97.7	101.3	60
25)	Borås	88.5	94.6	97.9	102.9	10
14)	Bäckefors	92.7	96.8	99.1	102.2	60
6)	Emmaboda	93.0	96.7	99.7	101.8	60
7)	Emmaboda				95.6	60
5)	Finnveden	90.1	94.2	99.9	103.4	30
24)	Gällivare	88.3	94.9	98.5	100.9	60
9)	Gävle	88.1	97.4	99.8	102.0	60
13)	Göteborg	89.3	96.3	99.4	101.9	60
12)	Halmstad	87.7	91.2	95.4	97.3	60
13)	Halmstad				102.6	3
11)	Helsingborg	89.8	95.7	98.4	103.2	6
20)	Hudiksvall	87.6	90.2	93.8	100.7	60
11)	Hörby	88.8	92.4	97.0	101.4	60
11)	Hörby				89.5	5
24)	Kalix	91.3	93.6	97.9	102.2	60
9)	Karlshamn	90.3	93.4	98.3	100.4	15
9)	Karlskrona	89.1	95.0	97.7	100.7	10
17)	Karlstad	90.5	94.2	96.5	103.5	15
24)	Kiruna	89.1	92.7	96.4	102.7	60
4)	Kisa	90.5	92.5	96.9	103.6	30
23)	Lycksele	92.9	95.4	98.7	103.3	60
11)	Malmö	87.9	93.3	98.0	102.0	6
11)	Malmö*				100.6	6
19)	Mora	92.2	96.7	99.0	101.0	60
4)	Motala	91.1	94.0	98.2	101.8	20
3)	Norrköping	90.0	93.5	98.7	102.3	60

FM (MHz)		1	2	3	4	kW
4)	Norrköping				94.8	60
5)	Nässjö	89.6	92.1	99.0	102.1	60
24)	Pajala	90.8	93.0	95.9	100.2	60
23)	Skellefteå	93.8	96.3	100.0	103.9	60
16)	Skövde	88.9	95.1	97.5	100.3	60
21)	Sollefteå	89.3	93.5	98.1	101.2	60
1)	Stockholm	92.4	96.2	99.3	103.3	60
1)	Stockholm**		89.6			0.9
1)	Stockholm***				93.8	0.9
23)	Storuman	87.6	91.2	99.0	102.5	60
21)	Sundsvall	92.7	96.9	99.2	102.8	60
16)	Sunne	90.9	94.5	98.5	101.8	60
22)	Sveg	90.6	94.9	97.9	102.2	60
22)	Tåsjö	88.9	94.7	97.5	100.8	60
23)	Tåsjö				88.2	60
2)	Uppsala	90.3	93.3	96.6	102.5	20
12)	Varberg	90.4	93.6	98.8	103.8	10
8)	Visby	87.6	94.1	97.2	100.2	60
6)	Vislanda	88.0	90.6	94.7	101.0	20
23)	Vännäs	88.5	92.1	95.8	103.6	60
7)	Västervik	88.3	91.8	96.0	102.7	60
15)	Västerås	90.7	95.8	98.0	100.5	60
21)	Ånge	93.2	95.6	99.6	103.1	60
22)	Ånge				94.5	60
24)	Älvsbyn	90.6	94.5	99.4	102.9	60
17)	Örebro	87.9	91.5	99.6	102.8	60
21)	Örnsköldsvik	90.8	94.4	97.8	100.1	60
22)	Östersund	87.9	91.5	94.0	100.4	60
2)	Östhammar	89.1	92.8	95.5	101.6	60
24)	Överkalix	88.9	91.7	99.0	103.2	15

+ 360 low power txs. A comprehensive list of all stns is available on **W:** www.teracom.se
*) Broadc. "Din Gata", a local P3-prgr for the Malmö-area. **) P6 Stockholm International. Prgr for immigrant and minority langs, mix of music and rel. of foreign broadc., BBC, Deutsche Welle, CBC etc. 24h. 2200-0200 and 0300-0600 rel. BBC WS. ***) SR Metropol. Music for young people, 24h (add. frqs in greater Stockholm area: 97.6, 102.9 MHz)

First Prgr. W: www.sr.se/p1 (news & spoken word): MF 0429-0045,SS0455-0030. News:MF 0430, 0500, 0530, 0600, 0630, 0700, 0800, 0900, 1000, 1130, 1300, 1400, 1445, 1500, 1545, 1645, 1800, 1900, 2000, 2100, 2200, 2300,2400. **Wrp** (incl. forecast for Swedish waters): 0455, 0555, 0655, 1155, 1455, 2050 – **Second Prgr. W:** www. sr.se/p2 24h: Classical music and jazz prgrs, Sami, Finnish and prgrs for immigrants – **Third Prgr. W:** www.sr.se/p3: light music, entertainment, current affairs, news for listeners under 40: 24h – **Fourth Prgr. W:** www.sr.se/p4 24h: Regional network 0459 - 1700. 1700-0500 relay of P4 network from Stockholm (frqs as above, addresses given below) – **P4 Radio Stockholm. W:** www.sr.se/stockholm 103.3 MHz Local prgrs for Stockholm area. 0503-2303. 2303-0503 Relay of main P4 prgr **Ann:** Nat. Prgr. "Sveriges Radio" and the sce e.g. "Sveriges Radio P1"

Digital Radio (DAB): Malmö 2kW, Göteborg 2kW, Stockholm/Nacka 4.0kW, Enköping 2.0kW, Uppsala 2.0kW, Södertälje 2.0kW, Älvsbyn 4.0kW, Sigtuna 0.2 kW. Single frequency network on 225.648MHz, block 12B with SR Atlas, SR Klassiskt, SR Minnen, SR P1, SR P7 Sisuradio, P3 Star and SR knattekanal. R.1 in Stockholm 12C. Commercial stns are using 12C, 12D, 13C and 13F.

Addresses of Regional Centres
1) SR Stockholm, Pipersgatan 45, 107 80 Stockholm. – **2)** SR Uppland, Box 1552, 751 45 Uppsala. – **3)** SR Storman, Box 641, 631 08 Eskilstuna. – **4)** SR Östergötland, Box 500, 601 07 Norrköping. – **5)** SR Jönköping, 551 92 Jönköping. – **6)** SR Kronoberg, Box 62, 351 03 Växjö. – **7)** SR Kalmar, 391 83 Kalmar. – **8)** SR Gotland, Box 1324, 621 24 Visby. – **9)** SR Blekinge, Box 305, 371 25 Karlskrona. – **10)** SR Kristianstad, Box 505, 291 25 Kristianstad. – **11)** SR Malmöhus, 211 01 Malmö. – **12)** SR Halland, Box 133, 301 04 Halmstad. – **13)** SR Göteborg, Pumpvägen 2, 405 13 Göteborg. – **14)** SR Väst, Box 654, 451 24 Uddevalla. – **15)** SR Västmanland, Box 850, 721 22 Västerås. – **16)** SR Skaraborg, 541 24 Skövde. – **17)** SR Värmland, Box 98, 651 03 Karlstad – **18)** SR Örebro, Västra Bangatan 15, 701 80 Örebro – **19)** SR Dalarna, Box 123, 791 23 Falun – **20)** SR Gävleborg, Box 6702, 801 74 Gävle – **21)** SR Västernorrland, 851 79 Sundsvall – **22)** SR Jämtland, Lingonvägen 7 B, 831 62 Östersund – **23)** SR Västerbotten, Mariehemsvägen 4, 906 15 Umeå – **24)** SR Norrbotten, Nygatan 3, 971 71 Luleå – **25)** SR Sjuhärad, Box 27, 503 05 Borås

Sami R., Österleden 21, SE-98131 Kiruna. MD: Ole-isak Mienna **W:** www.sverigesradio.se/sameradion **E:** sameradion@sverigesradio.se

Sisuradio, Oxenstiernsgatan 20 RH-4A, SE 10510 Stockholm. Regional prgrs in Finnish 1710-1800 via P4 transmitters, **E:** sisuradio@sr.se.
SR Metropol, Pipersgatan 45, SE-107 80 Stockholm **E:** metropol@sr.se
Further information about email addresses, tel numbers and prgrs can be found at **W:** www.sr.se & www.onair.nu

SVERIGES UTBILDNINGSRADIO AB (Pub)
(Swedish Educational Broadcasting Company)
☞ UR, Tulegatan 7, SE-113 95 Stockholm ☎ + 46 8 7840000
W: www.ur.se **E:** kundtjanst@ur.se **LP:** MD:Erik Fichtelius **FM:** See Swedish Radio **UR** produces educational prgrs for radio & television
Local Commercial Radio:

Location	MHz	kW	Net	Location	MHz	kW	Net
Skellefteå	92.4	1.5	C	Uddevalla	104.2	1	A
Vimmerby	100.0	1	C	Oskarström	104.2	1	A
Södertälje	100.8	3	C	Umeå	104.2	5	A
Skellefteå	101.9	1	C	Stockholm	104.3	1	A
Falun	103.2	3	A	Växjö	104.3	2	C
Östersund	104.0	3	C	Karlstad	104.4	10	C
Färjestaden	104.0	3	C	Visby	104.4	6	C
Eskilstuna	104.5	10	C	Västerås	106.1	3	A
Värnamo	104.6	1		Visby	106.1	6	A
Mora	104.6	5	C	Borlänge	106.3		C
Örebro	104.7	2	A	Stockholm	106.3	1	B
Örnsköldsvik	104.8	10	A	Karlshamn	106.4	1	C
Gävle	104.9	1	A	Skövde	106.4	3	C
Trollhättan	105.0	3	C	Karlskrona	106.4	1	C
Stockholm	105.1	1	B	Uppsala	106.5	4	D
Hudiksvall	105.1	3	C	Varberg	106.5	1	A
Jönköping	105.1	4	A	Norrköping	106.5	3	A
Stockholm	105.1	1.3	B	Gävle	106.7	1	A
Malmö	105.2	1	B	Malmö	106.7	1	C
Gällivare	105.2	10	A	Mora	106.8	1	A
Göteborg	105.3	1	B	Gnosjö	106.8	3	C
Uppsala	105.3	2	C	Luleå	106.9	3	A
Skellefteå	105.4	2	A	Linköping	106.9	3	A
Karlstad	105.4	5	A	Malmö	107.0	3	A
Kalmar	105.4	1	A	Hudiksvall	107.0	3	C
Borlänge	105.5	1	A	Kiruna	107.0	3	A
Sundsvall	105.5	1	A	Borås	107.1	3	C
Borås	105.5	1	A	Örnsköldsvik	107.1	5	C
Stockholm	105.5	2	C	Halmstad	107.2	1	C
Luleå	105.6	2	C	Göteborg	107.3	3	A
Nyköping	105.7	4	A	Kristianstad	107.3	1	A
Uddevalla	105.7	2	C	Eskilstuna	107.3	3	A
Växjö	105.8	1	A	Helsingborg	107.6	1	C
Göteborg	105.9	3	C	Skövde	107.6	5	C
Helsingborg	106.0	1	A	Nyköping	107.7	4	C
Jönköping	106.0	5	C				

+ 30 stns below 1kW. **NB:** These stns belong to networks. There are a number of commercial local stns on FM. A comprehensive list can be found on **W:** www.teracom.se & www.onair.nu
Addresses and other information:
A) MIX MEGAPOL, 115 78 Stockholm **W:** www.mixmegapol.se **E:** info@mixmegapol.se – **B) NRJ,** P.O. Box17179, SE-11867 Stockholm ☎ +46 8 6589800 **W:** www.nrj.se **E:** info@nrj.se – **C) RIX FM,** Box 17820, 118 94 Stockholm ☎ +46 8 56272000 🖷+46 8 56272082 **W:** www.rixfm.com **E:** rix@rixfm.com

MTG Modern Times Group
☞ Box 17115, 10462 Stockholm **W:** www.bandit.se
Bandit Rock Stockholm: 106.3 MHz 1 kW – **Bandit Rock Skåne**: 95.9 & 105.9 MHz 1 kW – **Bandit Rock Västra Götaland**: 90.8, 104.8, 106.8 & 106.9 MHz. 0.04 -1 kW – **Bandit Rock Norrbotten**: 95.3, 103.6 & 106.3 MHz. 0.25 – 5 kW

Private stations in the Stockholm area
FM(MHz): 88.0 City 1, 96.3 City 2, 97.3 Solna-Sundbyberg, 101.1 R. Sydost, 101.9 Star FM, 104.3 Mix Megapol, 104.7 Lugna Favoriter, 105.1 Energy, 105.5 Rix FM, 105.9 The Voice, 106.3 Bandit, 106.7 Rockklassiker, 107.1 Vinyl, 107.5 Studio

COMMUNITY STATIONS
Närradio is open for any non-commercial organization, whose main activity is other than broadcasting. The organization may obtain a permit for community radio broadcasting by PTS. The txs are made available at a nominal fee and built and operated by Teracom AB. The txs have powers of 10-400W and the target is the local community. There are more than 200 txs in operation. Frequency range: 88-108MHz. A few Närradio stns also broadcast commercial prgrs. A comprehensive list of Närradio-stns is at **W:** www.teracom.se

Närradio in greater Stockholm area:
FM(MHz):, 88.2 R. Sigtuna, 88.9 Sydväst, 90.5 MRS, 91.4 Tyresö, 91.6 BMU, 94.2 Järfälla, 94.5 Hit FM, 94.6 Sollentuna, 95.3 City 2, 97.3 Solna/Sbg, 97.8 Lidingö, 98.3 R. Nord, 08.5 Haninge, 99.9 Nacka, 101.4 R. Viking, 103.7 R. Österåker and 107.8 R. Roslagen.

SWITZERLAND

L.T: UTC +1h (31 Mar-27 Oct: +2h) — **Pop:** 7.6 million — **Pr.L:** German, Swiss-German dialects, French, Italian, Rumantsch — **E.C:** 50Hz, 230V — **ITU:** SUI

SRG SSR IDÉE SUISSE / SSR - Société Suisse de Radiodiffusion et Télévision (Pub.)
Giacomettistrasse 1, Postfach 570, CH-3000 Bern 31 ☎+41 31 3509111 ✉+41 31 3509256 **W:** srgssrideesuisse.ch **LP:** Pres: Jean Bernard Münch. DG: Armin Walpen. DG adj: Daniel Eckmann.

GERMAN LANGUAGE NETWORK
Schweizer Radio DRS (SR DRS)
Radiodirektion SR DRS, Novarastrasse 2, CH-4002 Basel ☎+41 61 365 3411 ✉ +41 61 365 3483 **W:** drs.ch **E:** radiofon@srdrs.ch
L.P: Dir: Iso Rechsteiner.

FM (MHz)	DRS 1	DRS 2	DRS 3	RR	kW
Bantiger	88.2	93.2	99.3		5
Biel-Magglingen		99.7			1
Castel S.Pietro	98.8				10
Celerina	91.9	100.3	106.3	89.1	0.75
Chalavornaire	93.2				1
Chasseral	103.0		105.3		20
Feschel	88.2	90.3	101.5		1.5
Froburg	96.0	98.7	91.3		1.2
Gebidem	89.4	93.9	103.9		2.4
Glarus	91.4				1
Haute-Nendaz	92.0				2.5
Leucel	88.1				6
Castel S. Pietro	98.8				10
Niederhorn	93.6	97.2	105.8		4.5
Paudo	96.9				2.2
Pfaender	96.3	97.7	107.5		4
Ravoire	102.1				1.9
Rigi	90.9	96.6	103.8		30
Salève	87.8				1
San Salvatore	96.3				17
Säntis	101.5	95.4	105.6		55
Schaltenrein	90.7				1
Solothurn	89.7	98.0			1.5
St. Chrischona	90.6	99.0	103.6		33
Tarasp	101.3	103.9	95.1	98.7	0.25
Uetliberg	94.6	99.6	105.8		1.6
Valzeina	93.8	102.5	104.3	90.3	0.75

+ numerous trs less than 1kW. – RR=Rumantsch (see below).
1st Prgr(DRS 1): 24h. **Local Broadc. in German:** MF 0532-0534,MF 0615-0617, MF 0632-0637,MF 0712-0714, Mon-Sat 1103-1113, MF + Sun1630-1700, Sat 1630-1640 – **2nd Prgr(DRS 2):** 24h. – **3rd Prgr(DRS 3):** 24h – **DRS Virus:** Satellite Hot Bird 12399 GHz, DAB and cable 24h – **DRS 4 News:** Satellite Hot Bird 12399 GHz, DAB and cable 24h. All prgrs also via Internet.

RUMANTSCH LANGUAGE NETWORK
Radio e Televisiun Rumantscha (RTR)
Theaterweg 1, CH-7002 Chur ☎+41 81 2557575 ✉ +41 81 2557500 **W:** www.rtr.ch **LP:** Dir: Mariano Tschuor.
FM: see RR netw. (above) **D.Prgr:** 0500-2300, 2300-0500 rel. DRS1.

FRENCH LANGUAGE NETWORK
Radio Télévision Suisse (RTS) - Radio Suisse Romande (RSR)
20 Quai Ernest-Ansermet, CP 234, CH-1211 Geneve 8 ☎+41 22 708 2020 ✉ +41 22 708 9800 **W:** rsr.ch **LP:** MD: Gilles Marchand.

FM (MHz)	RSR1	RRS2	RSR3	RSR4	kW
Anzere				106.5	0.5
Bantiger	95.1				5
Castel S.Pietro	87.8				10
Chasseral	102.3	100.3	104.2		20
Chamossaire	105.1/98.1	95.1	88.6		1
Chaux de Fo.	92.3	96.3	103.4		1.4
Dôle, La	91.2	100.1	105.6		19
Feschel	91.4	96.1	107.4		1.5
Gebidem	90.8				2.4
Gibloux	91.0	92.5	88.6		1.0
Hte Nendaz	94.4	96.5	106.0		2.5
Les Ordons	94.2	99.6	104.8		9
Leucel	102.6	96.2	98.5		6

FM (MHz)	RSR1	RRS2	RSR3	RSR4	kW
Martigny				90.8	0.6
Montmagny	92.3	92.0	89.1		4
Mt. Pélerin	91.6	101.5	90.6		2
Nendaz				97.5	0.5
Paudo	105.3				2.8
Premier	94.7	100.8	104.7		10
Ravoire	93.2	106.9	100.5		1.9
Salève	94.9	100.7	104.4	90.8	1
San Salvatore	104.0				17
Säntis	99.9				55
Schaltenrein	96.9				1
Vallée de Joux	99.5	87.6	101.4		1
Vercorin				98.5	0.5

+ many txs less than 1kW.
RSR1 (La Première): 24h. **N:** On the h. (exc. 2100, 2200). Also 0530, 0630, 1130, 2130 – **RSR2 (Espace 2):** 24h. **N:** 0500, 0600, 0700, 0800, 1200(M-F), 1600, 1800, 2130, 2300 – **RSR3 (Couleur 3):** 24h non-stop music and N – **RSR4 (Option Musique):** 24h.

ITALIAN LANGUAGE NETWORK
Radiotelevisione Svizzera (RSI)
Via Canevascini, Casella postale 235, CH-6903 Lugano-Besso ☎+41 91 803 5111 ✉ +41 91 803 5355 **W:** rsi.ch **E:** info@rsi.ch
L.P: Dir: Dino Balestra.

FM (MHz)	RSI I	RSI 2	RSI 3	kW
Celerina	104.3			2
Chasseral	107.3			20
Gebidem	96.7			2.4
Leucel	97.8			6
Castel S. Pietro	87.9	98.8	104.5	10
Paudo	89.4	93.5	107.4	2.8
Rigi	106.2			30
Salève	97.1			2
S. Salvatore	88.1	91.5	106.0	17
Valzeina	95.8			1.5

+ numerous txs less than 1kW.
RSI1 (Rete 1): 24h. **N:** hourly (not 1200, 1800) + 1130, 1730. – **RSI2 (Rete 2):** 24h. **N:** 0530, 0630, 0730, 0830, 0930, 1030, 1130, 1200, 1330, 1430, 1530, 1630, 1800, 2200, 2300. Classical music and cultural prgrs – **RSI3 (Rete 3):** 24h. **N:** 0530, 0630, 0730, 0830, 0930, 1330, 1530, 1800, 2130, 2300.

WORLD RADIO SWITZERLAND
Passage de la Radio 2, CH-1205 Geneva ☎+41 22 7087444 ✉ +41 22 7087454 **W:** www.worldradio.ch **E:** management@worldradio.ch
FM; Salève 101.7MHz 2kW. **D.Prgr** in English: 24h.

Private stations, main networks (FM, MHz):
R. Central: 89.3 Matt, 89.4 Steinberg, 89.4 Wangen, 89.6 Menzingen, 92.1 Weesen, 93.6 Stans, 97.7 Haslen, 97.7 Spiringen, 98.8 Seelisberg, 99.0 Giswil/Sarnen, 99.2 Küssnacht, 99.2 Zug, 100.1 Sonnenberg, 101.8 Andermatt, 101.8 Feusisberg, 101.8 Mattgratt, 102.6 Ingenbohl, 103.0 Attinghausen. **W:** www.radiocentral.ch
R. Grischa: 87.9 Avers, 89.3 Lohn, 89.4 Safien, 89.6 Ruschein, 89.8 Lenzerheide, 94.5 Sils i.D. Crap, 95.0 Sedrun, 95.1 Feldis, 97.2 Davos, 98.5 Arosa, 99.2 Malix, 99.7 Gotschnagrat, 102.3 Bergün, 102.4 Vals, 102.7 Splügen, 106.2 Mon, 107.0 Curaglia, 107.0 Valzeina, 107.4 Morissen. **W:** www.radiogrischa.ch
R. Pilatus: 87.6 Kussnacht/Schupfheim/Zug, 92.0 Kriens, 92.8 Dagmersellen, 93.0 Sursee, 95.7 Menzingen, 95.8 Beckenried/Ennetbürgen, 100.7 Willisau, 103.4 Igenbohl/Sarnen, 104.4 Engelberg/Ennetmoos/Giswil/Höchweidwald, 104.6 Seelisberg, 104.9 Sonnenberg, 106.5 Werthenstein. **W:** www.radiopilatus.ch
R. Sunshine: 88.0 Rooterberg/Zug, 88.8 Einsielden/Horgen/Widen/Willisau, 90.0 Igenbohl/Kriens, 93.4 Kriens/Menzingen, 93.6 Dagmersellen, 94.2 Giswil/Mattgratt/Sarnen/Sursee, 99.6 Seelisberg/Lopper/Werthenstein. **W:** www.sunshine.ch
R. Top: 87.9 Gossau, 88.2 Oberwinterthur, 88.5 St. Gallen, 90.0 St. Gallen, 93.1 Wil, 95.0 Feusisberg, 97.7 Strichboden, 98.9 Fluringen, 99.1 Ebnatt Kappel, 99.4 Niederhasli, 99.5 Kreuzlingen, 100.2 Reutenen Homburg, 101.9 Elgg, 103.3 Schaffhausen, 103.5 Winterthur, 104.5 Zürich. **W:** www.toponline.ch/radiotop.shtml
RJB: 90.0 Bienne, 90.3Sonceboz, 90.4 Plagne, 91.8 Lovresse, 95.5 Cormoret/Moutier, 95.9 Court Frête, 96.3 Gerolfingen, 97.5 Orvin, 101.2 Prêles/Tavannes, 102.0 Tramelan, 103.4 Delémont, 104.5 Péry, 104.9 Gals, **W:** www.rjb.ch
RTN: 87.9 Bôle, 90.2 Monts de Verrières, 93.2 Les Brenets, 93.4 Noiraigue, 94.2 Fleurier/Haut-Geneveys, 95.8 Marin, 97.5 Dombresson Clémesin, 97.5 La Brévine/Villiers, 98.0 Locle, 98.2 Montmagny/Neuchatel, 101.0 Brot, 101.7 Chaux-de-Fonds, 107.6 Yverdon. **W:** www.rtn.ch
NB: Tx powers vary from a few W to 5 kW. 40 more stns in operation.

DAB: Palette DeutschSchweiz: channel 12C 227.360MHz. Prgrs: DRS1, DRS2, DRS3, DRS Musigwälle, DRS Virus, R. Rumantsch, Swiss Pop, Swiss Classic, Swiss Jazz, RSR La Premiere+, RSI Rete Uno+ & DRS 4 News WRS+ – **Palette Suisse Romande:** channel 12A 225.648MHz. Prgrs: RSR La Première, RSR Espace 2, RSR Couleur 3, RSR Option Musique, Swiss Pop. Swiss Classic, Swiss Jazz, R. Rumantsch, DRS 1+, RSI Rete Uno+, DRS Musigwälle+ & World R. Switzerland – **Palette Svizzera Italiana:** channel 12 A 223.936 MHz. Prgrs: Rete Uno, Rete Due, Rete Tre, DRS Musigwälle, R. Rumantsch, Option Musique , Swiss Classic, Swiss Pop, Swiss Jazz & World R. Switzerland – **Palette Rumantsch:** channel 12 D 229.072 MHz. Prgrs: DRS1+ DRS2+, DRS3+, DRS Musigwälle, DRS Virus+, R. Rumantsch, Swiss Pop+, Swiss Classic+, Swiss Jazz+, RSR La Premiere+, RSI Rete Uno+ ,DRS 4 News, WRS+ – **Palette Privat SMC Deutschschweiz:** channel 7 D 194.064 MHz. Prgrs: Backstageradio+, Lifechannel+, Open Broadcast+,Radio Basel+, Radio Inside+ ,Energy+, Eviva+ ,Top Two+, Swissmountainholyday Radio+, R. Maria+, Option Musique +, Rete Tre+, DRS 4 News+, CH Classic+

SYRIA

L.T: UTC +2h (29 Mar-31 Oct: +3h) — **Pop:** 20 million — **Pr.L:** Arabic — **E.C:** 50Hz, 220V — **ITU:** SYR

MINISTRY OF INFORMATION
🖃 Mezzeh Autostrad, Dar al Ba'th Building, Damascus ☎+963 11 6664681 🖹 +963 11 6664681 **W:** www.moi.gov.sy **E:** info@moi.gov.sy **L.P:** Talib Qadi Amin, Asst. Minister.

SYRIAN RADIO AND TV (Gov.)
🖃 Radio & TV Directorate, Ommayad Square, Damascus ☎+963 11 2720700 🖹 +963 11 2234930 **W:** www.rtv.gov.sy **L.P:** DG: Fayez Al Sayegh. Dir. Eng: Adnan Salhah. Dir. Radio: Mahmoud Al Joma'at.

MW	kHz	kW	Prgr	MW	kHz	kW	Prgr
Adra	567	300	1	Al-Hassake	918	200	1
Homs	594	100	2	Homs	936	100	1
Sabboura	666	50	2	Deir ez-Zor	954	50	2
Sarakeb	747	100	1	Tartus	1071	100	*
Tartus	783	300	1/E	Sarakeb	1314	50	A/Y
Deir ez-Zor	828	200	1				

*relays R. Al-Nour, LBN

FM	1	2/M	Y	kW
Abu Kamal			92.6	
Afrin	93.0	90.3	96.6	
Al-Hassake	89.9	93.0	99.5	
Aleppo	96.1	99.4	89.9	10
Ayn al-Arab	89.4		105.1	
Bloudan	93.5		96.7	
Damascus	95.5	98.3	88.7	
Deir ez-Zor	90.0	94.1	87.8	150
Homs			99.3	
Maliqiyah	89.4	92.1	99.0	
Nabi Saleh	89.0	93.0	98.8	
Raqqah	103.7	96.9	93.7	
Slenfe	94.9	91.7	88.6	150
Suweida	92.6	87.8	100.9	150
Tartus			95.5	
Yabrud			93.0	

General Prgr (1): 24h. Incl. **VO Armed Forces:** 1630-1700 and **R. Palestine** prgr: 1700-1730.
Voice of the People (2): 0400-2000. **Voice of Youth (Y)** 0400-2400.
Aleppo local prgr (A): 1300-1600. **E:** External Service. **NB:** the segments and networks carried on each frequency may vary.
Ann: 1: "Idha'at Dimashq". 2: "Huna Idha'at Sowt as-Sha'ab min Dimashq". Y: "Huna Sowt ash-Shabab". R. Palestine: "Idha'at Falasteen min Dimashq". Aleppo: "Idha'at al-Halab".

EXTERNAL SERVICE: R. Damascus: see International Radio section.

Other stations:
Al Madina FM: Slenfe 100.5MHz, Aleppo/Damascus 101.5MHz. **W:** www.almadinafm.com – **Arabesque FM:** Aleppo/Damascus 102.3MHz, Slenfe 106.9MHz. **W:** arabesque.fm – **Fann FM:** Aleppo/Damascus 89.0MHz, Slenfe 106.1MHz. **W:** fann-fm.com – **Farah FM:** Aleppo/Damascus 97.3MHz. **W:** www.farah.fm – **R. Gecko (UN)**, Camp Faouar, Golan: 103.8MHz. **W:** www.radio-gecko.com – **Melody FM:** Aleppo/Damascus 97.9MHz. **W:** melodysyria.com – **Mix FM,** Damascus: 105.7MHz. **W:** mixfmsyria.com – **Ninar FM:** Aleppo 88.3MHz, Slenfe 89.6MHz, Damascus 93.8MHz. **W:** ninarweb.com – **Rotana Style FM:** Slenfe 103.3MHz, Aleppo/Damascus 105.0MHz. **W:** www.rotanastyle.com – **Sawt el-Ghad,** Damascus: 99.9MHz. **W:**

sawtelghad.com – **Shahba FM,** Aleppo 94.0MHz. **W:** www.shahbafm.com – **Sham FM:** Damascus 92.3MHz, Aleppo 95.3MHz, Slenfe 101.8MHz. **W:** www.shamfm.fm – **Syria Al-Ghad FM:** Damascus 104.2MHz, Aleppo 104.4MHz, Slenfe 107.4MHz. **W:** syriaalghad.com – **Version FM:** Damascus 94.4MHz. **W:** versionfm.com **NB:** many stns and transmitters reported off the air or operating irregularly. **Watan FM** reported in Damascus, operated by the opposition.

TAIWAN (Rep. of China)

L.T: UTC +8h — **Pop:** 23 million — **Pr.L:** Mandarin(Chinese), Taiwanese(Amoy), Hakka — **E.C:** 60Hz, 110V — **ITU:** CHN (**WRTH:** TWN)

NATIONAL COMMUNICATIONS COMISSION (NCC)
RenAi Rd. Office: 🖃 No. 50, Sec. 1, RenAi Rd., Taipei 10052 ☎ + 886 2 3343 7377 🖹 + 886 2 2343 3994 **W:** www.ncc.gov.tw **E:** po2@ncc.gov.tw **L.P:** Chairperson: Shyr, Howard S. H.

CHUNGKUO KUANGPO KUNGSSU (Broadcasting Corporation of China - BCC) (Priv. Comm.)
🖃 375 Sungchiang Rd, Chungshan Ward, Taipei 104 ☎ + 886 2 2501 9688 🖹 + 886 2 2501 8834 **W:** www.bcc.com.tw **E:** pr@bcc.com.tw **L.P:** Chairman: Chao Shao Kang
Call: BE followed by the callsign below

	MW Call	Location	kHz	kW	Netw.
1)	D57	Taipei (Tucheng)	531	10	L
10)	D65	Ilan	630	10	N
1)	D34	Taipei (Tucheng)	648	20	N
6)	D92	Tainan	711	10	C
4)	D58	Taichung	720	10	N
8)	D28	Taitung	819	10	N
9)	D27	Hualien	855	10	N
7)	D25	Kaohsiung	864	10	N
2)	G77	Hsinchu	882	10	N
6)	D24	Tainan	891	10	L
4)	D43	Taichung	927	10	C
1)	D55	Taipei (Tucheng)	963	20	C
8)	D88	Taitung	1008	10	C
2)	D53	Hsinchu	1017	10	C
5)	D26	Chia-i	1035	10	C
4)	D23	Taichung	1062	10	L
11)	D72	Yuli	1116	3.5	N
12)	D68	Puli*	1152	1	C
10)	D86	Ilan	1161	10	C
9)	D89	Miaoli	1161	10	C
4)	D32	Hualien	1188	10	C
7)	D52	Kaohsiung	1224	10	C
6)	D47	Tainan	1296	10	N
5)	D63	Chia-i	1350	10	N
11)	D74	Yuli*	1386	3.5	N
3)	D54	Miaoli	1413	10	N
12)	D67	Puli*	1413	1	N

N=News Netw, C=Country Netw, , L=local

	FM Location	P	F	M	kW
1)	Taipei	103.3	105.9	96.3	35/10/35
3)	Huoyenshan	102.9	101.5	96.1	10/10/10
4)	Taichung	102.1	106.9	96.3	10/10/35
5)	Chentoushan	103.1	104.3	96.1	10/10/5
7)	Kaohsiung	103.3	105.9	96.3	35/10/35
8)	Taitung	102.1	106.9	96.3	5/2.5/2.5
9)	Hualien	102.1	106.9	96.3	5/2.5/5
10)	Ilan	102.1	102.9	96.1	2.5/2.5/2.5
11)	Yuli*	103.3	105.7		1/2.5
12)	Puli*	107.3			1
13)	Kinmen*	96.3			10

P=Pop Netw, F=Formosa Netw, M=Music Netw. *) relay station.

D.Prgr: News Network: 24h in Mandarin. – **Country Network:** 24h in Amoy. – **Taipei Local R. (i go 531):** 24h Mainly in Hakka. – **Pop Network:** 24h in Mandarin. – **Formosa Network:** 24h in Amoy. – **Music Network (i radio):** 24h in Mandarin.
Addresses of local stations:
2) 3, 9th Flr, 55 Tungkuang Rd, Hsinchu 300. – **3)** 78, Lane 1008, Chungshan Rd, Kaomiao Li, Miaoli 360. – **4)** 35th Flr, 758 Chungming So. Rd, Taichung 402. – **5)** 121 Wufeng So. Rd, Chia-i 600. – **6)** 5, 19th Flr, 248, Sec. 2, Yunghua Rd, Anping, Tainan 708. – **7)** 1, 24th Flr, 91 Chungshan 2nd Rd, Chienchen, Kaohsiung 806. – **8)** 23, Lane 52, Kuilin No. Rd, Taitung 950. – **9)** 25 Shuiyuan Str, Hualien 970. – **10)** 8 Kuchie Rd, Chuangwei Village, Ilan 263. – **11)** Yuli (relay st.). – **12)** Puli (relay st.). – **13)** Kinmen (relay st.), relays also News Netw at certain times.
Ann: Mandarin: "Chungkuo Kuangpo Kungssu" or "Chungkuo Kuangpo Kungssu, (location) Kuangpo Tientai", Amoy: "Tiyon Gok Kon Po Kon Sih, (location) Kon Po Den Tai"

EXTERNAL SERVICES: Radio Taiwan International
see International Broadcasting section

HAN SHENG KUANGPO TIENTAI (Voice of Han Broadcasting Network) (Gov)
(operated by General Political Warfare Bureau, Ministry of National Defense)
B, 5th Flr, 3, Sec. 1, Hsin-i Rd, Chungcheng, Taipei 100 ☎ + 886 2 2321 5191 🖷 + 886 2 2396 2657 **W:** www.voh.com.tw

MW	Call	Location	kHz	kW
1)	C22	Taipei	684	10
1)	C25	Taoyuan	693	10
1c)	C32	Tainan	693	10
1e)	C33	Hualien	792	10
1f)	C38	Penghu	846	10
1)		Taoyuan	936	5
1)	C31	Yunlin	1089	10
1)	C22	Taipei	1116	10
1)	C30	Ilan	1116	10
1d)		Kaohsing	1251	10
1f)	C44	Penghu	1269	10
1b)	C27	Taichung	1287	10
1d)	C36	Kaohsing	1332	10
1e)	C40	Hualien	1359	5

FM	Call	Location	MHz	kW
1c)	C28	Tainan(Chentoushan)	101.3	35
1)	C26	Miaoli (Huoyenshan)	104.5	35
1e)	C35	Hualien	104.5	3
1)	C39	Taitung	105.3	3
1)	C24	Taipei	106.5	35
1)		Ilan*	106.5	
1d)	C34	Kaohsiung	107.3	35
1e)	C37	Hualien	107.3	3
1g)		Kinmen*	107.3	0.1

*) relay station

D.Prgr: MW: 2100-1600, FM 24h. Rel. RTI "Voice of Taiwan" domestic foreign language sce: **D:**1200-1400 on MW, Sun-Thu 2105-2200, Mon-Fri 0500-0600, Fri&Sat 2200-0000 on FM **–1b)** 178 Chenhsing Rd, Taichung 401– **1c)** 139 Fuhsing Rd, Yongkang, Tainan 710. **– 1d)** 40 Mingte New Village, Tsoying, Kaohsiung 813 – **1e)** 643 Chungcheng Rd, Hualien 970 – **1f)** Chukuang Ying, Makong, Penghu 880 – **1g)** Kinmen (relay st.)

BROADCASTS TO MAINLAND:
KUANGHUA CHIH SHENG (Voice of Kuanghua)
P.O.Box 1700, Taipei ☎ + 886 2 2603 0429 🖷 + 886 2 2603 0433 **W:** www.khmusic.com.tw

MW location	kHz	kW	Location	kHz	kW
Hsinfeng	711	250	Kuanyin	846	250
Kuanyin	801	250	Hsinfeng	981	250

D.Prgr. 24h

SW Location	kHz	kW
Kuanyin	9745	250

D.Prgr. 0755-0005 **Ann:** "Kuanghua chih Sheng."

FU HSING KUANGPO TIENTAI (Fu Hsing Broadcasting Station) (Gov)
(operated by Military Information Bureau, Ministry of National Defense)
5, Lane 280, Sec. 5, Chungshan No. Rd, Taipei 111 ☎ + 886 2 2882 3450 🖷 + 886 2 2881 8218 **W:** www.fhbs.com.tw

MW	Call	Location	kHz	kW
1)	H7	Taipei 1	558	1
1)	H2	Taipei 2	594	10
2)	H38	Taichung 2	594	5
3)	H44	Kaohsiung 1	594	10
3)	H56	Kaohsiung 2	846	10
1)	H3	Taipei 1	909	10
1)	H5	Taipei2	1089	5
2)	H34	Taichung 2	1089	10

SW	Call	Location	kHz	kW
1)		Kuanyin	9410	10
1)		Kuanyin	9774	10
1)		Kuanyin	15375	10

FM	Call	Location	MHz	kW
2)	I44	Taichung 1	107.8	10

D.Prgr. 1st Netw. on 558/909kHz, **2nd Netw**. on 594/1089kHz, both 24h. **Shortwave Netw**. on 9410/9774/15375kHz 2300-0100, 0400-0600, 0800-1000, 1100-1300 for China Mainland
Local Stations: 2) 81 Chungtai Rd, Chunshe Li, Nantun, Taichung 408. **1st Netw**. on 107.8MHz, **2nd Netw**. on 594/1089kHz. – **3)** 819 Chengching Rd, Niaosung Village, Kaohsiung 833. **1st Netw**. on 594kHz, **2nd Netw**. on 846kHz. **Ann:** "Fu Hsing Kuangpo Tientai, (location) Tai"

OTHER PUBLIC & COMMERCIAL STATIONS (Call: BE.)

MW	Call	Station	Location	kHz	kW
6a)		Taiwan	Tahsi	621	1
6c)		Taiwan	Sungling	630	10
7b)	V59	Cheng Sheng	Taichung 2	657	20
7c)		Cheng Sheng	Peikang	675	5
1b)	P24	Ching Cha	Taichung	702	10
8)	E43	Shih Hsin	Taipei	729	0.5
3)	L2	Yuyeh	Penghu	738	100
9)		Sheng Li	Makung	756	1
6b)	V94	Taiwan	Taichung	774	20
10)	V88	Hsien Sheng	Taoyuan	774	20
9)	V56	Sheng Li	Tainan 1	774	1
11)	V79	Keelung	Keelung	792	1
12)		Chien kuo	Hsinhua	801	1
13)	V54	Kuo Sheng	Changhua	810	10
7)	V35	Cheng Sheng	Taipei	819	5
1d)	P28	Ching Cha	Kaohsiung	819	10
7a)	V72	Cheng Sheng	Chia-i	855	1
14)	V24	Min Pen	Taipei 2	855	1
15)		Feng Ming	Penghu	882	1
16)	V98	Cheng Kung	Kaohsiung	936	1
12)	V85	Chien Kuo	Hsinying	954	10
6c)	V84	Taiwan	Chunghsing	963	10
15)	V68	Feng Ming	Kaohsiung 2	981	3
7b)	V58	Cheng Sheng	Taichung 1	990	20
1e)	P38	Ching Cha	Ilan	990	1
1f)	P34	Ching Cha	Hualien	990	10
17)	V92	Tien Nan	Taipei	999	1
7f)	V60	Cheng Sheng	Kaohsiung	1008	1
18)		Tien Sheng	Yuanli	1026	1
19)	V51	Chung Hua	Sanchung 2	1026	1
20)	V64	Yen Sheng	Hualien 1	1044	5
7d)	V82	Cheng Sheng	Ilan	1062	1
21)	V74	Min Li	Pingtung	1062	5
6a)		Taiwan	Kuanhsi	1062	1
22)	V96	Tien Sheng	Tainan	1071	1
5)	G28	Kaohsiung	Kaohsiung	1089	10
1a)	P26	Ching Cha	Hsinchu	1116	5
1d)	P25	Ching Cha	Kaohsiung	1116	5
7c)	V36	Cheng Sheng	Yunlin	1125	5
1g)	P40	Ching Cha	Taitung	1125	1
4)	G26	Taipei	Taipei	1134	10
3)	L3	Yuyeh	Penghu	1143	100
23)	V70	Hua Sheng	Taipei 1	1152	5
15)	V67	Feng Ming	Kaohsiung 1	1161	1
13)		Kuo Sheng	Erhlin	1179	2.5
6)	V46	Taiwan	Taipei 2	1188	1
9)	V57	Sheng Li	Tainan 2	1188	1
6a)	V62	Taiwan	Hsinchu	1206	10
18)		Tien Sheng	Pengshan	1215	1
23)	V71	Hua Sheng	Taipei 2	1224	1
19)		Chung Hua	Juifang	1233	1
20)		Yen Sheng	Hualien 2	1242	1
7a)		Cheng Sheng	Taipao	1260	1
1)	P22	Ching Cha	Taipei	1260	10
7e)	V37	Cheng Sheng	Taitung	1269	1
24)		Fuhsingkang	Peitou	1278	1
21)		Min Li	Fangliao	1287	1
14)	V23	Min Pen	Taipei 1	1296	1
1c)	P33	Ching Cha	Tainan	1314	1
18)	V76	Tien Sheng	Chunan	1314	10
6)	V45	Taiwan	Taipei 1	1323	1
6c)		Taiwan	Puli	1332	1
19)	V50	Chung Hua	Sanchung 1	1350	2.5
25)		Chin Hsi	Kaohsiung	1368	1
7f)		Cheng Sheng	Tafa	1395	1
26)	V78	Yi Shih	Keelung	1404	10
12)		Chien Kuo	Kuanyin	1422	1
2)	E32	Chiao Yu	Taipei	1494	10
2a)	E34	Chiao Yu	Changhua	1494	5
1a)		Ching Cha	Hsinchu	1512	10
3a)		Yuyeh	Ilan	1593	1

FM	Call	MHz	kW	FM	Call	MHz	kW	FM	Call	MHz	kW
8)		88.1		4)	G25	93.1	10	5)	G29	94.3	16
2f)		88.9	1	38)		93.3	3	1b)	P43	94.5	30
2l)		88.9	3	39)		93.5	3	45)		96.7	3
2n)		91.5		40)		93.5	3	46)		96.7	3
32)		92.1	3	41)		93.7	3	47)		96.9	3
33)		92.1	3	42)		93.7	3	48)		96.9	3
34)		92.3	3	43)		93.7	3	49)	N61	97.1	3
35)		92.7	3	44)		93.9	3	50)		97.1	3
36)		92.9	3	1)	P41	94.3	10	51)		97.1	3
37)		92.9	3	1f)	P44	94.3	5	2c)		97.3	3
1d)	P42	93.1	25	1g)	P45	94.3	5	52)		97.3	3

FM Call	MHz	kW
53)	97.3	3
54) N74	97.5	1
55)	97.5	3
56)	97.7	3
57)	97.7	3
58)	97.9	
59)	97.9	3
2i)	98.1	3
60) M23	98.1	3
61)	98.3	3
62)	98.3	3
63)	98.3	3
64)	98.5	3
65)	98.5	
66)	98.7	3
67)	98.7	3
68)	98.7	3
69) M31	98.9	3
70)	98.9	3
2k)	99.1	4
71)	99.1	3
72)	99.1	3
2m)	99.3	3
73)	99.3	3
74) M24	99.5	3

FM Call	MHz	kW
75) N77	99.5	3
76)	99.5	3
77)	99.7	3
78)	99.7	3
79) M30	99.9	3
2e)	100.1	1
31b)	100.1	13
2f) E39	100.3	1
80)	100.3	3
2d)	100.5	3
81) M26	100.7	3
31) M3	100.7	30
31a)	100.7	27
31c)	100.8	
82)	101.1	3
1f) P35	101.3	1.5
1e) P39	101.3	1
1g) P37	101.3	1.5
32) E33	101.7	30
2b) E36	101.7	30
83)	102.3	3
84) M27	102.5	3
2d) E38	102.9	5
2a) E35	103.5	30

FM	Call	MHz	kW
2g)	E40	103.5	10
2c)	E37	103.7	5
2h)	E41	103.9	3
85)		103.9	3
7)	M22	104.1	3
1)	P29	104.9	35
1c)	P31	104.9	3
1d)	P32	104.9	25
1c)		104.9	5
1b)	P30	105.1	35
2k)		105.3	3
86)		105.5	3
87)		105.5	3
88)		105.7	3
89)	M29	106.1	3
1f)	P36	106.5	1.5
90)		106.5	3
91)		106.7	3
92)	M28	106.9	3
93)		107.1	3
94)		107.3	3
95)		107.7	3
2j)		107.7	3
96)	M25	107.7	3

NB: + more than 80 low-powered community FM stns

Addresses and other information: under 30) AM or AM/FM stn(s), above 30) only FM stn(s)

1) Chingcha Broadc. St(Police R. Station),17 Kuangchou Str, Chungcheng, Taipei 10066. Four networks in 24h: AM Nat. Evergreen Netw. (ANE), AM Reg. Public Security Traffic Netw. (ARS), FM Nat. Public Security Traffic Netw. (FNS) and FM Reg. Public Security Traffic Netw. (FRS). ANE on 1260kHz, FNS on 104.9MHz,FRS on 94.3MHz – 1a) 1-1 Chiahsing Rd, Chupei City, Hsinchu 302. ANE on 1116kHz, ARS on 1512kHz – 1b) 99 Po-ai Str, Nantun, Taichung 408. ANE on 702kHz, FNS on 105.1MHz, FRS on 94.5MHz – 1c) 85-21, Nanshih, Nanshih Li, Matou, Tainan 721. ARS on 1314kHz, FNS on 104.9MHz – 1d) 455 Po-ai 4th Rd, Tsoying Ward, Kaohsiung 813. ANE on 1116kHz, FNS on 104.9MHz, FRS on 93.1MHz. – 1e) 48 Sec. 5, Chungshan Rd, Ilan 26054. ANE on 990kHz, FRS on 101.3MHz. – 1f) 21-2 Fuchien Rd, Hualien 970. , ANE on 990kHz, FNS on 101.3, 106.5MHz, FRS on 94.3MHz. – 1g) 289, Chungshan Rd. Taitung 950. ANE on 1125kHz, FNS on 101.3MHz, FRS on 94.3MHz. **W:** www.prs.gov.tw – 2) Chiao Yu Broadc. System – National Education R., 41 Nanhai Rd, Taipei 10066. On MW, FM both 24h. **Ann:** "Chiao Yu chih Sheng, Chiao Yu Kuangpo Tientai" – 2a) 5-1 Hukang Rd, Changhua 500 – 2b) 380 Kuangtung 3rd Rd, Kaohsiung 80656 – 2c) 457 Tunghsing Rd, Hualien 970. 1st prgr on 103.7MHz, 2nd prgr on 97.3MHz – 2d) 135, Ma Hengheng Rd, Taitung 95047. 1st prgr on 102.9MHz, 2nd prgr on 100.5MHz – **W:** www.ner.gov.tw – 2e) Keelung – 2f) Yuli (1st prgr on 100.3MHz, 2nd prgr on 88.9MHz) relay Hualien – 2g) Ilan – 2h) Miaoli – 2i) Nantou relay Changhua – 2j) Chia-I – 2k) Penghu (1st prgr on 99.1MHz, 2nd prgr on 105.3MHz) – 2l) Kinmen– 2m) Hengchun relay Kaohsiung – 2n) Matzu relay Taipei – 3) Yuyeh Broadc. St (Fishery R. Station), 5 Yukang No. 2nd Rd, Kaohsiung 806. 24h Weather rpt. at every h. **Ann:** "Hi-giap Kong-po'-tian-tai" **W:** www.frs.gov.tw – 3a) Ilan (relay st.) – 4) Taipei Broadc. St, 4th Flr, 62-2, Sec. 3, Chungshan No. Rd, Taipei 10452 (operated by Taipei City Council). AM "Ho Hi Yan" Ch. on 1134kHz, 2300-1600. FM "City Info" Ch. on 93.1MHz, 24h. **Rel: BBC-WS:** MF1400-1500, MF2200-2300. **W:** www.radio.taipei.gov.tw – 5) Kaohsiung Broadc. St, 90 Hsinchiang Rd, Kushan, Kaohsiung 804 (operated by Kaohsiung City Council). Two prgr on 1089kHz, 94.3MHz, both 2200-1600. **W:** www.kbs.gov.tw – 6) Taiwan Broadc. Co, 9th Flr, 2, Sec 2, Jen-ai Rd, Chungcheng, Taipei 100. 1st prgr on 1323kHz, 24h. 2nd prgr on 1188kHz, 24h. **W:** www.taiwanradio.com.tw – 6a) 2, Lane 506, Kaofeng Rd, Hsinchu 300. 24h. – 6b) 25th Flr, 787, Chungming So. Rd, Taichung. 24h. – 6c) 258-1 Fentsao Rd, Tsaotun Town, Nantou 542. 24h. – 7) Cheng Sheng Broadc. Corp., 7th Flr, 1, Lane 66, Sec. 1, Chungching So. Rd, Taipei 10045. 819kHz, 104.1MHz both 24h. – 7a) 17,Chuiyang Rd. Chia-i 60043. 24h. – 7b) 760, Sec. 2, Chunghsing Rd, Tali, Taichung 412. 1st prgr on 990kHz, 2nd prgr on 657kHz, both 24h. – 7c) 3rd Flr 32, Lane 416, 1 Sec. Linsen Rd, Huwei Town, Yunlin 63243. – 7d) 45 Chienchun Rd, Ilan 260. 24h. – 7e) 21, Lane 380, Hsinsheng Rd, Taitung 950. 24h. – 7f) 838 Chengching Rd, Niaosung , Kaohsiung 83347. Kaohsiung St. on 1008kHz, Tafa St. on 1395kHz, both 24h **W:** www.csbc.com.tw – 8) Shih Hsin Broadc. St, 1, Lane 17, Sec. 1, Mushan Rd, Wenshan Ward, Taipei 116. AM: and FM both 2255-1605(Sun 1305). **W:** www.shrs.shu.edu.tw – 9) Shengli chih Sheng (Voice of Victory) Broadc. Co, 22 Sec. 1, Chienkang Rd, Tainan 700. 1st Prgr on 774kHz, 24h. 2nd Prgr. on 1188kHz, 24h. Makung St. on 756kHz, 24h. **Ann:** "Tainan Sheng Li chih Sheng Kuangpo Tientai". **W:** www.e-go.org.tw/victor/ – 10) Hsien Sheng Broadc. Co, 1, 16th Flr, Lane 505, Chungshan Rd, Taoyuan 330. 24h.– 11) Keelung Broadc. St, 12th Flr, 13 Chungsu Rd, Keelung 200. 24h.– 12) Chien Kuo Broadc. St, 78 Chienkuo Rd, Hsinying , Tainan 730. 24h.– 13) Kuo Sheng Broadc. Co, 35 Wenchuan Rd, Pakuashan, Changhua 500. 24h. – 13a) 2 Taiping Rd, Erhlin Town, Changhua 526.– 14) Min Pen Broadc. Co, 6th Flr, 325, Sec. 3, Huanho So. Rd, Taipei 108. 1st Prgr on 1296kHz, 2nd Prgr on 855kHz, both 24h **W:** www.mingpen.com.tw – 15) Feng Ming Broadc. Co, 492 Chiuju 2nd Rd, Sanmin Ward, Kaohsiung 807. 1st Prgr on 1161kHz, 2nd Prgr on 981kHz, both 24h **W:** www.fengmin.com.tw – 15a) Chentieh Hsien, Li 38, Makung, Penghu.– 16) Chengkung Broadc. St, 63 Chunghua 3rd Rd, Kaohsiung 801. 24h (exc. Sun 1600-2100). – 17) Tien Nan Broadc. St, 1st Flr. 29-1, Sec. 2, Hangchou So. Rd, Taipei 106. 24h. – 18) T'ien Sheng Broadc. St, 285 Kungyi Rd, Chunan Town, Miaoli 350. 24h. – 18a) 8, Kozhuang, Chungshue Rd, Yuanli Town, Miaoli 358. Yuanli St. on 1026kHz, Pengshan St. on 1215kHz, both 24h. – 19) Chung Hua (China) Broadc. Co, 6th Flr, 238 Hopien No. Str, Sanchung, New Taipei 241. 1st Prgr on 1350kHz, 2nd prgr on 1026kHz, both 24h **Ann:** "Chung Hua Kuangpo Tientai Ti I/Erh Tai". Juifang St,. relays 2nd prgr on 1233kHz, 24h **W:** www.e-go.org.tw/chbc – 20) Yen Sheng Broadc. St, 31, Sec. 1, Nanpin Rd, Tungchang, Chi-an Village, Hualien 973. On 1044, 1242kHz, both 24h. – 21) Min Li Broadc. St, 57-20 Minsheng Rd, Pingtung 900. 24h – 22) Tien Sheng Broadc. St, 11, 15th Flr, 149, Sec. 1, Linsen Rd, Tainan 701. 24h (exc. Sun 1600-2155) **W:** www.am1071.com.tw – 23) Hua Sheng Broadc. Co, 18 Huasheng Str, Shihlin Ward, Taipei 111. 1st Prgr on 1152kHz, 2nd Prgr on 1224kHz, both 24h **W:** www.hsradio.com.tw – 24) Fuhsingkang Broadac. Stn. 70, Sec .2, Chungyang Rd, Peitou, Taipei 112. – 25) Chin Hsi Broadc. Co, 2nd Flr, 461 Wenfu Rd, Tsoying, Kaohsiung 804. 24h **W:** www.am1368@xuite.net – 26) Yi Shih Broadc. St, 75 Paisan Str, Chitu Ward, Keelung 206. 24h **Ann:** "Keelung Yi Shih Kuangpo Tientai". **W:** /yishih.ehosting.com.tw 31) International Community R. Taipei (ICRT), 19-5F, 107, Sec. 1, Chungshan Rd, Hsinchuang New Taipei 24250. 24h in English. **Rel. BBC News** Sun-Thu 2300-2330. – 31a) Kaohsiung. – 31b) Taichung – 31c) Chia-I **W:** www.icrt.com.tw – 32) Fei Tieh (UFO) Broadc. Co (UFO Netw), 25th Flr, 102, Sec. 2, Lossufou Rd, Taipei 100. 24h **W:** www.uforadio.com.tw UFO Netw: Miaoli 91.3MHz, Taitung 89.9MHz, Yunlin & Chia-i district 90.5MHz, Kaohusing 103.9MHz, Ilan 89.9MHz, Hualien 91.3MHz, Taitung 91.3MHz, Penghu 89.7MHz. – 33) Chin Sheng Broadc. St, 275 Flr, 206 Kuanghua 1st Rd, Lingya, Kaohsiung 802. 24h. – 34) Chia-i (Chia Le Broadc St), 1, 16th Flr, 193, Hsiaoya Rd, Chia-i 600. – 35) Yachou (Asia) Broadc. St (Asia FM Netw), 2, 22nd Flr, 102 Chungping Rd, Taoyuan 330. 24h **W:** www.asiafm.com.tw – 36) Cheng Shih Broadc. St, 28th Flr, 758 Chungming So. Rd, Taichung 402. **W:** www.goldfm.com.tw – Other Gold FM Netw st: Taipei 90.1MHz, Miaoli 98.3MHz, Tainan 97.1MHz – 37) Tiawu chih Chun Broadc. St, Lane 240, Sec. 1, Poyu Rd. Panglin, Chinning, Kinmen 893. – 38) Yun Chia Broadc. St, 9th Flr, 617 Chungshan Rd, Chia-i 600. 24h **W:** www.fm933.com.tw – 39) Hsin Kechia Broadc. St, 1, 16th Flr, 411 Huannan Rd, Pingchen City, Taoyuan 324. 24h– 40) Lien Hua Broadc. St. (Best 935) 3, 8th Flr. 65, Kuolienssu Rd. Hualien 970.– 41) Pao Tao Kechia Broadc. St, (Formosa Hakka R. Stn.) 2, 17th Flr, 91, Sec. 2, Lossufu Rd, Taipei 106. 24h **W:** www.formosahakka.org.tw – 42) Sheng Tu Broadc. Co, 233 Fentsao Rd, Tsaotun Town, Nantou 542. 24h **W:** www.fm937.com.tw – 43) Ling Hsiu Broadc. St, – 10, 20th Flr. 149, Sec. 1, Linsen Rd. Tainan 701 – 44) Ta Ti chih Sheng Broadc. St. 10, Chengpei Village, Huhsi, Penghu 885 – 45) Huan Yu Broadc. Co (Uni R.), 3, 6th Flr, 675, Sec. 1, Chingkuo Rd, Hsinchu 300. 24h **W:** www.turc967.com.tw – 46) Penghu Broadc. St. 2nd Flr. 1-204, I-lin Shihchuan-li, Makung, Penghu 880 – 47) Tien Tien (Sky) Broadc. St, 42nd Flr, 760 Chungming So. Rd, Taichung 402. 24h **W:** tw.myblog.yahoo.com/sky9692004 – 48) Chu Jen (Boss) Broadc. St, 16th Flr, 121-8 Tachang 2nd Rd, Kaohsiung 807. 24h – 49) Ta Han chih Yin (Voice of Hakka) Broadc. St, 1-1 Hsintung Rd, Toufen Town, Miaoli 351. 24h **W:** www.fm971.com.tw – 50) Tainan chih Yin Broadc. St, 18th Flr, 1-119 Chunghua Rd, Yongkang, Tainan 710 – 51) Ilan chih Sheng (Voice of Ilan) Chung Shan Broadc. Co, 12th Flr, 289-3 Kungcheng Rd, Lotung Town, Ilan 265. 24h **W:** www.super971.com.tw – 52) Green Peace Broadc. St, 1, 14th Flr, 97, Sec. 4, Chunghsing Rd, Sanchung New Taipei 241. 24h **W:** www.greenpeace.com.tw – 53) Ai Yu chih Sheng Broadc. St, 7, Lane 828, Sec. 3, Chinma Rd, Chungsha 500. 24h **W:** tw.myblog.yahoo.com/fm973-fm973 – 54) IC chih Yin, IC Broadc. Co. Ltd., 2, 11th Flr, 287, Sec. 2, Kuangfu Rd, Hsinchu 30071. 24h **W:** www.ic975.com – 55) Kuai Le (Happy) Broadc. St, 1st Flr, 70, Ling-an Rd, Lingya, Kaohsiung 802. 24h. Happy R. Netw: Taipei 89.3MHz, Taichung 89.5MHz, Chia-I 92.3MHz, Hualien 98.3MHz, Penghu 91.3MHz & 96.7MHz – 56) Taiwan Sheng Yin Broadc. St, 9th Flr. 76, Sec. 1, Minchuan Rd. Taipei, 104. 24h **W:** www.myblog.yahoo.com – 57) Hao Chia Ting Broadc. Co (Family 977 Broadc. Network), 37th Flr, 789 Chungming So. Rd, Taichung 402. 24h **W:** www.family977.com.tw – 58) Tainan Kaihsuan Broadc. St, 2, 21th Flr, 425 Chunghua Rd, Yungkang, Tainan 710 – 59) Ka Ma Lan Broadc. St, 36, Lane 175, Sec. 3, Chungcheng Rd, Wuchie Village, Ilan 268. – 60) Taiwan Chuan Min Broadc. St (News 98), 1, 25th Flr, 100, Sec. 2, Lossufou Rd, Taipei 100. 24h – 61) Ta Miaoli FM Broadc. St, 3, 16th Flr, 1 Chanchien, Shangmiao Li,

Miaoli 360. – **62)** Kang Tu Broadc. St (Best R.), 1, 34th Flr, 80 Mintsu 1st Rd, Kaohsiung 807. 24h **W:** www.bestradio.com.tw Haoshih (Best) Netw: Taipei 98.9MHz, Taichung 90.3MHz, Hualien 93.5MHz – **63)** Hualien (Huan Le Broadc St), 1, Lane 120, Tunghsing 2nd Str, Minhsiang Li, Hualien 970 – **64)** Pao Tao Hsin Sheng (Super FM 98.5) Broadc. St, 1, 2nd Flr, 3, Sec. 1, Tunhua So. Rd, Taipei 105. 24h **W:** www.superfm98-5.com.tw – **65)** Feifanyin Broadc. St (Libra R.), 40, Lane 40, Sec. 2, Shuangshih Rd. No. Ward, Taichung 40455. 24h **W:** www.libraradio.com.tw – **66)** Mei Jih Broadc. Co (Sakura R.), 1, 7th Flr, 1-67 Wuchuan Rd, Taichung 403. 24h **W:** www.fm987.com.tw – **67)** Ching Chun Broadc. St, 15-2, Sec. 2, Lin'an Rd, No. Ward, Tainan 704. – **68)** Tung Min Broadc. St. 156, Fuyu Rd. Chihpen, Taitung 950. – **69)** Chin Yue Broadc. St (Best 989), 6th Flr, 88, Sec. 2, Chunghsiao East Rd, Chungcheng, Taipei 100. 24h – **70)** Cheng Kang Broadc. St. 2, 4th Flr. 73, Taming Rd. Chia-i, 602 – **71)** Ta Chien Broadc. St (Super 99.1), 8th Flr, 83 Hsuehshih Rd, Taichung 404 **W:** www.superfm99-1.com.tw – **72)** Yang Kuang Broadc. St, 6, 21st Flr, 3, Tzuchang 3rd Rd, Lingya, Kaohsiung 802. – **73)** Hsin Sheng FM Broadc. St, 1, 19th Flr, 37 Chianchung 1st Rd, Hsinchu 300 **W:** www.ss-radio.com.tw – **74)** Shen Nong (Farmer R.) Broadc. Co, 10th Flr, 234 Peiping Rd, Huwei Town, Yunlin 632.24h **W:** www.fm995.com.tw – **75)** Tung Fang Broadc. St, 13rd Flr, 168, Sec. 3, Chunching Rd, Lotung Town, Ilan 265. 24h – **76)** Lan Yu Broadc. St, 147, Yujen, Hongtou, Lanyu Village, Taitung 95241.24h **W:** www.lanan.org.tw/radeo.htm – **77)** Taipei Ai Yue Broadc. Co, 7th Flr, 47 Tunghsing Rd, Hsin-i, Taipei 110. 24h **W:** www.prtmusic.com.tw – **78)** Nantou Broadc. St, 1A, 37th Flr, 760 Chungming So. Rd, Taichung 402. – **79)** Ta Chung Broadc. Co (Kiss R.), 2, 34th Flr, 6 Minchuan 2nd Rd, Kaohsiung 806. 24h **W:** www.kiss.com.tw – Kiss R. Netw: Nantou 99.7MHz. – **80)** Pao Tao Broadc. St. 1, 12th Flr. 287, Wenya St. Chia-i 600. – **81)** Taichung Broadc.Co, 21st Flr, 345, Sec. 1, Chungkang Rd, Taichung 403. 24h **W:** www.lucky7.com.tw – **82)** Ching Shan Broadc. St. A-12-7, 20, Talung Rd. Taichung 403. – **83)** Ai Miao Broadc. St, 78, Huatung Str, Chunan Town, Miaoli 360. 24h – **84)** Ku Tu Broadc. Co, 1, 15th Flr, 77, Sec. 2, Chunghua East Rd, Tainan 701. 24h **W:** www.fm1025.com.tw – **85)** Nan Taiwan chih Sheng (Voice of South Taiwan), 20th Flr, 12 Po-ai 3th Rd, Tsuying, Kaohsiung 813. – **86)** Huanhsi chih Sheng (Happy R.) Broadc. St, 37th Flr, 760 Chungming So. Rd, So. Ward, Taichung. 24h **W:** www.happy1055.com.tw – **87)** Tung Shan He FM Broadc. St, 13th Flr, 162-1, Sec. 3, Chunching Rd, Lotung Town, Ilan 265. – **88)** Tzumei (Sister R.) Broadc. St, 4th Flr, 32, Lane 416, Sec. 1, Linsen Rd, Huwei Town, Yunlin 632. 24h **W:** www.sister-radio.com.tw – **89)** Chuan Kuo Broadc. Co, 1, 10th Flr, 1-18, Sec. 2, Chungkang Rd, Taichung 407. 24h **W:** www.taichungnet.com.tw – **90)** Chih Nan Broadc. St, 6, 21st Flr, 3 Tzuchiang 3rd Rd, Lingya, Kaohsiung 802. – **91)** Kao Ping Hsi Broadc. St, 17th Flr, 161 Chiuta Rd, Chiuchu, Tashu Village, Kaohsiung 840 – **92)** Taoyuan Broadc. St (TBC R.), 9th Flr, 859, Sec. 1, Chunghua Rd, Chungli City, Taoyuan 320. 24h **W:** www.tbcradio.com.tw – **93)** Chia-i Huanchiu Broadc. St, 1, 19th Flr, 25 Pingtien, Chianghsi Village, Fanlu, Chia-i 600 – Other Smile Netw sts: Hsinchu on 90.3, Nantou on105.5, Tainan on 97.9, Kaohsiung on 90.5, Pingtung on 90.9/91.3/92.5MHz – **94)** Lan Yang FM Broadc. St, 12th Flr, 186, Sec. 3, Chungcheng Rd, Wuchie Village, Ilan. 24h – **95)** Taipei chih Yin Broadc. Co, (Hito R.) B, 1, 10th Flr, 15-1, Sec. 1, Hanchou So. Rd, Taipei 100. 24h. Hit FM Netw: Taichung 91.5MHz, Kaohsiung 90.1MHz **W:** www.hitfm.com – **96)** Tung Taiwan Broadc. St, 55 Chunghsing Rd, Hualien 970.

DAB: Pao Tao Hsin Sheng (Super FM 98.5, 213.360MHz) carries 3 prgrs plus Super FM 99.1 and R. Taiwan International. Taipei area.

TAJIKISTAN

L.T: UTC +5h — **Pop:** 7.6 million — **Pr.L:** Tajik, Uzbek — **E.C:** 50Hz, 220V — **ITU:** TJK

KUMITAI TELEVIZION VE RADIOI
(State Committee for Radio & TV)
📧 k. Sheroz 31, 734025 Dushanbe ☎ +992 37 2276569
🖷 +992 37 2213495 **W:** www.radiotoj.tj
L.P: Chmn: Asadullo Rakhmonov
NB: In addition to being a state broadcaster, the committee is also responsible for issuing licenses to private radio stations in Tajikistan.

LW/MW	kHz	kW	Prgr	MW	kHz	kW	Prgr
Dushanbe (a)	252	150	TR1	Khujand	819	15	TR1
Dushanbe	549	40	TR2	Orzu	1161	40	TR2
Orzu	702	150	TR1	Dushanbe	1323	7	TR1

SW	kHz	kW	Prgr	
Dushanbe (a)	4765	50	TR1	(a)=Yangiyul

FM (MHz)	TR1	TR2	TR1	TR2	TR3	kW
Ayvanj	-	-	-	107.8	-	-
Dushanbe	70.64	72.20	104.7	102.2	106.5	2x17/-
Khujand	72.56	69.80	102.7	-	106.1	2x17/-

FM (MHz)	TR1	TR2	TR1	TR2	TR3	kW
Khorugh	-	-	104.5	104.0	103.0	-
Panj	-	-	-	100.3	-	-
Qurghonteppa	67.88	66.32	-	-	-	17

+ low power txs.
D.Prgr: TR1 (Radioi Tojikiston) 24h on FM; on LW/MW/SW: 2300-2000. – **TR2 (Sadoi Dushanbe)** 0300-1500. – **TR3 (Radioi Farhang)** 0300-1500.
External Service (Ovozi Tojik): see International Radio section. On FM: Dushanbe 105.5.

OTHER STATIONS

MW	kHz	kW	Location	Station
C)	1296	300	Orzu	R.Rossii relay

FM	MHz	kW	Location	Station
4)	101.5	0.2	Kulob	R. Mavji ozod
9)	101.5	-	Dushanbe	R. Khovar
10)	101.5	-	Panjakent	Sadoi Panjakent
2)	102.4	-	Qurghonteppa	R. Vatan
7A)	103.0	-	Dushanbe	R. Rusii Oriyono
7B)	103.0	-	Khujand	R. Imruz
B)	103.7	-	Dushanbe	R. Zvezda
1A)	103.7	4	Khujand	R. Tiroz
5)	104.0	-	Dushanbe	AFM
3A)	104.5	0.3	Dushanbe	R. Aziya FM
4)	105.9	-	Isfara	R. Mavji ozod
2)	106.0	0.1	Dushanbe	R. Vatan
6)	106.1	-	Istaravshan	R. AVIS-Plus
1B)	106.7	-	Khujand	R. Tiroz Plus
3B)	107.0	0.1	Dushanbe	R. Aziya FM
7B)	107.4	-	Dushanbe	R. Imruz
8)	107.5	1	Ghafurov	R. Jahonoro

Addresses & other information:
1A,B) k. Tiroz 9, 735700 Khujand. **E:** radio@tiroz.org – **2)** pr. S.Sherozi 16, 734018 Dushanbe. **E:** info@vatan.tj – **3A,B)** pr. S.Sherozi 16, 734018 Dushanbe. **E:** radio@asiaplus.tj – **4)** k. Umari Hazom 18, 735330 Vose. – **5)** pr. S.Ayni 27/17, 734000 Dushanbe. **E:** info@afm.tj – **6)** k. A.Mirrajabov 10, 735610 Istaravshan. **E:** avis@avis.tj – **7A,B)** pr. Rudaki 100, 734001 Dushanbe. **E:** info@orionomedia.tj. 7A) rel. Russkoye R. (Russia) – **8)** k. Lenin 22, Ghafurov. – **9)** Dushanbe. **E:** sadr-shamsi67@mail.ru – **10)** Panjakent. – **A)** Rel. Voice of Russia (Russia). – **B)** Rel. R.Zvezda (Russia). – **C)** Rel. R.Rossii (Russia).

Int relays on MW: (txs operated by Teleradiokom) Dushanbe (Yangiyul) 1143kHz 150kW, 1251kHz 100kW; Orzu 648/801kHz 1000kW, 927kHz 300kW, 972/1503kHz 500kW & operated on behalf of IBB (USA): 972kHz 800kW. Other freqs may be used. See Int Radio section.

TANZANIA

L.T: UTC +3h — **Pop:** 41 million — **Pr.L:** Swahili, English — **E.C:** 50Hz, 230V — **ITU:** TZA

TANZANIA COMMUNICATIONS REGULATORY AUTHORITY (TCRA)
📧 Mawasiliano House, Plot 304, Ali Hassan Mwinyi/Nkomo Rd, P.O Box 474, Dar es Salaam ☎+255 22 2118947 🖷 +255 22 2116664
W: www.tcra.go.tz **E:** dg@tcra.go.tz
L.P: DG: John Nkoma. Dir. Broadc. Affairs: Habbi Gunze.

TANZANIA BROADCASTING CORPORATION (TBC, Gov)
📧 P. O. Box 9191, Nyerere Rd, Dar es Salaam ☎+255 22 2860760 🖷 +255 22 2866383 **W:** tbc.go.tz
L.P: DG: Dunstan Tido Mhando. Dir. Radio: Ms. Edah Sanga. TD: Harold Limo. Dir. News: Ms. Susan Mungi. Dir. PR: Ngalimecha Ngayoma

MW	kHz	kW	MW	kHz	kW
Dodoma	603	100/10	Mwanza	720	50/10
Nachingwea	648	100/10	Songea	990	100/10
Kunduchi+	657	2 x 50	Arusha	1215	50/10
Kigoma	711	100/10	+) near Dar es Salaam.		

FM (MHz): Arusha 91.6, Dar es Salaam 89.9/92.35, Dodoma 87.7, Kigoma 88.4, Lindi 93.5, Mbeya/Masasi/Nachingwea 92.3, Mwanza 89.2, Songea 98.7, Dar es Salaam 94.6 (includes **International Sce in English:** 0200-1915).
TBC Taifa in Swahili on MW: 24h. N. on the hour. Relayed also from Zanzibar at 1600. **TBC FM in Swahili:** 24h. MW & FM channels may opt out at times to carry regional prgrs.

PRIVATE STATIONS
RADIO ONE, P.O. Box 4374, Dar es Salaam. **W:** www.ippmedia.com/ipp/radio **E:** itv@ipp.co.tz **MW:** Moshi 1323kHz 10kW (Swahili), Dar es Salaam 1440kHz 10kW (English). **FM** (all 5kW): Dar es Salaam

89.5MHz, Mwanza 102.5MHz, Dodoma 100.8MHz, Arusha 95.3MHz.
RADIO FREE AFRICA, P.O. Box 1732, Post Road, Mwanza. **W:** radiofreeafricatz.com **E:** info@radiofreeafricatz.com Swahili Sce: **MW:** Mwanza 1377kHz 50kW. **FM:** Shinyanga 98.6MHz, Mbeya 99.3MHz, Arusha 89MHz, Mwanza 89.8MHz (also rel. BBC/VOA/RTD/DW). English sce: **Kiss FM:** Mbeya 88.2MHz, Mwanza 88.7MHz, Arusha 89.9MHz, Dar es Salaam 89MHz, Shinyanga 96.4MHz.

Other Stations: Clouds FM, P.O. Box 31513, Dar es Salaam. FM: Dar es Salaam 88.4MHz 2kW, Arusha 98.6MHz, Mwanza 99.4MHz. 0150 – **R. Five**, P.O. Box 11843, Arusha: 105.7MHz. **E:** impala@cybernet. co.tz – **R. Imaan** (Rlg.): Morogoro 96.0MHz – **R. Kheri** (Rlg.) Dar es Salaam 104.1MHz – **R. Kwizera**, P.O. Box 154, Ngara Field Office, Ngara. **W:** www.jrs.net/countries/eaf.php?lang=en **E:** eastern.africa@jrs.net - **FM:** 97.9MHz (in Swahili, also rel. RFI Afrique in English) – **East Africa R**, P.O.Box 4374, Dar es Salaam: 87.8MHz (also relayed on FM in Kampala, Uganda, & Nairobi, Kenya). **W:** www.eastafricafm. com **E:** admin@eastafricafm.com – **R. Maria Tanzania**, P.O. Box 34573, Dar es Salaam. FM: Songea 89.1MHz, Iringa 90.4MHz, Mbeya 91.9MHz, Morogoro 102.0MHz, Unguja/Pemba 103.5MHz, Mwanza 106.0MHz, Arusha 106,7MHz. Arusha 2kW, Pemba 0.5kW, others 1kW. **W:** www.radiomariatanzania.co.tz – **R. Sauti ya Injili** (Rlg.), Lutheran R. Centre, P.O. Box 777, Moshi **W:** www.elct.org/TechServ/Radio **E:** Redio@elct.org FM: Kidia 92.2MHz, Tanga 96.0MHz, Arusha 96.2MHz, Rombo 96.4MHz, Morogoro 99.6MHz, Same 100.4MHz, Usambara 102.6MHz, Kibaya 102.9MHz. F.PI: FM trs in Bukoba and Iringa and a low-power SW transmitter – **R. Sauti ya Quran** (Rlg.) Dar es Salaam: 102.0MHz – **Tanzanite R. FM**, Arusha: 96.1MHz – **R. Tumaini**: P.O. Box 9916, Dar es Salaam. FM: Dar es Salaam 96.3MHz, Kibahe 91.4MHz – **R.Tumaini 2:** Dar es Salaam: 105.9MHz.

ZANZIBAR & PEMBA
(autonomous islands)

ZANZIBAR BROADCASTING CORPORATION (Gov.)
✉ P.O. Box 1178, Zanzibar, Tanzania ☎ +255 54 31088/9 **E:** karumehouse@tvz.co.tv **L.P:** Dir. of Broadc: Yussuf Omar Chunda. CE: Ali Aboud Talib.
MW: Chumbuni 585kHz 50kW (rep. inactive).
SW: Dole: 6015/11735kHz 50kW.
FM: Unguja 97.4MHz, Pemba 90.5MHz.
D.Prgr in Swahili: 0900-2100 on 585kHz. FM ("Spice FM"): 0300-2100. **N:** Local bulletins at 0400, 1200, 1600, 1800, 1900. Rel. R.Tanzania from Dar es Salaam at 1700, 1900. **In English:** irr. 1800. **Ann:** "Hii ni Sauti Tanzania, Zanzibar". English: "Zanzibar Broadcasting Corporation."
Relays on shortwave: see International Radio section.

Other stations:
Al-Noor FM (Rlg.), Zanzibar: 92.6MHz 2kW. **W:** alnoorcharity.org
R. Maria Tanzania (Rlg.) Pemba: 103.5MHz.
R. Tumaini 2, Zanzibar: 105.9MHz.
BBC African Sce: Zanzibar 94.1MHz, Pemba 93.5MHz.
RFI Afrique: Dar es Salaam 94.6MHz in F/E/Swahili

THAILAND

L.T: UTC +7h — **Pop:** 67 million — **Pr.L:** Thai — **E.C:** 50Hz, 220V — **ITU:** THA

NATIONAL TELECOMMUNICATIONS COMMISSION (NTC)
✉ **Public Relations Bureau of the NTC:** 87 Phahonyotin Rd. Soi 8, Phayatai Bangkok 10400 ☎ +66 2271-3511 🖷 +66 2290-5240 **W:** eng. ntc.or.th **L.P:** Chmn: Prof. Prasit Prapinmongkolkarn.
The NTC controls administrative, legal, technical and programming aspects of broadcasting in Thailand pending the establishment of the National Broadcasting and Telecommunications Commission to supervise the broadcasting industry.

MW STATIONS:

	kHz	kW	Province +)		kHz	kW	Province +)
RT)	531	25	Maha Sarakham	32)	603	5	Khon Kaen
39)	540	5	Bangkok	10)	612	5	Lop Buri
RT)	549	100	Lampang (E)	25)	612	5	Chiang Mai
RT)	549	10	Mukdahan	RT)	621	100	Khon Kaen (E)
RT)	558	50	Songkhla (E)	1)	630	5	Bangkok
RT)	558	10	Kanchanaburi	RT)	639	10	Chiang Mai $
24)	567	5	Chaiyaphum	RT)	639	20	N. Si Thammarat
17)	576	5	Bangkok	RT)	648	25	Khon Kaen
7)	585	5	Phrae	24)	657	5	Bangkok
32)	585	5	Chumphon	7)	666	5	Tak
9)	594	5	Bangkok	6)	666	5	Surin

	kHz	kW	Province +)		kHz	kW	Province +)
29)	675	5	Bangkok	RT)	1116	10	Phangnga
8)	684	5	N. Si Thammarat	RT)	1125	25	Chanthaburi
39)	684	5	Udon Thani	RT)	1134	10	Lampang
11)	693	5	Saraburi	6)	1134	10	N. Ratchasima
19)	711	5	Chiang Mai	27)	1143	10	Bangkok
RT)	711	20	U. Ratchathani (E)	37)	1152	10	Chiang Mai
10)	711	5	Lop Buri	37)	1152	10	Khon Kaen
29)	720	10	Krabi	20)	1161	20	Bangkok
29)	720	5	Chon Buri	29)	1161	10	U. Ratchathani
32)	729	25	N. Ratchasima	29)	1170	10	Chanthaburi
32)	738	5	Chiang Mai	29)	1170	10	Phitsanulok
32)	738	5	Songkhla	36)	1179	10	Bangkok
32)	747	5	Bangkok	34)	1179	10	Chiang Rai
6)	747	5	Udon Thani	35)	1188	10	Sakon Nakhon
34)	756	5	Narathiwat	7)	1188	10	Phitsanulok
35)	756	5	Surin	5)	1188	10	Sa Kaeo
31)	765	5	Lampang	26)	1197	10	Lop Buri
12)	765	5	Lop Buri	RT)	1206	10	Satun
18)	774	5	Rayong	5)	1206	10	Prachuap KK
36)	774	5	Udon Thani	35)	1215	10	Phrae
RT)	783	10	Ranong	6)	1215	10	U. Ratchathani
7)	783	5	Kamphaeng Phet	RT)	1215	50	Surat Thani
19)	792	20	Bangkok	12)	1224	10	Chiang Rai
3)	801	5	N. Sawan	12)	1224	10	N. Sawan
12)	801	5	Chiang Rai	12)	1233	10	Bangkok
12)	801	5	U. Ratchathani	32)	1233	10	Udon Thani
RT)	810	20	Nong Khai	7)	‡1242	10	Lampang
RT)	810	10	Kanchanaburi	7)	1242	10	Phetchabun
RT)	810	10	Trang	RT)	1242	50	Surat Thani (E)
RT)	819	10	Pathum Thani#	24)	1251	10	Roi Et
32)	828	5	N. Si Thammarat	12)	1251	5	Bangkok
7)	828	5	Sukhothai	RT)	1260	25	Chiang Rai
34)	837	5	Sakon Nakhon	25)	1269	10	Songkhla
RT)	837	10	Pathum Thani#	15)	1269	10	Bangkok
RT)	846	10	Phetchabun	28)	1287	10	Samut Prakan#
2)	855	5	Prachin Buri	7)	‡1287	10	Uttaradit
RT)	864	10	Tak	32)	1287	10	U. Ratchathani
RT)	864	10	Si Sa Ket	RT)	1296	10	Pattani
RT)	864	10	Phatthalung	39)	1305	10	Bangkok
16)	873	5	Bangkok	25)	1314	10	Khon Kaen
RT)	891	1000	Sara Buri#	12)	1323	10	Chiang Mai
RT)	909	10	Loei	12)	1323	10	Surat Thani
RT)	909	25	Surin	14)	1332	10	Bangkok
30)	918	10	Chiang Mai	12)	1332	10	Maha Sarakham
RT)	918	100	Nakhon Pathom #	RT)	1341	20	Loei
RT)	927	20	Chanthaburi (E)	12)	1341	25	U. Ratchathani
RT)	927	10	Nong Khai	RT)	1341	10	Phangnga
8)	936	10	Pattani	4)	‡1350	10	Lampang
RT)	936	50	N. Sawan (E)	32)	1350	10	Trang
12)	945	10	Bangkok	33)	1350	10	Bangkok
6)	945	10	Kalasin	6)	1359	10	Sakhon Nakhon
12)	954	10	Phitsanulok	RT)	1368	25	Nan
12)	954	10	Chanthaburi	RT)	1368	10	Buri Ram
RT)	963	25	Krabi (E)	12)	1368	10	N. Pathom
18)	963	10	Bangkok	22)	1377	10	Phitsanulok
34)	972	10	Phetchabun	RT)	1377	10	Chumphon
38)	981	10	Pathum Thani#	13)	1386	10	Bangkok
RT)	981	25	Mae Hong Son	34)	1395	10	Chiang Rai
RT)	981	20	N. Phanom	RT)	1404	25	Songkhla
RT)	981	10	Yala	12)	1404	10	Yasothon
30)	990	10	N. Ratchasima	5)	1404	10	Suphan Buri
7)	999	10	Chiang Rai	RT)	1422	10	Amnat Charoen
33)	999	10	Bangkok	33)	‡1422	10	Bangkok
32)	1008	10	N. Ratchasima	30)	‡1422	10	Phitsanulok
12)	1017	10	Prachuap KK	12)	1431	10	N. Ratchasima
RT)	1026	50	Phitsanulok	29)	1431	5	Songkhla
RT)	1026	10	Yala	12)	1440	10	N. Phanom
31)	1035	10	Bangkok	32)	1440	10	Samut Sakhon
35)	1044	10	Khon Kaen	7)	1449	10	Phichit
8)	1044	10	N. Si Thammarat	10)	1449	10	Chumphon
4)	1053	10	Lampang	24)	1458	10	Si Sa Ket
1)	1053	10	Bangkok	29)	1458	10	Phuket
12)	1062	10	Udon Thani	RT)	1467	100	Pathum Thani (E)#
RT)	1062	10	Phuket	RT)	1476	50	Chiang Mai $
40)	1071	10	Bangkok	27)	1494	10	Bangkok
31)	1071	10	Tak	24)	1503	10	Surat Thani
32)	1080	10	Chiang Rai	RT)	1512	10	Yasothon (F.PI.)
32)	1080	10	N. Sawan	31)	1512	10	Phayao
32)	1080	10	Yala	12)	1512	10	Songkhla
31)	‡1089	10	Bangkok	34)	‡1512	5	Uthai Thani
31)	1089	10	Udon Thani	12)	1521	10	Bangkok
30)	1098	10	Songkhla	32)	1530	10	Uttaradit
RT)	1098	10	Tak	5)	1530	10	Chanthaburi
25)	1107	10	Samut Sakhon#	23)	1539	10	Kanchanaburi
6)	1107	10	Khon Kaen	11)	1557	10	Phetchabun
7)	1116	10	Phitsanulok	RT)	1557	10	Trat

kHz	kW	Province +)		kHz	kW	Province +)
−)	15751000	Ayutthaya		31)	‡1593	10	Buri Ram
RT)	‡1584	1	Loei		RT)	1593	10	Ratchaburi
8)	‡1584	1	Phatthalung				

*) r. inactive. +) N=Nakhon, U=Ubon, KK=Khiri Khan, RT=R. Thailand.
#) Bangkok area. $) Tr. located in Lamphun Province.
NB: Mobile 1kW units for Army use with no advertisements have been registered for 747, 1242, 1485, 1584, and 1602kHz

BANGKOK FM (MHz): (exc. R. Thailand and community radio stns): 87.5 Sathaanii Witthayu Ratthasapha (Parliament R. St.) – 88.5 Sor. Thor. Ror. 1, "Sabaidee R." – 89.0 Yaan Kraw "Chill FM" – 89.5 Rajamangala University of Technology "Sweet FM" – 90.0 Phon Neung Ror. Or. "Soft R." – 90.5 Wor. Phor. Thor. – 91.0 Sor. Wor. Phor. – 91.5 Yaan Kraw, "Hot Nine One Five" – 92.0 Wor. Sor. Sor. – 93.0 Sor. Thor. Ror. 1, "Cool 93 Fahrenheit" – 94.0 Thor. Thor. Bor. (Sathaanii Witthayu Thorathat Kongthap Bok, Army TV Station), "EFM" – 94.5 Jor. Sor, "Sanuk Sukniyom" – 95.0 Or. Sor. Mor. Thor "Luukthung Mahaanakhon" – 96.0 Ror. Dor, "Sport R." – 96.5 Or. Sor. Mor. Thor, "Modern Radio FM96.5" – 97.5 Or. Sor. Mor. Thor, "Modern Radio Seed 97.5 FM" – 98.0 Phon Neung Ror. Or. – 98.5 Neung Por. Nor, "Good FM" – 99.0 Or. Sor. Mor. Thor, "Active R." – 99.5 Sathaanii Witthayu 9-1-9, "Traffic Radio Society (TRS)" – 100.0 Jor. Sor. Roi – 100.5 Or. Sor. Mor. Thor, "News Station" – 101.0 Sathaanii Witthayu Kong Banchaakaan Thahaan Suungsut (Supreme Command HQ), "101 Radio Report One" – 101.5 Sathaanii Witthayu Chulaa or "Witthayu Chulaa" or "CU FM" – 102.0 Khor. Sor. Thor. Bor. "Working Station" – 102.5 Thor. Or, "Get 102.5" – 103.0 Jor. Sor "Like FM" – 103.5 Thor. Thor. Bor, "FM One" – 104.0 Or. Sor. – 104.5 Phon Por. Thor. Or. (Kong Phon Thahaan Peun Yai Tosue Akart Yaan, Anti-Aircraft Artillery Division) "Fat Radio" – 105.5 Or. Sor. Mor. Thor "Eazy FM" – 106.0 Sor. Thor. Ror. 1 – 106.5 Neung Por. Nor, "Green Wave" – 107.0 Or. Sor. Mor. Thor, "Met 107".
OTHER FM STATIONS: A large number of FM stns belonging to R. Thailand or other operators are on air throughout Thailand, including approx. 6,000 community radio stns in Bangkok and the provinces with max. permitted tx power 30W.

English language prgrs in Bangkok (freqs carrying substantial content in English): 918kHz R.Thailand Network 6 (English news & features, western light & classical music) – 88.0 Radio Thailand – 95.5MHz "Virgin Hitz" – 107.0MHz "Met 107" (Or Sor Mor Thor).

GOVERNMENT PUBLIC RELATIONS DEPT. (Gov.)
⌨ Soi Aree Samphan, Rama VI Road, Bangkok 10400
☎ +66 2618-2323 🖷 +66 2618-2364/2399 **W:** http://thailand.prd.go.th (general info in English). This body operates the NBT radio & TV services (R.Thailand & Television Thailand).
L.P: DG: Mr Grisanaporn Soempanich.

THE NATIONAL BROADCASTING SERVICES OF THAILAND (NBT) – RADIO THAILAND (Sathaanii Witthayu Krachaisiang Haeng Pratheet Thai, Sor. Wor. Thor.) (Gov.)
⌨ 236 Vibhavadi Rangsit Superhighway, Din Daeng, Huay Khwang, Bangkok 10320 ☎ +66 2277-4020 🖷 +66 2277-2809 **W:** http://nbt.prd.go.th **L.P:** Exec. Dir. R. Thailand: Paitoon Hiranpradith
D.Prgr: SWT=Sathaanii Witthayu Krachaisiang Haeng Pratheet Thai
AM 891/FM 92.5: 2200-1700 on 891kHz (tx site: Nong Khae, Sara Buri) and Bangkok 92.5MHz 10kW, and in full or in part on many RT regional AM stns. **N:** On the h –**AM 819**: 2200-1700 on 819kHz (tx site: Rangsit, Pathum Thani), also in part on many RT regional MW stns – **AM 837**: 2300-1700 on 837kHz (tx site: Bang Phun, Pathum Thani) .– **AM 918**: 2200-1700 **English & Thai** exc. **Malay:** 0600-0730, **Chinese:** 0730-0900, **Lao:** 0910-1000, **Burmese:** 1010-1100, **Khmer:** 1110-1200, on 918kHz (tx site: Salaya, Nakhon Pathom), also in part on some RT regional FM stns inc. Chiang Mai 98MHz, Phuket 90.5MHz, Samui 96.75MHz, Songkhla 102.25MHz – **Bangkok FM prgrs:** 88.0MHz Foreign Lang Prgr in English (10kW), 93.5MHz "Digital R. HD One" (10kW), 95.5MHz "Virgin Hitz" (10 kW), 97.0MHz (10kW) "Quality News Station.", 105.0MHz (10kW) prgr for children and families (SWT Pheua Dek Lae Khropkhrua). **Selected Reg. Stations:** ⌨ 49 Prachasamphan Rd., Tambon Chang Khlan, Muang Dist., **Chiang Mai** 50100 **FM:** 93.25 & 98.0MHz; 1476 kHz: Prgr in Thai and minority langs for hill tribes 2200-1600 ⌨ Kasikon Thungsang Rd, Muang Dist., **Khon Kaen** 40000 **FM:** 98.5 & 99.5MHz. ⌨ Soi Sathaban Ratchaphat Phuket, Thepkasatri Rd, Tambon Ratsada, Muang Dist., **Phuket** 83000 **FM:** 90.5 & 96.75MHz, ⌨ 439 Mu 2, Songkhla - Ko Yo Road, Tambon Phawong, Muang Dist., **Songkhla** 90100 **FM:** 89.5, 90.5, 102.25MHz

Addresses of other regional stations: Most stns can be reached by quoting "Sathaanii Witthayu Sor. Wor. Thor." or "R. Thailand" and the location given in the freq. list, followed by the phrase "Muang

District" and finally the city, which is generally the same as the location. Exceptions are the following: **Kanchanaburi** 810kHz: located in Sangkhlaburi district. **Loei** 909kHz: located in Dansai district. – **Nong Khai** 927kHz: located in Bung Kan district. – **Phangnga:** ⌨ for 1116kHz is Takua Pa District, Phangnga 82110. – **Saraburi:** Studios in Bangkok. ⌨ for the 1000kW tx on 891kHz is Rim Klong Hog Wa, Mu 4, Nong Rong, Nong Khae, Saraburi 18140. – **Tak:** ⌨ for 1098kHz is 14 Asia Hwy, Mae Sot District, Tak 63110. – **Yala:** ⌨ for 1026kHz is Betong District, Yala 95110, for 981kHz Raman District, Yala 95140.
D.Prgr of reg. sts: generally 2200-1700.

EXTERNAL SERVICE: Radio Thailand
see International Broadcasting section.

NATIONAL EDUCATION RADIO (Sathaanii Witthayu Krachaisiang Haeng Pratheet Thai Pheua Kaan Seuksaa, Sor. Wor. Sor.)
⌨ Soi Aree Samphan, Rama VI Rd, Samsen, Phaya Thai, Bangkok 10400
☎ +66 2271-3448 🖷 +66 2245-7083 **W:** http://edu.prd.go.th
D.Prgr: 2200-1700 on 1467kHz in the Bangkok area and nationwide on all "E" txs. Regional stns carry own prgrs and relay Bangkok.

OTHER STATIONS:
GENERAL NOTES: News: Stns are generally required to relay N. from R. Thailand at 0000 & 1200 daily, each 30 mins, and to relay time signal and national anthem at 0000 and 1100, if on the air at those times. **Station IDs:** Both short names, e.g. Wor. Por. Tho, and long names may serve as stn identifications, usually preceded by "Thiinii" ("This is"), "Thiinii Sathaanii Witthayu (Krachaisiang)" ("This is R. St.") or "Khun kamlang rap fang" ("You are listening to"). Changwat=province. Amphoe=district (dt.). prgrs are often supplied by separate production companies. The Thai name for Bangkok is 'Krung Thep' or 'Krung Thep Mahanakhon'. **Thai numerals:** 0 = suun, 1 = neung (et), 2 = song, 3 = saam, 4 = sii, 5 = haa, 6 = hok, 7 = jet, 8 = paet, 9 = kao, 10 = sip, 20 = yi sip, 100 = roi, 1000 = phan; thii = number, jut = decimal point.

RT) Radio Thailand see separate entry above – **1) Mor. Thor. Bor. Sip Et** (Monthon Thahaan Bok Thii Sip Et, 11th Military Circle). ⌨ 145 Rama V Rd, Dusit Region, Bangkok 10300. **Ann:** "Suan Mitsakawan". Prgrs produced by KCS R. – **2) Mor. Thor. Bor. Sip Song** (Monthon Thahaan Bok Thii Sip Song, "Siang Khai Chakkrapong", 12th Military Circle, "Voice of Chakkrapong Camp"). ⌨ Chakkrapong Camp, Dong Phra Ram, Prachin Buri 25000 – **3) Mor. Thor. Bor. Thii Saam Sip Et** (Monthon Thahaan Bok Thii Saam Sip Et, 31st Military Circle). ⌨ Jiraprawat Camp, Nakhon Sawan 60000 – **4) Mor. Thor. Bor. Saam Sip Song** (Monthon Thahaan Bok Thii Saam Sip Song, 32nd Military Circle). ⌨ Headquarters of the 32nd Army Area, Surasak Montri Camp, Phahonyothin Rd, Phichai, Lampang 52000 –. **5) Thor. Phor. Neung** (Kongthap Phaak Thii Neung, 1st Army Area). HQ: ⌨ Headquarters of the 1st Army Area, Suan Mitsakawan, Rajchadamnern Nok Ave, Dusit Region, Bangkok 10300. **Regional stns:** 9 Mu 4, Bang Kacha, Chanthaburi 22000 – Phairirayodet Camp, Suwansri Rd, Tha Kasem, Sa Kaeo 27000 – Kao Kuat, Kraw Plub Pla, Ratchaburi 70000 – Ban Sam Liam, Mu 4, Don Pho Thong, Suphan Buri 72000 – **6) Thor. Phor. Song** (Kongthap Phaak Thii Song, 2nd Army Area). HQ: ⌨ Suranari Camp, Ratchadamnoen Rd, Nong Phailom, Nakhon Ratchasima 30000. **Regional stns:** Aphai Rd, Nai Muang, Kalasin 46000 – Si Phatcharin Camp, Sila, Khon Kaen 40000 – Phra Yot Muang Khwang Camp, Nakhon Phanom-Sakon Nakhon Rd, Khurukhu, Nakhon Phanom 48000 – Krit Siwara Camp, That Naveng, Sakon Nakhon 47000 – Wirawatyothin Camp, Phakdichumphon Rd, Nok Muang, Surin 32000 – Sapphasiti Prasong Camp, Warin Chamrap District, Ubon Ratchathani 34190 – Yutthasin Prasit Camp, Non Sung Rd, Udon Thani 41330 – **7) Thor. Phor. Saam** (Kongthap Phaak Thii Saam, 3rd Army Area). ⌨ Headquarters of the 3rd Army Area, Somdet Phra Ekathosarot Camp, Aranyik, Phitsanulok 65000. **Regional stns:** Mengrai Maharat Camp, Chiang Rai 57000 – 236/5 Mu 3, Nakhon Sawan - Kamphaeng Phet Rd, Nakhon Chum, Kamphaeng Phet 62000 – Khalang Nakhon Camp, Nong Krating, Lampang 52000 – Phokun Pha Muang Camp, 166/1 Mu 1, Wat Pa, Lom Sak District, Phetchabun 67110 – 104/1 Mu 5, Ban Krot Ngam, Ban Na, Wachirabarami District, Phichit 66140 – Ban Mai, Ratsadon Uthit Rd, Nai Wiang, Phrae 54000 – Bypass Road, Pak Khwae, Sukhothai 64000 – Charot Withithong Rd, Nam Ruem, Tak 63000 – Phichai Dap Hak Camp, 109 Mu 8, Uttaradit 53000 – **8) Thor. Phor. Sii** (Kongthap Phaak Thii Sii, 4th Army Area). HQ: ⌨ Wachirahwud Camp, Ratchadamnoen-Pak Nun Rd, Nakhon Si Thammarat 80000. **Regional stns:** Aphai Borirak Rd, Chumphon, King-Ampoe Si Nakharin, Phatthalung 93000 – Senanarong Camp, Kho Hong, Hat Yai District, Songkhla 90110 – Ban Na San District, Surat Thani 84120 – Charoen Pradit Rd, Rusamilae, Pattani 94000 – **9) Phon Por. Thor. Or.** (Kong Phon Thahaan Peun Yai Tosue Akart Yaan, Anti-Aircraft Artillery

Division), ☞ Kiak Kay Junction, Thahaan Road, Bangsue, Dusit Region, Bangkok 10300 – **10) Wor. Sor. Por.** (Witthayu Suun Karn Thahaan Peun Yai, Artillery Centre R. St.). ☞ 301 Phahonyothin Camp, Artillery Centre, Khao Phra Ngam, Lop Buri 15160. **Regional st:** Khet Udomsak Camp, Wang Mai, Chumphon 86000 – **11) Siang Adison** (Suun Kaan Thahaan Maa, Cavalry Centre, "Voice of Adison"). ☞ Saraburi Cavalry Centre, Adison Camp, Mitraphap Rd, Pak Phrieo, Saraburi 18000. **Regional st:** Saraburi-Lom Sak Rd, Nong Khwai, Lom Sak District, Phetchabun 67110 – **12) Thor. Or.** (Thahaan Akart, Royal Thai Airforce). ☞ Tor. Or. 01, 1233kHz, Don Muang: 171 Mu 2, Phahonyothin Rd, Khlong Thanon, Sai Mai, Bangkok 0220. Tor. Or. 01, 945kHz, Min Buri: 74 Mu 2, Nimit Mai, Sai Kong Tin, Min Buri, Bangkok 10510. Tor. Or. 06, 1251kHz: The Empress Hotel,1091/343 Phetchaburi Tat Mai Road, Charurat, Makassan, Ratcha Thewi, Bangkok 10400. **Regional stns:** Thor. Or. 02: 301 Wing 2, 1st Air Division, Khao Phra Ngam Rd, Lop Buri 15160 – Thor. Or. 03: Wing 1, Mu 3, Nong Phai Lom, Nakhon Ratchasima 30000 – Thor. Or. 04: 305 Mu 4, Wing 4, 3rd Air Division, Takhli District, Nakhon Sawan 60140 – Thor. Or. 05: Wing 53, 4th Air Division, Ko Lak, Prachuap Khiri Khan 77000 – Thor. Or. 7: Surat Thani Airport Entrance, Huatoey, Phunphin District, Surat Thani 84130 – Thor. Or. 08: 38 Mu 14, Ban Nongphai, Chayangkun Rd, Khamyai, Ubon Ratchathani 34000 – Thor. Or. 09: 549 Mu 9, Wing 23, Thahaan Rd, Makkhaeng, Udon Thani 41000 – Thor. Or. 10: Wing 46, 3rd Air Division, Yaek Khok Matum, Phitsanulok - Wangthong Rd, Nai Muang, Phitsanulok 65000 – Thor. Or. 11: 99 Mu 8, Wing 56, Khok Muang, Khlong Hoykhong District, Songkhla 90110 – Thor. Or. 12: Flying Training School, Malaimaen Rd, Kratip, Kamphaeng Saen District, Nakhon Pathom 73180 – Thor. Or. 13: 90 Mu 3, Suthep, Chiang Mai 50200 – Thor. Or. 14: Wapiprathum Rd, Wangnang, Maha Sarakham 44000 – Thor. Or. 15, 141 Mu 1, Buasali, Mae Lao District, Chiang Rai 57250. 1st prgr: 801kHz. 2nd prgr: 1224kHz – Thor. Or. 16: 1049 Tha Chalaep Rd, Talat, Chanthaburi 22000 – **13) Sathaanii Witthayu Pheua Kaan Kaset** (Agricultural R. St.). ☞ Agricultural R. Section, Phahonyothin Road, Lat Yao, Bang Khen Region, Bangkok 10900 – **14) Or. Sor.** (Sathaanii Witthayu Amphon Sathaan, Phraratchawang Dusit, Amphon Sathan Throne R. Station). ☞ Dusit Palace, Ratchawithi Rd, Chitralada, Dusit Region, Bangkok 10303 **D.Prgr:** Tu-Sa 0330-0500, 0900-1200, Su 0230-0500, M silent – **15) Kho. Sor. Thor. Bor.** (Kromkarn Khon Song Thahaan Bok, Army Transportation Dept.). ☞ Army Transportation Broadcasting Station, Transport School Compound, Thahaan Road, Dusit Region, Bangkok 10300 – **16) Wor. Kor. Thor. Mor.** (Sathaanii Witthayu Krung Theep Mahaanakhon, Bangkok R. Station), ☞ 192 Sarasin Rd, Lumphini Park, Pathum Wan Region, Bangkok 10330 – **17) Tor. Chor. Dor.** (Tamruat Trawen Chaidaen, Border Patrol Police). ☞ Bang Khen Police Dept. Club, Vibhavadi-Rangsit Rd, Bang Khen Bangkok 10210 – **18) Phon Mor. Song** (Sathaanii Witthayu Kong Phan Thahaan Maa Thii Song, 2nd Cavalry Division), ☞ Samsen Rd, Bang Krabeu, Dusit Region, Bangkok 10300 Bangkok. **Regional st:** Rayong-Ban Khai Rd, Nam Khok, Rayong 21000 – **19) Wor. Phor. Thor.** (Witthayu Kromkarn Phalang Ngan Thahaan, Defence Energy Dept. R. St.). ☞ New Building, Sukhumvit 24, Phra Khanong, Bangkok 10250. **Regional st:** 141/3 Mu 4, Don Kaeo Rd, Chotana, Mae Rim District, Chiang Mai 50180 – **20) Wor. Sor. Sor.** (Witthayu Seuksa, Educational R.). ☞ Educational Technology Centre, Si Ayutthaya Rd, Ratcha Thewi, Bangkok 10400 – **22) Wor. Phon Sii** (Witthayu Kong Phon Thii Sii, 4th Infantry Division). ☞ Headquarters of the 4th Infantry Division, Somdet Phra Naresuan Maharat Camp, Phitsanulok 65000 – **23) Phon Ror. Kao** (Kong Phon Thahaan Raap Thii Kao, 9th Infantry Division), ☞ Surasi Camp, Kanchanaburi 71190 – **24) Jor. Sor.** (Krom Jaye Thahaan Suesarn, Army Signals Department). ☞ Jor. Sor. 1, Rama V Rd, Saphan Daeng, Bangsue, Dusit Region, Bangkok 10300. **Regional stns:** Jor. Sor. 2, Tharathibodi Rd, Thakham, Phunphin District, Surat Thani 84130 – Jor. Sor. 3, Prasert Songkhram Camp, Kongphon Si Rd, Nua Muang, Roi Et 45000 – Jor. Sor. 4, 104 Thetsaban 1 Rd, Nai Muang, Yasothon 35000 – Jor. Sor. 5, 5 Mu 2 Ban Lao, Ban Lao, Chaiyaphum 36000 – Jor. Sor. 6, 1543/23 Srisumang Rd, Muang Tai, Si Sa Ket 33000 – **25) Mor. Kor.** (Mahaawitthayalai Kasetsart, Kasetsart University). HQ: ☞ 50 Phahonyothin Rd, Bang Khen, Chatuchak, Bangkok 10900. Bangkok. Tr. located at Nongkhaem in Samut Sakhon province. **Regional stns:** 301/1 Mu 5, Paphai, Sansai District, Chiang Mai 50210 – 86/8 Maliwan Rd, Muang Kao, Sitan, Khon Kaen 40000 – 424 Mu 3, Kanchanawanit Rd, Phawong, Songkhla 90100 – **26) Jor. Tor. Lor.** (Jangwat Thahaan Bok Lop Buri, Lop Buri Army Province). ☞ 13th Military Circle, Narai Maharat Rd, Lop Buri 15000 – **27) Or. Sor. Mor. Thor.** (Ongkarn Suesarn Muanchon Haeng Pratheet Thai, Mass Communications Org. of Thailand, MCOT "Modern R."). ☞ 63/1 Rama IX Rd, Huay Khwang, Bangkok 10320 – **28) Sor. Or. Thor.** (Sathaanii Witthayu Krom Utiniyom Witthayaa, Meteorological Department R. St.), ☞ 4353 Sukhumvit Rd, Bangna, Bangkok 10260 – **29) Sor. Thor. Ror.** (Siang Chaak Thahaan Reua, Voice of the Navy). ☞ Sor. Thor. Ror. 2: Phutianan Stadium, Phra Khanong, Bangna District,

Bangkok 10260. **Regional stns:** Sor. Thor. Ror. 3: 99/1 Mu 1, Phuket 83000 – Sor. Thor. Ror. 4: 9/9 Thetsaban-Phatthana Rd, Wat Mai, Chanthaburi 22000 – Sor. Thor. Ror. 5: 652 Mu 2, Sattahip District, Chon Buri 20180 – Sor. Thor. Ror. 6: Songkhla Naval Station, Thale Luang Rd, Bo Yang, Songkhla 90000 – Sor. Thor. Ror. 7: Mae Klang River Operation Unit, Nakhon Phanom 48000 – Sor. Thor. Ror. 8: Ban Khlong Mek, Tha Chang, Phrom Phiram District, Phitsanulok 65150 – Sor. Thor. Ror. 9: Ban Thung Sawang, Ubon-Takan Rd, Rai Noi, Ubon Ratchathani 34000 – **30) Sor. Wor. Phor.** (Sathaanii Witthayu Phitaksantirat, Police R. St.). ☞ R. Broadcasting Section, 2nd Communication Division, Directorate of Police Communications, Police Department, Bang Khen Region, Bangkok 10900. **Regional stns:** 40 Mu 1, Chotana Rd, Maesa, Mae Rim District, Chiang Mai 50180 – Sor. Wor. Phor. 2, Suranarai Rd, Cho Ho, Nakhon Ratchasima 30310 – Sor. Wor. Phor. 3, Banphru, Hat Yai District, Songkhla 90250 – Sor. Wor. Phor. 4, Pracha Uthit Rd, Nai Muang, Phitsanulok – **31) Neung. Por. Nor.** (Krom Praisanii Thoralek, Post & Telegraph Dept.). ☞ Chaengwattana-Thungsonghong Rd, Don Muang, Bangkok 10210. 1035kHz=Phaak Phiset, 1089kHz=Mor. Sor. Thor. **Regional stns:** Bypass Rd, Nai Muang, Buri Ram 31000 – 219 Mu 4, Lampang-Hang Chat Rd, Pong Yang Khok, Hang Chat District, Lampang 52190 – 2/7 T. Nong Luang, Mahat Thai Bamrung Rd, Nong Luang, Tak 63000 – Ban Nong Bu, Rop Muang Rd, Samphrao, Udon Thani 41000 – **32) Wor. Por. Tho.** (Witthayu Prachaam Thin, Local R, Communications Division, Signals Dept, Royal Thai Army). ☞ Wor. Por. Tho. 8: Kamphaeng Phet Akkharayothin Camp, Suan Luang, Krathum Baen District, Samut Sakhon 74110. **Regional stns:** Wor. Por. Tho. 2: Kawila Camp, Kongsai, Wat Ket, Chiang Mai 50000 – Wor. Por. Tho. 3: 001 Na Khai Suranari, Phanibut Rd, Pho Klang, Nakhon Ratchasima 30000 – Wor. Por. Tho. 4: Thep Sattri Si Sunthon Camp, Kabang, Thung Song District, Nakhon Si Thammarat 80310 – Wor. Por. Tho. 5: 5 Kanchanawanit Rd, Hat Yai District, Songkhla 90110 – Wor. Por. Tho. 6: Sapphasiti Prasong Camp, Warin Chamrap District, Ubon Ratchathani 34190 – Wor. Por. Tho. 7: Khai Prachak Sinlaprakhom, Thahaan Rd, Mak Khaeng, Udon Thani 41000 – Wor. Por. Tho. 9: Chiraprawat Camp, Na Khai Chiraprawat Rd, Nakhon Sawan 60000 – Wor. Por. Tho. 10: Mengrai Maharat Barracks, Chiang Rai 57000 – Wor. Por. Tho. 12: 140 Kasikonthungsang Rd, Sila, Khon Kaen 40000 – Wor. Por. Tho. 14: Phichai Dap Hak Camp, 13/7 Prachanimit Rd, Tha It, Uttaradit 53000 – Wor. Por. Tho. 15, Khet Udomsak Camp, Wang Mai, Chumphon 86190– Wor. Por. Tho. 16: 35 Sukayang Rd, Sateng, Yala 95000 – Wor. Por. Tho. 17: Trang-Palian Rd, Ban Khuan, Trang 92000 – **33) Phon Neung Ror. Or.** (Kong Phon Thii Neung Raksaa Phra Ong, 1st Infantry Division, Royal Guard). ☞ Phitsanulok Rd, Dusit Region, Bangkok 10300. 999kHz=Phaak Phiset, 1350kHz=Phaak Pokkati. – **34) Nor. Thor. Phor.** (Nuai Bannachakaan Thahaan Phatthanaa, Armed Forces Development Command AFDC, Supreme Command HQ). ☞ Sathaanii Witthayu 919, Phitsanulok Rd, Dusit Region, Bangkok 10300. **Regional Stns:** Sathaanii Witthayu 914, Suan Sak Kieo Tap Yong, Ban Pong 00, Mae Chan, Mae Chan District, Chiang Rai 57110. 1395kHz in Thai, 1179kHz prgr in Thai and minority langs for hilltribes. – Sathaanii Witthayu 934, Mu 2 Ban Khao Kiw, Uthai-Thapthan Rd, Sakaekrang, Uthai Thani 61000 – Sathaanii Witthayu 912, 13 Chan Uthit Rd, Bang Nak, Narathiwat 96000 in Thai and Malay – Sathaanii Witthayu 921, 114 Mu 1, Na Saeng, Lom Kao District, Phetchabun 67120 – Sathaanii Witthayu 909, Ban Rung Phatthana, Sakon Nakhon-Nakhon Phanom Rd, That Naweng, Sakon Nakhon 47000 – **35) Kor. Wor. Sor.** (Kitkarn Witthayu Krachaisiang, R. & TV Division, Army Signals Dept). HQ: ☞ R. Broadcasting & Television Division, Signals Department, Royal Thai Army, Rama V Rd, Saphan Daeng, Bangsue, Dusit Region, Bangkok 10300. **Regional stns:** Kor. Wor. Sor. 1, Surin-Prasat Rd, Nok Muang, Surin 32000 – Kor. Wor. Sor. 2, Yantarakit Sokon Rd, Sung Men District, Phrae 54130 – Kor. Wor. Sor. 3, 1879 Mu 14, That Choeng Chum, Sakon Nakhon 47000 – Kor. Wor. Sor. 4, 383 Super Highway, Ban Dom, Phayao 56000 – Kor. Wor. Sor. 5, 252 Mitraphap Rd, Ban Phai District, Khon Kaen 40110 –**36) Sor. Sor. Sor.** (Siang Sam Yot, Crime Suppression Division, Royal Thai Police). ☞ Section 1, Superintendency 2, Command Division, Crime Suppression Division, Phahonyothin Rd, Bangkok 10900. **Regional st:** 195 Mu 8, Udon-Nong Samrong Rd, Mumon, Udon Thani 41000 – **37) Ror. Dor.** (Kromkarn Raksaa Dindaen, Territorial Defence Dept.). HQ: ☞ 2 Charoen Krung Rd, Suan Chaochet, Phra Nakhon Region, Bangkok 10200. **Regional stns:** Nong Ho, Chotana Rd, Chang Peuak, Chiang Mai 50000 – Sri Phatcharin Camp, Raat Khaneung Rd, Nai Muang, Khon Kaen 40000 – **38) Mahaawitthayalai Thammasat** (Thammasat University), ☞ Faculty of Journalism and Mass Communications, Thammasat University, Prachan Rd, Phra Nakhon Region, Bangkok 10200 – **39) Yaan Kraw** (4th Cavalry Battalion, Armoured Unit, Royal Guard). HQ: ☞ Military Armoured Car School, 1156 Samsen Road, Bangkabrue, Dusit Region, Bangkok 10300. **Regional st:** Mitraphap Rd, Nong Bua Udon Thani 41000 – **40) Sathaanii Witthayu Rattasapha** (Parliament R. Station). ☞ Parliament House, Uthong Nai Rd, Dusit Region, Bangkok 10300.

International Relays: R. Saranrom, R. Liberty, Voice of America, R. Farda, BBC – see International radio section

TIMOR-LESTE

L.T: UTC +9h — **Pop:** 1.1 million — **Pr.L:** Tetun, Portuguese, Indonesian — **E.C:** 50 Hz, 220V — **ITU:** TLS

AUTORIDADE REGULADORA DAS COMUNICAÇÕES (ARCOM)
⬚ Secretária de Estado dos Transportes, Equipamentos e Comunicações, Ministério das Infra-Estruturas, Av. Bispo de Medeiros, Díli ☎ +670 3339343 📠 +670 3339339 **E:** public.consultations@arcom.tl

RÁDIO E TELEVISÃO DE TIMOR-LESTE (RTTL) (Pub.)
⬚ Edifício da Rádio e Televisão, Rua Mercado Municipal, Díli ☎ +670 7231152 **L.P:** Acting Dir: Julio Manuel Correia. RTTL administers R. Timor-Leste (RTL) and TV Timor-Leste (TVTL).

RÁDIO TIMOR-LESTE (RTL) (Pub.)
⬚ Rua Mercado Municipal, Díli ☎ +670 3321827 or +670 7231158 **E:** radiotimorleste@gmail.com **L.P:** Dir: Rosário Maia Martins

MW (kHz)	kW	Location			
684	1	Díli (alt. freq. 680)			

FM (MHz)	kW	Location	FM (MHz)	kW	Location
88.7	0.5	Maliana	95.0	1	Baucau
90.1		Ermera	96.3		Ainaro
90.9	0.3	Aileu	96.3	1	Same
91.7	4	Díli	97.1	0.5	Lospalos
92.1	0.3	Oecussi	97.6		Díli (Antena 2)
93.1	0.3	Suai	98.5	0.3	Viqueque
94.5	0.3	Manatuto	99.5		Liquisa

D.Prgr in Tetun, Portuguese and Indonesian: 2045-1200. Regional stn hours may be limited due to restricted electricity supply.
N. in Tetun: 2200, 0800. **N. in Portuguese:** 2300, 0700. **N. in Indonesian:** 0000,1000. All N. Mon-Fri only.

RÁDIO MAUBERE (Operated by Fretilin Party)
⬚ Avenida dos Mártires da Pátria, Lurumata, Díli ☎ +670 3322599 **W:** www.mixcloud.com/radiomaubere **E:** radio-maubere@live.com
FM (MHz): Manatuto 93.8, Viqueque 94.8. Baucau 96.0 , Oecusse 96.2, Ermera 96.4, Suai 96.5, Aileu 97.9, Liquisa 97.9, Lospalos 98.0, Same 98.2, Ainaro 98.5, Maliana 99.5, Díli 99.9.

TIMOR-LESTE ASSOCIATION OF COMMUNITY RADIO STATIONS (Asosiasaun Radio Komunidade Timor-Leste - ARKTL)
⬚ c/o Timor-Leste Media Development Centre, Rua Sebastião, Colmera, Díli ☎ +670 3324475 **W:** http://arktl.wordpress.com ARKTL's main role is as advocate for all community and independent stns.

COMMUNITY RADIO CENTRE (Centru Radio Comunidade) (CRC)
⬚ CNE Building, Rua Bispo de Medeiros, Area of Quintal Boot, PO Box 160, Santa Cruz, Díli ☎ +670 3310127 or +670 7237890 **W:** www.crc-tl.org **E:** admin@crc-tl.org **L.P:** Mgr: Luis Evaristo dos Santos. CRC supports stns 2, 9, 11, 12, 13,14, 16, 19 and 21.

COMMUNITY AND INDEPENDENT STATIONS

MW	kHz	kW	Station
1)	1404	2.5/5	R. Timor Kmanek, Díli

FM	MHz	kW	Station
2)	87.9	0.1	R. Comunidade Raï Husar, Aileu
3)	88.8	0.15	Direitu FM, Díli
4)	89.5	0.5	Voz FM, Díli
5)	89.7		R. Comunidade Maubisse Mau-Loko, Maubisse
6)	90.0		R. Akademika, Universidade Nal de Timor-Leste, Díli
7)	91.2		R. Lalenok Ba Ema Hotu (Labeh), Díli
8)	91.7	0.2	R. Comunidade Maliana, Maliana
9)	92.3	0.1	R. Comunidade Café Ermera, Gleno
10)	92.3	0.1	R. Comunidade Tokodede, Liquisa
11)	93.3	0.1	R. Comunidade Atoni Lifau, Oecussi
12)	94.5	0.1	R. Comunidade Cova Taroman, Suai
13)	94.7	0.3	Centru R. Comunidade (CRC) R, Díli
14)	95.1	0.1	R. Comunidade 1912 Dom Boaventura, Same
15)	95.8		Liberdade FM, Díli
16)	96.1	0.1	R. Comunidade Ili Uai, Manatuto
17)	97.0		R. Suara Timor Lorosae, Díli
18)	97.9	0.8	R. Povo Viqueque, Viqueque
19)	98.1	0.1	R. Comunidade Lian Tatamailau, Ainaro
1)	98.5	0.1	R. Timor Kmanek, Díli
20)	99.5	0.16	R. Rakambia, Díli
21)	99.9	0.1	R. Comunidade Lian Matebian, Baucau
22)	100.1	0.3	R. Comunidade Lospalos, Lospalos

FM	MHz	kW	Station
23)	100.5	0.1	R. Lorico Lian, Díli
24)	102.0		R. Klibur, Díli
25)	102.5	0.15	R. Koulimai, Bukoli
26)	104.0		R. Sapientia, Díli*
27)	107.9		R. Fini Lorosae, Baucau

RELAYS OF INTERNATIONAL STATIONS:
RDP Internacional, Díli 105.3MHz 1 KW – **RDP Antena 1**, Díli 103.1MHz – **BBC World Service**, Díli 95.3vMHz – **R. Australia**, Díli 106.4MHz

TOGO

L.T: UTC — **Pop:** 6 million — **Pr.L:** French, Ewé, Kabyè, Kotokoli, Mina — **E.C:** 50Hz, 127(Lomé)/220V — **ITU:** TGO

HAUTE AUTORITÉ DE L'AUDIOVISUEL ET DE LA COMMUNICATION (HAAC)
⬚ Lomé. **L.P:** Pres: Philippe Evegno, Vice Pres: Wiyao Dadja Pouwi

RADIODIFFUSION-TÉLÉVISION TOGOLAISE (Gov.)
RADIO LOMÉ ⬚ B.P. 434, Lomé ☎+228 2221 2493 📠 +228 2221 3673 **W:** www.radiolome.tg **E:** radiolome@radiolome.tg
L.P: Dir: Bawa Semedo. CE: Dodzi Soares.
FM: Agou 88.3MHz, Alédjo 92.7MHz, Dapaong 88.3MHz, Badou 99.3MHz, Lomé 99.5MHz.
D.Prgr: French/Ethnic: 24h. **English:** 1940. **Ann:** "Radio Lomé". **IS:** Soft tempo chime.

RADIO KARA (Regional station)
⬚ B.P. 21, Kara. **L.P:** Dir: Kao Pérézi. CE: Tete Anani
FM: Kara 91.5MHz, Dapaong 91.9MHz, Agou 94.5MHz, Alédjo 99.3MHz, Lomé 101.5MHz.
D.Prgr: 0525-0905, 1200-1435, 1625-2105. **Ann:** "Radiodiffusion Kara".

Other Stations (FM MHz):
R. Avenir, 76 Blvd. de la Kara, Quartier Doumassessé, B.P. 20183, Lomé: 104.3 – **R. de L'Evangile**, Lomé: 100.3. – **R. Delta Santé,** Aneho: 106.1. (Also rel. RFI) – **R. Evangile Jésus Vous Aime**, Bretelle de Klimamé, B.P. 2313, Lomé. **FM:** Lomé 100.2, Agou 104.1 – **R. Maria Togo**, n°155 de la rue 158, Hédzranawoé, B.P. 30162, Lomé **W:** www. radiomaria.org **E:** rmariatg@ids.tg **FM:** Dapaong 88.5 0.25kW, Lomé 98.8, Kara 101.5, Kpalimé/Sokodé 104.5 – **R. Missionnaire**, Quartier Tomdé Kara, B.P. 170, Kara: 106.3. **E:** emc_kara@yahoo.com – **R. Nana FM**, Angle Rues Tanou et Djossi, B.P. 6035, Lomé: 95.5. **E:** petdog2@yahoo.fr – **Océan FM**, Aneho: 93.1 – **R. Rurale:** Pagouda 88.9, Notsè 100.1, Dapaong 102.5 – **Sport FM**, Tokoin Habitat, B.P. 8675, Lomé: 91.9 **W:** www.radiosportfm.com – **R. Tropik FM**, Quartier Wuiti, B.P. 2276, Lomé: 93.1. **E:** tropikfm@nomade.fr – **Zephyr FM**, B.P. 20017, Lomé. **W:** www.zephyr.tg **E:** zephyr@zephyr.tg **FM:** Lomé 92.3, Kara 95.5, Atakpamé 102.9 – **R. Zion**, Adidogomé, B.P. 13853, Lomé. **FM:** Lomé 94.3, Kpalimé 102.5.
Africa No 1: Lomé 102.
BBC African Sce in English/French: Lomé 97.5
RFI Afrique: Lomé 91.5, Aledjo 95.9, Agou 98.3

TOKELAU (New Zealand)

L.T: UTC +11h — **Pop:** 1,411 — **Pr.L:** Tokelauan, English — **E.C:** 50Hz, 240V — **ITU:** TOK

TOKELAU COMMUNITY RADIO
⬚ Office of the Council for the Ongoing Government, Tokelau Office, PO Box 3298 Apia, Samoa. **L.P:** GM: Jovilisi Suveinakama ☎ +685 20822 **W:** www.tokelau.org.nz **Prgr:** local community news and information, educational talks, weather reports and music. Each stn operates independently from studios on each individual atoll.

FM	MHz	kW	Station
Atafu Atoll	107.5	0.005	R. Atafu FM
Fakaofo Atoll	107.5	0.005	R. Fakaofo FM
Nukunonu Atoll	107.5	0.005	R. Nukunonu FM

TONGA

L.T: UTC +13h — **Pop:** 105,916 — **Pr.L:** Tongan, English — **E.C:** 50Hz, 240V — **ITU:** TON

MINISTRY OF INFORMATION & COMMUNICATIONS
⬚ P.O. Box 1380, Nuku'alofa ☎ +676 28170 📠 +676 24861 **W:** www.mic.gov.to **E:** enquiries@mic.gov.to **CEO:** Paula Ma'u

MIC is the government ministry responsible for broadcasting policy and radio spectrum administration.

TONGA BROADCASTING COMMISSION
(Independent Statutory Board, part-comm.)
✉ P.O. Box 36, Nuku'alofa ☎ +676 23295, 23555, 23556 🖃 +676 24417 Fangatongo, Neiafu, Vava'u ☎ +676 70827, 70843 **W:** www.tonga-broadcasting.net **E:** tbc_news@tonga-broadcasting.net
L.P: GM: 'Elenoa 'Amanaki DepGM: Nanise Fifita Chief Prgr Officer: Viola Ulakai C.E: Salomone Finau
Tongatapu: MW: A3Z 1017kHz 10kW **FM:** 90.0MHz 0.1kW (Kool FM)
Vava'u: 90.0MHz Vava'u Kool FM
R. Tonga "The Call of the Friendly Isles" on 1017kHz: **D.Prgr:** 1900-1100. **N. in English:** 1800 (BBC), 1900 (ABC), 0000 (ABC or RNZI), 0700 (local), 0715 (ABC) **Kool FM** "Kool 90FM" & "Vava'u Kool 90FM" **N:** local and RNZI **D.Prgr:** 24h

Other stations:
FM	Location	MHz	kW	Station
9)	Vaipoa	88.0		R. Niuatoputapu
10)	Nuku'alofa	88.1		FM 88.1
1)	Nuku'alofa	88.6		R. Nuku'alofa
6)	Neiafu, Vava"u	88.6		FM Peau Vava'u
11)	Nuku'alofa	87.5		F.P.I.
2)	Neiafu, Vava'u	89.0		Letio Faka-Kalistiana 89FM
3)	Nuku'alofa	89.1		Tonga R. Magic 89.1.
7)	Neiafu, Vava'u	89.3		PIG FM1
8)	Nuku'alofa	89.5		FM 89.5
4)	Nuku'alofa	93.1	0.2	Letio Faka-Kalistiane 93FM
12)	Nuku'alofa	98.0	0.1	Le'o 'o e Kakai
3)	Neiafu, Vava'u	101.1		Vava'u R.
5)	Nuku'alofa	103.0		R. Australia

Addresses and other information
1) Nuku'alofa. **ID:** '88.6 FM' ☎ +676 24901 Txt: +676 76511 **W:** www.bebo.com/radionukualofa **D.Prgr:** 24h – **2)** UCB Pacific Partners, P.O.Box 478, Nuku'alofa ☎ +676 27327 **W:** www.pacificpartners.org **E:** tonga@pacificpartners.org **LP:** Mgr Loni Akolo. **D.Prgr:** 24h **Call:** A3R – **3)** 13 Vaha'akolo Road, Kaipongipongi, Nuku'alofa ☎ +676 25891 🖃 +676 25600 **W:** www.tongaradio.com **E:** a3rv@tongaradio.com , magic@tongaradio.com **L.P:** Mgr Phillip Vea. **Call:** A3V – **4)** UCB Pacific Partners, P.O.Box 95, Neiafu, Vava'u ☎ +676 70223 **L.P:** Mgr Willy Florian **D.Prgr:** 24h – **5)** 24h English for the Pacific satellite relay – **6)** ☎ +676 71128/7129 – **7) ID:** "FM1" ☎ +676 71479 – **8)** BroadCom Ltd, Ngeieia, Nuku'alofa. **L.P:** MD Katalina Tohi, C.Ops Mgr: Siaosi Lavaka. **D.Prgr:** 24h in Tongan **N:** Tongan & English [RNZI]. **F.P.I:** nationwide FM coverage to other islands – **9)** Old Catholic Priest's residence, Vaipoa, Niuatoputapu, Northern Tonga. **Call:** A3NTT community radio funded by South Pacific Commission – **10)** Taimi Media Network, Vaiola Motu'a, Nuku'alofa ☎ +676 25133/27477 **W:** www.taimionline.com **E:** kalafim@yahoo.com.au **L.P:** CEO Kalafi Moala – **11)** Sovereign Distributors Ltd, P.O. Box 86, Nuku'alofa ☎ +676 23283 🖃 +676 22915 **L.P:** MD Lupe 'Ilaiu – **12)** Voice of the People, Ma'a Fafine moe Famili Inc, Community Media Centre, Fasi, Nuku'alofa. **L.P:** MD: Bale Huni.

TRINIDAD & TOBAGO

L.T: UTC -4h — **Pop:** 1.2 million — **Pr.L:** English — **E.C:** 60Hz, 115V — **ITU:** TRD

CARIBBEAN NEW MEDIA GROUP LTD. (Gov. Comm.)
✉ 11a Maraval Rd, Port of Spain ☎ +1 868 622 4141 **W:** www.talk-city91fm.com and www.next99fm.com and www.sweet100fm.com
FM: Talk City 91.1MHz – **Next** 99.1MHz – **Sweet** 100.1MHz

TRINIDAD BROADCASTING COMPANY (Comm.)
✉ Second Floor, Guardian Building, 22-24 St. Vincent St, P.O. Box 716, Port of Spain ☎ +1 868 623 3802-5 🖃 +1 868 625 1782 **W:** www.951thebestmix.co.tt and www.vibect105.co.tt
L.P: GM: Steve Dipnarine
MW: Inspirational 7-30 AM: 730kHz 20kW, 24h (Gospel). **N:** on the h 0600-1900
FM: The Best Mix: 95.1MHz 100kW (A/C) – **The Vibe CT 105:** 105.1MHz (Local music + sport) – **Sangeet:** 106.1MHz (Chutney + Current Affairs) – **Aakash Vani:** 106.5MHz (Easy Listening) – **SLAM:** 100.5MHz (Progressive Urban)

ONE CARIBBEAN MEDIA (Comm.)
✉ 5 Rosalina St, Woodbrook,, Port of Spain ☎ +1 868 625 8426 🖃 +1 868 624 3234 **L.P:** CEO: Vic Fernandes. GM: Richard Purcell. PD: Wayne LeBlanc **W:** www.ocmnet.net/hott93 and www.ocmnet.net/css

FM: Hott 93: 93.1MHz (Tobago), 93.5MHz (Port of Spain) – **Caribbean SuperStation (CSS):** 92.3MHz (Port of Spain) + tx's in Barbados, Grenada, St.Lucia, Montserrat (also serving Antigua), Virgin Islands (British), and St. Kitts – **The Wave:** Tx in St.Lucia

HCU COMMUNICATIONS GROUP (Comm.)
✉ 112 Montrose Main Rd, 3rd Floor, Chaguanas ☎ +1 868 665 3630 🖃 +1 868 672 1059 **W:** www.hotlikepepperradio.com and www.masala101.com **L.P:** Chmn: Mohan Jaikaran. CEO: Marcel Mahabir. SM: Joy Mahabir
FM: U97.5 Hot Like Pepper: 97.5MHz – **Masala Radio 101/Win Radio 101 Trinidad:** 101.1MHz 25kW. Format: East Indian

C.L. COMMUNICATIONS GROUP (Comm.)
✉ #3 Herbert St, St. Clair ☎ +1 868 622 3541. Radio 90.5: 622 0451, Music Radio 9-7: 622 9797, Heartbeat: 622 1035 & Ebony: 622 3104 🖃 +1 868 622 6693 **E:** radio90fm@homeviewtnt.com andradio97@wow.net, radio104@tstt.net.tt **W:** www.clcommunications.com
FM: Radio 90.5: 90.5MHz (East Indian Stn) – **Music Radio 9-7:** 97.1/97.9MHz – **Heartbeat 103.5:** 103.5MHz (For women) – **Ebony 104:** 104.1MHz

CITADEL LIMITED (Comm.)
✉ 47 Tragarete Rd, Newtown, Port of Spain ☎ +1 868 628 4107/4955 🖃 +1 868 628 0251 **W:** www.i955fm.com and www.hitz107fm.com **L.P:** CEO: Louis Lee Sing. PM: Tony Lee. VP Marketing: Ian Lee Sing. VP Fin: Charlene Quamina-Vincent
FM: i95.5 FM: 95.5MHz (News/talk/current affairs) – **Red 96.7:** 96.7MHz (Urban) – **Hitz 107.1:** 107.1MHz (AC)

TRINIDAD & TOBAGO RADIO NETWORK (Comm.)
✉ 153 Tragarete Rd, Newtown, Port of Spain ☎ +1 868 628 6937/6044 **W:** star947tt.com and 96wefm.com and 1077musicforlife.com **L.P:** MD: Tony Chow Lin On. SM: Robert Dash. PD: Paul Richards.
FM: Star 94.7 HD: 94.7MHz (Rock) – **W.E.F.M:** 96.1MHz (Urban Caribbean) – **Music for Life:** 107.7 (Soul)

RADIO VISION LIMITED (Comm.)
✉ 88-90 Abercromby St., Port of Spain ☎ +1 868 627 6937 **W:** www.city94fm.com and www.power102fm.com **L.P:** CEP: O'Brian Haynes. MD Brian Knight
FM: Boom Champions 94.1MHz – **POWER 102:** 102.1/102.5

Other stations:
BBC FM: 98.7MHz – **HERITAGE RADIO,** 104 Woodford St, New Town, Port of Spain ☎+1 868 622 3312 🖃+1 868 657 9248 **W:** heritageradiott.com **FM:** 101.7MHz (Multicultural/rlg.) – **ISAAC 98.1,** 105a Woodford Street, Newtown, Port of Spain ☎ +1 868 628 0904 **W:** www.isaac981.com **L.P:** CEO Margaret Elcock. **FM:** 98.1MHz (Rlg) – **LIFE RADIO,** 6A Naparima Mayaro Rd, Cocoyea Village, San Fernando ☎ +1 868 653 0237 **FM:** 99.5MHz (Rlg) – **MORE FM,** 177 Tragarete Rd., Woodbrook ☎ +1 868 628 9595 **W:** www.morefmtrinidad.com **FM:** 104.7/107.5MHz (Top 40) – **103FM,** Level 4, Long Circular Mall, Long Circular Road, St. James ☎ +1 868 628 9222/23/24 **W:** www.103fm.net **FM:** 103.1 (East Indian) – **PARLIAMENT OF THE REPUBLIC OF TRINIDAD & TOBAGO,** Abercromby St, Port of Spain: **FM:** 105.5MHz – **PULSE 91.5 FM,** Bolan Amar Building, Pole Carew Street, Woodbrook ☎+1 868 628 0827 **FM:** 91.5MHz – **RADIO JAAGRITI,** Corner Pasea Main Road Ext and Churchill Roosevelt Highway, Tunapuna ☎+1 868 663 8743 🖃+1 868 645 0613 **W:** www.jaagriti.com **L.P:** MD: Sat Maharaj. **FM:** 102.7MHz. (Rlg. hindu) – **RADIO TAMBRIN,** 3 Picton Street, Scarborough, Tobago ☎+1 868 639 3437 🖃+1 868 660 7351 **E:** tambrin@tstt.net.tt **W:** www.tambrintobago.com **L.P:** GM: George Leacock. **FM:** 92.7MHz – **RADIO TOCO,** Galera Road, Toco ☎+1 868 670 0068. **L.P:** CEO: Michael Als. **FM:** 106.7MHz 1.2kW Community Radio for NE Trinidad. Relays VoA 0200-1200 – **SIDEWALK RADIO,** Curepe Priority Mall, Curepe ☎ +1 868 662 2050 **FM:** 92.3MHz – **SOCA 91.9,** 56 Maraval Road, Port of Spain ☎ +1 868 628 3460 **W:** www.919socafm.com **FM:** 91.9MHz – **WACK FM,** 129c Coffee Street, San Fernando ☎ +1 868 652 9774 **W:** www.wackradio901fm.com **L.P:** CEO: Kenny Phillips **FM:** 90.1MHz – **WMJX FM,** 9 Long Circular Road, St. James ☎ +1 868 628 9561/3760 🖃 +1 868 622 2764 **W:** www.wmjxfm.com **L.P:** GM: Keith Cadet. **FM:** 100.5MHz (Smooth Jazz)

TRISTAN DA CUNHA (UK)

L.T: UTC — **Pop:** 275 — **Pr.L:** English — **E.C:** 50Hz, 220V — **ITU:** TRC

TRISTAN BROADCASTING SERVICE (Gov.)
✉ The Administrator, Tristan da Cunha, So. Atlantic via Cape

Town, South Africa. **E:** tristan.radio@yahoo.co.uk **L.P:** Head of Telecommunications: Andy Repetto.
FM: Atlantic FM, 93.5MHz 25W **D.Prgr:** Sun 1000-1200

Other stations:
Satellite relay of **BFBS 1** prob. rebroadcast on 93.5MHz

TUNISIA

L.T: UTC +1h — **Pop:** 10.5 million — **Pr.L:** Arabic — **E.C:** 50Hz, 115/220V — **ITU:** TUN

OFFICE NATIONAL DE LA TÉLÉDIFFUSION (ONT)
✉ Cité Ennasim I, Borjel, B.P. 399, 1080 Tunis Cedex ☎+216 71801177 ▤+216 71781927 **W:** www.telediffusion.net.tn **E:** ont@telediffusion.net.tn

RADIO TUNISIENNE (Gov.)
✉ 71 Ave. de la Liberté, TN-1002 Tunis ☎+216 71847300 ▤+216 71785146 **W:** rtci.tn **E:** ittisal@ertt.nat.tn
L.P: DG Radio: Chaouki Aloui. Dir. Tech. Radio: Moncef Fathallah.

MW	kHz	kW	Prgr.	Times
Gafsa	585	350	N	0400-2400
Tunis	630	300	N	24h
Mednine	684	10	N	0400-2400
Remada	882	1	N	0400-2400
Tunis	963	100	I/C	0400(Mon 0900)-2300

FM (MHz)	N	C	I	Y	kW
Ain Draham	90.3		93.4	96.6	6
Biadha		105.4	101.0	95.0	50
Gabes		93.3			1
Ghraba (Sfax)	93.0	103.0	99.5	93.0	60
Gorrâa	89.1		95.4	89.1	4
Harkoussia				92.5	
Kasserine			99.2	89.6	49
Kchabta	102.6		93.8	97.0	
Kef Errand	89.8			99.4	
Remada	103.4	99.9	93.4	90.3	80
Souk Jomaa				91.3	
Trozza		87.7		90.8	
Tunis	105.3		98.2	88.6	1
Zaghouan	94.3	101.1	94.3	96.5	20
Zarzis		90.7	97.2	93.9	72

National Channel (N) in Arabic: 24h. **N.** on the h. – **Cultural channel (C)** in Arabic: 1100-2300 on 963kHz & FM. – **R. Tunis Chaîne Internationale (RTCI) (I):** French/others: 0500-2300, 963kHz 0500-1100. – **R. Jeunes** (Youth R.) **(Y):** 24h.

Regional stations (FM MHz): R. Gafsa, Avenue Habib Bourguiba, 2100 **FM:** Gafsa: 88.3, 89.0 40kW, Biadha 91.8, Chambi 92.7 50kW, 93.5 – **R. Le Kef,** Rue Mongi Slim, 7100 Le Kef. **FM:** Souk-Jomaa 90.0, 92.2 50kW, Ain Draham 90.3, Ghardimaou 94.1, Sidi Youssef 95.8, Sidi Salem 96.2, Le Kef 96.8, Nefta 99.6, Nebeur 100.1, Goraa 102.2, 103.1, 106.7 – **R. Monastir,** Rue Farhat Hached, 5019 Monastir. **FM:** Harkoussia 95.7, Trozza 97.3 5kW, Sousse 99.0, Zaghouan 104.7, Monastir 106.1 – **R. Sfax,** Route de Menzel Chaker Road, 3058 Sfax. **FM:** Djerba 89.0, Ksour-Essaf 100.2, Trozza 100.8, Sfax 105.2 – **R. Tataouine,** Cité 7 Novembre, 3263 **FM:** Tataouine: 87.6 70kW, Techout 89.5, 92.2, 94.3 80kW, 96.6 80kW, 102.6.
Ann: National Channel: "Huna Tunis, Idha'atu-l-Wataniya at-Tunisiya". Cultural Channel: "Huna idha'at-Tunis at-thakafiya". F: "Ici Radio Tunisie Internationale"
Relays for abroad on shortwave: see International Radio section.

Other stations (FM MHz):
Cap FM: Kef-Errand 91.5, Hammamet 95.2/105.6. **W:** capradio.tn – **R. Express FM,** 1 rue Monastir 2045, l'Aouina, Tunis. FM: Tunis 103.6. **W:** radioexpressfm.com – **R. Mosaïque FM,** Immeuble Montplaisir, Tunis. Hammamet 88.9, Sidi Bou Said 90.3 0.1kW, Nabul 92.9, Tunis 94.9 5kW. D.Prgr: 24h in French and English. **W:** mosaiquefm.net – **R. Jawhara FM,** Kairouan 89.4, Sousse 102.5/107.3 1kW. 0500-2400. **W:** jawharafm.net – **Shems FM:** Gafsa 88.7, Monastir 90.6, Sousse 93.7, Bizerta 95.7, Sfax 96.2, Tunis 101.7, Cap Bon 106.5, Kairouan 107.0. **W:** shemsfm.net – **Zitouna FM:** El Ghraba 89.9 60kW, Nefta 91.4 1kW, Gorraa 92.2 3kW, Trozza 94.0 5kW, Tataouine 94.4 1kW, Ksour-Essaf 96.9, Zaghouan 97.6 80kW, Souk-Jomaa 97.8, Biadha 98.3 35 kW, Bizerte 99.1 5kW, Gabes 99.8 1kW, Ain Draham 100.4 5kW, Zarzis 100.7 63kW, Tozeur 102.3 1kW, Nabeul 102.9 7kW, Remada 103.4 80kW, Sidi Bou Said 106.9. **W:** zitounafm.net

TURKEY

L.T: UTC +2h (31 Mar-27 Oct: +3h) — **Pop:** 73 million — **Pr.L:** Turkish — **E.C:** 50Hz, 230V — **ITU:** TUR

SUPREME BOARD OF RADIO AND TELEVISION(RTÜK)
✉ Bilkent Plaza B2 Blok, 06530 Bilkent/Ankara ☎+90 312 2975000 **W:** www.rtuk.gov.tr **E:** rtuk@rtuk.gov.tr **L.P:** Pres: Davut Dursun.

TÜRKIYE RADYO-TELEVIZYON KURUMU (TRT) (Turkish Radio-Television Corporation)
✉ TRT Genel Mudurlugu, Turan Güneş Bulvarı, 06109 OR-AN, Ankara ☎+90 312 4634343 ▤ +90 312 4632335
W: www.trt.net.tr (Turkish), www. trt-world.com (E) **E:** aktifhat@trt.net.tr
Regional addr: TRT Çukurova Müdürlüğü,Inonu Bulvarı 30 Ocak Mah. No:48 Liman B Kapisi Karsisi, 33130 Mersin – TRT Antalya Müdürlüğü, Memur Evleri Tonguc Caddesi 19, 07050 Antalya – TRT Trabzon Müdürlüğü, Adnan Kahveci Bulvari 70, 61200 Sogutlu-Akcabat/Trabzon – TRT Diyarbakir Müdürlüğü, Istasyon Caddesi N:o 1, 21100 Diyarbakir.
L.P: DG: Ibrahim Sahin. Dep. DG (Eng.): Dr Zeki Çiftçi. Dep. DG (Radio Section): Ahmet Koyuncu. Dir. Radio Dept: Arif Koyuncu. Dir. Transmitters Dept: Recep Yurdusaven.

MW	kHz	kW	N	MW	kHz	kW	N
Mersin**	630	300	R	Izmir	927	200	1
Çatalca*	702	600	1	Trabzon	954	300	R
Antalya	891	300	R	Diyarbakir	1062	300	K

*) Istanbul, **Çukurova regional. 1=TRT1, 4=TRT4, R=Reg, K=Kurdish.

FM: Location	TRT1	TRT2	TRT3	TRT4	TürküHaber	Nagme	kW
Adana (c)	105.1	92.5	89.2	96.7	100.0		30
Adiyaman (d)	88.8	94.4		103.3	90.8	103.3	30
Afyon	97.0	93.0		94.0	92.0 96.2	94.0	5/30
Agri (e)	88.2	92.2			95.2	101.8	30
Amasya	94.7	93.9		107.3	101.9 99.6	98.9	30
Ankara-Cankaya	93.3	88.0		91.2 103.7	98.6 105.6	102.8	30
Ankara-Yenimehalle		100.3			107.8		30
Antalya (a)	100.6	95.6	91.6		88.4	92.1	30/1
Antalya-Alanya (a)	90.3	92.7			94.4		5
Antalya-Kas (a)	88.1	90.5	97.0	97.1			1/5
Aydin (a)	88.8	92.0	97.6	101.5 102.2		96.6	
Aydin-Kusadasi	98.7	90.2	93.5	103.5		96.6	5/30
Balikesir	92.6	98.4		99.3			30
Balikesir-Ayvalik	88.4	90.4		103.5 99.1	95.4	101.1	5
Bilecik	89.0	96.8	94.4	101.3			
Bingöl (d)	99.2	97.2		105.0 99.6		97.6	30
Bitlis (d)	98.0	94.2		100.0 94.3	96.3		5
Bolu	89.6	92.6		89.9	94.8		
Burdur (a)	94.0	89.6		102.4		99.2	5
Bursa	87.9	98.9	91.1	95.2	96.7		30/5
Çanakkale	93.0	89.5		97.0 100.3	106.3		30
Çankiri-Eldivan	88.4	91.6		98.8		100.8	30
Çorum	105.7	103.7		98.2		101.2	5
Denizli-Bozkurt	95.2	93.2	90.0	101.5			30/5
Diyarbakir (d)	98.4	95.5		107.3			30
Edirne	97.9	89.0		103.7 91.0		100.9 1/30
Elazig (d)	94.8	92.8		102.2 107.5	89.6	102.7	30
Erzincan (e)	88.0	93.2		91.2 96.7			30
Erzurum (e)	90.8	98.8		102.6	96.8	92.7 30/5	
Erzurum-Oltu (e)	95.6	93.6		89.1		98.1	5
Eskisehir	89.0	96.8	94.4	101.3			30
Eskisehir-Sivrihisar	90.2	98.4		104.4	96.2		30
Gaziantep (d)	92.0	97.6		101.9	95.2		30
Hatay (c)	93.6	91.2		88.0	100.0		30/5
Isparta (a)	94.0	89.6		105.5 102.4		99.2	30
Istanbul	95.6	91.4	88.2	103.4		101.6	100
Izmir	94.7	91.2	88.0	100.5			100
Izmir-Karaburun	90.8	93.8	99.1	101.6	99.1	88.7	5
Izmit-Kocaeli	90.5	96.0		100.5	93.6		30
Kahramanras (c)	99.8	105.8		87.8		107.9	5
Kahram.-Elbistan (c)	91.4	96.4		94.0			30
Karaman (c)	96.4	98.6		90.8		106.5	30
Kars (e)	100.8	89.5		103.3		91.3	30
Kastamonu	93.2	91.5		90.0		101.9 30/5	
Kastamonu-Bozkurt	101.5	97.5		103.5			30
Kayseri	89.4	97.2	93.3		99.2		30
Kilis (c)	94.4	90.8		98.3		88.8	5
Kirklareli	97.9	89.0		91.0		100.9	
Kirklareli-Demirköy	94.5	90.0		92.0	103.6		30
Kirsehir	97.6	92.0		88.8		102.5	30
Konya (c)	96.4	98.6		90.8		92.9	30
Konya-Tuzlukcu	89.2	95.8		92.4		101.0	30
Kütahya	90.2	95.4		88.1	92.1		30

FM: Location	TRT1	TRT2	TRT3	TRT4	Türkü	Haber	Nagme	kW
Mardin (d)	92.8	104.5		107.0				5
Mardin-Nusaybin(d)	96.8	93.4		91.0				30
Mersin-Icel (c)	93.1	90.0	95.8	92.0	104.3		102.1	5
Mersin-Silifke (c)	98.3	95.1		102.2			103.2	30/5
Mugla-Bodrum (a)	94.6	99.3	89.4	100.3			97.4	5
Mugla-Datça (a)	95.8	107.1	102.9	92.6	102.2		96.6	30
Mugla-Datça		92.0	104.7	92.6	102.2		96.6	30
Mugla-Fethiye (a)	97.7	94.5	89.3	93.7	103.1		93.7	5
Mugla-Köycegiz (a)	105.1	99.8	95.4	92.8				30
Mugla-Marmaris (a)	98.2	90.9	95.0	101.0				5
Mugla-Yatagan (a)	88.8	92.0		102.2			96.6	30
Mus (d)	99.2	97.2		105.0	102.7			5
Nevsehir-Avanos	99.6	95.0	93.7	103.0	88.8		102.5	5
Nigde (c)	90.0	95.6		93.2			105.7	30
Ordu-Persembe (t)	99.9	95.6		97.6				30
Samsun (t)	95.2	92.8	93.2	96.8	91.3	90.8	97.5	30
Sanliurfa (d)	98.1	102.5						5/30
Sanliurfa-Suruc (d)	90.4	100.3		105.5				30
Siirt-Kurtalan (d)	99.6	105.6		101.6				30
Sirnak (d)	101.6							30
Sirnak-Cizre (d)	101.9	97.7		103.8				30
Sivas	93.6	98.3	100.9		90.4			30
Trabzon (d)	88.8	95.0		97.0	103.7	92.0	105.7	30
Tunceli (d)	89.2	92.4		106.9			101.1	30
Usak	105.5	101.9		98.4			95.7	30
Van (d)	94.8	89.3		100.3	92.8			30/5
Van-Ozalp (d)	91.2	97.6		101.2			93.2	5
Yozgat	98.0	96.0		89.8	104.0			5
Zonguldak	88.8	97.2		93.4		99.2		5/30

+about 400 stations 1kW or less.

1 = Radyo Bir (spoken word): 24h on FM. **MW:** 0400-0800 on 702kHz, 0800-1100 on 927kHz. In Turkish exc. in Bosnian (Mon) Arabic (Tues), Kurdish (Wed/Fri) and Circassian (Thu): 0410-0445 – **2 = (TRT-FM)** (popular music): 24h in Turkish – **3 = Radyo Üc** (classical music): 24h in Turkish exc. N. in English/French/German (3 min's each): 0503, 0803, 1003, 1303, 1503, 1803. Tourist Prgrs (3 min's each on Saturdays): English: 1715, French: 1515, German: 2015 – **4= Radyo Dört** (art & folk music): 24h on FM, 1100 (927kHz from 0800)-1600 on 630/927/954kHz – **TRT Türkü** (Turkish folk music channel): 24h – **6= Radyo Sese in Kurdish:** 0400-1500 on 1062kHz & 24h on FM: Adiyaman 88.4, Bingöl 90.2, Bitlis 90.6, Diyarbakir 88.4, Mardin 102.1, Mus 90.2, Siirt 103.6, Sirnak 94.5 & Van 102.3MHz – **TRT Radyo Haber:** news network; 24h on FM – **TRT Nagme** (Turkish Art Music Channel): 24h – **Regional prgrs** (Bölgesel R): 0800-1100 on 630/891/954kHz & via FM1 on txs near Antalya (a(, Çukurova (c), Diyarbakir (e) and Trabzon (t) – **Armenian Sce.** on 106.25MHz: 0530-0600 & 1600-1630. – MW txs carry additional special prgr. during Ramazan month.

Ann: TRT-1: "Burasi TRT Radyo Bir", TRT-4: "Burasi TRT Radyo Dört". Reg.: e.g. Antalya: "Burasi TRT Antalya Radyosu."

EXTERNAL SERVICE: Voice of Turkey
See International Radio section.

Other stations; main networks:

FM (MHz)	1)	2)	3)	4)	5)	6)	7)	8)	9)	10)
Abant			104.5							104.8
Adana	105.4	89.6	102.9	103.8	96.0		106.3	90.8	101.9	92.0
Adiyaman						92.0		97.0	100.5	
Afyon			90.4			95.1	104.6	88.8	94.9	
Agri					100.4			88.8	96.2	
Akhisar		93.0					106.2		105.2	
Aksaray		93.0				90.5	97.2	92.0	105.0	
Aksehir							104.5	97.0	99.5	
Alanya		100.0	89.3	98.0			89.9	88.8	93.5	
Amasya							104.0	101.6		
Ankara	102.4	88.8	100.0	105.3	97.2	94.5	89.8	90.0	107.4	90.8
Antalya	90.2	89.7	100.0	89.3	102.6	90.9	101.2	97.6	95.3	94.2
Ardahan					95.5	98.0	88.8	99.0		
Artvin							99.0	100.4		
Aydin	100.2		92.3		95.8		94.5	91.0		
Ayvalik			98.3		93.6					105.2
Balikesir	98.7	88.8	100.0	90.7	93.5	94.3	97.2	106.8	88.5	100.8
Bandirma				89.3		107.7	106.2	94.4	107.0	
Bartin						95.5	98.4	98.8	100.0	
Batman								88.8	99.1	
Bayburt						91.5		98.0	95.0	
Bilecik							92.4	102.0		
Boyabat								88.8	99.0	
Bafra							101.0	105.5	96.0	
Bingol							96.0	103.3		
Bitlis					94.5			88.8	101.0	
Bodrum	104.8	103.5	100.0	90.3	92.4					89.0
Bolu	92.0		100.0	94.2		97.1	89.2	90.0	107.6	

FM (MHz)	1)	2)	3)	4)	5)	6)	7)	8)	9)	10)
Boyabat								88.8	99.0	
Bucak									100.0	
Burdur			92.0				88.0	88.8	104.5	
Bursa	92.0	89.8	100.0	89.2	97.2	101.6	104.6	88.8	104.5	90.8
Ceyhan							107.7	90.6	97.8	
Cizre					88.1			93.0		
Çanakkale			89.3			99.5	105.3	88.8	101.0	
Çankiri							90.1	104.0	92.8	
Çerkezkoy	101.9							100.2		
Çesme		89.6	100.0	89.3	97.2					93.3
Çorlu	100.3	100.0					101.6	91.3		
Çorum						91.3	97.7	89.5		
Demirci						104.6	97.4			
Denizli	92.0	88.0	100.0	89.3	96.0		107.7	88.8	96.8	90.8
Develi									99.0	
Didim		103.5								
Dinar								88.8	96.5	
Diyarbakir	92.0	89.7	100.3	92.3		90.4	98.0	88.7	101.0	97.5
Dogubeyazit						100.5				
Düzce	92.0						107.0	88.8	105.0	96.3
Edirne				101.3	102.6	90.5	103.0	104.3	91.3	98.4
Edremit						90.7		92.0	96.0	
Elazig						104.0	92.4	99.4	94.1	
Erzincan						89.5		88.8	93.8	
Erzurum	91.8	90.4	100.7	89.3		94.6	91.5	98.0	94.0	
Eskisehir	88.6	100.0	100.5	89.3		92.6	106.3	91.8	106.6	
Fethiye	102.0		100.3	96.7	96.4		99.0	90.7	98.5	93.2
Gaziantep	107.5	92.4	100.7	102.5	103.7	96.6	107.0	88.8	103.0	99.3
Gazipasa						97.5				
Gerede	104.0					94.5	102.7	88.8	107.4	104.8
Giresun						91.1		89.6	93.0	
Gölcük										90.8
Gümüshane						92.0		91.0	102.0	
Hakkari						98.0		88.8		
Hatay						88.5	106.7	105.0	101.0	
Igdir						95.5		88.8	95.5	
Iskenderun		101.0					94.6	100.6	95.5	
Isparta			91.8			96.0		88.8	100.0	
Istanbul	92.0	89.8	100.0	89.2	97.2	94.1	104.6	88.8	107.6	90.8
Izmir	96.2	89.6	100.0	89.3	97.2	96.7	101.3	95.2	96.9	90.8
K.Maras			89.0					92.5	94.0	
Karaman								88.8	103.9	
Kars						90.6		88.8	102.7	
Kayseri	93.9	105.0	100.0	88.7	98.9		100.2	92.5	88.5	96.2
Kirikkale						105.5	89.8	88.8	105.0	
Kirklareli								88.8	107.6	
Kirsehir								92.5	94.4	
Kocaeli	92.0	89.8	100.0	89.2		90.7	104.6	88.8	107.6	
Konya	95.1	89.9		89.3	101.7	98.0	92.1	92.6	102.0	93.4
Kusadasi	104.5		100.0	105.8	92.7			88.6		
Kütahya	93.5	94.1		91.3		92.6	107.0	88.4	93.8	90.8
Ladik	92.0									
Malatya	92.0	89.9	103.3	97.8		91.7	104.6	105.2	105.5	94.5
Manisa			89.1				101.3	99.1	103.3	105.4
Mardin								96.5	97.0	
Marmaris	109.6	105.5	100.0	89.3	96.1		97.9			
Mersin	98.1	88.1	105.0	90.3		94.5	103.0	106.8	105.3	
Milas							91.0	96.9		
Mugla	103.0		100.3	89.3			104.6	93.1	102.6	90.1
Mus							88.8	102.0		
Nevsehir						96.3		90.7	102.0	
Nigde						94.5		99.9	103.0	
Ordu								102.0	92.5	
Osmaniye	105.4	89.6				98.4	99.9	95.3	101.7	
Rize					94.6			106.5	101.0	
Sakarya	101.3		100.7	101.8	91.2		104.6	102.6	107.8	97.8
Samsun	99.7	106.2	100.0	88.0			94.1	92.0	103.0	96.3
Saraykoy						107.4				
Siirt								88.8	91.0	
Sinop						94.3		88.8	99.0	
Sivas	96.2			102.2			91.0	90.0	100.1	
Sivrihisar							97.5	102.2	94.9	
Soke									96.9	
Sanliurfa	92.5						92.0	103.0	93.5	105.4
Tekirdag	96.2			90.3	96.0		104.6	104.4	105.4	91.8
Tokat								104.0	96.5	
Trabzon	92.2	100.4		89.3		94.6	93.0	92.5	102.8	90.3
Tunceli						94.5			100.0	
Usak						106.0		105.0	99.0	
Van							104.6	92.0	96.0	
Yalova		100.0						94.1		
Yozgat								102.0	94.2	100.4
Zile								98.0	95.0	103.5
Zonguldak	92.7		90.0				104.6	100.0	107.0	91.0

Addresses and other information:
1) Kral FM ✉ Mehmet Akif Mah, Inönü Cad. Star Sk. No :2 Ikitelli (Merkez-Dr. Eminpasa Sokak No :20/3 Cagaloglu), Istanbul ☎+90 212 4489060 🖷 +90 212 4489158 **W:** www.kralfm.com.tr – **2) Show R.** ✉ Büyükdere Caddesi No 163, Zincirlikuyu, Istanbul ☎+90 212 2851260 🖷 +90 212 2851297 **W:** www.showradyo.com.tr – **3) Power FM** ✉ Power Media Center, Ali Riza Gürcan Cad. N. 27, 34173 Merter, Istanbul ☎+90 212 4490900 🖷 +90 216 4816364 **W:** www.powerfm.com.tr **E:** powerteknik@powerfm.com.tr – **4) Alem FM** ✉ Davutpasa Cad. Merkez Efende Mah. No 34, Topkapi, Zeytinburnu, Istanbul ☎+90 212 2305858 **W:** www.alemfm.com **E:** info@alemfm.com – **5) Metro FM** ✉ Mehmet Akif Mah. Basin Ekspres Yolu Star Sok. No 2, Ikitelli, Istanbul ☎+90 212 4489860 🖷 +90 212 4489365 **W:** www.metrofm.com.tr – **6) Polis Radyosu** ✉ Emniet Genel Müdürlügü, Haberlesma Dairesi, Baskanligi Radyo TV ve Foto Film, Sube Md. Necatibey caddes No. 105, Anittepe-Ankara ☎+90 312 4123000 **W:** www.polisradyosu.net **E:** polisradyosu@egm.gov.tr – **7) Radyo 7** ✉ Otakçilar Cad No: 60, Eyüp, Istanbul ☎+90 212 5675454 🖷 +90 212 5677797 **W:** www.radyo7.com **E:** radyo7@radyo7.com – **8) Burc FM** ✉ Ferah Mahallesi Resatbey Sokak No:12, 34692 Buyukcamlica, Istanbul ☎+90 216 4433470 **W:** www.burcfm.com **E:** burcfm@burcfm.com.tr – **9) Akra FM** ✉ Bulgurlu Mahallesi Duhanci Haci Mahmut Sokak No:35, Kucukcamlica, Istanbul ☎+90 216 3252265 🖷 +90 216 3277633 **W:** akradyo.nct **E:** akradyo@akradyo.net – **10) Super FM** ✉ Basin Ekspres Yolu Ikitelli, Istanbul ☎+90 212 368 6210 **W:** superfm.com.tr **E:** superfm@superfm.com.tr
In addition there are about 30 national, 100 regional and 1000 local stations in operation on FM.

AFN INCIRLIK AIR BASE BROADCASTING STN (Mil.)
☎+90 322 3166421 **W:** www.afrts.osd.mil **E:** 39abw.pa@incirlik.af.mil **MW:** 1590kHz 5W. **FM:** 107.1MHz on cable

TURKMENISTAN

L.T: UTC +5h — **Pop:** 5.1 million — **Pr.L:** Turkmen — **E.C:** 50Hz, 220V — **ITU:** TKM

TÜRKMEN RADIOSY (Gov)
✉ Magtymguly köçesi 89, 744000 Asgabat ☎ +993 12 351515 🖷 +993 12 394470

LW/MW	kHz	kW	Net	MW	kHz	kW	Net
Asgabat	279	150	1	Serhetabat	1080	5	1
Asgabat	576	150	1	Asgabat	1125	20	1
Türkmenbasy	675	10	2	Syrtagta	1233	40	1
Ekarça	720	1	1	Dasoguz	1233	5	1
Etrek	720	1	1	Türkmenbasy	1476	10	1
Türkmenabat	927	50	1				

FM (MHz)	Net 1	Net 2	Net 1	Net 2	Net 3	kW
Arlan	72.20	70.61	-	-	103.0	-
Asgabat	71.12	69.68	103.2	104.4	101.3	2x4/3x10
Baharly	-	70.64	-	-	-	4
Balkanabat	70.28	72.02	100.4	101.9	103.9	2x4/3x1
Bayramaly	-	70.27	-	-	-	4
Boldumsaz	-	-	105.6	106.9	-	4
Dasoguz	69.32	67.22	100.7	103.0	-	2x4/2x1
Magdanly	-	-	104.2	106.7	-	4
Mary	-	-	103.2	104.4	-	4
Tejen	70.52	72.14	-	-	-	4
Türkmenabat	66.95	68.77	104.4	106.0	-	4
Türkmenbasy	69.23	67.19	100.2	101.7	-	2x4/2x10

D.Prgr: Net 1 (Watan): 24h. – **Net 2 (Çar tarapdan/Miras):** Çar tarapdan: 0100-0400, 0700-0900, 1400-1700; **Miras:** 0400-0700, 0900-1400, 1700-2300. – **Net 3 (Owaz):** 24h in Turkmen, Russian, English.

TURKS & CAICOS ISLANDS (UK)

L.T: UTC -5h (10 Mar-3 Nov: -4h) — **Pop:** 46,000 — **Pr.L:** English — **E.C:** 60Hz, 110/220/440V — **ITU:** TCA

RADIO TURKS & CAICOS (Gov. Comm.)
✉ P.O. Box 69, Grand Turk ☎ +1 649 946 2010 🖷 +1 649 946 1600 **E:** teamrtc107fm.com **W:** www.rtc107fm.com **L.P:** MD: Yasmin Blues. PM: Audley Astwood
FM: 101.9MHz (Grand Turk/Salt Cay & South Caicos), 103.9MHz (North & Middle Caicos), 105.9MHz & 107.7MHz (Providenciales)
D.Prgr: 24h. Local prgr: 1100-0300; at other times relays country satellite stn. On 105.9: "RTC" (Official Government News Radio).
Ann: "This is Radio Turks & Caicos on Grand Turk, Turks & Caicos Islands"

RADIO VISIÓN CRISTIANA (Rlg.)
✉ North End, So. Caicos ☎ +1 649 946 6601 **W:** www.radiovision.net
L.P: Mgr. Bob Rodríguez. CEN: Peter Polano
MW: So. Caicos 530kHz (Lp.)
D.Prgr. in Spanish: rel. WWRV 1330, NY, USA

WIV FM RADIO (Comm.)
✉ WIV Building, Leeward Highway, Box 324, Providenciales ☎ +1 888 628 9391 **W:** www.praisehimfm.com www.939islandfm.com and www.power925fm.com **L.P.:** Kenny Caughlin
FM: PraiseHim FM: 90.5MHz (Gospel) – **Island FM:** 93.9MHz (Island music) – **KISS FM:** 102.5MHz (Light rock) – **Power 92.5 FM:** 92.5MHz (Hit music)

Other stations:
KIST (Rlg.), Providenciales: 106.3MHz. Grand Turk: 94.9MHz 2kW. Format: Gospel – **LIFE RADIO - ZIBF**, Communication Network, Basden Hill, So. Caicos. **FM:** Life R. 1:105.5MHz 0.6kW, Life R. 2: 107.1MHz – **TRADEWINDS RADIO** 104.5MHz – **TROPICAL REGGAE BREEZE**, The Bight, Providenciales **FM:** 105.5MHz – **WDDR RADIO,** Box 262, Providenciales: 88.7MHz (0.25kW) – **ZVIC (Victory In Christ)** (Rlg.), Providenciales: 96.7MHz

TUVALU

L.T: UTC +12h — **Pop:** 10,544 — **Pr.L:** Tuvaluan, English — **E.C:** 50Hz, 240V (Funafuti only) — **ITU:** TUV

TUVALU MEDIA CORPORATION (Gov.)
✉ Private Mail Bag, Vaiaku, Funafuti ☎ +688 20139 🖷 + 688 20732 **L.P:** GM Melali Taape. **Prgr Prod:** Ms Afasene Pese, Head of Tech. Sces: John Sammons
W: www.tuvalu-news.tv **F:** meltaape@govt.tv, apese@govt.tv
Radio Tuvalu AM: MW: 621kHz 5kW Funafuti (nationwide coverage) **FM:** Funafuti (local coverage) 100.1MHz 0.02kW
D.Prgr: 1830-2000, 2325-0100, 0625-10000 daily. **N. in English:** 1910, 0710 **Ann:** E: "This is Radio Tuvalu" **V.** by letter.
BBC Pacific stream via satellite at other times: 2000-2325, 0100-0625, 1000-1830

UGANDA

L.T: UTC +3h — **Pop:** 33 million — **Pr.L:** Luganda, Swahili, English — **E.C:** 50Hz, 240V — **ITU:** UGA

UGANDA COMMUNICATIONS COMMISSION (UCC)
✉ 12th Floor, Communications House, Plot 1, Colville Street, P. O. Box 7376, Kampala ☎+256 41 4339000 🖷 +256 41 4348832
W: www.ucc.co.ug **E:** ucc@ucc.co.ug

UBC RADIO (Pub.)
✉ P.O. Box 2038, Plot 17-19, Nile Ave, Kampala ☎+256 41 4257256 🖷 + 256 41 4257252 **W:** www.ubconline.co.ug **E:** ubc@ubconline.co.ug **L.P:** Chmn: Chris B. Katuramu. Man. Dir: Musinguzi Mugasa. Commissioners: Radio Broadc: Jack Turyamwijuka. Ag. Contr. of Prgrs (Radio): Charles Byekwaso. Ag. Principal Eng. (Radio): Yona Hamala.

MW: Most freqs rep. inactive, except Mityana 576kHz rep. carrying Blue Channel or Star FM and Palisa 729kHz, Kampala 909kHz & Kabale 999kHz for Red Channel, all irregular.

SW	kHz	kW	Ch.	Times
Kampala	‡4976	10	Red	0200-0600, 1300-2105
Kampala	‡7195	10	Red	0600-1300

NB: Both frequencies reported inactive.

FM (MHz)	Blue	Red	Butebo	Star FM	Magic
Fort Portal	98.8	-	-	-	-
Jinja	-	-	-	95.7	-
Kabale	93.7	-	-	-	-
Kampala	105.7	98.0	107.3	87.5	87.5
Lira	-	100.0	-	-	-
Masaka	99.5	-	-	96.9	-
Mbale	-	96.9	-	-	-
Mbarara	97.4	-	-	-	-
Masindi	105.0	-	-	-	-
Soroti	-	96.7	-	-	-

Red Channel in English, Swahili, 5 Northern languages: MF 0200-2105, SS 0345-2105 – **Blue Channel** in 6 ethnic langauges: MF 0300-2105, SS 0345-2105 – **Butebo Channel** in 10 ethnic languages – **Star FM** in Luganda. **Magic FM** in English.
Ann: E: "UBC Radio". **IS:** local xylophone.

DUNAMIS SHORTWAVE (Rlg.)
(a joint project by High Adventure Canada and Dunamis FM).
📧 P.O. Box 4260, Kampala. **W:** www.biblevoice.org **E:** dunamis4750@hotmail.com **LP:** CE: David Firth.
SW: Mukono 4750kHz 1kW. **D.Prgr:** in English/Ethnic 1500-1900v.

Other stations (FM MHz):
African R, Kampala: 104.5 – **All Karamoja FM,** Moroto: 94.7 – **Arua One FM,** Arua: 88.7 2kW – **Bamboo FM,** Jinja: 107.6 – **Basoga Bainho,** Jinja: 87.7 – **Beat FM,** Kampala: 96.3 – **Buddu BS,** Masaka: 98.8 – **Bukedde FM:** Kampala 100.5, Masaka 106.8 **W:** bukedde.co.ug – **Bunuyoro BS,** Masindi: 98.2 – **Busiro FM,** Kakiri: 107.5 – **Busoga FM,** Jinja: 96.0 – **Campus FM,** Kampala: 106.6 – **Capital FM:** Kampala 91.3, Mbale 90.9, Mbarara 88.7 – **City FM,** Kampala: 98.1 – **Continental FM,** Kumi: 94.7 – **Dembe FM,** Kampala: 90.4 – **Dunamis FM,** Kampala: 103.0 – **East Africa R,** Kampala: 99 (cf. Tanzania) – **Eastern Voice,** Bugiri: 102.3 – **Elgon FM,** Kapchorwa 89.2 – **Etop R,** Soroti: 99.4 – **Eye FM,** Iganga: 98.8 – **Impact & Alpha FM:** Mbale 98.5, Masaka 101.5 1kW, Kampala 102.1 4kW. **W:** www.victoryuganda.org – **Kibaale Community R:** 91.7 – **Kiira FM,** Jinja: 88.6 – **Liberty FM,** Hoima 89.0 – **Maranatha FM,** Lira: 104.7 – **Mbale FM:** 90.1 – **Mega FM,** Gulu: 102.1 – **Nile BS,** Jinja: 89.4 – **Open Gate FM,** Mbale: 103.2 – **Power FM,** Kampala: 104.1 – **Prime R,** Kampala: 91.9 – **R FM,** Iganga: 91.1 **W:** rfm.co.ug – **R. Apac,** Apac 92.9 0.4kW, Odokomit 106.5 0.1kW **W:** radioapac.tripod.com – **R. KFM,** Kampala: 93.3 **W:** kfm.co.ug – **R. Kitara,** Masindi: 101.8 – **Kyoga Veritas R,** Soroti: 91.5 1kW. **W:** facebook.com – **R. Lira,** Lira: 95.3 – **R. Mama,** Kampala: 101.7. **W:** interconnection.org/umwa/community_radio.html – **R. Maria Uganda,** Masaka 94 40W, Mbale 101.8, Kampala 103.7 40W, Fort Portal 104.6, Mbarara 105.4. **W:** www.radiomaria.org.ug – **R. One,** Kampala: 90.0 – **R. Pacis,** Arua: 90.9/94.5 1kW. **W:** radiopacis.org – **R. Paidha,** Nebbi: 87.8 – **R. Rukungiri:** 96.9 – **R. Rupiny:** Kampala 95.7, Lira 98.1 **W:** visiongroup.co.ug – **R. Sapientia,** Kampala: 94.4 5kW. **W:** radiosapientia.com – **R. Simba,** Kampala: 97.3 **W:** www.simba.fm – **R. Skynet,** Mityana: 96.9 – **R. Two,** Kampala: 87.9 – **R. Unity,** Lira: 97.7 – **R. Wa,** Lira: 89.8 – **R. West FM:** Mbarara 102.2, Tooro 91.0, Kabale & Masak – **Rhino FM,** Lira: 96.1 – **Rock Mamba FM,** Tororo 106,8 – **Sanyu FM,** Kampala 88.2 – **Speak FM,** Gulu 89.5 **W:** fowode.org – **Spirit FM,** Mukono: 96.6 – **Ssuubi FM,** Kampala 104.9, Masaka 88.1. **W:** ssuubifmradio.com – **Star FM,** Kampala: 100.0 – **Step FM,** Mbale: 99.8 – **Super FM,** Kampala: 88.5 – **Truth FM,** Mbale: 105.3 – **VO Africa:** Kampala 92.3 – **VO Kigezi,** Kabale 89.5 – **VO Teso,** Soroti: 88.4 – **Top R,** Kampala: 89.6 – **VO Toro,** Kampala 100.5, Fort Portal 101.0, Mbarara 95.0, Mubende 97.5 – **Touch FM,** Kampala: 95.9 1kW. **W:** touch.fm – **X FM:** Kampala: 94.8, Mbarara 96.6 **W:** xfm.co.ug

BBC African Sce Kampala 101.3MHz, Mbale/Mbarara 107.3MHz in English/Swahili/Kinyarwanda.

RFI Afrique: Kampala 93.7MHz in F/E/Swahili

UKRAINE

L.T: UTC +2h (31 Mar-27 Oct: +3h) — **Pop:** 45.9 million — **Pr.L:** Ukrainian, Russian — **E.C:** 50Hz, 220V — **ITU:** UKR

NATSIONALNA RADA UKRAINI ZA PYTAN TELEBACHENNIA I RADIOMOVLENNIA
(National Council for TV and Radio Broadcasting)
📧 vul. Prorizna 2, 01001 Kyiv ☎ +380 44 2786832 📠 +380 44 2787490 **E:** pressa@nrada.gov.ua **W:** www.nrada.gov.ua
LP: Chmn: Volodymyr Manzhosov
NB: The council is the regulatory authority for broadcasting.

DERZHAVNYI KOMITET TELEBACHENNIA I RADIOMOVLENNIA UKRAINY (DERZHTELERADIO)
(State Committee for TV and Radio Broadcasting)
📧 vul. Prorizna 2, 01001 Kyiv ☎ +380 44 2785349 📠 +380 44 2791170 **E:** pr@comin.gov.ua **W:** www.comin.kmu.gov.ua
LP: Chmn: Oleksandr Kurdinovych
NB: The committee is the administrative body for Natsionalna Radiokompania Ukrainy (NRKU), National TV, and the regional state broadcasting companies.

NATSIONALNA RADIOKOMPANIA UKRAINY (NRKU) (Gov)
(under the umbrella of Derzhteleradio)
📧 vul. Khreschatyk 26, 01001 Kyiv ☎ +380 44 2396224 📠 +380 44 2793477 **E:** int.rel@radioukr.com.ua **W:** radioukr.com.ua
LP: GD: Taras Avrakhov

MW	kHz	kW	Prgr	MW	kHz	kW	Prgr
Kyiv[1] (a)	549	150	UR2	Lviv[1] (b)	549	75	UR2

MW	kHz	kW	Prgr	MW	kHz	kW	Prgr
Mykolaiv[1] (c)	549	500	UR2	Mykolaiv[2] (c)	972	350	UR1
Chernivtsi4	657	25	UR3/F	Verkhovyna3*	1044	1	UR1,IF
Dokuchaievsk*	711	40	UR1,DO	Dokuchaievsk[1]242	40	UR2
Kharkiv (d)	837	150	UR1	Chernivtsi[1]	1377	50	UR2
Lviv (d)	936	1000	UR1	Mykolaiv (c)	1431	150	UR3

Tx Loc: (a) Brovary (b) Krasne (c) Luch (d) Taranivka. F=Ext. Serv. [1]=0400-2200 [2]=0800-1900 [3]=0800-2000 [4]=0800-2300 *) Txs are time-shared with reg. broadc. companies (see DO, IF in chapter below) **NB:** Subject to frequent change; some txs may run on reduced evening power.

FM: UR1 (Rg=Region: txs are time-shared with regional state b'casting companies, see below)

Rg	Location	MHz	kW	Rg	Location	MHz	kW
SU	Shostka	65.93	4	DN	Nikopol	69.38	1
VO	Kovel	66.02	4	DO	Kramatorsk	69.41	1
PO	Krasnohorivka	66.08	4	CH	Chernihiv	69.47	4
CH	Bakhmach	66.38	1	ZK	Uzhhorod	69.53	4
SU	Bilopillia	66.50	4	CV	Novodnistrovsk	69.59	1
RI	Antopil	66.53	4	DO	Donetsk	69.77	4
OD	Kamianske	66.59	4	MY	Mykolaiv	69.80	4
KR	Oktiabrske	66.68	4	ZH	Olevsk	69.80	4
CH	Kholmy	66.71	4	TE	Lozova	69.83	4
KR	Krasnoperekopsk	66.80	4	MY	Pervomaisk	69.92	4
KH	Kirovohrad	66.98	4	ZK	Khust	70.04	4
LV	Lviv	67.04	4	VI	Bershad	70.10	4
KA	Kharkiv	67.13	4	ZK	Rakhiv	70.19	2
KR	Sevastopol	67.25	4	OD	Odesa	70.52	4
OD	Kotovsk	67.25	4	ZP	Zaporizhia	70.73	4
DO	Mariupol	67.34	4	KM	Kulchiivtsi	70.76	4
KM	Khmelnytskyi	67.70	4	CH	Pryluky	71.00	4
CK	Buky	67.88	4	IF	Ivano-Frankivsk	71.24	4
LU	Rovenky	68.08	4	DN	Kryvyi Rih	71.63	1
LU	Starobilsk	68.08	4	KR	Kerch	71.66	4
DN	Dnipropetrovsk	68.36	4	VI	Vinnytsia	71.69	4
KY	Kyiv	68.51	5	KE	Kherson	71.90	4
ZP	Berdiansk	68.57	4	ZH	Andriivka	71.90	4
ZP	Melitopol	68.72	4	KA	Izium	72.08	4
LU	Luhansk	68.75	2	CK	Cherkasy	72.20	4
SU	Trostianets	68.75	4	KR	Sovietskyi	72.20	4
OD	Zhovten	68.99	4	OD	Izmail	72.53	1
ZP	Komysh-Zoria	68.99	4	ZH	Olevsk	100.2	1
KE	Vasylivka	69.23	4	ZH	Ovruch	104.2	1
CV	Chernivtsi	69.26	1	VI	Bershad	105.0	1

Also via Kyiv 105.0MHz (5kW), time-shared with UR2.
NB: Txs below 1kW not listed.
UR2: Liubeshiv 105.2MHz (1kW) & txs below 1kW. **UR3:** Kyiv 72.86 (5kW), Shaltsk 101.5 (1kW), Lutsk 101.9MHz (1kW) & txs below 1kW.
D.Prgr: UR1 (Persha prohrama): 0330 (SS 0400)-2300. – **UR2 (Promin):** 24h. – **UR3 (R. Kultura):** 0330 (SS 0400)-2300.
External Service (R. Ukraine Int.): see Int. Radio section.

REGIONAL STATE BROADCASTING SERVICES
(under the umbrella of Derzhteleradio)

MW	kHz	kW	Prgr	MW	kHz	kW	Prgr
Novodnistrovsk	819	7	CV	Dokuchaievsk	1359	40	DO
Chernivtsi	837	25	CV	Mykolaiv	1377	3.7	MY
Dnipropetrovsk	873	2.5	DN	Vinnytsia	1377	7	VI

MW/FM via txs shared with NRKU: see NRKU tx tables (UR1).
D.Prgr: see below. (*) = Via txs shared with the UR1 prgr of NRKU: 0410-0430 (SS), 0445-0455 (MF), 0610-0630, 1340-1400 (MF), 1345-1400 (Sat), 1610-1700, 1800-1830.
CH) Chernihivska ODTRK: pr. Peremohy 62, 14000 Chernihiv. **E:** tvodtrk@ukr.net. Reg. prgr "R. Siver-Tsentr": (*) – **CK) Cherkaska ODTRK:** vul. B.Vishnevetskoho 35/1, 18002 Cherkasy. **E:** tvros@icu.net.ua. Reg. prgr "R. Ros": (*). Local channel "R. 101 Dalmatin" (vul. Khreschatyk 195, 18002 Cherkasy, **E:** fm101@ukr.net) on 101.0 (Cherkasy): 24h. – **CV) Chernivetska ODTR:** vul. Holovna 91, 58001 Chernivtsi. **E:** bukdtrk-net@ukr.net. Reg. prgr "R. Bukovyna": (*). Reg. channel "R. Bukovyna" on 819 (Novodnistrovsk), 837 (Chernivtsi) + UR1 FM txs): 0800-1900.– **DN) Dnipropetrovska ODTRK:** vul. Televiziina 3, 49010 Dnipropetrovsk. **E:** dodtrk@email.ua. Reg. prgr: (*). Local channel "R. Mryia" on 873 (Dnipropetrovsk): 0600-1800. – **DO) Donetska OTDRK:** vul. Kuibysheva 61, 83016 Donetsk. **E:** office@k61.dn.ua. Reg. prgr "R. Donechyna" via UR1 FM txs + 711 (Dokuchaievsk): (*). Reg. channel "R. Tsentr" on 1359 (Dokuchaievsk): 0600-1900. – **IF) Ivano-Frankivska ODTRK:** vul. Sichovykh striltsiv 30a, 76000 Ivano-Frankivsk. **E:** radio@il.if.ua. Reg. prgr via UR1 FM txs & 1044 (Verkhovyna): (*) – **KA) Kharkivska ODTRK:** pl. Svobody 5, 61506 Kharkiv. **E:** info@otb.com.ua. Reg. prgr: (*). Local channel "R. Kharkiv" on 69.20 (Kharkiv 17kW): 0600-1500. – **KE) Khersonska ODTRK "Skifia":** vul. Perekopska 10, 73000 Kherson. **E:** khersonodtrk@skifiya.ks.ua. Reg. prgr "R. Dnipro": (*). Local channel "R. Tavria" on 100.6 (Kherson 1kW), 105.8 (Vasylivka 5kW): 0500-2100. – **KH) Kirovohradska ODTRK:** pl. Kirova 1, 25022

Kirovohrad. **E:** kodtrk@rambler.ru. Reg. prgr "R. Skifia-Tsentr": (*)
– **KM) Khmelnytska ODTRK "Podillia-Tsentr":** vul. Volodymyrska
92, 29000 Khmelnytskyi. **E:** tvradio@rp.km.ua. Reg. prgr: (*). Local
channel "R. Podillia-Tsentr" on 104.6 (Khmelnytskyi 1kW): 0500-2100.
– **KR) DTRK "Krym":** vul. Studentska 14, 95610 Simferopol. **E:** tv@
tv.crimea.com.ua. Reg. prgr "R. Krym": (*) – **KY) Kyivska DTRK:** vul.
Khreschatyk 5v, 01001 Kyiv. **E:** rtv@sl.net.ua. Reg. prgr "Holos Kyieva":
(*). Local channel on 72.08 (Kyiv): 0400-2000 – **LU) Luhanska ODTRK:**
vul. Demokhina 25, 91000 Luhansk. **E:** lgtrk@lep.lg.ua. Reg. prgr:
(*). Local channel "Puls" on 103.6 (Luhansk): 0400-2000. – **LV)**
Lvivska ODTRK: vul. Vysokyi Zamok 4, 79008 Lviv. **E:** lodtrk12@
gmail.com. Reg. prgr "Lvivske R.": (*) – **MY) Mykolaivska ODTRK:**
pr. Lenina 24-b, 54029 Mykolaiv. **E:** ogtrk@mksat.net. Reg. prgr "Buzka
khvylia": (*). Local channel "R. Mykolaiv" on 1377 (Mykolaiv): 0600-
1830 – **OD) Odeska ODTRK:** Fontanska doroha 3, 65963 Odesa. **E:**
odtrk@ukr.net. Reg. prgr "Chornomorskyi maiak": (*) – **PO) Poltavska**
ODTRK "Ltava": vul. R.Kyrychenko 1, 36000 Poltava. **E:** info@ltava.
poltava.ua. Reg. prgr "R. Ltava": (*). Reg. channel "Vasha khyvlia"
on 101.8 (Poltava 1kW), 102.5 (Perelisky 0.1kW), 103.1 (Hadiach
0.5kW), 105.4 (Kremenchuk 0.5kW), 106.3 (Krasnohorivka 3kW):
0500-2000. – **RI) Rivnenska ODTRK:** vul. Kotliarevskoho 20-a, 33028
Rivne. **E:** radiokraj@mail.ru. Reg. prgr "R. Krai": (*) – **SU) Sumska**
ODTRK: vul. Petropavlivska 125, 40030 Sumy. **E:** trksumy@ukr.net.
Reg. prgr: (*). Пeg. channel "Slobuda-FM" on 88.1 (Sumy 0.5kW),
91.6 (Bilipillia 0.25kW), 104.1 (Trostianets 0.5kW), 104.6 (Konotop
0.25kW), 104.8 (Lebedyn 0.1kW), 107.8 (Shostka 0.25kW): 0400-2000.
– **TE) Ternopilska ODTRK:** bul. T.Shevchenka 17, 46021 Ternopil. **E:**
todtrk@poshta.te.ua. Reg. prgr: (*). Local channel "R. Lad" on 71.03
(Lozova 1kW): 1000-1530. – **VI) Vinnytska ODTRK "Vintera":** vul.
Teatralna 15, 21100 Vinnytsia. mail@vodtrk.inut.ua. Reg prgr: (*).
Local channel "R. Khvylia" on 1377 (Vinnytsia): 0700-1115, 1300-1715
– **VO) Volynska ODTRK:** vul. Slovatskoho 9, 43025 Lutsk. **E:** admin@
voltv.lutsk.ua. Reg. prgr: (*). Reg. channel "R. Lutsk" on 100.4 (Tsumen
0.1kW), 101.6 (Novovolynsk 0.1kW), 105.2 (Horokhiv 0.1kW), 107.3
(Lutsk 1kW), 107.8 (Liubeshiv 0.1kW): 0455-1700. – **ZH) Zhytomyrska**
ODTRK: vul. Teatralna 7, 10014 Zhytomyr. **E:** tvradiozt@ukr.net. Reg.
prgr: (*). Reg. channel "Zhytomyrska khvylia" on 101.9 (Olevsk 0.1kW),
103.4 (Andriivka 5kW): 0500-2200. – **ZK) Zakarpatska ODTRK:**
Kyivska nab. 18, 88018 Uzhhorod. **E:** ztv@utel.net.ua. Reg. prgr: (*).
Reg. channel "Tysa FM" on 102.2 (Rakhiv 0.1kW), 103.0 (Uzhhorod
0.5kW), 104.3 (Velykyi Bereznyi 0.1kW), 106.6 (Mizhhiria 0.5kW), 106.8
(Khust 0.1kW): 0430-1500, 1800-1900, 2100-2200. – **ZP) Zaporizka**
ODTRK: vul. Matrosova 24, 69057 Zaporizhia. **E:** zdtrk@zp.ukrtel.net.
Reg. prgr "R. Zaporizhia": (*). Reg. channel "Zaporizhia FM" on 103.4
(Dniprorudne 1kW), 103.7 (Zaporizhia 1kW), 103.9 (Tokmak 2kW):
0200-1400.

OTHER STATIONS

MW	kHz	kW	Location	Station
70)	765	40	Petrivka	R. Maiak

SW	kHz	kW	Location	Station
71)§11980		0.25	Zaporizhia	Dniprovska khvylia (§=USB)

FM	MHz	kW	Location	Station
61)	69.68	1	Kyiv	R. Maria
30)	87.5	1	Odesa	FM1 - Pershe R.
11)	87.9	1	Odesa	Era FM
23)	88.0	1	Simferopol	R. Melodia
3C)	88.1	1	Dnipropetrovsk	R. Next
14)	88.5	1	Odesa	R. 5 - Retro FM
29)	88.5	1	Dnipropetrovsk	Music R.
11)	88.6	1	Lviv	Era FM
50)	89.7	1	Odesa	R. Pivdenna Stolitsia
14)	90.1	1	Simferopol	R. 5 - Retro FM
1)	90.2	1	Odesa	R. ROKS
7)	90.3	1	Sumy	Nashe R.
14)	90.4	1	Mariupol	R. 5 - Retro FM
17)	90.8	1	Luhansk	Stilne R. - Perets FM
11)	90.9	1	Sumy	Era FM
26)	90.9	1	Dnipropetrovsk	MFM
4)	91.0	1	Odesa	GALA-Radio
10)	91.1	1	Kryvyi Rih	Avtoradio-Ukraina
11)	91.1	1	Simferopol	Era FM
8A)	91.1	1	Lviv	R. Sharmanka
14)	91.3	1	Sumy	R. 5 - Retro FM
8A)	91.3	1	Vinnytsia	R. Sharmanka
32)	91.4	1	Odesa	R. 24
14)	91.5	1	Berdiansk	R. 5 - Retro FM
23)	91.5	1	Lviv	R. Melodia
12)	91.6	1	Kryvyi Rih	Lux FM
14)	92.4	1	Kyiv	R. 5 - Retro FM
3A)	92.8	1	Kyiv	Europa Plus Ukraina
8B)	93.8	1	Kyiv	Biznes R.
22)	94.2	1	Kyiv	R. Renesans

FM	MHz	kW	Location	Station
23)	95.2	1.5	Kyiv	R. Melodia
68)	95.6	2	Kyiv	Dzhem FM
11)	96.0	2	Kyiv	Era FM
12)	96.1	1	Donetsk	Lux FM
5)	96.4	2	Kyiv	Hit FM Ukraina
49)	96.8	2	Kyiv	DJ FM
41)	98.0	1	Kyiv	R. Kyiv
16)	98.5	1	Kyiv	Russkoye R. Ukraina
34)	99.0	2	Kyiv	R. Nostalgie 99FM
14)	99.1	1	Melitopol	R. 5 - Retro FM
14)	99.1	1	Poltava	R. 5 - Retro FM
3C)	99.3	1	Vinnytsia	R. Next
3C)	99.4	5	Kyiv	R. Next
46)	99.4	1	Kherson	R. Sofia
8A)	99.4	1	Donetsk	R. Sharmanka
12)	100.0	1	Poltava	Avtoradio-Ukraina
17)	100.0	1	Donetsk	Stilne R. - Perets FM
4)	100.0	5	Kyiv	GALA-Radio
10)	100.2	4	Kryvyi Rih	GALA-Radio
10)	100.3	1	Vinnytsia	Avtoradio-Ukraina
4)	100.3	1	Zaporizhia	GALA-Radio
10)	100.4	1	Odesa	Avtoradio-Ukraina
14)	100.4	1	Ivano-Frankivsk	R. 5 - Retro FM
1)	100.4	1	Luhansk	П. ROKS
3C)	100.5	1	Kharkiv	R. Next
12)	100.5	1	Dnipropetrovsk	Lux FM
18)	100.5	2	Kyiv	Narodne R.
25)	100.5	1	Donetsk	Mega-Radio
10)	100.6	1	Chernihiv	Avtoradio-Ukraina
13)	100.6	1	Simferopol	Super R.
53)	100.6	2	Korosten	R. Rekord FM
7)	100.7	1	Rivne	Nashe R.
24)	100.8	1	Lviv	Lvivska khvylia
5)	100.8	1	Mariupol	Hit FM Ukraina
1)	100.8	1	Zaporizhia	R. ROKS
14)	100.9	1	Kremenchuk	R. 5 - Retro FM
14)	100.9	1	Lutsk	R. 5 - Retro FM
14)	100.9	1	Vinnytsia	R. 5 - Retro FM
11)	101.0	1	Kramatorsk	Era FM
15)	101.0	1	Kryvyi Rih	R. Shanson
5)	101.0	1	Odesa	Hit FM Ukraina
54)	101.0	1	Sokal	R. Sokal
13)	101.1	2	Kyiv	Super R.
13)	101.1	1	Luhansk	Super R.
16)	101.1	1	Dnipropetrovsk	Russkoye R. Ukraina
3A)	101.1	1	Kharkiv	Europa Plus Ukraina
11)	101.2	1	Melitopol	Era FM
12)	101.2	1	Khmelnytskyi	Lux FM
5)	101.2	1	Donetsk	Hit FM Ukraina
6)	101.2	1	Kherson	Kiss FM
17)	101.3	1	Poltava	Stilne R. - Perets FM
13)	101.4	1	Rivne	Super R.
3A)	101.4	1	Kerch	Europa Plus Ukraina
57)	101.4	1	Sumy	R. SveSweet/MFM
13)	101.5	1	Dnipropetrovsk	Super R.
14)	101.5	1	Kirovohrad	R. 5 - Retro FM
14)	101.5	1	Ternopil	R. 5 - Retro FM
16)	101.5	1	Krasnohorivka	Russkoye R. Ukraina
17)	101.5	1	Kharkiv	Stilne R. - Perets FM
29)	101.5	4	Kyiv	Music R.
3C)	101.6	1	Cherkasy	R. Next
16)	101.6	1	Mykolaiv	Russkoye R. Ukraina
59)	101.6	1	Kholmets	R. Versiya
16)	101.7	1	Khmelnytskyi	Russkoye R. Ukraina
16)	101.7	1	Zhytomyr	Russkoye R. Ukraina
5)	101.7	1	Lviv	Hit FM Ukraina
1)	101.7	1	Kramatorsk	R. ROKS
6)	101.7	1	Mariupol	Kiss FM
7)	101.7	1	Simferopol	Nashe R.
10)	101.8	1	Luhansk	Avtoradio-Ukraina
6)	101.8	1	Odesa	Kiss FM
62)	101.8	1	Zaporizhia	R. Velykyi Luh
15)	101.9	4	Kyiv	R. Shanson
17)	101.9	1	Kherson	Stilne R. - Perets FM
55)	101.9	2	Khust	R. Zakarpattia FM
35)	102.0	1	Sevastopol	R. Bryz
5)	102.0	2	Dnipropetrovsk	Hit FM Ukraina
67)	102.0	1	Pryluky	R. Galaktika Plus
14)	102.1	1	Khmelnytskyi	R. 5 - Retro FM
6)	102.1	1	Mykolaiv	Kiss FM
69)	102.1	1	Donetsk	Klasne R.
37)	102.2	2	Odesa	Feel 102.2FM
26)	102.3	1	Luhansk	MFM
43)	102.3	1	Simferopol	Trans-M-Radio
5)	102.3	1	Poltava	Hit FM Ukraina

FM	MHz	kW	Location	Station
12)	102.4	1	Chernivtsi	Lux FM
4)	102.4	1	Kholmets	GALA-Radio
6)	102.4	1	Kharkiv	Kiss FM
13)	102.5	1	Khmelnytskyi	Super R.
14)	102.5	4	Lviv	R. 5 - Retro FM
36)	102.5	1	Tokmak	R. Nostalzhi Zaporizhia
3A)	102.5	1	Dnipropetrovsk	Europa Plus Ukraina
5)	102.5	1	Kherson	Hit FM Ukraina
9)	102.5	2	Kyiv	Prosto R.
13)	102.6	1	Donetsk	Super R.
14)	102.6	1	Lubyn	R. 5 - Retro FM
13)	102.7	1	Kovel	Super R.
7)	102.7	4	Kryvyi Rih	Nashe R.
7)	102.7	1	Zhytomyr	Nashe R.
13)	102.8	1	Kamianets-Pod.	Super R.
2)	102.8	1	Mariupol	Best FM
65)	102.8	1	Pryluky	R. Planeta
7)	102.8	1.2	Mykolaiv	Nashe R.
16)	102.9	1	Luhansk	Russkoye R. Ukraina
7)	102.9	1	Cherkasy	Nashe R.
7)	102.9	3	Dnipropetrovsk	Nashe R.
13)	103.0	1	Kharkiv	Super R.
14)	103.0	1	Rivne	R. 5 - Retro FM
8A)	103.0	1	Ivano-Frankivsk	R. Sharmanka
12)	103.1	3	Kyiv	Lux FM
3A)	103.1	1	Kherson	Europa Plus Ukraina
6)	103.1	1	Zaporizhia	Kiss FM
7)	103.1	1	Khmelnytskyi	Nashe R.
3C)	103.2	1	Kryvyi Rih	R. Next
13)	103.2	1	Melitopol	Super R.
18)	103.2	1	Odesa	Narodne R.
11)	103.3	1	Cherkasy	Era FM
22)	103.3	1	Dnipropetrovsk	R. Renesans
5)	103.4	1	Sumy	Hit FM Ukraina
15)	103.5	1	Kremenchuk	R. Shanson
1)	103.5	1	Ternopil	R. ROKS
1)	103.6	1	Kyiv	R. ROKS
6)	103.6	1	Khmelnytskyi	Kiss FM
8A)	103.6	2	Kryvyi Rih	R. Sharmanka
11)	103.7	1	Kherson	Era FM
16)	103.7	1	Cherkasy	Russkoye R. Ukraina
40)	103.7	1	Simferopol	R. Pilot
5)	103.7	1	Rivne	Hit FM Ukraina
63)	103.7	1	Vinnytsia	R. Takt
12)	103.8	1	Ivano-Frankivsk	Lux FM
16)	103.8	1	Kirovohrad	Russkoye R. Ukraina
17)	103.8	1	Bila Tserkva	Stilne R. - Perets FM
27)	103.8	5	Odesa	Moye Radio
3C)	103.9	1	Lviv	R. Next
11)	103.9	1	Zhytomyr	Era FM
14)	103.9	1	Evpatoria	R. 5 - Retro FM
14)	103.9	1	Kovel	R. 5 - Retro FM
16)	103.9	1	Kremenchuk	Russkoye R. Ukraina
69)	103.9	1	Kramatorsk	Klasne R.
2)	104.0	2	Kharkiv	Best FM
3A)	104.0	1	Mariupol	Europa Plus Ukraina
5)	104.0	1	Luhansk	Hit FM Ukraina
8A)	104.0	1	Dnipropetrovsk	R. Sharmanka
8A)	104.0	4	Kyiv	R. Sharmanka
16)	104.1	1	Vinnytsia	Russkoye R. Ukraina
17)	104.1	1	Mykolaiv	Stilne R. - Perets FM
26)	104.1	1	Donetsk	MFM
13)	104.2	1	Starobilsk	Super R.
36)	104.2	1	Polohy	R. Nostalzhi (R. Slavia)
17)	104.3	1	Simferopol	Stilne R. - Perets FM
20)	104.3	2	Odesa	Armianske R.
6)	104.3	1	Lviv	Kiss FM
7)	104.3	1	Chernihiv	Nashe R.
13)	104.4	1	Kherson	R. Melodia
19)	104.4	1	Novovolynsk	R. Nova
12)	104.5	1	Ternopil	Lux FM
16)	104.5	2	Sevastopol	Russkoye R. Ukraina
23)	104.5	1	Cherkasy	R. Melodia
6)	104.5	1	Zhytomyr	Kiss FM
7)	104.5	1	Kharkiv	Nashe R.
8A)	104.5	1	Zaporizhia	R. Sharmanka
11)	104.6	1	Kirovohrad	Era FM
32)	104.6	2	Kyiv	R. 24
9)	104.6	1	Mykolaiv	Prosto R.
12)	104.7	1	Lviv	Lux FM
13)	104.7	1	Kryvyi Rih	Super R.
16)	104.7	1	Donetsk	Russkoye R. Ukraina
16)	104.7	1	Melitopol	Russkoye R. Ukraina
5)	104.7	1	Chernihiv	Hit FM Ukraina
10)	104.8	1	Dnipropetrovsk	Avtoradio-Ukraina
16)	104.8	1	Kherson	Russkoye R. Ukraina
33)	104.8	1	Simferopol	R. Asol
3A)	104.8	1	Luhansk	Europa Plus Ukraina
7)	104.8	1	Lutsk	Nashe R.
16)	104.9	1	Odesa	Russkoye R. Ukraina
17)	104.9	1	Zarichne	Stilne R. - Perets FM
9)	104.9	1	Zhytomyr	Prosto R.
13)	105.0	1	Poltava	Super R.
14)	105.0	1	Chernivtsi	R. 5 - Retro FM
13)	105.1	1	Mykolaiv	Super R.
13)	105.1	1	Sumy	Super R.
15)	105.1	1	Zaporizhia	R. Shanson
6)	105.1	4	Donetsk	Kiss FM
12)	105.2	1	Uzhhorod	Lux FM
14)	105.2	1	Krasnohorivka	R. 5 - Retro FM
6)	105.2	1	Kryvyi Rih	Kiss FM
13)	105.3	1	Dubrovytsia	Super R.
14)	105.3	1	Shostka	R. 5 - Retro FM
15)	105.3	2	Dnipropetrovsk	R. Shanson
16)	105.3	1	Mariupol	Russkoye R. Ukraina
5)	105.3	1	Kirovohrad	Hit FM Ukraina
56)	105.3	1	Sieverodonetsk	R. STV
9)	105.3	4	Odesa	Prosto R.
10)	105.4	1	Lviv	Avtoradio-Ukraina
15)	105.4	1	Simferopol	R. Shanson
66)	105.4	1	Khmelnytskyi	OK FM
13)	105.5	1	Lutsk	Super R.
15)	105.5	1	Luhansk	R. Shanson
17)	105.5	2	Kyiv	Stilne R. - Perets FM
2)	105.5	1	Donetsk	Best FM
14)	105.6	1	Zhytomyr	R. 5 - Retro FM
16)	105.6	1	Sumy	Russkoye R. Ukraina
17)	105.6	1	Sevastopol	Stilne R. - Perets FM
5)	105.6	1	Krasnohorivka	Hit FM Ukraina
5)	105.6	1	Ternopil	Hit FM Ukraina
7)	105.6	1	Zaporizhia	Nashe R.
14)	105.7	1	Kamianets-Pod.	R. 5 - Retro FM
17)	105.7	1	Kramatorsk	Stilne R. - Perets FM
8A)	105.7	1	Kharkiv	R. Sharmanka
13)	105.8	1	Kirovohrad	Super R.
16)	105.8	1	Yalta	Russkoye R. Ukraina
17)	105.8	1	Mariupol	Stilne R. - Perets FM
9)	105.8	2	Dnipropetrovsk	Prosto R.
52)	105.8	1	Poltava	Klasyk R.
15)	105.9	1	Kryvyi Rih	Russkoye R. Ukraina
10)	106.0	1	Donetsk	Avtoradio-Ukraina
21)	106.0	1	Berdiansk	Azovska khvylia 106.4FM
39)	106.0	2	Kyiv	R. Dynamo
48)	106.0	1	Odesa	R. Odesa-Mama
7)	106.0	1	Lviv	Nashe R.
10)	106.1	1	Kharkiv	Avtoradio-Ukraina
12)	106.1	1	Cherkasy	Lux FM
47)	106.1	2	Zhytomyr	Z Radio 106.2FM
7)	106.1	1	Luhansk	Nashe R.
8A)	106.1	1	Ternopil	R. Sharmanka
14)	106.2	1	Bila Tserkva	R. 5 - Retro FM
17)	106.2	1	Kirovohrad	Stilne R. - Perets FM
28)	106.2	1	Kotovsk	R. Sanna
3A)	106.2	1	Zaporizhia	Europa Plus Ukraina
7)	106.2	2	Kherson	Nashe R.
36)	106.3	1	Melitopol	R. Nostalzhi Zaporizhia
10)	106.4	1	Ivano-Frankivsk	Avtoradio-Ukraina
15)	106.4	1	Donetsk	R. Shanson
3A)	106.4	1	Yalta	Europa Plus Ukraina
60)	106.4	2	Rivne	R. Trek
7)	106.4	1	Vinnytsia	Nashe R.
4)	106.5	1	Luhansk	GALA-Radio
6)	106.5	2	Kyiv	Kiss FM
7)	106.5	1	Mariupol	Nashe R.
15)	106.6	1	Kharkiv	R. Shanson
31)	106.6	1	Chernivtsi	Blysk FM
38)	106.6	2	Odesa	R. Glas
42)	106.6	1	Simferopol	R. Lider
5)	106.6	1	Zaporizhia	Hit FM Ukraina
14)	106.7	1	Kherson	R. 5 - Retro FM
45)	106.7	1	Lviv	R. Nezalezhnist
15)	106.8	1	Chernihiv	R. Shanson
15)	106.8	1	Poltava	R. Shanson
1)	106.8	5	Donetsk	R. ROKS
51)	106.8	2	Kolomyia	R. Siaivo
6)	106.8	3	Dnipropetrovsk	Kiss FM
12)	106.9	1	Lutsk	Lux FM
5)	106.9	1	Kryvyi Rih	Hit FM Ukraina

FM	MHz	kW	Location	Station
6)	106.9	1	Luhansk	Kiss FM
11)	107.0	1	Kharkiv	Era FM
14)	107.0	1	Zaporizhia	R. 5 - Retro FM
28)	107.0	1	Odesa	R. Sanna
3B)	107.0	2	Kyiv	Europa FM
5)	107.0	1	Sevastopol	Hit FM Ukraina
6)	107.0	1	Kramatorsk	Kiss FM
64)	107.0	1	Sumy	Diva R.
12)	107.1	1	Mykolaiv	Lux FM
13)	107.1	1	Zarichne	Super R.
28)	107.1	1	Izmail	R. Sanna
1)	107.1	1	Khmelnytskyi	R. ROKS
8A)	107.1	1	Cherkasy	R. Sharmanka
13)	107.2	1	Lviv	Super R.
14)	107.2	1	Kholmets	R. 5 - Retro FM
16)	107.2	1	Chernihiv	Russkoye R. Ukraina
4)	107.2	1	Donetsk	GALA-Radio
11)	107.3	1	Luhansk	Era FM
44)	107.3	1	Dnipropetrovsk	R. Mix
10)	107.4	2.5	Kyiv	Avtoradio-Ukraina
11)	107.4	1	Kryvyi Rih	Era FM
3A)	107.4	1	Odesa	Europa Plus Ukraina
4)	107.4	1	Kharkiv	GALA-Radio
17)	107.5	1	Dubrovytsia	Stilne R. - Perets FM
36)	107.5	1	Zaporizhia	R. Nostalzhi Zaporizhia
1)	107.6	1	Kherson	R. ROKS
7)	107.6	3	Donetsk	Nashe R.
12)	107.7	1	Zhytomyr	Lux FM
27)	107.7	1	Chernihiv	MFM
58)	107.7	1	Dnipropetrovsk	107.7FM - Dushevne R.
11)	107.8	1	Mykolaiv	Era FM
11)	107.8	1	Vinnytsia	Era FM
4)	107.8	1	Simferopol	GALA-Radio
10)	107.9	1	Sumy	Avtoradio-Ukraina
13)	107.9	1	Zaporizhia	Super R.
7)	107.9	1	Kirovohrad	Nashe R.
7)	107.9	5	Kyiv	Nashe R.
7)	107.9	2	Odesa	Nashe R.

NB: Txs less than 1kW not listed.

Addresses & other information:
1) vul. V.Khoiky 15/15, 04655 Kyiv. – **2)** pr-t Tychyny 2, 02098 Kyiv. – **3A-C)** vul. Frunze 39, 04080 Kyiv. – **4)** vul. Saksahanskoho 91, 01032 Kyiv. – **5)** vul. V.Khvoiky 15/15, 04655 Kyiv. – **6)** vul. V.Khvoiky 15/15, 04655 Kyiv. – **7)** vul. Otto Shmidta 6, 04107 Kyiv. – **8A,B)** b-r Shevchenka 54/1, 01032 Kyiv. – **9)** vul. Tereshkovoi 15, 65078 Odesa. – **10)** vul. Frunze 39, 04080 Kyiv. – **11)** b-r Verkhovnoy Rady 20, 02100 Kyiv. – **12)** vul. Volodymyrska 61/11, 01033 Kyiv. **13)** vul. Moskovskyi 9b, 04273 Kyiv. – **14)** vul. Frunze 39, 04080 Kyiv. – **15)** b-r Shevchenka 54/1, 01032 Kyiv. – **16)** vul. V.Khvoiky 15/15, 04655 Kyiv. – **17)** vul. Dovshenka 14, 03057 Kyiv. – **18)** b-r Lesi Ukrainki 34, 01133 Kyiv. – **19)** pr-t Druzhby 27, 45400 Novovolynsk. – **20)** vul. Saslavskoho 12/14, 65007 Odesa. – **21)** Melitopolska shose 20, 71100 Berdiansk. – **22)** b-r Shevchenka 54/1, 01032 Kyiv. – **23)** b-r Verkhovnoy Rady 20, 02100 Kyiv – **24)** vul. Hutsulska 9a, 79008 Lviv. – **25)** pr-t Illicha 100, 83052 Donetsk. – **26)** vul. Artema 145a, 83015 Donetsk. – **27)** vul. Artyleriyska 1, 65039 Odesa. – **28)** vul. Ak.Borobiova 1, 65031 Odesa. – **29)** vul. Frunze 39, 04080 Kyiv. – **30)** vul. Artyleriyska 1, 65039 Odesa. – **31)** vul Eminesku 2, 58000 Chernivtsi. – **32)** vul. Otto Shmidta 6, 04107 Kyiv. – **33)** vul. Radio 4, 95038 Simferopol. – **34)** vul. Saperno-Slobodska 25, 03039 Kyiv. – **35)** vul. 4-a Bastionna 5, 90011 Sevastopol. – **36)** vul. Sedova 12, 69044 Zaporizhia. – **37)** vul. Troiitska 50, 65045 Odesa. – **38)** vul. Kanatna 83, 65107 Odesa. – **39)** vul. Frunze 39, 04080 Kyiv. – **40)** vul. Kuibysheva 2, 95034 Simferopol. – **41)** vul. Dehtiarivska 37, 03680 Kyiv. – **42)** vul. Balaklavska 68, 95048 Simferopol. – **43)** vul. Marshala Zhukova 17, 95035 Sevastopol. – **44)** vul. Suchkova 2a, 49010 Novomoskovsk. – **45)** vul. Kn. Romana 12, 79005 Lviv. – **46)** vul. Lavrenova 25-2, 73000 Kherson. – **47)** vul. Yana Hamarnyka 6a, 10000 Zhytomyr. – **48)** vul. Saslavskoho 10/12, 65004 Odesa. – **49)** b-r Shevchenka 54/1, 01032 Kyiv. – **50)** vul. Uspenska 77, 65011 Odesa. – **51)** vul. Sichovykh Striltsiv 23, 78200 Kolomyia. – **52)** vul. Kotliarevskoho 1/27, 36020 Poltava. – **53)** vul. Peremohy 51-8, 10002 Zhytomyr. – **54)** vul. Sheptytskoho 105, 80000 Sokal. – **55)** vul. Magritycha 6, 89600 Mukachevo. – **56)** vul. Haharina 93, 93400 Severodonetsk. – **57)** vul. Kirova 25, 40030 Sumy. – **58)** vul. Robacha 23v, 49008 Dnipropetrovsk. – **59)** vul. Yerdeli 1, 88000 Uzhhorod. – **60)** vul. 16-ho Lypnia 38, 33000 Rivne. – **61)** vul. Sribnokilska 8, 01001 Kyiv. – **62)** vul. Matrosova 8a, 69057 Zaporizhia. – **63)** vul. Soborna 59, 21000 Vinnytsia. – **64)** vul. Kharkivska 5, 40024 Sumy. – **65)** vul. Pyriatynska 129, 17500 Pryluky. – **66)** pr-t Miru 69, 29015 Khmelnytskyi. – **67)** vul. Pyriatynska 129, 17500 Pryluky. – **68)** vul. Tymoshenka 2L, 04212 Kyiv. – **69)** vul. Artema 131a, 83015 Donetsk. – **70)** vul. Fontanska doroha 33, 65009 Odesa. **E:** mayak@radio.odessa.ua – **71)** TRK "Aleks TV", pr-t Motorobudivnykiv 48, 69068 Zaporizhia. **E:** radiodh@rambler.ru. SS

0700-0900; the b'casts consist of rel. UR1 exc. own ann's 0755-0800, 0855-0900 (irreg).

UNITED ARAB EMIRATES

L.T: UTC +4h — **Pop:** 5 million — **Pr.L:** Arabic — **E.C:** 50Hz, 220V — **ITU:** UAE

NATIONAL MEDIA COUNCIL
P.O. Box 17, Abu Dhabi ☎+971 2 4453000 🖷 +971 2 4452504 **W:** www.uaeinteract.com **L.P:** Chmn: Saqr Ghubash Saeed Ghubash.

ABU DHABI MEDIA COMPANY (Pub.)
4th St, Sector 18, Zone 1, Abu Dhabi ☎+971 2 4144000 🖷 +971 2 4144001 **W:** admedia.ae **L.P:** CEO: Ahmed Ali Mohamed Al Bloushi. Dir. Radio: Jaber Obaid. Head R&TV Eng: Mahmood Al-Redha.

MW	kHz	kW	Prgr.	Times
Al-Dhabbiya	657	100	AN	24h
Maqtaa	810	50	A	24h
Al-Ain	828	1	A	24h

AN=Asianet R. in Urdu: 24h. **A=Abu Dhabi FM** in Arabic: On MW & FM(MHz): Ras al-Khaimah 89.7, Abu Dhabi 90.0, Jabal Al-Dhanna 97.3, Dubai 98.4, Habshan 100.1, Liwa 103.7, Fujairah 106.0. **FM (MHz): Capital FM:** Dubai 88.8MHz, Abu Dhabi 97.3MHz – **Classic FM** (in English): Dubai 87.9. Abu Dhabi 91.6, Al Ain 105.2 – **Emarat FM:** 24h on FM (MHz): Ras al-Khaimah 88.5, Jabal al-Dhanna 92.4, Al-Ain 94.9, Abu Dhabi 95.8, Liwa 95.6, Dubai 97.1, Habshan 98.4, Fujairah 103.9 – **Holy Quran R:** 24h on FM (MHz) Jabel Dhana 87.7, Dubai 88.2, Al-Ain 88.6, Habshan 88.8, Liwa 89.3, Fujairah 97.6, Abu Dhabi 98.1MHz, Ras al-Khaimah 105.2 – **R. 1:** Abu Dhabi 100.5MHz 1kW, Dubai 104.1MHz 10kW – **R. 2:** Dubai 99.3MHz 10kW, Abu Dhabi 106.0MHz 1kW – **R. Mirchi:** Dubai/Sharjah 88.8MHz, Al-Ain 95.6MHz, Abu Dhabi 97.3MHz. **W:** radiomirchi.com – **Star FM:** Abu Dhabi 92.4MHz, Dubai 99.9MHz. Al-Ain 100.1MHz.

RAS AL-KHAIMAH BROADCASTING STATION
RAK Media, P.O. Box 141, Ras al Khaimah ☎+971 7 851151 🖷 +971 7 353441
MW: 1152kHz 200kW. **FM:** 95.3MHz (Arabic).
MW: rel. VO Kerala (radiovok.com)0200-2100v in Malayalam (Also r. two hours of Bangla R: banglaradiolive.com). **Ann:** A: "Idha'atu-l-Imarat min R'as al-Khaimah".

SHARJAH MEDIA CORPORATION
P.O. Box 111, Sharjah ☎+971 6 566 1111 🖷 +971 6 566 9999 **W:** smc.ae **E:** info@smc.ae
R. Sharjah in Arabic: Sharjah 94.4MHz, unk. loc 95.0MHz, Khor Fakkan 107.6MHz, Kalba 107.7MHz.

UMM AL QUWAIN BROADCASTING STATION
Shamal Media Services, P.O. Box 1106, Umm al Quwain ☎+971 6 5657106 🖷 +971 6 5651806
FM: UAQ FM: 97.8MHz in Arabic. **W:** uaqfm.com – **Hum FM:** 106.2MHz in Hindi/Urdu. **W:** humfm.com – **Holy Quran R:** MW 846kHz 20kW. D.Prgr: 0200-1900 in Arabic.

RADIO ASIA
Dolphin Recording Studio, P.O. Box 31876, Dubai ☎+971 4 3491011 🖷 +971 4 3421387 **L.P:** GM: Brij Bhalla. PD: Vettoor G. Sreedharan. **W:** www.radioasiauae.com **E:** admin@radioasia.ae
MW: Ras al Khaimah 1269kHz 200kW. **D.Prgr:** 24h in Malayalam.
FM: Super FM: Ras al-Khaimah 94.7MHz 20kW. **W:** super947.fm – **Suno FM:** 102.4MHz in Hindi & Urdu. **W:** suno1024.com **Ann:** "12-69 AM Radio Asia".

ARABIAN RADIO NETWORK (ARN)
P.O. Box 502255, CNN Bldg, Media City 103, Dubai ☎+971 4 3912000 🖷 +971 4 3912007 **W:** arnonline.com **E:** pr@arnonline.com **L.P:** GM: Mahmoud Al-Rasheed.
FM: Dubai 92: 92.0MHz 5kW in English – **Hit FM:** 96.7MHz 5kW in Malayalam – **Al-Arabiya:** 99.0MHz 10kW in Arabic – **Al-Khaleejiya:** 100.9MHz 5kW in Arabic – **City FM:** 101.6MHz 5kW in Hindi – **Dubai Eye:** 103.8MHz 5kW in English – **R. Shoma:** 93.4MHz – **Virgin R:** Dubai 104.4MHz 30kW.

DUBAI MEDIA INCORPORATED (DMI)
W: dmi.ae **Dubai FM:** 93.0MHz. **Noor Dubai:** 93.9MHz 5kW.

CHANNEL 4 RADIO NETWORK
P.O. Box 442, Ajman ☎+971 6 746 1444 **L.P:** MD: Mohammad Murad. Prgr. Controller: Peter Gowers. **W:** ch4network.com
FM: all in Ajman. **R. 4 FM:** 89.1MHz in English/Hindi – **Channel 4 FM:**

104.8 & 106.5MHz 1kW in English – **Gold FM:** 101.3MHz in Hindi – **Al Rabia FM:** 107.8MHz 1kW in Arabic.

FUJAIRAH MEDIA GROUP
✉ Fujairah ☎971 9 2244100 📠 +971 9 2244101 **W:** fmg.ae
FM: Coast FM: Ajman 103.2MHz (English) – **Fujairah FM:** 92.6MHz (Arabic) – **Hello FM:** 89.5MHz (Tamil) – **Jazz R.** 106.8MHz (German) – **R. Spice FM:** 105.4MHz (English/Hindi/Tamil) – **Rock R:** 90.9MHz – **Russkoye R:** 96.3MHz (Russian)

MBC FM & PANORAMA FM
✉ P.O. Box 75335, MBC Building, Media City, Dubai ☎+971 4 3919713 📠 +971 4 3916683 **W:** mbc.net **E:** contactus@mbc.ae
L.P: Dir: Hassan Muawad. **FM:** Txs in Bahrain, Iraq, Jordan, Kuwait, Qatar, Saudi Arabia, Sudan and Palestine West Bank.

R. Me: Dubai 100.3MHz in Malayalam. **W:** radiomeonline.com
Zayed R. for Quran: Fujairah 97.4 & 97.6MHz. **W:** zayedquran.gov.ae

BBC World Sce: Abu Dhabi 90.3MHz.
BBG - R. Sawa: MW: Al-Dhabbiya 1170kHz 800kW 24h. FM: Dubai 90.5MHz 5kW, Abu Dhabi 98.7MHz 10kW. For more details see Interational Radio section (USA).
BBG - R. Aap Ki Dunyaa: Al-Dhabbiya 1539kHz 600kW 1400-0200.
BBG - R. Farda: Al-Dhabbiya 1314kHz 1000kW 1400-0200 &1575kHz 800kW 24h. For further details see Int. radio section under USA.
Monte Carlo Doualiya: Dubai 95.3MHz

UNITED KINGDOM

L.T: UTC (31 Mar-27 Oct: +1h) — **Pop:** 63 million — **Pr.L:** English Welsh — **E.C:** 50Hz, 230V — **ITU:** G — **Int.Dialling Code:** +44

CROWN DEPENDENCIES
NB: The Channel Islands and the Isle of Man are dependencies of the British Crown and are not part of the United Kingdom. They are included here for editorial convenience.

BRITISH BROADCASTING CORPORATION (Pub)
The BBC is an independent body created by Royal Charter and operates under licence. ✉ Broadcasting House, Portland Place, London W1A 1AA. ☎ +44 20 7580 4468 **W:** www.bbc.co.uk **LP:** Chairman BBC Trust: Lord Patten; DG: George Entwistle; Dir Audio & Music: Tim Davie; Acting Dir Vision: Roger Mosey; Dir News: Helen Boaden; Dir Future Media: Ralph Rivera; CEO BBC Worldwide: Tim Davey.

LW/MW:

Radio 4	kHz	kW	Radio 4	kHz	kW
Burghead	198	50	Crystal Palace	720	0.8
Droitwich	198	500	Redruth	756	2
Westerglen	198	50	Enniskillen	774	1
Newcastle	603	2	Plymouth	774	1
Londonderry	720	0.25	Redmoss	1449	2
Lisnagarvey	720	10	Carlisle	1485	1

Radio 5 Live	kHz	kW	Radio 5 Live	kHz	kW
Barrow	693	1	Clevedon	909	50
Bexhill	693	1	Exeter	909	1
Brighton	693	1	Fareham	909	1
Burghead	693	25	Lisnagarvey	909	10
Droitwich	693	150	Londonderry	909	1
Enniskillen	693	1	Bournemouth	909	0.25
Folkestone	693	1	Moorside Edge	909	200
Postwick	693	10	Redruth	909	2
Redmoss	693	1	Westerglen	909	50
Stagshaw	693	50	Whitehaven	909	1
Start Point	693	50	Tywyn	990	1
Brookmans Park	909	150			

England, Isle of Man, Channel Is FM (all stereo)

FM	R1	R2	R3	R4	kW
Barnstaple	98.1	88.5	90.7	92.9	1
Beacon Hill	98.4	88.7	90.9	93.1	1
Belmont	98.3	88.8	90.9	93.1	16
Bilsdale	98.6	89.0	91.2	93.4	5
Bow Brickhill	98.2	88.6	90.8	93.0	10
Bristol	98.9	89.3	91.5	93.7	1.3
Chatton	99.7	90.1	92.3	94.5	5.6
Crystal Palace	98.5	88.8	91.0	93.2	4
Douglas (I.O.M.)	98.0	88.4	90.6	92.8	11
Guildford	97.7	88.1	90.3	92.5	3
Caversham	99.4	89.8	92.0	94.2	1
Holme Moss	98.9	89.3	91.5	93.7	250
Keighley	98.5	88.9	91.1	93.3	1
Les Platons (C.I.)	97.1	89.6	91.1	94.8	16
Manningtree	97.7	88.1	90.3	92.5	5

FM	R1	R2	R3	R4	kW
Morecambe Bay	99.6	90.0	92.2	94.4	10
North Hessary Tor	97.7	88.1	90.3	92.5	160
Oxford	99.1	89.5	91.7	93.9	46
Pendle Forest	97.8	90.2	92.6	94.6	1
Peterborough	99.7	90.1	92.3	94.5	40
Pontop Pike	98.1	88.5	90.7	92.9	134
Redruth	99.3	89.7	91.9	94.1	25
Ridge Hill	98.2	88.6	90.8	93.0	10
Rowridge	98.2	88.5	90.7	92.9	250
Sandale	97.7	88.1	90.3	92.5	250
Stanton Moor	99.4	89.8	92.0	94.2	1.2
Sutton Coldfield	97.9	88.3	90.5	92.7	250
Swingate (Dover)	99.5	90.0	92.4	94.4	11
Tacolneston	99.3	89.7	91.9	94.1	250
Winter Hill	98.2	88.6	90.8	93.0	4
Woolmoor	99.6	90.2	92.2	94.4	5
Wrotham	*98.8	89.1	91.3	93.5	125*/250

+ 74 low power txs less than 1kW

STATIONS: Radio 1: New music genres for youth audience 24h **N:** Newsbeat M-F 1245, 1745 – **Radio 1Xtra** (digital only) – **Radio 2:** Adult contemporary and specialist music: 24h **N:** on the h – **Radio 3:** Classical music, jazz, world music, arts: 24h **N:** 0700, 0800, 0900(SS), 1300, 1700(MF), 1800(MF) – **Radio 4:** News, documentaries, drama, entertainment, and cricket on LW/MW in season: 0520-0100; relays BBCWS 0100-0520. **N:** 0530, then on the h (not 1000 Sun, 1100 Sun, 1500 Sat) – **Radio 4Extra** (digital only) – **Radio 5 Live:** News & sport: 24h **N:** on the h and half h – **Radio 6 Music:** New and archive music: 24h (digital only)

BBC LOCAL RADIO

MW	Station	Location	kHz	kW
1)	Three Counties R.	Luton	630	0.2
6)	R. Cornwall	Redruth	630	2
6)	R. Cornwall	Bodmin	657	0.5
37)	R. York	Fulford	666	0.5
11)	Essex	Manningtree	729	0.2
15)	Hereford & Worcester	Worcester	738	0.037
8)	R. Cumbria	Carlisle	756	1
11)	Essex	Chelmsford	765	0.5
18)	R. Kent	Littlebourne	774	0.7
20)	R. Leeds	Farnley	774	0.5
10)	R. Devon	Barnstaple	801	2
8)	R. Cumbria	Barrow	837	1
19)	R. Lancashire	Preston	855	1
26)	R. Norfolk	Postwick	855	1.5
26)	R. Norfolk	West Lynn	873	0.3
10)	R. Devon	Exeter	990	1
33)	R. Solent	Fareham	999	1
4)	R. Cambridgeshire	Chesterton Fen	1026	0.5
17)	Jersey	Trinity	1026	1
31)	R. Sheffield	Sheffield	1035	1
9)	R. Derby	Burnaston Lane	1116	1
14)	Guernsey	Rohais	1116	0.5
30)	Sussex	Bexhill	1161	1
1)	Three Counties R.	Bedford	1161	0.1
37)	R. York	Scarborough	1260	0.5
36)	Wiltshire	Lacock	1332	0.4
33)	R. Solent for Dorset	Bournemouth	1359	0.85
30a)	Surrey	Duxhurst	1368	0.5
36)	Wiltshire	Swindon	1368	0.1
22)	R. Lincolnshire	Lincoln	1368	2
12)	R. Gloucestershire	Berkeley Heath	1413	0.5
12)	R. Gloucestershire	Bourton-on-the-Water	1413	0.5
8)	R. Cumbria	Whitehaven	1458	0.5
10)	R. Devon	Torquay	1458	2
25)	Newcastle	Wrekenton	1458	2
16)	R. Humberside	Hull	1485	2
30)	Sussex	Brighton	1485	1
23)	R. Merseyside	Wallasey	1485	2
34)	R. Stoke	Sideway	1503	1
11)	Essex	Southend-on-Sea	1530	0.15
3)	R. Bristol	Mangotsfield	1548	5
19)	R. Lancashire	Oxcliffe	1557	0.25
3)	Somerset & R. Bristol	Taunton	1566	1
28)	R. Nottingham	Clipstone	‡1584	1
15)	Hereford & Worcester	Woofferton	1584	0.3
18)	R. Kent	Rusthall	‡1602	0.25

NB: Some BBC local radio MW trs may close in 2013, ‡=inactive

FM	Station	Location	MHz	kW
31)	R. Sheffield	Sheffield	88.6	0.3
17)	Jersey	Les Platons	88.8	3.8
1)	Three Counties R.	Epping Green	90.4	0.1
20)	R. Leeds	Holme Moss	92.4	5.6

FM	Station	Location	MHz	kW
14)	Guernsey	Les Touillets	93.2	1
34)	R. Stoke	Alsagers Bank	94.6	6.1
2)	R. Berkshire	Henley	94.6	0.25
15)	Hereford & Worcester	Ridge Hill	94.7	2
1)	Three Counties R.	Aylesbury	94.7	0.2
31)	R. Sheffield	Chesterfield	94.7	0.4
7)	Coventry & Warwickshire	Meriden	94.8	2.2
10)	R. Devon	Huntshaw Cross	94.8	0.675
24)	London	Crystal Palace	94.9	4
3)	R. Bristol	Dundry Lane	94.9	0.5
22)	R. Lincolnshire	Belmont	94.9	6
30)	Sussex	Newhaven	95.0	0.1
5)	Tees	Bilsdale	95.0	10
12)	R. Gloucestershire	Stroud	95.0	0.1
13)	R. Manchester	Holme Moss	95.1	5.6
28)	R. Nottingham	Newark	95.1	0.2
26)	R. Norfolk	Stoke Holy Cross	95.1	4
6)	R. Cornwall	Caradon Hill	95.2	4.3
8)	R. Cumbria	Kendal	95.2	0.1
29)	Oxford	Beckley	95.2	5.8
11)	Essex	South Benfleet	95.3	1.2
30)	Sussex	Brighton	95.3	1.2
9)	R. Derby	Stanton Moor	95.3	1.2
20)	R. Leeds	Luddenden	95.3	0.083
2)	R. Berkshire	Windsor	95.4	0.5
25)	Newcastle	Pontop Pike	95.4	10
1)	Three Counties R.	Sandy Heath	95.5	1
2)	Somerset & R. Bristol	Mendip	95.5	9
19)	R. Lancashire	Hameldon Hill	95.5	1.6
28)	R. Nottingham	Mansfield	95.5	2
35)	R. Suffolk	Lowestoft	95.5	2
37)	R. York	Olivers Mount	95.5	0.25
26)	R. Norfolk	West Runton	95.6	2
8)	R. Cumbria	Sandale	95.6	15
38)	WM (West Midlands)	Sutton Coldfield	95.6	11
4)	R. Cambridgeshire	Peterborough	95.7	5.1
10)	R. Devon	Plymouth	95.7	1
23)	R. Merseyside	Allerton Park	95.8	8
5)	Tees	Whitby	95.8	0.1
10)	R. Devon	Exeter	95.8	0.4
35)	R. Suffolk	Aldeburgh	95.9	2
16)	R. Humberside	High Hunsley	95.9	9.6
4)	R. Cambridgeshire	Cambridge	96.0	1
9)	R. Derby	Buxton	96.0	1.5
32)	R. Shropshire	The Wrekin	96.0	4.8
25)	Newcastle	Chatton	96.0	5.6
8)	R. Cumbria	Morecambe Bay	96.1	3.2
33)	R. Solent	Rowridge	96.1	10
18)	R. Kent	Wrotham	96.4	8.7
18)	R. Kent	Folkestone	97.6	0.1
1)	Three Counties R.	High Wycombe	98.0	0.2
20)	R. Leeds	Keighley	102.7	0.5
10)	R. Devon	North Hessary Tor	103.4	15
11)	Essex	Great Braxted	103.5	12
36)	Wiltshire	Salisbury	103.5	1
3)	R. Bristol	Weston-S-Mare	103.6	0.1
36)	Wiltshire	Swindon	103.6	0.5
27)	R. Northampton	Geddington	103.6	0.8
7)	Coventry & Warwickshire	Lark Stoke	103.7	1.4
37)	R. York	Acklam Wold	103.7	2
25)	Newcastle	Hexham	103.7	0.1
1)	Three Counties R.	Zouches Farm	103.8	0.5
28)	R. Nottingham	Mapperley Ridge	103.8	1
33)	R. Solent for Dorset	Bincombe Hill	103.8	0.5
6)	R. Cornwall	Redruth	103.9	18
19)	R. Lancashire	Winter Hill	103.9	1
20)	R. Leeds	Beecroft Hill	103.9	0.1
35)	R. Suffolk	Manningtree	103.9	2
15)	Hereford & Worcester	Great Malvern	104.0	2
30a)	Surrey	Reigate	104.0	3.8
8)	R. Cumbria	Whitehaven	104.1	1
31)	R. Sheffield	Holme Moss	104.1	4.4
34)	R. Stoke	Stafford	104.1	0.075
2)	R. Berkshire	Hannington	104.1	3
18)	R. Kent	Swingate	104.2	10
27)	R. Northampton	Northampton	104.2	4
36)	Wiltshire	Naish Hill	104.3	0.6
10)	R. Devon	Beacon Hill	104.3	1
37)	R. York	Woolmoor	104.3	0.5
2)	R. Berkshire	Reading	104.4	1
26)	R. Norfolk	Great Massingham	104.4	4.2
15)	Hereford & Worcester	Redditch	104.4	0.1
30)	Sussex	Heathfield	104.5	10
1)	Three Counties R.	Bow Brickhill	104.5	2.2
9)	R. Derby	Drum Hill	104.5	5.4

FM	Station	Location	MHz	kW
19)	R. Lancashire	Lancaster	104.5	2
13)	R. Manchester	Saddleworth	104.6	0.1
15)	Hereford & Worcester	Kidderminster	104.6	0.5
30a)	Surrey	Guildford	104.6	3
3)	R. Bristol	Bath	104.6	0.082
35)	R. Suffolk	Great Barton	104.6	2
12)	R. Gloucestershire	Churchdown Hill	104.7	2
30)	Sussex	Burton Down	104.8	2
21)	R. Leicester	Copt Oak	104.9	8
36)	Wiltshire	Marlborough	104.9	0.1

+ 15 low power txs less than 0.1kW

Addresses

1) 1 Hastings St, Luton LU1 5XL ☎1582 637400 **E:** threecounties@ bbc.co.uk – **2)** Caversham Park, Peppard Rd, Reading RG4 8TZ ☎118 9464200 **E:** radioberkshirenews@bbc.co.uk – **3)** Whiteladies Rd, Bristol BS8 2LR ☎117 9741111 **E:** radio.bristol@bbc.co.uk; BBC Somerset, Broadcasting House, Park Street, Taunton TA1 4DA ☎1823 323956 **E:** somerset@bbc.co.uk – **4)** Cambridge Business Park, Cowley Rd, Cambridge CB4 0WZ ☎1223 259696 **E:** cambridgeshire@bbc.co.uk– **5)** Broadcasting House, Newport Rd, Middlesbrough TS1 5DG ☎1642 225211 **E:** tees@bbc.co.uk – **6)** Phoenix Wharf, Truro TR1 1UA ☎1872 275421 **E:** radio.cornwall@bbc.co.uk – **7)** Priory Place, Coventry CV1 5SQ ☎24 76551000 **E:** coventry.warwickshire@bbc.co.uk – **8)** Annetwell Street, Carlisle CA3 0DD ☎1228 592444 **E:** radio.cumbria@ bbc.co.uk – **9)** 56 St Helen's Str, Derby DE1 3HY ☎1332 361111 **E:** radio.derby@bbc.co.uk – **10)** PO Box 1034, Plymouth PL3 5YQ ☎1752 260323 **E:** radio.devon@bbc.co.uk – **11)** PO Box 765, Chelmsford CM2 9XB ☎1245 616000 **E:** essex@bbc.co.uk– **12)** London Rd, Gloucester GL1 1SW ☎1452 308585 **E:** radio.gloucestershire@bbc.co.uk – **13)** Quay House, BBC Media City UK, Salford M50 2QH ☎161 335 6000 **E:** radio.manchester@bbc.co.uk – **14)** Bulwer Ave, St Sampson, Guernsey GY2 4LA ☎ 1481 200600 **E:** bbcguernsey@bbc.co.uk – **15)** Hylton Rd, Worcester WR2 5WW ☎1905 748485 **E:** bbchw@bbc.co.uk and 43 Broad Street, Hereford HR4 9HH ☎1432 355255 – **16)** Queens Court, Queens Gardens, Hull HU1 3RH ☎1482 323232 **E:** radio.humberside@ bbc.co.uk – **17)** 18 Parade Rd, St. Helier, Jersey JE2 3PL ☎1534 870000 **E:** radiojersey@bbc.co.uk – **18)** The Great Hall, Mount Pleasant Rd, Tunbridge Wells TN1 1QQ ☎1892 670000 **E:** radio.kent@bbc. co.uk – **19)** 20-26 Darwen Street, Blackburn BB2 2EA ☎1254 262411 **E:** radio.lancashire@bbc.co.uk – **20)** 2 St Peters Square, Leeds LS9 8AH ☎113 244 2131 **E:** radioleeds@bbc.co.uk – **21)** 9 St Nicholas Place, Leicester LE1 5LB ☎116 251 6688 **E:** radioleicester@bbc.co.uk – **22)** Radion Buildings, Newport, Lincoln LN1 3XY ☎1522 511411 **E:** radio.lincolnshire@bbc.co.uk – **23)** 31 College Lane, Liverpool L1 3DS ☎151 708 6161 **E:** radio.merseyside@bbc.co.uk – **24)** Egton Wing, Broadcasting House, Portland Place, London W1A 1AA ☎20 8743 8000 **E:** yourlondon@bbc.co.uk – **25)** Broadcasting Centre, Barrack Rd, Newcastle-Upon-Tyne NE99 1RN ☎191 222 4141 **E:** bbcnewcastle@ bbc.co.uk – **26)** The Forum, Millennium Plain, Norwich NR2 1BH ☎1603 619331 **E:** norfolk@bbc.co.uk – **27)** Broadcasting House, Abington Street, Northampton NN1 2BH ☎1604 239100 **E:** northamptonshire@bbc.co.uk – **28)** London Rd, Nottingham NG2 4UU ☎115 955 0500 **E:** radio.nottingham@bbc.co.uk – **29)** 269 Banbury Rd, Oxford OX2 7DW ☎8459 311444 **E:** oxford@bbc.co.uk – **30)** Broadcasting House, 40-42 Queen's Rd, Brighton BN1 3XB ☎ sussex@bbc.co.uk – **30a)** Broadcasting Centre, Guildford GU2 7AP ☎1483 306306 **E:** surrey@ bbc.co.uk – **31)** 54 Shoreham Street, Sheffield S1 4RS ☎114 2731177 **E:** radio.sheffield@bbc.co.uk – **32)** 2-4 Boscobel Drive, Shrewsbury SY1 3TT ☎1743 248484 **E:** shropshire@bbc.co.uk – **33)** Broadcasting House, 10 Havelock Rd, Southampton SO14 7PW ☎23 8063 1311 **E:** radio.solent@bbc.co.uk – **34)** Cheapside, Hanley, Stoke-on-Trent ST1 1JJ ☎01782 08080 **E:** radio.stoke@bbc.co.uk – **35)** Broadcasting House, St. Matthew's Street, Ipswich IP1 3EP ☎1473 250000 **E:** suffolk@bbc.co.uk – **36)** 56-58 Prospect Place, Swindon SN1 3RW ☎ 1793 513626 **E:** wiltshire@bbc.co.uk – **37)** 20 Bootham Row, York YO30 7BR ☎1904 641 351 **E:** northyorkshire@bbc.co.uk – **38)** The Mailbox, Birmingham B1 1AY ☎121 567 6767 **E:** radio.wm@bbc.co.uk

D.Prgr: Stns generally carry local or regional prgrs from 0600-0100, then BBC Radio 5 Live overnight.

BBC SCOTLAND

⌂40 Pacific Quay, Glasgow G51 1DA ☎ 141 422 6000
W: www.bbc.co.uk/radioscotland
MW: R. Scotland: Burghead 810kHz 100kW, Westerglen 810kHz 100kW, Redmoss 810kHz 5kW, Dumfries 585kHz 2kW

FM stereo	R1	R2	R3	R4	RS/L	kW
Ashkirk	98.7	89.1	91.3	103.9	93.5f	50
Ben Gullipen	98.3	88.7	90.9	104.9	93.1	1
Black Hill	99.5	89.9	92.1	*95.8	94.3	250/200*
Bressay	97.9	88.3	90.5	94.9	92.7ac	43
Clettraval	97.7	88.1	90.3	95.1	92.5d	7

FM stereo	R1	R2	R3	R4	RS/L	kW
Daliburgh	98.9	89.3	91.5	95.9	93.7d	1
Darvel	99.1	89.5	91.7	104.3	93.9	10
Durris	99.0	89.4	91.6	95.9	93.8a	2.1
Eitshal	99.4	88.3	92.0	95.1	94.2d	2
Forfar	97.9	88.3	90.5	94.9	92.7	17
Fort William	98.9	89.3	91.5	95.9	93.7d	3
Glengorm	99.1	89.5	91.7	96.1	93.9d	5
Keelylang Hill	98.9	89.3	91.5	96.0	93.7ab	41
Kirkton Mailer	98.6	89.0	91.2	94.6	93.4	1
Meldrum	98.3	88.7	90.9	95.3	93.1a	150
Melvaig	98.7	89.1	91.3	95.7	93.5d	50
Oban	98.5	88.9	91.1	95.3	93.3d	3.6
Rosemarkie	99.2	89.6	91.8	103.6	94.0d	20
Rumster Forest	99.7	90.1	92.3	95.6	94.5d	10
Sandale	97.7	88.1	90.3	92.5	94.7e	250
Skriaig	98.1	88.5	90.7	94.8	92.9d	30
So. Knapdale	98.9	89.3	91.5	95.6	93.7	2.2

+ 32 low power txs less than 1kW
RS/L=R. Scotland + local news – a) RS: Aberdeen – b) RS: Orkney – c) RS: Shetland – d) RS: Inverness – e) RS: Dumfries – f) RS: Selkirk.

D.Prgr: 24h
Local Services (FM only). Freqs as above.
a) Beechgrove Terrace, Aberdeen AB15 5ZT. M-F: 0654, 0750, 0958, 1158, 1254, 1558, 1654, 1758. **W:** www.bbc.co.uk/northeastscotland – b) Castle Str, Kirkwall, Orkney KW15 1DF: M-F 0730-0800, Fri 1810-1900 – c) Pitt Lane, Lerwick, Shetland ZE1 0DW: M-F 1730-1800, Fri 1810-1900 – d) 7 Culduthel Rd, Inverness IV2 4AD M-F: 0654, 0750, 0958, 1158, 1254, 1558, 1654, 1758 – e) Elmbank, Lovers Walk, Dumfries DG1 1NZ: M-F: 0654, 0750, 0958, 1158, 1254, 1558, 1654. **W:** www.bbc.co.uk/southscotland – f) Ettrick Riverside, Dunsdale Rd, Selkirk TD7 5EB M-F: 0654, 0750, 0958, 1158, 1254, 1558, 1654

RADIO NAN GAIDHEAL

✉ 52 Church Street, Stornoway HS1 2LS ☎ 1851 705000 🖷 1851 704633 **W:** www.bbc.co.uk/radionangaidheal
MW: Redmoss 990kHz 1kW(a)

FM	MHz	kW	FM	MHz	kW
Glengorm	103.5	5	Meldrum	104.2	150
Clettraval	103.7	2	Eitshal	104.3	2
So. Knapdale	103.7	2.2	Kirkton Mailer	104.5	1
Forfar	103.7	17	Rumster Forest	104.5	10
Melvaig	103.9	50	Oban	104.6	3.6
Craigkelly	104.1	5	Black Hill	104.7	10
Daliburgh	104.2	1	Skriaig	104.7	30
Fort William	104.2	3	Rosemarkie	104.9	20

+ 16 low power txs less than 1kW
D.Prgr: Own prgrs in Gaelic and relays of BBC R. Scotland. (a) rel local news for Aberdeen in English M-F: 0958,1254, 1758.

BBC WALES

✉ Broadcasting House, Llantrisant Rd, Llandaff, Cardiff CF5 2YQ ☎ 29 2032 2000 🖷 29 2055 5960
E: radiowales@bbc.co.uk **W:** www.bbc.co.uk/wales

FM stereo	R1	R2	R3	R4	kW
Blaenplwyf	98.3	88.7	90.9	104.0	250
Carmel	98.0	88.4	90.6	92.8	2.5
Haverfordwest	98.9	89.3	91.5	104.9	20
Kilvey Hill	99.1	89.5	91.7	94.6	1
Llanddona	99.4	89.8	92.0	103.6	21
Llandrindod Wells	98.7	89.1	91.3	103.8	2.8
Llangollen	98.5	88.9	91.1	93.3	15.6
Wenvoe	99.5	89.9	92.1	94.3	250

FM stereo	R. Wales	R.Cymru	kW
Blaenplwyf	95.3	93.1	250/120
Carmel	95.1	104.6	3/3.2
Haverfordwest	95.9	93.7	20
Kilvey Hill	93.9	104.2	1
Llanddona	94.8	94.2	21/10
Llandrindod Wells		93.5	2.8
Llangollen		104.3	15.6
Wenvoe	103.9		40
Wenvoe		96.8	250

+ 42 low power txs less than 1kW
MW R. Wales: Forden 882kHz 1kW, Llandrindod Wells 1125kHz 1kW, Penmon 882kHz 10kW, Tywyn 882kHz 5kW, Washford 882kHz 100kW, Wrexham 657kHz 2kW.
D.Prgr: R Wales: 0530(SaSu0500)-0100. Rel. BBC WS overnight.
R Cymru: 0530(SaSu0500)-0100. Relays BBC Radio 5 overnight.

BBC NORTHERN IRELAND

✉ Broadcasting House, 25-27 Ormeau Avenue, Belfast BT2 8HQ ☎ 28 9033 8000 🖷 28 9032 6453 **W:** www.bbc.co.uk/northernireland

MW: Enniskillen 873kHz 1kW, Lisnagarvey 1341kHz 100kW

FM stereo	R1	R2	R3	R4	R.Ulster	kW
Brougher Mountain	99.0	89.4	91.6	95.6	93.8	9.8
Camlough	98.3	88.7	90.9	104.6	93.1	4
Divis	99.7	90.1	92.3	96.0	94.5	250/125
Limavady	99.2	89.6	91.8	94.0	95.4	3.4
Londonderry	98.3	88.7	90.9	94.9	93.1h	31/10

+ 5 low power txs of less than 1kW – h) **R. Foyle** (see below).
R. Ulster: Enniskillen 873kHz 1kW, Lisnagarvey 1341kHz 100kW.
D.Prgr: MF 0630-0000. Other times rel. BBC R5.

BBC RADIO FOYLE

✉ 8 Northland Rd, Londonderry BT48 7GD ☎ 28 7137 8600
E: radio.foyle@bbc.co.uk
MW: Londonderry 792kHz 1kW **FM:** 93.1MHz 31kW
D.Prgr: 24h.Own prgs. and relay BBC R. Ulster. Local N. M-F hourly 0700-1700

BBC ASIAN NETWORK

✉ The Mailbox, Birmingham B1 1AY ☎ 121 567 6767 **E:** asiannetworknews@bbc.co.uk **W:** www.bbc.co.uk/asiannetwork

MW	kHz	kW	MW	kHz	kW
Sedgley	828	0.2	Gunthorpe	1449	0.15
Freemen's Common	837	0.5	Langley Mill	1458	5

D.Prgr: 0600-2400, mainly in English. 2100-2400 in Bengali, Gujarati, Hindi, Urdu or Pubjabi. Relays BBC Radio 5 Live overnight.

BBC Asian Network relays

MW	kHz	kW	MW	kHz	kW
R. Leeds	774a	0.7	R. Derby	1116c	1
R. Sheffield	1035b	1			

Key: a) Mon-Fri 1900-0100, b) Mon-Fri 1600-0100, c) Mon-Fri 1900-0100, SS 1800-0030. Local Asian programming is also carried on many BBC local radio stns at various times.

ARQIVA

✉ Crawley Court, Winchester SO21 2QA ☎1962 823434
W: www.arqiva.com Operates most BBC domestic and many commercial radio tx sites. Formerly National Grid Wireless.

EXTERNAL SERVICE: BBC World Service

See International Broadcasting section.

OFFICE OF COMMUNICATIONS (Ofcom) (Regulatory Authority)

✉ Riverside House, 2A Southwark Bridge Rd, London SE1 9HA ☎20 7981 3040 🖷20 7981 3333 **W:** www.ofcom.org.uk **L.P:** CEO: Ed Richards. Ch Operating Officer: Jill Ainscough

RADIO CENTRE

✉ 6th Floor, 55 New Oxford Str., London W1A 1BS ☎20 7010 0600 🖷20 7306 7801 **W:** www.radiocentre.org - Radio Centre represents commercial radio to Government, Ofcom, Copyright Societies and other organizations concerned with radio.

DIGITAL RADIO (DAB): DAB trs are on Band 3. **BBC Digital Radio:** BBC Radios 1, 1Xtra, 2, 3, 4, 4 Extra, 5 Live, 5 Live Sports Extra, 6 Music, BBC Asian Network, BBC World Service and regional srvcs in Scotland, Wales and N.Ireland are in a single frequency network on 225.648MHz. **Digital One:** ✉ UK House, 4th Floor, 2-5 Gt Titchfield Str, London W1D 1NN **W:** www.ukdigitalradio.com Progr includes: Absolute, Absolute 80s, Absolute 90s, BFBS, Classic FM, Jazz FM, talkSPORT, Planet Rock, Premier Christian Radio, Smooth, Smooth 70s, UCB UK. **All prgrs** are in a single frequency network for England on 222.064MHz, block 11D, and for Scotland on 223.936MHz. **Local multiplexes: Arqiva:** Ayr. **Bauer,** Central Lancashire, Humberside, Leeds, Liverpool, South Yorkshire, Teesside, Tyne & Wear. **CE Digital,** Greater London, Birmingham, Manchester. **Digital Radio Group,** Greater London. **MXR,** North-East England, North-West England, South Wales/Severn Estuary, West Midlands, Yorkshire. **MuxCo** Chester & Wrexham*, Derbyshire*, Gloucestershire*, Lincolnshire*, Hereford & Worcester*, Mid & W Wales*, N Wales*, Northamptonshire*, Surrey, & N Sussex*, Somerset*, N Yorkshire*, Oxford* (*planned). **Now Digital,** Bournemouth, Bristol & Bath, Cambridge, Cardiff & Newport, Coventry, Exeter & Torbay, Kent, Leicester, Norwich, Nottingham, Peterborough, Reading & Basingstoke, So. Hampshire, Southend & Chelmsford, Sussex Coast, Swindon & West Wiltshire, Wolverhampton/Shrewsbury & Telford. **Score Digital,** Dundee & Perth, Edinburgh, Glasgow, Inverness, Northern Ireland. **South West Digital Radio,** Plymouth & Cornwall. **Switchdigital,** Aberdeen, Central Scotland, Greater London. **UTV-Bauer** Bradford & Huddersfield, Stoke-on-Trent, Swansea. **3G:** Isle of Man.

NATIONAL COMMERCIAL STATIONS:

ABSOLUTE RADIO

1 Golden Square, London W1F 9DJ ☎ 20 7434 1215 🖷 20 7434 1197 **W:** www.absoluteradio.co.uk

MW	kHz	kW	MW	kHz	kW
Bournemouth	1197	0.3	Plymouth	1215	1
Brighton	1197	1	Redmoss	1215	2.3
Cambridge	1197	0.2	Redruth	1215	2
Torbay	1197	1	Washford	1215	100
Trowell	1197	1	Westerglen	1215	100
Wallasey	1197	0.4	Wrekenton	1215	2
Gloucester	1197	0.3	Kings Heath	1233	1
Hoo (Kent)	1197	2	Manningtree	1233	1
Oxford	1197	0.3	Reading	1233	0.2
Brookmans Park	1215	125	Sheffield	1233	0.3
Dartford Tunnel	1215	0.004	Swindon	1233	0.1
Droitwich	1215	105	Boston	1242	2
Fareham	1215	1	Dundee	1242	1
Hull	1215	0.3	Sideway	1242	1
Lisnagarvey	1215	16	Stockton	1242	1
Moorside Edge	1215	200	Guildford	1260	1
Norwich	1215	1	Lydd	1260	1

D.Prgr: 24h (rock & contemporary music). **N:** on the h
FM: London 105.8MHz 4kW

CLASSIC FM

30 Leicester Square, London WC2H 7LA ☎ 20 7343 9000 **W:** www.classicfm.com

FM	MHz	kW	FM	MHz	kW
Cumbria	99.9	250	Blaen Plwyf	101.1	10
No.Hessary Tor	100.0	160	Holme Moss	101.1	250
Angus	100.1	10.3	Darvel	101.3	8
Sutton Coldfield	100.1	250	Oxford	101.3	46
Bath	100.2	0.2	Swansea	101.3	1
Douglas I.O.M.	100.2	1	Bristol	101.4	0.2
Bradford	100.3	0.5	Inverness	101.4	11
Pontop Pike	100.3	130	Tacolneston	101.5	250
Rowridge	100.3	250	Redruth	101.5	10
Milton Keynes	100.4	10	Gt. Ormes Head	101.6	2.5
Ridge Hill	100.4	5	Bilsdale	101.6	2
Belmont	100.5	6.2	Leeds	101.6	0.5
Londonderry	100.5	31	Black Hill	101.7	250
Meldrum	100.5	150	Sheffield	101.7	0.5
Presely	100.5	7.13	Wenvoe	101.7	250
Crystal Palace	100.6	2	Dover	101.8	5.2
Arton	100.7	18.75	Morecambe Bay	101.8	6.4
Swindon	100.8	0.72	Reading	101.8	0.5
Selkirk	100.9	10	Brighton	101.9	0.4
Wrotham	100.9	250	Divis	101.9	250
Fenham	101.0	0.05	Peterborough	101.9	35

D.Prgr: 24h **N:** on the h

GOLD

30 Leicester Square, London WC2H 7LA ☎ 20 7766 6000 🖷 20 7766 6100 **W:** www.mygoldmusic.co.uk

	MW	kHz	kW	Location		MW	kHz	kW	Location
40)	603	0.4	Littlebourne	104)	1251	0.76	Bury St.Eds.
76)	774	0.14	Gloucester	86)	1260	1.6	Bristol
72)	792	0.28	Bedford	100)	1260	0.64	Wrexham
43)	828	0.27	Bournemouth	42)	1305	0.2	Newport
72)	828	0.2	Luton	41)	1323	0.5	Brighton
87)	936	0.18	Naish Hill	88)	1332	0.6	Peterborough
41)	945	0.7	Bexhill	42)	1359	0.2	Cardiff
69)	945	0.4	Derby	92)	1359	0.28	Chelmsford
69)	999	0.25	Nottingham	89)	1431	0.14	Reading
104)	1152	0.83	Norwich	92)	1431	0.35	S'thend-on-Sea
82)	1152	0.32	Plymouth	45)	1458	5	Manchester
87)	1161	0.16	Swindon	89)	1485	1	Newbury
104)	1170	0.28	Ipswich	33)	1548	97.5	London
43)	1170	0.12	Portsmouth	72)	1557	0.76	Northampton
40)	1242	0.32	Maidstone	43)	1557	0.5	Southampton

D.Prgr: 24h (Numbers refer to local studio address - see list below)

HEART

30 Leicester Square, London WC2H 7LA ☎ 20 7766 6000 **W:** www.heart.co.uk

	FM	kHz	kW	Location		FM	kHz	kW	Location
40)	95.9	0.27	Thanet	100)	96.3	1.25	Llandudno
40)	96.1	0.2	Ashford	82)	96.4	1.6	Torbay
92)	96.1	0.5	Colchester	104)	96.4	2	Bury St.Eds
82)	96.2	2.5	N Devon	72)	96.6	4	Northampton
86)	96.3	2	Bristol	16)	96.6	0.5	Watford
92)	96.3	1	Southend	43)	96.7	0.5	Winchester

	FM	kHz	kW	Location		FM	kHz	kW	Location
72)	96.9	0.9	Bedford	41)	102.4	8.2	Eastbourne
41)	96.9	0.1	Newhaven	76)	102.4	2	Gloucester
40)	97.0	0.5	Dover	104)	102.4	3.3	Norwich
82)	97.0	1	Exeter	92)	102.6	2	Chelmsford
82)	97.0	2	Plymouth	89)	102.6	9	Oxford
89)	97.0	1	Reading	86)	102.6	4	Mendip
86)	97.1	0.2	W.Somerset	41)	102.7	3.6	Reigate
104)	97.1	3.4	Ipswich	88)	102.7	4	Peterborough
100)	97.1	1	Wirral	40)	102.8	1	Dunkirk
87)	97.2	0.7	Swindon	89)	102.9	3.4	Hannington
97.3	0.1		Ilfracombe	100)	103.0	5	Caernarfon
89)	97.4	0.3	Banbury	82)	103.0	1	Cambridge
43)	97.5	0.85	Portsmouth	82)	103.0	1	Stockland Hl
72)	97.6	1	Luton	76)	103.0	0.1	Stroud
82)	100.5	0.3	Totnes	86)	103.0	0.1	Weston-S-Mare
47)	100.7	11	Birmingham	40)	103.1	4	Maidstone
82)	100.8	0.1	Dartmouth	72)	103.3	2	Milton Keynes
82)	101.2	1.15	Salcombe	100)	103.4	1.4	Wrexham
92)	101.7	0.1	Harlow	89)	103.4	0.1	Henley-on-Th
82)	101.9	0.5	Ivybridge	41)	103.5	1	Brighton
41)	102.0	0.2	Hastings	85)	105.1	2.5	E.Cornwall
87)	102.2	0.5	W Wiltshire	85)	107.0	11	W.Cornwall
43)	102.3	2	Bournemouth	33)	106.2	4	London

D.Prgr: 24h **N:** on the h (No. refer to local studio address - see list)

SMOOTH RADIO

Laser House, Waterfront Quay, Salford M50 3XW ☎ 161 886 8800 **W:** www.smoothradio.co.uk

FM	MHz	kW	FM	MHz	kW
Newton	96.4	0.2	Glasgow	105.2	30
Burnhope	97.5	9	Sutton Coldfield	105.7	11
Winter Hill	100.4	5	Waltham	106.6	10.8
Derby	101.4	0.2	Eston Nab	107.7	5
Croydon	102.2	4			

D.Prgr: 24h **N:** on the h

TALKSPORT

18 Hatfields, London SE1 8DJ ☎ 20 7959 7800 🖷 20 7959 7808 **W:** www.talksport.net

MW	kHz	kW	MW	kHz	kW
Bournemouth	1053	1	Brookmans Park	1089	400
Brighton	1053	2	Dartford Tunnel	1089	0
Droitwich	1053	500	Lisnagarvey	1089	13
Dumfries	1053	10	Moorside Edge	1089	400
Londonderry	1053	1	Redmoss	1089	2
Plymouth	1053	1	Redruth	1089	2
Postwick	1053	18	Washford	1089	80
Stockton	1053	1	Westerglen	1089	125
Tonbridge	1053	4	Boston	1107	1
Dundee	1053	1	Fareham	1107	1
Exeter	1053	1	Lydd	1107	2
Hull	1053	1	Reigate/Crawley	1107	1
Inverness	1053	1	Torbay	1107	1
Clipstone	1071	1	Wallasey	1107	1
Newcastle	1071	1			

D.Prgr: 24h

COMMERCIAL RADIO STATIONS

	MW	kHz	kW	Station or Slogan	Location
-)	531	0.001	occasional RSLs	
175)	558	1	Spectrum R.	London
129)	756	0.63	R. Hafren	Newtown
56)	828	0.12	Magic 828	Leeds
128)	855	0.15	Sunshine R.	Ludlow
1)	963	0.95	Buzz Asia	E. London
93)	963	0.2	Asian Sound R.	Haslingden
1)	972	1	Buzz Asia	W. London
34)	990	0.09	Free R. 80s	Wolverhampton
53)	990	0.25	Magic AM	Doncaster
60)	999	0.8	Magic 999	Preston
34)	1017	0.63	Free R. 80s	Shrewsbury
153)	1026	1.7	Downtown R.	Belfast
155)	1035	0.78	Northsound Two	Aberdeen
160)	1035	0.32	West Sound AM	Ayr
18)	1035	2.5	Kismat R.	London
161)	1107	1.5	Moray Firth R.	Inverness
-)	1134	0.001	LPAMs	
33)	1152	23.5	LBC	London
158)	1152	3.6	Clyde 2	Glasgow
34)	1152	3	Free R. 80s	Birmingham
45)	1152	1.5	Magic 1152	Manchester
61)	1152	1.8	Magic 1152	Newcastle
54)	1161	0.35	Magic 1161	Hull
156)	1161	1.4	Tay AM	Dundee

MW	kHz	kW	Station or Slogan	Location
127)	1170	0.58	Swansea Sound	Swansea
59)	1170	0.32	Magic 1170	Stockton
35)	1170	0.2	Signal Two	Stoke-on-Trent
-)	1251	0.001	LPAMs	
151)	1260	0.29	Sabras R.	Leicester
106)	1278	0.43	Pulse 2	Bradford
-)	1278	0.001	LPAMs/RSLs	
-)	1287	0.001	LPAMs	
148)	1296	10	R. XL	Birmingham
53)	1305	0.15	Magic AM	Barnsley
98)	1305	0.5	Premier Christian R.	Epsom
98)	1305	0.5	Premier Christian R.	Chingford
98)	1332	1	Premier Christian R.	London
-)	1350	0.001	LPAMs	
34)	1359	0.27	Free R. 80s	Coventry
93)	1377	0.08	Asian Sound R.	Ashton Moss
24)	1386	0.003	R. JCom	Leeds
-)	1386	0.001	LPAMs	
-)	1404	0.001	LPAMs	
98)	1413	0.5	Premier Christian R.	Heathrow
98)	1413	0.5	Premier Christian R.	Dartford Marshes
-)	1431	0.001	LPAMs	
-)	1449	0.001	LPAMs	
167)	1458	125	Sunrise R.	W.London
81)	1503	0.1	Betar Bangla	E.London
234)	1521	0.07	Flame CCR	Wirral
106)	1530	0.74	Pulse 2	Huddersfield
109)	1530	0.01	Celtic Music R.	Glasgow
53)	1548	0.74	Magic AM	Sheffield
52)	1548	1	Magic 1548	Liverpool
159)	1548	2.2	Forth 2	Edinburgh
154)	1566	0.8	Eagle Extra	Guildford
-)	1575	0.001	LPAMs/RSLs	
156)	1584	0.21	Tay AM	Perth
11)	1584	0.2	London Turkish R.	N.London
83)	1602	0.07	Desi R.	Southall
-)	1602	0.001	occasional RSLs	

FM	MHz	kW	Name or Slogan	Location
-)	87.7	-	RSLs/LPFMs	
-)	87.9	-	RSLs	
123)	88.0	1.4	Real R. - Wales	Wrexham
91)	95.2	0.2	Kingdom FM	Dunfermline
33)	95.8	4	Capital FM	London
91)	96.1	0.5	Kingdom FM	Glenrothes
108)	96.1	0,.2	Rother FM	Rotherham
124)	96.2	4	SIBC	Shetland
63)	96.2	0.2	KMFM	Tonbridge
99)	96.2	1	Mix 96	Aylesbury
77)	96.2	2.6	North Norfolk R.	Stody
138)	96.2	0.1	The Revolution	Oldham
145)	96.2	0.625	Yorkshire Coast R.	Scarborough
169)	96.2	0.1	Touch R.	Coventry
69)	96.2	1	Capital FM	Nottingham
56)	96.3	2.5	R. Aire	Leeds
176)	96.3	0.2	Real R. XS	Paisley
36)	96.4	0.2	Real R. - NE	Hexham
153)	96.4	2	Downtown R.	Limavady
34)	96.4	10	Free R,	Birmingham
127)	96.4	1.5	The Wave	Swansea
154)	96.4	3	The Eagle	Guildford
156)	96.4	0.8	Tay FM	Perth
35)	96.4	0.25	Signal 1	Congleton
163)	96.4	3	CFM	Carlisle
96)	96.4	0.1	KMFM	Folkestone
112)	96.4	0.1	Compass FM	Grimsby
179)	96.5	0.4	R. Wave	Blackpool
157)	96.5	0.12	West Sound	Stranraer
153)	96.6	8.2	Downtown R.	Brougher Mountain
84)	96.6	0.1	The Breeze	Blandford
26)	96.6	0.2	RNA FM	Arbroath
59)	96.6	10	TFM R.	Bilsdale
31)	96.6	0.4	R. Ceredigion	Lampeter
142)	96.6	0.35	Nevis R.	Fort William
161)	96.6	0.45	Moray Firth R	Cairngorm
25)	96.6	0.4	Spirit FM	Chichester
160)	96.7	2.2	West FM	Ayr
52)	96.7	8	R. City	Liverpool
144)	96.7	0.55	City Beat	Belfast
115)	96.7	3	KL.FM	King's Lynn
171)	96.7	0.2	Ashbourne R.	Ashbourne
70)	96.7	0.1	Free R.	Kidderminster
161c)	96.7	0.1	Moray Firth R./Kinnaird	Fraserburgh
162)	96.8	5	R. Borders	Selkirk
125)	96.8	0.5	Lochbroom FM	Polbain

FM	MHz	kW	Name or Slogan	Location
54)	96.9	9.4	Viking FM	Hull
155)	96.9	11	Northsound One	Aberdeen
35)	96.9	0.2	Signal 1	Stafford
170)	96.9	3.2	The Bay	Morecambe Bay
142)	97.0	0.25	Nevis R.	Glencoe
157)	97.0	1	West Sound	Dumfries
34)	97.0	1.8	Free R.	Coventry
61)	97.1	10	Metro R.	Newcastle
121)	97.1	0.3	NECR	Braemar
121)	97.1	0.1	NECR	Turriff
133)	97.1	0.275	Kestrel FM	Haslemere
153)	97.1	0.08	Downtown R.	Larne
102)	97.1	3	R. Carmarthenshire	Carmel
64)	97.2	2	Free R.	Wolverhampton
58)	97.2	0.2	Kiss	Bristol
19)	97.2	0.31	Q Radio	Coleraine
118)	97.2	0.5	Wessex FM	Dorchester/Weymouth
147)	97.2	1	Stray FM	Harrogate
33)	97.3	4	LBC	London
159)	97.3	9.8	Forth 1	Edinburgh
161)	97.4	6.25	Moray Firth R.	Inverness
60)	97.4	2	Rock FM	Preston/Blackpool
153)	97.4	3.2	Cool FM	Belfast
42)	97.4	0.5	Capital FM	Newport
53)	97.4	0.4	Hallam FM	Sheffield
31)	97.4	0.4	R. Ceredigion	Penwaun
84)	97.4	0.125	The Breeze	Shaftesbury
134)	97.4	0.24	The Beach	Southwold
106)	97.5	0.5	The Pulse	Bradford
28)	97.5	0.4	Heartland FM	Pitlochry
160)	97.5	0.15	West FM	Girvan
66)	97.5	0.2	Scarlet FM	Llanelli
70)	97.6	0.8	Free R.	Hereford
159)	97.6	0.1	Forth 1	Edinburgh
45)	97.7	1	XFM	Manchester
15)	99.8	0.75	2BR	Burnley
68)	99.8	0.75	KCFM	Hull
50)	99.9	0.5	R. Norwich	Stoke Holy Cross
58)	100.0	4	Kiss	London
101)	100.1	0.2	Lakeland R.	Kendal
12)	100.2	2	Dream 100 FM	Clacton-on-Sea
122)	100.3	20	Real R - Scotland	Black Hill
135)	100.5	1	Q Radio	Newry
36)	100.7	10	Real R. - NE	Bilsdale
101)	100.8	0.12	Lakeland R.	Windermere
84)	100.8	0.13	The Breeze	Porlock
58)	101.0	40	Kiss	Mendip
122)	101.1	0.1	Real R – Scotland	Edinburgh
135)	101.1	0.4	Q Radio	Newry
178)	101.2	1.65	Waves R.	Peterhead
135)	101.2	6.26	Q Radio	Brougher Mountain
36)	101.2	0.2	Real R.-NE	Newton
133)	101.6	0.1	Kestrel FM	Alton
63)	101.6	0.4	KMFM	Wrotham
36)	101.8	8.5	Real R. - NE	Burnhope
133)	101.8	0.11	Kestrel FM	Petersfield
121)	101.9	0.22	NECR	Tullich
105)	102.0	1	Town FM	Ipswich
108)	102.0	0.45	Dearne FM	Barnsley
130)	102.0	0.1	Peak FM	Matlock
45)	102.0	0.5	Capital FM	Manchester
146)	102.0	1.25	Spire FM	Salisbury
133)	102.0	0.1	Kestrel FM	Alton
169)	102.0	2.6	Touch R.	Stratford upon Avon
177)	102.0	0.2	Wave 102	Dundee
121)	102.1	1.25	NECR	Inverurie
78)	102.1	1.2	Nation 80s	Swansea
159)	102.2	0.5	Forth 1	Penicuik
112)	102.2	6.4	Lincs FM	Belmont
165)	102.2	2.5	Pirate FM	Caradon Hill
47)	102.2	1	Capital FM	Birmingham
163)	102.2	0.815	CFM	Workington
125)	102.2	0.7	Lochbroom FM	Ullapool
158)	102.3	0.6	Clyde 1	Rothesay
25)	102.3	0.5	Spirit FM	Littlehampton
153)	102.3	0.5	Downtown R.	Ballymena
142)	102.3	0.8	Nevis R.	Fort William
123)	102.3	0.5	Real R. - Wales	Eglwysilan
20)	102.4	0.625	Touch R.	Tamworth
84)	102.4	2	The Breeze	Minehead
153)	102.4	10	Downtown R.	Londonderry
158)	102.4	0.6	Clyde 1	Rosneath
145)	102.4	0.5	Yorkshire Coast R.	Bridlington
22)	102.4	0.1	Wish FM	Wigan
142)	102.4	0.8	Nevis R.	Glenachulish

FM	MHz	kW	Name or Slogan	Location
158)	102.5	15	Clyde 1	Glasgow
106)	102.5	2	The Pulse	Halifax
161a)	102.5	1.2	Moray Firth R./Caithness	Thurso
102)	102.5	20	R. Pembrokeshire	Haverfordwest
163)	102.5	0.1	CFM	Penrith
35)	102.6	4	Signal 1	Stoke-on-Trent
61)	102.6	0.125	Metro R.	Alnwick
121)	102.6	0.3	NECR	Kildrummy
150)	102.6	0.1	Star R. NE	Richmond
62)	102.7	9	Cuillin FM	Isle of Skye
150)	102.8	0.5	Star R. NE	Burnhope
69)	102.8	0.9	Capital FM	Derby
70)	102.8	1	Free R.	Worcester
123)	102.8	0.2	Real R. - Wales	Long Mountain
156)	102.8	5	Tay FM	Dundee
165)	102.8	10	Pirate FM	Redruth
147)	102.8	1	Stray FM	Skipton
161d)	102.8	1	Moray Firth R./KCR	Keith
53)	102.9	0.45	Hallam FM	Barnsley
19)	102.9	3.14	Q102.9	Londonderry
51)	103.0	4	Key 103	Manchester
143)	103.0	4	Isles FM	Stornoway
155)	103.0	0.174	Northsound One.	Peterhead
174)	103.0	0.1	Your R.	Dumbarton
157)	103.0	0.7	West Sound	Kirkcudbright
64)	103.1	2.7	Free R.	Shrewsbury
14)	103.1	0.5	Central FM	Stirling
153)	103.1	1.8	Downtown R.	Newry
77)	103.2	0.25	North Norfolk R. (2 txs)	N. Norfolk
42)	103.2	2	Capital FM	Cardiff
43)	103.2	2	Capital FM	Southampton
32)	103.2	0.1	Mansfield 103.2	Mansfield
170)	103.2	0.1	The Bay	Kendal
168)	103.2	0.4	Sunrise FM	Bradford
150)	103.2	0.4	Star R - NE	Darlington
61)	103.2	0.12	Metro R.	Hexham
121)	103.2	0.3	NECR	Colpy
74)	103.3	0.17	High Peak R.	Buxworth
74)	103.3	0.1	High Peak R.	Hope Valley
114)	103.3	0.1	London Greek R.	London
31)	103.3	5.8	R. Ceredigion	Blaenplwyf
158)	103.3	0.1	Clyde 1	Rosneath
6)	103.3	0.4	Oban FM	Oban
122)	103.3	0.5	Real R.-Scotland	Penicuik
53)	103.4	1.6	Hallam FM	Doncaster
153)	103.4	0.2	Downtown R.	Newcastle
162)	103.4	0.5	R. Borders	Eyemouth
39)	103.4	0.16	Sun FM	Sunderland
163)	103.4	0.4	CFM	Whitehaven
134)	103.4	2	The Beach	Lowestoft
150)	103.5	0.2	Star R - NE	Northallerton
21)	103.7	4	Channel 103 FM	Jersey
141)	104.7	2.5	Minster FM	York
5)	104.7	1.25	Island FM	Guernsey
140)	104.9	0.64	Imagine FM	Stockport
33)	104.9	2.9	XFM	London
49)	105.1	3.1	Capital FM	Emley Moor
95)	105.1		Southend R.	Southend-on-Sea
73)	105.2	11	Kerrang!	Sutton Coldfield
164)	105.2	10	Wave 105	Solent
123)	105.2	3	Real R. - Wales	Carmel
48)	105.3	8.4	Capital FM	Burnhope
37)	105.4	5	Real R. - NE	Winter Hill
69)	105.4	5	Capital FM	Leicester
91)	105.4	0.1	Kingdom FM	Fife
58)	105.4	4	Magic 105.4	Croydon
123)	105.4	5	Real R. - Wales	Cardiff
111)	105.5	1.6	Palm FM	Torbay
58)	105.6	1	Kiss	Cambridge
49)	105.6	0.5	Capital FM	Bradford
49)	105.6	0.25	Capital FM	Sheffield
79)	105.6	0.25	The Breeze	Yeovil
63)	105.6	0.25	KMFM	Maidstone
29)	105.6	0.1	The Breeze	Newbury
44)	105.7	10	Capital FM	Edinburgh
123)	105.7	9.4	Real R. - Wales	Presely
123)	105.7	1.25	Real R. - Wales	Gt Ormes Head
10)	105.8	1.9	U105	Belfast
48)	105.8	0.2	Capital FM	Hexham
164)	105.8	0.625	Wave 105	Poole
49)	105.8	9.6	Capital FM	Hull
123)	105.9	1	Real R. - Wales	Newport
52)	105.9	7.5	City Talk	Liverpool
107)	106.0	4	Jack FM	Solent
38)	106.0	8	Gem 106	Copt Oak
135)	106.0	0.6	Q Radio	Cookstown
96)	106.0	0.1	KMFM	Canterbury
123)	106.0	1	Real R.- Wales	Swansea
75)	106.0	0.6	Two Lochs R.	Gairloch
58)	106.1	4	Kiss	Stoke Holy Cross
44)	106.1	20	Capital FM	Glasgow
37)	106.1	1	Real R. XS	Manchester
131)	106.2	3.12	Real R. Yorks	Emley Moor
123)	106.2	0.5	Real R.- Wales	Fishguard
103)	106.2	1.5	Sunshine R.	Hereford
91)	106.3	0.15	Kingdom FM	Fife
30)	106.3	0.9	Bridge FM	Bridgend
27)	106.3	0.2	Dee	Chester
58)	106.4	20	Kiss	Mendelsham
48)	106.4	10	Capital FM	Bilsdale
121)	106.4	0.3	NECR	Cock Bridge
94)	106.4	0.4	Bright FM	Haywards Heath
74)	106.4	0.25	High Peak R.(2 txs)	Buxton/Glossop
117)	106.4	0.1	The Breeze	Andover
13)	106.5	0.5	Argyll FM	Campbeltown
3)	106.5	0.5	Signal 107	Shrewsbury
84)	106.5	1	Jack FM	Bristol
15)	106.5	0.1	The Bee	Preston
107)	106.6	0.3	Jack FM	Poole
132)	106.6	0.25	Time	Slough
79)	106.6	0.25	The Breeze	Chard
75)	106.6	2	Two Lochs R.	Loch Ewe
25)	106.6	0.4	Spirit FM	Midhurst
28)	106.6	0.25	Heartland FM	Perth
23)	106.7	0.1	Jack FM	Stevenage
160)	106.7	0.6	West FM	Rothesay
173)	106.7	0.62	R Plymouth	Ft Staddon
8)	106.8	4	Nation R.	Cardiff
94)	106.8	0.1	Bright FM	Lewes
150)	106.8	0.2	Star R. - NE	Durham
96)	106.8	0.1	KMFM	Dover
136)	106.8	0.2	Connect FM	Peterborough
108)	106.8	0.5	Ridings FM	Wakefield
65)	106.8	0.3	Jack FM	Oxford
180)	106.8	19	Original FM	Aberdeen
123)	106.9	.044	Real R. - Wales	Moel-y-Parc
23)	106.9	0.28	Jack FM	Hertford
152)	106.9	0.1	Silk FM	Macclesfield
174)	106.9	0.1	Your R.	Helensburgh
15)	107.0	0.5	The Bee	Blackburn
113)	107.0	0.1	Isle of Wight R.	Chillerton Down
4)	107.0	0.1	Oak FM	Loughborough
90)	107.0	0.6	Reading 107	Reading
135)	107.0	0.62	Q Radio	Ballymena
103)	107.0	1	Sunshine R.	Monmouth
33)	107.1	0.16	Choice FM	N. London
108)	107.1	0.5	Trax FM	Doncaster
172)	107.1	0.14	Speysound R	Aviemore
46)	107.1	0.12	Star R.	Ely
13)	107.1	0.625	Argyll FM	Ballygroggan
169)	107.1	0.1	Rugby FM	Rugby
3)	107.1	0.1	Signal 107	Oswestry
123)	107.2	3.1	Real R. - Wales	Arfon
135)	107.2	0.25	Q Radio	Dungannon
107)	107.2	0.2	The Breeze	Winchester
22)	107.2	0.18	Wire FM	Warrington
110)	107.2	0.2	Rutland FM	Oakham
137)	107.2	0.2	Juice	Brighton
9)	107.2	0.1	KMFM	Thanet
84)	107.2	0.66	The Breeze	Bristol
3)	107.2	0.2	Signal 107	Kidderminster
119)	107.3	1	R. Exe	Exeter
123)	107.3	0.15	Real R. - Wales	Bargoed
169)	107.3	0.2	Touch R.	Warwick
8)	107.3	1.25	Nation R.	Swansea
136)	107.4	0.2	Connect FM	Kettering
84)	107.4	0.1	The Breeze	Bridgwater
130)	107.4	0.2	Peak FM	Chesterfield
3)	107.4	0.1	Signal 107	Telford
22)	107.4	0.18	Tower FM	Bolton
107)	107.4	0.2	The Breeze	Portsmouth
102)	107.5	0.1	R. Pembrokeshire	Fishguard
80)	107.5	0.1	Total Star	Cheltenham
126)	107.5	0.6	Time	Romford
7)	107.5	0.15	Sovereign FM	Eastbourne
84)	107.5	0.1	The Breeze	Warminster
17)	107.6	0.4	Juice FM	Liverpool
133)	107.6	0.1	Kestrel FM	Basingstoke
116)	107.6	1	Fire R.	Bournemouth
131)	107.6	0.2	Real R. - Yorks	Bradford

FM	MHz	kW	Name or Slogan	Location
67)	107.6	0.2	Banbury Sound	Banbury
96)	107.6	0.5	KMFM	Ashford, Kent
123)	107.6	10.25	Real R. - Wales	Blaenplwyf
2)	107.7	0.2	Jack FM	Swindon
120)	107.7	0.1	Nova R.	Weston Super Mare
95)	107.7	0.1	Chelmsford R.	Chelmsford
58)	107.7	0.2	Kiss	Peterborough
131)	107.7	0.2	Real R. - Yorks	Sheffield
55)	107.7	0.1	Splash FM	Worthing
3)	107.7	0.17	Signal 107	Wolverhampton
13)	107.7	0.5	Argyll FM	South Knapdale
149)	107.8	0.1	Arrow FM	Hastings
139)	107.8	0.8	R. Jackie	SW London
107)	107.8	0.9	The Breeze	Southampton
4)	107.9	0.2	Oak FM	Hinckley
108)	107.9	0.2	Trax FM	Worksop
198)	107.9	0.1	Star R.	Cambridge
57)	107.9	0.2	The Breeze	Bath
166)	107.9	0.2	Glide FM	Oxford
63)	107.9	0.2	KMFM	Medway

+approx 51 relays of less than 0.1kW

H. of tr: Most stns operate 24h Some stns carry automated prgrs outside peak hours

MAJOR COMMERCIAL RADIO GROUPS:
CELADOR RADIO ✉ 39 Long Acre, London WC2E 9LG ☎ 20 7845 6800 **W:** www.celador.co.uk
BAUER RADIO Ltd ✉ Mappin House, 4 Winsley Str, London W1W 8HF ☎ 207 182 8000 **W:** www.bauermedia.co.uk
GLOBAL RADIO ✉ 30 Leicester Square, London WC2H 7LA ☎ 20 7766 6000 🖷 20 7766 6111 **W:** www.thisisglobal.com/radio
TINDLE RADIO Ltd ✉ Radio House, Orion Court, Gt Blakenham IP5 0LW ☎ 1473 836100 🖷 1473 836136 **W:** www.tindleradio.com
UKRD GROUP Ltd ✉ Carn Brea Studios, Barncoose Ind. Est, Redruth TR15 3RQ ☎ 1209 310435 🖷 1209 310406 **W:** www.ukrd.com
UTV MEDIA plc ✉ 18 Hatfields, London SE1 8DJ ☎ 20 7959 7900 **W:** www.utvmedia.co.uk

Addresses & other information
1) Radio House, Bridge Rd, Southall UB2 4AT ☎ 20 8574 6666 **W:** www.buzzasiaonline.com – **2)** Lime Kiln, Royal Wootton Bassett, Swindon SN4 7HF ☎ 1793 851151 **W:** www.jackswindon.co.uk – **3)** 2nd Floor, Mander House, Wolverhampton WV1 3NB ☎ 1902 571070 **W:** www.signal107.co.uk – **4)** 3 Martins Court, Telford Way, Coalville LE67 3HD ☎ 1530 278200 **W:** www.oakfm.co.uk – **5)** 12 Westerbrook, St Sampsons, Guernsey GY2 4QQ ☎ 1481 242000 **W:** www.islandfm.com – **6)** 132 George Street, Oban PA34 5NT ☎ 1631 570057 **W:** www. obanfm.net – **7)** 14 St Mary's Walk, Hailsham BN27 1AF ☎ 1323 442700 **W:** www. sovereignfm.com – **8)** Media Centre, Culverhouse Cross, Cardiff CF5 6XJ ☎ 29 21414100 **W:** www.nationwales.com – **9)** 183 Northumberland Rd, Cliftonville, Margate, CT9 2TA ☎ 1843 220222 **W:** www.kmfm.co.uk – **10)** Haveland House, Ormeau Rd, Belfast BT7 1EB ☎ 28 9033 2102 **W:** www.u105.com – **11)** 185b High Rd, Wood Green, London N22 6BA ☎ 20 8888 3232 **W:** www.londraturkradyosu.net – **12)** Northgate House, St Peters Street, Colchester CO1 1HT ☎ 1206 764466 **W:** www.dream100.com – **13)** 27-29 Longrow, Campbeltown PA28 6ER ☎ 1586 551800 **W:** www.argyllfm.com – **14)** 201-203 High Street, Falkirk FK1 1DU ☎ 1324 611164 **W:** www.centralfm.co.uk – **15)** 2A Petre Court, Petre Rd, Clayton-le-Moors, Accrington BB5 5HH ☎ 1282 690000 **W:** www.2br.co.uk www.thebee.co.uk – **16)** Unit 5 Metro Centre, Dwight Rd, Watford WD18 9UD ☎ 1923 205480 **W:** www. heart.co.uk/watfordhemel – **17)** 33-39 Strand Str., Liverpool L1 8LT ☎ 151 242 0600 **W:** www.juicefm.com – **18)** Radio House, Bridge Rd, Southall UB2 4AT ☎ 20 8574 6666 **W:** www.kismatradio.com – **19)** 26 Balliniska Rd, Londonderry BT48 0NA ☎ 2871 296600 **W:** www.gra-dionetwork.com – **20)** 5-6 Aldergate, Tamworth, B79 7DJ ☎ 1827 318000 **W:** www.touchradio.co.uk – **21)** 6 Tunnell Street, St Helier, Jersey JE2 4LU ☎ 1534 888103 **W:** www.channel103.com – **22)** Orrell Lodge, Orrell Rd, Wigan WN5 8HJ ☎ 1942 761024 **W:** www.wishfm. net, www.towerfm.co.uk, www.wirefm.co.uk – **23)** The Pumphouse, Knebworth Park SG3 6HQ ☎ 1438 810900 **W:** www.106jack.com – **24)** MAZCC, 311 Stonegate Rd, Leeds LS17 6AZ ☎ 113 218 5836 **W:** www.radiojcom.com – **25)** 9/10 Dukes Court, Bognor Rd, Chichester PO19 8FX ☎ 1243 773600 **W:** www.spiritfm.net – **26)** Arbroath Infirmary, Rosemount Rd, Arbroath DD11 2AT ☎ 1241 879660 **W:** www.radionorthangus.co.uk – **27)** 2 Chantry Court, Chester CH1 4QN ☎ 1244 391000 **W:** www.dee1063.com – **28)** 9 Alba Place, Pitlochry PH16 5BH ☎ 1796 474040 **W:** www.heartlandfm.co.uk – **29)** Portway, Newbury RG14 1AY ☎ 1635 841600 **W:** www.thebreeze.com – **30)** PO Box 1063, Bridgend CF35 6WY ☎ 1656 838620 **W:** www.bridge.fm – **31)** Merlin House, Parc Merlin, Glan Yr Afon Ind. Est., Aberystwyth

SY23 3FF ☎ 1970 626991 **W:** www.ceredigionradio.co.uk – **32)** Unit 4, Brunts Business Centre, Samuel Brunts Way, Mansfield NG18 2AH ☎ 1623 646666 **W:** www.mansfield103.co.uk – **33)** 30 Leicester Square, London WC2H 7LA ☎ 20 7766 6000 **W:** www.capitalfm.com Choice: www.choice-fm.co.uk LBC: www.lbc.co.uk XFM: www.xfm.co.uk – **34)** 9 Brindleyplace, 4 Oozells Square, Birmingham B1 2DJ ☎ 121 566 5200 **W:** www.freeradio.co.uk, www.freeradio80s.co.uk – **35)** 67-73 Stoke Rd, Stoke-on-Trent ST4 2SR ☎ 1782 441 300 **W:** www.signal1. co.uk – **36)** Marquis Court, Team Valley Trading Estate, Gateshead NE11 0RU ☎ 191 440 7500 **W:** www.realradio.co.uk – **37)** Laser House, Waterfront Quay, Salford M50 3XW ☎ 161 886 8800 **W:** www.realradio.co.uk; www.realradioxs.co.uk – **38)** City Link, Nottingham NG2 4NG ☎ 115 910 6100 **W:** www.gem106.co.uk – **39)** PO Box 1034, Sunderland SR5 2YL ☎ 191 548 1034 **W:** www.sun-fm.com – **40)** Radio House, John Wilson Business Park, Whitstable CT5 3QX ☎ 1227 772004 – **41)** Radio House, Franklin Rd., Brighton BN41 1AF ☎ 1273 316900 – **42)** Radio House, Atlantic Wharf, Cardiff CF10 4DJ ☎ 29 2094 2900 **W:** www.capitalfm.co.uk – **43)** Apple Ind. Estate, Whittle Ave, Fareham PO15 5SX ☎ 1489 587600 **W:**www.capitalfm.co.uk – **44)** 4 Winds Pavilion, Pacific Quay, Glasgow G51 1EB ☎ 141 566 6106 **W:** www.capitalfm.co.uk – **45)** 4 Exchange Quay, Salford M5 3EE ☎ 161 662 4700 **W:** www.capitalfm.co.uk; www.xfmmanchester.co.uk – **46)** 20 Mercers Row, Cambridge CB5 8HY ☎ 1223 305107 **W:** www.star107.co.uk – **47)** 1 The Square, 111 Broad Street, Birmingham B15 1AS ☎ 121 226 5760 **W:** www.capitalfm.co.uk – **48)** Kingfisher Way, Silverlink Business Park, Wallsend NE28 9NX ☎ 191 444 2500 **W:** www.capitalfm.co.uk – **49)** 2a Joseph's Well, Hanover Walk, Leeds LS3 1AB ☎ 113 308 5100 **W:** www.capitalfm.co.uk – **50)** 29 Yarmouth Rd, Norwich NR7 0EE ☎ 1603 703300 **W:** www.norwich999.com – **51)** Castle Quay, Castlefield, Manchester M15 4PR ☎ 161 288 5000 **W:** www.key103.co.uk www.manchestersmagic.co.uk – **52)** St Johns Beacon, 1 Houghton Street, Liverpool L1 1RL ☎ 151 472 6800 **W:** www.magic1548.co.uk, www.radiocity.co.uk – **53)** 900 Herries Rd, Sheffield S6 1RH ☎ 114 2091000 **W:** www.magicam.co.uk, www.hallamfm.co.uk – **54)** The Boathouse, Commercial Rd, Hull HU1 2SG ☎ 1482 325141 **W:** Magic FM: www.magic1161.co.uk Viking FM: www.vikingfm.co.uk – **55)** Guildbourne Centre, Worthing BN11 1LZ ☎1903 210772 **W:** www.splashfm.com – **56)** PO Box 2000, 51 Burley Rd, Leeds LS3 1LR ☎ 113 283 5500 **W:** www.radioaire.co.uk, www.magic828. co.uk – **57)** The Tramshed, Beehive Yard, Walcot St, Bath BA1 5BB ☎ 1225 731318 **W:** www.thebreeze.com – **58)** Mappin House, 4 Winsley Street, London W1W 8HF ☎ 20 7182 8000 **W:** Magic: www.magic. co.uk Kiss: www.kissfmuk.com – **59)** Radio House, Yales Crescent, Thornaby, Stockton-on-Tees TS17 6AA ☎ 1642 888222 **W:** www.tfm-radio.co.uk www.magic1170.co.uk – **60)** PO Box 974, Preston PR1 1XA ☎ 1772 477700 **W:** Rock FM: www.rockfm.co.uk Magic 999: www.magic999.com – **61)** 55 Degrees North, Pilgrim St., Newcastle upon Tyne NE1 6BF ☎ 191 230 6100 **W:** www.magic1152.co.uk, www.metroradio.co.uk – **62)** Stormyhill Rd, Portree IV51 9DY ☎ 1478 611797– **W:** www.cuillinfm.co.uk – **63)** Medway House, Ginsbury Close, Strood, Rochester ME2 4DU ☎ 1634 711079 **W:** www.kmfm. co.uk – **64)** 267 Tettenhall Rd, Wolverhampton WV6 0DQ ☎ 1902 461300 **W:** www.freeradio.co.uk – **65)** 270 Woodstock Rd, Oxford OX2 7NW ☎ 1865 315980 **W:** www.jackfm.co.uk – **66)** PO Box 971, Llanelli SA15 1YH ☎ 845 8907000 **W:** www.radiocarmarthenshire.com www.scarletfm.com – **67)** Unit 9A Manor Park, Banbury OX16 3TB ☎ 1295 661070 **W:** www.banburysound.co.uk – **68)** Planet House, 2 Woodhouse St. Hull HU9 1RJ ☎ 1482 333999 **W:** www.kcfm.co.uk – **69)** Chapel Quarter, Maid Marian Way, Nottingham NG1 6HQ ☎ 115 873 1500 **W:** www.capitalfm.co.uk – **70)** Kirkham House, John Comyn Drive, Worcester WR3 7NS ☎ 1905 545510 **W:** www.freeradio.co.uk – **71)** 5 Abbey Court, Fraser Rd, Bedford, MK44 3WH ☎ 1234 235010 – **72)** 4th Floor CBX 11 East, Midsummer Blvd, Milton Keynes MK9 2EA ☎ 1908 591600 – **73)** 20 Lionel Street, Birmingham B3 1AQ ☎ 8450 531052 **W:** www.kerrangradio.co.uk – **74)** PO Box 106, High Peak SK23 0DJ ☎ 1298 813144 **W:** www.highpeakradio.co.uk – **75)** Mansegate, Gairloch IV21 2LR ☎ 870 712106 **W:** www.2lr.co.uk – **76)** Bridge Studios, Eastgate Centre, Gloucester GL1 1SS ☎ 1452 572400 – **77)** Breck Farm, Stody, Norfolk NR24 2ER ☎ 1263 860808 **W:** www.northnor-folkradio.com – **78)** 20 Llan Coed House, Llandarcy, SA10 6FG ☎ 1792 716200 **W:** www.nation80s.com – **79)** 72 Middle Street, Yeovil BA20 1DJ ☎ 1935 848480 **W:** www.thebreeze.com – **80)** 28 Knightsbridge Business Park, Cheltenham GL51 9TA ☎ 1242 680114 **W:** www.total-star.co.uk – **81)** Unit 6, 10-14 Hollybush Gdns., London E2 9QP ☎ 20 7729 4333 **W:** www.betarbangla.org.uk – **82)** Hawthorn Hse., Exeter Business Park, Exeter EX1 3OS ☎ 1392 354200 – **83)** Panjabi Centre, 30 Sussex Rd, Southall UB2 5EG ☎ 20 8564 9591 **W:** www.desiradio. org.uk – **84)** County Gates, Ashton Rd, Bristol BS3 2JH ☎ 117 966 6107 **W:** www.thebreeze.com www.jackbristol.com – **85)** 10 Wheal Kitty Workshops, St Agnes TR5 0RD ☎ 1872 554400 – **86)** 1 Passage Str., Bristol BS2 0JF ☎ 117 984 3200 – **87)** Chiseldon House, Stonehill

Green, Westlea, Swindon SN5 7HB ☎ 1793 663000 – **88)** 2 Enterprise House, Chivers Way, Histon, Cambridge CB24 9ZR ☎ 1233 623800 – **89)** The Chase, Calcot, Reading RG31 7RB ☎ 118 9454400 – **90)** Radio House, Madejski Stadium, Reading RG2 0FN ☎118 986 2555 **W:** www.reading107.com - **91)** Haig House, Haig Business Park, Markinch, Fife KY7 6AQ ☎ 1592 753753 **W:** www.kingdomfm.co.uk – **92)** 31 Glebe Rd, Chelmsford CM1 1QG ☎ 1254 524500 – **93)** 42 Southall Str, Manchester M3 1LQ ☎ 161 288 1000 **W:** asiansoundradio.co.uk – **94)** Market Place Shopping Centre, Burgess Hill RH15 9NP ☎1444 301064 **W:** www.brightfm.net – **95)** Icon Bldg., Western Esplanade, Southend-on-Sea SS1 1EE ☎ 1702 455070 **W:** www.southendradio.com www.chelmsfordradio.co.uk – **96)** 34-36 North Street, Ashford TN24 8JR ☎ 1233 623232 – **97)** The Stanley Centre, Kelvin Way, Crawley RH10 9SE ☎ 1293 636000 **W:** www.mercuryfm.co.uk – **98)** 22 Chapter Street, London SW1P 4NP ☎ 20 7316 1300 **W:** www.premier.org.uk – **99)** Friars Square Studios, 11 Bourbon Street, Aylesbury HP20 2PZ ☎ 1296 399396 **W:** www.mix96.co.uk – **100)** The Studios, Mold Rd, Wrexham LL11 4AF ☎ 1978 752200 – **101)** Lakeland Food Park, Plumgarths, Crook Rd, Kendal LA8 8QJ ☎1539 737 380 **W:** www.lakelandradio.co.uk – **102)** Unit 14, Old School Estate, Station Rd, Narberth SA67 7DU ☎1834 862010 **W:** www.radiopembrokeshire.com – **103)** Suite 5, Penn House, Broad Str. Hereford HR4 9AP ☎ 1432 360246 **W:** www.sunshineradio.co.uk – **104)** St George's Plain, 47-49 Colegate, Norwich NR3 1DB ☎ 1603 671100 **105)** Radio House, Orion Court, Gt Blakenham, Ipswich IP6 0LW ☎ 473 836102 **W:** www.town102.com – **106)** Forster Square, Bradford BD1 5NE ☎ 1274 203040 **W:** www.pulse.co.uk, www.pulsegold.co.uk – **107)** Roman Landing, Kingsway, Southampton SO14 1BN ☎ 845 466 1107 **W:** www.thebreeze.com www.jackradio.com – **108)** 5 Sidings Court, Doncaster DN4 5NU ☎ 1302 341166 **W:** www.dearnefm.co.uk www.ridingsfm.co.uk www.rotherfm.co.uk www.traxfm.co.uk – **109)** Livingstone Tower, 26 Richmond Rd, Glasgow G1 1XH ☎ 141 548 4041 **W:** www.celticmusicradio.net – **110)** 40 Melton Rd, Oakham LE15 6AY ☎ 1572 757868 **W:** www.rutlandradio.co.uk – **111)** Marble Court, Lymington Rd, Torquay TQ1 4FB ☎ 1803 321055 **W:** www.palm.fm – **112)** Witham Park, Waterside South, Lincoln LN5 7JN ☎ 1522 549900 **W:** www.lincsfm.co.uk www.compassfm.co.uk – **113)** Dodnor Park, Newport, Isle of Wight PO30 5XE ☎ 1983 822557 **W:** www.iwradio.co.uk – **114)** LGR house, 437 High Rd, London N12 0AP ☎ 20 8349 6950 **W:** www.lgr.co.uk – **115)** 18 Blackfriars Street, Kings Lynn PE30 1NN ☎ 1553 772777 **W:** www.klfmradio.co.uk – **116)** 307 Holdenhurst Rd, Bournemouth BH8 8BX ☎ 1202 385107 **W:** www.fireradio.co.uk – **117)** 3 Eastgate House, Andover SP10 1EP ☎ 11264 336000 **W:** www.thebreeze.com – **118)** 18 Trinity Street, Dorchester DT1 1DJ ☎ 1305 250333 **W:** www.wessexfm.co.uk – **119)** 6a Cranmere Court, Lustleigh Close, Exeter EX2 8PW ☎ 1392 823557 **W:** www.radioexe.co.uk – **120)** Knightstone Causeway, Weston-super-Mare BS23 2AD ☎ 1934 444900 **W:** www.thisisnova.com – **121)** The Shed, School Rd, Kintore, Inverurie AB51 0UX ☎ 1467 632909 **W:** www.necrfm.co.uk – **122)** Unit 1130, Parkway Court, Glasgow Business Park, Glasgow G69 6GA ☎ 141 781 1011 **W:** www.realradio.co.uk – **123)** Ty-Nant Court, Cardiff CF15 8LW ☎ 2920 315100 **W:** www.realradioco.uk – **124)** Market Street, Lerwick, Shetland ZE1 0JN ☎ 1595 695299 **W:** www.sibc.co.uk – **125)** Mill Street Industrial Estate, Ullapool IV26 2UN ☎ 1854 613131 **W:** www.lochbroomfm.co.uk – **126)** Lambourne House, 7 Western Rd, Romford RM1 3LD ☎ 1708 731643 **W:** www.time1075.com – **127)** Victoria Rd, Gowerton, Swansea SA4 3AB ☎ 1792 511964 **W:** www.swanseasound.co.uk www.thewave.co.uk – **128)** Unit 11, Burway Trading Estate, Ludlow SY8 1EN ☎ 1584 873795 **W:** www.sunshineradio.co.uk – **129)** The Studios, The Park, Newtown SY16 2NZ ☎ 1686 623777 **W:** www.radiohafren.co.uk – **130)** Radio House, Foxwood Rd, Chesterfield S41 9RF ☎ 1246 269107 **W:** www.peakfm.net – **131)** 1 Sterling Court, Tingley, Wakefield WF3 1EL ☎113 238 1114 **W:** www.realradio.co.uk – **132)** addr as stn 167) ☎ 845 194 1066 **W:** www.time1066.com – **133)** Paddington House, Festival Place, Basingstoke RG21 7LJ ☎ 1256 694000 **W:** www.kestrelfm.com – **134)** PO Box 103.4, Lowestoft NR32 2TL ☎ 845 3451035 **W:** www.thebeach.co.uk – **135)** Woodside Rd Industrial Estate, Ballymena BT42 4QJ ☎ 28 2564 8777 **W:** www.qradionetwork.com – **136)** 55 Headlands, Kettering NN15 7EY ☎ 1536 513664 **W:** www.connectfm.com – **137)** 170 North Street, Brighton BN1 1EA ☎ 1273 387107 **W:** www.juice-brighton.com – **138)** Sarah Moor Studios, Henshaw Str, Oldham OL1 3EN ☎ 161 621 6500 **W:** www.revolutiononline.co.uk – **139)** 110 Tolworth Broadway, Surbiton KT6 7JD ☎ 20 8288 1300 **W:** www.radiojackie.com – **140)** 1 Waterloo Place, Watson Square, Stockport SK1 3AZ ☎ 161 476 7340 **W:** www.imaginefm.net – **141)** PO Box 123, Dunnington, York YO19 5ZX ☎ 1904 488888 **W:** www.minsterfm.co.uk – **142)** Ben Nevis Estate, Claggan, Fort William PH33 6PR ☎ 1397 700007 **W:** www.nevisradio.co.uk – **143)** PO Box 333, Stornoway, Isle of Lewis HS1 2PU ☎ 1851 703333 **W:** www.isles.fm – **144)** Arena Bldg., 85 Ormeau Rd, Belfast BT7 1SH ☎ 28 9023 4967 **W:** www.city-

beat.co.uk – **145)** PO Box 962, Scarborough YO11 3ZP ☎ 1723 581700 **W:** www.yorkshirecoastradio.com – **146)** City Hall Studios, Malthouse Lane, Salisbury SP2 7QQ ☎ 1722 416644 **W:** www.spirefm.co.uk – **147)** The Hamlet, Hornbeam Park Avenue, Harrogate HG2 8RE ☎ 1423 522972 **W:** www.strayfm.com – **148)** KMS House, Bradford Street, Birmingham B12 0JD ☎ 121 753 5353 **W:** www.radioxl.net – **149)** Priory Meadow Centre, Queen Square, Hastings TN34 1PJ ☎ 1424 461177 **W:** www.arrowfm.co.uk – **150)** Radio House, 11 Woodland Rd, Darlington DL3 7BJ ☎ 1325 341801 **W:** www.thisisstar.co.uk – **151)** Radio House, 63 Melton Rd, Leicester LE4 6PN ☎ 116 261 0666 **W:** www.sabrasradio.com – **152)** 140 Moss Lane, Macclesfield SK11 7XE ☎ 1625 268000 **W:** www.silkfm.com – **153)** Kiltonga Ind. Estate, Newtownards, Co Down BT23 4ES ☎ 28 9181 5555 **W:** www.down-town.co.uk, www.coolfm.co.uk – **154)** Dolphin House, North Street, Guildford GU1 4AA ☎ 1483 300964 **W:** www.eagleextra.co.uk, www.964eagle.co.uk – **155)** Abbottswell Rd, West Tullos, Aberdeen AB12 3AJ ☎ 1224 337000 **W:** www.northsound1.co.uk – **156)** 6 North Isla Street, Dundee DD3 7JQ ☎ 1382 200800 **W:** www.radiotay.co.uk – **157)** Unit 40, The Loreburne Centre, High Street, Dumfries DG1 2BD ☎ 1387 250999 **W:** www.westsoundradio.com – **158)** Clydebank Business Park, Clydebank, Glasgow G81 2RX ☎ 141 565 2200 **W:** www.clyde1.com – **159)** Forth House, Forth Street, Edinburgh EH1 3LE ☎ 131 556 9255 **W:** www.forthone.com – **160)** Radio House, 54a Holmston Rd, Ayr KA/ 3BE ☎ 1292 283662 **W:** www.westsound.co.uk, www.westfm.co.uk – **161)** Scorguie Place, Inverness IV3 8UJ ☎ 1463 224433 **W:** www.mfr.co.uk – **161a)** Neil Gunn Drive, Thurso KW14 7QU ☎01847 890000 **W:** www.caithnessfm.co.uk – **161c)** Old Thomas Walker Hospital, Charlotte Street, Fraserburgh AB43 9LS ☎ 1346 512010 – **161d)** 59a Land Street, Keith AB55 5AN ☎ 1542 886080 **W:** www.kcr.fm – **162)** Tweedside Park, Galashiels TD1 3TD ☎ 1896 759444 **W:** www.radioborders.com – **163)** PO Box 964, Carlisle CA1 3NG ☎ 1228 818964 **W:** www.cfmradio.com – **164)** 5 Manor Court, Barnes Wallis Rd, Segensworth East, Fareham PO15 5TH ☎ 1489 481050 **W:** www.wave105.com – **165)** 102 Wilson Way, Redruth TR15 3XX ☎ 1209 314400 **W:** www.piratefm.co.uk – **166)** 270 Woodstock Rd, Oxford OX2 7NW ☎ 1865 315980 **W:** www.glidefm.co.uk – **167)** Radio House, Bridge Rd, Southall UB2 4AT ☎ 20 8574 6666 **W:** www.sunriseradio.com – **168)** 55 Leeds Rd, Bradford BD1 5AF ☎ 1274 735043 **W:** www.sunriseradio.fm – **169)** Holly Farm Business Park, Honily, Kenilworth CV8 1NP ☎ 1926 485600 **W:** www.touchradio.co.uk www.rugbyfm.co.uk – **170)** PO Box 969, 24 St George's Quay, Lancaster LA1 3LD ☎ 1524 848747 **W:** www.thebay.co.uk – **171)** St Monicas House, Windmill Lane, Ashbourne DE6 1EY ☎ 1335 346967 **W:** www.ashbourneradio.co.uk – **172)** Plot 4A, Dalfaber Industrial Estate, Aviemore PH22 1ST ☎ 1479 811888 **W:** www.speysoundradio.com – **173)** 3 Crescent Ave. Mews, Plymouth PL1 3AP ☎ 1752 389532 **W:** www.radioplymouth.com – **174)** Unit 3, 80 Castlegreen Str., Dumbarton G82 1JB ☎ 1389 734411 **W:** www.yourradio.com – **175)** 4 Inchgate Place, London SW8 3NS ☎ 20 7627 4433 **W:** www.spectrum-radio.net – **176)** Unit 1130, Parkway Court, Glasgow G69 6GA ☎ 141 781 0963 **W:** www.realradioxs.co.uk – **177)** 8 South Tay Street, Dundee DD1 1PA ☎ 1382 901000 **W:** www.wave102.co.uk – **178)** 7 Blackhouse Circle, Blackhouse Industrial Estate, Peterhead AB42 1BN ☎ 1779 491012 **W:** www.wavesfm.com – **179)** Mowbray Drive, Blackpool FY3 7JR ☎ 1253 650300 **W:** www.wave965.com – **180)** Craigshaw Rd, Aberdeen AB12 3AR ☎ 1224 294860 **W:** www.originalfm.com

MANX RADIO (Comm.)
⌨ Douglas Head, Douglas, Isle of Man IM1 5BW ☎ 1624 682600 📠 1624 682604 **W:** www.manxradio.com **LP:** MD: Anthony Pugh. **MW:** 1368kHz Foxdale 20kW **FM:** 89.0MHz Snaefell 4kW / 97.2MHz Carnane 11kW / 103.7MHz Jurby 4kW
D.Prgr: 24h. Separate prgrs on MW: MF 0730-0830, Sun 2100-2200, also during Manx motorcycle events.

ENERGY FM (Comm.)
⌨ 100 Market Street, Douglas, Isle of Man IM1 2PH ☎ 1624 611936 📠 1624 664699 **E:** mail@energyfm.net **W:** www.energyfm.net **FM:** 91.2MHz Snaefell 1.2kW, 93.4MHz Jurby 1.2kW, 98.6MHz Carnane 2kW (+ relays on 98.4/102.4/105.2) **D.Prgr:** 24h

3FM (Comm.)
⌨ 45 Victoria Street, Douglas, Isle of Man IM1 3RS ☎ 1624 616333 📠 1624 614333 **W:** www.three.fm
FM: 104.2MHz (Ramsey & Port St Mary), 105MHz (Carnane 2kW), 106.6MHz (Snaefell), 106.2MHz (Peel) **D.Prgr:** 24h

BRITISH FORCES BROADCASTING SCE.
(a division of Services Sound & Vision Corp.)
⌨ SSVC, Narcot Lane, Gerrards Cross SL9 8TN ☎ 1494 878354 📠 1494 878552 **E:** adminofficer@bfbs.com **W:** www.bfbs.com

L.P: Contr BFBS Radio: Nicky Ness
MW: BFBS Gurkha Radio in Nepali, news hourly in English on 1134kHz (Bramcote, Catterick & Sandhurst), 1251kHz (York), 1278kHz (Folkestone-main studio & Stafford), 1287kHz (Blandford, Brecon, Maidstone, Chippenham).
FM: BFBS on 100.6MHz (Lisburn) 101MHz (Belfast), 106.5MHz (Antrim), 107.5MHz (Ballykinlar) **DAB:** Digital One. See Afghanistan, Ascension Island, Belgium, Bosnia, Brunei, Canada, Cyprus, Falkland Islands, Germany, Gibraltar, Nepal, Netherlands for other sces.

GARRISON FM
🖃 Shute Rd, Catterick Garrison DL9 4AF ☎ 1748 830050 **E:** hq@garrisonfm.com **W:** www.garrisonfm.com **L.P:** MD: Mark Page.
MW: Low power sce on 1287kHz (Bassingbourn, Glencourse, Ripon, Thirsk, Topcliffe, Wattisham, Woodbridge) **FM:** 89.3MHz (Blandford), 98.5MHz (Edinburgh), 102.5MHz (Aldershot), 106.8MHz (Salisbury), 106.9MHz (Catterick), 107MHz (Colchester)

Restricted Service Licences (RSL) Licences are granted for low power special event stns operating for up to 28 days (occ. longer) usually on FM (occ. on MW)
LPAM (Low Power AM stations) There are currently about 60 stns on the air with txs of 0.001kW e.r.p. Freqs used: 1134, 1251, 1278, 1287, 1350, 1386, 1404, 1431, 1449, 1575kHz
LPFM (Low Power VHF/FM stations) There are currently about 18 stns on the air, most on 87.7MHz, with txs of typically 50mW

Community Radio Small-scale, low-power, non-profit community radio sces to serve a particular neighbourhood. Most on FM with 25W. approx 200 stns on air as of October 2012. For updated listing of short-term RSLs, long-term RSLs (LPAMs) and Community Radio see Radio Broadcast Licensing at **W:** www.ofcom.org.uk/radio

Community Audio Distribution Systems (CADS) licence-exempt service for religious and community events using 27MHz Citizens Band.

UNITED STATES OF AMERICA

L.T: See World Time Table (DST where applicable: 10 Mar-3 Nov) — **Pop:** 314 million — **Pr.L:** English — **E.C:** 60Hz, 110V — **ITU:** USA

FEDERAL COMMUNICATIONS COMMISSION (FCC)
Govt. licensing agency for broadcast stations
🖃 445 12th Street, SW, Washington, D.C. 20554 ☎ +1 202 418-0190 📠 +1 202 418-0232 **W:** www.fcc.gov **E:** fccinfo@fcc.gov
L.P: Chmn: Julius Genachowski. Commissioners: Michael J. Copps, Robert M. McDowell, Mignon Clyburn
The FCC is an independent federal agency composed of commissioners appointed by the President with the consent of the Senate. One of its major activities is the general regulation of broadcasting, visual as well as aural. This regulation may be divided into three phases: 1) The allocation of spectrum space to the different types of broadcast services 2) consideration of applications to build and operate individual stations 3) regulation of their operations. Broadcasting is handled by the FCC Media Bureau.

Call letter assignments: International agreement provides for the identification of the country of a radio stn by the first letter or first two letters of the stn's assigned call signal and for this purpose apportions the alphabet among different nations. USA nations use the initial letters K, N and W exclusively, and part of the A series. For broadcast stns, calls beginning with K are assigned to stns west of the Mississippi River, incl. Guam and No. Marianas Is, while W is assigned to broadcast stns east of the Mississippi, incl. Puerto Rico. Calls consist of four letters, to which FM or TV may be added, with a hyphen, for FM or TV stns.
    A few exceptions with stns east of the Mississippi using a "K" callsign and stns west of the Mississippi using a "W" callsign will be noted. These are old callsigns that were assigned before the geographical division was introduced and are retained by special permission. Similarly some very old callsigns using only three letters may be retained by the stns that once were assigned these callsigns.

Stations: More than 15,000 stns are operating on AM and FM. As of March 2012 there were 4,762 licensed AM stns.

MAJOR NETWORKS PROVIDING AM STATION PROGRAMMING:
CBS RADIO
🖃 1515 Broadway, New York, NY 10036 ☎ +1 212 846-3939 **W:** www.cbsradio.com **L.P:** Pres. & CEO: Dan Mason

CBS Radio is part of the CBS Corporation and operates 130 radio stns. The overall mix of each radio stn's programming is designed to fit the stns specific format and serve its local community. CBS Radio is home to stations across a number of formats including news (WCBS-AM), sports (WFAN-AM), alternative rock (KROQ-FM), classic hits (WCBS-FM), country (WUSN-FM) and adult hits (KCBS-FM). The Company also broadcasts play-by-play coverage of more than two dozen of the country's leading sports franchises amongst MLB, the NFL, the NBA, the WNBA and the NHL.

CUMULUS MEDIA NETWORKS
🖃 13725 Montfort Drive, Dallas, TX 75240 ☎ +1 972-991-9200 📠 261 Madison Avenue, New York, NY 10016 ☎ +1 212-735-1700
W: www.cumulusmedianetworks.com **L.P:** Chmn, Pres & CEO: Lewis W Dickey, Jr.
Cumulus Media Networks, which has has more than 4,000 affiliate radio stations, is owned and operated by Cumulus Media. It controls many of the radio assets formerly belonging to the American Broadcasting Company (ABC), which was broken up in 2007; Cumulus owns the portion of the network that was purchased by Citadel Broadcasting that year. The network adopted its current name in September 2011, following Cumulus's acquisition of Citadel; prior to this, it had been known as Citadel Media Networks since April 2009, after licensing the "ABC Radio Networks" name from The Walt Disney Company for nearly two years.

CLEAR CHANNEL MEDIA & ENTERTAINMENT
🖃 200 East Basse Road, San Antonio, TX 78209 ☎ +1 210 822-2828 **W:** www.clearchannel.com **L.P:** Pres/CEO, Clear Channel Media & Entertainment: John Hogan
Clear Channel operates over 850 radio stns in the USA. In addition, Clear Channel's Premiere Radio Network syndicates more than 90 prgrs to more than 5,000 radio affiliates, including The Rush Limbaugh Show, Coast to Coast AM, Jim Rome, Elvis Duran, Ryan Seacrest, Glenn Beck, Sean Hannity, and Randi Rhodes.

CNN RADIO
🖃 Box 105573, Atlanta, GA 30348. ☎ +1 404 827-1500 **W:** www.cnnradio.com **L.P:** Turner Chmn. & CEO: Philip Kent.
Cable News Network is owned by Turner Broadcasting System, Inc, a Time Warner Company. CNN Radio provides news, sports, business and feature reports. CNN and Westwood One are partnered together to distribute CNN Radio prgrs to radio stns across the U.S. Under the agreement, Westwood One syndicates the CNN Radio Network, the most widely distributed radio news network in North America.

DISNEY & ESPN MEDIA NETWORKS, INC
🖃 Walt Disney Comp., 500 S. Buena Vista St., Burbank, CA 91521-9722 ☎ +1-818-560-1000 **W:** disney.go.com **L.P:** Co-Chmn, Disney Media Networks and Pres, ESPN, Inc. & ABC Sports: John Skipper.
Disney Media Networks comprise a vast array of broadcast, cable, radio, publishing and Internet businesses. Key radio areas include Disney-ABC Television Group (which manages Radio Disney Network) and ESPN Inc.

FOX NEWS RADIO
🖃 Fox News Radio, 1211 Ave of the Americas, 18th Floor, New York, NY 10036 ☎ +1 212-301-5439 **W:** radio.foxnews.com **L.P:** Chmn & CEO: Roger Ailes.
Fox News Radio provides radio stns with hourly newscasts at top and bottom of the hour. Newscasts are anchored by Fox News Channel correspondents and provided 24 hours a day, 7 days a week. The service also provides radio stns with radio-anchored breaking news coverage of crisis events both nationally and internationally. Additionally, Fox News Radio syndicates talk prgrs to affiliates across the country.

IRN/USA RADIO NETWORK
🖃 USA Radio Network, Inc, PO Box 383230, Germantown, TN 38183. ☎ +1 800 325-0919 **W:** www.irnusaradio.com **L.P:** Pres.: Larry Bates.
USA Radio Network, inc. and Information Radio Network merged in Febraury 2008 to form a new company called IRN/USA Radio Network with a combined affiliate base of almost 2500 radio stns.

NATIONAL PUBLIC RADIO (NPR) (non-comm.)
🖃 635 Massachusetts Ave, NW, Washington, D.C. 20001 ☎ +1 202 513-2000 **W:** www.npr.org **L.P:** Interim CEO: Joyce Slocum.
NPR is a producer and distributor of non-commercial news, talk, and enter-tainment prgrs. A privately supported, not-for-profit membership organization, NPR serves an audience of 27.5 million Americans each week in partnership with more than 860 independently operated, non-commercial public radio sttns. Each NPR Member Station serves local

listeners with a distinctive combination of national and local prgrs.

TRITON RADIO NETWORKS/DIAL GLOBAL
Triton Radio Networks: 220 West 42nd Street.3rd Floor, New York, N.Y. 10036, ☎ +1 212 419-2900, 🖷 +1 212 896-5341 **W:** www.tritonradionetworks.com
Dial-Global: 11812 San Vicente Blvd., 3rd floor, Suite 350, Los Angeles, CA 90049 ☎ +1 310 820-8666 **W:** www.dial-global.com
LP: Pres/CEO Triton Radio Networks: Spencer Brown; Pres/CEO Dial Global: Ken Williams/David Landau
Dial Global, a division of Triton Radio Networks, is owned by the Triton Media Group, LLC. Dial Global owns the assets of Transtar Radio Networks, Jones Radio Networks, Waitt Radio Networks and more recently Westwood One. Dial Global Programming produces and syndicates approximately 100 music prgrs and prep services in a variety of formats to more than 6,000 radio stns nationwide.

OTHER NATIONAL ORGANIZATIONS:

NATIONAL ASSOCIATION OF BROADCASTERS
1771 N Str, NW, Washington, DC 20036 ☎ +1 202 429-5300 **W:** www.nab.org **LP:** Pres/CEO: Gordon H. Smith.
The NAB is a trade association that advocates on behalf of more than 8.300 free, local radio and television stns and also broadcast networks before Congress, the Federal Communications Commission and the Courts.

NATIONAL ASSOCIATION OF SHORTWAVE BROADCASTERS, INC.
10400 NW 240th Str, Okeechobee, FL 34972
☎ +1 863 763-0281 🖷 +1 863 763-1034 **W:** www.shortwave.org
LP: Pres: Glenn W. Tapley. Vice Pres: Brady Murray.
The NASB represents the interests of FCC-licensed broadcasters in the private sector of the US International Shortwave Broadcast community

COMMERCIAL STATIONS
Especially in multi-station markets, radio stns concentrate their prgrs to appeal to a given segment of the population or a given listening taste. Many stns devote their entire broadcast day to news and/or talk prgrs. Others specialize in hit music (adult contemporary, top 40), country music, oldies (e.g. hits of the fifties and sixties), big bands/standards, black (urban contemporary, jazz, rhythm & blues), religious services and inspirational music, classical music, ethnic prgrs.

Today satellites are widely used for the distribution of prgrs. Numerous such networks are in operation. Stns making extensive use of network prgrs may have only one local identification per hour, usually on top of the hour. The former "clear channel" stns today have a protected area extending to 700 miles. Outside this area, the frequencies are also used by other stns. A few stns have been granted temporary licenses for increased powers to combat interference from neighbouring countries. Many daytime stns may now operate after local sunset using low or very low powers.

With the large decrease in AM listening in favour of FM, an increasing number of AM stns go off the air for a longer or shorter period due to economic difficulties. The latest development is that stns on the so-called regional channels, previously limited to 5kW power, may now apply for up to 50kW, limited only by the required protection of other stns. Relaxed ownership rules have allowed groups of co-owned stns to form in larger markets with the group stns often broadcasting from a common studio address.

Digital broadcasting in the AM and FM bands is being tested by a number of stns, using the IBOC system. With this system digital signals are emitted on both sides of the stns analogue signal, so that both analogue and digital receivers can recover the audio. Analogue listeners may experience the IBOC signal as an increased noise level on the chs adjacent to the nominal channel of the emitting stn. There are currently 299 AM stns and 1716 FM stns licensed to transmit digital signals but actual transmission numbers are significantly lower.

MEDIUMWAVE
Explanations
Call: Station call letters. All stns are required to announce their actual call letters and city of licence once per hour as close as possible to the top of the hour.
Ant: Type of licence and use of directional antenna. The symbols mean as follows: **U** means Unlimited Time operation, i.e. up to 24 hours a day. **U1** without directional antenna, **U2** with directional antenna at night, **U3** with directional antenna at all hours, same pattern, day and night, **U4** with directional antenna at all hours, different patterns day and night, **U5** with directional antenna daytime,

non-directional at night, **U6** with directional antenna at night and during critical hours, **U7** with different directional patterns for day, critical hours and night, **U8** as U7 but non-directional day, **U9** means directional day and night (different patterns), but non-directional during critical hours (usually on reduced power), **U10** means directional during critical hours only, **U11** means separate patterns for daytime and critical hours, nondirectional nights. **D** is daytime operation (between local sunrise and local sunset. The symbols mean as follows: **D** is daytime operation (between local sunrise and local sunset), **D1** without directional antenna, **D2** with directional antenna during critical hours only, **D3** with directional antenna, **D4** with directional antenna, differenct patterns during critical and non-critical hours, **D5** with directional antenna except during critical hours. **L** is limited time, and means a st. West of the dominant st. can operate from as early as sunrise at the dominant sts location; A st. East of the dominant st. can operate as late as the dominant sts sunset. Number indicates directional pattern as under "U" above.
D: Daytime power in kW. **N:** Nighttime power in kW.
City of License and Sta: City and State that the license has been issued to. **N.B:** Hawaii and Alaska are listed under separate country headings.
Scope: Due to the large number of stns in operation, the following list has been limited to stns operating at 2.5kW or more during the daytime (and in some cases where power has been increased to 2.5kW or more at night). Stations on 1230, 1240, 1340, 1400, 1450, 1490 kHz have been omitted due to their low power.

STATES: AL Alabama, AR Arkansas, AZ Arizona, CA California, CO Colorado, CT Connecticut, DE Delaware, FL Florida, GA Georgia, IA Iowa, ID Idaho, IL Illinois, IN Indiana, KS Kansas, KY Kentucky, LA Louisiana, MA Massachusetts, MD Maryland, ME Maine, MI Michigan, MN Minnesota, MO Missouri, MS Mississippi, MT Montana, NC North Carolina, ND North Dakota, NE Nebraska, NH New Hampshire, NJ New Jersey, NM New Mexico, NV Nevada, NY New York, OH Ohio, OK Oklahoma, OR Oregon, PA Pennsylvania, RI Rhode Island, SC South Carolina, SD South Dakota, TN Tennessee, TX Texas, UT Utah, VA Virginia, VT Vermont, WA Washington, WI Wisconsin, WV West Virginia, WY Wyoming.

MW	Call	kHz	Ant.	D	N	Sta	City of License
1)	WASG	540	U1	2.5	0.01	AL	Daphne
2)	KRXA	540	U4	10	0.5	CA	Carmel Valley
3)	KVIP	540	U1	2.5	0.01	CA	Redding
4)	WFLF	540	U4	50	46	FL	Pine Hills
5)	WDAK	540	U1	4	0.03	GA	Columbus
6)	KWMT	540	U3	5	0.17	IA	Fort Dodge
7)	KMLB	540	U1	4	0.02	LA	Monroe
8)	WETC	540	U4	4	0.5	NC	Wendell-Zebulon
9)	WRGC	540	U1	5	0.14	NC	Sylva
10)	KNMX	540	U3	5	0.02	NM	Las Vegas
11)	WLIE	540	U4	2.5	0.22	NY	Islip
12)	WWCS	540	U4	5	0.5	PA	Canonsburg
13)	WKFN	540	U1	4	0.05	TN	Clarksville
14)	KFYI	550	U1	5	1	AZ	Phoenix
15)	KUZZ	550	U4	5	5	CA	Bakersfield
16)	KRAI	550	U2	5	0.5	CO	Craig
17)	WAYR	550	U3	5	0.06	FL	Orange Park
18)	WDUN	550	U2	10	2.5	GA	Gainesville
19)	KFRM	550	U3	5	0.11	KS	Salina
20)	KTRS	550	U4	5	5	MO	Saint Louis
21)	KBOW	550	U2	5	1	MT	Butte
22)	KFYR	550	U2	5	5	ND	Bismarck
23)	WGR	550	U2	5	5	NY	Buffalo
24)	WKRC	550	U4	5	1	OH	Cincinnati
25)	KOAC	550	U4	5	5	OR	Corvallis
26)	KCRS	550	U4	5	1	TX	Midland
27)	KTSA	550	U2	5	5	TX	San Antonio
28)	WSVA	550	U2	5	1	VA	Harrisonburg
29)	WDEV	550	U4	5	1	VT	Waterbury
30)	KARI	550	U4	5	2.5	WA	Blaine
31)	WSAU	550	U4	15	20	WI	Wausau
32)	WOOF	560	U1	5	0.11	AL	Dothan
33)	KSFO	560	U2	5	5	CA	San Francisco
34)	KLZ	560	U3	5	5	CO	Denver
35)	WQAM	560	U1	5	1	FL	Miami
36)	WIND	560	U4	5	5	IL	Chicago
37)	WMIK	560	U1	2.5	0.08	KY	Middlesboro
38)	WHYN	560	U3	5	1	MA	Springfield
39)	WFRB	560	U1	5	0.05	MD	Frostburg
40)	WGAN	560	U4	5	5	ME	Portland
41)	WEBC	560	U4	5	5	MN	Duluth
42)	KWTO	560	U4	5	4	MO	Springfield
43)	KMON	560	U2	5	5	MT	Great Falls
44)	WFIL	560	U4	5	5	PA	Philadelphia

MW	Call	kHz	Ant.	D	N	Sta	City of License
45)	WXBT	560	U2	5	5	SC	Columbia
46)	WHBQ	560	U4	5	1	TN	Memphis
47)	WNSR	560	U4	4.5	0.07	TN	Brentwood
48)	KLVI	560	U2	5	5	TX	Beaumont
49)	KPQ	560	U2	5	5	WA	Wenatchee
50)	WJLS	560	U2	4.5	0.47	WV	Beckley
51)	WAAX	570	U2	5	0.5	AL	Gadsden
52)	KCFJ	570	U1	5	0.04	CA	Alturas
53)	KLAC	570	U2	5	5	CA	Los Angeles
54)	WTBN	570	U4	5	5	FL	Pinellas Park
55)	WSPZ	570	U4	5	1	MD	Bethesda
56)	WWNC	570	U2	5	5	NC	Asheville
57)	KSNM	570	U1	5	0.15	NM	Las Cruces
58)	WMCA	570	U4	5	5	NY	New York
59)	WSYR	570	U4	5	5	NY	Syracuse
60)	WKBN	570	U2	5	5	OH	Youngstown
61)	WNAX	570	U2	5	5	SD	Yankton
62)	KLIF	570	U4	5	5	TX	Dallas
63)	KNRS	570	U3	5	5	UT	Salt Lake City
64)	KVI	570	U1	5	5	WA	Seattle
65)	KSAZ	580	U2	5	0.39	AZ	Marana
66)	KMJ	580	U3	50	50	CA	Fresno
67)	KUBC	580	U2	5	1	CO	Montrose
68)	WDBO	580	U2	5	5	FL	Orlando
69)	WGAC	580	U2	5	0.84	GA	Augusta
70)	KIDO	580	U2	5	5	ID	Nampa
71)	WILL	580	U3	5	0.1	IL	Urbana
72)	WIBW	580	U2	5	5	KS	Topeka
73)	KJMJ	580	U2	5	1	LA	Alexandria
74)	WTAG	580	U4	5	5	MA	Worcester
75)	WTCM	580	U4	50	1.1	MI	Traverse City
76)	WKSK	580	U1	5	0.03	NC	West Jefferson
77)	WHP	580	U2	5	5	PA	Harrisburg
78)	WYHM	580	U1	5	0.04	TN	Rockwood
79)	WKTY	580	U4	5	0.74	WI	La Crosse
80)	WCHS	580	U2	5	5	WV	Charleston
81)	KZHS	590	U1	5	0.06	AR	Hot Springs
82)	KTHO	590	U2	2.5	0.5	CA	South Lake Tahoe
83)	KTIE	590	U4	2.5	0.96	CA	San Bernardino
84)	WDIZ	590	U2	1.7	2.5	FL	Panama City
85)	WDWD	590	U4	12	4.5	GA	Atlanta
86)	KID	590	U4	5	1	ID	Idaho Falls
87)	WVLK	590	U4	5	1	KY	Lexington
88)	WEZE	590	U2	5	5	MA	Boston
89)	WJMS	590	U2	5	1	MI	Ironwood
90)	WKZO	590	U2	5	5	MI	Kalamazoo
91)	KXSP	590	U1	5	5	NE	Omaha
92)	WROW	590	U4	5	1	NY	Albany
93)	KUGN	590	U2	5	5	OR	Eugene
94)	WARM	590	U3	5	5	PA	Scranton
95)	KLBJ	590	U2	5	1	TX	Austin
96)	KSUB	590	U2	5	1	UT	Cedar City
97)	KQNT	590	U1	5	5	WA	Spokane
98)	KOGO	600	U4	5	5	CA	San Diego
99)	KCOL	600	U4	5	0.5	CO	Wellington
100)	WBOB	600	U2	5	1.8	FL	Jacksonville
101)	WMT	600	U2	5	5	IA	Cedar Rapids
102)	WKYH	600	U1	5	0.04	KY	Paintsville
103)	WCAO	600	U3	5	5	MD	Baltimore
104)	WFST	600	U1	5	0.12	ME	Caribou
105)	KGEZ	600	U4	5	1	MT	Kalispell
106)	WSJS	600	U4	5	5	NC	Winston-Salem
107)	KSJB	600	U3	5	5	ND	Jamestown
108)	WREC	600	U4	5	5	TN	Memphis
109)	KROD	600	U2	5	5	TX	El Paso
110)	KTBB	600	U4	5	2.5	TX	Tyler
111)	WAGG	610	U2	5	1	AL	Birmingham
112)	KAVL	610	U4	4.9	4	CA	Lancaster
113)	KEAR	610	U1	5	5	CA	San Francisco
114)	KVLE	610	U1	5	0.21	CO	Vail
115)	WIOD	610	U4	5	5	FL	Miami
116)	KDAL	610	U2	5	5	MN	Duluth
117)	KCSP	610	U1	5	5	MO	Kansas City
118)	WFNZ	610	U4	5	1	NC	Charlotte
119)	WGIR	610	U4	5	1	NH	Manchester
120)	KNML	610	U2	5	5	NM	Albuquerque
121)	WTVN	610	U2	5	5	OH	Columbus
122)	KRTA	610	U4	2.5	5	OR	Medford
123)	WIP	610	U3	5	5	PA	Philadelphia
124)	KILT	610	U4	5	5	TX	Houston
125)	KVNU	610	U2	10	1	UT	Logan
126)	WVBE	610	U4	5	1	VA	Roanoke
127)	KONA	610	U4	5	5	WA	Kennewick-Richland-Pasco
128)	WJHX	620	U1	5	0.09	AL	Lexington
129)	KTAR	620	U2	5	5	AZ	Phoenix
130)	KJOL	620	U1	5	0.07	CO	Grand Junction
131)	WDAE	620	U2	5.6	5.5	FL	Saint Petersburg
132)	WTRP	620	U1	2.5	0.12	GA	La Grange
133)	WZON	620	U2	5	5	ME	Bangor
134)	WJDX	620	U2	5	1	MS	Jackson
135)	WDNC	620	U4	5	1	NC	Durham
136)	WSNR	620	U4	3	7.6	NJ	Jersey City
137)	WHEN	620	U2	5	1	NY	Syracuse
138)	KPOJ	620	U2	25	10	OR	Portland
139)	WKHB	620	U1	5.5	0.05	PA	Irwin
140)	WGCV	620	U1	2.5	0.12	SC	Cayce
141)	WRJZ	620	U2	5	5	TN	Knoxville
142)	KMKI	620	U2	5	4.5	TX	Plano
143)	WVMT	620	U4	5	5	VT	Burlington
144)	WTMJ	620	U4	50	10	WI	Milwaukee
145)	WWNR	620	U1	5	0.02	WV	Beckley
146)	KHOW	630	U4	5	5	CO	Denver
147)	WMAL	630	U4	10	5	DC	Washington
148)	WBMQ	630	U1	4.8	0.04	GA	Savannah
149)	WNEG	630	U1	5	0.04	GA	Toccoa
150)	KFXD	630	U4	5	5	ID	Boise
151)	WLAP	630	U4	5	1	KY	Lexington
152)	WREY	630	U4	1	2.5	MN	Saint Paul
153)	KJSL	630	U4	5	5	MO	Saint Louis
154)	KPLY	630	U2	5	1	NV	Reno
155)	KWRO	630	U1	5	0.04	OR	Coquille
156)	WPRO	630	U2	5	5	RI	Providence
157)	KSLR	630	U4	5	4.3	TX	San Antonio
158)	KCIS	630	U2	5	2.5	WA	Edmonds
159)	KFI	640	U1	50	50	CA	Los Angeles
160)	WMEN	640	U2	7.5	0.46	FL	Royal Palm Beach
161)	WGST	640	U4	50	1	GA	Atlanta
162)	WOI	640	U2	5	1	IA	Ames
163)	KTIB	640	U4	5	1	LA	Thibodaux
164)	WNNZ	640	U4	50	1	MA	Westfield
165)	KGVW	640	U4	10	1	MT	Belgrade
166)	WFNC	640	U1	10	1	NC	Fayetteville
167)	WWJZ	640	U4	50	0.95	NJ	Mount Holly
168)	WHLO	640	U4	5	0.5	OH	Akron
169)	KWPN	640	U4	5	1	OK	Moore
170)	WCRV	640	U2	50	0.48	TN	Collierville
171)	WXSM	640	U2	10	0.81	TN	Blountville
172)	KSTE	650	U4	21.4	0.92	CA	Rancho Cordova
173)	WNMT	650	U2	10	1	MN	Nashwauk
174)	WSM	650	U1	50	50	TN	Nashville
175)	KMTI	650	U4	10	0.9	UT	Manti
176)	KGAB	650	U2	8.5	0.5	WY	Orchard Valley
177)	WXQW	660	U2	10	0.85	AL	Fairhope
178)	KTNN	660	U2	50	50	AZ	Window Rock
179)	KWVE	660	U4	8	6	CA	Oildale
180)	WBHR	660	U4	10	0.5	MN	Sauk Rapids
181)	KEYZ	660	U4	5	5	ND	Williston
182)	WFAN	660	U1	50	50	NY	New York
183)	KXOR	660	U1	10	0.07	OR	Junction City
184)	WLFJ	660	D1	50		SC	Greenville
185)	KSKY	660	U4	20	0.7	TX	Balch Springs
186)	KAPS	660	U4	10	1	WA	Mount Vernon
187)	WYLS	670	D1	4.8		AL	York
188)	KWXI	670	D1	5		AR	Glenwood
189)	KIRN	670	U3	5	3	CA	Simi Valley
190)	KLTT	670	U4	50	1.4	CO	Commerce City
191)	WWFE	670	U4	50	1	FL	Miami
192)	KBOI	670	U2	50	50	ID	Boise
193)	WSCR	670	U1	50	50	IL	Chicago
194)	KMZQ	670	U4	30	0.6	NV	Las Vegas
195)	WIEZ	670	U4	5.4		PA	Lewistown
196)	WMTY	670	D1	2.5		TN	Farragut
197)	WRJR	670	U5	20	0.003	VA	Claremont
198)	KNBR	680	U1	50	50	CA	San Francisco
199)	WCNN	680	U4	50	10	GA	North Atlanta
200)	WRKO	680	U4	50	50	MA	Boston
201)	WCBM	680	U4	50	20	MD	Baltimore
202)	WDBC	680	U4	10	1	MI	Escanaba
203)	KFEQ	680	U4	5	5	MO	Saint Joseph
204)	KKGR	680	D1	5		MT	East Helena
205)	WPTF	680	U2	50	50	NC	Raleigh
206)	WINR	680	U4	5	0.5	NY	Binghamton
207)	WMFS	680	U4	10	5	TN	Memphis
208)	KKYX	680	U2	50	10	TX	San Antonio
209)	KOMW	680	D1	5		WA	Omak
210)	WOGO	680	U4	2.5	0.5	WI	Hallie
211)	WKAZ	680	U4	10	0.22	WV	Charleston
212)	WJOX	690	U2	50	0.6	AL	Birmingham
213)	WADS	690	D3	3.2		CT	Ansonia
214)	WOKV	690	U4	50	25	FL	Jacksonville
215)	KGGF	690	U4	10	5	KS	Coffeyville
216)	WIST	690	U4	10	5	LA	New Orleans

MW	Call	kHz	Ant.	D	N	Sta	City of License
217)	WNZK	690	D3	2.5		MI	Dearborn Heights
218)	KTSM	690	U4	10	10	TX	El Paso
219)	WZAP	690	U1	10	0.01	VA	Bristol
220)	WELD	690	U1	3	0.01	WV	Fisher
221)	KMBX	700	U1	2.5	0.7	CA	Soledad
222)	WTUB	700	D1	2.5		MA	Orange-Athol
223)	WDMV	700	D3	5		MD	Walkersville
224)	WLW	700	U1	50	50	OH	Cincinnati
225)	KGRV	700	U1	23	0.47	OR	Winston
226)	KSEV	700	U4	15	1	TX	Tomball
227)	KALL	700	U4	50	10	UT	North Salt Lake City
228)	KXLX	700	U2	10	0.6	WA	Airway Heights
229)	KBMB	710	U4	22	3.9	AZ	Black Canyon City
230)	KFIA	710	U4	25	1	CA	Carmichael
231)	KSPN	710	U2	50	10	CA	Los Angeles
232)	KNUS	710	U3	5	5	CO	Denver
233)	WAQI	710	U4	50	50	FL	Miami
234)	WUFF	710	D1	2.5		GA	Eastman
235)	WEKC	710	D1	4.2		KY	Williamsburg
236)	KEEL	710	U4	50	5	LA	Shreveport
237)	KCMO	710	U4	10	5	MO	Kansas City
238)	WEGG	710	D1	2.5		NC	Rose Hill
239)	KXMR	710	U7	50	4	ND	Bismarck
240)	WOR	710	U4	50	50	NY	New York
241)	KGNC	710	U4	10	10	TX	Amarillo
242)	WFNR	710	D3	10		VA	Blacksburg
243)	KIRO	710	U2	50	50	WA	Seattle
244)	WDSM	710	U2	10	5	WI	Superior
245)	WRZN	720	U2	10	0.25	FL	Hernando
246)	WVCC	720	D1	7.97		GA	Hogansville
247)	WGN	720	U1	50	50	IL	Chicago
248)	WGCR	720	U1	50		NC	Pisgah Forest
249)	KDWN	720	U2	50	50	NV	Las Vegas
250)	KFIR	720	U1	10	0.18	OR	Sweet Home
251)	KSAH	720	U4	10	0.89	TX	Universal City
252)	WSTT	730	U1	5	0.02	GA	Thomasville
253)	KINF	730	U4	15	0.5	ID	Boise
254)	WMTC	730	U3	5	0.05	KY	Vancleve
255)	WACE	730	U1	5	0.008	MA	Chicopee
256)	KYYA	730	U1	5	0.23	MT	Billings
257)	WZGV	730	U1	10	0.19	NC	Cramerton
258)	WPIT	730	U1	5	0.02	PA	Pittsburgh
259)	WLTQ	730	U1	5	0.1	SC	Charleston
260)	WTNT	730	U1	8	0.02	VA	Alexandria
261)	WMSP	740	U4	10	0.23	AL	Montgomery
262)	KBRT	740	U3	10	0.11	CA	Avalon
263)	KCBS	740	U4	50	50	CA	San Francisco
264)	KVOR	740	U4	3.3	1.5	CO	Colorado Springs
265)	WSBR	740	U3	2.5	0.94	FL	Boca Raton
266)	WYGM	740	U4	50	50	FL	Orlando
267)	WNOP	740	U4	2.5	0.03	KY	Newport
268)	WPAQ	740	U1	10	0.007	NC	Mount Airy
269)	KVOX	740	U7	50	0.94	ND	Fargo
270)	WNYH	740	U3	25	0.04	NY	Huntington
271)	KRMG	740	U4	50	25	OK	Tulsa
272)	KTRH	740	U4	50	50	TX	Houston
273)	WDGY	740	D3	2.5		WI	Hudson
274)	WSB	750	U1	50	50	GA	Atlanta
275)	WNDZ	750	D3	15		IN	Portage
276)	KBNN	750	D1	5		MO	Lebanon
277)	KERR	750	U2	50	1	MT	Polson
278)	KMMJ	750	L3	10.5		NE	Grand Island
279)	KHWG	750	U1	10	0.25	NV	Fallon
280)	KXTG	750	U4	50	20	OR	Portland
281)	KAMA	750	U4	10	1	TX	El Paso
282)	KOAL	750	U2	10	6.8	UT	Price
283)	KMTL	760	D1	10		AR	Sherwood
284)	KFMB	760	U2	5	50	CA	San Diego
285)	KKZN	760	U4	50	1	CO	Thornton
286)	WEFL	760	U4	3	1.5	FL	Tequesta
287)	WLCC	760	U4	10	1	FL	Brandon
288)	KCCV	760	U4	6	0.2	KS	Overland Park
289)	WVNE	760	D1	25		MA	Leicester
290)	WJR	760	U1	50	50	MI	Detroit
291)	WCIS	760	D1	3.5		NC	Morganton
292)	WCHP	760	U4	35	0.01	NY	Champlain
293)	KTKR	760	U4	50	1	TX	San Antonio
294)	WVNN	770	U2	7	0.25	AL	Athens
295)	KCBC	770	U4	50	4.1	CA	Manteca
296)	WWCN	770	U4	10	0.63	FL	North Fort Myers
297)	KUOM	770	D1	5		MN	Minneapolis
298)	KATL	770	U2	10	1	MT	Miles City
299)	WLWL	770	D1	5		NC	Rockingham
300)	KKOB	770	U2	50	50	NM	Albuquerque
301)	WABC	770	U1	50	50	NY	New York
302)	WTOR	770	D3	13		NY	Youngstown

MW	Call	kHz	Ant.	D	N	Sta	City of License
303)	KAAM	770	U4	10	1	TX	Garland
304)	WYRV	770	D1	5		VA	Cedar Bluff
305)	KTTH	770	U4	50	5	WA	Seattle
306)	WZZX	780	D1	5		AL	Lineville
307)	KAZM	780	U2	5	0.25	AZ	Sedona
308)	WBBM	780	U1	50	50	IL	Chicago
309)	WTME	780	U1	10	0.01	ME	Rumford
310)	WXME	780	U1	5	0.06	ME	Monticello
311)	WIIN	780	D1	5		MS	Ridgeland
312)	WCKB	780	U1	7	0.001	NC	Dunn
313)	WWOL	780	D1	10		NC	Forest City
314)	KKOH	780	U2	50	50	NV	Reno
315)	WAVA	780	D1	12		VA	Arlington
316)	WTSK	790	U1	5	0.03	AL	Tuscaloosa
317)	KURM	790	U2	5	0.5	AR	Rogers
318)	KNST	790	U4	5	0.5	AZ	Tucson
319)	KABC	790	U4	5	5	CA	Los Angeles
320)	KEJY	790	U1	5	0.11	CA	Eureka
321)	KFPT	790	U4	5	2.5	CA	Clovis
322)	WAXY	790	U4	5	5	FL	South Miami
323)	WLBE	790	U2	5	1	FL	Leesburg
324)	WQXI	790	U2	28	1	GA	Atlanta
325)	KXXX	790	U1	5	0.02	KS	Colby
326)	WKRD	790	U4	5	1	KY	Louisville
327)	WSGW	790	U4	5	1	MI	Saginaw
328)	KGHL	790	U1	5	1.8	MT	Billings
329)	WBLO	790	U1	10	0.02	NC	Thomasville
330)	KFGO	790	U2	5	5	ND	Fargo
331)	WAEB	790	U4	3.6	1.5	PA	Allentown
332)	WPRV	790	U2	5	5	RI	Providence
333)	WETB	790	U1	5	0.07	TN	Johnson City
334)	WMC	790	U2	5	5	TN	Memphis
335)	KBME	790	U4	5	5	TX	Houston
336)	KFYO	790	U4	5	1	TX	Lubbock
337)	WNIS	790	U3	5	5	VA	Norfolk
338)	KGMI	790	U2	5	1	WA	Bellingham
339)	KJRB	790	U4	5	3.8	WA	Spokane
340)	WAYY	790	U2	5	5	WI	Eau Claire
341)	KBRV	800	U1	10	0.15	ID	Soda Springs
342)	WNNW	800	U1	3	0.24	MA	Lawrence
343)	WVAL	800	U4	2.6	0.85	MN	Sauk Rapids
344)	WTMR	800	U4	5	0.5	NJ	Camden
345)	KQCV	800	U4	2.5	1	OK	Oklahoma City
346)	WSVS	800	U1	10	0.27	VA	Crewe

MW	Call	kHz	Ant.	D	N	Sta	City of License
347)	WDUX	800	U3	5	0.5	WI	Waupaca
348)	WVHU	800	U1	5	0.18	WV	Huntington
349)	WCKA	810	U4	50	0.5	AL	Jacksonville
350)	KGO	810	U3	50	50	CA	San Francisco
351)	WRSO	810	U4	10	0.4	FL	Orlovista
352)	WTHV	810	D1	2.5		GA	Hahira
353)	WEKG	810	D1	5		KY	Jackson
354)	WMJH	810	D1	3.6		MI	Rockford
355)	WHB	810	U2	50	5	MO	Kansas City
356)	WSJC	810	U2	50	0.5	MS	Magee
357)	KSWV	810	U1	5	0.01	NM	Santa Fe
358)	WGY	810	U1	50	50	NY	Schenectady
359)	WQIZ	810	D1	5		SC	Saint George
360)	KBHB	810	U1	25	0.06	SD	Sturgis
361)	WMGC	810	U1	5	0.006	TN	Murfreesboro
362)	WPIN	810	D1	4.2		VA	Dublin
363)	KTBI	810	D1	50		WA	Ephrata
364)	WWBA	820	U4	50	1	FL	Largo
365)	WCPT	820	U2	5	1.5	IL	Willow Springs
366)	WWFD	820	U4	4.3	0.43	MD	Frederick
367)	WNYC	820	U4	10	1	NY	New York
368)	WWLZ	820	U4	4.1	0.85	NY	Horseheads
369)	WVSG	820	U2	5	0.79	OH	Columbus
370)	WBAP	820	U1	50	50	TX	Fort Worth
371)	KUTR	820	U8	50	2.5	UT	Taylorsville
372)	WGGM	820	U1	10	1	VA	Chester
373)	KGNW	820	U4	50	5	WA	Burien-Seattle
374)	KFLT	830	U2	50	1	AZ	Tucson
375)	KLAA	830	U2	50	20	CA	Orange
376)	KNCO	830	U2	5	5	CA	Grass Valley
377)	WFNO	830	U4	5	0.75	LA	Norco
378)	WCRN	830	U4	50	50	MA	Worcester
379)	WCCO	830	U1	50	50	MN	Minneapolis
380)	WTRU	830	U4	10	10	NC	Kernersville
381)	WEEU	830	U4	20	6	PA	Reading
382)	KOTC	830	D1	3		TN	Memphis
383)	KUYO	830	D1	25		WY	Evansville
384)	WBHY	840	D1	10		AL	Mobile
385)	KMPH	840	U4	5	5	CA	Modesto
386)	WHAS	840	U1	50	50	KY	Louisville
387)	KWDF	840	D1	8		LA	Ball
388)	KTIC	840	D1	5		NE	West Point
389)	KXNT	840	U4	50	25	NV	North Las Vegas
390)	WCEO	840	D3	50		SC	Columbia
391)	KVJY	840	U4	5	1	TX	Pharr
392)	WKTR	840	D3	8.2		VA	Earlysville
393)	KMAX	840	U1	10	0.28	WA	Colfax
394)	WXJC	850	U4	50	1	AL	Birmingham
395)	KOA	850	U1	50	50	CO	Denver
396)	WAXB	850	D1	2.5		CT	Ridgefield
397)	WFTL	850	U4	5	1	FL	West Palm Beach
398)	WRUF	850	U2	5	5	FL	Gainesville
399)	WAIT	850	D3	2.5		IL	Crystal Lake
400)	WEEI	850	U4	50	50	MA	Boston
401)	WWJC	850	D1	10		MN	Duluth
402)	KFUO	850	D1	5		MO	Clayton
403)	WQST	850	D1	10		MS	Forest
404)	WPTK	850	U2	10	5	NC	Raleigh
405)	WKNR	850	U4	50	4.7	OH	Cleveland
406)	WKGE	850	U3	10	10	PA	Johnstown
407)	WKVL	850	D3	50		TN	Knoxville
408)	KEYH	850	U4	10	0.18	TX	Houston
409)	KJON	850	D3	5		TX	Carrollton
410)	WTAR	850	U4	50	25	VA	Norfolk
411)	KHHO	850	U4	10	1	WA	Tacoma
412)	KTRB	860	U2	50	50	CA	San Francisco
413)	WGUL	860	U4	5	1.5	FL	Dunedin
414)	WAEC	860	U12	5	0.5	GA	Atlanta
415)	WDMG	860	U2	5	5	GA	Douglas
416)	KKOW	860	U2	10	5	KS	Pittsburg
417)	WSBS	860	U2	2.7	0.004	MA	Great Barrington
418)	WFSI	860	U4	2.5	0.06	MD	Baltimore
419)	KPAM	860	U2	50	15	OR	Troutdale
420)	WWDB	860	D3	10		PA	Philadelphia
421)	KONO	860	U2	5	0.9	TX	San Antonio
422)	KKAT	860	U1	10	0.19	UT	Salt Lake City
423)	WOAY	860	U1	10	0.01	WV	Oak Hill
424)	WQRX	870	D1	10		AL	Valley Head
425)	KRLA	870	U4	50	3	CA	Glendale
426)	WWL	870	U3	50	50	LA	New Orleans
427)	WLVP	870	U4	10	1	ME	Gorham
428)	WKAR	870	D3	10		MI	East Lansing
429)	KPRM	870	U2	25	1	MN	Park Rapids
430)	WTCG	870	D1	5		NC	Mount Holly
431)	KLSQ	870	U2	5	0.43	NV	Whitney
432)	WHCU	870	U2	5	1	NY	Ithaca
433)	WPWT	870	D1	10		TN	Colonial Heights
434)	KFLD	870	U1	10	0.25	WA	Pasco
435)	KLRG	880	U2	50	0.22	AR	Sheridan
436)	KKMC	880	U4	10	10	CA	Gonzales
437)	WZAB	880	U4	4	5	FL	Sweetwater
438)	WBKZ	880	D1	5		GA	Jefferson
439)	KJJR	880	U1	10	0.5	MT	Whitefish
440)	WPEK	880	D1	5		NC	Fairview
441)	KRVN	880	U2	50	50	NE	Lexington
442)	KHAC	880	U1	10	0.43	NM	Tse Bonito
443)	WCBS	880	U1	50	50	NY	New York
444)	WRFD	880	D1	23		OH	Columbus-Worthington
445)	KWIP	880	U1	5	1	OR	Dallas
446)	WMDB	880	U1	2.5	0.002	TN	Nashville
447)	KJOZ	880	U4	10	1	TX	Conroe
448)	KIXI	880	U4	50	10	WA	Mercer Island-Seattle
449)	WMEQ	880	U2	10	0.21	WI	Menomonie
450)	WYAM	890	D1	2.5		AL	Hartselle
451)	KLFF	890	U4	5	5	CA	Arroyo Grande
452)	KJME	890	U4	5	0.58	CO	Fountain
453)	WJTP	890	D1	5		GA	Lithia Springs
454)	KYWN	890	U2	50	0.25	ID	Meridian
455)	WLS	890	U1	50	50	IL	Chicago
456)	WAMG	890	U4	25	6	MA	Dedham
457)	WHJA	890	D1	10		MS	Laurel
458)	WBAJ	890	D1	50		SC	Blythewood
459)	KTXV	890	U4	20	0.25	TX	Mabank
460)	KVOZ	890	U2	10	1	TX	Del Mar Hills
461)	KDXU	890	U2	10	10	UT	Saint George
462)	WKNV	890	D3	10		VA	Fairlawn
463)	WJWL	900	U4	10.5	1.08	DE	Georgetown
464)	WMOP	900	U1	2.7	0.02	FL	Ocala
465)	WJLG	900	U1	4.35	0.15	GA	Savannah
466)	WLSI	900	U1	3.5	0.12	KY	Pikeville
467)	KTIS	900	U4	50	0.5	MN	Minneapolis
468)	WYCV	900	U1	2.5	0.25	NC	Granite Falls
469)	WCPA	900	U4	2.5	0.5	PA	Clearfield
470)	WKDA	900	U1	5	0.13	TN	Lebanon
471)	KREH	900	U4	5	0.01	TX	Pecan Grove
472)	WKDW	900	U1	2.5	0.12	VA	Staunton
473)	KLCN	910	U1	5	0.08	AR	Blytheville
474)	KGME	910	U2	5	5	AZ	Phoenix
475)	KECR	910	U4	5	5	CA	El Cajon
476)	KKSF	910	U2	20	5	CA	Oakland
477)	KOXR	910	U3	5	1	CA	Oxnard
478)	KPOF	910	U1	5	1	CO	Denver
479)	WLAT	910	U2	5	5	CT	New Britain
480)	WTWD	910	U3	5	5	FL	Plant City
481)	WRFV	910	U2	5	5	GA	Valdosta
482)	WSUI	910	U2	5	4	IA	Iowa City
483)	WAEI	910	U2	5	5	ME	Bangor
484)	WFDF	910	U4	50	25	MI	Farmington Hills
485)	WALT	910	U1	5	1	MS	Meridian
486)	WSRP	910	U2	5	5	NC	Jacksonville
487)	KCJB	910	U4	5	5	ND	Minot
488)	KBIM	910	U2	5	0.5	NM	Roswell
489)	WLTP	910	U5	5	0.04	OH	Marietta
490)	WAVL	910	U4	5	0.06	PA	Apollo
491)	WSBA	910	U4	5	1	PA	York
492)	WOLI	910	U4	3.6	0.89	SC	Spartanburg
493)	WEPG	910	U1	5	0.09	TN	South Pittsburg
494)	WJCW	910	U2	5	1	TN	Johnson City
495)	KRIO	910	U2	5	5	TX	McAllen
496)	KWDZ	910	U4	5	1	UT	Salt Lake City
497)	WRNL	910	U2	5	1.5	VA	Richmond
498)	KKSN	910	U4	3.3	4.3	WA	Vancouver
499)	WHSM	910	U1	5	0.07	WI	Hayward
500)	KARN	920	U2	5	5	AR	Little Rock
501)	KPSI	920	U2	5	1	CA	Palm Springs
502)	KVIN	920	U4	0.5	2.5	CA	Ceres
503)	KLMR	920	U2	5	0.5	CO	Lamar
504)	WDMC	920	U2	5	1	FL	Melbourne
505)	WGKA	920	U1	14	0.49	GA	Atlanta
506)	KYFR	920	U4	5	2.5	IA	Shenandoah
507)	WBAA	920	U2	5	1	IN	West Lafayette
508)	WTCW	920	U1	4.2	0.04	KY	Whitesburg
509)	KDHL	920	U2	5	5	MN	Faribault
510)	WPCM	920	U1	5	0.05	NC	Burlington-Graham
511)	KBAD	920	U2	5	0.5	NV	Las Vegas
512)	KIHM	920	U4	4.6	0.85	NV	Reno
513)	WGHQ	920	U2	5	0.07	NY	Kingston
514)	WIRD	920	U1	10	0.08	NY	Lake Placid
515)	WHJJ	920	U2	5	5	RI	Providence
516)	KKLS	920	U3	5	0.11	SD	Rapid City
517)	KYST	920	U2	5	1	TX	Texas City
518)	KVEL	920	U2	5	1	UT	Vernal

MW	Call	kHz	Ant.	D	N	Sta	City of License	MW	Call	kHz	Ant.	D	N	Sta	City of License
519)	WURA	920	U4	7	0.97	VA	Quantico	605)	KJR	950	U4	50	50	WA	Seattle
520)	KGTK	920	U2	3	0.007	WA	Olympia	606)	WBES	950	U2	5	1	WV	Charleston
521)	KXLY	920	U1	20	5	WA	Spokane	607)	WERC	**960**	U2	5	5	AL	Birmingham
522)	WOKY	920	U4	5	1	WI	Milwaukee	608)	WLPR	960	U1	6	0.03	AL	Prichard
523)	WMMN	920	U1	5	0.2	WV	Fairmont	609)	KCGS	960	U1	5	0.04	AR	Marshall
524)	WEZZ	**930**	U1	5	0.04	AL	Monroeville	610)	KKNT	960	U2	5	5	AZ	Phoenix
525)	WJBY	930	U2	5	0.5	AL	Rainbow City	611)	KIXW	960	U1	5	0.02	CA	Apple Valley
526)	KAFF	930	U1	5	0.03	AZ	Flagstaff	612)	KNEW	960	U3	5	5	CA	Oakland
527)	KAPR	930	U1	2.5	0.07	AZ	Douglas	613)	WELI	960	U2	5	5	CT	New Haven
528)	KHJ	930	U2	5	5	CA	Los Angeles	614)	WJYZ	960	U4	5	0.39	GA	Albany
529)	KIUP	930	U1	5	0.1	CO	Durango	615)	WRFC	960	U2	5	2.5	GA	Athens
530)	KRKY	930	U1	4.5	0.12	CO	Granby	616)	KMA	960	U2	5	5	IA	Shenandoah
531)	WFXJ	930	U2	5	5	FL	Jacksonville	617)	WSBT	960	U4	5	5	IN	South Bend
532)	WLSS	930	U4	5	3	FL	Sarasota	618)	WPRT	960	U1	3.8	0.01	KY	Prestonsburg
533)	WMGR	930	U2	5	0.5	GA	Bainbridge	619)	WFGL	960	U4	2.5	1	MA	Fitchburg
534)	KSEI	930	U2	5	5	ID	Pocatello	620)	WTGM	960	U4	5	5	MD	Salisbury
535)	WAUR	930	U4	2.5	4.2	IL	Sandwich	621)	WHAK	960	U1	5	0.13	MI	Rogers City
536)	WTAD	930	U2	5	1	IL	Quincy	622)	KLTF	960	U1	5	0.03	MN	Little Falls
537)	WKCT	930	U2	5	0.5	KY	Bowling Green	623)	KZIM	960	U2	5	0.5	MO	Cape Girardeau
538)	WFMD	930	U4	5	2.5	MD	Frederick	624)	KFLN	960	U1	5	0.09	MT	Baker
539)	WBCK	930	U4	5	1	MI	Battle Creek	625)	WCRU	960	U4	10	0.5	NC	Dallas
540)	KKIN	930	U1	2.5	0.36	MN	Aitkin	626)	WRNS	960	U2	5	1	NC	Kinston
541)	KWOC	930	U2	5	0.5	MO	Poplar Bluff	627)	KNEB	960	U4	5	0.35	NE	Scottsbluff
542)	WSFZ	930	U2	3.8	3.1	MS	Jackson	628)	KNDN	960	U1	5	0.16	NM	Farmington
543)	KMPT	930	U2	5	1	MT	East Missoula	629)	WEAV	960	U4	5	5	NY	Plattsburgh
544)	WDLX	930	U2	5	1	NC	Washington	630)	KLAD	960	U2	5	5	OR	Klamath Falls
545)	WYFQ	930	U2	5	1	NC	Charlotte	631)	WATS	960	U1	5	0.05	PA	Sayre
546)	KOGA	930	U4	5	0.5	NE	Ogallala	632)	WHYL	960	U4	5	0.02	PA	Carlisle
547)	WPKX	930	U2	5	5	NH	Rochester	633)	KGKL	960	U2	5	1	TX	San Angelo
548)	WPAT	930	U4	5	5	NJ	Paterson	634)	KOVO	960	U2	5	1	UT	Provo
549)	WBEN	930	U2	5	5	NY	Buffalo	635)	WFIR	960	U2	5	5	VA	Roanoke
550)	WKY	930	U2	5	5	OK	Oklahoma City	636)	KALE	960	U2	5	1	WA	Richland
551)	KAGI	930	U1	5	0.12	OR	Grants Pass	637)	WERH	**970**	D1	5		AL	Hamilton
552)	KSDN	930	U4	5	1	SD	Aberdeen	638)	WTBF	970	U1	5	0.04	AL	Troy
553)	WSEV	930	U1	5	0.14	TN	Sevierville	639)	KVWM	970	U1	5	0.19	AZ	Show Low
554)	KLUP	930	U2	5	1	TX	Terrell Hills	640)	KHTY	970	U1	1	5	CA	Bakersfield
555)	WLLL	930	U1	9	0.04	VA	Lynchburg	641)	KNWZ	970	U4	5	1	CA	Coachella
556)	KYAK	930	U1	10	0.12	WA	Yakima	642)	KFEL	970	U1	3.2	0.18	CO	Pueblo
557)	WLBL	930	U1	5	0.07	WI	Auburndale	643)	WFLA	970	U4	25	11	FL	Tampa
558)	WRVC	930	U2	5	1	WV	Huntington	644)	WNIV	970	U1	5	0.03	GA	Atlanta
559)	KROE	930	U1	5	0.11	WY	Sheridan	645)	WVOP	970	U1	4	0.06	GA	Vidalia
560)	KYNO	**940**	U4	50	50	CA	Fresno	646)	KFTA	970	U2	2.5	0.9	ID	Rupert
561)	WINZ	940	U2	50	10	FL	Miami	647)	WFSR	970	U1	5	0.02	KY	Harlan
562)	WMAC	940	U2	50	10	GA	Macon	648)	WGTK	970	U2	5	5	KY	Louisville
563)	KPSZ	940	U2	10	5	IA	Des Moines	649)	WZAN	970	U2	5	5	ME	Portland
564)	WMIX	940	U4	5	1.5	IL	Mount Vernon	650)	WZAM	970	U1	5	0.06	MI	Ishpeming
565)	WYLD	940	U4	10	0.5	LA	New Orleans	651)	KQAQ	970	U3	5	0.5	MN	Austin
566)	WIDG	940	U1	5	0.004	MI	Saint Ignace	652)	KBUL	970	U2	5	5	MT	Billings
567)	WCPC	940	U4	50	0.25	MS	Houston	653)	WYSE	970	U1	5	0.03	NC	Canton
568)	WKYK	940	U2	4.6	0.01	NC	Burnsville	654)	WDAY	970	U2	5	5	ND	Fargo
569)	KVSH	940	U1	5	0.01	NE	Valentine	655)	KJLT	970	U1	5	0.05	NE	North Platte
570)	KICE	940	U4	10	0.06	OR	Bend	656)	WNYM	970	U4	50	50	NJ	Hackensack
571)	WECO	940	U1	5	0.01	TN	Wartburg	657)	KNUU	970	U4	5	0.5	NV	Paradise
572)	KIXZ	940	U4	5	1	TX	Amarillo	658)	WNED	970	U3	5	5	NY	Buffalo
573)	KTFS	940	U1	2.5	0.01	TX	Texarkana	659)	WFUN	970	U4	5	1	OH	Ashtabula
574)	KOBY	940	U1	10	0.03	UT	Cedar City	660)	KCFO	970	U4	2.5	1	OK	Tulsa
575)	WKGM	940	U2	10	3.1	VA	Smithfield	661)	KUFO	970	U2	5	5	OR	Portland
576)	WNRG	940	U1	5	0.01	VA	Grundy	662)	WBGG	970	U4	5	5	PA	Pittsburgh
577)	KXJK	**950**	U1	5	0.08	AR	Forrest City	663)	WJMX	970	U2	10	3	SC	Florence
578)	KAHI	950	U4	5	5	CA	Auburn	664)	WKCI	970	U1	5	1	VA	Waynesboro
579)	KRWZ	950	U3	5	5	CO	Denver	665)	KTTO	970	U2	5	1	WA	Spokane
580)	WTLN	950	U2	12	5	FL	Orlando	666)	WHA	970	U1	5	0.05	WI	Madison
581)	WGOV	950	U1	3.5	0.06	GA	Valdosta	667)	KCAB	**980**	U1	5	0.03	AR	Dardanelle
582)	WGTA	950	U1	5	0.11	GA	Summerville	668)	KDBV	980	U4	10	10	CA	Salinas
583)	KOEL	950	U4	5	0.5	IA	Oelwein	669)	KFWB	980	U1	5	5	CA	Los Angeles
584)	KMHR	950	U1	3.5	0.03	ID	Boise	670)	KWSW	980	U2	5	0.5	CA	Eureka
585)	KOZE	950	U4	5	1	ID	Lewiston	671)	WTEM	980	U4	50	5	DC	Washington
586)	WNTD	950	U2	1	5	IL	Chicago	672)	WDVH	980	U1	5	0.16	FL	Gainesville
587)	WXLW	950	U1	5	0.11	IN	Indianapolis	673)	WHSR	980	U4	5	2.2	FL	Pompano Beach
588)	WROL	950	U1	5	0.09	MA	Boston	674)	WRNE	980	U2	4	1	FL	Gulf Breeze
589)	WCTN	950	U3	2.5	0.06	MD	Potomac-Cabin John	675)	WPGA	980	U1	2.6	0.08	GA	Perry
590)	WWJ	950	U4	50	50	MI	Detroit	676)	KSPZ	980	U4	5	1	ID	Ammon
591)	KWOS	950	U2	5	0.5	MO	Jefferson City	677)	KOKA	980	U1	5	0.07	LA	Shreveport
592)	WHSY	950	U1	5	0.06	MS	Hattiesburg	678)	WCAP	980	U4	5	5	MA	Lowell
593)	KMTX	950	U2	5	5	MT	Helena	679)	KKMS	980	U3	5	5	MN	Richfield
594)	KDCE	950	U1	4.2	0.08	NM	Española	680)	KMBZ	980	U2	5	5	MO	Kansas City
595)	KNFT	950	U1	5	0.22	NM	Bayard	681)	WAKK	980	U1	5	0.15	MS	McComb
596)	WIBX	950	U3	5	5	NY	Utica	682)	WAAV	980	U2	5	5	NC	Leland
597)	KTBR	950	U1	3.4	0.02	OR	Roseburg	683)	KVLV	980	D1	5		NV	Fallon
598)	WPEN	950	U4	43	21	PA	Philadelphia	684)	WOFX	980	U2	5	5	NY	Troy
599)	WJKB	950	U4	10	6	SC	Moncks Corner	685)	WONE	980	U2	5	5	OH	Dayton
600)	WORD	950	U2	5	5	SC	Spartanburg	686)	WILK	980	U2	5	1	PA	Wilkes-Barre
601)	WAKM	950	U1	5	0.08	TN	Franklin	687)	WBZK	980	U3	3	0.16	SC	York
602)	KJTV	950	U4	5	0.5	TX	Lubbock	688)	KDSJ	980	U2	5	1	SD	Deadwood
603)	KPRC	950	U2	5	5	TX	Houston	689)	WYFN	980	U2	5	5	TN	Nashville
604)	WXGI	950	U1	3.9	0.04	VA	Richmond	690)	KRTX	980	U4	5	4	TX	Rosenberg-Richmond

MW	Call	kHz	Ant.	D	N	Sta	City of License
691)	KSVC	980	U2	10	1	UT	Richfield
692)	WFHG	980	U2	5	1	VA	Bristol
693)	KBBO	980	U4	5	0.5	WA	Selah
694)	WCUB	980	U4	5	5	WI	Two Rivers
695)	WHAW	980	U1	25	0.04	WV	Lost Creek
696)	KTKT	990	U4	10	1	AZ	Tucson
697)	KATD	990	U4	10	5	CA	Pittsburg
698)	KTMS	990	U5	5	0.5	CA	Santa Barbara
699)	KRKS	990	U2	6.5	0.39	CO	Denver
700)	WXCT	990	U4	2.5	0.08	CT	Southington
701)	WDYZ	990	U4	50	14	FL	Orlando
702)	WMYM	990	U4	5	5	FL	Miami
703)	WDEO	990	U4	9.2	0.25	MI	Ypsilanti
704)	KRMO	990	U1	2.5	0.04	MO	Cassville
705)	WEEB	990	U1	10	0.02	NC	Southern Pines
706)	WDCX	990	U4	5	2.5	NY	Rochester
707)	WNTP	990	U4	50	10	PA	Philadelphia
708)	WNTW	990	U3	10	0.1	PA	Somerset
709)	WALE	990	U4	5	5	RI	Greenville
710)	KWAM	990	U4	10	0.45	TN	Memphis
711)	WNML	990	U2	10	10	TN	Knoxville
712)	KFCD	990	U4	7	0.92	TX	Farmersville
713)	WNRV	990	U1	5	0.01	VA	Narrows-Pearisburg
714)	KCEO	1000	U4	2.5	0.25	CA	Vista
715)	WYBT	1000	D1	5		FL	Blountstown
716)	WMVP	1000	U4	50	50	IL	Chicago
717)	WXTN	1000	D1	5		MS	Benton
718)	KKIM	1000	U1	10	0.03	NM	Albuquerque
719)	WLNL	1000	D1	5		NY	Horseheads
720)	KTOK	1000	U4	5	5	OK	Oklahoma City
721)	KXRB	1000	U4	10	0.1	SD	Sioux Falls
722)	WRQR	1000	D4	5		TN	Paris
723)	KOMO	1000	U2	50	50	WA	Seattle
724)	WCOC	1010	U1	5	0.04	AL	Dora
725)	KXXT	1010	U5	15	0.25	AZ	Tolleson
726)	KCHJ	1010	U4	5	1	CA	Delano
727)	KIQI	1010	U3	10	0.5	CA	San Francisco
728)	KXPS	1010	U4	3.6	0.4	CA	Thousand Palms
729)	KSIR	1010	U3	25	0.28	CO	Brush
730)	WHFS	1010	U4	5	5	FL	Seffner
731)	WJXL	1010	U4	50	30	FL	Jacksonville Beach
732)	WGUN	1010	U1	50	0.07	GA	Atlanta
733)	KXEN	1010	U4	50	0.5	MO	Saint Louis
734)	WMOX	1010	U4	10	1	MS	Meridian
735)	WFGW	1010	U7	50	0.5	NC	Black Mountain
736)	WCNL	1010	U1	10	0.03	NH	Newport
737)	WINS	1010	U3	50	50	NY	New York
738)	KOOR	1010	D1	4.5		OR	Milwaukie
739)	WHIN	1010	U1	5	0.04	TN	Gallatin
740)	KBBW	1010	U4	10	2.5	TX	Waco
741)	KLAT	1010	U4	5	3.6	TX	Houston
742)	KTNZ	1010	U4	10	1	TX	Amarillo
743)	KIHU	1010	U13	50	0.19	UT	Tooele
744)	WPMH	1010	U3	5	0.44	VA	Portsmouth
745)	KTNQ	1020	U4	50	50	CA	Los Angeles
746)	WHDD	1020	D1	2.5		CT	Sharon
747)	WURN	1020	U4	8.9	0.98	FL	Kendall
748)	WSBX	1020	D1	10		GA	Ochlocknee
749)	KMMQ	1020	U4	5	1.4	NE	Plattsmouth
750)	KCKN	1020	U4	50	50	NM	Roswell
751)	KDKA	1020	U1	50	50	PA	Pittsburgh
752)	WRIX	1020	D1	10		SC	Homeland Park
753)	KDYK	1020	U5	4	0.4	WA	Union Gap
754)	KFAY	1030	U4	10	1	AR	Farmington
755)	KVOI	1030	U4	10	1	AZ	Cortaro
756)	KJDJ	1030	U4	2.5	0.7	CA	San Luis Obispo
757)	WONQ	1030	U2	45	1.7	FL	Oviedo
758)	WEBS	1030	U1	5	0.003	GA	Calhoun
759)	WNVR	1030	U7	10	0.12	IL	Vernon Hills
760)	KBUF	1030	U2	2.5	1.2	KS	Holcomb
761)	WBZ	1030	U3	50	50	MA	Boston
762)	WWGB	1030	D3	50		MD	Indian Head
763)	WUFL	1030	D3	5		MI	Sterling Heights
764)	WCTS	1030	U4	50	1	MN	Maplewood
765)	KCWJ	1030	U4	5	0.5	MO	Blue Springs
766)	WDRU	1030	D3	50		NC	Creedmoor
767)	WNOW	1030	D3	9.4		NC	Mint Hill
768)	KDUN	1030	U1	50	0.63	OR	Reedsport
769)	WGSF	1030	U12	50	1	TN	Memphis
770)	KCTA	1030	D1	50		TX	Corpus Christi
771)	KMAS	1030	U1	10	1	WA	Shelton
772)	WBGS	1030	D5	10		WV	Point Pleasant
773)	KTWO	1030	U2	50	50	WY	Casper
774)	KCBR	1040	D1	15		CO	Monument
775)	WHBO	1040	U2	3.6	0.42	FL	Pinellas Park
776)	WLVJ	1040	U4	25	1.1	FL	Boynton Beach
777)	WPBS	1040	D1	50		GA	Conyers
778)	WHO	1040	U1	50	50	IA	Des Moines
779)	WSGH	1040	U4	9.1	0.18	NC	Lewisville
780)	WNJE	1040	U7	15	1.5	NJ	Flemington
781)	WYSL	1040	U7	20	0.5	NY	Avon
782)	WJTB	1040	D1	5		OH	North Ridgeville
783)	WZSK	1040	D1	10		PA	Everett
784)	WKTI	1040	D1	10		TN	Powell
785)	KGGR	1040	D1	3.3		TX	Dallas
786)	KJPG	1050	U5	10	0.007	CA	Frazier Park
787)	KTCT	1050	U4	50	10	CA	San Mateo
788)	WJSB	1050	D1	3.1		FL	Crestview
789)	WROS	1050	U4	5	0.01	FL	Jacksonville
790)	WFAM	1050	U1	5	0.08	GA	Augusta
791)	WBQH	1050	U1	10	0.04	MD	Silver Spring
792)	WTKA	1050	U3	10	0.5	MI	Ann Arbor
793)	KLOH	1050	U4	9.38	0.43	MN	Pipestone
794)	KMTA	1050	U1	10	0.13	MT	Miles City
795)	WFSC	1050	U1	5	0.15	NC	Franklin
796)	WEPN	1050	U4	50	50	NY	New York
797)	WSEN	1050	U3	2.5	0.01	NY	Baldwinsville
798)	KORE	1050	U1	5	0.14	OR	Springfield-Eugene
799)	WHSC	1050	U3	5	0.47	SC	Conway
800)	WBRG	1050	U4	3.8	0.09	VA	Lynchburg
801)	WVXX	1050	U3	5	0.35	VA	Norfolk
802)	KBLE	1050	U1	5	0.44	WA	Seattle
803)	KEYF	1050	U1	5	0.26	WA	Dishman
804)	WADC	1050	U1	10	0.14	WV	Parkersburg
805)	KDUS	1060	U2	5	0.5	AZ	Tempe
806)	KTNS	1060	U1	5	0.02	CA	Oakhurst
807)	KRCN	1060	U1	50	0.11	CO	Longmont
808)	WIXC	1060	U7	50	5	FL	Titusville
809)	WKNG	1060	D1	50		GA	Tallapoosa
810)	KBGN	1060	D1	10		ID	Caldwell
811)	WMCL	1060	U3	2.5	0.002	IL	McLeansboro
812)	WLNO	1060	U4	50	5	LA	New Orleans
813)	WQOM	1060	U4	50	2.5	MA	Natick
814)	WHFB	1060	U1	5	0.001	MI	Benton Harbor-St Joseph
815)	WXNC	1060	D1	4		NC	Monroe
816)	KKVV	1060	U4	5	0.04	NV	Las Vegas
817)	WILB	1060	D4	15		OH	Canton
818)	KYW	1060	U3	50	50	PA	Philadelphia
819)	KGFX	1060	U4	10	1	SD	Pierre
820)	KIJN	1060	D3	10		TX	Farwell
821)	KXPL	1060	D1	10		TX	El Paso
822)	KDYL	1060	U1	10	0.14	UT	South Salt Lake
823)	WAPI	1070	U2	50	5	AL	Birmingham
824)	KNX	1070	U1	50	50	CA	Los Angeles
825)	WFRF	1070	U4	50	5	FL	Tallahassee
826)	WNVY	1070	U1	15	0.02	FL	Cantonment
827)	WFNI	1070	U4	50	10	IN	Indianapolis
828)	KLIO	1070	U2	10	1	KS	Wichita
829)	KVKK	1070	U2	10	5	MN	Verndale
830)	KHMO	1070	U4	5	1	MO	Hannibal
831)	KATQ	1070	U1	5	0.05	MT	Plentywood
832)	WNCT	1070	U4	50	10	NC	Greenville
833)	WSCP	1070	D1	2.5		NY	Sandy Creek-Pulaski
834)	WTWK	1070	D1	5		NY	Plattsburgh
835)	WKOK	1070	U4	10	1	PA	Sunbury
836)	WCSZ	1070	U4	50	1.5	SC	Sans Souci
837)	WDIA	1070	U4	50	5	TN	Memphis
838)	WFLI	1070	U4	50	2.5	TN	Lookout Mountain
839)	KNTH	1070	U4	10	5	TX	Houston
840)	KWEL	1070	D1	2.5		TX	Midland
841)	WINA	1070	U2	5	5	VA	Charlottesville
842)	WTSO	1070	U4	10	5	WI	Madison
843)	WBKW	1070	U4	10		WV	Beckley
844)	WKAC	1080	D1	5		AL	Athens
845)	KSCO	1080	U2	10	5	CA	Santa Cruz
846)	WTIC	1080	U2	50	50	CT	Hartford
847)	WHIM	1080	U4	50	10	FL	Coral Gables
848)	WHOO	1080	U7	19	0.19	FL	Kissimmee
849)	WFTD	1080	D4	50		GA	Marietta
850)	KVNI	1080	U2	10	1	ID	Coeur d'Alene
851)	WNWI	1080	U2	3	2.6	IL	Oak Lawn
852)	WKJK	1080	U4	10	1	KY	Louisville
853)	WKGX	1080	D1	5		NC	Lenoir
854)	KFXX	1080	U4	50	9	OR	Portland
855)	WWNL	1080	D4	50		PA	Pittsburgh
856)	WALD	1080	D1	9		SC	Johnsonville
857)	KRLD	1080	U2	50	50	TX	Dallas
858)	KSLL	1080	D1	10		UT	Price
859)	KAAY	1090	U2	50	50	AR	Little Rock
860)	KNCR	1090	D1	10		CA	Fortuna
861)	KMXA	1090	U4	50	0.5	CO	Aurora
862)	WFCV	1090	D4	2.5		IN	Fort Wayne

MW	Call	kHz	Ant.	D	N	Sta	City of License
863)	WILD	1090	D1	4.8		MA	Boston
864)	WBAL	1090	U2	50	50	MD	Baltimore
865)	KEXS	1090	D4	8		MO	Excelsior Springs
866)	KBOZ	1090	U2	5	5	MT	Bozeman
867)	WTSB	1090	D1	9		NC	Selma
868)	KLWJ	1090	D1	2.5		OR	Umatilla
869)	WCZZ	1090	D1	5		SC	Greenwood
870)	WHGG	1090	D1	10		TN	Kingsport
871)	KVOP	1090	U4	5	0.5	TX	Plainview
872)	KPTK	1090	U4	50	50	WA	Seattle
873)	WAQE	1090	D1	5		WI	Rice Lake
874)	KFNX	**1100**	U4	50	1	AZ	Cave Creek
875)	KAFY	1100	U2	4.2	0.8	CA	Bakersfield
876)	KFAX	1100	U3	50	50	CA	San Francisco
877)	KNZZ	1100	U12	50	10	CO	Grand Junction
878)	WCGA	1100	D1	10		GA	Woodbine
879)	WWWE	1100	D1	5		GA	Hapeville
880)	WZFG	1100	U2	50	0.44	MN	Dilworth
881)	KKLL	1100	D1	5		MO	Webb City
882)	KWWN	1100	U4	22	2	NV	Las Vegas
883)	WHLI	1100	D3	10		NY	Hempstead
884)	WTAM	1100	U1	50	50	OH	Cleveland
885)	KDRY	1100	U2	11	1	TX	Alamo Heights
886)	WTWN	1100	D1	5		VT	Wells River
887)	WISS	1100	D1	2.5		WI	Berlin
888)	WTOF	**1110**	D1	10		AL	Bay Minette
889)	KGFI	1110	D1	5		AR	Clinton
890)	KDIS	1110	U4	50	20	CA	Pasadena
891)	KLIB	1110	U4	5	0.5	CA	Roseville
892)	WTIS	1110	D3	10		FL	Tampa
893)	WMBI	1110	D1	4.2		IL	Chicago
894)	WUPE	1110	D3	5		MA	Pittsfield
895)	WJML	1110	U3	10	0.01	MI	Petoskey
896)	WBT	1110	U2	50	50	NC	Charlotte
897)	KFAB	1110	U2	50	50	NE	Omaha
898)	WCCM	1110	D3	5		NH	Salem
899)	KYKK	1110	D1	5		NM	Humble City
900)	WGNZ	1110	U7	5	0.002	OH	Fairborn
901)	KBND	1110	U12	10	5	OR	Bend
902)	WNAP	1110	D5	4.8		PA	Norristown
903)	WPMZ	1110	D3	5		RI	East Providence
904)	WSLV	1110	D1	2.5		TN	Ardmore
905)	KTEK	1110	D3	2.5		TX	Alvin
906)	KVTT	1110	D4	50		TX	Mineral Wells
907)	WYRM	1110	D3	50		VA	Norfolk
908)	KZSJ	**1120**	U1	5	0.15	CA	San Martin
909)	WUST	1120	D1	20		DC	Washington
910)	WDNW	1120	U4	5	I	MA	Concord
911)	KMOX	1120	U1	50	50	MO	Saint Louis
912)	WTWZ	1120	D1	10		MS	Clinton
913)	WSME	1120	D1	6		NC	Camp Lejeune
914)	KPNW	1120	U3	50	50	OR	Eugene
915)	KANN	1120	U4	10	1.1	UT	Roy
916)	WALQ	1130	D1	25		AL	Carrville
917)	KRDU	1130	U4	5	6.2	CA	Dinuba
918)	KSDO	1130	U4	10	10	CA	San Diego
919)	WWBF	1130	U2	2.5	0.5	FL	Bartow
920)	WLBA	1130	D1	10		GA	Gainesville
921)	KWKH	1130	U2	50	50	LA	Shreveport
922)	WDFN	1130	U4	50	10	MI	Detroit
923)	KTCN	1130	U4	50	25	MN	Minneapolis
924)	WPYB	1130	D1	6.5		NC	Benson
925)	KBMR	1130	U1	10	0.02	ND	Bismarck
926)	WBBR	1130	U2	50	50	NY	New York
927)	KQRR	1130	U4	25	0.49	OR	Mount Angel
928)	WEAF	1130	U1	5	0.007	SC	Camden
929)	KTMR	1130	D3	25		TX	Converse
930)	WISN	1130	U4	50	10	WI	Milwaukee
931)	WBXR	**1140**	D4	15		AL	Hazel Green
932)	KLTK	1140	D1	5		AR	Centerton
933)	KHTK	1140	U4	50	50	CA	Sacramento
934)	KNWQ	1140	U4	10	2.5	CA	Palm Springs
935)	WQBA	1140	U4	50	10	FL	Miami
936)	WRMQ	1140	U2	5	0.008	FL	Orlando
937)	KGEM	1140	U2	10	10	ID	Boise
938)	WVEL	1140	D1	5		IL	Pekin
939)	WVHF	1140	D3	5		MI	Kentwood
940)	KCXL	1140	U1	4	0.006	MO	Liberty
941)	WSAO	1140	D1	5		MS	Senatobia
942)	KYDZ	1140	U2	10	2.5	NV	North Las Vegas
943)	WCJW	1140	D3	2.5		NY	Warsaw
944)	KSOO	1140	U2	10	5	SD	Sioux Falls
945)	KHFX	1140	U4	5	0.71	TX	Cleburne
946)	KYOK	1140	D3	5		TX	Conroe
947)	WRVA	1140	U3	50	50	VA	Richmond
948)	WXLZ	1140	D1	2.5		VA	Saint Paul
949)	KZMQ	1140	D1	10		WY	Greybull
950)	WJRD	**1150**	U2	20	1	AL	Tuscaloosa
951)	KCKY	1150	U4	5	1	AZ	Coolidge
952)	KTLK	1150	U4	50	44	CA	Los Angeles
953)	KNRV	1150	U4	10	1	CO	Englewood
954)	WMRD	1150	U1	2.5	0.04	CT	Middletown
955)	WDEL	1150	U4	5	5	DE	Wilmington
956)	WTMP	1150	U4	10	0.5	FL	Egypt Lake
957)	WJEM	1150	U3	5	0.1	GA	Valdosta
958)	KWKY	1150	U4	2.5	1	IA	Des Moines
959)	WGGH	1150	U4	5	0.04	IL	Marion
960)	KSAL	1150	U2	5	5	KS	Salina
961)	WMST	1150	U1	2.5	0.05	KY	Mount Sterling
962)	WJBO	1150	U3	5	5	LA	Baton Rouge
963)	WWDJ	1150	U4	5	5	MA	Boston
964)	KSEN	1150	U4	10	5	MT	Shelby
965)	WGBR	1150	U4	5	0.8	NC	Goldsboro
966)	KDEF	1150	U2	5	0.5	NM	Albuquerque
967)	WUTI	1150	U4	5	1	NY	Utica
968)	WCUE	1150	U3	5	0.5	OH	Cuyahoga Falls
969)	KAGO	1150	U4	5	1	OR	Klamath Falls
970)	KXET	1150	U1	5	0.01	OR	Portland
971)	WLLI	1150	U1	5	0.03	PA	Huntingdon
972)	WAVO	1150	U1	5	0.05	SC	Rock Hill
973)	KIMM	1150	U2	5	0.5	SD	Rapid City
974)	WCRK	1150	U2	5	0.5	TN	Morristown
975)	WGOW	1150	U2	5	1	TN	Chattanooga
976)	KHRO	1150	U1	5	0.38	TX	El Paso
977)	WNLR	1150	U1	2.5	0.03	VA	Churchville
978)	KKNW	1150	U2	10	6	WA	Seattle
979)	KQQQ	1150	U1	11	0.02	WA	Pullman
980)	WEAQ	1150	U1	5	0.04	WI	Chippewa Falls
981)	WHBY	1150	U4	20	25	WI	Kimberly
982)	WELC	1150	D1	5		WV	Welch
983)	WEWC	**1160**	U5	5	0.25	FL	Callahan
984)	WIWA	1160	U4	2.5	0.5	FL	Saint Cloud
985)	WCFO	1160	U5	50	0.16	GA	East Point
986)	WYLL	1160	U4	50	50	IL	Chicago
987)	WKCM	1160	U2	2.5	1	KY	Hawesville
988)	WQRT	1160	U4	5	0.99	KY	Florence
989)	WMET	1160	U4	50	1.5	MD	Gaithersburg
990)	WSKW	1160	U1	10	0.73	ME	Skowhegan
991)	KCTO	1160	U4	5	0.23	MO	Cleveland
992)	WJFJ	1160	U2	10	0.5	NC	Tryon
993)	WTEL	1160	U1	5	0.25	NC	Red Springs
994)	WOBM	1160	U4	50	8.9	NJ	Lakewood Township
995)	WVNJ	1160	U4	20	2.5	NJ	Oakland
996)	WABY	1160	U1	5	0.57	NY	Mechanicville
997)	WPIE	1160	U4	5	0.31	NY	Trumansburg
998)	WBYN	1160	U4	4	1	PA	Lehighton
999)	WCCS	1160	U4	10	1	PA	Homer City
1000)	WCRT	1160	U2	50	1	TN	Donelson
1001)	KRDY	1160	U4	10	1	TX	San Antonio
1002)	KVCE	1160	U4	35	1	TX	Highland Park
1003)	KSL	1160	U1	50	50	UT	Salt Lake City
1004)	WODY	1160	U2	5	0.25	VA	Fieldale
1005)	WGMP	**1170**	U4	10	1	AL	Montgomery
1006)	KCBQ	1170	U4	50	2.9	CA	San Diego
1007)	KLOK	1170	U4	50	5	CA	San Jose
1008)	WAVS	1170	U2	5	0.25	FL	Davie
1009)	WLBH	1170	D3	5		IL	Mattoon
1010)	KRUE	1170	U1	2.5	0.005	MN	Waseca
1011)	WCLN	1170	D1	5		NC	Clinton
1012)	WCXN	1170	D1	7.7		NC	Claremont
1013)	KFAQ	1170	U2	50	50	OK	Tulsa
1014)	WDEK	1170	D1	10		SC	Lexington
1015)	KPUG	1170	U2	10	5	WA	Bellingham
1016)	WWVA	1170	U2	50	50	WV	Wheeling
1017)	KXIQ	**1180**	U7	5	0.02	AR	Turrell
1018)	KYET	1180	U1	10	0.25	AZ	Williams
1019)	KERN	1180	U4	50	10	CA	Wasco-Greenacres
1020)	VOA	1180	U3	100	100	FL	Marathon
1021)	WZQZ	1180	D1	5		GA	Trion
1022)	WXLA	1180	D4	5		MI	Dimondale
1023)	KYES	1180	U7	50	5	MN	Rockville
1024)	WJNT	1180	U12	50	0.5	MS	Pearl
1025)	KOFI	1180	U2	50	10	MT	Kalispell
1026)	WSFM	1180	D3	10		NC	Carolina Beach
1027)	KZOT	1180	U4	25	1	NE	Bellevue
1028)	WHAM	1180	U1	50	50	NY	Rochester
1029)	WFGN	1180	D1	2.5		SC	Gaffney
1030)	WVLZ	1180	D1	10		TN	Knoxville
1031)	KGOL	1180	U4	50	3	TX	Humble
1032)	KLAY	1180	U2	5	1	WA	Lakewood
1033)	WEUV	**1190**	D1	2.5		AL	Moulton
1034)	KJJI	1190	U2	25	0.35	AR	White Hall

MW	Call	kHz	Ant.	D	N	Sta	City of License	MW	Call	kHz	Ant.	D	N	Sta	City of License
1035)	KREB	1190	D1	5		AR	Bentonville-Bella Vista	1119)	KZDC	1250	U4	25	1	TX	San Antonio
1036)	KNUV	1190	U4	5	0.25	AZ	Tolleson	1120)	KNEU	1250	U1	5	0.12	UT	Roosevelt
1037)	KGBN	1190	U4	20	1.3	CA	Anaheim	1121)	WDVA	1250	U2	5	5	VA	Danville
1038)	KVCU	1190	U1	6.8	0.11	CO	Boulder	1122)	WKDL	1250	U3	3	0.12	VA	Warrenton
1039)	WAMT	1190	U2	4.7	0.23	FL	Pine Castle-Sky Lake	1123)	KKDZ	1250	U2	5	5	WA	Seattle
1040)	WAFS	1190	D1	25		GA	Atlanta	1124)	KWSU	1250	U1	5	5	WA	Pullman
1041)	WOWO	1190	U2	50	9.8	IN	Fort Wayne	1125)	WSSP	1250	U4	5	5	WI	Milwaukee
1042)	KKOJ	1190	D3	5		MN	Jackson	1126)	WYKM	1250	D1	5		WV	Rupert
1043)	KPHN	1190	U2	5	0.5	MO	Kansas City	1127)	WYDE	1260	U1	5	0.04	AL	Birmingham
1044)	KQQZ	1190	U4	10	0.02	MO	Desoto	1128)	KBSZ	1260	U1	3.5	0.05	AZ	Apache Junction
1045)	WMEJ	1190	D1	5		MS	Bay Saint Louis	1129)	KMZT	1260	U4	20	7.5	CA	Beverly Hills
1046)	WIXE	1190	U1	5	0.07	NC	Monroe	1130)	KSFB	1260	U1	5	1	CA	San Francisco
1047)	KXKS	1190	U1	10	0.02	NM	Albuquerque	1131)	WWRC	1260	U4	25	5	DC	Washington
1048)	WLIB	1190	U4	10	30	NY	New York	1132)	WFTW	1260	U1	2.5	0.13	FL	Fort Walton Beach
1049)	KEX	1190	U2	50	50	OR	Portland	1133)	WSUA	1260	U4	50	20	FL	Miami
1050)	WSDQ	1190	D1	5		TN	Dunlap	1134)	WTJH	1260	U1	5	0.03	GA	East Point
1051)	KFXR	1190	U4	50	5	TX	Dallas	1135)	WUFE	1260	D1	5		GA	Baxley
1052)	WCRW	1190	D3	50		VA	Leesburg	1136)	KDLF	1260	U3	5	0.03	IA	Boone
1053)	WNWC	1190	U7	4.8	0.02	WI	Sun Prairie	1137)	KBLY	1260	U1	5	0.06	ID	Idaho Falls
1054)	WVUS	1190	U1	4.5	0.02	WV	Grafton	1138)	KTRP	1260	U1	8.4	0.03	ID	Weiser
1055)	KPSF	**1200**	U4	5	1.3	CA	Desert Hot Springs	1139)	WSDZ	1260	U4	20	5	IL	Belleville
1056)	KYAA	1200	U2	25	10	CA	Soquel	1140)	WNDE	1260	U2	5	5	IN	Indianapolis
1057)	WINK	1200	U4	50	1	FL	Pine Island Center	1141)	KBRH	1260	U1	5	0.12	LA	Baton Rouge
1058)	WRTO	1200	U4	20	4.5	IL	Chicago	1142)	WMKI	1260	U2	5	5	MA	Boston
1059)	WXKS	1200	U4	50	50	MA	Newton	1143)	WPNW	1260	U4	10	1	MI	Zeeland
1060)	WCHB	1200	U4	50	15	MI	Taylor	1144)	KSGF	1260	U2	5	5	MO	Springfield
1061)	WSML	1200	U2	10	1	NC	Graham	1145)	WKXR	1260	U4	5	0.5	NC	Asheboro
1062)	WXIT	1200	D1	10		NC	Blowing Rock	1146)	WFJS	1260	U4	5	2.5	NJ	Trenton
1063)	KFNW	1200	U4	50	13	ND	West Fargo	1147)	KTRC	1260	U1	5	1	NM	Santa Fe
1064)	WKST	1200	U2	5	1	PA	New Castle	1148)	WSKO	1260	U2	5	5	NY	Syracuse
1065)	WRKK	1200	U4	10	0.25	PA	Hughesville	1149)	WNXT	1260	U4	5	1	OH	Portsmouth
1066)	WMIR	1200	U1	6.5	0.01	SC	Atlantic Beach	1150)	WWMK	1260	U4	10	5	OH	Cleveland
1067)	WAMB	1200	D1	50		TN	Nashville	1151)	WPHB	1260	U1	5	0.03	PA	Philipsburg
1068)	WOAI	1200	U1	50	50	TX	San Antonio	1152)	WRIE	1260	U4	5	5	PA	Erie
1069)	WEMM	1200	U1	22	0.009	WV	Huntington	1153)	WHYM	1260	U1	5	0.05	SC	Lake City
1070)	WTXK	**1210**	U1	10	0.003	AL	Pike Road	1154)	WPJF	1260	U1	5	0.01	SC	Greenville
1071)	KEVT	1210	U2	10	1	AZ	Sahuarita	1155)	KWYR	1260	U1	5	0.14	SD	Winner
1072)	KEBR	1210	U5	5	0.5	CA	Rocklin	1156)	WDKN	1260	U1	5	0.01	TN	Dickson
1073)	KPRZ	1210	U4	20	10	CA	San Marcos	1157)	WNOO	1260	U1	5	0.02	TN	Chattanooga
1074)	KQEQ	1210	U5	5	0.37	CA	Fowler	1158)	KSML	1260	U1	4.5	0.07	TX	Diboll
1075)	WNMA	1210	U4	47	2.5	FL	Miami Springs	1159)	WCHV	1260	U4	25	2.5	VA	Charlottesville
1076)	WDGR	1210	D1	10		GA	Dahlonega	1160)	WWVT	1260	U1	5	0.02	VA	Christiansburg
1077)	WILY	1210	U11	10	0.003	IL	Centralia	1161)	WXCE	1260	U1	5	5	WI	Amery
1078)	WLRO	1210	U2	10	1	LA	Denham Springs	1162)	KPOW	1260	U2	5	1	WY	Powell
1079)	WJNL	1210	D1	50		MI	Kingsley	1163)	WIJD	**1270**	U1	5	0.1	AL	Prichard
1080)	KGYN	1210	U2	10	10	OK	Guymon	1164)	KDJI	1270	U1	5	0.13	AZ	Holbrook
1081)	WANB	1210	D1	5		PA	Waynesburg	1165)	KFUT	1270	U4	5	0.75	CA	Thousand Palms
1082)	WPHT	1210	U1	50	50	PA	Philadelphia	1166)	KJUG	1270	U2	5	1	CA	Tulare
1083)	KOKK	1210	U4	5	0.87	SD	Huron	1167)	WNLS	1270	U1	5	0.11	FL	Tallahassee
1084)	WMPS	1210	U2	10	0.25	TN	Bartlett	1168)	WNOG	1270	U4	5	5	FL	Naples
1085)	WSBI	1210	D1	10		TN	Static	1169)	WRLZ	1270	U4	25	5	FL	Eatonville
1086)	KUBR	1210	U4	10	5	TX	San Juan	1170)	WJJC	1270	U1	5	0.17	GA	Commerce
1087)	KUNF	1210	U1	10	0.25	UT	Washington	1171)	WSHE	1270	U1	5	0.18	GA	Columbus
1088)	KMIA	1210	U4	27.5	10	WA	Auburn-Federal Way	1172)	KXOZ	1270	U1	5	1	ID	Twin Falls
1089)	KHAT	1210	U2	10	1	WY	Laramie	1173)	WKBF	1270	U2	5	5	IL	Rock Island
1090)	KRSV	1210	U1	5	0.25	WY	Afton	1174)	WCMR	1270	U4	5	1	IN	Elkhart
1091)	KDOW	**1220**	U1	5	0.14	CA	Palo Alto	1175)	KSCB	1270	U1	5	0.02	KS	Liberal
1092)	WSLM	1220	U3	5	0.08	IN	Salem	1176)	WSPR	1270	U1	5	1	MA	Springfield
1093)	KLBB	1220	U1	5	0.25	MN	Stillwater	1177)	WCBC	1270	U1	5	1	MD	Cumberland
1094)	WDYT	1220	U5	25	0.1	NC	Kings Mountain	1178)	WMKT	1270	U2	27	5	MI	Charlevoix
1095)	WENC	1220	U1	5	0.15	NC	Whiteville	1179)	WXYT	1270	U4	50	50	MI	Detroit
1096)	WGNY	1220	U4	10	0.18	NY	Newburgh	1180)	KFAN	1270	U4	5	1	MN	Rochester
1097)	WHKW	1220	U3	50	50	OH	Cleveland	1181)	WWWI	1270	U2	5	5	MN	Baxter
1098)	WFAX	1220	U1	5	0.04	VA	Falls Church	1182)	WCGC	1270	U4	10	0.5	NC	Belmont
		1230	various stns of less than 1kW					1183)	WMPM	1270	U1	5	0.14	NC	Smithfield
		1240	various stns of less than 1kW					1184)	WTSN	1270	U4	5	5	NH	Dover
1099)	WRBZ	**1250**	U1	5	0.08	AL	Wetumpka	1185)	KBZZ	1270	U2	13	5	NV	Sparks
1100)	WZOB	1250	U1	5	0.12	AL	Fort Payne	1186)	WDLA	1270	U1	5	0.08	NY	Walton
1101)	KHIL	1250	U1	5	0.19	AZ	Willcox	1187)	WHLD	1270	U3	5	1	NY	Niagara Falls
1102)	KLLK	1250	U4	5	2.5	CA	Willits	1188)	KRVT	1270	U4	5	1	OK	Claremore
1103)	KZER	1250	U4	2.5	1	CA	Santa Barbara	1189)	KAJO	1270	U1	10	0.04	OR	Grants Pass
1104)	WHNZ	1250	U4	25	5.9	FL	Tampa	1190)	WLBR	1270	U4	5	1	PA	Lebanon
1105)	KYYS	1250	U4	25	3.7	KS	Kansas City	1191)	WHGS	1270	U1	10	0.21	SC	Hampton
1106)	WARE	1250	U4	5	2.5	MA	Ware	1192)	KNWC	1270	U4	5	2.3	SD	Sioux Falls
1107)	WNEM	1250	U4	5	1.1	MI	Bridgeport	1193)	WLIC	1270	U2	5	0.5	TN	Newport
1108)	KBRF	1250	U4	5	2.2	MN	Fergus Falls	1194)	KFLC	1270	U4	50	5	TX	Fort Worth
1109)	WHNY	1250	U2	5	1	MS	McComb	1195)	WHEO	1270	D1	5		VA	Stuart
1110)	KIKC	1250	U1	5	0.13	MT	Forsyth	1196)	KBAM	1270	U1	5	0.08	WA	Longview
1111)	WBRM	1250	U1	5	0.05	NC	Marion	1197)	KIML	1270	U2	5	1	WY	Gillette
1112)	WGHB	1250	U4	5	2.5	NC	Farmville	1198)	WMXB	**1280**	U2	5	0.5	AL	Tuscaloosa
1113)	WGAM	1250	U4	5	5	NH	Manchester	1199)	KXEG	1280	U1	2.5	0.04	AZ	Phoenix
1114)	WMTR	1250	U4	5	7	NJ	Morristown	1200)	KXTK	1280	U4	10	2.5	CA	Arroyo Grande
1115)	WDDZ	1250	U2	5	5	PA	Pittsburgh	1201)	KBNO	1280	U4	5	5	CO	Denver
1116)	WLEM	1250	U1	2.5	0.03	PA	Emporium	1202)	WDSP	1280	U1	5	0.04	FL	De Funiak Springs
1117)	WTMA	1250	U2	5	1	SC	Charleston	1203)	WIBB	1280	U1	5	0.09	GA	Macon
1118)	KDEI	1250	U2	5	1	TX	Port Arthur	1204)	WGBF	1280	U2	5	1	IN	Evansville

MW	Call	kHz	Ant.	D	N	Sta	City of License
1205)	WODT	1280	U3	5	5	LA	New Orleans
1206)	WPKZ	1280	U4	5	1	MA	Fitchburg
1207)	WFAU	1280	U2	5	5	ME	Gardiner
1208)	KVXR	1280	U4	5	5	MN	Moorhead
1209)	WWTC	1280	U2	5	5	MN	Minneapolis
1210)	WYAL	1280	D1	5		NC	Scotland Neck
1211)	KRZE	1280	U1	5	0.1	NM	Farmington
1212)	KQLL	1280	U1	5	0.02	NV	Henderson
1213)	WADO	1280	U4	50	7.2	NY	New York
1214)	WHTK	1280	U2	5	5	NY	Rochester
1215)	KRVM	1280	U4	5	1.5	OR	Eugene
1216)	WHVR	1280	U4	5	0.5	PA	Hanover
1217)	WJST	1280	U2	4.9	1	PA	New Castle
1218)	WANS	1280	U2	5	1	SC	Anderson
1219)	WJAY	1280	U1	4.2	0.27	SC	Mullins
1220)	WMCP	1280	U4	5	0.5	TN	Columbia
1221)	KZNS	1280	U4	50	0.67	UT	Salt Lake City
1222)	WYVE	1280	U1	2.5	0.16	VA	Wytheville
1223)	KIT	1280	U1	5	1	WA	Yakima
1224)	KPTQ	1280	U4	5	0.12	WA	Spokane
1225)	WNAM	1280	U4	5	5	WI	Neenah-Menasha
1226)	WOPP	1290	U4	2.5	0.5	AL	Opp
1227)	KDMS	1290	U1	2.5	0.1	AR	El Dorado
1228)	KUOA	1290	U1	5	0.03	AR	Siloam Springs
1229)	KAZA	1290	U4	5	0.08	CA	Gilroy
1230)	KKDD	1290	U4	5	5	CA	San Bernardino
1231)	KPAY	1290	U2	5	5	CA	Chico
1232)	WWTX	1290	U1	2.5	0.03	DE	Wilmington
1233)	WJNO	1290	U4	10	4.9	FL	West Palm Beach
1234)	WCHK	1290	U2	10	0.5	GA	Canton
1235)	WTKS	1290	U2	5	5	GA	Savannah
1236)	KOUU	1290	U5	50	0.02	ID	Pocatello
1237)	WIRL	1290	U4	5	5	IL	Peoria
1238)	KMMM	1290	U4	5	0.5	KS	Pratt
1239)	WCBL	1290	U1	5	0.05	KY	Benton
1240)	WKI R	1290	U1	5	0.03	KY	Manchester
1241)	WNBN	1290	U1	2.5	0.09	MS	Meridian
1242)	KGVO	1290	U2	5	5	MT	Missoula
1243)	WHKY	1290	U4	50	1	NC	Hickory
1244)	WJCV	1290	U1	5	0.04	NC	Jacksonville
1245)	KOIL	1290	U2	5	5	NE	Omaha
1246)	WKBK	1290	U3	5	5	NH	Keene
1247)	WNBF	1290	U2	9.3	5	NY	Binghamton
1248)	WHIO	1290	U2	5	5	OH	Dayton
1249)	KUMA	1290	U2	5	5	OR	Pendleton
1250)	WFBG	1290	U2	5	1	PA	Altoona
1251)	WRNI	1290	U4	10	10	RI	Providence
1252)	KIVY	1290	U1	2.5	0.17	TX	Crockett
1253)	KRGE	1290	U2	5	5	TX	Weslaco
1254)	KWFS	1290	U1	5	0.07	TX	Wichita Falls
1255)	WDZY	1290	U1	25	0.04	VA	Colonial Heights
1256)	WKLJ	1290	U1	5	0.05	WI	Sparta
1257)	WMCS	1290	U1	5	5	WI	Greenfield
1258)	WVOW	1290	U2	5	1	WV	Logan
1259)	KOWB	1290	U4	5	1	WY	Laramie
1260)	WKXM	1300	U1	5	0.03	AL	Winfield
1261)	KWCK	1300	D1	5		AR	Searcy
1262)	KAZN	1300	U2	23	1	CA	Pasadena
1263)	KPMO	1300	U1	5	0.07	CA	Mendocino
1264)	KWRU	1300	U2	5	1	CA	Fresno
1265)	KCSF	1300	U1	5	1	CO	Colorado Springs
1266)	WFFG	1300	U3	2.5	2.5	FL	Marathon
1267)	WMEL	1300	U4	5	1	FL	Cocoa Beach
1268)	WQBN	1300	U5	5	0.16	FL	Temple Terrace
1269)	WMTM	1300	U1	5	0.06	GA	Moultrie
1270)	KGLO	1300	U4	5	5	IA	Mason City
1271)	KLER	1300	U2	5	1	ID	Orofino
1272)	WRDZ	1300	U4	4.5	4	IL	La Grange
1273)	WLXG	1300	U2	2.5	1	KY	Lexington
1274)	KSYB	1300	U1	5	0.03	LA	Shreveport
1275)	WIBR	1300	U2	5	1	LA	Baton Rouge
1276)	WJZ	1300	U4	5	5	MD	Baltimore
1277)	WOOD	1300	U3	20	20	MI	Grand Rapids
1278)	KPMI	1300	U2	2.5	0.6	MN	Bemidji
1279)	WOAD	1300	U1	5	1	MS	Jackson
1280)	WSYD	1300	U2	5	1	NC	Mount Airy
1281)	KBRL	1300	U3	5	0.13	NE	McCook
1282)	WPNH	1300	U1	5	0.08	NH	Plymouth
1283)	WIMG	1300	U4	3.2	1.3	NJ	Ewing
1284)	KCMY	1300	U2	5	0.5	NV	Carson City
1285)	WGDJ	1300	U2	10	8	NY	Rensselaer
1286)	WXRL	1300	U4	5	2.5	NY	Lancaster
1287)	WJMO	1300	U3	5	5	OH	Cleveland
1288)	KAKC	1300	U4	5	1	OK	Tulsa
1289)	KAPL	1300	U2	20	5	OR	Phoenix
1290)	WKZN	1300	U4	5	0.5	PA	West Hazleton
1291)	KOLY	1300	U1	5	0.11	SD	Mobridge
1292)	WMTN	1300	U1	5	0.09	TN	Morristown
1293)	WNQM	1300	U1	50	5	TN	Nashville
1294)	KVET	1300	U4	5	1	TX	Austin
1295)	WKCY	1300	U1	6.4	0.005	VA	Harrisonburg
1296)	KKOL	1300	U4	50	47	WA	Seattle
1297)	WCLG	1300	U1	2.5	0.04	WV	Morgantown
1298)	WHEP	1310	U1	2.5	0.04	AL	Foley
1299)	WJUS	1310	U1	5	0.03	AL	Marion
1300)	KIHP	1310	U2	5	0.5	AZ	Mesa
1301)	KIQO	1310	U3	5	0.11	CA	Barstow
1302)	KMKY	1310	U3	5	5	CA	Oakland
1303)	KFKA	1310	U2	5	1	CO	Greeley
1304)	WICH	1310	U4	5	5	CT	Norwich
1305)	WAUC	1310	U3	5	0.5	FL	Wauchula
1306)	WYND	1310	U1	10.4	0.11	FL	Deland
1307)	WOKA	1310	U1	3.9	0.03	GA	Douglas
1308)	WPBC	1310	U1	2.5	0.03	GA	Decatur
1309)	KLIX	1310	U2	5	2.5	ID	Twin Falls
1310)	WTLC	1310	U2	5	1	IN	Indianapolis
1311)	WDOC	1310	U1	5	0.02	KY	Prestonsburg
1312)	KMBS	1310	U1	5	0.04	LA	West Monroe
1313)	WORC	1310	U4	5	1	MA	Worcester
1314)	WLOB	1310	U4	5	5	ME	Portland
1315)	WCCW	1310	U4	15	7.5	MI	Traverse City
1316)	WDTW	1310	U4	5	5	MI	Dearborn
1317)	KTWN	1310	U4	2.5	0.27	MN	Glencoe
1318)	KZRG	1310	U4	5	1	MO	Joplin
1319)	KEIN	1310	U1	5	1	MT	Great Falls
1320)	WGSP	1310	U1	5	0.24	NC	Charlotte
1321)	WISE	1310	U2	5	1	NC	Asheville
1322)	WTIK	1310	U4	5	1	NC	Durham
1323)	KNOX	1310	U2	5	5	ND	Grand Forks
1324)	WADB	1310	U4	2.5	1	NJ	Asbury Park
1325)	KKNS	1310	U2	5	0.5	NM	Corrales
1326)	WRVP	1310	U3	5	0.03	NY	Mount Kisco
1327)	WTLB	1310	U4	5	0.5	NY	Utica
1328)	KNPT	1310	U2	5	1	OR	Newport
1329)	WBFD	1310	U1	2.5	0.08	PA	Bedford
1330)	WNAE	1310	U1	5	0.09	PA	Warren
1331)	WDKD	1310	U1	5	0.06	SC	Kingstree
1332)	WDXI	1310	U2	5	1	TN	Jackson
1333)	KAHL	1310	U3	5	0.28	TX	San Antonio
1334)	KTCK	1310	U4	25	5	TX	Dallas
1335)	WDCT	1310	U4	5	0.5	VA	Fairfax
1336)	WGH	1310	U4	20	5	VA	Newport News
1337)	KZXR	1310	U1	5	0.06	WA	Prosser
1338)	WIBA	1310	U2	5	5	WI	Madison
1339)	WSLW	1310	U1	5		WV	White Sulphur Springs
1340)	WENN	1320	U1	5	0.11	AL	Birmingham
1341)	KWHN	1320	U1	5	5	AR	Fort Smith
1342)	KCTC	1320	U4	5	5	CA	West Sacramento
1343)	WATR	1320	U4	5	1	CT	Waterbury
1344)	WDDV	1320	U4	5	1	FL	Venice
1345)	WJNJ	1320	U2	50	5	FL	Jacksonville
1346)	WLQY	1320	U4	5	5	FL	Hollywood
1347)	WHIE	1320	U1	5	0.08	GA	Griffin
1348)	KNCB	1320	U1	5	0.05	LA	Vivian
1349)	WARL	1320	U4	5	5	MA	Attleboro
1350)	WDMJ	1320	U1	5	0.13	MI	Marquette
1351)	WILS	1320	U4	25	1.9	MI	Lansing
1352)	KOZY	1320	U2	5	5	MN	Grand Rapids
1353)	KSIV	1320	U2	4.6	0.27	MO	Clayton
1354)	WRJW	1320	U1	5	0.07	MS	Picayune
1355)	WCOG	1320	U1	5	5	NC	Greensboro
1356)	WKRK	1320	U1	5	0.06	NC	Murphy
1357)	KHRT	1320	U1	2.5	0.31	ND	Minot
1358)	KOLT	1320	U2	5	1	NE	Scottsbluff
1359)	WDER	1320	U4	10	1	NH	Derry
1360)	WJAS	1320	U4	7	3.3	PA	Pittsburgh
1361)	WISW	1320	U2	5	2.5	SC	Columbia
1362)	KELO	1320	U2	5	5	SD	Sioux Falls
1363)	WGOC	1320	U2	5	0.5	TN	Kingsport
1364)	WMSR	1320	U1	5	0.07	TN	Manchester
1365)	KXYZ	1320	U2	5	5	TX	Houston
1366)	KFNZ	1320	U3	5	5	UT	Salt Lake City
1367)	WVNZ	1320	U4	5	0.008	VA	Richmond
1368)	KXRO	1320	U2	5	1	WA	Aberdeen
1369)	WFHR	1320	U2	5	0.5	WI	Wisconsin Rapids
1370)	WZCT	1330	U1	5	0.03	AL	Scottsboro
1371)	KWFM	1330	U2	2	5	AZ	South Tucson
1372)	KLBS	1330	U2	0.42	5	CA	Los Banos
1373)	KWKW	1330	U2	5	5	CA	Los Angeles
1374)	WCVC	1330	D1	5		FL	Tallahassee
1375)	WEBY	1330	U5	25	0.07	FL	Milton
1376)	WJNX	1330	U4	5	1	FL	Fort Pierce

MW	Call	kHz	Ant.	D	N	Sta	City of License
1377)	WMLT	1330	U2	5	0.5	GA	Dublin
1378)	KWLO	1330	U4	5	5	IA	Waterloo
1379)	WKTA	1330	U4	5	0.11	IL	Evanston
1380)	WVHI	1330	U4	5	1	IN	Evansville
1381)	KNSS	1330	U2	5	5	KS	Wichita
1382)	WKDP	1330	U4	5	0.01	KY	Corbin
1383)	KVOL	1330	U2	5	1	LA	Lafayette
1384)	WRCA	1330	U4	25	17	MA	Watertown
1385)	WJSS	1330	U2	5	0.5	MD	Havre de Grace
1386)	WTRX	1330	U4	5	1	MI	Flint
1387)	WLOL	1330	U4	9.7	5.1	MN	Minneapolis
1388)	KGAK	1330	U2	5	1	NM	Gallup
1389)	WEBO	1330	U1	5	0.03	NY	Owego
1390)	WWRV	1330	U4	10	5	NY	New York
1391)	KKPZ	1330	U3	5	5	OR	Portland
1392)	WFNN	1330	U4	5	5	PA	Erie
1393)	WPJS	1330	U1	3.2	0.02	SC	Conway
1394)	WYRD	1330	U4	5	5	SC	Greenville
1395)	KCKM	1330	U2	5	1	TX	Monahans
1396)	WBTM	1330	U2	5	1	VA	Danville
1397)	WESR	1330	U1	5	0.05	VA	Onley-Onancock
1398)	WITM	1330	U1	5	0.03	VA	Marion
1399)	KMBI	1330	D1	5		WA	Spokane
1400)	WHBL	1330	U4	5	1	WI	Sheboygan
1401)	KOVE	1330	U1	5	0.25	WY	Lander
		1340	various stns of less than 1kW				
1402)	WGAD	**1350**	U2	5	5	AL	Gadsden
1403)	KZTD	1350	U1	2.5	0.07	AR	Cabot
1404)	KSRO	1350	U2	5	5	CA	Santa Rosa
1405)	KTDD	1350	U4	5	0.6	CA	San Bernardino
1406)	WINY	1350	U1	5	0.07	CT	Putnam
1407)	WFNS	1350	U3	2.5	0.11	GA	Blackshear
1408)	WRWR	1350	U2	15	0.5	GA	Warner Robins
1409)	KRNT	1350	U2	5	5	IA	Des Moines
1410)	KRLC	1350	U2	5	1	ID	Clarkston WA-Lewiston
1411)	KTIK	1350	U2	5	0.6	ID	Nampa
1412)	WIOU	1350	U4	5	1	IN	Kokomo
1413)	WWWL	1350	U2	5	5	LA	New Orleans
1414)	WZGM	1350	U1	10	0.05	NC	Black Mountain
1415)	WEZS	1350	U1	5	0.11	NH	Laconia
1416)	WHWH	1350	U4	5	5	NJ	Princeton
1417)	KABQ	1350	U2	5	0.5	NM	Albuquerque
1418)	WARF	1350	U3	5	5	OH	Akron
1419)	WOYK	1350	U2	5	1	PA	York
1420)	KCOR	1350	U2	5	5	TX	San Antonio
1421)	KCOX	1350	U1	5	0.03	TX	Jasper
1422)	WBLT	1350	U1	5	0.04	VA	Bedford
1423)	WGPL	1350	U1	5	5	VA	Portsmouth
1424)	WNVA	1350	U1	5	0.03	VA	Norton
1425)	WIXI	**1360**	U1	12	0.04	AL	Jasper
1426)	WMOB	1360	U3	5	0.21	AL	Mobile
1427)	KPXQ	1360	U2	50	1	AZ	Glendale
1428)	KFIV	1360	U4	4	0.95	CA	Modesto
1429)	KLSD	1360	U1	5	1	CA	San Diego
1430)	KHNC	1360	U4	10	1	CO	Johnstown
1431)	WDRC	1360	U2	5	5	CT	Hartford
1432)	WCGL	1360	U4	5	0.08	FL	Jacksonville
1433)	WHNR	1360	U4	5	2.5	FL	Cypress Gardens
1434)	WKAT	1360	U1	5	1	FL	North Miami
1435)	KSCJ	1360	U2	5	5	IA	Sioux City
1436)	WKMI	1360	U2	5	1	MI	Kalamazoo
1437)	KKBJ	1360	U2	5	2.5	MN	Bemidji
1438)	WCHL	1360	U2	5	1	NC	Chapel Hill
1439)	WNJC	1360	U4	5	0.8	NJ	Washington Twnshp
1440)	KBUY	1360	U1	5	0.2	NM	Ruidoso
1441)	WYOS	1360	U4	5	0.5	NY	Binghamton
1442)	WSAI	1360	U2	5	5	OH	Cincinnati
1443)	WWOW	1360	U1	5	0.03	OH	Conneaut
1444)	KOHU	1360	U2	4.3	0.5	OR	Hermiston
1445)	KUIK	1360	U2	5	5	OR	Hillsboro
1446)	WMNY	1360	U2	5	1	PA	McKeesport
1447)	WPPA	1360	U4	5	0.5	PA	Pottsville
1448)	WELP	1360	U1	5	0.03	SC	Easley
1449)	KDJW	1360	U4	6	0.32	TX	Amarillo
1450)	KMNY	1360	U4	50	0.89	TX	Hurst
1451)	KWWJ	1360	U4	5	1	TX	Baytown
1452)	WHBG	1360	U1	5	0.009	VA	Harrisonburg
1453)	WWWJ	1360	U1	5	0.03	VA	Galax
1454)	KKMO	1360	U1	5	5	WA	Tacoma
1455)	WTAQ	1360	U4	10	5	WI	Green Bay
1456)	WMOV	1360	D1	5		WV	Ravenswood
1457)	KRKK	1360	U2	5	1	WY	Rock Springs
1458)	KRAC	**1370**	U4	5	0.5	CA	Quincy
1459)	KWRM	1370	U1	5	2.5	CA	Corona
1460)	KZSF	1370	U3	5	5	CA	San Jose
1461)	WCOA	1370	U2	5	5	FL	Pensacola
1462)	WOCA	1370	U1	5	0.03	FL	Ocala
1463)	WLOP	1370	U1	5	0.03	GA	Jesup
1464)	KDTH	1370	U2	5	5	IA	Dubuque
1465)	WGCL	1370	U4	5	0.5	IN	Bloomington
1466)	KGNO	1370	U1	5	0.23	KS	Dodge City
1467)	WGOH	1370	U1	5	0.02	KY	Grayson
1468)	WQLL	1370	U4	50	24	MD	Pikesville
1469)	WDEA	1370	U4	5	5	ME	Ellsworth
1470)	WLJW	1370	U4	5	1	MI	Cadillac
1471)	KXTL	1370	U1	5	5	MT	Butte
1472)	WGIV	1370	U1	16	0.04	NC	Pineville
1473)	WLLN	1370	U3	5	0.04	NC	Lillington
1474)	WTAB	1370	U1	5	0.1	NC	Tabor City
1475)	KWTL	1370	U1	12	0.27	ND	Grand Forks
1476)	WFEA	1370	U4	5	5	NH	Manchester
1477)	WJIP	1370	D1	5		NY	Ellenville
1478)	WXXI	1370	U2	5	5	NY	Rochester
1479)	WSPD	1370	U2	5	5	OH	Toledo
1480)	WKMC	1370	U3	5	0.03	PA	Roaring Spring
1481)	WDEF	1370	U2	5	5	TN	Chattanooga
1482)	KJCE	1370	U4	5	0.5	TX	Rollingwood
1483)	KSOP	1370	U2	5	0.5	UT	South Salt Lake
1484)	WHEE	1370	D1	5		VA	Martinsville
1485)	WSHV	1370	U1	4.2	0.41	VA	South Hill
1486)	WCCN	1370	U1	5	0.04	WI	Neillsville
1487)	WVLY	1370	U1	5	0.02	WV	Moundsville
1488)	WMMR	1370	D1	5		WV	Frost
1489)	WVSA	**1380**	U1	5	0.03	AL	Vernon
1490)	KDXE	1380	U4	5	2.5	AR	North Little Rock
1491)	KLPZ	1380	U1	2.5	0.05	AZ	Parker
1492)	KTKZ	1380	U4	5	5	CA	Sacramento
1493)	WFNW	1380	U4	5	0.5	CT	Naugatuck
1494)	WELE	1380	U4	5	2.5	FL	Ormond Beach
1495)	WWMI	1380	U2	5	5	FL	Saint Petersburg
1496)	WAOK	1380	U2	25	4.2	GA	Atlanta
1497)	WTJK	1380	U2	5	5	IL	South Beloit
1498)	WKJG	1380	U4	5	5	IN	Fort Wayne
1499)	KCNW	1380	U1	2.5	0.02	KS	Fairway
1500)	WMJR	1380	U1	5	0.03	KY	Nicholasville
1501)	WPYR	1380	U4	5	0.06	LA	Baton Rouge
1502)	WPHM	1380	U4	5	5	MI	Port Huron
1503)	KLIZ	1380	U2	5	5	MN	Brainerd
1504)	KXFN	1380	U4	5	1	MO	Saint Louis
1505)	WKJV	1380	U2	25	1	NC	Asheville
1506)	WTOB	1380	U4	5	2.5	NC	Winston-Salem
1507)	WABH	1380	U4	10	0.45	NY	Bath
1508)	WKDM	1380	U3	5	5	NY	New York
1509)	KMUS	1380	U4	7	0.25	OK	Sperry
1510)	KSRV	1380	U2	5	1	OR	Ontario
1511)	WNRI	1380	U1	2.5	0.01	RI	Woonsocket
1512)	WNRR	1380	U1	4	0.07	SC	North Augusta
1513)	KOTA	1380	U2	5	5	SD	Rapid City
1514)	WHEW	1380	D1	2.8		TN	Franklin
1515)	WLRM	1380	U4	2.5	1	TN	Millington
1516)	KHEY	1380	U1	5	0.5	TX	El Paso
1517)	KRCM	1380	U1	2.8	0.06	TX	Shenandoah
1518)	KWMF	1380	U5	4	0.16	TX	Pleasanton
1519)	WBTK	1380	U4	5	5	VA	Richmond
1520)	WSYB	1380	U2	5	1	VT	Rutland
1521)	KRKO	1380	U2	5	5	WA	Everett
1522)	WOTE	1380	U3	3.9	1.8	WI	Clintonville
1523)	WHMA	**1390**	U2	5	1	AL	Anniston
1524)	KFFK	1390	U1	5	0.03	AR	Rogers
1525)	KLOC	1390	U4	5	5	CA	Turlock
1526)	KLTX	1390	U4	5	3.6	CA	Long Beach
1527)	KGNU	1390	U1	5	0.13	CO	Denver
1528)	WAJD	1390	U1	5	0.05	FL	Gainesville
1529)	WGRB	1390	U4	5	5	IL	Chicago
1530)	WZQQ	1390	D1	5		KY	Hazard
1531)	WPLM	1390	U1	5	5	MA	Plymouth
1532)	WEGP	1390	U4	25	10	ME	Presque Isle
1533)	WLCM	1390	U2	5	4.5	MI	Holt
1534)	KXSS	1390	U4	2.5	1	MN	Waite Park
1535)	KJPW	1390	U1	5	0.11	MO	Waynesville
1536)	WMER	1390	U1	5	0.1	MS	Meridian
1537)	WROA	1390	U1	5	5	MS	Gulfport
1538)	WEED	1390	U1	5	0.03	NC	Rocky Mount
1539)	KRRZ	1390	U1	5	1	ND	Minot
1540)	KENN	1390	U2	5	1.3	NM	Farmington
1541)	KHOB	1390	U2	5	0.5	NM	Hobbs
1542)	WEOK	1390	U3	5	0.1	NY	Poughkeepsie
1543)	WFBL	1390	U4	5	5	NY	Syracuse
1544)	WMPO	1390	U1	5	0.12	OH	Middleport-Pomeroy
1545)	WNIO	1390	U2	9.5	4.8	OH	Youngstown
1546)	KWOD	1390	U1	5	0.69	OR	Salem
1547)	WSPO	1390	U2	5	5	SC	Charleston

MW	Call	kHz	Ant.	D	N	Sta	City of License
1548)	WTJS	1390	U2	5	1	TN	Jackson
1549)	WYXI	1390	U1	2.5	0.06	TN	Athens
1550)	KLGN	1390	U2	5	0.5	UT	Logan
1551)	WKPA	1390	U1	4.7	0.03	VA	Lynchburg
1552)	WZHF	1390	U4	5	5	VA	Arlington
1553)	WCAT	1390	U2	5	5	VT	Burlington
1554)	KTCR	1390	U4	5	0.39	WA	Yakima
1555)	WRIG	1390	U4	10	7.2	WI	Schofield
		1400		various stns of less than 1kW			
1556)	WIQR	**1410**	U2	5	1	AL	Prattville
1557)	WNGL	1410	U2	5	4.6	AL	Mobile
1558)	KCAL	1410	U2	5	4	CA	Redlands
1559)	KMYC	1410	U4	5	1	CA	Marysville
1560)	WPOP	1410	U4	5	5	CT	Hartford
1561)	WDOV	1410	U4	5	5	DE	Dover
1562)	WHBT	1410	U1	5	0.01	FL	Tallahassee
1563)	WMYR	1410	U2	5	5	FL	Fort Myers
1564)	WQBQ	1410	U1	5	0.09	FL	Leesburg
1565)	WKKP	1410	U1	2.5	0.05	GA	McDonough
1566)	KGSO	1410	U4	5	1	KS	Wichita
1567)	KKLO	1410	U4	5	0.5	KS	Leavenworth
1568)	WHLN	1410	U1	5	0.04	KY	Harlan
1569)	WRJD	1410	U1	5	0.29	NC	Durham
1570)	KOOQ	1410	U2	5	0.5	NE	North Platte
1571)	WELM	1410	U1	5	1	NY	Elmira
1572)	WNER	1410	U1	3.5	0.05	NY	Watertown
1573)	WING	1410	U2	5	5	OH	Dayton
1574)	KBNP	1410	U1	5	0.009	OR	Portland
1575)	KQV	1410	U4	5	5	PA	Pittsburgh
1576)	WLSH	1410	D3	5		PA	Lansford
1577)	WRIS	1410	U1	5	0.07	VA	Roanoke
1578)	WIZM	1410	U2	5	5	WI	La Crosse
1579)	WSCW	1410	D1	5		WV	South Charleston
1580)	KWYO	1410	U1	5	0.35	WY	Sheridan
1581)	WACT	**1420**	U1	5	1	AL	Tuscaloosa
1582)	KBHS	1420	U1	5	0.08	AR	Hot Springs
1583)	KMOG	1420	U2	2.5	0.5	AZ	Payson
1584)	KSTN	1420	U4	5	1	CA	Stockton
1585)	WLIS	1420	U2	5	0.5	CT	Old Saybrook
1586)	WBRD	1420	U4	2.5	1	FL	Palmetto
1587)	WDJA	1420	U1	5	0.5	FL	Delray Beach
1588)	WKWN	1420	U1	5	0.11	GA	Trenton
1589)	WRCG	1420	U1	5	0.07	GA	Columbus
1590)	WOC	1420	U4	5	5	IA	Davenport
1591)	KIGO	1420	U1	32	0.01	ID	Saint Anthony
1592)	WIMS	1420	U1	5	1	IN	Michigan City
1593)	WBSM	1420	U3	5	1	MA	New Bedford
1594)	KTOE	1420	U2	5	5	MN	Mankato
1595)	WIGG	1420	U1	5	0.07	MS	Wiggins
1596)	WASR	1420	U1	5	0.13	NH	Wolfeboro
1597)	WACK	1420	U2	5	0.5	NY	Newark
1598)	WLNA	1420	U4	5	1	NY	Peekskill
1599)	WHK	1420	U2	5	5	OH	Cleveland
1600)	WCED	1420	U1	4.2	0.005	PA	Du Bois
1601)	WCOJ	1420	U2	5	5	PA	Coatesville
1602)	WEMB	1420	U1	5	0.02	TN	Erwin
1603)	WKCW	1420	U1	22	0.06	VA	Warrenton
1604)	KITI	1420	U4	5	5	WA	Centralia - Chehalis
1605)	KUJ	1420	U1	5	0.9	WA	Walla Walla
1606)	WTCR	1420	U2	5	0.5	WV	Kenova
1607)	WFHK	**1430**	D1	5		AL	Pell City
1608)	KFIG	1430	U3	5	5	CA	Fresno
1609)	KMRB	1430	U4	50	9.8	CA	San Gabriel
1610)	KVVN	1430	U4	1	2.5	CA	Santa Clara
1611)	KEZW	1430	U2	10	5	CO	Aurora
1612)	WLKF	1430	U2	5	1	FL	Lakeland
1613)	WLTG	1430	U4	5	5	FL	Panama City
1614)	WOIR	1430	U2	5	0.5	FL	Homestead
1615)	WTMN	1430	U1	10	0.04	FL	Gainesville
1616)	WDAL	1430	U1	2.5	0.07	GA	Dalton
1617)	WGFS	1430	U1	3.9	0.21	GA	Covington
1618)	WXNT	1430	U2	5	5	IN	Indianapolis
1619)	WCWC	1430	U1	5.7	0.03	KY	Williamsburg
1620)	WKOX	1430	U2	5	1	MA	Everett
1621)	WPNI	1430	U4	5	0.01	MA	Amherst
1622)	WNAV	1430	U2	5	1	MD	Annapolis
1623)	WION	1430	U2	4.7	0.33	MI	Ionia
1624)	KZQZ	1430	U4	5	5	MO	Saint Louis
1625)	WDEX	1430	U4	2.5	2.5	NC	Monroe
1626)	WDJS	1430	U4	10	5	NC	Mount Olive
1627)	WMNC	1430	U1	2.7	0.04	NC	Morganton
1628)	KRGI	1430	U2	5	1	NE	Grand Island
1629)	WNSW	1430	U4	10	7	NJ	Newark
1630)	KCRX	1430	U2	5	1	NM	Roswell
1631)	WENE	1430	U2	5	5	NY	Endicott
1632)	KTBZ	1430	U4	25	5	OK	Tulsa
1633)	KYKN	1430	U2	5	5	OR	Keizer
1634)	WVAM	1430	U2	5	1	PA	Altoona
1635)	WBLR	1430	U1	5	0.16	SC	Batesburg
1636)	WOWW	1430	U2	2.5	2.5	TN	Germantown
1637)	WPLN	1430	U2	15	1	TN	Madison
1638)	KCOH	1430	U4	5	1	TX	Houston
1639)	KEES	1430	U2	5	1	TX	Gladewater
1640)	KLO	1430	U4	25	5	UT	Ogden
1641)	WDIC	1430	D1	5		VA	Clinchco
1642)	KBRC	1430	U2	5	1	WA	Mount Vernon
1643)	KCLK	1430	U2	5	1	WA	Asotin
1644)	WLWI	**1440**	U2	5	1	AL	Montgomery
1645)	KTUV	1440	U2	5	0.24	AR	Little Rock
1646)	KAZG	1440	U1	5	0.05	AZ	Scottsdale
1647)	KUHL	1440	U2	5	1	CA	Santa Maria
1648)	KVON	1440	U4	5	1	CA	Napa
1649)	KRDZ	1440	U1	5	0.21	CO	Wray
1650)	WPRD	1440	U2	5	1	FL	Winter Park
1651)	WWCL	1440	U4	5	1	FL	Lehigh Acres
1652)	WGIG	1440	U2	5	1	GA	Brunswick
1653)	WGMI	1440	U1	2.5	0.06	GA	Bremen
1654)	KPTO	1440	U4	2.5	0.35	ID	Pocatello
1655)	WGEM	1440	U4	5	1	IL	Quincy
1656)	WROK	1440	U5	5	0.27	IL	Rockford
1657)	KMAJ	1440	U3	5	1	KS	Topeka
1658)	WVEI	1440	U2	5	5	MA	Worcester
1659)	WRED	1440	U2	5	5	ME	Westbrook
1660)	WKPR	1440	U1	2.7	0.02	MI	Kalamazoo
1661)	WMAX	1440	U4	5	2.5	MI	Bay City
1662)	KDIZ	1440	U2	5	0.5	MN	Golden Valley
1663)	WVGG	1440	D1	5		MS	Lucedale
1664)	WBLA	1440	U1	5	0.19	NC	Elizabethtown
1665)	WLXN	1440	U2	5	1	NC	Lexington
1666)	WFNY	1440	U2	5	0.5	NY	Gloversville
1667)	WHKZ	1440	U4	5	5	OH	Warren
1668)	KMED	1440	U1	5	1	OR	Medford
1669)	KODL	1440	U2	5	1	OR	The Dalles
1670)	WCDL	1440	U1	5	0.03	PA	Carbondale
1671)	WNPV	1440	U4	2.5	0.5	PA	Lansdale
1672)	WGVL	1440	U2	5	5	SC	Greenville
1673)	WZYX	1440	U1	5	0.06	TN	Cowan
1674)	KETX	1440	U1	5	0.09	TX	Livingston
1675)	KPUR	1440	U2	5	1	TX	Amarillo
1676)	KTNO	1440	U4	50	0.35	TX	University Park
1677)	WKLV	1440	U1	5	0.07	VA	Blackstone
1678)	WNFL	1440	U4	5	0.5	WI	Green Bay
1679)	WAJR	1440	U4	5	0.5	WV	Morgantown
1680)	WHIS	1440	U2	5	0.5	WV	Bluefield
		1450		various stns of less than 1kW			
1681)	WHAL	**1460**	U1	4	0.14	AL	Phenix City
1682)	WMCJ	1460	U2	5	0.5	AL	Cullman
1683)	KION	1460	U3	10	10	CA	Salinas
1684)	KTYM	1460	U4	5	0.5	CA	Inglewood
1685)	KZNT	1460	U2	5	0.54	CO	Colorado Springs
1686)	WNPL	1460	U4	7	2	FL	Golden Gate
1687)	WQOP	1460	U2	15	5	FL	Jacksonville
1688)	WZEP	1460	U1	10	0.18	FL	Defuniak Springs
1689)	WXEM	1460	U1	5	0.19	GA	Buford
1690)	KXNO	1460	U2	5	5	IA	Des Moines
1691)	WKAM	1460	U2	2.5	0.5	IN	Goshen
1692)	WEKB	1460	U1	5	0.11	KY	Elkhorn City
1693)	WXOK	1460	U1	4.7	0.29	LA	Port Allen
1694)	WXBR	1460	U2	5	1	MA	Brockton
1695)	WBRN	1460	U2	5	2.5	MI	Big Rapids
1696)	KKAQ	1460	U1	2.5	0.15	MN	Thief River Falls
1697)	KHOJ	1460	U4	5	0.21	MO	Saint Charles
1698)	WEWO	1460	U4	5	5	NC	Laurinburg
1699)	WHBK	1460	U1	5	0.13	NC	Marshall
1700)	KLTC	1460	U2	5	5	ND	Dickinson
1701)	KXPN	1460	U2	5	0.05	NE	Kearney
1702)	WIFI	1460	U3	5	0.5	NJ	Florence
1703)	KENO	1460	U1	10	0.62	NV	Las Vegas
1704)	WDDY	1460	U2	5	5	NY	Albany
1705)	WHIC	1460	U2	3.7	5	NY	Rochester
1706)	WBNS	1460	U2	5	1	OH	Columbus
1707)	WGMF	1460	U4	5	1	PA	Tunkhannock
1708)	WTKT	1460	U2	5	4.2	PA	Harrisburg
1709)	KBRZ	1460	U1	5	0.12	TX	Missouri City
1710)	KCLE	1460	U4	11	0.7	TX	Burleson
1711)	WKDV	1460	U4	5	5	VA	Manassas
1712)	WRAD	1460	U2	5	0.5	VA	Radford
1713)	KARR	1460	U4	5	2.5	WA	Kirkland
1714)	KUTI	1460	U4	5	3.7	WA	Yakima
1715)	WBUC	1460	U1	5.5	0.02	WV	Buckhannon
1716)	KNXN	**1470**	U1	2.5	0.03	AZ	Sierra Vista
1717)	KIID	1470	U4	5	1	CA	Sacramento

MW	Call	kHz	Ant.	D	N	Sta	City of License
1718)	KUTY	1470	U4	5	5	CA	Palmdale
1719)	WMMW	1470	U4	2.5	2.5	CT	Meriden
1720)	WMGG	1470	U1	5	0.5	FL	Dunedin
1721)	WWNN	1470	U4	50	2.5	FL	Pompano Beach
1722)	WRGA	1470	U2	5	5	GA	Rome
1723)	KWSL	1470	U4	5	5	IA	Sioux City
1724)	WMBD	1470	U4	5	5	IL	Peoria
1725)	WBFC	1470	U1	2.5	0.02	KY	Stanton
1726)	KLCL	1470	U1	5	0.5	LA	Lake Charles
1727)	WAZN	1470	U4	1.4	3.4	MA	Watertown
1728)	WJDY	1470	U3	5	0.04	MD	Salisbury
1729)	WLAM	1470	U3	5	5	ME	Lewiston
1730)	WFNT	1470	U4	5	1	MI	Flint
1731)	KMNQ	1470	U4	5	5	MN	Brooklyn Park
1732)	WNAU	1470	U2	2.5	0.5	MS	New Albany
1733)	WJPI	1470	D1	5		NC	Plymouth
1734)	WTOE	1470	U1	5	0.1	NC	Spruce Pine
1735)	WWBG	1470	U4	10	5	NC	Greensboro
1736)	WNYY	1470	U2	5	1	NY	Ithaca
1737)	WSAN	1470	U2	5	5	PA	Allentown
1738)	WQXL	1470	U1	11	0.1	SC	Columbia
1739)	WVOL	1470	U4	5	1	TN	Berry Hill
1740)	KWRD	1470	D1	5		TX	Henderson
1741)	KYYW	1470	U2	5	1	TX	Abilene
1742)	WBTX	1470	U1	5	0.03	VA	Broadway-Timberville
1743)	WTZE	1470	D1	5		VA	Tazewell
1744)	KBSN	1470	U4	5	1	WA	Moses Lake
1745)	KELA	1470	U1	5	1	WA	Centralia-Chehalis
1746)	WBKV	1470	U4	2.5	2.5	WI	West Bend
1747)	WABB	**1480**	U2	5	4.4	AL	Mobile
1748)	WQOH	1480	U1	5	0.02	AL	Irondale
1749)	KTHS	1480	U1	5	0.06	AR	Berryville
1750)	KPHX	1480	U2	5	0.5	AZ	Phoenix
1751)	KGOE	1480	U1	5	1	CA	Eureka
1752)	KVNR	1480	U4	5	5	CA	Santa Ana
1753)	KYOS	1480	U2	5	5	CA	Merced
1754)	WKGC	1480	U1	5	0.03	FL	Southport
1755)	WCHZ	1480	U2	5	5	GA	Augusta
1756)	WYZE	1480	U1	10	0.04	GA	Atlanta
1757)	KRXR	1480	U1	5	0.09	ID	Gooding
1758)	WPFR	1480	U4	5	1	IN	Terre Haute
1759)	KQAM	1480	U4	5	1	KS	Wichita
1760)	WIZD	1480	D1	5		KY	Neon
1761)	WSAR	1480	U3	5	5	MA	Fall River
1762)	WGVU	1480	U2	2	5	MI	Kentwood
1763)	WSDS	1480	U4	0.75	3.8	MI	Salem Township
1764)	KKCQ	1480	U1	5	0.09	MN	Fosston
1765)	WGFY	1480	U4	4.4	5	NC	Charlotte
1766)	WPFJ	1480	U1	5	0.01	NC	Franklin
1767)	WQTM	1480	U1	10	0.04	NC	Fair Bluff
1768)	WLEA	1480	U1	2.5	0.01	NY	Hornell
1769)	WRCK	1480	D1	5		NY	Remsen
1770)	WZRC	1480	U4	5	5	NY	New York
1771)	WDJO	1480	U4	4.5	0.3	OH	Cincinnati
1772)	WHBC	1480	U4	15	5	OH	Canton
1773)	WDAS	1480	U4	5	1	PA	Philadelphia
1774)	WBBP	1480	U1	5	0.04	TN	Memphis
1775)	KBXD	1480	U4	5	1.9	TX	Dallas
1776)	KCHL	1480	U3	2.5	0.09	TX	San Antonio
1777)	KLVL	1480	U4	5	0.5	TX	Pasadena
1778)	WPWC	1480	U4	5	0.5	VA	Dumfries-Triangle
1779)	WTOX	1480	U4	6.3	1.5	VA	Glen Allen
1780)	WTOY	1480	U1	5	0.02	VA	Salem
1781)	WCFR	1480	U1	5	0.02	VT	Springfield
1782)	KBMS	1480	U2	1	2.5	WA	Vancouver
1783)	WLMV	1480	U4	5	5	WI	Madison
		1490	various stns of less than 1kW				
1784)	KSJX	**1500**	U4	10	5	CA	San Jose
1785)	WFIF	1500	D3	5		CT	Milford
1786)	WFED	1500	U4	50	50	DC	Washington
1787)	WDPC	1500	D4	5		GA	Dallas
1788)	WBRI	1500	D3	5		IN	Indianapolis
1789)	WLQV	1500	U4	50	10	MI	Detroit
1790)	KSTP	1500	U2	50	50	MN	Saint Paul
1791)	KFNN	**1510**	U3	22	0.1	AZ	Mesa
1792)	KIRV	1510	D3	10		CA	Fresno
1793)	KSFN	1510	U4	8	2.4	CA	Piedmont
1794)	KSPA	1510	U4	10	1	CA	Ontario
1795)	KCKK	1510	U4	10	25	CO	Littleton
1796)	WWBC	1510	D4	50		FL	Cocoa
1797)	WWZN	1510	U7	50	50	MA	Boston
1798)	WJKN	1510	D3	5		MI	Jackson
1799)	KCTE	1510	D3	10		MO	Independence
1800)	KMRF	1510	D4	5		MO	Marshfield
1801)	WFAI	1510	D3	2.5		NJ	Salem
1802)	KOAZ	1510	U1	5	0.02	NM	Isleta

MW	Call	kHz	Ant.	D	N	Sta	City of License
1803)	WPGR	1510	U4	5	0.001	PA	Monroeville
1804)	WWSM	1510	D3	5		PA	Annville-Cleona
1805)	KMSD	1510	U1	5	0.01	SD	Milbank
1806)	WLAC	1510	U2	50	50	TN	Nashville
1807)	KBED	1510	D3	5		TX	Nederland
1808)	KLLB	1510	D1	10		UT	West Jordan
1809)	KGA	1510	U4	50	15	WA	Spokane
1810)	WRRD	1510	D4	23		WI	Waukesha
1811)	KMPG	**1520**	D4	5		CA	Hollister
1812)	KVTA	1520	U4	10	1	CA	Port Hueneme
1813)	WBZW	1520	U4	5	0.35	FL	Apopka
1814)	WEXY	1520	U2	5	0.8	FL	Wilton Manors
1815)	WDCY	1520	D1	2.5		GA	Douglasville
1816)	WHOW	1520	D1	5		IL	Clinton
1817)	WLGC	1520	D1	5		KY	Greenup
1818)	KFXZ	1520	U6	10	0.5	LA	Lafayette
1819)	WIZZ	1520	D3	10		MA	Greenfield
1820)	WTRI	1520	D3	17		MD	Brunswick
1821)	KOLM	1520	U8	10	0.8	MN	Rochester
1822)	KRHW	1520	U7	5	1.6	MO	Sikeston
1823)	WARR	1520	D1	5		NC	Warrenton
1824)	WDSL	1520	D1	5		NC	Mocksville
1825)	WWKB	1520	U3	50	50	NY	Buffalo
1826)	KOKC	1520	U2	50	50	OK	Oklahoma City
1827)	KGDD	1520	U3	50	15	OR	Oregon City
1828)	KQOB	1520	D3	2.5		TX	Stockdale
1829)	KYND	1520	D5	3		TX	Cypress
1830)	KKXA	1520	U6	20	50	WA	Snohomish
1831)	KVDW	**1530**	D1	2.5		AR	England
1832)	KFBK	1530	U4	50	50	CA	Sacramento
1833)	KCMN	1530	U1	15	0.01	CO	Colorado Springs
1834)	WDJZ	1530	D3	5		CT	Bridgeport
1835)	WYMM	1530	D3	50		FL	Jacksonville
1836)	WTTI	1530	D4	10		GA	Dalton
1837)	WLCO	1530	D3	5		MI	Lapeer
1838)	KQSP	1530	U3	8.6	0.01	MN	Shakopee
1839)	WLLQ	1530	D3	10		NC	Chapel Hill
1840)	WCKY	1530	U2	50	50	OH	Cincinnati
1841)	KXTD	1530	D3	5		OK	Wagoner
1842)	KCLR	1530	D1	5		TX	Ralls
1843)	KGBT	1530	U8	50	10	TX	Harlingen
1844)	KLBW	1530	D1	2.5		TX	New Boston
1845)	KZNX	1530	U7	10	0.22	TX	Creedmoor
1846)	KASA	**1540**	U3	10	10	AZ	Phoenix
1847)	KMPC	1540	U4	50	37	CA	Los Angeles
1848)	WKVQ	1540	D1	10		GA	Eatonton
1849)	KXEL	1540	U2	50	50	IA	Waterloo
1850)	WACA	1540	D1	5		MD	Wheaton
1851)	WYNC	1540	D1	2.5		NC	Yanceyville
1852)	WXEX	1540	U1	5	0.003	NH	Exeter
1853)	WDCD	1540	U3	50	50	NY	Albany
1854)	WECZ	1540	D1	5		PA	Punxsutawney
1855)	WNWR	1540	D3	50		PA	Philadelphia
1856)	WTBI	1540	D1	10		SC	Pickens
1857)	KEDA	1540	U4	5	1	TX	San Antonio
1858)	KGBC	1540	U4	2.5	0.25	TX	Galveston
1859)	KZMP	1540	U4	32	0.75	TX	University Park
1860)	WREJ	1540	U4	10	0.007	VA	Richmond
1861)	KXPA	1540	U2	5	5	WA	Bellevue
1862)	WLOR	**1550**	U4	50	0.04	AL	Huntsville
1863)	KUAZ	1550	D1	50		AZ	Tucson
1864)	KWRN	1550	U2	5	0.5	CA	Apple Valley
1865)	KXEX	1550	U4	5	2.5	CA	Fresno
1866)	KZDG	1550	U4	10	10	CA	San Francisco
1867)	WSDK	1550	U4	5	2.4	CT	Bloomfield
1868)	WAMA	1550	U1	10	0.13	FL	Tampa
1869)	WNZF	1550	U2	11	0.25	FL	Bunnell
1870)	WRHC	1550	U4	10	5	FL	Coral Gables
1871)	WAZX	1550	U5	50	0.01	GA	Smyrna
1872)	WKTF	1550	U1	10	0.02	GA	Vienna
1873)	WTHB	1550	U1	5	0.01	GA	Augusta
1874)	WPFC	1550	U1	5	0.04	LA	Baton Rouge
1875)	WNTN	1550	U1	10	0.003	MA	Newton
1876)	KAPE	1550	U3	5	5	MO	Cape Girardeau
1877)	KESJ	1550	U2	2.5	0.5	MO	Saint Joseph
1878)	KLFJ	1550	U1	5	0.04	MO	Springfield
1879)	KIVA	1550	U1	10	0.02	NM	Albuquerque
1880)	KXTO	1550	U1	2.5	0.09	NV	Reno
1881)	KYAL	1550	U3	2.5	0.04	OK	Sapulpa
1882)	WITK	1550	U4	10	0.5	PA	Pittston
1883)	WBSC	1550	U2	10	5	SC	Bennettsville
1884)	WIGN	1550	U1	35	0.006	TN	Bristol
1885)	KMRI	1550	U1	10	0.34	UT	West Valley City
1886)	WKBA	1550	D3	10		VA	Vinton
1887)	WVAB	1550	U1	5	0.009	VA	Virginia Beach
1888)	KKOV	1550	U2	50	12	WA	Vancouver

MW	Call	kHz	Ant.	D	N	Sta	City of License
1889)	KRPI	1550	U4	50	10	WA	Ferndale
1890)	WHIT	1550	D3	5		WI	Madison
1891)	WMRE	1550	U1	5	0.006	WV	Charles Town
1892)	KNZR	**1560**	U2	25	10	CA	Bakersfield
1893)	WINV	1560	D1	5		FL	Beverly Hills
1894)	WLZR	1560	D1	5		FL	Melbourne
1895)	KLNG	1560	D1	10		IA	Council Bluffs
1896)	WPAD	1560	U7	10	5	KY	Paducah
1897)	WNWN	1560	D3	4.1		MI	Portage
1898)	WQEW	1560	U4	50	50	NY	New York
1899)	WCNW	1560	D3	5		OH	Fairfield
1900)	WAGL	1560	D3	50		SC	Lancaster
1901)	KKAA	1560	U4	10	10	SD	Aberdeen
1902)	KGOW	1560	U4	46	15	TX	Bellaire
1903)	KTXZ	1560	U4	2.5	2.5	TX	West Lake Hills
1904)	WSBV	1560	D1	2.5		VA	South Boston
1905)	KVAN	1560	U4	10	0.7	WA	Burbank
1906)	KZIZ	1560	U2	5	0.9	WA	Pacific
1907)	WCRL	**1570**	U1	2.5	0.06	AL	Oneonta
1908)	KCVR	1570	U4	5	0.5	CA	Lodi
1909)	KPRO	1570	U3	5	0.19	CA	Riverside
1910)	KTGE	1570	U4	5	0.5	CA	Salinas
1911)	KPIO	1570	U1	7	0.01	CO	Loveland
1912)	WTWB	1570	U1	5	0.01	FL	Auburndale
1913)	WVOJ	1570	U1	10	0.03	FL	Fernandina Beach
1914)	WIGO	1570	U1	5	0.05	GA	Morrow
1915)	WFRL	1570	U3	5	0.5	IL	Freeport
1916)	WNSH	1570	U1	30	0.08	MA	Beverly
1917)	WNST	1570	U1	5	0.23	MD	Towson
1918)	KAKK	1570	U1	9.5	0.25	MN	Walker
1919)	KYCR	1570	U1	3.8	0.23	MN	Golden Valley
1920)	KBCV	1570	U4	5	3	MO	Hollister
1921)	WIZK	1570	D1	3.2		MS	Bay Springs
1922)	WECU	1570	U1	8	0.2	NC	Winterville
1923)	WNCA	1570	U1	5	0.28	NC	Siler City
1924)	WFLR	1570	U1	5	0.44	NY	Dundee
1925)	WISP	1570	U4	5	0.9	PA	Doylestown
1926)	WPGM	1570	U1	2.5	0.22	PA	Danville
1927)	WCLE	1570	U1	5	0.08	TN	Cleveland
1928)	WYTI	1570	U1	2.5	0.22	VA	Rocky Mount
1929)	WLKD	1570	U1	5	0.5	WI	Minocqua
1930)	WVOK	**1580**	U1	2.5	0.02	AL	Oxford
1931)	KMIK	1580	U2	50	50	AZ	Tempe
1932)	KBLA	1580	U4	50	50	CA	Santa Monica
1933)	KREL	1580	U1	10	0.14	CO	Colorado Springs
1934)	WNTF	1580	D3	10		FL	Bithlo
1935)	WSRF	1580	U4	10	5	FL	Fort Lauderdale
1936)	WTCL	1580	D1	10		FL	Chattahoochee
1937)	WGVN	1580	U3	10	0.04	KY	Georgetown
1938)	WNEW	1580	U4	50	0.27	MD	Morningside
1939)	WPMO	1580	U4	5	0.05	MS	Pascagoula-Moss Point
1940)	WLIM	1580	U8	10	0.5	NY	Patchogue
1941)	WVKO	1580	U4	3.2	0.29	OH	Columbus
1942)	WDAB	1580	U1	5	0.01	SC	Travelers Rest
1943)	WLIJ	1580	U1	5	0.01	TN	Shelbyville
1944)	WNPZ	1580	D1	5		TN	Knoxville
1945)	WTTN	1580	U5	5	0.004	WI	Columbus
1946)	WVNA	**1590**	U2	5	1	AL	Tuscumbia
1947)	KBJT	1590	U1	4.7	0.03	AR	Fordyce
1948)	KYNG	1590	U1	2.5	0.05	AR	Springdale
1949)	KLIV	1590	U2	5	5	CA	San Jose
1950)	KUNX	1590	U4	5	5	CA	Ventura
1951)	WPSL	1590	U1	5	0.06	FL	Port Saint Lucie
1952)	WRXB	1590	U4	5	1	FL	Saint Pete Beach
1953)	WALG	1590	U4	5	1	GA	Albany
1954)	WQCH	1590	D1	5		GA	Lafayette
1955)	WXRS	1590	U1	2.5	0.02	GA	Swainsboro
1956)	WAIK	1590	U3	5	0.05	IL	Galesburg
1957)	WCGO	1590	U2	7	2.5	IL	Evanston
1958)	WNTS	1590	U4	5	0.5	IN	Beech Grove
1959)	KVGB	1590	U4	5	5	KS	Great Bend
1960)	WHGT	1590	U4	15	0.05	MD	Maugansville
1961)	WTVB	1590	U2	5	1	MI	Coldwater
1962)	KGFK	1590	U4	5	1	MN	East Grand Forks
1963)	WZRX	1590	U2	5	1	MS	Jackson
1964)	WCSL	1590	U1	10	0.03	NC	Cherryville
1965)	WHPY	1590	U3	5	0.02	NC	Clayton
1966)	KTCH	1590	U3	2.5	0.04	NE	Wayne
1967)	WSMN	1590	U3	5	5	NH	Nashua
1968)	KQLO	1590	U1	5	0.06	NV	Sun Valley
1969)	WGGO	1590	U1	5	0.01	NY	Salamanca
1970)	WAKR	1590	U2	5	5	OH	Akron
1971)	KTIL	1590	U2	5	1	OR	Tillamook
1972)	WPSN	1590	U1	2.5	0.01	PA	Honesdale
1973)	WPWA	1590	U2	2.5	1	PA	Chester
1974)	WARV	1590	U4	5	5	RI	Warwick

MW	Call	kHz	Ant.	D	N	Sta	City of License
1975)	WKTP	1590	U3	5	5	TN	Jonesborough
1976)	KELP	1590	U4	5	0.8	TX	El Paso
1977)	KGAS	1590	U1	2.5	0.12	TX	Carthage
1978)	KLRK	1590	U1	2.5	0.06	TX	Mexia
1979)	KMIC	1590	U2	5	5	TX	Houston
1980)	WFTH	1590	U1	5	0.01	VA	Richmond
1981)	KLFE	1590	U2	5	5	WA	Seattle
1982)	WGBW	1590	U4	10	0.05	WI	Denmark
1983)	WIXK	1590	U1	5	0.09	WI	New Richmond
1984)	WHIY	**1600**	U2	5	0.5	AL	Huntsville
1985)	WXVI	1600	U4	5	1	AL	Montgomery
1986)	KNWA	1600	U1	5	0.05	AR	Bellefonte
1987)	KAHZ	1600	U2	5	5	CA	Pomona
1988)	KGST	1600	U2	5	5	CA	Fresno
1989)	KUBA	1600	U2	5	2.5	CA	Yuba City
1990)	KEPN	1600	U2	5	5	CO	Lakewood
1991)	WRJE	1600	U4	5	1	DE	Dover
1992)	WHTY	1600	U4	5	4.7	FL	Riviera Beach
1993)	WZNZ	1600	U1	5	0.08	FL	Atlantic Beach
1994)	WAOS	1600	U1	20	0.06	GA	Austell
1995)	KGYM	1600	U2	5	5	IA	Cedar Rapids
1996)	KLEB	1600	U4	5	0.25	LA	Golden Meadow
1997)	WHNP	1600	D1	2.5		MA	East Longmeadow
1998)	WUNR	1600	U3	20	20	MA	Brookline
1999)	WAAM	1600	U4	5	5	MI	Ann Arbor
2000)	KPNP	1600	U3	5	5	MN	Watertown
2001)	KATZ	1600	U2	6	3.5	MO	Saint Louis
2002)	WIDU	1600	U4	5	0.14	NC	Fayetteville
2003)	KRKE	1600	U1	10	0.17	NM	Albuquerque
2004)	WEHH	1600	U4	5	0.17	NY	Elmira Heights-Horseheads
2005)	WWRL	1600	U4	25	5	NY	New York
2006)	KOPB	1600	U2	5	1	OR	Eugene
2007)	WAYC	1600	U1	2.7	0.01	PA	Bedford
2008)	WKZK	1600	U1	4	0.02	SC	North Augusta
2009)	WATX	1600	U1	2.5	0.02	TN	Algood
2010)	WMQM	1600	U1	50	0.03	TN	Lakeland
2011)	KOKE	1600	U1	5	0.7	TX	Pflugerville
2012)	KRVA	1600	U4	25	0.93	TX	Cockrell Hill
2013)	KTUB	1600	U2	5	1	UT	Centerville
2014)	WCPK	1600	U1	4.2	0.02	VA	Chesapeake
2015)	WXMY	1600	D1	5		VA	Saltville
2016)	KVRI	1600	U4	50	10	WA	Blaine
2017)	WRPN	1600	U4	5	5	WI	Ripon
2018)	WKKX	1600	U1	5	0.03	WV	Wheeling
2019)	WZZW	1600	U1	5	0.02	WV	Milton
2020)	KSMH	**1620**	U1	10	1	CA	West Sacramento
2021)	WNRP	1620	U1	10	1	FL	Gulf Breeze
2022)	WDND	1620	U1	10	1	IN	South Bend
2023)	KOZN	1620	U1	10	1	NE	Bellevue
2024)	WTAW	1620	U1	10	1	TX	College Station
2025)	KYIZ	1620	U1	10	1	WA	Renton
2026)	WRDW	**1630**	U1	10	1	GA	Augusta
2027)	KCJJ	1630	U1	10	1	IA	Iowa City
2028)	KKGM	1630	U1	10	1	TX	Fort Worth
2029)	KRND	1630	U1	10	1	WY	Fox Farm
2030)	KDIA	**1640**	U2	10	10	CA	Vallejo
2031)	WTNI	1640	U1	10	1	MS	Biloxi
2032)	KFXY	1640	U4	10	1	OK	Enid
2033)	KDZR	1640	U1	10	1	OR	Lake Oswego
2034)	KBJA	1640	U1	10	1	UT	Sandy
2035)	WKSH	1640	U1	10	1	WI	Sussex
2036)	KYHN	**1650**	U1	10	1	AR	Fort Smith
2037)	KFOX	1650	U1	10	0.49	CA	Torrance
2038)	KBJD	1650	U1	10	1	CO	Denver
2039)	KCNZ	1650	U1	10	1	IA	Cedar Falls
2040)	KSVE	1650	U1	8.5	0.85	TX	El Paso
2041)	WHKT	1650	U1	10	1	VA	Portsmouth
2042)	KTIQ	**1660**	U1	10	1	CA	Merced
2043)	WCNZ	1660	U1	10	1	FL	Marco Island
2044)	KUDL	1660	U1	10	1	KS	Kansas City
2045)	WQLR	1660	U1	10	1	MI	Kalamazoo
2046)	WBCN	1660	U1	10	1	NC	Charlotte
2047)	KQWB	1660	U1	10	1	ND	West Fargo
2048)	WWRU	1660	U4	10	10	NJ	Jersey City
2049)	KRZI	1660	U1	10	1	TX	Waco
2050)	KXOL	1660	U1	10	1	UT	Brigham City
2051)	KHPY	**1670**	U4	10	9	CA	Moreno Valley
2052)	KNRO	1670	U1	10	1	CA	Redding
2053)	WPLA	1670	U1	10	1	GA	Dry Branch
2054)	WTDY	1670	U1	10	1	WI	Madison
2055)	KGED	**1680**	U1	10	1	CA	Fresno
2056)	WOKB	1680	U1	10	1	FL	Winter Garden
2057)	KRJO	1680	U1	10	1	LA	Monroe
2058)	WPRR	1680	U1	10	0.68	MI	Ada
2059)	WTTM	1680	U1	10	1	NJ	Lindenwold
2060)	KNTS	1680	U1	10	1	WA	Seattle

MW	Call	kHz	Ant.	D	N	Sta	City of License
2061)	KFSG	1690	U1	10	1	CA	Roseville
2062)	KDDZ	1690	U1	10	1	CO	Arvada
2063)	WMLB	1690	U1	10	1	GA	Avondale Estates
2064)	WVON	1690	U1	10	1	IL	Berwyn
2065)	WPTX	1690	U1	10	1	MD	Lexington Park
2066)	WEUP	1700	U1	10	1	AL	Huntsville
2067)	WJCC	1700	U1	10	1	FL	Miami Springs
2068)	KBGG	1700	U1	10	1	IA	Des Moines
2069)	KKLF	1700	U1	10	1	TX	Richardson
2070)	KVNS	1700	U1	8.8	0.88	TX	Brownsville

1) 273 Azalea Rd, Mobile, AL 36609-1970 – **2)** 495 Elder Ave #7, Sand City, CA 93955-3547 – **3)** 1139 Hartnell Ave, Redding, CA 96002-2113 – **4)** 2500 Maitland Center Pkwy #401, Maitland, FL 32751-4122 – **5)** 1501 13th Ave, Columbus, GA 31901-1908 – **6)** 200 N 10th St, Fort Dodge, IA 50501-3925 – **7)** 1109 Hudson Lane, Monroe, LA 71201-6003 – **8)** 3305 Durham Dr #111, Raleigh, NC 27603-3579 – **9)** 1846 Skyland Dr, Sylva, NC 28779-8008 – **10)** 304 South Grand Ave, Las Vegas, NM 87701-3873 – **11)** 2395 Ocean Ave #3, Ronkonkoma, NY 11779-5670 – **12)** 400 Ardmore Dr, Pittsburgh, PA 15221-3019 – **13)** 1640 Old Russellville Pike, Clarksville, TN 37043-1709 – **14)** 4686 E Van Buren St #300, Phoenix, AZ 85008-6967 – **15)** 3223 Sillect Ave, Bakersfield, CA 93308-6329 – **16)** 1111 W Victory Way, Craig, CO 81625-2950 – **17)** 2500 Russell Rd, Green Cove Springs, FL 32043-9492 – **18)** 1102 Thompson Bridge Rd, Gainesville, GA 30501-1706 – **19)** 1815 Meadowlark Rd, Clay Center, KS 67432-8201 – **20)** 638 West Port Plaza, Saint Louis, MO 63146-3106 – **21)** 660 Dewey Blvd, Butte, MT 59701-2318 – **22)** 3500 E Rosser Ave, Bismarck, ND 58501-3398 – **23)** 500 Corporate Pkwy #200, Buffalo, NY 14226-1263 – **24)** 8044 Montgomery Rd #650, Cincinnati, OH 45236-2959 – **25)** 7140 SW Macadam Ave, Portland, OR 97219-3013 – **26)** 1330 East 8th St #207, Odessa, TX 79761-4731 – **27)** 4050 Eisenhauer Rd, San Antonio, TX 78218-3409 – **28)** 1820 Heritage Center Way, Harrisonburg, VA 22801-8451 – **29)** 9 Stowe St, Waterbury, VT 05670-1820 – **30)** 4840 Lincoln Rd, Blaine, WA 98230-9602 – **31)** 557 Scott St, Wausau, WI 54403-4829 – **32)** 2518 Columbia Hwy, Dothan, AL 36303-5402 – **33)** 900 Front St, San Francisco, CA 94111-1427 – **34)** 2821 S Parker Rd #1205, Aurora, CO 80014-2708 – **35)** 194 NW 187th St, Miami, FL 33169-4050 – **36)** 25 NW Point Blvd #400, Elk Grove, IL 60007-1030 – **37)** P.O. Box 608, Middlesboro, KY 40965-0608 – **38)** 1331 Main St, Springfield, MA 01103-1669 – **39)** 242 Finzel Rd, Frostburg, MD 21532-4009 – **40)** 420 Western Ave, South Portland, ME 04106-1704 – **41)** 14 East Central Entrance, Duluth, MN 55811-5508 – **42)** 3000 Chestnut Expressway, Springfield, MO 65802-2528 – **43)** 20 3rd St N #231, Great Falls, MT 59401-3188 – **44)** 117 Ridge Pike, Lafayette Hill, PA 19444-1900 – **45)** 316 Greystone Blvd, Columbia, SC 29210-8007 – **46)** 6080 Mount Moriah Rd Ext., Memphis, TN 38115-2698 – **47)** 1815 Division St #110, Nashville, TN 37203-2753 – **48)** 2885 Interstate 10 E, Beaumont, TX 77702-1001 – **49)** 231 N Wenatchee Ave, Wenatchee, WA 98801-2009 – **50)** 102 N Kanawha St, Beckley, WV 25801-4715 – **51)** 304 South 4th St, Gadsden, AL 35901-5213 – **52)** P.O. Box 580, Alturas, CA 96101-0580 – **53)** 3400 Olive Ave #550, Burbank, CA 91505-5544 – **54)** 5211 West Laurel St #101, Tampa, FL 33607-1725 – **55)** 1801 Rockville Pike #405, Rockville, MD 20852-5604 – **56)** 13 Summerlin Rd, Asheville, NC 28806-2800 – **57)** 1355 California Ave, Las Cruces, NM 88001-4130 – **58)** 777 Terrace Ave #602, Hasbrouck Heights, NJ 07604-3113 – **59)** 500 Plum St #410, Syracuse, NY 13204-1427 – **60)** 7461 South Ave, Youngstown, OH 44512-5789 – **61)** WNAX Bldg - 1609 East Hwy 50, Yankton, SD 57078-6406 – **62)** 3500 Maple Ave #1600, Dallas, TX 75219-3945 – **63)** 2801 Decker Lake Dr, West Valley City, UT 84119-2330 – **64)** 140 4th Ave North #340, Seattle, WA 98109-4932 – **65)** 1110 S Park Ave, Tucson, AZ 85719-6745 – **66)** 1071 West Shaw St, Fresno, CA 93771-3702 – **67)** 106 Rose Lane, Montrose, CO 81401-3823 – **68)** 4192 North John Young Pkwy, Orlando, FL 32804-2696 – **69)** 4051 Jimmie Dyess Pkwy, Augusta, GA 30909-9469 – **70)** 827 Park Blvd #1001, Boise, ID 83712-7781 – **71)** Campbell Hall - 300 N Goodwin Ave, Urbana, IL 61801-2316 – **72)** 1200 SW Executive Dr, Topeka, KS 66615-3850 – **73)** 601 Washington St, Alexandria, LA 71301-8028 – **74)** 96 Stereo Lane, Paxton, MA 01612-1376 – **75)** 314 E Front St, Traverse City, MI 49684-2528 – **76)** 240 Radio Rd, West Jefferson, NC 28694-ND – **77)** 600 Corporate Cir #100, Harrisburg, PA 17110-9787 – **78)** 319 W Rockwood St, Rockwood, TN 37854-2245 – **79)** 201 State St, La Crosse, WI 54601-3246 – **80)** 1111 Virginia St East, Charleston, WV 25301-2406 – **81)** 208 Buena Vista Rd, Hot Springs, AR 71913-8208 – **82)** 900 Ski Run Blvd Ste 200, South Lake Tahoe, CA 96150-9000 – **83)** 701 N Brand Blvd #550, Glendale, CA 91203-1235 – **84)** 1834 Lisenby Ave, Panama City, FL 32405-3713 – **85)** 900 Circle 75 Pkwy SE #1320, Atlanta, GA 30339-3095 – **86)** 1406 Commerce Way, Idaho Falls, ID 83401-1233 – **87)** 300 W Vine St 3rd Flr, Lexington, KY 40507-1807 – **88)** 500 Victory Rd #2, Quincy, MA 02171-3132 – **89)** 222 S Lawrence St, Ironwood, MI

49938-2524 – **90)** 4200 W Main St, Kalamazoo, MI 49006-2766 – **91)** 5030 North 72nd St, Omaha, NE 68134-2363 – **92)** 6 Johnson Rd, Latham, NY 12110-5638 – **93)** 1200 Executive Pkwy #440, Eugene, OR 97401-2169 – **94)** 600 Baltimore Dr, Wilkes-Barre, PA 18702-7901 – **95)** 8309 North Interstate 35, Austin, TX 78753-5771 – **96)** 750 Ridgeview Dr #204, St George, UT 84770-2697 – **97)** 808 East Sprague Ave, Spokane, WA 99202-2126 – **98)** 9660 Granite Ridge Dr, San Diego, CA 92123-2657 – **99)** 4270 Byrd Dr, Loveland, CO 80538-7074 – **100)** 4190 Belfort Rd #450, Jacksonville, FL 32216-1405 – **101)** 600 Old Marion Rd NE, Cedar Rapids, IA 52402-2152 – **102)** 330 2nd Ave, Paintsville, KY 41240-1034 – **103)** 711 West 40th St #350, Baltimore, MD 21211-2190 – **104)** 670 Sweden St, Caribou, ME 04736-3419 – **105)** 2995 US Highway 93 South, Kalispell, MT 59901-8640 – **106)** 875 W 5th St, Winston-Salem, NC 27101-2505 – **107)** 2400 8th Ave SW, Jamestown, ND 58401-6623 – **108)** 2650 Thousand Oaks Blvd #4100, Memphis, TN 38118-2451 – **109)** 4180 North Mesa St, El Paso, TX 79902-1420 – **110)** 1001 E Southeast Loop 323 #455, Tyler, TX 75701-9600 – **111)** 2700 Corporate Dr #115, Birmingham, AL 35242-2735 – **112)** 352 "E" Ave #K4, Lancaster, CA 93535-4505 – **113)** 260 Hegenberger Rd, Oakland, CA 94621-1491 – **114)** 614 Kimbark St, Longmont, CO 80501-4911 – **115)** 7601 Riviera Blvd, Miramar, FL 33023-6574 – **116)** 715 East Central Entrance, Duluth, MN 55811-5596 – **117)** 7000 Squibb Rd, Mission, KS 66202-3233 – **118)** 1520 South Blvd #300, Charlotte, NC 28203-3701 – **119)** 195 McGregor St #810, Manchester, NH 03102-3755 – **120)** 500 4th St NW, Albuquerque, NM 87102-5324 – **121)** 2323 West 5th Ave #200, Columbus, OH 43204-4988 – **122)** 511 Rossanley Dr, Medford, OR 97501-1771 – **123)** 400 Market St 9th Flr, Philadelphia, PA 19106-2530 – **124)** 24 East Greenway Plaza #1900, Houston, TX 77046-2428 – **125)** 810 West 200 North, Logan, UT 84321-3726 – **126)** 3934 Electric Rd, Roanoke, VA 24018-4513 – **127)** 2823 W Lewis St, Pasco, WA 99301-6700 – **128)** 100 Yeager Pkwy, Pelham, AL 35124-1859 – **129)** 7740 N 16th St #200, Phoenix, AZ 85020-4482 – **130)** 1354 E Sherwood Dr, Grand Junction, CO 81501-7546 – **131)** 4002 W Gandy Blvd, Tampa, FL 33611-3410 – **132)** 806 New Franklin Rd, La Grange, GA 30240-1859 – **133)** 861 Broadway, Bangor, ME 04401-2916 – **134)** 1375 Beasley Rd, Jackson, MS 39206-2018 – **135)** 3100 Highwoods Blvd #140, Raleigh, NC 27604-1065 – **136)** 2508 Coney Island Ave 2nd Flr, Brooklyn, NY 11223-5026 – **137)** 500 Plum St #100, Syracuse, NY 13204-1427 – **138)** 4949 SW Macadam Ave, Portland, OR 97201-3912 – **139)** 1918 Lincoln Hwy, North Versailles, PA 15137-2706 – **140)** 2440 Millwood Ave, Columbia, SC 29205-1128 – **141)** 1621 E Magnolia Ave, Knoxville, TN 37917-7825 – **142)** 13725 Montfort Dr, Dallas, TX 75240-4455 – **143)** 118 Malletts Bay Ave, Colchester, VT 05446-2009 – **144)** 720 E Capitol Dr, Milwaukee, WI 53212-1308 – **145)** 306 S Kanawha St, Beckley, WV 25801-5619 – **146)** 4695 S Monaco St, Denver, CO 80237-3403 – **147)** 4400 Jenifer St NW #400, Washington, DC 20015-2183 – **148)** 214 Television Circle, Savannah, GA 31406-4519 – **149)** 145 N Alexander St, Toccoa, GA 30577-2371 – **150)** 827 Park Blvd #100, Boise, ID 83712-7782 – **151)** 2601 Nicholasville Rd, Lexington, KY 40503-3307 – **152)** 2619 East Lake St, Minneapolis, MN 55406-1925 – **153)** 10845 Olive Blvd #160, Saint Louis, MO 63141-7792 – **154)** 2900 Sutro St, Reno, NV 89512-1616 – **155)** 320 Central Ave #519, Coos Bay, OR 97420-2272 – **156)** 1502 Wampanoag Trail, Riverside, RI 02915-1075 – **157)** 9601 McAllister Freeway #1200, San Antonio, TX 78216-4686 – **158)** 19319 Fremont Ave N, Shoreline, WA 98133-3800 – **159)** 3400 Olive Ave #550, Burbank, CA 91505-5544 – **160)** 2100 Park Central Blvd #100, Pompano Beach, FL 33064-2219 – **161)** 1819 Peachtree Rd NE #700, Atlanta, GA 30309-1849 – **162)** 204 Communications Bldg - Iowa State Univ, Ames, IA 50011-0001 – **163)** 108 Green St, Thibodaux, LA 70301-3144 – **164)** 131 County Circle, Amherst, MA 01003-9257 – **165)** 2050 Amsterdam Rd, Belgrade, MT 59714-8957 – **166)** 1009 Drayton Rd, Fayetteville, NC 28303-3887 – **167)** 501 Office Center Dr #190, Fort Washington, PA 19034-3268 – **168)** 7755 Freedom Ave NW, North Canton, OH 44720-6905 – **169)** 4045 NW 64th St #600, Oklahoma City, OK 73116-2615 – **170)** 6401 Poplar Ave #640, Memphis, TN 38119-4808 – **171)** 162 Free Hill Rd, Gray, TN 37615-3144 – **172)** 1440 Ethan Way #200, Sacramento, CA 95825-2214 – **173)** 807 West 37th St, Hibbing, MN 55746-2856 – **174)** 2804 Opryland Dr, Nashville, TN 37214-1209 – **175)** 1600 West 500 North, Manti, UT 84642-5503 – **176)** 1912 Capitol Ave #300, Cheyenne, WY 82001-3659 – **177)** 2800 Dauphin St #104, Mobile, AL 36606-2400 – **178)** P.O. Box 2569, Window Rock, AZ 86515-2569 – **179)** 3000 W MacArthur Blvd #500, Santa Ana, CA 92704-7947 – **180)** 1010 2nd St North, Sauk Rapids, MN 56379-2527 – **181)** 410 E 6th St, Williston, ND 58801-5552 – **182)** 345 Hudson St Fl11, New York, NY 10014-4502 – **183)** 2911 Tennyson Ave, #400, Eugene, OR 7408-4811 – **184)** 2420 Wade Hampton Blvd, Greenville, SC 29615-1107 – **185)** 6400 North Belt Line Rd #110, Irving, TX 75063-6065 – **186)** 2029 Freeway Dr, Mount Vernon, WA 98273-5470 – **187)** 11474 US Hwy 11, York, AL 36925-9764 – **188)** 108 Highway 70 East #11, Glenwood, AR

71943-8800 – **189)** 3301 Barham Blvd #300, Los Angeles, CA 90068-1477 – **190)** 2821 S Parker Rd #1205, Aurora, CO 80014-2708 – **191)** 330 SW 27th Ave #207, Miami, FL 33135-2957 – **192)** 1419 W Bannock St, Boise, ID 83702-5234 – **193)** 180 North Stetson St #1250, Chicago, IL 60601-6732 – **194)** 3999 Las Vegas Blvd S #K, Las Vegas, NV 89119-1097 – **195)** 12½ E Market St, Lewistown, PA 17044-2123 – **196)** 517 Watt Rd, Knoxville, TN 37922-1110 – **197)** 2202 Mt. Jolliff Rd, Chesapeake, VA 23321-1416 – **198)** 55 Hawthorne St #1100, San Francisco, CA 94105-3932 – **199)** 780 Johnson Ferry Rd NE #500, Atlanta, GA 30342-1436 – **200)** 20 Guest St 3rd Flr, Brighton, MA 02135-2040 – **201)** 1726 Reisterstown Rd #117, Pikesville, MD 21208-2986 – **202)** 604 Ludington St, Escanaba, MI 49829-3830 – **203)** 4104 Country Lane, Saint Joseph, MO 64506-4921 – **204)** 1400 11th Ave #3, Helena, MT 59601-7996 – **205)** 3012 Highwoods Blvd #201, Raleigh, NC 27604-1031 – **206)** 320 N Jensen Rd, Vestal, NY 13850-2111 – **207)** 1835 Moriah Woods Blvd, Memphis, TN 38117-7122 – **208)** 8122 Datapoint Dr #600, San Antonio, TX 78229-3446 – **209)** 320 Emery Dr, Omak, WA 98841-9237 – **210)** 2396 Hallie Rd, Chippewa Falls, WI 54729-7519 – **211)** 1111 Virginia St East, Charleston, WV 25301-2406 – **212)** 244 Goodwin Crest Dr. #300, Birmingham, AL 35209-3700 – **213)** 261 Portsea St, New Haven, CT 06519-2104 – **214)** 8000 Belfort Pkwy #100, Jacksonville, FL 32256-6971 – **215)** 306 W 8th St, Coffeyville, KS 67337-5829 – **216)** 1218 Decatur St #B, New Orleans, LA 70116-2608 – **217)** Tower 14-21700 Northwestern Hwy #1190, Southfield, MI 48075-4923 – **218)** 4045 N Mesa St, El Paso, TX 79902-1526 – **219)** 11373 Wallace Pike, Bristol, VA 24202-2743 – **220)** 126 Kessel Rd, Fisher, WV 26818-4012 – **221)** 67 Garden Court, Monterey, CA 93940-5302 – **222)** 362 Green St, Gardner, MA 01440-1348 – **223)** 5028 Wisconsin Ave NW #304, Washington, DC 20016-4118 – **224)** 8044 Montgomery Rd #650, Cincinnati, OH 45236-2959 – **225)** 196 Main St, Winston, OR 97496-ND – **226)** 11451 Katy Freeway #125, Houston, TX 77079-2004 – **227)** 1903 W Research Way, Salt Lake City, UT 84119-5684 – **228)** 500 West Boone Ave, Spokane, WA 99201-2404 – **229)** 501 North 44th St #425, Phoenix, AZ 85008-6587 – **230)** 1425 River Park Dr. #520, Sacramento, CA 95815-4524 – **231)** 800 W Olympic Blvd #A-200, Los Angeles, CA 90015-1360 – **232)** 3131 S Vaughn Way #601, Aurora, CO 80014-3516 – **233)** 800 S Douglas Rd #111, Coral Gables, FL 33134-3187 – **234)** 855 College St, Eastman, GA 31023-6771 – **235)** 402 Main St, Williamsburg, KY 40769-1126 – **236)** 6341 West Port Ave, Shreveport, LA 71129-2415 – **237)** 5800 Foxridge Dr #600, Mission, KS 66202-2347 – **238)** 3228 South US Hwy 117, Rose Hill, NC 28458-8498 – **239)** 3500 E Rosser Ave, Bismarck, ND 58501-3398 – **240)** 111 Broadway 3rd Flr, New York, NY 10006-1992 – **241)** 3505 Olsen Blvd #117, Amarillo, TX 79109-3096 – **242)** 7080 Lee Highway, Fairlawn, VA 24141-8416 – **243)** 1820 Eastlake Ave East, Seattle, WA 98102-3711 – **244)** 715 East Central Entrance, Duluth, MN 55811-5596 – **245)** 3988 N Roscoe Rd, Hernando, FL 34442-3141 – **246)** 154 Boone Dr, Newman, GA 30263-2801 – **247)** 435 N Michigan Ave, Chicago, IL 60611-4076 – **248)** 3232 Hendersonville Hwy, Pisgah Forest, NC 28768-7806 – **249)** 1455 East Tropicana Ave #800, Las Vegas, NV 89119-8326 – **250)** 28041 Pleasant Valley Rd, Sweet Home, OR 97386-9599 – **251)** 4050 Eisenhauer Rd, San Antonio, TX 78218-3409 – **252)** 2194 US Hwy 319 South, Thomasville, GA 31792-1417 – **253)** 5660 E Franklin Rd # 200, Nampa, ID 83687-5133 – **254)** 1036 Highway 541, Jackson, KY 41339-9434 – **255)** 326 Chicopee St, Chicopee, MA 01013-1197 – **256)** 2075 Central Ave, Billings, MT 59102-4956 – **257)** 1366 Startown Rd, Lincolntown, NC 28152-5033 – **258)** 7 Parkway Center - 875 Greentree Rd #625, Pittsburgh, PA 15220-3508 – **259)** 2 Beeco Rd, Greer, SC 29650-1004 – **260)** 9540 Godwin Dr, Manassas, VA 20110-4165 – **261)** 1 Commerce St #300, Montgomery, AL 36104-3542 – **262)** 3183 Airway Ave #D, Costa Mesa, CA 92626-4611 – **263)** 865 Battery St, San Francisco, CA 94111-1503 – **264)** 6805 Corporate Dr #130, Colorado Springs, CO 80919-5903 – **265)** 1650 S Dixie Hwy, Boca Raton, FL 33432-7462 – **266)** 2500 aitland Center Pkwy #401, Maitland, FL 32751-4179 – **267)** 5440 Moeller Ave, Cincinnati, OH 45212-1211 – **268)** 2147 Springs Rd, Mount Airy, NC 27030-2447 – **269)** 1020 South 25th St, Fargo, ND 58103-2312 – **270)** 100-25 Queens Blvd #1CC, Forest Hills, NY 11375-6217 – **271)** 7136 S Yale Ave #500, Tulsa, OK 74136-6325 – **272)** 2000 West Loop South #300, Houston, TX 77027-3510 – **273)** 300 St Croix Trail South, Lakeland, MN 55043-ND – **274)** 1601 W Peachtree St NE, Atlanta, GA 30309-2663 – **275)** 5625 North Milwaukee Ave, Chicago, IL 60646-6221 – **276)** 18553 Gentry Rd, Lebanon, MO 65536-5748 – **277)** 36581 N Reservoir Rd, Polson, MT 59860-8677 – **278)** 128 South 4th St, O'Neill, NE 68763-1814 – **279)** 1050 W Williams Ave, Fallon, NV 89406-2634 – **280)** 1211 SW 5th Ave 6 Flr, Portland, OR 97204-3735 – **281)** 2211 E Missiouri Ave # S-300, El Paso, TX 79903-3831 – **282)** 1899 Carbonville Rd, Helper, UT 84526-ND – **283)** P.O. Box 215, Clarksville, AR 72830-0215 – **284)** 7677 Engineer Rd, San Diego, CA 92111-1582 – **285)** 4695 S Monaco St, Denver, CO 80237-3408 – **286)** 2090 Palm Beach Lake Blvd #701, West Palm Beach, FL 33409-6508 – **287)** 3514 W Arch St #200, Tampa, FL 33607-4901 – **288)** 10550

Barkley St, Overland Park, KS 66212-1824 – **289)** 70 James St #140, Worcester, MA 01603-1038 – **290)** 3011 W Grand Blvd #800, Detroit, MI 48202-3086 – **291)** 2828 NC 126, Morganton, NC 28655-8264 – **292)** 137 Rapids Rd, Champlain, NY 12919-4945 – **293)** 6222 West Interstate 10, San Antonio, TX 78201-2097 – **294)** 1717 US Hwy 72 E, Athens, AL 35611-4413 – **295)** 10948 Cleveland Ave, Oakdale, CA 95361-9709 – **296)** 20125 S Tamiami Trail, Estero, FL 33928-2117 – **297)** 330 21st Ave South #610, Minneapolis, MN 55455-4550 – **298)** 818 Main St, Miles City, MT 59301-3221 – **299)** 275 River Rd, Rockingham, NC 28380-1536 – **300)** 500 4th St Ne, Albuquerque, NM 87102-2102 – **301)** 2 Penn Plaza #1700, New York, NY 10121-1701 – **302)** 904 Center St, Lewiston, NY 14092-1737 – **303)** 3201 Royalty Row, Irving, TX 75062-4961 – **304)** 504 Middle Creek Rd, Cedar Bluff, VA 24609-ND – **305)** 1820 Eastlake Ave East, Seattle, WA 98102-3711 – **306)** 801 Noble St #30, Anniston, AL 36201-5698 – **307)** 3400 W Highway 89a, Sedona, AZ 86336-4914 – **308)** 180 North Stetson St #1100, Chicago, IL 60601-6723 – **309)** 243 Main St, Norway, ME 04268-5914 – **310)** 274 Britton Rd, Monticello, ME 04760-3110 – **311)** 265 Highpoint Dr, Ridgeland, MS 39157-6018 – **312)** 17336 US Highway 421 South, Dunn, NC 28334-5580 – **313)** 1381 W Main St, Forest City, NC 28043-2525 – **314)** 595 E Plumb Lane, Reno, NV 89502-3503 – **315)** 1901 North Moore St #200, Arlington, VA 22209-1746 – **316)** 142 Skyland Blvd. East, Tuscaloosa, AL 35405-4096 – **317)** 113 East New Hope Rd, Rogers, AR 72758-6058 – **318)** 3202 North Oracle Rd, Tucson, AZ 85705-3820 – **319)** 3321 S La Cienega Blvd, Los Angeles, CA 90016-3114 – **320)** 1101 Marsh Rd, Eureka, CA 95501-1574 – **321)** 351 W Cromwell Ave #108, Fresno, CA 93711-6115 – **322)** 20450 NW 2nd Ave, Miami, FL 33169-2505 – **323)** 32900 Radio Rd, Leesburg, FL 34788-3903 – **324)** 3350 Peachtree Rd NE #1610, Atlanta, GA 30326-1040 – **325)** 1065 S Range Ave, Colby, KS 67701-3505 – **326)** 4000 Radio Dr #1, Louisville, KY 40218-4568 – **327)** 1795 Tittabawassee Rd, Saginaw, MI 48604-9431 – **328)** 600 First Ave North, Billings, MT 59101-2654 – **329)** 1607 Country Club Dr, High Point, NC 27626-4559 – **330)** 1020 U S 25th St, Fargo, ND 58103-3212 – **331)** 1541 Alta Dr #400, Whitehall, PA 18052-5632 – **332)** 1502 Wampanoag Trail, Riverside, RI 02915-1075 – **333)** 231 Brandonwood Dr, Johnson City, TN 37604-2156 – **334)** 1835 Moriah Woods Blvd, Memphis, TN 38117-7122 – **335)** 2000 West Loop South #300, Houston, TX 77027-3510 – **336)** 4413 82nd St #300, Lubbock, TX 79424-3395 – **337)** 500 Dominion Tower - 999 Waterside Dr, Norfolk, VA 23510-3300 – **338)** 2219 Yew St Rd, Bellingham, WA 98229-8898 – **339)** 1601 E 57th Ave, Spokane, WA 99223-6623 – **340)** 944 Harlem St, Altoona, WI 54720-1127 – **341)** 213 East 2nd St, Soda Springs, ID 83276-1411 – **342)** 462 Merrimack St, Methuen, MA 01844-5804 – **343)** 1010 2nd St North, Sauk Rapids, MN 56379-2527 – **344)** 2775 Mt Ephraim Ave, Camden, NJ 08104-3295 – **345)** 1919 North Broadway Ave, Oklahoma City, OK 73103-4499 – **346)** 1032 Melody Lane, Crewe, VA 23930-ND – **347)** 200 Tower Rd, Waupaca, WI 54981-1699 – **348)** 134 4th Ave, Huntington, WV 25701-1253 – **349)** 188 John Turner Broadcast Blvd., Jacksonville, AL 36265-6659 – **350)** 900 Front St, San Francisco, CA 94111-1450 – **351)** 999 Douglas Ave #3318, Altamonte Springs, FL 32714-5213 – **352)** 4198 Rebecca Circle, Valdosta, GA 31606-2201 – **353)** 1501 Hargis Lane, Jackson, KY 41339-1102 – **354)** 2422 Burton St SE, Grand Rapids, MI 49546-4806 – **355)** 6721 West 121st St, Overland Park, KS 66209-2003 – **356)** 130 Radio Station Dr, Magee, MS 39111-4399 – **357)** 102 Taos St, Santa Fe, NM 87505-3832 – **358)** 1203 Troy-Schenectady Rd #201, Latham, NY 12205-5579 – **359)** 2 Beeco Rd, Greer, SC 29650-1004 – **360)** 1612 Junction Ave, Sturgis, SD 57785-2149 – **361)** 2514 Eugenia Ave, Nashville, TN 37211-2117 – **362)** 145 Jackson St NE, Blacksburg, VA 24060-3931 – **363)** 55 Alder St NW #3, Ephrata, WA 98823-1663 – **364)** 800 8th Ave SE, Largo, FL 33771-2162 – **365)** 5475 N Milwaukee Ave, Chicago, IL 60630-1249 – **366)** 3400 Idaho Ave NW #200, Washington, DC 20016-3000 – **367)** 160 Varick St, New York, NY 10013-1220 – **368)** 2205 College Ave, Elmira, NY 14903-1201 – **369)** 4673 Winterset Dr, Columbus, OH 43220-8113 – **370)** 2221 E Lamar Blvd #300, Arlington, TX 76006-7419 – **371)** 3701 Harrison Rd, Ogden, UT 84403-2059 – **372)** 4301 W Hundred Rd, Chester, VA 23831-1737 – **373)** 2201 6th Ave #1500, Seattle, WA 98121-1840 – **374)** 7355 N Orcale Rd #102, Tucson, AZ 85704-6353 – **375)** 2000 E Gene Autry Way, Anaheim, CA 92806-6143 – **376)** 1255 E Main St #A, Grass Valley, CA 95945-5711 – **377)** 3500 N Causeway Blvd #830, Metairie, LA 70002-3561 – **378)** 82 Franklin St, Worcester, MA 01608-1917 – **379)** 625 2nd Ave South #200, Minneapolis, MN 55402-1961 – **380)** 4405 Providence Lane #D, Winston-Salem, NC 27106-3226 – **381)** 34 North 4th St, Reading, PA 19601-3996 – **382)** 932 County Rd 448, Poplar Bluff, MO 63901-9018 – **383)** 1423 S Beverly St, Casper, WY 82609-4131 – **384)** 6530 Spanish Fort Blvd #B, Spanish Fort, AL 36527-5014 – **385)** 1192 Norwegian Ave, Modesto, CA 95350-3643 – **386)** 4000 Radio Dr #1, Louisville, KY 40218-4568 – **387)** 3735 Rigolette Rd, Pineville, LA 71360-7365 – **388)** 1011 N Lincoln St, West Point, NE 68788-1003 – **389)** 7255 S Tenaya Way #100, Las Vegas, NV 89113-1900 – **390)** 4801

East Independence Blvd #815, Charlotte, NC 28212-5490 – **391)** 1201 North Jackson Ave #900, McAllen, TX 78501-5764 – **392)** P.O. Box 7111, Charlottesville, VA 22906-7111 – **393)** 1114 North Almon St, Moscow, ID 83843-8507 – **394)** 120 Summit Pkwy #200, Birmingham, AL 35209-4741 – **395)** 4695 S Monaco St, Denver, CO 80237-3403 – **396)** 198 Main St, Danbury, CT 06810-6662 – **397)** 2100 Park Central Blvd #100, Pompano Beach, FL 33064-2219 – **398)** 1200 Weimer Hall, Gainesville, FL 32611 – **399)** 5625 N Milwaukee Ave, Chicago, IL 60646-6221 – **400)** 20 Guest St 3rd Flr, Brighton, MA 02135-2040 – **401)** 1120 E McCuen St, Duluth, MN 55808-2199 – **402)** 85 Founders Lane, Saint Louis, MO 63105-3085 – **403)** 18844 Highway 80, Forest, MS 39074-4410 – **404)** 3012 Highwoods Blvd #201, Raleigh, NC 27604-1031 – **405)** 1301 E 9th St #252, Cleveland, OH 44114-1800 – **406)** 104 South Center St #400, Ebensburg, PA 15931-1656 – **407)** 261 Hannum St, Alcoa, TN 37701-2451 – **408)** 3000 Bering Dr, Houston, TX 77057-5708 – **409)** 8828 N Stemmons Fwy #106, Dallas, TX 75247-3720 – **410)** 500 Dominion Tower - 999 Waterside Dr, Norfolk, VA 23510-3300 – **411)** 351 Elliott Ave West #300, Seattle, WA 98119-4150 – **412)** 300 Broadway #8, San Francisco, CA 94133-4545 – **413)** 5211 W Laurel St #101, Tampa, FL 33607-1725 – **414)** 1465 Northside Dr. NW #218, Atlanta, GA 30318-4239 – **415)** 601 West Roanoke St, Fitzgerald, GA 31750-3633 – **416)** 1162 East Hwy 126, Pittsburg, KS 66762-8712 – **417)** 425 Stockbridge Rd, Great Barrington, MA 01230-1233 – **418)** 305 Washington Ave 4th Flr, Towson, MD 21204-4748 – **419)** 6605 SE Lake Rd, Portland, OR 97222-2161 – **420)** 555 East City Ave #330, Bala Cynwyd, PA 19004-1137 – **421)** 8122 Datapoint Dr. #600, San Antonio, TX 78229-3446 – **422)** 434 Bearcat Dr, Salt Lake City, UT 84115-2520 – **423)** 240 Central Ave, Oak Hill, WV 25901-3006 – **424)** 2278 Wortham Lane, Grovetown, GA 30813-5103 – **425)** 701 N Brand Blvd #550, Glendale, CA 91203-1235 – **426)** 400 Poydras St #800, New Orleans, LA 70130-3245 – **427)** 477 Congress St #900, Portland, ME 04101-3432 – **428)** 283 Comm. Arts Bldg. - M.S.U., East Lansing, MI 48824-1212 – **429)** P.O. Box 49, Park Rapids, MN 56470-0049 – **430)** P.O. Box 107, Keene, TX 76059 – **431)** 6767 W Tropicana Ave #102, Las Vegas, NV 89103-4755 – **432)** 1751 Hanshaw Rd, Ithaca, NY 14850-9105 – **433)** 340 Martin Luther King Blvd, Bristol, TN 37620-3996 – **434)** 2621 West A St, Pasco, WA 99301-4702 – **435)** 10000 Warden Rd, North Little Rock, AR 72120-3656 – **436)** 30 East San Joaquin St #105, Salinas, CA 93901-2946 – **437)** 2828 W Flagler St, Miami, FL 33135-1337 – **438)** 1186 West Broad St, Athens, GA 30606-3050 – **439)** 2432 US Hwy 2 East, Kalispell, MT 59901-2310 – **440)** 13 Summerlin Rd, Asheville, NC 28806-2800 – **441)** 1007 Plum Creek Pkwy, Lexington, NE 68850-2621 – **442)** P.O. Box 9090, Window Rock, AZ 86515-9090 – **443)** 345 Hudson St Flr 11, New York, NY 10014-4502 – **444)** 8101 N High St #360, Columbus, OH 43235-1442 – **445)** 1405 E Ellendale Ave, Dallas, OR 97338-1709 – **446)** 209 10th Ave South #342, Nashville, TN 37203-0758 – **447)** 912 Curtis Ave, Pasadena, TX 77502-2402 – **448)** 3650 131st St SE #550, Bellevue, WA 98006-1334 – **449)** 619 Cameron St, Eau Claire, WI 54703-4700 – **450)** 1301 Central Pkwy SW, Decatur, AL 35601-4817 – **451)** 560 Higuera St #G, San Luis Obispo, CA 93401-3850 – **452)** Fountain, CO – **453)** 2800 Shallowford Rd NE, Atlanta, GA 30341-5217 – **454)** 1050 Clover Dr, Boise, ID 83703-5714 – **455)** 190 N State St, Chicago, IL 60601-3398 – **456)** 122 Green St #2, Worcester, MA 01604-4138 – **457)** 6555 US Hwy 98 #8, Hattiesburg, MS 39402-8699 – **458)** 243 Riverchase Way #A, Lexington, SC 29072-9470 – **459)** 10613 Bellaire Blvd #900, Houston, TX 77072-5221 – **460)** 4501 North McColl Rd, McAllen, TX 78504-2431 – **461)** 750 Ridgeview Dr #204, Saint George, UT 84770-2665 – **462)** 145 Jackson St NE, Blacksburg, VA 24060-3931 – **463)** 233 NE Front St, Milford, DE 19963-1431 – **464)** 2320 NE 2nd St #5, Ocala, FL 34470-6992 – **465)** 214 Television Circle, Savannah, GA 31406-4519 – **466)** 1240 Radio Dr, Pikeville, KY 41501-4779 – **467)** 3003 Snelling Ave North, Saint Paul, MN 55113-1599 – **468)** 398 South Main St, Granite Falls, NC 28630-8535 – **469)** 801 E DuBois Ave, DuBois, PA 15801-3643 – **470)** 2514 Eugenia Ave, Nashville, TN 37211-2117 – **471)** 10613 Bellaire Blvd #900, Houston, TX 77072-5221 – **472)** 207 University Blvd #200, Harrisonburg, VA 22801-3752 – **473)** 125 South 2nd St, Blytheville, AR 72315-3413 – **474)** 4686 E Van Buren St #300, Phoenix, AZ 85008-6967 – **475)** 11865 Moreno Ave, Lakeside, CA 92040-1110 – **476)** 340 Townsend St #4, San Francisco, CA 94107-1698 – **477)** 200 South A St #400, Oxnard, CA 93030-5717 – **478)** 3455 W 83rd Ave Westminster, Denver, CO 80030-4005 – **479)** 135 Burnside Ave, East Hartford, CT 06108-3466 – **480)** 5211 West Laurel St, Tampa, FL 33607-1736 – **481)** 3765 N John Young Pkwy, Orlando, FL 32804-3213 – **482)** 710 S Clinton St Bldg, Iowa City, IA 52242-4214 – **483)** 184 Target Industrial Circle #207, Bangor, ME 04401-5718 – **484)** 1000 Town Center #2810, Southfield, MI 48075-1183 – **485)** 4307 Highway 39 N, Meridian, MS 39301-1007 – **486)** 1223 W New Bern Rd, Kinston, NC 28504-4713 – **487)** 1000 20th Ave SW, Minot, ND 58701-6447 – **488)** 1301 North Main St, Roswell, NM 88201-5013 – **489)** 6006 Grand Central Ave, Parkersburg, WV 26105-9125 – **490)** 120 Beale Rd, Sarver, PA 16055-9403 – **491)** 5989

Susquehanna Plaza Dr, Hellam, PA 17406-8910 – **492)** 225 S Pleasantburg Dr #3B, Greenville, SC 29607-2533 – **493)** 105 N Ash Ave, South Pittsburg, TN 37380-1565 – **494)** 162 Freehill Rd, Gray, TN 37615-3144 – **495)** 4300 S US Highway 281, Edinburg, TX 78539-9650 – **496)** 2801 Decker Lake Dr #100, West Valley City, UT 84119-2330 – **497)** 3245 Basie Rd, Richmond, VA 23228-3404 – **498)** 0700 SW Bancroft St, Portland, OR 97239-4226 – **499)** 16880 West US Highway 63, Hayward, WI 54843-7186 – **500)** 700 Wellington Hills Rd, Little Rock, AR 72211-2026 – **501)** 2100 E Tahquitz Canyon Way, Palm Springs, CA 92262-7046 – **502)** 961 N Emerald Ave #A, Modesto, CA 95351-1556 – **503)** 7350 US Hwy 50, Lamar, CO 81052-9563 – **504)** 1800 Turtle Mound Rd, Melbourne, FL 32934-8105 – **505)** 2970 Peachtree Rd NW #700, Atlanta, GA 30305-4919 – **506)** 290 Hegenberger Rd, Oakland, CA 94621-1436 – **507)** 712 3rd St, West Lafayette, IN 47907-2005 – **508)** P.O. Box 228, Mayking, KY 41837-0228 – **509)** 601 Central Ave North, Faribault, MN 55021-1307 – **510)** 1109 Tower Dr, Burlington, NC 27215-4425 – **511)** 8755 W Flamingo Rd, Las Vegas, NV 89147-8667 – **512)** 3256 Penryn Rd #100, Loomis, CA 95650-8052 – **513)** 715 Route 52, Beacon, NY 12508-1047 – **514)** 159 Santanoni Ave, Saranac Lake, NY 12983-2478 – **515)** 75 Oxford St, Providence, RI 02905-4722 – **516)** 660 Flormann St #100, Rapid City, SD 57701-4679 – **517)** 7322 Southwest Frwy #500, Houston, TX 77074-2084 – **518)** 2495 N Vernal Ave, Vernal, UT 84078-ND – **519)** 1770 Van Buren Dr, Dumfries, VA – **520)** 1700 SE Mile Hill Dr #201A, Port Orchard, WA 98366-3553 – **521)** 500 W Boone Ave, Spokane, WA 99201-2497 – **522)** 12100 W Howard Ave, Greenfield, WI 53228-1851 – **523)** 450 Leonard Ave Extension, Fairmont, WV 26554-3878 – **524)** 2711 Pelham Pkwy, Pelham, AL 35124-1704 – **525)** 301 N 12th St #1, Gadsden, AL 35901-3058 – **526)** 1117 West Route 66, Flagstaff, AZ 86001-6213 – **527)** 3222 South Richey Ave, Tucson, AZ 85713-5453 – **528)** 1845 W Empire Ave, Burbank, CA 91504-3402 – **529)** 190 Turner Dr #G, Durango, CO 81303-8231 – **530)** P.O. Box 7069, Breckenridge, CO 80424-7069 – **531)** 11700 Central Pkwy, Jacksonville, FL 32224-2600 – **532)** 5211 West Laurel St, Tampa, FL 33607-1736 – **533)** 203 West Shotwell St, Bainbridge, GA 39819-3903 – **534)** 544 N Arthur Ave, Pocatello, ID 83204-3002 – **535)** 1496 Bellevue St #202, Green Bay, WI 54311-4205 – **536)** 329 Maine St, Quincy, IL 62301-3928 – **537)** 804 College St, Bowling Green, KY 42101-2133 – **538)** 5966 Grove Hill Rd, Frederick, MD 21703-6012 – **539)** 390 Golden Ave, Battle Creek, MI 49015-4598 – **540)** 37208 US Hwy 169, Aitkin, MN 56431-4195 – **541)** 1015 W Pine St, Poplar Bluff, MO 63901-4839 – **542)** 574 Hwy 51 N #F, Ridgeland, MS 39157-2607 – **543)** 3250 South Reserve St #200, Missoula, MT 59801-8236 – **544)** 525 Evans St, Greenville, NC 27858-2311 – **545)** 11530 Carmel Commons Blvd, Charlotte, NC 28226-3976 – **546)** 113 W 4th St, Ogallala, NE 69153-2508 – **547)** 815 Lafayette Rd, Portsmouth, NH 03801-5406 – **548)** 27 William St 11th Flr, New York, NY 10005-2718 – **549)** 500 Corporate Pkwy #200, Buffalo, NY 14226-1263 – **550)** 4045 NW 64th St #600, Oklahoma City, OK 73116-2615 – **551)** 1250 Siskiyou Blvd., Ashland, OR 97520-5010 – **552)** 3304 S Highway 281, Aberdeen, SD 57401-8792 – **553)** 430 State Highway 165 #C, Branson, MO 65616-3541 – **554)** 9601 McAllister Freeway #1200, San Antonio, TX 78216-6486 – **555)** 105 Whitehall Rd, Lynchburg, VA 24501-6706 – **556)** P.O. Box 31000, Spokane, WA 99223-3016 – **557)** 821 University Ave, Madison, WI 53706-1412 – **558)** 401 11th St #200, Huntington, WV 25701-2225 – **559)** 1716 KROE Lane, Sheridan, WY 82801-9681 – **560)** 1415 Fulton St, Fresno, CA 93721-1609 – **561)** 7601 Riviera Blvd, Miramar, FL 33023-6574 – **562)** 544 Mulberry St #500, Macon, GA 31201-8258 – **563)** 1416 Locust St, Des Moines, IA 50309-3014 – **564)** 3501 Broadway St, Mount Vernon, IL 62864-2202 – **565)** 929 Howard Ave, New Orleans, LA 70113-1148 – **566)** 7119 W M-68, Indian River, MI 49749-9472 – **567)** 1189 North Jackson St, Houston, MS 38851-8273 – **568)** 401 Saw Mill Hollow Rd, Burnsville, NC 28714-9789 – **569)** 126 W 3rd St, Valentine, NE 69201-1826 – **570)** 345 SW Cyber Dr #100, Bend, OR 97702-1045 – **571)** 305 N Church St, Wartburg, TN 37887-3164 – **572)** 6214 West 34th Ave, Amarillo, TX 79109-4006 – **573)** 615 Olive St, Texarkana, TX 75501-5512 – **574)** 1105 N Iron Springs Rd, Cedar City, UT 84720-6526 – **575)** 13379 Great Springs Rd, Smithfield, VA 23430-6930 – **576)** 1011 Radio Dr, Grundy, VA 24614-6157 – **577)** 501 E Broadway St, Forrest City, AR 72335-3801 – **578)** 985 Lincoln Way #103, Auburn, CA 95603-5255 – **579)** 7800 East Orchard Rd #400, Greenwood Village, CO 80111-2599 – **580)** 1188 Lake View Rd, Altamonte Springs, FL 32714-2713 – **581)** 2973 US Hwy 84 West, Valdosta, GA 31601 – **582)** 1800 Lake Park Dr #99, Smyrna, GA 30080-7689 – **583)** 501 Sycamore St #300, Waterloo, IA 50703-4651 – **584)** 624 3rd St South, Nampa, ID 83651- 3840 – **585)** 2560 Snake River Ave, Lewiston, ID 83501-9685 – **586)** 541 North Fairbanks Court #1260, Chicago, IL 60611-3319 – **587)** 645 Industrial Dr, Franklin, IN 46131-9617 – **588)** 500 Victory Rd #2, Quincy, MA 02171-3132 – **589)** 7825 Tuckerman Ln #217, Potomac, MD 20854-3241 – **590)** 26495 American Dr, Southfield, MI 48034-6114 – **591)** 3109 South 10 Mile Dr, Jefferson City, MO 65109-1012 – **592)** 63 Braswell Rd, Hattiesburg, MS

39401-9730 – **593)** 516 Fuller Ave, Helena, MT 59601-3301 – **594)** 403 W Pueblo Dr, Española, NM 87532-2530 – **595)** 1560 North Corbin St, Silver City, NM 88061-6526 – **596)** 9418 State Route 49, Marcy, NY 13403-2342 – **597)** 1250 Siskiyou Blvd, Ashland, OR 97520-5010 – **598)** 1 Bala Plaza #424, Bala Cynwyd, PA 19004-1403 – **599)** 60 Markfield Dr #4, Charleston, SC 29407-7907 – **600)** 25 Garlington Rd, Greenville, SC 29615-4613 – **601)** 222 Mallory Station Rd, Franklin, TN 37067-0201 – **602)** 9800 University Ave, Lubbock, TX 79423-5302 – **603)** 2000 West Loop South #300, Houston, TX 77027-3510 – **604)** 701 German School Rd, Richmond, VA 23225-5357 – **605)** 351 Elliott Ave West #300, Seattle, WA 98119-4150 – **606)** 817 Suncrest Place, Charleston, WV 25303-2302 – **607)** 600 Beacon Pkwy W #400, Birmingham, AL 35209-3118 – **608)** 6530 Spanish Fort Blvd #B, Spanish Fort, AL 36527-5014 – **609)** 260 Battle St, Marshall, AR 72650-9440 – **610)** 2425 E Camelback Rd #570, Phoenix, AZ 85016-4250 – **611)** 12370 Hesperia Rd #16, Victorville, CA 92392-5808 – **612)** 340 Townsend St #4, San Francisco, CA 94107-1698 – **613)** 495 Benham St, Hamden, CT 06514-2009 – **614)** 809 S Westover Blvd, Albany, GA 31707-4953 – **615)** 1010 Tower Place, Bogart, GA 30622-3052 – **616)** 209 N Elm St, Shenandoah, IA 51601-1139 – **617)** 1301 E Douglas Rd, Mishawaka, IN 46545-1732 – **618)** 1240 Radio Dr, Pikeville, KY 41501-4779 – **619)** 356 Broad St, Fitchburg, MA 01420-3030 – **620)** 351 Tilghman Rd, Salisbury, MD 21804-1920 – **621)** 1491 M-32 West, Alpena, MI 49707-8194 – **622)** 16405 Haven Rd, Little Falls, MN 56345-6400 – **623)** 324 Broadway St, Cape Girardeau, MO 63701-7331 – **624)** 3600 Highway 7 North, Baker, MT 59313-ND – **625)** 4405 Providence Lane #D, Winston-Salem, NC 27106-3226 – **626)** 1361 Colony Dr, New Bern, NC 28562-4129 – **627)** 1928 East Portal Place, Scottsbluff, NE 69361-2727 – **628)** 1515 W Main St, Farmington, NM 87401-3896 – **629)** 265 Hegeman Ave, Colchester, VT 05446-3174 – **630)** 404 Main St, Klamath Falls, OR 97601-6021 – **631)** 193 S Keystone Ave, Sayre, PA 18840-1330 – **632)** 1703 Walnut Bottom Rd, Carlisle, PA 17015-9151 – **633)** 1301 South Abe St, San Angelo, TX 76903-7245 – **634)** 515 South 700 East #1C, Salt Lake City, UT 84102-2802 – **635)** 3934 Electric Rd, Roanoke, VA 24018-4513 – **636)** 830 N Columbia Center Blvd #B2, Kennewick, WA 99336-7756 – **637)** 1597 Military St South, Hamilton, AL 35570-5026 – **638)** 67 W Court Square, Troy, AL 36081-2611 – **639)** 1838 Commerce Dr #A, Lakeside, AZ 85929-7007 – **640)** 1100 Mohawk St #280, Bakersfield, CA 93309-7417 – **641)** 1321 North Gene Autry Trail, Palm Springs, CA 92262-5473 – **642)** 201 N Industrial Park Rd, Excelsior Springs, MO 64024-1736 – **643)** 4002 West Gandy Blvd #A, Tampa, FL 33611-3410 – **644)** 2970 Peachtree Rd NW #700, Atlanta, GA 30305-4919 – **645)** 1501 Mount Vernon Rd, Vidalia, GA 30474-3031 – **646)** 120 South 300 West, Rupert, ID 83350-9667 – **647)** 125 S Main St, Harlan, KY 40831-2109 – **648)** 9960 Corporate Campus Dr #3600, Louisville, KY 40223-4070 – **649)** 420 Western Ave, South Portland, ME 04106-1704 – **650)** 121 North Front St, Marquette, MI 49855-4300 – **651)** 109 East Clark St, Albert Lea, MN 56007-2420 – **652)** 27 N 27th St, Billings, MT 59101-2357 – **653)** 1190 Patton Ave, Asheville, NC 28806-2706 – **654)** 301 8th St South, Fargo, ND 58103-1826 – **655)** 201 S Bailey Ave, North Platte, NE 69101-5406 – **656)** 777 Terrace Ave #402, Hasbrouck Heights, NJ 07604-3113 – **657)** 1455 E Tropicana Ave #550, Las Vegas, NV 89119-6592 – **658)** 140 Lower Terrace, Buffalo, NY 14202-4303 – **659)** 3226 Jefferson Rd, Ashtabula, OH 44004-9112 – **660)** 5800 East Skelly Dr #150, Tulsa, OK 74135-6416 – **661)** 211 SW 5th Ave 6th Fl, Portland, OR 97204-3735 – **662)** 200 Fleet St 4th Flr, Pittsburgh, PA 15220-2910 – **663)** 181 E Evans St #311, Florence, SC 29506-2512 – **664)** 207 University Blvd #200, Harrisonburg, VA 22801-3752 – **665)** P.O. Box 2482, Kirkland, WA 98083-2482 – **666)** 821 University Ave, Madison, WI 53706-1412 – **667)** 2705 E Parkway Dr, Russellville, AR 72802-2006 – **668)** 229 Pajaro St #205, Salinas, CA 93901-3499 – **669)** 5670 Wilshire Blvd #200, Los Angeles, CA 90036-5611 – **670)** 1101 Marsh Rd, Eureka, CA 95501-1574 – **671)** 1801 Rockville Pike #405, Rockville, MD 20852-5604 – **672)** 100 NW 76th Dr #2, Gainesville, FL 32607-6659 – **673)** 1650 S Dixie Hwy, Boca Raton, FL 33432-7462 – **674)** 312 East Nine Mile Rd #29D, Pensacola, FL 32514-1475 – **675)** 1691 Forsyth St, Macon, GA 31201-1407 – **676)** 854 Lindsay Blvd., Idaho Falls, ID 83402-1820 – **677)** 208 North Thomas Dr, Shreveport, LA 71107-6520 – **678)** 243 Central St, Lowell, MA 01852-2214 – **679)** 2110 Cliff Rd, Eagan, MN 55122-2347 – **680)** 7000 Squibb Rd, Mission, KS 66202-3233 – **681)** 206 North Front St, McComb, MS 39648-3916 – **682)** 3233 Burnt Mill Rd #4, Wilmington, NC 28403-2655 – **683)** 1155 Gummow Dr, Fallon, NV 89406-9453 – **684)** 1203 Troy-Schenectady Rd #201, Latham, NY 12110-1046 – **685)** 101 Pine St, Dayton, OH 45402-2925 – **686)** 305 Hwy 315, Pittston, PA 18640-3987 – **687)** 4405 Providence Ln, Winston Salem, SC 27106-3226 – **688)** 745 Main St, Deadwood, SD 57732-1015 – **689)** 11530 Carmel Commons Blvd, Charlotte, NC 28226-3976 – **690)** 912 Curtis Ave, Pasadena, TX 77502-2402 – **691)** 390 East Annabella Rd, Richfield, UT 84701-2692 – **692)** 901 E Valley Dr, Bristol, VA 24201-4903 – **693)** 1200 Chesterly Dr #160, Yakima, WA 98902-7345 – **694)** 1915 Mirro Dr, Manitowoc, WI 54220-

6715 – **695)** 300 Harrison Ave, Weston, WV 26452-2100 – **696)** 3871 North Commerce Dr, Tucson, AZ 85705-2983 – **697)** 145 Natoma St, San Francisco, CA 94105-3734 – **698)** 414 E Cota St, Santa Barbara, CA 93101-1624 – **699)** 3131 S Vaughn Way #601, Aurora, CO 80014-3516 – **700)** 34 Sylvan St, West Springfield, MA 01089-3444 – **701)** 610 Sycamore St #220, Celebration, FL 34747-4996 – **702)** 2150 W 68th St #202, Hialeah, FL 33016-1802 – **703)** 24 Frank Lloyd Wright Dr, Ann Arbor, MI 48105-9755 – **704)** 1569 N Central Ave, Monett, MO 65708-1104 – **705)** 1560 Midland Rd, Southern Pines, NC 28387-2111 – **706)** 2494 Browncroft Blvd, Rochester, NY 14625-1410 – **707)** 117 Ridge Pike, Lafayette Hill, PA 19444-1900 – **708)** 109 Plaza Dr #2, Johnstown, PA 15905-1212 – **709)** 1185 North Main St, Providence, RI 02904-1824 – **710)** 5495 Murray Rd, Memphis, TN 38119-3703 – **711)** 4711 Old Kingston Pike, Knoxville, TN 37919-5207 – **712)** 12900 Preston Rd #100, Dallas, TX 75230-1312 – **713)** 1848 Clay St SE, Roanoke, VA 24013-2614 – **714)** 3256 Penryn Rd #100, Loomis, CA 95650-8052 – **715)** 20872 NE Kelley Ave, Blountstown, FL 32424-1115 – **716)** 190 N State St, Chicago, IL 60601-3302 – **717)** P.O. Box 369, Lexington, MS 39095-0369 – **718)** 4125 Carlisle Blvd NE, Albuquerque, NM 87107-4848 – **719)** 3134 Lake Rd, Horseheads, NY 14845-3103 – **720)** 1900 NW Expressway St #1000, Oklahoma City, OK 73118-1854 – **721)** 5100 South Tennis Lane, Sioux Falls, SD 57108-2212 – **722)** 110 India Rd, Paris, TN 38242-7565 – **723)** 140 4th Ave North #340, Seattle, WA 98109-4932 – **724)** 6475 Highway 78 #73, Cordova, AL 35550-4101 – **725)** 2800 North 44th St #100, Phoenix, AZ 85008-1560 – **726)** 5100 Commerce Dr, Bakersfield, CA 93309-0684 – **727)** 145 Natoma St, San Francisco, CA 94105-3734 – **728)** 75-153 Merle Dr #D, Palm Desert, CA 92211-5197 – **729)** 220 State St, Fort Morgan, CO 80701-2116 – **730)** 9721 Executive Circle Dr North #200, Saint Petersburg, FL 33702-2439 – **731)** 9090 Hogan Rd, Jacksonville, FL 32216-4648 – **732)** 2901 Mountain Industrial Blvd., Tucker, GA 30084-3011 – **733)** 5615 Pershing Ave #12, Saint Louis, MO 63112-1757 – **734)** 451 Highway 11 & 80, Meridian, MS 39301-2779 – **735)** 3 Porters Cove Rd, Asheville, NC 28805-2834 – **736)** 103 Hanover St, Newport, NH 03766-1098 – **737)** 345 Hudson St Fl11, New York, NY 10014-4502 – **738)** 5110 SE Stark St, Portland, OR 97215-1751 – **739)** 1625 Hwy 109 North, Gallatin, TN 37066-8135 – **740)** 1019 Washington Ave, Waco, TX 76701-1256 – **741)** 5100 Southwest Freeway, Houston, TX 77056-7308 – **742)** 3639 Wolfin Ave, Amarillo, TX 79102-2119 – **743)** 3256 Penryn Rd #100, Loomis, CA 95650-8052 – **744)** 2202 Jolliff Rd, Chesapeake, VA 23321-1416 – **745)** 655 N Central Ave #2500, Glendale, CA 91203-1447 – **746)** 67 Main St, Sharon, CT 06069-2018 – **747)** 2555 Ponce De Leon Blvd #225, Coral Gables, FL 33134-6033 – **748)** 131 Doe Run Circle, Thomasville, GA 31757-0923 – **749)** 5011 Capitol Ave, Omaha, NE 68132-2921 – **750)** 1700 La Luz Rd, Roswell, NM 88201-ND – **751)** Foster Plaza 5, 651 Holiday Dr, Pittsburgh, PA 15220-2740 – **752)** 100 E Shockley Ferry Rd, Anderson, SC 29624-3746 – **753)** 706 Butterfield Rd, Yakima, WA 98901-2021 – **754)** 4209 N Frontage Rd, Fayetteville, AR 72703-5002 – **755)** 3222 S Richey Ave, Tucson, AZ 85704-7738 – **756)** 121 W Alvin Ave, Santa Maria, CA 93458-3002 – **757)** 1355 E Altamonte Dr, Altamonte Springs, FL 32701-5011 – **758)** 427 S Wall Sreet, Calhoun, GA 30701-2431 – **759)** 3656 W Belmont Ave, Chicago, IL 60618-5328 – **760)** 1402 E Kansas Ave, Garden City, KS 67846-5806 – **761)** 1170 Soldiers Field Rd, Boston, MA 02134-1004 – **762)** 5210 Auth Rd #600, Suitland, MD 20746-4354 – **763)** 42669 Garfield Rd #328, Clinton Township, MI 48038-5024 – **764)** 900 Forestview Lane North, Plymouth, MN 55441-5934 – **765)** 18920 E Valley View Pkwy #C, Independence, MO 64055-7020 – **766)** 4405 Providence Lane #D, Winston-Salem, NC 27106-3226 – **767)** 4321 Stuart Andrew Blvd #E, Charlotte, NC 28217-1588 – **768)** 136 North 7th St, Reedsport, OR 97467-1503 – **769)** 3654 Park Ave, Memphis, TN 38111-5626 – **770)** 1602 South Brownlee Blvd, Corpus Christi, TX 78404-3134 – **771)** 210 West Cota St, Shelton, WA 98584-2264 – **772)** 303 8th St, Point Pleasant, WV 25550-1209 – **773)** 150 Nichols Ave, Casper, WY 82601-1816 – **774)** 5050 Edison Ave #218, Colorado Springs, CO 80915-3450 – **775)** 800 8th Ave SE, Largo, FL 33771-2162 – **776)** 2100 Park Central Blvd #100, Pompano Beach, FL 33064-2219 – **777)** 1885 Beaver Ridge Cir NW, Norcross, GA 30071-3847 – **778)** 2141 Grand Ave, Des Moines, IA 50312-5303 – **779)** 4321 Stuart Andrew Blvd #E, Charlotte, NC 28217-1588 – **780)** Two Penn Plaza 17th Floor, New York, NY 10121-0101 – **781)** 5620 S Lima Rd, Avon, NY 14414-9791 – **782)** 105 Lake Ave, Elyria, OH 44035-5013 – **783)** 151 E 1st Ave, Everett, PA 15537-1351 – **784)** 1533 Amherst Rd, Knoxville, TN 37909-1204 – **785)** 5787 South Hampton Rd #285, Dallas, TX 75232-2290 – **786)** 3256 Penryn Rd #100, Loomis, CA 95650-8052 – **787)** 55 Hawthorne St #1100, San Francisco, CA 94105-3914 – **788)** 506 West 1st Ave, Crestview, FL 32536-2420 – **789)** 5590 Rio Grande Ave, Jacksonville, FL 32254-1354 – **790)** 552 Laney-Walker Extension, Augusta, GA 30901-3014 – **791)** 3400 Idaho Ave NW #200, Washington, DC 20016-3000 – **792)** 1100 Victors Way #100, Ann Arbor, MI 48108-5220 – **793)** 608 State Highway 30, Pipestone, MN 56164-1458 – **794)** 508 Main St, Miles

City, MT 59301-3047 – **795)** 180 Radio Hill Rd, Franklin, NC 28734-6927 – **796)** Two Penn Plaza 17th Floor, New York, NY 10121-0101 – **797)** 8456 Smokey Hollow Rd, Baldwinsville, NY 13027-8222 – **798)** 2080 Laura St, Springfield, OR 97477-2197 – **799)** 11640 Highway 17 Bypass, Murrells Inlet, SC 29576-9332 – **800)** 539 Ragland Rd, Madison Heights, VA 24572-ND – **801)** 700 Monticello Ave #301, Norfolk, VA 23510-2538 – **802)** P.O. Box 2482, Kirkland, WA 98083-2482 – **803)** 1601 E 57th Ave, Spokane, WA 99223-6623 – **804)** 5 Rosemar Circle, Parkersburg, WV 26104-1203 – **805)** 1900 W Carmen St, Guadalupe, AZ 85283-2559 – **806)** 40356 Oak Park Way, Oakhurst, CA 93612-8872 – **807)** 614 Kimbark St, Longmont, CO 80501-4911 – **808)** 800 8th Ave SE, Largo, FL 33771-2162 – **809)** 102 Parkwood Circle, Carrollton, GA 30117-8353 – **810)** 3303 E Chicago St, Caldwell, ID 83605-6904 – **811)** P.O. Box 818, Benton, IL 62812-0818 – **812)** 401 Whitney Ave #160, Gretna, LA 70056-2573 – **813)** 6325 Sheridan Dr, Williamsville, NY 14221-4801 – **814)** 2100 Fairplain Ave, Benton Harbor, MI 49022-6828 – **815)** 4801 East Independence Blvd #815, Charlotte, NC 28212-5490 – **816)** 3185 S Highland Dr #13, Las Vegas, NV 89109-1029 – **817)** 4365 Fulton Dr NW, Canton, OH 44718-2823 – **818)** 400 Market St, Philadelphia, PA 19106-2530 – **819)** 214 W Pleasant Dr, Pierre, SD 57501-2472 – **820)** 205 9th St, Farwell, TX 79325-ND – **821)** 2211 E Missiouri Ave #N-300, El Paso, TX 79903-3807 – **822)** 3606 South 500 West, Salt Lake City, UT 84115-4208 – **823)** 244 Goodwin Crest Dr #300, Birmingham, AL 35209-3700 – **824)** 5670 Wilshire Blvd #200, Los Angeles, CA 90036-5611 – **825)** 4015 North Monroe St, Tallahassee, FL 32303-2139 – **826)** 2070 N Palafox St, Pensacola, FL 32501-2145 – **827)** 40 Monument Circle #600, Indianapolis, IN 46204-3011 – **828)** 4200 N Old Lawrence Rd, Wichita, KS 67219-3211 – **829)** 11 Bryant Ave SE, Wadena, MN 56482-1543 – **830)** 119 N 3rd St, Hannibal, MO 63401-0711 – **831)** 112 East 3rd Ave, Plentywood, MT 59254-2223 – **832)** 2929 Radio Station Rd, Greenville, NC 27834-0864 – **833)** 235 Walton St, Syracuse, NY 13202-1533 – **834)** 372 S Dorset St, South Burlington, VT 05403-6363 – **835)** 1227 County Line Rd, Selinsgrove, PA 17870-8188 – **836)** 6304 White Horse Rd #B-5, Greenville, SC 29611-3203 – **837)** 2650 Thousand Oaks Blvd #4100, Memphis, TN 38118-2451 – **838)** 621 O'Grady Dr, Chattanooga, TN 37419-1305 – **839)** 6161 Savoy Dr #1200, Houston, TX 77036-3363 – **840)** 310 West Wall St #104, Midland, TX 79701-5123 – **841)** 1140 Rose Hill Dr, Charlottesville, VA 22903-5128 – **842)** 2651 S Fish Hatchery Rd, Fitchburg, WI 53711-5410 – **843)** 306 S Kanawha St, Beckley, WV 25801-5619 – **844)** 19245 Hwy 127, Athens, AL 35614-6805 – **845)** 2300 Portola Dr, Santa Cruz, CA 95062-4203 – **846)** 10 Executive Dr, Farmington, CT 06032-2841 – **847)** 2828 W Flagler St, Miami, FL 33135-1337 – **848)** 1160 S Semoran Blvd #A, Orlando, FL 32807-1461 – **849)** 3405 Duluth Park Lane, Duluth, GA 30096-3259 – **850)** 500 W Boone Ave, Spokane, WA 99201-2404 – **851)** 934 West 138th St, Riverdale, IL 60827-1673 – **852)** 4000 Radio Dr #1, Louisville, KY 40218-1568 – **853)** 827 Fairview Dr SW, Lenoir, NC 28645-6023 – **854)** 0700 SW Bancroft St, Portland, OR 97239-4226 – **855)** 5316 William Flynn Hwy #3N, Gibsonia, PA 15044-9646 – **856)** P.O. Box 2355, West Columbia, SC 29171-2355 – **857)** 4131 North Central Expressway, Dallas, TX 5204-2102 – **858)** 63 East Main St, Price, UT 84501-3031 – **859)** 700 Wellington Hills Rd, Little Rock, AR 72211-2026 – **860)** 2200 Smith Lane, Fortuna, CA 95540-2771 – **861)** 777 Grant St, Denver, CO 80203-3501 – **862)** 3737 Lake Ave, Fort Wayne, IN 46805-5554 – **863)** 500 Victory Rd, Quincy, MA 02171-3139 – **864)** 3800 Hooper Ave, Baltimore, MD 21211-1313 – **865)** 201 Industrial Park Rd, Excelsior Springs, MO 64024-1736 – **866)** 5445 Johnson Rd, Bozeman, MT 59718-8333 – **867)** P.O. Box 90, Smithfield, NC 27577-0090 – **868)** 80898 Powerline Rd, Umatilla, OR 97882-9309 – **869)** 210 Montague Ave, Greenwood, SC 29649-1935 – **870)** 340 Martin Luther King Blvd, Bristol, TN 37620-2313 – **871)** 3218 Quincy St, Plainview, TX 79072-1906 – **872)** 1000 Dexter Ave North #100, Seattle, WA 98109- 582 – **873)** 1859 211 Lake Ave, Rice Lake, WI 54868-9502 – **874)** 2001 N 3rd St #102, Phoenix, AZ 85004-1439 – **875)** 4043 Geer Rd, Hughson, CA 95326-9715 – **876)** 39138 Fremont Blvd 3rd Flr, Fremont, CA 94538-1305 – **877)** 1360 E Sherwood Dr, Grand Junction, CO 81501-7546 – **878)** 714 Narrow Way, Saint Simons Island, GA 31522-9712 – **879)** 1465 Northside Dr. NW #218, Atlanta, GA 30318-4220 – **880)** 64 Broadway N, Fargo, ND 58102-4934 – **881)** 1411 Locust St, Saint Louis, MO 63103-2332 – **882)** 8755 W Flamingo Rd, Las Vegas, NV 89147-8667 – **883)** 234 Airport Plaza Blvd #5, Farmingdale, NY 11735-3938 – **884)** 6200 Oak Tree Blvd 4th Flr, Independence, OH 44131-2510 – **885)** 16414 San Pedro Ave #575, San Antonio, TX 78232-2277 – **886)** 1047 Route 302, Wells River, VT 05081-9742 – **887)** 112 North Pearl St, Berlin, WI 54923-1570 – **888)** 2500 Battleship Pkwy, Mobile, AL 36602-8003 – **889)** 360 Main St, Clinton, AR 72031-6622 – **890)** 3800 West Alameda Ave, Burbank, CA 91505-4300 – **891)** 3463 Ramona Ave #15, Sacramento, CA 95826-3827 – **892)** 311 112th Ave NE, St Petersburg, FL 33716-3394 – **893)** 820 N LaSalle St, Chicago, IL 60610-3214 – **894)** 211 Jason St, Pittsfield, MA 01201-5998 – **895)** 2175 Click Rd, Petoskey, MI 49770-8818 – **896)** 1 Julian Price Place, Charlotte, NC

28208-5211 – **897)** 5010 Underwood Ave, Omaha, NE 68132-2297 – **898)** 462 Merrimack St, Methune, MA 01844-5804 – **899)** 1423 West Bender Blvd, Hobbs, NM 88240-9252 – **900)** 8010 North Main St, Dayton, OH 45405-2249 – **901)** 63088 NE 18th St #200, Bend, OR 97701-7102 – **902)** 2311 Old Arch Rd, Norristown, PA 19401-2013 – **903)** 1270 Mineral Spring Ave, North Providence, RI 02904-4637 – **904)** 26321 Stateline Rd West, Ardmore, TN 38449-3083 – **905)** 6161 Savoy Dr #1200, Houston, TX 77036-3363 – **906)** 919 N Main St, Cleburne, TX 76033-3853 – **907)** 700 Monticello Ave #305, Norfolk, VA 23510-2517 – **908)** 2670 S White Rd #165, San Jose, CA 95148-2083 – **909)** 2131 Crimmins Lane, Falls Church, VA 22043-1962 – **910)** 144 Gould St #155, Needham Heights, MA 02494-2338 – **911)** 1 South Memorial Dr #600, Saint Louis, MO 63102-2498 – **912)** 4611 Terry Rd #C, Jackson, MS 39212-5646 – **913)** 410 New Bridge St #3B, Jacksonville, NC 28540-4759 – **914)** 1500 Valley River Dr #350, Eugene, OR 97401-2163 – **915)** 2201 S 6th St, Las Vegas, NV 89104-2999 – **916)** 320 Barnett Blvd, Tallassee, AL 36078-1506 – **917)** 83 East Shaw Ave #150, Fresno, CA 93710-7622 – **918)** 136 South Oak Knoll Ave #300, Pasadena, CA 1101-2624 – **919)** 1130 Radio Rd, Bartow, FL 33830-7600 – **920)** 5815 Westside Rd, Austell, GA 30106-3179 – **921)** 6341 West Port Ave, Shreveport, LA 71129-2415 – **922)** 27675 Halsted Rd, Farmington Hills, MI 48331-3511 – **923)** 1600 Utica Ave South #400, Minneapolis, MN 55416-1480 – **924)** 2234 Hodges Chapel Rd, Benson, NC 27504 – **925)** 3500 E Rosser Ave, Bismarck, ND 58501-3398 – **926)** 731 Lexington Ave, New York, NY 10022-1331 – **927)** 5110 SE Stark St, Portland, OR 97215-1751 – **928)** 2440 Millwood Ave, Columbia, SC 29205-1128 – **929)** 3050 Post Oak Blvd #1688, Houston, TX 77056-6527 – **930)** 12100 W Howard Ave, Milwaukee, WI 53228-1851 – **931)** 2926 Huntsville Hwy #D, Fayetteville, TN 37334-6687 – **932)** 1504 W Persimmon St, Rogers, AR 72756-3350 – **933)** 5244 Madison Ave, Sacramento, CA 95841-3004 – **934)** 1321 North Gene Autry Trail, Palm Springs, CA 92262-5473 – **935)** 800 S Douglas Rd #111, Coral Gables, FL 33134-3187 – **936)** 1355 E Altamonte Dr, Altamonte Springs, FL 32701-5011 – **937)** 5601 Cassia St, Boise, ID 83705-1836 – **938)** 120 Eaton St, Peoria, IL 61603-4217 – **939)** 2504 Ardmore St SE, Grand Rapids, MI 49506-4901 – **940)** 310 S La Frenz Rd, Liberty, MO 64068-7944 – **941)** 15963 Highway 4 East, Senatobia, MS 38668-5786 – **942)** 7255 S Tenaya Way #100, Las Vegas, NV 89113-1900 – **943)** 3258 Merchant Rd, Warsaw, NY 14569-9320 – **944)** 5100 South Tennis Lane, Sioux Falls, SD 57108-2212 – **945)** 2251 Double Creek Dr #302, Round Rock, TX 78664-3831 – **946)** 300 Bryant Rd, Conroe, TX 77303-1796 – **947)** 3245 Basie Rd, Richmond, VA 23228-3404 – **948)** P.O. Box 1299, Lebanon, VA 24266-1299 – **949)** 1949 Mountain View Dr, Cody, WY 82414-4932 – **950)** 5455 Jug Factory Rd, Tuscaloosa, AL 35405-4213 – **951)** 1445 West Baseline Rd, Phoenix, AZ 85041-7010 – **952)** 3400 Olive Ave #550, Burbank, CA 91505-5544 – **953)** 1582 S Parker Rd #204, Denver, CO 80231-2716 – **954)** 777 River Rd, Middletown, CT 06457-3922 – **955)** 2727 Shipley Rd, Wilmington, DE 19810-3299 – **956)** 407 N Howard Ave #200, Tampa, FL 33606-1575 – **957)** 118 N Patterson St, Valdosta, GA 31601-5570 – **958)** 6626 Dubuque Trail, Norwalk, IA 50211-9645 – **959)** 1801 East Main St, Marion, IL 62959-5115 – **960)** 131 N Santa Fe Ave, Salina, KS 67401-2615 – **961)** 22 West Main St, Mount Sterling, KY 40353-1314 – **962)** 5555 Hilton Ave #500, Baton Rouge, LA 70808-2564 – **963)** 500 Victory Rd #2, Quincy, MA 02171-3132 – **964)** 830 Oilfield Ave, Shelby, MT 59474-1641 – **965)** 2581 US Hwy 70 West, Goldsboro, NC 27530-9553 – **966)** 10424 Edith Blvd NE, Albuquerque, NM 87113-2408 – **967)** 8456 Smokey Hollow Rd, Baldwinsville, NY 13027-8222 – **968)** 290 Hegenberger Rd, Oakland, CA 94621-1436 – **969)** 404 Main St, Klamath Falls, OR 97601-6021 – **970)** 5110 SE Stark St, Portland, OR 97215-1751 – **971)** 1 Forever Dr, Holidaysburg, PA 16648-3029 – **972)** 5732 N Tryon St, Charlotte, NC 28213-6802 – **973)** 11 Main St, Rapid City, SD 57701-2831 – **974)** 510 West Economy Rd, Morristown, TN 37814-3223 – **975)** 821 Pineville Rd, Chattanooga, TN 37405-2633 – **976)** 5426 North Mesa St, El Paso, TX 79912-5421 – **977)** 35 Eagle Rock Lane, Churchville, VA 24421 – **978)** 3650 131st Ave #550, Bellevue, WA 98006-1334 – **979)** 801 Old Wawawai Rd, Pullman, WA 99163-9002 – **980)** 944 Harlem St, Altoona, WI 54720-1127 – **981)** 2800 East College Ave, Appleton, WI 54915-3255 – **982)** 18385 Coal Heritage Rd, Welch, WV 24801-9773 – **983)** 4565 St Augustine Rd #A, Jacksonville, FL 32207-7229 – **984)** 4365 Kennedy Ave, Orlando, FL 32812-8214 – **985)** 1100 Spring St #610, Atlanta, GA 30309-2828 – **986)** 25 NW Point Blvd #400, Elk Grove Village, IL 60007-1030 – **987)** 1115 Tamarack Rd #500, Owensboro, KY 42301-6988 – **988)** 635 West 7th St #400, Cincinnati, OH 45203-1549 – **989)** 8121 Georgia Ave #806, Silver Spring, MD 20910-4945 – **990)** 208 Middle Rd, Skowhegan, ME 04976-5023 – **991)** 813 S 7th St, Kansas City, MO 66105-2003 – **992)** 60 Courthouse St, Columbus, NC 28722 – **993)** P.O. Box 711, Red Springs, NC 28377-0711 – **994)** 1015 Atlantic City Blvd, Bayville, NJ 08721-3541 – **995)** 1086 Teaneck Rd #4F, Teaneck, NJ 07666-4858 – **996)** 100 Saratoga Village Blvd #21, Malta, NY 12020-3703 – **997)** 3100 N Triphammer Rd #100, Lansing,

NY 14882-8906 – **998)** 619 Alexander Rd, Princeton, NJ 08540-6000 – **999)** 840 Philadelphia St #100, Indiana, PA 15701-3922 – **1000)** 15 Century Blvd #101, Nashville, TN 37214-3692 – **1001)** 84 NE Loop 410 #143, San Antonio, TX 78216-5835 – **1002)** 6400 N Belt Line Rd #110, Irving, TX 75063-6065 – **1003)** 55 North 300 West, Salt Lake City, UT 84180-1109 – **1004)** 1675 Grandview Rd, Martinsville, VA 24112-2319 – **1005)** 4101 Wall St #A, Montgomery, AL 36106-3656 – **1006)** 9255 Towne Centre Dr #535, San Diego, CA 92121-3038 – **1007)** 2905 King St, San Jose, CA 95122-1518 – **1008)** 6360 SW 41st Place, Davie, FL 33314-3412 – **1009)** P.O. Box 322, Mattoon, IL 61938-0322 – **1010)** 255 Cedardale Dr SE, Owatonna, MN 55060-4425 – **1011)** 118 E Main St, Clinton, NC 28328-4029 – **1012)** 785 US Highway 70 SW, Hickory, NC 28602-5096 – **1013)** 4590 E 29th St, Tulsa, OK 74114-6208 – **1014)** 109 Old Chapin Rd #Q, Lexington, SC 29072-2065 – **1015)** 2219 Yew St Rd, Bellingham, WA 98229-8855 – **1016)** 1015 Main St, Wheeling, WV 26003-2782 – **1017)** 113 Jackson Ave, Memphis, TN 38103-1509 – **1018)** 812 East Beale St, Kingman, AZ 86401-5925 – **1019)** 1400 Easton Dr #144B, Bakersfield, CA 93309-9404 – **1020)** VOA - 330 Independence Ave SW, Washington, DC 20547-0003 – **1021)** 10143 Commerce St, Summerville, GA 30747-1356 – **1022)** 600 Cavanaugh Rd, Lansing, MI 48910-5299 – **1023)** 1310 2nd St NW #A, Sauk Rapids, MN 56379-2532 – **1024)** 731 S Pear Orchard Rd #27, Ridgeland, MS 39157-4839 – **1025)** 317 First Ave East, Kalispell, MT 59901-9601 – **1026)** 122 Cinema Dr, Wilmington, NC 28403-1490 – **1027)** 5011 Capitol Ave, Omaha, NE 68132-2921 – **1028)** 100 Chestnut St #1700, Rochester, NY 14604-2418 – **1029)** 470 Leadmine Rd, Gaffney, SC 29340-4037 – **1030)** 802 S Central Ave, Knoxville, TN 37902-1207 – **1031)** 6161 Savoy Dr #1140, Houston, TX 77036-3323 – **1032)** 10025 Lakewood Dr SW #B, Tacoma, WA 98499-3897 – **1033)** 2609 Jordan Lane NW, Huntsville, AL 35816-1030 – **1034)** 5183 N 35th St, Milwaukee, WI 53209-5399 – **1035)** 1780 West Holly St, Fayetteville, AR 72703-1307 – **1036)** 4041 N Central Ave #1000, Phoenix, AZ 85012-3310 – **1037)** 621 S Virgil Ave #400, Los Angeles, CA 90005-4043 – **1038)** UMC Campus Box 207, Boulder, CO 80309-1001 – **1039)** 1160 S Semoran Blvd, Orlando, FL 32807-1461 – **1040)** 2970 Peachtree Rd NW #700, Atlanta, GA 30305-4919 – **1041)** 2915 Maples Rd, Fort Wayne, IN 46816-3199 – **1042)** 71991 US Hwy 71 South, Jackson, MN 56143-ND – **1043)** 1100 Main St #1950, Kansas City, MO 64105-5173 – **1044)** 6500 West Main St #315, Belleville, IL 62223-3700 – **1045)** 1190 Hollywood Blvd, Bay Saint Louis, MS 39520-1662 – **1046)** 1700 Buena Vista Dr, Monroe, NC 28112-6306 – **1047)** 2000 Randolph Rd SE #103, Albuquerque, NM 87106-2146 – **1048)** 3 Park Ave FL 41, New York, NY 10016-5902 – **1049)** 4949 SW Macadam Ave, Portland, OR 97239-3997 – **1050)** 105 Ash Ave, South Pittsburg, TN 37380-1513 – **1051)** 14001 Dallas Pkwy #300, Dallas, TX 75240-7369 – **1052)** 2131 Crimmins Lane, Falls Church, VA 22043-1962 – **1053)** 5606 Medical Circle, Madison, WI 53719-1232 – **1054)** 132 Carubia Dr, Core, WV 26541-7137 – **1055)** 75-153 Merle Dr #D, Palm Desert, CA 92211-5197 – **1056)** 1976 Fremont Blvd #D, Seaside, CA 93955-3169 – **1057)** 2824 Palm Beach Blvd, Fort Myers, FL 33916-1503 – **1058)** 625 N Michigan Ave #300, Chicago, IL 60611-3163 – **1059)** 10 Cabot Rd #302, Medford, MA 02155-5173 – **1060)** 3250 Franklin St, Detroit, MI 48207-4219 – **1061)** 875 W 5th St, Winston-Salem, NC 27101-2505 – **1062)** 738 Blowing Rock Rd, Boone, NC 28607-4840 – **1063)** 5702 52nd Ave South, Fargo, ND 58104-5605 – **1064)** 219 Savannah-Gardner Rd, New Castle, PA 16101-5546 – **1065)** 1559 W 4th St, Williamsport, PA 17701-5650 – **1066)** 4337 Big Barn Dr, Little River, SC 29566-6802 – **1067)** 1617 Lebanon Rd, Nashville, TN 37210-3217 – **1068)** 6222 West Interstate 10, San Antonio, TX 78201-2097 – **1069)** 703 3rd Ave, Huntington, WV 25701-1421 – **1070)** 1359 Carmichael Way, Montgomery, AL 36106-3629 – **1071)** 2919 E Broadway Blvd #235, Tucson, AZ 85716-5301 – **1072)** 4135 Northgate Blvd, Sacramento, CA 95834-1226 – **1073)** 9255 Towne Centre Dr #535, San Diego, CA 92121-3038 – **1074)** 139 West Olive Ave, Fresno, CA 93728-3035 – **1075)** 350 NW 71st St, Miami, FL 33138-5530 – **1076)** 4325 Steve Reynolds Blvd, Norcross, GA 30093-3362 – **1077)** 302 S Poplar St, Centralia, IL 62801-3900 – **1078)** 5555 Hilton Ave #500, Baton Rouge, LA 70808-2564 – **1079)** 2175 Click Rd, Petoskey, MI 49770-8818 – **1080)** 2300 North Lelia St, Guymon, OK 73942-2840 – **1081)** 369 Tower Rd, Waynesburg, PA 15370-3663 – **1082)** 2 Bala Plaza #800, Bala Cynwyd, PA 19004-1501 – **1083)** 1726 Dakota Ave South, Huron, SD 57350-4024 – **1084)** 9245 Poplar Ave #8-101, Germantown, TN 38138-7931 – **1085)** 1079 East Trinity Lane, Nashville, TN 37216-3043 – **1086)** 4501 North McColl Rd, McAllen, TX 78504-2431 – **1087)** 750 Ridgeview Dr #204, Saint George, UT 84770-2665 – **1088)** 1400 West Main St, Auburn, WA 98001-5230 – **1089)** 302 South 2nd St #204, Laramie, WY 82070-3650 – **1090)** 10399 State Hwy 238, Afton, WY 83110-ND – **1091)** 39138 Fremont Blvd 3rd Flr, Fremont, CA 94538-1305 – **1092)** 1308 East Hwy 56, Salem, IN 47167-9690 – **1093)** 104 Main St North, Stillwater, MN 55082-5076 – **1094)** 6223 Old Mendenhall Rd, High Point, NC 27263-3940 – **1095)** 108 Radio Station Rd, Whiteville, NC 28472-4906 – **1096)** 661 Little Britain Rd, Newburgh,

NY 12553-6150 – **1097)** 4 Summit Park Dr #150, Independence, OH 44131-6921 – **1098)** 161 Hillwood Ave #B, Falls Church, VA 22046-2983 – **1099)** 2821 US Highway 231, Wetumpka, AL 36093-1222 – **1100)** P.O. Box 680748, Fort Payne, AL 35968-1608 – **1101)** 900 Patte Rd, Willcox, AZ 85643-3408 – **1102)** 140 North Main, Lakeport, CA 95453-4815 – **1103)** 200 South "A" St #400, Oxnard, CA 93030-5717 – **1104)** 4002 W Gandy Blvd, Tampa, FL 33611-3410 – **1105)** 1701 S 55th St, Kansas City, KS 66106-2241 – **1106)** 3 Converse St #101, Palmer, MA 01069-1538 – **1107)** 107 North Franklin St, Saginaw, MI 48607-1263 – **1108)** 728 Western Ave, Fergus Falls, MN 56537-1095 – **1109)** 63 Braswell Rd, Hattiesburg, MS 39401-9730 – **1110)** 210 W Front St, Forsyth, MT 59327-ND – **1111)** 147 N Garden St, Marion, NC 28752-3709 – **1112)** 525 Evans St, Greenville, NC 27858-2311 – **1113)** 149 Main St #210, Nashua, NH 03060-2725 – **1114)** 55 Horsehill Rd, Cedar Knolls, NJ 07927-2003 – **1115)** 400 Ardmore Blvd, Pittsburgh, PA 15221-3019 – **1116)** 241 W 4th St, Emporium, PA 15834-1047 – **1117)** 4230 Faber Place Dr #100, North Charleston, SC 29405-8512 – **1118)** 601 Washington St, Alexandria, LA 71301-8028 – **1119)** 4050 Eisenhauer Rd, San Antonio, TX 78218-3409 – **1120)** RR2 Box 2384, Roosevelt, UT 84066-9523 – **1121)** 1 Radio Lane, Danville, VA 24541-5235 – **1122)** 1901 N Moore St #200, Arlington, VA 22209-1746 – **1123)** 200 1st Ave West #104, Seattle, WA 98119-4291 – **1124)** Murrow Comm Cntr - WSU, Pullman, WA 99163-ND – **1125)** 11800 W Grange Ave, Hales Corners, WI 53130-1099 – **1126)** 714 Nicholas St, Rupert, WV 25984 – **1127)** 120 Summit Pkwy #200, Birmingham, AL 35209-4719 – **1128)** 4301 North 75th St #105, Scottsdale, AZ 85251-3501 – **1129)** 1500 Cotner Ave, Los Angeles, CA 90025-3303 – **1130)** 3256 Penryn Rd #100, Loomis, CA 95650-8052 – **1131)** 1901 N Moore St #200, Arlington, VA 22209-1706 – **1132)** 225 Hollywood Blvd NW, Fort Walton Beach, FL 32548-4725 – **1133)** 2100 Coral Way, Coral Gables, FL 33145-2635 – **1134)** 3079 Campbellton Rd SW #104, Atlanta, GA 30311-5400 – **1135)** 4005 Golden Isle West, Baxley, GA 31513-7972 – **1136)** 924 W Second St, Boone, IA 50036-3904 – **1137)** 400 W Sunnyside Rd, Idaho Falls, ID 83402-4613 – **1138)** 1156 N Orchard St, Boise, ID 83706-2234 – **1139)** 1978 Interbelt Business Center Dr, Saint Louis, MO 63114-5760 – **1140)** 6161 Fall Creek Rd, Indianapolis, IN 46220-5032 – **1141)** 1105 Lee Dr, Baton Rouge, LA 70808-8714 – **1142)** 309 Waverly Oaks Rd #103, Waltham, MA 02452-8403 – **1143)** 425 Centerstone Ct #1, Zeeland, MI 49464-2249 – **1144)** 2330 W Grand St, Springfield, MO 65802-4900 – **1145)** 1119 Eastview Dr, Asheboro, NC 27203-4576 – **1146)** P.O. Box 7509, Trenton, NJ 08628-0509 – **1147)** 2502 Camino Entrada #C, Santa Fe, NM 87507-4911 – **1148)** 1064 James St, Syracuse, NY 13203-2704 – **1149)** 604 Chillicothe St #405, Portsmouth, OH 45662-4024 – **1150)** 175 Ken Mar Industrial Pkwy, Broadview Heights, OH 44147-2950 – **1151)** 315 S Atherton St, State College, PA 16801-4045 – **1152)** 471 Robison Rd West, Erie, PA 16509-5425 – **1153)** 51 Commerce St, Sumter, SC 29150-5014 – **1154)** 20 Grand Ave #C, Greenville, SC 29607-2161 – **1155)** 346 South Main St, Winner, SD 57580-1832 – **1156)** 106 E College St, Dickson, TN 37055-1828 – **1157)** 1108 Hendricks St, Chattanooga, TN 37406-3159 – **1158)** 121 South Cotton Square, Lufkin, TX 75904-2933 – **1159)** 1150 Pepsi Place #300, Charlottesville, VA 22901-2865 – **1160)** 3520 Kingsbury Circle, Roanoke, VA 24014-1356 – **1161)** 328 100th St, Amery, WI 54001-4024 – **1162)** 912 Lane 11½, Powell, WY 82435-9222 – **1163)** 273 Azalea Rd #403, Mobile, AL 36609-1970 – **1164)** 1838 Commerce Dr #A, Lakeside, AZ 85929-7007 – **1165)** 1321 North Gene Autry Trail, Palm Springs, CA 92262-5473 – **1166)** 1401 West Caldwell Ave, Visalia, CA 93277-7725 – **1167)** 325 John Knox Rd #G, Tallahassee, FL 32303-4161 – **1168)** 2824 Palm Beach Blvd, Ft Myers, FL 33916-1503 – **1169)** 6106 Hoffner Ave, Orlando, FL 32822-4906 – **1170)** 1801 North Elm St, Commerce, GA 30529-2347 – **1171)** 1501 13th Ave, Columbus, GA 31901-1908 – **1172)** 21361 Highway 30, Twin Falls, ID 83301-0197 – **1173)** 1035 Lincoln Rd #205, Bettendorf, IA 52722-4149 – **1174)** 25802 County Rd 26, Elkhart, IN 46517-9132 – **1175)** 1410 N Western Ave, Liberal, KS 67901-2212 – **1176)** 34 Sylvan St, West Springfield, MA 01089-3444 – **1177)** 35 Baltimore St, Cumberland, MD 21502-3024 – **1178)** 2095 South US Highway 131, Petoskey, MI 49770-9216 – **1179)** 31555 W 14 Mile Rd #102, Farmington Hills, MI 48334-1286 – **1180)** 1530 Greenview Dr SW #200, Rochester, MN 55902-1080 – **1181)** 305 West Washington St, Brainerd, MN 56401-2923 – **1182)** 5732 N Tryon St, Charlotte, NC 28607-4835 – **1183)** P.O. Box 57, Smithfield, NC 27577-0057 – **1184)** 101 Back Rd, Dover, NH 03820-5012 – **1185)** 961 Matley Lane #120, Reno, NV 89502-2119 – **1186)** 34 Chestnut St, Oneonta, NY 13820-2466 – **1187)** 50 James E Casey Dr, Buffalo, NY 14206-2367 – **1188)** 5807 S Garnett Rd #K, Tulsa, OK 74146-6847 – **1189)** 888 Rogue River Highway, Grants Pass, OR 97527-5209 – **1190)** 440 Rebecca Lane, Lebanon, PA 17046-1734 – **1191)** 1816 Savannah Hwy, Hampton, SC 29924-6545 – **1192)** 6300 South Tallgrass Ave, Sioux Falls, SD 57108-8184 – **1193)** 640 W Hwy 25/70, Newport, TN 37821-8068 – **1194)** 7700 Carpenter Freeway Fl2, Dallas, TX 75247-4829 – **1195)** 3824 Wayside Rd, Stuart, VA 24171-2506 – **1196)** 1130 14th Ave, Longview,

WA 98632-3017 – **1197)** 2810 Southern Dr, Gillette, WY 82718-9369 – **1198)** 601 Greensboro Ave #507, Tuscaloosa, AL 35401-1795 – **1199)** 2800 North 44th St #100, Phoenix, AZ 85008-1559 – **1200)** 880 Via Esteban #C, San Luis Obispo, CA 93420-2462 – **1201)** 600 Grant St #600, Denver, CO 80203-3540 – **1202)** 21 Miracle Strip Pkwy SE, Ft. Walton Beach, FL 32548-5815 – **1203)** 7080 Industrial Way, Macon, GA 31206-7538 – **1204)** 117 SE 5th St, Evansville, IN 47708-1639 – **1205)** 929 Howard Ave, New Orleans, LA 70113-1148 – **1206)** 762 Water St, Fitchburg, MA 01420-6481 – **1207)** 125 Community Dr #201, Augusta, ME 04330-8157 – **1208)** 216 Belmont Rd, Grand Forks, ND 58201-4620 – **1209)** 2110 Cliff Rd, Saint Paul, MN 55122-2347 – **1210)** 25539 NC Hwy 125, Scotland Neck, NC 27874-ND – **1211)** 204 E Broadway, Farmington, NM 87401-6418 – **1212)** 150 Spectrum Blvd, Las Vegas, NV 89101-4860 – **1213)** 485 Madison Ave, New York, NY 10022-5803 – **1214)** 100 Chestnut St #1700, Rochester, NY 14604-2418 – **1215)** PMB 2371574 1574 Coburg Rd #237, Eugene, OR 97401-4802 – **1216)** 275 Radio Rd, Hanover, PA 17331-1140 – **1217)** 219 Savannah-Gardner Rd, New Castle, PA 16101-5546 – **1218)** 100 E Shockley Ferry Rd, Anderson, SC 29624-3746 – **1219)** 3004 East Highway 76, Mullins, SC 29574-7396 – **1220)** 886 Mt Olivet Rd, Columbia, TN 38401-8031 – **1221)** 515 South 700 East #1C, Salt Lake City, UT 84102-2802 – **1222)** 110 West Spiller Ave, Wytheville, VA 24382-1953 – **1223)** 4010 Summitview Ave, Yakima, WA 98908-2966 – **1224)** 808 East Sprague Ave, Spokane, WA 99202-2126 – **1225)** 491 South Washburn St #400, Oshkosh, WI 54904-6733 – **1226)** 1101 Cameron Rd, Opp, AL 36467-2407 – **1227)** 1904 W Hillsboro St, El Dorado, AR 71730-6806 – **1228)** 2250 West Sunset Ave #3, Springdale, AR 72762-5187 – **1229)** 1820 Cochrane Rd, Morgan Hill, CA 95037-9029 – **1230)** 2030 Iowa Ave #A, Riverside, CA 92507-7412 – **1231)** 2654 Cramer Lane, Chico, CA 95928-8838 – **1232)** 920 West Basin Rd #400, New Castle, DE 19720-1013 – **1233)** 3071 Continental Dr, West Palm Beach, FL 33407-3274 – **1234)** 1176 Satellite Blvd NW #200, Suwanee, GA 30024-2868 – **1235)** 245 Alfred St, Savannah, GA 31408-3205 – **1236)** 436 N Main St, Pocatello, ID 83204-3018 – **1237)** 331 Fulton St #1200, Peoria, IL 61602-1475 – **1238)** 30129 East US Hwy 54, Pratt, KS 67124-8304 – **1239)** 1039 Eggners Ferry Rd, Benton, KY 42025-8070 – **1240)** P.O. Box 448, Manchester, KY 40962-0448 – **1241)** 266 23rd St, Meridian, MS 39301-1728 – **1242)** 3250 South Reserve St #200, Missoula, MT 59801-8236 – **1243)** 526 Main Ave SE, Hickory, NC 28602-1103 – **1244)** 907 Lejeune Blvd, Jacksonville, NC 28540-5916 – **1245)** 5011 Capitol Ave, Omaha, NE 68132-2921 – **1246)** 69 Stanhope Ave, Keene, NH 03431-1577 – **1247)** 59 Court St #100, Binghamton, NY 13901-3293 – **1248)** 1611 S Main St, Dayton, OH 45409-2547 – **1249)** 2003 NW 56th St, Pendleton, OR 97801-4593 – **1250)** 1 Forever Dr, Holidaysburg, PA 16648-3029 – **1251)** 1246 Cranston St, Cranston, RI 02920-7318 – **1252)** 102 South 5th St, Crockett, TX 75835-2037 – **1253)** 2720 Highway 83, Weslaco, TX 78596-1225 – **1254)** 2525 Kell Blvd #200, Wichita Falls, TX 76308-1008 – **1255)** 413 Stuart Circle #110, Richmond, VA 23220-3754 – **1256)** 113 W Oak St, Sparta, WI 54656-1712 – **1257)** N72W12922 Good Hope Rd, Menomonee Falls, WI 53051-4441 – **1258)** 204 Main St #201, Logan, WV 25601-3943 – **1259)** 3525 Soldier Springs Rd, Laramie, WY 82070-8903 – **1260)** 655 Fairview Rd, Winfield, AL 35594-4755 – **1261)** 111 N Spring St, Searcy, AR 72143-7712 – **1262)** 747 E Green St #400, Pasadena, CA 91101-2148 – **1263)** 1250 Siskiyou Blvd, Ashland, OR 97520-5010 – **1264)** 4910 E Clinton Ave, Fresno, CA 93727-1560 – **1265)** 6805 Corporate Dr #130, Colorado Springs, CO 80919-1977 – **1266)** 1 Boot Key, Marathon, FL 33050 – **1267)** 2355 Pluckebaum Rd, Cocoa, FL 32926-5179 – **1268)** 4023 North Armenia Ave #400, Tampa, FL 33607-1053 – **1269)** 100 WMTM Rd, Moultrie, GA 31788-4104 – **1270)** 341 South Yorktown Pike, Mason City, IA 50401-4533 – **1271)** 3110 Upper Fords Creek Rd, Orofino, ID 83544-9629 – **1272)** 401 North Michigan Ave #2010, Chicago, IL 60611-4206 – **1273)** 401 West Main St #301, Lexington, KY 40507-1646 – **1274)** 1526 Corporate Dr, Shreveport, LA 71107-6338 – **1275)** 650 Wooddale Blvd, Baton Rouge, LA 70806-2980 – **1276)** 1423 Clarkview Rd, Baltimore, MD 21209-2134 – **1277)** 77 Monroe Center NW #1000, Grand Rapids, MI 49503-2912 – **1278)** Bemidji, MN – **1279)** 731 S Pear Orchard Rd #27, Ridgeland, MS 39157-4839 – **1280)** 2147 Springs Rd, Mount Airy, NC 27030-ND – **1281)** 1811 West O St, McCook, NE 69001-4264 – **1282)** 110 Babbitt Rd, Franklin, NH 03235-2105 – **1283)** 1842 S Broad St, Trenton, NJ 08610-6002 – **1284)** 1960 Idaho St, Carson City, NV 89701-5324 – **1285)** 51 S Pearl St, Albany, NY 12207-1500 – **1286)** 5426 William St, Lancaster, NY 14086-9320 – **1287)** 2510 St Clair Ave NE, Cleveland, OH 44114-4013 – **1288)** 2625 South Memorial Dr #A, Tulsa, OK 74129-2623 – **1289)** 7590 Highway 238, Jacksonville, OR 97530-9728 – **1290)** 305 Hwy 315, Pittston, PA 18640-3987 – **1291)** 118 E 3rd St East, Mobridge, SD 57601-2511 – **1292)** 510 W Economy Rd, Morristown, TN 37814-3223 – **1293)** 1300 WWCR Ave, Nashville, TN 37218-3800 – **1294)** 3601 South Congress Ave #F, Austin, TX 78704-7280 – **1295)** 207 University Blvd #200, Harrisonburg, VA 22801-3752 – **1296)** 2201 6th Ave #1500, Seattle, WA 98121-1840 – **1297)** 343 High St, Morgantown,

WV 26505-5515 – **1298)** P.O. Box 1747, Foley, AL 36536-1747 – **1299)** 16 Martin Luther King St, Selma, AL 36703-3109 – **1300)** 3256 Penryn Rd #100, Loomis, CA 95650-8052 – **1301)** 650 S E St #H, San Bernadino, CA 92408-1946 – **1302)** 963 Industrial Rd #I, San Carlos, CA 94070-4146 – **1303)** 820 11th Ave, Greeley, CO 80631-3246 – **1304)** P. O. Box 551, Norwich, CT 06360-0551 – **1305)** 1310 S Florida Ave, Wauchula, FL 33873-9479 – **1306)** 316 E Taylor Rd, Deland, FL 32724-7817 – **1307)** 1310 Walker St West, Douglas, GA 31533-7952 – **1308)** 2215 Perimeter Park Dr, Atlanta, GA 30341-1307 – **1309)** 415 Park Ave, Twin Falls, ID 83301-7752 – **1310)** 21 East St Joseph St, Indianapolis, IN 46204-1025 – **1311)** 95 Jackson St, Prestonsburg, KY 41653-1010 – **1312)** 613 N 5th St, West Monroe, LA 71291-1726 – **1313)** 122 Green St #2R, Worcester, MA 01604-4138 – **1314)** 779 Warren Ave, Portland, ME 04103-1176 – **1315)** 300 East Front St #450, Traverse City, MI 49684-5720 – **1316)** 27675 Halsted Rd, Farmington Hills, MI 48331-3511 – **1317)** 5300 Edina Industrial Blvd #200, Minneapolis, MN 55439-2922 – **1318)** 2702 East 32nd St, Joplin, MO 64804-4307 – **1319)** 3313 15th St #F, Great Falls, MT 59405-ND – **1320)** 4801 East Independence Blvd #815, Charlotte, NC 28212-5497 – **1321)** 1190 Patton Ave, Asheville, NC 28806-2706 – **1322)** 707 Leon St, Durham, NC 27704-4125 – **1323)** 1185 9th St NE, Thompson, ND 58278-9343 – **1324)** 2401 State Route 66, Ocean, NJ 07712-3962 – **1325)** 1606 Central Ave SE #104, Albuquerque, NM 87106-4478 – **1326)** 419 Broadway, Paterson, NJ 07501-2104 – **1327)** 39 Kellogg Rd, New Hartford, NY 13413-2849 – **1328)** 906 SW Alder St, Newport, OR 97365-4712 – **1329)** 134 East Pitt St, Bedford, PA 15522-1311 – **1330)** 310 2nd Ave, Warren, PA 16365-2407 – **1331)** 51 Commerce St, Sumter, SC 29150-5014 – **1332)** 1 Radio Park Dr, Jackson, TN 38305-4124 – **1333)** 8023 Vantage Dr #840, San Antonio, TX 78230-4771 – **1334)** 3500 Maple Ave #1310, Dallas, TX 75219-3931 – **1335)** 3231 Old Lee Highway, Fairfax, VA 22030-1501 – **1336)** 5589 Greenwich Rd #200, Virginia Beach, VA 23462-6565 – **1337)** 152101 W County Rd 12, Prosser, WA 99350-7265 – **1338)** 2651 S Fish Hatchery Rd, Madison, WI 53711-5400 – **1339)** 276 Seneca Trail, Ronceverte, WV 24970-1343 – **1340)** 2700 Corporate Dr Ste 115, Birmingham, AL 35242-2735 – **1341)** 311 Lexington Ave, Fort Smith, AR 72901-3842 – **1342)** 5345 Madison Ave, Sacramento, CA 95841-3141 – **1343)** 79 Baldwin Ave, Waterbury, CT 06706-1854 – **1344)** 1779 Independence Blvd, Sarasota, FL 34234-2106 – **1345)** 2360 St Johns Bluff Rd S #2, Jacksonville, FL 32246-2310 – **1346)** 1055 NE 125th St, North Miami, FL 33161-5804 – **1347)** 1000 Memorial Dr, Griffin, GA 30223-4446 – **1348)** 17525 Highway 1, Vivian, LA 71082-9526 – **1349)** 127 Dorrance St, Providence, RI 02903-2828 – **1350)** 1009 West Ridge St #A, Marquette, MI 49855-3963 – **1351)** 600 Cavanaugh Rd, Lansing, MI 48910-5299 – **1352)** 507 SE 11th St, Grand Rapids, MN 55744-3990 – **1353)** 1750 S Brentwood Blvd #811, Saint Louis, MO 63144-1344 – **1354)** 2438 Highway 43 South, Picayune, MS 39466-7486 – **1355)** 875 W 5th St, Winston Salem, NC 27101-2505 – **1356)** 427 Hill St, Murphy, NC 28906-3509 – **1357)** 3600 County Rd 19 South, Minot, ND 58701-ND – **1358)** 2002 Char Ave, Scottsbluff, NE 69361-2255 – **1359)** 8 Lawrence Rd, Derry, NH 03038-4191 – **1360)** 900 Parish St, 3rd FLR, Pittsburgh, PA 15220-3407 – **1361)** 1801 Charleston Hwy #J, Cayce, SC 29033-2019 – **1362)** 500 S Phillips Ave, Sioux Falls, SD 57104-6825 – **1363)** 162 Free Hill Rd, Gray, TN 37615-3144 – **1364)** 1030 Oakdale St, Manchester, TN 37355-5618 – **1365)** 1782 W Sam Houston Pkwy North, Houston, TX 77043-2723 – **1366)** 434 Bearcat Dr, Salt Lake City, UT 84115-2520 – **1367)** 306 West Broad St, Richmond, VA 23220-4219 – **1368)** 1308 Coolidge Rd, Aberdeen, WA 98520-6317 – **1369)** 645 25th Ave North, Wisconsin Rapids, WI 54495-3294 – **1370)** 1111 East Willow St, Scottsboro, AL 35768-2210 – **1371)** 4433 E Broadway Blvd #210, Tucson, AZ 85711-3536 – **1372)** 401 Pacheco Blvd., Los Banos, CA 93635-4227 – **1373)** 3301 Barham Blvd #201, Los Angeles, CA 90068-1477 – **1374)** 201 West Park Ave #11, Tallahassee, Fl 32301-7760 – **1375)** 7179 Printers Alley, Milton, FL 32583-5347 – **1376)** 4100 Metzger Rd, Fort Pierce, FL 34947-1712 – **1377)** 807 Bellevue Ave, Dublin, GA 31021-4847 – **1378)** 514 Jefferson St, Waterloo, IA 50701-5422 – **1379)** 4320 Dundee Rd, Northbrook, IL 60062-1703 – **1380)** 2207 E Morgan Ave #J, Evansville, IN 47711-4355 – **1381)** 2120 N Woodlawn St #352, Wichita, KS 67208-1881 – **1382)** 821 Adams Rd, Corbin, KY 40701-4708 – **1383)** 514 Guilbeau Rd #B, Lafayette, LA 70506-8416 – **1384)** 552 Massachusetts Ave #201, Cambridge, MA 02139-4088 – **1385)** 1605 Level Rd, Havre de Grace, MD 21078-1727 – **1386)** 6317 Taylor Dr, Flint, MI 48507-4683 – **1387)** 919 Lilac Dr North, Golden Valley, MN 55422-4615 – **1388)** 401 E Coal Ave, Gallup, NM 87301-6099 – **1389)** 57 North Ave, Owego, NY 13827-1392 – **1390)** 419 Broadway, Paterson, NJ 07501-2104 – **1391)** 9700 SE Eastview Dr, Happy Valley, OR 97086-6975 – **1392)** 1 Boston Store Place, Erie, PA 16501-2312 – **1393)** 1516 4th Ave #B, Conway, SC 29526-5032 – **1394)** 25 Garlington Rd, Greenville, SC 29615-4613 – **1395)** 1200 S Stockton Ave, Monahans, TX 79756-4060 – **1396)** 710 Grove St, Danville, VA 24541-1704 – **1397)** 22479 Front St, Accomac, VA 23301-1641 – **1398)** 804 N Broadway, Knoxville, TN 37917-7203 –

1399) 5408 S Freya St, Spokane, WA 99223-7114 – **1400)** 2100 Washington Ave, Sheboygan, WI 53081-7042 – **1401)** 1530 Main St, Lander, WY 82520-2658 – **1402)** 301 N 12th St #1, Gadsden, AL 35901-3058 – **1403)** 308 S Broadway St, Cabot, AR 72201-2324 – **1404)** 1410 Neotomas Ave #200, Santa Rosa, CA 95405-7533 – **1405)** 2030 Iowa Ave #A, Riverside, CA 92507-7412 – **1406)** 45 Pomfret St, Putnam, CT 06260-1827 – **1407)** 7515 Blythe Island Hwy, Brunswick, GA 31523-6261 – **1408)** 1350 Radio Loop, Warner Robins, GA 31088-3626 – **1409)** 1416 Locust St, Des Moines, IA 50309-3014 – **1410)** 805 Stewart Ave, Lewiston, ID 83501-4709 – **1411)** 1419 W Bannock St, Boise, ID 83702-5234 – **1412)** 671 East County Rd 400 South, Kokomo, IN 46902-8101 – **1413)** 400 Poydras St #800, New Orleans, LA 70130-3245 – **1414)** 101 West St #2, Black Mountain, NC 28711-3161 – **1415)** 277 Union Ave #205, Laconia, NH 03246-3114 – **1416)** 27 Wiliam St 11th Flr, New York, NY 10005-2718 – **1417)** 5411 Jefferson St NE #100, Albuquerque, NM 87109-3485 – **1418)** 7755 Freedom Ave NW, North Canton, OH 44720-6905 – **1419)** 1051 Dairy Lane, Elizabethtown, PA 17022-9547 – **1420)** 1777 NE Loop 410 #400, San Antonio, TX 78217-5217 – **1421)** 1408 E Gibson St, Jasper, TX 75951-6123 – **1422)** 1035 Avalon Dr, Forest, VA 24551-2970 – **1423)** 645 Church St #400, Norfolk, VA 23510-1712 – **1424)** 214 Walnut Dr SE, Wise, VA 24293-ND – **1425)** 409 9th Ave, Jasper, AL 35501-3731 – **1426)** 2500 Battleship Pkwy, Mobile, AL 36602-8003 – **1427)** 2425 East Camelback Rd #570, Phoenix, AZ 85016-4250 – **1428)** 2121 Lancey Dr, Modesto, CA 95355-3000 – **1429)** 9660 Granite Ridge Dr, San Diego, CA 92123-2657 – **1430)** 2 S Parish Ave, Johnstown, CO 80534-7800 – **1431)** 869 Blue Hills Ave, Bloomfield, CT 06002-3710 – **1432)** 3890 Dunn Ave #804, Jacksonville, FL 32218-6429 – **1433)** 1505 Dundee Rd, Winter Haven, FL 33884-1013 – **1434)** 2828 W Flagler St, Miami, FL 33135-1337 – **1435)** 2000 Indian Hills Dr, Sioux City, IA 51104-1602 – **1436)** 4154 Jennings Dr, Kalamazoo, MI 49048-1087 – **1437)** 2115 Washington Ave S, Bemidji, MN 56601-8918 – **1438)** 88 Vilcom Center #130, Chapel Hill, NC 27514-1660 – **1439)** 123 Egg Harbor Rd Ste 302, Sewell, NJ 08080-9406 – **1440)** 1096 Mechem Dr #G3, Ruidoso, NM 88345-7057 – **1441)** 59 Court St #100, Binghamton, NY 13901-3293 – **1442)** 8044 Montgomery Rd #650, Cincinnati, OH 45236-2959 – **1443)** 229 Broad St, Conneaut, OH 44030-2616 – **1444)** 80404 Cooney Lane, Hermiston, OR 97838-6613 – **1445)** 3355 NE Cornell Rd, Hillsboro, OR 97124-5018 – **1446)** 900 Parish St, Pittsburgh, PA 15220-3425 – **1447)** 212 S Centre St, Pottsville, PA 17901-3532 – **1448)** 100 Cross Hill Way, Easley, SC 29640-8854 – **1449)** 701 S Pierce St #101, Amarillo, TX 79101-2428 – **1450)** 5801 Marvin D Love Freeway #409, Dallas, TX 75237-2319 – **1451)** 4638 Decker Dr, Baytown, TX 77520-1418 – **1452)** 1820 Heritage Center Way, Harrisonburg, VA 22801-8451 – **1453)** 325 Poplar Knob Rd, Galax, VA 24333-4106 – **1454)** 2201 6th Ave #1500, Seattle, WA 98121-1840 – **1455)** 1420 Bellevue St, Green Bay, WI 54311-5649 – **1456)** 527 Gibbs St, Ravenswood, WV 26164-1011 – **1457)** 2717 Yellowstone Rd, Rock Springs, WY 82901-2813 – **1458)** PO Box 669, Marysville, CA 95901-0018 – **1459)** 210 Radio Rd, Corona, CA 92879-1722 – **1460)** 2347 Bering Dr, San Jose, CA 95131-1125 – **1461)** 6565 N W St #270, Pensacola, FL 32505-1797 – **1462)** 1515 E Silver Springs Blvd #134, Ocala, FL 34470-6830 – **1463)** 2420 Waycross Highway, Jesup, GA 31545-2332 – **1464)** 346 West 8th St, Dubuque, IA 52001-4649 – **1465)** 120 West 7th St #400, Bloomington, IN 47404-3869 – **1466)** 2601 Central Ave #C, Dodge City, KS 67801-6212 – **1467)** P.O. Box 487, Grayson, KY 41143-0487 – **1468)** 1726 Reisterstown Rd #117, Pikesville, MD 21208-2986 – **1469)** 49 Acme Rd, Brewer, ME 04412-1545 – **1470)** 1101 South Cass St, Traverse City, MI 49684-3235 – **1471)** 750 Dewey Blvd #1, Butte, MT 59701-3200 – **1472)** 9349 China Grove Church Rd, Pineville, NC 28134-8531 – **1473)** 910 E McNeill St, Lillington, NC 27546-7483 – **1474)** P.O. Box 127, Tabor City, NC 28463-0127 – **1475)** 216 Belmont Rd, Grand Forks, ND 58201-4620 – **1476)** 500 North Commercial St, Manchester, NH 03101-1511 – **1477)** 20 Tucker Dr, Poughkeepsie, NY 12603-1644 – **1478)** 280 State St, Rochester, NY 14614-1033 – **1479)** 125 S Superior St, Toledo, OH 43602-1790 – **1480)** 2513 6th Ave, Altoona, PA 16602-2129 – **1481)** 2615 Broad St, Chattanooga, TN 37408-3100 – **1482)** 4301 Westbank Dr #301, Austin, TX 78746-4400 – **1483)** 1285 West 2320 South, Salt Lake City, UT 84119-1448 – **1484)** 1129 Chatham Heights, Martinsville, VA 24112-2149 – **1485)** 26256 Highway Forty Seven, South Hill, VA 23970-ND – **1486)** 1201 E Division St, Neillsville, WI 54456-2123 – **1487)** 1143 Main St, Wheeling, WV 26003-2722 – **1488)** RR1 Box 139, Dunmore, WV 24934-9712 – **1489)** P.O. Box 630, Vernon, AL 35592-0630 – **1490)** PO Box 55450, North Little Rock, AR 72215-5450 – **1491)** 816 West 6th St, Parker, AZ 85344-4599 – **1492)** 1425 River Park Dr #520, Sacramento, CA 95815-4524 – **1493)** 182 Grand St #215, Waterbury, CT 06702-1914 – **1494)** 432 S Nova Rd, Ormond Beach, FL 32174-6121 – **1495)** 11300 4th St N, Saint Petersburg, FL 33716-2918 – **1496)** 400 Colony Square NE #800, Atlanta, GA 30361-6318 – **1497)** 1 Parker Place #485, Janesville, WI 53545-4078 – **1498)** 2915 Maples Rd, Fort Wayne, IN 46816-3199 – **1499)** 4535 Metropolitan Ave, Kansas City, KS 66106-

2599 – **1500)** 195 Moore Dr, Lexington, KY 40503-2918 – **1501)** 8230 Summa Ave, Baton Rouge, LA 70809-3421 – **1502)** 808 Huron Ave, Port Huron, MI 48060-3705 – **1503)** 13225 Dogwood Dr, Baxter, MN 56425-8669 – **1504)** 8045 Big Bend Blvd, Saint Louis, MO 63119-2714 – **1505)** 70 Adams Hill Rd, Asheville, NC 28806-3841 – **1506)** 4321 Stuart Andrew Blvd #E, Charlotte, NC 28217-1588 – **1507)** 7035 E Washington St Ext, Bath, NY 14810-ND – **1508)** 27 Wiliam St 11th Flr, New York, NY 10005-2718 – **1509)** 1232 E 2nd St, Tulsa, OK 74120-2010 – **1510)** 1725 N Oregon St, Ontario, OR 97914-1541 – **1511)** 786 Diamond Hill Rd, Woonsocket, RI 02895-1499 – **1512)** 445 Carolina Springs Rd, North Augusta, SC 29841-8801 – **1513)** 518 St Joseph St, Rapid City, SD 57701-2717 – **1514)** 1811 Carters Creek Pike, Franklin, TN 37064-6823 – **1515)** 6960 Bucknell Rd, Millington, TN 38053-7502 – **1516)** 4045 N Mesa St, El Paso, TX 79902-1526 – **1517)** 912 Curtis Ave, Pasadena, TX 77502-2402 – **1518)** 3308 Broadway #401, San Antonio, TX 78209-6550 – **1519)** 2809 Emerywood Pkwy #540, Henrico, VA 23294-3745 – **1520)** 67 Merchants Row, Rutland, VT 05701-5910 – **1521)** 2707 Colby Ave #1380, Everett, WA 98201-3568 – **1522)** 1456 East Green Bay St, Shawano, WI 54166-2258 – **1523)** 801 Noble St #30, Anniston, AL 36201-5698 – **1524)** 1780 West Holly St, Fayetteville, AR 72703-1307 – **1525)** 4043 Geer Rd, Hughson, CA 95326-9715 – **1526)** 136 South Oak Knoll Ave #300, Pasadena, CA 91101-2624 – **1527)** 4700 Walnut St, Boulder, CO 80301-2548 – **1528)** 7120 SW 24th Ave, Gainesville, FL 32607-3705 – **1529)** 233 N Michigan Ave #2800, Chicago, IL 60601-5519 – **1530)** 516 Main St, Hazard, KY 41701-1775 – **1531)** 17 Columbus Rd, Plymouth, MA 02360-4810 – **1532)** 28 Houlton Rd, Presque Isle, ME 04769-5206 – **1533)** 1613 Lawrence Hwy, Charlotte, MI 48813-8844 – **1534)** 640 Lincoln Ave SE, Saint Cloud, MN 56304-1024 – **1535)** 313 Old Route 66, Saint Robert, MO 65584-ND – **1536)** 1106 18th Ave, Meridian, MS 39301-4101 – **1537)** 10250 Lorraine Rd, Gulfport, MS 39503-6005 – **1538)** 115 North Church St, Rocky Mount, NC 27804-5402 – **1539)** 1000 20th Ave SW, Minot, ND 58701-6447 – **1540)** 212 W Apache St, Farmington, NM 87401-6235 – **1541)** 3301 North Densing Rd, Hobbs, NM 88240-8803 – **1542)** 2 Pendell Rd, Poughkeepsie, NY 12601-1500 – **1543)** 8456 Smokey Hollow Rd, Baldwinsville, NY 13027-8222 – **1544)** 39540 Bradbury Rd, Middleport, OH 45760-9703 – **1545)** 7461 South Ave, Youngstown, OH 44512-5789 – **1546)** 5110 SE Stark St, Portland, OR 97215-1751 – **1547)** 2294 Clements Ferry Rd, Charleston, SC 29492-7729 – **1548)** 122 Radio Rd, Jackson, TN 38301-3445 – **1549)** 104 Cherry St, Athens, TN 37303-ND – **1550)** 810 West 200 North, Logan, UT 84321-3726 – **1551)** 2043 10th St NE, Roanoke, VA 24012-5309 – **1552)** 12216 Parklawn Dr, Rockville, MD 20852-1710 – **1553)** 372 Dorset St, South Burlington, VT 05403-6212 – **1554)** 1200 Chesterly Dr #160, Yakima, WA 98902-7345 – **1555)** 557 Scott St, Wausau, WI 54403-4829 – **1556)** 800 County Rd 4 East, Prattville, AL 36067-6610 – **1557)** 366 S Section St, Fairhope, AL 36532-ND – **1558)** 1950 S Sunwest Lane #302, San Bernadino, CA 92408-3227 – **1559)** 1605 Simpson Lane, Marysville, CA 95901-9747 – **1560)** 10 Columbus Blvd #24, Hartford, CT 06106-1973 – **1561)** 1575 McKee Rd #206, Dover, DE 19904-1382 – **1562)** 3411 W Tharpe St, Tallahassee, FL 32303-1139 – **1563)** 5043 Tamiami Trail East, Naples, FL 34113-4127 – **1564)** 3765 N John Young Pkwy, Orlando, FL 32804-3213 – **1565)** 940 Brownlee Rd, Jackson, GA 30233-2418 – **1566)** 1632 South Maize Rd, Wichita, KS 67209-3912 – **1567)** 1411 Locust St, Saint Louis, MO 63103-2332 – **1568)** 100 Eversole St #1, Harlan, KY 40831-2346 – **1569)** 707 Leon St, Durham, NC 27704-4125 – **1570)** 1301 E 4th St, North Platte, NE 69101-4302 – **1571)** 1705 Lake St, Elmira, NY 14901-1299 – **1572)** 134 Mullin St, Watertown, NY 13601-3616 – **1573)** 717 E David Rd, Dayton, OH 45429-5218 – **1574)** 278 SW Arthur St, Portland, OR 97201-4745 – **1575)** Centre City Towers - 650 Smithfield St #620, Pittsburgh, PA 15222-3913 – **1576)** 2147 Market St, Nesquehoning, PA 18240-1422 – **1577)** 219 Luckett St NW, Roanoke, VA 24017-6812 – **1578)** 201 State St, La Crosse, WI 54601-3246 – **1579)** 100 Kanawha Terrace, Saint Albans, WV 25177-2771 – **1580)** 1716 KROE Lane, Sheridan, WY 82801-9681 – **1581)** 3900 11th Ave, Tuscaloosa, AL 35401-7056 – **1582)** 208 Buena Vista Rd, Hot Springs, AR 71913-8208 – **1583)** 500 E Tyler Pkwy, Payson, AZ 85541-3276 – **1584)** 2171 Ralph Ave, Stockton, CA 95206-3699 – **1585)** 777 River Rd, Middletown, CT 06457-3922 – **1586)** 3912 US Highway 301 North, Ellenton, FL 34222-2333 – **1587)** 2710 W Atlantic Ave, Delray Beach, FL 33445-4431 – **1588)** 12544 North Main St, Trenton, GA 30752-2227 – **1589)** 1820 Wynnton Rd, Columbus, GA 31906-2930 – **1590)** 3535 E Kimberly Rd, Davenport, IA 52807-2583 – **1591)** P.O. Box 84, Jerome, ID 83338-0084 – **1592)** 685 E 1675 N, Michigan City, IN 46360-9503 – **1593)** 22 Sconticut Neck Rd, Fairhaven, MA 02719-1930 – **1594)** 59346 Madison Ave, Mankato, MN 56001-8518 – **1595)** 959 Magnolia Dr North, Wiggins, MS 39577-3630 – **1596)** 73 Varney Rd #A, Wolfeboro, NH 03894-ND – **1597)** 187 Vienna Rd, Newark, NY 14513-9124 – **1598)** 715 Route 52, Beacon, NY 12508-1047 – **1599)** 4 Summit Park Dr #150, Independence, OH 44131-6921 – **1600)** 12 West Long Ave, Du Bois, PA 15801-2100 – **1601)** 40 Rickert Rd, Doylestown, PA 18901-2326 – **1602)**

101 Riverview Rd, Erwin, TN 37650-8722 – **1603)** 9540 Godwin Dr, Manassas, VA 20110-4165 – **1604)** 1133 Kresky Ave, Centralia, WA 98531-3789 – **1605)** 45 Campbell Rd, Walla Walla, WA 99362-9597 – **1606)** 134 4th Ave, Huntington, WV 25701-1220 – **1607)** 22 Cogswell Ave, Pell City, AL 35125-2438 – **1608)** 351 W Cromwell Ave #108, Fresno, CA 93711-6115 – **1609)** 747 E Green St #400, Pasadena, CA 91101-2148 – **1610)** 342 Day St, San Francisco, CA 94131-2313 – **1611)** 4700 S Syracuse St #1050, Denver, CO 80237-2713 – **1612)** 404 West Lime St, Lakeland, FL 33815-4651 – **1613)** 3100 E 15th St, Panama City, FL 32405-7421 – **1614)** 13085 SW 133rd Ct, Miami, FL 33186-5850 – **1615)** 100 NW 76th Dr #2, Gainesville, FL 32607-6659 – **1616)** 613 Silver Circle, Dalton, GA 30721-4551 – **1617)** 3589 North Decatur Rd, Scottdale, GA 30079-1867 – **1618)** 9245 N Meridian St #300, Indianapolis, IN 46260-1832 – **1619)** 522 Main St, Williamsburg, KY 40769-1127 – **1620)** 10 Cabot Rd #302, Medford, MA 02155-5173 – **1621)** 100 William T Morrissey Blvd, Dorchester, MA 02125-3300 – **1622)** 236 Admiral Dr, Annapolis, MD 21401-3123 – **1623)** 1150 Haynor Rd, Ionia, MI 48846-8532 – **1624)** 6500 West Main St #315, Belleville, IL 62223-3700 – **1625)** 3901 Weddington Rd, Monroe, NC 28110-9513 – **1626)** 990 North Center St Extension, Mount Olive, NC 28365-2704 – **1627)** 1103 North Green St, Morganton, NC 28655-9003 – **1628)** 3205 West North Front St, Grand Island, NE 68803-4024 – **1629)** 27 Wiliam St 11th Flr, New York, NY 10005-2718 – **1630)** 200 West 1st St, Roswell, NM 88203-4668 – **1631)** 320 N Jensen Rd, Vestel, NY 13850-2111 – **1632)** 2625 South Memorial Dr, Tulsa, OK 74129-2600 – **1633)** 4205 Cherry Ave NE, Keizer, OR 97303-4856 – **1634)** 1 Forever Dr, Holidaysburg, PA 16648-3029 – **1635)** 2278 Wortham Lane, Grovetown, GA 30813-5103 – **1636)** 6080 Mount Moriah Rd Extension, Memphis, TN 38115-2698 – **1637)** 630 Mainstream Dr, Nashville, TN 37228-1204 – **1638)** 5011 Almeda Rd, Houston, TX 77004-5996 – **1639)** 4638 Decker Dr, Baytown, TX 77520-1418 – **1640)** 257 E 200 S #400, Salt Lake City, UT 84111-2073 – **1641)** 2298 Rose Ridge, Clintwood, VA 24228-7738 – **1642)** 2029 Freeway Dr, Mount Vernon, WA 98273-5470 – **1643)** 403 Capital St, Lewiston, ID 83501-1815 – **1644)** 1 Commerce St #300, Montgomery, AL 36104-3549 – **1645)** 8211 Geyer Springs Rd #P6, Little Rock, AR 72209-4909 – **1646)** 4343 East Camelback Rd #200, Phoenix, AZ 85018-8306 – **1647)** 1101 S Broadway, Santa Maria, CA 93463-2689 – **1648)** 1124 Foster Rd, Napa, CA 94558-6520 – **1649)** 32992 US Highway 34, Wray, CO 80758-9161 – **1650)** 222 Hazard St, Orlando, FL 32804-3030 – **1651)** 419 Broadway, Paterson, FL 07501-2104 – **1652)** 3833 US Highway 82, Brunswick, GA 31523-7735 – **1653)** 613 Tallapoosa St W, Bremen, GA 30110-1838 – **1654)** c/o Klien Assc 299 S Main St #1300, Salt Lake City, UT 84111 – **1655)** 513 Hampshire St, Quincy, IL 62301-2928 – **1656)** 3901 Brendenwood Rd, Rockford, IL 61107-2200 – **1657)** 825 S Kansas Ave #100, Topeka, KS 66612-1233 – **1658)** 20 Guest St 3rd Flr, Brighton, MA 02135-2040 – **1659)** 79 Warren Avene, Portland, ME 04103-1007 – **1660)** 2244 Ravine Rd , Kalamazoo, MI 49004-3506 – **1661)** 24 Frank Lloyd Wright Dr, Ann Arbor, MI 48105-9755 – **1662)** 2000 Elm Sreet SE, Minneapolis, MN 55414-2531 – **1663)** 3276 Highway 198 West, Lucedale, MS 39452-7947 – **1664)** 512 Peanut Rd, Elizabethtown, NC 28337-8811 – **1665)** 200 Radio Dr, Lexington, NC 27292-8010 – **1666)** 101 South Main St, Gloversville, NY 12078-3820 – **1667)** 4 Summit Park Dr #150, Independence, OH 44131-6921 – **1668)** 3624 Avion Dr, Medford, OR 97504-4011 – **1669)** 404 East 2nd St, The Dalles, OR 97058-2412 – **1670)** 1049 N Sekol Ave, Carbondale, PA 18504-1098 – **1671)** 1210 Snyder Rd, Lansdale, PA 19446-4614 – **1672)** 105 N Spring St #113, Greenville, SC 29601-2859 – **1673)** 540 Cumberland St West, Cowan, TN 37318-3115 – **1674)** 115 Radio Rd, Livingston, TX 77351-7702 – **1675)** 301 South Polk St #100, Amarillo, TX 79101-1404 – **1676)** 6400 N Belt Line Rd #110, Irving, TX 75063-6065 – **1677)** 950 Kenbridge Rd, Blackstone, VA 23824-3105 – **1678)** 1420 Bellevue St, Green Bay, WI 54311-5649 – **1679)** 1251 Earl L. Core Rd, Morgantown, WV 26505-5881 – **1680)** 900 Bluefield Ave, Bluefield, WV 24701-2760 – **1681)** 1501 13th Ave, Columbus, GA 31901-1908 – **1682)** 1707 Warnke Rd NW, Cullman, AL 35055-2231 – **1683)** 903 N Main St, Salinas, CA 93906-3912 – **1684)** 6803 West Blvd, Inglewood, CA 90302-1895 – **1685)** 7150 Campus Dr #150, Colorado Springs, CO 80920-3157 – **1686)** 2824 Palm Beach Blvd, Fort Myers, FL 33916-1503 – **1687)** 1611 Atlantic Blvd, Atlantic Beach, FL 32233-2516 – **1688)** 449 North 12th St, Defuniak Springs, FL 32433-0411 – **1689)** 5815 Westside Rd, Austell, GA 30106-3179 – **1690)** 2141 Grand Ave, Des Moines, IA 50312-5303 – **1691)** 930 East Lincoln Ave, Goshen, IN 46528-3504 – **1692)** 1240 Radio Dr, Pikeville, KY 41501-4779 – **1693)** 650 Wooddale Blvd, Baton Rouge, LA 70806-2930 – **1694)** 60 Main St, Brockton, MA 02301-4040 – **1695)** 18720 16 Mile Rd, Big Rapids, MI 49307-9303 – **1696)** 1433 Main Ave North, Thief River Falls, MN 56701-1141 – **1697)** 4424 Hampton Ave, Saint Louis, MO 63109-2232 – **1698)** 1338 Bragg Blvd, Fayetteville, NC 28301-4202 – **1699)** 1055 Skyway Dr, Marshall, NC 28753-3809 – **1700)** 11291 39th St SW, Dickinson, ND 58601-9206 – **1701)** 403 E 25th St, Kearney, NE 68847-5515 – **1702)** 123 Egg Harbor

Rd #302, Sewell, NJ 08080-9406 – **1703)** 8755 West Flamingo Rd, Las Vegas, NV 89147-8667 – **1704)** 52 Corporate Circle #K, Albany, NY 12203-5176 – **1705)** 6325 Sheridan Dr, Williamsville, NY 14221-4801 – **1706)** 605 South Front St #300, Columbus, OH 43215-5626 – **1707)** P.O. Box 701, Tunkhannock, PA 18657-0701 – **1708)** 600 Corporate Cir #100, Harrisburg, PA 17110-9787 – **1709)** 10614 Rockley Rd, Houston, TX 77099-3514 – **1710)** 919 N Main St, Cleburne, TX 76033-3853 – **1711)** 9540 Godwin Dr, Manassas, VA 20110-4165 – **1712)** 7080 Lee Highway, Fairlawn, VA 24141-8416 – **1713)** 290 Hegenberger Rd, Oakland, CA 94621-1436 – **1714)** 4010 Summitview Ave, Yakima, WA 98908-2966 – **1715)** 1 Washington Ave, Elkins, WV 26241-3160 – **1716)** 3222 S Richey Ave, Tucson, AZ 85713-5453 – **1717)** 8265 Sierra College Blvd #312, Roseville, CA 95661-9403 – **1718)** 570 E Ave Q9, Palmdale, CA 93550-2354 – **1719)** 869 Blue Hills Ave, Bloomfield, CT 06002-3789 – **1720)** 800 8th Ave SE, Largo, FL 33771-2162 – **1721)** 1650 S Dixie Hwy, Boca Raton, FL 33432-7462 – **1722)** 20 John Davenport Dr NW, Rome, GA 30165-2536 – **1723)** 1113 Nebraska St, Sioux City, IA 51105-1438 – **1724)** 331 Fulton St #1200, Peoria, IL 61602-1475 – **1725)** 2401 Paint Creek Rd, Stanton, KY 40380-9272 – **1726)** 900 North Lake Shore Dr, Lake Charles, LA 70601-2120 – **1727)** 500 West Cummings Park #2600, Woburn, MA 01801-6503 – **1728)** 351 Tilghman Rd, Salisbury, MD 21804-1920 – **1729)** 447 Congress St #3B, Portland, ME 04101-3505 – **1730)** 3338 E Bristol Rd, Burton, MI 48529-1408 – **1731)** 1516 E Lake St #200, Minneapolis, MN 55407-1997 – **1732)** 240 Moss Hill Dr, New Albany, MS 38652-3400 – **1733)** 126 E Water St, Plymouth, NC 27962-1330 – **1734)** 401 Saw Mill Hollow Rd, Burnsville, NC 28714-9789 – **1735)** 4321 Stuart Andrew Blvd #E, Charlotte, NC 28217-1588 – **1736)** 1751 Hanshaw Rd, Ithaca, NY 14850-9105 – **1737)** 1541 Alta Dr #400, Whitehall, PA 18052-5622 – **1738)** 2440 Millwood Ave, Columbia, SC 29205-1128 – **1739)** 1320 Brick Church Pike, Nashville, TN 37207-5038 – **1740)** 1101 Kilgore Dr, Henderson, TX 75652-5129 – **1741)** 3911 South 1st St, Abilene, TX 79605-1639 – **1742)** 166 North Main St, Broadway, VA 22815-9702 – **1743)** 900 Bluefield Ave, Bluefield, WV 24701-2760 – **1744)** 2241 W Main St, Moses Lake, WA 98837-2826 – **1745)** 1635 S Gold St, Centralia, WA 98531-8997 – **1746)** 2410 S Main St #A, West Bend, WI 53095-5270 – **1747)** 1551 Springhill Ave #A, Mobile, AL 36604-3283 – **1748)** 40 Park Rd #B, Pleasant Grove, AL 35127-1910 – **1749)** 1 Radio Dr, Berryville, AR 72616-ND – **1750)** 824 E Washington St, Phoenix, AZ 85034-1088 – **1751)** 5640 S Broadway St, Eureka, CA 95503-6997 – **1752)** 13749 Beach Blvd, Westminster, CA 92683-3204 – **1753)** 1020 West Main St, Merced, CA 95340-4521 – **1754)** 5230 W Highway 98, Panama City, FL 32401-1058 – **1755)** 4051 Jimmie Dyess Pkwy, Augusta, GA 30909-9469 – **1756)** 1111 Boulevard SE, Atlanta, GA 30312-3895 – **1757)** 501 S Lincoln Ave, Jerome, ID 83338-3026 – **1758)** 18889 N 2350th St, Dennison, IL 62423-2523 – **1759)** 1632 South Maize Rd, Wichita, KS 67209-3912 – **1760)** 486 Lakeside Dr, Jenkins, KY 41537-8917 – **1761)** 1 Home St, Somerset, MA 02720-5229 – **1762)** 301 Fulton St West, Grand Rapids, MI 49404-6492 – **1763)** 580 West Clark Rd, Ypsilanti, MI 48198-3488 – **1764)** 35006 US Highway 2 East, Fosston, MN 56542-9268 – **1765)** 1100 South Tryon St #210, Charlotte, NC 28203-4297 – **1766)** 292 Old Clarkesville Rd, Toccoa Falls, NC 30577-ND – **1767)** 804 Perryman St, Fair Bluff, NC 36401-1902 – **1768)** 5942 County Route 64, Hornell, NY 14843-9730 – **1769)** 185 Genesee St, Utica, NY 13501-2102 – **1770)** 27 Wiliam St 11th Flr, New York, NY 10005-2718 – **1771)** 635 W 7th St #201A, Cincinnati, OH 45203-1513 – **1772)** 550 Market Ave South, Canton, OH 44702-2103 – **1773)** 111 Presidential Blvd #100, Bala Cynwyd, PA 19004-1009 – **1774)** 369 East GE Patterson Ave, Memphis, TN 38126-3301 – **1775)** 771 Helena St, Dallas, TX 75217-5129 – **1776)** 1211 West Hein Rd, San Antonio, TX 78220-3301 – **1777)** 1302 N Shepherd Dr, Houston, TX 77008-3752 – **1778)** 4415 39th Place, Brentwood, MD 20772-1106 – **1779)** 306 West Broad St, Richmond, VA 23220-4219 – **1780)** 504 23rd St NW, Roanoke, VA 24017-5414 – **1781)** 10 Clinton St #10, Springfield, VT 05156-3310 – **1782)** 601 Main St #400, Vancouver, WA 98660-3404 – **1783)** 730 Ray O Vac Lane, Madison, WI 53711-2472 – **1784)** 501 Wooster Ave, San Jose, CA 95116-1046 – **1785)** 90 Kay Ave, Milford, CT 06460-5495 – **1786)** 3400 Idaho Ave NW #200, Washington, DC 20016-3000 – **1787)** 8451 S Cherokee Blvd. #B, Douglasville, GA 30134-8520 – **1788)** 4802 E 62nd St, Indianapolis, IN 46220-5296 – **1789)** 2 Radio Plaza St, Ferndale, MI 48220-ND – **1790)** 3415 University Ave West, Saint Paul, MN 55114-2099 – **1791)** 4800 N Central Ave Phoenix, Mesa, AZ 85012-1722 – **1792)** 3401 Holland Ave, Fresno, CA 93722-4197 – **1793)** 459 Hamilton Ave #300, Palo Alto, CA 94301-1811 – **1794)** 8729 9th St #110, Rancho Cucamonga, CA 91730-4312 – **1795)** 11203 E Peakview Ave, Greenwood Village, CO 80111-6811 – **1796)** 1150 W King St, Cocoa, FL 32922-8618 – **1797)** 308 Victory Rd, Quincy, MA 02171-3129 – **1798)** 106 E Main St, Spring Arbor, MI 49283-9701 – **1799)** 6721 West 121st St, Overland Park, KS 66209-2003 – **1800)** 1411 Locust St, Saint Louis, MO 63103-2332 – **1801)** 704 North King St #604, Wilmington, DE 19801-3535 – **1802)** P.O. Box 907, Magdalena, NM 87825-0907 – **1803)** 151 Penns

Grove Lane, Latrobe, PA 15650-3745 – **1804)** 277 Gravel Hill Rd, Palmyra, PA 17078-8535 – **1805)** 15096 South Dakota Highway 15, Milbank, SD 57252-5954 – **1806)** 55 Music Square West, Nashville, TN 37203-3207 – **1807)** 755 South 11th St #102, Beaumont, TX 77701-3723 – **1808)** 868 East 5900 South, Murray, UT 84107-7650 – **1809)** 1601 E 57th Ave, Spokane, WA 99223-6623 – **1810)** 310 W Wisconsin Ave #100, Milwaukee, WI 53203-2224 – **1811)** P.O. Box 369, Hollister, CA 95024-0369 – **1812)** 2284 S Victoria Ave #2-G, Ventura, CA 93003-6626 – **1813)** 1188 Lake View Rd, Altamonte Springs, FL 32714-2713 – **1814)** 412 W Oakland Park Blvd, Wilton Manors, FL 33311-1712 – **1815)** 8451 S Cherokee Blvd. #B, Douglasville, GA 30134-8520 – **1816)** 2980 US Highway 51, Clinton, IL 61727-9479 – **1817)** 1401 Winchester Ave, Ashland, KY 41101-7555 – **1818)** 3225 Ambassadore Caffery Pkwy, Lafayette, LA 70506-7214 – **1819)** 369 Shelburne Rd, Greenfield, MA 01301-9653 – **1820)** 10 Radio Lane, Brunswick, MD 21788-1645 – **1821)** 122 4th Ave SW, Rochester, MN 55902-3339 – **1822)** 125 S Kingshighway St, Sikeston, MO 63801-2943 – **1823)** 824 US Hwy 158 West Bypass, Warrenton, NC 27589-9796 – **1824)** 431 Eaton Rd, Mocksville, NC 27028-8653 – **1825)** 500 Corporate Pkwy #200, Buffalo, NY 14226-1265 – **1826)** 400 E Britton Rd, Oklahoma City, OK 73114-7507 – **1827)** 5110 SE Stark St, Portland, OR 97215-1751 – **1828)** 111 North Main St, Hallettsville, TX 77964-2796 – **1829)** 16620 Cypress Rosehill Rd, Cypress, TX 77429-1424 – **1830)** 2707 Colby Ave #1380, Snohomish, WA 98201-3568 – **1831)** 204 Bucky Beaver St, England, AR 72076-4907 – **1832)** 1440 Ethan Way #200, Sacramento, CA 95825-2214 – **1833)** 5050 Edison Ave #218, Colorado Springs, CO 80915-3540 – **1834)** 177 State St, Bridgeport, CT 06604-4872 – **1835)** 4190 Belfort Rd #450, Jacksonville, FL 32254-1172 – **1836)** P.O. Box 216, Dalton, GA 30722-0216 – **1837)** 3338 East Bristol Rd, Burton, MI 48529-1408 – **1838)** 1107 Hazeltine Blvd #301, Chaska, MN 55318-1065 – **1839)** 3025 Waughtown St #G, Winston-Salem, NC 27107-1634 – **1840)** 8044 Montgomery Rd #650, Cincinnati, OH 45236-2959 – **1841)** 5807 S Garnett St #K, Tulsa, OK 74146-6847 – **1842)** 4501 North McColl Rd, McAllen, TX 78504-2431 – **1843)** 200 South 10th #600, McAllen, TX 70501-4869 – **1844)** 1190 Daniels Chapel Rd, New Boston, TX 75570-ND – **1845)** 912 S Capital of Texas Hwy #400, Austin, TX 78746-6176 – **1846)** 1445 W Baseline Rd, Phoenix, AZ 85041-7010 – **1847)** 3700 Wilshire Blvd #670, Los Angeles, CA 90010-3013 – **1848)** 869 Church St, Eatonton, GA 31024-6452 – **1849)** 514 Jefferson St, Waterloo, IA 50701-5422 – **1850)** 11141 Georgia Ave #310, Wheaton, MD 20902-4658 – **1851)** 545 Fire Tower Rd, Yanceyville, NC 27379-ND – **1852)** PO Box 1540, Exeter, NH 03833-1540 – **1853)** 4243 Albany St, Albany, NY 12205-4609 – **1854)** 904 North Main St, Punxsutawney, PA 15767-2641 – **1855)** 200 Monument Rd #6, Bala Cynwyd, PA 19004-1726 – **1856)** 3931 Whitehorse Rd, Greenville, SC 29611-5599 – **1857)** 1246 W Laurel #200, San Antonio, TX 78201-6431 – **1858)** 1302 N Shepherd Dr, Houston, TX 77008-3752 – **1859)** 400 Las Colinas Blvd E #1033, Irving, TX 75039-5599 – **1860)** 306 West Broad St, Richmond, VA 23220-4219 – **1861)** 114 Lakeside Ave, Seattle, WA 98122-6542 – **1862)** 1550 The Boardwalk #1, Huntsville, AL 35816-ND – **1863)** Univ. of Arizona, Tucson, AZ 85721-0067 – **1864)** 15165 7th St #D, Victorville, CA 92392-3816 – **1865)** 139 West Olive Ave, Fresno, CA 93728-3035 – **1866)** 40931 Freemont Blvd, Freemont, CA 94538-4307 – **1867)** 160 Chapel Rd #103, Manchester, CT 06042-8929 – **1868)** 4201 N Armenia Ave, Tampa, FL 33607-6446 – **1869)** 2405 E Moody Blvd #402, Bunnell, FL 32110-5994 – **1870)** 330 SW 27th Ave #207, Miami, FL 33135-2957 – **1871)** 2460 Atlanta Rd SE, Smyrna, GA 30080-2000 – **1872)** 7120 US Highway 41, Vienna, GA 31092-4605 – **1873)** 411 Radio Station Rd, North Augusta, SC 29841-9411 – **1874)** 6943 Titian Dr, Baton Rouge, LA 70806-2767 – **1875)** 143 Rumford Ave, Auburndale, MA 02466-1311 – **1876)** 901 S Kingshighway, Cape Girardeau, MO 63703-8003 – **1877)** 4104 Country Lane, Saint Joseph, MO 64506-4921 – **1878)** 430-C State Highway 165 South, Branson, MO 65616-3541 – **1879)** 1213 San Pedro Dr NE, Albuquerque, NM 87110-6725 – **1880)** 5166 Meadowood Mall Circle, Reno, NV 89502-6502 – **1881)** 2448 East 81st St #5500, Tulsa, OK 74137-4201 – **1882)** 944 Exeter Ave, Exeter, PA 18643-1215 – **1883)** 226 Radio Rd, Bennettsville, SC 29512-6183 – **1884)** 101 Lee St, Bristol, VA 24201-4355 – **1885)** 314 S Redwood Rd, Salt Lake City, UT 84104-3536 – **1886)** 2043 10th St NE, Roanoke, VA 24012-5309 – **1887)** 2202 Jolliff Rd, Chesapeake, VA 23321-1416 – **1888)** 6605 SE Lake Rd, Portland, OR 97222-2161 – **1889)** P.O. Box 3213, Ferndale, WA 98248-3213 – **1890)** 730 Ray O Vac Lane, Madison, WI 53711-2472 – **1891)** 510 Pegasus Court, Winchester, VA 22602-4596 – **1892)** 3561 Pegasus Dr #107, Bakersfield, CA 93308-0658 – **1893)** 4554 S Suncoast Blvd, Homosassa, FL 34446-1103 – **1894)** 1800 W Hibiscus Blvd #138, Melbourne, FL 32901-2624 – **1895)** 120 South 35th St #2, Council Bluffs, IA 51501-3203 – **1896)** 6000 Bristol Dr, Paducah, KY 42003-9213 – **1897)** 4200 W Main St, Kalamazoo, MI 49006-2766 – **1898)** 2 Penn Plaza 17th Floor, New York, NY 10121-0101 – **1899)** 8686 Michael Lane, Fairfield, OH 45014-3096 – **1900)** 101 S Woodland Dr, Lancaster, SC 29720-2244 – **1901)** 3980 S Dakota St, Aberdeen, SD 57401-8585

– **1902)** 5353 West Alabama #415, Houston, TX 77056 – **1903)** 9434 Parkfield Dr, Austin, TX 78758-6227 – **1904)** P.O. Box 778, South Boston, VA 24592-0778 – **1905)** 216 N 11th Ave, Pasco, WA 99301-5461 – **1906)** 2600 S Jackson St, Seattle, WA 98144-2499 – **1907)** 908 2nd Ave East, Oneonta, AL 35121-2506 – **1908)** 6820 Pacific Ave #3A, Stockton, CA 95207-2604 – **1909)** 7351 Lincoln Ave, Riverside, CA 92504-4618 – **1910)** 548 E Alisal St, Salinas, CA 93905-2760 – **1911)** 201 N Industrial Park Rd, Excelsior Springs, MO 64024-1736 – **1912)** 127 Glenn Rd, Auburndale, FL 33823-2401 – **1913)** 4565 St Augustine Rd #A, Jacksonville, FL 32207-7229 – **1914)** 2424 Old Rex Morrow Rd, Ellenwood, GA 30294-3901 – **1915)** 834 N Tower Rd, Freeport, IL 61032-8650 – **1916)** 462 Merrimack St, Methuen, MA 01844-5804 – **1917)** 1550 Hart Rd, Towson, MD 21286-1697 – **1918)** P.O. Box 49, Park Rapids, MN 56470-0049 – **1919)** 2110 Cliff Rd, Eagan, MN 55122-2347 – **1920)** 1111 S Glenstone Ave #3-102,, Springfield, MO 65804 – **1921)** 150 Bay Ave, Laurel, MS 39440-4510 – **1922)** P.O. Box 1534, Greenville, NC 27835-1534 – **1923)** 17890 US Hwy 64 West, Siler City, NC 27344-1631 – **1924)** 3568 Lenox Rd, Geneva, NY 14456-2058 – **1925)** 40 Rickert Rd, Doylestown, PA 18901-2326 – **1926)** 8 East Market St, Danville, PA 17821-2917 – **1927)** 1860 Executive Park NW #E, Cleveland, TN 37312-2743 – **1928)** 275 Glenwood Dr, Rocky Mount, VA 24151-2136 – **1929)** 3616 State Highway 47, Rhinelander, WI 54501-8819 – **1930)** 1215 Church St, Oxford, AL 36203-1639 – **1931)** 4602 E University Dr #150, Phoenix, AZ 85034-7423 – **1932)** 747 E Green St #400, Pasadena, CA 91101-2148 – **1933)** 614 Kimbark St, Longmont, CO 80501-4911 – **1934)** 3765 N John Young Pkwy, Orlando, FL 32804-3213 – **1935)** 1510 NE 162nd St, North Miami Beach, FL 33162-4716 – **1936)** P.O. Box 300, Greensboro, FL 32330-0300 – **1937)** 2601 Nicholasville Rd, Lexington, KY 40503-3307 – **1938)** 4200 Parliament Place #300, Lanham, MD 20706-1881 – **1939)** 5115 Telephone Rd, Pascagoula, MS 39567-1130 – **1940)** 41 Pennsylvania Ave, Medford, NY 11763-3717 – **1941)** 1 Radio Place, Painesville, OH 44077-4458 – **1942)** 830 Old Buncombe Rd, Travelers Rest, SC 29690-9467 – **1943)** 236 Woodland Dr, Shelbyville, TN 37160 6750 – **1944)** 804 N Broadway St, Knoxville, TN 37917-7203 – **1945)** 100 Stoddart St, Beaver Dam, WI 53916-1306 – **1946)** 509 North Main St, Tuscumbia, AL 35674-2048 – **1947)** 303 N Spring St, Fordyce, AR 71742-3317 – **1948)** 4209 N Frontage Rd, Fayetteville, AR 72703-5002 – **1949)** 750 Story Rd, San Jose, CA 95122-2604 – **1950)** 2284 Victoria Ave #2-G, Ventura, CA 93003-6626 – **1951)** 4100 Metzger Rd, Fort Pierce, FL 34947-1712 – **1952)** 3551 42nd Ave S #B106, Saint Petersburg, FL 33711-4369 – **1953)** 1104 W Broad Avene, Albany, GA 31707-4340 – **1954)** P.O. Box 746, Lafayette, GA 30728-0746 – **1955)** 2 Radio Loop, Swainsboro, GA 30401-5673 – **1956)** 55 Public Square, Monmouth, IL 61462-1755 – **1957)** 2100 Lee St, Evanston, IL 60202-1539 – **1958)** 3745 W Washington St, Indianapolis, IN 46241-1503 – **1959)** 1200 Baker Ave, Great Bend, KS 67530-4523 – **1960)** 16221 National Pike, Hagerstown, MD 21740-2150 – **1961)** 182 N Angola Rd, Coldwater, MI 49036-9554 – **1962)** 1185 9th St NE, Thompson, ND 58278-9343 – **1963)** 1375 Beasley Rd, Jackson, MS 39206-2018 – **1964)** 1366 Startown Rd, Lincolnton, NC 28092-8038 – **1965)** 911 W Main St, Clayton, NC 27520-1620 – **1966)** 85592 574th Ave, Wayne, NE 68787-7043 – **1967)** 149 Main St #210, Nashua, NH 03060-2725 – **1968)** 2450 Wrondell Way #G, Reno, NV 89502-3767 – **1969)** 231 N Union St, Olean, NY 14760-2663 – **1970)** 1795 West Market St, Akron, OH 44313-7001 – **1971)** 170 3rd St, Tillamook, OR 97141-9489 – **1972)** 575 Grove St, Honesdale, PA 18431-1041 – **1973)** 12 Kent Rd, Aston, PA 19014-1498 – **1974)** 19 Luther Ave, Warwick, RI 02886-4615 – **1975)** 222 Commerce St, Kingsport, TN 37660-4319 – **1976)** 6900 Commerce Ave, El Paso, TX 79915-1102 – **1977)** 215 South Market St, Carthage, TX 75633-2623 – **1978)** 5501 Bagby Ave, Waco, TX 76711-2300 – **1979)** 3120 Southwest Freeway #610, Houston, TX 77098-4521 – **1980)** 227 E Belt Blvd, Richmond, VA 23224-1205 – **1981)** 2201 6th Ave #1500, Seattle, WA 98121-1840 – **1982)** 1414 16th St, Two Rivers, WI 54241-3031 – **1983)** 125 East 3rd St, New Richmond, WI 54017-1800 – **1984)** 2609 Jordan Lane NW, Huntsville, AL 35816-1030 – **1985)** 912 South Perry St, Montgomery, AL 36104-5002 – **1986)** 600 South Pine St, Harrison, AR 72601-5828 – **1987)** 747 E Green St #400, Pasadena, CA 91101-2148 – **1988)** 1110 E Olive Ave, Fresno, CA 93728-3535 – **1989)** 1479 Sanborn Rd, Yuba City, CA 95993-6042 – **1990)** 7800 East Orchard Rd #400, Greenwood Village, CO 80111-2599 – **1991)** 1076 S Chapel St, Newark, DE 19702-1304 – **1992)** 5840 Corporate Way #101A, West Palm Beach, FL 33407-2080 – **1993)** 1611 Atlantic Blvd, Atlantic Beach, FL 32233-2516 – **1994)** 5815 Westside Rd SW, Austell, GA 30106-3179 – **1995)** 1110 26th Ave SW, Cedar Rapids, IA 52404-3430 – **1996)** 11603 Highway 308, Larose, LA 70373 – **1997)** 15 Hampton Ave, Northampton, MA 01060-3809 – **1998)** 60 Temple Place #200, Boston, MA 02111-1324 – **1999)** 4230 Packard St, Ann Arbor, MI 48108-1597 – **2000)** 6500 Brooklyn Blvd, Brooklyn Center, MN 55429-1754 – **2001)** 1001 Highlands Plaza Dr West #100, Saint Louis, MO 63110-1339 – **2002)** 1338 Bragg Blvd, Fayetteville, NC 28301-4202 – **2003)** 1213 San

Pedro Dr NE, Albuquerque, NM 87110-6725 – **2004)** 1705 Lake St, Elmira, NY 14901-1299 – **2005)** 333 7th Ave #1401, New York, NY 10001-5021 – **2006)** 7140 SW Macadam Ave, Portland, OR 97219-3013 – **2007)** 134 East Pitt St, Bedford, PA 15522-1311 – **2008)** 2 Milledge Rd, Augusta, GA 30904-3063 – **2009)** 259 S Willow Ave #A, Cookeville, TN 38501-3140 – **2010)** 3704 Whittier Rd, Memphis, TN 38108-2649 – **2011)** 9434 Parkfield Dr, Austin, TX 78758-6227 – **2012)** 9780 Walnut St #TE405, Dallas, TX 75243-2389 – **2013)** 2722 South Redwood Rd #1, Salt Lake City, UT 84119-8410 – **2014)** 645 Church St #400, Norfolk, VA 23510-1712 – **2015)** 188 Valley Rd, Saltville, VA 24370-ND – **2016)** 4840 Lincoln Rd, Blaine, WA 98230-9602 – **2017)** N7502 Radio Rd, Ripon, WI 54971-9231 – **2018)** 1201 Main St, Wheeling, WV 26003-2844 – **2019)** 134 4th Ave, Huntington, WV 25701-1253 – **2020)** 3256 Penryn Rd #100, Loomis, CA 95650-8052 – **2021)** 7251 Plantation Rd, Pensacola, FL 32504-6334 – **2022)** 3371 W Cleveland Rd Ext. #300, South Bend, IN 46628-9780 – **2023)** 5011 Capitol Ave, Omaha, NE 68132-2921 – **2024)** 2700 Earl Rudder Freeway South #5000, College Station, TX 77845-5011 – **2025)** 2600 S Jackson St, Seattle, WA 98144-2499 – **2026)** 4051 Jimmie Dyess Pkwy, Augusta, GA 30909-9469 – **2027)** 845 Quarry Rd #120, Iowa City, IA 52241-2212 – **2028)** 5787 South Hampton Rd #108, Dallas, TX 75232-6377 – **2029)** 415 E 3rd St, Cheyenne, WY 82007-1479 – **2030)** 3260 Blume Dr #520 Plaza II, Richmond, CA 94806-5715 – **2031)** 1909 East Pass Rd #D11, Gulfport, MS 39507-3778 – **2032)** 316 E Willow Rd, Enid, OK 73701-1514 – **2033)** 3030 SW Moody Ave #210, Portland, OR 97201-4868 – **2034)** 1762 S Main St, Salt Lake City, UT 84115-1912 – **2035)** W223 N3251 Shady Lane, Pewaukee, WI 53072-4194 – **2036)** 311 Lexington Ave, Fort Smith, AR 72901-3842 – **2037)** 4525 Wilshire Blvd 3rd Flr, Los Angeles, CA 90010-3845 – **2038)** 3131 S Vaughn Way #601, Aurora, CO 80014-3516 – **2039)** 721 Shirley St, Cedar Falls, IA 50613-1513 – **2040)** 5426 North Mesa St, El Paso, TX 79912-5442 – **2041)** 2202 Mt. Jolliff Rd, Chesapeake, VA 23321-1416 – **2042)** 1020 West Main St, Merced, CA 95340-4521 – **2043)** 5043 Tamiami Trail East, Naples, FL 34113-4127 – **2044)** 7000 Squibb Rd, Mission, KS 66202-3233 – **2045)** 4200 W Main St, Kalamazoo, MI 49006-2994 – **2046)** 1520 South Blvd #300, Charlotte, NC 28203-3701 – **2047)** 2720 South 7th Ave SW, Fargo, ND 58103-8710 – **2048)** 27 Wiliam St 11th Flr, New York, NY 10005-2718 – **2049)** 5501 Bagby Ave, Waco, TX 76711-2300 – **2050)** 515 S 700 E #1C, Salt Lake City, UT 84102-2802 – **2051)** 2636 N Ontario St, Burbank, CA 91504-2514 – **2052)** 3360 Alta Mesa Dr, Redding, CA 96002-2831 – **2053)** 7080 Industrial Way, Macon, GA 31216-7538 – **2054)** 730 Ray O Vac Lane, Madison, WI 53711-2472 – **2055)** 139 W Olive Ave, Fresno, CA 93728-3035 – **2056)** 3765 N John Young Pkwy, Orlando, FL 32804-3213 – **2057)** 1109 Hudson Lane, Monroe, LA 71201-6003 – **2058)** 3777 44th St SE, Grand Rapids, MI 49512-3945 – **2059)** 1341 N Delaware Ave #405, Philadelphia, PA 19125-4347 – **2060)** 2201 6th Ave #1500, Seattle, WA 98121-1840 – **2061)** 3463 Ramona Ave #15, Sacramento, CA 95826-3827 – **2062)** 12136 Bayaud Ave #125, Lakewood, CO 80228-2115 – **2063)** 1100 Spring St #610, Atlanta, GA 30309-2828 – **2064)** 1000 East 87th St, Chicago, IL 60619-6397 – **2065)** 28095 Three Notch Rd #2B, Mechanicsville, MD 20659-3373 – **2066)** 2609 Jordan Lane NW, Huntsville, AL 35816-1030 – **2067)** 7250 NW 58th St, Miami, FL 33166-3719 – **2068)** 4143 109th St, Urbandale, IA 50322-7925 – **2069)** 3500 Maple Ave #1600, Dallas, TX 75219-3945 – **2070)** 901 East Pike Blvd, Weslaco, TX 78596-4937.

FM STATIONS IN MAJOR METROPOLITAN AREAS

FM Callsign	MHz	Location	kW
Atlanta Area			
W201CC	88.1	Buford	0.02
WRAS	88.5	Atlanta	100
WRFG	89.3	Atlanta	65
WYFW	89.5	Winder	6
W209CD	89.7	Buford	0.03
W209CG	89.7	Tallapoosa	0.01
WWBM	89.7	Yates	1
WABE	90.1	Atlanta	96
W213BE	90.5	Snellville	0.01
WUWG	90.7	Carrollton	0.43
WMVV	90.7	Griffin	18
WREK	91.1	Atlanta	40
WWEV-FM	91.5	Cumming	8.9
WMVW	91.7	Peachtree City	13
WCLK	91.9	Atlanta	6
WBTR-FM	92.1	Carrollton	0.58
W221CG	92.1	Kennesaw	0.04
W221AZ	92.1	Lilburn	0.03
W222AF	92.3	Marietta	0.02
WZGC	92.9	Atlanta	66
W229AG	93.7	Atlanta	0.22
WSTR	94.1	Smyrna	100
W233BF	94.5	Social Circle	0.12

FM Callsign	MHz	Location	kW
WUBL	94.9	Atlanta	100
WSBB-FM	95.5	Doraville	100
WWPW	96.1	Atlanta	100
W243CE	96.5	Winder	0.25
WWLG	96.7	Peachtree City	2.15
WSRV	97.1	Gainesville	100
WUMJ	97.5	Fayetteville	7.9
W250BC	97.9	Atlanta	0.25
WSB-FM	98.5	Atlanta	100
W255CJ	98.9	Atlanta	0.25
W256BO	99.1	Atlanta	0.10
WWWQ	99.7	Atlanta	100
W261BG	100.1	Morrow	0.01
WNNX	100.5	College Park	13.5
W265AV	100.9	Woodstock	0.25
W266BW	101.1	Winder	0.25
WKHX-FM	101.5	Marietta	100
W270AS	101.9	Carrollton	0.01
WLKQ-FM	102.3	Buford	4.2
WPZE	102.5	Mableton	3
W275BK	102.9	Decatur	0.16
WVEE	103.3	Atlanta	100
WALR-FM	104.1	Greenville	100
WFSH-FM	104.7	Athens	23.5
WBZY	105.3	Bowdon	70
WWVA-FM	105.7	Canton	20
W290AG	105.9	Griffin	0.03
WHLE-LP	106.3	Atlanta	0.1
WZHB-LP	106.3	Douglasville	0.1
WYAY	106.7	Gainesville	77
W296BB	107.1	Jonesboro	0.01
WAMJ	107.5	Roswell	33
WPCG-LP	107.9	Canton	0.1
WHTA	107.9	Hampton	33
Baltimore Area			
WYPR	88.1	Baltimore	15.5
WMUC-FM	88.1	College Park	0.01
WAMU	88.5	Washington	50
WEAA	88.9	Baltimore	12.5
W205BL	88.9	Frederick	0.2
WPFW	89.3	Washington	50
WTMD	89.7	Towson	10
WCSP-FM	90.1	Washington	36
WKHS	90.5	Worton	17.5
WZXY	90.7	Spring Grove	0.2
W215BY	90.9	Church Hill	0.03
WETA	90.9	Washington	75
WHFC	91.1	Bel Air	1.1
WBJC	91.5	Baltimore	50
WGTS	91.9	Takoma Park	27
WERQ-FM	92.3	Baltimore	37
WWXT	92.7	Prince Frederick	2.85
WPOC	93.1	Baltimore	19.5
WD2XAB	93.5	Columbia	2
WKYS	93.9	Washington	25
W231BG	94.1	Sunnyburn	0.03
WIAD	94.7	Bethesda	50
WRBS-FM	95.1	Baltimore	50
WPGC-FM	95.5	Morningside	50
WWIN-FM	95.9	Arbutus	6
WSOX	96.1	Red Lion	13.5
W241AO	96.1	Wye Mills	0.08
WHUR-FM	96.3	Washington	16.5
WCEI-FM	96.7	Easton	12.5
WASH	97.1	Washington	17.5
W248AO	97.5	Baltimore	0.25
WRYR-LP	97.5	Sherwood	0.1
WIYY	97.9	Baltimore	13.5
W252BR	98.3	Edgemere	0.25
WYCR	98.5	York-Hanover	10.5
WMZQ-FM	98.7	Washington	50
WNEW	99.1	Bowie	45
WIHT	99.5	Washington	50
W260BV	99.9	Aberdeen	0.01
W260BM	99.9	Annapolis	0.01
W261CD	100.1	Baltimore	0.00
WBIG-FM	100.3	Washington	50
WZBA	100.7	Westminster	25
W265BG	100.9	North East	0.01
WWDC	101.1	Washington	25
WLIF	101.9	Baltimore	13.5
WMMJ	102.3	Bethesda	2.9
W272BJ	102.3	Fairlee	0.004
WQSR	102.7	Baltimore	50
WRNR-FM	103.1	Grasonville	6
WTOP-FM	103.5	Washington	44

FM Callsign	MHz	Location	kW	FM Callsign	MHz	Location	kW
WXCY	103.7	Havre de Grace	37	WRHJ-LP	93.1	Rock Hill	0.04
WPRS-FM	104.1	Waldorf	0.45	WOGR-FM	93.3	Salisbury	0.01
WZFT	104.3	Baltimore	29	WYFQ-FM	93.5	Wadesboro	8.7
W284BE	104.7	Havre de Grace	0.01	WWLV	94.1	Lexington	43
W285EJ	104.9	White Marsh	0.25	W232AX	94.3	Rock Hill	0.05
WAVA-FM	105.1	Arlington	33	WNKS	95.1	Charlotte	100
W288BS	105.5	Reston	0.10	WXRC	95.7	Hickory	100
WJZ-FM	105.7	Catonsville	50	WHQC	96.1	Shelby	100
WVRX	105.9	Woodbridge	40	W243BY	96.5	Charlotte	0.25
W291BA	106.1	Baltimore	0.24	WKKT	96.9	Statesville	100
WWMX	106.5	Baltimore	16.5	WPEG	97.9	Concord	95
WJFK-FM	106.7	Manassas	22.5	W252BU	98.3	Dallas	0.25
WMVK-LP	107.3	Perryville	0.01	W253BA	98.5	Indian Trail	0.02
WRQX	107.3	Washington	21.5	W254AZ	98.7	Belmont	0.09
WGTY	107.7	Gettysburg	16	W256BP	99.1	Charlotte	0.01
WLZL	107.9	Annapolis	50	WBT-FM	99.3	Chester	7.7
Boston Area				WRFX	99.7	Kannapolis	84
WMBR	88.1	Cambridge	0.72	W261AP	100.1	Kings Mountain	0.01
WBMT	88.3	Boxford	0.66	W262BM	100.3	Charlotte	0.01
WIQH	88.3	Concord	0.1	WPZS	100.9	Indian Trail	6
WGAO	88.3	Franklin	0.18	WWGT-LP	100.9	Lincolnton	0.1
WRPS	88.3	Rockland	0.11	W267AG	101.3	Salisbury	0.04
WERS	88.9	Boston	4	WBAV-FM	101.9	Gastonia	100
WHAB	89.1	Acton	0.01	WGSP-FM	102.3	Pageland	2.55
WGBH	89.7	Boston	100	WLKO	102.9	Hickory	31
WZBC	90.3	Newton	1	W277CB	103.3	Charlotte	0.25
WBUR-FM	90.9	Boston	40	WSOC-FM	103.7	Charlotte	100
WSHL-FM	91.3	Easton	0.1	W282BP	104.3	Charlotte	0.25
WDJM-FM	91.3	Framingham	0.1	WKQC	104.7	Charlotte	100
WBIM-FM	91.5	Bridgewater	0.18	WNOW-FM	105.3	Gaffney	51
WUML	91.5	Lowell	1.4	W289BO	105.7	Rock Hill	0.25
WMFO	91.5	Medford	0.13	WOLS	106.1	Waxhaw	21
WMLN-FM	91.5	Milton	0.17	WEND	106.5	Salisbury	84
WZLY	91.5	Wellesley	0.01	WRHM	107.1	Lancaster	2.4
WUMT	91.7	Marshfield	1.1	WLNK	107.9	Charlotte	100
WAVM	91.7	Maynard	0.5	**Chicago Area**			
WMWM	91.7	Salem	0.13	WWTG	88.1	Carpentersville	2
WUMG	91.7	Stow	0.5	WSSD	88.1	Chicago	0.01
WUMB-FM	91.9	Boston	0.66	WCRX	88.1	Chicago	0.1
W275BH	92.1	Newton	0.06	WBMF	88.1	Crete	0.09
WBOS	92.9	Brookline	18.5	WLTL	88.1	La Grange	0.18
WSNE	93.3	Taunton	31	WAES	88.1	Lincolnshire	0.15
WEEI-FM	93.7	Lawrence	42	WLRA	88.1	Lockport	0.14
WJMN	94.5	Boston	9.2	WTZI	88.1	Rosemont	0.3
WHRB	95.3	Cambridge	3	WETN	88.1	Wheaton	0.25
WATD-FM	95.9	Marshfield	1.6	WNTH	88.1	Winnetka	0.1
W242AA	96.3	Beacon Hill	0.01	WCLR	88.3	Arlington Hts.	1
WTKK	96.9	Boston	22.5	WDSU	88.3	Chesterton	0.4
WKAF	97.7	Brockton	2.7	WZRD	88.3	Chicago	0.1
WYAJ	97.7	Sudbury	0.004	WXAV	88.3	Chicago	0.15
WBZ-FM	98.5	Boston	16	WDGC-FM	88.3	Downers Grove	0.25
WPLM	99.1	Plymouth	50	WHCM	88.3	Palatine	0.1
WCRB	99.5	Lowell	37	WHPK-FM	88.5	Chicago	0.1
WHHB	99.9	Holliston	0.02	WHFH	88.5	Flossmoor	1.5
WBRS	100.1	Waltham	0.03	WGBK	88.5	Glenview	0.19
WZLX	100.7	Boston	21.5	WHSD	88.5	Hinsdale	0.13
WWBB	101.5	Providence	13.5	W203AJ	88.5	Michigan City	0.01
WHBA	101.7	Lynn	1.7	WSEH	88.5	South Elgin	0.67
WKLB-FM	102.5	Waltham	14	WLUW	88.7	Chicago	0.1
W275BH	102.9	Lawrence	0.25	WRSE	88.7	Elmhurst	0.32
WODS	103.3	Boston	15.5	WGVE-FM	88.7	Gary	2.1
W279BQ	103.7	Gloucester	0.08	WCSF	88.7	Joliet	0.1
WBMX	104.1	Boston	21	WEGN	88.7	Kankakee	5
WXLO	104.5	Fitchburg	37	WSRI	88.7	Sugar Grove	0.6
WRBB	104.9	Boston	0.02	WIIT	88.9	Chicago	0.01
WBOQ	104.9	Gloucester	3.2	WEPS	88.9	Elgin	0.74
WROR-FM	105.7	Framingham	23	WMXM	88.9	Lake Forest	0.35
WMJX	106.7	Boston	21.5	WMXM	88.9	Lake Forest	0.29
WAAF	107.3	Worcester	9.6	WOTW	88.9	Monee	0.1
WXKS-FM	107.9	Medford	20.5	WRRG	88.9	River Grove	0.1
Charlotte Area				WARG	88.9	Summit	0.5
WPIR	88.1	Hickory	26.5	W206AI	89.1	Lake Villa	0.08
W201DI	88.1	Monroe	0.17	WLPR-FM	89.1	Lowell	2.4
W202BW	88.3	Harrisburg	0.01	W206BL	89.1	Mount Prospect	0.12
WNSC	88.9	Rock Hill	97.9	WONC	89.1	Naperville	1.5
WDAV	89.9	Davidson	100	WJLV	89.1	Round Lake Bch.	1.9
WRBK	90.3	Richburg	7.5	WKKC	89.3	Chicago	0.28
WFAE	90.7	Charlotte	100	WNUR-FM	89.3	Evanston	7.2
W217AX	91.3	Harrisburg	0.01	W207BI	89.3	University Park	0.01
WFBK	91.5	Fort Mill	0.14	WBEW	89.5	Chesterton	4
WSGE	91.7	Dallas	7.5	WMBI-FM	90.1	Chicago	100
W219CH	91.7	Lowrys	0.01	WRTE	90.5	Chicago	0.07
W220DL	91.9	Statesville	0.04	WRTW	90.5	Crown Point	3.1
WRCM	91.9	Wingate	30	WMTH	90.5	Park Ridge	0.01
WPZS	92.7	Harrisburg	6	WDCB	90.9	Glen Ellyn	5
W225BD	92.9	Statesville	0.25	W216AC	91.1	Valparaiso	0.001

FM Callsign	MHz	Location	kW
W217BM	91.3	Elgin	0.01
WBEZ	91.5	Chicago	7.5
W219CD	91.7	Elgin	0.01
WJCH	91.9	Joliet	50
W221BY	92.1	Elgin	0.02
WPWX	92.3	Hammond	50
WCPT-FM	92.7	Arlington Hts.	1.8
WXRT	93.1	Chicago	14
WVIX	93.5	Lemont	6
WITW-LP	93.5	Valparaiso	0.05
WLIT-FM	93.9	Chicago	6
WJKL	94.3	Glendale Hts.	3.5
W232BL	94.3	Joliet	0.01
WLS-FM	94.7	Chicago	20.5
W236BD	95.1	Michigan City	0.01
WIIL	95.1	Union Grove	50
WVUR-FM	95.1	Valparaiso	0.03
WNUA	95.5	Chicago	8.3
WERV-FM	95.9	Aurora	3
W240BJ	95.9	Crown Point	0.01
WEFM	95.9	Michigan City	3
WBBM-FM	96.3	Chicago	19
WSSR	96.7	Joliet	3.1
WCOE	96.7	La Porte	3
W244BQ	96.7	Park Ridge	0.01
WWDV	96.9	Zion	50
WDRV	97.1	Chicago	8.3
W248AP	97.5	Chesterton	0.1
W248BB	97.5	Hillside	0.25
WLUP-FM	97.9	Chicago	6
WCCQ	98.3	Crest Hill	3
W252AW	98.3	Ridgefield	0.25
WRLR-LP	98.3	Round Lake Hts.	0.09
WVLP-LP	98.3	Valparaiso	0.1
WFMT	98.7	Chicago	6
WUSN	99.5	Chicago	24.2
WCPQ	99.9	Park Forest	50
W260BJ	99.9	Waukegan	0.01
WILV	100.3	Chicago	8.3
WRXQ	100.7	Coal City	2.45
W264BF	100.7	Englewood	0.002
WIQI	101.1	Chicago	8.3
WLGS-LP	101.5	Lake Villa	0.1
W268AY	101.5	Seward Township	0.02
WTMX	101.9	Skokie	4.2
WYCA	102.3	Crete	1.05
W272BZ	102.3	Portage	0.03
WXLC	102.3	Waukegan	3
WVAZ	102.7	Oak Park	35
WVIV-FM	103.1	Highland Park	6
W276BM	103.1	Park Forest	0.01
WKSC-FM	103.5	Chicago	17
WLMM-LP	103.9	Channahon	0.1
WXRD	103.9	Crown Point	3
WWYW	103.9	Dundee	2.55
WJMK	104.3	Chicago	24.2
WOJO	105.1	Evanston	8.4
WLJE	105.5	Valparaiso	1.25
WZSR	105.5	Woodstock	1.6
WCFS-FM	105.9	Elmwood Park	25.1
W292DJ	106.3	Lake Bluff	0.01
WSRB	106.3	Lansing	4.1
WPPN	106.7	Des Plaines	50
W294BA	106.7	Valparaiso	0.05
W295AF	106.9	La Porte	0.01
WZVN	107.1	Lowell	2.65
WGCI-FM	107.5	Chicago	6
WLEY-FM	107.9	Aurora	21
Dallas & Fort Worth Area			
KNTU	88.1	McKinney	100
KJRN	88.3	Keene	23
KEOM	88.5	Mesquite	61
KTCU-FM	88.7	Fort Worth	10
KNON	89.3	Dallas	55
KERA	90.1	Dallas	100
KTXG	90.5	Greenville	38
KCBI	90.9	Dallas	100
K218EB	91.5	Greenville	0.25
KKXT	91.7	Dallas	100
KZPS	92.5	Dallas	100
KLIF-FM	93.3	Haltom City	50
KLNO	94.1	Fort Worth	100
KSOC	94.5	Gainesville	9.8
KLTY	94.9	Arlington	100
K240DS	95.9	Garland	0.12
KSCS	96.3	Fort Worth	100

FM Callsign	MHz	Location	kW
WBAP	96.7	Flower Mound	90
KEGL	97.1	Fort Worth	100
K248BC	97.5	Dallas	0.05
KBFB	97.9	Dallas	100
K252EB	98.3	Cleburne	0.01
KLUV	98.7	Dallas	100
KPLX	99.5	Fort Worth	100
K260BP	99.9	Irving	0.25
KJKK	100.3	Dallas	100
WRR	101.1	Dallas	100
KDGE	102.1	Fort Worth-Dallas	100
K273BJ	102.5	Dallas	0.25
KDMX	102.9	Dallas	100
KVIL	103.7	Highland Park-Dallas	100
KTDK	104.1	Sanger	6.2
KKDA-FM	104.5	Dallas	100
KRLD-FM	105.3	Dallas	100
KRNB	105.7	Decatur	4.3
KHKS	106.1	Denton	100
K295BF	106.9	Greenville	0.25
KDXX	107.1	Benbrook	0.2
KMVK	107.5	Fort Worth	53
KESS-FM	107.9	Lewisville	5
Denver Area			
KVOD	88.1	Lakewood	1.2
KGNU-FM	88.5	Boulder	4
KDAB	88.9	Central City	0.01
KUVO	89.3	Denver	22.5
KCFR-FM	90.1	Denver	50
K213EG	90.5	Littleton	0.003
KGUD	90.7	Longmont	0.1
KLDV	91.1	Morrison	100
K219LF	91.7	Idaho Springs	0.03
K220IY	91.9	Lafayette	0.12
KJMN	92.1	Castle Rock	42
KWOF	92.5	Broomfield	57
KTCL	93.3	Wheat Ridge	71
K229BS	93.7	Lakewood	0.10
K229AC	93.7	Ward	0.03
K231AA	94.1	Boulder	0.21
KRKS-FM	94.7	Lafayette	100
KPTT	95.7	Denver	100
KXPK-FM1	96.5	Boulder	0.5
KXPK	96.5	Evergreen	100
K245AD	96.9	Arvada	0.2
KBCO	97.3	Boulder	100
K251AB	98.1	Longmont	0.25
KYGO-FM1	98.5	Boulder	0.5
KYGO-FM	98.5	Denver	100
KQMT	99.5	Denver	100
K260AL	99.9	Arvada	0.25
KIMN-FM1	100.3	Boulder	0.58
KIMN	100.3	Denver	100
KOSI	101.1	Denver	100
KJHM-FM1	101.5	Commerce City	20
K269AE	101.7	Boulder	0.10
K269CL	101.7	Evergreen	0.04
KAMV-LP	101.9	Brighton	0.1
KXWA	101.9	Centennial	9.5
KRKY-FM	102.1	Estes Park	0.18
KDSP-FM2	102.3	Boulder	0.25
KDSP	102.3	Greenwood Village	1
K274BW	102.7	Berthoud	0.25
KYGT-LP	102.7	Idaho Springs	0.1
K276FK	103.1	Pinecliffe	0.25
KRFX	103.5	Denver	100
KKFN	104.3	Longmont	100
KXKL-FM1	105.1	Boulder	1.5
KXKL-FM	105.1	Denver	100
KJAC-FM1	105.5	Boulder	0.10
KALC	105.9	Denver	100
K292FM	106.3	Denver	0.10
KBPI	106.7	Denver	100
KDHT-FM3	107.1	Aurora	20
KQKS	107.5	Lakewood	100
K232EF	94.3	Estes Park	0.05
Detroit Area			
WBFH	88.1	Bloomfield Hills	0.36
WHPR-FM	88.1	Highland Park	0.01
WSMF	88.1	Monroe	1.2
WSDP	88.1	Plymouth	0.2
WCBN-FM	88.3	Ann Arbor	0.2
WCBN-FM	88.3	Ann Arbor	3
WXOU	88.3	Auburn Hills	0.11
WDTE	88.3	Grosse Pt. Shores	5.5
WSHJ	88.3	Southfield	0.11

FM Callsign	MHz	Location	kW
WSHM	88.3	Wixom	0.1
WDTR	88.9	Imlay City	6
W206BI	89.1	Hamtramck	0.01
WPHS	89.1	Warren	0.1
WEMU	89.1	Ypsilanti	16
WHFR	89.3	Dearborn	0.27
WBLD	89.3	Orchard Lake	0.02
WAHS	89.5	Auburn Heights	0.1
WDTP	89.5	Huron Township	0.7
WOVI	89.5	Novi	0.1
W208BB	89.5	Royal Oak	0.05
WDTP	90.1	Huron Township	0.7
WRCJ-FM	90.9	Detroit	42
WVMV	91.5	China Township	1.05
WUOM	91.7	Ann Arbor	93
WMXD	92.3	Detroit	45
W244CC	92.7	Detroit	0.25
WDRQ	93.1	Detroit	26.5
W228CJ	93.5	Detroit	0.04
W284BQ	93.9	Detroit	0.25
W232CA	94.3	Detroit	0.10
W232BH	94.3	Holly	0.01
WCSX	94.7	Birmingham	14
WKQI	95.5	Detroit	100
WDVD	96.3	Detroit	21
WXYT-FM	97.1	Detroit	50
W248AQ	97.5	Harrison	0.001
WYDM	97.5	Monroe	41
WJLB	97.9	Detroit	50
W252BX	98.3	Detroit	0.17
WDZH	98.7	Detroit	50
W256AY	99.1	Detroit	0.04
WYCD	99.5	Detroit	17.5
W206CB	99.9	Hamtramck	0.25
WNIC	100.3	Dearborn	50
WRIF	101.1	Detroit	27
WDET-FM	101.9	Detroit	48
W272CA	102.3	Detroit	0.04
WPZR	102.7	Mount Clemens	50
WWWW-FM	102.9	Ann Arbor	15
WMUZ	103.5	Detroit	50
WOMC	104.3	Detroit	190
W284BQ	104.7	Detroit	0.25
WMGC-FM	105.1	Detroit	50
W288BK	105.5	Rochester Hills	0.04
WDMK	105.9	Detroit	20
W292DK	106.3	Westland	0.01
WDTW-FM	106.7	Detroit	61
WQKL	107.1	Ann Arbor	3
WGPR	107.5	Detroit	50
WCRZ	107.9	Flint	50

+16 Canadian stations within 65 kilometers (see Canada listing)

Houston-Galveston Area

FM Callsign	MHz	Location	kW
K201FA	88.1	Freeport	0.05
201EU	88.1	Katy	0.25
KFTG	88.1	Pasadena	0.7
K201DZ	88.1	Port Bolivar	0.12
KAFR	88.3	Conroe	100
KUHF	88.7	Houston	100
KSBJ	89.3	Humble	100
KZBJ	89.5	Bay City	35
K208DG	89.5	Galveston	0.25
KACC	89.7	Alvin	5.6
K210DF	89.9	Lake Jackson	0.25
KPFT	90.1	Houston	100
KJIC	90.5	Santa Fe	36
KGBV	90.7	Hardin	0.45
KTSU	90.9	Houston	18.5
KYBJ	91.1	Lake Jackson	17.5
K217DP	91.3	Barker	0.25
K217DJ	91.3	Kemah	0.18
KPVU	91.3	Prairie View	31
K218EJ	91.5	Galveston	0.25
K218DA	91.5	Houston	0.01
KUHA	91.7	Houston	50
KROI	92.1	Seabrook	24
KKBQ-FM	92.9	Pasadena	100
K227BD	93.3	Freeport	0.2
KQBU-FM	93.3	Port Arthur	100
KKRW	93.7	Houston	100
KTBZ-FM	94.5	Houston	100
K236AR	95.1	Angleton	0.04
KKHH	95.7	Houston	100
KHMX	96.5	Houston	100
KTHT	97.1	Cleveland	0.8
KFNC	97.5	Beaumont	8

FM Callsign	MHz	Location	kW
KBXX	97.9	Houston	100
KTJM	98.5	Port Arthur	100
KODA	99.1	Houston	100
K258BZ	99.5	Sugar Land	0.10
KVST	99.7	Willis	2.95
KSHN	99.9	Liberty	26.5
KILT-FM	100.3	Houston	100
KKHT-FM	100.7	Winnie	100
KLOL	101.1	Houston	100
KSTB	101.5	Crystal Beach	6
KMJQ	102.1	Houston	100
KLTN	102.9	Houston	100
KHJK	103.7	La Porte	100
KRBE	104.1	Houston	100
KAMA-FM	104.9	Deer Park	10.6
KORG-LP	105.3	Cleveland	0.07
KPTY	105.3	Crystal Beach	6
KTWL	105.3	Hempstead	92
KHCB-FM	105.7	Houston	100
KOVE-FM	106.5	Galveston	100
K294BH	106.7	Simonton	0.25
KHPT	106.9	Conroe	100
KGLK	107.5	Lake Jackson	100
KQQK	107.9	Beaumont	100
KBCP-LP	107.9	Brookshire	0.06

Los Angeles Area

FM Callsign	MHz	Location	kW
KKJZ	88.1	Long Beach	41
KQRU	88.3	Acton	0.1
KCLU-FM	88.3	Thousand Oaks	3.2
K203FC	88.5	North Edwards	0.25
KCSN	88.5	Northridge	0.37
KCSN-FM1	88.5	West Los Angeles	1.28
KISL	88.7	Avalon	0.2
KSPC	88.7	Claremont	3
KUCI	88.9	Irvine	0.2
K205EP	88.9	La Canada	0.01
KXLU	88.9	Los Angeles	2.9
K206AA	89.1	Laguna Beach	0.04
KCRU	89.1	Oxnard	0.92
KPCC	89.3	Pasadena	0.6
KPCC-FM1	89.3	Santa Clarita	0.01
K208AM	89.5	Newport Beach	0.08
KCRW	89.9	Santa Monica	6.9
K210EO	89.9	Santa Paula	0.01
KBPK	90.1	Buena Park	0.02
K211EY	90.1	Palmdale	0.01
K211DK	90.1	Santa Ana	0.01
KSAK	90.1	Walnut	0.004
KMRO-FM1	90.3	Camarillo	2
KMRO-FM3	90.3	Camarillo	0.02
K205DZ	90.3	Devore	0.002
K212FA	90.3	Temple City	0.01
KPFK	90.7	Los Angeles	110
KPFK-FM1	90.7	Malibu	1.5
K216EM	91.1	Arcadia	0.01
K216FA	91.1	Quartz Hill	0.01
K216FM	91.1	Van Nuys	0.01
KUSC	91.5	Los Angeles	39
KUSC-FM1	91.5	Santa Clarita	0.2
K220FR	91.9	Simi Valley	0.01
K220HC	91.9	Sun Valley	0.01
KHHT	92.3	Los Angeles	40
KJLL-FM	92.7	Fountain Valley	0.69
KHJL-FM1	92.7	Malibu Vista	0.04
KLSI	92.7	Thousand Oaks	3.1
KCBS-FM	93.1	Los Angeles	27.5
KXRN-LP	93.5	Laguna Niguel	0.05
KDEY-FM	93.5	Ontario	5
KDAY	93.5	Redondo Beach	4.2
KDAY	93.5	Redondo Beach	0.75
KXOS	93.9	Los Angeles	35
KXOS-FM1	93.9	Santa Clarita	0.25
KEBN	94.3	Garden Grove	6
KBUA	94.3	San Fernando	6
KBUA-FM1	94.3	Valencia & Newhall	0.04
KTWV	94.7	Los Angeles	58
K236AW	95.1	Lancaster	0.01
KBBY-FM	95.1	Ventura	12.5
KLOS	95.5	Los Angeles	72
KFSH-FM	95.9	La Mirada	6
K241AJ	96.1	Palmdale	0.01
KXOL-FM	96.3	Los Angeles	22
KWIZ	96.7	Santa Ana	6
KLJR-FM	96.7	Santa Paula	0.28
KAMP-FM	97.1	Los Angeles	21
KLAX-FM	97.9	East Los Angeles	33

FM Callsign	MHz	Location	kW
KRCV-FM1	98.3	San Dimas	0.75
KRCV	98.3	West Covina	6
KYSR	98.7	Los Angeles	75
KKLA-FM	99.5	Los Angeles	10
K261AB	100.1	Newhall, etc.	0.01
KSWD	100.3	Los Angeles	15
K264AF	100.7	Guasti	0.01
KHAY	100.7	Ventura	39
KRTH	101.1	Los Angeles	54
KORM-LP	101.5	Corona	0.1
KWVS-LP	101.5	Malibu	0.1
KOCI-LP	101.5	Newport Beach	0.04
KSCA	101.9	Glendale	11.5
KJLH	102.3	Compton	5.6
K272DI	102.3	Fillmore	0.01
KJLH-FM1	102.3	Hollywood	0.01
KIIS-FM	102.7	Los Angeles	8
K276EF	103.1	Muscoy	0.01
KDLE	103.1	Newport Beach	0.3
KDLD	103.1	Santa Monica	3.7
KOST	103.5	Los Angeles	12.5
KRCD	103.9	Inglewood	4.1
K280DT	103.9	Thousand Oaks	0.01
KBIG-FM	104.3	Los Angeles	65
KCAQ-FM1	104.7	Calabasas	0.09
KCAQ-FM2	104.7	Granada Hills	0.5
KXRN-LP	104.7	Laguna Niguel	0.04
KCAQ-FM5	104.7	Las Flores Canyon	0.5
KCAQ	104.7	Oxnard	4.5
KKGO	105.1	Los Angeles	35
KKGO-FM1	105.1	Santa Clarita	0.06
KGIC-LP	105.5	Corona	0.06
KBUE	105.5	Long Beach	3.9
KBUE	105.5	Long Beach	3
KPWR	105.9	Los Angeles	25
KGMX	106.3	Lancaster	3
KALI-FM	106.3	Santa Ana	6
K292CR	106.3	Simi Valley	0.004
KROQ-FM	106.7	Pasadena	6.5
KSSE	107.1	Arcadia	6
KSSE-FM1	107.1	San Fernando	0.02
KLVE	107.5	Los Angeles	32
KWVE-FM	107.9	San Clemente	0.53
KWVE-FM4	107.9	San Clemente	0.02
KNJR-LP	107.9	Thousand Oaks	0.1
Miami-Fort Lauderdale Area			
WRGP	88.1	Homestead	0.17
WGNK	88.3	Pennsuco	6
WMFL	88.5	Florida City	7.7
WKPX	88.5	Sunrise	25
WDNA	88.9	Miami	7.4
WRMB	89.3	Boynton Beach	100
WKCP	89.7	Miami	100
WYBP	90.3	Ft Lauderdale	3
WVUM	90.5	Coral Gables	5.9
WLFE	90.9	Cutler Bay	100
WLRN-FM	91.3	Miami	47
W220DU	91.7	W Deerfield Bch	0.25
WMKL	91.9	Hammocks	25
WCMQ-FM	92.3	Hialeah	31
WFEZ	93.1	Miami	100
W228BY	93.5	Allapattah	0.12
W228BV	93.5	Ft Lauderdale	0.17
W228AY	93.5	Key Largo	0.02
WMIA-FM	93.9	Miami Beach	100
W233AP	94.5	Oakland Park	0.09
WMGE	94.9	Miami Beach	100
WURN-FM	95.3	Key Largo	21
W237CP	95.3	Miami	0.07
W237BD	95.3	Pompano Beach	0.25
WXDJ	95.7	N Miami Beach	40
W241AX	96.1	Boca Raton	0.25
WPOW	96.5	Miami	100
W245BC	96.9	Lauderdale Lks.	0.07
W245BF	96.9	North Miami	0.10
WFLC	97.3	Miami	100
WRTO-FM	98.3	Goulds	100
WEDR	99.1	Miami	100
WKIS	99.9	Boca Raton	100
W262AN	100.3	Tamarac	0.19
WHYI-FM	100.7	Ft Lauderdale	100
WLYF	101.5	Miami	100
WKLG	102.1	Rock Harbor	100
WMXJ	102.7	Pompano Beach	100
WSHE	103.5	Ft Lauderdale	100
WORZ-LP	104.3	Key Largo	0.1

FM Callsign	MHz	Location	kW
WAXY	104.3	West Palm Beach	100
WHQT	105.1	Coral Gables	100
WWWK	105.5	Islamorada	50
WBGG-FM	105.9	Ft Lauderdale	100
WRAZ-FM	106.3	Leisure City	50
WRMA	106.7	Ft Lauderdale	100
WAMR-FM	107.5	Miami	95
Minneapolis-St Paul Area			
WAJC	88.1	Newport	1.2
KRLX	88.1	Northfield	0.1
KJGT	88.3	Waconia	11
KBEM-FM	88.5	Minneapolis	2.9
WUSG-LP	88.7	Cambridge	0.1
WRFW	88.7	River Falls	3
KCMP	89.3	Northfield	100
KPCS	89.7	Princeton	40
KMOJ	89.9	Minneapolis	6.2
KFAI	90.3	Minneapolis	0.9
KMKL	90.3	North Branch	15
K214DF	90.7	Golden Valley	0.01
KNOW-FM	91.1	Minneapolis	100
K218DK	91.5	Bloomington	0.22
WMCN	91.7	St. Paul	0.01
K220JP	91.9	Minneapolis	0.01
W220DO	91.9	North Branch	0.04
K221ES	92.1	Albertville	0.25
W221BS	92.1	Waite	0.06
KQRS-FM	92.5	Golden Valley	100
W225AP	92.9	St. Paul	0.17
W227BF	93.3	Shoreview	0.01
KXXR	93.7	Minneapolis	100
KSTP-FM	94.5	St. Paul	100
KNOF	95.3	St. Paul	6
KRDS-FM	95.5	New Prague	6
WDMO	95.7	Baldwin	4
W239AM	95.7	Hudson	0.25
KQCL	95.9	Faribault	3
WLKX-FM	95.9	Forest Lake	3
WLKX-FM	95.9	Forest Lake	3
KHTC	96.3	Edina	19
W239AM	96.7	Hudson	0.17
KTCZ-FM	97.1	Minneapolis	100
K249ED	97.7	Albertville	0.17
KTIS-FM	98.5	Minneapolis	100
KSJN	99.5	Minneapolis	100
K260BA	99.9	Coon Rapids	0.25
KFXN-FM	100.3	Minneapolis	100
W264BR	100.7	Falcon Heights	0.09
KDWB-FM	101.3	Richfield	100
KEEY-FM	102.1	St. Paul	100
K273BH	102.5	Fridley	0.25
KMNB	102.9	Minneapolis	100
K277AS	103.3	Big Lake	0.01
K278BP	103.5	Cottage Grove	0.17
KZJK	104.1	St. Louis Park	100
K283BG	104.5	Minneapolis	0.10
WGVX	105.1	Lakeville	2.6
WGVY	105.3	Cambridge	25
WGVZ	105.7	Eden Prarie	3.8
KLCI	106.1	Elk River	9.1
WEVR-FM	106.3	River Falls	6
K293BA	106.5	Elko	0.20
KDXL	106.5	St. Louis Park	0.01
KUOM-FM	106.5	St. Louis Park	0.01
K294AM	106.7	West St. Paul	0.17
KTMY	107.1	Coon Rapids	22
KQQL	107.9	Anoka	100
New York Area			
WYGG	88.1	Asbury Park	0.92
WXBA	88.1	Brentwood	0.18
WCWP	88.1	Brookville	0.1
WDNJ	88.1	Hopatcong	0.5
WARY	88.1	Valhalla	0.04
WBGO	88.3	Newark	4.5
W202AR	88.3	Newburgh	0.01
WVOF	88.5	Fairfield	0.1
W203BB	88.5	Norwalk	0.01
WPOB	88.5	Plainview	0.12
WEDW-FM	88.5	Stamford	2
WNJP	88.5	Sussex	0.45
WKWZ	88.5	Syosset	0.12
WRHU	88.7	Hempstead	0.47
WRSU-FM	88.7	New Brunswick	1.35
WNYK	88.7	Nyack	0.01
WPSC-FM	88.7	Wayne	0.2
WMNJ	88.9	Madison	0.01

FM Callsign	MHz	Location	kW
WWES	88.9	Mount Kisco	0.2
WFRS	88.9	Smithtown	1.5
WSIA	88.9	Staten Island	0.01
WMCX	88.9	W. Long Branch	1
WNYU-FM	89.1	New York	8.3
WNYU-FM1	89.1	New York	0.01
WFDU	89.1	Teaneck	0.55
WGSS	89.3	Copiague	0.03
WFJS-FM	89.3	Freehold	3.8
WDDM	89.3	Hazlet	0.01
WLJP	89.3	Monroe	1.58
WNJY	89.3	Netcong	0.52
W208AU	89.5	Massapequa	0.23
WSOU	89.5	South Orange	2.4
WRDR	89.7	Freehold Township	5
WOBH	89.7	Lindenhurst	1.8
W209CJ	89.7	Mount Kisco	0.03
WKCR-FM	89.9	New York	1.35
WJZZ	90.1	North Salem	0.1
W211AI	90.1	Stamford	0.25
WUSB	90.1	Stony Brook	3.6
WKRB	90.3	Brooklyn	0.01
WHPC	90.3	Garden City	0.5
WRPR	90.3	Mahwah	0.1
WHCR-FM	90.3	New York	0.01
W212CC	90.3	Newburgh	0.01
WDFH	90.3	Ossining	0.05
WVPH	90.3	Piscataway	0.1
WKNJ-FM	90.3	Union Township	0.01
WMSC	90.3	Upper Montclair	0.001
WWPT	90.3	Westport	0.33
WBJB-FM	90.5	Lincroft	0.9
WJSV	90.5	Morristown	0.12
WFUV	90.7	New York	47
WFUV-FM3	90.7	New York	2.5
WFMU	91.1	East Orange	1.25
WFMU-FM1	91.1	New York	0.02
WOSS	91.1	Ossining	0.01
W217AF	91.3	Huntington Stn.	0.25
WNYE	91.5	New York	2
WXCI	91.7	Danbury	3
W219DQ	91.7	Dillyville	0.04
W220AC	91.9	Fairfield	0.01
WNTI	91.9	Hackettstown	5.6
WSHR	91.9	Lk. Ronkonkoma	6
WSLX	91.9	New Canaan	0.01
W219DQ	91.9	New City	0.01
W220AA	91.9	Parlin	0.01
WXRK	92.3	New York	18
WQBU-FM2	92.7	Brooklyn	1.2
WQBU-FM	92.7	Garden City	2
WQBU-FM1	92.7	New York	0.08
WPAT-FM	93.1	Paterson	22
WVIP	93.5	New Rochelle	1.75
W228CG	93.5	Warwick	0.25
W229BH	93.7	Newburgh	0.01
WNYC-FM	93.9	New York	11
W231BP	94.1	Chester	0.25
WJLK	94.3	Asbury Park	1.3
W232AL	94.3	Pomona	0.03
WIGX	94.3	Smithtown	3
W233BM	94.5	Beacon	0.01
WFME	94.7	Newark	37.2
W235BB	94.9	Hauppauge	0.01
WRKI-FM2	95.1	Bridgeport	0.23
WRKI-FM1	95.1	Norwalk	0.6
WPLJ	95.5	New York	19
WFOX	95.9	Norwalk	3
WRAT	95.9	Point Pleasant	6
WXNY-FM	96.3	New York	26
W244AS	96.7	Oakhurst	0.01
WKLV-FM	96.7	Port Chester	3.1
W245AS	96.9	Manorville	0.01
WQHT	97.1	New York	29.5
WALK-FM	97.5	Patchogue	39
WSKQ-FM	97.9	New York	6
WDAQ	98.3	Danbury	1.3
WKJY	98.3	Hempstead	3
WMGQ	98.3	New Brunswick	1.2
WEPN	98.7	New York	6
WAWZ	99.1	Zarephath	28
WBAI	99.5	New York	4.3
WHTZ	100.3	Newark	13
W264BT	100.7	Edison	0.01
WHUD	100.7	Peekskill	50
WCBS-FM	101.1	New York	16.8
W268AN	101.5	Plainview	0.01
WRXP	101.9	New York	29.5
WUPC-LP	102.3	Arrowhead Vlg	0.1
WBAB	102.3	Babylon	6
WSUS	102.3	Franklin	0.6
WWFS	102.7	New York	50
WBZO	103.1	Bay Shore	3
W276AQ	103.1	Fort Lee	0.04
W276BV	103.1	Greenwich	0.002
WJGK	103.1	Newburgh	6
W276AV	103.1	Stamford	0.003
WKTU	103.5	Lake Success	17
WNNJ	103.7	Newton	0.5
W280DJ	103.9	Beacon	0.01
WFAS-FM	103.9	Bronxville	1.3
WAXQ	104.3	New York	17
W283BA	104.5	Selden	0.01
W284BW	104.7	Franklin Township	0.01
W284AQ	104.7	Hackettstown	0.21
WSPK	104.7	Poughkeepsie	7.4
W285DE	104.9	Bridgeport	0.02
WWPR-FM	105.1	New York	17
W287AZ	105.3	Southport	0.05
WDHA-FM	105.5	Dover	1
W289AD	105.7	Selden	0.25
WQXR-FM	105.9	Newark	1.59
WBLI	106.1	Patchogue	49
WKMK	106.3	Eatontown	1.1
WFAF	106.3	Mount Kisco	0.98
W292DV	106.3	New York	0.09
W293AE	106.5	Newburgh	0.01
WLTW	106.7	New York	17
WXPK	107.1	Briarcliff Manor	1.9
WWZY	107.1	Long Branch	5
W296BD	107.1	Warwick	0.01
W297AN	107.3	Danbury	0.02
WBLS	107.5	New York	4.2
W299AG	107.7	Newburgh	0.01
WMDI-LP	107.9	Lakewood	0.1
WMNJ	107.9	Madison	0.01
WWPH	107.9	Princeton Jct.	0.02
WEBE	107.9	Westport	50

Philadelphia Area

FM Callsign	MHz	Location	kW
WNJS-FM	88.1	Berlin	0.08
WPEB	88.1	Philadelphia	0.001
WMHS	88.1	Pike Creek	0.09
WNJT-FM	88.1	Trenton	0.11
WXPN	88.5	Philadelphia	3.2
WBZC	88.9	Pemberton	10
WBYO	88.9	Sellersville	4.5
WXHL-FM	89.1	Christiana	1.2
WYBF	89.1	Radnor Township	0.7
WWFM	89.1	Trenton	1.15
WXVU	89.1	Villanova	0.1
WNJB-FM	89.3	Bridgeton	2.5
WRTJ	89.3	Coatesville	0.46
WRDV	89.3	Warminster	1.6
WKVP	89.5	Cherry Hill	2
WDNR	89.5	Chester	0.01
WGLS-FM	89.7	Glassboro	0.75
WRTI	90.1	Philadelphia	11
WVBV	90.5	Medford Lakes	21
WHYY-FM	90.9	Philadelphia	13.5
WVUD	91.3	Newark	6.8
WTSR	91.3	Trenton	1.5
WDBK	91.5	Blackwood	0.1
WSRN-FM	91.5	Swarthmore	0.11
WLBS	91.7	Bristol	0.1
WKDU	91.7	Philadelphia	0.8
WBMR	91.7	Telford	0.5
WCUR	91.7	West Chester	0.1
WMPH	91.7	Wilmington	0.1
W220AG	91.9	Lawrenceville	0.01
WVLT	92.1	Vineland	6
WXTU	92.5	Philadelphia	15
WMMR	93.3	Philadelphia	25
WSTW	93.7	Wilmington	47.1
WIP-FM	94.1	Philadelphia	15
WPST	94.5	Trenton	50
WRSD	94.9	Folsom	0.01
W235AP	94.9	Radnor	0.002
W236AF	95.1	Burlington	0.12
WBEN-FM	95.7	Philadelphia	11
WCTO	96.1	Easton	50
WRDW-FM	96.5	Philadelphia	9.6
W245AG	96.9	Gladwyne	0.01

FM Callsign	MHz	Location	kW
W246AR	97.1	Bensalem	0.07
W246AQ	97.1	Collingswood	0.01
WZZE	97.3	Glen Mills	0.02
WPEN-FM	97.5	Burlington	26
W249BY	97.7	Bridgeton	0.01
WOGL	98.1	Philadelphia	10
WZFI-LP	98.5	Bridgeton	0.08
WUSL	98.9	Philadelphia	32
WJBR-FM	99.5	Wilmington	50
W260BW	99.9	Egg Harbor	0.12
WHHS	99.9	Havertown	0.01
WRNB	100.3	Media	33
W264BH	100.7	Mount Holly	0.02
WBEB	101.1	Philadelphia	14
WKXW	101.5	Trenton	15.5
WJKS	101.7	Canton	4.1
W269BL	101.7	Coatesville	0.003
W269BT	101.7	Pottstown	0.02
WIOQ	102.1	Philadelphia	32
WMGK	102.9	Philadelphia	43
W277BA	103.3	Millville	0.02
W277BL	103.3	New Castle	0.003
WPRB	103.3	Princeton	14
W278AK	103.5	Village Green	0.08
WPPZ-FM	103.9	Jenkintown	0.37
W280CP	103.9	Wagontown	0.01
WRFF	104.5	Philadelphia	11
WSJO	104.9	Egg Harbor City	10
WDAS-FM	105.3	Philadelphia	42
W289AZ	105.7	Trenton	0.01
WISX	106.1	Philadelphia	22.5
WWIQ	106.9	Camden	38
W297AD	107.3	Philadelphia	0.02
WBYN-FM	107.5	Boyertown	5.5
WRRC	107.7	Lawrenceville	0.02
W299BH	107.7	Marshallton	0.25
WPOV-LP	107.7	Vineland	0.04
W300AC	107.9	Chatsworth, etc.	0.04
WPHI-FM	107.9	Pennsauken	0.78

Phoenix Area

FM Callsign	MHz	Location	kW
KNAI	88.3	Phoenix	22.5
KPHF	88.3	Phoenix	22.5
K204DR	88.7	Laveen	0.01
K205CI	88.9	Phoenix	0.01
KLVK	89.1	Fountain Hills	30
KBAQ	89.5	Phoenix	30
K209DV	89.7	Scottsdale	0.01
K210DY	89.9	Black Canyon City	0.25
KZAI	89.9	Superior	45
KFLR-FM	90.3	Phoenix	100
KVIT	90.7	Apache Jct	2
K214DN	90.7	Surprise	0.01
K216FO	91.1	Guadalupe	0.01
KJZZ	91.5	Phoenix	100
K219DZ	91.7	Rio Verde	0.01
KTAR-FM	92.3	Glendale	100
K224CJ	92.7	Phoenix	0.01
KDKB	93.3	Mesa	100
KOOL-FM	94.5	Phoenix	100
KVIB	95.1	Sun City West	41
KYOT-FM	95.5	Phoenix	100
K240DC	95.9	Buckeye	0.06
K241BQ	96.1	Ft Mcdowell	0.25
KSWG	96.3	Wickenburg	6.4
KMXP	96.9	Phoenix	100
K247BH	97.3	Goodyear	0.04
KMVA	97.5	Dewey	42
KUPD	97.9	Tempe	100
KKFR	98.3	Mayer	41
KPKX	98.7	Phoenix	100
K257CD	99.3	Phoenix	0.02
K258BY	99.5	Tortilla Flat	0.01
K258BY	99.5	Tortilla Flat	0.12
KRPH-FM1	99.5	Wittmann	0.45
KESZ	99.9	Phoenix	100
KCWG-LP	100.3	Crown King	0.001
KSLX-FM	100.7	Scottsdale	100
KNRJ	101.1	Cordes Lakes	40
KZON	101.5	Phoenix	100
K270BA	101.9	Wickenburg	0.12
KAHM	102.1	Spring Valley	25.5
KNIX-FM	102.5	Phoenix	100
KLNZ	103.5	Glendale	62
KEXX	103.9	Gilbert	43
KAJM	104.3	Camp Verde	40
K282BC	104.3	Sunflower	0.01

FM Callsign	MHz	Location	kW
KZZP	104.7	Mesa	100
K282BC	104.9	Sunflower	0.01
KLVA	105.5	Casa Grande	50
KHOT-FM	105.9	Paradise Valley	36
KOMR	106.3	Sun City	23
KKMR	106.5	Arizona City	8.6
KWSS-LP	106.7	Scottsdale	0.01
KDVA	106.9	Buckeye	6
KVVA-FM	107.1	Apache Jct	23.5
KMLE	107.9	Chandler	100

Portland Area

FM Callsign	MHz	Location	kW
KBVM	88.3	Portland	3.5
KMUZ	88.5	Turner	0.04
KTFH	88.7	Lees Camp	0.1
KLVP	88.7	Sandy	3.7
KMHD	89.1	Gresham	7.9
KJVH	89.5	Longview	0.1
KPFR	89.5	Pine Grove	7
KQAC	89.9	Portland	5.9
KLWO	90.3	Longview	0.4
KSLC	90.3	Mcminnville	0.75
KWBX	90.3	Salem	0.14
KBOO	90.7	Portland	26.5
KZME	91.1	Brightwood	0.13
K216EH	91.1	Colton	0.01
KOPB-FM	91.5	Portland	73
K220IN	91.9	Portland	0.01
KGON	92.3	Portland	100
K224DL	92.7	Portland	0.02
K225BF	92.9	Turner	0.02
KRYP	93.1	Gladstone	1.6
KKJC-LP	93.5	Mcminnville	0.1
K228EU	93.5	Portland	0.10
KPDQ-FM	93.9	Portland	52
K231AM	94.1	Woodland	0.12
KZZR	94.3	Government Camp	3.4
KLYK	94.5	Kelso	3
KNRK	94.7	Camas	6.3
KBFF	95.5	Portland	100
K240DA	95.9	Stevenson	0.09
K240CZ	95.9	Tigard	0.02
KQRZ-LP	96.3	Hillsboro	0.1
KKJC-LP	96.3	Mcminnville	0.1
KQSO-LP	96.3	Newberg	0.001
K242AF	96.3	Portland	0.03
K242AB	96.3	Salem	0.25
KWLZ-FM	96.3	West Linn	4.1
KPVN-LP	96.3	Woodburn	0.03
KYCH-FM	97.1	Portland	100
K248BS	97.5	Newberg	0.003
KNRQ-FM	97.9	Aloha	10
K250AE	97.9	Longview	0.25
KRRC	97.9	Portland	0.01
KPPK	98.3	Rainier	1.6
KUPL	98.7	Portland	25
KWJJ-FM	99.5	Portland	52
KKRZ	100.3	Portland	100
KXL-FM	101.1	Portland	100
K268BN	101.5	Eufaula/Longview	0.25
KINK	101.9	Portland	100
K272EL	102.3	Portland	0.10
K273AI	102.5	Ariel	0.01
K273AJ	102.5	Elwood	0.01
K274AR	102.7	Gresham	0.01
KKCW	103.3	Beaverton	100
KXPC-FM	103.7	Lebanon	0.6
KFIS	104.1	Scappoose	7
K283BL	104.5	Portland	0.10
K284BM	104.7	Longview	0.04
KRSK	105.1	Molalla	22.5
KUKN	105.5	Longview	0.7
K288FT	105.5	Portland	0.05
KFBW	105.9	Vancouver	22.5
KLTH	106.7	Lake Oswego	100
KLVU-FM2	107.1	Family Camp	0.05
KRQT-FM1	107.1	Longview	2
K296FT	107.1	West Haven	0.03
KXJM	107.5	Banks	71

San Diego Area

FM Callsign	MHz	Location	kW
KSDS	88.3	San Diego	22
KSBR	88.5	Mission Viejo	0.6
KSDW	88.9	Temecula	1.15
KNSJ	89.1	Descanso	0.33
K206AC	89.1	San Diego	0.004
K206AC	89.1	San Diego	0.04
KPBS-FM	89.5	San Diego	26

     United States of America

FM Callsign	MHz	Location	kW
K210CL	89.9	Lemon Grove	0.001
KOPA	91.3	Pala	0.1
KSOQ-FM	92.1	Escondido	0.58
K225BA	92.9	Borrego Springs	0.05
KXFG	92.9	Sun City	6
KHTS-FM	93.3	El Cajon	50
K229BO	93.7	Rancho Bernardo	0.01
KMYI	94.1	San Diego	77
KMYT	94.5	Temecula	0.54
KBZT	94.9	San Diego	26.5
KOGO	95.7	Carlsbad	28
KSIQ	96.1	Campo	25
KSIQ-FM1	96.1	Santee	5
KYXY	96.5	San Diego	26.5
K245AI	96.9	San Pasqual	0.01
KSON	97.3	San Diego	50
KIFM	98.1	San Diego	26.5
K252BF	98.3	Temecula	0.003
K253AD	98.5	Oceanside	0.01
KLVJ	100.1	Julian	0.11
KFMB-FM	100.7	San Diego	30
KGB-FM	101.5	San Diego	50
KPRI	102.1	Encinitas	30
KLQV	102.9	San Diego	30
KTMQ	103.3	Temecula	1.25
KEGY	103.7	San Diego	26.5
KIOZ	105.3	San Diego	26
KLNV-FM1	106.5	Rancho Bernardo	0.004
KLNV	106.5	San Diego	50
KSSD	107.1	Fallbrook	3
KHHS-LP	107.5	San Diego	0.04
KRLY-LP	107.9	Alpine	0.002

+15 Mexican stations, within 65 kilometers (see Mexico listing)

San Francisco Area

FM Callsign	MHz	Location	kW
KSFH	87.9	Mountain View	0.01
K201RV	88.1	Benicia Martinez	0.004
KECG	88.1	El Cerrito	0.02
K215FB	88.1	Napa	0.01
KSRH	88.1	San Rafael	0.01
KQED-FM	88.5	San Francisco	110
KQED-FM2	88.5	Walnut Creek	0.06
K205BM	88.9	San Rafael	0.01
KCEA	89.1	Atherton	0.1
KPFB	89.3	Berkeley	0.46
K207EP	89.3	Concord	0.01
KOHL	89.3	Fremont	0.15
KARC	89.3	Moss Beach	0.04
KPDO	89.3	Pescadero	0.1
KSMC	89.5	Moraga	0.8
KPOO	89.5	San Francisco	0.3
KZCT	89.5	Vallejo	0.01
KFJC	89.7	Los Altos	0.11
K210EH	89.9	Bolinas	0.01
KCRH	89.9	Hayward	0.02
KZSU	90.1	Stanford	0.5
K212BJ	90.3	Dublin	0.2
KUSF	90.3	San Francisco	2.85
KVHS	90.5	Concord	0.41
KWMR-FM2	90.5	Inverness Pk.	0.004
KWMR	90.5	Pt. Reyes Stn.	0.24
KALX	90.7	Berkeley	0.5
K214CS	90.7	Sonoma	0.004
K215FB	90.9	Napa	0.01
K216FV	91.1	Concord	0.01
KCSM	91.1	San Mateo	11
KDVZ	91.3	Point Reyes	0.1
KSVY	91.3	Sonoma	2.5
KXCF	91.5	Marshall	0.1
KALW	91.7	San Francisco	1.9
K220JV	91.9	Byron	0.01
KKDV-FM3	92.1	Martinez	0.25
K221DQ	92.1	Petaluma	0.01
KKDV	92.1	Walnut Creek	3
KSJO	92.3	San Jose	32
KREV	92.7	Alameda	3.6
KRZZ-FM1	93.3	Pleasanton	0.19
KRZZ	93.3	San Francisco	33
KPFA	94.1	Berkeley	59
KPFA-FM3	94.1	Oakley	0.04
KYLD-FM1	94.9	Pleasanton	0.18
KYLD	94.9	San Francisco	30
KUIC-FM2	95.3	Vallejo	0.17
KGMZ	95.7	San Francisco	6.9
KGMZ-FM1	95.7	Walnut Creek	0.18
KOIT-FM3	96.5	Martinez	3.3
KOIT	96.5	San Francisco	24

FM Callsign	MHz	Location	kW
KLLC-FM2	97.3	Pleasanton	4.8
KLLC	97.3	San Francisco	82
KFFG	97.7	Los Altos	3.3
K249DJ	97.7	San Pablo	0.01
KISQ-FM2	98.1	Pleasanton	10
KISQ	98.1	San Francisco	75
KUFX-FM3	98.5	Pleasanton	0.15
KSOL-FM3	98.9	Pleasanton	0.18
KSOL	98.9	San Francisco	6.1
KSOL-FM2	98.9	Sausalito	0.15
KVYN-FM1	99.3	Cordelia	0.01
K257BE	99.3	Los Gatos	0.01
KMVQ-FM	99.7	San Francisco	45
KMVQ-FM3	99.7	Walnut Creek	0.18
KZST-FM1	100.1	Petaluma	0.04
K264AQ	100.7	Mountain View	0.002
KVVZ	100.7	San Rafael	6
K265CV	100.9	Fremont	0.01
K265DI	100.9	Sausalito	0.08
KIOI	101.3	San Francisco	125
KIOI-FM1	101.3	Walnut Creek	0.15
K269FB	101.7	Daly City	0.01
KKIQ-FM1	101.7	Hayward	0.85
KHTH-FM1	101.7	Petaluma	0.04
KUZX	102.1	San Francisco	33
KUZX-FM2	102.1	San Francisco	1
KBLX-FM	102.9	Berkeley	7
KBLX-FM2	102.9	Pleasanton	0.18
KSCU	103.3	Santa Clara	0.03
KOSF-FM1	103.7	Pleasanton	0.18
KOSF	103.7	San Francisco	10
K281BB	104.1	Vacaville	0.01
KFOG-FM3	104.5	Pleasanton	0.18
KFOG	104.5	San Francisco	13.5
KMHX-FM2	104.9	Glen Ellen	0.95
KITS-FM4	105.3	Antioch	0.33
KITS-FM2	105.3	Pleasanton	0.04
KITS-FM3	105.3	San Francisco	0.03
KITS	105.3	San Francisco	16.5
KITS-FM1	105.3	Walnut Creek	0.61
K289AS	105.7	Napa	0.25
KVVF	105.7	Santa Clara	50
KMEL	106.1	San Francisco	69
KMEL-FM2	106.1	Walnut Creek	6.5
KFRC-FM1	106.9	Pleasanton	4.8
KFRC-FM	106.9	San Francisco	80
KIVS	107.3	Livermore	8.1
KSAN-FM1	107.7	Pleasanton	0.18
KSAN	107.7	San Mateo	8.9

Seattle-Tacoma Area

FM Callsign	MHz	Location	kW
K201EN	88.1	Everett	0.01
K201EX	88.1	Greenwater	0.01
KWAO	88.1	Ocean Park	76
K201EM	88.1	Olympia	0.14
K201AB	88.1	West Seattle	0.12
KPLU-FM	88.5	Tacoma	68
KMIH	88.9	Mercer Island	0.03
K206DM	89.1	Bremerton	0.01
K206DO	89.1	Cape George	0.002
K206DL	89.1	Granite Falls	0.01
K206CJ	89.1	Issaquah	0.003
K207AZ	89.3	Gig Harbor	0.03
KAOS	89.3	Olympia	1.25
K207AP	89.3	Sumner & Lake Tapps	0.02
KNHC	89.5	Seattle	15
KWFJ	89.7	Roy	1
KGRG-FM	89.9	Auburn	0.25
KASB	89.9	Bellevue	0.06
KXIR	89.9	Freeland	1.8
KGHP	89.9	Gig Harbor	1.35
KPLI	90.1	Olympia	0.1
K211FH	90.1	Shelton	0.05
KUPS	90.1	Tacoma	0.1
KEXP-FM	90.3	Seattle	4.7
KSER	90.7	Everett	5.8
KVTI	90.9	Tacoma	51
KROH	91.1	Port Townsend	1.15
KBCS	91.3	Bellevue	8
KQXI	91.5	Granite Falls	1.6
KSQM	91.5	Sequim	2.4
KXOT	91.7	Tacoma	23
K220HD	91.9	Fall City	0.004
K221FJ	92.1	Tacoma	0.15
KQMV	92.5	Bellevue	60
KUBE	93.3	Seattle	100
K229BP	93.7	Auburn	0.09

FM Callsign	MHz	Location	kW
K229BL	93.7	Gig Harbor	0.06
KANY	93.7	Montesano	14
KMPS-FM	94.1	Seattle	73
K233BU	94.5	White Center	0.06
KUOW-FM	94.9	Seattle	100
KJR-FM	95.7	Seattle	100
KJAQ	96.5	Seattle	53
KWPA-LP	96.9	Coupeville	0.03
KGY-FM	96.9	Mccleary	11
KIRO-FM	97.3	Tacoma	55
KOMO-FM	97.7	Belfair	69
K249DX	97.7	Redmond	0.08
KING-FM	98.1	Seattle	68
KLCK-FM	98.9	Seattle	68
KDDS-FM	99.3	Elma	64
K258BJ	99.5	Everett	0.01
KISW	99.9	Seattle	68
KKWF	100.7	Seattle	68
KPLZ-FM	101.5	Seattle	100
K271AH	102.1	Camano	0.12
K272ER	102.3	Sequim	0.2
KZOK-FM	102.5	Seattle	73
K277AE	103.3	Seattle	0.25
KMTT	103.7	Tacoma	68
K281AD	104.1	Olympia	0.05
KMCQ	104.5	Covington	7.1
KZFX-LP	104.5	Fall City	0.1
KKBW	104.9	Eatonville	17
KCMS	105.3	Edmonds	54
K289AK	105.7	Orting	0.01
KBKS-FM	106.1	Tacoma	73
K293AY	106.5	Enumclaw	0.01
KOWA-LP	106.5	Olympia	0.02
KRWM	106.9	Bremerton	49
K201EX	107.3	Greenwater	0.002
KNDD	107.7	Seattle	68

St Louis Area

FM Callsign	MHz	Location	kW
KDHX	88.1	St. Louis	42
WSIE	88.7	Edwardsville	50
W206AN	89.1	Carlinville	0.08
KCLC	89.1	St. Charles	50
KTBJ	89.3	Festus	25
KNLH	89.5	Cedar Hill	0.06
WARW	89.5	Dorsey	1.5
KCFV	89.5	Ferguson	0.1
WGRN	89.5	Greenville	0.3
KGNX	89.7	Ballwin	0.12
WCBW-FM	89.7	East St. Louis	0.25
KGNA-FM	89.9	Arnold	0.15
WLCA	89.9	Godfrey	1.5
KGNV	89.9	Washington	1
W211AD	90.1	Granite City	0.06
KRHS	90.1	Overland	0.01
KWUR	90.3	Clayton	0.01
KWMU	90.7	St. Louis	100
KSIV-FM	91.5	St. Louis	85
K220HT	91.9	St. Louis	0.09
WIL-FM	92.3	St. Louis	100
W224BJ	92.7	Carlyle	0.17
W226BC	93.1	Brighton	0.02
KBDZ	93.1	Perryville	50
KQQX	93.3	Hermann	50
KSD	93.7	St. Louis	74
KSHE	94.7	Crestwood	100
K236AZ	95.1	Gray Summit	0.02
WFUN-FM	95.5	Bethalto	24.5
WOLG	95.9	Carlinville	6
KIHT	96.3	St. Louis	100
WCXO	96.7	Carlyle	2.1
K241BS	96.7	St. Louis	0.1
KFTK	97.1	Florissant	100
WDLJ	97.5	Breese	2.5
KHZR	97.7	Potosi	26.5
KYKY	98.1	St. Louis	90
KLJY	99.1	Clayton	100
WZJM-LP	99.9	Freeburg	0.1
KFAV	99.9	Warrenton	10.5
KDJR	100.1	De Soto	2
KBWX	100.3	Bridgeton	17
KFNS-FM	100.7	Troy	6
WXOS	101.1	East St. Louis	100
K268BF	101.5	Bellefontaine	0.09
KXQX	101.7	Elsberry	3.1
WGEL	101.7	Greenville	6
KEZK-FM	102.5	St. Louis	100
KLOU	103.3	St. Louis	90

FM Callsign	MHz	Location	kW
W279AQ	103.7	Mascoutah	0.01
W280DR	103.9	Greenville	0.25
WHHL	104.1	Hazelwood	50
KSLQ-FM	104.5	Washington	3
WNSV	104.7	Nashville	3.4
KMJM-FM	104.9	Columbia	7.8
W286AJ	105.1	Jerseyville	0.12
K286BG	105.1	Washington	0.01
WAOX	105.3	Staunton	6
KPNT	105.7	St. Genevieve	100
WSMI-FM	106.1	Litchfield	39
WARH	106.5	Granite City	90
KSLZ	107.7	St. Louis	100

Tampa-St Petersburg Area

FM Callsign	MHz	Location	kW
WJIS	88.1	Bradenton	100
W202CB	88.3	Bayonet Point	0.03
WMNF	88.5	Tampa	7
WMYZ	88.7	Clermont	1.2
WYFE	88.9	Tarpon Springs	60
WSMR	89.1	Sarasota	54
W207BU	89.3	Bayonet Point	0.01
W207BU	89.3	Bayonet Point	0.25
WFLJ	89.3	Frostproof	10
WKFA	89.3	St. Catherine	3.9
WUSF	89.7	Tampa	100
WJUF	90.1	Inverness	21
WLVF-FM	90.3	Haines City	0.75
WBVM	90.5	Tampa	77
WKES	91.1	Lakeland	100
WCIE	91.5	New Port Richey	16.5
WFTI-FM	91.7	St. Petersburg	3
WHGN	91.9	Crystal River	41
WYFO	91.9	Lakeland	25
WLTQ-FM	92.1	Venice	11.5
W221CE	92.1	Wesley Chapel S.	0.124
WYUU	92.5	Safety Harbor	50
WFLZ-FM	93.3	Tampa	100
W229BM	93.7	Riverview	0.23
WLLD	94.1	Lakeland	100
W233AV	94.5	Gulfport	0.25
WWRM	94.9	Tampa	100
WXCV	95.3	Homosassa Spgs	6
W237CW	95.3	Pinellas Park	0.01
W237DI	95.3	West Tampa	0.12
WBTP	95.7	Clearwater	100
W254AI	95.9	Auburndale	0.25
WAPQ-LP	95.9	Avon Park	0.1
WLAS-LP	96.1	Bartow	0.1
WTMP-FM	96.1	Dade City	2.8
W242AK	96.3	Lakeland	0.25
W243AK	96.5	Bradenton	0.08
WVVD-LP	96.5	East Tampa	0.1
WSLR-LP	96.5	Sarasota	0.02
W244BE	96.7	Brandon	0.08
WEKJ-LP	96.7	Chassahowitzka	0.05
WZPH-LP	96.7	Dade City	0.1
W244BJ	96.7	Frostproof	0.02
WCFQ-LP	96.7	Inverness	0.08
W244BJ	96.9	Frostproof	0.25
WSUN-FM	97.1	Holiday	22
W247AF	97.3	Sarasota	0.08
WPCV	97.5	Winter Haven	100
WXTB	97.9	Clearwater	100
WWRZ	98.3	Fort Meade	27
W254AI	98.7	Auburndale	0.05
WHFS	98.7	Holmes Beach	50
W255CC	98.9	Sarasota	0.05
WWOJ	99.1	Avon Park	10
WQYK-FM	99.5	St. Petersburg	100
WXJB	99.9	Homosassa	2.3
W260CA	99.9	Sebring	0.05
WMTX	100.7	Tampa	100
W265BJ	100.9	Crystal River	0.05
W266AI	101.1	Chassahowitzka	0.17
WPOI	101.5	St. Petersburg	100
WHPT	102.5	Sarasota	100
WKJO-LP	102.7	Brooksville	0.08
W274BB	102.7	Haines City	0.01
W275AX	102.9	Fort Meade	0.14
WHKQ	103.1	Windermere	22
WFUS	103.5	Gulfport	100
W280DK	103.9	Inverness	0.25
W280DW	103.9	Tampa	0.25
W283AM	104.3	Arcadia	0.03
WKZM	104.3	Sarasota	25
W283AM	104.5	Arcadia	0.02

FM Callsign	MHz	Location	kW
WRBQ-FM	104.7	Tampa	100
WCFQ-LP	104.9	Inverness	0.08
WVDV-LP	104.9	Sebring	0.07
WZSP	105.3	Nocatee	4.1
WDUV	105.5	New Port Richey	47
WTZB	105.9	Englewood	25
W290BJ	105.9	West Tampa	0.25
W291AG	106.1	Highland City	0.17
WJQB	106.3	Spring Hill	25
WCTQ	106.5	Sarasota	13
W295BH	106.9	Sarasota	0.05
WZZS	106.9	Zolfo Springs	5
WXGL	107.3	St. Petersburg	100
W298AV	107.5	Englewood	0.08
W299AU	107.7	Zolfo Springs	0.01
WWMA-LP	107.9	Avon Park	0.1
WEKJ-LP	107.9	Chassahowitzka	0.05
WSRZ-FM	107.9	Coral Cove	47
Washington DC Area			
WYPR	88.1	Baltimore	15.5
WMUC-FM	88.1	College Park	0.01
WAMU	88.5	Washington	50
WPFW	89.3	Washington	50
W209BY	89.7	Woodbridge	0.01
WCSP-FM	90.1	Washington	36
WETA	90.9	Washington	75
WGTS	91.9	Takoma Park	27
WERQ-FM	92.3	Baltimore	37
WWXT	92.7	Prince Frederick	2.8
WPOC	93.1	Baltimore	19.5
WD2XAB	93.5	Columbia	2
WKYS	93.9	Washington	25
WIAD	94.7	Bethesda	50
WRBS-FM	95.1	Baltimore	50
WPGC-FM	95.5	Morningside	50
WWIN-FM	95.9	Arbutus	6
W240BH	95.9	Gainesville	0.004
WHUR-FM	96.3	Washington	16.5
WASH	97.1	Washington	17.5
W249BE	97.7	Alexandria	0.01
W252BR	98.3	Edgemere	0.25
WSMD-FM	98.3	Mechanicsville	3
WMZQ-FM	98.7	Washington	50
WNEW	99.1	Bowie	45
WIHT	99.5	Washington	50
W260BM	99.9	Annapolis	0.01
W261CD	100.1	Baltimore	0.002
WBIG-FM	100.3	Washington	50
WWDC	101.1	Washington	25
WMJS-LP	102.1	Prince Frederick	0.08
WMMJ	102.3	Bethesda	2.9
W275BO	102.9	Chantilly	0.01
WTOP-FM	103.5	Washington	44
WPRS-FM	104.1	Waldorf	50
W282BA	104.3	Leesburg	0.1
WAVA-FM	105.1	Arlington	33
W288BS	105.5	Reston	0.09
WJZ	105.7	Catonsville	50
WMAL	105.9	Woodbridge	40
W291BA	106.1	Baltimore	0.23
WJFK-FM	106.7	Manassas	40
WROX	107.3	Washington	21.5
WWWT	107.7	Manassas	29
WLZL	107.9	Annapolis	50

URUGUAY

LT: UTC -3h (7 Oct 12-10 Mar 13, 6 Oct 13-9 Mar 14: -2h) — **Pop:** 3.3 million — **Pr.L:** Spanish — **E.C:** 50Hz, 220V — **ITU:** URG — **Int. dialling code:** +598

DIRECCION NACIONAL DE TELECOMUNICACIONES
Ministerio de Industria, Energía y Minería.
⌨ Av. Uruguay 988 (Casilla de Correo 927), 11100 Montevideo Edificio Ciudadela Sarandí 690 D, 2º entrepiso ☎ 2915 0856 **E:** info@dinatel.miem.gub.uy **W:** www.dinatel.gub.uy

UNIDAD REGULADORA DE SERVICIOS DE COMUNICACIONES (URSEC)
⌨ Av. Uruguay 988 (Casilla de Correo 927), 11100 Montevideo ☎ 2902 8082, 2900 5708 **E:** radiodifusion@ursec.gub.uy
W: www.ursec.gub.uy **L.P:** Presidente: Sr. Ing. Gabriel Lombide

ASOCIACION NACIONAL DE BROADCASTERS URUGUAYOS (ANDEBU)
⌨ Carlos Quijano 1264, 11100 Montevideo ☎ 2902 1525, 2908 0037 📠 2902 1540 **E:** andebu@adinet.com.uy **W:** www.andebu.com.uy

COOPERATIVA DE RADIO EMISORAS DEL INTERIOR (CORI)
⌨ Av. 18 de Julio 948, Oficina 603, 11000 Montevideo 📠 2902 9047 **W:** http://www.cori.com.uy **E:** coriamfm@adinet.com.uy

RADIOS AM DEL INTERIOR (RAMI)
⌨ Nueva York 1618, 11800 Montevideo 📠 29047279
W: www.ramiradiosdelinterior.com.uy **E:** rami@adinet.com.uy

RED ORO
⌨ Rio Negro 1337, Esc. 209, 11100 Montevideo ☎ 2903 1678 📠 2 900 3916 **E:** redoro@adinet.com.uy

SERVICIO OFICIAL DE DIFUSIÓN, RADIOTELEVISIÓN Y ESPECTÁCULOS (S.O.D.R.E.) (Gov)
⌨ Sarandí 450, 11000 Montevideo ☎ 2 915 5378 **W:** www.sodre.gub.uy **E:** dirradio@sodre.gub.uy
L.P: Dir: Sergio Sacomani. Tech. Dir: José Cuello

MW Call		kHz	kW	Station, location, h. of tr.
CO01)	CW1	550	25	R. Colonia, Colonia: 24h
MO01)	CX58	580	2	R. Clarín, Montevideo: 24h
MO02)	CX4	610	50	R. Rural, Montevideo: 0900-0400
MO03)	CX6	650	50/25	S.O.D.R.E. "R. Clásica", Montevideo: 24h
RN01)	CW68	680	1	R. Young, Young: 0900-0300
MO04)	CX8	690	10/15	R. Sarandí, Montevideo: 24h
MO05)	CX10	730	5/2.5	R. Continente, Montevideo: 24h
SA01)	CW27	740	5	R. Tabaré, Salto: 0900-0300
MO06)	CX12	770	100/25	R. Oriental, Montevideo: 24h
MO07)	CX14	810	50/25	R. El Espectador, Montevideo: 0800-0500
SA02)	CW23	‡820	1/0.5	R. Cultural, Salto
MO08)	CX16	850	50	R. Carve, Montevideo: 0825-0300
MO09)	CX18	890	25	R. Sport 890, Montevideo: 24h
AR1)	CW17	900	3	R. Frontera, Artigas
MO10)	CX20	930	50	R. Monte Carlo, "la Super R.", Montevideo: 24h
DU01)	CW96	960	2/1	R. Yi, Durazno: 1000-0200
MO11)	CX22	970	20/3	R. Universal, Montevideo: 1030-0100
MO12)	CX24	1010	20	R. 1010AM, Montevideo: 0900-0400
SA03)	CW102	1020	0.1	R. Libertadores, Salto: 0700-0300
MO03)	CX26	1050	25	S.O.D.R.E. "R. Uruguay", Montevideo: 24h
MO14)	CX28	1090	15	R. Imparcial, Montevideo: 24h
TA01)	CX111	1110	3	R. Paso de los Toros, Paso de los Toros: 1100-0200
SA04)	CW31	1120	10	R. Salto, Salto: 0900-0300
MO15)	CX30	1130	20	R. Nacional, Montevideo: 24h
TT01)	CW116	1160	2/1	R. Agraria del Uruguay, Cerro Chato: 0800-0100
MO16)	CX32	1170	10	Radiomundo, Montevideo: 1100-0300
AR02)	CW118	1180	10	LV de Artigas, Artigas: 0900-0300
FL01)	CW33	1200	1	La Nueva R., Florida: 24h
SO02)	CX121	1210	2/1	Difusora Soriano, Mercedes: 24h
MA01)	CV121	1210	2/1	R. RBC, Piriápolis: 24h
TT02)	CX121	1210	0.25	R. El Libertador, Villa Vergara
RI05)	CX122	1220	1/0.5	R. Reconquista, Rivera: 1100-0400
PA01)	CW35	1240	5/1	R. Paysandú, Paysandú: 0900-0400
MO17)	CX36	1250	10	R. Centenario, Montevideo:24h
AR03)	CW125	1250	5	R. Bella Unión, Bella Unión: 0900-0300
RO01)	CW37	1260	3	Dif. Rochense, Rocha: 0900-0300
AR04)	CV127	1270	4/2	R. Cuareim, Artigas: 0900-0300
TA02)	CX128	1280	3/1	R. Tacuarembó, Tacuarembó: 0845-0300
MO18)	CX38	1290	10	S.O.D.R.E. "Em. del Sur", Montevideo: 24h
PA02)	CW39	1320	1/0.5	R. LV de Paysandú, Paysandú: 0900-0300
RO02)	CW132	1320	1/0.5	R. Fortaleza, Rocha: 1000-0200
MO19)	CX40	1330	5	R. Fénix, Montevideo: 1000-0600
CL01)	CW53	1340	10/1	LV de Melo, Melo: 0800-0300
CL02)	CW136	1360	1	R. Río Branco, Río Branco: 1055-0200
SJ01)	CW41	1360	2.5	R. 41, San José: 24h
MO20)	CX42	1370	5.3/2.5	Em. Ciudad de Montevideo: 1100-0300
RI01)	CV137A	1370	0.5	R. Real, Minas de Corrales: 0930-0130
RN02)	CW137	1370	0.5	R. Nueva R. San Javier, San Javier: 24h
TT03)	CW45	±1390	5	Dif. Treinta y Tres, Treinta y Tres: 0800-0300
TA03)	CX140	1400	25	R. Zorrilla de San Martín, Tacuarembó: 0900-0300
MO21)	CX44	1410	10/5	AM Libre, Montevideo: 24h
SA05)	CW141	1410	2/0.5	R. Turística, Salto: 0900-0300
LA01)	CW43	1420	5	R. Lavalleja, Minas: 0900-0300
PA03)	CX142	1420	1/0.5	R. Felicidad, Paysandú: 0830-0130
DU02)	CW25	1430	20/5	R. Durazno, Durazno: 0830-0300
RI02)	CW144	1440	3/0.5	R. Rivera, Rivera: 0830 (Su: 1000)-0300)
MO22)	CX46	1450	10/5	R. América, Montevideo: (0930-0630)

MW	Call	kHz	kW	Station, location, h. of tr.
SA06)	CW145	1450	1/0.25	R. Arapey, Salto: 24h
CO02)	CX146	1460	1	R. Carmelo, Carmelo: 0930-0030 (Su: 1000-0100)
LA02)	CV146	1460	0.25	R. José Batlle y Ordóñez, José Batlle y Ordóñez
CA01)	CX147	1470	2	R. Cristal del Uruguay,Las Piedras: 24h
CL03)	CW147	1470	1	R. Maria, Melo: 24h
RO04)	CW148	1480	3	R. Universo, Castillos: 0900-0300
RI03)	CW43B	1480	3/0.5	R. Internacional, Rivera: 0800-0300
RN03)	CX148	1480	1	Difusora Rio Negro, Young:0900-0300
AR05)	CV149	1490	1/0.25	R. del Centro, Baltasar Brum: 0900-0100
CO03)	CX149	1490	5	R. del Oeste, Nueva Helvecia: 0930-0300
RN04)	CX151	1510	1/0.5	R. Rincón, Fray Bentos: 0915-0230
MA02)	CW57	1510	2/0.5	R. San Carlos, San Carlos: 0800-0400
TA04)	CW151	1510	0.5	R. Ibirapitá, San Gregorio de Polanco: 1000-0200
CL04)	CV152	1520	2	R. Acuarela, Melo: 0900-0300
SO03)	CV152	1520	1/0.5	R. Paz, "La Nueva R.", Guichón: 1000-0030
CO4)	CW153	1530	0.25	Em. Cono Sur, Nueva Palmira: 0900-0300
PA04)	CW154	1540	0.1	R. Charrúa, Paysandú: 1000-0300
TT04)	CX154	1540	0.5/0.25	R. Patria, Treinta y Tres: 0800-0300
CO05)	CV154	1540	1	R. Centro, Cardona: 0900-0200
SO04)	CV155	1550	0.25	R. Agraciada, Mercedes: 24h
DU03)	CW155	1550	2/0.5	R. Sarandí del Yí, Sarandí del Yí: 1030-0130
MA03)	CW151	1550	3/0.5	R. Maldonado, Maldonado: 24h
FO01)	CX156	1560	2/0.5	Dif. Americana, Trinidad: 0930-0130
RI04)	CV156	1560	1	R. Vichadero: 1000-0200
CA02)	CX157	1570	2/0.5	R. Canelones: 0930-0300
AR06)	CW15A	1570	0.25	Em. Celeste, Tomás Gomensoro: 0930-0300
LA03)	CW54	1580	2/0.5	Emisoras del Este, Minas: 0800-0200
SO05)	CW158	1580	1/0.5	R. San Salvador, Dolores: 0900(SS 0800)-0300
RO05)	CW159	1590	1/0.25	R. Regional, Lascano
CO06)	CX159	1590	1	R. Real, Colonia: 0930-0300
CA03)	CV160	1600	2	R. Continental, Pando: 0915-0300
RN05)	CX160	1600	1	R. Litoral, Fray Bentos: 0900-0300

SW	Call	kHz	kW	Station, location
TA05)	#	±5900	0.03	Em. Chaná, Tacuarembó: 1200-0200
MO20)	CXA142A	‡6010	10	Em. Ciudad de Montevideo
MO09)	CXA61	6045	0.3	R. Sport 890, Montevideo: (LSB) rel. MO04
RO04)	CWA148	6055	0.3	R. Universo, Castillos
AR02)	CXA3	6075	1	LV de Artigas, Artigas: irr.
MO18)	CXA4	6125	0.35	S.O.D.R.E, Montevideo: irr (rel. MO03)
MO10)	CXA20	‡6140	1	R. Montecarlo, Montevideo
DU03)	CWA155	‡6140	2	Banda Oriental, Sarandí del Yí
MO20)	CXA142A	‡9650	10	Em. Ciudad de Montevideo
MO10)	CXA72	‡9595	1	R. Montecarlo, Montevideo
NO18)	CXA6	‡9620	0.35	S.O.D.R.E., Montevideo
MO06)	CXA7	‡11735	1	R. Oriental, Montevideo

‡ = inactive, ± = varying freq, #=unofficial

Addresses and other information
AR00) ARTIGAS
AR01) Av Lecueder 815, 55000 Artigas ☎4772 1230 - **FM:** 88.3MHz "Frontera FM" – **AR02)** Av Lecueder 483, 55000 Artigas ☎4772 2447 ☎4772 4744 **W:** www.radioartigas.com **E:** radioartigas118@gmail.com - **FM:** 90.7MHz "Amatista FM", 105.5MHz "Norte FM" – **AR03)**Enrique Ferreira 1550, 55100 Bella Unión ☎4779 2058 ☐4772 4744 **W:** www.radiobellaunion.com **E:** radiobellaunion@gmail.com - **FM:** 105.5MHz "Stereo Norte FM" – **AR04)** Av Lecueder 167, 55000 Artigas ☎4772 2867 **W:** www.radiocuareim.com **E:** racua@adinet. com.uy – **AR05)** Batlle y Ordóñez y 25 de Agosto, 55001 Baltasar Brum, Artigas ☎4776 2109 **W:** www.radiodelcentro.com **E:** radiodelcentro_95@hotmail.com – **AR06)** 18 de Julio y 19 de Abril, 55002 Tomás Gomensoro ☎4777 2157

CA00) CANELONES
CA01) Av Artigas 781, 90200 Las Piedras, Canelones ☎4236 44775 ☐4236 44814 **W:** www.radiocristaldeluruguay.com **E:** cx147cristal@hotmail.com or info@radiocristaldeluruguay.com – **CA02)** Tolentino González 434, 90000 Canelones ☎4332 2589 ☐4332 2040 **E:** cx157@adinet.com.uy - **FM:** 101.1MHz – **CA03)** Av Artigas 977, 91000 Pando ☎4229 22512 ☐4229 24440 **W:** www.radiocontinental.com.uy **E:** gerencia@radiocontinental.com.uy

CL00) CERRO LARGO
CL01) Remigio Castellanos 721, 37000 Melo ☎4642 2105 ☐4642 3226 **W:** www.lavozdemelo.com **E:** director@lavozdemelo.com – **CL02)** Virrey Arredondo 986, 37100 Rio Branco ☎4675 2009 **E:** am1360@adinet.com.uy – **CL03)** Treinta y Tres 949, 37100 Melo ☎4642 2387 **W:** www.radiomaria.org.uy **E:** info.ury@radiomaria.org – **CL04)** José Pedro Varela 750, Melo ☎4642 2051 ☐4642 1264 **E:** acuarelaradio@yahoo.com or correo@radioacuarela

CO00) COLONIA
CO01) Rivadavia 383, 70000 Colonia ☎4522 2006 ☐4522 2961 **W:** radiocolonia.com **E:** cw1@adinet.com.uy - **FM:** 93.5MHz "FM Mágica"

– **CO02)**19 de Abril 444, 70100 Carmelo ☎4542 3558 ☐4542 2520 **W:** www.radiocarmelo.com **E:** radiocarmelo@adinet.com.uy – **CO03)** Calle Berna 1375, 70201 Nueva Helvecia **W:** www.ro.com.uy ☎4554 4217 ☐4554 4409 **E:**1490@ro.com.uy - **FM:** 90.7MHz "Reflejos" – **CO04)** Chile 1162 y Gral Artigas, 70101 Nueva Palmira, Depto de Colonia ☎4544 6053 **E:** emisoraconosur@gmail.com – **CO05)** Boulevard Cardona s/n y Rivera, 75.200 Cardona ☎4536 9315 – **CO06)** Av Gral Flores 472, 70000 Colonia ☎4522 2030 **W:** www.radioreal.com.uy **E:** radioreal@adinet.com.uy

DU00) DURAZNO
DU01) Zorrilla de San Martín 875, 97000 Durazno ☎4362 2701 ☐4362 3297 **E:** multimyi@adinet.com.uy – **DU02)** Artigas 487, 97000 Durazno ☎4362 2015 ☐4362 2058 **W:** www.radiodurazno.com **E:** am1430@adinet.com.uy, info@radiodurazno.com - **FM:** 95.1MHz "Radio City" – **DU03)** Calle Sarandí del Yí 428, 97100 Sarandí del Yí ☎4367 9155 **E:** norasan@adinet.com.uy - **FM:** 89.5MHz "Scala FM"

FL00) FLORIDA
FL01) Antonio Ma Fernández 800, 94000 Florida ☎4352 2026 **W:** www.cw33florida.com.uy **E:** cw33@adinet.com.uy - **FM:** 88.7MHz "Claridad"

FO00) FLORES
FO01) 25 de Agosto 724, 85000 Trinidad ☎4364 2229 ☐364 37550

LA00) LAVALLEJA
LA01) José E Rodó 530, 30000 Minas ☎4442 2304 – **LA02)** Camino Nacional s/n, 30200 José Batlle y Ordóñez ☎4469 2132 – **LA03)** Treinta y Tres 632, 30000 Minas **W:** http://www.federalfm.com.uy/cw54.php ☎4442 3092 ☐442 8714 **E:** federalfm@federalfm.com.uy - **FM:** 107.3MHz "Federal FM".

MA00) MALDONADO
MA01) Chacabuco y Moreno, 20200 Piriápolis ☎☐4432 2771 **W:** www.radiobc.com.uy **E:** rbc1210@adinet com.uy – **MA02)** Calle Sarandí 775, entre 18 de Julio y Treinta y Tres, 20400 San Carlos ☎4266 9162 ☐4426 69575 **W:** www.radiosancarlos.8k.com **E:** radiosancarlos@adinet.com.uy & rsc@adinet.com.uy – **MA03)** Zelmar Michelini 819, 20000 Maldonado ☎4422 3872 ☐4422 2555 **E:** am1560@adinet.com.uy **N:** every ½h - **FM:** 103.5MHz "Aspen FM"

MO00) MONTEVIDEO
MO01) Av 18 de Julio 1516, P.9, Esc 7, 11200 Montevideo ☎240 06877 ☐240 15841 **W:** www.radioclarin.com **E:** clarinam580@adinet.com.uy – **MO02)** Joaquín Suárez 3409, 11700 Montevideo ☎233 60610 **W:** www.cx4radiorural.com **E:** rural@cx4radiorural.com – **MO03)** Sarandí 430, 11000 Montevideo **W:** www.sodre.gub.uy ☎291 5387 ☐291 61933 - CX6: - Clásica: - 1000-0300 - CX26: - Uruguay - 0900-0300 - CX38 Uruguayan music Media Prgr: SS1400-1500, 0200-0300 "Radioactividades" on 1050kHz Rpt. to Cas, 7011, 11000 Montevideo. **E:** radioactividades@sodre.gub.uy – **MO04)** Enriqueta Compte y Riquet 1250, 11800 Montevideo ☎220 82612 ☐220 36906 **W:** www.sarandi.com.uy **E:** direccion@sarandi690.com.uy – **MO05)** Germán Barbato 1472, 11100 Montevideo ☎2902 4038 ☐290 24038 **E:** cx10.730.continente@adinet.com.uy – **MO06)** Cerrito 475, 11000 Montevideo **W:** www.oriental.com.uy **E:** via http://www.oriental.com.uy/php/contacto.php ☎291 61130 – **MO07)** Río Branco 1481, 11100 Montevideo ☎290 23531 ☐290 83044 **W:** www.espectador.com **E:** am810@espectador.com.uy – **MO08)** Mercedes 973, 11100 Montevideo ☎202 6162 ☐290 20126 **W:** www.carve850.com **E:** programacion@sadrep.com.uy – **MO09)** Enriqueta Compte y Riquet 1250, 11800 Montevideo ☎220 4163 ☐220 3786 **W:** sport890.com.uy **E:** sport890@sport890.com - Rpt. to: fgopar34@gmail.com – **MO10)** Av 18 de Julio 1224, 11100 Montevideo ☎290 14433 **W:** www.radiomontecarlo.com.uy **E:** cx20@radiomontecarlo.com.uy – **MO11)** Av 18 de Julio, 1220, 3er piso, 11100 Montevideo ☎290 26022 ☐290 26050 **W:** www.22universal.com **E:** info@22universal.com – **MO12)** Mercedes 973, 11100 Montevideo **W:** http://www.radio1010.com.uy ☎2902 6712 ☐2902 9110 **E:** programacion@sadrep.com.uy – **MO14)** Av del Libertador Brig Gral. Lavalleja 1708, ap 101, Edificio Carioca, 11800 Montevideo ☎292 41514 ☐292 42323 **E:** radioimparcial@net-gate.com.uy – **MO15)** Plaza Independencia 846, EP, 11100 Montevideo ☎290 25640 **W:** www.la30.com.uy **E:** prensa@radionacional.com.uy – **MO16)** Rambla Armenia 1647, Montevideo ☎262 89626 ☐262 89627 – **MO17)** Av 18 de Julio 1357, Oficina 202, 11000 Montevideo ☎290 30302 ☐290 30307 **E:** radio36@gmail.com **W:** www.radio36.com.uy – **MO19)** Canelones 1969, 11200 Montevideo ☎☐240 83292 **W:** www.cx40radiofenix.com **E:** radiofenix@adinet.com.uy – **MO20)** Arenal Grande 2093, 11800 Montevideo ☎292 40142 ☐292 40700 **W:** www.emisoraciudaddemontevideo.com.uy **E:** CX42@emisoraciudaddemontevideo.com.uy – **MO21)** Garibaldi 2579, Montevideo **W:** www.1410amlibre.com.uy **E:** via http://www3.1410amlibre.com/contacto.php ☎248 73565 – **MO22)** Emilio Frugoni 1312, Montevideo **W:** www.cx46.com ☎240 90094 ☐240 89314 **E:** correo@cx46.com

PA00) PAYSANDÚ
PA01) Av España 1629, 60000 Paysandú **E:** correo@radiocw39.com

☎4722 3617 🖷4722 2954 **W:** www.radiocw39.com – **PA02)** 18 de Julio 614, 60000 Paysandú ☎4722 2267 🖷4722 4970 **E:** cw39@adinet. com.uy – **PA03)** 33 Orientales 946,1° piso, 60000 Paysandú ☎4722 4020 🖷4722 4020 **W:** www.paysandu.com/radiofelicidad **E:** radiofelicidad@adinet.com.uy – **PA04)** Tte. Cnl Francisco Bicuda y Ruta 3 Gral Artigas, 60000 Paysandú ☎4722 4856 **E:** cw154@adinet.com.uy

RI00) RIVERA

RI01) Dr Dávison s/n, 40002 Minas de Corrales ☎4658 2073 – **RI02)** Dr Gabriel Anolles 441, 40000 Rivera ☎🖷4622 3230 - **E:** radiorivera@ gmail.com – **RI03)** Av Sarandí 792, 40000 Rivera ☎4622 3259 🖷4622 3422 **E:** internac@gmail.com – **FM:** 94.5MHz – **RI04)** Bulevar Artigas casi Rivera, 40003 Vichadero ☎🖷4654 2018 **E:** radiosamfm@hotmail. com – **RI05)** Francisco Acuña de Figueroa 887, 40000 Rivera ☎4622 5893 **W:** www.multimediadelnorte.com/reconquista **E:** reconquista1220@hotmail.com – **FM:** 90.6MHz

RN00) RIO NEGRO

RN01) Rincón 1689, 65100 Young 🖷4567 2071 **E:** am680@adinet. com.uy – **RN02)** 27 de Julio casi Basilio Lubkov, San Javier ☎4569 2005 🖷4569 2089 **E:** radiosanjavier@hotmail.com – **RN03)** Rincón 1811, 65100 Young ☎🖷4567 5143 **E:** imagenfm@adinet.com.uy - **FM:** 89.1MHz "Imágen FM" – **RN04)** 25 de Mayo 3164 al 3168, 65000 Fray Bentos ☎4562 2022 🖷4562 2653 **W:** www.agenda.org.uy/radiorincon **E:** rinconprensa@adinet.com or prensa.rincon@gmail.com – **RN05)** 18 de Julio y 25 de Agosto, 65000 Fray Bentos ☎4562 3100 & 4562 3100 🖷4562 3528 **W:** www.radiolitoral.com.uy **E:** litoral@adinet.com.uy

RO00) ROCHA

RO01) Ramírez 127, 27000 Rocha ☎4472 2250 🖷4472 2650 **W:** www. difusararochense.com.uy **E:** difusora1260am@hotmail.com – **FM:** 91.5MHz & 106.3MHz – **RO02)** Zorrilla de S Martin 200, 27000 Rocha ☎4472 2460 🖷4472 3973 – **RO04)** 18 de Julio 1322, 27200 Castillos ☎4475 8054 🖷4475 8755 **W:** www.universoam.com **E:** am1480@adinet.com.uy (radio) grupouniverso@adinet.com.uy (dir.) – **RO05)** Nicolás Corbo 1152, 27300 Lascano. **W:** www.lanuevaradiolascano.com **E:** lanuevaradio@adinet.com.uy ☎🖷4456 9280 & 4456 4380

SA00) SALTO

SA01) Uruguay 1416, 50000 Salto ☎4734 0298 🖷4733 3222 **W:** www. saltouruguay.com/radiotabre **E:** amtabare@adinet.com.uy, radiotabare. hotmail.com – **SA02)** Lavalleja 48, 50000 Salto ☎🖷4732 4330 - **FM:** 106.5MHz "Emisora del Éxodo." – **SA03)** Uruguay 1416, 50000 Salto ☎🖷4733 3222 **W:** http://amlibertadores **E:** amlibertadores@ adinet.com.uy – **SA04)** Brasil 715, 50000 Salto ☎4733 2615 🖷4733 3414 **W:** www.agenda.org.uy/radiosalto **E:** cw31salt@adinet.com.uy & radiosalto@adinet.com.uy – **FM:** 88.3MHz "Emisora del Lago" – **SA05)** Calle Artigas 1014, 50000 Salto ☎4732 7759 🖷4732 6264 **W:** http//agenda.org.uy/radioturistica/ – **SA06)** Artigas 101, 50000 Salto ☎4732 6264 **W:** www.10minutos.com.uy **E:** amarapey@adinet.com.uy

SJ00) SAN JOSÉ

SJ01) Evaristo Ciganda 511, 80000 San José ☎🖷4342 6444 **W:** www. radio41.com.uy **E:** radionoticias41@adinet.com.ut

SO00) SORIANO

SO02) De Castro y Careaga 568, 75000 Mercedes ☎4532 3430 🖷4532 2977 **W:** www.difusorasoriano.com **E:** difusorasoriano@adinet.com. uy - **FM:** 89.3MHz "Em del Hum" – **SO03)** Luis Alberto de Herrera 346, 60008 Guichón, Depto de Paysandú ☎4742 2053 🖷4742 2297 **W:** www.pazlanuevaradio.net **E:** lanuevapaz@adinet.com.uy – **SO04)** Colón 86, 75000 Mercedes ☎4532 8536 (Adm.), 4532 8538 (AM Studio) **W:** http://agenda.org.uy/radioagraciada@ adinet.com.uy - **FM:** 100.3MHz "Galicia" – **SO05)** Av Asencio 1695, 75100 Dolores, Depto de Soriano ☎4534 2110 🖷4534 2691 **W:** www. radiosansalvador.com.uy **E:** administracion@radiosansalvador.com.uy - **FM:** 89.7MHz "Skorpio".

TA00) TACUAREMBÓ

TA01) 18 de Julio 743, 45100 Paso de los Toros ☎🖷4664 2333 **W:** www.pasodelostoros.com **E:** am1110@adinet.com.uy or radio-pasodelostoros@pasodelostoros.com - **FM:** 91.9MHz "Toros FM" – **TA02)** 18 de Julio 112, 45000 Tacuarembó ☎4263 20214 🖷4263 2495 **W:** radiotacuarembo.com **E:** radiotacuaremboam@radiotacuarembo.com - **FM:** 92.5MHz, 104.5MHz – **TA03)** 18 de Julio 302, 45000 Tacuarembó ☎4632 2605 🖷4622 2779 – **W:** www.radiozorrilla.com **E:** zsm@adinet.com.uy - **FM:** 88.9MHz "Em de la Música" – **TA04)** Gral Artigas 193, 42500 San Gregorio de Polanco, Tacuarembó ☎4639 4547 🖷4639 2495 – **TA05)** Sr. Omar Lima, Barragué 395, Barrio La Palma, 45000 Tacuarembó **E:** emisorachanatacuarembo@hotmail.com

TT00) TREINTA Y TRES

TT01) Juan Muñoz s/n, 30204 Cerro Chato, Depto Treinta y Tres ☎4466 2200 🖷4466 2225 **E:** radioagraria@hotmail.com Rpts. to: cx2ua@hotmail.com – **TT02)** Marcelo Barreto s/n, Villa Vergara, 33000 Treinta y Tres ☎4458 2917 **W:** www.ellibertador.com.uy **E:** ellibertador@adinet.com.uy – **TT03)** Pablo Zufriátegui 1076, 33000 Treinta y Tres ☎4452 22476 🖷4452 2340 **W:** difusoratreintaytres. com.uy **E:** cw45@adinet.com.uy – **TT04)** Juan A.Lavallea 1530, 33000

Treinta y Tres ☎4452 3532 🖷452 2423 **W:** www.radiopatria.com.uy **E:** radiopatria@adinet.com.uy

FM in Montevideo (MHz): all stns 10-100kW

89.1 Uni-Radio (LP stn) – 90.3 FM Oldies – 91.1 R.Futura – 91.5 ZOE Gospel Music – **6)** 91.9 R.Disney – 92. MO7)93. Urbana FM – MO7) 92.5 El Espectador **19)** 93.9 Océano – **MO03)** 94.7 Emisora del Sur (SODRE) – 95.5 Em. Del Plata – 96.3 Alfa FM – **MO03)** 97.1 Babel (SODRE) – 97.9 M24 – 98.7 Diamante FM – 99.5 Em. del Sol – 100.3 Aire FM – 101.3 LV de la Esperanza – 101.9 Azul FM – 103.7 Latina FM – **8)** 104.3 Radiocero – 105.9 Galaxia FM – 106.7 La Ley FM.

In the rest of the country there are 165 FM outlets. There are 111 Community FM low-power authorized stns in the country.

UZBEKISTAN

LT: UTC +5h — **Pop:** 29.6 million — **Pr.L:** Uzbek — **E.C:** 50Hz, 220V — **ITU:** UZB

O'ZBEKISTON ALOQA VA AXBOROTLASHTIRISH AGENTLIGI (O'zAAA)

(Communications and Information Agency of Uzbekistan)

🖃 A. Navoiy ko'chasi, 28A, 100011 Toshkent ☎ +998 71 2384107 🖷 +990 71 2398782 **E:** info@aci.uz **W:** www.aci.uz

L.P: DG: Xurshid Mirzaxidov

NB: O'zAAA is the licensing authority for broadcasting.

O'ZBEKISTON MILLY TELERADIOKOMPANIYASI (Gov)

🖃 A. Navoiy ko'chasi 69, 100011 Toshkent ☎ +998 71 2141250 🖷 +998 71 2441332.**E:** info@mtrk.uz **W:** www.mtrk.uz

🖃 Radio studios: Xorazm ko'chasi 49, 100047 Toshkent

L.P: Pres: Alisher Xadjayev

FM	UZR1*	UZR2	UZR3	kW
Andijon	-	105.2	-	1
Buxoro	102.0c	103.9	105.4	2
Navoiy	106.6g	-	105.8	2
Qarshi	102.3e	103.1	105.6	1
Termiz	103.1k	104.6	-	-
Toshkent	103.1	104.0	107.8	4
Samarqand	105.2i	101.9	-	0.1
Urganch	103.5l	101.5	-	4

NB: Selected district capitals shown *) incl. reg prgrs (see below)

D.Prgr: UZR1 (O'zbekiston): 0000-2200. – **UZR2 (Yoshlar):** 2300-2100. – **UZR3 (Mash'al):** 0000-2200. – **Local Station: "Toshkent"** on Toshkent 87.9 (4kW): 24h in Uzbek, Russian.

O'zbekiston MTRK Regional Services

D.Prgr: via UZR1 txs. **a) Andijon TRK:** Istiqlol ko'chasi 9, 170120 Andijon. – **b) Buxoro TRK:** Eshanov ko'chasi 20, 200120 Buxoro. – **c) Farg'ona TRK:** 150100 Farg'ona. – **d) Jizzax TRK:** Rashidov maydon, 130100 Jizzax. – **e) Qashqadaryo TRK:** 180100 Qarshi. – **f) Qoraqalpog'iston TRK:** Dustnazarov ko'chasi 20, 230100 Nukus. – **g) Navoiy TRK:** Xalklar Do'stligi ko'chasi 32, 210100 Navoiy. – **h) Namangan TRK:** Holhanov ko'chasi 1, 160136 Namangan. – **i) Samarqand TRK:** 140100 Samarqand. – **j) Sirdaryo TRK:** 120100 Guliston. – **k) Surxandaryo TRK:** 190100 Termiz. – **l) Xorazm TRK:** 220100 Urganch.

OTHER STATIONS

FM	MHz	kW	Location	Station
8)	88.4	1	Toshkent	Navro'z FM
4C)	90.0	1	Toshkent	A'lo FM
1B)	100.5	2	Toshkent	Oriat FM
10)	100.5	1	Farg'ona	Ruxsor FM
3)	101.0	1	Toshkent¹	O'zbegim taronasi
2)	101.5	1	Toshkent	R. Grand
5)	102.0	2	Toshkent	R. Hamroh
6)	102.7	1	Toshkent¹	Vodiy sadosi
9A)	103.5	1	Toshkent	R. Poytaxt
9A)	104.5	1	Samarqand	R. Poytax
4A)	105.0	4	Toshkent	R. Terra
10)	105.8	1	Toshkent	Zamin FM
1A)	106.5	4	Toshkent	Oriat Dono
6)	106.9	1	Angren¹	Vodiy sadosi
9B)	107.2	1	Toshkent	R. Poytaxt-Inform
7)	107.2	1	Samarqand	STV Radio
4B)	107.3	1	Andijon	Zamin FM
4B)	107.4	1	Buxoro	Zamin FM

¹) + txs in other towns on same freq. (synchr. network)

NB: Txs below 1kW not listed.

Addresses & other information:

1A,B) Istikbol ko'chasi 6, 100000 Toshkent. 1A) in Uzbek, **E:** radio@

oriatdono.uz; 1B) in Russian, **E:** fm@oriat.uz – **2)** Bunyodkor ko'chasi 15, 100043 Toshkent. **E:** radio@grand.uz – **3)** Shaxrisabz ko'chasi 16a, 100000 Toshkent. **E:** ut101@mail.ru – **4A-C)** Xamid Olimjon maydon 13A, 100000 Toshkent. – **5)** Shayxontohur ko'chasi 36, 100007 Toshkent. **E:** hamroh@mail.ru – **6)** Mirobod ko'chasi 39/1A, 100000 Toshkent. **E:** mtrk@intal.uz – **7)** Firdavskiy ko'chasi 1, 140100 Samarqand. – **8)** Muqumiy ko'chasi 178, 100096 Toshkent. **E:** info@navruzfm.uz – **9A,B)** Movaraunnahr ko'chasi 14, 100000 Tashkent. **E:** radio1072@rambler.ru – **10)** Marg'ilon ko'chasi 76, 150100 Farg'ona

VANUATU

L.T. UTC + 11h — **Pop:** 224,564 — **Pr.L:** Bislama, English, French — **E.C:** 50Hz, 230V — **ITU:** VUT

VANUATU BROADCASTING AND TELEVISION CORPORATION (VBTC)
PMB 049, Port Vila ☎ +678 22999 ▤ +678 22026 **L.P:** GM: Fred Vurobaravu, Mgr Radio: Samuel Seiragi, Mgr-Tech. Srvcs: Warren Robert **E:** technical@vbtc.com.vu
MW: Emten Lagoon (Port Vila) 1125kHz 10kW, Santo (Luganville) 1179kHz 10kW
SW: Emten Lagoon (Port Vila) 3945kHz 10kW 5055kHz 10kW 7260kHz 10kW **Schedule:** A10 - 3945 0700-2000, 5055 0700-1800; B10 – 3945 0700-2000, 7260 0700-1800. Relays MW.
FM: Paradise FM, Luganville 98.1MHz 0.2kW, **Tudei FM**, Port Vila 98.0MHz 0.25kW
D.Prgr: 1125/1179 1900-1115 (Sun -1000)
Other stations:

FM	MHz	kW	Station
6) Aniwa Is	89.0	0.1	CREST FM
7) Siviri	89.0		Taleva 89 FM
1) Port Vila	90.0	0.3	FM90 Christian R.
2) Port Vila	99.0	0.25	BBC
2) Luganville	99.0	0.25	BBC
3) Port Vila	100.0	0.2	France-Inter
4) Port Vila	102.0		China R. International
4) Luganville	102.0		China R. International
9) Port Vila	103.0	0.2	R. Australia
6) Isangel	104.0	0.1	CREST FM
5) Lakatoro	106.0		China R. International
5) Port Vila	107.0	0.3	Capital FM107
8) Saratamata	-	-	-

Addresses and other information:
1) Vanuatu Christian Broadcasting Network [VCBN], P.O.Box 674, Port Vila ☎ +678 26408 **E:** nenes@vanuatu.com.vu **W:** www.vcbn.com **L.P:** CEO: Jenny Joy James (r. inactive] – **2)** 24h Pacific stream satellite relay – **3)** 24h French service satellite relay from Paris – **4)** 24h English/Chinese service satellite relay from Beijing – **5)** Top Flr, Laguna Bldg, Port Vila. ☎ +678 23847 **E:** sales@fm107vanuatu.com **W:** www.fm107vanuatu.com **L.P:** GM Arthur Knight Dir. Sabie Natonga **ID:** "Capital FM107" **D.Prgr:** 24h – **6)** CREST R. Society of Tafea, Isangel Station, Tanna Island ☎ +678 68054 **E:** gudfella@vanuatu.com.vu **L.P:** Mgr: David Kiel. **Network:** 3 community FM stns in Tafea Province – **7)** community FM stn, Siviri, North Efate – **8) F.PL:** new community FM stn, Penama Province – **9)** 24h English for the Pacific and French service satellite relay

VATICAN CITY STATE

L.T: UTC +1h (31 Mar-27 Oct: +2h) — **Pop:** 900 — **E.C:** 50Hz, 220V — **ITU:** CVA

RADIO VATICANA (RIg.)
Vatican Radio, 00120 Vatican City ☎ +39 06 6988 3551 Int. Rel: ☎ +39 06 6988 3551 ▤ +39 06 6988 4565 **W:** www.radiovaticana.org **E:** promo@vatiradio.va
L.P: DG: Rev. Federico Lombardi S.J.; TD: Sandro Piervenanzi; CE: Maurizio Venuti; Head of Int. Rel: Giacomo Ghisani; Vatican Radio Museum, guided visiting tour c/o Palazzo Pio XII, Piazza Pia 3, **E:** contact museo_rv@vaticanradio.org **W:** www.radiovaticana.org/museo_tecnico/it/index.asp
MW: 585kHz 5kW, 1260kHz 5kW, **FM:** 93.3/105.0MHz 10kW
Progr: Europa Programma 1 93.3MHz 24h; 1260kHz (0210-1650); 1611kHz (0520-0030); **One-o-Five Live** 105.0MHz 24h (Multil.) **W:** http://it.radiovaticana.va/105/index.asp (Relay Studio A 2330-0530); 585kHz 24h (Classical Music & relay One-o-Five Live105).
DRM+: Radio Vaticana International Service: Roma area 103.8MHz 0.2kW 24h **W:** www.radiovaticana.org/it1/sched_eur1.asp

Ann: Before all transmissions: Latin: "Laudetur Jesus Christus"

(Praised be Jesus Christ), repeated in the language of the broadcast, then stn identification. **IS:** "Christus Vincit". **V.** by QSL-card.

EXTERNAL SERVICE: Vatican Radio see International Radio section

VENEZUELA

L.T: UTC -4½h — **Pop:** 26.4 million — **Pr.L:** Spanish — **E.C:** 60Hz, 120V — **ITU:** VEN

COMISION NACIONAL DE TELECOMUNICACIONES (CONATEL)
Avenida Veracruz con Calle Cali, Edificio CONATEL, Urb. Las Mercedes, Caracas 1060 ▤ 212 993 8801 **W:** www.conatel.gob.ve **E:** conatel@conatel.gob.ve

CAMARA VENEZOLANA DE LA INDUSTRIA DE RADIODIFUSION
Ap. 3955, Caracas 1060 ☎ +58 212 2634855, 2634528 ▤ +58 212 2614783

In 2009, the Venezuelan authorities announced the closure of some 240 AM and FM stns for failure to comply with licensing requirements. At time of editing, these measures have mostly still not been carried out. Those known to have closed are marked with an ‡.

MW	Call	kHz	kW	Station, location, h. of tr.
AM01		540	10	LV de Manapiare, San Juan de Manapiare
ZU01	OY	540	50/25	R. Perijá, La Villa del Rosario: 0900-0400
DC01	KE	550	50	R. Mundial, Caracas
DC02	RH	560	50	RNV Canal Informativo, Puerto Ordaz: 1030-0430
TA01	PJ	560	20/10	CNB Tachirense, Rubio
AR09	LX	570	100	R. La Villa, Villa de Cura
ZU02	MJ	580	50/10	LV de la Fe, Maracaibo
DC04	KL	590	20	R. Continente, Caracas
BA01	SW	600	15	R. Alto Llano, Sta Bárbara de Barinas
SU01	QB	‡600	10	R. Sucre, Cumaná
AN01	XY	610	10	R. Centro 6-10, Cantaura
LA01	SE	610	10	R. Cristal, Barquisimeto
AP01	ZC	620	50/25	R. Fe y Alegría,Guasdualito 0900-0400
ZU03	NO	620	10	R. Libertad, Cabimas: 0900-0400
DC02	KA	630	50/25	RNV Canal Informativo, Caracas: 1030-0430
AN02	QO	‡640	30	Actualidad 640, Puerto La Cruz
LA02	MU	640	10/5	R. Carora, Carora: 1000-0400
AR01	LH	‡650	50/20	Aragüeña 650, Maracay: 0900-0500
AN03	QZ	660	10	R. Anaco, Anaco: 0900-0400
FA01	NA	660	10	Ondas de los Medanos, Coro: 0900-0400
DC03	LL	670	100	R. Rumbos, Caracas
BA02	ZJ	680	10	R. Llanera "R. 1400", Barinas: 0900-0500
SU02	QR	680	10	R. Continente Cumaná, Cumaná: 1000-0500
LA03	MR	690	50/20	R. Barquisimeto, Barquisimeto
B001	PQ	700	5/2	R. Sur, Puerto Ordaz
ZU04	MH	700	10	R. Popular, Maracaibo: 1000-0400
DC05	KY	710	50/20	R. Capital, Caracas: 1000-0600
AP02	XE	720	10	R. Elorza, Elorza
NE01	QE	720	50	R. Venezuela Oriente, Porlamar
LA04	MT	730	10	R. Universo, Barquisimeto
TA02	OO	‡730	10	R. Frontera, San Antonio del Táchira
B002	NQ	740	50	R. Caroni "Q-FM", Puerto Ordaz
ZU05	NC	740	10	CNB 740 La Zuliana, Maracaibo: 0900-0400
DC06	KS	750	100	RCR 750 "Radio Caracas", Caracas
AN04	QQ	‡760	10	R. Puerto La Cruz, Pto. La Cruz:
TR01	SO	760	10	R. Simpática 760, Trujillo
DC02	KK	770	50/20	RNV Canal Informativo, Campo Carabobo: 1030-0430
FA02	MN	780	15	R. Coro, Coro
TA03	OD	780	50/20	Ecos del Torbes, San Cristóbal: 0900-0400(SS -0600)
DC02)		790		RNV Canal Informativo, Cd. Bolívar: 1030-0430
DC07	KC	790	10	R. Caracas 790, Caracas
LA05	XM	790	10	R. Minuto, Barquisimeto
CA01	PV	‡810	50	Super Radio 810, Valencia
B003	SH	820	50	R. Guayana, Upata
FA03	XG	‡820	25/10	R. Guadalupana, Coro: 0900-0400
TA04	KU	820	10	R. Altura 820, La Grita: 1000-0400
DC08	LT	830	25	R. Nueva Sensación, Caracas: 0900-0500
LA04	MY	840	10	8-40 AM, Barquisimeto
M001	UZ	840	10/5	Guarapiche 8-40 "La Primera", Maturín
CA02	RV	‡850	10	RV-850, Valencia
ZU06	ZC	850	10	R. Fe y Alegría, Maracaibo: 0900-0500
GU01	YE	860	20/10	Enlace 8-60, Valle de la Pascua
TA05	OL	860	10	Mundial 8-60, San Cristóbal: 0900-0500

MW	Call	kHz	kW	Station, location, h. of tr.
AN06)	RU	‡870	10	Unión R. Deportes 870, Puerto La Cruz
LA11)	MP	870	10	Unión R. Notícias, Barquisimeto: 1000-0300
BA04)	ZD	880	20/10	R. Venezuela Barinas, Barinas
BO04)	YM	880	20/10	R. Venezuela Guayana, Puerto Ordaz
DC02)	KV	880	10	RNV Canal Musical, Caracas: 1030-0430
FA04)		880	10	R. Paraguaná, Punto Fijo
AN07)	VO	‡890	10	R. Oriente, El Tigre
CA03)	LW	890	25	R. América, Valencia: 0900-0400
ZU07)	MD	900	25	R. Venezuela Mara Ritmo, Maracaibo
DC10)	RQ	910	50/20	R. AM Center, Caracas
CO01)	QU	920	10/5	R. San Carlos, San Carlos
NE02)	QX	920	20	R. Nueva Esparta, Porlamar: 1000-0400
AR02)	LJ	930	10	R. Maracay, Maracay: 1000-0600
AN08)	LU	‡940	10	R. Fe y Alegría El Tigre, El Tigre: 0900-0300
BA03)	ZR	940	15	R. Continental, Barinas: 0900-0500
FA05)	NN	940	10	R. Punto Fijo, Punto Fijo: 0900-0500
DC11)	KG	950	50	AM Popular, Caracas: 1000-0400
MO02)	RB	960	50/20	R. Monagas, Maturín
PO01)		960	25	R. Venezuela Llanera, Acarigua
TA06)	SS	960	10	R. San Sebastián, San Cristóbal: 1000-0500
AN09)		‡970	10	Mundial 970, Barcelona
AR03)	LR	970	10	R. Continente 970, Maracay: 0900-0400
TR02)	SD	970	15	R. Turismo, Valera: 0900-0400
AN10)	OM	980	10	Unión R. Notícias, El Tigre: 1000-0300
DC12)	RT	990	20	R. Tropical "99-0", Caracas
LA06)	TA	990	10	R. Venezuela Tricolor, Barquisimeto
CA04)	NM	1000	10	R. Caribeña Mil AM (Continente), Morón: 0900-0400
TA11)	OA	1000	10	R. Táchira, San Cristóbal: 1000-0400
AR04)	PC	1010	10	R. Aragua, Cagua: 0900-0400
BO05)	QF	1010	10	R. Venezuela Bolívar, Cd. Bolívar
NE03)	RS	1020	10	R. Mundial Margarita, La Asunción: 1000-0500
YA01)	TW	1020	25	R. Alegría, Chivacoa
ZU08)	MX	1020	50/10	R. Calendario Zulia, Maracaibo
MI01)	TD	1020	25/10	R. Valles del Iuy, Ucumare del Tuy: 0930-0400
PO02)	QY	1030	10	R. Onda 1030, Guanare: 0900-0600
CA05)	LB	1040	20	LV de Carabobo, Valencia: 0900-0400
ME01)	ON	1040	20/10	Mundial Los Andes, Mérida
DC02)	KZ	1050	25	RNV "R. Educativa", Caracas: 1030-0430
DC02)	PO	1050	20	RNV Canal Informativo, Cabudare: 1030-0430
GU02)	LN	1060	10	R. Guárico, San Juan de los Morros: 1030-0330
TA07)	OE	1060	10	Unión R. Notícias, San Cristóbal
AP03)		1070	10	Superior 1070 Biruaca, S. Fernando de Apure
PO03)		1070	25	Contacto 1070, Ospino: 1000-0400
TA08)	PX	1070	5	R. El Sol, La Fría
ZU09)	MA	1070	10	Mundial Zulia, Maracaibo
AN11)	QJ	1080	10	R. Barcelona, Barcelona
AR05)	NR	1080	10	R. Venezuela Universal, Maracay
DC13)	SZ	1090	20	Deportes Unión R., Caracas
YA02)	PB	1090	10	R. Yaracuy "Operadora 1090 AM", S. Felipe
ZU10)	TG	1090	3	Melódica 1090, Machiques: 0900-0500
BO06)	SV	1100	10	R. Angostura, Cd.Bolívar
ME02)	OP	‡1100	10	R. Occidente, Tovar: 0900-0300
CA06)	RX	1110	10	Deportes Unión R., Valencia
SU03)	QT	1110	10	R. Venezuela Carúpano, Carúpano: 0900-0400
AP04)	SK	1120	20/10	R. Dif.del Sur, San Fernando de Apure
MO03)	XZ	1120	5	R. República "La Estación Feliz", Maturín
ZU11)	MF	1120	10	Ondas del Lago "Super Ondas", Maracaibo
AM02)	PY	‡1130	15	R. Amazonas, Puerto Ayacucho: 0830-0400
LA07)	KQ	1130	10	R. Popular, Barquisimeto: 0900-0300
DC16)	RL	1130	20/10	R. Ideal, Maiquetía
NE04)		‡1140		R. Porlamar "LV del Caribe", Porlamar 1000-0400
BO07)	QD	1150	10	Ecos del Orinoco, Cd.Bolívar
FA06)	MV	1150	10	R. Venezuela Caribe, Punto Fijo
ME03)	OK	1160	1	R. Universidad, Mérida
MI02)	RR	1160	10	R. Industrial, Guarenas
PO04)	QV	‡1170	20/10	R. Acarigua, Acarigua
VA01)	KW	1170	10	R. Bolivariana "R. 1070", Maiquetía: 1000-0300
AR06)	LQ	1180	10	Super Suave 11-80, La Victoria
MO04)	OR	1180	10	R. Maturín, Maturín: 0900-0400
ZU12)	NJ	1180	10	R. Petrolera, Cd.Ojeda: 0900-0700
BA04)	RE	‡1190	20/10	R. Barinas, Barinas
BO08)	PF	1190	20/10	Ondas de Libertad, San Felix: 0900-0300
TA09)	ZD	1190	10	R. Dif. Cult. del Táchira, San Cristóbal: 1000-0400
DC14)	OZ	1200	10	R. Tiempo, Caracas
MO05)	SF	1200	10	R. Dimensión, Caripito: 1000-0300
ZU13)	NH	‡1200	1	Ondas del Escalante, Sta Bárbara del Zulia 1000-0300
AN12)	ZT	‡1210	10	R. Anzoátegui, Barcelona
AP05)	RD	1220	10	LV de Apure, San Fernando de Apure
CA07)	VM	1220	10/5	R. Venezuela Valencia, Valencia

MW	Call	kHz	kW	Station, location, h. of tr.
ZU14)	ZO	1220	20/10	R. Aeropuerto 1220, Maracaibo
MI03)	NT	‡1230	10	R. Barlovento, Caucagua
TR03)	OH	1230	10	R. Valera, Valera: 0900-0400
BO09)	PZ	1250	20/10	Latina 12-50, Pto Ordaz: 0900-0400
ZU15)	ML	1250	1	R. Cabimas, Cabimas: 1000-0300
DC15)	RM	1260	10	BBN R, Caracas
YA03)	RY	1260	10	R. Horizonte, Nirgua: 1000-0200
DA01)	TR	‡1270	5	R. Tucupita, Tucupita: 0900-0500
DC02)		‡1270		R. Nacional, Ureña: (r. 630): 1030-0430
ME04)	OU	1270	10	R. Ondas Panamericanas, El Vigía
GU03)	QS	1280	10/5	R. Zaraza, Zaraza: 1000-0300
TR04)	OF	1280	10	R. Trujillo, Trujillo
CA08)	LF	1290	10	R. Puerto Cabello, Puerto Cabello
DC10)	KH	1300	10/8	R. Recuerdos 1300, Caracas
ZU16)	NS	1300	10	R. Reloj, Maracaibo
DC02)	SM	1310	10	RNV Canal Informativo, Barcelona: 1030-0430
DC02)	SL	1310	1	RNV Canal Informativo, Guri: 1030-0430
DC02)		1310		RNV Canal Informativo, Santa Elena: 1030-0430
TR05)	TS	1310	5	R. Andina "Sonido 13-10", Isnotú: 0900-0500
AR07)	WP	1320	10/5	R. Apolo, Turmero
LA08)	SG	1320	10	R. Colonial, El Tocuyo
DC02)		1330		RNV Canal Informativo, La Paragua: 1030-0430
GU04)	OY	1330	5	R. Los Llanos, Calabozo: 0900-0300
ZU17)	TU	‡1330	10	R. Regional, Cd. Ojeda: 0900-0500
DC17)	NE	1340	10	R. Uno, Caracas
AN13)	ZZ	1350	5	R. Eclipse, El Tigrito
FA07)	TJ	1350	5	R. Falcón, Puerto Cumarebo
MI04)	TZ	1360	10	AM Center, Charallave: 1000-0300
ZU18)	TI	1360	10	R. Internacional, Maracaibo
GU05)	OQ	1370	5	Unión R. Notícias, Valle de la Pascua: 1000-0400
ME05)	JI	1370	10	R. Continente Cumbre, Mérida: 1000-0400
PO05)	SV	1370	5	RNV Portuguesa, Acarigua: 1000-0400
BO10)	ME	1380	5	R. Revelación, Cd.Bolívar
CA09)	NG	1380	10	Ondas del Mar, Puerto Cabello: 0900-0400
ZU19)	TL	1380	10	R. Triunfo 13-80, Caja Seca: 0900-0400
DC18)	ZA	1390	20	R. Fe y Alegría, Caracas
LA09)	TT	1390	10	R. Terepaima, Cabudare
ZU20)	ZO	1390	10	R. Lumen, Maracaibo: 1030-0500
GU06)	NF	1400	1	R. Sabana, El Sombrero: 1000-0200
PO06)	ST	1410	5	R. Turén, Turén: 0900-0400
TR01)	SP	1410	10	R. Simpatía, Valera
DC21)		1420	5	R. Sintonía, Caracas
LA10)	RW	1420	10/5	R. Cardenal, Carora: 1000-0400
ZU21)	NZ	‡1420	5	R. Marabina 1420, Maracaibo
AN14)	TP	1430	25	R. Bahía, Puerto La Cruz
BO11)	TM	1430	10	R. Caicara, Caicara del Orinoco
CA10)	NB	1430	10	Llanerísima, Guacara: 0930-0400
GU07)	RF	1440	5	R. Orituco, Altagracia del Orituco
PO07)	ZI	1440	10	R. Estelar 14-40, Guanare: 0900-0400
TA10)	TY	1440	1	R. Sucesos, Táriba: 0950-0400
BO12)	XC	1450	10/5	R. Mega Visión, San Felix
VA02)	KJ	1450	10/8	R. María, Caracas
ZU22)	ZQ	1450	10	Informativa 14-50, Los Puertos de Altagracia: 0900-0500
TR07)	RJ	1460	5	R. Jardín, Boconó
CA11)	JW	‡1470	10	Union R. Cultural, Valencia
SU04)	SY	1470	10	R. Vibración, Carúpano (also r. Unión R.)
FA08)		1480		R. Cumarebo, Cumarebo
DC19)	XD	1490	10	La Dinámica, Caracas
ME06)	SQ	1490	1	R. Mérida 14-90, Mérida
ZU11)	RP	1490	10/5	R. El Sol, Maracaibo
AR08)		‡1500		R. Galaxia, San Mateo
SU05)	RZ	1500	10/5	R. 2000 AM, Cumaná: 1000-0400
CA12)		‡1510	20	Informativa "LV del Centro", Güigüe
YA04)	NP	1530	10	R. San Felipe, San Felipe
MI05)	MW	‡1550	10	R. Metropolitana, Los Teques
ZU24)	XO	1550	10/5	R. Impacto La Poderosa, Cd. Ojeda
ME07)	LZ	1560	10/5	R. Dif. Andina, Mérida
GU08)	YV	1580	10	R. Venezolana, Calabozo: 1000-0200
SU06)	TK	‡1580	10/5	Manzanares 15-80, Cumaná
ZU25)	YO	1580	10	R Celestial, San Francisco, Maracaibo
DC20)	UD	1590	10	R. Deporte, Caracas

Hrs of tr 24h unless shown Call YV–, *=inactive, (r)=repeater v=varying fq

Other Stations

CNB - CIRCUITO NACIONAL BELFORT
Quinta CNB, Av.Los Naranjos, La Florida, Caracas W: cnb.com.ve
CIRCUITO AM CENTER
CentroComercialConcresa, Nivel 1, Circuito Center, Prados del Este, Caracas 1080, Edo.Miranda ☎ +58 212 976-2013
E: feloespinosa@cantv.et.

CIRCUITO RADIAL ALFA OMEGA
Calle 25, Con Calle 67, Sector El Paraíso, frente Al Colegio La Epifanía, Maracaibo, Edo.Zulia ☎ +58 261 783-2524

CIRCUITO POPULAR
Boulevard de Sabana Grande, Torre Provincial, P10, Sabana Grande, Caracas 1050 ☎ +58 212 762 5052

CIRCUITO RADIO CARACAS RADIO
Av.Páez, Quinta RCR, El Paraíso, Caracas 1021 ☎ +58 212 481-3590

CIRCUITO RADIAL CONTINENTE
Calle La Joya, Edif.Cosmos, PH, Chacao, Caracas 1060, Edo. Miranda ☎ +58 212 267-3132 ▤ +58 212 267-1223 **W:** radiocontinente.jimdo.com **E:** produccion@radiocontinente zzn.com

CIRCUITO RADIO VENEZUELA
Av.Rómulo Gallegos, Edif.KLM, P12, Ofcs CyD, Los Palos Grandes, Caracas 1062, Edo.Miranda ☎ +58 212 286-8492 **W:** radiovenezuela.com.ve **E:** radiovenezuela@hotmail.com

CIRCUITO SATELITAL RUMBOS
Av.Francisco de Miranda, Multicentro Empresarial del Este, Edif. Libertador, Núcleo A, P7, Chacao, Caracas 1060, Edo.Miranda ☎ +58 212 263-3236 ▤ 212 263-2212 **E:** radiorumbos@ip-net.work.net

CORPORACIÓN REGIONAL BRADCASTING
Calle 74, Entre Av. 3Dy3E, Edif.Televisa, Sector La Lago, Maracaibo 4002, Edo. Zulia ☎ +58 261 792-9217

GRUPO RADIAL DE ORIENTE
Urb.Tricentenaria, Centro ComercialTricentenaria, P2, Ofcs 03y09, Barcelona 6001, Edo.Anzoátegui ☎ +58 281 277-1743 ▤ 281 277-1776 **E:** radioanzoategui@hotmail.com

RADIO CADENA MUNDIAL
Calle Nueva York, Edif.Manzanillo, P2, Las Mercedes, Caracas 1060, Edo.Miranda ☎ 212 993-9391 **W:** radiomundial.com.ve **E:** prensayvke@cantv.net

UNION RADIO
Av.Mohedano, Entre Calle Los Granados y 1ª transversal, Edif. Splendor, La Castellana, Caracas 1060, Edo.Miranda ☎ +58 212 263-5133 **W:** unionradio.net

State abbreviations: AM = Amazonas, AN = Anzoátegui, AP = Apure, AR = Aragua, BA = Barinas, BO = Bolívar, CA = Carabobo, CO = Cojedes, DA = Delta Amacuro, DC = Distrito Capital, FA = Falcón, GA = Guárico, LA = Lara, ME = Mérida, MI = Miranda, MO = Monagas, NE = Nueva Esparta, PO = Portuguesa, SU = Sucre, TA = Táchira, TR = Trujillo, VA = Vargas, YA = Yaracuy, ZU = Zulia.
N.B: These abbreviations are not officially recognized by the Venezuelan Post Office. Letters should therefore carry the full name.

Addresses and other information:
AM00) AMAZONAS
AM01) San Juan de Manapiare.
AAN00) ANZOÁTEGUI
AN01) Av Hospital cruce con Calle Freites, Edif.Radio Centro, Cantura 6007 – **AN02)** Av 5 de Julio, Edif Los Angeles, Sotanos 1y2, Puerto La Cruz 6023. **W:** unionradio.net – **AN03)** Calle Cajigal cruce con Av.Nueva Esparta N° 39, Edif.Radio City, planta baja, Anaco 6003 – **AN04)** Calle Arismendi N° 20, Edif.Radio Puerto La Cruz, PB, Puerto La Cruz 6023 – **AN06)** Av.Municipal,Torre Porteñas, Mezzanina, Ofc 2-4, Puerto La Cruz 6023 – **AN07)** Calle Guayana, Centro Comercial Bleu Hill, P1, Local 4, El Tigre 6034 – **AN08)** Av.Simon Rodríguez con 8va Calle Norte, Complejo Cultural Simón Rodríguez, El Tigre 6034 **W:** feyalegria.org – **AN09)** Av.Intercomunal "Andrés Bello", Centro Comercial Géminis, P3, Local 9, Barcelona 6001 – **AN10)** Av Francisco de Miranda N° 196, Al lado del Banco Provincial, El Tigre 6034 – **AN11)** Av Miranda cruce con Av.San Carlos, Edif.Radio Barcelona, P2, Barcelona 6001 – **AN12)** Urb Tricentenaria, Centro Comercial Tricente-naria, P2, Ofc 3y9, Barcelona 6001 – **AN13)** Av.Intercomunal El Tigre El Tigrito, Detrás de Elite Motors, Casa Amarilla,El Tigrito 6035 – **AN14)** Av Municipal, Torre Pelicano, P8, Apto 8-4, Puerto La Cruz 6023.
AP00) APURE
AP01) Carr Nacional, Vía Elorza La Arenosa, Edif. Fe y Alegría, Guasdualito 5063. **W:** feyalegria.org – **AP02)** Calle 9 con Cra 4, Municipio Rómulo Gallegos, Elorza 7007 – **AP03)** Av.Fuerzas Armadas, Edif.Superior, P1, San Fernando de Apure 7001 0930-0400 – **AP04)** Calle Carlos Rodríguez Rincones, Gobernación del Estado Apure, San Fernando de Apure 7001 – **AP05)** Av Miranda, Edif.Don António Cestari, San Fernando de Apure 7001.
AR00) ARAGUA
AR01) Calle Coromoto, Urb.Calicanto, Torre Capitolio, P9, Ofc.B-9, Urb. Calicanto, Maracay 2101 **W:** unionradio.net – **AR02)** Calle Boyacá,

Edif Centro, P9, Ofc 1, Maracay 2101 – **AR03)** Av Miranda Oeste N° 149, Entre Carabobo y Pinhincha, Edif.Canaobre, PH, Maracay 2101 **W:** radiocontinente.jimdo.com – **AR04)** Calle Sucre, Edificio Comercial y Profesional Sucre, Piso 2, Oficina #3, Cagua 2122 **W:** radioaragua.com – **AR05)** Urb.Calicanto, Calle Coromoto, Norte 6, Detrás de la Maestranza Cesar Girón, Maracay 2101 **W:** radiovenezuela.com.ve – **AR06)** Edif Veliz, Calle Aldao, frente a la Plaza Rivas, La Victoria 2126 – **AR07)** Av.Bermúdez, Torre Apolo, PB, entre Mariño y Bolívar, Turmero 2115 – **AR08)** San Mateo – **AR09)** Calle Páez, N° 138, Detrás del Teatro de La Opera, Maracay 2126
BA00) BARINAS
BA01) Cra 3 N° 7-39, entre Calles 7 y 8, Santa Bárbara de Barinas 5210 – **BA02)** Av Sucre Quinta Claret N° 17-46, Barinas 5201 – **BA03)** Av Marqués del Pumar, Edif.Radio Continental, Barinas 5201 – **BA04)** Av. 23 de Enero, Centro Comercial Central Plaza, Local 27, Barinas 5201 **W:** radiovenezuela.com.ve
BO00) BOLÍVAR
BO01) Av.Guasipati, Edif Piarde, PH, Puerto Ordaz 8015 – **BO02)** Urb. Altavista Calle Caura, Edif Los Bancos, P4, Puerto Ordaz 8015 – **BO03)** Av.Raúl Leoni, Edif.Antonelli, PB, Upatá 8026 – **BO04)** Av.Venezuela, Centro Comercial Venezuela, Local 14-15, P1, Urb Villa Colombia, Puerto Ordaz 8015 **W:** radiovenezuela.com.ve – **BO05)** Calle Dalla Costa, Alto N° 5, Cd Bolívar 8001 - 0900-0400 **W:** radiovenezuela.com.ve – **BO06)** Final Paseo Heres, Edif.Tovar, P2, Cd Bolívar 8001 – **BO07)** Paseo Meneses, Centro Comercial Meneses, PA, Locales 11 y 12, Cd Bolívar 8001 – **BO08)** Calle México, Parcela El Roble, Detrás de la Estación de Servicio Volfo, Sector La Antena, San Félix 8024 – **BO09)** Calle El Tocuyo, Centro Comercial Plaza, P2, Pto Ordaz 8015 – **BO10)** Av 19 de Abril, Edif La Disinca, P.B., Cd Bolívar 8001 – **BO11)** Calle Constitución N° 78, Caicara del Orinocco 7107 – **BO12)** Av.Della Costa, Edif.Flor Motors, PB, San Felix 8024.

CA00) CARABOBO
CA01) Av.Girardot con Calle Montes de Oca, Edif.Normal, Piso PH, Valencia 2001 – **CA02)** Av Bolívar Norte, Edif Felpo, P7, Ofc 3-3, Valencia 2001 – **CA03)** Calle Girardot, Entre Urdaneta y Boyacá N° 98-28, Valencia 2001 **W:** www.america890.net – **CA04)** Carr. Panamericana, Edif.Radio Mil, Morón – **CA05)** Av Rosarito, Torre Trebol, P1, Ofc 13, Urb Lomas del Este, Valencia 2001 – **CA06)** Av.Bolívar Norte, Torre Banavén, P12, Ofc.12-9, Valencia 2001 **W:** deportesunionradio.net – **CA07)** Av.Rosario, Edif.El Parque, PB Local 2, Urb.Lomas del Este, Valencia 2001 **W:** radiovenezuela.com.ve – **CA08)** Av.Marina, Edif.Diproca, PB, Local 3, Puerto Cabello 2024. **W:** radiopuertocabello.com – **CA09)** Av Bolívar, Edif Sabatino, P1, Urb.Rancho Grande, Puerto Cabello 2024 – **CA10)** Final de la Calle Jacinto con Calles Ricaurte y Girardot, Edif.Radio Satélite, Guacara 2015 – **CA11)** Av.Montes de Oca, Edif.Don Pelayo, P12, Valencia 2001 **W:** unionradio.net/cultural - **FM:** 99.1MHz – **CA12)** Av Miranda,Edif Padre Cecilio Ávila, PH, Güigüe 2010.
CO00) COJEDES
CO01) Av.Sucre, Edif.General Manuel Manrique, P3, Local 46, San Carlos 2201 - 0955-0400 **W:** unionradio.net
DA00) DELTA AMACURO
DA01) Calle Petión cruse con Calle La Paz, Tucupita 6401
DC00) DISTRITO CAPITAL
DC01) Calle Nueva York Cruce con Av.Rio de Janeiro, Edif YVKE Mundial, P1, Las Mercedes, Caracas 1060, Edo.Miranda **W:** radiomundial.com.ve – **DC02)** Final Calle Las Marías, Edif. Radio Nacional de Venezuela, entre Chapellín y Country Club, La Frorida, Caracas 1050, Edo. Miranda **W:** rnv.gov.ve – **DC03)** Av.Francisco de Miranda, Multicentro Empresarial del Este, Edif.Libertador, P7, Núcleo A Chacao, Caracas 1060, Edo Miranda – **DC04)** Calle La Joya, Edif Cosmos PH, Chacao, Caracas 1060, Edo Miranda **W:** radiocontinente.jimdo.com – **DC05)** Av.Francisco de Miranda, Centro Comercial Los Ruices, P3, Los Ruices, Caracas 1071, Edo Miranda – **DC06)** Av José A Paez, Quinta RCR, El Paraiso, Caracas 1021, Distrito Capital – **DC07)** Av.Rómulo Gallegos, Edif.KLM, P12, Ofc CyD, Los Palos Grandes, Caracas 1062, Edo Miranda. **W:** radiovenezuela.com.ve – **DC08)** Av Santiago de Chile, Quinta Radio Sensación, Los Caobos, Caracas 1050 – **DC10)** Centro Comercial Concresa, Nivel 1, Circuito Center, Prados del Este, Caracas 1080, Edo.Miranda. **W:** fmcenter.com.ve/amcenter.aspx – **DC11)** Edif Provincial, Boulevard de Sabana Grande (frente al Gran Café)Caracas 1050, Distrito Capital – **DC12)** Puente Nuevo a Puerto Escondido, Edif.Torre del Oeste, P1, El Silencio, Caracas 1010, Distrito Capital (or: Ap.3674, Caracas 1010-A) – **DC13)** Av.Mohedano, Entre Calle Los Granados y 1ª transversal, Edif.Splendor, La Castellana, Caracas 1060, Edo.Miranda **W:** unionradio.net – **DC14)** Av Los Mangos N° 49, Qta. Radio Tiempo, La Florida, Caracas 1050-A, Edo.Miranda **W:** radiotiempo.com.ve – **DC15)** Av Los Mangos con Av.Valencia Parpacén, Qta. Marisabel (BBN), La Florida, Caracas 1050, Edo.Miranda **W:** bbnradio.org/wcm4/spanish/Radio/Emisoras/tabid/646/StationID/236/Default.

aspx – **DC16)** Centro Comercial Uslar, P15, Ofc 152, Montalbán, Caracas 1021, Distrito Capital **W:** radioideal.com.ve – **DC17)** Edif Mundial, Av Tamanaco, El Rosal, Caracas 1060. **W:** radiouno.com.ve – **DC18)** Calle 3B, Edif.C-207, P2, (detrás del McDonald's), La Urbina, Caracas 1070, Edo.Miranda **W:** feyalegria.org – **DC19)** Av.Boulevard Brasil N° 74, de Santa Ana a Providencia La Pastora, Caracas 1010, Distrito Capital. **W:** radiodinamica.com – **DC20)** Av Circunvalación del Sol, Centro Profesional Sta Paula, Torre A, P5 Ofc 51, Caracas 1061, Edo.Miranda. **W:** radiodeporte.com – **DC21)** Calle La Joya, Torre Cosmos, P9, Ofc 9A, Chacao, Caracas 1060, Edo.Miranda (or: Centro Comercial El Pichacho, P8, San António de los Altos 1204). **W:** radiosintonia1420.com.ve

FA00) FALCÓN
FA01) Calle Bolívar, Edif.Don Cosme, P2, Coro 4101 – **FA02)** Avenida Manaure esquina Maparari, Edificio Pepelupe, Coro 4101. **W:** radio-coro.com – **FA03)** Calle Palmasola cruce Con Calle Federación, Edif. Arquidiocesano, Coro 4101 **W:** radioguadalupana.com – **FA04)** Urb Los Caciques, Calle Falcón, Qta.Paraguaná, Punto Fijo 4102 – **FA05)** Calle Talavera, entre Calles Comercio y Arismendi, Edif.Radio Punto Fijo, Punto Fijo 4102 – **FA06)** Av.Ecuador, Entre Calles Comercio y Arismendi, Punto Fijo 4102 – **FA07)** Av.Bolívar, Edif.Colonial Planta Baja, Urb.Alta Vista, Puerto Cumarebo 4167 – **FA08)** Centro Ciudad Comercial Tamanaco (CCCT), Torre B, P7, Ofc 704, Chuao, Caracas 1060, Edo Miranda

GU00) GUÁRICO
GU01) Av RómuloGallegos, Edif.Flor de Pascua, Loc 2, Valle de la Pascua 2307. **W:** enlace860am.tk – **GU02)** Av Principal La Moreras, Edif.Ghersy N° 28, San Juan de los Morros 2301 – **GU03)** Calle Concordia, Qta Puerto Arturo N° 35, Zaraza 2332 – **GU04)** Cra 12, Altos del Teatro Paez, Frente a La Bomba, Calabozo 2312 – **GU05)** Av 5 de Julio N° 20, Valle de la Pascua 2307 **W:** unionradio.net – **GU06)** Calle Alegría, Qta.Galia, El Sombrero 2319 – **GU07)** Calle Andrés Eloy Blanco, Altagracia de Orituco 2320 – **GU08)** Cra 12, Entre Calles 3 y 4 N° 3-57, Calabozo 2312

LA00) LARA
LA01) Av Venezuela con Calles 13 y 14, Edif.Radio Cristal, Barquisimeto 3001 – **LA02)** Calle Sucre Entre Cras 7 y 8, La Casita, Carora 3040 - **FM:** 100.5MHz – **LA03)** Calle 4 con Cra 3, Qta.Técnica, Urb.del Este, Barquisimeto 3002 – **LA04)** Av Venezuela con Calles 32 y 33, Edif.Don Martín, P4, Apto 4-A, Barquisimeto 3001 – **LA05)** Av.Pedro León Torres, Centro Comercial Venrol, locales 29 y 30, Barquisimeto 3001. **W:** radiominuto.net – **LA06)** Av Vargas, Cra 16, Edif Tricolor, Barquisimeto 3001 **W:** radiovenezuela.com.ve – **LA07)** Calle 29, Entre Calles 18 y 19, Casa N° 18-74, Barquisimeto 3001 – **LA08)** Calle 10 cruce con Calle 9, Casa S/N, El Tocuyo 3018 – **LA09)** Av.Libertador, altos de la Farmacia San Rafael, Cabudare 3023 – **LA10)** Av Bolívar, Edif Guillermo, Locales 2 y 3, Carora 3040 – **LA11)** Av Los Leones, Centro Empresarial Caracas, P5, Ofc 5-2, Barquisimeto 3002 **W:** unionradio.net

ME00) MÉRIDA
ME01) Calle 44 N° 3-57, Diagonal al Colegio de Médicos, Mérida 5101 – **ME02)** Cra 4 N° 6-46, Frente a La Plaza Bolívar, Tovar 5143 – **ME03)** Av Gonzalo Pico, Bajando por La Facultad de Ingeniería, Qta. Radio Universidad, Mérida 5101 – **ME04)** Av Bolívar, Esquina Calle 11, N° 10-87, El Vigía 5145 – **ME05)** Av.Andrés Bello, Centro Comercial Las Tapias, P3, Ofc.40-41, Mérida 5101 **W:** radiocontinente.jimdo. ve – **ME06)** Av 3, Esquina con Calle 22, Mérida 5101 – **ME07)** Av Urdaneta, Calle La Huaca, PH, Mérida 5101

MI00) MIRANDA
MI01) Calle Urdaneta N° 29, Edif Radio Valles del Tuy, P1, Ocumare del Tuy 1209 – **MI02)** Edif. Electricidad De Caracas, Semi Sotano, Frente a La Plaza Bolívar, Guarenas 1220 – **MI03)** Calle Real Pantoja, al lado del Estadium De Barlovento, Caucagua 1246 – **MI04)** Final Av.Tosta Gracía, Resd.Boal, Mezz.2, Charallave 1200 **W:** fmcenter.com.ve/amcenter. aspx – **MI05)** Calle Rivas, Edif Centro Empresarial, Torre Chocolate, P7, Ofc.7-A y 7-B, Los Teques 1201.

MO00) MONAGAS
MO01) Cra 5 N° 33, Antigua Calle Boyacá, Maturín 6201 – **MO02)** Av Bolívar,Edif.Radio Monagas, P1, Maturín 6201 - **FM:** 93.5MHz – **MO03)** Calle Monagas, Edif Isotú, PB, Maturín 6201 – **MO04)** Calle Sucre, Edif.Radio Maturín, PB, Maturín 6201 – **MO05)** Av Bolívar, Edif.Radio Dimensión, PB, Caripito 6211

NE00) NUEVA ESPARTA
NE01) Calle La Marina, Edif.Sta Rita, Nivel 3, Porlamar 6301 **W:** radiovenezuela.com.ve – **NE02)** Av Miranda, Edif.Best, P2, Porlamar 6301 – **NE03)** Calle Girardot, Urb.Cocheima, Edif Doña Teresa, P3, La Asunción 6311 – **NE04)** Av 4 de Mayo, Centro Comercial Real, Local 2, Porlamar 6301

PO00) PORTUGUESA
PO01) Av 36-A, cruce con Av.Las Lagrimas, Qta. Mundial, frente al Parque Mario Nerio, Acarigua 3301. **W:** radiovenezuela.com. ve – **PO02)** Cra 9, Esq Calle 15, Edif D'Zonno, P3, Apto 8, Guanare

3310 – **PO03)** Intercepción de la Autopista José António Páez con Carr.Nacional, Ospino 3319 – **PO04)** Av 35 con Calle 29, Edif.Radio Acarigua, Acarigua 3301 – **PO05)** Av. 28 entre calles 26 y 27 del sector Campo Lindo del Municipio Páez, Acarigua – **PO06)** Av Peñalver con Calle 31, Edif.Los Andes, PB, Turén 3308 – **PO07)** Av Los Próceres, Urb. Francisco de Miranda, Edif.Radial, Guanare 3310

SU00) SUCRE
SU01) Av.Perimetral, Edif.Libertad, P2, Cumaná 6101 – **SU02)** Av.Gran Mariscal Sucre N° 30, Cumaná 6101 **W:** circuitoradiocontinente. com – **SU03)** Calle Independencia con Calle Páez, Multinacional, P5, Radio Venezuela, Carúpano 6124 **W:** radiovenezuela.com.ve – **SU04)** Av Independencia 141, Edif Plaza, PB, Carúpano 6124 **W:** unionradio. net – **SU05)** Av Santa Rosa 18, Sector La Copita, frente a la Iglesia Santa Rosa de Lima, Cumaná 6101 **W:** radio2000.com.ve – **SU06)** Av Miranda, Qta.Tere, Cumaná 6101.

TA00) TÁCHIRA
TA01) Av 19 N° 13-61, Rubio 5030 - 1000-0400 – **TA02)** Av.1 de Mayo (Cra 3), Edif.Centro Civico, P7, San Antonio del Táchira 5007 – **TA03)** Calle 9 N° 8-16, San Cristóbal 5001 **W:** ecosdeltorbes.net – **TA04)** Av Fco de Cáceres 9-88, Qta Delia Mercedes, La Grita 5022 – **TA05)** Av Las Lomas, Edif.Primo Centro, Locales 3-12 y 3-13, San Cristóbal 5001 – **TA06)** Av 19 de Abril, Qta.Circuito Lider, San Cristóbal 5001 – **TA07)** Pasaje Acueducto N° 24-60, Barrio Obrero, San Cristóbal 5001 **W:** unionradio.net – **TA08)** Calle 2, Edif Illinois, P2, La Fria 5020 – **TA09)** Av 19 de Abril con Av 8, La Concordia, San Cristóbal 5001 – **TA10)** Cra 4 N° 1-35, Táriba 5017 – **TA11)** Cra 9 cruce con Calle 9, Edif.El Ciclón, P4, San Cristóbal 5001.

TR00) TRUJILLO
TR01) Av 11, entre Calles 12y13 N° 12-56, Valera 3101 – 1045-0400 **W:** radiosimpatia.com.ve – **TR02)** Av Bolívar con Calle 15, Edif.Grasso, P1, Valera 3101 – **TR03)** Av 10 entre Calles 9y10, Edif.Radio Valera, Local 9-31, Valera 3101 – **TR04)** Calle Independencia N° 10-11, Trujillo 3102 – **TR05)** Calle Iglesia, José Gregorio Hernández, Isnotu 3109 – **TR07)** CalleBolívar, Plaza la Alameda, Edif.Radio Jardín, Boconó 3103.

VA00) VARGAS
VA01) Av Soublette, Edif Las Américas B, P16, Maiquetía 1161 – **VA02)** 3era Norte Av Guaicaipuro, Quinta Mirna, Caracas **W:** radi-omaria.org.ve

YA00) YARACUY
YA01) Av 10, Entre Calles 7y8, Edif.Alegría, Chivacoa 3202 – **YA02)** Prolongación 5ta Av.Urb.Andrés Eloy Blanco, Sector la Aduana, San Felipe 3201 – **YA03)** Urb Las Tunitas, Av 4, entre Calles 4 y 5, Nirgua 3205 – **YA04)** Av.Cartagena, entre Calles 19 y 20, Edif.Radio San Felipe, San Felipe 3201.

ZU00) ZULIA
ZU01) Calle Central, Edif.Radio Perijá, P2, La Villa del Rosario 4047 – **ZU02)** Calle 64 Esq.Av 3e, Edif.La Voz de la Fe, Sector Don Bosco, Maracaibo 4002 (or: P.O.Box 459, Maracaibo 4002-A) – **ZU03)** Av El Muelle N° 1, Edif.Radio Libertad, frente a la Plaza Bolívar, Cabimas 4013 – **ZU04)** Av 11 N° 87-46, Edif 95.5, PB, Sector Veritas, Maracaibo 4002 – **ZU05)** Av 25 con Calle Paraíso N° 24-88, Maracaibo 4005 – **ZU06)** Av 3-E N° 63-50, Sector Don Bosco, Maracaibo 4002 **W:** feyalegria.org – **ZU07)** Calle 67 cruce con Av 27, detrás del Colegio La Epifanía, Sector Santa María, Maracaibo 4005 **W:** radiovenezuela.com. ve – **ZU08)** Av Edif.Radio Calendario, Sector Grano de Oro, frente al Stadium Alejandro Borges, Maracaibo 4005. **W:** radiocontinente.jimdo. ve – **ZU09)** Edif Radio Zulia, Av 23 con Calle 79 1 de Mayo,Maracaibo 4005 – **ZU10)** Av Gral Trias, Machiques 4021, Distrito Perijá – **ZU11)** Calle 74, Entre Av 3Dy3E, Edif.Televisa, Sector La Lago, Maracaibo 4002 – **ZU12)** Calle Manrique, Edif.Raquel, PB, Cd.Ojeda 4019 – **ZU13)** Av 5 N° 2-21, Sta Bárbara del Zulia 5148 – **ZU14)** Av 3H, Edif.Plaza, Local 2, Sierra Maestra, Maracaibo 4008 – **ZU15)** Calle 74, Entre Av 3Dy3E, Edif Televisa, Sector La Lago, Maracaibo 4002 (or: Av Radio Bello, Edif Ambrosio, Cabimas 4013) (Office in Maracaibo, tx site Cabimas) – **ZU16)** Av 8 Esq Calle 73, N° 72-75, Edif Radiolandia, Sector Santa Rita, Maracaibo 4020 – **ZU17)** Av.Intercomunal Cabimas-Cd.Ojeda, con Calle La Planta, Cd.Ojeda 4019 – **ZU18)** Calle 27 con Av.12 N° 12-10, Edif.Camsa, Maracaibo 4002 (or: Calle Bello Lago, Santa Cruz de Mara 4045) (Office in Maracaibo, tx site Santa Cruz de Mara) – **ZU19)** Av El Terminal, Centro Comercial Nuevo Mundo, Local 2, Caja Seca 3156 – **ZU20)** Iglesia de María en Pentecostés, Urb.San Jacinto, primera entrada, vía El Moján, Maracaibo 4005 – **ZU21)** Edif. R. Marabina, Av 25 con Calle 67 N° 24-88, Sector Paraiso, Maracaibo 4002 – **ZU22)** Sector La Salina, Los Puertos de Altagracia 4036 – **ZU24)** Cra N Con Av.51, Zona Industrial, Cd.Ojeda 4019 – **ZU25)** Calle 13, Edif.La Linda, Sector Sierra Maestra, Municipio San Francisco, Maracaibo 4008.

FM in Caracas (MHz): 88.1 Imagen – 88.9 Romántica – 89.7 X FM – 90.3 Unión Noti – 91.1 Nacional (classical) – 91.9 Candela Pura Estrella – 92.9 Tu FM – 93.5 Melodía Stereo – 94.1 Hot 94 – 94.9 Clásicos FM – 95.5 Jazz – 96.3 Alba Ciudad – 96.9 X FM – 97.7 Em.Cultural – 98.5 La Radio del Sur – 99.1 La Nueva Mágica – 99.9

Éxitos – 100.7 Ateneo – 101.5 Kys – 101.9 Tiuna – 102.3 AN Radio, La Voz de la Asamblea Nacional –.7 Original –103.3 Radiorama Stereo – 103.9 R. Activa/Canal Juvenil (RNV) – 104.5 Rumbera – 105.3 Planeta – 105.9 Sonera – 106.5 Fiesta 106 – 106.9 Playa 107 – 107.3 La Mega Estación107 – 107.9 Onda

VIETNAM

L.T: UTC +7h — **Pop:** 91 million — **Pr.L:** Vietnamese, ethnic — **E.C:** 50Hz, 220V — **ITU:** VTN

DÀI TIẾNG NÓI VIỆT NAM
(VOV, RADIO THE VOICE OF VIETNAM) (Gov.)
✉ 58 Quan Su Str, Hanoi ☎ +84 (4) 8255694 📠 +84 4 8265875
W: vov.vn **E:** qhqt.vov@hn.vnn.vn
LP: DG: Vu Van Hien. Deputy DG (Int. Rel): Hoang Minh Nguyet. Deputy DG (Tech): Doan Viet Trung.

MW	kHz	Net	kW	Station, location, h of tr
1)	549	2	200	Hung Yen, (Site: My Hao): 2145-1700
1)	558	2	100	Ho Chi Minh C., Quan Tre: 2145-1700
2)	576	2,P	50	Khanh Hoa, Nha Trang: 2145-1700
1)	594	1	50	Danang, (Site: An Hai): 2145-1700
3)	610	H	200	Ho Chi Minh City, Tang Nhon Phu: 2100-1700
1)	630	1	200	Quang Binh, Dong Hoi: 2145-1700
1)	648	1	50	Binh Dinh, Quy Nhon, (Site: An Nhon): 2145-1700
1)	657	1	100	Ho Chi Minh C., Quan Tre: 2145-1700
1)	666	1	50	Khanh Hoa, Nha Trang: 2145-1700
1)	675	1	500	Hung Yen, (Site: My Hao): 2145-1700
1)	702	2,Q,D	50	Danang, (Site: An Hai): 2145-1700
1)	711	1	500	Can Tho, Thoi Long: 2145-1700
5)	±720	P	10	Dong Nai: 2200-1500 (Site: Quan Tre, Ho Chi Minh C)
1)	729	2	200	Quang Binh, Dong Hoi: 2145-1700
6)	740	2,P	50	Binh Dinh, Quy Nhon, (Site: An Nhon): 2145-1700
1)	‡±747	1,4	100	Ho Chi Minh C., Quan Tre: 2145-1330
7)	756	P	10	Long An, Tan An: 2200-1100†
1)	783	2	500	Can Tho, Thoi Long: 2145-1700
1)	819	4	20	Dac Lac, Buon Ma Thuot: 2200-1600†
8)	828	P	50	Son La: 2200-1400†
9)	837	P	10	Can Tho: 2200-1200†
10)	846	P	10	Thanh Hoa: 0400-1600†
1)	873	1,3,4	500	Can Tho, Thoi Long: 2155-1700
11)	‡891	1,P	10	Lam Dong, Da Lat: 2200-1600†
12)	±900	P	10	Ha Tinh: 2200-1200†
13)	900	1,P	10	Kon Tum: 2200-1600†
14)	‡909	P	10	Ca Mau: 2200-1330†
15)	972	1,P	10	Quang Ngai: 2155-1600†
16)	‡1035	P	10	Hoa Binh: 2215-1100†
17)	1089	P	10	Kien Giang, Rach Gia: 2200-1200†
18)	1089	P	10	Cao Bang
19)	1098	1,P	10	Binh Thuan (Phan Thiet): 2200-1100†
20)	1098	P	10	Thua Thien Hue, Hue: 2145-1145/1310†
21)	1125	P	5	Tay Ninh: 2200-1200†
22)	1170	P	10	An Giang, Long Xuyen: 2200-1330†
1)	1242	E	2000	Can Tho, Thoi Long: 1300-1600 +

‡) r. inactive ±) variable fq. †) Split schedule, see Regional stns below for details. +) Recently r. on reduced power.

SW	kHz	Net	kW	Location, h. of tr
1)	5925	2	50	Xuan Mai: 2145-1700
1)	5975	1	50	Hanoi: 2145-1700
1)	6020	4	20	Buon Ma Thuot: 2200-1600
1)	6165	4	50	Xuan Mai: 2200-2300, 2330-2400, 1130-1400
1)	7210	1	20	Buon Ma Thuot: 2145-1700
1)	7435	1	100	Son Tay: 24h+
1)	9530	1	50	Xuan Mai: 2145-1700
1)	9635	1	100	Son Tay: 24h+
1)	9850	4	50	Xuan Mai: 0400-0600
1)	‡9875	2	50	Hanoi: 0150v-1000
1)	11720	1	100	Son Tay: 24h+

+) transmission for Gulf of Tonkin area.
SW Stations: Hanoi 50kW (Me Tri, G.C: 105.47E 21.01N). Xuan Mai (also known as CK2) 50kW (GC: 105.36E 20.53N). Buon Ma Thuot 2x20kW (G.C: 108.03E 12.41N). Son Tay (see Int Radio section)
Netw.: 1/2/3: Voice of Vietnam 1st/2nd/3rd national prgr – **4:** Voice of Vietnam minorities network – **D:** Radio & TV Danang – **E:** Voice of Vietnam external sces – **H:** Voice of the People of Ho Chi Minh City – **P:** Provincial sce – **Q:** Radio & TV Quang Nam (Hoi An, Quang Nam Province).
FM: Most services are also carried by numerous FM stns. Details for Hanoi and Ho Chi Minh City are shown here, others in the address section where known. All FM powers shown are TRP.

FM(MHz) Local kW VOV1 kW VOV2 kW VOV3 kW VOV5 kW

		Local	kW	VOV1	kW	VOV2	kW	VOV3	kW	VOV5	kW
Hanoi		90.0	10	100.0m	10	96.5t	10	102.7t	20	105.5m	5

FM(MHz) Local kW VOV1 kW VOV2 kW VOV3 kW VOV5 kW

		Local	kW	VOV1	kW	VOV2	kW	VOV3	kW	VOV5	kW
Hanoi		96.0h	2								
HCMC		99.9	20	94.0d	10	-		104.5q	10	105.7q	10
HCMC		95.6	20								

Hanoi Radio & TV Station: ✉ 5 Huynh Thuc Khang, Dong Da District, Hanoi. d) Dong Hung Thuan, Hoc Mon. h) 2nd prgr, tx in Ha Dong. m) Me Tri. q) Quan Tre. t) Tam Dao in Vinh Phuc province.

Prgrs. from Hanoi
VOV1, news & current affairs: 2145-1700. **FM:** Hanoi 100.0MHz, Ho Chi Minh C. 94.0MHz, and also relayed in part by many regional sts. **N:** 2205, 2300, 0100, 0300, 0500, Mon-Sat 0630, 0700, Mon-Sat 0730, 0800, Mon-Sat 1000, 1100, 1230, MF 1330, 1430. SW freqs marked + relay VOV3 1700-2145.
VOV2, economic, social, cultural & education prgrs: 2145-1700. **FM:** Hanoi 96.5MHz 10kW, Son La (Deo Pha Din) 93.5MHz 20kW, Phu Yen 102.7MHz 5kW, Buon Ma Thuot 102.7MHz 5kW. **LL:** English 0600, French 0615, Chinese/Japanese/Vietnamese through English 0630 (repeated Mon-Sat 1600-1645).
VOV3, news & music prgrs: 24h on FM (freqs in MHz) Hanoi 102.7 20kW, Quang Binh 100.0 MHz 5kW, Vinh 98.0 0.5kW, Hue 106.1MHz 10kW, Danang (Ba Na) 102.5MHz 10kW, Qui Nhon 103.1 10kW, Phu Yen (Tuy Hoa) 96.0 2.5kW, Dac Nong (Gia Nghia) 96.6 5kW, Bing Thuan (Phan Thiet) 102.0MHz 5kW, Ho Chi Minh C. 104.5MHz 10kW, Tay Ninh 10.0MHz 20kW, An Giang (Nui Cam) 91.5MHz 20kW. Inc. **Xone FM:** music prgrs for young people, MF 2300-0200, 0900-1600, SS 0600-1600.
VOV4, prgrs for ethnic minorities: Bana, Ede, Giarai, Hmong, K'Hor (Koho), Sedang, Thai, M'Nong: 2200-1600 on 819kHz, 6020kHz, Dac Lac (Buon Ma Thuot) 100.0MHz 5kW & Dac Nong (Gia Nghia) 101.5MHz 5kW for Central Highlands. **Dao, H'Mong (Ho Mong), Thai:** 2150-2300, 0000-0030, 1145-1400 on 6165kHz, 0400-0530 on 9850kHz for Northern Vietnam, also in whole or in part on Cao Bang (Phan Thanh) 97.0MHz 10kW, Dien Bien Phu 98.0MHz 2kW, Ha Giang (Quan Ba) 103.2MHz 10kW, Lai Chau (Muong Te) 101.5MHz 2kW, Lang Son (Mau Son) 101.0MHz 10kW, Son La (Deo Pha Din) 104.3MHz 10kW (FM freqs relay VOV1 or provincial stns at other times). **Co Tu:** 2330-2400, 0420-0450, 1230-1300 on Danang (Ba Na) 100.0MHz 10kW (freq. relays VOV1 at other times). **Cham, Khmer (Kho Me), Vietnamese:** 2155-1330 on 873kHz for the Mekong Delta (inc. relays of VOV1).
VOV5, prgrs for foreigners: Hanoi 105.5MHz, Ho Chi Minh City 105.7MHz. **Cambodian:** 0800-0830. **Chinese:** 0400-0430, 1100-1130. **English:** 0030-0130, 0500-0600, 0900-1030, 1200-1300, 1400-1500, 1600-1730. **French:** 0130-0230, 0600-0700, 1300-1330. **German:** 0000-0030 **Indonesian:** 0730-0800. **Japanese:** 0430-0500, 1330-1400. **Lao:** 0700-0730. **Russian:** 0230-0300, 0830-0900. **Spanish:** 1030-1100. **Thai:** 1130-1200. **Vietnamese:** 0300-0400, 1500-1600.
VOV Traffic Channel (VOV Giao Thong): 2230-1800. **FM:** Hanoi (Me Tri) 91.0MHz 5kW, Ho Chi Minh C. (Quan Tre)91.0MHz 5kW.
Ann: "Dây là Tiếng Nói Việt Nam, phát thanh từ Hà Nội, thu dô nước Công Hòa Xá Hôi Chu Nghia Việt Nam"". Khmer: "Thini Vithayu Samlang Vietnam".

Regional stations
General remarks: Schedules shown are for provincial services on MW. Stns may also relay VOV1, especially at 2300-2330, 0500-0545/0600 and 1100-1130/1145 if they are on air at those times, but relays of VOV as a rule are not included in the schedules below. Several hundred FM stns are operated by local governmnts of county-level administrative divisions (huyen or counties, thi xa or county-level towns, or quan or urban districts). These generally transmit with powers in the 50-500W range and with limited hours, and in many cases relay the provincial stn or Hanoi at times.
Ann: Provincial sces usually identify as "Radio & TV (name of province)", in Vietnamese: "Dài Phàt Thanh Truyên Hình (name)".

Addresses and other information:
1) National freqs. See above for details– **2)** 70 Tran Phu, Nha Trang. 2230-2200, 0430-0500, 1030-1100 - **FM:** 103.3MHz 0.1kW/106.5MHz 2kW + relays– **3)** 3 Nguyen Dinh Chieu, Dist. 1, Ho Chi Minh City. H: 2100-1700 in Vietnamese/Khmer - **FM:** 95.6/99.9MHz. Districts: Hoc Mon 93.0MHz, Nha Be 96.5MHz, Binh Chanh 103.4MHz, Can Gio 105.0MHz, Cu Chi 106.5MHz. – **4)** Q: Tran Phu Road, Tan Thanh Ward, Tam Ky Town, Quang Nam: 2220-2245, 0400-0430, 1145-1215. - **FM:** 97.6MHz 2kW. **D:** 33 Le Loi, Hai Chau Ward, Da Nang. 2245-2300, 0430-0445, 1215-1315(SS 1400) - **FM:** 96.3MHz 5kW – **5)** Dong Khoi Road, Tam Hoa, Bien Hoa, Dong Nai - **FM:** 97.5MHz 10kW. – **6)** 23 Mai Xuan Thuong, Quy Nhon City. 2230-2300, 0430-0500, 1145-1230. - **FM:** 97.0MHz 5kW, (Huai Nhon)99.9MHz 1kW – **7)** 125 National Road 1A, Ward 4, Tan An City. 2200-0030(Sat 0100, Sun 0315), 0430-0530, 1000-1110/1210 - **FM:** 96.9MHz 3kW – **8)** Group 12, Quyet Thang Ward, Son

La Town. 2200-2400, 0400-0600, 1200-1400 in Vietnamese/Hmong-
FM: 96.0MHz 2kW + relays– **9)** 213 30 Thang 4 St, Can Tho City.
2200-2400, 0400-0600, 0900-1100 - **FM:** 97.3MHz 5kW – **10)** 8 Hac
Thanh St, Thanh Hoa City. 2200-2300, 0250-0600, 0930-1045 –**11)** 10
Tran Hung Dao, Da Lat City, Lam Dong Province. 2330-0030, 0400-0630,
0900-1100, 1230-1330 in Vietnamese/Koho – **FM:** 97.0MHz 2kW +
relays – **12)** 28 Phan Dinh Phung, Ha Tinh Town. 2200-2330, 0400-0600,
1000-1200 - **FM:** 93.6MHz 0.05kW – **13)** 258A Phan Dinh Phung St, Kon
Tum. 2215-2300, 2330-2400, 0345-0500, 1015-1100, 1145-1215 - **FM:**
95.1MHz 2kW– **14)** 413 Nguyen Trai, Ward 9, Ca Mau City. 2200-2400,
0400-0500, 1000-1330 - **FM:** 94.6MHz 5kW –**15)** 165 Hung Vuong St,
Quang Ngai City. 2230-2300, 0200-0300, 0400-0500, 0530-0545/0600,
0830-0900, 1000-1100 in Vietnamese/Kor - **FM:** 102.9MHz 5kW
– **16)** 115 Tran Hung Dao St, Phuong Lam Ward, Hoa Binh City - **FM:**
97.5MHz 0.2kW– **17)** 39 Dong Da, Vinh Lac, Rach Gia Town. 2230-
0030(Sun 0230), 0400-0600, 0900-1145/1200 in Vietnamese/Khmer
- **FM:** 99.4MHz 5kW **18)** 87 Be Van Dan Rd, Cao Bang Town. 2200-2300,
0300-0500, 1000-1200 - **FM:** 99.0MHz 5kW – **19)** 339-341 Thu Khoa
Huan, Phan Thiet City, Binh Thuan Province. 2200-2300, 0400-0500,
1000-1100 - **FM:** 92.3MHz 5kW – **20)** 58 Huong Vong St, Hue. 2230-
2300, 0400-0500, 0955-1100, occ. 1145-1310 - **FM:** 93.0MHz 2kW &
96.0MHz 0.02kW –**21)** 188 Ward 3, 30/4 Rd, Tay Ninh. 2200-2400(Sun
0230), 0400-0500, 0900-1330 in Vietnamese/Khmer - **FM:** 103.1MHz 0.05kW – **22)** 45/1 Tran
Hung Dao, Long Xuyen City, An Giang Province. 2200-0015 (Sun 0145),
0330-0600, 0900-1330 in Vietnamese/Khmer. **FM:** 90.1MHz 0.1kW

Provincial sces operating on FM only (MHz):
Bac Giang 98.4 5kW; Bac Kan 99.3 2kW; Bac Lieu 93.8 2kW; Bac Ninh
92.1 2kW; Ba Ria Vung Tau (Vui Nho) 92.0 5kW; Ben Tre 97.9 2kW; Binh
Duong (Thu Dau Mot) 92.5 10kW; Binh Phuoc (Dong Xoai) 89.4 2kW; Dac
Lac (Buon Ma Thuot) 94.7 5kW; Dac Nong (Gia Nghia) 88.8 2kW, (Dak
Mil) 95.5 2kW; Dien Bien (Dien Bien Phu) 96.3 1kW; Gia Lai (Pleiku) 93.7
2kW + relays; Ha Giang 92.0 2kW + relays; Hai Duong 104.5 5kW; Hai
Phong 93.7 3kW; Ha Nam (Phu Ly) 93.3 2kW; Hau Giang 89.6 3kW; Hung
Yen 92.7 2kW; Lang Son 88.2MHz 1kW, (Mau Son) 101.0MHz 10kW;
Lao Cai 91.0 5kW, 95.2 1kW & 97.0 10kW; Nam Dinh 95.1 2kW; Nghe
An (Vinh) 99.6 10kW + relays; Ninh Binh 98.1 2kW; Ninh Thuan (Phan
Rang Thap Cham) 95.0 5kW & 99.6 2kW; Phu Tho (Viet Tri) 106.0 5kW;
Phu Yen 96.0 2.5kW; Quang Binh (Dong Hoi) 94.1 1kW; Quang Ninh (Ha
Long) 97.8 10kW; Quang Tri (Dong Ha) 92.5 5kW;Soc Trang 100.4 2kW;
Thai Binh 91.7 3.3kW; Tieng Giang (My Tho) 96.2 2kW; Thai Nguyen
106.5MHz 1kW; Tra Vinh 92.7 2kW; Tuyen Quang 95.6 2kW,Vinh Long
90.2 1kW; Vinh Phuc 102.7 2kW; Yen Bai 92.1 2kW + relays.

VIRGIN ISLANDS (AMERICAN) (USA)

L.T: UTC -4h — **Pop:** 105,000 — **Pr.L:** English, Spanish, Creole
— **E.C:** 60Hz, 110V — **ITU:** VIR

FEDERAL COMMUNICATIONS COMMISSION (FCC)
see USA for details

	MW Call	kHz	kW		MW	Call	kHz	kW
1)	WSTX	970	5/1		5)	WSTA	1340	1
2)	WVWI	1000-	5/1		4)	WDHP	1620	10/1
3)	WGOD	1090	0.25					

	FM Call	MHz	kW		FM	Call	MHz	kW
6)	WIVH	89.9	1.4		2)	WWKS	101.3	50
7)	WXZT	90.7	10		11)	WEVI	101.7	0.9
8)	WVVI	93.5	9.6		12)	WIUJ	102.9	1.5
9)	WJKC	95.1	50		4)	WAXJ	103.5	6
7)	WIVI	96.1	2.4		13)	WZIN	104.3	44
3)	WGOD	97.9	50		14)	WMNG	104.9	6
10)	WMYP	98.3	1.9		2)	WVJZ	105.3	30
9)	WVIQ	99.5	32		15)	WVGN	107.3	1.7
1)	WSTX	100.3	50		16)	WLDV	107.9	3.6

Addresses and other information
1) 2111 Company St, Suite 3, Christiansted, St. Croix 00820 ☎ +1 340
773-7284 **W:** www.wstxam.com www.wstxfm.com Stns: WSTX-AM on
970kHz (news/sport/talk) & WSTX-FM on 100.3MHz (reggae) – **2)** Gark
LLC, 13 Crown Bay Fill, PO Box 302179, Charlotte Amalie, St. Thomas
00803 ☎ +1 340 776 1000. Stn's: Hitz 96 on 96.1 (Top 40), KISS 101.3
FM (A/C), 105 JAMZ on 105.3 (CHR/rythmic) & Radio One on 1000kHz
(News/talk/sport) – **3)** 3AGN, Box 305012, Charlotte Amalie, St.
Thomas 00803-5012 ☎ +1 340 774 4498 **W:** www.godradio.org Stn:
'3ABN Radio' (Rlg.) – **4)** Reef Broadcasting Inc., 79A Castle Coakley,
Christiansted, St. Croix 00820 ☎ +1 340 719 1620 🗎 +1 340 778 1686
W: www.reefbroadcasting.com. Stn's: WAXJ 'The Reef' on 103.5MHz
(News/talk) & WDHP on 1620kHz (Local Information/Music) – **5)** PO
Box 1340, Charlotte Amalie, St. Thomas 00801 ☎ +1 340 774 4500 **W:**
www.wsta.com Ann: "Lucky 13 - WSTA" – **6)** Missionary Radio, 5007

Mt. Washington, Christiansted, St. Croix 00820 ☎ +1 340 718 2852.
Ann: "WIVH The Voice Of Hope" (Rlg.) – **7)** PO Box 8294, Christiansted
00823, St, Croix ☎ +1 340 277 7821 **W:** papiloveradio.com Ann:
"Radio Latino 90.7" – **8)** PO Box 25387, Christiansted, St. Croix 00824
☎ +1 340 773 5935 **W:** www.wvifm.com Ann: "Caribbean Country"
– **9)** JKC Communications/Radio 95, 5020 Anchors Way, PO Box 25680,
Christiansted, St. Croix 00824 ☎ +1 340 773 0995 **W:** www.isle95.com
Stns: Isle 95 on 95.1MHz (Urban/reggae) & Sunny 99.5 (A/C) – **10)** PO
Box 25387, Christiansted, St. Croix 00824. ☎ +1 340 772 0098 Ann:
"Latino 98.3"(Spanish/Tropical/Variety) – **11)** Frontline Missions Int'l,
4449 Peter's Rest, 7D, Suite 2, PO Box 892, Christiansted 00821 – ☎ +1
340 719 9384 **W:** www.wevifm.org Ann: "Power 101.7 FM" (Rlg.) – **12)**
Virgin Isl. Youth Development Radio, PO Box 2477, Charlotte Amalie, St.
Thomas 00803 ☎ +1 340 776 1029 **W:** www.wiuj.com (Pub./Educ.) –
13) PO Box 306117, Charlotte Amalie, St. Thomas 00803 ☎ +1 340 776
1043 **W:** www.buzzrocks.com Ann: "The Buzz" (Active Rock) – **14)** Clara
Communications Corp., PO Box 25680, Christiansted, St. Croix 00824 ☎
+1 340 713 9666 **W:** www.mongoose1049.com Ann: "Mongoose 104.9
FM" (Classic hits) – **15)** Caribbean Community Broadcasting, 8000 Nisky
Center, Suite 714, St. Thomas 00802 ☎ +1 800 275 6437 **W:** www.
wvgn.org (Pub.) – **16)** Da Vybe, Frederiksted, St. Croix.

VIRGIN ISLANDS (BRITISH) (UK)

L.T: UTC -4h — **Pop:** 31,000 — **Pr.L:** English — **E.C:** 60Hz, 110V
— **ITU:** VRG

VIRGIN ISLANDS BROADCASTING LTD. (Comm.)
🖃 Baughers Bay, P.O. Box 78, Road Town, Tortola, BVI ☎ +1 284 494
2250/2430/6994 🗎 +1 284 494 1139 **E:** zbvi@surfbvi.com **W:** www.
zbviradio.com www.zbvi.vi **L.P:** MD: Meritt Herbert. GM: Harvey
Herbert. Ops Mgr: Sandra Warrican. Production: Iris Jones
MW: ZBVI 780kHz 10kW
D.Prgr: MF 0930-0200, Sat 1000-0300, Sun 1100-0200. **Ann:** "This is
ZBVI Radio from Tortola"

Other stations:
CSS - CARIBBEAN SUPER STATION: 90.9MHz 1kW (rel. Trinidad)
– **ZCBN**, 2nd Floor Cheville Center, Road Town, Tortola ☎ +1 284 440
3633 🗎 +1 284 494 7815 **W:** www.cbnbvi.com **FM:** 92.3MHz **Ann.:**
CBN Radio – **ZCCR**, Little Dix Hill Rd, East End, PO Box 41, Tortola ☎
+1 284 495 2861/2161/0461 🗎 +1 284 495 1461 **FM:** 94.1MHz 8.5kW
Ann: CCR Your Caribbean Christian Station. Format: Rlg. – **ZROD**, 19
Flemming St.,P.O. Box 992, Road Town, Tortola ☎ +1 284 494 1037
🗎 +1 284 494 4564 **W:** www.zrodfm.com L.P: GM: Rodney Herbert.
FM: 103.7MHz **Ann.:** Z-Rod – **Z.V.C.R.**, Main St., P.O.Box 43, Road
Town, Tortola ☎ +1 284 494 6995/7305 **W:** www.zvcr1069fm.com
FM: 106.9MHz

WAKE ISLAND (USA)

L.T: UTC +12h — **Pop:** 150 — **Pr.L:** English — **E.C:** 60Hz, 110V
— **ITU:** WAK

THE QUAKE
🖃 USAF Detachment 3, 13AF, PACAF/Chugach Federal Solutions Inc.
PO Box 187, Wake Island 96898 ☎ +1 808 424 2101 **E:** baseops@
wakeisland.net **L.P:** Comms Mgr: Colin Bradley. **Prgr:** Local prgrs and
automated music 24/7.
FM: 104.5MHz
NB: Another 4 FM satellite radio prgr feeds are supplied from Armed
Forces Radio.

WALLIS & FUTUNA (France)

L.T: UTC +12h — **Pop:** 13,000 — **Pr.L:** French, Wallisian — **E.C:**
50Hz, 220V — **ITU:** WAL

WALLIS ET FUTUNA PREMIÈRE (Gov)
🖃 B.P.102, Pointe Matala, 98600 Mata-Utu, Uvea, Iles de Wallis et
Futuna (par Nouméa, Nouvelle-Calédonie) ☎ +681 72 13 00 🗎 +681
72 23 46 **W:** www.wallisfutuna.la1ere.fr (live streaming) **D.Prgr:** 24h
local and satellite relay from Paris

FM	MHz	FM	MHz
Sigave, Futuna	89.0	Hihifo, Uvea	101.0
Sigave, Futuna	90.0	Mua/Hahake, Uvea	103.0
Alo, Futuna	91.0		

RADIO Ô (Gov)
W: www.radioo.fr **D.Prgr:** 24h satellite relay from Paris
FM: Mua/Hahake, Uvea, 100.0MHz

YEMEN

L.T: UTC +3h — **Pop:** 24 million — **Pr.L:** Arabic — **E.C:** 50Hz, 220/230V — **ITU:** YEM

MINISTRY OF INFORMATION
✉ P.O. Box 19560, Al-Zubairy St, San'a ☎+967 1 215116/7/8 🖷 +967 1 207716 **W:** www.yemeninfo.gov.ye **E:** yemen-info@y.net.ye
L.P: Hassan al-Lawzi, Minister.

YEMEN RADIO & TV CORPORATION (YRTC) (Gov)
✉ Tech. Dept, 26 September St, PO Box 2371, San'a ☎+967 1 282060 🖷 +967 1 282053 **W:** yemenrt.com aden radio.net **E:** info@yemenradio.net, adenradio@yemen.net.ye
L.P: Tech. Dir: Mohammed H. Bather. Dir. Eng: Ali Ahmed Altashi. Head Tr. Station: Ismail Hussein Al-Nono.

MW	kHz	kW	Netw.	Times
Unknown location	602		G	-2300
San'a	711	200	G	0300-1900
Mukalla	756	50	G/L	1500-2300
Al-Hiswah	792	100	2	0300-0800,1100-2100
San'a	837	30	Y	0300-2300
Taiz	891		L	0300-2100
Hudaydah	909	750	G	1500-2300
San'a	±1008	600	G	1400-2100
Taiz	1071	30	G	0300-2300
Hudaydah	1125	50	L	0300-2300
Al-Hiswah	1188	100	G	0300-2300

FM (MHz): Ad-Dali 96.7 5kW, Ad-Damigh 99.9 5kW, Aden 99.0 (G)/102.5 (2), Al-Ashmur 92.6 5kW, Al Hudah 88.6/98.0, Hudaydah 90.4 (L)/107.0 (G), Ibb 96.0 (G)/98.4 (L), Mukalla 91.5 (L)/98.5 (G), Riam 92.4 5kW, San'a 88.1 (G)/89.9 (L)/92.5 (2)/96.5 (Y), Sayun 89.5 (G)/954 (L), Taiz 88.1 (G)/89.0 (L).
G=General prgr. from San'a: 0300-2215. **English:** 1800-1900.
2=Second prgr. from Aden: 0300-0800, 1100-2130 (Fri 0255-2130). **English:** 1600-1630. **French:** 1705-1725.
Y=Youth prgr. on 89.9/96.5MHz + 3 other trs.
L=Local prgr; times vary by station, between 0600-2100, also rel. General prgr. Mukalla R. frequencies are shared by Sayun R.
IS: Flute. **Ann:** "Idha'atu-l-Jumhuriyah al-Yamaniyah min San'a", Huna Adan, Idha'atu-l-Jumhuriyah al-Yamaniyah, il-barnamig at-thani". E: "This is Republic of Yemen Radio broadcasting from (town: San'a/Aden)".
Relays for abroad on shortwave: see International radio section

ZAMBIA

L.T: UTC +2h — **Pop:** 12 million — **Pr.L:** English, Bemba, Lozi, Lunda, Nyanja, Tonga, Chichewa, others — **E.C:** 50Hz, 230V — **ITU:** ZMB

MINISTRY OF INFORMATION AND BROADCASTING SERVICES (MIBS)
✉ P.O. Box 32020, Lusaka ☎+260 211 235 🖷 +260 211 235410 **W:** www.mibs.gov.zm **L.P:** Minister: Mike Mulongoti.

ZAMBIA NATIONAL BROADCASTING CORPORATION (ZNBC, Pub)
✉ P.O. Box 50015, Mass Media Complex, Alick Nkhata Rd, Lusaka 10101 ☎+260 21 1251983 🖷 +260 21 1254920 **W:** www.znbc.co.zm **L.P:** DG: Chibamba Kanyama. Actg. Dir. Tech. Sces: Mr. Malolela Lusambo. PD: Kenneth Maduma. PR Officer: Masuzyo Ndhlovu.

SW	kHz	kW	Sce.	Times
Lusaka	5915	100	R1	0245-2205
Lusaka	6165	100	R2	0245-2205

FM(MHz)	R1	R2	N	R4	kW
Chipata	93.3	96.5	94.9		1
Choma		105.7			
Kabwe			92.1		0.5
Kapiri Mposhi	97.5	94.3	91.1		1
Kasama	88.3	92.3	91.5		1
Kitwe	98.5	95.7	94.1	88.1	2
Livingstone	89.3	97.3	100.5	95.7	1/0.5
Lusaka	102.9	95.7	92.5	88.1	2
Mansa	88.3	92.3	91.5		1
Mongu	94.9	91.7	98.1		1
Solwezi	91.3	95.7	93.3		1

R. One in 7 Zambian languages: 0245-2205. – **R. Two in English:** 0245-2205. Relays VOA 2000-2100. – **N=National Assembly Channel – R. Four (music channel) in English:** 0240-2205. Also rel. VOA.

Ann: E: "This is Radio Two of ZNBC broadcasting from Lusaka". Chichewa: "Kuno ndi ku Zambia National Broadcasting Corporation wa Lusaka." **IS:** "Call of the Fish Eagle".

Other stations (FM: MHz):
Breeze FM, Chipata: 99.6. **W:** www.breezefm.com – **Chikuni Community R,** Monze: 91.8 0.5kW. **W:** www.chikuniradio.org – **Choice FM,** Lusaka: 107.8. **E:** choice@microlink.zm – **Falls FM,** Livingstone: 90.1 – **Five FM,** Lusaka: 105.1 – **Flava FM,** Kitwe: 96.4. **W:** www.flavafm.co.zm – **Horn FM,** Lusaka: 94.2 – **R. Christian Voice:** FM: Ndola 98.9, Kapiri 101.5, Kitwe 105.3, Lusaka 106.1. **W:** radiochristianvoicezambia.com – **R. Icengelo,** Kitwe: 89.1 – **R. Liambayi,** Mongu 101.9 – **R. Maria Zambia,** Chipata. FM: Kanjala 90 0.3kW. E: info.zam@radiomar.org F.PI: another tr in Lusaka – **R. Musi O Tunya,** Livingstone: 106 – **R. Phoenix,** 12th Floor, ZIMCO House, Cairo Rd, Private Bag E702, Lusaka. **W:** www.radiophoenix.co.zm FM: Lusaka 89.5, Kabwe 100, Kitwe 100.5, Chingola 104, Kapiri/Mposhi 104.5, Ndola/Luanshya 107.6 – **R. Q-FM,** 15th floor Indeco House, P.O. Box 30896, Lusaka **W:** www.qfmradio.com FM: Lusaka 93.2, Kabwe 96.7, Choma 89.8, Kitwe 90.0, Mumbwa 89, Namwala 90.6 – **Sky FM,** P.O. Box 31165, Plot 55, Luwato Rd, Roma, Lusaka. FM: Choma 88.8, Zimba 93.8, Monze 95.1, Livingstone 102.4, Lusaka 104. E: skyfmbcast@zamtel.zm – **Yatsani R,** P.O. Box 320147, Bauleni, Lusaka: 99.1 2kW. **W:** www.yatsani.com
BBC African Sce: Kitwe/Lusaka 98.1 2kW.
RFI Afrique: Lusaka 100.5 2kW, Kitwe 92.5 1kW.

ZIMBABWE

L.T: UTC +2h — **Pop:** 11 million — **Pr.L:** English, Shona, Ndebele, Chewa — **E.C:** 50Hz, 220V — **ITU:** ZWE

BROADCASTING AUTHORITY OF ZIMBABWE (BAZ)
✉ Block A, Emerald Park 30, The Chase, P.O. Box MP 843, Mt. Pleasant, Harare ☎+263 4 333032/48 🖷 +263 4 333041 **E:** baz@comone.co.zw **L.P:** Acting Chairperson: Pikirai Deketeke.

ZIMBABWE BROADCASTING CORPORATION (ZBC, Gov)
✉ P.O. Box HG 444, Broadcasting Centre, Pockets Hill, Highlands, Harare +263 4 498610, SW station: ☎+263 4 22104 🖷 +263 4 498613 **W:** www.zbc.co.zw **L.P:** DG: Henry Muradzikwa. CEO: Happison Muchechetere. Head Radio & TV: Abigail Mvududu.

SW	kHz	kW	Prgr	Times		
Gweru	6045	100	2	24h (irregular)		

FM (MHz)	R1	R2	R3	R4	kW
Beithbridge		98.1		105.2	-
Bulawayo	90.0	96.3	99.6	103.1	10
Chiredzi	93.3	95.5	98.8	102.3	-
Chivhu	93.3	96.5	103.3	106.8	-
Gokwe		96.8	89.6	103.5	-
Gwanda	105.8	95.4	98.7	102.2	-
Gweru	90.7	93.9	97.2	100.7	5
Harare	92.8	96.0	99.3	102.8	10
Hwange	91.5	98.2	94.7		-
Kadoma	88.5	94.8	98.1	101.6	10
Karoi	99.9	96.6	93.4	90.3	-
Kenmur	90.4	93.5	96.7		-
Lowveld	101.1	88.0	91.1	94.3	-
Masvingo	106.5	92.9	99.4	102.9	-
Mount Darwin		95.2	99.2	102.0	-
Mutare	105.3	89.1	98.7	105.8	3
Mutorashanga	104.7	94.3	91.1	101.1	-
Nyanga	105.5	91.7	94.9	101.7	-
Sabi/Chipinge	94.5	97.8	101.3		-
Victoria Falls	92.9	96.1	99.4		-

F.PI: community radio stations: Sunshine R. in Harare and Skies R. in Bulawayo.

1) S-FM: mainly in English: 24h – **2) R. Zimbabwe:** in Shona/Ndebele/English: 24h – **3) Power FM:** youth programme in English: 24h. **N:** on the h. – **4) National FM:** in 14 minority languages: 24h.
Ann: In addition to programme names: "ZBC".

EXTERNAL SERVICE: Voice of Zimbabwe; see Int. radio section.

Other stations:
Star FM: Harare 89.7MHz, Bulawayo 93.1MHz. **W:** starfm.co.zw
Zi FM: Mutare 95.4MHz, Masvingo 96.1MHz, Mutorashanga 97.6MHz, Nyanga 98.2MHz, Beitbridge 101.6MHz, Gweru 104.3MHz, Kadoma 1052.MHz, Harare 106.4MHz, Victoria Falls 106.5MHz, Bulawayo 106.7MHz. **W:** zifmstereo.co.zw

INTERNATIONAL RADIO

Section Contents

Initial entries for each letter,
see Main Index for full details.

NB: The copy deadline for this section was 12 November 2012

Features & Reviews

National Radio

International Radio

Frequency Lists

Terrestrial Television

Reference

Notes for the International Radio section

Country abbreviation codes are shown after the country name. The three-letter codes after each frequency are transmitter site codes. These, and the Area/Country codes in the Area column, can all be decoded by referring to the tables in the Reference Section.

Where a frequency has an asterisk (*) etc. after it, see the '**KEY**' section at the end of the schedule entry.

The following symbols are used throughout this section:
† = Irregular transmissions/broadcasts;
‡ = Inactive at editorial deadline;
± = variable frequency;
+ = DRM (Digital Radio Mondiale) transmission.

Where transmitter details are given for a particular entity, the number of units shown represent the installed capability of the site, but do not reflect any details of txs being coupled/bridged (to increase overall power output), run at reduced power or remaining unused.
Should a site become decommissioned or dismantled, it is removed from the entry but if a site is merely dormant/inactive, it is then marked with the 'inactive' symbol, shown above.

If **Webcast:** is shown, the letter(s) after indicate the type of service(s) available: **D** = On Demand audio; **L** = Live audio; **P** = Podcast. For international services we have shown, where possible, languages available only via webcast. We do not include those broadcasters that have a foreign service available only via the internet, and are no longer broadcasting via MW/SW radio.

An alphabetical listing of **Religious Broadcasters**, cross-referenced by country, is given at the end of the section.

AFGHANISTAN (AFG)

RADIO TELEVISION AFGHANISTAN ‡ (Gov)
🖃 See National Radio section.
E: radioafghanistan@yahoo.com **W:** www.rta.org.af
L.P: DG (R. Afghanistan): Abdul Ghaney Mudaqiq.
MW: [KAB] Kabul, Pol-e Charkhi: 1296kHz 400kW; [KHO] Khost, Tani: 621kHz 200kW (Both txs operated on behalf of IBB).
SW: [KAB] Kabul, Yakatut: 1 x 100kW
Ann: Engish: "This is the National Radio of Afghanistan"; Urdu: "Yeh Radio Afganistan ke Urdu Service hai".
Notes: International Service on SW since July 2011. Inactive at time of publication. RTA continues to provide MW facilities for IBB (USA).

ALASKA (ALS)

KNLS INTERNATIONAL (Rlg)
🖃 P.O. Box 473, Anchor Point, AK 99556, USA. (Transmitting station)
☎ +1 907 2352326. 🖷 +1 907 2352326.
E: knls@aol.com **W:** www.knls.org (English); www.knls.net (Russian); www.smzg.org (Mandarin)
Webcast: D
🖃 605 Bradley Court, Franklin, TN 37067, USA. (World Christian Broadcasting HQ & studios)
☎ +1 615 3718707. 🖷 +1 615 3718791.
L.P: SM: Dave Dvorak; Chief Engineer: Kevin K. Chambers.
SW: [NLS] Anchor Point, AK: 2 x 100kW.
kHz: 6190, 9615, 9655, 9680

Chinese	Days	Area	kHz
0900-1000	daily	CHN	9655nls
1100-1200	daily	CHN	9615nls
1300-1400	daily	CHN	9680nls
1400-1500	daily	CHN	9615nls
English	**Days**	**Area**	**kHz**
1000-1100	daily	EAs	9615nls
1200-1300	daily	EAs	9615nls
1500-1600	daily	EAs	9655nls
Russian	**Days**	**Area**	**kHz**
0800-0900	daily	RUS	9655nls
1600-1800	daily	RUS	6190nls

Winter Schedule 2012/2013

Ann: English: "Broadcasting from the top of the world, this is your new life station - KNLS, Anchor Point, Alaska, USA".
V: QSL-card.

Notes: On air since 23 Jul 1983. KNLS is a SW transmitting station owned by World Christian Broadcasting, Inc. (WCB). See under USA for corporate details.

ALBANIA (ALB)

RADIO TIRANA (Pub)
🖃 Rruga Ismail Qemali 11, Tirana, Albania.
☎ +355 4 2223650. 🖷 +355 4 2223650.
E: radiotiranaenglish@live.com **W:** www.rtsh.al
Webcast: L
L.P: Dir: Alfons Zeneli; Technical Dir, RTSH: Agron Aranitasi; Head of RTV Monitoring: Mrs. Drita Çiço. (drita.cico@yahoo.com)
MW: [FLA] Fllaka: 1215/1395/1458kHz 500kW.
SW: [SHI] Shijak: 2 x 100kW.
kHz: 1395, 1458, 6040, 6100, 7390, 7465

Winter Schedule 2012/2013

Albanian	Days	Area	kHz
0000-0100	daily	NAm	7465shi
0800-1000	daily	Eu	7390shi
0900-1000	daily	Eu	1395fla
1500-1630	daily	Eu	1458fla
English	**Days**	**Area**	**kHz**
0230-0300	.twtfss	NAm	6100shi
2100-2130	mtwtfs.	Eu	7465shi
French	**Days**	**Area**	**kHz**
1830-1900	mtwtfs.	Eu	7465shi
German	**Days**	**Area**	**kHz**
2030-2100	mtwtfs.	Eu	7465shi
Greek	**Days**	**Area**	**kHz**
1645-1700	mtwtfs.	Eu	1458fla
Italian	**Days**	**Area**	**kHz**
1800-1830	mtwtfs.	Eu	6040shi
Serbian	**Days**	**Area**	**kHz**
2115-2130	mtwtfs.	Eu	1458fla
Turkish	**Days**	**Area**	**kHz**
1930-2000	mtwtfs.	ME	1458fla

Ann: Albanian: "Radio Tirana per Bashkatdhetaret"; English: "This is Radio Tirana"; French: "Ici Tirana"; German: "Hier ist Radio Tirana"; Greek: "Sas milun ta Tirana"; Italian: "Parla Tirana"; Serbian: "Govori Tirana"; Turkish: "Burasi Tiran Radyosu".
V: QSL-card.
Notes: Radio Tirana is the External Sce of the public broadcaster Albanian Radio & TV (Radiotelevizioni Shqiptar - RTSH).

CHINA RADIO INTERNATIONAL (CRI) RELAY
L.P: Mgr: Zhang Tianwei.
SW: [CER] Cërrik, Shtërmen: 6 x 150kW.
Notes: The Cërrik transmitting stn is owned by Radiotelevizioni Shqiptar (RTSH), and was leased to China Radio International for 15 years in 2003.

ALGERIA (ALG)

RADIO ALGÉRIENNE (Pub)
✉ 21 Boulevard des Martyrs, 16000 Algiers, Algeria.
☎ +213 21483790. 🖷 +213 21230823.
W: www.radioalgerie.dz
Webcast: L
L.P: (ENRS) DG: Chabane Lounakel; Dir, Technical Services: Mohamed Salah Saidi.
SW: Leased from TDA (planned from late 2013) & via foreign relays.
SAT: Atlantic Bird 3, Badr 6, Galaxy 25, Hot Bird 6, Nilesat 102, NSS 7.
kHz: 5865, 7295, 7495, 9390, 9395, 11775, 11955

Winter Schedule 2012/2013

Arabic/French	Days	Area	kHz
0400-0700	daily	CAf,WAf	5865iss
0500-0600	daily	CAf,WAf	7295iss
1800-1900	daily	CAf,WAf	11955iss
1900-2100	daily	NAf,WAf	11775iss
1900-2100	daily	CAf,WAf	9390iss
2100-2200	daily	CAf,WAf	9395iss
2100-2300	daily	NAf,WAf	7495iss

Ann: Arabic: "Huna Al-Djazair".
V: QSL-card.
Notes: Relays of FNRS (Entreprise Nationale de Radiodiffusion Sonore) Home Sce 'Koran' prgr and Chaîne 1/3.

TÉLÉDIFFUSION D'ALGÉRIE (TDA) (Tx Operator)
✉ BP 50, 16340 Alger, Algeria.
☎ +213 21 901717. 🖷 +213 21 901522.
E: contact@tda.dz **W:** www.tda.dz
L.P: DG: Houyou Abdelmalek.
SW: [BEC] Béchar: 1 x 250kW ‡; [ORG] Ouargla: 1 x 250kW ‡.
Notes: Télédiffusion d'Algérie is the national transmitter network operator. Transmissions from the Béchar and Ouargla sites are expected to start in late 2013.

ANGOLA (AGL)

ANGOLAN NATIONAL RADIO (Gov)
✉ C.P. 1329, Luanda, Angola.
☎ +244 22 2323172. 🖷 +244 22 2324647.
E: rna@rna.ao **W:** www.rna.ao
L.P: DG: Eduardo Magalhães; Dir, Technical: Ale Fernandes.
MW: [MUL] Luanda, Mulenvos: 945kHz 25kW.
SW: [MUL] Luanda, Mulenvos: 1 x 15kW.
kHz: 945, 7217

Winter Schedule 2012/2013

English	Days	Area	kHz
2100-2200	daily	Af	945mul, 7217mul†

French	Days	Area	kHz
2000-2100	daily	Af	945mul, 7217mul†

Key: † Irregular.
Ann: English: "International Service of Angolan National Radio".
V: QSL-card.

ANGUILLA (AIA)

CARIBBEAN BEACON
(UNIVERSITY NETWORK RELAY)
✉ P.O. Box 690, The Valley, Anguilla.
☎ +1 809 4974340. 🖷 +1 809 4974311.
E: beacon@anguillanet.com
L.P: SM/Chief Engineer: Eddie Sutton.
MW: [AIA] The Valley: 690kHz 10kW, 1610kHz 25kW (run at 8/10kW).
SW: [AIA] The Valley: 1 x 100kW.
FM/DAB: FM: 100.1MHz (The Valley, 35kW).

V: QSL-card.
Notes: Transmitting station owned by Melissa Scott (USA), carrying "University Network" programming (see main entry under "USA" for schedules).

ARGENTINA (ARG)

RADIODIFUSIÓN ARGENTINA AL EXTERIOR (RAE) (Pub)
✉ Casilla de Correo 555, Correo Central, C1000WAF Buenos Aires, Argentina.
☎ +54 11 43256368. 🖷 +54 11 43259433.
E: rae@radionacional.gov.ar; argentinainternationalradio@gmail.com (English Sce)
W: rae.radionacional.com.ar
Webcast: L
L.P: Dir: Luis María Barassi.
SW: [BUE] Buenos Aires, General Pacheco: 2 x 50, 1 x 100kW.
kHz: 6060, 11710, 15345

Winter Schedule 2012/2013

English	Days	Area	kHz
0200-0300	.twtfs.	Am	11710bue
1800-1900	mtwtf..	Eu	15345bue
French	**Days**	**Area**	**kHz**
0300-0400	.twtfs.	Am	11710bue
2000-2100	mtwtf..	Eu	15345bue
German	**Days**	**Area**	**kHz**
1700-1800	mtwtf..	Eu	15345bue
2100 2200	mtwtf..	Eu	15345bue
Italian	**Days**	**Area**	**kHz**
1900-2000	mtwtf..	Eu	15345bue
Japanese	**Days**	**Area**	**kHz**
0100-0200	.twtfs.	As	11710bue
1000-1100	mtwtf..	SAm	6060bue
1000-1100	mtwtf..	As	15345bue
Portuguese	**Days**	**Area**	**kHz**
0000-0100	mtwtf..	Am	11710bue
1100 1200	mtwtf..	Am	6060bue, 15345bue
Spanish	**Days**	**Area**	**kHz**
1200-1400	mtwtf..	am	6060bue, 15345bue
1800-0300	......s	Am	6060bue*, 15345bue*
2000-0230	.....s.	Am	6060bue*
2000-0230	.....s.	Eu	15345bue*
2200-2400	mtwtf..	Eu	15345bue
2200-2400	mtwtf..	Am	6060bue, 11710bue

Key: * Relay of RNA 870kHz.
Ann: English: "This is RAE, the International Service of the Argentine Radio", "RAE, Buenos Aires".
V: QSL-card.
Notes: RAE is the External Sce of the national public-service broadcaster Radio y Televisión Argentina (RTA S.E.).

ARMENIA (ARM)

PUBLIC RADIO OF ARMENIA (FOREIGN SERVICE) (Pub)
✉ A. Manoogian Street 5, 0025 Yerevan, Armenia.
☎ +374 10 558010. 🖷 +374 10 551513.
E: ak@arradio.am **W:** www.int.armradio.am
Webcast: D
L.P: Dir, Foreign Service: Amasia Hovhannisyan.
MW/SW: Via Gavar transmitting station.
kHz: 1314, 4810

Winter Schedule 2012/2013

Arabic	Days	Area	kHz
1900-1930	daily	ME	4810erv
Assyrian	**Days**	**Area**	**kHz**
1530-1545	daily	ME	4810erv
Azeri	**Days**	**Area**	**kHz**
1145-1200	daily	ME	1314erv, 4810erv
1200-1215	mtwtf..	ME	1314erv, 4810erv
Farsi	**Days**	**Area**	**kHz**
1430-1500	daily	ME	4810erv
Kurdish	**Days**	**Area**	**kHz**
1230-1300	daily	ME	1314erv, 4810erv

Turkish	Days	Area	kHz
1200-1215	.....ss	ME	1314erv, 4810erv
1215-1230	daily	ME	1314erv, 4810erv

Yezidi*	Days	Area	kHz
0600-0630	daily	ME	1314erv
1500-1530	daily	ME	4810erv

Key: * Kurmanji (designated "Yezidi" in Armenia).
Ann: Arabic: "Huna Idha'at Jumhuriyat al-Yermaniyah min Yerevan".
V: QSL-card. Rp. (1 IRC)
Notes: Times may be changed or broadcasts may be cancelled without notice. In some languages the prgrs identify as "Voice of Armenia".

AR RADIO INTERCONTINENTAL (Tx Operator)
⌨ A.Manoogian Street 5, 0025 Yerevan, Armenia.
☎ +374 10 551143. 📄 +374 10 554600.
E: aa@arradio.am **W:** www.arradio.am
L.P: DG: Armen Amiryan; CEO: Hrachya Kostanyan.
MW: [ERV] Gavar, Noratus: 864/1350/1377kHz 1000kW.

RADIO CJSC (Tx Operator)
⌨ 3333 Noratus, Armenia.
☎ +374 264 62640. 📄 +374 264 30440.
E: info@radio-int.am **W:** www.radio-int.am
L.P: Dir: Gagik Aloyan.
MW: [ERV] Gavar, Noratus: 1314kHz 1000kW, 1395kHz 500kW.
SW: [ERV] Gavar, Noratus: 4 x 100, 3 x 1000kW
Notes: Radio CJSC is the operator of high power transmitting facilities in Armenia.

ASCENSION ISLAND (ASC)

BBC ATLANTIC RELAY STATION
⌨ English Bay, Ascension Island, ASCN 1ZZ.
☎ +247 4458. 📄 +247 6117.
L.P: Transmitter Engineer: Nicola Nicholls.
SW: [ASC] English Bay: 6 x 250kW.
V: QSL-letter. (For direct report)
Notes: Owned by the BBC and operated by Babcock International Group PLC (see under United Kingdom).

AUSTRALIA (AUS)

RADIO AUSTRALIA (Pub)
⌨ P.O. Box 428G, Melbourne, VIC 3001, Australia.
☎ +61 3 96261500. 📄 +61 3 96261899.
E: english@ra.abc.net.au **W:** www.radioaustralia.net.au
Webcast: D/L/P
L.P: CEO: Dr Michael McCluskey; Senior Editor: Hanh Tran; Transmission Mgr: Nigel Holmes.
SW: Leased from Broadcast Australia.
SAT: Intelsat 5/8/10, SES 7.
kHz: *5940, 5995, 6020, 6080, 6140, 7240, 7410, 9475, 9490, 9500, 9540, 9580, 9660, 9695, 9710, 9855, 9965, 11650, 11660, 11695, 11700, 11780, 11880, 11945, 12005, 12080, 13630, 15160, 15230, 15240, 15415, 15515, 17750, 17795, 17800, 19000, 21725, 21740*

Winter Schedule 2012/2013

Burmese	Days	Area	kHz
0100-0130	daily	SEA	11780sng
2300-2330	daily	SEA	9490dha

Chinese	Days	Area	kHz
1300-1430	daily	EAs	9475shp, 9965hbn, 11660shp

English	Days	Area	kHz
0000-0900	daily	Pac	15240shp
0030-0400	daily	As	17750shp
0100-0500	daily	Pac	15160shp
0300-0330	.....ss	Pac	12080brn, 15515shp
0300-0700	daily	As,Pac	21725shp
0330-0600	daily	Pac	15515shp
0330-0900	daily	Pac	12080brn
0500-0800	daily	Pac	13630shp
0530-0700	daily	As	17750shp
0600-1530	daily	Pac	11945shp
0700-0900	daily	Pac	7410shp, 9475shp, 9710shp

English	Days	Area	kHz
0800-0900	daily	Pac	5995brn
0800-1500	daily	Pac	9580shp
1000-1100	.....ss	Pac	5995brn, 6020shp, 6080shp, 9475shp, 9710shp, 12080brn
1100-1200	daily	Pac	5995brn, 12080brn+
1100-1300	daily	As	9475shp, 11945shp
1100-1300	daily	Pac	6080shp
1100-1300	daily	SEA	6140sng
1100-1400	daily	Pac	6020shp
1200-1400	daily	Pac	5995brn+
1300-1700	daily	As	5940shp
1400-1800	daily	Pac	5995shp
1430-1730	daily	As	11660shp
1430-1900	daily	As	9475shp
1500-1700	daily	Pac	7240shp
1530-2000	daily	Pac	11880shp
1600-1630	daily	EAs	9540sng
1700-2100	daily	Pac	9580shp
1700-2200	daily	Pac	9500shp
1730-2030	daily	Pac	6080shp
1800-2000	daily	Pac	9710shp
1900-2100	daily	Pac	11660shp
2000-0300	daily	Pac	12080brn
2000-2200	daily	Pac	11650shp
2000-2300	daily	Pac	15515shp
2030-2200	daily	As	11695shp
2100-0100	daily	Pac	21740shp
2100-0800	daily	Pac	9660brn
2100-2300	daily	Pac	13630shp
2200-0700	daily	As	15415shp
2200-2400	daily	EAs	9855dha
2200-2400	daily	Pac	15230shp
2300-0300	daily	Pac	17795shp, 19000shp
2330-2400	daily	As	17750shp

French	Days	Area	kHz
0300-0330	mtwtf..	Pac	12080brn, 15515shp

Indonesian	Days	Area	kHz
0000-0030	daily	SEA	12005dha, 17750shp
0400-0500	daily	SEA	17840hbn
0400-0530	daily	SEA	17750shp
0500-0530	daily	SEA	11700sng
2200-2330	daily	SEA	9695dha, 11695shp

Tok Pisin	Days	Area	kHz
0900-1000	daily	Pac	5995brn, 6020shp, 6080shp, 9475shp, 9710shp, 12080brn
1000-1100	mtwtf..	Pac	5995brn, 6020shp, 6080shp, 9475shp, 9710shp, 12080brn

Key: + DRM. Schedule may be subject to occasional variation.
Ann: English: "This is Radio Australia broadcasting from studios in Melbourne, Victoria".
IS: "Waltzing Matilda" prior to opening, on all freqs. Foreign language broadcasts start with the laugh of the Kookaburra.
V: QSL-card.
Notes: Radio Australia is the External Sce of the public service Australian Broadcasting Corporation (ABC).

HCJB GLOBAL VOICE AUSTRALIA (Rlg)
⌨ P.O. Box 291, Kilsyth, VIC 3137, Australia.
☎ +61 3 87208000. 📄 +61 3 87208020.
E: office@hcjb.org.au **W:** www.hcjb.org.au
Webcast: P
⌨ 579 Packsaddle Rd, Kununurra, WA 6743. (Transmitter Site)
L.P: CEO: Dale Stagg; Frequency Mgr: Ian Williams; Transmitter Ste Mgr: Peter Michalke.
SW: [KNX] Kununurra, two sites: New Site: 1 x 100kW (another 100kW tx, a refurbished unit from the former HCJB Pifo site in Ecuador, to be shipped); Old Site: 1 x 100kW (temporary backup tx during transition period; site to be dismantled)
kHz: *11750, 15340, 15400, 15525*

Winter Schedule 2012/2013

Amoy	Days	Area	kHz
2300-2330	mtwtf..	SEA	15525knx

Amoy/Cantonese	Days	Area	kHz
1030-1100	mtwtf..	SEA	15400knx
Bengali	**Days**	**Area**	**kHz**
1430-1445	m......	SEA	15340knx
Bhojpuri	**Days**	**Area**	**kHz**
0115-0130	..t...	SEA	15400knx
1315-1330	.....s	SEA	15340knx
Chhattisgarhi	**Days**	**Area**	**kHz**
0230-0245	.....ss	SEA	15400knx
1430-1445	.....ss	SEA	15340knx
Chinese	**Days**	**Area**	**kHz**
1030-1130	.....ss	SEA	15400knx
2230-2300	mtwt..s	SEA	15525knx
2300-2330	.....ss	SEA	15525knx
Dzongkha	**Days**	**Area**	**kHz**
1300-1315	...f..	SEA	15340knx
English	**Days**	**Area**	**kHz**
0245-0300	daily	SEA	15400knx
0730-0830	daily	SEA	11750knx
1445-1530	mtwtf.s	SEA	15340knx
1515-1530	.....s.	SEA	15340knx
Gujarati	**Days**	**Area**	**kHz**
0115-0130	m......	SEA	15400knx
1430-1445	....f..	SEA	15340knx
Hindi	**Days**	**Area**	**kHz**
0200-0230	daily	SEA	15400knx
1330-1400	daily	SEA	15340knx
Hmar	**Days**	**Area**	**kHz**
0230-0245	...f..	SEA	15400knx
1315-1330	...f..	SEA	15340knx
Indonesian	**Days**	**Area**	**kHz**
0000-0030	mtwtfs.	SEA	15400knx
1145-1200	daily	SEA	15340knx
1200-1230	mtwtfs.	SEA	15340knx
2345-2400	mtwtfs.	SEA	15400knx
Japanese	**Days**	**Area**	**kHz**
2230-2300	.....fs.	SEA	15525knx
Kuruk	**Days**	**Area**	**kHz**
0230-0245	m..t...	SEA	15400knx
1430-1445	..w....	SEA	15340knx
Malayalam	**Days**	**Area**	**kHz**
0000-0030	......s	SEA	15400knx
0115-0130	3	SEA	15400knx
1200-1230	......s	SEA	15340knx
1315-1330	...t...	SEA	15340knx
Marathi	**Days**	**Area**	**kHz**
0115-0130	..w....	SEA	15400knx
1315-1330	..w....	SEA	15340knx
Marawari	**Days**	**Area**	**kHz**
0230-0245	.t.....	SEA	15400knx
1430-1445	.t.....	SEA	15340knx
Nepali	**Days**	**Area**	**kHz**
0100-0115	daily	SEA	15400knx
1300-1315	mtwt...	SEA	15340knx
1445-1515	.....s.	SEA	15340knx
Oriya	**Days**	**Area**	**kHz**
1300-1315	.....s.	SEA	15340knx
Punjabi	**Days**	**Area**	**kHz**
0115-0130	....f..	SEA	15400knx
1300-1315	......s	SEA	15340knx
Rawang	**Days**	**Area**	**kHz**
0030-0100	daily	SEA	15400knx
1230-1300	daily	SEA	15340knx
Tamil	**Days**	**Area**	**kHz**
0115-0130	.....s.	SEA	15400knx
1315-1330	mt.....	SEA	15340knx
Telugu	**Days**	**Area**	**kHz**
0230-0245	..w....	SEA	15400knx
1430-1445	...t...	SEA	15340knx
Urdu	**Days**	**Area**	**kHz**
0115-0130	.t.....	SEA	15400knx
0130-0200	daily	SEA	15400knx
1315-1330	.....s.	SEA	15340knx
1400-1430	daily	SEA	15340knx

Ann: English: "You are listening to HCJB Global Voice, Melbourne, Australia".
V: QSL-card.

Notes: HCJB Global branch and transmitting stn; for corporate details see under USA. Txs are to be moved to new site near the existing facility and is expected to be operational in the near future.

BROADCAST AUSTRALIA (Tx Operator)
✉ P.O. Box 1212, Crows Nest, NSW 1585, Australia.
☎ +61 2 8113 4666. 🖷 +61 2 8113 4646.
E: info@broadcastaustralia.com.au
W: www.broadcastaustralia.com.au
✉ Level 10, Tower A, 799 Pacific Highway, Chatswood, NSW 2067, Australia. (HQ)
L.P: Chmn: Gerry Moriarty; Group CEO: Graeme Barclay.
SW: [BRN] Brandon: 3 x 10kW; [SHP] Shepparton: 7 x 100kW.
Notes: Broadcast Australia is the national transmitter network operator and is owned by Canada Pension Plan Investment Board (CPPIB). Has purchased 2 x100kW DRM-ready transmitters for use at Shepparton and Tenant Creek.

AUSTRIA (AUT)

RADIO Ö1 INTERNATIONAL (ORF) (Pub)
✉ Argentinierstrasse 30a, A-1040 Wien, Austria.
☎ +43 1 5010116060. 🖷 +43 1 5010116066.
E: roi.service@orf.at **W:** oe1.orf.at
Webcast: D/L/P
L.P: DG: Dr. Monika Lindner; Dir, Technical: Peter Moosmann.
SW: Uses txs provided by ORS.
SAT: Astra 1H.
kHz: *6155, 17360, 18910*

	Winter Schedule 2012/2013		
German	**Days**	**Area**	**kHz**
0600-0715	daily	Eu,NAf,ME	6155mos
0900-0935	mtwtfs.	AUS,NZL	17360mos, 18910mos

V: QSL-letter.
Notes: Relays of ORF's domestic service "Österreich 1" (Ö1).

TWR EUROPE (Rlg)
✉ Postfach 141, A-1235 Wien, Austria.
☎ +43 1 863120. 🖷 +43 1 8631220.
E: twre@twr.org **W:** www.twreurope.org
✉ Other European branches: P.O. Box 176, 3780 BD Voorthuizen, The Netherlands; P.O. Box 12, 820 02 Bratislava 22, Slovakia.
L.P: Dir: Felix Widme.
SAT: Eutelsat 28A (TWR UK).
kHz: *864, 999, 1035, 1233, 1350, 1377, 1395, 1467, 1548, 5910, 6105, 7210, 7225, 7295, 7400, 9495*

	Winter Schedule 2012/2013		
Adyghe	**Days**	**Area**	**kHz**
1740-1755	...t...	Cau	864erv
Arabic	**Days**	**Area**	**kHz**
0300-0330	mtwtf..	NAf,ME	1233cgr
2000-2015	.....ss	ME	1377erv
2015-2230	..t...	ME	1377erv
2025-2155	daily	NAf,ME	1233cgr
2030-2100	daily	ME	1377erv
2130-2300	daily	NAf	1467rou
2300-2315	...tfs.	NAf	1467rou
Assyrian	**Days**	**Area**	**kHz**
2015-2030	.t.....	ME	1377erv
Belarusian	**Days**	**Area**	**kHz**
1500-1530	m......	Eu	7295wer, 9495mos
2000-2030	m......	Eu	999kch
Bosnian	**Days**	**Area**	**kHz**
2045-2130	.....s.	Eu	1395fla
Bulgarian	**Days**	**Area**	**kHz**
1800-1830	daily	Eu	1548kch
Chechen	**Days**	**Area**	**kHz**
1740-1755	.....s.	Cau	864erv
Croatian	**Days**	**Area**	**kHz**
2015-2130	.....s.	Eu	1395fla
2030-2045	.....s.	Eu	1395fla
2030-2100	mtwtf..	Eu	1395fla
English	**Days**	**Area**	**kHz**
0800-0850	daily	Eu	6105wer, 7400mos
1445-1500	daily	Eu	1467bis
1845-1915	.....s.	ME	1350erv

English	Days	Area	kHz
2300-2315	mtw....	NAf	1467rou
2300-2345	......s	NAf	1467rou

Farsi	Days	Area	kHz
1830-1845	.twt...	ME	1377erv
1830-1900	m...fss	ME	1377erv
1845-1900	.twt...	ME	1377erv
1900-1930	daily	ME	1377erv
1932-2000	daily	ME	1377erv

Gilaki	Days	Area	kHz
1815-1830	...t...	ME	1377erv

Hebrew	Days	Area	kHz
1845-1915	mtwt..s	ME	1350erv

Hungarian	Days	Area	kHz
0930-1000	daily	Eu	7210wer
1925-2000	daily	Eu	1395fla

Kabyle	Days	Area	kHz
2045-2115	mtw.fs.	NAf	1467rou
2045-2130	...t..s	NAf	1467rou

Karalpak	Days	Area	kHz
1915-1945	.....ss	ME	864erv

Kazakh	Days	Area	kHz
1500-1515	daily	CAs	1467bis
1625-1640	daily	CAs	864erv

Kumyk	Days	Area	kHz
1740-1755	....f..	Cau	864erv

Kurdish (Kurmanji)	Days	Area	kHz
1800-1815	daily	ME	1350erv

Kurdish (Sorani)	Days	Area	kHz
1800-1815	daily	ME	1377erv

Kyrgyz	Days	Area	kHz
1545-1600	daily	CAs	1467bis
1630-1645	daily	CAs	1467bis

Lak	Days	Area	kHz
1740-1755	..w....	Cau	864erv

Lezgi	Days	Area	kHz
1740-1755	.t.....	Cau	864erv

Montenegrin	Days	Area	kHz
1945-2000	......s	Eu	1548kch

Polish	Days	Area	kHz
0645-0700	mtwtf..	Eu	5910wer, 7225mos
2000-2015	.....s.	Eu	1395fla
2000-2030	mtwtf.s	Eu	1395fla

Qashqai	Days	Area	kHz
1815-1830	...f..	ME	1377erv

Romani (Balkan)	Days	Area	kHz
1830-1845	daily	Eu	1548kch

Romani (Vlax)	Days	Area	kHz
1915-1945	mtwtf..	Eu	1548kch

Romanian	Days	Area	kHz
1100-1130	.....s.	Eu	6105wer
1629-1659	.....s.	Eu	6105wer
1845-1915	mtwtf..	Eu	1548kch
1845-1945	.....ss	Eu	1548kch

Russian	Days	Area	kHz
0200-0400	daily	RUS	1035ttu
1500-1530	.twtfss	RUS	7295wer, 9495mos
1515-1545	....ss	CAs	1467bis
1600-1700	m.w.f.	RUS	1035ttu
1640-1710	mtwtf..	CAs	864erv
1645-1700	daily	CAs	1467bis
1655-1710	.....s.	CAs	864erv
1800-2000	daily	RUS	1035ttu
1845-1915	...f...	ME	1350erv
1930-2000	m......	RUS	999kch
1930-2030	.t...s	RUS	999kch
1945-2015	.....s.	RUS	999kch
2000-2030	..wtf..	RUS	999kch

Serbian	Days	Area	kHz
1945-2000	mtwtfs.	Eu	1548kch, 1548kch
2100-2130	mtwtf..	Eu	1395fla

Tabasaran	Days	Area	kHz
1740-1755	m......	Cau	864erv

Tachawit	Days	Area	kHz
2115-2130	.....s.	NAf	1467rou

Tachelhit (Sous)	Days	Area	kHz
2115-2130	...f..	NAf	1467rou

Tajik	Days	Area	kHz
1700-1715	daily	CAs	1467bis

Tamazight	Days	Area	kHz
2115-2130	m.w....	NAf	1467rou

Tarifit	Days	Area	kHz
2115-2130	.t.....	NAf	1467rou

Tatar	Days	Area	kHz
1740-1755	.....s.	Cau	864erv

Turkish	Days	Area	kHz
1815-1845	.....s.	ME	864erv
1815-1845	mtwtf.s	ME	1350erv

Turkmen	Days	Area	kHz
1610-1625	m.wt.ss	CAs	864erv

Uighur	Days	Area	kHz
1600-1630	daily	CAs	1467bis

Ukrainian	Days	Area	kHz
1900-1930	mt....s	Eu	999kch
1900-1945	.....s.	Eu	999kch
1900-2000	..wtf..	Eu	999kch
2015-2030	.....s.	Eu	999kch

Uzbek	Days	Area	kHz
1515-1545	mtwtf..	CAs	1467bis
1655-1710	.....s	CAs	864erv
1710-1725	......s	CAs	864erv
1715-1745	mtwt.ss	CAs	1467bis

Ann: English: "This is Trans World Radio. The following programme is in the ... language"; "This is TWR UK".
V: QSL-card.
Notes: TWR regional division, covering Europe, Russia, Central Asia, the Near & Middle East. For corporate details, see under TWR (USA).

ÖSTERREICHISCHE RUNDFUNKSENDER GMBH & CO KG (ORS) (Tx Operator)

⌂ Würzburggasse 309, A-1136 Wien, Austria.
☎ +43 1 870400. 🖷 +43 1 8704012773.
E: office@ors.at **W:** www.ors.at
L.P: CEO: Michael Wagenhofer, MD: Norbert Grill.
SW: [MOS] Moosbrunn: 4 x 100, 2 x 500kW.
Notes: ORS is the national transmitter network operator.

BAHRAIN (BHR)

RADIO BAHRAIN (Gov)
⌂ See National Radio section.
Webcast: L (www.bna.bh/portal/radio)
L.P: CEO: Ahmed Najim; Dir, Broadcasting: Hamad Al-Manai; Dir, Technical: Abdulla Ahmed Al-Balooshi.
SW: [ABH] Abu Hayan: 2 x 60kW.
SAT: Badr 4.
kHz: 6010, 9745

		Winter Schedule 2012/2013	
Arabic	Days	Area	kHz
0000-2400	daily	ME	9745abh*
English	Days	Area	kHz
0000-2400	daily	ME	6010abh‡

Key: * AM/U; ‡ Inactive at time of publication.
Ann: Arabic: "Idhaat al-Bahrain".
IS: Local composition, played on guitar and violin.
V: QSL-letter.
Notes: Relays of Home Sce prgrs.

BANGLADESH (BGD)

BANGLADESH BETAR (Pub)
⌂ 121 Kazi Nazrul Islam Avenue, Shah Bagh, Dhaka-1000, Bangladesh.
☎ +880 2 8618119. (Ext. Sce) 🖷 +880 2 8612012.
E: ts-betar@bdonline.com; betar.external@yahoo.com (Dir, Ext Sce)
W: www.betar.org.bd
Webcast: D/L
☎ +880 2 8651083. (DG) 🖷 +880 2 9662600. (DG)

L.P: DG: Kazi Akhtar Uddin Ahmed; Deputy DG (Prgr): A. S. M. S. Apel Mahmood; Dir, External Sce: Setab Uddin Ahmed.
SW: [DKA] Dhaka, Khabirpur: 2 x 250kW. The first tx is a recent replacement, the second tx is also due to be replaced.
kHz: *7250, 15105, 15505*

Winter Schedule 2012/2013

Arabic	Days	Area	kHz
1600-1630	daily	ME	7250dka
Bengali	**Days**	**Area**	**kHz**
1630-1730	daily	ME	7250dka
1915-2000	daily	Eu	7250dka
English	**Days**	**Area**	**kHz**
1230-1300	daily	SEA	15105dka
1745-1900	daily	Eu	7250dka
Hindi	**Days**	**Area**	**kHz**
1515-1545	daily	SAs	15505dka
Nepali	**Days**	**Area**	**kHz**
1315-1345	daily	SAs	7250dka
Urdu	**Days**	**Area**	**kHz**
1400-1430	daily	SAs	15505dka

Ann: English: "This is the External Service of Bangladesh Betar".
IS: Local composition, played on violin and tanpura.
V: QSL-card (Rpt to Senior Engineer, Research and Receiving Centre. Email rpt to: rrc@dhaka.net)
Notes: External service of the national public broadcaster Bangladesh Betar, which began broadcasting on 1 Jan 1972.

BELARUS (BLR)

BELARUSKAJE RADYJO (Gov)
⌨ See National Radio section.
Webcast: L
kHz: *1170, 7255*

Winter Schedule 2012/2013

Belarusian	Days	Area	kHz
0400-0700	daily	RUS	7255mns
0400-0700	daily	Eu	1170sas
1500-1700	daily	RUS	7255mns

V: QSL-card.
Notes: SW frequencies for domestic coverage: see National Radio section.

RADIO BELARUS (Gov)
⌨ Cyrvonaja Street 4, 220807 Minsk, Belarus.
☎ +375 17 2395852. 🖨 +375 17 2848574.
E: radio_belarus@tvr.by **W:** www.radiobelarus.tvr.by
Webcast: D/L
L.P: Dir: Navum Halpiarovic; Head, Foreign Language Dept: Vjacaslaú Lakcjušyn.
MW/SW: Leased from Belaruski Radyjotelevizijny Peredajucy Centr.
FM/DAB: See National Radio section.
kHz: *1170, 6155, 11730*

Winter Schedule 2012/2013

Belarusian	Days	Area	kHz
1100-1400	daily	Eu	11730mns
English	**Days**	**Area**	**kHz**
2000-2020	mtwtfs.	Eu	6155mns, 11730mns
2020-2200	daily	Eu	6155mns, 11730mns
French	**Days**	**Area**	**kHz**
1940-2000	daily	Eu	11730mns
German	**Days**	**Area**	**kHz**
1800-1940	daily	Eu	11730mns
1800-2000	daily	Eu	6155mns
Polish	**Days**	**Area**	**kHz**
1600-1700	daily	Eu	11730mns
1600-1800	daily	Eu	1170sas
1705-1800	daily	Eu	6155mns
Russian	**Days**	**Area**	**kHz**
1400-1600	daily	Eu	11730mns
2200-2300	daily	Eu	6155mns, 11730mns
Spanish	**Days**	**Area**	**kHz**
2000-2020	......s	Eu	6155mns, 11730mns

Ann: Belarusian: "Havoryc Radyjo Belarus"; English: "This is Radio Belarus", "You are listening to Radio Belarus"; German: "Hier ist die Radio Belarus".
V: QSL-card.

Notes: Radio Belarus is the External Sce of the National State Radio-TV Company of Belarus.

BELARUSKI RADYJOTELEVIZIJNY PEREDAJUCY CENTR (Tx Operator)
⌨ vul. Engelsa 22, 220030 Minsk, Belarus.
☎ +375 17 2270845. 🖨 +375 17 2271084.
E: inbox@brtpc.by **W:** www.brtpc.by
L.P: Dir: Andrej Karaim.
MW: [SAS] Sasnovy: 1170kHz 1000kW (run at 700kW).
SW: [MNS] Minsk, Kalodziščy: 1 x 75, 1 x 150, 1 x 250kW.
Notes: Belaruski Radyjotelevizijny Peredajucy Centr, a subsidiary of the Ministry of Telecommunications & Informatisation, is the national transmitter network operator.

BELGIUM (BEL)

RTBF INTERNATIONAL (Pub)
⌨ Local 3P09, 52 Bd Reyers, B-1044 Bruxelles, Belgium.
☎ +32 2 7374014. 🖨 +32 2 7373032.
E: rtbfi@rtbf.be **W:** www.rtbf.be/rtbfi
Webcast: L
L.P: Dir/GM (RTBF): Jean-Paul Philippot.
MW: [WAV] Wavre: 621kHz 300kW.
FM/DAB: FM: 99.2MHz (Kinshasa, Dem. Rep. of Congo).
SAT: Eutelsat 5WA.
kHz: *621*

Winter Schedule 2012/2013

French	Days	Area	kHz
0400-2310	daily	WEu	621wav

V: Email only. Does not send QSL-cards via regular mail.
Notes: Transmissions are relays of RTBF Home Sce prgrs.

RADIO 700 (Comm)
⌨ Trierer Str. 26, B-4750 Bütgenbach, Belgium.
☎ +32 87 480200.
E: info@radio700.eu **W:** www.radio700.eu; www.radio700.de
Webcast: L
SW: Via Radio 700 Kurzwellendienst. (Germany)
FM/DAB: see National Radio section. (Belgium, Germany)
kHz: *3955, 6085*

Winter Schedule 2012/2013

German	Days	Area	kHz
0500-1600	daily	Eu	6085kll
0500-1800	daily	Eu	3955kll
2130-2300	daily	Eu	3955kll

V: QSL-card.
Notes: Radio 700 - "Schlager und Oldies" is licensed to VoG Privater Rundfunk in Ostbelgien (PRiO) and is primarily targeting German speaking listeners on both sides of the Belgian-German border. Radio 700 was founded 2002 as local radio project of Funkhaus Euskirchen e.V. in Euskirchen, Germany.

TDPRADIO ‡
Notes: TDPradio was a music station created by the former TDP to promote DRM shortwave broadcasting. The project was discontinued in summer 2012. Sister station "The Disco Palace", see under USA, remains active.

BROADCAST BELGIUM (Consultants) (Broker)
⌨ P.O. Box 1, B-2310 Rijkevorsel, Belgium.
☎ +32 33 147800.
E: info@broadcast.be **W:** www.broadcast.be
L.P: Managing Director: Ludo Maes.
V: QSL-card (For brokered transmissions). Rp.
Notes: Broadcast Belgium (formerly TDP) are an international radio consultation company that, in conjunction with their sister company Alyx & Yeyi (see under USA) provide services and broker airtime etc. for radio stations with political, religious, commercial and NGO background.

BENIN (BEN)

TWR RELAY STATION
⌨ B.P. 1039, Parakou, Benin.
☎ +214 7643929.
E: 1566@twr.org **W:** www.cox-net.com (unofficial)

L.P: SM: Paul Cox.
MW: [PAR] Parakou: 1566kHz 100kW.
SW: [PAR] Parakou: 1 x 100kW (Planned). ‡
Notes: Owned by TWR. For corporate details, see under TWR (USA). For schedule, see TWR Africa (South Africa). F.PI: SW tx to be installed at site (pending license/construction permit and funding).

BONAIRE (BES)

TWR BONAIRE (Rlg)
✉ P.O. Box 388, Kralendijk, Bonaire, Carribean Netherlands..
☎ +599 7178800. 🖷 +599 7178808.
E: 800am@twr.org **W:** www.twr.org/americas.html
MW: [TWB] Bonaire, Belnem: 800kHz 100kW.
FM/DAB: FM: 89.5MHz (Bonaire).
kHz: 800

	Winter Schedule 2012/2013		
Baniua	**Days**	**Area**	**kHz**
0845-0900	.....s.	SAm	800twb
English	**Days**	**Area**	**kHz**
2300-0030	daily	CAm	800twb
Macuxi	**Days**	**Area**	**kHz**
0845-0900	......s	SAm	800twb
Portuguese	**Days**	**Area**	**kHz**
0700-0845	daily	SAm	800twb
0845-0900	mtwtf..	SAm	800twb
Spanish	**Days**	**Area**	**kHz**
0030-0700	daily	CAm,SAm	800twb
0900-1215	daily	CAm,SAm	800twb
2130-2300	daily	CAm,SAm	800twb

Ann: English: "This is the international sound of the Caribbean, Trans World Radio, Bonaire".
V: QSL-card.
Notes: branch and transmitting station. Owned by TWR, for corporate details, see under USA.

RADIO NETHERLANDS WORLDWIDE (RNW) RELAY STATION
✉ P.O. Box 45, Kralendijk, Bonaire.
SW: [BON] Bonaire, Tolo: 3 x 250kW.
V: QSL-card. (For direct rpt)
Notes: Owned by Radio Netherlands Worldwide.

BOSNIA AND HERZEGOVINA (BIH)

INTERNATIONAL RADIO SERBIA RELAY STATION
✉ KTCB, 76300 Bijeljina, Bosnia & Herzegovina.
SW: [BIJ] Bijeljina, Jabanuša: 2 x 500kW.
Notes: Owned and operated by International Radio Serbia.

BOTSWANA (BOT)

IBB RELAY STATION BOTSWANA
✉ IBB Transmitting Station, Private Bag 38, Selebi-Phikwe, Botswana.
☎ +267 2610932. 🖷 +267 2610185.
L.P: SM: George O. Miller.
MW: [BOT] Selebi-Phikwe, Moepeng Hill: 909kHz 600kW. Reserve: 50kW.
SW: [BOT] Selebi-Phikwe, Moepeng Hill: 4 x 100kW.
V: QSL-card.

BULGARIA (BUL)

SPACELINE LTD (Broker)
✉ P.O. Box 812, 1000 Sofia, Bulgaria.
☎ +359 2 9625962. 🖷 +359 2 9633428.
E: info@spaceline.bg **W:** www.spaceline.bg
L.P: GM: Dimitar Todorov.
Notes: Spaceline Ltd brokers air time for SW facilities in Bulgaria and Armenia.

NURTS BULGARIA (Tx Operator)
✉ bul. Peyo K. Yavorov 2, 1164 Sofia, Bulgaria.
☎ +359 2 8069300. 🖷 +359 2 8069309.
E: office@nurts.bg **W:** www.nurts.bg

L.P: CEO's: Emil Atanasov, Svilen Popov.
SW: [SOF] Sofia, Kostinbrod: 1 x 15, 4 x 50, 3 x 100, 1 x 250kW.
Notes: NURTS is the Bulgarian national transmitter operator, a joint-venture of Bulsat Partners (Bulgaria) and Mancelord Ltd (Cyprus).

CANADA (CAN)

RADIO CANADA INTERNATIONAL (RCI) ‡ (Pub)
✉ 1400, boulevard René-Lévesque Est, Montréal, QC H2L 2M2, Canada.
☎ +1 514 5977500. 🖷 +1 514 5977760.
E: info@rcinet.ca **W:** www.rcinet.ca
Webcast: D/L/P
L.P: Dir: Helene Parent; Dir, Programming: Roger Tetrault; Dir, Engineering: Jaques Bouliane; Audience Relations: Bill Westenhaver; Schedules: Steve Lemay.
SW: Sackville site is being dismantled.
SAT: Hot Bird 6.
Ann: English: "This is Radio Canada International"; French: "Ici Radio Canada Internationale".
IS: First bar of Canadian National Anthem.
V: QSL-card.
Notes: Radio Canada International is the External Sce of the public service Canadian Broadcasting Corporation (CBC). Ceased SW broadcasts in June 2012.

BIBLE VOICE BROADCASTING (BVB) (Rlg)
✉ P.O. Box 425, Station E, Toronto, Ontario M6H 4E3, Canada.
☎ +1 800 5504670.
E: sales@bvbroadcasting.org **W:** www.bvbroadcasting.org
Webcast: D/P
✉ 569 Bristol Road, Newmarket, ON L3Y 6TZ, Canada. (HAGCM)
☎ +1 905 8985447. 🖷 +1 905 8982500.
W: www.hagcm.org
L.P: GM, HAGCM: Marty Mclaughlin.
kHz: 5940, 5945, 5950, 5980, 6030, 6095, 7325, 7365, 7395, 9440, 9450, 9470, 9515, 9665, 9715, 9925, 11700, 11875, 11915, 13740, 15180, 15215, 15335, 15390, 15470, 17545

	Winter Schedule 2012/2013		
Amharic	**Days**	**Area**	**kHz**
1630-1800	.....ss	Af	15335iss
1700-1800	.t.tf..	Af	15335iss
1730-1800	m.w....	Af	15335iss
Arabic	**Days**	**Area**	**kHz**
0300-0315	daily	ME	7325nau
0430-0445	daily	ME	5980nau
0500-0515	....f..	ME	9450wer
0500-0530	...t...	ME	9450wer
0900-1000	....f..	Af	17545wer
1700-1720	mt.tf..	ME	11915iss
1700-1730	daily	Af	9440wer
1700-1735	..w....	ME	11915iss
1700-1800	.t.t...	ME	11700wer
1715-1800	m.w.f..	ME	11700wer
2000-2015	daily	Af	5940nau
2030-2045	daily	Af	9515nau
Cantonese	**Days**	**Area**	**kHz**
1100-1115	.twtf..	EAs	15390trm
Chinese	**Days**	**Area**	**kHz**
1100-1130	m......	EAs	15390trm
Dinka	**Days**	**Area**	**kHz**
1700-1730	daily	SDN	11875wer
English	**Days**	**Area**	**kHz**
0100-0115	.....ss	As	7395wer
0800-0830	......s	Eu	5945wer
0800-0845	......s.	Eu	5945wer
1100-1115	......s	EAs	15390trm
1100-1130	.....s.	EAs	15390trm
1115-1130	......s	EAs	15390trm
1115-1130	....f..	EAs	15390trm
1400-1500	......s	As	15470wer
1430-1500	......s.	As	15470wer
1500-1530	......s	ME	13740iss
1515-1530	.....s.	ME	13740nau
1530-1600	...t...	ME	13740nau
1745-1800	m.w....	ME	9715wer
1745-1815	....f..	ME	9715wer

English	Days	Area	kHz
1745-1845	...t....	ME	9715wer
1745-1900	.t.....	ME	9715wer
1745-2000	.....ss	ME	9715wer
1800-1815	.....s.	ME	7365nau
1900-2000	......s	Eu	6030nau
1900-2000	.....s.	ME	9470nau
1915-1945	......s	ME	9470nau
1915-1945	.....s.	Eu	6030nau

Hebrew	Days	Area	kHz
1800-1830	m.w....	ME	9715wer

Japanese	Days	Area	kHz
1130-1145	......s	J	15390trm
1145-1200	......s	J	15390trm

Korean	Days	Area	kHz
1230-1400	......s	EAs	15180trm
1300-1400	mtwtfs.	EAs	15180trm

Luri	Days	Area	kHz
0400-0430	m....ss	ME	5950nau

Nuer	Days	Area	kHz
1630-1700	daily	SDN	11875wer

Oromo	Days	Area	kHz
1600-1630	m..tf.s	Af	15335iss

Persian	Days	Area	kHz
0330-0345	..wtfss	ME	6095nau
1600-1615	..wtfss	ME	9665wer
1630-1830	daily	ME	9925wer
1800-1830	...f..	ME	7365nau
1800-1900	.t.t..	MF	7365nau
1830-1900	......s	ME	7365nau

Punjabi	Days	Area	kHz
1515-1530	...f..	As	13740nau

Russian	Days	Area	kHz
1900-1915	...f..	RUS	6030nau
1900-1930	.t.....	RUS	6030nau

Somali	Days	Area	kHz
1800-1830	...fss	Af	15335iss

Tamil	Days	Area	kHz
1630-1645	......s	As	15215wer

Tigrinya	Days	Area	kHz
1700-1730	m.w....	Af	15335iss

Ukrainian	Days	Area	kHz
1900-1915	...t...	Eu	6030nau

Urdu	Days	Area	kHz
1530-1600	..w.f..	As	13740nau

V: QSL-card.
Notes: BVB is operated by High Adventure Gospel Communication Ministries (Canada), in cooperation with Bible Voice (UK) and High Adventure Gospel Communication Ministries, Inc (USA). BVB's SW transmissions consist of religious paid programming, produced by small religious organisations, or individuals.

CHILE (CHL)

CVC LA VOZ ‡ (Rlg)
🖅 Casilla 395 Talagante, Santiago, Chile.
☎ +56 2 8557046. 📠 +56 2 8557053.
E: ondacorta@cvclavoz.cl **W:** www.cvclavoz.cl (Shortwave)
 W: www.cvclavoz.com
L.P: Senior Engineer (Transmitting station): Mathias Svensson.
SW: Santiago site closed.
V: QSL-card.
Notes: The SW transmitting station at Calera de Tango, owned by Voz Cristiana S.A. (a subsidiary of Christian Vision, see under United Kingdom), was closed in August 2012. It was transmitting La Voz (Radio Cristiana), a Spanish-language service for listeners in Latin America, produced in the Miami studio of Christian Vision (USA), Inc. (a subsidiary of Christian Vision, UK)

CHINA (CHN)

CHINA RADIO INTERNATIONAL (CRI) (Gov)
🖅 16a, Shijingshan Rd, Beijing 100040, P.R. China.
☎ +86 10 68891001. 📠 +86 10 68891582.
E: crieng@cri.com.cn **W:** www.cri.cn
Webcast: D/L

L.P: GD: Wang Gengnian; CE: Zhou Yi; Dir, English Sce: Yang Lei.
MW: See SARFT for tx information.
SW: See SARFT for tx information.
SAT: Amos 5, Apstar 6, ChinaSat 6B, Eutelsat Hot Bird 13B, Intelsat 7/8/9/10, Superbird C2, Telstar 11N, Yamal 202.

kHz: *603, 684, 702, 900, 963, 1017, 1044, 1080, 1170, 1188, 1215, 1269, 1296, 1323, 1341, 1422, 1440, 1458, 1521, 5905, 5910, 5915, 5955, 5960, 5965, 5970, 5980, 5985, 5990, 6005, 6010, 6020, 6025, 6040, 6055, 6060, 6065, 6070, 6075, 6080, 6090, 6095, 6100, 6110, 6115, 6135, 6140, 6145, 6150, 6155, 6160, 6165, 6170, 6175, 6180, 6185, 6415, 7205, 7210, 7215, 7220, 7225, 7230, 7235, 7245, 7250, 7255, 7260, 7265, 7275, 7285, 7290, 7295, 7300, 7305, 7310, 7315, 7320, 7325, 7330, 7335, 7340, 7345, 7350, 7360, 7365, 7380, 7390, 7395, 7400, 7405, 7410, 7415, 7420, 7425, 7430, 7435, 7440, 7445, 7410, 7415, 7420, 7425, 7430, 9435, 9440, 9450, 9455, 9460, 9470, 9490, 9515, 9525, 9535, 9540, 9550, 9555, 9560, 9565, 9570, 9580, 9585, 9590, 9600, 9610, 9615, 9620, 9640, 9645, 9650, 9655, 9665, 9670, 9675, 9685, 9690, 9695, 9705, 9710, 9720, 9730, 9745, 9760, 9765, 9770, 9785, 9790, 9795, 9800, 9825, 9855, 9860, 9865, 9870, 9875, 9880, 11610, 11620, 11640, 11650, 11665, 11680, 11690, 11700, 11710, 11720, 11725, 11730, 11750, 11760, 11770, 11780, 11785, 11790, 11795, 11820, 11830, 11845, 11855, 11860, 11870, 11875, 11880, 11885, 11900, 11920, 11935, 11945, 11955, 11975, 11980, 11990, 12015, 12070, 13580, 13590, 13600, 13610, 13620, 13625, 13640, 13645, 13650, 13655, 13665, 13670, 13680, 13715, 13720, 13735, 13740, 13750, 13780, 13790, 13810, 13850, 13855, 15110, 15120, 15130, 15135, 15140, 15145, 15160, 15170, 15190, 15205, 15210, 15220, 15225, 15245, 15250, 15335, 15340, 15350, 15425, 15435, 15440, 15445, 15465, 15505, 15525, 15565, 15600, 15620, 15625, 15665, 15485, 15490, 17495, 17500, 17505, 17540, 17560, 17570, 17630, 17640, 17650, 17670, 17680, 17690, 17710, 17720, 17725, 17735, 17740, 17750, 17800, 17830, 17855*

Winter Schedule 2012/2013

Albanian	Days	Area	kHz
1600-1700	daily	Eu	1215fla
1900-2000	daily	Eu	6020szg, 7315kas
2100-2130	daily	Eu	6145iss
Amoy	**Days**	**Area**	**kHz**
0100-0200	daily	Eu	9860bei
0100-0200	daily	Pac	9460kun
0100-0200	daily	SAs	9610kun
0100-0200	daily	SEA	9550kun, 11945kun, 11980kun
0100-0300	daily	SEA	15425xia, 17495bei
1400-1500	daily	SEA	9655kun, 11650kun
Arabic	**Days**	**Area**	**kHz**
0500-0700	daily	NAf	5985cer, 7210cer
0500-0700	daily	ME	9590cer
0500-0700	daily	ME,NAf	17485kas
1600-1800	daily	ME,NAf	7300kas
1600-1800	daily	NAf	9555cer, 11725cer
1830-1930	daily	CAf,EAf	11640bko
2000-2200	daily	ME,NAf	6100xia, 6185cer, 7215cer
Bengali	**Days**	**Area**	**kHz**
0200-0300	daily	SAs	9655kun, 11640kun
1300-1400	daily	SAs	9600bji
1300-1500	daily	SAs	9490kun, 11610kun
1400-1500	daily	SAs	1269xuw
1500-1600	daily	SAs	9610kun, 9690kun
Bulgarian	**Days**	**Area**	**kHz**
1100-1200	daily	Eu	7220cer
1700-1800	daily	Eu	1458fla
1830-1900	daily	Eu	6020szg, 7265uru, 9695jin
2030-2100	daily	Eu	7320kun, 9720uru
Burmese	**Days**	**Area**	**kHz**
0200-0300	daily	MYA	900deh
0700-0800	daily	MYA	900deh
1100-1200	daily	SEA	1188kun, 9880kun
1300-1400	daily	SEA	1188kun, 9880kun
1300-1500	daily	SEA	11780kun
1400-1500	daily	MYA	900deh
Cantonese	**Days**	**Area**	**kHz**
0000-0100	daily	SEA	11820xia, 17495bei

Cantonese	Days	Area	kHz
0400-0500	daily	EAs	15160jin
0400-0500	daily	NAm	9790hab
0400-0600	daily	EAs	13655xia
0500-0600	daily	EAs	15170jin
0700-0800	daily	EAs	11640jin, 13610xia
1000-1100	daily	Pac	15440kun, 17670kun
1100-1200	daily	SEA	603dof, 9590kun, 9645bei
1100-1200	daily	Pac	7440nnn, 9540bei, 13580kun
1200-1300	daily	NAm	9570hab
1700-1800	daily	EAf	7220kas
1700-1800	daily	SAf	7325uru
1900-2000	daily	Eu	7215szg, 9770kas
2300-2400	daily	SEA	6140kun, 7325kun, 9425jin, 9460kun, 11935kun

Chaozhou	Days	Area	kHz
0700-0800	daily	SEA	15145xia, 17750xia
1100-1200	daily	SEA	9440kun, 11875kun
1800-1900	daily	Eu	6010uru, 7285xia

Chinese	Days	Area	kHz
0000-0100	daily	SEA	9435kun, 11845xia, 11975kun
0000-0100	daily	EAs	11780jin, 11900bei
0000-0200	daily	SEA	13580bei
0000-0300	daily	EAs	13655xia
0100-0200	daily	SAs	7250uru, 7300kas, 9560kas
0100-0200	daily	SEA	9600nnn, 11640xia, 11770nnn
0100-0400	daily	EAs	15160jin
0200-0300	daily	NAm	9580hab
0200-0300	daily	NAm,CAm	9690nob
0200-0300	daily	SAm	7330kas
0200-0300	daily	SAs	9825kas
0200-0400	daily	Eu	6020cer
0200-0400	daily	NAm	9570cer
0300-0400	daily	SAs	9450kas, 17540bei
0300-0600	daily	EAs	15130bei
0400-0500	daily	SAs	13640kas, 15170kas
0500-0600	daily	SAs	15140kas
0500-0700	daily	EAs	13620xia, 15120bei
0600-0700	daily	EAs	13655xia, 15170jin
0600-0800	daily	SEA	9655nnn, 13750kun, 17740xia
0600-0800	daily	Eu	17650kas
0700-0800	daily	Eu	11785nnn
0700-0900	daily	Eu	11855cer
0700-0900	daily	SAs	17830kas
0800-0900	daily	EAs	9880bei, 11640jin, 13610xia
0800-1000	daily	CAs,ME	15565xia, 17560xia
0800-1100	daily	EAs	9880bei
0900-1000	daily	SEA	11750nnn
0900-1000	daily	Pac	15440kun, 17670kun
0900-1000	daily	EAs	7430jin, 9440xia
0900-1100	daily	SAs	15525uru, 17500kas
0900-1100	daily	SEA	5965bei, 9460nnn, 11980kun, 13850bei, 15250kun
0900-1100	daily	SEA,EAs	15340xia
1000-1100	daily	EAs	7255xia, 9880bei
1000-1300	daily	Eu	17650kas
1100-1200	daily	EAs	7435bei
1100-1200	daily	Pac	11620bei, 15440kun
1100-1200	daily	SAs	9515kas
1100-1200	daily	SEA	11980kas
1200-1300	daily	EAs	7395bei
1200-1300	daily	SAs	7205kas, 9655kas
1200-1300	daily	SEA	11640xia

Chinese	Days	Area	kHz
1200-1400	daily	CAs	9540kun
1200-1400	daily	ME,NAf	11790kas*, 13810bei*
1200-1400	daily	SEA	7440nnn, 9855bei
1300-1400	daily	EAs	7205bei
1300-1400	daily	Eu	13855kas
1300-1400	daily	ME	13650uru
1300-1400	daily	SEA	7215xia
1300-1500	daily	Eu	702cdm
1400-1500	daily	SEA	6040xia
1400-1500	daily	SAs	7400bei, 7445kas, 9730kas
1400-1500	daily	EAs	7410bei
1400-1500	daily	Eu	11785kas
1400-1500	daily	ME	9430kas, 11610uru
1500-1600	daily	EAs	7255bei
1500-1600	daily	Eu	9590kas, 9705kas
1500-1600	daily	SAs	7235kas, 9560kas
1500-1600	daily	SEA	5910bei, 9455kun
1730-1830	daily	Eu	6150szg, 7445uru
1730-1830	daily	ME,NAf	7275uru, 7315kun, 9695kun
2000-2100	daily	Eu	7245kas, 7335szg, 7440bei
2000-2100	daily	ME	9865kun
2000-2100	daily	SAf	7305xia
2200-2300	daily	EAs	7305jin
2200-2300	daily	SEA	6100kun, 6140kun, 7325kun, 7440kun
2200-2300	daily	SAf	7430jin
2200-2300	daily	ME	5965kas
2200-2300	daily	NAf,ME	7220kun, 7405uru
2230-2300	daily	CAf,WAf	15505bko
2300-2400	daily	EAs	9555bei
2300-2400	daily	Eu	7300uru
2300-2400	daily	SEA	7425kun
2300-2400	daily	WAf	7295bko

Croatian	Days	Area	kHz
1700-1800	daily	Eu	7335bei, 9610kas
2100-2200	daily	Eu	6135xia, 7225uru

Czech	Days	Area	kHz
1100-1200	daily	Eu	15225kas, 17570kas
1900-1930	daily	Eu	7325bei
1900-2000	daily	Eu	7415uru
1930-2000	daily	Eu	7305iss
2000-2100	daily	Eu	963por
2230-2330	daily	Eu	1458fla

English	Days	Area	kHz
0000-0100	daily	EAs	9425bei
0000-0100	daily	SAs	6005kas, 6180kas, 7425kas
0000-0200	daily	NAm	6020cer, 9570cer
0000-0200	daily	SEA	11885xia, 15145bei
0100-0200	daily	Eu	9410kas
0100-0200	daily	NAm	9580hab
0100-0200	daily	SAs	6075kas, 6175kas, 9420kas
0200-0300	daily	SAS	13640kas
0200-0400	daily	SAs	11785kas
0300-0400	daily	NAm	9790hab
0300-0400	daily	NAm,CAm	9690nob
0300-0400	daily	SAs	15110kas
0300-0500	daily	EAs	13590bei, 13620xia, 15120bei
0400-0600	daily	CAs,ME	17725xia, 17855bei
0500-0600	daily	NAf,WAf	7220cer
0500-0700	daily	ME,NAf	17505kas
0500-0900	daily	SAs	11880kas, 15465kas, 17540kas
0500-1100	daily	SAs	15350kas
0600-0700	daily	ME	11770kas, 15145kas
0600-0700	daily	NAf	11750cer

English	Days	Area	kHz
0600-0800	daily	SEA	13645xia, 17710bei
0700-0800	daily	ME,NAf	17800kas
0700-0900	daily	Eu	1215fla, 11785cer
0700-1300	daily	Eu	17490kas
0800-0900	daily	ME,Af	15625kas
0800-1000	daily	EAs	9415xia
0900-1000	daily	Eu	17570uru, 17650kas
0900-1000	daily	SAs	17750kas
0900-1100	daily	Pac	15210kun, 17690jin
1000-1100	daily	EAs	5955xia, 7215xia, 11640bei
1000-1100	daily	SAs	15190uru
1000-1200	daily	SEA	13590bei, 13720xia
1100-1200	daily	SAs	9570kas, 11795kas, 13645kas
1100-1300	daily	Eu	13665cer
1100-1300	daily	SAs	1269xuw, 11650uru
1100-1600	daily	EAs	5955bei
1200-1300	daily	SEA	684dof, 1188kun, 9600kun, 9645bei, 9730kun
1200-1300	daily	SAs	7250kas, 9460kas, 12015kas
1200-1300	daily	Pac	9760kun
1200-1300	daily	CAs,ME	11690xia
1200-1300	daily	Eu	13790uru
1200-1400	daily	Pac	11760kun
1200-1400	daily	SEA	1341hdu, 11980kun
1200-1500	daily	Eu	13790uru
1300-1400	daily	SEA	9730bei
1300-1400	daily	Eu	13670kas, 13790kas
1300-1400	daily	NAm	9570hab
1300-1400	daily	Pac	11900kas
1300-1400	daily	SAs	7300kas, 9655kas
1300-1500	daily	CAs,ME	9765xia
1300-1600	daily	SAs	9870xia
1400-1500	daily	CAs	11665uru
1400-1500	daily	Eu	9795uru, 13625kas
1400-1500	daily	SAs	7300uru, 9460uru
1400-1600	daily	CAf,WAf	17630bko
1400-1600	daily	NAm	13740hab
1400-1600	daily	SEA	1188kun
1500-1600	daily	NAf,ME	6095kas, 9525kas, 9720uru
1500-1600	daily	SAs	7405uru, 9785jin
1500-1600	daily	SEA	7325bei, 9650nnn
1500-1700	daily	Eu	9435kas
1500-1800	daily	SAs	1323uru
1600-1700	daily	SEA	6060kun
1600-1700	daily	SAs	7235kas
1600-1700	daily	NAf,ME	7420uru
1600-1700	daily	Eu	9875kas
1600-1700	daily	ME	6100kas, 9600jin
1600-1800	daily	EAf,SAf	7435jin, 9570bei
1600-1800	daily	Eu	7255kas
1600-1800	daily	SEA	1080xuw, 6155nnn, 9460nnn
1700-1800	daily	Eu	7205bei
1700-1800	daily	ME	6165bei
1700-1800	daily	SAs	6140kas, 7410kas, 7425uru
1700-1800	daily	SEA	6090kun, 7420kun
1700-1900	daily	Eu	6100bei
1800-1900	daily	Eu	7405bei
1900-2100	daily	ME,NAf	7295kas, 9440kun
2000-2100	daily	EAf,SAf	5985bei
2000-2200	daily	Eu	5960cer, 7285cer, 7415kas, 9600kas
2100-2200	daily	SAf	7205xia, 7405bei
2200-2300	daily	EAs	5915bei

English	Days	Area	kHz
2200-2400	daily	Eu	1440mrn
2300-0100	daily	SEA	11790xia
2300-0100	daily	Eu	7350kas
2300-2400	daily	SEA	9535kun
2300-2400	daily	SAs	5915kas, 7415kas
2300-2400	daily	CAm	5990hab
2300-2400	daily	EAs	6145bei

Esperanto	Days	Area	kHz
1100-1200	daily	EAs	7210uru, 9450uru
1300-1400	daily	SEA	9440nnn, 11650bei
1700-1800	daily	Eu	1215fla, 7245xia
1930-2030	daily	Eu	7265uru, 9745uru
2200-2300	daily	SAm	7315kas, 9860kas

Farsi	Days	Area	kHz
1500-1530	daily	ME	6165uru, 9600kas, 9765kun
1800-1900	daily	ME	7295bei, 7325bei

Filipino	Days	Area	kHz
1130-1200	daily	SEA	1341hdu, 6060bei, 7410jin, 12070xia
1130-1230	daily	SEA	11955kun
1200-1230	daily	SEA	9720xia
1430-1500	daily	SEA	1341hdu, 7325xia, 11830kun

French	Days	Area	kHz
0600-0800	daily	Eu	15220uru
0800-1300	daily	Eu	702cdm
1200-1400	daily	Eu	15205kas
1400-1600	daily	WAf	11920cer, 13670cer
1600-1800	daily	Eu	7350kas
1800-2000	daily	Eu	702cdm
1830-2030	daily	WAf	9645kun
1830-2030	daily	CAf	7350uru
2030-2230	daily	Eu	6115bei, 7350uru
2100-2200	daily	Eu	1440mrn

German	Days	Area	kHz
0500-0700	daily	Eu	15245uru, 17720kas
1600-1800	daily	Eu	5970cer, 7380cer
1800-2000	daily	Eu	6160xia, 7395kas, 9615uru
1900-2100	daily	Eu	1440mrn
2100-2300	daily	Eu	963por

Hakka	Days	Area	kHz
0000-0100	daily	SEA	9460kun, 9550kun, 9860jin
0000-0100	daily	SAs	9610kun
0400-0500	daily	SEA	17505xia, 17710bei
0400-0500	daily	SAs	15350kas, 17540kas
1600-1700	daily	EAf	6090xia
1600-1700	daily	SAf	7325uru

Hausa	Days	Area	kHz
0800-0900	daily	WAf	7295bko
1630-1730	daily	WAf	9620kun, 9670kun
1730-1830	daily	WAf	9450kas, 9685kun
1800-1830	daily	WAf	11640bko

Hindi	Days	Area	kHz
0300-0400	daily	SAs	11640kas, 13720kas, 15210kas, 15350kas
1300-1400	daily	SAs	1269xuw, 1422kas, 7265uru, 9450kas
1500-1600	daily	SAs	7225uru, 7265kas
1500-1700	daily	SAs	1269xuw
1600-1700	daily	SAs	1422kas, 5915kas, 7395kun

Hungarian	Days	Area	kHz
1000-1100	daily	Eu	15220kas, 17570kas
1900-1930	daily	Eu	7440xia, 9560uru
2000-2100	daily	Eu	1458fla
2030-2100	daily	Eu	7390jin, 9585kas
2130-2200	daily	Eu	6145iss, 7250uru

Indonesian	Days	Area	kHz
0830-0930	daily	SEA	15135kun, 17735kun
1030-1130	daily	SEA	11700kun, 15135kun
1330-1430	daily	SEA	11955kun, 15135kun
Italian	**Days**	**Area**	**kHz**
0600-0700	daily	Eu	15620kas
1500-1800	daily	Eu	702cdm
1800-1900	daily	Eu	1458fla, 7340kas, 7435jin
2030-2130	daily	Eu	7265uru, 7310kas
Japanese	**Days**	**Area**	**kHz**
1000-1300	daily	EAs	7325jin, 9440xia
1100-1600	daily	EAs	1044hnl
1300-1400	daily	EAs	7215jin
1400-1500	daily	EAs	7210xia, 7410jin
1500-1600	daily	EAs	5980xia, 7220jin
2200-2300	daily	EAs	5985xia, 7440bei
2300-2400	daily	EAs	9435xia, 9695jin
Khmer	**Days**	**Area**	**kHz**
1030-1130	daily	SEA	684dof, 15160nnn, 17680kun
1200-1300	daily	SEA	9440kun, 11680nnn
1400-1500	daily	SEA	6055nnn, 9600nnn
2300-0100	daily	SEA	9765nnn, 11990nnn
Korean	**Days**	**Area**	**kHz**
1100-1500	daily	EAs	1017cah, 1323hdn
1400-1500	daily	EAs	5965xia
2100-2300	daily	EAs	1323hdn, 7210xia
Lao	**Days**	**Area**	**kHz**
1230-1330	daily	SEA	7360kun, 9785kun
1430-1530	daily	SEA	1080xuw, 7360kun, 9675kun
Malay	**Days**	**Area**	**kHz**
0930-1030	daily	SEA	15135kun, 17680kun
1230-1330	daily	SEA	11955kun, 15600kun
Mongolian	**Days**	**Area**	**kHz**
0000-0100	daily	EAs	9470uru, 11875bei
1100-1200	daily	EAs	6110uru, 7400huh
1200-1300	daily	EAs	1323uru, 5915huh, 5990huh
1300-1400	daily	EAs	6100uru, 7285bei
1400-1500	daily	EAs	5915huh, 5990huh
2300-2400	daily	EAs	6185xia, 7205xia
Nepali	**Days**	**Area**	**kHz**
0130-0230	daily	SAs	11860kun
0130-0330	daily	SAs	13780kun
0230-0330	daily	SAs	11730kun
1400-1500	daily	SAs	7220kun, 7435kun
1500-1600	daily	SAs	7215kun, 9535kun
Pashto	**Days**	**Area**	**kHz**
0200-0230	daily	WAs	6065kas, 7350kas, 15435xia
1500-1600	daily	WAs	7435kun, 9620kas
1530-1600	daily	WAs	6165uru
Polish	**Days**	**Area**	**kHz**
1900-2000	daily	Eu	963por
2000-2100	daily	Eu	6020szg, 6145iss, 7405uru
2130-2230	daily	Eu	1458fla
Portuguese	**Days**	**Area**	**kHz**
0000-0100	daily	SAm	9435kas
1900-2000	daily	CAf,SAf	5985bei, 7365kas, 7405xia, 9535bji
1900-2000	daily	Eu	7335jin, 9730kas
2200-2300	daily	Eu	6175cer, 7260uru, 9410kas
2200-2300	daily	SAm	9685kas
2300-0100	daily	SAm	6100bei
2300-2400	daily	SAm	13650hab
Romanian	**Days**	**Area**	**kHz**
0900-1000	daily	Eu	7285cer, 9460cer
1800-1900	daily	Eu	1215fla
1900-1930	daily	Eu	7305iss

Romanian	Days	Area	kHz
1900-2000	daily	Eu	6145uru
1930-2000	daily	Eu	7440xia
Russian	**Days**	**Area**	**kHz**
0000-0200	daily	CAs	1521uru
0100-0200	daily	CAs,Eu	13600xia
0100-0200	daily	EAs	5905kas
0200-0300	daily	CAs,Eu	17640xia
0200-0400	daily	CAs	5915kas
0300-0400	daily	CAs	11710uru
0300-0400	daily	CAs,Eu	17710jin
0300-0500	daily	Eu	963por
0300-0500	daily	CAs,Eu	15435xia
0400-0500	daily	CAs	17640xia
0400-0600	daily	CAs,Eu	15445kas, 15665kas
0800-1000	daily	CAs,Eu	15335kas, 15665kas
1000-1100	daily	EAs	7400huh
1000-1200	daily	EAs	5915huh
1000-1300	daily	EAs	7290szg
1000-1600	daily	EAs	963hdn‡
1100-1200	daily	CAs	6080bei
1100-1200	daily	EAs	1323uru
1100-1600	daily	EAs	1323hei
1100-2000	daily	CAs	1521uru
1200-1300	daily	EAs	6100bei
1200-1300	daily	RUS	7215xia, 7410szg, 9590szg, 9685szg
1200-1400	daily	CAs	5905kas
1300-1400	daily	SEA	9870xia
1300-1400	daily	EAs	5915huh, 5990huh, 7255szg
1300-1500	daily	EAs	1323uru
1400-1500	daily	EAs	9450szg
1400-1500	daily	CAs	7330xia
1400-1600	daily	CAs	6005kas
1500-1600	daily	EAs	5915huh, 5965bei, 5990huh
1500-1600	daily	Eu	6025xia
1500-1600	daily	Eu,CAs	6180uru
1600-1700	daily	CAs,Eu	7215szg
1600-1700	daily	Eu	6070kas
1600-1800	daily	CAs,Eu	6040uru, 7265uru
1700-1800	daily	RUS	5915kas, 7410bji
1700-1900	daily	Eu	963por
1700-1900	daily	RUS	6070xia
1800-1900	daily	RUS	6170kas, 7210uru, 7255szg, 9535iss
1900-2000	daily	Eu	6110xia, 7245bji
1900-2100	daily	Eu	6100bei
2000-2100	daily	Eu	7255bji, 9525bei
2300-0100	daily	EAs	5990huh, 7405huh
Serbian	**Days**	**Area**	**kHz**
1200-1300	daily	Eu	7345cer
2000-2030	daily	Eu	7315uru, 7390xia, 9585kas, 9585kas
2100-2130	daily	Eu	7325xia, 7425jin, 7440kun
2200-2300	daily	Eu	1215fla
Sinhala	**Days**	**Area**	**kHz**
1400-1500	daily	SAs	7265kas, 9610jin
2330-0030	daily	SAs	6100kun, 7260kas
Spanish	**Days**	**Area**	**kHz**
0000-0100	daily	CAm	5990hab
0000-0100	daily	SAm	15120hab
0100-0300	daily	SAm	9590xia, 9710kas
0600-0800	daily	Eu	15135kas
2100-2300	daily	Eu	6020szg, 9640kas
2200-2300	daily	SAm	6100bei
2200-2400	daily	Eu	7210cer, 7250uru
2300-0100	daily	Eu	9800kas
2300-0100	daily	SAm	9590kas
2300-2400	daily	Eu	6175cer
Swahili	**Days**	**Area**	**kHz**
1600-1700	daily	EAf	7320xia

Swahili	Days	Area	kHz
1600-1800	daily	EAf	5985bei
1700-1800	daily	EAf	7400xia

Tamil	Days	Area	kHz
0200-0300	daily	SAs	11870kas, 13715kas
0300-0400	daily	SAs	13600kun, 13735kas
1400-1500	daily	SAs	9570kas, 9665kas
1500-1600	daily	SAs	9730kas, 13600kas

Thai	Days	Area	kHz
1130-1230	daily	SEA	1080xuw, 7360kun, 9785kun
1330-1430	daily	SEA	1080xuw, 7360kun, 9785kun

Turkish	Days	Area	kHz
1500-1600	daily	ME	7230cer, 9565cer
1600-1700	daily	ME	6165uru, 7325kun
1900-2000	daily	ME	7255kun, 9655kun
1930-2000	daily	ME	1170arm

Urdu	Days	Area	kHz
0100-0200	daily	SAs	6020kas, 7360kas
0200-0300	daily	SAs	6020kas, 7290kas
1400-1600	daily	SAs	1422kas, 6075kas, 7285kas

Vietnamese	Days	Area	kHz
0000-0100	daily	SEA	11770bei, 13680xia
0400-0500	daily	SEA	11650kun
0400-0600	daily	SEA	11740xia
0500-0600	daily	SEA	11640kun
1100-1200	daily	SEA	11785bei, 11990xia
1100-1500	daily	SEA	1296kun
1100-1600	daily	SEA	9550bei
1200-1300	daily	SEA	11720bji
1300-1600	daily	SEA	603dof
1400-1500	daily	SEA	9685bji
1400-1600	daily	SEA	684dof
1600-1700	daily	SEA	6010bei, 7360kun
2300-0100	daily	SEA	603dof
2300-2400	daily	SEA	6415bei, 7220xia

Ann: Arabic: "Idha'at as-Sin ad-Duwaliyah"; English: "This is China Radio International, broadcasting from Beijing"; German: "Hier ist Radio China International"; Indonesian: "Inilah Radio CRI, China Radio International"; Japanese: "Kochirawa Pekin Hoso, Chugoku Kokusai Hosokyoku desu"; Korean: "Jungguk gukje bangsonggugimnida"; Malay: "Inilah Radio Antarabangsa China, dalam bahasa Melayu"; Mandarin: "Zhongguo guoji guangbo diantai"; Mongolian: "Hyatadyn Olon Ulsyn Radio"; Russian: "Govorit Meždunarodnoye Radio Kitaya"; Spanish: "Esta es Radio Internacional de China"; Swahili: "Hii ni Radio China kimataifa"; Vietnamese: "Day la dai phatthanh quoc te Trung quoc".

IS: First bars of the National Anthem.

V: QSL-card.

Notes: Founded on 3 Dec 1941. China Radio International is the External Sce produced under the roof of the State Administration of Radio, Film and Television of the P.R. of China (SARFT). Some MW programme content provided by Radio86 (Futuvision), see under Finland for schedule.

VOICE OF GUANGXI BEIBU WAN, BEIBU BAY RADIO (Gov)
🖃 75 Minzu Dadao, Nanning, Guangxi 530022, P.R.China.
☎ +86 771 5802999. 🖷 +86 771 5802555.
W: bbr.bbrtv.com; www.bbrtv.com/english
Webcast: L
SW: See SARFT, for tx information.
kHz: 5050, 9820

Winter Schedule 2012/2013			
Cantonese	Days	Area	kHz
1000-1100	daily	SEA	5050nnn, 9820nnn
Chinese	Days	Area	kHz
0100-0400	mtwtf..	SEA	5050nnn, 9820nnn
0400-0800	daily	SEA	5050nnn, 9820nnn
2300-0200	.....ss	SEA	5050nnn, 9820nnn
English	Days	Area	kHz
0800-1000	daily	SEA	5050nnn, 9820nnn

Thai	Days	Area	kHz
1100-1130	mtwtf..	SEA	5050nnn, 9820nnn
Vietnamese	Days	Area	kHz
0200-0400	.....ss	SEA	5050nnn, 9820nnn
1100-1130	....ss	SEA	5050nnn, 9820nnn
1130-1600	daily	SEA	5050nnn, 9820nnn
2300-0100	mtwtf..	SEA	5050nnn, 9820nnn

Ann: English: "Learn about the world. Know China. This is Beibu Bay Radio"; Mandarin: "Guangxi Bei-bu Wan zhi sheng"; Vietnamese: "Tieng noi vinh bac phong guang tay".
V: QSL-letter.
Notes: Beibu Bay Radio is a joint External Service project of the provincial Guanxi People's Broadcasting Station and China Radio International.

YUNNAN PEOPLE'S BROADCASTING STATION – THE VOICE OF SHANGRI–LA (Gov)
🖃 Voice of Shangri-La, 182 Renmin Xi Lu, Kunming, Yunnan 650031, P.R.China.
☎ +86 871 5310211. 🖷 +86 871 5361744.
E: admin@ynradio.net **W:** www.ynradio.com
Webcast: D/L
SW: See SARFT for tx information.
kHz: 6035

Winter Schedule 2012/2013			
Chinese	Days	Area	kHz
1100-1200	daily	SEA	6035sha
1300-1400	daily	SEA	6035sha
Vietnamese	Days	Area	kHz
1000-1100	daily	SEA	6035sha
1200-1300	daily	SEA	6035sha
1400-1500	daily	SEA	6035sha

Ann: English: "This is the Voice of Shangri-La brought to you by Yunnan Radio"; Mandarin: "Xianggelila zhi sheng".
V: QSL-letter.
Notes: External Service of the provincial Yunnan People's Broadcasting Station.

STATE ADMINISTRATION OF RADIO, FILM AND TV (SARFT) (Tx Operator)
🖃 2 Fuxingmenwai Street, Xicheng District, Beijing 100866, P.R.China.
☎ +86 10 66093114. 🖷 +86 10 86092437.
E: sarft@chinasarft.gov.cn **W:** www.sarft.gov.cn; www.chinasarft.gov.cn
L.P: Minister: Cai Fuchao.
MW: [CAH] Changchun, Jilin prov.: 1017kHz 100kW; [DEH] Luxi, Dehong pref., Yunnan prov.: 900kHz 100kW; [DOF] Dongfang, Hainan prov.: 603/684kHz 600kW; [HDN] Huadian, Jilin prov.: 963/1323kHz 600kW; [HDU] Guangzhou, Liantang, Huadu district, Guangdong prov.: 1341kHz 300kW; [HEI] Shuangyashan, Heilongjiang prov.: 1323 kHz 200kW; [HNL] Changzhou, Henglin, Jiangsu prov.: 1044kHz 600kW; [KAS] Kashgar (Kashi), Sayibage, Xinjiang Uighur autonomous region: 1422kHz 600kW; [KUN] Kunming, Anning, Yunnan prov.: 1188/1296kHz 300kW; [URU] Ürümqi, Hutubi, Xinjiang Uighur autonomous region: 1323/1521kHz 500kW; [XUW] Xuanwei, Yunnan prov.: 1080/1269kHz 600kW.
SW: [BEI] Beijing, Doudian: 150/500kW; [BJI] Baoji, Qishan, Shaanxi prov.: 150kW; [HUH] Hohhot, Bikeqi, Nei Menggu autonomous region: 4 x 100kW; [JIN] Jinhua, Lanxi, Zhejiang prov.: 2 x 100, 3 x 500kW; [KAS] Kashgar (Kashi), Sayibage, Xinjiang Uighur autonomous region: 2 x 100, 8 x 500kW; [KUN] Kunming, Anning, Yunnan prov.: 1 x 50; 2 x 100, 5 x 500kW; [NNN] Nanning, Guangxi Zhuang autonomous region: 2 x 15; 2 x 100kW; [SHA] Kunming, Shalang, Yunnan prov.: 1 x 500kW; [SZG] Shijiazhuang, Nanpozhuang, Hebei prov.: 2 x 500kW; [URU] Ürümqi, Hutubi, Xinjiang Uighur autonomous region: 9 x 100, 8 x 500kW; [XIA] Xi'an, Xianyang, Shaanxi prov.: 150/500kW.
Notes: SARFT in an executive branch under the State Council of the Peoples Republic of China.

COSTA RICA (CTR)

RADIO EXTERIOR DE ESPAÑA (REE) RELAY STATION
🖃 RNE Centro Emisor de Onda Corta, 500 Oeste Palí, Cariari de Pococí, Limón, Costa Rica.
☎ +506 22904620.
SW: [CRI] Guápiles, Cariari de Pococí: 3 x 100kW.

CROATIA (HRV)

VOICE OF CROATIA (GLAS HRVATSKE) (Pub)
✉ Prisavlje 3, 10000 Zagreb, Croatia.
☎ +385 1 6342602. ▤ +385 1 6343305.
E: voiceofcroatia@hrt.hr; hrt@hrt.hr **W:** www.hrt.hr
Webcast: D/L
LP: GM, HRT: Josip Popovac.
SW: Uses txs provided by Odašiljaci i veze d.o.o. and leased foreign relays.
SAT: Eutelsat Hot Bird 13A, Optus D2.
kHz: *1134, 3985, 7370, 7375, 17860*

Winter Schedule 2012/2013

Croatian/Various	Days	Area	kHz
0000-0600	daily	NAm	7375nau
0600-1650	daily	Eu	7370dea
0700-1100	daily	AUS,NZL	17860sng
1655-0555	daily	Eu	3985dea
1700-2345	daily	Eu	1134zad
2300-0400	daily	SAm	7375nau

Ann: Croatian: "Hrvatska Radio, kratki val"; "Glas Hrvatske"; English: "This is Croatian Radio, you are listening to the Voice of Croatia"; Spanish: "La Voz de Croacia".
IS: Tune to Dubrovnik's poem "Lovely, Dear, Sweet Liberty", played on celeste.
V: QSL-card. Email rpt to qsl@hrt.hr
Notes: A service of the public broadcaster Hrvatska Radiotelevizija (HRT) for listeners abroad. "Glas Hrvatske" consists of Home Sce prgrs in Croatian (partly relay HR1), plus newscasts in English 0300-0315, 0700-0705, 1100-1005, 1700-1715, 1805-1815, 2315-2330; Spanish 0330-0345, 1300-1305, 2330-2345; Italian 1500-1520 (HRT R.Rijeka); Hungarian 1830-1840 (HRT R.Osijek) & German 1900-1905.

ODAŠILJACI I VEZE D.O.O. (OIV) (Tx Operator)
✉ ul. grada Vukovara 269d, 10000 Zagreb, Croatia.
☎ +385 1 6186000. ▤ +385 1 6186100.
E: oiv@oiv.hr **W:** www.oiv.hr
LP: Chmn: Denis Nikola Kulišic.
MW: [ZAD] Zador 1134kHz 600kW.
SW: [DEA] Deanovec: 2 x 10, 1 x 100kW.
Notes: Odašiljaci i veze is the national transmitter network operator.

CUBA (CUB)

RADIO HABANA CUBA (RHC) (Gov)
✉ Apartado 6240, La Habana 10600, Cuba.
☎ +53 7 877 5524. ▤ +53 7 8776531.
E: inforhc@enet.cu **W:** www.radiohc.cu
Webcast: L
LP: DG: Lic. Isidro Fardales; Chief Eng: Ing. Luis Pruna Amer; Advisor Consultant to DG: Prof. Arnaldo Coro Antich.
SW: Uses txs operated by Radiocuba.
SAT: Hispasat 1D.
kHz: *5040, 6000, 6010, 6060, 6120, 6125, 6150, 6165, 9550, 9640, 9710, 9810, 9850, 11680, 11690, 11750, 11760, 11840, 11860, 11880, 13680, 13780, 15230, 15340, 15370, 17580, 17705, 17730, 17750*

Winter Schedule 2012/2013

Arabic	Days	Area	kHz
2030-2100	daily	Eu	15340hab

Creole	Days	Area	kHz
0100-0130	daily	Car	5040hab
2300-2330	daily	SAm	15370hab

English	Days	Area	kHz
0000-0100	daily	Car	5040hab
0100-0500	daily	NAm	6000hab
0100-0700	daily	NAm	6165hab
0500-0700	daily	Am	6125hab
0500-0700	daily	NAm	6010hab, 6060hab
0600-0700	daily	Car	5040hab
2000-2100	daily	Am	11760hab
2200-2300	daily	Af	11880hab*

Esperanto	Days	Area	kHz
0700-0730	......s	NAm	6010hab

Esperanto	Days	Area	kHz
1600-1630	......s	Am	11760hab
2230-2300	......s	SAm	15370hab

French	Days	Area	kHz
0130-0200	daily	Car	5040hab
1930-2000	daily	Eu	15340hab
2100-2130	daily	Af	11880hab*
2100-2130	daily	CAm	11760hab
2230-2300	mtwtfs.	SAm	15370hab

Portuguese	Days	Area	kHz
2000-2030	daily	Eu	15340hab
2130-2200	daily	Af	11880hab*
2300-2400	daily	SAm	15230hab
2330-2400	daily	SAm	15370hab

Quecha	Days	Area	kHz
0000-0030	daily	SAm	15370hab

Spanish	Days	Area	kHz
0000-0100	mtwtf..	NAm	6000hab**, 9640hab**
0000-0500	daily	Am	11760hab
0000-0500	daily	NAm	6060hab
0000-0500	daily	SAm	11680hab
0000-0600	daily	Car	6120hab
0000-0600	daily	SAm	15230hab
0200-0600	daily	Car	5040hab
1200-1300	daily	Am	6150hab
1200-1300	daily	NAm	9550hab, 9850hab
1200-1600	daily	NAm	11860hab
1200-1600	daily	SAm	15230hab, 17580hab, 17730hab
1200-1600	daily	Car	11690hab
1200-1600	daily	Am	11760hab
1300-1500	daily	NAm	13780hab
1300-1600	daily	CAm	11750hab
1300-1600	daily	NAm	15340hab
1400-1800	......s	CAm	13680hab‡
1400-1800	......s	Car	11690hab‡
1400-1800	......s	NAm	15340hab‡
1400-1800	......s	SAm	15370hab‡, 17750hab‡
2200-0600	daily	CAm	9810hab
2200-0600	daily	SAm	11840hab, 17705hab
2200-2400	daily	Eu	15340hab
2200-2400	daily	Car	5040hab, 9710hab

Key: ‡ Aló Presidente prgr, (off air at time of publication); * Planned; ** Mesa Redonda Prgr.
Ann: English: "This is Radio Havana, Cuba".
V: QSL-card and letter. (Email to: radiohc@enet.cu)
Notes: Radio Habana Cuba is the External Sce of the state-owned Instituto Cubano de Radio y Television (ICRT). Frequencies and schedule are variable.

RADIOCUBA (Tx Operator)
✉ Habana No 406, e/ Obispo y Obrapía, Habana Vieja, Ciudad de La Habana, Cuba.
☎ +53 7 8607181. ▤ +53 7 8603107.
E: dirgeneral@radiocuba.cu
LP: DG: Justo Moreno García.
SW: [HAB] La Habana, three sites: Bauta, Corralillo (G.C. 22N57 082W33): 1 x 50, 6 x 100kW; Bejucal, Casualidad (G.C. 22N52 082W20): 3 x 50, 1 x 100kW; Quivicán, San Felipe (G.C. 22N50 082W18): 5 x 250kW. The status of the Bejucal site is uncertain.
Notes: Radiocuba, a state operated company that forms part of the Ministry of Information and Communications, is the national transmitter network operator.

CYPRUS (CYP)

CYPRUS BROADCASTING CORPORATION (CYBC) (Pub)
✉ P.O. Box 24824, 1397 Nicosia, Cyprus.
☎ +357 22862000. ▤ +357 22314050.
E: rik@cybc.com.cy **W:** www.cybc.com.cy
Webcast: L
LP: DG/CEO: Themis Themistocleous.
SW: via BBC East Mediterranean Relay Station.

SAT: Hellas Sat 2.
kHz: 6135, 7220, 9760

Winter Schedule 2012/2013

Greek	Days	Area	kHz
2215-2245	....fss	Eu	6135cyp, 7220cyp, 9760cyp

Ann: Greek: "Radiofoniko Idrima Kyprou".
IS: "Avkoritssa" (guitar).
V: QSL-card.
Notes: The transmissions are relays of CBC's Home Sce prgrs.

BBC EAST MEDITERRANEAN RELAY STATION
✉ P.O. Box 54912, 3729 Limassol, Cyprus.
☎ +357 24332511. 🖷 +357 24332595.
E: Via Babcock website.
L.P: SM: Andreas Themistocleous.
MW: [CYP] Zygi: 1323kHz 200kW (‡ after late March 2013); [ZAK] Zakaki (located at Lady's Mile in the Akrotiri Sovereign Base Area): 639/720kHz 500kW.
SW: [CYP] Zygi: 2 x 250, 8 x 300kW. (‡ after late March 2013)
V: QSL-card. (For direct report)
Notes: Owned by the BBC and operated by Babcock International Group PLC (see under United Kingdom). Transmissions from the Zygi site are due to cease at the end of March 2013.

MONTE CARLO RADIODIFFUSION RELAY STATION
✉ Cape Gkreko, Cyprus.
MW: [CGR] Cape Gkreko: 990kHz 600kW (leased by IBB), 1233kHz 1200kW.
Notes: Transmitting station owned by Monte Carlo Radiodiffusion, see under Monaco for corporate details.

CYPRUS

Northern

RADIO BAYRAK INTERNATIONAL ‡ (Gov)
✉ Bayrak Radio Television Corporation, P.O. Box 417, Lefkosa, via Mersin 10, Turkey.
☎ +90 392 2255555. 🖷 +90 392 2254581.
E: brt@brtk.net **W:** www.brtk.net; www.brtk.eu
Webcast: L
L.P: Chmn, BRTC: Yilmaz Baskaya; Head of R.Bayrak Int: Ülfet Kortmaz.
SW: [ISK] Yeni Iskele: 1 x 25kW. ‡
FM/DAB: FM: 87.8MHz (Sinandagi, 10kW); 105.0MHz (Selvilitepe, 5kW).
SAT: Türksat 3A.
Ann: English: "This is Bayrak International, the Voice of the Turkish Republic of Northern Cyprus".
V: QSL-letter.
Notes: Foreign language channel of the state broadcaster Bayrak Radyo Televizyon Kurumu (BRTK). News broadcasts in the following languages/times:- English: 1200, 1700; Greek: 1230, 1730; Arabic, French, German & Russian: Mon-Wed and Fri, 1215-1240; Headlines in English/Greek: Mon-Fri, 1000 and 1400.No transmissions at time of publication.

CZECH REPUBLIC (CZE)

RADIO PRAGUE (Pub)
✉ Vinohradská 12, 120 99 Praha 2, Czech Republic.
☎ +420 2 21552933. 🖷 +420 2 21552903.
E: cr@radio.cz **W:** www.radio.cz
Webcast: L. Web only languages: Czech, English, French, German, Russian, Spanish.
L.P: Dir: Miroslav Krupi?ka; Editor in Chief: Gerald Schubert.
SW: Leases airtime on WRMI (See under USA).
SAT: Astra 3A (Also on WRN via Eurobird 1, Galaxy 25, Hot Bird 6).
kHz: 9955

Winter Schedule 2012/2013

English	Days	Area	kHz
1000-1030	mtwtfs.	LAm	9955rmi
1530-1600	.....ss	LAm	9955rmi

Spanish	Days	Area	kHz
0300-0330	daily	LAm	9955rmi
0630-0700	daily	LAm	9955rmi
0930-1000	daily	LAm	9955rmi
1300-1330	daily	LAm	9955rmi

Key: Can be heard via WRN Broadcast, in some areas.
Ann: English: "Welcome to Radio Prague, the External Service of Czech Radio".
IS: Fanfare from Dvorák's 9th Symphony ("From the New World"), played on French horn.
V: QSL-card. Rec. acc. (Online form at: www.radio.cz/en/report)
Notes: Radio Prague (Ceský Rozhlas 7) is the External Sce of the public service Czech Radio (Ceský Rozhlas). Can be heard via WRN on MW in some areas.

DJIBOUTI (DJI)

IBB RELAY STATION DJIBOUTI
✉ IBB Transmitting Station, Djibouti.
MW: [DJI] Djibouti, Dorale: 1431kHz 600kW.

ECUADOR (EQA)

HCJB – LA VOZ DE LOS ANDES (Rlg)
✉ Postal address: Casilla 17-17-691, Quito, Ecuador.
☎ +593 2 2266808. 🖷 +593 2 2267263.
E: vozandes@hcjb.org.ec **W:** www.vozandes.org; www.radiohcjb.org
Webcast: L/P
✉ Street address: Villalengua OE2-52 y Av. 10 de Agosto, Quito, Ecuador.
SW: [QUI] Quito, Mount Pichincha: 1 x 10kW.
kHz: 1251, 6050, 9835, 11920, 12025, 13740

Winter Schedule 2012/2013

Arabic	Days	Area	kHz
2115-2145	daily	NAf	12025wof
Cha-palaa	**Days**	**Area**	**kHz**
2130-2200	mtwtf..	SAm	6050qui
Cofan	**Days**	**Area**	**kHz**
0000-0030	daily	SAm	6050qui
Dari	**Days**	**Area**	**kHz**
1530-1600	m .tfss	CAs	1251dsb
German	**Days**	**Area**	**kHz**
2300-2330	daily	SAm	9835wer
Kulina	**Days**	**Area**	**kHz**
2245-2300	daily	SAm	11920nau
Portuguese	**Days**	**Area**	**kHz**
2300-0045	daily	SAm	11920nau
Quichua	**Days**	**Area**	**kHz**
0030-0100	mtwtf..	SAm	6050qui
0030-0300	.....ss	SAm	6050qui
Russian	**Days**	**Area**	**kHz**
1530-1630	.....s.	RUS	13740nau
Shuar	**Days**	**Area**	**kHz**
2330-2400	mtwtf..	SAm	6050qui
Spanish	**Days**	**Area**	**kHz**
0130-0500	mtwtf..	SAm	6050qui
0300-0500	.....ss	SAm	6050qui
1100-1500	mtwtf..	SAm	6050qui
1130-1500	.....ss	SAm	6050qui
1900-2130	mtwtf..	SAm	6050qui
1900-2400	.....ss	SAm	6050qui
Tachelhit	**Days**	**Area**	**kHz**
2100-2115	daily	NAf	12025wof
Turkmen	**Days**	**Area**	**kHz**
1545-1600	.tw....	CAs	1251dsb
1600-1615	daily	CAs	1251dsb
Uzbek	**Days**	**Area**	**kHz**
1530-1545	.tw....	CAs	1251dsb
Waorani	**Days**	**Area**	**kHz**
0100-0130	mtwtf..	SAm	6050qui

V: QSL-card. Rp (1 IRC). Rec. acc.
Notes: HCJB Global branch and transmitting stn; for corporate details see under USA.

EGYPT (EGY)

RADIO CAIRO (Gov)
P.O. Box 1186, 11511 Cairo, Egypt.
+20 2 25789461. +20 2 25789461.
E: egyptianoverseas_english@hotmail.com; enginfo@ertu.org (ERTU Engineering) **W:** ertu.org
L.P: Pres, ERTU: Tharwat Mekky; Chmn, Broadcasting Sector: Ismael El Sheshtawy; Chmn, Engineering Sector: Hamdy Mounir.
MW: [ELA] El Arish: 1008kHz, 100kW
SW: [ABS] Abis: 8 x 250, 1 x 500kW; [ABZ] Abu Zaabal: 13 x 100, 1 x 250, 4 x 500kW.
kHz: 1008, 9280, 9655, 9720, 9855, 9885, 9905, 9965, 11540, 11560, 11890, 13580, 13620, 13855, 15160, 15205, 15245, 15285, 15290, 15345, 15365, 15450, 15480, 15545, 15610, 15710, 15800, 17480, 17510, 17585, 17625, 17810, 17870

Winter Schedule 2012/2013

Afar	Days	Area	kHz
1600-1700	daily	EAf	15450abz
Albanian	**Days**	**Area**	**kHz**
1500-1600	daily	Eu	13580abs
Amharic	**Days**	**Area**	**kHz**
1730-1900	daily	EAf	15285abz
Arabic	**Days**	**Area**	**kHz**
0030-0430	daily	NAm	9965abs
0200-0700	daily	Eu,NAm	9905abs*
0600-1500	daily	ISR	1008ela
0700-1100	daily	WAf	17510abz*
1015-1215	daily	ME,SEA	17480abz
1300-1600	daily	WAf	15800abs
1900-0030	daily	CAf,EAf	11540abz**
2000-2200	daily	Pac	9855abz
2330-0045	daily	LAm	13855abs, 15480abz
Dari	**Days**	**Area**	**kHz**
1300-1400	daily	WAs	15365abz
English	**Days**	**Area**	**kHz**
0200-0330	daily	NAm	9720abz
1215-1330	daily	SAs	17870abz
1600-1640	daily	ISR	1008ela
1600-1800	daily	CAf,SAf	15345abs
1900-2030	daily	WAf	15290abz
2115-2245	daily	Eu	11890abz
2300-0030	daily	NAm	9965abz
Farsi	**Days**	**Area**	**kHz**
1330-1530	daily	WAs	15245abz
French	**Days**	**Area**	**kHz**
1640-1700	daily	ISR	1008ela
2000-2115	daily	Eu	11560abz
2100-2300	daily	WAf	15205abs
Fulani	**Days**	**Area**	**kHz**
1845-2000	daily	WAf	17625abs
German	**Days**	**Area**	**kHz**
1900-2000	daily	Eu	11560abz
Hausa	**Days**	**Area**	**kHz**
1800-2100	daily	WAf	15710abs
Hebrew	**Days**	**Area**	**kHz**
1700-2200	daily	ISR	1008ela
Indonesian	**Days**	**Area**	**kHz**
1230-1400	daily	SEA	15710abs
Italian	**Days**	**Area**	**kHz**
1800-1900	daily	Eu	9655abs
Pashto	**Days**	**Area**	**kHz**
1400-1600	daily	WAs	15545abz
Portuguese	**Days**	**Area**	**kHz**
2215-2330	daily	SAm	15480abz
Russian	**Days**	**Area**	**kHz**
1500-1600	daily	ISR	1008ela
1900-2000	daily	Eu	9885abs
Somali	**Days**	**Area**	**kHz**
1700-1730	daily	EAf	15285abz
Spanish	**Days**	**Area**	**kHz**
0045-0200	daily	LAm	9720abz, 13620abs, 13855abs

Swahili	Days	Area	kHz
0400-0600	daily	EAf,CAf	15610abz
1530-1730	daily	EAf,CAf	17810abz
Turkish	**Days**	**Area**	**kHz**
1700-1900	daily	ME	9280abs
Urdu	**Days**	**Area**	**kHz**
1600-1800	daily	SAs	17585abz
Uzbek	**Days**	**Area**	**kHz**
1500-1600	daily	CAs	15160abs

Key: * General prgr; ** "Voice of the Arabs" prgr
Ann: English: "You are tuned to Radio Cairo"; Arabic: "Sout al-Arab, min al Qahira", "Sowt-il Afrikiy min al-Qahira".
V: QSL-card. Email rpt to freqmeg@yahoo.com
Notes: Radio Cairo is the External Sce of the Egyptian Radio & TV Union (ERTU).

EQUATORIAL GUINEA (GNE)

RADIO AFRICA (Rlg)
CP 851, Malabo, Equatorial Guinea.
E: radioafrica@myway.com
W: www.radioafricanetwork.com; radiopanam.com/africa.htm
Suite 250, 7011 Koll Center Parkway, Pleasanton, CA 94566-3253, USA. (Pan American Broadcasting); P.O. Box 3741, Cantonments, Accra, Ghana. (Radio Africa); P.O.Box 698, 60400 Chuka, Kenya. (Radio East Africa)
E: info@panambc.com **W:** www.panambc.com
L.P: Pres, Pan American Broadcasting: Gene Bernald.
SW: [BAT] Bata: 1 x 50kW (R. Nacional de Guinea Ecuatorial site)
kHz: 15190

Winter Schedule 2012/2013

English	Days	Area	kHz
0500-0900	daily	Af	15190bat†
1400-2030	daily	Af	15190bat†

Key: † Irregular.
Ann: English: "Radio Africa", "Radio Africa 2", "Radio East Africa".
V: QSL-card. Online form available on www.panambc.com
Notes: Run by Pan American Broadcasting, Inc. (see USA for corporate details). Transmits religious paid programming. Times vary considerably, depending on airtime sales. Because of this, the station may be off the air for varying amounts of time, until the next airtime booking. The tx is leased from Radio Nacional de Guinea Ecuatorial (see National Radio section).

ESTONIA (EST)

TARTU PERERAADIO (Rlg)
See National Radio section.
Webcast: D/L (radioeli.ru)
MW: [TTU] Tartu, Kavastu: 1035kHz 200kW.
Notes: Tartu Pereraadio is an Estonian evangelical broadcaster. Its transmissions include TWR broadcasts, see TWR Europe schedule (under Austria).

ETHIOPIA (ETH)

RADIO ETHIOPIA (Gov)
P.O. Box 654, Addis Ababa, Ethiopia.
+251 11 5524079. +251 11 5512686.
E: info@erta.gov.et **W:** www.ertagov.com
L.P: Head, Foreign Languages Dept: Melesse Edea Beyi.
SW: [GJW] Geja: 3 x 100kW.
kHz: 7235, 9560

Winter Schedule 2012/2013

Afar	Days	Area	kHz
1300-1400	daily	EAf,ME	7235gjw±, 9560gjw±
Arabic	**Days**	**Area**	**kHz**
1400-1500	daily	EAf,ME	7235gjw±, 9560gjw±
English	**Days**	**Area**	**kHz**
1600-1700	daily	EAf,ME	7235gjw±, 9560gjw±
French	**Days**	**Area**	**kHz**
1700-1800	daily	EAf,ME	7235gjw±, 9560gjw±
Somali	**Days**	**Area**	**kHz**
1200-1300	daily	EAf,ME	7235gjw±, 9560gjw±

Key: ± Variable Frequency.
Ann: English: "You are tuned to the External Service of Radio Ethiopia".

V: QSL-card.
Notes: External Sce of the national state broadcaster Radio Ethiopia.

FINLAND (FIN)

RADIO86
Pinninkatu 55, FI-33100 Tampere, Finland.
☎ +358 3 4108 9035. 🖷 +358 3 4108 9001.
W: gbtimes.com
L.P: (GBTIMES Ltd) CEO: Zhao Yinong; Editor-in-Chief: Juhanna Tommila.
MW: Leased from Digita Oy.
kHz: 963

Winter Schedule 2012/2013

Estonian	Days	Area	kHz
0500-0600	daily	Eu	963por

Lithuanian	Days	Area	kHz
0600-0700	daily	Eu	963por

Notes: In 2007, GBTIMES Ltd was formed as a joint venture of Global Media Consulation Co. Ltd (P.R.China) and FutuVision Media Ltd (Finland). GBTIMES is a partner of China Radio International (CRI), and among other activities, the media company produces and manages prgrs for CRI in Estonian and Lithuanian under the label "Radio86".

SCANDINAVIAN WEEKEND RADIO (SWR)
P.O. Box 99, FI-34801 Virrat, Finland.
☎ +358 400 995559. (During broadcast) 🖷 +358 3 4755776.
E: info@swradio.net **W:** www.swradio.net
L.P: Chief Editor: Esa Saunamäki; QSL Mgr: Alpo Heinonen.
MW: [VIR] Virrat, Liedenpohja: 1602kHz 0.4kW.
SW: [VIR] Virrat, Liedenpohja: 2 x 0.1kW.
kHz: 1602, 5980, 6170, 11690, 11720

Winter Schedule 2012/2013

English/Finnish	Days	Area	kHz
0600-0900	.....s.	Eu	5980vir*
0800-1400	.....s.	Eu	11720vir*
0900-1500	.....s.	Eu	6170vir*
1400-1700	.....s.	Eu	11690vir*
1500-1900	.....s.	Eu	5980vir*
1700-1900	.....s.	Eu	11720vir*
1900-2200	.....s.	Eu	6170vir*, 11690vir*
2200 0600	....fs.	Eu	6170vir*
2200-2200	....fs.	Eu	1602vir*
2200-2300	....f..	Eu	11720vir*
2300-0800	....fs.	Eu	11690vir*

Key: * 1st Fri/Sat of each month.
Ann: English: "You are listening to Scandinavian Weekend Radio".
V: QSL-card. Rp (2 IRCs/2 EUR/2 USD); Rpt form on website (down-loadable form for QSL-card; online form for QSL-email).
Notes: On air since 1 July 2000. Run by radio hobbyists, organized in the association Vaihtoehtoisen radiotoiminnan tukiyhdistys ry. Usually broadcasts for 24h every first Friday/Saturday of the month and on Christmas Day.

DIGITA OY (Tx Operator)
P.O. Box 135, FI-00521 Helsinki, Finland.
☎ +358 20 4117234.
E: communications@digita.fi **W:** www.digita.fi
Jämsänkatu 2, FI-00520 Helsinki, Finland.
L.P: CEO: Sirpa Ojala.
MW: [POR] Pori: 963kHz 600kW.
Notes: Digita Oy is the Finnish national transmitter operator. In August 2012, Digita was sold to the Australian private equity firm Colonial First State, after having been part of the TDF group (France) since 2000.

FRANCE (F)

MONTE CARLO DOUALIYA (Gov)
Maison de la Radio, 116 Avenue du Président Kennedy, F-75220 Paris Cedex 16, France.
☎ +33 1 56401717. 🖷 +33 1 56401700.
E: Via website. **W:** www.france24.com/ar
Webcast: D/L/P

L.P: Dir: Nahida Nakad.
MW: Leased from Monte Carlo Radiodiffusion.
FM/DAB: FM: Txs in Bahrain, Djibouti, Iraq, Jordan, Kuwait, Lebanon, Mauritania, Palestinian Territories and Qatar. (See National Radio section)
SAT: Astra 1L, Badr 4/6, Eutelsat 5WA/9A, Galaxy 19, Nilesat 101.
kHz: 1233

Winter Schedule 2012/2013

Arabic	Days	Area	kHz
0330-2020	daily	NAf,ME	1233cgr

Ann: Arabic: "Monte Carlo Doualiya".
V: QSL-card.
Notes: Produced under the roof of the External Services holding Audiovisuel extérieur de la France (AEF).

RADIO FRANCE INTERNATIONALE (RFI) (Gov)
Maison de la Radio, 116 Avenue du Président-Kennedy, F-75762 Paris Cedex 16, France.
☎ +33 1 56401212. 🖷 +33 1 42303071.
E: english.service@rfi.fr **W:** www.rfi.fr
Webcast: L/P
B.P. 9516, F-75016 Paris Cedex 16, France.
L.P: Pres/DG (AEF): Alain de Pouzilhac; Dir (RFI): Anne-Marie Capomaccio.
MW/SW: Leased from TDF & foreign relays.
SAT: AB4, Afristar, Astra1H, Asiasat 3, AsiaStar, Anik F1/F1R, Atlantic Bird 3, Badr 6, Echostar 3, Eutelsat W2/W3/W4, Galaxy 3C/19, Hispasat 1C, Hot Bird 8, Intelsat 701/903/907, IS7/10, NIMIQ 1, NSS7, Optus D2, Sirius, Solidaridad 2.
kHz: 684, 1008, 1098, 1296, 1503, 3965, 5915, 5925, 6180, 7205, 7295, 7310, 7325, 7380, 7390, 9565, 9665, 9790, 9805, 9835, 9870, 9955, 11605, 11670, 11700, 11790, 11860, 11875, 11955, 11995, 13650, 13685, 13695, 13740, 15170, 15300, 15315, 15360, 15530, 15680, 17615, 17620, 17660, 17850, 21580, 21690

Winter Schedule 2012/2013

Chinese	Days	Area	kHz
0930-1030	daily	EAs	7325tnn, 11875tnn
2200-2300	daily	EAs	1098kou
2200-2400	daily	EAs	1008luk
2300-2400	daily	EAs	7310tnn, 9955tnn

French	Days	Area	kHz
0400-0600	daily	CAf,EAf	7390iss*, 9700iss, 11700iss**
0500-0600	daily	CAf	11605mey
0600-0700	daily	NAf,WAf	5925iss*, 7390iss
0600-0800	daily	CAf	15170mey
0600-0800	daily	NAf,WAf	9790iss*
0600-0900	daily	WAf,CAf	15300iss
0700-0800	daily	NAf,WAf	11700iss
0700-0800	daily	CAf	17850iss, 21580iss**
0700-0900	daily	NAf,WAf	13695iss
0800-0900	daily	WAf	17620iss
0800-0900	daily	CAf	21580iss
1100-1130	daily	SEA	15680tnn
1200-1300	daily	CAf	17660mey, 21580iss
1200-1300	daily	NAf,WAf	17620iss
1200-1300	daily	WAf	21690guf
1300-1400	daily	SEA	684dof
1600-1700	daily	SEA	1296kun
1700-1800	daily	CAf	17850iss
1700-1800	daily	NAf,WAf	13740iss*
1700-1800	daily	WAf	17620iss**
1700-1900	daily	WAf,CAf	15300iss
1700-2000	daily	NAf,WAf	21690guf
1800-1900	daily	NAf,WAf	13740iss
1800-2000	daily	WAf,CAf	11995iss*
1900-2000	daily	Eu	3965iss+
1900-2000	daily	NAf,WAf	13740iss**
1900-2200	daily	WAf,CAf	9790iss
2000-2100	daily	WAf	11995iss
2000-2200	daily	NAf,WAf	7205iss
2200-1800	daily	Eu	3965iss+

Hausa	Days	Area	kHz
0600-0630	daily	WAf,CAf	7295iss*, 9805iss, 11995iss**

Hausa	Days	Area	kHz
0700-0730	daily	WAf,CAf	13685iss, 15315iss
1600-1700	daily	WAf,CAf	17615iss
Khmer	**Days**	**Area**	**kHz**
1200-1300	daily	SEA	1503fan
Persian	**Days**	**Area**	**kHz**
1430-1500	daily	ME	17850iss, 21580iss
1700-1800	daily	ME	11955iss
Portuguese	**Days**	**Area**	**kHz**
1700-1730	daily	CAf	9870mey
1900-1930	daily	WAf	6180mey
Russian	**Days**	**Area**	**kHz**
1400-1430	daily	Eu	11860iss*, 15530iss, 17850iss**
1600-1630	daily	Eu	11670iss, 13650iss
1900-2000	daily	Eu	5915iss, 9835iss
Swahili	**Days**	**Area**	**kHz**
0430-0500	daily	EAf,CAf	9665mey
0530-0600	daily	EAf,CAf	11790mey
1500-1600	daily	CAf,EAf	15360mey
Vietnamese	**Days**	**Area**	**kHz**
1400-1500	daily	SEA	7380tnn
1500-1600	daily	SEA	1296kun, 9565tsh

Key: + DRM; * to Feb 23;** From Feb 24.
Ann: French: "Ici Paris, Radio France Internationale".
V: QSL-card.
Notes: RFI is produced under the roof of the External Services holding Audiovisuel extérieur de la France (AEF). For AEF programming in Arabic, see Monte Carlo Doualiya.

TÉLÉDIFFUSION DE FRANCE S.A.S. (TDF) (Tx Operator)
✉ 106 Avenue Marx Dormoy, 92541 Montrouge Cedex, France.
☎ +33 149651000. 🖷 +33 146574850.
W: www.tdf.fr; www.tdf-group.com
✉ 10 rue d'Oradour-sur-Glane, F-75732 Paris Cedex 15, France. (Radio Division)
☎ +33 155951000. 🖷 +33 155952233.
L.P: GD: Patrick Puy.
SW: [ISS] Issoudun: 21 x 500kW.
V: QSL-card. (For RFI and other broadcaster relays via ISS)
Notes: TDF S.A.S., part of the TDF group, is the national French transmitter network operator with shortwave transmitting facilities in Issoudun and Montsinéry (French Guiana). For other members of the TDF group, see under Germany (Media Broadcast) and Monaco (Monte Carlo Radiodiffusion).

FRENCH GUIANA (GUF)

TÉLÉDIFFUSION DE FRANCE RELAY STATION
✉ TDF Outre-Mer, BP 7024, F-97307 Cayenne Cedex, French Guiana.
☎ +594 594350550. 🖷 +594 594350555.
E: germinal.cerda@tdf.fr
L.P: Dir (TDF branch): Germinal Cerda.
SW: [GUF] Cayenne, Montsinéry: 1 x 250, 4 x 500kW.
V: QSL-card.

GABON (GAB)

AFRICA NO.1 (Comm)
✉ Blvd Triomphal Omar Bongo, BP 1, Libreville, Gabon.
☎ +241 1760001. 🖷 +241 1742133.
E: Via website. **W:** www.africa1.com
Webcast: L/P
✉ 33 Rue du Faubourg Saint Antoine, F-75011 Paris, France.
☎ +33 155075801. 🖷 +33 155079748.
SW: [GAB] Moanda, Moyabi: 3 x 500kW.
FM/DAB: Local FM relays in francophone African countries.
SAT: Eutelsat 5WA.
kHz: 9580

Winter Schedule 2012/2013			
French	**Days**	**Area**	**kHz**
0500-2300	daily	Af	9580gab
2300-2315	.....ss	Af	9580gab

Ann: French: "Africa Numéro Un".
V: QSL-card.

Notes: Africa N°1 (Gabon) owns 20% of the shares of Africa Média, in France, that is producing a different (partly joint) channel of Africa N°1 from Paris.

GERMANY (D)

RADIO ANDERNACH ‡ (Gov)
✉ General-Delius-Kaserne, Kürrenberger Steig 34, D-56727 Mayen, Germany.
☎ +49 2651 4972601. 🖷 +49 2651 4972635.
E: radioandernach@bundeswehr.org **W:** www.radio-andernach. bundeswehr.de
Webcast: L (authorized access only)
L.P: Editor-in-chief: Oberstleutnant Markus Herholt.
V: QSL-card.
Notes: Radio Andernach is the radio station of the German Armed Forces (Bundeswehr). DRM test transmissions in autumn 2012; no SW transmissions at time of publication.

DEUTSCHE WELLE (DW) (Pub)
✉ Kurt-Schumacher-Str. 3, D-53113 Bonn, Germany.
☎ +49 228 4290. 🖷 +49 228 4293000.
E: info@dw.de **W:** www.dw.de
Webcast: D/L/P. Web only languages (some of which may also be broadcast on local FM affiliate stns): Albanian, Arabic, Bosnian, Bulgarian, Croatian, Farsi, Greek,. Hindi,Macedonian, Polish, Portuguese, Romanian, Russian, Serbian, Spanish, Turkish, Ukrainian.
L.P: DG: Erik Bettermann; PD: Christian Gramsch; MD, Strategy, Marketing and Distribution: Guido Baumhauer.
SW: Via DW Relay Station Kigali (Rwanda) and leased foreign relays.
SAT: AMC 1, AsiaSat 3S, Badr 4, Eutelsat 5WA/Hot Bird 13B, Intelsat 7, Nilesat 102.
kHz: 5905, 5925, 7265, 7285, 7300, 9420, 9470, 9655, 9795, 9800, 11600, 11800, 11865, 12045, 12055, 12070, 13700, 13780, 15275, 15440, 15640, 15700, 17700, 17710, 17800, 17860, 21780

Winter Schedule 2012/2013			
Amharic	**Days**	**Area**	**kHz**
1600-1700	daily	ETH	9800kig, 12070kig, 15275kig
Chinese	**Days**	**Area**	**kHz**
1300-1330	daily	CHN	11600sng, 13700dha
1330-1400	daily	CHN	11600sng, 13700dha
Dari	**Days**	**Area**	**kHz**
0830-0900	daily	AFG	15640dha, 17710dha
1330-1400	daily	AFG	15640sng, 17860dha
English	**Days**	**Area**	**kHz**
0400-0500	daily	Af	5905kig, 7285kig, 9420kig, 9470kig
0500-0530	daily	Af	5905kig, 9420kig, 9800kig, 11800kig
0530-0600	daily	Af	9420kig, 11800kig
0600-0630	daily	WAf	12045kig, 13780kig, 17800kig
0630-0700	daily	WAf	13780kig, 17800kig
1900-1930	daily	Af	11800kig, 12070kig, 15275kig
1930-2000	daily	Af	12070kig, 15275kig
2000-2100	daily	Af	9655kig, 11800kig, 12070kig
2100-2200	daily	Af	9655kig, 11800kig, 12070kig
French	**Days**	**Area**	**kHz**
1200-1300	daily	Af	9800kig, 15275kig, 15440kig, 17820wof, 21780kig
1700-1800	daily	Af	9795kig, 12070kig, 15275kig, 15700wof
Hausa	**Days**	**Area**	**kHz**
0630-0700	daily	WAf	12045kig, 15275kig, 21780dha
1300-1400	daily	WAf	15275kig, 17800kig, 21780kig

Hausa	Days	Area	kHz
1800-1900	daily	WAf	12070kig, 15275kig, 15700dha, 17800kig

Pashto	Days	Area	kHz
0800-0830	daily	AFG	15640dha, 17710dha
1400-1430	daily	AFG	15640sng, 17860dha

Portuguese	Days	Area	kHz
0530-0600	daily	Af	9800kig, 12045kig, 17800dha
1930-2000	daily	Af	11800kig, 11865kig, 12045mey

Swahili	Days	Area	kHz
0300-0400	daily	EAf	5905kig, 5925kig, 7265kig, 12070asc
1000-1100	daily	EAf	9800kig, 12070kig, 15275kig, 15700kig
1500-1600	daily	EAf	7300kig, 9800kig, 12055kig, 12070kig

Urdu	Days	Area	kHz
1430-1500	daily	SAs	15275kig, 15640sng, 17860dha

Ann: English: "DW - Deutsche Welle".
V: QSL-card. (Rpt to DW Customer Service)
Notes: Deutsche Welle is a public service External broadcaster.

EVANGELISCHE MISSIONS–GEMEINDEN (Rlg)
✉ Jahnstrasse 9, D-89182 Bernstadt, Germany.
☎ +49 7348 948026. 🖷 +49 7348 948027.
kHz: *6055, 9605, 13730*

Winter Schedule 2012/2013

German	Days	Area	kHz
1130-1200	.....ss	Eu	6055wer

Russian	Days	Area	kHz
1200-1230	.....s.	RUS	13730wer
1600-1630	.....s.	RUS	9605wer

V: QSL-card.
Notes: Rebroadcasts prgrs of various Protestant missions.

HCJB GERMANY (Rlg)
✉ Radio HCJB c/V., Postfach 8025, D-32736 Detmold, Germany.
☎ +49 5232 803009.
E: info@hcjb.de; hoffnungswelle@gmx.de **W:** www.hcjb.de
Webcast: L
✉ Casilla 17-17-691, Quito, Ecuador.
☎ +593 2 2266808. 🖷 +593 2 2267263.
E: deutsch@andenstimme.org **W:** www.andenstimme.org
L.P: Dir: Marco Schaa.
SW: [WNM] Weenermoor: 1 x 1.5kW
kHz: *3995*

Winter Schedule 2012/2013

English	Days	Area	kHz
2330-0400	daily	Eu	3995wnm*

German	Days	Area	kHz
0430-1700	daily	Eu	3995wnm*
1730-2000	daily	Eu	3995wnm*
2030-2330	daily	Eu	3995wnm*

German (Low)	Days	Area	kHz
1700-1730	daily	Eu	3995wnm
2000-2030	daily	Eu	3995wnm

Russian	Days	Area	kHz
0400-0430	daily	Eu	3995wnm

Key: * Includes rebroadcasts of prgrs by other religious prgr producers (pre-recorded or live).
V: QSL-card.
Notes: German branch of HCJB Global Voice / Vozandes Media (Ecuador), and transmitting station.

LUTHERISCHE STUNDE (Rlg)
✉ Postfach 1162, D-27363 Sottrum, Germany.
☎ +49 4264 2436. 🖷 +49 4264 2437.
E: info@lutherischestunde.de **W:** www.lutherischestunde.de
Webcast: D
L.P: MD (Lutherische Stunde e.V.): Petra Schmid.

kHz: *558, 630, 693, 1323, 1431, 7310*

Winter Schedule 2012/2013

German	Days	Area	kHz
1755-1800	m.w..s.	Eu	558cen*, 630klu, 693bln, 1323wbr, 1431dsd, 7310sam

Key: * Until 31 Dec 2012.
V: QSL-card. (Email to: p.schmid@lutherischestunde.de)
Notes: Produced by Lutherische Stunde e.V.

MISSIONSWERK HEUKELBACH (Rlg)
✉ Sülemickerstraße 15, D-51700 Bergneustadt, Germany.
☎ +49 2261 9450. 🖷 +49 2261 94537.
E: info@missionswerk-heukelbach.de
W: www.missionswerk-heukelbach.de
Webcast: D/L (live on: rtl1440.com)
L.P: Head of missionary organisation: Rudi Joas.
kHz: *558, 630, 693, 1323, 1431, 1440, 3995, 7310*

Winter Schedule 2012/2013

German	Days	Area	kHz
0415-0430	mtwtf..	Eu	1440mrn
0445-0500	.....s.	Eu	1440mrn
0500-0515	......s	Eu	1440mrn
0600-0630	daily	Eu	3995wnm
0615-0630	......s	Eu	1440mrn
1630-1700	daily	Eu	3995wnm
1840-1900	mt.tfss	Eu	7310sam
1845-1900	mt.tfss	Eu	558cen*, 630klu, 693bln, 1323wbr, 1431dsd
1845-1900	daily	Eu	1440mrn

Key: * until 31 Dec 2012.
V: QSL-card.
Notes: Produced by Missionswerk Werner Heukelbach e.V.

HAMBURGER LOKALRADIO
✉ Max-Eichholz-Ring 18, D-21031 Hamburg, Germany. (Editorial Office)
☎ +49 40 7382417. 🖷 +49 40 7382417.
E: redaktion@hamburger-lokalradio.de **W:** www.hhlr.de
✉ c/o Kulturzentrum Lola, Lohbrügger Landstrasse 8, D-21031 Hamburg, Germany. (Studio)
☎ +49 40 72692422. 🖷 +49 40 72692423.
L.P: Editor-in-Chief: Michael Kittner.
kHz: *7265*

Winter Schedule 2012/2013

English	Days	Area	kHz
0600-0700	..w..s.	Eu	7265goh*
1600-1700	..w..s.	Eu	7265goh*

German	Days	Area	kHz
0700-1600	..w..s.	Eu	7265goh*

Key: * AM/U, Alternate freq: 6190kHz
V: QSL-card.
Notes: Community radio prgr, produced by Anbietergemeinschaft Hamburger Lokalradio e.V.

MV BALTIC RADIO
✉ Seestrasse 17, D-19089 Göhren, Germany.
☎ +49 3861 301380. 🖷 +49 3861 3029720.
E: info@mvbalticradio.de **W:** www.mvbalticradio.de
L.P: Producer: Roland Rohde.
SW: [GOH] Göhren: 1 x 2kW & via leased tx from Media Broadcast GmbH
kHz: *6190, 7265*

Winter Schedule 2012/2013

German	Days	Area	kHz
0500-1100	......s	Eu	7265goh*†
1100-1700	......s	Eu	6190goh*†

Key: * AM/U; † Irregular.
V: QSL-card.
Notes: Produced by R&R Medienservice. Varying schedule. Own prgrs and/or rebroadcasts of shows by other prgr producers (see also Hamburger Lokalradio).

RADIO 6150
Rudolf-Diesel-Str. 1, D-85296 Rohrbach, Germany.
E: info@radio-6150.de **W:** www.radio-6150.de
L.P: CEO: Rainer Ebeling.
SW: [ROB] Rohrbach: 1 x 0.75kW.
kHz: *6070*

Winter Schedule 2012/2013
English	Days	Area	kHz
0000-2400	daily		6070rob*

Key: * Test transmissions (recordings of former offshore radio prgrs).
V: QSL-email. Rpt to qsl@radio-6150.de
Notes: Expected relaunch and name change did not occur as anticipated.

RADIO 700 KURZWELLENDIENST
Kuchenheimer Str. 155, D-53881 Euskirchen, Germany.
☎ +49 2251 921300. 🖷 +49 2251 921303.
E: info@funkhaus-euskirchen.de **W:** www.shortwaveservice.com;
www.classicbroadcast.de; www.radio700.info
Webcast: L/P (P: www.radio700.info)
L.P: Project coordinator: Christian Millig.
SW: [KLL] Kall, Krekel: 4 x 1, 1 x 20kW (PEP).
kHz: *3955, 6005, 6085*

Winter Schedule 2012/2013
German	Days	Area	kHz
1730-1745	mtwtfs.	Eu	6005kll

German/Various	Days	Area	kHz
0500-1600	daily	Eu	6085kll
0700-1700	daily	Eu	6005kll
2130-1900	daily	Eu	3955kll

V: QSL-card. (for relayed prgrs)
Notes: Shortwave relay service and podcast Internet portal, provided by Funkhaus Euskirchen e.V. Frequently changing schedule, details at www.shortwaveservice.com

RADIO ÖÖMRANG
Tanenwai 24, D-25946 Nebel-Westerheide, Germany.
☎ +49 4682 2688. 🖷 +49 4682 2262.
E: familie-koelzow@t-online.de
L.P: Producer: Arjan Kölzow.
kHz: *15215*

Winter Schedule 2012/2013
Frisian
(Low German)	Days	Area	kHz
1600-1700	...t...	NAm	15215wer*

Key: * 21st February 2013, annual broadcast.
Ann: English: "This is Radio Öömrang, the free voice of the Frisian people".
Notes: Radio Öömrang ("Radio Amrum") is on the air each year on 21 February, produced by the radio amateur Arjan Kölzow, on the island of Amrum in North Germany. First broadcast on 21 February 2006. The prgr is in the Frisian language and is aimed at the Frisian diaspora in North America.

IBB RELAY STATIONS GERMANY
IBB Transmitting Station Lampertheim, Postfach 1145, D- 68601 Lampertheim, Germany.
L.P: SM: Michael R. Hardegen.
SW: [BIB] Biblis: 11 x 100kW; [LAM] Lampertheim: 9 x 100kW.
V: QSL-card.

MEDIA BROADCAST GMBH (Tx Operator)
Joseph-Schumpeter-Allee 17, D-53227 Bonn, Germany.
☎ +49 228 55055022. 🖷 +49 228 55055019.
E: info@media-broadcast.com **W:** www.media-broadcast.com
L.P: CEO: Bernd Kraus.
MW: [BLN] Berlin, Zehlendorf: 693kHz 250kW; [DSD] Dresden, Wilsdruff: 1431kHz 150/250kW; [KLU] Königslutter: 630kHz 16/100kW; [WBR] Wachenbrunn: 1323kHz 150/1000kW.
SW: [NAU] Nauen: 2 x 100, 4 x 500kW; [WER] Wertachtal: 2 x 100, 14 x 500kW.
V: QSL-card. (For relayed stns. Email rpts: qsl-shortwave@media-broadcast.com).
Notes: Media Broadcast GmbH, part of the TDF Group (France), is a major transmitter network operator in Germany and owns the SW transmitting centres in Nauen and Wertachtal.

RADIOFONIKOS STATHMOS MAKEDONIAS (ERT3) (Pub)
Aggelaki 2, 546 36 Thessaloniki, Greece. (Admin)
☎ +30 2310299400. 🖷 +30 2310299655.
E: programc@ert3.gr **W:** www.ert3.gr
Webcast: L
Aggelaki 14, 546 36 Thessaloniki, Greece. (Studio)
L.P: GD: Kostas Bliatkas.
SW: Via ERT transmitting station at Vathy (Avlida municipality), see Voice of Greece (ERA5).
SAT: Hellas Sat 2.
kHz: *7450, 9935*

Winter Schedule 2012/2013
Greek	Days	Area	kHz
1300-1650	daily	Eu	9935avl
1700-2250	daily	Eu	7450avl

Ann: Greek: "Edo Thessaloniki, Radiofonikos Stathmos Makedonias, Trito Programma, Vrahea".
V: QSL-card.
Notes: ERT3 ("Radio Station Macedonia") is a regional station of the public broadcaster ERT, transmitting on MW & FM in the Macedonia region in Northern Greece (see National Radio section) and on SW for Greek listeners in Europe.

VOICE OF GREECE (ERA5) (Pub)
Messogion 432, 15342 Aghia Paraskevi Attikis, Athens, Greece.
☎ +30 2106066310. 🖷 +30 2106066309.
E: era5@ert.gr **W:** www.ert.gr/voiceofgreece
Webcast: L
L.P: Dir: Zinovia Sirivli; Head, Foreign Language Broadcast Dept: Sihanis Zilber; Head, Greeks Living Abroad Dept: Ageliki Barka; Frequency Mgr: Demetri Vafeas.
SW: [AVL] Vathy (Avlida municipality), Kalochori-Pantichi: 2 x 100kW, 1 x 250kW. One 100kW tx is used for the ERT3 prgr (see Radiofonikos Stathmos Makedonias).
SAT: Anik F3, Apstar 2R, EchoStar 15, Eutelsat Hot Bird 13A, Hellas Sat 2, Intelsat 8/10-02, NSS 806, Optus D2.
kHz: *7475, 9420, 11645, 15630, 15650*

Winter Schedule 2012/2013
Greek	Days	Area	kHz
0300-0900	daily	Af	11645avl*
1300-0900	daily	Eu,Am	9420avl*
1300-1850	daily	As	15630avl*
1900-0250	daily	SAm	15650avl*
2300-0900	daily	Eu,Am	7475avl*

Key: * Schedule Variable
Ann: Greek: "ERA pente, Foni tis Elladas".
IS: The opening notes of the Greek folk song "Tsopanakos imouna" (Once I was a Shepherd Boy), played on flute and sheep bells.
V: QSL-card. (Also accepts email rpt to: apodimos_era5@ert.gr)
Notes: The Voice of Greece (ERA5) is the External Sce of the public broadcaster Elliniki Radiofonia Teleorassi (ERT). Some prgrs are relays of ERT's domestic multilingual channel R.Filia.

KSDA (AWR ASIA/PACIFIC RELAY STATION)
P.O. Box 8990, Agat, Guam 96928. (Transmitting station)
☎ +1 671 5652289. 🖷 +1 671 5652983.
E: guam@awr.org
Ruko Palm Spring, Blok A-4, # 6-8, Batam Center, Batam 29461, Indonesia (AWR Asia/Pacific branch & studios)
☎ +62 778 460318. 🖷 +62 778 460597.
W: www.awr.org
L.P: SM: Victor Shepherd; Chief Engineer: Brook Powers.
SW: [SDA] Agat, Facpi Point: 5 x 100kW.
Ann: English: "From the beautiful island of Guam in the West Pacific, this is Adventist World Radio, the Voice of Hope".
V: No own QSL-card. (Rpt to AWR Asia/Pacific branch in Indonesia)
Notes: Transmitting station owned by Adventist Broadcasting Service, Inc., see USA for corporate details. For schedules, see AWR Asia/Pacific (Indonesia).

KTWR (TWR RELAY STATION)

✉ P.O. Box 8780, Agat, Guam 96928. (Transmitting station)
☎ +1 671 8288637. 🖷 +1 671 8288636.
E: ktwrfcd@twr.org **W:** www.ktwr.net
✉ 85 Playfair Road #04-01, Tong Yuan Industrial Building, Singapore 368000. (TWR Asia branch & studios)
☎ +65 65015150. 🖷 +65 64443053.
E: info@twr.asia **W:** www.twr.asia
L.P: Chief Engineer: Mike Sabin.
SW: [TWR] Merizo: 3 x 100, 2 x 250kW.
Ann: English: "This is your Station for Inspiration, KTWR, Agana".
IS: "We've a story to tell the Nations", played on an organ.
V: QSL-card. Rp. (3 IRCs)
Notes: Transmitting station owned by TWR, Inc. See USA for corporate details. For schedule, see TWR Asia (Singapore).

INDIA (IND)

ALL INDIA RADIO (AIR) (Pub)

✉ External Services Division, P.O. Box 500, New Delhi-110001, India.
☎ +91 11 23715411. 🖷 +91 11 23710057.
E: airlive@air.org.in **W:** www.allindiaradio.org
✉ Akashvani Bhavan, 1 Sansad Marg, New Delhi-110001, India. (Studio)
E: gosesdair@yahoo.co.in **W:** www.newsonair.com (News)
L.P: (Prasar Bharati Corp) Chmn: Mrinal Pande; CEO: Jawhar Sircar; DG, AIR Ext Sces: J.K. Das; Head of Engineering: H.R.Singh.
MW: [JAL] Jalandhar: 702kHz 300kW; [KKT] Chinsurah: 594/1134kHz 1000kW; [RAJ] Rajkot 1071kHz 1000kW; [TUT] Tuticorin. 1053kHz 200kW.
SW: [ALG] Aligarh: 4 x 250kW; [BGL] Bengalaru, Doddaballapur: 6 x 500kW; [DEL] Dellhi, two sites: Khampur (G.C. 28N49 077E07): 7 x 250kW; Kingsway (G.C. 28N43 077E12): 3 x 50‡, 2 x 100kW; [GKP] Gorakhpur: 1 x 50kW; [GUW] Guwahati: 50/200kW; [MUM] Mumbai: 1 x 100kW; [PAN] Panaji: 2 x 250kW. New DRM-ready txs are being installed: 2 x 250kW at Aligarh, 1 x 500kW at Bengalaru, 2 x 100kW at Dehli Kingsway.
kHz: 594, 702, 1053, 1071, 1134, 3945, 4870, 5990, 6045, 6055, 6155, 6165, 7250, 7270, 7340, 7370, 7420, 7550, 9415, 9445, 9575, 9595, 9620, 9635, 9690, 9705, 9810, 9820, 9835, 9910, 9950, 11580, 11620, 11645, 11670, 11710, 11715, 11735, 11740, 11775, 11840, 11850, 11935, 11985, 12025, 13605, 13640, 13645, 13695, 13710, 13795, 15030, 15040, 15050, 15120, 15140, 15175, 15185, 15210, 15410, 15770, 15795, 17510, 17670, 17715, 17875, 17895

Winter Schedule 2012/2013

Arabic	Days	Area	kHz
0430-0530	daily	ME	11670alg, 15210pan, 15770del
1730-1945	daily	ME	9620alg, 11710del, 13640bgl

Baluchi	Days	Area	kHz
1500-1600	daily	SAs	1071raj, 6165del, 7340mum, 9620alg

Bengali	Days	Area	kHz
0300-0430	daily	SAs	594kkt*, 7420guw
0800-1100	daily	SAs	594kkt*, 7420guw
1445-1515	daily	SAs	1134kkt*, 7420guw
1600-1730	daily	SAs	7420guw

Burmese	Days	Area	kHz
1215-1315	daily	SEA	11710del, 15040del

Chinese	Days	Area	kHz
1145-1315	daily	EAs	11840del, 13605bgl, 15795bgl

Dari	Days	Area	kHz
0300-0345	daily	WAs	9835del, 9910alg, 11740alg
1315-1415	daily	WAs	9910del, 11670pan

English	Days	Area	kHz
1000-1100	daily	EAs	13605bgl, 15030alg, 15410bgl
1000-1100	daily	Pac	13695bgl, 17510del, 17895bgl
1000-1100	daily	SAs	1053tut, 7270cni

English	Days	Area	kHz
1330-1500	daily	SEA	9690bgl, 11620del, 13710bgl
1530-1545	daily	SAs	9910alg
1745-1945	daily	EAf	9415del, 11935mum, 17670del
1745-1945	daily	Eu	7550bgl, 9950del+, 11670bgl
1745-1945	daily	NAf,WAf	9445del, 11580alg, 13695bgl
2045-2230	daily	Eu	7550bgl, 9445bgl, 9950del+, 11670bgl
2045-2230	daily	Pac	9910alg, 11620bgl, 11740pan
2245-0045	daily	SEA	6055del, 9705pan, 11710del
2245-0045	daily	EAs	9690bgl, 11645del+, 13605bgl

Farsi	Days	Area	kHz
0400-0430	daily	ME	11670alg, 15210pan, 15770del
1615-1730	daily	ME	9620del, 11710del, 13640bgl

French	Days	Area	kHz
1945-2030	daily	NAf,WAf	9620alg, 11710del, 13640bgl

Gujarati	Days	Area	kHz
0415-0430	daily	EAf	15120del, 15185pan , 17715del+
1515-1600	daily	EAf	11620bgl, 13640bgl, 15175pan

Hindi	Days	Area	kHz
0315-0415	daily	EAf	15120bgl, 15185pan, 17715del+
0315-0415	daily	ME	11840del, 13695bgl
0430-0530	daily	EAf	15120del, 15185pan , 17715del+
1615-1730	daily	ME	9445del, 12025pan
1615-1730	daily	EAf	7250pan, 9950del, 1360bgl, 17670bgl
1945-2045	daily	Eu	7550bgl, 9950del+, 11670bgl
2300-2400	daily	SEA	9910alg, 11740pan, 13795bgl

Indonesian	Days	Area	kHz
0845-0945	daily	SEA	15770alg, 17510del, 17875bgl

Kannada	Days	Area	kHz
0215-0300	daily	ME	13695bgl, 15120bgl

Malayalam	Days	Area	kHz
1730-1830	daily	ME	7250pan, 12025pan

Nepali	Days	Area	kHz
0130-0230	daily	SAs	594kkt**, 3945gkp, 7420guw, 9810del, 11715del+
0700-0800	daily	SAs	7250gkp, 7420guw, 9595del, 11850del
1330-1430	daily	SAs	1134kkt*, 3945gkp, 4870del, 7420guw, 11775pan

Pashto	Days	Area	kHz
0215-0300	daily	WAs	9835del, 9910alg, 11735alg
1415-1530	daily	WAs	9910del, 11670pan

Punjabi	Days	Area	kHz
0800-0830	daily	SAs	702jal
1130-1230	daily	SAs	702jal
1300-1430	daily	SAs	702jal

Russian	Days	Area	kHz
1615-1715	daily	Eu	9595bgl, 15140del+

Saraiki	Days	Area	kHz
1230-1300	daily	SAs	702jal

Sindhi	Days	Area	kHz
0100-0200	daily	SAs	1071raj, 5990del, 7370del, 9635alg
1230-1500	daily	SAs	1071raj, 6165del, 7340mum, 9620alg

Sinhala	Days	Area	kHz
0045-0115	daily	SAs	1053tut, 7270cni, 11740pan, 11985del
1300-1500	daily	SAs	1053tut, 7270cni, 9820pan, 15050del+

Swahili	Days	Area	kHz
1515-1615	daily	EAf	9950del, 13605bgl, 17670del

Tamil	Days	Area	kHz
0000-0045	daily	SAs	1053tut, 7270cni, 9835del, 11985del
0000-0045	daily	SEA	9910alg, 11740pan, 13795bgl
0115-0330	daily	SAs	1053tut
1100-1300	daily	SAs	1053tut
1115-1215	daily	SAs	7270cni, 15050del, 17510del
1115-1215	daily	SEA	9810pan, 13695bgl, 15770alg
1500-1530	daily	SAs	1053tut

Telugu	Days	Area	kHz
1215-1245	daily	SEA	9810pan, 13695bgl, 15770alg

Thai	Days	Area	kHz
1115-1200	daily	SEA	11670bgl, 13645alg, 15410pan

Tibetan	Days	Area	kHz
1215-1330	daily	SAs	1134kkt*, 7420guw, 9575bgl, 11775pan

Urdu	Days	Area	kHz
0015-0100	daily	SAs	1071raj
0015-0430	daily	SAs	702jal, 6155alg, 7340mum, 9595del, 11620bgl
0200-0430	daily	SAs	1071raj
0800-1130	daily	SAs	1071raj
0830-1130	daily	SAs	702jal, 7250gkp, 7340mum, 9595del, 11620del
1430-1740	daily	SAs	3945gkp
1430-1930	daily	SAs	702jal, 6045del
1600-1930	daily	SAs	1071raj, 6155bgl

Key: + DRM; * Planned.
Ann: Dari: "Inja Delhi"; English: "This is the General Overseas Service of All India Radio"; Hindi: "Yeh Akashvani ki videsh prasaran sewa hai"; Nepali: "Yo All India Radio ho"; Sinhala: "Me All India Radio videshiya sevayai"; Tamil: "Idi Akashvani videsh sewai".
V: QSL-card. (Rpt to the Director of Spectrum Management, All India Radio, Room No.204, Akashvani Bhavan, New Delhi-110001, India. Email rpt to: spectrum-manager@air.org.in - downloadable reception report form available at allindiaradio.gov.in/Contact Us/Reception)
Notes: External Sce of the national public broadcaster Prasar Bharati Corporation. Began broadcasting on 1 October 1939.

ATHMIK YATRA RADIO (Rlg)
⌨ P.O. Box 12, Manjadi Junction P.O., Tiruvalla-5, Kerala 689 105, India.
☎ +91 469 2630654.
E: ayradio4567@gmail.com; info@athmeeyayathra.org; info@ayasia.org **W:** www.athmeeyayathra.org; www.ayasia.org
Webcast: D
⌨ P.O.Box 3342, Kathmandu, Nepal.
E: atmikyatra@aynepal.com **W:** www.aynepal.com
L.P: Pres: Dr K.P. Yohannan.
kHz: *1548, 7215, 7240, 15150, 15235, 15285*

Winter Schedule 2012/2013			
Ao	Days	Area	kHz
1400-1415	.....s.	As	15235trm

Awadhi	Days	Area	kHz
1600-1615	mtw....	As	15150trm

Bagheli	Days	Area	kHz
1545-1600	..wtf..	As	15150trm

Bagri	Days	Area	kHz
0030-0045	mt.....	As	7215trm

Banjara	Days	Area	kHz
0015-0030	m......	As	1548trm
1415-1430	.....ss	As	15285trm

Bantawa	Days	Area	kHz
2330-2345	......s	As	7240trm

Bengali	Days	Area	kHz
0015-0030	.....ss	As	7240trm
1515-1530	....fss	As	15235trm
1515-1530	mtwt...	As	1548trm

Bengali (Muslimi)	Days	Area	kHz
1515-1530	....f..	As	1548trm

Bhaojpuri	Days	Area	kHz
1445-1500	.....ss	As	15285trm

Bhili	Days	Area	kHz
0115-0130	m......	As	7215trm
1400-1415	...t..	As	15285trm

Bhojpuri	Days	Area	kHz
1415-1430	....fs.	As	1548trm

Bodo	Days	Area	kHz
0000-0015	mt.....	As	7240trm

Bondo	Days	Area	kHz
1400-1415	..w....	As	15285trm

Bundelkhandi	Days	Area	kHz
0030-0045	...f..	As	7215trm
1545-1600	mt.....	As	15150trm

Burmese	Days	Area	kHz
1330-1345	......s	As	1548trm
2345-2400	.twt...	As	7240trm

Chakma	Days	Area	kHz
0015-0030	mt.....	As	7240trm
1415-1430	......s	As	1548trm

Chhattisgarhi	Days	Area	kHz
1345-1400	mt.....	As	1548trm
1530-1545	mt.....	As	15150trm

Chin	Days	Area	kHz
1345-1400	......s	As	1548trm
2345-2400	m....s	As	7240trm

Chowdhari	Days	Area	kHz
1330-1345	...t..	As	1548trm

Dari	Days	Area	kHz
1545-1615	.....s.	As	15150trm

Deori	Days	Area	kHz
1345-1400	...tf..	As	15235trm

Deshiya	Days	Area	kHz
1345-1400	..wt...	As	15285trm

Dogri	Days	Area	kHz
0045-0100	...tf..	As	7215trm

Dzongkha	Days	Area	kHz
1430-1445	mtw....	As	15235trm

Gamit	Days	Area	kHz
1400-1415	...t...	As	1548trm
1415-1430	..wt...	As	15285trm

Garhwali	Days	Area	kHz
0030-0045	.....ss	As	7215trm

Garo	Days	Area	kHz
1415-1430	.....ss	As	15235trm

Gojri	Days	Area	kHz
1230-1245	m......	As	15285trm

Gondi	Days	Area	kHz
1400-1415	...f..	As	15285trm

Gujarati	Days	Area	kHz
1245-1300	...tf..	As	15285trm
1345-1400	..wt...	As	1548trm

Gurung	Days	Area	kHz
2330-2345	.tw....	As	7240trm

Halam	Days	Area	kHz
1400-1415	mt.....	As	15235trm
1430-1445	......s	As	1548trm
Haryanvi	**Days**	**Area**	**kHz**
1430-1445	.....ss	As	15285trm
Hindi	**Days**	**Area**	**kHz**
1315-1330	.....ss	As	15285trm
1445-1500	.....ss	As	1548trm
1445-1500	mtwtf..	As	15285trm
1500-1515	...fss	As	1548trm
1615-1630	daily	As	15150trm
Ho	**Days**	**Area**	**kHz**
0015-0030	...f..	As	7240trm
1445-1500	..w...	As	1548trm
Kangri	**Days**	**Area**	**kHz**
0045-0100	.....ss	As	7215trm
Kannada	**Days**	**Area**	**kHz**
0000-0015	.wtfss	As	1548trm
Karbi	**Days**	**Area**	**kHz**
1400-1415	..tf..	As	15235trm
2345-2400	....fs.	As	7240trm
Kashmiri	**Days**	**Area**	**kHz**
1230-1245	..wt...	As	15285trm
Kaubru	**Days**	**Area**	**kHz**
1345-1400	..w...	As	15235trm
Khandesi	**Days**	**Area**	**kHz**
1315-1330	..w...	As	15285trm
Khariya	**Days**	**Area**	**kHz**
0030-0045	..w...	As	7215trm
1415-1430	..w...	As	1548trm
Khasi	**Days**	**Area**	**kHz**
1430-1445	.....ss	As	15235trm
Khota	**Days**	**Area**	**kHz**
1415-1430	m......	As	1548trm
Khurukh	**Days**	**Area**	**kHz**
0000-0015	..wt...	As	7240trm
1430-1445	mt.....	As	1548trm
Kinnauri	**Days**	**Area**	**kHz**
0100-0115	.....ss	As	7215trm
Kokborok	**Days**	**Area**	**kHz**
1345-1400	mt.....	As	15235trm
1400-1415	.....ss	As	1548trm
Konkani	**Days**	**Area**	**kHz**
0000-0015	.t.....	As	1548trm
Konyak	**Days**	**Area**	**kHz**
1430-1445	..tf..	As	15235trm
Kotwali	**Days**	**Area**	**kHz**
0115-0130	..w...	As	7215trm
1415-1430	...t...	As	1548trm
Kotwalia	**Days**	**Area**	**kHz**
1430-1445	...f..	As	15285trm
Koya	**Days**	**Area**	**kHz**
0015-0030	.t.....	As	1548trm
1245-1300	.....ss	As	15285trm
Kui	**Days**	**Area**	**kHz**
1330-1345	...fs.	As	1548trm
1415-1430	mt.....	As	15285trm
Kukna	**Days**	**Area**	**kHz**
0115-0130	.t.....	As	7215trm
1415-1430	...f..	As	1548trm
1430-1445	...t...	As	1548trm
Kupiya	**Days**	**Area**	**kHz**
1400-1415	......s	As	15285trm
Ladakhi	**Days**	**Area**	**kHz**
1230-1245	.t.....	As	15285trm
Lepcha	**Days**	**Area**	**kHz**
1500-1515	.tw...	As	15235trm
Limbu	**Days**	**Area**	**kHz**
2330-2345	....fs.	As	7240trm
Lungeli-Magar	**Days**	**Area**	**kHz**
2330-2345	m......	As	7240trm

Magahi	Days	Area	kHz
0045-0100	..w...	As	7215trm
1430-1445	....fs.	As	1548trm
1500-1515	...tf..	As	15235trm
Maithili	**Days**	**Area**	**kHz**
1530-1545	..wtf..	As	15150trm
Malayalam	**Days**	**Area**	**kHz**
0030-0045	daily	As	1548trm
Malto	**Days**	**Area**	**kHz**
1330-1345	...tf..	As	15285trm
1415-1430	.t.....	As	1548trm
Marathi	**Days**	**Area**	**kHz**
1315-1330	...tf..	As	15285trm
1330-1345	mtw...	As	1548trm
Marwari	**Days**	**Area**	**kHz**
0100-0115	mt.....	As	7215trm
1345-1400	mt.....	As	15285trm
Meitei	**Days**	**Area**	**kHz**
1330-1345	mtw...	As	15285trm
1500-1515	.....ss	As	15235trm
Mising	**Days**	**Area**	**kHz**
0000-0015	...fss	As	7240trm
1415-1430	..wtf..	As	15235trm
Mouchi	**Days**	**Area**	**kHz**
1430-1445	...t...	As	15285trm
Mundari	**Days**	**Area**	**kHz**
1430-1445	..w...	As	1548trm
1515-1530	..wt...	As	15235trm
Nepali	**Days**	**Area**	**kHz**
1300-1315	daily	As	15285trm
Netakani	**Days**	**Area**	**kHz**
1345-1400	......s	As	15285trm
Newari	**Days**	**Area**	**kHz**
1445-1500	...tf..	As	15235trm
Nockte	**Days**	**Area**	**kHz**
1330-1345	mt.....	As	15235trm
Oriya	**Days**	**Area**	**kHz**
1230-1245	....fss	As	15285trm
1345-1400	...fs.	As	1548trm
Pashto	**Days**	**Area**	**kHz**
1545-1615	......s	As	15150trm
Punjabi	**Days**	**Area**	**kHz**
0100-0115	...tf..	As	7215trm
1245-1300	mtw...	As	15285trm
Rajasthani	**Days**	**Area**	**kHz**
0045-0100	mt.....	As	7215trm
Rengma	**Days**	**Area**	**kHz**
1400-1415	..w...	As	15235trm
Rongmei	**Days**	**Area**	**kHz**
1330-1345	......s	As	15235trm
Sadri	**Days**	**Area**	**kHz**
1445-1500	mt.....	As	1548trm
1600-1615	...tf..	As	15150trm
Sambalpuri	**Days**	**Area**	**kHz**
1400-1415	....f..	As	1548trm
1430-1445	mt.....	As	15285trm
Santhali	**Days**	**Area**	**kHz**
0015-0030	..wt...	As	7240trm
1315-1330	m......	As	15285trm
1400-1415	mtw...	As	1548trm
1415-1430	mt.....	As	15235trm
Sarchopa	**Days**	**Area**	**kHz**
1445-1500	mtw...	As	15235trm
Sherpa	**Days**	**Area**	**kHz**
1500-1515	m......	As	15235trm
2330-2345	...t...	As	7240trm
Sindhi	**Days**	**Area**	**kHz**
0100-0115	..w...	As	7215trm
1530-1545	.....ss	As	15150trm
Sinhala	**Days**	**Area**	**kHz**
2345-2400	m.....s	As	1548trm

Soura	Days	Area	kHz
1400-1415	mt.....	As	15285trm
1445-1500	....f..	As	1548trm
Sumi	**Days**	**Area**	**kHz**
1400-1415	.....s	As	15235trm
Tamang	**Days**	**Area**	**kHz**
1515-1530	mt.....	As	15235trm
Tamil	**Days**	**Area**	**kHz**
2345-2400	.twtfs.	As	1548trm
Tangkhul	**Days**	**Area**	**kHz**
1330-1345	....fs.	As	15235trm
Telugu	**Days**	**Area**	**kHz**
0015-0030	..wtfss	As	1548trm
Thadou-Kuki	**Days**	**Area**	**kHz**
1345-1400	.....ss	As	15235trm
Tharu	**Days**	**Area**	**kHz**
1330-1345	..wt...	As	15235trm
Tibetan (Amdo)	**Days**	**Area**	**kHz**
1330-1345	.....s.	As	15285trm
Tibetan (Khams)	**Days**	**Area**	**kHz**
1445-1500	.....ss	As	15235trm
Tibetan (Lhasa)	**Days**	**Area**	**kHz**
1330-1345	.....s	As	15285trm
Tulu	**Days**	**Area**	**kHz**
0000-0015	m......	As	1548trm
Urdu	**Days**	**Area**	**kHz**
1345-1400	...fs.	As	15285trm
1515-1530	.....ss	As	1548trm
Vadari	**Days**	**Area**	**kHz**
0115-0130	..t....	As	7215trm
1315-1330	.t.....	As	15285trm
Varli	**Days**	**Area**	**kHz**
0115-0130	....f..	As	7215trm
Varti	**Days**	**Area**	**kHz**
1430-1445	..w....	As	15285trm
Vasavi	**Days**	**Area**	**kHz**
0030-0045	..t....	As	7215trm
1445-1500	..t....	As	1548trm
Yerukala	**Days**	**Area**	**kHz**
1400-1415	.....s.	As	15285trm

Ann: Malayalam: "Athmeeya Yathra".
V: QSL-card.
Notes: Athmik Yatra Radio ("AY Radio") is the radio mission of the Believers Church (a network of Pentecostal Churches in India). Successor station to "Gospel For Asia" (GFA). The name of the service originates in the prgr "Athmik Yatra" ("Spiritual Journey"), hosted by K.P. Yohannan, and transmitted for Malalayam speakers in India via Trans World Radio since 1985.

TWR INDIA (Rlg)
✉ P.O. Box 4310, Delhi 110019, India.
☎ +91 11 26515790. 📠 +91 11 6868049.
E: info@twr.in; **W:** twr.in; radio882.com
Webcast: D/L
L.P: CEO: George Philip.
kHz: *882, 5930, 6115, 7285, 7505, 11965, 15360*

Winter Schedule 2012/2013

Awadhi	Days	Area	kHz
1400-1415	.t.....	As	7505tac
Banjara	**Days**	**Area**	**kHz**
0115-0130	..w....	SAs	882put
1230-1245	.....s.	SAs	882put
Bengali	**Days**	**Area**	**kHz**
0030-0045	mtwtf.s	As	11965irk
1315-1330	.....s.	As	5930irk
2230-2300	daily	SAs	882put
Bhili	**Days**	**Area**	**kHz**
1500-1515	.....ss	As	5930irk
Bhojpuri	**Days**	**Area**	**kHz**
0045-0115	mtwtf..	As	11965irk
Bondo	**Days**	**Area**	**kHz**
1330-1345	......s	As	5930irk

Braj Bhasha	Days	Area	kHz
1315-1330	....f..	As	5930irk
Bundeli	**Days**	**Area**	**kHz**
1345-1415	.....s.	As	5930irk
Chattisgarhi	**Days**	**Area**	**kHz**
1230-1245	m......	SAs	882put
1245-1315	mtwtf..	SAs	882put
1300-1315	.....ss	SAs	882put
Chodri	**Days**	**Area**	**kHz**
1445-1500	.....ss	As	5930irk
Dari	**Days**	**Area**	**kHz**
1615-1630	.....s.	As	7285sam
Deccani	**Days**	**Area**	**kHz**
1315-1330	.....s	SAs	882put
1330-1345	mtwtf..	SAs	882put
Dhodia	**Days**	**Area**	**kHz**
1515-1530	..wt...	As	5930irk
Dogri	**Days**	**Area**	**kHz**
1315-1330	mtwtf..	As	7505tac
Dzonkha	**Days**	**Area**	**kHz**
0115-0130	mtw...s	As	11965irk
English	**Days**	**Area**	**kHz**
0030-0045	..tfss	SAs	882put
0045-0100	daily	SAs	882put
0100-0130	..t...	SAs	882put
0115-0130	...f..	SAs	882put
1545-1615	.....s	SAs	882put
Gamith	**Days**	**Area**	**kHz**
1500-1515	mtw....	As	5930irk
Garhwali	**Days**	**Area**	**kHz**
1330-1345	.....s.	As	5930irk
1415-1430	mtwtf..	As	7505tac
Gondi	**Days**	**Area**	**kHz**
1230-1245	....f..	SAs	882put
1545-1615	mtwtf..	SAs	882put
Gujarati	**Days**	**Area**	**kHz**
1230-1245	..w....	SAs	882put
1330-1345	.....s.	SAs	882put
1345-1400	.....s	SAs	882put
1400-1415	.....ss	SAs	882put
1545-1615	.....s.	SAs	882put
2300-2330	..wtfss	SAs	882put
Haryanvi	**Days**	**Area**	**kHz**
1330-1345	....f..	As	5930irk
Hindi	**Days**	**Area**	**kHz**
0045-0115	......s	As	11965irk
1315-1430	.....ss	As	7505tac
1330-1400	mtwtf..	As	7505tac
1400-1415	m.wtf..	As	7505tac
1430-1445	daily	As	7505tac
1445-1515	mtwtfs.	As	7505tac
Ho	**Days**	**Area**	**kHz**
1300-1315	.....s.	As	5930irk
Kannada	**Days**	**Area**	**kHz**
0100-0115	....fs.	SAs	882put
0115-0130	.....s.	SAs	882put
1415-1445	mtwtf..	SAs	882put
Kashmiri	**Days**	**Area**	**kHz**
1330-1345	..w....	As	5930irk
Kharia	**Days**	**Area**	**kHz**
1400-1415	.....s	As	5930irk
Konkani	**Days**	**Area**	**kHz**
0030-0045	.t.....	SAs	882put
Kotuwalia	**Days**	**Area**	**kHz**
2315-2330	m......	SAs	882put
Koya	**Days**	**Area**	**kHz**
1230-1245	...t...	SAs	882put
Kui	**Days**	**Area**	**kHz**
1245-1300	.....s.	As	5930irk
Kukna	**Days**	**Area**	**kHz**
2300-2315	mt.....	SAs	882put

Kumaoni

	Days	Area	kHz
1300-1315	.....s	As	5930irk

Kurukh

	Days	Area	kHz
1345-1400	.....s	As	5930irk
1415-1430	...tfs.	As	5930irk

Kutchi

	Days	Area	kHz
2315-2330	.t.....	SAs	882put

Maghi

	Days	Area	kHz
1415-1430	m.....s	As	5930irk

Maithili

	Days	Area	kHz
1330-1345	mt.....	As	5930irk
1345-1415	mtwtf..	As	5930irk

Malayalam

	Days	Area	kHz
0100-0130	.....s	SAs	882put
1230-1245	.....s	SAs	882put
2330-2400	daily	SAs	882put

Marathi

	Days	Area	kHz
1430-1500	.....s.	SAs	882put
1445-1500	.....s	SAs	882put
1445-1515	mtwtf..	SAs	882put

Marwari

	Days	Area	kHz
1315-1330	mt....s	As	5930irk

Mewadi

	Days	Area	kHz
1315-1330	..wt...	As	5930irk

Mouchi

	Days	Area	kHz
1515-1530	mt.....	As	5930irk

Mundari

	Days	Area	kHz
1415-1430	.tw....	As	5930irk

Nepali

	Days	Area	kHz
0045-0115	.....s.	As	11965irk

Oriya

	Days	Area	kHz
0100-0115	..w....	SAs	882put
1415-1430	.....s.	SAs	882put
1500-1530	.....s.	SAs	882put
1500-1545	.....s	SAs	882put
1515-1545	mtwtf.s	SAs	882put

Pashto

	Days	Area	kHz
1600-1615	daily	As	7285sam
1615-1630	mtwtf..	As	7285sam

Punjabi

	Days	Area	kHz
1445-1515	.....s	As	7505tac
1515-1545	.....ss	As	7505tac
1515-1615	mtwtf..	As	7505tac

Sadari

	Days	Area	kHz
1430-1445	.....ss	As	5930irk

Santhali

	Days	Area	kHz
1245-1300	.....s	As	5930irk

Sindhi

	Days	Area	kHz
1430-1500	mtwtf..	As	5930irk

Soura

	Days	Area	kHz
1245-1300	....ss	SAs	882put

Tamil

	Days	Area	kHz
0030-0045	m......	SAs	882put
0100-0130	mt.....	SAs	882put
2400-0030	daily	SAs	882put

Telugu

	Days	Area	kHz
1345-1400	mtwtfs.	SAs	882put
1530-1545	.....s.	SAs	882put

Tibetan

	Days	Area	kHz
1330-1345	...t...	As	5930irk

Tulu

	Days	Area	kHz
0030-0045	..w....	SAs	882put

Urdu

	Days	Area	kHz
1400-1415	daily	As	15360man
1500-1530	daily	As	6115sam

Varli

	Days	Area	kHz
1230-1245	.t.....	SAs	882put

Vasavi

	Days	Area	kHz
1500-1515	...tf..	As	5930irk

V: QSL-card. (Online form for reception reports)

Notes: TWR regional division, covering the Indian subcontinent. For corporate details, see under TWR (USA).

INDONESIA (INS)

VOICE OF INDONESIA (VOI) (Pub)

✉ P.O. Box 1157, Jakarta 10110, Indonesia.
☎ +62 21 3456811. 📠 +62 21 3500990.
E: english@voi.co.id **W:** www.voi.co.id
Webcast: D/L
✉ Physical address: 4-5 Jalan Medan Merdeka Barat, Jakarta 10110, Indonesia.
LP: Dir: Kabul Budiono.
SW: [JAK] Jakarta, Cimanggis: 2 x 50, 3 x 100, 9 x 250kW.
kHz: *9526*

Winter Schedule 2012/2013

	Days	Area	kHz
Arabic			
1600-1700	daily	Eu,NAf,ME	9526jakt
Chinese			
1100-1200	daily	As,Pac	9526jakt
1500-1600	daily	As,Pac	9526jakt
English			
1000-1100	daily	As,Pac	9526jakt
1300-1400	daily	As,Pac	9526jakt
1900-2000	daily	Eu,NAf,ME	9526jakt
French			
2000-2100	daily	Eu,NAf,ME	9526jakt
German			
1800-1900	daily	Eu,NAf,ME	9526jakt
Indonesian			
1400-1500	daily	As,Pac	9526jakt
Japanese			
1200-1300	daily	As,Pac	9526jakt
Spanish			
1700-1800	daily	Eu,NAf,ME	9526jakt

Key: † Irregular.
Ann: English: "This is the Voice of Indonesia, in Jakarta"; Spanish: "La Voz de Indonesia en Jakarta".
V: QSL-card.
Notes: The Voice of Indonesia is the External Sce of the state broadcaster Radio Republik Indonesia.

AWR ASIA/PACIFIC (Rlg)

✉ Ruko Palm Spring, Blok A-4, # G-8, Batam Center, Batam 29461, Indonesia.
☎ +62 778 460318. 📠 +62 778 460597.
LP: Dir, Asia/Pacific Region: Jonathan Wagiran.
kHz: *5970, 9565, 9650, 9720, 9880, 9890, 11670, 11685, 11690, 11700, 11730, 11825, 11855, 11935, 11955, 12035, 15215, 15250, 15255, 15260, 15270, 15320, 15330, 15370, 15420, 15440, 15445, 15480, 15495, 15605, 15640, 15660, 17540, 17590, 17605, 17635, 17670, 17680, 17700, 17880*

Winter Schedule 2012/2013

	Days	Area	kHz
Amoy			
1200-1230	.....ss	As	11825sda, 11855sda, 15420sda
Asho Chin			
1400-1430	daily	SEA	17590sda
Assamese			
1330-1400	..w...s	As	15660sda
Bengali			
1230-1300	mt.t.s.	As	11670trm
1300-1330	daily	As	15215sda
Burmese			
0000-0030	daily	As	17700sda
1430-1500	daily	SEA	15660sda
Cambodian			
1300-1330	daily	As	17680sda
1330-1400	.....s	As	17680sda
Cantonese			
1000-1100	.....s	As	11955sda, 15260sda
2100-2157	.....s.	As	9565sda
2100-2200	.....s.	As	9720sda
Chinese			
0000-0200	daily	CHN	12035sda, 17880sda

Chinese	Days	Area	kHz
0100-0200	daily	CHN	17700sda
1000-1100	mtwtfs.	CHN	11955sda, 15260sda
1100-1200	daily	CHN	11730sda, 11825sda, 12035sda
1200-1230	mtwtf..	CHN	11825sda, 11855sda, 15420sda
1230-1300	daily	CHN	11825sda, 11855sda, 15420sda
1300-1330	mtwtf..	SEA	15480trm
1300-1400	daily	CHN	11935sda
1330-1500	daily	SEA	15480trm
1400-1500	daily	CHN	11935sda, 15495sda
2100-2157	mtwtf.s	CHN	9565sda
2100-2200	mtwtf.s	CHN	9720sda
2200-2300	daily	CHN	11685sda, 15370sda
2300-2400	daily	CHN	11700sda, 15370sda

English	Days	Area	kHz
1600-1630	daily	As	15215sda, 15660sda
1630-1700	m.w.f..	As	15660sda
2230-2330	daily	SEA	15320sda
2330-2400	.tw....	As	17700sda

Hiligaynon	Days	Area	kHz
1030-1100	..wt...	SEA	17540sda

Hindi	Days	Area	kHz
1530-1600	daily	As	15270trm, 15605sda

Hmong	Days	Area	kHz
1330-1400	...tf..	SEA	15660sda

Ilocano	Days	Area	kHz
1030-1100	....f.s	SEA	17540sda

Indonesian	Days	Area	kHz
1100-1130	daily	SEA	15495sda
2200-2230	daily	SEA	15320sda

Javanese	Days	Area	kHz
1130-1200	m.w.f..	SEA	15495sda
2200-2230	.t.t..s	SEA	15260sda

Kachin	Days	Area	kHz
1300-1330	daily	SEA	17605sda

Kannada	Days	Area	kHz
1530-1600	daily	As	11690sda

Karen	Days	Area	kHz
0030-0100	daily	SEA	17700sda
1500-1530	daily	SEA	15660sda

Karen (Pwo)	Days	Area	kHz
1430-1500	daily	SEA	17590sda

Korean	Days	Area	kHz
1200-1300	daily	EAs	9880sda
2100-2200	daily	EAs	9890sda

Laotian	Days	Area	kHz
1330-1357	...t.s.	SEA	17605sda

Malay	Days	Area	kHz
1330-1400	mt...s.	SEA	15660sda

Malayalam	Days	Area	kHz
1530-1600	daily	As	15640sda

Marathi	Days	Area	kHz
1530-1600	daily	As	15330sda

Mizo	Days	Area	kHz
1500-1530	daily	As	15605sda

Nepali	Days	Area	kHz
1500-1530	daily	As	15255trm

Russian	Days	Area	kHz
0300-0330	daily	RUS	17635sda
1330-1400	daily	RUS	9650sda

Sindhi	Days	Area	kHz
1630-1700	.t.t.ss	As	15660sda

Sinhala	Days	Area	kHz
1400-1430	daily	As	15255sda

Sundanese	Days	Area	kHz
1130-1200	.t.t.ss	SEA	15495sda
2200-2230	m.w.ts.	SEA	15260sda

Tagalog	Days	Area	kHz
1030-1100	mt...s.	SEA	17540sda

Tamil	Days	Area	kHz
1500-1530	daily	As	11685sda

Telugu	Days	Area	kHz
1500-1530	daily	As	15495sda

Thai	Days	Area	kHz
1330-1357	mtw.f..	SEA	17605sda

Tibetan	Days	Area	kHz
1530-1600	...tf..	As	15255trm

Urdu	Days	Area	kHz
0200-0230	daily	As	5970mos
1400-1430	daily	As	15440mos
1600-1627	daily	As	15605sda
1600-1630	daily	As	15250mos

Uyghur	Days	Area	kHz
1300-1330	.....ss	As	15480trm

Vietnamese	Days	Area	kHz
0100-0200	.....s.	SEA	15445tsu
1300-1400	daily	SEA	17670mdc
2300-2330	.tw....	SEA	17700sda
2300-2400	m..tfss	SEA	17700sda

V: QSL-card.

Notes: Regional branch of Adventist Broadcasting Service, Inc (USA), see USA for corporate details. The individual AWR prgrs are produced by a large number of partner studios within the region.

IRAN (IRN)

VOICE OF THE ISLAMIC REPUBLIC OF IRAN (VOIRI) (Gov)

✉ P.O. Box 19395-6767, Tehran, Iran.
☎ +98 21 22013687; +98 21 22162731. 🖷 +98 21 22044287.
E: englishradio@irib.ir; bm@irib.ir; prworld@irib.ir
W: www.worldservice.irib.ir
Webcast: D/L
☎ +98 21 22013720.

LP: Pres (IRIB): Ezatollah Zarghami; GD (IRIB): Gholamali Ramezani; DG, Int. Affairs (IRIB): Mohammad Jafar Safi.

MW: [AHW] Ahwaz, Bandar-e Mahshar: 576/1080kHz 750kW; 1530kHz 50kW; [BNB] Bonab: 639kHz 400kW; [BNT] Bandar-e Torkaman: 1449kHz 400kW; [CHB] Chabahar: 765kHz 1000kW; [JOL] Jolfa 1323kHz 600kW; [KER] Kerman: 1224kHz 600kW; [KIA] Bandar-e Kiashahr: 702kHz 500kW; [QSH] Qasr-e Shirin: 612/1161kHz 600kW; [TYB] Tayebad: 720kHz 400kW; [ZAB] Zabol: 1098kHz 200kW

SW: [AHW] Ahwaz, Bandar-e Mahshar: 2 x 250kW; [KAM] Tehran, Kamalabad: 10 x 100, 3 x 250, 1 x 350, 12 x 500kW; [SIR] Sirjan: 10 x 500kW; [ZAH] Zahedan: 2 x 500kW.

SAT: Express AM22, Intelsat 10.

kHz: *576, 612, 639, 702, 720, 765, 1080, 1098, 1161, 1224, 1323, 1449, 1530, 3965, 4005, 5915, 5920, 5940, 5950, 5985, 5995, 6005, 6010, 6040, 6060, 6080, 6085, 6090, 6095, 6100, 6110, 6140, 6145, 6165, 6175, 6185, 6205, 7205, 7230, 7270, 7285, 7295, 7300, 7315, 7320, 7325, 7335, 7345, 7350, 7370, 7380, 7385, 7395, 7420, 7435, 9500, 9510, 9515, 9540, 9570, 9605, 9610, 9630, 9665, 9685, 9710, 9715, 9725, 9740, 9755, 9775, 9785, 9850, 9895, 11685, 11700, 11720, 11770, 11800, 11805, 11820, 11830, 11860, 11870, 11925, 12015, 12025, 12085, 13650, 13670, 13680, 13690, 13725, 13730, 13740, 13750, 13785, 13810, 15085, 15150, 15170, 15220, 15260, 15300, 15330, 15360, 15400, 15450, 15500, 15515, 15525, 15550, 17550, 17560, 17600, 17650, 17680, 17690, 17715, 17810, 17820, 17865, 21480, 21500, 21510, 21575, 21600, 21610, 21640, 21800*

Winter Schedule 2012/2013

Albanian	Days	Area	kHz
0630-0730	daily	Eu	13810kam, 15500sir
1830-1930	daily	Eu	6040sir, 9605kam
2030-2130	daily	Eu	6165sir, 9605kam

Arabic	Days	Area	kHz
0000-2400	daily	ME	1224ker
0130-0330	daily	ME	1161qsh
0230-0530	daily	NAf,ME	7350kam, 9740kam, 9895zah
0230-1300	daily	ME	765chb
0230-1530	daily	ME	576ahw
0330-0430	daily	ME	7295kam*, 9500sir*
0430-1530	daily	ME	612qsh
0530-0830	daily	ME	13690kam

Arabic	Days	Area	kHz
0530-1030	daily	NAf,ME	17820sir
0530-1430	daily	ME	17650zah
0830-1030	daily	ME	15400sir
0830-1430	daily	ME	13750kam
1030-1130	daily	NAf,ME	11925ahw, 13725kam
1030-1630	daily	NAf,ME	17550kam
1430-1730	daily	ME	9515kam
1430-2230	daily	ME	1530ahw***
1530-0230	daily	ME	1080ahw
1530-2030	daily	ME	1161qsh
1630-0230	daily	NAf,ME	6060sir
1730-0130	daily	ME	765chb
1730-2030	daily	ME	7285kam

Armenian	Days	Area	kHz
0300-0330	daily	Cau	5915sir, 7300sir
0930-1000	daily	Cau	11820sir, 15220sir
1630-1730	daily	Cau	6090kam, 7230sir

Azeri	Days	Area	kHz
0330-0530	daily	Cau	702kia
0330-0530	daily	ME	1323jol, 7335sir
1430-1700	daily	ME	702kia, 1323jol, 12015zah

Azeri (Aran)	Days	Area	kHz
0530-0930	daily	Cau	702kia

Bengali	Days	Area	kHz
1430-1530	daily	ME	7320kam
1430-1530	daily	SAs	7335kam, 9630kam, 9785kam, 11805kam

Bosnian	Days	Area	kHz
0530-0630	daily	Eu	15500kam, 17560sir
1730-1830	daily	Eu	6080sir, 9850kam
2130-2230	daily	Eu	5950sir, 9710kam

Chinese	Days	Area	kHz
1200-1300	daily	EAs	15150kam, 15360sir, 15525kam, 17560sir
2330-0030	daily	EAs	5915sir, 6110sir, 7325kam

Dari	Days	Area	kHz
0300-0630	daily	ME	1098zab
0300-0630	daily	WAs	720tyb, 9570kam, 11860ahw
0830-1200	daily	WAs	15170kam
0830-1430	daily	WAs	15300ahw
0830-1500	daily	WAs	720tyb, 1098zab
1200-1500	daily	WAs	12085kam

English	Days	Area	kHz
0330-0430	daily	NAm	9710kam**, 11770sir**
1030-1130	daily	ME	702kia
1030-1130	daily	SAs	21575kam, 21610kam
1530-1630	daily	SAs	13785sir, 15525kam
1930-2030	daily	Eu	6040kam, 7345sir
1930-2030	daily	SAf	13670sir, 15450sir

French	Days	Area	kHz
0630-0730	daily	Eu,NAf	17560kam, 17865kam
1830-1930	daily	Eu	6085kam, 7380sir
1830-1930	daily	WAf	13650kam

Georgian	Days	Area	kHz
1700-1800	daily	ME	702kia

German	Days	Area	kHz
0730-0830	daily	Eu	17690kam, 21500kam
1730-1830	daily	Eu	6205sir, 7420kam

Hausa	Days	Area	kHz
0600-0700	daily	WAf	17810sir
1130-1200	daily	WAf	21480sir, 21800sir
1830-1930	daily	WAf	9570kam, 13730sir

Hebrew	Days	Area	kHz
0430-0500	daily	ME	9755kam, 11870sir
1200-1230	daily	ME	13740sir, 15515kam

Hindi	Days	Area	kHz
0230-0300	daily	SAs	9510sir, 11820sir
1430-1530	daily	SAs	11700kam, 13750sir

Indonesian	Days	Area	kHz
1230-1330	daily	SEA	15450kam, 17715sir
2230-2330	daily	SEA	9775kam, 11800sir

Italian	Days	Area	kHz
0630-0730	daily	Eu	15085kam, 17600sir
1930-2000	daily	Eu	6085kam, 7385sir

Japanese	Days	Area	kHz
1330-1430	daily	EAs	9540kam, 9785sir
2100-2200	daily	EAs	6145sir, 7395sir

Kazakh	Days	Area	kHz
0130-0230	daily	CAs	6040sir, 7205sir
1530-1630	daily	CAs	7380kam, 9850sir

Kurdish	Days	Area	kHz
0430-0530	daily	ME	612qsh, 639bnb, 7370kam, 9610sir
1330-1630	daily	ME	639bnb, 5920kam

Pashto	Days	Area	kHz
0230-0330	daily	WAs	5950sir, 6095kam
0730-0830	daily	WAs	1098zab
1230-1330	daily	WAs	7435sir, 9725zah
1300-1330	daily	WAs	765chb
1430-1530	daily	WAs	5985sir
1630-1730	daily	WAs	6005sir, 7345ahw

Russian	Days	Area	kHz
0300-0330	daily	Eu	702kia
0300-0330	daily	Eu,CAs	9510sir, 11925kam
0500-0530	daily	Eu,NAs	12025kam, 13680sir, 17680sir, 21600sir
1430-1530	daily	RUS	1449bnt
1430-1530	daily	Eu,CAs	7285kam, 9685ahw, 11860sir
1700-1800	daily	Eu,CAs	3965ahw, 5920ahw
1800-1900	daily	Eu	6140kam, 7350sir
1930-2030	daily	Eu	4005kam, 7205sir
1930-2030	daily	RUS	702kia

Spanish	Days	Area	kHz
0030-0230	daily	LAm	7345kam
0030-0330	daily	LAm,Eu	6010kam
0530-0630	daily	Eu	15330sir, 15550kam
2030-2130	daily	Eu	6080kam, 963Usir

Swahili	Days	Area	kHz
0400-0500	daily	CAf,EAf	13680sir, 15260sir
0830-0930	daily	CAf,EAf	21510kam, 21640sir
1730-1830	daily	CAf,EAf	11830sir
1730-1830	daily	EAf,ME	9665kam

Tajik	Days	Area	kHz
0100-0230	daily	CAs	720tyb, 5950sir, 7435kam
1600-1730	daily	CAs	720tyb, 5995sir, 7435kam

Talysh	Days	Area	kHz
1330-1430	daily	ME	702kia

Turkish	Days	Area	kHz
0430-0600	daily	ME	6085kam, 7270kam
1600-1730	daily	ME	6175kam, 7315kam
1830-1930	daily	ME	639bnb, 702kia

Turkmen	Days	Area	kHz
1330-1430	daily	CAs	1449bnt
1530-1930	daily	CAs	1449bnt

Urdu	Days	Area	kHz
0130-0230	daily	ME	1098zab
0130-0230	daily	SAs	765chb, 3965zah, 6100kam, 6185ahw
1300-1430	daily	ME	11685kam
1300-1430	daily	SAs	9715sir, 11720kam
1330-1430	daily	SAs	765chb
1530-1730	daily	SAs	765chb, 5940sir

Uzbek	Days	Area	kHz
0230-0300	daily	CAs	6175kam, 7300sir
1500-1600	daily	SAs	5995kam, 7395sir

Key: * "VO Palestine" prgr; ** "VO Justice" prgr; ***Al-Amal TV sound ((Site presumed). **W:** alalam.ir)

Ann: Arabic: "Huna Tahran - Sawt al Jumhuriya al Islamiya fi Iran"; English: "This is the Voice of the Islamic Republic of Iran", V.O.J. prgr: "This is the Voice of Justice"; Farsi: "Inja Tehran ast, sedaye jomhuriye eslamiye Iran"; French: "Ici Tehran, la Voix de la République Islamique de l'Iran"; Russian: "Govorit Tegeran, Golos Islamskoy Respubliki Iran".
IS: "Love's Rainfall", by Nasser Cheshmazar.
V: QSL-card.
Notes: The Voice of the Islamic Republic of Iran is the External Sce of the state broadcaster IRIB. The prgr "Voice of Justice" is aimed at listeners in the USA. The "Voice of the Palestinian Islamic Revolution" prgr targets listeners in the territories under Palestinian Authority. External Sce in Farsi/Persian is known as "Seda-ye Ashena" (www.sedayeashna.ir) and is not available via terrestrial broadcasting methods.

IRELAND (IRL)

RTÉ RADIO WORLDWIDE (Pub)
✉ RTÉ, Donnybrook, Dublin 4, Ireland.
☎ +353 1 208 3111. 🖷 +353 1 208 3080.
E: hearus@rte.ie **W:** www.rte.ie/radio/worldwide.html
Webcast: D/L/P
L.P: DG, RTÉ: Noel Goan; MD, Radio: Clare Duignan.
SAT: (via WRN English) Eutelsat 28A/36B/Hot Bird 13A, Intelsat 7/10, Galaxy 19, Sirius FM 5, Superbird C2, Telstar 18, XM3/4.
kHz: 5820

Winter Schedule 2012/2013

English/ Irish Gaelic	Days	Area	kHz
1930-2000	daily	Af	5820mey

Ann: English: "RTÉ Ireland, a production of RTÉ Radio One".
V: QSL-card.
Notes: RTÉ is Ireland's national Public Service broadcaster.

ISRAEL (ISR)

KOL ISRAEL (VOICE OF ISRAEL) (Pub)
✉ P.O. Box 1082, Jerusalem 91010, Israel.
☎ +972 2 6248715. 🖷 +972 2 5302327.
E: radio-int@iba.org.il; reception@iba.org.il
W: www.iba.org.il/world; www.radis.org (Farsi)
Webcast: D/L
L.P: Dir, Intl Broadcasting: Shmuel Ben-Zvi; Head, Foreign Languages Dept: Alegra Amado Ben-Itzhak.
SW: Leased from Bezeq.
SAT: Amos 3, Eutelsat Hot Bird 13A. (Via Globecast Persian language sat-feed Radio Jahani)
kHz: 13850, 15760

Winter Schedule 2012/2013

Persian	Days	Area	kHz
1500-1600	daily	ME	13850isr, 15760isr*
1600-1630	mtwt..s	ME	13850isr, 15760isr*

Key: * alternate freq: 9985kHz.
Ann: Farsi: "Inja Sedaye Israel".
V: Does not verify.
Notes: Kol Israel is the national broadcaster in Israel, under the roof of the Israel Broadcasting Authority (IBA). The prgrs in Persian are part of domestic immigrant channel Kol Israel Reka.

GALEI TZAHAL
✉ See National Radio section.
Webcast: L
SW: [LOD] Lod: 2 x 10kW.
kHz: 6885, 15850

Winter Schedule 2012/2013

Hebrew	Days	Area	kHz
0000-2400	daily	Eu	6885lod, 15850lod

V: QSL-card.
Notes: Relay of domestic channel.

BEZEQ (THE ISRAEL TELECOMMUNICATIONS CORP. LTD.) (Tx Operator)
✉ P.O. Box 1088, Jerusalem 91010, Israel.
☎ +972 3 6800029. 🖷 +972 3 6800030.
E: mosheor@bezeq.com **W:** www.bezeq.com
L.P: CEO: Avi Gabbay.
SW: [ISR] Yavne: 2 x 500kW.

Notes: Established in 1984. Bezeq is the national transmitter network operator in Israel.

ITALY (I)

IRRS–SHORTWAVE (NEXUS–IBA)
✉ P.O. Box 10980, I-20110 Milano, Italy.
☎ +39 02 2666971. 🖷 +39 02 70638151.
E: info@nexus.org **W:** www.nexus.org (General); www.egradio.org (Religious relays)
Webcast: L (mp3.nexus.org)
L.P: Pres: Alfredo E. Cotroneo.
SW: Via tx leased from Radiocom (Romania).
kHz: 7290, 9510

Winter Schedule 2012/2013

English	Days	Area	kHz
0900-1000	.....s.	Eu,ME,NAf	9510tig
1030-1300	......s	Eu,ME,NAf	9510tig
1900-2000	....fss	Eu,ME,NAf	7290tig
2000-2100	daily	Eu,ME,NAf	7290tig

Ann: English: "This is IRRS shortwave in Milano - signing on".
IS: S/on: Triumphal Scene from Aida (Verdi); S/off: Prisoners' Chorus (Verdi).
V: QSL-card. Rp. (Rpt by email to: reports@nexus.org)
Notes: NEXUS-IBA is a provider of relay services for prgr producers and broadcasters, via Internet (24/7) and leased tx facilities in Romania.

JAPAN (J)

RADIO JAPAN (NHK WORLD) (Pub)
✉ 2-1, Jinnan 2-chome, Shibuya-ku, Tokyo. 150-8001, Japan.
☎ +81 3 34651111. 🖷 +81 3 34811350.
E: nhkworld@nhk.jp **W:** www.nhk.or.jp/nhkworld
Webcast: D/L/P
L.P: DG (NHK): T. Wakita; Pres (NHK): M.Matsumoto; DG, Broadcasting: S.Kaneda.
SW: Leased from KDDI & foreign relays.
SAT: Badr 4, Eutelsat Hot Bird 13A, Intelsat 8/9/10.
kHz: 927, 1350, 1386, 5960, 5970, 6075, 6090, 6115, 6130, 6165, 6190, 6195, 7395, 9560, 9620, 9625, 9655, 9670, 9700, 9750, 9760, 9770, 9785, 9795, 9835, 9860, 11665, 11695, 11730, 11740, 11760, 11815, 11850, 11860, 11880, 11910, 11925, 11935, 11945, 11975, 12035, 12045, 13650, 13725, 13730, 13840, 13870, 15190, 15195, 15290, 15325, 15445, 15720, 17660, 17735, 17810

Winter Schedule 2012/2013

Arabic	Days	Area	kHz
0600-0630	ME,NAf	daily	11975iss
2000-2030	ME	daily	1350erv*
Bengali	**Days**	**Area**	**kHz**
1300-1345	daily	SAs	12035sng
Burmese	**Days**	**Area**	**kHz**
1030-1100	daily	SEA	11740sng
1430-1500	daily	SEA	11740sng
2340-2400	daily	SEA	13650yam
Chinese	**Days**	**Area**	**kHz**
0900-0930	daily	As	6090yam
1200-1230	daily	As	6090yam
1300-1330	daily	As	6190yam
1400-1430	daily	As	6190yam
1600-1630	daily	As	9655yam
2230-2250	daily	As	9560yam
English	**Days**	**Area**	**kHz**
0500-0530	daily	NAm	11740guf
0500-0530	daily	SAf	9770iss
0500-0530	Eu	daily	17660dha
1000-1030	daily	Pac	9625yam
1000-1030	daily	SEA	11740sng
1100-1130	....f..	WEu	9760wof+
1200-1230	daily	NAm	15190guf
1200-1230	daily	SEA	11740sng
1300-1330	daily	SAs	11730tac
1400-1430	daily	SEA	11925hbn
1400-1430	daily	SAs	11695tac
1800-1830	daily	CAf	15720mdc

French	Days	Area	kHz
0530-0600	daily	CAf,WAf	11730iss, 13840mdc
2030-2100	daily	WAf	11850mdc

Hindi	Days	Area	kHz
0130-0200	daily	SAs	9785tac
1430-1515	daily	SAs	15720mdc

Indonesian	Days	Area	kHz
0945-1030	daily	SEA	9860sng
1315-1400	daily	SEA	11925hbn
2300-2330	daily	SEA	11665yam

Japanese	Days	Area	kHz
0200-0300	daily	SEA	11860sng
0200-0400	daily	CAm	5960guf
0200-0400	daily	SAm	11935guf
0200-0500	daily	As	15145yam
0200-0500	daily	SAs	15325yam
0200-0500	ME,NAf	daily	9620wer
0300-0500	daily	SEA	17810yam
0700-0800	EAs	daily	6165yam
0800-0900	daily	SAm	5970guf
0800-1000	daily	SEA	11740sng
0800-1000	daily	WAf	15290iss
0800-1700	daily	As	9750yam
0900-1500	daily	SEA	11815yam
1500-1700	daily	CAf	17735iss
1500-1700	daily	SAs	12045sng
1700-1900	daily	SAf	11945iss
1700-1900	daily	SAm	9835yam
1700-1900	ME,NAf	daily	15445wer
1900-2200	ME,NAf	daily	9670yam
2000-2100	daily	Pac	9625yam
2100-2200	daily	SEA	6075yam
2100-2400	daily	As	11910yam
2200-2300	daily	SEA	11665yam
2200-2300	ME,NAf	daily	9620wer

Korean	Days	Area	kHz
0915-0945	EAs	daily	9700yam
1130-1200	EAs	daily	6090yam
1230-1300	EAs	daily	6190yam
1330-1400	EAs	daily	6190yam
1430-1500	EAs	daily	6190yam
2209-2230	EAs	daily	9560yam

Persian	Days	Area	kHz
0400-0430	ME,NAf	daily	11730tac
1430-1500	ME,NAf	daily	13725iss**
1630-1700	ME,NAf	daily	927dsb

Portuguese	Days	Area	kHz
0900-0930	daily	SAm	6130guf
2130-2200	daily	SAm	11880guf

Russian	Days	Area	kHz
0330-0400	Eu	daily	1386sit
0430-0500	Eu	daily	6115sit
0530-0600	EAs	daily	11760yam
0800-0830	EAs	daily	6165yam
1100-1130	EAs	daily	6090yam
1130-1200	....f..	WEu	9760wof+
1600-1630	Eu	daily	927dsb

Spanish	Days	Area	kHz
0400-0430	daily	SAm	6195guf
0500-0530	daily	CAm	6195hri
0930-1000	daily	CAm	9795guf
0930-1000	daily	SAm	6195hri

Swahili	Days	Area	kHz
0315-0400	EAf	daily	7395mdc
1730-1800	EAf	daily	13730mdc***

Thai	Days	Area	kHz
1130-1200	daily	SEA	11740sng
1230-1300	daily	SEA	11740sng
2259-2320	daily	SEA	13650yam

Urdu	Days	Area	kHz
1515-1600	daily	SAs	13870dha
1700-1745	daily	SAs	927dsb

Vietnamese	Days	Area	kHz
1100-1130	daily	SEA	11740sng
1300-1330	daily	SEA	11740sng
2320-2340	daily	SEA	13650yam

Key: + DRM; Relayed in parts of the Middle East and Africa on FM: * 89.3MHz (Jenin) and 87.8MHz (Ramallah) in the West Bank; ** 88.0MHz (Kabul and Herat, Afghanistan); *** 94.6MHz (Dar es Salaam, Tanzania and 22 other cities).

Ann: English: "This is NHK World, Radio Japan in Tokyo"; Indonesian: "Inilah Radio Jepang, NHK World, siaran bahasa Indonesia"; Japanese: "Kochirawa NHK Warudo, Rajio Nippon, NHK no kokusaihoso desu"; Korean: "Yeogineun NHK World, Radio Ilbonimnda"; Mandarin: "Zheli shi riben guoji guangbo diantai, NHK huanqiu guangbowang".

IS: Melody "Kazoe Uta".

V: QSL-card.

Notes: Radio Japan is the External Sce of the public broadcaster NHK. The Japanese programmes include relays of NHK domestic Radio 1. Indonesian is broadcast daily from 1406-1451 on 89.2MHz FM in Jakarta, plus 34 other cities in Indonesia. Bengali is broadcast daily from 1500-1545 on 97.6MHz FM in Dhaka, plus 6 other cities in Bangladesh.

KDDI CORPORATION (Tx Operator)

Garden Air Tower, 10-10, Iidabashi 3-chome, Chiyoda-ku, Tokyo 102-8460, Japan.
☎ +81 3 33470077. 🖷 +81 3 33475845.
W: www.kddi.com
LP: Pres: Takashi Tanaka.
SW: [YAM] Koga, Yamata, Ibaraki prefecture: 4 x 100, 7 x 300kW.
Notes: KDDI Corporation is a major national telecommunications provider.

KOREA, (D.P.R.) (KRE)

VOICE OF KOREA (VOK) (Gov)

Pyongyang, Democratic People's Republic of Korea.
☎ +850 2 3816035. 🖷 +850 2 3814416.
E: vok@star-co.net.kp **W:** www.vok.rep.kp
Webcast: D
MW/SW: Uses txs provided by the Ministry of Post & Telecommunications.
SAT: Thaicom 5.
kHz: *621, 3250, 3560, 4405, 6070, 6170, 6185, 7210, 7220, 7235, 7570, 7580, 9325, 9335, 9345, 9650, 9730, 9850, 9975, 9990, 11535, 11545, 11710, 11735, 11910, 12015, 13650, 13760, 15100, 15180, 15245*

Winter Schedule 2012/2013

Arabic	Days	Area	kHz
1500-1600	daily	ME,NAf	9990kuj, 11545kuj
1700-1800	daily	ME,NAf	9990kuj, 11545kuj

Chinese	Days	Area	kHz
0300-0400	daily	EAs	3560kuj†
0300-0400	daily	SEA	13650kuj, 15100kuj
0500-0600	daily	EAs	4405kuj†, 7220kuj, 9345kuj, 9730kuj
0600-0700	daily	EAs	3560kuj†
0600-0700	daily	SEA	13650kuj, 15100kuj
0800-0900	daily	EAs	3560kuj†, 7220kuj, 9345kuj
1100-1200	daily	EAs	3560kuj†, 7220kuj, 9345kuj
1300-1400	daily	SEA	6185kuj, 9850kuj
2100-2300	daily	EAs	7235kuj, 9345kuj, 9975kuj, 11535kuj

English	Days	Area	kHz
0400-0500	daily	EAs	4405kuj†, 7220kuj, 9345kuj, 9730kuj
0400-0500	daily	LAm	11735kuj, 13760kuj, 15180kuj
0500-0600	daily	EAs	3560kuj†
0500-0600	daily	SEA	13650kuj, 15100kuj
0600-0700	daily	EAs	4405kuj†, 7220kuj, 9345kuj, 9730kuj
1000-1100	daily	LAm	6170kuj†, 9335kuj
1000-1100	daily	SEA	6185kuj, 9850kuj
1300-1400	daily	NAm	9335kuj, 11710kuj

English	Days	Area	kHz
1300-1400	daily	EAs	3560kuj†
1300-1400	daily	Eu	7570kuj, 12015kuj
1500-1600	daily	NAm	9335kuj, 11710kuj
1500-1600	daily	Eu	7570kuj, 12015kuj
1500-1600	daily	EAs	3560kuj†
1600-1700	daily	ME,NAf	9990kuj, 11545kuj
1800-1900	daily	EAs	3560kuj†
1800-1900	daily	Eu	7570kuj, 12015kuj
1900-2000	daily	ME,NAf	9975kuj, 11535kuj
1900-2000	daily	SAf	7210kuj, 11910kuj
2100-2200	daily	EAs	3560kuj†
2100-2200	daily	Eu	7570kuj, 12015kuj

French	Days	Area	kHz
0400-0500	daily	EAs	3560kuj†
0400-0500	daily	SEA	13650kuj, 15100kuj
0600-0700	daily	LAm	11735kuj, 13760kuj, 15180kuj
1100-1200	daily	LAm	6170kuj†, 9335kuj
1100-1200	daily	SEA	6185kuj, 9850kuj
1400-1500	daily	EAs	3560kuj†
1400-1500	daily	Eu	7570kuj, 12015kuj
1400-1500	daily	NAm	9335kuj, 11710kuj
1600-1700	daily	NAm	9335kuj, 11710kuj
1600-1700	daily	EAs	3560kuj†
1600-1700	daily	Eu	7570kuj, 12015kuj
1800-1900	daily	ME,NAf	9975kuj, 11535kuj
1800-1900	daily	SAf	7210kuj, 11910kuj
2000-2100	daily	EAs	3560kuj†
2000-2100	daily	Eu	7570kuj, 12015kuj

German	Days	Area	kHz
1600-1700	daily	EAs	4405kuj†
1600-1700	daily	Eu	6170kuj†, 9325kuj
1800-2000	daily	EAs	4405kuj†
1800-2000	daily	Eu	6170kuj†, 9325kuj

Japanese	Days	Area	kHz
0700-1250	daily	EAs	621chj, 3250pyo, 4405kuj†, 7580kuj, 9650kuj
0900-1250	daily	EAs	6070kng
2100-2350	daily	EAs	621chj, 3250pyo, 4405kuj†, 7580kuj, 9650kuj

Korean	Days	Area	kHz
0300-0350	daily	EAs	4405kuj**,†, 7220kuj**, 9345kuj**, 9730kuj**
0700-0750	daily	EAs	3560kuj**,†, 7220kuj**, 9345kuj**
0900-0950	daily	EAs	3560kuj*,†, 7220kuj*, 9345kuj*, 9975kuj**, 11735kuj**
0900-0950	daily	Eu	13760kuj**, 15245kuj**
1000-1050	daily	EAs	3560kuj**,†, 7220kuj**, 9345kuj**
1200-1250	daily	EAs	3560kuj*,†, 7220kuj**, 9345kuj**
1200-1250	daily	LAm	6170kuj*,†, 9335kuj*
1200-1250	daily	SEA	6185kuj*, 9850kuj*
1300-1350	daily	Eu	6170kuj*,†, 9325kuj**
1300-1350	daily	EAs	4405kuj**,†
1400-1450	daily	SEA	6185kuj*, 9850kuj*
1700-1750	daily	EAs	3560kuj*,†
1700-1750	daily	Eu	7570kuj*, 12015kuj*
1700-1750	daily	NAm	9335kuj*, 11710kuj*
2000-2050	daily	EAs	4405kuj*,†
2000-2050	daily	Eu	6170kuj*,†, 9325kuj*
2000-2050	daily	ME,NAf	9975kuj*, 11535kuj*
2000-2050	daily	SAf	7210kuj*, 11910kuj*
2300-2350	daily	EAs	3560kuj*,†, 7235kuj*, 9345kuj*, 9975kuj*, 11535kuj*
2300-2350	daily	Eu	7570kuj*, 12015kuj*

Russian	Days	Area	kHz
0700-0900	daily	EAs	9975kuj, 11735kuj
0700-0900	daily	Eu	13760kuj, 15245kuj
1400-1600	daily	Eu	6170kuj†, 9325kuj
1400-1600	daily	EAs	4405kuj†
1700-1800	daily	EAs	4405kuj†
1700-1800	daily	Eu	6170kuj†, 9325kuj

Spanish	Days	Area	kHz
0300-0400	daily	LAm	11735kuj, 13760kuj, 15180kuj
0500-0600	daily	LAm	11735kuj, 13760kuj, 15180kuj
1900-2000	daily	EAs	3560kuj†
1900-2000	daily	Eu	7570kuj, 12015kuj
2200-2300	daily	Eu	7570kuj, 12015kuj
2200-2300	daily	EAs	3560kuj†

Key: † Irregular; * Produced by KCBS; ** Produced by Pyongyang BS.
Ann: Arabic: "Huna Sowt al Koriya"; English: "This is the Voice of Korea"; French: "La Voix de la Corée"; German: "Hier ist die Stimme Koreas"; Japanese: "Choson no koe hoso desu"; Korean: "Joson Jung-ang Pangsong-imnida", "Pyongyang Pangsong-imnida"; Mandarin: "Chaoxian zhi sheng guangbo diantai"; Russian: "Govorit Golos Korei"; Spanish: "Aqui la Voz de Corea".
IS: Song of General Kim Il Sung. Opening music: National Anthem.
V: QSL-card.
Notes: Voice of Korea is the External Sce of the Radio & TV Broadcasting Committee of the Democratic People's Republic of Korea.

PYONGYANG BROADCASTING STATION (PYONGYANG PANGSONG)

Pyongyang, Democratic People's Republic of Korea.
MW/SW: Uses txs provided by the Ministry of Post & Telecommunications.
kHz: 621, 657, 684, 729, 801, 855, 1053, 3250, 3320, 6250, 6400

Winter Schedule 2012/2013

Korean	Days	Area	kHz
0000-0700	daily	EAs	621chj, 3250pyo
0755-1400	daily	EAs	1053hju
1300-1800	daily	EAs	621chj
1300-1800	daily	EAs	3250pyo
2100-1800	daily	EAs	684sag
2100-1900	daily	EAs	801hwd, 3320pyo, 6250pyo, 6400kng
2100-2030	daily	EAs	657kan, 729sep, 855swo
2155-0405	daily	EAs	1053hju

Ann: Korean: "Pyongyang Pangsong-imnida".
IS: Song of General Kim Il Sung. Opening & closing music: National Anthem.
Notes: Timings and frequency use variable.

MINISTRY OF POST & TELECOMMUNICATIONS (Tx Operator)

Oesong-dong, Central District, Pyongyang, Democratic People's Republic of Korea.
☎ +850 2 3813180. 📠 +850 2 3814418.
E: mptird@co.chesin.com
L:P: Minister: Ryu Yong Sop.
MW: [CHJ] Chongjin: 621kHz 500kW; [HJU] Haeju: 1053kHz 1000kW; [HWD] Kimchaek, Hwadae county: 801kHz 500kW; [KAN] Kangnam: 657kHz 1500kW; [SAG] Samgo: 684kHz 250kW; [SEP] Sepo: 729kHz 50kW; [SWO] Sangwon: 855kHz 500kW.
SW: [KNG] Kanggye: 1 x 250kW; [KUJ] Kujang: 10 x 200kW; [PYO] Pyongyang: 1 x 100kW. New Chinese-made txs (20/50/100/150kW) are currently being installed.
Notes: The Ministry of Post and Telecommunications owns and operates the transmitter network in the Democratic People's Republic of Korea.

KOREA, Rep. of (KOR)

KBS WORLD RADIO (Pub)

International Broadcasting, Korean Broadcasting System, 18 Yeouido-dong, Yeongdeungpo-gu, Seoul 150-790, Republic of Korea.

☎ +82 2 7813885. (English) 🖷 +82 2 7813694.
E: rki@kbs.co.kr; english@kbs.co.kr **W:** world.kbs.co.kr
Webcast: D/L/P
L.P: Pres: Kim In-Kyu; Exec. Producer, World Radio: Paek Seung Yeop.
MW: [DAN] Dangjin (HLCA): 972kHz 1500kW; [KIM] Gimje (HLSR): 1170kHz 500kW.
SW: [KIM] Gimje: 8 x 100, 3 x 250kW; [HWA] Hwaseong: 1 x 100kW.
kHz: *972, 1170, 3955, 5950, 6015, 6045, 6095, 6155, 7235, 7275, 9515, 9570, 9580, 9640, 9690, 9740, 9760, 9770, 9805, 9840, 11635, 11795, 11810, 15160, 15575*

Winter Schedule 2012/2013

Arabic	Days	Area	kHz
2000-2100	daily	ME,Af	9840dha

English	Days	Area	kHz
0200-0300	daily	SAm	9580kim, 9640kim
0800-0900	daily	SEA	9570kim
1100-1130	.....s.	Eu	9760wof+
1200-1300	daily	NAm	15575kim
1230-1330	daily	CHN	6095kim
1300-1400	daily	SEA	9570kim
1400-1500	daily	SEA	9640kim
1600-1700	daily	Eu	9515kim
1600-1700	daily	SEA	9640kim
1800-1900	daily	Eu	7275kim
2200-2230	daily	Eu	3955skn

French	Days	Area	kHz
2000-2100	daily	ME,Af	5950iss
2100-2200	daily	Eu	3955skn

Gorman	Days	Area	kHz
2000-2100	daily	Eu	3955skn

Indonesian	Days	Area	kHz
1200-1300	daily	SEA	9570kim
1400-1500	daily	SEA	9570kim
2200-2300	daily	SEA	9805kim

Japanese	Days	Area	kHz
0100-0200	daily	SAm	9580kim
0200-0300	daily	SAm	11810kim
0800-0900	daily	FE	6155kim, 7275kim
0900-1100	daily	FE	9805kim
1100-1300	daily	FE	1170kim

Korean	Days	Area	kHz
0000-0400	daily	FE	1170kim**
0300-0400	daily	SAm	11810kim
0400-2400	daily	EAs	6015hwa*
0400-2400	daily	FE	972dan*
0700-0800	daily	Eu	6045wof
0900-1000	daily	ME,Af	15160kim
0900-1100	daily	FE	7275kim
0900-1100	daily	SEA	9570kim
1000-1100	daily	FE	1170kim
1200-1300	daily	FE	7275kim
1400-1500	daily	NAm	15575kim
1400-2400	daily	FE	1170kim**
1600-1800	daily	Eu	7275kim
1600-1800	daily	ME,Af	9740kim
1700-1900	daily	Eu	9515kim

Mandarin	Days	Area	kHz
1130-1230	daily	CHN	6095kim
1130-1230	daily	SEA	9770kim
1300-1400	daily	FE	1170kim, 7275kim
2200-2300	daily	CHN	7275kim
2300-2400	daily	SEA	9805kim

Russian	Days	Area	kHz
1800-1900	daily	Eu	7235wof

Spanish	Days	Area	kHz
0100-0200	daily	SAm	11635guf, 11810kim
0200-0230	daily	NAm	15575kim
0600-0700	daily	Eu	6045kim
1100-1200	daily	SAm	11795kim

Vietnamese	Days	Area	kHz
0100-0200	daily	SEA	9690kim
1030-1130	daily	SEA	9770kim
1500-1600	daily	SEA	9640kim

Key: + DRM; * 1st Global Korean Network; ** 2nd Global Korean Network.
Ann: Arabic: "Huna KBS World Radio min Si'ul"; English: "This is KBS World Radio, the overseas service of the Korean Broadcasting System, coming to you from Seoul, the capital of the Republic of Korea"; German: "Hier ist KBS World Radio aus Seoul, der Auslandssender der Republik Korea"; Indonesian: "Inilah siaran bahasa Indonesia, KBS World Radio, yang dipancarkan langsung dari ibu kota Republik Korea, Seoul"; Japanese: "Kochirawa Kankoku Souru kara okurishiteimasu KBS no rajio kokusai hoso, KBS warudo rajio desu"; Korean: "Yeogineun Daehan Minguk Seoul-eseo bonaedeurineun KBS World Radio urimal bangsong-imnida"; Mandarin: "Zheli shi Hanguo guoji guangbo diantai, zai Dahanminguo shoudu Shou'er wei nin boyin"; Spanish: "Esto es KBS World Radio, emitiendo desde Seúl, Republica de Corea."; Vietnamese: "Day la chuong trinh phat thanh tieng Viet cua dai KBS World Radio phat thanh tu Seoul Han quoc".
IS: Korean children's song "Dar-a Dar-a Balgeun Dar-a (Oh, Bright Moon)", played on a glockenspiel. Original music "Dawn" composed by Kim Hee Jyo, with KBS symphony orchestra.
V: QSL-card.
Notes: KBS World Radio is the External Sce of the public broadcaster Korean Broadcasting System (KBS). KBS Global Korean Network Programmes are services for ethnic Koreans living outside of the Republic of Korea. Indonesian is broadcast daily from 1200-1300 on 102.6MHz in Jakarta (Indonesia) and Spanish is broadcast mon-fri from 0100-0200 on 94.7MHz in Buenos Aires (Argentina).

FEBC KOREA (Rlg)
🖃 P.O. Box 88, Seoul 121-707, Republic of Korea.
☎ +82 2 3200114. 🖷 +82 2 3200229.
E: febcadm@febc.net **W:** www.febc.or.kr; www.febc.net (Korean); english.febc.net (English)
Webcast: L
🖃 Yeongdeungpo-dong 6-ga 8-1, Yeongdeungpo-gu, Seoul 150-036, Republic of Korea.
L.P: Chmn: Dr Billy Kim; Pres: Sanwoong Min.
MW: [JEJ] Jeju (HLAZ): 1566kHz 250kW; [SEO] Seoul, Incheon (HLKX): 1188kHz 100kW.
kHz: *1188, 1566*

Winter Schedule 2012/2013

Chinese	Days	Area	kHz
1100-1230	daily	CHN	1566jej
1345-1730	daily	CHN	1566jej
1500-1700	daily	CHN	1188seo
1730-1830	daily	CHN	1566jej

English	Days	Area	kHz
1100-1200	daily	EAs	1188seo

Japanese	Days	Area	kHz
1230-1345	daily	J	1566jej

Korean	Days	Area	kHz
1700-2200	daily	EAs	1188seo
1900-1100	daily	EAs	1566jej
2200-1100	daily	EAs	1188seo

Russian	Days	Area	kHz
1830-1900	daily	RUS	1566jej

Key: * VOA English language lesson.
Ann: English: "It's 8 o'clock and time for daily English segment on HLKX 1188 on your am radio dial"; Japanese: "Kochirawa kirisutokyo hosokyoku FEBC desu"; Korean: "Jungpa Cheonbaek-palsip-pal (1188) kHz, Pyojun FM Paeng-nyuk-jeom-gu (106.9) MHz, Areumdaun Chanyanggwa Guwon-eui Gibbeun Sosigeul Jeonhaneun Geukdong Bangsong-imnida.", "Yeogineun Daehan Minguk Jeju Geukdong Bangsong-imnida"; Mandarin: "HLKX. Zheli shi zhongpo 1188 (yao yao ba ba) qianhe, Yiyou Diantai di 2 (er) dai.", "HLAZ. Zheli shi zhongbo 1566 (yao wu liu liu) qianhe, Yiyou Diantai di 1 (yi) dai".
V: QSL-card.
Notes: FEBC Korea is a regional division of Far East Broadcasting Company, Inc (FEBC) (USA), targeting Korea, China, Mongolia, and the Far Eastern parts of Russia. See USA for FEBC corporate details. The transmissions may include prgrs provided by small religious prgr producers and broadcast under own labels.

KUWAIT (KWT)

RADIO KUWAIT (Gov)
See National Radio section.
SW: [KBD] Kuwait, Kabd: 5 x 500kW.
SAT: AsiaSat 5, Badr 4, Eutelsat Hot Bird 13C, Express AM22, Galaxy 19, Hispasat 1E, Nilesat 201.
kHz: 5960, 6080, 7250, 9750, 11630, 13650, 15515, 15540, 17550, 21540

Winter Schedule 2012/2013

Arabic	Days	Area	kHz
0200-0900	daily	ME	5960kbd
0500-0900	daily	EAs	15515kbd
0930-1600	daily	WAf,CAf	11630kbd*
1005-1500	daily	Eu,NAm	21540kbd
1100-1600	daily	NAf	9750kbd
1600-2100	daily	ME	6080kbd
1700-2000	daily	NAm	13650kbd
2000-2400	daily	NAm	17550kbd
English	**Days**	**Area**	**kHz**
1800-2100	daily	Eu,NAm	15540kbd
Filipino	**Days**	**Area**	**kHz**
1000-1200	daily	SEA	15540kbd
Persian	**Days**	**Area**	**kHz**
0800-1000	daily	ME	7250kbd
Urdu	**Days**	**Area**	**kHz**
1600-1800	daily	SAs	15540kbd

Key: * May carry Quran prgr.
Ann: Arabic: "Huna al-Kuwait".
V: QSL-card.
Notes: Arabic prgrs are relays of Home Sce networks.

IBB RELAY STATION KUWAIT
IBB Transmitting Station, c/o US Embassy, P.O. Box 77, Safat 13001, Kuwait City, Kuwait.
L.P: SM: Walter Patterson.
MW: [KWT] Kuwait, Umm Al-Rimam: 1548kHz 600kW; 1593kHz 150kW. Backup tx: 50kW. Additional 600kW tx under installation.
SW: [KWT] Kuwait, Umm Al-Rimam: 4 x 250kW; two additional 250kW txs under installation.
V: QSL-card.

KYRGYZSTAN (KGZ)

SHORTWAVE RELAY SERVICE (Rlg)
Bishkek, Kyrgyzstan.
SW: Leased from Kyrgyztelekom.
kHz: 5130

Winter Schedule 2012/2013

Persian	Days	Area	kHz
1500-1800	daily	WAs	5130bis†

Key: † Irregular.
Notes: Rebroadcasts paid religious programming in Central Asian languages. Activity and schedule varies acc. to airtime sales.

KYRGYZTELECOM (Tx Operator)
Chui avenue 96, 720000 Bishkek, Kyrgyzstan.
+996 312 681616. +996 312 662424.
E: info@kt.kg **W:** www.kt.kg
L.P: Pres: Marat M.Mambetaliev.
MW: [BIS] Bishkek, Krasnaya Rechka: 1467kHz 150kW.
SW: [BIS] Bishkek, Krasnaya Rechka: 1 x 15kW. (Estimated power)
Notes: Kyrgyztelekom is the national tx operator.

LAOS (LAO)

LAO NATIONAL RADIO (Gov)
See National Radio Section.
Webcast: D
MW: [VIE] Vientiane 567kHz 200kW.
SW: [VIE] Vientiane 1 x10kW.
FM/DAB: FM: 97.25MHz (Vientiane, 2kW).
kHz: 567, 6130

Winter Schedule 2012/2013

English	Days	Area	kHz
1400-1430	daily	SEA	567vie, 6130vie
French	**Days**	**Area**	**kHz**
1430-1500	daily	SEA	567vie, 6130vie
Khmer	**Days**	**Area**	**kHz**
1530-1600	daily	SEA	567vie, 6130vie
Thai	**Days**	**Area**	**kHz**
1330-1400	daily	SEA	567vie, 6130vie
Vietnamese	**Days**	**Area**	**kHz**
1500-1530	daily	SEA	567vie, 6130vie

IS: National Anthem.
V: QSL-Card.
Notes: Times variable.

LESOTHO (LSO)

LESOTHO NATIONAL BROADCASTING SERVICE (Tx Operator)
See National Radio section.
MW: [MSU] Maseru, Lancer's Gap: 1197kHz 50kW (2 x 50kW, 1 only in operation).
Notes: The transmitter is leased to Family Stations, Inc (see "Family Radio", under USA, for corporate details and schedule).

LIBYA (LBY)

RADIO LIBYA (Gov)
El Fath Rd, Tripoli, Libya,
SW: [SAB] Sabrata: 2 x 500kW.
kHz: 11600

Winter Schedule 2012/2013

Arabic	Days	Area	kHz
1500-2000	daily	Af	11600sabt†

Key: † Irregular.
Ann: Arabic: "Radio Libya min Tarabulus alasema".
Notes: Known as Voice of Africa, prior to Libyan regime change in October 2011.

LITHUANIA (LTU)

RADIO BALTIC WAVES INTERNATIONAL (RBWI)
Švitrigailos g. 11a-211, LT-03228 Vilnius, Lithuania.
+370 5 2652532. +370 5 2652532.
E: radio@balticwaves.cjb.net
L.P: Dir: Rolandas Stirblys; Project Coordinator: Rimantas Pleikys.
MW: Leased from LRTC.
V: QSL-card. (For relayed stns)
Notes: RBWI markets air time on MW relay facilities in Lithuania for foreign broadcasters.

ZILIONIS RADIO TV CONSULTING (Broker)
P.O. Box 3300, LT-02003 Vilnius 13, Lithuania.
+370 685 76840. +370 526 52532.
E: consult@zilionis.com **W:** www.zilionis.com/airtime
L.P: Dir: Sigitas Zilionis.

LIETUVOS RADIJO IR TELEVIZIJOS CENTRAS (LRTC) (Tx Operator)
Sausio 13-osios g. 10, LT-04347 Vilnius, Lithuania.
+370 5 2040300. +370 5 2040325.
E: info@telecentras.lt **W:** www.telecentras.lt
L.P: GD: Gediminas Stirbys.
MW: [SIT] Kaunas, Sitkunai: 1386kHz 150/500kW; [VLN] Vilnius: 612kHz 100kW.
SW: [SIT] Kaunas, Sitkunai: 1 x 100kW.
Notes: LRTC is the national transmitter network operator.

LUXEMBOURG (LUX)

RTL RADIO (Comm)
45, boulevard Pierre Frieden, L-1543 Luxembourg.
+352 421423500. +352 421422738.
E: oliver.fahlbusch@rtlgroup.com **W:** www.rtlgroup.com
Webcast: L (rtl1440.com)
L.P: (RTL Group) CEO: Guillaume de Posch; Corporate Communications: Oliver Fahlbusch.
MW/SW: Uses txs provided by Broadcasting Center Europe.
SAT: Astra 1M.

kHz: *234, 1440*

Winter Schedule 2012/2013

French	Days	Area	kHz
0000-2400	daily	F	234bdw*

German	Days	Area	kHz
0400-1900	daily	Eu	1440mrn

Key: * Rel. RTL France (see National Radio section)
Ann: German: "RTL Radio".
Notes: RTL Radio is part of RTL Group, a multinational TV, radio and media production holding, majority-owned by Bertelsmann AG (Germany).

BROADCASTING CENTER EUROPE (BCE)
(Tx Operator)
✉ 45, boulevard Pierre Frieden, L-1543 Luxembourg.
☎ +352 24806605. 🖷 +352 24806609.
E: contact@bce.lu **W:** www.bce.lu
L.P: CEO: Alain Flammang.
LW: [BDW] Beidweiler: 234kHz 2 x 1000kW.
MW: [MRN] Marnach: 1440kHz 1200kW. (site to be closed in 2014)
V: QSL-card.
Notes: BCE is part of RTL Group's Technical Division. It was founded in January 2000, as a result of the merger of various technical entities of the RTL Group.

MACEDONIA (MKD)

RADIO MAKEDONIJA (Pub)
✉ Blvd. "Goce Delcev" bb, 1000 Skopje, FYR Macedonia.
☎ +389 2 3112200.. 🖷 +389 2 3227529.
E: radiomakedonija@mr.com.mk **W:** www.mtv.com.mk
L.P: Dir (MRT): Grigori Popovski.
MW: Leased from Makedonska Radiodifuzija.
kHz: 810

Winter Schedule 2012/2013

Albanian	Days	Area	kHz
2000-2030	mtwtf..	Eu	810sko
Bulgarian	**Days**	**Area**	**kHz**
1900-1930	mtwtf..	Eu	810sko
Greek	**Days**	**Area**	**kHz**
1930-2000	mtwtf..	Eu	810sko
Macedonian	**Days**	**Area**	**kHz**
1830-1900	mtwtf..	Eu	810sko
1900-2100	.....s.	Eu	810sko
2100-0200	mtwtf..	Eu	810sko
Serbian	**Days**	**Area**	**kHz**
2030-2100	mtwtf..	Eu	810sko

Ann: Macedonian: "Radio Makedonija".
V: QSL-letter.
Notes: External Sce of the public service broadcaster Makedonska Radio Televizija (MRT).

MAKEDONSKA RADIODIFUZIJA (Tx Operator)
✉ blvd. "Goce Delcev" bb, 1000 Skopje, FYR Macedonia.
☎ +389 2 3297100. 🖷 +389 2 3225520.
E: radiodifuzija@jpmrd.gov.mk **W:** www.jpmrd.gov.mk
MW: [SKO] Skopje, Sveti Nikole: 810kHz 1200kW.
V: QSL-letter.
Notes: Makedonska Radiodifuzija is the national transmitter network provider.

MADAGASCAR (MDG)

MADAGASCAR WORLD VOICE ‡ (Rlg)
✉ World Christian Broadcasting, Immeuble Assist, 7ème etage, 101 Antananarivo, Madagascar.
W: For planned services: www.africanpathways.com
✉ 4344 Livingston Ave, Dallas, TX 75205-2608, USA.
E: info@worldchristian.org **W:** www.worldchristian.org
L.P: Pres/CEO: Earl Young; Engineer: Kevin Chambers.
SW: [MWV] Mahajanga: 3 x 100kW. (txs not yet shipped) ‡
Notes: Transmitting station under construction, owned World Christian Broadcasting, Inc. (WCB). See USA for corporate details. Due to delays in the construction process, the station's initial license expired, and the project is currently on hold. After a recent regime change in Madagascar, the time frame for a license renewal is uncertain; no date has been set for a possible completion of the construction works.

MALAGASY GLOBAL BUSINESS S.A. (MGLOB)
(Tx Operator)
✉ Lot Bonnet 88, Ivandry, 101 Antananarivo, Madagascar.
☎ +261 202242222. 🖷 +261 202243184.
E: flore@mglob.mg
L.P: Director: Ms. Flore Ravelojaona; Technical Mgr: Tovonirina Razananaivo (tovo@mglob.mg).
SW: [MDC] Talata Volonondry: 1 x 50, 1 x 250, 2 x 300kW.
Notes: Malagasy Global Business S.A. (MGlob) was established by staff members of the former Radio Netherlands Worldwide Relay Station at Talata Volonondry and is the new operator of the transmitting station,from November 2012..

MALI (MLI)

CHINA RADIO INTERNATIONAL (CRI) RELAY
SW: [BKO] Bamako, Kati: 2 x 100kW.
V: QSL-card. (Rpt to CRI, in China)
Notes: The shortwave facilities are leased to CRI by Radiodiffusion-Télevision du Mali.

MOLDOVA (MDA)

Transnistria

RADIO PMR (Gov)
✉ ul. Pravdy 31, MD-3300 Tiraspol, Moldova.
☎ +373 533 73772. 🖷 +373 533 77758.
E: radiopmr@inbox.ru **W:** radiopmr.org
L.P: Dir. Anatoliy A. Kirsa; Editor-In-Chief: Yekaterina N. Poshelyuk.
MW/SW: Leased from Pridnestrovskiy Radioteletsentr.
kHz: 999, 7290

Winter Schedule 2012/2013

English	Days	Area	kHz
1800-1830	mtwtf..	Eu	7290kch
2000-2030	mtwtf..	Eu	7290kch
2200-2230	mtwt..s	Eu	7290kch
French	**Days**	**Area**	**kHz**
1930-2000	mtwtf..	Eu	7290kch
2130-2200	mtwtf..	Eu	7290kch
German	**Days**	**Area**	**kHz**
1830-1900	mtwtf..	Eu	7290kch
2030-2100	mtwtf..	Eu	7290kch
2230-2300	mtwt..s	Eu	7290kch
Russian	**Days**	**Area**	**kHz**
0300-0500	mtwtf..	Eu	999kch
1900-1930	mtwtf..	Eu	7290kch
2100-2130	mtwtf..	Eu	7290kch

Ann: English: "Here is Tiraspol, the capital of the Pridnestrovian Moldavian Republic", "Radio PMR"; German: "Hier ist Tiraspol"; Russian: "Vy slushaete programmu Pridnestrovya Radio Pridnestrovsko-Moldavskoy Respubliki".
V: QSL-Card.
Notes: Produced by the state broadcaster of the self-proclaimed Pridnestrovian Moldavian Republic, in Eastern Moldova.

PRIDNESTROVSKIY RADIOTELETSENTR
(Tx Operator)
✉ MD-4006 Maiac, Pridnestrovian Moldavian Republic, Moldova.
☎ +373 210 66500.
E: prtc@idknet.com
L.P: DG: Vitaliy Kucherenko.
MW: [KCH] Grigoriopol, Maiac: 621kHz 150kW, 999/1413/1548kHz 1000kW.
SW: [KCH] Grigoriopol, Maiac: 5 x 1000kW.
Notes: Pridnestrovskiy Radioteletsentr (owned by RTRN, Russia) provides high power MW & SW transmitting facilities.

MONACO (MCO)

RADIO MONACO (Comm)
✉ 7 rue du Gabian, Gildo Pastor Center, 98000 Monaco.
☎ +377 97985050. 🖷 +377 97985051.

E: info@radio-monaco.com **W:** radio-monaco.com
SW: Via Monaco Radio (NAYA) utility station.
kHz: *4363, 8728, 13146, 17260*

Winter Schedule 2012/2013

French	Days	Area	kHz
1200-1203	mtwtf..	Atl,Med	4363mco*, 8728mco*,
			13146mco*, 17260mco*

Key: * USB
Ann: French: "Radio Monaco".
V: QSL-email.
Notes: Relay of newscasts, for ships, via Monaco Radio/Naya Radio
utility station.

MONACO RADIO (NAYA) (Tx Operator)
⬚ 1, Chemin du Fort Antoine, 98000 Monte Carlo, Monaco.
☎ +377 97980000. 🖺 +377 93301300.
E: info@naya.mc **W:** www.naya.mc
SW: [MCO] Fontbonne, Mont Agel (France): 4 x 10kW.
Notes: Monaco Radio (call sign 3AC) is a costal radio utility station,
operated by NAYA.

MONTE CARLO RADIODIFFUSION (MCR) (Tx
Operator)
⬚ 10-12 quai Antoine 1er, MC-98000 Monte Carlo, Monaco.
☎ +377 97974700. 🖺 +377 97974707.
E: mcradiodiffusion@mcr.mc **W:** www.mcr.mc
L.P: DG: Jean-Pierre Margossian.
LW: [ROU] Roumoules (France): 216kHz 2000kW.
MW: [CDM] Col de la Madone (France): 702kHz 400kW (run at
200kW); [ROU] Roumoules (France): 1467kHz 1000kW.
SW: [MCO] Fontbonne, Mont Agel (France): 2 x 100, 1 x 500kW. ‡
Notes: MCR (a subsidiary of Télédiffusion de France) is the national
transmitter network owner in Monaco and also maintains high power
transmitting centres in France and Cyprus.

MONGOLIA (MNG)

VOICE OF MONGOLIA (Pub)
⬚ P.O. Box 365, Ulaanbaatar 13, Mongolia.
☎ +976 11 327900. 🖺 +976 11 323096.
E: info@vom.mn; english@vom.mn **W:** www.vom.mn; www.mnb.mn
Webcast: D
L.P: Dir, Foreign Sce: Mrs Narantuya B; Mail Editor: Bolorchimeg E.
MW/SW: Leased from MRTBN.
kHz: *990, 12015, 12085*

Winter Schedule 2012/2013

Chinese	Days	Area	kHz
1000-1030	daily	As	990uba, 12085uba
1430-1500	daily	As	990uba, 12015uba
English	**Days**	**Area**	**kHz**
1030-1100	daily	As	12085uba
1530-1600	daily	As	12015uba
Japanese	**Days**	**Area**	**kHz**
0900-0930	daily	As	12085uba
1500-1530	daily	As	12015uba
Mongolian	**Days**	**Area**	**kHz**
0930-1000	daily	As	990uba, 12085uba
1400-1430	daily	As	990uba, 12015uba

Ann: English: "This is the Voice of Mongolia"; Mongolian:
"Ulaanbaataraas yarij baina".
V: QSL-card. Rp (2 IRCs or 1 USD) appreciated.
Notes: The Voice of Mongolia is the External Sce of the Mongolian
National Radio & TV.

MONGOLIAN RADIO AND TELEVISION
BROADCASTING NETWORK (MRTBN) (Tx Operator)
⬚ P.O.Box 1530, Ulaanbaatar 15160, Mongolia.
☎ +976 11 351043. 🖺 +976 11 350008.
E: rnts@mongol.net **W:** rtbn.gov.mn
L.P: Dir: T. Gantömör.
MW: [CHO] Choybalsan: 1350kHz 500kW ‡; [UBA] Ulaanbaatar,
Honhor: 990kHz 500kW.
SW: [UBA] Ulaanbaatar, Honhor: 3 x 50, 1 x 100, 1 x 250, 1 x 500kW.
Notes: MRTBN is the national transmitter operator in Mongolia.

MOROCCO (MRC)

RADIO MAROCAINE ‡ (Gov)
⬚ BP 1042, 10000 Rabat, Morocco.
☎ +212 537700319. 🖺 +212 537722047.
W: www.snrt.ma
Webcast: L
L.P: Pres/CEO (SNRT): Faiçal Laraichi.
SW: Uses tx of Radio Méditerranée Internationale/Medi 1.
SAT: Arabsat 5A, Badr 4, Eutelsat Hot Bird 13A, Nilesat 102/201.
kHz: *15349*

Winter Schedule 2012/2013

Arabic	Days	Area	kHz
0900-2100	daily	Af	15349nad‡

Key: ‡ Inactive at time of publication.
Ann: Arabic: "Huna Ribat, idha'atu-l-mamlaka al Maghribiyya".
V: QSL-card.
Notes: Relays of Home Sce prgrs for listeners abroad.

RADIO MÉDITERRANÉE INTERNATIONALE (MEDI
1) (Comm)
⬚ 3/5 Rue M'Sallah, 90000 Tanger, Morocco.
☎ +212 539936363. 🖺 +212 539936363.
E: medi1@medi1.com **W:** www.medi1.com
Webcast: D/L
L.P: CEO: Hassan Khiyar.
LW: [NAD] Nador: 171kHz 2000kW.
SW: [NAD] Nador: 2 x 250kW.
FM/DAB: FM: Transmitters in Morocco, France and Belgium.
SAT: Arabsat 5A, Eutelsat Hot Bird 13A, Nilesat 101.
kHz: *171, 9579*

Winter Schedule 2012/2013

Arabic/French	Days	Area	kHz
0000-2400	daily	NAf,ME,Eu	171nad, 9579nad*

Key: * Nominal freq 9575kHz.
Ann: Arabic: "Mahataat Medi an"; French: "Ici Medi 1, Radio
Méditerranée Internationale".
V: QSL-card.
Notes: Medi 1 is produced by the Moroccan-French joint venture
Société Radio Méditerranée Internationale.

NETHERLANDS (HOL)

TRANSPORT RADIO (Comm)
⬚ P.O. Box 1010, 8200 BA Lelystad, The Netherlands.
☎ +33 653 367364.
E: info@transportradio.nl **W:** www.transportradio.nl
Webcast: L/P
L.P: Producer: Eric van Willegen.
kHz: *6095*

Winter Schedule 2012/2013

Dutch	Days	Area	kHz
0900-1600	mtwtf..	Eu	6095wer

Ann: Dutch: "Transport Radio".
Notes: Internet radio station aimed at Dutch hauliers, focussing on
transport related news and information.

RADIO NETHERLANDS WORLDWIDE (RNW)
⬚ P.O. Box 222, 1200 JG Hilversum, Netherlands.
☎ +31 35 6724211. (Switchboard, open 24 hours) 🖺 +31 35 6724239.
(English language service)
E: letters@rnw.nl **W:** www.radionetherlands.nl
Webcast: D/L/P. Web only languages (some of which may also be
broadcast on local FM affiliate stns): Arabic, Chinese, French (to
Africa), Portuguese.
☎ +31 35 6724784. (For journalists/media professionals)
L.P: Chmn, Supervisory Board: Dr B.R. Bot; GD: Jan C. Hoek; Editor in
Chief: Rik R. Rensen; Frequency Mgr: Jan Peter Werkman.
SW: Via leased relay.
SAT: Astra 1L/4A, Hot Bird 6/8, Intelsat 10/11, Optus D2, SatMex 6,
SES 1, Thaicom 5, Yamal 201.
kHz: *9895*

Winter Schedule 2012/2013

Spanish	Days	Area	kHz
0000-0030	mtwtf..	LAm	9895hri

Ann: Spanish: "Transmite R. Nederland desde la ciudad de Hilversum en Holanda".
V: QSL-card.
Notes: RNW is a government funded public broadcaster serving Dutch citizens abroad, listeners in the former Dutch colonies and an international audience around the world.

THE MIGHTY KBC
Argonstraat 6, NL-6718 WT Ede, Netherlands.
☎ +31 318 552491. 🖷 +31 318 437801.
E: themightykbc@gmail.com **W:** www.kbcradio.eu
Webcast: L
L.P: Producer: Eric van Willegen.
kHz: 6095

Winter Schedule 2012/2013

English	Days	Area	kHz
0000-0200	......s	NAm	9450sof
0900-1600	.....ss	Eu	6095wer

V: QSL-card. Rp. ($2 USD/2 IRCs)
Notes: Produced by KBC Import/Export. Resumed SW broadcasts in October 2011, after a period of over 2 years on MW only.

XVRB RADIO
De Klerkstraat 69, 3067 BL Rotterdam, The Netherlands.
☎ +31 10 2207965.
E: xvrbradio@gmail.com **W:** www.xvrb.org
L.P: Producer: Marcel Strücker.
kHz: 6045

Winter Schedule 2012/2013

German	Days	Area	kHz
0900-1000	......s	Eu	6045wer*

Key: * 3rd Sunday of the month.
Ann: English: "XVRB Radio, the Music Museum".
V: QSL-email.
Notes: Ceasing transmissions 1 January 2013.

NEW ZEALAND (NZL)

RADIO NEW ZEALAND INTERNATIONAL (RNZI) (Pub)
P.O. Box 123, Wellington, New Zealand.
☎ +64 4 4741437. 🖷 +64 4 4741433.
E: info@rnzi.com **W:** www.rnzi.com
Webcast: D/L/P
L.P: CEO & Chief Editor: Peter Cavanagh; Technical Mgr: Adrian Sainsbury; Transmission Engineer: Andy Anderson.
SW: [RAN] Rangitaiki: 2 x 100kW. F.pl: new 300kW tx (DRM-capable)
kHz: 5950, 7440, 9765, 9870, 9890, 11657, 11725, 13730, 15720, 17675

Winter Schedule 2012/2013

English	Days	Area	kHz
0500-0650	daily	Pac	13730ran+
0500-0800	daily	Pac	11725ran
0650-0800	daily	Pac	11657ran+
0800-1100	daily	Pac	9765ran
0800-1300	daily	Pac	9870ran+
1100-1300	daily	Pac	17675ran
1300-1550	daily	Pac	5950ran
1550-1650	daily	Pac	7440ran+
1550-1845	daily	Pac	9765ran
1650-1845	daily	Pac	9890ran+
1845-2050	daily	Pac	11725ran
1845-2150	daily	Pac	15720ran+
2050-2150	daily	Pac	17675ran
2150-0500	daily	Pac	15720ran, 17675ran+

Key: + DRM
Ann: English: "This is Radio New Zealand International, the Voice of the Pacific"; Maori: "Te reo irirangi o Aotearoa, o te Moana-nui-a-Kiwa".
V: QSL-card. Rp (2 IRC or 2 USD)
Notes: Schedule is variable. RNZI is the External Sce of the public broadcaster Radio New Zealand. The SW transmissions are in English, with news in various Pacific languages. Increased programming and languages, plus local FM relays in major Pacific urban centers are planned. 1st & 3rd Thursdays of each month are site maintenance days and transmissions may be reduced or there may be test transmissions during this period.

NIGERIA (NIG)

VOICE OF NIGERIA (VON) (Pub)
6th and 7th Floors, Radio House, Herbert Macaulay Way, Area 10, Garki, Abuja, Nigeria. (Headquarters)
☎ +234 9 2344016. 🖷 +234 9 2346970.
E: info@voiceofnigeria.org **W:** www.voiceofnigeria.org
Webcast: L/P
Broadcasting House, Ikoyi, P.M.B. 40003, Falomo, Lagos, Nigeria.
☎ +234 1 2693076. 🖷 +234 1 2691944.
L.P: Chmn: Stella Effah Attoe; DG: Mallam Abubakar B. Jijiwa; PD: Alh. Kabir M. Ahmed.
SW: [AJA] Abuja, Lugbe: 3 x 250kW; [IKO] Ikorodu: 3 x 250kW.
kHz: 7255, 9690, 11770, 15120

Winter Schedule 2012/2013

Arabic	Days	Area	kHz
0730-0800	mtwtf..	NAf,ME	15120iko†
1730-1800	mtwtf..	NAf,ME	15120iko†
English	**Days**	**Area**	**kHz**
0455-0700	mtwtf..	Eu	15120iko†
0800-0900	mtwtf..	WAf	15120iko†
0900-1500	mtwtf..	WAf	9690iko†
1500-1600	mtwtf..	WAf	15120iko†
1800-1900	mtwtf..	Eu,Af	15120iko†
1830-2000	mtwtf..	Eu,Af	15120aja+
1900-2000	mtwtf..	WAf	7255iko†
French	**Days**	**Area**	**kHz**
0700-0730	mtwtf..	Eu	15120iko†
2000-2100	mtwtf..	WAf	7255iko†
Fulfulde	**Days**	**Area**	**kHz**
2100-2200	mtwtf..	WAf	7255iko†
Hausa	**Days**	**Area**	**kHz**
2200-2300	mtwtf..	WAf	7255iko†
Igbo	**Days**	**Area**	**kHz**
1700-1730	mtwtf..	WAf	9690iko†
Swahili	**Days**	**Area**	**kHz**
1600-1630	mtwtf..	EAf	11770iko†
Yoruba	**Days**	**Area**	**kHz**
1630-1700	mtwtf..	WAf	9690iko†

Key: + DRM; † Irregular
Ann: English: "You're listening to the Voice of Nigeria, Lagos".
IS: As Home Sce. Also bells playing the first bars of the National Anthem, 15 minutes before the commencement of each transmission block.
V: QSL-card.
Notes: The Voice of Nigeria is the External Sce of the Federal Radio Corporation of Nigera (FRCN).

NORTHERN MARIANA ISL. (MRA)

IBB "ROBERT E. KAMOSA" TRANSMITTING STATION
P.O. Box 504969, Saipan, MP 96950, USA.
☎ +1 670 2331624. 🖷 +1 670 2331614.
L.P: SM: David Strawman.
SW: [SAI] Saipan, Agingan Point: 3 x 100kW; [TIN] Tinian: 2 x 250, 6 x 500kW.
V: QSL-card.
Notes: IBB owned transmitting station. Maintained & operated by Rome Research Corporation (RRC).

OMAN (OMA)

RADIO SULTANATE OF OMAN (Gov)
P.O. Box 397, 113 Muscat, Oman.
☎ +968 24603888. 🖷 +968 24604629.
E: feedback_rd@oman-radio.gov.om **W:** www.oman-tv.gov.om
Webcast: L
English FM, P.O.Box 398, 113 Muscat, Oman. (English prgr)
L.P: Dir, Foreign Sce: Shakar Al-Araimi; Dir, Engineering: Mohd Salim Al Morhouby; Frequency Mgr: Salim Al-Nomani.
SW: [THU] Thumrait: 1 x 100kW.
SAT: Arabsat 5C, AsiaSat 5, Badr 6, Hispasat 1C, Eutelsat Hot Bird 13C, Galaxy 19, Nilesat 201, NSS 7, Optus D2.
kHz: 15140

Winter Schedule 2012/2013

Arabic	Days	Area	kHz
1500-2200	daily	Eu,ME	15140thu

English	Days	Area	kHz
1400-1500	daily	Eu,ME	15140thu

Key: † Irregular.
Ann: Arabic: "Idha'atu Saltanat Oman min Muscat"; English: "Radio Sultanate of Oman".
V: QSL-folder.
Notes: Relays of Home Sce programmes in Arabic and English.

BBC EASTERN RELAY STATION
P.O. Box 40, 422 Al Ashkarah, Oman.
E: opsaseela@yahoo.com; rebers@omantel.net.com
L.P: Resident Engineer: Dave Batty.
MW: [SLA] A'Seela: 702/1413kHz 800kW.
SW: [SLA] A'Seela: 3 x 250kW.
V: QSL-card. (For direct report)
Notes: Owned by the BBC and operated by Babcock International Group PLC (see under United Kingdom).

PAKISTAN (PAK)

RADIO PAKISTAN (Gov)
Broadcasting House, Constitution Avenue, Islamabad 44000, Pakistan.
☎ +92 51 9210689. (News Room) 🖷 +92 51 9222432.
E: info@radio.gov.pk **W:** www.radio.gov.pk
L.P: DG, PBC: Murtaza Solangi; GD: S Auwar Mehmood; Dir, Technical: Muhammad Iqbel; Dir, Overseas Liaison: Muhammad Sharif Shad; Mgr, Eng: Shahid Hameed; Mgr, Freq: Iftikhar Chuadry.
SW: [ISL] Islamabad, Rawat: 5 x 100, 2 x 250kW; [KAC] Karachi, Landhi: 2 x 100kW. ‡ (Under construction)
kHz: 5080, 5900, 6280, 7465, 7475, 9560, 11570, 11645, 11865, 11870, 11880, 15105, 15325, 15425, 15490, 15700, 15725, 15735, 17700, 17830

Winter Schedule 2012/2013

Balti	Days	Area	kHz
0445-0530	daily	SAs	7465isl

Bengali	Days	Area	kHz
0900-1000	daily	SAs	11870isl, 15105isl‡

Chinese	Days	Area	kHz
1200-1300	daily	EAs	11570isl, 15700isl

Dari	Days	Area	kHz
1445-1545	daily	WAs	5080isl‡

Farsi	Days	Area	kHz
1700-1800	daily	ME	5900isl, 6280isl‡

Gujarati	Days	Area	kHz
1145-1215	daily	SAs	7475isl‡, 11865isl

Hindi	Days	Area	kHz
1045-1145	daily	SAs	7475isl‡, 11865isl

Nepali	Days	Area	kHz
1000-1030	daily	SAs	11870isl, 15105isl‡

Pashto	Days	Area	kHz
1345-1445	daily	WAs	5080isl‡

Sheena	Days	Area	kHz
0530-0615	daily	SAs	7465isl

Sinhala	Days	Area	kHz
1230-1300	daily	SAs	11880isl, 15325isl‡

Tamil	Days	Area	kHz
1300-1330	daily	SAs	11880isl, 15325isl‡

Urdu	Days	Area	kHz
0045-0215	daily	SEA	11570isl, 15490isl
0500-0700	daily	ME	15735isl, 17830isl
0830-1105	daily	Eu	15725isl*, 17700isl*
1330-1530	daily	ME	11645isl, 15425isl
1700-1900	daily	Eu	9560isl**, 11570isl**

Key: * News in English: 0904-0910 &1100-1104; ** News in English: 1700-1710; ‡ Inactive at time of publication.
Ann: English: "This is Radio Pakistan"; Urdu: "Ye Radio Pakistan hai".
V: QSL-card. Email reports to: fmcell@radio.gov.pk
Notes: Some transmissions are irregular.

PALAU (PLW)

T8WH – WORLD HARVEST RADIO (WHR) (Rlg)
P.O. Box 66, Koror, PW 96940, Republic of Palau.
E: whr@lesea.com **W:** www.whr.org
61300 S Ironwood Rd, South Bend, IN 46614, USA (LeSEA, Inc)
W: www.lesea.com (LeSEA, Inc)
L.P: Chief Engineer: Gary Shirk.
SW: [HBN] Medorm, Babeldaob Island: 4 x 100kW.
SAT: Galaxy 16.
kHz: 9930, 15680, 17650

Winter Schedule 2012/2013

English	Days	Area	kHz
0100-0130	......s	As	17650hbn
0130-0200	......s	As	17650hbn
0300-0400	daily	As	17650hbn
0800-1000	mtwtf.s	As	9930hbn
0900-0930	.t...s.	As	17650hbn
0900-1000	......s	As	9930hbn
0930-0945	.t.....	As	17650hbn
0930-1000	......s.	As	17650hbn
0945-1000	.t.....	As	17650hbn
1200-1400	.....ss	As	9930hbn
1600-1630	......s.	As	15680hbn

Japanese	Days	Area	kHz
0800-0900	......s.	As	9930hbn

Ann: English: "This is T8WH, Palau. This is World Harvest Radio, the international voice of LeSEA Broadcasting".
V: QSL-card.
Notes: Transmitting station owned by LeSEA, Inc. Historical callsigns (licensed to previous owners): T8BZ, KHBN. Registered freqs shown, actual usage depends on airtime sales/tx lease. T8WH transmits prgrs of World Harvest Radio (see USA); some tx capacity is leased to International Broadcasting Board (IBB), USA.

PHILIPPINES (PHL)

RADYO PILIPINAS OVERSEAS (DZRP) (Gov)
4th Floor, PIA Bldg, Visayas Ave, Quezon City, Metro Manila 1100, Philippines.
☎ +63 2 9242267. 🖷 +63 2 9242745.
E: dzrp_pbs@yahoo.com; radyo_pilipinas_overseas@yahoo.com
W: www.pbs.gov.ph
Webcast: L
L.P: SM: Evelyn Agato.
SW: Uses facilities provided by IBB.
kHz: 9825, 11890, 15190, 15285, 17700, 17820

Winter Schedule 2012/2013

English	Days	Area	kHz
0200-0330	daily	ME	15285pht, 17700pht, 17820pht

Filipino	Days	Area	kHz
1730-1930	daily	ME	9825pht, 11890pht, 15190pht

Ann: English: "This is Radyo Pilipinas, the Overseas Service of the Philippines Broadcasting Service, PBS. Radyo Pilipinas is reaching you from Manila, Philippines", "Radyo Pilipinas Overseas Service, The Voice of the Philippines".
V: QSL-card. Rp (2 IRCs). Rec. acc.
Notes: Radyo Pilipinas Overseas is the External Sce of the Philippine Broadcasting Service (PBS), organized under the Philippine government Bureau of Broadcast Services (BBS). Broadcasts include relays of PBS's domestic services Radyo ng Bayan and Radyo Magasin.

FEBC PHILIPPINES (Rlg)
P.O.Box 1, 0560 Valenzuela City, Philippines.
☎ +63 2 2936445. 🖷 +63 2 6500859.
E: info@febc.org.ph **W:** febc.ph
62 Karuhatan Road, 1441 Valenzuela City, Philippines.
L.P: Pres: Dan Andrew S. Cura.
SW: [BOC] Bocaue, Bulacan prov: 4 x 100kW; [IBA] Iba, Zambales prov: 2 x 100kW.
kHz: 5990, 7410, 7480, 9345, 9400, 9405, 9430, 9435, 9445, 9550, 9795, 9855, 9890, 9920, 11650, 11750, 11820, 11825, 11880, 11895,

11905, 12055, 12070, 12095, 12120, 15225, 15320, 15330, 15435, 15450, 15455, 15525, 15560, 15580, 15600, 15620

Winter Schedule 2012/2013

	Days	Area	kHz
Achang			
1230-1245	mtw.fss	As	12095boc
Akha	**Days**	**Area**	**kHz**
1215-1230	daily	As	12120boc
Bahnar	**Days**	**Area**	**kHz**
1130-1200	m.w.f..	As	9920boc
Banjar	**Days**	**Area**	**kHz**
0830-0900	m.w.f..	As	11820boc
1530-1600	daily	As	11880boc
Batak Toba	**Days**	**Area**	**kHz**
1000-1030	daily	As	15450boc
Bru	**Days**	**Area**	**kHz**
1200-1230	...t.s.	As	9920boc
Buginese	**Days**	**Area**	**kHz**
0930-1000	daily	As	15580boc
Burmese	**Days**	**Area**	**kHz**
1330-1430	daily	As	12120boc
2330-0100	daily	As	15600boc
Cambodian	**Days**	**Area**	**kHz**
1200-1300	daily	As	7410iba
2300-2400	daily	As	9445iba
Cham	**Days**	**Area**	**kHz**
1200-1230	......s	As	9920boc
Chin Asho	**Days**	**Area**	**kHz**
0100-0115	mtw...s	As	15600boc
Chin Khumi	**Days**	**Area**	**kHz**
0100-0115	...tfs.	As	15600boc
Chin-Daai	**Days**	**Area**	**kHz**
1245-1300	daily	As	12120boc
Chinese	**Days**	**Area**	**kHz**
0000-0100	daily	As	15320iba
0030-0200	daily	As	15455boc
0600-0800	daily	As	15450iba
0700-0900	daily	As	15525boc
0900-1400	daily	As	9400iba
0900-1700	daily	As	9430boc
1400-1600	daily	As	9345iba
2230-0030	daily	As	9405boc
2300-0100	daily	As	12070iba
Chin-Mro	**Days**	**Area**	**kHz**
0130-0200	daily	As	15435boc
Chin-Thado	**Days**	**Area**	**kHz**
0100-0115	daily	As	15435boc
Chrau	**Days**	**Area**	**kHz**
1130-1200	.t....s	As	9920boc
Chru	**Days**	**Area**	**kHz**
1130-1200	...t.s.	As	9920boc
Gorontalo	**Days**	**Area**	**kHz**
0830-0900	.t.t.s.	As	11820boc
Hmong-Black	**Days**	**Area**	**kHz**
1100-1130	daily	As	12095boc
Hmong-Blue/Njua	**Days**	**Area**	**kHz**
1300-1330	.....ss	As	12095boc
2300-2330	.....ss	As	12095boc
Hmong-White/Daw	**Days**	**Area**	**kHz**
1300-1330	mtwtf..	As	12095boc
2300-2330	mtwtf..	As	12095boc
Hre	**Days**	**Area**	**kHz**
1330-1400	.t.t.s.	As	7480iba
Hu	**Days**	**Area**	**kHz**
0800-0830	daily	As	15450iba
Indonesian	**Days**	**Area**	**kHz**
0900-0930	daily	As	15450boc
1430-1530	daily	As	15620boc
2230-2330	daily	As	9435boc
Iu Mien	**Days**	**Area**	**kHz**
1200-1230	daily	As	12095boc
1230-1300	...t.s.	As	12095boc
2230-2300	daily	As	5990boc
Jarai	**Days**	**Area**	**kHz**
1100-1130	...tfs.	As	9920boc
Javanese	**Days**	**Area**	**kHz**
0100-0130	daily	As	15560boc
1400-1430	daily	As	15620boc
Jeh	**Days**	**Area**	**kHz**
1300-1330	...t.s.	As	7480iba
Jingpho	**Days**	**Area**	**kHz**
1145-1200	daily	As	15330boc
Karen (Pao)	**Days**	**Area**	**kHz**
1100-1115	daily	As	15330boc
Karen (Pwo)	**Days**	**Area**	**kHz**
0115-0130	...tfs.	As	15600boc
Katu	**Days**	**Area**	**kHz**
1330-1400	m.w....	As	7480iba
Khmu	**Days**	**Area**	**kHz**
0000-0015	daily	As	9795iba
1330-1400	daily	As	12095boc
Koho	**Days**	**Area**	**kHz**
1230-1300	daily	As	9920boc
Komering	**Days**	**Area**	**kHz**
0730-0800	daily	As	15580boc
Lahu	**Days**	**Area**	**kHz**
0015-0045	daily	As	12055boc
1000-1030	daily	As	12095boc
1400-1430	daily	As	11750boc
Laotian	**Days**	**Area**	**kHz**
1130-1200	daily	As	12095boc
2330-2400	daily	As	9795boc
Lisu	**Days**	**Area**	**kHz**
1300-1330	daily	As	12120boc
Lum	**Days**	**Area**	**kHz**
0015-0100	daily	As	15225iba
Madurese	**Days**	**Area**	**kHz**
0800-0830	mtw....	As	15320boc
Makassarese	**Days**	**Area**	**kHz**
0900-0930	daily	As	15580boc
Maru	**Days**	**Area**	**kHz**
0130-0145	mtw...s	As	15600boc
Meitei	**Days**	**Area**	**kHz**
0115-0130	daily	As	15435boc
Minangkabau	**Days**	**Area**	**kHz**
0930-1000	daily	As	15450boc
Mnong Central	**Days**	**Area**	**kHz**
1300-1330	m.w....	As	7480iba
Mon	**Days**	**Area**	**kHz**
1115-1145	daily	As	15330boc
2300-2330	daily	As	9795boc
Mongolian	**Days**	**Area**	**kHz**
0830-0900	daily	As	15450iba
Muong	**Days**	**Area**	**kHz**
1300-1330	....f..	As	7480iba
Naga	**Days**	**Area**	**kHz**
1230-1245	daily	As	12120boc
Nung	**Days**	**Area**	**kHz**
1330-1400	....f..	As	7480iba
Palaung, Pale	**Days**	**Area**	**kHz**
2330-2345	daily	As	12055boc
Pasemah	**Days**	**Area**	**kHz**
0700-0730	daily	As	15580boc
Rade	**Days**	**Area**	**kHz**
1100-1130	mtw...s	As	9920boc
Rawang	**Days**	**Area**	**kHz**
1200-1215	daily	As	12120boc
Roglai	**Days**	**Area**	**kHz**
1200-1230	m.w....	As	9920boc

Russian	Days	Area	kHz
1500-1600	daily	As	11650boc

Sasak	Days	Area	kHz
0800-0830	...tfss	As	15320boc
1030-1100	daily	As	15580boc

Sedang	Days	Area	kHz
1200-1230	.t.....	As	9920boc

Shan	Days	Area	kHz
0000-0045	daily	As	15435boc

Stieng Bulo	Days	Area	kHz
1300-1330	.t....s	As	7480iba

Sunda	Days	Area	kHz
1000-1030	daily	As	15580boc

Tai Dam	Days	Area	kHz
1200-1230	....f..	As	9920boc

Tai Nua	Days	Area	kHz
0045-0100	daily	As	15435boc

Tai-Lu	Days	Area	kHz
1030-1100	daily	As	12095boc
2345-0015	daily	As	12055boc

Tibetan (Khams)	Days	Area	kHz
1300-1330	daily	As	11825boc

Uyghur	Days	Area	kHz
1430-1500	daily	As	11905boc

Vietnamese	Days	Area	kHz
1100-1200	daily	As	9855iba
2230-2300	daily	As	9550iba
2300-2330	daily	As	11895boc

Wa	Days	Area	kHz
0045-0100	daily	As	12055boc

Yunnan	Days	Area	kHz
1330-1400	daily	As	9890boc

Zaiwa	Days	Area	kHz
0130-0145	...tfs.	As	15600boc

Zhuang	Days	Area	kHz
0530-0600	daily	As	15455iba

Ann: English: "This is FEBC Radio, broadcasting from Manila, Philippines".
V: QSL-card. Rp. preferred (3 IRCs)
Notes: Far East Broadcasting Company (Philippines), Inc is a regional division of Far East Broadcasting Company, Inc (FEBC) (USA), targeting Asia and Russia. See USA for FEBC corporate details. The transmissions may include prgrs provided by small religious prgr producers and broadcast under own labels.

RADIO VERITAS ASIA (Rlg)
✑ P.O. Box 2642, Quezon City, Manila 1166, Philippines.
☎ +63 2 9390011. 🖷 +63 2 9390011.
E: rvaprogram@rveritas-asia.org **W:** www.rveritas-asia.org
Webcast: D/L
L.P: GM: Fr. Roberto M. Ebisa; PD: Rev. Msgr. Gabriel Htun Myint; Technical Dir: Engr. Alex M. Movilla.
SW: [PUG] Palauig: 1 x 50, 2 x 250kW.
kHz: *6115, 9520, 9645, 9670, 9720, 11750, 11850, 11855, 11870, 11935, 11945, 15225, 15255, 15265, 15280, 15320, 15330, 15450, 15460, 15530, 17860*

Winter Schedule 2012/2013

Bengali	Days	Area	kHz
0030-0057	daily	As	15265pug
1400-1430	daily	As	11870pug

Burmese	Days	Area	kHz
1130-1157	daily	SEA	15450pug
2330-2357	daily	SEA	9720pug

Chin	Days	Area	kHz
0130-0157	daily	SEA	15255pug
1430-1457	daily	SEA	11870pug

Chinese	Days	Area	kHz
1000-1157	daily	CHN	11945pug
2100-2257	daily	CHN	6115pug

Hindi	Days	Area	kHz
0030-0057	daily	As	15280pug

Hindi	Days	Area	kHz
1330-1400	daily	As	11870pug

Hmong	Days	Area	kHz
1200-1227	daily	SEA	11935pug

Kachin	Days	Area	kHz
1230-1257	daily	SEA	15225pug
2330-2357	daily	SEA	9645pug

Karen	Days	Area	kHz
0000-0027	daily	SEA	11935pug
1200-1230	daily	SEA	15225pug

Khmer	Days	Area	kHz
1000-1027	daily	SEA	11850pug

Sinhala	Days	Area	kHz
0000-0027	daily	SEA	11855pug, 15460pug
1330-1357	daily	SEA	9520pug

Tagalog	Days	Area	kHz
1500-1553	daily	SEA	15320smg
2300-2327	daily	SEA	9720pug

Tamil	Days	Area	kHz
0030-0057	daily	As	11935pug
1400-1427	daily	As	9520pug

Telugu	Days	Area	kHz
0100-0127	daily	As	15530pug
1430-1457	daily	As	11750pug

Urdu	Days	Area	kHz
0100-0127	daily	As	15280pug, 17860pug
1430-1457	daily	As	15330smg

Vietnamese	Days	Area	kHz
0130-0227	daily	SEA	15530pug
1030-1127	daily	SEA	11850pug
1300-1327	daily	SEA	11850pug
2330-2357	daily	SEA	9670pug

V: QSL-card.
Notes: Catholic station, on air since 11 April 1969. Owned by the "Philippine Radio Educational and Information Center" (PREIC), composed of Filipino bishops and professionals.

IBB RELAY STATIONS PHILIPPINES
✑ Station Manager, IBB Philippines Transmitting Station, PSC 500 Box 28, DPO AP 96515-1000, USA.
☎ +63 45 9820254. 🖷 +63 45 9821402.
✑ IBB Transmitting Station (Poro Point), San Fernando, La Unión, Philippines.
☎ +63 72 8882747. 🖷 +63 72 8885133.
L.P: SM: David J. Strawman.
MW: [PHP] Poro Point (DWVA): 1170kHz 1000kW.
SW: [PHT] Tinang: 3 x 50, 12 x 250kW.
V: QSL-card.

POLAND (POL)

POLISH RADIO (EXTERNAL SERVICE) (Pub)
✑ P.O. Box 46, 00-977 Warszawa, Poland.
☎ +48 22 6453302. 🖷 +48 22 6453952.
E: zagranica@polskieradio.pl **W:** external.polskieradio.pl
Webcast: D/L/P
 W: www.thenews.pl
L.P: Dir: Marek Cajzner.
SAT: Eutelsat Hot Bird 13C.
kHz: *1386, 9755, 12095*

Winter Schedule 2012/2013

Belarusian	Days	Area	kHz
1430-1500	daily	Eu	12095sof
1730-1830	daily	BLR	1386sit, 9755sof

Polish	Days	Area	kHz
1500-1600	daily	Eu	12095sof
1630-1730	daily	Eu	9755sof

Russian	Days	Area	kHz
1400-1430	daily	Eu	12095sof
1830-1900	daily	Eu	9755sof

Ann: Polish: "Polskie Radio dla zagranicy".
V: QSL-card.

Notes: External Sce of the public broadcaster Polskie Radio.

PORTUGAL (POR)

RDP INTERNACIONAL ‡
✉ Av. Marechal Gomes da Costa, 37 – bloco B – 2º, 1849-030 Lisboa, Portugal.
☎ +351 21 7947000. 📠 +351 21 7947570.
E: rdp.internacional@rtp.pt **W:** www.rtp.pt
Webcast: D/L/P. Webcast languages: Portuguese.
LP: Dir: Jorge Oliveira Gonçalves. Dir, EngineEring Technology: Teresa Beatriz Abreu.
SW: [LIS] São Gabriel: 4 x 300kW.‡
SAT: Hotbird 8; Intelsat 805/907; Asiasat 5; AMC4; Galaxy 28.
Key: ‡ Inactive at time of publication, however broadcasts on SW may possibly resume in the future.
Ann: Portuguese: "RDP Internacional - Rádio Portugal".
IS: Opens with tune on Portuguese guitar, followed by stn ID, national anthem and fqs. announcement. Closes with frequency announcement.
V: QSL-card.
Notes: SW transmissions suspended as of June 2011, no decision regarding the complete cessation of SW has been made. Broadcasts continue to be available via webcasts.

ROMANIA (ROU)

RADIO ROMANIA INTERNATIONAL (RRI) (Pub)
✉ P.O. Box 1-111, 014700 Bucuresti, Romania.
☎ +40 21 3031357; +40 21 3031465. 📠 +40 21 2232613.
E: rri@rri.ro **W:** www.rri.ro
Webcast: L/P
LP: Deputy DG,SRR & Head of RRI: Doru Vasile Ionescu.
MW/SW: Leased from Radiocom.
SAT: Eutelsat 16A/Hot Bird 13A, Optus D2.
kHz: 5910, 5960, 5975, 5990, 5995, 6010, 6015, 6030, 6060, 6090, 6130, 6145, 6170, 6175, 7210, 7220, 7300, 7305, 7310, 7315, 7325, 7340, 7345, 7350, 7370, 7380, 7390, 7415, 7420, 7425, 7430, 9435, 9450, 9525, 9530, 9600, 9650, 9655, 9690, 9725, 9765, 9780, 9805, 9810, 9895, 11620, 11635, 11690, 11700, 11740, 11790, 11810, 11825, 11850, 11870, 11955, 13590, 13630, 13860, 15110, 15150, 15155, 15160, 15170, 15220, 15255, 15260, 15280, 15330, 15370, 15380, 15430, 15460, 15735, 17500, 17530, 17540, 17745, 17765, 17775, 17780, 17820, 17850, 17860, 17870, 21500, 21570, 21600

Winter Schedule 2012/2013

Arabic	Days	Area	kHz
0730-0800	daily	NAf,ME	15155gal, 15330tig, 17500tig
1500-1600	daily	NAf,ME	9655gal, 11620gal, 15280tig, 17540tig

Aromanian	Days	Area	kHz
1530-1600	daily	Eu	6060tig*
1730-1800	daily	Eu	5960tig*
1930-2000	daily	Eu	7345tig*

Chinese	Days	Area	kHz
0500-0530	daily	As	17870tig+, 21500tig
1400-1430	daily	As	9725tig, 11825tig

English	Days	Area	kHz
0100-0200	daily	NAm	6145gal, 7325gal
0400-0500	daily	ME	15220gal, 17870tig
0400-0500	daily	NAm	6130gal, 7305tig
0630-0700	daily	AUS,NZL	17780gal, 21600tig
0630-0700	daily	Eu	7310tig, 9600gal+
1200-1300	daily	Af	17765gal, 21570tig
1200-1300	daily	Eu	15460gal, 17530tig
1800-1900	daily	Eu	9780tig+, 11955tig
2130-2200	daily	NAm	7310tig, 9435tig
2130-2200	daily	Eu	6030gal+, 7380gal
2300-2400	daily	Eu	6015gal, 7220gal
2300-2400	daily	SEA	9530tig, 11810tig

French	Days	Area	kHz
0200-0300	daily	NAm	5975gal, 7325gal
0600-0630	daily	Af	9690tig, 11790tig
0600-0630	daily	Eu	9650gal+, 11740gal
1000-1100	......s	Eu	15260gal, 17870gal
1100-1200	daily	Af	17870tig
1100-1200	daily	Eu	15150tig, 15255gal, 17820gal
1700-1800	daily	Eu	9690tig, 11635tig
1800-1900	daily	Eu	7350gal
2000-2100	daily	Eu	7380gal
2100-2130	daily	Eu	6030gal, 7370gal+

German	Days	Area	kHz
0700-0730	daily	Eu	9450tig+, 11810tig
1300-1400	daily	Eu	9810tig, 11700tig
1900-2000	daily	Eu	6010tig, 9805tig+

Italian	Days	Area	kHz
1500-1530	daily	Eu	7390tig*
1700-1730	daily	Eu	7415tig*
1900-1930	daily	Eu	7345tig*,+

Romanian	Days	Area	kHz
0100-0300	daily	NAm	5910tig, 7340tig
0500-0600	daily	Eu	6145gal, 7220gal
0800-0900	......s	Af	15370tig, 17860tig
0800-0900	......s	ME	15430gal, 17850gal
0900-1000	......s	Af	17745gal
0900-1000	......s	ME	15380gal, 15430tig, 17775tig
1000-1100	......s	Af	17780tig, 21500tig
1300-1400	daily	Eu	7420tig*
1300-1500	daily	Eu	11870gal, 15170gal
1600-1700	daily	Eu	9655gal, 11870gal
1700-1800	daily	Af	5995gal, 7325gal
1800-2000	daily	Eu	5990gal
1900-2000	daily	Eu	7430gal

Russian	Days	Area	kHz
0530-0600	daily	RUS	6175tig+, 7210tig
1430-1500	daily	RUS	11690tig, 15735tig
1600-1700	daily	RUS	7300tig+, 9810tig

Serbian	Days	Area	kHz
1630-1700	daily	Eu	6030tig*
1830-1900	daily	Eu	6030tig*
2030-2100	daily	Eu	7425tig*

Spanish	Days	Area	kHz
0000-0100	daily	SAM,CAm	7315gal, 9525gal, 13590tig, 15110tig
0300-0400	daily	SAm	9765gal, 11825tig, 11850gal, 13630tig
2000-2100	daily	Af	6010tig
2000-2100	daily	Eu	9895tig
2200-2300	daily	SAm	13860tig, 15160tig

Ukrainian	Days	Area	kHz
1600-1630	daily	Eu	5960tig*
1800-1830	daily	Eu	6090tig*
2000-2030	daily	Eu	6170tig*

Key: + DRM; * Via Saftica.
Ann: English: "You are tuned to Radio Romania International, broadcasting from Bucharest".
V: QSL-card. (Online reception report form available)
Notes: Radio Romania International is the External Sce of the public broadcaster Radio Romania. Romanian language prgrs includes relays of Home Sce networks. Transmissions may be shortened, or cancelled, at times.

RADIOCOM (Tx Operator)
✉ sos. Oltenitei nr. 103, sector 4, 041303 Bucuresti, Romania.
☎ +40 31 5003001. 📠 +40 31 5003013.
E: office@radiocom.ro **W:** www.radiocom.ro
LP: DG: Cristian Nitu.
SW: [GAL] Bacau, Galbeni: 2 x 300kW; [TIG] Bucuresti, two sites: Tiganesti (G.C. 44N45 026E06): 3 x 300kW; Saftica (G.C. 44N38 026E05): 1 x 100kW.
Notes: Radiocom is the national transmitter network owner.

RUSSIA (RUS)

GTRK "ADYGEYA" (Gov)
⌨ ul. Zhukovskogo 24, 385000 Maykop, Russia.
☎ +7 87722 23542. 🖷 +7 87722 203039.
E: adigradio@mail.ru **W:** www.adygtv.ru/radio
Webcast: D
LP: Dir: Vyacheslav Zhachemuk.
SW: Leased from RTRN.
kHz: *6005*

Winter Schedule 2012/2013

Adyghe	Days	Area	kHz
1700-1800	m...f..	ME	6005arm*
1800-1900	......s	ME	6005arm

Key: * Mondays also in Arabic and Turkish.
Notes: Special prgr for Circassian communities in the Near East, produced by the regional state broadcasting company GTRK "Adygeya". Prgrs for domestic audience: see National Radio section.

RADIO ROSSII (Gov)
⌨ See National Radio section.
Webcast: L
SW: Leased from RTRN.
kHz: *5905, 7310, 9840, 12075*

Winter Schedule 2012/2013

Russian	Days	Area	kHz
0400-0700	daily	Eu,Atl	9840msk
0725-1200	daily	Eu,Atl	12075msk
1225-1500	daily	Eu,Atl	7310msk
1525-2100	daily	Eu,Atl	5905msk

VOICE OF RUSSIA (VOR) (Gov)
⌨ Pyatnitskaya 25, 115326 Moscow, Russia.
☎ +7 495 9506331. 🖷 +7 495 9512017.
E: world@ruvr.ru **W:** www.ruvr.ru
Webcast: D/L/P
LP: Chmn: Andrey Bystritskiy.
MW/SW: Leased from RTRN.
SAT: Eutelsat Hot Bird 13A, Express A4/AM22/AM33/MD1, Yamal 201/202.
kHz: *558, 612, 621, 630, 648, 693, 720, 801, 927, 972, 999, 1026, 1080, 1089, 1143, 1170, 1215, 1314, 1323, 1350, 1377, 1395, 1413, 1431, 1494, 1503, 1548, 4950, 5885, 5900, 5920, 5940, 5945, 5955, 5975, 5980, 5995, 6005, 6015, 6030, 6090, 6110, 6120, 6130, 6135, 6145, 6235, 7205, 7210, 7220, 7225, 7230, 7240, 7250, 7260, 7290, 7295, 7305, 7310, 7315, 7330, 7340, 9340, 9395, 9400, 9405, 9455, 9475, 9480, 9560, 9625, 9680, 9715, 9720, 9735, 9750, 9765, 9825, 9830, 9840, 9865, 9880, 11635, 11640, 11655, 11680, 11830, 11895, 11915, 11985, 12055, 12060, 12070, 12075, 13790, 15470, 15630, 15740, 15745, 17500, 17665, 17690, 21800, 21820*

Winter Schedule 2012/2013

Arabic	Days	Area	kHz
1600-1700	daily	ME,NAf	5945nvs, 6005arm
1600-2000	daily	NAf	9825spb
1600-2100	daily	ME	1314erv
1600-2100	daily	ME,NAf	9340dsb
1700-1800	daily	ME	6015spb
1700-1900	daily	ME	5920arm
1800-2100	daily	ME	6235dsb
1800-2100	daily	ME,NAf	5975nvs

Chinese	Days	Area	kHz
1000-1300	daily	As	5900vld
1000-1400	daily	As	648vld, 7305irk
1200-1300	daily	As	801tch, 1080irk

English	Days	Area	kHz
0100-0200	daily	As,ME	801dsb
0100-0400	daily	As,ME	927dsb
0100-0400	daily	ME	648dsb
0200-0400	daily	As,ME	972dsb
0200-0400	daily	ME	1377erv
0200-0400	daily	NAm	17665ppk, 17690vld
0200-0600	daily	NAm	15630ppk
0300-0500	daily	ME	1314erv
0400-0600	daily	NAm	9830ppk

English	Days	Area	kHz
0500-0900	daily	Eu	1323wbr
0600-0900	daily	Eu	11635msk+
0600-1000	daily	AUS,NZL,Pac	21800irk, 21820nvs
0700-1100	daily	As	15745dsb
0800-0900	daily	Eu	9625klg*,+
0900-1200	daily	SEA	7205tch
0900-1200	daily	Eu	9625klg*,+
1000-1200	daily	As	11680tch
1000-1200	daily	As,SEA	7260vld
1100-1200	daily	As	11640irk+, 15740sam
1100-1400	daily	As,SEA	9560nvs*,+
1200-1300	daily	As	5885dsb
1200-1400	daily	As,ME	972dsb
1200-1400	daily	Eu	9625klg*,+
1200-1500	daily	As	12075dsb
1300-1400	daily	SEA	7205tch
1300-1500	daily	As,SEA	7260vld
1400-1500	daily	ME	648dsb, 13790sam
1400-1900	daily	As,ME	4950dsb
1500-1600	daily	As,ME	927dsb
1500-1600	daily	ME	11985erv
1500-1800	daily	As,SEA	9880ppk
1500-1900	daily	ME,Af	9735msk
1600-1700	daily	As	5885dsb, 5955nvs
1700-1800	daily	As	7240ppk
1700-1900	daily	As,ME	801dsb
1700-1900	daily	ME	648dsb
1700-2100	daily	Eu	7330msk
1800-1900	daily	As,ME	927dsb
1800-1900	daily	ME,Af	11985erv
2100-2200	daily	Eu	5940sam
2200-0400	daily	NAm,CAm	7240arm
2200-2300	daily	NAm	11830ppk
2300-0400	daily	NAm,CAm	7290kch

Farsi	Days	Area	kHz
1500-1700	daily	ME	648dsb, 1377erv, 6015spb, 6235dsb, 7205spb

French	Days	Area	kHz
1600-1700	daily	Af	9405kch
1600-1700	daily	Eu	7330msk
1600-1800	daily	Af	7295tch, 11985erv
1600-2100	daily	Eu,Af	6130msk, 11655msk
1700-2100	daily	Af	9400kch
1700-2100	daily	Eu,Af	12060msk
1800-1900	daily	Eu	6145klg+
1900-2100	daily	Eu	558cen**, 1323wbr

German	Days	Area	kHz
0900-1000	daily	Eu	9720klg, 11635msk+
0900-1200	daily	Eu	630klu, 693bln, 1323wbr, 1431dsd, 9625klg*,+
1000-1200	daily	Eu	558cen**
1500-1700	daily	Eu	558cen**, 7220sam
1500-1900	daily	Eu	630klu, 693bln, 1323wbr, 1431dsd
1700-1900	daily	Eu	7310sam
1800-1900	daily	Eu	558cen**

Hindi	Days	Area	kHz
1300-1400	daily	As	972dsb, 5885dsb, 5995tch, 7315irk+
1500-1600	daily	As	801dsb, 5885dsb, 5955nvs, 7315irk+

Italian	Days	Area	kHz
1700-1800	daily	Eu	558cen**, 6145irk+, 9480msk, 9715arm
2130-2230	daily	Eu	1548kch

Japanese	Days	Area	kHz
1200-1400	daily	As	720iuj, 5980irk, 6110ppk

Kurdish	Days	Area	kHz
0500-0600	daily	ME	1314erv

Kurdish	Days	Area	kHz
1500-1600	daily	ME	1314erv, 5945nvs, 11830spb

Mongolian	Days	Area	kHz
1300-1400	daily	As	801tch, 1080irk, 5900vld

Pashto/Dari	Days	Area	kHz
1200-1400	daily	WAs	648dsb, 801dsb, 4950dsb, 15470sam

Polish	Days	Area	kHz
1700-1800	daily	Eu	693bln, 1143klg, 7220sam

Portuguese	Days	Area	kHz
2100-2200	daily	Eu	6090arm, 6120klg
2200-2400	daily	SAm	9750erv
2300-2400	daily	SAm	9865sam

Russian	Days	Area	kHz
0000-0100	daily	ME	1314erv
0000-2300	daily	CAs,ME	1503dsb
0100-0300	daily	ME	7225sam
0100-0400	daily	ME	1395erv***
0200-0600	daily	CAs	12070msk
0400-0800	daily	Eu	1548kch
0400-1600	daily	Eu	621kch
0500-0700	daily	Eu	9680sam
0500-0900	daily	Eu	630klu, 693bln, 1431dsd
0500-1900	daily	Eu	999kch
0600-1200	daily	MF	1314erv
0800-0900	daily	Eu	9625klg*,+
1200-1400	daily	Eu,ME	11915msk
1200-1400	daily	As,AUS,NZL	9455irk
1200-1400	daily	CAs,As,Pac	9840msk
1200-1400	daily	Eu	9625klg*,+
1200-1500	daily	Eu	630klu, 693bln, 1323wbr, 1431dsd
1200-1500	daily	ME,CAs	5945nvs
1300-1500	daily	As,CAs	12055msk
1400-1500	daily	Eu	612vln, 1548kch
1400-1500	daily	ME	6235dsb, 11830spb
1400-1600	daily	ME	17500msk
1400-2000	daily	Eu	5940sam
1500-1700	daily	ME,CAs	5900sam
1500-1700	daily	Eu	1143klg, 9865kch
1500-1900	daily	CAs	1026nvs
1500-2000	daily	ME	1089arm
1600-1700	daily	As	7240ppk
1600-1700	daily	ME	11830spb
1600-1900	daily	Eu	7230msk
1600-2200	daily	Eu	1215klg
1600-2200	daily	ME	1170arm
1700-1800	daily	ME	6235dsb
1700-1900	daily	Eu	1494spb
1800-2000	daily	Eu	1413kch
1800-2000	daily	ME,CAs	5995irk
1800-2100	daily	Eu	1143klg
1900-2100	daily	ME	11985erv
1900-2100	daily	Eu	7250msk
1900-2300	daily	Eu	630klu, 693bln, 1431dsd
2100-2200	daily	Eu	1323wbr
2100-2300	daily	Eu	999kch
2100-2400	daily	ME	1314erv
2200-2400	daily	CAm,SAm	9395erv
2300-0300	daily	CAm,SAm	7260kch

Serbian	Days	Area	kHz
1500-1700	daily	Eu	1548kch, 7340klg, 9480msk
2000-2130	daily	Eu	1548kch, 6030sam

Spanish	Days	Area	kHz
0000-0200	daily	SAm	9865sam
0000-0400	daily	SAm	9750erv
0000-0500	daily	CAm	9395erv
0000-0500	daily	SAm	7210msk
0100-0300	daily	SAm	6135spb
0100-0400	daily	SAm	9475dsb
0400-0500	daily	SAm	9765erv
2000-2100	daily	Eu	5940sam, 6090arm, 6120klg

Turkish	Days	Area	kHz
0100-0300	daily	ME	1314erv
0300-0500	daily	ME	1350erv
1300-1500	daily	ME	1314erv, 1350erv
1400-1600	daily	ME	1170arm, 6005arm, 11895spb, 11915msk
2100-2230	daily	ME	1314erv

Urdu	Days	Area	kHz
1400-1500	daily	As	801dsb, 927dsb, 5885dsb, 5900sam, 5995tch, 7315irk+

Vietnamese	Days	Area	kHz
1200-1300	daily	SEA	7205tch, 7260vld

Key: + DRM; *,+ DRM (with dual channel audio); ** To 31 Dec 2012; *** R. Kavkaz

Ann: English: "This is The Voice of Russia World Service"; French: "Vous ecoutez la Voix de la Russie".

V: QSL-card.

Notes: External Service produced by the Russian state broadcasting company "Golos Rossii". R. Kavkaz: additional LW/MW freqs for the domestic audience can be found in the National Radio section.

YEVANGELSKIYE CHTENIYA (Rlg)

✉ 2-y Raushskiy per. 4, 115035 Moskva, Russia.

☎ +7 485 9515793.

L.P: Chief Editor: Fyodor V. Kalinin.

MW: Leased from RTRN.

kHz: *612, 1089*

Winter Schedule 2012/2013			
Russian	Days	Area	kHz
1500-1600	mt.t.ss	RUS	612msk
2000-2100	daily	RUS	612msk
2000-2100	daily	ME	1089arm

Notes: Produced by the Russian Orthodox brotherhood "Bratstvo Svyatitelya Aleksiya".

RADIOAGENCY–M (Broker)

✉ Novokhoroshevskiy proyezd 18, 123308 Moskva, Russia.

☎ +7 499 1919161. 📠 +7 499 1918591.

E: abat@radioagency.ru

L.P: Dir: Anatoliy Batyushkin.

V: QSL-card. (For brokered stns)

Notes: Radioagency-M brokers air time for high power medium and shortwave txs owned by RTRN in Russia.

RUSSIAN TELEVISION AND RADIO BROADCASTING NETWORK (RTRN) (Tx Operator)

✉ ul. Nikolskaya 7, 109012 Moscow, Russia.

☎ +7 495 6480111. 📠 +7 495 6480111.

E: glavred@rtrn.ru **W:** www.rtrs.ru; www.rtrn.ru

L.P: GD: Andrey Yu. Romanchenko

MW: [ARM] Krasnodar, Tbilisskaya: 1089/1170kHz 1200kW; [IRK] Angarsk, Odinsk: 1080kHz 1000kW; [IUJ] Yuzhno-Sakhalinsk, Vestochka: 720kHz 1000kW; [KLG] Kaliningrad, Bolshakovo: 1143kHz 150kW, 1215kHz 1200kW; [MSK] Moskva 612kHz 20kW; [NVS] Novosibirsk, Oyash: 1026kHz 500kW; [SPB] St.Peterburg, Krasnyy Bor: 1494kHz 600kW; [TCH] Chita, Kruchina: 801kHz 1200kW; [VLD] Vladivostok, Razdolnoye: 648kHz 1000kW.

SW: [ARM] Krasnodar, Tbilisskaya: 8 x 100, 1 x 250, 4 x 1000kW; [IRK] Angarsk, Odinsk: 2 x 100, 4 x 250, 2 x 2000kW; [KHB] Khabarovsk: 7 x 100, 4 x 120kW; [KLG] Kaliningrad, Bolshakovo: 9 x 80kW; [MSK] Moskva, three sites: Kurovskaya (G.C. 55N35 039E08): 2 x 80, 8 x 100, 1 x 150, 6 x 250kW; Taldom (G.C. 55N45 037E37): 3 x 40kW (DRM), 5 x 250, 2 x 500kW; Lesnoy (G.C. 56N04 037E57): 1 x 150, 15 x 250kW; [NVS] Novosibirsk, two sites: Novosibirsk (G.C. 54N55 082E51): 23 x 100kW; Oyash (G.C. 55N29 083E41): 3 x 1000kW; [PPK] Petropavlovsk-Kamchatskiy, Yelizovo: 4 x 100, 2 x 250kW; [SAM] Samara: 8 x 250kW; [SPB] St.Peterburg, Krasnyy Bor: 18 x 200kW; [TCH] Chita, Kruchina: 1 x 100, 2 x 250, 2 x 1000kW; [VLD] Vladivostok, two sites: Razdolnoye

(G.C. 43N32 131E56): 2 x 250kW; Tavrichanka (G.C. 43N23 131E54): 2 x 100, 2 x 250kW.

Notes: RTRN is the national transmitter network operator in Russia.

RWANDA (RRW)

DEUTSCHE WELLE (DW) RELAY STATION
✉ 420 Kinyinya, Rwanda.
SW: [KIG] Kigali, Kinyinya: 1 x 100, 4 x 250kW.
V: QSL-card (Rpt to DW, Germany).

SÃO TOMÉ E PRÍNCIPE (STP)

IBB RELAY STATION SÃO TOMÉ
✉ IBB Transmitting Station, CP 522, São Tomé, São Tomé e Príncipe.
☎ +239 2223406. 🖷 +239 2223406.
L.P: SM: Kenneth Tripp.
MW: [SAO] Pinheira: 1530kHz 600kW.
SW: [SAO] Pinheira: 5 x 100kW.
V: QSL-card. Email rpt to hmenezes@sto.ibb.gov

SAUDI ARABIA (ARS)

SAUDI RADIO (BSKSA) (Gov)
✉ P.O. Box 60059, Riyadh-11545, Saudi Arabia.
☎ +966 1 4425170. 🖷 +966 1 4041692.
E: eng@saudiradio.net.sa (English Service)
W: www.saudiradio.net.sa; www.saudiradio.net
Webcast: L
L.P: Minister, Culture and Information: Abdulaziz bin Modieddin Khoja; Deputy Minister, Culture and Information (Engineering Affairs): Riyadh Najm.
SW: [JED] Jeddah, Al Khumra: 4 x 250kW ‡; [RIY] Riyadh: 4 x 350, 8 x 500kW.
SAT: Arabsat 5A/C, AsiaSat 5, Badr 4, Galaxy 19, Hispasat 1C, Eutelsat Hot Bird 13B/C, Nilesat 102, NSS 7.
kHz: 7240, 9555, 9675, 9715, 9870, 9885, 11820, 11915, 11930, 11935, 13710, 13775, 15120, 15150, 15205, 15225, 15250, 15285, 15380, 15435, 15490, 17560, 17570, 17615, 17625, 17660, 17705, 17730, 17740, 17785, 17805, 17895, 21505, 21670

Winter Schedule 2012/2013

Arabic	Days	Area	kHz
0300-0600	daily	Eu,CAs,WAs	15170riy*
0300-0800	daily	CAs,EAs	17895riy*
0300-1000	daily	ME	9715riy*
0600-0900	daily	Eu	17740riy**
0600-0900	daily	ME	15380riy*
0600-0900	daily	NAf	17730riy*
0900-1200	daily	Eu	15490riy**
0900-1200	daily	SAs,SEA	17615riy*
0900-1200	daily	ME	11935riy*
0900-1200	daily	EAs,SEA	17570riy*
0900-1200	daily	NAf	17805riy**
1200-1400	daily	ME	15380riy*
1200-1400	daily	SAs,SEA	17625riy*
1200-1500	daily	Eu	17705riy*
1200-1500	daily	NAf	17895riy*, 21505riy**
1300-1600	daily	SAf	17615riy*
1500-1800	daily	Eu	15435riy**
1500-1800	daily	NAf	13710riy*, 15225riy**
1600-1800	daily	Eu	15205riy*
1600-1800	daily	WAf,CAf	17560riy*
1800-2300	daily	Eu	9870riy**, 11820riy*
1800-2300	daily	NAf	9555riy**, 11915riy*
1800-2300	daily	WAf,CAf	11930riy*

Bengali	Days	Area	kHz
1200-1500	daily	SAs	15120riy

English	Days	Area	kHz
1000-1230	daily	WAf,CAf	15250riy

French	Days	Area	kHz
0800-1000	daily	WAf	17785riy
1400-1800	daily	WAf	17660riy

Indonesian	Days	Area	kHz
0900-1200	daily	SEA	21670riy

Persian	Days	Area	kHz
1500-1800	daily	ME	7240riy

Swahili	Days	Area	kHz
0400-0700	daily	EAf	15285riy

Tajik/Turkmen/ Uyghur/Uzbek	Days	Area	kHz
1500-1800	daily	CAs	9885riy

Turkish	Days	Area	kHz
1800-2100	daily	ME	9675riy

Urdu	Days	Area	kHz
1200-1500	daily	SAs	13775riy

Key: * Quran prgr; ** General prgr.
Ann: Arabic (General Prgr): "Idha'at al mamlaka alarabiya al saudiyah min al Riyadh"; English: "Radio Riyadh", "Broadcasting Service of the Kingdom of Saudi Arabia".
IS: 'Ud' (Oriental Lute). Opens and closes with National Anthem.
V: No longer issues QSL-cards.
Notes: The SW transmissions in Arabic are relays of Home Sce prgrs.

SERBIA (SRB)

INTERNATIONAL RADIO SERBIA (Gov)
✉ P.O. Box 72, Hilandarska 2, 11000 Beograd, Serbia.
☎ +381 11 3244455. 🖷 +381 11 3232014.
E: radioju@sbb.rs **W:** www.voiceofserbia.org; glassrbije.org
Webcast: D/L
L.P: Dir/Editor-in-Chief: Milorad Vujovic; Deputy Dir: Igor Mladenovic; Deputy Editor-in-Chief: Vukomir Petric.
SW: [BEO] Beograd, Stubline: 1 x 10kW & via own relay station, see under Bosnia-Herzegovina.
kHz: 6100, 6190, 9635

Winter Schedule 2012/2013

Albanian	Days	Area	kHz
1745-1800	daily	Eu	9635beo‡

Arabic	Days	Area	kHz
1530-1600	daily	Eu	9635beo‡

Chinese	Days	Area	kHz
1730-1745	daily	Eu	9635beo‡

English	Days	Area	kHz
0130-0200	.twtfs.	NAm,Eu	6190bij
1400-1430	daily	Eu	9635beo‡
1930-2000	daily	Eu	6100bij
2200-2230	daily	Eu	6100bij

French	Days	Area	kHz
1630-1700	daily	Eu	9635beo‡
2130-2200	daily	Eu	6100bij

German	Days	Area	kHz
1700-1730	daily	Eu	9635beo‡
2100-2130	mtwtf.s	Eu	6100bij

Greek	Days	Area	kHz
1815-1830	daily	Eu	9635beo‡

Hungarian	Days	Area	kHz
1800-1815	daily	Eu	9635beo‡

Italian	Days	Area	kHz
1830-1900	daily	Eu	9635beo‡

Russian	Days	Area	kHz
1600-1630	daily	Eu	9635beo‡
1900-1930	daily	RUS	6100bij

Serbian	Days	Area	kHz
0100-0130	mtwtfs.	NAm,Eu	6190bij
0100-0200	......s	NAm,Eu	6190bij
0130-0230	m......	NAm,Eu	6190bij
0200-0230	.twtfs.	NAm,Eu	6190bij
1430-1500	daily	Eu	9635beo‡
2030-2100	mtwtf.s	Eu	6100bij
2030-2130	.....s.	Eu	6100bij
2230-2300	....f..	Eu	6100bij

Spanish	Days	Area	kHz
1500-1530	daily	Eu	9635beo‡

Spanish	Days	Area	kHz
2000-2030	daily	Eu	6100bij

Key: ‡ Inactive at time of publication.
Ann: English: "This is the Engish Service of International Radio Serbia"; Serbian: "Medjunarodni Radio Srbija"; Spanish: "Esta es Radio Serbia".
V: QSL-card.

SEYCHELLES (SEY)

BBC INDIAN OCEAN RELAY STATION
✉ P.O. Box 448, Victoria, Mahé, Seychelles.
☎ +248 4378496. 🖷 +248 4378500.
LP: Senior Engineer: Herve Cherry.
SW: [SEY] Mahé: 2 x 250kW.
V: QSL-card. (For direct report)
Notes: Owned by the BBC and operated by Babcock International Group PLC (see under United Kingdom).

SINGAPORE (SNG)

TWR ASIA (Rlg)
✉ 85 Playfair Road #04-01, Tong Yuan Industrial Building, Singapore 368000.
☎ +65 65015150. 🖷 +65 64443053.
E: info@twr.asia **W:** www.twr.asia
Webcast: D
LP: Int Dir: Sebastian Chan.
SW: Via TWR Guam relay station (KTWR) & leased foreign relays.
kHz: 9910, 9975, 11580, 11675, 11840, 13765, 15200, 15225, 15235, 15240, 15265, 15390, 15550

Winter Schedule 2012/2013

Assamese	Days	Area	kHz
1315-1345	mtwtf.s	SAs	15265twr
Balinese	**Days**	**Area**	**kHz**
0930-0940	......s	INS	15200twr
0930-1000	.....s.	INS	15200twr
Bengali (Muslimi)	**Days**	**Area**	**kHz**
1230-1245	.....ss	SAs	15240twr
Burmese	**Days**	**Area**	**kHz**
1200-1240	mtwt...	BRM	15390twr
1200-1300	...fss	BRM	15390twr
Cantonese	**Days**	**Area**	**kHz**
1330-1400	mtwtf..	CHN	11675twr
Chinese	**Days**	**Area**	**kHz**
0945-1100	mtwtfs	CHN	15235twr
1045-1200	mtwtfs	CHN	11580twr
1100-1145	daily	CHN	13765twr
1100-1230	daily	CHN	9910twr
1215-1245	mtwtf..	CHN	9975twr
1330-1430	mtwtf..	CHN	9975twr
1430-1500	daily	CHN	9975twr
English	**Days**	**Area**	**kHz**
0850-0930	mtwtf..	SEA	15200twr
1000-1010	mtwtf..	Pac	11840twr
1000-1030	.....s.	Pac	11840twr
1400-1420	mt.tf..	SAs	15225twr
1400-1430	..w..ss	SAs	15225twr
Hui	**Days**	**Area**	**kHz**
1330-1400	.....ss	CHN	11675twr
Indonesian	**Days**	**Area**	**kHz**
1000-1030	mtwtf.s	INS	15200twr
Javanese	**Days**	**Area**	**kHz**
1000-1030	.....s.	INS	15200twr
Karen (Sgaw)	**Days**	**Area**	**kHz**
1300-1330	daily	BRM	15390twr
Kokborok	**Days**	**Area**	**kHz**
1230-1300	mtwtf..	SAs	15240twr
1245-1300	......s	SAs	15240twr
Korean	**Days**	**Area**	**kHz**
1345-1430	......s	KRE,KOR	11580twr

Korean	Days	Area	kHz
1345-1440	.....s	KRE,KOR	11580twr
1345-1500	mtwtf..	KRE,KOR	11580twr
Madurese	**Days**	**Area**	**kHz**
0930-1000	mtwtf..	INS	15200twr
Manipuri	**Days**	**Area**	**kHz**
1330-1345	.....s	SAs	15240twr
Nosu Yi	**Days**	**Area**	**kHz**
1200-1215	daily	CHN	11580twr
Santhali	**Days**	**Area**	**kHz**
1300-1315	daily	SAs	15240twr
1315-1330	.....s	SAs	15240twr
Sundanese	**Days**	**Area**	**kHz**
1030-1100	daily	INS	15200twr
Vietnamese	**Days**	**Area**	**kHz**
1245-1330	mtwtf.s	VTN	15550twr
1245-1340	.....s.	VTN	15550twr

V: QSL-card. (Online form on website)
Notes: TWR regional branch for Asia. For corporate details, see under TWR (USA).

BBC FAR EASTERN RELAY STATION
✉ 51 Turut Track, Singapore 718930.
☎ +65 67937511. 🖷 +65 67937834.
SW: [SNG] Singapore: 4 x 100, 5 x 250kW.
V: QSL-card. (For direct report)
Notes: Owned by the BBC and operated by Babcock International Group PLC (see under United Kingdom).

SLOVAKIA (SVK)

RADIO SLOVAKIA INTERNATIONAL (Pub)
✉ Mýtna 1, P.O. Box 55, 817 55 Bratislava 15, Slovak Republic.
☎ +421 2 57273734. 🖷 +421 2 52496282.
E: drahoslava.valocka@slovakradio.sk; englishsection@slovakradio.sk
W: www.rozhlas.sk/radio-international-en
Webcast: L. Webcast languages: English, French, German, Russian, Slovak, Spanish.
LP: Dir: Vincent Štofaník; Chief Editor: Mária Mikušová.
SW: Leases airtime on WRMI (See under USA).
SAT: Astra 3A.
kHz: 9955

Winter Schedule 2012/2013

English	Days	Area	kHz
0130-0200	.twtfs.	LAm	9955rmi
Spanish	**Days**	**Area**	**kHz**
0330-0400	daily	LAm	9955rmi
0600-0630	daily	LAm	9955rmi
1030-1100	mtwtfs	LAm	9955rmi
1330-1400	daily	LAm	9955rmi

Ann: English: "You are listening to Radio Slovakia International".
V: QSL-card.
Notes: Began broadcasting in 1993. Radio Slovakia International is the External Sce of the public-service Slovak Radio (Slovenský Rozhlas). Can be heard via WRN Broadcast on MW in some areas.

SOUTH AFRICA (AFS)

CHANNEL AFRICA (Pub)
✉ P.O. Box 91313, Auckland Park 2006, South Africa.
☎ +27 11 7142255. 🖷 +27 11 7142072.
E: matemm@sabc.co.za (Gen Mgr); dawetimj@sabc.co.za (Prgr Mgr)
W: www.channelafrica.co.za
Webcast: D/L/P
LP: GM: Maurice Mate; Managing Editor: Moshongwa Matsena; Prgr Mgr: Lungi Daweti.
SW: Leased from Sentech.
SAT: Intelsat 10.
kHz: 3345, 6155, 7230, 9625, 15235, 15255, 17770

Winter Schedule 2012/2013

English	Days	Area	kHz
0300-0400	mtwtf..	SAf	3345mey
0300-0400	mtwtf..	EAf	6155mey
0400-0700	mtwtf..	SAf	7230mey

English	Days	Area	kHz
0600-0700	mtwtf..	WAf	15255mey
0700-1200	mtwtf..	SAf	9625mey
1500-1600	mtwtf..	SAf	9625mey
1700-1800	mtwtf..	WAf	15235mey
French	**Days**	**Area**	**kHz**
1600-1700	mtwtf..	WAf	15235mey
Lozi	**Days**	**Area**	**kHz**
1300-1400	mtwtf..	SAf	9625mey
Nyanja	**Days**	**Area**	**kHz**
1200-1300	mtwtf..	SAf	9625mey
Portuguese	**Days**	**Area**	**kHz**
1400-1500	mtwtf..	SAf	9625mey
Swahili	**Days**	**Area**	**kHz**
1500-1600	mtwtf..	EAf	17770mey

Ann: English: "You're listening to Channel Africa coming to you from Johannesburg"; "You are listening to Channel Africa, the voice of the African Renaissance, broadcasting live from Johannesburg, South Africa".
IS: Birds chirping and native melody.
V: Does not verify. Rpts should be sent to Sentech.
Notes: Channel Africa is the External Sce of the public-service South African Broadcasting Corporation (SABC).

CVC 1AFRICA RADIO (Rlg)
✉ P.O. Box 3933, Tygervalley 7536, South Africa.
☎ +27 21 9506900. 🖷 +27 21 9419261.
E: 1africa@cvc.tv; radio@1africa.tv **W:** www.1africa.tv
Webcast: L/P
E: radio@cvcmedia.tv **W:** www.cvcmedia.tv
L.P: Dir, Christian Vision South Africa: Oliver J. Raper.
SW: For tx details see CVC Radio Christian Voice, under Zambia.
SAT: Intelsat 10.
kHz: *13590*

Winter Schedule 2012/2013

English	Days	Area	kHz
0600-2200	daily	Af	13590lus

Ann: English: "Number 1 Africa - CVC"; "One Life, One Way, One Africa".
V: QSL-letter.
Notes: Produced by Christian Vision South Africa, a subsidiary of Christian Vision (see under United Kingdom).

TWR AFRICA (Rlg)
✉ P.O. Box 4232, 1620, Kempton Park, South Africa. (Postal)
☎ +27 11 9742885. 🖷 +27 11 9749960.
E: info@twrafrica.org **W:** www.twrafrica.org
Webcast: D/L/P
✉ San Croy Business Park, Die Agora Road, Croydon 1619, South Africa. (Physical Address)
L.P: Dir: Dr Emmanuel D. Mbennah; Dir (Tech Sces) James Burnett.
MW: Via TWR Benin relay station.
SW: Via TWR Swaziland relay station & leased foreign relays.
SAT: Intelsat 10.
kHz: *1170, 1566, 3200, 3240, 4760, 4775, 5965, 5995, 6025, 6120, 6130, 7215, 7300, 7315, 9475, 9500, 9525, 9585, 9940, 11635, 13660, 15105*

Winter Schedule 2012/2013

Afar	Days	Area	kHz
1300-1315	...tfss	EAf	13660kig
Amharic	**Days**	**Area**	**kHz**
0330-0345	m...f.s	EAf	9525man
1630-1645	mt.....	EAf	9500man
1700-1715	.....s	EAf	9500man
1700-1730	mtwtfs.	EAf	9500man
1730-1800	.....s.	EAf	9500man
1830-1845	......s	EAf	5965dha
Bambara	**Days**	**Area**	**kHz**
2025-2040	....f..	WAf	1566par
Chewa	**Days**	**Area**	**kHz**
0400-0445	.....ss	SAf	5995man
Chokwe	**Days**	**Area**	**kHz**
1820-1835	daily	SAf	6130man

Dendi/Fon/			
Various	**Days**	**Area**	**kHz**
2010-2025	daily	WAf	1566par
English	**Days**	**Area**	**kHz**
0255-0325	......s	SAf	3200man
0315-0330	mtwtf..	WAf	1566par
0335-0345	.....ss	WAf	1566par
0430-0500	daily	WAf	1566par
0500-0800	daily	EAf	9500man
0500-0800	daily	SAf	4775man
0501-0800	daily	SAf	6120man
0530-0545	daily	WAf	1566par
1425-1455	daily	SAf	6025man
1525-1555	.....ss	SAf	6025man
1700-2105	daily	SAf	1170man
1745-1820	daily	WAf	1566par
1745-2045	daily	SAf	3200man
1800-1900	daily	EAf	9500man
Ewe	**Days**	**Area**	**kHz**
0515-0530	.....ss	WAf	1566par
Fiote	**Days**	**Area**	**kHz**
1905-1920	...f..	SAf	6130man
Fon	**Days**	**Area**	**kHz**
1855-1910	......s	WAf	1566par
1940-2010	mtwtf..	WAf	1566par
Fongbe	**Days**	**Area**	**kHz**
1725-1745	daily	WAf	1566par
French	**Days**	**Area**	**kHz**
1455-1525	.....s.	SAf	9585man
1935-1950	daily	Af	9940man
1950-2020	.....s.	Af	9940man
2040-2215	daily	WAf	1566par
2215-2230	mtwtf..	WAf	1566par
Fulfulde	**Days**	**Area**	**kHz**
1940-2010	.....ss	WAf	1566par
Fulfulde/Various	**Days**	**Area**	**kHz**
1925-1940	daily	WAf	1566par
German	**Days**	**Area**	**kHz**
0400-0430	mtwtf..	SAf	3200man, 4775man
0400-0500	.....ss	SAf	3200man, 4775man
Hadiyya	**Days**	**Area**	**kHz**
1645-1700	...fs.	EAf	9500man
Hausa	**Days**	**Area**	**kHz**
0330-0430	mtwtf..	WAf	1566par
0345-0430	.....ss	WAf	1566par
1855-1910	mtwtf..	WAf	1566par
Igbo	**Days**	**Area**	**kHz**
2025-2040	.....ss	WAf	1566par
Jula	**Days**	**Area**	**kHz**
2025-2040	...t...	WAf	1566par
Kambaata	**Days**	**Area**	**kHz**
1630-1645	...fs.	EAf	9500man
Kanuri	**Days**	**Area**	**kHz**
1910-1925	daily	WAf	1566par
KiKongo	**Days**	**Area**	**kHz**
1850-1905	.twtf.s	SAf	6130man
Kimbundu	**Days**	**Area**	**kHz**
1950-2005	daily	SAf	6130man
Kirundi	**Days**	**Area**	**kHz**
1555-1625	mtwtf..	EAf	15105man
Kuanyama	**Days**	**Area**	**kHz**
1905-1920	......s	SAf	6130man
Kunama	**Days**	**Area**	**kHz**
1800-1830	......s	EAf	5965dha
Lingala	**Days**	**Area**	**kHz**
1905-1935	daily	Af	9525man, 9940man
Lomwe	**Days**	**Area**	**kHz**
0342-0358	daily	SAf	4775man
1510-1555	daily	SAf	7315man
Luchazi	**Days**	**Area**	**kHz**
1905-1920	..w....	SAf	6130man

Lunyaneka	Days	Area	kHz
1905-1920	.....s.	SAf	6130man
Luvale	**Days**	**Area**	**kHz**
1850-1905	m......	SAf	6130man
1905-1920	..t...	SAf	6130man
Makhuwa	**Days**	**Area**	**kHz**
1355-1425	.....s	SAf	7315man
1455-1510	daily	SAf	7315man
Malagasy	**Days**	**Area**	**kHz**
1455-1525	mtwtf.s	SAf	9585man
Moore	**Days**	**Area**	**kHz**
2025-2040	mtw....	WAf	1566par
Ndau	**Days**	**Area**	**kHz**
0325-0340	daily	SAf	3240man
1600-1630	.....s.	SAf	4760man
1615-1645	.....s	SAf	4760man
1645-1700	daily	SAf	4760man
Ndebele	**Days**	**Area**	**kHz**
0255-0310	.....s.	SAf	3200man
0255-0325	mtwtf..	SAf	3200man
1455-1510	daily	SAf	6025man
1525-1555	mtwtf..	SAf	6025man
Oromo	**Days**	**Area**	**kHz**
0330-0345	.t.....	EAf	7215mey
1630-1700	..wt...	EAf	9500man
1645-1700	mt...s	EAf	9500man
1715-1745	.....s	EAf	9500man
1730-1800	mtwtf..	EAf	9500man
Portuguese	**Days**	**Area**	**kHz**
1355-1425	.....s	SAf	7315man
1425-1455	daily	SAf	7315man
1630-1645	m..t...	SAf	4760man
1850-1905	...s.	SAf	6130man
1905-1920	mt.....	SAf	6130man
1920-1950	daily	SAf	6130man
Shangaan	**Days**	**Area**	**kHz**
1545-1615	.....s	SAf	4760man
1630-1645	.tw.fs.	SAf	4760man
Shona	**Days**	**Area**	**kHz**
0255-0325	daily	SAf	3240man
1510-1525	daily	SAf	6025man
1555-1625	daily	SAf	6025man
Sidamo	**Days**	**Area**	**kHz**
0330-0345	..wt...	EAf	9525man
Somali	**Days**	**Area**	**kHz**
1630-1645	.....s	Af	11635kig
1630-1655	mtwtf..	Af	11635kig
Swahili	**Days**	**Area**	**kHz**
1700-1745	daily	Af	9475man
1745-1815	.....ss	Af	9475man
Tigre	**Days**	**Area**	**kHz**
1800-1830	.....s.	EAf	5965dha
Tigrinya	**Days**	**Area**	**kHz**
1800-1815	mtwt...	EAf	5965dha
1815-1845	mtwtf..	EAf	5965dha
Tshwa	**Days**	**Area**	**kHz**
1600-1630	mtwtf..	SAf	4760man
Twi	**Days**	**Area**	**kHz**
0500-0515	.....ss	WAf	1566par
0500-0530	mtwtf..	WAf	1566par
Umbundu	**Days**	**Area**	**kHz**
1750-1820	mtwtf..	SAf	6130man
1835-1850	daily	SAf	6130man
Yao	**Days**	**Area**	**kHz**
1705-1735	daily	SAf	7300man
Yoruba	**Days**	**Area**	**kHz**
1820-1855	daily	WAf	1566par
1855-1910	.....s.	WAf	1566par
Zulu	**Days**	**Area**	**kHz**
1630-1700	daily	SAf	1170man

Ann: English: "You are listening to TWR Broadcasting from Manzini, Swaziland".

IS: Last bar of "We've a story to tell the Nations", played on hand bells.
V: QSL-folder. Rp. (IRCs appreciated, 3 IRCs for airmail reply)
Notes: TWR regional division for Africa. For corporate details, see under TWR (USA). TWR Africa administrates the TWR transmitting stations in Benin and Swaziland.

AMATEUR RADIO MIRROR INTERNATIONAL
✉ P.O. Box 90438, Garsfontein 0042, South Africa.
☎ +27 11 6752393. 🖷 +27 11 6752793.
E: armi@sarl.org.za
W: www.amateurradio.org.za/armi.htm; www.sarl.org.za/public/armi/armi.asp
Webcast: P
SW: Leased from Sentech.
kHz: *4895, 7205, 17760*

Winter Schedule 2012/2013			
English	**Days**	**Area**	**kHz**
0800-0900	.....s	SAf	7205mey
0800-0900	.....s	EAf	17760mey
1630-1730	m......	SAf	4895mey

V: QSL-card.
Notes: ARMI is a weekly prgr about amateur radio, shortwave listening and electronics produced by the South African Radio League.

SENTECH (PTY) LTD. (Tx Operator)
✉ Private Bag X06, Honeydew 2040, South Africa.
☎ +27 11 4388883. 🖷 +27 11 6917107.
E: support@sentechsa.com
W: www.sentech.co.za; www.sentechsa.com
✉ P.O. Box 234, Meyerton 1960, South Africa. (Transmitter site)
☎ +27 16 3661055. 🖷 +27 16 3660709.
L.P: Board Chairperson: Thabo Mongake; CEO: Setumo Mohapi; HF Coverage Planning: Sikander Hoosen.
SW: [MEY] Meyerton, Bloemendal: 10 x 100, 4 x 250, 2 x 500kW.
V: QSL-Letter. Reception reports for all Meyerton transmissions should be sent to: Mr Sikander Hoosen, at the transmitter site address shown above.
Notes: Sentech (Pty) Ltd. is the operator of the transmitter networks in South Africa.

SPAIN (E)

RADIO EXTERIOR DE ESPAÑA (REE) (Pub)
✉ Casa de la Radio, Avenida de la Radio y la Televisión 4, Pozuelo de Alarcón, 28223 Madrid, Spain.
☎ +34 91 3461034. 🖷 +34 91 3461815.
E: ree@rtve.es; secretariatecnica.ree@rtve.es
W: www.rtve.es/radio/radio-exterior
Webcast: D/L/P
☎ +34 91 3461149.
L.P: Dir: Josefina Benéitez; Head, Foreign Language prgrs: Jose J. Amorena Zabalza.
SW: [NOB] Noblejas: 6 x 250kW.
SAT: Asiasat 5, Eutelsat 5WA/Hot Bird 13B, Hispasat 1C.
kHz: *3350, 5965, 5970, 6055, 6125, 7265, 7275, 9535, 9570, 9590, 9605, 9620, 9630, 9665, 9675, 9690, 9765, 9780, 11625, 11680, 11755, 11780, 11815, 11895, 11910, 11940, 12030, 12035, 13720, 15110, 15125, 15170, 15385, 15585, 17595, 17715, 17755, 17850, 21540, 21610*

Winter Schedule 2012/2013			
Arabic	**Days**	**Area**	**kHz**
1700-1900	daily	ME	21610nob
1900-2100	mtwtf..	NAf	7265nob
2000-2200	.....ss	NAf	7265nob
English	**Days**	**Area**	**kHz**
0000-0100	daily	NAm	6055nob
1900-2000	mtwtf..	Af	9605nob
1900-2000	mtwtf..	Eu	9665nob
2200-2300	.....ss	Eu	6125nob
French	**Days**	**Area**	**kHz**
1800-1900	mtwtf..	Eu	9665nob
1900-2000	.....s	ME	12030nob
1900-2000	.....s.	Af	9590nob
2000-2100	mtwtf..	Af	9570nob
2000-2100	mtwtf..	ME	9605nob

French	Days	Area	kHz
2300-2400	.....ss	Eu	5970nob
2300-2400	daily	NAm	6055nob

Ladino	Days	Area	kHz
0115-0145	.t.....	SAm	11780nob
0415-0445	.t.....	NAm	9690nob
1425-1455	m......	ME	15385nob

Portuguese	Days	Area	kHz
2100-2200	mtwtf..	SAm	11680nob

Russian	Days	Area	kHz
1700-1730	mtwtf..	Eu	11755nob

Spanish	Days	Area	kHz
0000-0100	daily	SAm	11815cri+
0000-0200	daily	NAm	9630cri+
0000-0400	daily	SAm	9765cri
0100-0600	daily	NAm	6055nob
0200-0600	daily	CAm	3350cri
0200-0600	daily	NAm	9675cri
0400-0800	daily	SAm	5965cri
0500-0600	mtwtf..	Eu	12035nob
0500-0700	daily	ME	11895nob
0500-0900	daily	Eu	9780nob+
0600-0900	daily	Eu	12035nob
0900-1500	daily	Af	21540nob*
0900-1700	daily	Eu	15585nob*
1100-1300	daily	Eu	13720nob+
1100-1700	daily	ME	21610nob*
1200-1400	daily	SEA	11910xia*
1200-1500	mtwtf..	CAm	9765cri*
1200-1500	mtwtf..	SAm	11815cri*
1200-1500	mtwtf.s	NAm	15170cri*
1200-2300	......s	SAm	15125cri
1200-2300	......s	CAm	9765cri
1300-1500	daily	Am	17595nob*
1500-1700	mtwtf..	SAm	17715nob
1500-1700	mtwtfs.	Af	15385nob
1500-1700	.....ss	LAm	17595nob
1500-2200	......s	Af	17755nob
1500-2300	......s	NAm	17850cri
1600-2300	.....s.	SAm	15125cri
1600-2300	.....s.	NAm	17850cri
1600-2300	.....s.	CAm	9765cri
1700-1900	mtwtf..	Af	17755nob
1700-1900	daily	SAm	17715nob
1700-2200	......s.	Af	17755nob
1700-2200	.....ss	Eu	9665nob
1700-2300	daily	Eu	7275nob
1800-2000	mtwtf..	NAm	17850cri
1800-2000	mtwtf..	SAm	15125cri
1800-2000	mtwtf..	CAm	9765cri
1900-2300	daily	NAm	15110nob
1900-2300	.....ss	LAm	11940nob
2200-2300	...ss	Af	11625nob
2200-2300	daily	Af	7265nob
2300-0500	daily	SAm	9620nob**
2300-0500	daily	LAm	6125nob**
2300-0500	daily	NAm,CAm	9535nob**

Key: + DRM; * Basque (irregular); ** Includes news Mon-Fri, in Galician & Catalan, at 2330-2345.
Ann: Arabic: "Idha'atu Isbania al-Jariyia"; English: "Radio Exterior de España, English language service"; French: "Radio Exterior de España, émmisión en Français"; Spanish: "Radio Exterior de España".
V: Does not verify.
Notes: REE is the External Sce of the public broadcaster Radio Nacional de España.

SRI LANKA (CLN)

SRI LANKA BROADCASTING CORPORATION (SLBC) (Pub)
P.O. Box 574, Colombo 7, Sri Lanka.
☎ +94 11 2697491. 🖷 +94 11 2691568.

E: chmnslbc@slbc.lk (Chairman); ddge@slbc.lk (DG, Engineering)
W: www.slbc.lk
Webcast: L
Independence Square, Colombo 7, Sri Lanka. (Studio)
☎ +94 26 2222097.
L.P: Chmn: Hudson Samarasinghe; DG: Samantha Weliweriya; Deputy DG, Engineering: H.M Jacson.
MW: [PUT] Puttalam: 873/882kHz 400kW, 1125kHz 50kW. 873kHz used for SLBC relays; 882kHz leased to TWR (see TWR India schedule, under India), 1125kHz leased to WRN; [TRM] Trincomalee, Perkara (Former DW Relay Station): 1548kHz 400kW.
SW: [EKA] Colombo, Ekala: 10 x 10, 3 x 35, 2 x 100, 2 x 300kW; [TRM] Trincomalee, Perkara (Former DW Relay Station): 1 x 250, 3 x 300kW.
kHz: 1125, 6005, 7190, 9770, 11750, 11905, 15745

Winter Schedule 2012/2013			
Bengali	Days	Area	kHz
0110-0130	daily	SAs	7190eka, 11905eka
English	Days	Area	kHz
0120-0300	mtwtfs.	SAs	6005eka, 9770eka, 15745eka
0300-0330	......s.	SAs	9770eka, 15745eka
0300-0500	......s	SAs	6005eka, 9770eka, 15745eka
Hindi	Days	Area	kHz
0200-0330	daily	SAs	7190eka, 11905eka
Malayalam	Days	Area	kHz
1000-1100	daily	SAs	6005eka, 11905eka
Sinhala	Days	Area	kHz
1630-1830	daily	ME	11750trm
Tamil	Days	Area	kHz
0000-0100	daily	SAs	1125put*
0130-0200	daily	SAs	7190eka, 11905eka
1100-1215	daily	SAs	6005eka, 11905eka
1330-1430	daily	SAs	1125put*
1430-1530	daily	SAs	1125put
Telugu	Days	Area	kHz
0930-1000	daily	SAs	6005eka, 11905eka

Key: * FEBA Prgr.
Ann: English: "This is the Sri Lanka Broadcasting Corporation".
IS: Melody on drums.
V: QSL-card. Rp.

DEUTSCHE WELLE (DW) RELAY STATION
Notes: The transmitting station was closed by Deutsche Welle on 1 November 2011 and handed over to the Sri Lanka Broadcasting Corporation (SLBC). See SLBC entry for details.

IBB RELAY STATION SRI LANKA
IBB Transmitting Station, P.O. Box 14, Negombo, Sri Lanka.
☎ +94 32 2255931. 🖷 +94 32 2255822.
L.P: SM:William S.Martin.
SW: [IRA] Iranawila: 3 x 250, 4 x 500kW.
V: QSL-card.

SUDAN (SDN)

VOICE OF AFRICA – SUDAN RADIO (Gov)
See National Radio section (under SRTC, Sudan).
W: sudanradio.info
SW: [ALF] Al Aitahab 1 x 100kW.
kHz: 9505

Winter Schedule 2012/2013			
Multilingual	Days	Area	kHz
0500-0800	daily	Af	9505alf*
1600-1900	daily	Af	9505alf*

Key: * Test Transmissions.
Ann: Arabic: "Saut Afrikya min Idaa-tu Sudanya"; French: "La Voix de L'Afrique, Radio National de Soudan".
Notes: The Voice of Africa is the external prgr of the state controlled Sudan Radio and Television Corporation (SRTC). Began test transmissions, consisting of Sudanese music and multilingual identifications, in October 2012.

SWAZILAND (SWZ)

TWR RELAY STATION
✉ P.O. Box 64, Manzini, Swaziland.
☎ +268 25052781. 📠 +268 25055333.
L.P: SM: Mark Blosser; Chief Engineer: Steve Stavropoulos.
MW: [MAN] Manzini, Mpangela Ranch: 1170kHz 50kW.
SW: [MAN] Manzini, Mpangela Ranch: 1 x 50, 3 x 100kW.
Notes: Owned by TWR. For corporate details, see under USA. For schedule, see TWR Africa, under South Africa.

SWEDEN (S)

IBRA RADIO (Rlg)
✉ SE-141 99 Stockholm, Sweden.
☎ +46 8 6089680. 📠 +46 8 6089650.
E: info@ibra.se **W:** www.ibra.org (English); www.ibra.se (Swedish)
✉ P.O. Box 2899, Stoke-on-Trent, ST4 9EL, United Kingdom.
☎ +44 1782 623759.
E: info@ibra-uk.org **W:** ibra-uk.org
L.P: Dir, IBRA Media: Lars Anderås; Public Relations: Maria Levander.
kHz: *7445, 9635, 11610, 11785, 12045*

Winter Schedule 2012/2013

Arabic	Days	Area	kHz
1700-1800	daily	Af	12045wof
1900-1930	daily	Af	9635wof
Beja	**Days**	**Area**	**kHz**
1800-1830	daily	Af	9635wof
Fulfulde	**Days**	**Area**	**kHz**
1900-1930	daily	Af	7445skn
Fur	**Days**	**Area**	**kHz**
1830-1900	daily	Af	9635wof
Jula	**Days**	**Area**	**kHz**
1945-2000	mt.fss	Af	7445skn
Malinke	**Days**	**Area**	**kHz**
1945-2000	..wt...	Af	7445skn
Moore	**Days**	**Area**	**kHz**
1930-1945	mtw...s	Af	7445skn
Sara Ngambai	**Days**	**Area**	**kHz**
1930-1945	m.....s	Af	9635wof
Shuwa	**Days**	**Area**	**kHz**
1930-1945	...tfs	Af	9635wof
Somali	**Days**	**Area**	**kHz**
1730-1800	daily	Af	11610mey
Swahili	**Days**	**Area**	**kHz**
1730-1800	daily	Af	11785dha
Tamajeq	**Days**	**Area**	**kHz**
1930-1945	...tfs.	Af	7445skn
Zaghawa	**Days**	**Area**	**kHz**
1930-1945	.tw....	Af	9635wof

V: QSL-card.
Notes: IBRA Radio (part of IBRA Media), is the radio ministry of the Swedish Pentecostal Movement. On air since July 1955.

SWITZERLAND (SUI)

RADIO FREUNDES–DIENST (Rlg)
✉ Missionswerk Freundes-Dienst International, Quellmattweg 2, CH-5023 Biberstein, Switzerland.
☎ +41 62 8272727. 📠 +41 62 8393003.
E: info@freundesdienst.org **W:** www.freundesdienst.org
Webcast: D
L.P: Pres (Freundes-Dienst International): Joseph Schmid.
kHz: *558, 630, 693, 1431, 1440, 6005, 7310*

Winter Schedule 2012/2013

German	Days	Area	kHz
0415-0430	......s	Eu	1440mrn
0430-0445	mtwtfs.	Eu	1440mrn
0600-0615	......s	Eu	1440mrn
1100-1115	daily	Eu	6005kll
1715-1745	daily	Eu	1440mrn

German	Days	Area	kHz
1730-1745	mtwtfs.	Eu	6005kll
1830-1845	daily	Eu	1440mrn
1925-1940	.t....s	Eu	558cen*, 630klu, 693bln, 1431dsd, 7310sam

Key: * until 31 Dec 2012.
V: QSL-card.
Notes: The prgr "Licht und Leben" (Radio Freundes-Dienst) is produced by the evangelical missionary organisation Freundes-Dienst International since 1959.

STIMME DES TROSTES (Rlg)
✉ Missionwerk Arche, Rosenbüelstrasse 48, CH-9642 Ebnat-Kappel, Switzerland.
☎ +41 71 9922500. 📠 +41 71 9922555.
E: info@missionswerk-arche.ch **W:** www.missionswerk-arche.ch
kHz: *1440, 6055*

Winter Schedule 2012/2013

German	Days	Area	kHz
0415-0430	.....s.	Eu	1440mrn
1200-1215	......s	Eu	6055wer
1815-1830	.....s.	Eu	1440mrn*

Key: * Every second week
V: QSL-card.
Notes: Produced by Missionshaus Arche.

SWISSCOM BROADCAST AG (Tx Operator)
✉ Ostermundigenstrasse 99, CH-3050 Bern, Switzerland.
☎ +41 58 8929292. 📠 +41 58 2218120.
E: info.broadcasting@swisscom.com **W:** www.swisscom.ch
L.P: CEO: Jean-Paul de Weck.
MW: [CEN] Monte Ceneri: 558kHz 300kW (run at 200kW).
Notes: Swisscom Broadcast is the national transmitter operator in Switzerland. Transmissions on 558kHz due to cease on 31 Dec 2012.

SYRIA (SYR)

RADIO DAMASCUS (Gov)
✉ P.O. Box 4702, Damascus, Syria.
☎ +963 11 2720700. 📠 +963 11 2234336.
E: radiodamascusenglish@yahoo.com **W:** www.radio-damascus.net
Webcast: D/P (Podcasts are at: radiodamascusenglish.podomatic.com)
W: www.syriaonline.sy
L.P: DG (ORTAS): Mohammad Ramez Al-Torjan; Dir, Radio: Mahmoud Al Joma'at; Dir, Public Rel: Marwan Nasseh.
MW: [HMS] Homs, Saraqeb: 594kHz 100kW ‡; [TTS] Tartus: 783kHz 300kW.
SW: [ADR] Adra: 2 x 500kW.
SAT: Badr 4, Nilesat 201.
kHz: *783, 9330*

Winter Schedule 2012/2013

English	Days	Area	kHz
2100-2200	daily	Eu,NAm,Pac	9330adr‡
French	**Days**	**Area**	**kHz**
1900-2000	daily	Eu,NAm	9330adr‡
German	**Days**	**Area**	**kHz**
1800-1900	daily	Eu	9330adr‡
Hebrew	**Days**	**Area**	**kHz**
0400-0630	daily	ME	783tts†
Russian	**Days**	**Area**	**kHz**
0630-0700	daily	ME	783tts†
1700-1800	daily	Eu	9330adr‡
Spanish	**Days**	**Area**	**kHz**
2200-2300	daily	Eu,LAm	9330adr‡
Turkish	**Days**	**Area**	**kHz**
1600-1700	daily	ME	9330adr‡

Key: † Irregular; ‡ Inactive at time of publication.
Ann: Arabic: "Idha'atu-l-jumhuriyati-l'arabiyya as-suriyya min dimashq"; English: "You are listening to Radio Damascus, the External Service of the Syrian Broadcasting System", "Welcome to the Broadcasting Service of the Syrian Arab Republic calling from Damascus"; French: "Ici Damas"; Hebrew: "Kol Damasek".
IS: Guitar.
V: QSL-card.

Notes: Radio Damascus is the External Sce of the state broadcaster Organisme de la Radio-TV Arabe Syrienne (ORTAS).

TAIWAN (Rep. of China) (TWN)

RADIO TAIWAN INTERNATIONAL (RTI) (Gov)
✉ 55 Pei An Road, Taipei 10462, Taiwan. or P.O. Box 123-199, Taipei 11199, Taiwan.
☎ +886 2 28856168. 🖷 +886 2 28862382.
E: rti@rti.org.tw **W:** www.rti.org.tw
Webcast: D/L
✉ Post Box 4914, P.O. Safdarjung Enclave, New Delhi 110029 India. (RTI India)
L.P: Chmn: Chang Jung-Kung; Pres: Lee Yu-Lung.
MW: [FAN] Fangliao: 1359/1503kHz 600kW; [KOU] Kouhu: 1098/1557kHz 300kW; [LUK] Lukang: 612kHz 1000kW, 1008kHz 600kW; [MIN] Minhsiung: 1206kHz 100kW, 1422kHz 50kW; [TSU] Taiwan (see note below).
SW: [HUW] Huwei: 4 x 100, 1 x 300kW; [KOU] Kouhu: 3 x 100kW; [PAO] Paochung: 5 x 100kW; [TNN] Tainan: 4 x 250kW; [TSH] Tanshui: 3 x 300kW; [TSU] Taiwan (see note below).
SAT: Intelsat 902, SatMex 5.
kHz: 612, 1008, 1098, 1206, 1359, 1422, 1503, 1557, 3955, 3965, 6075, 6085, 6105, 6115, 6145, 6150, 7365, 7380, 7385, 7445, 7465, 7555, 9440, 9465, 9625, 9660, 9665, 9680, 9685, 9690, 9735, 9780, 9840, 9895, 9930, 11520, 11550, 11605, 11625, 11635, 11640, 11655, 11700, 11715, 11720, 11765, 11875, 11885, 11915, 11985, 11995, 15180, 15245, 15265, 15270, 15290, 15320, 15440, 15465, 15485, 15690

Winter Schedule 2012/2013

Amoy	Days	Area	kHz
0500-0600	daily	EAs	1206min, 1422min
0800-0900	..w....	EAs	15290tnn*
0900-1000	..w....	EAs	11550tnn*
0900-1000	daily	EAs	1422min
1000-1100	daily	EAs	1206min, 15465pao
1200-1300	daily	EAs	1206min
1200-1300	daily	SEA	11715tnn
1300-1400	daily	EAs	11625pao

Cantonese	Days	Area	kHz
0000-0100	daily	NAm	15440yfr
0230-0300	daily	EAs	1422min
0430-0500	daily	EAs	15320pao
0900-1000	.....ss	EAs	15465pao
1000-1030	daily	SEA	11625pao, 15270pao
1200-1230	daily	EAs	6105kou, 11915tnn
1500-1530	daily	SEA	11605tnn
1500-1600	.....ss	SEA	7380pao

Chinese	Days	Area	kHz
0000-0100	daily	EAs	1422min
0300-0800	.....ss	EAs	1557kou
0400-0500	daily	EAs	1008luk, 1206min
0400-0600	daily	EAs	11640kou
0400-0600	daily	SEA	15245tsh
0900-1000	mtwtf..	EAs	15465pao
0900-1000	daily	EAs	1206min
1000-1100	daily	EAs	1422min, 6105kou
1000-1200	daily	EAs	1503fan
1000-1400	daily	EAs	9780kou, 11640kou
1000-1500	daily	EAs	6085huw
1000-1700	daily	EAs	7385kou
1100-1200	daily	EAs	1206min
1100-1200	daily	SEA	11625pao
1100-1300	daily	EAs	11720tnn
1100-1700	daily	EAs	612luk, 1008luk, 9680huw
1200-1300	daily	EAs	9665pao
1300-1330	daily	EAs	1503fan
1300-1400	daily	SEA	15265tsh
1300-1500	daily	SEA	7445pao
1300-1700	daily	EAs	1098kou
1400-1500	daily	EAs	1206min
1400-1800	daily	EAs	6075kou, 6145pao

Chinese	Days	Area	kHz
1500-1600	mtwtf..	SEA	7380pao
1500-1700	daily	EAs	7365tsh
1600-1700	daily	EAs	1503fan
2200-2400	daily	EAs	6105kou, 6150kou, 11700tnn, 11885huw
2200-2400	daily	SEA	11635pao
2300-0300	daily	EAs	9660kou
2300-2400	daily	EAs	1206min, 9685kou
2300-2400	daily	NAm	15440yfr

English	Days	Area	kHz
0100-0200	daily	SEA	11875tnn
0300-0400	daily	SEA	15320pao
1100-1200	daily	EAs	1359fan
1100-1200	daily	SEA	7445pao, 9465tnn
1600-1700	daily	SAs	9440tnn, 15485iss
1700-1800	daily	Af	15690iss
1800-1900	daily	Eu	3965iss
2200-2300	daily	NAm	6115yfr, 15440yfr

French	Days	Area	kHz
1900-2000	daily	Af	11875iss
1900-2000	daily	Eu	9895dha

German	Days	Area	kHz
1900-2000	daily	Eu	3955skn
2100-2200	daily	Eu	3965iss

Hakka	Days	Area	kHz
0030-0100	daily	NAm	15440yfr
0200-0230	daily	EAs	1422min
0430-0500	daily	SEA	15320pao
1030-1100	daily	SEA	11625pao, 15270pao
1230-1300	daily	EAs	6105kou, 11915tnn
1530-1600	daily	SEA	11605tnn

Indonesian	Days	Area	kHz
0300-0400	daily	EAs	1206min
0300-0500	daily	EAs	1422min
1000-1100	daily	SEA	11520pao, 11915tnn
1200-1300	daily	SEA	11625pao
1200-1300	daily	EAs	1422min
1400-1500	daily	SEA	11875tnn

Japanese	Days	Area	kHz
0800-0900	daily	EAs	11605tnn
1100-1200	daily	EAs	9735tnn
1300-1400	daily	EAs	9735tnn

Russian	Days	Area	kHz
1100-1200	daily	EAs	11985huw
1400-1500	daily	CAs	15180iss
1700-1800	daily	Eu	7465iss**, 9840iss***

Spanish	Days	Area	kHz
0100-0200	daily	LAm	9930yfr
0200-0300	daily	SAm	11995guf
2000-2100	daily	Eu	3965iss
2300-2400	daily	LAm	9690yfr

Thai	Days	Area	kHz
1300-1500	daily	EAs	1422min
1400-1600	daily	SEA	11635pao
1500-1600	daily	SEA	1503fan, 7555pao
2200-2300	daily	SEA	1503fan
2200-2400	daily	SEA	7445pao
2300-2400	daily	EAs	1422min

Vietnamese	Days	Area	kHz
0900-1000	daily	SEA	15270pao
1100-1200	daily	EAs	1422min
1200-1300	daily	EAs	1359fan
1200-1300	daily	SEA	11765tnn
1300-1400	daily	EAs	1206min
1400-1500	daily	SEA	9625tnn
2330-0030	daily	SEA	11655tnn

Key: * Relay of Taiwan Fishery R. Stn; ** Nov 2012-Feb 2013; *** March 2013.
Ann: English: "This is Radio Taiwan International"; Indonesian: "Inilah Radio Taiwan Internasional"; Japanese: "Kochirawa Taiwan Kokusai

Hoso, RTI, Chukaminkoku Chuohosokyoku no nihongobangumi desu"; Mandarin: "Cheli shih Chungyang Kuangpo Tientai, Taiwan chih Yin".
V: QSL-card. Rec. acc.
Notes: Formed in 1998, when the former Central Broadcasting System (owned by the Ministry of Defense? was joined with the international section of the Broadcasting Corporation of China ?Voice of Free China). Schedule includes some CBS networks. [TSU] (Taiwan, Site Unknown, rather than the confusing TAI code previously used, which was associated with the ex-site of Taipei.) is used as a general term for Taiwanese sites when the exact site is unknown. Some RTI programmes are transmitted by local US stations situated in Baltimore, MD and Sacramento, CA. Programmes to mainland China are jammed by "China National Radio (CNR)" 1st programme transmissions.

TAJIKISTAN (TJK)

VOICE OF TAJIK (OVOZI TOJIK) (Gov)
✉ Sheroz St. 31, 734025 Dushanbe, Tajikistan.
☎ +992 37 2277417. 🖷 +992 37 2211198.
W: radiotoj.tj
MW/SW: Leased from Teleradiokom.
SAT: ABS 1.
kHz: 1143, 7245

		Winter Schedule 2012/2013	
Arabic	**Days**	**Area**	**kHz**
1200-1300	daily	ME	1143dsb, 7245dsb
Dari	**Days**	**Area**	**kHz**
0600-0800	daily	WAs	1143dsb, 7245dsb
English	**Days**	**Area**	**kHz**
1300-1400	daily	WAs, ME	1143dsb, 7245dsb
Farsi	**Days**	**Area**	**kHz**
0400-0600	daily	ME	1143dsb, 7245dsb
1600-1800	daily	ME	1143dsb, 7245dsb
Hindi	**Days**	**Area**	**kHz**
1100-1200	daily	As	1143dsb, 7245dsb
Russian	**Days**	**Area**	**kHz**
0800-1000	daily	CAs	1143dsb, 7245dsb
Tajik	**Days**	**Area**	**kHz**
0200-0400	daily	CAs	1143dsb, 7245dsb
1400-1600	daily	CAs	1143dsb, 7245dsb
Uzbek	**Days**	**Area**	**kHz**
1000-1100	daily	CAs	1143dsb, 7245dsb

V: QSL-letter.
Notes: External Sce under the roof of the State Committee for TV and Radio Broadcasting.

TELERADIOKOM (Tx Operator)
✉ Internatsionalnaya Street 85, 734001 Dushanbe, Tajikistan.
☎ +992 37 2210912. 🖷 +992 37 2217974.
E: info@teleradiocom.tj **W:** www.teleradiocom.tj
LP: DG: Suhrob Aliyev.
MW: [DSB] Two sites: Dushanbe, Yangiyul (G.C: 38N29 068E48): 1143kHz 150kW; 1251kHz 100kW; Orzu (G.C: 37N32 068E48): 648/801kHz 1000kW, 927kHz 300kW; 972/1503kHz 500kW. Operated on behalf of IBB (USA): 972kHz 800kW.
SW: [DSB] Two sites: Dushanbe, Yangiyul (G.C: 38N29 068E48): 1 x 50, 5 x 100kW; Orzu (G.C: 37N32 068E48): 2 x 1000kW. Operated on behalf of IBB (USA): 2 x 250kW.
Notes: Teleradiokom, a subsidiary of the Telecommunications Ministry, is the national transmitter network owner.

TANZANIA (TZA)

ZANZIBAR BROADCASTING CORPORATION (Gov)
✉ P.O. Box 1178, Zanzibar, Tanzania.
☎ +255 54 31088.
E: karumehouse@tvz.co.tv
LP: Dir, Broadcasting: Yussuf Omar Chunda; CE: Ali Aboud Talib.
kHz: 6015, 11735

		Winter Schedule 2012/2013	
Swahili	**Days**	**Area**	**kHz**
0300-0600	daily	EAf	6015dol†
1500-2100	daily	EAf,ME	11735dol†

Key: † Irregular.

Ann: English: "Zanzibar Broadcasting Corporation"; "ZBC".

THAILAND (THA)

RADIO SARANROM (Gov)
✉ 443 Sri Ayudhya Road, Bangkok 10400, Thailand.
☎ +66 26435094. 🖷 +66 26435093.
E: radio_saranrom@mfa.go.th; information05@mfa.go.th
Webcast: D
LP: Dir, Broadcasting Division (Information Dept): Jesda Katavetin.
MW: Uses tx operated by IBB.
kHz: 1575

		Winter Schedule 2012/2013	
Thai	**Days**	**Area**	**kHz**
1030-1100	daily	SEA	1575bph
1100-1130	mtwtf..	SEA	1575bph
1200-1230	mtwtf..	SEA	1575bph
1500-1530	daily	SEA	1575bph
2230-2400	mtwt..s	SEA	1575bph

V: QSL-card.
Notes: Service for Thai's living in South East Asia, produced by the Information Department of the Thai Ministry of Foreign Affairs.

RADIO THAILAND WORLD SERVICE (HSK9) (Gov)
✉ Public Relations Department, Royal Thai Government, 236 Vibhavadi Rangsit Road, Ding Daeng, Bangkok 10400, Thailand.
☎ +66 26919917. 🖷 +66 22776139.
E: english@hsk9.org; feedback@hsk9.org **W:** www.hsk9.org
Webcast: D/L
LP: Dir: Amaraporn Rathavinij.
SW: Uses txs operated by IBB.
SAT: Thaicom 5.
kHz: 5875, 7460, 9535, 9585, 9720, 9950, 11870, 12015, 13745, 17630

		Winter Schedule 2012/2013	
Burmese	**Days**	**Area**	**kHz**
1145-1200	daily	SEA	5875udo
Chinese	**Days**	**Area**	**kHz**
1315-1330	daily	EAs	7460udo
English	**Days**	**Area**	**kHz**
0000-0100	daily	NAm	13745udo
0200-0230	daily	NAm	13745udo
0530-0600	daily	Eu	12015udo
1230-1300	daily	As,Pac	9720udo
1400-1430	daily	As,Pac	9950udo
1900-2000	daily	Eu	9585udo
2030-2045	daily	Eu	9535udo
German	**Days**	**Area**	**kHz**
2000-2015	daily	Eu	9535udo
Japanese	**Days**	**Area**	**kHz**
1300-1315	daily	EAs	7460udo
Khmer	**Days**	**Area**	**kHz**
1115-1130	daily	SEA	5875udo
Lao	**Days**	**Area**	**kHz**
1130-1145	daily	SEA	5875udo
Malay	**Days**	**Area**	**kHz**
1200-1215	daily	SEA	11870udo
Thai	**Days**	**Area**	**kHz**
0100-0200	daily	NAm	13745udo
0230-0330	daily	NAm	13745udo
1000-1100	daily	ME	17630udo
1330-1400	daily	EAs	7460udo
1800-1900	daily	Eu	9585udo
2045-2115	daily	Eu	9535udo
Vietnamese	**Days**	**Area**	**kHz**
1100-1115	daily	SEA	5875udo

Ann: English: "This is HSK9, Radio Thailand's World Service broadcasting from the Public Relations Department in Bangkok".
IS: Gongs and chimes.
V: QSL-card.
Notes: Radio Thailand World Service is the External Sce and is produced by the Thai Government Public Relations Department.

BBC ASIA RELAY STATION
P.O. Box 20, Muang, Nakhon Sawan 60000, Thailand.
☎ +66 56227275. 📠 +66 56227277.
SW: [NAK] Nakhon Sawan: 4 x 250kW.
V: QSL-card. (For direct report)
Notes: Owned by the BBC and operated by Babcock International Group PLC (see under United Kingdom).

IBB RELAY STATIONS THAILAND
IBB Transmitting Station, Rangsit-Bangpoon Road, Bangkok, Thailand.
☎ +66 25815191.
IBB Transmitting Station (Udon Thani), P.O. Box 99, Amphur Muang, Udon Thani 41000, Thailand.
L.P: SM: Dennis G.Brewer.
MW: [BPH] Ban Phachi, Rasom: 1575kHz 1000kW.
SW: [UDO] Udon Thani (Udorn), Ban Dung: 7 x 500kW.
V: QSL-card. (Email to manager_thailand@tha.ibb.gov)

TUNISIA (TUN)

RADIO TUNISIENNE (Gov)
See National Radio section.
Webcast: L (www.radiotunisienne.tn)
SW: Uses txs provided by ONT.
SAT: Badr 6, Eutelsat 7WA/12WA/Hot Bird 13B, Galaxy 19.
kHz: 7225, 7275, 7335, 7345, 12005, 17735

Winter Schedule 2012/2013

Arabic	Days	Area	kHz
0300-0510	daily	NAf,ME	12005sfa, 17735sfa
0400-0625	daily	Eu	7275sfa
0600-0810	daily	NAf	7335sfa
1600-2000	daily	NAf,ME	12005sfa
1600-2010	daily	NAf,ME	17735sfa
1700-2110	daily	NAf	7225sfa
1900-2310	daily	NAf	7345sfa

Ann: Arabic: "Huna Tunis, Idha'al-wataniya at-Tunisiya".
V: Does not verify. Rpt to Office National de la Télédiffusion (ONT).
Notes: Relay of the domestic "National Channel".

OFFICE NATIONAL DE LA TÉLÉDIFFUSION (ONT) (Tx Operator)
Cité Ennassim 1, Montplaisir, BP 399, Tunis 1080, Tunisia.
☎ +216 71908177. 📠 +216 71904923.
E: ont@telediffusion.net.tn **W:** www.telediffusion.net.tn
L.P: Chmn/CEO: Sadok Toumi.
SW: [SFA] Sfax, Sidi Mansour: 4 x 500kW.
V: QSL-card. (Email rpt to ecoute@telediffusion.net.tn)
Notes: ONT is the national transmitter network owner.

TURKEY (TUR)

VOICE OF TURKEY (VOT) (Pub)
P.O. Box 333, Yenisehir, Ankara 06443, Turkey.
☎ +90 312 4909809. 📠 +90 312 4909845.
E: tsr@trt.net.tr **W:** www.trt-world.com
Webcast: D/L/P
TRT/Oran Sitesi A Blok No: 427, Ankara 06109, Turkey. (Studio)
☎ +90 312 4633372. (English Desk)
L.P: Dir, Foreign Broadcasting: Süleyman Köksoy.
SW: [EMR] Emirler: 5 x 500kW.
SAT: Eutelsat Hot Bird 13B, Galaxy 19, Türksat 2A/3A.
kHz: 5960, 5965, 5970, 5980, 6000, 6050, 6120, 6185, 7205, 7240, 7245, 9410, 9460, 9495, 9530, 9610, 9650, 9655, 9665, 9700, 9785, 9820, 9840, 11680, 11730, 11795, 11805, 11815, 11835, 11925, 11955, 11965, 11985, 12035, 13625, 13685, 15200, 15350, 15360, 15480, 17755

Winter Schedule 2012/2013

Arabic	Days	Area	kHz
1000-1100	daily	NAf,ME	11955emr
1500-1600	daily	ME,NAf	9665emr
1500-1600	daily	NAf,WAf	15200emr
Azeri	**Days**	**Area**	**kHz**
0800-0900	daily	ME	11835emr
1630-1730	daily	ME	5965emr

Bulgarian	Days	Area	kHz
1200-1230	daily	Eu	7245emr
Chinese	**Days**	**Area**	**kHz**
1200-1300	daily	EAs	11805emr
Dari	**Days**	**Area**	**kHz**
1600-1630	daily	WAs	11680emr
English	**Days**	**Area**	**kHz**
0400-0500	daily	Eu,NAm	9655emr
0400-0500	daily	ME,NAf	7240emr
1330-1430	daily	Eu	12035emr
1730-1830	daily	CAs,SAs	11730emr
1930-2030	daily	Eu	6050emr
2130-2230	daily	SEA,Pac	9610emr
2300-2400	daily	Eu,NAm	5960emr
Farsi	**Days**	**Area**	**kHz**
0930-1100	daily	ME	11795emr
1600-1700	daily	ME	9530emr
French	**Days**	**Area**	**kHz**
2030-2130	daily	Eu	5970emr
2030-2130	daily	NAf,WAf	6050emr
Georgian	**Days**	**Area**	**kHz**
1100-1200	daily	Cau	9840emr
German	**Days**	**Area**	**kHz**
1230-1330	daily	Eu	17755emr
1830-1930	daily	Eu	7205emr
Italian	**Days**	**Area**	**kHz**
1500-1530	daily	Eu	6185emr
Kazakh	**Days**	**Area**	**kHz**
1430-1500	daily	CAs	9785emr
Pashto	**Days**	**Area**	**kHz**
1630-1700	daily	WAs	11680emr
Russian	**Days**	**Area**	**kHz**
1400-1500	daily	RUS	9410emr
Spanish	**Days**	**Area**	**kHz**
0200-0300	daily	LAm,Eu	9410emr, 9650emr
1730-1830	daily	Eu	9495emr
Tatar	**Days**	**Area**	**kHz**
1100-1130	daily	Eu,CAs	15360emr
Turkish	**Days**	**Area**	**kHz**
0100-0300	daily	CAs	6000emr
0500-0700	daily	Eu	9700emr
0500-0700	daily	ME	9820emr
0700-1000	daily	ME	11925emr
0700-1300	daily	ME,NAf	15480emr
0700-1400	daily	Eu	15350emr
1400-1700	daily	Eu	11815emr
1700-2200	daily	Eu	5980emr
1700-2200	daily	ME,NAf	6120emr
Turkmen	**Days**	**Area**	**kHz**
1300-1330	daily	CAs	11965emr
Urdu	**Days**	**Area**	**kHz**
1300-1400	daily	SAs	11985emr
Uyghur	**Days**	**Area**	**kHz**
0300-0400	daily	CAs	9460emr
1330-1430	daily	CAs	13685emr
Uzbek	**Days**	**Area**	**kHz**
1130-1200	daily	CAs	13625emr
1700-1730	daily	CAs	11680emr

Ann: English: "This is the Voice of Turkey's English transmission"; German: "Hier ist der Kurzwellensender Die Stimme der Türkei"; Spanish: "Esta es La Voz de Turquia"; Turkish: "Burasi Türkiye'nin Sesi Radyosu".
V: QSL-card.
Notes: The Voice of Turkey is the External Sce of the public service Turkish Radio-TV Corporation, TRT (Türkiye Radyo-Televizyon Kurumu).

UKRAINE (UKR)

RADIO UKRAINE INTERNATIONAL (RUI) (Gov)
vul. Kreschatyk 26, 01001 Kyiv, Ukraine.
☎ +380 44 2782534. 📠 +380 44 2287356.
E: via website. **W:** radioukr.com.ua

Webcast: L. Webcast languages: English, German, Romanian, Ukrainian.
L.P: Dir: Zhanna Mescherska.
MW: Leased from Concern RRT.
SAT: Astra 4A.
kHz: *657*

Winter Schedule 2012/2013

Romanian	Days	Area	kHz
1800-1900	daily	Eu	657crn
2000-2100	daily	Eu	657crn
2200-2225	daily	Eu	657crn

V: QSL-card.
Notes: Radio Ukraine International is the External Sce of the state broadcaster Natsionalna Radiokompaniia Ukraini (NRKU).

CONCERN RRT (Tx Operator)
✉ vul. Dorohozhytska 10, 04112 Kyiv, Ukraine.
☎ +380 44 2262260. 🖷 +380 44 4408722.
E: rrt@rrt.ua **W:** www.rrt.ua
L.P: GD: Anatolyi M. Antonenko.
MW: [CRN] Chernivtsi: 657kHz 25kW.
Notes: Concern RRT is the national transmitter network operator.

UNITED ARAB EMIRATES (UAE)

ABU DHABI MEDIA (Tx Operator)
✉ 4th St, sector 18, Abu Dhabi, United Arab Emirates.
☎ +971 2 4144000. 🖷 +971 2 4144001.
E: communications@admedia.ae **W:** www.admedia.ae
L.P: Chmn: Mohamed Mubarak Al Mazrouei; CEO: Ayman Al Safadi; Exec. Dir, Radio: Abdul Rahman Al Harti.
MW: [DHA] Dhabbaya: 1170/1539/1575kHz 800kW; 1314kHz 1000kW.
SW: [DHA] Dhabbaya: 4 x 500kW.
Notes: Abu Dhabi Media is a state media company and transmitter operator. Under special appointment, the Dhabbaya transmitting station is currently operated and maintained by Babcock International Group PLC (UK).

UNITED KINGDOM (G)

BBC WORLD SERVICE (Pub)
✉ Broadcasting House, Portland Place, London W1A 1AA, United Kingdom.
☎ +44 20 72403456. 🖷 +44 20 75571258.
E: worldservice.letters@bbc.co.uk **W:** www.bbc.co.uk/worldservice
Webcast: D/L/P. Web only languages (some of which may also be broadcast on local FM affiliate stns): Azeri, Russian, Turkish, Ukrainian, Vietnamese.
L.P: Dir: Peter Horrocks; Head of Asia-Pacific Region: Behrouz Afagh; Head of Americas-Europe: Nikki Clarke; Head of Africa Region & International Relations: Jerry Timmins; Head of Middle East Region: Liliane Landor.
MW/SW: Uses txs provided by Babcock International Group plc & foreign relays.
SAT: Apstar 7, Astra 1L/2B, Badr 4, Eutelsat 36B/Hot Bird 13B, Express AM33, Intelsat 7/10/10-02/907, Koreasat 6, Nilesat 101, NSS 806, Optus C1, Palapa D, SES 4/7, Sirius FM 5, Superbird C2, Telstar 18, Thaicom 5, XM 3/4, Yamal 201.
kHz: *198, 639, 675, 702, 720, 1251, 1323, 1413, 3255, 3915, 3955, 5790, 5845, 5865, 5875, 5885, 5905, 5910, 5915, 5940, 5945, 5955, 5970, 5975, 5980, 5985, 6005, 6040, 6055, 6110, 6135, 6140, 6155, 6165, 6170, 6175, 6190, 6195, 7255, 7285, 7305, 7325, 7350, 7355, 7360, 7375, 7400, 7410, 7415, 7425, 7435, 7445, 7465, 7490, 7505, 7600, 7610, 9430, 9440, 9460, 9490, 9505, 9510, 9560, 9605, 9615, 9650, 9695, 9740, 9790, 9800, 9810, 9815, 9820, 9855, 9870, 9900, 9915, 9920, 11680, 11685, 11750, 11760, 11770, 11800, 11810, 11820, 11850, 11860, 11890, 11895, 11925, 11950, 11955, 11965, 11970, 11975, 11995, 12015, 12025, 12035, 12045, 12065, 12095, 13660, 13695, 13725, 13820, 13865, 15105, 15150, 15180, 15270, 15285, 15310, 15335, 15360, 15400, 15420, 15490, 15510, 15575, 15710, 15755, 15790, 17510, 17640, 17660, 17685, 17720, 17745, 17760, 17780, 17790, 17830, 17870, 17885, 21470, 21590, 21595, 21630, 21660, 21720*

Winter Schedule 2012/2013

Arabic	Days	Area	kHz
0300-0400	daily	NAf	6040skn

Arabic	Days	Area	kHz
0300-0400	daily	ME	6040cyp
0300-0500	daily	ME,NAf	5790wof, 5875cyp
0300-2100	daily	ME	720zak
0330-2100	daily	ME	639zak
0400-0500	daily	ME	9915cyp, 11820sla
0400-0600	daily	ME	7325cyp
0400-0600	daily	NAf	5915skn
0400-0700	daily	NAf	7325wof
0500-0600	daily	ME	15790sla
0500-0700	daily	ME,NAf	13660cyp, 15790cyp
0500-0700	daily	NAf	5790wof
0600-0700	daily	ME	9915cyp
0700-0800	daily	ME	17885cyp
0700-0800	daily	NAf	11680skn
1500-2100	daily	ME	702sla
1700-1800	daily	ME	9915skn
1700-1900	daily	NAf	6110wof
1700-2100	daily	ME	6195sla
1700-2100	daily	ME,NAf	5790skn, 7375cyp, 9915cyp
1900-2000	daily	NAf	6170wof
2000-2100	daily	NAf	5875cyp, 5875wof

Bengali	Days	Area	kHz
0030-0100	daily	SAs	7325nak, 9510sng, 12025sng
0130-0200	daily	SAs	9510nak, 15270sng
1330-1400	daily	SAs	5865nak, 9510sla, 11850sng
1630-1700	daily	SAs	5865nak, 7465sng, 9650sng

Burmese	Days	Area	kHz
0000-0030	daily	SEA	5875nak, 9510sng, 12025sng
0200-0230	daily	SEA	9460nak, 11975nak, 11995sng
1345-1430	daily	SEA	7400sng, 9900sng, 11685sng

Dari	Days	Area	kHz
0030-0100	daily	WAs	1413sla, 5875cyp, 7435wof
0130-0200	daily	WAs	5875cyp, 6195cyp, 7445wof
0200-0230	daily	CAs	1251dsb
0230-0300	daily	WAs	6140sla, 6195cyp, 7445cyp
0930-1030	daily	CAs	1251dsb
0930-1030	daily	WAs	15710sla, 17720nak
1400-1500	daily	CAs	1251dsb
1400-1500	daily	WAs	9810sla, 11950cyp
1400-1500	daily	WEu	15710cyp
1700-1730	daily	WAs	5865nak, 5875cyp, 5910sla
1800-1830	daily	CAs	1413sla, 5910cyp, 7505nak
1800-1830	daily	WAs	5865nak
1800-1900	daily	CAs	1251dsb

English	Days	Area	kHz
0000-0100	daily	FE	13725nak
0000-0100	daily	SAs	5970sla, 6195sng, 7360cyp, 9410nak, 12095sng
0000-0200	daily	FE	15755nak
0000-0200	daily	SAs	11750sng, 12095nak
0000-0200	daily	SEA	15335sng
0000-2400	daily	CHN	675hkg
0100-0200	daily	SAs	5970sla
0100-0200	daily	SEA	17685sng
0100-0300	daily	SAs	15310nak
0100-0400	daily	CAs	5940cyp
0100-0520	daily	Eu	198dro
0200-0230	daily	SAs	1413sla

English	Days	Area	kHz
0200-0300	daily	EAf	7435sey
0200-0300	daily	ME	5875cyp
0200-0300	daily	SAs	12095sla
0200-0730	mtwtf..	ME	1323cyp
0200-2300	.....ss	ME	1323cyp
0300-0330	daily	ME	639zak
0300-0400	daily	SAf	7435asc
0300-0400	daily	CAf	6140mey
0300-0400	daily	CAs	12095sla
0300-0400	daily	EAf	9460sey, 12035sey
0300-0400	daily	ME	1413sla, 5940skn
0300-0500	daily	ME	9410cyp
0300-0600	daily	SAf	3255mey
0300-0600	daily	SAs	15310sla
0300-0600	daily	CAf	7255asc
0300-0700	daily	SAs	17790nak
0300-2200	daily	SAf	6190mey
0400-0500	daily	CAf	12015mey
0400-0500	daily	EAf	12035cyp
0400-0600	daily	EAf	12095sey
0400-0600	daily	ME	11760cyp
0400-0700	daily	WAf	6005asc
0500-0600	daily	CAs	15360sla
0500-0600	mtwtf..	EAf	15420sey
0500-0600	.....ss	EAf	15420cyp
0500-0700	daily	CAf	15400mey
0500-0700	daily	EAf	17640cyp
0500-0700	daily	Eu	3955skn+
0600-0700	.....ss	EAf	15420sey
0600-0700	daily	ME	15360cyp
0600-0700	daily	WAf	9410asc, 9460asc
0600-0700	mtwtf..	EAf	15420cyp
0600-1400	daily	SAs	15310nak
0600-1500	daily	SAf	12095mey
0700-0800	daily	WAf	11770asc, 13820asc
0700-0800	mtwtf..	EAf	17640cyp
0700-0800	daily	CAf	17830mey
0700-0800	.....ss	EAf	17640sey
0700-0900	daily	WEu	5875wof+, 7355mos+
0700-1000	daily	ME	15575sla, 17660cyp
0700-1000	daily	WAf	15400asc
0700-1300	daily	SAs	17790nak
0800-1000	daily	CAf	17830asc
0800-1400	daily	EAf	17640sey
0800-1400	daily	SAf	21470sey
0900-1100	daily	FE	17760nak
0900-1100	daily	SEA	9740nak
0900-1200	daily	FE	15285sng
0900-1300	daily	FE	11895nak
0900-1300	daily	SEA	6195sng, 9740sng
0900-2300	mtwtf..	ME	1323cyp
1000-1100	.....ss	CAf	17830asc
1000-1100	.....ss	WAf	15400asc
1000-1400	daily	ME	11760sla, 15575cyp
1100-1130	daily	WAf	15400asc
1100-1800	daily	CAf	17830asc
1200-1600	daily	FE	5875nak
1300-1400	daily	SAs	1413sla
1300-1500	daily	FE	11890nak
1300-1700	daily	SAs	9410sla
1400-1600	daily	ME	11760cyp
1400-1700	daily	SAs	5975sng
1400-1700	daily	EAf	17640cyp, 21470cyp
1400-1800	daily	SAs	5845nak+
1430-1500	daily	SAs	1413sla
1500-1600	daily	SAf	9490mey
1500-1700	daily	SAs	9505cyp
1500-1800	daily	EAf	12095sey
1500-2100	daily	WAf	15400asc
1600-1700	daily	ME	9915cyp
1600-1800	daily	WAf	21660wof

English	Days	Area	kHz
1600-2200	daily	SAf	3255mey
1630-1800	daily	SAs	1413sla
1700-1800	daily	EAf	15420cyp
1700-1800	.....ss	CAs	1251dsb
1700-1830	daily	SAs	5975sla, 7600nak, 9505sng
1700-1900	daily	EAf	17640mey
1800-2000	daily	CAs	5945sla
1800-2000	daily	ME	5875cyp
1800-2100	daily	CAf	11810asc
1800-2100	daily	EAf	12095cyp
1800-2100	daily	WAf	9430wof
1830-2200	daily	EAf	9410sey
1900-2100	daily	EAf	6005sey
1930-2100	daily	ME	1413sla
2100-2200	daily	SEA	6195nak
2100-2200	daily	SAf	5955sey
2100-2300	daily	FE	5905sla
2100-2300	daily	WAf	9915asc, 12095asc
2100-2400	daily	FE	5875nak
2100-2400	daily	SEA	3915sng
2200-0100	daily	SEA	6195sng
2200-2300	daily	CAf	5885mey
2200-2400	daily	FE	6135kim, 7490nak
2300-0200	daily	SEA	9740sng
2300-2400	daily	FE	5980sla
2300-2400	daily	SEA	11955sng

Farsi	Days	Area	kHz
0230-0300	daily	ME	1413sla
0230-0330	daily	ME	5985wof, 6165skn, 7410cyp
0230-0330	daily	CAs	1251dsb, 9800tac
0330-0430	daily	ME	7445cyp, 9695cyp, 11975sla
0330-0430	daily	CAs	1251dsb
1600-1700	daily	ME	5875cyp, 6155sla
1830-1900	daily	ME	5865nak, 5910cyp, 7505nak
1830-1930	daily	ME	1413sla

French	Days	Area	kHz
0430-0500	daily	EAf	15490sey
0430-0500	daily	CAf	6135asc, 7415asc
0600-0630	daily	WAf	6135asc
0600-0630	daily	NAf	6055skn, 7350wof
0600-0630	daily	CAf	11800asc
0700-0730	daily	CAf	15105asc
0700-0730	daily	WAf	11800asc
1200-1230	daily	CAf	21630asc
1200-1230	daily	NAf	21720wof
1200-1230	daily	WAf	17780asc
1800-1830	daily	NAf	9605skn
1800-1830	daily	WAf	11860asc, 17885wof
1800-1830	daily	SAf	7465mey
1800-1830	daily	CAf	15105asc

Hausa	Days	Area	kHz
0530-0600	daily	WAf	5975wof, 6135asc, 7305asc
0630-0700	daily	WAf	9440asc, 9870wof, 11800asc
1230-1500	.....s.	WAf	17780asc
1400-1430	daily	WAf	15105asc, 21630asc
1400-1430	mtwtf.s	WAf	17780asc
1930-2000	daily	WAf	11890asc, 15105asc, 17885asc
2000-2030	....f..	WAf	11890asc, 15105asc, 17885asc

Hindi	Days	Area	kHz
0100-0130	daily	SAs	1413sla, 6165sla, 7285cyp, 11995nak, 15510sng
0230-0300	daily	SAs	9560cyp, 11995sla, 15510nak, 17510nak

Hindi

	Days	Area	kHz
1400-1430	daily	SAs	1413sla, 5865nak, 7600nak, 9510sla, 12065sng, 13865cyp
1600-1630	daily	SAs	1413sla, 5865nak, 9790sng, 13695cyp, 15710cyp

Kinyarwanda/ Kirundi

	Days	Area	kHz
0500-0600	.....s.	EAf	11925sey, 15490cyp
0530-0600	......s	EAf	11925sey, 15490cyp
1630-1700	mtwtf..	EAf	11860sey, 15790cyp
1830-1900	mtwtf..	EAf	6140sey, 7425cyp, 9815cyp

Pashto

	Days	Area	kHz
0100-0130	daily	WAs	5875cyp, 6195sla, 7445wof
0200-0230	daily	WAs	6140sla, 6195cyp, 7445cyp
0300-0330	daily	WAs	7445wof, 9820cyp, 11970sla
0830-0930	daily	WAs	15710sla, 17720nak
1030-1130	daily	WAs	15710sla, 17720nak
1500-1600	daily	WAs	7360cyp, 9810cyp
1500-1600	daily	WEu	15710cyp
1730-1800	daily	WAs	5865nak, 5875cyp, 5910sla

Sinhala

	Days	Area	kHz
1630-1700	daily	SAs	6135sng, 7600nak, 9615sla

Somali

	Days	Area	kHz
0400-0430	daily	EAf	9815cyp, 15490sey
1100-1130	daily	EAf	17780cyp, 21595dha
1130-1230	.....s.	EAf	12065cyp, 15180cyp, 17745cyp
1230-1500	.....s.	EAf	15510cyp, 17745cyp
1400-1500	mtwtf.s	EAf	12045sey, 15150sey, 17870cyp
1800-1830	daily	EAf	6140sey, 9410sey, 9815cyp

Tamil

	Days	Area	kHz
1545-1615	daily	SAs	6135sng, 7600nak, 9855sla, 11965skn

Urdu

	Days	Area	kHz
0130-0200	daily	SAs	1413sla, 5980sla, 6165sla, 15510nak
0130-0200	daily	WAs	7285cyp
0300-0330	daily	SAs	9695cyp, 11995dha, 17510nak, 17760nak
1500-1545	daily	SAs	7600nak
1500-1600	daily	SAs	1413sla, 6175sla, 9920nak, 12065cyp

Uzbek

	Days	Area	kHz
1300-1330	daily	CAs	13865sla, 17790cyp, 21590cyp
1300-1400	daily	CAs	1251dsb

Key: + DRM
Ann: English: "BBC World Service"; "This is the BBC".
V: Does not verify reception reports.
Notes: BBC World Sce prgrs in English and other languages are relayed by local stns in many countries. Transmissions in some Asian languages are jammed.

AWR AFRICA/EUROPE (Rlg)
✉ 1 Milbanke Court, Milbanke Way, Bracknell, Berks. RG12 1RP, United Kingdom.
☎ +44 1344 401401. 🖷 +44 1344 401419.
L.P: Dir, Africa Region: Ray Allen; Dir, Europe Region: Tihomir Zestic.
kHz: 3215, 5970, 5975, 6045, 6100, 6145, 6155, 7315, 9535, 9610, 9630, 9770, 9805, 9830, 11645, 11670, 11690, 11750, 11755, 11760, 11795, 11830, 11860, 11925, 11955, 11975, 15125, 15145, 15240, 15255, 15270, 15290, 15480, 17575, 17605

Winter Schedule 2012/2013

Afar

	Days	Area	kHz
1430-1500	daily	Af	17605mos

Amharic

	Days	Area	kHz
0330-0400	daily	Af	9610wer

Arabic

	Days	Area	kHz
0400-0600	daily	ME	15480mey
0700-0800	daily	NAf	11975wer
1830-1900	daily	NAf	11860mos
1900-1930	daily	NAf	11760wer
1900-2000	daily	NAf	9535nau
1900-2100	daily	NAf	15480mey

Bulgarian

	Days	Area	kHz
0400-0430	daily	Eu	5975wer
1600-1630	daily	Eu	6100wer

Dyula

	Days	Area	kHz
2000-2030	daily	Af	9770mos

English

	Days	Area	kHz
1200-1230	daily	SEA	11670trm
1530-1600	mtw..ss	As	15255trm
1830-1900	daily	Af	11830mey
2100-2130	daily	Af	9830mos

French

	Days	Area	kHz
0430-0500	daily	Af	6045mos
0800-0830	daily	Af	15145wer
1930-2000	daily	Af	11690mos
2000-2030	daily	Af	9805wer, 11755mey
2030-2100	daily	Af	9805mos

Fulfulde

	Days	Area	kHz
1900-1930	daily	Af	15240mey

Hausa

	Days	Area	kHz
0500-0530	daily	Af	9630mos
1900-1930	daily	Af	11690mos

Ibo

	Days	Area	kHz
1930-2000	daily	Af	11750mey

Italian

	Days	Area	kHz
1000-1100	......s	Eu	9610nau

Kabyle

	Days	Area	kHz
0800-0830	daily	Af	15125wer
1730-1800	daily	Af	11860wer

Maasai

	Days	Area	kHz
1730-1800	daily	Af	11925mey

Malagasy

	Days	Area	kHz
0230-0330	daily	Af	3215mdc
1430-1530	daily	Af	6155mdc

Meitei

	Days	Area	kHz
1230-1300	..w.f.s	As	11670trm

Oromo

	Days	Area	kHz
0300-0330	daily	Af	9610wer
1730-1800	daily	Af	11795nau

Persian

	Days	Area	kHz
0330-0430	daily	ME	6145mos
1630-1730	daily	ME	11645mos

Punjabi

	Days	Area	kHz
0230-0300	daily	As	5970mos
1500-1530	daily	As	15270trm
1530-1600	daily	As	15290mos

Somali

	Days	Area	kHz
1630-1700	daily	Af	17575wer

Swahili

	Days	Area	kHz
1700-1730	daily	Af	11925mey

Tachelhit

	Days	Area	kHz
0830-0900	daily	Af	15145wer
1930-2000	daily	Af	11760wer

Tigrinya

	Days	Area	kHz
0300-0330	daily	Af	7315nau

Turkish

	Days	Area	kHz
1500-1530	daily	ME	11955mos

Wolof

	Days	Area	kHz
1900-1930	daily	Af	11860wer

Yoruba

	Days	Area	kHz
2030-2100	daily	Af	11755mey

Notes: Regional branch of Adventist Broadcasting Service, Inc (USA), covering Europe, Africa and the Middle East. See USA for corporate details. The individual AWR prgrs are produced by a large number of partner studios within the region.

CHRISTIAN VISION (Rlg)

📧 The Pavilion, Manor Drive, Coleshill, West Midlands, B46 1DL, United Kingdom.
☎ +44 1675 435500. 📠 +44 1675 435501.
E: admin@cvuk.org **W:** www.christianvision.com
L.P: Dir, Int Broadcasting: Andrew Flynn.
V: QSL-card.
Notes: Christian Vision is an evangelical charitable company. For international radio broadcasting activities, see CVC La Loz (Chile), CVC 1Africa Radio (South Africa), CVC The Voice Asia (United Kingdom), CVC Radio Christian Voice (Zambia). Christian Vision owns shortwave transmitting stations in Chile and Zambia.

CVC THE VOICE ASIA (Rlg)

📧 P.O.Box 3040, West Bromwich, B70 0AY, United Kingdom.
☎ +44 121 5578098.
E: mail@thevoiceasia.com **W:** www.thevoiceasia.com
Webcast: L/P
📧 P.O.Box 2, Ludhiana-141008, Punjab, India; GPO 770, Rawalpindi 46000, Pakistan.
L.P: Dir: Daniel Choranji; Ops Mgr: Narinder Choranji.
SAT: Eutelsat Hot Bird 13A.
kHz: 6260, 9500, 13630

Winter Schedule 2012/2013

Hindi	Days	Area	kHz
0000-0400	daily	As	6260tac
0400-1100	daily	As	13630tac
1100-1400	daily	As	9500tac
1400-2000	daily	As	6260tac

V: QSL-card. Rp.
Notes: Produced by The Voice Asia Ltd, a subsidiary of the charity Christian Vision (see separate entry). Internet radio station since 1 June 2002, on shortwave since 2010.

FEBA RADIO (Rlg)

📧 Ivy Arch Road, Worthing, West Sussex, BN14 8BX, United Kingdom.
☎ +44 1903 237281. 📠 +44 1903 205294.
E: info@feba.org.uk; lifechange@feba.org.uk **W:** www.feba.org.uk
W: www.febaradio.net (Schedules)
L.P: CEO: Jonathan Frank.
kHz: 6125, 6180, 7230, 7315, 7510, 9390, 9400, 9540, 9550, 9595, 9850, 11875, 11985, 12125, 15215, 15220, 15250

Winter Schedule 2012/2013

Afar	Days	Area	kHz
1600-1630	daily	Af	11875kig
Amharic	**Days**	**Area**	**kHz**
1600-1630	...tfss	Af	12125erv
1630-1700	...tfs.	Af	9850dha
1630-1700	daily	Af	12125erv
Arabic	**Days**	**Area**	**kHz**
0800-0830	daily	ME	15220mos
1800-1927	daily	ME	9550kig
Balti	**Days**	**Area**	**kHz**
1430-1445	m...fss	As	7230tac
Baluchi	**Days**	**Area**	**kHz**
0215-0230	mtw....	As	7315dha
Bengali	**Days**	**Area**	**kHz**
0000-0030	daily	As	9390tac
1500-1530	daily	As	9390tac
Dari	**Days**	**Area**	**kHz**
0230-0300	daily	WAs	6125dha
1500-1530	daily	WAs	9400erv
French	**Days**	**Area**	**kHz**
1830-1845	daily	Af	15250asc
Guragena	**Days**	**Area**	**kHz**
1600-1630	mtw....	Af	12125erv
Hassinya	**Days**	**Area**	**kHz**
2145-2200	mt.tfss	Af	11985asc
Hindi	**Days**	**Area**	**kHz**
1430-1500	daily	As	9540tac
Oromo	**Days**	**Area**	**kHz**
1700-1730	daily	Af	9595kig

Pashto	Days	Area	kHz
0300-0315	daily	WAs	6125dha
1530-1558	daily	WAs	9400erv
Pulaar	**Days**	**Area**	**kHz**
2200-2215	mt.tfss	Af	11985asc
Silte	**Days**	**Area**	**kHz**
1730-1800	daily	As	7510erv
Sindhi	**Days**	**Area**	**kHz**
0215-0230	...tfs.	As	7315dha
Somali	**Days**	**Area**	**kHz**
1700-1730	daily	Af	6180dha
Tibetan	**Days**	**Area**	**kHz**
1200-1230	daily	EAs	15215dha
Tigrinya	**Days**	**Area**	**kHz**
1630-1700	mtw...s	Af	9850dha
1730-1757	daily	Af	9595kig
Urdu	**Days**	**Area**	**kHz**
0200-0215	mtwtfs.	As	7315dha
0200-0230	......s	As	7315dha
1400-1430	daily	As	7230tac
1430-1445	.twt...	As	7230tac

V: Does not verify reception reports.
Notes: Associated regional partner of Far East Broadcasting Company, Inc (FEBC) (USA), targeting Africa, the Middle East and the Indian subcontinent. See USA for FEBC corporate details. FEBA Radio transmissions may include prgrs provided by small religious prgr producers and broadcast under own labels.

WRN BROADCAST LTD

📧 Wyvil Court, 10 Wyvil Road, London, SW8 2TG, United Kingdom.
☎ +44 20 78969000. 📠 +44 20 78969007.
E: contactus@wrn.org **W:** www.wrnbroadcast.com; www.wrn.org
Webcast: D/L
L.P: MD: David Treadway; Dir, Technology: Tim Ashburner; Dir, Development: Jeff Cohen; Dir: Karl Miosga; Head of Operations: Michael Ward.
SAT: Astra 1L, Eutelsat 28A/36B/Hot Bird 13A, Intelsat 7/10, Galaxy 19, Sirius FM 5, Superbird C2, Telstar 18, XM3/4.
Ann: English: "This is the WRN".
V: QSL-card. (Email to freqdept@wrn.org)
Notes: WRN Broadcast Ltd provides a multichannel 24h news and information network via satellite and Internet, carrying prgrs from major world broadcasters. WRN Broadcast feeds can be heard on numerous AM/FM radio stations and cable around the globe. WRN Broadcast also brokers shortwave transmitter air time.

BABCOCK INTERNATIONAL GROUP PLC (Tx Operator)

📧 33 Wigmore Street, London, W1 1QX, United Kingdom. (Corporate HQ)
☎ +44 20 7355 5300. 📠 +44 20 7355 5360.
E: broadcast@babcock.co.uk **W:** www.babcockinternational.com; www.babcock-online.co.uk
📧 Blue Fin Building, 110 Southwark Street, London, SE1 0TA, United Kingdom. (Media Management Centre)
☎ +44 20 79690000. 📠 +44 20 73555360.
L.P: CEO: Peter Rogers.
SW: [SKN] Skelton: 11 x 250, 6 x 300kW; [WOF] Woofferton: 6 x 250, 4 x 300kW.
Notes: Babcock International Group PLC is the owner and operator of the medium and shortwave transmitting centres in the UK that are used by the BBC World Service, it also operates the BBC overseas relay stations, under a management contract.

UNITED STATES OF AMERICA (USA)

AMERICAN FORCES RADIO AND TELEVISION SERVICE (AFRTS) (Gov)

📧 NMC DET AFRTS-DMC, 23755 Z St., Bldg. 2730, Riverside, CA 92518-2017, USA.
☎ +1 951 4132236. 📠 +1 951 4132457.
E: afrtops1@dma.mil; technologist@dma.mil
W: afrts.dodmedia.osd.mil; myafn.dodmedia.osd.mil
📧 601 N. Fairfax Street, Room 360, Alexandria, VA 22314, USA. (HQ/Engineering)
L.P: Dir (DMA): Bryan G. Whitman.

SW: Relayed by the following U.S. Navy utility sites: [BAR] Barrigada, Guam: 3kW; [DGA] Diego Garcia, British Indian Ocean Territory: 3kW
SAT: Eutelsat 9A, Galaxy 16, Intelsat 10-02/906, NSS 6, SES 4.
kHz: *4319, 5765, 12759, 13362*

Winter Schedule 2012/2013

English	Days	Area	kHz
0200-1400	daily	IOc	12759dga*
0800-2000	daily	Pac	5765bar*
1400-0200	daily	IOc	4319dga*
2000-0800	daily	Pac	13362bar*

Key: * SSB
Ann: English: "You're listening to AFN", "This is National Public Radio".
V: QSL-card.
Notes: The AFRTS prgrs are produced by the American Forces Network Broadcast Center (AFN-BC), part of the Defense Media Activity (DMA) under the U.S. Department of Defense (DoD). The current SW transmissions (resumed in 2000), carrying the AFN Voice Channel in USB (incl. relays of National Public Radio - NPR), are provided by the U.S. Navy as an option for their ships without the Navy's Direct-to-Sailor (DTS) satellite capability, as well as a backup for ships with DTS. They are also an option for land-based U.S. Navy listeners in remote locations that do not have access to local or satellite-delivered AFRTS full Satellite Network (SATNET) services.

BBG – AFIA DARFUR RADIO (Gov)
✉ 7600 Boston Boulevard, Springfield, VA 22153, USA.
☎ +1 703 8529000. 🖷 +1 703 9125499..
E: info@afiadarfur.com **W:** www.afiadarfur.com
Webcast: D
L.P: Dir (Middle East Broadcasting Networks): Brian Conniff.
SW: Via txs provided by IBB, plus other relays.
kHz: *5885, 7275, 9645, 9780, 9815, 9845, 11615, 11975*

Winter Schedule 2012/2013

Arabic	Days	Area	kHz
0300-0330	daily	SDN	5885smg, 7275sao, 9845bot
1800-1830	daily	SDN	9645wer, 11615smg, 11975lam
1900-1930	daily	SDN	9780smg, 9815wer, 11975sao

Ann: Arabic: "Afia Darfur".
V: QSL-card
Notes: BBG funded service for listeners in the Darfur region of Sudan and Eastern Chad, launched on 29 Sept 2008. Produced in the studios of Middle East Broadcasting Network, Inc.

BBG – RADIO FARDA (Gov)
✉ 1201 Connecticut Avenue NW, Washington, D.C. 20036, USA.
☎ +1 202 8287220. 🖷 +1 202 8287235.
E: comment@radiofarda.com; info@radiofarda.com
W: www.radiofarda.com
Webcast: D/L/P
✉ Vinohradská 159A, 100 00 Prague 10, Czech Republic. (Studio)
☎ +420 2 21124113. 🖷 +420 2 21122622.
L.P: Dir: Armand Mostofi.
MW/SW: Via txs provided by IBB, plus other relays.
SAT: AsiaSat 3S, Badr 4, Eutelsat Hot Bird 7WA/13B, Intelsat 907, Nilesat 101, NSS 12/806, Telstar 12, Türksat 3A.
kHz: *1575, 5850, 5860, 7520, 7580, 9395, 9430, 9990, 11750, 12005, 12035, 13615, 13680, 13800, 15410, 15535, 15690*

Winter Schedule 2012/2013

Farsi	Days	Area	kHz
0000-0100	daily	IRN	5860lam
0000-2400	daily	IRN	1575dha
0100-0300	daily	IRN	5860ira
0200-0500	daily	IRN	9430lam
0230-1400	daily	IRN	15690ira
0300-0500	daily	IRN	13615ira
0300-0830	daily	IRN	5860kwt
0500-0730	daily	IRN	13615wer
0500-0930	daily	IRN	15535ira
0730-1100	daily	IRN	13800ira
0730-1530	daily	IRN	12005lam
0830-1200	daily	IRN	11750bib
0930-1300	daily	IRN	9990kwt
1100-1500	daily	IRN	13800lam
1200-1400	daily	IRN	15410bib
1300-1430	daily	IRN	9990ira
1400-1600	daily	IRN	15410wof
1400-1700	daily	IRN	15690bib
1430-1500	daily	IRN	13680lam
1500-1630	daily	IRN	13680wer
1500-1730	daily	IRN	13615lam
1530-1700	daily	IRN	12005bib
1600-2300	daily	IRN	7580ira
1700-1900	daily	IRN	12035bib
1730-1900	daily	IRN	9395lam
1730-2100	daily	IRN	7520udo
1900-2130	daily	IRN	5850ira
2100-2400	daily	IRN	7520lam
2130-0300	daily	IRN	5850kwt

Ann: Farsi: "Radyo Farda".
V: QSL-card.
Notes: BBG funded station for listeners in Iran, launched in December 2002. 24h on satellite & FM. Transmissions on medium wave are jammed.

BBG – RADIO FREE AFGHANISTAN (Gov)
✉ 1201 Connecticut Avenue NW, Washington, D.C. 20036, USA.
☎ +1 202 4576900. 🖷 +1 202 4576992.
E: afghan@rferl.org **W:** www.azadiradio.org; pa.azadiradio.org (Pashto); da.azadiradio.org (Dari)
Webcast: D/L/P
✉ Vinohradská 159A, 100 00 Prague 10, Czech Republic. (Studio)
☎ +420 2 21122370. 🖷 +420 2 21123245.
L.P: Dir: Hashem Mohmand.
MW/SW: Via txs provided by IBB, plus other relays.
FM/DAB: See National Radio section. (Afghanistan)
SAT: AsiaSat 3S, Eutelsat Hot Bird 13B.
kHz: *1296, 9335, 12140, 19010*

Winter Schedule 2012/2013

Dari	Days	Area	kHz
0300-0330	daily	AFG	1296kab, 9335kwt, 12140kwt
0430-0530	daily	AFG	1296kab, 12140kwt, 19010kwt
0630-0730	daily	AFG	1296kab, 12140kwt, 19010kwt
0830-0930	daily	AFG	1296kab, 12140kwt, 19010kwt
1030-1130	daily	AFG	1296kab, 12140kwt, 19010kwt
1230-1330	daily	AFG	1296kab, 9335kwt, 12140kwt
1400-1430	daily	AFG	1296kab, 9335kwt, 12140kwt

Pashto	Days	Area	kHz
0230-0300	daily	AFG	1296kab, 9335kwt, 12140kwt
0330-0430	daily	AFG	1296kab, 9335kwt, 12140kwt
0530-0630	daily	AFG	1296kab, 12140kwt, 19010kwt
0730-0830	daily	AFG	1296kab, 12140kwt, 19010kwt
0930-1030	daily	AFG	1296kab, 12140kwt, 19010kwt
1130-1230	daily	AFG	1296kab, 9335kwt, 12140kwt
1330-1400	daily	AFG	1296kab, 9335kwt, 12140kwt

Ann: Dari: "Inja Radyoi Azadi"; Pashto: "Da Azadi Radyo".
V: QSL-card.
Notes: BBG funded station for listeners in Afghanistan, launched in January 2001. Produced in the RFE/RL studios in Prague, Czech Republic.

BBG – RADIO FREE ASIA (RFA) (Gov)
✉ 2025 M Street NW, Suite 300, Washington, D.C. 20036, USA.
☎ +1 202 5304900. 🖷 +1 202 5307794.
E: contact@rfa.org; info@rfa.org **W:** www.rfa.org
Webcast: D/L/P
L.P: Chmn: Michael P. Meehan; Pres: Libby Liu; Dir, Programme & Ops
Support: A.J. Janitschek; Dir, Communications & External Relations:
John A. Estrella.
MW/SW: Via txs provided by IBB, plus other relays.
SAT: NSS 12, Telstar 18.
kHz: 648, 1098, 1503, 5810, 5825, 5840, 5855, 5860, 6005, 6010, 6020, 6025, 6095, 7210, 7250, 7310, 7355, 7385, 7415, 7445, 7460, 7470, 7480, 7495, 7540, 7550, 9325, 9350, 9355, 9385, 9400, 9455, 9480, 9585, 9605, 9645, 9670, 9690, 9700, 9725, 9780, 9790, 9825, 9835, 9875, 9905, 9940, 9955, 11545, 11585, 11590, 11605, 11695, 11775, 11790, 11795, 11850, 11905, 11945, 11965, 11975, 11980, 11995, 12035, 12085, 12105, 12115, 12130, 13620, 13625, 13710, 13725, 13735, 13765, 15120, 15140, 15150, 15160, 15170, 15375, 15520, 15550, 15610, 15665, 15690, 15700, 17515, 17675, 17730, 17770, 17805, 17810, 17835, 17880, 21540, 21610, 21695, 21700, 21710, 21745, 21755, 21765, 21775, 21785

Winter Schedule 2012/2013

Burmese	Days	Area	kHz
0030-0130	daily	SEA	12115tin, 15700tin, 17835tin
1230-1330	daily	SEA	11795tin
1230-1400	daily	SEA	13735tin
1230-1430	daily	SEA	12105ira
1330-1400	daily	SEA	11795ira
1400-1430	daily	SEA	11795kwt
1630-1730	daily	SEA	9940tin

Cantonese	Days	Area	kHz
1400-1500	daily	CHN	6025tin, 7470tin
2200-2300	daily	CHN	7250tin, 9780sai, 11775tin

Chinese	Days	Area	kHz
0300-0400	.....ss	CHN	21755tin
0300-0400	m......	CHN	21765tin
0300-0400	.t.....	CHN	21775tin
0300-0400	..w....	CHN	21785tin
0300-0400	...f...	CHN	21710tin
0300-0400	.....s.	CHN	21745tin
0300-0400	...t...	CHN	21700tin
0300-0700	..w....	CHN	11980tin
0300-0700	daily	CHN	13710tin, 15665sai, 17880tin, 21540tin
0300-0700	mt.tfss	CHN	11980dsb
0400-0500	..w....	CHN	21700tin
0400-0500	.....s.	CHN	21755tin
0400-0500	m......	CHN	21775tin
0400-0500	.t.....	CHN	21785tin
0400-0500	.....ss	CHN	21765tin
0400-0500	...f...	CHN	21745tin
0400-0500	...t...	CHN	21710tin
0500-0600	..w....	CHN	21710tin
0500-0600	.t.....	CHN	21700tin
0500-0600	...t...	CHN	21745tin
0500-0600	...f...	CHN	21755tin
0500-0600	.....ss	CHN	21775tin
0500-0600	.....s.	CHN	21765tin
0500-0600	m......	CHN	21785tin
0600-0700	daily	CHN	15150tin
1500-1600	daily	CHN	6025tin, 9790sai
1500-1700	daily	CHN	9605sai, 13725tin
1500-1800	daily	CHN	9905hbn
1500-1900	daily	CHN	7445tin
1500-2200	daily	CHN	11945dsb
1600-1800	daily	CHN	6020tin
1600-1900	daily	CHN	7415tin
1600-2200	daily	CHN	9455sai
1700-1900	daily	CHN	11965tin
1700-2200	daily	CHN	9355sai
1800-2000	daily	CHN	7385kou, 9905tin, 11790sai

Chinese	Days	Area	kHz
1800-2200	daily	CHN	6025tin
1900-2100	daily	CHN	5860tin
1900-2200	daily	CHN	1098kou, 6095tin, 9875hbn
2000-2200	daily	CHN	7355kou, 7495tin
2300-2400	daily	CHN	7540dsb, 9585sai, 9825tin, 11775tin, 11975sai, 15550tin

Khmer	Days	Area	kHz
1230-1330	daily	SEA	13765ira, 15160tin
2230-2330	daily	SEA	5840tin, 11850ira

Korean	Days	Area	kHz
1500-1700	daily	KRE	7210irk, 11585tin
1500-1900	daily	KRE	648vld, 5855tin
1700-1900	daily	KRE	9385ira
2100-2200	daily	KRE	648vld, 7460uba, 9385tin, 11995tin

Lao	Days	Area	kHz
0000-0100	daily	LAO	15690tin, 17770sai
1100-1130	daily	LAO	15120ira
1100-1200	daily	LAO	9325ira
1130-1200	daily	LAO	15120sai

Tibetan	Days	Area	kHz
0100-0200	daily	CHN	13620kwt, 15610tin
0100-0300	daily	CHN	9670dsb, 11695dha, 17730uba
0200-0300	daily	CHN	9700kwt, 15520tin
0600-0700	daily	CHN	17515dsb, 17675kwt, 21610tin, 21695dha
1000-1100	....f..	CHN	17810bib
1000-1100	daily	CHN	9690sit, 15140lam
1100-1200	daily	CHN	11545tin, 15375dha
1100-1400	daily	CHN	7470uba, 9350dsb
1200-1400	daily	CHN	11590kwt, 13625tin, 15375dsb
1500-1600	daily	CHN	5825dsb, 9955tin, 11905dha, 12085kwt
2200-2300	daily	CHN	6005tin, 9835lam
2200-2400	daily	CHN	7470dsb
2300-2400	daily	CHN	6010dha, 7550kwt, 9875sit

Uyghur	Days	Area	kHz
0100-0200	daily	CHN	7480dsb, 9480kwt, 9645dha, 9690dha, 17805tin
1600-1700	daily	CHN	5810dsb, 7310ira, 9725dha, 12035sai

Vietnamese	Days	Area	kHz
0000-0030	daily	VTN	11965tin
1400-1430	daily	VTN	1503fan
1400-1500	daily	VTN	9400tin, 11605tsh, 12130ira, 13735ira
2300-2400	daily	VTN	1503fan
2330-0030	daily	VTN	11605tsh, 15170tin
2330-2400	daily	VTN	11965tin

Ann: At the start of the transmission period on each frequency in English: "This is Radio Free Asia. The following program is in ...".
V: QSL-card. (Rpt to 'Reception Reports', Radio Free Asia, 2025 M. Street NW, Washington, DC 20036, USA. Email: qsl@rfa.org or www.techweb.rfa.org)
Notes: BBG funded station, launched in September 1996 and aimed at listeners in East & South East Asia. Transmissions are jammed in parts of the target area. Burmese language prgr includes segments in Arakanese, Chin Kachin, Karen, Karenni, Mon and Shan.

BBG – RADIO FREE EUROPE/RADIO LIBERTY (RFE/RL) (Gov)
✉ 1201 Connecticut Avenue NW, Washington, D.C. 20036, USA. (Corporate Office)
☎ +1 202 4576900. 🖷 +1 202 4576992.
E: zvanersm@rferl.org **W:** www.rferl.org
Webcast: D/L Web-only languages (some of which may also be broadcast on local FM affiliate stns): Albanian (Kosovo), Armenian,

Bosnian, Georgian, Macedonian, Montenegrin, Serbian, Ukrainian. ✉ Vinohradská 159A, 100 00 Prague 10, Czech Republic. (HQ/Studios)
☎ +420 2 21121111. 🖷 +420 2 21123013.
E: knappj@rferl.org **W:** Most language services have own dedicated websites, see www.rferl.org for details.
L.P: Pres/CEO: Steven Korn; Associate Dir of Communications (Washington, D.C.): Martins Zvaners; Deputy Dir of Communications (Prague): Julian Knapp.
MW/SW: Via txs provided by IBB, plus other relays.
SAT: AsiaSat 2, Hot Bird 3, Intelsat 907, NSS 703.
kHz: 612, 864, 5820, 5885, 5895, 5930, 5945, 5975, 5995, 6060, 6075, 6105, 6120, 6135, 7215, 7220, 7225, 7235, 7260, 7275, 7390, 7400, 7425, 7430, 7470, 7480, 7485, 7550, 9360, 9405, 9445, 9515, 9520, 9535, 9540, 9585, 9595, 9680, 9695, 9760, 9790, 11610, 11705, 11775, 11790, 11795, 11850, 11870, 11890, 11975, 11990, 11995, 12015, 12025, 12060, 13645, 13775, 13790, 15130, 15205, 15265, 15525, 15530, 15650, 17735, 17770

Winter Schedule 2012/2013

Avar	Days	Area	kHz
0300-0320	daily	Cau	5975bib, 5995kwt
1500-1520	daily	Cau	11775lam, 13775nau

Azeri	Days	Area	kHz
1600-1700	daily	Cau,ME	7480ira, 11610lam

Belarusian	Days	Area	kHz
0300-0400	daily	BLR	6075smg
0300-0500	daily	BLR	612vln, 6105wer
0400-0500	daily	BLR	6075wer
1500-1700	daily	BLR	6120wer, 11890wof
1500-2100	daily	BLR	612vln
1700-1800	daily	BLR	9515lam
1700-2100	daily	BLR	5930bib
1800-1900	daily	BLR	9515smg
1900-2100	daily	BLR	5895lam

Chechen	Days	Area	kHz
0320-0340	daily	Cau	5975bib, 5995kwt
1520-1540	daily	Cau	11775lam, 13775nau

Circassian	Days	Area	kHz
0340-0400	daily	Cau	5975bib, 5995kwt
1540-1600	daily	Cau	11775lam, 13775nau

Kazakh	Days	Area	kHz
0100-0200	daily	KAZ	7235lam, 9790udo
1300-1400	daily	KAZ	12025bib, 15525lam

Kyrgyz	Days	Area	kHz
1200-1230	daily	KGZ	11990udo, 15265wer, 17735ira
1500-1530	daily	KGZ	7485udo, 11790wer

Moldovan (Romanian)	Days	Area	kHz
0500-0530	mtwtf..	MDA	5945bib
1600-1630	.....ss	MDA	9760bib
1700-1730	mtwtf..	MDA	7430bib
1900-1930	mtwtf..	MDA	6135bib

Russian	Days	Area	kHz
0300-0400	daily	RUS	9520bib
0300-0700	daily	RUS	7425lam, 17770udo
0400-0500	daily	RUS	9520kwt
0500-0600	daily	RUS	9520bib
0600-0700	daily	RUS	15205pht
0800-1000	daily	RUS	9360pht, 11705bib
1200-1400	daily	RUS	9360sai
1200-1600	daily	RUS	15130lam
1400-1500	daily	RUS	11995bib
1400-1600	daily	RUS	9515bib
1600-1700	daily	RUS	5930lam, 12060bib
1600-1800	daily	RUS	11850bib
1700-1800	daily	Cau	5885udo*, 9585wer*
1700-1800	daily	RUS	9405lam, 9540bib
1800-1900	daily	RUS	7220lam
1800-2000	daily	RUS	9405wof
1900-2000	daily	RUS	7235lam
2000-2100	daily	RUS	5885udo, 7235kwt

Tajik	Days	Area	kHz
0100-0300	daily	CAs	7275lam
0100-0400	daily	CAs	11795udo
0300-0400	daily	CAs	15530pht
1400-1500	daily	CAs	7215udo
1400-1600	daily	CAs	11975lam
1500-1600	daily	CAs	7260udo
1600-1700	daily	CAs	9445wer, 9695lam

Tatar-Bashkir	Days	Area	kHz
0300-0400	daily	CAs,RUS	7235bib, 7400lam
0500-0600	daily	CAs,RUS	9535kwt
1500-1600	daily	CAs,RUS	9445bib, 11870bib
1900-2000	daily	CAs,RUS	7470ira

Turkmen	Days	Area	kHz
0200-0300	daily	CAs	864erv
0200-0400	daily	CAs	7390lam, 12015udo
1400-1500	daily	CAs	12025bib
1400-1600	daily	CAs	6060wkt
1500-1600	daily	CAs	12025wof
1530-1600	daily	CAs	864erv
1600-1800	daily	CAs	5820udo, 7225kwt

Uzbek	Days	Area	kHz
0200-0300	daily	CAs	9680ira, 12025udo
0200-0400	daily	CAs	15650udo
0300-0400	daily	CAs	12025kwt, 13790pht
1400-1500	daily	CAs	9595wer, 13645wer, 15265lam
1500-1530	daily	CAs	864erv
1600-1700	daily	CAs	7550kwt, 9540lam, 11975lam

Key: * Special service for Caucasus: "Ekho Kavkaza" ("Echo of the Caucasus").
Ann: Radio Free Europe: Romanian (Moldovan) to Moldova: "Europa Libera"; Radio Liberty: Belarusian: "Havoryc Radyjo Svaboda"; Kazakh: "Azattyq Radiosinan sövlep turmiz"; Kyrgyz: "Azattiq Radioyosinan söylöbüz"; Russian: "Govorit Radio Svoboda"; Tajik: "Injo Radioi Ozodi"; Tatar: "Azatliq Radiosi söyli"; Turkmen: "Gepleýär Azatlyk Radiosy"; Uzbek: "Ozodlik Radiosidan gapiramiz".
V: QSL-card.
Notes: BBG funded station for listeners in Eastern Europe and the successor states to the former USSR. Radio Free Europe (launched 1949, targeting Eastern Europe incl. prgrs in Baltic languages) and Radio Liberty (launched 1953, targeting the USSR) merged into a single broadcaster, RFE/RL, in 1976. Since the 1990s, the task of RFE/RL has been expanded to produce services targeting the Middle East and Afghanistan, see BBG-Radio Farda, BBG-Radio Free Afghanistan, BBG-Radio Free Iraq, BBG-Radio Mashaal. The following schedule lists Russian language segments that are broadcast within other language transmissions: Azeri: 1635-1700 Sat (in summer, schedule one hour earlier); Kazakh: 1335-1400 Sun, 0135-0200 Mon; Kyrgyz: 1500-1530 Sun; Tajik: 1635-1700 Sun; Turkmen: 1435-1500, 1535-1600, 1635-1700, 1735-1800 Sun, 0235-0300, 0335-0400 Mon; Uzbek: 1435-1500, 1635-1700 Sat, 0235-0300, 0335-0400 Sun.

BBG – RADIO FREE IRAQ (Gov)
✉ 1201 Connecticut Avenue NW, Washington, D.C. 20036, USA.
☎ +1 202 4576900. 🖷 +1 202 4576992.
E: iraq@rferl.org **W:** www.iraqhurr.org
Webcast: D/L/P
✉ Vinohradská 159A, 100 00 Prague 10, Czech Republic. (Studio)
☎ +420 2 21121111. 🖷 +420 2 21123013.
L.P: Dir: Sergei Danilochkin.
MW: Via tx provided by IBB.
SAT: Eutelsat Hot Bird 13B.
kHz: 1593

Winter Schedule 2012/2013

Arabic	Days	Area	kHz
0200-0700	daily	IRQ	1593kwt
1500-1530	daily	IRQ	1593kwt
1830-2000	daily	IRQ	1593kwt
2100-2300	daily	IRQ	1593kwt

Ann: Arabic: "Idha'at al-Iraq al-hurrah".
V: QSL-card.
Notes: BBG funded station for listeners in Iraq, launched in October 1998. Produced in the RFE/RL studios in Prague, Czech Republic. 24h on satellite and Internet.

BBG – RADIO MARTÍ (Gov)

P.O. Box 521868, 2200 NW 72 Avenida, Miami, FL 33152-9998, USA.
☎ +1 305 4377000. 📠 +1 305 4377016.
E: info@martinoticias.com W: www.martinoticias.com
Webcast: L
L.P: Dir: Carlos A García-Pérez.
MW/SW: Via txs provided by IBB, plus other relays.
SAT: Hispasat 1C, NSS 806.
kHz: 1180, 5745, 5980, 6030, 7365, 7405, 9565, 9805, 9825, 11930, 13820, 15330

Winter Schedule 2012/2013

Spanish	Days	Area	kHz
0000-0300	daily	CUB	7365grv, 9825grv
0000-2400	daily	CUB	1180mth
0300-0500	.twtfss	CUB	7365grv
0300-0700	.twtfss	CUB	7405grv
0300-0900	.twtfss	CUB	6030grv
0700-0900	.twtfss	CUB	5980grv
0900-1200	daily	CUB	6030grv
0900-1300	daily	CUB	5980grv
1100-1300	daily	CUB	9805grv
1200-1400	daily	CUB	7405grv
1300-1400	daily	CUB	5745grv
1300-2200	daily	CUB	11930grv
1400-2000	daily	CUB	15330grv
1400-2200	daily	CUB	13820grv
2000-2400	daily	CUB	9565grv
2200-0300	daily	CUB	6030grv
2200-2400	daily	CUB	7405grv

Ann: Spanish: "Radio Martí, retransmitiendo para Cuba desde Miami, Estados Unidos de America".
V: QSL-card.
Notes: BBG funded station for listeners in Cuba, launched in May 1985. Produced in the studios of Office of Cuba Broadcasting. Jammed.

BBG – RADIO MASHAAL (Gov)

1201 Connecticut Avenue NW, Washington, D.C. 20036, USA.
☎ +1 202 4576900. 📠 +1 202 4576992.
E: mashaalradio@rferl.org W: www.mashaalradio.com; www.mashaalradio.org
Webcast: L/D/P
Vinohradská 159A, 100 00 Prague 10, Czech Republic. (Studio)
☎ +420 2 21121111. 📠 +420 2 21123013.
L.P: Dir: Amanullah Ghilzai.
MW/SW: Via txs provided by IBB, plus other relays.
FM/DAB: See National Radio section. (Afghanistan)
SAT: Eutelsat Hot Bird 13B.
kHz: 621, 12130, 13580, 13700, 15760

Winter Schedule 2012/2013

Pashto	Days	Area	kHz
0400-0500	daily	WAs	12130udo, 13580ira
0400-1300	daily	WAs	621kho, 15760ira
0500-0700	daily	WAs	12130lam
0500-0900	daily	WAs	13580nau
0700-0800	daily	WAs	12130udo
0800-1300	daily	WAs	12130kwt
0900-1100	daily	WAs	13580udo
1100-1300	daily	WAs	13700ira

Ann: Pashto: "Daa Mashaal Radyo".
V: QSL-card.
Notes: BBG funded service of RFE/FL for Pashto speaking listeners in the Pakistani border region with Afghanistan. 24h on satellite and Internet. Radio Mashaal was launched on 15 January 2010 in order to counter the growing number of Islamic extremist radio stations in the region.

BBG – RADIO SAWA (Gov)

7600 Boston Boulevard, Springfield, VA 22153, USA.
☎ +1 703 6885200. 📠 +1 703 6885255.
E: comments@radiosawa.com W: www.radiosawa.com
Webcast: L
L.P: Managing Editor: Maha Rabie.
MW: Via txs provided by IBB, plus other relays.

SAT: Badr 4, Eutelsat Hot Bird 13B, Intelsat 907, Nilesat 101, NSS 12.
kHz: 990, 1170, 1431, 1548

Winter Schedule 2012/2013

Arabic	Days	Area	kHz
0000-2400	daily	ME,NAf	990cgr
0000-2400	daily	ME	1170dha, 1548kwt
1645-0400	daily	NAf	1431dji

Ann: Arabic: "Radio Sawa".
V: QSL-card.
Notes: BBG funded station for young Arab listeners in the Middle East & North Africa, launched on 23 March 2002. Produced in the studios of Middle East Broadcasting Network, Inc. 24h on satellite, FM, Internet.

BBG – VOA ASHNA RADIO (Gov)

Room 3200, 330 Independence Avenue SW, Washington, D.C. 20237, USA.
☎ +1 202 6193136 (Dari); +1 202 0327619. (Pashto) 📠 +1 202 3825193 (Dari); +1 202 2125260. (Pashto)
E: dari@voanews.com (Dari); pashto@voanews.com (Pashto)
W: www.darivoa.com; www.pashtovoa.com
Webcast: D/L/P
L.P: Chief (VOA Afghanistan Service): Beth Mendelson.
MW/SW: Via txs provided by IBB, plus other relays.
FM/DAB: See National Radio section. (Afghanistan)
kHz: 1296, 5810, 5925, 7560, 9335, 9440, 9770, 9975, 12140, 13830

Winter Schedule 2012/2013

Dari	Days	Area	kHz
0130-0230	daily	WAs	1296kab, 7560ira, 9335kwt
1530-1630	daily	WAs	1296kab, 9770wer, 9975kwt, 12140kwt
1730-1830	daily	WAs	1296kab, 5810kwt, 7560udo, 9440udo
1930-2030	daily	WAs	1296kab, 5810kwt, 7560kwt

Pashto	Days	Area	kHz
0030-0130	daily	WAs	1296kab, 5925ira, 7560kwt
1430-1530	daily	WAs	1296kab, 9335kwt, 12140kwt, 13830ira
1630-1730	daily	WAs	1296kab, 9770wer, 9975kwt, 12140kwt
1830-1930	daily	WAs	1296kab, 5810kwt, 7560udo

Ann: Dari: "In Radyoi Ashna"; Pashto: "Da VOA Ashna Radyo".
V: QSL-card.
Notes: BBG funded service for listeners in Afghanistan, launched April 2004. Produced in the VOA studios.

BBG – VOA DEEWA RADIO (Gov)

330 Independence Avenue SW, Washington, D.C. 20237, USA.
☎ +1 202 2050403. 📠 +1 202 3825218.
E: deewaradio@voanews.com W: www.voadeewaradio.com; www.voanews.com/deewa/news
Webcast: D/L
L.P: Managing Editor: Nafees Talkar.
MW/SW: Via txs provided by IBB, plus other relays.
FM/DAB: See National Radio section. (Afghanistan)
SAT: AsiaSat 3S, Eutelsat Hot Bird 13B.
kHz: 621, 5835, 7455, 7495, 9370, 9565, 9955, 11895

Winter Schedule 2012/2013

Pashto	Days	Area	kHz
0100-0400	daily	WAs	621kho, 9370ira, 9955udo, 11895ira
1300-1400	daily	WAs	7455ira, 9370bib, 9565udo
1300-1900	daily	WAs	621kho, 7495udo
1400-1500	daily	WAs	9565wer
1400-1800	daily	WAs	7455udo
1400-1900	daily	WAs	9370pht
1500-1900	daily	WAs	5835ira
1800-1900	daily	WAs	7455kwt

Ann: Pashto: "Deewa Radio".
V: QSL-card.

Notes: BBG funded service for Pashto speaking listeners in the Afghanistan-Pakistan border area. Launched 29 September 2006. Produced in the VOA studios.

BBG – VOA RADIO AAP KI DUNYAA (Gov)
☒ 330 Independence Avenue SW, Washington, D.C. 20237, USA.
☎ +1 202 6191933. ▤ +1 202 6190339.
E: urdu@voanews.com **W:** www.urduvoa.com
Webcast: D/L/P
L.P: Chief (VOA Urdu Service): Brian Q. Silver.
MW/SW: Via txs provided by IBB, plus other relays.
kHz: 972, 1539, 7460, 7480, 11675, 12020

Winter Schedule 2012/2013			
Urdu	**Days**	**Area**	**kHz**
0100-0200	daily	ME	7460ira, 12020kwt
1400-0200	daily	ME	972dsb, 1539dha
1400-1500	daily	ME	7480ira, 11675ira

Ann: Urdu: "Radyo Aap Ki Dunyaa".
V: QSL-card.
Notes: BBG funded station for listeners in Pakistan, launched May 2004. Produced in the VOA studios. Between 1900-0100 a trilingual service is carried, consisting of VOA news in English, VOA R. Aap Ki Dunya in Urdu and VOA Deewa R. in Pashto.

BBG – VOA STUDIO 7 (Gov)
☒ Voice of America, Africa Division, 330 Independence Avenue SW, Washington, D.C. 20237, USA.
☎ +1 202 2059942. (Then select #11) ▤ +1 202 2034230.
E: studio7@voanews.com **W:** www.voanews.com/zimbabwe
Webcast: D/P
MW/SW: Via txs provided by IBB, plus other relays.
kHz: 909, 4930, 12080, 15775

Winter Schedule 2012/2013			
English	**Days**	**Area**	**kHz**
1720-1740	.....ss	ZWE	909bot, 4930bot, 12080sao, 15775sao
1730-1800	mtwt...	ZWE	909bot, 4930bot, 12080sao, 15775sao
English/Ndebele/			
Shona	**Days**	**Area**	**kHz**
1800-1830	...f..	ZWE	909bot, 4930bot, 12080sao, 15775sao
1830-1900	mtwtf..	ZWE	909bot, 12080sao, 15775sao
Ndebele	**Days**	**Area**	**kHz**
1730-1800	...f..	ZWE	909bot, 4930bot, 12080sao, 15775sao
1740-1800	.....ss	ZWE	909bot, 4930bot, 12080sao, 15775sao
1800-1830	mtwt...	ZWE	909bot, 4930bot, 12080sao, 15775sao
Shona	**Days**	**Area**	**kHz**
1700-1720	.....ss	ZWE	909bot, 4930bot, 12080sao, 15775sao
1700-1730	mtwtf..	ZWE	909bot, 4930bot, 12080sao, 15775sao

Ann: English: "You're listening to Studio 7 for Zimbabwe, coming to you live from the Voice of America in Washington".
V: QSL-card.
Notes: BBG funded station for listeners in Zimbabwe, launched in April 2003. Produced in the VOA studios.

BBG – VOICE OF AMERICA (VOA) (Gov)
☒ 330 Independence Avenue SW, Washington, D.C. 20237, USA.
☎ +1 202 2034959. (Public Relations) ▤ +1 202 2034960.
E: askvoa@voanews.com **W:** www.voanews.com
Webcast: D/L/P. Web only languages (some of which may also be broadcast on local FM affiliate stns): Armenian, Bosnian, Creole, Greek, Indonesian, Macedonian, Russian, Serbian, Thai, Turkish, Ukrainian.
L.P: Dir: David Ensor; Chief of Staff: Barbara Brady; Associate Dir, Operations: Mark L. Prahl.
MW/SW: Via txs provided by IBB, plus other relays.
SAT: AsiaSat 3S, Eutelsat Hot Bird 13B, Intelsat 7, Nilesat 101, NSS 12/806, SES 7, Superbird C2, Telstar 12.
kHz: 648, 909, 1170, 1188, 1296, 1431, 1530, 1575, 1593, 4930, 4940, 4960, 5820, 5830, 5835, 5885, 5890, 5895, 5945, 5955, 5960, 5980, 6020, 6035, 6045, 6060, 6080, 6100, 6105, 6140, 6170, 7235, 7255, 7260, 7275, 7290, 7295, 7315, 7365, 7390, 7405, 7425, 7430, 7440, 7460, 7465, 7480, 7495, 7520, 7530, 7560, 7570, 7575, 9315, 9320, 9325, 9355, 9390, 9395, 9400, 9435, 9445, 9480, 9485, 9490, 9495, 9515, 9530, 9545, 9550, 9570, 9585, 9595, 9640, 9645, 9655, 9670, 9680, 9690, 9705, 9715, 9755, 9760, 9775, 9780, 9790, 9800, 9810, 9815, 9825, 9860, 9875, 9880, 9885, 9930, 9945, 11560, 11635, 11640, 11695, 11705, 11720, 11750, 11775, 11820, 11840, 11855, 11860, 11880, 11885, 11905, 11915, 11920, 11925, 11965, 11990, 12000, 12005, 12045, 12060, 12070, 12080, 12120, 12150, 13570, 13580, 13625, 13650, 13735, 13740, 13750, 13755, 13765, 15110, 15115, 15125, 15155, 15205, 15225, 15265, 15290, 15385, 15460, 15470, 15555, 15560, 15580, 15590, 15620, 15670, 17530, 17645, 17655, 17680, 17725, 17780, 17850, 17860, 17895, 21570, 21590

Winter Schedule 2012/2013			
Albanian	**Days**	**Area**	**kHz**
0600-0630	daily	Eu	5945bib
1700-1730	daily	Eu	5955bib
1930-2000	daily	Eu	5885bib
Amharic	**Days**	**Area**	**kHz**
1600-1630	mtwtf..	EAf	1431dji
1800-1900	daily	EAf	9320ira, 9485nau, 9860mey, 11905kwt, 13625wer
Azeri	**Days**	**Area**	**kHz**
1830-1900	daily	Cau,ME	7315bib, 9435wer, 9595ira
Bengali	**Days**	**Area**	**kHz**
1600-1700	daily	SAs	1575pph, 7405udo, 9490pht
Burmese	**Days**	**Area**	**kHz**
0000-0030	daily	SEA	1575bph, 9325pht
0130-0300	daily	SEA	12120udo, 15115pht, 17780pht
1130-1230	daily	SEA	11965pht, 15555pht, 17850ira
1430-1500	daily	SEA	1575bph
1430-1530	daily	SEA	11965pht, 12120pht
1430-1630	daily	SEA	9355pht
1530-1600	daily	SEA	1575bph
1530-1630	daily	SEA	1150Upht
2300-0030	daily	SEA	7430ira, 12120pht
2300-2400	daily	SEA	9325pht
Cantonese	**Days**	**Area**	**kHz**
1300-1500	daily	EAs	1170php, 7390pht, 9705sai
Chinese	**Days**	**Area**	**kHz**
0000-0100	daily	EAs	7495udo, 9545udo, 11925pht, 15125sai, 15385pht, 17645pht
0900-1000	daily	EAs	11855udo
0900-1100	daily	EAs	9880pht, 12120udo, 13765udo, 21590pht
0900-1200	daily	EAs	11720dsb, 13650tin, 15670udo
1000-1400	daily	EAs	9530pht
1100-1200	daily	EAs	9825sai
1100-1300	daily	EAs	12045pht
1200-1300	daily	EAs	15110pht
1200-1400	daily	EAs	6045udo, 11635udo
1200-1500	daily	EAs	9825pht
1300-1400	daily	EAs	9390pht, 12045sai
1300-1500	daily	EAs	7295nvs
1400-1500	daily	EAs	6105dsb, 9390tin, 9490pht, 9550pht
2200-2300	daily	EAs	6045udo, 7440udo, 9545pht, 9755udo, 9875udo, 11925pht
English	**Days**	**Area**	**kHz**
0030-0100	daily	EAs	9490pht, 11695pht, 15290pht
0030-0100	daily	SAs	6170kwt, 9325udo
0030-0100	daily	SAs,SEA	12005pht, 15155pht

English	Days	Area	kHz
0030-0100	daily	SEA	1575bph, 9715udo, 15205pht
0100-0200	daily	SAs	9435udo, 11705udo, 15155pht
0130-0200	.twtfs.	LAm	5960grv, 7465grv
0300-0430	daily	Af	1530sao, 9885bot
0300-0500	daily	Af	15580sao
0300-0600	daily	Af	4930bot
0300-0700	daily	Af	909bot, 6080sao
0400-0500	daily	Af	4960sao
0430-0600	daily	Af	9885sao
0500-0630	daily	EAf,SAf	15580bot
0600-0700	daily	Af	1530sao, 9885mey
0630-0700	daily	EAf,SAf	15580sao
1100-1200	.....ss	SEA	1575bph
1200-1300	daily	EAs	7520ira, 11750pht, 12150udo
1200-1300	daily	SEA	1170php, 9640pht
1300-1400	.....ss	EAs	7520pht, 12150udo
1300-1400	.....ss	SEA	9640pht, 11750pht
1400-1500	daily	Af	15580mey, 17530sao, 17725sao
1400-1500	mtwtf..	SAs	7520udo, 9760udo, 12150pht
1400-1530	daily	Af	6080sao
1400-1700	daily	Af	4930bot
1500-1600	daily	Af	15580ira, 17725bot, 17895sao
1500-1600	daily	EAs	6140udo, 9945ira
1500-1600	daily	ME	11840lam, 13570lam
1500-1600	daily	SAs	7520udo, 9930ira, 12150ira
1500-1600	daily	SAs,SEA	7575pht
1500-1600	daily	SEA	9760pht
1530-1700	daily	Af	6080mey
1600-1700	daily	Af	909bot, 1530sao, 9395ira, 13755sao, 15470lam, 15580sao, 17895wer
1600-1700	mtwtf..	SEA	1170php
1630-1700	mtwtf..	Af	9790bot**, 11905wer**, 13625wer**
1700-1800	daily	Af	13755bot, 17895smg
1700-1800	daily	EAf	15580smg
1700-2200	daily	Af	6080sao
1800-1830	.....ss	SAf	4930bot
1800-1830	daily	Af	15580sao
1800-1900	.....ss	Af	909bot
1800-1900	daily	Af	13755ira
1830-2000	daily	Af	15580bot
1830-2100	daily	Af	4930bot
1900-2000	daily	ME	7480udo, 9515lam
1900-2030	daily	Af	4940sao
1900-2100	daily	Af	909bot
2000-2100	daily	Af	15580grv
2000-2100	mtwtf..	ME	7480lam, 9480lam
2000-2200	daily	Af	1530sao
2030-0030	daily	AFG	1296kab*, 7560kwt*
2030-2100	.....ss	Af	4940sao
2100-2200	daily	Af	15580bot
2200-2300	mtwt..s	SEA	5895pht
2200-2300	mtwt..s	EAs	7365kwt, 7425kwt, 7480pht, 11860sai
2230-2300	daily	EAs	7460udo, 9570ira
2230-2400	....fs.	SEA	1575bph
2230-2400	daily	EAs	5820udo
2300-0200	daily	ME	1593kwt
2300-2400	daily	SEA	5830pht, 5895pht, 7460pht

English	Days	Area	kHz
2300-2400	daily	EAs	7365pht, 7480pht, 9490pht, 11840pht, 11860sai

French	Days	Area	kHz
0530-0600	mtwtf..	Af	1530sao
0530-0630	mtwtf..	Af	4960sao, 6020bot, 9480sao, 12060bot
1100-1130	.....s.	Af	11915sao, 13735sao, 15620sao, 17850smg
1830-1900	daily	Af	15620grv
1830-2000	daily	Af	1530sao
1830-2030	daily	Af	15225grv
1900-2030	daily	Af	12080bot
2000-2030	daily	Af	9815bot, 9885sao, 15620sao
2030-2100	.....ss	Af	9815sao, 9885bot, 12080ira, 15225bot
2100-2130	mtwtf..	Af	9435wof, 9680smg, 9815bot, 9885sao

Georgian	Days	Area	kHz
1600-1700	daily	Cau	11840wof
1600-1800	daily	Cau	11775wer
1700-1800	daily	Cau	11840lam

Hausa	Days	Area	kHz
0500-0530	daily	WAf	1530sao, 4960sao, 6020sao, 6035asc
0700-0730	daily	WAf	4960sao, 12070sao, 17680kwt
1500-1530	daily	WAf	9780sao, 11750sao, 17680bot
2030-2100	mtwtfs.	WAf	6035sao
2030-2100	.....s.	WAf	9815sao, 15225bot
2030-2100	mtwtf..	WAf	4940sao, 9690wer, 11860mey, 11885sao

Khmer	Days	Area	kHz
1330-1430	daily	SEA	1575bph, 9325pht, 11965pht
2200-2230	daily	SEA	1575bph, 6060pht, 7260pht, 9435tin

Kinyarwanda/ Kirundi	Days	Area	kHz
0330-0430	daily	CAf	7275sao, 9400bot, 9775sao
1600-1630	.....s.	CAf	12080mey, 13740sao, 15460sao

Korean	Days	Area	kHz
1200-1500	daily	EAs	1188seo, 5890tin, 7235tin, 9800pht
1900-2100	daily	EAs	648vld, 5835pht, 6060udo, 7460udo

Kurdish	Days	Area	kHz
0500-0600	daily	ME	7290bib, 9690lam, 9760nau
1400-1500	daily	ME	1593kwt, 11840lam, 11880bib, 13580wer
1700-1800	daily	ME	7480ira, 9655bib, 11820lam
2000-2100	daily	ME	1593kwt

Lao	Days	Area	kHz
1230-1300	daily	SEA	1575bph, 9810sai, 11965pht

Oromo	Days	Area	kHz
1730-1800	mtwtf..	EAf	9320ira, 9485nau, 9860wer, 11905kwt, 13625bot

Persian	Days	Area	kHz
0230-0330	daily	ME	9445bib, 9495bib

Portuguese	Days	Area	kHz
1000-1030	.....ss	Af	11915sao, 17850ira
1630-1700	....f..	Af	9880mey, 15670wer, 17655grv

Portuguese	Days	Area	kHz
1700-1800	daily	Af	1530sao, 9880bot, 15670sao, 17655grv
1800-1830	mtwtf..	Af	1530sao, 9880bot, 15670bot, 17655grv

Somali	Days	Area	kHz
0330-0400	daily	EAf	11990smg, 13580ira, 15620ira
1300-1400	daily	EAf	13580ira, 15620bot
1600-1630	.....ss	EAf	1431dji, 13580ira, 15620bot
1630-1700	daily	EAf	15620wer
1630-1800	daily	EAf	13580ira
1700-1730	daily	EAf	15620ira
1730-1800	daily	EAf	15620smg

Spanish	Days	Area	kHz
0030-0100	mtwtf..	LAm	5890grv, 9885grv, 12000grv
0100-0200	.twtfs.	LAm	5890grv, 9885grv, 12000grv
1300-1400	daily	LAm	9885grv, 13750grv, 15590grv

Swahili	Days	Area	kHz
1630-1700	daily	EAf	13740bot, 15265sao, 15460sao

Tibetan	Days	Area	kHz
0000-0100	daily	EAs	5980ira, 7255udo, 9645udo
0300-0400	daily	EAs	15560pht
0300-0600	daily	EAs	17860pht, 21570pht
0400-0600	daily	EAs	15560udo
1400-1500	daily	EAs	7255kwt, 7530pht, 9315udo, 9670lam
1600-1700	daily	EAs	7560udo, 7570pht, 11920pht

Tigrinya	Days	Area	kHz
1900-1930	mtwtf..	EAf	9320ira, 9485nau, 9860dha, 11905kwt, 13625smg

Uzbek	Days	Area	kHz
1500-1530	daily	CAs	6100udo, 9570smg, 9585lam, 11640kwt

Vietnamese	Days	Area	kHz
1300-1330	daily	SEA	1575bph
1500-1600	daily	SEA	1170php

Key: * Separate VOA English Sce for Afghanistan incl. news in Dari 0000-0005; ** Special sce for Sudan.

Ann: At the start and end of the transmission period on each frequency, English: "This is the Voice of America, Washington D.C., signing on/off". Before all foreign language programs: "This is the Voice of America. The following program is in... (language)".

V: QSL-card. (Email to: letters@voa.gov)

Notes: Launched in 1942, under the roof of the U.S. Foreign Information Service (FIS). From 1953-1994, financed by the U.S. Information Agency (USIA). BBG funded since April 1994. Some transmissions in Asian languages are jammed. Some programmes in Portuguese, directed to Angola, are from the "Vision Angola/VOA Multipress" service.

BROADCASTING BOARD OF GOVERNORS (BBG) (Gov)

⌨ 330 Independence Avenue SW, Washington, D.C. 20237, USA.
☎ +1 202 2034400. 🖹 +1 202 2034585.
E: publicaffairs@bbg.gov **W:** www.bbg.gov
L.P: Chmn: Jeff Shell; Chief Financial Officer: Maryjean Buhler.
Notes: On 1 October 1999, the Broadcasting Board of Governors (BBG) became the independent, autonomous entity responsible for all U.S. government and government sponsored, non-military, international broadcasting.

INTERNATIONAL BROADCASTING BUREAU (IBB) (Gov)

⌨ 330 Independence Avenue SW, Washington, D.C. 20237, USA.
☎ +1 202 4017000. 🖹 +1 202 6191241.
E: pubaff@ibb.gov

⌨ 3919 VOA Site B Road, Grimesland, NC 27837, USA (Edward R. Murrow Transmitting Station).
L.P: Dir: Richard M. Lobo; Deputy Dir: Jeffrey N. Trimble; Dir, Engineering/Technical Sces: André V. Mendes; Chief of Staff: Marie Skiba Lennon; SM, Edward R. Murrow Transmitting Station (Greenville): Wilfred Cooper (tbc).
MW: [MTH] Marathon Key, FL: 1180kHz 100kW.
SW: [GRV] Greenville, NC: 3 x 250, 5 x 500kW. (Three 500kW txs are currently run at 250kW)
V: QSL-card.
Notes: Under the supervision of the Broadcasting Board of Governors (BBG), the International Broadcasting Bureau (IBB) provides the administrative and engineering support for U.S. government funded non-military international broadcast services. The IBB Office of Engineering and Technical Services manages, operates, and maintains a network of domestic and overseas transmitting stations in Botswana, Djibouti, Germany, Kuwait, Philippines, Northern Mariana Islands, São Tomé, Sri Lanka, Thailand and USA.

ADVENTIST WORLD RADIO (AWR) (Rlg)

⌨ 12501 Old Columbia Pike, Silver Spring, ML 20904-6600, USA.
☎ +1 301 6806304. 🖹 +1 301 6806303.
E: info@awr.org **W:** www.awr.org
Webcast: D/L/P
L.P: Pres: Dowell W. Chow; Freq Manager: Claudius Dedio.
SAT: Eutelsat Hot Bird 13A.
Ann: English: "You're listening to Adventist World Radio, the Voice of Hope"; French: "Ici la Radio Mondiale Adventiste, la Voix de l'Esperance"; German: "Sie hören Adventist World Radio, die Stimme der Hoffnung"; Italian: "La Voce della Speranza".
IS: Various arrangements of the melody "Lift Up the Trumpet".
V: QSL-card.
Notes: AWR the international broadcast ministry of the Seventh-day Adventist Church. Produced by Adventist Broadcasting Service, Inc. which also is the owner of the SW transmitting station KSDA in Guam. For schedules, see AWR Asia/Pacific (Indonesia), AWR Africa/ Europe (United Kingdom).

CHRISTIAN SCIENCE SENTINEL (Rlg)

⌨ 1 Norway Street C04-10, Boston, MA 02115-3195, USA.
☎ +1 617 4502893. 🖹 +1 617 4502893.
E: herald@csps.com; csradio.d@gmx.de **W:** christianscience.com
Webcast: D
kHz: *5960*

Winter Schedule 2012/2013

Russian	Days	Area	kHz
1900-2000	.....s.	Eu	5960wer

Notes: Produced by the Christian Science Publishing Society (The First Church of Christ, Scientist).

ETERNAL GOOD NEWS (Rlg)

⌨ P.O. Box 5333, Edmond, OK 73083-5333, USA.
☎ +1 405 3591235.
E: gabry@cox.net
W: eternalgoodnews.info; www.oldpaths.net/works/radio/wilshire (outdated)
Webcast: D (limited archive only).
kHz: *15525*

Winter Schedule 2012/2013

English	Days	Area	kHz
1130-1145	....f..	As	15525dha

V: QSL-letter.
Notes: Produced by the religious organisation "Eternal Good News".

FAMILY RADIO (Rlg)

⌨ 290 Hegenberger Rd., Oakland, CA 94621, USA. (HQ/Studios)
☎ +1 510 5686200. 🖹 +1 510 6337983.
E: international@familyradio.com; info@familyradio.org
W: www.familyradio.com
Webcast: D/L
⌨ 10400 NW 240th Street, Okeechobee, FL 34972, USA. (Transmitting Station)
☎ +1 863 7630281. 🖹 +1 863 7631034.
L.P: Pres: Vacant; International Mgr: David Hoff.
SW: [YFR] Okeechobee, FL (WYFR): 2 x 50, 12 x 100kW & via leased foreign relays.
SAT: Eutelsat 7WA/28A, Yamal 201.
kHz: *1197, 5985, 6115, 6220, 6240, 7540, 9280, 11520, 11825, 11885, 13695, 17575*

Winter Schedule 2012/2013

Burmese	Days	Area	kHz
1100-1200	daily	SEA	6220huw

Chinese	Days	Area	kHz
1100-1300	daily	CHN	6240pao, 9280pao

English	Days	Area	kHz
1600-1900	daily	SAf	1197msu
2000-2300	daily	SAf	1197msu
2330-0400	daily	NAm	6115yfr

Portuguese	Days	Area	kHz
2200-2300	daily	SAm	17575yfr
2300-0100	daily	SAm	11885yfr

Spanish	Days	Area	kHz
0000-0200	daily	CAm,SAm	5985yfr
0100-0200	daily	SAm	11825yfr
2300-0100	daily	SAm	13695yfr

Tagalog	Days	Area	kHz
1100-1200	daily	SEA	11520pao

Vietnamese	Days	Area	kHz
1300-1400	daily	SEA	7540tsu

Ann: English: "You are listening to Family Radio, the Sound of the New Life", "This is your Family Radio, International Broadcast Station WYFR, Okeechobee, Florida, the United States of America".
V: QSL-card.
Notes: Began International SW broadcasts in 1973. Owned by Family Stations, Inc. The callsign WYFR is used only for transmissions from the Okeechobee, FL facility.

FAR EAST BROADCASTING COMPANY INC (FEBC) (Rlg)
✉ P.O. Box 1, La Mirada, CA 90637-0001, USA.
☎ +1 562 9474651. 🖷 +1 562 9430160.
E: info@febc.org **W:** www.febc.org
Webcast: D
✉ FEBC International Ltd, 30 Lorong Ampas, #07-01 Skywaves Industrial Bldg., Singapore 328783.
☎ +65 63923154. 🖷 +65 63923156.
E: info@febcintl.org **W:** www.febcintl.org
LP: Chmn: Dr Douglas Pennoyer; Pres: Edward W. Cannon.
Notes: Far East Broadcasting Company, Inc (FEBC) is a global evangelical media enterprise. For schedules, see FEBC Philippines (Philippines), FEBC Korea (South Korea), and the associated partner FEBA Radio (United Kingdom). FEBC owns transmitting stations in several countries, incl. the Philippines and South Korea.

HCJB GLOBAL VOICE (Rlg)
✉ P.O. Box 39800, Colorado Springs, CO 80949-9800, USA.
☎ +1 719 5909800. 🖷 +1 719 5909801.
E: info@hcjb.org **W:** www.hcjb.org
LP: Pres, HCJB Global: Wayne Pederson; SM: John E. Beck; PD: Alex Saks; Frequency Mgr: Douglas Weber.
V: QSL-card.
Notes: HCJB Global Voice is the media ministry of HCJB Global, owned by World Radio Missionary Fellowship, Inc. HCJB Global owns SW transmitting stations in Australia, Ecuador and Germany.

HMONG WORLD CHRISTIAN RADIO (Rlg)
✉ P.O. Box 600402, St. Paul, MN 55105, USA.
☎ +1 651 3034386.
E: giatoulee@comcast.net; voiceofhope@comcast.net
W: www.hwcr.us
Webcast: D/L
✉ P.O. Box 132, Cottage Grove, St. Paul, MN 55106, USA.
LP: Pres: Rev. Gia Tou Lee.
kHz: 9930

Winter Schedule 2012/2013

Hmong	Days	Area	kHz
2200-2300	....f..	SEA	9930hbn

Notes: Founded August 2005. Religious prgr for Hmong speakers.

KJES RADIO (Rlg)
✉ Our Lord's Ranch, 230 High Valley Rd., Vado, NM 88072-7221, USA.
☎ +1 505 2332090. 🖷 +1 505 2333019.
E: kjesroots@gmail.com
LP: Pres: Fr Rick Thomas; GM: Michael Reuter.
SW: [JES] Vado, NM: 1 x 50kW, Reserve tx:1 x 5kW.

kHz: 7555, 11715, 15385

Winter Schedule 2012/2013

English	Days	Area	kHz
0200-0330	daily	NAm	7555jest
1400-1600	daily	NAm	11715jest
2000-2100	daily	CAm	15385jest

Spanish	Days	Area	kHz
1600-1700	daily	CAm	11715jest
1830-2000	daily	SEA,AUS	15385jest

Key: † Irregular.
Ann: English: "This is KJES Radio, broadcasting from the Lord's Ranch".
V: QSL-card. Rp.
Notes: Catholic station. Transmissions are part of a rehabilitation programme for young people. KJES ("King Jesus Eternal Savior") has been licensed since November 1992.

PAN AMERICAN BROADCASTING (Rlg)
✉ Suite 250, 7011 Koll Center Parkway, Pleasanton CA 94566-3253 USA.
☎ +1 925 4629800. 🖷 +1 925 4629808.
E: info@panambc.com
W: www.panambc.com; www.radiopanam.com
Webcast: L (unrelated to SW broadcasts)
LP: Pres: Gene Bernald.
SW: Via leased foreign relays.
kHz: 9410, 9685, 15205

Winter Schedule 2012/2013

English	Days	Area	kHz
1400-1445	......s	IND	15205wer
1415-1430	mtwtfs.	IND	15205wer
1530-1545	......s	IND	9410iss
1930-2000	......s	NAf	9685nau

V: QSL-card. Online form available.
Notes: Pan American Broadcasting, Inc sells air time for religious paid programming, broadcast via international tx providers and via its service 'Radio Africa' (see Equatorial Guinea).

RADIO PAYAM–E DOOST (Rlg)
✉ P.O. Box 765, Great Falls, VA 22066, USA.
☎ +1 703 6718888. 🖷 +1 301 2926947.
E: payam@bahairadio.org **W:** www.bahairadio.org
Webcast: D/L
SAT: Eutelsat Hot Bird 13B, Galaxy 19.
kHz: 7460, 7480

Winter Schedule 2012/2013

Farsi	Days	Area	kHz
0230-0315	daily	ME	7460kch
1800-1845	daily	ME	7480kch

Ann: Farsi: "Payam-e Doost".
Notes: Payam-e Doost ("Message from a friend") is an Internet/satellite radio station run by members of the Baha'i Faith in the USA. Regular relays on shortwave started 21 April 2001 and on satellite from May 2002. Jammed.

SUAB XAA MOO ZOO (Rlg)
✉ Hmong District, 12287 Pennsylvania St, Thornton, CO 80241-3113, USA.
☎ +1 303 2521793. 🖷 +1 303 2527911.
E: suabxaamoozoo@yahoo.com **W:** www.suabxaamoozoo.org
Webcast: D
E: radio@hmongdistrict.org **W:** www.hmongdistrict.org
LP: Head, Radio Ministry (Hmong District): Num Nyaj Hawj.
kHz: 7530, 11570

Winter Schedule 2012/2013

Hmong	Days	Area	kHz
1130-1200	daily	SEA	11570tsu
2230-2300	daily	SEA	7530tsu

V: QSL-card.
Notes: Christian missionary programming targeting Hmong listeners, produced by the Hmong District of the Christian & Missionary Alliance.

THE OVERCOMER MINISTRY (Rlg)
✉ P.O. Box 691, Walterboro, SC 29488, USA.

☎ +1 843 5384202. 🖷 +1 843 5384202.
E: brotherstair@overcomerministry.org
W: www.overcomerministry.org
Webcast: L
L.P: Owner: Ralph G. Stair.
SAT: Amos 3/5, Eutelsat Hot Bird 13A, Galaxy 19, Optus D2, Thaicom 5.
kHz: *1548, 3185, 5890, 7290, 7490, 9370, 9460, 9700, 9835, 9980, 9990, 11900, 13570, 13810, 15420, 15565*

Winter Schedule 2012/2013

English	Days	Area	kHz
0000-1300	daily	NAm	3185wrb
0100-0400	mtwt...	NAm	7490bcq
0200-0400	....f..	NAm	7490bcq
0400-1300	mtwtf..	NAm	5890wcr
0500-1200	.....ss	NAm	5890wcr
1100-1500	.....ss	FE	15565erv
1200-1530	mtwtf..	CAm	13570inb
1300-2100	mtwtf..	NAm	9980wcr
1300-2400	daily	NAm	9370wrb
1400-1600	daily	WFu	9460wer
1400-1600	daily	ME	13810wer
1500-1600	.....s.	NAm	15420bcq
1500-1800	daily	ME	11900erv
1500-2300	.....ss	NAm	9980wcr
1530-1730	.....ss	FE	1548trm
1700-1800	.....s.	NAm	15420bcq
1900-2000	daily	NAf	9835wer
1900-2030	mtwtf..	CAm	13570inb
1900-2200	daily	WEu	9700sof
2000-2100	daily	WEu	7290tig
2000-2300	daily	EAf	9990erv
2200-2400	mtwtf..	NAm	9980wcr

Ann: English: "You have been listening to the International Broadcast - The Overcomer".
V: QSL-card. (Rpt to: overcomer@overcomerministry.com)
Notes: Owned by Faith Cathedral Fellowship, Inc. Schedule is subject to change.

TWR (Rlg)
🖃 P.O. Box 8700, Cary, NC 27512, USA.
☎ +1 919 4603700. 🖷 +1 919 4603702.
E: info2@twr.org **W:** www.twr.org
Webcast: D/L
L.P: Chmn: Dr Thomas J. Lowell; Pres/CEO: Lauren Libby.
V: QSL-card.
Notes: Trans World Radio, Inc (TWR) is a global Christian media enterprise. For TWR's regional divisions and schedules, see under Austria (TWR Europe), India (TWR India), Singapore (TWR Asia) and South Africa (TWR Africa). TWR owns transmitting facilities in Benin, Bonaire, Guam and Swaziland.

UNIVERSITY NETWORK (Rlg)
🖃 P.O. Box 1, Los Angeles, CA 90053-0001, USA.
☎ +1 818 2408151.
E: pastor@pastormelissascottvideos.com **W:** : www.worldwideuniversitynetwork.com; www.pastormelissascott.com; www.drgenescott.com
Webcast: L
SW: See "Caribbean Beacon", under Anguilla.
kHz: *6090, 11775*

Winter Schedule 2012/2013

English	Days	Area	kHz
1000-2200	daily	NAm	11775aiat
2200-1000	daily	NAm	6090aiat

Key: † Irregular.
V: Does not verify reception reports.
Notes: Run by (Pastor) Melissa Scott, who took over the operation in 2005 after the death of her husband, (Pastor) Dr. William Eugene "Gene" Scott. The service consists of 24/7 broadcasts of sermons by Melissa Scott and archived material from the period of Gene Scott.

WEWN – EWTN SHORTWAVE RADIO (Rlg)
🖃 5817 Old Leeds Rd., Irondale, AL 35210-2164, USA.

☎ +1 205 2712900. 🖷 +1 205 2712926.
E: radio@ewtn.com **W:** www.ewtn.com
Webcast: D/L/P
🖃 P.O. Box 157, Station A, Etobicoke, ON M9C 4V2, Canada.
L.P: Pres/CEO: Michael P.Warsaw; Exec. Vice Pres/Chief Operating Officer: Doug Keck; Vice Pres, Engineering: Terry L Borders; Freq Manager: Glen Tapley.
SW: [EWN] Vandiver, AL: 3 x 500kW. Backup tx: 1 x 500kW.
SAT: Eutelsat 28A, Galaxy 15, Intelsat 8/9, Sirius FM 5.
kHz: *5810, 7555, 11520, 11550, 11870, 12050, 13830, 15610*

Winter Schedule 2012/2013

English	Days	Area	kHz
0000-0900	daily	Af	11520ewn
0900-1300	daily	SEA	11520ewn
1300-1700	daily	Eu	15610ewn
1700-2400	daily	ME	15610ewn
Spanish	**Days**	**Area**	**kHz**
0000-0500	daily	CAm	5810ewn
0000-1000	daily	SAm	11870ewn
0500-1300	daily	CAm	7555ewn
1000-1700	daily	SAm	12050ewn
1300-1800	daily	CAm	11550ewn
1700-2400	daily	SAm	13830ewn
1800-2400	daily	CAm	12050ewn

Ann: English: "This is WEWN, Global Catholic Radio, Birmingham, Alabama, USA".
V: QSL-card.
Notes: Owned by the Eternal Word TV Network, Inc. Catholic station, began broadcasting in December 1992.

WHRI – WORLD HARVEST RADIO (WHR) (Rlg)
🖃 P.O. Box 12, South Bend, IN 46624, USA.
☎ +1 574 2918200. 🖷 +1 574 2919043.
E: whr@lesea.com **W:** www.whr.org
Webcast: L
🖃 61300 S Ironwood Rd, South Bend, IN 46614, USA.
W: www.lesea.com
L.P: GM: Peter Sumrall; Dir, Engineering: Larry Vehorn.
SW: [HRI] Furman, SC: 1 x 100, 3 x 500kW.
SAT: Galaxy 16.
kHz: *5920, 7315, 7335, 7385, 7465, 7520, 9490, 9495, 9505, 9595, 9605, 9615, 9640, 9840, 11565, 15180, 15665, 17520, 17570, 21600, 21630*

Winter Schedule 2012/2013

English	Days	Area	kHz
0000-0030	.....ss	SAm	7335hri
0000-0100	daily	NAm	7385hri
0000-0300	daily	NAm,Eu	5920hri
0030-0100	daily	SAm	7335hri
0100-0200	m......	CAm	9605hri
0100-1300	daily	NAm	7385hri
0330-0400	mtwtf..	CAm	5920hri
0400-0500	.....s.	Af	9640hri
0430-0800	mtwtf..	CAm	5920hri
0500-0700	.....ss	Af	9615hri
0500-0700	mtwtf..	NAm,Eu	7465hri
0700-1000	daily	NAm,Eu	7465hri
0800-0830	mtwtf..	Eu,Af	11565hri
0800-0930	.....s	SAm	7315hri
0830-0900	.twtf..	Eu,Af	11565hri
0900-1030	.....s	Eu,Af	11565hri
1000-1200	daily	NAm	7520hri
1030-1100	.....s	Eu,Af	11565hri
1200-1400	daily	Eu,Af	15665hri
1300-1400	.....ss	NAm	7385hri, 9840hri
1300-1400	.....ss	SAm	9495hri
1300-1900	mtwtf..	SAm	9495hri
1400-1500	daily	Af	21600hri
1400-2200	daily	NAm	9840hri
1400-2300	.....ss	SAm	15665hri
1500-1600	.....s	NAm,Eu	17570hri
1500-1600	mtwtfs.	Af	21630hri

English	Days	Area	kHz
1600-2000	daily	Af	21630hri
1900-2300	mtwtf..	SAm	9595hri
2000-2200	...tfs.	Af	21630hri
2000-2300	mtw..s	NAm,Eu	9505hri
2100-2200	mtw...s	NAm,Eu	9490hri
2200-2300	...tfs.	Af	17520hri
2200-2300	daily	NAm	15180hri
2300-2400	daily	NAm,Eu	9505hri
2300-2400	mtwtf..	SAm	7315hri
2300-2400	daily	NAm	7385hri

Russian/English	Days	Area	kHz
0300-0400	daily	NAm,Eu	7520hri
0400-0500	mtwtf.s	NAm,Eu	7520hri

Spanish/English	Days	Area	kHz
0100-0200	.twtfss	SAm	7315hri
0200-0300	daily	SAm	7315hri
0300-0500	.....s.	SAm	7315hri
0530-0800	.....s.	SAm	7315hri
0800-0900	.....s.	CAm	5920hri
0900-1100	mtwtf..	CAm	5920hri
1000-1100	......s	SAm	7315hri
1100-1200	daily	SAm	7315hri
1200-1300	daily	CAm	5920hri
2300-2400	.....ss	SAm	5920hri

Ann: English: "This is World Harvest Radio".
V: QSL-card. (Online reception report form)
Notes: World Harvest Radio is a service of LeSEA, Inc. and part of LeSEA Broadcasting Network. On air since 25 Dec 1985. LeSEA, Inc. owns the shortwave transmitting stations WHRI (Furman, SC) and T8WH (Palau). WHR transmits mainly own and paid religious programming; certain airtime is leased to non-religious broadcasters or prgr producers. Registered freqs shown, actual usage varies, depending on airtime sales.

WINB (Rlg)
⌨ P.O. Box 88, Red Lion, PA 17356, USA.
☎ +1 717 2445360. 🖷 +1 717 2460363.
E: info@winb.com **W:** www.winb.com
Webcast: L
L.P: Sales/Frequency Mgr: Hans Johnson.
SW: [INB] Red Lion, PA: 1 x 50kW.
kHz: *9265, 13570*

	Winter Schedule 2012/2013		
English	Days	Area	kHz
1000-1200	daily	CAm	9265inb**
1100-1300	daily	CAm	9265inb*
1200-2100	daily	CAm	13570inb**
1300-2200	daily	CAm	13570inb*
2100-0400	daily	CAm	9265inb**
2200-0500	daily	CAm	9265inb*

Key: * To 9 Mar; ** From 10 Mar.
Ann: English: "This is WINB, Red Lion, Pennsylvania in the United States of America".
V: QSL-card.
Notes: Owned by World International Broadcasters, Inc. Operational since October 1962. The station transmits religious paid programming. Registered freqs shown, actual usage varies, depending on airtime sales.

WJHR RADIO INTERNATIONAL (Rlg)
⌨ 5920 Oak Manor Drive, Milton, FL 32570, USA.
E: wjhr@usa.com **W:** calvaryscall.org/Radio.html
L.P: Owner: George Scott Mock.
SW: [JHR] Milton, FL: 1 x 50kW.
kHz: *15550*

	Winter Schedule 2012/2013		
English	Days	Area	kHz
1400-2200	daily	NAm	15550jhr*

Key: * USB
Ann: English: "WJHR Radio International, Milton, Florida".
V: QSL-email.
Notes: WJHR ("John Hill Radio") is owned by Hill Radio International (George Scott Mock), and operated by members of the Mt. Calvary Baptist Church. On the air since November 2009.

WMLK ‡ (Rlg)
⌨ P.O. Box C, Bethel, PA 19507, USA.
☎ +1 717 9334518.
E: aoy@wmlkradio.net **W:** www.wmlkradio.net
L.P: Directing Elder: Jacob O. Meyer (d. April 2010); Operating Engineer: Gary A. McAvin.
SW: [MLK] Bethel, PA: 1 x 50kW ‡. Installed 250kW tx not in use.
Ann: English: "This is Radio Station WMLK".
V: QSL-card. Rp.
Notes: Owned by the Assemblies of Yahweh. Off air due to antenna damage.

WORLD CHRISTIAN BROADCASTING INC. (Rlg)
⌨ 605 Bradley Court, Franklin, TN 37067, USA.
☎ +1 615 3718707.
E: info@worldchristian.org **W:** www.worldchristian.org
L.P: Chmn: Dr. John Tyson; Pres: Charles H. Caudill; Vice Pres, Development: Andy Baker; Dir, Engineering: Kevin K. Chambers.
Notes: World Christian Broadcasting, Inc owns the shortwave transmitting station KNLS (see under Alaska), and is constructing a SW transmitting station in Southern Africa (see under Madagascar).

WRNO WORLDWIDE (Rlg)
⌨ P.O. Box 895, Fort Worth, TX 76101, USA.
☎ +1 817 8509990. 🖷 +1 817 8509994.
E: wrnoradio@mailup.net
W: wrnoradio.com; wrnoradionetwork.com
Webcast: L
E: info@goodnewsworldoutreach.com
W: goodnewsworldoutreach.com
L.P: Chmn, Good News World Outreach: Robert E. Mawire.
SW: [RNO] New Orleans, LA: 1 x 50kW.
kHz: *7506*

	Winter Schedule 2012/2013		
English	Days	Area	kHz
0200-0500	daily	NAm,CAm	7506rno†±

Key: † Irregular; ± Variable frequency.
Ann: English: "From New Orleans, Louisiana, you're listening to WRNO Worldwide broadcasting from the United States of America".
IS: "When the Saints go marching in".
V: QSL-card. Rp. (2 IRCs).
Notes: Owned by Good News World Outreach. The station transmits religious paid programming. Office is being relocated to Nashville, TN.

WTWW (Rlg)
⌨ 1784 West Northfield Blvd, #305 Murfreesboro, TN 37129-1702, USA.
E: george@wtww.us **W:** wtww.us
Webcast: L
⌨ 6611 Osmond Dr, Nashville, TN 37205, USA. (HQ)
L.P: Owner/GM: George McClintock; SM: Dan Dixon.
SW: [TWW] Lebanon, TN: 1 x 50, 2 x 100kW.
kHz: *5085, 5745, 9479, 9990, 12105*

	Winter Schedule 2012/2013		
Arabic	Days	Area	kHz
1400-1700	daily	NAm,Eu,Af	12105tww
English	**Days**	**Area**	**kHz**
0100-1100	daily	NAm,Eu,Af	5745tww*
0100-1300	daily	CAm,SAm	5085tww*
0200-1100	daily	NAm,Eu,Af	5745tww**
0200-1300	daily	CAm,SAm	5085tww**
1100-0100	daily	NAm	9479tww*
1100-0200	daily	NAm	9479tww**
1300-0100	daily	CAm,SAm	9990tww*
1300-0200	daily	CAm,SAm	9990tww**
French	**Days**	**Area**	**kHz**
1700-2000	daily	NAm,Eu,Af	12105tww
Portuguese	**Days**	**Area**	**kHz**
2100-0500	daily	NAm,Eu,Af	12105tww
Russian	**Days**	**Area**	**kHz**
1100-1400	daily	NAm,Eu,Af	12105tww
Spanish	**Days**	**Area**	**kHz**
2300-0200	daily	NAm,Eu,Af	12105tww

Key: * To 31 Jan 2013; ** From 1 Feb 2013.

Ann: English: "This is WTWW, Lebanon, Tennessee, USA".
V: QSL-card.
Notes: Owned by Leap of Faith, Inc. On the air since Feb 2010 (tests during Jan 2010). WTWW ("We Transmit World Wide") transmits own and paid religious programming. Registered freqs shown, actual usage may vary, depending on airtime sales.

WWCR – WORLDWIDE CHRISTIAN RADIO (Rlg)
⌨ 1300 WWCR Avenue, Nashville, TN 37218, USA.
☎ +1 615 2551300. 🖷 +1 615 2551311.
E: wwcr@wwcr.com **W:** www.wwcr.com
L.P: GM: Eric Westenberger; Ops Mgr: Brady Murray; Frequency Mgr: Dr Jerry Plummer.
SW: [WCR] Nashville, TN: 4 x 100kW.
kHz: 3195, 3215, 4840, 5070, 5890, 5935, 6875, 7490, 9350, 9980, 12160, 13845, 15825

Winter Schedule 2012/2013

English	Days	Area	kHz
0000-1200	daily	NAm,Eu	4840wcr** , 4840wcr°
0000-1200	daily	Af	5935wcr** , 5935wcr°
0100-0900	daily	NAm,Af	3215wcr** , 3215wcr°
0100-1100	daily	NAm,CAm,Af	5890wcr°
0100-1200	daily	NAm,CAm,Af	5890wcr* , 5890wcr**
0100-1300	daily	Af	5935wcr*
0100-1300	daily	NAm,Eu	4840wcr*
0200-1200	daily	NAm,Af	3215wcr*
0600-1000	daily	NAm,Af	3195wcr* , 3195wcr** , 3195wcr°
0700-1200	daily	NAm,CAm,Af	5070wcr* , 5070wcr** , 5070wcr°
0900-1100	daily	NAm,Af	6875wcr** , 6875wcr°, 7490wcr** , 7490wcr°
1000-1200	daily	NAm,Af	6875wcr* , 7490wcr*
1100-0100	daily	NAm,CAm,Af	9980wcr°
1100-2000	daily	NAm,Af	15825wcr°
1100-2100	daily	NAm,Af	15825wcr**
1200-0100	daily	NAm,CAm,Af	9980wcr*, 9980wcr**
1200-1500	daily	Af	7490wcr* , 7490wcr°
1200-2100	daily	NAm,Af	15825wcr*
1200-2400	daily	NAm,Eu	13845wcr** , 13845wcr°
1300-0100	daily	Af	13845wcr*
1300-1600	daily	Af	7490wcr*
1500-2000	daily	Af	12160wcr°
1500-2100	daily	Af	12160wcr**
1600-2100	daily	Af	12160wcr*
2000-2200	daily	Af	9350wcr°
2000-2200	daily	NAm,Af	6875wcr°
2100-0100	daily	NAm,Af	3195wcr** , 6875wcr**
2100-2300	daily	Af	9350wcr*
2100-2300	daily	NAm,Af	6875wcr*
2100-2400	daily	Af	9350wcr**
2200-0100	daily	NAm,Af	3195wcr°
2200-2400	daily	Af	5070wcr°
2300-0100	daily	Af	5070wcr*
2300-0200	daily	NAm,Af	3195wcr*

Key: * To 9 Mar 2013; ** From 10 Mar 2013; ° To 31 Dec 2012
Ann: English: "This is World Wide Christian Radio-WWCR, Nashville, Tennessee, USA".
V: QSL-card. Rp. preferred (1 IRC). Rec. acc.
Notes: Owned by F.W. Robert Broadcasting Co., Inc. The station transmits religious paid programming.

COMMANDO SOLO (U.S. MILITARY)
⌨ Pennsylvania Air National Guard, 193rd Special Operations Wing, 81 Constellation Court, Middletown, PA 17057-5086, USA.
☎ +1 717 9482490. 🖷 +1 717 9482490.
E: Via website. **W:** www.193sow.ang.af.mil
MW/SW: 10kW MW/SW txs onboard airplane.
FM/DAB: FM:1kW txs onboard airplane.
V: QSL-card.
Notes: The 193rd Special Operations Wing, under the U.S. Air Force Special Operations Command, conducts airborne radio/tv transmissions ("PsyOps") from Lockheed EC130J Commando Solo III aircraft,

upon demand. Schedules of the broadcasts - when active - can be found in the section "Clandestine and Other Target Broacasts".

THE DISCO PALACE
⌨ c/o Alyx & Yeyi, LLC, 5201 Blue Lagoon Drive, 8th Floor, Miami, FL 33126, USA.
☎ +1 305 5728070.
E: info@thediscopalace.com **W:** www.thediscopalace.com
Webcast: L
kHz: 12115, 17875

Winter Schedule 2012/2013

English	Days	Area	kHz
1530-1630	daily	SAs	12115iss+
2000-2100	daily	NAm	17875guf+

Key: + DRM
Ann: English: "Feel the Music- The Disco Palace!".
V: QSL-card. Rp.
Notes: Music station created to promote DRM shortwave broadcasting. 24h on the Internet. Sister station of the now defunct TDPradio, see under Belgium. On SW since February 2010.

WBCQ – THE PLANET
⌨ 274 Britton Road, Monticello, ME 04760, USA.
☎ +1 207 5389180.
E: wbcq@wbcq.com **W:** www.wbcq.com
Webcast: D/L
L.P: Owner: Allan Weiner.
SW: [BCQ] Monticello, ME: 4 x 50kW.
kHz: 5110, 7490, 9330, 15420

Winter Schedule 2012/2013

English	Days	Area	kHz
0000-2400	daily	NAm,CAm	5110bcq*
1200-0600	daily	NAm,CAm	9330bcq*
1200-2300	daily	NAm,CAm	15420bcq*
1900-0500	daily	NAm,CAm	7490bcq*

Key: * AM/U
Ann: English: "This is WBCQ, Monticello, Maine, the United States of America. The Planet".
V: QSL-card. (SASE)
Notes: Owned by A. Weiner/Becker Broadcast Systems, Inc. Leases air time to religious and other prgr producers. Schedule is subject to daily variation (according to bookings) and start/end times are approximate. On air since 8 September 1998.

WRMI – RADIO MIAMI INTERNATIONAL
⌨ 175 Fontainebleau Blvd., Suite 1N4, Miami, FL 33172 USA.
☎ +1 305 5599764. 🖷 +1 305 5598186.
E: info@wrmi.net **W:** www.wrmi.net
Webcast: L
L.P: GM: Jeff White; Dir, Technical: Jose Raul Mena.
SW: [RMI] Hialeah, FL: 1 x 50kW, Reserve tx: 1 x 5kW.
kHz: 9955

Winter Schedule 2012/2013

English/Spanish	Days	Area	kHz
1500-2300	.....ss	CAm,SAm	9955rmi
2300-1500	daily	CAm,SAm	9955rmi

Ann: English: "This is WRMI, Radio Miami International".
V: QSL-card.
Notes: Owned by Radio Miami International, Inc. On air since June 1994. WRMI provides air time for prgrs by various production companies (mainly in English and Spanish) and rebroadcasts international radio stations (R. Prague, R. Slovakia, etc. It also relays World Radio Network programming at times. See WRMI web site for detailed schedule. Some prgrs aimed at a Cuban audience are jammed.. Some prgrs aimed at a Cuban audience are jammed.

WWRB
⌨ Airline Transport Communications Inc., Listener Services, P.O. Box 7, Manchester, TN 37349-0007, USA.
☎ +1 931 7286063. 🖷 +1 931 7286087.
E: dfrantz@wwrb.org **W:** www.wwrb.org
Webcast: L
⌨ 6755 Shady Grove Road, Morrison, TN 37355, USA. (Studio)
L.P: Owner & CE: Dave Frantz.
SW: [WRB] Manchester, TN: 4 x 100kW. (plus 1 x 100kW backup tx).

kHz: *3185, 3195, 3215, 5050, 9370*

Winter Schedule 2012/2013

English	Days	Area	kHz
0000-1300	daily	NAm	3185wrb
0100-0400	daily	NAm	3195wrb**
0200-0500	daily	NAm	3195wrb*
1300-2400	daily	NAm	9370wrb
2100-0100	daily	NAm	3215wrb**
2100-0200	daily	NAm	3215wrb*
2200-1300	daily	NAm	5050wrb

V: QSL-card. (Email rpts not accepted)
Notes: A subsidiary of Airline Transport Communications Inc. The station transmits religious paid programming. Registered freqs shown, actual usage may vary, depending on airtime sales. Occ uses unregistered freqs such as 3145kHz.

ALYX & YEYI (TECHNICAL SERVICE PROVIDER) (Broker)
5201 Blue Lagoon Drive, 8th Floor, Miami, FL 33126, USA.
☎ +1 305 5728070.
E: info@alyx-yeyi.com **W:** www.alyx-yeyi.com
L.P: MD: Ludo Maes.
Notes: Alyx & Yeyi is a Technical Service Provider and brokers airtime for programs on shortwave, satellite and the internet, for radio stations with political, religious, commercial and NGO background. Latest broadcasting schedule can be found at www.airtime.org/schedule.asp

RED TELECOM (Broker)
300 East 75th Street, Suite 50, New York, NY 10021, USA.
☎ +1 917 5392494. 🖷 +1 208 4603547.
E: d.robinson@dtholdings.com; sales@dtholdings.com
W: www.dtholdings.com
L.P: MD: Daniel Robinson.
Notes: Red Telecom brokers air time for transmitter facilities in Tajikistan and Uzbekistan.

UZBEKISTAN (UZB)

RADIOALOQA, RADIOESHITTIRISH VA TELEVIDENIYE MARKAZI (RRTM) (Tx Operator)
Amir Timur Street 109a, 100084 Toshkent, Uzbekistan.
☎ +998 71 2356516. 🖷 +998 71 2344517.
E: info@crrt.uz **W:** www.crrt.uz
L.P: GD: Shomansur Sh. Abidxodjayev.
SW: [TAC] Toshkent: 11 x 100kW.
Notes: RRTM, a division of the State Communications and Information Agency of Uzbekistan, is the national transmitter network operator in Uzbekistan.

VATICAN CITY STATE (CVA)

VATICAN RADIO (Rlg)
Piazza Pia 3, I-00120 Vatican City.
☎ +39 06 69883945. 🖷 +39 06 69883463.
E: sedoc@vatiradio.va **W:** www.radiovaticana.va
Webcast: D/L/P
L.P: GD: Fr Federico Lombardi; PD: Fr Andrzej Koprowski; Dir, Technical: Sandro Piervenanzi; Int Rel: Giacomo Ghisani.
MW: [SMG] Santa Maria di Galeria: 1530kHz 600kW ‡, 1611kHz 50kW ‡; [VAT] Vatican City: 585/1260kHz 5kW.
SW: [SMG] Santa Maria di Galeria: 4 x 100, 5 x 500kW; [VAT] Vatican City: 1 x 10, 1 x 80kW.‡
SAT: Galaxy 19.
kHz: *585, 1260, 3975, 6020, 6040, 6070, 6075, 6185, 7250, 7290, 7305, 7335, 7360, 7365, 7395, 7410, 7585, 9560, 9600, 9635, 9645, 9660, 9695, 9755, 9850, 11625, 11715, 11740, 11835, 11850, 11865, 11935, 12035, 13765, 15460, 15495, 15570, 15595, 15775, 17590, 21650, 21680*

Winter Schedule 2012/2013

Albanian	Days	Area	kHz
0620-0640	daily	Eu	1260vat
2000-2020	daily	Eu	1260vat

Amharic	Days	Area	kHz
0400-0415	daily	Af	7360smg, 13765mdc
1630-1645	daily	Af	13765smg, 15570smg

Amharic/Armenian/ Russian/Ukrainian (Liturgy)	Days	Area	kHz
0930-1050	......s	Eu	11740smg, 15595smg, 17590smg

Angelus	Days	Area	kHz
1100-1130	......s	Eu	585vat

Arabic	Days	Area	kHz
0500-0530	daily	NAf,ME	9645smg, 11715smg
0500-0530	daily	Eu	1260vat
0745-0805	mtwtfs.	Eu	6075smg
0745-0805	mtwtfs.	NAf,ME	9645smg, 11740smg, 15595smg
1630-1700	daily	Eu	1260vat
1630-1700	daily	NAf	11935smg
1630-1700	daily	NAf,ME	9635smg
2140-2200	daily	Eu	3975smg
2140-2200	daily	NAf	6040smg, 6040smg
2140-2200	daily	NAf,ME	7250smg

Armenian	Days	Area	kHz
0310-0330	daily	Eu	1260vat
0310-0330	daily	ME	6185smg, 7335smg
1650-1710	daily	ME	6185smg, 7360smg

Belarusian	Days	Area	kHz
0420-0440	daily	Eu	1260vat
1800-1820	daily	Eu	1260vat, 6185smg

Bulgarian	Days	Area	kHz
0540-0600	daily	Eu	1260vat
1920-1940	daily	Eu	1260vat

Chinese	Days	Area	kHz
1230-1300	mtwtf.s	As	6020irk, 11865pht, 15495pug
1230-1315	.....s.	As	6020irk, 11865pht, 15495pug
2200-2245	daily	As	7395pht, 9600pht, 15460tin

English	Days	Area	kHz
0140-0200	daily	As	7410tac, 9560smg
0300-0320	daily	As	15460pug
0300-0330	daily	Af	9660smg, 11625mdc
0500-0528	daily	Af	13765mdc
0500-0530	daily	Af	7360smg
0630-0658	daily	Af	13765smg
0630-0700	daily	Af	11625smg
0730-0745	mtwtfs.	Eu	585vat
0730-0745	mtwtfs.	NAf,ME	15595smg
1530-1550	mtwtf.s	As	7585tac, 11850smg, 15595tin, 15775smg+
1530-1558	.....s.	As	7585tac, 15595tin, 15775smg+
1530-1600	.....s.	As	11850smg
1715-1730	daily	Eu	585vat, 7290smg
1730-1758	daily	Af	11625smg, 13765smg
1730-1800	daily	Af	15570smg
2000-2028	daily	Af	7365smg, 11625smg

English (Liturgy)	Days	Area	kHz
1130-1200	...f..	Af	17590smg
1130-1200	...f..	ME	21650smg

Finnish	Days	Area	kHz
0600-0620	m....s.	Eu	1260vat
1940-2000	....fs.	Eu	1260vat

French	Days	Area	kHz
0230-0300	daily	Af	9660smg
0430-0458	daily	Af	7360smg, 13765mdc
0600-0628	daily	Af	9660smg
0600-0628	mtwtfs.	Af	11625smg, 13765smg
0715-0730	mtwtfs.	Eu	585vat
0715-0730	mtwtfs.	NAf,ME	15595smg
1700-1715	daily	Af	11935smg
1700-1715	daily	Eu	585vat
1700-1728	daily	Af	13765smg
1700-1730	daily	Af	15570smg
2030-2058	daily	Af	11625smg, 13765smg

Hindi	Days	Area	kHz
0040-0100	daily	As	7410tac, 9560smg
0200-0220	daily	As	15460pug
1430-1450	daily	As	7585tac, 11850smg, 15595tin

Italian	Days	Area	kHz
0700-0715	mtwtf..	Af	15595smg
0700-0715	mtwtfs.	Eu	585vat
1300-1320	daily	Af	21680smg
1300-1320	daily	Eu	585vat
1300-1320	daily	NAf,ME	15595smg
1630-1700	daily	Eu	585vat
2200-2220	daily	Eu	585vat
2240-2300	daily	Eu	585vat

Italian (Angelus)	Days	Area	kHz
1050-1130	......s	Eu	6075smg, 7250smg, 11740smg
1050-1130	......s	ME	11740smg
1050-1130	......s	NAf,ME	9645smg, 15595smg
1050-1130	......s	Af	17590smg, 21680smg

Italian (Liturgy)	Days	Area	kHz
0830-0930	......s	Eu	7250smg

Italian (Mass)	Days	Area	kHz
0830-0913	......s	Eu	585vat

Italian (Papal Audience)	Days	Area	kHz
0905-1100	..w....	Eu	585vat, 6075smg

Latin (Compline)	Days	Area	kHz
2220-2240	daily	Eu	585vat

Latin (Liturgy)	Days	Area	kHz
1940-2000	daily	Eu	3975smg, 6075smg
1940-2000	daily	NAf,ME	9755smg
1940-2000	daily	Af	11625smg, 13765smg

Latin (Mass)	Days	Area	kHz
0630-0700	daily	Eu	585vat, 3975smg
0630-0710	daily	Eu	6075smg, 6075smg, 7250smg, 9645smg
0630-0710	daily	NAf,ME	15595smg

Latvian	Days	Area	kHz
1840-1900	daily	Eu	1260vat

Lithuanian	Days	Area	kHz
0440-0500	daily	Eu	1260vat
1820-1840	daily	Eu	1260vat

Malayalam	Days	Area	kHz
0120-0140	daily	As	7410tac, 9560smg
0240-0300	daily	As	15460pug
1510-1530	daily	As	7585tac, 11850smg, 15595tin

Oriental Liturgy	Days	Area	kHz
0930-1050	......s	Eu	585vat

Portuguese	Days	Area	kHz
0030-0100	daily	SAm	7305grv
0030-0100	daily	Eu	1260vat
0530-0558	daily	Af	7360smg, 11625smg, 13765mdc
0900-0930	mtwtfs.	Eu	1260vat
1000-1030	mtwtfs.	Eu	1260vat
1415-1430	daily	Eu	1260vat
1500-1530	...t...	Eu	1260vat
1600-1630	daily	Eu	1260vat
1800-1830	daily	Af	11625smg, 13765smg, 15570smg

Romanian	Days	Area	kHz
1900-1920	daily	Eu	1260vat

Romanian (Liturgy)	Days	Area	kHz
0715-0830	......s	Eu	7250smg

Rosary	Days	Area	kHz
1940-2000	daily	Eu	585vat

Russian	Days	Area	kHz
0330-0400	daily	Eu	1260vat
1330-1400	daily	CAs	6070tac
1330-1400	daily	Eu	1260vat
1330-1400	daily	RUS	9695smg
1710-1740	daily	RUS	6185smg, 7360smg
2100-2130	daily	Eu	1260vat

Somali	Days	Area	kHz
0345-0358	.....s.	Af	11625mdc
0345-0359	.....s.	Af	7360smg
1615-1630	.....s.	Af	13765smg, 15570smg

Spanish	Days	Area	kHz
0100-0145	daily	Eu	1260vat
0200-0245	daily	SAm	7305grv
1130-1200	mtwtfs.	Eu	1260vat
1130-1200	daily	SAm	7305grv
1400-1415	daily	Eu	1260vat
1500-1530	m...f..	Eu	1260vat
1700-1730	daily	Eu	1260vat
1900-1930	.....s.	Af	11625smg, 13765smg

Swahili	Days	Area	kHz
0330-0345	......s	Af	9660smg, 11625mdc
0330-0358	mtwtfs.	Af	9660smg
0330-0400	mtwtfs.	Af	11625mdc
1600-1615	.....s.	Af	13765smg, 15570smg
1600-1628	mtwtf.s	Af	13765smg
1600-1630	mtwtf.s	Af	15570smg

Swedish	Days	Area	kHz
0600-0620	.twtf.s	Eu	1260vat
1940-2000	.twt..s	Eu	1260vat

Tagalog	Days	Area	kHz
2020-2040	......s	Eu	1260vat

Tamil	Days	Area	kHz
0100-0120	daily	As	7410tac, 9560smg
0220-0240	daily	As	15460pug
1450-1510	daily	As	7585tac, 11850smg, 13765smg, 15595tin

Tigrinya	Days	Area	kHz
0415-0428	daily	Af	7360smg, 13765mdc
1645-1658	..wtfss	Af	13765smg
1645-1700	daily	Af	15570smg

Ukrainian	Days	Area	kHz
0400-0420	daily	Eu	1260vat
1740-1800	daily	Eu	6185smg, 7360smg

Ukrainian (Liturgy)	Days	Area	kHz
0710-0845	......s	Eu	9850smg, 11740smg

Urdu	Days	Area	kHz
0025-0040	m..t...	As	7410tac, 9560smg
1415-1430	..w..s	As	7585tac, 15595tin

Vietnamese	Days	Area	kHz
1315-1400	daily	SEA	11835pht, 15495tin
2315-2400	daily	SEA	9600pht, 12035pht

Key: + DRM

Ann: Before all transmissions: Latin: "Laudetur Jesus Christus" (Praised be Jesus Christ), repeated in the language of the broadcast, then station identification. English: "This is the English program of Vatican Radio".

V: QSL-card.

Notes: On air since 12 Feb 1931. Certain schedule variations apply on Catholic Holy Days.

VIETNAM (VTN)

VOICE OF VIETNAM (OVERSEAS SERVICE) (VOV) (Gov)
✉ 45 Ba Trieu Street, Hanoi, Vietnam.
☎ +84 4 38266809. 🖷 +84 4 38266707..
E: vovworld@vov.org.vn; btdn.vov@hn.vnn.vn
W: vovworld.vn; tnvn.gov.vn; vov.vn
Webcast: L
L.P: Dir (VOV5): Doan Thi Trung.
MW: [OMO] Can Tho, Ô Môn: 1242kHz 2000kW (Run at lower power - est. approx 100kW) .

SW: [HAN] Hanoi, Me Tri: 2 x 50kW; [VNI] Son Tay: 11 x 100kW & via leased foreign relays.
FM/DAB: FM: 105.5MHz (Hanoi); 105.7MHz (Ho Chi Minh City).
SAT: Vinasat 1.
kHz: 1242, 5955, 6135, 6175, 7220, 7280, 7285, 7345, 7370, 9550, 9640, 9730, 9840, 12000, 12020

Winter Schedule 2012/2013

Chinese	Days	Area	kHz
1100-1130	daily	As	7220vni, 12000vni
1200-1230	daily	As	7220vni, 12000vni
1300-1330	daily	As	7220vni, 12000vni
2200-2230	daily	As	7220vni, 12000vni
2230-2300	daily	As	9840vni, 12020vni

English	Days	Area	kHz
0100-0130	daily	NAm	9640wof
0230-0300	daily	NAm	9640wof
0330-0400	daily	NAm	9640wof
1000-1030	daily	As	9840vni, 12020vni
1100-1130	daily	As	7285han
1130-1200	daily	As	9840vni, 12020vni
1230-1300	daily	As	9840vni, 12020vni
1330-1400	daily	As	9840vni, 12020vni
1500-1530	daily	As	7285han, 9840vni, 12020vni
1600-1630	daily	ME	7220vni, 9550vni
1600-1630	daily	Eu	7280vni, 9730vni
1800-1830	daily	Eu	5955mos
1900-1930	daily	Eu	7280vni, 9730vni
2030-2100	daily	Eu	7280vni, 9730vni
2030-2100	daily	ME	7220vni, 9550vni
2330-2400	daily	As	9840vni, 12020vni

French	Days	Area	kHz
1200-1230	daily	As	7285han
1300-1330	daily	As	7285han
1630-1700	daily	ME	7220vni, 9550vni
1830-1900	daily	Eu	7280vni, 9730vni
1930-2000	daily	Eu	5955mos, 7280vni, 9730vni
2100-2130	daily	Eu	7280vni, 9730vni
2100-2130	daily	ME	7220vni, 9550vni

German	Days	Area	kHz
2030-2100	daily	Eu	6175dha
2100-2130	daily	Eu	6175dha

Indonesian	Days	Area	kHz
1030-1100	daily	As	9840vni, 12020vni
1300-1330	daily	As	9840vni, 12020vni
1430-1500	daily	As	9840vni, 12020vni
2300-2330	daily	As	9840vni, 12020vni

Japanese	Days	Area	kHz
1100-1130	daily	As	9840vni, 12020vni
1200-1230	daily	As	9840vni, 12020vni
1400-1430	daily	As	9840vni, 12020vni
2200-2230	daily	As	9840vni, 12020vni

Khmer	Days	Area	kHz
1030-1100	daily	As	7285han
1230-1300	daily	As	7285han
1300-1330	daily	SEA	1242omo
1430-1500	daily	SEA	1242omo
2230-2300	daily	As	7285han

Lao	Days	Area	kHz
1330-1430	daily	As	7285han
1330-1430	daily	SEA	1242omo
2300-2400	daily	As	7285han

Russian	Days	Area	kHz
1130-1200	daily	As	7220vni, 12000vni
1230-1300	daily	As	7220vni, 12000vni
1630-1700	daily	Eu	7280vni, 9730vni
2000-2030	daily	Eu	6135wof, 7280vni, 9730vni

Spanish	Days	Area	kHz
0300-0330	daily	NAm	6175hri
0400-0430	daily	NAm	6175hri
1800-1830	daily	Eu	7280vni, 9730vni

Thai	Days	Area	kHz
1130-1200	daily	As	7285han
1430-1500	daily	As	7285han
1530-1600	daily	As	7285han
2200-2230	daily	As	7285han

Vietnamese	Days	Area	kHz
0000-0100	daily	As	7285han
0130-0230	daily	NAm	9640wof
0430-0530	daily	NAm	7345wof
1500-1600	daily	ME	7220vni, 9550vni
1500-1600	daily	SEA	1242omo
1700-1800	daily	Eu	7280vni, 9730vni
1830-1930	daily	Eu	5955mos
2130-2230	daily	Eu	7370wof

Ann: English: "You are listening to Radio The Voice of Vietnam".
V: QSL-card.
Notes: The External Sce (VOV5) of the national broadcaster, Voice of Vietnam. Schedule and frequency usage variable. Chinese prgr consists of Mandarin with some segments in Cantonese.

YEMEN (YEM)

REPUBLIC OF YEMEN RADIO (Gov)
⌕ See National Radio section.
Webcast: L (www.sanaaradio.net)
SW: [SAN] Sana'a: 1 x 50, 1 x 100kW.
kHz: 6135, 9780

Winter Schedule 2012/2013

Arabic	Days	Area	kHz
0500-1500	daily	ME	6135san
1200-1700	daily	ME	9780san†

Key: † Irregular.
V: QSL-card.
Notes: All broadcasts are a simulcast of the domestic "General Prgr" from Sana'a.

ZAMBIA (ZMB)

CVC RADIO CHRISTIAN VOICE ‡ (Rlg)
⌕ Private Bag E606, Lusaka, Zambia.
☎ +260 21 1256466. 🖷 +260 21 1257206.
E: voicefm@zamnet.zm
W: www.rcvoice.co.zm; radiochristianvoicezambia.com
Webcast: P
LP: SM: Mwiza Sinyangwe; Head of Transmissions: Edward Phiri.
SW: [LUS] Lusaka, Makeni Ranch: 2 x 100kW.
FM/DAB: See National Radio section.
Ann: English: "Radio Christian Voice".
V: QSL-card
Notes: Radio Christian Voice is produced by Christan Voice Ltd, a subsidiary of Christian Vision (see under United Kingdom), but is no longer aired on SW. The Christian Vision owned SW transmitting station at Lusaka continues to rebroadcast prgrs of CVC 1Africa Radio (see under South Africa).

ZIMBABWE (ZWE)

VOICE OF ZIMBABWE (Gov)
⌕ No 3, 5th Street, Gweru, Zimbabwe,
☎ +263 54 22600.
E: voiceof_zimbabwe@yahoo.com **W:** www.zbc.co.zw
Webcast: P
LP: SM: Paul Mtangadura; Exec. producer: Donald Mukota.
SW: [GWE] Gweru, Guinea Fowl: 1 x 100kW.
kHz: 999, 4828

Winter Schedule 2012/2013

English/Ndebele/ Shona	Days	Area	kHz
0000-2400	daily	SAf	999-†
1600-2200	daily	Af	4828gwe†

Key: † Irregular.
Ann: English: "This is the Voice of Zimbabwe".
Notes: External Service under the roof of the state-run "Zimbabwe Broadcasting Holdings" (ZBH). On the air since 25 May 2007, officially launched on 30 July 2010.

CLANDESTINE AND OTHER TARGET BROADCASTS

Clandestine Broadcasts (Clan) are politically-motivated broadcasts produced by groups opposed to the government of the target country.

Other Target Broadcasts are produced by non-governmental or governmental organisations and targetted at zones of regional or local conflict. Most COTBs are transmitted via the facilities of international transmitter operators.

The following symbols are used in this section: † Irregular transmsission; ‡ Inactive at editorial deadline. ± variable frequency.

Where a station is no longer broadcasting, the inactive symbol appears next to the station name.

Target: CAMBODIA (CBG)

THE KHMER POST RADIO
✉ P.O. Box 4073, Long Beach, CA 90804, USA.
☎ +1 562 7288972.
E: sovannara@thekhmerpost.com **W:** www.thekhmerpost.com
Webcast: D/L/P
LP: Pres (KPMC/KPR): Sovannara Meach.
kHz: *9930*

Winter Schedule 2012/2013
Khmer	Days	Area	kHz
1200-1300	mtwtf..	SEA	9930hbn

Notes: On shortwave, sporadically, since 15 March 2011. Produced by the oppositional "The Khmer Post Media Center" (KPMC).

KPPM RADIO (Clan)
✉ P.O. Box 5952, Fresno, CA 93755, USA.
☎ +1 562 5953634.
E: info@kppmradio.org **W:** www.kppmradio.org
Webcast: D
✉ P.O. Box 8074, Cranston, RI 02920, USA.
kHz: *9960*

Winter Schedule 2012/2013
Khmer	Days	Area	kHz
1200-1300	.....ss	CBG	9960hbn

Notes: KPPM Radio began SW broadcasts on 17 September 2011 and is produced by Khmer People Power Movement (KPPM).

Target: CAMEROON (CME)

SAWTU LINJIILA (VOICE OF THE GOSPEL) (Rlg)
✉ B.P. 02, Ngaoundéré, Cameroon.
E: administration@sawtulinjiila.org; sawtulinjiila@yahoo.fr
W: www.sawtulinjiila.org; www.lutheranworld.org/lwf (LWF)
LP: Dir: Rev Yaya Bournang.
kHz: *9800*

Winter Schedule 2012/2013
Fulfulde	Days	Area	kHz
1830-1900	daily	CAf	9800wer

Ann: Fulfulde: "Sawtu Linjiila".
V: QSL-email.
Notes: Radio ministry of the Evangelical Lutheran Church of Cameroon (EELC), a member of the Lutheran World Federation (LWF). Launched in November 1966; prgrs are re-transmitted on various local stns in Africa.

Target: CHINA (CHN)

MINGHUI RADIO
✉ P.O. Box 250759, New York, NY 10025, USA.
E: editor@minghui.org **W:** www.mhradio.org
Webcast: D
kHz: *6030*

Winter Schedule 2012/2013
Chinese	Days	Area	kHz
1300-1400	daily	CHN	6030tsh

Ann: Mandarin: "Zhe shi Minghui Guangbo Diantai".

Notes: Falun Gong-affiliated and sister station to Sound of Hope Radio. On air since 30 Dec 2005.

SOUND OF HOPE RADIO INTERNATIONAL
✉ 6-4, Lane 84, GuóTài St, North District, Taichung 404, Taiwan.
E: contact@soundofhope.org; allenz@soundofhope.org
W: www.soundofhope.org
Webcast: D/L/P
✉ P.O. Box 70456, Sunnyvale, CA 94086, USA; 1010 Corporation Way, Palto Alto, CA 94303, USA.
☎ +1 866 432 7764. ▯ +1 415 2765861.
E: 9ping@soundofhope.org
W: sohnetwork.com; asia-cast.com/shortwave-broadcasts (English)
LP: Dir: Allen Zeng.
kHz: *6280, 7105, 7280, 7310, 7600, 7630, 7970, 9375, 9450, 9540, 9635, 9970, 9995, 10960, 11230, 11300, 11550, 11760, 11765, 11970, 12230, 12320, 12370, 12670, 12800, 12870, 12980, 13130, 13270, 13350, 13430, 13530, 13775, 13820, 13920, 13970, 14370, 14400, 14600, 14700, 14750, 14800, 14870, 14980, 15750, 15780, 15800, 15870, 15900, 15940, 15970, 16100, 16250, 16360, 16600, 16920, 17100, 17170, 17250, 17300, 17370, 17450, 17900, 18200, 18250, 18970*

Winter Schedule 2012/2013
Chinese	Days	Area	kHz
0000-2400	daily	CHN	7970tsu*±, 9970tsu*±, 10960tsu*±, 12230tsu*±, 12670tsu*±, 12800tsu*±, 13270tsu*±, 15940tsu*±, 16920tsu*±, 17900tsu*±
0900-1100	.....ss	CHN	9540tsh, 11760tsh
1100-1300	daily	CHN	7280tsh
1130-1330	daily	CHN	15750dsb±
1230-1300	daily	CHN	9375dsb±
1300-1400	daily	CHN	7310tsh
1300-1500	daily	CHN	11760tsh
1330-1400	daily	CHN	11550dsb±
1400-1430	daily	CHN	9995dsb±
1400-1600	daily	CHN	9450pao
1430-1500	daily	CHN	15780dsb±
1500-1600	daily	CHN	7630dsb±
1600-1700	daily	CHN	11765tsh
2000-1700	daily	CHN	11230tsu*±, 11300tsu*±, 11970tsu*±, 12320tsu*±, 12370tsu*±, 12870tsu*±, 12980tsu*±, 13130tsu*±, 13350tsu*±, 13430tsu*±, 13530tsu*±, 13775tsu*±, 13820tsu*±, 13920tsu*±, 13970tsu*±, 14370tsu*±, 14400tsu*±, 14600tsu*±, 14700tsu*±, 14750tsu*±, 14800tsu*±, 14870tsu*±, 14980tsu*±, 15800tsu*±, 15870tsu*±, 15900tsu*±, 15970tsu*±, 16100tsu*±, 16250tsu*±, 16360tsu*±, 16600tsu*±, 17100tsu*±, 17170tsu*±, 17250tsu*±, 17300tsu*±, 17370tsu*±,

Chinese	Days	Area	kHz
			17450tsu*±, 18200tsu*±,
			18250tsu*±, 18970tsu*±
2200-2300	daily	CHN	7105tsh, 9635tsh
2200-2400	....fs.	CHN	6280tsh
2200-2400	daily	CHN	7600dsb±
2300-2400	daily	CHN	7310tsh

Key: * Cantonese 0200-0300 & 0600-0700; ± Variable Frequency.
Ann: Mandarin: "Xiwang zhi sheng guoji guangbo diantai".
V: QSL-card.
Notes: Established in June 2003. Falun Gong-related Sound of Hope Radio International is the shortwave programme of Sound of Hope Radio Network Inc. It is a global provider of Chinese language news and cultural programming for the Chinese community in over 20 major cities in USA, Canada, Australia, Germany, Sweden, Denmark, Taiwan and mainland China. SW broadcasts are subject to 'Firedragon',aka 'Firedrake', Chinese music jammer. At the top of the hour the jammer is off air for 15 minutes. Also reported on 1053kHz at approx 1700-1900. Relays Falun Dafa Radio broadcasts.

VOICE OF TIBET
✉ Voice of Tibet Foundation, Kirkegata 5, 0153 Oslo, Norway. (Administration)
☎ +47 22111209; +47 22112700.
E: info@vot.org; oystalme@gmail.com **W:** www.vot.org
Webcast: D
✉ Narthang Building, Gangchen Kyishong, Dharamsala, 176215 H.P., India. (Main Editorial Office)
☎ +91 1892 228179; +91 1892 222384. 🖷 +91 1892 224913.
L.P: Dir: Øystein Alme; Editor-in-Chief: Tenzin Paldon.
SAT: Intelsat 10.
kHz: 15485, 15487, 15488, 15497, 15553, 15558, 15562, 15567, 17535

Winter Schedule 2012/2013			
Mandarin	Days	Area	kHz
1200-1213	daily	CHN	15488dsb±
1213-1230	daily	CHN	15497dsb±
1300-1313	daily	CHN	15487dsb±
1313-1338	daily	CHN	15497dsb±
1338-1400	daily	CHN	15487dsb±
Tibetan	Days	Area	kHz
1230-1237	daily	CHN	15558dsb±
1237-1303	daily	CHN	15553dsb±
1303-1317	daily	CHN	15562dsb±
1317-1332	daily	CHN	15567dsb±
1332-1400	daily	CHN	15562dsb±
1400-1430	daily	CHN	15562dsb±
1430-1500	daily	IND,NPL	17535mdc
1530-1600	daily	IND,NPL	15485mdc

Key: ± Varible Frequency.
Ann: Mandarin: "Zheli shi Nuowei Xizang zhi Sheng Guangbo Diantai huayu jiemu"; Tibetan: "Di nor we bod kyi rlung 'phrin khang yin".
V: QSL-card.
Notes: On air since July 1996. Licensed radio station in Norway, run by the "Voice of Tibet Foundation". Established by the organisations "Worldview Rights", the "Norwegian Human Rights House" and the "Norwegian Tibet Committee". Jammed. Frequencies are often changed.

VOICE OF CHINA (Clan)
✉ 2261 Morello Avenue, Suite A, Pleasant Hill, CA 94523, USA.
☎ +1 510 6872354. 🖷 +1 510 6877396.
E: info@china21century.org **W:** www.china21century.org
L.P: Exec Producer: Hu Juying (Lily Hu).
kHz: 7270

Winter Schedule 2012/2013			
Chinese	Days	Area	kHz
1400-1500	daily	CHN	7270tsu
2300-2400	daily	CHN	7270tsu

Ann: Mandarin: "Zhongguo zhi yin".
V: QSL-card.
Notes: On air since April 1991. Produced by the "Foundation for China in the 21st Century", a U.S.-based non-profit organisation. Jammed.

Target:CONGO (Dem. Rep. of) (COD)

RADIO OKAPI
✉ See National Radio section.
Webcast: D/P (radiookapi.net)
kHz: 11690

Winter Schedule 2012/2013			
French/Various	Days	Area	kHz
0400-0500	daily	COD	11690mey

Ann: French: "Radio Okapi".
V: QSL-card.

Target:CUBA (CUB)

WRMI – RADIO MIAMI INTERNATIONAL
✉ See International Radio section, under "USA".
SW: See International Radio section, under USA.
Notes: WRMI relays a number of anti-Government broadcasts to Cuba, usually on 9955kHz, in Spanish, from various programmme producers. For full programme details, see www.wrmi.net

RADIO REPÚBLICA (Clan)
✉ P.O. Box 110235, Hialeah, FL 33011, USA.
☎ +1 305 2794416.
E: radiorepublica@gmail.com
L.P: Asst to Prgr Coordinator: Maria A. Lima.
SW: [CRR] Cariari (Costa Rica): 1 x 50kW.
kHz: 5954, 9490

Winter Schedule 2012/2013			
Spanish	Days	Area	kHz
0000-0200	daily	CUB	9490guf
0100-0200	.twtfs.	CUB	5954crr
2300-0200	.....ss	CUB	5954crr

Ann: Spanish: "Esta es Radio República. La voz del Directorio Democrático Cubano", "Radio República, la voz de Cuba libre".
V: QSL-card.
Notes: On air since August 2005. Produced by Directorio Democrático Cubano. Jammed. Freqs/schedules may be changed without notice to escape from jamming.

Target:ERITREA (ERI)

DIMTSI WEGAHTA (VOICE OF THE DAWN) (Clan)
✉ Based in Mekelle, Ethiopia.
E: selamwegahta@sallina.com **W:** www.sallina.com
Webcast: D
kHz: 918

Winter Schedule 2012/2013			
Arabic/Tigrinya	Days	Area	kHz
0300-0600	daily	ERI	918mek
1400-2100	daily	ERI	918mek

Ann: Tigrinya: "Dimtsi Wegahta".
Notes: Established on 19 July 2007. Mahbersebawit Dimtsi Wegahta ("Community Voice of Dawn") is produced by the oppositional "Charity of Civic Society of Eritrea". Successor station to "Eastern Radio", which transmitted via a tx in Sudan 2006-2007.

VOICE OF ASENA (Clan)
✉ Based in London, United Kingdom.
E: aseye.asena@gmail.com **W:** www.assenna.com
Webcast: D
L.P: Dir: Amanuel Eyasu.
kHz: 15245

Winter Schedule 2012/2013			
Tigrinya	Days	Area	kHz
1700-1800	m.w.f..	ERI	15245sam

Ann: Tigrinya: "Ezi dimtsi Asena Eyu".
Notes: Started broadcasts on 16 Feb 2009.

VOICE OF DEMOCRATIC ALLIANCE (Clan)
✉ c/o Eritrean Democratic Alliance P.O. Box 13043, Khartoum, Sudan.

E: erit_alliance_2008@yahoo.com
W: www.erit-alliance.com (EDA)
SW: Via txs of the Ethiopian state broadcaster, Radio Ethiopia.
kHz: *7235, 9560*

Winter Schedule 2012/2013

Afar	Days	Area	kHz
1530-1600	.t.t.s.	EAf	7235gjw±, 9560gjw±

Arabic	Days	Area	kHz
1500-1530	m.w.f.s	EAf	7235gjw±, 9560gjw±

Kunama	Days	Area	kHz
1530-1600	m.w.f..	EAf	7235gjw±, 9560gjw±

Tigrinya	Days	Area	kHz
1500-1530	.t.t.s	EAf	7235gjw±, 9560gjw±
1530-1600	......s	EAf	7235gjw±, 9560gjw±

Key: ± Variable frequency.
Ann: Arabic: "Sawt al-Tahalufa al-Dimuqrati".
Notes: On air since April 2005. Produced by the "Eritrean Democratic Alliance" (EDA).

VOICE OF ERITREA (Clan)
E: hizbawii@gmail.com
W: www.mahta.net; www.harnnet.org (EPDP)
Webcast: D
SW: Via txs of the Ethiopian state broadcaster, Radio Ethiopia.
kHz: *7235, 9560*

Winter Schedule 2012/2013

Tigrinya	Days	Area	kHz
0400-0430	.t.t.s.	ERI	7235gjw±, 9560gjw±
1800-1830	.t.t.s.	ERI	7235gjw±, 9560gjw±

Key: ± Variable Frequency.
Ann: Tigrinya: "Dimtsi Ertrai".
V: QSL-email.
Notes: Produced by "Eritrean People's Democratic Party" (EPDP). Formerly produced by the "Eritrean Democratic Party" (EPM), which in 2010 merged with other oppositional organisations to form the EPDP.

VOICE OF PEACE AND DEMOCRACY OF ERITREA (Clan)
c/o Radio Ethiopia, P.O. Box 1020, Addis Ababa, Ethiopia.
SW: Via txs of the Ethiopian state broadcaster, Radio Ethiopia.
kHz: *7235, 9560*

Winter Schedule 2012/2013

Tigrinya	Days	Area	kHz
0400-0500	m.w.f..	ERI	7235gjw±, 9560gjw±
1800-1830	m.w.f..	ERI	7235gjw±, 9560gjw±

Key: ± Varible Frequency.
Ann: Tigrinya: "Yeh Radio Demtsi Selaman Demokratia Ertrai".
Notes: On air since February 1999.

Target:ETHIOPIA (ETH)

ESAT RADIO
P.O. Box 11261, Alexandria, VA 22312, USA.
☎ +1 571 3354024.
E: radio@ethsat.com **W:** www.ethsat.com
Webcast: D
SAT: Eutelsat 7WA.
kHz: *15375*

Winter Schedule 2012/2013

Amharic	Days	Area	kHz
1700-1800	daily	ETH	15375*

Key: * Operates between 15355-15395 kHz, to avoid jamming.
Notes: Began tests on SW in September 2011, regular programming commenced on 7 October 2011. 24h on satellite. ESAT Radio is produced by the U.S. NGO Advocates for Democracy and Media, Inc., and is a project under the roof of the Netherlands-based NGO "Task Force on Promoting Ethiopian Democracy and Human Rights" (TEDH).

GINBOT 7 DIMTS RADIO (Clan)
P.O. Box 56281, London, N4 9BH, United Kingdom.
☎ +44 20 32869661.
E: g7radio@ginbot7.org; info@ginbot7.org **W:** www.ginbot7.org

Webcast: D
SW: Broadcast via txs of "The Voice of the Broad Masses of Eritrea" in Asmara, Eritrea.
kHz: *837, 5980, 6025, 7120, 7185, 9700*

Winter Schedule 2012/2013

Amharic	Days	Area	kHz
0500-0530	.t.t...	ETH	837asm, 5980asm±, 6025asm±, 7120asm±, 7185asm±, 9700asm±
0530-0600	.....s.	ETH	837asm, 5980asm±, 6025asm±, 7120asm±, 7185asm±, 9700asm±
1430-1500	.t.t.s.	ETH	837asm, 5980asm±, 6025asm±, 7120asm±, 7185asm±, 9700asm±

Key: ± Variable Frequency.
Ann: Amharic: "Yeh Ginbot Sabat Dimtse now".
V: QSL-email.
Notes: On air since September 2008. Produced by the Ethiopian oppositional party "Ginbot 7 - Movement for Justice, Freedom and Democracy".

RADIO XORIYO (Clan)
P.O. Box 27618, Toronto, ON M3A 3B8, Canada.
E: raadioxoriyo@yahoo.com **W:** www.radioxoriyo.com
Webcast: D
kHz: *17630, 17870*

Winter Schedule 2012/2013

Somali	Days	Area	kHz
1600-1630	m..f..	ETH	17870sof
1600-1630	.t..s.	EAf	17630iss

Ann: Somali: "Ku soo dhawaada Radio Xoriyo codkii ummadda Ogadeniya".
V: QSL-email.
Notes: On air, intermittently, since May 2000. Produced by the "Ogaden National Liberation Front" (ONLF).

VOICE OF OROMO LIBERATION (Clan)
Postfach 510620, D-13366 Berlin, Germany.
☎ +49 30 4943372. ▤ +49 30 4943372.
E: sbo13366@aol.com **W:** www.oromoliberationfront.org/sbo.html
Webcast: D
kHz: *11810, 13810*

Winter Schedule 2012/2013

Amharic	Days	Area	kHz
1730-1800	..w....	ETH	11810wer

Oromo	Days	Area	kHz
1700-1730	..w...	ETH	11810wer
1700-1800	..w..s	ETH	13810wer
1700-1800	.....s	ETH	11810wer

Ann: Amharic: "Radio Bilisummaa Oromoo"; Oromo: "Kun Sagalee Bilisummaa Oromoo".
V: QSL-letter.
Notes: On air since July 1988 (transmitted from outside of Ethiopian territory since 1996). Produced by the "Oromo Liberation Front" (OLF); sister prgr: "Voice of Oromo Liberation Front". Also carried via "Voice of the Broad Masses of Eritrea" transmitters (Eritrea).

VOICE OF OROMO LIBERATION FRONT (Clan)
E: sabo@gemel.com.er
W: www.oroomoliberationfront.org/SABO/sabo.php
Webcast: D
kHz: *15315*

Winter Schedule 2012/2013

Oromo	Days	Area	kHz
1600-1630	......s	ETH	15315wer

Notes: Produced by the "Oromo Liberation Front" (OLF). Sister prgr of "Voice of Oromo Liberation".

Target:FIJI (FJI)

FIJI FREEDOM AND DEMOCRACY MOVEMENT (Clan)
9 Florence Terrace, Rosewater, Adelaide SA 5014, Australia.
☎ +61 48 8046249.

E: fijidemocracy@hotmail.com
W: sites.google.com/site/fijidemocracyfreedommovement
kHz: 11565

Winter Schedule 2012/2013

Fijian	Days	Area	kHz
0830-0900	m......	FJI	11565hri

Ann: Fijian: "Domo I Viti".
Notes: Produced by the Adelaide based "Fiji Freedom and Democracy Movement". On SW since 4 June 2012.

Target:INDIA (IND)

VOICE OF JAMMU & KASHMIR FREEDOM MOVEMENT ‡ (Clan)
✉ P.O. Box 102, Muzaffarabad 13100, Pakistan.
L.P: PM: J. Rehan.
SW: via tx of Pakistan Broadcasting Corp. in Rewat (Islamabad), Pakistan.
Ann: Urdu: "Ye Sadayee Hurriyat Jammu Kashmir hai".
V: QSL-letter. No rp.
Notes: On air since 1999. Produced by the "Jammu and Kashmir Freedom Movement" (JKFM). Reported inactive at the editorial deadline.

Target:IRAN (IRN)

RADIO RANGINKAMAN
✉ Based in Los Angeles, USA.
E: radioranginkaman@gmail.com
SAT: Eutelsat Hot Bird 13A.(via Globecast Persian sat-feed Radio Jahani)
kHz: 7530

Winter Schedule 2012/2013

Persian	Days	Area	kHz
1700-1730	m...f..	ME, CAs	7530kch

Notes: Prgr targetting the LGBT (lesbian, gay, bisexual and transgender) communities in Iran, Afghanistan and Tajikistan. The name translates in English as 'Radio Rainbow'. On SW since 24 September 2012. Also carried by KIRN Simi Valley, CA 670kHz (USA).

RADIO VOICE OF KURDISTAN (Clan)
✉ Based in Northern Iraq.
☎ +964 77 01597268. 📠 +964 77 01597268.
E: info@kurdistanradio.net **W:** kurdistanradio.net
Webcast: L
E: kdpsecretariat@gmail.com (KDP.Iran)
W: www.kurdistanukurd.com (KDP.Iran)
SW: Transmitters are located in Northern Iraq.
FM/DAB: See National Radio section, under Iraq.
SAT: Eutelsat Hot Bird 13A (via Tishk TV audio).
kHz: 3930

Winter Schedule 2012/2013

Farsi	Days	Area	kHz
0300-0330	daily	IRN	3930±

Kurdish	Days	Area	kHz
0200-0300	daily	IRN	3930±

Key: ± Variable Frequency.
Ann: Farsi: "In Radyo Sedaye Kordestane"; Kurdish: "Era Radyo Dengi Kurdistana".
Notes: Produced by the Iran branch of the "Kurdistan Democratic Party" (KDP.Iran). The Iraq branch of the KDP is a registered political party in Iraq. The station was launched on 28 September 1963 as "Voice of Iraqi Kurdistan". Jammed.

VOICE OF IRANIAN KURDISTAN (Clan)
✉ Reportedly based in Salah Al-Din, Iraqi Kurdistan.
☎ +964 75 01531826.
E: info@rdkiran.com **W:** www.rdkiran.com
Webcast: D
✉ c/o 17 Avenue d'Italie, 75013 Paris, France. (PDKI)
☎ +33 145856431. (PDKI) 📠 +33 145852093. (PDKI)
SW: Transmitter reported to be in the Salah Al Din area of Northern Iraq.
SAT: Eutelsat Hot Bird 13A (via Tishk TV audio).

kHz: 3965, 4875

Winter Schedule 2012/2013

Farsi	Days	Area	kHz
0230-0300	daily	IRN	3965±, 4875±
1230-1330	daily	IRN	3965±, 4875±

Kurdish	Days	Area	kHz
0300-0430	daily	IRN	3965±, 4875±
1330-1430	daily	IRN	3965±, 4875±

Key: ± Variable frequency
Ann: Farsi: "In Seda-ye Kordestan-e Iran"; Kurdish: "Erê Dengê Kurdistana Îranê".
V: QSL-letter. (Rpt to France address)
Notes: On air 1973-1975, and again since 1980. Produced by the "Democratic Party of Iranian Kurdistan" (PDKI). Jammed.

Target:KOREA, (D.P.R.) (KRE)

VOICE OF THE MARTYRS (Rlg)
✉ P.O. Box 92, Yangcheon, Yangcheon-gu, Seoul, Republic of Korea.
☎ +82 2 20650703. 📠 +82 2 20650704.
W: vomkorea.co.kr
✉ 14960 Woodcarver Road, Colorado Springs, CO 80923, USA.
☎ +1 719 4814408.
E: pastorfoley@seoulusa.org
W: www.seoulusa.org; seoulusa.co.kr
L.P: CEO, Soul USA: Eric Foley.
kHz: 7515

Winter Schedule 2012/2013

Korean	Days	Area	kHz
1600-1730	daily	KOR,KRE	7515tac

Ann: Korean: "I-bangsong-oen Daehan-Minguk Seoul-eseo bonae deurineun Sungyo sori Tansaeng sori bangsong-imnida" (Translation: "This broadcast from Republic of Korea, Seoul. This is Voice of Martyrdom-Voice of the Birth").
Notes: On air since 31 October 2009. Produced by the U.S. Christian missionary organisation USA Seoul. Earlier transmitted under the label "Voice of Free Radio" between 8 March 2008 and 30 September 2009.

VOICE OF WILDERNESS (Rlg)
✉ P.O. Box 8, Yeongdong, Seoul, 135-660, Republic of Korea.
☎ +82 2 7968846. 📠 +82 2 7927567.
E: main@cornerstone.or.kr **W:** www.cornerstone.or.kr
Webcast: D
✉ Cornerstone Ministries Int., P.O. Box 4002, Tustin, CA 92781, USA.
☎ +1 714 4840042. 📠 +1 714 4840046.
E: info@cornerstoneusa.org (USA) **W:** cornerstoneusa.org
kHz: 1566, 9920, 15180

Winter Schedule 2012/2013

Korean	Days	Area	kHz
1300-1330	mtwtfs.	KRE	9920dsb
1300-1400	mtwtfs.	KRE	15180trm*
1300-1430	......s	KRE	9920dsb
1330-1400	......s	KRE	15180trm*
1900-1930	m.w...	KRE	1566jej**
1900-2000	.....s.	KRE	1566jej**

Key: * via Bible Voice Broadcasting; ** via HLAZ.
Ann: Korean: "Gwangya-e Sori Bangsong-imnida".
Notes: Produced by Cornerstone Ministries International. Initially listed in WRTH as "North Korea Missionary Broadcast".

FURUSATO NO KAZE/ILBON–E BARAM
✉ Policy Planning Division, Headquarters for the Abduction Issue, Cabinet Secretariat, 6-1 Nagata-cho 1-chome, Chiyoda-ku, Tokyo 100-8968, Japan.
☎ +81 3 52532111. 📠 +81 3 3592 2300.
E: info@rachi.go.jp **W:** www.rachi.go.jp/jp/shisei/radio
Webcast: D

kHz: *9780, 9950, 9965, 9975*

Winter Schedule 2012/2013

Japanese	Days	Area	kHz
1330-1400	daily	KRE	9950tsu
1430-1500	daily	KRE	9950hbn
1600-1630	daily	KRE	9780tnn
Korean	**Days**	**Area**	**kHz**
1300-1330	daily	KRE	9950tsu
1500-1530	daily	KRE	9975hbn
1530-1600	daily	KRE	9965hbn

Ann: Japanese: "Furusato no Kaze"; Korean "Ilbon-e Baram".
V: QSL-letter.
Notes: Produced by the Japanese government agency "Headquarters for the Abduction Issue", targeting abducted Japanese citizens in North Korea. On the air since July 2007. "Furusato no Kaze" is the name of the Japanese broadcast; "Ilbon-e Baram" is the name of the Korean broadcast (translated to Japanese: "Nippon no Kaze").

MND RADIO

🖃 Ministry of National Defence, #1 Yongsandong 3ga, Yongsangu, Seoul 140-701, Republic of Korea.
☎ +82 2 7950071. 🖷 +82 2 7033109.
E: cyber@mnd.go.kr
W: www.mnd.go.kr/mndEng_2009/main/index.jsp
SW: [CHC] Chuncheon: 1 x 100kW; [JAA] Jongan: power unknown.
kHz: *5150, 5410, 5900, 6270, 6300, 6435, 6550, 6650, 6670*

Winter Schedule 2012/2013

Korean	Days	Area	kHz
0400-0440	daily	KRE	5150chc*, 6300chc*
0500-0540	daily	KRE	5410chc*, 6550chc*
0600-0640	daily	KRE	6270chc*, 6670chc*
0700-0740	daily	KRE	5900chc*, 6435chc*
1000-1040	daily	KRE	5410chc*, 6650chc*
1100-1140	daily	KRE	6270chc*, 6670chc*
1200-1240	daily	KRE	5150chc*, 6300chc*

Key: * Times and frequencies may vary.
IS: Opens and closes with one of 3 sets of music (different tunes for open/close).
Notes: On the air since March, 2011. Thought to be operated by the Ministry of National Defense (MND). Jammed.

RADIO FREE CHOSUN

🖃 3rd Floor, 384-20 Mangwon-dong, Mapo-gu, Seoul 121-821, Republic of Korea.
☎ +82 505 8702012. 🖷 +82 505 8702012.
E: rfchosun@rfchosun.org **W:** www.rfchosun.org
Webcast: D
W: nknet.org
LP: Pres: Lee Kwang Baek.
kHz: *7505, 11560*

Winter Schedule 2012/2013

Korean	Days	Area	kHz
1200-1300	daily	KRE	11560dsb
1300-1400	daily	KRE	11560dsb
2000-2100	daily	KRE	7505dsb

Ann: Korean: "Inmin-e sori, jeongni-e hamseong, Jayu Joseon Bangsong-imnida".
V: QSL-email.
Notes: On SW since 5 December 2005. Produced by the NGO "Network for North Korean Democracy and Human Rights" (NKnet). The project is funded through U.S. government / U.S. Congress grants.

SHIOKAZE (SEA BREEZE)

🖃 c/o COMJAN, Dairoku Matsuya Building 301, 3-8, Koraku 2-chome, Bunkyo-ku, Tokyo 112-0004, Japan.
☎ +81 3 56845058. 🖷 +81 3 56845059.
E: chosakai@circus.ocn.ne.jp **W:** www.chosa-kai.jp/SWR.html
Webcast: D (very limited archive)
LP: Dir, COMJAN & Producer/Editor: Tatsuru Murao.
kHz: *5910, 6110*

Winter Schedule 2012/2013

English/Korean/Japanese/Mandarin	Days	Area	kHz
1330-1430	daily	KRE	5910yam
2000-2100	daily	KRE	6110yam

Ann: English: "JSR. This is Shiokaze, Sea Breeze, the shortwave radio program from Tokyo, Japan. This program is broadcast by the Japanese private organization COMJAN"; Japanese: "JSR, Kochirawa Shiokaze desu"; Korean: "Yeogineun Shiokaze, Badatbaramimnida"; Mandarin: "Zheshi Shiokaze, Chaofeng Bosong".
V: QSL-card. (Issued if a $10 (US) money order donation is sent together with report)
Notes: Operational since 20 October 2005, produced by the "Investigation Commission on Missing Japanese Probably Related to North Korea" (COMJAN). Aimed at reaching Japanese citizens believed to have been abducted to North Korea. Jammed. Frequencies subject to change without notice. Chinese is broadcast, irregularly, twice a month.

VOICE OF FREEDOM

🖃 1, 3-ga, Yongsan-dong, Yongsan-gu, Seoul, Republic of Korea.
☎ +82 2 7484662.
FM/DAB: FM: 101.7MHz, 107.3MHz (Republic of Korea, exact location unknown).
Ann: Korean: "Yeogineun Jayu-eui Sori Bang-imnida".
Notes: Station re-activated on 24 May 2010, after 6 years off air. Reported to be administered by the Republic of Korea Government Defense Department. In the future may also use MW, to replace FM. Uperates to the following daily schedule, in Korean, targeting the Democratic People's Republic of Korea: 0300-0500, 0900-1400, 1500-2000 and 2100-2400 on both 101.7MHz and 107.3MHz FM. No SW broadcasts at time of publication.

ECHO OF HOPE (VOH) (Clan)

🖃 c/o National Intelligence Service (NIS), Seongnam, Sinchon-dong, Seoul, Rep. of Korea.
W: www.nis.go.kr (NIS); en.nis.go.kr (NIS, English)
SW: [JAA] Hwaseong, Jeongnam 3 x 100kW.
kHz: *3985, 6003, 6348*

Winter Schedule 2012/2013

Korean	Days	Area	kHz
0555-2400	daily	KRE	3985jaa, 6003jaa, 6348jaa

Ann: Korean: "Huimang-e meari pangsong-imnida, VOH".
Notes: Echo of Hope (alternative translation: Voice of Hope - VOH) was broadcast under the name "The Voice of Reunification" prior to 1973. Operated by the South Korean National Intelligence Service (NIS), though claiming to be a prgr of the (non-existent) "General Union of Overseas Compatriots". Jammed.

FREE NORTH KOREA RADIO (Clan)

🖃 P.O. Box 92, Mok-dong, Yangcheon-gu, Seoul 158-600, Republic of Korea.
☎ +82 2 26990977. 🖷 +82 2 26990978.
E: mini6915@hanmail.net **W:** www.fnkradio.com
Webcast: D
LP: Dir: Kim Seong Min.
kHz: *11550*

Winter Schedule 2012/2013

Korean	Days	Area	kHz
1200-1400	daily	KRE	11550dsb

Ann: Korean: "Jigeumbuteo Daehan Minguk sudo Seoul-eso bonae-neun Jayu Bukhan Bangsong-eul sijakhagesseumnida".
V: QSL-letter.
Notes: Founded on 20 April 2004 by North Korean defectors, on SW since 7 December 2005. Produced by the "North Korea People's Liberation Front" (NKPLF).

NORTH KOREA REFORM RADIO (Clan)

☎ +82 2 22426512. 🖷 +82 2 22426512.
E: nkreform@naver.com **W:** www.nkreform.com
Webcast: D
LP: Pres: Kim Seung Cheol.
kHz: *7590*

Winter Schedule 2012/2013

Korean	Days	Area	kHz
1500-1700	daily	KRE	7590tac

Ann: Korean: "Inmini baraneun saeroun sesang-ul hamgge ggumg-guneun Joseon Gyaehyeok Bangsong-imnida".
Notes: On SW since December 2007. Produced by the NGO "North Korea Reform Institute" (NKRI). The project is funded through U.S. government / U.S. Congress grants.

OPEN RADIO FOR NORTH KOREA (Clan)
✉ P.O. Box 158, Mapo-dong, Mapo-gu, Seoul, 121-600, Republic of Korea.
☎ +82 505 4707470; +82 10 71512785. 🖷 +82 505 4717470.
E: nkradio@nkradio.org; nkradio@naver.com; opennk@naver.com
W: www.nkradio.org; english.nkradio.org
Webcast: D/L (L: www.chmbc.co.kr (MBC Chuncheon), 1900-2000 broadcast only)
LP: Pres: Young Howard (Tae Kung Ha)
MW: [CHC] Relayed by MBC Chuncheon, South Korea: HLAN 774kHz 10kW (1900-2000 broadcast only).
FM/DAB: FM: Relayed by MBC Chuncheon, South Korea: HLAN-FM 92.3MHz 3kW (1900-2000 broadcast only)
kHz: 774, 7480, 7540

Winter Schedule 2012/2013

Korean	Days	Area	kHz
1400-1500	daily	KRE,CHN	7540dsb
1500-1600	daily	KRE,CHN	7540dsb
1900-1955	daily	KRE	774chc
2100-2200	daily	KRE,CHN	7480dsb

Ann: Korean: "Jayue gwangjang, huimang-e sori, Yeollin Bukhan Bangsong-imnida".
V: QSL-card.
Notes: On SW since 7 December 2005, targeting listeners in North Korea, and the Korean minority in the NE of PR.China. The project is funded thru U.S. government / U.S. Congress grants.

VOICE OF THE PEOPLE (Clan)
✉ Based in, and transmitted from, Republic of Korea.
SW: [GOY] Goyang 5 x 50kW (presumed site).
kHz: 3480, 3912, 4450, 4557, 6518, 6600

Winter Schedule 2012/2013

Korean	Days	Area	kHz
0455-2305	daily	KRE	3480goy, 3912goy,
			4450goy, 4557goy,
			6518goy, 6600goy

Ann: Korean: "Inmin-e sori pangsong-imnida".
Notes: On air since June 1985. Claims to be run by the Korean Workers Union, but is operated by the South Korean National Intelligence Service. Jammed.

Target:LEBANON (LBN)

RADIO MASHREQ (Clan)
✉ P.O. Box 52341, 4062 Limassol, Cyprus. (Correspondence)
E: contactus@radioalmachrek.org; almachrek@gmail.com
W: www.radioalmachrek.org
MW: [MEA] Metula (Israel): 756kHz 50kW.
FM/DAB: FM: Metula, Israel: 99.9MHz. Also reported on 90.3MHz.
kHz: 756

Winter Schedule 2012/2013

Arabic	Days	Area	kHz
0000-2400	daily	LBN	756mea

Ann: Arabic: "Al-idha'at al-Mashriqiyah".
V: QSL-email.
Notes: On air since January 2001 (tests since December 2000). Presumed to be run by the Israeli Army.

Target:MADAGASCAR (MDG)

RADIO FEON'NY FILAZANTSARA ‡ (Rlg)
✉ P.O. Box 1741, 101 Antananarivo, Madagascar.

☎ +261 202221001. 🖷 +261 202233767.
Notes: Produced by Fiangonana Loterana Malagasy or FLM (Malagasy Lutheran Church). Inactive at time of publication.

Target:MALAYSIA (MLA)

RADIO FREE SARAWAK
✉ Based in London, United Kingdom.
☎ +60 82 237191. (Malaysia)
E: info@radiofreesarawak.org **W:** radiofreesarawak.org
Webcast: D/P
kHz: 15420

Winter Schedule 2012/2013

English/Iban/ Malay	Days	Area	kHz
1000-1200	daily	MLA	15420hbn

Ann: Iban: "Radio Free Sarawak".
Notes: On air since November 2010. Oppositional prgr for listeners in rural Sarawak. Linked with Sarawak tycoon and former MP S'ng Chee Hua.

Target:MYANMAR (BRM)

DEMOCRATIC VOICE OF BURMA
✉ P.O. Box 6720, St Olavs Pass, N-0130 Oslo, Norway.
☎ +47 22868486. 🖷 +47 22868471.
E: acn@dvb.no **W:** www.dvb.no
Webcast: D/L
☎ +66 81 9518786. (Thailand Office)
LP: Exec Dir/Chief Editor: Aye Chan Naing; Head, Thailand Office: Toe Zaw Latt.
SAT: Apstar 7.
kHz: 7510, 11560

Winter Schedule 2012/2013

Burmese	Days	Area	kHz
1430-1530	daily	BRM	11560erv
2330-0030	daily	BRM	7510erv

Ann: Burmese: "Democratic Myanmar a-Than".
V: QSL-card.
Notes: On the air since July 1992. Produced by members of the exile organisation "National Coalition Government of the Union of Burma". DVB holds a Norwegian broadcasting license. Broadcasts are in Burmese, with 15 mins per transmission allocated to the Arakan, Chin, Karen, Karenni, Kayan, Kachin, Mon and Shan languages. Plans to move its operation from Norway via Thailand to Myanmar.

Target:NIGERIA (NIG)

HAMADA RADIO INTERNATIONAL
✉ Based in Spain.
E: abd2t@yahoo.com
kHz: 7350

Winter Schedule 2012/2013

Hausa	Days	Area	kHz
0530-0600	mtwtf..	NIG	7350nau

Ann: Hausa: "Hamada Radio International".
Notes: On air since Dec 2010. Station was known as "Aso Radio International" during 2009.

RADIO BIAFRA LONDON
✉ 72 Dovehouse Mead, Barking, IG11 7EB, United Kingdom.
☎ +44 7831 308376.
E: contact@radiobiafralondon.com
W: www.radiobiafralondon.com; www.radiobiafralondononline.com
Webcast: D
LP: Dir/Presenter: Nnamdi Kanu; Editor/Presenter: Amarachi Gloria Okpara; Research Analyst/Presenter: Uche Mefor. .
kHz: 11830

Winter Schedule 2012/2013

English/Igbo	Days	Area	kHz
1900-2000	...t.s.	NIG	11830wer

Ann: English: "Radio Biafra broadcasting live from London".
Notes: On air since 21 April 2012. Returned to SW after a 2.5 year hiatus. Produced by Biafra Media Group (United Kingdom) and supported by public donations.

Target:PAKISTAN (PAK)

RADIO SEDAYEE KASHMIR (Clan)
✉ c/o All India Radio (AIR), Akashvani Bhavan, Sansad Marg, New Delhi-110001, India.
kHz: *4870, 6100*

Winter Schedule 2012/2013

Dogri	Days	Area	kHz
0310-0330	daily	PAK	4870del
0810-0830	daily	PAK	6100del
1510-1530	daily	PAK	4870del

Kashmiri	Days	Area	kHz
0230-0310	daily	PAK	4870del
0730-0810	daily	PAK	6100del
1430-1510	daily	PAK	4870del

Ann: Urdu: "Ye Radio Sedayee Kashmir".
Notes: On air since early 2003. Radio Sedayee Kashmir is a prgr representing the views of the Indian government in the dispute with Pakistan over Kashmir.

Target:SOMALIA (SOM)

RADIO DAMAL ‡
✉ P.O. Box 104668, Nairobi 00100, Kenya.
☎ +254 718 239415.
E: yourvoice@radiodamal.com; radiodamal@gmail.com
W: www.radiodamal.com
Webcast: L
L.P: SM: Faith Kwamboka.
Ann: Somali: "Idaacada Codka Bulshada Soomalyeed".
V: Does not verify.
Notes: On the air since 4 Nov 2010. Radio Damal ("The Voice of the Somali People") is produced in the studios of the public service Kenya Broadcasting Corp. (KBC), allegedly financed through P.R.China government funds. Inactive at time of publication.

RADIO ERGO
✉ P.O.Box 2234, 00621 Nairobi, Kenya.
☎ +254 20 4002102.
E: info@radioergo.org **W:** www.radioergo.org
Webcast: D/P
✉ Nørregade 18, DK-1165 København K, Denmark. (IMS)
☎ +45 88327000. 🖷 +45 33120099.
E: ims@i-m-s.dk **W:** www.i-m-s.dk
L.P: Exec. Dir, IMS: Jesper Højberg.
kHz: *17680*

Winter Schedule 2012/2013

Somali	Days	Area	kHz
0830-0930	daily	SOM	17680dha

Ann: Somali: "Halkalee Walanta Somalia Radio Ergo".
Notes: Produced by IMS Productions Aps (a branch of IMS - International Media Support). Originally aired under the name "IRIN Radio" by the UN Office for the Coordination of Humanitarian Affairs (OCHA) since 2008. IMS Productions took over the operation on 1 July 2011 and rebranded the service "Radio Ergo".

Target:SOUTH SUDAN (SSD)

VOICE OF SOUTH SUDAN REVOLUTIONARY RADIO ‡ (Clan)
Ann: English: "This is the Voice of South Sudan Revolutionary Radio", "The Voice of South Sudan".
Notes: On SW since April 2012. Broadcasting in support of the "South Sudan Liberation Army". Inactive at time of publication.

Target:SRI LANKA (CLN)

VOICE OF TIGERS RADIO
☎ +94 21 2285702. 🖷 +94 21 2285015.
E: info@pulikalinkural.com
W: www.votradio.com; www.pulikalinkural.com
Webcast: D/L
kHz: *11550*

Winter Schedule 2012/2013

Tamil	Days	Area	kHz
1530-1630	.....s.	CLN	11550tac

Notes: Satellite/web radio stn. On SW since July 2012.

Target:SUDAN (SDN)

MIRAYA FM
✉ Station details under South Sudan in National Radio Section.
Webcast: D/L (www.mirayafm.org)
kHz: *9940*

Winter Schedule 2012/2013

Arabic/English	Days	Area	kHz
0300-0600	daily	SDN	9940-

Ann: English: "Radio Miraya".

RADIO DABANGA
✉ c/o Free Press Unlimited, Witte Kruislaan 55, 1217 AM Hilversum, The Netherlands.
☎ +31 35 6254350. 🖷 +31 35 6254310.
E: radiodabanga@yahoo.com **W:** www.radiodabanga.org
Webcast: D
W: www.freepressunlimited.org
L.P: Dir: Hildebrand Bijleveld.
kHz: *7315, 11940, 13780, 13800, 15535*

Winter Schedule 2012/2013

Arabic (Darfuri)	Days	Area	kHz
0430-0500	daily	SDN	13780mdc
0430-0600	daily	SDN	7315smg, 11940mdc, 13800dha
1500-1530	daily	SDN	13800mdc, 15535smg
1530-1630	daily	SDN	13800mdc, 15535smg
1700-1730	daily	SDN	13780mdc

Ann: All languages: "Radio Dabanga".
V: QSL-card.
Notes: On air since 15 November 2008, produced by the Dutch NGO "Press Unlimited" (a merger of the NGOs "Press Now" and "Free Voice"). Radio Dabanga is aimed at listeners in the Darfur area in Western Sudan.

RADIO TAMAZUJ
✉ c/o Free Press Unlimited, Witte Kruislaan 55, 1217 AM Hilversum, The Netherlands.
☎ +31 35 6254300.
E: info@freepressunlimited.org **W:** radiotamazuj.org
kHz: *7315, 11940, 13800*

Winter Schedule 2012/2013

Arabic	Days	Area	kHz
0400-0430	daily	SDN	7315smg, 11940mdc, 13800dha

Notes: Produced by the Dutch foundation "Free Press Unlimited". Daily broadcasts began in January 2012 and targets audiences in The Republic of Sudan and Republic of Southern Sudan, with an emphasis on the conflict affected regions.

SUDAN RADIO SERVICE
✉ Postal Address: c/o Education Development Center, P.O. Box 4392, 00100 Nairobi, Kenya.

☎ +254 20 2346217.
E: srs@edc.org; srs@sudanradio.org
Webcast: D (www.sudanradio.org)
▣ Physical address: Umeme Plaza, Old Naivasha Road, Dagoretti Corner, Nairobi, Kenya.
kHz: *13720, 17745*

Winter Schedule 2012/2013

Arabic	Days	Area	kHz
0400-0420	m.....s	SDN	13720dha
0400-0430	.twtf..	SDN	13720dha
0400-0530	.....s.	SDN	13720dha
0435-0530	m.....s	SDN	13720dha
0445-0530	.twtf..	SDN	13720dha
1600-1620	.....ss	SDN	17745wof
1600-1630	mtwt...	SDN	17745wof
1600-1730	....f..	SDN	17745wof
1635-1730	.....ss	SDN	17745wof
1645-1730	mtwt...	SDN	17745wof
Fur	**Days**	**Area**	**kHz**
0430-0445	.t..f..	SDN	13720dha
1630-1645	m..t...	SDN	17745wof
Masalit	**Days**	**Area**	**kHz**
0420-0435	m......	SDN	13720dha
0430-0445	...t...	SDN	13720dha
1620-1635	.....s	SDN	17745wof
1630-1645	..w....	SDN	17745wof
Zaghawa	**Days**	**Area**	**kHz**
0420-0435	.....s	SDN	13720dha
0430-0445	..w....	SDN	13720dha
1620-1635	.....s.	SDN	17745wof
1630-1645	.t.....	SDN	17745wof

V: QSL-letter.
Notes: On air, intermittently, since July 2003. SRS is a project of Education Development Center, Inc. (USA). It is funded by the U.S. State Department's Bureau of Democracy, Human Rights, and Labor.

Target:TURKEY (TUR)

DENGÊ KURDISTANÊ
▣ Stiftelsen Kurdisk Media, Tre Kronors väg 33, S-13131 Nacka, Sweden.
☎ +46 8 6562038. 🖷 +46 8 6567919.
E: info@denge-kurdistane.com **W:** www.denge-kurdistane.com
Webcast: D/L
W: www.kongrakurdistan.net (KNC)
SAT: Eutelsat 9A.
kHz: *11510*

Winter Schedule 2012/2013

Kurdish	Days	Area	kHz
0400-1600	daily	ME	11510kch
1600-2000	daily	ME	11510sof

Ann: Kurdish: "Era Dengê Kurdistanê".
Notes: Dengê Kurdistanê ("Voice of Kurdistan") is produced under the roof of the foundation Kurdisk Media. The prgr was launched on 1 Sep 2012 (on shortwave since 7 Sep), replacing Dengê Mezopotamya. The station broadcasts in various Kurdish dialects and is targeting Kurdish listeners across the Near East (Turkey, Iran, Iraq, Syria).

Target:VIETNAM (VTN)

QUÊ ME RADIO
▣ BP 60063, F-94472 Boissy Saint Léger Cedex, France.
☎ +33 145983085. 🖷 +33 145983261.
E: queme.democracy@gmail.com; queme@free.fr
W: www.queme.net
kHz: *9930*

Winter Schedule 2012/2013

Vietnamese	Days	Area	kHz
1200-1230	....f..	VTN	9930hbn

RADIO CHÂN TRÒI MÓI
▣ P.O. Box 18031, Spokane, WA 99228-0031, USA.
☎ +1 509 4897017.
E: lienlac@radiochantroimoi.com **W:** www.radiochantroimoi.com
Webcast: D/P
▣ P.O. Box 48, Hishi Yodogawa, Osaka 555, Japan. (Correspondence)
W: www.viettan.org (Viet Tan)
kHz: *1503*

Winter Schedule 2012/2013

Vietnamese	Days	Area	kHz
1330-1400	daily	VTN	1503fan

Ann: Vietnamese: "Dài là dai phat thanh Chân Tròi Mói".
V: QSL-card.
Notes: Radio Chân Tròi Mói ("New Horizont Radio") is produced by the "Vietnam Reform Party" (Viet Tan). On air since 1992.

RADIO DLSN
▣ c/o LLDTCNTQ, P.O.Box 6005, Torrance, CA 90504, USA.
E: vpll.llcq@gmail.com **W:** radiodlsn.com; www.lldtcntq.org
kHz: *1503*

Winter Schedule 2012/2013

Vietnamese	Days	Area	kHz
1430-1500	daily	VTN	1503fan

Ann: Vietnamese: "Ðây là dây phát thanh Ðáp Lòi Sông Núi".
Notes: On air since 15 May 2011. The transmissions of Radio DLSN (Ðáp Lòi Sông Núi - "Fatherland") are arranged by the "Foundation for Democracy of Vietnam".

Target:WEST BANK & GAZA (PSE)

RADIO AL–QUDS
▣ P.O. Box 5092, Damascus, Syria.
W: www.palestinesons.com (PFLP-GC)
MW: [SBB] Damascus, Sabboura (Syria): 702kHz 200kW.
FM/DAB: FM: Aleppo, Syria: 90.6MHz; unknown locations, Syria: 96.7 (10kW), 105.4MHz (10kW).
kHz: *702*

Winter Schedule 2012/2013

Arabic	Days	Area	kHz
0500-1800	daily	PSE	702sbb†

Key: † Irregular
Ann: Arabic: "Idha'at Al-Quds".
V: QSL-card.
Notes: On air since 1 January 1988. Operated by "Popular Front for the Liberation of Palestine - General Command" (PFLP-GC), with approval by Syrian authorities. The txs are provided by the Syrian state broadcaster General Organisation of Radio and TV. 24h on FM.

Target:WESTERN SAHARA (AOE)

RADIO NACIONAL DE LA R.A.S.D.
▣ BP 470, 37000 Tindouf, Algeria.
☎ +213 49 923525.
E: rasdradio@yahoo.es **W:** web.jet.es/rasd/radionacional
▣ c/o Mission de la R.A.S.D., BP 10, El Mouradia, 16000 Algiers, Algeria.
MW: [RBN] Rabouni (Algeria): 1550kHz 50kW (estimated power).
SW: [RBN] Rabouni (Algeria): 1 x 20kW. ‡
kHz: *1550*

Winter Schedule 2012/2013

Arabic	Days	Area	kHz
0600-1200	daily	NAf	1550rbn*
1800-2330	daily	NAf	1550rbn*
Spanish	**Days**	**Area**	**kHz**
1200-1300	daily	NAf	1550rbn*
1700-1800	daily	NAf	1550rbn*

Key: * Alternate Freq 702kHz.
Ann: Arabic: "Huna el-estudiohaay al-markaziya al-wataniya, Sowt al-sha'ab a-Sahraui al-mukafa"; Spanish: "Ésta es la Radio Nacional de la República Arabe Saharaui Democrática".
V: QSL-letter.

Notes: On air since 28 December 1975, founded by the "Polisario Front". Operated by the Ministry of Information of the government-in-exile of the Sahrawi Arab Democratic Republic, with approval by the Algerian authorities. Jammed.

Target:ZIMBABWE (ZWE)

RADIO DIALOGUE (ZIMBABWE COMMUNITY RADIO)
⌨ Box FM 100, Famona, Bulawayo, Zimbabwe.
☎ +263 9 884858. 🖷 +263 9 884828.
E: via website **W:** www.radiodialogue.com
Webcast: D/P
L.P: Dir (ZACRAS): Henry Masuku.
kHz: 12115

Winter Schedule 2012/2013
Shona/Ndebele/

English	Days	Area	kHz
1600-1700	daily	SAf	12115mdc

Ann: English: "Radio Dialogue - giving you a voice".
Notes: Produced by the local radio station Radio Dialogue for the Zimbabwe Association of Community Radio Stations (ZACRAS).

SW RADIO AFRICA
⌨ P.O. Box 243, Borehamwood, Herts, WD6 4WA, United Kingdom.
☎ +44 20 83871441. 🖷 +44 20 83871416.
E: tech@swradioafrica.com **W:** www.swradioafrica.com
Webcast: D/L/P
L.P: SM: Ms Gerry Jackson.
kHz: 4880

Winter Schedule 2012/2013
English/Ndebele/

Shona	Days	Area	kHz
1700-1900	daily	ZWE	4880mey

Ann: English: "SW Radio Africa, Zimbabwe's Independent Voice".
V: QSL-card.
Notes: On air since December 2001. Produced by a London based group of Zimbabwean exiles. Funded by the U.S. Agency for International Development (USAID).

RADIO VOICE OF THE PEOPLE (Clan)
⌨ P.O. Box 5750, Harare, Zimbabwe.
☎ +263 91 308052. 🖷 +263 4 707123.
E: voxpop@ecoweb.co.zw **W:** www.radiovop.com
Webcast: D/L/P
L.P: MD: John Masuku.
kHz: 9345

Winter Schedule 2012/2013
English/Ndebele/

Shona	Days	Area	kHz
1800-1900	daily	ZWE	9345mdc

Ann: English: "This is Radio VOP, Zimbabwe's Alternative Voice", "You are tuned to Radio Voice of the People".
V: QSL-letter.
Notes: On air since June 2000, founded by former journalists of the Zimbabwe Broadcasting Corporation (ZBC). Funded by the "Soros Foundation" and the Dutch NGO "HIVOS".

INTERNATIONAL & CLANDESTINE UPDATES

Pdfs containing updates of the B12 schedules in this edition will be uploaded to *www.wrth.com* in early February 2013. The A13 schedules will be uploaded in early May 2013, and an A12 update in mid-July 2013.

Religious Broadcasters Cross Reference Table

This table shows the names of religious broadcasters in the International Radio and COTB sections, together with a cross reference to enable the station and/or schedule to be looked up, by country. Where ✓ appears in the **Admin/Relay** column, this means that the entry contains corporate details of the broadcaster and is usually the company HQ. If the word 'Relay' appears in that coulmn, this indicates that this is just a transmitting site, the schedule can be found under the parent station as indicated. ✗ indicates that the schedule is located elsewhere. ‡ indicates a broadcaster that was inactive at ediitorial deadline (and, therefore, will not have a schedule).

Station Name	Country	Code	Schedule	Admin/Relay	Section
Adventist World Radio (AWR)	United States of America	USA	✗	✓	International Radio
Athmik Yatra Radio	India	IND	✓		International Radio
AWR Africa/Europe	United Kingdom	G	✓		International Radio
AWR Asia/Pacific	Indonesia	INS	✓		International Radio
Bible Voice Broadcasting (BVB)	Canada	CAN	✓		International Radio
Christian Science Sentinel	United States of America	USA	✓		International Radio
Christian Vision	United Kingdom	G	✗	✓	International Radio
CVC 1Africa Radio	South Africa	AFS	✓		International Radio
CVC La Voz ‡	Chile	CHL	✗	✓	International Radio
CVC Radio Christian Voice ‡	Zambia	ZMB	✗	✓	International Radio
CVC The Voice Asia	United Kingdom	G	✓		International Radio
Eternal Good News	United States of America	USA	✓		International Radio
Evangelische Missions-Gemeinden	Germany	D	✓		International Radio
Family Radio	United States of America	USA	✓		International Radio
Far East Broadcasting Company Inc (FEBC)	United States of America	USA	✗	✓	International Radio
FEBA Radio	United Kingdom	G	✓		International Radio
FEBC Korea	Korea, Rep. of	KOR	✓		International Radio
FEBC Philippines	Philippines	PHL	✓		International Radio
HCJB - La Voz de Los Andes	Ecuador	EQA	✓		International Radio
HCJB Germany	Germany	D	✓		International Radio
HCJB Global Voice	United States of America	USA	✗	✓	International Radio
HCJB Global Voice Australia	Australia	AUS	✓		International Radio
Hmong World Christian Radio	United States of America	USA	✓		International Radio
IBRA Radio	Sweden	S	✓		International Radio
KJES Radio	United States of America	USA	✓		International Radio
KNLS International	Alaska	ALS	✓		International Radio
KSDA (AWR Asia/Pacific Relay Station)	Guam	GUM	✗	Relay	International Radio
KTWR (TWR Relay Station)	Guam	GUM	✗	Relay	International Radio
Lutherische Stunde	Germany	D	✓		International Radio
Madagascar World Voice ‡	Madagascar	MDG	✗	✓	International Radio
Minghui Radio	China	CHN	✓		COTB
Missionswerk Heukelbach	Germany	D	✓		International Radio
Pan American Broadcasting	United States of America	USA	✓		International Radio
Radio Africa	Equatorial Guinea	GNE	✓		International Radio
Radio Chân Tròi Mói	Vietnam	VTN	✓		COTB
Radio Feon'ny Filazantsara ‡	Madagascar	MDG	✗	✓	COTB
Radio Freundes-dienst	Switzerland	SUI	✓		International Radio
Radio Payam-e Doost	United States of America	USA	✓		International Radio
Radio Veritas Asia	Philippines	PHL	✓		International Radio
Sawtu Linjiila (Voice of The Gospel)	Cameroon	CME	✓		COTB
Shortwave Relay Service	Kyrgyzstan	KGZ	✓		International Radio
Stimme Des Trostes	Switzerland	SUI	✓		International Radio
Suab Xaa Moo Zoo	United States of America	USA	✓		International Radio
T8WH - World Harvest Radio (WHR)	Palau	PLW	✓		International Radio
Tartu Pereraadio	Estonia	EST	✗	✓	International Radio
The Overcomer Ministry	United States of America	USA	✓		International Radio
TWR	United States of America	USA	✗	✓	International Radio
TWR Africa	South Africa	AFS	✓		International Radio
TWR Asia	Singapore	SNG	✓		International Radio
TWR Bonaire	Bonaire	BES	✓		International Radio
TWR Europe	Austria	AUT	✓		International Radio
TWR India	India	IND	✓		International Radio
TWR Relay Station	Benin	BEN	✗	Relay	International Radio
TWR Relay Station	Swaziland	SWZ	✗	Relay	International Radio
University Network	United States of America	USA	✓		International Radio
Vatican Radio	Vatican City State	CVA	✓		International Radio
Voice of The Martyrs	Korea, (D.P.R.)	KRE	✓		COTB
Voice of Wilderness	Korea, (D.P.R.)	KRE	✓		COTB
WEWN - EWTN Shortwave Radio	United States of America	USA	✓		International Radio
WHRI - World Harvest Radio (WHR)	United States of America	USA	✓		International Radio
WINB	United States of America	USA	✓		International Radio
WJHR Radio International	United States of America	USA	✓		International Radio
WMLK ‡	United States of America	USA	✗	✓	International Radio
World Christian Broadcasting Inc.	United States of America	USA	✗	✓	International Radio
WRNO Worldwide	United States of America	USA	✓		International Radio
WTWW	United States of America	USA	✓		International Radio
WWCR - Worldwide Christian Radio	United States of America	USA	✓		International Radio
WWRB	United States of America	USA	✓		International Radio
Yevangelskiye Chteniya	Russia	RUS	✓		International Radio

FREQUENCY LISTS

Section Contents

Features & Reviews

MW Listings:

National Radio

SW Listings:

International Radio

Frequency Lists

(For country codes and transmitter codes, please see the decode tables in the Reference section)

Please note that the North America MW listing has been removed in order to increase the number of MW stations in the main USA listing

Terrestrial Television

Reference

EUROPE, AFRICA, NEAR & MIDDLE EAST

Abbreviations: AFN=American Forces Network, BBCWS=British Broadcasting Corporation World Service, COPE= Cadena de Ondas Populares Espanolas, DRM=Digital Radio Mondiale, LPAMs=Low Power AM station, OCR=Onda Cero Radio, RFI=Radio France International, RSL=Restricted Service Licences, TWR=Trans World Radio, VOA=Voice of America.

kHz	kW	Ctry	Station, location	kHz	kW	Ctry	Station, location
25	300	BLR	STFT Station, Vileyka (CW)	549	600	ALG	R. Algérienne Jil FM, Sidi Hamadouche
	900	RUS	STFT Station, 3 stns (CW)		51	ARS	BSKSA General prgr, Qurayyat +3 stns
60	15	G	STFT Station, Anthorn (CW)		200	D	Deutschlandfunk, Nordkirchen/Thurnau
66.66	10	RUS	STFT Station, Moscow (AM)		20	GAB	RTG 2, Oyem
77.5	50	D	STFT Station, Mainflingen (CW/PSK)		25	IRL	Spirit R, Carrickroe
153	2000/1000	ALG	R. Algérienne 1, Béchar		400/100	IRN	IRIB R. Iran, Sirjan
	500/250	D	Deutschlandfunk, Donebach		25	NIG	Broadc. Sce of the Ekiti State, Ado
	100	NOR	NRK P1/Troms og Finnmark, Ingøy		25	NIG	Kano State BC, Tukun Tawa
	200	ROU	Antena Satelor, Brasov		10	RKS	RTK Radio Kosova, Prishtinë
162	2000/1000	F	France Inter, Allouis		50	RUS	R. Mayak, Kaliningrad
171	1600	MRC	Medi 1, Nador		600	RUS	R. Mayak, Krasnyy Bor (St. P.)
	1200	RUS	GR Prgr. Kavkaz/Checnya Sv, Tbilisskaya		75	RUS	R. Mayak, Noginsk (Moskva)
	150	RUS	R. Rossii, Bolshakovo		50	RUS	R. Mayak, Novocherkassk
177	500	D	Deutschlandradio Kultur, Zehlendorf		150	RUS	R. Mayak, Syktyvkar
183	2000	D	Europe 1, Felsberg (Saarlouis)		15	SVN	R. Koper, Beli Kriz
189	300	ISL	RUV Rás 2, Gufuskálar		725	UKR	UR2, Kyiv/Lviv/Mykolaiv
198	2000/1000	ALG	R. Algérienne 1, Ouargla	558	10	ALG	R. Algérienne 1/R. Ouargla, Touggourt
	50	G	BBC R4, Burghead		50	ARS	BSKSA Quran prgr, Jeddah
	500	G	BBC R4, Droitwich		50	BOT	R. Botswana, Muchenje
	50	G	BBC R4, Westerglen		10	CYP	CyBC 1, Paphos
	150	RUS	R. Mayak, Kurovskaya (Moskva)		20	E	RNE5 TN, A Coruña
	150	RUS	R. Mayak, Olgino (Sankt-Peterburg)		20	E	RNE5 TN, San Sebastián
207	500/250	D	Deutschlandfunk, Aholming		50	E	RNE5 TN, Valencia
	100	ISL	RUV Rás 1, Eidar		100	EGY	ERTU Educ. prgr, Cairo (Abu Zaabal)
	400	MRC	SNRT National Netw, Azilal		1	G	Spectrum Radio, London
216	900	F	RMC Info, Roumoules		1000	IRN	IRIB R. Farhang, Gheslagh
225	1000	POL	Polksie R. 1, Solec Kujawski		25	KEN	KBC Western Sce, Kapsimotwa (inactive)
234	1500	LUX	RTL, Beidweiler		10	MWI	MBC R. 1, Karonga
243	50	DNK	DR P4 news & weather, Kalundborg		50	NIG	Cross River State BC, Calabar
252	1500/750	ALG	R. Algérienne 3, Tipaza		400	ROU	R. România Actualitati, Tirgu Jiu
	300	IRL	RTE Radio 1, Summerhill (Clarkstown)		-	SSD	South Sudan R, Bentiu
	150	RUS	R. Rossii/Reg, Kazan		10	SVN	MMR / R. Slovenija 1, Nemcavci
261	75	BUL	Horizont, Sofia Vakarel	567	25	AFS	Cape Talk, Cape Town
	500	RUS	R. Rossii, Taldom (Moskva)		20	ARS	BSKSA Quran prgr, Afif/Abha
270	650	CZE	CRo 1, Uherské Hradišt		50	E	RNE5 TN, Murcia
279	500	BLR	BR 1, Sasnovy		50	KEN	KBC Swahili Sce, Garissa
531	600	ALG	R. Algérienne Jil FM, F'Kirina		50	NIG	FRCN Ibadan, Alaho
	10	ARS	BSKSA Quran prgr, Bisha		50	NIG	Imo BC, Owerri
	50	BOT	R. Botswana, Maun		-	NIG	Zamfara State R, Gusau
	10	E	RNE5 TN, Cordoba		100	ROU	R. România Actualitati, Brasov/Satu Mare
	20	E	RNE5 TN, Oviedo		250	RUS	R. Rossii/Reg, Volgograd
	10	E	RNE5 TN, Pamplona		300	SYR	Syrian R. 1, Damascus Adra
	10	E	RNE5 TN, Pontevedra	576	50	AFS	R. Veritas, Meyerton
	25	FRO	Kringvarp Føroya Útvarpið, Akraberg		400/200	ALG	R. Algérienne R. Béchar
	0.001	G	RSLs		20	ARS	BSKSA Quran prgr, Gizan
	500	IRN	IRIB R. Iran, Azarshahr		20	CNR	RNE R. Nacional, Las Palmas
	600	IRN	IRIB R. Iran, Iranshahr		100	E	RNE5 TN, Barcelona
	50	ISR	KI Reshet Alef, Yavne		750	IRN	IRIB R. Iran/VOIRI, Mahshahr
	50	NIG	Ondo State R. Corp, Akure		25	NIG	FRCN Ibadan, Moniya
	0.8	POL	Twoje R, Wlodawa		100	OMA	R. Sultanate of Oman, Haima
	0.8	POL	Twoje R, Zywiec		10	POR	R. Sim, Braga
	15	ROU	Antena Satelor, Urziceni		100	UGA	UBC Blue Channel, Mityana
	15	ROU	R. România Actualitati, Petrosani	584	5	AFG	R. Badakhshan, Faizabad (inactive)
	30	RUS	R. Mayak/Reg, Cheboksary	585	1200	ARS	BSKSA General prgr, Riyadh
540	50	E	OCR Catalunya, Barcelona		5	CVA	Vatican R, Vatican City
	2000/1000	HNG	MR Kossuth R, Solt		600	E	RNE R. Nacional, Madrid
	200	IRN	IRIB R. Iran, Mashhad		2	G	BBC R. Scotland, Dumfries
	100	KEN	KBC Swahili Sce, Voi (inactive)		600	IRN	IRIB R. Quran, Tehran
	600	KWT	R. Kuwait Main prgr, Kabd		50	NIG	Enugu State BC, Abakaliki
	600	MRC	SNRT National Netw./Reg, Sidi Bennour		150	RUS	R. Rossii/Reg, Perm
	10	MWI	MBC R. 1, Mangochi		350	TUN	ERTT National prgr, Gafsa
	50	NIG	Sokoto State BC, Sokoto		50	TZA	VO Tanzania Zanzibar, Chumbuni (inactive)
	50	RUS	R. Mayak, Orenburg	594	5	AFG	R. Faryab, Maimana
	50	SDN	SRTC Regional, Nyala		2000	ARS	BSKSA General prgr, Duba + 1 stn

kHz	kW	Ctry	Station, location
	50	ARS	BSKSA General/Pilgrimage prgr, Makkah
	100	ETH	R. Ethiopia, Bahir Dar
	400	IRN	IRIB Regional, Shiraz (Dehnow)
	30	MWI	MBC R. 1, Lilongwe
	200	NIG	FRCN Kaduna, Jaji
	70	POR	R. Sim, Muge
	40	RUS	R. Rossii, Izhevsk
	0.6	SVN	R.Odmev, Cerkno
	100	SYR	Syrian R. 2, Homs
595	50	MRC	SNRT A/R, Oujda (alt. on 594kHz)
602	-	YEM	YRTC General prgr, (unknown location)
603	100	CYP	CyBC 3, Nicosia
	20	D	CRI relay, Zehlendorf (F.P.I.)
	10	E	RNE5 TN, Palencia
	50	E	RNE5 TN, Sevilla
	50	EGY	ERTU Koran prgr, Sohag
	300	F	France Info, Lyon
	2	G	BBC R. 4, Newcastle
	0.4	G	Gold, Littlebourne
	100	IRN	IRIB R. Iran, Zahedan + 1 stn
	20	IRQ	IMN Republic of Iraq R, Mosul
	50	NIG	Borno R. & TV Corp, Maiduguri
	25	NIG	Ogun State BC, Abeokuta
	30	ROU	Antena Satelor, Bucuresti
	100	ROU	R. România Actualitati, Botosani/Oradea
	15	ROU	R. România Actualitati, Drobeta-T. Severin
	100/10	TZA	R. Tanzania, Dodoma
612	20	ARS	BSKSA Quran prgr, Al-Aflaj/Hail
	100	BHR	R. Bahrain Quran prgr, Manama
	10	E	RNE R. Nacional, Lleida
	10	E	RNE R. Nacional, Vitoria
	600	IRN	VOIRI, Qasr-e-Shirin
	200	JOR	R. Jordan Main prgr, Shobak
	100	KEN	KBC Swahili Sce, Ngong
	100	LTU	R. Liberty via R. Baltic Waves, Vilnius
	300	MRC	SNRT National Netw, Sebaa-Aioun
	50	NIG	Kwara State BC, Ilorin
	150	RUS	R. Mayak, Pedaselga (Petrozavodsk)
	20	RUS	R. Radonezh/Narodnoye R, Kurkino, (Moskva)
621	200	AFG	BBG Deewa R./R. Mashal, Khost
	300	BEL	RTBF International, Wavre
	100	BOT	R. Botswana, Selebi-Phikwe
	100	CNR	RNE R. Nacional, Santa Cruz de Tenerife
	10	E	RNE R. Nacional, Avila
	10	E	RNE R. Nacional, Jaén
	10	E	RNE R. Nacional, Palma de Mallorca
	1000	EGY	ERTU VO Arabs, Batra (Al-Mansura)
	50	IRN	IRIB Regional, Bandar Abbas
	200	IRN	IRIB Regional, Birjand
	150	MDA	R. PMR, Grigoriopol
	20	NIG	Anambra BS, Akwa
	5	RUS	R. Rossii/Reg, Kochubey
	50	RUS	R. Rossii/Reg, Makhachkala
	50	RUS	R. Rossii/Reg, Syktyvkar
630	20	ARS	BSKSA 2nd prgr, Gizan
	10	ARS	BSKSA Quran prgr, Najran
	100/16	D	VOR, Scheppau (Braunschweig)
	2	G	BBC R. Cornwall, Redruth
	0.2	G	BBC Three Counties R, Luton
	10	KWT	R. Kuwait Quran prgr, Kuwait city
	75	MDG	RNM, Antananarivo (irregular)
	14	POR	RTP Antena 1, Montemor-o-Velho + 2 stns
	50	ROU	Antena Satelor, Voinesti
	400	ROU	R. Timisoara/R.R. Act, Ortisoara
	300	TUN	ERTT National prgr, Tunis Djedeida
	300	TUR	TRT Çukurova Reg, Mersin Kazanli
638	25	NIG	Kaduna State Media Corp, Katabu
639	500	CYP	BBC Arabic Sce, Zakaki (Ladies Mile)
	780	CZE	CRo 2/CRo 6, Praha (Liblice) + Ostrava
	300	E	RNE R. Nacional, A Coruña
	10	E	RNE R. Nacional, Albacete
	20	E	RNE R. Nacional, Almeria

kHz	kW	Ctry	Station, location
	50	E	RNE R. Nacional, Bilbao
	50	E	RNE R. Nacional, Zaragoza
	400	IRN	VOIRI, Bonab
	50	KEN	KBC English/Northern Sce, Garissa (inactive)
	100	LSO	LNBS R. Lesotho, Lancer's Gap
	1	MKD	R. Stip
	10	SDN	SRTC Regional, El Obeid
	50	UGA	UBC R, Kampala (inactive)
648	2000	ARS	BSKSA General prgr, Jeddah Khumra
	50	BOT	R. Botswana, Mopipi
	50	E	RNE R. Nacional, Badajoz
	50	GMB	GRTS, Bonto (inactive)
	50	IRN	IRIB R. Iran, Shahr-e-Kord
	10	SVN	R. Murski Val, Nemcavci
	100/10	TZA	R. Tanzania, Nachingwea
657	50	AFS	R. Pulpit / R. Kansel, Meyerton
	20	ARS	BSKSA Quran prgr, Rafha
	50	E	RNE5 TN, Madrid
	0.5	G	BBC R. Cornwall, Bodmin
	2	G	BBC R. Wales, Wrexham
	25	I	RAI Radiouno/Reg, Bolzano
	55	I	RAI Radiouno/Reg, Pisa (Coltano)
	100	IRN	IRIB R. Iran, Zahedan
	100	IRN	IRIB Regional, Kiashahr
	1	IRQ	IMN Republic of Iraq R, Kirkuk
	100	ISR	KI Reshet Bet, Yavne
	100	NIG	FRCN Ibadan, Ibadan
	50	RUS	GR Prgr Kavkaz/Chechya Sv, Groznyy
	150	RUS	R. Rossii/Reg, Murmansk
	100	TZA	R. Tanzania, Dar-es-Salaam
	100	UAE	Asianet R, Al-Dhabbiya
	25	UKR	UR3/RUI, Chernivtsi
666	10	ALG	R. Algérienne 1/R. Tindouf
	50	E	SER R. Barcelona, Barcelona
	0.5	G	R. York, Fulford
	100	GRC	ERA R. Filia/Kosmos, Athína Megara
	50	IRN	IRIB R. Iran, Shushtar
	50	NIG	Edo State BS, Benin City
	52	POR	RTP Antena 1, 6 stns
	20	REU	R. Réunion, St. Pierre
	25	RUS	R. Mayak, Sochi
	10	SDN	SRTC Regional, Kassala
	50	SYR	Syrian R. 2, Damascus Adra
675	25	ARS	BSKSA General prgr, Abha/Afif
	120	HOL	R. Maria Nederland, Lopik
	50	IRN	IRIB Regional, Hamadan
	1	IRQ	IMN Republic of Iraq R, Baghdad
	50	KEN	KBC Swahili Sce, Marsabit
	100	LBY	R. Free Libya, Benghazi
	50	MWI	MBC R. 1, Ekwendeni
	25	NIG	R. Oyo, Ojeowode
	20	NOR	NRK P1/Nordland, Røst (until end of 2012)
	600	QAT	Qatar RTC, Al Arish
	1	SRB	RTS Beograd 1, Bosilegrad
684	60	ARS	BSKSA 2nd prgr, Jeddah/Riyadh
	600	E	RNE R. Nacional, Sevilla
	100	ETH	R. Ethiopia, Metu
	100	IRN	IRIB Regional, Mashhad
	10	MAU	MBC R. Maurice, Malherbes
	50	NIG	Yobe BC, Damaturu
	10	RUS	R. Radonezh, Sankt-Petersburg
	10	SRB	RTS Beograd 1, Aleksinac
	10	TUN	ERTT National prgr, Mednine
693	10	ALG	R. Algérienne 1/R. Adrar, Reggane
	5	ALG	RA 2, Aboudid (Ain el Hammam)
	20	ARS	BSKSA Quran prgr, Tabuk
	3	AZR	RDP Açores, Santa Barbara
	25	BOT	R. Botswana, Shakawe
	10	CYP	CyBC 1, Limassol
	250	D	VOR, Zehlendorf (Oranienburg)
	5	E	RNE R. Nacional, Boal
	20	E	RNE R. Nacional, Toledo
	10	E	RNE R. Nacional, Tortosa

kHz	kW	Ctry	Station, location
	50/1	G	BBC R. 5 Live, 10 stns
	150	G	BBC R. 5 Live, Droitwich
	20	I	RAI Radiouno/Reg, Potenza
	100	IRN	IRIB Regional, Bandar Lengeh
	10	NIG	Kogi State BC, Ochaja
	20	RUS	Deutsche Welle, Kurkino (Moskva)
	150	RUS	R. Rossii, Yazykovo (Ufa)
	1	SOM	R. Hargeisa, Hargeisa
	0.5	SRB	RTS Beograd 1, Negotin
	100	SSD	South Sudan R, Juba
702	25	ALG	R. Algérienne 3/R. Laghouat
	50	ARS	BSKSA 2nd prgr, Bisha/Duba
	5	D	NDR Info Spezial, Flensburg
	10	EGY	ERTU Reg./Koran prgr, Asswan
	10	EGY	ERTU Reg./Koran/Sports, El Kharga
	200	F	China R. Int, Col de la Madone
	100	IRN	IRIB R. Iran, Bushehr
	500	IRN	VOIRI, Kiashahr
	100	KEN	KBC Swahili Sce, Marania (inactive)
	25	NIG	Taraba State BS, Wukari
	800	OMA	BBC Arabic Service, A'Seela
	5	SVK	SR R. Patria/Devín, Kosice
	200	SYR	R. Al-Quds, Damascus Sabboura
	600	TUR	TRT1, Çatalca (Istanbul)
711	25	E	COPE Murcia
	100	EGY	ERTU Youth & Sports prgr, Tanta
	300	F	France Info, Rennes
	200	IRN	IRIB Regional, Ahwaz
	300	MRC	SNRT National Netw./R, Laâyoune
	50	ROU	R. România Actualitati, Sighetul Marmatiei
	7	RUS	R. Rossii/Reg, Naryan-Mar
	10	SRB	RTS Beograd 1/R. Niš
	100/10	TZA	R. Tanzania, Kigoma
	40	UKR	UR1/Reg, Dokuchaievsk
	200	YEM	YRTC General prgr, San'a
720	10	CNR	RNE5 TN, Santa Cruz de Tenerife
	500	CYP	BBC Arabic Sce, Zakaki (Ladies Mile)
	85	D	WDR 2/VERA, Langenberg
	10/0.3	G	BBC R. 4, Lisnagarvey + 2 stns
	750	IRN	IRIB R. Iran, Mahidasht
	400	IRN	IRIB Regional/VOIRI, Tayebad
	50	NIG	Imo BC, Owerri
	60	POR	RTP Antena 1, 6 stns
	40	ROU	R. România Actualitati, Isaccea + 2 stns
	50/10	TZA	R. Tanzania, Mwanza
729	1.2	D	BR Bayern Plus, Hof/Würzburg
	10	E	RNE R. Nacional, Alicante
	10	E	RNE R. Nacional, Cuenca
	20	E	RNE R. Nacional, Logroño
	20	E	RNE R. Nacional, Málaga
	100	E	RNE R. Nacional, Oviedo
	10	E	RNE R. Nacional, Valladolid
	0.2	G	BBC Essex, Manningtree
	100	GRC	ERA NET, Athína Bogiati
	50	NIG	Kano State BC, Jogana
	100	UGA	UBC R. Red Channel, Palisa (inactive)
738	5	ALG	R. Algérienne 1/R. Illizi, In Amenas
	600	E	RNE R. Nacional, Barcelona
	0.04	G	BBC Hereford & W, Worcester
	50	IRN	IRIB Regional, Dayyer
	10	ISR	KI Arabic prgr, Akko (Acre)
	50	MOZ	Antena Nacional, Maputo
	100	OMA	R. Sultanate of Oman, Salalah
	10	RUS	WRN Relay, Kurkino (Moskva)
747	10	ARS	BSKSA General prgr, Najran
	10	BUL	Horizont/Turkish Sce, Shumen Salmanovo
	25	CNR	RNE5 TN, Las Palmas
	10	E	RNE5 TN, Cádiz
	10	GMB	GRTS, Basse
	400/200	HOL	NOS Radio 5 Nostalgia, Zeewolde
	150	IRN	IRIB R. Iran, Gonbad
	100	IRN	IRIB Regional, Kerman
	100	KEN	KBC English/Central Sce, Ngong

kHz	kW	Ctry	Station, location
	60	NIG	Nagarta R, Kaduna
	10/5	SDN	SRTC Regional, Khartoum/Port Sudan
	100	SYR	Syrian R. 1, Sarakeb
756	300	D	DLF, Ravensburg/Scheppau
	10	E	R. Euskadi, Bilbao
	10	EGY	ERTU Reg./Koran prgr, Qena
	2	G	BBC R 4, Redruth
	1	G	R. Cumbria, Carlisle
	0.6	G	R. Maldwyn, "Magic 756", Newtown
	10	IRQ	R. Al-Amal, Basra
	3	IRQ	R. Dar as-Salam, Basra
	50	ISR	R. Mashreq, Metulla
	10	MWI	MBC R. 1, Blantyre
	25	NIG	Borno Radio & TV Corp, Damagum
	100	NIG	R. Oyo, Ibadan
	2	POR	RTP Antena 1, Lamego
	400	ROU	R. România Actualitati, Lugoj (Boldur)
	50	YEM	YRTC Local/General prgr, Mukalla
765	50	ARS	BSKSA Quran prgr, 3 stns
	0.5	G	BBC Essex, Chelmsford
	200/50	IRN	IRIB Regional, Sepid Dasht
	1000/400	IRN	VOIRI/IRIB, Chabahar
	50	MOZ	EP de Nampula, Nampula
	75	RUS	R. Rossii/Reg, Pedaselga (Petrozavodsk)
	50	SDN	SRTC General prgr, Omdurman
	1	SRB	RTS Beograd 1, Medvedja
	40	UKR	R. Maiak, Odesa (Petrivka)
774	50	AGL	EP de Benguela, Benguela
	2	BIH	R. 7, Tuzla
	75	BUL	R. Varna
	5	D	WDR Event, Bonn
	40	E	RNE R. Nacional, 4 stns
	60	E	RNE R. Nacional, Cáceres
	20	E	RNE R. Nacional, Ourense
	50	E	RNE R. Nacional, San Sebastián
	100	E	RNE R. Nacional, Valencia
	1000	EGY	ERTU Middle East prgr, Alexandria (Abis)
	1	G	BBC R4, Enniskillen/Plymouth
	0.1	G	Gold, Gloucester
	0.7	G	R. Kent, Littlebourne
	0.5	G	R. Leeds/BBC Asian Network, Farnley
	100	IRN	IRIB Regional, Arak
	10	NIG	Taraba State BS, Wukari
	30	RUS	R. Mayak/Reg, Voronezh
783	5	ALG	R. Algérienne 1/R. Illizi, Djanet
	10	ALG	R. Algérienne 1/R. Souf, El Oued
	100	ARS	BSKSA 2nd prgr, Ras al-Zawr
	100	D	MDR Info, Wiederau (Leipzig)
	50	E	COPE Miramar/Rock & Gol, Barcelona
	150	IRN	IRIB Regional, Iranshahr
	50	MTN	R. Mauritanie, Nouakchott
	50	NIG	R. Kogi, Okene
	5	SDN	SRTC Regional, Atbara
	300	SYR	Syrian R. 1/Ext. Sce, Tartus
792	50	ARS	BSKSA Quran prgr, Jeddah
	1	BIH	R. Banovici
	5	D	NDR Info Spezial, Lingen
	50	E	SER R. Sevilla
	300	F	France Info, Limoges
	1	G	BBC R. Foyle, Londonderry
	0.3	G	Gold, Bedford
	100	GRC	ERA Spor, Thessaloniki Malgara (irreg.)
	50	IRN	IRIB Regional, Sohravard (Zanjan)
	25	NIG	R. Oyo, Gambari
	100	YEM	YRTC 2nd prgr, Al-Hiswah
801	150	AZE	Azärbaycan R, Haciqabul (Pirsaat)
	100	BHR	R. Bahrain General prgr, Manama
	110	D	BR Bayern Plus, München/Nürnberg
	40	E	RNE R. Nacional, 4 stns
	25	E	RNE R. Nacional, Ciudad Real
	20	E	RNE R. Nacional, Lugo
	100	ETH	VO Amhara State, Bahir Dar
	2	G	R. Devon, Barnstaple

kHz	kW	Ctry	Station, location
	50	IRN	IRIB R. Iran, Kashmar
	10	JOR	R. Jordan Main prgr, Ajlun
	1	NIG	R. Kebbi, Zuru
	20	NIG	Yobe BC, Damaturu
810	20	ARS	BSKSA 2nd prgr, Abha
	20	E	SER R. Madrid
	100	G	BBC R. Scotland, Burghead
	5	G	BBC R. Scotland, Redmoss
	100	G	BBC R. Scotland, Westerglen
	100	IRN	IRIB R. Iran, Khorramabad
	50	IRN	IRIB Regional, Shahr-e-Kord
	5/2.5	IRQ	R. Um al-Qura, Baghdad
	1200	MKD	MR 1 & R. Makedonija, Sveti Nikole
	50	MOZ	EP de Gaza, Xai-Xai
	10	MWI	MBC R. 1, Bangula
	500	RUS	R. Mayak, Volgograd
	20	RUS	VOA relay, Kurkino (Moskva)
	50	UAE	Abu Dhabi FM, Maqtaa
	100	UGA	UBC R, Gulu (inactive)
819	10	E	R. Euskadi, Vitoria-Gasteis
	1000	EGY	ERTU General prgr, Batra (Al-Mansura)
	20	I	RAI Radiouno/Reg, Trieste
	30	IRN	IRIB Regional, Sari
	10	MAU	MBC R. Mauritius, Malherbes
	10	SDN	SRTC Regional, Dongola
	7	UKR	R. Bukovyna, Novodnistrovsk
828	20	ARS	BSKSA General prgr, Medinah
	1	AZR	RDP Açores, Monte das Cruzes
	20/5	D	NDR Info Spezial, Hannover
	5	E	Hit FM Catalunya, Terrassa
	100	ETH	R. Ethiopia, Arba Minch
	0.2	G	BBC Asian Network, Sedgley
	0.3	G	Gold, Bournemouth
	0.2	G	Gold, Luton
	0.1	G	Magic 828, Leeds
	20	HOL	R. 10 Gold, Heinenoord
	50	IRN	IRIB Regional, Tabas
	100	NIG	FRCN Enugu
	10	RUS	Rgazeta Slovo/Pravoslavnoye R, Skt-P.
	200	SYR	Syrian R. 1, Deir-ez-Zor
	1	UAE	Abu Dhabi FM, Al-Ain
837	5	ALG	R. Algérienne 3, Béchar
	10	CNR	COPE, Las Palmas
	10	E	COPE, Burgos
	5	E	COPE, Eivissa
	5	E	COPE, El Ferrol
	10	E	COPE, Sevilla
	100	ERI	Vo the Broad Masses 2, Asmara
	100	ETH	R. Oromiya, Robe (Bale)
	200	F	France Info, Nancy
	0.5	G	BBC Asian Netw, Freemen's Common
	1	G	R. Cumbria, Barrow
	300	IRN	IRIB Isfahan Reg, Habibabad
	30	UKR	R. Bukovyna, Chernivtsi
	150	UKR	UR1, Kharkiv (Taranivka)
	30	YEM	YRTC Youth prgr, San'a
840	20	TCD	ONRTV, N'djamena-Gredia (irregular)
846	100	AFS	SABC Umhlobo Wenene FM, Komga
	20	ARS	BSKSA Quran prgr, Buraida
	1	IRL	R. North, Redcastle
	10	IRN	IRIB R. Iran, Mianeh
	20	IRQ	IMN Republic of Iraq R, Nasiriya (inactive)
	100	KEN	KBC Swahili Sce, Nyamninia (inactive)
	10	NIG	Bauchi R. Corp, Azare
	150	RUS	R. Radonezh/Podmoskovya, Noginsk
	42	RUS	R. Rossii/Reg, Elista
	20	UAE	Holy Quran Radio, Umm al Qiwain
855	100	ARS	BSKSA Quran prgr, Ras al-Zawr
	55	E	RNE R. Nacional, 6 stns
	300	E	RNE R. Nacional, Murcia
	20	E	RNE R. Nacional, Pontevedra
	50	E	RNE R. Nacional, Santander
	20	E	RNE R. Nacional, Tarragona

kHz	kW	Ctry	Station, location
	100	ETH	R. Ethiopia, Harar
	1	G	BBC R. Lancashire, Preston
	1.5	G	BBC R. Norfolk, Postwick
	0.2	G	Sunshine R, Ludlow
	10	JOR	R. Jordan Quran prgr, Amman
	400	ROU	R. România Actualitati, Tancabesti
	50	RUS	R. Rossii, Kamenka
864	1000	ARM	BBG/TWR relay, Gavar
	10	BUL	Horizont/Turkish Sce, Samuil
	75	BUL	R. Blagoevgrad
	10	E	RNE R. Nacional, Socuellamos
	500	EGY	ERTU Koran prgr, Santah
	300	F	France Bleu Ile de France, Paris (stereo)
	50	IRN	IRIB Regional, Qasr-e-Shirin
	10	IRQ	IMN Republic of Iraq R, Ramadi (inactive)
873	10	ALG	R. Algérienne 1/R. Ghardaïa
	10	ARS	BSKSA Quran prgr, Ar-Rass
	50	BOT	R. Botswana, Gantsi
	60	BUL	Hristo Botev/R. Stara Zagora
	150	D	AFN Power Network, Weisskirchen
	10	E	SER R. Galicia, Stgo. de Compostela
	25	E	SER R. Zaragoza
	100	ETH	R. Ethiopia, Addis Ababa
	0.3	G	BBC R. Norfolk, West Lynn
	1	G	BBC R. Ulster, Enniskillen
	40	HNG	Magyar R. 4, Lakihegy/Pécs
	1	I	RAI Radiouno/Reg, Taranto
	50	IRN	IRIB Regional, Bojnurd
	100	IRN	IRIB Regional, Mazandaran prov.
	75	MDA	R. Moldova Actualitati, Chisinau
	50	MOZ	EP de Sofala, Beira
	50	RUS	R. Rossii, Kaliningrad
	250	RUS	R. Rossii, Lesnoy (Moskva)
	75	RUS	R. Rossii, Olgino (Sankt-Peterburg)
	100	RUS	R. Rossii/Reg, Samara
	10/5	SDN	SRTC Reg, Wad Madani/Wadi Halfa
	10	UKR	R. Mryia, Dnipropetrovsk
882	100	ARS	BSKSA Quran prgr, Dammam
	20	CNR	COPE Tenerife, La Laguna (irreg.)
	10	E	COPE, Alicante
	5	E	COPE, Gijón
	5	E	COPE, Málaga
	5	E	COPE, Valladolid
	50	E	Xarxa R, Barcelona
	10	EGY	ERTU General prgr, Matruh
	10/5/1	G	BBC Wales, Penmon/Tywyn/Forden
	100	G	BBC Wales, Washford
	60	IRN	IRIB Regional, Mahabad
	5	IRQ	R. Dar as-Salam, Mosul
	10	ISR	KI Reshet Bet, She'ar Yashuv
	50	KEN	KBC Swahili Sce, Kitale (inactive)
	5	MNE	R. Crne Gore 1, Podgorica
	25	NIG	Capital Sound, Kafanchan
	7	RUS	R. Mayak/Reg, Stavropol
891	600/300	ALG	R. Algérienne 1, Ouled Fayet
	30	AZE	Azärbaycan R, Baki
	100	ETH	R. Ethiopia, Dese
	20	HOL	R. 538, Hulsberg
	50	IRN	IRIB Regional, Yasuj/Dehdasht
	50	LSO	LNBS Ultimate FM, Lancer's Gap
	-	NIG	Osun State BC, Osu
	10	POR	R. Sim, Vilamoura
	5	SDN	SRTC Sennar Reg, Singa
	300	TUR	TRT Reg, Antalya
900	1000	ARS	BSKSA General prgr, Qurayyat II
	10	E	COPE Alta Extremadura, Cáceres/Plasencia
	5	E	COPE, Granada
	5	E	COPE, Vigo
	10	E	R. Popular, Bilbao
	600	I	RAI Radiouno, Milano
	600	IRN	IRIB R. Iran, Tehran
	100	KEN	KBC English Sce, Marania (inactive)
	25	NIG	Ogun State BC, Abeoukuta

kHz	kW	Ctry	Station, location
	20	RUS	R. Mayak/Reg, Sovietskiy
909	10	AFG	R. Kunduz
	0.05	AFG	R. Paktia, Gardez
	10	ALG	R. Algérienne 1, Tamanrasset
	600	BOT	VOA, Mopeng Hill (Selebi-Phikwe)
	0.1	D	biteXpress, Dillberg (DRM)
	10	E	RNE5 TN, Palma de Mallorca
	50/1	G	BBC R.5 Live, 9 stns
	150	G	BBC R.5 Live, Brookmans Park
	200	G	BBC R.5 Live,Moorside Edge
	50	IRN	IRIB R. Iran, Lar
	25	IRQ	IMN Republic of Iraq R, Basra
	50	NIG	FRCN Abuja, Gwagwalada
	200	ROU	R. Cluj, Jucu
	25	ROU	R. Constanta, Valu lui Traian
	50	ROU	R. România Actualitati, Timisoara
	5	SSD	South Sudan R, Malakal
	20	UGA	UBC R, Kampala
	750	YEM	YRTC General prgr, Hudaydah
917	50	NIG	R. Gotel, Yola
918	10	CYP	CyBC 3, Paphos
	20	E	R. Intereconomia, Madrid
	10	EGY	ERTU General prgr, Bawiti
	100	ETH	VO the Dawn, Mekele
	50	IRN	IRIB Regional, Jiroft
	50	NIG	R. Benue, Makurdi
	50	RUS	R. Mayak/Reg, Makhachkala
	150	RUS	R. Rossii/Reg, Arkhangelsk
	300	SVN	R. Slovenija 1, Domzale
	100	SYR	Syrian R. 1, Al-Hassake
927	10	ALG	R. Algérienne 1/R. Adrar, Timimoun
	20	ARS	BSKSA 2nd prgr, Al-Hufuf
	5	GRC	ERA Regional, Zakynthos
	50	IRN	IRIB Regional, Dorud
	100	KEN	KBC Swahili Sce, Malindi
	1	POR	R. Sim, Évora
	200	TUR	TRT 1, Izmir
936	10	AFG	R. Zabul, Qalat
	100	ARS	BSKSA Quran prgr, Makkah/Riyadh
	20	E	RNE5 TN, Alicante
	20	E	RNE5 TN, Valladolid
	20	E	RNE5 TN, Zaragoza
	10	EGY	ERTU General prgr, Salum
	100	EGY	ERTU Om Kalthoum prgr, Cairo
	0.2	G	Gold, Naish Hill
	10	I	RAI Radiouno/Reg, Trapani
	20	I	RAI Radiouno/Reg, Venezia
	100	IRN	IRIB Regional, Urumiyeh
	20	IRQ	R. As-Safir, Basra
	100	MRC	SNRT C/R, Agadir
	5	RUS	R. Rossii/Reg, Matveyevka
	100	SYR	Syrian R. 1, Homs
	500	UKR	UR1, Lviv (Krasne)
945	5	ARS	BSKSA General prgr, Hail
	25	BOT	R. Botswana, Mmathethe
	100	ERI	Vo the Broad Masses 1, Asmara
	300	F	France Info, Toulouse
	0.7	G	Gold, Bexhill
	0.2	G	Gold, Derby
	100	IRN	IRIB Regional, Dehgolan
	100	ISR	Galei Tzahal, Yavne
	10	NIG	R. Kebbi, Birnin Kebbi
	15	ROU	R. România Actualitati, Miercurea Ciuc
	40	RUS	R. Rossii/Reg, Novocherkassk
	5	SDN	SRTC Regional, Al-Foula
	20	STP	R. Nacional, Pinheira
954	250	CZE	CRo 2/CRo 6, Dobrochov (Brno) + 2 stns
	50	E	Onda Cero R, Madrid
	3	ETH	R. Sidama, Yirgalem
	100	KEN	KBC English Sce, Nyamninia (inactive)
	1500	QAT	Qatar RTC (Al-Jazeera TV sound), Al Arish
	50	SYR	Syrian R. 2, Deir ez-Zor
	300	TUR	TRT Reg, Trabzon

kHz	kW	Ctry	Station, location
963	40	BUL	Horizont, Sofia Dragoman
	50	BUL	Horizont/Turkish Sce, Kardzhali
	100	CYP	CyBC 1, Nicosia
	10	E	R. Euskadi, Donostia-San Sebastián
	600	FIN	CRI relay, Pori
	0.2	G	Asian Sound R, Haslingden
	1	G	Buzz Asia, East London
	50	IRN	IRIB R. Iran, Birjand
	20	KWT	R. Kuwait Multilingual/Main prgr, K. City
	50	MOZ	EP de Tete, Tete
	0.5	POL	Twoje R, Brzesko
	0.1	POL	Twoje R, Lipsko
	0.1	POL	Twoje R, Lubliniec
	10	POR	R. Sim, Seixal
	100	SDN	SRTC Peace R./Koran prgr, Khartoum
	100	TUN	ERTT Int. & Cultural ch, Tunis Djedeida
972	100	D	NDR Info Spezial, Hamburg
	5	E	RNE R. Nacional, Cabra
	2	E	RNE R. Nacional, Monforte de Lemos
	100	ETH	R. Ethiopia, Robe (Bale)
	1	G	Buzz Asia, West London
	100	IRN	IRIB Regional, Ilam
	5	MEL	RNE R. Nacional, Mellilla
	25	NIG	Katsina State R, Katsina
	10	NIG	R. Kogi, Otite
	350	UKR	UR1, Mykolaiv
981	100	ALG	R. Algérienne 2, Ouled Fayet (Algér)
	20	ARS	BSKSA Quran prgr, Madinah
	2	EGY	ERTU General prgr, Abu Simbel/Baris
	10	EGY	ERTU Reg./Koran prgr, Assiut
	200	GRC	ERA Spor, Athína Megara
	10	I	RAI Reg. "Trst A", Trieste
	1	IRL	R. Star Country, Emmyvale
	100	IRN	IRIB R. Iran, Hamadan
	100	KEN	KBC English Sce, Voi (inactive)
	13	POR	R. Sim, Coimbra + 3 stns
989	1	ETH	R. Ethiopia FS relay, Addis Ababa
990	50	AGL	EP do Bié, Kuito
	600	CYP	R. Sawa, Cape Greco
	100	D	Deutschlandradio Kultur, Berlin-Britz
	10	E	SER R. Bilbao
	5	E	SER R. Cádiz
	1	G	BBC R. 5 Live, Tywyn
	1	G	BBC R. Devon, Exeter
	1	G	BBC R. Nan Gaidheal, Redmoss
	0.1	G	Free R. 80s, Wolverhampton
	0.3	G	Magic AM, Doncaster
	400	IRN	IRIB R. Iran, Shiraz (Dehnow)
	50	NIG	Bauchi R. Corp, Bauchi
	10	NIG	Lagos State BC, Ikeja
	1	RUS	R. Mayak, Yuryuzan
	100/10	TZA	R. Tanzania, Songea
999	5	AFG	R. Helmand, Lashkar Ga (inactive)
	20	ARS	BSKSA Quran prgr, Duba
	50	E	COPE, Madrid
	0.3	G	Gold, Nottingham
	0.8	G	Magic 999, Preston
	1	G	R. Solent, Fareham
	20	I	RAI Radiouno/Reg, Perugia
	20	I	RAI Radiouno/Reg, Rimini
	10	I	RAI Radiouno/Reg, Torino (Volpiano)
	2	I	RAI Radiouno/Reg, Vibo Valentia
	50	IRN	IRIB R. Iran, Baneh
	20	IRQ	R. Bilad, Baghdad
	500	MDA	R. PMR/Relays, Grigoriopol
	5	MLT	R. Malta, Bizbizja
	0.5	SRB	RTS Beograd 1, Kladovo
	100	UGA	UBC R Red Channel, Kabale
	-	ZWE	Voice of Zimbabwe (irregular)
1008	10	CNR	ABC Punto R, Las Palmas
	5	E	SER R. Alicante
	5	E	SER R. Extremadura, Badajoz
	10	E	SER R. Girona

kHz	kW	Ctry	Station, location
	1	EGY	ERTU General prgr, El Farafra
	100	EGY	ERTU Palestine/Hebrew prgr, El Arish
	10	EGY	ERTU Reg. prgr, El Fayoum
	100	GRC	ERA Regional, Kerkyra (Corfu)
	200	HOL	Groot Nieuws R, Zeewolde
	100	IRN	IRIB Regional, Semnan
	20	IRQ	Sowt al-Fadhila, Najaf
	50	MOZ	EP de Maputo, Maputo
	10	NIG	Niger State Media Corp, Kontagora
	10	NIG	Osun State BC, Iree
	5	RUS	R. Mayak, Tuapse
	0.5	SRB	RTS Beograd 2/3, Beograd
	600	YEM	YRTC General prgr, San'a
1017	10	AFG	R. Ghazni
	20	ARS	BSKSA Pilgrimage R, Madinah
	10	E	RNE5 TN, Burgos
	10	E	RNE5 TN. Granada
	0.6	G	Free R. 80s, Shrewsbury
	50	IRN	IRIB R. Iran, Bandar Abbas
	50	IRN	IRIB R. Iran, Zahedan
	10	IRQ	R. Karbala, Karbala
1026	10	ALG	RA 1/R. Ouargla, Hassi Messaoud
	5	E	SER R. Asturias, Oviedo
	5	E	SER R. Jaén
	5	E	SER R. Jerez, J. de la Frontera
	10	E	SER R. Reus
	5	E	SER R. Salamanca
	5	E	SER R. Vigo
	1	G	BBC Jersey, Trinity
	0.5	G	BBC R. Camhrigeshire, Chesterton Fcn
	1.7	G	Downtown R, Belfast
	100	IRN	IRIB Regional, Tabriz
	50	MOZ	EP de Manica, Chimoio
	25	NIG	Jigawa BC, Dutse
	7	RUS	R. Mayak, Nyandoma + 2 stns
	5	SDN	SRTC Regional, Al-Damazin
	10	UGA	UBC R, Mbale (inactive)
1035	20	ARS	BSKSA 2nd prgr, Yanbu al-Bahr
	25/100	EST	R. Eli/TWR, Tartu
	10	ETH	R. Oromiya, Adama (Nazret)
	1	G	BBC R. Sheffield/Asian Netw, Sheffield
	1	G	Kismat Radio, London
	0.8	G	Northsound Two, Aberdeen
	0.3	G	West Sound AM, Ayr
	2	I	RAI Radiouno/Reg, Lecce
	10	I	RAI Radiouno/Reg, Pescara
	50	IRN	IRIB Regional, Yazd
	20	JOR	R. Jordan Main prgr, Amman
	10	POR	Star FM, Benavente
1044	7	AFG	R. Farah (inactive)
	10	CYP	CyBC 3, Limassol
	20	D	MDR Info, Wilsdruff (Dresden)
	10	E	SER R. San Sebastian, Donostia-S.S.
	5	E	SER R. Valladolid
	200	ETH	R. Ethiopia, Mekele
	50	IRN	IRIB R. Iran, Dehloran
	100	KEN	KBC English Sce, Malindi (inactive)
	300	MRC	SNRT C, Sebaa-Aioun
	1	UKR	UR1/Reg, Verkhovyna
1053	5	E	COPE, Vila Real
	25	E	COPE, Zaragoza
	100	ETH	R. Oromiya, Nekemte
	500	G	TalkSport, Droitwich + 12 stns
	100	IRN	IRIB R. Iran, Khorramabad
	25	IRN	IRIB Regional, Saravan
	3	IRQ	R. As-Salam, Baghdad
	100	LBY	VO Homeland, Tripoli
	400	ROU	R. Iasi, Uricani
	10	RUS	R. Mariya, Sankt-Peterburg
1062	20/1	CZE	Country R, Praha
	10	I	RAI Radiouno/Reg, Ancona
	25	I	RAI Radiouno/Reg, Cagliari
	2	I	RAI Radiouno/Reg, Catania

kHz	kW	Ctry	Station, location
	2	I	RAI Radiouno/Reg, Trento
	200	IRN	IRIB R. Iran, Kerman
	10	NIG	Enugu State BS, Onitsha
	0.8	POL	Twoje R, Cmolas
	0.5	POL	Twoje R, Jaroslaw
	0.8	POL	Twoje R, Pulawy
	0.8	POL	Twoje R, Skarzysko
	1	SRB	RTS Beograd 1/R. Novi Pazar
	300	TUR	TRT Kurdish prgr, Diyarbakir
1071	5	ALG	R. Algérienne 1, Illizi
	20	ARS	BSKSA General prgr, Bisha
	25	BOT	R. Botswana, Jwaneng
	100	EGY	ERTU Adults/Wadi al Nil, Cairo (Abu Zaabal)
	1	G	TalkSport, Clipstone/Newcastle
	100	IRN	IRIB R. Ma'aref, Qom
	20	IRQ	IMN R. Babil, Hilla
	5	SDN	South Sudan R, Wau
	100	SYR	R. Al-Nour (LBN) relay, Tartus
	30	YEM	YRTC General prgr, Taiz
1080	10	ARS	BSKSA 2nd prgr, Najran
	10	E	Onda Cero R, Toledo
	5	E	SER R. Coruña, A Coruña
	5	E	SER R. Granada
	10	E	SER R. Huesca
	5	E	SER R. Mallorca, Palma de M.
	20	EGY	ERTU General prgr, El Minya/Luxor
	3	ETH	R. Fana, Addis Ababa
	750	IRN	IRIB Regional/VOIRI, Mahshahr
	50	ISR	KI Arabic prgr, Yavne
	100	RUS	R. Rossii/Reg, Kovylkino
1088	25	AGL	RNA Canal A, Mulenvos
1089	10	ALG	R. Algérienne 1/R. Adrar
	20	ARS	BSKSA 2nd prgr, Qurayyat
	400	G	TalkSport, Brookmans Park
	400	G	TalkSport, Moorside Edge
	80/1	G	TalkSport, Washford + 4 stns
	125	G	TalkSport, Westerglen
	50	IRN	IRIB Regional, Biarjmand
	50	RUS	R. Teos, Krasnyy Bor (Sankt-Peterburg)
	1200	RUS	VOR, Tbilisskaya
1098	100	ARS	BSKSA 2nd prgr, Dammam
	2x50	CYP	BRT Bayrak Radyo 1, Iskele (Trikomo)
	25	E	RNE5 TN, Almeria
	10	E	RNE5 TN, Avila
	5	E	RNE5 TN, Huelva
	20	E	RNE5 TN, Lugo
	200/100	IRN	VOIRI/IRIB, Zabol
	12	RUS	R. Rossii/Reg, Chagoda/Nikolsk
	10	SVK	SR R. Patria/Devín, Nitra
1107	400	AFG	RTV Afghanistan, Pol-e-Charkhi
	10	D	AFN Bavaria, Vilseck
	10	D	AFN Power Network, Kaiserslautern
	20	E	RNE5 TN, Caceres
	20	E	RNE5 TN, Camargo
	25	E	RNE5 TN, Logroño
	10	E	RNE5 TN, Ponferrada
	10	E	RNE5 TN, Teruel
	1.5	G	Moray Firth R, Inverness
	2/0.5	G	TalkSport, 6 stns
	10	I	RAI Radiouno, Roma
	50	IRN	IRIB Regional, Sabzevar
	100	KEN	KBC Swahili Sce, Maralal
	25	NIG	FRCN Kaduna, Jaji
	50	SRB	RTN, rel. of Beograd 1, Orlovat
1116	20	ARS	BSKSA 2nd prgr, Madinah
	50	DJI	RTD, Djibouti
	5	E	SER R. Albacete
	5	E	SER R. Pontevedra
	0.5	G	BBC Guernsey, Rohais
	1	G	BBC R Derby/Asian N, Burnaston Lane
	15	HNG	Magyar R. 6/7, Miskolc
	5	HNG	Magyar R. 6/7, Mosonmagyaróvár
	0.5	HOL	R. Bloemendaal, Bloemendaal

kHz	kW	Ctry	Station, location
	2	I	RAI Radiouno/Reg, Aosta
	20	I	RAI Radiouno/Reg, Cuneo
	10	I	RAI Radiouno/Reg, Palermo
	200	IRN	IRIB R. Iran, Ardekan
	20	IRQ	R. Dar as-Salam, Baghdad
	30	RUS	R. Rossii/Reg, Sochi
1125	10	BEL	RTBF Vivacité, Wavre
	5	E	RNE5 TN, Badajoz
	10	E	RNE5 TN, Castelló
	10	E	RNE5 TN, Soria
	10	E	RNE5 TN, Toledo
	10	E	RNE5 TN, Vitoria
	1	G	R. Wales, Llandrindod Wells
	50	IRN	IRIB Regional, Qazvin
	500	LBY	R. Free Libya, El Beida
	20	NGR	ORTN La Voix du Sahel, Niamey
	100	SYR	Syrian R. 2, Al-Hassake
	50	YEM	YRTC Local prgr, Hudaydah
1134	10	AGL	EP do Bengo, Mulenvos
	5	E	COPE, Astorga
	5	E	COPE, Ciutadella
	5	E	COPE, Jerez de la Frontera
	5	E	COPE, Pamplona
	5	E	COPE, Puertollano
	10	E	COPE, Salamanca
	0.003	G	BFBS Gurkha R, 3 stns
	0.001	G	LPAMs
	600	HRV	HR Voice of Croatia, Zadar
	50	IRN	IRIB Fars reg, unk. location
	50	IRN	IRIB R. Iran, Bojnurd
	10	IRN	IRIB R. Iran, Kalibar
	50	KEN	KBC English Sce, Kitale
	100	KWT	R. Kuwait Sports/Main prgr, Kabd
	20	NIG	Cross River State BC, Ugaga
	75	RUS	R. Mayak, Murmansk + 2 stns
	5	RUS	R. Rossii/Reg, Salsk + 2 stns
	20	RUS	R. Teos, Kurkino (Moskva)
1143	0.31	D	AFN Bavaria, Bamberg/Schweinfurt
	1	D	AFN Benelux, Mönchengladbach
	12	D	AFN Power Network, Stuttgart + 2 stns
	5	E	COPE, Jaén
	2	E	COPE, Ourense
	5	E	COPE, Oviedo
	2	E	COPE, Reus
	10	I	RAI Radiouno/Reg, Sassari
	50	IRN	IRIB R. Iran, Yasuj
	10	NIG	Niger State Media Corp, Bida
	100	RUS	R. Mayak, Samara
	150	RUS	R. Mayak/VOR, Bolshakovo
1152	10	AGL	EP do Zaire, Mbanza Congo
	10	E	RNE5 TN, Albacete
	10	E	RNE5 TN, Cartagena
	10	E	RNE5 TN, Lleida
	20	E	RNE5 TN, Málaga
	10	E	RNE5 TN, Zamora
	4	G	Clyde 2, Glasgow
	3	G	Free R. 80s, Birmingham
	0.8	G	Gold, Norwich
	0.3	G	Gold, Plymouth
	24	G	LBC News, London
	1.5	G	Magic 1152, Manchester
	2	G	Magic 1152, Newcastle
	50	KEN	KBC Swahili Sce, Wajir
	400	ROU	R. România Actualitati, Cluj (Jucu)
	200	UAE	Voice of Kerala, Ras al-Khaimah
1161	5	ALG	RA 1/R. Tamanrasset, In Salah
	20	BUL	Horizont/Turkish Sce, Dulovo/Targovishte
	100	EGY	ERTU Reg. prgr, Tanta
	1	G	BBC Sussex, Bexhill
	0.1	G	BBC Three Counties R, Bedford
	0.2	G	Gold, Swindon
	0.4	G	Magic 1161, Hull

kHz	kW	Ctry	Station, location
	1	G	Tay AM, Dundee
	600	IRN	VOIRI, Qasr-e-Shirin
	75	RUS	R. Orfey, Dubovka (Volgograd)
1170	25	AGL	EP do Huambo, Huambo
	700	BLR	R. Belarus/VOR relay, Sasnovy
	0.3	G	Gold, Ipswich
	0.1	G	Gold, Portsmouth
	0.3	G	Magic 1170, Stockton
	0.2	G	Signal Two, Stoke-on-Trent
	0.6	G	Swansea Sound, Swansea
	400	IRN	IRIB R. Iran, Eshtehard
	50	IRN	IRIB R. Iran, Semnan (Damghan)
	1200	RUS	VOR/Relays, Tbilisskaya
	15	SVN	R. Capodistria/R. Slovenija Int, Beli Kriz
	50	SWZ	TWR Mpangela Ranch (Manzini)
	800	UAE	R. Sawa, Al-Dhabbiya
1179	25	CNR	SER R. Club Tenerife, Santa Cruz
	10	D	SR Antenne Saar, Heusweiler
	2	E	SER R. Rioja, Logroño
	50	E	SER R. València
	10	EGY	ERTU General prgr, Qena
	0.05	G	R. BGWS, Farnborough
	50	GRC	RSM 1, Thessaloniki Malgara (irreg.)
	50	IRN	IRIB R. Iran, Chabahar
	50	IRN	IRIB Regional, Gonbad
	30	IRQ	R. Voice of Iraq, Baghdad
	50	MOZ	EP da Zambézia, Quelimane
	400	ROU	R. România Actualitati, Bacau (Galbeni)
	10	ROU	R. România Actualitati, Resita
1188	3	D	MDR Info, Reichenbach (Görlitz)
	10	EGY	ERTU General prgr, Ras Gharib
	400	HNG	Magyar R. 4, Marcali/Szolnok
	300	IRN	IRIB R. Payam, Tehran
	100	YEM	YRTC General prgr, Al-Hiswah
1197	10	AGL	EP de Malange, Malange
	50	E	Euskadi Irratia, Gasteiz-Vitoria
	6	G	Absolute R, 9 stns
	50	IRN	IRIB Regional, Dasht
	50	IRN	IRIB Regional, Moghan
	1	IRQ	R. Dar as-Salam, Kirkuk
	50	LSO	LM R./Family R, Lancer´s Gap
	1	MKD	R. Kriva Palanka
	15	ROU	R.Târgu Mures/Ant. Brasovului, Brasov
	15	RUS	R. Rossii/Reg, Balakovo/Balashov/Ershov
1200	0.5	AFG	R. Day Kundi, Nili (inactive)
1206	300	F	France Info, Bordeaux
	50	IRN	IRIB Birjand regional
	50	ISR	KI Reshet Bet, Akko (Acre)
	50	MOZ	EP de Inhambane, Inhambane
	1	ROD	Mauritius BC R. Rodrigues, Citronelle
	5	RUS	R. Mayak, Plesetsk
1215	500	ALB	CRI relay, Fllakë
	20	ARS	BSKSA General prgr, Madinah
	50	BOT	R. Botswana, Mahalapye
	5	E	COPE, Córdoba
	5	E	COPE, Léon
	5	E	COPE, Lorca
	5	E	COPE, Santander
	660	G	Absolute R, 14 stns
	50	IRN	IRIB Regional, Chalus
	-	IRQ	IMN Republic of Iraq R, Tikrit
	5	REU	R. Réunion, St. André
	1200	RUS	VOR, Bolshakovo
	10	TZA	R. Tanzania, Arusha
1224	5	E	COPE, Albacete
	5	E	COPE, Almería
	5	E	COPE, Huelva
	5	E	COPE, Lleida
	5	E	COPE, Lugo
	5	E	COPE, Palma de Mallorca
	10	E	COPE, San Sebastián
	-	IRN	IRIB R. Iran, unknown location

kHz	kW	Ctry	Station, location
	300	IRN	VOIRI, Kish Island
	20	ISR	Galei Tzahal, Beersheba
	50	MOZ	EP de Cabo Delgado, Pemba
	50	NIG	Plateau RTV Corp, Jos
	30	RUS	R. Ura, Elista
1232	10	AGL	EP da Huíla, Lubango
1233	600	CYP	Monte-Carlo Doualiya/TWR, Cape Greco
	1.6	G	Absolute R, 5 stns
	50	IRN	IRIB Regional, Abadeh
	50	KEN	KBC English Sce, Marsabit
1242	150	F	France Info, Marseille
	4	G	Absolute R, 4 stns
	0.3	G	Gold, Maidstone
	50	IRN	IRIB R. Iran, Zanjan
	200	OMA	R. Sultanate of Oman, Seeb
	40	UKR	UR2, Dokuchaievsk
1251	-	G	BFBS Gurkha Service, York
	0.8	G	Gold, Bury St. Edmunds
	0.001	G	LPAMs
	25	HNG	Magyar R. 6/7, Nyíregyháza
	25	HNG	Magyar R. 6/7, Szombathely
	5	HOL	NOS Radio 5 Nostalgia, Hulsberg
	100	IRN	IRIB R. Iran, Kiashahr
	22	POR	R. Sim, Valongo/Viseu + 2 stns
	6	RUS	R. Mayak, Letnaya Stavka/Neftekumsk
	8	RUS	R. Rossii/Reg, Cherkessk/Urup
1260	10	AGL	EP do Kuanza Norte, N'dalatando
	500	ARS	BSKSA General prgr, Dammam
	2.5	CVA	Vatican R, Vatican City
	5	E	SER R. Algeciras
	5	E	SER R. Murcia
	1.5	G	Absolute R, Lydd/Guildford
	0.5	G	BBC R. York, Scarborough
	2	G	Gold, Bristol
	0.6	G	Gold, Wrexham
	0.3	G	Sabras R, Leicester
	10	IRN	IRIB R. Iran, Khur
	50	MOZ	EP do Niassa, Lichinga
1269	20	CNR	R. ECCA, Las Palmas
	300	D	Deutschlandfunk, Neumünster
	5	E	COPE, Badajoz
	10	E	COPE, Ciudad Real
	10	E	COPE, Figueres
	5	E	COPE, Zamora
	50	IRN	IRIB R. Iran, Khalkhal
	100	KWT	R. Kuwait Classical music, Kabd
	10	NIG	Taraba State BS, Jalingo
	3	SRB	RTN Serbian Sce, Srbobran
	200	UAE	R. Asia, Ras al-Khaimah
1278	25	AGL	EP de Cabinda, Tenda
	10	EGY	ERTU General prgr, Asswan
	300	F	France Bleu Alsace, Strasbourg
	0.002	G	BFBS Gurkha R, Folkestone/Stafford
	0.001	G	LPAMs/RSLs
	0.4	G	Pulse 2, Bradford
	10	GRC	ERA Regional, Florina
	100	IRN	IRIB R. Iran, Kermanshah
1287	2	AFS	SABC Ligwalagwala FM, Welgedacht
	5	ARS	BSKSA Quran prgr, Makkah
	5	E	SER R. Castilla, Burgos
	10	E	SER R. Lleida
	5	E	SER R. Lugo
	0.003	G	BFBS Gurkha R, 3 stations
	0.004	G	Garrison Radio, 4 stations
	0.001	G	LPAMs
	100	IRN	IRIB Regional, Lar
	2	POR	RTP Antena 1, Portalegre
	50	RUS	R. Rossii/Reg, Groznyy
1296	400	AFG	R. Free Afgh. / VOA, Pol-e-Charkhi
	10	AGL	EP do Uíge, Uíge
	-	AZE	VO Azerbaijan, Haciqabul (Pirsaat)
	50	E	COPE, Valencia

kHz	kW	Ctry	Station, location
	10	G	R. XL, Birmingham
	50	IRN	IRIB Regional, Zabol
	600	SDN	SRTC General prgr, Reiba
	8	SRB	RTS Beograd 1, Vranje
1305	10	AFG	R. Kandahar
	1	ARS	BSKSA 2nd prgr, Taif
	20	E	RNE5 TN, Bilbao
	20	E	RNE5 TN, Ciudad Real
	10	E	RNE5 TN, León
	25	E	RNE5 TN, Ourense
	10	EGY	ERTU General prgr, Assiut
	0.2	G	Gold, Newport
	0.2	G	Magic AM, Barnsley
	0.5	G	Premier Christian R, Chingford/Epsom
	50	IRN	IRIB Regional, Bushehr
	50	ISR	Galei Tzahal, Rosh-Pina
	50	KEN	KBC Swahili/Eastern Sce, Wajir
	7	RUS	R. Mayak, Serov
1314	10	AGL	EP do Namibe, Namibe
	1000	ARM	PRA FS/VOR relay, Gavar
	20	E	RNE5 TN, Cuenca
	10	E	RNE5 TN, Salamanca
	10	E	RNE5 TN, Tarragona
	1	EGY	ERTU General prgr, Nag Hamadi
	1	EGY	ERTU Reg./Koran prgr, Abu Simbel
	10	GRC	ERA Regional, Tripolis
	2	I	RAI Radiouno/Reg, Matera
	50	IRN	IRIB R. Iran, Ardabil + 1 stn
	50	ROU	Antena Satelor, Constanta (Valu lui Traian)
	25	ROU	Antena Satelor, Timisoara
	15	ROU	R. Oltenia Craiova, Craiova
	1	RUS	R. Rossii/Reg, Pleshanovo
	50	SYR	Syrian R. Youth/Aleppo R, Sarakeb
1323	200	CYP	BBC World Sce, Zyyi
	1000/150	D	VOR, Wachenbrunn
	0.5	G	Gold, Brighton
	50	IRN	IRIB Regional, Jolfa
	15	ROU	R. Târgu Mures
	10	TZA	R. One Swahili channel, Moshi
1332	50	CZE	CRo2/CRo6, Moravské Budejovice
	0.4	G	BBC R. Wiltshire, Lacock
	0.6	G	Gold, Peterborough
	1	G	Premier Christian R, London
	300	IRN	IRIB Tehran City R, Tehran
	0.5	POL	Twoje R, Pinczów
	50	ROU	R. România Actualitati, Galati
1341	10	E	Onda Cero R, Almeria
	5	E	Onda Cero R, Ciudad Real
	5	E	SER R. León
	100	EGY	ERTU Cult./Songs prgr, Cairo (Abu Zaabal)
	20	EGY	ERTU General prgr, Idfu/Siwa
	10	EGY	ERTU Koran/Educ./Sports prgr, Bawiti
	100	G	BBC R. Ulster, Lisnagarvey
	20	IRN	IRIB R. Iran, Bam
	100	KWT	R. Kuwait Quran/2nd prgr, Magwa
1350	1000	ARM	TWR/NHK relay, Gavar
	50	BOT	R. Botswana, Tshabong
	10	EGY	ERTU General prgr, Quseir
	10	F	R. Orient, Nice (Fontbonne)
	0.001	G	LPAMs
	30	GEO	Abkhaz State Radio, Soxum
	5	HNG	Magyar R. 6/7, Györ
1359	10	E	RNE R. Nacional, Madrid (inactive)
	100	ETH	VO Tigray Revolution, Mekele
	0.8	G	BBC R. Solent, Bournemouth
	0.3	G	Free R. 80s, Coventry
	0.2	G	Gold, Cardiff
	0.3	G	Gold, Chelmsford
	50	IRN	IRIB Regional, Darab
	25	NIG	Capital Sound, Zaria
	10	NIG	Osun State BC, Iwo
	50	RUS	R. Mayak, Perm

kHz	kW	Ctry	Station, location
	40	UKR	Donetske Oblasne Radio, Dokuchaievsk
1368	10	EGY	ERTU General prgr, El Kharga
	1	EGY	ERTU Koran/Educ./Sports, El Farafra
	2	G	BBC R. Lincolnshire, Lincoln
	0.1	G	BBC R. Wiltshire, Swindon
	0.5	G	BBC Surrey, Duxhurst
	20	G	Manx Radio, Foxdale
	10	I	Challenger R, Villa Estense
	100	IRN	IRIB Regional, Gorgan
	20	ISR	Galei Tzahal, Shivta
	10	SEY	SBC Radio, Victoria (inactive)
1377	1000	ARM	VOR/TWR relay, Gavar
	300	F	France Info, Lille
	0.1	G	Asian Sound R, Ashton Moss
	50	IRN	IRIB Regional, Chabahar
	50	IRN	IRIB Regional, Paveh
	50	TZA	R. Free Africa, Mwanza
	7	UKR	R. Khvylia, Vinnytsia
	5	UKR	R. Mykolaiv
	50	UKR	UR2, Chernivtsi
1386	5	AFG	R. Paktin Voice, Shakin
	10	AGL	EP da Lunda Sul, Saurimo
	50	E	Euskadi Irratia, Bilbao
	10	EGY	ERTU Reg./Koran prgr, Luxor
	0.001	G	LPAMs
	0.003	G	R Jcom, Leeds
	50	GUI	R. Rurale, Labé (inactive)
	100	KEN	KBC English/Northern Sce, Maralal
	500/150	LTU	VOIRI via R. Baltic Waves Int, Sitkunai
1395	500	ALB	R. Tirana/TWR relay, Fllakë
	500	ARM	VOR relay, Gavar
	10	HOL	R. Seagull, Harlingen
	0.4	IRL	Energy, Dublin (irreg.)
	50	IRN	IRIB R. Iran, Hajiabad
	10	NIG	Akwa Ibom BC, Abak
	10	NIG	R. Kogi, Egbe
	5	RUS	R. Rossii/Reg, Buguruslan
1404	10	AGL	EP do Bié, Kuito
	20	F	France Bleu Frequenza Mora, Ajaccio
	45	F	France Info, Brest/Dijon/Grenoble
	0.001	G	LPAMs/RSLs
	100	GRC	ERA Regional, Komotini
	1	I	R. Luna, Dinazzano di Casalgrande
	10	IRN	IRIB R. Iran, Dasht
	-	IRQ	R. Kull al-Iraq, Maysan
	10	MWI	MBC R. 1, Chitipa
	10	NIG	Gombe State BS, Gombe
	0.8	POL	Twoje R. RCH Plus, Chojnice
	15	ROU	R. România Actualitati, Sibiu
	50	ROU	R.Cluj/R. Sighet, Sighetul Marmatiei
1413	5	E	RNE5 TN, Girona
	10	E	RNE5 TN, Jaén
	20	E	RNE5 TN, Vigo
	1	G	BBC R. Gloucestershire, 2 stns
	1	G	Premier Christian R, 2 stns
	10	IRN	IRIB Regional, Estahban
	500	MDA	VOR, Grigoriopol
	750	OMA	BBC World Sce, A'Seela
1422	1	AFS	Hellenic R, Bedfordview
	50	ALG	R. Algérienne C, Ouled Fayet (Algér)
	20	ARS	BSKSA Call of Islam, Riyadh
	400	D	Deutschlandfunk, Heusweiler
	10	EGY	ERTU Koran/Educ./Sports, Ras Gharib
	10	EGY	ERTU Reg./Koran prgr, Salum
	10	MWI	MBC R. 1, Matiya
	10	ROU	R.România Actualitati, Olanesti
1431	250/150	D	VOR/Relays, Wilsdruff (Dresden)
	600/300	DJI	R. Sawa, Djibouti (Pk 12)
	0.1	G	Gold, Reading
	0.4	G	Gold, Southend
	0.001	G	LPAMs
	0.35	GRC	1431 AM, Thessaloniki

kHz	kW	Ctry	Station, location
	2	I	RAI Radiouno, Foggia
	200	IRN	IRIB R. Iran, Habibabad (Isfahan)
	50	IRN	IRIB Regional, Lamerd
	150	UKR	UR3, Mykolaiv
1440	10	AFG	R. Nangarhar, Jalalabad
	10	AGL	EP da Lunda Norte, Dundo
	1600	ARS	BSKSA General prgr, Ras al-Zawr
	50	CAF	R. Centrafrique, Bangui
	600	LUX	RTL R./CRI/KBS World R, Marnach
	10	NIG	Adamawa BC, Yola
	10	RUS	R. Zvezda, Sankt-Peterburg
	4	SRB	RTS Beograd 1, Jagodina
	10	TZA	R. One English channel, Dar es Salaam
1449	100	ARS	BSKSA General prgr, Yanbu al-Bahr
	0.2	G	BBC Asian Network, Gunthorpe
	2	G	BBC R.4, Redmoss
	0.001	G	LPAMs
	2	I	RAI Radiouno/Reg, Biella
	4	I	RAI Radiouno/Reg, Bolzano
	2	I	RAI Radiouno/Reg, Sondrio
	400	IRN	VOIRI, Bandar-e-Torkamen
	500	LBY	R. Misrata, Misrata
	70	RUS	R. Mayak, Monchegorsk + 6 stns
1458	10	AGL	EP do Moxico, Luena
	500	ALB	R. Tirana/CRI relay, Fllakë
	10	BHR	R. Bahrain General prgr, Manama
	5	G	BBC Asian Network, Langley Mill
	2	G	BBC Newcastle, Wrekenton
	0.5	G	BBC R. Cumbria, Whitehaven
	2	G	BBC R. Devon, Torquay
	5	G	Gold, Manchester
	125	G	Sunrise Radio, London
	2	GIB	GBC R. Gibraltar, Wellington Front
	10	IRN	IRIB Regional, Birjand
	20	ISR	KI Reshet Alef, Eilat/She'ar Yashuv
	5	MYT	RFO Mayotte, Pamandzi
	100	ROU	R. România Actualitati, Constanta
	7	RUS	R. Rossii/Reg, Kudymkar
	1	SRB	R. Kladovo
1467	10	AGL	EP do Kuando-Kubango, Menongue
	50	ARS	BSKSA General prgr, Hafar Al-Batin
	40	F	R. Maria France, Col de la Madone
	1000	F	Trans World R, Roumoules
	100	IRN	IRIB Regional, Qom (Alborz)
1476	50	E	Euskadi Irratia, Donostia-San Sebastián
	10	EGY	ERTU Reg./Koran prgr, El Minya
	10	I	R. Medjugorje Italia, Villa Estense
	20	IRN	IRIB Regional, Marivan
1485	1	AFS	R. Today, Honeydew
	10	AGL	EP do Kuanza Sul, Sumbe
	0.3	D	AFN Bavaria, Hohenfels
	0.6	D	AFN Power Netw, Ansbach/G.-Partenkirchen
	5	E	ABC Punto R, Vilanova
	6	E	Onda Cero R, Antequera
	5	E	SER R. Alcoi
	10	E	SER R. Santander
	10	E	SER R. Zamora
	10/1	EGY	ERTU Educ./Koran/Sports prgr, El Tur
	1	G	BBC R 4, Carlisle
	2	G	BBC R. Humberside, Hull
	2	G	BBC R. Merseyside, Wallasey
	1	G	BBC Sussex, Brighton
	1	G	Gold, Newbury
	0.2	HNG	Régió R, Mohács
	1	HOL	R. Marina, Harlingen (F.PI.)
	1	IRN	IRIB R. Iran, Damghan
	10	IRN	IRIB Regional, Abadan
	10	IRN	IRIB Regional, Jahrom
	10	IRN	IRIB Regional, Khoy
	1	LVA	R. Merkurs, Riga
	1	MEL	SER R. Melilla, Melilla
	1	NOR	NRK P1/Troms og Finnmark, Longyearbyen

kHz	kW	Ctry	Station, location
	0.5	POL	Twoje R, Zakopane
	4	ROU	R. Vocea Sperantei, Bacau + 3 stns
	5	SDN	SRTC Regional, Al-Gadarif
	1	SRB	R. Priboj, Priboj
	0.5	SRB	RTN Serbian Sce, Novi Sad
	0.5	SRB	RTS Beograd 1, Crna Trava
	0.6	SRB	RTS Beograd 1/R. Tutin
1494	20	F	France Bleu Frequenza Mora, Bastia
	24	F	France Info, Bayonne/Clermont Ferrand
	100	GRC	ERA Regional, Rhodos
	-	IRN	IRIB Razavi Khorasan reg, unk. location
	50	MDA	R. Moldova Actualitati, Cahul/Edinet
1500	0.1	AFG	R. Nuristan
	0.1	AFG	R. Samangan, Aybak (inactive)
	-	AFG	R. Sar-e-Pol
	6	AFG	RTA R. Badghis, Qalay-e-Naw
1503	10	AGL	EP de Benguela, Benguela
	0.1	AZR	AFN, Lajes
	1	BIH	R. 1503 Zavidovici, Zavidovici
	5	E	RNE5 TN, La Linea
	2	E	RNE5 TN, Monforte de Lemos
	25	EGY	ERTU Reg. prgr, El Arish
	1	G	BBC R. Stoke, Sideway
	0.5	I	Onda Media Broadcast, San Pietro in Casale
	200	IRN	IRIB R. Iran, Bushehr
	20/10	RUS	R. Tsentr, Kurkino (Moskva)
	10	SRB	RTS Beograd 202, Beograd
1512	1000	ARS	BSKSA Quran prgr, Jeddah Khumra
	100	GRC	ERA Regional, Chania
	0.5	I	Onda Media Broadcast, San Pietro in Casale
	0.2	IRL	Tyrone Community R, Lifford
	50	IRN	IRIB Regional, Ardabil
1521	2000	ARS	BSKSA General prgr, Duba
	10	BHR	R. Bahrain 2nd prgr, Manama
	5	E	SER R. Castelló
	0.07	G	Flame Christian & Community R, Wirral
	7	RUS	R. Mayak, Zapolyarnyy
1530	10	AGL	EP de Cabinda, Tenda
	0.2	G	BBC Essex, Southend-on-Sea
	0.1	G	Celtic Music R, Glasgow
	0.7	G	Pulse 2, Huddersfield
	50	IRN	IRIB R. Iran, Yazd
	3	MDR	Posto Emissor do Funchal, Poiso
	15	ROU	R. România Actualitati, Radauti
	15	ROU	R.Constanta, Mahmudia (Nufaru)
	600	STP	VOA, Pinheira
1539	50	DJI	RTD, Djibouti (inactive)
	6	E	SER R. Elche, Elx
	5	E	SER R. Manresa
	50	IRN	IRIB Regional, Gorgan
	600	UAE	VOA R. Aap Ki Dunyaa, Al-Dhabbiya
1548	10	AFS	R. Islam, Lenasia
	5	G	BBC R. Bristol, Mangotsfield
	2	G	Forth 2, Edinburgh
	97	G	Gold, London
	1	G	Magic 1548, Liverpool
	0.7	G	Magic AM, Sheffield
	70	IRN	IRIB R. Iran, 3 sites
	10	IRN	IRIB Regional, Ferdows/Larijan
	300/600	KWT	R. Sawa, Kuwait
	500	MDA	VOR/TWR, Grigoriopol
1550	0.1	AFG	R. Herat
	50	ALG	R. Nacional de la RASD, Rabouni
1557	300	F	France Info, Nice (Fontbonne)
	0.8	G	Gold, Northampton
	0.5	G	Gold, Southampton
	0.3	G	R. Lancashire, Oxcliffe
	4	HOL	Vahon FM, Haag (Stompwijk)
	50	IRN	IRIB R. Iran, Zabol
1566	100	BEN	TWR Africa, Parakou
	0.6	G	BBC Somerset, Taunton
	0.8	G	Eagle Extra, Guildford

kHz	kW	Ctry	Station, location
	1	I	Challenger R, Roma
	0.1	I	R. Kolbe, Schio
	100	IRN	IRIB R. Iran, Bandar Abbas
1575	10	AFG	R. Kunar, Asadabad
	5	E	SER R. Córdoba
	10	E	SER R. Pamplona
	10	EGY	ERTU Koran/Educ./Sports, Quseir
	0.001	G	LPAMs/RSLs
	2	I	RAI Radiouno/Reg, Campobasso
	50	I	RAI Radiouno/Reg, Genova
	2	I	RAI Radiouno/Reg, Gorizia
	1	I	RAI Radiouno/Reg, Nuoro
	400/800	IRN	IRIB R. Iran, Abadan
	2	MAU	BBC WS, Bigara
	800	UAE	R. Farda, Al-Dhabbiya
1584	10	AFG	R. Balkh, Mazar-e-Sharif
	0.5	AFG	R. Ghor, Chaghcharan
	2	AFG	R. Nimroz, Zaranj
	1	BHR	R. Bahrain English prgr, Manama
	1	BIH	R. Bosanski Petrovac
	5	CEU	SER Radiolé, Ceuta
	5	E	SER R. Gandía
	5	E	SER R. Ourense
	10	EGY	ERTU Reg./Koran prgr, Idfu
	1	EGY	ERTU Reg./Koran/Sports prgr, Baris
	1	FIN	R Hami (occ. operation)
	0.3	G	DDC Hereford & Worcester, Woofferton
	0.2	G	London Turkish R, London
	0.2	G	Tay AM, Perth
	1	GRC	RS Amaliadas, Kastro
	0.1	HOL	R. Paradijs, Utrecht (irreg.)
	2.5/12	I	R. Studio X, Momigno
	2	I	RAI Radiouno/Reg, Terni
	1	IRL	Zenith Classic Rock, Waterford (temp. stn)
	50/10	IRN	IRIB Regional, Semnan
	0.1	POL	Twoje R, Andrychów
	0.5	POL	Twoje R, Busko-Zdrój
	0.8	POL	Twoje R, Chelm
	5	ROU	R. Vocea Sperantei, Bistrita + 4 stns
	0.1	RUS	R. MTUCI/Zelyoniy Glaz, Moskva
	7	RUS	R. Rossii, Khunzakh
	5	SDN	SRTC Regional, Kosti
1590	0.005	TUR	AFN Incirlik (Adana)
1593	10/0.5	D	R. 700, Kall-Krekel (irregular)
	10	EGY	ERTU Reg./Koran prgr, Matruh
	150	KWT	VOA/R. Free Iraq, Kuwait
	10	ROU	Antena Sibiului/R. Cluj, Sibiu
	15	ROU	R. Cluj, Oradea
	15	ROU	R. Constanta, Ion Corvin
	15	ROU	R. Târgu Mures, Miercurea Ciuc
	0.01	RUS	R. SPBGUT/Bonch, Sankt-Peterburg
1602	10	AFG	R. Khost
	25	E	R. Vitoria
	5	E	SER R. Cartagena
	5	E	SER R. Linares
	5	E	SER R. Ontinyent
	5	E	SER R. Segovia
	10/1	EGY	ERTU Reg./Koran prgr, Nag Hamadi
	10	EGY	ERTU Reg./Koran/Sports, Siwa
	1	F	R. Orient, Nîmes
	0.4	FIN	Scandinavian Weekend R, Virrat
	0.1	G	Desi R, Southall
	0.001	G	RSLs
	1	HOL	R. Seagull/Waddensee, Pietersbierum
	1	IRN	IRIB R. Iran, Bafq/Estahban/Kazerun
	1	IRN	IRIB Regional, Dezful
	1	IRN	IRIB Regional, Semnan
	0.5	POL	Twoje R, Krakow
	2	ROU	R. Vocea Sperantei, Bistrita + 1 stn
	5	SDN	SRTC Regional, Kadogli
	0.7	SRB	RTS Beograd 1, Sjenica

EAST ASIA & PACIFIC

Abbreviations peculiar to the E.Asia/Pacific section of MW freq. lists: AF = allocated freq. C. = City. PO = Present operation on. Proj. = Projected station. Rptr. = repeater. Trtr = translator.
Australia: The numeral preceding the call letters indicates the state: 2 = New South Wales. 3 = Victoria. 4 = Queensland. 5 = South Australia. 6 = Western Australia. 7 = Tasmania. 8 = Northern Territory. ACT = Australian Capital Territory. **China, P.R:** If several locations are listed for one frequency, the power listed applies to the first entry. For full details see country section. **Indonesia:** Only RRI stns included. For details of other stns see country section. **Philippines:** Province Abbreviations: Ag Nte = Agusan del Norte; Ag Sur = Agusan del Sur; Ant = Antique; Boh = Bohol; Bat = Batangas; Buk = Bukidnon; Bul = Bulacan; Cag = Cagayan; Cam Nte = Camarines Norte; Cam Sur = Camarines Sur; Dvo Nte = Davao del Norte; Dvo Sur = Davao del Sur; Isa = Isabela; I.Nte = Ilocos Norte; I.Sur = Ilocos Sur; LU = La Union; Lanao Nte = Lanao del Norte; Lanao Sur = Lanao del Sur; Mag = Maguindanao; Mas = Masbate; M Octal = Mindoro Occidental; Mind Or = Mindoro Oriental; Mis Octal = Misamis Occidental; Mis Or = Misamis Oriental; Mt Prov = Mountain Province; Neg Occ = Negros Occidental; Neg Or = Negros Oriental; Nva Viz = Nueva Vizcaya; Pam = Pampanga; Pang = Pangasinan; Que = Quezon; Riz = Rizal; S Cot = South Cotabato; S Leyte = Southern Leyte; S Sur = Surigao del Sur; Sor = Sorsogon; Tar = Tarlac; Z Nte = Zamboanga del Norte; Z Sib = Zamboanga Sibugay; Z Sur = Zamboanga del Sur; Zamb = Zambales. **Russia:** Regions in the Asian parts of Russia: Sib. = Siberia. FE = Far East.

kHz	kW	Ctry	Call	Station, location	kHz	kW	Ctry	Call	Station, location
153	1200	RUS		R. Rossii + Reg., Komsomolsk, FE		5	NZL		NZ's Rhema, Tauranga
162	150	RUS		R. Rossii + Reg., Norilsk, Sib.		1.5	NZL		The Word/Bible Radio, Christchurch
164	500	MNG		MRT (1), Ulaanbaatar		300	PAK		PBC, Peshawar
171	250	RUS		R. Rossii + Reg., Oyash, Sib.		1	PHL	DYRB	DWRL Radio, Inc., Cebu C
	150	RUS		R. Rossii + Reg., Yakutsk, FE		10	PHL	DZWT	Mt. Province BC, Baguio C, Benguet
180	150	RUS		R. Rossii + Reg., Yelizovo, FE		50	RUS		R. Mayak, Orenburg
189	1200	RUS		R. Rossii + Reg., Konstantinogradovka, FE		5	SMO		National Radio 2AP, Apia
209	75	MNG		MRT (1), Dalanzadgad/Choybalsan		5	THA		Yaan Kraw, Bangkok
	30	MNG		MRT (1), Ölgiy	549	50	AUS	2CR	ABC (LR), Orange
	150	RUS		R. Mayak, Tynda, FE		25	CHN		EN; NM (2 stns)
216	30	RUS		R. Rossii + Reg., Birobidzhan, FE		1200	CHN		FJ (CNR5)
	150	RUS		R. Rossii + Reg., Krasnoyarsk, Sib.		100	IND		AIR, Ranchi A
225	1000	RUS		R. Rossii + Reg., Surgut, Sib.		10	J	JOAP	NHK (1), Okinawa
227	75	MNG		MRT (1), Altay		3	NZL		NZ's Rhema, Kaitaia
234	500	RUS		R. Rossii + Reg., Angarsk, Sib.		1	NZL		R. Sport, Nelson
	500	RUS		R. Rossii + Reg., Arman, FE		1	NZL		R. Trackside/LiveSPORT, Napier-Hastings
252	150	TJK		TR (1), Yangiyul		5	PHL	DXHM	Catholic Media Netw., Madong, Mind Or
270	150	RUS		R. Slovo, Novosibirsk, Sib.		10	PHL	DWRP	Philippine Bc. Sce., Naga C, Cam. Sur
279	50	RUS		R. Rossii + Reg., Gorno-Altaysk, Sib.		25-500	RUS		R. Mayak, FE , 4 stns (sync.)
	150	RUS		R. Rossii + Reg., Selenginsk, Sib.		100	THA		R. Thailand, Lampang
	150	RUS		R. Rossii + Reg., Yekaterinburg, Sib.		10	THA		R. Thailand, Mukdahan
	500	RUS		R. Rossii + Reg., Yuzhno-Sakhalinsk, FE		40	TJK		TR (2), Dushanbe
	150	TKM		Turkmen Radio (1), Asgabat		200	VTN		Hung Yen (2), My Hao
531	10	AUS	6DL	ABC (LR), Dalwallinu	550	5	HWA	KMVI	Wailuku, Maui
	0.5	AUS	5RTI	Adelaide (HPONS)	558	5	AUS	4AM	Atherton (Mareeba)
	5	AUS	4KZ	Innisfail		50	AUS	6WA	ABC (LR), Wagin
	5	AUS	2PM	Kempsey		2	AUS	7BU	Burnie
	5	AUS	3GG	Warragul		5	AUS	4GY	Gympie
	10	CHN		ZJ		100	BGD		Bangladesh Betar, Khulna
	300	IND		AIR, Jodhpur A		120	CHN		XJ + 7 stns
	10	J	JOQG	NHK (1), Morioka		10	FJI		Fiji Bc. Corp. Ltd. (1), Suva
	1	J		NHK (1), Nago		100	IND		AIR, Mumbai B
	5	NZL		531pi, Auckland		20	J	JOCR	CRK, Kobe
	2	NZL		More FM, Alexandra		250	KOR	HLQH	KBS, Daegu (2)
	5	PHL	DZBR	Kumintang Bc. System, Batangas C, Bat.		5	NZL		R. Sport, Invercargill
	5	PHL	DXGH	Pacific Bc. System, Gen. Santos C, S Cot		50	PHL	DZXL	R. Mindanao Netw., Pasig C, NCR
	10	PHL	DYDW	Word Bc. Corp., Tacloban C, Leyte		10	THA		R. Thailand, Kanchanaburi
	5	RUS		Avtoradio, Yuzhno-Sakhalinsk, FE		50	THA		R. Thailand, Songkhla
	25	THA		R. Thailand, Maha Sarakham		1	TWN	BEH7	Fu Hsing BS (1), Taipei
	10	TWN	BED57	BCC (L), Taipei		100	VTN		Ho Chi Min C. (2), Quan Tre
540	10	AUS	4QL	ABC (LR), Longreach	565	10	MLA		RTM Labuan, Tenom
	5	AUS	7SD	Scottsdale	567	10	AUS	4JK	ABC (LR), Julia Creek
	10	CHN		CNR1		0.1	AUS	6...	ABC (LR), W. A., 4 stns
	10	CHN		NM; QH		0.5	AUS	2BH	Broken Hill
	20	IND		AIR, Aizawl		10	CHN		JS (CNR1)
	2/10	INS		RRI, Bandung (4)		20	CHN		TJ; EN
	1	J	JOSK	NHK (1), Kitakyushu		10	GUM	KGUM	Agana
	1	J		NHK (1), Matsumoto		20	HKG		RTHK (3), Golden Hill
	5	J	JOMG	NHK (1), Miyazaki		300	IND		AIR, Dibrugarh
	1	J		NHK (1), Nanao/Ishigaki		100	J	JOIK	NHK (1), Sapporo
	5	J	JOJG	NHK (1), Yamagata		100	KOR	HLKF	KBS, Jeonju
	10	KOR		KBS, Hongseong		200	LAO		Lao National Radio, Vientiane
	1	KOR		KBS, Jangsu/Jangheung/Jeomchon		50	NZL		RNZ National, Wellington
	3	NZL		NZ's Rhema, New Plymouth		150	PAK		PBC, Khuzdar

kHz	kW	Ctry	Call	Station, location
	5	PHL	DXCH	Pacific Bc. System, Cotabato C, Mag.
	150	RUS		R. Rossii + Reg., Kyzyl, Sib.
	5	THA		Jor. Sor. 5, Chaiyaphum
570	1	HWA	KQNG	Lihu'e, Kauai
576	50	AUS	2RN	ABC (RN), Sydney
	200	BRM		MRTV, Yangon
	10	CHN		YN; ZJ(v); EN; FJ
	200	IND		AIR, Alappuzha
	1	J	JODG	NHK (1), Hamamatsu
	10	J	JOHG	NHK (1), Kagoshima
	40	KGZ		R. DDD, Osh
	5	KOR		AFNK, Munsan
	1	KOR		KBS, Suncheon (3)
	100	NPL		R. Nepal, Surkhet
	2.5	NZL		The Word/Bible Radio, Hamilton
	5	PHL	DZHR	Cebu Bc. Co., Tuguegarao, Cag.
	10	PHL	DXMF	People's Bc. Sce., Davao C, Dvo Sur
	10	PHL	DYMR	Philippine Bc. Sce., Cebu C
	5	PHL	DZMQ	Philippine Bc. Sce., Dagupan C, Pang.
	150	RUS		R. Mayak, FE, 2 stns, (sync)
	250 500	RUS		R. Mayak, Sib., 2 stns, (sync)
	5	THA		Tor. Chor. Dor., Bangkok
	150	TKM		Turkmen Radio (2), Asgabat
	50	VTN		Khanh Hoa (2/P), Nha Trang
585	10	AUS	6PB	ABC (PNN), Perth
	10	AUS	7RN	ABC (RN), Hobart
	10	AUS	2WEB	W. Region Educ. Bc., Bourke
	50	CHN		JS + 11 stns
	200	CHN		Southeast BC, FJ
	300	IND		AIR, Nagpur A
	50	INS		RRI, Surabaya (4)
	10	J	JOPG	NHK (1), Kushiro
	20	LAO		Lao National Radio, Khantabouly
	2	NZL		R. Ngati Porou, Ruatoria
	500	PAK		PBC, Islamabad (Faqeerabad)
	5	PHL	DXCP	Catholic Media Netw., Gen. Santos C, S Cot
	1	PHL	DYLL	Philippine Bc. Sce., Iloilo C
	10	PNG		NBC Port Moresby
	5	SMA	KJAL	Asia Pac. Media Min., Tafuna (r. 580/inactive)
	5	THA		Thor. Phor. 3, Phrae
	5	THA		Wor. Por. Tho. 15, Chumphon
590	7.5	HWA	KSSK	Honolulu, Oahu
594	50	AUS	3WV	ABC (LR), Horsham
	200	BRM		MRTV, Nay Pyi Taw
	300	CHN		XZ; SD
	1000	IND		AIR, Chinsurah, FS
	300	J	JOAK	NHK (1), Tokyo
	10	KOR		KBS, Yeongju
	5	NZL		NZ's Rhema, Timaru
	2	NZL		NZ's Rhema, Wananqui
	5	PHL	DXDB	Catholic Media Netw., Malaybalay, Buk.
	20	PHL	DZBB	GMA Network, Inc., Quezon C, NCR
	150	RUS		R. Mayak, Krasnoyarsk, Sib.
	1000	RUS		R. Mayak, Surgut, Sib.
	5	THA		Phon. Por. Thor. Or., Bangkok
	10	TWN	BEH44	Fu Hsing BS (1), Kaohsiung
	5	TWN	BEH38	Fu Hsing BS (2), Taichung
	10	TWN	BEH2	Fu Hsing BS (2), Taipei
	50	VTN		Danang (1), An Hai
603	10	AUS	2RN	ABC (RN), Nowra
	10	AUS	4CH	ABC (LR), Charleville
	2	AUS	6PH	ABC (LR), Port Hedland
	200	CHN		EN + 41 stns
	600	CHN		China R. International, Dongfang, Hainan
	200	IND		AIR, Ajmer
	5	J	JOOG	NHK (1), Obihiro
	5	J	JOKK	NHK (1), Okayama
	500	KOR	HLSA	KBS, Namyang (Seoul)
	5	NZL		R. Waatea, Auckland
	10	PHL	DZLL	Bicol Bc. System, Naga C, Cam Sur
	5	PHL	DZVV	Consolidated Bc. Syst., Inc., Vigan, I. Sur
	5	PHL	DXPR	R. Mindanao Netw., Pagadian C, Z Sur
	30	RUS		R. Mayak, Belogorsk/Skovorodino, FE

kHz	kW	Ctry	Call	Station, location
	5	THA		Wor. Por. Tho. 12, Khon Kaen
610	200	VTN		Ho Chi Minh C. (H), Tang Nhon Phu
612	50	AUS	4QR	ABC (LR), Brisbane
	10	AUS	6RN	ABC (RN), Dalwallinu
	100	CHN		FJ; LN; SC: SD
	200	IND		AIR, Bengaluru A
	100	J	JOLK	NHK (1), Fukuoka
	150	KGZ		Kyrgyz R. (2), Bishkek
	2	NZL		NZ's Rhema, Christchurch
	1.5	NZL		Southern Star, Nelson
	10	PAK		PBC (2), Karachi (Landhi)
	5	PHL	DWSP	Philippine Bc. Corp., Itogon, Benguet
	10	PHL	DYHP	R. Mindanao Netw., Cebu C
	25	RUS		R. Mayak, Norilsk, Sib.
	5	THA		Mor. Kor., Chiang Mai
	5	THA		Wor. Sor. Por., Lop Buri
	1000	TWN		RTI, RFI relay, Lukang
620	5	HWA	KHNU	Hilo, Hawaii
	10	HWA	KHNU	Kalaoa, Hawaii (rptr)
	5	HWA	KHNU	Na'alehu, Hawaii (rptr)
621	200	AFG		BBG - R. Mashaal/VOA, Khost, Tani
	50	AUS	3RN	ABC (RN), Melbourne
	2	AUS	6EL	Bunbury
	200	CHN		HL; QH; HB; SC; YN; SD
	20	HKG		RTHK (2), Golden Hill
	100	IND		AIR, Patna A
	3	J	JOCG	NHK (1), Asahikawa
	1	J		NHK (1), Iida/Nobeoka
	1	J	JOOK	NHK (1), Kyoto
	10	KOR		KBS, Seogwipo
	10	KOR		KBS, Taebaek
	1	KOR		KBS, Yeongdong
	500	KRE		Pyongyang BS/VoK, Chongjin
	2	NZL		NZ's Rhema, Dunedin
	2	NZL		NZ's Rhema, Whangarei
	1	PHL	DZVC	Philippine Bc. Sce., Virac, Catanduanes
	10	PHL	DXDC	R. Mindanao Netw., Davao C, Dvo Sur
	5	PHL	DZTG	R. Philippines Netw., Tuguegarao, Cag.
	50	RUS		R. Rossii + Reg., Khabarovsk, FE
	100	THA		H. Thailand, Khon Kaen
	5	TUV		R. Tuvalu, Funafuti
	1	TWN		Taiwan BC, Tahsi
630	10	AUS	2PB	ABC (PNN), Sydney
	0.4	AUS	7RN	ABC (RN), Queenstown
	5	AUS	6AL	ABC (LR), Albany
	50	AUS	4QN	ABC (LR), Townsville
	100	BGD		Bangladesh Betar (B), Dhaka
	200	CHN		JX (CNR2); HEN (CNR2)
	2.5	CKH		R. Cook Is. AM, Rarotonga
	10	GUM	KUAM	Agana
	100	IND		AIR, Thrissur
	50	INS		RRI, Makassar
	5	KOR		KBS, Inje
	10	KOR		KBS, Yeosu
	10	NZL		RNZ National, Napier-Hastings
	100	PAK		PBC (1), Lahore
	35	PHL	DZMM	ABS-CBN Bc. Corp., Quezon C, NCR
	5	PHL	DYAG	Cadiz R. And TV Netw., Cadiz C, Cam. Sur
	500	RUS		VoR, Komsomolsk, FE
	5	THA		Mor. Thor. Bor. 11, Bangkok
	10	TWN	BED65	BCC (N), Ilan
	10	TWN		Taiwan BC, Sungling
	200	VTN		Quang Binh (1), Dong Hoi
639	2	AUS	8RN	ABC (RN), Katherine
	1	AUS	4MS	ABC (LR), Mossman
	10	AUS	5CK	ABC (LR), Port Pirie
	5	AUS	2HC	Coff's Harbour
		BRM		Thazin Radio
	200	CHN		BJ (CNR1)
	100	IND		AIR, Kohima
	5	J	JOIP	NHK (1), Oita
	10	J	JOPB	NHK (2), Shizuoka
	5	J	JOWN	STV, Hakodate

kHz	kW	Ctry	Call	Station, location
	2	NZL		RNZ National, Alexandra
	100	PAK		PBC, Karachi (Landhi)
	5	PHL	DXKR	R. Mindanao Netw., Koronadal, Cot. Sur
	1	PHL	DZRL	R. Philippines Netw., Batac, I. Nte
	75	RUS		R. Rossii + Reg., Omsk, Sib.
	10	THA		R. Thailand, Chiang Mai
	20	THA		R. Thailand, N. Si Thammarat
648	2	AUS	6GF	ABC (LR), Kalgoorlie
	10	AUS	2NU	ABC (LR), Tamworth
	150	CHN		GD + 6 stns
	200	IND		AIR, Indore A
	10	J		AFN, Okinawa C.
	5	J	JOIG	NHK (1), Toyama
	1	KOR		KBS, Boseong
	100	NPL		R. Nepal, Dhankuta
	5	PHL	DYRC	Manila Bc. Co., Cebu C
	10	PHL	DWRH	Pacific Bc. System, Santiago C, Isa.
	10	PHL	DWRM	Philippine Bc. Sce., Pto. Princesa, Palawan
	5	PHL	DXMB	R. Mindanao Netw., Malaybalay, Buk.
	1000	RUS		VoR/VOA/R. Free Asia, Razdolnoye, FE
	25	THA		R. Thailand, Khon Kaen
	500	TJK		VO Russia, Dushanbe
	20	TWN	BED34	BCC (N), Taipei
	50	VTN		Binh Dinh (1), An Nhon
650	10	HWA	KRTR	Honolulu, Oahu
657	2	AUS	8RN	ABC (RN), Darwin
	10	AUS	2BY	ABC (LR), Byrock
	2	AUS	6RF	Perth (HPONS)
	300	CHN		EN; JL; ZJ
	200	IND		AIR, Kolkata A
	50	KOR	HLKM	KBS, Chuncheon
	1500	KRE		Pyongyang BS, Kangnam
	10	NZL		RNZ AM/So. Star, Tauranga
	50	NZL		RNZ AM/So. Star, Wellington
	5	PHL	DXDD	Dan-ag sa Dakbayan Bc. Corp., Ozamis C, Mis. Occ.
	1	PHL	DYES	Philippine Bc. Sce., Borongan, E. Samar
	5	PHL	DWRN	Philippine R. Corp., Naga C, Cam. Sur
	5	PHL	DYVR	R. Mindanao Netw., Roxas C, Capiz
	1	PHL	DZLU	Satellite Bc. Corp., S. Fernando C, LU
	75	RUS		R.Mayak, Kruchina, Sib.
	5	THA		Jor. Sor. 1, Bangkok
	20	TWN	BEV59	Cheng Sheng BC (2), Taichung
	100	VTN		Ho Chi Minh C. (1), Quan Tre
666	5	AUS	2CN	ABC (LR), Canberra
	2	AUS	4CC	Biloela (trtr)
	1	AUS	4LN	Carnarvon
	2	AUS	4LM	Mt. Isa
	200	CHN		QH + 9 stns
	600	CHN		VO Strait, FJ
	100	IND		AIR, New Delhi B
	100	J	JOBK	NHK (1), Osaka
	20	NCL		NouvelleCaledonie la 1ere, Noumea
	50/25	PHL	DZRH	Manila Bc. Co., Makati C, NCR
	10	PHL	DXRP	Philippine Bc. Sce., Davao C, Dvo Sur
	150	RUS		R. Mayak, Komsomolsk, FE
	5	THA		Thor. Phor. 2, Surin
	5	THA		Thor. Phor. 3, Tak
	50	VTN		Khanh Hoa (1), Nha Trang
670	5	HWA	KPUA	Hilo, Hawaii
675	10	AUS	2CO	ABC (LR), Albury
	5	AUS	6BE	ABC (LR), Broome
	200	CHN		NM + 5 stns
	10	HKG		RTHK (6), Peng Chau
	20	IND		AIR, Bhadravathi
	20	IND		AIR, Chhattarpur
	100	IND		AIR, Itanagar
	5	J	JOVK	NHK (1), Hakodate
	5	J	JOUG	NHK (1), Yamaguchi
	10	KOR		KBS, Jeonju (3)
	10	NZL		RNZ National, Christchurch
	5	PHL	DWLW	Intercontinental Bc. Corp., Laoag C, I. Nte
	5	PHL	DYKC	R. Philippines Netw., Mandaue, Cebu
	1	PHL	DXGD	Sulu Tawi-Tawi Bc. Found., Bongao, Tawi-Tawi
	10	PNG		NBC Wewak
	10	PNG		NBC Morobe, Lae
	5	THA		Sor. Thor. Ror. 2, Bangkok
	150	TKM		Turkmen R. (1), Asgabat
	10	TKM		Turkmen R. (2), Türkmenbasy
	5	TWN		Cheng Sheng BC, Peikang
	500	VTN		Hung Yen (1), My Hao
684	1	AUS	8RN	ABC (RN), Tennant Creek
	5	AUS	6BS	ABC (LR), Busselton
	10	AUS	2KP	ABC (LR), Kempsey
	1200	CHN		FJ (CNR6)
	600	CHN		CRI/RFI relay, Dongfang, Hainan prov.
	50	CHN		HL + 8 stns
	200	IND		AIR, Kargil A
	100	IND		AIR, Kozhikode A
	100	IND		AIR, Port Blair
	5	J	JODF	IBC, Morioka
	1	J	JOLO	IBC, Ofunato
	5	J	JOAG	NHK (1), Nagasaki
	250	KRE		Pyongyang BS, Samgo
	100	NPL		R. Nepal, Pokhara
	5	NZL		NZ's Rhema, Gisborne
	5	PHL	DZCV	Filipinas Bc. Netw.,., Tuguegarao, Cag.
	5	PHL	DWJJ	Kaissar Bc. Netw., Cabanatuan, Nva. Ecija
	10	PHL	DYEZ	Manila Bc. Co., Bacolod, Neg. Occ.
	5	THA		Thor. Phor. 4, N. Si Thammarat
	5	THA		Yaan Kraw, Udon Thani
	1	TLS		R. Timor-Leste, Díli (Mt. Kutulau)
	10	TWN	BEC22	VO Han Bc. Netw., Taipei
690	10	HWA	KHNR	Honolulu, Oahu
693	2	AUS	5SY	ABC (LR), Streaky Bay
	10/5	AUS	4KQ	Brisbane (Newstead)
	0.5	AUS	4LM	Cloncurry (trtr)
	5	AUS	3AW	Melbourne
	5	AUS	6WR	R. Stn. 6WR, Kununurra
	0.5	AUS	4KZ	Tully (trtr)
	1000	BGD		Bangladesh Betar (A), Dhaka
	300	CHN		SN; HL
	500	J	JOAB	NHK (2), Tokyo
	5	NZL		R. Sport, Dunedin
	1	PHL	DYKX	Manila Bc. Co., Kalibo, Aklan
	10	PHL	DYPH	Manila Bc. Co., Pto. Princesa, Palawan
	10	PHL	DXBC	R. Mindanao Netw., Butuan, Ag. Nte
	1	PHL	DXDX	R. Philippines Netw., Gen. Santos C, S. Cot.
	10	PHL	DZTP	Tirad Pass R/TV Bc. Netw., Candon, I. Sur
	150	RUS		R. Rossii, Yazykovo, Sib.
	5	THA		Siang Adison, Saraburi
	10	TWN	BEC32	VO Han Bc. Netw., Tainan
	10	TWN	BEC25	VO Han Bc. Netw., Taoyuan
702	50	AUS	2BL	ABC (LR), Sydney
	10	AUS	6KP	ABC (LR), Karratha
		CHN		GD (CRI DS)
	200	CHN		JS + 8 stns
	200	IND		AIR, Jalandhar A, FS
	2/10	INS		RRI, Manokwari
	10	J	JOFB	NHK (2), Hiroshima
	10	J	JOKD	NHK (2), Kitami
	50	KRE		Korean Central BS (C/R), Chongjin
	10	NZL		R. Live, Auckland
	1	NZL		R. Sport, Ashburton
	50	PHL	DZAS	FEBC, Valenzuela, NCR
	7	RUS		R. Mayak, Bratsk, Sib.
	150	TJK		TR (1), Orzu
	10	TWN	BEP24	Ching Cha BS, Taichung
	50	VTN		Danang (2/Q/D), An Hai
705	10	LAO		Lao National Radio, Luang Prabang
711	10	AUS	4QW	ABC (LR), Roma/St. George
	400	BRM		MRTV, Nay Pyi Taw
	10	CHN		QH + 7 stns
	200	IND		AIR, Siliguri

kHz	kW	Ctry	Call	Station, location
	500	KOR	HLKA	KBS, Sorae (Seoul)
	5	NZL		Trackside/LiveSPORT, Wellington
	5	PHL	DZVR	Newsounds Bc. Netw., Laoag, I. Nte
	10	PHL	DZLW	Peñafrancia Bc. Corp., Naga C, Cam. Sur
	5	PHL	DXIC	R. Mindanao Netw., Iligan C, Lanao Nte
	5	PHL	DXRD	Swara Sug Media Corp., Davao C, Dvo. Sur
	5	PHL	DZYI	Swara Sug Media Corp., Ilagan, Isa.
	5	RUS		R. Rossii + Reg., Nikolayevsk, FE
	20	THA		R. Thailand, U. Ratchathani
	5	THA		Wor. Por. Thor., Chiang Mai
	5	THA		Wor. Sor. Por., Lop Buri
	10	TWN	BED92	BCC (C), Tainan
	250	TWN		VO Kuanghua, Hsinfeng
	500	VTN		Can Tho (1), Thoi Long
720	50	AUS	6WF	ABC (LR), Perth
	0.05	AUS	2RN	ABC (RN), Armidale
	4	AUS	4AT	ABC (LR), Atherton
	0.4	AUS	2ML	ABC (LR), Murwillumbah
	2	AUS	3MT	ABC (LR), Omeo
	200	CHN		BJ (CNR2)
		CHN		CNR13
	1	CHN		SC; AH
	5	HWA	KUAI	'Ele'ele, Kauai
	200	IND		AIR, Chennai A
	10	INS		RRI, Ambon
	1	J	JOIL	KBC, Kitakyushu
	500	KRE		Korean Central BS (C/R), Wiwon (Kanggye)
	10	NZL		HNZ National, Invercargill
	5	PHL	DZJO	Bayanihan Bc. Corp., San Juan, NCR
	10	PHL	DYOK	Manila Bc. Co., Iloilo C
	5	PHL	DZSO	Newsounds Bc. Netw., San Fernando, LU
	1000	RUS		VoR, Vestochka, FE
	10	THA		R. Thailand, Krabi
	5	THA		Sor. Thor. Ror. 5, Chon Buri
	1	TKM		Turkmen Radio (1), Ek-Arça/Etrek
	1	TWN	BED58	BCC (N), Taichung
	10	VTN		Dong Nai (P), Quan Tre (v)
729	50	AUS	5RN	ABC (RN), Adelaide
	100	BRM		MRTV, Yangon
	200	CHN		JX; EN
	100	IND		AIR, Guwahati A
		INS		RRI, Nabire
	50	J	JOCK	NHK (1), Nagoya
	50	KRE		Pyongyang BS, Sepo
	5	NCL		NouvelleCaledonie la 1ere, Touho
	0.1	NZL		Burn 729AM, Ranfurly
	3	NZL		R. Sport, Whangarei
	2.5	NZL		RNZ National, Tokoroa
	5	PHL	DYEH	Katigbak Enterprises, Pto. Princesa, Palawan
	5	PHL	DXOR	Pedro N. Roa Bc., Cagayan de Oro C, Mis. Or.
	5	PHL	DZGB	People's Bc. Netw., Legaspi C, Albay
	10	PHL	DWPE	Philippine Bc. Sce., Tuguegarao, Cag.
	5	PHL	DXMY	R. Mindanao Netw., Cotabato C, Mag.
	25	THA		R. Thailand, N. Ratchasima
	0.5	TWN	BEE43	Shih Hsin BS, Taipei
	200	VTN		Quang Binh (2), Dong Hoi
738	50	AUS	2NR	ABC (LR), Grafton
	5	AUS	6MJ	ABC (LR), Manjimup
	200	CHN		HN; EN; JL; XJ; ZJ
	200	IND		AIR, Hyderabad A
	1	J		KNB, Takaoka
	5	J	JOLR	KNB, Toyama
	10	J	JORR	RBC, Naha, Okinawa
	100	KOR	HLKG	KBS, Daegu
	10	MAC		R. Vilaverde
	5	NZL		R. Live, Christchurch
	20	OCE		Polynesie La 1ere, Mahina
	60	PHL	DZRB	Philippine Bc. Sce., Quezon C, NCR
	50	RUS		R. Radonnezh, Tavrichanka, Sib.
	40	RUS		R. Rossii + Reg., Chelyabinsk, Sib.
	25	RUS		R. Rossii + Reg., Palana, FE
	5	THA		Wor. Por. Tho. 2, Chiang Mai
	5	THA		Wor. Por. Tho. 5, Songkhla

kHz	kW	Ctry	Call	Station, location
	100	TWN	BEL2	Yuyeh BS, Penghu
740	50	VTN		Binh Dinh (2/P), An Nhon
747	10/5.5	AUS	7PB	ABC (PNN), Hobart
	0.2	AUS	8JB	ABC (LR), Jabiru
	10	AUS	4QS	ABC (LR), Toowoomba
	5	AUS	6SE	Esperance
	1	AUS	6FMS	Exmouth
		CHN		BJ (CNR12)
	200	CHN		SC + 26 stns
	300	IND		AIR, Lucknow
	10	INS		RRI, Bengkulu
	500	J	JOIB	NHK (2), Sapporo
	20	KAZ		R. Liberty, Qaraghandy
	100	KOR	HLKH	KBS, Gwangju
	0.4	NZL		NewstalkZB, Rotorua
	10	PHL	DZJC	Manila Bc. Co., Laoag C, I. Nte
	5	PHL	DXND	Notre Dame Bc. Corp., Kidapawan, N. Cot.
	10	PHL	DYHB	R. Mindanao Netw., Bacolod, Neg. Occ.
	5	SMO		National Radio 2AP, Apia
	5	THA		Ror. Dor., Bangkok
	5	THA		Thor. Phor. 2, Udon Thani
750	1	CHN		SX
756	10	AUS	3RN	ABC (RN), Wangaratta (rptr)
	2	AUS	2TR	ABC (LR), Taree
	2	AUS	6TZ	Margaret River
	150	CHN		HL (CNR1)
	100	IND		AIR, Jagdalpur
	2/10	INS		RRI, Purwokerto
	10	J	JOGK	NHK (1), Kumamoto
	100	KOR		KBS, Yeoju
	0.8	NZL		Puketapu R., Palmerston
	10	NZL		RNZ National, Auckland
	150	PAK		PBC (1), Quetta (Pishin)
	10	PHL	DXBZ	Baganian Bc. Corp., Pagadiani, Z Sur
	1	PHL	DWHL	Beta Bc. Syst., Olongapo C, Zamb.
	5	PHL	DWNW	Intercontinental Bc. Corp., Naga C, Cam. Sur
	10	PHL	DWRS	Philippine Bc. Sce., Tayug, Pang.
	2	PHL	DXJM	R. Corp. of the Philippines, Butuan C, Ag. Nte
	5	THA		Kor. Wor. Sor. 1, Surin
	5	THA		Nor. Thor. Phor., Narathiwat
	1	TWN		Sheng Li chih Sheng BC, Makung
	10	VTN		Long An (P), Tan An
760	10	HWA	KGU	Honolulu, Oahu
765	5	AUS	2EC	Bega
	0.5	AUS	4GC	Hughenden (trtr)
	0.5	AUS	8HOT	Katherine (trtr)
	5	AUS	5CC	Port Lincoln
	0.1	AUS	6SAT	Tom Price/Paraburdoo (trtr)
	10	CHN		EN + 5 stns
	600	CHN		FJ (CNR5)
	200	IND		AIR, Dharwad A
	1	INS		RRI, Tual
	5	J	JOPF	KRY, Shunan
	5	J	JOJF	YBS, Kofu
	10	KOR	HLCQ	MBC, Daejeon
	50	KRE		Korean Central BS (C/R), Hyesan
	2.5	NZL		R. Kahungunu, Napier-Hastings
	5	PHL	DXGS	DWRL Radio, Inc., Gen. Santos C, S. Cot.
	10	PHL	DYPR	Palawan Bc. Corp., Pto. Princesa, Palawan
	5	PHL	DYAR	Swara Sug Media Corp., Cebu C
	5	PHL	DZYT	Swara Sug Media Corp., Tuguegarao, Cag.
	5	RUS		R. Vostok Rossii, Bikin, FE (sync)
	20	RUS		R. Vostok Rossii, Khabarovsk, FE (sync)
	5	THA		Neung. Por. Nor., Lampang
	5	THA		Thor. Or. 2, Lop Buri
774	50	AUS	3LO	ABC (LR), Melbourne
	5	AUS	4TO	Townsville
	10	CHN		BJ (Bejing Foreign)
	100	CHN		HB; SX; LN; XJ
	100	IND		AIR, Shimla
		INS		RRI, Fak-Fak
	500	J	JOUB	NHK (2), Akita
	10	KOR	HLAN	Open R. For North Korea, Chuncheon

kHz	kW	Ctry	Call	Station, location
	10	KOR	HLAJ	MBC, Jeju
	5	NZL		R. Sport, New Plymouth
	25	PHL	DWWW	Interactive Bc. Media, Inc., Quezon C, NCR
	10	PHL	DXSM	Philippine Bc. Sce., Jolo, Sulu
	10	PHL	DXSO	Philippine Bc. Sce., Marawi C, Lanao Sur
	10	PHL	DYRI	R. Mindanao Netw., Iloilo C
	5	THA		Phon. Mor. 2, Rayong
	5	THA		Sor. Sor. Sor., Udon Thani
	20	TWN	BEV88	Hsien Sheng BC, Taoyuan
	1	TWN	BEV56	Sheng Li chih Sheng BC (1), Tainan
	20	TWN	BEV94	Taiwan BC, Taichung
783	2	AUS	8AL	ABC (LR), Alice Springs
	2	AUS	6VA	Albany
	100	CHN		EB(3 stns); GD
		CHN		VO Strait, FJ
	20	HKG		RTHK (5), Golden Hill
	20	IND		AIR, Chennai C
	2/10	INS		RRI, Ende
	10	KOR		KBS, Yeongwol
	10	NZL		Samoan Cap. R., Wellington (CAS)
	5	PHL	DYME	Masbate Comm. Bc. Co., Masbate C
	5	PHL	DZNL	Philippine Bc. Corp., San Fernando, LU
	10	PHL	DXRA	RMC Bc. Co., Inc., Davao C, Dvo Sur
	75	RUS		R. Lemma, Vladivostok, FE
	10	THA		R. Thailand, Ranong
	5	THA		Thor. Phor. 3, Kamphaeng Phet
	500	VTN		Can Tho (2), Thoi Long
790	5	HWA	KKON	Kealakekua, Hawaii
792	25	AUS	4RN	ABC (RN), Brisbane
	200	CHN		GX + 7 stns
	100	IND		AIR, Pune A
	1	J		NHK (1), Takada/Naze
	1	J		NHK (1), Takayama/Enbetsu
	50	KOR	HLSQ	Seoul Bc. System, Goyang (Seoul)
	100	NPL		R. Nepal, Kathmandu
	5	NZL		R. Sport, Hamilton
	150	PAK		Azad Kashmir R., Muzaffarabad (r. inactive)
	5	PHL	DWGV	GV Bc. System, Angeles C, Pampanga
	5	PHL	DYRR	Ormoc Bc. Co., Ormoc C, Leyte
	5	PHL	DXPD	People's Bc. Co., Pagadian, Z. Sur
	10	PHL	DXBN	Philippine Bc. Sce., Butuan, Ag. Nte
	5	PHL	DWES	Rolin Bc. Enterprises, Narra, Palawan
	25	RUS		R. Rossii + Reg., Abakan, Sib.
	50	RUS		R. Rossii + Reg., Aleksandrovsk-Sakh., FE
	20	THA		Wor. Por. Thor., Bangkok
	10	TWN	BEC33	VO Han Bc. Netw., Hualien
	1	TWN	BEV79	Keelung BS, Keelung
801	2	AUS	4QY	ABC (LR), Cairns
	2	AUS	5RM	Berri
	5	AUS	2RF	Gosford (HPONS)
	25	CHN		EB + 25 stns
	50	CHN		Zhujiang EBS, GD
	10	GUM	KTWG	TWR, Agana
	200	IND		AIR, Jabalpur
	1	INS		RRI, Medan (4)
	10	INS		RRI, Semarang
	500	KRE		Pyongyang BS, Hwadae
	10	MLA		RTM Labuan, Kudat
	2	NZL		NZ's Rhema, Nelson
	5	PHL	DYKA	Catholic Media Netw., San José, Ant.
	5	PHL	DXES	Consolidated Bc. Syst., Inc., Gen. Santos C, S. Cot.
	5	PHL	DYWC	Franciscan Bc. Corp., Dumaguete, Neg. Or.
	5	PHL	DWFA	Hypersonic Bc. Center, Sorsogon C
	10	PHL	DZNC	Newsounds Bc. Netw., Cauayan, Isa.
	1	PHL	DXBL	Swara Sug Media Corp., Bislig, Surigao S.
	1200	RUS		VoR, Chita (Atamanovka), Sib.
	5	THA		Mor. Thor. Bor. No. 31, N. Sawan
	5	THA		Thor. Or. 15, Chiang Rai
	5	THA		Thor. Or. 8, U. Ratchathani
	500	TJK		VO Russia, Dushanbe
	1	TWN		Chien Kuo BS, Hsinhua
	250	TWN		VO Kuanghua, Kuanyin

kHz	kW	Ctry	Call	Station, location
810	20	AUS	6RN	ABC (RN), Perth
	10	AUS	2BA	ABC (LR), Bega
	200	CHN		ZJ + 6 stns
	300	IND		AIR, Rajkot A
	7.5	INS		RRI, Merauke
	50	J		AFN, Tokyo
	20	KOR	HLCT	MBC, Daegu
	50	KRE		Korean Central BS (C/R), Kaesong
	10	NPL		R. Nepal, Dipayal
	2	NZL		BBC WS NZ, Auckland
	10	NZL		RNZ National, Dunedin
	10	PHL	DZRJ	Rajah Bc. Netw., Manila, NCR
	2	PNG		NBC Rabaul
	10	RUS		Avtoritetnoye R., K., Sib.
·	50	RUS		R. Mayak, Yekaterinburg, Sib.
	150	RUS		R. Rossii + Reg., Razdolnoye, FE
	10	THA		R. Thailand, Kanchanaburi
	20	THA		R. Thailand, Nong Khai
	10	THA		R. Thailand, Trang
	10	TWN	BEV54	Kuo Sheng BC, Changhua
819	10	AUS	2GL	ABC (LR), Glen Innes
	5	AUS	6KW	ABC (LR), Kununurra
	200	CHN		SX; XJ(3 stns)
	200	IND		AIR, New Delhi A
	5	J	JONK	NHK (1), Nagano
	20	KOR	HLCN	MBC, Gwangju
	500	KRE		Korean Central BS (C), Pyongyang
	10	NZL		RNZ National, Tauranga
	10	PHL	DYVL	Manila Bc. Co., Tacloban, Leyte
	1	PHL	DXSC	So. Philippines Mass. Comm., Zamboanga C, Z. Sur
	5	PHL	DWAR	Swara Sug Media Corp., Laoag C, I. Nte
	10	PHL	DXUM	Univ. of Mindanao Bc. Netwk, Davao C, Dvo Sur
	1	PHL	DWMG	Vanguard R. Netw., Solano, Nva Viz
	10	THA		R. Thailand, Pathum Thani
	15	TJK		TR (1), Khujand
	10	TWN	BED28	BCC (N), Taitung
	5	TWN	BEV35	Cheng Sheng BC, Taipei
	10	TWN	BEP28	Ching Cha BS, Kaohsiung
	20	VTN		Dac Lac (4), Buon Ma Tuhot
828	10	AUS	6GN	ABC (LR), Geraldton
	10	AUS	3GI	ABC (LR), Sale
	1	AUS	4GC	Charters Towers
	50	CHN		BJ + 6 stns
	20	IND		AIR, Panaji B
	20	IND		AIR, Silchar
	300	J	JOBB	NHK (2), Osaka
	2	NZL		R. Trackside/LiveSPORT, Palmerston No.
	100	PAK		PBC (1), Karachi
	1	PHL	DZTC	Govt of Tarlac Prov., Tarlac C
	5	PHL	DWZR	Hypersonic Bc. Center, Legaspi C, Albay
	10/5	PHL	DYER	Pto. Princesa Bc. Co., Pto. Princesa, Palawan
	10	PHL	DXCC	R. Mindanao Netw., Cagayan de Oro C, Mis. Or.
	150	RUS		R. Mayak, Kyzyl, Sib.
	5	THA		Thor. Phor. 3, Sukhothai
	5	THA		Wor. Por. Tho. 4, N. Si Thammarat
	50	VTN		Son La (P)
830	10	HWA	KHVH	Honolulu, Oahu
837	1	AUS	6ED	ABC (LR), Esperance
	10	AUS	4RK	ABC (LR), Rockhampton
	0.5	AUS	7XS	Queenstown
		CHN		CNR1
		CHN		FJ (CNR5)
	20	CHN		HL; EN; FJ (2 stns); LN; XJ;
	100	IND		AIR, Vijayawada A
	1	J		NHK (1), Nayoro
	10	J	JOQK	NHK (1), Niigata
	50	KOR	HLKY	CBS, Seoul
	2	NZL		RNZ National, Kaitaia
	2.5	NZL		RNZ National, Whangarei
	10	PHL	DYFM	Consolidated Bc. Syst., Inc., Iloilo C

kHz	kW	Ctry	Call	Station, location
	10	PHL	DXJS	Philippine Bc. Sce., Tandag, S Sur
	5	PHL	DXRE	Swara Sug Media Corp., Gen. Santos C, S. Cotab.
	5	THA		Nor. Thor. Phor., Sakon Nakhon
	10	THA		R. Thailand, Pathum Thani
	10	VTN		Can Tho (P)
846	10	AUS	2RN	ABC (RN), Canberra
	2.5	AUS	6CA	ABC (LR), Carnarvon
	5	AUS	4EL	Cairns
	100	BGD		Bangladesh Betar, Rajshahi (Bogra)
	10	CHN		BJ (CRI DS4)
	100	CHN		EN + 30 stns
	200	IND		AIR, Ahmedabad A
	5	J		NHK (1), Koriyama
	1	J		NHK (1), Uwajima/Hitoyoshi
	5	KOR		KBS, Yanggu
	10	KOR	HLAU	MBC, Ulsan
	2	NZL		NewstalkZB, Masterton
	50	PHL	DZRV	R. Veritas, Quezon C, NCR
	10	THA		R. Thailand, Phetchabun
	10	TWN	BEH56	Fu Hsing BS (2), Kaohsiung
	10	TWN	BEC38	VO Han Bc. Netw., Penghu
	250	TWN		VO Kuanghua, Kuanyin
	10	VTN		Thanh Hoa (P)
850	5	HWA	KHLO	Hilo, Hawaii
855	10	AUS	4QO	ABC (LR), Eidsvold
	10	AUS	4QB	ABC (LR), Pialba
	2	AUS	3CR	Community R. Fed. Ltd., Melbourne
	50	CHN		YN (CNR2); XJ (CNR13)
	20	CLN		SLBC, Irattaperiyakulam
	2/10	INS		RRI, Mataram
	10	KOR	HLCX	MBC, Jeonju
	500	KRE		Pyongyang BS, Sangwon
	2	NZL		NZ's Rhema, Hamilton
	5	PHL	DXZH	Cebu Bc. Co., Zamboanga C, Z. Sur
	10	PHL	DZGE	Filipinas Bc. Netw., Naga C, Cam. Sur
	10	PHL	DXGO	Pacific Bc. System, Davao C, Dvo Sur
	5	THA		Mor. Thor. Bor. 12, Prachin Buri
	10	TWN	BED27	BCC (N), Hualien
	1	TWN	BEV72	Cheng Sheng BC, Chia-i
	1	TWN	BEV24	Min Pen BC (2), Taipei
864	2	AUS	7RPH	Bc. Sce. for Handicapped Inc., Hobart
	2	AUS	6AM	Northam
	2	AUS	4GR	Toowoomba
	50	CHN		AH; EN; EB; SD; ZJ (2 stn's)
	10	HKG		Hong Kong Comm. Bc. Co., Peng Chau
	100	IND		AIR, Shillong
	2/10	INS		RRI, Cirebon
	1	J	JOXN	CRT, Nasu
	5	J	JOPR	FBC, Fukui
	3	J	JOHE	HBC, Asahikawa
	1	J		HBC, Enbetsu
	3	J	JOQF	HBC, Muroran
	10	J	JOXR	ROK, Naha, Okinawa
	1	J	JOSO	SBC, Matsumoto
	100	KOR	HLKR	KBS, Gangneung
	10	NZL		NewstalkZB, Invercargill
	10	PHL	DZWM	Alaminos City Bc. Corp., Alaminos, Pang.
	10	PHL	DYHH	Philippine Air Force, Bogo, Cebu
	5	PHL	DZSP	Swara Sug Media Corp., San Pablo C, Laguna
	5	PHL	DWSI	Swara Sug Media Corp., Santiago, Isa.
	10	PHL	DZIP	R.Palaweño, Pto. Princesa, Palawan
	10	PNG		NBC Madang
	25	RUS		Yakutsk (Reg.), Sib.
	10	THA		R. Thailand, Phattahalung
	10	THA		R. Thailand, Si Sa Ket
	10	THA		R. Thailand, Tak
	10	TWN	BED25	BCC (N), Kaohsiung
873	2	AUS	6DB	ABC (LR), Derby
	2	AUS	4AY	Innisfail (HPONS)
	5	AUS	2GB	Sydney
	100	BGD		Bangladesh Betar, Chittagong

kHz	kW	Ctry	Call	Station, location
	200	CHN		China Huayi BC, FJ
	200	CHN		HL + 7 stns
	400	CLN		SLBC/Family R, Puttalam
	300	IND		AIR, Jalandhar B
	500	J	JOGB	NHK (2), Kumamoto
	250	KRE		Korean Central BS (C/R), Sinuiju
	1	NZL		Newstalk ZB, Ashburton
	1	NZL		R. Trackside/LiveSPORT, Tauranga
	5	PHL	DZPA	Abra Comm. Bc. Corp., Bangued, Abra
	5	PHL	DZRC	Filipinas Bc. Netw., Legaspi C, Albay
	5	PHL	DXRB	Swara Sug Media Corp., Butuan C, Ag. Nte
	5	PHL	DXRT	Swara Sug Media Corp., Jolo, Sulu
	5	PHL	DYUP	Univ. of the Philippines in the Visyas, Miagao, Iloilo
	5	THA		Wor. Kor. Thor. Mor., Bangkok
	500	VTN		Can Tho (1/3/4), Thoi Long
880	2	HWA	KHCM	Honolulu, Oahu
882	5	AUS	4BH	Brisbane
	10	AUS	6PR	Perth
	2	AUS	3YB	Warrnambool
	100	CHN		FJ + 11 stns
	400	CLN		TWR, Puttalam
	300	IND		AIR, Imphal
	10	J	JOPK	NHK (1), Shizuoka
	1	J		STV, Esashi
	3	J	JOWS	STV, Kushiro
		KGZ		R. Rossii relay, Bishkek
	20	KOR	HLKI	KBS, Daejon
	250	KRE		Korean Central BS (C/R), Wonsan
	75	MNG		MRT (1), Mörön
	10	NZL		RNZ AM /So. Star, Auckland
	50	PHL	DWIZ	Aliw Bc. Corp., Navotas, NCR
	10	PHL	DXMS	Notre Dame Bc. Corp., Cotabato C, Mag.
	10	PHL	DYOG	Philippine Bc. Sce., Calbayog, W. Samar
	1	PHL	DXRG	Philippine Bc. Sce., Gingoog, Mis. Or.
	10	TWN	BEG77	BCC (N), Hsinchu
	1	TWN		Feng Ming BC, Penghu
891	50	AUS	5AN	ABC (LR), Adelaide
	5	AUS	4TAB	Townsville (HPONS)
	200	CHN		NX; LN; NM; SD; XJ
	20	IND		AIR, Rampur
	10	INS		RRI Ternate
	10	INS		RRI, Malang
	20	J	JOHK	NHK (1), Sendai
	250	KOR	HLKB	KBS, Busan
	5	NZL		The Breeze, Wellington
	5	PHL	DZGR	People's Bc. Sce., Tuguegarao, Cag.
	1	RUS		R. Mayak + Reg., Tyumen, Sib.
	1000	THA		R. Thailand, Sara Buri
	10	TWN	BED24	BCC (L), Tainan
	10	VTN		Lam Dong (1/P), Da Lat (r inactive)
900	2	AUS	8HA	Alice Springs
	2	AUS	6BY	Bridgetown
	2	AUS	7AD	Devonport
	5	AUS	2LM	Lismore
	5	AUS	2LT	Lithgow
		CHN		BJ (CRI DS5)
	10	CHN		QH (CNR2)
	100	CHN		YN/CRI + 33 stns
	5	HWA	KNUI	Kahului, Maui
	100	IND		AIR, Kadapa
	5	J	JOHF	BSS, Yonago
	5	J	JOHO	HBC, Hakodate
	5	J	JOZR	RKC, Kochi
	50	KOR	HLKV	MBC, Seoul
	2.5	NZL		Coast, Whangarei
	10	NZL		RNZ AM /So. Star, Dunedin
	5	PHL	DYOW	Consolidated Bc. Syst., Inc., Roxas, Capiz
	5	PHL	DWNE	Nueva Ecija Prov. Gov. Cabanatuan C, Nva Viz.
	5	PHL	DXRZ	R. Mindanao Netw., Zamboanga C, Z . Sur
	5	PHL	DXIP	Southern Bc. Netw., Davao C
	10	PNG		NBC Kimbe

kHz	kW	Ctry	Call	Station, location
	10	VTN		Kon Tum (1/P)
	10	VTN		Ha Tinh (P) (v)
909	100	CHN		FJ (CNR6)
	50	CHN		TJ + 6 stns
	100	IND		AIR, Gorakhpur
	5/10	INS		RRI, Sorong
	10	J	JOCB	NHK (2), Nagoya
	5	J	JOVX	STV, Abashiri
	10	KOR		KBS, Gumi
	5	NZL		RNZ AM /So. Star, Napier-Hastings
	5	PHL	DZEA	Catholic Media Netw., Laoag C, I. Nte
	5	PHL	DYSP	Republic Bc. System, Pto. Princesa, Palawan
	5	PHL	DYLA	Visayas Mindanao C. of TU, Cebu C
	10	THA		R. Thailand, Loei
	25	THA		R. Thailand, Surin
	10	TWN	BED79	BCC (C), Kaohsiung
	10	TWN	BEH3	Fu Hsing BS (1), Taipei
	10	VTN		Ca Mau (P) (r inactive)
918	2/2.5	AUS	4VL	Charleville
	2	AUS	2XL	Cooma
	2	AUS	6NA	Narrogin
	200	CBG		Nat. R. of Kampuchea, Steung Meanchey
	200	CHN		SD
	300	IND		AIR, Suratgarh
	1	J	JOPN	KRY, Iwakuni
	1	J	JOPM	KRY, Shimonoseki
	1	J		YBC, Shinjo
	1	J		YBC, Tsuruoka/Yonezawa
	5	J	JOEF	YBC, Yamagata
	50	KOR		KBS, Yeoncheon
	2.5	NZL		RNZ National, New Plymouth
	2.5	NZL		RNZ National, Timaru
	10	PHL	DZSR	Philippine Bc. Sce., Quezon C, NCR
	5	PHL	DXRS	R. Mindanao Netw., Surigao C, S. Nte
	5/7	RUS		R. Mayak, Sib., 3stns, (synch)
	100	THA		R. Thailand, Nakhon Pathom
	10	THA		Sor. Wor. Phor. 1, Chiang Mai
927	5	AUS	4CC	Gladstone
	5	AUS	3UZ	Melbourne
		CHN		FJ (CNR6)
	200	CHN		GZ + 24 stns
	100	IND		AIR, Visakhapatnam
	25	INS		RRI, Pekanbaru (4)
	5	J	JOFG	NHK (1), Fukui
	5	J	JOKG	NHK (1), Kofu
	1	J		NHK (1), Wakkanai/Tsuyama
	10	KOR		KBS, Buyeo
	1	KOR		KBS, Hongcheon/Hadong
	50	KRE		Korean Central BS (C/R), Hwangju (Sariwon)
	2	NZL		NewstalkZB, Palmerston No.
	5	PHL	DXDA	Office of the Governor, San Francisco, Ag. Sur
	5	PHL	DZLG	People's Bc. Sce., Legaspi, Albay
	5	PHL	DXMD	R. Mindanao Netw., Gen. Santos C, S. Cot.
	10	PHL	DWRS	Solidnorth Bc.Syst., Vigan, I. Sur
	5	PHL	DXMM	Sulu Tawi-Tawi Bc. Found., Jolo,Sulu
	20	THA		R. Thailand, Chanthaburi
	10	THA		R. Thailand, Nong Khai
	300	TJK		R. Japan (NKH World)/relays, Dushanbe
	10	TWN	BED43	BCC (C), Taichung
930		CHN		ZJ
936	5	AUS	6FX	Fitzroy Crossing (PBS)
	10	AUS	7ZR	ABC (LR), Hobart
	10	AUS	4PB	ABC (PNN), Brisbane
	200	CHN		AH; NM
	100	IND		AIR, Tiruchirapalli A
	5	J	JOTR	ABS, Akita
	1	J		MRT, 4 stns
	5	J	JONF	MRT, Miyazaki
	10	KOR		KBS, Changwon (3)
	1	NZL		New Supremo, Auckland
	100	PAK		Azad Kashmir R., Mirpur (r. 930 inactive)
	5	PHL	DWIM	Insular Bc. System, Calapan, Mind. Or.
	10	PHL	DXIM	Philippine Bc. Sce., Cagayan de Oro C,

kHz	kW	Ctry	Call	Station, location
				Mis. Or.
	1	PHL	DZXT	R. Corp. of the Philippines, Tarlac C
	1	PHL	DYCC	R. Mindanao Netw., Calbayog C, W. Samar
	1	PHL	DYKW	R. Philippines Netw., Binalbagan, Neg. Occ.
	5	PHL	DXDN	Univ. of Mindanao, Tagum C, Dvo Nte
	50	THA		R. Thailand, N. Sawan
	10	THA		Thor. Phor. 4, Pattani
	1	TWN	BEV98	Cheng Kung BS, Kaohsiung
	5	TWN		VO Han Bc. Netw., Taoyuan
940	10	HWA	KKNE	Honolulu, Oahu
945	2	AUS	3UZ	Bendigo (HPONS)
	1	AUS	4HI	Dysart (trtr)
		CHN		CNR13
	50	CHN		HL; HB (2 stns)
	400	CHN		JL (CNR 1)
	100	IND		AIR, Sambalpur
	1	J		NHK (1), Fukue
	1	J	JOQP	NHK (1), Hikone
	3	J	JOIQ	NHK (1), Muroran
	5	J	JOXK	NHK (1), Tokushima
	10	KOR		KBS, Boeun
	2	NZL		NewstalkZB, Gisborne
	10	PHL	DWFB	Philippine Bc. Sce., Laoag C, I. Nte
	5	PHL	DXRO	Swara Sug Media Corp., Cotabato C, Mag.
	10	PHL	DXDV	Vismin R. and TV Bc. Net, Butuan C, Ag. Nte
	10	SLM		R. Hapi Lagun (SIBC), Gizo (r inactive)
	10	THA		Thor. Or. 1, Bangkok
	10	THA		Thor. Phor. 2, Kalasin
954	0.35	AUS	4EL	Gordonvale (trtr)
	5	AUS	2UE	Sydney
	50	CHN		NM + 7 stns
	200	IND		AIR, Najibabad
	10	INS		RRI, Kendari
	100	J	JOKR	TBS Radio, Tokyo
	1	NZL		Coast, Dunedin
	2	NZL		R. Trackside/LiveSPORT, Hamilton
	40	PHL	DZEM	Christian Era Bc. Sce., Quezon City, NCR
	1	PHL	DXJT	Philippine Bc. Sce., Tangub C, Mis Octal
	5	PHL	DZAL	Rinconada Bc. Corp., Iriga C, Cam Sur
	10	THA		Thor. Or. 10, Phitsanulok
	10	THA		Thor. Or. 16, Chantaburi
	10	TWN	BEV85	Chien Kuo BS, Hsinying
963	2	AUS	6TZ	Bunbury
	5	AUS	2RG	Griffith
	5	AUS	5SE	Mt. Gambier
	5	AUS	4WK	Warwick
	20	BGD		Bangladesh Betar, Sylhet
	600	CHN		CRI, Huadian, Jilin
	50	CHN		LN; EB; HB; XJ; ZJ
	20	IND		AIR, Jalgaon
	2/10	INS		RRI, Jember
	5	J	JOTG	NHK (1), Aomori
	5	J	JOZK	NHK (1), Matsuyama
	1	J	JOSP	NHK (1), Saga
	1	J		NHK (1), Yonago/Hagi
	10	KOR	HLCR	KBS, Andong
	10	KOR	HLKS	KBS, Jeju
	10	NZL		RNZ AM /So. Star, Christchurch
	5	PHL	DZNS	Archdiocese of Nueva Segovia, Vigan, I. Sur
	10	PHL	DYMF	People's Bc. Sce., Cebu C
	5	PHL	DXYZ	Swara Sug Media Corp., Zamboanga C, Z. Sur
	1	RUS		R. Rossii, Guzino-Ozersk, Sib.
	20	RUS		R. Rossii, Zakamensk, Sib.
	10	THA		Phon Mor. 2, Bangkok
	25	THA		R. Thailand, Krabi
	10	TWN	BEV84	Taiwan BC, Chunghsing
	20	TWN	BED55	BCC (C), Taipei
972	2	AUS	5PB	ABC (PNN), Adelaide
	0.3	AUS	2DU	Cobar (trtr)
	5	AUS	2MW	Murwillumbah
	150	CHN		EN; HL; XJ
	300	IND		AIR, Cuttack A

kHz	kW	Ctry	Call	Station, location
	50	INS		RRI, Surakarta
	1500	KOR	HLCA	KBS, Dangjin
	5	NZL		NZ's Rhema, Wellington
	5	PHL	DXKH	Cebu Bc. Co., Cagayan de Oro C, Mis. Or.
	1	PHL	DYSM	Cebu Bc. Co., Catarman, N. Samar
	5	PHL	DWTI	Katigbak Enterprises, Lucena C, Que.
	5	PHL	DWFR	Philippine Bc. Sce., Bontoc, Mt. Prov.
	10	THA		Nor. Thor. Phor., Phetchabun
	800	TJK		VOA/VOR relays, Dushanbe
	10	VTN		Quang Ngai (1/P)
981	2	AUS	3HA	Hamilton
	2	AUS	6KG	Kalgoorlie
	5	AUS	2NM	Muswellbrook
	200	CHN		JL (CNR1); JX (CNR1)
	5	CHN		SD
	100	IND		AIR, Raipur
	1	J		NHK (1), Kisofukushima/Sasebo
	2	NZL		RNZ National, Kaikohe
	2.5	NZL		Southern Star, Timaru
	10	PHL	DXBR	Consolidated Bc. Syst., Inc., Butuan C, Ag. Nte
	10	PHL	DYBQ	Intercontinental Bc. Corp., Iloilo C
	5	PHL	DWMT	Philippine Bc. Corp., Naga C, Cam. Sur
	5	PHL	DXDR	R. Mindanao Netw., Dipolog, Z. Nte
	10	PHL	DXOW	R. Pilipino Corp., Davao C, Dvo Sur
	5	PHL	DZRD	Swara Sug Media Corp., Dagupan C, Pang.
	10	THA		Mahaawittayalai Thammasat, Pathum Thani
	25	THA		R. Thailand, Mae Hong Son
	20	THA		R. Thailand, Nakhon Phanom
	25	THA		R. Thailand, Yala
	3	TWN	BEV68	Feng Ming BC (2), Kaohslung
990	250	TWN		VO Kuanghua, Hsinfeng
	0.5	AUS	3RN	ABC (RN), Albury-Wodonga
	0.5	AUS	8GO	ABC (LR), Gove
	5	AUS	6RPH	Perth (PBS)
	5	AUS	4RO	Rockhampton
	100	CHN		SH; EB; YN
	5	HWA	KIKI	Honolulu, Oahu
	300	IND		AIR, Jammu A
	10	J	JORK	NHK (1), Kochi
	10	KOR	HLAP	MBC, Changwon
	500	MNG		MRT (FS), Ulaanbaatar
	1	NZL		Apna 990, Auckland
	1	NZL		R. Trackside/LiveSPORT, Nelson
	5	PHL	DZMT	Pacific Bc. System, Laoag, I. Nte
	5	PHL	DYTH	Pacific Bc. System, Tacloban C, Leyte
	5	PHL	DXBM	Republic Bc. System, Cotabato C, Mag.
	10/5	PHL	DZIQ	Trans-Radio Bc. Corp., Makati C, NCR
	10	THA		Sor. Wor. Phor. 2, N. Ratchasima
	20	TWN	BEV58	Cheng Sheng BC (1), Taichung
	10	TWN	BEP34	Ching Cha BS, Hualien
	1	TWN	BEP38	Ching Cha BS, Ilan
999	2	AUS	2NB	ABC (LR), Broken Hill
	5	AUS	2ST	Nowra
	10	BGD		Bangladesh Betar, Thakurgaon
	200	CHN		LN + 7 stns
	1	FSM	V6AF	Baptist R. Pohnpei, Kolonia
	1	IND		AIR, Almora
	20	IND		AIR, Coimbatore
	1/150	INS		RRI, Jakarta (3)
	1	J		NHK (1), Fukuyama/Hachinoe
	1	J		NHK (1), Nakamura
	10	KOR	HLCL	CBS, Gwangju
	250	KRE		Korean Central BS (C/R), Hamhung
	1.5	NZL		Manawatu Access R., Palmerston No. (CAS)
	5	PHL	DWMI	Katigbak Enterprises, Calapan, Mind. Or.
	5	PHL	DZEQ	Philippine Bc. Sce., Baguio C, Benguet
	1	PHL	DXPT	Philippine Bc. Sce., Bongao, Tawi-Tawi
	1	PHL	DXHP	R. Mindanao Netw., Bislig, S. Sur
	5	PHL	DYSS	Republic Bc. System, Cebu C
	10	THA		Phon. Neung Ror. Or., Bangkok
	10	THA		Thor. Phor. 3, Chiang Rai
	1	TWN	BEV92	Tien Nan BS, Taipei

kHz	kW	Ctry	Call	Station, location
1008	10	AUS	4TAB	Brisbane
	0.3	AUS	2TAB	Canberra (HPONS)
	5	AUS	7TAB	Launceston (HPONS)
		CHN		BJ (CNR DS3)
	3	CHN		XJ (CNR DS)
	50	CHN		TJ + 20 stns
	200	CHN		YN (CNR1)
	100	IND		AIR, Kolkata B
		INS		RRI, Gorontalo
	10	INS		RRI, Madiun
	50	J	JONR	ABC, Osaka
	50	KOR		KBS, Gangneung (3)
	10	NZL		NewstalkZB, Tauranga
	120	PAK		PBC (1), Hyderabad
	5	PHL	DWBS	Catholic Media Netw., Sto. Domingo, Albay
	10	PHL	DXXX	R. Philippines Netw., Zamboanga C, Z. Sur
	5	PHL	DWGO	Subic Bc. Corp., Olongapo C, Zamb.
	10	THA		Wor. Por. Tho 3, N. Ratchasima
	10	TWN	BED88	BCC (C), Taitung
	600	TWN		RTI, Lukang
	1	TWN	BEV60	Cheng Sheng BC, Kaohsiung
1017	0.5	AUS	6WH	ABC (LR), Wyndham
	1	AUS	6TAB	Bunbury (HPONS)
	5	AUS	2KY	Sydney
	10	CHN		EB; GD
	200/100	CHN		JL(CNR8/CRI)
		CHN		ZJ (CNR1)
	20	IND		AIR, Chennai B
	10	IND		AIR, New Delhi
	50	J	JOIR	NHK (2), Fukuoka
	10	KOR	HLAW	MBC, Andong
	2.5	NZL		R. Sport/NewstalkZB, Christchurch
	10	PHL	DWDC	Intercontinental Bc. Corp., Dagupan C, Pang.
	10	PHL	DXAM	Kalayaan Bc. System, Davao C, Dvo Sur
	10	PHL	DWLC	Philippine Bc. Sce., Lucena C, Que.
	5	PHL	DXSN	Silangan Bc. Corp., Surigao C, S. Nte
	10	THA		Thor. Or. 5, Prachuap KK
	10	TON	A3Z	Tonga Bc. Comm., Nuku'alofa
	10	TWN	BED53	BCC (C), Hsinchu
1026	10	AUS	3PR	ABC (PNN), Melbourne
	5	AUS	4AA	Mackay
	2	AUS	6NW	Port Hedland
	200	CHN		GZ; BJ + 4 stns
	20	IND		AIR, Allahabad A
	5	INS		RRI, Serui
	1	KOR		KBS, Geochang/Hwacheon
	2	NZL		Newstalk ZB, Kaitaia/Whangarei
	2.5	NZL		The Word Bible Radio, Invercargill
	5	PHL	DXMC	People's Bc. Sce., Koronadal, S. Cot.
	10	PHL	DZAR	Swara Sug Media Corp., Quezon C, NCR
	250	RUS		VoR, Novosibirsk, Sib.
	50	THA		R. Thailand, Phitsanulok
	10	THA		R. Thailand, Yala
	1	TWN	BEV51	Chung Hua BC (2), Sanchung
	1	TWN		Tien Sheng BS, Yuanli
1035	2	AUS	2EA	Wollongong (SBS)
	50	CHN		CNR1
	10	IND		AIR, Guwahati B
	1/5	INS		RRI, Bandar Lampung
		INS		RRI, Palu
	1	J	JOHD	NHK (2), Takamatsu
	1	J	JOIC	NHK (2), Toyama
	1	J		NHK (2), Tsuruoka
	10	KOR	HLCP	KBS, Pohang
	20	NZL		Newstalk ZB, Wellington
	120	PAK		PBC, Multan
	5/1	PHL	DXUZ	Univ. de Zamboanga, Ipil, Z. Sib
	5	PHL	DZWX	Consolidated Bc. Syst., Inc., Baguio C, Benguet
	10	PHL	DYRL	R. Pilipino Corp., Bacolod C, Neg. Occ.
	6	SLM		R. Happy Isles (SIBC), Honiara
	10	THA		Phaak Phiset, Bangkok
	10	TWN	BED26	BCC (C), Chia-i

kHz	kW	Ctry	Call	Station, location
	20	IND		AIR, Rewa
	2/10	INS		RRI, Padang
	50	J	JOOR	MBS, Osaka
	5	NZL		R. Ake, Auckland
	5	PHL	DYCX	Newsounds Bc. Netw., S. J. de Buenavista, Antique
	1	PHL	DZRS	R. Sorsogon Netw., Inc., Sorsogon C
	5	PHL	DXYK	Republic Bc. System, Butuan C, Ag. Nte
	5	PHL	DYSB	GMA Netw., Inc., Bacolod C, Neg. Occ
	10	THA		Nor. Thor. Phor, Chiang Rai
	10	THA		Sor. Sor. Sor., Bangkok
	2.5	TWN		Kuo Sheng BC, Erhlin
	10	VUT		VBTC, Santo
1180	1	HWA	KORL	Honolulu , Oahu
1188	2	AUS	6XM	ABC (LR), Exmouth
	2	AUS	2NZ	Inverell
	10	CHN		EB(2 stns); JL
	300	CHN		CRI, Kunming, Yunnan
	50	IND		AIR, Mumbai C
	10	INS		RRI, Manado (4)
	10	J	JOKP	NHK (1), Kitami
		KAZ		BBCWS relay, Abay
	50/100	KOR	HLKX	VOA/FEBC, Seoul
	0.4	NZL		RNZ National, Rotorua
	5	PHL	DXLX	Consolidated Bc. Syst., Inc., Iligan, Lanao Nte
	10	PHL	DXIF	Newsounds Bc. Netw., Cagayan de Oro C, Mis. Or.
	5	PHL	DZLT	R. Corp. of the Philippines, Lucena C, Que.
	5	PHL	DZXO	Vanguard R. Netw., Cabanatuan, Nva. Ecija
	5	RUS		R. Teos, Khabarovsk, FE
	10	THA		Kor. Wor. Sor. 3, Sakon Nakhon
	10	THA		Thor. Phor. 3, Phitsanulok
	10	THA		Thor. Phor. 1, Sa Kaeo
	10	TWN	BED32	BCC (C), Hualien
	1	TWN	BEV57	Sheng Li chih Sheng BC (2), Tainan
	1	TWN	BEV46	Taiwan BC (2), Taipei
1197	2	AUS	5RPH	R. 5RPH, Adelaide
	0.5/1	AUS	4BI	Switch FM, Brisbane
	10	CHN		HL; FJ(v); SD; SH; YN
	1	IND		AIR, Shillong (stand-by)
	20	IND		AIR, Tirunelveli
	10	INS		RRI, Palangkaraya
	5	J	JOYF	IBS, Mito
	1	J	JOFO	RKB, Kitakyushu
	1	J		RKC, Nakamura
	1	J		RKK, 3 stns
	10	J	JOBF	RKK, Kumamoto
	1	J		STV, 3 stns
	3	J	JOWL	STV, Asahikawa
	10	KAZ		BBCWS relay, Astana
	1	KOR		AFNK, Dongducheon
	10	MLA		RTM Labuan, Kudat (v)
	2	NZL		NewstalkZB, Wanganui
	5	PHL	DXFE	FEBC, Davao C, Dvo Sur
	5	PHL	DWBA	Satellite Bc. Corp., Bangued, Abra
	0.2	RUS		R. Rossii + Reg., Sib., 4stns
	10	THA		Jor. Tor. Lor, Lop Buri
1206	5	AUS	2CC	Canberra, ACT
	5	AUS	2GF	Grafton
	2	AUS	6TAB	Perth (HPONS)
	150	CHN		JL + 9 stns
	200	IND		AIR, Bhawanipatna
	1	KOR		KBS, Jeongseon/Cheongsong
	0.5	NZL		Free FM89, Hamilton (CAS)
	2	NZL		Trackside/LiveSPORT, Dunedin
	10	THA		R. Thailand, Satun
	10	THA		Thor. Phor. 1, Prachuap KK
	100	TWN		RTI, Minhsiung
	10	TWN	BEV62	Taiwan BC, Hsinchu
1210	1	HWA	KZOO	Honolulu, Oahu
1215	0.5	AUS	6NM	ABC (LR), Northam
	0.35	AUS	2TAB	Bowral (HPONS)
	0.25	AUS	4HI	Moranbah (trtr)

kHz	kW	Ctry	Call	Station, location
	50	CHN		GD (CNR7)
	20	CHN		LN (CNR2)
	10	CHN		XJ; HB; HL
	20	IND		AIR, New Delhi (Kingsway) N
	20	IND		AIR, Pudducherri
		INS		RRI, Bandung (3)
	0.5/10	INS		RRI, Samarinda
	1	J	JOBW	KBS, Hikone
	2	J	JOBO	KBS, Maizuru
	10	KOR	HLAK	MBC, Jinju
	2	NZL		NewstalkZB, Kaikohe
	10	PHL	DYRF	Word Bc. Corp., Cebu C
	10	THA		Kor. Wor. Sor. 2, Phrae
	50	THA		R. Thailand, Surat Thani
	10	THA		Thor. Phor. 2, U. Ratchathani
	1	TWN		Tien Sheng BS, Pengshan
1224	5	AUS	6RN	ABC (RN), Busselton
	5	AUS	3EA	Melbourne (SBS)
	5	AUS	2RPH	R. for the Print-Handicapped, Sydney
		CHN		FJ (CNR6)
	100	CHN		GX; JS
	20	IND		AIR Srinagar C
	10	J	JOJK	NHK (1), Kanazawa
	20	KOR		KBS, Gwangju (3)
	1	MHL		AFN, Kwajalein
	2	NZL		R. Trackside/LiveSPORT, Invercargill
	10	PHL	DXED	Eagle Bc. Corp., Davao C, Dvo Sur
	5	PHL	DWSR	Manila Bc. Co., Lucena, Que.
	10	PHL	DZAG	Philippine Bc. Sce., Agoo, LU
	10	THA		Thor. Or. 15, Chiang Rai
	10	THA		Thor. Or. 4, N. Sawan
	10	TWN	BED52	BCC (C), Kaohsiong
	1	TWN	BEV71	Hua Sheng BC (2), Taipei
1233	10	AUS	2NC	ABC (LR), Newcastle
	120	CHN		XJ (2stns); HN; JS
	20	IND		AIR, Tura
	0.2/1/5	INS		RRI,Pontianak
	5	J	JOUR	NBC, Nagasaki
	5	J	JOGR	RAB, Aomori
	1	KOR		KBS, Pyeongchang
	2	NZL		R. Live, Wellington
	5	PHL	DYVS	FEBC, Bacolod, Neg. Occ.
	5	PHL	DWRV	R. Veritas, Bayombong, Nva Viz.
	20	RUS		Yumor FM, Yelizovo, FE
	10	THA		Thor. Or. 1, Bangkok
	10	THA		Wor. Por. Tho. 7, Udon Thani
	40	TKM		Turkmen Radio (1), Syrtagta
	1	TWN		Chung Hua BC, Juifang
1242	2	AUS	8TAB	Darwin (HPONS)
	2	AUS	5AU	Port Augusta
	5	AUS	3GV	Sale
	2	AUS	4AK	Toowoomba
	1	CHN		LN + 5 stns
	100	IND		AIR, Varanasi
	10	INS		RRI, Bogor
	100	J	JOLF	NBS, Tokyo
	10	KOR	HLSB	MBC, Wonju
	2	NZL		1XX – One Double X, Whakatane
	1	NZL		R. Trackside/LiveSPORT, Timaru
	5	PHL	DXZB	DXZB/TV13 Coop., Inc., Zamboanga C, Z. Sur
	20	PHL	DWBL	FBS R. Netw., Pasig C, NCR
	5	PHL	DXSY	Times Bc. Corp., Ozamis C, Mis. Occ.
	50	THA		R. Thailand, Surat Thani
	10	THA		Thor. Phor. 3, Phetchabun
	1	TWN		Yen Sheng BS (2), Hualien
	100	VTN		VO Vietnam, Can Tho, Ô Môn
1250	1	CHN		ZJ
1251	2	AUS	2DU	Dubbo
		CHN		BJ(CRI DS1)
	100	CHN		QH + 25 stns
	20	IND		AIR, Sangli
	10	INS		RRI, Banda Aceh
	10	KOR	HLKT	CBS, Daegu

kHz	kW	Ctry	Call	Station, location
	5	NZL		NZ's Rhema, Auckland
	10	PAK		PBC, Loralai
	1	PHL	DYRG	Intercontinental Bc. Corp., Kalibo, Aklan
	2.5	PHL	DZMS	People's Bc. Netw., Sorsogon C
	10	THA		Jor. Sor. 3, Roi Et
	5	THA		Thor. Or. 6, Bangkok
	100	TJK		BBCWS/HCJB/VOR relays, Dushanbe
	10	TWN		VO Han Bc. Netw., Kaohsiung
1260	1	AUS	6KA	Karratha
	2	AUS	3SR	Shepparton
	2	AUS	4MW	Thursday Island (PBS)
	1	CHN		HN; LN; XZ
	20	IND		AIR, Ambikapur
	20	J	JOIR	TBC, Sendai
	5	KOR		AFNK, Busan
	10	KOR		KBS, Namwon
	2	NZL		R. Trackside/LiveSPORT, Christchurch
	5	PHL	DZEL	Eagle Bc. Corp., Lucena C, Que.
	5	PHL	DWMC	Magiliw Comm. Bc. Co., Rosales, Pang.
	5	PHL	DXRF	Manila Bc. Co., Davao C, Dvo Sur
	10	PHL	DYDD	Siam Bc. Netw. Corp., Lapu-Lapu C, Cebu
	25	THA		R. Thailand, Chiang Rai
	1	TWN		Cheng Sheng BC, Taipao
	10	TWN	BEP22	Ching Cha BS, Taipei
1269	5	AUS	6RN	ABC (RN), Busselton
	5	AUS	2SM	Sydney
	10	CHN		SX; JL; JS
	600	CHN		CRI, Xuanwei, Yunnan
	20	IND		AIR, Agartala
	20	IND		AIR, Madurai
	1	J	JOFM	HBC, Esashi
	5	J	JOHW	HBC, Obihiro
	1	J		JRT, Ikeda
	5	J	JOJR	JRT, Tokushima
	1	KOR		KBS, Gurye
	10	KOR		KBS, Yangju
	0.4	NZL		Classic Hits, Takaka
	10/5	PHL	DYWB	Consolidated Bc. Syst., Inc., Bacolod, Neg. Occ
	5	PHL	DZVX	Newsounds Bc. Netw., Daet, Cam. Nte
	10	PHL	DWRC	Republic Bc. System, San Nicolas, I. Nte
	5	RUS		R. Ussuri, Ussuryisk, FE
		RUS		R. Vostok Rossii, Komsomolsk, FE
	10	THA		Kho. Sor. Thor. Bor., Bangkok
	10	THA		Mor. Kor., Songkhla
	1	TWN	BEV37	Cheng Sheng BC, Taitung
	10	TWN	BEC44	VO Han Bc. Netw., Penghu
	50	UZB		UZR (2), Zarafshon
1270	5	HWA	KNDI	Honolulu, Oahu
1278	5	AUS	3EE	Melbourne
	100	CHN		EB (2 stns); HL; JX
	10	IND		AIR, Lucknow C
	50	J	JOFR	RKB, Fukuoka
	1	KOR		KBS, Hapcheon
	2	NZL		Newstalk ZB, Napier-Hastings
	10	PHL	DZRM	Philippine Bc. Sce., Quezon C, NCR
	7	RUS		R. Rossii + Reg., Severobaykalsk, Sib.
	5	RUS		R. Rossii, Bagdarin, Sib.
	1	TWN		Fuhsingkang BS, Peitou
1287	2	AUS	2TM	Tamworth
	10	BGD		Bangladesh Betar, Barishal
		CHN		CNR1
	30	CHN		GD + 8 stns
	100	IND		AIR, Panaji A
	50	J	JOHR	HBC, Sapporo
	150	KGZ		KGR (1), Bishkek
	10	KOR	HLAX	MBC, Cheongju
	10	KOR	HLAF	MBC, Gangneung
	2	NZL		R. Sport, Westport
	5	PHL	DZZH	Manila Bc. Co., Sorsogon C
	5	RUS		R. Rossii + Reg., Kyakhta, Sib.
	10	THA		Sor. Or. Thor., Samut Prakan (Bangkok)
	10	THA		Wor. Por. Tho. 6, U. Ratchathani

kHz	kW	Ctry	Call	Station, location
	10	TWN	BEC27	VO Han Bc. Netw., Taichung
	1	TWN		Min Li BS, Fangliao
1296	400	AFG		BBG, Kabul
	10	AUS	6RN	ABC (RN), Wagin
	5	AUS	4RPH	Queensland R. for the Print-H., Brisbane
	25	CHN		SH + 5 stns
	300	CHN		CRI/RFI, Kunming, Yunnan
	10	IND		AIR, Darbhanga
	10	J	JOTK	NHK (1), Matsue
	500	KGZ		R.Rossii relay, Bishkek
	2.5	NZL		NewstalkZB, Hamilton
	10	PHL	DXAB	ABS-CBN Bc. Corp., Davao C, Dvo Sur
	5	PHL	DYJJ	Intercontinental Bc. Corp., Roxas C, Capiz
	5	PHL	DWPR	Multipoint Broadc. Netw., Dagupan C, Pang.
	10	THA		R. Thailand, Pattani
	300	TJK		R.Rossii relay, Dushanbe
	10	TWN	BED47	BCC (N), Tainan
	1	TWN	BEV23	Min Pen BC (1), Taipei
1305	2	AUS	5RN	ABC (RN), Renmark/Loxton
		CHN		CNR2
		CHN		Jinan,SD
	20	IND		AIR, Parbhani
	10	KOR		KBS, Uljin
	2.5	NZL		R. Dunedin
	7	RUS		R. Mayak, Ust-Kut, Sib.
	10	THA		Yaan Kraw, Bangkok
1314	10	BGD		Bangladesh Betar, Cox's Bazar
	5	AUS	3BT	Ballarat
	5	AUS	2TAB	Wollongong (HPONS)
	50	CHN		CU + 5 stns
	1	IND		AIR, Cuttack B
	20	IND		AIR, Bhuj
	50	J	JOUF	OBC, Osaka
	10	KOR	HLCM	CBS, Jeonbuk
	5	NZL		RNZ AM /So. Star, Invercargill
	2	NZL		RNZ National, Gisborne
	10	PHL	DWXI	Delta Bc. System, Parañaque, NCR
	10	THA		Mor. Kor., Khon Kaen
	1	TWN	BEP33	Ching Cha BS, Tainan
	10	TWN	BEV76	Tien Sheng BS, Chunan
1322	5	PHL	DXAD	Mindanao DMPC, Marawi, Lanao Sur (v)
1323	2	AUS	5DN	Adelaide
	0.4	AUS	1--	Canberra (HPONS)
	600	CHN		CRI, Huadian, Jilin
	600	CHN		CRI, Shuangyashan, Heilongjiang
	500	CHN		CRI, Ürümqi, Hutubi
	20	CHN		ZJ + 5 stns
	20	IND		AIR, Kolkata C
	1	J	JOFP	NHK (1), Fukushima
	1	J		NHK (1), Yamada
	1	KOR		KBS, Yeonggwang/Ulleung
	3	NZL		Newstalk ZB, Hawera
	10	PHL	DYSI	GMA Netw., Inc., Iloilo C
	10	PHL	DZRK	Philippine Bc. Sce., Tabuk, Kalinga
	10	THA		Thor. Or. 13, Chiang Mai
	10	THA		Thor. Or. 7, Surat Thani
	7	TJK		Tajik R1, Dushanbe
	1	TWN	BEV45	Taiwan BC (1), Taipei
1332	5	AUS	4BU	Bundaberg
	2	AUS	3SH	Swan Hill
	100	CHN		EN (3 stns) + 4 stns
	10	IND		AIR, Tezu
	10	INS		RRI, Jakarta (4)
	50	J	JOSF	Tokai R., Nagoya
	10	KOR	HLAO	MBC, Chungju
	10	NZL		R. Sport, Auckland
	100	PAK		PBC (2), Lahore
	1	PHL	DZKI	R. Philippines Netw., Iriga C, Cam. Sur
	5	PHL	DWAY	Swara Sug Media Corp., Cabanatuan, Nva. Ecija
	10	THA		Or. Sor., Bangkok
	10	THA		Thor. Or. 14, Maha Sarakham
	10	TWN	BEC36	VO Han Bc. Netw., Kaohsiung

kHz	kW	Ctry	Call	Station, location
	1	TWN		Taiwan BC, Puli
1341	5	AUS	3CW	Geelong (HPONS)
	5	AUS	2TAB	Newcastle (HPONS)
	100/200	CHN		GD(CNR 1/CRI)
	100	CHN		HL + 6 stns
	1	IND		AIR, Kohima
	1/5	INS		RRI, Tanjung Pinang
	1	J		NHK (1), Iwaki/Minamata
	25	KAZ		Qazaq Radiosi, Aqtaw
	30	KAZ		RFE/RL relay, Almati
	2	NZL		NewstalkZB, Nelson
	10	PAK		PBC, Bahawalpur
	20	THA		R. Thailand, Loei
	10	THA		R. Thailand, Phangnga
	25	THA		R. Thailand, Ubon Ratchathani
1350	5	AUS	2LF	Young
	50	CHN		YN + 5 stns
	1	FSM	V6A	Baptist Church, Weno, Chuuk
	0.25	GUM	KUSG	Managament Adv. Sce., Agana
	1	IND		AIR, Jalandhar C
	20	IND		AIR, Kupwara
	10	INS		RRI, Tarakan
	20	J	JOER	RCC, Hiroshima
	10	KOR	HLAQ	MBC, Samcheok
	1	NZL		R. Sport, Rotorua
	10	PHL	DWUN	Prog.Bc.Corp., Quezon, C, NCR
	5	RUS		R. Rossii + Reg., Ust-Kan/Ust-Ulagan, Sib.
	10	THA		Phon. Neung Ror. Or., Bangkok
	10	THA		Wor. Por. Tho. 17, Trang
	10	TWN	BED63	BCC (N), Chia-i
	2.5	TWN	BEV50	Chung Hua BC (1), Sanchung
1359	0.2	AUS	3UZ	Mildura (HPONS)
	0.25	AUS	4WK	Toowoomba (trtr)
		CHN		CNR1; YN
	1	KOR		AFNK, Songtan
	2.5	NZL		Coast, New Plymouth
	1	NZL		More FM, Queenstown
	1	PHL	DYSJ	Inter-Island Broadc. Corp., S. J. de Buenavista, Antique
	5	PHL	DZYR	Philippine R. Corp., S. Fernando, LU
	1	RUS		R. Mayak, Choya/Shebalino, Sib.
	5	RUS		R. Mayak, Onguday, Sib.
	7	RUS		R. Mayak, Ust-Ilimsk, Sib.
	10	THA		Thor. Phor. 2, Sakhon Nakhon
	5	TWN	BEC40	VO Han Bc. Netw., Hualien
	600	TWN		RTI/WYFR, Fangliao
1368	2	AUS	2GN	Goulburn
	10	CHN		HL; FJ (v); HB (2 stns)
	20	IND		AIR, New Delhi C
	1	J	JOTS	HBC, Wakkanai
	5	J	JOHP	NHK (1), Takamatsu
	1	J	JOLG	NHK (1), Tottori
	1	J		NHK (1), Tsuruoka
	1	KOR		KBS, Muju
	2	KRE		Korean Central BS (E), Pyongyang
	0.8/0.1	NZL		1XT Village R., Tauranga
	1	NZL		R. Live, Napier-Hastings
	1	PHL	DZRA	Catanduanes State College, Virac, Catanduanes
	2.5	PHL	DZBS	R. Philippines Netw., Baguio C, Benguet
	10	PHL	DXKO	R. Philippines Netw., Cagayan de Oro C, Mis. Or.
	10	THA		R. Thailand, Buri Ram
	25	THA		R. Thailand, Nan
	10	THA		Thor. Or. 12, N. Pathom
	1	TWN		Chin Hsi BC, Kaohsiung
1370	6.2	HWA	KUPA	Pearl City, Oahu
1377	5	AUS	3MP	Melbourne
	600	CHN		HEN (CNR1)
	10	CHN		SD + 5 stns
	20	IND		AIR, Hyderabad B
	10	INS		RRI, Tolitoli
	1	J		NHK (2), Hachinohe

kHz	kW	Ctry	Call	Station, location
	1	J	JOAC	NHK (2), Nagasaki
	5	J	JOUC	NHK (2), Yamaguchi
	2	NZL		R. Sport, Levin
	3	NZL		The Word/Bible R., Dunedin
	10	PHL	DXKP	R. Philippines Netw., Pagadian C, Z. Sur
	10	THA		R. Thailand, Chumphon
	10	THA		Wor. Phon 4, Phitsanulok
1386	50	CHN		TJ + 6 stns
	20	IND		AIR, Gwalior
	10	J	JOHC	NHK (2), Kagoshima
	10	J	JOJB	NHK (2), Kanazawa
	10	J	JOQC	NHK (2), Morioka
	5	J	JOKB	NHK (2), Okayama
	10	KOR	HLAM	MBC, Mokpo
	10	NZL		R. Tarana, Auckland
	5	PHL	DYVW	Catholic Media Netw., Borongan, E. Samar
	25	PHL	DZTV	Intercontinental Bc. Corp., Quezon C, NCR
	10	PHL	DXCR	Mt. View College, Valencia, Buk.
	5	SLM		R. Temotu (SIBC), Lata, Sta. Cruz Is. (r inactive)
	10	THA		SW Pheua Kaan Kaset, Bangkok
	3.5	TWN	BED74	BCC (C), Yuli
1395	0.2	AUS	2LG	ABC (LR), Lithgow
	5	AUS	5AA	Adelaide
	50	CHN		AH; FJ; NM (2 stns); YN
	20	IND		AIR, Bikaner
	1	INS		RRI, Wamena
	1	J	JOCE	CRK, Toyooka
	1	J	JOWE	RFC, Wakamatsu
	10	KOR		KBS, Cheorwon
	2	NZL		NewstalkZB, Oamaru
	5	PHL	DZVT	Apostolic Vicariate of S. J., San Jose, Min. Occ.
	10	PHL	DYCH	Cebu Bc. Co., Talisay C, Cebu
	10	THA		Nor. Thor. Phor., Chiang Rai
	1	TWN		Cheng Sheng BC, Tafa
1404	4	AUS	6TAB	Busselton (HPONS)
	2	AUS	2PK	Parkes/Forbes
	50	CHN		FJ (3 stns); HB; LN; ZJ
	20	IND		AIR, Gangtok
	5	J	JOQL	HBC, Kushiro
	1	J	JOVO	SBS, Hamamatsu
	10	J	JOVR	SBS, Shizuoka
	1	KGZ		KGR (1), Cholpon-Ata
	7	KGZ		KGR (1), Haidarkan/Naryn
	20	KGZ		KGR (1), Jojomel
		KGZ		KGR (1), Orgochor
	10	KOR	HLKP	CBS, Busan
	5	NZL		NZ's Rhema, Invercargill
		PHL	DXAQ	End Time Mission, Lucena C, Que
	1	PHL	DYKB	R. Philippines Netw., Bacolod, Neg. Occ.
	10	THA		Jor. Sor. 4, Yasothon
	25	THA		R. Thailand, Songkhla
	10	THA		Thor. Phor. 1, Suphan Buri
	2.5/5	TLS		R. Timor Kmanek, Dili
	10	TWN	BEV78	Yi Shih BS, Keelung
1413	5	AUS	2EA	Newcastle (SBS)
	0.5	AUS	3UCB	Shepparton (HPONS)
	10	BGD		Bangladesh Betar, Comilla
	5	CHN		XJ + 4 stns
	20	IND		AIR, Kota
	5	INS		RRI, Sungai Liat
	50	J	JOIF	KBC, Fukuoka
	1	NZL		3XP R. Ferrymead, Christchurch
	2	NZL		NewstalkZB, Tokoroa
	5	PHL	DYXW	Filipinas Bc. Netw.., Tacloban C, Leyte
	5	PHL	DWRA	Republic Bc. System, Bauio C, Benguet
	5	RUS		R. Rossii, Sangar, FE
	10	TWN	BED54	BCC (N), Miaoli
	1	TWN	BED67	BCC (N), Puli
1420	5	HWA	KKEA	Honolulu, Oahu
1422	5	AUS	3XY	Melbourne (HPONS)
	1	AUS	4AM	Port Douglas (trtr)
	2	AUS	6GS	Wagin (HPONS)

kHz	kW	Ctry	Call	Station, location
	20	CHN		SH (2 stns); SX; SC
	600	CHN		XJ (CNR1/8/13/CRI)
	0.5	CHR	6ABCRN	ABC Radio National relay, Phosphate Hill
	50	J	JORF	RF, Yokohama
	5	PHL	DYZD	Bohol Chronicle R. Corp., Ubay, Bohol
	5	PHL	DXMU	Central Mindanao Univ., Musuan, Buk.
	5	RUS		R. Rossii, Kuanda, Sib.
	10	THA		Phon. Neung Ror. Or., Bangkok
	10	THA		R. Thailand, Amnat Charoen
	100	TWN		RTI, Minhsiung
	1	TWN		Chien Kuo BS, Kuanyin
1431	2	AUS	2RN	ABC (RN), Wollongong
	2	AUS	6TAB	Kalgoorlie (HPONS)
	10	BGD		Bangladesh Betar, Bandorban
	10	CHN		EB + 6 stns
	1	J		BSS, Izumo
	1	J	JOHL	BSS, Tottori
	5	J	JOZF	GBS, Gifu
	1	J		NBC, Fukue
	1	J	JOWW	RFC, Iwaki
	5	J	JOVT	WBS, Wakayama
	40	KGZ		KGR1, Jalal-Abad
	2	NZL		R. Kidnappers, Napier-Hastings (CAS)
	5	PHL	DYRS	Ragde, Vicente & Sons, San Carlos, Neg. Occ.
	5	THA		Sor. Thor. Ror. 6, Songkhla
	10	THA		Thor. Or. 3, N. Ratchasima
1440	2	AUS	1SBS	Canberra (SBS)
	50	CHN		NM (2); GX; LN
	1	IND		AIR, Kurseong
	3	J		STV, Muroran
	50	J	JOWF	STV, Sapporo
	1	J		STV, Tomakomai
		KAZ		BBCWS relay, Qizilorda
	10	KIR		R. Kiribati, Bairiki
	1-0.25	KOR		AFNK, 4 stns
	1.1	MHA	KKMP	Blue Continent Comm., Rota
	1	NZL		Goldrush R., Lawrence
	0.2	NZL		Moana AM, Tauranga
	10	PHL	DWDH	Manila Bc. Co., Dagupan C, Pang.
	0.01	PHL	DXSI	So. Inst. of Tech., Cagayan de Oro C, Mis. Or.
	5	RUS		R. Rossii + Reg., Turachak, Sib.
	5	RUS		R. Rossii + Reg., Ust-Koksha/Kosh-Agach, Sib.
	10	THA		Thor. Phor. 2, N. Phanom
	10	THA		Wor. Por. Tho. 8, Samut Sakhon
1449	2	AUS	6TAB	Mandurah (HPONS)
	5	AUS	2MG	Mudgee
	20	CHN		JX; FJ; SD(2 stns)
	10	FSM	V6AH	FSMBS R. Pohnpei, Kolonia
	1	IND		AIR, Kanpur
	5	J	JOQM	HBC, Abashiri
	1	J		RNC, Marugame
	5	J	JOKF	RNC, Takamatsu
	10	KOR	HLQB	KBS, Ulsan
	5	MLD		Raajje Radio, Malé
	2.5	NZL		RNZ National, Palmerston No.
	10	PAK		PBC, Zhob
	5	PHL	DYAC	Leyte State University, Baybay, Leyte (v)
	5	PHL	DXSA	Mindanao Bc. Co., Inc., Marawi C, Lanao Sur
	10	THA		Thor. Phor. 3, Phichit
	10	THA		Wor. Sor. Por., Chumphon
1458	2	AUS	2PB	ABC (PNN), Newcastle
	200	CHN		NM; JS; LN
	20	IND		AIR, Barmer
	20	IND		AIR, Bhagalpur
	1	J		IBS, Sekijo
	1	J	JOYL	IBS, Tsuchiura
	1	J	JOUO	NBC, Saga
	1	J		RCC, Shobara
	1	J	JOWR	RFC, Fukushima
	1	KOR		KBS, Hamyang/Bonghwa
	2.5	NZL		RNZ National, Westport

kHz	kW	Ctry	Call	Station, location
	10	PHL	DYZZ	Siam Bc. Netw. Corp., Gihulngan, Neg. Occ.
	10	PHL	DZJV	ZOE Bc. Netw., Calamba, Laguna
	10	THA		Jor. Sor. 6, Si Sa Ket
	10	THA		Sor. Thor. Ror. 3, Phuket
1460	5	HWA	KRHA	Honolulu, Oahu
1467	2	AUS	3ML	Mildura
	10	CHN		EB; JX; SD
	100	IND		AIR, Jeypore
	1	J	JOVB	NHK (2), Hakodate
	1	J	JOMC	NHK (2), Miyazaki
	1	J	JONB	NHK (2), Nagano
	1	J	JOID	NHK (2), Oita
	1	J		NHK (2), Wakkanai
	150	KGZ		TWR relay, Bishkek
	50	KOR	HLKN	KBS, Mokpo
	1	PHL	DWVR	R. Veritas, San Jose C, Nva Ecija
	5	PHL	DXVP	RCA-ZBN, Zamboanga C, Z. Sur
	100	THA		R. Thailand, Pathum Thani
1476	1	AUS	5MG	ABC (LR), Mt. Gambier
	0.18	AUS	2KA	Penrith (HPONS)
	2	AUS	4ZR	Roma
	200	CHN		HL (CNR2)
	10	CHN		HL + 9 stns
	1	IND		AIR, Jaipur A
	1	J		NHK (2), Iida
	700	MLA		RTM Labuan, Tuaran (r1475)
	5	NZI		R. Trackside/LiveSPORT, Auckland
	10	PAK		PBC, Faisalabad
	1	PHL	DZYA	R. Pilipino Corp., Angeles C, Pamp.
	10	PHL	DXRJ	Rajah Bc. Netw., Iligan C, Lanao Nte
	1	PHL	DWRB	Ribbon Bc. Netw., Lipa C, Bat
	20	RUS		R. Rossii + Reg., Onguday, Sib.
	50	THA		R. Thailand, Chiang Mai
	10	TKM		Turkmen R. (1), Türkmenbasy
1485	0.1	AUS	2RN	ABC (RN), Wilcannia
	0.05-0.2	AUS		ABC (LR), 2 stns
	0.15	AUS	2EA	Shellharbour (SBS)
	10	CHN		HB + 15 stns
	0.25	DGA		AFRTS, Diego Garcia
	1	IND		AIR, 10 stns
	1	J	JOPL	KRY, Hagi
	1	J	JOGO	RAB, Hachinohe
	1	KOR		KBS, Gongju/Goheung
	1	NZL		R. Trackside/LiveSPORT, Gisborne
	5	PHL	DYDH	Pacific Bc. System, Iloilo C
	1/2	RUS		R. Mayak, FE, 2 stns (sync.)
	1	RUS		R. Rossii + Reg., Kamenskoye, FE
	1	RUS		R. Rossii + Reg., Tyumen, FE
	0.2-1	RUS		R. Rossii, FE, 2 stns (sync.)
	1	RUS		R. Rossii, Sib., 2 stns (sync.)
1494	2	AUS	2AY	Albury
	1	CHN		AH + 4 stns
	5	FSM	V6AI	FSMBS R. Yap, Colonia
	1	J	JOTL	HBC, Nayoro
	1	J		RSK, 5 stns
	10	J	JOYR	RSK, Okayama
	2.5	NZL		RNZ AM /So. Star, Hamilton
	2.5	NZL		R. Sport, Timaru
	5	PHL	DXOC	DWRL Radio, Inc., Ozamis C, Mis. Occ.
	10	PHL	DWSS	Supreme Bc. Systems DWSS, Pasig C, NCR
	10	THA		Or. Sor. Mor. Thor., Bangkok
	5	TWN	BEE34	Chiao Yu Bc. System, Changhua
	10	TWN	BEE32	Chiao Yu Bc. System, Taipei
1500	10	HWA	KHKA	Honolulu, Oahu
1503	5	AUS	3KND	Port Melbourne (PBS)
	5	AUS	2BS	Bathurst
	10	CHN		HN; AH(v); LN; ZJ
	1	FSM	V6AJ	FSMBS R. Kosrae, Tofol
	1	IND		AIR, Vijayawada B
	10	J	JOUK	NHK (1), Akita
	1	J		NHK (1), Aso
	1	KOR		KBS, Gimcheon
	2.5	NZL		R. Sport, Christchurch

kHz	kW	Ctry	Call	Station, location
	5	NZL		R. Sport, Wellington
	5	RUS		R. Mayak, Salekhard, Sib.
	1	RUS		R. Rossii + Reg., Magistralnyy, Sib.
	10	THA		Jor. Sor. 2, Surat Thani
	500	TJK		VoR, Dushanbe
	600	TWN		RTI/RFI/VOR/BBG/relays, Fangliao
1512	10	AUS	2RN	ABC (RN), Newcastle
	5	AUS	6BAY	Geraldton
	10	CHN		GS; NM; SD
	20	IND		AIR, Kokrajhar
	10	INS		RRI, Bukittinggi
	1	J		NHK (2), Koriyama/Matsumoto
	5	J	JOZB	NHK (2), Matsuyama
	0.25-0.1	KOR		AFNK, 5 stns
	10	PAK		PBC, Gilgit
	10	PHL	DYAB	ABS-CBN Bc. Corp., Cebu C
	10	PHL	DZAT	End Time Mission, Lucena C, Que
	10	THA		Kor. Wor. Sor. 4, Phayao
	10	THA		Thor. Or. 11, Songkhla
	10	TWN		Ching Cha BS, Hsinchu
1521	2	AUS	2QN	Deniliquin
	10	CHN		NM + 25 stns
	500	CHN		CRI, Ürümqi, Hutubi
	10	IND		AIR, Tawang
	1	J	JOTC	NHK (2), Aomori
	1	J	JOFC	NHK (2), Fukui
	1	J	JODC	NHK (2), Hamamatsu
	1	J		NHK (2), Ishigaki/Nakamura
	1	J	JOJC	NHK (2), Yamagata
	1	J		NHK (2), Yonago
	1	NZL		R. Sport, Tauranga
	5	RUS		R. Rossii, Boguchany, Sib.
	10	THA		Nor. Thor. Phor, Bangkok
1530	2	AUS	2VM	Moree
	50	CHN		ZJ; JL; SX
	0.25	GUM	KVOG	Agana
	20	IND		AIR, Agra
	1	J	JODO	BSN, Joetsu
	5	J	JOXF	CRT, Utsunomiya
	1	J	JOEO	RCC, Fukuyama
	1	J		RCC, Mihara
	5	KOR		AFNK, Seoul (Yongsan)
	1	NZL		The Wireless Station, Napier-Hastings
	10	PHL	DZME	Capitol Bc. Center, Quezon C, NCR
	5	RUS		R. Mayak, Krasnyy Chikoy, Sib.
	10	THA		Thor. Phor. 1, Chanthaburi
	10	THA		Wor. Por. Tho. 14, Uttaradit
1539	5	AUS	5TAB	Adelaide (HPONS)
	1	AUS	2RF	Sydney (HPONS)
	10	CHN		CNR1
	1	KOR		KBS, Gosan
	0.4	NZL		Classic Hits, Picton
	5	PHL	DZYM	Philippine R. Corp., San José, Mind. Occ.
	10	THA		Phon Ror. Kao, Kanchanaburi
1540	5	HWA	KREA	Honolulu, Oahu
1548	50	AUS	4QD	ABC (LR), Emerald
	200	CHN		SD; HN
	400	CLN		Athmik Yatra R., Trincomalee
	1	NZL		Coast, Palmerston No
	0.9	NZL		R. Trackside/LiveSPORT, Rotorua
	5	PHL	DYDM	Catholic Media Netw., Maasin C, So. Leyte
	10	PHL	DZSD	GMA Netw., Inc., Dagupan C, Pang.
1557	0.5	AUS	5TAB	Renmark/Loxton (HPONS)
	2	AUS	2RE	Taree
	25	CHN		EB (2 stns); LN
	2	NZL		Coast, Hawera
	10	PAK		PBC, Skardu
	10	THA		R. Thailand, Trat
	10	THA		Siang Adison, Phetchabun
	300	TWN		RTI/WYFR, Kouhu
1566	0.2	AUS	4GM	ABC (LR), Gympie
	5	AUS	3NE	Wangaratta
	10	CHN		EB + 5 stns
1000	IND			AIR, Nagpur (Buttibori) N
	250	KOR	HLAZ	FEBC/VO Wilderness, Jeju
	0.1	NFK	VL2NI	R.Norfolk
	10	PHL	DXID	Asc. of Islamic Dev. Coop., Pagadian C, Z. Sur
1570	15	HWA	KUAU	Ha'iku, Maui
1575	5	AUS	2RF	Wollongong (HPONS)
	2	CHN		LN; GX; JL
	1	J		AFN, Iwakuni
	0.6	J		AFN, Misawa
	0.25	J		AFN, Sasebo
	2.5	NZL		OAR 105.4 FM, Dunedin (CAS)
	1000	THA		R. Saranrom/BBG, Ban Phachi, Rasom
1584	0.05-0.1	AUS		ABC (LR), 3 stns
	0.2	AUS	4VL	Cunnamulla (trtr)
	0.2	AUS	2EC	Narooma (trtr)
	0.5	AUS	4CC	Rockhampton (trtr)
	10	CHN		SX (2 stns) + 8 stns
	0.1	HKG		RTHK (3), Chung Hom Kok
	1	IND		AIR, 10 stns
	1	KOR		KBS, Danyang/Geumsan/Sancheong
	1	NZL		Coast, Napier-Hastings
	0.25	PAK		PBC, Turbat/Chitral/Sibi
	1	PHL	DWBR	Dawnbreaker's Found., Talavera, Nva Ecija
	5	PLW	T8AA	Voice of Palau, Malakal Island, Koror
	1/5	RUS		R. Mayak, Aykhal/Ust-Nera, FE
	1	RUS		R. Rossii + Reg., Klyuchi/Tigil, FE
	0.2	RUS		R. Rossii, B. Gora/Khandyra, Sib.
	1	RUS		R. Rossii, Taksimo, Sib.
1593	5	AUS	3RG	Melbourne (HPONS)
	0.2	AUS	2TAB	Murwillumbah (HPONS)
	10	CHN		HL (2 stns); XJ
	600	CHN		JS (CNR1)
	5	FSM	V6AK	FSMBS R. Chuuk, Weno
	10	IND		AIR, Bhopal A
	10	J	JOTB	NHK (2), Matsue
	10	J	JOQB	NHK (2), Niigata
	2.5	NZL		Coast, Christchurch
	5	NZL		R. Samoa, Auckland
	10	PHL	DXFM	Ranao Radio & TV Bc. Sys. Corp, Marawi C, Lanao Sur
	50	RUS		R. Yunost, Sib.
	10	THA		R. Thailand, Ratchaburi
	10	TWN		Yuyeh BS, Ilan
1602	0.05-0.25	AUS		ABC (LR), 3 stns
	1	CHN		Jiangsu N,JS
	1	IND		AIR, 11 stns
	1	J		NHK (2), 6 stns
	1	J	JOCC	NHK (2), Asahikawa
	1	J	JOFD	NHK (2), Fukushima
	1	J	JOSB	NHK (2), Kitakyushu
	1	J	JOKC	NHK (2), Kofu
	1	KOR		KBS, Sabuk
	2.5	NZL		R. Reading Service, Levin
	0.25	PAK		PBC, Abbottabad
	1	PHL	DZUP	Univ. of the Philippines, Quzon C, NCR
	1	RUS		Ekho Moskvy, Zeleznogorsk-Ilimskiy, Sib.
	0.2	RUS		R. Rossii, Chumikan, FE
	1	RUS		R. Rossii, Sib., 2 stns (sync.)
1611	0.05-0.4	AUS		16 stns (HPONS)
1613		KRE		Frontline Soldiers Radio (v)
1620	0.4	AUS		5 stns (HPONS)
1629	0.1-0.4	AUS		11 stns (HPONS)
1638	0.4	AUS		6 stns (HPONS)
	0.6	PHL	DWGI	Guzman Inst. Of Tech., Manila, NCR
1647	0.4	AUS		3 stns (HPONS)
1656	0.4	AUS		3 stns (HPONS)
1665	0.4	AUS	2MM	Sydney (HPONS)
	0.4	AUS	3UCB	Melbourne (HPONS)
1674	0.4	AUS	3---	Melbourne (HPONS)
	1	PHL	DZBF	Mun. of Marikina, Marikina C, NCR
1683	0.4	AUS	2---	Sydney (HPONS)

NORTH AMERICA

The North American MW frequency listing has been removed from this edition in order to make space for over 1,000 extra MW stations and their addresses in the main USA listing. To find the stations previously listed here, please go to the entries for Alaska, Canada and United States of America in the National Radio section.

CENTRAL AMERICA, CARIBBEAN, BERMUDA & MEXICO

Abbreviations: Broadc.=Broadcasting, Corp.=Corporation, Em=Emisora, LV=La Voz, Nal=Nacional, Nat=National, Sce=Service.
Call signs: Costa Rica TI_, Cuba CM_, Dominican Republic HI_, El Salvador YS_, Guatemala TG_, Honduras HR_, Mexico XE_, Nicaragua YN_, Panama HO_

kHz	kW	Ctry	Call	Station, location
530	10	CTR	RI	R. Sinfonola, Cartago
	10	CUB	BQ	R. Enciclopedia, HA
	1	CUB	BA	R. Rebelde, Guantánamo, GU
		TCA		R. Visión Cristiana, So. Caicos
540	10	CUB	BA	R. Rebelde, Maisí, GU
	1	CUB	BA	R. Rebelde, Sancti Spíritus, SS
	5	DOM	CM	R. ABC, Sto Domingo
	10	GRD		G.B.N. R., Klassic AM, St. George's
	0.02	GTM		R. Amistad, San Pedro de Laguna
		GTM		R. Cobán, Cobán
	5/2.5	MEX	HS	La Mejor, Los Mochis
	20/2.5	MEX	WF	La Poderosa, Ixtapaluca
	5	MEX	TX	La TX/La Ranchera de Paquime, Nuevo Casas Grandes
	5/1	MEX	MIT	LV de BalúnCanán, Comitán
	0.1	MEX	SURF	R. Zion, Tijuana
	1	MEX	WA	W R., Monterrey
	150	MEX	WA	W R., San Luis Potosí
	25	NCG	A3OW	R. Corporación, Managua
	10	PNR	PU	R. Lider, Panamá
	10	PNR	U23	R. Mía Chiriqui, David
	5	SLV	HV	La Estación de la Palabra, San Salvador
550	5	CTR	SCL	R. Santa Clara, Cd. Quesada
	12	CUB	BA	R. Rebelde, Pinar del Río, PR
	0.5	HND	XD	R. Manantial, Sta Rosa de Copán
	1	HND	XT	R. X, Tegucigalpa
	5/0.15	MEX	PL	La Super Estación, Cd. Cuauhtémoc
	1	MEX	ACD	Los 40 Principales, Acapulco
	1.5/0.25	MEX	HLL	Los40 Principales, Salina Cruz
	2/0.35	MEX	QW	Mexicanísima, Mérida
	2.5/1	MEX	ZK	Poder 55, Tepatitlán
	2.5/0.15	MEX	TNC	R. Nayarit, Tepic
	5/0.25	MEX	KL	W Radio, Xalapa
	5	PTR	WPAB	WPAB 550, Ponce
	2	SLV	FG	R. Cristo Te Llama, Sonsonate
555	10	SCN		R. ZIZ, Basseterre, St. Kitts
560	10	CUB	BA	R. Rebelde, Ciego de Avila, CA
	10	GTM	RV	R. 560, Guatemala
	1	GTM		R. Quetzal, Malacatán
	1	HND	KL	R. Reloj, San Pedro Sula
	1	HND	VF	R. Valladolid, Comayagua
	5	HND	RZ	VRZ R. Juticalpa, Juticalpa

kHz	kW	Ctry	Call	Station, location
	10/1	MEX	MZA	Fórmula Melódica del Pacífico, Manzanillo
	5/1	MEX	XZ	Ke Buena, Zacatecas
	1.4/0.25	MEX	GIK	La Acerera, Monclova
	5/1	MEX	QAA	La Poderosa, Chetumal
	10/0.1	MEX	SRD	La Tremenda, Santiago Papasquiaro
	2/0.25	MEX	IN	LV del Valle, Cintalapa
	0.75/0.5	MEX	OC	R. Chapultepec, México
	1/0.5	MEX	YO	R. Lobo, Huatabampo
	3	PNR	H2	RPC R., Colón
570	5	CTR	ELR	R. Libertad, San José
	1	CUB	BA	R. Rebelde, Pilón, GR
	25	CUB	BD	R. Reloj, Santa Clara, VC
	10/5	DOM	MS	R. Crystal, Sto Domingo
	1	GTM	PA	R. Palmeras, Escuintla
		HND	LP	R. América, Tela
	1	HND	OX	R. El Triunfo, Choluteca
	1	MEX	TJ	Estereo Vida, Torreón
	10/2.5	MEX	VX	La Grande de Tabasco, Villahermosa
	2.5	MEX	ME	La Poderosa del Oriente, Valladolid
	5/2.5	MEX	OA	O-A R. Mexicana, Oaxaca
	5/0.5	MEX	BJB	R. 570, Monterrey
	2/1.7	MEX	LQ	R. 5-70, Morelia
	5/1	MEX	TD	R. Red, Tecuala
	0.5	MEX	VJP	R. Xicotepec, Xicotepec de Juárez
	0.5/0.25	MEX	UK	TuExpresión, Caborca
	5	NCG	A2RQ	R. Veritas 5-70, Chinandega
	5	PNR	S	R. Soberana, Panamá
	10	SLV	KT	R. Exus "YXR Radio", San Salvador
580	2.5	CUB	BA	R. Rebelde, Mabujabo, GU
	5	DOM	FS	R. Montecristi, Montecristi
	5	GTM	Y	R. Progreso, Guatemala
	3	HND	ZQ	R. Notícias STC, Tegucigalpa
		HND	EO	Super Estrella de Occidente, Sta Rosa de Copán
	10/1	MEX	AV	Canal 58, Guadalajara
	1/0.5	MEX	DZ	Imagen R, Córdoba
	1/0.25	MEX	HO	La Fuerza de la Palabra, Cd.Obregón
	1/0.25	MEX	UE	La Más Perrona, Tuxtla Gutiérrez
	1	MEX	HP	La Más Prendida, Cd.Victoria
	5/0.5	MEX	MU	La Rancherita del Aire, Piedras Negras
	1/0.25	MEX	YI	Mix FM, Cancún
	5/0.7	MEX	FI	R. Mexicana, Chihuahua

kHz	kW	Ctry	Call	Station, location
	0.25	MEX	UAQ	R. Universidad, Querétaro
	10	NCG	A3LP	R. 5-80, Managua
	10	PNR	H4	RPC R., David
	10/5	PTR	WKAQ	R. KAQ, San Juan
590	5	CTR	RN	R. Nacional, San José
	25	CUB	BF	R. Musical Nacional, La Julia, MB
	10	CUB	BA	R. Rebelde, Guantánamo, GU
	10/5	DOM	DV	R. Santa María, La Vega
	5	GTM	RQ	R. Quiché, Sta Cruz del Quiché
		HND	SA	R. América, San Pedro Sula
		HND	RE	R. Renacer, Catacamas
	10/1	MEX	CJU	La Explosiva 590, Puerto Vallarta
	1	MEX	BH	La Mejor, Hermosillo
	5/0.5	MEX	FD	La Mejor, Reynosa
	1	MEX	OM	R. Fórmula, Coatzacoalcos
	1	MEX	E	R. Fórmula, Primera Cad., Durango
	2.5	MEX	PH	Sabrosita 590, México
	5/1	MEX	ZZZ	Triple Z, Tapachula
	10/0.25	MEX	GTO	TuRecuerdo, León
	10	PNR	H3	RPC R., Chitré
600	5	CUB	BC	R. Progreso, Santiago de Cuba, SC
	50	CUB	BA	R. Rebelde, San Germán, HO
		DOM		Celestial 600, Santo Domingo
		DOM	SD	R. Santo Domingo, El Seybo
	1	GTM	RC	R. Campesina, Escuintla
		HND	EK	R. Orion, La Ceiba
	1	MEX	TA	600 Solo Hits, Zitácuaro
	10/1	MEX	OCH	K'in Radio, Ococingo
	5/1	MEX	BB	La Comadre, Puros Éxitos, Acapulco
	5/1	MEX	CV	La Gran Compañía, Cd.Valles
	5/1	MEX	HW	La Kañona, Rosario
	2.5	MEX	LAZ	La Mejor, Cd.Guzmán
	1	MEX	DN	La Mexicana, Torreón
	1/0.5	MEX	MN	La Regiomontaña, Monterrey
	20/1	MEX	Z	R. Fórmula, Segunda Cad., Mérida
	10	NCG	A3MD	La Nueva R. Ya, Managua
	5	PTR	WYEL	WYEL, Mayagüez
	3	SLV	NK	Vox FM, San Salvador
610	15	CTR	RMV	R. María, San José
	10	CUB	BA	R. Rebelde, Bueycito, GR
	1	CUB	BA	R. Rebelde, Cienfuegos, CI
	10	CUB	BA	R. Rebelde, Guane, PR
	1	CUB	BD	R. Reloj, Trinidad, SS
	5	DOM	JR	R. Amanecer, Santiago
	1	DOM	SD	R. Santo Domingo, Pedernales
	5	GTM	GA	R. Alianza, Guatemala
	10	HND	LP	R. América, Sta Rosa de Copán
	10	HND	LD	R. América,Tegucigalpa
	10	MEX	UM	Candela FM, Valladolid
	5/0.1	MEX	EL	El Super Canal 610, Fresnillo
	1/0.5	MEX	JA	Ke Buena, Xalapa
	1/0.5	MEX	GS	La GS/La Ley, Guasave
	1/0.5	MEX	KZ	La Poderosa, Tehuantepec
	5/0.5	MEX	BX	La Primera, Sabinas
	1	MEX	SAC	R. Lobo, Saltillo
	5/1	MEX	UF	Variadísima, Uruapan
	10	PNR	HM	RPC R., Panamá
	1/0.25	PTR	WEXS	X AM, Patillas
620	10	ATG		ABS Radio, St. John's
	25	CUB	BA	R. Rebelde, Colón, MA
	10	DOM	SD	R. Santo Domingo, Sto Domingo
	5	GTM	PQ	R. 6-20, San Cristóbal
	1	HND	LP5	R. América, Comayagua
	1	HND	LP	R. América, Juticalpa
	1	HND	LP17	R. Continental, San Pedro Sula
		HND	LO	R. Litoral, Tocoa
	5	MEX	SS	ESPN Deportes, Ensenada
	1/0.25	MEX	GH	La Lupe, Reynosa
	5/1	MEX	BU	La Norteñita, Chihuahua
	1/0.5	MEX	CK	R. 6-20, Durango
	50/5	MEX	NK	R. 6-20, México (Ecatepec ME)
	2.5/1	MEX	HGR	R. Fórmula 620, Villahermosa
	2.5/0.5	MEX	WZ	R. Novedades, San Luis Potosí
	5/1	MEX	OO	W Radio, Tepic
	50	NCG	N	R. Nicaragua, Managua

kHz	kW	Ctry	Call	Station, location
630	5	CUB	BC	R. Progreso, Camagüey, CM
	1	DOM	SD	R. Santo Domingo, San Juan
		GTM	EL	R. Cultural Porvenir, Sta Elena
	1	HND	LP	R. América, Choluteca
	1	HND	LP7	R. América, La Ceiba
	1	HTI		Rdif. Jérémienne, Jérémie
	5	MEX	JR	Coral 630, Zihuatanejo
	1/0.25	MEX	FX	Doble X, Guaymas
	5/0.25	MEX	OPE	Exa, Mazatlán
	10	MEX	FB	F-B La - "Estación que da las notícias", Monterrey
	0.5	MEX	CCQ	Frecuencia Turquesa, Cancún
	10/0.5	MEX	JB	Jalisco R., Guadalajara
	10/0.75	MEX	FU	La Nueva Voz, Cosamaloapan
	1/0.15	MEX	ERO	R. Tamaulipas, Altamira
	2	PNR	J35	R. Provincias, Chitré
	5	PTR	WUNO	NotiUno, San Juan
	10	SLV	LN	R. Promesa, San Salvador
640	20	CTR	ALY	R. Rica, San José
	50	CUB	BC	R. Progreso, Guanabacoa, CH
	10	CUB	BC	R. Progreso, Las Tunas, LT
	10	DOM	SD	R. Santo Domingo, Santiago
	1	HND	UP	R. Centro, Tegucigalpa
		HND	JT	R. Jerusalen, Sta Bárbara
	5/1	MEX	HDL	Aro-AM, Huajuapán de León
	1/0.25	MEX	TAM	Ke Buena, Cd.Victoria
	5/1	MEX	YQ	La Tremenda, Fresnillo
	5	MEX	JUA	Milenio TV, Cd.Juárez
	10	MEX	NQ	N-Q La Superestación, Tulancingo
	10/1	MEX	HHI	R. Uno/La Número Uno, Hidalgo del Parral
	5/1	MEX	WM	Suprema 64, San Cristóbal de las Casas
	10	NCG	A4LR	La Mera Mera , Managua
	2.5	PNR		R. Panamá, La Palma
	2.5	PNR	K22	R.CPR, Colón
	40			Guadeloupe Première, Point-à-Pitre
650	10	CUB	BC	R. Progreso, Ciego de Avila, CA
	5	CUB	BA	R. Rebelde, Stgo de Cuba, SC
	15/5	DOM	AT	R. Universal, Sto Domingo
	25	HND	VS	Nuestra Señora de La Esperanza, San Pedro Sula
	15	HND	LP	R. América, Danlí
	1	HND	VS	R. Católica Olancho, Olanchito
		HND	TA	R. Turquesa, Siguatepeque
	1/0.5	MEX	VILL	650 Notícias, Villahermosa
	5	MEX	CHH	Capital Máxima, Chilpancingo
	1	MEX	IY	Espectacular, Río Verde
	10/2.5	MEX	EJ	La Z, Puerto Vallarta
	5	MEX	ZM	La Zamorana, Zamora
	5/0.2	MEX	PX	LV de Ángel/R. Fórmula, Puerto Ángel
	1/0.25	MEX	VSS	R. 13, Hermosillo
	1	MEX	VG	R. Fórmula, Primera Cad, Mérida
	5	MEX	RCG	R. Vida, Cd. Acuña
	5/1	MEX	TNT	W R., R. 65, Los Mochis
	10/8	NCG	RD	R. Diriangén "La Super D", Granada
	5	PNR	S22	R. Mía "Cadena Nacional", Panamá
660	12	CUB	BC	R. Progreso, Jovellanos, MA
	3	DOM	AM	R. Visión Cristiana, Santiago
	3	GTM	Q	LV de Quetzaltenango
	3	HND	NN18	LV de Honduras, La Ceiba
		HND	KV	R. Betania, Choluteca
	5	HTI		R. Lumiere, Port-au-Prince
	50/10	MEX	EY	6-60 La Consentida, Aguascalientes
	10/1	MEX	FZ	ABC R., Monterrey
	2.5/0.25	MEX	SJC	KVOZ, San José del Cabo
	5	MEX	AR	La Mexicana, Tampico
	5	MEX	ACB	R. 6-60/La Tremenda N:o Uno, Cd. Delicias
	1/0.5	MEX	YG	R. 660/R. Fiesta Mexicana, Matías Romero
	1	MEX	CPR	R. Chan Santa Cruz - "LV de los Mayas", Felipe Carrillo Puerto
	50	MEX	DTL	R. Ciudadana, México
	1/0.5	MEX	WX	R. Mexicana, Durango
	5	NCG		R. Máxima, Managua
	5	PNR		La Nueva Exitosa, Sabana Grande
	1	PNR	F33	RPC R., Bocas del Toro

kHz	kW	Ctry	Call	Station, location
670	10	CTR	TNT	R. Managua, San José
	1	CUB	BQ	R. Enciclopedia, Cárdenas, MA
	50	CUB	BA	R. Rebelde, Arroyo Arenas, CH
	5	CUB	BA	R. Rebelde, Bahía Honda, PR
	10	CUB	BA	R. Rebelde, C. Brasil, CM
	10	CUB	BA	R. Rebelde, Camagüey, CM
	5	CUB	BA	R. Rebelde, Ciego de Avila, CA
	5	CUB	BA	R. Rebelde, Circunvalación, MA
	10	CUB	BA	R. Rebelde, El Coco, HO
	1	CUB	BA	R. Rebelde, Los Palacios, PR
	1	CUB	BA	R. Rebelde, Pinar del Río, PR
	50	CUB	BA	R. Rebelde, Santa Clara, VC
	1	CUB	BA	R. Rebelde, Santa Lucía, LT
	10	CUB	BA	R. Rebelde, Victoria de LT, LT
	5	DOM	BS	R. Dial, San Pedro de Macorís
	1	DOM	SD	R. Santo Domingo, Barahona
	1	HND	NN20	LV de Honduras, Sta Rosa de Copán
	10	HND	N	LV de Honduras, Tegucigalpa
	1/0.1	MEX	OG	ABC R. 670, Querétaro
	5/0.5	MEX	OB	La Máquina Musical, Pichucalco
	5/1	MEX	IS	La Rancherita Consentida, Cd.Guzmán
	5/0.1	MEX	LH	La Zeta 670, Acaponeta
	5/0.25	MEX	TOR	R. Ranchito, Torreón
	1/0.1	MEX	SIC	Tu Recuerdo, Córdoba
		NCG	RC	R. Caribe, Pto Cabezas
	5	PNR	LY	R. Hogar, Panamá
680	3	DOM	JX	R. Zamba, San Ignacio de Sabaneta
	10	GTM	VP	R. Norte, Cobán
	1	HND	NN7	LV de Honduras, Danlí
	1	HND	NN10	LV de Honduras, Juticalpa
	10	HND	NN8	LV de Honduras, San Pedro Sula
	10	HND	NN2	LV de Honduras, Siguatepeque
	1	HND	NN9	LV de Honduras, Tela
	10	HND	NN11	LV de Honduras, Tocoa
	5	MEX	OAX	Aro AM "la radio que une a Oaxaca", Oaxaca
	1/0.25	MEX	FO	Éxtasis Digital, Chihuahua
	1	MEX	SON	Éxtasis, Hermosillo
	5/2.5	MEX	CHG	Ke Buena, Chilpancingo
	1/0.1	MEX	FJ	La Consentida, Teziutlán
	1/0.5	MEX	ORO	La Mera Jefa, Guasave
	5/3	MEX	KQ	La Mexicana, Tapachula
	10/3	MEX	LG	LG, La Grande, León
	2.5/1	MEX	PY	Retro 103 FM, Mérida
	10/2	NCG	AM	R. La Primerísima, Managua
	5	PNR	F32	Mujer AM, David
	5	PNR		Voz Sin Fronteras, Metetí
	0.4	PTR	WAPA	Arecibo
	10	PTR	WAPA	Cadena WAPA, San Juan
690	50	AIA		The Caribbean Beacon, The Valley
		CUB	BC	R. Progreso, MA
	10	CUB	BC	R. Progreso, Santa Clara, VC
	10	DOM	AW	R. Guarachita "La Poderosa", Sto Domingo
	1	GTM	VB	R. Tamazulapa, Jutiapa
	1	HND	NN3	LV de Honduras, Choluteca
	2.5	MEX	AFA	Ke Buena, Coatzacoalcos
	50/5	MEX	N	La 69, México
	10/1	MEX	RG	La Deportiva 6-90/La R-G, Monterrey
	2/0.25	MEX	ST	La Invasora, Mazatlán
	2.5	MEX	XL	La Ley, Pátzcuaro
	5/1	MEX	CS	La Mejor, Manzanillo
	50/2	MEX	MA	M-A/La Madre de Todas, Fresnillo
	78/50	MEX	WW	W R. América, LV del Pueblo, Tijuana
	10/5	NCG	RH	R. Hermanos, Matagalpa
	5	PNR		R. Evangelio Vivo, Panamá
	10	PNR	R43	R. Veraguas, Santiago
700	10	CTR	JC	FCNRadio.com, San José
	0.6	DOM	DC	R. Mao, Mao, Valverde
	1	GTM	AJ	R. Inspiración, Escuintla
	15	GTM	HR	R. Mundial, Guatemala
		HND		LV de Honduras, Olanchito
	5	HND	KL	R. Reloj, Tegucigalpa
	5	MEX	LX	La Ke Buena, Zitácuaro
	2.5/0.1	MEX	VC	La Más Buena, Córdoba
	5/0.25	MEX	GD	La Poderosa, Hidalgo del Parral
	5d	MEX	ETCH	LV de los Tres Ríos, Etchojoa

kHz	kW	Ctry	Call	Station, location
	5	MEX	XPUJ	LV del Corazón de la Selva, X'pujil
	1	MEX	DKR	R. Red, Guadalajara
	2.5/0.5	MEX	RV	Yo FM, Villahermosa
	30	NCG	MM	R. La Poderosa, Managua
	12	SLV	JW	R. Mi Gente, San Miguel
	12	SLV	JW	R. Mi Gente, San Salvador
	10	VCT		R. St Vincent & The Grenadines, Kingstown
710	10	CUB	AM	R. Guamá, La Palma, PR
	50	CUB	BA	R. Rebelde, Cacocúm, HO
	25	CUB	BA	R. Rebelde, Camagüey, CM
	200	CUB	BA	R. Rebelde, Chambas, CA
	50	CUB	BA	R. Rebelde, La Julia, MB
	50	CUB	BA	R. Rebelde, Martí, MA
	50	CUB	BA	R. Rebelde, Santa Clara, VC
	1	CUB	BA	R. Rebelde, Yaguajay, SS
		DOM	P	Onda del Caribe, San Cristóbal
		DOM		Red Nacional Cristiana, Santo Domingo
	1	GTM	XL	R. Tecún Umán, Quetzaltenango
	1	HND	NN13	LV de Honduras, Yoro
	3	HND	RH	LV de Occidente, Sta Rosa de Copán
	2.5	HND	KN	LV de Olancho, Catacamas
	2	HND	LK	R. Comayagua/LV Católica, Comayagua
	1	HND	UP3	R. Rock 'n Pop, San Pedro Sula
	1	MEX	MAR	Amor, Acapulco
	1	MEX	OLA	Huasteca, Tampico
	10	MEX	MP	Interferencia 7 Diez, Mexico
	5/0.25	MEX	BL	La Ke Buena, Culiacán
	5/0.5	MEX	RPO	La Ley 710, Oaxaca
	7/0.1	MEX	DP	La Ranchera de Cuauhtémoc, Cd. Cuauhtémoc
	5/0.25	MEX	LZ	La Reina, Torreón
	1	MEX	RL	La R-L de Colima, Colima
	1/0.25	MEX	PS	La Super Grupera, Guaymas
	5/0.25	MEX	YK	La Z, Mérida
	1/0.25	MEX	SMR	R. Fórmula, San Luis Potosí
	1	MEX	RK	R. Korita, Tepic
	4.5/1	MEX	ON	R. Mexicana, Tuxtla Gutiérrez
	10	PNR	Q51	KW R. Continente, Panamá
	5	PNR	B52	Ondas del Caribe, Bocas del Toro
	10/0.75	PTR	WKJB	KJB"R. Isla", Mayagüez
720	2.5	CUB	BC	R. Progreso, Mabujabo, GU
	5	DOM	EF	R. Cayacoa, Higüey
	1.5	DOM	AQ	R. Norte, Santiago
	1	GTM	RO	R. Corona, Morales
	1	HND	NN3	R. Caribe, La Ceiba
		HND	ZN	R. San Lorenzo, San Lorenzo
	1	HTI		R. Lumière, Petite Riv.
	1	MEX	JCC	Extremo 7-20, Cd. Juárez
	2d	MEX	CPQ	La Estrella Maya Que Habla, Felipe Carillo Puerto
	8/0.25	MEX	DE	La Kaliente, Saltillo
	1/0.5	MEX	VU	Magia, Mazatlán
	10/0.25	MEX	AVR	R.Fórmula, Primera Cadena, Veracruz
	1/0.25	MEX	QZ	Ritmo 720/La Máquina Musical, San Juan de los Lagos
	25	NCG	A3RC	R. Católica, Managua
	10	PNR	B50	R. República, Chitré
	1	SLV	RA	Qué Buena, San Salvador
730	1	CTR		R. Pacífico, Puntarenas
	20	CTR	HB	Sin Fronteras, Desamparados
	10	CUB	BC	R. Progreso, La Fe, IJ
	10	DOM	Z	R. HIZ/Zulu R, Sto Domingo
	10	GTM	N	R. Cultural, Guatemala
	0.25	HND	XG	R. Cadena Dial, Sta Bárbara
	1	HND	NN4	R. Exitos, Tegucigalpa
	1/0.25	MEX	EBC	Ke Buena, Ensenada
	50/1	MEX	HB	Ke Buena, Hidalgo del Parral
	5/0.1	MEX	PQ	La 73/La Sabrosita, Cd.Muzquiz
	5/1	MEX	GDL	La Explosiva, Guadalajara
	10d	MEX	PET	LV de los Mayas, Peto
	10/1	MEX	LBC	R. La Giganta 730 AM, Loreto
	10	MEX	SOS	R. Uno, Agua Prieta
	10/5	MEX	VF	R. Villaflores, Villaflores
	100	MEX	X	TDW Radio, México
	3	PNR		Asamblea Nacional, Fort Sherman, Colón

kHz	kW	Ctry	Call	Station, location
	20	TRD		Trinidad Broadcasting Company, Port of Spain
740	10	CUB	KO	R. Angulo, Sagua de Tanamo, HO
	1	HND	IH	7-40 La Super Grande, Juticalpa
		HND	VC	LV Evangélica, Olanchito
	1	HND	QQ	R. Intibuca, La Esperanza
	1	HND	TG2	R. Satélite, San Pedro Sula
	1	HTI		R. Lumière, Pignon
	1	MEX	VAY	Amor, Puerto Vallarta
	10/1	MEX	KV	Exa FM, Villahermosa
	1	MEX	LTZ	FM Globo, Aguascalientes
	5/1	MEX	OF	Hit FM, Celaya
	5/1	MEX	POR	La Explosiva/R. Fórmula, Putla de Guerrero
	2/0.25	MEX	GF	La Ley, Gutiérrez Zamora
	10/1	MEX	QN	R. Fórmula Primera Cadena, Torreón
	20/10	MEX	CAQ	R. Fórmula QR Cancún, Cancún
	10/1	MEX	CW	R. Variedades, Los Mochis
	50	NCG	A3LS	R. Sandino "La S Grande", Managua
	2.6	PNR	R44	La Exitosa de Chorrera, La Chorrera
	5	PNR	N26	R. Cristal, David
	0.5/0.1	PTR	WIAC	Acción 740, Ponce
	10	PTR	WIAC	Acción 740, San Juan
750	10	CUB	BC	R. Progreso, Palmira, CI
	5	DOM	DB	R. Jesús AM, Santiago
	1/0.1	MEX	RASA	Candela 750/Candela Pasión Grupera, San Luis Potosí
	5/0.25	MEX	KOK	Éxtasis Digital, Acapulco
	1/0.1	MEX	CORO	Ke Buena, Loma Bonita
	10/0.25	MEX	TI	LaHuasteca, Tempoal
	1/0.25	MEX	MG	La Ke Buena, Arriaga
	1/0.75	MEX	OH	La Pantera, Camargo
	10/1	MEX	URM	Los 40 Principales, Uruapán
	10d	MEX	JMN	LV de los Cuatro Pueblos, Jesús María
	1/0.25	MEX	CSI	Vida 750, Culiacán
	5	PNR		R. La Inolvidable, Chitré
760	5	CTR	LX	R. Columbia, San José
	10	CUB	BC	R. Progreso, Guane, PR
		CUB	BC	R. Progreso, Mayarí Arriba, SC
	5	DOM	CO	R. Cordillera, Sto Domingo
	5	GTM	HB	Nueva R. Super, Guatemala
	2.5	HND	XW	R. Comayagüela/Stereo Azul, Comayagüela
		HND	IJ	R. Jicatuyo, San José de Colinas
	2	HTI		R. Lumière, Cayes
	70/10	MEX	ABC	ABC Radio, México (La Paz ME)
	10	MEX	ES	Antena Musical 7-60, Chihuahua
	5/5	MEX	DGO	La Mejor, Durango
	5/1	MEX	EB	Preciosa, Cd.Obregón
	5/1	MEX	ZZ	R. Gallito, Guadalajara
	5/0.1	MEX	NY	R. Geny, Nogales
	2.5/0.5	MEX	YW	R. María, Mérida
	5/0.5	MEX	RA	R. Uno, San Cristóbal las Casas
	10	NCG	A3AR	R. Magic, Managua
	3	PNR		Asamblea Nacional, Bocas del Toro
	5	PNR	XO	LV del Istmo, Panamá
	5	PTR	WORA	NotiUno, Mayagüez
	5	SLV	KL	YSKL La Poderosa, San Miguel
	1	SLV	KL	YSKL La Poderosa, Sonsonate
		SLV	KL	YSKL La Poderosa, Zacateluca
770	5	CUB	BA	R. Rebelde, Victoria de LT, LT
	5	DOM	MD	R. Águila, Santiago
	1	GTM	BX	R. Nueva Fraternidad, Quetzaltenango
	0.5	HND	MV	R. Aguán, Olanchito
	1	HND	RD	R. Majestad "LV del Guayape", Juticalpa
	10	HND	NN21	R. Norte, San Pedro Sula
		HND	PI	R. Sui Generis, Comayagua
	1	MEX	MRO	Aro-AM, Matias Romero
	1	MEX	HUA	Aro-AM, Sta Cruz Huatulco
	5/1.5	MEX	ML	La Ranchera, Apatzingán
	10/1	MEX	IH	La Unica, Fresnillo
	1/0.1	MEX	REV	Los 40 Principales, Los Mochis
	10	MEX	ANT	LV de las Huastecas, Tancanhuitz de los Santos
	7	MEX	ACH	R. Fórmula Primera Cadena, Monterrey
	5/1	MEX	SUR	Tu Ritmo Musical, Chilapa
	5/0.5	MEX	QRV	Ultra, Veracruz
	10	PNR	L83	R. Nacional Herrera, Chitré
	10	SLV	KL	YSKL La Poderosa, San Salvador
780	10	CTR	RA	R. América, San José
	0.5	DOM	BO	R. Constanza, Constanza
	1	GTM	CK	Sultana La Cristiana, Zacapa
	1	HND	SE	Alabanza Estéreo, Choluteca
		HND	QN	R. Sonora, La Ceiba
	10	HTI		Eben-Ezer, Mirebalais
	0.5	HTI		R. Lumière, Jérémie
	5/1	MEX	ZN	EXA FM, Celaya
	10/0.25	MEX	WGR	Exa FM, Monclova
	5/1	MEX	TS	Ke Buena, Tapachula
	5/1	MEX	SFT	La Triple T/La Caliente, San Fernando
	10	MEX	GLO	LV de la Sierra Juárez, Guelato de Juárez
	2. 5/1	MEX	XY	LV del Balsas, Cd.Altamirano
	5/0.5	MEX	LD	R. Costa, Autlán
	2.3/0.25	MEX	MTS	R.Fórmula, Tampico
	10	PNR	B55	R. Chiriquí, David
	5	PNR		R. Recuerdo, Panamá
	1	SLV	KL	YSKL La Poderosa, Sta Ana
	1	SLV	KL	YSKL La Poderosa, Usulután
	10	VRG	ZBVI	Virgin Is Broadcasting, Road Town, Tortola
790	10	CUB	BD	R. Reloj, Holguín, HO
	25	CUB	BD	R. Reloj, Pinar del Río, PR
	5	DOM	L	R. Centro, Sto Domingo
	3	GTM	O	R. Festival, Guatemala
	1	HND	FI	R. Feliz, Sta Bárbara
	3	HND	TG	R. Satélite, Tegucigalpa
	2. 5/1	MEX	UP	Candela, Tizimín
	1	MEX	GZ	Colorín Colorradio, Torreón
	50/1	MEX	RC	Formato 21, México
	1/0.5	MEX	FE	La Fiesta, Nuevo Laredo
	1/0.25	MEX	SU	R. 790/La Dinámica, Mexicali
	10/5	MEX	BI	R. B-I, La Estación que da las Notícias, Aguascalientes
	0.25	MEX	GAJ	R. Fórmula, Primera Cadena, Guadalajara
	5/0.75	MEX	NT	R. La Paz/R. Fórmula, La Paz
	1/0.5	MEX	COV	R. Lobo, Poza Rica
	5/0.4	MEX	RPC	R. Ranchito, Chihuahua
	25/5	MEX	VA	R. Tabasco, La Em. del Hogar, Villahermosa
	6	PNR		R. Panamá, Santiago
800	100	BES	PJB	Trans World R., Kralendijk, Bonaire
	3	CTR	SD	R. La Gigante, San José
	1	DOM	VM	R. Bonao, Bonao
	1	GTM	YZ	R. Rosa, Chiquimulilla
	1	HND	DL	R. Corporación, Comayagua
	3	HND	MA	R. Moderna, San Pedro Sula
		HND	GW	R. Patria, Catacamas
	1	HND	QN	R. Sonora, Danlí
		HND	MD	R. Yoro, Jocon
	5/1	MEX	GX	Fiesta Mexicana , San Luis de la Paz
	1	MEX	QT	La Poderosa, Veracruz
	2/0.25	MEX	ZR	La Traviesa de Coahuila, Zaragoza
	10/2.5	MEX	DD	La Tremenda, Montemorelos
	5d	MEX	ZV	LV de la Montaña, Tlapa de Comonfort
	0.5/0.25	MEX	SPN	Notícias800 Con Imagen, Tijuana
	1/0.1	MEX	AN	R. Alegría, Ocotlán
	50	MEX	ROK	R. Cañon, Cd.Juárez
	5/1	MEX	UI	R. Comitán, Comitán
	10	NCG	A3RO	R. 800, Managua
	3	PNR		Tropical 800, Los Santos
	12	SLV	AX	R. María El Salvador, San Salvador
810	1	BAH		ZNS3, Freeport
	10	CUB	BC	R. Progreso, Guantánamo, GU
	5	DOM	AV	R. Salvación Internacional, Baní
		GTM		R. Circuito San Juan, San Juan
		GTM	END	R. Constelación, San Marcos
		GTM		R. Moapán, Sta Elena
	6	HND	VC	LV Evangélica, La Ceiba
	3	HND	LP24	R. Valle, Choluteca
	0.05	HTI		R. Atlantique, Gonaives
	1/0.5	MEX	IM	Fiesta Mexicana, Saltillo
	10/0.25	MEX	UX	LaLegendaria, Tepic
	50/1	MEX	FW	R. Estrella, Tampico
	5/1	MEX	ZC	R. Felicidad, Río Grande
	7/0.6	MEX	AGR	R. Fórmula, Primera Cad., Acapulco

kHz	kW	Ctry	Call	Station, location
	5/1	MEX	HT	R. Huamantla, Huamantla
	0.1	MEX	IC	R. I-C, Campeche
	1/0.5	MEX	EMM	R. La Salmantina, Salamanca
	1	MEX	SB	R. Mexicana/La S B, Santa Bárbara
	1/0.1	MEX	RI	R. Rey, Reynosa
	3/0.25	MEX	MAX	Radiomax, Tecomán
	2.5/1.5	MEX	OE	Romántica, Tapachula
	2.5/0.25	MEX	RB	SolEstéreo, Cozumel
	5d	MEX	RSV	Tribuna R., Cd. Obregón
	2/0.25	MEX	MQ	W R., Mérida
	1	PNR	G	R. 10, Panamá
	50	PTR	WKVM	R. Paz 810 AM, San Juan
	1.5	SLV	DA	R. Imperial, Sonsonate
	2	SLV	FA	R. Lorenzana, San Vicente
820	2.5	CTR	GC	R. Centro AM, San José
	10	CUB	BE	R. Ciudad de la Habana, Arroyo Arenas, CH
	10	CUB	BC	R. Progreso, Ciego de Avila, CA
	10	CUB	BC	R. Progreso, Ciego de Avila, CA
	1	CUB	BC	R. Progreso, Moa, HO
	3	DOM	AZ	R. Vida, Santiago
	10	GTM	TO	R. Kyrios/R. Internacional, Guatemala
	5	HND	LP16	R. Moderna, Tegucigalpa
	7/3	HND	KW	R. Sultana, Sta Rosa de Copán
	10/1	MEX	BA	La Consentida, Guadalajara
	2.5/0.1	MEX	KG	La Dorada, Córdoba
	10/1	MEX	BM	La Mera Mera, San Luis Potosí
	1/0.5	MEX	YN	Los 40 Principales, Oaxaca
	1/0.25	MEX	UDO	R. Cultural, Los Mochis
	0.75d	MEX	ESC	R. Escárcega, Escárcega
	3.5/0.5	MEX	ABCA	R. Frontera, Mexicali
	1d	MEX	GRC	Soy Guerrero, Coyuca do Catalán
	10/0.5	MEX	DRD	W R., Durango
	20	NCG	FAOL	R. Ondas de Luz, Managua
	3	PNR	F28	R. Ritmo Chiriquí, David
	50	SCN		R. Paradise, St Kitts
830	10	DOM	JB	R. HIJB, Sto Domingo
	5	GTM	AV	R. Satélite, Mazatenango
	1	HND	JB	Cadena Radial Impacto, Comayagua
		HND	TB	R. Colón, Tocoa
	1	HND	VQ	R. Excelsior, Juticalpa
	1	HND	RU	R. Uno, San Pedro Sula
	5	MEX	DR	Digital 99, Guaymas
	10/0.5	MEX	LK	Digital, Zacatecas
	3/0.25	MEX	LN	La Caliente 830 AM, Linares
	5	MEX	IK	La Norteñita 8-30AM/R. Fórmula, Piedras Negras
	6	MEX	TLX	La Poderosa/R. Tlaxiaco, Tlaxiaco
	5/1	MEX	VQ	La Superestación - "La Grande de Sinaloa",Culiacán
	8d	MEX	PUR	LV de los P'urhepechas, Cheran
	1	MEX	DQ	R. Alegría, San Andrés Tuxtla
	10/5	MEX	ITE	R. Capital, México
	5/1	MEX	ZQ	R. Futurama, Villahermosa
	5	PNR	R56	R. Península, Macaracas
	5	SLV	PX	R. Pax, San Miguel
840	10	CUB	HW	CMHW, Santa Clara, VC
	1	CUB	KC	R. Revolución, Palma Soriano, SC
	1	DOM	AB	R. Isabel de Torres, Puerto Plata
		GTM		R. Idea 840, Jutiapa
	2.5	GTM		R. Luz, San Pedro Carchá
	1	HND	CR	Dif. Cristiana de R. "DCR", Choluteca
		HND		LV Evangélica, Tela
	10	HTI		R. 4VEH, Cap Haitien
	5/1	MEX	XXX	Fiesta Mexicana/Fiesta Digital, Tamazula
	2.5/0.1	MEX	PV	La Fiera Grupera, Papantla
	1d	MEX	MY	La Jefa, Cd.Mante
	10/2.5	MEX	IO	La Más Picuda, Tuxtla Gutiérrez
	5/0.5	MEX	FG	La Pachanga, Celaya
	1/0.25	MEX	TEY	R. Sensación, Tepic
	5	NCG	A3NT	R. Noticias, Managua
	10	PNR	L80	R. Nacional, Panamá
	5/1	PTR	WXEW	NotiUno/R. Victoria, Yabucoa
	10	SLV	FB	R. Santa Biblia, San Salvador
850	2	CTR	RDR	R. Cartago, Cartago
	1	CUB	BC	R. Progreso, Trinidad, SS

kHz	kW	Ctry	Call	Station, location
	1	CUB	BD	R. Reloj, Nueva Gerona, IJ
	5	DOM	UA	R. Clarín, Santiago
	5	DOM	GA	R. Guarocuya, Barahona
	10	GTM	X	R. Ciro, Guatemala
	0.5	HND	IF	R. Inspiración, La Entrada
	10	HND	UP	R. Televisión, Tegucigalpa
	0.25d	MEX	ZF	Éxtasis Digital, Mexicali
	1d	MEX	ZI	Maxistar, Zacapu
	3/1	MEX	MIA	Mundo de Ofertas, Guadalajara
	1	MEX	JAQ	R. Joya, Jalpan
	1/0.2	MEX	US	R. Univ. de Sonora, Hermosillo
	5/0.5	MEX	RTM	R. Variedades, Macuspana
	5/1	MEX	M	Renacimiento 850 , Chihuahua
	10/1	MEX	TQ	Romántica, Orizaba
	5	PNR	T61	La Exitosa de Chiriquí, David
	1	PNR		La Exitosa de Colón, Colón
	5/1	PTR	WABA	Waba "La Grande", Aguadilla
860	5	CUB	BD	R. Reloj, Jovellanos, MA
	10	CUW	PJZ-86	R. Curom, Willemstad
	10	DOM	UA	R. Clarín, Sto Domingo
		HND	NZ	La Respuesta es la Cruz, Olanchito
	0.5	HND	LS	R. Dinorama, La Paz
		HND	BV	R. Piedra Blanca-LV de Nuestra Gente, Catacamas
	10	HND	BS	R. San Pedro, San Pedro Sula
	3	HTI		R. Men Kontre, Cayes
	5/0.5	MEX	RRF	860 AM, Mérida
	1/0.5	MEX	DU	D-U la que le gusta a Usted, Durango
	5/0.25	MEX	DB	La Máquina Musical, Tonalá
	2.5	MEX	PLA	La Mexicana, Aguascalientes
	5/0.25	MEX	HX	La Mia, Ciudad Obregón
	10/7.5	MEX	MO	La Poderosa 860, Tijuana
	1/0.15	MEX	ZX	LV de Usumacinta, Tenosique
	1/0.25	MEX	NW	Máxima 103.3, Culiacán
	1	MEX	IW	R. 860, Uruapan
	5	MEX	CCN	R. Caribe, Cancún
	5/1	MEX	CTL	R. Chetumal, Presencia Mexicana en el Caribe, Chetumal
	1/0.25	MEX	TW	R. Fiesta, Tampico
	5/0.1	MEX	AI	R. Mundo/R. Fórmula, Manzanillo
	1/0.5	MEX	ZOL	R. Noticias 860, Cd.Juárez
	5/2	MEX	NL	R. Recuerdo, Monterrey
	4.5	MEX	UN	R. UNAM, México
	5	NCG	A3CO	La Gran Cadena, Managua
	10	PNR	L55	R. Reforma, Chitré
	10	SCN		Voice of Nevis, Charlestown, Nevis
	1	SLV	RC	R. Tecana, Sta Ana
870	10	CTR	UCR	R. 870 UCR, San Pedro Montes de Oca
	10	CUB	BD	R. Reloj, Baracoa, GU
	10	CUB	BD	R. Reloj, Bueycito, GR
	1	CUB	BD	R. Reloj, Sancti Spíritus, SS
	4	DOM	VG	R. La Vega, La Vega
	0.5	GTM	L	R. Victoria, Mazatenango
	5	HND	H9	R. Nacional de Honduras, La Ceiba
	3	HND	H4	R. Nacional de Honduras, Nacaome
	5	HND	H10	R. Nacional de Honduras, Puerto Lempira
	1	HTI		R. Express, Jacmel
	1/0.5	MEX	AMO	AMO 870, Irapuato
	1/0.1	MEX	NG	Canal 87, Huauchinango
	1/0.1	MEX	LY	Candela, Morelia
	10d	MEX	TAR	LV de la Sierra Tarahumara, Guachochi
	5/0.25	MEX	ACC	R. Fórmula/LV del Puerto, Puerto Escondido
	1/0.25	MEX	FIL	R. Notícias, Mazatlán
	1	MEX	GRO	Soy Guerrero, Chilpancingo
	10	NCG	CD	R. Centro, Juigalpa
	5.5	PNR	HO	R. Libre, Panamá
	5	PTR	WQBS	La Gran Cadena QBS, San Juan
	10	SLV	AR	R. Renacer, San Salvador
880	12	CUB	BC	R. Progreso, Mantua, PR
		CUB	BD	R. Reloj, Mayarí Arriba, SC
	10	GTM	J	R. Nuevo Mundo, Guatemala
	5	HND	H5	R. Nal de Honduras, Sta Rosa de Copán
	10	HND	H	R. Nacional de Honduras, Tegucigalpa
	0.3	HTI		R. Independance, Gonaives
	10/1	MEX	TC	880 AM/Estéreo Mayran, Torreón

kHz	kW	Ctry	Call	Station, location
	10/2	MEX	PNK	Canal 88/Superestación, Los Mochis
	10/1	MEX	YV	El Patrón, Córdoba
	10/0.5	MEX	QQQ	Ke Buena, Villahermosa
	5/1	MEX	EM	La M Mexicana, Río Verde
	1	MEX	RTP	La Poderosa, S. M. Texmelucan
	2.5/1	MEX	IG	Los 40 Principales, Iguala
	20/1	MEX	AAA	R. 880/La Triple A, Guadalajara
	5/0.25	MEX	V	R. Fórmula, Primera Cadena Nacional, Chihuahua
	10	NCG	A3EP	R. El Pensamiento, Managua
	2.5	PNR		R. Panamá, Bocas del Toro
	2.5	PNR		R. Panamá, Chiriquí
	1	PNR	B51	R. Visión Panamá, Colón
	1/0.5	PTR	WYKO	La Poderosa 880, Sabana Grande
	1	SLV	CD	R. Ritmo, Stgo de María
890	10	CTR	BAS	R. Heredia, Heredia
	200	CUB	BC	R. Progreso, Chambas, CA
		CUB	KC	R. Revolución, Santiago de Cuba, SC
	3	DOM	OR	R. 8-90/La Consentida, Valverde
	4/5	DOM	PJ	R. Continental, Sto Domingo
	1	GTM	HU	R. Escuintla, Escuintla
	1	HND	H2	R. Nacional de Honduras, Comayagua
	1	HND	H	R. Nacional de Honduras, Danlí
	1	HND	H6	R. Nacional de Honduras, El Paraíso
	3	HND	H7	R. Nacional de Honduras, Juticalpa
	5	HND	H8	R. Nacional de Honduras, Olanchito
	10	HND	H9	R. Nacional de Honduras, Siguatepeque
	10	HND	H3	R. Nal de Honduras, San Pedro Sula
	0.5	HTI		R. Trans Artibonite, Gonaives
	1	HTI		Voix du Nord'est, Forte Liberte
	1/0.3	MEX	BY	Extasis Digital, Tuxpan
	10/0.5	MEX	NZ	La Sinaloense, Culiacán
	5/0.5	MEX	AK	R. Consentida, Acámbaro
	10/1	MEX	FRT	R. Frontera, Comitán
	1/0.25	MEX	PNA	R. Joya/R. Fórmula, Tepic
	5/1	MEX	PC	Sonido Estrella, Zacatecas
	5	PNR	Q62	R. Ritmo Stereo, Chitré
	0.25	PTR	WFAB	La Nave 890, Ceiba
	3	SLV	LA	R. Renacimiento, Sta Ana
900	5	BRB		Caribbean Broadcasting Corp, St. Michael
	50	CUB	BC	R. Progreso, San Germán, HO
		DOM	FK	R. Amanecer, Neiba
	5/1	DOM	EN	R. Puerto Plata, Puerto Plata
	1	GTM	MA	R. Amatique, Puerto Barrios
	1	HND	UP	R. Centro, Choluteca
	1	HND	UP6	R. Satélite, La Ceiba
	1/0.75	MEX	TAK	Éxtasis, Tapachula
	5/1	MEX	DT	Hits FM, Cuahtémoc
	1	MEX	ED	La Líder 900 AM, Arneca
	50/10	MEX	WB	Los 40 Principales, Veracruz
	10/2.5	MEX	OK	OK Notícias/R. Tráfico, Monterrey
	250	MEX	W	W R., México
	5	NCG	A3RT	R. Tiempo, Managua
	10	PNR	HA	R. Panamá, Panamá
	2	SLV	QJ	R. Cristo Te Llama, San Salvador
910	5	CTR	UM	BBN, San José
	25	CUB	HA	R. Cadena Agramonte, Camagüey, CM
	5	CUB	BL	R. Metropolitana, V. María, CH
	5	CUB	BD	R. Reloj, Bolondron, MA
	3	DOM	LB	Tiempo 910, Bonao
	10	GTM	KL	R. Fe y Esperanza, Guatemala
	10	HND	VS	R. Católica "LV de Suyapa", Tegucigalpa
	2.5	HND	NM	R. Comunidad, Ocotepeque
	5/1	MEX	ACM	R. Exitos, Cárdenas
	10/2.5	MEX	OL	R. Impacto, Teziutlán
	5/0.1	MEX	ACN	R. Metrópoli, León
	0.25	MEX	AO	R. Mexicana, Mexicali
	10/1	MEX	NAY	W R., Puerto Vallarta
	5	NCG		R. Jinotega, Jinotega
	3	PNR	L85	R. Nacional, Colón
	10	PNR		R. Nacional, Darién
	10	PNR	L81	R. Nacional, David
	4.4	PTR	WPRP	NotiUno, Ponce
920	1	CUB	BC	R. Progreso, Pilón, GR
	10	DOM	BA	R. 9-20 AM-Stereo "Power", Sto Domingo

kHz	kW	Ctry	Call	Station, location
	0.2	GTM	RS	R. Cultural, Escuintla
	5	HND	SK	R. Catacamas, Catacamas
		HND	VS	R. Católica, Tocoa
	1	HND	H11	R. Nacional de Honduras, Danlí
	1	HND	RM	R. Sistema, Comayagua
	1	HND	ZV	Una Voz que clama en el desierto, San Pedro Sula
	5/1	MEX	RE	La Comadre, Puros Éxitos, Celaya
	1/0.25	MEX	MJ	La Más Jóven, Piedras Negras
	10/0.5	MEX	VV	La Mejor, Tuxtla Gutiérrez
	5/0.5	MEX	CQ	La Nueva Ranchera, Culiacán
	10	MEX	LE	La Preferida, Tampico
	1	MEX	ZAR	La Z, Puebla
	5/0.2	MEX	RCA	Planeta, Torreón
	5/1	MEX	HQ	R. Capital, Hermosillo
	1/0.15	MEX	PNX	R. Costa/Ke Buena, Santiago Pinotepa Nal
	5/2.5	MEX	LCM	R. La Mexicana, Cd.Lázaro Cárdenas
	10	MEX	LT	R. María, Tlaquepaque
	1/0.25	MEX	QD	R. Noticias 920, Chihuahua
	1.5/0.5	MEX	TEB	Voces, Campeche
	10	NCG	W	R. Mundial, Managua
	5	PNR	S56	R. Mía Centrales, Los Santos
930	5	CTR	RCR	R. Costa Rica, Guadalupe
	1	CUB	BD	R. Reloj, Cienfuegos, CI
	1	CUB	BD	R. Reloj, La Jaiba, MA
	1	CUB	BD	R. Reloj, Stgo de Cuba, SC
	10	CUB	IP	R. Surco, Ciego de Ávila, CA
	10	DOM	CK	Ondas del Yaque, Santiago
		HND	CQ	Cadena R. Samaritano, La Ceiba
		HND	LD	R. Estéreo Leed, Nacaome
	5	HTI		R. Cap Haitien, Cap Haitien
	0.1	HTI		R. Echo 2000, Val. de Jacmel
	2.5/0.2	MEX	UL	Átomo, Mérida
	1	MEX	ZU	La Explosiva, Zacapu
	1/0.25	MEX	SHT	La Poderosa, Saltillo
	10/1	MEX	U	La U de Veracruz, Veracruz
	5d	MEX	TLA	LV de la Mixteca, Tlaxiaco
	1	MEX	TTT	Magia, Colima
	5/2.5	MEX	MK	M-K R. Mexicana, Huixtla
	2/1	MEX	CY	R. Diversión, Colima
	10/3	MEX	QS	Romance en Radio/R. Fórmula, Fresnillo
	10	PNR	R46	La Nueva Exitosa, Panamá
	2	PNR	K85	Mi Preferida Estéreo, Pto Armuelles
	2.5	PTR	WYAC	Acción 740, Cabo Rojo
		SLV		R. Rey de Gloria, San Salvador
940	1	CUB	BC	R. Progreso, Sancti Spíritus, SS
	3	DOM	AS	R. Metro, Montecristi
	10	GTM	TL	Eventos Católicos R., San Pedro Sacatepéquez, Guatemala
	1	HND	BO	R. Cadena Occidental, La Entrada
	1	HND	CR	R. Dif. Cristiana de R. "DCR", Tegucigalpa
	0.25	HTI		R. St Marc, St Marc
	0.2	HTI		Rdif. Jacmelienne, Jacmel
	1/0.1	MEX	MMM	940 AM Oldies/R. Fórmula, Mexicali
	50	MEX	Q	Bésame 9-40, México
	1d	MEX	HE	La Melódica, Atotonilco
	1d	MEX	RKS	La Poderosa, Reynosa
	15/0.5	MEX	YJ	La YJ Mexicana, Sabinas
	10/1	MEX	RLA	R. Santa Rosalía, Santa Rosalía
	1/0.25	MEX	REC	Romántica, Villahermosa
	5	PNR		Asamblea Nacional, Darien
	10	PTR	WIPR	Máxima 940 AM, San Juan
950	1	CUB	KC	R. R. Revolución, Mayarí Arriba, SC
	10	CUB	BD	R. Reloj, Arroyo Arenas, HA
	10	CUB	BD	R. Reloj, Camagüey, CM
	10	DOM	IG	R. Popular, Sto Domingo
	1	GTM	AF	R. Indiana, Mazatenango
	1	HND	QL	Centro Radial Hondureño, Siguatepeque
		HND	QJ	R. Agalta, San Esteban
	6	HND		R. Choloma, Choloma
	1.5	HND	ZE	R. Cortés AM, Puerto Cortés
		HND	XI	R. El Camino, Olanchito
	1/0.25	MEX	TUG	Éxtasis, Tuxtla Gutiérrez
	10/0.1	MEX	PB	La Grande/R. Amor, Hermosillo
	5/0.5	MEX	MEX	La Mexicana, Cd.Guzmán

kHz	kW	Ctry	Call	Station, location
	3/0.9	MEX	MAB	La Poderosa, Cad. del Carmen
	1/0.5	MEX	FA	La Poderosa, Chihuahua
	2.5/1	MEX	ZE	La Poderosa, Santiago Ixcuintla
	1	MEX	CAA	Life FM, Aguascalientes
	10d	MEX	OJN	LV de la Chinantla, San Lúcas Ojitlán
	5/0.5	MEX	ORF	R. Exitos, Los Mochis
	20/5	MEX	KAM	R. Fórmula Californias, Tijuana
	5/1	MEX	ACA	R. Fórmula, Segunda Cadena, Acapulco
	10/1	MEX	CEL	R. Lobo Bajío, Celaya
	5/1	MEX	RN	R. Naranjera, Monterey
	5/2	MEX	TO	Romántica, Tampico
	3	PNR	L84	R. Nacional, Penonomé
	2.5	PNR		R. Panamá, Las Mercedes, Colón
	1	SLV	HG	R. Chaparrastique, San Miguel
960	5	CTR	SD	R. Actual 960, San José
	10	CUB	BD	R. Reloj, Guantánamo, GU
	5/1	DOM	FF	LV del Atlántico, Puerto Plata
		HND	XB	R. Bautista Buenas Nuevas, Puerto Lempira
	1	HND	YF	R. Fergusón, Choluteca
	1	MEX	MM	960 Notícias, Morelia
	1	MEX	XC	ABC R. 960, Taxco
	1	MEX	CZ	ABC R., San Luis Potosí
	1/0.25	MEX	OZ	Amor, Xalapa
	1/0.5	MEX	IQ	Éxtasis, Cd.Obregón
	5/0.5	MEX	ROO	La Guadalupana, Chetumal
	5/1	MEX	TAP	La Poderosa, Tapachula
	5/1	MEX	K	La Radio 9-60/La Estación Grande, Laredo
	10/2.5	MEX	HK	LV de Guadalajara, Guadalajara
	10/1	MEX	FAMA	R. Fama, Cd.Camargo
	1/0.5	MEX	UQ	R. Variedades, Zihuatanejo
	1/0.5	MEX	GB	Stereo Vida, Coatzacoalcos
	0.5/0.1	MEX	KS	XEKS 960/LV del Tiempo, Saltillo
	2.5	NCG	ACTH	LV del Trópico Húmedo, San Carlos
	1	PNR	M33	CHT Stereo Digital, David
	1	PNR		R. Capital, Panamá
	1/1.7	PTR	WDNO	La Radio Que Te Bendice, Quebradillas
	0.5	SLV	TW	R. Centro, Sonsonate
970	5	CUB	AM	R. Guamá, Los Palacios, PR
	1	CUB	BA	R. Rebelde, Trinidad, SS
	5/1	DOM	CV	R. Barahona, Barahona
	6	DOM	VP	R. Olímpica, La Vega
	5	GTM	AX	R. Continental, Guatemala
		HND	KI	La Picosa, N. Ocotepeque
	2	HND	LY	R. Milenium, Tegucigalpa
	5/0.5	MEX	MH	Candela FM, Mérida
	1/0.5	MEX	ZAZ	De Mil Amores 9-70, Zacatecas
	10/1	MEX	VOX	Fiesta Mexicana, Mazatlán
	1	MEX	BJ	Imagen, Cd. Victoria
	10/5	MEX	J	La J Mexicana, Cd.Juárez
	5/0.25	MEX	EZ	La Mejor, Caborca
	1/0.5	MEX	MF	La Mejor, Monclova
	1	MEX	O	NotiGape 970 AM, Matamoros
	1/0.25	MEX	CJ	R. Apatzingán, Apatzingán
	50/4	MEX	RFR	R. Fórmula, Primera Cadena, México
	1/0.5	MEX	SW	R. Madera/La Mera Mera, Cd. Madera
	1	MEX	UG	R. Universidad de Guanajuato, Guanajuato
	10/5	MEX	VT	VT, Villahermosa
	3	PNR	S97	Ondas Centrales, Santiago
	5	SLV	MS	R. UTEC-R. Universidad Tecnológica, San Salvador
	5/1	VIR		WSTX-AM, Christiansted, St. Croix
980	10	CTR	RC	R. Alajuela, Alajuela
	2.5	CUB	B	R. COCO, L. Cruz, CH
	1	CUB	BD	R. Reloj, Moa, HO
	1	GTM	MQ	R. Retama, San Marcos
		HND	VC	LV Evangélica, Siguatepeque
	2	HND	ZC	R. Monumental, San Pedro Sula
	1	HND	AO	R. Tocoa, Tocoa
		HND	UI	Super 10, Catacamas
	5/0.2	MEX	LC	Dual Stereo, La Piedad
	5	MEX	TU	Estéreo Vida, Tampico
	1/0.25	MEX	KE	KE-98, Solo para it, Navojoa
	1	MEX	JK	La Poderosa, Cd.Delicias
	2.5/0.5	MEX	FQ	LV de la Ciudad del Cobre, Cananea
	5/0.5	MEX	NR	R. 980, Nueva Rosita

kHz	kW	Ctry	Call	Station, location
	1	MEX	XT	R. Capital/Capital Máxima, Tepic
	5	MEX	FS	R. Matamoros, Izúcar de Matamoros
	5/1	MEX	QO	R. Romance, Cosamaloapan
	1	NCG	A3NO	R. Redención Internac., Managua
990	25	CUB	AM	R. Guamá, Pinar del Río, PR
	1	DOM	SA	R. Cibao, Santiago
	1	GTM	AL	R. Perla de Oriente, Chiquimula
	1	HND	OJ	R. La Voz de Jesús, La Ceiba
	3.5	HND	PR	R. Paz, Choluteca
	1	MEX	IU	Amor, Oaxaca
	5/0.25	MEX	HZ	HZ La Pura Sabrosura, La Paz
	1/0.1	MEX	BC	La Buena Onda, Cd.Guzmán
	20/1	MEX	TG	La Grande del Sureste, Tuxtla Gutiérrez
	50	MEX	T	La T Grande, Monterrey
	10/3	MEX	FP	R. Alegría, Xalpa
	1	MEX	ATM	R. Fórmula, Morelia
	10/2.5	MEX	ID	R. K-ñon, Álamo
	5/0.25	MEX	ER	R. Lobo, Cd.Cuauhtémoc
	1.4/3	MEX	CL	Rockola 990, Mexicali
	20/5	MEX	PI	W R., Chilpancingo
	5	PNR		Asamblea Nacional, Chiriquí
	5	PNR		R. Impacto, Panamá
	0.91	PTR	WPRA	La Primera, Mayagüez
1000	1	CTR	MIL	100.7/Mil FM, San José
	10	CUB	SW	R. Artemisa, Artemisa, AR
	5	CUB	NM	R. Granma, Media Luna, GR
	25	CUB	AM	R. Guamá, Pinjar del Río, PR
	5/1	DOM	HG	R. Beller, Dajabón
		GTM		R. Cultural y Educativa, Patzún
		GTM		R. Revelación y Verdad, Guatemala
	1	HND	XZ	R. Alfa, Tegucigalpa
	6	HND		R. Río de Piedras, Lempira
	10/1	MEX	TAC	Exa FM, Tapachula
	1	MEX	MMS	Ke Buena, Mazatlán
	1	MEX	FV	La Rancherita, Cd.Juárez
	5/0.25	MEX	MYL	Los 40 Principales, Mérida
	1	MEX	CSV	Máxima FM, Coatzacoales
	1/0.25	MEX	MIL	Planeta Mil, Los Mochis
	1/0.1	MEX	NLT	R. Fórmula/Laredo R., Nuevo Laredo
	50/20	MEX	OY	R. Mil, México
	1/0.5	MEX	HPC	R. Mil/R Fórmula, Hidalgo del Parral
	1/0.5	MEX	RZ	W R., León
	10	NCG	FF	R. Mil, Managua
	10	PNR	K36	R. Poderosa "La Fuerte", Aguadulce
	1	SLV	HH	Estación H, Sta Ana
	5/1	VIR	WWMI	R. One, Charlotte Amalie, St. Thomas
1010		DOM	JA	R. Comercial, Salcedo
		DOM	JA	R. Comercial, San Juan de la Maguana
	10	DOM	JA	R. Comercial, Sto Domingo
	1	GTM		R. Caribe, Izabal
	1	GTM	XI	R. Ixil, Nebaj
		HND	AE	R. Apaguiz, Danlí
	1	HND	CD	R. Constelación. Juticalpa
		HND	QN	R. Sonora, San Pedro Sula
		HND		R. Visión Cristiana, Tocoa
	2/0.5	MEX	DX	Cadena 1010 AM, Ensenada
	50/5	MEX	HL	Estadio W, Guadalajara
	5/0.5	MEX	FM	La Máquina Tropical, Veracruz
	0.5/0.25	MEX	KD	LaMejor, Cd.Acuña
	5/1	MEX	VK	La Poderosa 10-10 AM, Torreón
	5/0.5	MEX	LO	La X/Lobo Latino, Chihuahua
	5d	MEX	TUMI	LV Mazahua Otomi/LV de la Sierra Oriente, Tuxpán
	20/2	MEX	PA	Punto 10 R, Puebla
	1d	MEX	HGO	R. Hidalgo, Huejutla
	0.5/0.2	MEX	XN	R. Ures, Ures
	5/1	MEX	WS	Romántica, Culiacán
	5	NCG	FAVP	R. LV del Pinar, Ocotal
	3	PNR	L86	R. Nacional, Bocas del Toro
1020	5	CTR	TIC	LV de la Liberación, San José
	10	CUB	M	Cadena CMKS, Baracoa, GU
		CUB	AM	R. Artemisa, AR
	10	CUB	AM	R. Guamá, Bahía Honda, PR
	10	CUB	BD	R. Reloj, Victoria de LT, LT
	10	DOM	TS	R. Enriquillo, Neyba

kHz	kW	Ctry	Call	Station, location
	5	GTM	CM	R. Frontera, Pajapita
		HND	PN	R. Visión Cristiana Roca de Salvación, Marcovia
	1/0.1	MEX	WO	97.7, Chetumal
	5/1	MEX	OU	La Primera, Huajuapan de León
	5/0.5	MEX	PR	Los 40 Principales, Poza Rica
	1	MEX	PIC	R. Hits, Tepic
	1	MEX	KH	Top Music 91.7, Querétaro
	1	MEX	VE	W R., Colima
	5	PNR		R. Ancón, Panamá
	1/0.28	PTR	WOQI	R. Coquí/La Señal de la Montaña, Adjuntas
	5	SLV	CA	R. Int. /La Máxima, San Salvador
1030	5	DOM	DL	R. Novedades, Santiago
	10	GTM	UX	R. Panamericana, Guatemala
	1	HND	UP3	R. Rock 'n Pop, Tegucigalpa
	1	HND	RJ	R. Ticante, Ocotepeque
		HTI		R. Ginen, Port-au-Prince
	10/1	MEX	MPM	Exa FM, Los Mochis
	20/2	MEX	LJ	Ke Buena, Lagos de Moreno
	1/0.5	MEX	PAV	La Picosita, Tampico
	10	MEX	SSD	La Tremenda, Ensenada
	1/0.25	MEX	BCC	Los 40 Principales, Cad. del Carmen
	10/0.25	MEX	VFS	LVde la Frontera Sur, Las Margaritas
	5d	MEX	NKA	LV del Gran Pueblo, Felipe Carillo Puerto
	5/1	MEX	IE	R. Alegría, Matehuala
	50/5	MEX	QR	R. Centro, México
	5/0.5	MEX	YC	R. Fórmula, Cd.Juárez
	1/0.5	MEX	TEKA	R. T-K, Juchitán
	1/0.5	MEX	VP	W R., Acapulco
	10	PTR	WOSO	Total R. El Oso, San Juan
	1	SLV	RM	R. Frontera, Ahuachapán
1040	5	CTR	AC	R. Fides, San José
	2	CTR	HG	R. Nosara, Hojancha
	10	CUB	CL	R. Mayabeque, Güines, MB
	10	DOM	ON	CDN Radio, Sto Domingo
	1	GTM	JP	R. Revelación, Jalapa
	3	HND	NNY	Exitos, San Pedro Sula
		HND	VC	LV Evangélica, Danlí
		HND	VC	LV Evangélica, Juticalpa
	1	HND	MJ	R. Renovación, Comayagua
	5/0.25	MEX	HES	Éxtasis Digital, Chihuahua
	5/0.25	MEX	GYS	La Primera/La Número Uno, Guaymas
	2.5/1	MEX	GR	OK Radio, Xalapa
	5/0.75	MEX	CH	R. Capital, Toluca
	1/0.25	MEX	SAG	R. Lobo, Irapuato
	10/1	MEX	BBB	R. Mujer, Guadalajara
	5/0.5	MEX	PLE	R. Palanque, Palenque
	2	NCG	VJ	LV de Jinotega, Jinotega
	3	PNR		LV del Mamoni, Panamá
	2.5	PNR	J2	Ondas del Canajagua, Las Tablas
	9/0.25	PTR	WZNA	Zona 1040, Moca
1050	1	CUB	AM	R. Guamá, Santa Lucía, PR
	10	CUB	LL	R. Victoria, Victoria de LT, LT
	1.5	DOM	CB	R. Hispaniola, Santiago
	5/1	GTM	SL	LV de los Cuchumatanes, Huehuetenango
		HND	OK	R. Roatán, Roatán
	10/5	MEX	TAB	¡Ya! FM, Villahermosa
	15	MEX	ZUM	ABC R., Chilpancingo
	1	MEX	DC	Amor, Aguascalientes
	5	MEX	RIO	La Poderosa, Ixtlán del Río
	1/0.5	MEX	IP	La Poderosa, Uruapán
	100	MEX	G	La Ranchera 1050, Monterrey
	10/1	MEX	BCS	R. Cultura Surcalifornia, La Paz
	35/2.5	MEX	QOO	R. Imagen, Cancún
	5d	MEX	JF	R. Max, Tierra Blanca
	10	MEX	D	Radiorama Siglo 21/W R., Mexicali
	3	NCG	LL	R. Masaya, Masaya
1060	1	CTR	LX	R. Columbia, San Isidro del General
	25	CUB	DL	R. 26, Jovellanos, MA
		DOM	AJ	R. Amanecer, San Pedro de Macorís
	1	DOM	XF	R. Azua, Azua
	10	GTM		R. Favorita, Guatemala
	2	HND	KT	La Catracha, Tegucigalpa
	0.5	HND	FA	R. Peña Blanca, Sta Barbara
	100/20	MEX	EP	R. Educación, México

kHz	kW	Ctry	Call	Station, location
	1	NCG		LV del Atlántico, Bluefields
	3.5	PNR	J60	R. LV de Panamá "La Auténtica", Panamá
	5/0.5	PTR	WCGB	La Roca, Rock R. Netw., Juana Díaz
1070	10	CUB	M	Cadena CMKS, Guantánamo, GU
	10	CUB	AM	R. Guamá, Guane, PR
	5/1	DOM	BI	HIBI R. 1070, San Francisco de Macorís
	3/2	GTM	D	LV de Occidente, Quetzaltenango
	3	HND	GR	Cadena Guaymuras, El Paraíso
	2.5	HND	QN	R. Sonora, Siguatepeque
	1	HND	LE	R. Unica AM, San Pedro Sula
		HND	BB	R. Unidad Evangélica, Catacamas
	10/1	MEX	SP	10-70 R. Notícias, Guadalajara
	5/0.25	MEX	EI	Antena, San Luis Potosí
	1/0.2	MEX	AGS	Digital 101.3,/Solo Exitos Acapulco
	1/0.25	MEX	IT	Exa FM, Cad. del Carmen
	1/0.25	MEX	GY	La Mejor, Tehuacán
	0.5/0.1	MEX	MI	La Poderosa, Minatitlán
	2.5	MEX	RPR	Oye, Siempre Hits, Tuxtla Gutiérrez
	1/0.25	MEX	OBS	R. Fórmula, Cd.Obregón
	3	PNR		R. Estéreo Mi Favorita, Penonomé
	10	PNR		R. Nacional, Los Santos
	0.5/2.5	PTR	WMIA	R. Arecibo del Norte, Arecibo
	1	SLV	AN	LV de los Ausoles, Ahuachapán
1080	1	CTR	FC	Faro del Caribe, San José
	5	CUB	CH	R. Cadena Habana, V. María, CH
	1	DOM	MC	R. RPQ Sport, Sto Domingo
	1	GTM	LU	R. Novedad, Zacapa
		HND	IE	R. Evangélica Senda de Vida, Nacaome
	1	HND	ID	R. Miramar, Tela
	20	HTI		R. Nationale, Port-au-Prince
	1/0.5	MEX	UU	La Mejor, Colima
	1/0.5	MEX	CN	Los 40 Principales, Irapuato
	0.5/0.25	MEX	PAB	R.Celebridad, La Paz
	5/0.5	MEX	AX	R. Fórmula Oaxaca, Oaxaca
	10/0.25	MEX	XK	R.Fórmula, Poza Rica
	1/0.25	MEX	DY	R. Gallo, San LuisRíoColorado
	5/0.25	MEX	TUL	R. Mexiquense Valle de México, Tultitlán
	5d	MEX	JLV	Sistema Jaliscience, Puerto Vallarta
	10	NCG	A3LC	R. 15 de Septiembre, Managua
	5	PNR	J24	R. Mundo Internacional, Panamá
	0.25	PTR	WLEY	R. Isla 1080, Cayey
	6	SLV	ME	R. CRET, San Salvador
1090	1	CUB	LL	R. Victoria, Amancio, LT
	3	DOM	JM	R. Amistad, Santiago
	1	HND	CQ	Cad. Radial Samaritano, Tegucigalpa
	1	HND	LB	R. La Mejor, Sta Rosa de Copán
	5/1	MEX	LB	La Buenísima, La Barca
	10	MEX	MCA	La Grande de las Huastecas, Pánuco
	1	MEX	HR	La HR, Puebla
	1/0.5	MEX	IL	La Nueva Mix, Veracruz
	1d	MEX	WL	La Romántica, Nuevo Laredo
	5/0.5	MEX	AU	Milenio TV, Monterrey
	2.5/1	MEX	XE	R. Grupo Fórmula Querétaro, Querétaro
	10/0.25	MEX	FC	SuperStereo, Mérida
	50	MEX	PRS	XX 1090 AM, Rosarito
	5	NCG	HAAL	R. Alma Latina, Estelí
	10	PNR		R. Nacional, La Peña
	0.25/0.7	PTR	WSOL	LaNueva Sol 1090, San Germán
	3	SLV	MG	R. 1090, Atiquizaya
	1	SLV		R. CRET, Sta Ana
	0.25	VIR	WGOD	3ABN R., Charlotte Amalie, St. Thomas
1100	5	CTR	SCR	R. Chorotega, Santa Cruz
	5	CTR	SBC	R. Guápiles, Guápiles
	1	CUB	KO	R. Angulo, Mayarí, HO
	1	DOM	PS	R. Comercial, Nagua
	1	DOM	RB	R. Jimaní, Jimaní
	1	DOM	MP	R. Ocoa, San José de Ocoa
	1	DOM	HD	R. Oriente, San Pedro de Macorís
	1	GTM	SR	R. Superior, Coatepeque
		HND	AJ	R. Antena 5, Catacamas
	1	HND	ND	R. Esperanza, La Esperanza
	1	HND	FQ	R. Máxima, Olanchito
	1	HND	VA	R. Tiempo/R. Fama, San Pedro Sula
	1/0.25	MEX	PO	Imagen, San Luis Potosí
	1/0.1	MEX	HTY	La Mejor, Tlapacoyan

kHz	kW	Ctry	Call	Station, location
	5	MEX	BV	R. Alegría, Moroleón
	1	MEX	BAC	R. Asunción/R. Sur California, Bahía Asunción
	5/0.5	MEX	TGO	R. Cañón, Tlaltenango
	4	MEX	CAN	R. Mundo Maya Turquesa, Cancún
	1d	MEX	GRM	Soy Geurrero, Ometepec
	1/0.5	MEX	NAS	Única 1100 AM, Navojoa
	5	PNR	M92	R. Sabrosa, Panamá
	3	SLV	RF	R. Don Bosco, San Salvador
1110	10	CUB	KO	R. Angulo, Holguín, HO
	2.5	DOM	TC	R. Jarabacoa, Jarabacoa
	1/0.5	DOM	OS	R. Marién, Dajabón
	1	GTM	MK	R. Verapaz, Cobán
		HND	QN	R. Sonora, Choluteca
	0.4	MEX	TEO	ARO AM, Teotitlán de Flores Magon
	0.5	MEX	TUX	ARO AM, Tuxtepec
	1/0.2	MEX	PVJ	Ke Buena, Puerto Vallarta
	10	MEX	HTY	La Mejor, Tlapacayan
	5/1	MEX	LEO	La Rancherita, León
	1/0.25	MEX	VS	Maxima 96, Hermosillo
	1	MEX	OQ	Notigape 11-10/R. Fórmula, Reynosa
	0.25	MEX	PU	Patronato Cultural Monclova, Monclova
	1/0.5	MEX	WR	R. Guadalupana, Cd.Juárez
	100	MEX	RED	R. Red, México (Tlalnepantla ME)
	1	NCG	F2MT	R. Momotombo, La Paz Centro
	2.5/0.5	PTR	WVJP	R. Caguas, Caguas
	2.5	SLV	CL	R. Horizonte, San Miguel
1120	1	BES	PJE-3	R. Statia, Oranjestad, St Eustatius
	1	CTR	ACE	R. Miel, Alajuela
		DOM		R. Antillas, Barahona
		DOM	CN	R. Metro Hit, Samaná
	10	DOM	CN	R. Metro Hit, Sto Domingo
	0.5	GTM	C	R. Poderosa "La Voz de la Liberación", Guatemala
	2	HND	TL	R. Fiesta, Tegucigalpa
		HND	VR	R. Marchala, Ocotepeque
	1/0.5	MEX	GV	11-20 Notícias, Querétaro
	5	MEX	POP	Fórmula 11-20 AM, Puebla
	5/0.5	MEX	TQE	La Morena 1230 AM, La Más Choca de Todas, Tenosique
	0.4/0.1	MEX	MX	MIC R., Mexicali
	2/0.25	MEX	ZB	R. Oro/La Tremenda, Oaxaca
	1	MEX	TR	R. Panorámica, Cd.Valles
	1	MEX	RUY	R. Universidad, Mérida
	0.5	MEX	UNO	R. Uno La Popular , Guadalajara
	5	NCG	A3CP	R. CEPAD "El Arco Iris del Amor", Managua
	5	PNR	M21	R. Sonora, Panamá
	2.6/5	PTR	WWSW	R. Once, Hatillo
	3	SLV	LR	Una Voz que Clama en el Desierto, San Salvador
1130	10/1	DOM	RL	CDN R., Santiago
	1	GTM	VR	Em. Unidas LV de la Costa Sur, Retalhuleu
	1	HND	HP	R. Pinares, Siguatepeque
		HND		R. Pirata, Sonaguera
	5	HND	PL	R. Progreso, El Progreso
	1	HND	BT	R. San Francisco, San Francisco de la Paz
	10/5	MEX	TOL	11-30 Notícias, Toluca
	1	MEX	HN	Ke Buena/Mariachi Estéreo, Nogales
	1/0.25	MEX	MOS	La Invasora, Los Mochis
	10/2.5	MEX	YZ	La Poderosa, Aguascalientes
	1	MEX	LUP	R. Lupita, Las Varas
	1/0.1	MEX	FN	R. Moderna, Uruapan
	10/1	MEX	ZL	Yo FM, Xalapa
	0.5	NCG		Voz Evangélica de Jalapa, Jalapa
	2.5	PNR	U80	R. Sensación, Aguadulce
	0.2/0.7	PTR	WOIZ	R. Antillas, Guayanilla
	1	SLV	LG	R. Chaparrastique, San Miguel
	1	SLV	AJ	R. Moderna, Sta Ana
1140	5	CTR	DKN	R. Nueva, Guápiles
	1	CUB	NL	R. Bayamo, Media Luna, GR
	1	CUB	DP	R. Ciudad Bandera, Cárdenas, MA
	1	CUB	BQ	R. Enciclopedia, Camagüey, CM
	25	CUB	CL	R. Mayabeque, La Salud, MB
	10	CUB	BF	R. Musical Nacional, Santa Clara, VC
	10	CUB	BA	R. Rebelde, Aguada, CI
	5	CUB	BA	R. Rebelde, Circunvalación, MA

kHz	kW	Ctry	Call	Station, location
	25	CUB	BA	R. Rebelde, Morón, CA
	5	DOM	RA	R. Anacaona, San Juan de la Maguana
		HND	VC	LV Evangélica, Choluteca
	1	HND	UL	R. Pico Bonito1140 AM, La Ceiba
	5	MEX	TE	1140 Punto Digital, Tehuacán
	1	MEX	PEC	Hidalgo R., San Bartolo Tutotepec
	5/0.5	MEX	LIA	La Tremenda, Morelia
	50	MEX	MR	R. Esperanza, Monterrey
	5/1	MEX	XF	R. Felicidad, León
	1/0.5	MEX	TEC	R. Tecpatán, Tecpatán
	5	PNR	B49	R. Panamericana, Panamá
	10	PTR	WQII	Once Q, San Juan
1150	10	CUB	NL	R. Bayamo, Entronque Bueycito, GR
	5	DOM	AS	Onda Musical, Sto Domingo
	10	GTM	T	R. Sonora, Guatemala
	5	HND	AV	Ondas del Ulúa, Sta Bárbara
		HND	LP12	R. Universal, Tegucigalpa
	50/10	MEX	JP	El Fonógrafo, México
	10/1	MEX	XP	La Mejor, Tuxtepec
	1.5/0.5	MEX	TVR	La Nueva Azul, Tuxpán
	5/0.3	MEX	SO	La Poderosa, Cd.Obregón
	1/0.5	MEX	JS	R. Exitos/JS Digital, Hidalgo del Parral
	2. 5/1	MEX	BF	R. Extremo, San Pedro
	1	MEX	RM	R. Fórmula, Mexicali
	5/1	MEX	XM	R. Jerez, Jerez de García Salinas
	50/1	MEX	AD	R. Metrópoli, Guadalajara
	10/0.15	MEX	UAS	R.Universidad/ R. UA Sinaloa, Culiacán
	1	SLV	CF	R. María Zona Oriental, San Miguel
1160	10	ATG		Caribbean Radio Lighthouse, St.John's
	1	BER		Defontes Broadcasting Co., Hamilton
	1	CTR	CA	R. Columbia, Puntarenas
	1	CUB	NL	R. Bayamo, Pilón, GR
	5	DOM	BE	Radiolandia, Santiago
	1	GTM	RI	R. Izabal, Morales
	0.5	HND	GF	R. El Paraíso, El Paraíso
	1	HND	VZ	R. Juan Pablo II, Siguatepeque
		HND	HZ	R. Liberación, Tocoa
		HND	BJ	R. Nueva Palestina, Nueva Palestina
		HND	FJ	R. País "LV del Valle de Sula", Progreso
	2.5	MEX		Canal Stereo Juvenil, Aruapan
	10	MEX	QIN	LV del Valle, San Quintín
	5/0.1	MEX	BE	Que tal R, Perote
	1/0.1	MEX	GI	R. Reyna – "La Gigante del Cuadrante", Tamazunchale
	2.5/0.5	MEX	VW	R. Sensación, Acámbaro
	1	NCG	HM	R. Satélite, Estelí
	5	PNR	C20	Ondas Chiricanas, David
	10	PNR	WK	R. Metrópolis, Panamá
	5/2.5	PTR	WBQN	Super Borinquén, Barceloneta-Manatí
	1	SLV	RG	R. Corporación, Sta Ana
1170	10	CUB	M	Cadena CMKS, Maisí, GU
		DOM	JS	Cadena Espacial, Azua
	5	GTM	RL	R. Cadena Landívar, Quetzaltenango
	2	HND	AF	R. Campeonísima, Choluteca
		HTI		R. Tropicale Internationale, Jérémie
	5	MEX	RT	Ke Buena, Reynosa
	1/0.5	MEX	MDA	La Ley 11-70, Monclova
	1	MEX	IB	La Primera/La Número Uno, Caborca
	1/0.1	MEX	JTF	Prisma La Poderosa/Prisma Musical, Zacoalco de Torres
	2. 5/1	MEX	ZS	R. Hits, Coatzacoalcos
	5/0.1	MEX	FEM	R. Manantial, Hermosillo
	10/2.5	MEX	CD	R. Oro, Puebla
	1/0.25	MEX	RLK	Super Stereo Miled, Atlacomulco
	10/2.5	MEX	UVA	UVA, Aguascalientes
	0.2	PTR	WLEO	R. Leo, Ponce
		SLV	CR	R. Cristo Viene, San Miguel
	0.5	SLV	CB	R. Pentecostés, Sonsonate
1180	5	CTR	PJ	R. Victoria, Heredia
	10	CUB	BA	R. Rebelde, Arroyo Arenas, CH
	10	CUB	BA	R. Rebelde, Artemisa, AR
	5	CUB	BA	R. Rebelde, Bahía Honda, PR
	1	CUB	BA	R. Rebelde, Banes, HO
	10	CUB	BA	R. Rebelde, C. Brasil, CM
	50	CUB	BA	R. Rebelde, Cacocúm, HO

kHz	kW	Ctry	Call	Station, location
	50	CUB	BA	R. Rebelde, Camagüey, CM
	5	CUB	BA	R. Rebelde, Cárdenas, MA
	50	CUB	BA	R. Rebelde, Chambas, CA
	1	CUB	BA	R. Rebelde, Ciego de Avila, CA
	1	CUB	BA	R. Rebelde, Cienfuegos, CI
	25	CUB	BA	R. Rebelde, Colón, MA
	50	CUB	BA	R. Rebelde, Guanabacoa, CH
	1	CUB	BA	R. Rebelde, Guantánamo, GU
	10	CUB	BA	R. Rebelde, Güines, MB
	5	CUB	BA	R. Rebelde, Ja Jaiba, MA
	10	CUB	BA	R. Rebelde, La Palma, PR
	10	CUB	BA	R. Rebelde, Los Palacios, PR
	1	CUB	BA	R. Rebelde, Mabujabo, GU
	200	CUB	BA	R. Rebelde, Martí, MA
	1	CUB	BA	R. Rebelde, Mayarí Arriba, SC
	1	CUB	BA	R. Rebelde, Moa, HO
	5	CUB	BA	R. Rebelde, Nueva Gerona, IJ
	10	CUB	BA	R. Rebelde, Pinar del Río, PR
	1	CUB	BA	R. Rebelde, Puerto Padre, LT
	5	CUB	BA	R. Rebelde, Sagua de Tánamo, HO
	10	CUB	BA	R. Rebelde, Sagua La Grande, VC
	1	CUB	BA	R. Rebelde, San Cristóbal, PR
	1	CUB	BA	R. Rebelde, Sancti Spíritus, SS
	10	CUB	BA	R. Rebelde, Santa Clara, VC
	1	CUB	BA	R. Rebelde, Santa Lucía, PR
	10	CUB	BA	R. Rebelde, Sta Cruz del Norte, MB
	5	CUB	BA	R. Rebelde, Tulipán, CI
	10	CUB	BA	R. Rebelde, Victoria de LT, LT
	10	DOM	BE	R. Mil, Sto Domingo
		GTM		R. 10, Guatemala
	1/0.8	HND	VS	R. Congolon, Gracias
	1	HND	AZ	R. La Tigre, Tegucigalpa
	0.5	MEX	AH	Hits, Juchitán
	5/1.5	MEX	DCH	Ke Buena, Cd. Delicias
	10/1	MEX	GN	La Gigante, Piedras Negras
	1/0.8	MEX	YA	La Picosa, Irapuato
	10/5	MEX	FR	R. Felicidad, México
	10	MEX	UBS	R. Universidad Autonoma de Baja California Sur, La Paz
	10	PNR	U	AM Original, Santiago
	10	PNR		China Visión Panamá, Panamá
	5	SLV	VG	R. VEA-Voz Evangélica de América, San Salvador
1190	10	CUB	JD	R. Coral/R. Revolución, Chivirico, SC
	1	CUB	GL	R. Sancti Spíritus, Trinidad, SS
	10	DOM	AG	Azul 11-90 Bachatisima, Santiago
	1	HND	GK	R. Brassabola, Minas de Oro
		HND		R. Ecológica de Olancho, Catacamas
		HND	ZQ	R. Notícias STC, El Progreso
	0.3	HTI		R. Grand Anse, Jérémie
	10/2.5	MEX	TOT	ABC R., Tampico
	0.25/0.1	MEX	MBC	Canal1190 AM, Mexicali
	10/0.1	MEX	CT	Contacto 11-90, Monterrey
	5	MEX	PP	La Comadre, Orizaba
	5	MEX	JPA	La Poderosa, Cuernavaca
	5/0.1	MEX	PZ	R. Norteña, Cd.Juárez
	5/1	MEX	SOL	R. Sol, la pura ley, Cd.Hidalgo
	7	MEX	XQ	R. Universidad, San Luís Potosí
	50/10	MEX	WK	W R./W Guadalajara, Guadalajara
	1	NCG	A6RB	R. Bendición, Cayanlipe
	10/5	PTR	WBMJ	WBMJ Rock R. Netw. "La Roca", San Juan
1200	5	CTR	TQ	R. Cucú, San José
	1	CUB	GL	R. Sancti Spíritus, Yaguajay, SS
	1	DOM	MR	R. Caracol, Azua
		DOM	AH	R. VEN - Voz Evangélica Nal, Sto Domingo
	12	GTM	RJ	R. Unción, Jutiapa
	1	HND	SI	R. Impacto, Tela
		HTI		Voix de la Paix, Port de Paix
	1	MEX	AGA	La Bonita, Aguascalientes
	2.5	MEX	QY	La Mexicana, Toluca
	1/0.25	MEX	YF	R. Fórmula Hermosillo, Hermosillo
	1	MEX	PAS	R. Punta Abreojos, Punta Abreojos
	5	MEX	QJAL	R. Querétaro, Jalpán
	1/0.25	MEX	WT	W R., Culiacán
	1/0.3	MEX	PW	W R., Poza Rica

kHz	kW	Ctry	Call	Station, location
		NCG	A3AC	1200 La Radio, Managua
	0.25/1	PTR	WGDL	La mejor AM, Lares
	1	SLV	KJ	R. Sirama, San Miguel
1210	10	CUB	GL	R. Sancti Spíritus, Sancti Spíritus, SS
	5	DOM	CJ	R. Merengue, San Francisco de Macorís
	10/5	GTM	MX	R. Miel, Guatemala
	1	HND	MY	LV Evangélica, La Entrada
	1	HND	RO	R. Capital, Comayagüela
	10/0.25	MEX	BD	ElPatrón, Xalapa
	5/1	MEX	VZ	Ke Buena, Acayucan
	5d	MEX	COPA	LV de los Vientos, Copainalá
	5/1	MEX	PUE	Méxicana, Puebla
	1	MEX	ITC	R. Tecnológico, Celaya
	1	PNR	E91	R. Diez, Panamá
	5	PTR	WHOY	La Señal Activa de PR, Salinas
	1	SLV	CG	R. América/R. La Paz, Zacatecoluca
1220	1	CTR	Q	R. Fe y Poder, Limón
		CUB	BY	R. Caribe, IJ
	10	CUB	BY	R. Caribe, La Fe, IJ
		DOM		R. HIN, Sto Domingo
	1	HND	OP	R. Costeña Ebenezer, San Pedro Sula
	3	HND	SD	R. Destellos de Luz, Sabá
		HND		R. Sintonía, Juticalpa
	1	HND	YS	R. Suari, Marcala
	1	HTI		Voix du Plateau Central, Hinche
	100	MEX	B	La B Grande, México
	2.5d	MEX	SAL	R. Universidad Agraria, Saltillo
	1	NCG	A3RA	R. América, Managua
	5	PNR		Asamblea Nacional, Veraguas
1230		CUB	BC	R. Progreso, La Palma, PR
		DOM	PM	R. Moca, Moca
		GTM		R. América, Cuyotenango
	1	GTM	AT	R. Atlántida, Puerto Barrios
	0.25	HND	CQ	R. Samaritano, San Marcos de Colón
	10	HND	QW	R. Tela, Tela
	1	HTI		Voix de l'ave Maria, Cap Haitien
	20/1	MEX	TVH	La Morena 1230, La Más Choca de Todas, Villahermosa
	1	MEX	IZ	R. Fórmula Cadena 3, Monterrey
	10/2	MEX	EX	R. Fórmula, Culiacán
	1/0.25	MEX	DKN	R. Fórmula, Segunda Cadena, Guadalajara
	1	MEX	LP	R. Pía, La Piedad
	1	MEX	TCP	W R. La Romántica, Tehuacán
	5	NCG	MNG	R. Manantial, Nueva Guinea
	1	PTR	WNIK	Única R., Arecibo
1240	1	BAH		ZNS2, Freeport
	1	CTR	WC	R. Corobici, Cañas
	1	DOM		R. María, Santo Domingo
	1	DOM	AU	R. Vida, Puerto Plata
	5	GTM	K	R. Luz, Guatemala
	1	HND	ZC	R. Vanguardial, Tegucigalpa
	1	HND	VN	R. Venus, Sta Bárbara
	1	MEX	VM	Amor 107, Piedras Negras
	1	MEX	WG	Cambio 1240, Cd.Juárez
	1	MEX	BQ	FM 105, Guaymas
	2.5/1	MEX	CE	Ke Buena, Oaxaca
	3	MEX	RD	La Comadre, Pachuca
	10/2.5	MEX	RO	La Invasora, Aguascalientes
	2.5/0.5	MEX	OV	La Picosa, Orizaba
	1	MEX	SI	R. Positiva, Santiago Ixcuintla
	25/2	MEX	RPA	R. Ranchito, Morelia
	1	MEX	BN	Radiola, Cd.Delicias
	2.5	MEX	LM	Romántica 12-40, Tuxtla Gutiérrez
	1	MEX	CG	Romántica, Nogales
	1/0.25	MEX	S	W R., Tampico
	5	NCG	A3RR	R. Vida Managua
	1	PNR		Comunicación de Masas, Panamá
	3	PNR	M56	Faro de David, David
	1	PTR	WALO	R. Oriental/Cad. R. Puerto Rico,Humacao
	0.5	SLV	MT	R. Metapán, Metapán
	1	SLV	QN	R. Norteña, San Miguel
1250	1	CUB	M	Cadena CMKS, Imías, GU
	5	DOM	BC	LV del Progreso, San Francisco de Macorís
	5	DOM	RJ	R. Juventud, La Romana
	1	GTM		LV Cristiana, Totonicapán

kHz	kW	Ctry	Call	Station, location
	1	GTM	PY	R. Payakí, Esquipulas
	1	HND	DG	R. Oriental, Danlí
	1	HND	YF	R. Renacimiento, Comayagua
		HND	YL	R. Sonaguera, Sonaguera
		HND		Super R., San Pedro Sula
	5/1	MEX	JX	Cadena R. Uno, Grupo Fórmula, Querétaro
	10/1	MEX	DK	DK 12-50, Guadalajara
	5/0.5	MEX	ZT	La Mejor, Puebla
	1/0.5	MEX	SC	La Pantera/R. 1250, Sabinas
	5/0.5	MEX	SJ	La Sarapera, Saltillo
	1/0.5	MEX	DL	R. 13/DL/Fuerza de la Palabra, Hermosillo
	10	MEX	TF	R. Fórmula Segunda Cadena, Veracruz
	5/0.25	MEX	AT	R. Imagen/Nueva Imagen, Hidalgo del Parral
	1/0.25	MEX	TEJ	R. Mexiquense, Tejupilco
	2.5	NCG	CR	Cad. Radial Samaritano, Condega
	5	PNR	LY	R. Hogar, Penonomé
	0.25/1	PTR	WJIT	R. Hit, Sabana
1260	5	CTR	DIO	R. Emaús, San Vito de Coto Brus
	2.5	CUB	BC	R. Progreso, Media Luna, GR
	1	DOM	T	R. Recuerdos, Sto Domingo
	1	HND	FP	R. Amistad, San Marcos de Colón
	1	MEX	QL	Catedral de la Música, Zamora
	1/0.25	MEX	R	Hits 12-60, Linares
	1	MEX	TBV	Ke Buena, Tierra Blanca
	20/10	MEX	L	La 12-60, México (La Paz ME)
	1/0.25	MEX	ZH	La Estación que se Escucha, Salamanca
	5/1	MEX	JY	La Mejor, Autlán
	5/0.5	MEX	SA	La Mexicana, Culiacán
	10d	MEX	JAM	LV de la Costa Chica, Santiago Jamiltepec
	1	MEX	MTV	R. Lobo de Mina, Minatitlán
	5/1	MEX	XR	R. Mensajera, Cd.Valles
	5/0.25	MEX	OG	R. Ranchito, Ojinaga
	1/0.25	MEX	MW	R. San Luis/Sonido Z, San Luis Río Colorado
	2.5/0.9	PTR	WISO	R. Wiso/Cadena WAPA, Aguadilla
	5/1.8	PTR	WISO	R. Wiso/Cadena WAPA, Mayagüez
	2.5	PTR	WISO	R. Wiso/Cadena WAPA, Ponce
	12	SLV	AA	R. Abba, San Salvador
1270	2.5	ABW		R. 1270 AM, San Nicolas
	1	DOM	TA	R. Ambiente, Baní
	1.2	DOM	DA	R. Metro-Hit 12-70, Santiago
	2.5	GTM	CQ	R. Exclusiva, Guatemala
	1	HND	OF	Ecos del Celaque, Gracias
	1	HND	QN	R. Sonora, Tegucigalpa
	0.5	MEX	AZ	Canal 1270, Zeta 13, Tijuana
	1/0.5	MEX	GL	Digital 12-70, Navojoa
	0.5/0.15	MEX	WN	ElFonógrafo del Recuerdo, Torreón
	10/0.15	MEX	RPL	LaPoderosa RPL, León
	3	MEX	QH	Milenium R., Ixmiquilpán
	1.5/0.5	MEX	HD	R. Universidad, Durango
	1/0.25	MEX	RRR	Romántica, Papantla
	2/0.5	MEX	RRT	Sport R., Cd.Madero
	1	MEX	VHT	W R., Villahermosa
	3	NCG	RA	R. Amistad, Matagalpa
	3	PNR	J22	R. Tipy Q, Panamá
	1	SLV	QZ	R. W "LV de la Verdad en Oriente", San Miguel
1280	1	BER		Defontes Broadcasting Co., Hamilton
	2	CTR	GV	Visión 1280, San José
		CUB	BQ	R. Enciclopedia, Varadero, MA
	1	CUB	KW	R. Mambí, Stgo de Cuba, SC
	10	CUB		R. Trinidad Digital, Sancti Spíritus, SS
		DOM	JH	Cadena Espacial, Sto Domingo
	2.5	GTM	VY	R. Zamaneb "LV del Urram", Salamá
		HND		R. Armonía, Juticalpa
	1	HND	RF	R. Cadena de Notícias, San Pedro Sula
	1	HND	BN	R. San Miguel, Marcala
	1	HND	AM	R. Unción AM, Olanchito
		HTI		R. Transcaribbean International, Jean Rabel
	1/0.5	MEX	EG	ABC Radio, Puebla
	2.5/1	MEX	CAM	Kiss FM, Campeche
	2/1	MEX	AG	La Mejor, Córdoba
	1/0.1	MEX	KY	Oye 1280, Siempre Hits, Huixtla
	1/0.5	MEX	BW	Palabra Viva, Chihuahua
	0.5/0.25	MEX	BON	R. Fórmula, Tercera Cadena, Guadalajara
	2.5/1.15	MEX	SQ	R. San Miguel. San Miguel de Allende

kHz	kW	Ctry	Call	Station, location
	1	MEX	TUT	R. Tamaulipas, Tula
	10/1	MEX	AW	Teleradio A-W, Monterrey
	5/1	PTR	WCMN	NotiUno 1280, Arecibo
	1	SLV	QV	R. CRET, Sta Ana
		SLV		R. Emaús, San Vicente
1290	0.5	DOM	BD	R. Jánico, Santiago
		GTM		R. Miramundo "LV del Ejercito", Zacapa
	1	HND	NN26	R. Choluteca, Choluteca
	1	HND	GS	R. HRGS/Bay Island Christian Network, Utila
	1/0.5	MEX	IX	Enlace Digital 12-90/La Pantera, Sahuayo
	5/0.25	MEX	FAC	La Mera Mera, Salvatierra
	10/1	MEX	NX	R. Mujer, Mazatlán
	0.25d	MEX	TH	R. Palizada, Palizada
	20/5	MEX	DA	R. Trece, México
	1/0.25	MEX	AP	Romántica 1290, Cd.Obregón
	3	PNR	S23	R. Única, Chiriquí
	5.5	PNR		R. Unica, Los Santos
	5	PNR		R. Unica, Panama
	1	SLV	MA	R. Chalatenango, Chalatenango
1300	1	CTR	GL	La Fuente Musical, Cartago
	1	CUR	KO	R. Angulo, Danes, HO
	1	DOM	KQ	R. Doz 1300, Sto Domingo
	1	HND	IV	R. C.C.I., Tegucigalpa
	5	HND	LR	R. Sta Rosa, Sta Rosa de Copán
	1/0.25	MEX	JL	La 130, La Ley, Guamuchil
	1	MEX	KW	La Guadalupana, Morelia
	1	MEX	HU	La Que Manda, Martinez de la Torre
	10/0.75	MEX	XV	LaZ, León
	50	MEX	P	R. 13/R. Centro, Cd.Juárez
	1/0.25	MEX	AWL	R. Jacala/Hidalgo R.,Jacala
	1/0.1	MEX	XW	W R., Nogales
	1	NCG	A2CC	Canal 130 AM, Managua
	5	PNR	I417	R. Baha'ís, Boca del Monte
	1	PTR	WTIL	La Voz Romántica, Mayagüez
		SLV	KG	R. Llanera "La Campechana", San Miguel
	6	SLV	LV	W-LV de la Verdad, San Salvador
	1	SXM	PJD-2	The Voice of St Maarten, Philipsburg
1310	1	CUB	BQ	R. Enciclopedia, Nueva Gerona, IJ
	1	DOM	MH	R. Real, La Vega
	1	GTM	AN	R. LV de los Altos, Quetzaltenango
	2.5	HND	VC	LV Evangélica, San Pedro Sula
	1	HND	RL	R. Libertad, Marcala, La Paz
	5	HND	CM	R. Universidad de Agricultura, Catacamas
	2. 5/1	MEX	HV	La Fiera, Veracruz
	5/0.25	MEX	AM	La M Grande, Matamoros
	5	MEX	HY	Mia 93.9, Querétaro
	1d	MEX	BTS	R. Bahía de Tortugas, Bahía de Tortugas
	1	MEX	C	R. Enciso, Tijuana
	5/1	MEX	HIT	R. Felicidad, Puebla
	1	MEX	LPZ	R. La Paz, La Paz
	5/0.25	MEX	VB	R. Mujer, Monterrey
	1/0.1	MEX	FH	R. Plan de Agua Prieta, Agua Prieta
	1/0.25	MEX	RU	R. Universidad, Chihuahua
	10/1	MEX	TIA	R. Vital, Guadalajara
	1d	MEX	GRT	Soy Guerrero, Taxco
	5	MRT		Martinique Première, Lamentin
	10/1	NCG	SC	R. San Cristóbal, Chinandega
	12	PNR		R. María, Panamá
	5	SLV	RV	R. Veritas, Stgo de María
1320	1	CTR	LX	R. Columbia, San Carlos
	1	CUB	DL	R. 26, La Jaiba, MA
	1	CUB	CW	R. Artemisa, Artemisa, AR
	1/0.5	DOM	BZ	R. Centro, San Juan de la Maguana
	0.5	GTM	ME	R. Quezada, Jutiapa
	1	HND	MG	R. Bahía "La Super Grande", La Ceiba
	2.5/0.25	MEX	JZ	La Campera/R. Fórmula, Cd.Jimenez
	10/2	MEX	RJ	La Nueva Ranchera, Mazatlán
	10/0.1	MEX	CPN	La Poderosa, Piedras Negras
	2.5/1	MEX	PAR	Los 40 Principales, Villahermosa
	1/0.5	MEX	NM	R. 1320, Estación sin fronteras, Aguascalientes
	0.5/0.25	MEX	SR	R. Cachanía, Santa Rosalia
	10/1	MEX	NI	Stereo Vida, Uruapán
	10/2	MEX	UH	X R., Tuxtepec
	5/2.3	PTR	WSKN	R. Isla 1320, San Juan

kHz	kW	Ctry	Call	Station, location
	1	SLV	AH	R. Emanuel, La Unión
1330	3	DOM	VC	R. Visión Cristiana, Sto Domingo
	5	GTM	MU	Unión R, Guatemala
		HND		R. Emisora Evangélica, Tegucigalpa
	1	HND	FL	R. Florida, La Entrada
	10	HTI		R. Haiti Inter, Port-au-Prince
	10	MEX	MAC	Ke Buena, Manzanillo
	5/0.9	MEX	AJ	La Explosiva, Saltillo
	1/0.1	MEX	RP	La Tremenda, Cd.Madero
	0.5d	MEX	EV	R. Festival, Izúcar de Matamoros
	4/0.25	MEX	WQ	R. Triunfadora, Monclova
	5/1	MEX	BO	R. Variedades, Irapuato
	5	NCG	A6RM	R. Matagalpa, Matagalpa
	5	PNR		LV Poderosa, Panamá
	2/1.4	PTR	WENA	La Buena del Sur, Yauco
1340	5	SLV	HQ	R. Cristo Te Llama, San Salvador
	5	CTR	HR	R. Sideral, San Ramón
	0.25	CUB		AFRTS, Guantánamo Bay
	10	CUB	FL	R. Ciudad del Mar, Palmira, CI
	1	HND	CQ	Cadena Radial Samaritano, Comayagua
	10	HND	TQ	R. 1430/R. El Mundo, San Pedro Sula
		HND		Telecolor R, Catacamas
	1	MEX	AA	13-40 AM, Mexicali
	1	MEX	NV	91X La Experiencia, Monterrey
	1	MEX	APM	Candela, Apatzingán
	10/5	MEX	LU	Ke Buena Puebla, Cd. Serdán
	2	MEX	SL	Ke Buena, San Luis Potosí
	1	MEX	RPV	La Cotorra, Cd.Victoria
	1	MEX	QB	La Divertida/R. Fórmula, Tulancingo
	1d	MEX	QE	La Kañona, Escuinapa
	1	MEX	CR	La Zeta, Morelia
	1	MEX	BK	Mega ¡Sí pega!, Nuevo Laredo
	1	MEX	MT	Mi Radio 13-40 - Nostalgia, Matamoros
	1	MEX	DH	R. Amistad, Cd.Acuña
	1/0.5	MEX	RCH	R. Exitos, Ojinaga
	1	MEX	OS	R. Mujer, Cd.Obregón
	5/1	MEX	DKT	R. Ranchito, Guadalajara
	5	MEX	ASM	Romántica 107.7, Cuernavaca
	1	MEX	CI	Romántica 13-40, Acapulco
	1	NCG	OS	R. Ondas Sonoras, Managua
	2.5	PNR		R. Tipikal, Las Tablas
	0.95	PTR	WWNA	R. Una 1340, Aguadilla
	1	SLV	XW	R. Novedades, Usulután
	1	VIR		WSTA, Charlotte Amalie, St. Thomas
1350	10	CUB	FL	R. Ciudad del Mar, Aguada, CI
	1	CUB	LM	R. Libertad, Puerto Padre, LT
	1	DOM	JD	Ondas del Yuna, Bonao
	1	DOM	PM	R. Rutas Musical, La Romana
	1	GTM	MC	R. Monja Blanca, Cobán
		HND	EL	R. Estelar, La Ceiba
	1	HND	JV	R. Henecan, San Lorenzo
	0.25	HTI		R. Dame Marie, Dame Marie
	5/1	MEX	CAH	La Popular 13-50/La Voz de Soconusco, Cacahoatán
	10d	MEX	CTZ	LV de la Sierra Norte, Cuetzalán
	1/0.25	MEX	ZD	Mi Radio 1350, La Preferida, Camargo
	8	MEX	LBL	R. Centro, San Luis Río Colorado
	5/0.5	MEX	TB	R. Laguna, Torreón
	5/1	MEX	QK	Tropicalísima 13-50, México
	5	PNR	Z38	BBN R., Panamá
	2.5	PTR	WEGA	Nueva Victoria, Vega Baja
1360	5	CTR	DS	R. Radio 1360, San José
		DOM	XZ	R. Tropical, Sto Domingo
	10	GTM	LK	R. Tic Tac "LV del Evangelio", Guatemala
	1	HND	BS	R. San Pedro, Tegucigalpa
	5	HND	BH	R. Sta Bárbara, Sta Bárbara
	5/0.5	MEX	UD	Ke Buena, Tuxtla Gutiérrez
	1/0.4	MEX	DI	La Nueva, Chihuahua
	1	MEX	KF	La Z, Iguala
	10d	MEX	ZON	LV de la Sierra, Zongolica
	1/0.25	MEX	Y	R. Fiesta Retro, Celaya
	5	SLV	FM	Super Radio, San Salvador
1370	5	DOM	RP	R. Seybo, El Seybo
	1	GTM	AC	LV de Colomba, Colomba
	1	HND	SQ	R. El Shaddai R., Siguatepeque

kHz	kW	Ctry	Call	Station, location
	1	HND	ST	R. Fraternidad, San Pedro Sula
		HND	ZG	R. Guayapeña, Catacamas
		HND		R. Regional, Tocoa
	0.5	HTI		R. Citadelle, Cap Haitien
	1	HTI		Rdif. Cayenne, Cayes
	10/1	MEX	PJ	Frecuencia Deportiva, Guadalajara
	1	MEX	A	Ke Buena, Campeche
	1/0.25	MEX	RPU	La Z, Durango
	5/0.5	MEX	GNK	Mariachi Estéreo, Nuevo Laredo
	5	MEX	HF	R. Fórmula, Nogales
	10	MEX	MON	R. Fórmula, Segunda Cadena, Monterrey
	1/0.5	MEX	SV	R. Nicolaíta, Morelia
	5/1.5	MEX	JE	R. Reyna, Dolores Hidalgo
	0.5	MEX	HG	Romántica, Mexicali
	1	NCG	AARS	R. Fronteras, Somoto
	1	PNR	B64	R. Sitrachilco, Pto Armuelles
	5/1	PTR	WIVV	WIVV Rock R. Network, Vieques Isl.
	1	SLV	KO	R. Lluvias de Bendición, San Miguel
1380	1	CTR	MS	R. Guanacaste, Liberia
	1	DOM	SC	R. Nacional, Santiago
	0.5	GTM	EB	R. Momostenango Educativa, Momost
	1	HND	EJ	R. Monjaras, Choluteca
	0.5	HND	AH	R. Redención, Jutiapa
	5/1	MEX	GW	Mazz W, Cd.Victoria
	1/0.5	MEX	RS	R. Señal, Torreón
	1/0.1	MEX	VD	R. Sensación, Allende
	50/5	MEX	CO	Romántica AM Digital, México
	10/1	MEX	TP	Sensación FM, Xalapa
	10	PNR		Mujer AM, Panamá
	1	PTR	WOLA	Prócer, Voz de la Montaña, Barranquitas
1390	1	DOM	AR	R. San Cristóbal
	1	HND	VC	LV Evangélica, Sta Rosa de Copán
	10/5	HND	VC	LV Evangélica, Tegucigalpa
	10/0.25	MEX	RW	Almade México, León
	5/1	MEX	XO	La Super Buena, Cd.Mante
	5/0.1	MEX	KT	La Súper Estación, Tecate
	10/2.5	MEX	TY	Los 40 Principales, Tecomán
	1/0.15	MEX	QC	LV de Pto Peñasco/La Reyna del Mar, Pto Peñasco
	1	MEX	OR	NotiGape 1390 AM, Reynosa
	0.5d	MEX	ZG	R. Mezquital y Huasteca Hidalguense, Ixmiquilpán
	5/1	MEX	TL	R. Ola, Tuxpan
	1	MEX	CTA	Retro FM, Cuautla
	5	PNR		R. Mundo Internacional, Colón
	1	PTR	WISA	Acción 740, Isabela
		SLV		R. Fraternidad de Jesucristo, Chalchuapa
		SLV		R. Getsemaní, La Unión
1400	1	CTR	GJ	R. Sinaí, San Isidro del General
	1	CUB		R. Sagua, Sagua La Grande, VC
	1	DOM	AC	Ondas del Valle, La Vega
	5	GRD		Harbour Light of the Windwards, Carriacou
	1	GTM	RB	R. Porteña, Puerto Barrios
	1	HND	AU	R. Alegre, Sava Colón
	1	HND	YT	R. Estrella de Oro, San Pedro Sula
		HND	BO	R. Punto, Comayagua
		HND	UV	R. Universitaria, Catacamas
	1	MEX	VI	EXA FM 99.1, San Juan del Río
	1	MEX	AC	Ke Buena, Aguascalientes
	2. 5/1	MEX	XI	La "I" de Ixtapan, Ixtapan de la Sal
	1	MEX	PF	La Efectiva/La Rancherita, Ensenada
	0.25	MEX	WU	La Poderosa, Matehuala
	1	MEX	KJ	Mariachi Stereo, Acapulco
	5/1	MEX	OJ	R. Horizonte/R. Fórmula, Cd.Lázaro Cárdenas
	51	MEX	SH	R. Sabinas, Cd.Sabinas
	0.25	MEX	AB	R. Santa Ana, Santa Ana
	5	MEX	I	R. Trece, Morelia
	1	MEX	UBJ	R. Universidad Benito Juárez, Oaxaca
	10	NCG	A3MA	R. María, Managua
	10	PNR	T40	Digital R. Luz, La Chorrera
	1	PTR	WIDA	R. Vida AM, Carolina
	1	SLV	JI	LV del Litoral, Usulután
1410	3/0.5	DOM	CH	R. 14-10 Cristiana, Barahona
	1/0.5	DOM	JJ	R. Grí-Grí, Río San Juan
	1	DOM	AE	R. Tricolor, Sto Domingo

kHz	kW	Ctry	Call	Station, location
	5	GTM	GH	Nueva R. Xelajú, Quetzaltenango
	3	HTI		Voix de Nord-ouest, Port de Paix
	2/1	MEX	ZHO	Aquamarina R., Zihuatanejo
	2.5	MEX	KB	Canal 14-10, Guadalajara
	1/0.25	MEX	AS	Ke Buena, Nuevo Laredo
	1/0.1	MEX	YD	La Grande de Madero, Torreón
	7	MEX	BS	La Más Perrona, México
	10/0.5	MEX	CF	La Mexicana, Los Mochis
	1/0.25	MEX	CUA	R. Universidad, Campeche
	5/0.5	MEX	IR	XEIR, La Señal Perfecta, Cd.Valles
	3/1	NCG	RA	La Estación de la Amistad, León
	5	PNR	H779	R. Mensabé, Las Tablas
	1	PTR	WRSS	R. Progreso, San Sebastián
1420	1	CTR	RPN	R. Pampa, Liberia
	1.5	DOM	FD	R. Oro, Cotuí
	1	GTM	RP	R. Capital, Guatemala
		HND	GB	R. Sabanagrande, Sabanagrande
	1	HND	SL	R. Stereo Actualidad, Trinidad
	0.5	HTI		R. Messie Continental, Dessalines
	2.5	MEX	WJ	Exa FM, Tehuacán
	10/1	MFX	WF	La Estación Familiar, Irapuato
	5/1	MEX	H	La H, Antología Vallenata, Monterrey
	1d	MEX	KMX	La Super X, Sayula
	1	MEX	PK	R. Felicidad 14-20, Pachuca
	2	MEX	XX	R. Mexicana/R. Fórmula 1420, Tijuana
	1	MEX	AFQ	Romántica, Minatitlan
	5/0.5	MEX	F	Tu Recuerdo, Cd.Juárez
	1	MEX	EW	W1420/LV del Bajo Bravo, Matamoros
	1	PTR	WUKQ	Ponce
1430	3	CTR	RDVC	R. San Carlos, Cd. Quesada
	5	DOM	JC	R. Emanuel, Santiago
	1.2	GTM	AG	LV de Huehuetenango
		HND	QV	La Nueva Potencia, Olanchito
	1	HND	FO	LV Evangélica, Puerto Cortés
		HND		Ministerios Cristianos Fuente de Vida, Juticalpa
	1	HND	VM	R. Maranatha, La Paz
	5/0.5	MEX	OX	Exa FM 106.5, Cd.Obregón
	1	MEX	COC	Inolvidable, Colima
	5/0.15	MEX	WD	La Grande de Ciudad Miguel Alemán, Cd. Miguel Alemán
	0.25	MEX	RAC	La Número Uno en Campeche/R. Fórmula, Campeche
	5/1	MEX	LL	Latido, Veracruz
	5/1	MEX	TT	R. Tlaxcala, Tlaxcala
	5	NCG	AARL	R. Liberación "La Tayacana", Estelí
	7.5	PNR		R. Kids, Panamá
	5	PTR	WNEL	NotiUno/R. Tiempo, Caguas
1440	5	DOM	AK	R. Impactante, Sto Domingo
	5	DOM	AD	R. San Juan, San Juan de la Maguana
	0.5	GTM	MS	R. Nacional, Mazatenango
	5	HND	RD	R. Belén, La Ceiba
	0.5	HND	RY	R. Ekklesia Int./R. Mía, San Marcos de Colón
	10/1	MEX	ABCJ	ABC Radio/Corazón , Guadalajara
	1/0.15	MEX	VSD	La Señal del Progreso, Cd. Constitución
	25/5	MEX	EST	Quiéreme 14-40, México
	25	NCG	A3MR	R. Maranatha, Managua
1450	1	BER		Defontes Broadcasting Co., Hamilton
	1	CUB	LN	R. Maboas, Amancio Rodríguez, LT
	1	CUB	CL	R. Mayabeque, Güines, MB
		DOM		R. Alfa y Omega, Sto Domingo
	10	DOM	AC	R. Util, Salcedo
	1	GTM	LG	R. Hosanna, Guatemala
	1	HND	BR	R. Cultural, La Entrada
		HND	GB	R. Sabanagrande, Tegucigalpa
	0.4	MEX	PNO	ARO AM, Santiago Pinotepa Nal
	1	MEX	CM	Bonita, Cd.Mante
	1	MEX	BP	Bonita, Torreón
	1	MEX	KM	KM-FM/R. Mina, Minatitlán
	5/1	MEX	JM	La Caliente, Monterrey
	2/1	MEX	RY	La Poderosa V del Sur, Arcelia
	5/1	MEX	RDO	La Radio 14-50, Reynosa
	10/1	MEX	CU	La Rancherita, Los Mochis
	0.5	MEX	DJ	R. Clave, Magdalena
	1	MEX	RNB	R. Impacto, Sahuayo y Jiquilpan

kHz	kW	Ctry	Call	Station, location
	1	MEX	JD	R. Mundo, Poza Rica
	1/0.25	MEX	ARE	R. Pegüis/R. Lobo, Ojinaga
	5/1	MEX	NA	Yo FM, Querétaro
	5	PNR		R. Melodía, Panamá
	1	PTR	WCPR	R. Coamo, Coamo
	1	SLV	KR	R. Restauración, San Miguel
1460	1	CTR	LX	R. Columbia, Ciudad Quesada
	0.5	DOM	AN	R. Renacimiento, Hato Mayor del Rey
	2.5	GTM	RN	R. Petén, Flores
	0.5	HND	CX	LV de Patuca, Catacamas
		HND	FR	R. Firmamento, La Paz
	0.5	HND	KS	R. Ministerio Bautista, Yoro
	2.5	HND	GC	R. Reino, San Pedro Sula
	0.2	HTI		Voix du Nord, Cap Haitien
	1/0.1	MEX	JH	ABC R., Xalapa
	5/0.5	MEX	KC	Estéreo Exitos, Oaxaca
	10/1	MEX	CB	R. Ranchito, San Luis Río Colorado
	0.5	PNR	D42	LV de Almirante, Bocas del Toro
	0.5	PTR	WLRP	R. Raíces, San Sebastián
	0.5/0.3	PTR	WRRE	Sonido Santidad, Juncos
1470	1	CUB	LM	R. Libertad, Puerto Padre, LT
	1	DOM	DE	LV de la Alabanza, San Francisco de Macorís
		DOM	CV	R. Barahona, Provincia Independencia
		DOM	CH	R. Vibra "La Deportiva", Barahona
		HND	XH	R. Globo Grupera/R. Nacaome, Nacaome
	50/5	MEX	AI	Fórmula Femenina, México
	1	MEX	IRG	La Campirana, Irapuato
	1/0.5	MEX	IND	LV Sierra Hidalguense, Tlanchinol
	10/0.25	MEX	HI	MiRadio 1470, Puro Cañonazo, Ciudad Miguel Alemán
	5/1	MEX	CAV	Play 14-70, Tocando Tu Memoria, Durango
	1/0.1	MEX	ACE	R. Fórmula Mazatlán, Mazatlán
	10/5	MEX	RCN	R. Hispana 14-70 San Diego y Tijuana, Tijuana
	2.5/0.5	MEX	BAL	R. Voz Maya de México, Bécal
	1	NCG	RY	R. Yarrince, Boaco
	5	PNR		R. La Primerísima, Panamá
	2.4/2.5	PTR	WKCK	R. Cumbre, Orocovis
1480	2	CTR	AW	R. El Sol, Puntarenas
	5	DOM	AH	R. Villa, Sto Domingo
	5	GTM	HB	R. Horizontes, Guatemala
	1	HND	EZ	LV de Misiones "R. MI", Comayagüela
	1	HND	WP	R. Soberanía, San Marcos, Ocotepeque
	2/1	MEX	ZJ	Ciudad 1480, Guadalajara
	1/0.5	MEX	HM	H-M Radio, Cd.Delicias
	1/0.1	MEX	XU	La Poderosa, Monclova
	2.5	MEX	CARH	LV del Pueblo Hña-hñu, Cárdonal
	5/0.15	MEX	VIC	R. Tamaulipas, Cd.Victoria
	10/1	MEX	TKR	TKR Rancherita y Regional, Monterrey
	5/0.25	MEX	NS	Z14, Solo Exitos, Navojoa
	5	PTR	WMDD	El 14-80 AM, Fajardo
1490	1	CUB	KN	R. Mayarí, Mayarí, HO
	3	DOM		La Voz del Cibao, Santiago
	1	GTM	RE	R. Modelo, Retalhuleu
		HND		R. Así se informa, La Unión
	1	HND	OM	R. Omega "Sonido Internacional", La Esperanza
		HND	OE	R. Pijol, Morazán
	1.2	HND	GO	R. Porteña, Puerto Cortés
	1	MEX	AQ	La Caliente, Agua Prieta
	1/0.25	MEX	SK	La Super K/La Costeñita, Cd.Ruiz
	1	MEX	MS	R. Mexicana, Matamoros
	1	MEX	CJC	R. Net, Cd.Juárez
	1/0.25	MEX	FF	R. Norteña, Matehuala
	1	MEX	YT	R. Teocelo, Teocelo
	1	MEX	KN	R. Variedades, Huetamo
	5/1	MEX	GT	W R., Zamora
	3	PNR		Asamblea Nacional, Cocle
	5/1	PTR	WDEP	R. Isla, Ponce
1500	1	CTR	ASF	R. Radio1500, Sarapiqui
	0.5	DOM	PA	R. Higüey, Higüey
	3	DOM	RD	R. Juan Pablo Duarte, Elías Piña
		HND		R. MI-EL, Sabá
		HND	VP	R. Sion, La Ceiba
	1	HND	TX	R. Victoria, Choluteca
	0.4	MEX	JQ	La Explosiva, Parras

kHz	kW	Ctry	Call	Station, location
	50	MEX	DF	R. Fórmula 1500, Segunda Cadena, México
	1/0.5	MEX	FL	R. Santa Fe, Guanajuato
	1	NCG	PT	R. Minuto, Managua
	1/0.25	PTR	WMNT	R. Atenas, Manatí
	1	SLV	CS	R. Pentecostal, Usulután
1510	10/3	DOM	BL	R. Pueblo, Sto Domingo
	5	GTM	DX	R. Centroamericana del Amor, Guatemala:
	1	HND	EM	R. Emanuel, Ocotepeque
	1	HND	PG	R. Gualcho, Tegucigalpa
	10	MEX	QI	La Nueva Radio, Monterrey
	0.25	MEX	HUI	R. Huichapán, Huichapán
	5	PNR	A95	Hosanna R., Panamá
	1	PTR	WBSG	R. Voz, Lajas
1520	1	CTR	LX	R. Columbia, Cartago
	1	DOM	WJ	R. Samaná "R. 15-20", Samaná
	1	GTM	RS	R. Superior, Coatepeque
		GTM		R. Taysal, Sta Elena de la Cruz
	1	HND	CR	Dif. Cristiana de R. "DCR", San Pedro Sula
		HND	MQ	R. Manantial de Vida Eterna, Juticalpa
		HND	DF	R. Rios de Agua Viva, Siguatepeque
	1	HND	HJ	R. Santiago, Yoro
	1/0.5	MEX	YP	Imagen, Cd. Mante
	1d	MEX	VO	La Furia, San Rafael
	1	MEX	VUC	La Norteñita, Allende
	1	MEX	EH	R. Exitos, San Luis Río Colorado
	1/0.25	MEX	ATL	R. Mexiquense, Atlacomulco
	2	MEX	ART	Señal 152, Jojutla
	25	PTR	WVOZ	R. Voz/La Voz Boricua, San Juan
1530	0.25	DOM	JN	Canal 25, Santiago
		HND		La Guarachera, Choluteca
	1	MEX	GQ	La Reyna de los Reyes, Los Reyes
	10/0.1	MEX	SD	Los 40 Principales, Silao
	50/1	MEX	UR	R. Fiesta 15-30, México
	0.5	NCG	A4TS	LV de Sta Teresa, Sta Teresa
	10	PNR		R. Avivamiento, Panamá
	1/0.25	PTR	WUPR	Exitos 15-30, Utuado
1540	8	BAH		ZNS1, Nassau
	1	CTR	CUB	Enlace R., Pavas
	1	DOM	BU	LV de La Romana, La Romana
	1	DOM	FP	R. Criolla Comercial, Sto Domingo
	1	GTM		R. Cultura y Deportes, Guatemala
		HND	VK	R. Nuevo Mundo "Cadena Radial Reloj", Tegucigalpa
	1/0.25	MEX	NC	La Auténtica 15-40, Celaya
	5	MEX	HOS	La Poderosa, Hermosillo
	1/0.5	MEX	STN	R. Red, Monterrey
	1	PTR	WIBS	R. Voz/R. Caribe, Guayama
1550	5	CUB	BA	R. Rebelde, Cárdenas, MA
	5	CUB	BA	R. Rebelde, Circunvalación, MA
	1	CUB	BA	R. Rebelde, Guantánamo, GU
	1	CUB	BA	R. Rebelde, Sagua La Grande, VC
	10	CUB	BA	R. Rebelde, Santa Clara, VC
	5	CUB	BA	R. Rebelde, Tulipán, CI
	1	CUB	BA	R. Rebelde, Guayajay, SS
	1	HND	JO	R. Campeona, Comayagua
	1	HND	JX	R. Cristiana Nueva Vida, San Pedro Sula
		HND		R. Wuampu, Dulce Nombre de Culmi
	1	MEX	BG	Cadena 1550 AM, Tijuana
	5/0.25	MEX	NU	La Rancherita, Nuevo Laredo
	1	MEX	REL	R. Michoacán, Morelia
	10	MEX	RUV	R. Universidad Veracruzana, Xalapa
	0.25	PTR	WKFE	La Isla/R. Café Dinámica Yauco
	5	SLV		R. Sanidad Divina, San Salvador
1560	5	CTR	OAR	R. Nicoya, Nicoya
	1/0.5	DOM	PZ	R. Pedernales, Pedernales
	1	DOM	GL	R. Única, Santiago
	1	DOM		R. Universidad UASD, Santo Domingo
		GTM		R. Inspiración, Quetzaltenango
		HND	FD	R. Mi Preferida, Choluteca
	50/10	MEX	INFO	15-60 AM, México
	1/0.25	MEX	MAS	Ke Buena, Salamanca
	0.25	MEX	SE	LV de Campeche, Champotón
	5/1	MEX	LAC	R. Azul/LV del Balsas, Cd.Lázaro Cárdenas
	20/0.15	MEX	CHZ	R.Lagarto/LV Viva de Chiapas, Chiapa de Corzo

kHz	kW	Ctry	Call	Station, location
	1	MEX	JPV	R. Viva, Cd. Juárez
	10	PNR		R. Adventista de Panamá, Panamá
	5/0.75	PTR	WRSJ	La Bachatera del Norte, Bayamón
1570	10	GTM	VE	VEA-Voz Evengélica de América, Guatemala
		HND	TF	Difusora Cristiana Torre Fuerte, Gracias
	2.5	HND	RF	R. Cad Nal de Noticias "RCN", Tegucigalpa
	100	MEX	RF	La Poderosa, Cd.Acuña
	1/0.1	PTR	WPPC	R. Felicidad, Peñuelas
1580	0.25	CTR	RCVT	LV de Talamanca, Talamanca
	1	CTR	LG	R. Casino, Siguirres, Limón
	0.25	CTR	RCC	R. Cultural de Corredores,
	0.25	CTR	RCLS	R. Cultural Los Santos
	0.25	CTR	RSCM	R. Cultural Maleku
	0.5	CTR	RCS	R. Cultural Santiago
	0.5	CTR	RCP	R. Cultural, Pérez Zeledón
	0.5	CTR	RCT	R. CulturalTilarán
	0.25	CTR	RCLC	R. Sistema Cultural de La Cruz
	0.25	CTR	RCL	R. Sistema Cultural de Los Chiles
	10	DOM	AJ	R. Amanecer, Sto Domingo
	1	DOM	PK	R. Neiba, Neiba
		HND		R. La Voz Lenca, La Esperanza
	10	MEX	DM	DM Notícias, Hermosillo
	1/0.5	MEX	AF	La Temeraria 15-80, Celaya
	1/0.25	MEX	LI	Super 94.7, Chilpancingo
	20	MEX	VAB	Super Stereo Miled, Valle del Bravo
	1	PNR		Hosanna Oeste, Panamá
	5/2.5	PTR	WEKO	R. Voz 1580, Morovis
		SLV		R. Poder y Gloria, Santa Ana
1590	1.5	CTR	LGJ	R. 16, Grecia
	1	DOM	SF	R. Libertad, Santiago
	1	GTM	XC	R. Triunfadora, Chimaltenango
		HND	BX	R. Perla, El Progreso
		HND	ZL	R. Zol, Choluteca
	1/0.25	MEX	BZ	Extasis Digital, Cd.Delicias
	1/0.1	MEX	PT	La Nueva Misantla R, Misantla
	1	MEX	HC	R. Bahía, Ensenada
	20/10	MEX	VOZ	R. Mexicana, México (La Paz ME)
	1	PTR	WXRF	R. Voz, Guayama
1600	2.5	CTR	RCCH	R. Cultural Chirripó
	0.25	CTR	RCBA	R. Cultural de Buenos Aires
	0.25	CTR	RCP	R. Cultural de Pital
	0.25	CTR	RCT	R. Cultural de Turrialba
	0.25	CTR	RCU	R. Cultural de Upala
	2.5	CTR	RCPV	R. Cultural Puerto Viejo
	0.5	CTR	RCSG	R. Cultural San Gabriel
	1.5	CTR	MQ	R. Pococí, Guápiles
	0.5	CTR	RPQ	R. Quepos, Pto Quepos
	2.5	CTR	CC	R. Radio Cima, Pto Golfito
	0.25	CTR	RSCN	R. Sistema Cultural Nicoyano
	5	DOM	FG	R. Revelación en América, Sto Domingo
	1	HND	PC	R. Luz y Vida, San Luís
		HND	PQ	R. Poderosa, Tegucigalpa
	5	MEX	GEM	R. Mexiquense, Metepec
	1	MEX	TPA	Soy Guerrero, Tlapa de Comonfort
	5	PTR	WOVA	Cima 1600, Bayamón
1610	30	AIA		The Caribbean Beacon, The Valley
		BER		Bermuda Broadcasting Co., Prospect (emergencies only)
	0.25	MEX	UACH	R. Chapingo, Chapingo
1620		CUB	NL	R. Bayamo, Bayamo GR
	5	CUB	BA	R. Rebelde, Guanabacoa, CH
	1	CUB	BA	R. Rebelde, Guantánamo, GU
		DOM	SR	R. Taina/Planeta, San Pedro de Macorís
	10/1	VIR		WDHP, Christiansted, St. Croix
1630	10/1	MEX	UT	R. Universidad UABC, Mexicali
1640	1/0.5	DOM	C80	R. Juventus Don Bosco, Sto Domingo
1650	5/3	DOM		RADECO, Santiago
	5	MEX	ARZ	ZER R. 16-50, México
1660	5/1	DOM		Fundación Lama, Sto Domingo
	10/1	PTR	WGIT	Noticias 16-60, Canóvanas
1670	1	MEX	ANAH	R. Anáhuac, Huixquilucan
1680	1	DOM	SV	R. Senda 1680 AM, San Pedro de Macorís
1700	5/1	DOM		R. Eternidad, Sto Domingo
	10	MEX	PE	ESPN R., Tecate

SOUTH AMERICA
(excluding Brazil)

NB: Brazil has been excluded to save space – see country entry for frequencies

Abbreviations: Dif=Difusora, Em=Emisora, LV=La Voz, Nal=Nacional, SF=Santafé.

kHz	kW	Ctry	Call	Station, location
530	25/5	ARG		LV de las Madres, Buenos Aires
	1	EQA	DC1	R. Iris/530 AM "LV de la Comunidad", Quito
	15	FLK		Falkland Is R. Sce/KTV R., Bush Rincon
540	10/5	ARG	LU17	R. Golfo Nuevo, Pto. Madryn
	25	ARG	LRA14	R. Nal., Santa Fé
	5	ARG	LRA25	R. Nal.,Tartagal
		ARG		R.Italia, Villa Martelli
	25/5	ARG		Ushuaia (F.Pl.)
		BOL		Radiodifusora Victoria, La Paz
	1	CHL	CB54	R. Ignacio Serrano, Melipilla
	10	CLM	KA	R. Auténtica Básica, Bogotá
	25	EQA	FA2	R. Tropicana "Canal 540", Guayaquil
	1	PRU	OBX4E	R. Inca del Perú, Lima
	1	PRU	OCX2D	R. San Antonio, Trujillo
	10	VEN		LV de Manapiare, San Juan de Manapiare
	50/25	VEN	OY	R. Perijá, La Villa del Rosario
550	5/0.5	ARG		Neuquén (F.Pl.)
	1	CHL	CD55	R. LV. de la Tierra, Angol
	50	CLM	HF	R. Nal., Marinilla
	30	CLM	R36	Vida AM, Mitú
	50	EQA	GM1	R. Reloj "5-50", Quito
	4	FLK		BFBS, Bush Rincon
	20/12	PRG	ZP16	R. Parque, Ciudad del Este
	25	URG	CW1	R. Colonia, Colonia
	50	VEN	KE	R. Mundial, Caracas
560	25/5	ARG	LV1	R. Colón, San Juan
	10/5	ARG	LT15	R. del Litoral, Concordia
	25/5	ARG	LRA13	R. Nal., Bahia Blanca
	25	ARG	LRA9	R. Nal., Esquel
	25	ARG	LRA16	R. Nal., La Quiaca
	15	BOL		R. El Mundo, La Paz
	25/10	CLM	PF	LV de la Pampa, Maicao
	10	CLM	GS	R. Nal., Tunja
	25	EQA	RN2	C. R. E. Satelital, Guayaquil
	10	GUY		NCN, Georgetown
	2	PRU	OBZ4L	R. Oriente, Lima
		PRU	OBX1H	Radiomar, Chiclayo
	20/10	VEN	PJ	CNB Tachirense, Rubio
	50	VEN	RH	RNV Canal Informativo, Puerto Ordaz
570		ARG		R. Argentina, Buenos Aires
	100	CLM	ND	R. Nal de Colombia, Bogotá
	10	EQA	CE1	R. El Sol, Quito
	1	PRG	ZP15	R. LV del Amambay, Pedro Juan Caballero
	1	PRG	ZP39	R. San Roque, Ayolas
		PRU	OCU2B	Huamachuco
	1	PRU	OAU1M	R. Univ. Nal. Pedro Ruiz Gallo, Lambayeque
	100	VEN	LX	R. La Villa, Villa de Cura
580	10/5	ARG	LU20	R. Chubut, Trelew
	25/5	ARG	LW1	R. Univ. Nal. de Córdoba, Córdoba
		ARG		R.Andina, San Rafael
	10	BOL		R. Panamericana, La Paz
	50/10	CLM	HP	R. Nal., Cali
	10	EQA	PC2	R. Uno, Guayaquil
	1	PRU	OCY2L	R. El Sol, La Esperanza
	10	PRU	OAX2E	R. Marañón, Jaén
		PRU	OAX4M	R. Maria, Lima
	2	URG	CX58	R. Clarín, Montevideo
	50/10	VEN	MJ	LV de la Fe, Maracaibo
590	50	ARG	LS4	R. Continental, Buenos Aires
	4	ARG	LV12	R. Independencia, San Miguel de Tucumán
	25	ARG	LRA30	R. Nal., San Carlos de Bariloche
	10	CHL	CD59	R. Pingüino, Punta Arenas
	50	CLM	CR	W Radio, Medellín
	10	EQA	SP1	R. Carrusel, Quito
	5	PRG	ZP32	R. Ycuámandyyú, Villa de S. Pedro
	1	PRU	OCX6V	R. Catedral, Miraflores, Arequipa
	20	VEN	KL	R. Continente, Caracas
600	20/5	ARG	LU5	R. Neuquén, Neuquén
	10	BOL		R. ACLO, Sucre
	1	BOL		Radioemisoras del Recobro, La Paz
	10	CHL	CB60	R. Monumental, Santiago
	1	CLM	Z95	LV de los Awas, Ricaurte el Diviso
	50	CLM	HJ	R. Libertad, Barranquilla
	50	EQA	XY2	R. Ciudadana, Guayaquil
	10	PRU	OBZ4W	R. Cora, Lima
		PRU	OAX6S	R. Cultura Toquepala, Ilabaya
		PRU	OCX6D	R. Cultural, Ilabaya
	1	PRU	OBX2B	R. Star, Trujillo
	15	VEN	SW	R. Alto Llano, Sta Bárbara de Barinas
	10	VEN	QB	R. Sucre, Cumaná
610	1	ARG	LRK201	R. Solidaridad, Añatuya
	5/1	ARG		R.General San Martin, San Martin
	30	CLM	KL	La Cariñosa, Bogotá
	50	CLM	D90	R. Nal., Uribia
	10	EQA	MJ1	R. Caravana AM, Quito
	25	PRG	ZP30	LV del Chaco Paraguayo, Filadelfia
	5	PRU	OCY2I	R. Santa Monica, Chota
	1	PRU	OBU1E	R. Santa Rosa, Sullana
	50	URG	CX4	R. Rural, Montevideo
	10	VEN	XY	R. Centro 6-10, Cantaura
	10	VEN	SE	R. Cristal, Barquisimeto
620	25	ARG	LRA18	R. Nal,. Río Turbio
	10	ARG	LRA26	R. Nal., Resistencia
	25/5	ARG	LT17	R. Provincia de Misiones, Posadas
	10/5	ARG	LV4	R. San Rafael, San Rafael
	10	BOL		R. San Gabriel, El Alto
	10	CHL	CC62	R. Bío-Bío, Concepción
	1	CHL	CA62	R. Norte Verde, Ovalle
	50/20	CLM	EL	Colmundo, Cali
	10	CLM	VP	Colmundo, Cartagena
	10	EQA	HA2	Ondas Quevedeñas, Quevedo
	50	EQA	XY3	R. Ciudadana, Loja
	5	PRG	ZP40	R. Ñasaindý, San Estanislao
		PRU	OAR7H	Apostol de Yanaoca, Yanaoca
	0.4	PRU	OAX2M	R. Chepen, Chepen
		PRU	OCX6B	R. Maria, Arequipa
	10	PRU	OBU4B	R. Ovación, San Isidro
	50/25	VEN	ZC	R. Fe y Alegría,Guasdualito
	10	VEN	NO	R. Libertad, Cabimas
630	10/5	ARG	LU4	R. Patagonia Argentina, Comodoro Rivadavia
	25/5	ARG	LS5	R. Rivadavia, Buenos Aires
	25	ARG	LW8	R. San Salvador de Jujuy
	10	CHL	CB63	R. Stela Maris, Valparaíso
	10	CLM	E69	LV del Guainía, Puerto Inírida
	10	CLM	FD	R. Manizales, Manizales
	50/25	VEN	KA	RNV Canal Informativo, Caracas
634		PRU	OAU2R	R. Cajamarca, Cajamarca
640	10/5	ARG	LU18	R. El Valle, "640 AM", GeneralRoca
	25/5	ARG	LRA24	R. Nal., Río Grande
	10/5	ARG	LV15	R. Villa Mercedes
		BOL		R. ALCO, Sucre
	15	BOL		R. Dif. Integración, El Alto
	10	CHL	CD64	R. Cooperativa AM, Temuco
	0.25	CHL	CC64	R. Portales, Curico

kHz	kW	Ctry	Call	Station, location
	10	CLM	BJ	RCN, Santa Marta
	50	EQA	XY1	R. Ciudadana, Quito
	15	PRG	ZP19	R. Caaguazú, Coronel Oviedo
	10	PRU	OAZ4K	R. Del Pacífico, Lima
	1	PRU	OAU1Y	R. La Luz, José Leonardo Ortiz
	10	PRU	OBX7B	R. Onda Azul, Puno
	30	VEN	QO	Actualidad 640, Puerto La Cruz
	10/5	VEN	MU	R. Carora, Carora
650		ARG		R. Belgrano AM 650, Buenos Aires
	50	CLM	KH	RCN Antena 2, Bogotá
	5	EQA	FD4	R. Visión Manta, Manta
	50	PRG	ZP4	R. Uno, Asunción
		PRU	OAU9D	Neiva
	3	PRU	OBU2P	R. Bendición Cristiana, Chota
	1	PRU	OAX2N	R. Regional del Norte, Trujillo
	50/25	URG	CX6	S.O.D.R.E. "R. Clásica", Montevideo
	50/20	VEN	LH	Aragüeña 650, Maracay
660		ARG		Amplitud 660, San Justo
	1/0.5	ARG	LT41	R. LV del Sur Entrerriano, Gualeguaychú
		ARG		R. Popular, Claypole
	1	BOL		R. ABC, Santa Cruz
	50	CHL	CB66	R. UC, Santiago
	25	CLM	QS	Colmundo, Cúcuta
	10	CLM	EZ	R. Auténtica, Cali
	30	EQA	LG2	R. Carrusel, Guayaquil
	5	PRG	ZP26	R. Itapirú, Cd. del Este
	1	PRU	OCX4L	R. Chinchaycocha, Junin
	5	PRU	OCX1U	R. J.H.C., Chiclayo
	10	PRU	OCX4R	R. La Inolvidable, Lima
	10	VEN	NA	Ondas de los Medanos, Coro
	10	VEN	QZ	R. Anaco, Anaco
670	1	ARG	LT4	R. Dif. Misiones, Posadas
	25/5	ARG	LRI209	R. Mar del Plata, Mar del Plata
	10	ARG	LRA52	R. Nal., Chos Malal
	25/5	ARG	LRA11	R. Nal., Comodoro Rivadavia
		ARG		R. Republica, Lomas de Mirador
	10	CLM	R33	R. U.I.S, Bucaramanga
	50	CLM	PL	RCN Antena 2, Medellín
	12/5	EQA	FF1	R. Jesús del Gran Poder, Quito
	10	PRU	OAX7H	R. Nacional del Perú, Puno
	100	VEN	LL	R. Rumbos, Caracas
680	5	ARG	LT3	R. Cerealista, Rosario
		ARG		R. Magna, San Martin
	25/5	ARG	LV6	R. Nihuil, Mendoza
	25/5	ARG	LU12	R. Río Gallegos, Río Gallegos
		BOL		R. ACLO, Potosi
	5	BOL		R. Andina, La Paz
	10	CHL	CC68	R. Cooperativa, Concepción
	50	CLM	ZO	R. Nal., Barranquilla Sabanagrande
	25/12	EQA	VP2	R. Atalaya, Guayaquil
	50	PRG	ZP11	R. Caritas, Asunción
	5	PRU	OAX5E	Emisora del Pacífico, Ica
	0.5	PRU	OBX2L	R. Amauta, Chócope
	5	PRU	OCY2Y	R. San Luis, Jaén
	20	PRU	OBX4A	R. Tigre, San Isidro
	1	URG	CW68	R. Young, Young
	10	VEN	QR	R. Continente Cumaná, Cumaná
	10	VEN	ZJ	R. Llanera "R. 1400", Barinas
690		ARG		K -24 en Radio, Buenos Aires
	10/3	ARG	LU19	R. LV de Comahue, Cipolletti
	25/5	ARG	LRA4	R. Nal., Salta
	10	CHL	CD69	R. Estrella del Mar, Ancud
	10	CHL	CB69	R. Santiago, Santiago
	1	CLM	Z73	LV Indígena de Uberaba, Apartado
	35	CLM	CZ	R. Recuerdos, Bogotá
	50	EQA	JB1	LV de los Andes, Quito
	5	EQA	FA4	Sucre Portoviejo, Portoviejo
	1/10	URG	CX8	R. Sarandí, Montevideo
	50/20	VEN	MR	R. Barquisimeto, Barquisimeto
693	1.5	PRU	OCX1T	R. Horizonte, Chiclayo
700	25/5	ARG	LV3	R. Córdoba - "Caden 3 Argentina"
		ARG		Rawson (F.P.I.)
		BOL		R. Pacha Qamasa, El Alto
	5	CHL	CD70	R. Magallanes, Punta Arenas

kHz	kW	Ctry	Call	Station, location
	1	CHL	CA70	R. Nibsan, Copiapó
	1	CHL	CD70	R. Valdivia, Valdivia
	30	CLM	CX	W Radio, Cali
	50	EQA	RS2	Sucre Guayaquil, Guayaquil
	1	GUY		NCN, Linden
	12	PRG	ZP12	R. Carlos Antonio López, Pilar
	10	PRU	OAU9A	R. Canal Catolica San Gabriel, Moyobamba
	10	PRU	OBX1U	R. Cutivalú "LV del Desierto", Castilla
	1	PRU	OBU4J	R. La Luz, Huancayo
	1	PRU	OBU7K	R. La Salle, Urubamba
	25	PRU	OBZ4H	R. Integridad, San Miguel
	1	PRU	OCY2H	R. Sausal Superior, Sausal
		PRU	OCU1B	Sechura
	10	VEN	MH	R. Popular, Maracaibo
	5/2	VEN	PQ	R. Sur, Puerto Ordaz
710	50	ARG	LRL202	R. Diez, Buenos Aires
	25/5	ARG	LRA19	R. Nal., Pto. Iguazú
	1 2/3	ARG	LRA17	R. Nal., Zapala
	1	CLM	YD	R. La Paz, Paipa
	10	CLM	NX	R. Super, Medellín
	8	EQA	ER5	Escuelas Radiofónicas Populares, Riobamba
	1	PRU	OAU6L	R. Amor, Arequipa
	10	PRU	OCX7I	R. Nacional del Peru, Puerto Maldonado
	5	PRU	OBX5Q	R. Programas del Perú - RPP, Ica
		PRU		R. Surupana, Azángaro
	50/20	VEN	KY	R. Capital, Caracas
720	25/5	ARG	LV10	R. de Cuyo, Mendoza
	1 2/3	ARG	LRA59	R. Nal., Gobernador Gregores
	10	BOL		R. La Cruz del Sur, La Paz
	10	BOL		R. Pío XII, Siglo Veinte
	2.5	BOL		R. Yungas, Chulumani
	1	CHL	CA72	R. Portales, Iquique
	30	CLM	AN	Emisoras Unidas, Barranquilla
	50	CLM	ZX	R. Dif. Nal., Rionegro
	25	CLM	VO	Transmisora Quindío, Armenia
	10	EQA	GB4	LV de Portoviejo, Portoviejo
	5	EQA	MO3	R. Matovelle "HCM-3", Loja
	5	EQA	IC1	R. Municipal, Quito
	10	EQA	UE3	R. Única, Machala
	25	PRG	ZP17	R. Pai Puku, Teniente Irala Fernández
	1	PRU	OBU7D	R. Alegria, Wanchaq
	1	PRU	OAU1Q	R. Frecuencia Oceánica, Lambayque
	25	PRU	OAX2J	R. Nacional del Perú, Trujillo
	10	PRU	OAU4E	R. Sideral, La Oroya
	10	VEN	XE	R. Elorza, Elorza
	50	VEN	QE	R. Venezuela Oriente, Porlamar
730	10/5	ARG		Concepto AM, Gregorio de Laferrere
	10/1	ARG	LU23	R. Lago Argentino, El Calafate
	25/5	ARG	LRA27	R. Nal., Catamarca
	20/5	ARG	LRA3	R. Nal., Santa Rosa
	1	CHL	CD73	R. Angelina, Los Angeles
	10	CHL	CB73	R. Cooperativa AM, Valparaíso
	10	CLM	CU	Melodía Stéreo, Bogotá
	15	CLM	TJ	R. Uno, Montería
	10	EQA	MG2	R. Guayaquil, Guayaquil
	30	PRG	ZP7	R. Cardinal, Asunción
	10	PRU	OAX1D	R. del Pacifico, Piura
	5	PRU	OBU2Q	R. Maria, Cajamarca
	50	PRU	OAX4G	R. Programas del Perú, San Isidro
	5/2.5	URG	CX10	R. Continente, Montevideo
	10	VEN	OO	R. Frontera, San Antonio del Táchira
	10	VEN	MT	R. Universo, Barquisimeto
740	10	ARG		AM 740 La Carretera, Allen
	25/5	ARG	LRH251	R. Chaco, Resistencia
	10/1	ARG	LRI200	R. Municipal
	25	ARG	LRA55	R. Nal., Alto Río Senguer
	5/0.5	ARG		R. Nal., Neuquén - F.P.I.
		ARG		R. Rebelde, Buenos Aires
	10	CLM	HB	Ecos de Pasto, Pasto
	50	CLM	NS	R. Guatapurí, Valledupar
	10	EQA	SE4	R. Libertad, Chone
	10	EQA	GC1	R. Melodía "Canal 7-40", Quito
	10	PRU	OAX6C	R. Continental, Arequipa

kHz	kW	Ctry	Call	Station, location
	1	PRU	OCX2X	R. El Puerto, Pascamayo
		PRU	OCU4X	R. Vision, Huancayo
	1	PRU	OBU7C	Red Latino, Cusco
	5	URG	CW27	R. Tabaré, Salto
	10	VEN	NC	CNB 740 La Zuliana, Maracaibo
	50	VEN	NQ	R. Caroni "Q-FM", Puerto Ordaz
750	1/0.25	ARG		R. AM 7-50, Lomas de Zamora
	100/10	ARG	LRA7	R. Nal., Córdoba
	50	CLM	DK	Caracol R, Medellín
	5	CLM	LH	LV de Yopal, Yopal
	30	EQA	RC2	Caravana AM, Guayaquil
	5	PRG	ZP42	LV de la Policía Nal, Asunción
	5	PRU	OCX4X	R. Altura, Cerro de Pasco
	100	VEN	KS	RCR 750 "Radio Caracas", Caracas
760	25/5	ARG	LU6	Emisora Atlántica, Mar del Plata
		BOL		R. Casachun Coca, Lauca Ñ
	5	BOL		R. Cosmos, Cochabamba
	50	BOL		R. Fides, La Paz
	50	CHL	CB76	R. Cooperativa, Santiago
	25	CLM	AJ	RCN La Radio, Barranquilla
	25	EQA	QR1	R. Quito "LV de la Capital", Quito
	10	GUY		NCN, Georgetown
	0.5	PRU	OBX2K	R. Andino, Otuzco
	10	PRU	OBZ4X	R. Mar Plus, Chorillos
	10	VEN	QQ	R. Puerto La Cruz, Pto. La Cruz:
	10	VEN	SO	R. Simpática 760, Trujillo
770	5/1	ARG		R. Cooperativa, Valentín Alsina
	1	CHL	CD77	R. Cooperativa, Castro
	100	CLM	JX	RCN L Radio, Bogotá
	25/12	EQA	MF2	R. El Telégrafo, Guayaquil
	5	PRU	OAX8M	LV de la Selva, Iquitos
	2.5	PRU	OAU7D	R. LV del Allinccapac, Macusani
	1.5	PRU	OCX1T	R. Vision, Chiclayo
	5	PRU	OBX6H	Radiomar, Uchumayo
	100/25	URG	CX12	R. Oriental, Montevideo
	50/20	VEN	KK	RNV Canal Informativo, Campo Carabobo
780	25/5	ARG	LV8	R. Libertador, Mendoza
	5	ARG	LRA12	R. Nal., Santo Tomé
	25	ARG	LRA10	R. Nal., Ushuaía
	10/5	ARG	LRF210	R. Tres "Cadene Patagoni", Trelew
		BOL		R. Sol, Santa Cruz
	10	CLM	C21	Antena del Río, Barrancabermeja
	10	CLM	ZG	LV del Valle, Cali
	30	CLM	ZW	R. Almirante, Riohacha
	10/2	EQA	CM1	R. Colón AM, Quito
	30	PRG	ZP70	R. Primero de Marzo, Asunción
	1	PRU	OBU2N	R. Coremarca, Bambamarca
	10	PRU	OAX1K	R. Nacional del Perú, Tumbes
	10	PRU	OAZ7S	R. Nuevo Tiempo, Juliaca
	3	PRU	OAX4X	R. Victoria,Lima
	50/20	VEN	OD	Ecos del Torbes, San Cristóbal
	15	VEN	MN	R. Coro, Coro
790	5	ARG	LV19	R. Malargüe
	25/5	ARG	LR6	R. Mitre "AM 80," Buenos Aires
	25/5	ARG	LRA22	R. Nal, San Salvador de Jujuy
	15	CLM	DC	Caracol R, Medellín
	1	CLM	NC	Ecos del Combeima, Ibagué
	50	CLM	ZR	R. Nal., Villavicencio
	50	CLM	BU	R. Nal., Zambrano
		EQA		R. Paraíso, Maldonado
		EQA		Su Radio 790 AM, Otavalo
	5	PRU	OAZ7H	R. La Luz, Cusco
	10	PRU	OAX2I	R. Programas del Perú, Trujillo
	50	VEN	XM	R. Minuto, Barquisimeto
	10	VEN	KC	R. Venezuela 790, Caracas
		VEN		RNV Canal Informativo, Cd. Bolívar
800	1/0.25	ARG	LT43	R. Mocoví, Charata
	1/0.25	ARG	LV23	R. Rio Atuel, General Alvear
	24/5	ARG	LU15	R. Viedma
	5	BOL		R. Libertad, La Paz
	5/1	CHL	CB80	R. Maria, Viña del Mar
	1	CLM	JH	R. Ciudad Milagro, Armenia
	100	CLM	BW	RCN, Bucaramanga
	25	EQA	ML2	K 800, Guayaquil

kHz	kW	Ctry	Call	Station, location
	5	EQA	FB1	R. Sensación 800, Quito
	5/3	PRG	ZP27	R. Mbaracayá, Salto del Guairá
	0.5	PRU	OAU4H	R. La Luz, Huaral
	0.3	PRU	OBX6A	R. Porteña, Arequipa
	1	PRU	OBX5B	R. Sur, Ica
	1	PRU	OBU4D	R. Vida, Huancayo
		PRU		R. Vision, Cajamarca
	1	PRU	OCX1P	Telecom del Norte, Piura
810		ARG		R. La Gauchita, Morón
	10/1	ARG		R. Mitre AM 810, Córdoba
	60	CLM	CY	Caracol R., Bogotá
	5	EQA	VT2	R. Atalaya, El Milagro
		EQA		Sucre Ambato, Ambato
	5	PRU	OAM7E	Cusco, Gregorio Huallapamayta Quispe
		PRU	OBU5E	Huamanga
	1	PRU	OAU2G	R. Apocali, Trujillo
	10	PRU	OAX7V	R. Programas del Perú, Juliaca
	50/25	URG	CX14	R. El Espectador, Montevideo
	50	VEN	PV	Super Radio 810, Valencia
820	5/1	ARG	LRI208	Estacion 820, Lomas de Zamora
	1/0.25	ARG	LRK221	R. Ciudad Perico, Perico
	25/5	ARG	LRA8	R. Nal., Formosa
	5/1	ARG	LU24	R. Tres Arroyos
	10	BOL		R. Altiplano, La Paz
	1	CHL	CD82	R. Concordia, La Unión
	1	CHL	CC82	R. Maria Inmaculada, Concepción
	10/1	CHL	CA82A	R. Portales, Santiago
	10/5	CHL	CB82	Radioem. Carabineros de Chile, Santiago
	50	CLM	ED	Caracol R., Cali
	10	CLM	AD	R. Vigía, Cartagena
	1	EQA	RF4	Canal Manabita, Portoviejo
	5	EQA	VI5	LV de Ingapirca, Cañar
	25	EQA	UP1	R. Unión, Quito
	20	PRU	OAX4O	R. Libertad, Lima
	0.5	PRU	OBX2J	R. Nuevo Continente, Cajamarca
		PRU	OBU1X	R. Vision, Piura
	1/0.5	URG	CW23	R. Cultural, Salto
	10	VEN	KU	R. Altura 820, La Grita
	25/10	VEN	XG	R. Guadalupana, Coro
	50	VEN	SH	R. Guayana, Upata
830	5	ARG		R. Del Pueblo, Buenos Aires
	1/0.5	ARG	LT21	R. Municipal, Alvear
	0.25	ARG	LV18	R. Municipal, San Rafael
	25	ARG	LU14	R. Provincia de Santa Cruz, Río Gallegos
	10/5	ARG	LT8	R. Rosario, Rosario
	15	CLM	DM	R. Reloj, Medellín
	25	EQA	RM2	R. Huancavilca, Guayaquil
	4.5	EQA	RP5	R. Promoción, Riobamba
	1	PRU	OAU4C	CPN R., El Tambo
	1	PRU	OCX2Y	CPN R., Trujillo
		PRU	OCU2M	R. Ebenezer, Bambamarca
	1	PRU	OAZ7U	R. Inti Raimi, Santiago
	1	PRU	OAX3Y	R. La Selva, Rupa-Rupa
	10	PRU	OAX6D	R. Nacional del Perú, Tacna
	25	VEN	LT	R. Nueva Sensación, Caracas
840	25/5	ARG	LU2	R. Bahía Blanca, Bahía Blanca
	3	ARG		R. General Belgrano, Buenos Aires
	10/5	ARG	LT12	R. General Madariaga, Paso de los Libres
	25/5	ARG	LV9	R. Salta AM 840, Salta
	3	BOL		R. Atipiri, El Alto
	10	CHL	CB84	R. Portales, Valparaíso
	10	CHL	CD84	R. Santa María, Coyhaique
	30	CLM	KK	H J Doble K, Neiva
	10	CLM	BI	Ondas del Caribe, Santa Marta
	1	EQA	EM4	R. Costa Azul, Portoviejo
	50	EQA	PN1	R. Vigía "LV de la Policía Nacional", Quito
	5	PRG	ZP6	R. Guairá, Villarrica
		PRU	OAU3Q	Casma
	1	PRU	OBX6Y	R. Azul, Arequipa
		PRU	OCU1C	R. Campesina
		PRU		R. Campesina, Cajamarca
		PRU		R. Campesina, Huari
	1	PRU	OAU2E	R. Nuevo Continente, San Ignacio
		PRU	OCU7I	R. Santa Cruz, Kunturkanki

kHz	kW	Ctry	Call	Station, location
	1	PRU	OAX3S	R. Vision, Casma
	10	VEN	MY	8-40 AM, Barquisimeto
	10/5	VEN	UZ	Guarapiche 8-40 "La Primera", Maturín
850	10	ARG		LV de Amérca, San Miguel Oeste
	5	BOL		R. María, Montero
	35	CLM	KC	W Radio, Bogotá
	20/12	EQA	VS2	R. San Francisco, Guayaquil
	40	PRU	OAX4A	R. Nacional del Perú, Lima
		PRU	OAU6S	R. Nacional del Peru, Tarata
		PRU	OBU7Z	R. Pachamama, Puno
		PRU		R. San Juan, El Tambo
	50	URG	CX16	R. Carve, Montevideo
	10	VEN	ZC	R. Fe y Alegría, Maracaibo
	10	VEN	RV	RV-850, Valencia
860		ARG		R. Digital, Lanus
	5/1	ARG		R. Municipal, Chilecito
	25	ARG	LRA56	R. Nal., Perito Moreno
	10	BOL		R.Nuava America, La Paz
	10	CHL	CC86	R. Inés de Suárez, Concepción
	50	CLM	NJ	W Radio, Valledupar
	10	EQA	PC1	R. Positiva AM, Quito
	25	PRG	ZP28	LV de la Cordillera, Caacupé
	5	PRU	OAU5Q	R. Educativo Macedonia, Ayacucho
		PRU	OAU2J	R. Nor Andina, Cajamarca
	3	PRU	OCX1M	R. Nuevo Norte, Sullana
	20/10	VEN	YE	Enlace 8-60, Valle de la Pascua
	10	VEN	OL	Mundial 8-60, San Cristóbal
870	100	ARG	LRA1	R. Nal., Buenos Aires
	1	CLM	GD	Em. Reina de Colombia, Chiquinquirá
	10	CLM	LA	LV del Tolima, Ibagué
	25	CLM	SB	R. Mar Caribe Int., Barranquilla
	5	CLM	ZH	Vida AM, Medellín
	20	EQA	NY2	R. Cristal "RCQ", Guayaquil
	1	EQA	GS6	R. Píllaro, Píllaro
	2.5	PRU	OCX4D	R. Huancayo, Huancayo
	5	PRU	OAU7O	R. Libertad, Puno
	1	PRU	OCX7R	R. Mundo, Wanchaq
	10	PRU	OBX1F	R. Programas del Perú, Chiclayo
	1	PRU	OAU1G	R. San Pedro Chanel, Sullana
	10	VEN	RU	Unión R. Deportes 870, Puerto La Cruz
	10	VEN	MP	Unión R. Notícias, Barquisimeto
880	10	ARG	LU14	R. Provincia de Santa Cruz, Las Heras
		ARG		R. Provincial de Sierra Colorada, Sierra Colorada (F.P.I.)
		ARG		Radiar AM 880, ZS GBA
		BOL		R. Inca, El Alto
		BOL		Rdif. Oriente, Santa Cruz
	10	CHL	CB88	R. Colo Colo, Santiago
	20	CLM	GE	Caracol R, Bucaramanga
	10	CLM	FH	R. Regional Independiente, Anserma
	50/40	EQA	RP1	R. Católica Nacional, Quito
		PRU	OBU5W	Huamanga, Augusto Palomino Ramos
	1	PRU	OAX2P	R. Sintonia, Trujillo
	10	PRU	OBZ4N	R. Union, Lima
	10	VEN		R. Paraguaná, Punto Fijo
	20/10	VEN	ZD	R. Venezuela Barinas, Barinas
	20/10	VEN	YM	R. Venezuela Guayana, Puerto Ordaz
	10	VEN	KV	RNV Canal Musical, Caracas
890	25/5	ARG	LV11	Em. Santiago del Estero, Santiago del Estero
	25/5	ARG	LU33	Emisora Pampeana, Santa Rosa
		ARG		R.Libre, San Justo
	10	CHL	CC89	R. Interamericana, Concepción
	20	CHL	CD89	R. Nal., Punta Arenas
	10	CLM	CE	R. Continental, Bogotá
	0.25	CLM	HKO93	R. Ecos de Soledad, Soledad
	20	CLM	PM	R. Galeón, Santa Marta
	1	EQA	TL5	Ondas del Chimborazo, Riobamba
	25/20	EQA	RS3	R. Superior, Machala
	5/0.5	PRG	ZP33	R. Tres de Febrero, Itá
	1	PRU	OBX7S	R. Bahá´í del Lago Titicaca, Chiucuito
		PRU	OCU7C	R. Laramani, Espinar
	1	PRU	OAU2N	R. Panorama, Cajamarca
	25	URG	CX18	R. Sport 890, Montevideo

kHz	kW	Ctry	Call	Station, location
	25	VEN	LW	R. América, Valencia
	10	VEN	VO	R. Oriente, El Tigre
900	1	ARG		R. Municipal, 25 de Mayo
	25/5	ARG	LT7	R. Provincia de Corrientes, Corrientes
	0.25	BOL		R. LV Nacional, Tarija
	5/0.1	BOL		R. Popular, La Paz
	1	CHL	CB90	Cablenoticias, Valparaíso
	1	CHL	CD90	R. LV de la Costa, Osorno
	1	CHL	CC90	R. Mayor, Chillán
	10	CLM	EY	LV de Cali, Cali
	10	CLM	DD	RCN Fiesta, Cúcuta
	1	EQA	RR5	R. Carrusel, Cuenca
	5	EQA	OF4	R. Chone, Chone
	10	EQA	VA1	Sucre Quito, Quito
	1	PRU	OCU1P	Huarmaca
	10	PRU	OBX4X	R. Felicidad, Lima
	1	PRU	OBX6K	R. Nevada, Uchumayo
	1	PRU	OAU2Q	R. Nor Oriental, Jaén
		PRU	OAX3E	R. Ribereña, Aucaycu
	1	PRU	OCX1D	R. Sensacional, Ferreñafe
	3	URG	CW17	R. Frontera, Artigas
	25	VEN	MD	R. Venezuela Mara Ritmo, Maracaibo
902	1	BOL		R. Central Misionera, Cochabamba
910	150	ARG	LR5	R. La Red, Buenos Aires
	50/5	ARG	LRA23	R. Nal.,San Juan
		CHL	CC91	R. Tropical Latina (RTL), Talca
	15	CLM	S52	Colombia Estereo, Florencia
	10	CLM	DO	LV del Rio Grande, Medellín
	1	CLM	TT	Ondas del Porvenir, Samacá
	30	CLM	MY	RCN, San Andrés
	2	EQA	BO2	Colón AM,Guayaquil
	5	EQA	GE5	R. Mundial, Riobamba
	1	PRU	OAU5M	R. Estacion Wari, Ayacucho
	1	PRU	OAU7M	R. Regional, Sicuani
	1	PRU	OAU7G	R. Vision del Altiplano, Juliaca
	50/20	VEN	RQ	R. AM Center, Caracas
920		BOL		R. Bartolina Sisa, El Alto
		BOL		R. El Mana, Santa Cruz
	3	BOL		R. Encuentro, Sucre
	1	BOL		R. San Andres de Topohoco, Topohoco
	1	CHL	CD92	R. 920, Temuco
	10	CLM	SJ	Colmundo, Ibagué
	10	CLM	AA	Em. Fuentes, Cartagena
	10	CLM	JN	Ondas del Mayo, Pasto
	10	EQA	RU3	CRO - Compañia Radiofónica Orense, Machala
	1	EQA	AB1	R. Demócracia "La Cariñosa", Quito
	100	PRG	ZP1	R. Nal. del Paraguay, Asunción
		PRU		R. Campesina, Juli
	1	PRU	OAX9V	R. Marginal, Tocache
	1	PRU	OBX2S	R. Ollantay, Virú
	1	PRU	OCX7H	R. Programas del Perú, Cusco
	10	PRU	OBX1J	R. Programas del Peru, Piura
	0.1	PRU	OCX5C	R. Stelar, Chinca Alta
		PRU	OAM2G	R. Vision, Samangay
	20	VEN	QX	R. Nueva Esparta, Porlamar
	10/5	VEN	QU	R. San Carlos, San Carlos
930		ARG		R. Nativa - "LV de Nuestra Gente", Ciudad Madero
	25/5	ARG	LV7	R. Tucumán, San Miguel de Tucumán
	5/1	ARG	LV28	R. Villa María, Villa María
	10	CHL	CB93	R. Nuevo Mundo, Santiago
	10	CHL	CD93	R. Reloncaví, Puerto Montt
	10	CLM	CS	LV de Bogotá, Bogotá
	5	EQA	VI2	Canal Tropical, Guayaquil
	5	EQA	BA6	R. Ambato, Ambato
	1	PRU	OAM7J	Espinar
	3	PRU	OCU1U	Olmos
		PRU	OBU7T	R. Cadena Colca, Juliaca
	1	PRU	OCX2V	R. Inti, Chepén
	5	PRU	OAX4E	R. Moderna, Lima
	2.5	PRU	OBX6T	R. Yaravi, Arequipa
	50	URG	CX20	R. Monte Carlo, Montevideo
	10	VEN	LJ	R. Maracay, Maracay

kHz	kW	Ctry	Call	Station, location
940	3/5	ARG	LRH200	R. Chajarí, Chajarí
	20/5	ARG	LRJ241	R. Dimensión, San Luís
	1	BOL		R. Chuquisaca XXI, Sucre
		BOL		R. Metropolitana, La Paz
		CHL	CC94	R. Armonia, Viña del Mar
	1	CHL	CB94	R. Valentín Letelier, Valparaíso
	5	CLM	A76	Frecuencia U, Medellín
	10	CLM	GB	R. Calima, Cali
	25	CLM	TL	RCN, Cúcuta
		EQA		R. Austral del Ecuador, Cuenca
	5	EQA	BZ1	R. Dif. de la Casa de la Cultura Ecuatoriana, Quito
	1	PRU	OBU4E	R. Comericial, Jauja
	1	PRU	OBX2G	R. R.Cutervo, Cutervo
	1	PRU	OBU1Y	R. Studio Satelite, Tambo Grande
	1.5	PRU	OBX7L	W.R., Wanchaq
	15	VEN	ZR	R. Continental, Barinas
	10	VEN	LU	R. Fe y Alegría El Tigre, El Tigre
	10	VEN	NN	R. Punto Fijo, Punto Fijo
950	25/5	ARG	LR3	R. 9am - La Deportiva, Buenos Aires
	25/5	ARG	LT16	RSP - R. Sáenz Peña (Cadena Eco), Roque Saénz Peña
	5	CLM	UJ	Armonias Boyacenses, Tunja
	15	CLM	FN	Caracol R, Pereira
		EQA		Chaskis del Norte, Ibarra
	10	EQA	DE2	GRD R. Internacional, Guayaquil
	3	EQA	UE5	R. Colta "LV de la Asociación", Colta
	1	PRU	ODU5R	Cutabambas
	1	PRU	OBX9L	R. Estacón Láser, Rioja
	1	PRU	OBX3S	R. Programas del Perú, Chimbote
	50	VEN	KG	AM Popular, Caracas
960	25/5	ARG	LRA6	R. Nal., Mendoza
	10/1	ARG	LU13	R. Necochea, Necochea
	1	BOL		R. Kollasuyo, Potosí
	10	BOL		R. Santa Cruz, Santa Cruz
	10	CHL	CB96	R. Carrera, Santiago
	10	CHL	CD96	R. Polar, Punta Arenas
	5	CLM	HX	Candela AM, Bucaramanga
	15	CLM	R31	Candela, San Andrés
	10	CLM	HN	Caracol R, Magangué
	1	EQA	NC1	La Pantera, Quito
	1	EQA	JX6	LV del Santuario, Baños
	1	EQA	SA5	Sono Onda Internacional, Cuenca
		PRU	OBU7P	R. Concierto Santa Monica, Espinar
	1	PRU	OBX8H	R. Diez, Iquitos
	12	PRU	OBX6S	R. Hispania, Mariano Melgar
	1	PRU	OCY4V	R. Manantial, Huancayo
	10	PRU	OAX4D	R. Panamericana, Lima
	3	PRU	OBX1Y	R. WSP, Chiclayo:
	2/1	URG	CW96	R. Yi, Durazno
	50/20	VEN	RB	R. Monagas, Maturín
	10	VEN	SS	R. San Sebastián, San Cristóbal
	25	VEN		R. Venezuela Llanera, Acarigua
962	1	BOL		R. Huayna Potosí, Milluni
965	10	EQA	OT1	R. Católica Nacional, Sto Domingo de los Colorados
970	25/5	ARG	LV2	R. General Paz "AM 970", Córdoba
		ARG		R. Génesis, Buenos Aires
	1/0.25	ARG	LT25	R. Guaraní, Curuzú Cuatiá
	1	CHL	CD97	R. Austral, Valdivia
	1	CHL	CA97	R. Calama, Calama
	1	CHL	CC97	R. Lautaro, Talca
	1	CHL	CD97A	R. Patagonia Chilena, Coyhaique
	15	CLM	VK	Armonias del Caquetá, Florencia
	1	CLM	HKX59	Ecos del Cacique, Calarca
	10	CLM	CI	R. Super, Bogotá
	10	CLM	ME	RCN Guajira, Maicao
	20	EQA	AW2	R. Católica Nal. del Ecuador, Guayaquil
	1	EQA	MB1	R. Imperio, Ibarra
	80	PRG	ZP9	R. 9-70 , Asunción
	1	PRU	OBX5A	R. Comericial Sonora, Ica
	1	PRU	OBX1V	R. La Capullana, Sullana
	1	PRU	OAU2K	R. Lider del Norte, Cajamarca
	1	PRU	OBU7B	R. Qollasuyo, Juliaca

kHz	kW	Ctry	Call	Station, location
	1	PRU	OAU7A	R. Tropicana, Wanchaq
	20/3	URG	CX22	R. Universal, Montevideo
	10	VEN		Mundial 970, Barcelona
	10	VEN	LR	R. Continente 970, Maracay
	15	VEN	SD	R. Turismo, Valera
980		ARG		F.Pl., Rio Gallegos
	3/1	ARG	LU37	R. General Pico "Radio37",
	1	ARG	LRG387	R. Luján AM, Valcheta
	2/1	ARG		R. Regional, San Miguel
	5	ARG	LT39	R. Victoria, Victoria
	3	BOL		R. Esperanza, Aiquile
		BOL		R. La Bohemia, Sucre
	2.5	BOL		R. Mar, La Paz
	5	CHL	CB98	R. Agricultura, Valparaíso
	15	CLM	JV	Bésame, Cúcuta
	100	CLM	ES	RCN, Cali
	5	EQA	CL3	R. Cariamanga, Cariamanga
	1	EQA	JI5	R. El Prado, Riobamba
	5	PRG	ZP31	R. Mburucuyú, Pedro Juan Caballero
	1	PRU	OCX2R	Andina R., Chota
		PRU	OBU1N	R. Campesina, Huancabamba
		PRU		R. Campesina, Tarata
		PRU	OAX5K	R. LV de Huamanga, Huamanga
	1	PRU	OBU4H	R. OBU4H, Huancayo
	1	PRU	OAU1N	R. Primavera, Chiclayo
	1	PRU	OAU6F	R. Universidad, Arequipa
	10	VFN	QM	Unión R. Notícias, El Tigre
990	25/5	ARG	LRH203	AM 990, Formosa
	1	ARG	LRJ201	R. Calingasta, Tamberías
	26/5	ARG	LN4	R. Splendid AM 990, Villa Domínico
	5	CLM	HI	LV de Garagoa, Garagoa
	50	CLM	CH	RCN, Medellín
	15	EQA	EW2	Frecuencia Mil, Guayaquil
	25	EQA	GH1	R. Tarquí, Quito
		PRU	OCU4A	Huayllay
	10	PRU	OAX6K	R. Continental, Tacna
	0.5	PRU	OBX2M	R. Contumaza, Contumaza
	12	PRU	OBX4J	R. Latina, Miraflores
	1	PRU	OBU1C	R. OBU1C, Sechuar
		PRU	OBX3L	R. Peruana, Chimbote
	20	VEN	RT	R. Tropical "99-0", Caracas
	10	VEN	TA	R. Venezuela Tricolor, Barquisimeto
1000	5/1	ARG		Comodoro Rivadavia (F.Pl.)
	1/0.25	ARG	LT42	R. Del Iberá, Mercedes
	1/0.25	ARG	LU16	R. Río Negro, Villa Regina
		ARG		R.Sintonia, José C.Paz
	10	BOL		R. Bahá'í de Bolivia, Caracollo
		BOL		R. LV del Arrebatamiento , Guaqui
	1	BOL		R. Mística, La Paz
	1	BOL		Rdif, Oriente, Santa Cruz
	10	CHL	CB100	BBN Radio, Santiago
		CHL	CD100	Nuevo Mundo, Punta Arenas
	10	CLM	JG	R. Nal., Manizales
	50	CLM	ZP	R. Nal., Yopal
	0.8	CLM		R. Panamericana, Cajibío
	15	CLM	AQ	RCN, Cartagena
	20	CLM	Q98	Vida AM, San José del Guaviare
	1	EQA	NT3	Dinamita Mil AM, Catamayo
	5/0.5	PRG	ZP36	R. Mil, San Antonio
	2	PRU	OAU2P	R. Bambamarca, Bambamarca
	1	PRU	OBX6R	R. Edesa, Paucarpata
		PRU	OBX3V	R. Huanuco
	1	PRU	OBX5W	R. Lircay, Lircay
	2	PRU	OAZ7P	R. Prensa al Dia, Cusco
	1	PRU	OAU1P	R. San Jose, Lambayque
	10	VEN	NM	R. Caribeña Mil AM, Morón
	10	VEN	OA	R. Táchira, San Cristóbal
1010	1/0.25	ARG	LW2	R. Emis. Tartagal
		ARG		R. Onda Latina, Buenos Aires
	20/10	ARG	LV16	R. Rio Cuarto, Rio Cuarto
	15	CLM	JR	Caracol R, Neiva
	10/5	CLM	BN	LV del Galeras, Pasto
	10	CLM	OP	Oxígeno, Barranquilla
	15	CLM	ZD	R. Panzenú, Montería

kHz	kW	Ctry	Call	Station, location
	10	CLM	CC	R. Reloj, Bogotá
	10	CLM	IX	R. Yarima, Barrancabermeja
	3	EQA	RZ2	R. Amiga, Guayaquil
	2.5	EQA	RV5	R. Visión AM, Cuenca
	15	EQA	NR6	TSB R. Líder, Ambato
		PRU	OBU1L	LV de las Huaringas, Huancabamba
	1	PRU	OAU5G	R. Amistad, Abancay
		PRU		R. Bella, Tingo Maria
	10	PRU	OAX4U	R. Cielo, Lima
		PRU	OBX9T	R. Ministerio Mundial, Utcubamba
	1.5	PRU	OBX2P	R. San Francisco, Cajamarca
	1	PRU	OBZ1C	R. Sonora, Tumbes
	20	URG	CX24	R. 1010AM, Montevideo
	10	VEN	PC	R. Aragua, Cagua
	10	VEN	QF	R. Venezuela Bolívar, Cd. Bolívar
1020	25/5	ARG	LRJ214	AM Mil 20 - La R. de la Gente, San Juan
	1	ARG	LRA58	R. Nacional, Río Mayo
	10/5	ARG	LT10	R. Univ. Nal. del Litoral, Santa Fé
		BOL		R. Illimani - R.Patria Nueva, Achacachi
		BOL		R. Illimani - R.Patria Nueva, Aiquila
		BOL		R. Illimani - R.Patria Nueva, Bermejo
		BOL		R. Illimani - R.Patria Nueva, Camiri
		BOL		R. Illimani - R.Patria Nueva, Carabuco
		BOL		R. Illimani - R.Patria Nueva, Caranavi
		BOL		R. Illimani - R.Patria Nueva, Catavi
		BOL		R. Illimani - R.Patria Nueva, Chapare
		BOL		R. Illimani - R.Patria Nueva, Chulumani
		BOL		R. Illimani - R.Patria Nueva, Cochabamba
		BOL		R. Illimani - R.Patria Nueva, Copacabana
		BOL		R. Illimani - R.Patria Nueva, Guaqui
		BOL		R. Illimani - R.Patria Nueva, Kami
	10	BOL		R. Illimani - R.Patria Nueva, La Paz
		BOL		R. Illimani - R.Patria Nueva, Oruro
		BOL		R. Illimani - R.Patria Nueva, Potosi
		BOL		R. Illimani - R.Patria Nueva, San Borja
		BOL		R. Illimani - R.Patria Nueva, Santa Cruz
		BOL		R. Illimani - R.Patria Nueva, Sucre
		BOL		R. Illimani - R.Patria Nueva, Tarija
		BOL		R. Illimani - R.Patria Nueva, Trinidad
		BOL		R. Illimani - R.Patria Nueva, Valle Alto
		BOL		R. Illimani - R.Patria Nueva, Vallegrande
		BOL		R. Illimani - R.Patria Nueva, Yapacani
		BOL		R. Illimani - R.Patria Nueva, Tarata
	5	CHL	CC102	R. Amiga, Talca
	10	CLM	DQ	Emisora Claridad, Medellín
	10	CLM	KS	LV del Llano, Villavicencio
	15	CLM	DZ	R. Primavera, Bucaramanga
	10	CLM	FT	R. Super, Ibagué
	10	CLM	FQ	RCN, Pereira
	5/3	EQA	CR6	R. Surcos, Guaranda
	5	EQA	HR1	RTU
	25	PRG	ZP14	R. Ñandutí, Asunción
	2	PRU	OAU2P	R. Bambamarca, Bambamarca
	1	PRU	OBU4F	R. Cristo Vive, Huancayo
	5	PRU	OBX1G	R. Heroica, Chiclayo
	1	PRU	OBU7O	R. Informes, Sicuani
	1	PRU	OAU6J	R. Internacional, Tacna
	1	PRU	OBU1D	R. La Luz, Piura
	1	PRU	OBX3U	R. Nacional, Chimbote
	0.1	URG	CW102	R. Libertadores, Salto
	25	VEN	TW	R. Alegría, Chivacoa
	50/10	VEN	MX	R. Calendario Zulia, Maracaibo
	10	VEN	RS	R. Mundial Margarita, La Asunción
1030	25/5	ARG	LS10	R. del Plata, Buenos Aires
		BOL		R. Comunitaria Colquechaca (RPO), Colquechaca
		BOL		R. Comunitaria Mojocoya (RPO), Mojocoya
	3	BOL		R. Comunitaria Orinaca (RPO), Orinaca
	3	BOL		R. Comunitaria Riberalte - RPO, Riberalta
	3	BOL		R. Independencia, Ayopaya (RPO)
		BOL		R. Totora (RPO) Totora
		CHL	CC103	R. Chilena, Concepción
	1	CHL	CD103	R. Chiloé, Castro
	1	CHL	CD103A	R. Payne AM, Puerto Natales
	1	CHL	CB103	R. Progreso, Talagante
	1	CLM	GX	CARACOL, Lorica
	15	CLM	RF	Ondas del Cesar, Aguachica
	5	CLM		Ondas del Vaupés, Mitú
	30	CLM	DT	RCN Antena 2, Cali
	10	CLM	DJ	RCN LV de los Libertadores, Duitama
	5	EQA	RF2	R. Punto 1030/Ecuantena, Guayaquill
	1	PRU	OCX6L	R. Cumbia, Arequipa
	1	PRU	OCX7O	R. HG-AM, Cusco
	3	PRU	OAX2U	R. Los Andes, Huamachuco
	1	PRU	OAX7N	R. LV del Altiplano, Puno
		PRU		R. Sillustani, Atuncolla
	20	VEN	QY	R. Onda 1030, Guanare
	25/10	VEN	TD	R. Valles del Tuy, Ocumare del Tuy
1040		BOL		R. 12 de Marzo (RPO), Tarabuco
	0.25	BOL		R. Atlántida, Oruro
	1	BOL		R. Bolivianíssima, La Paz
		BOL		R. Comunitaria Libertad (RPO), Villamontes
		BOL		R. Comunitaria Qaqachaca (RPO), Qaqachaca
		BOL		R. Comunitaria San Juan (RPO), San Julián
		BOL		R. Nanduti (RPO), Camiri
		BOL		R. San José (RPO), San José de Chiquitos
	0.25	BOL		R. Sipe Sipe, Quillacollo
	1	CHL	CD104	R. Raíces, Curacautín
	15	CLM	CJ	Colmundo, Bogotá
	15	CLM	UB	Colmundo, Pasto
	15	CLM	FM	LV de Armenia, Armenia
	15	CLM	BF	LV del Norte, Cúcuta
	10	CLM	SY	R. 1040/La Caucana 10-40, Popayán
	15	CLM	AI	R. Tropical, Barranquilla
	3	EQA	CW1	LV del Valle, Machachi
	3	EQA	GB6	R. Colosal, Ambato
	10/5	EQA	EV5	R. Splendit, Cuenca
	5	PRG	ZP43	R. Arapisandú, San Ignacio
	1	PRU	OAU7H	Multimedio Sistena de R., Espinar
	1	PRU	OBX5U	R. La Luz, Ica
	10	PRU	OBX4O	R. Metropolitiana, Miraflores
	1	PRU	OBX2O	R. Nor Oriente, Jaén
	1	PRU	OAZ1D	R. Vecinal, Piura
	20	VEN	LB	LV de Carabobo, Valencia
	20/10	VEN	ON	Mundial Los Andes, Mérida
1050	1.3	ARG		R. General Güemes "La Radio Mundial", Villa Lynch
	10	ARG	LV27	R. San Francisco - LV de San Justo, San Francisco
		BOL		R. Comunitaria Caiza (RPO), Caiza D
		BOL		R. Em.Comunitaria (RPN), Independencia
	3	BOL		R. Sabaya (RPN) Sabaya
	1	CHL	CD105	R. Armonía, Osorno
	10	CLM	BB	Caracol R, Valledupar
	15	CLM	S62	Cusiana R., Yopal
	10	CLM	FZ	La Cariñosa del Centro, Espinal
	5	CLM	IO	LV de la Conquista, Granada
	10	CLM	E73	LV del Cinaruco/Caracol, Arauca
	10	CLM	GU	R. Bucarica, Bucaramanga
	5	CLM	NG	R. Palmira, Palmira
	10	CLM	DR	R. Unica, Medellín
	5/3	EQA	IM1	LV de Imbabura, Ibarra
	5	EQA	RQ2	R. Águila, Guayaqui
	1	PRU	OBX8F	CPN R., Iquitos
	3	PRU	OCU1C	R. Bendición Cristiana, Chiclayo
	1	PRU	OBX6D	R. Bethel, Arequipa
	1	PRU	OBZ4J	R. Bolognesi, Huancayo
		PRU		R. Campesina, Cajamarca
	1	PRU	OCX2B	R. Maria, Chepen
	1	PRU	OAZ7Q	R. San Augustín, Juliaca
	25	URG	CX26	S.O.D.R.E. "R.Uruguay", Montevideo
	25	VEN	KZ	RNV "R. Educativa", Caracas
	20	VEN	PO	RNV Canal Informativo, Cabudare
1058	5	PRU	OAU1C	CPN R., Tumbes
1060		ARG		R. Las Naciones, Monte Grande
	1	BOL		R. Dif. Colosal, Sucre
	10	BOL		R. Eco Loyola, La Paz
	1.5	BOL		R. Noticias, Oruro

kHz	kW	Ctry	Call	Station, location
		BOL		R. Quana, Caranavi
	50	CHL	CB106	R. Maria, Santiago
	1	CLM	YX	Caracoli, Sincelejo
	10	CLM	LY	R. Delfín, Riohacha
	10	CLM	MV	R. Furatena, Chiquinquirá
	1	CLM	MG	R. Litoral, Turbo
	15	CLM	OV	R. Surcolombiana, Neiva
	15	CLM	FJ	RCN Caldas, Manizales
	5	EQA	MG6	R. Ecos del Pueblo, Saquisilí
		EQA		R. Fiesta, Machala
		EQA		R. Richi, El Empalme
	3	PRU	OAU3S	Angelica Julian Human Lourdes, Chimbote
	5	PRU	OAU1C	CPN R., Tumbes
		PRU	OAU7U	R. 1060, Cusco
		PRU	OBU1F	R. 1060. Piura
	1	PRU	OCY4D	R. Exito, Lima
		PRU	OAU6R	R. La Luz, Ilo
	5	PRU	OCY2O	R. Sudamerica, Cutervo
	10	VEN	LN	R. Guárico, San Juan de los Morros
	10	VEN	OE	Unión R. Noticias, San Cristóbal
1070	25/5	ARG	LR1	R. El Mundo, Buenos Aires
	20	CLM	AH	Em. Atlántico, Barranquilla
	30	CLM	CG	R. Santa Fé, Bogotá
	15	CLM	VR	R. Super, Popayán
	1	EQA	VP1	R. Libertad, Quito
	1	EQA	RS1	R. Lubakán, Santo Domingo de los Colorados
	5	EQA	CJ5	R. LV de Tomebamba, Cuenca
	1	PRU	OAU3N	Huánuco
	3	PRU	OBX9J	R. Andes, Tarapoto
	0.2	PRU	OAX5A	R. San Juan, San Juan de Marcona
	1	PRU	OAU6K	R. Trinidad, Arequipa
	1	PRU	OAU1J	R. Vida, Chiclayo
	1	PRU	OBX4G	R. Visión, San Ramón
	25	VEN		Contacto 1070, Ospino
	10	VEN	MA	Mundial Zulia, Maracaibo
	5	VEN	PX	R. El Sol, La Fría
	10	VEN		Superior 1070 Biruaca, S. Fernando de Apure
1080	25/5	ARG	LU3	Ondas del Sur, Bahía Blanca
		ARG		R. Claridad, Monte Grande
	25/5	ARG	LW4	R. Orán/R.Maria
		BOL		LV de la Mayoria, Caranavi
	1	CHL	CD108	R. Los Confines, Angol
	1	CHL	CA108	R. Río Elqui, Vicuña
	10	CLM	AX	LV de la Nostalgia, Medellín
	10	CLM	AW	LV de Montería, Montería
	10	CLM	AW	LV de Montería, Montería
	10	CLM	MH	Melodía AM, Floridablanca
	10	CLM	KT	R. Autentica, Villavicencio
	10	CLM	JF	R. Eco, Cali
	15	CLM	JS	R. Pontoná, La Dorada
	1	EQA	AB4	R. Contacto, Manta
	10	EQA	BH6	R. Latacunga AM, Latacunga
	10	EQA	KD2	Sistema 2, Guayaquil
	10	PRG	ZP25	R. Monumental, Luque
		PRU	OCU7O	R. 1080, Puno
	1	PRU	OCX6X	R. Futura, Ilo
	10	PRU	OAU4I	R. La Luz, Lima
	1	PRU	OAU2L	R. Nueva Vida, Cajamarca
	2.2	PRU	OAX7S	R. Salkantay, Cusco
	1.5	PRU	OBX1D	R. San Miguel, Piura
	10	VEN	QJ	R. Barcelona, Barcelona
	10	VEN	NR	R. Venezuela Universal, Maracay
1090	0.5	ARG		Libertad AM 1100, Rosario
		ARG		R. Décadas, Hurlingham
	2	ARG		R. Popular, Valentín Alsina
		BOL		R. Cliza (RPN), Cliza
		BOL		R. Comunitaria Pachakuti
	3	BOL		R. Cultura, Cochabamba
	5/1	CHL	CC	R. Chilena (R. Familia), Talca
	15	CLM	BC	Caracol R, Cúcuta
	8	CLM	IH	Caracol R, Sogamoso
	5	CLM	OM	Fuego AM, Cartagena
	10	CLM	JB	HJ Doble K, Libano
	10	CLM	IA	Oxígeno, Manizales
	10	CLM	IG	R. Autentica, Florencia
	5	EQA	VI1	R. Irfeyal "Fe y Alegría", Quito
	1	PRU	OBX6X	R. Amistad, Arequipa
	1	PRU	OBX2A	R. Cajabamba, Cajabamba
	1	PRU	OAU5F	R. Inti Andina, Aucara
	15	URG	CX28	R. Imparcial, Montevideo
	20	VEN	SZ	Deportes Unión R., Caracas
	3	VEN	TG	Melódica 1090, Machiques
	10	VEN	PB	R. Yaracuy "Operadora 1090 AM", S. Felipe
1100	1.3	ARG		R. Estilo, Glew
		BOL		R. Cultural Chaka, Pucarani
	1	BOL		R. Universidad de Oruro
	10	CHL	CB110	BBN Radio, Viña del Mar
	10	CLM	CN	BBN R, Bogotá
	15	CLM	AT	Caracol R, Barranquilla
	5	CLM	MK	Emisora Ideal, Planeta Rica
	1	CLM	GI	LV de Colombia, Socorro
	2	CLM	EF	LV del Vichada, Puerto Carreño
	15	CLM	YZ	R. Uno, Neiva
	5	CLM	GQ	Transmisora Surandes, Andes
	5/2	EQA	GR6	R. Novedades, Latacunga
	1.5	EQA	LE7	R. Oriental, Tena
	5	PRG	ZP71	R. Ñú Verá, Capitán Bado
		PRU	OCU2E	R. 1000, Julcan
		PRU	OCX4S	R. Imperial, Cañete
	1	PRU	OBX7Z	R. LTC, Juliaca
	1	PRU	OAZ4W	R. Programas del Peru, Barranca
	1	PRU	OBX1L	R. Star, Chiclayo
	1	PRU	OCY4G	Sonorama R., Huancayo
	10	VEN	SV	R. Angostura, Cd.Bolívar
	10	VEN	OP	R. Occidente, Tovar
1110	25/5	ARG	LS1	R. de la Ciudad, Buenos Aires
	10	CHL	CD111	R. La Frontera, Temuco
	1	CLM	PA	LV de las Islas, San Andrés
	5	CLM	GP	LV del Río Arauca, Arauca
	10	CLM	EW	Oxígeno, Cali
	9	CLM	DI	R. Bolivariana, Medellín
	15	CLM	ZE	R. Piragua, Sincelejo
	10	CLM	JP	RCN, Villavicencio
	10	EQA	JR1	R. Clásica, Quito
	5	EQA	JC5	R. Ondas Azuayas, Cuenca
	5	EQA	RP6	R. Pelileo, Pelileo
	1	PRU	OCX6F	R. Austral, Ilo
	0.5	PRU	OCX1R	R. Centro Popular, La Union
	5	PRU	OCX7T	R. Comer, Cusco
	1	PRU	OAZ4W	R. Feliz, Lima
	1	PRU	OCX2U	R. Jaén, Jaén
	3	URG	CX111	R. Paso de los Toros, Paso de los Toros
	10	VEN	RX	Deportes Unión R., Valencia
	10	VEN	QT	R. Venezuela Carúpano, Carúpano
1120		ARG		AM Tango, Buenos Aires
		ARG		Em. Santiago y Copla, Gregoria de Laferrere
	25/5	ARG	LV5	R. Sarmiento, San Juan
		ARG		R.Sudamericana, San Martin
		BOL		R. Celestial El Milagro, El Alto
		BOL		R. El Porvenir, Tiquipaya
	1.5	BOL		R. Norte, Montero
		BOL		R. Wiñay Khantatt, Tiahuanacu
	10	CLM	KQ	Bésame, Tunja
	5	CLM	Q92	Colombia Mía, Yopal, CS
	15	CLM	GH	Oxígeno, Bucaramanga
	5	CLM	JC	R. Matecaña, Pereira
	10	CLM	TI	Vox Dei, Cúcuta
	2	EQA	EB1	Canal 1120, San Gabriel
	5	EQA	FV2	Estación Intercontinental, Guayaquil
	3	EQA	AS7	R. Variedades del Puyo, El Puyo
	10	PRG	ZP24	R. Nuevo Mundo, San Lorenzo
		PRU	OAM2F	R. Dif. Cultura, Chota
	1	PRU	OAU5H	R. Dif. Sonora Comunal - R. Quispillaccta,
	1.5	PRU	OBX2I	R. Dinamica, Trujillo
		PRU	OAU5W	R. Huayllahuara
	1	PRU	OCX6U	R. Municipal, Cerro Colorado
		PRU	OBX8R	Rios Perez Zosimo, Campoverde

kHz	kW	Ctry	Call	Station, location
	10	URG	CW31	R. Salto, Salto
	10	VEN	MF	Ondas del Lago "Super Ondas", Maracaibo
	20/10	VEN	SK	R. Dif.del Sur, San Fernando de Apure
	5	VEN	XZ	R. República "La Estación Feliz", Maturín
1130		ARG		AM 1130 El Manantial, Buenos Aires
	10	ARG		R. Cadena Vida, Buenos Aires
	5/1	ARG	LRG203	R. Capital "Antena 10", Santa Rosa
	25/5	ARG	LRA21	R. Nal., Santiago del Estero
		ARG		R.Popular, Buenos Aires
	10	CLM	AC	Em. Riomar, Barranquilla
	1	CLM	NN	Ondas del Río, Magangué
	10	CLM	QQ	Oxígeno, Pasto
	15	CLM	VA	Vida AM, Bogotá
	5	EQA	PV6	R. Centro, Ambato
	5/3	EQA	RD1	R. Punto, Ibarra
		EQA		R. Sibimbe AM, Ventanas
		EQA		Romántica AM, Machala
	3	PRU	OBU6Q	Angelica Julian Human Lourdes, Moquegua
	5	PRU	OAM7F	Cusco
		PRU	OCU1R	Huarmaca
	1	PRU	OAU5A	R. Armonia, Abancay
	2.6	PRU	OAX4N	R. Bacán, Lince
	1	PRU	OAZ4S	R. Chanchamayo, Chanchamayo
	1.2	PRU	OAX2V	R. Los Andes
	1	PRU	OAU7B	R. San Gabriel, Juliaca
	20	URG	CX30	R. Nacional, Montevideo
	15	VEN	PY	R. Amazonas, Puerto Ayacucho
	20/10	VEN	RL	R. Ideal, Maiquetía
	10	VEN	KQ	R. Popular, Barquisimeto
1140		ARG		R. Independencia, Lanús
		ARG		R. La Luna, El Palomar
	10/1	ARG	LU22	R. Tandil, Tandil
	2	BOL		R. Pico Verde, Chulumani
		BOL		R. Sol Poder de Dios, Huanca
		BOL		R. Sol Poder de Dios, La Paz
	75	CHL	CB114	R. Nal., Santiago
	10	CLM	E67	Caracol R, Villavicencio
	10	CLM	KO	R. Esperanza, Cartagena
	10	CLM	DL	R. Paisa, Medellín
	10	CLM	CL	R. Panamericana, Girardot
		CLM		R. Piendamo, Piendamo
	10	CLM	RN	RCN, Barbosa
	1	EQA	AZ5	R. Alfa Musical, Cuenca
	1.5	EQA	FB2	R. Cóndor, Guayaquil
	4	EQA	MF4	R. Rumbos, Portoviejo
	5	EQA	IR1	Raíz 11-40, Quito
	5/2	PRG	CP22	R. Central de Notícias, Atyrá
		PRU	OCU2D	Chami R., Otuzco
	1	PRU	OAX3R	R. Bahia, Chimbote
	0.5	PRU	OAX5W	R. Chinchaysuyo, Chinca Alta
	1	PRU	OAX6L	R. Concordia, Arequipa
		PRU	OAU1T	R. Fraternal, Ferreñafe
	1.5	PRU	OBX1W	R. Piura, Piura
	1	PRU	OCY4C	R. Programas del Perú, Pilcomayo
		VEN		R. Porlamar "LV del Caribe", Porlamar
1150	60	ARG	LT9	R. Brigadier López, Santa Fé
	5	ARG	LRA51	R. Nal., Jáchal
	25	ARG	LRA2	R. Nal., Viedma
	5	ARG		R. Sagrada Familia
	10	ARG	LRH202	R. Tupá Mbaé, Posadas
	0.3	BOL		R. Guaqui, Puerto de Guaqui
	15	CLM	FI	Caracol R, Armenia
	1	CLM	TE	LV del Chocó, Quibdó
	10	CLM	BT	R. Catatumbo, Ocaña
	10	CLM	FP	RCN, Neiva
	1	CLM	GJ	W Radio, Duitama
	10	EQA	GB5	LV de Riobamba "Antena 1", Riobamba
	10	EQA	AV3	R. Luz y Vida, Loja
	0.5	PRU	OCY2E	R. Chasqui Llacta, San Marcos
	2.5	PRU	OAU7K	R. Frontera, Juliaca
	10	PRU	OAX8D	R. Loreto, Iquitos
	5	PRU	OBU4K	R. Mineria, Cerro de Pasco
	2.5	PRU	OCX7Q	R. Universal, Santa Monica
	10	VEN	QD	Ecos del Orinoco, Cd.Bolívar
	10	VEN	MV	R. Venezuela Caribe, Punto Fijo
1153		PRU		R. Ayabaca , Ayabaca
1160	5/10	ARG	LRH253	R. Cataratas, Pto. Iguazú
	10/2.5	ARG	LU32	R. Coronel Olavarría, Olavarría
		ARG		R. Excelsior, Monte Grande
	1	ARG	LRA57	R. Nal., El Bolsón
	5	BOL		R. Centenario, Sta. Cruz
	10	BOL		R. Continental, La Paz
	1	BOL		R. Nuevo Mundo, Sucre
	3/1	BOL		R. RTC, Cochabamba
	1	CHL	CC116	R. Ancoa, Linares
	1	CHL	CD116A	R. Baha'i, Temuco
		CHL	CD116	R. El Espectador de America, La Serena
	10	CLM	S31	Colombia Mía, Barrancabermeja
	5	CLM	AZ	Frecuencia Bolivariana, Montería
	15	CLM	OC	Fuego AM, Bogotá
	15	CLM	AU	Ondas del Orteguaza, Florencia
		CLM		Ondas del Puerto, La Virginia
	10	CLM	BL	R. Aeropuerto, Barranquilla
	10	CLM	EC	R. San José de Cúcuta, Cúcuta
	10	CLM	EV	R. Unica, Cali
	5	CLM	ZV	RCN R. Las Lajas, Ipiales
		EQA		LV del Pueblo, Azoguez
	1	EQA	WD4	R. Cenit, Portoviejo
	1	EQA	UR6	R. Runatacuyaj "LV de la Asociación", Latacunga
	2	EQA	VR3	R. Vía, Machala
	5	EQA	CP1	Super Auténtica, La Radio 11-60, Quito
	10	PRG	ZP72	R. Antena Dos, Asunción
	5	PRU	OAX4C	R. 1160, Lima
	1	PRU	OCX7Z	R. del Sur, Puerto Maldonado
	1	PRU	OBX5O	R. Huanta 2000, Huanta
	0.3	PRU	OAX2C	R. Libertad Mundo, Trujillo
	1	PRU	OBX6G	R. Nacional del Perú, Moquegua
	1	PRU	OAU2T	R. Siglo 21, Chota
	1	PRU	OCX1S	Radiales Nor Oriental del Marañon, Chiclayo
	2/1	URG	CW116	R. Agraria del Uruguay, Cerro Chato
	20/10	VEN	RR	R. Industrial, Guarenas
	1	VEN	OK	R. Universidad, Mérida
1170	5	ARG		R. Mi País, Hurlingham
	10	ARG	LRA29	R. Nal., San Luis
	3	CHL	CD117	R. Natales, Puerto Natales
	10	CLM	NW	Caracol R, Cartagena
	10	CLM	GA	Caracol R, Tunja
	10	CLM	E74	Meridiano 70, Arauca
	10	CLM	PB	Ondas de Macondo, Valledupar
	10	CLM	BX	Ondas del Meta, Villavicencio
	10	CLM	FW	R. Nutibara, Medellín
	1	CLM	JE	RCN, Tuluá
	5	EQA	JV5	R. Central, Riobamba
	5	EQA	RV2	R. Filadelfia, Guayaquil
		PRU	OBU7F	R. Bethel, Cusco
	0.5	PRU	OCX7Y	R. Constelación, Puno
	1	PRU	OCX4Y	R. COSAT, Satipo
		PRU	OAU5V	R. Horizonte La Voz del Agro, Pueblo Nuevo
	1	PRU	OBX8M	R. La Luz, Iquitos
	1	PRU	OAU2M	R. Layzon, Cajamarca
	1	PRU	OAZ3K	R. Nor Peruana Chimbote
	10	PRU	OBX6L	R. Programas del Perú, Arequipa
	1	PRU	OCX1B	R. San Juan, Talara
	10	URG	CX32	Radiomundo, Montevideo
	20/10	VEN	QV	R. Acarigua, Acarigua
	10	VEN	KW	R. Bolivariana "R. 1070", Maiquetía
1180		ARG	LRI230	R. de la Sierra, Tandil
	1	BOL		R. Independencia, Quillacollo
	1	BOL		R. Ingavi, Viacha
	50	CHL	CB118	R. Portales, Santiago
	15	CLM	FX	Caracol R, Manizales
		CLM		Em. Coorpurabá, Apartadó
	5	CLM	WA	LV del Guaviare, San José del Guaviare
	20	CLM	GK	R. Santander 2, Bucaramanga
	10/5	CLM	JT	RCN, Ibagué
		EQA		LV del Volante, Portoviejo

kHz	kW	Ctry	Call	Station, location
	12.5	EQA	LR1	Nueva Em. Central, Quito
	4	EQA	DP5	R. Cuenca "LV de los 4 Ríos", Cuenca
	5/1	PRG	ZP52	R. Coronel Oviedo, Coronel Oviedo
		PRU	OCE4K	NSE Radio, Lima
	1	PRU	OCX2A	R. Americana, Quiruvilca
	1	PRU	OAZ1C	R. Chulucanas, Chulucanas
		PRU	OBU6J	R. Corporacion Plus & Plus, Pocoally
	1	PRU	OBU2E	R. La Luz, Jaen
	1	PRU	OCY4Z	R. Libertad, Junin
	10	URG	CX118	LV de Artigas, Artigas
	10	VEN	OR	R. Maturín, Maturín
	10	VEN	NJ	R. Petrolera, Cd.Ojeda
	10	VEN	LQ	Super Suave 11-80, La Victoria
1190	25/5	ARG	LR9	R. América, Buenos Aires
	50	ARG	LRA15	R. Nal., San Miguel de Tucumán
	10	CLM	CT	LV de la Costa, Barranquilla
	15	CLM	EO	Ondas del Valle, Cartago
	10	CLM	CV	R. Cordillera, Bogotá
	10	CLM	KG	R. Mira, Tumaco
	2	EQA	DE2	Estudio Universidad Católica, Guayaquil
	1	EQA	RF6	R. El Sol, Pujilí
	5	PRG	ZP45	LV de la Libertad, Henendarias
	1.5	PRU	OCX6G	R. Alas Peruanas
	5	PRU	OBX3D	R. Ancash, Huaraz
	10	PRU	OAX1E	R. Em. del Pacifico, Chiclayo
	3	PRU	OCU1S	R. OCU1S. Tumbes
	2	PRU	OAX7B	R. Tawantinsuyo, Cusco
	20/10	VEN	PF	Ondas de Libertad, San Felix
	20/10	VEN	RE	R. Barinas, Barinas
	10	VEN	ZD	R. Dif. Cult. del Táchira, San Cristóbal
1195		CLM		Ondas del Ranchería, Barrancas
1200		ARG		Esquel (F.P.I.)
	1	ARG	LT6	R. Goya, Goya
	1	ARG	LRA6	R. Nal. Mendoza, Valle de Uspallata
	25/5	ARG		Rio Grande (F.P.I.)
		BOL		Cuarzo Comunicaciones, La Paz
	0.25	BOL		R. 24 de Noviembre, Arani
		BOL		R. Capital, Oruro
		BOL		R. Carlos Palenque, La Paz
		BOL		R. Maria de la Candelaria, Copacabana
		BOL		R. Mauro Nuñes, Villa Serrano
	5	BOL		R. Oriental, Santa Cruz
	10	CLM	CD	Em. Nueva Epoca, Fusagasugá
	10	CLM	GC	La Cariñosa, Antena2, Sogamoso
	10	CLM	BZ	Ondas del Riohacha, Riohacha
	15	CLM	IJ	R. 1200 "LV de la Raza", Medellín
	10	CLM	BV	R. Príncipe, Cartagena
	10	CLM	NF	R. Super, Cali
	5	EQA	RE2	LV del Trópico, Quevedo
	5	EQA	RM5	R. El Mercurio, Cuenca
	5	EQA	CS1	R. Super K, La Líder, Sangolquí
		EQA		R. U Cadena Sur, Sta Rosa
	10	PRG	ZP44	R. Libre, Fernando de la Mora
	3	PRU	OAX4B	Cadena R. 1200, Lima
	1	PRU	OAU2A	Frecuencia Pedagogica, Cajamarca
	3	PRU	OAU4G	R. Andes, Huancayo
	1	PRU	OBX5X	R. Comercial, Abancay
	1	PRU	OCX7S	R. Cultura, Juliaca
		PRU	OBX8N	R. La Luz, Pucallapa
		PRU	OAU6P	R. La Luz, Tacna
	1	PRU	OAU1Q	R. San Andres, Tambogrande
	1	URG	CW33	La Nueva R., Florida
	1	VEN	NH	Ondas del Escalante, Sta Bárbara del Zulia
	10	VEN	SF	R. Dimensión, Caripito
	10	VEN	OZ	R. Tiempo, Caracas
1210	5	ARG		am Doce Diez, La Tablada
	5/1	ARG	LRI229	R. Las Flores, Las Flores
		ARG		R. Mailín, Gregorio de Laferrere
	5	CHL	CD121	R. Armonía, Puerto Montt
	1	CHL	CC121	R. Universidad de Talca, Talca
		CHL	CB121	R. Valparaiso, Valparaiso
	10	CLM	E65	La Cariñosa, Antena 2, Cúcuta
	10	CLM	BQ	La Cariñosa, Pereira
	10	CLM	FR	Oxígeno, Neiva

kHz	kW	Ctry	Call	Station, location
	10	EQA	VC3	R. Centinela del Sur "CDS", Loja
	20	EQA	BJ2	R. El Mundo, Guayaquil
	3	EQA	JM6	R. Sira, Ambato
		PRU	OBX3X	Huanuco (F.P.I.)
	1	PRU	OCY4T	R. Galaxia, Satipo
	1	PRU		R. Municipalidad, Ayabaca
	5	PRU	OAX8A	R. Nacional del Perú, Iquitos
	1	PRU	OAX7M	R. Quillabamba, Quillabamba
		PRU	OCU7B	R. Santo Tomas
	1	PRU	OAX2Q	R. Universo, Trujillo
	2/1	URG	CX121	Difusora Soriano, Mercedes
	0.25	URG	CW121	R. El Libertador, Villa Vergara
	2/1	URG	CV121	R. RBC, Piriápolis
	10	VEN	ZT	R. Anzoátegui, Barcelona
1220		ARG		LRC R., Pres. Roque Sanez Peña
	5/1	ARG	LRL328	R. Cadena Eco, Buenos Aires
	1	ARG	LRI224	R. Onda Marina, Mar del Plata (Cad. Eco)
	1	BOL		R. Batallón Topáter, Oruro
	1	BOL		R. Splendid, La Paz
	10	CHL	CD122	R. Maria, Temuco
	10	CLM	KR	R. María, "LV Católica de su Hogar", Bogotá
	10	CLM	NM	R. Viva Cultural Bolívar, Ipiales
	10	CLM	MT	RCN La Radio, San Gil
	10	CLM	AV	RCN, Montería
	3/5	EQA	EB6	Ecos de Bolívar, Guaranda
	10	EQA	AP1	R. Marañón, Quito
		PRU	OBU5I	R. Amor y Paz, Pisco
		PRU	OCU4H	R. Fe, Lima
	1	PRU	OAU5N	R. La Luz, Ica
	3	PRU	OCX1X	R. Libertad, Chiclayn
	4	PRU	OAX6X	R. Melodia, Arequipa
	1	PRU	OAU7N	R. Univ. Nal. San Antonio Abad, Cusco
	1/0.5	URG	CX122	R. Reconquista, Rivera
	10	VEN	RD	LV de Apure, San Fernando de Apure
	20/10	VEN	ZO	R. Aeropuerto 1220, Maracaibo
	10/5	VEN	VM	R. Venezuela Valencia, Valencia
1230		ARG		R. Claridad, Monte Grande
		ARG		R. Creativa, CA Buenos Aires
	25/5	ARG	LT2	R. Gen. San Martín "R.Dos", Rosario
		ARG		R. La Bendición, General Pico
	5/1	ARG	LW5	R. Libertador, General San Martin
		ARG		R. Litoral, Isidro Casanova
	15	CLM	EH	Colmundo, Bucaramanga
	10	CLM	IL	Minuto de Dios, Medellín
	6	CLM	BR	Oxígeno, Tunja
	10	CLM	LK	R. Calidad "La Cariñosa", Cali
	1	CLM	TP	R. Colina, Girardot
	1	CLM	MJ	RCN Antena 2, Maicao
	3	CLM	RI1	CRI-Centro Radiofónico de Imbabura, Ibarra
	1	EQA	RL6	LV de Saquisilí y Libertador, Saquisilí
	15	EQA	FV2	R. Galáctica, Guayaquil
	3	EQA	MV5	R. Popular, Cuenca
	5	EQA	FG4	Sucre Esmeraldas, Esmeraldas
	1	PRU	OAX2T	R. Albújar, Guadalupe
		PRU	OAU7V	R. Frecuencia Amistad, Juliaca
		PRU	OCU4C	R. La Luz, Huacho
	1	PRU	OBX4Z	R. LV de Oxapampa, Oxapampa
	0.5	PRU	OBX7J	R. Madre de Dios, Puerto Maldonado
	1	PRU	OBZ4Y	R. Selecciones,Tarma
	10	VEN	NT	R. Barlovento, Caucagua
	10	VEN	OH	R. Valera, Valera
1240		ARG		R. Cadena Uno, Buenos Aires
		ARG	LRI218	R. Universidad Nacional del Sur, Bahia Blanca
		BOL		R. Indoamerica, Potosi
	2	BOL		R. Los Andes, Tarija
		BOL		Rdif. Achocalla, Achocalla
	0.25	CHL	CA124	R. Principal Chuquicamata, Calama
	5	CLM	GN	R. Barrancabermeja, Barrancabermeja
	3	CLM	JA	R. Buenaventura, Buenaventura
	1	CLM	GO	R. Caribabere, Saravena
	10	CLM	FG	RCN, Calarcá
	5	EQA	RF3	R. Fenix, Zaruma
	1	EQA	PA1	R. Metropolitana, Yaraquí

kHz	kW	Ctry	Call	Station, location
		PRU	OBX9O	R. Bagua Grande
		PRU	OAU5U	R. Eco, Ica
	1	PRU	OAU3C	R. La Luz, Chimbote
	5	PRU	OAU6D	R. Lider, Arequipa
	10	PRU	OAU4V	R. Maria, Chilca
	1	PRU	OAU2Y	R. Nor Andino, Santiago de Chuco, Trujillo
		PRU	OBX7M	R. Pachatusán, Sicuani
		PRU	OCX1C	R.Campesina, Ayaviri
	5	URG	CW35	R. Paysandú, Paysandú
1250	1	ARG		R. Estirpe Nacional., San Justo
	0.1	BOL		R. Frontera, Cobija
	2.5	BOL		R. La Plata, Sucre
	10	CHL	CD125	R. Armonía, Valdivia
	10	CLM	CA	Capital Radio, Bogotá
	10	CLM	OK	Em. ABC, Barranquilla
	1	CLM	EM	LV de Corozal, Corozal
	15	CLM	HS	Oxígeno/W Radio, Cúcuta
	5	CLM	FV	R. Viva, Pasto
	3	EQA	MY1	LV del Triunfo, Sto Domingo de los Colorados
	10	EQA	EM1	Ondas Carchenses, Tulcán
	10	EQA	HB2	R. Tricolor, Guayaquil
	5	PRG	ZP3	R. Asunción, Asunción
	3	PRU	OBX8S	Angelica Julian Human Lourdes, De Calleria
	1	PRU	OAU2V	HGV, Santa Cruz
		PRU	OAX9C	R. Americana, Rioja
		PRU	OAU6I	R. Campesina, Omate
	5	PRU	OAX4L	R. Miraflores, Miraflores
	1	PRU	OAX8P	R. Pucallapa, Pucallapa
	3	PRU	OBX7A	R. Solar, Cusco
	1	PRU	OBZ1B	R.B.N.S., Talara Alta
	5	URG	CW125	R. Bella Unión, Bella Unión
	10	URG	CX36	R. Centenario, Montevideo
	20/10	VEN	PZ	Latina 12-50, Pto Ordaz
	1	VEN	ML	R. Cabimas, Cabimas
1258		PRU		R. Centinela, Huancabamba
1260	10/5	ARG	LT14	R. General Urquiza, Paraná
	2	ARG		R. Oasis, Victoria
		ARG		R. Oliva - "Unicon del Cielo", Buenos Aires
		ARG		R. Panamericana, CA Buenos Aires
		ARG		R. y Television del Neuquén, Neuquén
		BOL		R. LV de la Esperanza, Quillacollo
	10	BOL		R. Nacional de Huanuni, Hunanuni
	2	CHL	CC126	R. Condell, Curicó
	5	CLM	CO	Caracol R, Ibagué
	1	CLM	HU	Caracol R, San Andrés
	5	CLM	LX	Minuto de Dios Eco Llanero, Villavicencio
	2	CLM	OU	Ondas del Amazonas, Leticia
	5	CLM	NO	Oxígeno, Duitama
	5	CLM	DA	R. Auténtica, Medellín
	5	CLM	ET	R. María, Cali
	5	CLM	TM	R. Sonar, Ocaña
	5	CLM	OH	RCN Cesar, Valledupar
	10	EQA	MO1	LV del Santuario del Quinche, Quito
	1	EQA	RB3	R. Benemérita, Sta Rosa
	3	EQA	RO6	R. Calidad, Ambato
	2	EQA	PB5	R. Contacto XG, Cuenca
	5	PRG	ZP34	R. Panambi Vera, Villarrica
	1	PRU	OAZ1A	R. Ferrañafe, Ferrañafe
	1	PRU	OAU3F	R. La Luz, Huanuco
		PRU		R. Mahanaim, Mollendo
	1	PRU	OBX6D	R. Mundial, Arequipa
	0.3	PRU	OBX5S	R. Nacional del Perú, Ayacucho
	1	PRU	OCX10	R. Nor Puruana, Chiclayo
		PRU	OAU3G	R. Pregonero Cristiano, Chimbote
		PRU	OBX2C	Telesistema Peruano, Otuzco
	3	URG	CW37	Dif. Rochense, Rocha
	10	VEN	RM	BBN R, Caracas
	10	VEN	RY	R. Horizonte, Nirgua
1265	0.4	BOL		R. Uncía, Uncía
1270	25/5	ARG	LRA20	R. Nal., Las Lomitas
	100	ARG	LS11	R. Provincia de Buenos Aires, La Plata
	10	CHL	CB127	R. Festival, Viña del Mar
	5	CLM	TX	Bésame, Bucaramanga
	1	CLM	IM	Colmundo, Pereira

kHz	kW	Ctry	Call	Station, location
	5	CLM	Q99	Colombia Mía, San José del Guaviare
	2	CLM	AR	La Cariñosa, Antena 2,Cartagena
	1	CLM	XQ	LV Amiga, Ubaté
	1.5	CLM	KJ	LV de Curumaní, Curumaní
	1	CLM	SV	LV de Orito, Orito
	5	CLM	BM	R. Internacional, Honda
	3	EQA	LD4	R. Junín, Junín
	15	EQA	UM2	R. Universal, Guayaqui
	1	PRU	OAX8T	R. Eco, Iquitos
	1	PRU	OCX2Z	R. Estacion Latina, Cepén
	2	PRU	OAU7S	R. Horizonte, Cusco
	0.4	PRU	OAZ4H	R. Huacho, Huacho
	0.4	PRU	OBZ4T	R. La Merced, Chanchamayo
	1	PRU	OAU1S	R. Nor Paita, Paita
	4/2	URG	CV127	R. Cuareim, Artigas
		VEN		R. Nacional, Ureña
	10	VEN	OU	R. Ondas Panamericanas, El Vigía
	5	VEN	TR	R. Tucupita, Tucupita
1276	1	PRU	OAU1R	R. Gotas del Oro, Urrunaga
1280		ARG		AM 1530, CA Buenos Aires
		ARG		R. Mística, Libertad
		ARG		R. Punto, Buenos Aires
	10/5	ARG	LU11	R. Trenque Lauquen, Tr. Lauquen
		BOL		R. Ondas del Titicaca, Huarina
	1	CHL	CC128	R. Arturo Prat Chacón AM, San Carlos
	10	CHL	CD128	R. del Sur, Osorno
	5	CLM	LR	Caracol R, Pasto
	5	CLM	RP	Ecos de Tibú, Tibú
	5	CLM	CM	HJ Doble K, Pitalito
	5	CLM	HO	Impacto Popular, San Juan del Cesar
	1	CLM	NQ	LV del Río Suárez, Barbosa
	5	CLM	SO	R. Playa Mendoza, Barranquilla
	5	CLM	TK	R. Super, Caicedonia
	5	CLM	MB	R. Suroeste, Concordia
	5	CLM	KN	R. Única, Bogotá
	1	EQA	IN4	LV del Sur de Manabí, Jipijapa
	1	EQA	NW5	R. Canal Tropical, Riobamba
		EQA		R. Universitaria, Quito
	1/0.25	PRG	ZP53	R. LV del Este, Cd. del Este
		PRU	OBX3C	R. Alopesa, Chimbote
	0.5	PRU	OBX6P	R. Fénix, Camaná
	1	PRU	OAU1R	R. Gotas del Oro, Urrunaga
	1	PRU	OAX3Y	R. La Selva, Rupa-Rupa
		PRU	OCU7R	R. Ministerio Mundial, Sicuani
	1	PRU	OBX2F	R. Moderna, Cajamarca
		PRU	OAU7K	R. Stereo Nevada, Espinar
	1	PRU	OCX6B	R. Trebol, Mariano Melgar
	3/1	URG	CX128	R. Tacuarembó, Tacuarembó
	10	VEN	OF	R. Trujillo, Trujillo
	10/5	VEN	QS	R. Zaraza, Zaraza
1290	1	ARG	LRI371	R. Amanecer, Reconquista
		ARG		R. Interactiva, Gregorio de la Ferrere
	5/1	ARG	LRJ212	R. Murialdo, Villa Nueva de Guaymallén
		ARG		R. Provinciana, San Miguel
	1	BOL		Radiodifusoras Minería, Oruro
	0.25	CHL	CA129	R. Coya, María Elena
	5	CLM	SZ	Colombia Mía, Saravena, AR
	5	CLM	TH	LV de las Estrellas, Medellín
	5	CLM	NE	LV del Ariari, Granada
	5	CLM	EB	LV del Turismo, Santa Marta
	5	CLM	OI	R. Chacurí, Sampués
	5	CLM	MC	R. Viva 12-90, Cali
	5	CLM	KY	RCN, Girardot
	1	EQA	OF2	Canal Milagreño, El Milagro
	3	EQA	JA5	LV del Río Tarqui, Cuenca
	0.5	EQA	VM6	R. Once de Noviembre, Latacunga
	1	EQA	NS1	R. Popular, Atuntaqui
	1	PRU	OBU5W	Ayacucho
		PRU	OBU4S	R. 1290, La Oroya
		PRU	OAM2C	R. Esetlar, Chota
	0.3	PRU	OAX7X	R. Juliaca, Juliaca
	10	PRU	OAX9N	R. Nor Oriental, Bagua Grande
	1	PRU	OCX1Q	R. Programas del Perú, Tumbes
		PRU		R. Satelite, La Union

kHz	kW	Ctry	Call	Station, location
	1	PRU	OCX6B	R. Trebol, Mariano Melgar
	1	PRU	OBU4Q	S & RD, Hualmay
	10	URG	CX38	S.O.D.R.E. "Em. del Sur". Montevideo
	10	VEN	LF	R. Puerto Cabello, Puerto Cabello
1300		ARG		Plus Radio, Lanús
		ARG		R. Identidad, Buenos Aires
	5	ARG	LRA5	R. Nal., Villa Gobernador Gálvez
	5	BOL		R. Bandera Beniana, Trinidad
	1	BOL		R. Fuerzas Armadas, Sta. Cruz
	2.5	BOL		R. Loyola, Sucre
	15/6	BOL		R. Sol, El Alto
	5	CHL	CB130	R. Tierra, Santiago
	5	CLM	RB	CRB Cadena Radial Boyacense, Tunja
	5	CLM	OG	LV de las Antillas, Cartagena
	5	CLM	NB	Onda 5, Bucaramanga
	5	CLM	LD	Oxígeno, Pereira
	5	CLM	IN	R. Eucha, Belalcázar
	5	CLM	EA	R. Lumbí, Mariquita
	5	CLM	UA	R. Sindamanoy, Mocoa
	5	EQA	DC2	R. Cenit, Guayaqui
	5	EQA	RV1	R. Festival, Sto Domingo de los Colorados
		EQA		R. La Paz, Guaranda
	2/1	EQA	RS7	R. Sucumbios, Nueva Loja
	5	PRG	ZP10	R. Fe y Alegria, Villa Hayes
	1	PRU	OAZ4B	R. Andina, Huancayo
	5	PRU	OAX4S	R. Comas, Comas
	0.4	PRU	OAX6P	R. Comercial Latina, Tacna
	1	PRU	OAU1U	R. Frecuencia Lider, Morrop
	0.5	PRU	OAX3O	R. Huascarán, Independencia
	0.3	PRU	OAX7X	R. Juliaca, Juliaca
		PRU	ORX9P	R. La Luz, Tarapoto
		PRU	OAZ8B	R. Nuevo Mundo, Pucallapa
	5	PRU	OAX7P	R. Onda Imperial, Cusco
	1	PRU	OAU2I	R. Paraiso, Cajabamba
	10/8	VEN	KH	R. Recuerdos 1300, Caracas
	10	VEN	NS	R. Reloj, Maracaibo
1310		ARG		Gesell R., Villa Gesell
	1	ARG		R. Dr. Gregorio Alvarez (Cad Eco), Piedra del Aguila
		ARG		R. Imagen, Castelar
	10	ARG	LRA42	R. Nal., Gualeguaychú
	1	ARG		Rdif. Antártida Argentina, Buenos Aires
	10	BOL		R. San Rafael, Cochabamba
	5	CLM	JZ	Aviva 2, Bogotá
	5	CLM	DG	Caracol R, Monteria
	5	CLM	TQ	G12 Radio, Cúcuta
	5	CLM	AK	LV de la Patria Celestial, Barranquilla
	5	CLM	WD	Micrófono Cívico, Palermo
	5	CLM	LM	R. Santa Bárbara
	5	CLM	IR	RCN Urabá, Apartadó
	0.5	EQA	AI5	Eco de los Andes, Cumanda
	1	EQA	CP3	LV de El Oro, Pasaje
	20	EQA	GB1	R. Nal. Espejo, Quito
	3	EQA	CI5	T. V. O. "El Poder Mágico de la Fé", Biblián
	2	PRU	OBU5X	Ayacucho
	1	PRU	OBX2D	R. Chota, Chota
	1	PRU	OBX4L	R. Irvisa, Huacho
	6	PRU	OUA6N	R. Libertad, Arequipa
	1	PRU	OBX8L	R. Vision Amazonia, Iquitos
	5	VEN	TS	R. Andina "Sonido 13-10", Isnotú
	10	VEN	SM	RNV Canal Informativo, Barcelona
	1	VEN	SL	RNV Canal Informativo, Guri
		VEN		RNV Canal Informativo, Santa Elena
1320	5/3	ARG	LU10	R. Azul, Azul
	0.25	ARG	LV24	R. Manantiales, Tunuyán
		ARG		R. Máster, Luján
		ARG		R. Mística, Libertad
		ARG		R.Area Uno, Tres de Febrero
		ARG		R.Ciudad, Remedios de Escalada
		BOL		R. Em. Septima Voz, Achocalla
		BOL		R. Sucre, Sucre
		BOL		R. Taipichullo, Taraco
		BOL		R. Tawantinsuyo, Taraco
		BOL		R.Comunitaria La Lumberia, La Paz
	0.25	CHL	CA132	R. Estrella del Norte, Vallenar
	1	CHL	CD132	R. Lincoyan, Mulchén
	5	CLM	MS	La Cariñosa, Barrancabarmeja
	5	CLM	NV	La Cariñosa, Girardot
	5	CLM	HT	R. Guateque, Guateque
	10	CLM	QI	R. Leda Int., San Andrés
	1	CLM	NK	R. Luna, Palmira
	5	CLM	TA	R. María, Medellín
	5	CLM	LV	R. Onda Fantastica, Fundación
	10	EQA	JD6	R. Continental, Ambato
	3	EQA	FR2	R. Guayaquil, Babahoyo
	1	EQA	VO4	R. Stéreo Carrizal, Calceta
	1	PRU	OBU4T	R. Corporacion, Huancayo
		PRU	OBU1S	R. Frecuencia Popular, Olmos
		PRU	OAX4I	R. La Cronica, Lima//R. Nacional 850
	1	PRU	OAX3U	R. Miramar, Chimbote
	3	PRU	OAU7W	R. Peru, Juliaca
	1/0.5	URG	CW132	R. Fortaleza, Rocha
	1/0.5	URG	CW39	R. LV de Paysandú, Paysandú
	10/5	VEN	WP	R. Apolo, Turmero
	10	VEN	SG	R. Colonial, El Iocuyo
1330	1/0.25	ARG		AM Rosario, Rosario
		ARG		R. Mailín, Gregorio de Laferrere
	3	CHL	CB133	La Mexicana, Santiago
	3/1.5	CHL	CD133	R. Vicente Pérez Rosales, Puerto Montt
	0.25	CLM	HKR33	Alcadía de Salamina, Salamina
	5	CLM	FE	Antena 2, Pereira
	5	CLM	LS	Caracol R, Popayán
	5	CLM	NR	La Caliente 13-30, San Gil
	1	CLM	MP	LV de Aguachica, Aguachica
	5	CLM	AP	R. Auténtica, Cartagena
	1	CLM	RD	R. Fénix de Oriente 1330 AM, El Peñol
		EQA		Lomas Stereo 2000, Guayaquil
	5	EQA	RV3	Nacional El Oro, Machala
	2	EQA	LW5	R. Visión Cristiana, Cuenca
	3	EQA		R. Visión Cristiana, Quito
	10	PRG	ZP13	R. Chaco Boreal, Asunción
	0.5	PRU	OAU5L	R. Bethel, Huamanga
	1	PRU	OAU1A	R. Dos Mil, Chiclayo
	1	PRU	OVX6E	R. Ondas del Misti, Mariano Melgar
	1	PRU	OCX/K	R. San Miguel, Wanchaq
	5	URG	CX40	R. Fénix, Montevideo
	5	VEN	OY	R. Los Llanos, Calabozo
	10	VEN	TU	R. Regional, Cd. Ojeda
		VEN		RNV Canal Informativo, La Paragua
1340		ARG		AM Renacer, Moreno
	1/0.25	ARG		Goya (F.PI.)
		ARG		R. Mediterránea, Rosario del Tala
		ARG		R.Tradicional Conurbano Norte
		BOL		R. Comunitario Taipichullo
	0.5	BOL		R. Copacabana, Copacabana
	1	BOL		R. Grigotá, Santa Cruz
	0.5	BOL		R. Jach'a Suyu, Corocoro
	10	CHL	CB134	R. Colo Colo, Valparaíso
	1	CHL	CC134	R. La Discusión, Chillán
	1	CHL	CD134	R. Panguipulli, Panguipulli
	5	CLM	FB	Amor, Bogotá
	0.5	CLM	VL	Brisas del Catatumbo, Tibú
	5	CLM	KD	La Cariñosa/Antena 2, Neiva
	5	CLM	FA	R. Alegre, Barranquilla
	1	CLM	NP	R. Comunal, Nariño
	5	CLM	IS	R. El Sol, Buenaventura
	5	CLM	PY	R. Lemas, Cúcuta
	4	CLM	NY	R. Unica, Bucaramanga
	5	CLM	HA	RCN Nariño, Pasto
	5	CLM	HY	RCN Sucre, Sincelejo
		EQA		LV de su amigo "Esté Musical", Esmeraldas
	1	EQA		Ondas de Esperanza, Loja
	5	EQA	RT6	H. Paz y Bien, Ambato
		PRU	OAU3E	Assn. Iglesia de Dios, Chimbote
	2	PRU	OAQ4Q	R. Alegria, Pucasana
	0.5	PRU	OAX5D	R. Chinca, Chinca Alta
		PRU	OAU6T	R. Comercial, Mollendo
	1	PRU	OAU4N	R. Jauja, Jauja

kHz	kW	Ctry	Call	Station, location
	1	PRU	OAU2S	R. Shalom, Cajamarca
		PRU	OBU7V	R. Sudamericana, Juliaca
	10/1	URG	CW53	LV de Melo, Melo
	10	VEN	NE	R. Uno, Caracas
1350	1/0.25	ARG		Juan José Castelli (F.PI.)
	25/5	ARG	LS6	R. Buenos Aires, Buenos Aires
	5/1	ARG	LRJ747	R. Sucesos, Villa Carlos Paz
	1	BOL		R. America, Sucre
		BOL		R. Comunitario Inti, Contorno/Viacha
	1	CHL	CA135	R. Riquelme, Coquimbo
	1	CLM	HW	Em. Ecos del Río, Puerto Boyacá
	5	CLM	DS	Ondas de la Montaña, Medellín
	5	CLM	HL	Oxígeno, Ibagué
	5	CLM	EN	R. Armonía, Cali
	1	CLM		R. Cultural 2001, Pailitas
	1	CLM	MN	R. Perijá, Codazzi
	5	CLM	OA	R. Uno, Santa Marta
	5	CLM	LO	RCN Antena 2/La Cariñosa, Caucasia
	2/1	EQA	SF5	LV de San Fernando, San Fernando
	3	EQA	VP2	Teleradio 13-50 AM Digital , Guayaquil
		PRU	OBU5O	Huamanga
	1	PRU	OBX6F	R. Ilo, Ilo
		PRU	OBX8D	R. Super, Pucallpa
	1	PRU	OAU1H	R. Vision, Chiclayo
	1	PRU	OBU7E	R.Santa Beatriz, Cusco
	5	VEN	ZZ	R. Eclipse, El Tigrito
	5	VEN	TJ	R. Falcón, Puerto Cumarebo
1352	1	PRU	OAX3N	R. Ondas del Huallaga, Huanuco
1355	0.25	BOL		R. Armonía, Cliza
1360		ARG		R. Nuestra Señora de Itatí, Morón
		BOL		R. 24 de Septiembre, Santa Cruz
	2.5	BOL		R. Cochabamba, "CBA"
		BOL		R. Coral, Oruro
		BOL		R. Em. Tunupa, Tiahuanacu
		BOL		R. Instituto Politécnico Tomás Katari, Sucre
	5	BOL		Radiodifusoras Jiménez, El Alto
	5	CLM	RA	Eco 13-60 "La Superestación", Pereira
	10/5	CLM	PK	LV de Abejorral, Abejorral
	5	CLM	UO	Oxígeno, Cartagena
	5	CLM	MI	R. Auténtica, Melgar
	1	CLM	KV	R. Láser, Zapatoca
	0.5	CLM		R. Segovia, Segovia
	3	EQA	MT	Oyambaro AM, Tumbaco
	1	EQA	RJ5	R. América, Riobamba
	5	EQA	HG3	R. Jerusalem AM, Machala
	1	PRG	ZP37	R. Yby Ya'u, Ybu Ya'u
	2.5	PRU	OUA7L	R. Continente, Juliaca
	1	PRU	OBZ5Z	R. Cruz del Sur, Palpa
	1	PRU	OBZ1A	R. del Norte, Sullana
	1	PRU	OAU4O	R. Hecaburt, Tarma
	0.2	PRU	OAU3A	R. Intercontinental, Yungay
	1	PRU	OCX6T	R. Luza, Paucarpata
		PRU	OAX4I	R. Nueva Q-FM, Lima
	2.5	PRU	OAX7R	R. Sicuani, Sicuani
	1	PRU	OBX2N	R. Super Uno, Santiago de Cao
	2.5	URG	CW41	R. 41, San José
	1	URG	CW136	R. Río Branco, Río Branco
	5	VEN	TZ	AM Center, Charallave
	10	VEN	TI	R. Internacional, Maracaibo
1370	1/0.25	ARG		Aire de Santa FeRafaela
	5/3	ARG		AM Trece-70, Isidro Casanova
		ARG		Junin (F.PI.)
	10	ARG	LRA54	R. Nal., Ingeniero Jacobacci
	0.15	BOL		R. Libertad, Cliza
	5	CLM	BO	Minuto de Dios, Barranquilla
	1	CLM	BD	R. Guaimaral, Cúcuta
	5	CLM	KI	R. Mundial, Bogotá
	1	CLM	NI	R. Sabana, Sincelejo
	1	CLM	JQ	RCN Antena 2, Zarzal
	5	CLM	EQ	RCN Cauca, Popayán
	2.5	CLM	NU	RCN, Rionegro
	2	EQA	JS1	Ecos Andinos, Pimampiro
	5	EQA	VO2	LV del Milagro, El Milagro
		EQA	AO5	R. El Rocio, Biblián
	5	EQA	ER3	R. Progreso, Loja
	1	PRU	OCX5A	Inti R., Abanacy
	1	PRU	OAU1W	R. Chiclayo, Chiclayo
		PRU	OAX6T	R. Moquegua, Moquegua
		PRU	OBX9A	R. Palmera
	1	PRU	OAZ7J	R. Santa Monica, Wanchaq
		PRU	OBU2U	R. Satelite, Santa Cruz
	0.5	PRU	OAZ40	R. Tres de Octubre
	5.3/2.5	URG	CX42	Em. Ciudad de Montevideo
	1/0.5	URG	CW137	Nueva R. San Javier, San Javier
	0.5	URG	CV137A	R. Real, Minas de Corrales
	10	VEN	JI	R. Continente, Mérida
	5	VEN	SV	RNV Portuguesa, Acarigua
	5	VEN	OQ	Unión R. Notícias, Valle de la Pascua
1380	5/1	ARG	LRI231	LV del Sudeste, Necochea
		ARG		R. Buenas Nuevas, Merlo
		ARG		R. Los Toldos, Los Toldos
		ARG		R. Redentor, Claypole
	1.5	BOL		R. Bandera Tricolor, Cochabamba
		BOL		R. Global, Sucre
		BOL		R. Horizontes, Huanuni
	0.5	BOL		R. Luis de Fuentes, Tarija
		BOL		R. Maria, La Paz
	50	CHL	CB138	R. Corporación, Santiago
	1	CLM	EJ	Armonías del Palmar, Palmira
	3	CLM	LG	LV de La Dorada, La Dorada
	3	CLM	JD	R. Nuestra Señora del Encuentro con Dios, Medellín
	5	CLM	ID	R. Potencia Latina, La Plata
	5	CLM	EE	RCN, Tunja
	5	CLM	MM	Vida AM, Valledupar
	1	EQA	OA3	La Mejor, Balsas
	5	EQA	CV1	R. Cristal "RCQ", Quito
	5	EQA		R. Mera, Ambato
	1	PRG	ZP8	R. Concepción, "LV del Norte"
	1	PRU	OAX2W	R. Atahualpa, Cajamarca
	1	PRU	OBZ1D	R. Bellavista, Bellavista
		PRU	OBU4L	R. Chilca, Huancayo
		PRU		R. Fraternidad, Trujillo
	1	PRU	OCY4U	R. Nuevo Tiempo, Lima
	2.5	PRU	OAX6O	R. San Martin, Arequipa
	10	VEN	NG	Ondas del Mar, Puerto Cabello
	5	VEN	ME	R. Revelación, Cd. Bolivar
	10	VEN	TL	R. Triunfo 13-80, Caja Seca
1382	1	PRU	OBX3I	R. Pilco Mozo, Huanuco
1390		ARG		R. General Paz, José C. Paz
	10	ARG	LR11	R. Univ. Nacional, La Plata
		BOL		R. Andina (CEPRA), Pongo K´asa
	1	CLM	ZY	La Primera, Bucaramanga
	5	CLM	FY	Oxígeno, Espinal
	5	CLM	YW	R. Auténtica, Pacho
	0.1	CLM		R. Ciudad de Antioquia, Santa Fé de Antioquia
	5	CLM	FO	Red de los Andes, Manizales
	1	EQA	HE4	LV de Esmeraldas, Esmeraldas
	5	EQA	EA5	R. Tropicana "Canal 13-90", Cuenca
	1.5	EQA	IE1	R. Uno, Urcuquí
		PRU	OAU6Q	Difusora Neptuno, Mollendo
		PRU	OBU2U	Frecuencia del Norte, Santa Cruz
	1	PRU	OCX7U	R. Cultura, Yunguyo
	1	PRU	OAU7T	R. Enlace, Kunturkanki
		PRU	OCU1G	R. Fe, Chiclayo
	1	PRU	OBX5O	R. Huanta 2000, Huanta
	1	PRU	OAU2Z	R. La Luz, Trujillo
	1	PRU	OAU1V	R. Tropical, Morrope
	3	PRU	OAM7A	Telecom Ingenieros S.A.C., Sicuani
	5	URG	CW45	Dif. Treinta y Tres, Treinta y Tres
	20	VEN	ZA	R. Fe y Alegría, Caracas
	10	VEN	ZO	R. Lumen, Maracaibo
	10	VEN	TT	R. Terepaima, Cabudare
1400	1/0.25	ARG		Charata (F.PI.)
		ARG		R. AM 1400, Luján
	5/1	ARG	LRG202	R. Cumbre, Neuquén

kHz	kW	Ctry	Call	Station, location
		ARG		R. Gama, Lanús
		ARG		R. Malvinas Argentina, Rosario
		ARG		R.Gen. Lavalle, General Lavalle (F.Pl.)
		BOL		R. Antena 2000, Sucre
	5	BOL		R. Nacional de Bolivia, La Paz
	5	CHL	CD140	R. La Amistad, Los Angeles
	5	CHL	CD140A	R. Viento del Sur, Puerto Montt
	0.25	CLM	HKZ22	Alcaldía de Majagual, Majagual
	0.25	CLM	HKZ25	Alcaldía de Ovejas, Ovejas
	0.25	CLM		Brisas del Sinú, Tierralta
	1	CLM	ER	Ecos del Atrato, Quibdó
	5	CLM	KM	Em. Mariana, Bogotá
	5	CLM	HM	La Cariñosa de Armenia, Calarcá
	1	CLM	D31	LV de Cimitarra, Cimitarra
	1	CLM	BK	LV de la Gran Colombia, Cúcuta
	1	CLM	WY	LV de los Samanes
	5	CLM	DF	LV de Niquel, Montelíbano
	1.5	CLM		LV de Samaniego, Samaniego
	0.45	CLM		R. Cañaveral, Morales
	1	CLM	JJ	R. Ipiales, Ipiales
	5	CLM	AS	R. Uno/RCN Antena 2, Barranquilla
	1	CLM	LL	RCN Antena 2, Santa Bárbara
		EQA		Impacto 1400 AM, Latacunga
	10	EQA	FL2	R. Z Uno, Guayaquil
	2.5	PRU	OBX4W	R. Callao Super, Lima
	1	PRU	OCX5B	R. Interandina, Pisco
	1	PRU	OAX7I	R. La Hora, Cuzco
	0.5	PRU	OAX6J	R. Landa, Arequipa
	1	PRU	OBX4H	R. Luz, Tarma
	1	PRU	OCX1A	R. MDY, Talara Alta
	1	PRU	OAU2H	R. OAU2H, Cajamarca
	25	URG	CX140	R. Zorrilla de San Martín, Tacuarembó
	1	VEN	NF	R. Sabana, El Sombrero
1410	5/1	ARG		R. Folclorismo, José Léon Suárez
		ARG		R. Fundacion, Rafael Calzada
		ARG		R. María de La Paz, Villa Mercedes
		ARG		R.Cope, Chivilcoy (F.Pl)
	1	CHL	CD141	R. Loncoche, Loncoche
	3	CHL	CB141	R. Quinta Región, Valparaíso
	0.25	CLM	HKP86	Alcaldía de Chiquinquira, Chiquinquira
	1	CLM	TY	Caracol R, Vélez
	5	CLM	DU	Em. Cultural Univ. de Antioquia, Medellín
	2	CLM	P79	R. Evangélica, Uribia
	5	CLM	EI	R. Guadalajara, Buga
	1	CLM	HKP79	R. Universidad, Tunja
	5	CLM	FS	RCN, Honda
	1	EQA	FR4	LV de Quinindé, Quinindé
	1	EQA		Ondas Cisnerinas, Riobamba
	1	EQA	GC5	R. Centro Gualaceo, Gualaceo
	1	EQA	EC1	R. El Tiempo "Em.del Amor", Quito
	1	EQA	CQ2	R. Net AM, El Milagro
	2	PRG	ZP35	R. Mangore, S. Juan Bautista
		PRU	OBX8I	Dif. Comercial, Pucallapa
		PRU	OBZ4C	R. Bethel, Huacho
	1	PRU	OAX2Y	R. Heróica, Trujillo
		PRU	OBU7A	R. La Luz, Juliaca
	1	PRU	OBU1H	R. La Luz, Tumbes
		PRU	OBU1G	R. Olmos, Olomos
	1	PRU	OBZ4V	R. Universal, Santa Maria
		PRU	OCU2Q	San Marcos
	10/5	URG	CX44	AM Libre, Montevideo
	2/0.5	URG	CW141	R. Turística, Salto
	10	VEN	SP	R. Simpatía, Valera
	5	VEN	ST	R. Turén, Turén
1420	1/0.25	ARG	LRI220	R. AM 1420, Buenos Aires
		ARG		R. Génesis 2000, General Conesa
	1	BOL		R. Centro, Cochabamba
		BOL		R. Creo en Milagros, Murillo
	1.5	BOL		R. Guadalquivir, Tarija
		BOL		R. Omasuyos Andina, Achacachi
	1	BOL		R. Real Audiencia, Sucre
	1	CHL	CC142	R. Maule, Cauquenes
	1	CHL	CB142	R. Panamericana, Santiago
	5	CLM	BH	Caracol R/R. Magdalena, Santa Marta

kHz	kW	Ctry	Call	Station, location
	1	CLM	D23	Ecos de Frontino, Frontino
	1	CLM	LE	La Cariñosa, Antena 2, Ibagué
	2	CLM	SN	R. Lenguerque, Zapatoca
	5	CLM	HK	Vida AM, Manizales
		EQA		Corazón AM, Machala
		EQA	VN7	LV del Napo, Tena
	1	EQA	MA6	R. Alternativa, Salcedo
	3	EQA	RN1	R. Bahá'í, Otavalo
	5	PRG	ZP42	R. Güyrá Campana, Horqueta
		PRU	OAU2R	R. Cajamarca, Cajamarca
	5	PRU	OBX2V	R. Ilucan, Cutervo
		PRU	OBU7L	R. OBU7L, Yanaoca
	1	PRU	OAZ8Z	R. Oriente, Yurimaguas
	1	PRU	OBZ4G	R. San Isidro, Lima
	1/0.5	URG	CX142	R. Felicidad, Paysandú
	5	URG	CW43	R. Lavalleja, Minas
	10/5	VEN	RW	R. Cardenal, Carora
	5	VEN	NZ	R. Marabina 1420, Maracaibo
	5	VEN		R. Sintonía, Caracas
1426	0.2	PRU	OCX1H	R. San Jose, La Union
1430	0.25	ARG	LRI235	R. Balcarce, Balcarce
		ARG		R. Cunumi Guazú
	1/0.25	ARG	LV26	R. Río Tercero (Cad. 26), Río Tercero
	1/0.25	ARG	LT24	R. San Nicolás, San Nicolás
		ARG		R. Shekinah, Merlo
		ARG		R.Victoria, La Plata
	1	ARG		Red La Pampeana, General Pico
	5	CLM	KU	1430 AM "Sonríele a Jesús R.", Bogotá
	1	CLM	IU	Armonías del Ingrumá, Riosucio
	5	CLM	PW	Colmundo, Barranquilla
	0.25	CLM	X61	L U FM Estéreo, Armenia
	5	CLM	MF	La Ribereña, Puerto Berrío
	1	CLM	EG	LV de Belalcázar, Popayán
	0.5	CLM	G42	R. Alejandría, Alejandría
	2	CLM	BP	R. Cariongo, Pamplona
	1	CLM	HKX73	R. Ciudad de Pereira, Pereira
	5	CLM	QX	R. Majagual, Sincelejo
	0.5	CLM	HKK38	R. Manantial, Sibundoy
	1	CLM	CK	R. Sensación, Yarumal
	5	EQA	CV3	Ondas del Zamora, Canal Juvenil, Loja
	10	EQA	MB2	R. Federal, Virgen de Fátima
	3.5	EQA	GF1	R. Futura 14-30, Quito
	5	EQA	JC6	R. Guaranda, Guaranda
	1	PRU	OAZ7M	CPN R., Cusco
	1	PRU	OAZ3H	R. Chavin, Chimbote
	1	PRU	OBX3E	R. Huarmey, Huarmey
	1	PRU	OAU6M	R. Lider, Tacna
		PRU		R. Nueva Juventud, Tucumé
		PRU	OBU7U	R. Red, Andina
	1	PRU	OBX2T	R. Santa Bárbara, Ascope
	0.5	PRU	OAZ4V	R. Universal, El Tambo
	1	PRU	OBX9H	R. Utcubamba, Bagua Grande
		PRU	OCU4L	San Vicente de Cañete
	20/5	URG	CW25	R. Durazno, Durazno
	10	VEN	NB	Llanerísima, Guacara
	25	VEN	TP	R. Bahía, Puerto La Cruz
	10/5	VEN	TM	R. Caicara, Caicara del Orinoco
1440	1	ARG	LU36	R. Coronel Suárez, Coronel Suárez
		ARG		R. Cristo Viene, Mar del Plata
	5/1	ARG	LRI221	R. General Obligado, Reconquista
		ARG		R. Impacto, Tapiales
	1/0.25	ARG	LV20	R. Laboulaye, Laboulaye
	1	ARG	LRA53	R. Nal., San Martín de los Andes
	1	BOL		R. Batallón Colorados, La Paz
	0.25	BOL		R. Bolivia, Cochabamba
	1	BOL		R. Em. Bolivia, Oruro
	2/1	BOL		R. Yaguary, Vallegrande
		BOL		R.Dif. Tropico, Trinidad
	1	CHL	CC144	R. El Sembrador, Chillán
	0.25	CLM	HKT58	Alcaldía de Ubala, Ubala
	5	CLM	EK	Caracol R, Tuluá
	5	CLM	NZ	Colmundo, Medellín
	5	CLM	IB	RCN Caqueta, Florencia
	5	CLM	GM	RCN, Sogamoso

kHz	kW	Ctry	Call	Station, location
		EQA		Mi Radio AM, Machala
	2.8	EQA	OV5	Ondas del Volante, Azogues
	3/5	EQA	AQ6	R. Fenix, Latacunga
	2.5	EQA	DY4	R. Iris, Esmeraldas
	5	EQA	DF1	R. Panorama, Ibarra
	1	PRU	OAU2O	LV de Celendin, Celendin
	2	PRU	OBX1T	R. Cooperativa Tumán, Chiclayo
	1	PRU	OAX4K	R. Imperial 2, Lima
	1	PRU	OAZ3O	R. LV de Pomabamba, Pomabamba
		PRU	OAX6R	R. Santa Monica, Arequipa
		PRU	OAM7L	R. Solar, Espinar
	3/0.5	URG	CX144	R. Rivera, Rivera
	10	VEN	ZI	R. Estelar 14-40, Guanare
	5	VEN	RF	R. Orituco, Altagracia del Orituco
	1	VEN	TY	R. Sucesos, Táriba
1445	0.5	CLM		Em. R. Unión, La Palma
1450	5/1	ARG		Corrientes (F.P.I.)
	5/1	ARG	LRI213	R. El Sol, Porción Quilmes
	1/0.25	ARG	LRI211	R. Las 40, Villa Aberastain
		BOL		R. Litoral, Guaqui
	1	CHL	CB145	R. Universidad Técnica, Valparaíso
	5	CLM	NL	La Cariñosa, Ant. 2, Manizales
	0.5	CLM		LV del Cauca, El Bordo
	5	CLM	BY	Oxígeno, Flandes
	5	CLM	HH	R. Católica Metropolitana, Bucaramanga
	0.2	CLM		R. LV del Nordeste, Remedios
	1	CLM	MX	R. Mancomoján, Carmen de Bolívar
	1	CLM	E20	R. María, Urrao
	1	EQA	SC1	AS La Radio, Tabacundo
	10	EQA	SC5	R. Calidad, Riobamba
	1	EQA	DR	R. Minutera, Guayaquil
	1	EQA	SE2	R. Santa Elena, Santa Elena
	5	PRG	ZP29	R. Vallemi, Vallemi
	1	PRU	OBX4K	R. Fortaleza, Barranca
	1.5	PRU	OCX2J	R. San Juan, Trujillo
		PRU	OAU2W	R. San Miguel, Cajamarca
	1	PRU	OCX7W	R. Santa Rosa, Santa Ana
		PRU		R. Super Nueva Sencacion, Chirinos
		PRU	OBU4Y	Rdif. E.G.C S.R.L., Huancayo
	1	PRU	OAM4A	Tinyahuarco
	10/5	URG	CX46	R. América, Montevideo
	1/0.25	URG	CW145	R. Arapey, Salto
	10	VEN	ZQ	Informativa 14-50, Los Puertos de Altagracia
	10/8	VEN	KJ	R. María, Caracas
	10/5	VEN	XC	R. Mega Visión, San Felix
1455	0.5	BOL		R. Magnal, Capinota
1457	1	PRU	OAX1V	R. Sullana, Sullana
1458	1	PRU	OAU2W	R. San Miguel, San Miguel
1460	1	ARG	LRK204	R. 21 (Cad. Eco), Yerba Buena
		ARG		R. Contacto, Merlo
		ARG		R. Jerusalén, Jerusalen
	0.25	ARG	LU30	R. Maipú (Cad. Eco), Maipú
	0.1	ARG	LU34	R. Pigüé, Pigüé
	1/0.25	ARG	LT29	R. Venado Tuerto, Venado Tuerto
		BOL		R. Morochata (CEPRA), Morochata
		BOL		R. Plenitud de Vida, El Alto
	10	CHL	CA146	R. Antofagasta, Antofagasta
	1	CHL	CC146	R. Armonía, Concepción
	1	CHL	CB146	R. Yungay, Santiago
	1	CLM	FL	Agustiniana Minuto de Dios, San Agustín
	0.25	CLM	HKY73	Alcaldía de San Andrés, San Andrés
	5	CLM	JW	Em. Nuevo Continente, Bogotá
	1	CLM	MU	LV de Amalfi "La Primera", Amalfi
	1	CLM	E26	R. Capiro, La Ceja
	5	CLM	TN	R. María, Turbo
	1	CLM	IW	R. Monumental, Cúcuta
	1	CLM	AL	R. Sincelejo, Sincelejo
	5	CLM	VH	R. Uno/RCN Antena 2, Barranquilla
	5	CLM	ZU	RCN Antena 2, Pasto
	5	EQA	AA7	LV de Gualaquiza, Gualaquiza
	5	EQA	IC6	R. Nuevos Horizontes, Latacunga
	1	PRU	OBX6C	R. Bahia, Mollendo
	1	PRU	OBU2E	R. Comercial, Jaén
	10	PRU	OAX7W	R. El Sol de los Andes, Juliaca

kHz	kW	Ctry	Call	Station, location
	0.5	PRU	OCY4I	R. Imperial, Junin
	2.5	PRU	OAX5K	R. Internacional, Pisco
	1	PRU	OAZ4F	R. La Oroya, La Oroya
		PRU	OBU7M	R. OBU7M, Marcapata
	1	PRU	OAX1V	R. Sullana, Sullana
	1	URG	CX146	R. Carmelo, Carmelo
	0.25	URG	CV146	R. José Batlle y Ordoñez, José Batlle y Ordoñez
	5	VEN	RJ	R. Jardín, Boconó
1470		ARG		Cadena 1470, Lanús
	0.25	ARG	LU26	Em. Coronel Dorrego, Coronel Dorrego
	1/0.25	ARG	LT20	R. Junín
		ARG		R. Lider, Mariano Acosta
		ARG		R. Mburucuya, José León Suarez
	1	ARG		R. Municipal, Luis Beltrán
	1/0.25	ARG	LT26	R. Nuevo Mundo, Colón
	1/0.25	ARG	LT28	R. Rafaela, Rafaela
		BOL		R. Em. Ayni, Corapata
	1	BOL		R. Integración, Padilla
	0.25	CLM	HKO96	Alcaldía de Baranoa, Baranoa
	5	CLM	PX	Colmundo, Cartagena
	0.25	CLM	JS20	Ecos de Palo Cabildo, Palo Cabildo
	5	CLM	TB	Ondas de Ibagué, Ibagué
	5	CLM	HQ	R. Futurama, Pacho
	5	CLM	NT	R. Huellas, Cali
	5	CLM	II	R. Popular, Medellín
	1	CLM	JIF	R. Tres Fronteras, Puerto Asís
	1	CLM	HJB63	R. Uno, Iza
	5	EQA	JC1	Ecos de Cayambe, Cayambe
	1.5	EQA	LD2	R. Ecos de Naranjito, Naranjito
	20	PRU	OAU4B	R. Amor, Lima
	1	PRU	OCX2G	R. Occidente, Quiruvilca
	0.8	PRU	OAX6M	R. Tacna, Tacna
	1	PRU	OAU6E	R. Victoria, Arequipa
		PRU	OCY4Y	R. Voz Cristiana, Huancayo
	2	URG	CX147	R. Cristal del Uruguay,Las Piedras
	1	URG	CW147	R. Maria, Melo
	10	VEN	SY	R. Vibración, Carúpano
	10	VEN	JW	Union R. Cultural, Valencia
1476	5	PRU	OBX2V	R. Ilucan, Cutervo
1480	1	ARG	LU27	R. Centro, Dolores
		ARG		R. Sensaciones, Tapiales
		BOL		L de los Andes, Carabuco
		BOL		R. Amor de Diós, El Alto
		BOL		R. Charcas, Sucre
	1/0.8	BOL		R. Chiwalaki, Vacas
		BOL		R. Comunitaria Waley, Saguadero
		BOL		R. Domingo Savio, Villa Independencia
	0.1	BOL		R. Patrimonio del Sur, Potosí
	1	BOL		R. San José, San José, Oruro
	1	CHL	CC148	R. La Amistad AM, Tomé
	1	CHL	HKR44	Alcaldía de Victoria, Victoria
	0.25	CLM		LV del Samán, Bochalema
	1	CLM	VB	R. Guayabal, Armero, Guayabal
	5	CLM	OD	R. Rodadero, Santa Marta
	1	CLM	TC	R. Sonsón, Sonsón
	5	CLM	FC	R. Unica, Pereira
	5	CLM	TZ	RCN Antena 2, Bucaramanga
	3	EQA	BS3	Oro Radio AM, Machala
	3	EQA	WP5	R. Atlántida, Alausí
	3	EQA	JV4	R. LV de Jipijapa, Jipijapa
	1	EQA	MC1	R. Municipal, Cotacachi
	5	EQA	CY6	R. Popular de La Maná, La Maná
	5	PRG	ZP20	R. América, Nemby
	1	PRG	ZP23	R. Dos Fronteras, Bella Vista Norte
	0.6	PRU	OCX2C	R. Comercial, Virú
	1	PRU	OAZ7G	R. Espinar, Yauri
	1	PRU	OCX4V	R. K´ler, Paramonga
	1	PRU	OAU4A	R. Laser, Santa Rosa de Sacco
	0.5	PRU	OBU2H	R. San Lorenzo, Socota
	1	PRU	OCX1L	R. Supercontinental, Chulucanas
	1	URG	CX148	Difusora Rio Negro, Young
	3/0.5	URG	CW43B	R. Internacional, Rivera
	3	URG	CW148	R. Universo, Castillos

kHz	kW	Ctry	Call	Station, location
		VEN		R. Cumarebo, Cumarebo
1490		ARG		AM Vida en el Espíritu, Mar del Plata
		ARG		R. AM Vida, Córdoba
	0.1	ARG	LU25	R. Carhué, Carhué
		ARG		R. Emanuel, Partido de Ezieza
	1	ARG	LV22	R. Huinca Renancó, Huinca Renancó
		ARG		R. Unidad, José Mármol
	1	CHL	CA149	R. Alicante, El Salvador
	1	CHL	CB149	R. El Canelo de Nos AM, San Bernardo
	5	CHL	CD149A	R. Malleco, Victoria
	0.2	CLM	J76	Alcaldía de El Peñon, El Peñon
	0.2	CLM	HKW24	Alcaldía de Guaitarilla, Guaitarilla
	4	CLM	BS	Em. Punto Cinco, Bogotá
	1	CLM	JO	LV de San Marcos, San Marcos
	1	CLM	E62	R. Garzón, Garzón
	5	CLM	AY	R. Vida Nueva, Barranquilla
	5	CLM	ZB	Robles 14-90, La Nueva, Tuluá
	1	EQA	VY2	La R. Dinámica, Guayaquil
		EQA		Poderosa 14-90, Quito
	3	EQA	AI6	R. Moderna, Píllaro
	5	EQA	SM5	R. Santa María, Azogues
	2.5	EQA	AE4	R. Unión, Esmeralda
	1	PRU	OBU7I	R. Chaski, Maras
	1	PRU	OCX7P	R. Emisora Frontera, Puno
	1	PRU	OBU4N	R. La Luz, Cerro de Pasco
	1.3	PRU	OAX6Q	R. Minuto, Cerro Colorado
	0.3	PRU	OAX5N	R. Nazca, Nazca
	1	PRU	OAX1L	R. Vision, Chiclayo
		PRU	OBU5C	Radiodifusora los Chankas, Andahuaylas
	1/0.25	URG	CV149	R. del Centro, Baltasar Brum
	5	URG	CX149	H. del Oeste, Nueva Helvecia
	10	VEN	XD	La Dinámica, Caracas
	10/5	VEN	RP	R. El Sol, Maracaibo
	1	VEN	SQ	R. Mérida 14-90, Mérida
1500	5/1	ARG	LRI214	R. Bonaerense, Lavallol
	1/0.25	ARG		R. Municipal, Gral. Conesa
	0.25	ARG	LT34	R. Nuclear, Zárate
	5/1	BOL		R. Chuquisaca, El Alto
	1	BOL		R. Sagrado Corazón, Mineros
	1	CHL	CC150	R. Centenario, San Javier
	1	CHL	CB150	R. Trasandina, Los Andes
	1	CLM	HKT71	Macheta
	5	CLM	UW	R. María, Manizales
	5	CLM	TW	R. Sumapaz, Fusagasugá
	5	CLM	LJ	Sonora, La Voz de la Red, Cali
	5	EQA	HG2	LV del Río Vinces, Vinces
	1	EQA	RO1	R. Otavalo, Otavalo
	1	PRU	OAU6B	R. Bulevar, Tacna
	1	PRU	OBX2X	R. Comercial, Trujillo
	1	PRU	OBX3J	R. Luz y Sonido, Huanuco
		PRU	OBU2J	R. San Pablo, San Pablo
	10	PRU	OBX4I	R. Santa Rosa, Lima
	1	PRU	OAU4W	R. Wanka, Huancayo
	10/5	VEN	RZ	R. 2000 AM, Cumaná
		VEN		R. Galaxia, San Mateo
1510		ARG		LV del Oeste, Libertad
		ARG		R. Alabanza, Guernica
	1/0.25	ARG	LRI253	R. Belgrano, Suardi
		ARG		R. RBN, Lomas de Zamora
		ARG		R. Urkupiña, Buenos Aires
	0.05	CHL	CD151	R. La Trompeta de Dios, Loncoche
	1/0.5	CHL	CA151	R. Luís Alvarez Sierra, Illapel
	1	CHL	CC151	R. Poder Pentecostal, Rancagua
	0.25	CLM	HKZ94	Alcaldía de Buenaventura, Buenaventura
	1	CLM	HKZ93	Alcaldía de Versalles, Versalles
	1	CLM	HX	Candela AM, Bucaramanga
	1	CLM	HKY41	Colombia Mía, Barrancabermeja
	5	CLM	D24	LV de La Unión, La Unión
	0.5	CLM		LV de los Cedros, Líbano
	1	CLM	A22	LV de San Luis, San Luis de Gaceno
	1	CLM	ZA	R. Cristal, Armenia:
	0.5	EQA	HD2	Inst. Oceanográfico de la Armada, Guayaquil
	3	EQA	JV7	R. Ecos del Oriente, Lago Agrio
	5	EQA		R. Monumental, Quito
		EQA		R. Net, Ambato
	2	EQA	RC5	R. Punto C 1510 AM, Cañar
	1	EQA	RY6	R. Runacunapac Yachana "R. El Saber del Hombre", Simiátug
	3	PRU	OCU4M	Cerro Laguna
	1	PRU	OCX6Q	R. Alegría, Arequipa
	1	PRU	OBX8K	R. Centro de los Medios, Sepahua
		PRU	OCX2O	R. Inca, Los Baños del Inca
	1	PRU	OAX5F	R. LV Huamanga, Nazca
	1	PRU	OBU1B	R. Super Real, Olmos
	1	PRU	OCX4J	R. Tarma, Tarma
	1	PRU	OCX1V	R. Tumbes, Tumbes
	2.5	PRU	OAU2U	R. Virgin de la Alta Gracia, Huamachuco
	0.5	URG	CW151	R. Ibirapitá, San Gregorio de Polanco
	1/0.5	URG	CX151	R. Rincón, Fray Bentos
	2/0.5	URG	CW57	R. San Carlos, San Carlos
	20	VEN		Informativa "LV del Centro", Güigüe
1517	1	PRU	OCX2O	R. Inca, Los Baños del Inca
1520		ARG		Cadena D, Monte Chingolo
	5/1	ARG		R. Chascomús, Chascomús
		ARG		R. Cielo Nuevo, Isidro Casanova
	0.25	ARG	LT38	R. Gualeguay, Gualeguay
		ARG		R. Metropolitana, Ciudadela
	3	ARG		R. Norteña, Los Polvorines
		ARG		R. Visión Fortaleza, Ezeiza
	1	BOL		R. la Chiwana, Cochabamba
		BOL		R. La Luz del Tiempo, El Alto
	0.25	BOL		R. Litoral, Llica
		BOL		R. San Pedro, Tiahuanacu
	1	CHL	CC152	R. Soberanía, Linares
	0.25	CLM	HKT20	Alcaldía de Montería, Montería
	0.1	CLM	HKW43	Alcaldía de Tangua, Tangua
	1	CLM	RL	Antena de los Andes, Santa Rosa de Cabal
	0.3	CLM		Brisas del Palmar, Caucasia
	0.25	CLM	T21	Colombia Mía, Tierralta
	1	CLM	MZ	Ecos de la Sierra Flor, Sincelejo
	1	CLM	J98	Em. Una Voz de la Frontera, Puerto Santander
	5	CLM	LI	Libertad, Bogotá
	1	CLM	MA	LV de Suroeste, Jericó
	1	CLM	AM	R. Altamizal, Dolores
	0.5	CLM	HKS24	R. Cristalares Timbío, Timbío
	5	CLM	LQ	R. Minuto, Barranquilla
	1	CLM	V37	R. Pueblo Viejo, Zipacon
	1	CLM	HKW37	R. Universidad, Pasto
		CLM		Sonoradio 1520 AM, Viterbo
	2.5	EQA	RI5	LV de Guamote, Guamote
	1	EQA	RN2	LV de Naranjal, El Naranjal
	1	EQA	TI1	R. Ibarra, Ibarra
		PRU	OAU1H	R. Cristal, Chiclayo
		PRU	OBU7X	R. Fuentes Mollo, Espinar
	5	PRU	OAU7Y	R. OAU7Y, Juliaca
	1	PRU	OAX9X	R. Vision, Janjui
	2	URG	CX152	R. Acuarela, Melo
	1/0.5	URG	CV152	R. Paz, "La Nueva R.", Guichón
1530		ARG		AM 1530 Cadena UOCRA, Buenos Aires
	1	ARG	LRJ200	R. Centro Morteros, Morteros
		ARG		R. Eco, CA Buenos Aires
		ARG		R. El Faro, Gregorio de Laferrere
		ARG		R. Esencia "LV del Litoral", San Miguel Oeste
	0.5	BOL		R. Em. Ballivián, San Borja
	1	CHL	CA153	R. Juan Godoy, Copiapó
	1	CHL	CB153	R. Nexo, Quillota
	1	CHL	CD153	R. Nuvo Mundo, Puerto Montt
	0.25	CLM	HKN85	Alcaldía de Anza, Anza
	0.1	CLM	HKS58	Alcaldía de El Copey, El Copey
	0.25	CLM	HKN57	Alcaldía de San Juan de Uraba, San Juan de Uraba
	0.25	CLM	HKN79	Alcaldía de Uramita, Uramita
	1	CLM	HKV82	Alcaraván Radio, Puerto Lleras
	1	CLM	EU	Caracol Sevilla, Sevilla
	0.25	CLM	HKN65	Colombia Mía, Caucasia, AN
	1	CLM	HKR73	Ecos del Pacífico, Guapí
		CLM	HKS56	Fascinación AM, Becerril

kHz	kW	Ctry	Call	Station, location
	5	CLM	OZ	LV de la Prov. de Padilla, San Juan del Cesar
		CLM		R. Integración, Morales
	5	CLM	DN	Yeshu'a LV de Jesucristo, Medellín
	5	EQA	MP2	LV de la Península, La Libertad
	5	EQA	CC5	Ondas Cañaris AM, R. Universitaria Católica, Azogues
	1	EQA	MZ6	R. Deportes 15-30, Pelileo
	3	EQA	VP5	R. LV de Pallatanga, Pallatanga
	1	PRU	OBX3H	CPN R., Chimbote
	1	PRU	OBZ4S	R. 15-50, Huancayo
		PRU		R. Capachica, Capachica
	1	PRU	OCX1Y	R. Leomar, Bellavista
	10	PRU	OBU4C	R. Milenia, Lima
		PRU	OBU7N	R. Ondas del Sur Oriente, Quillabamba
	3	PRU	OBX2R	R. Oriental, Jaén
		PRU	OAU5R	R. Universidad, San Juan Bautista
	0.5	PRU	OAZ7F	Rdif. Espinar, Yauri
	0.25	URG	CW153	Em. Cono Sur, Nueva Palmira
	10	VEN	NP	R. San Felipe el Fuerte, San Felipe
1540		ARG		R. AM Líder, José León Suárez
		ARG		R. Amanecer, CA Buenos Aires
		ARG		R. Cotidiana, Merlo
	0.25	ARG	LT35	R. Mon, Pergamino
	0.25	ARG	LU28	R. Tuyú
		ARG		R. Zorobabel, Esteban Echeverría
		BOL		R. Bendita Trinidad y Espíritu Santo, El Alto
		BOL		R. Comunitario Tutuka, Vilaque
	0.8	BOL		R. Sariri, Escoma
	1	CHL	CC154	R. Colocolo, Chillán
	1	CHL	CD154	R. San José de Alcudia, Río Bueno
	1	CHL	CB154	R. Sudamérica, Santiago
	0.25	CLM	HKP50	Alcaldía de Arjona, Arjona
	0.15	CLM	HKR80	Alcaldía de Sacama, Sacama
	1	CLM	HKZ52	Colombia Mía, Chaparral
	1	CLM	A26	Em. Brisas del Río Chico, Belmira
	1	CLM	HD	LV del Petróleo, Barrancabermeja
	0.25	CLM		LV Dorada, Segovia
	2	CLM	RQ	R. Austral, Túquerres
	5	CLM	ZF	R. Cóndor, Manizales
	0.25	CLM		R. El Sur, San Vicente de Chucurí
	0.5	EQA	MH	Cotopaxi Digital, Latacunga
	0.25	EQA	VB7	LV del Upano, Macas
	1	EQA	DP1	R. Caracol, Quito
	3	EQA	FM2	R. Cristal de Ventanas, Babahoyo
		EQA		R. Flecha AM, Machala
	1	PRU	OBZ4U	R. Barranca, Barranca
	0.3	PRU	OBX4N	R. Corporacion, Cerro de Pasco
	1	PRU	OCX7V	R. Los Andes, Cusco
	1	PRU	OBX1B	R. LV de la Frontera, Tumbes
	1	PRU	OAU6A	R. Milenio Universal, Arequipa
	2	PRU	OBU2A	R. Mundial AM, Trujillo
	5	PRU	OCU2X	R.Turbomix, Cajamarca
	1	URG	CV154	R. Centro, Cardona
	0.1	URG	CW154	R. Charrúa, Paysandú
	0.5/0.25	URG	CX154	R.Patria, Treinta y Tres
1545	1	PRU	OAX9X	R. Vision, Janjui
1550	0.25	ARG	LT32	R. Chivilcoy, Chivilcoy
		ARG		R. Esperanza, Gregorio de Laferrere
	1	ARG	LT40	R. LV de la Paz, La Paz
		ARG		R. Popular, José León Suárez
	5/0.25	ARG	LT23	R. Regional, San Jenaro Norte
		ARG		R. Urkupiña, Buenos Aires
	10	BOL		R. Caranavi, Caranavi
	1	CHL	CC155	R. Manuel Rodríguez, San Fernando
	1	CHL	CB155	R. Provincial AM, Putaendo
	0.1	CLM	HKW53	Alcaldía de El Tablón, El Tablón
	0.1	CLM	HKW55	Alcaldía de Guachucal, Guachucal
	0.25	CLM	HKW50	Alcaldía de Mallama, Mallama
	1	CLM	HKV38	Colombia Mía, Pitalito
	5	CLM	HKX29	Colombia Mía, Tibú
	5	CLM	LT	Em. Revivir en Cristo, Cali
	5	CLM	ZI	G12 Radio, Bogotá

kHz	kW	Ctry	Call	Station, location
	5	CLM	UN	LV del Río Arma, Aguadas
	0.5	CLM		Ondas del Nechí, Campamento
	5	CLM	CB	R. El Sol "La Cariñosa", Barranquilla
	5	CLM	QD	Sistema Vida, Armenia
	5	EQA	AD5	LV de Chaguarurco, Santa Isabel
	2	EQA	AD2	LV del Triunfo, El Triunfo
	2	EQA	EI6	R. Montalvo, Ambato
	1	PRU	OBZ4S	R. 15-50, Huancayo
	1	PRU	OAU3D	R. Cruz, Chimbote
	1	PRU	OBX4P	R. Independencia, Lima
	1	PRU	OBX5J	R. Maria
	1	PRU	OAX1D	R. Superior, Monsefú
	0.25	URG	CV155	R. Agraciada, Mercedes
	2/0.5	URG	CW155	R. Sarandí del Yí, Sarandí del Yí
	10/5	VEN	XO	R. Impacto La Poderosa, Cd. Ojeda
	10	VEN	MW	R. Metropolitana, Los Teques
1555	0.5	CLM		R. Parroquial, El Santuario
1560	05/0.25	ARG		AM 1560 "La R. de la Gente", Tandil
	1/0.25	ARG		Mendoza (F.P.I.)
	1	ARG		R. Antena Lobos, Lobos
		ARG		R. Castañares, Ituzaingó
	2.5/1.5	ARG	LT11	R. Gral. Francisco Ramírez, Villaguay
	0.25	ARG	LT33	R. Nueve de Julio, 9 de Julio
		ARG		R. Restauración, Llavallol
	1	BOL		R. Occidental, Oruro
	0.5	BOL		R. Urkupiña, Quillacollo
	1	CHL	CB156	R. Manantial, Talagante
	5/3	CHL	CA156	R. Parinacota, Putre
	1	CHL	CD156	R. Parque Nacional, Villarrica
	0.25	CLM	HKO35	Alcaldía de Cañasgordas, Cañasgordas
	0.25	CLM	HKV90	Alcaldía de Villavicencio, Villavicencio
	5	CLM	LP	La Cariñosa, Antena 2, Tuluá
	1	CLM	PZ	R. Codazzi, Codazzi
	0.5	CLM	HKS65	R. Tamalameque, Tamalameque
	5	CLM	CP	RCN Antena 2, Arbelaez
	5	CLM	XZ	Santa María de la Paz R., Medellín
	5	CLM	HE	Voces Rovirenses, Málaga
	1.5	EQA	ZD1	Ecos Culturales de Urcuquí, Urcuquí
	2	EQA	TR3	LV del Guabo, El Guabo
	2	EQA	CS2	R. Sideral, Daule
	1.5	PRU	OAU7Z	R. Carráviz, Juliaca
	1	PRU	OCX6N	R. La Luz, Arequipa
	1	PRU	OAZ7N	R. Maria, Wanchaq
		PRU	OBX80	R. Nuevo Mundo, Iquitos
	0.5	PRU	OBX2J	R. Nuvo Continente, Cajamarca
	1	PRU	OBU4G	R. San Sebastian, Yauyos
	2/0.5	URG	CX156	Dif. Americana, Trinidad
	3/0.5	URG	CW51	R. Maldonado, Maldonado
	1	URG	CV156	R. Vichadero
	10/5	VEN	LZ	R. Dif. Andina, Mérida
1564	0.5	PRU	OBU2H	R. San Lorenzo, Socota
1570	5/1	ARG	LRI223	Lomas de Zamora (F.P.I.)
		ARG		R. Alegría Regional, Luis Palacio
	2	ARG		R. AM Rocha, La Plata
		ARG		R. La Morena de Itatí, Grand Bourg
		ARG		R. Melody, Remedios de Escalada
		BOL		R. Comunitaria Tawantinsuyo, Taraco
		BOL		R. Pedro Ignacio Muiba
	7	CHL	CC157A	R. Familia Chilena, Talca
	1	CHL	CC157	R. Niebla, Rancagua
	0.25	CLM	HKX78	Alcaldía de Balboa, Balboa
	0.15	CLM	HKU42	Alcaldía de Cajica, Cajica
	0.25	CLM	HKQ83	Alcaldía de Maripi, Maripi
	0.25	CLM	HKQ82	Alcaldía de Sta María, Sta María
	0.25	CLM	HKP58	Alcaldía de Sta Rosa Sur, Sta Rosa Sur
	2	CLM	HKX52	Arc. Armada de Colombia, Pto Leguizamo
	1	CLM	E96	Colombia Mía, Palmira
		CLM		LV de Fomeque, Fomeque
	1	CLM	E70	R. Auténtica, Manizales
	1	CLM	HKO22	R. Ciudad Dabeiba, Dabeiba
	1	CLM	TG	R. María, Machetá
	0.1	CLM	HKX80	R. Marsella, Marsella

kHz	kW	Ctry	Call	Station, location
	0.2	CLM	HKR66	R. Universidad de la Amazonia, Florencia
	0.5	CLM	HJR66	Timbiqui Estéreo, Timbiqui
	0.5	EQA		Ondas Quereñas, Quero
	1	EQA		R. LV Espíritu Santo de Dios, Manta
	10	EQA	PG1	R. Nucanchic, Maldonado
		PRU		R. Bethel, Lima
	1	PRU	OBX3N	R. Chasqui, Yungay
		PRU	OBU2L	R. Colonial, Contumaza
	1	PRU	OCX1Z	R. La Nueva Esperanza, Tambo Grande
	1	PRU	OBX3M	R. San Martin, Huanuco
	1	PRU	OCU7L	R. Vilcanota, Sicuani
	1	PRU	OCX6I	R. Willy, Uraca
		PRU	OCU2C	Radiodifusora Julcan
	0.25	URG	CW157A	Em. Celeste, Tomás Gomensoro
	2/0.5	URG	CX157	R. Canelones
1575	3/1	PRU	OAZ1F	R. Naylamp, Lambayeque
	1	PRU	OAU2E	R. Nuevo Continente, San Ignacio
1580		ARG		AM Tradición, San Martín
	1	ARG		R. 26. de Julio, Longchamps
	0.25	ARG	LT36	R. Chacabuco, Chacabuco
	1	ARG	LT27	R. LV del Montiel, Villaguay
		ARG		R. Provincial de Sierra Colorada, Sierra Colorada: (F.pl.)
		ARG		R. Tradición, Isidro Casanova
	1	BOL		R. Adonai, Santa Cruz
	3	BOL		R. Bermejo, Bermejo
		BOL		R. Contacto, Sucre
		BOL		R. El Fuego del Espíritu Santo, El Alto
		BOL		R. Kollasuyo Marka, Tiawanaku
	1	CHL	CC158	R. Colchagua, Santa Cruz
	0.5	CHL	CD158A	R. Continental, Collipulli
	0.25	CLM	HKU42	Alcaldía de Cajica, Cajica
	0.1	CLM	HKW74	Alcaldía de Pupiales, Pupiales
	0.25	CLM	HKT34	Alcaldía de San Antero, San Antero
		CLM		Alcaldía de Yaguará, Yaguará
	5	CLM	QT	Aviva R., Bogotá
	5	CLM	RM	Caracol R, Sincelejo
	1	CLM	LC	LV del Banco, El Banco
	0.15	CLM	HKS46	R. Alcaldía de Padilla, Padilla
	5	CLM	QZ	R. María, Barranquilla
	1	CLM	E66	R. Miraflores, Rovira
	5	CLM	NA	R. Robledo/RCN Antena 2, Cartago:
	1	CLM	KB	R. Zulima, Villa del Rosario
	1	EQA	LF1	Ecos de Orellana, Machach
	3	EQA	TP5	Ecos del Portete, Girón
	5	EQA	VA4	Estación de la Alegría, Esmeraldas
	0.25	EQA	AB3	Ondas de Paltas, Catacocha
	1	PRU		R. Central, Bellavista
	3/1	PRU	OBX1M	R. Naylamp, Lambayeque
	1	PRU	OAU4P	R. San Juan, Tarma
	1	PRU	OAU5J	R. Virgen del Carmen, Huancavelica
	2/0.5	URG	CW54	Emisoras del Este, Minas
	1/0.5	URG	CW158	R. San Salvador, Dolores
	10/5	VEN	TK	Manzanares 15-80, Cumaná
	10	VEN	YO	R Celestial, San Francisco, Maracaibo
	10/5	VEN	YV	R. Venezolana, Calabozo
1584	0.5	PRU	OBX7Q	R. El Triunfo, Cusco
1587	1	PRU	OAU5A	R. Armonia, Abancay
1590		ARG		AM 1590 La Radio de la Region, Dolores
		ARG		R. Cristiana Adonal, Bánfield Oeste
		ARG		R. Olivera, General Rodriguez
		ARG		R.Stentor, Buenos Aires
	1	BOL		R. Wayana Songo, Pongo K´asa
	1	CHL	CB159	R. Carnaval, San Felipe
		CLM	HKS72	Alcaldía de La Gloria, La Gloria
	5	CLM	IP	BBN 15-90 R., Envigado
	1	CLM	QM	Ecos de la Miel, Samaná
	5	CLM	WB	Em Nuestra Sra del Socorro, Socorro
		CLM		Ondas del Rioseco, Rioseco
		CLM		R. Espacial, Andalucía
	1	EQA	RZ1	R. Mensaje, Cayambe

kHz	kW	Ctry	Call	Station, location
	1	EQA	QT6	R. Panamericana, Quero
	0.25	EQA	AS2	R. Record, La Libertad
	1	PRU	OBU2C	Agro R., Trujillo
	2	PRU	OAZ4Z	R. Agricultura "La Peruanísima", Lima
	1	PRU	OAU7C	R. Huaynaroque, Juliaca
	1	PRU	OCX6S	R. Mundo, Arequipa
		PRU		R. Municipal, San Marcos
	1	URG	CX159	R. Real, Colonia
	1/0.25	URG	CW159	R. Regional, Lascano
	10	VEN	UD	R. Deporte, Caracas
1600	0.25	ARG		AM 1600 R. del Centro, Montes de Oca
	1.2	ARG		R. Armonia, Caseros
		ARG		R. Metropolitana - "La Radio", Luís Guillón
	0.5	BOL		R. Continental, Punata
	0.25	CHL	CC160	R. Llacolén, Concepción
	0.25	CHL	CB160	R. Nuevo Tiempo, Santiago
	0.25	CHL	CB160A	R. Positiva, Viña del Mar
	0.15	CLM	HKZ79	Alcaldía de Cajamarca, Cajamarca
	0.25	CLM	HKO63	Alcaldía de Jardín, Jardín
	0.25	CLM	HKX83	Alcaldía de La Celia, Celia
	0.25	CLM	HKT39	Alcaldía de Valencia, Valencia
	0.15	CLM	HKZ77	Alcaldía de Venadillo, Venadillo
	5	CLM	HJO72	Colombia Mía, Carepa
		CLM	HKX84	Em. Mundial, Dosquebradas
	5	CLM	HV	Emisora Armoniaz, Zipaquirá
	0.25	CLM		LV de Aranzazu, Aranzazu
	0.25	CLM	HKR52	LV de Colina, Risaralda
	1	CLM		LV del Rosario, Junín
		CLM		R. Bello Horizonte, Pesca
		CLM		R. Fortaleza, Sogamoso
	0.25	CLM		R. Impacto Cristiano, Popayán
	0.25	CLM	F33	R. Restauración, Cali
		EQA		Ondas de Caluma "R.del Pueblo", Caluma
		EQA		R. Ilusión 1600 AM, Puembo
	1	PRU	OCY2D	R. Int., San Pablo
		PRU	OBU4R	R. Nuevo Tiempo, Huancayo
		PRU		R. San Juan, Catacaos
	1	URG	CV160	R. Continental, Pando
	1	URG	CX160	R. Litoral, Fray Bentos
1610	0.2	ARG		R. Fósil, Rosario
		ARG		R. Guabiyú, Gregorio de Laferrere
	0.05	ARG		R. Luz del Mundo, Rafael Calzada
	0.5	ARG		R. Regional, Laboulaye
		CLM		Armonías de Occidente, Medellín
		CLM		R. Estelar, Santuario
		PRU		R. Carabamba, Julcán
	0.5	PRU	OAU6O	R. Flor de los Andes, Arequipa
1613	1	CLM		R. Ideal, Umbita
1620	10/1	ARG		AM 16-20 La Radio, Mar del Plata
		ARG		R. Italia, Villa Martelli
		ARG		R. Sentir,Merlo
		ARG		R. Vida, Monte Grande
1630	10	ARG		AM Diagonal, La Plata
		ARG		R. AM Súper Sport, Lomas de Zamora
		ARG		R. Restauración, Hurlingham
	1/0.25	ARG		R.America, San José
1640		ARG		Hosanna AM 1640, Isidro Casanova
		ARG		R. Nueva Bolivia, Buenos Aires
1650	1/0.5	ARG	LRI227	Antares AM 1650, Pilar
		ARG		R. Guarani AM, San Justo
		ARG		R.Fenix. Temperley
1660	5/0.25	ARG		Nogoyá (F.P.I.)
	1/0.25	ARG		Paso de los Libres (F.P.I.)
		ARG		R. Reivir, Gregorio de la Ferrere
1670		ARG		R. Bethel, Banfield
1680		ARG		R.Hosanna Tropical, Ezeiza
1690	1/0.25	ARG		R. Cristo la Solución, San Justo
1700	5/1	ARG		R. Fantastico, Tigre
1710	0.3	ARG		AM 1710 - R.Urquiza, Buenos Aires

SHORTWAVE STATIONS OF THE WORLD

November 2012 - World Copyright WRTH Publications Ltd

For country and site codes, see relevant tables in reference section. Stations marked as '**dom**' in the site column are domestic/national broadcasts. Stations marked with '**STF**' in the site column are Standard Time/Frequency transmissions. The column '**N**' indicates Notes. Symbols used in the '**N**' column are '**+**', indicating DRM transmissions; '**±**' which indicates variable frequency; '**†**' for irregular transmissions and **‡** for frequencies that were inactive at the editorial deadline.

kHz	N	kW	Ctry	Site	Station, location
2310		50	AUS	dom	N. Terr. SW Sce, Alice Springs
2325		50	AUS	dom	N. Terr. SW Sce, Tennant Creek
2350			KRE	dom	KCBS/Reg., Sariwon
2368	‡	1	AUS	dom	R. Symban, Sydney
2380		0.25	B	dom	R. Educadora, Limeira
2485		50	AUS	dom	N. Terr. SW Sce, Katherine
2500		10	CHN	STF	BPM, Kinshan
		2.5	USA	STF	WWV NIST, Fort Collins, CO
		5	HWA	STF	WWVH NIST, Kauai, HI
2850			KRE	dom	KCBS, Pyongyang
3025	†		KRE	dom	Frontline Soldiers Radio
3185		100	USA	WRB	The Overcomer Ministry
		100	USA	WRB	WWRB
3195		100	USA	WCR	WWCR
		100	USA	WCR	WWCR
		100	USA	WRB	WWRB
3200		25	SWZ	MAN	TWR Africa
		50	SWZ	MAN	TWR Africa
3205		10	PNG	dom	NBC Sandaun, Vanimo
3215		50	MDG	MDC	AWR Africa/Europe
		50	MDG	dom	R. Feon'ny Filazantsara, Talata V
		100	USA	WCR	WWCR
		100	USA	WCR	WWCR
		100	USA	WRB	WWRB
3220		5	KRE	dom	KCBS/Reg., Hamhung
3235	†	10	PNG	dom	NBC West New Britain, Kimbe
3240		50	SWZ	MAN	TWR Africa
3250		50	KRE	PYO	Pyongyang Broadcasting Stn.
	†	1	HND	dom	R. Luz y Vida, San Luís
		100	KRE	PYO	Voice of Korea
3255		100	AFS	MEY	BBC World Service
3260	†	10	PNG	dom	NBC Madang, Madang
3275	‡	10	PNG	dom	NBC Sthn Highlands, Mendi
3280		2	EQA	dom	LV del Napo, Tena
		50	CHN	dom	VO Pujiang, Shanghai
3290	‡	10	PNG	dom	NBC Central, Port Moresby
	†	5	GUY	dom	NCN VO Guyana, Georgetown
3305	‡	10	PNG	dom	NBC Western, Daru
3310		10	BOL	dom	R. Mosoj Chaski, Cochabamba
3315	†	10	PNG	dom	NBC Manus, Lorengau
3320		50	KRE	PYO	Pyongyang Broadcasting Stn.
		100	AFS	dom	R. Sonder Grense, Meyerton
3325		10	PNG	dom	NBC Bougainville, Buka
		2.5	B	dom	R. Mundial, São Paulo
		10	INS	dom	RRI, Palangkaraya
3329		5	PRU	dom	R. Ondas d. Huallaga, Huánuco
3330		10	CAN	STF	CHU, Ottawa
3335	‡	10	PNG	dom	NBC East Sepik, Wewak
3340		2	HND	dom	R. Misiones Int., Comayagüela
3345		100	AFS	MEY	Channel Africa
	†	10	PNG	dom	NBC Northern, Popondetta
	†	10	INS	dom	RRI, Ternate
3350			KRE	dom	KCBS/Reg., Pyongsong

kHz	N	kW	Ctry	Site	Station, location
		100	CTR	CRI	R. Exterior de España (REE)
3355	‡	10	PNG	dom	NBC Simbu, Kundiawa
		1	B	dom	R. Educadora, Xapuri
	†		PRU	dom	R. JPJ, Lima
3365		10	PNG	dom	NBC Milne Bay, Alotau
		1	B	dom	R. Cultura, Araraquara
3375		1	B	dom	R. Municipal, São Gabriel Cach.
3385	†	10	PNG	dom	NBC E. New Britain, Rabaul
3390	†	1	BOL	dom	R. Emisora, Camargo
	‡	1	CAF	dom	R. ICDI, Boali
3396		100	ZWE	dom	ZBC R. Zimbabwe, Gweru
3480		50	KOR	GOY	Voice of the People
3560	†	50	KRE	KUJ	Voice of Korea
3810		1	EQA	STF	HD2IOA, Guayaquil
3900		5	CHN	dom	Hulun Buir-Ch, Hailar
3905	†	10	PNG	dom	NBC New Ireland, Kavieng
3912		50	KOR	GOY	Voice of the People
3915		100	SNG	SNG	BBC World Service
		1	PNG	dom	R. Fly, Kiunga
3920			KRE	dom	KCBS/Reg., Hyesan
3925		10	J	dom	R. Nikkei 1, Sapporo
		50	J	dom	R. Nikkei 1, Tokyo
3930	±				Radio Voice of Kurdistan
3940			KRE	dom	KCBS/Reg., Chongjin
3945		50	IND	dom	All India R., Gorakhpur
		50	IND	GKP	All India Radio (AIR)
		10	J	dom	R. Nikkei 2, Tokyo
		10	VUT	dom	R. Vanuatu, Port Vila
3950		50	CHN	dom	Xinjiang PBS, Urumqi
3955	+	100	G	SKN	BBC World Service
		250	G	SKN	KBS World Radio
		1	D	KLL	Radio 700
		1	D	KLL	Radio 700 Kurzwellendienst
		250	G	SKN	Radio Taiwan International
3959			KRE	dom	KCBS/Reg., Kanggye
3960	‡	2.5	LBR	dom	Star R., Monrovia
3963	±	10	INS	dom	RRI, Palu
3965	+	1	F	ISS	Radio France Int. (RFI)
		250	F	ISS	Radio Taiwan International
		500	F	ISS	Radio Taiwan International
		500	IRN	KAM	VO the Islamic Rep. of Iran
		500	IRN	ZAH	VO the Islamic Rep. of Iran
	±				Voice of Iranian Kudistan
3975	‡	100	PAK	dom	Azad Kashmir R., Islamabad
			KRE	dom	KCBS/Reg., Wonsan
		100	CVA	SMG	Vatican Radio
		250	CVA	SMG	Vatican Radio
3976	‡	10	INS	dom	RRI, Pontianak
3985		100	CHN	dom	CNR2 Business R, Golmud
		100	KOR	JAA	Echo of Hope (VOH)
		10	HRV	DEA	Voice of Croatia
3990		15	CHN	dom	Gannan PBS, Hezuo
		50	CHN	dom	Xinjiang PBS, Urumqi

kHz	N	kW	Ctry	Site	Station, location
3995		1	D	WNM	HCJB Germany
		1	D	WNM	Missionwerk Heukelbach
	†	5	INS	dom	RRI, Kendari
4005		500	IRN	KAM	VO the Islamic Rep. of Iran
4010		100	KGZ	dom	KGR1, Bishkek
4050		100	KGZ	dom	R. Rossii relay, Bishkek
4055		0.7	GTM	dom	R. Verdad, Chiquimula
4111	†	0.5	BOL	dom	R. Virgen de Remedios, Tupiza
4220		15	CHN	dom	Qinghai, Xining
4319		3	DGA	DGA	AFRTS (AFN Feeder)
4363		10	F	MCO	Radio Monaco
4405	†	50	KRE	KUJ	Voice of Korea
4410		0.5	BOL	dom	R. Eco, Reyes
4413	‡	1	LAO	dom	R. Nationale Lao, Sam Neua
4450		50	KOR	GOY	Voice of the People
4451		1	BOL	dom	R. Santa Ana, Santa Ana
4500		50	CHN	dom	Xinjiang PBS, Urumqi
4557		50	KOR	GOY	Voice of the People
4605	‡	1	INS	dom	RRI, Serui
4700		1	BOL	dom	R. San Miguel, Riberalta
4717		1	BOL	dom	R. Yura, Yura
4747		0.5	PRU	dom	R. Huanta 2000, Huanta
4750		100	BGD	dom	Bangladesh Betar, Savar
		100	CHN	dom	CNR1 VO China, Hailar
		1	UGA	dom	Dunamis SW, Mukono
		15	CHN	dom	Qinghai PBS, Xining
	‡	20	INS	dom	RRI, Makassar
4755	±	1	FSM	dom	PMA The Cross, Kolonia
		10	B	dom	R. Imaculada Conceição, C. G.
4760		10	IND	dom	All India R., Leh
		8	IND	dom	All India R., Port Blair
		50	SWZ	MAN	TWR Africa
4765	†	10	B	dom	R. Integração, Cruzeiro do Sul
		50	TJK	dom	Tajik R, Yangiyul
4775		50	IND	dom	All India R., Imphal
		1	B	dom	R. Congonhas, Congonhas
		0.5	PRU	dom	R. Tarma, Tarma
		50	SWZ	MAN	TWR Africa
4780		50	DJI	dom	RTD, Djibouti
4781		3	EQA	dom	R. Oriental, Tena
4785		10	B	dom	R. Caiari, Porto Velho
4790		0.5	PRU	dom	R. Visión, Chiclayo
		10	INS	dom	RRI, Fak-Fak
4795		15	KGZ	dom	KGR1, Bishkek
4796			BOL	dom	R. Lípez, Uyuni
4800		50	IND	dom	All India R., Hyderabad
		100	CHN	dom	CNR1 VO China, Golmud
	‡	1	MEX	dom	R. Transcontinental, México
4805		5	B	dom	R. Dif. do Amazonas, Manaus
4810		50	IND	dom	All India R., Bhopal
		100	ARM	ERV	Public Radio of Armenia (FS)
		1	PRU	dom	R. Logos, Chazuta
4815		10	B	dom	R. Dif. Londrina, Londrina
		1	EQA	dom	R. El Buen Pastor, Saraguro
4820		50	IND	dom	All India R., Kolkata
		100	CHN	dom	Xizang PBS, Lhasa
4824		10	PRU	dom	LV de la Selva, Iquitos
4825	†	10	B	dom	R. Canção Nova, Cach. Paulista
	†	5	B	dom	R. Educadora, Bragança
4827		0.3	PRU	dom	R. Sicuani, Sicuani
4828	†	100	ZWE	GWE	Voice of Zimbabwe
4830		10	MNG	dom	Mongolian R. 1, Altay
		50	CHN	dom	VO Strait, Fuzhou
4835		10	IND	dom	All India R., Gangtok
		50	AUS	dom	N. Terr. SW Sce, Alice Springs
	†	1	PRU	dom	R. Marañón, Jaén
4840		50	IND	dom	All India R., Mumbai
		100	USA	WCR	WWCR
		100	USA	WCR	WWCR
4845		10	B	dom	R. Cultura, Manaus
	†	1	B	dom	R. Met. Paulista, Ibitinga
4850		50	IND	dom	All India R., Kohima
		50	CHN	dom	Xinjiang PBS, Urumqi
4851		1	PRU	dom	R. Genesis, Huanta
4857		2	PRU	dom	R. La Hora, Cusco
4860		50	IND	dom	All India R., Shimla
4865		5	B	dom	R. Alvorada, Londrina
		5	BOL	dom	R. Logos, Santa Cruz
		5	B	dom	R. Verdes Florestas, Cruzeiro
4870		100	IND	DEL	All India Radio (AIR)
		100	IND	DEL	Radio Sedayee Kashmir
		10	INS	dom	RRI, Wamena
4875	±				Voice of Iranian Kudistan
4878	†	10	B	dom	R. Dif. Roraima, Boa Vista
4880		50	IND	dom	All India R., Lucknow
		100	AFS	MEY	SW Radio Africa
4885		2	B	dom	R. Clube do Pará, Belém
	†	5	B	dom	R. Dif. Acreana, Rio Branco
	†	1	B	dom	R. Maria, Anápolis
4895		50	IND	dom	AIR Kolkata, Kurseong
		100	AFS	MEY	Amateur R. Mirror Int.
		10	MNG	dom	Mongolian R. 2, Mörön
		5	B	dom	R. Novo Tempo, Campo Grande
4905		1	B	dom	R. Anhanguera, Araguaína
		100	CHN	dom	Xizang PBS, Lhasa
4910		50	IND	dom	All India R., Jaipur
		50	AUS	dom	N. Terr. SW Sce, Tennant Creek
4915		10	B	dom	R. Daquí, Goiânia
	†	10	B	dom	R. Dif., Macapá
4920		50	IND	dom	All India R., Chennai
	†	12	EQA	dom	R. Quito "LV de la Capital", Quito
		100	CHN	dom	Xizang PBS, Lhasa
4925		5	B	dom	R. Educação Rural, Tefé
	‡	10	INS	dom	RRI, Jambi
4930		100	BOT	BOT	BBG - VO America (VOA)
		100	BOT	BOT	BBG - VOA Studio 7
4935		1	B	dom	R. Capixaba, Vitória
4940		50	IND	dom	All India R., Guwahati
		100	STP	SAO	BBG - VO America (VOA)
	†	1	PRU	dom	R. San Antonio, Villa Atalaya
		50	CHN	dom	VO Strait News Ch, Fuzhou
4950		50	IND	dom	AIR Kashmir, Srinagar
		5	PRU	dom	R. Madre de Dios, Pto M.
		25	AGL	dom	R. Nal de Angola, Mulenvos
		50	CHN	dom	VO Pujiang, Shanghai
		100	TJK	DSB	Voice of Russia (VOR)
4955		5	PRU	dom	R. Cultural Amauta, Huanta
4960		100	STP	SAO	BBG - VO America (VOA)
4965		5	B	dom	R. Alvorada, Parintins
4970		50	IND	dom	All India R., Shillong
4975		10	CHN	dom	Fujian PBS, Fuzhou
		5	PRU	dom	Pacífico R., Lima
		1	B	dom	R. Iguatemi, Osasco
4976	‡	10	UGA	dom	UBC R. Red channel, Kampala
4980		50	CHN	dom	Xinjiang PBS, Urumqi
4985		10	B	dom	R. Brasil Central, Goiânia
4986		1	PRU	dom	R. Voz Cristiana, Huancayo
4990		50	IND	dom	All India R., Itanagar
		100	CHN	dom	Hunan PBS, Xiangtan
	†	1	SUR	dom	R. Apintie, Paramaribo
4996		5	RUS	STF	RWM, Moscow
5000		20	CHN	STF	BPM, Kinshan

kHz	N	kW	Ctry	Site	Station, location
		10	USA	STF	WWV NIST, Fort Collins, CO
		10	HWA	STF	WWVH NIST, Kauai, HI
5005	‡	5	NPL	dom	R. Nepal, Khumaltar
	†	50	GNE	dom	Rdif Guinea Ecuatorial, Bata
5010		50	IND	dom	AIR, Thiruvananthapuram
	†	10	MDG	dom	R. Nal Malagasy, Ambohidrano
	†	100	MDG	dom	R. Nal Malagasy, Ambohidrano
5014		1	PRU	dom	R. Altura, Cerro de Pasco
5015	‡	20	TKM	dom	Türkmen R. 1st prgr, Asgabat
5020		10	SLM	dom	Solomon Islands BC, Honiara
5025		50	AUS	dom	N. Terr. SW Sce, Katherine
		10	BEN	dom	ORT Benin, Parakou
		5	PRU	dom	R. Quillabamba, Quillabamba
		50	CUB	dom	R. Rebelde, La Habana
5030		100	BTN	dom	Bhutan BS, Thimpu
	‡	100	BFA	dom	RTB, Ouagadougou
5035	†	5	B	dom	R Educação Rural, Coari
		10	B	dom	R. Aparecida, Aparecida
	†	1	CAF	dom	R. Centrafrique, Bangui
5039		1	PRU	dom	R. Libertad, Junín
5040		50	IND	dom	All India R., Jeypore
		10	CHN	dom	Fujian PBS, Fuzhou
		100	CUB	HAB	Radio Habana Cuba
5045		10	B	dom	R. Cultura do Pará, Belém
	†	0.25	B	dom	R. Guarujá AM, Guarujá
5050	†	10	IND	dom	All India R., Aizawl
		15	CHN	NNN	Beibu Bay Radio
		100	USA	WRB	WWRB
5055	†	5	B	dom	R Jornal A Crítica, Manaus
		1	B	dom	R. Difusora, Cáceres
5060		1	PRU	dom	LV de Huarinjas, Huancabamba
	±	10	ERI	dom	VO Broad Masses 1, Asmara
		50	CHN	dom	Xinjiang PBS, Urumqi
5066		1	COD	dom	R. Télé Candip, Bunia
5070		100	USA	WCR	WWCR
		100	USA	WCR	WWCR
5075			CHN	dom	VO Pujiang, Shanghai
5080	‡	100	PAK	ISL	Radio Pakistan
5085		100	USA	TWW	WTWW
5110		50	USA	BCQ	WBCQ
5120	†	1	PRU	dom	Ondas Suroriente, Quillabamba
5130	†	15	KGZ	BIS	Shortwave Relay Sce.
5150		100	KOR	CHC	MND Radio
5410		100	KOR	CHC	MND Radio
5460			PRU	dom	R. LV Bolivar, Bolivar
5486	†	1	PRU	dom	R. Frecuencia Popular, Olmos
5487		0.06	PRU	dom	La Reyna de la Selva, Chachap.
5580		0.25	BOL	dom	R. San José, S. José
5745		250	USA	GRV	BBG - R. Martí
		100	USA	TWW	WTWW
5765		3	GUM	BAR	AFRTS (AFN Feeder)
	†	10	BOL	dom	R. Panamericana, La Paz
5770		10	BRM	dom	Defence Forces BC, Taunggyi
5790		250	G	WOF	BBC World Service
		300	G	SKN	BBC World Service
5810		200	TJK	DSB	BBG - R. Free Asia (RFA)
		250	KWT	KWT	BBG - VOA Ashna Radio
		250	USA	EWN	WEWN - EWTN Shortwave
5820		250	THA	UDO	BBG - RFE/RL
		250	THA	UDO	BBG - VO America (VOA)
		100	AFS	MEY	RTÉ Radio Worldwide
5825		200	TJK	DSB	BBG - R. Free Asia (RFA)
5830		250	PHL	PHT	BBG - VO America (VOA)
5835		250	PHL	PHT	BBG - VO America (VOA)
		250	CLN	IRA	BBG - VOA Deewa Radio
5840		250	MRA	TIN	BBG - R. Free Asia (RFA)
5845	+	250	THA	NAK	BBC World Service
5850		250	CLN	IRA	BBG - R. Farda
		250	KWT	KWT	BBG - R. Farda
5855		250	MRA	TIN	BBG - R. Free Asia (RFA)
5860		250	CLN	IRA	BBG - R. Farda
		100	D	LAM	BBG - R. Farda
		250	KWT	KWT	BBG - R. Farda
		250	MRA	TIN	BBG - R. Free Asia (RFA)
		50	CHN	dom	VO Jinling, Nanjing
5865		250	THA	NAK	BBC World Service
		500	F	ISS	Radio Algeriénnne
5875		300	CYP	CYP	BBC World Service
	+	250	G	WOF	BBC World Service
		250	G	WOF	BBC World Service
		250	THA	NAK	BBC World Service
		250	THA	UDO	R. Thailand World Service
5885		100	AFS	MEY	BBC World Service
		250	CVA	SMG	BBG - Afia Darfur Radio
		250	THA	UDO	BBG - RFE/RL
		100	D	BIB	BBG - VO America (VOA)
		100	TJK	DSB	Voice of Russia (VOR)
5890		250	MRA	TIN	BBG - VO America (VOA)
		250	USA	GRV	BBG - VO America (VOA)
		100	USA	WCR	The Overcomer Ministry
		100	USA	WCR	WWCR
		100	USA	WCR	WWCR
5895		100	D	LAM	BBG - RFE/RL
		250	PHL	PHT	BBG - VO America (VOA)
5900		100	KOR	CHC	MND Radio
		100	PAK	ISL	Radio Pakistan
		100	RUS	VLD	Voice of Russia (VOR)
		250	RUS	SAM	Voice of Russia (VOR)
5905		250	OMA	SLA	BBC World Service
		100	CHN	KAS	China Radio Int. (CRI)
		250	RRW	KIG	Deutsche Welle
		250	RUS	MSK	Radio Rossii
5910		5	CLM	dom	Alcaraván R, Puerto Lleras
		250	CYP	CYP	BBC World Service
		250	OMA	SLA	BBC World Service
		500	CHN	BEI	China Radio Int. (CRI)
		300	ROU	TIG	Radio Romania International
		300	J	YAM	Shiokaze
		100	D	WER	TWR Europe
5915		300	G	SKN	BBC World Service
		100	CHN	HUH	China Radio Int. (CRI)
		100	CHN	KAS	China Radio Int. (CRI)
		500	CHN	BEI	China Radio Int. (CRI)
		500	CHN	KAS	China Radio Int. (CRI)
		50	BRM	dom	Myanma R., Naypyitaw
		500	F	ISS	Radio France Int. (RFI)
		500	IRN	SIR	VO the Islamic Rep. of Iran
		100	ZMB	dom	ZNBC R. One, Lusaka
5920		250	IRN	AHW	VO the Islamic Rep. of Iran
		500	IRN	KAM	VO the Islamic Rep. of Iran
		100	RUS	ARM	Voice of Russia (VOR)
		250	USA	HRI	WHRI - World Harvest R.
5921		1	PRU	dom	R. Bethel, Arequipa
5925		250	CLN	IRA	BBG - VOA Ashna Radio
		100	CHN	dom	CNR5 VO Zhonghua, Beijing
		250	RRW	KIG	Deutsche Welle
		500	F	ISS	Radio France Int. (RFI)
		50	VTN	dom	VO Vietnam 2, Xuan Mai
5930		100	D	BIB	BBG - RFE/RL
		100	D	LAM	BBG - RFE/RL
		50	RUS	dom	R. Rossii/Reg., Monchegorsk
		100	RUS	dom	R. Rossii/Reg., Yelizovo

kHz	N	kW	Ctry	Site	Station, location
		250	RUS	IRK	TWR India
5935		100	USA	WCR	WWCR
		100	USA	WCR	WWCR
		100	CHN	dom	Xizang PBS, Lhasa
5940		250	CYP	CYP	BBC World Service
		300	G	SKN	BBC World Service
		250	D	NAU	Bible Voice Broadcasting (BVB)
		100	RUS	dom	R. Rossii/Reg., Arman
		100	AUS	SHP	Radio Australia
		500	IRN	SIR	VO the Islamic Rep. of Iran
		250	RUS	SAM	Voice of Russia (VOR)
		10	B	dom	Voz Missionária, Camboriú
5945		250	OMA	SLA	BBC World Service
		100	D	BIB	BBG - RFE/RL
		100	D	BIB	BBG - VO America (VOA)
		100	D	WER	Bible Voice Broadcasting (BVB)
		100	CHN	dom	CNR1 VO China, Beijing
		250	RUS	NVS	Voice of Russia (VOR)
5950		100	D	NAU	Bible Voice Broadcasting (BVB)
		500	F	ISS	KBS World Radio
		100	NZL	RAN	R. New Zealand Int. (RNZI)
		500	IRN	SIR	VO the Islamic Rep. of Iran
		100	ETH	dom	VO Tigray Revolution, Geja
5952		5	BOL	dom	R. Pío XII, Siglo Veinte
5954		50	CTR	CRR	Radio República
5955		250	SEY	SCY	BBC World Service
		100	D	BIB	BBG - VO America (VOA)
		150	CHN	BEI	China Radio Int. (CRI)
		500	CHN	XIA	China Radio Int. (CRI)
		100	CHN	dom	CNR8 VO Minorities, Beijing
		50	CHN	dom	CNR8 VO Minorities, Beijing
	†	10	B	dom	R. Gazeta, São Paulo
		250	RUS	NVS	Voice of Russia (VOR)
		100	AUT	MOS	Voice of Vietnam (VOV)
5960		250	USA	GRV	BBG - VO America (VOA)
		150	ALB	CER	China Radio Int. (CRI)
		100	D	WER	Christian Science Sentinel
	‡	1	PNG	dom	R. Fly, Kiunga
		250	GUF	GUF	Radio Japan (NHK World)
		250	KWT	KBD	Radio Kuwait
		100	ROU	TIG	Radio Romania International
		500	TUR	EMR	Voice of Turkey (VOT)
		50	CHN	dom	Xinjiang PBS, Urumqi
5965		100	CHN	KAS	China Radio Int. (CRI)
		500	CHN	BEI	China Radio Int. (CRI)
		500	CHN	XIA	China Radio Int. (CRI)
		100	CTR	CRI	R. Exterior de España (REE)
	†	8	B	dom	R. Transmundial, Santa Maria
		100	MLA	dom	RTM Klasik Nal FM, Kajang
		250	UAE	DHA	TWR Africa
		500	TUR	EMR	Voice of Turkey (VOT)
5970		300	AUT	MOS	AWR Africa/Europe
		300	AUT	MOS	AWR Asia/Pacific
		250	OMA	SLA	BBC World Service
		150	ALB	CER	China Radio Int. (CRI)
		15	CHN	dom	Gannan PBS, Hezuo
		250	E	NOB	R. Exterior de España (REE)
		10	B	dom	R. Itatiaia, Belo Horizonte
		250	GUF	GUF	Radio Japan (NHK World)
		500	TUR	EMR	Voice of Turkey (VOT)
5975		100	D	WER	AWR Africa/Europe
		250	G	WOF	BBC World Service
		250	OMA	SLA	BBC World Service
		250	SNG	SNG	BBC World Service
		100	D	BIB	BBG - RFE/RL
		100	CHN	dom	CNR8 VO Minorities, Beijing

kHz	N	kW	Ctry	Site	Station, location
		300	ROU	GAL	Radio Romania International
		50	VTN	dom	VO Vietnam 1, Hanoi
		250	RUS	NVS	Voice of Russia (VOR)
5980		250	OMA	SLA	BBC World Service
		250	USA	GRV	BBG - R. Martí
		250	CLN	IRA	BBG - VO America (VOA)
		125	D	NAU	Bible Voice Broadcasting (BVB)
		500	CHN	XIA	China Radio Int. (CRI)
	±	10	ERI	ASM	Ginbot 7 Dimts Radio
		0.1	FIN	VIR	Scandinavian Weekend R.
	±	10	ERI	dom	VO Broad Masses 2, Asmara
		250	RUS	IRK	Voice of Russia (VOR)
		250	TUR	EMR	Voice of Turkey (VOT)
5985		250	G	WOF	BBC World Service
		150	ALB	CER	China Radio Int. (CRI)
		500	CHN	BEI	China Radio Int. (CRI)
		500	CHN	XIA	China Radio Int. (CRI)
		100	USA	YFR	Family Radio
		500	IRN	SIH	VO the Islamic Rep. of Iran
5986		50	BRM	dom	Myanmar R., Yangon
5990		250	IND	DEL	All India Radio (AIR)
		100	CHN	HUH	China Radio Int. (CRI)
		250	CUB	HAB	China Radio Int. (CRI)
		100	PHL	BOC	FEBC Philippines
		300	ROU	GAL	Radio Romania International
5995		250	KWT	KWT	BBG - RFE/RL
		50	MLI	dom	R. Mali, Damaku (Katl)
		10	AUS	BRN	Radio Australia
		100	AUS	SHP	Radio Australia
	+	8	AUS	BRN	Radio Australia
		300	ROU	GAL	Radio Romania International
		100	SWZ	MAN	TWR Africa
		500	IRN	KAM	VO the Islamic Rep. of Iran
		500	IRN	SIR	VO the Islamic Rep. of Iran
		250	RUS	IRK	Voice of Russia (VOR)
		500	RUS	TCH	Voice of Russia (VOR)
6000		10	IND	dom	All India R., Leh
		100	CHN	dom	CNR1 VO China, Beijing
		150	CHN	dom	CNR2 Business R, Xianyang
		10	B	dom	R. Guaíba, Porto Alegre
		100	CUB	HAB	Radio Habana Cuba
		500	TUR	EMR	Voice of Turkey (VOT)
6003		100	KOR	JAA	Echo of Hope (VOH)
6005		250	ASC	ASC	BBC World Service
		250	SEY	SEY	BBC World Service
		250	MRA	TIN	BBG - R. Free Asia (RFA)
		100	CHN	KAS	China Radio Int. (CRI)
	‡	4	CME	dom	CRTV Buea, Buea
		100	RUS	ARM	GTRK "Adygeya"
		1	D	KLL	R. Freundes-Dienst
		1	D	KLL	Radio 700 Kurzwellendienst
		10	CLN	EKA	Sri Lanka Broadcasting Corp.
		500	IRN	SIR	VO the Islamic Rep. of Iran
		100	RUS	ARM	Voice of Russia (VOR)
6010		500	UAE	DHA	BBG - R. Free Asia (RFA)
		500	CHN	BEI	China Radio Int. (CRI)
		500	CHN	URU	China Radio Int. (CRI)
		100	CHN	dom	CNR11 Tibetan Sce, Xi'an
		5	CLM	dom	LV Conciencia, Puerto Lleras
		5	B	dom	R. Inconfidência, Belo Horizonte
	†	1	MEX	dom	R. Mil Onda Corta, México
		100	RUS	dom	R. Rossii/Reg., Yelizovo
	‡	10	BHR	ABH	Radio Bahrain
		100	CUB	HAB	Radio Habana Cuba
		300	ROU	TIG	Radio Romania International
		500	IRN	KAM	VO the Islamic Rep. of Iran

kHz	N	kW	Ctry	Site	Station, location
6015		100	KOR	HWA	KBS World Radio
		300	ROU	GAL	Radio Romania International
		400	RUS	SPB	Voice of Russia (VOR)
		100	CHN	dom	Xinjiang PBS, Urumqi
	†	50	TZA	DOL	Zanzibar Broadcasting Corp.
6019		3	PRU	dom	R. Victoria, Lima
6020		50	IND	dom	All India R., Shimla
		250	MRA	TIN	BBG - R. Free Asia (RFA)
		100	BOT	BOT	BBG - VO America (VOA)
		100	STP	SAO	BBG - VO America (VOA)
		300	ALB	CER	China Radio Int. (CRI)
		100	CHN	KAS	China Radio Int. (CRI)
		500	CHN	SZG	China Radio Int. (CRI)
		100	CHN	dom	CNR8 VO Minorities, Beijing
	†	10	B	dom	R. Gaúcha, Porto Alegre
		100	AUS	SHP	Radio Australia
		100	RUS	IRK	Vatican Radio
		20	VTN	dom	VO Vietnam 1, Buôn Ma Thuôt
6025		250	MRA	TIN	BBG - R. Free Asia (RFA)
		500	CHN	XIA	China Radio Int. (CRI)
	‡	10	NIG	dom	FRCN, Enugu
	±	10	ERI	ASM	Ginbot 7 Dimts Radio
	‡	1		dom	R. Amanecer Int., Sto domingo
		10	BOL	dom	R. Patria Nueva, La Paz
		100	SWZ	MAN	TWR Africa
		100	CHN	dom	Xizang PBS, Lhasa
6030		100	IND	dom	All India R., Delhi
		250	IND	dom	All India R., Delhi
		250	USA	GRV	BBG - R. Martí
		100	D	NAU	Bible Voice Broadcasting (BVB)
		0.1	CAN	dom	CKMX, Calgary, AB
		100	CHN	dom	CNR1 VO China, Beijing
		100	TWN	TSH	Minghui Radio
		1	CAF	dom	R. ICDI, Boali
		1	CAF	dom	R. Ndeke Luka, Boali
		100	ETH	dom	R. Oromiya, Geja
		100	ROU	TIG	Radio Romania International
	+	300	ROU	GAL	Radio Romania International
		300	ROU	GAL	Radio Romania International
		50	BRM	dom	Thazin R, Pyin Oo Lwin
		250	RUS	SAM	Voice of Russia (VOR)
6035		250	ASC	ASC	BBG - VO America (VOA)
		100	STP	SAO	BBG - VO America (VOA)
		30	BTN	dom	Bhutan BS, Thimpu
		5	CLM	dom	LV Guaviare, San José del G
		50	CHN	SHA	Yunnan PBS
6040		50	IND	dom	All India R., Jeypore
		250	CYP	CYP	BBC World Service
		300	G	SKN	BBC World Service
		500	CHN	URU	China Radio Int. (CRI)
		500	CHN	XIA	China Radio Int. (CRI)
		150	CHN	dom	CNR2 Business R, Beijing
		50	CHN	dom	Nei Menggu-Mo, Hohhot
		100	ALB	SHI	RadioTirana
		250	CVA	SMG	Vatican Radio
		500	IRN	KAM	VO the Islamic Rep. of Iran
		500	IRN	SIR	VO the Islamic Rep. of Iran
6045		100	IND	DEL	All India Radio (AIR)
		300	AUT	MOS	AWR Africa/Europe
		250	THA	UDO	BBG - VO America (VOA)
		250	G	WOF	KBS World Radio
		250	KOR	KIM	KBS World Radio
	†	0.3	URG	dom	R. Sarandi, Montevideo
	‡	0.45	MEX	dom	R. Universidad, San Luis Potosí
		100	D	WER	XVRB Radio
		100	ZWE	dom	ZBC R. Zimbabwe, Gweru
6047		10	PRU	dom	R. Santa Rosa, Lima
6050		10	EQU	QUI	HCJB La Voz de los Andes
		100	MLA	dom	RTM Asyik FM, Kajang
		250	TUR	EMR	Voice of Turkey (VOT)
		500	TUR	EMR	Voice of Turkey (VOT)
		100	CHN	dom	Xizang PBS, Lhasa
6055		250	IND	DEL	All India Radio (AIR)
		300	G	SKN	BBC World Service
		100	CHN	NNN	China Radio Int. (CRI)
		125	D	WER	Ev. Missions-Gemeinden
		250	E	NOB	R. Exterior de España (REE)
		3	BOL	dom	R. Juan XXIII, San Ignacio
		50	J	dom	R. Nikkei 1, Tokyo
		50	RRW	dom	Rdif. de Rep. Rwandaise, Kigali
		250	D	WER	Stimme Des Trostes
6060			PRU	dom	Aroma Café R, Pichanaki
		250	KWT	KWT	BBG - RFE/RL
		250	PHL	PHT	BBG - VO America (VOA)
		250	THA	UDO	BBG - VO America (VOA)
		150	CHN	KUN	China Radio Int. (CRI)
		500	CHN	BEI	China Radio Int. (CRI)
		100	CUB	HAB	Radio Habana Cuba
		100	ROU	TIG	Radio Romania International
		50	ARG	BUE	Rdif. Argentina al Exterior
		15	CHN	dom	Sichuan PBS, Xichang
		10	B	dom	Super R. Deus é Amor, Curitiba
		500	IRN	SIR	VO the Islamic Rep. of Iran
6065		50	IND	dom	All India R., Kohima
		100	CHN	KAS	China Radio Int. (CRI)
		150	CHN	dom	CNR2 Business R, Beijing
6070		1	CAN	dom	CFRX, Toronto ON
		500	CHN	KAS	China Radio Int. (CRI)
		500	CHN	XIA	China Radio Int. (CRI)
		7.5	B	dom	R. Capital, Rio de Janeiro
		1	D	ROB	Radio 6150
		100	UZB	TAC	Vatican Radio
		200	KRE	KNG	Voice of Korea
6075		250	CVA	SMG	BBG - RFE/RL
		250	D	WER	BBG - RFE/RL
		100	CHN	KAS	China Radio Int. (CRI)
		300	J	YAM	Radio Japan (NHK World)
		100	TWN	KOU	Radio Taiwan International
		100	CVA	SMG	Vatican Radio
6076	†	1	URG	dom	LV de Artigas, Artigas
	†		BOL	dom	R. Causachun Coca, Lauca Ñ
6080		100	AFS	MEY	BBG - VO America (VOA)
		100	STP	SAO	BBG - VO America (VOA)
		150	BLR	dom	Belaruskaje R. 1, Minsk
		500	CHN	BEI	China Radio Int. (CRI)
		100	CHN	dom	CNR1 VO China, Golmud
		7	CHN	dom	Hulun Buir, Hailar
		7	CHN	dom	Hulun Buir-Mo, Hailar
		5	B	dom	R. Daquí, Goiânia
		10	B	dom	R. Marumby, Curitiba
		100	AUS	SHP	Radio Australia
		500	KWT	KBD	Radio Kuwait
		500	IRN	KAM	VO the Islamic Rep. of Iran
		500	IRN	SIR	VO the Islamic Rep. of Iran
6085		50	RUS	dom	R. Rossii/Reg., Krasnoyarsk
		1	D	KLL	Radio 700
		1	D	KLL	Radio 700 Kurzwellendienst
		100	TWN	HUW	Radio Taiwan International
		500	IRN	KAM	VO the Islamic Rep. of Iran
6089			PRU	dom	R. Universal, Cusco
6090		150	CHN	KUN	China Radio Int. (CRI)
		500	CHN	XIA	China Radio Int. (CRI)

kHz	N	kW	Ctry	Site	Station, location
		100	CHN	dom	CNR2 Business R, Golmud
	†	50	NIG	dom	FRCN, Kaduna
		10	B	dom	R. Bandeirantes, São Paulo
		300	J	YAM	Radio Japan (NHK World)
		100	ROU	TIG	Radio Romania International
	†	100	AIA	AIA	University Network
		100	ETH	dom	VO Amhara State, Geja
		500	IRN	KAM	VO the Islamic Rep. of Iran
		200	RUS	ARM	Voice of Russia (VOR)
6095		250	MRA	TIN	BBG - R. Free Asia (RFA)
		125	D	NAU	Bible Voice Broadcasting (BVB)
		500	CHN	KAS	China Radio Int. (CRI)
		250	KOR	KIM	KBS World Radio
		100	D	WER	The Mighty KBC
		100	D	WER	Transport Radio
		500	IRN	KAM	VO the Islamic Rep. of Iran
6100	†	10	IND	dom	AIR Delhi (DRM)
		100	D	WER	AWR Africa/Europe
		250	THA	UDO	BBG - VO America (VOA)
		100	CHN	URU	China Radio Int. (CRI)
		150	CHN	KUN	China Radio Int. (CRI)
		250	CHN	BEI	China Radio Int. (CRI)
		500	CHN	BEI	China Radio Int. (CRI)
		500	CHN	KAS	China Radio Int. (CRI)
		500	CHN	XIA	China Radio Int. (CRI)
		250	BIH	BIJ	International Radio Serbia
		125	KRE	dom	KCBS, Kanggye
		1	RUS	dom	R. Rossii/Reg., Kyzyl
		250	IND	DEL	Radio Sedayee Kashmir
		100	ALB	SHI	RadioTirana
		500	IRN	KAM	VO the Islamic Rep. of Iran
6105		250	D	WER	BBG - RFE/RL
		250	TJK	DSB	BBG - VO America (VOA)
	‡	0.25	MEX	dom	Candela FM, Mérida
		5	B	dom	R. Filadélfia, Foz de Iguaçu
		100	TWN	KOU	Radio Taiwan International
		100	D	WER	TWR Europe
6110	†	50	IND	dom	AIR Delhi
		50	IND	dom	AIR Kashmir, Srinagar
		250	G	WOF	BBC World Service
		100	CHN	URU	China Radio Int. (CRI)
		500	CHN	XIA	China Radio Int. (CRI)
	†	100	ETH	dom	R. Fana, Geja
		300	J	YAM	Shiokaze
		500	IRN	SIR	VO the Islamic Rep. of Iran
		250	RUS	PPK	Voice of Russia (VOR)
		100	CHN	dom	Xizang PBS, Lhasa
6115		500	CHN	BEI	China Radio Int. (CRI)
		100	USA	YFR	Family Radio
	†	50	COG	dom	R. Congo, Brazzaville
		50	J	dom	R. Nikkei 2, Tokyo
		100	LTU	SIT	Radio Japan (NHK World)
		100	USA	YFR	Radio Taiwan International
		250	PHL	PUG	Radio Veritas Asia
		250	RUS	SAM	TWR India
		50	CHN	dom	VO Strait, Fuzhou
6120		250	D	WER	BBG - RFE/RL
		100	CUB	HAB	Radio Habana Cuba
		10	B	dom	Super R. Deus é Amor, São Paulo
		50	SWZ	MAN	TWR Africa
		120	RUS	KLG	Voice of Russia (VOR)
		500	TUR	EMR	Voice of Turkey (VOT)
		50	CHN	dom	Xinjiang PBS, Urumqi
6125		100	CHN	dom	CNR1 VO China, Beijing
		100	CHN	dom	CNR1 VO China, Shijiazhuang
		250	UAE	DHA	FEBA Radio

kHz	N	kW	Ctry	Site	Station, location
		250	E	NOB	R. Exterior de España (REE)
		100	CUB	HAB	Radio Habana Cuba
6130		50	LAO	VIE	Lao National Radio
		50	LAO	dom	R. Nationale Lao, Vientiane
		250	GUF	GUF	Radio Japan (NHK World)
		300	ROU	GAL	Radio Romania International
		100	SWZ	MAN	TWR Africa
		200	RUS	MSK	Voice of Russia (VOR)
		100	CHN	dom	Xizang PBS, Lhasa
6135		250	ASC	ASC	BBC World Service
		250	KOR	KIM	BBC World Service
		250	SNG	SNG	BBC World Service
		100	D	BIB	BBG - RFE/RL
		500	CHN	XIA	China Radio Int. (CRI)
		250	CYP	CYP	Cyprus Broadcasting Corp.
		10	B	dom	R. Aparecida, Aparecida
	‡	30	MDG	dom	R. Nal Malagasy, Ambohidrano
		10	BOL	dom	R. Santa Cruz, Santa Cruz
		50	YEM	SAN	Republic of Yemen Radio
		800	RUS	SPB	Voice of Russia (VOR)
		250	G	WOF	Voice of Vietnam (VOV)
6140		100	AFS	MEY	BBC World Service
		250	OMA	SLA	BBC World Service
		250	SEY	SEY	BBC World Service
		250	THA	UDO	BBG - VO America (VOA)
		100	CHN	KAS	China Radio Int. (CRI)
		100	CHN	KUN	China Radio Int. (CRI)
		100	SNG	SNG	Radio Australia
		500	IRN	KAM	VO the Islamic Rep. of Iran
6145		300	AUT	MOS	AWR Africa/Europe
		150	CHN	BEI	China Radio Int. (CRI)
		500	CHN	URU	China Radio Int. (CRI)
		250	F	ISS	China Radio Int. (CRI)
		500	F	ISS	China Radio Int. (CRI)
		100	CHN	dom	CNR8 VO Minorities, Lingshi
		15	CHN	dom	Qinghai PBS, Xining
		300	ROU	GAL	Radio Romania International
		100	TWN	PAO	Radio Taiwan International
		500	IRN	SIR	VO the Islamic Rep. of Iran
	+	15	RUS	IRK	Voice of Russia (VOR)
	+	15	RUS	KLG	Voice of Russia (VOR)
6150	†	50	IND	dom	All India R., Itanagar
		500	CHN	SZG	China Radio Int. (CRI)
		8	B	dom	R. Record, São Paulo
		100	CUB	HAB	Radio Habana Cuba
		100	TWN	KOU	Radio Taiwan International
6155		250	IND	ALG	All India Radio (AIR)
		500	IND	BGL	All India Radio (AIR)
		50	MDG	MDC	AWR Africa/Europe
		250	OMA	SLA	BBC World Service
		250	AFS	MEY	Channel Africa
		100	CHN	NNN	China Radio Int. (CRI)
		150	CHN	dom	CNR2 Business R, Beijing
		100	KOR	KIM	KBS World Radio
		10	BOL	dom	R. Fides, La Paz
		250	BLR	MNS	Radio Belarus
		300	AUT	MOS	Radio Ö1 International
6160		1	CAN	dom	CBC R. One, St. John's, NL
		1	CAN	dom	CBC R. One, Vancouver, BC
		500	CHN	XIA	China Radio Int. (CRI)
	†	10	B	dom	R. Boa Vontade, Porto Alegre
		20	RUS	dom	R. Rossii/Reg., Arkhangelsk
6161	†	10	B	dom	R. Rio Mar, Manaus
6165		250	IND	DEL	All India Radio (AIR)
		300	G	SKN	BBC World Service
		250	OMA	SLA	BBC World Service

kHz	N	kW	Ctry	Site	Station, location
		100	CHN	URU	China Radio Int. (CRI)
		250	CHN	BEI	China Radio Int. (CRI)
		500	CHN	URU	China Radio Int. (CRI)
		100	CHN	dom	CNR6 VO Shenzhou, Beijing
	†	250	TCD	dom	ONRT du Tchad, N'Djamena
	†	1	BOL	dom	R. Logos, Santa Cruz
		100	CUB	HAB	Radio Habana Cuba
		300	J	YAM	Radio Japan (NHK World)
		500	IRN	SIR	VO the Islamic Rep. of Iran
		50	VTN	dom	VO Vietnam Min, Xuan Mai
		100	ZMB	dom	ZNBC R. Two, Lusaka
6170		250	G	WOF	BBC World Service
		250	KWT	KWT	BBG - VO America (VOA)
		500	CHN	KAS	China Radio Int. (CRI)
		100	ROU	TIG	Radio Romania International
		0.1	FIN	VIR	Scandinavian Weekend R.
	†	200	KRE	KUJ	Voice of Korea
6174		1	PRU	dom	R. Tawantinsuyo, Cusco
6175		250	OMA	SLA	BBC World Service
		150	ALB	CER	China Radio Int. (CRI)
		100	CHN	KAS	China Radio Int. (CRI)
		100	CHN	dom	CNR1 VO China, Beijing
	+	300	ROU	TIG	Radio Romania International
		500	IRN	KAM	VO the Islamic Rep. of Iran
		250	UAE	DHA	Voice of Vietnam (VOV)
		250	USA	HRI	Voice of Vietnam (VOV)
6180		100	CHN	KAS	China Radio Int. (CRI)
		500	CHN	URU	China Radio Int. (CRI)
		100	CHN	dom	CNR1 VO China, Lingshi
		100	CHN	dom	CNR8 VO Minorities, Beijing
		100	CHN	dom	CNR8 VO Minorities, Lingshi
		250	UAE	DHA	FEBA Radio
	†	250	B	dom	R. Nal da Amazônia, Brasília
		100	AFS	MEY	Radio France Int. (RFI)
6185		15	CHN	dom	China Huayi BC, Fuzhou
		150	ALB	CER	China Radio Int. (CRI)
		500	CHN	XIA	China Radio Int. (CRI)
		10	MEX	dom	R. Educación, México
		100	CVA	SMG	Vatican Radio
		250	CVA	SMG	Vatican Radio
		250	IRN	AHW	VO the Islamic Rep. of Iran
		200	KRE	KUJ	Voice of Korea
		500	TUR	EMR	Voice of Turkey (VOT)
6190		100	AFS	MEY	BBC World Service
		100	CHN	dom	CNR2 Business R, Golmud
		250	BIH	BIJ	International Radio Serbia
		100	ALS	NLS	KNLS International
	†	1	D	GOH	MV Baltic Radio
		300	J	YAM	Radio Japan (NHK World)
		50	CHN	dom	Xinjiang PBS, Urumqi
6192	†	1	PRU	dom	R. Cusco, Cusco
6195		300	CYP	CYP	BBC World Service
		250	OMA	SLA	BBC World Service
		250	SNG	SNG	BBC World Service
		250	THA	NAK	BBC World Service
		50	RUS	dom	R. Rossii/Reg., Selenginsk
		250	GUF	GUF	Radio Japan (NHK World)
		250	USA	HRI	Radio Japan (NHK World)
6200		100	CHN	dom	Xizang PBS, Lhasa
6205		500	IRN	SIR	VO the Islamic Rep. of Iran
6210		1	COD	dom	R. Kahuzi, Bukavu
6220		100	TWN	HUW	Family Radio
6235		100	TJK	DSB	Voice of Russia (VOR)
6240		100	TWN	PAO	Family Radio
6250		50	KRE	PYO	Pyongyang Broadcasting Stn.
	‡	20	GNE	dom	Rdif Guinea Ecuatorial, Malabo

kHz	N	kW	Ctry	Site	Station, location
6260		100	UZB	TAC	CVC The Voice Asia
6270		100	KOR	CHC	MND Radio
6280	‡	100	PAK	ISL	Radio Pakistan
		300	TWN	TSH	Sound of Hope Radio Int.
6300		100	KOR	CHC	MND Radio
6348		100	KOR	JAA	Echo of Hope (VOH)
6400		50	KRE	KNG	Pyongyang Broadcasting Stn.
6415		500	CHN	BEI	China Radio Int. (CRI)
6435		100	KOR	CHC	MND Radio
6518		50	KOR	GOY	Voice of the People
6550		100	KOR	CHC	MND Radio
6600		50	KOR	GOY	Voice of the People
6650		100	KOR	CHC	MND Radio
6670		100	KOR	CHC	MND Radio
6875		100	USA	WCR	WWCR
		100	USA	WCR	WWCR
6885		10	ISR	LOD	Galei Tzahal
7105		100	TWN	TSH	Sound of Hope Radio Int.
7110		50	BRM	dom	Thazin R, Pyin Oo Lwin
7120	±	10	ERI	ASM	Ginbot 7 Dimts Radio
	†	100	SOM	dom	R. Hargeisa
	±	10	ERI	dom	VO Broad Masses 2, Asmara
7125	†	50	GUI	dom	R. Guineé, Conakry
7165	±	10	ERI	dom	VO Broad Masses 2, Asmara
7175	±	10	ERI	dom	VO Broad Masses 2, Asmara
7185	±	10	ERI	ASM	Ginbot 7 Dimts Radio
	±	10	ERI	dom	VO Broad Masses 2, Asmara
7190		10	CLN	EKA	Sri Lanka Broadcasting Corp.
7195	‡	10	UGA	dom	UBC R. Red channel, Kampala
7200		50	BRM	dom	Myanma R., Yangon
	†	100	SDN	dom	SRTC, Khartoum
7205		100	AFS	MEY	Amateur R. Mirror Int.
		100	CHN	KAS	China Radio Int. (CRI)
		150	CHN	BEI	China Radio Int. (CRI)
		500	CHN	BEI	China Radio Int. (CRI)
		500	CHN	XIA	China Radio Int. (CRI)
		500	F	ISS	Radio France Int. (RFI)
	±	100	ERI	dom	VO Broad Masses 1, Asmara
		500	IRN	SIR	VO the Islamic Rep. of Iran
		250	RUS	TCH	Voice of Russia (VOR)
		400	RUS	SPB	Voice of Russia (VOR)
		250	TUR	EMR	Voice of Turkey (VOT)
		50	CHN	dom	Xinjiang PBS, Urumqi
7210		50	IND	dom	All India R., Kolkata
		250	RUS	IRK	BBG - R. Free Asia (RFA)
		150	ALB	CER	China Radio Int. (CRI)
		100	CHN	URU	China Radio Int. (CRI)
		500	CHN	URU	China Radio Int. (CRI)
		500	CHN	XIA	China Radio Int. (CRI)
	†	100	ETH	dom	R. Fana, Geja
		300	ROU	TIG	Radio Romania International
		100	D	WER	TWR Europe
		20	VTN	dom	VO Vietnam 1, Buôn Ma Thuôt
		200	KRE	KUJ	Voice of Korea
		500	RUS	MSK	Voice of Russia (VOR)
		20	CHN	dom	Yunnan PBS, Kunming
7215		250	CLN	TRM	Athmik Yatra Radio
		250	THA	UDO	BBG - RFE/RL
		150	ALB	CER	China Radio Int. (CRI)
		500	CHN	JIN	China Radio Int. (CRI)
		500	CHN	KUN	China Radio Int. (CRI)
		500	CHN	SZG	China Radio Int. (CRI)
		500	CHN	XIA	China Radio Int. (CRI)
		100	CHN	dom	CNR1 VO China, Shijiazhuang
		250	AFS	MEY	TWR Africa
7217	†	15	AGL	MUL	Angolan National Radio

kHz	N	kW	Ctry	Site	Station, location
		15	AGL	dom	R. Nal de Angola, Mulenvos
7220		100	D	LAM	BBG - RFE/RL
		150	ALB	CER	China Radio Int. (CRI)
		100	CHN	KAS	China Radio Int. (CRI)
		500	CHN	JIN	China Radio Int. (CRI)
		500	CHN	KUN	China Radio Int. (CRI)
		500	CHN	XIA	China Radio Int. (CRI)
		100	CHN	dom	CNR2 Business R, Golmud
		300	CYP	CYP	Cyprus Broadcasting Corp.
		300	ROU	GAL	Radio Romania International
		200	KRE	KUJ	Voice of Korea
		250	RUS	SAM	Voice of Russia (VOR)
		100	VTN	VNI	Voice of Vietnam (VOV)
7225		250	KWT	KWT	BBG - RFE/RL
		500	CHN	URU	China Radio Int. (CRI)
		500	TUN	SFA	Radio Tunisienne
		10	CHN	dom	Sichuan PBS, Chengdu
		100	AUT	MOS	TWR Europe
		250	RUS	SAM	Voice of Russia (VOR)
7230		50	IND	dom	AIR Kolkata, Kurseong
		100	AFS	MEY	Channel Africa
		150	ALB	CER	China Radio Int. (CRI)
		100	CHN	dom	CNR1 VO China, Xi'an
		100	UZB	TAC	FEBA Radio
		100	RUS	dom	R. Rossii/Reg., Yakutsk
‡		100	BFA	dom	RTB, Ouagadougou
		500	IRN	SIR	VO the Islamic Rep. of Iran
		250	RUS	MSK	Voice of Russia (VOR)
		50	CHN	dom	Xinjiang PBS, Urumqi
7235		100	D	BIB	BBG - RFE/RL
		100	D	LAM	BBG - RFE/RL
		250	KWT	KWT	BBG - RFE/RL
		250	MRA	TIN	BBG - VO America (VOA)
		100	CHN	KAS	China Radio Int. (CRI)
		500	CHN	KAS	China Radio Int. (CRI)
		300	G	WOF	KBS World Radio
+		100	ETH	GJW	Radio Ethiopia
±		100	ETH	GJW	VO Peace & Dem. of Eritrea
±		100	ETH	GJW	Voice of Democratic Alliance
±		100	ETH	GJW	Voice of Eritrea
		200	KRE	KUJ	Voice of Korea
7240		50	IND	dom	All India R., Mumbai
		250	CLN	TRM	Athmik Yatra Radio
		100	AUS	SHP	Radio Australia
		500	ARS	RIY	Saudi Radio (BSKSA)
		250	RUS	PPK	Voice of Russia (VOR)
		500	RUS	ARM	Voice of Russia (VOR)
		500	TUR	EMR	Voice of Turkey (VOT)
		100	CHN	dom	Xizang PBS, Lhasa
7245		150	CHN	BJI	China Radio Int. (CRI)
		500	CHN	KAS	China Radio Int. (CRI)
		500	CHN	XIA	China Radio Int. (CRI)
		150	CHN	dom	CNR2 Business R, Beijing
†		100	MTN	dom	R. Mauritanie, Nouakchott
†		20	MDG	dom	R. Nal Malagasy, Ambohidrano
		100	TJK	DSB	Voice of Tajik (Ovozi Tojik)
		250	TUR	EMR	Voice of Turkey (VOT)
7250		50	IND	dom	All India R., Gorakhpur
		250	IND	PAN	All India Radio (AIR)
		50	IND	GKP	All India Radio (AIR)
		250	BGD	DKA	Bangladesh Betar
		250	MRA	TIN	BBG - R. Free Asia (RFA)
		100	CHN	KAS	China Radio Int. (CRI)
		500	CHN	URU	China Radio Int. (CRI)
		500	KWT	KBD	Radio Kuwait
		100	CVA	SMG	Vatican Radio

kHz	N	kW	Ctry	Site	Station, location
		250	CVA	SMG	Vatican Radio
		250	RUS	MSK	Voice of Russia (VOR)
7255		250	IND	dom	All India R., Aligarh
		250	ASC	ASC	BBC World Service
		250	KWT	KWT	BBG - VO America (VOA)
		250	THA	UDO	BBG - VO America (VOA)
		250	BLR	MNS	Belaruskaje Radyjo
		150	CHN	BJI	China Radio Int. (CRI)
		500	CHN	BEI	China Radio Int. (CRI)
		500	CHN	KAS	China Radio Int. (CRI)
		500	CHN	KUN	China Radio Int. (CRI)
		500	CHN	SZG	China Radio Int. (CRI)
		500	CHN	XIA	China Radio Int. (CRI)
		100	CHN	dom	CNR2 Business R, Baoji
†		250	NIG	IKO	Voice of Nigeria
		100	CHN	dom	Xizang PBS, Lhasa
7260		250	THA	UDO	BBG - RFE/RL
		250	PHL	PHT	BBG - VO America (VOA)
		100	CHN	KAS	China Radio Int. (CRI)
		500	CHN	URU	China Radio Int. (CRI)
		50	MNG	dom	Mongolian R. 2, Ulaanbaatar
		10	VUT	dom	R. Vanuatu, Port Vila
		500	MDA	KCH	Voice of Russia (VOR)
		500	RUS	VLD	Voice of Russia (VOR)
		50	CHN	dom	Xinjiang PBS, Urumqi
7265	‡	100	PAK	dom	Azad Kashmir R., Islamabad
		100	CHN	KAS	China Radio Int (CRI)
		500	CHN	URU	China Radio Int. (CRI)
		100	CHN	dom	CNR2 Business R, Baoji
		250	RRW	KIG	Deutsche Welle
		1	D	GOH	Hamburger Lokalradio
†		1	D	GOH	MV Baltic Radio
		250	E	NOB	R. Exterior de España (REE)
7270		100	IND	dom	All India R., Chennai
		100	IND	CNI	All India Radio (AIR)
		50	CHN	dom	Nei Menggu-Mo, Hohhot
		500	IRN	KAM	VO the Islamic Rep. of Iran
		100	TWN	TSU	Voice of China
7275		100	STP	SAO	BBG - Afia Darfur Radio
		100	D	LAM	BBG - RFE/RL
		100	STP	SAO	BBG - VO America (VOA)
		500	CHN	URU	China Radio Int. (CRI)
		100	CHN	dom	CNR1 VO China, Beijing
†		100	NIG	dom	FRCN, Abuja
		250	KOR	KIM	KBS World Radio
		250	E	NOB	R. Exterior de España (REE)
		500	TUN	SFA	Radio Tunisienne
		50	CHN	dom	Xinjiang PBS, Urumqi
7280		50	IND	dom	All India R., Guwahati
		300	TWN	TSH	Sound of Hope Radio Int.
		100	VTN	VNI	Voice of Vietnam (VOV)
7285		300	CYP	CYP	BBC World Service
		150	ALB	CER	China Radio Int. (CRI)
		100	CHN	KAS	China Radio Int. (CRI)
		500	CHN	BEI	China Radio Int. (CRI)
		500	CHN	XIA	China Radio Int. (CRI)
		250	RRW	KIG	Deutsche Welle
		50	MLI	dom	R. Mali, Bamako (Kati)
		100	AFS	dom	R. Sonder Grense, Meyerton
		250	RUS	SAM	TWR India
		500	IRN	KAM	VO the Islamic Rep. of Iran
		50	VTN	HAN	Voice of Vietnam (VOV)
7290		50	IND	dom	AIR, Thiruvananthapuram
		100	D	BIB	BBG - VO America (VOA)
		100	CHN	KAS	China Radio Int. (CRI)
		500	CHN	SZG	China Radio Int. (CRI)

kHz	N	kW	Ctry	Site	Station, location
		100	CHN	dom	CNR1 VO China, Beijing
		150	ROU	TIG	IRRS Shortwave
		500	MDA	KCH	Radio PMR
		10	INS	dom	RRI, Nabire
		100	ROU	TIG	The Overcomer Ministry
		250	CVA	SMG	Vatican Radio
		500	MDA	KCH	Voice of Russia (VOR)
7295		10	IND	dom	All India R., Aizawl
		250	RUS	NVS	BBG - VO America (VOA)
		500	CHN	BEI	China Radio Int. (CRI)
		500	CHN	KAS	China Radio Int. (CRI)
		100	MLI	BKO	China Radio Int. (CRI)
		500	F	ISS	Radio Algeriénne
		500	F	ISS	Radio France Int. (RFI)
	†	100	MLA	dom	RTM Traxx FM, Kajang
		100	D	WER	TWR Europe
		500	IRN	KAM	VO the Islamic Rep. of Iran
		500	RUS	TCH	Voice of Russia (VOR)
		50	CHN	dom	Xinjiang PBS, Urumqi
7300		100	CHN	KAS	China Radio Int. (CRI)
		500	CHN	KAS	China Radio Int. (CRI)
		500	CHN	URU	China Radio Int. (CRI)
		250	RRW	KIG	Deutsche Welle
	+	300	ROU	TIG	Radio Romania International
		50	SWZ	MAN	TWR Africa
		500	IRN	SIR	VO the Islamic Rep. of Iran
7305		250	ASC	ASC	BBC World Service
		500	CHN	JIN	China Radio Int. (CRI)
		500	CHN	XIA	China Radio Int. (CRI)
		250	F	ISS	China Radio Int. (CRI)
		100	CHN	dom	CNR1 VO China, Shijiazhuang
		300	ROU	TIG	Radio Romania International
		250	USA	GRV	Vatican Radio
		250	RUS	IRK	Voice of Russia (VOR)
7310		250	CLN	IRA	BBG - R. Free Asia (RFA)
		500	CHN	KAS	China Radio Int. (CRI)
		250	RUS	SAM	Lutherische Stunde
		250	RUS	SAM	Missionswerk-Heukelbach
		250	RUS	SAM	R. Freundes-Dienst
		100	TWN	TNN	Radio France Int. (RFI)
		300	ROU	TIG	Radio Romania International
		250	RUS	MSK	Radio Rossii
		300	TWN	TSH	Sound of Hope Radio Int.
		250	RUS	SAM	Voice of Russia (VOR)
		50	CHN	dom	Xinjiang PBS, Urumqi
7315		50	IND	dom	All India R., Shillong
		250	D	NAU	AWR Africa/Europe
		100	D	BIB	BBG - VO America (VOA)
		500	CHN	KAS	China Radio Int. (CRI)
		500	CHN	KUN	China Radio Int. (CRI)
		500	CHN	URU	China Radio Int. (CRI)
		150	CHN	dom	CNR2 Business R, Xi'an
		250	UAE	DHA	FEBA Radio
		250	CVA	SMG	Radio Dabanga
		300	ROU	GAL	Radio Romania International
		250	CVA	SMG	Radio Tamazuj
		50	SWZ	MAN	TWR Africa
		500	IRN	KAM	VO the Islamic Rep. of Iran
	+	15	RUS	IRK	Voice of Russia (VOR)
		250	USA	HRI	WHRI - World Harvest R.
7320		500	CHN	KUN	China Radio Int. (CRI)
		500	CHN	XIA	China Radio Int. (CRI)
		100	RUS	dom	R. Rossii/Reg., Arman
		500	IRN	KAM	VO the Islamic Rep. of Iran
7325		50	IND	dom	All India R., Jaipur
		300	CYP	CYP	BBC World Service

kHz	N	kW	Ctry	Site	Station, location
		250	G	WOF	BBC World Service
		250	THA	NAK	BBC World Service
		250	D	NAU	Bible Voice Broadcasting (BVB)
		150	CHN	KUN	China Radio Int. (CRI)
		500	CHN	BEI	China Radio Int. (CRI)
		500	CHN	JIN	China Radio Int. (CRI)
		500	CHN	KUN	China Radio Int. (CRI)
		500	CHN	URU	China Radio Int. (CRI)
		500	CHN	XIA	China Radio Int. (CRI)
		100	TWN	TNN	Radio France Int. (RFI)
		300	ROU	GAL	Radio Romania International
		500	IRN	KAM	VO the Islamic Rep. of Iran
		1	PNG	dom	Wantok R. Light, Port Moresby
7330		500	CHN	KAS	China Radio Int. (CRI)
		500	CHN	XIA	China Radio Int. (CRI)
		250	RUS	MSK	Voice of Russia (VOR)
7335		50	IND	dom	All India R., Imphal
		500	CHN	BEI	China Radio Int. (CRI)
		500	CHN	JIN	China Radio Int. (CRI)
		500	CHN	SZG	China Radio Int. (CRI)
		100	CHN	dom	CNR2 Business R, Baoji
		500	TUN	SFA	Radio Tunisienne
		100	CVA	SMG	Vatican Radio
		500	IRN	KAM	VO the Islamic Rep. of Iran
		500	IRN	SIR	VO the Islamic Rep. of Iran
		250	USA	HRI	WHRI - World Harvest R.
7340		100	IND	dom	All India R., Mumbai
		100	IND	MUM	All India Radio (AIR)
		500	CHN	KAS	China Radio Int. (CRI)
		300	ROU	TIG	Radio Romania International
		60	RUS	KLG	Voice of Russia (VOR)
		100	CHN	dom	Xinjiang PBS, Urumqi
7345		150	ALB	CER	China Radio Int. (CRI)
		100	CHN	dom	CNR1 VO China, Beijing
		100	ROU	TIG	Radio Romania International
	+	100	ROU	TIG	Radio Romania International
		500	TUN	SFA	Radio Tunisienne
		50	BRM	dom	Thazin R, Pyin Oo Lwin
		250	IRN	AHW	VO the Islamic Rep. of Iran
		500	IRN	KAM	VO the Islamic Rep. of Iran
		500	IRN	SIR	VO the Islamic Rep. of Iran
		250	G	WOF	Voice of Vietnam (VOV)
7350		250	G	WOF	BBC World Service
		100	CHN	KAS	China Radio Int. (CRI)
		500	CHN	KAS	China Radio Int. (CRI)
		500	CHN	URU	China Radio Int. (CRI)
		100	CHN	dom	CNR11 Tibetan Sce, Xi'an
		100	D	NAU	Hamada Radio International
		300	ROU	GAL	Radio Romania International
		500	IRN	KAM	VO the Islamic Rep. of Iran
		500	IRN	SIR	VO the Islamic Rep. of Iran
7355	+	100	AUT	MOS	BBC World Service
		100	TWN	KOU	BBG - R. Free Asia (RFA)
		100	CHN	dom	CNR5 VO Zhonghua, Beijing
7360		300	CYP	CYP	BBC World Service
		100	CHN	KAS	China Radio Int. (CRI)
		100	CHN	KUN	China Radio Int. (CRI)
		100	CHN	dom	CNR11 Tibetan Sce, Xi'an
		100	CVA	SMG	Vatican Radio
		125	CVA	SMG	Vatican Radio
		250	CVA	SMG	Vatican Radio
		500	CVA	SMG	Vatican Radio
7365		250	USA	GRV	BBG - R. Martí
		250	PHL	PHT	BBG - VO America (VOA)
		100	D	NAU	Bible Voice Broadcasting (BVB)
		500	CHN	BEI	China Radio Int. (CRI)

kHz	N	kW	Ctry	Site	Station, location
		100	CHN	dom	CNR1 VO China, Shijiazhuang
		300	TWN	TSH	Radio Taiwan International
		250	CVA	SMG	Vatican Radio
7370		100	IND	DEL	All India Radio (AIR)
		150	CHN	dom	CNR2 Business R, Beijing
	+	300	ROU	GAL	Radio Romania International
		500	IRN	KAM	VO the Islamic Rep. of Iran
		10	HRV	DEA	Voice of Croatia
		250	G	WOF	Voice of Vietnam (VOV)
7375		300	CYP	CYP	BBC World Service
		150	CHN	dom	CNR2 Business R, Beijing
		100	D	NAU	Voice of Croatia
7380		50	IND	dom	All India R., Chennai
		150	ALB	CER	China Radio Int. (CRI)
		100	TWN	TNN	Radio France Int. (RFI)
		300	ROU	GAL	Radio Romania International
		100	TWN	PAO	Radio Taiwan International
		500	IRN	KAM	VO the Islamic Rep. of Iran
		500	IRN	SIR	VO the Islamic Rep. of Iran
7385		100	TWN	KOU	BBG - R. Free Asia (RFA)
		100	CHN	dom	CNR5 VO Zhonghua, Beijing
		100	TWN	KOU	Radio Taiwan International
		500	IRN	SIR	VO the Islamic Rep. of Iran
		100	USA	HRI	WHRI - World Harvest R.
		250	USA	HRI	WHRI - World Harvest R.
		100	CHN	dom	Xizang PBS, Lhasa
7390	9		IND	dom	All India R., Port Blair
		100	D	LAM	BBG - RFE/RL
		250	PHL	PHT	BBG - VO America (VOA)
		500	CHN	JIN	China Radio Int. (CRI)
		500	CHN	XIA	China Radio Int. (CRI)
		500	F	ISS	Radio France Int. (RFI)
		100	ROU	TIG	Radio Romania International
		100	ALB	SHI	RadioTirana
7395		250	D	WER	Bible Voice Broadcasting (BVB)
		150	CHN	BEI	China Radio Int. (CRI)
		500	CHN	KAS	China Radio Int. (CRI)
		500	CHN	KUN	China Radio Int. (CRI)
		250	MDG	MDC	Radio Japan (NHK World)
		250	PHL	PHT	Vatican Radio
		500	IRN	SIR	VO the Islamic Rep. of Iran
7400		100	SNG	SNG	BBC World Service
		100	D	LAM	BBG - RFE/RL
		100	CHN	HUH	China Radio Int. (CRI)
		500	CHN	BEI	China Radio Int. (CRI)
		500	CHN	XIA	China Radio Int. (CRI)
		100	AUT	MOS	TWR Europe
7405		250	USA	GRV	BBG - R. Martí
		250	THA	UDO	BBG - VO America (VOA)
		100	CHN	HUH	China Radio Int. (CRI)
		500	CHN	BEI	China Radio Int. (CRI)
		500	CHN	URU	China Radio Int. (CRI)
		500	CHN	XIA	China Radio Int. (CRI)
7410		300	CYP	CYP	BBC World Service
		100	CHN	BJI	China Radio Int. (CRI)
		100	CHN	KAS	China Radio Int. (CRI)
		150	CHN	BEI	China Radio Int. (CRI)
		500	CHN	JIN	China Radio Int. (CRI)
		500	CHN	SZG	China Radio Int. (CRI)
		100	CHN	dom	CNR8 VO Minorities, Beijing
		100	PHL	IBA	FEBC Philippines
		100	AUS	SHP	Radio Australia
		100	UZB	TAC	Vatican Radio
7415		250	ASC	ASC	BBC World Service
		250	MRA	TIN	BBG - R. Free Asia (RFA)
		100	CHN	KAS	China Radio Int. (CRI)

kHz	N	kW	Ctry	Site	Station, location
		500	CHN	KAS	China Radio Int. (CRI)
		500	CHN	URU	China Radio Int. (CRI)
		100	ROU	TIG	Radio Romania International
7420		50	IND	dom	All India R., Guwahati
		50	IND	dom	All India R., Hyderabad
		50	IND	GUW	All India Radio (AIR)
		150	CHN	KUN	China Radio Int. (CRI)
		500	CHN	URU	China Radio Int. (CRI)
		100	CHN	dom	Nei Menggu-Ch, Hohhot
		100	ROU	TIG	Radio Romania International
		500	IRN	KAM	VO the Islamic Rep. of Iran
7425		250	CYP	CYP	BBC World Service
		100	D	LAM	BBG - RFE/RL
		250	KWT	KWT	BBG - VO America (VOA)
		100	CHN	KAS	China Radio Int. (CRI)
		100	CHN	KUN	China Radio Int. (CRI)
		150	CHN	KUN	China Radio Int. (CRI)
		500	CHN	JIN	China Radio Int. (CRI)
		150	CHN	dom	CNR2 Business R, Xianyang
		100	ROU	TIG	Radio Romania International
7430		50	IND	dom	All India R., Bhopal
		100	D	BIB	BBG - RFE/RL
		250	CLN	IRA	BBG - VO America (VOA)
		500	CHN	JIN	China Radio Int. (CRI)
		300	ROU	GAL	Radio Romania International
7435		250	ASC	ASC	BBC World Service
		250	G	WOF	BBC World Service
		250	SEY	SEY	BBC World Service
		500	CHN	BEI	China Radio Int. (CRI)
		500	CHN	JIN	China Radio Int. (CRI)
		500	CHN	KUN	China Radio Int. (CRI)
		500	IRN	KAM	VO the Islamic Rep. of Iran
		500	IRN	SIR	VO the Islamic Rep. of Iran
		50	VTN	dom	VO Vietnam 1, Son Tay
7440		50	IND	dom	All India R., Lucknow
		250	THA	UDO	BBG - VO America (VOA)
		100	CHN	KUN	China Radio Int. (CRI)
		100	CHN	NNN	China Radio Int. (CRI)
		500	CHN	BEI	China Radio Int. (CRI)
		500	CHN	KUN	China Radio Int. (CRI)
		500	CHN	XIA	China Radio Int. (CRI)
	+	50	NZL	RAN	R. New Zealand Int. (RNZI)
7445		300	CYP	CYP	BBC World Service
		250	G	WOF	BBC World Service
		250	MRA	TIN	BBG - R. Free Asia (RFA)
		100	CHN	KAS	China Radio Int. (CRI)
		500	CHN	URU	China Radio Int. (CRI)
		100	CHN	dom	CNR8 VO Minorities, Beijing
		300	G	SKN	IBRA Radio
		100	TWN	PAO	Radio Taiwan International
7450		100	GRC	AVL	RS Makedonias (ERT3)
		100	CHN	dom	Xizang PBS, Lhasa
7455		250	CLN	IRA	BBG - VOA Deewa Radio
		250	KWT	KWT	BBG - VOA Deewa Radio
		250	THA	UDO	BBG - VOA Deewa Radio
7460		250	MNG	UBA	BBG - R. Free Asia (RFA)
		250	PHL	PHT	BBG - VO America (VOA)
		250	THA	UDO	BBG - VO America (VOA)
		250	CLN	IRA	BBG - VOA R. Aap Ki Dunyaa
		250	THA	UDO	R. Thailand World Service
		500	MDA	KCH	Radio Payam-e Doost
7465		250	AFS	MEY	BBC World Service
		100	SNG	SNG	BBC World Service
		250	USA	GRV	BBG - VO America (VOA)
		100	PAK	ISL	Radio Pakistan
		500	F	ISS	Radio Taiwan International

kHz	N	kW	Ctry	Site	Station, location
		100	ALB	SHI	RadioTirana
		250	USA	HRI	WHRI - World Harvest R.
7470		250	MNG	UBA	BBG - R. Free Asia (RFA)
		250	MRA	TIN	BBG - R. Free Asia (RFA)
		250	TJK	DSB	BBG - R. Free Asia (RFA)
		250	CLN	IRA	BBG - RFE/RL
7475	‡	100	PAK	ISL	Radio Pakistan
		100	GRC	AVL	Voice of Greece (ERA5)
7480		200	TJK	DSB	BBG - R. Free Asia (RFA)
		250	CLN	IRA	BBG - RFE/RL
		250	CLN	IRA	BBG - VO America (VOA)
		100	D	LAM	BBG - VO America (VOA)
		250	PHL	PHT	BBG - VO America (VOA)
		250	THA	UDO	BBG - VO America (VOA)
		250	CLN	IRA	BBG - VOA R. Aap Ki Dunyaa
		100	PHL	IBA	FEBC Philippines
		300	TJK	DSB	Open Radio for North Korea
		500	MDA	KCH	Radio Payam-e Doost
7485		250	THA	UDO	BBG - RFE/RL
7490		250	THA	NAK	BBC World Service
		50	USA	BCQ	The Overcomer Ministry
		50	USA	BCQ	WBCQ
		100	USA	WCR	WWCR
		100	USA	WCR	WWCR
7495		250	MRA	TIN	BBG - R. Free Asia (RFA)
		250	THA	UDO	BBG - VO America (VOA)
		250	THA	UDO	BBG - VOA Deewa Radio
		500	F	ISS	Radio Algeriénnne
7505		250	THA	NAK	BBC World Service
		100	TJK	DSB	Radio Free Chosun
		100	UZB	TAC	TWR India
7506	†±	50	USA	RNO	WRNO Worldwide
7510		300	ARM	ERV	Democratic VO Burma
		300	ARM	ERV	FEBA Radio
7515		100	UZB	TAC	Voice of the Martyrs
7520		100	D	LAM	BBG - R. Farda
		250	THA	UDO	BBG - R. Farda
		250	CLN	IRA	BBG - VO America (VOA)
		250	PHL	PHT	BBG - VO America (VOA)
		250	THA	UDO	BBG - VO America (VOA)
		250	USA	HRI	WHRI - World Harvest R.
7530		250	PHL	PHT	BBG - VO America (VOA)
		100	MDA	KCH	Radio Ranginkaman
		100	TWN	TSU	Suab Xaa Moo Zoo
7540		500	TJK	DSB	BBG - R. Free Asia (RFA)
		100	TWN	TSU	Family Radio
		100	TJK	DSB	Open Radio for North Korea
7550		500	IND	BGL	All India Radio (AIR)
		250	KWT	KWT	BBG - R. Free Asia (RFA)
		250	KWT	KWT	BBG - RFE/RL
7555	†	50	USA	JES	KJES Radio
		100	TWN	PAO	Radio Taiwan International
		250	USA	EWN	WEWN - EWTN Shortwave
7560		250	KWT	KWT	BBG - VO America (VOA)
		250	THA	UDO	BBG - VO America (VOA)
		250	CLN	IRA	BBG - VOA Ashna Radio
		250	KWT	KWT	BBG - VOA Ashna Radio
		250	THA	UDO	BBG - VOA Ashna Radio
7570		250	PHL	PHT	BBG - VO America (VOA)
		200	KRE	KUJ	Voice of Korea
7575		250	PHL	PHT	BBG - VO America (VOA)
7580		250	CLN	IRA	BBG - R. Farda
		200	KRE	KUJ	Voice of Korea
7585		100	UZB	TAC	Vatican Radio
7590		100	UZB	TAC	North Korea Reform Radio
7600		250	THA	NAK	BBC World Service

kHz	N	kW	Ctry	Site	Station, location
	±	100	TJK	DSB	Sound of Hope Radio Int.
7630	±	100	TJK	DSB	Sound of Hope Radio Int.
7850		3	CAN	STF	CHU, Ottawa, ON
7970	±	1	TWN	TSU	Sound of Hope Radio Int.
8728		10	F	MCO	Radio Monaco
9265		50	USA	INB	WINB
9280		100	TWN	PAO	Family Radio
		250	EGY	ABS	Radio Cairo
9315		250	THA	UDO	BBG - VO America (VOA)
9320		250	CLN	IRA	BBG - VO America (VOA)
9325		250	CLN	IRA	BBG - R. Free Asia (RFA)
		250	PHL	PHT	BBG - VO America (VOA)
		250	THA	UDO	BBG - VO America (VOA)
		200	KRE	KUJ	Voice of Korea
9330	‡	500	SYR	ADR	Radio Damascus
		50	USA	BCQ	WBCQ
9335		250	KWT	KWT	BBG - R. Free Afghanistan
		250	KWT	KWT	BBG - VOA Ashna Radio
		200	KRE	KUJ	Voice of Korea
9340		500	TJK	DSB	Voice of Russia (VOR)
9345		100	PHL	IBA	FEBC Philippines
		250	MDG	MDC	Radio VOP
		200	KRE	KUJ	Voice of Korea
9350		200	TJK	DSB	BBG - R. Free Asia (RFA)
		100	USA	WCR	WWCR
		100	USA	WCR	WWCR
9355		100	MRA	SAI	BBG - R. Free Asia (RFA)
		250	PHL	PHT	BBG - VO America (VOA)
9360		100	MRA	SAI	BBG - RFE/RL
		250	PHL	PHT	BBG - RFE/RL
9370		250	CLN	IRA	BBG - VOA Deewa Radio
		100	D	BIB	BBG - VOA Deewa Radio
		125	PHL	PHT	BBG - VOA Deewa Radio
		100	USA	WRB	The Overcomer Ministry
		100	USA	WRB	WWRB
9375	±	100	TJK	DSB	Sound of Hope Radio Int.
9385		250	CLN	IRA	BBG - R. Free Asia (RFA)
		250	MRA	TIN	BBG - R. Free Asia (RFA)
9390		250	MRA	TIN	BBG - VO America (VOA)
		250	PHL	PHT	BBG - VO America (VOA)
		100	UZB	TAC	FEBA Radio
		500	F	ISS	Radio Algeriénnne
9395		100	D	LAM	BBG - R. Farda
		250	CLN	IRA	BBG - VO America (VOA)
		500	F	ISS	Radio Algeriénnne
		500	ARM	ERV	Voice of Russia (VOR)
9400		250	MRA	TIN	BBG - R. Free Asia (RFA)
		100	BOT	BOT	BBG - VO America (VOA)
		300	ARM	ERV	FEBA Radio
		100	PHL	IBA	FEBC Philippines
		500	MDA	KCH	Voice of Russia (VOR)
9405		100	D	LAM	BBG - RFE/RL
		300	G	WOF	BBG - RFE/RL
		100	PHL	BOC	FEBC Philippines
		500	MDA	KCH	Voice of Russia (VOR)
9410		250	ASC	ASC	BBC World Service
		300	CYP	CYP	BBC World Service
		250	OMA	SLA	BBC World Service
		250	SEY	SEY	BBC World Service
		250	THA	NAK	BBC World Service
		500	CHN	KAS	China Radio Int. (CRI)
		100	CHN	dom	CNR5 VO Zhonghua, Beijing
		10	TWN	dom	Fu Hsing BS, Kuanyin
		250	F	ISS	Pan American Broadcasting
		250	TUR	EMR	Voice of Turkey (VOT)
		500	TUR	EMR	Voice of Turkey (VOT)

kHz	N	kW	Ctry	Site	Station, location
9415		250	IND	DEL	All India Radio (AIR)
		500	CHN	XIA	China Radio Int. (CRI)
9420		500	CHN	KAS	China Radio Int. (CRI)
		100	CHN	dom	CNR1 VO China, Lingshi
		100	CHN	dom	CNR13 Uyghur Sce, Lingshi
		250	RRW	KIG	Deutsche Welle
		170	GRC	AVL	Voice of Greece (ERA5)
9425		250	IND	dom	All India R., Delhi
		500	CHN	BEI	China Radio Int. (CRI)
		500	CHN	JIN	China Radio Int. (CRI)
9430		250	G	WOF	BBC World Service
		100	D	LAM	BBG - R. Farda
		500	CHN	KAS	China Radio Int. (CRI)
		100	PHL	BOC	FEBC Philippines
9435		250	D	WER	BBG - VO America (VOA)
		300	G	WOF	BBG - VO America (VOA)
		250	MRA	TIN	BBG - VO America (VOA)
		500	THA	UDO	BBG - VO America (VOA)
		100	CHN	KUN	China Radio Int. (CRI)
		500	CHN	KAS	China Radio Int. (CRI)
		500	CHN	XIA	China Radio Int. (CRI)
		100	PHL	BOC	FEBC Philippines
		300	ROU	TIG	Radio Romania International
9440		250	ASC	ASC	BBC World Service
		250	THA	UDO	BBG - VOA Ashna Radio
		125	D	WER	Bible Voice Broadcasting (BVB)
		100	CHN	NNN	China Radio Int. (CRI)
		150	CHN	KUN	China Radio Int. (CRI)
		500	CHN	KUN	China Radio Int. (CRI)
		500	CHN	XIA	China Radio Int. (CRI)
		50	CHN	dom	CNR8 VO Minorities, Beijing
		300	TWN	TNN	Radio Taiwan International
9445		250	IND	DEL	All India Radio (AIR)
		500	IND	BGL	All India Radio (AIR)
		100	D	BIB	BBG - RFE/RL
		250	D	WER	BBG - RFE/RL
		100	D	BIB	BBG - VO America (VOA)
		100	PHL	IBA	FEBC Philippines
9450		250	D	WER	Bible Voice Broadcasting (BVB)
		100	CHN	KAS	China Radio Int. (CRI)
		100	CHN	URU	China Radio Int. (CRI)
		500	CHN	KAS	China Radio Int. (CRI)
		500	CHN	SZG	China Radio Int. (CRI)
	+	300	ROU	TIG	Radio Romania International
		100	TWN	PAO	Sound of Hope Radio Int.
		50	BUL	SOF	The Mighty KBC
9455		100	MRA	SAI	BBG - R. Free Asia (RFA)
		150	CHN	KUN	China Radio Int. (CRI)
		100	CHN	dom	CNR1 VO China, Lingshi
		100	CHN	dom	CNR8 VO Minorities, Lingshi
		250	RUS	IRK	Voice of Russia (VOR)
9460		250	ASC	ASC	BBC World Service
		250	SEY	SEY	BBC World Service
		250	THA	NAK	BBC World Service
		150	ALB	CER	China Radio Int. (CRI)
		100	CHN	KAS	China Radio Int. (CRI)
		100	CHN	NNN	China Radio Int. (CRI)
		150	CHN	KUN	China Radio Int. (CRI)
		500	CHN	URU	China Radio Int. (CRI)
		50	BRM	dom	Thazin R, Pyin Oo Lwin
		100	D	WER	The Overcomer Ministry
		500	TUR	EMR	Voice of Turkey (VOT)
9465		250	TWN	TNN	Radio Taiwan International
9470		250	IND	dom	All India R., Aligarh
		250	D	NAU	Bible Voice Broadcasting (BVB)
		100	CHN	URU	China Radio Int. (CRI)

kHz	N	kW	Ctry	Site	Station, location
		100	CHN	dom	CNR1 VO China, Beijing
		250	RRW	KIG	Deutsche Welle
		100	CHN	dom	Xinjiang PBS, Urumqi
9475		100	AUS	SHP	Radio Australia
		100	SWZ	MAN	TWR Africa
		500	TJK	DSB	Voice of Russia (VOR)
9479		100	USA	TWW	WTWW
9480		250	KWT	KWT	BBG - R. Free Asia (RFA)
		100	D	LAM	BBG - VO America (VOA)
		100	STP	SAO	BBG - VO America (VOA)
		100	CHN	dom	CNR11 Tibetan Sce, Xi'an
		250	RUS	MSK	Voice of Russia (VOR)
9485		125	D	NAU	BBG - VO America (VOA)
9490		250	AFS	MEY	BBC World Service
		250	PHL	PHT	BBG - VO America (VOA)
		150	CHN	KUN	China Radio Int. (CRI)
		500	UAE	DHA	Radio Australia
		250	GUF	GUF	Radio República
		250	USA	HRI	WHRI - World Harvest R.
		100	CHN	dom	Xizang PBS, Lhasa
9495		100	D	BIB	BBG - VO America (VOA)
		100	AUT	MOS	TWR Europe
		250	TUR	EMR	Voice of Turkey (VOT)
		250	USA	HRI	WHRI - World Harvest R.
9500		100	CHN	dom	CNR1 VO China, Shijiazhuang
		100	UZB	TAC	CVC The Voice Asia
		100	AUS	SHP	Radio Australia
		100	SWZ	MAN	TWR Africa
		500	IRN	SIR	VO the Islamic Rep. of Iran
9505		300	CYP	CYP	BBC World Service
		250	SNG	SNG	BBC World Service
		8	B	dom	R. Record, São Paulo
		50	SDN	ALF	VO Africa
		50	CHN	dom	VO Strait News Ch, Fuzhou
		250	USA	HRI	WHRI - World Harvest R.
9510		250	OMA	SLA	BBC World Service
		250	SNG	SNG	BBC World Service
		250	THA	NAK	BBC World Service
		150	ROU	TIG	IRRS Shortwave
		500	IRN	SIR	VO the Islamic Rep. of Iran
		50	CHN	dom	Xinjiang PBS, Urumqi
9515		250	CVA	SMG	BBG - RFE/RL
		100	D	BIB	BBG - RFE/RL
		100	D	LAM	BBG - RFE/RL
		100	D	LAM	BBG - VO America (VOA)
		250	D	NAU	Bible Voice Broadcasting (BVB)
		100	CHN	KAS	China Radio Int. (CRI)
		150	CHN	dom	CNR2 Business R, Beijing
		100	KOR	KIM	KBS World Radio
		250	KOR	KIM	KBS World Radio
		10	B	dom	R. Marumby, Curitiba
		500	IRN	KAM	VO the Islamic Rep. of Iran
9520		100	D	BIB	BBG - RFE/RL
		250	KWT	KWT	BBG - RFE/RL
		50	CHN	dom	Nei Menggu-Ch, Hohhot
		250	PHL	PUG	Radio Veritas Asia
9525		500	CHN	BEI	China Radio Int. (CRI)
		500	CHN	KAS	China Radio Int. (CRI)
		300	ROU	GAL	Radio Romania International
		100	SWZ	MAN	TWR Africa
		50	SWZ	MAN	TWR Africa
9526	†	250	INS	JAK	Voice of Indonesia
9530		250	PHL	PHT	BBG - VO America (VOA)
		100	CHN	dom	CNR11 Tibetan Sce, Xi'an
		10	B	dom	R. Transmundial, Santa Maria
		300	ROU	TIG	Radio Romania International

kHz	N	kW	Ctry	Site	Station, location
		50	VTN	dom	VO Vietnam 1, Xuan Mai
		500	TUR	EMR	Voice of Turkey (VOT)
9535	†	5	GEO	dom	Abkhaz State R., Soxum
		100	D	NAU	AWR Africa/Europe
		250	KWT	KWT	BBG - RFE/RL
		100	CHN	KUN	China Radio Int. (CRI)
		150	CHN	BJI	China Radio Int. (CRI)
		500	CHN	KUN	China Radio Int. (CRI)
		500	F	ISS	China Radio Int. (CRI)
		250	E	NOB	R. Exterior de España (REE)
		250	THA	UDO	R. Thailand World Service
9540		100	D	BIB	BBG - RFE/RL
		100	D	LAM	BBG - RFE/RL
		500	CHN	BEI	China Radio Int. (CRI)
		500	CHN	KUN	China Radio Int. (CRI)
		100	UZB	TAC	FEBA Radio
		100	SNG	SNG	Radio Australia
		100	TWN	TSH	Sound of Hope Radio Int.
		500	IRN	KAM	VO the Islamic Rep. of Iran
9545		250	PHL	PHT	BBG - VO America (VOA)
		250	THA	UDO	BBG - VO America (VOA)
9550		250	PHL	PHT	BBG - VO America (VOA)
		150	CHN	KUN	China Radio Int. (CRI)
		500	CHN	BEI	China Radio Int. (CRI)
		250	RRW	KIG	FEBA Radio
		100	PHL	IBA	FEBC Philippines
		10	B	dom	R. Boa Vontade, Porto Alegre
		100	CUB	HAB	Radio Habana Cuba
		100	VTN	VNI	Voice of Vietnam (VOV)
9555		150	ALB	CER	China Radio Int. (CRI)
		150	CHN	BEI	China Radio Int. (CRI)
		500	ARS	RIY	Saudi Radio (BSKSA)
9560		250	CYP	CYP	BBC World Service
		100	CHN	KAS	China Radio Int. (CRI)
		500	CHN	URU	China Radio Int. (CRI)
	±	100	ETH	GJW	Radio Ethiopia
		300	J	YAM	Radio Japan (NHK World)
		250	PAK	ISL	Radio Pakistan
		250	CVA	SMG	Vatican Radio
	±	100	ETH	GJW	VO Peace & Dem. of Eritrea
	±	100	ETH	GJW	Voice of Democratic Alliance
	±	100	ETH	GJW	Voice of Eritrea
	+	250	RUS	NVS	Voice of Russia (VOR)
		50	CHN	dom	Xinjiang PBS, Urumqi
9565		100	GUM	SDA	AWR Asia/Pacific
		250	USA	GRV	BBG - R. Martí
		250	D	WER	BBG - VOA Deewa Radio
		250	THA	UDO	BBG - VOA Deewa Radio
		150	ALB	CER	China Radio Int. (CRI)
		250	TWN	TSH	Radio France Int. (RFI)
		20	B	dom	Super R. Deus é Amor, Curitiba
9570		250	CLN	IRA	BBG - VO America (VOA)
		250	CVA	SMG	BBG - VO America (VOA)
		300	ALB	CER	China Radio Int. (CRI)
		100	CHN	KAS	China Radio Int. (CRI)
		500	CHN	BEI	China Radio Int. (CRI)
		250	CUB	HAB	China Radio Int. (CRI)
		100	CHN	dom	CNR2 Business R, Golmud
		100	KOR	KIM	KBS World Radio
		250	E	NOB	R. Exterior de España (REE)
		500	IRN	KAM	VO the Islamic Rep. of Iran
9575		500	IND	BGL	All India Radio (AIR)
9579		0.25	PHL	dom	Philippine BS, Marulas
		250	MRC	NAD	Radio Méditerranée Int.
9580		250	GAB	GAB	Africa No.1
		250	CUB	HAB	China Radio Int. (CRI)

kHz	N	kW	Ctry	Site	Station, location
		250	KOR	KIM	KBS World Radio
		100	AUS	SHP	Radio Australia
		100	CHN	dom	Xizang PBS, Lhasa
9585		100	MRA	SAI	BBG - R. Free Asia (RFA)
		250	D	WER	BBG - RFE/RL
		100	D	LAM	BBG - VO America (VOA)
		500	CHN	KAS	China Radio Int. (CRI)
		250	THA	UDO	R. Thailand World Service
		10	B	dom	Super R. Deus é Amor, São Paulo
		100	SWZ	MAN	TWR Africa
9590		150	ALB	CER	China Radio Int. (CRI)
		150	CHN	KUN	China Radio Int. (CRI)
		500	CHN	KAS	China Radio Int. (CRI)
		500	CHN	SZG	China Radio Int. (CRI)
		250	E	NOB	R. Exterior de España (REE)
		50	BRM	dom	Thazin R, Pyin Oo Lwin
9595		100	IND	dom	All India R., Delhi
		100	IND	DEL	All India Radio (AIR)
		250	IND	DEL	All India Radio (AIR)
		500	IND	BGL	All India Radio (AIR)
		250	D	WER	BBG - RFE/RL
		250	CLN	IRA	BBG - VO America (VOA)
		250	RRW	KIG	FEBA Radio
		50	J	dom	R. Nikkei 1, Tokyo
		250	USA	HRI	WHRI - World Harvest R.
9600		100	CHN	NNN	China Radio Int. (CRI)
		150	CHN	BJI	China Radio Int. (CRI)
		150	CHN	KUN	China Radio Int. (CRI)
		500	CHN	JIN	China Radio Int. (CRI)
		500	CHN	KAS	China Radio Int. (CRI)
	+	300	ROU	GAL	Radio Romania International
		250	PHL	PHT	Vatican Radio
		50	CHN	dom	Xinjiang PBS, Urumqi
9605		300	G	SKN	BBC World Service
		100	MRA	SAI	BBG - R. Free Asia (RFA)
		250	D	WER	Ev. Missions-Gemeinden
		250	E	NOB	R. Exterior de España (REE)
		500	IRN	KAM	VO the Islamic Rep. of Iran
		250	USA	HRI	WHRI - World Harvest R.
9610		100	D	NAU	AWR Africa/Europe
		250	D	WER	AWR Africa/Europe
		100	CHN	KUN	China Radio Int. (CRI)
		150	CHN	KUN	China Radio Int. (CRI)
		250	CHN	JIN	China Radio Int. (CRI)
		500	CHN	KAS	China Radio Int. (CRI)
		50	CHN	dom	CNR8 VO Minorities, Beijing
		500	IRN	SIR	VO the Islamic Rep. of Iran
		500	TUR	EMR	Voice of Turkey (VOT)
9615		250	OMA	SLA	BBC World Service
		500	CHN	URU	China Radio Int. (CRI)
		50	CHN	dom	CNR8 VO Minorities, Beijing
		100	ALS	NLS	KNLS International
		250	USA	HRI	WHRI - World Harvest R.
9620		250	IND	ALG	All India Radio (AIR)
		250	IND	DEL	All India Radio (AIR)
		100	CHN	KAS	China Radio Int. (CRI)
		500	CHN	KUN	China Radio Int. (CRI)
		150	CHN	dom	CNR2 Business R, Beijing
		50	CHN	dom	CNR6 VO Shenzhou, Beijing
		250	E	NOB	R. Exterior de España (REE)
		250	D	WER	Radio Japan (NHK World)
		500	D	WER	Radio Japan (NHK World)
9625		100	AFS	MEY	Channel Africa
		300	J	YAM	Radio Japan (NHK World)
		300	TWN	TNN	Radio Taiwan International
	+	15	RUS	KLG	Voice of Russia (VOR)

kHz	N	kW	Ctry	Site	Station, location
9630		300	AUT	MOS	AWR Africa/Europe
		100	CHN	dom	CNR1 VO China, Golmud
		100	CHN	dom	CNR1 VO China, Lingshi
		100	CHN	dom	CNR8 VO Minorities, Beijing
		100	CHN	dom	CNR8 VO Minorities, Lingshi
		10	B	dom	R. Aparecida, Aparecida
	+	30	CTR	CRI	R. Exterior de España (REE)
		500	IRN	KAM	VO the Islamic Rep. of Iran
		500	IRN	SIR	VO the Islamic Rep. of Iran
9635		250	IND	ALG	All India Radio (AIR)
		250	G	WOF	IBRA Radio
	‡	10	SRB	BEO	International Radio Serbia
		50	MLI	dom	R. Mali, Bamako (Kati)
		100	TWN	TSH	Sound of Hope Radio Int.
		100	CVA	SMG	Vatican Radio
		100	VTN	dom	VO Vietnam 1, Son Tay
9640		250	PHL	PHT	BBG - VO America (VOA)
		500	CHN	KAS	China Radio Int. (CRI)
		100	KOR	KIM	KBS World Radio
		250	KOR	KIM	KBS World Radio
		100	CUB	HAB	Radio Habana Cuba
		250	G	WOF	Voice of Vietnam (VOV)
		250	USA	HRI	WHRI - World Harvest R.
9645		250	D	WER	BBG - Afia Darfur Radio
		500	UAE	DHA	BBG - R. Free Asia (RFA)
		250	THA	UDO	BBG - VO America (VOA)
		500	CHN	BFI	China Radio Int. (CRI)
		500	CHN	KUN	China Radio Int. (CRI)
		100	CHN	dom	CNR1 VO China, Beijing
		100	CHN	dom	CNR8 VO Minorities, Beijing
		8	B	dom	R. Bandeirantes, São Paulo
		250	PHL	PUG	Radio Veritas Asia
		100	CVA	SMG	Vatican Radio
		250	CVA	SMG	Vatican Radio
9650		100	GUM	SDA	AWR Asia/Pacific
		250	SNG	SNG	BBC World Service
		100	CHN	NNN	China Radio Int. (CRI)
		100	AFS	dom	R. Sonder Grense, Meyerton
	+	300	ROU	GAL	Radio Romania International
		200	KRE	KUJ	Voice of Korea
		500	TUR	EMR	Voice of Turkey (VOT)
9655		100	D	BIB	BBG - VO America (VOA)
		100	CHN	KAS	China Radio Int. (CRI)
		100	CHN	KUN	China Radio Int. (CRI)
		100	CHN	NNN	China Radio Int. (CRI)
		150	CHN	KUN	China Radio Int. (CRI)
		500	CHN	KUN	China Radio Int. (CRI)
		100	CHN	dom	CNR1 VO China, Lingshi
		100	CHN	dom	CNR13 Uyghur Sce, Lingshi
		250	RRW	KIG	Deutsche Welle
		100	ALS	NLS	KNLS International
		250	EGY	ABS	Radio Cairo
		300	J	YAM	Radio Japan (NHK World)
		300	ROU	GAL	Radio Romania International
		500	TUR	EMR	Voice of Turkey (VOT)
9660		10	AUS	BRN	Radio Australia
		100	TWN	KOU	Radio Taiwan International
		250	CVA	SMG	Vatican Radio
		500	CVA	SMG	Vatican Radio
9665		250	D	WER	Bible Voice Broadcasting (BVB)
		100	CHN	KAS	China Radio Int. (CRI)
		100	CHN	dom	CNR5 VO Zhonghua, Beijing
		50	KRE	dom	KCBS, Pyongyang
		250	E	NOB	R. Exterior de España (REE)
		250	AFS	MEY	Radio France Int. (RFI)
		100	TWN	PAO	Radio Taiwan International
		500	IRN	KAM	VO the Islamic Rep. of Iran
		250	TUR	EMR	Voice of Turkey (VOT)
		10	B	dom	Voz Missionária, Camboriú
9670		250	TJK	DSB	BBG - R. Free Asia (RFA)
		100	D	LAM	BBG - VO America (VOA)
		500	CHN	KUN	China Radio Int. (CRI)
		300	J	YAM	Radio Japan (NHK World)
		250	PHL	PUG	Radio Veritas Asia
9675		150	CHN	KUN	China Radio Int. (CRI)
		100	CHN	dom	CNR1 VO China, Beijing
	†	5	PRU	dom	Pacífico R., Lima
		10	B	dom	R. Canção Nova, Cach. Paulista
		100	CTR	CRI	R. Exterior de España (REE)
		500	ARS	RIY	Saudi Radio (BSKSA)
9677		5	AZE	dom	Ädälän Säsi Rad., Stepanakert
9680		250	CLN	IRA	BBG - RFE/RL
		250	CVA	SMG	BBG - VO America (VOA)
		100	ALS	NLS	KNLS International
		300	TWN	HUW	Radio Taiwan International
		250	INS	dom	RRI Prgr. 4, Jakarta
		250	RUS	SAM	Voice of Russia (VOR)
9685		150	CHN	BJI	China Radio Int. (CRI)
		500	CHN	KAS	China Radio Int. (CRI)
		500	CHN	KUN	China Radio Int. (CRI)
		500	CHN	SZG	China Radio Int. (CRI)
		100	CHN	dom	CNR5 VO Zhonghua, Beijing
		250	D	NAU	Pan American Broadcasting
	‡	8	B	dom	R. Gazeta, São Paulo
		100	TWN	KOU	Radio Taiwan International
		250	IRN	AHW	VO the Islamic Rep. of Iran
9690		500	IND	BGL	All India Radio (AIR)
		100	LTU	SIT	BBG - R. Free Asia (RFA)
		500	UAE	DHA	BBG - R. Free Asia (RFA)
		100	D	LAM	BBG - VO America (VOA)
		250	D	WER	BBG - VO America (VOA)
		150	CHN	KUN	China Radio Int. (CRI)
		350	E	NOB	China Radio Int. (CRI)
		250	KOR	KIM	KBS World Radio
		250	E	NOB	R. Exterior de España (REE)
		300	ROU	TIG	Radio Romania International
		100	USA	YFR	Radio Taiwan International
	†	250	NIG	IKO	Voice of Nigeria
9695		250	CYP	CYP	BBC World Service
		100	D	LAM	BBG - RFE/RL
		500	CHN	JIN	China Radio Int. (CRI)
		500	CHN	KUN	China Radio Int. (CRI)
	†	8	B	dom	R. Rio Mar, Manaus
		500	UAE	DHA	Radio Australia
		250	CVA	SMG	Vatican Radio
9700		250	KWT	KWT	BBG - R. Free Asia (RFA)
	±	10	ERI	ASM	Ginbot 7 Dimts Radio
		300	J	YAM	Radio Japan (NHK World)
		50	BUL	SOF	The Overcomer Ministry
		500	TUR	EMR	Voice of Turkey (VOT)
9704	±	40	NGR	dom	La Voix du Sahel, Niamey
9705		250	IND	PAN	All India Radio (AIR)
		100	MRA	SAI	BBG - VO America (VOA)
		500	CHN	KAS	China Radio Int. (CRI)
		100	ETH	dom	R. Ethiopia, Geja
		15	CHN	dom	VO Pujiang, Shanghai
		50	CHN	dom	Xinjiang PBS, Urumqi
9710		500	CHN	KAS	China Radio Int. (CRI)
		100	CHN	dom	CNR1 VO China, Shijiazhuang
		100	AUS	SHP	Radio Australia
		100	CUB	HAB	Radio Habana Cuba
		500	IRN	KAM	VO the Islamic Rep. of Iran

kHz	N	kW	Ctry	Site	Station, location
9715		250	THA	UDO	BBG - VO America (VOA)
		100	D	WER	Bible Voice Broadcasting (BVB)
		250	ARS	RIY	Saudi Radio (BSKSA)
		500	IRN	SIR	VO the Islamic Rep. of Iran
		100	RUS	ARM	Voice of Russia (VOR)
9720		100	GUM	SDA	AWR Asia/Pacific
		500	CHN	URU	China Radio Int. (CRI)
		500	CHN	XIA	China Radio Int. (CRI)
		150	CHN	dom	CNR2 Business R, Baoji-Xinjie
		250	THA	UDO	R. Thailand World Service
		1	PRU	dom	R. Victoria, Lima
		250	EGY	ABZ	Radio Cairo
		250	PHL	PUG	Radio Veritas Asia
		120	RUS	KLG	Voice of Russia (VOR)
9725		500	UAE	DHA	BBG - R. Free Asia (RFA)
		300	ROU	TIG	Radio Romania International
		500	IRN	ZAH	VO the Islamic Rep. of Iran
9730		100	CHN	KAS	China Radio Int. (CRI)
		100	CHN	KUN	China Radio Int. (CRI)
		500	CHN	BEI	China Radio Int. (CRI)
		500	CHN	KAS	China Radio Int. (CRI)
		50	CHN	dom	CNR6 VO Shenzhou, Beijing
		50	BRM	dom	Myanma R., Yangon
		200	KRE	KUJ	Voice of Korea
		100	VTN	VNI	Voice of Vietnam (VOV)
9735		250	TWN	TNN	Radio Taiwan International
		500	RUS	MSK	Voice of Russia (VOR)
9740		250	SNG	SNG	BBC World Service
		250	THA	NAK	BBC World Service
		250	KOR	KIM	KBS World Radio
		500	IRN	KAM	VO the Islamic Rep. of Iran
9745		500	CHN	URU	China Radio Int. (CRI)
		10	BHR	ABH	Radio Bahrain
9750		50	CHN	dom	Nei Menggu-Mo, Hohhot
		300	J	YAM	Radio Japan (NHK World)
		300	KWT	KBD	Radio Kuwait
		500	ARM	ERV	Voice of Russia (VOR)
9755		250	THA	UDO	BBG - VO America (VOA)
		100	CHN	dom	CNR2 Business R, Baoji
		50	BUL	SOF	Polish Radio (Ext Sce)
		500	CVA	SMG	Vatican Radio
		500	IRN	KAM	VO the Islamic Rep. of Iran
9760		100	D	BIB	BBG - RFE/RL
		125	D	NAU	BBG - VO America (VOA)
		250	PHL	PHT	BBG - VO America (VOA)
		250	THA	UDO	BBG - VO America (VOA)
		100	CHN	KUN	China Radio Int. (CRI)
		250	CYP	CYP	Cyprus Broadcasting Corp.
	+	90	G	WOF	KBS World Radio
		50	J	dom	R. Nikkei 2, Tokyo
	+	100	G	WOF	Radio Japan (NHK World)
9765		100	CHN	KUN	China Radio Int. (CRI)
		100	CHN	NNN	China Radio Int. (CRI)
		500	CHN	XIA	China Radio Int. (CRI)
		100	CTR	CRI	R. Exterior de España (REE)
		100	NZL	RAN	R. New Zealand Int. (RNZI)
		300	ROU	GAL	Radio Romania International
		500	ARM	ERV	Voice of Russia (VOR)
9770		300	AUT	MOS	AWR Africa/Europe
		250	D	WER	BBG - VOA Ashna Radio
		500	CHN	KAS	China Radio Int. (CRI)
		100	KOR	KIM	KBS World Radio
		500	F	ISS	Radio Japan (NHK World)
		10	CLN	EKA	Sri Lanka Broadcasting Corp.
9774		10	TWN	dom	Fu Hsing BS, Kuanyin
9775		100	STP	SAO	BBG - VO America (VOA)

kHz	N	kW	Ctry	Site	Station, location
		150	CHN	dom	CNR2 Business R, Beijing
		500	IRN	KAM	VO the Islamic Rep. of Iran
9780		250	CVA	SMG	BBG - Afia Darfur Radio
		100	MRA	SAI	BBG - R. Free Asia (RFA)
		100	STP	SAO	BBG - VO America (VOA)
		100	TWN	TNN	Furustato/Ilbon-E Baram
		15	CHN	dom	Qinghai PBS, Xining
	+	100	E	NOB	R. Exterior de España (REE)
	+	300	ROU	TIG	Radio Romania International
		100	TWN	KOU	Radio Taiwan International
	†	50	YEM	SAN	Republic of Yemen Radio
9785		150	CHN	KUN	China Radio Int. (CRI)
		500	CHN	JIN	China Radio Int. (CRI)
		100	CHN	dom	CNR8 VO Minorities, Beijing
		100	UZB	TAC	Radio Japan (NHK World)
		500	IRN	KAM	VO the Islamic Rep. of Iran
		500	IRN	SIR	VO the Islamic Rep. of Iran
		500	TUR	EMR	Voice of Turkey (VOT)
9790		250	SNG	SNG	BBC World Service
		100	MRA	SAI	BBG - R. Free Asia (RFA)
		250	THA	UDO	BBG - RFE/RL
		100	BOT	BOT	BBG - VO America (VOA)
		250	CUB	HAB	China Radio Int. (CRI)
		500	F	ISS	Radio France Int. (RFI)
9795		500	CHN	URU	China Radio Int. (CRI)
		250	RRW	KIG	Deutsche Welle
		100	PHL	BOC	FEBC Philippines
		100	PHL	IBA	FEBC Philippines
		250	GUF	GUF	Radio Japan (NHK World)
9800		100	UZB	TAC	BBC World Service
		250	PHL	PHT	BBG - VO America (VOA)
		500	CHN	KAS	China Radio Int. (CRI)
		150	RRW	KIG	Deutsche Welle
		250	RRW	KIG	Deutsche Welle
		500	RRW	KIG	Deutsche Welle
		500	D	WER	Sawtu Linjiila
9805		300	AUT	MOS	AWR Africa/Europe
		100	D	WER	AWR Africa/Europe
		250	USA	GRV	BBG - R. Martí
		100	KOR	KIM	KBS World Radio
		500	F	ISS	Radio France Int. (RFI)
	+	300	ROU	TIG	Radio Romania International
9810		250	IND	DEL	All India Radio (AIR)
		250	IND	PAN	All India Radio (AIR)
		300	CYP	CYP	BBC World Service
		250	OMA	SLA	BBC World Service
		100	MRA	SAI	BBG - VO America (VOA)
		100	CHN	dom	CNR1 VO China, Nanning
		100	CHN	dom	CNR2 Business R, Baoji
		100	CUB	HAB	Radio Habana Cuba
		300	ROU	TIG	Radio Romania International
9815		250	CYP	CYP	BBC World Service
		250	D	WER	BBG - Afia Darfur Radio
		100	BOT	BOT	BBG - VO America (VOA)
		100	STP	SAO	BBG - VO America (VOA)
9820		250	IND	dom	All India R., Panaji
		250	IND	PAN	All India Radio (AIR)
		300	CYP	CYP	BBC World Service
		15	CHN	NNN	Beibu Bay Radio
		150	CHN	dom	CNR2 Business R, Xianyang
		10	B	dom	R. Nove de Julho, São Paulo
		250	TUR	EMR	Voice of Turkey (VOT)
9825		250	MRA	TIN	BBG - R. Free Asia (RFA)
		250	USA	GRV	BBG - R. Martí
		100	MRA	SAI	BBG - VO America (VOA)
		250	PHL	PHT	BBG - VO America (VOA)

kHz	N	kW	Ctry	Site	Station, location
		100	CHN	KAS	China Radio Int. (CRI)
		250	PHL	PHT	Radyo Pilipinas Overseas
		200	RUS	SPB	Voice of Russia (VOR)
9830		300	AUT	MOS	AWR Africa/Europe
		100	CHN	dom	CNR1 VO China, Beijing
		250	RUS	PPK	Voice of Russia (VOR)
9835		250	IND	DEL	All India Radio (AIR)
		100	D	LAM	BBG - R. Free Asia (RFA)
		100	D	WER	HCJB La Voz de los Andes
		500	F	ISS	Radio France Int. (RFI)
		300	J	YAM	Radio Japan (NHK World)
	†	100	MLA	dom	RTM Sarawak, Kajang
		500	D	WER	The Overcomer Ministry
		50	CHN	dom	Xinjiang PBS, Urumqi
9840		250	UAE	DHA	KBS World Radio
		250	RUS	MSK	Radio Rossii
		500	F	ISS	Radio Taiwan International
		250	RUS	MSK	Voice of Russia (VOR)
		250	TUR	EMR	Voice of Turkey (VOT)
		100	VTN	VNI	Voice of Vietnam (VOV)
		250	USA	HRI	WHRI - World Harvest R.
9845		100	BOT	BOT	BBG - Afia Darfur Radio
		100	CHN	dom	CNR1 VO China, Beijing
9850		250	UAE	DHA	FEBA Radio
		15	CHN	dom	Qinghai-Ib, Xining
		100	CUB	HAB	Radio Habana Cuba
		100	CVA	SMG	Vatican Radio
		500	IRN	KAM	VO the Islamic Rep. of Iran
		500	IRN	SIR	VO the Islamic Rep. of Iran
		100	VTN	dom	VO Vietnam Min, Xuan Mai
		200	KRE	KUJ	Voice of Korea
9855		250	OMA	SLA	BBC World Service
		500	CHN	BEI	China Radio Int. (CRI)
		100	PHL	IBA	FEBC Philippines
		500	UAE	DHA	Radio Australia
		250	EGY	ABZ	Radio Cairo
9860		100	AFS	MEY	BBG - VO America (VOA)
		250	D	WER	BBG - VO America (VOA)
		250	UAE	DHA	BBG - VO America (VOA)
		500	CHN	BEI	China Radio Int. (CRI)
		500	CHN	JIN	China Radio Int. (CRI)
		500	CHN	KAS	China Radio Int. (CRI)
		100	CHN	dom	CNR1 VO China, Beijing
		250	SNG	SNG	Radio Japan (NHK World)
9865		500	CHN	KUN	China Radio Int. (CRI)
		500	MDA	KCH	Voice of Russia (VOR)
		500	RUS	SAM	Voice of Russia (VOR)
9870		500	IND	dom	All India R., Bengaluru
		250	G	WOF	BBC World Service
		500	CHN	XIA	China Radio Int. (CRI)
	+	50	NZL	RAN	R. New Zealand Int. (RNZI)
		100	AFS	MEY	Radio France Int. (RFI)
		500	ARS	RIY	Saudi Radio (BSKSA)
9875		100	LTU	SIT	BBG - R. Free Asia (RFA)
		80	PLW	HBN	BBG - R. Free Asia (RFA)
		250	THA	UDO	BBG - VO America (VOA)
		500	CHN	KAS	China Radio Int. (CRI)
9880		100	GUM	SDA	AWR Asia/Pacific
		100	AFS	MEY	BBG - VO America (VOA)
		100	BOT	BOT	BBG - VO America (VOA)
		250	PHL	PHT	BBG - VO America (VOA)
		100	CHN	KUN	China Radio Int. (CRI)
		150	CHN	BEI	China Radio Int. (CRI)
		500	CHN	BEI	China Radio Int. (CRI)
		250	RUS	PPK	Voice of Russia (VOR)
9885		100	AFS	MEY	BBG - VO America (VOA)
		100	BOT	BOT	BBG - VO America (VOA)
		100	STP	SAO	BBG - VO America (VOA)
		250	USA	GRV	BBG - VO America (VOA)
		250	EGY	ABS	Radio Cairo
		500	ARS	RIY	Saudi Radio (BSKSA)
9890		100	GUM	SDA	AWR Asia/Pacific
		100	CHN	dom	CNR1 VO China, Lingshi
		100	CHN	dom	CNR13 Uyghur Sce, Lingshi
		100	PHL	BOC	FEBC Philippines
	+	50	NZL	RAN	R. New Zealand Int. (RNZI)
9895		250	USA	HRI	R. Netherlands Worldwide
		300	ROU	TIG	Radio Romania International
		250	UAE	DHA	Radio Taiwan International
		500	IRN	ZAH	VO the Islamic Rep. of Iran
9900		100	SNG	SNG	BBC World Service
9905		250	MRA	TIN	BBG - R. Free Asia (RFA)
		80	PLW	HBN	BBG - R. Free Asia (RFA)
		250	EGY	ABS	Radio Cairo
9910		250	IND	ALG	All India Radio (AIR)
		250	IND	DEL	All India Radio (AIR)
		500	IND	ALG	All India Radio (AIR)
		100	GUM	TWR	TWR Asia
9915		250	ASC	ASC	BBC World Service
		250	CYP	CYP	BBC World Service
		300	CYP	CYP	BBC World Service
		300	G	SKN	BBC World Service
9920		250	THA	NAK	BBC World Service
		100	PHL	BOC	FEBC Philippines
		100	TJK	DSB	Voice of Wilderness
9925		100	D	WER	Bible Voice Broadcasting (BVB)
9930		250	CLN	IRA	BBG - VO America (VOA)
		100	PLW	HBN	Hmong World Christian Radio
		100	PLW	HBN	Quê Me Radio
		100	USA	YFR	Radio Taiwan International
		100	PLW	HBN	T8WH - World Harvest Radio Int
		100	PLW	HBN	The Khmer Post Radio
9935		100	GRC	AVL	RS Makedonias (ERT3)
9940		250	MRA	TIN	BBG - R. Free Asia (RFA)
		70	-	-	Miraya FM
		100	SWZ	MAN	TWR Africa
9945		250	CLN	IRA	BBG - VO America (VOA)
9950		250	IND	DEL	All India Radio (AIR)
	+	50	IND	DEL	All India Radio (AIR)
		100	PLW	HBN	Furustato/Ilbon-E Baram
		100	TWN	TSU	Furustato/Ilbon-E Baram
		250	THA	UDO	R. Thailand World Service
9955		250	MRA	TIN	BBG - R. Free Asia (RFA)
		250	THA	UDO	BBG - VOA Deewa Radio
		100	TWN	TNN	Radio France Int. (RFI)
		50	USA	RMI	Radio Prague
		50	USA	RMI	Radio Slovakia Int.
		50	USA	RMI	WRMI - R. Miami Int.
9960		100	PLW	HBN	KPPM Radio
9965		100	PLW	HBN	Furustato/Ilbon-E Baram
		100	PLW	HBN	Radio Australia
		250	EGY	ABS	Radio Cairo
		250	EGY	ABZ	Radio Cairo
9970	±	1	TWN	TSU	Sound of Hope Radio Int.
9975		250	KWT	KWT	BBG - VOA Ashna Radio
		100	PLW	HBN	Furustato/Ilbon-E Baram
		100	GUM	TWR	TWR Asia
		200	KRE	KUJ	Voice of Korea
9980		100	USA	WCR	The Overcomer Ministry
		100	USA	WCR	WWCR
		100	USA	WCR	WWCR
9990		250	CLN	IRA	BBG - R. Farda

kHz	N	kW	Ctry	Site	Station, location
		250	KWT	KWT	BBG - R. Farda
		300	ARM	ERV	The Overcomer Ministry
		200	KRE	KUJ	Voice of Korea
		100	USA	TWW	WTWW
9995	±	100	TJK	DSB	Sound of Hope Radio Int.
9996		5	RUS	STF	RWM, Moscow
10000		20	CHN	STF	BPM, Kinshan
		2	ARG	STF	LOL, Buenos Aires
		1	B	STF	Observatório Nal, Rio de Janeiro
		10	USA	STF	WWV NIST, Fort Collins, CO
		10	HWA	STF	WWVH NIST, Kauai, HI
10960	±	1	TWN	TSU	Sound of Hope Radio Int.
11230	±	1	TWN	TSU	Sound of Hope Radio Int.
11300	±	1	TWN	TSU	Sound of Hope Radio Int.
11510		70	BUL	SOF	Dengê Kurdistanê
		250	MDA	KCH	Dengê Kurdistanê
11520		100	TWN	PAO	Family Radio
		100	TWN	PAO	Radio Taiwan International
		250	USA	EWN	WEWN - EWTN Shortwave
11535		200	KRE	KUJ	Voice of Korea
11540		100	EGY	ABZ	Radio Cairo
11545		250	KWT	KWT	BBG - R. Free Asia (RFA)
		200	KRE	KUJ	Voice of Korea
11550		300	TJK	DSB	Free North Korea Radio
		250	TWN	TNN	Radio Taiwan International
	±	100	TJK	DSB	Sound of Hope Radio Int.
		100	UZB	TAC	Voice of Tigers Radio
		250	USA	EWN	WEWN - EWTN Shortwave
11560		250	PHL	PHT	BBG - VO America (VOA)
		100	ARM	ERV	Democratic VO Burma
		250	EGY	ABZ	Radio Cairo
		300	TJK	DSB	Radio Free Chosun
11565		250	USA	HRI	Fiji Freedom Democracy Mov.
		250	USA	HRI	WHRI - World Harvest R.
11570		250	PAK	ISL	Radio Pakistan
		100	TWN	TSU	Suab Xaa Moo Zoo
11580		250	IND	ALG	All India Radio (AIR)
		100	GUM	TWR	TWR Asia
11585		250	MRA	TIN	BBG - R. Free Asia (RFA)
11590		250	KWT	KWT	BBG - R. Free Asia (RFA)
11600		250	SNG	SNG	Deutsche Welle
	†	500	LBY	SAB	Radio Libya
11605		250	TWN	TSH	BBG - R. Free Asia (RFA)
		100	AFS	MEY	Radio France Int. (RFI)
		250	TWN	TNN	Radio Taiwan International
		300	TWN	TNN	Radio Taiwan International
11610		100	D	LAM	BBG - RFE/RL
		150	CHN	KUN	China Radio Int. (CRI)
		500	CHN	URU	China Radio Int. (CRI)
		150	CHN	dom	CNR2 Business R, Beijing
		100	AFS	MEY	IBRA Radio
11615		250	CVA	SMG	BBG - Afia Darfur Radio
11620		250	IND	dom	All India R., Delhi
		250	IND	DEL	All India Radio (AIR)
		500	IND	BGL	All India Radio (AIR)
		500	IND	DEL	All India Radio (AIR)
		500	CHN	BEI	China Radio Int. (CRI)
		100	CHN	dom	CNR5 VO Zhonghua, Beijing
		300	ROU	GAL	Radio Romania International
11625		250	E	NOB	R. Exterior de España (REE)
		100	TWN	PAO	Radio Taiwan International
		100	CVA	SMG	Vatican Radio
		250	CVA	SMG	Vatican Radio
		500	CVA	SMG	Vatican Radio
		250	MDG	MDC	Vatican Radio
11630		100	CHN	dom	CNR1 VO China, Lingshi
		100	CHN	dom	CNR8 VO Minorities, Lingshi
		250	KWT	KBD	Radio Kuwait
	‡	100	MLA	dom	RTM Sarawak, Kajang
11635		250	THA	UDO	BBG - VO America (VOA)
		250	GUF	GUF	KBS World Radio
		300	ROU	TIG	Radio Romania International
		100	TWN	PAO	Radio Taiwan International
		250	RRW	KIG	TWR Africa
	+	40	RUS	MSK	Voice of Russia (VOR)
11640		250	KWT	KWT	BBG - VO America (VOA)
		100	CHN	KAS	China Radio Int. (CRI)
		100	CHN	KUN	China Radio Int. (CRI)
		150	CHN	KUN	China Radio Int. (CRI)
		500	CHN	BEI	China Radio Int. (CRI)
		500	CHN	JIN	China Radio Int. (CRI)
		500	CHN	XIA	China Radio Int. (CRI)
		100	MLI	BKO	China Radio Int. (CRI)
		100	TWN	KOU	Radio Taiwan International
	+	15	RUS	IRK	Voice of Russia (VOR)
11645	+	50	IND	DEL	All India Radio (AIR)
		300	AUT	MOS	AWR Africa/Europe
		250	PAK	ISL	Radio Pakistan
		170	GRC	AVL	Voice of Greece (ERA5)
11650		100	CHN	KUN	China Radio Int. (CRI)
		150	CHN	KUN	China Radio Int. (CRI)
		500	CHN	BEI	China Radio Int. (CRI)
		500	CHN	URU	China Radio Int. (CRI)
		100	PHL	BOC	FEBC Philippines
		100	AUS	SHP	Radio Australia
11655		100	TWN	TNN	Radio Taiwan International
		250	RUS	MSK	Voice of Russia (VOR)
11657	+	50	NZL	RAN	R. New Zealand Int. (RNZI)
11660		150	CHN	dom	CNR2 Business R, Xi'an
		100	AUS	SHP	Radio Australia
11665		500	CHN	URU	China Radio Int. (CRI)
		300	J	YAM	Radio Japan (NHK World)
	†	100	MLA	dom	RTM Sarawak, Kajang
11670		250	IND	ALG	All India Radio (AIR)
		250	IND	PAN	All India Radio (AIR)
		500	IND	BGL	All India Radio (AIR)
		250	CLN	TRM	AWR Africa/Europe
		250	CLN	TRM	AWR Asia/Pacific
		150	CHN	dom	CNR2 Business R, Beijing
		500	F	ISS	Radio France Int. (RFI)
11675		250	CLN	IRA	BBG - VOA R. Aap Ki Dunyaa
		100	GUM	TWR	TWR Asia
11680		300	G	SKN	BBC World Service
		100	CHN	NNN	China Radio Int. (CRI)
		50	KRE	dom	KCBS, Kanggye
		250	E	NOB	R. Exterior de España (REE)
		100	CUB	HAB	Radio Habana Cuba
		500	RUS	TCH	Voice of Russia (VOR)
		250	TUR	EMR	Voice of Turkey (VOT)
11685		100	GUM	SDA	AWR Asia/Pacific
		100	SNG	SNG	BBC World Service
		100	CHN	dom	CNR11 Tibetan Sce, Xi'an
		500	IRN	KAM	VO the Islamic Rep. of Iran
11690		300	AUT	MOS	AWR Africa/Europe
		100	GUM	SDA	AWR Asia/Pacific
		500	CHN	XIA	China Radio Int. (CRI)
		100	CUB	HAB	Radio Habana Cuba
	‡	100	CUB	HAB	Radio Habana Cuba
		250	AFS	MEY	Radio Okapi
		300	ROU	TIG	Radio Romania International
		0.5	FIN	VIR	Scandinavian Weekend R.
11695		500	UAE	DHA	BBG - R. Free Asia (RFA)

kHz	N	kW	Ctry	Site	Station, location
		250	PHL	PHT	BBG - VO America (VOA)
		100	AUS	SHP	Radio Australia
		100	UZB	TAC	Radio Japan (NHK World)
11700		100	GUM	SDA	AWR Asia/Pacific
		100	D	WER	Bible Voice Broadcasting (BVB)
		150	CHN	KUN	China Radio Int. (CRI)
		100	SNG	SNG	Radio Australia
		500	F	ISS	Radio France Int. (RFI)
		300	ROU	TIG	Radio Romania International
		300	TWN	TNN	Radio Taiwan International
		500	IRN	KAM	VO the Islamic Rep. of Iran
11705		100	D	BIB	BBG - RFE/RL
		250	THA	UDO	BBG - VO America (VOA)
11710		100	IND	DEL	All India Radio (AIR)
		250	IND	DEL	All India Radio (AIR)
		500	CHN	URU	China Radio Int. (CRI)
		100	CHN	dom	CNR1 VO China, Beijing
		100	ARG	BUE	Rdif. Argentina al Exterior
		200	KRE	KUJ	Voice of Korea
11715+		50	IND	DEL	All India Radio (AIR)
	†	50	USA	JES	KJES Radio
		250	TWN	TNN	Radio Taiwan International
		100	CVA	SMG	Vatican Radio
11720		250	TJK	DSB	BBG - VO America (VOA)
		150	CHN	BJI	China Radio Int. (CRI)
		100	CHN	dom	CNR1 VO China, Shijiazhuang
		300	TWN	TNN	Radio Taiwan International
		0.5	FIN	VIR	Scandinavian Weekend R.
		500	IRN	KAM	VO the Islamic Rep. of Iran
	†	100	VTN	dom	VO Vietnam 1, Son Tay
11725		150	ALB	CER	China Radio Int. (CRI)
	‡	10	B	dom	R. Marumby, Curitiba
		100	NZL	RAN	R. New Zealand Int. (RNZI)
11730		100	GUM	SDA	AWR Asia/Pacific
		500	CHN	KUN	China Radio Int. (CRI)
		150	BLR	MNS	Radio Belarus
		250	BLR	MNS	Radio Belarus
		500	F	ISS	Radio Japan (NHK World)
		100	UZB	TAC	Radio Japan (NHK World)
		500	TUR	EMR	Voice of Turkey (VOT)
11735		250	IND	ALG	All India Radio (AIR)
		50	B	dom	R. Transmundial, Santa Maria
		200	KRE	KUJ	Voice of Korea
	†	50	TZA	DOL	Zanzibar Broadcasting Corp.
11740		250	IND	dom	All India R., Panaji
		250	IND	ALG	All India Radio (AIR)
		250	IND	PAN	All India Radio (AIR)
		100	CHN	dom	CNR2 Business R, Lingshi
		250	GUF	GUF	Radio Japan (NHK World)
		250	SNG	SNG	Radio Japan (NHK World)
		300	ROU	GAL	Radio Romania International
		100	CVA	SMG	Vatican Radio
		250	CVA	SMG	Vatican Radio
11750		250	AFS	MEY	AWR Africa/Europe
		100	SNG	SNG	BBC World Service
		100	D	BIB	BBG - R. Farda
		250	PHL	PHT	BBG - VO America (VOA)
		100	STP	SAO	BBG - VO America (VOA)
		150	ALB	CER	China Radio Int. (CRI)
		100	CHN	NNN	China Radio Int. (CRI)
		100	CHN	dom	CNR1 VO China, Shijiazhuang
		100	PHL	BOC	FEBC Philippines
		50	AUS	KNX	HCJB Global Voice Australia
		100	CUB	HAB	Radio Habana Cuba
		250	PHL	PUG	Radio Veritas Asia
		250	CLN	TRM	Sri Lanka Broadcasting Corp.
	‡	10	B	dom	Voz Missionária, Camboriú
11755		250	AFS	MEY	AWR Africa/Europe
		250	E	NOB	R. Exterior de España (REE)
11760		100	D	WER	AWR Africa/Europe
		250	CYP	CYP	BBC World Service
		300	CYP	CYP	BBC World Service
		250	OMA	SLA	BBC World Service
		500	CHN	KUN	China Radio Int. (CRI)
		100	CHN	dom	CNR1 VO China, Shijiazhuang
		100	CUB	HAB	Radio Habana Cuba
		300	J	YAM	Radio Japan (NHK World)
		300	TWN	TSH	Sound of Hope Radio Int.
11765		100	TWN	TNN	Radio Taiwan International
		100	TWN	TSH	Sound of Hope Radio Int.
		20	B	dom	Super R. Deus é Amor, Curitiba
11770		250	ASC	ASC	BBC World Service
		100	CHN	NNN	China Radio Int. (CRI)
		500	CHN	RFI	China Radio Int. (CRI)
		500	CHN	KAS	China Radio Int. (CRI)
		500	IRN	SIR	VO the Islamic Rep. of Iran
	†	250	NIG	IKO	Voice of Nigeria
		50	CHN	dom	Xinjiang PBS, Urumqi
11775		250	IND	PAN	All India Radio (AIR)
		250	MRA	TIN	BBG - R. Free Asia (RFA)
		100	D	LAM	BBG - RFE/RL
		250	D	WER	BBG - VO America (VOA)
		500	F	ISS	Radio Algeriénnne
	†	100	AIA	AIA	University Network
11780		100	CHN	KUN	China Radio Int. (CRI)
		500	CHN	JIN	China Radio Int. (CRI)
		100	CHN	dom	CNR8 VO Minorities, Beijing
		250	E	NOB	R. Exterior de España (REE)
		250	B	dom	R. Nal da Amazônia, Brasília
		100	SNG	SNG	Radio Australia
11785		150	ALB	CER	China Radio Int. (CRI)
		100	CHN	KAS	China Radio Int. (CRI)
		100	CHN	NNN	China Radio Int. (CRI)
		500	CHN	BEI	China Radio Int. (CRI)
		500	CHN	KAS	China Radio Int. (CRI)
		250	UAE	DHA	IBRA Radio
11790		100	MRA	SAI	BBG - R. Free Asia (RFA)
		250	D	WER	BBG - RFE/RL
		100	CHN	KAS	China Radio Int. (CRI)
		500	CHN	XIA	China Radio Int. (CRI)
		100	AFS	MEY	Radio France Int. (RFI)
		300	ROU	TIG	Radio Romania International
11795		250	D	NAU	AWR Africa/Europe
		250	CLN	IRA	BBG - R. Free Asia (RFA)
		250	KWT	KWT	BBG - R. Free Asia (RFA)
		250	MRA	TIN	BBG - R. Free Asia (RFA)
		250	THA	UDO	BBG - RFE/RL
		100	CHN	KAS	China Radio Int. (CRI)
		250	KOR	KIM	KBS World Radio
		500	TUR	EMR	Voice of Turkey (VOT)
11800		250	ASC	ASC	BBC World Service
		150	CHN	dom	CNR2 Business R, Beijing
		250	RRW	KIG	Deutsche Welle
		500	IRN	SIR	VO the Islamic Rep. of Iran
11805	†	10	B	dom	Super R. Deus é Amor, Rio de J.
		500	IRN	KAM	VO the Islamic Rep. of Iran
		500	TUR	EMR	Voice of Turkey (VOT)
11810		250	ASC	ASC	BBC World Service
		100	CHN	dom	CNR8 VO Minorities, Beijing
		250	KOR	KIM	KBS World Radio
		300	ROU	TIG	Radio Romania International
		100	D	WER	Voice of Oromo Liberation

kHz	N	kW	Ctry	Site	Station, location
11815		50	CHN	dom	CNR8 VO Minorities, Beijing
		8	B	dom	R. Brasil Central, Goiânia
		100	CTR	CRI	R. Exterior de España (REE)
	+	30	CTR	CRI	R. Exterior de España (REE)
		300	J	YAM	Radio Japan (NHK World)
		250	TUR	EMR	Voice of Turkey (VOT)
11820		250	OMA	SLA	BBC World Service
		100	D	LAM	BBG - VO America (VOA)
		500	CHN	XIA	China Radio Int. (CRI)
		100	PHL	BOC	FEBC Philippines
		500	ARS	RIY	Saudi Radio (BSKSA)
		500	IRN	SIR	VO the Islamic Rep. of Iran
11825		100	GUM	SDA	AWR Asia/Pacific
		100	USA	YFR	Family Radio
		100	PHL	BOC	FEBC Philippines
		300	ROU	TIG	Radio Romania International
11830		250	AFS	MEY	AWR Africa/Europe
		100	CHN	KUN	China Radio Int. (CRI)
		10	B	dom	R. Daqui, Goiânia
		125	D	WER	Radio Biafra London
		500	IRN	SIR	VO the Islamic Rep. of Iran
		200	RUS	SPB	Voice of Russia (VOR)
		250	RUS	PPK	Voice of Russia (VOR)
11835		150	CHN	dom	CNR2 Business R, Xianyang
		250	PHL	PHT	Vatican Radio
		250	TUR	EMR	Voice of Turkey (VOT)
11840		250	IND	DEL	All India Radio (AIR)
		100	D	LAM	BBG - VO America (VOA)
		300	G	WOF	BBG - VO America (VOA)
		250	PHL	PHT	BBG - VO America (VOA)
		100	CUB	HAB	Radio Habana Cuba
		100	GUM	TWR	TWR Asia
11845		500	CHN	XIA	China Radio Int. (CRI)
		150	CHN	dom	CNR2 Business R, Xianyang
11850		100	IND	DEL	All India Radio (AIR)
		100	SNG	SNG	BBC World Service
		250	CLN	IRA	BBG - R. Free Asia (RFA)
		100	D	BIB	BBG - RFE/RL
		250	MDG	MDC	Radio Japan (NHK World)
		300	ROU	GAL	Radio Romania International
		250	PHL	PUG	Radio Veritas Asia
		100	CVA	SMG	Vatican Radio
		250	CVA	SMG	Vatican Radio
11855		100	GUM	SDA	AWR Asia/Pacific
		250	THA	UDO	BBG - VO America (VOA)
		150	ALB	CER	China Radio Int. (CRI)
	†	1	B	dom	R. Aparecida, Aparecida
		250	PHL	PUG	Radio Veritas Asia
11860		300	AUT	MOS	AWR Africa/Europe
		100	D	WER	AWR Africa/Europe
		250	ASC	ASC	BBC World Service
		250	SEY	SEY	BBC World Service
		250	AFS	MEY	BBG - VO America (VOA)
		100	MRA	SAI	BBG - VO America (VOA)
		500	CHN	KUN	China Radio Int. (CRI)
		500	F	ISS	Radio France Int. (RFI)
		100	CUB	HAB	Radio Habana Cuba
		250	SNG	SNG	Radio Japan (NHK World)
		250	IRN	AHW	VO the Islamic Rep. of Iran
		500	IRN	SIR	VO the Islamic Rep. of Iran
		100	CHN	dom	Xizang PBS, Lhasa
11865		250	RRW	KIG	Deutsche Welle
		100	PAK	ISL	Radio Pakistan
		250	PHL	PHT	Vatican Radio
11870		100	D	BIB	BBG - RFE/RL

kHz	N	kW	Ctry	Site	Station, location
.		100	CHN	KAS	China Radio Int. (CRI)
		250	THA	UDO	R. Thailand World Service
		100	PAK	ISL	Radio Pakistan
		300	ROU	GAL	Radio Romania International
		250	PHL	PUG	Radio Veritas Asia
		500	IRN	SIR	VO the Islamic Rep. of Iran
		250	USA	EWN	WEWN - EWTN Shortwave
11875		100	D	WER	Bible Voice Broadcasting (BVB)
		500	CHN	BEI	China Radio Int. (CRI)
		500	CHN	KUN	China Radio Int. (CRI)
		250	RRW	KIG	FEBA Radio
		100	TWN	TNN	Radio France Int. (RFI)
		500	F	ISS	Radio Taiwan International
		250	TWN	TNN	Radio Taiwan International
11880		100	D	BIB	BBG - VO America (VOA)
		100	CHN	KAS	China Radio Int. (CRI)
		100	PHL	BOC	FEBC Philippines
		100	AUS	SHP	Radio Australia
		100	CUB	HAB	Radio Habana Cuba
		250	GUF	GUF	Radio Japan (NHK World)
		100	PAK	ISL	Radio Pakistan
11885		100	STP	SAO	BBG - VO America (VOA)
		500	CHN	XIA	China Radio Int. (CRI)
		100	USA	YFR	Family Radio
		100	TWN	HUW	Radio Taiwan International
		50	CHN	dom	Xinjiang PBS, Urumqi
11890		250	ASC	ASC	BBC World Service
		250	THA	NAK	BBC World Service
		300	G	WOF	BBG - RFE/RL
		250	EGY	ABZ	Radio Cairo
		250	PHL	PHT	Radyo Pilipinas Overseas
11895		250	THA	NAK	BBC World Service
		250	CLN	IRA	BBG - VOA Deewa Radio
		100	PHL	BOC	FEBC Philippines
	†	10	B	dom	R. Boa Vontade, Porto Alegre
		100	E	NOB	R. Exterior de España (REE)
		200	RUS	SPB	Voice of Russia (VOR)
11900		100	CHN	KAS	China Radio Int. (CRI)
		500	CHN	BEI	China Radio Int. (CRI)
		300	ARM	ERV	The Overcomer Ministry
11905		500	UAE	DHA	BBG - R. Free Asia (RFA)
		250	D	WER	BBG - VO America (VOA)
		250	KWT	KWT	BBG - VO America (VOA)
		100	CHN	dom	CNR6 VO Shenzhou, Beijing
		100	PHL	BOC	FEBC Philippines
		200	CLN	EKA	Sri Lanka Broadcasting Corp.
		35	CLN	EKA	Sri Lanka Broadcasting Corp.
11910		500	CHN	XIA	R. Exterior de España (REE)
		300	J	YAM	Radio Japan (NHK World)
		200	KRE	KUJ	Voice of Korea
11915		100	STP	SAO	BBG - VO America (VOA)
		250	F	ISS	Bible Voice Broadcasting (BVB)
		100	CHN	dom	CNR2 Business R, Baoji
		10	B	dom	R. Gaucha, Porto Alegre
		250	TWN	TNN	Radio Taiwan International
		500	ARS	RIY	Saudi Radio (BSKSA)
		250	RUS	MSK	Voice of Russia (VOR)
11920		250	PHL	PHT	BBG - VO America (VOA)
		150	ALB	CER	China Radio Int. (CRI)
		100	D	NAU	HCJB La Voz de los Andes
11925		250	AFS	MEY	AWR Africa/Europe
		250	SEY	SEY	BBC World Service
		250	PHL	PHT	BBG - VO America (VOA)
		100	CHN	dom	CNR1 VO China, Lingshi
		10	B	dom	R. Bandeirantes, São Paulo

kHz	N	kW	Ctry	Site	Station, location
		100	PLW	HBN	Radio Japan (NHK World)
		500	IRN	AHW	VO the Islamic Rep. of Iran
		500	IRN	KAM	VO the Islamic Rep. of Iran
		500	TUR	EMR	Voice of Turkey (VOT)
11930		250	USA	GRV	BBG - R. Martí
		500	ARS	RIY	Saudi Radio (BSKSA)
11935		100	IND	MUM	All India Radio (AIR)
		100	GUM	SDA	AWR Asia/Pacific
		100	CHN	KUN	China Radio Int. (CRI)
		100	CHN	dom	CNR5 VO Zhonghua, Beijing
		250	GUF	GUF	Radio Japan (NHK World)
		250	PHL	PUG	Radio Veritas Asia
		500	ARS	RIY	Saudi Radio (BSKSA)
		250	CVA	SMG	Vatican Radio
11940		250	E	NOB	R. Exterior de España (REE)
		250	MDG	MDC	Radio Dabanga
		250	MDG	MDC	Radio Tamazuj
11945		250	TJK	DSB	BBG - R. Free Asia (RFA)
		150	CHN	KUN	China Radio Int. (CRI)
		100	AUS	SHP	Radio Australia
		500	F	ISS	Radio Japan (NHK World)
		250	PHL	PUG	Radio Veritas Asia
11950		300	CYP	CYP	BBC World Service
		100	CHN	dom	Xizang PBS, Lhasa
11955		300	AUT	MOS	AWR Africa/Europe
		100	GUM	SDA	AWR Asia/Pacific
		100	SNG	SNG	BBC World Service
		100	CHN	KUN	China Radio Int. (CRI)
		500	CHN	KUN	China Radio Int. (CRI)
		500	F	ISS	Radio Algeriénnne
		500	F	ISS	Radio France Int. (RFI)
		300	ROU	TIG	Radio Romania International
		500	TUR	EMR	Voice of Turkey (VOT)
11960		100	CHN	dom	CNR1 VO China, Beijing
11965		300	G	SKN	BBC World Service
		250	MRA	TIN	BBG - R. Free Asia (RFA)
		250	PHL	PHT	BBG - VO America (VOA)
		250	RUS	IRK	TWR India
		250	TUR	EMR	Voice of Turkey (VOT)
11970		250	OMA	SLA	BBC World Service
±	1	TWN	TSU	Sound of Hope Radio Int.
11975		100	D	WER	AWR Africa/Europe
		250	OMA	SLA	BBC World Service
		250	THA	NAK	BBC World Service
		100	D	LAM	BBG - Afia Darfur Radio
		100	STP	SAO	BBG - Afia Darfur Radio
		100	MRA	SAI	BBG - R. Free Asia (RFA)
		100	D	LAM	BBG - RFE/RL
		500	CHN	KUN	China Radio Int. (CRI)
		500	F	ISS	Radio Japan (NHK World)
		50	CHN	dom	Xinjiang PBS, Urumqi
11980		250	MRA	TIN	BBG - R. Free Asia (RFA)
		250	TJK	DSB	BBG - R. Free Asia (RFA)
		100	CHN	KAS	China Radio Int. (CRI)
		100	CHN	KUN	China Radio Int. (CRI)
		150	CHN	KUN	China Radio Int. (CRI)
†	0.3	UKR	dom	Dniprovska Khvylia, Zaporizhia
11985		250	IND	DEL	All India Radio (AIR)
		250	ASC	ASC	FEBA Radio
		100	TWN	HUW	Radio Taiwan International
		500	ARM	ERV	Voice of Russia (VOR)
		500	TUR	EMR	Voice of Turkey (VOT)
11990		250	THA	UDO	BBG - RFE/RL
		250	CVA	SMG	BBG - VO America (VOA)
		100	CHN	NNN	China Radio Int. (CRI)

kHz	N	kW	Ctry	Site	Station, location
		500	CHN	XIA	China Radio Int. (CRI)
11995		250	OMA	SLA	BBC World Service
		100	SNG	SNG	BBC World Service
		250	THA	NAK	BBC World Service
		250	UAE	DHA	BBC World Service
		250	MRA	TIN	BBG - R. Free Asia (RFA)
		100	D	BIB	BBG - RFE/RL
		500	F	ISS	Radio France Int. (RFI)
		500	GUF	GUF	Radio Taiwan International
12000		250	USA	GRV	BBG - VO America (VOA)
		100	VTN	VNI	Voice of Vietnam (VOV)
12005		100	D	BIB	BBG - R. Farda
		100	D	LAM	BBG - R. Farda
		250	PHL	PHT	BBG - VO America (VOA)
		500	UAE	DHA	Radio Australia
		500	TUN	SFA	Radio Tunisienne
12015		100	AFS	MEY	BBC World Service
		500	TIIA	UDO	BBG - RFE/RL
		100	CHN	KAS	China Radio Int. (CRI)
		250	THA	UDO	R. Thailand World Service
		500	IRN	ZAH	VO the Islamic Rep. of Iran
		200	KRE	KUJ	Voice of Korea
		250	MNG	UBA	Voice of Mongolia
12020		250	KWT	KWT	BBG - VOA R. Aap Ki Dunyaa
		100	VTN	VNI	Voice of Vietnam (VOV)
12025		250	IND	PAN	All India Radio (AIR)
		100	SNG	SNG	BBC World Service
		250	SNG	SNG	BBC World Service
		100	D	BIB	BBG - RFE/RL
		300	G	WOF	BBG - RFE/RL
		250	KWT	KWT	BBG - RFE/RL
		250	THA	UDO	BBG - RFE/RL
		250	G	WOF	HCJB La Voz de los Andes
		500	IRN	KAM	VO the Islamic Rep. of Iran
12030		250	E	NOB	R. Exterior de España (REE)
12035		100	GUM	SDA	AWR Asia/Pacific
		250	CYP	CYP	BBC World Service
		250	SEY	SEY	BBC World Service
		100	D	BIB	BBG - R. Farda
		100	MRA	SAI	BBG - R. Free Asia (RFA)
		250	E	NOB	R. Exterior de España (REE)
		250	SNG	SNG	Radio Japan (NHK World)
		250	PHL	PHT	Vatican Radio
		500	TUR	EMR	Voice of Turkey (VOT)
12045		250	SEY	SEY	BBC World Service
		100	MRA	SAI	BBG - VO America (VOA)
		250	PHL	PHT	BBG - VO America (VOA)
		100	CHN	dom	CNR1 VO China, Beijing
		100	AFS	MEY	Deutsche Welle
		250	RRW	KIG	Deutsche Welle
		300	G	WOF	IBRA Radio
		250	SNG	SNG	Radio Japan (NHK World)
12050		250	USA	EWN	WEWN - EWTN Shortwave
12055		100	CHN	dom	CNR1 VO China, Lingshi
		100	CHN	dom	CNR8 VO Minorities, Lingshi
		250	RRW	KIG	Deutsche Welle
		100	PHL	BOC	FEBC Philippines
		250	RUS	MSK	Voice of Russia (VOR)
12060		100	D	BIB	BBG - RFE/RL
		100	BOT	BOT	BBG - VO America (VOA)
		250	RUS	MSK	Voice of Russia (VOR)
12065		300	CYP	CYP	BBC World Service
		100	SNG	SNG	BBC World Service
12070		100	STP	SAO	BBG - VO America (VOA)
		500	CHN	XIA	China Radio Int. (CRI)

kHz	N	kW	Ctry	Site	Station, location
		250	ASC	ASC	Deutsche Welle
		250	RRW	KIG	Deutsche Welle
		100	PHL	IBA	FEBC Philippines
		250	RUS	MSK	Voice of Russia (VOR)
12075		250	RUS	MSK	Radio Rossii
		500	TJK	DSB	Voice of Russia (VOR)
12080		100	AFS	MEY	BBG - VO America (VOA)
		100	BOT	BOT	BBG - VO America (VOA)
		250	CLN	IRA	BBG - VO America (VOA)
		100	STP	SAO	BBG - VOA Studio 7
		100	CHN	dom	CNR2 Business R, Baoji
		10	AUS	BRN	Radio Australia
+		8	AUS	BRN	Radio Australia
12085		250	KWT	KWT	BBG - R. Free Asia (RFA)
		500	IRN	KAM	VO the Islamic Rep. of Iran
		250	MNG	UBA	Voice of Mongolia
12095		100	AFS	MEY	BBC World Service
		250	ASC	ASC	BBC World Service
		250	CYP	CYP	BBC World Service
		250	OMA	SLA	BBC World Service
		250	SEY	SEY	BBC World Service
		100	SNG	SNG	BBC World Service
		250	THA	NAK	BBC World Service
		100	PHL	BOC	FEBC Philippines
		50	BUL	SOF	Polish Radio (Ext Sce)
12105		250	CLN	IRA	BBG - R. Free Asia (RFA)
		100	USA	TWW	WTWW
12115		250	MRA	TIN	BBG - R. Free Asia (RFA)
		250	MDG	MDC	Radio Dialogue (ZCR)
+		100	F	ISS	The Disco Palace
12120		250	PHL	PHT	BBG - VO America (VOA)
		250	THA	UDO	BBG - VO America (VOA)
		100	PHL	BOC	FEBC Philippines
12125		300	ARM	ERV	FEBA Radio
12130		250	CLN	IRA	BBG - R. Free Asia (RFA)
		100	D	LAM	BBG - Radio Mashaal
		250	KWT	KWT	BBG - Radio Mashaal
		500	THA	UDO	BBG - Radio Mashaal
12140		250	KWT	KWT	BBG - R. Free Afghanistan
		250	KWT	KWT	BBG - VOA Ashna Radio
12150		250	CLN	IRA	BBG - VO America (VOA)
		250	PHL	PHT	BBG - VO America (VOA)
		250	THA	UDO	BBG - VO America (VOA)
12160		100	USA	WCR	WWCR
		100	USA	WCR	WWCR
12230±		1	TWN	TSU	Sound of Hope Radio Int.
12320±		1	TWN	TSU	Sound of Hope Radio Int.
12370±		1	TWN	TSU	Sound of Hope Radio Int.
12670±		1	TWN	TSU	Sound of Hope Radio Int.
12759		3	DGA	DGA	AFRTS (AFN Feeder)
12800±		1	TWN	TSU	Sound of Hope Radio Int.
12870±		1	TWN	TSU	Sound of Hope Radio Int.
12980±		1	TWN	TSU	Sound of Hope Radio Int.
13130±		1	TWN	TSU	Sound of Hope Radio Int.
13146		10	F	MCO	Radio Monaco
13270±		1	TWN	TSU	Sound of Hope Radio Int.
13350±		1	TWN	TSU	Sound of Hope Radio Int.
13362		3	GUM	BAR	AFRTS (AFN Feeder)
13430±		1	TWN	TSU	Sound of Hope Radio Int.
13530±		1	TWN	TSU	Sound of Hope Radio Int.
13570		100	D	LAM	BBG - VO America (VOA)
		50	USA	INB	The Overcomer Ministry
		50	USA	INB	WINB
13580		250	CLN	IRA	BBG - Radio Mashaal
		250	D	NAU	BBG - Radio Mashaal
		250	THA	UDO	BBG - Radio Mashaal
		250	CLN	IRA	BBG - VO America (VOA)
		250	D	WER	BBG - VO America (VOA)
		500	CHN	BEI	China Radio Int. (CRI)
		500	CHN	KUN	China Radio Int. (CRI)
		250	EGY	ABS	Radio Cairo
13590		500	CHN	BEI	China Radio Int. (CRI)
		100	ZMB	LUS	CVC 1Africa Radio
		300	ROU	TIG	Radio Romania International
13600		100	CHN	KAS	China Radio Int. (CRI)
		100	CHN	KUN	China Radio Int. (CRI)
		500	CHN	XIA	China Radio Int. (CRI)
13605		500	IND	BGL	All India Radio (AIR)
13610		500	CHN	XIA	China Radio Int. (CRI)
		100	CHN	dom	CNR1 VO China, Nanning
13615		250	CLN	IRA	BBG - R. Farda
		100	D	LAM	BBG - R. Farda
		250	D	WER	BBG - R. Farda
13620		250	KWT	KWT	BBG - R. Free Asia (RFA)
		500	CHN	XIA	China Radio Int. (CRI)
		250	EGY	ABS	Radio Cairo
13625		250	MRA	TIN	BBG - R. Free Asia (RFA)
		100	BOT	BOT	BBG - VO America (VOA)
		250	CVA	SMG	BBG - VO America (VOA)
		250	D	WER	BBG - VO America (VOA)
		500	CHN	KAS	China Radio Int. (CRI)
		500	TUR	EMR	Voice of Turkey (VOT)
13630		100	UZB	TAC	CVC The Voice Asia
		100	AUS	SHP	Radio Australia
		300	ROU	TIG	Radio Romania International
13640		500	IND	BGL	All India Radio (AIR)
		100	CHN	KAS	China Radio Int. (CRI)
13645		250	IND	ALG	All India Radio (AIR)
		250	D	WER	BBG - RFE/RL
		100	CHN	KAS	China Radio Int. (CRI)
		500	CHN	XIA	China Radio Int. (CRI)
13650		250	MRA	TIN	BBG - VO America (VOA)
		500	CHN	URU	China Radio Int. (CRI)
		250	CUB	HAB	China Radio Int. (CRI)
		500	F	ISS	Radio France Int. (RFI)
		300	J	YAM	Radio Japan (NHK World)
		500	KWT	KBD	Radio Kuwait
		500	IRN	KAM	VO the Islamic Rep. of Iran
		200	KRE	KUJ	Voice of Korea
13655		500	CHN	XIA	China Radio Int. (CRI)
13660		250	CYP	CYP	BBC World Service
		250	RRW	KIG	TWR Africa
13665		150	ALB	CER	China Radio Int. (CRI)
13670		150	ALB	CER	China Radio Int. (CRI)
		500	CHN	KAS	China Radio Int. (CRI)
		500	IRN	SIR	VO the Islamic Rep. of Iran
		50	CHN	dom	Xinjiang PBS, Urumqi
13680		100	D	LAM	BBG - R. Farda
		250	D	WER	BBG - R. Farda
		500	CHN	XIA	China Radio Int. (CRI)
‡		100	CUB	HAB	Radio Habana Cuba
		500	IRN	SIR	VO the Islamic Rep. of Iran
13685		500	F	ISS	Radio France Int. (RFI)
		500	TUR	EMR	Voice of Turkey (VOT)
13690		500	IRN	KAM	VO the Islamic Rep. of Iran
13695		500	IND	BGL	All India Radio (AIR)
		300	CYP	CYP	BBC World Service
		100	USA	YFR	Family Radio
		500	F	ISS	Radio France Int. (RFI)
13700		250	CLN	IRA	BBG - Radio Mashaal

kHz	N	kW	Ctry	Site	Station, location
		100	CHN	dom	CNR1 VO China, Lingshi
		100	CHN	dom	CNR13 Uyghur Sce, Lingshi
		250	UAE	DHA	Deutsche Welle
13710		500	IND	BGL	All India Radio (AIR)
		250	MRA	TIN	BBG - R. Free Asia (RFA)
		500	ARS	RIY	Saudi Radio (BSKSA)
13715		100	CHN	KAS	China Radio Int. (CRI)
13720		100	CHN	KAS	China Radio Int. (CRI)
		500	CHN	XIA	China Radio Int. (CRI)
	+	100	E	NOB	R. Exterior de España (REE)
		250	UAE	DHA	Sudan Radio Service
13725		250	THA	NAK	BBC World Service
		250	MRA	TIN	BBG - R. Free Asia (RFA)
		500	F	ISS	Radio Japan (NHK World)
		500	IRN	KAM	VO the Islamic Rep. of Iran
13730		250	D	WER	Ev. Missions-Gemeinden
	+	50	NZL	RAN	R. New Zealand Int. (RNZI)
		250	MDG	MDC	Radio Japan (NHK World)
		500	IRN	SIR	VO the Islamic Rep. of Iran
13735		250	CLN	IRA	BBG - R. Free Asia (RFA)
		250	MRA	TIN	BBG - R. Free Asia (RFA)
		100	STP	SAO	BBG - VO America (VOA)
		100	CHN	KAS	China Radio Int. (CRI)
13740		100	BOT	BOT	BBG - VO America (VOA)
		100	STP	SAO	BBG - VO America (VOA)
		100	D	NAU	Bible Voice Broadcasting (BVB)
		100	F	ISS	Bible Voice Broadcasting (BVB)
		250	CUB	HAB	China Radio Int. (CRI)
		100	D	NAU	HCJB La Voz de los Andes
		500	F	ISS	Radio France Int. (RFI)
		500	IRN	SIR	VO the Islamic Rep. of Iran
13745		250	THA	UDO	R. Thailand World Service
13750		250	USA	GRV	BBG - VO America (VOA)
		500	CHN	KUN	China Radio Int. (CRI)
		500	IRN	KAM	VO the Islamic Rep. of Iran
		500	IRN	SIR	VO the Islamic Rep. of Iran
13755		100	BOT	BOT	BBG - VO America (VOA)
		250	CLN	IRA	BBG - VO America (VOA)
		100	STP	SAO	BBG - VO America (VOA)
13760		200	KRE	KUJ	Voice of Korea
13765		250	CLN	IRA	BBG - R. Free Asia (RFA)
		250	THA	UDO	BBG - VO America (VOA)
		100	GUM	TWR	TWR Asia
		100	CVA	SMG	Vatican Radio
		250	CVA	SMG	Vatican Radio
		500	CVA	SMG	Vatican Radio
		250	MDG	MDC	Vatican Radio
13775		250	D	NAU	BBG - RFE/RL
		500	ARS	RIY	Saudi Radio (BSKSA)
	±	1	TWN	TSU	Sound of Hope Radio Int.
13780		500	CHN	KUN	China Radio Int. (CRI)
		250	RRW	KIG	Deutsche Welle
		250	MDG	MDC	Radio Dabanga
		100	CUB	HAB	Radio Habana Cuba
13785		500	IRN	SIR	VO the Islamic Rep. of Iran
13790		250	PHL	PHT	BBG - RFE/RL
		100	CHN	KAS	China Radio Int. (CRI)
		500	CHN	URU	China Radio Int. (CRI)
		250	RUS	SAM	Voice of Russia (VOR)
13795		500	IND	BGL	All India Radio (AIR)
13800		250	CLN	IRA	BBG - R. Farda
		100	D	LAM	BBG - R. Farda
		250	MDG	MDC	Radio Dabanga
		500	UAE	DHA	Radio Dabanga
		500	UAE	DHA	Radio Tamazuj

kHz	N	kW	Ctry	Site	Station, location
13810		100	CHN	BEI	China Radio Int. (CRI)
		100	D	WER	The Overcomer Ministry
		500	IRN	KAM	VO the Islamic Rep. of Iran
		100	D	WER	Voice of Oromo Liberation
13820		250	ASC	ASC	BBC World Service
		250	USA	GRV	BBG - R. Martí
	±	1	TWN	TSU	Sound of Hope Radio Int.
13830		250	CLN	IRA	BBG - VOA Ashna Radio
		250	USA	EWN	WEWN - EWTN Shortwave
13840		250	MDG	MDC	Radio Japan (NHK World)
13845		100	USA	WCR	WWCR
		100	USA	WCR	WWCR
13850		500	CHN	BEI	China Radio Int. (CRI)
		250	ISR	ISR	Kol Israel
13855		500	CHN	KAS	China Radio Int. (CRI)
		250	EGY	ABS	Radio Cairo
13860		300	ROU	TIG	Radio Romania International
13865		300	CYP	CYP	BBC World Service
		250	OMA	SLA	BBC World Service
13870		250	UAE	DHA	Radio Japan (NHK World)
13920	±	1	TWN	TSU	Sound of Hope Radio Int.
13970	±	1	TWN	TSU	Sound of Hope Radio Int.
14370	±	1	TWN	TSU	Sound of Hope Radio Int.
14400	±	1	TWN	TSU	Sound of Hope Radio Int.
14600	±	1	TWN	TSU	Sound of Hope Radio Int.
14670		10	CAN	STF	CHU, Ottawa, ON
14700	±	1	TWN	TSU	Sound of Hope Radio Int.
14750	±	1	TWN	TSU	Sound of Hope Radio Int.
14800	±	1	TWN	TSU	Sound of Hope Radio Int.
14870	±	1	TWN	TSU	Sound of Hope Radio Int.
14951	†		CLM	dom	Salem Stereo, Rioblanco
14980	±	1	TWN	TSU	Sound of Hope Radio Int.
14996		5	RUS	STF	RWM, Moscow
15000		20	CHN	STF	BPM, Kinshan
		10	USA	STF	WWV NIST, Fort Collins, CO
		10	HWA	STF	WWVH NIST, Kauai, HI
15030		250	IND	ALG	All India Radio (AIR)
15040		100	IND	DEL	All India Radio (AIR)
15050		250	IND	DEL	All India Radio (AIR)
	+	50	IND	DEL	All India Radio (AIR)
15085		500	IRN	KAM	VO the Islamic Rep. of Iran
15100		200	KRE	KUJ	Voice of Korea
15105		250	BGD	DKA	Bangladesh Betar
		250	ASC	ASC	BBC World Service
	‡	100	PAK	ISL	Radio Pakistan
		100	SWZ	MAN	TWR Africa
15110		250	PHL	PHT	BBG - VO America (VOA)
		100	CHN	KAS	China Radio Int. (CRI)
		250	E	NOB	R. Exterior de España (REE)
		300	ROU	TIG	Radio Romania International
15115		250	PHL	PHT	BBG - VO America (VOA)
15120		500	IND	BGL	All India Radio (AIR)
		250	CLN	IRA	BBG - R. Free Asia (RFA)
		100	MRA	SAI	BBG - R. Free Asia (RFA)
		500	CHN	BEI	China Radio Int. (CRI)
		250	CUB	HAB	China Radio Int. (CRI)
		500	ARS	RIY	Saudi Radio (BSKSA)
	+	250	NIG	AJA	Voice of Nigeria
	†	250	NIG	IKO	Voice of Nigeria
15125		100	D	WER	AWR Africa/Europe
		100	MRA	SAI	BBG - VO America (VOA)
		100	CTR	CRI	R. Exterior de España (REE)
15130		100	D	LAM	BBG - RFE/RL
		150	CHN	BEI	China Radio Int. (CRI)
15135		100	CHN	KUN	China Radio Int. (CRI)

kHz	N	kW	Ctry	Site	Station, location
		500	CHN	KAS	China Radio Int. (CRI)
		500	CHN	KUN	China Radio Int. (CRI)
15140	+	50	IND	DEL	All India Radio (AIR)
		100	D	LAM	BBG - R. Free Asia (RFA)
		100	CHN	KAS	China Radio Int. (CRI)
		100	OMA	THU	Radio Sultanate of Oman
15145		100	D	WER	AWR Africa/Europe
		100	CHN	KAS	China Radio Int. (CRI)
		500	CHN	BEI	China Radio Int. (CRI)
		500	CHN	XIA	China Radio Int. (CRI)
15150		250	CLN	TRM	Athmik Yatra Radio
		250	SEY	SEY	BBC World Service
		250	MRA	TIN	BBG - R. Free Asia (RFA)
		300	ROU	TIG	Radio Romania International
		500	IRN	KAM	VO the Islamic Rep. of Iran
15155		250	PHL	PHT	BBG - VO America (VOA)
		300	ROU	GAL	Radio Romania International
15160		250	MRA	TIN	BBG - R. Free Asia (RFA)
		100	CHN	NNN	China Radio Int. (CRI)
		500	CHN	JIN	China Radio Int. (CRI)
		100	KOR	KIM	KBS World Radio
		100	AUS	SHP	Radio Australia
		250	EGY	ABS	Radio Cairo
		300	ROU	TIG	Radio Romania International
15170		250	MRA	TIN	BBG - R. Free Asia (RFA)
		100	CHN	KAS	China Radio Int. (CRI)
		500	CHN	JIN	China Radio Int. (CRI)
		100	CTR	CRI	R. Exterior de España (REE)
		250	AFS	MEY	Radio France Int. (RFI)
		300	ROU	GAL	Radio Romania International
		500	ARS	RIY	Saudi Radio (BSKSA)
		500	IRN	KAM	VO the Islamic Rep. of Iran
15175		250	IND	PAN	All India Radio (AIR)
15180		300	CYP	CYP	BBC World Service
		125	CLN	TRM	Bible Voice Broadcasting (BVB)
		500	F	ISS	Radio Taiwan International
		200	KRE	KUJ	Voice of Korea
		250	CLN	TRM	Voice of Wilderness
		100	USA	HRI	WHRI - World Harvest R.
15185		250	IND	PAN	All India Radio (AIR)
15190		500	CHN	URU	China Radio Int. (CRI)
	†	5	B	dom	R. Inconfidência, Belo Horizonte
	†	50	GNE	BAT	Radio Africa
		250	GUF	GUF	Radio Japan (NHK World)
		250	PHL	PHT	Radyo Pilipinas Overseas
15195		300	J	YAM	Radio Japan (NHK World)
15200		100	GUM	TWR	TWR Asia
		500	TUR	EMR	Voice of Turkey (VOT)
15205		250	PHL	PHT	BBG - RFE/RL
		250	PHL	PHT	BBG - VO America (VOA)
		500	CHN	KAS	China Radio Int. (CRI)
		100	D	WER	Pan American Broadcasting
		250	EGY	ABS	Radio Cairo
		500	ARS	RIY	Saudi Radio (BSKSA)
15210		250	IND	PAN	All India Radio (AIR)
		100	CHN	KAS	China Radio Int. (CRI)
		500	CHN	KUN	China Radio Int. (CRI)
15215		100	GUM	SDA	AWR Asia/Pacific
		125	D	WER	Bible Voice Broadcasting (BVB)
		250	UAE	DHA	FEBA Radio
		500	D	WER	Radio Öömrang
15220		500	CHN	KAS	China Radio Int. (CRI)
		500	CHN	URU	China Radio Int. (CRI)
		300	AUT	MOS	FEBA Radio
		300	ROU	GAL	Radio Romania International

kHz	N	kW	Ctry	Site	Station, location
		500	IRN	SIR	VO the Islamic Rep. of Iran
15225		100	BOT	BOT	BBG - VO America (VOA)
		250	USA	GRV	BBG - VO America (VOA)
		500	CHN	KAS	China Radio Int. (CRI)
		100	PHL	IBA	FEBC Philippines
		250	PHL	PUG	Radio Veritas Asia
		500	ARS	RIY	Saudi Radio (BSKSA)
		100	GUM	TWR	TWR Asia
15230		100	AUS	SHP	Radio Australia
		100	CUB	HAB	Radio Habana Cuba
15235		250	CLN	TRM	Athmik Yatra Radio
		250	AFS	MEY	Channel Africa
		100	GUM	TWR	TWR Asia
15240		500	AFS	MEY	AWR Africa/Europe
		100	AUS	SHP	Radio Australia
		100	GUM	TWR	TWR Asia
15245		500	CHN	URU	China Radio Int. (CRI)
		100	EGY	ABZ	Radio Cairo
		300	TWN	TSH	Radio Taiwan International
		250	RUS	SAM	Voice of Asena
		200	KRE	KUJ	Voice of Korea
15250		300	AUT	MOS	AWR Asia/Pacific
		100	CHN	KUN	China Radio Int. (CRI)
		250	ASC	ASC	FEBA Radio
		500	ARS	RIY	Saudi Radio (BSKSA)
15255		250	CLN	TRM	AWR Africa/Europe
		250	CLN	TRM	AWR Asia/Pacific
		100	GUM	SDA	AWR Asia/Pacific
		250	AFS	MEY	Channel Africa
		300	ROU	GAL	Radio Romania International
		250	PHL	PUG	Radio Veritas Asia
15260		100	GUM	SDA	AWR Asia/Pacific
		300	ROU	GAL	Radio Romania International
		500	IRN	SIR	VO the Islamic Rep. of Iran
15265		100	D	LAM	BBG - RFE/RL
		250	D	WER	BBG - RFE/RL
		100	STP	SAO	BBG - VO America (VOA)
		250	TWN	TSH	Radio Taiwan International
		250	PHL	PUG	Radio Veritas Asia
		100	GUM	TWR	TWR Asia
15270		250	CLN	TRM	AWR Africa/Europe
		250	CLN	TRM	AWR Asia/Pacific
		250	SNG	SNG	BBC World Service
		150	CHN	dom	CNR2 Business R, Beijing
		100	TWN	PAO	Radio Taiwan International
15275		150	RRW	KIG	Deutsche Welle
		250	RRW	KIG	Deutsche Welle
15280		300	ROU	TIG	Radio Romania International
		250	PHL	PUG	Radio Veritas Asia
15285		250	CLN	TRM	Athmik Yatra Radio
		100	SNG	SNG	BBC World Service
		100	EGY	ABZ	Radio Cairo
		250	PHL	PHT	Radyo Pilipinas Overseas
		500	ARS	RIY	Saudi Radio (BSKSA)
15290		300	AUT	MOS	AWR Africa/Europe
		250	PHL	PHT	BBG - VO America (VOA)
		250	EGY	ABZ	Radio Cairo
		500	F	ISS	Radio Japan (NHK World)
		250	TWN	TNN	Radio Taiwan International
15300		500	F	ISS	Radio France Int. (RFI)
		250	IRN	AHW	VO the Islamic Rep. of Iran
15310		250	OMA	SLA	BBC World Service
		250	THA	NAK	BBC World Service
15315		500	F	ISS	Radio France Int. (RFI)
		125	D	WER	VO Oromo Liberation Front

kHz	N	kW	Ctry	Site	Station, location
15320		100	GUM	SDA	AWR Asia/Pacific
		100	PHL	BOC	FEBC Philippines
		100	PHL	IBA	FEBC Philippines
		100	TWN	PAO	Radio Taiwan International
		250	CVA	SMG	Radio Veritas Asia
15325		300	J	YAM	Radio Japan (NHK World)
	‡	100	PAK	ISL	Radio Pakistan
15330		100	GUM	SDA	AWR Asia/Pacific
		250	USA	GRV	BBG - R. Martí
		100	PHL	BOC	FEBC Philippines
		300	ROU	TIG	Radio Romania International
		250	CVA	SMG	Radio Veritas Asia
		500	IRN	SIR	VO the Islamic Rep. of Iran
15335		100	SNG	SNG	BBC World Service
		100	F	ISS	Bible Voice Broadcasting (BVB)
		500	CHN	KAS	China Radio Int. (CRI)
15340		500	CHN	XIA	China Radio Int. (CRI)
		100	AUS	KNX	HCJB Global Voice Australia
		100	CUB	HAB	Radio Habana Cuba
	‡	100	CUB	HAB	Radio Habana Cuba
15345		250	EGY	ABS	Radio Cairo
		100	ARG	BUE	Rdif. Argentina al Exterior
15349	‡	250	MRC	NAD	Radio Marocaine
15350		100	CHN	KAS	China Radio Int. (CRI)
		500	TUR	EMR	Voice of Turkey (VOT)
15360		250	CYP	CYP	BBC World Service
		250	OMA	SLA	BBC World Service
		250	AFS	MEY	Radio France Int. (RFI)
		100	SWZ	MAN	TWR India
		500	IRN	SIR	VO the Islamic Rep. of Iran
		500	TUR	EMR	Voice of Turkey (VOT)
15365		250	EGY	ABZ	Radio Cairo
15370		100	GUM	SDA	AWR Asia/Pacific
		100	CHN	dom	CNR1 VO China, Shijiazhuang
	‡	100	CUB	HAB	Radio Habana Cuba
		100	CUB	HAB	Radio Habana Cuba
		300	ROU	TIG	Radio Romania International
15375		250	TJK	DSB	BBG - R. Free Asia (RFA)
		500	UAE	DHA	BBG - R. Free Asia (RFA)
		50	-	-	Esat Radio
		10	TWN	dom	Fu Hsing BS, Kuanyin
15380		100	CHN	dom	CNR1 VO China, Beijing
		300	ROU	GAL	Radio Romania International
		500	ARS	RIY	Saudi Radio (BSKSA)
15385		250	PHL	PHT	BBG - VO America (VOA)
	†	50	USA	JES	KJES Radio
		250	E	NOB	R. Exterior de España (REE)
15390		125	CLN	TRM	Bible Voice Broadcasting (BVB)
		100	CHN	dom	CNR1 VO China, Lingshi
		100	CHN	dom	CNR13 Uyghur Sce, Lingshi
		100	GUM	TWR	TWR Asia
15400		250	AFS	MEY	BBC World Service
		250	ASC	ASC	BBC World Service
		100	AUS	KNX	HCJB Global Voice Australia
		500	IRN	SIR	VO the Islamic Rep. of Iran
15410		250	IND	PAN	All India Radio (AIR)
		500	IND	BGL	All India Radio (AIR)
		100	D	BIB	BBG - R. Farda
		300	G	WOF	BBG - R. Farda
15415		100	CHN	dom	CNR8 VO Minorities, Beijing
		50	CHN	dom	CNR8 VO Minorities, Beijing
		100	AUS	SHP	Radio Australia
15420		100	GUM	SDA	AWR Asia/Pacific
		250	CYP	CYP	BBC World Service
		300	CYP	CYP	BBC World Service

kHz	N	kW	Ctry	Site	Station, location
		250	SEY	SEY	BBC World Service
		100	PLW	HBN	Radio Free Sarawak
		50	USA	BCQ	The Overcomer Ministry
		50	USA	BCQ	WBCQ
15425		500	CHN	XIA	China Radio Int. (CRI)
		250	PAK	ISL	Radio Pakistan
15430		300	ROU	GAL	Radio Romania International
		300	ROU	TIG	Radio Romania International
15435		500	CHN	XIA	China Radio Int. (CRI)
		100	PHL	BOC	FEBC Philippines
		500	ARS	RIY	Saudi Radio (BSKSA)
15440		300	AUT	MOS	AWR Asia/Pacific
		500	CHN	KUN	China Radio Int. (CRI)
		250	RRW	KIG	Deutsche Welle
		100	USA	YFR	Radio Taiwan International
15445		100	TWN	TSU	AWR Asia/Pacific
		500	CHN	KAS	China Radio Int. (CRI)
		250	D	WER	Radio Japan (NHK World)
15450		100	PHL	BOC	FEBC Philippines
		100	PHL	IBA	FEBC Philippines
		250	EGY	ABZ	Radio Cairo
		250	PHL	PUG	Radio Veritas Asia
		500	IRN	KAM	VO the Islamic Rep. of Iran
		500	IRN	SIR	VO the Islamic Rep. of Iran
15455		100	PHL	BOC	FEBC Philippines
		100	PHL	IBA	FEBC Philippines
15460		100	STP	SAO	BBG - VO America (VOA)
		300	ROU	GAL	Radio Romania International
		250	PHL	PUG	Radio Veritas Asia
		250	MRA	TIN	Vatican Radio
		250	PHL	PUG	Vatican Radio
15465		100	CHN	KAS	China Radio Int. (CRI)
		100	TWN	PAO	Radio Taiwan International
15470		100	D	LAM	RRG - VO America (VOA)
		250	D	WER	Bible Voice Broadcasting (BVB)
		250	RUS	SAM	Voice of Russia (VOR)
15480		250	AFS	MEY	AWR Africa/Europe
		250	CLN	TRM	AWR Asia/Pacific
		100	CHN	dom	CNR1 VO China, Beijing
		250	EGY	ABZ	Radio Cairo
		500	TUR	EMR	Voice of Turkey (VOT)
15485		500	F	ISS	Radio Taiwan International
		250	MDG	MDC	Voice of Tibet
15487	±	100	TJK	DSB	Voice of Tibet
15488	±	100	TJK	DSB	Voice of Tibet
15490		250	CYP	CYP	BBC World Service
		250	SEY	SEY	BBC World Service
		250	PAK	ISL	Radio Pakistan
		500	ARS	RIY	Saudi Radio (BSKSA)
15495		100	GUM	SDA	AWR Asia/Pacific
		250	MRA	TIN	Vatican Radio
		250	PHL	PUG	Vatican Radio
15497	±	100	TJK	DSB	Voice of Tibet
15500		150	CHN	dom	CNR2 Business R, Beijing
		500	IRN	KAM	VO the Islamic Rep. of Iran
		500	IRN	SIR	VO the Islamic Rep. of Iran
15505		250	BGD	DKA	Bangladesh Betar
		100	MLI	BKO	China Radio Int. (CRI)
15510		250	CYP	CYP	BBC World Service
		250	SNG	SNG	BBC World Service
		250	THA	NAK	BBC World Service
15515		100	AUS	SHP	Radio Australia
		500	KWT	KBD	Radio Kuwait
		500	IRN	KAM	VO the Islamic Rep. of Iran
15520		250	MRA	TIN	BBG - R. Free Asia (RFA)

kHz	N	kW	Ctry	Site	Station, location
15525		100	D	LAM	BBG - RFE/RL
		500	CHN	URU	China Radio Int. (CRI)
		250	UAE	DHA	Eternal Good News
		100	PHL	BOC	FEBC Philippines
		100	AUS	KNX	HCJB Global Voice Australia
		500	IRN	KAM	VO the Islamic Rep. of Iran
15530		250	PHL	PHT	BBG - RFE/RL
		500	F	ISS	Radio France Int. (RFI)
		250	PHL	PUG	Radio Veritas Asia
15535		250	CLN	IRA	BBG - R. Farda
		250	CVA	SMG	Radio Dabanga
15540		500	KWT	KBD	Radio Kuwait
15545		250	EGY	ABZ	Radio Cairo
15550		250	MRA	TIN	BBG - R. Free Asia (RFA)
		100	CHN	dom	CNR1 VO China, Beijing
		100	GUM	TWR	TWR Asia
		500	IRN	KAM	VO the Islamic Rep. of Iran
		50	USA	JHR	WJHR Radio International
15553±		100	TJK	DSB	Voice of Tibet
15555		250	PHL	PHT	BBG - VO America (VOA)
15558±		100	TJK	DSB	Voice of Tibet
15560		250	PHL	PHT	BBG - VO America (VOA)
		250	THA	UDO	BBG - VO America (VOA)
		100	PHL	BOC	FEBC Philippines
15562±		100	TJK	DSB	Voice of Tibet
15565		500	CHN	XIA	China Radio Int. (CRI)
		300	ARM	ERV	The Overcomer Ministry
15567±		100	TJK	DSB	Voice of Tibet
15570		100	CHN	dom	CNR11 Tibetan Sce, Xi'an
		250	CVA	SMG	Vatican Radio
		500	CVA	SMG	Vatican Radio
15575		250	CYP	CYP	BBC World Service
		250	OMA	SLA	BBC World Service
		250	KOR	KIM	KBS World Radio
15580		250	AFS	MEY	BBG - VO America (VOA)
		100	BOT	BOT	BBG - VO America (VOA)
		250	CLN	IRA	BBG - VO America (VOA)
		250	CVA	SMG	BBG - VO America (VOA)
		100	STP	SAO	BBG - VO America (VOA)
		250	USA	GRV	BBG - VO America (VOA)
		100	PHL	BOC	FEBC Philippines
15585		250	E	NOB	R. Exterior de España (REE)
15590		250	USA	GRV	BBG - VO America (VOA)
15595		100	CVA	SMG	Vatican Radio
		250	CVA	SMG	Vatican Radio
		250	MRA	TIN	Vatican Radio
15600		100	CHN	KUN	China Radio Int. (CRI)
		100	PHL	BOC	FEBC Philippines
15605		100	GUM	SDA	AWR Asia/Pacific
15610		250	MRA	TIN	BBG - R. Free Asia (RFA)
		250	EGY	ABZ	Radio Cairo
		250	USA	EWN	WEWN - EWTN Shortwave
15620		100	BOT	BOT	BBG - VO America (VOA)
		250	CLN	IRA	BBG - VO America (VOA)
		250	CVA	SMG	BBG - VO America (VOA)
		250	D	WER	BBG - VO America (VOA)
		100	STP	SAO	BBG - VO America (VOA)
		250	USA	GRV	BBG - VO America (VOA)
		500	CHN	KAS	China Radio Int. (CRI)
		100	PHL	BOC	FEBC Philippines
15625		500	CHN	KAS	China Radio Int. (CRI)
15630		100	GRC	AVL	Voice of Greece (ERA5)
		250	RUS	PPK	Voice of Russia (VOR)
15640		100	GUM	SDA	AWR Asia/Pacific
		250	SNG	SNG	Deutsche Welle

kHz	N	kW	Ctry	Site	Station, location
		250	UAE	DHA	Deutsche Welle
15650		250	THA	UDO	BBG - RFE/RL
		100	GRC	AVL	Voice of Greece (ERA5)
15660		100	GUM	SDA	AWR Asia/Pacific
15665		100	MRA	SAI	BBG - R. Free Asia (RFA)
		500	CHN	KAS	China Radio Int. (CRI)
		250	USA	HRI	WHRI - World Harvest R.
15670		100	BOT	BOT	BBG - VO America (VOA)
		250	D	WER	BBG - VO America (VOA)
		100	STP	SAO	BBG - VO America (VOA)
		250	THA	UDO	BBG - VO America (VOA)
		100	CHN	dom	CNR8 VO Minorities, Beijing
15680		100	TWN	TNN	Radio France Int. (RFI)
		100	PLW	HBN	T8WH - World Harvest Radio Int
15690		250	CLN	IRA	BBG - R. Farda
		100	D	BIB	BBG - R. Farda
		250	MRA	TIN	BBG - R. Free Asia (RFA)
		500	F	ISS	Radio Taiwan International
15700		250	MRA	TIN	BBG - R. Free Asia (RFA)
		250	G	WOF	Deutsche Welle
		250	RRW	KIG	Deutsche Welle
		250	UAE	DHA	Deutsche Welle
		250	PAK	ISL	Radio Pakistan
15710		300	CYP	CYP	BBC World Service
		250	OMA	SLA	BBC World Service
		50	CHN	dom	CNR6 VO Shenzhou, Beijing
		250	EGY	ABS	Radio Cairo
15720		100	NZL	RAN	R. New Zealand Int. (RNZI)
	+	50	NZL	RAN	R. New Zealand Int. (RNZI)
		250	MDG	MDC	Radio Japan (NHK World)
15725		250	PAK	ISL	Radio Pakistan
15735		250	PAK	ISL	Radio Pakistan
		300	ROU	TIG	Radio Romania International
15740		250	RUS	SAM	Voice of Russia (VOR)
15745		35	CLN	EKA	Sri Lanka Broadcasting Corp.
		500	TJK	DSB	Voice of Russia (VOR)
15750±		100	TJK	DSB	Sound of Hope Radio Int.
15755		250	THA	NAK	BBC World Service
15760		250	CLN	IRA	BBG - Radio Mashaal
		250	ISR	ISR	Kol Israel
15770		250	IND	ALG	All India Radio (AIR)
		250	IND	DEL	All India Radio (AIR)
		100	CHN	dom	CNR2 Business R, Lingshi
15775		100	STP	SAO	BBG - VOA Studio 7
	+	125	CVA	SMG	Vatican Radio
15780±		100	TJK	DSB	Sound of Hope Radio Int.
15790		250	CYP	CYP	BBC World Service
		250	OMA	SLA	BBC World Service
15795		500	IND	BGL	All India Radio (AIR)
15800		250	EGY	ABS	Radio Cairo
	±	1	TWN	TSU	Sound of Hope Radio Int.
15825		100	USA	WCR	WWCR
		100	USA	WCR	WWCR
15850		10	ISR	LOD	Galei Tzahal
15870±		1	TWN	TSU	Sound of Hope Radio Int.
15896+		0.1	D	dom	BiteXpress, Erlangen
15900±		1	TWN	TSU	Sound of Hope Radio Int.
15940±		1	TWN	TSU	Sound of Hope Radio Int.
15970±		1	TWN	TSU	Sound of Hope Radio Int.
16100±		1	TWN	TSU	Sound of Hope Radio Int.
16250±		1	TWN	TSU	Sound of Hope Radio Int.
16360±		1	TWN	TSU	Sound of Hope Radio Int.
16600±		1	TWN	TSU	Sound of Hope Radio Int.
16920±		1	TWN	TSU	Sound of Hope Radio Int.
17100±		1	TWN	TSU	Sound of Hope Radio Int.

kHz	N	kW	Ctry	Site	Station, location
17170±	1		TWN	TSU	Sound of Hope Radio Int.
17250±	1		TWN	TSU	Sound of Hope Radio Int.
17260		10	F	MCO	Radio Monaco
17300±	1		TWN	TSU	Sound of Hope Radio Int.
17360		100	AUT	MOS	Radio Ö1 International
17370±	1		TWN	TSU	Sound of Hope Radio Int.
17450±	1		TWN	TSU	Sound of Hope Radio Int.
17480		250	EGY	ABZ	Radio Cairo
17485		500	CHN	KAS	China Radio Int. (CRI)
17490		500	CHN	KAS	China Radio Int. (CRI)
17495		500	CHN	BEI	China Radio Int. (CRI)
17500		100	CHN	KAS	China Radio Int. (CRI)
		300	ROU	TIG	Radio Romania International
		500	RUS	MSK	Voice of Russia (VOR)
17505		100	CHN	KAS	China Radio Int. (CRI)
		500	CHN	XIA	China Radio Int. (CRI)
17510		250	IND	DEL	All India Radio (AIR)
		250	THA	NAK	BBC World Service
		100	EGY	ARZ	Radio Cairo
17515		200	TJK	DSB	BBG - R. Free Asia (RFA)
17520		250	USA	HRI	WHRI - World Harvest R.
17530		100	STP	SAO	BBG - VO America (VOA)
		300	ROU	TIG	Radio Romania International
17535		250	MDG	MDC	Voice of Tibet
17540		100	GUM	SDA	AWR Asia/Pacific
		100	CHN	KAS	China Radio Int. (CRI)
		500	CHN	BEI	China Radio Int. (CRI)
		300	ROU	TIG	Radio Romania International
17545		125	D	WER	Bible Voice Broadcasting (BVB)
17550		100	CHN	dom	CNR1 VO China, Beijing
		500	KWT	KBD	Radio Kuwait
		500	IRN	KAM	VO the Islamic Rep. of Iran
17560		500	CHN	XIA	China Radio Int. (CRI)
		500	ARS	RIY	Saudi Radio (BSKSA)
		500	IRN	KAM	VO the Islamic Rep. of Iran
		500	IRN	SIR	VO the Islamic Rep. of Iran
17565		100	CHN	dom	CNR1 VO China, Beijing
17570		500	CHN	KAS	China Radio Int. (CRI)
		500	CHN	URU	China Radio Int. (CRI)
		500	ARS	RIY	Saudi Radio (BSKSA)
		250	USA	HRI	WHRI - World Harvest R.
17575		250	D	WER	AWR Africa/Europe
		100	USA	YFR	Family Radio
17580		100	CHN	dom	CNR1 VO China, Lingshi
		100	CUB	HAB	Radio Habana Cuba
17585		250	EGY	ABZ	Radio Cairo
17590		100	GUM	SDA	AWR Asia/Pacific
		100	CVA	SMG	Vatican Radio
		250	CVA	SMG	Vatican Radio
17595		100	CHN	dom	CNR1 VO China, Shijiazhuang
		250	E	NOB	R. Exterior de España (REE)
17600		500	IRN	SIR	VO the Islamic Rep. of Iran
17605		300	AUT	MOS	AWR Africa/Europe
		100	GUM	SDA	AWR Asia/Pacific
		100	CHN	dom	CNR1 VO China, Beijing
17615		500	F	ISS	Radio France Int. (RFI)
		500	ARS	RIY	Saudi Radio (BSKSA)
17620		500	F	ISS	Radio France Int. (RFI)
17625		150	CHN	dom	CNR2 Business R, Beijing
		250	EGY	ABS	Radio Cairo
		500	ARS	RIY	Saudi Radio (BSKSA)
17630		100	MLI	BKO	China Radio Int. (CRI)
		250	THA	UDO	R. Thailand World Service
		500	F	ISS	R. Xoriyo
17635		100	GUM	SDA	AWR Asia/Pacific

kHz	N	kW	Ctry	Site	Station, location
17640		250	AFS	MEY	BBC World Service
		250	CYP	CYP	BBC World Service
		250	SEY	SEY	BBC World Service
		500	CHN	XIA	China Radio Int. (CRI)
17645		250	PHL	PHT	BBG - VO America (VOA)
17650		500	CHN	KAS	China Radio Int. (CRI)
		100	PLW	HBN	T8WH - World Harvest Radio Int
		500	IRN	ZAH	VO the Islamic Rep. of Iran
17655		250	USA	GRV	BBG - VO America (VOA)
17660		250	CYP	CYP	BBC World Service
		250	AFS	MEY	Radio France Int. (RFI)
		250	UAE	DHA	Radio Japan (NHK World)
		500	ARS	RIY	Saudi Radio (BSKSA)
17665		250	RUS	PPK	Voice of Russia (VOR)
17670		250	IND	DEL	All India Radio (AIR)
		500	IND	BGL	All India Radio (AIR)
		250	MDG	MDC	AWR Asia/Pacific
		500	CHN	KUN	China Radio Int. (CRI)
17675		250	KWT	KWI	BBG - R. Free Asia (RFA)
		100	NZL	RAN	R. New Zealand Int. (RNZI)
+		50	NZL	RAN	R. New Zealand Int. (RNZI)
17680		100	GUM	SDA	AWR Asia/Pacific
		100	BOT	BOT	BBG - VO America (VOA)
		250	KWT	KWT	BBG - VO America (VOA)
		100	CHN	KUN	China Radio Int. (CRI)
		150	CHN	KUN	China Radio Int. (CRI)
		250	UAE	DHA	Radio ERGO
		500	IRN	SIR	VO the Islamic Rep. of Iran
17685		250	SNG	SNG	BBC World Service
17690		500	CHN	JIN	China Radio Int. (CRI)
		100	CHN	dom	CNR1 VO China, Nanning
		500	IRN	KAM	VO the Islamic Rep. of Iran
		250	RUS	VLD	Voice of Russia (VOR)
17700		100	GUM	SDA	AWR Asia/Pacific
		250	PAK	ISL	Radio Pakistan
		250	PHL	PHT	Radyo Pilipinas Overseas
17705		100	CUB	HAB	Radio Habana Cuba
		500	ARS	RIY	Saudi Radio (BSKSA)
17710		500	CHN	BEI	China Radio Int. (CRI)
		500	CHN	JIN	China Radio Int. (CRI)
		250	RRW	KIG	Deutsche Welle
17715+		50	IND	DEL	All India Radio (AIR)
		250	E	NOB	R. Exterior de España (REE)
		500	IRN	SIR	VO the Islamic Rep. of Iran
17720		250	THA	NAK	BBC World Service
		500	CHN	KAS	China Radio Int. (CRI)
17725		100	BOT	BOT	BBG - VO America (VOA)
		100	STP	SAO	BBG - VO America (VOA)
		500	CHN	XIA	China Radio Int. (CRI)
17730		250	MNG	UBA	BBG - R. Free Asia (RFA)
		100	CUB	HAB	Radio Habana Cuba
		500	ARS	RIY	Saudi Radio (BSKSA)
17735		250	CLN	IRA	BBG - RFE/RL
		100	CHN	KUN	China Radio Int. (CRI)
		500	F	ISS	Radio Japan (NHK World)
		250	TUN	SFA	Radio Tunisienne
17740		500	CHN	XIA	China Radio Int. (CRI)
		500	ARS	RIY	Saudi Radio (BSKSA)
17745		250	CYP	CYP	BBC World Service
		300	CYP	CYP	BBC World Service
		300	ROU	GAL	Radio Romania International
		300	G	WOF	Sudan Radio Service
17750		100	CHN	KAS	China Radio Int. (CRI)
		500	CHN	XIA	China Radio Int. (CRI)
		100	AUS	SHP	Radio Australia

kHz	N	kW	Ctry	Site	Station, location
‡		100	CUB	HAB	Radio Habana Cuba
17755		250	E	NOB	R. Exterior de España (REE)
		500	TUR	EMR	Voice of Turkey (VOT)
17760		250	AFS	MEY	Amateur R. Mirror Int.
		250	THA	NAK	BBC World Service
17765		300	ROU	GAL	Radio Romania International
17770		100	MRA	SAI	BBG - R. Free Asia (RFA)
		250	THA	UDO	BBG - RFE/RL
		250	AFS	MEY	Channel Africa
17775		300	ROU	TIG	Radio Romania International
17780		250	ASC	ASC	BBC World Service
		300	CYP	CYP	BBC World Service
		250	PHL	PHT	BBG - VO America (VOA)
		300	ROU	GAL	Radio Romania International
		300	ROU	TIG	Radio Romania International
17785		500	ARS	RIY	Saudi Radio (BSKSA)
17790		300	CYP	CYP	BBC World Service
		250	OMA	SLA	BBC World Service
		250	THA	NAK	BBC World Service
17795		100	AUS	SHP	Radio Australia
17800		500	CHN	KAS	China Radio Int. (CRI)
		250	RRW	KIG	Deutsche Welle
		250	UAE	DHA	Deutsche Welle
17805		250	MRA	TIN	BBG - R. Free Asia (RFA)
		500	ARS	RIY	Saudi Radio (BSKSA)
17810		100	D	BIB	BBG - R. Free Asia (RFA)
		250	EGY	ABZ	Radio Cairo
		300	J	YAM	Radio Japan (NHK World)
		500	IRN	SIR	VO the Islamic Rep. of Iran
17820		250	G	WOF	Deutsche Welle
		250	PHL	PHT	Radyo Pilipinas Overseas
		300	ROU	GAL	Radio Romania International
		500	IRN	SIR	VO the Islamic Rep. of Iran
17830		250	AFS	MEY	BBC World Service
		250	ASC	ASC	BBC World Service
		100	CHN	KAS	China Radio Int. (CRI)
		250	PAK	ISL	Radio Pakistan
17835		250	MRA	TIN	BBG - R. Free Asia (RFA)
17840		100	PLW	HBN	Radio Australia
17845		100	CHN	dom	CNR1 VO China, Shijiazhuang
17850		250	CLN	IRA	BBG - VO America (VOA)
		250	CVA	SMG	BBG - VO America (VOA)
		100	CTR	CRI	R. Exterior de España (REE)
		500	F	ISS	Radio France Int. (RFI)
		300	ROU	GAL	Radio Romania International
17855		500	CHN	BEI	China Radio Int. (CRI)
17860		100	IND	dom	All India R., Delhi
		250	PHL	PHT	BBG - VO America (VOA)
		250	UAE	DHA	Deutsche Welle
		300	ROU	TIG	Radio Romania International
		250	PHL	PUG	Radio Veritas Asia
		100	SNG	SNG	Voice of Croatia
17865		500	IRN	KAM	VO the Islamic Rep. of Iran
17870		250	CYP	CYP	BBC World Service
		50	BUL	SOF	R. Xoriyo
		250	EGY	ABZ	Radio Cairo
		300	ROU	GAL	Radio Romania International
+		300	ROU	TIG	Radio Romania International
		300	ROU	TIG	Radio Romania International
17875		500	IND	BGL	All India Radio (AIR)
+		100	GUF	GUF	The Disco Palace
17880		100	GUM	SDA	AWR Asia/Pacific
		250	MRA	TIN	BBG - R. Free Asia (RFA)
17885		250	ASC	ASC	BBC World Service
		250	CYP	CYP	BBC World Service
		250	G	WOF	BBC World Service
17890		100	CHN	dom	CNR1 VO China, Beijing
17895		500	IND	BGL	All India Radio (AIR)
		250	CVA	SMG	BBG - VO America (VOA)
		250	D	WER	BBG - VO America (VOA)
		100	STP	SAO	BBG - VO America (VOA)
		500	ARS	RIY	Saudi Radio (BSKSA)
17900±		1	TWN	TSU	Sound of Hope Radio Int.
18200±		1	TWN	TSU	Sound of Hope Radio Int.
18250±		1	TWN	TSU	Sound of Hope Radio Int.
18910		100	AUT	MOS	Radio Ö1 International
18970±		1	TWN	TSU	Sound of Hope Radio Int.
19000		100	AUS	SHP	Radio Australia
19010		250	KWT	KWT	BBG - R. Free Afghanistan
20000		2.5	USA	STF	WWV NIST, Fort Collins, CO
21470		250	CYP	CYP	BBC World Service
		250	SEY	SEY	BBC World Service
21480		500	IRN	SIR	VO the Islamic Rep. of Iran
21500		300	ROU	TIG	Radio Romania International
		500	IRN	SIR	VO the Islamic Rep. of Iran
21505		500	ARS	RIY	Saudi Radio (BSKSA)
21510		500	IRN	KAM	VO the Islamic Rep. of Iran
21540		250	MRA	TIN	BBG - R. Free Asia (RFA)
		250	E	NOB	R. Exterior de España (REE)
		500	KWT	KBD	Radio Kuwait
21570		250	PHL	PHT	BBG - VO America (VOA)
		300	ROU	TIG	Radio Romania International
21575		500	IRN	KAM	VO the Islamic Rep. of Iran
21580		500	F	ISS	Radio France Int. (RFI)
21590		300	CYP	CYP	BBC World Service
		250	PHL	PHT	BBG - VO America (VOA)
21595		250	UAE	DHA	BBC World Service
21600		300	ROU	TIG	Radio Romania International
		500	IRN	SIR	VO the Islamic Rep. of Iran
		250	USA	HRI	WHRI - World Harvest R.
21610		250	MRA	TIN	BBG - R. Free Asia (RFA)
		250	E	NOB	R. Exterior de España (REE)
		500	IRN	KAM	VO the Islamic Rep. of Iran
21630		250	ASC	ASC	BBC World Service
		250	USA	HRI	WHRI - World Harvest R.
21640		500	IRN	SIR	VO the Islamic Rep. of Iran
21650		100	CVA	SMG	Vatican Radio
21660		250	G	WOF	BBC World Service
21670		500	ARS	RIY	Saudi Radio (BSKSA)
21680		250	CVA	SMG	Vatican Radio
21690		500	GUF	GUF	Radio France Int. (RFI)
21695		500	UAE	DHA	BBG - R. Free Asia (RFA)
21700		250	MRA	TIN	BBG - R. Free Asia (RFA)
21710		250	MRA	TIN	BBG - R. Free Asia (RFA)
21720		250	G	WOF	BBC World Service
21725		100	AUS	SHP	Radio Australia
21740		100	AUS	SHP	Radio Australia
21745		250	MRA	TIN	BBG - R. Free Asia (RFA)
21755		250	MRA	TIN	BBG - R. Free Asia (RFA)
21765		250	MRA	TIN	BBG - R. Free Asia (RFA)
21775		250	MRA	TIN	BBG - R. Free Asia (RFA)
21780		250	RRW	KIG	Deutsche Welle
		250	UAE	DHA	Deutsche Welle
21785		250	MRA	TIN	BBG - R. Free Asia (RFA)
21800		500	IRN	SIR	VO the Islamic Rep. of Iran
		250	RUS	IRK	Voice of Russia (VOR)
21820		500	RUS	NVS	Voice of Russia (VOR)
25000		0.1	FIN	STF	Centre for Metrology, Espoo
26000		0.25	I	dom	R. Maria, Andrate
26010+		0.25	I	dom	R. Maria, Andrate
26060+		0.2	CVA	dom	Raiway, Vatican City

International Broadcasts
in English, French, German,
Portuguese and Spanish

English

0000	English	Area	kHz
0000-0030	WHRI	SAm	7335hri
0000-0100	BBC World Sce	FE	13725nak
0000-0100	BBC World Sce	SAs	5970sla, 6195sng, 7360cyp, 9410nak, 12095sng
0000-0100	CRI	SAs	6005kas, 6180kas, 7425kas
0000-0100	CRI	EAs	9425bei
0000-0100	REE	NAm	6055nob
0000-0100	R. Habana Cuba	Car	5040hab
0000-0100	R. Thailand WS	NAm	13745udo
0000-0100	WHRI	NAm	7385hri
0000-0200	BBC World Sce	SAs	11750sng, 12095nak
0000-0200	BBC World Sce	SEA	15335sng
0000-0200	BBC World Sce	FE	15755nak
0000-0200	CRI	SEA	11885xia, 15145bei
0000-0200	CRI	NAm	6020cer, 9570cer
0000-0200	The Mighty KBC	NAm	9450sof
0000-0300	WHRI	NAm,Eu	5920hri
0000-0900	R. Australia	Pac	15240shp
0000-0900	WEWN - EWTN SW	Af	11520ewn
0000-1200	WWCR	NAm,Eu	4840wcr**, 4840wcr
0000-1200	WWCR	Af	5935wcr**, 5935wcr
0000-1300	Overcomer Min.	NAm	3185wrb
0000-1300	WWRB	NAm	3185wrb
0000-2400	BBC World Sce	CHN	675hkg
0000-2400	R. 6150	Eu	6070rob*
0000-2400	R. Bahrain	ME	6010abh‡
0000-2400	WBCQ	NAm,CAm	5110bcq*
0030-0045	TWR India	SAs	882put
0030-0100	BBG-VOA	SAs,SEA	12005pht, 15155pht
0030-0100	BBG-VOA	SEA	1575bph, 9715udo, 15205pht
0030-0100	BBG-VOA	SAs	6170kwt, 9325udo
0030-0100	BBG-VOA	EAs	9490pht, 11695pht, 15290pht
0030-0100	WHRI	SAm	7335hri
0030-0400	R. Australia	As	17750shp
0045-0100	TWR India	SAs	882put
0100	**English**		
0100-0115	BVB	As	7395wer
0100-0130	T8WH - WHR Int	As	17650hbn
0100-0130	TWR India	SAs	882put
0100-0130	VO Vietnam	NAm	9640wof
0100-0200	BBC World Sce	SEA	17685sng
0100-0200	BBC World Sce	SAs	5970sla
0100-0200	BBG-VOA	SAs	9435udo, 11705udo, 15155pht
0100-0200	CRI	SAs	6075kas, 6175kas, 9420kas
0100-0200	CRI	Eu	9410kas
0100-0200	CRI	NAm	9580hab

0100	English	Area	kHz
0100-0200	R.Romania Int	NAm	6145gal, 7325gal
0100-0200	R.Taiwan Int.	SEA	11875tnn
0100-0200	VO Russia (VOR)	As,ME	801dsb
0100-0200	WHRI	CAm	9605hri
0100-0300	BBC World Sce	SAs	15310nak
0100-0400	BBC World Sce	CAs	5940cyp
0100-0400	Overcomer Min.	NAm	7490bcq
0100-0400	VO Russia (VOR)	ME	648dsb
0100-0400	VO Russia (VOR)	As,ME	927dsb
0100-0400	WWRB	NAm	3195wrb**
0100-0500	R. Australia	Pac	15160shp
0100-0500	R. Habana Cuba	NAm	6000hab
0100-0520	BBC World Sce	Eu	198dro
0100-0700	R. Habana Cuba	NAm	6165hab
0100-0900	WWCR	NAm,Af	3215wcr**, 3215wcr
0100-1100	WTWW	NAm,Eu,Af	5745tww*
0100-1100	WWCR	NAm,CAm,Af	5890wcr
0100-1200	WWCR	NAm,CAm,Af	5890wcr*, 5890wcr**
0100-1300	WHRI	NAm	7385hri
0100-1300	WTWW	CAm,SAm	5085tww*
0100-1300	WWCR	NAm,Eu	4840wcr*
0100-1300	WWCR	Af	5935wcr*
0115-0130	TWR India	SAs	882put
0120-0300	SLBC	SAs	6005eka, 9770eka, 15745eka
0130-0200	BBG-VOA	LAm	5960grv, 7465grv
0130-0200	Int. R. Serbia	NAm,Eu	6190bij
0130-0200	R. Slovakia Int	LAm	9955rmi
0130-0200	T8WH - WHR Int	As	17650hbn
0140-0200	Vatican Radio	As	7410tac, 9560smg
0200	**English**		
0200-0230	BBC World Sce	SAs	1413sla
0200-0230	R. Thailand WS	NAm	13745udo
0200-0300	BBC World Sce	SAs	12095sla
0200-0300	BBC World Sce	ME	5875cyp
0200-0300	BBC World Sce	EAf	7435sey
0200-0300	CRI	SAS	13640kas
0200-0300	KBS World R.	SAm	9580kim, 9640kim
0200-0300	RAE	Am	11710bue
0200-0330	KJES Radio	NAm	7555jes†
0200-0330	R. Cairo	NAm	9720abz
0200-0330	R. Pilipinas	ME	15285pht, 17700pht, 17820pht
0200-0400	CRI	SAs	11785kas
0200-0400	Overcomer Min.	NAm	7490bcq
0200-0400	VO Russia (VOR)	ME	1377erv
0200-0400	VO Russia (VOR)	NAm	17665ppk, 17690vld
0200-0400	VO Russia (VOR)	As,ME	972dsb
0200-0500	WRNO Worldwide	NAm,CAm	7506mo1±
0200-0500	WWRB	NAm	3195wrb*
0200-0600	VO Russia (VOR)	NAm	15630ppk
0200-0730	BBC World Sce	ME	1323cyp
0200-1000	WWCR	NAm,Af	3215wcr*
0200-1100	WTWW	NAm,Eu,Af	5745tww**
0200-1300	WTWW	CAm,SAm	5085tww**

0200	English	Area	kHz
0200-1400	AFRTS (AFN)	IOc	12759dga*
0200-2300	BBC World Sce	ME	1323cyp
0230-0300	R. Tirana	NAm	6100shi
0230-0300	VO Vietnam	NAm	9640wof
0245-0300	HCJB Australia	SEA	15400knx
0255-0325	TWR Africa	SAf	3200man
0300	**English**		
0300-0320	Vatican Radio	As	15460pug
0300-0330	BBC World Sce	ME	639zak
0300-0330	R. Australia	Pac	12080brn, 15515shp
0300-0330	SLBC	SAs	9770eka, 15745eka
0300-0330	Vatican Radio	Af	9660smg, 11625mdc
0300-0400	BBC World Sce	CAs	12095sla
0300-0400	BBC World Sce	ME	1413sla, 5940skn
0300-0400	BBC World Sce	CAf	6140mey
0300-0400	BBC World Sce	SAf	7435asc
0300-0400	BBC World Sce	EAf	9460sey, 12035sey
0300-0400	Channel Africa	SAf	3345mey
0300-0400	Channel Africa	EAf	6155mey
0300-0400	CRI	SAs	15110kas
0300-0400	CRI	NAm,CAm	9690nob
0300-0400	CRI	NAm	9790hab
0300-0400	R.Taiwan Int.	SEA	15320pao
0300-0400	T8WH - WHR Int	As	11650hbn
0300-0430	BBG-VOA	Af	1530sao, 9885bot
0300-0500	BBC World Sce	ME	9410cyp
0300-0500	BBG-VOA	Af	15580sao
0300-0500	CRI	EAs	13590bei, 13620xia, 15120bei
0300-0500	SLBC	SAs	6005eka, 9770eka, 15745eka
0300-0500	VO Russia (VOR)	ME	1314erv
0300-0600	BBC World Sce	SAs	15310sla
0300-0600	BBC World Sce	SAf	3255mey
0300-0600	BBC World Sce	CAf	7255asc
0300-0600	BBG-VOA	Af	4930bot
0300-0700	BBC World Sce	SAs	17790nak
0300-0700	BBG-VOA	Af	909bot, 6080sao
0300-0700	R. Australia	As,Pac	21725shp
0300-2200	BBC World Sce	SAf	6190mey
0315-0330	TWR Africa	WAm	1566par
0330-0400	VO Vietnam	NAm	9640wof
0330-0400	WHRI	CAm	5920hri
0330-0430	VOIRI	NAm	9710kam**, 11770sir**
0330-0600	R. Australia	Pac	15515shp
0330-0900	R. Australia	Pac	12080brn
0335-0345	TWR Africa	WAf	1566par
0400	**English**		
0400-0500	BBC World Sce	CAf	12015mey
0400-0500	BBC World Sce	EAf	12035cyp
0400-0500	BBG-VOA	Af	4960sao
0400-0500	Deutsche Welle	Af	5905kig, 7285kig, 9420kig, 9470kig
0400-0500	R.Romania Int	ME	15220gal, 17870tig
0400-0500	R.Romania Int	NAm	6130gal, 7305tig
0400-0500	VO Korea	LAm	11735kuj, 13760kuj, 15180kuj
0400-0500	VO Korea	EAs	4405kuj†, 7220kuj, 9345kuj, 9730kuj
0400-0500	VO Turkey	ME,NAf	7240emr
0400-0500	VO Turkey	Eu,NAm	9655emr
0400-0500	WHRI	Af	9640hri
0400-0600	BBC World Sce	ME	11760cyp
0400-0600	BBC World Sce	EAf	12095sey
0400-0600	CRI	CAs,ME	17725xia, 17855bei
0400-0600	VO Russia (VOR)	NAm	9830ppk
0400-0700	BBC World Sce	WAf	6005asc
0400-0700	Channel Africa	SAf	7230mey

0400	English	Area	kHz
0400-1300	Overcomer Min.	NAm	5890wcr
0430-0500	TWR Africa	WAf	1566par
0430-0600	BBG-VOA	Af	9885sao
0430-0800	WHRI	CAm	5920hri
0455-0700	VO Nigeria	Eu	15120ikot
0500	**English**		
0500-0528	Vatican Radio	Af	13765mdc
0500-0530	Deutsche Welle	Af	5905kig, 9420kig, 9800kig, 11800kig
0500-0530	R. Japan	NAm	11740guf
0500-0530	R. Japan	daily	17660dha
0500-0530	R. Japan	SAf	9770iss
0500-0530	Vatican Radio	Af	7360smg
0500-0600	BBC World Sce	CAs	15360sla
0500-0600	BBC World Sce	EAf	15420cyp
0500-0600	BBC World Sce	EAf	15420sey
0500-0600	CRI	NAf,WAf	7220cer
0500-0600	VO Korea	SEA	13650kuj, 15100kuj
0500-0600	VO Korea	EAs	3560kuj†
0500-0630	BBG-VOA	EAf,SAf	15580bot
0500-0650	RNZI	Pac	13730ran+
0500-0700	BBC World Sce	CAf	15400mey
0500-0700	BBC World Sce	EAf	17640cyp
0500-0700	BBC World Sce	Eu	3955skn+
0500-0700	CRI	ME,NAf	17505kas
0500-0700	R. Habana Cuba	NAm	6010hab, 6060hab
0500-0700	R. Habana Cuba	Am	6125hab
0500-0700	WHRI	NAm,Eu	7465hri
0500-0700	WHRI	Af	9615hri
0500-0800	R. Australia	Pac	13630shp
0500-0800	RNZI	Pac	11725ran
0500-0800	TWR Africa	SAf	4775man
0500-0800	TWR Africa	EAf	9500man
0500-0900	CRI	SAs	11880kas, 15465kas, 17540kas
0500-0900	R. Africa	Af	15190batt
0500-0900	VO Russia (VOR)	Eu	1323wbr
0500-1100	CRI	SAs	15350kas
0500-1200	Overcomer Min.	NAm	5890wcr
0501-0800	TWR Africa	SAf	6120man
0530-0545	TWR Africa	WAf	1566par
0530-0600	Deutsche Welle	Af	9420kig, 11800kig
0530-0600	R. Thailand WS	Eu	12015udo
0530-0700	R. Australia	As	17750shp
0600	**English**		
0600-0630	Deutsche Welle	WAf	12045kig, 13780kig, 17800kig
0600-0700	BBC World Sce	ME	15360cyp
0600-0700	BBC World Sce	EAf	15420cyp
0600-0700	BBC World Sce	EAf	15420sey
0600-0700	BBC World Sce	WAf	9410asc, 9460asc
0600-0700	BBG-VOA	Af	1530sao, 9885mey
0600-0700	Channel Africa	WAf	15255mey
0600-0700	CRI	NAf	11750cer
0600-0700	CRI	ME	11770kas, 15145kas
0600-0700	Hamburger LR	Eu	7265goh*
0600-0700	R. Habana Cuba	Car	5040hab
0600-0700	VO Korea	EAs	4405kuj†, 7220kuj, 9345kuj, 9730kuj
0600-0800	CRI	SEA	13645xia, 17710bei
0600-0900	VO Russia (VOR)	Eu	11635msk+
0600-1000	VO Russia (VOR)	AUS,NZL,Pac	21800irk, 21820nvs
0600-1000	WWCR	NAm,Af	3195wcr*, 3195wcr** , 3195wcr
0600-1400	BBC World Sce	SAs	15310nak
0600-1500	BBC World Sce	SAf	12095mey
0600-1530	R. Australia	Pac	11945shp
0600-2200	1Africa Radio	Af	13590lus
0630-0658	Vatican Radio	Af	13765smg

0600	English	Area	kHz
0630-0700	BBG-VOA	EAf,SAf	15580sao
0630-0700	Deutsche Welle	WAf	13780kig, 17800kig
0630-0700	R.Romania Int	AUS,NZL	17780gal, 21600tig
0630-0700	R.Romania Int	Eu	7310tig, 9600gal+
0630-0700	Vatican Radio	Af	11625smg
0650-0800	RNZI	Pac	11657ran+
0700	**English**		
0700-0800	BBC World Sce	WAf	11770asc, 13820asc
0700-0800	BBC World Sce	EAf	17640cyp
0700-0800	BBC World Sce	EAf	17640sey
0700-0800	BBC World Sce	CAf	17830mey
0700-0800	CRI	ME,NAf	17800kas
0700-0900	BBC World Sce	WEu	5875wof+, 7355mos+
0700-0900	CRI	Eu	1215fla, 11785cer
0700-0900	R. Australia	Pac	7410shp, 9475shp, 9710shp
0700-1000	BBC World Sce	WAf	15400asc
0700-1000	BBC World Sce	ME	15575sla, 17660cyp
0700-1000	WHRI	NAm,Eu	7465hri
0700-1100	VO Russia (VOR)	As	15745dsb
0700-1200	Channel Africa	SAf	9625mey
0700-1200	WWCR	NAm,CAm,Af	5070wcr*, 5070wcr**, 5070wcr
0700-1300	BBC World Sce	SAs	17790sla
0700-1300	CRI	Eu	17490kas
0730-0745	Vatican Radio	NAf,ME	15595smg
0730-0745	Vatican Radio	Eu	585vat
0730-0830	HCJB Australia	SEA	11750knx
0800	**English**		
0800-0830	BVB	Eu	5945wer
0800-0830	WHRI	Eu,Af	11565hri
0800-0845	BVB	Eu	5945wer
0800-0850	TWR Europe	Eu	6105wer, 7400mos
0800-0900	Am.R.Mirr Int.	EAf	17760mey
0800-0900	Am.R.Mirr Int.	SAf	7205mey
0800-0900	CRI	ME,Af	15625kas
0800-0900	KBS World R.	SEA	9570kim
0800-0900	R. Australia	Pac	5995brn
0800-0900	VO Nigeria	WAf	15120iko†
0800-0900	VO Russia (VOR)	Eu	9625klg*,+
0800-0930	WHRI	SAm	7315hri
0800-1000	BBC World Sce	CAf	17830asc
0800-1000	CRI	EAs	9415xia
0800-1000	T8WH - WHR Int	As	9930hbn
0800-1000	Beibu Bay Radio	SEA	5050nnn, 9820nnn
0800-1100	RNZI	Pac	9765ran
0800-1300	RNZI	Pac	9870ran+
0800-1400	BBC World Sce	EAf	17640sey
0800-1400	BBC World Sce	SAf	21470sey
0800-1500	R. Australia	Pac	9580shp
0800-2000	AFRTS (AFN)	Pac	5765bar*
0830-0900	WHRI	Eu,Af	11565hri
0850-0930	TWR Asia	SEA	15200twr
0900	**English**		
0900-0930	T8WH - WHR Int	As	17650hbn
0900-1000	CRI	Eu	17570uru, 17650kas
0900-1000	CRI	SAs	17750kas
0900-1000	IRRS Shortwave	Eu,ME,NAf	9510tig
0900-1000	T8WH - WHR Int	As	9930hbn
0900-1030	WHRI	Eu,Af	11565hri
0900-1100	BBC World Sce	FE	17760nak
0900-1100	BBC World Sce	SEA	9740nak
0900-1100	CRI	Pac	15210kun, 17690jin
0900-1100	WWCR	NAm,Af	6875wcr**, 6875wcr, 7490wcr**, 7490wcr
0900-1200	BBC World Sce	FE	15285sng
0900-1200	VO Russia (VOR)	SEA	7205tch
0900-1200	VO Russia (VOR)	Eu	9625klg*,+
0900-1300	BBC World Sce	FE	11895nak

0900	English	Area	kHz
0900-1300	WEWN - EWTN SW	SEA	11520ewn
0900-1500	VO Nigeria	WAf	9690iko†
0900-1600	BBC World Sce	SEA	6195sng, 9740sng
0900-1600	The Mighty KBC	Eu	6095wer
0900-2300	BBC World Sce	ME	1323cyp
0930-0945	T8WH - WHR Int	As	17650hbn
0930-1000	T8WH - WHR Int	As	17650hbn
0945-1000	T8WH - WHR Int	As	17650hbn
1000	**English**		
1000-1010	TWR Asia	Pac	11840twr
1000-1030	R. Japan	SEA	11740sng
1000-1030	R. Japan	Pac	9625yam
1000-1030	R. Prague	LAm	9955rmi
1000-1030	TWR Asia	Pac	11840twr
1000-1030	VO Vietnam	As	9840vni, 12020vni
1000-1100	All India R.	SAs	1053tut, 7270cni
1000-1100	All India R.	EAs	13605bgl, 15030alg, 15410bgl
1000-1100	All India R.	Pac	13695bgl, 17510del, 17895bgl
1000-1100	BBC World Sce	WAf	15400asc
1000-1100	BBC World Sce	CAf	17830asc
1000-1100	CRI	SAs	15190uru
1000-1100	CRI	EAs	5955xia, 7215xia, 11640bei
1000-1100	KNLS Int.	EAs	9615nls
1000-1100	R. Australia	Pac	5995brn, 6020shp, 6080shp, 9475shp, 9710shp, 12080brn
1000-1100	VO Indonesia	As,Pac	9526jak†
1000-1100	VO Korea	LAm	6170kuj†, 9335kuj
1000-1100	VO Korea	SEA	6185kuj, 9850kuj
1000-1200	CRI	SEA	13590bei, 13720xia
1000-1200	VO Russia (VOR)	As	11680tch
1000-1200	VO Russia (VOR)	As,SEA	7260vld
1000-1200	WHRI	NAm	7520hri
1000-1200	WINB	CAm	9265inb**
1000-1200	WWCR	NAm,Af	6875wcr*, 7490wcr*
1000-1230	Saudi R (BSKSA)	WAf,CAf	15250riy
1000-1400	BBC World Sce	ME	11760sla, 15575cyp
1000-2200	University Netw	NAm	11775aia†
1030-1100	VO Mongolia	As	12085uba
1030-1100	WHRI	Eu,Af	11565hri
1030-1130	VOIRI	SAs	21575kam, 21610kam
1030-1130	VOIRI	ME	702kia
1030-1300	IRRS Shortwave	Eu,ME,NAf	9510tig
1100	**English**		
1100-0100	WTWW	NAm	9479tww*
1100-0100	WWCR	NAm,CAm,Af	9980wcr
1100-0200	WTWW	NAm	9479tww**
1100-1115	BVB	EAs	15390trm
1100-1130	BBC World Sce	WAf	15400asc
1100-1130	BVB	EAs	15390trm
1100-1130	KBS World R.	Eu	9760wof+
1100-1130	R. Japan	WEu	9760wof+
1100-1130	VO Vietnam	As	7285han
1100-1200	BBG-VOA	SEA	1575bph
1100-1200	CRI	SAs	9570kas, 11795kas, 13645kas
1100-1200	FEBC Korea	EAs	1188seo
1100-1200	R. Australia	Pac	5995brn, 12080brn+
1100-1200	R.Taiwan Int.	EAs	1359fan
1100-1200	R.Taiwan Int.	SEA	7445pao, 9465trn
1100-1200	VO Russia (VOR)	As	11640irk+, 15740sam
1100-1300	CRI	SAs	1269xuw, 11650uru
1100-1300	CRI	Eu	13665cer
1100-1300	R. Australia	Pac	6080shp
1100-1300	R. Australia	SEA	6140sng
1100-1300	R. Australia	As	9475shp, 11945shp

1100	English	Area	kHz
1100-1300	RNZI	Pac	17675ran
1100-1300	WINB	CAm	9265inb*
1100-1400	R. Australia	Pac	6020shp
1100-1400	VO Russia (VOR)	As,SEA	9560nvs*,+
1100-1500	Overcomer Min.	FE	15565erv
1100-1600	CRI	EAs	5955bei
1100-1800	BBC World Sce	CAf	17830asc
1100-2000	WWCR	NAm,Af	15825wcr
1100-2100	WWCR	NAm,Af	15825wcr**
1115-1130	BVB	EAs	15390trm
1130-1145	Etern.Good News	As	15525dha
1130-1200	VO Vietnam	As	9840vni, 12020vni
1200	**English**		
1200-0100	WWCR	NAm,CAm,Af	9980wcr*, 9980wcr**
1200-0600	WBCQ	NAm,CAm	9330bcq*
1200-1230	AWR Af/Eu	SEA	11670trm
1200-1230	R. Japan	SEA	11740sng
1200-1230	R. Japan	NAm	15190guf
1200-1300	BBG-VOA	SEA	1170php, 9640pht
1200-1300	BBG-VOA	EAs	7520ira, 11750pht, 12150udo
1200-1300	CRI	CAs,ME	11690xia
1200-1300	CRI	Eu	13790uru
1200-1300	CRI	SEA	684dof, 1188kun, 9600kun, 9645bei, 9730kun
1200-1300	CRI	SAs	7250kas, 9460kas, 12015kas
1200-1300	CRI	Pac	9760kun
1200-1300	KBS World R.	NAm	15575kim
1200-1300	KNLS Int.	EAs	9615nls
1200-1300	R.Romania Int	Eu	15460gal, 17530tig
1200-1300	R.Romania Int	Af	17765gal, 21570tig
1200-1300	VO Russia (VOR)	As	5885dsb
1200-1400	CRI	Pac	11760kun
1200-1400	CRI	SEA	1341hdu, 11980kun
1200-1400	R. Australia	Pac	5995brn+
1200-1400	T8WH - WHR Int	As	9930hbn
1200-1400	VO Russia (VOR)	Eu	9625klg*,+
1200-1400	VO Russia (VOR)	As,ME	972dsb
1200-1400	WHRI	Eu,Af	15665hri
1200-1500	CRI	Eu	13790uru
1200-1500	VO Russia (VOR)	As	12075dsb
1200-1500	WWCR	Af	7490wcr**, 7490wcr
1200-1530	Overcomer Min.	CAm	13570inb
1200-1600	BBC World Sce	FE	5875nak
1200-2100	WINB	CAm	13570inb**
1200-2100	WWCR	NAm,Af	15825wcr*
1200-2300	WBCQ	NAm,CAm	15420bcq*
1200-2400	WWCR	NAm,Eu	13845wcr**, 13845wcr
1215-1330	R. Cairo	SAs	17870abz
1230-1300	Bangladesh Bet.	SEA	15105dka
1230-1300	R. Thailand WS	As,Pac	9720udo
1230-1300	VO Vietnam	As	9840vni, 12020vni
1230-1330	KBS World R.	CHN	6095kim
1300	**English**		
1300-0100	WTWW	CAm,SAm	9990tww*
1300-0100	WWCR	Af	13845wcr*
1300-0200	WTWW	CAm,SAm	9990tww**
1300-1330	R. Japan	SAs	11730tac
1300-1400	BBC World Sce	SAs	1413sla
1300-1400	BBG-VOA	EAs	7520pht, 12150udo
1300-1400	BBG-VOA	SEA	9640pht, 11750pht
1300-1400	CRI	Pac	11900kas
1300-1400	CRI	Eu	13670kas, 13790kas
1300-1400	CRI	SAs	7300kas, 9655kas
1300-1400	CRI	NAm	9570hab
1300-1400	CRI	SEA	9730bei
1300-1400	KBS World R.	SEA	9570kim

1300	English	Area	kHz
1300-1400	VO Indonesia	As,Pac	9526jak†
1300-1400	VO Korea	EAs	3560kuj†
1300-1400	VO Korea	Eu	7570kuj, 12015kuj
1300-1400	VO Korea	NAm	9335kuj, 11710kuj
1300-1400	VO Russia (VOR)	SEA	7205tch
1300-1400	VO Tajik	WAs, ME	1143dsb, 7245dsb
1300-1400	WHRI	NAm	7385hri, 9840hri
1300-1400	WHRI	SAm	9495hri
1300-1500	BBC World Sce	FE	11890nak
1300-1500	CRI	CAs,ME	9765xia
1300-1500	VO Russia (VOR)	As,SEA	7260vld
1300-1550	RNZI	Pac	5950ran
1300-1600	CRI	SAs	9870xia
1300-1600	WWCR	Af	7490wcr*
1300-1700	BBC World Sce	SAs	9410sla
1300-1700	R. Australia	As	5940shp
1300-1700	WEWN-EWTN SW	Eu	15610ewn
1300-1900	WHRI	SAm	9495hri
1300-2100	Overcomer Min.	NAm	9980wcr
1300-2200	WINB	CAm	13570inb*
1300-2400	Overcomer Min.	NAm	9370wrb
1300-2400	WWRB	NAm	9370wrb
1330-1400	VO Vietnam	As	9840vni, 12020vni
1330-1430	VO Turkey	Eu	12035emr
1330-1500	All India R.	SEA	9690bgl, 11620del, 13710bgl
1400	**English**		
1400-0200	AFRTS (AFN)	IOc	4319dga*
1400-1420	TWR Asia	SAs	15225twr
1400-1430	Int. R. Serbia	Eu	9635beo‡
1400-1430	Lao National R.	SEA	567vie, 6130vie
1400-1430	R. Japan	SAs	11695tac
1400-1430	R. Japan	SEA	11925hbn
1400-1430	R. Thailand WS	As,Pac	9950udo
1400-1430	TWR Asia	SAs	15225twr
1400-1445	PanAm Bc	IND	15205wer
1400-1500	BBG-VOA	Af	15580mey, 17530sao, 17725sao
1400-1500	BBG-VOA	SAs	7520udo, 9760udo, 12150pht
1400-1500	BVB	As	15470wer
1400-1500	CRI	CAs	11665uru
1400-1500	CRI	SAs	7300uru, 9460uru
1400-1500	CRI	Eu	9795uru, 13625kas
1400-1500	KBS World R.	SEA	9640kim
1400-1500	R. Sult.of Oman	Eu,ME	15140thu
1400-1500	VO Russia (VOR)	ME	648dsb, 13790sam
1400-1500	WHRI	Af	21600hri
1400-1530	BBG-VOA	Af	6080sao
1400-1600	BBC World Sce	ME	11760cyp
1400-1600	CRI	SEA	1188kun
1400-1600	CRI	NAm	13740hab
1400-1600	CRI	CAf,WAf	17630bko
1400-1600	KJES Radio	NAm	11715jes†
1400-1600	Overcomer Min.	ME	13810wer
1400-1600	Overcomer Min.	WEu	9460wer
1400-1700	BBC World Sce	EAf	17640cyp, 21470cyp
1400-1700	BBC World Sce	SAs	5975sng
1400-1700	BBG-VOA	Af	4930bot
1400-1800	BBC World Sce	SAs	5845nak+
1400-1800	R. Australia	Pac	5995shp
1400-1900	VO Russia (VOR)	As,ME	4950dsb
1400-2030	R. Africa	Af	15190batt
1400-2200	WHRI	NAm	9840hri
1400-2200	WJHR	NAm	15550jhr*
1400-2300	WHRI	SAm	15665hri
1415-1430	PanAm Bc	IND	15205wer
1425-1455	TWR Africa	SAf	6025man
1430-1500	BBC World Sce	SAs	1413sla

1400	English	Area	kHz
1430-1500	BVB	As	15470wer
1430-1730	R. Australia	As	11660shp
1430-1900	R. Australia	As	9475shp
1445-1500	TWR Europe	Eu	1467bis
1445-1530	HCJB Australia	SEA	15340knx
1500	**English**		
1500-1530	BVB	ME	13740iss
1500-1530	VO Vietnam	As	7285han, 9840vni, 12020vni
1500-1600	BBC World Sce	SAf	9490mey
1500-1600	BBG-VOA	ME	11840lam, 13570lam
1500-1600	BBG-VOA	Af	15580ira, 17725bot, 17895sao
1500-1600	BBG-VOA	EAs	6140udo, 9945ira
1500-1600	BBG-VOA	SAs	7520udo, 9930ira, 12150ira
1500-1600	BBG-VOA	SAs,SEA	7575pht
1500-1600	BBG-VOA	SEA	9760pht
1500-1600	Channel Africa	SAf	9625mey
1500-1600	CRI	NAf,ME	6095kas, 9525kas, 9720uru
1500-1600	CRI	SEA	7325bei, 9650nnn
1500-1600	CRI	SAs	7405uru, 9785jin
1500-1600	KNLS Int.	EAs	9655nls
1500-1600	Overcomer Min.	NAm	15420bcq
1500-1600	VO Korea	EAs	3560kuj†
1500-1600	VO Korea	Eu	7570kuj, 12015kuj
1500-1600	VO Korea	NAm	9335kuj, 11710kuj
1500-1600	VO Nigeria	WAf	15120iko†
1500-1600	VO Russia (VOR)	ME	11985erv
1500-1600	VO Russia (VOR)	As,ME	927dsb
1500-1600	WHRI	NAm,Eu	17570hri
1500-1600	WHRI	Af	21630hri
1500-1700	BBC World Sce	SAs	9505cyp
1500-1700	CRI	Eu	9435kas
1500-1700	R. Australia	Pac	7240shp
1500-1800	BBC World Sce	EAf	12095sey
1500-1800	CRI	SAs	1323uru
1500-1800	Overcomer Min.	ME	11900erv
1500-1800	VO Russia (VOR)	As,SEA	9880ppk
1500-1900	VO Russia (VOR)	ME,Af	9735msk
1500-2000	WWCR	Af	12160wcr
1500-2100	BBC World Sce	WAf	15400asc
1500-2100	WWCR	Af	12160wcr**
1500-2300	Overcomer Min.	NAm	9980wcr
1515-1530	BVB	ME	13740nau
1515-1530	HCJB Australia	SEA	15340knx
1525-1555	TWR Africa	SAf	6025man
1530-1545	All India R.	SAs	9910alg
1530-1545	PanAm Bc	IND	9410iss
1530-1550	Vatican Radio	As	7585tac, 11850smg, 15595tin, 15775smg+
1530-1558	Vatican Radio	As	7585tac, 15595tin, 15775smg+
1530-1600	AWR Af/Eu	As	15255trm
1530-1600	BVB	ME	13740nau
1530-1600	R. Prague	LAm	9955rmi
1530-1600	Vatican Radio	As	11850smg
1530-1600	VO Mongolia	As	12015uba
1530-1630	Disco Palace	SAs	12115iss+
1530-1630	VOIRI	SAs	13785sir, 15525kam
1530-1700	BBG-VOA	Af	6080mey
1530-1730	Overcomer Min.	FE	1548trm
1530-2000	R. Australia	Pac	11880shp
1545-1615	TWR India	SAs	882put
1550-1650	RNZI	Pac	7440ran+
1550-1845	RNZI	Pac	9765ran
1600	**English**		
1600-1630	AWR As/Pacific	As	15215sda, 15660sda

1600	English	Area	kHz
1600-1630	R. Australia	EAs	9540sng
1600-1630	T8WH - WHR Int	As	15680hbn
1600-1630	VO Vietnam	ME	7220vni, 9550vni
1600-1630	VO Vietnam	Eu	7280vni, 9730vni
1600-1640	R. Cairo	ISR	1008ela
1600-1700	BBC World Sce	ME	9915cyp
1600-1700	BBG-VOA	SEA	1170php
1600-1700	BBG-VOA	Af	909bot, 1530sao, 9395ira, 13755sao, 15470lam, 15580sao, 17895wer
1600-1700	CRI	SEA	6060kun
1600-1700	CRI	ME	6100kas, 9600jin
1600-1700	CRI	SAs	7235kas
1600-1700	CRI	NAf,ME	7420uru
1600-1700	CRI	Eu	9875kas
1600-1700	Hamburger LR	As	7265goh*
1600-1700	KBS World R.	Eu	9515kim
1600-1700	KBS World R.	SEA	9640kim
1600-1700	R. Ethiopia	EAf,ME	7235gjw±, 9560gjw±
1600-1700	R.Taiwan Int.	SAs	9440tnn, 15485iss
1600-1700	VO Korea	ME,NAf	9990kuj, 11545kuj
1600-1700	VO Russia (VOR)	As	5885dsb, 5955nvs
1600-1800	BBC World Sce	WAf	21660wof
1600-1800	CRI	SEA	1000xuw, 6155nnn, 9460nnn
1600-1800	CRI	Eu	7255kas
1600-1800	CRI	EAf,SAf	7435jin, 9570bei
1600-1900	R. Cairo	CAf,SAf	15345abs
1600-1900	Family Radio	SAf	1197msu
1600-2000	WHRI	Af	21630hri
1600-2100	WWCR	Af	12160wcr*
1600-2200	BBC World Sce	SAf	3255mey
1630-1700	AWR As/Pacific	As	15660sda
1630-1700	BBG-VOA	Af	9790hot**, 11905wer**, 13625wer**
1630-1730	Am.R.Mirr Int.	SAf	4895mey
1630-1800	BBC World Sce	SAs	1413sla
1650-1845	RNZI	Pac	9890ran+
1700	**English**		
1700-1800	BBC World Sce	CAs	1251dsb
1700-1800	BBC World Sce	EAf	15420cyp
1700-1800	BBG-VOA	Af	13755bot, 17895smg
1700-1800	BBG-VOA	EAf	15580smg
1700-1800	Channel Africa	WAf	15235mey
1700-1800	CRI	SEA	6090kun, 7420kun
1700-1800	CRI	SAs	6140kas, 7410kas, 7425kun
1700-1800	CRI	ME	6165bei
1700-1800	CRI	Eu	7205bei
1700-1800	R.Taiwan Int.	Af	15690iss
1700-1800	Overcomer Min.	NAm	15420bcq
1700-1800	VO Russia (VOR)	As	7240ppk
1700-1830	BBC World Sce	SAs	5975sla, 7600nak, 9505sng
1700-1900	BBC World Sce	EAf	17640mey
1700-1900	CRI	Eu	6100bei
1700-1900	VO Russia (VOR)	ME	648dsb
1700-1900	VO Russia (VOR)	As,ME	801dsb
1700-2100	R. Australia	Pac	9580shp
1700-2100	VO Russia (VOR)	Eu	7330msk
1700-2105	TWR Africa	SAf	1170man
1700-2200	BBG-VOA	Af	6080sao
1700-2200	R. Australia	Pac	9500shp
1700-2400	WEWN - EWTN SW	ME	15610ewn
1715-1730	Vatican Radio	Eu	585vat, 7290smg
1720-1740	BBG-VOA Studio7	ZWE	909bot, 4930bot, 12080sao, 15775sao

1700	English	Area	kHz
1730-1758	Vatican Radio	Af	11625smg, 13765smg
1730-1800	BBG-VOA Studio7	ZWE	909bot, 4930bot, 12080sao, 15775sao
1730-1800	Vatican Radio	Af	15570smg
1730-1830	VO Turkey	CAs,SAs	11730emr
1730-2030	R. Australia	Pac	6080shp
1745-1800	BVB	ME	9715wer
1745-1815	BVB	ME	9715wer
1745-1820	TWR Africa	WAf	1566par
1745-1845	BVB	ME	9715wer
1745-1900	Bangladesh Bet.	Eu	7250dka
1745-1900	BVB	ME	9715wer
1745-1945	All India R.	Eu	7550bgl, 9950del+, 11670bgl
1745-1945	All India R.	EAf	9415del, 11935mum, 17670del
1745-1945	All India R.	NAf,WAf	9445del, 11580alg, 13695bgl
1745-2000	BVB	ME	9715wer
1745-2045	TWR Africa	SAf	3200man
1800	**English**		
1800-1815	BVB	ME	7365nau
1800-1830	BBG-VOA	Af	15580sao
1800-1830	BBG-VOA	SAf	4930bot
1800-1830	R. Japan	CAf	15720mdc
1800-1830	R. PMR	Eu	7290kch
1800-1830	VO Vietnam	Eu	5955mos
1800-1900	BBG-VOA	Af	13755ira
1800-1900	BBG-VOA	Af	909bot
1800-1900	CRI	Eu	7405bei
1800-1900	KBS World R.	Eu	7275kim
1800-1900	R.Romania Int	Eu	9780tig+, 11955tig
1800-1900	R.Taiwan Int.	Eu	3965iss
1800-1900	RAE	Eu	15345bue
1800-1900	TWR Africa	EAf	9500man
1800-1900	VO Korea	EAs	3560kuj†
1800-1900	VO Korea	Eu	7570kuj, 12015kuj
1800-1900	VO Nigeria	Eu,Af	15120iko†
1800-1900	VO Russia (VOR)	ME,Af	11985erv
1800-1900	VO Russia (VOR)	As,ME	927dsb
1800-2000	BBC World Sce	ME	5875cyp
1800-2000	BBC World Sce	CAs	5945sla
1800-2000	R. Australia	Pac	9710shp
1800-2100	BBC World Sce	CAf	11810asc
1800-2100	BBC World Sce	EAf	12095cyp
1800-2100	BBC World Sce	WAf	9430wof
1800-2100	R. Kuwait	Eu,NAm	15540kbd
1830-1900	AWR Af/Eu	Af	11830mey
1830-2000	BBG-VOA	Af	15580bot
1830-2000	VO Nigeria	Eu,Af	15120aja+
1830-2100	BBG-VOA	Af	4930bot
1830-2200	BBC World Sce	EAf	9410sey
1845-1915	TWR Europe	ME	1350erv
1845-2050	RNZI	Pac	11725ran
1845-2150	RNZI	Pac	15720ran+
1900	**English**		
1900-0500	WBCQ	NAm,CAm	7490bcq*
1900-1930	Deutsche Welle	Af	11800kig, 12070kig, 15275kig
1900-1930	VO Vietnam	Eu	7280vni, 9730vni
1900-2000	BBG-VOA	ME	7480udo, 9515lam
1900-2000	BVB	Eu	6030nau
1900-2000	BVB	ME	9470nau
1900-2000	IRRS Shortwave	Eu,ME,NAf	7290tig
1900-2000	REE	Af	9605nob
1900-2000	REE	Eu	9665nob
1900-2000	R. Thailand WS	Eu	9585udo
1900-2000	Overcomer Min.	NAf	9835wer
1900-2000	VO Indonesia	Eu,NAf,ME	9526jak†

1900	English	Area	kHz
1900-2000	VO Korea	SAf	7210kuj, 11910kuj
1900-2000	VO Korea	ME,NAf	9975kuj, 11535kuj
1900-2000	VO Nigeria	WAf	7255iko†
1900-2030	BBG-VOA	Af	4940sao
1900-2030	R. Cairo	WAf	15290abz
1900-2030	Overcomer Min.	CAm	13570inb
1900-2100	BBC World Sce	EAf	6005sey
1900-2100	BBG-VOA	Af	909bot
1900-2100	CRI	ME,NAf	7295kas, 9440kun
1900-2100	R. Australia	Pac	11660shp
1900-2200	Overcomer Min.	WEu	9700sof
1900-2300	WHRI	SAm	9595hri
1915-1945	BVB	Eu	6030nau
1915-1945	BVB	ME	9470nau
1930-2000	Deutsche Welle	Af	12070kig, 15275kig
1930-2000	Int. R. Serbia	Eu	6100bij
1930-2000	PanAm Bc	NAf	9685nau
1930-2030	VOIRI	SAf	13670sir, 15450sir
1930-2030	VOIRI	Eu	6040kam, 7345sir
1930-2030	VO Turkey	Eu	6050emr
1930-2100	BBC World Sce	ME	1413sla
2000	**English**		
2000-0300	R. Australia	Pac	12080brn
2000-0800	AFRTS (AFN)	Pac	13362bar*
2000-2020	R. Belarus	Eu	6155mns, 11730mns
2000-2028	Vatican Radio	Af	7365smg, 11625smg
2000-2030	R. PMR	Eu	7290kch
2000-2100	BBG-VOA	Af	15580grv
2000-2100	BBG-VOA	ME	7480lam, 9480lam
2000-2100	CRI	EAf,SAf	5985bei
2000-2100	Deutsche Welle	Af	9655kig, 11800kig, 12070kig
2000-2100	IRRS Shortwave	Eu,ME,NAf	7290tig
2000-2100	KJES Radio	CAm	15385jes†
2000-2100	R. Habana Cuba	Am	11760hab
2000-2100	Disco Palace	NAm	17875guf+
2000-2100	Overcomer Min.	WEu	7290tig
2000-2200	BBG-VOA	Af	1530sao
2000-2200	CRI	Eu	5960cer, 7285cer, 7415kas, 9600kas
2000-2200	R. Australia	Pac	11650shp
2000-2200	WHRI	Af	21630hri
2000-2200	WWCR	NAm,Af	6875wcr
2000-2200	WWCR	Af	9350wcr
2000-2300	Family Radio	SAf	1197msu
2000-2300	R. Australia	Pac	15515shp
2000-2300	Overcomer Min.	EAf	9990erv
2000-2300	WHRI	NAm,Eu	9505hri
2020-2200	R. Belarus	Eu	6155mns, 11730mns
2030-0030	BBG-VOA	AFG	1296kab*, 7560kwt*
2030-2045	R. Thailand WS	Eu	9535udo
2030-2100	BBG-VOA	Af	4940sao
2030-2100	VO Vietnam	ME	7220vni, 9550vni
2030-2100	VO Vietnam	Eu	7280vni, 9730vni
2030-2200	R. Australia	As	11695shp
2045-2230	All India R.	Eu	7550bgl, 9445bgl, 9950del+, 11670bgl
2045-2230	All India R.	Pac	9910alg, 11620bgl, 11740pan
2050-2150	RNZI	Pac	17675ran
2100	**English**		
2100-0100	R. Australia	Pac	21740shp
2100-0100	WWCR	NAm,Af	3195wcr**, 6875wcr**
2100-0100	WWRB	NAm	3215wrb**
2100-0200	WWRB	NAm	3215wrb*
2100-0400	WINB	CAm	9265inb**
2100-0800	R. Australia	Pac	9660brn
2100-2130	AWR Af/Eu	Af	9830mos

2100	English	Area	kHz
2100-2130	R. Tirana	Eu	7465shi
2100-2200	Angolan Nat R.	Af	945mul, 7217mul†
2100-2200	BBC World Sce	SAf	5955sey
2100-2200	BBC World Sce	SEA	6195nak
2100-2200	BBG-VOA	Af	15580bot
2100-2200	CRI	SAf	7205xia, 7405bei
2100-2200	Deutsche Welle	Af	9655kig, 11800kig, 12070kig
2100-2200	R .Damascus	Eu,NAm,Pac	9330adr‡
2100-2200	VO Korea	EAs	3560kuj†
2100-2200	VO Korea	Eu	7570kuj, 12015kuj
2100-2200	VO Russia (VOR)	Eu	5940sam
2100-2200	WHRI	NAm,Eu	9490hri
2100-2300	BBC World Sce	FE	5905sla
2100-2300	BBC World Sce	WAf	9915asc, 12095asc
2100-2300	R. Australia	Pac	13630shp
2100-2300	WWCR	NAm,Af	6875wcr*
2100-2300	WWCR	Af	9350wcr*
2100-2400	BBC World Sce	SEA	3915sng
2100-2400	BBC World Sce	FE	5875nak
2100-2400	WWCR	Af	9350wcr**
2115-2245	R. Cairo	Eu	11890abz
2130-2200	R.Romania Int	Eu	6030gal+, 7380gal
2130-2200	R.Romania Int	NAm	7310tig, 9435tig
2130-2230	VO Turkey	SEA,Pac	9610emr
2150-0500	RNZI	Pac	15720ran, 17675ran+
2200	**English**		
2200-0100	BBC World Sce	SEA	6195sng
2200-0100	WWCR	NAm,Af	3195wcr
2200-0400	VO Russia (VOR)	NAm,CAm	7240arm
2200-0500	WINB	CAm	9265inb*
2200-0700	R. Australia	As	15415shp
2200-1000	University Netw	NAm	6090aia†
2200-1300	WWRB	NAm	5050wrb
2200-2230	Int. R. Serbia	Eu	6100bij
2200-2230	KBS World R.	Eu	3955skn
2200-2230	R. PMR	Eu	7290kch
2200-2300	BBC World Sce	CAf	5885mey
2200-2300	BBG-VOA	SEA	5895pht
2200-2300	BBG-VOA	EAs	7365pht, 7425kwt, 7480pht, 11860sai
2200-2300	CRI	EAs	5915bei
2200-2300	REE	Eu	6125nob
2200-2300	R. Habana Cuba	Af	11880hab*
2200-2300	R.Taiwan Int.	NAm	6115yfr, 15440yfr
2200-2300	VO Russia (VOR)	NAm	11830ppk
2200-2300	WHRI	NAm	15180hri
2200-2300	WHRI	Af	17520hri
2200-2400	BBC World Sce	FE	6135kim, 7490nak
2200-2400	CRI	Eu	1440mrn
2200-2400	R. Australia	Pac	15230shp
2200-2400	R. Australia	EAs	9855dha
2200-2400	Overcomer Min.	NAm	9980wcr
2200-2400	WWCR	Af	5070wcr
2230-2300	AWR As/Pacific	SEA	15320sda
2230-2300	BBG-VOA	EAs	7460udo, 9570ira
2230-2400	BBG-VOA	SEA	1575bph
2230-2400	BBG-VOA	EAs	5820udo
2245-0045	All India R.	SEA	6055del, 9705pan, 11710del
2245-0045	All India R.	EAs	9690bgl, 11645del+, 13605bgl
2300	**English**		
2300-0030	R. Cairo	NAm	9965abz
2300-0030	TWR Bonaire	CAm	800twb
2300-0100	CRI	SEA	11790xia
2300-0100	CRI	Eu	7350kas
2300-0100	WWCR	Af	5070wcr*
2300-0200	BBC World Sce	SEA	9740sng

2300	English	Area	kHz
2300-0200	BBG-VOA	ME	1593kwt
2300-0200	WWCR	NAm,Af	3195wcr*
2300-0300	R. Australia	Pac	17795shp, 19000shp
2300-0400	VO Russia (VOR)	NAm,CAm	7290kch
2300-2315	TWR Europe	NAf	1467rou
2300-2345	TWR Europe	NAf	1467rou
2300-2400	BBC World Sce	SEA	11955sng
2300-2400	BBC World Sce	FE	5980sla
2300-2400	BBG-VOA	SEA	5830pht, 5895pht, 7460pht
2300-2400	BBG-VOA	EAs	7365pht, 7480pht, 9490pht, 11840pht, 11860sai
2300-2400	CRI	SAs	5915kas, 7415kas
2300-2400	CRI	CAm	5990hab
2300-2400	CRI	EAs	6145bei
2300-2400	CRI	SEA	9535kun
2300-2400	R.Romania Int	Eu	6015gal, 7220gal
2300-2400	R.Romania Int	SEA	9530tig, 11810tig
2300-2400	VO Turkey	Eu,NAm	5960emr
2300-2400	WHRI	SAm	7315hri
2300-2400	WHRI	NAm	7385hri
2300-2400	WHRI	NAm,Eu	9505hri
2330-0400	Family Radio	NAm	6115yfr
2330-0400	HCJB Germany	Eu	3995wnm*
2330-2400	AWR As/Pacific	As	17700sda
2330-2400	R. Australia	As	17750shp
2330-2400	VO Vietnam	As	9840vni, 12020vni
0600	**English/Finnish**		
0600-0900	Scan.Weekend R.	Eu	5980vir*
0800	**English/Finnish**		
0800-1400	Scan.Weekend R.	Eu	11720vir*
0900	**English/Finnish**		
0900-1500	Scan.Weekend R.	Eu	6170vir*
1400	**English/Finnish**		
1400-1700	Scan.Weekend R.	Eu	11690vir*
1500	**English/Finnish**		
1500-1900	Scan Weekend R.	Eu	5980vir*
1700	**English/Finnish**		
1700-1900	Scan.Weekend R.	Eu	11720vir*
1900	**English/Finnish**		
1900-2200	Scan.Weekend R.	Eu	6170vir*, 11690vir*
2200	**English/Finnish**		
2200-0600	Scan.Weekend R.	Eu	6170vir*
2200-2200	Scan.Weekend R.	Eu	1602vir*
2200-2300	Scan.Weekend R.	Eu	11720vir*
2300	**English/Finnish**		
2300-0800	Scan.Weekend R.	Eu	11690vir*
1900	**English/Irish Gaelic**		
1930-2000	RTÉ R.Worldwide	Af	5820mey
1300	**English/Korean/Japanese/Mandarin**		
1330-1430	Shiokaze	KRE	5910yam
2000	**English/Korean/Japanese/Mandarin**		
2000-2100	Shiokaze	KRE	6110yam
0000	**English/Ndebele/Shona**		
0000-2400	VO Zimbabwe	SAf	999-†
1600	**English/Ndebele/Shona**		
1600-2200	VO Zimbabwe	Af	4828gwe†
1700	**English/ndebele/shona**		
1700-1900	SW Radio Africa	ZWE	4880mey
1800	**English/ndebele/shona**		
1800-1830	BBG-VOA Studio7	ZWE	909bot, 4930bot, 12080sao, 15775sao
1800-1900	R. VOP	ZWE	9345mdc
1830-1900	BBG-VOA Studio7	ZWE	909bot, 12080sao, 15775sao
1500	**English/Spanish**		
1500-2300	WRMI	CAm,SAm	9955rmi

2300	English/Spanish	Area	kHz
2300-1500	WRMI	CAm,SAm	9955rmi

FRENCH

0000	French	Area	kHz
0000-2400	RTL Radio	F	234bdw*
0100	**French**		
0130-0200	R. Habana Cuba	Car	5040hab
0200	**French**		
0200-0300	R.Romania Int	NAm	5975gal, 7325gal
0230-0300	Vatican Radio	Af	9660smg
0300	**French**		
0300-0330	R. Australia	Pac	12080brn, 15515shp
0300-0400	RAE	Am	11710bue
0400	**French**		
0400-0500	VO Korea	SEA	13650kuj, 15100kuj
0400-0500	VO Korea	EAs	3560kuj†
0400-0600	RFI	CAf,EAf	7390iss*, 9790iss, 11700iss**
0400-2310	RTBF Int.	WEu	621wav
0430-0458	Vatican Radio	Af	7360smg, 13765mdc
0430-0500	AWR Af/Eu	Af	6045mos
0430-0500	BBC World Sce	EAf	15490sey
0430-0500	BBC World Sce	CAf	6135asc, 7415asc
0500	**French**		
0500-0600	RFI	CAf	11605mey
0500-2300	Africa No.1	Af	9580gab
0530-0600	BBG-VOA	Af	1530sao
0530-0600	R. Japan	CAf,WAf	11730iss, 13840mdc
0530-0630	BBG-VOA	Af	4960sao, 6020bot, 9480sao, 12060bot
0600	**French**		
0600-0628	Vatican Radio	Af	11625smg, 13765smg
0600-0628	Vatican Radio	Af	9660smg
0600-0630	BBC World Sce	CAf	11800asc
0600-0630	BBC World Sce	NAf	6055skn, 7350wof
0600-0630	BBC World Sce	WAf	6135asc
0600-0630	R.Romania Int	Eu	9650gal+, 11740gal
0600-0630	R.Romania Int	Af	9690tig, 11790tig
0600-0700	RFI	NAf,WAf	5925iss*, 7390iss
0600-0700	VO Korea	LAm	11735kuj, 13760kuj, 15180kuj
0600-0800	CRI	Eu	15220uru
0600-0800	RFI	CAf	15170mey
0600-0800	RFI	NAf,WAf	9790iss*
0600-0900	RFI	WAf,CAf	15300iss
0630-0730	VOIRI	Eu,NAf	17560kam, 17865kam
0700	**French**		
0700-0730	BBC World Sce	WAf	11800asc
0700-0730	BBC World Sce	CAf	15105asc
0700-0730	VO Nigeria	Eu	15120iko†
0700-0800	RFI	NAf,WAf	11700iss
0700-0800	RFI	CAf	17850iss, 21580iss**
0700-0900	RFI	NAf,WAf	13695iss
0715-0730	Vatican Radio	NAf,ME	15595smg
0715-0730	Vatican Radio	Eu	585vat
0800	**French**		
0800-0830	AWR Af/Eu	Af	15145wer
0800-0900	RFI	WAf	17620iss
0800-0900	RFI	CAf	21580iss
0800-1000	Saudi R (BSKSA)	WAf	17785riy
0800-1300	CRI	Eu	702cdm
1000	**French**		
1000-1100	R.Romania Int	Eu	15260gal, 17870gal
1100	**French**		
1100-1130	BBG-VOA	Af	11915sao, 13735sao, 15620sao, 17850smg

1100	French	Area	kHz
1100-1130	RFI	SEA	15680tnn
1100-1200	R.Romania Int	Eu	15150tig, 15255gal, 17820gal
1100-1200	R.Romania Int	Af	17870tig
1100-1200	VO Korea	LAm	6170kuj†, 9335kuj
1100-1200	VO Korea	SEA	6185kuj, 9850kuj
1200	**French**		
1200-1203	R. Monaco	Atl,Med	4363mco*, 8728mco*, 13146mco*, 17260mco*
1200-1230	BBC World Sce	WAf	17780asc
1200-1230	BBC World Sce	CAf	21630asc
1200-1230	BBC World Sce	NAf	21720wof
1200-1230	VO Vietnam	As	7285han
1200-1300	Deutsche Welle	Af	9800kig, 15275kig, 15440kig, 17820wof, 21780kig
1200-1300	RFI	NAf,WAf	17620iss
1200-1300	RFI	CAf	17660mey, 21580iss
1200-1300	RFI	WAf	21690guf
1200-1400	CRI	Eu	15205kas
1300	**French**		
1300-1330	VO Vietnam	As	7285han
1300-1400	RFI	SEA	684dof
1400	**French**		
1400-1500	VO Korea	EAs	3560kuj†
1400-1500	VO Korea	Eu	7570kuj, 12015kuj
1400-1500	VO Korea	NAm	9335kuj, 11710kuj
1400-1600	CRI	WAf	11920cer, 13670cer
1400-1800	Saudi R (BSKSA)	WAf	17660riy
1430-1700	Lao National R.	SEA	567vie, 6130vie
1455-1525	TWR Africa	SAf	9585man
1600	**French**		
1600-1700	Channel Africa	WAf	15235mey
1600-1700	RFI	SEA	1296kun
1600-1700	VO Korea	EAs	3560kuj†
1600-1700	VO Korea	Eu	7570kuj, 12015kuj
1600-1700	VO Korea	NAm	9335kuj, 11710kuj
1600-1700	VO Russia (VOR)	Eu	7330msk
1600-1700	VO Russia (VOR)	Af	9405kch
1600-1800	CRI	Eu	7350kas
1600-1800	VO Russia (VOR)	Af	7295tch, 11985erv
1600-2100	VO Russia (VOR)	Eu,Af	6130msk, 11655msk
1630-1700	Int. R. Serbia	Eu	9635beo‡
1630-1700	VO Vietnam	ME	7220vni, 9550vni
1640-1700	R. Cairo	ISR	1008ela
1700	**French**		
1700-1715	Vatican Radio	Af	11935smg
1700-1715	Vatican Radio	Eu	585vat
1700-1728	Vatican Radio	Af	13765smg
1700-1730	Vatican Radio	Af	15570smg
1700-1800	Deutsche Welle	Af	9795kig, 12070kig, 15275kig, 15700wof
1700-1800	R. Ethiopia	EAf,ME	7235gjw±, 9560gjw±
1700-1800	RFI	NAf,WAf	13740iss*
1700-1800	RFI	WAf	17620iss**
1700-1800	RFI	CAf	17850iss
1700-1800	R.Romania Int	Eu	9690tig, 11635tig
1700-1900	RFI	WAf,CAf	15300iss
1700-2000	RFI	NAf,WAf	21690guf
1700-2000	WTWW	NAm,Eu,Af	12105tww
1700-2100	VO Russia (VOR)	Eu,Af	12060msk
1700-2100	VO Russia (VOR)	Af	9400kch
1800	**French**		
1800-1830	BBC World Sce	WAf	11860asc, 17885wof
1800-1830	BBC World Sce	CAf	15105asc
1800-1830	BBC World Sce	SAf	7465mey
1800-1830	BBC World Sce	NAf	9605skn

1800	French	Area	kHz
1800-1900	REE	Eu	9665nob
1800-1900	RFI	NAf,WAf	13740iss
1800-1900	R.Romania Int	Eu	7350gal
1800-1900	VO Korea	SAf	7210kuj, 11910kuj
1800-1900	VO Korea	ME,NAf	9975kuj, 11535kuj
1800-1900	VO Russia (VOR)	Eu	6145klg+
1800-2000	RFI	WAf,CAf	11995iss*
1800-2300	CRI	Eu	702cdm
1830-1845	FEBA Radio	Af	15250asc
1830-1900	BBG-VOA	Af	15620grv
1830-1900	R. Tirana	Eu	7465shi
1830-1900	VO Vietnam	Eu	7280vni, 9730vni
1830-1930	VOIRI	WAf	13650kam
1830-1930	VOIRI	Eu	6085kam, 7380sir
1830-2030	BBG-VOA	Af	1530sao
1830-2030	BBG-VOA	Af	15225grv
1830-2030	CRI	CAf	7350uru
1830-2030	CRI	WAf	9645kun
1900	**French**		
1900-2000	R .Damascus	Eu,NAm	9330adr‡
1900-2000	REE	ME	12030nob
1900-2000	REE	Af	9590nob
1900-2000	RFI	NAf,WAf	13740iss**
1900-2000	RFI	Eu	3965iss+
1900-2000	R.Taiwan Int.	Af	11875iss
1900-2000	R.Taiwan Int.	Eu	9895dha
1900-2000	BBG-VOA	Af	12080bot
1900-2100	VO Russia (VOR)	Eu	558cen**, 1323wbr
1900-2200	RFI	WAf,CAf	9790iss
1930-2000	AWR Af/Eu	Af	11690mos
1930-2000	R. Habana Cuba	Eu	15340hab
1930-2000	R. PMR	Eu	7290kch
1930-2000	VO Vietnam	Eu	5955mos, 7280vni, 9730vni
1935-1950	TWR Africa	Af	9940man
1940-2000	R. Belarus	Eu	11730mns
1945-2030	All India R.	NAf,WAf	9620alg, 11710del, 13640bgl
1950-2020	TWR Africa	Af	9940man
2000	**French**		
2000-2030	AWR Af/Eu	Af	9805wer, 11755mey
2000-2030	BBG-VOA	Af	9815bot, 9885sao, 15620sao
2000-2100	Angolan Nat R.	Af	945mul, 7217mul†
2000-2100	KBS World R.	ME,Af	5950iss
2000-2100	REE	Af	9570nob
2000-2100	REE	ME	9605nob
2000-2100	RFI	WAf	11995iss
2000-2100	R.Romania Int	Eu	7380gal
2000-2100	RAE	Eu	15345bue
2000-2100	VO Indonesia	Eu,NAf,ME	9526jak†
2000-2100	VO Korea	EAs	3560kuj†
2000-2100	VO Korea	Eu	7570kuj, 12015kuj
2000-2100	VO Nigeria	WAf	7255iko†
2000-2115	R. Cairo	Eu	11560abz
2000-2200	RFI	NAf,WAf	7205iss
2030-2058	Vatican Radio	Af	11625smg, 13765smg
2030-2100	AWR Af/Eu	Af	9805mos
2030-2100	BBG-VOA	Af	9815sao, 9885bot, 12080ira, 15225bot
2030-2100	R. Japan	WAf	11850mdc
2030-2130	VO Turkey	Eu	5970emr
2030-2130	VO Turkey	NAf,WAf	6050emr
2030-2230	CRI	Eu	6115bei, 7350uru
2040-2215	TWR Africa	WAf	1566par
2100	**French**		
2100-2130	BBG-VOA	Af	9435wof, 9680smg, 9815bot, 9885sao

2100	French	Area	kHz
2100-2130	R. Habana Cuba	CAm	11760hab
2100-2130	R. Habana Cuba	Af	11880hab*
2100-2130	R.Romania Int	Eu	6030gal, 7370gal+
2100-2130	VO Vietnam	ME	7220vni, 9550vni
2100-2130	VO Vietnam	Eu	7280vni, 9730vni
2100-2200	CRI	Eu	1440mrn
2100-2200	KBS World R.	Eu	3955skn
2100-2300	R. Cairo	WAf	15205abs
2130-2200	Int. R. Serbia	Eu	6100bij
2130-2200	R. PMR	Eu	7290kch
2200	**French**		
2200-1800	RFI	Eu	3965iss+
2215-2230	TWR Africa	WAf	1566par
2230-2300	R. Habana Cuba	SAm	15370hab
2300	**French**		
2300-2315	Africa No.1	Af	9580gab
2300-2400	REE	Eu	5970nob
2300-2400	REE	NAm	6055nob
0400	**French/Various**		
0400-0500	R. Okapi	COD	11690mey

GERMAN

0400	German	Area	kHz
0400-0430	TWR Africa	SAf	3200man, 4775man
0400-0500	TWR Africa	SAf	3200man, 4775man
0400-1900	RTL Radio	Eu	1440mrn
0415-0430	Miss.Heukelbach	Eu	1440mrn
0415-0430	R. Freundes-D.	Eu	1440mrn
0415-0430	Stimme Des Tr.	Eu	1440mrn
0430-0445	R. Freundes-D.	Eu	1440mrn
0430-1700	HCJB Germany	Eu	3995wnm*
0445-0500	Miss.Heukelbach	Eu	1440mrn
0500	**German**		
0500-0515	Miss.Heukelbach	Eu	1440mrn
0500-0700	CRI	Eu	15245uru, 17720kas
0500-1100	MV Baltic Radio	Eu	7265goh*†
0500-1600	R. 700	Eu	6085kll
0500-1800	R. 700	Eu	3955kll
0600	**German**		
0600-0615	R. Freundes-D.	Eu	1440mrn
0600-0630	Miss.Heukelbach	Eu	3995wnm
0600-0715	R. Öl Int.	Eu,NAf,ME	6155mos
0615-0630	Miss.Heukelbach	Eu	1440mrn
0700	**German**		
0700-0730	R.Romania Int	Eu	9450tig+, 11810tig
0700-1600	Hamburger LR	Eu	7265goh*
0730-0830	VOIRI	Eu	17690kam, 21500sir
0900	**German**		
0900-0935	R. Öl Int.	AUS,NZL	17360mos, 18910mos
0900-1000	VO Russia (VOR)	Eu	9720klg, 11635msk+
0900-1000	XVRB Radio	Eu	6045wer*
0900-1200	VO Russia (VOR)	Eu	630klu, 693bln, 1323wbr, 1431dsd, 9625klg*,+
1000	**German**		
1000-1200	VO Russia (VOR)	Eu	558cen**
1100	**German**		
1100-1115	R. Freundes-D.	Eu	6005kll
1100-1700	MV Baltic Radio	Eu	6190goh*†
1130-1200	Ev.Miss.Gemeind	Eu	6055wer
1200	**German**		
1200-1215	Stimme Des Tr.	Eu	6055wer
1230-1330	VO Turkey	Eu	17755emr
1300	**German**		
1300-1400	R.Romania Int	Eu	9810tig, 11700tig

1500	German	Area	kHz
1500-1700	VO Russia (VOR)	Eu	558cen**, 7220sam
1500-1900	VO Russia (VOR)	Eu	630klu, 693bln, 1323wbr, 1431dsd
1600	**German**		
1600-1700	VO Korea	EAs	4405kuj†
1600-1700	VO Korea	Eu	6170kuj†, 9325kuj
1600-1800	CRI	Eu	5970cer, 7380cer
1630-1700	Miss.Heukelbach	Eu	3995wnm
1700	**German**		
1700-1730	Int. R. Serbia	Eu	9635beo‡
1700-1800	RAE	Eu	15345bue
1700-1900	VO Russia (VOR)	Eu	7310sam
1715-1745	R. Freundes-D.	Eu	1440mrn
1730-1745	R700 KWD	Eu	6005kll
1730-1745	R. Freundes-D.	Eu	6005kll
1730-1830	VOIRI	Eu	6205sir, 7420kam
1730-2000	HCJB Germany	Eu	3995wnm*
1755-1800	Lutherische Std	Eu	558cen*, 630klu, 693bln, 1323wbr, 1431dsd, 7310sam
1800	**German**		
1800-1900	R .Damascus	Eu	9330adr‡
1800-1900	VO Indonesia	Eu,NAf,ME	9526jak†
1800-1900	VO Russia (VOR)	Eu	558cen**
1800-1940	R. Belarus	Eu	11730mns
1800-2000	CRI	Eu	6160xia, 7395kas, 9615uru
1800-2000	R. Belarus	Eu	6155mns
1800-2000	VO Korea	EAs	4405kuj†
1800-2000	VO Korea	Eu	6170kuj†, 9325kuj
1815-1830	Stimme Des Tr.	Eu	1440mrn*
1830-1845	R. Freundes-D.	Eu	1440mrn
1830-1900	R. PMR	Eu	7290kch
1830-1930	VO Turkey	Eu	7205emr
1840-1900	Miss.Heukelbach	Eu	7310sam
1845-1900	Miss.Heukelbach	Eu	1440mrn
1845-1900	Miss.Heukelbach	Eu	558cen*, 630klu, 693bln, 1323wbr, 1431dsd
1900	**German**		
1900-2000	R. Cairo	Eu	11560abz
1900-2000	R.Romania Int	Eu	6010tig, 9805tig+
1900-2000	R.Taiwan Int.	Eu	3955skn
1900-2100	CRI	Eu	1440mrn
1925-1940	R. Freundes-D.	Eu	558cen*, 630klu, 693bln, 1431dsd, 7310sam
2000	**German**		
2000-2015	R. Thailand WS	Eu	9535udo
2000-2100	KBS World R.	Eu	3955skn
2030-2100	R. PMR	Eu	7290kch
2030-2100	R. Tirana	Eu	7465shi
2030-2100	VO Vietnam	Eu	6175dha
2030-2330	HCJB Germany	Eu	3995wnm*
2100	**German**		
2100-2130	Int. R. Serbia	Eu	6100bij
2100-2130	VO Vietnam	Eu	6175dha
2100-2200	R.Taiwan Int.	Eu	3965iss
2100-2200	RAE	Eu	15345bue
2100-2300	CRI	Eu	963por
2130-2300	R. 700	Eu	3955kll
2200	**German**		
2230-2300	R. PMR	Eu	7290kch
2300	**German**		
2300-2330	HCJB Equador	SAm	9835wer
1700	**German (Low)**		
1700-1730	HCJB Germany	Eu	3995wnm
2000	**German (Low)**		
2000-2030	HCJB Germany	Eu	3995wnm

PORTUGUESE

0000	Portuguese	Area	kHz
0000-0100	CRI	SAm	9435kas
0000-0100	RAE	Am	11710bue
0030-0100	Vatican Radio	Eu	1260vat
0030-0100	Vatican Radio	SAm	7305grv
0500	**Portuguese**		
0530-0558	Vatican Radio	Af	7360smg, 11625smg, 13765mdc
0530-0600	Deutsche Welle	Af	9800kig, 12045kig, 17800dha
0700	**Portuguese**		
0700-0845	TWR Bonaire	SAm	800twb
0800	**Portuguese**		
0845-0900	TWR Bonaire	SAm	800twb
0900	**Portuguese**		
0900-0930	R. Japan	SAm	6130guf
0900-0930	Vatican Radio	Eu	1260vat
1000	**Portuguese**		
1000-1030	BBG-VOA	Af	11915sao, 17850ira
1000-1030	Vatican Radio	Eu	1260vat
1100	**Portuguese**		
1100-1200	RAE	Am	6060bue, 15345bue
1300	**Portuguese**		
1355-1425	TWR Africa	SAf	7315man
1400	**Portuguese**		
1400-1500	Channel Africa	SAf	9625mey
1415-1430	Vatican Radio	Eu	1260vat
1425-1455	TWR Africa	SAf	7315man
1500	**Portuguese**		
1500-1530	Vatican Radio	Eu	1260vat
1600	**Portuguese**		
1600-1630	Vatican Radio	Eu	1260vat
1630-1645	TWR Africa	SAf	4760man
1630-1700	BBG-VOA	Af	9880mey, 15670wer, 17655grv
1700	**Portuguese**		
1700-1730	RFI	CAf	9870mey
1700-1800	BBG-VOA	Af	1530sao, 9880bot, 15670sao, 17655grv
1800	**Portuguese**		
1800-1830	BBG-VOA	Af	1530sao, 9880bot, 15670bot, 17655grv
1800-1830	Vatican Radio	Af	11625smg, 13765smg, 15570smg
1850-1905	TWR Africa	SAf	6130man
1900	**Portuguese**		
1900-1930	RFI	WAf	6180mey
1900-2000	CRI	CAf,SAf	5985bei, 7365bei, 7405xia, 9535bji
1900-2000	CRI	Eu	7335jin, 9730kas
1905-1920	TWR Africa	SAf	6130man
1920-1950	TWR Africa	SAf	6130man
1930-2000	Deutsche Welle	Af	11800kig, 11865kig, 12045mey
2000	**Portuguese**		
2000-2030	R. Habana Cuba	Eu	15340hab
2100	**Portuguese**		
2100-0500	WTWW	NAm,Eu,Af	12105tww
2100-2200	REE	SAm	11680nob
2100-2200	VO Russia (VOR)	Eu	6090arm, 6120klg
2130-2200	R. Habana Cuba	Af	11880hab*
2130-2200	R. Japan	SAm	11880guf
2200-2300	CRI	Eu	6175cer, 7260uru, 9410kas
2200-2300	CRI	SAm	9685kas
2200-2300	Family Radio	SAm	17575yfr

2200	Portuguese	Area	kHz
2200-2400	VO Russia (VOR)	SAm	9750erv
2215-2330	R. Cairo	SAm	15480abz
2300	**Portuguese**		
2300-0045	HCJB Equador	SAm	11920nau
2300-0100	CRI	SAm	6100bei
2300-0100	Family Radio	SAm	11885yfr
2300-2400	CRI	SAm	13650hab
2300-2400	R. Habana Cuba	SAm	15230hab
2300-2400	VO Russia (VOR)	SAm	9865sam
2330-2400	R. Habana Cuba	SAm	15370hab

SPANISH

0000	Spanish	Area	kHz
0000-0030	RNW	LAm	9895hri
0000-0100	CRI	SAm	15120hab
0000-0100	CRI	CAm	5990hab
0000-0100	REE	SAm	11815cri+
0000-0100	R. Habana Cuba	NAm	6000hab**, 9640hab**
0000-0100	R.Romania Int	SAM,CAm	7315gal, 9525gal, 13590tig, 15110tig
0000-0200	Family Radio	CAm,SAm	5985yfr
0000-0200	REE	NAm	9630cri+
0000-0200	R. República	CUB	9490guf
0000-0200	VO Russia (VOR)	SAm	9865sam
0000-0300	BBG-R.Martí	CUB	7365grv, 9825grv
0000-0400	REE	SAm	9765cri
0000-0400	VO Russia (VOR)	SAm	9750erv
0000-0500	R. Habana Cuba	SAm	11680hab
0000-0500	R. Habana Cuba	Am	11760hab
0000-0500	R. Habana Cuba	NAm	6060hab
0000-0500	VO Russia (VOR)	SAm	7210msk
0000-0500	VO Russia (VOR)	CAm	9395erv
0000-0500	WEWN-EWTN SW	CAm	5810ewn
0000-0600	R. Habana Cuba	SAm	15230hab
0000-0600	R. Habana Cuba	Car	6120hab
0000-1000	WEWN-EWTN SW	SAm	11870ewn
0000-2400	BBG-R.Martí	CUB	1180mth
0030-0100	BBG-VOA	LAm	5890grv, 9885grv, 12000grv
0030-0230	VOIRI	LAm	7345kam
0030-0330	VOIRI	LAm,Eu	6010kam
0030-0700	TWR Bonaire	CAm,SAm	800twb
0045-0200	R. Cairo	LAm	9720abz, 13620abs, 13855abs
0100	**Spanish**		
0100-0145	Vatican Radio	Eu	1260vat
0100-0200	BBG-VOA	LAm	5890grv, 9885grv, 12000grv
0100-0200	Family Radio	SAm	11825yfr
0100-0200	KBS World R.	SAm	11635guf, 11810kim
0100-0200	R. República	CUB	5954crr
0100-0200	R.Taiwan Int.	LAm	9930yfr
0100-0300	CRI	SAm	9590kas, 9710kas
0100-0300	VO Russia (VOR)	SAm	6135spb
0100-0400	VO Russia (VOR)	SAm	9475dsb
0100-0600	REE	NAm	6055nob
0130-0500	HCJB Equador	SAm	6050qui
0200	**Spanish**		
0200-0230	KBS World R.	NAm	15575kim
0200-0245	Vatican Radio	SAm	7305grv
0200-0300	R.Taiwan Int.	SAm	11995guf
0200-0300	VO Turkey	LAm,Eu	9410emr, 9650emr
0200-0600	REE	CAm	3350cri
0200-0600	REE	NAm	9675cri
0200-0600	R. Habana Cuba	Car	5040hab
0300	**Spanish**		
0300-0330	R. Prague	LAm	9955rmi

0300	Spanish	Area	kHz
0300-0330	VO Vietnam	NAm	6175hri
0300-0400	R.Romania Int	SAm	9765gal, 11825tig, 11850gal, 13630tig
0300-0400	VO Korea	LAm	11735kuj, 13760kuj, 15180kuj
0300-0500	BBG-R.Martí	CUB	7365grv
0300-0500	HCJB Equador	SAm	6050qui
0300-0700	BBG-R.Martí	CUB	7405grv
0300-0900	BBG-R.Martí	CUB	6030grv
0330-0400	R. Slovakia Int	LAm	9955rmi
0400	**Spanish**		
0400-0430	R. Japan	SAm	6195guf
0400-0430	VO Vietnam	NAm	6175hri
0400-0500	VO Russia (VOR)	SAm	9765erv
0400-0800	REE	SAm	5965cri
0500	**Spanish**		
0500-0530	R. Japan	CAm	6195hri
0500-0600	REE	Eu	12035nob
0500-0600	VO Korea	LAm	11735kuj, 13760kuj, 15180kuj
0500-0700	REE	ME	11895nob
0500-0900	REE	Eu	9780nob+
0500-1300	WEWN-EWTN SW	CAm	7555ewn
0530-0630	VOIRI	Eu	15330sir, 15550kam
0600	**Spanish**		
0600-0630	R. Slovakia Int	LAm	9955rmi
0600-0700	KBS World R.	Eu	6045kim
0600-0800	CRI	Eu	15135kas
0600-0900	REE	Eu	12035nob
0630-0700	R. Prague	LAm	9955rmi
0700	**Spanish**		
0700-0900	BBG-R.Martí	CUB	5980grv
0900	**Spanish**		
0900-1200	BBG-R.Martí	CUB	6030grv
0900-1215	TWR Bonaire	CAm,SAm	800twb
0900-1300	BBG-R.Martí	CUB	5980grv
0900-1500	REE	Af	21540nob*
0900-1700	REE	Eu	15585nob*
0930-1000	R. Japan	SAm	6195hri
0930-1000	R. Japan	CAm	9795guf
0930-1000	R. Prague	LAm	9955rmi
1000	**Spanish**		
1000-1700	WEWN-EWTN SW	SAm	12050ewn
1030-1100	R. Slovakia Int	LAm	9955rmi
1100	**Spanish**		
1100-1200	KBS World R.	SAm	11795kim
1100-1300	BBG-R.Martí	CUB	9805grv
1100-1300	REE	Eu	13720nob+
1100-1500	HCJB Equador	SAm	6050qui
1100-1700	REE	ME	21610nob*
1130-1200	Vatican Radio	Eu	1260vat
1130-1200	Vatican Radio	SAm	7305grv
1130-1500	HCJB Equador	SAm	6050qui
1200	**Spanish**		
1200-1300	R. Habana Cuba	Am	6150hab
1200-1300	R. Habana Cuba	NAm	9550hab, 9850hab
1200-1300	R. Nac.RASD	NAf	1550rbn*
1200-1400	BBG-R.Martí	CUB	7405grv
1200-1400	REE	SEA	11910xia*
1200-1400	RAE	am	6060bue, 15345bue
1200-1500	REE	SAm	11815cri*
1200-1500	REE	NAm	15170cri*
1200-1500	REE	CAm	9765cri*
1200-1600	R. Habana Cuba	Car	11690hab
1200-1600	R. Habana Cuba	Am	11760hab
1200-1600	R. Habana Cuba	NAm	11860hab
1200-1600	R. Habana Cuba	SAm	15230hab, 17580hab, 17730hab
1200-2300	REE	SAm	15125cri

1200	Spanish	Area	kHz
1200-2300	REE	CAm	9765cri
1300	**Spanish**		
1300-1330	R. Prague	LAm	9955rmi
1300-1400	BBG-R.Martí	CUB	5745grv
1300-1400	BBG-VOA	LAm	9885grv, 13750grv, 15590grv
1300-1500	REE	Am	17595nob*
1300-1500	R. Habana Cuba	NAm	13780hab
1300-1600	R. Habana Cuba	CAm	11750hab
1300-1600	R. Habana Cuba	NAm	15340hab
1300-1800	WEWN - EWTN SW	CAm	11550ewn
1300-2200	BBG-R.Martí	CUB	11930grv
1330-1400	R. Slovakia Int	LAm	9955rmi
1400	**Spanish**		
1400-1415	Vatican Radio	Eu	1260vat
1400-1800	R. Habana Cuba	Car	11690hab‡
1400-1800	R. Habana Cuba	CAm	13680hab‡
1400-1800	R. Habana Cuba	NAm	15340hab‡
1400-1800	R. Habana Cuba	SAm	15370hab‡, 17750hab‡
1400-2000	BBG-R.Martí	CUB	15330grv
1400-2200	BBG-R.Martí	CUB	13820grv
1500	**Spanish**		
1500-1530	Int. R. Serbia	Eu	9635beo‡
1500-1530	Vatican Radio	Eu	1260vat
1500-1700	REE	Af	15385nob
1500-1700	REE	LAm	17595nob
1500-1700	REE	SAm	17715nob
1500-2200	REE	Af	17755nob
1500-2300	REE	NAm	17850cri
1600	**Spanish**		
1600-1700	KJES Radio	CAm	11715jes†
1600-2300	REE	SAm	15125cri
1600-2300	REE	NAm	17850cri
1600-2300	REE	CAm	9765cri
1700	**Spanish**		
1700-1730	Vatican Radio	Eu	1260vat
1700-1800	R. Nac.RASD	NAf	1550rbn*
1700-1800	VO Indonesia	Eu,NAf,ME	9526jak†
1700-1900	REE	SAm	17715nob
1700-1900	REE	Af	17755nob
1700-2200	REE	Af	17755nob
1700-2200	REE	Eu	9665nob
1700-2300	REE	Eu	7275nob
1700-2400	WEWN - EWTN SW	SAm	13830ewn
1730-1830	VO Turkey	Eu	9495emr
1800	**Spanish**		
1800-0300	RAE	Am	6060bue*, 15345bue*
1800-1830	VO Vietnam	Eu	7280vni, 9730vni
1800-2000	REE	SAm	15125cri
1800-2000	REE	NAm	17850cri
1800-2000	REE	CAm	9765cri
1800-2400	WEWN - EWTN SW	CAm	12050ewn
1830-2000	KJES Radio	SEA,AUS	15385jes†
1900	**Spanish**		
1900-1930	Vatican Radio	Af	11625smg, 13765smg
1900-2000	VO Korea	EAs	3560kuj†
1900-2000	VO Korea	Eu	7570kuj, 12015kuj
1900-2130	HCJB Equador	SAm	6050qui
1900-2300	REE	LAm	11940nob
1900-2300	REE	NAm	15110nob
1900-2400	HCJB Equador	SAm	6050qui
2000	**Spanish**		
2000-0230	RAE	Eu	15345bue*
2000-0230	RAE	Am	6060bue*
2000-2020	R. Belarus	Eu	6155mns, 11730mns
2000-2030	Int. R. Serbia	Eu	6100bij
2000-2100	R.Romania Int	Af	6010tig
2000-2100	R.Romania Int	Eu	9895tig
2000-2100	R.Taiwan Int.	Eu	3965iss

2000	Spanish	Area	kHz
2000-2100	VO Russia (VOR)	Eu	5940sam, 6090arm, 6120klg
2000-2400	BBG-R.Martí	CUB	9565grv
2030-2130	VOIRI	Eu	6080kam, 9630sir
2100	**Spanish**		
2100-2300	CRI	Eu	6020szg, 9640kas
2130-2300	TWR Bonaire	CAm,SAm	800twb
2200	**Spanish**		
2200-0300	BBG-R.Martí	CUB	6030grv
2200-0600	R. Habana Cuba	SAm	11840hab, 17705hab
2200-0600	R. Habana Cuba	CAm	9810hab
2200-2300	CRI	SAm	6100bei
2200-2300	R .Damascus	Eu,LAm	9330adr‡
2200-2300	REE	Af	11625nob
2200-2300	REE	Af	7265nob
2200-2300	R.Romania Int	SAm	13860tig, 15160tig
2200-2300	VO Korea	EAs	3560kuj†
2200-2300	VO Korea	Eu	7570kuj, 12015kuj
2200-2400	BBG-R.Martí	CUB	7405grv
2200-2400	CRI	Eu	7210cer, 7250uru
2200-2400	R. Habana Cuba	Eu	15340hab
2200-2400	R. Habana Cuba	Car	5040hab, 9710hab
2200-2400	RAE	Eu	15345bue
2200-2400	RAE	Am	6060bue, 11710bue
2300	**Spanish**		
2300-0100	CRI	SAm	9590kas
2300-0100	CRI	Eu	9800kas
2300-0100	Family Radio	SAm	13695yfr
2300-0200	R. República	CUB	5954crr
2300-0200	WTWW	NAm,Eu,Af	12105tww
2300-0500	REE	LAm	6125nob**
2300-0500	REE	NAm,CAm	9535nob**
2300-0500	REE	SAm	9620nob**
2300-2400	CRI	Eu	6175cer
2300-2400	R.Taiwan Int.	LAm	9690yfr
0100	**Spanish/English**		
0100-0200	WHRI	SAm	7315hri
0200	**Spanish/English**		
0200-0300	WHRI	SAm	7315hri
0300	**Spanish/English**		
0300-0500	WHRI	SAm	7315hri
0500	**Spanish/English**		
0530-0800	WHRI	SAm	7315hri
0800	**Spanish/English**		
0800-0900	WHRI	CAm	5920hri
0900	**Spanish/English**		
0900-1100	WHRI	CAm	5920hri
1000	**Spanish/English**		
1000-1100	WHRI	SAm	7315hri
1100	**Spanish/English**		
1100-1200	WHRI	SAm	7315hri
1200	**Spanish/English**		
1200-1300	WHRI	CAm	5920hri
2300	**Spanish/English**		
2300-2400	WHRI	SAm	5920hri

NB: not all transmissions are daily, please check main schedules under the appropriate country for full details

For *, ** and *** please see Notes under the Country entry for that station in the International Radio section

Key: + = DRM broadcast; † = irregular; ‡ = inactive at time of publication.

© WRTH Publications Ltd, November 2012

Notes

DRM International Broadcasts

0000	Language	Area	Station	kHz
0000-0200	Spanish	NAm	REE	9630cri
0000-0100	Spanish	SAm	REE	11815cri
0100				
0130-0230	Nepali	SAs	All India R.	11715del
0300				
0315-0415	Hindi	EAf	All India R.	17715del
0400				
0415-0430	Gujarati	EAf	All India R.	17715del
0430-0530	Hindi	EAf	All India R.	17715del
0500				
0500-0530	Chinese	As	R.Romania Int	17870tig
0500-0650	English	Pac	RNZI	13730ran
0500-0700	English	Eu	BBC World Sce	3955skn
0530-0600	Russian	RUS	R.Romania Int	6175tig
0500-0900	Spanish	Eu	REE	9780nob
0600				
0650-0800	English	Pac	RNZI	11657ran
0600-0900	English	Eu	VO Russia (VOR)	11635msk
0630-0700	English	Eu	R.Romania Int	9600gal
0600-0630	French	Eu	R.Romania Int	9650gal
0700				
0700-0900	English	WEu	BBC World Sce	7355mos
0700-0900	English	WEu	BBC World Sce	5875wof
0700-0730	German	Eu	R.Romania Int	9450tig
0800				
0800-0900	English	Eu	VO Russia (VOR)	9625klg
0800-1300	English	Pac	RNZI	9870ran
0800-0900	Russian	Eu	VO Russia (VOR)	9625klg
0900				
0900-1200	English	Eu	VO Russia (VOR)	9625klg
0900-1000	German	Eu	VO Russia (VOR)	11635msk
0900-1200	German	Eu	VO Russia (VOR)	9625klg
1100				
1100-1130	English	Eu	KBS World R.	9760wof
1100-1130	English	WEu	R. Japan	9760wof
1100-1200	English	Pac	R. Australia	12080brn
1100-1200	English	As	VO Russia (VOR)	11640irk
1100-1400	English	As,SEA	VO Russia (VOR)	9560nvs
1130-1200	Russian	WEu	R. Japan	9760wof
1100-1300	Spanish	Eu	REE	13720nob
1200				
1200-1400	English	Pac	R. Australia	5995brn
1200-1400	English	Eu	VO Russia (VOR)	9625klg
1200-1400	Russian	Eu	VO Russia (VOR)	9625klg
1300				
1300-1400	Hindi	As	VO Russia (VOR)	7315irk
1300-1500	Sinhala	SAs	All India R.	15050del
1400				
1400-1800	English	SAs	BBC World Sce	5845nak
1400-1500	Urdu	As	VO Russia (VOR)	7315irk
1500				
1530-1550	English	As	Vatican Radio	15775smg
1550-1650	English	Pac	RNZI	7440ran
1530-1630	English	SAs	Disco Palace	12115iss
1530-1558	English	As	Vatican Radio	15775smg
1500-1600	Hindi	As	VO Russia (VOR)	7315irk
1600				
1650-1845	English	Pac	RNZI	9890ran
1600-1700	Russian	RUS	R.Romania Int	7300tig
1615-1715	Russian	Eu	All India R.	15140del
1700				
1745-1945	English	Eu	All India R.	9950del
1700-1800	Italian	Eu	VO Russia (VOR)	6145irk
1800-1900	English	Eu	R.Romania Int	9780tig

1800	Language	Area	Station	kHz
1830-2000	English	Eu,Af	VO Nigeria	15120aja
1845-2150	English	Pac	RNZI	15720ran
1800-1900	French	Eu	VO Russia (VOR)	6145klg
1900				
1900-2000	French	Eu	RFI	3965iss
1900-2000	German	Eu	R.Romania Int	9805tig
1945-2045	Hindi	Eu	All India R.	9950del
1900-1930	Italian	Eu	R.Romania Int	7345tig
2000				
2045-2230	English	Eu	All India R.	9950del
2000-2100	English	NAm	Disco Palace	17875guf
2100				
2130-2200	English	Eu	R.Romania Int	6030gal
2150-0500	English	Pac	RNZI	17675ran
2100-2130	French	Eu	R.Romania Int	7370gal
2200				
2245-0045	English	EAs	All India R.	11645del
2200-1800	French	Eu	RFI	3965iss

Note: Not all broadcasts are daily.
Key: * Dual channel audio (e.g., simultaneous English and French).
© WRTH Publications Ltd. November 2012.

TERRESTRIAL TELEVISION

Section Contents

Initial entries for each letter,
see Main Index for full details

Features & Reviews

National Radio

International Radio

Frequency Lists

Terrestrial Television
(incl. Radio via DTT)

Reference

CHARACTERISTICS OF ANALOGUE TELEVISION SYSTEMS
(Recommendation ITU-R BT.470-6, Revision 2005)

System	Number of lines	Channel width MHz.	Vision band-width MHz.	Vision/Sound separation MHz.	Vestigial side-band MHz.	Vision mod.	Sound mod.
B	625	7	5	+5.5	0.75	Neg.	FM
B1	625	8	5	+5.5	0.75	Neg.	FM
D	625	8	6	+6.5	0.75	Neg.	FM
D1	625	8	5	+6.5	0.75	Neg.	FM
G	625	8	5	+5.5	0.75	Neg.	FM
H	625	8	5	+5.5	1.25	Neg.	FM
I	625	8	5.5	+5.996	1.25	Neg.	FM
I1	625	8	5.5	+5.996	1.25	Neg.	FM
K	625	8	6	+6.5	0.75	Neg.	FM
K1	625	8	5	+6.5	0.75	Neg.	FM
L	625	8	6	+6.5	1.25	Pos.	AM
M	525	6	4.2	+4.5	0.75	Neg.	FM
N	625	6	4.2	+4.5	0.75	Neg.	FM

ANALOGUE CHANNEL INFORMATION
(Vision carrier frequencies in MHz)
(† = being phased out)

VHF Channels

[A] Channels

(Americas, parts of Asia & Pacific)

A2 = 55.25	A6 = 83.25	A10 = 193.25
A3 = 61.75	A7 = 175.25	A11 = 199.25
A4 = 67.25	A8 = 181.25	A12 = 205.25
A5 = 77.25	A9 = 187.25	A13 = 211.25

[E] Channels

(Most of Europe, Greenland, Africa, most of Asia & Pacific)

E2 = 48.25	E6 = 182.25	E11 = 217.25
E3 = 55.25	E7 = 189.25	E12 = 224.25
E4 = 62.25	E9 = 203.25	
E5 = 175.25	E10 = 210.25	

[K] Channels

(Parts of Africa)

K4 = 175.25	K7 = 199.25	K10 = 223.25
K5 = 183.25	K8 = 207.25	
K6 = 191.25	K9 = 215.25	

[R] Channels

(Parts of Europe, Russia, parts of Asia)

R1 = 49.75	R5 = 93.25	R9 = 199.25
R2 = 59.25	R6 = 175.25	R10 = 207.25
R3 = 77.25	R7 = 183.25	R11 = 215.25
R4 = 85.25	R8 = 191.25	R12 = 223.25

Specific national parameters:

Morocco (†)

M4 = 163.25	M7 = 187.25	M9 = 203.25
M5 = 171.25	M8 = 195.25	M10 = 211.25
M6 = 179.25		

South Africa & Namibia

SA4 = 175.25	SA7 = 199.25	SA10 = 223.25
SA5 = 183.25	SA8 = 207.25	SA11 = 231.25
SA6 = 191.25	SA9 = 215.25	SA13 = 247.43

Japan

J1 = 91.25	J5 = 177.25	J9 = 199.25
J2 = 97.25	J6 = 183.25	J10 = 205.25
J3 = 103.25	J7 = 189.25	J11 = 211.25
J4 = 171.25	J8 = 193.25	J12 = 217.25

China (P.R.)

DS1 = 49.75	DS5 = 85.25	DS9 = 192.25
DS2 = 57.75	DS6 = 168.25	DS10 = 200.25
DS3 = 65.75	DS7 = 176.25	DS11 = 208.25
DS4 = 77.25	DS8 = 184.25	DS12 = 216.25

Australia & parts of Pacific

AU0 = 46.25 (†)	AU5 = 102.25 (†)	AU9 = 196.25
AU1 = 57.25 (†)	AU5A = 138.25 (†)	AU9A = 203.25
AU2 = 64.25 (†)	AU6 = 175.25	AU10 = 209.25
AU3 = 86.25 (†)	AU7 = 182.25	AU11 = 216.25
AU4 = 95.25 (†)	AU8 = 189.25	AU12 = 224.25

New Zealand (†) & parts of Pacific

NZ1 = 45.25	NZ5 = 182.25	NZ9 = 210.25
NZ2 = 55.25	NZ6 = 189.25	NZ10 = 217.25
NZ3 = 62.25	NZ7 = 196.25	NZ11 = 224.25
NZ4 = 175.25	NZ8 = 203.25	

UHF Channels

"A" Channels
(Americas, parts of Asia & Pacific)

14 = 471.25	33 = 585.25	52 = 699.25
15 = 477.25	34 = 591.25	53 = 705.25
16 = 483.25	35 = 597.25	54 = 711.25
17 = 489.25	36 = 603.25	55 = 717.25
18 = 495.25	37 = 609.25	56 = 723.25
19 = 501.25	38 = 615.25	57 = 729.25
20 = 507.25	39 = 621.25	58 = 735.25
21 = 513.25	40 = 627.25	59 = 741.25
22 = 519.25	41 = 633.25	60 = 747.25
23 = 525.25	42 = 639.25	61 = 753.25
24 = 531.25	43 = 645.25	62 = 759.25
25 = 537.25	44 = 651.25	63 = 765.25
26 = 543.25	45 = 657.25	64 = 771.25
27 = 549.25	46 = 663.25	65 = 777.25
28 = 555.25	47 = 669.25	66 = 783.25
29 = 561.25	48 = 675.25	67 = 789.25
30 = 567.25	49 = 681.25	68 = 795.25
31 = 573.25	50 = 687.25	69 = 801.25
32 = 579.25	51 = 693.25	

[E], [R] Channels
(Europe, Greenland, Russia, Africa, most of Asia & Pacific)

21 = 474.25	38 = 607.25	55 = 743.25
22 = 479.25	39 = 615.25	56 = 751.25
23 = 487.25	40 = 623.25	57 = 759.25
24 = 495.25	41 = 631.25	58 = 767.25
25 = 503.25	42 = 639.25	59 = 775.25
26 = 511.25	43 = 647.25	60 = 783.25
27 = 519.25	44 = 655.25	61 = 791.25
28 = 527.25	45 = 663.25	62 = 799.25
29 = 535.25	46 = 671.25	63 = 807.25
30 = 543.25	47 = 679.25	64 = 815.25
31 = 551.25	48 = 687.25	65 = 823.25
32 = 559.25	49 = 695.25	66 = 831.25
33 = 567.25	50 = 703.25	67 = 839.25
34 = 575.25	51 = 711.25	68 = 847.25
35 = 583.25	52 = 719.25	69 = 855.25
36 = 591.25	53 = 727.25	
37 = 599.25	54 = 735.25	

[J] Channels
(Japan)

13 = 471.25	30 = 573.25	47 = 675.25
14 = 477.25	31 = 579.25	48 = 681.25
15 = 483.25	32 = 585.25	49 = 687.25
16 = 489.25	33 = 591.25	50 = 693.25
17 = 495.25	34 = 597.25	51 = 699.25
18 = 501.25	35 = 603.25	52 = 705.25
19 = 507.25	36 = 609.25	53 = 711.25
20 = 513.25	37 = 615.25	54 = 717.25
21 = 519.25	38 = 621.25	55 = 723.25
22 = 525.25	39 = 627.25	56 = 729.25
23 = 531.25	40 = 633.25	57 = 735.25
24 = 537.25	41 = 639.25	58 = 741.25
25 = 543.25	42 = 645.25	59 = 747.25
26 = 549.25	43 = 651.25	60 = 753.25
27 = 555.25	44 = 657.25	61 = 759.25
28 = 561.25	45 = 663.25	62 = 765.25
29 = 567.25	46 = 669.25	

[NZ] Channels
(New Zealand & parts of Pacific)

27 = 519.25	42 = 639.25	57 = 759.25
28 = 527.25	43 = 647.25	58 = 767.25
29 = 535.25	44 = 655.25	59 = 775.25
30 = 543.25	45 = 663.25	60 = 783.25
31 = 551.25	46 = 671.25	61 = 791.25
32 = 559.25	47 = 679.25	62 = 799.25
33 = 567.25	48 = 687.25	
34 = 575.25	49 = 695.25	
35 = 583.25	50 = 703.25	
36 = 591.25	51 = 711.25	
37 = 599.25	52 = 719.25	
38 = 607.25	53 = 727.25	
39 = 615.25	54 = 735.25	
40 = 623.25	55 = 743.25	
41 = 631.25	56 = 751.25	

[DS] Channels
(China, P.R., exc. SAR Macau, SAR Hong Kong)

13 = 471.25	36 = 695.25	59 = 879.25
14 = 479.25	37 = 703.25	60 = 887.25
15 = 487.25	38 = 711.25	61 = 895.25
16 = 495.25	39 = 719.25	62 = 903.25
17 = 503.25	40 = 727.25	
18 = 511.25	41 = 735.25	
19 = 519.25	42 = 743.25	
20 = 527.25	43 = 751.25	
21 = 534.25	44 = 759.25	
22 = 543.25	45 = 767.25	
23 = 551.25	46 = 775.25	
24 = 559.25	47 = 783.25	
25 = 607.25	48 = 791.25	
26 = 615.25	49 = 799.25	
27 = 623.25	50 = 807.25	
28 = 631.25	51 = 815.25	
29 = 639.25	52 = 823.25	
30 = 647.25	53 = 831.25	
31 = 655.25	54 = 839.25	
32 = 663.25	55 = 847.25	
33 = 671.25	56 = 855.25	
34 = 679.25	57 = 863.25	
35 = 687.25	58 = 871.25	

DIGITAL TERRESTRIAL TELEVISION (DTT) SYSTEMS

ATSC
ATSC (**A**dvanced **T**elevision **S**ystems **C**ommittee) is the digital television standard developed in the USA. ATSC transmits with MPEG-2 video- and audio compression. It produces wide screen 16:9 images up to 1920×1080 pixels in size; up to six standard TV channels can be broadcast from a single TV transmitter using an existing 6MHz channel. ATSC uses the Dolby Digital AC-3 format to provide 5.1-channel surround sound. Numerous auxiliary services can also be provided, incl. radio programmes.

DVB-T
DVB-T (**D**igital **V**ideo **B**roadcasting - **T**errestrial) is the standard of the European DVB consortium for the transmission of digital terrestrial television. This system transmits a compressed digital audio/video stream, using OFDM modulation with concatenated channel coding (COFDM). The source coding methods are MPEG-2 and MPEG-4. The modulation method in DVB-T is COFDM with either 64 or 16 state Quadrature Amplitude Modulation (QAM). 16 and 64QAM constellations can be combined in a single multiplex, providing a controllable degradation for more important programme streams. Several radio programmes can be transmitted as well.

DTMB
DTMB (**D**igital **T**errestrial **M**ultimedia **B**roadcast) is the DTT standard of the P.R. China. It is understood to be a fusion of TDS-OFDM (**T**ime **D**omain **S**ynchronous OFDM), developed by the Beijing Tsinghua university and based on the standard used by multi-carriers (similar to DVB-T), and ADTB-T (**A**dvanced **D**igital **T**elevision **B**roadcast - **T**errestrial) developed by the Shanghai Jiatong University.

ISDB-T / SBTVD (ISDB-Tb)
ISDB-T (**I**ntegrated **S**ervices **D**igital **B**roadcasting - **T**errestrial) was developed in Japan and works similar to the European DVB-T. It uses COFDM modulation with PSK/QAM. The compression system is MPEG-2. ISDB-T can also transmit radio programmes in addition to TV channels. ISDB-Tb or SBTVD (**S**istema **B**rasileiro de **T**elevisão **D**igital) is a version of ISDB-T developed in Brazil, with MPEG4 compression.

T-DMB
T-DMB (**T**errestrial **D**igital **M**ultimedia **B**roadcast) is the DTT standard developed in the Republic of Korea.

INTRODUCTION

The TV section contains information about terrestrial TV stations and radio prgrs via DTT, in a compact format. If applicable, each country entry is devided into subsections: "National Stations", "Regional Stations", "Local Stations", "Foreign TV Relays", "Foreign Military Stations". The subsection "DTT Transmitters" contains details of DTT transmitter operators or licensees, and DTT transmitter networks. Contact info for domestic prgrs included in the DTT multiplexes is found in the subsections mentioned above.
Keys: "Systems": # = txs to be phased out, † = analogue txs are being phased out (tx details no longer listed) ⍓ = analogue shutdown date; [A], [DS], [E], [J], [K], [R], [AU], [NZ], [SA] refer to the channel characteristics as shown in the "Channel Information" table. Tx networks for national stations are listed either with main txs (power limit applied) or with key tx(s). Local Stations (if included) are listed in full; if no tx location is given, the site refers to the city of the station's headquarters. (-) = tx details not received at editorial deadline.

AFGHANISTAN

Systems: PAL-B/G [E]. BFBS-TV: DVB-T (MPEG4)

National Stations
RTA TV (Gov) ✉ P.O.Box 544, Kabul ☎ +93 20 2102487 🖷 +93 20 2101086 **E:** info@rta.org.af **Web:** www.rta.org.af **L.P:** DG (RTA): Ghulam Hassan Hazrati **Txs:** Kabul ch11 (2kW) & relay txs. NB. Local stations in Herat, Kandahar, Khost. – **AFGHAN TV (Comm)** ✉ Kabul **E:** info@afghantv.af **Web:** www.afghantv.af **L.P:** Dir: Ahmed Shah Afghanzai. **Txs:** Kabul ch24 & relay txs. – **ARIANA TELEVISION NETWORK (ATN) (Comm)** ✉ Darlaman Street, Kabul ☎ +93 70 151515 **E:** marketing@arianatelevision.com **W:** arianatelevision.com **L.P:** Dir: Ehsanollah Aryanzai **Txs:** Kabul ch4 & relay txs. – **TOLO TV (Comm)** ✉ P.O.Box 225, Kabul **E:** info@tolo.tv **W:** www.tolo.tv **L.P:** Dir: Saad Mohseni **Txs:** Kabul ch9 & relay txs.

Local Stations not shown.

Foreign Military Station
BFBS-TV (British Mil) ✉ Chalfont Grove, Narcot Lane, Chalfont St Peter, Buckinghamshire, SL9 8TN, United Kingdom. **Mux✪:** BFBS1, BFBS2, BFBS3 Kids, BFBS4, BFBS1 One Day Later, BFBS+, Sky Sports 1, Sky Sports 2 ⌘ BFBS R. 1+2, BFBS Afghanistan **Txs:** ch27 (SFN).

ALASKA (USA)

System: ATSC [A]

Local Stations*
KAKM (Pub) 3877 University Dr, Anchorage, AK 99508-4676. °PBS. Tx: Anchorage ch8 (50kW). **KATN (Comm):** 516 2nd Ave Ste 400, Fairbanks, AK 99701-4729. °ABC. Tx: ch18 (16kW). **KDMD (Comm):** 1310 E 66th Ave, Anchorage, AK 99518-1915. °ION, Telemundo, HSN. Tx: ch32 (50kW). Mux: KDMD, Telemundo. **KFXF (Comm):** 3650 Braddock St Ste 2, Fairbanks, AK 99701-7617. °Fox. Tx: ch22 (11kW). **KIMO (Comm):** 2700 E Tudor Rd, Anchorage, AK 99507-1136. °ABC, CW. Tx: ch12 (41kW). Mux: KIMO-DT (ABC), KWBX-DT (CW). **KJNP-TV (Rlg):** 2501 Mission Rd, North Pole, AK 99705-6361. °TBN. Tx: ch20 (15kW). **KJUD (Comm)** 175 S Franklin St, Juneau, AK 99801-1384. °Fox, CW. Tx: ch11 (0.14kW). Mux: KJUD, CW. **KTBY (Comm):** 440 E Benson Blvd Ste 1, Anchorage, AK 99503-4121. °Fox. Tx: ch20 (234.4kW). **KTNL-TV (Comm):** 520 Lake St, Sitka, AK 99835-7403. °CBS. Tx: ch2 (1kW). **KTOO-TV (Pub):** 360 Egan Dr, Juneau, AK 99801-1748. °PBS. Tx: ch10 (1kW). **KTUU-TV (Comm):** 701 E Tudor Rd Ste 220, Anchorage, AK 99503-7488. °NBC. Tx: ch10 (21kW). **KTVA (Comm):** 1007 W 32nd Ave, Anchorage, AK 99503-3728. °CBS. Tx: ch28 (28.9kW). **KTVF (Comm):** 3528 International Way, Fairbanks, AK 99701-7382. °NBC. Tx: ch26 (12kW). **KUAC-TV (Pub):** 312 Tanana Dr, Fairbanks, AK 99775-2004. °PBS. Tx: ch24 (69kW). **KYES-TV (Comm)** 3700 Woodland Dr Ste 800, Anchorage, AK 99517-2588. °MyNetworkTV. Tx: ch6 (45kW). Mux: KYES-DT, audio channels, Wealth TV. **KYUK-TV (Pub)** 640 Radio St, Bethel, AK 99559. °PBS. Tx: ch3 (4.68kW).
*) Full power licenses (lp licenses not listed); °) Network affiliation.

ALBANIA

Systems: PAL-B/G [E]; DVB-T (MPEG2) [E]

National Stations
RADIOTELEVISIONI SHQIPTAR (RTSH) (Pub) ✉ Rr. "Ismail Qemali" 11, Tirana ☎ +355 4 2256059 🖷 +355 4 2227745 **W:** www.rtsh.al **L.P:** DG: Petrit Beci; Dir TV: Mirela Oktrova. **Chs:** TVSH1, TVSH2. **Txs: TVSH1:** Dajt ch4 (10kW) & ch57 (5kW), Gllava ch9 (2kW), Cervenake ch11 (5kW), Mide ch12 (5kW), Durres ch25 (1kW) & txs below 1kW; **TVSH2:** Dajt ch11 (1kW). – **TOP CHANNEL (Comm)** ✉ Blv. "Deshmoret e Kombit, Qendra Nderbombetare e Kultures", Tirana ☎ +355 4 2253177 🖷 +355 4 2253178 **E:** info@top-channel.tv

W: www.top-channel.tv. **Txs:** Tirana ch36 & network. – **TV KLAN (Comm)** ✉ Rr. "Aleksander Moisiu" 97, Tirana ☎ +355 4 2347805 🖷 +355 4 2347808 **E:** info@tvklan.al **W:** www.tvklan.al **L.P:** Dir: Pandi Laço **Txs:** Tirana ch28 & network.

Local Stations not shown.

Foreign TV Relay
TV5 Monde Europe (France): Tirana ch43.

DTT Transmitters (under construction)
Licensee: DigitALB ✉ Rr. "Themistokli Germenji" 10, Tirana ☎+355 4 2255813 🖷 +355 4 2274831 **E:** info@digitalb.al **W:** www.digitalb.al **Mux 1-5✪:** multiprgr **Txs: Mux 1:** ch62 (SFN), **Mux 2:** ch64 (SFN), **Mux 3:** ch67 (SFN), **Mux 4:** ch69 (SFN). **Mux 5 (DVB-H):** ch38 (Tirana). – **Licensee:** Tring Digital ✉ Kompleksi Don Bosko, Kulla 7, kati II, Tirana ☎+355 4 4800008 🖷 +355 4 4800001 **E:** info@tring.tv **W:** www.tring.tv **Mux 1+2✪:** multiprgr **Txs: Mux 1:** ch47 (Dajt) **Mux 2:** ch59 (Dajt).

ALGERIA

Systems: DVB-T (MPEG2); # PAL-B [E] ⍓2014

ENTREPRISE NATIONALE DE TÉLÉVISION (ENTV) (Gov)✉ 21, Boulevard des Martyrs, Alger ☎ +213 21 602300 🖷 +213 21 230914 **E:** commerciale@entv.dz **W:** www.entv.dz **L.P:** DG: Toufik Kheladi **Chs:** Chaîne Nationale, Canal Algérie, A3, Chaîne 4/5, Regional stns **Txs: Chaîne Nationale:** Alger (Bordj El Bahri) ch11 (32kW) & network; **Chaîne 4/5:** Alger (Bordj El Bahri) ch49 (47kW) & netw.

DTT Transmitters (under construction)
Operator: Télédiffusion d'Algérienne (TDA) ✉ BP 50, 16340 Alger ☎ +213 21 901717 🖷 +213 21 902424 **E:** info@tda.dz **W:** www.tda.dz **Mux:** Chaîne Nationale, Canal Algérie, A3, Chaîne 4/5, Regional stns ⌘ Chaîne I, II, III, R.Algérie Internationale

Location	ch	kW	Location	ch	kW
Kef El Akhal	28	1.5	Chréa	43	100
Akfadou	33	1.5	Tessala	43	100
Bordj El Bahri	41	1.5			
+ sites with txs below 1kW.					

Sahrawi Refugee Camps
TV RASD (Gov) ✉ BP 470, 37000 Tindouf ☎ +213 49 923525 **W:** www.rasd-tv.com **Tx:** Rabouni ch22 (10kW).

ANDORRA

System: DVB-T (MPEG2) [E]

ANDORRA TELEVISIÓ (Pub)✉ Baixada del Molí 24, AD500 Andorra la Vella ☎ +376 873777 🖷 +376 863242 **E:** rtva@rtva.ad **W:** www.rtva.ad **L.P:** DG (RTVA): Francesc Robert Ribes.

DTT Transmitters
Licensee: Andorra Telecom ✉ C/ Mossèn Lluís Pujol, numero 8-14, AD500 Santa Coloma ☎ +376 875274 🖷 +376 863667 **E:** comunicacio@andorratelecom.ad **W:** www.andorratelecom.ad **Mux 1:** BBC World, RTP Intl, Tele 5, Arte, 3/24 **Tx:** ch28 (La Vella) **Mux 2:** CNN Int., Cuatro, C33, La Sexta, NRJ12 **Tx:** ch36 (La Vella). **Mux 3:** Andorra Televisió, La 2, M6, TF1, TV3 **Tx:** ch42 (La Vella) **Mux 4:** Antena 3, France 2, France 3, La 1, Super 3/3XL **Tx:** ch45 (La Vella).

ANGOLA

Systems: # PAL-I [E]; ISDB-T [E] planned

TELEVISÃO PÚBLICA DE ANGOLA (Pub)✉ CP 2604, Luanda ☎ +244 222 320326 🖷 +244 222 323622 **E:** tpa.informatica@netangola.com

W: www.tpa.ao **LP:** Pres: Hélder Manuel Bárber Dias dos Santos **Chs:** TPA1, TPA2 **Txs: TPA 1:** Luanda ch9 (13kW) & relay txs. **TPA2:** Luanda ch4 & relay txs.

Local Station
TV Zimbo: Avenida de Talatona, Luanda Sul; ch45.

Foreign TV Relay
RTP Africa (Portugal): (-).

DTT Transmitters (trial planned)
Operator: TPA **Mux:** tbd **Txs:** ch31 (Luanda)

ANGUILLA (UK)

System: NTSC-M [A]

KREATIVE COMMUNICATIONS NETWORK (KCN) (Comm) P.O.Box 154, The Valley ☎ +1 264 5843519 🖷 +1 264 4973367 **E:** kcn@caribcable.com **W:** kcntv4.com **LP:** CEO: Carlton Pickering **Stns:** ZJF-TV3 ch3 (0.003kW), ZJF-TV9 ch9 (0.03kW).

ANTARCTICA

NB: No terrestrial TV station.

ANTIGUA & BARBUDA

System: NTSC-M [A]

ABS-TV (Gov) Public Information Division, Galstron's Palace, Old Parnham Road, St. John's ☎ +1 268 4620010 🖷 +1 268 4624442 **E:** absradio@caribmail.com **LP:** SM. Trevor Parker. **Tx:** ch10V (5kW).

ARGENTINA

Systems: # PAL-N [A] ⇩1 Sep 2019; # DVB-T (MPEG2); SBTVD (MPEG4) [A]

National Stations
TV PÚBLICA (CANAL 7) (Gov) Avenida Figueroa Alcorta 2977, 1425 Buenos Aires ☎+54 11 8026001 **W:** www.tvpublica.com.ar; canal7.com. ar **Txs:** ch7 (212kW) & relay txs. – **CANAL 9 (Comm)** Av. Dorrego 1708, 1414 Buenos Aires ☎ +54 11 50936838 **W:** www.canal9.com. ar **Txs:** ch9 (62kW) & relay txs. – **EL TRECE (Comm)** Lima 1261, Constitucion, Capital Federal ☎ +54 11 3050013 🖷 +54 11 3318559 **W:** www.eltrecetv.com.ar **Txs:** ch13 (116kW) & relay txs. – **TELEFE (Comm)** Pavón 2495, 1248 Buenos Aires ☎ +54 11 43080145 🖷 +54 11 4301522 **W:** www.telefe.com **Txs:** ch11 (180kW) & relay txs.

Local Stations not shown.

DTT Transmitters (SBTVD)
Licensee: Radio y Televisión Argentina **Mux 1:** Encuentro, Encuentro Movil, Paka Paka, TaTeTi **Txs:** ch22 (Buenos Aires) & netw. **Mux 2:** TV Pública HD, TV Pública Movil, Construir TV **Txs:** ch23 (Buenos Aires) & netw. **Mux 3:** Gol TV, Go TV Movil, V!vra, Suri TV, Vídeo Éxito **Txs:** ch24 (Buenos Aires) & netw. **Mux 4:** CN23, C5N, Telesur, 360 TV **Txs:** ch25 (Buenos Aires) & netw. – **Licensee:** Telefe **Mux:** Telefe, Telefe HD **Tx:** ch34 (Buenos Aires) & netw. – **Licensee:** El Trece **Mux:** El Trece **Tx:** ch33 (Buenos Aires) & netw. – **Licensee:** Canal 9 **Mux:** Canal 9, Canal9 HD,Canal 9 Movil **Txs:** ch35 (Buenos Aires) & netw. **Local licensees** not shown. Some local operators use DVB-T (MPEG2) and will migrate to SBTVD.

ARMENIA

Systems: # SECAM-D/K [R], PAL-D/K [R] ⇩2015; DVB-T [E] planned

National Stations
ARMENIAN PUBLIC TELEVISION (Pub) 26, G. Hovsepyan St., Nork 47, 0047 Yerevan ☎ +374 10 569574 🖷 +374 10 562460 **E:** info@ armtv.am **W:** www.armtv.am **LP:** CEO: Gagik Buniatyan **Txs:** Yerevan ch8 (5kW) & network. – **ARMENIA TV (Comm)** Yeghvard Highway N1, 0054 Yerevan ☎ +374 10 369344 🖷 +374 10 366852 **E:** info@ armeniatv.am **W:** www.armeniatv.am **Txs:** Yerevan ch25 (1.5kW) & network. – **h2 (Comm)** 3/1, Quarter # G-3, 0088 Yerevan ☎ +374 10 398831 🖷 +374 10 395640 **E:** lraber@tv.am **W:** www.tv.am **LP:** Dir:

Samvel Mayrapetyan **Txs:** Yerevan ch12 (5kW) & network.

Local Stations
Abovyan: 20, Hanrapetutyan St., Abovyan; ch24 (0.1kW). **Achin:** 1, Tumanyan St., Nor-Hachin; ch33 (0.1kW). **Ankyun Gumarats 3:** 2/26, Sarahart St., Alaverdy; ch37 (0.1kW). **Anna:** H.62,23 Ogostosi St., Artashat; ch30. **AR:** 5a, Tumanyan St., 0010 Yerevan; ch3 (5kW). **ArmenAkob TV:** Radiotun, 5, A. Manukyan St., Yerevan; ch31 (1kW). **Armenia TV:** 1, Yeghvard Highway, 0045 Yerevan; ch25 (1.5kW). **Armnews:** 2 floor,1 Yeghvard Highway St., Yerevan; ch63 (1kW). **DAR 21:** 4, Hrazdan Canyon St., Yerevan; ch27 (1.3kW) **Echmiadzin:** 5a, Araratyan St., Echmiadzin; ch29 (0.1kW). **Fortuna:** 21, Garegin Nzhdeh St., # 32, Stepanavan; ch29 (0.01kW). **Hai TV:** 78, Hanrapetutyan St., # 37, Yerevan; ch45 (1kW). **Hayrenik:** 13, Frunze St., Yerevan; ch21 (1kW). **Hrazdan:** Marzpetaran building, Hrazdan; ch12 (0.1kW). **Ijevan:** 5, Yerevanyan St., Ijevan; ch12 (0.1kW). **Knetron:** 2, Alikhanyan Yeghbayrneri St., Yerevan; ch37 (1.3kW). **Kyavar:** 20, Zoravar Andranik St., Gavar; ch27 (0.2kW). **Last:** 38/1a, Komitas St., Goris; ch38 (0.1kW). **Lori TV:** 10, Batumi St., Vanadzor; ch2 (0.2kW). **Lusalik:** Culture House, Karen Demirchyan Sq., Charentsavan; ch32 (0.05kW). **Mig TV:** 46a, Abeghyan St., Vanadzor; ch32 (0.1kW). **Mir TV:** 2 Arshakunyats Avenue, 6th floor, Yerevan; ch61 (1kW). **Narek TV:** 23, Ogostosi St., Abovyan; ch26 (0.15kW). **Nig-Aparan:** 1, Shahumyan, St., Aparan; ch10 (0.025kW). **Noy Hayastan:** 22, Yerevanyan St., hotel "Armavir", Armavir; ch32 (0.01kW). **Paradise:** 18, Abovyan St., Yerevan; ch23 (1kW). **Qamut:** 3, Kamo St., 1st floor, Noyemberyan; ch12 (0.015kW). **RTV:** 66, Myasnikyan St., Dilijan; ch2 (0.05kW). **Shant:** Vazgen Sargsyan St., TV Center, Gyumri; ch2 (0.1kW), Yerevan ch41 (1kW). **Shirak:** 248, Abovyan St., Gyumri; ch6. **Shoghakat:** 8, Hayk Hovsepyan Str., Yerevan; ch35 (1kW). **Sosi:** 8, R. Meliqyan St., Kapan; Kajaran ch22 (0.1kW), Kapan ch30 (0.2kW). **STV:** 15, Shahumyan St., Spitak; ch7 (0.01kW). **STV1:** 6, Sargis Sevanetsi St., Sevan; ch21 (0.1kW) **Syuni:** 5, Shirvanzade St., Sisian; ch27 (0.1kW). **Tashirk:** 4, Jahukyan St., Tashir; ch21 (0.035kW). **Tsayg TV:** 248, Abovyan St., 3rd floors, Gyumri; ch6 (0.1kW), ch28 (0.5kW) **TV5:** 1, Yoghvard Highway, Yerevan; ch39 (1kW). **Yerevan TV:** 2, Arshakunyats Avenue, Yerevan; ch51 (1kW). **Yerkir Media:** 94, Charents St., Yerevan; ch56 (2.5kW). **Zangak:** 43, Getapnya St., Martuni; ch25 (0.025kW).

Foreign TV Relays not shown.

ARUBA (Netherlands)

System: NTSC-M [A]

ARUBA BROADCASTING CO. N.V. (ATV) (Comm) P.O.Box 5040, Oranjestad ☎+297 5838150 🖷 +297 5838110 **W:** www.15atv.com **Tx:** Oranjestad ch15. – **CANAL 22 (Comm)** Oranjestad. **Tx:** Oranjestad ch22. – **TELE ARUBA (Comm)** P.O.Box 392, Oranjestad ☎ +297 5857302 🖷 + 297 5851683 **E:** info@telearuba.aw **W:** www.telearuba.aw **LP:** Dir: Toko Winklaar. **Tx:** Oranjestad ch13 (3kW H).

ASCENSION ISLAND (UK)

System: PAL-I [E]

BFBS-TV (British Mil) Chalfont Grove, Narcot Lane, Chalfont St Peter, Buckinghamshire, SL9 8TN, United Kingdom. **Txs: BFBS1:** Travellers Hill ch64, Cross Hill ch50 & ch61 **BFBS2:** Travellers Hill ch64, Cross Hill ch46.

AUSTRALIA

Systems: DVB-T (MPEG2) [VHF=AU, UHF=E]; † PAL-B/G [B=AU, G=E] ⇩31 Dec 2013

National Stations
AUSTRALIAN BROADCASTING CORPORATION (ABC) (Pub) ABC Ultimo Centre, 700 Harris St, Ultimo, NSW 2007 ☎ +61 2 83331500 🖷 +61 2 83335305 **E:** comments@your.abc.net.au **W:** www.abc.net.au **LP:** MD: Mark Scott **Chs:** ABC1, ABC2, ABC3, ABC News 24. – **SPECIAL BROADCASTING SERVICE (SBS) (Pub)** Locked bag 028, Crows Nest, NSW 1585 ☎+61 2 94302828 🖷 +61 2 94303700 **E:** comments@sbs.com.au **W:** www.sbs.com.au **LP:** MD: Michael Ebeid – **NATIONAL INDIGIOUS TELEVISION (NITV) (Pub)** 5 Parsons Street, Alice Springs, NT 0870 ☎ +61 8 89534763 🖷 +61 8 89534764 **E:** admin@nitv.org.au **W:** nitv.org.au.

Regional Stations
IMPARJA TELEVISION (Pub) P.O.Box 2924, Alice Springs, NT 0871 ☎ +61 89 523744, 🖷 +61 89 531014 **W:** www.imparja.com.

au – **NETWORK TEN (Comm)** P.O. Box 10, Lane Cove, NSW 2066 ☎ +61 2 8870222 **W:** www.ten.com.au; tencorporate.com.au (corporate) – **NINE NETWORK (Comm)** P.O.Box 27, Willoughby, NSW 2068 ☎ +61 2 99069999 +61 2 99582279 **W:** channelnine. ninemsn.com.au – **PRIME TELEVISION (Comm)** PO Box 878, Dickson, ACT 2602 ☎ +61 2 62423700 +61 2 62423764 **W:** www. primetv.com.au; www.primemedia.com.au (corporate) – **SEVEN NETWORK (Comm)** Television Centre, Mobbs Lane, Epping, NSW 2121 ☎ +61 2 8587777 +61 2 8587888 **W:** au.tv.yahoo.com; www.sevencorporate.com.au (corporate) – **SOUTHERN CROSS TELEVISION (Comm)** 70 Park Street, South Melbourne, VIC 3205 ☎ +61 3 92432100 +61 3 96825158 **W:** www.sctv.com.au – **WIN TELEVISION (Comm)** Television Ave, Mt St Thomas, Wollongong, NSW 2500 ☎ +61 2 42234199 +61 2 42273682 **W:** www.wintv.com.au.

Local Stations not shown.

DTT Transmitters
Licensee: ABC **Mux:** ABC1, ABC2/ABC4 Kids, ABC3, ABC News 24 ✲ ABC DigMusic, ABC Jazz – **Licensee:** Seven Network **Mux:** Seven Digital, 7Two, 7mate – **Licensee:** Nine Network **Mux:** Nine Digital, GEM, GO! – **Licensee:** Network Ten **Mux:** One HD, One Digital, Ten Digital, Eleven – **Licensee:** SBS **Mux:** SBS One, SBS One HD, SBS Two, SBS 3, SBS 4 ✲ SBS Radio 1, 2.

Location	ABC	7N	9N	N10	SBS	kW
Sydney	12	6	8	11	34	50

+ nationwide tx networks

Systems: DVB-T (MPEG2) [E], DVB-T2 (MPEG4) [E]

National Stations
ÖSTERREICHISCHER RUNDFUNK (ORF) (Pub) Würzburgasse 30, 1136 Wien ☎ +43 1 878780 **E:** presse@orf.at **W:** www.orf.at **LP:** DG: Dr.Alexander Wrabetz **Chs:** ORF eins, ORF2 incl. reg. stns: a) ORF Burgenland (Buchgraben 51, 7000 Eisenstadt), b) ORF Kärnten (Sponheimer Straße 13, 9020 Klagenfurt), c) ORF Niederösterreich (Radioplatz 1, 3109 St.Pölten), d) ORF Oberösterreich (Europaplatz 3, 4010 Linz), e) ORF Salzburg (Nonntaler Hauptstraße 49d, 5020 Salzburg), f) ORF Steiermark (Marburgerstr. 20, 8042 Graz), g) ORF Tirol (Rennweg 14, 6010 Innsbruck), h) ORF Vorarlberg (Höchsterstraße 38, 6850 Dornbirn), i) ORF Wien (Argentinierstr. 30a, 1040 Wien), ORF III – **ATV (Comm)** Aspernbrückengasse 2, 1020 Wien ☎ +43 1 213640 +43 1 21364999 **E:** atv@atv.at **W:** www.atv.at **LP:** CEO: Franz Prenner. – **PULS 4 (Comm)** Maria Jacobi Gasse 1, 1030 Wien ☎ +43 1 999880 +43 1 999888888 **E:** post@pulstv.at **W:** www.pulstv.at **LP:** CEO: Markus Breitenecker. – **SERVUS TV (Comm)** Ludwig-Bieringer-Platz 1, 5073 Wals-Himmelreich +43 662 84224428181 **E:** office@servustv.at **W:** www.servustv.com **LP:** CEO: Martin Blank.

Local Stations not shown (via Mux 3 txs).

DTT Transmitters (DVB-T/MPEG2 unless indicated otherwise)
Licensee Mux 1+2: Österreichische Sender GmbH & Co KG (ORS) Würzburggasse 309, 1136 Wien ☎ +43 1 8704012680 +43 1 874012773 **E:** office@ors.at **W:** www.ors.at **Mux 1:** ORF eins, ORF2 incl. reg. prgrs, ATV **Mux 2:** ORF III, ORF Sport Plus, 3sat, Puls 4, ServusTV. – **Licensee Mux 3:** Regional licensees (not shown). – **Licensee Mux 4+5:** ORS **Mux 4, 5 (DVB-T2/MPEG4):** tbd.

Location	M1	M2	M4*	M5*	kW
Bregenz (Pfänder)	24	21	31	-	2x56/32
Bruck a.d.M. (Mugel)	41	25	-	-	45/56
Freilassing (Högl)°	47V	-	-	-	20
Graz (Schöckl)	26	23	39V	-	2x48/20
Innsbruck (Patscherkofel)	23	27	37	-	2x63/25
Klagenfurt (Dobratsch)	24	30	54	-	80/76/10
Linz (Lichtenberg)	43	37	-	-	50
Mattersburg (Heuberg)	52V	-	36	-	20
Rechnitz (Hirschenstein)	43	23	36V	-	25/10/20
Salzburg (Gaisberg)	32	29	47V	-	2x40/13
St.Pölten (Jauerling)	31	21	-	-	50
Schärding (Schardenberg)	43	-	-	-	16
Schladming (Hauser Kaibling)	40	-	-	-	20
Viktring (Stifterkogel)	24	30	46	-	2x16/14
Waidhofen/Ybbs (Sonntagberg)	43	-	-	-	12
Weitra (Wachberg)	31	-	-	-	14
Wien (Kahlenberg)	24	34	36	-	2x63/16

+ sites with txs below 10kW. °) Tx located in Germany *) under construction

Systems: DVB-T (MPEG4) [E]; † PAL-D/K [R] ⇩2013

National Stations
AZƏRBAYCAN TELEVIZIYA VÄ RADIO VERISLÄRI (Gov) Mehdi Hüseyn St. 1, AZ 1011 Baki ☎ +994 12 4984720 +994 12 4972020 **E:** info@aztv.az **W:** www.aztv.az **LP:** Dir: Nizami Xudiyev. **Chs:** AzTV, Idman Azärbaycan, Mädäniyyät. – **ICTIMAI TELEVIZIYA (ITV) (Pub)** Serifzade St. 241, AZ 1012 Baki ☎ +994 12 4335525 +994 12 4302958 **E:** info@itv.az **W:** www.itv.az **LP:** Dir: Ismail Omarov. **Ch:** 1-ci kanal – **ANS-TV (Comm)** Matbuat ave. 28/11, Baki ☎ +994 12 4977267 +994 12 4989498 **E:** ans@ans. az **W:** www.ans.az – **AZAD AZƏRBAYCAN TV (ATV) (Comm)** A.Abbaszadä St. 8, AZ 1073 Baki ☎ +994 12 4974621 +994 12 4932522 **E:** atv@azadazerbaijan.com – **LIDER TV (Comm)** Ä.Äläkbärov St. 83/23, AZ 1141 Baki ☎ +994 12 4978899 +994 12 4978898 **E:** mail@lidermedia.az **W:** www.lidertv.com – **SPACE TV (Comm)** Hüseyn Cavid ave. 8, AZ 1073 Baki ☎ +994 12 4921256 +994 12 4927665 **E:** info@spacetv.az **W:** www.spacetv.az – **XÄZAR TV (Comm)** Atatürk ave. 28, AZ 1000 Baki ☎ +994 12 5621647 +994 12 5621623 **E:** info@xazar.tv **W:** www.xazar.tv.

Local Stations (all analogue)
Alternativ TV: Tagi Arani 6, AZ 2000 Gäncä; ch44. **Aygün TV:** Azadliq St 1, AZ 6200 Zaqatala; ch12. **Cänub TV:** Azad Mirzäyev St. 70, AZ 4200 Länkaran; ch29. **Dünya TV:** 10-su mikrorayon, AZ 5000 Sumgayit; ch42. **Kanal-S MMC:** Q.Qarayev St. 11, Säki; ch53. **Käpäz TV:** Ali Näzmi St. 4, AZ 2000 Gäncä; ch46. **Mingäçevir TV:** S.Vurgun St. 19, AZ 4500 Mingäçevir; ch12. **Qütb TV:** H.Aliyev pr. 156, AZ 4000 Quba; ch27. **Simurq M TV:** S. Mämädov St. 1, AZ 6000 Tovuz; ch45. **RTV:** H.Z.Tagiyev St. 10, Xaçmaz; ch43. **Xäyal TV:** F.Xan 133, AZ 4000 Quba; ch39. **Yevlax TV:** Zärdabi St. 1/6, Yevlax; ch57.

Foreign TV Relays not shown.

DTT Transmitters (under construction)
Operator: RITN Teleradio IB A.Abbaszadä 2, AZ 1073 Baki ☎ +994 12 4988066 +994 12 4988397 **E:** teleradio@azerin. com **W:** www.teleradio.rabita.az **Mux 1:** AzTV, Idman Azärbaycan, Mädäniyyät, 1-ci kanal **Mux 2:** multiprgr.

Location	M1	M2	kW
Baki	37	48	0.8/1.2

+ nationwide network (txs being installed at all main sites)

Mountainous Karabagh

LERNAYIN GHARABAGH HANRAYIN HERUSTARADIOYIN KERUTYUN Tigran Mets St. 23a, Stepanakert ☎ +374 47 945261 **E:** artv_or@ktsurf.net **W:** www.artsakh.tv **LP:** Chmn: Norek A. Gasparyan **Txs:** (-).

Systems: DVB-T (MPEG4) [E]

RTP AÇORES (Pub) Rua Ernesto do Canto 40, 9500-312 Ponta Delgada ☎ +351 296202700 +351 296202771 **E:** rtpa@rtp.pt **LP:** Dir: Antonio Mauricio Sousa.

DTT Transmitters
Licensee: Portugal Telecom **Mux:** RTP1, RTP2, RTP Açores, SIC, TVI **Txs:** ch47 (São Jorge), ch50 (Pico), ch61 (S.Miguel, Graciosa), ch64 (Faial), ch67 (Terceira, S.Maria, Flores, Carvo).

System: NTSC-M [A]

ZNS TV (Pub) P.O. Box N-1347, Nassau ☎ +1 242 5023800 +1 242 3226598 **E:** info@znsbahamas.com **W:** www.znsbahamas.com **LP:** GM: Edwin Lightbourn **Tx:** Nassau ch13 (50kW).

System: PAL-B/G [E]; DVB-T [E] planned

BAHRAIN TELEVISION (BTV) (Gov) P.O.Box 1075, Bahrain ☎ +973 17686000 +973 17681544 **Chs:** BTV (Arabic), Channel 55

(English) **Txs: BTV:** ch4 (5kW), ch44* (500kW), **Channel 55:** ch55 (0.03kW).*) tx to change to DTT.

Foreign TV Relay
BBC World News (UK): ch57 (1kW)

BANGLADESH

Systems: # PAL-B [E]; ⇩2015; DVB-T [E] planned

BANGLADESH TELEVISION (BTV) (Pub)▣ TV Bhaban, Rampura, Dhaka 1219 ☎ +880 2 8618606 🖷 +880 2 8312927 **L.P:** DG: M. Hamid. **Txs:** Dhaka ch9 (20kW) & netw. – **EKUSHEY TELEVISION (ETV) (Comm)**▣ Jahangir Tower, 10, Karwan Bazar, Dhaka 1215 ☎ +880 2 8126535 🖷 +880 2 8121270 **E:** info@ekushey-tv.com **W:** www.ekushey-tv.com **Txs:** Dhaka ch6 (20kW) & netw.

DTT Transmitters (trial planned)
Operator: BTV **Mux:** tbd **Txs:** Dhaka, Chittagong, Khulna (3.5kW)

BARBADOS

System: NTSC-M [A]

CARIBBEAN BROADCASTING CORP. (CBC-TV) (Gov)▣ P.O. Box 900, Pine Hill, Bridgetown ☎ +1 246 4675400 🖷 +1 246 4294795 **E:** sales@cbcbarbados.bb **W:** www.cbc.bb **L.P:** GM: Lars Soderstrom **Txs:** Bridgetown ch8 (60kW).

BELARUS

Systems: DVB-T (MPEG4) [E]; † SECAM-D/K [R] ⇩2015

National Stations
BELARUSKAJE TELEBACANNE (BT) (Gov)▣ Makaionka St. 9, 220807 Minsk ☎ +375 17 2634301 🖷 +375 17 2648182 **E:** pr@tvr.by **W:** www.tvr.by **Chs:** Belarus 1, Belarus 2, Regional prgrs. Also provides relays of NTV-Belarus. – **OBSHCHENATSIONALNOYE TELEVIDENIYE (ONT) (Gov)**▣ Kamunistycny St. 6, 220029 Minsk ☎ +375 17 2170424 **E:** w@ont.by **W:** www.ont.by **L.P:** Pres: Grigoriy L. Kisol. – **STOLICHNOYE TV (STV) (Gov)** ▣ Kamunistycny St. 6, 220029 Minsk ☎ +375 17 2906272 🖷 +375 17 2906432 **E:** reklama@ctv.by **W:** www.ctv.by.

Local Stations (all Comm, all analogue)
Bug TV: Brest; ch9 (0.1kW). **Inteks:** Baranavicy; ch23. **Nireja:** Homiel; ch35 (0.1kW). **Njuans TV:** Zlobin; ch29 (0.1kW). **MPKET:** Kobrin; ch25. **Ranak:** Svetlahorsk; ch29. **Skif TV:** Babrujsk ch3, Viciebsk; ch48 (0.1kW), Palack ch21 (0.1kW), Vorša ch34 (0.1kW). **STK:** Salihorsk; ch30 (0.1kW). **Televid:** Recica; ch12. **TRK Pinsk:** Pinsk; ch39. **TV2:** Mahilioú; Palykovicy ch2 (0.1kW). **Varjag:** Pinsk; ch7 (0.2kW). **1-horadski:** Homiel; ch1. **12-iy kanal:** Barysaú; ch12 (0.5kW).

DTT Transmitters
Operator: Ministry of Communications **Mux:** Belarus 1 (incl. reg prgrs), Belarus 2, ONT, NTV-Belarus, RTR-Belarus, STV, Mir ⌘ Belaruskaje R. 1, 2, R. Stalica, Radyus FM

Location	Ch	kW	Location	Ch	kW
Svislac	21	2	Miadziel	44	2
Vorša	25	1	St. Darohi	44	2
Kapyl	34	2	Trokeniki	44	0.2
Salihorsk	34	2	Smetanicy	46	1
Baranavicy	38	2	Babrujsk	47	2
Berazino	41	1	Minsk	48	1
Krupski	41	2	Heraniony	49	2
Luki	41	1	Mahiliou	49	1
Slonim	41	2	Mscislaúl	49	2
Hrodna	42	1	Kastjukovicy	50	1
Brahin	43	2	Homiel	51	1
Braslaú	43	1	Rakitnica	51	2
Bycycha	43	2	Pinsk	56	1
Šarkaúšcyna	43	0.2	Drahicyn	57	2
Viciebsk	43	0.2	Zlobin	57	2
Zaščobye	43	1	Asveja	61	1

Local licensee: Kosmos TV ▣ Minsk **Mux 1+2✪:** multiprgr **Txs:**

Mux 1: ch32 (Minsk), **Mux 2:** ch57 (Minsk).

BELGIUM

System: DVB-T2 (MPEG4) [E]

Flanders

National Station
VLAAMSE RADIO EN TELEVISIEOMROEP (VRT) (Pub)▣ A. Reyerslaan 52, 1043 Brussel ☎ +32 2 7413111 🖷 +32 2 7349351 **E:** info@vrt.be **W:** www.vrt.be **L.P:** CEO: Sandra de Preter **Chs:** (in Flemish) Één, Één +, Canvas/Ketnet, Canvas+/Ketnet+.

DTT Transmitters
Operator: Norkring België ▣ Jules Bordetlaan 160, 1140 Evere ☎ +32 2 3639900 🖷 +32 2 7454537 **E:** info@norkring.be **W:** www.norkring.be **Mux 1:** Één, Één+, Canvas/Ketnet, Canvas+/Ketnet+ ⌘ VRT Radio 1, 2 Carrousel, Klara, Klara continuo, Studio Brussel, MNM, NMN Hits, Sporza, nieuws+. **Mux 2-4✪:** tbd.

Location	M1	M2	M3	M4	kW
Antwerpen	25V	-	-	-	10
Brussel	22V	-	-	-	20
Egem	22V	40V	43V	46V	20
Genk	25V	-	-	-	20
Gent	22	-	-	-	7
Sint-Peeters-Leeuw	22V	-	-	-	20
Schoten	25V	-	-	-	20
Veltem	22V	40V	43V	46V	20

Wallonia

National Stations
RADIO TÉLÉVISION BELGE DE LA COMMUNAUTÉ FRANÇAISE (RTBF) (Pub)▣ Cité Reyers - Local 11M31, Boulevard A. Reyers 52, 1044 Bruxelles ☎ +32 2 7372111 🖷 +32 2 7374210 **W:** www.rtbf.be **L.P:** Dir TV: François Tron **Chs:** (in French) La une, La deux, La troix. – **BELGISCHER RUNDFUNK (BRF) (Pub)**▣ Kehrweg 11, 4700 Eupen ☎ +32 87 591111 🖷 +32 87 591199 **E:** info@brf.be **W:** www.brf.be **L.P:** Dir: Arthur Spoden. **Ch:** (News-magazine in German) Blickpunkt.

DTT Transmitters
Operator: RTBF **Mux:** La Une, La Deux, La Troix, Euronews (via Liège tx: Euronews/BRF Blickpunkt) ⌘ RTBF La Première, Vivacité, Musiq3, Classic 21, Pure FM, BRF.

Location	Ch	kW	Location	Ch	kW
Liège	45	100	Tournai	56V	40
Anderlues	56	80	Wavre	56	80
Bruxelles	56	2	Léglise	66	100
Namur	56	5	Marche-en-Famene	66	12.5
Profondville	56	50			

+ txs below 1kW

Local Licensees: Be TV ▣ chaussée de Louvain 656, 1030 Bruxelles ☎ +32 2 7304050 🖷 +32 2 7300379 **E:** abonnesweb@betv.be **W:** www.betv.be **Mux✪:** Be 1, Be Ciné, Be Séries **Tx:** ch55V (Bruxelles 2kW). – Télé Bruxelles (TLB) ▣ rue Gabrielle Petit 32/34, 1080 Bruxelles ☎ +32 2 4212121 🖷 +32 2 4212122 **E:** contact@telebruxelles.net **W:** www.telebruxelles.net **Mux:** TLB **Tx:** ch60 (Bruxelles 0.5kW).

BELIZE

Systems: NTSC-M [A]. BFBS-TV: DVB-T (MPEG4) [E]

BELIZE BROADCASTING NETWORK (Comm) ▣ Belize City ☎ +501 2232008 **E:** ramon@bbn9.com **W:** www.bbn9.com **L.P:** Chmn/CEO: Ramon Vasquez **Tx:** ch9. – **CHANNEL 5 (Comm)**▣ P.O.Box 679, Belize City ☎ +501 2277781 🖷 +501 2274936 **E:** gbtz@btl.net **W:** edition.channel5belize.com **Tx:** ch5. – **CHANNEL 7 (Comm)**▣ P.O.Box 89, Belize City ☎ +501 2277246 🖷 +501 2275040 **E:** tvseven@btl.net **W:** www.7newsbelize.com **Tx:** ch7. – **TBN (Rlg)** ▣ Belize City **Tx:** ch13.

Foreign Military Station
BFBS-TV (British Mil) ▣ BFBS Belize, Airport Camp, BFPO 12, United Kingdom. **Mux✪:** BFBS1, BFBS2, BFBS3 Kids, BFBS4, Sky Sports 1, Sky Sport 2, Sky News ⌘ BFBS R. 1+2, BFBS Belize **Tx:** ch27 (Price Barracks).

BENIN

System: SECAM-K1 [VHF=K, UHF=E]

National Station
ORTB - TÉLÉVISION NATIONALE (Gov) ✉ BP 366, Cotonou ☎+229 21301096 📠 +229 21301437 **E:** ortb@intnet.bj **W:** www.ortb.info **LP:** Dir: Pierette Amoussou **Txs:** Cotonou (Kandi) ch5 (20kW) & relay txs. **LC2 (Comm)** ✉ 05 BP 427 Cotonou. ☎+229 21334749 📠 +229 21334675 **E:** lc2@intnet.bj **W:** lc2international.tv **Txs:** Cotonou (Kandi) ch8 & relay txs.

Local Stations
Canal 3: 02 BP 371, Cotonou; ch42. **Carrefour TV:** 01BP 440 Bohicon; ch67. **Golfe TV:** 06 BP 1624, Cotonou; ch38. **Imalè Africa:** Puerto-Novo; ch68. **LC2:** 05 BP 427, Cotonou; ch44.

BERMUDA (UK)

Systems: NTSC-M [A]; DVB-T [A]

BERMUDA BROADCASTING CO. LTD. (Gov) ✉ P.O.Box HM452, Hamilton ☎ +1 441 2952828 📠 +1 441 2954282 **LP:** Chmn: Fernance B. Perry **Chs:** ZFB-TV (ABC affiliate), ZBM-TV (CBS affiliate) **Txs:** ZFB-TV: Hamilton ch7 (32.5kW); ZBM-TV: Hamilton ch9 (17.5kW) – **VSB-TV (Comm)** ✉ P.O.Box HM 1450, Hamilton HM FX ☎ +1 441 2761111 📠 +1 441 2923375 **W:** www.vsbbermuda.com **Tx:** Hamilton ch11 (NBC affiliate, also relays BBC World News).

DTT Transmitters
Licensee: The World in Wireless Ltd. **W:** www.wow.bm **Mux:** multiprgr **Tx:** (-).

BHUTAN

System: PAL-B/G [E]

BHUTAN BROADCASTING SERVICE (BBS) (Pub) ✉ P.O.Box 101, Thimphu ☎ +975 2 323580 📠 +975 2 323073 **E:** md@bbs.bt **W:** www. bbs.bt **LP:** CEO: Thinley Dorji **Chs:** BBS 1, BBS 2 **Txs:** **BBS 1:** Thimpu ch5 (1kW) & relay txs. **BBS 2:** (-).

BOLIVIA

Systems: SBTVD (MPEG4) [A]; † NTSC-M [A]

National Stations
TELEVISIÓN BOLIVIANA (TVB) (Gov) ✉ Av. Camacho 1485, Ed. La Urbana, La Paz ☎ +591 2 2203404 📠 +591 2 2203015 **W:** www. boliviatv.bo **Txs:** La Paz ªch7 & relay txs. – **ATB (ASOCIACIÓN TELEVISIÓN BOLIVIANO) (Comm)** ✉ Av. Argentina 2057, La Paz ☎ +591 2 2229922 📠 +591 2 227935 **E:** atbcbb@atb.com.bo **W:** www.atb. com.bo **Tx:** La Paz ªch9 & relay txs. – **RED BOLIVISIÓN (Comm)** ✉ Av Santa Cruz esq, Tres pasos al frente, Santa Cruz ☎ +591 3 3524544 📠 +591 3 3530707 **W:** www.redbolivision.tv.bo **Tx:** La Paz ªch5 & relay txs. – **RED UNO DE BOLIVIA (Comm)** ✉ Romecin Campos 592, Sopocachi, 14976 La Paz ☎ +591 2 2421111 📠 +591 2 2415101 **E:** notivision@ reduno.com.bo **W:** www.reduno.com.bo **Tx:** La Paz ªch11 & relay txs. – **TELEVISIÓN UNIVERSITARIA (Educ)** ✉ Av. 6 de Agosto No. 2170, 13383 La Paz ☎ +591 2 359297 📠 +591 2 359491 **E:** canal13@umsa. bo **W:** tvu.umsa.bo. **Txs:** La Paz ªch13 (10kW) & relay txs. – **UNITEL (UNIVERSAL DE TELEVISIÓN) (Comm)** ✉ A83 La Paz ☎ +591 2 359297 📠 +591 2 359491 **W:** www.unitel.tv. **Txs:** La Paz ch2 (10kW) & relay txs. (ª=analogue)

Local Stations not shown.

BONAIRE (Netherlands)

NB: No terrestrial TV station.

BOSNIA & HERZEGOVINA

Systems: # PAL-B/G [E]; DVB-T (MPEG4) [E] planned

National (Federal) Station
RADIO TELEVIZIJA BOSNE I HERCEGOVINE (BHRT) (Pub) ✉ Bulevar Meše Selimovica 12, 71000 Sarajevo ☎+387 33 455124 📠 +387 33 461523 **E:** sptrgov@bhrt.ba **W:** www.bhrt.ba **LP:** DG:

Muhamed Bakarevic **Ch:** BHT.

Location	Ch	Location	Ch
Ilincica	7	H.Brdo	21
Hum	8	Brekovica	23
V. Gomila	10	Fortica	26
C.Brdo	11	Kozara	27
Vlašic	11	Leotar	37
Lisac	12	Lisin	47
+ repeaters			

Federacija Bosna i Hercegovina

National Station
FTV (Pub) ✉ Bulevar Meše Selimovica 12, 71000 Sarajevo ☎ +387 33 461539 📠 +387 33 461539 **E:** press@rtvfbih.ba **W:** www.rtvfbih.ba **LP:** Dir TV: Vladimir Bilic.

Location	Ch	Location	Ch
Fortica	7	V.Gomila	47
Brekovica	21	Ilincica	51
Vlašic	29	Hum	52
Lisac	39	Lisin	54
H.Brdo	43		
+ repeaters			

Local Stations not shown.

Republika Srpska

National Station
RADIO TELEVIZIJA REPUBLIKE SRPSKE (RTRS) (Pub) ✉ ul. Kralja Petra I Karadordevica 129, 78000 Banja Luka ☎ +387 51 301660 **E:** tv@rtrs.tv **W:** www.rtrs.tv **LP:** DG: Dragan Davidovic. **Txs:** Udrigovo ch5, Kmur ch6, Kozara ch6, Banja Luka I ch10, Leotar I ch10, Duge Njive ch12, Trebevic I ch12, Banja Luka II ch31, Trebevic II ch33, Leotar II ch37.

Local Stations not shown.

BOTSWANA

Systems: # PAL-I [E]; DVB-T2 [E] planned

BOTSWANA TV (BTV) (Gov) ✉ P.O.Box 0060, Gaborone ☎ +267 3658000 📠 +267 3900051 **E:** marketing@btv.gov.bw **W:** www.btv.gov. bw **LP:** GM: Molefhe Sejoe. **Txs:** (-). – **E-BOTSWANA (Comm)** ✉ P.O.Box 921, Gaborone **LP:** GM: David Coles; **Txs:** Gaborone ch23 & relay txs.

BRAZIL

Systems: SBTVD (MPEG4) [A]; † PAL-M [A] ↓31 Dec 2013

National Stations
TV BRAZIL (BTV) ✉ An. Gomes Freire 474, Centro, 20231-010 Rio de Janeiro, RJ ☎ +55 21 21176208 **E:** contacto@tvbrasil.org.br **W:** tvbrasil.ebc.com.br – **CENTRAL NACIONAL DE TELEVISÃO (CNT) (Comm)** ✉ Rua Francisco Caron 29, Pilarzinho, 82120-200 Curitiba, PR ☎ +55 41 3383377 📠 +55 41 3384878 **E:** cnt@cnt.com.br **W:** www. cnt.com.br – **REDE BRASIL DE TELEVISÃO (RBTV) (Comm)** ✉ Alameda dos Uapés, 313 - Saúde, 04067-030 São Paulo, SP **W:** www. rbtv.com.br – **REDE CULTURA (Comm)** ✉ Rua Vladimir Herzog 75, Agua Branca, SP 05036-900 São Paulo ☎ +55 11 38743122 📠 +55 11 36112014 **E:** dirprog@tvcultura.com.br **W:** tvcultura.cmais.com.br **LP:** Pres: Antonio Carlos Caruso-Ronca. – **REDE GLOBO (Comm)** ✉ Rua Lopes Quintas 303, Jardim Botanico, 22460-010 Rio de Janeiro, RJ ☎ +55 21 25402000 📠 +55 21 22942092 **E:** wm@redeglobo.com. br **W:** redeglobo.globo.com – **REDE RECORD (Comm)** ✉ Rua da Várzea 240, 01140-080 São Paulo, SP ☎ +55 11 36604761 📠 +55 11 36604756 **E:** tvrecord@rederecord.com.br **W:** rederecord.r7.com – **SISTEMA BRASILEIRO DE TELEVISÃO (SBT) (Comm)** ✉ Av. das Comunicações 4, Vila Jaraguá, 06278-905 Osasco, SP ☎ +55 11 70873000 📠 +55 11 70873509 **E:** marketing@sbt.com.br **W:** www. sbt.com.br.

Local Stations not shown.

DTT Transmitters
Nationwide & local multiprgr DTT networks under construction.

BRITISH INDIAN OCEAN TERRITORY

NB: No terrestrial TV stations.

BRUNEI

Systems: # PAL-B [E] ⇩2014; DVB-T [E]

RADIO TELEVISYEN BRUNEI (RTB) (Gov) ✒ Bandar Seri Begawan, BS8610, Negara ☎ +673 2243111 🖷 +673 2220884 **E:** rtbdir@rtb.gov.bn **W:** www.rtb.gov.bn **L.P:** Dir: Awang Haji Mohamad Yunos bin Haji Bolhassan **Chs:** RTB1, RTB2, RTB3, RTB3 HD, RTB4 International, RTB5 **Txs: RTB1:** Bt. Subok ch5 (10kW H), Bt. Andulau ch8 (20kW H); **RTB2:** Subok ch10, Kuala Belait ch11.

DTT Transmitters (under construction)
Operator: RTB **Mux:** RTB1, RTB2, RTB3, RTB3 HD, RTB4 International, RTB5 **Txs:** ch(-) (Bt. Subok 5kW, Bt. Andulau)

BULGARIA

Systems: # PAL-D/K [R] ⇩1 Jan 2015; DVB-T (MPEG4) [E]

National Stations
BALGARSKA NATSIONALNA TELEVIZIYA (BNT) (Pub) ✒ ul. San Stefano 29, 1504 Sofiya ☎ +359 2 9661149 🖷 +359 2 9634045 **E:** press@bnt.bg **W:** www.bnt.bg **L.P:** DG: Vyara Ankova **Chs (terr.):** BNT1 BNT2 & reg. studios. – **bTV (Comm)** ✒ Natsionalen Dvorets na Kulturata, 1463 Sofiya ☎ +359 2 9176800 🖷 +359 2 9521483 **E:** pr@btv.bg **W:** www.btv.bg – **NOVA TELEVIZIYA (Comm)** ✒ bul. N. Vabtsarov 55, Expo 2000 P.K., 1507 Sofiya ☎ +359 2 9151200 **E:** office@novatv.bg **W:** www.novatv.bg

Location	BNT1	BNT2	bTV	Nova TV	kW
Belogradchik	12	-	30	46	10/20/10
Burgas	7	32	26	38	20/0.1/40/40
Dobrich	12	35	28	51	5/-/2x10
Gotse Delchev	9	-	25	42	10/20/20
Kardzhali	9	49	34	53	10/0.1/20/20
Kyustendil	10	-	32	51	5/2x20
Montana	9	-	26	-	10/5
Ruse	-	40	-	44	0.2/10
Sliven	12	-	31	48	10/2x20
Smolyan	6	50	38	-	5/0.05/10
Sofiya	7	43	29	36	10/1/2x10
Shumen	5	-	39	-	50/40
Varna	9	21	33	50	5/0.5/5/10
Vrh Botev	11	-	25	-	20/40

+ sites with txs below 5kW.
BBT (Comm) ✒ bul. "Tsarskoe shose" 113-A, 1784 Sofiya ☎ +359 2 8159701 🖷 +359 2 8159707 **E:** office@bbt.tv **W:** www.bbt.tv **Txs:** Sofiya ch55 (1kW) & network. – **BULGARIA ON AIR (Comm)** ✒ bul. Bryuksel 1, 1000 Sofiya ☎ +359 2 4484070 **E:** office@bulgarionair.bg **W:** www.bulgariaonair.bg **Txs:** network. – **TV7 (Comm)** ✒ bul. Dzheyms Baucher 100, Sofiya ☎ +359 2 8162740 🖷 +359 2 8162714 **E:** tv7@tv7.bg **W:** www.tv7.bg **Txs:** Sofiya ch53 (1kW) & network.

Local Stations
Kanal 0: ul. Odrin 15, etazh 2, 1800 Burgas; ch28 (0.1kW). **Rekording TV:** bul. Hakovski 9, 6300 Haskovo; ch51 (0.5kW). **SKAT+:** 8200 Pomorie; ch41. **TV Cherno More:** kv. Chayka, do blok 23, 9005 Varna; Shabla ch31 (0.25kW), Beloslav ch48 (0.01kW), Varna ch48 (0.1kW). **TV Karnobat:** ul. Asparuh 5, Hotel Karnobat, etazh 8, 8400 Karnobat; ch52 (0.01kW). **TV Rodopi:** Kompleks Vazrozhdenci, blok 14, etaz 15, 6600 Kardzhali; ch21 (0.03kW). **TV Sopot:** ul. Osmi mart 10, 4330 Sopot; ch35. **TV Shumen:** ul. Sedinenie 105, 9700 Shumen; Divdyadovo ch47, Shumen ch52 (0.1kW). **TV Varna:** bul. Slivnitsa 2, 9000 Varna; ch64 (0.5kW). **The Voice:** bul. Cherni vrah 43, 1407 Sofiya; ch53 (1kW).

DTT Transmitters (under construction)
Licensee Mux 1+2: NURTS Bulgaria ✒ bul. P. Yavorov 2, 1164 Sofiya **W:** www.nurts.bg **Mux 1: Mux 2:** bTV, TV7 **Licensee Mux 3:** Hannu Pro Bulgaria ✒ bul. Shipchenski prohod 63, 1574 Sofiya ☎ +359 2 8707350 🖷 +359 2 8077114 **Mux 3:** BNT1, BNT2 & regional stns, BNT Svyat ⌘ Horizont, Hristo Botev .

Location	M1	M2	M3
Belogradchik	32	49	53
Blagoevgrad	31	29	33
Burgas	42	49	55
Dobrich	22	29	64
Gabrovo	26	49	-
Kardzhali	26	42	48
Karlovo	25	35	-
Kyustendil	23	40	52
Pleven	41	51	57
Plovdiv	25	35	41
Ruse	26	49	64
Sliven	22	37	-
Smolyan	34	49	58
Sofiya	23	40	52
St. Zagora	22	37	64
Shumen	28	40	51
Varna	22	29	64
Vidin	32	49	53

+ translators
NB. Local test muxes not shown.

BURKINA FASO

System: SECAM-K1 [VHF=K, UHF=E]

National Station
RTB TV (Gov) ✒ 01 BP 2530, Ouagadougou 01 ☎ +226 50318353 🖷 +226 50318393 **E:** television@rtb.bf **W:** tv.rtb.bf **L.P:** Dir: Pascal Yemboini Thiombiano **Txs:** Ouagadougou ch4 (10kW H) & relay txs.

Local Stations
Canal Viim Koeega (Rlg): 01 BP 108, Ouagadougou 01; ch24. **Canal 3 (Comm):** 11 BP 340, Ouagadougou 11; ch43.

BURUNDI

System: SECAM-K1 [VHF=K, UHF=E]

TÉLÉVISION NATIONALE DU BURUNDI (Gov) ✒ RP 1900, Bujumbura ☎ +257 2222476U 🖷 +257 22244877 **E:** rtnb@cbinf.com **W:** www.rtnb.bi **L.P:** Dir: Nestor Bankumukunzi **Tx:** Bujumbara ch25 (4kW) & relay txs.

CAMBODIA

Systems: # PAL-B/G [E] ⇩2015; DVB-T [E]

National Stations
NATIONAL TV OF CAMBODIA (TVK) (Gov) ✒ 62 Preah Monivong Boulevard, Sangkat Sras Chork, Khan Daun Penh, Phnon Penh 12202 ☎ +855 23 724149 🖷 +855 23 426407 **E:** tvk@camnet.gov.kh **W:** www.tvk.gov.kh **L.P:** DG: Kem Gunnawadh **Txs:** Phnom Penh ch7 (10kW) & relay txs. – **BAYON TV (Comm)** ✒ National Road No 1, Boeung Snoa, Chbar Ampeou, Phnom Penh 12357 ☎ +855 23 363695 🖷 +855 23 726619 **E:** bayontv@camnet.gov.kh **W:** www.bayontv.com.kh **Txs:** Phnom Penh ch27 (250kW) & relay txs. – **CAMBODIAN TV NETWORK (CTN) (Comm)** ✒ National Highway 5, Phum Krol Ko, Sangkat Kilomet 6, Khan Russei Keo, Phnom Penh 12104 ☎ +855 12 800800 🖷 +855 12 801801 **E:** wmaster@ctncambodia.com **W:** www.ctn.com.kh **Chs:** CTN, MyTV **Txs: CTN:** Phnom Penh ch21 & relays txs; **MyTV:** Phnom Phenh ch29. – **TV3 (Comm)** ✒ 2 Bvd Confédération de la Russie (Rue 112), Sangat Monorom, Khan 7 Makra, Phnom Penh ☎ 🖷 +855 23 360800 **W:** www.tv3.com.kh **Txs:** Phnom Penh ch5 (10kW) & relay txs. – **TV FARK (Comm)** ✒ rue 169, Borei Keila, Phnom Penh 12253 ☎ +855 23 366061 🖷 +855 23 366063 **W:** www.ch5cambodia.com **Txs:** Phnom Penh ch5 (10kW) & relay txs.

Local Stations
Apsara TV (Comm): 69, rue 57, Sangat Beung Keng Kang 1, Khan Chamcarmon, Phnom Penh; ch11 (10kW). **CTV9 (Comm):** 18 rue 562, Toul Kok, Phnom Penh 12151; ch9 (10kW).

Foreign TV Relays
TV5 Monde Asie (France): Phnom Penh ch23. **VTV1 (Vietnam):** Phnom Penh ch25.

DTT Transmitters
Licensee: PPCTV **W:** www.ppctv.com.kh **Mux:** multiprgr **Tx:** (-).

CAMEROON

System: PAL-B/G [E]

National Stations
CAMEROON RADIO AND TELEVISION (CRTV) (Gov) ✒ BP 1634, Yaoundé ☎ +237 2214088 🖷 +237 2204340 **E:** infos@crtv.cm **W:** www.crtv.cm **L.P:** DG: Amadou Vamoulké **Txs:** Yaoundé ch5 (150kW)

& relay txs. – **SPECTRUM TÉLÉVISION (Comm)** BP 4883, Douala ☎ +237 3433045 ▤ +237 3433048 **E:** spectrum1@camnet.cm **W:** www.stvgroup.com **Chs:** STV1, SVT2 **Txs: STV1:** Douala ch2 (5kW) & relay txs, **STV 2:** (-).

Local Stations (all Comm)
Equinoxe Télévision (E.TV): BP 212, Douala; tx: (-). **RTV Lumière:** Yaoundé; tx: (-). **TV Max:** BP 4527, Douala; tx: (-).

CANADA

Systems: ATSC [A]; † NTSC-M [A] (small markets only)

National Networks (ᵃ=analogue, to be replaced by DTT)
CANADIAN BROADCASTING CORP. (CBC) (Pub) 181 Queen St, Box 3220 Stn C, Ottawa ON K1Y 1E4 ☎ +1 613 2886000 **W:** www.cbc.radio-canada.ca **LP:** Pres/CEO: Hubert T. Lacroix. **Chs:** National English and French networks. **Stations:** CBAT Fredericton NB ch31 (7.36kW), CBCT Charlottetown PE ch13 (13kW), CBET Windsor ON ch9 (26kW), CBHT Halifax NS ch39 (157.54kW), CBIT Sydney NS ch39 (157.54kW), CBKST Saskatoon SK ᵃch11 (325kW), CBKT Regina SK ch9 (60kW), CBLT Toronto ON ch20 (106.9kW), CBMT Montréal PQ ch21 (107kW), CBNT St. John's NF ch8 (14.54kW), CBOT Ottawa ON ch25 (165kW), CBRT Calgary AB ch21 (23.5kW), CBUT Vancouver BC ch43 (103.34kW), CBWT Winnipeg MB ᵃch6 (100kW), CBXT Edmonton AB ch42 (131.71kW) & relay txs. NB: Stns identify as 'CBC'. **French Network (Télévision de Radio-Canada):** 1400 René-Lévesque Boul. E, Box 6000, Montréal PQ H3C 3A8 ☎ +1 514 5976000 **W:** www.radio-canada.ca **LP:** Vice Pres. (French Networks): Sylvain Lafrance. **Stations:** CBAFT Moncton NB ch11 (17.65kW), CBFT Montréal PQ ch19 (230kW), CBKFT Regina SK ch13 (27.1kW), CBOFT Ottawa ON ch9 (3.5kW), CBVT Québec PQ ch25 (2.45kW), CBUFT Vancouver BC ch26 (27.52kW), CBWFT Winnipeg MB ᵃch3 (59kW), CBXFT Edmonton AB ch47 (15.18kW) & relay txs. NB: Stns identify as 'Radio-Canada'. – **CTV TELEVISION NETWORK (Comm)** (Div. of Bell Media) 9 Channel Nine Court, Scarborough ON M1S 4B5 ☎ +1 416 3325000 ▤ +1 416 3325283 **E:** bellmediapr@bellmedia.ca **W:** www.ctv.ca **LP:** Pres (Bell Media): Kevin Crull. **Stations:** CFCF Montréal QC ch12 10.6kW), CFCN Calgary AB ch29 (220kW), CFCN-5 Lethbridge AB ch13 (139kW), CFQC Saskatoon SK ch8 (13kW), CFPL London ON ch10 (45kW), CFRN Edmonton AB ch12 (25kW), CFTO Toronto ON ch9 (10.2kW), CHBX Sault Ste. Marie ON ᵃch2 (100kW), CHRO Ottawa/Pembroke ON ᵃch5 (100kW), CHWI Windsor ON ch16 (3.4kW), CICC Yorkton SK ᵃch10 (56kW), CICI Sudbury ON ᵃch5 (100kW), CIPA Prince Albert SK ᵃch9 (325kW), CITO Timmins ON ᵃch3 (100kW), CIVI Victoria BC ch23 (1.5kW), CIVT Vancouver BC ch32 (33W), CJCB Sydney NS ᵃch4 (180kW), CJCH Halifax NS ch48 (400kW), CJOH Ottawa ON ch13 (19kW), CKCK Regina SK ch8 (23kW), CKCO Kitchener ON ch13 (12kW), CKCW Moncton NB ch29 (390kW), CKLT St. John NB ch9 (7.6kW), CKNY North Bay ON ᵃch10 (132.6kW), CKVR Barrie ON ch10 (11kW), CKY Winnipeg MB ch7 (24kW) & smaller txs. NB: Stns identify 'CTV' or 'CTV TWO'. – **GLOBAL TV NETWORK (Comm)** (Div. of Shaw Media Inc.) 121 Bloor St. East, Toronto, ON M4W 3M5 ☎ +1 416 0671174 **E:** corporate.inquiries@shawmedia.ca **W:** www.globaltv.com **LP:** Pres (Shaw Media): Paul Robertson. **Stations:** CFRE Regina SK ch11 (17.3kW), CFSK Saskatoon SK ch42 (30kW), CHAN Vancouver BC ch22 (40kW, CHBC Kelowna BC ᵃch2 (3.7kW), CICT Calgary AB ch41 (50kW), CIHF Halifax/Dartmouth NS ch8 (1kW), CIHF-2 St. John NB ch12 (6kW), CIII Toronto ON ch41 (100kW), CISA Lethbridge AB ch17 (19.7kW), CITV Edmonton AB ch13 (25kW), CKMI Québec PQ ch15 (8kW), CKMI-1 Montréal/Sherbrooke PQ ch11 (1kW), CKND Winnipeg MB ch40 (25.1kW) & relay txs. NB: Stns identify as 'Global'.

Major Regional Networks (ᵃ=analogue)
SOCIÉTÉ DE TÉLÉDIFFUSION DU QUEBEC (TÉLÉ-QUÉBEC) (Pub) 1000 rue Fullum, Montréal PQ H2K 3L7 ☎ +1 514 5212424 ▤ +1 514 5255511 **W:** www.telequebec.tv **LP:** CEO: Michèle Fortin. **Stations (French):** CIVM Montréal QC ch26 (889.5kW) & relay txs (QC only). – **TVO (Pub)** Box 200 Stn Q, Toronto ON M4T 2T1 ☎ +1 416 4842600 ▤ +1 416 4847771 **W:** www.tvo.org **LP:** CEO: Lisa de Wilde. **Stations:** CICA Toronto ON ch19 (107kW) & relay txs (ON only). – **CHANNEL ZERO INC. (Comm)** Box 6143 Stn A, Toronto ON M5W 1P6 ☎ +1 416 4921595 ▤ +1 416 4929539 **W:** www.tvchannelzero.com **LP:** Pres/CEO: Romen Podzhyhun. **Stations:** CHCH Hamilton ON ch11 (325kW), CJNT Montréal PQ ch49 (4kW) – **CORUS ENTERTAINMENT INC. (Comm)** 630-3rd Ave SW Suite 501, Calgary AB T2P 4L4 ☎+1 403 4444244 ▤ +1 403 4444242 **W:** www.corusent.com **LP:** Pres/CEO: John M. Cassaday. **Stations:** CKWS (CBC affiliate) Kingston ON ᵃch11 (325kW), CHEX (CBC affiliate) Peterborough ON ᵃch12 (185kW) & relay

txs (ON only). – **GROUPE TVA INC. (Comm)** (Div. of Québecor Media) 1600 boul. de Maisonneuve Est, Montréal PQ H2L 4P2☎ +1 514 5269251 **W:** tva.canoe.com **L.P:** Pres/CEO: Pierre Dion. **Stations (English):** CKXT Toronto ON ch66 (3kW) (F.pl ch40) (rebroadcasting Sun News); **Stations (French):** CFCM Québec QC ch17 (210kW), CFEM Rouyn-Noranda QC ch13 (10.5kW), CFER Rimouski QC ᵃch11 (325kW), CFTM Montréal QC ch10 (11kW), CHAU Carleton-sur-Mer QC ᵃch5 (81.7kW), CHEM Trois-Rivières QC ch8 (325kW), CHLT Sherbrooke QC ch7 (300kW), CHOT Hull QC ch40 (111.5kW), CIMT Rivière-du-Loup QC ch9 (275.4kW), CJPM Chicoutimi QC ch46 (89.3kW) & relay txs. – **JIM PATTISON BROADCAST GROUP (Comm)** 460 Pemberton Terrace, Kamloops BC V2C 1T5 ☎ +1 250 3723322 ▤ +1 250 3740445 **W:** www.jimpattison.com **LP:** Pres: Rick Arnish. **Stations:** CKPG Prince George BC ᵃch2 (8.3kW), CFJC Kamloops BC ᵃch4 (3.7kW), CHAT Medicine Hat AB ᵃch6 (58kW) & relay txs (AB & BC only). – **NEWFOUNDLAND BROADCASTING CO. LTD (Comm)** Box 2020, St. John's NL, A1C 5S2 ☎ +1 709 7225015 ▤ +1 709 7265107 **W:** www.ntv.ca **LP:** Pres: Scott Sterling. **Stations:** CJON St. John's NL ch21 (266kW) & relay txs (NL only). NB: Stns identify as 'NTV'. – **ROGERS MEDIA INC. (Comm)** 333 Bloor St. E, 7th flr, Toronto ON M4W 1G9 ☎ +1 416 9358200 **W:** www.rogers.com **LP:** Pres: Ken Whyte. **Stations:** CFMT Toronto ON ch47 (15kW), CHMI Portage LaPrairie/Winnipeg MB ch13 (8.3kW), CHNM-TV Vancouver BC ch20 (1.5kW), CITY Toronto ON ch44 (15kW), CJMT Toronto ON ch51 (15kW), CJCO-TV Calgary AB ch38 (25kW), CJEO-TV Edmonton AB ch44 (58kW), CKAL Calgary AB ch49 (100kW), CKEM Edmonton AB ch17 (107kW), CKVU Vancouver ch33 (8.3kW) & relay txs. NB: Stns identify as 'Citytv', 'OMNI' or 'OMNI.2'. – **V (Comm)** 612, rue St-Jacques bureau 100, Montréal PQ H3C 5R1 ☎ +1 514 3906035 **W:** vtele.ca **LP:** Pres/CEO: Maxime Rémillard **Stations (French):** CFJP Montréal QC ch35 (13.9kW) & relay txs (QC only).

Other Regional Networks & Local Stations not shown.

CANARY ISLANDS (Spain)

System: DVB-T (MPEG2, MPEG4) [E]

National (Regional) Stations
TELEVISION ESPAÑOLA EN CANARIAS (TVE) (Pub) Plazoleta de Milton 1, 35005 Las Palmas de Gran Canaria ☎ +34 928 293096. – **RADIOTELEVISIÓN CANARIA (RTCV) (Pub)** Mariucha 2, 35012 Las Palmas de Gran Canaria ☎ +34 928 280188 **W:** www.rtvc.es. **Chs:** TV Canaria, TV Canaria Dos. – **ANTENA 3 TELEVISIÓN (Comm)** Alcalde José Ramírez Bethencourt 25, 35004 Las Palmas de Gran Canaria ☎ +34 928 297300. – **POPULAR TV CANARIAS (Rlg)** Las Palmas de Gran Canaria.

Local Stations not shown.

DTT Transmitters (MPEG2 exc. *=MPEG4)
Operator: n/a **Mux 1:** La 1, La 2, 24 Horas, Clan ⌘ RNE R. Nacional, RNE R.5 Todo Noticias **Txs:** ch60 (SFN). **Mux 3:** Cuatro, la Sexta, laSexta 3, Divinity, La Tienda en Casa, Gol Televisión◉ **Txs:** ch67 (SFN) **Mux 4:** Telecinco, La Siete, FDF, Disney Channel, Intereconomía ⌘ R. Interecononomía, esRadio, ABC Punto R. **Txs:** ch68 (SFN). **Mux 5:** Veo TV, Antena 3, Neox, Nova, AXN◉ ⌘ R.Marca, Vaughan R. **Txs:** ch69 (SFN). **Mux 6:** TVE HD, TDP ⌘ RNE R. Clásica HQ, RNE R.3 **Txs:** ch28 (SFN) **Mux 7:** Xplora, laSexta 3, LaSexta HD, Quatro HD, Energy **Txs:** ch35 (SFN). **Mux 8:** Telecinco HD, Boing, Paramount Channel, MTV **Txs:** ch32 (SFN). **Mux 9:** Antena 3 HD, Nitro, Marca TV, 13TV ⌘ Cope, R. María, Onda Cero, Europa FM, Onda Melodía **Txs:** ch38 (SFN). **Mux 10*:** TVE HD, TDP ⌘ RNE R. Clásica HQ, R.3 **Txs:** ch28 (SFN), ch45 (SFN).
Local muxes not shown.

CAPE VERDE

Systems: # SECAM-K1 [VHF=K, UHF=E]; DVB-T (MPEG2) [E]

TELEVISÃO DE CABO VERDI (TCV) (Pub) Rua 13 de Janeiro, 1-A, Achada Santo António, Praia ☎ +238 2605200 ▤ +238 2605256 **E:** tcv@rtc.cv **W:** www.rtc.cv **LP:** Dir: Waldemar Pires **Txs:** Praia ch9 (0.5kW H) & relay txs.

Foreign TV Relay
RTP África (Portugal): (-).

DTT Transmitters
Licensee: CV Telecom **W:** www.cvtelecom.cv **Mux:** Televisão de Cabo Verde, SIC Noticias, TV Record, Rai Uno, BBC World, TV5, TV Galicia, Infinito, Fox Life, Fashion TV, Euronews, Eurosport, Extreme Sport, TVE Internacional, CNBC, MCM, RTP Africa, Lusomundo Premium, Lusomundo Gallery, Playboy, SportTv, RTP1, RTP2, SIC, TVI. **Txs:** (-)

CAYMAN ISLANDS (UK)

System: NTSC-M [A]

CAYMAN INTERNATIONAL TV NETWORK (CITN) (Comm) ✉ P.O. Box 30563 SMB, Grand Cayman ☎ +1 345 9452739 🖷 +1 345 9490021 **E:** citn@cayman27.com.ky **W:** www.cayman27.com.ky **Tx:** ch27. – **CAYMAN TELEVISION SERVICE (CTS) (Comm)** ✉ P.O.Box 3117 SMB, Grand Cayman. **Tx:** ch24. – **CAYMAN ADVENTIST TELEVISION NETWORK (CATN) (Rlg)** ✉ P.O.Box 515 GT, Grand Cayman. **E:** mission@candw.ky **Tx:** ch30. Rel. 3ABN (USA). – **CAYMAN CHRISTIAN TELEVISION (CCT) (Rlg)** ✉ Grand Cayman. **Tx:** ch21. Rel. TBN (USA).

CENTRAL AFRICAN REPUBLIC

System: SECAM-K1 [VHF=K, UHF=E]

TÉLÉVISION CENTRAFRICAINE (TVCA) (Gov) ✉ BP 940, Bangui ☎ +236 75501412 🖷 +236 21615985 **L.P:** DG: Michel Ouambéti **Txs:** Bangui ch9 (2kW) & relay txs.

CHAD

System: SECAM-K1 [VHF=K, UHF=E]

TÉLÉ TCHAD (Gov) ✉ BP 5123, N'Djamena ☎ +235 22522923 🖷 +235 22525163 **E:** tele.tchad@intnet.td **L.P:** DG (ONRTV): Doubaye Kleoutouin**Txs:** N'Djamena ch6V (50kW) & relay txs.

CHILE

Systems: # NTSC-M [A] ⇓2017; SBTVD (MPEG4) [A] planned

National Stations
TVN CHILE (Gov) ✉ Bellavista 0990, Providencia, Santiago ☎ +56 +56 2 7077130 🖷 +56 2 7077750 **E:** tvngprog@tvn.cl **W:** www.tvchile. cl **Txs:** Valparaíso ch12 & network. – **CANAL 13 (Rlg, Comm)** ✉ Inés Matte Urrejola 0825, Providencia, Santiago ☎ +56 2 6302356 🖷 +56 2 6302341 **E:** mailbag@13.cl **W:** www.13.cl **Txs:** Concepción ch5, Valparaíso ch8, Santiago ch13. – **CHILEVISION (Comm)** ✉ Inés Matte Urrejola 0890, Providencia, Santiago ☎ +56 2 4615100 🖷 +56 2 4615456 **E:** rcarmi@chilevision.cl **W:** www.chilevision.cl. **Txs:** ch11 (60kW) & relays. – **MEGA (Comm)** ✉ Av. Vicuña Mackenna 1348, Santiago ☎ +56 2 8108000 🖷 +56 2 5518916 **E:** mega@mega.cl **W:** www.mega.cl **Txs:** Santiago ch8 & relays. – **RED TV (Comm)** ✉ Av. Manquehue Sur 1201, Las Condes, Santiago ☎ +56 2 3854000 🖷 +56 2 3854060 **E:** rrpp@redtv.cl **W:** www.redtv.cl **Txs:** Santiago ch4 & relays. – **TELE CANAL (Comm)** ✉ Nueva Tajamar 481, Oficina 201, Torre Central, Las Condes, Santiago ☎ +56 2 4115600 🖷 +56 2 4115608 **E:** telecanal@telecanal.cl **W:** www.telecanal.cl **Tx:** Santiago ch2 & relays. – **UCV TV (Comm)** ✉ Av. 11 Septiembre 2155 Óf. 1402, Edificio Panorámico Torre A, Santiago ☎ +56 2 5864350 🖷 +56 2 5864351 **E:** direccion@ucv.cl **W:** www.ucvtv.cl **Txs:** Valparaíso ch4, Santiago ch5, Puerto Montt ch7, La Serena ch8.

Local Stations not shown.

CHINA (People's Rep. of)

Systems: DTMB (MPEG2, MPEG4) [DS]; † PAL-D [DS] ⇓2020

National Stations
CHINA CENTRAL TELEVISION (CCTV) (Gov) ✉ 11 Fuxing Lu, Haidian Qu, Beijing 100859 ☎ +86 10 68500114 🖷 +86 10 68508743 **W:** www.cntv.cn **L.P:** Pres: Hu Zhanfan. **Chs (national, terr.):** CCTV1, CCTV2, CCTV HD, CCTV-Children, CCTV-Music – **CHINA EDUCATION TELEVISION (CETV) (Gov)** ✉ 160 Fuxingmennei Dajie, Xicheng Qu, Beijing 100031 ☎ +86 10 66419055. 🖷 +86 10 66084298 **L.P:** Pres: Kang Ning. **W:** www.cetv.edu.cn **Chs:** CETV1, CETV2, CETV3.

Regional Stations (all Gov)
AH) Anhui TV: 355 Tongcheng Nanlu, Hefei, Anhui 230011. **W.** www.ahtv.cn **BJ)** Beijing TV: 98 A Jianguo Lu, Chaoyang QAu, Beijing 100022. **W:** www.btv.com.cn **CQ)** Chongqing TV: 68 Yuzhou Lu, Chongqing 400041. **W:** www.cbg.cn **EB)** Hebei TV: 100 Jianhua Nandajie, Shijiazhuang, Hebei 050031. **W:** www.hebtv.cn **EN)** Henan TV: 18 Zhenghua Lu, Zhengzhou, Henan 450008. **W:** www.hntv.

ha.cn **FJ)** Fujian TV: 2 Gutian Lu, Fuzhou, Fujian 350001. **W:** www.fjtv. net **GD)** Guangdong TV: 331 Huangshi Donglu, Guangzhou, Guangdong 510066. **W:** www.gdtv.com.cn; Guangdong Southern TV: 331 Huangshi Donglu, Guangzhou, Guangdong 510066. **W:** www.tvscn.com **GS)** Gansu TV: 561 Zhangsutan, Chengguan Qu, Lanzhou, Gansu 730010. **W:** www.gstv.com.cn **GX)** Guangxi TV: 73 Minzu Dadao, Nanning, Guangxi 530022. **W:** www.gxtv.com.cn **GZ)** Guizhou TV: 261 Qingyun Lu, Guiyang, Guizhou 550002. **W:** www.gzstv.com **HA)** Hainan TV: 61 Nansha Lu, Haikou, Hainan 570206. **W:** www.bluehn.com **HB)** Hubei TV: Zijin Cun, Liangdao Jie,Wuchang Qu, Wuhan, Hubei 430071. **W:** www.hbtv.com.cn **HL)** Heilongjiang TV: 181 Zhongshan Lu, Harbin, Heilongjiang 150001. **W:** www.hljtv.com **HN)** Hunan TV: Liuyang He Daqiao Dong, Changsha, Hunan 410003. **W:** www.hunantv.com **JL)** Jilin TV: 2066 Weixing Lu, Changchun, Jilin 130051. **W:** www.jilintv. cn **JS)** Jiangsu TV: 48 Xi Citang Xiang, Zhongshan Donglu, Nanjing, Jiangsu 210002. **W:** www.jsbc.com **JX)** Jiangxi TV: 207 Hongdu Zhong Dadao, Nanchang, Jiangxi 330046. **W:** www.jxgdw.com **LN)** Liaoning TV: 79 Wenhua Lu, Heping Qu, Shenyang, Liaoning 110003. **W:** www. lntv.cn **NM)** Nei Menggu TV: 55 Xinhua Dajie, Hohhot, Nei Menggu 010058. **W:** www.nmtv.cn **NX)** Ningxia TV: 66 Beijing Zhonglu, Jinfeng Qu, Yinchuan, Ningxia 750005. **W:** www.nxtv.cn **QH)** Qinghai TV: 6 Kunlun Lu, Xining, Qinghai 810001. **W:** qht.hunanyv.com **SD)** Shandong TV: 81 Jingshi Lu, Jinan, Shandong 250001. **W:** www.sdtv. com.cn **SC)** Sichuan TV: 40 Dongsheng Jie, Chengdu, Sichuan 610015. **W:** www.sctv.com **SH)** Shanghai TV: 651 Nanjing Xilu, Shanghai 200041. **W:** www.smg.cn **SN)** Shaanxi TV: 336 Chang'an Nanlu, Xi'an, Shaanxi 710061. **W:** www.sxtvs.com **SX)** Shanxi TV: 318 Yingze Dajie, Taiyuan, Shanxi 030001. **W:** www.sxrtv.com **TJ)** Tianjin TV: 143 Weijin Lu, Heping Qu, Tianjin 300071. **W:** www.tjtv.com.cn **XJ)** Xinjiang TV: 84 Tuanjic Lu, Urumqi, Xinjiang 830044. **W:** www.xjtvs.com.cn **XZ)** Xizang TV: 149 Beijing Zhonglu, Lhasa, Xizang 850000. **W:** www. tibetinfor.com/tibetzt/xztv **YN)** Yunnan TV: 182 Renmin Xilu, Kunming, Yunnan 650031. **W:** www.yntv.cn **ZJ)** Zhejiang TV: 111 Moganshan Lu, Hangzhou, Zhejiang 310005. **W:** www.cztv.com.cn.
NB. Keys to regional codes see National radio section.

DTT Transmitters (under construction)
Operator: SARFT **Mux 1:** CCTV1, CCTV2, CCTV-Children, CCTV-Music, CETV3 **Mux 2:** CCTV HD

Location	M1	M2
Beijing	33	32

+ national network under construction
Local muxes not shown. Also the content of the muxes 1+2 varies from region to region.

CHRISTMAS ISLAND (Australia)

NB: No terrestrial TV station.

COCOS (Keeling) ISLANDS (Australia)

NB: No terrestrial TV station.

COLOMBIA

Systems: # NTSC-M [A] ⇓1 Jan 2017; DVB-T [A]

National Stations
RADIO TELEVISIÓN NACIONAL DE COLOMBIA (RTVC) (Pub) ✉ Avenida El Dorado No. 46 - 76, Bogotá ☎ +57 1 5978000 🖷 +57 1 2222765 **E:** info@rtvc.gov.co **W:** www.rtvc.gov.co **Chs:** Canal Uno, Canal Institucional, Señal Colombia. **Txs: Canal Uno:** Bogotá ch8 & relay txs, **Canal Institucional:** Bogotá ch13 & relay txs, **Señal Colombia:** Bogotá ch11 & relay txs. – **CARACOL TELEVISION (Comm)** ✉ Calle 103 #69 B 43, Bogota ☎ +57 1 6430430 🖷 +57 1 6430444 **E:** serviciocliente@caracol.com.co **W:** www.caracoltv.com **Txs:** Bogotá ch5 & relay txs. – **RCN TELEVISIÓN (Comm)** ✉ Av Americas 65-82, Bogotá ☎ +57 1 4269292 🖷 +57 1 4140412 **W:** www.canalrcnmsn.com **Txs:** Bogotá ch4 & relay txs.

Local Stations not shown.

DTT Transmitters

Location	RTVC*	Caracol	RCN
Bogotá	16	14	15

+ nationwide netw. under construction
*) Mux: Canal Uno, Canal Institucional, Señal Columbia
Local muxes not shown.

COMOROS

System: SECAM-K1 [VHF=K, UHF=E]

National Station
OFFICE DE RADIO ET TÉLÉVISION DES COMORES (ORTC) (Pub) ✉ BP 250, Moroni ☎ +269 7744045 🖷 +269 7731079 **W**: www.ortc.fr **Txs:** (-).

Local Stations (all Comm)
Djabal TV: Iconi; tx: (-). **TV-Sha:** Moroni; tx: (-). **MTV:** Moroni; tx: (-). **Radio Télévision Anjouanaise (RTA):** Mbouyoujou-Ouani, Ile Autonome d'Anjouan; tx: (-).

CONGO (Dem. Rep. of)

System: # SECAM-K1 [VHF=K, UHF=E]; DTT planned

National Station
RADIOTÉLÉVISION NATIONALE CONGOLAISE (RTNC) (Pub) ✉ BP 3164, Kinshasa-Gombe ☎ +243 1 5260601 🖷 +243 1 5220655 **E:** ica@ic.cd **LP:** DG: Christophe Kolomonyi Ndibu **Chs:** RTNC1, RTNC2. **Txs:** RTNC1: Kananga ch4 (2kW), Kamina ch4 (2kW), Kinshasa ch5 (27kW), Kolwezi ch5 (1kW), Mbuji Mayi ch6 (2kW). **RTNC2:** Kinshasa ch37.

Local Stations not shown.

CONGO (Rep. of)

System: # SECAM-K1 [VHF=K, UHF=E]; DTT planned

TÉLÉ CONGO (Gov) ✉ BP 1046, Brazzaville ☎ +242 222810116 🖷 +242 222814128 **LP:** DG: Jean Obambi **Txs:** (pol.H): Loubomo ch5 (1kW), Brazzaville ch7 (9kW), Pointe Noire ch9 (4.7kW) & relay txs.

COOK ISLANDS

System: PAL-B [NZ]

COOK ISLANDS TELEVISION (CITV) (Comm) ✉ P.O.Box 126, Avarua, Rarotonga ☎ +682 29460 🖷 +682 21907 **E:** watchus@citv.co.ck **W:** www.citv.co.ck **LP:** Dir: Shona Pitt **Txs:** Airport ch4, Works Depot, TV studio, Mauke ch5, Matavera ch6, Titikaveka ch7, Aitutaki & Rarotonga ch9, Tu Papa ch10, Hospital & Ngatangiia ch11.

COSTA RICA

Systems: # NTSC-M [A] ⇩Dec 2018; SBTVD (MPEG4) [A] planned

National Stations
CANAL 13 (Pub) ✉ Apt 7-1908-1000, San José ☎ +506 22313333 🖷 +506 22200072 **E:** canal13@sinart.go.cr **W:** www.sinart.go.cr **LP:** DG: Dr. Ch. Zelaya Goodman **Txs:** San José ch13 & relay txs. – **REPRETEL (Comm)** ✉ Apartado 2860, 1000 San José ☎ +506 22906665 🖷 +506 22324203 **E:** info@repretel.com **W:** www.repretel.com **Chs:** Canal 4, 6, 11. **Txs:** San José ch4 & ch6 & ch11. – **TELETICA (Comm)** ✉ Sabana Oeste, San José ☎ +506 22101201 🖷 +506 22321107 **E:** info@teletica.com **W:** www.teletica.com **Tx:** San José ch7.

Local Stations not shown.

CROATIA

System: DVB-T (MPEG2, MPEG4). DVB-T (MPEG4) [E]

National Stations
HRVATSKA TELEVIZIJA (HRT) (Pub) ✉ Prisavlje 3, 10000 Zagreb. ☎ + 385 1 6163366 🖷 + 385 1 6163392 **W:** www.hrt.hr **LP:** Dir (TV): Damir Novinic. **Chs:** HRT1, HRT2, HRT3, HRT4, HRT HD – **NOVA TV (Comm)** ✉ Remetinecka cesta 139, 10000 Zagreb ☎ +385 1 6008300 🖷 +385 1 6008333 **E:** novatv@novatv.hr **W:** www.novatv.hr **LP:** Chmn: Drazen Mavric **Chs:** Nova TV, Doma TV. – **RTL TELEVIZIJA (Comm)** ✉ Krapinska 45, 10000 Zagreb ☎ +385 1 3660000 🖷 +385 1 3660609 **E:** rtl@rtl.hr **W:** www.rtl.hr **LP:** Chmn: Johannes Züll. **Chs:** RTL Televizija, RTL2.

Local Stations (via Mux 4, DTT regions: a-i)
Gradska TV: Molatska bb, 23000 Zadar (g) **Kanal RI:** Trg rijecke rezolucije 3, 51000 Rijeka (e). **Nezavisna Istarska Televizija (NIT):** Trg pod lipom 1, 52000 Pazin (e). **RI-TV:** Uzarska 17/3, 51000 Rijeka (e). **Slavonskobrodska Televizija:** Mile Budaka 1/IV, 35 000 Slavonski Brod (b). **TV Cakovec:** Kralja Tomislava 6, 40000 Cakovec (c). **TV Jadran:** Split (h). **TV Nova:** M. Laginje 5, 52100 Pula (e). **TV Slavonije i Baranje:** Hrvatske republike 20, 31000 Osijek (a). **Varazdinska Televizija (VTV):** Kralja P. Kresimira IV 6a, 42000 Varazdin (c). **Vinkovacka Televizija (VKTV):** Trg dr.F.Tudmana 2, Vinkovci (a).

DTT Transmitters (DVB-T/MPEG2 exc. where indicated)
Operator: OIV ✉ ul. grada Vukovara 269d, 10000 Zagreb ☎ +385 1 6186000 🖷 +385 1 6186100 **E:** dvbt@oiv.hr **W:** www.oiv.hr **Mux 1:** HRT1, HRT2, RTL Televizija, Nova TV **Mux 2:** HRT3, HRT4, RTL2, Doma TV **Mux 3 (DVB-T2/MPEG4)✪:** tbd **Mux 4:** Local stns. **Mux 5 (DVB-T2/MPEG4)✪:** tbd

Location	M1	M2	M3	M4º	M5
Belje	38	44	51	21a	56
Biokovo	33	53	-	34h	-
Borinci	38	44	51	21a	56
Brac	33	53	41	53h	23
Celevac	51	59	-	31g	-
Drenovci	38	-	-	-	-
Gruda	51	59	-	-	-
Ivanščica	44V	48V	21V	36Vc	56V
Kalnik	44	48	-	-	-
Krk	28	53	-	45	-
Labinština	33	53	41	34h	23
Lastovo	33	-	-	-	-
Licka Plješevica	30	44	-	54	-
Mali Losinj	28	53	-	-	-
Mirkovica	30	44	-	54	-
Moslavacka Gora	23	39	-	-	-
Pag	51	59	-	-	-
Papuk	23	39	-	58	-
Petrova Gora	25	48	-	-	-
Promina	51	59	-	31g	-
Psunj	23	39	-	58	-
Pula	28	53	-	45e	-
Razromir	28	53	-	-	-
Rota	33	59	-	-	-
Sljeme	25	48	53	42d	28
Srd	51	59	22	28i	45
Stipanov Gric	30	44	36	54	34
Sveta Gera	25	48	-	-	-
Sveta Nedjelja	25	48	56	-	-
Šibenik	51	59	21	31g	45
Ucka	28	53	57	29e	39
Ugljan	51	59	21	31g	45
Uljenje	51	59	-	-	-
Zagreb (HRT HQ)	25	48	56	-	-

+ repeaters. º) DTT regions a-i, see under "Local Stations".

CUBA

System: NTSC-M [A]; DVB-T [A] planned

National Stations
INSTITUTO CUBANO DE RADIO Y TELEVISIÓN (ICRT) (Gov) ✉ Televisión Cubana, Calle M No. 313, Vedado, La Habana 10400 ☎ +53 7 8309705 🖷 +53 7 8309705 **E:** tvcubana@icrt.cu **W:** www.tvcubana.icrt.cu **LP:** Pres (ICRT): Danylo Sirio López **Chs:** Canal Educativo, Canal Educativo 2, Cubavisión, Tele Rebelde. **Txs: Canal Educativo:** La Habana ch4 & network; **Canal Educativo 2:** La Habana ch15 & network; **Cubavisión:** La Habana ch6 & network; **Tele Rebelde:** La Habana ch2 & network.

Local Stations not shown.

CURAÇAO (Netherlands)

System: NTSC-M [A]

TELECURAÇAO (Gov) ✉ Berg Ararat zn., Willemstad ☎ +599 9 7771688 🖷 +599 9 4614138 **E:** info@telecuracao.com **W:** www.telecuracao.com **LP:** GM: Norbert Hendrikse; TD: J. Rufina. **Txs** ch8 (20kW H).

CYPRUS

System: DVB-T (MPEG4) [E]. Northern Cyprus: # PAL-B/G [E], DVB-T (MPEG4, MPEG4) [E]

National Stations
CYPRUS BROADCASTING CORP. (CYBC) (Pub) ✉ P.O.Box 24824, 1397 Lefkosia ☎ +357 22862000 🖷 +357 223175 85 E: rik@cybc.com.cy W: www.cybc.com.cy LP: DG: Themis Themistocleous Chs: RIK1, RIK 2 – **ALFA TV (Comm)** ✉ P.O.Box 26811, 1648 Lefkosia ☎ +357 22763000 🖷 +357 22760001 LP: Pres/DG: Socratis Hassikos. – **ANT1 (Comm)** ✉ P.O.Box 20923, 1665 Lefkosia ☎+357 22200200 🖷 +357 22200210 E: hr@antenna.com.cy W: www.ant1iwo.com LP: GM: Stelios Malekos. – **EXTRA TV (Comm)** ✉ P.O.Box 70651, 3801 Limassol ☎ +357 25715111 🖷 +357 25715333 E: harnic@cytanet.com.cy W: www.extratv.com.cy LP: Exec. Chmn: Koullis Constantinou – **LUMIERE TV (LTV) (Comm)** ✉ P.O.Box 25614, 1311 Lefkosia ☎ +357 22357272 🖷 +357 22354622 E: administration@ltv.com.cy W: www.lumieretv.com LP: MD: George Xinaris. – **MEGA TV (Comm)** ✉ P.O.Box 27400, 1644 Lefkosia ☎ +357 22477777 🖷 +357 22355138 E: newsdpt@megatv.com.cy W: www.megatv.com.cy LP: GM: George Chouliaras. – **PLUS TV (Comm)** ✉ Neas Engomis St. 8, 2409 Lefkosia ☎ +357 22600600 🖷 +357 22600512 LP: GM: Costakis Constantinou. – **SIGMA TV (Comm)** ✉ P.O.Box 21836, 1513 Lefkosia ☎ +357 22580100 🖷 +357 22580252 E: info@sigmatv.com W: www.sigma.com.cy LP: GM: Antis Hadjicostis.

Local stations not shown.

DTT Transmitters (MPEG4)
Operator Mux 1: CYBC **Mux:** RIK1, RIK2, RIK HD, ERT World, Euronews ⌘ RIK1-4 **Operator Mux 2+3:** Velister ✉ Evaggelistrias St. 68, Helen Hall, 2057 Strovolos ☎ +357 22267222 🖷 +357 22267233 E: info@velister.com.cy W: www.velister.com.cy **Mux 2:** Alfa TV, ANT1, Sigma, Plus TV, Extra TV, Capital TV, Mad TV, Music TV **Mux 3♻:** LTV, LTV1, LTV2, LTV3, LTV Sports 1, LTV Sport 2 **Mux 4+5:** F.pl

Location	M1	M2	M3	M4*	M5*	kW
Troodos	33	49	50	56	59	5
Vavatsinia	33	49	50	56	59	5

+ txs below 5kW (*= F.pl)

Northern Cyprus

National Station
BAYRAK RADIO TELEVISYON KURUMU (BRTK) (Gov) ✉ Dr. Fazil Küçük Bulvari, BRT Sitesi, Lefkosa, via Mersin 10, Turkey ☎ +90 392 2254577 🖷 +90 392 2254577 E: info@brtk.net W: www.brtk.net LP: Pres: Ahmet Okan Chs: Bayrak-Haber TV, Bayrak-Aile TV. Txs: Bayrak-Haber TV: Sinandagi ch21 (15kW), Selvilitepe ch44 (390kW); Bayrak-Aile TV: Sinandagi ch50 (15kW), Selvilitepe ch52 (200kW).

Local Stations not shown.

Foreign TV Relays
TRT (Turkey): TRT1: Sinandagi ch8 (100kW), Selvilitepe ch11 (15kW); TRT2: Selvilitepe ch41 (200kW).

DTT Transmitters (MPEG4 exc. *=MPEG2)
Operator: BRT **Mux:** Bayrak-Haber TV*, TRT1, TRT2, Genç TV, Ada TV, ART, Kanal T, NTV ⌘ Bayrak R*., Bayrak FM* **Txs:** ch33 (Selvilitepe 1.25kW).

AKROTIRI & DHEKELIA (UK)

System: DVB-T (MPEG2) [E]

BFBS-TV Relay (British Mil) ✉ BFPO 57, Dhekelia Mil 381 ☎ +357 24748518 **Mux♻:** BFBS1, BFBS2, BFBS 3 Kids, BFBS4 ⌘ BFBS Radio 1+2, BFBS Cyprus **Txs:** ch27 (SFN).

CZECH REPUBLIC

Systems: DVB-T (MPEG2, MPEG4) [E]

National Stations
CESKÁ TELEVIZE (CT) (Pub) ✉ Kavcí Hory, 140 70 Praha 4 ☎ +420 261131111 🖷 +420 261212891 E: info@ceskatelevize.cz W: www.ceskatelevize.cz LP: DG: Petr Dvorak Chs: CT1, CT2, Reg prgrs, CT24, sport – **PETKA (Comm)** ✉ Francouzská 4, 120 00 Praha 2 ☎ +420 222515999 E: info@petka.cz W: www.petka.cz – **PRIMA TV (Comm)** ✉ Na Zertvách 24, 180 00 Praha 8 ☎ +420 266700111 🖷 +420 266700201 E: informace@iprima.cz W: www.iprima.cz **Chs:** TV

Prima, Prima COOL, Prima love – **TV NOVA (Comm)** ✉ Krízeneckého nám. 5, 152 52 Praha 5 ☎ +420 233100111 🖷 +420 242424525 E: info@nova.cz W: tv.nova.cz – **TV BARRANDOV (Comm)** ✉ Krízeneského nám. 322, 15200 Praha 5 🖷 +420 267071771 W: www.barrandov.tv – **TV OCKO (Comm)** ✉ Vrchlického 29, 150 00 Praha ☎ +420 257222256 🖷 +420 257222094 E: ocko@ocko.tv W: www.ocko.tv.

Regional & Local Stations not shown.

DTT Transmitters (MPEG2 exc. where stated)
Licensee Mux 1: Ceské Televize **Mux:** CT1, CT2, Reg. prgrs, CT24, sport **Licensee Mux 2:** Ceské Radiokomunikace a.s. ✉ Mahlerovy sady 1, 130 00 Praha 3 🖷 +420 242411111 E: digital@radiokomunikace.cz W: www.radiokomunikace.cz **Mux:** TV Nova, Nova Cinema, Prima TV, Prima COOL, TV Barrandov – **Licensee Mux 3:** Czech Digital Group a.s. ✉ Skokanská 2117/1, 169 00 Praha 6 ☎+420 242411411 E: mail@digitv.cz W: www.digitv.cz **Mux:** Prima love, Ócko, Petka, local stns. – **Licensee Mux 4:** Digital Broadcasting s.r.o. ✉ Stavební 992/1, 708 00 Ostrava W: www.multiplex4.cz **Mux (MPEG4):** CT1 HD, TV Nova HD, Nova Fanda, TV Pohoda.

Location	M1	M2	M3	M4	kW
Benčšov (Kozmice)	-	-	-	44	40
Brno (Barvicova)	-	-	-	46	10
Brno (Kojál)	29	40	59	-	100
Brno (Hády)	29	40	59	-	10
Brno (mesto)	29V	40V	59V	-	10
C.Budejovice (Kleť)	49	39	22	25	100
Cheb (Zelená hora)	36	35	-	-	20
Chomutov (Jedlová hora)	33	58	-	-	32
Domazlice (Vraní vrch)	34	48	-	-	10
Frýdek (Lysá hora)	54	37	-	-	25
Hradec Kralové (Chlum)	-	-	-	45	10
Jablonec nad Nisou	-	-	-	25	10
Jáchymov (Klínovec)	36	35	-	-	50
Jeseník (Praded)	36	53	51	-	100
Jihlava (Javorice)	33	35	30	-	100
Jihlava (Vetrny Jenikov)	-	-	-	42	10
Kraslice (Snezná)	36	35	-	-	10/0.01
Liberec (Jeŝted)	43	52	60	-	2x50/20
Mikolov (Devín)	29	40	-	-	25
Olomouc (Slavonín)	-	-	-	44	10
Ostrava (Hoŝtálkovice)	54	37	48	-	100
Ostrava (Hladnov)	54	37	48	-	10
Pardubice	32	39	34	-	2x100/10
Plzen (Kraŝov)	34	48	52	-	100
Praha (Cukrák)	53	41	59	-	100
Praha (Ládví)	-	-	-	42	20
Praha (Olŝanská)	-	-	-	64	10
Praha (Zizkov)	53V	41V	59V	-	32
Sušice (Svatobor)	49	48	52	-	100/71/100
Trutnov (Cerná hora)	40	61	60	-	100
Ústí n.L. (Buková hora)	33	58	55	-	100
Valašské Klobouky	33	49	-	-	25
Velké Popovice (Batoŝky)	-	-	-	64	20
Vimperk	49	39	-	-	20
Votice (Mezivrata)	53	41	-	-	32
Zlín (Tlustá hora)	33	49	25	-	2x100/10

+ sites with txs below 10kW
Regional/Local Licensees not shown.

DENMARK

System: DVB-T (MPEG4) [E], DVB-T2 (MPEG4) [E]

National Stations
DR (Pub) ✉ TV Byen, Emil Holms Kanal 20, 0999 København C ☎ +45 35203040 🖷 +45 35202644 E: presse@dr.dk W: www.dr.dk LP: DG: Maria Rørbye Rønn **Chs:** DR1, DR2, DR Update, DR K, DR Ramasjang, DR HD. – **TV 2 DANMARK (Pub)** ✉ Rugaardsvej 25, 5100 Odense C ☎ +45 65919191 🖷 +45 65913322 E: tv2@tv2.dk W: www.tv2.dk LP: Chmn: Lars Liebst. **Chs:** TV 2, regional stns (W: www.tv2regionerne.dk): a) TV 2/Bornholm (Brovangen 1, 3720 Aakirkeby), b) TV 2/Fyn (Olfert Fischers Vej 31, 5220 Odense SØ), c) TV 2/Lorry (Allégade 7-9, 2000 Frederiksberg), d) TV/Midt-Vest (Søvej 2, 7500 Holstebro), e) TV 2/Nord (Søparken 4, 9440 Åbybro), f) TV Syd (El-vej 2 B, Seest, 6000 Kolding), g) TV2 Øst (Kildemarksvej 1, 4760 Vordingborg), h) TV 2 / Østjylland (Skejbyparken 1, 8200 Århus N).

Local Stations not shown (via Mux 1).

DTT Transmitters (DVB-T exc. where indicated)
Licensee Mux 1+2: DIGI-TV I/S ✉ Banestrøget 21, 2630 Taastrup **E:** info@digi-tv.dk **W:** www.digi-tv.dk **Mux 1:** DR1, DR2, TV 2 Regional stns / indep. local stations. **Mux 2:** DR HD, DR K, DR Ramasjang, DR Update, Folketinget. – **Licensee Mux 3-6:** Boxer TV A/S ✉ Admiralgade 24, 1066 København K **E:** info@boxertv.dk **W:** www. boxertv.dk **Mux 3✪:** TV 2, Kanal 4, Kanal 5, Animal Planet, Canal 9, TLC, CNN, Discovery Science, History Channel, Travel Channel, Disney Channel, Disney XD, The Voice **Mux 4✪:** TV 2 Charlie, TV 2 Film, TV 2 NEWS, TV2 Sport, TV 2 Zulu, 6'eren, Discovery, DK4, Nickelodeon, Cartoon Network, MTV, VH1 **Mux 5 (DVB-T2✪):** TV 2 HD, TV 2 Film HD, TV 2 Sport HD, C More First, C More Hits, TV4 Sverige, TV2 Norge, ZDF, Star!, 6'eren HD. – **Licensee Mux 6-8✪:** tbd.

Location	M1*	M2	M3	M4	M5	M6¹	M7¹	M8¹	kWº
Hadsten	26hV	44	69V	56V	55V	36V	24V	5	50
Hedensted	30f	44	33	46	55	36	68	7	50
Jyderup	58g	51	42	31	60	23	65	6	50
København (1)	53c	51	54	31	60	23	67	6	50
København (2)	53c	51	54	31	60	23	67	6	10
Nakskov	58g	34	43	38	66	48	63	6	16
Nibe	29e	57	50	37	35	39	63	5	50
Rø	59a	56	51	32	65	39	62	9	25
Svendborg	25b	49	27	22	43	41	61	7	25
Thisted	31dV	42V	21V	43V	22V	49V	62V	10	25
Tolne	29e	57	50	37	35	39	63	5	10
Tommerup	25b	49	27	22	43	41	61	7	50
Varde	30f	54	33	46	53	28	68	7	50
Viborg	40d	59	66	56	52	45	24	10	50
Videbæk	40d	59	66	48	52	28	34	10	50
Vordingborg	58g	34	42	38	66	48	63	6	50
Åbenrå	37f	50	42	31	44	41	67	7	50
Århus	26hV	44V	69V	56V	55V	36V	24V	5	1

+ sites with txs below 1kW. (1) Søborg (2) Gladsaxe º) Power refers to muxes 1-7 *) incl. TV 2 reg stns (a-h) ¹) F.pl.

System: SECAM-B/G [E]

RADIO TÉLÉVISION DE DJIBOUTI (Gov) ✉ BP 97, Djibouti ☎ +253 21352294 🖷 +253 21356502 **E:** rtd@intnet.dj **W:** www.rtd.dj **L.P:** DG: Kadar Ali Diraneh **Tx:** Djibouti ch7 (10kW H) & relay txs.

NB: No terrestrial TV stations.

System: # NTSC-M [A] ⇩ Sep 2015; ATSC [A] planned

National Station
CORPORACIÓN ESTATAL DE RADIO Y TELEVISIÓN (CERTV) (Pub) ✉ Av. Dr. Tejeda Florentino 8, Sto. Domingo ☎ +1 829 6891220 🖷+1 829 6886208 **W:** www.certvdominicana.com **L.P:** Dir: George Rodriguez. **Txs:** Sto. Domingo ch4 & relay txs.

Local Stations
Antena Latina: Av. Independencia, Sto. Domingo; ch7. **Cadena de Noticias:** C/ Dr Defillo 4, Sto. Domingo; ch37. **Canal 25:** Av. General Lopez, Santiago; ch25. **Canal 27:** Av. Luperon, Sto. Domingo; ch27. **Color Vision:** Corporación Dominicana de Radio & TV, Av. Emilio Morel, Sto. Domingo; ch9. **Digital 15:** Av. San Martin, Sto. Domingo; ch15. **Digital Vision:** Av. Constitución 101, San Cristobal; ch63. **Mango TV:** Av. 27 de Febrero 308, Sto. Domingo; ch59. **Medios Educativa/Canal del Sol:** C/ Cub Scout 19, Sto. Domingo; ch6, ch65. **Radioemisoras Unidas:** Av. Tirandentes 35, Sto. Domingo; ch57. **Supercanal 33:** C/ Rafael A Sanchz, Sto. Domingo; ch33. **Teleamerica:** Av. Abraham Lincoln 1015, Sto. Domingo; ch47. **Teleantillas:** Autopista Duarte Km.7½, Sto. Domingo; ch2. **Telecoral:** Av. Independencia 59, Sto. Domingo; ch39. **Telecentro/Transmisiones y Proyecciones:** Av. Pasteur 204, Sto. Domingo; ch13, ch31. **Telefuturo:** Av. 27 de Febrero 371, Sto. Domingo; ch23. **Telemicro:** Av. San Martin, Sto. Domingo; ch5. **Telesistema:** Av. 27 de Febrero 52, Sto. Domingo; ch11. **Teleuniverso:** Av. Las Carreras 1, Santiago; ch29. **Televida:** Expreso V Centenario, Sto. Domingo; ch41.

System: NTSC-M [A]

TV RAPA NUI ✉ Hanga Roa, Isla de Pascua. **Tx:** ch13.

System: NTSC-M [A]

National Stations
SISTEMA ECUATORIANA DE RADIO Y TELEVISIÓN (Pub)✉ San Salvador E6-49 y Eloy Alfaro, Edificio Medias Públicos, Quito. **W:** www. tctelevision.com; www.gamatv.ec **Chs:** TC Televisión, Gama TV. **Txs:** TC Televisión: Quito ch10 & relay txs, Gama TV: Quito ch2 & relay txs. – **CANAL UNO (Comm)** ✉ Av. del Bosque Mz 112, Ciudadela Kennedy Norte, Guayaquil ☎ +593 4 2680200 🖷 +593 4 2680185 **E:** relad_sa@canal1tv.com **W:** www.canal1tv.com. **Txs:** Quito ch13 & relay txs. – **ECUAVISA (Comm)** ✉ Bosmediano 447, José Carb, Quito 1 ☎ +593 2 2995300 🖷 +593 2 2445488 **W:** www.ecuavisa.com. **Txs:** Quito ch8 & relay txs. – **RTS (RED TELESISTEMA) (Comm)** ✉ Av. de los Shyris y Suecia, Edificio Renazzo Plaza #202, Quito. **W:** +593 2 2272086 🖷 +593 2 2272086 **E:** rts@rts.com.ec **W:** www.rts.com.ec. **Txs:** Quito ch5 & relay txs. – **RTU (RADIO Y TELEVISIÓN UNIDAS) (Comm)** ✉ Carrión 555 y Juan León Mera, Quito. **W:** www.rtu.com.ec **Txs:** Quito ch46 & relay txs. – **TELEAMAZONAS (Comm)** ✉ Av. A. Granda C. 529 y Av. Brasil, Quito ☎ +593 2 2430350 🖷 +593 2 2441620 **E:** contactenos@teleamazonas.com **W:** www.teleamazonas.com. **Txs:** Quito ch4 & relay txs.

Local Stations not shown.

System: # PAL-B/G [E] ⇩ 2015; DVB-T

EGYPTIAN RADIO AND TV UNION (ERTU) (Pub) ✉ TV Bldg, Corniche El Nil, Cairo 11511 ☎ +20 2 25757155 🖷 +20 2 25746989 **W:** www.ertu.org **L.P:** Head of TV: Essam El Amir **Chs:** Prgr 1+2 (National), Prgr 3-8 (Regional), Nile TV, Nile Comedy, Nile Culture, Nile Drama, Nile Family, Nile Life, Nile News, Nile Sport

Location	P1	P2	kW	Location	P1	P2	kW
Abu Znima	26	29	15.5	Isna	6	9	18
Alamain	46	48	126	Kom Ombo	10	7	40
Alexandria	6	11	110	Luxor	11	7	19
Assiut	10	6	60	Mahalla	8	10	1600
Asswan	5	9	67	Matruh	10	8	39.2
Baris	7V	5V	10	Mokattem	5	9	200
Barnis	24	29	830	Nag Hamadi	5	8	17
Bawiti	10	8	22.4	Natron	41	44	36.4
Beni Ali	6V	9V	5	Negila	22	25	74
Beni Suef	11V	7V	110	Port Said	5V	7V	200
Dahab	6V	8V	9.3	Qena	9	6	30
Dumyat	58	61	15.2	Quser	7	5	50
El Arish	6V	10V	182	Rafah	45	48	350
El Dakhla	8	6	23	Ras Gharib	9	11	66
El Farafra	5V	7V	10	Ras Sedr	58	61	66.2
El Hammam	39	42	69.2	Ras El Hekma	32	35	31.6
El Kharga	10V	8V	40	Safaga	11V	9V	50
El Minya	8V	5V	165	Salum	9	11	6
El Tur	10	8	33	Sharm El Sheikh	27	33	8.9
Halayeb	9V	11V	31.6	Sidy Barany	49	52	74
Hassana	34	31	35.5	Siwa	6V	8V	10
Hurghada	5V	7V	89	Sohag	7	11	52
Idfu	8	11	165	Suez	7	5	200
Ismailia	11V	9V	260	Taba	32	37	25.7

+ sites with txs below 5kW. P=Prgr.
ERTU Regional Services
Prgr 3 (Cairo): Mokattem ch7 (200kW) **Prgr 4 (Ismailia):** Negila ch28 (74kW), Ismailia ch33V (79.4kW), Port Said ch42V (20.3kW), Zagazig ch52 (158kW), Suez ch30 (20.3kW) **Prgr 5 (Alexandria):** Matruh ch5 (11kW), Siwa ch7V (11kW), Negila ch28 (74kW), Alexandria ch36 (678kW), Ras Hekma ch39 (31.6kW), Hammam ch51 (69kW), Sidi Barany ch55 (74kW) **Prgr 6 (Tanta):** Mahalla ch49 (321kW) **Prgr 7 (El Minya):** Beni Ali ch22V (13.2kW), El Minya ch39V (56kW), Assiut ch48 (117kW), Beni Suef ch51V (43kW), Fayoum ch55 (107kW) **Prgr 8 (Asswan):** Asswan ch21 (67.6kW), Luxor ch22 (69.2kW), Sohag

ch27 (340kW), Kom Ombo ch29 (33.9kW), Qena ch30 (85.1kW), Nag Hamady ch32 (77.6kW), Idfu ch40 (66kW), Isna ch49 (70.9kW).

ERTU Nile TV Network
Nile TV: Sharm El Sheikh ch31 (79.4kW), Mokattem ch46 (282kW)
Nile Cinema: Alexandria ch21 (74kW), Sohag ch23 (340kW), Asswan ch24 (67.6kW), Luxor ch25 (69.2kW), Mokkatem ch28 (282kW), Ismailia ch31 (20.7kW) **Nile Comedy:** Mokattem ch30 (282kW)
Nile Culture: Mokattem ch43 (91kW) **Nile Drama:** Mokattem ch34 (282kW) **Nile Family:** Mokattem ch40 (89kW) **Nile Life:** Mokattem ch22 (282kW) **Nile News:** Alexandria ch24 (74kW); Mokattem ch26 (282kW) **Nile Sport:** Mokattem ch38 (316kW).
(Txs below 5kW not mentioned; Pol=H exc. where indicated)

DTT Transmitters (under construction)
Operator: ERTU **Mux 1:** multiprgr **Tx:** ch27 (Alexandria 10kW), ch32 Mokattem (50kW) **Mux 2:** multiprgr **Tx:** ch36 (Mokattem 30kW).

EL SALVADOR

Systems: # NTSC-M [A] ↓1 Jan 2019; ATSC [A] planned

National Stations
TELEVISION CULTURAL EDUCATIVA CANAL 10 (Pub) ✉ Ap. Postal No. 104, Neuva San Salvador ☎ +503 2280499 🖷 +503 2280973 **E:** tydiez@es.com.sv **Tx:** S.Salvador ch10 (109kW). – **CANAL 12 (Comm)** ✉ Boulevard Santa Elena Sur #12, Antiguo Custatlan, La Libertad, San Salvador ☎ +503 25101212 🖷 +503 25101222 **E:** canal12@canal12.com.sv **W:** www.canal12.com.sv **Tx:** S.Salvador ch12. – **TELECORPORACIÓN SALVADOREÑA (TCS) (Comm)** ✉ Alameda Manuel Enrique Araújo, Edifício Canales 2, 4 y 6, San Salvador ☎ +503 22092000 🖷 +503 22092065 **W:** esmitv.com **LP:** CEO: Boris eserski. **Chs:** teledos, Canal Cuatro, Canal Seis. **Txs:** S.Salvador Teledos ch2 (100kW), Canal Cuatro ch4 (75kW), Canal Seis ch6 (150kW). – **AGAPE TV CANAL 8 (Rlg)** ✉ Calle Gerardo Barrios No. 1511, Col. Cucumacayán, Santa Salvador ☎ +503 22812828 🖷 +503 22110799 **E:** dircomunicaciones@agapetv8.com **W:** www.agapetv8.com **Tx:** S.Salvador ch8 (109kW).

Local Stations not shown.

EQUATORIAL GUINEA

System: PAL-B/G [E]

RTVGE (Gov) ✉ Calle 3 Augusto, Malabo ☎ +240 222515335 **E:** info@rtvge.com **W:** www.rtvge.com **LP:** DG: Téobaldo Nchaso. **Txs:** Santa Isabel ch2 (50kW H) & relay txs. – **RTV ASONGA (Comm)** ✉ Malabo. **Txs:** (-).

ERITREA

System: PAL-B/G [E]

ERITREA TELEVISION (ERI-TV) (Gov) ✉ Asmara ☎ +291 1 116033 🖷 +291 1 124847 **W:** www.eri.tv **LP:** DG: Asmelash Abraha **Chs:** ERI-TV1, ERI-TV2 **Txs:** **ERI-TV1:** (Pol.=H) Asmara ch5 (5kW), Assab ch11 (5kW) & relay txs. **ERI-TV2:** (-).

ESTONIA

System: DVB-T (MPEG4) [E]

EESTI TELEVISIOON (ETV) (Pub) ✉ Faehlmanni 12, 15029 Tallinn ☎ +372 6284133 🖷 +372 6284155 **E:** etv@etv.ee **W:** etv.err.ee **LP:** Chmn (ERR): Margus Allikmaa. **Chs:** ETV, ETV2 – **KANAL 2/KANAL 11/KANAL 12 (Comm)** ✉ Maakri 23a, 10145 Tallinn ☎ +372 6662450 🖷 +372 6662451 **E:** info@kanal2.ee / info@kanal11.ee / info@kanal12.ee **W:** kanal2.ee / kanal11.ee / kanal12.ee **LP:** DG: Urmas Oru – **TV3/TV6 (Comm)** ✉ Peterburi tee 81, 11415 Tallinn ☎ +372 6220200 🖷 +372 6220201 **E:** tv3@tv3.ee / tv6@tv6.ee **W:** www.tv3.ee / www.tv6.ee **LP:** CEO: Priit Leito. – **TALLINNA TV (TTV)** ✉ Rävala pst 12, 10143 Tallinn ☎ +372 6005523 **E:** info@tallinnatv.eu **W:** www.tallinnatv.eu **LP:** Chmn: Allan Alaküla.

DTT Transmitters
Operator Mux 1: Levira AS ✉ Kloostrimetsa tee 58 A, 15026 Tallinn ☎ +372 6804000 🖷 +372 6804001 **E:** levira@levira.ee **W:** www.levira.ee **Mux:** ETV, ETV2, Kanal 2, TV3, TTV, Kanal 12. **Licensee Mux 2+3:** Starman AS ✉ Akadeemia tee 28, 12618 Tallinn ☎ +372 6779977

🖷 +372 6779907 **E:** pressiinfo@starman.ee **W:** www.starman.ee
Mux 2✪: TV6, TV3+, Sony TV, Discovery, Discovery Investigation, Universal, Animal Planet, Cartoon Network/TCM, Eurosport, Fashion TV, PBK Estonia, Ren-TV Estonia **Mux 3✪:** Kanal 11, Seitse, Fox Life, Fox Crime, Showtime, National Geographic, Nickelodeon, Eurosport 2, MTV Europe, Euronews, CNN, Hustler TV.

Location	M1	M2	M3	kW
Ellamaa	45	-	-	8.8
Koeru	57	60	63	5/1.7/1.8
Kohtla-Nõmme	33	48	58	12/2x2.3
Pehka	45	-	-	6.6
Pärnu	53	56	62	12.7/2x2.3
Tallinn (TV-tower)	45	59	64	18.8
Valgjärve	47	52	61	14/2x7

+ sites with txs below 5kW

ETHIOPIA

Systems: #PAL-B/G [E] ↓June 2015; DTT planned

National Station
ETHIOPIAN TELEVISION (ETV) (Gov) ✉ P.O.Box 5544, Addis Ababa ☎ +251 11 5505483 🖷 +251 11 5505174 **E:** info@erta.gov. et **W:** www.ertagov.com **LP:** DG (ERTA): Desta Tesfaw **Chs (Terr.):** ETV1, ETV2, ETV3, reg. stns **Txs:** **ETV1:** (pol.H) Shashemene ch5 (1kW), Debrebirhan ch6 (1kW), Debre Markos ch6 (1kW), Goba ch6 (1kW), Addis Ababa ch7 (25kW), Harar ch7 (1kW), Mekele ch7 (1kW), Gambella ch8 (1kW), Araminch ch9 (1kW), Assaita ch9 (1kW), Axum ch9 (1kW), Dessie ch9 (1kW), Godie ch9 (1kW), Assosa ch11 (1kW), Nazereth ch11 (1kW) & txs below 1kW; **ETV2:** Addis Ababa ch(-) (25kW); **ETV3:** Addis Ababa ch42 (10kW), to be converted to DTT.

Local Stations (all Gov)
Dire TV: Dire Dawa; ch9. **Harari TV:** Harar; tx. (-). **Oromia Radio & TV (ORTV):** P.O.Box 2919, Adama; Adama ch9 & netw. **Somali TV:** Jijiga; tx: (-).

DTT Transmitters (under construction)
Operator: ETV **Mux:** ETV1, ETV2, ETV3, ETV4 **Txs:** ch42 (Addis Ababa 10kW) & network.

FALKLAND ISLANDS (UK)

System: DVB-T (MPEG4) [E]

BFBS-TV (British Mil) ✉ BFBS Falkland Islands, Mt. Pleasant, BFPO 655 ☎ +500 32179 🖷 +500 32193 **Mux:** BFBS1, BFBS2, BFBS3 Kids, BFBS4, BFBS1 One Day Later, BFBS+, Sky Sports 1, Sky Sports 2 ❊ BFBS Radio 1+2, BFBS Falkland Islands **Txs:** ch27 (SFN).

FAROE ISLANDS (Denmark)

Systems: # PAL-B/G [E]; DVB-T (MPEG2) [E]

KRINGVARP FØROYA - SJÓNVARP (Pub) ✉ P.O.Box 1299, 110 Tórshavn ☎ +298 347500 🖷 +298 347501 **E:** kringvarp@kringvarp.fo **W:** www.kringvarp.fo **LP:** GM: Dia Midjord. **Tx:** Húsareyn ch6 (10kW) & netw. – **IKTUS (Rlg)** ✉ c/o Anja Hansen, Landsvegur 9, 511 Gøtugjógv **E:** iktus@iktus.fo **W:** www.iktus.fo.

DTT Transmitters
Licensee Mux 1-4: Televarpið ✉ P.O.Box 3128, 110 Tórshavn ☎ +298 340340 🖷 +298 340341 **E:** televarp@televarp.fo **W:** www.televarp.fo **Mux 1✪:** 3+, 3 Plus, National Geographic, BBC Entertainement, BBC World News, Kanal 4, Kanal 5 **Mux 2 (partly✪):** SvF, DR1, DR2, TV3, NRK1, Vision Norge **Mux 3✪:** Canal+ First, Canal+ Comedy, Canal+ Sport, Canal+ Sport 1, DR Ramasjang/TCM, Disney Channel, Discovery **Mux 4✪:** TV2 Danmark, TV2 Sport, Eurosport, Animal Planet, VH1, Kanal 6, Rás 1. **Licensee Mux 5:** R2 Net ✉ Søldarfjarðarvefur 11, 660 Søldarfjørður ☎ +298 409999 🖷 +298 409990 **E:** petur@r2net.fo **W:** www.r2net.fo **Mux 5:** 10'arlig, IKTUS.

Location	M1	M2	M3	M4	M5	kW
Brúnaskarð	57	59	65	67	-	0.25
Klakk	57	59	65	67	31	0.25
Knúkur	53	55	61	63	-	0.04
Stongin	46	48	50	52	34	0.04
Støðlafjall	52	50	48	46	-	0.04
Velbastaður	60	66	68	58	-	0.04

+ repeaters.

FIJI

System: PAL-B [NZ]

FIJI TELEVISION (Comm) ✉ P.O.Box 2442, Suva ☎ +679 3305100 🖷 +679 3305077 **E:** fijitv@is.com.fj **W:** fijitv.info **Chs:** Fiji 1; Sky Fiji (✪) **Txs:** (-).

FINLAND

System: DVB-T (MPEG2) [E], DVB-T2 (MPEG4) [E]

National Stations
YLEISRADIO OY (Pub) ✉ P.O.Box 66, 00024 Yleisradio ☎ +358 9 14801 🖷 +358 9 14805148 **W:** www.yle.fi **LP:** CEO: Pekka Karhuvaara. **Chs:** Yle HD, Yle TV1, Yle TV2 (✉P.O.Box 196, 33101 Tampere; Yle Teema; Yle Fem in Swedish (✉P.O.Box 83, 00024 Yleisradio). – **CANAL DIGITAL (Comm)** ✉ P.O.Box 2, 00381 Helsinki ☎ +358 9 54264200 🖷 +358 9 54264270 **E:** asiakaspalvelu@ canaldigital.fi **W:** www.canaldigital.fi – **MTV3 (Comm)** ✉ 00033 MTV3 ☎ +358 10 300300 🖷 +358 10 3005164 **W:** www.mtv3.fi **LP:** CEO (MTV3 Media): Pekka Karhuvaara. **Chs:** MTV3, MTV3 Max, MTV3 Fakta, JIM, Sub, MTV3 Juniori, MTV3 Leffa – **NELONEN (Comm)** ✉ P.O.Box 350, 00151 Helsinki ☎ +358 9 4545414 **W:** www.nelonen.fi **LP:** Pres (Nelonen Media): Hans Edin. **Chs:** Nelonen, Nelonen Kino, Nelonen Maailma, Nelonen Perhe, Nelonen Pro 1, Nelonen Pro 2.

DTT Transmitters (DVB-T/MPEG2 unless stated otherwise) **Operator:** Digita Oy ✉ P.O.Box 135, 00521 Helsinki ☎ +358 20 411711 **E:** info@digita.fi **W:** www.digita.fi **Mux 1:** Yle TV1, Yle TV2, Yle Teema, Yle Fem/SVT World✪ (via selected txs, see chart), FOX, AVA ✠ Ylen Klassinen, Yle Puhe, Yle Mondo **Mux 2:** MTV3, MTV3 Max✪, Nelonen, JIM, Sub, Estradi, MTV3 Juniori/Leffa✪, URHOtv✪ **Mux 3 (✪exc.*):** TV5*, Iskelmä TV/Harju & Pöntinen*, C More First, C More Series, C More Urheilu, C More Aitio, Disney Channel, Nelonen Pro 1, Nelonen Pro 2, Digaviihde, BC-TV **Mux 4 (DVB-T2/MPEG4)✪:** Estradi HD, MTV3 HD **Mux 5 (✪exc.*):** Liv*, Kutonen*, MTV3 Fakta, Discovery, Eurosport, MTV, Nickelodeon, Nelonen Kino, Nelonen Perhe, Nelonen Maailma.

Location	M1	M2	M3	M4	M5	kW
Anjalankoski	22°	27	53	56	-	50
Espoo	32°	44	46	53	35	50
Eurajoki	38°	45	52	55	36	50
Fiskars	32°	44	46	58	-	10
Haapavesi	34	42	53	57	-	50
Iisalmi	26	38	-	-	-	30
Inari	48	25	-	-	-	50
Joutseno	47	35	57	32	26	50
Jyväskylä	30	60	55	41	25	50
Karigasniemi	50	49	-	-	-	30
Kerimäki	30	37	33	58	-	50
Kiihtelysvaara	26	59	-	-	-	30
Koli	25	40	47	51	-	60
Kruunupyy	27°	22	41	44	30	50
Kuopio	24	31	39	52	46	50
Kuttanen	53	58	-	-	-	30
Lahti	33°	47	57	51	40	50
Lapua	38°	37	55	48	24	50
Mikkeli	29	43	59	38	-	50
Oulu	41	51	54	37	24	50
Pernaja	23°	50	-	39	-	10
Pihtipudas	50	45	58	-	-	50
Posio	31	39	-	-	-	50
Pyhätunturi	60	41	-	-	-	50
Pyhävuori	28°	41	-	35	-	50
Rovaniemi	43	46	-	53	-	50
Ruka	33	48	59	-	-	50
Taivalkoski	32	38	-	-	-	50
Tammela	22°	27	50	43	30	60
Tampere	34°	23	58	59	42	60
Tervola	40	42	-	44	-	50
Turku	51°	54	57	60	29	50
Utsjoki	44	51	-	-	-	30
Vaasa	38°	37	-	57	-	10
Vuokatti	30	52	55	59	-	80
Vuotso	31	50	-	-	-	30
Ylläs	30	36	-	-	-	50
Ähtäri	52	44	-	-	-	50

+ sites with txs below 10kW. °) mux includes SVT World

FRANCE

System: DVB-T (MPEG2, MPEG4) [E]

National Stations
FRANCE TÉLÉVISIONS (Pub) ✉ 7 esplanade Henri de France, 75907 Paris Cedex 15 ☎ +33 156226000 **W:** www.francetelevisions.fr; www. francetv.fr **LP:** Pres: Rémy Pflimlin. ✉ France 5: 10 rue Horace Vernet, 92785 Issy-les-Moulineaux Cedex 9 ☎ +33 156229191 🖷 +33 141080222. ✉ France Ô: 35/37 rue Danton, 92240 Malakoff ☎ +33 155227100. **Chs: France 2** (www.france2.fr), **France 3** (www.france3.fr) & regional stations, **France 4** (www.france4.fr), **France 5** (www.france5.fr), **France Ô** (www.franceo.fr), **La 1ère** (for French overseas territories, www.la1ere. fr) – **ARTE (Pub)** ✉ 8 rue Marceau, 92785 Issy-les-Moulineaux Cedex 9 ☎ +33 155007772 🖷 +33 155007700 **W:** www.arte.tv **LP:** Pres: Véronique Cayla. – **LA CHAÎNE PARLEMENTAIRE - ASSEMBLÉE NATIONALE (LCP) (Pub)** ✉ 106 rue de l'Université, 75007 Paris ☎ +33 140639050 🖷 +33 140639019 **W:** www.lcpan.fr **LP:** DG: Gérard Leclerc. – **PUBLIC SÉNAT (Pub)** ✉ 92 boulevard Raspail, 75006 Paris ☎ +33 142344400 🖷 +33 142344469 **W:** www.publicsenat.fr **LP:** DG: Gilles Leclerc. – **BFM TV (Comm)** ✉ 12 rue d'Oradour-sur-Glane, 75740 Paris Cedex 15 ☎ +33 171191360 **W:** www.bfmtv.com **LP:** Pres: Alain Weill. – **CANAL PLUS (Comm)** ✉ 1 place du spectacle, 92863 Issy les Moulineaux Cedex 9 ☎ +33 171353535 **W:** www.canalplus.fr **LP:** Pres.: Bertrand Meheut. **Chs (Terr.):** Canal+, Canal+ Cinéma, Canal+ Sport. – **DIRECT 8 / DIRECT STAR (Comm)** ✉ 31/32 quai de Dion Bouton, 92811 Puteaux Cedex ☎ +33 146964888 **W:** www.direct8.fr / www.directstar.fr **LP:** Pres: Jean-Christophe Thiery. – **EUROSPORT FRANCE (Comm)** ✉ 3, rue Gaston et René Caudron, 92798 Issy-les-Moulineaux Cedex 9 ☎ +33 140938000 **W:** www.eurosport.fr **LP:** DG: Laurent-Eric Le Lay. – **GULLI (Comm)** ✉ 28 rue François 1er, 75008 Paris ☎ +33 156365555 🖷 +33 156365535 **W:** www.gulli.fr **LP:** DG: Antoine Villeneuve. – **I>TELE (Comm)** ✉ 6 allée de la 2ème DB, 75015 Paris ☎ +33 153915000 **W:** www.itele.fr **LP:** DG: Cécilia Ragueneau. – **LCI (Comm)** ✉ 54 avenue de la Voie Lactée, 92656 Boulogne-Billancourt Cedex ☎ +33 141412345 **W:** lci.tf1.fr **LP:** Eric Revel. – **M6 (Comm)** ✉ 89/91 avenue Charles de Gaulle, 92575 Neuilly sur Seine Cedex ☎ +33 141926666 🖷 +33 141926610 **W:** www.m6.fr **LP:** Pres: Nicolas de Tavernost. – **NRJ 12 (Comm)** ✉ 46/50 av. Théophile Gautier, 75016 Paris ☎ +33 140713929 **W:** www.nrj12.fr **LP:** DG: Gérard-Brice Viret. – **PARIS PREMIÈRE (Comm)** ✉ 60 avenue Charles de Gaulle, 92575 Neuilly sur Seine Cedex ☎ +33 141925700 **W:** www.paris-premiere. fr **LP:** Pres: Karine Blouët. – **PLANÈTE+ (Comm)** ✉ 1 place du Spectacle, 92823 Issy le Moulineaux Cedex 9 ☎ +33 171353535 **W:** www.plan-eteplus.com **LP:** DG: Arielle Saracco. – **TF1 / NT1 (Comm)** ✉ 1 quai du Point du Jour, 92656 Boulogne-Billancourt, Cedex ☎ +33 141411234 🖷 +33 141412793 **W:** www.tf1.fr / www.nt1.tv **LP:** Pres/DG: Nonce Paolini. – **TF6 (Comm)** ✉ 120 avenue Charles de Gaulle, 92522 Neuilly sur Seine Cedex ☎ +33 147382530 **W:** www.tf6.fr **LP:** DG: Laurent de Lorme. – **TMC (Comm)** ✉ 6 bis quai Antoine 1er, 98000 Monaco ☎ +377 93151415 🖷 +377 93151436 **W:** www.tmc.tv **LP:** DG: Jean Pastorelli. – **W9 (Comm)** ✉ 89/91 avenue Charles de Gaulle, 92575 Neuilly sur Seine Cedex ☎ +33 141927373 **W:** www.w9.fr **LP:** Pres: Jérôme Lefébure.

Local Stations
The stns generally transmit via Mux 1 in their regions. Txs are only mentioned if they are not part of the Mux 1 network. (*) Via Paris Local Mux: ch33 (Paris 5kW, Coulommiers 0.006kW). PoI=H.
Alsace 20: 17 rue Nuée Bleue, 67000 Strasbourg. **BDM TV:** 50 rue de Clignancourt, 75018 Paris; (*). **BFM Business:** 12 rue d'Oradour sur Glane, 75015 Paris; (*). **BIP TV:** Rue des Noues Chaudes, 36100 Issoudun; ch30 (Issoudun 0.075kW). **Canal 32:** 7 rue Raymond Aron, 10120 Saint André les Vergers; ch25 (Troyes 2kW). **CÉLA TV:** 17 place des Coureauleurs, 17004 La Rochelle Cedex. **CINAPS TV:** 17 rue des Tiphoines, 91240 Saint Michel sur Orge; (*). **Clermont1ère:** 40 rue Morel Ladeuil, 63006 Clermont-Ferrand Cedex 01. **Demain IDF:** 1 rue Patry, 92220 Bagneux; (*). **Grand Lille TV:** 101 boulevard Descat, 59200 Tourcoing; ch36 (Lille 1kW). **IDF1:** 7 rue des Bretons, 93210 La Plaine Saint Denis; (*). **La Chaîne Normande:** 4 passage de la Luciline, Le Vauban - Immeuble A, 76000 Rouen. **LCM:** 37/41 rue Guibal, 13331 Marseille Cedex 3. **LDVTV:** Lycée Léonard de Vinci, site du Mazel, 43120 Monistrol sur Loire; ch43 (0.005kW). **LM TV Sarthe:** 21/25 rue Pasteur, 72015 Le Mans Cedex 2. **Mirabelle TV:** 2 rue Saint Vincent, 57140 Woippy. **N7 TV:** 42 rue de la Tour d'Auvergne, 44200 Nantes. **Normandie TV:** 3 square du Théâtre, 14200 Hérouville Saint Clair. **NRJ Paris:** 40/50 avenue Théophile Gautier, 75016 Paris; (*). **Opal'TV:** 19 rue des Fusiliers Marins, 59140 Dunkerque. **Tébéo:** 19 rue Jean Macé, 29200 Brest. **Télé Bocal:** 12 villa Ribérolle, 75020 Paris; (*). **TéléGrenoble:** 109 rue Hilaire de Chardonnet, 38100 Grenoble. **TéléPaese:** 36 chemin de Palazzi, 20220 Santa Reparata di Balagna; ch29 (Calvi 0.002kW, L'Île Rousse 0.001kW). **TELIM TV:** 15 rue du Général Catroux, 87000 Limoges. **Territorial TV:** rue Louis Lepitre, 52200 Langres. **TLC (Télévision**

Locale du Choletais): La Novathèque, boulevard Pierre Lecoq, 49300 Cholet; ch56 (Nantes 8kW) + lps. **TLM (Télé Lyon Métropole):** 227 cours Lafayette, 69006 Lyon Cedex 07; ch32 (Lyon/Taluyers 1kW). **TLP (Télé Locale Provence):** Les prés Combaux, 04100 Manosque; ch56 (Villemus 0.001kW), Gréoux les Bains 0.008kW). **TLT (Télé Toulouse):** 1 allée Jacques Chaban-Delmas, 31500 Toulouse. **TL7 Horizon Numérique:** 2 bis rue Joseph Cugnot 42160 Andrézieux Bouthéon. **TV Rennes 35 Bretagne:** 19 rue de la Quintaine, 35000 Rennes. **TV Sud Camargue Cévennes:** 240 rue Le Corbusier, 30000 Nîmes; ch28 (Nîmes 1kW). **TV Sud Montpellier:** 753 avenue de la Pompignane, 34170 Castelnau Le Lez. **TV Tours:** 232 avenue de Grammont, 37019 Tours Cedex 1. **TV Vendée:** ZI le Séjour, 85170 Dompierre sur Yon; ch56 (Nantes 8kW) + lps. **TVPI:** route de Bayonne, 64210 Bidart. **TV7 Bordeaux:** 73 av. Thiers, 33000 Bordeaux. **TV8 Mont-Blanc:** route des Pontets, 74320 Sevrier Cedex; + lps. **Ty Télé:** 8 Auguste Nayel, 56100 Lorient. **VOO TV:** 20 rue des Ardennes, 21000 Dijon; ch40 (Dijon 0.134kW). **Vosges Télévision Images Plus:** 2 rue de la Chipotte, BP 267, 88007 Epinal. **Wéo La Télé Nord Pas de Calais:** 17 place Mendès France, 59000 Lille.

DTT Transmitters (MPEG2, exc.⚙ and HD channels: MPEG4)
Licensee Mux 1: Société de gestion du réseau R1 ⌨ 7 esplanade Henri-de-France, 75015 Paris ☎ +33 156224302 ▤ +33 156225818 **Mux:** France 2, France 3 + reg stns, France 5, France Ô, LCP/Public Sénat, local stations. – **Licensee Mux 2:** Nouvelles télévisions numériques ⌨ 1/32 quai de Dion Bouton, 92800 Puteaux ☎ +33 146962956 **Mux:** BFM TV, Direct 8, Direct Star, France 4, Gulli, i>TELE. – **Licensee Mux 3:** Compagnie du numérique hertzien 1 ⌨ place du Spectacle, 92863 Issy-les-Moulineaux ☎ +33 171350130 ▤ +33 171350626 **Mux⚙:** Canal+ HD*, Canal+ Cinéma, Canal+, Sport**, Planète. – **Licensee Mux 4:** Multi 4 ⌨ 89 avenue Charles de Gaulle, 92200 Neuilly-sur-Seine ☎ +33 141926140 ▤ +33 141925954 **Mux:** Arte HD, M6, NT1, Paris Première⚙*, W9. – **Licensee Mux 5:** MR5 ⌨ 1 quai du Point-du-Jour, 92100 Boulogne-Billancourt ☎ +33 141411234 ▤ +33 141411234 **Mux:** TF1 HD, France 2 HD, M6 IID. – **Licensee Mux 6:** SMR6 ⌨ 1 quai du Point-du-Jour, 92100 Boulogne-Billancourt ☎ +33 141411234 ▤ +33 141413046 **Mux:** Arte, Eurosport France⚙, LCI⚙, NRJ 12, TF1, TF6⚙, TMC. – **Operator Mux 7+8:** TDF **Mux 7:** Chérie HD, HD1, L'Équipe HD **Txs:** ch42 (Paris) & netw. **Mux 8:** 6 ter HD, RMC Découverte HD, Tvous la Diversité HD **Txs:** ch58 (Paris) & netw.
*) incl. unencrypted sequences. **) in MPEG2-SD during unencrypted sequences

Location	M1	M2	M3	M4	M5	M6	kW
Abbeville	57	25	33	55	37	39	80/4x30/80
Ajaccio	21	51	34	44	37	31	64
Amiens	41	52	49	47	59	44	40/29/4x40
Aurillac (Labastide)	54	45	43	51	42	48	40/35.2/4x40
Autun	48	51	39	35	42	32	40/20/32/40/36/40
Auxerre	52	50	49	34	58	44	4x40/10/40
Avignon	45	36	33	47	39	42	50/33/4x50
Bar le Duc	48	30	57	44	51	54	12/6
Bastia	21	51	34	44	37	31	32/2x37/2x32/36
Bayonne	56	42	45	49	57	58	25
Bergerac	33	41	56	31	35	50	40/23/4x40
Besançon (Lomont)	47	44	54	23	29	26	50
Besançon (Montfaucon)	47	44	54	23	29	26	25
Bordeaux	23	37	60	39	57	30	63/37/4x63
Bourges	56	46	43	24	40	36	4x63/40/63
Brest	43	58	35	39	34	191/144/107/140/120/118
Caen	25	42	22	29	45	28	100/50/100/94/2x100
Carcassonne	60	31	43	57	41	46	50/27/4x50
Chambéry	23	29	51	54	57	26	13
Charleville-Mézières	44	32	26	22	29	23	100/27/51/54/2x50
Chartres	47	21	49	50	55	44	4x25/11/25
Cherbourg-Octeville	35	34	59	37	60	36	10/7/2x11/8/11
Clermont-Ferrand	25	41	22	30	52	28	50
Dijon	37	50	59	33	28	32	32
Dunkerque	42	52	27	45	31	21	13/6/2x13/4/13
Gex	45	21	27	55	58	24	63/39/4x63
Hirson	48	32	27	51	35	54	80/3x22/80
Laval	33	58	43	57	60	51	9/14/4x10
Le Havre	43	44	57	32	41	46	20/15/6/3x20
Le Mans	26	23	22	31	37	36	79/32/79/2x32/79
Lille	24	23	27	26	21	31	80/20/80/14/2x80
Limoges	49	47	50	34	44	29	100/70/4x100
Longwy	59	47	31	22	39	25	2x10/5/10/2x7
Lyon (Mt Pilat)	43	44	59	40	49	46	126
Marseille	23	59	30	35	22	29	100/58/32/10/45/100
Metz	36	37	31	22	39	24	100/64/80/85/62/80
Montpellier	40	52	51	23	49	56	100/32/35/100/32/100
Mulhouse	24	27	54	37	53	21	100
Nancy	53	26	23	22	29	52	50/31/4x50
Nantes	47	23	30	54	44	29	98/43/65/83/2x65
Niort	25	52	22	40	27	28	70

Location	M1	M2	M3	M4	M5	M6	kW
Paris	35	25	22	30	28	32	50
Parthenay	48	49	33	55	60	36	13/6/3x13/6
Reims	53	56	43	46	45	40	4x80/30/80
Rennes	21	40	27	49	55	24	80
Rouen	26	34	33	53	23	51	40/25/10/3x40
Saint-Raphaël	39	54	28	25	22	48	63
Sarrebourg	50	47	25	22	56	34	50/20/40/50/40/50
Sens	47	50	49	34	58	44	4x10/4/10
Strasbourg	48	47	43	22	56	51	50/2x20/10/2x21
Toulon	58	54	28	25	22	48	10
Toulouse	21	38	24	27	25	36	50
Tours	42	23	45	24	37	29	78
Troyes	26	21	27	24	29	36	5x100/63/100
Vannes	57	25	53	48	22	50	20
Verdun	59	47	31	22	39	25	100/41/4x65
Vittel	60	58	59	40	45	32	10/3/7/9/2x10

+ sites with txs below 10kW.

FRENCH GUIANA

System: DVB-T (MPEG4) [E]

GUYANE 1ÈRE (Pub) ⌨ Avenue le grand boulevard, BP 7013, F-97307 Cayenne Cedex ☎ +594 594299900 ▤ +594 594302649 **W:** guyane.1ere.fr **LP:** Dir: Henri Neron.

DTT Transmitters
Operator: TDF **Mux:** Guyane 1ère, France 2-5, France Ô, France 24, Arte **Txs:** MFN.

FRENCH POLYNESIA

System: DVB-T (MPEG4) [E]

POLYNÉSIE 1ÈRE (Pub) ⌨ BP 60125, F-98702 Faa'a ☎ +689 689861616 ▤ +689 689861611 **W:** polynesie.1ere.fr **LP:** Dir: Gilles Cozanet. – **TAHITI NUI TV (TNTV) (Comm)** ⌨ BP 348, F-98713 Papeete ☎ +689 689473636 ▤ +689 689532721 **E:** tntv@tntv.pf **W:** www.tntv.pf.

DTT Transmitters
Operator: TDF **Mux:** Polynésie 1ère, France 2-5, France Ô, France 24, Arte. TNTV **Txs:** MFN.

FRENCH SO. & ANTARTIC LANDS

NB: No terrestrial TV station.

GABON

System: # SECAM-K1 [VHF=K, UHF=E]; DVB-T, DVB-T2

RADIODIFFUSION-TÉLÉVISION GABONAISE (RTG) (Gov) ⌨ BP 10150, Libreville ☎ +241 1732152 ▤ +241 1732153 **LP:** DG (TV): David Ella Mintsa **Chs:** RTG1, RTG2 **Txs: RTG1:** Libreville ch4 (2kW H) & relay txs. **RTG2:** Libreville ch7 (2kW H). – **TV+ CHAÎNE 3 (Comm)** ⌨ BP 8344, Libreville ☎ +241 1775740 ▤ +241 1729204 **Txs:** Libreville ch(-), Franceville ch41.

DTT Transmitters
Operator: Digital TV ⌨ BP 7331, Libreville ☎ +241 6663666 **W:** www.tntafrica.com **Muxes 1-6 (partly ⚙):** multichannel **Txs:** Libreville, Gentil, Oyen ch(-).

GALAPAGOS ISLANDS (Ecuador)

System: NTSC-M [A]

TELEGALAPAGOS (Rlg) ⌨ Misión Franciscana, Puerto Baquerizo Moreno, Isla San Cristobal, Galapagos, Ecuador ☎ +593 5 2520144 **Tx:** ch13.

GAMBIA

System: PAL-I [E]

GAMBIA TELEVISION (Gov) ⌨ P.O.Box 2380, Serekunda ☎ +220 4374251 ▤ +220 4374242 **E:** grts@gamtel.gm **W:** www.grts.gm **LP:** DG: Alhaji Momodou Sanyang **Txs:** Banjul ch11V (100kW) & relay txs.

GEORGIA

Systems: # PAL-D/K [R] ⇩2015; DVB-T [E]

National Stations
GEORGIAN PUBLIC BROADCASTER (Pub) ✉ M. Kostava Street 68, Tbilisi ☎ +995 32 2362294 🖷 +995 32 2368665 **E:** info@gpb.ge **W:** www.gbp.ge **L.P:** GD: Giorgi Chanturia **Chs:** Public TV 1, Channel 2. **Txs: Public TV1:** Tbilisi ch6 (490kW) & network; **Channel 2:** Tbilisi ch4 (228kW) & network. – **RUSTAVI 2 (Comm)** ✉ Vazha Pshavela Avenue 4, Tbilisi ☎ +995 32 2201111 🖷 +995 32 2200012 **E:** tv@rustavi2.com.ge **W:** www.rustavi2.com.ge. **L.P:** DG: Koba Davarashvili. **Txs:** Tbilisi ch9 (478kW) & network.

Local Stations
ATV12: M. Mashtots St. 56, Akhalkalaki; ch12. **Kvemo Kartlis Tele-Radio Kompania:** Megobroba Ave. 32, 9th Fl, Rustavi; ch8. **Kvemo Kartlis TRC-s Marneulis Philiali:** Maisi St. 40, Marneuli. Tx: ch43. **L-TV:** Zakatala St. 29, Lagodekhi; ch27. **Mega TV:** Solomon Meore St. 7, Khoni. Tx: ch2. **TV Argo:** Argonavtebi St. 1, Zestaphoni; ch9. **TV Borjomi:** Rustaveli Sq. 1, 9th Fl, Borjomi; ch7. **TV Dia:** Tamar Mepe St. 1, 4th Fl, Khashuri; ch11. **TV Edelweiss:** Rustaveli St. 20, Tskaltubo; ch3 (shares tx with TV Imervizia). **TV Egrisi:** Akhalgazrdobis Kheivani St. 9, 2nd Fl, Senaki; ch1. **TV Evrika:** Tsinamdzghvrishvili St. 95, Tbilisi; ch25. **TV Guria:** Aghmashenebeli St. 120, Ozurgeti; ch21 (shares tx with TV Madi). **TV Gurjaani:** Ninoshvili St. 14, Gurjaani; ch11. **TV Imedi:** Lubliana St. 5, Tbilisi; ch30. **TV Imervizia:** Ninoshvili St. 7, Tchiatura; ch3 (shares tx with TV Edelweiss). **TV Jikha:** Gamsakhurdia St. 9, Tsalenjikha; ch5. **TV Kartli:** Chavchavadze St. 51, Gori; ch10. **TV Kavkazia:** Kostava St. 14, Tbilisi; ch28. **TV Kolkheti:** Chavchavadze St. 4, Chkhorotsku; ch4. **TV Kutaisi:** Gelati St. 1, Kutaisi; ch1. **TV Lomsia:** Didmamishvili St. 3, Akhaltsikhe; ch2. **TV Madi:** Ramishvili St. 120, Ozurgeti; ch21 (shares tx with TV Guria). **TV Metormete Arkhi:** Svanuri Koshki, Davit Aghmashenebeli St., Bolnisi; ch12. **TV Metskhre Arkhi:** Tamar Mepe St. 6, Akhaltsikhe; ch9. **TV Mze:** Kostava St. 75b, Tbilisi; ch45. **TV Odishi:** Aghmashenebeli St. 17, Zugdidi; ch39. **TV Parvana:** Freedom St. 39, Ninotsminda; ch12. **TV Rioni:** Tamar Mepe St. 14, Kutaisi; ch31. **TV Sameba:** 19 Kakhetis Gzatketsili St. 19, Sagarejo; tx (-) **TV Samegrelo:** Rustaveli St. 90, Zugdidi; ch21, ch30. **TV Stereo One:** Aleksidze St. 1, 2nd Fl, Tbilisi; ch40. **TV Tanamgzavri:** Sanapiro St. 1, Telavi; ch4. **TV Trialeti:** Chavchavadze St. 45, Gori; ch1. **TV Tvali:** David Aghmashenebeli St. 15, Sagarejo; ch34. **TV Zari:** Javakhishvili St. 8, Samtredia; ch4. **TV 202:** Tsereteli St. 144, Tbilisi; ch12. **TV-1:** Leselidze St. 44, Akhmeta; ch10. **V Channel:** Sulkhan-Saba Orbeliani St. 115, Bolnisi; ch5. **9th Talgha:** Rekvava St. 22, Poti; ch35.

ABKHAZIA
APSUA XÖYNTKARRATÄ TELERADIOKOMPANIA (Gov) ✉ Lasuria St. 16, Sokhumi ☎ +7 840 2266144 🖷 +7 840 2266144 **E:** info@apsua.tv **W:** www.apsua.tv **L.P:** Dir: Zurab Argun **Txs:** Sokhumi ch26 & netw.

SOUTH OSSETIA
PTRK "IR" (Gov) ✉ Geroev St. 48, Tskhinvali ☎ +7 9974 451218 **E:** radio-ir@yandex.ru **L.P:** Dir: Robert Kulumbegov **Txs:** (-)

GERMANY

System: DVB-T (MPEG2, MPEG4) [E], DVB-T2 (MPEG4) [E]

National Stations
ARBEITSGEMEINSCHAFT DER ÖFFENTLICH-RECHTLICHEN RUNDFUNKANSTALTEN DEUTSCHLANDS (ARD) (Pub) ✉ Arnulfstrasse 42, 80335 München ☎ +49 89 590001 🖷 +49 89 59003249 **L.P:** Chairwoman: Monika Piel. **W:** www.ard.de; www. daserste.de **Chs (terr.):** Das Erste, regional stns. **NB.** ARD is the head organisation for the regional public service broadcasters: **Bayerischer Rundfunk (BR):** Rundfunkplatz 1, 80335 München ☎ +49 89 59002433 🖷 +49 89 59003199. **Hessischer Rundfunk (HR):** Bertramstrasse 8, 60320 Frankfurt ☎ +49 69 1551 🖷 +49 69 1552900. **Mitteldeutscher Rundfunk (MDR):** Kantstrasse 71-73, 04275 Leipzig ☎ +49 341 22760 🖷 +49 341 5663544. **Norddeutscher Rundfunk (NDR):** Rothenbaumchaussee 132, 20149 Hamburg ☎ +49 40 4131 🖷 +49 40 447602. **Rundfunk Berlin-Brandenburg (RRB)** Masurenallee 8-14, 14057 Berlin ☎ +49 30 9799330141 🖷 +49 30 9799330149. **Radio Bremen Fernsehen (RB),** Diepenau 10, 28195 Bremen ☎ +49 421 2460 🖷 +49 421 2462010. **Saarländischer Rundfunk (SR),** Funkhaus Halberg, 66100 Saarbrücken ☎ +49 681 6020 🖷 +49 681 6023874. **Südwestrundfunk (SWR),** Neckarstrasse 230, 70190 Stuttgart ☎ +49 711 92910001 🖷 +49 711 9291010.

Westdeutscher Rundfunk (WDR), Appellhoffplatz 1, 50667 Köln ☎ +49 221 2202100 🖷 +49 221 22085724. – **ZWEITES DEUTSCHES FERNSEHEN (ZDF) (Pub)** ✉ Postfach 4040, 55030 Mainz ☎ +49 6131 701 🖷 +49 6131 702157 **E:** info@zdf.de **W:** www.zdf.de **L.P:** CEO: Markus Schächter **Chs (terr.):** ZDF, ZDF_neo, ZDFinfo – **PRO7SAT1 MEDIEN AG (Comm)** ✉ Medienallee 7, 85774 Unterföhring ☎ +49 89 950710 🖷 +49 89 950711227 **E:** stefanie.prinz@pro7sat1.de **W:** www. pro7sat1.de **L.P:** CEO: Thomas Ebeling **Chs (terr.):** Pro7, Sat1, Kabel 1, N24 – **RTL TELEVISION GMBH (Comm)** ✉ Picasoplatz 1, 50679 Köln ☎ +49 221 45600 🖷 +49 221 45669999 **E:** ukomm@rtl.de **W:** www.rtl.de **L.P:** CEO: Anke Schäferkordt **Chs (terr.):** RTL Television, RTL2, SuperRTL, Vox, n-tv.

Local Stations not shown.

DTT Transmitters (DVB-T/MPEG2 unless indicated otherwise)
Licensee Mux 1: ARD **Mux:** Das Erste, other public channels. – **Licensee Mux 2:** ARD **Mux:** public regional stns. – **Licensee Mux 3:** ZDF **Mux:** ZDF, 3Sat, KiKa/ZDF_neo, ZDFinfo. – **Licensee Mux 4:** ProSiebenSat.1 **Mux:** Sat1 (incl. reg. prgrs), Pro7, Kabel1, N24. – **Licensee Mux 5:** RTL Group **Mux:** RTL (incl. reg. prgrs), RTL2, SuperRTL, Vox.
NB: The content of the muxes is licensed individually by each federal state and varies accordingly.

RE	Location	M1	M2	M3	M4	M5	kW
BB	Cottbus (Calau)	53	57	36	-	-	100
BB	Frankfurt/O.	53V	57V	33V	-	-	50
BE	Berlin (Mitte)	27	47	33	44	25	120/10/50/120/20
BE	Berlin (Charlottenburg)	27	47	-	-	-	10
BE	Berlin (Wannsee)	27	47V	33	44	25	50/5/3x50
BW	Aalen	59	50	23	-	-	50
BW	Baden-Baden	60	49	33	-	-	50
BW	Bad Mergentheim	26	50	23	-	-	5/10/5
BW	Brandenkopf	52	39	33	-	-	50
BW	Donaueschingen	54	41	22	-	-	50
BW	Freiburg	52	39	33	-	-	50
BW	Heidelberg	60	49	21	-	-	50
BW	Hochrhein	52	39	33	-	-	50
BW	Pforzheim	60	49	33	-	-	50
BW	Ravensburg	43	40	22	-	-	50
BW	Raichberg	43	40	22	-	-	50
BW	Stuttgart	26	50	23	-	-	50
BW	Ulm	43	40	22	-	-	50
BW	Waldenburg	26	50	23	-	-	50
BY	Augsburg	36	25	44	-	-	100
BY	Bamberg	29	40	34	-	-	50
BY	Brotjacklriegel	40V	27V	33V	-	-	25/100/50
BY	Büttelberg	55	47	-	-	-	50
BY	Dillberg	55V	47V	34V	-	-	25/2x50
BY	Gelbelsee	36	25	44	-	-	50
BY	Grünten	45	46	28	-	-	50
BY	Hirschau	29	28	23	-	-	50
BY	Hohe Linie	42V	28V	53V	-	-	25/2x100
BY	Hoher Bogen	42V	28V	33V	-	-	25/100/50
BY	Hohenpeißenberg	47	53	28	-	-	2x100/50
BY	Landshut	40	27	33	-	-	20
BY	München	54V	56V	35V	48V	34V	20/5x100
BY	Nürnberg	55V	47V	34V	52V	-	25/2x50/20
BY	Ochsenkopf	29	40	23	-	-	50
BY	Pfaffenberg	36	46	25	-	-	2x100/50
BY	Pfaffenhofen	36	25	44	-	-	50
BY	Pfarrkirchen	40	27	33	-	-	50
BY	Pfänder°	45	-	46	-	-	10
BY	Rhön	36	46	25	-	-	2x100/50
BY	Wassertrüdingen	55	47	44	-	-	2x100/50
BY	Wendelstein	54V	56V	35V	48V	34V	25/4x100
BY	Würzburg	36V	46	25	-	-	25/2x50
HB	Bremerhaven	22	29	32	49	42	2x10/3x5
HB	Bremen (Walle)	22	29	32	49	42	40/50/32/2x50
HE	Angelburg	32	24	45	-	-	50
HE	Frankfurt (Ginnheim)	37V	59V	22V	54V	34V	50/20/3x50
HE	Großer Feldberg	37V	59V	22V	54V	34V	50/10/3x50
HE	Habichtswald	32	55	42	-	-	50
HE	Heidelstein	43	35	25	-	-	50
HE	Hohe Wurzel	37V	59V	22V	54V	34V	100/20/2x100
HE	Hoher Meißner	32	55	42	-	-	50
HE	Rimberg	32	35	22	-	-	50
HE	Würzberg	31	53	21	-	-	50
HH	Hamburg	33	54	23	30	40	3x50/2x100
HH	Hamburg (Rahlstedt)	33	54	23	30	40	20/25/3x20
HH	Hamburg (Moorfleet)	-	54V	-	-	-	25

RE	Location	M1	M2	M3	M4	M5	kW
MV	Garz	29	40	-	-	-	20
MV	Helpterberg	22	23	-	-	-	20
MV	Marlow	29V	46V	-	-	-	20
MV	Schwerin	26	53	-	-	-	50
NI	Aurich	48	43	35	-	-	2x50/20
NI	Braunschweig	47V	36V	23V	44V	24V	10/8/3x5
NI	Braunschweig (Broitzem)	47V	36V	23V	44V	24V	2x10/3x5
NI	Cuxhaven	26	29	31	-	-	2x10/5
NI	Dannenberg	43	58	-	-	-	10/2
NI	Göttingen	59	21	42	-	-	50
NI	Göttingen (Hetjersh.)	59V	21V	-	-	-	40/25
NI	Hannover (Buchholz)	47	36	23	44	24	10/4x20
NI	Hildesheim	47V	36V	23V	-	-	10/8/5
NI	Lingen	41	37	59	-	-	20
NI	Osnabrück	41	37	59	-	-	50
NI	Rosengarten	33	56	23	-	-	5/20/5
NI	Stadthagen	47	36	-	-	-	10
NI	Steinkimmen	55	29	32	49	42	100/4x5
NI	Torfhaus	59V	46V	-	-	-	32
NI	Uelzen	43	58	27	-	-	20/2x50
NI	Visselhövede	43V	58V	27V	-	-	20
NW	Aachen	50V	37V	26V	-	-	2x10/5
NW	Aachen (Stolberg)	50V	37V	26V	-	-	2x50/20
NW	Bielefeld	26	31	33	-	-	20
NW	Bonn	50V	49V	26V	53V	29V	3x50/2x20
NW	Dortmund	48V	25V	35V	55V	29V	50
NW	Düsseldorf	48V	46V	35V	55V	29V	50
NW	Düsseldorf	46V	-	-	-	-	50
NW	Essen	48V	57V	35V	55V	29V	50
NW	Hochsauerland	60	27	30	-	-	50
NW	Köln	50V	49V	26V	53V	29V	3x50/2x20
NW	Langenberg	48V	46V	35V	55V	29V	50
NW	Langenberg	46V	25V	-	-	-	50
NW	Münster	21V	45V	59V	-	-	50
NW	Nordhelle	60V	27V	30V	-	-	100/2x50
NW	Siegen	60	27	30	-	-	50
NW	Teutoburger Wald	26V	31	33	-	-	50
NW	Wesel	48V	46V	35V	55V	29V	50
NW	Wesel	46V	-	-	-	-	50
NW	Wuppertal	48	22	35	-	-	20
RP	Ahrweiler	56	33	28	-	-	10
RP	Bad Marienberg	56	33	28	-	-	20
RP	Donnersberg	57	44	30	-	-	50
RP	Eifel	46	48	30	-	-	50
RP	Haardtkopf	46	48	30	-	-	50
RP	Kaiserslautern	57	44	30	-	-	20
RP	Kettrichshof	60	44	30	-	-	50
RP	Koblenz	56	33	28	-	-	50
RP	Saarburg	46	48	30	-	-	50
SH	Bredstedt	26	24	31	-	-	25
SH	Bungsberg	47V	39V	21V	-	-	50
SH	Flensburg	47V	39V	21V	-	-	50
SH	Heide	32	24	31	-	-	32/2x20
SH	Kiel	47	39	21	35	45	2x50/20
SH	Lübeck (Berkenthin)	33	28	23	30	40	20
SH	Lübeck (Stockelsdorf)	33V	28V	23V	30V	40V	20
SH	Mölln	-	28	-	-	-	10
SH	Neumünster	-	28	-	-	-	20
SH	Wedel	-	28	-	-	-	25
SL	Göttelborner Höhe	42V	44V	30V	-	-	50
SL	Schocksberg	42V	-	30V	-	-	20
SL	Spiesen	42V	-	-	-	-	25
ST	Brocken	29V	34V	30V	-	-	50
ST	Dequede	41V	34V	31V	-	-	50
ST	Magdeburg	29V	34V	30V	-	-	2x100/50
ST	Halle	24V	35V	22V	-	-	50
ST	Wittenberg	24V	38V	30V	-	-	50
SN	Chemnitz (Geyer)	25V	32V	22V	-	-	50
SN	Chemnitz (Reichenhain)	25V	32V	22V	-	-	2x20/5
SN	Dresden (Wachwitz)	39V	29V	36V	-	-	100
SN	Leipzig	24V	37V	22V	-	-	100
SN	Löbau	39V	27V	36V	-	-	50
SN	Schöneck	25V	32V	22V	-	-	50
TH	Erfurt	21V	27V	50V	-	-	50
TH	Gera	25V	27V	22V	-	-	50
TH	Inselsberg	53V	48V	50V	-	-	50
TH	Jena	21V	27V	50V	-	-	2x10/5
TH	Sonneberg	21V	27V	50V	-	-	2x10/20
TH	Weimar	21V	27V	50V	-	-	25

+ sites with txs below 10kW. °) tx located in Austria
RE) Region codes (federal states): BB=Brandenburg, BE=Berlin, BW=Baden-Württemberg, BY=Bayern, HB=Bremen, HE=Hessen, HH=Hamburg, MV=Mecklenburg-Vorpommern, NI=Niedersachsen, NW=Nordrhein-Westfalen, RP=Rheinland-Pfalz, SH=Schleswig-Holstein, SL=Saarland, ST=Sachsen-Anhalt, SN=Sachsen, TH=Thüringen.

Regional & Local Licensees not shown.

GHANA

Systems: # PAL-B/G [E]; DVB-T2 (MPEG4) [E]

GHANA BROADCASTING CORP. (GBC) (Gov) ⌧ P.O. Box 1633, Accra ☎ +233 30 2221161 ▤ +233 30 2773240 **E:** info@gbcghana. comh **W:** www.gbcghana.com **L.P:** DG: Berifi Afari Apenteng. **Chs:** GTV, GBC 24, GBC Life, GTV Sports+ **Txs:** (-). **E.TV GHANA (Comm)** ⌧ P.O.Box CT 5976, Accra ☎ +233 30 2912071 **E:** info@etvghana. com **W:** www.etvghana.com **Txs:** (-) – **METRO TV (Semi-Gov, Comm)** 59 Josiah Tongara Street, Labone, Accra ☎ +233 30 2765701 ▤ +233 30 2765703 **E:** admin@metroworld.tv **W:** www. metroworld.tv **Txs:** (-). – **TV3 (Comm)** ⌧ Box M83, Accra ☎ +233 30 2763458 ▤ +233 30 2763450 **E:** info@tv3.com.gh **W:** www.tv3. com.gh **LP:** CEO: Santokh Singh. **Txs:** (-). – **TV AFRICA (Comm)** ⌧ P.O.Box 7151, Accra-North ☎ +233 30 2224323 ▤ +233 30 2223320 **Txs:** (-). – **VIASAT 1 (Comm)** ⌧ House 25/8 Abafun Crescent, North Labone, Accra ☎ +233 30 2760516 **Tx:** ch30.

DTT Transmitters
Operator: GBC **Mux 1 (❂exc.*):** GTV, GBC 24, GBC Life, GTV Sports+,TV3, Viasat 1, TV Africa, NET2, BBC World News, God TV, FOX Entertainment❂, Showtime❂, Hi Nolly❂, Homebase❂, Setanta Africa❂, Kiss❂, KidsCo❂ **Mux 2❂:** Skyy One, Music World, Channel D, Sports24, Cinimax, Heaven, Planet Kidz, Fiesta, Skyy World, e.TV Ghana ✼ Skyy Power FM, Citi FM **Txs:** (-).

GIBRALTAR (UK)

System: DVB-T [E]

GBC TELEVISION ⌧ Broadcasting House, 18 So. Barrack Rd, Gibraltar ☎ +350 20079760 ▤ +350 20078673 **E:** info@gbc.gi **W:** www.gbc.gi **L.P:** CEO (Gibraltar B'casting Corp): Allan King.

DTT Transmitters
Operator: GBC **Muxes 1+2:** multiprgr. **Txs:** Mux 1: ch30 (Upper Rock) **Mux 2:** ch56 (Upper Rock).

GREECE

Systems: DVB-T (MPEG2, MPEG4) [E]; † PAL-B/G [E] ⇩2015

National Stations
ELLINIKI TILEORASSI (ET) (Pub) ⌧ HQ: 432 Messogion Ave., 15342 Agia Paraskevi ☎ +30 2106075704 ▤ +30 2106075714 **E:** nkarra@ert.gr **W:** www.ert.gr **L.P:** Chmn: Athanassios Papageorgiou. **Chs (terr.):** ET1, NET, ET3, ERT HD, Vouli TV. ⌧ (ET1) 136 Messogion Ave., 15342 Agia Paraskevi ☎ +2107761000 ▤ +30 2107797776; ⌧ (ET3) Aggelaki 16, 54621 Thessaloniki ☎ +30 2310299400 ▤ +30 2310299750 **E:** pr@ert3.gr **W:** www.ert3.gr – **ALPHA TV (Comm)** ⌧ 40,2km Attiki Odos, SEA Mesogion, Building 6, 19002 Paiania ☎ +30 2122124000 ▤ +30 2122124356 **E:** pr@alphatv.gr **W:** www.alphatv. gr – **ALTER CHANNEL (Comm)** ⌧ Agia Paraskevi 36-38, 12132 Peristeri ☎ +30 2105707000 ▤ +30 2105707078 **E:** info@alter.gr **W:** www.alter.gr – **ANTENNA TV (ANT1) (Comm)** ⌧ Leof. Kifisias 10-12, 15125 Marousi ☎ +30 2106886100 ▤: +30 2106890304 **E:** pr@antenna.gr **W:** tv.antenna.gr – **m. (MAKEDONIA TV) (Comm)** ⌧ 26hs Oktovriou 90, 54621 Thessaloniki ☎ +30 2310504300 ▤ +30 2310504344 **E:** info@maketv.gr **W:** www.maketv.gr – **MAD TV (Comm)** ⌧ Eth. Antistaseos 253 & E. Kotsopoulou, 15331 Pallini ☎ +30 2106665669 ▤ +30 2106665812 **E:** info@mad.tv **W:** www.mad. tv – **MEGA CHANNEL (Comm)** ⌧ Roussou 4 & Leof. Messogion, 11526 Ambelokipoi ☎ +30 2106903000 ▤ +30 2106983600 **E:** publ_rel@megatv.com **W:** www.megatv.com **L.P:** Chmn: Elias Tsigas – **MTV GREECE (Comm)** ⌧ Leof. Kifisias 304, 15232 Halandri ☎ +30 2106835056 **W:** www.mtvgreece.gr – **NOVA CINEMA / NOVA SPORTS (Comm)** ⌧ Proektasi Odou Manis, Kantza, 15351 Pallini ☎ +30 2106602000 ▤ +30 2106722961 **W:** www.cinema. gr / www.novasports.gr – **SKAI TV (Comm)** ⌧ Eth. Makariou & Falireos 2, 18547 Neo Faliro ☎ +30 2104800170 ▤ +30 2104800120

E: technicaltv@skai.gr **W:** www.skai.gr **L.P:** CEO: John Alafouzos. – **STAR CHANNEL (Comm)** ☒ Viltanioti 36, 14564 Kifisia ☎ +30 2111891000 ▤ +30 2111892000 **E:** info@star.gr **W:** www.star.gr – **TILEASTY (Comm)** ☒ Praxitelous 58, 17674 Kalithea ☎ +30 2109407000 ▤ +30 2109407024 – **902 TV (Comm)** ☒ Leof. Irakliou 145, 14231 Nea Ionia ☎ +30 2102592902 ▤ +30 2102592532 **E:** mailbox@902.gr **W:** www.902.gr.

Regional & Local Stations not shown.

DTT Transmitters (under construction) (MPEG4 exc. *=MPEG2) **Licensee Mux 1-3:** ERT **Mux 1:** Vouli TV, BBC World News, DW-TV, RIK Sat **Mux 2:** ET1, NET, ET3, ERT HD ❤ NET FM, ERA2, ERA3, ERA Spor, Kosmos 93.6 **Mux 3:** Nova Cinema 1✪, Nova Sports 1/Disney XD✪, Euronews, TV5 Monde Europe. – **Licensee Mux 4+5:** Digea ☒ Artemidos 3, 15124 Athens ☎ +30 2106838700 ▤ +30 2106823205 **E:** info@digea.gr **W:** www.digea.gr **Mux 4:** Alter Channel, Alpha TV, ANT1, m. (Makedonia TV). **Mux 5:** Mega Channel, Skai TV, Star Channel. – **Licensee Mux L1:** Digital Union ☒ Ginosati 88, 1st Fl., 14452 Metamorfosi ☎ +40 2102850880 **E:** info@digital-union.eu **W:** www.digital-union.eu **Mux L1*:** relays of local stns.

Location	M1	M2	M3	M4	M5	L1
Agrinio (Akarnanika)	46	28	43	31	37	47
Alexandroupoli (Plaka)	64	58	46	24	32	47
Athens (Aigina I.)	48	52	22	46	47	-
Athens (Mt. Ymittos)	48	52	22	46	47	-
Athens (Mt. Parnitha)	48	-	-	-	-	-
Drama (Korivilos)	37	-	-	-	-	-
Hania (Malaxa)	32	-	39	-	-	-
Ioannina (Liggiades)	49	-	33	-	-	-
Irakleio (Rogdia)	42	-	37	-	-	61
Kalamata (Likodimo)	43	-	-	-	-	53
Kastoria (Mt. Vitsi)	23	-	-	-	-	-
Kavala (Thassos I.)	47	-	-	-	-	-
Korinthos (Xylokastro)	61	55	-	37	43	-
Larissa (Mt. Dovroutsi)	48	43	56	22	29	47
Livadia (Hlomo)	22	-	-	-	-	-
Mitilini (Profitis Ilias)	31	-	-	-	-	-
Patra (Mt. Panahaiko)	42	25	24	44	46	53
Rhodos I. (Mt. Smith)	-	-	24	27	38	-
Thessaloniki (Mt. Hortiati)	56	23	46	25	29	59
Thessaloniki (Filippio)	56	23	46	25	29	-
Tripoli (Doliana)	39	-	-	-	-	-
Volos (Mt. Pílio)	53	-	-	-	-	-

Local licensees: not shown.

GREENLAND (Denmark)

System: DVB-T (MPEG2, MPEG4) [E]

National Station
KNR-TV (Pub) ☒ P.O.Box 1007, 3900 Nuuk ☎ +299 361500 ▤ +299 325042 **W:** www.knr.gl **E:** knr@knr.gl **L.P:** Head (TV): Malîñánguaq Marcussen Mølgaard.

DTT Transmitters
Operator: TELE Greenland **Mux (MPEG4):** KNR-TV, DR HD, DR Ramasjang, DR K ❤ KNR Radio, DR P1, DR P2, DR P3 **Txs:** Nationwide network.
Other local licensees not shown.

GRENADA

System: NTSC-M [A]

GBN-TV (Gov) ☒ P.O.Box 535, St. George's ☎ +1 473 4445521 ▤ +1 473 4445054 **E:** gbn@spiceisle.com **W:** www.klassicgrenada.com **L.P:** GM: Ruel Edwards **Txs:** North/East ch7 (4kW), Saint George's ch11 (5kW).

GUADELOUPE (France)

System: DVB-T (MPEG4) [E]

GUADELOUPE 1ÈRE (Pub) ☒ BP 180, F-97122 Baie-Mahault ☎ +590 590939696 ▤ +590 590939682 **W:** guadeloupe.la1ere.fr **L.P:** Dir: Liliane Francil – **A1 GUADELOUPE (Comm)** ☒ 20 rue Henri Becquerel, F-97122 Baie Mahault ☎ +590 590380606 ▤ +590 590380607 **E:** aurelie.

bancet@guadeloupe-television.com **W:** www.guadeloupe-television.com. – **CANAL 10 (Comm)** ☒ Bd Marquisart De Houelbourg, BP 416, F-97122 Baie-Mahault. ☎ +590 590267303 ▤ +590 590266125 **E:** contact@canal10-tv.com **W:** www.canal10-tv.com.

DTT Transmitters
Operator: TDF **Mux:** Guadeloupe 1ère, France 2-5, France Ô, France 24, Arte, A1, Canal 10. **Txs:** MFN.

GUAM (USA)

System: ATSC [A]

Local Stations*
KGTF (Pub): P.O.Box 21449, GMF, Agana, GU 96921. °PBS. Tx: Agana ch5 (8.26kW). **KTGM (Comm):** 692 N Marine Dr, Tamuning, GU 96913-4454. °ABC. Tx: Tamuning ch17 (2kW). **KUAM-TV (Comm):** 600 Harmon Loop Rd, #102, Dededo, GU 96912-2536. °NBC. Tx: Agana ch2 (0.035kW).
*) Full power licenses (lp licenses not listed). °) Network affiliation.

GUATEMALA

Systems: NTSC-M [A]; ATSC [A]

CORPORACIÓN ESTATAL DE RADIO Y TELEVISIÓN (CERTV) (Gov) ☒ 30, Av. 3-40, Zona 11, 01011 Guatemala ☎ +502 25945320 **Chs:** Canal 19, El Súper Canal, Televisiete **W:** www.canal3.com.gt; www.canal7.com.gt **L.P:** DG: Hector Olivo. **Txs:** Canal 19: °ch19; **El Súper Canal:** °ch3 (240kW); **Televisiete:** °ch7 (180kW). – **MAZATELEVISIÓN (Comm)** ☒ Guatemala.**Tx:** °ch58. – **TELEONCE (Comm) / TRECEVISIÓN (Comm)** ☒ 20, Calle 5-02, Zona 10, 01010 Guatemala ☎ +502 23682532 ▤ +502 23682221 **W:** www.canaltrece.tv; www.gatotv.com **Txs:** **TeleOnce:** °ch11 (316kW); **Trecevisión:** °ch13 (25kW). – **TELEVISIÓN AZTECA GUATEMALA (Comm)** ☒ 12 Avenida 1-96, Zona 2 de Mixco, Colonia Alvarado, Guatemala ☎ +502 24111140 ▤ +502 24111200 **E:** festrada@tvaguatemala.tv **W:** www.azteca.com.gt **Tx:** °ch31. – **TV USAC (Educ)** ☒ **W:** www.usac.edu.gt **Tx:** °ch33. – **CANAL 27 (Rlg)** ☒ Carretera Vieja a Antigua 2 Calle 23-70, Zona 1 de Mixco, Guatemala ☎ +502 24213434 **E:** canal27@motivacioncristiana.org **W:** www.canal27.org **Tx:** °ch27. – **CANAL 63 (Rlg)** ☒ Guatemala. **W:** www.canalcatolico.tv **Tx:** °ch63. – **CANAL 65 (Rlg)** ☒ Guatemala. **Tx:** °ch65. Rel. ETWN (USA). – **ENLACE CANAL 21 (Rlg)** ☒ Guatemala. **Tx:** °ch21. Rel. TBN (USA). (°=analogue)

GUINEA

System: PAL-K1 [VHF=K, UHF=E]

TÉLÉVISION NATIONALE DE GUINÉE (Gov) ☒ BP 391, Conakry. ☎ +224 30452786 ▤ +224 30451408 **W:** rtg-conakry.com **L.P:** Dir: Sam Mamadou **Txs:** Kindia ch4 (0.2kW), Conakry ch5 (1kW), Faranah ch5 (0.5kW), Labé ch7 (8kW), Mamou/Mali ch9 (0.2kW), Kankan ch9 (1kW).

GUINEA-BISSAU

System: PAL-B/G [E]

TELEVISÃO DA GUINÉ-BISSAU (TGB) (Gov) ☒ CP 178, Bissau ☎ +245 5603333 **E:** infotgb@televisao-gb.net **W:** www.televisao-gb.net **L.P:** DG: Luís Domingos Camará de Barros **Txs:** Nhacra ch7 (200kW) & relay txs.

Foreign TV Relay
RTP África (Portugal): (-).

GUYANA

System: NTSC-M [A]

National Station
NATIONAL COMMUNICATIONS NETWORK (NCN) (Gov) ☒ Homestretch Ave, D'Urban Park, Georgetown ☎ +592 2271566 ▤ +592 2262253 **E:** gmgtv@sdnp.org.gy **W:** www.ncnguyana.com **L.P:** CEO: Michael Gordon **Tx:** ch10.

Local Stations not shown.

HAITI

System: NTSC-M [A]

National Station
TÉLÉVISION NATIONALE D'HAITI (TNH) (Pub) ✉ BP 13400, Delmas 33, Port-au-Prince ☎ +509 2460200 🖷 +509 2463889 **E:** info@tnhtv.ht **W:** www.tnhtv.ht **L.P:** DG: Bernier Sylvain **Txs:** Port-au-Prince ch8 (0.3kW), unknown location ch10 (5kW), Cap. Haïtien ch12.

Local Stations not shown.

HAWAII (USA)

System: ATSC [A]

Local Stations*
KAAH-TV (Rlg): 1152 Smith St, Honolulu, HI 96817-5101.°TBN. Tx: ch27 (262kW). **KAII-TV (Comm):** satellite of KHON-TV. Tx: Wailuku 36 (50kW). Mux: Fox, CW. **KALO (Rlg):** 875 Waimanu St, Ste 110, Honolulu, HI 96813-5271. °ETV. Tx: ch10 (21kW). **KBFD (Comm):** 1188 Bishop St PH-1, Honolulu, HI 96813-3300. Tx: ch33 (108kW). **KFVE (Comm):** 150-B Puuhale Rd, Honolulu, HI 96819-2233. Tx: ch23 (50kW). °MNI. **KGMB (Comm):** 1534 Kapiolani Blvd, Honolulu, HI 96814-3715. Tx: ch22 (1000kW). °CBS. **KGMD-TV (Comm):** satellite of KGMB. Tx: Hilo ch8 (3.2kW). **KGMV (Comm):** satellite of KGMB. Tx: Wailuku ch24 (72.4kW). **KHAW-TV (Comm):** satellite of KHON-TV. Tx: Hilo ch21 (50kW). Mux: Fox, CW. **KHBC-TV (Comm):** satellite of KHNL. Tx: Hilo ch22 (84kW). **KHET (Pub):** 2350 Dole St, Honolulu, HI 96822-2410. Tx: ch18 (9.5kW). °PBS. **KHNL (Comm):** 150-B Puuhale Rd, Honolulu, HI 96819-2233. Tx: ch35 (5.9kW). °NBC. **KHON-TV (Comm):** 88 Piikoi St, Honolulu, HI 96814-4245. °Fox, CW. Tx: ch8 (7.2kW). Mux: Fox, CW. **KHVO (Comm):** satellite of KITV. Tx: Hilo ch10 (50kW). **KIKU (Comm):** 737 Bishop St Ste 1430, Honolulu, HI 96813-3204. Tx: ch19 (60.7kW). **KITV (Comm):** 801 S King St, Honolulu, HI 96813-3013. Tx: ch40 (85kW). °ABC. **KKAI (Rlg):** 875 Waimanu St, Ste 110, Honolulu, HI 96813-5271. °Faith TV. Tx: Kailua ch15 (19kW). **KLEI (Comm):** satellite of KPXO. Tx: Kailua-Kona ch25 (700kW). **KMAU (Comm):** satellite of KITV. Tx: Wailuku ch29 (51.2kW). **KMEB (Pub):** satellite of KHET. Tx: Wailuku ch30 (50kW). **KOGG (Comm):** satellite of KHNL. Tx: Wailuku ch16 (50kW). **KPXO (Comm):** 875 Waimanu St Ste 630, Honolulu, HI 96813-5267. Tx: Kane'ohe ch41 (34kW). °ION. **KUPU (Rlg):** 1188 Bishop St Ste 502, Honolulu, HI 96813-3302. Tx: Waimanalo ch23 (19kW). **KWBN (Rlg):** 3901 S Hwy 121 S, Bedford, TX 76021-2066. °ETV. Tx: ch43 (6.46kW). **KWHE (Rlg):** 1188 Bishop St Ste 502, Honolulu, HI 96813-3302. °LeSEA. Tx: ch31 (20.1kW). **KWHH (Rlg):** satellite of KWHE. Tx: Hilo ch23 (14.9kW). **KWHM (Rlg):** rel. KWHE. Tx: Wailuku 45 (87kW).
*) Full power license (lp licenses not listed); °) Network affilation
NB: Txsites are Honolulu unless mentioned otherwise.

HONDURAS

System: NTSC-M [A]

HRJS-TV (Comm) ✉ Apt. Postal 120, San Pedro Sula. **W:** www.vicatv.hn **Txs:** ch2, ch9 & relays. – **HRNQ-TV (Comm)** ✉ Casilla 3424, Tegucigalpa. **Tx:** ch13. – **HRGJ-TV (Comm)** ✉ Apt. Postal 882, Barrio Rio Piedras ☎ +504 5505009 🖷 +504 5531810 **W:** canal6.com.hn **Tx:** ch6. – **TELEVICENTRO (Comm)** ✉ Boulevard Suyapa, Tegucigalpa ☎ +504 2327835 🖷 +504 2320097 **W:** www.televicentro.hn **Chs:** Canal Cinco, Canal 3, Telecadenas Canales 7 y 4. **Txs:** ch3 (Canal 3), ch5 (Canal Cinco), ch4, ch7.

Local Stations not shown.

HONG KONG (China, SAR)

Systems: DTMB (MPEG2, MPEG4) [E]; # PAL-I [E] ⇩2015

RADIO TELEVISION HONG KONG (RTHK) (Pub) ✉ 30 Broadcast Drive, Kowloon, Hong Kong ☎ +852 23396330 🖷 +852 33800279 **E:** ccu@rthk.hk **W:** www.rthk.hk **L.P:** Assistant Dir of Broadcasting (TV): Man-sun Cheung. **NB.** Uses airtime on ATV and TVB. – **ASIA TELEVISION LTD. (ATV) (Comm)** ✉ 25-31 Dai Shing Street, Tai Po, Hong Kong ☎ +852 31682288 🖷 +852 27191654 **E:** atv@hkatv.com **W:** www.hkatv.com **L.P:** CEO (acting): Kwong Hoi Ying **Chs:** ATV Home (Chinese), ATV World (English), ATV HD **Txs:** Temple Hill ch23 (10kW) (ATV Home) & ch27 (10kW) (ATV World), and lp txs.

– **TELEVISION BROADCASTS LTD. (TVB) (Gov)** ✉ TV City, 77 Chun Choi Street, Tseung Kwan O Industrial Estate, Kowloon Hong Kong ☎ +852 23359123 🖷 +852 23581300 **E:** tvbpr@tvb.com.hk **W:** www.tvb.com **L.P:** Chmn: Run Run Shaw. **Chs:** TVB Jade, TVB Jade J2, TVB Jade HD, TVB Pearl **Txs:** Temple Hill ch21 (10kW) (TVB Jade) & ch25 (10kW) (TVB Pearl), and lp txs.

DTT Transmitters (MPEG4 exc. *=MPEG2)
Operator: n/a **Mux 1*:** TVB Jade, TVB Pearl, ATV, ATV World. **Mux 2:** TVB Jade J2, TVB Jade HD. **Mux 3:** ATV Financial News Channel, ATV Home, CCTV4, ATV HD. **Mux 4:** HD channels.

Location	M1	M2	M3	M4
SFN	22	35	37	43

HUNGARY

Systems: DVB-T (MPEG4) [E]; † PAL-D/K [R] ⇩2015

National Stations
MAGYAR TELEVÍZIÓ (MTV) (Pub) ✉ Szabadság tér 17, 1810 Budapest 5 ☎ +36 1 3734303 🖷 +36 1 3734133 **E:** info@mtv.hu **W:** www.mtv.hu **L.P:** DG: Balazs Medveczky **Chs:** m1, m2, reg. prgrs: a) Budapesti stúdió, b) Debreceni stúrió, c) Miskolci stúdió, d) Pécsi stúdió, e) Soproni stúdió, f) Szegedi stúdió – **DUNA TELEVÍZIÓ (Pub)** ✉ Mészáros u. 48-54, 1016 Budapest ☎ +36 1 4891200 🖷 +36 1 4891366 **E:** info@dunatv.hu **W:** www.dunatv.hu **L.P:** DG: László Cselényi **Chs (terr.):** Duna, Duna World. – **RTL KLUB (Comm)** ✉ Fehérvári út 84, 1117 Budapest ☎ +36 1 3828282 🖷 +36 1 3828283 **E:** rtlklub@rtlklub.hu **W:** www.rtlklub.hu **L.P:** Dirk Gerkens. – **TV2 (Comm)** ✉ Róna u. 174, 1145 Budapest ☎ +36 1 4676400 🖷 +36 1 4676500 **E:** info@tv2.hu **W:** www.tv2.hu **L.P:** CEO: Gábor Kereszty.

Local Stations not shown.

DTT Transmitters (under construction)
Operator: Antenna Hungária ✉ Petzvál József u. 31-33, 1119 Budapest ☎ +36 1 2036060 🖷 +36 1 4642525 **E:** antennadigital@ahrt.hu **W:** www.ahrt.hu; www.antennadigital.hu **Mux 1:** m1 HD, m2 HD, reg prgrs, Duna, Duna World ✂ Kossuth R., Petöfi R., Bartók R. **Mux 2✪:** Viasat 3, Comedy Central, Universal, Spektrum, History, Minimax, Cartoon Network, Prizma, Musika TV, Sport 1, Sport 2, Pro 4, Dorcel TV **Mux 3 (✪ exc.*):** RTL Klub*, TV2*, Euronews*, Info Csatorna*, National Geographic Channel, Film, Disney Channel, SportKlub, Hír TV, ATV, HBO, Private Spice ✂ Neo FM*.

Location	M1	M2	M3	kW
Aggtelek	45c	31	63	39/34/48
Budapest	38a	55	62	100/40/50
Csengöd	45f	-	68	50/43
Debrecen	45b	51	62	15/13/15
Gerecse	64e	29	63	97/16/97
Györ	42e	25	61	27/19/34
Kabhegy	64e	-	61	100
Kékes	56c	39	69	15/8/28
Komádi	46b	51	62	80/88/102
Nagykanizsa	24e	55	-	35/20
Pécs	52d	-	67	62/40
Salgótarján	38e	55	62	17/15.1/18.5
Sopron	42e	40	68	83/61/80
Szeged	60f	22	65	20/9.5/19
Szentes	60f	-	65	100
Szombathely	38e	58	68	14.5/17/15.5
Tokaj	60c	31	63	55/13/47
Úzd	52d	37	67	29/25/33
Vásvar	38e	58	68	98/85/72

+ site with txs below 10kW. °) incl. reg prgrs (a-f), see above
NB. Subject to changes while the transition to DTT is progressing.

ICELAND

Systems: # PAL-B/G [E]; DVB-T (MPEG2) [E]

National Stations
RÚV (Pub) ✉ Efstaleiti 1, 150 Reykjavík ☎ +354 5153000 🖷 +354 5153010 **E:** istv@ruv.is **W:** www.ruv.is **L.P:** Dir: Páll Magnússon

Location	ch	kW	Location	ch	kW
Stykkishólmur	3	90	Háfell	8	1100
Gagnhæði	4	80	Hegranes	8	12
Skáfafell	4	300	Blönduós	9	20
Stóra Klif	5	39	Vatnsendi	10	20
Heiðárfjall	5	10	Auðsholt	49	10
Vaðlaheiði	6	490	+ txs below 10kW		

365 MIÐLAR (Comm) ⌨ Skaftahlíð 24, 105 Reykjavík ☎ +354 5156000 **E:** 365@365midlar.is **W:** www.365midlar.is **L.P:** Chair: Ingibjörg S Pálmadóttir **Chs:** Stöð 2 (partly◐), Stöð 2 Bíó◐, Stöð 2 Sport◐ **Txs: Stöð 2:** Reykjavík ch6 (10kW) & netw.; **Stöð 2 Bíó:** Reykjavík ch49 (2kW); **Stöð 2 Sport:** Reykjavík ch12 (1kW) & netw. – **SKJÁRINN (Comm)** ⌨ Skipholti 31, 105 Reykjavík ☎ +354 5956000 **E:** info@skjarinn.is **W:** www.skjarinn.is. **Txs: Skjár Einn** ◐ : Reykjavík ch55 (1kW). **L.P:** CEO: Friðrik Friðriksson.

Local Stations
Extra: 600 Akureyri; Vaðlaheidi ch53 (0.1kW) **Omega (Rlg)** Grensásvegi 8 108 Reykjavík; Bláfjöll ch45 (0.1kW), Reykjavík ch45 (0.002kW) & ch51 (1kW), Mosfellsbær ch57 (0.1kW). **Sjónvarp Flensborg:** Brekkugötu 17-19, 220 Hafnarfjörður; ch58 (0.01kW). **Sjónvarp Ólafsvík:** 355 Ólafsvík; ch63 (0.01kW).

DTT Transmitters
Licensee: Og Fjarskipti (Vodafone Digital Ísland) ⌨ Skútuvogi 2, 104 Reykjavík **E:** vodafone@vodafone.is **W:** www.vodafone.is **Mux 1◐:** RÚV, Stöð 2, Stöð 2 Bíó, Stöð 2 Sport, Stöð Sport 2, Stöð 2 Extra, Stöð 2+, Skjár Einn **Mux 2◐:** Discovery Channel, E! Entertainement, Sky News, DR1, Cartoon Network, ÍNN, Skjár Golf, Blue Hustler.

Location	M1	M2	kW
Reykjavík	27	28	0.3

+ nationwide tx network

INDIA

Systems: # PAL-B/G [E] ⇩2015; DVB-T (MPEG2) [E], DVB-T2 (MPEG4) [E]

DOORDARSHAN (DD) (Pub) ⌨ Doordarshan Bhawan, Copernicus Marg, New Delhi-110001 ☎ +91 11 23386055 🖷 +91 11 23385843 **E:** dddirect@dd.nic.in **W:** www.ddindia.gov.in **L.P:** DG: Tripurari Sharan **Chs (terr.):** DD-National, DD-News, DD-Sports, DD-Barathi, DD-Regional Channels **Txs: DD-1:** New Delhi ch5 (20kW) & network; **DD-News:** New Delhi ch7 (20kW) & network.

DTT Transmitters (under construction)
Operator: Doordardshan **Mux 1:** DD-National, DD-News, DD-Sports, DD-Barathi, DD-Regional **Mux 2 (DVB-T2/MPEG4):** tbd **Mux 3 (DVB-H):** 16 prgrs.

Location	M1	M2	M3	kW
New Delhi	32	29	26	6/50

+ nationwide netw. under construction, mainly Mux 1 (ca. 230 HP sites)

INDONESIA

Systems: # PAL-B/G [E] ⇩2018; DVB-T (MPEG2) [E]

National Stations
TELEVISI REPUBLIK INDONESIA (TVRI) (Gov) ⌨ Jalan Gerbang Pemuda, Senayan, Jakarta 10270 ☎ +62 21 3846740 🖷 +62 21 5737152 **E:** wmaster@tvri.co.id **W:** www.tvri.co.id **L.P:** MD: Azis Husein **Chs:** TVRI1, TVRI2. **Txs:** TVRI1: Jakarta ch6 (5kW) & network; TVRI2: Jakarta ch9. – **TELEVISIE EDUKASIE (Gov)** ⌨ Jakarta. **W:** www.televisiedukasi.com **Txs:** Bandung ch7 (0.1kW) & netw. – **ANTEVE (PT CAKRAWALA ANDALAS TELEVISI) (Comm)** ⌨ Mulia Center Building, 19th Floor, Jl. HR Rasuna Said Kav. X-6 No.8, Jakarta 12940 ☎ +62 21 5222084 🖷 +62 62 215222087 **E:** sales@anteve.co.id **W:** www.an.tv **Txs:** Jakarta ch47 (40kW) & network. – **GLOBAL TV (PT GLOBAL INFORMASI BERMUTU) (Comm)** ⌨ Jl Jend. Ahmad Yani 31, Jakarta 13230☎+62 21 5360601 🖷 +62 21 5360602 **E:** globaltv@globaltv.co.id **W:** www.globaltv.co.id **Txs:** Jakarta ch51 & network. – **INDOSIAR (PT. INDOSIAR VISUAL MANDIRI) (Comm)** ⌨ Jl. Damai No 11, Daan Mogot, Jakarta 11510 ☎ +62 21 5672222 🖷 +62 21 5652221 **E:** program@indosiar.com **W:** www.indosiar.com **Txs:** Jakarta ch41 & network. – **METRO TV (PT MEDIA TELEVISI INDONESIA) (Comm)** ⌨ Jl. Pilar Mas Raya Kav. A-D., Kedoya, Kebon Jeruk, Jakarta 11520 ☎ +62 21 58300077 🖷 +62 21 5816365 **E:** info@metrotvnews.com **W:** www.metrotvnews.com **Txs:** Jakarta ch57 & network. – **MNC TV (PT MEDIA NUSANTARA CITRA TV) (Comm)** ⌨ Jalan Pintu II - Taman Mini Indonesia Indah, Pondok Gede, Jakarta Timur 13810 ☎ +62 21 8409475 🖷 +62 21 8412471 **E:** info@mnctv.com **W:** www.mnctv.com **L.P:** GM: Syamsudin C. Haesy **Txs:** Jakarta ch37 (80kW) & network. – **RCTI (PT RAJAWALI CITRA TELEVISI INDONESIA) (Comm)** ⌨ Jl. Raya Perjuangan No. 3, kb. Jeruk, Jakarta 11000 ☎ +62 21 5303540 🖷 +62 21 5493852 **E:** pr@rcti.tv **W:** www.rcti.tv **L.P:** Pres Dir: Muchamad Ralie Siregar; TM: Doopy Irwan **Txs:** Jakarta ch43 & network. – **SCTV (PT SURYA CITRA TELEVISI) (Comm)** ⌨ Graha SCTV 2nd floor,

Jl. Gatot Subroto Kav 21, Jakarta 12930 ☎ +62 21 5225555 🖷 +62 21 5224777 **E:** pr@sctv.co.id **W:** www.sctv.co.id **L.P.:** Dir. Op.: Lanny Ratulangi **Txs:** Jakarta ch45 (120kW) & network. – **TRANS TV (PT TELEVISI TRANSFORMASI INDONESIA) (Comm)** ⌨ Jl. Kapten Tendean Kav. 12-14A, Jakarta 12790 ☎ +62 21 7944240 🖷 +62 21 7992600 **E:** wmaster@transtv.co.id **W:** www.transtv.co.id **Txs:** Jakarta ch29 (80kW) & network. – **TRANS 7 (PT DUTA VISUAL NUSANTARA TIVI TUJUH) (Comm)** ⌨ Menara Bank Mega Lt. 20, Jl. Kapt. P. Tendean Kav.12-14A, Jakarta 12790 ☎+62 21 79177000 🖷 +62 21 79184684 **E:** info@trans7.co.id **W:** www.trans7.co.id **Txs:** Jakarta ch49 (60kW) & network. – **TVONE (PT LATIVI MEDIA KARYA (Comm)** ⌨ Kawasan Industri Pulo Gadung, Jl Rawa Teratai II No 2, Jakarta Timur 13260 ☎+62 21 4613545 🖷+62 21 4616255 **E:** info@tvone.co.id **W:** www.tvone.co.id **Txs:** Jakarta ch53 & network.

Local Stations not shown.

DTT Transmitters (under construction)
Licensee: TVRI/PT Telekom **Mux:** TVRI1, TVRI2, TV Edukasi, MNC TV/Global TV **Licensee:** Televisi Digital Indonesie **W:** www.ktdi.tv **Mux 2:** SCTV, Anteve, tvOne, Trans TV, Trans7, Metro TV

Location	M1	M2	kW
Jakarta	44	46	1.5/5

+ nationwide netw. under construction

IRAN

Systems: # PAL-B/G [E] ⇩2015; DVB-T (MPEG4) [E]

ISLAMIC REPUBLIC OF IRAN BROADCASTING (IRIB) (Gov) ⌨ P.O.Box 19395 3333, 19395 Tehran ☎ +98 21 22041093 🖷 +98 21 22014802 **E:** tv@irib.ir **W:** www.iribtv.ir **L.P:** Pres: Seyed Ezzatollah **Chs (Terr.):** IRIB TV1, IRIB TV2, IRIB TV3, IRIB TV5, IRINN, IRIB Bazar, regional stations, Al-Alam (in Arabic for viewers in Iraq). **Txs:** (-). **Al-Alam:** ch4.

DTT Transmitters (under construction)
Operator: IRIB **Mux:** IRIB TV1, IRIB TV2, IRIB TV3, IRIB TV4, IRIB TV5, IRIB Bazar, IRINN **Txs:** ch37 (Tehran) & netw. (nationwide netw. under construction).

IRAQ

System: PAL-B/G [E]

National Stations
AL-IRAQIYA TV (Pub) ⌨ Salhiya, Baghdad ☎ +964 1 8844412 🖷 +964 1 5410480 **W:** www.imn.iq **Chs:** Al-Iraqiya TV, Al-Iraqiya Sport Channel, Al-Iraqiya Atyaf. **Txs: Al-Iraqiya TV:** Najaf area ch5 & ch11, Sinjar ch5, Kirkuk ch6, Tikrit ch6, Amara ch7, Nasirya ch7, Samawa area ch8 & ch10, Ali Al-Gharbi ch9, Baghdad ch9, Basra area ch9 & ch25, Falluja ch9, Karbala area ch5 & ch8, Kut ch9, Mosul ch9, Dewanya ch12, Baquba ch23, Suq Ashiukh ch26, Beiji ch27, Nasir ch33, Al-Hillah area ch38 & ch41, Samarra ch39; **Al-Iraqiya Sport Channel:** Nasirya ch5, Baghdad ch7, Mosul ch7, Nasir ch9, Suq Ashiukh ch10, Amara ch11, Ali Al-Gharbi ch12, Basra ch52; **Al-Iraqiya Atyaf:** Baghdad ch37 – **AL-FORAT (Comm)** ⌨ Baghdad. **E:** info@alforattv.com **W:** www.alforattv.net **Txs:** Baghdad ch26, Najaf ch28, Basra ch46, Kerbala ch57. – **AL-SHARQIYA (Comm)** ⌨ Baghdad. **E:** alsharqiya@alsharqiya.com **W:** www.alsharqiyatv.com **Txs:** Mosul ch42, Basra ch44, Baghdad ch48.

Local Stations
Al-Furatain: Hilla; ch36. **Al-Ghadeer:** Najaf; ch25. **Al-Huda:** Karbala; ch23. **Al-Hurriya:** Baghdad; ch37. **Al-Masar:** Baghdad; ch46. **Al-Mashriq:** Baghdad; ch54. – **Al-Merbad:** Basra; ch5: Amara ch42, Nasiriya ch46, Basra ch52. **Al-Nahrain:** Kut; ch6. **Al-Nakheel:** Basra; ch57. **Al-Rasheed:** Baghdad; ch34. **Al-Salam:** Baghdad; ch5. **Al-Sumaryia:** Qadisay; ch56. **Al-Yaum:** Baghdad; ch26. **Ashur:** Baghdad; ch44. **Kurdistan TV:** ch33. **Kurdsat TV:** Sulaimaniyah ch30. **Nahrian:** Baghdad; ch41. **TV Baghdad:** Baghdad; ch51.

Foreign TV Relays
MBC (Saudi Arabia): Baghdad ch61.

IRELAND

Systems: DVB-T (MPEG4) [E]

RTÉ TELEVISION (Pub) ⌨ Donnybrook, Dublin 4 ☎ +353 1 208 3111 🖷 +353 1 2082772 **E:** info@rte.ie **W:** www.rte.ie **L.P:** DG

(RTÉ): Noel Curran **Chs:** RTÉ1, RTÉ TWO, RTE News Now, TG4 (Irish-language service) **W:** www.tg4.ie) – **TV3 (Comm)** ▭ Westgate Business Park, Ballymount, Dublin 24 ☎ +353 1 4193333 🖷 +353 1 4193300 **E:** info@tv3.ie **W:** www.tv3.ie **Chs:** TV3, 3e **L.P:** CEO (TV3 Group): David McRedmond.

DTT Transmitters
Operator: RTÉ Network Ltd **Mux 1:** RTÉ1, RTÉ1 +1, RTÉ TWO HD, RTÉ News Now/Euronews, RTÉ jr., 3e, TV3, TG4 ✛ RTÉ R. 1, R. 1 Extra, 2FM, Lyric FM, Raidio na Gaeltachta, Pulse, 2XM, Choice, Gold, Chill, Junior. **Mux 2:** tbd

Location	M1	M2	kW	Location	M1	M2	kW
Cairn Hill	47	44	160	Mount Leinster	23	39	160
Clermont Carn	52	57	160	Mullaghanish	21	24	160
Dungarvan	55	59	10	Spur Hill	45	49	50
Holywell Hill	30	20	20	Three Rock	54	58	63
Kippure	54	58	63	Truskmore	53	57	160
Maghera	48	55	160	Woodcock Hill	47	44	10

+ sites with txs below 10kW.

ISRAEL

System: DVB-T (MPEG4) [F]

ISRAEL BROADCASTING AUTHORITY (IBA) (Pub) L.P: Chmn: Amir Gilat **W:** www.iba.org.il **Chs:** Channel 1, Channel 33. **Channel 1** ▭ P.O.Box 7139, Jerusalem 91071 ☎ +972 2 5301333 🖷 +972 2 6291862 **E:** tvdep@iba.org.il **Channel 33** ▭ P.O.Box 13172, Jerusalem 91131 ☎ +972 2 5013800 **E:** arutz33@iba.org.il – **THE SECOND AUTHORITY FOR TELEVISION AND RADIO (Pub)** P.O.Box 3445, Jerusalem **L.P:** Chmn: Ilan Avishar. **NB.** The Second Authority for Television and Radio supervises the commercial TV channels Channel 2, Channel 10. **Channel 2 (Comm)** P.O.Box 34122, Jerusalem 95464 ☎ +972 2 6556222 🖷 +972 2 6556286 **E:** rashut@rashut2.org.il **W:** www.rashut2.org.il. **Channel 10 (Comm)** ▭ 53 Derech Hashalom St., Givatayim 53454 ☎ +972 3 7331000 🖷 +972 3 7331040 **W:** www.nana10.co.il **L.P:** CEO Yoav Heldman. – **CHANNEL 99 - KNESSET CHANNEL (Gov)** ▭ Kiryat Ben-Gurion, Jerusalem 91950 ☎ +972 2 6541636 **E:** feedback@knesset.gov.il **W:** www.knesset.gov.il.

DTT Transmitters
Operator: Bezeq ▭ P.O.Box 1088, Jerusalem 91010 ☎ +972 36 264562 🖷 +972 36 264559 **W:** www.bezeq.com **Mux:** IBA Channel 1, IBA Channel 33, Channel 2, Channel 10, Channel 99 **Txs:** ch26 (SFN, Central Israel), ch29 (SFN, Northern/Southern Israel).

WEST BANK & GAZA (Palestinian Authority)

System: PAL-B/G [E]

National Station
PALESTINIAN BROADCASTING CORP. TV (Gov) ▭ P.O.Box 984, Ramallah Albereih, West Bank ☎ +970 2 2987903 🖷 +970 2 29879031 **E:** pbcinfo@pbc.gov.ps **W:** www.pbc.gov.ps **L.P:** Chmn: Radwan Abu Ayyash **Txs:** Nablus ch5, Khan Yunis ch21, Ariha (Jericho) ch21, Kasser-Elhakim (Gaza) ch23, Ramallah ch25, Halhul ch30, Jenin ch31, Betjala ch34.

Local Stations not shown.

ITALY

Systems: DVB-T (MPEG2) [E], DVB-T2 (MPEG4)

National Stations
RADIOTELEVISIONE ITALIANA (RAI) (Pub) ▭ Direzione Centrale TV, Viale Mazzini 14, 00195 Roma ☎ +39 06 36864046 🖷 +39 06 36226422 **E:** portale@rai.it **W:** www.rai.it **L.P:** DG: Mauro Masi **Chs:** RaiUno, RaiDue, RaiTre, Rai 4, RaiNews24, Rai Sport 1, RAI Sport 2, Rai Storia, Rai Move, Rai Gulp, Rai YoYo – **LA 7 (Comm)** ▭ Via della Pineta Sacchetti 229, 00166 Roma (RM) ☎ +39 06 35584 🖷 +39 06 355 84257 **E:** la7@la7.tv **W:** www.la7.tv – **MEDIASET (Comm)** ▭ Viale Europa 48, Palazzo dei Cigni, 20093 Cologno Monzese (MI) ☎ +39 02 21021 🖷 +39 02 85414283 **W:** www.mediaset.it **Chs:** Italia 1, Rete 4, Canale 5. – **MTV ITALIA (Comm)** ▭ Corso Europa 7, 20122 Milano (MI). ☎ +39 02-7621171 🖷 +39 02 7621227 **E:** segreteria@mtvne.com **W:** www.mtv.it – **SAT2000 (Comm)** ▭ Via Aurelia 786, 00165 Roma (RM) ☎ +39 06 665081 🖷 +39 06 66508581 **E:** sat2000@sat2000.it **W:** www.sat2000.it.

Local Stations not shown.

DTT Transmitters
Licensee: RAIWAY **Mux 1:** Rai 1, Rai 2, Rai 3, RAI News ✛ RAI R.1-3 **Txs:** Roma (Monte Cavo) ch11 & netw. **Mux 2:** Rai Sport 1, Rai Sport 2, Rai Scuola ✛ Rai radiofd4, Rai radiofd5, Rai Notturno Italiano, Radio Isoradio **Txs:** Roma (Monte Cavo) ch30 & netw. – **Mux 3:** Rai 4, Rai Gulp, Rai Movie, Rai Premium, Rai YoYo **Txs:** Roma (Monte Cavo) ch26 & netw. **Mux 4:** Rai 5, Rai HD, Rai Storia **Txs:** Roma (Monte Cavo) ch40 & netw. – **Licensee:** Dfree **E:** tecnici@dfree.tv **W:** www.dfree.tv **Mux✪:** Disney Channel, BBC Knowledge, Universal, Cinema, Crime, Emotion, Energy, Premium Joi, Mya, NetTV **Txs:** Roma (Monte Cavo) ch50 & netw. – **Licensee:** Mediaset **Mux✪:** Cartoon Network, Disney Junior, Disney Channel +1, Moto GP, Calcio HD 1, Calcio 1-6, Extra 1, Extra 2, Steel **Txs:** Roma (Monte Cavo) ch52 & netw. – **Licensee:** TIMB **Mux 1:** HSE24, Gallio, Mediaset Extra, Mediasat Italia, QVC, Real Time, DMAX, CUBOVISIONE **Txs:** Roma (Monte Cavo) ch47 & netw. **Mux 2:** LA7 HD, Super!, Focus, Sportitalia, Sportitalia2, Sportitalia24, VERO TV, PADRE PIO TV ✛ RTL 102.5 **Txs:** Roma (Monte Cavo) ch60 & netw. **Mux 3:** La7, La7D, K2, FriSBEE, MTV, MTV Music, VERO CAPRI, Cinquantacinque, various VOD **Txs:** Roma (Monte Cavo) ch48 & netw.
Other licensees: Regional and licensees not shown (except below).

South Tyrol

Regional Licensee: Rundfunk-Anstalt Südtirol (RAS) ▭ Europallee 164A, 39100 Bozen ☎ +39 0471 546666 🖷 +39 0471 200378 **E:** info@ras.bz.it **W:** www.ras.bz.it **Mux 1:** ORF eins, ORF2, Das Erste, ZDF **Mux 2:** SF1, SF ZWEI, Bayerisches Fernsehen, KiKa/ZDF_neo **Mux 3:** ZDF HD*, 3sat, ARTE, RSI La 1 **Mux 4*:** ORF 1 HD, ORF Zwei HD **Txs: Mux 1:** ch34 (SFN), **Mux 2:** ch51 (SFN) **Mux 3:** ch27 (SFN) **Mux 4:** ch59 (SFN). (*=MPEG4)

IVORY COAST

System: SECAM-K1 [VHF=K, UHF=E]

TÉLÉVISION IVOIRIENNE (Gov) ▭ 08 BP 883, Abidjan 08 ☎ +225 22449039 🖷 +225 22447339 **E:** dgrti@aviso.ci **W:** www.rti.ci **L.P:** Pres: Pascal Brou Aka **Chs:** RTI1, RTI2. **Txs: RTI1:** Koun ch4 (10kW), Tiémé ch4 (10kW), Séguéla ch5 (10kW), Digo ch5 (2kW), Dimbroko ch6 (2kW), Touba ch6 (1kW), Man ch7 (10kW), Dabakala ch7 (2kW), Abidjan ch8 (10kW), Niangbo ch8 (10kW), Niangué ch8 (10kW), Bouaflé ch9 (10kW) & repeaters. **RTI2:** (-).

JAMAICA

System: NTSC-M [A]

PUBLIC BROADCASTING CORP. OF JAMAICA (Pub) ▭ 5-9 South Odeon Avenue, Kingston ☎ +1 876 7549123 🖷 +1 876 9060435 **E:** info@ pbcjamaica.org **W:** www.pbcjamaica.org **Txs:** (-) – **CVM TELEVISION LTD (Comm)** ▭ 69 Constant Spring Rd, Kingston 10 ☎ +1 876 9319400 🖷 +1 876 9311573 **E:** customerservice@cvmtv.com **W:** www.cvmtv. com **L.P:** Chmn: Neville Blythe **Txs:** Marley Hill ch4, Coopers Hill ch9, Ochos Rios ch10, Montego Bay ch11, Cabbage Hill ch12, Port Antonio ch13. – **TELEVISION JAMAICA LTD (TVJ) (Comm)** ▭ P.O.Box 100, Kingston 10. ☎ +1 876 9265620 🖷 +1 876 9291029 **E:** tvjadmin@ cwjamaica.com **W:** www.televisionjamaica.com **L.P:** GM: Claire C. Grant **Txs:** ZQI-TV: Coopers Hill ch7, Port Antonio ch8, Yallahs ch9, Montego Bay ch9, Kingston ch11, Oracabessa ch12, Spur Tree ch13. – **LOVE TV (Rlg)** ▭ 12 Carlton Cresent, Kingston ☎ +1 876 9689596 🖷 +1 876 9685379 **Txs:** Montego Bay ch2, Ochos Rios ch3, Kingston ch6, Huntley ch8, Kingston ch17.

JAPAN

System: ISDB-T [J]

National Stations
NIPPON HOSO KYOKAI (NHK) (Pub) ▭ 2-1, Jinnan 2-chome, Shibuya-ku, Tokyo 150-8001 ☎ +81 3 34651111 **W:** www.nhk.or.jp **Chs:** NHK General, NHK Educational **L.P:** Pres: Masayuki Matsumoto – **ALL-NIPPON NEWS NETWORK (ANN) (Comm)** ▭ 9-1, Roppongi 6-chome, Minato-ku, Tokyo 106-8001 ☎ +81 3 61061111 **W:** www. tv-asahi.co.jp **L.P:** Pres: Masao Kimiwada. – **FUJI TELEVISION NETWORK (FTN) (Comm)** ▭ 4-8, Daiba 2-chome, Minato-ku, Tokyo 137-8088 ☎ +81 3 55008888 **W:** www.fujitv.co.jp **L.P:** Chmn: Hisashi Hieda. – **JAPAN NEWS NETWORK (JNN) (Comm)** ▭ 3-6, Akasaka 5-chome, Minato-ku, Tokyo 107-8006. ☎ +81 3 37461111 **W:** news. tbs.co.jp **L.P:** Chmn: Hiroshi Inoue – **NIPPON NEWS NETWORK (NNN) (Comm)** ▭ 6-1, Higashi Shimbashi 1-chome, Minato-ku,

Tokyo 105-7444 ☎ +81 3 62154444 **W:** www.ntv.co.jp **L.P:** Pres: Noritada Hosokawa – **TV TOKYO NETWORK (TXN) (Comm)** 3-12, Toranomon 4-chome, Minato-ku, Tokyo 105-8012 ☎ +81 3 54707777 **W:** www.tv-tokyo.co.jp. **L.P:** Pres/CEO: Masayuki Shimada. **NB.** Commercial stns are relayed nationwide via local affiliates.

Local Stations not shown.

DTT Transmitters (National Stations)

Location	NHK[1]	NHK[2]	ANN	FTN	JNN	NNN	TXN
Tokyo (Tokyo Tower)	1	2	24	21	22	25	23

+ nationwide tx network [1]) NHK General [2]) NHK Educational

JORDAN

System: PAL-B/G [E]

JORDAN TELEVISION (JTV) (Pub) ✉ P.O.Box 1041, 11118 Amman ☎ +962 6 4749171 🖷 +962 6 4778578 **E:** tv@jrtv.gov.jo **W:** www.jrtv. jo **L.P:** Chmn/CEO (JRTV): Saleh Al-Kallab **Chs:** JTV1, JTV2 **Txs** (pol. H): **JTV1:** Suweilih ch3 (104kW), Aqaba ch9 (5kW), Ras Munif-Ajlun ch9 (500kW), Deir Alla ch26 (6kW) & repeaters. **JTV2:** Aqaba ch5 (5kW), Suweilih ch6 (108kW), Ras Munif-Ajlun ch11 (500kW), Deir Alla ch29 (6kW) & repeaters.

KAZAKHSTAN

Systems: SECAM-D/K [R], PAL-D/K [R]; DVB-T2 (MPEG4) [E]

National Stations
QAZAQ TELEVIZIYASY (Gov) ✉ Jeltoqsan 177, 050013 Almaty ☎ +7 727 2635579 🖷 +7 727 2631207 **W:** www.kaztrk.kz **Txs:** Almaty ch5 & network. – **XABAR (Gov)** ✉ Jeltoqsan 185, 050013 Almaty ☎ +7 727 2700001 🖷 +7 727 2627805 **E:** khabar@khabar.kz **W:** www. khabar.kz **Chs:** Xabar, Yel Arna. **Txs: Xabar:** Almaty ch3 (25kW) & network.**Yel Arna:** (-). – **KTK (Comm)** ✉ Respwblïk alana 13, 050013 Almaty ☎ +7 727 2583657 🖷 +7 727 2583693 **E:** ktk@ktk-tv.kz **W:** www.ktk-tv.kz **L.P:** Dir: Andrey Osadtsyuk. **Txs:** Almaty ch12 (5kW) & network. – **NTK (Comm)** ✉ Respwblïk alana 13, 050013 Almaty ☎ +7 727 2672750 🖷 +7 727 2721154 **E:** office@ntk.kz **W:** www.ntk.kz **L.P:** GD: Saida Igenbek. **Txs:** Almaty ch7 & network.

Local Stations, Foreign TV Relays not shown.

DTT Transmitter (Trial)
Operator: Kazteleradio **Mux:** Test **Txs:** ch49 (Qaragandi 1kW)

KENYA

System: DVB-T2 (MPEG4) [E]

National Stations
KENYA BROADCASTING CORP. (Gov) ✉ P.O.Box 30456, Harry Thuku Road, 00100 Nairobi ☎ +254 20 334567 🖷 +254 20 220675 **E:** kbctv@swiftkenya.com **W:** www.kbc.co.ke **L.P:** Chmn: Charles Musyoki Muoki **Chs:** Channel 1, Channel 2, Metro TV. – **CITIZEN TV (Comm)** ✉ P.O.Box 7468, 00300 Nairobi ☎ +254 20 2721415 🖷 +254 20 2724220 **E:** news@royalmedia.co.ke **W:** www.citizentv. co.ke – **FAMILY TV (Rlg)** ✉ P.O.Box 2330 KNH, Nairobi ☎ +254 20 4200000 🖷 +254 20 4200100 **E:** info@familymedia.com **W:** www. familymedia.tv – **KENYA TELEVISION NETWORK (KTN) (Comm)** ✉ P.O.Box 56985, 00100 Nairobi ☎ +254 20 227122 🖷 +254 20 3114467 **E:** admin@ktnkenya.com **W:** www.standardmedia.co.ke **L.P:** Chmn: Mwakio Sio. – **K24 (Comm)** ✉ 3rd Floor, Longonot Place, Kijabe St., 00100 Nairobi. ☎ +254 21 248000 – **NATION TV (NTV) (Comm)** ✉ P.O.Box 49010, Nairobi 00100 GPO ☎ +254 20 3208000 **E:** views@ntv. co.ke **W:** www.ntv.co.ke – **OXYGEN TV (Comm)** ✉ P.O.Box 48445, 00100 Nairobi. **L.P:** MD: Kass Khimji. – **STELLA VISION (STV) (Comm)** ✉ P.O. Box 20190, Nairobi ☎ +254 20 2712982 🖷 +254 20 2713146.

Local Stations not shown.

DTT Transmitters
Operator: Signet Ltd (KBC) **Mux:** KBC Channel One, KBC Channel 2, Metro TV, NTV, KTN, CNBC Africa, K24, STV, EATN, EATV, Oxygen TV, Family TV, God TV, Kiss TV, Classic TV, Citizen TV, GBS ✻ KBC English Service, KBC Idha FM, Metro FM, Coro FM **Txs:** (-).

KIRIBATI

NB: No terrestrial TV station.

KOREA, North (D.P.R. of Korea)

System: PAL-D/K [R]

RADIO AND TELEVISION BROADCASTING COMMITTEE OF THE DEM.PEOPLE'S REPUBLIC OF KOREA (Gov) ✉ Jonsung-dong, Moranbong District, Pyongyang ☎ +850 2 816035 🖷 +850 2 812100 **L.P:** Chmn: Sung Su Cha **Chs:** Korean Central Television (KCTV), Korean Educational and Cultural Television (KECTV), Kaesong Television, Mansudae Television. **Txs: KCTV:** Sangmasan ch1 (10kW), Chayubong ch2 (30kW), Suryongsan ch2 (30kW), Pegebong ch3 (30kW), Hamhung ch3 (70kW), Wonsan ch4 (10kW), Songjinsan ch4 (20kW), Jajiryong ch5 (30kW), Peakam ch5 (10kW), Sambongsan ch5 (10kW), Kangryong ch5 (30kW), Kumgungsan ch5 (30kW), Chongjin ch6 (70kW), Hyangsan ch6 (10kW), Sepo ch6 (70kW), Sinuiju ch6 (70kW), Sariwon ch7 (30kW), Chayubong ch8 (30kW), Haksongsan ch8 (20kW), Kanggye ch8 (70kW), Jaedoksan ch9 (30kW), Unjubong ch9 (70kW), Wangjesan ch9 (30kW), Sepo ch9 (70kW), Sinyang ch9 (30kW), Wonsan ch10 (70kW), Haeju ch11 (70kW), Sambongsan ch11 (10kW), Jonchon ch11 (10kW), Songsan ch12 (10kW), Jajiryong ch12 (30kW), Chongjin ch12 (70kW), Haksongsan ch12 (20kW), Misan ch12 (70kW), Pyongyang ch12 (700kW), Rimbong ch12 (10kW), Robaeksan ch12 (30kW), Tokusan ch12 (20kW) & relay txs below 10kW; **KECTV:** Pyongyang ch9 (140kW); **Kaesong Television:** Kaesong ch8 (30kW); **Mansudae Television:** Pyongyang ch5 (350kW).

KOREA, South (Rep. of Korea)

Systems: T-DMB [A]. AFN: # NTSC-M [A]

National Stations
KOREAN BROADCASTING SYSTEM (KBS) (Pub) ✉ 113, Yeouigongwon-ro, Yeoungdeungpo-gu, Seoul 150-790 ☎ +82 2 7812001 🖷 +82 2 7812099 **W:** www.kbs.co.kr **L.P:** Pres: In-Kyu Kim **Chs:** KBS 1TV, KBS 2TV. – **EDUCATIONAL BROADCASTING SYSTEM (EBS) (Pub)** ✉ 2748, Nambusunhwan-ro, Seocho-gu. Seoul 137-791 ☎ +82 2 5211586 🖷 +82 2 5210241 **W:** www.ebs.co.kr **L.P:** Pres: Duk Hoon Kwak. – **MUNHWA BROADCASTING CORP. (MBC) (Comm)** ✉ 96, Yeouinaru-ro, Yeoungdeungpo-gu, Seoul 150-728 ☎ +82 2 7892851 🖷 +82 2 7823094 **W:** www.imbc.com **L.P:** Pres/CEO: Jae-Cheol Kim. – **SBS (Comm)** ✉ 161, Mokdongseo-ro, Yangcheon-gu, Seoul 158-725 ☎ +82 2 20610006 🖷 +82 2 21133169 **W:** www. sbs.co.kr **L.P:** Chmn: Se-young Yoon. **Affiliates:** CJB (Cheongju), GTB (Chuncheon), JIBS (Jeju), JTV (Jeonju), KBC (Gwangju), KNN (Busan), TBC (Daegu), TJB (Daejeon), UBC (Ulsan).

Local Stations not shown.

DTT Transmitters (National Stations)

Location	KBS 1TV	KBS 2TV	EBS	MBC	SBS
Seoul	10	8	9	13	16

+ nationwide tx network

Foreign Military Station
AFN Korea (U.S. Mil) ✉ Unit #15324, APO AP 96205-0097, USA ☎ +82 2 79146495 **W:** www.afnkorea.net **Txs:** Daegu ch12 (1kW), Seoul (Yongsan-gu) ch34 (30kW), Munsan ch49 (5kW), Dongducheon ch49 (1kW), Gunsan ch49 (2.5kW) & txs below 1kW.

KOSOVO

System: PAL-B/G [E]

National Stations
RADIO TELEVIZIONE I KOSOVËS (RTK) (Pub) ✉ Rr. Xhe Prishtina 12, 10000 Prishtinë ☎ +381 38 230102 🖷 +381 38 235336 **E:** post@rtklive.com **W:** www.rtklive.com **L.P:** DG (RTK): Bekim Hasani **Txs:** Crnusha ch7, Zatriq ch9, Maja e Gjelbërt ch12, Prishtinë ch23. – **KOHAVISION TV (KTV) (Comm)** ✉ Rr. Nene Tereza, 10000 Prishtinë ☎ +381 38 248014 🖷 +381 38 248015 **E:** kohavision@koha. net **W:** www.kohavision.net **Txs:** (-). – **TV 21 (Comm)** ✉ Pallati i Mediave, Aneks II, 10000 Prishtinë ☎ +381 38 241526 🖷 +381 38 241526 **E:** lajmet@rtv21.tv **W:** rtv21.tv **Txs:** Prishtinë ch37 & network.

Local Stations
TV Besa: Rr. Kater Kullat n.n., 20000 Prizereni; ch30. **TV Dukagjini:** Rr. Fehmi Agani 16, Pejë; ch36. **TV Festina:** Rr. Deshmoret e Kombit n.n., Ferizaj; ch40. **TV Herc:** 73000 Shterpcë; ch35. **TV Iliria:** Rr. Hoxhë Jonuzi n.n., 61000 Viti; ch28. **TV Liria:** Rr. Reçak n.n., Ferizaj; ch29. **TV Men:** Rr. Nene Tereza 52, Gjilan; ch47. **TV Mir:** Rr. Vojske

Jugoslavije n.n., Leposaviq; ch23. **TV Mitrovica:** Mitrovicë; ch42. **TV Most:** Rr. Nemanjica 14, Zveqan; ch61. **TV Opinion:** Rr. Asdreni 1, 20000 Prizereni; Zym ch28. **TV Prizren:** Rr. Papa Gjon Pali II 1A, Prizereni; ch60. **TV Puls:** Shillovë; Gjilan ch36. **TV Syri Vision:** Rr. Sadik Pozhegu 28, Gjakovë; ch33. **TV Tema:** Rr. Sadik Bega n.n., Ferizaj; ch50. **TV Vali:** Pasjak; Gjilan ch39. **TV Zoom:** Kuvcë e Epërme; ch43. **TV Yeni Donem:** Rr. Gjeravica 13A, 20000 Prizereni; ch53. **TV 3K:** 38217 Soqanicë; ch52.

KUWAIT

Systems: PAL-B/G [E]. BFBS-TV: DVB-T (MPEG4) [E]

KUWAIT TELEVISION (Gov) ✉ P.O. Box 621, 13007 Safat ☎ +965 22415300 🖷 +965 22454233 **W:** www.moinfo.kw.gov **Chs:** KTV1, KTV2, KTV3, KTV4, KTV5 **Txs: KTV1:** Failaka ch8 (950kW), Failaka ch24 (4500kW), Moi ch26 (25kW), Rawdatein ch38 (4700kW), Ahmadi ch59 (100kW). **KTV2:** Failaka ch10 (1000kW), Moi ch28 (6kW), Failaka ch39 (4800kW), Dibdibah ch65 (400kW). **KTV3:** Mutlaa ch5 (455kW), Mutlaa ch47 (2200kW). **KTV4:** Mutlaa ch12 (600kW), Mutlaa ch45 (2200kW). **KTV5:** ch5.

Foreign Military Station
BFBS-TV (British Mil) ✉ Chalfont Grove, Narcot Lane, Chalfont St Peter, Buckinghamshire, SL9 8TN, United Kingdom. **Mux✪:** BFBS1, BFBS2, BFBS3 Kids, BFBS4, BFBS1 One Day Later, BFBS+, Sky Sports 1, Sky Sports 2 ✪ BFBS R. 1+2, BFBS Gurkha R. **Tx:** ch27 (Camp Beuhring)

KYRGYZSTAN

Systems: # SECAM-D/K [R], # PAL-D/K [R]; DVB-T (MPEG4) [E]

KYRGYZ TELEVISION (Gov) ✉ blvd. Jash Gvardiya 59, 720010 Bishkek ☎ +996 312 253404 🖷 +996 312 651064 **W:** www.ktrk.kg **L.P:** DG: Kubat Otorbaev **Ch:** 1 Kanal Kyrgyzstan **Txs:** Bishkek ch11 & netw. – **ELTR (Pub)** ✉ blvd. Erkindik 122, 720040 Bishkek ☎ +996 312 906144 **L.P:** Dir: Shayyrbek Abdrakhmanov **E:** eltr@ktnet.kg **Txs:** Bishkek ch41 & netw. – **5 KANAL (Pub)** ✉ Ibraimov St 24, 720000 Bishkek ☎ +996 312 592066 **L.P:** Dir: Yevgeniy Berdnikov. **Txs:** Bishkek ch5 (5kW) & netw.

Local Stations, Foreign TV Relays not shown.

DTT Transmitters (under construction)
Operator: Kyrgyztelecom ✉ Chui avenue 96, 720000 Bishkek ☎ +996 312 681616 🖷 +996 312 662424 **E:** info@kt.kg **W:** www.kt.kg **Mux:** 1 Kanal Kyrgyzstan, ELTR, 5 Kanal, 1 Kanal Russia, Rossiya 1, Rossiya 24, TV Mir **Txs:** ch25 (Bishkek) & netw.

LAOS

Systems: # PAL-B/G [E] ⬇2015; DTMB [E]

National Station
TÉLÉVISION NATIONALE LAO (LNTV) (Gov) ✉ BP 5635, Vientiane ☎ +856 21 710643 🖷 +856 21 710182 **E:** tnlinfo@tnl.gov.la **W:** www.tnl.gov.la **L.P:** DG: Bounchom Vongphet. **Chs:** TV1, TV3, Provincial stns **Txs: TV1:** Vientiane ch9 (5kW) & relay txs **TV3:** Vientiane ch5 (10kW). Provincial stns not shown.

Foreign TV Relays
VTV4 (Vietnam): Vientiane ch11 (20kW).

DTT Transmitters (under construction)
Operator: LNTV **Mux 1-3:** n/a **Txs: Mux 1:** ch21 (Savannakhet 2.5kW) **Mux 2:** ch23 (Savannakhet 2.5kW) **Mux 3:** ch25 (Savannakhet 2.5kW). Additional txs at Pakse and Luangprabang.

LATVIA

Systems: DVB-T (MPEG4) [E]; Local stns: † PAL-D/K [R]

National Stations
LATVIJAS TELEVIZIJA (LTV) (Pub) ✉ Zakusalas krastmala 3, 1509 Riga ☎ +371 67200314 🖷 +371 67200025 **E:** ltv@ltv.lv **W:** www.ltv.lv **L.P:** DG: Edgars Kots **Chs:** LTV1, LTV7. – **LATVIJAS NEATKARIGA TELEVIZIJA (LNT) (Comm)** ✉ Elijas iela 17, 1050 Riga ☎ +371 67070200 🖷 +371 67821128 **E:** lnt@lnt.lv **W:** www.lnt.lv **L.P:** DG: Andrejs Ekis. – **TV3 VIASAT / TV6 VIASAT (Comm)** ✉ Maskavas iela 322, 1063 Riga ☎ +371 67629366 🖷 +371 67600599 **E:** tv3@tv3.

lv / tv6@tv6.lv **W:** www.tv3.lv / www.tv6.lv **L.P:** CEO: Baiba Zuzena. – **TV5 (Comm)** ✉ Elijas iela 17, 1050 Riga ☎ +371 67503924 🖷 +371 67503925 **E:** info@tv5.lv **W:** www.tv5.lv **L.P:** GD: Mihaels Šeitelmans. – **TV24 (Comm)** ✉ Vecpilsetas iela 19, 1050 Riga, ☎ +371 67490050 **E:** zinas@tv24.lv **W:** www.tv24.lv.

Local Stations (all Comm, all analogue)
Livanu TV: Rigas iela 112, 5316 Livani; ch12 (0.6kW). **Ogres Televizija:** Rigas iela 98a, 5001 Ogre; ch2 (0.1kW). **Smiltenes TV:** Dakteru iela 73, 4729 Smiltene; ch7 (0.15kW). **TV Jelgava:** Aviacijas iela 18, 3001 Jelgava; ch33 (0.85kW). **TV Spektrs:** Nakotnes iela 1, 2152 Malpils; Allazi ch12 (0.15kW). **Valmieras TV:** Rigas iela 4, 4201 Valmiera; Valmiera ch9 (0.16kW), Cesis ch46 (1.25kW), Madona ch56 (1.25). **Vidusdaugavas Televizija:** Brivibas iela 2d, 5200 Jekabpils; ch34 (0.4kW).

DTT Transmitters
Licensee: Lattelcom SIA ✉ Dzirnavu iela 105, 1011 Riga **E:** lattelecom@lattelecom.lv **W:** www.lattelecom.lv **Mux 1:** LTV1, LTV7, LNT, TV3 **Mux 2✪:** TV5, TV3+, TV6, Perviy Baltiyskiy, Diva Universal, Ren-TV Baltic, Eurosport, National Geographic **Mux 3✪:** Cartoon Network/TCM, OE, LMK, Euronews, RTR Planeta, Okhota i Rybalka, NTV Mir, PBMK, TVXXI, Šlagermuzikas kanals **Mux 4✪:** Discovery Travel & Living, Discovery Channel, Discovery Science, Animal Planet, ID Investigation Discovery, Travel Channel, Discovery World, BBC Entertainment, Nickelodeon, MTV Europe **Mux 5✪:** Fox Crime, Fox Life, Universal Channel, Syfy Universal, Silver Baltic, Sony Entertainment Television, Dom Kino, VH-1 Europe, iConcerts, Hustler TV **Mux 6 ✪:** ESPN America, KHL, Motors TV, NBA TV, Sportacentrs.com, Eurosport 2, KimJam, Disney Channel, Playhouse Disney/Boomerang.

Location	M1	M2	M3	M4	M5	M6	kW
Cesvaine	41	58	22	69	30	-	2x200/3x50
Dagda	44	-	-	-	-	-	10
Daugavpils	47	51	64	27	39	-	2x158/50/2x158
Dundaga	30	-	-	-	-	-	20
Kuldiga	30	40	47	52	25	-	100
Liepaja	21	61	62	69	33	-	50
Rezekne	44	50	62	27	39	-	158/126/50/2x158
Riga	28	31	43	45	48	59	200/125/3x200/125
Valmiera	21	51	54	50	33	-	2x100/50/2x100
Viesite	38	46	60	67	26	-	50/40/50/20/50

+ sites with txs below 10kW.

LEBANON

Systems: PAL-B/G [E]; DVB-T [E]

TÉLÉ-LIBAN (Pub) ✉ BP 115054, Hazmieh, 4848 Beirut ☎ +961 1 792000 🖷 +961 1 786921 **E:** tl@tele-liban.com **W:** www.tele-liban.com **L.P:** Pres/DG: Ibrahim El Khoury. **Txs:** Beirut ch5 (50kW) & network. – **AL-JADEED TV (Comm)** ✉ BP 110, 5958 Beirut ☎ +961 1 303300 🖷 +961 1 303300 **E:** info@aljadeed.tv **W:** www.aljadeed.tv. **Txs:** (-). – **AL-MANAR TV (Comm)** ✉ BP 354/25, Beirut ☎ +961 1 276000 🖷 +961 1 823794 **E:** info@almanar.com.lb **W:** www.almanar.com.lb **Txs:** (-). – **FUTURE TELEVISION (Comm)** ✉ BP 13-6052, Sanayeh, Beirut ☎ +961 1 355355 🖷 +961 1 753232 **W:** www.futuretvnetwork.com **Txs:** (-). – **LEBANESE BROADCASTING CORP. (LBC) (Comm)** ✉ BP 165853, Zouk 111, Beirut ☎ +961 9 850850 🖷 +961 9 850916 **E:** info@lbcgroup.tv **W:** www.lbcgroup.tv **L.P:** SM: Pierre Al Daher. **Txs:**(-). – **MURR TELEVISION (MTV) (Comm)** ✉ Ashrafieh Fouad Chehab Street, RML Building, Beirut ☎ +961 1 841020 🖷 +961 1 841029 **W:** mtv.com.lb **L.P:** Chmn/CEO: Michel El Murr. **Txs:** (-). – **NATIONAL BROADCASTING NETWORK (NBN) (Comm)** ✉ BP 13-6633 Chouran, Beirut ☎ +961 1 841020 🖷 +961 1 841029 **E:** info@nbn.com.lb **W:** www.nbn.com.lb **Txs:** (-).

LESOTHO

Systems: # PAL-I [E] ⬇2015 ; DVB-T [E] planned

LESOTHO TELEVISION (LTV) (Gov) ✉ P.O.Box 552, Maseru 100 ☎ +266 22323561 🖷 +266 22310003 **L.P:** Dir: Dyke Sehloho **Txs:** Katse (Terata), Semongkong (Thaba-Nts'o), Hilton Hill (Maseru) ch25; Quthing, Hilton Hill (Maseru) ch29; Mokhotlong ch36; Masite ch39; Berea Plateau ch47; Mohale's Hoek, Thabe-Putsoa ch51; Thaba-Tseke ch54; Leribe, Souru (Qacha's Nek) ch58; Baking, Mafeteng ch62.

Foreign TV Relay
TBN (USA): Berea Plateau ch21, Leribe ch41.

LIBERIA

System: PAL-B [E]

CLAR TV (Comm) ✉ Ashmun & Mechlin Street, Monrovia **E:** royal-comlr@yahoo.com **Tx:** Monrovia ch5. – **DC TV (Comm)** ✉ P.O.Box 1312, Monrovia. **Tx:** Monrovia ch11. – **POWER TV (Comm)** ✉ Broad & Gurley Street, Monrovia ☎ +231 6514343 **Tx:** Monrovia ch9. – **REAL TV (Comm)** ✉ Monrovia. **Tx:** Monrovia ch3.

LIBYA

System: PAL-B/G [E]

LIBYAN TELEVISION (Gov) ✉ P.O.Box 80237, Tripoli ☎ +218 21 3402153 🖷 +218 21 3403458 **Txs:** (pol.H exc. where stated) Benghazi ch5 (10kW V), Tripoli ch6 (20kW), Derna ch6V (5kW), Elmarj ch7V (5kW), Houn ch7 (1kW), Sirte ch7 (1kW), Khoms ch8 (5kW), Tobruk ch8 (5kW), Yevren ch9 (20kW), El Beida ch9 (5kW), Misurata ch10 (5kW), Egdabia ch11 (15kW) & repeaters.

LIECHTENSTEIN

NB: No terrestrial TV station.

LITHUANIA

Systems: DVB-T (MPEG2, MPEG4) [E]; Local stns: † PAL-D/K [R]

National Stations
LIETUVOS TELEVIZIJA (LTV) (Pub) ✉ Konarskio g. 49, 03123 Vilnius ☎ +370 5 2363100 🖷 +370 5 2363208 **E:** lrt@lrt.lt **W:** www.lrt.lt **LP:** Dir: Rimvydas Paleckis. **Chs (terr.):** LRT Televizija, LRT Kultura. – **BALTIJOS TELEVIZIJA (BTV) (Comm)** ✉ Laisves pr. 60, 05120 Vilnius ☎ +370 5 2780805 🖷 +370 5 2428907 **E:** info@btv.lt **W:** www.btv.lt **LP:** Dir: Liutaras Elkimavicius. – **LAISVES IR NEPRIKLAUSOMAS KANALAS (LNK) (Comm)** ✉ Šeškines g. 20, 07156 Vilnius ☎ +370 5 2431058 🖷 +370 5 2123924 **E:** lnk@lnk.lt **W:** www.lnk.lt **LP:** DG: Zita Sarakiene **Chs:** LNK, TV1, Info TV, Liuks! – **LIETUVOS RYTAS TV (Comm)** ✉ Gedimino pr. 12 A, 01103 Vilnius ☎ +370 5 2743718 🖷 +370 5 68307 **W:** tv.lrytas.lt **LP:** Dir: Edmundas Jakilaitis – **TV3 / TV6 (Comm)** ✉ Kalvariju g. 143, 08221 Vilnius ☎ +370 5 2030101 🖷 +370 5 2030103 **E:** info@@tv3.lt **W:** www.tv3.lt / www.6tv.lt

Local Stations (all Comm) (ª=analogue)
Aidas: Birutes g. 42, 21117 Trakai; ch24 (Trakai, Papliauškai). **Aukštaitijos krašto televizija:** Pazagieniu g. 29, Pazagieniai, 35185 Panevežio raj.; ch56 (Pazagienai, Viešintos). **Dzukijos televizija:** Naujoji g. 124, 62001 Alytus; ªch35 (0.4kW). **Kedainiu krašto televizija:** Basanaviciaus g. 36, 57288 Kedainiai; ch46. **KTV plius:** Nemuno g. 79, 37355 Panevezys; ch56 (Pazagienai, Viešintos). **Kupiškenu studija:** Krantines g. 2-28, 40126 Kupiškis; ch56 (Pazagienai, Viešintos). **LN Televizija:** Plateliu g. 17, Plunge; ch40. **Marijampoles televizija:** Gedimino g. 11, 68307 Marijampole; ch41. **PAN TV:** Respublikos g. 19-8, 35185 Panevezys; ch56 (Pazagienai, Viešintos). **PTV:** Peršekininku kaimas, Miroslavo sen., 64262 Alytus r.; Peršekininkai ªch12 (0.03kW). **Pukas-TV:** Ringuvos g. 61, 45242 Kaunas; ch54 (Juragiai). **Raseiniu krašto televizija:** Vaižganto g. 20, 60130 Raseiniai; ªch31 (0.15kW). **Roventos TV:** Draugystes g. 18, 89168 Mazeikiai; ªch37 (0.5kW). **Šiauliu televizija:** Liejyklos g. 10, 78147 Šiauliai; ch30 (Bubai). **S Plius:** Tilzes g. 74, 78140 Šiauliai; ch30 (Bubai). **Vakaru Lietuvos televizija:** Zveju g. 2, 91248 Klaipeda; ch45 (Girulai). **Ventos regionine televizija:** Ventos g. 32a, Venta, 85316 Akmenes r.; Venta ªch9 (0.1kW).

DTT Transmitters
Licensee Mux 1+2: Lietuvos radijo ir televizijos centras (LRTC) ✉ Sausio 13-osios g. 10, 04347 Vilnius ☎ +370 5 2621511 🖷 +370 5 2040396 **E:** info@lrtc.lt **W:** www.lrtc.lt **Mux 1:** LRT Televizija, LRT Kultura, LNK, TV3, TV1, BTV, TV6, Info TV, Liuks! **Mux 2(✪exc.*):** BBC World News*, CNN International, MTV, Cartoon Network, RTL, NBA TV, RTR Planeta, Ren-TV, RTVi, Balticum Auksinis. – **Licensee Mux 3-5:** Teo LT ✉ Savanoriu pr. 28, 03501 Vilnius ☎ +370 5 2621511 🖷 +370 5 2126665 **E:** info@teo.lt **W:** www.teo.lt **Mux 3 (✪exc.*):** Lietuvos rytas TV*, Animal Planet, Discovery Channel, Discovery World, Discovery Science, Eurosport, National Geographic, Travel Channel/Playboy, Diva Universal, SHOWTIME **Mux 4 (✪exc.*):** TV Polonia*, VH1, Sony Entertainement, Eurosport

2, Nickelodeon, Fashion TV, Euronews, LOLO TV, TLC, Baby TV **Mux 5✪:** Discovery HD, National Geographic HD, Eurosport HD.

Location	M1	M2	M3	M4	M5	kW
Bubiai	57	63	36	53	-	2x1.3/2x1.2
Girulai	60	38	36	53	-	2x0.8/2x1.2
Juragai	44	33	59	60	25	2x1.3/1.2/2x1.3
Viešintos	58	62	36	-	-	2x1/0.8
Vilnius	57	64	50	60	37	19.5/7.6/22.9/19.1/1.9/6.3

+ sites with txs below 1kW

Licensee: Balticum TV ✉ Taikos pr. 101, 94198 Klaipeda ☎ +370 46 390709 🖷 +370 46 342815 **E:** info@balticum-tv.lt **W:** www.balticum-tv.lt **Mux✪ (MPEG2):** Balticum TV, Balticum Auksinis, TV1000, Eurosport, Discovery Channel, Discovery Wild, RTR Planeta, NTV Mir. **Txs:** ch45 (Girulai), ch53 (Vilnius 0.6kW).

LORD HOWE ISLAND (Australia)

NB: No terrestrial TV station.

LUXEMBOURG

System: DVB-T (MPEG2) [E]

RTL GROUP (Comm) ✉ 45, blvd Pierre Frieden, 1543 Luxembourg ☎ +352 24865200 🖷 +352 24865139 **W:** www.rtlgroup.com; www.rtl.lu **LP:** Chmn (RTL Group): Thomas Rabe. **NB:** RTL Group is the company holding for several radio & TV enterprises. Prgrs distributed terrestrially via txs in Luxembourg: **RTL Télé Lëtzebuerg, den 2ten RTL** (in Luxembourgish); **RTL4, RTL5, RTL7, RTL8** (in Dutch, for viewers in the Netherlands); **Club RTL** (in Flemish, for viewers in Belgium); **Plug RTL, RTL TVI** (in French, for viewers in Belgium).

DTT Transmitters
Operator: BCE **Mux 1:** Club RTL, Plug RTL, RTL TVI, RTL4, RTL5, RTL7 **Tx:** ch24 (Dudelange 200kW) **Mux 2:** RTL Télé Lëtzebuerg, RTL Télé Lëtzebuerg HD, den 2ten RTL **Tx:** ch27 (Dudelange 200kW) **Mux 3:** RTL8, Luxe TV **Tx:** ch7 (Dudelange 25kW).

MACAU (China, SAR)

Systems: DTMB (MPEG2) [E]; # PAL-I [E]

TELEDIFUSÃO DE MACAU S.A. (TDM) (Gov) ✉ CP 446, Macau ☎ +853 28520206 🖷 +853 28520208 **E:** tdmadm@tdm.com.mo **W:** www.tdm.com.mo **LP:** Chmn: João Leong Kam Chun **Txs:** Aoshi Puwen (Portuguese): Monte da Guia ch30 (0.2kW) & 1 repeater; Aoshi Macau (Chinese): Monte da Guia ch32 (0.2kW) & 1 repeater.

DTT Transmitters
Operator: TDM **Mux 1:** Aoshi Macau, Aoshi Puwen, Aoshi Life, TDM Satellite Channel Macau **Mux 2:** CCTV News, CCTV English, Hunan Satellite TV **Mux 3:** Aoshi HD, Aoshi Sports

Location	M1	M2	M3
SFN	24	43	48

MACEDONIA

Systems: # PAL-B/G [E] ⇩2015; DVB-T (MPEG4) [E]

National Stations
MAKEDONSKA TELEVIZIJA (MTV) (Pub) ✉ ul. Dolno Nerezi bb, 1000 Skopje ☎ +389 2 258230 🖷 +389 2 3112578 **W:** www.mtv.com.mk **LP:** Dir (TV): Mirjana Dimovska **Chs:** MTV1, MTV2, MTV3 (Sobraniski kanal).

Location	MTV1	MTV2	MTV3	kW
Belasica	7	35	54	6/-/-
Boskija	8	57	54	10/20/2
Crn Vrv	6	30	40	100/-/10
Golak	5	38	44	10/-/-
Mali Vlaj	9	44	50	10/-/-
Ohrid	6	21	-	-/4
Pelister	4	29	33	30/-/10
Popova Šapka	10	38	34	10/-/-
Stogovo	6	31	37	10/-/-
Turtel	11	22	32	50/1000/-
Vodno	9	26	36	5/2/20

+ sites with txs below 1kW.

A1 TELEVIZIJA (Comm) ☐ ul. Pero Nakov bb, 1000 Skopje ☎ +389 2 2550301.🖷 +389 2 2550330 **E:** a1tv@a1.com.mk **W:** www.a1.com.mk **L.P:** GM: Gordana Stošic **Txs:** Vodno (Skopje) ch47 & network. – **ALSAT-M (Comm)** ☐ ul. Krste Misirkov 7, DTC Mavrovka Iom. C kat 9, 1000 Skopje ☎ +389 2 3290364 🖷 +389 2 3290365 **W:** www.alsat. tv **Txs:** Vodno (Skopje) ch45 & network. NB: relays Alsat-M (Albania). – **KANAL 5 (Comm)** ☐ ul. Skupi bb, 1000 Skopje ☎ +389 2 3091551 🖷 +389 2 3091560 **E:** kanal5@kanal5.com.mk **W:** kanal5.com.mk **Txs:** Vodno (Skopje) ch50 & network. – **TV SITEL (Comm)** ☐ ul. Gradski stadion bb, 1000 Skopje ☎ +389 2 3116566 🖷 +389 2 3229799 **E:** marketing@sitel.com.mk **W:** www.sitel.com.mk **Txs:** Vodno (Skopje) ch57 & network. – **TV TELMA (Comm)** ☐ ul. Nikola Parapunov bb, 1000 Skopje ☎ +389 2 3076677 🖷 +389 2 3070040 **E:** telma@telma.com.mk **W:** telma.com.mk.**Txs:** Vodno (Skopje) ch43 & network.

Local Stations
TV Alfa: Gradski stadion, 1000 Skopje; Raštak ch37, Sredno Vodno ch63. **TV Amazon:** ul. Gemdziska 135-b, 1000 Skopje; Raštak ch58, Sredno Vodno ch65 (time shared with TV Edo/TV KRT). **TV Anisa:** 6530 Plasnica; ch35. **TV Art:** ul. Ohridska 18, 1200 Tetovo; Kaleto ch36. **TV Art Kanal:** ul. Kuzman Šapkarev 12, 6330 Struga; ch22. **TV Boem:** ul. Cvetan Jakovlevski 3, 6250 Kicevo; ch42. **TV BTR Nacional:** ul. 376 br.108, 1000 Skopje; Sredno Vofno ch21. **TV Dalga-KRT:** ul. Partizanska 1, 1321 Kumanovo; Stari Lozja ch34. **TV Due:** ul. Mara Ugrinova bb, 1230 Gostivar; ch59. **TV Edo:** ul. 103 br, 50, 1000 Skopje; Raštak ch58, Sredno Vodno ch65 (time shared with TV Amazon/TV KRT). **TV EMI:** ul. 1-vi maj 34, 2420 Radoviš; ch48. **TV Era:** ul. Dzon Kennedi 9-a, 1010 Skopje-Cair; Sredno Vodno ch29, Gazi Baba ch53. **TV Gurra:** ul. Maršal Tito 172, 6250 Kicevo; Kaleto ch45. **TV Hana:** ul. Sima Pogacarevic bb, 1300 Kumanovo; Stari Lozja ch28. **TV Intel:** ul. Gorgi Trajcev 54, 2400 Strumica; ch24. **TV Iris:** ul. Goce Delcev 44, 2000 Štip; ch30. **TV Kaltrina:** ul. Boro Šain 19-A, 6330 Struga; ch38. **TV Kanal Festa:** ul. Kiro Antevski 15, 1300 Kumanovo; ch29. **TV Kanal 21:** ul. Alekso Deminevski-Bauman hh, 1400 Veles; Bašino ch21. **TV Kiss:** ul. Blagoja Toska 10, 1200 Tetovo; ch31. **TV Ko-Bra:** bul. Aleksandar Makedonski bb, 2420 Radoviš; ch43. **TV Koha:** ul. GTC Trijada 2-ri kat, lok.77, 1200 Tetovo; ch45. **TV KTV-41:** ul. Ploštad Maršal Titobb, 1430 Kavadarci; ch25. **TV KRT:** ul. Anton Popov 103-b, 1000 Skopje-Gazi Baba; Raštak ch58, Sredno Vodno ch65 (time shared with TV Amazon/TV Edo) **TV Medi:** ul. Jorgo Kostovski bb, 7000 Bitola; Brusnik ch51. **TV Menada:** ul. Maršal Tito 36, 1200 Tetovo; Kaleto ch29. **TV Moris:** ul. Pariska komuna 34, 6000 Ohrid; Kaleto ch52. **TV MS (MakSpot):** ul. Nikola Rusinski bb, 1000 Skopje; Raštak ch35, Sredno Vodno ch55. **TV MTM:** ul. Blagoja Stefkovski 40, 1000 Skopje; Gazi Baba ch27, Sredno Vodno ch25. **TV Nova:** ul. Ilindenska bb, 1300 Kumanovo; Stari Lozja ch25. **TV NTV:** ul. Kej Maršal Tito bb, 6000 Ohrid; Gorenicka cuka ch32. **TV Orbis:** ul. Rieka 7a, 7000 Bitola; Kopanki ch39, Pirava ch48. **TV Protel:** ul. Jordan Stojanov 2, 2210 Probištip; ch34. **TV SkajNet:** ul. Vasil Glavinov 16-6, 1000 Skopje; Gazi Baba ch48, Sredno Vodno ch61. **TV Star:** ul. Banco Prke bb, 2000 Štip; ch27. **TV Super Skaj:** ul. 169 br.162, 1201 Maka Recica; ch43. **TV Svet:** ul. Makedonska 29, 2220 Sveti Nikole; ch27. **TV Šutel:** ul. Ce Gevara 37, 1000 Skopje; Sredno Vodno ch59. **TV Tera:** ul. Milton Manaki 21, 7000 Bitola; Pirava ch32, Brusnik ch37. **TV Uskana:** bul. Osloboduvanje 33, 6250 Kicevo; Kicevo ch35, Cocon ch49. **TV Vis:** ul. Blagoj Jankov-Muceto 54, 2400 Strumica; Bair ch28. **TV VTV:** ul. Bojmija 10, 2460 Valandovo; ch47. **TV Zdravkin:** ul. Dimce Mircev 1, 1400 Veles; ch27. **TV Zupa:** 1258 Mal. Papradnik; ch29 & ch55. **TVM:** ul.Nada Fileva 40, 6000 Ohrid; Kaleto ch28.

DTT Transmitters (under construction)
Licensee: ONE Telecommunication Services ☐ bul. Kuzman Josifovski Pitu 15, 1000 Skopje ☎ +389 2 441000 🖷 +389 2 441122 **E:** info@one.mk **W:** www.one.mk **Mux 1:** MTV1, MTV2, MTV3 **Mux 2-4✪:** multiprgr.

Location	M1	M2	M3	M4
Crn Vrv	-	20	25	41
Pelister	-	20	55	63
Popova Šapka	-	20	49	64
Turtel	-	20	-	-
Vodno	39	20	25	41

+ national network under construction

System: SECAM-K1 [VHF=K, UHF=E]

National Station
TELEVISIONA MALAGASY (TVM) (Pub) ☐ BP 271, 101 Antananarivo ☎ +261 20 2221784 🖷 +261 20 2232815 **E:** tvm@dts.mg **W:** www.

televisionmalagasy.sitew.com **LP:** DG: Herinirina Lalao Razafimahefa **Txs:** Antanarivo ch5 (1kW H) & relay txs.

Local Stations
CANAL F+ Fianarantsoa: Près Lot 408 IB Andohan'Ivory, 301 Fianarantsoa; ch28. **MATV:** BP 1414, 101 Antananarivo; ch23, ch27. **M3TV:** 29 rue de la Libération, Mahajanga; ch55. **OTV:** BP 4100, 101 Antananarivo; ch39, ch43. **R.T.T. Toamasina:** BP 12170, 101 Antananarivo; ch34. **RTVA:** BP 258, 110 Antsirabe; ch32. **RTV Analamanga:** BP 12170, 101 Antananarivo; ch30, ch33, ch47. **RTV Kalizy:** Zone Zital Ankorondrano, Antananarivo; ch30. **RTV Record:** BP 7522, 101 Antananarivo; ch51. **RTV Soafia:** Zorozoroana Ambalakosoa; ch47. **RTV Soavinandriana:** FKT Ambatombositra Soavinandriana Ambany, Soavinandriana; ch38. **TV Plus Madagascar:** Lot IVW 3D Anosizato - Est, 101 Antananarivo; ch31. **TV Ny Antsika Antalaha:** BP 101, 206 Antalaha; ch21. **TV Soa Menabe:** BP 405 619 Morondava; ch32. **TV Viva:** Parcelle 34; Zone Tana Water Front, 101 Antananarivo; ch53, ch57.

System: DVB-T (MPEG4) [E]

RTP MADEIRA (Pub) ☐ Rua Caminho de Santo António 145, 9020-002 Funchal ☎ +351 291709100 🖷 +351 291741859 **E:** martim.santos@rtp.pt **L.P:** Dir: Martim Santos.

DTT Transmitters
Licensee: Portugal Telecom **Mux:** RTP1, RTP2, RTP Madeira, SIC, TVI **Txs:** ch67 (SFN).

System: PAL-I [E]

MALAWI BROADCASTING CORP. (Pub) ☐ Private bag 268, Blantyre ☎ +265 1675033 🖷 +265 1672627 **E:** tvmalawi@malawi.net **LP:** DG: Benson Tembo **Txs:** (-). – **AFJ TV (Rlg)** ☐ Blantyre. **Txs:** (-). – **TBN MALAWI (Rlg)** ☐ Blantyre. **Txs:** Lilongwe ch32, Blantyre ch60.

Systems: # PAL-B/G [E]; DVB-T (MPEG4) [E]

RADIO TELEVISYEN MALAYSIA (RTM) (Gov) ☐ Dept. of Broadc, Angkasapuri, Kuala Lumpur 50614 ☎ +60 3 22825333 🖷 +60 3 22825103 **E:** programtv@rtm.net.my **W:** www.rtm.net.my **L.P:** DG: Dato Norhyati Ismail **Chs:** TV1 (mainly in Malay) iTV2 (in Chinese, English, Malay and Tamil), regional stns. **Txs:** TV1: Kuala Lumpur ch50 & netw.; **iTV:** Kuala Lumpur ch53 & netw.. – **METROPOLITAN TV (8TV)** ☐ Metropolitan TV sdn bhd, Sri Pentas, 3 Persiaran Bandar Utama, 47800 Petaling Jaya, Selangor Darul Ehsan ☎ +60 3 77288282 🖷 +60 3 77268282 **E:** info@8tv.com.my **W:** www.8tv.com.my. **Txs:** Kuala Lumpur ch58 & netw. NB. 8TV is affiliated to TV3. – **NAT SEVEN (NTV7) (Comm)** ☐ 7, Jalan Jurubina U1/18, Hicom-Glenmarie Industrial Park, 40000 Shah Alam, Selangor Darul Ehsan ☎ +60 3 55691777 🖷 +60 3 55692515 **E:** feedback@ntv7.com.my **W:** www.ntv7.com.my. **Txs:** Kuala Lumpur ch7 & netw. – **SYSTEM TV MALAYSIA BERHAD (TV3)** ☐ Sri Pentas (Ground Floor, South Wing) No. 3, Persiaran Banjar Utama, 47800 Petaling Jaya Selangor Darul Ehsan ☎ +60 3 7166333 🖷 +60 3 77278455 **E:** query@tv3.com.my **W:** www.tv3.com.my **L.P:** MD: Hisham Abdul Rahman. **Txs:** Kuala Lumpur ch12 & netw. – **TV9 (Comm)** ☐ Lot 31, Jalan Pelukis U1/46, Temasya Industrial Park, 40150 Shah Alam, Selangor Darul Ehsan ☎ +60 3 55685999 **W:** www.tv9.com.my. **Txs:** Kuala Lumpur ch33 & netw.

DTT Transmitters (under construction)
Licensee: MiTV ☐ 3rd Floor, KL Plaza, 179 Jalan Bukit Bintang, 55100 Kuala Lumpur **Mux✪:** multiprgr. **Txs:** (-).

System: PAL-B [E]

MALDIVES BROADCASTING CO. (Gov) ☐ Buruzu Magu, 20-04 Malé ☎ +960 3323105 🖷 +960 3325083 **E:** info@mbc.mv **W:** www.mbc.mv **Chs:** MNBC One, MNBC Plus. **Txs:** **MNBC One:** Malé ch7 (1kW H); **MNBC Plus✪:** (-).

MALI

System: SECAM-B/G [VHF=K, UHF=E]

RADIODIFFUSION TÉLÉVISION DU MALI (ORTM) (Pub) ✉ BP 171, Bamako ☎ +223 20210737 🖷 +223 20214205 **E:** info@ortm-mali.tv **W:** www.ortm-mali.tv **L.P:** Dir (TV): Youssouf Touré **Txs:** Bamako ch4 (10kW) & relay txs.

Foreign TV Relay
TV5 Monde (France): Bamako ch49.

MALTA

System: DVB-T (MPEG2) [E]

TELEVISION MALTA (TVM) (Pub) ✉ PBS, 75, Triq San Luqa, Gwardamangia, Pieta', PTA 1024 ☎ +356 21225051 🖷 +356 21244601 **E:** info@tvm.com.mt **W:** tvm.com.mt **L.P:** Chmn: Joseph Mizzi. **Chs:** TVM, TVM2 – **CALYPSO MUSIC TV (Comm)** ✉ 28, New Street in Valletta Road, Luqa, LQA 2000 ☎ +356 21578022 🖷 +356 21578026 **E:** info@calypsomusictv.com **W:** www.calypsomusictv.com **L.P:** Dirs: Frank Camilleri, Alfred Cacciatolo – **FAVOURITE CHANNEL (Comm)** ✉ Gudja Road, Luqa, LQA 2022 ☎ +356 21664566 **E:** info@favouritechannel.tv **W:** www.favouritechannel.tv – **NET TV (Comm)** ✉ Media.Link Communications, Dar Centrali, Triq Herbert Ganado, Pieta', PTA 1450 ☎ +356 21243641 🖷 +356 21242886 **E:** news@media.link.com.mt **W:** www.nettv.com.mt **L.P:** Chmn: Joe Saliba. – **ONE TV (Comm)** ✉ ONE Productions Ltd., A28b, Qasam Industrijali, Marsa, MRS 3000 ☎ +356 25682568 🖷 +356 21248249 **E:** info@one.com.mt **W:** www.one.com.mt **L.P:** Chmn: Jason Micallef. – **SMASH TV (Comm)** ✉ 2, Triq Tax-Xewk, Paola, PLA 1341 ☎ +356 21697829 🖷 +356 21697830 **E:** info@smashmalta.com **W:** www.smash.com.mt **L.P:** Head: Jesmond Saliba.

DTT Transmitters
Licensee: PBS **Mux:** TVM, TVM2, Net TV, One TV, Smash TV, Favourite Channel **Txs:** ch66 (SFN). – **Licensee:** GO ✉ Gnien Spencer, Marsa, MRS 1990 ☎ +356 21212121 🖷 +356 21248925 **E:** info@go.com.mt **W:** www.go.com.mt **Muxes⊙:** multiprgr (incl. Calypso Music TV) **Txs:** MFN.

MARSHALL ISLANDS (USA associated)

NB: No terrestrial TV station.

MARTINIQUE (France)

System: DVB-T (MPEG4) [E]

MARTINIQUE 1ÈRE (Pub) ✉ BP 662, F-97263 Fort-de-France Cedex ☎ +596 596595200 **W:** martinique.la1ere.fr **L.P:** Dir: Fred Jouhoud. **ANTILLES TÉLÉVISION (ATV) (Comm)** ✉ 28 rue Arawaks, F-97200 Fort-de-France ☎ +596 596754444 🖷 +596 596755565 **E:** accueil@atv.mq **W:** atv.mq – **KANAL MARTINIQUE TÉLÉVISION (KMT) (Comm)** ✉ Voie n° 7, Renéville, F-97200 Fort-de-France ☎ +596 596718604 🖷 +596 596636485 **E:** webmaster@kmttelevision.com **W:** kmttelevision.com.

DTT Transmitters
Operator: TDF **Mux:** Martinique 1ère, France 2-5, France Ô, France 24, Arte, ATV, KMT **Txs:** MFN.

MAURITANIA

System: SECAM-B [E]

TÉLÉVISION DE MAURITANIE (Pub) ✉ BP 5522, Nouakchott ☎ +222 45258017 🖷 +222 45254069 **E:** dgtvm@tvmsat.mr **W:** www.tvm.mr **L.P:** DG: Sidi Mohamed Ould Bouna **Chs:** TVM, TVM Plus **Txs:** **TVM:** Nouakchott ch5 (2kW H) & relay txs; **TVM Plus:** (-).

MAURITIUS

System: DVB-T (MPEG2) [E]

MAURITIUS BROADCASTING CORP. (MBC) (Pub) ✉ BP 48, Curepipe ☎ +230 6755001 🖷 +230 6757332 **E:** dirgen@mbc.intnet.

mu **W:** mbc.intnet.mu **L.P:** DG: Dhanjay Callikan.

DTT Transmitters
Licensee: Multi Carrier (Mauritius) Ltd ✉ Clement Charoux Street, Malherbes, Curepipe ☎ +230 6753234 🖷 +230 6746547 **E:** mcml@multi-carrier.net **W:** www.multi-carrier.net **Mux 1:** MBC1, MBC2, MBC3, Movie Channel, TV5 Monde, DD India ✿ RM1, RM2, Kool FM **Mux 2:** Sports Channel, CCTV9, France 24, Knowledge Channel, DD Bharati, BBC World News **Mux 3:** Tourism Channel, DD Télugu Channel, DD Marathi Channel, DD Urdu Channel, DD Tamil Channel ✿ Best FM **Txs:** MFN

MAYOTTE (France)

System: DVB-T (MPEG4) [E]

MAYOTTE 1ÈRE (Pub) ✉ BP 103, F-97610 Pamandzi, Ile de Mayotte ☎ +262 269601017 🖷 +262 269601852 **W:** mayotte.la1ere.fr **L.P:** Dir: Gérald Prufer.

DTT Transmitters
Operator: TDF **Mux:** Mayotte 1ère, France 2-5, France Ô, France 24, Arte **Txs:** ch27 (SFN), ch41 (Handréma), ch44 (SFN).

MEXICO

Systems: # NTSC-M [A] ⇩2015; ATSC [A]

National Stations (ᵃ=analogue)
TELEVISIÓN AZTECA SA DE CV (Comm) ✉ Periférico Sur 4121, Col. Fuentes del Pedregal, Mexico, DF 14140 ☎ +52 55 30991313 🖷 +52 55 30991418 **E:** webtv@tvazteca.com **W:** www.tvazteca.com **L.P:** CEO: Mario San Román. **Chs:** Azteca 7, Azteca Trece. **Txs: Azteca 7:** XHIMT-TV Mexico City ᵃch7 (267kW)/ch24 & relay txs; **Azteca Trece:** XHDF-TV Mexico City ᵃch13 (320kW)/ch25 & relay txs. – **TELEVISA SA DE CV (Comm)** ✉ 2000 Avenida Vasco De Quiroga Santa Fe, Mexico, DF 01210 ☎ +52 55 52612000 🖷 +52 55 52612494 **W:** www.televisa.com **L.P:** CEO: Emilio Azcarraga Jean. **Chs:** Canal 2, Canal 5, Galavisión, Foro TV. **Txs: Canal 2:** XEW-TV Mexico City ᵃch2 (64kW)/ch48 & relay txs; **Canal 5:** XHGC-TV Mexico City ᵃch5 (54kW)/ch50 & relay txs; **Foro TV:** XHTV Mexico City ᵃch4 (64kW)/ch49 & relay txs; **Galavisión:** XEQ-TV Mesico City ᵃch9 (325kW)/ch44 & relay txs.

Regional Networks, Local Stations not shown.

MICRONESIA (USA associated)

System: NTSC-M [A]

KPON-TV (Comm)✉ Central Micronesia Communications, P.O.Box 460, Colonia, Pohnpei, FM 96941. **L.P:** Pres: Bernard Hegenberger. DirTech: David Cliffe. **Tx:** Pohnpei ch7 (1kW). – **TTTK (Comm)** ✉ Chuuk, FM 96942. **Tx:** Moen ch7 (0.1kW). – **WAAB-TV (Gov)** ✉ Department of Youth and Civic Affairs, P.O.Box 30, Colonia, Yap, FS 96943 ☎ +1 691 3502502 **Tx:** ch7 (1kW).

MOLDOVA

Systems: # SECAM-D/K [R], # PAL-D/K [R] ⇩17 Jun 2015; DVB-T/DVB-T2 (MPEG4) [E]

National Stations
TELERADIO-MOLDOVA (Pub) ✉ str. Hâncesti nr. 64, 2018 Chisinau ☎ +373 22 723380 🖷 +373 22 723329 **E:** tvdir@trm.md **W:** www.trm.md **L.P:** Dir (TV) Angela Sirbu **Ch:** Moldova 1. **Txs:** Straseni ch3 (912kW) & netw. – **CANAL 3 (Comm)** ✉ Str. Banulescu-Bodoni nr. 57/1, 2102 Chisinau ☎ +373 22 854615 **E:** info@mediaproduction.md **W:** canal3.md **Txs:** Chisinau ch45 (1kW) & netw. – **EURO-TV (Comm)** ✉ str. Columna nr. 106, 2012 Chisinau ☎ +373 22 221149 🖷 +373 22 221147 **E:** eurotv@yahoo.com **W:** www.eutv.md **Txs:** Straseni ch23 (354kW) & netw. (Rel. Antena 1, Romania). – **MEGA TV (Comm)** ✉ str. Sciusev nr. 93, 2012 Chisinau ☎+373 22 233505 🖷: +373 22 273588 **E:** www.info@dixi.md **W:** www.dixi.md **Txs:** Chisinau ch26 (0.6kW) & netw. (Rel. STS, Russia) – **MUZ-TV (Comm)** ✉ str. Ismail nr. 88/1, 2001 Chisinau ☎ +373 22 207906 🖷 +373 22 270755 **E:** info@muztv.md **W:** www.muztv.md **Txs:** Chisinau ch53 (0.3kW) & netw. – **NOROC TV (Comm)** ✉ bd. Negruzzi 6s, 2001 Chisinau ☎+373 22 500995 **E:** noroctv@gmail.com **W:** www.noroc.tv – **N4 (Comm)** ✉ str. Miorita nr. 3/5, 2028 Chisinau ☎ +373 22 924275 **Txs:** Chisinau ch51 (3.2kW) & netw. – **PRIME (Comm)** ✉str.

Banulescu-Bodoni nr. 57/1, 2005 Chisinau ☎ +373 22 244746 🖷 +373 22 244746 **E:** info@prime.md **W:** prime.md **Txs:** Straseni ch30 (602kW) & netw. (Rel. Pervyy kanal, Russia) – **PRO TV (Comm)** 🖳 str. Maior Petru nr. 7, 2001 Chisinau ☎+373 22 213645 🖷: +373 22 213642 **E:** office@protv.md **W:** www.protv.md **Txs:** Chisinau ch37 (2.5kW) & netw. (Rel. Pro TV, Romania) – **SUPER TV (Comm)** 🖳 bd. Moscova nr. 21, sectia 3, 2068 Chisinau ☎ +373 22 601715 **W:** super-tv.md (Rel. SET, Russia) – **TV7 (Comm)** 🖳 str. Alecu Russo nr. 1, of. 21, 2068 Chisinau ☎+373 22 438434 🖷: +373 22 438434 **E:** office@amg.md **W:** www.tv7.md **Txs:** Chisinau ch43 (7.9kW) & netw. (Rel. NTV, Russia) – **2 PLUS (Comm)** 🖳 bd. D.Cantemir nr. 1/1, 2001 Chisinau ☎+373 22 809112 🖷: +373 22 809110 **W:** www.2plus.md **Txs:** Straseni ch11 (151kW) & netw. (Rel. TVR1, Romania).

Local Stations
Albasat: str. Suveranitatii nr. 1, 6401 Nisporeni; ch8 (0.2kW). **ART-TV:** str. Eminescu nr.37, 3736 Straseni; Zubresti ch7 (0.01kW). **AVM:** str. Puskin nr. 16, 4601 Edinet; ch25 (0.1kW). **BAS TV:** str. K. Marx nr. 67, 7401 Basarabeasca; ch26 (0.3kW). **Canal-X:** bd. Independentei nr. 48, 4701 Briceni; ch3 (0.1kW). **Drochia TV:** str. Sorocii nr. 44, ap. 7, 5201 Drochia; ch28 (0.3kW). **Elita:** str. 1 mai nr. 2, 5400 Rezina; Rezina ch21 (0.3kW), Soldanesti ch45 (0.4kW). **Euronova:** str. Suveranitatii nr. 1, 6401 Nisporeni; Ungheni ch39 (5kW). **FLOR-TV:** str. Stefan cel Mare nr. 30 A, 5003 Floresti; Vadeni ch38 (0.2kW), Floresti ch48 (0.1kW). **Impuls TV:** str. 31 august nr. 1, of. 304, 7201 Soldanesti; ch7 (0.3kW). **Media TV:** str. Stefan cel Mare nr. 14, 4101 Cimislia; ch43 (0.4kW). **NTS:** str. Mira nr. 12/67, 7401 Taraclia; Ciumai ch38 (0.3kW), Taraclia ch41 (0.3kW). **SOR-TV:** str. Banulescu-Bodoni nr. 2, 3000 Soroca; ch43 (0.3kW). **Studio-L:** bd. M. Eminescu nr. 23, 4301 Causeni; ch35 (0.2kW). **TV Prim:** str. Suveranitatii nr. 5, of. 94, 4901 Glodeni; ch35 (0.4kW). **TV6 Balti:** str. 31 August nr. 20-B, 3121 Balti; ch26 (0.3kW). **Gagauzia (autonomous region): Ain-Aciic:** str. Cikalov, nr. 59/7, 6101 Ceadir-Lunga; ch37 (0.03kW). **ATV Comrat:** str. Tretiacov nr. 4, of. 36, 3801 Comrat; ch38 (0.2kW). **Eni Ai:** str. Tretiacov nr. 4, 3801 Comrat; ch23 (0.2kW). **TV Gagauzia (Pub):** str. Lenin nr. 134, 3802 Comrat; Vulcanesti ch24 (0.2kW), Comrat ch36 (0.2kW), Copceac ch47 (0.03kW).

Foreign TV Relay
TV5 Monde (France): Chisinau ch8 (0.2kW).

DTT Transmitters (under construction)
Operator: Radiocomunicatii 🖳 str. Drumul Viilor nr. 28/2, 2021 Chisinau ☎ +373 22 733914 🖷 +373 22 733874 **E:** crtvr@cni.md **Mux 1 (DVB-T2):** Moldova 1, Prime (Pervyy kanal), 2 Plus (TVR1), TVC21, N4 **Mux 2:** Alt TV, Publika TV, Jurnal TV, Ru TV Moldova, TV5 Monde, Mega TV, Super TV.

Location	M1	M2	kW
Chisinau	61	58	10

+ nationwide network under construction

TRANSNISTRIA

TV PMR (Gov) 🖳 ul. Yunosti 1, 3300 Tiraspol ☎ +373 533 25708 **W:** www.tv-pmr.com **L.P:** Dir: Igor Nikitenko **Ch:** Pervyy respublikan-skiy **Txs:** Maiac ch5 (1kW), Dnestrovsc ch6, Grigoriopol ch6, Bender & Camenca ch10, Dubasari ch12, Tiraspol ch31, Ribnita ch35. – **TSV (Comm)** 🖳ul. Karl Libknekhta 1/2, 3300 Tiraspol ☎ +373 533 63632 🖷 +373 533 63632 **E:** inform@tsv-tv.idknet.com **Txs:** Ribnita ch44, Camenca & Dubasari ch45, Maiac ch47, Dnestrovsc ch49, Tiraspol ch54.

Local Station
BTV (TV Bender): ul. Lenina 17, 3200 Bender; ch26 (0.3kW) (Rel. Domashnyy, Russia)

DTT Transmitters (under construction)
Operator: Ministry of Communications **Mux 1:** NTV, TNT, MTV Russia, Rossiya 1, Rossiya K, STS, TV Zvezda, Rossiya 24 **Mux 2:** Pervyy kanal, Euronews, TV PMR, Rossiya 2, TVTsi, Karusel **Mux 3:** TV3, 8 kanal, TRO, TV Mir, Ren TV, Europa Plus TV **Mux 4:** Muz-TV, Ru Music, STsi, Otkrytyy Mir, Vsegda s toboy, Domashnyy, TV Podmoskovye, 7TV **Mux 5:** Sport 2, ReMusic, Sarafan, Shanson, Znanye, DTV, RVTs-TV.

Location	M1	M2	M3	M4	M5
SFN	59	61	63	44	56

MONACO

System: DVB-T (MPEG2) [E]

TÉLÉ MONTE-CARLO (TMC) (Comm) 🖳 6 Quai Antoine 1ᵉʳ, 98000 Monaco ☎ +377 93151415 🖷 +377 92165481 **E:** tmc@ fr.multithematiques.com **W:** www.tmc.tv **L.P:** Pres: Jean Claude Riey.

DTT Transmitters
Operator: Monaco Telecom 🖳 25 Boulevard de Suisse, 98000 Monaco ☎ +377 99663497 **E:** a.segala@monaco-telecom.mc **W:** www.monaco.mc **Mux:** TMC, Monaco Info, TF1, France 2-5, M6, Arte, Canal+ (unencrypted sequences), BFM TV, I>télé, Euronews, RAI 1-3, Canale 5, CNBC **Tx:** ch10 (Mont Agel).

MONGOLIA

Systems: PAL-D/K [R]; DVB-T [E] planned

National Station
MONGOLIN ÜNDESNIY TELEVIZ (Pub) 🖳 Huvsgalin zam 3, Ulaanbaatar 11☎ +976 11 323801 🖷 +976 11 327234 **E:** mrtv@ magicnet.mn **W:** www.mnb.mn **L.P:** Dir: Ts. Enkhbat. **Txs:** (-).

Local Stations not shown.

MONTENEGRO

Systems: DVB-T2 (MPEG4) [E]; # PAL-B/G [E] ⬇2013

National Stations
TELEVIZIJA CRNE GORE (TVCG) (Pub) 🖳 Bul. revolucije 19, 81000 Podgorica ☎ +382 20 225602 🖷 +382 20 225640 **E:** kontakt@rtcg.me **W:** www.rtcg.me **L.P:** Dir TV: Radojka Rutovic **Chs:** TVSG1, TVSG2 **Txs: TVSG1:** Sjenica ch23 (15kW) & netw.; **TVSG2:** Sjenica ch29 (15kW) & netw. – **PINK M (Comm)** 🖳 bul. Ivana Crnojevica 97, 81000 Podgorica ☎ +382 20 403511 🖷 +382 20 403525 **E:** redakcija@pink.co.me **W:** www.pink.co.me **Txs:** Sjenica ch62 (1kW) & netw. – **NTV MONTENA (Comm)** 🖳 Djoka Miraševica G1, 81000 Podgorlca ☎ +382 20 266543 **E:** montena@montena.me **W:** www.montena.me **L.P:** Dir: Djuro Vucinic. **Txs:** Sjenica ch53 (0.3kW) & netw. – **RTV ATLAS (Comm)** 🖳 Vaka Djurovica bb, 81000 Podgorica ☎ +382 20 409300 🖷 +382 20 409305 **E:** info@rtvatlas.tv **W:** www.rtvatlas.tv **Txs:** (-) – **TV IN (Comm)** 🖳 13. Jula 2, 81000 Podgorica. ☎ +382 20 237890 🖷 +382 20 237766 **E:** produkcija@rtvin.com **W:** www.rtvin.com **Txs:** Podgorica ch37 (0.01kW) & netw. – **TV VIJESTI (Comm)** 🖳 Trg Republike bb, 81000 Podgorica ☎ +382 20 404601 🖷 +382 20 404636 **E:** desk@rtv-vijesti.com **W:** rtvvijesti.com **Txs:** Podgorica ch64 & netw.

Local Stations not shown.

DTT Transmitters (under construction)
Operator: Radio-difuzni centar d.o.o. 🖳 Bulevar Svetlog Petra Cetinjskog 130/V, 81000 Podgorica ☎ +382 20 408000 🖷 +382 20 408005 **E:** rdc@rdc.co.me **W:** www.rdc.co.me **Mux:** TVCG1, TVCG2 **Tx:** ch67 (Podgorica) & national network.

MONTSERRAT (UK)

System: NTSC-M [A]

ZJB-TV (Gov) 🖳 Sweeney's, Montserrat. ☎ +1 664 4912885 🖷 +1 664 4919250 **E:** zjb@gov.ms **W:** www.zjb.gov.ms **Tx:** Chance Pic ch13. – **ANTILLES TV LTD (Comm)** 🖳 P.O. Box 342, Plymouth, Montserrat ☎ +1 664 4912226 🖷 +1 664 4914511 **L.P:** GM: K. Osborne; TD: Z.A. Joseph. **Tx:** Chance Pic ch7 (48kW).

MOROCCO

Systems: # SECAM-B/G [VHF=M; UHF=E] ⬇2015; DVB-T (MPEG2) [E]

SOCIÉTÉ NATIONALE DE RADIODIFFUSION ET DE TÉLÉVISION (SNRT) (Gov) 🖳 BP 1042, Rabat ☎ +212 37700319 🖷 +212 37722047 **W:** www.snrt.ma **L.P:** DG: Faiçal Laraichi. **Chs:** Al Aoula, Arriadia, Arradia 2, Arrabia, Assadissa, Aflam TV, Tamazight TV

Location	ch	kW	Location	ch	kW
Zerhoun	4	120	Figuig	6	9
Zaio	4	9	Rabat	7	180
Oujda	5	316	Izeft	7	14
Boukhouali	5	150	Tan Tan	8	11
Tanger	5	20	Safi	8	20
Sidi Bounouara	5	11	Tazerkount	8	90
Oukaimeden	6	18	Touzarine	9	9
Azougar	6	9	Tiguelamine	9	9
Dakhla	6	11	S.Bounoara	9	11

Location	ch	kW	Location	ch	kW
Biougra	9	4	Ourzazate	10	267
Casablanca	10	180	Bouarfa	10	267
Hafa Safa	10	9	Essaouira	11	20

Regional stn: Lâayoune TV. Tx: chE4 Lâayoune (We. Sahara), 316kW.
TÉLÉVISION 2M (Semi-Gov, Comm) ✉ Km 7,3 route de Rabat Ain Sebaa, Casablanca 20250 ☎ +212 22354444 🖷 +212 22343390 **E:** 2m@tv2m.co.ma **W:** www.2m.tv **L:P:** MD: Tawfik Bennani-Smires. **Txs:** Rabat ch21 & netw.

DTT Transmitters (under construction)
Operator: SNRT **Mux 1:** Al Aoula, 2M, Arriadia, Arradia 2, Arrabia, Assadissa, Aflam TV **Mux 2:** Aflam TV, Tamazight TV

Location	M1	M2
Rabat	30	23

+ nationwide network (txs being installed at all main sites)

CEUTA & MELILLA (Spain)

Systems: DVB-T (MPEG2, MPEG4) [E]

Local Stations
Ceuta Televisión (Comm): Ceuta. **Radio Televisión de Ceuta (RTVCE) (Pub)**: Alcalde Sanchez Prados nº 5, 51001 Ceuta. **Melilla Televisión (Comm)**: Los Castaños, Urb Los Balandros nº 33, Aguadulce, 04720 Roquetas de Mar. **TV Melilla (TVM) (Comm)**: Miguel Zazo, 31, 2º 52004 Pontevedra.

DTT Transmitters (MPEG2 exc. *=MPEG4)
Operator: n/a **Mux 1:** La 1, La 2, 24 Horas, Clan ⌘ RNE R. Nacional, RNE R.5 Todo Noticias **Txs:** ch52 (Ceuta), ch64 (Melilla). **Mux 3:** Cuatro, la Sexta, laSexta 3, Divinity, La Tienda en Casa, Gol Televisión✪ **Txs:** ch67 (SFN) **Mux 4:** Telecinco, La Siete, FDF, Disney Channel, Interecononomía ⌘ R. Intereconomía, esRadio, ABC Punto R. **Txs:** ch68 (SFN). **Mux 5:** Veo TV, Antena 3, Neox, Nova, AXN✪ ⌘ R.Marca, Vaughan R. **Txs:** ch69 (SFN). **Mux 6:** TVE HD, TDP ⌘ RNE R. Clásica HQ, RNE R.3 **Txs:** ch27 (Melilla), ch55 (Ceuta) **Mux 7:** Xplora, laSexta 3, LaSexta HD, Quatro, Energy ⌘ SER, 40 Principales, Cadena Dial **Txs:** ch21 (Melilla), ch53 (Ceuta) **Mux 8:** Telecinco HD, Boing, Paramount Channel, MTV **Txs:** ch41 (Melilla), ch44 (Ceuta) **Mux 9:** Antena 3 HD, Nitro, Marca TV, 13TV ⌘ Cope, R. María, Onda Cero, Europa FM, Onda Melodía **Txs:** ch45 (Melilla), ch49 (Ceuta). **Mux 10*:** TVE HD, TDP ⌘ RNE R. Clásica HQ, R.3 **Txs:** ch22 (Melilla), 55 (Ceuta). **Local Mux Ceuta:** RTVCE, Ceuta TV, Canal Sur ⌘ Radio Ceuta **Tx:** ch62 (Ceuta). **Local Mux Melilla:**TV Melilla, Popular TV, Canal Sur. **Tx:** ch61 (Melilla).

MOZAMBIQUE

System: PAL-G [E]

TELEVISÃO DE MOÇAMBIQUE (TVM) (Gov) ✉ CP 2675, Maputo ☎ +258 21 308117 🖷 +258 21 308122 **E:** tvm@tvm.co.mz **W:** www.tvm.co.mz **L:P:** Chmn/CEO: Armindo Chavana **Txs:** Maputo ch33 (1kW) & relay txs. – **KTV (Comm)** ✉ Av. Julius Nyerere 390, Maputo ☎ +258 21 491744 🖷 +258 21 491745 **Txs:** (-). – **SOICOS TELEVISÃO (STV) (Comm)** ✉ Rua de Timor Leste 108, Maputo ☎ +258 21 315117 🖷 +258 21 301865 **E:** stv@soico.co.mz **W:** www.stv.co.mz **L:P:** DG: Daniel David **Txs:** (-). – **TELEVISÃO MIRAMAR (Comm)** ✉ Rua Pereira Lago, 221 - 11o. Andar, Maputo. ☎🖷 +258 21 486813 **Txs:** (-).

Foreign TV Relay
RTP África (Portugal): (-).

MYANMAR

Systems: # PAL-B/G [E]; DVB-T (MPEG2) [E]

MYANMA RADIO AND TELEVISION (MRTV) (Gov) ✉ Naypyidaw ☎ +95 67 79483 **E:** mrtv@mptmail.net.mm **Chs:** MRTV1, MRTV2, MRTV3, MRTV4 **Txs: MRTV1:** Yangon ch6 (17kW H) & relay txs. – **MYAWADY TV (Gov)** ✉ Naypyidaw **Chs:** MWD1, MWD2, MWD3, MWD4 **Txs:** (-).

DTT Transmitters
Operator: MRTV **Muxes:** MRTV1, MRTV2, MRTV3, MRTV4 **Txs:** ch(-). National network planned. – **Licensee:** Myawady TV **Mux:** MWD1, MWD2, MWD3, MWD4 **Tx:** ch(-) (Yangon/Tarmwe 0.4kW). National network planned.

NAMIBIA

Systems: # PAL-I [SA] ⇩2013; DVB-T (MPEG2) [SA]

NAMIBIAN BROADCASTING CORP. (Gov) ✉ P.O.Box 321, Windhoek 9000 ☎ +264 61 2913111 🖷 +264 61 216209 **E:** pr@nbc.na **W:** www.nbc.na **L:P:** DG: Albertus Aochamub **Txs:** Rundu ch4, Keetmanshoop ch4, Paresis ch5, Windhoek ch6, Erongo ch7 & repeaters. – **ONE AFRICA TV (Comm)** ✉ Storch House, Storch Street, Windhoek ☎ +264 61 253190 🖷 +264 61 220410 **E:** paul@mac.com. na **W:** www.oneafrica.tv **L:P:** MD: Paul van Schalkwyk **Txs:** Windhoek ch48 & netw. – **TBN NAMIBIA (Rlg)** ✉ P.O.Box 1587, Swakopmund ☎ +264 64 401100 🖷 +264 64 403752 **E:** comments@tbnnamibia.tv **W:** www.tbnnamibia.tv **Txs:** Walvis Bay ch37, Windhoek ch40, Rehoboth ch40, Okahandja ch40, Swakopmund ch65.

DTT Transmitters
Licensee: MultiChoice Namibia Pty. ✉ P.O.Box 2662, Windhoek ☎ +264 61 2705111 🖷 +264 61 2705247 **Mux✪:** M-Net, SuperSport 1, SABC Africa, Discovery, Channel O. **Tx:** Windhoek ch13 (0.06kW).

NAURU

System: PAL-B [NZ]

NAURU TELEVISION (NTV) (Gov) ✉ Government Offices, Yaren District ☎ +674 4443113 🖷 +674 4443153 **Txs:** Command Ridge ch4 (0.1kW), NTV studio building ch10 (0.01kW).

NEPAL

System: PAL-B/G [E]; DTT planned

NEPAL TELEVISION (Gov) ✉ P.O.Box 3826, Singha Durbar, Kathmandu ☎ +977 1 4200348 🖷 +977 1 4200212 **E:** neptv@ccsl. com **W:** www.ntv.org.np **L:P:** GM: Deepak Mani Dhital **Chs:** NTV, NTV Plus **Txs: NTV:** Kathmandu (Pulchowki) ch5 (5kW), Namje ch5 (2kW), Chamere Danda ch5 (1kW), Sarangkot ch7 (5kW), Jaleshwar ch11 (2kW), Ilam ch12 (5kW) + txs below 1kW; **NTV Plus:** Kathmandu (Pulchowki) ch21 (1kW). – **KANTIPUR TELEVISION (Comm)** ✉ P.O.Box 7368, Subidhanagar, Kathmandu ☎ +977 1 4466300 🖷 +977 1 4466321 **E:** info@kantipurtv.com **W:** www.kantipurtv.com **Txs:** Lalitpur ch23 (5kW), Namje ch23 (5kW).

Local Stations not shown.

NETHERLANDS

System: DVB-T (MPEG2) [E]

National Stations
NEDERLANDSE PUBLIEKE OMROEP (NPO) (Pub) ✉ P.O.Box 26444, 1202 JJ Hilversum ☎ +31 35 6779222 🖷 +31 35 6774188 **E:** voorlichting@publiekeomroep.nl **W:** www.publiekeomroep.nl **L:P:** Chmn: Henk Hagoort. **Chs:** Nederland 1, Nederland 2, Nederland 3. Prgrs for the NPO are provided by **Nederlandse Omroep Stichting (NOS):** Sumatralaan 45, 1217 GP Hilversum; **NTR:** P.O.Box 29000, 1202 MA Hilversum; and the following major broadcasting organizations: **AVRO (Algemene Vereniging Radio Omroep):** P.O.Box 2, 1200 JA Hilversum; **BNN (Bart's Neverending Network):** P.O.Box 646, 1200 AP Hilversum; **BOS (Boeddhistische Omroep Stichting):** P.O.Box 61, 1200 AB Hilversum; **EO (Evangelische Omroep):** P.O.Box 21000, 1202 BB Hilversum; **HUMAN (Humanistische Omroep):** P.O.Box 135, 1200 AC Hilversum; **IKON:** P.O.Box 10009, 1201 DA Hilversum; **Joodse Omroep:** P.O.Box 450, 1200 AL Hilversum; **KRO (Katholieke Radio Omroep):** P.O.Box 23000, 1202 EA Hilversum; **MAX:** P.O.Box 554, 2700 AM Hilversum; **NCRV (Nederlandse Christelijke Radio Vereniging):** P.O.Box 25000, 1202 HB Hilversum; NTR: P.O.Box 29000, 1202 MA Hilversum; **OHM (Organisatie voor Hindoe Media):** Koninneweg 8, 1217 KX Hilversum; **PowNed:** P.O.Box 92109, 1090 AC Amsterdam; **RKK: (Katoliek Nederland Radio):** P.O.Box 23000, 1202 EA Hilversum; **TROS (Televisie en Radio Omroep Stichting):** P.O.Box 28450, 1202 LL Hilversum; **VARA (Vereniging Arbeiders Radio Amateurs):** P.O.Box 175, 1200 AD Hilversum; **VPRO (Vrijzinnig Protestantse Radio Omroep):** P.O.Box 11, 1200 JC Hilversum; **WNL (Wakker Nederland):** P.O.Box 376, 1000 EB Amsterdam; **ZvK (Zendtijd voor Kerken):** P.O.Box 94, 1200 AB Hilversum. In addition, a number of smaller broadcasting organisations is contributing with prgr production. – **RTL.NL (Comm)**

P.O.Box 20, 1200 AA Hilversum ☎ +31 35 6718711 🗎 + 31 35 6236892 **E:** info@rtl.nl **W:** www.rtl.nl **Chs:** RTL4, RTL5, RTL7, RTL8 – **SBS BROADCASTING NEDERLAND (Comm)** 🖃 P.O.Box 18179, 1001 ZB Amsterdam ☎ +31 20 8007000 🗎 +31 20 8007001 **E:** info@ sbs.nl **W:** www.sbs.nl **Chs:** NET5, SBS6, Veronica TV. – **TMF (Comm)** 🖃 P.O.Box 999, 1400 AZ Bussum ☎ +31 35 6996666 🗎 +31 35 6947775 **E:** tmfinteractive@tmf.nl **W:** www.tmf.nl.

Regional Stations (Pub) (via DTT Mux 1)
a) L1TV: P.O.Box 31, 6200 AA Maastricht; **b) Omroep Brabant TV:** Postbus 108, 5600 AC Eindhoven; **c) Omroep Fryslân TV:** P.O.Box 7600, 8903 JP Leeuwarden; **d) Omroep Zeeland TV:** P.O.Box 1090, 4388 ZH Oost-Souburg; **e) Regio TV Utrecht:** P.O.Box 9043, 3506 GA Utrecht; **f) TV Drenthe:** P.O.Box 999, 9400 AZ Assen; **g) TV Flevoland:** P.O.Box 567, 8200 AN Lelystad; **h) TV Gelderland:** P.O.Box 747, 6800 AS Arnhem; **i) TV Noord:** P.O.Box 30101, 9701 BH Groningen; **j) TV Noord-Holland:** P.O.Box 9823, 1006 AM Amsterdam; **k) TV Oost:** P.O.Box 1000, 7550 BA Hengelo; **l) TV Rijmond:** P.O.Box 350, 3000 AJ Rotterdam; **m) TV West:** P.O.Box 24012, 2490 AA Den Haag.

Local Stations
AT5: P.O.Box 3976, 1001 AT Amsterdam; via DTT Mux 3. **Haarlem 105:** P.O.Box 3355, 2001 DJ Haarlem; ch46V (0.025kW).

DTT Transmitters
Licensee: KPN 🖃 P.O.Box 30000, 2516 CK Den Haag ☎ +31 70 3434343 **W:** www.kpn.com **Mux 1:** Nederland 1, Nederland 2, Nederland 3, Public Regional Stations (a-m) ⌘ R.1, 2, 3FM, 4, 5, 6, FunX, Public reg. radio stns **Mux 2✪:** RTL4, RTL5, RTL7/RTL2, NET5, SBS6 ⌘ Classic FM, Q-Music, R.Veronica, R.10 Gold, Sky R. 101 FM, Slam!FM, 100%NL **Mux 3✪:** Animal Planet/TLC, BBC1, BBC2, CNN, MTV, NGC, Eredivisie Live 1, Eredivisie Live/Cartoon Netw./AT5, 24Kitchen ⌘ Arrow Classic Rock, BNR Nieuwsradio, R.538 **Mux 4✪:** Eén, Canvas/Ketnet, Discovery Channel, Eurosport, Kindernet/Comedy Central, HIL8, Veronica TV/Disney HD, Meiden van Holland Hard **Mux 5✪:** CNN, Nickelodeon/TeenNick, Slam!TV, 13th Street ⌘ Arrow Jazz FM, BBC Radio 1-4.

Location	M1*	M2	M3	M4	M5	kW
Alkmar	39j	45	34	35	44	20
Alphen a.d.R.	52m	49	57	24	27	10/15/3x2
Amsterdam	39j	49	57	24	27	10
Apeldoorn	42h	36	58	66	28	20
Arnhem	42h	36	58	66	28	20/2x40/2x20
Breda	30b	60	31	32	33	2x20/3x15
Den Bosch	30b	60	31	56	33	2x10/5/10/5
Den Haag	52m	49	57	24	27	10
Den Haag (Zichtenb.)	52m	49	57	24	27	10
Deventer	22k	36	23	47	-	10
Doetinchem	42h	36	58	53	28	20/100/2x20
Eindhoven Oost	30b	60	31	56	33	15/10/3x15
Eindhoven West	30b	60	31	56	33	4x10/5
Enschede	22k	36	23	47	28	10/4x20
Goes	54d	48	29	32	35	10
Groningen	46i	30	54	33	25	20
Haarlem	39j	49	57	24	27	20
Heerlen	54a	34	51	51	27	40/20/2x40/20
Helmond	30b	60	31	56	33	20
Hengelo	22k	36	23	47	28	3x40/2x20
Hilversum	39j	49	57	24	27	15
Ijsselstein	50e	49	57	24	27	3x15/10
Krimpen a.d.IJ.	21l	49	57	24	27	10
Leeuwarden	32c	55	34	21	44	20
Lelystad	26g	36	23	47	44	2x20/10/2x20
Loon op Zand	30b	60	31	56	33	15
Maarssen	50e	49	57	24	27	10
Maastricht	54a	34	51	51	27	20/2x10/15/10
Nijmegen	42h	60	31	56	33	10/20/10/20/15
Oegstgeest	52m	49	57	24	27	15
Oss	42h	60	31	56	33	20/4x10
Oss	30b	-	-	-	-	10
Roermond	54a	34	24	51	27	20
Rosendaal	30b	48	29	32	35	20
Rotterdam (Waalhaven)	21l	49	57	24	27	10
Sittard	54a	34	24	51	27	20
Sliedrecht	21l	49	57	24	27	10
Smilde**	60f	30	54	33	25	3x40/30/40
Utrecht	50e	49	57	24	27	10/5/3x4
Veenendal	50e	36	58	53	28	20
Veenendal	42h	-	-	-	-	20
Venlo	54a	34	31	56	27	20/40/20/40/20
Zoetermeer	52m	49	57	24	27	10
Zwolle	22k	36	23	47	28	20

+ sites with txs below 10kW. Pol=V. *) incl. regional stns (see above).
**) Currently out of service; temporarily replaced by tx in Assen

NEW CALEDONIA (France)

System: DVB-T (MPEG4) [E]

NOUVELLE CALEDONIE 1ÈRE (Pub) 🖃 BP G3 Mont Coffin, F-98848 Nouméa Cedex ☎ +687 687274327 🗎 +687 687281252 **W:** nouvellecaledonie.1ere.fr **L.P:** Dir: Wallès Kotra.

DTT Transmitters
Operator: TDF **Mux:** Nouvelle Caledonie 1ère, France 2-5, France Ô, France 24, Arte **Txs:** MFN

NEW ZEALAND

Systems: DVB-T (MPEG4) [NZ]; † PAL-B/G [NZ] ⬇1 Dec 2013

National Stations
TELEVISION NEW ZEALAND (TVNZ) (Pub) 🖃 P.O.Box 3819, Auckland ☎ +64 9 9167000 🗎 +64 9 9167934 **L.P:** Chmn: Wayne Walden **Chs:** TV One, TV One Plus 1, TV2, TVNZ U. – **PRIME TELEVISION (Comm)** 🖃 1 John Glenn Ave., North Harbour, Auckland ☎ +64 9 4140700 🗎 +64 9 4140701 **E:** info@ primetv.co.nz **W:** primetv.co.nz – **TAB TRACKSIDE (Comm)** 🖃 P.O. Box 388-99, Wellington Mail Centre, Wellington ☎ +64 4 5766999 🗎 +64 4 5766996 **E:** corporate@tab.co.nz **W:** www.tab.co.nz – **TV3 (Comm)** 🖃 P.O. Box 5185, Auckland ☎ +64 9 779730 🗎 +64 9 3G67029 **W:** www.tv3.co.nz

Local Stations not shown.

DTT Transmitters
Licensee Mux 1: TVNZ **Mux:** TV One, TV One Plus 1, TV2, TVNZ U – **Licensee Mux 2:** MediaWorks 🖃 P.O.Box 92624, Symonds Street, Auckland ☎ +69 9 3779730 🗎 +69 9 3665999 **W:** www.mediaworks. co.nz **Mux:** TV3, TV3+, C4 – **Licensee Mux 3:** Kordia 🖃 P.O.Box 2495, Auckland ☎ +64 9 9166400 🗎 +64 9 9166403 **W:** www.kordia-solutions.com **Mux:** Parliament TV, Maori TV, CTV8, Prime.

Location	M1	M2	M3
Auckland (Waiatarua)	29	33	45

+ nationwide tx network

NICARAGUA

System: NTSC-M [A]; SBTVD (MPEG4) [A] planned

CANAL 6 (Comm) 🖃 3 1/2 Carretera Sur Contig o Shell, Managua ☎ +505 22660118 🗎 +505 22666522 **Tx:** Managua ch6 (25kW). – **CANAL 10 (Comm)** 🖃 Hotel Mansión Teodolinda, 2c, Abajo ☎ +505 22227788 **W:** canal10.com.ni **Tx:** Managua ch10. – **CANAL 15 (Comm)** 🖃 Lomas de Tiscapa, frente al Hospital Militar, Managua ☎ +505 22669086 **W:** www.canal15.com.ni **Tx:** Managua ch15. – **CANAL DE NOTICIAS DE NICARAGUA (CDNN) (Comm)** 🖃 Carretera a Masaya Km. 4½, Motorama ½c al Su, Managua ☎ +505 22670170 **W:** www.cdnn23.com **Tx:** Managua ch23. – **MULTINOTICIAS (CANAL 4)** 🖃 Del Montoya, 1c al Sur, 1c al Este, Managua ☎ +505 22663420 🗎 +505 22663467 **W:** www. multinoticiastv4.com **Tx:** Managua ch4. – **NICAVISIÓN (Comm)** 🖃 Apdo 2766, Managua ☎ +505 22660691 🗎 +505 22661424 **Tx:** ch12. – **TELENICA (CANAL 8) (Comm)** 🖃 Apdo Postal 3611, Hotel Mansión Teodolinda 1c al Sur, y ½ Abajo ☎ +505 22665021 🗎 +505 22665024 **W:** tn8.tv **Tx:** Managua ch8. – **TELEVICENTRO (CANAL 2) (Comm)** 🖃 Apdo Postal 688, Managua ☎ +505 22682222 **E:** canal2@canal2.com.ni **W:** www.canal2.com.ni **Tx:** Managua ch2 (25kW). – **ENLACE NICARAGUA (CANAL 21) (Rlg)** 🖃 De la Casa de Obrero, 5c. al Sur y 2c. Arriba ☎ +505 22668688 🗎 +505 22683132 **W:** www.enlacenicaragua.org **Tx:** Managua ch21. Rel. TBN (USA).

NIGER

System: SECAM-K1 [VHF=K, UHF=E]

TÉLÉ-SAHEL (Gov) 🖃 BP 309, Niamey ☎ +227 20723686 🗎 +227 20723153 **E:** ortny@intnet.net **W:** www.ortn.ne **L.P:** Dir TV: Moussa Abdou Saley. **Chs:** Télé Sahel, Tal TV. **Txs:** (pol.H exc. where stated) **Télé Sahel:** Agadez ch4 (10kW), Dosso ch4 (10kW), Zinder ch5 (10kW), Arlit ch6 (1kW), Maradi ch7V (10kW), Dogondoutchi ch7

(1kW), Gaya ch8V (1kW), Niamey ch9 (10kW), Konni ch9 (10kW), Diffa ch9 (10kW) & repeaters. **Tal TV:** (-). – **TÉNÉRÉ TV (Comm)** ☒ BP 13600, Niamey ☎ +227 20736576 🖷 +227 20737775 **E:** tenerefm@ intnet.net **Txs:** (-).

NIGERIA

System: PAL-B/G [E]; DVB-T

NIGERIAN TELEVISION AUTHORITY (NTA) (Pub) ☒ P.M.B 113, Garki, Abuja ☎ +234 9 2346907 🖷 +234 9 2345914 **E:** servicom@nta. com.ng **W:** www.nta.com.ng **L.P:** Chmn: Alhaji Ibrahim Buba **Chs:** NTA, NTA2, reg. stns. **Txs: NTA:** ch10 (100kW) & relay txs; **NTA 2:** ch5 (100kW) & relay txs. – **DBN TELEVISION (Comm)** ☒ The Dream Centre, Durosinmi etti Drive, Lekki Phase 1, Lagos ☎+234 1 2130800 **W:** www.dbntelevision.com **L.P:** CEO: Osa Sonny Adun. **Txs:** Lagos ch32 & relay txs. – **GALAXY TV (Comm)** ☒ Lagos **W:** www.galaxyonline.com **Tx:** Lagos ch27. – **LAGOS TV (Comm)** ☒ Lagos. **Tx:** Lagos ch8. – **MINAJ BROADCAST INTERNATIONAL (Comm)** ☒ P.O.Box 3975, Mushin, Lagos ☎ +234 1 4529203 🖷 +234 1 4528500 **E:** info@minajgroup.com **W:** www.minajgroup.com **L.P:** Exec. Chairman: Mike Ajegbo **Txs:** ch41, ch43.

NIUE

System: PAL-B [NZ]

TV NIUE ☒ P.O.Box 68, Alofi ☎ +683 4026 🖷 +683 4217 **E:** gm.bcn@ mail.gov.nu **L.P:** GM: Trever Tiakia **Txs:** Makefu ch4 (0.01kW), Alofi ch6 (0.75kW), Mutulau ch8 (0.04kW).

NORFOLK ISLAND (Australia)

System: PAL-B [AU]

NORFOLK ISLAND TELEVISION SCE. (Gov) ☒ New Cascade Rd, Norfolk Island 2899, Australia ☎ +672 22137 🖷 +672 23298 **Chs:** rel. ABC, SBS & Central 7 TV from Australia. **Txs:** Mt. Pitt ch7V (0.02kW); ch10 (local).

NO. MARIANA IS (USA associated)

System: ATSC [A]

WSZE-TV (Comm) ☒ Saipan. **Tx:** ch10 (0.5kW). **Mux:** NBC; CBS / KUAM-TV (Guam).

NORWAY

System: DVB-T (MPEG4)

National Stations
NORSK RIKSKRINGKASTING (NRK) (Pub) ☒ 0340 Oslo ☎ +47 23047000 🖷 +47 23047799 **E:** info@nrk.no **W:** www.nrk.no **L.P:** DG: Hans-Tore Bjerkaas. **Chs:** NRK1, NRK2, NRK3/NRK Super, regional stns – **CANAL DIGITAL (Comm)** ☒ 4896 Grimstad ☎ +47 81559600 🖷 +47 22939305 **E:** kundeservice@canaldigital.no **W:** www.canaldigital. no – **TV2 (Comm)** ☒ Postboks 7222, 5002 Bergen ☎ +47 55908070 🖷 +47 55908090 **E:** info@tv2.no **W:** www.tv2.no **L.P:** CEO: Alf Hildrum. – **TV Norge (Comm)** ☒ Postboks 11 Sentrum, 0101 Oslo ☎ +47 21022000 🖷 +47 22051000 **E:** tvnorge@tvnorge.no **W:** www.tvnorge. no **L.P:** CEO: Harald Strømme.

Local Stations (all Comm) (via DTT Mux 3)
a) BTV: P.O.Box 7240, 5020 Bergen; **b) TV Aust-Agder (TV-A):** P.O.Box 349, 4801 Arendal; **c) TV-Adressa:** Industriveien 13, 7003 Trondheim; **d) TV Budstikka*:** P.O.Box 133, 1376 Billingstad; **e) TV Drammen*:** P.O.Box 7033, 3007 Drammen; **f) TV Follo*:** Idrettsveien 11, 1400 Ski. **g) TV Haugaland:** P.O.Box 408, 5501 Haugesund; **h) TV Hålogaland:** P.O.Box 85, 9481 Harstad; **i) TV Innlandet:** P.O.Box 94, 2801 Gjøvik; **j) TV Nord:** P.O.Box 1193 Sentrum, 9504 Alta; **k) TV Nordland:** P.O.Box 564, 8601 Mo i Rana; **l) TV Nord-Trøndelag:** Drivhuset, Skippergata 11 d, 7725 Steinkjer; **m) TV Nordvest*:** P.O.Box 471, 6501 Kristiansund. **n) TV Oslo:** P.O.Box 11, Sentrum, 0101 Oslo; **o) TV Romerike:** Roseveien 1, 2007 Kjeller; **p) TV Sunnmøre:** Kirkegata 10, 6004 Ålesund; **q) TV Sør:** P.O.Box 342, 4663 Kristiansand; **r) TV Telemark:** P.O.Box 2833, 3702 Skien; **s) TV Tromsø:** P.O.Box 815, 9258 Tromsø; **t) TV Vest:** Auglendsmyrå 6, 4016 Stavanger; **u) TV**

Vestfold*: P.O.Box 2003, 3103 Tønsberg. **v) TV Østfold:** P.O.Box 48, 1701 Sarpsborg.
NB: all stns relay TV Norge outside own prgrs, except (*).

DTT Transmitters
Licensee: Norges televisjon AS ☒ P.O.Box 313, 0511 Oslo ☎ +47 22883780 🖷 +47 22883781 **E:** info@ntv.no **W:** www.ntv.no **Mux (❖exc.*):** NRK1 (incl. reg prgrs)*, NRK2*, NRK3/NRK Super*, TV3, Viasat 4, Disney Channel. **Mux 2 (❖exc.*):** TV2*, TV2 Filmkanalen, TV2 Nyhetskanalen, TV2 Sport, TV2 Zebra, Animal Planet, The Voice TV. **Mux 3 (❖exc.*):** TVNorge, FEM, National Geographic, BBC World News, Canal+ First, Canal+ Hits, Canal+ Sport 1, Åpen kanal*, Local Stations*. **Local Mux Oslo:** TV Oslo, TV Follo og TV Budstikka **Tx:** Oslo ch46.

Location	M1	M2	M3	kW
Bagn	32	39	42	50
Bergen	33	49	39	50
Bjerkreim	23	26	30	50
Bokn	36	54	57	50
Bremager	25	28	31	50
Gamlemsveten	37	38	54	50
Gausta	25	27	35	10
Greipstad	51	54	47	50
Grong	21	31	35	50
Gulen	37	42	26	50
Hadsel	45	48	58	50
Halden	38	42	62	60
Hammerfest	33	37	48	50
Hemnes	42	45	48	50
Hovdefjell	41	52	48	40
Jetta	45	48	58	50
Kautokeino	46	56	59	50
Kistefjell	26	46	43	50
Kongsberg	60	66	51	50
Kongsvinger	24	48	55	50
Kopparen	26	40	45	50
Lyngdal	25	53	47	50
Lønahorgi	31	41	44	50
Melhus	55	28	25	50
Mosvik	44	47	46	50
Narvik	21	27	37	50
Nordfjordeid	40	44	33	10
Nordhue	33	43	56	50
Nordkapp	30	40	43	50
Oslo	52	58	61	50
Reinsfjell	39	42	35	50
Salten	50	43	60	50
Skien	60	66	54	50
Sogndal	21	24	34	50
Steigen	31	41	44	50
Stord	55	58	60	50
Trolltind	27	39	42	50
Tron	26	34	49	50
Varanger	28	33	50	50
Vega	25	32	37	50

+ sites with txs below 10kW.

OMAN

System: PAL-B/G [E]

SULTANATE OF OMAN TELEVISION (Gov) ☒ P.O.Box 600, 113 Muscat, Oman ☎ +968 24603888 🖷 +968 24604629 **E:** tvradio@ omantel.net.om **W:** www.oman-tv.gov.om **L.P:** DG: Abdullah Bin Said Al Abri **Chs:** Bahlah ch5 (4kW), Shinas ch5 (7kW), Sur ch7 (15kW), Thamret ch8V (100kW), Al-Amirat ch10, Nizwa ch10 (100kW), Quriat ch11 (0.3kW), Saham ch11 (200kW), Al-Berami ch12, Ibra ch12 (6kW), Maserah ch24, Dhank ch25 (2kW), Haima ch28, Adam ch40, Madha ch48, Barka ch51, Ibri ch55, Jabal Qahwi ch60 & low power txs.

PAKISTAN

System: PAL-B/G [E]

PAKISTAN TELEVISION CORP. LTD (PTV) (Gov) ☒ P.O.Box 1221, Islamabad 44000 ☎ +92 51 9208651 🖷 +92 51 9203406 **E:** ptvhq@

hotmail.com **W:** www.ptv.com.pk **L.P:** MD: Yousaf Baig Mirza **Chs (terr.):** PTV Home, PTV News, regional stns, PTV Bolan, AJK TV **Txs: PTV Home:** Islamabad ch6 (50kW) & network; **PTV News:** (-) – **ATV (Comm)** ▣ 11 -F, Model Town, Lahore ☎ +92 42 5853669 ▤ +92 42 5853668 **E:** info@atv.com.pk **W:** www.atv.com.pk **L.P:** Chmn: Abdul Jabbar. **Txs:** (-).

PALAU (USA associated)

NB: No terrestrial TV station.

PANAMA

Systems: # NTSC-M [A]; DVB-T (MPEG2) [A]

National Stations
SYSTEMA ESTATAL DE RADIO Y TELEVISIÓN (Pub) ▣   Apt. 0843-0256, Curundu, diagonal al Ministerio de Obras Públicas, Panamá ☎ +507 5071500 ▤ +507 2362987 **E:** administracion@sertv.gob.pa **W:** www.sertv.gob.pa **Chs:** SERTV, TV Educativa **Txs: SERTV:** (-), **TV Educativa:** Panamá ch11. – **CADENA MILENIUM RCM (CANAL 21) (Comm)** ▣ Via Espana Sector de Carrasquilla, Apdo. postal 87-1989, Zona 7, Panamá **Tx:** Panamá ch21 (20kW). – **FETV (CANAL 5) (Comm)** ▣Ave Ricardo J. Alfaro Contiguo al Gimnasio de la USMA, Apdo.6-7295, El Dorado, Panamá ☎ +507 2308000 ▤ +507 2301955 **W:** www.fetv.org **L.P:** DG: Manuel Santiago Blanquer i Planells **Tx:** Panamá ch5 (30kW). – **RPC TELEVISION (CANAL 4) (Comm)** ▣Ave 12 de Octubre, Apartado 1-1425, Panamá 8 ☎ +507 2104104 **W:** www.rpctv.com **Tx:** Panamá ch4 (30kW). – **TELEMETRO (CANAL 13) (Comm)** ▣ Ave 12 de Octubre, Apartado 1-1425, Panama 8, Panamá ☎ +507 2106845 ▤ +507 2106929 **W:** www.telemetro.com.pa **L.P:** Pres: Fernando Eleta Almarán **Tx:** Panamá ch13 (30kW). **TELEVISORA NACIONAL S.A. (Comm)** ▣ Apt. 0819-07129, El Dorado, Panamá ☎ +507 2793700 ▤ +507 2362987 **E:** tvn@tvn-2.com **W:** www.tvn-2.com **L.P:** DG: Agustin De La Guardia **Chs:** TVN, TV Max **Txs: TVN:** Panamá ch2 (18kW); **TV Max:** Panamá ch9.

Local Stations
Canal +23 (Comm): Plaza Hispanidad, Ave. 12 de Octubre, (Ap. 6A-9292 El Dorado), Panamá; ch23 (30kW). **Canal 29 (Comm):** Avenida Ricardo J. Alfaro, Sun Tower Mall, Piso 2, Apdo. postal 1465, Balboa, Ancón Panamá; ch29. **Hosanna Vision (Canal 37) (Rlg):** Ave. Martin Sosa, Ed. Hosanna Vision (A.P. Hosanna, El Dorado 6-7981), Panamá; ch37 (20kW).

DTT Transmitters
Licensee: SERTV **Mux:** SERTV, TV Educativa **Tx:** ch41 (Panamá). – **Licensee:** Televisora National S.A. **Mux:** TVN, TV Max, TV Max HD **Tx:** ch45 (Panamá).

PAPUA NEW GUINEA

System: PAL-B/G [NZ]

EM TV (Comm) ▣ P.O.Box 443, Boroko NCD 111 ☎ +675 3257322 ▤ +675 3254450 **E:** emtv@datec.com.pg **W:** www.emtv.com.pg **L.P:** CEO (Media Niugini Ltd): Ken Clark. **Txs:** Burns Peak ch9 (1.1kW), Air Niugini Hill ch31 (0.17kW), Garden City ch68 (0.02kW) (all Port Moresby area).

PARAGUAY

Systems: # PAL-N [A]; SBTVD (MPEG4) [A] planned

National Stations
ARANDU RAPE (Pub) ▣ Av. Avda. Eusebio Ayala km. 4 1/2, Asunción ☎ +594 21 506794 **E:** marandu@arandurape.edu.py **W:** www.arandurape.edu.py **Txs:** time-shared via txs of Latele, Telefuturo. – **LATELE (Comm)** ▣ Av. Eusebio Ayala No. 2995, Esq. Pasaje Tembetary, Asunción ☎ +595 21 4157400 **E:** info@latele.com. py **W:** www.latele.com.py **Txs:** Asunción ch11 (40kW) & relays. – **PARAVISION (Comm)** ▣ Av. Mariscal López esq. Bélgica, Asunción ☎ +595 21 664380 **E:** info@paravision.com.py **W:** www.paravision. com.py **Txs:** Asunción ch5 (20kW) & relays. – **RED GUARANÍ (Comm)** ▣ Gral. Santos 1024 c/Concordia, Asunción ☎ +595 21 205444 **E:** info@redguarani.com.py **W:** www.redguarani.com.py **Txs:** Asunción ch2 (20kW) & relays. – **RED PRIVADA DE COMUNICACIÓN (RPC) (Comm)** ▣ Calles Comendador Nicolás Bó y Guaranies, Lambaré, Asunción ☎ +595 21 332823 ▤ +595 21 331695 **E:** commercial@rpc. com.py **W:** www.rpc.com.py **Txs:** Asunción ch13 (40kW) & relays.

– **SISTEMA NACIONAL DE TELEVISIÓN (SNT) (Comm)** ▣ Av. Carlos Antonio Lopez 572, Asunción ☎ +595 21 424222 ▤ +595 21 480230 **E:** snt@snt.com.py **W:** www.snt.com.py **Txs:** Asunción ch9 (40kW) & relays. – **TELEFUTURO (Comm)** ▣ Andrade c/ O'Higgins, Villa Morra, Asunción ☎ +595 21 608756 **W:** www.telefuturo.com.py **Txs:** Asunción ch4 (60kW) & relays.

Local Stations not shown.

PERU

Systems: # NTSC-M [A] ⇩2020; SBTVD (MPEG4) [A]

National Stations (ᵃ=analogue)
TV PERU (Gov) ▣ Av. Jose Galvez 1040, Santa Beatriz, Líma ☎ +51 1 6190707 ▤ +51 1 6190711 **W:** www.tvperu.gob.pe **L.P:** Dir: Juan Carlos Vicente **Txs:** Líma ᵃch7 (10kW)/ch16 (0.24kW) & relays txs. – **AMÉRICA TELEVISIÓN (Comm)** ▣ Montero Rosas 1099, Santa Beatriz, Líma ☎ +51 1 2657361 ▤ +51 1 2656976 **E:** americanoticias@ americatv.com.pe **W:** www.americatv.com.pe **L.P:** CEO: Eric Jurgensen **Txs:** Líma ᵃch4 (2kW)/ch24 (0.24kW) & relay txs. – **ATV (ANDINA DE RADIODIFUSIÓN) (Comm)** ▣ Arequipa 3570, San Isidro, Apartado 270077, Líma ☎ +51 1 2212261 ▤ +51 1 4217263 **W:** atv.tuteve. tv **Txs:** Líma ch9 (315kW)/ch18 (1kW) & relay txs. – **FRECUENCIA LATINA (Comm)** ▣ Av. San Felipe 968, Jesús Mariá, Líma 11 ☎ +51 1 4707272 ▤ +51 1 4712688 **E:** flatina@frecuencialatina.com.pe **W:** frecuencialatina.com.pe **Txs:** Líma ᵃch2 (22,5kW)/ch20 (0.24kW) & relays txs. – **PANAMÉRICANA TELEVISIÓN (Comm)** ▣ Av. Arequipa 1110, Líma ☎ +51 1 4113200 ▤ +51 1 4113309 **E:** pantel@ pantel.com.pe **W:** www.pantel.com.pe **Txs:** Líma ᵃch5 (290kW)/ch26 (0.24kW)& relay txs. – **RBC TELEVISIÓN (Comm)** ▣ Manco Capac 333, La Victoria, Líma ☎ +51 1 4337674 ▤ +51 1 4331237 **W:** www. rbctelevision.com **Txs:** Líma ᵃch11 (30kW)/ch38 (0.24kW) & relays.

Local Stations not shown.

PHILIPPINES

Systems: # NTSC-M [A] ⇩31 Dec 2015; ISDB-T [A]

National Stations (ᵃ=analogue)
INTERCONTINENTAL BROADCASTING CORP. (IBC) (Gov)▣ Broadcast City, Capitol Hills, Diliman, Quezon City ☎ +63 2 9318781 ▤ +63 2 9324611 **L.P:** Pres/CEO: Eric Canoy **Txs:** DZTV-TV Manila ᵃch13 (50kW) & relay stns. – **PEOPLE'S TELEVISION NETWORK, INC (PTV) (Gov)**▣ Broadcast Complex, Visayas Ave, Quezon City 1100 ☎ +63 2 9206521 ▤ +63 2 9204342 **W:** www.ptv.ph **L.P:** GM: Renato Caluag. **Txs:** DGWT-TV Manila ᵃch4 (50kW)/ch48 & relay stns. – **PROGRESSIVE BROADCASTING CORP. (UNTV) (Pub)**▣ #907 ESDA Philam, Quezon City. **W:** www.untvweb.com **L.P:** Pres: Alfredo L. Henares. **Txs:** DWAO-TV Manila ᵃch37 (2058kW) & relay stns. – **ABS-CBN BROADCASTING CORP. (Comm)**▣Eugenio Lopez Jnr St, Quezon C. ☎+63 2 4111166 ▤ +63 2 4152272 **W:** www.abs-cbn.com **L.P:** Chmn/CEO: Eugenio Lopez III. **Txs:** DWAC-TV Manila ᵃch23 (1125kW)/ch47 & relay stns. – **ASSOCIATED BROADCASTING CO., INC. (TV5) (Comm)**▣ AMPC Bldg., 136 Amorsolo cor. Gamboa Sts., Legaspi Village, Makati City ☎ +63 2 8923801 ▤ +63 2 8154314 **W:** www.tv5.com.ph **L.P:** Chmn: Manny V. Pangilinan. **Txs:** DWET-TV Manila ᵃch5 (55kW) & relay stns. – **RADIO MINDANAO NETWORK (RMN) (Comm)**▣ 4F State Condominium I, Salcedo St., Legaspi Village, Makati City ☎ +63 2 8120540 ▤ +63 2 8163680 **W:** www.rmnnews.com **L.P:** Pres/CEO: Eric S. Canoy. **Txs:** DWKC-TV Manila ᵃch31 (50kW) & relay stns (rel. BEAM TV). – **RADIO PHILIPPINES NETWORK (RPN) (Comm)**▣ Broadcast City, Capitol Hills, Quezon City ☎+63 2 9315080 ▤ +63 2 9321470 **W:** www.etc. com.ph **L.P:** Chmn: Wilson Tieng **Txs:** DZKB-TV Manila ᵃch9 (50kW) & relay stns. – **RAJAH BROADCASTING NETWORK, INC. (RJTV) (Comm)**▣ 3/F Save-A-Lot Mall, 2284 Pasong Tamo Ext., Makati City ☎ +63 2 8933404 ▤ +63 2 8932360 **E:** rjofc@compass.com.ph **W:** www.rjplanet.com **Txs:** DZRJ-TV Manila ᵃch29 (1354kW) & relay stns. – **GMA NETWORK, INC (Comm)**▣ EDSA, Diliman, Quezon City, Metro Manila ☎ +63 2 9285041 ▤ +63 2 9285041 **W:** www.gmanetwork.com **L.P:** Chmn/CEO: Filipe Gozon. **Txs:** DZBB-TV Manila ᵃch7 (100kW) & relay stns. – **SOUTHERN BROADCASTING NETWORK, INC (SBN) (Comm)**▣ Suite 2901 Jollibee Plaza, Emerald Ave., Ortigas Center, Pasig City ☎ +63 2 6363286 ▤ +63 2 6363288 **E:** genceo@sbnphilippines.net **W:** www. talktv.ph **L.P:** Pres/CEO: Teofilo A. Henson **Txs:** DWCP-TV Manila ᵃch21 (40kW) & relay stns. – **STUDIO 23 (Comm)**▣ 3rd/F, Main Building, ABS-CBN Broadcasting Center, Mo. Ignacia Street cor. Sgt Esguerra, Quezon City, Philippines 1103 ☎ +63 2 4152272

E: studio23@abs-cbn.com **W:** www.studio23.tv **L.P:** MD: Antonio Ventosa. **Txs:** DWAC-TV Manila °ch23 (1126kW) & relay stns. Owned by ABS-CBN. – **ACQ KINGDOM BROADCASTING NETWORK (ACQ-KBN) (Rlg)** Suite 3102 31/F Jollibee Plaza, F. Ortigas Jr. Road, Ortigas Center, Pasig City, 1600 ☎ +63 2 6830772 ▤ +63 2 6830775 **E:** sonshine@sonshinemedia.com **W:** www.acqkbn.tv **Txs:** DWBP-TV Manila °ch39 (50kW) & relay stns. – **GATEWAY UHF BROADCASTING (3ABN) (Rlg)** Sumulong Highway, Block 5, Brgy. Sta. Cruz, Antipolo City **Txs:** DWVN-TV Manila °ch45 (5kW) & relay stns. – **ZOE BROADCASTING NETWORK (Rlg)** 22F Strata 2000 Bldg., F. Ortigas Road, Ortigas Ctr, Pasig City ☎ +63 6383469 **W:** www.lightnetwork.ph **L.P:** Chmn: Eddie Villanueva. **Txs:** DZOZ-TV Manila °ch33 & relay stns (rel. Light 33 TV); DZOE-TV Manila °ch11 & relay stns (rel. GMA News TV).

Local Stations not shown.

PITCAIRN ISLANDS (UK)

System: PAL-G [NZ]

Foreign TV Relay
Hope Channel (USA): ch29 (0.003.5kW).

POLAND

Systems: DVB-T (MPEG4) [E]; † PAL-D/K [R] ⇩31 Jul 2013

National Stations
TELEWIZJA POLSKA S.A. (TVP) (Pub) ul. Woronicza 17, 00-999 Warszawa ☎ +48 225478000 ▤ +48 225478000 **W:** www.tvp.pl **L.P:** Chmn: Juliusz Braun. **Chs (terr.):** TVP1, TVP2, TVP Info/TVP Regionalna, TVP Historia, TVP Kultura **TVP2:** Warszawa (Raszyn) ch27 (800kW) & netw. – **TV4-CZWÓRKA (Comm)** ul. Gen. Okulickiego 6, 05-500 Piaseczno ☎ +48 227569711 ▤ +48 227503090 **E:** sekretariat@tv4.pl **W:** www.tv4.pl **L.P:** Chmn: Piotr Fajks. – **TVN (Comm)** ul. Wiertnicza 166, 02-952 Warszawa ☎ +48 228566060 ▤ +48 228566666 **E:** widzowie@tvn.pl **W:** www. tvn.pl **L.P:** Chmn: Markus Tellenbach. – **TV POLSAT (Comm)** ul. Ostrobramska 77, 04-175 Warszawa ☎ +48 225145533 ▤ +48 225145550 **E:** poczta@polsat.pl **W:** www.polsat.pl **L.P:** Chmn: Dominik Libicki – **TV PULS (Comm)** ul. Chelmska 21, 00-724 Warszawa ☎ +48 225597300 ▤ +48 225597305 **E:** recepcja@pulstv. pl **W:** pulstv.pl **L.P:** Chmn: Dariusz Dabski. **Chs:** TV Puls, TV Puls 2.

Local Stations (all Comm)
NTL Radomsko*: ul. 11-go Listopada 2, 97-500 Radomsko; ch9 (1kW). Rel. TVN. **Telewizja Luzyce*:** ul. Bracka 12,59-800 Luban; ch51 (10kW). **Telewizja Odra**:** ul. Muchoborska 6, 54-424 Wroclaw; Lubin ch22 (1kW), Opole ch30 (0.2kW), Wroclaw ch31 (1kW), Swidnica ch39 (1kW), Gorzów Wlkp. ch40 (1kW), Jelenia Góra ch43 (1kW), Zielona Góra ch51 (1kW), Glogów ch56 (1kW), Legnica ch57 (1kW). **Telewizja TVT*:** ul. Rynek 1, 44-200 Rybnik; Rybnik ch22 (0.2kW), Zory ch30 (0.2kW). *) Rel. TVN + Local prgrs **) Rel. Czwórka + Local prgrs

DTT Transmitters (under construction)
Operator: EmiTel ul. Kamienna 21, 30-403 Kraków ☎ +48 126273100 ▤ +48 126273102 **E:** sekretariat@emitel.pl **W:** www. emitel.pl **Mux 1:** Temp. allocations: TVP1, TVP2, TVP INFO/TVP Regionalna; to be replaced by comm. stns **Mux 2:** Polsat, TVN, TV4-Czwórka, TV Puls, TV Puls 2, TVN7, Polsat Sport News, TV6 **Mux 3:** TVP1, TVP2, TVP INFO/Regional stns, TVP Historia, TVP Kultura.

Location	M1	M2	M3	kW
Bialogard (Slawoborze)	45	50	-	50
Bialystok (Krynice)	46	49	-	58/63
Bydgoszcz (Trzeciewiec)	49	32	-	100
Czestochowa (Bleszno)	35	39	41	2x100/2
Elblag (Jagodnik)	43	25	45	10
Gdansk (Chwaszczyno)	64	35	48	2x100/15
Gizycko (Milki)	48	29	-	100/20
Gorlice	-	61	-	20
Ilawa (Kisielice)	38	24	46	2x100/50
Jelenia Gora (Sniezne Kotly)	48	-	-	100
Kalisz (Mikstat)	38	44	-	100
Katowice (Kosztowy)	55	49	51	25/63/2.5
Kielce (Swiety Krszyz)	62	36	-	50
Klodzko (Czarna Góra)	55	58	-	50/20
Konin (Zolwieniec)	55	45	-	100
Koszalin (Gologóra)	44	47	-	100
Kraków (Choragwica)	25	64	48	29/63/2

Location	M1	M2	M3	kW
Krosno (Sucha Góra)	42	32	-	25/100
Lebork (Skórowo Nowe)	38	45	-	10
Lezajsk (Giedlarowa)	37	61	-	40
Lodz	46	24	-	100
Lublin (Piaski)	33	21	-	100
Olsztyn (Pieczewo)	28	33	44	10/100/2.5
Opole (Chrzelice)	46	34	43	2x100/2.5
Plock (Rachocin)	25	57	35	2x100/20
Poznan (Srem)	23	39	28	2x100/20
Przemysl (Tatarska Góra)	48	61	-	20
Przysucha (Kozlowiec)	50	37	-	50
Ryki (Janiszewska)	22	24	-	20
Siedlce (Losice)	36	43	56	20/50/5
Solina (Góra Jawor)	60	32	-	20
Suwalki (G. Krzemianucha)	64	20	-	20
Swinoujscie	58	34	-	10
Szczawnica (Góra Prehyba)	45	-	-	20
Szczecin (Kolowo)	41	34	49	2x100/10
Tarnobrzeg	37	-	-	15
Tarnów (G. Sw.Marcina)	45	23	-	50
Wagrowiec (Chojna)	42	43	-	20
Walcz (Rusinowo)	42	43	51	2x100/20
Warszawa (Raszyn)	58	48	55	2x100/50
Wisla (G. Skrzyczne)	62	38	62	25/1.25/10
Wroclaw (G. Sleza)	64	58	-	100
Zagan (Wichów)	45	41	-	50
Zakopane (G. Gubalówka)	60	63	-	20
Zamosc (Tarnawatka)	50	52	-	50/25
Zielona Góra (Jemiolów)	45	46	-	80

+ sites with txs below 10kW. Pol.=H.
Temporary/Local muxes not shown.

PORTUGAL

System: DVB-T (MPEG4) [E]

RÁDIO E TELEVISÃO DE PORTUGAL, SGPS, S.A. (RTP) (Pub) Av. Marechal Gomes da Costa 37, 1849-030 Lisboa ☎ +351 217947000 ▤ +351 217947570 **E:** rtp@rtp.pt **W:** www.rtp.pt **L.P:** Pres: Guilherme Costa **Chs (terr.):** RTP1, RTP2; RTP Açores and RTP Madeira (see Azores, Madeira), RTP África (see Angola, Cape Verde, Guinea-Bissau, Mozambique, São Tomé e Príncipe). – **SOCIEDADE INDEPENDENTE DE COMUNICAÇÃO, S.A. (SIC) (Comm)** Estrada da Outurela 119, 2794-052 Carnaxide ☎ +351 214179550 ▤ +351 214173118 **E:** contacto@siconline.pt **W:** www.sic.pt **L.P:** Pres: Pedro Norton de Matos. – **TELEVISÃO INDEPENDENTE, S.A. (TVI) (Comm)** R. Mário Castelhano, 40, Queluz de Baixo, 2749-502 Barcarena ☎ +351 214347500 ▤ +351 214355076 **E:** relacoes.exteriores@iol.pt **W:** www.tvi.iol.pt **L.P:** Pres: Miguel Pais do Amaral.

DTT Transmitters
Licensee: Portugal Telecom Av. Casal Ribeiro, nº 14 1°, 1000-092 Lisboa ☎ +351 213308100 ▤ +351 213308160 **E:** contact@ptcontact.pt **W:** www.telecom.pt **Mux:** RTP1, RTP2, SIC, TVI **Txs:** ch67 (SFN)

PUERTO RICO (USA Commonwealth)

Systems: ATSC [A]

Local Stations*
WAPA-TV (Comm): Carr 19 Kilometro 0.5, Guaynabo, PR 00966. **Txs:** ch27 (1000kW). Mux: WAPA-TV, El Canal del Tiempo. **WCCV-TV (Rlg):** Carr No 2 K92.6, Camuy, PR 00627-2348. Tx: Arecibo ch46 (50kW). **WDWL (Rlg):** Ave Sabana Seca Section 5, Toa Baja, PR 00949. °TBN. Tx: Bayamon ch30 (50kW). **WECN (Rlg):** Carr 167 KM 18.9, Bayamon, PR 00957. Tx: Naranjito ch18 (23kW). **WELU (Rlg):** Carr #2 Km162.8, Hormigueros, PR 00660. Tx: ch34 (250kW). **WIDP (Rlg):** Loma Verde San Jose 1820, Rio Piedras, PR 00926. Tx: ch45 (50.1kW). **WIMN-CA (Rlg):** PO Box 1350, Hatillo, PR 00659. Tx: Arecibo ch20 (0.035kW). **WIPM-TV (Pub):** satellite of WIPR-TV. Tx: Mayagüez ch35 (620kW). **WIPR-TV (Pub):** 570 Ave.Hostos U.Baldrich, Hato Rey, PR 00918. °PBS. Tx: ch43 (790kW). **WIRS (Comm):** satellite of WJPX. Tx: Jauco ch41 (185kW). **WJPX (Comm):** Carr 19 Kilometro 0.5, Guaynabo, PR 00966. °CaribeVisión. Tx: ch21 (1000kW). **WJWN-TV (Comm):** satellite of WJPX. Tx: San Sebastán ch39 (700kW). **WKAQ-TV (Comm):** 383 Roosevelt Ave, Hato Rey, PR 00919. °Telemundo Tx: ch28 (924kW). **WKPV (Comm):** satellite of WJPX. Tx: Ponce ch19 (700kW). **WLII (Comm):** Calle Carazo 62, Guaynabo, PR 00969. °Univision. Tx: Caguas ch56 (71kW). **WMEI (Comm):** 1095 Avenida Wilson, Edificio Puerta

del Condado, Suite 2, San Juan, PR 00907. Tx: Arecibo ch14 (50kW). **WMTJ (Pub):** Isodoro Colon Estatal176, San Juan, PR 00928-1345. °PBS. Tx: ch16 (140kW). **WNJX-TV (Comm):** satellite of WAPA-TV. Tx: Mayagüez ch23 (400kW). Mux: WAPA-TV, El Canal del Tiempo. **WOLE-TV (Comm):** Carr 111 Bario Palmar, Aguadilla, PR 00603-5125. Repeater for WKAQ-TV. Tx: Aguadilla ch69 (120kW). **WORA-TV (Comm):** satellite of WLII. Tx: Mayagüez ch29 (650kW). **WORO-TV (Rlg):** Ave Iturreguy/ Baldorioti, Carolina, PR 00902. Tx: ch33 (6kW). **WQHA (Rlg):** satellite of WUJA. Tx: Aguada ch50 (50kW). **WQQZ-CA (Comm):** satellite of WMEI. Tx: Ponce ch33 (3kW). **WQTO (Pub):** satellite of WMTJ. Tx: Ponce ch25 (200kW). **WRFB (Comm):** #21Clle B Sabana Abajo Ind, Carolina, PR 00982. Tx: ch51 (16kW). **WRUA (Rlg):** satellite of WECN. Tx: Fajardo ch33 (37kW). **WSJN-CA (Rlg):** Carr 861 KM 4.4, Toa Alta, PR 00953. Tx: ch15 (38.8kW). **WSJU-TV (Comm):** 1508 Calle Bori Urb Antonsant, San Juan, PR 00927-6116. Tx: ch31 (66kW). **WSTE (Comm):** Calle Carazo 64, Guaynabo, PR 00969. Tx: Ponce ch8 (50kW). Boosters in San Juan (WSTE1), Mayagüez (WSTE2), Arecibo (WSTE3). **WSUR-TV (Comm):** satellite of WLII. Tx: Ponce 43 (68kW). **WTCV (Comm):** Calle Bori # 1554, San Juan, PR 00927-6113. Tx: ch32 (50kW). **WTIN (Comm):** satellite of WAPA-TV. Tx: Ponce ch15 (380.2kW). Mux: WAPA-TV, El Canal del Tiempo. **WUJA (Rlg):** Calle B #24 Urb Ind, Sabana Abajo Carolina, PR 00984-4039. Tx: Caguas ch48 (2.5kW). **WVEO (Comm):** satellite of WTCV. Tx: Aguadilla ch17 (42kW). **WVOZ-TV (Comm):** satellite of WTCV. Tx: Ponce ch47 (50.1kW). **WVSN (Rlg):** Satellite of WCCV-TV. Tx· Humaco ch49 (46kW).
*) Full power licenses (Ip licenses not shown). °) Network affiliation. Tx sites are San Juan, unless indicated otherwise.

QATAR

System: PAL-B/G [E]

QATAR TELEVISION (Gov) P.O.Box 1944, Doha ☎ +974 44894444 ▤ +974 44864611 **W:** www.qatarmedialive.com **Che:** Prgr 1 (Arabic), Prgr 2 (English). **Txs: Prgr 1:** Jumaliyah ch11 (200kW) & netw. **Prgr 2:** Jumaliyah ch52 (400kW) & netw.

RÉUNION (France)

System: DVB-T (MPEG4) [E]

RÉUNION 1ÈRE (Pub) 1 rue Jean-Chatel, F-97716 Saint Denis ☎ +262 262406767 ▤ +262 262406771 **W:** reunion.1ere.fr **LP:** Dir: Gérard Christian Hoarau – **ANTENNE RÉUNION (Comm)** BP 80 001, F-97801 Saint-Denis Cedex 009 ☎ +262 262482828 ▤ +262 262482829 **W:** www.antennereunion.fr **LP:** DG: Christophe Ducasse – **TÉLÉ KRÉOL (Comm)** 16 rue du Fangourin, F-97460 Savannah ☎ +262 262452017

DTT Transmitters
Operator: TDF **Mux:** Réunion 1ère, France 2-5, France Ô, France 24, Arte, Antenne Réunion, Télé Kréol **Txs:** MFN.

ROMANIA

Systems: # PAL-D/G [R/E] ⇩31 Dec 2015; DVB-T (MPEG4) [E]

National Stations
TELEVIZIUNEA ROMÂNA (TVR) (Pub) Calea Dorobantilor nr. 191, sector 1, Bucuresti ☎ +40 21 3199112 ▤ +40 21 3199264 **E:** office@tvr.ro **W:** www.tvr.ro **LP:** DG: Claudiu Saftoiu. **Chs (terr.):** TVR1, TVR2, TVR HD, Regional stns.

Location	TVR1	TVR2	REG	kW
Balota	51	-	-	5
Bucuresti	34	51	57	10
Cerbu Novaci	8	-	-	20
Comanesti	23	40	-	5
Costila	6	22	-	10/20
Cozia	44	27	-	2/10
Craiova	-	-	50	10
Dobrogea Sud	46	-	-	5
Feleac	11	21	42	10
Gheorghieni	32	-	-	5
Heniu	59	21	-	5
Magura Boiu	27	-	-	5
Magura Odobesti	9	38	-	2/5
Mogosa	10	37	-	5
Paltinis	7	-	-	5
Pietriarie	-	-	59	10
Saveni	22	-	-	5

Location	TVR1	TVR2	REG	kW
Semenic	58	-	-	20
Siria	52	-	-	5
Terghirghiol	8	42	-	5/10
Urseni	9	21	53	10/40/10
Vacareni	43	26	-	5

+ sites with txs below 5kW.
ANTENA 1 (Comm) Bd. Ficusului 44A, sector 1, Bucuresti ☎ +40 21 2303202 ▤ +40 21 2327707 **E:** office@a1.ro **W:** a1.ro **LP:** DG: F. Bratescu. **Txs:** Bucuresti ch57 (1kW) & network. – **NATIONAL TV (Comm)** Str, Fabricii nr. 46B, Sector 6, 060825 Bucuresti ☎ +40 21 4042570 ▤ +40 21 4042429 **E:** office@nationaltv.ro **W:** www. nationaltv.ro **Txs:** via Bucuresti DTT & netw. – **PRO TV (Comm)** Bd. Pache Protopopescu 109, Bucuresti ☎ +40 21 2501430 ▤ +40 21 3124218 **E:** doinita@protv.ro **W:** www.protv.ro. **Txs:** Bucuresti ch31 (1kW) & network. – **REALITATEA TV (Comm)** Sos. Dudesti Pantelimon 1-3, 033091 Bucuresti ☎ 402 1 3160019 ▤ 402 1 3160019 **E:** office@realitatea.net **W:** www.realitatea.net **L.P:** DG: Sorin Enache. **Txs:** Bucuresti ch42 (1kW) & network.

Local & Regional Stations not shown.

DTT Transmitters (under construction)
Operator: Radiocom ▤ Bd. Libertatii 14, sector 5, 050706 Bucuresti ☎ +40 31 5003007 ▤ +40 21 3149798 **W:** www.radiocom.ro **Mux 1:** TVR1, TVR2, TVR HD, Pro TV HD **Mux 2:** TVR3, TVR Cultural, Antena 1, Antena 3, Realitatea TV, National TV. – **Licensee:** Media Pro **Mux 3:** Pro TV HD, sport.ro HD

Location	M1	M2	M3	kW
Bucuresti (Herastrau)	54	59	30	5

+ nationwide tx network under construction

RUSSIA

Systems: # SECAM-D/K [R] ⇩2015; DVB-T (MPEG2, MPEG4) [E], DVB-T2 (MPEG4) [E]

National Stations
VSEROSSIYSKAYA GOSUDARSTVENNAYA TELEVIZIONNAYA I RADIOVESHCHATELNAYA KOMPANIYA (VGTRK) (Gov) HQ: 125040 Moskva, 5-ya Yamskogo Polya ul. 19/21 ☎ +7 495 2326333 **W:** www.vgtrk.com **LP:** GD: Oleg B. Dobrodeyev. Studios: Rossiya 1, Rossiya 2, Rossiya 24: 15162 Moskva, ul. Shabolovka 37; Rossiya K: 119902 Moskva, ul. Zubovskiy bul. 4; Karusel: 127427 Moskva, ul. Ak. Korolyova 19. **Chs:** Rossiya 1 (rutv.ru), Rossiya 2 (rutv.ru), Rossiya K (www.tvkultura.ru), Rossiya 24 (www.vesti.ru), Karusel (www.karusel-tv.ru); Regional Stations (see chapter below) **Txs: Rossiya 1:** Moskva ch11 (60kW) & network; **Rossiya 2:** Moskva ch6 (1kW) & network; **Rossiya 24:** via DTT; **Rossiya K:** Moskva ch33 (20kW) & network; **Karusel:** via DTT. – **PERVYY KANAL (Gov/ Comm)** 127000 Moskva, ul. Ak. Korolyova 12 ☎ +7 495 2179838 ▤ +7 495 2151976. **E:** dip@1tv.ru **W:** www.1tv.ru **LP:** DG: Konstantin Ernst. **Txs:** Moskva ch1 (40kW) & network. – **TV TSENTR (Gov)** 115184 Moskva, ul. Bolshaya Tatarskaya 33-1 ☎ +7 495 9593900 **E:** press@tvc.ru **W:** www.tvc.ru **LP:** DG: Aleksandr S. Ponomayov. **Txs:** Moskva ch3 (40kW) & network. – **TV ZVEZDA (Gov)** 129110 Moskva, Suvorovskaya pl. 2 ☎ +7 495 6316883 **E:** info@tvzvezda.ru **W:** www.tvzvezda.ru **LP:** DG: Vladimir Zhelonkin. **Txs:** Moskva ch57 (5kW) & network. – **5 KANAL (Comm)** 197376 St.Peterburg, ul. Chapygina 6 ☎ +7 812 3351560 ▤ +7 812 2343846 **E:** trk@spbtv. ru **W:** www.5-tv.ru **LP:** DG: Aleksey Brodskiy. **Txs:** St.Peterburg ch3 (50kW) & network. – **NTV (Comm)** 127000 Moskva, ul. Ak. Korolyova 12 ☎ +7 495 2177895 ▤ +7 495 2175103 **E:** ntv@ntv.ru **W:** www.ntv.ru **LP:** DG: Vladimir Kulistikov. **Txs:** Moskva ch8 (40kW) & network. – **PERETS (Comm)** 129226 Moskva, Leningradskiy pr. 31a ☎ +7 495 7856347 **W:** www.peretz.ru **LP:** DG: Dmitriy Troitskiy. **Txs:** Moskva ch23 (10kW) & network. – **REN-TV (Comm)** 119847 Moskva, Zubovskiy bul. 17-1 ☎ +7 495 2465933. ▤ +7 495 2460655. **E:** site@ren-tv.com **W:** www.ren-tv.com **LP:** DG Aleksandr Ordzhonikidze. **Txs:** Moskva ch49 (20kW) & network. – **STS (Comm)** 123298 Moskva, ul. 3-ya Khoroshevskaya 12 ☎ +7 495 7974126. ▤ +7 495 7974101 **E:** ctc@ctc.ru **W:** ctc.ru **LP:** DG: Vyacheslav Murugov. **Txs:** Moskva ch27 (5kW) & network. – **TNT (Comm)** 129272 Moskva, ul. Trifonovskaya 57-3 ☎ +7 495 2178188 ▤ +7 495 7481490 **E:** info@tnt-tv.ru **W:** tnt-online.ru **LP:** DG: Roman Petrenko. **Txs:** Moskva ch35 (5kW) & network. – **TV3 (Comm)** 129515 Moskva, ul. Ak. Korolyova 4-4 ☎ +7 495 9374039 **W:** tv3.ru **LP:** DG Aleksandr Karpov. **Txs:** Moskva ch46 (5kW) & network.

State Regional Stations (Branches of VGTRK)
AD) GTRK "Adygeya": 385000 Maykop, ul. Zhukovskogo 24. **AK)** GTRK "Altay": 656045 Barnaul, Zmeinogorskiy trakt 27a. **AM)** GTRK "Amur":

675000 Blagoveshchensk, per. Svyatitelya Innokentiya 15. **AR)** GTRK "Pomorye": 163061 Arkhangelsk, ul. Popova 2. **AS)** GTRK "Lotos": 414000 Astrakhan, ul. Molodoy Gvardii 17. **BA)** GTRK "Bashkortostan": 450076 Ufa, ul. Gafuri 9/1. **BE)** GTRK "Belgorod": 308000 Belgorod, pr. Slavy 60. **BR)** GTRK "Bryansk": 241033 Bryansk, ul. Stanke Dimitrova 77. **BU)** GTRK "Buryatiya": 670000 Ulan-Ude, ul. Erbanova 7. **CB)** GTRK "Yuzhnyy Ural": 454000 Chelyabinsk, ul. Ordzhonikidze 54b. **CC)** GTRK "Vaynakh": 364000 Groznyy, ul. B.Khmelnitskogo 147, korpus 5. **CK)** GTRK "Chukotka": 686710 Anadyr, ul. Lenina 18. **CV)** GTRK "Chuvashiya": 428003 Cheboksary, ul. Nikolayeva 4. **DA)** GTRK "Dagestan": 367032 Makhachkala, ul. Magomeda Gadzhieva 182. **IN)** GTRK "Ingushetiya": 366720 Nazran, pr. Bazorkina 72. **IR)** GTRK "Irkutsk": 664003 Irkutsk, ul. Gorkogo 15. **IV)** GTRK "Ivteleradio": 153647 Ivanovo, ul. Teatralnaya 31. **KA)** GTRK "Kaliningrad": 236016 Kaliningrad, ul. Klinicheskaya 19. **KB)** GTRK "Kabardino-Balkariya": 360000 Nalchik, pr. Lenina 3. **KC)** GTRK "Karachayevo-Cherkesiya": 357100 Cherkessk, ul. Krasnoarmeyskaya 51. **KD)** GTRK "Kuban": 350038 Krasnodar, ul. Radio 5. **KE)** GTRK "Kuzbass": 650099 Kemorovo, ul. Krasnoarmeyskaya 137a. **KG)** GTRK "Kurgan": 640018 Kurgan, ul. Sovetskaya 105. **KH)** GTRK "Dalnevostochnaya": 682632 Khabarovsk, ul. Lenina 4. **KL)** GTRK "Kaluga": 248021 Kaluga, Pole Svobody 40a. **KM)** GTRK "Kamchatka": 683000 Petropavlovsk-Kamchatskiy, ul. Sovetskaya 62. **KN)** GTRK "Krasnoyarsk": 660028 Krasnoyarsk, ul. Mechnikova 44a. **KO)** GTRK "Komi Gor": 167610 Syktyvkar, Oktyabrskiy pr. 164. **KS)** GTRK "Kostroma": 156005 Kostroma, ul. Nikitskaya 10. **KT)** GTRK "Kareliya": 185630 Petrozavodsk, ul. Pirogova 2. **KU)** GTRK "Kursk": 305016 Kursk, ul. Sovetskaya 32. **KV)** GTRK "Vyatka": 610002 Kirov, ul. Uritskogo 34. **KX)** GTRK "Kalmykiya": 358000 Elista, ul. M. Gorkogo 34. **KY)** GTRK "Yugoriya": 626200 Khanty-Mansiysk, ul. Mira 7. **LI)** GTRK "Lipetsk": 398050 Lipetsk, pl. Plekhanova 1. **MA)** GTRK "Magadan": 685024 Magadan, ul. Kommuny 8/12. **MD)** GTRK "Mordoviya": 430000 Saransk, ul. Dokuchayeva 29. **ME)** GTRK "Mariy-El": 424014 Yoshkar-Ola, ul. Osipenko 50. **MU)** GTRK "Murman": 183032 Murmansk, per. Rusanova 7. **NE)** Territorialnoye otdeleniya GTRK "Pomorye", 164700 Naryan-Mar, ul. Smidovicha 19. **NN)** GTRK "Nizhniy Novgorod": 603600 Nizhniy Novgorod, ul. Belinskogo 9a. **NO)** GTRK "Slaviya": 173620 Velikiy Novgorod, ul. B.Moskovskaya 106. **NS)** GTRK "Novosibirsk", 630048 Novosibirsk, ul. Rimskogo-Korsakova 9. **OB)** GTRK "Orenburg": 460024 Orenburg, per. Televizionnyy 3. **OL)** GTRK "Oryol": 302028 Oryol, ul. 7 Noyabrya 43. **OM)** GTRK "Irtysh": 644050 Omsk, pr. Mira 2. **PM)** GTRK "Vladivostok": 690091 Vladivostok, ul. Uborevicha 20a. **PR)** GTRK "Perm": 614070 Perm, ul. Tekhnicheskaya 7. **PS)** GTRK "Pskov": 180000 Pskov, ul. Nekrasova 50. **PZ)** GTRK "Penza": 440602 Penza, ul. Lermontova 39. **RA)** GTRK "Gornyy Altay": 659700 Gorno-Altaysk, ul. Choros-Gurkina 38. **RK)** GTRK "Khakasiya": 662000 Abakan, ul. Vyatkina 12. **RO)** GTRK "Don-TR": 344101 Rostov-na-Donu, ul. 1-ya Barrikadnaya 18. **RS)** GTRK "Sakha" (NVK "Sakha"): 677007 Yakutsk, ul. Ordzhonikidze 48. **RT)** GTRK "Tyva": 667003 Kyzyl, ul. Gornaya 31. **RY)** GTRK "Oka": 390006 Ryazan, ul. Skomoroshinskaya 20. **SA)** GTRK "Samara": 443011 Samara, ul. Sovetskoy Armii 205. **SL)** GTRK "Sakhalin": 693000 Yuzhno-Sakhalinsk, ul. Komsomolskaya 209. **SM)** GTRK "Smolensk": 214025 Smolensk, ul. Nakhimova 13. **SO)** GTRK "Alaniya": 362007 Vladikavkaz, Osetinskaya gorka 2. **SP)** GTRK "Sankt-Peterburg": 197022 St.Peterburg, nab. reki Karpovki 43. **SR)** GTRK "Saratov": 410004 Saratov, 2-ya Sadovaya ul. 7. **ST)** GTRK "Stavropolye": 355000 Stavropol, ul. Artema 36a. **SV)** GTRK "Ural": 620026 Yekaterinburg, ul. Lunacharskogo 212. **TA)** GTRK "Tambov": 392720 Tambov, ul. Michurinskaya 8a. **TL)** GTRK "Tula": 300600 Tula, Staronikitskaya ul. 1. **TO)** GTRK "Tomsk": 634050 Tomsk, ul. Pushkina 19. **TS)** GTRK "Tatarstan": 420015 Kazan, ul. M. Gorkogo 15. **TV)** GTRK "Tver": 170000 Tver, ul. Vagzhanova 9. **TY)** GTRK "Region-Tyumen": 625013 Tyumen, ul. Permyakova 6. **UD)** GTRK "Udmurtiya": 426004 Izhevsk, ul. Komunarov 216. **UL)** GTRK "Volga": 432030 Ulyanovsk, ul. Simbirskaya 5. **VG)** GTRK "Volgograd-TRV": 400066 Volgograd, ul. Mira 9. **VL)** GTRK "Vladimir": 600000 Vladimir, ul. Bol. Moskovskaya 62. **VN)** GTRK "Voronezh": 394625 Voronezh, ul. Karl Marksa 114. **VO)** GTRK "Vologda": 160000 Vologda, ul. Predtecheskaya 32. **YA)** GTRK "Yaroslavye": 150014 Yaroslavl, ul. Bogdanovicha 20. **YN)** GTRK "Yamal": 626600 Salekhard, ul. Lambinykh 3. **YV)** GTRK "Bira": 679016 Birobidzhan, ul. Oktyabrskaya 15. **ZB)** GTRK "Chita": 672090 Chita, ul. Kostyushko-Grigorovicha 27.

NB. Keys to region codes: see National Radio section (see also below)

Other Regional & Local Stations not shown.

DTT Transmitters (under construction)
Operator: RTRS ⌨ Moskva, ul. Ak. Korolyova 13 ☎ +7 495 6480111 🖷 +7 495 6480111 **E:** glavred@rtrn.ru **W:** www.rtrs.ru **Mux 1:** Rossiya 1, Rossiya 2, Rossiya 24, Rossiya K, Karusel, Pervyy kanal, NTV, 5-kanal, VGTRK Regional TV stns ⌘ R.Rossii, R. Mayak, Vesti FM. **Mux 2:** tbd

Re	Location	M1	M2	Re	Location	M1	M2
AD	Maykop	45	22	NN	N.Novgorod	28	53
AK	Barnaul	27	58	NO	V.Novgorod	30	56
AM	Blagoveshchensk	34	36	OB	Orenburg	22	31
AR	Arkhangelsk	33	44	OL	Oryol	26	44
BA	Ufa	31	43	OM	Omsk	31	49
BE	Belgorod	46	43	PM	Vladivostok	37	56
BR	Bryansk	39	23	PR	Perm	23	58
BU	Ulan-Ude	30	56	PS	Pskov	49	56
CB	Chelyabinsk	59	40	PZ	Penza	44	53
CC	Groznyy	57	59	RA	Gorno-Altaysk	24	32
CK	Anadyr	32	34	RK	Abakan	24	60
CV	Cheboksary	46	57	RO	Rostov-na-Donu	37	38
DA	Makhachkala	22	53	RS	Yakutsk	51	58
IN	Nazran	38	46	RT	Kyzyl	33	37
IR	Irkutsk	33	57	RY	Ryazan	43	27
IV	Ivanovo	59	57	SA	Samara	21	51
KA	Kaliningrad	47	41	SL	Yuzhnyy Sakhalinsk	21	51
KB	Nalchik	34	59	SM	Smolensk	39	46
KC	Cherkessk	58	59	SO	Vladikavkaz	35	50
KD	Krasnodar	60	56	SP	Sankt-Peterburg	35	45
KE	Kemerovo	23	56	SR	Saratov	56	40
KH	Khabarovsk	30	38	ST	Stavropol	57	32
KL	Kaluga	44	58	SV	Yekaterinburg	60	46
KM	Petropavlovsk-K.	22	26	TA	Tambov	46	56
KN	Krasnoyarsk	25	53	TL	Tula	60	56
KO	Syktyvkar	26	34	TO	Tomsk	21	44
KS	Kostroma	46	43	TS	Kazan	36	53
KT	Petrozavodsk	25	39	TV	Tver	47	58
KU	Kursk	24	53	TY	Tyumen	35	59
KV	Kirov	44	51	UD	Izhevsk	57	36
KX	Elista	46	39	UL	Ulyanovsk	56	59
KY	Khanty-Mansiysk	38	44	VG	Volgograd	44	60
LI	Lipetsk	30	40	VL	Vladimir	58	36
MA	Magadan	27	29	VN	Voronezh	52	43
MD	Saransk	43	46	VO	Vologda	34	35
ME	Yoshkar-Ola	34	56	YA	Yaroslavl	56	36
MO	Moskva	30	24	YN	Nakhodka	21	22
MU	Murmansk	23	34	YV	Birobidzhan	34	58
NE	Naryan-Mar	26	30	ZB	Chita	24	34

NB. Only txs in top-level administrative capitals shown.
Regional/Local licensees not shown.

RWANDA

Systems: # PAL-B/G [E] ⇩2015; DVB-T [E]

TÉLÉVISION RWANDAISE (TVR) (Gov)⌨ BP 83, Kigali ☎ +250 2577519 🖷 +250 2577520 **E:** telerwa@rwanda1.com **W:** www.orinfor.gov.rw **LP:** Dir: Rodgers Kayihura. **Txs:** (-). – **TELE 10 (Comm)** ⌨ BP 4307, Kigali ☎ +250 2512022 🖷 +250 2512024 **E:** info@tele10group.com **W:** www.tele10group.com **LP:** CEO: Eugene Nyagahene. **Txs:** (-).

DTT Transmitters (Trial)
Licensee: n/a **Mux:** TVR, CNN, TV5 **Tx:** Kigali ch(-). National network planned.

SABA (Netherlands)

NB: No terrestrial TV station.

SAMOA

System: PAL-B [E]

SBC TELEVISION (Gov) ⌨ P.O.Box 3691, Apia ☎ +685 626641 🖷 +685 624789 **E:** ceotvsamoa@samoa.ws **LP:** CEO: Faiesea Lei Sam Matafeo **Ch:** TV1 **Txs:** Mount Aflau ch4 (0.05kW), Api Park ch5 (0.005kW), Mount Fiamoe ch6 (0.01kW), Mount Vaea ch8 (0.05kW), Faleasiu ch10 (0.01kW), Apia ch11 (0.01kW). – **STAR (Comm)** ⌨ Apia. **LP:** SM: George Pitt. – **TV3 (Comm)** ⌨ Apia. **LP:** CEO: Atanoa Herbert Crichton. **Txs:** (-) – **VAIALA BEACH TELEVISION (VBTV) (Comm)** ⌨ Apia. **LP:** SM: Muaausa Shane Rivers **Txs:** ch31, ch35.

Foreign TV Relay
CCTV-9 (China): (-).

SAMOA (AMERICAN) (USA)

Systems: ATSC [A]; lp stns only: # NTSC-M [A]

KVZK-TV (Gov) ⌨ P.O.Box 3511, Pago Pago AS 96799, USA ☎ +1 684 6334191 🖷 +1 684 6331044 **E:** kvzk-tv@samoatelco.com **LP:** Dir: Paolo Sivia **Tx:** Pago Pago ch5. **Mux:** KVZK, KGMB/CBS, PBS, BBC World.
NB: Full power license (lp licenses not listed)

SAN MARINO

System: DVB-T (MPEG2) [E]

SAN MARINO RTV (Pub) ⌨ Viale J.F.Kennedy 13, San Marino A-3, SM-43031 ☎ +378 0549 882000 🖷 +378 0549 882850 **E:** amministrazione@sanmarinortv.sm **W:** www.smtvsanmarino.sm **LP:** DG: Carmen Lasorella **Tx:** San Marino ch51 (10kW).

SÃO TOMÉ & PRÍNCIPE

System: PAL-B [E]

TELEVISÃO SÃO-TOMENSE (TVS) (Pub) ⌨ CP 420, São Tomé ☎ +239 2221041 🖷 +239 2221942 **E:** tvs@cstome.net **LP:** DG: Óscar Medeiros **Txs:** São Tomé ch11 (10kW) & repeaters.

Foreign TV Relay
RTP África (Portugal): (-).

SAUDI ARABIA

Systems: DVB-T (MPEG2) [E]; † SECAM-B/G [E], PAL-B/G [E]

SAUDI ARABIAN TELEVISION (Gov) ⌨ P.O.Box 570, Riyadh 11421 ☎ +966 1 4014440 🖷 +966 1 4044192 **Chs:** Saudi TV 1, Saudi TV2, Al-Riyadih, Al-Ekhbariya.

DTT Transmitters (under construction)
Licensee: Ministry of Culture and Information **Mux:** Saudi TV1, Saudi TV2, Arriyadiya, Al-Ekhbariya (+3 prgrs) ⌘ General prgr, R.Qu'ran, Second prgr, European prgr **Txs:** ch30 (Jeddah) & netw.

SENEGAL

System: SECAM-K1 [VHF=K, UHF=E]

RADIODIFFUSION TÉLÉVISION SÉNÉGALAISE (Pub) ⌨ BP 1765, Dakar ☎ +221 338217801 🖷 +221 338223490 **E:** rts@rts.sn **W:** www.rts.sn **LP:** DG: Guila Thiam; Dir TV: Babacar Diagne **Chs:** RTS1, SN2 **Txs:** RTS1: (pol.H) Kédougou ch4 (10kW), Kolda ch4 (5kW), Linguère ch4 (5kW), Kaolack ch5 (10kW), Richard Toll ch6 (10kW), Bakel ch7 (5kW), Thiès ch7 (10kW), Ndioum ch8 (10kW), Tambacounda ch9 (10kW), Ziguinchor ch9 (10kW), Louga ch10 (10kW), Ourossogui ch10 (10kW), Dakar ch21 (3kW), Sedhiou ch62 (200kW), Dakar ch21 (3kW) & txs below 2kW. **SN2:** Dakar ch34. – **TÉLÉ FUTURS MÉDIAS (TFM) (Comm)** ⌨ BP 17795, Dakar ☎ +221 338491644 **LP:** DG: Mamoudou Ibra Kane **Tx:** Dakar ch42; network planned, pending national licence.

SERBIA

Systems: DVB-T2 (MPEG4) [E]; † PAL-B/G [E]

National Stations
RADIOTELEVIZIJA SRBIJE (RTS) (Pub) ⌨ Takovska 10, 11000 Beograd ☎ +381 11 3212000 🖷 +381 11 3212211 **E:** rtstv@rts.rs **W:** www.rts.rs **LP:** DG: Aleksandar Tijanic **Chs:** RTS1, RTS2, RTS Digital, RTS HD – **B92 (Comm)** ⌨ Bulevar AVNOJ-a 64, 11000 Beograd ☎ +381 11 3012000 🖷 +381 11 3012001 **E:** tvpitanja@b92.net **W:** www.b92.net **LP:** DG: Manja Grcic. – **HAPPY TV (Comm)** ⌨ Aleksandra Dubceka 14, 11080 Zemun ☎ +381 11 3778373 🖷 +381 11 3778053 **E:** office@happytv.rs **W:** www.happytv.rs **LP:** GD: Aleksandra Krstic. – **PINK TV (Comm)** ⌨ Neznanog junaka 1, 11000 Beograd ☎ +381 11 3063400 🖷 +381 11 3063500 **E:** marketing@rtvpink.com **W:** www.rtvpink.com **LP:** GD: Svetislav Milicevic. – **PRVA SRBSKA TELEVIZIJA (Comm)** ⌨ Autoput 22, 11080 Zemun ☎ +381 11 2091000 🖷 +381 11 2091001 **E:** produkcija@prva.rs **W:** www.prva.rs **LP:** GD: Dejan Jocic. – **TV AVALA (Comm)** ⌨ Bulevar Vojvode Mišica 39a, 11000 Beograd

☎ +381 11 3644100 🖷 +381 11 3644153 **E:** office@tv-avala.com **W:** www.tv-avala.com **LP:** GM: Bojana Lekic.

Local Stations not shown.

DTT Transmitters (under construction)
Operator: JP Emisiona Technika i Veze ⌨ Jovana Ristica 1, 11000 Beograd ☎ +381 11 3693251 🖷 +381 11 3693260 **E:** office@etv.rs **W:** www.etv.rs **Mux:** RTS1, RTS2, RTS Digital, RTS HD + others tbd ⌘ R.Beograd 1, 2, 202.

Location	Ch	kW	Location	Ch	kW
Avala	27	1	Ovcar	64	1

+ sites with txs below 1kW

Vojvodina

RADIOTELEVIZIJA VOJVODINE (RTV) (Pub) ⌨ Sutjecka 1, 21000 Novi Sad ☎ +381 21 422829 🖷 +381 21 420139 **E:** office@rtv.rs **W:** www.rtv.rs. **Chs:** RTV1, RTV2.

Local Stations not shown.

DTT Transmitters (under construction)
Operator: JP Emisiona Technika i Veze ⌨ Jovana Ristica 1, 11000 Beograd ☎ +381 11 3693251 🖷 +381 11 3693260 **E:** office@etv.rs **W:** www.etv.rs **Mux:** RTS1, RTS2, RTS Digital, RTS HD, RTV1, RTV2 + others tbd ⌘ R.Beograd 1, 2, 202.

Location	Ch	kW	Location	Ch	kW
Crveni Cot	31	3	Subotica	47	1

+ sites with txs below 1kW

SEYCHELLES

System: PAL-B [E]

SEYCHELLES BROADCASTING CORP. (SBC-TV) (Pub) ⌨ P.O.Box 321, Hermitage, Mahé ☎ +248 4289670 🖷 +248 4225641 **E:** sbcradtv@seychelles.sc **W:** www.sbc.sc **LP:** CEO: Antoine Onezime **Txs:** La Misère ch5 (1kW), St. Louis ch7 (6kW) & repeaters.

SIERRA LEONE

System: PAL-G [E]

SIERRA LEONE BROADCASTING CORP. (SLBC-TV) (Pub) ⌨ New England Ville, Freetown ☎ +232 22 240123 🖷 +232 22 240922 **E:** contactus@slbc.sl **W:** www.slbc.sl **LP:** DG: Elvis Gbanabom Hallowell **Txs:** Freetown ch24 & relay txs.

SINGAPORE

Systems: # PAL-B/G [E] ⇩2015/2020; DVB-T (MPEG4) [E]

MEDIACORP TV HOLDINGS PTE. LTD (Comm) ⌨ Caldecott Broadcast Centre, Andrew Rd. Singapore, 299939 ☎ +65 63333888 🖷 +65 62538119 **W:** www.mediacorp.sg **LP:** CEO: Shaun Seow. **Txs:** Channel 5 (English): Bukit Batok ch5 (120kW); Channel 8 (Chinese): Bukit Batok ch8 (120kW); Suria (Malay): ch12 (120kW); Vasantham: ch24; Channel U: ch28; okto: ch30; NewsAsia: ch32.

DTT Transmitters
Operator: Mediacorp **Mux 1:** Channel 5, Channel 8, Channel U, Suria, Vasantham, okto, NewsAsia **Txs:** ch29 (SFN). **Mux 2:** Channel 5 (HD5) **Txs:** ch38 (SFN).

SLOVAKIA

Systems: DVB-T (MPEG2) / DVB-T2 (MPEG4) [E]; local stns: † PAL-B/G [E]

National Stations
SLOVENSKÁ TELEVÍZIA (Pub) ⌨ Mlynská Dolina 28, 845 45 Bratislava ☎ +421 2 60611111 **W:** www.stv.sk **LP:** DG: Miloslava Zemkova **Chs:** STV1, STV2, reg prgrs. – **TV JOJ (Comm)** ⌨ P.O.Box 33, 830 07 Bratislava 37 ☎ +421 2 59888111 🖷 +421 2 59888112 **E:** joj@joj.sk **W:** www.joj.sk **LP:** CEO: Fratišek Borovský. **Chs:** TV JOJ, Plus. – **TV MARKIZA TV (Comm)** ⌨ Bratislavská 1/a, 843 56 Bratislava 48 ☎ +421 2 68274111 🖷 +421 2 65956824 **E:** sekretariatgr@markiza.sk **W:** www.markiza.sk **LP:** GD Zuzana Tapáková. **Chs:** Markíza TV, Doma.

Local Stations
Bardejovská TV: Radnicné nám. 16, 08501 Bardejov; ch24 (0.025kW). **Kysucké televízne vysielanie:** Podvysoká 370, 023 57 Podvysoká; Cadka ch55 (0.03kW). Rel. TV JOJ. **MTT Trnava:** Hlavná 1, 917 01 Trnava; ch53 (0.2kW). **MsTV Komárno:** P.O.Box 136, 945 01 Komárno; ch53 (0.2kW). **RTV Banská Bystrica:** Skuteckého 3, 974 00 Banská Bystrica; ch51 (0.5kW).**Štúrovská TV:** Petöfiho 9, 943 01 Štúrovo; ch34 (0.01kW). **Teleprior:** Slovenskej jednoty 8, 040 01 Košice; ch33 (0.2kW). **TV B52:** Stanicná 1329, 093 01 Vranov n. Topľou; ch49 (0.1kW). Rel. TV JOJ. **TV Liptov:** Štúrova 1989/41, 031 42 Liptovský Mikuláš; ch60 (0.1kW). **TV Naša:** Hutnóicka 1, 040 01 Košice; ch50 (1kW). **TV Myjava:** Parizánska 290/17, 907 01 Myjava; ch30 (0.01kW). **TV Nové Zámky:** Radnicná 3, 940 01 Nové Zámky; ch52 (0.2kW). **TV Pezinok:** Holubyho 42, 902 01 Pezinok; ch55 (0.1kW). **TV Poprad:** Podtatranská 1/149, 058 01 Poprad; ch52 (0.2kW). **TV Prievidza:** Hviezdoslavova 3, 971 01 Prievidza; ch46 (0.05kW). **TV Púchov:** Nám. slobody 1400, 020 01 Púchov; ch40 (0.05kW). **TV Reduta:** Radicné nám. 4, 052 01 Spišská Nová Ves; ch26 (0.25kW). **TV Sen:** Nám. oslobodenia 11, 905 01 Senica; Skalica ch32 (0.05kW), Senica ch48 (0.03kW). **TV Trencín:** Mierové nám. 22, 911 01 Trencín; Trencín ch60 (0.3kW), Púchov ch60 (0.04kW). **Zilinská TV:** Horný val 3, 010 01 Zilina; ch55 (0.2kW).

DTT Transmitters (MPEG2)
Operator: Towercom, a.s. ✉ Cesta na Kamzík 14, 831 01 Bratislava ☎ +421 2 49220111 🖳: +421 2 44461042 **E:** info@towercom.sk **W:** www.towercom.sk **Mux 1:** STV1, STV2, reg. prgrs ⌘ Slovensko, Regina, R. Devín, Radio_FM, Patria, Klasika, Litera, Junior, R. Slovakia International **Mux 2:** TV JOJ, Plus, TV Markíza TV, Doma.

Location	M1	M2	kW
Banská Bystrica	33	51	25
Banská Štiavnica	48	21	17/13
Bardejov	54	40	16
Bratislava	27	56	50
Košice (Dubník)	25	59	31/20
Košice (Heringeš)	25	59	16
Královský Chlmec	25	59	10
Lucenec	33	60	20/16
Námestovo	26	59	10/16
Nitra	48	21	40/44
Nové Mesto n.V.	57	-	50
Poprad	54	56	20
Roznava	54	27	14.3/10
Ruzomberok	26	59	20
Snina	25	59	20
Stará Ľubovna	24	55	35/25
Štúrovo	48	21	16/0.9
Trencin	57	52	50/40
Zilina	32	52	5/18

+ sites with txs below 10kW. Pol=V.
Local licensees not shown.

SLOVENIA

System: DVB-T (MPEG4) [E]

National Stations
TELEVIZIJA SLOVENIJA (TVS) (Pub) ✉ Kolodvorska 2-4, 1000 Ljubljana ☎ +38 61 1311333 🖳 +38 61 1319171 **E:** info@rtvslo.si **W:** www.rtvslo.si **L.P:** DG: Marko Filli **Chs:** TV SLO1, TV SLO2, TV SLO3, TV Koper/Capodistria, Tele M. – **PINK SI (Comm)** ✉ Ljubljana **E:** info@tvpink.si **W:** www.tvpink.si. – **POP TV (Comm)** ✉ Kranjceva 26, 1113 Ljubljana ☎ +386 1 5893200 🖳 +386 1 5893200 **E:** info@pop-tv.si **W:** www.pop-tv.si **L.P:** GD: Marjan Jurenec.

Local Stations not shown.

DTT Transmitters
Licensee: TVS **Mux:** TV SLO1, TV SLO2, TV SLO3, TV SLO [1]TV Kapodistria, [2]Tele M, Pop TV, Pink SI, Local stns

Location	ch*	kW	Location	ch*	kW
Beli Kriz	27[1]	5	Tinjan	27[1]	5
Golo Brdo	27[1]	5	Trstelj	27[1]	25
Nanos	27[1]	200	Krim	32	5
Pecarovci	27[2]	5	Krvavec	32	100
Plešivec	27[2]	25	Kuk	32[1]	5
Pohorje	27[2]	100	Kum	32	5
Skalnica	27[1]	5	Trdinov vrh	32	20
Slavnik	27[1]	5	Boc	66[2]	5

+ sites with txs below 5kW. *) Incl. reg. channels: [1] [2] see above
Local licensees not shown.

NB: No terrestrial TV station.

System: PAL-B/G [E]

National Stations
SOMALI NATIONAL TELEVISION (SNTV) (Gov) ✉ Mogadishu. **Txs:** (-). – **SHABELLE TV (Comm)** ✉ Mogadishu ☎ +252 5 933111 **E:** info@shabelle.net **W:** www.shabelle.net **Txs:** (-). – **SOMALI BROADCASTING CORP. (SBC) (Comm)** ✉ SBC Building, Airport Road, Bossaso ☎ +252 5 824600 **E:** sbc@allsbc.com **W:** www.allsbc.com **Txs:** (-).

Local Stations not shown.

Systems: # PAL-I [SA] ⇩2013; DVB-T (MPEG2) [SA], DVB-T2 (MPEG4) [SA] planned

SOUTH AFRICAN BROADCASTING CORP. (SABC) (Pub) ✉ Private Bag XI, Auckland Park 2006 ☎ +27 11 7149111 🖳 +27 11 7143106 **E:** info@sabc.co.za **W:** www.sabc.co.za **L.P:** Chmn: Ben Ngubane. **Chs:** SABC1, SABC2, SABC3, Bop TV. – **E.TV (Comm)** ✉ Block B, Longkloof Studios, Darters Road, Gardens, Cape Town 8001 ☎ +27 21 4814500 🖳 +27 21 4814510 **E:** info@e.tv **W:** www.etv. co.za **L.P:** CEO: Marcel Golding. – **M-NET (Comm)** ✆ ✉ P.O.Box 4950, Randburg 2125 ☎ +27 11 2893000 🖳 +27 11 7875763 **E:** inquiries@mnet.co.za **W:** mnet.dstv.com **L.P:** CEO: Patricia van Rooyen.

DTT Transmitters (DVB-T/MPEG2, under construction)
Licensee: Sentech **W:** www.sentech.co.za **Mux:** SABC1, SABC2, SABC3, e.tv **Txs:** ch65 (Johannesburg) & netw. – **Licensee:** Multichoice **W:** www.multichoice.co.za **Mux✪:** multiprgr (Orbicom/ M-Net) **Txs:** ch62V (Johannesburg, Kyalami, Helderkruin).
NB: Nationwide networks with 2 multiplexes under construction.

System: PAL-B/G [E]

SOUTH SUDAN TELEVISION (SSTV) (Gov) ✉ Juba **L.P:** Dir: Moyiga Korokoto Nduru **Txs:** (-)

System: DVB-T (MPEG2, MPEG4) [E]

National Stations
TELEVISION ESPAÑOLA (TVE) (Pub) ✉ Prado del Rey, 28223 Pozuelo de Alarcon (Madrid) ☎ +34 91 5817000 🖳 +34 91 5815476 **E:** direccion.comunicacion@rtve.es **W:** www.rtve.es **L.P:** Dir: Santiago Gonzalez. **Chs:** La 1, La 2, 24 horas, Clan, TDP – **ANTENA 3 (Comm)** ✉ Carretera San Sebastian de los Reyes, 28700 Madrid ☎ +34 1 6320500 🖳 +34 1 6327144 **W:** www.antena3.com **L.P:** Pres: Javier de Godó. **Chs:** Antena 3, Neox, Nitro – **CUATRO (Comm)** ✉ Avenida de los Artesanos 6, 28760 Madrid ☎ +34 91 7367000 **E:** internet@ cuatro.com **W:** www.cuatro.com – **LA SEXTA (Comm)** ✉ C/ Virgilio, 2 Edificio 4, 28223 Pozuelo de Alarcón ☎ +34 91 8382960 **E:** rr.hh@lasexta.com **W:** www.lasexta.com **L.P:** Pres: Emilio Aragón **Chs:** laSexta, laSexta 3, Xplora – **TELECINCO (Comm)** ✉ Ctra de Irún, Km 11,700, 28049 Madrid ☎ +34 902 155555 **E:** inversores@ telecinco.es **W:** www.telecinco.es **Chs:** Telecinco, Divinity, Energy.

Public Regional Stations
AN) Radio y Televisión de Andalucía (RTVA): Edificio Cana Sur, Avda. Josó Gálvez 1, 41092 Isla de la Cartuja (Sevilla) **W:** www.rtva.es. Chs: Canal Sur, Canal Sur 2, Andalusía TV. **AR)** Corporación Aragonesa de Radio y Televisión (CARTV): Avda. Maria Zambrano 2, 50018 Zaragoza. **W:** www.cartv.es. Chs: Aragón TV. **AS)** Radioelevisión del Principado de Asturias (RTPA): Edificio RTPA, Parque Científico y Tecnológico de Gijon, c/ Luis Blanco 82, 33203 Gijon. **W:** www.rtpa.es. Chs: TPA7, TPA8. **BA)** Ente Público de Radiotelevisión de las Islas Baleares (EPRTVIB): c/ Madalena, 21 Polígon Son Bugadelles, 07180 Santa Ponça **W:** www.ib3noticies.es. Ch: IB3 TV. **CA)** Corporació Catalana de Mitjans Audivisuals (CCMA): HQ: Via Augusta 252, 4a planta, 08817 Barcelona;

Televisió de Catalunya: Carrer de la TV3, s/n, 08970 Sant Joan Despi (Barcelona) **W**: www.ccma.cat. Chs: TV3, TV3 HD, 33, Canal Super3, 324, Canal 3XL, Esport 3. **CL)** Castilla y León Televisión: c/Monasterio San Millán de la Cogolla 30, 47015 Valladoid **W**: www.rtvcyl.es Chs: CyLTV, La 8. **CM)** Radio Televisión de Castilla-La Mancha (RTVCM): C/ Río Alberche, s/n Polígono Santa Mª de Benquerencia, 45007 Toledo **W**: www.rtvcm.es. Chs: CMT, CMT 2. **EU)** Euskal Irrati Telebista (EITB): Capuchinos de Basurto 2, 48013 Bilbao **W**: www.eitb.com. Chs: ETB1, ETB2, ETB3. **GA)** Compañía de Radio-Televisión de Galicia (CRTVG): Bando - San Marcos s/n, 15820 Santiago de Compostela **W**: www.crtvg.es. Chs: TVG, tvG2. **MA)** Ente Público Radio Televisión Madrid (EPRTVM): Paseo del Príncipe 3, 28223 Pozuelo de Alarcón (Madrid). **W**: www.telemadrid.es. Chs: Telemadrid, Telemadrid HD, LaOtra. **MU)** Radiotelevisión de la Región de Murcia (RTRM): Plaza de San Agustín 5, 30005 Murcia. **W**: www.rtrm.es Chs: 7RM, 7RM HD. **VA)** Ràdio Televisió Valenciana (RTVV): Polígon Accés Ademús s/n; 46100 Burjassot, València. **W**: www.rtvv.es. Chs: Canal Nou, Canal Nou Dos, Canal Nou 24. **NB.** Keys to region codes see National radio section.

Local Stations not shown.

DTT Transmitters (MPEG2 exc. *=MPEG4)
Operator: n/a **Mux 1:** La 1, La 2, 24 Horas, Clan ⌘ RNE R. Nacional, RNE R.5 Todo Noticias **Txs:** ch66 (SFN), ch57-65 (MFN). **Mux 3:** Cuatro, laSexta, laSexta 3, Divinity, l a Tienda en Casa, Gol Televisión◒ **Txs:** ch67 (SFN). **Mux 4:** Telecinco, La Siete, FDF, Disney Channel, Intereconomía ⌘ R. Interecononomía, esRadio, ABC Punto R. **Txs:** ch68 (SFN). **Mux 5:** Antena 3, Neox, Nova, Discovery Max, AXN◒ ⌘ R.Marca, Vaughan R. **Txs:** ch69 (SFN). **Mux 6*:** TVE HD, TDP ⌘ RNE R. Clásica HQ, RNE R.3 **Txs:** ch55 (Madrid) & netw. **Mux 7:** Xplora, laSexta 3, LaSexta HD, Quatro HD, Energy **Txs:** ch33 (Madrid) & netw. **Mux 8*:** Telecinco HD, Boing, Paramount Channel, MTV **Txs:** ch59 (Madrid) & netw. **Mux 9*:** Antena 3 HD, Nitro, Marca TV, 13TV ⌘ Cope, R. María, Onda Cero, Europa FM, Onda Melodía **Txs:** ch49 (Madrid) & netw. **Mux 10*:** TVE HD, TDP ⌘ RNE R. Clásica HQ, R.3 **Txs:** ch55 (Madrid) & netw. *) currently only available in selected areas.
Regional/Local muxes not shown.

SRI LANKA

Systems: # PAL-B/G [E] ⇩2018; DVB-T2 [E]

National Stations
SRI LANKA RUPAVAHINI CORP. (SLRC) (Pub) ✉ P.O. Box 2204, Colombo 7 ☎ +94 11 2697491 🖷 +94 11 2695488 **L.P:** CEO: Gamini Somachandra Rasaputhra **E:** dg@rupavahini.lk **W:** www.rupavahini.lk **Chs:** Rupavahini, Channel Eye/Nethra TV, NTV. **Txs: Rupavahini:** Pidurutalagala ch5 (20kW), Kokavil ch8 (20 kW) & relay txs; **Channel Eye/Nethra TV:** Pidurutalagala ch7 (20kW) & network; **NTV:** Colombo ch52. – **INDEPENDENT TELEVISION NETWORK (ITN) (Comm)** ✉ Wickramasinghepura, Battaramulla ☎ +94 11 2774424 🖷 +94 11 2774591 **E:** itnadm@slt.lk **W:** www.itn.lk **L.P:** Chmn: Rosmund Senaratne **Chs:** Prime TV (English)/ Vasantham TV (Tamil) **Txs:** Deniyaya ch9 (20kW), Colombo ch12 (100kW), Yatiyantota ch12 (100kW), Nayabedde ch12 (3kW). – **MTV CHANNEL (PVT) LTD. (Comm)** ✉ 7, Braybrook Pl., Colombo 2 ☎ +94 11 4792600 🖷 +94 11 2447308 **E:** info@media.maharaja.lk **L.P:** CEO: Gayirika Perusignhe. **Chs:** MTV (English), Shakhti TV (Tamil), Sirasa TV (Singalese). **Txs: Channel One/Shakhti:** Colombo ch25 (5kW) & net-work; **Sirasa:** Colombo ch23 (5kW) & network. – **SWARNAVAHINI (EAP NETWORKS (PVT) LTD.) (Comm)** ✉ 676 Galle Rd, Colombo 3 ☎ +94 11 2599642 🖷 +94 11 2503788 **E:** admin@swarnavahini.lk **W:** www.swarnavahini.lk **L.P:** Chmn: Soma Edirisinghe. **Txs:** Colombo ch34 (5kW) & network. – **TELSHAN NETWORK (PVT) LTD. (TNL) (Comm)** ✉ Innagale Estate Dampe-Piliyandala ☎ +94 11 2501681 🖷 +94 11 2575436 **E:** tnltvtr@slt.lk **W:** www.tnltvisira.com **L.P:** Chmn/MD: Shantilal Nilkant Wickremesinghe **Txs:** Piliyandala ch3 (20kW), Polgahawela ch3 (1kW), Nuweraeliya ch4 (40kW), Colombo ch21 (22kW), Hantana (Kandy) ch21 (22kW), Piliyandala ch26 (22kW), Ratnapura ch26 (1kW). – **TV LANKA (Comm)** ✉ 68 Attidiya Road, Ratmalana ☎ +94 11 4213771 🖷 +94 11 4213980 **Txs:** Colombo ch48, Badulla & Kandy & Vauniya ch53.

Local Stations
Art TV: 451 Kandy Road, Kelaniya; Colombo ch28, Kandy ch52. **Derana TV:** 1072/1 5th Lane, Kotte Road, Rajagiriya; Matale ch28, Matara ch31, Badulla ch32, Nuwara Eliya ch36, Colombo ch37, Kalutara ch56. **Extra Terrestrial Vision:** 31 Shady Grove Avenue, Colombo 08; Colombo ch35, Kalutara ch40. **Max TV:** 221 Stanley Thilakaratne Mawatha, Nugedoga; Colombo ch30, Ratnapura ch32, Karagahatenna ch46, Nayabedda ch47, Hunnasgiriya & Kandy ch56.

TV2: Media House, 594/1 Galle Road, Colombo 03; Karagahatenna ch42, Colombo ch53. **Voice of Asia Networks:** Manila. Chs: Siyatha TV (Sinhala), Vettri TV (Tamil); Siyatha TV: Gongala ch28, Gammaduwa ch31, Colombo ch32, Kandy ch35; Vettri TV: Colombo ch46.

DTT Transmitters (Trial)
Licensee: Dialog Telekom PLC ✉ 475, Union Place, Colombo 02 ☎ +94 11 2678700 **W:** www.dialog.lk **Mux:** Rupavahini, ITN, Channel C, CSN, Citi Hitz, Kalaignar TV, The Buddhist **Txs:** ch50 (Colombo).

ST BARTHÉLEMY (France)

System: DVB-T (MPEG4) [E]

CARRIB'IN TV (Comm) ✉ BP 658 Gustavia Cedex, F-97099 Saint-Barthélemy ☎ +590 590874362 🖷 +590 590510787.

DTT Transmitters
Operator: TDF **Mux:** Guadeloupe 1ère, France 2-5, France Ô, France 24, Arte, Caribb'In TV **Txs:** SFN

ST EUSTATIUS (Netherlands)

NB: No terrestrial TV station.

ST HELENA (UK)

System: PAL-I [E]

NB: Cable & Wireless St. Helena is distributing satellite TV prgrs in St. Helena on three UHF channels: Channel A (Supersport), Channel B (MNET), Channel C (BBC World/Discovery Channel).

ST KITTS & NEVIS

System: NTSC-M [A]

ZIZ TELEVISION (Gov) ✉ P.O.Box 331, Basseterre, St. Kitts ☎ +1 869 4652621 🖷 +1 869 4652159 **E:** info@zizonline.com **W:** www.zizonline.com **L.P:** GM: Viere Galloway **Txs:** (pol.H) Basseterre ch2 (0.2kW), Bayfords (St. Kitts) ch5 (20kW), Brimstone ch9 (0.15kW), Ottleys Mount ch11 (0.04kW), Nevis ch13 (0.01kW).

ST LUCIA

System: NTSC-M [A]

NATIONAL TELEVISION NETWORK (NTN) (Gov) ✉ Greaham Louisy Administrative Building, The Waterfront, Castries, Saint Lucia ☎ +1 758 4682116 🖷 +1 758 4531614 **E:** ntn@candw.lc **Txs:** Castries ch2. – **HELEN TELEVISION (HTS) (Comm)** ✉ P.O. Box 621, The Morne, Castries ☎ +1 758 4524982 🖷 +1 758 4531737 **E:** news@htsstlucia.org **W:** www.htsstlucia.org **L.P:** MD: Linford Fevrier; CE: Stephenson Anius. **Txs:** Castries ch4 (20kW H) & ch5 (20kW H).

ST MAARTEN (Netherlands)

System: NTSC-M [A]

LEEWARD BROADCASTING CORP. (LBC) ✉ P.O.Box 375, Philipsburg. **Tx:** ch7 (5kW).

ST MARTIN (France)

System: DVB-T (MPEG4) [E]

DTT Transmitters
Operator: TDF **Mux:** Guadeloupe 1ère, France 2-5, France Ô, France 24, Arte, Caribb'In TV **Txs:** SFN.

ST PIERRE & MIQUELON (France)

System: DVB-T (MPEG4) [E]

SAINT-PIERRE ET MIQUELON 1ÈRE (Pub) ✉ BP 4227, F-97500 Saint-Pierre et Miquelon ☎ +508 508411111 🖷 +508 508412219 **W:** saintpierremiquelon.la1ere.fr **L.P:** Dir: Joseph Eden.

DTT Transmitters
Operator: TDF **Mux:** Saint-Pierre et Miquelon 1ère, France 2-,5, France Ô, France 24, Arte **Txs:** SFN.

ST VINCENT & THE GRENADINES

System: NTSC-M [A]

SVG-TV (Gov) P.O.Box 705, Kingstown, St. Vincent ☎ +1 784 457111 +1 784 4562759 **E:** svgbc@vincysurf.com **W:** www.svgbc.com **LP:** MD: R. Paul MacLeish. **Txs:** (pol.H) Dorsetshirehill ch9 (0.4kW), Layouhill ch7 (0.04kW), Maroonhill ch7 (0.04kW), Belleislehill ch11 (0.06kW), Mustique ch11 (0.06kW), Bequia ch13 (0.06kW).

Foreign TV Relay
TBN (USA): Kingstown ch4.

SUDAN

System: PAL-B/G [E]

SUDAN TELEVISION (Gov) P.O.Box 1094, Omdurman ☎ +249 183557398 +249 183553538 **E:** sudantvlive@sudanmail.net **W:** www.sudantv.net **LP:** DG: Mohammed Hatem Suleiman **Txs:** Omdurman ch5 (5kW H), Gezira ch7 (10kW) & relay txs.

SURINAME

System: NTSC-M [A]

National Stations
SURINAAMSE TELEVISIE STICHTING (STVS) (Gov) P.O.Box 535, Paramaribo ☎ +597 473032 +597 477216 **E:** info@stvs.sr **W:** www.stvs.sr **Txs:** Wageningen ch7 (0.10kW), Paramaribo ch8 (1kW), Moango ch9 (0.01kW), Caranis ch10 (0.10kW), Nickerie ch11 (1kW). – **ALGEMENE TELEVISIE VERZORGING (ATV) (Comm)** P.O.Box 1839, Paramaribo ☎ +597 404661 +597 402660 **E:** info@atv.sr **W:** www.atv.sr **Txs:** Borokopondo ch2 (1kW), Wageningen ch6 (0.25kW), Moengo ch7, Paramaribo ch12 (0.4kW), Nickerie ch13 (0.5kW).

Local Stations (all Comm)
Ampies Broadcasting Corp: P.O.Box 885, Paramaribo; ch4 (1kW). **Garuda TV:** Goudstraat 20, Paramaribo; ch23. **Radika TV:** P.O.Box 1083, Paramaribo; ch14 (1kW). **Rapar Broadcasting Network:** P.O.Box 975, Paramaribo. Tx: ch5 (2kW). **Rasonic:** Bataviastraat 2, Nickerie; ch7 (1kW). **TV Apinti:** P.O.Box 595, Paramaribo; ch10 (1kW). **TV Sookha:** Bataviaistraat 25, Nickerie; tx: (-).

SWAZILAND

System: PAL-B/G [E]

SWAZI TV (Gov) Private Bag A146, Mbabane ☎ +268 24043036 +268 24042093 **E:** info@swazitv.co.sz **W:** www.swazitv.co.sz **LP:** CEO: Austin B. Dlamini **Chs:** 2 national networks **Txs:** (pol. H exc. where stated) **Prgr 1:** Bulembu ch5 (1.5kW), Ntondozi ch25 (15kW), Mbabane ch27V (1kW) & relay txs. **Prgr 2:** Unknown loc. ch4, unknown loc. ch9, Ntondozi ch21 (50kW).

SWEDEN

System: DVB-T (MPEG2, MPEG4), DVB-T2 (MPEG4) [E]

National Stations
SVERIGES TELEVISION AB (SVT) (Pub) Oxenstiernsgatan 26-34, 105 10 Stockholm ☎ +46 8 7840000 +46 8 7841500 **E:** info@svt.se **W:** www.svt.se **LP:** CEO: Eva Hamilton. **Chs:** SVT1, SVT2, SVT24, regional stns. – **CANAL DIGITAL (Comm)** Tegeluddsvägen 7, 115 80 Stockholm ☎ +46 8 7722700 +46 8 7722555 **E:** kundservice@canaldigital.se **W:** www.canaldigital.se. – **TV4 AB (Comm)** Tegeluddsvägen 3-5, 115 79 Stockholm ☎ +46 8 4594000 +46 8 4594444 **E:** info@tv4.se **W:** www.tv4.se **LP:** CEO: Jan Scherman – **VIASAT AB (Comm)** P.O.Box 17115, 104 62 Stockholm ☎ +46 8 56241060 +46 8 56202330 **E:** info@viasat.se **W:** www.viasat.se.

Local Stations not shown.

DTT Transmitters (MPEG2 exc. where stated)
Licensee: Boxer TV Access AB Esplanaden 3c, 3 tr, 172 67

Sundbyberg ☎ +46 8 58789900 +46 8 58789999 **E:** kundtjanst@boxer.se **W:** www.boxer.se **Mux 1:** SVT1 (incl. reg. prgrs), SVT2 (incl. reg. prgrs), Kunskapskanalen, SVTB/SVT24 **Mux 2 (✪exc.*):** TV4 (incl. reg. prgrs)*, TV4 Fakta, TV4 Film, Sjuan, TV6, TV11, CNN International. **Mux 3✪:** TV3 (incl. reg. prgrs), Kanal 5 (incl. reg. prgrs), TV8, Disney Channel/VH1, C More First, C More Hits, SF-kanalen/C More Sport 1. **Mux 4✪:** Eurosport, Discovery Channel, Nickelodeon/Comedy Central, Kanal 9, MTV, TLC, TV10, Eurosport 2 (MPEG4), Star! (MPEG4) **Mux 5 (MPEG4) (✪exc.*):** Axess TV, Canal Global, Silver, TNT, TV4 Sport, Local stns*, TV Finland* (Stockholm region only), BBC World News, Silver, Animal Planet, Cartoon Network/TCM, Disney XD/Showtime, C More Series. **Mux 6 (DVB-T2/MPEG4) (✪exc.*):** SVT1 HD*, SVT2 HD*, TV3 HD, TV4 HD, Kanal 5 HD **Mux 7 (DVB-T2/MPEG4)✪** C More HD, MTV Live HD, National Geographic HD.

Location	M1	M2	M3	M4	M5	M6	M7[1]	kW[1]
Arvidsjaur (Julträsk)	21	24	30	34	42	57	51	50
Bollnäs	29	49	34	39	23	53	6	50
Borlänge (Idkerberget)	47	52	43	41	54	60	28	50
Borås (Dalsjöfors)	44	54	29	42	55	36	41	50
Bäckefors	26	22	35	25	56	49	7	50
Emmaboda (Bälshult)	31	28	46	21	53	47	8	50
Filipstad (Klockarhöjden)	33	23	30	42	40	27	59	50
Finnveden	26	56	52	60	48	58	7	50
Gällivare	33	26	40	28	46	43	22	50
Gävle (Skogmur)	27	24	32	30	46	50	9	50
Göteborg (Brudaremossen)	30	27	46	40	59	33	9	50
Halmstad (Oskarström)	21	28	38	45	47	32	7	10
Helsingborg (Olympia)	33	43	41	25	30	30	10	10
Hudiksvall (Forsa)	31	44	34	39	23	53	60	50
Hörby (Sallerup)	33	43	41	25	61	30	10	50
Jönköping (Bondberget)	31	28	35	33	51	26	6	50
Kalix	35	29	60	55	50	58	27	50
Karlshamn	27	24	42	55	56	30	8	50
Karlskrona (Vämö)	27	24	42	55	26	30	8	50
Karlstad (Sörmon)	43	46	30	42	40	27	59	50
Kiruna (Kirunavaara)	39	35	32	49	42	29	44	50
Kisa	29	55	50	56	59	49	6	50
Lycksele (Knaften)	45	53	22	28	48	58	38	50
Malmö (Jägersro)	33	43	41	25	27	27	10	50
Mora (Eldris)	22	25	35	42	44	51	38	50
Motala (Ervasteby)	27	40	21	42	52	39	53	50
Norrköping (Krokek)	36	46	60	28	54	32	5	50
Nässjö	22	23	35	33	51	25	6	50
Pajala	34	23	31	37	54	47	51	50
Skellefteå	23	26	49	43	59	46	6	50
Skövde	37	24	32	34	57	69	47	50
Sollefteå (Multrå)	46	24	31	26	44	49	59	50
Stockholm (Nacka)	23	42	56	50	55	59	53	50
Storuman	33	43	36	46	56	60	49	50
Sundsvall (S Stadsberget)	47	27	30	43	56	50	58	50
Sunne (Blåbärskullen)	36	39	50	53	47	60	7	50
Sveg (Brickan)	21	24	46	41	36	59	9	50
Trollhättan	23	43	31	25	56	53	9	50
Tåsjö	37	40	51	41	50	57	30	50
Uddevalla (Herrestad)	23	43	31	25	56	53	9	50
Uppsala (Vedyxa)	40	21	43	49	33	58	52	50
Varberg (Grimeton)	21	28	38	45	47	32	7	10
Visby (Follingbo)	41	44	48	37	58	51	9	50
Vislanda (Nydala)	40	49	34	37	39	57	8	50
Vännäs (Granlundsberget)	47	50	56	36	52	60	8	50
Västervik (Fårhult)	26	34	24	30	40	43	57	50
Västerås (Lillhärad)	37	31	22	34	38	51	57	50
Västerås (Lillhärad)	44	-	-	-	-	-	-	-
Ange (Snöberg)	42	37	57	28	55	52	22	50
Älvsbyn	36	39	47	32	38	52	56	50
Örebro (Lockhyttan)	35	29	49	55	49	58	6	50
Örnsköldsvik (Ås)	23	21	34	23	39	29	60	50
Östersund (Brattåsen)	27	45	58	53	54	46	48	50
Östhammar (Valö)	40	21	43	26	48	58	6	50
Överkalix	45	48	60	55	50	58	27	50

+ sites with txs below 10kW. [1] Power refers to UHF chs

SWITZERLAND

System: DVB-T (MPEG2) [E]

SCHWEIZERISCHE RUNDFUNK- UND FERNSEHGESELLSCHAFT (SRG SSR) (Pub) Giacomettistrasse 3, 3000 Bern 15 ☎ +41 31 3509111 +41 31 3509256 **E:** info@srg-ssr.ch **W:** www.srg-ssr.ch **LP:** DG: Roger de Weck.
NB: SRG SSR is the holding institution for the regional radio & TV enterprises SRF, RTS, RSI and RTR.
Schweizer Radio und Fernsehen (SRF): Fernsehstrasse 1-4, 8052 Zürich ☎ +41 44 3056611 +41 44 3055001 **E:** srf@srf.ch **W:** www.

srf.ch; www.sf.tv **L.P:** Dir: Ruedi Matter **Chs (in German):** SF1, SF ZWEI, SF Info. **Radio Télévision Suisse (RTS):** 20 Quai Ernest Ansermet, 1205 Genève ☎ +41 22 7082020 🖹 +41 22 7089800 **E:** info@rts.ch **W:** www.rts.ch **L.P:** DG: Gilles Marchand **Chs (in French):** RTS Un, RTS Deux. **Radiotelevisione svizzera (RSI):** Casella postale, 6949 Comano ☎ +41 91 8035111 🖹 +41 91 803 9314 **E:** info@rsi.ch **W:** www.rsi.ch **L.P:** Dir: Dino Balestra **Chs (in Italian):** LA 1, LA 2. **Radiotelevisiun Svizra Rumantscha (RTR):** Via da Masans 2, 7002 Cuira ☎ +41 81 2557575 🖹 +41 81 2557500 **E:** info@rtr.ch **W:** www.rtr.ch **L.P:** Dir: Mariano Tschuor **Prgrs (in Rumansh):** via SF1.

DTT Transmitters
Licensee: SRG-SSR **Mux 1:** SF1, SF ZWEI, SF Info, RTS Un, LA 1 **Mux 2:** RTS Un, RTS Deux, SF1, LA 1 **Mux 3:** LA 1, LA 2, SF1, RTS Un.

Location	M1	M2	M3	kW	Location	M1	M2	M3	kW
Bantiger	48V	51V	-	10	M.Ceneri	-	-	49	34
Brüelberg	34V	-	-	10	Mt.Pelerin	-	-	47V	16
Buclards	-	-	34V	10	Pizzo Matro	-	29	-	14
Champ Lequet	-	56V	-	14	Rigi Kulm	32V	-	-	16
Chasseral	62V	56V	-	10	Säntis	34	-	-	42
Gebidem	45V	-	-	10	Tremblex	-	-	56V	10
Gibloux	-	56V	-	11	Tüllingen*	31V	-	-	20
Hoher Kasten	34V	-	-	21	Uetliberg	32	-	-	45

+ sites with txs below 10kW. *) 1x located in Germany
Other licensees: Local/regional licensees not shown.

SYRIA

System: # PAL-B/G [E]

SYRIAN TELEVISION (Gov) 🖃 pl. Ommayad, Damas ☎ +963 11 2720700 🖹 +963 11 2234930 **L.P:** Dir TV: Diana Jabbour **E:** contact@rtv.gov.sy **W:** www.rtv.gov.sy **Txs:** (pol H) **Prgr 1:** Abou-Kmal ch3 (200kW), Nabi-Saleh ch3 (100kW), Hassakeh ch4 (200kW), Aleppo ch4 (200kW), Damas ch4 (100kW), Deir-Al Zoor ch6 (100kW), Saroukhieh ch6 (10kW), Soueida ch7 (350kW), Al Soweida ch7 (200kW), Homs ch7 (200kW), Aein-Al-Arab ch7 (100kW), Tabqua ch8 (100kW), Kaldoun ch8 (10kW), Slenfeh ch9 (200kW), Salhieh ch11 (30kW), Afrien ch11 (10kW), Palmyra ch11 (10kW) & txs below 10kW; **Prgr 2:** Al-Malkeih ch12 (200kW), Lattakia ch26 (60kW) & txs below 10kW.

TAIWAN

System: DVB-T [A] (MPEG2, MPEG4)

CHINESE TELEVISION SYSTEM (CTS) (Pub) 🖃 100, Kuang Fu South Rd, Taipei 106 ☎ +886 2 27510321 🖹 +886 2 27775414 **E:** wwwpub@mail.cts.com.tw **W:** www.cts.com.tw **L.P:** Chair: Yaly Chao. **Chs:** CTS, CTS Education, CTS Recreation. – **PUBLIC TELEVISION SERVICE (PTS) (Pub)** 🖃 50, Lane 75, Kang-Ning Rd., Section 3, Taipei 114 ☎ +886 2 26339122 🖹 +886 2 26338124 **E:** pub@mail.pts.org.tw **W:** www.pts.org.tw **L.P:** Chair: Yaly Chao **Chs:** PTS, Dimo TV, Hakka TV, Hi-HD. – **CHINA TELEVISION CO., LTD (CTV) (Comm)** 🖃 120, Chung-Yang Rd, Taipei 115 ☎ +886 2 27838308 🖹 +886 2 2782 6007 **E:** pubr@mail.chinatv.com.tw **W:** www.ctv.com.tw **L.P:** Chmn: Shengfen Lin. **Chs:** CTV, CTV News, CTV MyLife. – **FORMOSA TELEVISION, INC (FTV) (Comm)** 🖃 24/F, 30, Pa Te Road, Section 3, Tapei 105 ☎ +886 2 25702570 🖹 +886 2 25796633 **E:** service@ftv.com.tw **W:** www.ftv.com.tw **Chs:** FTV, Follow Me TV, FTV News, FTV HD. – **TAIWAN TELEVISION ENTERPRISE CO., LTD (TTV) (Comm)** 🖃 10, Pa Te Rd, Section 3, Taipei 10560 ☎ +886 2 25781515 🖹 +886 2 25799625 **E:** ref@email.ttv.com.tw **W:** www.ttv.com.tw **L.P:** GM: Zhou Faxun. **Chs:** TTV, TTV Family, TTV Finance.

DTT Transmitters (MPEG2 exc. *=MPEG4)
Licensee: PTS **Mux 1:** PTS, Dimo TV, Hakka TV **Mux 2*:** Hi-HD. – **Licensee:** CTV **Mux:** CTV, CTV News, CTV MyLife. – **Licensee:** CTS **Mux:** CTS, CTS Education, CTS Recreation. – **Licensee:** FTV **Mux:** FTV, Follow Me TV, FTV News, FTV HD*. – **Licensee:** TTV **Mux:** TTV, TTV Financial, TTV Family/TTV Finance.

Location	PTS M1	PTS M2	CTS	CTV	FTV	TTV
SFN	26	30	34	24	28	31

TAJIKISTAN

Systems: SECAM-D/K [R], PAL-D/K [R]; DVB-T planned

National Stations
TAJIK TELEVISION (TVT) (Gov) 🖃 Bekhzod St. 7a, 734013

Dushanbe ☎ +992 37 2224357 🖹 +992 37 2213459 **E:** administrator@tvt.tj **W:** www.tvt.tj. **Ch:** Shabakai 1 **Txs:** (-). – **TV SAFINA (Gov)** 🖃 Bukhoro St. 43, 734025 Dushanbe ☎ +992 37 2278029 🖹 +992 37 2277905 **E:** tv_safina@mail.tj **W:** www.safina.tj. **Txs:** (-).

Local Stations, Foreign TV Relays not shown.

TANZANIA

System: PAL-B/G [E]

National Stations
TANZANIA BROADCASTING CORP. (TBC) (Gov) 🖃 P.O.Box 31519, Dar es Salaam ☎ +255 22 2700062 🖹 +255 22 2121315 **E:** tvt-dg@africaonline.co.tz **W:** www.tbc.go.tz **L.P:** DG: Clement Mshana **Ch:** TBC 1 **Txs:** Dar es Salaam ch5 & relay txs. – **CHANNEL 10 TV (Comm)** 🖃 P.O.Box 21122, Dar es Salaam. **Txs:** Dar es Salaam ch10 & relay txs. – **INDEPENDENT TV (ITV) (Comm)** 🖃 P.O.Box 4374, Dar es Salaam ☎ +255 22 2775914 🖹 +255 22 2775915 **E:** info@itv.co.tz **W:** www.itv.co.tz **Txs:** (-) – **STAR TV (Comm)** 🖃 P.O.Box 1732, Mwanza ☎ +255 28 2503262 🖹 +255 28 2500713 **E:** marketing@startvtz.com **W:** www.startvtz.com **Txs:** Lake Victoria zone ch31, Arusha ch34, Dar es Salaam ch42.

Local Stations not shown.

THAILAND

Systems: # PAL-B/G [E] ⇩2015; DVB-T (MPEG2), DVB-T2 (MPEG4) [E]

MASS COMMUNICATIONS ORGANISATION OF THAILAND (MCOT) (MODERNINE TV) (Gov) 🖃 63/1 Rama IX Road, Huay Khwang, Bangkok 10320 ☎ +66 2 2201G000 🖹 +66 2 22451960 **E:** tnanews@mcot.or.th **W:** www.mcot.net **Txs:** Bangkok ch9 (200kW) & network. – **ROYAL ARMY TELEVISION (TV5) (Gov)** 🖃 210 Phaholyothin Rd, Sanam Pao, Bangkok 10400 ☎ +66 2 22710060 🖹 +66 2 22712515 **E:** army@tv5.co.th **W:** www.tv5.co.th **L.P:** DG: Maj. Gen. Vijit Junapart. **Txs:** Bangkok ch5 (20kW) & network. – **TELEVISION OF THAILAND (TVT) (Gov)** 🖃 90-91 New Phetchaburi Road, Huay Khwang, Bangkok 10320 ☎ +66 2 3182110 🖹 +66 2 3182991 **E:** tv11@prd.go.th **W:** tv11.prd.go.th **Txs:** Bangkok ch11 (200kW) & relays. – **THAI PUBLIC BROADCASTING SERVICE (TTPBS) (Pub)** 🖃 1010 Shinawatra Tower III, 13 Vibhavadi Rangsit Road, Chatchuchak, Bangkok 10900 ☎ +66 2 27911000 🖹 +66 2 27911010 **E:** webmaster@thaipbs.or.th **W:** www.thaipbs.or.th **Txs:** Bangkok ch29 (1000kW) & network. – **BANGKOK BROADCASTING & TELEVISION (BBTV) (Comm)** 🖃 P.O.Box 4-56, Bangkok 10900 ☎ +66 2 2720010 🖹 +66 2 27202106 **E:** marketing@ch7.com **W:** www.ch7.com. **L.P:** SM: Chatchur Karnasuta **Txs:** Bangkok ch7 (20kW) & network. – **BANGKOK ENTERTAINMENT CO. Ltd. (THAI COLOR CHANNEL 3) (Comm)** 🖃 Floors 7, 15, 16, The Emporium Tower, Sukhumvit Road, Khlong Tan, Khlong Toey, Bangkok 10110 ☎ +66 2 22623333 🖹 +66 2 22041384 **E:** internet@tv3.co.th **W:** www.thaitv3.com **L.P:** PD: Pravit Maleenont. **Txs:** Bangkok ch32 (650kW) & network.

DTT Transmitters (Trial)
Licensee: TVT **Mux 1:** multiprgr **Txs:** ch56 (Bangkok SFN) **Mux 2 (DVB-T2/MPEG4):** multiprgr **Txs:** ch43 (Bangkok SFN).

TIMOR-LESTE

System: PAL-B [E]

RÁDIO E TELEVISÃO DE TIMOR-LESTE (RTTL) (Gov) 🖃 Rua de Kaikoli 2, Díli ☎+670 3321825 **L.P:** Pres: Expedito Dias Ximenes **Txs:** Díli ch7 (1.5 kW), Baucau ch12.

TOGO

System: SECAM-K1 [VHF=K, UHF=E]; DVB-T2 planned

National Stations
TÉLÉVISION TOGOLAISE (Gov) 🖃 BP 3286, Lomé ☎ +228 22215357 🖹 +228 22215786 **E:** televisiontogolaise@yahoo.fr **W:** www.tvt.tg **L.P:** Dir: Kuessan Yovodévi **Txs:** Mt. Agou ch6 (10kW H), Lomé ch8V (10kW), Aledjo-Kadara ch8 (10kW H) & relay txs. – **RTV DELTA SANTÉ (RTDS) (Comm)** 🖃 BP 202, Aneho, Lomé ☎ +228 3310573 🖹 +228 2221477 **E:** tvdeltasante@wanadoo.fr. **Txs:** (-).

Local Stations
TV2: Hotel du 2 février, Lomé; tx: (-) **TV7:** BP 81104, Lomé; tx: (-).

TOKELAU (New Zealand)

NB: No terrestrial TV station.

TONGA

Systems: DVB-T (MPEG4) [NZ]; # PAL-B [NZ] ⇩2014

TONGA BROADCASTING COMMISSION (Gov) ✉ P.O.Box 36, Nuku'alofa ☎ +676 23555 🖷 +676 24417 **E:** tbc_news@tonga-broadcasting.net **W:** www.tonga-broadcasting.net **L.P:** GM: 'Elenora 'Amanaki **Chs:** TV Tonga, TV Tonga 2 (incl. relay CCTV9) **Txs: TV Tonga:** Nuku'alofa ch6 (0.5kW), **TV Tonga 2:** Nuku'alofa ch8 (0.5kW). – **DOULOS BROADCASTING NETWORK (Rlg)** ✉ P.O.Box 91, Nuku'alofa ☎ +676 23314 🖷 +676 23658 **E:** a3mtonga@kalianet.to **Tx:** Nuku'alofa ch33 (1kW).

DTT Transmitters
Operator: DigiTV (Tonga) Ltd. ✉ P.O.Box 875, Nuku'alofa **E:** custom-ercare.tonga@digicelgroup.com **W:** www.digiceltonga.com **Mux✪:** multiprgr **Tx:** ch45V (Nuku'alofa 1kW).

TRINIDAD & TOBAGO

Systems: NTSC-M [A]; DVB-T (MPEG4) [A]

NCC-TV (Gov) ✉ 11A Maraval Rd., P.O. Box 665, Port-of-Spain, Trinidad ☎ +1 868 62241414 🖷 +1 868 6220344 **E:** nbnl@nbn.co.tt **W:** www.ncctt.org **Txs:** ch4, ch16. – **ADVANCED COMMUNITY TV STATION (ACTS)** ✉ 538, Circular Road, San Fernando, Trinidad ☎ +1 868 6524855 **E:** info@acts25tt.com **W:** www.acts25tt.com **L.P:** CEO/Pres: Nelson Sammy-Guilarte **Tx:** ch25. – **CCN TV6 (Comm)** ✉ 35 Independence Sq, Port-of-Spain, Trinidad ☎ +1 868 6278806 🖷 +1 868 6271451 **W:** www.tv6tnt.com **L.P:** CEO: Craig Reynald **Txs:** ch6 & ch18 (Trinidad), ch19 (Tobago). – **C TELEVISION (CNMG) (Comm)** ✉ 11A Maraval Road, Port-of-Spain, Trinidad **W:** www.ctntworld.com **L.P:** CEO: Dominic Beaubrun **Txs:** ch9, ch13. – **GAYELLE TV (Comm)** ✉ 161 Western Main Road, St. James, Port-of-Spain, Trinidad ☎ +1 868 6227954 🖷 +1 868 6224601 **W:** www.gayelletv.com **L.P:** CEO: Christopher Laird **Tx:** ch23. – **WIN TV (Comm)** ✉ Mulchan Seuchan & Endeavors Road, Lange Park, Chaguanas, Trinidad ☎ +1 809 6716937 🖷 +1 809 6721059 **E:** feedback@wintvworld.com **W:** www.wintvworld.com **L.P:** Chmn: Mohan Jaikaran **Tx:** ch37, ch39.

DTT Transmitters (under construction)
Licensee: Green Dot Ltd ✉ 61 Mucurapo Road, St James, Trinidad ☎ +868 6284388 🖷 +868 6285197 **E:** info@gd.tt **W:** www.gd.tt **Mux 1-4:** multiprgr **Txs:** SFN.

TRISTAN DA CUNHA (UK)

NB: No terrestrial TV station.

TUNISIA

Systems: DVB-T (MPEG4) [E]; † PAL-B [E], SECAM-B/G [E] ⇩2015

ENTREPRISE DE LA RADIODIFFUSION-TÉLÉVISION TUNISIENNE (E.R.T.T.) (Gov) ✉ 71 Ave de la Liberté, 1002 Tunis Belvedere ☎ +216 71287300 🖷 +216 71781058 **E:** info@watania1.tn; info@.watania2.tn **W:** www.watania1.tn; www.watania2.tn **L.P:** DG (ERTT): Imen Bahroun. **Chs:** Al Watanya 1; Al Watanya 2. – **HANNIBAL TV (HTV) (Comm)** ✉ 85 Avenue du 13 Aout, Choutrana 2 - La Soukra, 2036 Tunis ☎ +216 70944944 🖷 +216 70944411 **E:** info@hannibaltv.com.tn **W:** www.hannibaltv.com.tn.

DTT Transmitters
Operator: Office National de la Télédiffusion (ONT) ✉ BP 399, Tunis 1080 ☎ +216 71801177 🖷 +216 71781927 **E:** ont@telediffusion.net.tn **W:** www.telediffusion.net.tn **Mux:** Al Watanya 1, Al Watanya 2, HTV, RAI 1.

Location	ch	Location	ch
Trozza	21	Zarzis	28
Kchabta	23	Nefta	28
Ain Draham	28	Chaambi	29

Location	ch	Location	ch
Kef Errand	30	Souk Ejomaa	44
Zaghouan	36	Boukornine	45
Remada	36	Brourmet	51
Biadha	37	Goraa	52
Ksour Essaf	38	Tozeur	55
Ghraba	41		

TURKEY

Systems: # PAL-B/G [E] ⇩2015; DVB-T2 (MPEG4) [E] planned

National Stations
TÜRKIYE RADYO TELEVIZYON KURUMU (TRT) (Pub) ✉ TRT-TV Department, TRT Sitesi A Blok 427 Oran, 06109 Ankara ☎ +90 312 4901058 🖷 +90 312 4901109 **E:** genel.sekreterlik@trt.net.tr **W:** www.trt.net.tr. **L.P:** Head of TV Dept: Nimet Ersin **Chs (terr.):** TRT1, TRT Haber, TRT3, TRT4 / TRT Çocuk, TRT Avaz, TRT TÜRK, TV Gap, Regional stns.

Location	TRT1	TRT Haber	TRT3	TRT4	kW
Adana (Yüregir)	33	22	6	25	2x450/30/450
Agri	5	32	35	38	30/3x450
Aksehir	9	23	26	29	30/3x450
Amasya	9	22	25	28	100/3x450
Ankara (Çankaya)	5	47	40	50	100/3x450
Ankara (Çankaya)	44	-	-	-	450
Antalya	5	47	50	53	30/3x450
Bingöl	46	42	49	36	450
Bursa	26	23	11	29	2x450/100/450
Çanakkale	8	22	25	43	30/3x450
Cizre	5	27	43	21	30/3x450
Denizli	8	28	32	35	100/3x450
Diyarbakir	59	56	9	49	2x450/100/450
Edirne	9	28	31	41	30/3x450
Eskisehir	7	22	25	33	100/3x450
Elazig	7	21	24	31	100/3x450
Elbistan	5	34	37	44	30/3x450
Erzincan	8	42	39	45	100/3x450
Erzurum	6	23	26	29	30/3x450
Gaziantep (Sehitkamil)	10	27	30	40	30/3x450
Isparta	22	26	39	33	450
Istanbul (Üsküdar)	48	51	23	54	450
Izmir (Karsiyaka)	57	23	26	29	450
Izmit	10	21	24	27	30/3x450
Kars	9	21	24	27	100/3x450
Kastamonu (Çatalzeytin)	45	48	10	-	2x450/30
Kayseri	8	26	23	29	30/3x450
Kirsehir	7	42	45	49	30/3x450
Konya (Cihanbeyli)	22	12	35	28	450/100/2x450
Mugla (Yatagan)	7	55	58	52	30/3x450
Ordu (Fatsa)	5	57	60	44	30/3x450
Samsun	7	52	49	55	30/3x450
Silifke	10	52	55	47	30/3x450
Sivas	50	47	10	54	2x450/30/450
Trabzon	9	28	31	35	30/3x450
Van	7	22	25	28	30/3x450
Zonguldak	37	33	26	57	30/2x450

+ sites with txs below 30kW.
Additional txs in Ankara (Çankaya): TRT Avaz ch11, ch37 (450kW), TRT TÜRK ch34 (450kW).

ATV (Comm) ✉ Barbaros Bulvari 125, Cam Han, Besiktas, Istanbul ☎ +90 216 4742020 **E:** editor@atv.com.tr **W:** www.atv.com.tr **Txs:** Ankara (Çankaya) ch51 & netw. – **CINE 5 (Comm)** ✉ Halaskargazi Cad. 180, Pangalti, Istanbul ☎ +90 212 3361515 🖷 +90 212 2171986 **E:** cine5@cine5.com.tr **W:** www.cine5.com.tr **Txs:** Ankara (Çankaya) ch42 & netw. – **CNBC-E (Comm)** ✉ Eskibüyükdere Cad. 61, USO Center, Maslak, 80660 Istanbul ☎ +90 212 3350000 🖷 +90 212 3350035 **E:** insankaynaklari@cnbce.com **W:** www.cnbce.com **Txs:** Ankara (Polatli) ch54 & netw. – **CNN TÜRK (Comm)** ✉ Hürriyet Media Towers, Evren Mah. Günesli, Bagcilar, 34204 Istanbul ☎ +90 212 4785876 🖷 +90 212 5500239 **E:** info@cnnturk.com **W:** www.cnnturk.com **Txs:** netw. – **FLASH TV (Comm)** ✉ Catmamescit Mah., Tepebasi Cad., Elektrik Sok. 11, Istanbul ☎🖷+90 212 2568282 🖷 +90 212 2569992 **E:** flashtv-w@flashtv.com.tr **W:** www.flashtv.com.tr **Txs:** Ankara (Çankaya) ch32 & netw. – **FOX (Comm)** ✉ Kazlicesme Mah. Kennedy Cad 44, Zeytinburnu, 34020 Istanbul ☎ +90 212 4149000 **E:** info@fox.com.tr **W:** www.fox.com.tr **Txs:** Ankara (Çankaya) ch30 & netw. – **HABER TÜRK (Comm)** ✉ Tevfik Bey Mah. 20 Temmuz Cad 24, Sefaköy-Küçükçekmece, Istanbul ☎ +90 212 5805267 🖷 +90 212 4264241 **W:** www.haberturk.com.tr **Txs:** Ankara (Polatli) ch45 & netw. – **KANAL A (Comm)** ✉ Subayevleri

Güzin Sokak 40, Kiçiören, Ankara ☎ +90 313 3186970 🖥 +90 312 3181752 **E:** iletisim@kanala.com.tr **W:** www.kanala.com.tr **Txs:** Ankara (Çankaya) ch68 & netw. – **KANAL D (Comm)** 🖥 Kanal D TV Center, 100. Yil Mahallesi, Bagcilar, 34204 Istanbul ☎ +90 212 4135111 🖥 +90 212 4135550 **E:** bizeyazin@kanald.com.tr **W:** www. kanald.com.tr **Txs:** Ankara (Çankaya) ch38 & netw. – **KANAL 7 (Comm)** 🖥 Otakçilar Cad. 78, Eyüp, 34030 Istanbul ☎ +90 212 4378080 🖥 +90 212 4378599 **E:** kanal7@kanal7com **W:** www.kanal7. com **Txs:** Ankara (Çankaya) ch6 & netw. – **MELTEM TV (Comm)** 🖥 Imönü Cad. 96, Besyol, Florya, 34295 Istanbul ☎ +90 212 6240999 🖥 +90 212 4246977 **E:** bilgi@meltemtv.com.tr **W:** www.meltemtv. com.tr **Txs:** Ankara (Çankaya) ch39 & netw. – **NTV (Comm)** 🖥 Eskibüyükdere Cad. 61, Uso Center, Maslak, 80660 Istanbul ☎ +90 212 3350000 🖥 +90 212 3350099 **W:** www.ntvmsnbc.com **Chs:** NTV, NTV Spor **Txs: NTV:** Ankara (Çankaya) ch38 & netw.; **NTV Spor:** Ankara (Çankaya) ch48 & netw. – **SHOW TV (Comm)** 🖥 AKS Televizyon, Yapi Kredi Plaza, E Blok 1, Levent, 80620 Istanbul ☎ +90 212 3550101 🖥 +90 212 2806302 **E:** info@showtv.com **W:** www. showtv.com.tr **Txs:** Ankara (Polatli) ch35 & netw. – **STAR TV (Comm)** 🖥 Dogan TV Center, 100. Yil Mahallesi, 34204 Bagcilar, Istanbul ☎: +90 212 4135000 **E:** izleyicitemsilcisi@startv.com.tr **W:** www. startv.com **Txs:** Ankara (Çankaya) ch28 & netw. – **STV (Comm)** 🖥 Ferah Mah. Resatbey Sok. 12, Büyükçamlica, 34692 Istanbul ☎ +90 216 5249524 🖥 +90 216 3443803 **E:** haber@stv.com.tr **W:** www. stv.com.tr **Txs:** Ankara (Çankaya) ch36 & netw. – **TNT (Comm)** 🖥 Türkali Mah. Odalar Sok 9, Besiktas, Istanbul **W:** www.tnttv.com.tr **Txs:** Ankara (Çankaya) ch53 & netw. – **TV8 (Comm)** 🖥 Ihlamurdere Cad., Yesilçimen Sok. 5, OTIM, Besiktas, 80820 Istanbul ☎ +90 212 2885152 🖥 +90 212 2880413 **E:** tv8@tv8.com.tr **W:** www.tv8.com.tr **Txs:** Ankara (Polatli) ch21 & netw.

Local Stations not shown.

DTT Transmitters (under construction)
Operator: TRT **Mux:** multiprgr **Txs:** Nationwide netw. in preparation.

TURKMENISTAN

Systems: SECAM-D/K [R], PAL-D/K [R]

TURKMEN TELEVISION (Gov) 🖥 2003 St. 3, 744000 Asgabat ☎ +993 12 351515 🖥 +993 12 356850 **LP:** Chmn: Murad Orazov. **Chs:** Altyn Asyr Türkmenistan, Miras, Yaslyk, TV4-Türkmenistan, Türkmen Owaz, Asgabat. **Txs:** (-).

TURKS & CAICOS ISLANDS (UK)

NB: No terrestrial TV station.

TUVALU

System: PAL-B [E]

TUVALU MEDIA CORP. (TMC) (Pub) 🖥 Private Mail Bag, Funafuti ☎ +688 20139 🖥 +688 20732 **E:** media@tuvalu.tv **W:** www.tuvalu-news.tv **Tx:** Funafuti ch n/a (0.02kW).

UGANDA

Systems: # PAL-B/G [E]; DVB-T2 (MPEG4) [E]

National Stations
UGANDA BROADCASTING CORP. (UBC) (Pub) 🖥 P.O.Box 2038, Kampala ☎ +256 41 4257034 🖥 +256 41 4257252 **E:** ubc@ubconline. co.ug **W:** www.ubc.ug; ubconline.co.ug **LP:** MD: Paul Kihika Txs: Kampala ch5 (100kW) & netw. – **WBS TELEVISION (Comm)** 🖥 P.O.Box 5914, Kampala ☎ +256 41 4344313 🖥 +256 41 4345672 **E:** inquiry@wbs-tv.co.ug **W:** www.wbs-tv.co.ug. Txs: Kampala ch25 & netw.

Local Stations (all analogue)
Bukedde TV (Comm): Kampala; ch(-) **Capital TV (Comm):** Kampala; ch10. **East Africa TV (EATV) (Comm):** P.O.Box 26445, Kampala; ch31. **Lighthouse TV (Rlg):** P.O.Box 23934, Kampala; ch22. **Nation TV (NTV) (Comm):** Kampala; ch54. **NB TV (Comm):** Lira; ch61. **Pulse TV (Comm):** P.O.Box 25705, Kampala; ch12. **Sports TV (Comm):** P.O.Box 27, Kampala; ch43. **Top TV (Rlg):** P.O.Box 9816, Kampala; ch28. **TV West (Comm):** Mbarara; ch(-).

DTT Transmitters

Operator: n/a **Mux:** multiprgr **Txs:** (-)

UKRAINE

Systems: # SECAM-D/K [R], # PAL-D/K [R] ⇩Jul 2015; DVB-T (MPEG2, MPEG4) [E], DVB-T2 (MPEG4) [E]

National Stations
NATSIONALNA TELEKOMPANIA UKRAINY (Gov) 🖥 vul. Melnykova 42, 04119 Kyiv ☎ +380 44 2413909 🖥 +380 44 2468848 **E:** pr@ntu.com. ua **W:** 1tv.com.ua **LP:** GD: Egor Benkendorf. **Chs:** Pershyi Natsionalnyi, regional stns – **1+1 (Comm)** 🖥 vul. Kreschatyk 7/11, 01001 Kyiv ☎ +380 44 4900101 🖥 +380 44 4907097 **E:** feedback@1plus1.ua **W:** www.1plus1.ua **LP:** DG: Oleksandr Rodnianskyi – **INTER (Comm)** 🖥 vul. Dmytrivska 30, 01601 Kyiv ☎ +380 44 4906765 🖥 +380 44 4906765 **E:** program@inter.ua **W:** www.inter.ua

Location	PN	1+1	Inter	kW
Andriivka	12	7	21	2x5/1
Bershad	22	34	32	2x20/0.1
Bilopillia	5V	7	24	2x25/20
Buky	5	28	1V	5
Cherkasy	12	3	33	5
Chernihiv	6	11	28	2x5/1
Dnipropetrovsk	5	7	28	25/2x5
Donetsk	4	30	10	50/20/50
Ivano-Frankivsk	7	9	40	5
Izium	11	29	40	2x25/20
Kamyanets-Podilsky	21	33	-	20
Kamyanske	4	7	29	2x5/1
Kerch	12	25	30	5/2x1
Kharkiv	3	9	32	2x5/20
Kherson	3	12	26	2x5/0.1
Khmelnitskyi	28	30	33	2x20/0.1
Kholmy	21	33	-	20
Khust	22	34	28	25/20/5
Kirovohrad	6	21	11	5
Komysh-Zoria	8V	3	22	2x5/0.1
Kotovsk	6	39		5
Kovel	6	5	26	25/5/1
Kramatorsk	22	34	37	20
Krasnohorivka	8	10	28	25/50/10
Krasnoperekopsk	32	12V	39	25/5/20
Kryvyi Rih	9	1	40	5
Kyiv	2	4	9	50
Luhansk	6	2	3	5
Lviv	8	1	6	25/40/5
Mariupol	5V	25	31	5
Melitopol	11	29	41	5/2x20
Mykolaiv	10	33	2	5
Novodnistrovsk	38	26	9	2x5/0.1
Odesa	5	9	12	5
Olevsk	34	22	36	2x20/1
Pervomaysk	7	29	12	2x5/0.1
Pryluky	34	22	41	25/5/-
Rivne	3	27	39	50/25/20
Rovenky	12	6	29	2x5/0.1
Sevastopol	5	31	11	5/20/5
Shostka	35	38	51	2x5/0.1
Simferopol	6	3V	1	2x5/25
Sovietske	2V	7	38	2x5/0.1
Starobilsk	28	8	35	25/5/0.1
Ternopil	5V	11V	38	2x25/20
Trostianets	1	11V	25	5
Uzhhorod	2	11	33	5
Vasylivka	4	8	28	2x5/0.1
Vinnitsia	8	10	40	40/35/20
Zaporizhia	6	12	33	5

+ sites with txs below 5kW.

Local Stations not shown.

DTT Transmitters (under construction) (DVB-T2/MPEG4)
Licensee Mux 1-3, 5: Zeonbud 🖥 P.O.Box 110, 01054 Kyiv. **E:** office@zeonbud.com.ua **W:** www.zeonbud.com.ua **Mux 1:** Pershyi Natsionalnyi, Inter, Ukraina, 1+1, NTN, K1, ICTV, T2, Enter-Film **Mux 2:** MTV-Ukraina, Kinotochka, STB, TET, K2, Novyi kanal, M1, 5-yi kanal **Mux 3:** Mega, Piksel TV, Khokei, NLO-TB, 2+2, Star TV, Pogoda TB **Mux 5:** Goldberry, Bank-TV, Vintage, Eskulap-TV, KDRTK. **Licencee Mux 4:** UDTVN 🖥 P.O.Box 266, 03150 Kyiv ☎🖥 +380 44 3538643 **E:** office@udtvn.com.ua **W:** www.udtvn.com.ua **Mux 4:** Music Box

UA, Humor/Babai, M2, Unian, Business, Ukrainian Fashion, Dobro-TV, A-One Ukraina. NB: Regional variations may apply.

Location	M1	M2	M3	M4	M5	kW
Kyiv	26	31	49	51	29	2

+ nationwide network under construction
Local licensees (DVB-T/MPEG2, MPEG4) not shown.

UNITED ARAB EMIRATES

Systems: # PAL-B/G [E] ⬇2013; DVB-T [E]

ABU DHABI TV (Gov) ✉ P.O.Box 637, Abu Dhabi ☎ +971 2 44451111 **E:** adtv@emi.co.ae **W:** www.adtv.ae **Txs: Prgr 1:** Abu Dhabi ch11 (2kW) & network, **Prgr 2:** Abu Dhabi ch5 & network. – **AJMAN TV (Gov)** ✉ P.O.Box 422, Ajman ☎ +971 6 7465000 📠 +971 6 7465135 **E:** progajtv@ajmantv.com **W:** www.ajmantv.com **Tx:** Ajman ch26 (100kW) – **DUBAI TV (Gov)** ✉ P.O.Box 1695, Dubai ☎ +971 4 3077245 📠 +971 4 3374111 **W:** www.dmi.ae **Txs: Prgr 1:** Dubai ch2 (150kW), Zabeel ch10 (455kW), Jebel Hatta ch41 (1600kW); **Prgr 2:** Zabeel ch33 (1700kW). – **SHARJAH TV (Gov)** ✉ P.O.Box 111, Sharjah ☎ +971 6 5661111 📠 +971 6 5669999 **E:** admin@ sharjahtv.ae **W:** www.sharjahtv.ae **Txs: Prgr 1** (Arabic): Sharjah ch54 (199kW); **Prgr 2** (English): Jabel ch22 (398kW).

DTT Transmitters (under construction)
Operator: Dubai TV **Mux:** multiprgr **Txs:** (-)

UNITED KINGDOM

Systems: DVB-T (MPEG2) [E], DVB-T2 (MPEG4) [E]

National Stations
BRITISH BROADCASTING CORP. (BBC) (Pub) ✉ BBC Television Centre, 80 Wood Lane, London W12 4RJ ☎ +44 20 87438000 📠 +44 20 87497520 **W:** www.bbc.co.uk/tv **LP:** DG: George Entwistle. **Chs:** BBC One, BBC Two, BBC Three, BBC Four, CBBC, BBC News Channel, BBC Parliament, BBC HD, regional stns: **a) BBC Channel Islands:** 18-21 Parade Road, St Helier JE2 3PL; **b) BBC East:** The Forum, Millennium Plain, Norwich NR2 1BH; **c) BBC East Midlands:** London Road, Nottingham NG2 4UU; **d) BBC East Yorkshire & Lincolnshire:** Queen's Court, Hull HU1 3RH; **e) BBC London:** Marylebone High St., London W1A 6FL; **f) BBC North East & Cumbria:** Broadcasting Centre, Barrack Rd, Newcastle upon Tyne NE99 2NE; **g) BBC North West:** New Broadcasting House, Oxford Road, Manchester M60 1SJ; **h) BBC Northern Ireland:** Ormeau Avenue, Belfast BT2 8HQ; **i) BBC Scotland:** 40 Pacific Quay, Glasgow G51 1DA; **j) BBC South:** Broadcasting House, 10 Havelock Road, Southampton SO14 7PU; **k) BBC South East:** The Great Hall, Mount Pleasant Road, Tunbridge Wells TN1 1QQ; **l) BBC South West:** Broadcasting House, Seymour Road, Plymouth PL3 5BD; **m) BBC Wales:** Llantrisant Rd, Cardiff CF5 2YQ; **n) BBC West:** Broadcasting House, Whiteladies Road, Bristol BS8 2LR; **o) BBC West Midlands:** Level 7, The Mailbox, Birmingham B1 1RF; **p) BBC Yorkshire:** 2 St Peter's Square, Leeds LS9 8AH. – **CHANNEL FOUR TELEVISION CORP. (Pub)** ✉ 124 Horseferry Road, London SW1P 2TX ☎ +44 20 73964444 📠 +44 20 73068366 **W:** www.channel4.com **LP:** CEO: David Abraham. – **S4C (WELSH FOURTH CHANNEL AUTHORITY) (Pub)** ✉ Park Ty Glas, Llanishen, Caerdydd/Cardiff CF14 5DU ☎ +44 2920 747444 📠 +44 2920 754444 **E:** s4c@s4c.co.uk **W:** www.s4c.co.uk **LP:** CEO: Ian Jones. – **INDEPENDENT TELEVISION NETWORK (ITV) (Comm)** ✉ London Television Centre, Upper Ground, London SE1 9LT ☎ +44 20 76201620 **W:** www.itv.com **LP:** CEO: Adam Crozier. **Chs:** ITV1 (incl. regional prgrs), ITV2, ITV3, ITV4. **Reg: a) ITV1 Anglia:** Anglia House, Norwich NR1 3JG; **b) ITV1 Border:** The Television Centre, Carlisle CA1 3NT; **c) ITV Central:** Gas Street, Birmingham B1 2JT; **d) ITV Channel Television:** Television Centre, St Helier, Jersey, Channel Islands JE1 3ZD; **e) ITV Granada:** Quay Street, Manchester M60 9EA; **f) ITV London:** 200 Gray's Inn Road, London WC1X 8XZ; **g) ITV Meridian:** Solent Business Park, Whiteley PO15 7PA; **h) ITV Thames Valley:** 9 Windrush Court, Abingdon Business Park, Abingdon OX14 1SA; **i) ITV Tyne Tees:** Television House, The Watermark, Gateshead, Tyne and Wea NE11 9SZ; **j) ITV Wales:** The Television Centre, Culverhouse Cross, Cardiff CF5 6XJ; **k) ITV West:** 470 Bath Road, Bristol BS4 3HG; **l) ITV Westcountry:** Langage Science Park, Western Wood Way, Plymouth PL7 5BQ; **m) ITV Yorkshire:** The Television Centre, 104 Kirkstall Rd, Leeds LS3 1JS; **n1) STV:** Pacific Quay, Glasgow G51 1PQ; **o) UTV:** Havelock House, Ormeau Road, Belfast BT7 1EB. – **CHANNEL 5 BROADCASTING LTD (Comm)** ✉ 22 Long Acre, London WC2E 9LY ☎ +44 20 75505555 📠 +44 20 75505554 **W:** www.channel5. com – **BRITISH SKY BROADCASTING LTD (Comm)** ✉ Grant Way,

Isleworth, London TW7 5QD ☎ +44 20 77053000 📠 +44 20 77053453 **W:** www.sky.com **LP:** CEO: Jeremy Darroch.

DTT Transmitters (MPEG2 except where indicated otherwise)
Licensee Mux 1+3: BBC **Mux 1:** BBC One (incl. reg. prgrs a-p), BBC Two, BBC Three, BBC Four, CBBC, BBC News Channel, BBC Parliament ✂ BBC R.1, 1Xtra, R.2,R.3, R.4, R. 4 Extra, R.5 Live, R.5 Live Sports Extra, R.6 Music, BBC Asian Network, BBCWS **Mux 3 (DVB-T2/ MPEG4):** BBC One HD, BBC HD, ITV1 HD, Channel 4 HD. – **Licensee Mux 2:** Digital 3&4 Ltd. **Mux:** ITV1 (incl. reg. prgrs a-o), ITV1 +1, ITV2, Channel 4, Channel 4 +1, Channel 5, Channel 5 +1✪, Rabbit✪, Gay Rabbit✪ – **Licensee Mux 4:** SDN Ltd. **Mux:** ITV 3, ITV 2 +1, 5*, 5USA, Quest, The Zone, Channel 5 +1, CITV, QVC, Bid TV, The Jewellery Channel, 1-2-1 Dating, Mail Travel TV, Christian, CONNECT 2, VISION2, CONNECT 4, God TV, Sony SAB TV Asia, ADULT Section✪, Television X✪, ADULT Playboy✪ ✂ Capital R., Absolute R., Heart – **Licensee Mux 5+6:** Arqiva **Mux 5:** PICK TV, Dave, Really, E4+1, Challenge, Food Network, TV Stars, Sky News, Community Channel, TV News, Big Deal, Create and Craft, Price Drop TV, Gems TV 1, ADULT smileTV3✪, ADULT PARTY✪, ADULT Blue✪, ADULT Blue✪, Babestation Xtra✪ ✂ talkSPORT **Mux 6:** ITV4, Film 4, 4Music, Yesterday, VIVA, 4seven, Al Jazeera English, Russia Today English, Ideal World, QVC Beauty, Rocks and Co 1, Argos TV, CCTV, Sports, Racing TV, Channel Zero, ADULT smileTV2✪, Babestation✪, ADULT Section, VISION✪ ✂ The Hits R., Smash Hits!, Kiss R., heat, Magic, Q, Smooth R., Kerrang!, Premier X. **NB.** Some regional variations may apply.

Location	M1°	M2°	M3	M4	M5	M6	kW
Angus	60i	53n	57	54	58	61	3x20/3x10
Beacon Hill	60l	53l	57	42	45	51	3x20/3x10
Belmont	22d	25m	28	30	53	60	3x150/50/2x100
Bilsdale	26f	29i	23	43	46	40	3x100/3x50
Black Hill	46i	43n	40	41	44	47	100
Blaenplwyf	27m	24j	21	25	22	28	3x40/3x10
Bluebell Hill	46f	43q	40	45	39	54	20
Brougher Mt.	28h	22o	25	21	24	27	20
Caldbeck	25f	28b	30	27	24	22	3x100/3x50
Caradon Hill	28l	25l	22	21	24	27	3x100/3x50
Carmel	60m	53j	57	54	58	61	3x20/3x10
Chatton	45f	42i	49	41	44	47	3x20/3x10
Craigkelly	27i	24n	21	42	45	39	3x20/3x10
Crystal Palace	23e	26f	30	25	22	28³	200
Darvel	22i	25n	28	23	26	29	3x100/3x50
Divis	27h	21o	24	23	26	29	3x100/3x50
Dover	50f	51g	53	55	59	48	3x80/3x40
Durris	28i	25n	22	23	26	29	3x100/3x50
Emley More	47b	44a	41	51	52	48	5x174/87
Hannington	45j	42h	39	41	44	47	4x50/3x25
Heathfield	52k	49g	47	42	44	41	20
Huntshaw Cross	62l	59l	55	48	52	56	3x20/3x10
Keelylang Hill	46i	43n	50	42	45	49	3x20/3x10
Knock More	26i	23n	29	53	57	60	3x20/3x10
Limavady	50h	59o	55	54	58	49	3x20, 3x10
Llanddona	57m	60j	53	43	46	50	3x20/3x10
Mendip	61n	54k	58	48	52	56	100
Midhurst	55j	56g	58	54	59	50	3x20/3x10
Moel-y-Parc	45m	49j	42	51	52	48	3x20/3x10
Oxford	53j	60h	57	62	59	55	3x100/3x50
Pontop Pike	58f	54i	49	50	59	55	3x100/3x50
Presely	43m	46j	50	42	45	49	3x20/3x10
Redruth	44l	41l	47	48	52	51	3x20/3x10
Ridge Hill	28o	25c	22	21	24	27	3x20/3x10
Rosemarkie	45i	49n	42	43	46	50	3x20/3x10
Rowridge	34j	32g	28	30	37	33	200¹
Rumster Forest	27i	24n	21	30	59	62	3x20/3x10
Sandy Heath	27b	24a	21	51	52	48	3x180/3x170
Selkirk	62i	59n	55	57	53	60	3x10/3x5
Stockland Hill	26l	23l	29	25	22	28	3x50/3x25
Sudbury	44b	41a	47	58	60	56	100
Sutton Coldfield	43o	46c	40	42	45	39	200
Talconeston	55b	59a	62	42	45	50	100
The Wrekin	26o	23c	30	41	44	47	3x20/3x10
Waltham	61c	54c	58	29	56	57	3x50/3x25
Wenvoe	41m	44j	47	42	45	49	3x100/3x50
Winter Hill	62g	59e	54	58	61	55	100

+ sites with txs below 10kW. ° incl. reg. prgrs
Pol=H exc. ¹) also V (3x200/3x50kW)

UNITED STATES OF AMERICA

Systems: ATSC [A]

Main National Networks
PUBLIC BROADCASTING SERVICE (PBS) (Pub) ✉ 1320 Braddock Place, Alexandria, VA 22314-1698 ☎ +1 703 7395000 📠

+1 703 7390775 **W:** www.pbs.org **L.P:** Pres/CEO: Paula A. Kerger. **Member Stations:** ca 350. – **ABC, Inc. (Comm)** (Subsidiary of Walt Disney Co.) ◻ 77 W. 66th St., New York, NY 10023-6298 ☎ +1 212 4567777 🖃 +1 212 4566850 **W:** abc.go.com **L.P:** Pres (Disney ABC Television Group): Anne Sweeney. **O&O Stations¹:** KABC-TV Los Angeles, CA: ch7 (28.7kW); KFSN-TV Fresno, CA: ch30 (260kW); KGO-TV San Francisco, CA: ch7 (24kW); KTRK-TV Houston, TX: ch13 (32.4kW); WABC-TV New York, NY: ch7 (26.9kW); WJRT-TV Flint, MI: ch12 (30kW); WLS-TV Chicago, IL: ch44 (346kW); WPVI-TV Philadelphia, PA: ch6 (30kW); WTVD Durham, NC: ch11 (45kW); WTVG-TV Toledo, OH: ch13 (16.7kW). **Full-Power Affiliates:** ca 209. – **CBS BROADCASTING, Inc. (Comm)** (Subsidiary of CBS Corporation) ◻ 51 W 52nd St, New York, NY 10019-6119 ☎ +1 212 9754321 🖃 +1 212 9754516 **W:** www.cbs.com **L.P:** CEO (CBS Corp.): Leslie Moonves. **O&O Stations¹:** KCBS-TV Los Angeles, CA: ch43 (1000kW); KCNC-TV Denver, CO: ch35 (1000kW), KDKA-TV Pittsburgh, PA: ch25 (1000kW); KOVR-TV Sacramento, CA: ch25 (760kW); KPIX-TV San Francisco, CA: ch29 (1000kW); KTVT-TV Dallas, TX: ch11 (23kW); KYW-TV Philadelphia, PA: ch26 (790kW); WBBM-TV Chicago, IL: ch12 (8kW); WBZ-TV Boston, MA: ch30 (825kW); WCBS-TV New York, NY: ch33 (349kW); WFOR-TV Miami, FL: ch22 (1000kW); WJZ-TV Baltimore, MD: ch13 (28.8kW); WCCO-TV Minneapolis, MN: ch32 (1000kW); WKBD-TV Detroit, MI: ch14 (180kW); WWJ-TV Detroit, MI: ch44 (425kW) **Full-Power Affiliates:** ca 215. – **FOX BROADCASTING CO. (Comm)** (Subsidiary of Fox Entertainment Group, Inc.) ◻ 10201 W. Pico Blvd., Los Angeles, CA 90035 ☎ +1 310 3693716 🖃 +1 310 9693300 **W:** www.fox.com **L.P:** Pres/CEO (Fox Networks Group): Peter Rice **O&O Stations¹:** KDFW Dallas/Fort Worth, TX: ch35 (857kW); KMSP-TV Minneapolis, MN: ch9 (30kW); KRIV Houston, TX: ch26 (1000kW); KSAZ-TV Phoenix, AZ: ch10 (1000kW); KTBC Austin, TX: ch7 (30kW); KTTV Los Angeles, CA: ch11 (115kW); WAGA Atlanta, GA: ch27 (1000kW); WFLD Chicago, IL: ch31 (690kW); WFXT Boston, MA: ch31 (1000kW); WHBQ-TV Memphis, TN: ch13 (95kW); WJBK Detroit, MI: ch7 (20kW); WOFL Orlando, FL: ch22 (607kW); WOGX Ocala/Gainesville, FL: ch31 (500kW); WNYW New York, NY: ch44 (246kW); WTTG Washington, D.C.: ch36 (1000kW); WTVT Tampa Bay, FL: ch12 (17.5kW); WTXF-TV Philadelphia, PA: ch42 (1000kW). **Full-Power Affiliates:** ca 223. – **NBC UNIVERSAL, Inc. (Comm)** (Subsidiary of NBCUniversal Media, LLC) ◻ 30 Rockefeller Plaza, New York, NY 10112 ☎ +1 212 6644444 🖃 +1 212 6644085 **W:** www.nbc.com **L.P:** Chmn (NRC Entertainement): Robert Greenblatt. **O&O Stations:** KNBC Los Angeles, CA: ch36 (380kW); KNSD San Diego, CA: ch40 (370kW); KNTV San Francisco, CA: ch12 (103.1kW); KXAS-TV Dallas/Fort Worth, TX: ch41 (891kW); WCAU Philadelphia, PA: ch34 (790kW); WMAQ-TV Chicago, IL: ch29 (350kW); WNBC New York, NY: ch28 (200.2kW); WRC-TV Washington, D.C: ch48 (813kW); WTVJ Miami, FL: ch31 (1000kW); WVIT Hartford, CT: ch35 (250kW). **Full-Power Affiliates:** ca 209. – **THE CW NETWORK, LLC (Comm)** (Subsidiary of WB Communications, Inc. and CBS Corporation) ◻ 4000 Warner Blvd., Burbank, CA 91522 ☎ +1 818 9775000 🖃 +1 818 9778310 **W:** www.cwtv.com **L.P:** Pres: Mark Pedowitz. **Full-Power Affiliates:** ca 204.

¹) O&O = owned-and-operated.

Other Major Networks
V-ME (Pub) (V-me Media Inc.; Spanish-language netw.) ◻ 450 West 33 St., 6th Floor, New York, NY 10016 ☎ +1 212 5608700 🖃 +1 212 5608720 **W:** www.vmetv.com **Full-Power Affiliates:** ca 45. – **ION TELEVISION (Comm)** (Subsidiary of ION Media Networks, Inc.) ◻ 601 Clearwater Park Road, West Palm Beach, FL 33401 ☎ +1 561 6594122 🖃 +1 561 6594252 **W:** www.iontelevision.com **L.P:** Pres/CEO (ION Media Networks): Brandon Burgess. **Full-Power Affiliates:** ca 64. – **MYNETWORKTV, Inc. (Comm)** (Subsidiary of Fox Entertainment Group, Inc.) ◻ 1999 S. Bundy Dr., Los Angeles, CA 90025-5203 ☎ +1 310 5842000 🖃 +1 310 5842085 **W:** www.mynetworktv.com **L.P:** CEO: Jack Abernethy. **Full-Power Affiliates:** ca 162. – **TELEFUTURA NETWORK (Comm)** (Subsidiary of Univision Communications, Inc.; Spanish-language netw.) ◻ 9405 NW 41st Street, Miami, FL 33178-2301 ☎ +1 305 4713900 🖃 +1 305 4714065 **W:** www.telefutura.com **L.P:** Pres/CEO (Univision): Randy Falco. **Full-Power Affiliates:** ca 43. – **TELEMUNDO NETWORK GROUP, LLC (Comm)** (Subsidiary of Telemundo Holdings, Inc.; Spanish-language netw.) ◻ 2290 West 8th Avenue, Hialeah, FL 33010 ☎ +1 305 8848200 🖃 +1 305 8897950 **W:** www.telemundo.com **L.P:** Pres: Emilio Romano. **Full-Power Affiliates:** ca 42. – **UNIVISION NETWORK, LP (Comm)** (Subsidiary of Univision Communications, Inc.; Spanish-language netw.) ◻ 9405 NW 41 St., Miami, FL 33178-2301 ☎ +1 305 4713900 🖃 +1 305 4714065 **W:** www.univision.com **L.P:** Pres/CEO: Randy Falco. **Full-Power Affiliates:** ca 44. – **JCTV (Rlg)** (TBN channel) ◻ 2442 Michelle Dr, Tustin, CA 92780 ☎ +1 714 8322950 🖃 +1 714 6652191 **W:** www.jctv.org **Full-Power Affiliates:** ca 33.

– **SMILE OF A CHILD (Rlg)** (TBN channel) ◻ P.O.Box 10700, Santa Ana, CA 92711-0700 ☎ +1 714 6652100 🖃 +1 714 7085428 **W:** www.smileofachildtv.org **Full-Power Affiliates:** 33. – **THE WORSHIP NETWORK (Rlg)** (The Christian Network, Inc.) ◻ P.O.Box 428, Safety Harbor, FL 34695 ☎ +1 877 2967744 **W:** worship.net **L.P:** CEO: Bruce Koblish. **Full-Power Affiliates:** ca 58. – **TBN ENLACE USA (Rlg)** (Spanish-language TBN channel) ◻ 2823 West Irving Blvd., Irving, TX 75061 ☎ +1 972 3139500 **W:** www.tbnenlaceusa.com **Full-Power Affiliates:** ca 33. – **THE CHURCH CHANNEL (Rlg)** (TBN channel) ◻ 14171 Chambers Rd., Tustin, CA 92780 ☎ +1 714 6652153 **W:** www.churchchannel.tv **Full-Power Affiliates:** ca 33. – **TRINITY BROADCASTING NETWORK (TBN) (Rlg)** ◻ P. O.Box A, Santa Ana, CA 92711 ☎ +1 714 8322950 **W:** www.tbn.org **L.P:** Chmn/Pres: Paul Crouch. **Full-Power Affiliates:** ca 37.

Other Networks, Local Stations not shown.

Systems: # PAL-N [A]; SBTVD (MPEG4) [A]

Key Local Stations (ª=analogue)
TELEVISIÓN NACIONAL URUGUAY (TNU) (Gov) ◻ Bvrd. Artigas 2552,11600 Montevideo ☎ +598 2 4871129 **E:** contacto@tnu.com.uy **W:** www.tnu.com.uy. **Tx:** Montevideo ªch5 (96kW). – **MONTE CARLO TELEVISIÓN (Comm)** ◻ Paraguay 2253, 11800 Montevideo ☎ +598 2 9247924 🖃 +598 2 9244444 **W:** www.montecarlotv.com.uy **Tx:** Montevideo ªch4 (300kW). – **SAETA CANAL 10 (Comm)** ◻ Lorenzo Carnelli 1234, 11200 Montevideo ☎ +598 2 4002120 🖃 +598 2 4095812 **W:** www.canal10.com.uy **Tx:** Montevideo ªch10 (600kW)/ch7. – **TELEDOCE (Comm)** ◻ Enriqueta Compte y Rique 1276, 11800 Montevideo ☎ +598 2 2083363 🖃 +598 2 2083555 **E:** teledoce@teledoce.com **W:** www.teledoce.com **Tx:** Montevideo ch12 (600kW).

Other Local Stations not shown.

Systems: # SECAM-D/K [R], # PAL-D/K [R] ⇩ 2015; DVB-T (MPEG4) [E]

National Stations
UZBEK TELEVISION (Gov) ◻ Navoiy Str. 69, 100011 Toshkent ☎ +998 71 1141250 🖃 +998 71 1441332 **E:** info@mtrk.uz **W:** www.mtrk.uz **L.P:** Chmn: Alisher Djurakulovich Hadjayev. **Chs:** O'zbekiston, Yoshlar, TV Toshkent, regional stns. **Txs: O'zbekiston:** Toshkent ch5 (20kW) & network; **Yoshlar:** Toshkent ch9 (20kW) & network; **TV Toshkent:** Toshkent ch12.

Local Stations, Foreign TV Relays not shown.

DTT Transmitters (under construction)
Licensee: Uzdigital TV ◻ Amir Timur St. 109-A, 100084 Toshkent ☎ +998 71 1299000 🖃 +998 71 1505884 **E:** info@uzdtv.uz **W:** www.uzdigitaltv.uz **Mux 1:** O'zbekiston, Yoshlar, TV Toshkent, Sport TV, 1 kanal, NTV, Telenyanya, dom kino, Home, Vremya, MzTV, TNT, Test **Mux 2:** 5 kanal, 7 TV, BBC World News, DTV, Euronews, Yumor TV, Luxe TV HD, Rossiya 1, Rossiya 2, Rossiya 24, TV3, TV Zvezda **Mux 3:** tbd.

Location	M1	M2	M3	kW
Toshkent	42	41	37	2

+ national network under construction

System: PAL-B [E]

TV BLONG VANUATU (Gov) ◻ P.M.B. 049, Port Vila **L.P:** GM (VBTC): Fred Vurobaravu. **Txs:** (-).

Foreign TV Relay
CCTV9 (China): (-).

System: DVB-T (MPEG4) [E]

CENTRO TELEVISIVO VATICANO (CTV) ◻ Via del Pellegrino, I-00120 Vatican City ☎ +39 06 69885467 🖃 +39 06 69885192 **E:** ctv@ctv.va **L.P:** Dir: Fr. Federico Lombardi, S.I. **Mux:** CTV HD ✳ R. Vaticana 105 Live, R. Vaticana Europa/America, R. Vaticana Africa/Asia **Tx:** ch45 (Castel Gandolfo).

VENEZUELA

Systems: # NTSC-M [A]; SBTVD (MPEG4) [A]

National Stations (ᵃ=analogue)
TVES (TELEVISORA VENEZOLANA SOCIAL) (Gov) ⌨ Caraças W: www.tves.gob.ve **Txs:** Caracas ch2 & relay txs. – **VIVE (VISIÓN VENEZUELA) (Gov)** ⌨ Final Av. Panteón, Foro Libertador, Edf. Biblioteca Nacional, AP-4, Altagracia, Caracas ☎ +58 212 5051611 **E:** atencionciudadana@vive.gob.ve **W:** www.yive.gob.ve **Txs:** Caracas ᵃch25 & relay tx. – **VTV (CORPORACIÓN VENEZOLANA DE TELEVISIÓN) (Gov)** ⌨ Ap. 2979, Caracas 1050. ☎ +58 212 2349581 **E:** atencionciudadano@vtv.gob.ve **W:** www.vtv.gob.ve **Txs:** Caracas ᵃch8 (190kW) & relay txs. – **TELESUR (Pub)** ⌨ Calle Vargas con Calle Santa Clara, edificio TeleSUR, Boleita Norte, Caracas ☎ +58 212 6000202 **E:** contactenos@telesurtv.net **W:** www.telesurtv.net **Txs:** Caracas ᵃch49 & relay txs. – **GLOBOVISIÓN (Comm)** ⌨ av. Los Pinos, cruce con Calle Alameda, Qta. Globovisión, Urb. Alta Florida, Caracas ☎ +58 212 7301134 **E:** info@globovision.com **W:** globovision.com. **Txs:** Caracas ᵃch33 & relay txs. – **MERIDIANO TELEVISÓN (Comm)** ⌨ Final av. San Martin con Av. La Paz, Edificio Bloque De Armas, Caracas ☎ +58 212 4064516 🖷 +58 212 4515627 **E:** meridianotv@internet.ve **W:** www.meridiano.com.ve **Txs:** Caracas ᵃch39 & relay txs. – **TELEVEN (Comm)** ⌨ Av. Romulo Gallegos con 4ta. transversal de horizonte, Edificio Televen, Caracas 1071 ☎ +58 212 2800151 **E:** webmaster@televen.com **W:** www.televen.com. **Txs:** Caracas ᵃch10 & relay txs. – **VENEVISIÓN (Comm)** ⌨ La Salle, Edif, Venevision,Colinas de Los Caobos, Caracas 1050 ☎ +58 212 7089444 **W:** www.venevision. net. **Txs:** Caracas ᵃch4 (132kW) & relay txs. – **VALE TV (Rlg)** ⌨ Final Av. La Salle, Quinta ValeTV, Colinas de los Caobos, Caracas ☎ +58 212 7939215 🖷 +58 212 7089743 **E:** webmaster@valetv.com **W:** www. valetv.com **Txs:** Caracas ᵃch5 (210kW) & relay txs.

Local Stations (Comm. exc. where stated)
Amavision (Rlg): Calle Selesiano, Colegio Pio XI, Puerto Ayacucho, Amazonas; Puerto Ayacucho ᵃch7 (6kW). **La Tele:** Calle Republica Dominicana, Boleita Sur, Caracas; ᵃch12. **Canal Metropolitano de Televisión:** Av. Circumvalacion El Sol, Centro Professional Santa Paula, Torre B, Piso 4, Santa Paula, Caracas;ᵃch51. **NCTV:** Urv. La Paz, Avenida 57 y Maracaibo, Maracaibo; ᵃch11 (108kW). **Omnivision:** Calle Milan, Edif. Omnivision, Los Ruices Sur, Caracas. Puma TV: Av. Sanatorio del Avila, Boleíta Norte, Caracas 1071; Maracaibo ᵃch53, Caracas ᵃch57. **Televisora Andina de Merida (Rlg):** Av. Bolivar, Calle 23 entre Av. 4-5, Merida 5101; Tachira ᵃch3 (33kW), Merida ᵃch6 (20kW). **Tele Bocono (Cult):** Calle 3, Qta. Caleuche, El Saman. Bocono; Trujillo ᵃch13 (4kW). **Telecaribe:** Centro Banaven (Cubo Negro), Torre C, Piso 1, of C-12, Chuao, Caracas; Anzoategui ᵃch9 (50kW), Nueva Esparta ᵃch12 (30kW). **Telecentro:** Avenide Pedro León Torres, esquina de la calle 47, Edificio Telecentro, Barquisimeto, (3001) Lara; ᵃch11 (100kW). **TV Guyana:** Puerto Ordaz, Bolivar; ch12 (125kW). **Telesol:** Calle Sucre no 15, Cumana, Sucre; ᵃch7 (12kW). **Televisora Regional del Tachira:** Av. Libertador, edif. Servicios Unidos, Piso 3, San Cristobal, Tachira; ᵃch6 (144kW). **Televisora de Oriente (TVO):** Puerto la Cruz, Anzoategui; ᵃch5 (50kW).

VIETNAM

Systems: # PAL-D/K [R] ⇩2015; DVB-T (MPEG2) [E]

National Stations
VIETNAM TELEVISION (Gov) ⌨ 43 Nguyen Chi Thanh, Ba Dinh District, Hanoi ☎ +84 8 8224403 🖷 +84 8 8223422 **E:** banbientap@ vtv.vn **W:** www.vtv.vn **LP:** DG: Vu Van Hien **Chs (terr.):** VTV1, VTV2, VTV3. **Txs:** VTV1: Hanoi ch9 (10kW) & netw. **VTV2:** Hanoi ch11 (10kW) & netw. **VTV3:** Hanoi ch22 (20kW) & netw.

Regional and Local Stations not shown.

DTT Transmitters (under construction)
Licensee: VTCi Media ⌨ 67B Ham Long Street, Hoan Kiem District, Hanoi ☎ +84 4 9433409 🖷 +84 4 9439867 **E:** tv.vtc@hn.vnn.vn **W:** vtci.com.vn **Mux:** VTV1-7, Hanoi TV 1, HTV1 **Txs:** ch26 (Hanoi 1.3kW) & nationwide netw. under construction.

VIRGIN ISLANDS (USA)

Systems: ATSC [A]

Local Stations*
WCVI-TV (Comm): 1 k Little Princess, St. Croix, VI 00820-4027. °CW. Tx: St. Croix ch23 (0.66kW). **WSVI (Comm):** Sunny Isle Shopping Cente,

St Croix, VI 00820-4493. °ABC. Tx: St. Croix ch20 (459kW). **WTJX-TV (Pub):** 58-158A Hay Place Hill S, St. Thomas, VI 20801. °PBS. Tx: Charlotte Amalie ch44 (50kW). **WVIF (Comm):** 4200 United Shipping Plaza #3, St Croix, VI 00820. Tx: Christiansted ch15 (16.2kW). **WVXF (Comm):** 8000 Nisky Center, Suite 714, Saint Thomas, VI 00802. °CBS. Tx: Charlotte Amalie ch48 (50kW). **WZVI (Comm):** satellite of WSVI. Tx: Charlotte Amalie ch43 (1.4kW).
*) Full power licenses (lp licenses not listed); °) Network affiliation

VIRGIN ISLANDS (UK)

System: NTSC-M [A]

VIRGIN ISLANDS BROADCASTING LTD (Comm) ⌨ P.O.Box 78, Road Town, Tortola ☎ +1 284 4942250 **LP:** GM: Harvey Herbert **Tx:** ch5 (30kW).

WAKE ISLAND (USA)

NB: No terrestrial TV station.

WALLIS & FUTUNA (France)

System: DVB-T (MPEG4) [E]

WALLIS ET FUTUNA 1ÈRE (Pub) ⌨ BP 102, Pointe Matala, F-98600 Mata Utu ☎ +681 681722020 🖷 +681 681722346 **W:** wallisfutuna.la1ere.fr

DTT Transmitters
Operator: TDF **Mux:** Wallis et Futuna 1ère, France 2-5, France Ô, France 24, Arte **Txs:** ch34 (SFN).

YEMEN

System: PAL-B [E]

REPUBLIC OF YEMEN TELEVISION (Gov) Yemen TV: ⌨ P.O.Box 1140, al-Guraf, Sana'a ☎ +967 1 332001 🖷 +967 1 332086 **E:** info@ yemen-tv.net **W:** www.yemen-tv.net **Channel 2:** ⌨ P.O.Box 1264, Tawahi, Aden ☎ +967 2 202481 🖷 +967 2 221121. **Txs:** (-).

ZAMBIA

Systems: #PAL-B [E] ⇩2015; DVB-T2 (MPEG4) [E]

National Stations
ZAMBIA NATIONAL BROADCASTING CORP. (Gov) ⌨ P.O.Box 50015, Lusaka 10101 ☎ +260 21 1254989 🖷 +260 21 1254317 **E:** znbctv@znbc.co.zm **W:** www.znbc.co.zm **LP:** DG: Chibamba Kanyama **Chs:** ZNBC TV1, ZNBC TV2 **Txs: TV1:** Kapiri Mposhi ch6 (200kW H), Pemba ch8 (200kW V), Kasama ch8 (16kW H), Kitwe ch9 (200kW H), Lusaka ch10 (200kW H), Senkobo ch10 (200kW V), Chipata ch11 (16kW H) & translators **TV2:** (-) – **MUVI TV (Comm)** ⌨ P.O.Box 33932, Lusaka ☎ +260 21 1253271 **E:** frontoffice@muvitv.com **W:** www.muvitv.com **Txs:** Lusaka ch(-) (2kW) & relay txs.

Local Stations (all Comm)
CBC: 22nd Floor, Findeco House, Lusaka; tx: Lusaka ch(-) 2kW. **Copperbelt Broadcasting Services:** Ndola; tx: Ndola ch(-) 2kW. **Mobi TV:** 25 Mwambula Rd, Lusaka; tx: Lusaka ch(-) 2kW. **Northrise TV:** Lusaka; tx: Lusaka ch(-).

Foreign TV Relay
TBN (USA): Lusaka ch(-).

DTT Transmitters
Licensee: Multichoice Zambia ⌨ P.O.Box 320011, Lusaka ☎ +260 21 1368300 🖷 +260 21 1261533 **E:** mczambia@zambia.multichoice. co.za **Mux✪:** multiprgr **Txs:** (-)

ZIMBABWE

Systems: #PAL-B/G [E] ⇩2013; DVB-T [E] planned

ZIMBABWE TELEVISION (ZTV) (Gov) ⌨ P.O.Box HG 444, Highlands, Harare ☎ +263 4 498610 🖷 +263 4 498613 **E:** zbc@zbc. co.zw **W:** www.zbc.co.zw **LP:** CEO (Zimbabwe Broadcasting Corp.): Happison Muchechetere **Chs:** ZTV1, ZTV2 **Txs: ZTV1:** Gweru ch2 (17.6kW H), Bulawayo ch3 (3kW H) & relay txs; **ZTV2:** (-).

REFERENCE

Section Contents

Features & Reviews

National Radio

International Radio

Frequency Lists

Terrestrial Television

Reference

MAIN COUNTRY INDEX

	Nat	Int	CTB	TV		Nat	Int	CTB	TV
Afghanistan	66	434		612	Djibouti	179	447		622
Alaska	67	434		612	Dominica	179			622
Albania	67	434		612	Dominican Republic	179			622
Algeria	68	435		612	Easter Island	181			622
Andorra	69			612	Ecuador	181	447		622
Angola	69	435		612	Egypt	185	448		622
Anguilla	70	435		613	El Salvador	186			623
Antarctica	70			613	Equatorial Guinea	187	448		623
Antigua & Barbuda	70			613	Eritrea	188		502	623
Argentina	70	435		613	Estonia	188	448		623
Armenia	78	435		613	Ethiopia	188	448	503	623
Aruba	78			613	Falkland Islands	189			623
Ascension Island	79	436		613	Faroe Islands	189			623
Australia	79	436		613	Fiji	189		503	624
Austria	88	437		614	Finland	190	449		624
Azerbaijan	89			614	France	191	449		624
Azores	89			614	French Guiana	200	450		625
Bahamas	90			614	French Polynesia	200			625
Bahrain	91	438		614	French So. & Antarctic Lands	201			625
Bangladesh	91	438		615	Gabon	201	450		625
Barbados	91			615	Galapagos Islands	201			625
Belarus	92	439		615	Gambia	201			625
Belgium	93	439		615	Georgia	202			626
Belize	95			615	Germany	203	450		626
Benin	95	439		616	Ghana	217			627
Bermuda	95			616	Gibraltar	217			627
Bhutan	96			616	Greece	217	452		627
Bolivia	96			616	Greenland	219			628
Bonaire	99	440		616	Grenada	219			628
Bosnia & Herzegovina	100	440		616	Guadeloupe	220			628
Botswana	101	440		616	Guam	220	452		628
Brazil	101			616	Guatemala	220			628
British Indian Ocean Territory	132			616	Guinea	222			628
Brunei	132			617	Guinea-Bissau	222			628
Bulgaria	133	440		617	Guyana	223			628
Burkina Faso	133			617	Haiti	223			629
Burundi	134			617	Hawaii	223			629
Cambodia	134		501	617	Honduras	225			629
Cameroon	135		501	617	Hong Kong	228			629
Canada	136	440		618	Hungary	228			629
Canary Islands	142			618	Iceland	230			629
Cape Verde	143			618	India	230	453	504	630
Cayman Islands	143			619	Indonesia	235	457		630
Central African Rep.	144			619	Iran	240	458	504	630
Chad	144			619	Iraq	241			630
Chile	144	441		619	Ireland	243	460		630
China	147	441	501	619	Israel	244	460		631
Christmas Island	163			619	Italy	245	460		631
Cocos Islands	163			619	Ivory Coast	248			631
Colombia	163			619	Jamaica	248			631
Comoros	169			620	Japan	248	460		631
Congo (Dem. Rep.)	169		502	620	Jordan	252			632
Congo (Rep. of)	170			620	Kazakhstan	252			632
Cook Islands	170			620	Kenya	253			632
Costa Rica	170	445		620	Kiribati	254			632
Croatia	171	446		620	Korea (DPR) (North)	254	461	504	632
Cuba	173	446	502	620	Korea (Rep) (South)	254	462		632
Curaçao	174			620	Kosovo	258			632
Cyprus	175	446		621	Kuwait	258	464		633
Czech Republic	176	447		621	Kyrgyzstan	259	464		633
Denmark	178			621	Laos	259	464		633

GEOGRAPHICAL AREA CODES USED IN WRTH

Codes assigned by the International Telecommunications Union ITU (except * = WRTH code)

Code	Country	Code	Country	Code	Country	Code	Country
ABW	Aruba	D	Germany	LBY	Libya	SDN	Sudan
AFG	Afghanistan	DGA	Diego Garcia	LCA	St. Lucia	SEN	Senegal
AFS	South Africa	DJI	Djibouti	LHW*	Lord Howe Island	SEY	Seychelles
AGL	Angola	DMA	Dominica	LIE	Liechtenstein	SHN	St. Helena
AIA	Anguilla	DNK	Denmark	LSO	Lesotho	SLM	Solomon Islands
ALB	Albania	DOM	Dominican Republic	LTU	Lithuania	SLV	El Salvador
ALG	Algeria	E	Spain	LUX	Luxembourg	SMA	American Samoa
ALS	Alaska	EGY	Egypt	LVA	Latvia	SMO	Samoa
AND	Andorra	EQA	Ecuador	MAC	Macao	SMR	San Marino
AOE	Western Sahara	ERI	Eritrea	MAF	St. Martin	SNG	Singapore
ARG	Argentina	EST	Estonia	MAU	Mauritius	SOM	Somalia
ARM	Armenia	ETH	Ethiopia	MCO	Monaco	SPM	St. Pierre & Miquelon
ARS	Saudi Arabia	F	France	MDA	Moldova	SRB	Serbia
ASC	Ascension Island	FIN	Finland	MDG	Madagascar	SRL	Sierra Leone
ATA	Antarctica	FJI	Fiji	MDR	Madeira	SSD	South Sudan
ATG	Antigua & Barbuda	FLK	Falkland Islands	MEX	Mexico	STP	São Tomé & Príncipe
AUS	Australia	FRO	Faroe Islands	MHL	Marshall Islands	SUI	Switzerland
AUT	Austria	FSA*	French So. & Ant. Lands	MKD	Macedonia	SUR	Suriname
AZE	Azerbaijan	FSM	Micronesia	MLA	Malaysia	SVK	Slovakia
AZR	Azores	G	United Kingdom	MLD	Maldives	SVN	Slovenia
B	Brazil	GAB	Gabon	MLI	Mali	SWZ	Swaziland
BAH	Bahamas	GAL*	Galapagos Islands	MLT	Malta	SXM	St Maarten
BDI	Burundi	GEO	Georgia	MNE	Montenegro	SYR	Syria
BEL	Belgium	GHA	Ghana	MNG	Mongolia	TCA	Turks & Caicos Islands
BEN	Benin	GIB	Gibraltar	MOZ	Mozambique	TCD	Chad
BER	Bermuda	GLP	Guadeloupe	MRA	Northern Mariana Is	TGO	Togo
BES	Bonaire / St Eustatius / Saba	GMB	Gambia	MRC	Morocco	THA	Thailand
		GNB	Guinea-Bissau	MRT	Martinique	TJK	Tajikistan
BFA	Burkina Faso	GNE	Equatorial Guinea	MSR	Montserrat	TKM	Turkmenistan
BGD	Bangladesh	GRC	Greece	MTN	Mauritania	TKL	Tokelau
BHR	Bahrain	GRD	Grenada	MWI	Malawi	TLS	Timor-Leste
BIH	Bosnia & Herzegovina	GRL	Greenland	MYT	Mayotte	TON	Tonga
BIO	British Indian Ocean Territory	GTM	Guatemala	NCG	Nicaragua	TRC	Tristan da Cunha
		GUF	French Guiana	NCL	New Caledonia	TRD	Trinidad & Tobago
BLM	St. Barthélemy	GUI	Guinea	NFK	Norfolk Island	TUN	Tunisia
BLR	Belarus	GUM	Guam	NGR	Niger	TUR	Turkey
BLZ	Belize	GUY	Guyana	NIG	Nigeria	TUV	Tuvalu
BOL	Bolivia	HKG	Hong Kong	NIU	Niue	TWN*	Taiwan
BOT	Botswana	HND	Honduras	NMB	Namibia	TZA	Tanzania
BRB	Barbados	HNG	Hungary	NOR	Norway	UAE	United Arab Emirates
BRM	Myanmar	HOL	Netherlands	NPL	Nepal	UGA	Uganda
BRU	Brunei	HRV	Croatia	NRU	Nauru	UKR	Ukraine
BTN	Bhutan	HTI	Haiti	NZL	New Zealand	URG	Uruguay
BUL	Bulgaria	HWA	Hawaii	OCE	French Polynesia	USA	United States of America
CAF	Central African Republic	I	Italy	OMA	Oman	UZB	Uzbekistan
CAN	Canada	ICO	Cocos (Keeling) Islands	PAK	Pakistan	VCT	St. Vincent & the Grenadines
CBG	Cambodia	IND	India	PAQ	Easter Island		
CHL	Chile	INS	Indonesia	PHL	Philippines	VEN	Venezuela
CHN	China (People's Rep. of)	IRL	Ireland	PLW	Palau	VIR	Virgin Islands
CHR	Christmas Island	IRN	Iran	PNG	Papua New Guinea	VRG	British Virgin Islands
CKH	Cook Islands	IRQ	Iraq	PNR	Panama	VTN	Vietnam
CLM	Colombia	ISL	Iceland	POL	Poland	VUT	Vanuatu
CLN	Sri Lanka	ISR	Israel	POR	Portugal	WAL	Wallis & Futuna
CME	Cameroon	J	Japan	PRG	Paraguay	WAK	Wake Island
CNR	Canary Islands	JMC	Jamaica	PRU	Peru	XGZ	Gaza Strip[1]
COD	Congo (Dem. Rep. of the)	JOR	Jordan	PSE*	Palestine[1]	XWB	West Bank[1]
COG	Congo (Rep. of the)	KAZ	Kazakhstan	PTC	Pitcairn Islands	YEM	Yemen
COM	Comoros	KEN	Kenya	PTR	Puerto Rico	ZMB	Zambia
CPV	Cape Verde	KER	Iles Kerguelen	QAT	Qatar	ZWE	Zimbabwe
CTI	Côte d'Ivoire	KGZ	Kyrgyzstan	REU	Réunion		
CTR	Costa Rica	KIR	Kiribati	RKS*	Kosovo		
CUB	Cuba	KOR	Korea, South	ROD	Rodrigues		
CUW	Curaçao	KRE	Korea, North	ROU	Romania		
CVA	Vatican City State	KWT	Kuwait	RRW	Rwanda		
CYM	Cayman Islands	LAO	Laos	RUS	Russia		
CYP	Cyprus	LBN	Lebanon	S	Sweden		
CZE	Czech Republic	LBR	Liberia	SCN	St. Kitts & Nevis		

[1] The code "PSE" is used as target designation in the "COTB" section of "International Radio/COTB"; otherwise the codes "XGZ"/"XWB" are used.

ABBREVIATIONS & SYMBOLS USED IN WRTH

- ✉ = Address
- ☎ = Telephone
- 🖷 = Fax
- ✪ = Encrypted
- ⌘ = Radio via DTT
- ‡ = inactive
- ± = variable
- acc. = accepted
- Admin. = Administration
- alt. = alternate, alternative
- AM = Amplitude Modulation
- Ann. = Announcement
- Ap. = Apartado
- approx. = approximate(ly)
- Assoc. = Association
- Asst. = Assistant
- Ave = Avenue, Avenida
- B.P. = Boîte Postale
- B'caster = Broadcaster
- Bldg = Building
- Broadc. = Broadcast(ing)
- BS = Broadc. Stn/Sce
- C = Chinese
- C.P. = Case/Caixa Postal, Construction Permit
- Cad. = Cadena
- Cas. = Casilla
- Cd. = Ciudad
- Ce. = Central
- CEO = Chief Exec. Officer
- cf. = refer to
- Ch. = Channel
- Chmn. = Chairman/Chair
- Cl. = Club(e)
- Clan. = Clandestine
- Co. = Company
- Com. = Comunicações
- comm. = commercial
- Contr. = Controller
- Corp. = Corporation
- Cra. = Carrera
- Cult. = Cultura, Cultural
- D = Daily
- d = directional antenna
- D.Prgr = Daily Programme(s)
- DAB = Digital Audio Broadc.
- DMB = Digital Multimedia Broadcasting
- Dem. = Democratic
- Dep. = Deputy
- Dept. = Department
- Depto. = Departamento
- Desp. = Despacho
- DG = Director General
- Dif. = Difusora, Difusão
- Diff. = Diffusion
- Dir. = Director
- Div. = Division
- dom = domestic
- DRM = Digital Radio Mondiale
- DSB = Double Side Band
- DST = Daylight Saving Time
- DTT = Digital Terrestrial TV

- DVB = Digital Video Broadc.
- DX = Long Distance (Reception)
- E = English
- E: = Email
- E.C = Electric Current
- Ea. = East(ern)
- Edif. = Edificio
- Educ. = Education(al), Educación
- e.g. = for example
- Em. = Emis(s)ora
- Eng. = Engineer(ing)
- ERP = Effective Radiated Power
- Esq. = Esquina
- est. = estimated
- Est. = Estado
- exc. = except
- excl. = excluding
- exec. = executive
- ext. = external
- F = French
- F.Pl. = Future Plan(s)
- fed. = federal
- FM = Frequency Modulation
- Fr. = Father
- Freq. = Frequency
- Fri = Friday
- FS = Foreign Service
- Ft. = Fort
- G = German
- G.C = Geographical Coordinates
- GD = General Director
- gen. = general
- GM = General Manager
- Gov. = Government(al)
- Gte. = Gerente
- H = Horizontal Pol.
- h(rs) = hour(s)
- HD = High Definition
- HQ = Headquarters
- HS = Home Service
- I = Italian
- ID = (Station) Identification
- i.e. = that is
- Inc. = Incorporated
- incl. = including
- Inf. = Information
- int. = international
- IRC = Int. Reply Coupon
- irr. = irregular
- IS = Interval Signal
- I./Is = Island/Islands
- kHz = kiloHertz
- L = Local
- L.P = Leading Personnel
- L.T = Local Time
- Langs. = Languages
- Lp. = Low power (transmitter)
- LSB = Lower Side Band
- Ltd = Limited
- LV = La Voz, La Voce

- LW = Longwave
- max. = maximum
- MD = Managing Director
- MF = Mondays-Fridays
- MFN = Multiple Freq. Netw.
- Mgr = Manager
- MHz = MegaHertz
- mil. = military
- Min. = Ministry, Ministerio, Ministério
- min(s) = minute(s)
- Mon = Monday
- Mpal. = Municipal
- Mpo. = Município
- Mt = Mount, Mountain
- Mux = Multiplex
- MW = Mediumwave
- N. = News
- NB = Note (Nota Bene)
- n.f. = nominal frequency
- n/a = not available, not applicable
- nal. = nacional
- nat. = national
- nd = nondirectional antenna
- NE = North East(ern)
- Netw. = Network
- No. = North(ern), Number
- nom. = nominal
- Ntc = Norte
- NW = North West(ern)
- occ. = occasional(ly)
- Op(s) = Operation(s)
- Org. = Organisation
- Ote. = Oeste
- P = Portuguese
- P.O. = Post Office
- P.R. = Public Relations, People's Republic
- PD = Programme Director
- pl. = planned
- Pol. = Polarisation
- Pop. = Population
- Pr. = Praça
- Pr.L = Principal Language(s)
- Pres. = President
- Priv. = Private
- Prgr(s). = Programme(s)
- Prod. = Production
- Prov. = Province, Provincial
- Pt. = Point
- Pte. = Presidente
- Pto. = Puerto
- Pub = Public service
- Pub(s) = Publication(s)
- QSL = Reception Confirmation
- R. = Radio, Rádio, Rádió Radyjo, Radyo
- r. = reported, repeater
- Rdif. = Radiodifusion
- R. Dif. = Radio Difusora
- Rec. = Recording(s)
- Reg. = Region(al)
- Rel. = Relay(s), Relations

- Rep. = Republic
- Rev. = Reverend
- rlg = religious
- Rp. = Return Postage
- Rpt. = (Reception) Report
- S. = San(ta), Sán, Santo
- s/off = sign off
- s/on = sign on
- SAE = Self Addressed Envelope
- SAR = Special Administrative Region
- Sat = Saturday, satellite
- Sce. = Service
- Sched. = Schedule
- SE = South East(ern)
- Secr. = Secretary
- Sen. = Senior
- SFN = Single Freq. Netw.
- Sist. = Sistema
- SM = Station Manager
- So. = South(ern)
- Soc. = Sociedad(e)
- Sp. = Spanish
- SS = Sat/Sun
- SSB = Single Side Band
- St = Saint, Street
- Stn = Station
- Str. = Street, Straße
- Su. = Summer
- Sun = Sunday
- Superv. = Supervisor
- SW = Shortwave South West(ern)
- Syst. = System
- tbd = to be defined
- TD = Technical Director
- techn. = technical
- terr. = terrestrial
- Thu = Thursday
- tr(s) = transmission(s)
- TRP = Transmitter Power
- Tue = Tuesday
- tx(s) = transmitter(s)
- ul. = ulitsa, ulica
- u.c. = under construction
- Univ. = University
- unk. = unknown
- UHF = Ultra High Frequency
- USB = Upper Side Band
- UTC = Coordinated Universal Time
- V = Vertical Pol.
- V. = Verification
- v. = varying/variable
- VHF = Very High Frequency
- VO = Voice of
- W = Weekdays (Mon-Sat)
- W: = Web
- We. = West(ern)
- Wed = Wednesday
- Wi. = Winter
- Wrp. = Weather Report

TRANSMITTER SITES
Location & Decode Tables

INTERNATIONAL TRANSMITTER SITES

Code	Site	Ctry	Lat	Long	SW	MW
-	unidentified	-	-	-	✓	✓
ABH	Abu Hayan	BHR	26N02	050E37	✓	✗
ABS	Abis	EGY	31N08	030E04	✓	✗
ABZ	Abu Zaabal	EGY	30N16	031E22	✓	✗
ADR	Adra	SYR	33N33	036E34	✓	✗
AHW	Ahwaz, Bandar-e Mahshar	IRN	30N37	049E12	✓	✓
AIA	The Valley	AIA	18N13	063W01	✓	✓
AJA	Abuja, Lugbe	NIG	08N58	007E22	✓	✗
ALF	Al Aitahab	SDN	15N35	032E27	✓	✗
ALG	Aligarh	IND	28N00	078E06	✓	✗
ARM	Krasnodar, Tbilisskaya	RUS	45N28	040E06	✗	✓
ASC	English Bay	ASC	07S54	014W23	✓	✗
ASM	Asmara	ERI	15N13	038E52	✓	✗
AVL	Vathy (Avlida municipality)	GRC	38N23	023E36	✓	✗
BAR	Barrigada	GUM	13N29	144E50	✓	✗
BAT	Bata	GNE	01N50	009E47	✓	✗
BCQ	Monticello, ME	USA	46N20	067W49	✓	✗
BDW	Beidweiler	LUX	49N44	006E19	✗	✓
BEC	Béchar ‡	ALG	31N34	002W21	✓	✗
BEI	Beijing, Doudian	CHN	39N38	116E06	✓	✗
BEO	Beograd, Stubline	SRB	44N34	020E09	✓	✗
BGL	Bengaluru, Doddaballapur	IND	13N15	077E29	✓	✗
BIB	Biblis	D	49N41	008E29	✓	✗
BIJ	Bijeljina, Jabanuša	BIH	44N42	019E10	✓	✗
BIS	Bishkek, Krasnaya Rechka	KGZ	42N53	074E59	✓	✓
BJI	Baoji, Qishan, Shaanxi prov.	CHN	34N42	106E57	✓	✗
BKO	Bamako, Kati	MLI	12N45	008W03	✓	✗
BLN	Berlin, Zehlendorf	D	52N47	013E23	✗	✓
BNB	Bonab	IRN	37N18	046E03	✗	✓
BNT	Bandar-e Torkaman	IRN	36N54	054E03	✗	✓
BOC	Bocaue, Bulacan prov.	PHL	14N48	120E55	✓	✗
BON	Bonaire, Tolo	BES	12N13	068W19	✓	✗
BOT	Selebi-Phikwe, Moepeng Hill	BOT	21S57	027E38	✓	✗
BPH	Ban Phachi, Rasom	THA	14N24	100E47	✗	✓
BRA	Brasília, Brazlândia ‡	B	15S36	048W08	✓	✗
BRN	Brandon	AUS	19S31	147E20	✓	✗
BUE	Buenos Aires, General Pacheco	ARG	34S26	058W37	✓	✗
CAH	Changchun, Jilin prov.	CHN	43N44	125E24	✗	✓
CDM	Col de La Madone	F	43N47	007E25	✗	✓
CEN	Monte Ceneri	SUI	46N08	008E59	✗	✗
CER	Cërrik, Shtërmen	ALB	41N00	020E00	✓	✗
CGR	Cape Gkreko	CYP	34N58	034E05	✓	✗
CHB	Chabahar	IRN	25N29	060E32	✗	✓
CHC	Chuncheon	KOR	37N56	127E46	✓	✓
CHJ	Chongjin	KRE	41N45	129E42	✗	✓
CHO	Choybalsan ‡	MNG	48N00	114E27	✗	✓
CLZ	Calabozo ‡	VEN	08N55	067W23	✓	✗
CNI	Chennai	IND	13N08	080E07	✓	✗
CRI	Guápiles, Cariari de Pococí	CTR	10N25	083W43	✓	✗
CRN	Chernivtsi	UKR	48N16	025E53	✗	✓
CRR	Cariari (R. República)	CTR	10N22	083W43	✓	✗
CYP	Zygi	CYP	34N43	033E19	✓	✗
DAN	Dangjin (HLCA)	KOR	36N58	126E37	✗	✓
DEA	Deanovec	HRV	45N42	016E28	✓	✗
DEH	Luxi, Dehong pref., Yunnan prov.	CHN	24N27	098E36	✗	✓
DEL	Delhi	IND	28N43	077E12	✓	✗
DGA	Diego Garcia, British Indian Ocean Terr.	DGA	07S26	072E26	✓	✗
DHA	Dhabbaya	UAE	24N10	054E15	✓	✗
DJI	Djibouti, Dorale	DJI	11N34	043E04	✗	✓
DKA	Dhaka, Khabirpur	BGD	24N00	090E15	✓	✗
DOF	Dongfang, Hainan prov.	CHN	18N53	108E39	✗	✓
DOL	Dole	TZA	06S06	039E15	✗	✓
DRO	Droitwich	G	52N18	002W06	✗	✓
DSB	Dushanbe	TJK	38N29	068E48	✓	✗
DSD	Dresden, Wilsdruff	D	51N04	013E31	✗	✓
EKA	Colombo, Ekala	CLN	07N06	079E54	✓	✗
ELA	El Arish	EGY	31N07	033E42	✗	✓
EMR	Emirler	TUR	39N24	032E51	✓	✗
ERV	Gavar, Noratus	ARM	40N25	045E11	✓	✗
EWN	Vandiver, AL	USA	33N30	086W29	✓	✗
FAN	Fangliao	TWN	22N23	120E34	✗	✓
FLA	Fllaka	ALB	41N22	019E30	✗	✓
GAB	Mouanda, Moyabi	GAB	01S41	013E18	✓	✗
GAL	Bacau, Galbeni	ROU	46N45	026E51	✗	✓
GJW	Geja	ETH	08N47	038E39	✓	✗
GKP	Gorakhpur	IND	26N53	083E28	✓	✗
GOH	Göhren	D	53N32	011E36	✗	✓
GOY	Goyang	KOR	37N36	126E51	✗	✓
GRV	Greenville, NC	USA	35N28	077W12	✗	✓
GUF	Cayenne, Montsinéry	GUF	04N54	052W30	✓	✗
GUW	Guwahati	IND	26N09	091E39	✓	✗
GWE	Gweru, Guinea Fowl	ZWE	19S31	029E56	✓	✗
HAB	La Habana	CUB	22N57	082W33	✓	✗
HAN	Hanoi, Me Tri	VTN	21N00	105E47	✓	✗
HBN	Medorm, Babeldaob Island	PLW	07N27	134E29	✓	✗
HDN	Huadian, Jilin prov.	CHN	43N07	126E31	✗	✓

Code	Site	Ctry	Lat	Long	SW	MW
HDU	Guangzhou, Liantang, Huadu dist.	CHN	23N24	113E14	×	✓
HEI	Shuangyashan, Heilongjiang prov.	CHN	46N43	131E13	×	✓
HJU	Haeju	KRE	38N02	125E43	✓	✓
HKG	Hongkong, Peng Chau	CHN	22N17	114E03	×	✓
HMS	Homs, Saraqeb ‡	SYR	35N52	036E48	×	✓
HNL	Changzhou, Henglin, Jiangsu prov.	CHN	31N42	120E07	×	✓
HRI	Furman, SC	USA	32N41	081W08	✓	×
HUH	Hohhot, Bikeqi, Nei Menggu aut. reg.	CHN	40N48	111E12	✓	×
HUW	Huwei	TWN	23N43	120E25	✓	×
HWA	Hwaseong	KOR	37N13	126E47	✓	×
HWD	Kimchaek, Hwadae county	KRE	40N41	129E12	×	✓
IBA	Iba, Zambales prov.	PHL	15N22	119F57	✓	×
IKO	Ikorodu	NIG	06N36	003E30	✓	×
INB	Red Lion, PA	USA	39N54	076W35	✓	×
IRA	Iranawila	CLN	07N30	079E48	✓	×
IRK	Angarsk, Odinsk	RUS	52N25	103E40	✓	✓
ISK	Yeni Iskele ‡	CYP	35N18	033E55	✓	×
ISL	Islamabad, Hawat	PAK	33N28	073E12	✓	×
ISR	Yavne	ISR	31N54	034E45	✓	×
ISS	Issuudun	F	46N56	001E53	✓	×
IUJ	Yuzhno-Sakhalinsk, Vestochka	RUS	46N51	142E53	✓	×
JAA	Hwaseong, Jeongnam	KOR	37N09	126E59	✓	×
JAK	Jakarta, Cimanggis	INS	06S24	106E52	✓	×
JAL	Jalandhar	IND	31N09	075E47	×	✓
JED	Jeddah, Al Khumra ‡	ARS	21N23	039E25	✓	×
JEJ	Jeju (HLAZ)	KOR	33N29	126E23	×	✓
JES	Vado, NM	USA	32N08	106W36	✓	×
JHR	Milton, FL	USA	30N39	087W05	✓	×
JIN	Jinhua, Lanxi, Zhejiang prov.	CHN	29N07	119E19	✓	×
JOL	Jolfa	IRN	38N56	045E36	×	✓
KAB	Kabul	AFG	34N32	069E20	✓	✓
KAC	Karachi, Landhi ‡	PSK	24N55	067E00	✓	×
KAM	Tehran, Kamalabad	IRN	35N50	050E52	✓	×
KAN	Kangnam	KRE	38N50	125E40	×	✓
KAS	Kashgar (Kashi), Sayibage, Xinjiang Uighur	CHN	39N21	075E46	✓	✓
KBD	Kuwait, Kabd	KWT	29N09	047E46	✓	×
KCH	Grigoriopol, Maiac	MDA	47N17	029E25	✓	✓
KER	Kerman	IRN	30N17	057E05	✓	×
KHO	Khost, Tani	AFG	33N20	069N56	×	✓
KIA	Bandar e-Kiashahr	IRN	37N25	050E01	✓	×
KIG	Kigali, Kinyinya	RRW	01S55	030E07	✓	×
KIM	Gimje	KOR	35N49	126E52	✓	×
KKT	Chinsurah	IND	23N02	088E21	×	✓
KLG	Kaliningrad, Bolshakovo	RUS	54N55	021E42	✓	✓
KLL	Kall, Krekel	D	50N29	006E31	✓	×
KLU	Königslutter	D	52N17	010E44	×	✓
KNG	Kanggye	KRE	41N01	126E39	✓	×
KNX	Kununurra	AUS	15S49	128E40	✓	×
KOU	Kouhu	TWN	23N32	120E10	✓	×
KUJ	Kujang	KRE	40N05	126E07	✓	×
KUN	Kunming, Anning, Yunnan prov.	CHN	24N53	102E30	✓	✓
KWT	Kuwait, Umm Al-Rimam	KWT	29N31	047E40	✓	✓
LAM	Lampertheim	D	49N36	008E32	✓	×
LIS	São Gabriel ‡	POR	38N47	008W42	✓	×
LOD	Lod	ISR	32N00	034E50	✓	×
LRA	Base Antártica Esperanza ‡	ATA	63S24	057W00	✓	×
LUK	Lukang	TWN	24N03	120E25	×	✓
LUS	Lusaka, Makeni Ranch	ZMB	15S32	028E00	✓	×
MAN	Manzini, Mpangela Ranch	SWZ	26S20	031E36	✓	×
MCO	Fontbonne, Mont Agel	F	43N46	007E26	✓	×
MDC	Talata Volonondry	MDG	18S45	047E37	✓	×
MEA	Metula	ISR	33N17	035E34	×	✓
MEK	Mek'ele	ETH	13N30	039E29	×	✓
MEY	Meyerton, Bloemendal	AFS	26S35	028E08	✓	×
MIN	Minhsiung	TWN	23N34	120E26	×	✓
MLK	Bethel, PA ‡	USA	40N29	076W17	✓	×
MNS	Minsk, Kalodziscy	BLR	53N58	027E47	✓	×
MOS	Moosbrunn	AUT	48N00	016E28	✓	×
MRN	Marnach	LUX	50N03	006E05	×	✓
MSK	Moskva	RUS	55N45	037E37	✓	×
MSU	Maseru, Lancer's Gap	LSO	29S19	027E33	×	✓
MTH	Marathon Key, FL	USA	24N42	081W05	×	✓
MUL	Luanda, Mulenvos	AGL	08S51	013E19	✓	×
MUM	Mumbai	IND	19N11	072E48	✓	×
MWV	Mahajanga ‡	MDG	15S43	046E26	✓	×
NAD	Nador	MRC	35N03	002W55	✓	×
NAK	Nakhon Sawan	THA	15N49	100E04	✓	×
NAU	Nauen	D	52N39	012E55	✓	×
NLS	Anchor Point, AK	ALS	59N45	151W44	✓	×
NNN	Nanning, Guangxi Zhuang aut. reg.	CHN	22N48	108E11	✓	×
NOB	Noblejas	E	39N57	003W26	✓	×
NVS	Novosibirsk	RUS	55N55	082E51	✓	✓
OMO	Can Tho, Ô Môn	VTN	10N07	105E34	×	✓
ORG	Ourgla ‡	ALG	31N55	005E04	✓	×
PAN	Panaji	IND	15N27	073E51	✓	×
PAO	Paochung	TWN	23N43	120E18	✓	×
PAR	Parakou	BEN	09N21	002E37	✓	✓
PHP	Poro Point	PHL	16N37	120E17	×	✓
PHT	Tinang	PHL	15N22	120E37	✓	×
POR	Pori	FIN	61N29	021E34	×	✓
PPK	Petropavlovsk-Kamchatskiy, Yelizovo	RUS	53N11	158E25	✓	×
PUG	Palauig	PHL	15N28	119E55	✓	×
PUT	Puttalam	CLN	07N58	079E48	×	✓
PYO	Pyongyang	KRE	39N03	125E42	✓	×
QSH	Qasr-e Shirin	IRN	34N27	045E37	×	✓
QUI	Quito, Mount Pichincha	EQU	00S10	078W32	✓	×
RAJ	Rajkot	IND	22N22	070E41	✓	×
RAN	Rangitaiki	NZL	38S51	176E26	✓	×
RBN	Rabouni	ALG	27N33	008W06	✓	✓
RIY	Riyadh	ARS	24N49	046E52	✓	×
RMI	Hialeah, FL	USA	25N54	080W22	✓	×
RNO	New Orleans, LA	USA	29N50	090W07	✓	×
ROB	Rohrbach	D	48N36	011E33	✓	×
ROU	Roumoules	F	43N48	006E10	×	✓
SAB	Sabrata	LBY	32N36	012E21	✓	×

Code	Site	Ctry	Lat	Long	SW	MW
SAG	Samgo	KRE	38N02	126E32	✗	✓
SAI	Saipan, Agingan Point	MRA	15N07	145E42	✓	✗
SAM	Samara	RUS	53N17	050E14	✓	✗
SAN	Sana'a	YEM	15N23	044E12	✓	✗
SAO	Pinheira	STP	00N18	006E45	✓	✓
SAS	Sasnovy	BLR	53N25	028E31	✗	✓
SBB	Damascus, Sabboura	SYR	33N30	036E07	✗	✓
SDA	Agat, Facpi Point	GUM	13N20	144E39	✓	✗
SEO	Seoul, Incheon (HLKX)	KOR	37N25	126E45	✗	✓
SEP	Sepo	KRE	38N40	127E22	✗	✓
SEY	Mahé	SEY	04S41	055E27	✓	✗
SFA	Sfax, Sidi Mansour	TUN	34N49	010E51	✓	✗
SHA	Kunming, Shalang, Yunnan prov.	CHN	25N41	102E41	✓	✗
SHI	Shijak	ALB	41N20	019E33	✓	✗
SHP	Shepparton	AUS	36S19	145E25	✓	✗
SIR	Sirjan	IRN	29N36	055E47	✓	✗
SIT	Kaunas, Sitkunai	LTU	55N03	023E49	✓	✓
SKN	Skelton	G	54N44	002W53	✓	✗
SKO	Skopje, Sveti Nikole	MKD	41N47	021E53	✗	✓
SLA	A'Seela	OMA	21N55	059E37	✓	✗
SMG	Santa Maria di Galeria	CVA	42N03	012E19	✓	✗
SNG	Singapore	SNG	01N25	103E43	✓	✗
SOF	Sofia, Kostinbrod	BUL	42N49	023E11	✓	✗
SPB	St. Peterburg, Krasnyy Bor	RUS	59N40	030E41	✓	✓
SWO	Sangwon	KRE	38N53	126E06	✗	✓
SZG	Shijiazhuang, Nanpozhuang, Hebei prov.	CHN	38N13	114E06	✓	✗
TAC	Toshkent	UZB	41N13	069E09	✓	✗
TCH	Chita, Kruchina	RUS	51N50	113E43	✓	✓
THU	Thumrait	OMA	17N38	053E56	✓	✗
TIG	Bucuresti	ROU	44N45	026E06	✓	✗
TIN	Tinian	MRA	15N03	145E36	✓	✗
TNN	Tainan	TWN	23N03	120E10	✓	✗
TRM	Trincomalee, Perkara (Former DW Relay)	CLN	08N45	081E08	✓	✓
TSH	Tanshui	TWN	25N11	121E25	✓	✗
TSU	Taiwan (exact site unknown)	TWN	-	-	✓	✓
TTS	Tartus	SYR	34N57	035E53	✗	✓
TTU	Tartu, Kavastu	EST	58N25	027E06	✗	✓
TUT	Tuticorin	IND	08N49	078E05	✗	✓
TWB	Bonaire, Belnem	BES	12N06	068W17	✗	✓
TWR	Merizo	GUM	13N17	144E40	✓	✗
TWW	Lebanon, TN	USA	36N17	086W06	✓	✗

Code	Site	Ctry	Lat	Long	SW	MW
TYB	Tayebad	IRN	34N44	060E48	✗	✓
UBA	Ulaanbaatar, Honhor	MNG	47N48	107E11	✓	✓
UDO	Udon Thani (Udorn), Ban Dung.	THA	17N40	103E12	✓	✗
URU	Ürümqi, Hutubi, Xinjiang Uighur aut. reg.	CHN	44N09	086E54	✓	✓
VAT	Vatican City	CVA	41N54	012E27	✓	✓
VIE	Vientiane	LAO	18N00	102E38	✓	✗
VIR	Virrat, Liedenpohja	FIN	62N23	023E37	✓	✗
VLD	Vladivostok, Razdolnoye	RUS	43N32	131E56	✓	✗
VLN	Vilnius	LTU	54N42	025E13	✗	✓
VNI	Son Tay	VTN	21N12	105E22	✓	✗
WAV	Wavre	BEL	50N45	004E35	✗	✓
WBR	Wachenbrunn	D	50N29	010E33	✗	✓
WCR	Nashville, TN	USA	36N12	086W54	✓	✗
WER	Wertachtal	D	48N05	010E42	✓	✗
WNM	Weenermoor	D	53N12	007E19	✓	✗
WOF	Woofferton	G	52N19	002W43	✓	✗
WRB	Manchester, TN	USA	35N37	086W01	✓	✗
XIA	Xi'an, Xianyang, Shaanxi prov.	CHN	34N22	108E37	✓	✗
XUW	Xuanwei, Yunnan prov.	CHN	26N08	104E01	✗	✓
YAM	Koga, Yamata, Ibaraki prefecture	J	36N10	139E49	✓	✗
YFR	Okeechobee, FL	USA	27N27	080W56	✓	✗
ZAB	Zabol	IRN	31N02	061E33	✗	✓
ZAD	Zadar	HRV	44N14	015E14	✗	✓
ZAH	Zahedan	IRN	29N28	060E52	✓	✗
ZAK	Zakaki (located at Lady's Mile, Akrotiri SBA)	CYP	34N37	033E00	✗	✓

Where the symbol ‡ appears after a site name, this indicates that the site is currently inactive but in a potentially usable, but dormant, state. If a site is known to have been decommissioned or dismantled, it is then removed from the table.

TARGET AREA CODES

Code	Target Area	Code	Target Area	Code	Target Area	Code	Target Area
Af	Africa	Cau	Caucasia	IOc	Indian Ocean	SAf	Southern Africa
Am	Americas	CEu	Central Europe	LAm	Latin America	SAm	South America
As	Asia	EAf	Eastern Africa	ME	Middle East	SAs	Southern Asia
Atl	Atlantic Ocean	EAs	Eastern Asia	Med	Mediterranean	SEA	South East Asia
CAf	Central Africa	EEu	Eastern Europe	NAf	Northern Africa	SEu	Southern Europe
CAm	Central America	Eu	Europe	NAm	North America	WAf	Western Africa
Car	Caribbean	FE	Far East	NEu	Northern Europe	WAs	West Asia
CAs	Central Asia	FER	Far Eastern Russia	Pac	Pacific Ocean	WEu	Western Europe

DOMESTIC SW TRANSMITTER SITES

Coordinate System: WGS84 (rounded)
NB: For coordinates of sites that are jointly used for National and International/COTB services, see the International
Transmitter Sites table
*) Sites not co-located with Int. services: (a) ORTB (b) ZNBC °) unconfirmed locations

Ctry	Site	Lat	Long	Ctry	Site	Lat	Long
AFG	Qalat	32N07	66E56	BOL	S. Ana del Yac.	13S45	065W32
AGL	Luena	11S47	19E55	BOL	Santa Cruz	17S46	063W11
ARG	Malargüe	35S30	069W35	BOL	Siglo Veinte	18S23	066W38
ARG	Mendoza	32S50	068W47	BOL	Trinidad	14S48	064W48
AUS	Alice Springs	23S42	133E53	BOL	Tumupasa	14S09	067W55
AUS	Katherine	14S28	132E16	BOL	Tupiza	21S27	065W43
AUS	Sydney	33S53	151E13	BOL	Uyuni	20S27	066W49
AUS	Tennant Creek	19S40	134E10	BOL	Yura	20S02	066W10
AZE	Stepanakert	39N49	046E44	BRM	Naypyitaw	19N45	096E11
R	Anápolis	16S20	048W58	BRM	Pyin U Lwin	22N01	096E33
B	Aparecida	23S00	045W00	BRM	Taunggyi	20N49	097E02
B	Araguaína	07S16	048W18	BRM	Yangon	16N52	096E09
B	Araraquara	21S47	048W10	BTN	Thimphu	27N29	089E37
B	Belém	01S27	048W29	CAF	Bangui	04N20	018E31
B	Belo Horizonte	19S54	043W54	CAF	Boali	04N53	018E01
B	Boa Vista	02N51	060W43	CAN	Calgary	50N54	113W53
B	Bragança	01S02	046W46	CAN	St. John's	47N34	052W49
B	Cáceres	16S05	057W40	CAN	Toronto	43N30	079W38
B	Cachoeira Paul.	22S39	045W01	CAN	Vancouver	49N08	123W12
B	Camboriú	26S59	048W38	CHL	Putre	18S12	069W35
B	Campinas	22S54	047W06	CHL	Temuco	38S41	072W35
B	Campo Grande	20S24	054W35	CHN	Bayanhot	38N58	105E35
B	Coari	04S08	063W07	CHN	Changsha	28N12	112E58
B	Congonhas	20S30	043W53	CHN	Fuzhou	26N06	119E24
B	Cruzeiro do Sul	07S40	072W39	CHN	Gejiu	23N21	103E08
B	Curitiba	25S23	049W10	CHN	Guiyang	26N25	106E36
B	Florianópolis	27S35	048W31	CHN	Hailar	49N02	119E45
B	Goiânia	16S43	049W18	CHN	Hezuo	35N06	102E54
B	Guajará Mirim	10S50	065W21	CHN	Nanjing	32N02	118E44
B	Guarulhos	23S28	046W32	CHN	Shanghai	31N15	121E29
B	Ibitinga	21S43	048W47	CHN	Shangzhi	45N02	128E00
B	Limeira	22S34	047W25	CHN	Wuchang	44N54	127E11
B	Londrina	23S18	051W13	CHN	Xichang	27N49	102E14
B	Macapá	00N04	051W04	CHN	Xining	36N38	101E36
B	Manaus	03S04	060W00	CLM	Bogotá	04N38	074W05
B	Marília	22S13	049W56	CLM	Puerto Lleras	03N16	073W22
B	Porto Alegre	30S03	051W10	CLM	S. José del Guav.	02N34	072W38
B	Porto Velho	08S45	063W54	CME	Buea	04N10	009E14
B	Rio de Janeiro	22S57	043W13	COD	Bunia	01N32	030E11
B	Santa Maria	29S42	053W42	CTR	San José	09N56	084W05
B	S. Gabriel da Ca.	00S09	067W03	D	Erlangen	49E58	011E00
B	São Paulo	23S33	046W39	DJI	Doraleh	11N35	043E05
B	Tefé	03S24	064W45	DOM	Santo Domingo	18N30	069W57
B	Vitória	20S19	040W21	EQA	Ibarra	00N21	078W08
B	Xapuri	10S40	068W30	EQA	Otavalo	00N18	078W11
BEN	Parakou* (a)	09N20	002E32	EQA	Quito	00S11	078W32
BFA	Ouagadougou	12N26	001W33	EQA	Saquisilí	00S58	078W24
BGD	Savar	23N52	090E16	EQA	Saraguro	03S42	079W18
BOL	Camargo	20S38	065W15	EQA	Tena	01S00	077W48
BOL	Camp. Bolívar	18S29	066W53	ERI	Asmara	15N13	038E53
BOL	Cobija	11S01	068W45	ETH	Addis Ababa	08N58	038E43
BOL	Cochabamba	17S23	066W11	ETH	Geja Dera	08N46	038E40
BOL	La Paz	16S30	068W08	ETH	Adama	08N33	039E14
BOL	Reyes	14S18	067W23	FSM	Ninseitamw	06N58	158E12
BOL	Riberalta	10S59	066W06	GEO	Sokhumi	43N00	041E04
BOL	S. Ignacio de Vel.	16S22	060W57	GNE	Malabo	03N45	008E47
BOL	S. José de Chiqu.	17S53	060W45	GTM	Chiquimula	14N48	089W32

Ctry	Site	Lat	Long	Ctry	Site	Lat	Long
GTM	Guatemala City	14N37	090W31	PNG	Lae	06S41	146E54
GTM	S. Pedro La Lag.	14N46	091W11	PNG	Lorengau	02S01	147E15
GTM	S. Sebastián Coa.	15N30	091W30	PNG	Madang	05S14	145E45
GUI	Conakry	09N41	013W32	PNG	Mendi	06S13	143E39
GUY	Georgetown	06N46	058W14	PNG	Popondetta	08S45	148E15
HND	Comayagüela	14N15	087W20	PNG	Port Moresby	09S26	147E11
HND	San Luís	15N05	088W23	PNG	Rabaul	04S13	152E07
I	Andrate	45N31	007W53	PNG	Tabubil	05S17	141E14
IND	Aizawl	23N43	092E43	PNG	Vanimo	02S42	141E18
IND	Bhopal	23N15	077E29	PNG	Wabag	05S28	143E40
IND	Gangtok	27N20	088E40	PNG	Wewak	03S35	143E40
IND	Guwahati	26N09	091E39	PRG	Asunción	25S16	057W38
IND	Hyderabad	17N20	078E34	PRG	Ypané	25S27	057W32
IND	Imphal	24N37	093E54	PRU	Arequipa	16S25	071W32
IND	Itanagar	27N05	093E35	PRU	Atalaya	10S44	073W46
IND	Jaipur	26N55	075E45	PRU	Bolívar	07S16	077W47
IND	Jammu	32N47	074E49	PRU	Callalli	15S51	072W51
IND	Jeypore	18N55	082E34	PRU	Cerro de Pasco	10S41	076W16
IND	Kohima	25N43	094E02	PRU	Chachapoyas	06S10	077W50
IND	Kolkata	22N22	088E17	PRU	Chiclayo	06S47	079W47
IND	Kurseong	26N55	088E19	PRU	Cusco	13S32	071W57
IND	Leh	34N07	077E35	PRU	Huancabamba	05S14	079W24
IND	Lucknow	26N53	081E03	PRU	Huancavelica	12S45	075W03
IND	Port Blair	11N37	092E45	PRU	Huancayo	12S05	075W12
IND	Shillong	25N34	091E56	PRU	Huanta	12S54	074W13
IND	Shimla	31N10	077E12	PRU	Huánuco	09S55	076W11
IND	Srinagar	34N02	074E54	PRU	Huaraz	09S33	077W31
IND	Thiruvananthap.	08N27	076E56	PRU	Iquitos	03S51	073W13
INS	Fakfak	02S55	132E18	PRU	Jaén	05S43	078W48
INS	Jambi	01S38	103E34	PRU	Junín	11S11	076W00
INS	Kendari	03S58	122E34	PRU	Líma	12S06	077W03
INS	Makassar	05S10	119E25	PRU	Panao	09S54	075W58
INS	Nabire	03S22	135E29	PRU	Puerto Maldon.	12S37	069W11
INS	Palangkaraya	02S12	113E50	PRU	Quillabamba	12S49	072W41
INS	Pontianak	00S05	109E16	PRU	Santa Cruz	06S40	079W00
INS	Serui	01S53	136E14	PRU	Santa Monica	07S10	078W30
INS	Ternate	00N48	127E23	PRU	Sicuani	14S15	071W12
INS	Wamena	04S06	138E57	PRU	Sóndor	05S19	079W25
IRQ	Salah ad-Din°	33N58	044E10	PRU	Tarma	11S28	075W41
IRQ	Sulaimaniyah°	35N34	045E19	PRU	Wanchaq	13S31	071W58
J	Nagara	35N28	140E12	PRU	Yurimaguas	05S54	076W07
J	Nemuro	43N17	145E34	RUS	Arkhangelsk	64N21	041E23
KRE	Hamhung	39N55	127E31	RUS	Arman	59N42	150E10
KRE	Hyesan	41N23	128E10	RUS	Krasnoyarsk	56N02	092E45
KRE	Pyongsong	40N14	125E49	RUS	Kyzyl	51N41	094E36
KRE	Sariwon	38N31	125E46	RUS	Monchegorsk	68N04	032E58
LAO	Sam Neua	20N25	104E04	RUS	Selenginsk	52N02	106E56
LBR	Monrovia	06N14	010W42	RUS	Yakutsk	62N14	129E49
MDG	Ambohidrano	18S47	047E29	SDN	Omdurman	15N35	032E26
MEX	Mérida	20N58	089W37	SLM	Honiara	09S25	160E03
MEX	México	19N26	099W08	SOM	Hargaysa	09N34	44E04
MEX	San Luis Potosí	22N01	100W59	TCD	N'Djaména	12N07	015E05
MNG	Altay	46N19	096E15	TWN	Guanyin	25N02	121E06
MNG	Mörön	49N37	100E10	TZA	Dole	06S06	039E15
MTN	Nouakchott	18N08	015W60	UGA	Kampala	00N19	032E37
NGR	Niamey	13N32	002E04	UGA	Mukono	00N21	032E45
NIG	Kaduna	10N45	007E33	URG	Artigas	30S25	056W29
NPL	Khumaltar	27N39	085E20	URG	Castillos	34S16	053W56
PNG	Alotau	10S18	150E28	URG	Montevideo	34S50	056W18
PNG	Buka	05S25	154E40	URG	Sarandí del Yi	33S22	055W38
PNG	Daru	09S05	143E10	URG	Tacuarembó	31S43	055W59
PNG	Kavieng	02S34	150E48	VTN	Buôn Mê Thuôt	12N40	108E12
PNG	Kerema	07S59	145E46	VTN	Xuân Mai	20N53	105E34
PNG	Kimbe	05S36	150E10	VUT	Port-Vila	17S45	168E22
PNG	Kundiawa	06S00	144E57	ZMB	Lusaka* (b)	15S30	028E15

CLUBS FOR DXERS & INTERNATIONAL LISTENERS

This section lists non-commercial hobby clubs serving international radio enthusiasts. Most clubs are orientated to DXing, the reception of distant radio stations, some are oriented to programme listening. Many clubs produce bulletins on a regular basis. Sample copies of printed periodicals are generally available for return postage (3 or 4 IRCs, or equivalent currency). For officially multilingual countries, the language(s) used in club publications (and/or activities) is indicated when known; for non-English speaking countries also if a publication is partly or entirely in English: EE = English, FF = French, GG = German, II = Italian, JJ = Japanese, SS = Spanish. This list does not include clubs run by commercial publications or by individual broadcasters.

EUROPE

European DX Council (EDXC) (Umbrella organization of DX Clubs in Europe) c/o Tibor Szilagyi, Ringvägen 86, 13731 Västerhaninge, Sweden. General Secretary: Tibor Szilagyi (**E:** tiszi2035@yahoo.com), Vice General Secretary: Ingvar Kohlström (**E:** ingvar.kohlstrom@telia.com) **W:** www.edxc.org; edxcnews.wordpress.com (blog)

AUSTRIA: Austrian DX Board (ADXB-OE) (Club der Freunde elektronischer Medien - Rundfunk global) , Postfach 1000, 1082 Wien. **E:** office@adxb-oe.org **W:** www.adxb-oe.org Pub: *Rundbrief* (quarterly). Annual DX camp. Member of AGDX (Germany)

BELGIUM: DX-Antwerp, Steynstraat 104, 2660 Hoboken. (Flemish) **E:** info@dx-antwerp.com **W:** www.dx-antwerp.com – **Belgique Radio-Loisirs**, B.P. 12, 7160 Chapelle-lez-Herlaimont. (FF)

BULGARIA: Association of Balkan Cross-band DXers (ABCDX), c/o Rumen Pankov, P.O.Box 199, 1000 Sofia-C **E:** rumen_pankov@yahoo.co.uk – **Bulgarian DX Club plus Satellite**, c/o Ivan Penev, Simeon Radev 40-V, 1618 Sofia **☎** +359 2 855/143 **E:** ipenev@mail.orbitel.bg

CZECH REPUBLIC/SLOVAKIA: Czechoslovak DX Club (CSDXC), c/o Václav Dosoudil, Horní 9, 768 21 Kvasice, Czech Republic. **E:** mail@dx.cz **W:** www.dx.cz Pub: *Radio revue*

DENMARK: Danish Shortwave Club International (DSWCI), Tavleager 31, 2670 Greve. **E:** kaj.bredahl@mail.dk **W:** www.dswci.org Pub (all EE): *Shortwave News*, *DX-Window* (bi-weekly by email), *Tropical Bands Monitor* (monthly), *Domestic Broadcasting Survey* (Annual) – **Dansk DX Lytter Klub (DDXLK)**, P.O.Box 112, 8960 Randers SØ. **E:** ddxlk@ddxlk.net **W:** ddxlk.net Pub: *DX-FOKUS* (bimonthly)

FINLAND: Suomen DX-liitto ry (SDXL), P.O.Box 454, 00100 Helsinki (Umbrella organization of Finnish language DX clubs) **E:** toimisto@sdxl.org **W:** www.sdxl.org Pub: *Radiomaailma* (Finnish/EE) – **Finlands Svenska DX-Förbund rf (FSDXF)**, P.O.Box 9, 68601 Jakobstad (Umbrella organization of Swedish language DX clubs in Finland). **E:** info@fsdxf.org **W:** uk.groups.yahoo.com/group/fsdxf (newsgroup)

FRANCE: Monde & Radiodiffusion, 65 Montée des Princes, 84100 Orange. – **Radio Club de la Poste**, c/o Marcel Lecerf, 13 avenue St Michel, 54220 Malzéville. – **Radio Club du Perche**, 12 rue du Grand Thuret, 72320 Greez sur Roc. – **Radio Club International Ondes Courtes**, 19 lot Saturne, 26120 Malissard. – **Radio DX Club d'Auvergne**, Centre Municipal P. et M. Curie, 2 bis, Rue du Clos Perret, 63100 Clermont-Ferrand. – **Union des Écouteurs Français**, BP 31, 92242 Malakoff Cédéx. **E:** tsfinfo@u-e-f.net **W:** www.u-e-f.net

GERMANY: Arbeitsgemeinschaft DX e.V. (AGDX), Postfach 1214, 61282 Bad Homburg (Umbrella organization for the German DX clubs adxb-DL, Kurzwellenfreunde Sachsen, UKW/TV Arbeitskreis der AGDX, Worldwide DX Club, and for the Austrian DX-Board) **E:** mail@agdx.de **W:** www.agdx.de – **Assoziation Deutschsprachiger Kurzwellenhörer e.V. (ADDX)**, Scharsbergweg 14, 41189 Mönchengladbach. **E:** kurier@addx.de **W:** www.addx.de Pub: *Radio-Kurier* – **Assoziation Junger DXer e.V. (adxb-DL)**, c/o Thomas Schubaur, Neufnachstr. 30, 86850 Fischach. **E:** dl1ts@t-online.de **W:** www.adxb-dl.de – **Deutscher Welt-Radioclub e.V. (DWRC)**, c/o Bernd Schilling, Hüling 11, 53332 Bornheim. – **Eastside DX (EDX)**, c/o Jens Adolph, 04159 Leipzig-Wahren (Pittler) **E:** eastsidedx@mail.com – **Freundeskreis Berliner Empfangsamateure e.V.**, Postfach 200113, 13511 Berlin. **E:** mittelwelle@genion.de – **Hamburger Freunde des Rundfunkfernempfangs**, c/o Dieter Schäfer, Am Sportplatz 18, 24629 Kisdorf. **E:** dl1lad@darc.de – **Kurzwellenfreunde Brand**, c/o Hans-Jürgen Schmelzer, Mitterteicher Str. 15, 95643 Tirschenreuth. **E:** hugotir@t-online.de – **Kurzwellenclub Schwalmtal e.V.**, c/o Helmut Reitzer Jr, Willy-Rösler-Str. 41, 41366 Schwalmtal. **E:** dk0kws@qsl.net **W:** www.qsl.net/dk0kws – **Kurzwellenfreunde Rhein/Ruhr e.V.**, c/o U. Schnelle, Kurfürstenstr. 37, 45883 Gelsenkirchen. **E:** infohq@kwfr.de **W:** www.kwfr.de – **Kurzwellenfreunde Sachsen (KWFS)**, c/o AGDX e.V., Postfach 1214, 61282 Bad Homburg. **E:** dk5tl@qsl.net – **Kurzwellenfreunde Wuppertal (KWFW)**, c/o Worner Kortmann, Postfach 220342, 42373 Wuppertal. – **Kurzwellenring Süd (KWRS)**, c/o Thomas Schubaur, Neufnachstr. 30, 86850 Fischach. **E:** adxbld@kwrs.de **W:** www.kwrs.de – **Oldenburger Kurzwellenfreunde**, c/o Olaf C. Hänßler, Sandweg 98, 26135 Oldenburg. **E:** olaf.haenssler@informatik.uni-oldenburg.de **W:** www.member.uni-oldenburg.de/olaf.haenssler/olaf/OKF – **Radio Japan Club Brilon (RJCB)**, c/o Reinhard Reese, Niederbeckstr. 23, 40472 Düsseldorf. **E:** rreese@gmx.net **W:** radio-japan-club-brilon.gmxhome.de – **Rhein-Main-Radio-Club e.V. (RMRC)**, Postfach 700849, 60558 Frankfurt. **E:** mail@rmrc.de **W:** www.rmrc.de. **UKW/TV Arbeitskreis der AGDX**, c/o H.-J. Kuhlo, Wilhelm-Leuschner-Str. 293B, 64347 Griesheim. (FM/TV only) **E:** sekretariat@ukwtv.de **W:** www.ukwtv.de – **Worldwide DX Club (WWDXC)**, Postfach 1214, 61282 Bad Homburg. **E:** mail@wwdxc.de **W:** www.wwdxc.de. Pub: *DX-Magazine* (EE)

HUNGARY: FM DX Club, **E:** fmdx@ha5kfu.hu **W:** fmdx.ha5kfu.hu – **Hungarian DX Club**, Beke utca 85, 2519 Piliscsév. **E:** tiszi2035@yahoo.com

IRELAND: Irish DX Radio Club, c/o Edward Dunne, 17 Anville Drive, Kilmacud, Stillorgan, Co. Dublin **E:** irishdxclub@live.ie Pub: *MediaWatch* (by email)

ITALY: Associazione Italiana Radioascolto (A.I.R.), C.P. 1338, 10100 Torino (AD). **E:** info@air-radio.it **W:** www.air-radio.it Pub: *Radioarama* (monthly) – **BCL Sicilia Club**, c/o Roberto Scaglione, C.P. 119, Succ. 34, 90144 Palermo (PA). **E:** bclsiciliaclub@inwind.it **W:** www.bclnews.it – **Coordinamento del Radioascolto (Co. Rad)**, c/o Dario Monferini (Web-based umbrella organisation of various Italian DX clubs) **E:** info@corad.net **W:** www.corad.net – **FM-DX Italy**, c/o Fabrizio Carnevalini (Web-based, FM-TV DX only) **E:** fabrizio58it@yahoo.it **W:** www.fmdx.altervista.org – **Gruppo d'Ascolto della Marca Trevigiana**, C.P. 3, Succ. 10, 31100 Treviso (TV). – **Gruppo d'Ascolto Radio dello Stretto**, c/o Giovanni Sergi, Via Sibari 40, 98149 Messina (Camaro Inferiore). **E:** gsergi5050@hotmail.com **W:** www.polistenaweb.it/gars (II) Pub: *Radio Notizie* (quarterly - print & pdf) – **Gruppo d'Ascolto Radio Televisivo della Sicilia**, c/o Gioacchino Stallone, Via G.Falcone 11, Lotto 27, interno 3, 91025 Marsala (TP). (local activity) – **Gruppo Radio Ascolto Bologna**, c/o Elio Antonucci (Web-based) **E:** radioascolto@elio.org **W:** www.elio.org/radioascolto – **Play-DX**, c/o Dario Monferini, Via Davanzati 8, 20158 Milano (MI). (II/EE/SS) (specialises in difficult DX) **E:** info@playdx.com **W:** www.playdx.com Pub: *PLAY-DX* (weekly)

NETHERLANDS: Benelux DX Club (BDXC), Rietdekkerstraat 40,

1445 KG Purmerend. **E:** secretaris@bdxc.nl **W:** www.bdxc.nl Pub: *BDXC-Bulletin* (Dutch/EE)

NORWAY: DX Listeners' Club (DXLC), c/o Jan Alvestad, Vigdelsveien 637B, 4054 Tjelta. **E:** sveinope@online.no **W:** dxlc. wordpress.com Pub: *DX-News*

RUSSIA: Club of DX-ers, c/o Vadim Alexeew, P.O.Box 65, 125581 Moscow. **E:** gusev@itep.ru **W:** www.radio.hobby.ru — **Irkutsk DX Club:** c/o Feodor Brazhnikov, P.O.Box 3036, 664059 Irkutsk. **E:** brazhnikov@yahoo.com **W:** www.irkutsk.com/radio — **Novosibirsk DX Club**, c/o Igor Yaremenko, Novosibirsk. **E:** dx@ngs.ru **W:** www. novosibdx.info — **Russian DX League**, c/o Anatoly Klepov, ul. Tvardovskogo 23-365, 123458 Moscow. **E:** rusdx@yandex.ru **W:** rusdx.narod.ru — **Sankt-Peterburg DX Club**, c/o Alexey Osipov, P.O.Box 46, 195213 Sankt-Peterburg. **E:** dxspb@vfemail.net — **Tomsk DX Club**, c/o Vladimir Kovalenko, Tomsk. **E:** tomskdx@mail.ru

SPAIN: Asociación DX Barcelona (ADXB), P.O. Box 335, 08080 Barcelona. **E:** info@mundodx.net **W:** www.mundodx.net Pub: *Mundo DX* - multimedia (SS/Catalan) — **Asociación Española de Radioescucha (AER)**, Apartado 10014, 50080 Zaragoza. **E:** sedano@lander.es **W:** www.aer-dx.org — **S500 DX Club**, c/o Álvaro López Osuma, c/ Santa Micaela, 1 2° Derecha, 18015 Granada. **E:** alvak7@yahoo.es **W:** www.upv.es/~csahuqui/julio/s500. Pub: *SW DX newsletter* (four-monthly)

SWEDEN: Arctic Radio Club (ARC), c/o Tore Larsson, Frejagatan 14A, 52143 Falköping (MW only) **E:** tore.larsson@beta.telenordia. se Pub: *MV-Eko* (Swedish/EE, by email) — **Sveriges DX Förbund (SDXF)**, Box 1097, 40523 Göteborg (Umbrella organization). **E:** sdxf@ sdxf.se **W:** www.sdxf.se Pub: *Eter-aktuellt*

SWITZERLAND: Radio- und Fernseh-Club Basel und Umgebung (RFCB), Postfach 354, 4015 Basel. (GG) **E:** hb9b@rfcb. ch **W:** www.rfcb.ch

UNITED KINGDOM: British DX Club (BDXC), 10 Hemdean Hill, Caversham, Reading RG4 7SB. **E:** bdxc@bdxc.org.uk **W:** www.bdxc. org.uk Pub: *Communication* — **International Shortwave League (ISWL)**, c/o Peter Lewis, 18 Bittaford Wood, Ivybridge, Devon, PL21 0ET. **E:** vfgnsu@yahoo.co.uk **W:** www.iswl.org.uk — **Medium Wave Circle (MWC)**, c/o Herman Boel, Papeveld 3, 9320 Erembodegem-Aalst, Belgium (LW/MW only) **E:** herman@hermanboel.eu **W:** www. mwcircle.org

AFRICA

IVORY COAST: DX-Ivoire, c/o Jibirila Liasu, B.P. 197, Abidjan 20. (FF)

KENYA: DX Listeners' Club, c/o Oscar Machuki, PO Box 646, Kisii 4-0200. (EE/Swahili) (SW only) ☎ +254 721 534171 **E:** oscarmogire@yahoo.com

NIGERIA: Africa DX Association, c/o Mr. Friday I. Okoloise, NITEL, P.M.B. 23, Lafia, Plateau State. (EE) — **International DX Club**, Emmanuel Ezeani, P.O.Box 1633, Sokoto, Sokoto State. (EE) **E:** idxerclub@yahoo.com; emmanuel_ezeani@yahoo.com

SÃO TOMÉ & PRÍNCIPE: Clube DX-STP, c/o Leal Bouças, Av. 12 de Julho, Vila Maria (C.P. 490), São Tomé. **E:** petterboudx@ hotmail.com

TANZANIA: Kemogemba DX Listeners Club, c/o Ras Franz Manko Ngogo, P.O.Box 71, Tarime, Mara. (EE/Swahili)☎ + 255 755 814704 **E:** kemogemba@yahoo.com

TOGO: Club Inter Amitié Radio, CCF, B.P. 2090, Lomé. (FF) — **Groupe Endoc**, B.P. 2667, Lomé. (FF)

TUNISIA: Club des Auditeurs et de l'Amitié, c/o De Riadh Sakka, Route de Gremda Merkez Sahnoun, 3012 Sfax. (FF)

UGANDA: International DX Club of East Africa, c/o Samuel Ouma, P.B.Box 565, Iganga. (EE) ☎ +256 772 444201 **E:** samuel. ouma@talk21.com

ASIA

BANGLADESH: Aurora Listeners' Club, c/o Miss Kakali Rani, Harida Khalsi-6403, Madhnagar-Natore-6400 — **Basupara DX Listeners Club**, c/o Asfaqul Alam, Basupara, Nandangachi, Rajshahi 6260. **E:** bdxls@uymail.com — **International Radio Listeners Club**, Konabari, P.O.Nilnagor, Gazipur, Dhaka. (EE/Bengali) — **Online DX Forum**, c/o MD Azizul Alam Al-Amin, Gourhanga, Ghoramara, Rajshahi 6100. **E:** mtech@rajbd.com. — **Rose DW Listeners Club**, c/o Ashik Eqbal "Tokon", Luximpur Greater Rd, G.P.O.Box 56, Rajshahi 6000. **E:** rosedwlc@yahoo.com **W:** rosedwlc.webs.com. Pub: *DX-Net* (Bengali)

INDIA: Apollo DX International, c/o Deepak Kumar Das, Dholi Sakra 843105, Dist. Muzaffarpur, Bihar. **E:** deepakdx@rediffmail. com — **Ardic DX Club**, c/o Jaisakthivel, T., Dept of Communication, Manonmaniam Sundranar University, Abishekapatti Post, Tirunelveli 627012, Tamil Nadu. ☎ +91 98413 66086 Pub: *DXers Guide* (EE quarterly), *Sarvadesa Vanoli* (Tamil monthly). DX Prgr: Vaanoli Ulagam on AIR (Tamil) and Gyanvani 105.6MHz Tirunelvedi (EE). **E:** ardicdx-club@yahoo.co.in **W:** dxersguide.blogspot.com — **Chaudhary Srota Sangh**, c/o Santosh Kumar (President), Kharauna Jairam, Kharauna Dih 843113, Dist. Muzaffarpur, Bihar — **Chennai DX Club**, c/o K. Raja, 21 JP Koil St, Old Washermenpet, Chennai 600021, Tamil Nadu. **E:** chennaidxclub@gmail.com — **El Nino Electronics DX Club**, c/o Partha Sarathi Goswami, Kishalay, College Road, Siliguri 734001, Darjeeling, West Bengal. **E:** elnino@dxinginfo.com **W:** www. dxinginfo.com ☎ +91 94343 27414 — **Foreign Radio Listeners' Club**, c/o Prasenjit Bhakat, 313/8 Ghoradhara, P.O Jhargram 721507, West Bengal. ☎ +91 3221 256084 **E:** frlclub@gmail.com — **Globe Radio DX Club (GRDXC)**, c/o Harjot Singh Brar, P.O.Box 158, Chandigarh 160017, Chandigarh. **E:** grdxc@yahoo.co.in — **India DX Club International**, GPO Box 646, Kolkata 700001, West Bengal. **E:** idxc.international@gmail.com **W:** www.idxci.in — **International DX Association**, c/o Bedanta Das, 1-No,Galiahati, Near Night School, Barpeta 781301, Assam. ☎ +91 3665 236267 **E:** das884@gmail.com Pub: *DX Times* (EE) — **Metali Listeners' Club**, c/o Mr Shivendu Paul, 49/36, Dr SG Dhar Lane, P.O. Khagra, Dist. Murshidabad 742103, West Bengal. **E:** metalilistenersclub@gmail.com ☎ +91 94348 58497 — **Minnakkal Kurinji DX Club**, c/o E. Selvaraj, Choolaimedu Street, Minnakkal Post, Dist. Namakkal 637505, Tamil Nadu. **E:** selvarajminnakkal@gmail.com — **Paribar Bandhu SWL Club**, c/o Mr Anand Mohan Bain, UCO Bank, 47/6, Nehru Nagar, P.O. Nehru Nagar, Bhilai, Dist. Durg 490020, Chattisgarh. **E:** anand_mohan10@ yahoo.com ☎ +91 94255 21083, +91 78840 31648. — **Pollachi Radio Club**, c/o Mr. N. Lakshmanan, Sri Mugha Bhavan, 44/77 Lac Colony, Dr Ansari Street, Pollachi 642001, Tamil Nadu. ☎ +91 98650 16402 **E:** pollachidxclub@yahoo.co.in **W:** pollachiradioclub. blogspot.com (blog) — **Span Radio Listeners' Club**, c/o A Ragu, Nandavankula Theru, Vedaraniam 614810, Tamil Nadu. ☎ +91 4369 318808 — **Utkarna Shrota Sangha**, c/o Mr. Rajib Bandopadhyay, Amrita Bhaban, P.O. Makardah 711409, Dist. Howrah, West Bengal ☎ +91 94334 28609, **E:** ussrajib@gmail.com — **World DX Club & Library**, c/o Baidyanath Upadhyaya, At Khairabarigaon, P.O. Khawrang, Udalguri 784509, Darrang, Assam. — **World DXing Club**, c/o Mr Madhab Ch. Sagour, 93/1, Mitrapara Road, P.O. Naihati 743 165, 24 Parganas (North), West Bengal. — **World Radio Club**, c/o Mr. Biswanath Mandal, Chak Harharia, P.O. Islampur 742304, Dist. Murshidabad, West Bengal ☎ +91 3481 236534 **E:** bmandalwrc@ rediffmail.com — **Young Stars Radio Club**, c/o Mr Hari Madugula, 40 Hastinapura Colony, Raghavendra Residency-FF4, Sainikpuri, Secunderabad 500094, Andhra Pradesh. **W:** http://ysrc.webs.com — **Youth International Radio Listeners' Club**, c/o Mr. Pranab Kumar Roy, Vill + PO, Shyamnagar, 741 155, Via Palashipara, Nadia, West Bengal. ☎ +91 3471 252163 **E:** etherbarta@gmail.com Pub: *Etherbarta* (Bengali), *Radio Monitors' Guide* (EE)

INDONESIA: Borneo Listeners Club, Jalan Timur Penjajap 3 A, Pemangka Kab. Sambas 79453, Kalimantan Barat. (Indonesian/ EE). **E:** h.rudi@yahoo.co.id **W:** www.bielsiklub.blogspot.com Pub: *Mediator* — **Indonesian DX Club (IDXC)**, P.O.Box 50, Kutoarjo 54201. (EE/Indonesian). **E:** contact@idxc.org **W:** www.idxc.org — **MAPEM Club**, c/o M. Jayadi D., 02 Tromolpos Pringgabaya, East Lombok, West Nusa Tenggara 83654. **E:** mapemclub2020@gmail. com **W:** mapem-club.org — **Media Monitoring Club**, c/o Summase A. Sanjaya, P.O.Box 1157 MKS, Makassar 90000. **E:** monitoringclub@ yahoo.co.id **W:** monitoringclub.org

JAPAN: Asian Broadcasting Institute (ABI), P.O.Box 2334, Ginza Branch, Japan Post, Tokyo 100-8698. **E:** info@abiweb.jp **W:** www.abiweb.jp – **Indonesian DX Circle Japan**, c/o Atusnori Ishida, 1-16-201 Teranishi, Saichi-cho, Iwakura-shi, Aichi 42-0036 – **Japan BCL Federation**, 1-9-23 Tadao, Machida City, Tokyo 194-0035. **E:** mywave@m2.ocv.ne.jp – **Japanese Association of DXers**, P.O.Box 1766, Tokyo 100-91. (JJ/EE) – **Japan Short Wave Club (JSWC)**, P.O.Box 44, Kamakura 248-8691. (JJ/EE) ☎🖷 +81 467 43 2167 **E:** jswchq@live.jp Pub: *SW DX Guide* (JJ/EE) – **Nagoya DXers Circle (NDXC)**, c/o Shigenori Aoki, 302 Yanagimori, Nakagawa-ku, Nagoya 454-0871. **W:** www.ndxc.org – **Radio Nuevo Mundo**, Tetsuyu Hirahara, 5-6-6 Nukuikita, Koganei-shi, Tokyo 184-0015

KOREA (SOUTH): Northeast Asian Broadcasting Institute (NEABI), c/o SeKyung Park, #103-302, Geumho Apt, 240-32 Yeomchang-dong, Gangseo-gu, Seoul 157-861. **E:** neabipress@gmail.com **W:** www.neabi.com Pub: *Reports* (Korean, monthly)

NEPAL: Friendship Radio Club, c/o Mr Umesh Regmi, Tanki Sinuwari 5, District Morang, Biratnagar. **E:** friendshipradioclub@yahoo.com – **Listeners' Club of Nepal** (Reg. No.144), P.O.Box 126, Biratnagar-4. – **Small Giant Radio Listener Club** (Reg. No.17), P.O.Box 21110, Kathmandu

PAKISTAN: International Radio Listeners Club, Karachi. **E:** irl-club@hotmail.com **W:** irlclub.googlepages.com – **National Society of Pakistani DXers**, E-161/1, Iqbal Park, opposite Adil Hospital, Defence Housing Society Rd, Lahore Cantt. – **Pakistan Aafaqie Lehrain Society (PALS)**, c/o Asrar Chaudhary, Dusehra Ground, Shoikhupura 39350, Punjab. Pub: *Newsletter Aafaqie Lehrain* (Urdu with EE section) **E:** pals_swlc@yahoo.com **W:** www.pals2000.webs.com – **Pakistani Shortwave Listeners' Association**, c/o Muhammad Imran Mehr, 38/2 Habib Colony, Bahawalpur 63108, Punjab. ☎ +92 334 6865847, +92 300 6801719. **E:** imran.mehr@gmail.com Pub: *Radio World* (bi-monthly by email) – **Wonderful World of Shortwave (WWSW)**, c/o Baber Shehzad, 43 Habib Colony, Bahawalpur 63108, Punjab. **E:** baber73@yahoo.com. Pub: *News Letter of Pakistani DX-ers* (by email)

SRI LANKA: Union of Asian DXers (UADX), c/o Victor Goonetilleke, "Shangri-La" 298 Kolamunne, Piliyandala. **E:** victor.goonetileke@gmail.com Blog: dxasia-uadx.blogspot.com (EE)

PACIFIC

AUSTRALIA: Australian Radio DX Club (ARDXC), c/o John Wright, 29 Milford Road, Peakhurst, NSW 2210. **E:** dxer1234@gmail.com **W:** www.ardxc.info – **The Electronic DX Press Radio Monitoring Association (EDXP)**, c/o Bob Padula, 404 Mont Albert Road, Mont Albert, VIC 3127. (Web-based club). **E:** bobpadula@mydesk.net.au **W:** edxp.yolasite.com

NEW ZEALAND: New Zealand Radio DX League, P.O.Box 39-596, Howick, Manukau 2145. **E:** secretary@radiodx.com **W:** radiodx.com Pub: *NZ DX Times* (monthly)

NORTH AMERICA

CANADA: Canadian International DX Club (CIDX), P.O.Box 67063-Lemoyne, St. Lambert, QC J4R 2T8. **E:** cidxclub@yahoo.com **W:** www.cidx.ca – **Club d'Ondes Cortes du Québec**, c/o Dominique Duplessis, 5120 35ème rue, Grand-Mère, QC G9T 3N6. (FF) **E:** dduplessis@infoteck.qc.ca – **Ontario DX Association (ODXA)**, 3211 Centennial D., Apt. 23, Vernon, BC V1T 2T8. **E:** odxa@rogers.com **W:** www.odxa.on.ca – **Vancouver Shortwave Association**, P.O.Box 500, 2245 Eton St., Vancouver, BC V5L 1C9

MEXICO: Audio Pico DX Club, c/o César Granillo, Ap. Postal 309, 94301 Orizaba, Veracruz – **Club DX Miguel Auza**, c/o Luis Antero Aguilar, Ap. Postal 38, 98330 Miguel Auza, Zacatecas – **Consultorio DX**, c/o Miguel Ángel Rocha Gámez, Ap. Postal 31, 31820 Ascensión, Chihuahua – **Nayarit DX Club**, Ap. Postal 62, 63001 Tepic, Nayarit. **W:** www.naydx.8m.com – **Sociedad de Ingenieros Radioescuchas**, c/o Rafael Gustavo Grajeda Rosado, Ap. Postal 203, Admon. No.1, 91701 Veracruz, Veracruz. **E:** rggr681121@hotmail.com

USA: American Shortwave Listeners Club (ASWLC), c/o Stewart MacKenzie, 16182 Ballad Lane, Huntington Beach, CA

92649. – **Boston Area DXers**, c/o Paul Graveline, 9 Stirling St., Andover, MA 01810-1408. – **Central Indiana Shortwave Club**, c/o Steve Hammer, 2517 E. DePauw Road, Indianapolis, IN 46227-4404. – **Chicago Area DX Club**. Now defunct. Archive of articles at http://home.earthlink.net/~dxchicago/ – **DecaloMania**, c/o Phil Bytheway, 9705 Mary NW, Seattle, WA 98117-2334. (Club for collectors of station promo, items and airchecks). **E:** phil_tekno@yahoo.com **W:** www.anarc.org/decal Pub: *DecalcoMania* – **Hampton Roads DX Association**, c/o Dr. Marc Fink, P.O.Box 2681, Chesapeake, VA 23327-2681. ☎ +1 757 547 3668 **E:** familyfoot@msn.com (LW, MW, SW, FM/TV)– **Indiana Recording Club**, c/o Bill Davies, 1729 E. 77th St., Indianapolis, IN 46240. (Club for airchecks and recordings of mediumwave stations). – **International Radio Club of America (IRCA)**, P.O.Box 60241, Lafayette, LA 70596. (MW only) **E:** ircamember@ircaonline.org **W:** www.ircaonline.org Pub: *DX Monitor* (by online or hardcopy subscription) – **Longwave Club of America (LWCA)**, 45 Wildflower Road, Levittown, PA 19057. **E:** bil-loliver@verizon.net **W:** www.lwca.org Pub: *The Lowdown* – **Miami Valley DX Club (MVDXC)**, P.O.Box 292132, Columbus, OH 43229. **W:** www.anarc.org/mvdxc Pub: *DX World*. – **Michigan Area Radio Enthusiasts Inc**, P.O.Box 200, Manchester, MI 48158. **E:** mare.radio@gmail.com **W:** mare.radio.tripod.com – **Minnesota DX Club (MDXC)** c/o James Dale, 16330 Germane Ct W, Rosemount, MN 55068. **E:** mndxclub@charter.net **W:** www.frontiernet.net/~jadale Pub: *MDXC Newsletter* – **National Radio Club Inc (NRC)**, P.O.Box 473251, Aurora, CO 80047-3251. (MW only) **E:** sales@nrcdxas.org **W:** www.nrcdxas.org Pub: *DX News* – **North American Shortwave Association (NASWA)**, 45 Wildflower Road, Levittown, PA 19057. **E:** billoliver@verizon.net **W:** www.naswa.net Pub: *The Journal* (by post) and *Flashsheet* (by email) – **Pacific Northwest/British Columbia DX Club**, c/o Bruce Portzer, 6546 19th Ave NE, Seattle WA 98115. **E:** phil_tekno@yahoo.com **W:** www.anarc.org/pnbcdxc Pub: *PNBCDXC newsletter* (every one or two months) – **Puna DX Club**, c/o Jerry Witham, P.O.Box 596, Keaau, HI 96749. – **Rocky Mountain Radio Listeners**, c/o Mike Curta, P.O.Box 470776, Aurora, CO 80047-0776. – **Southern California Area DXers**, c/o Bill Fisher Sr., 6398 Pheasant Drive, Buena Park, CA 90620-1356. **E:** billfishernow@netzero.net – **Worldwide TV-FM DX Association (WFTDA)**, P.O.Box 501, Somersville, CT 06072 (FM/TV only). **E:** sales@wtfda.org **W:** www.wtfda.org Pub: *VHF-UHF Digest*.

SOUTH AMERICA

ARGENTINA: Asociación DX del Litoral, c/o Emilio Pedro Povrzenic, 1 de Mayo 1071, 2124 Villa Diego, Santa Fé. **E:** adx-lboletin@yahoo.com.ar – **Grupo DX Suquía**, c/o Carolina J.G. Vandenberghe, Estafeta Rivera Indarte, C.C. No.26, 5149 Córdoba. **E:** gdxs@hotmail.com – **Grupo Radioescucha Argentino (GRA)**, c/o Marcelo A. Cornachioni, Alvarez Thomas 248, B1832DNF Lomas de Zamora, Buenos Aires. **E:** info@conexiongra.com.ar **W:** grupora-dioescuchaargentino.wordpress.com

BRAZIL: DX Clube do Brasil (DXCP), C.P. 1594, 09571-970 São Caetano do Sul (SP). **E:** dxcb@bol.com.br **W:** www.ondascurtas.com – **Associação DX do Brasil**, C.P. 4, 58300-970 Santa Rita, Paraiba. **E:** cartas@adxb.com.br **W:** www.adxb.com.br

CHILE: Club Diexista de Chile, Calle 3 Ponienta 55, Talca. **E:** chiledxclub@mixmail.com **W:** www.galeon.com/chiledxclub Pub: *Radiograma* – **Federación de Clubes de Radioaficionados de Chile (FEDERACHI)**, c/o Héctor Frías Jofre, Dr. Eduardo Cruz Coke 389, Oficina D, Casilla 9570, Santiago 21. **E:** federachi@federachi.cl **W:** www.federachi.cl

COLOMBIA: Grupo Internacional de Diexistas y Radioaficionados, c/o Miguel Bayona. **E:** m-bayona@hotmail.com

URUGUAY: DX Club Montevideo, Calle Batovi 2068, 11800 Montevideo. **E:** dxclubmontevideo@yahoo.com **W:** groups.yahoo.com/group/dxclubmontevideo (newsgroup)

VENEZUELA: Asociación Diexista de Venezuela, Ap. Postal 65657, Caracas 1066-A. **E:** marl1@hotmail.com – **Club Diexistas de la Amistad**, c/o Ing. Santiago San Gil Gonzáles, Ap. Postal 202, Barinas 5201-A, Estado Barinas. **E:** cdxainternacional@hotmail.com **W:** diexismovenezolano.blogspot.com – **Venezuelan QSL Help**, c/o Winter Monges, Ap. Postal 1.116, Barquisimeto 3001-A, Lara. (SS/EE) **E:** wintermonges@yahoo.com

STANDARD TIME & FREQUENCY TRANSMISSIONS

What are STFTs?

Standard Time and Frequency Transmissions (STFTs) are transmissions aimed at testing and calibrating radio receivers and synchronizing clocks. When broadcast on shortwave, STFTs usually consist of continuous AM and/or SSB transmissions of 'beeps' or 'pips' every second (often referred to as 'Time Signals'), with the time in UTC (or local time) announced at certain intervals. Some stations broadcast for 24 hours a day while other stations run for up to a few hours daily or on certain days of the week.

Also listed in this chapter is a selection of standard broadcast and VLF utility stations that broadcast regular timechecks in modes other than AM/SSB. The VLF transmitters of the maritime navigation networks Loran-C/Chayka on 100kHz and similar VLF txs primarily used for navigation purposes, except for txs of the "Beta" system of the Russian Navy, are not included.

Using STFTs

STFTs are invaluable aids for the SW radio user. Not only do they allow listeners to synchronise clocks to UTC but they are also a handy tool for checking propagation and reception paths. Their most useful role for serious shortwave listeners, however, is for checking that equipment is performing as it should and to test for receiver frequency calibration errors.

Checking Performance

It is possible to carry out tests on a variety of frequencies ranging from 2500 to 20000kHz. First select an appropriate set of STFTs, perhaps by saving them into a set of memory channels if your radio has the facility. A quick check can be made for the characteristic ticks and pulses to ensure that there is a good reception path and that the STFT is currently active, before moving on to the tests themselves. Don't forget that it is essential to allow the radio to warm up for at least one hour before starting these tests.

The object of the exercise is to mix the incoming STFT signal with an internally generated signal from the radio's Beat Frequency Oscillator (BFO) and then tune the radio until the resulting whistle, or heterodyne as it is known, drops down to zero. This process of tuning for 'zero beat' then ensures that the radio is on exactly the same frequency as the transmission – any error shown on the dial will be the receiver error and any drift in tone will be receiver drift.

For most radios it will suffice to select either upper or lower sideband mode with a wide filter setting and use a loudspeaker or pair of headphones with a good low frequency audio performance. Many SW receivers have internal speakers which are not good when it comes to reproducing low notes so are useless for this procedure.

As you carefully tune down and hear the note drop, you should find that the S-meter needle starts to fluctuate. This means that you are very close to 'zero beat'. The lower the rate of S-meter needle movement, the nearer you are to the end point. At this stage you will probably not be able to hear much in the headphones apart from a near silent carrier, and the meter will be your best guide as it will be indicating the 'phase error' between the STFT and your BFO. When your needle moves at its slowest rate, you have reached zero beat. Make a note of the dial reading as this will show the receiver error.

For those radios with particularly good filters, which may prevent a 'zero beat' approach, a similar technique can be used by switching to CW mode. This method requires the use of an audio digital frequency meter – ask around at your radio club and you will probably find one. First of all, refer to the manual and find the 'CW offset' frequency. This is the audio frequency which the receiver will produce when it is exactly tuned to the carrier of the STFT. Common values are 600Hz to 800Hz. Some radios allow the user to programme the CW offset, so make sure that it has not been changed before you start the tests.

The procedure is essentially the same as has just been described, except that you will be tuning the radio until the DFM reads 600Hz exactly, then the receiver dial will show you any error. By repeating this test on a number of frequencies, you can be confident that your radio is accurate, or at least be aware of any errors or developing problems, and of course these are handy techniques for testing a radio you are considering buying.

STFT Stations, Schedules and Contact Information

ARGENTINA

Servicio de Hidrografía Naval, Observatorio Naval, Av. España 2099, 1107 Buenos Aires, Argentina ☎ +54 11 43611162 🖅 +54 11 43611162 **E:** onba@hidro.gov.ar **W:** www.hidro.gov.ar

Location	Call	kHz	kW	Mode	Schedule
Buenos Aires	LOL	10000	2	AM	1400-1500 (MF)

BELARUS

43-y uzel svyazi Voenno-morskogo Flota RF, Vileyka, Belarus.

Location	Call	kHz	kW	Mode	Schedule
Vileyka	RJH69	*25	300	CW	0406-0447

Key: *) :06-:25 on 25.0, :27-:30 on 25.1, :32-:35 on 25.5, :38-:41 on 23.0, :44-:47 on 20.5kHz.
NB: Site is operated by Russian Navy; see Russia for HQ.

BRAZIL

Divisão Serviço da Hora (DSHO), Observatório Nacional, R. Gal. José Cristino 77, São Cristóvão, Rio de Janeiro, CEP 20921-400, Brazil ☎ +55 21 35049100 🖅 +55 21 25806041 **E:** dsh@on.br **W:** www.horalegalbrasil.mct.on.br

Location	Call	kHz	kW	Mode	Schedule
Rio de Janeiro	PPE	10000	1	AM/U	24h

CANADA

Institute for National Measurement Standards, National Research Council of Canada (NRC-INMS), 1200 Montreal Road, Bldg M-36, Ottawa, Ontario, K1A 0R6, Canada ☎ +1 613 9935698 🖅 +1 613 9521394 **E:** radio.chu@nrc-cnrc.gc.ca **W:** www.nrc-cnrc.gc.ca

Location	Call	kHz	kW	Mode	Schedule
Ottawa	CHU	3330	10	AM/U	24h
	CHU	7850	3	AM/U	24h
	CHU	14670	3	AM/U	24h

CHINA (P.R.)

National Time Service Center (NTSC), Chinese Academy of Sciences, P.O.Box 18, Lintong 710600, Shaanxi, P.R.China ☎ +86 29 83890326 🖅 +86 29 83890196 **E:** kyc@ntsc.ac.cn **W:** www.ntsc.ac.cn

Location	Call	kHz	kW	Mode	Schedule
Shangqiu	BPC	68.5	-	CW	0000-2100
Lintong	BPM	2500	10	AM	0730-0100
(Mt. Li)	BPM	5000	20	AM	24h
	BPM	10000	20	AM	24h
	BPM	15000	20	AM	0100-0900

ECUADOR

Instituto Oceanográfico de la Armada, Casilla 5940, Guayaquil, Ecuador ☎+593 4 2481300 🖅 +593 4 2485166 **E:** inocar@inocar.mil.ec **W:** www.inocar.mil.ec

Location	Call	kHz	kW	Mode	Schedule
Guayaquil	HD2IOA	3810	1	AM/U	0000-1200

FINLAND

✉ Centre for Metrology and Accreditation (MIKES), P.O.Box 9, Tekniikantie 1, 02151 Espoo, Finland ☎+358 29 5054000 🖷 +358 29 5054299 **E**: kalevi.kalliomaki@mikes.fi **W**: www.mikes.fi

Location	Call	kHz	kW	Mode	Schedule
Espoo	(none)	25000	0.1	AM	24h

NB: Tx is intended for local service only.

FRANCE

✉ Laboratoire national de métrologie et d'essais - Système de Références Temps-Espace (LNE-SYRTE), 61 avenue de l'Observatoire, 75014 Paris, France ☎+33 140512070 🖷 +33 143255542 **E**: info.syrte@obspm.fr **W**: syrte.obspm.fr

Location	Call	kHz	kW	Mode	Schedule
Allouis	(none)	162	2000*	PSK	24h

Key: *) 1000kW evening/nighttime
NB: Tx is provided by Télédiffusion de France (TDF) and carries the France Inter radio prgr.

GERMANY

✉ Physikalisch-Technische Bundesanstalt (PTB), Bundesallee 100, 38116 Braunschweig, Germany ☎ +49 531 5923006 🖷 +49 531 5923008 **E**: time@ptb.de **W**: www.ptb.de

Location	Call	kHz	kW	Mode	Schedule
Mainflingen	DCF77	77.5	50	CW/PSK	24h

NB: Tx is leased from Media Broadcast.

HAWAII (USA)

✉ NIST radio station WWVH, P.O.Box 417, Kekaha, HI 96752, USA **E**: wwvh@boulder.nist.gov

Location	Call	kHz	kW	Mode	Schedule
Kekaha, HI	WWVH	2500	5	AM	24h
	WWVH	5000	10	AM	24h
	WWVH	10000	10	AM	24h
	WWVH	15000	10	AM	24h

NB: Time announced in female voice. NIST HQ: see USA.

JAPAN

✉ National Institute of Information and CommunicationsTechnology (NICT), Applied Electromagnetic Research Institute, Japan Standard Time Group, 4-2-1, Nukui-Kitamachi, Koganei, Tokyo 184-8795, Japan ☎ +81 42 3277567 🖷 +81 42 3276689 **E**: horonet @ nict.go.jp **W**: jjy.nict.go.jp

Location	Call	kHz	kW	Mode	Schedule
Mt. Ohtakadoya	JJY	40	10	CW	24h
Mt. Hagane	JJY	60	10	CW	24h

KOREA, SOUTH

✉ Center for Time and Frequency, Korea Research Institute of Standards & Science (KRISS), P.O.Box 102, Yusong, Daejeon 305-600, Rep. of Korea ☎ +82 42 8685114 🖷 +82 42 8611494 **E**: hslee@kriss.re.kr **W**: www.kriss.re.kr

Location	Call	kHz	kW	Mode	Schedule
Daejeon	HLA	5000	2	AM	24h

KYRGYZSTAN

✉ Sukhoputnyy uzel svyazi Tikhookeanskogo flota VMF RF, Chaldybar, Kyrgyzstan.

Location	Call	kHz	kW	Mode	Schedule
Chaldybar	RJH66	*25	300	CW	0206-0247,0806-0847

Key: *) :06-:25 on 25.0, :27-:30 on 25.1, :32-:35 on 25.5, :38-:41 on 23.0, :44-:47 on 20.5kHz.
NB: Site is operated by Russian Navy; see Russia for HQ.

RUSSIA

✉ Generalniy Shtab Voenno-morskogo Flota RF (Russian Navy), St.Petersburg, Russia **W**: www.navy.ru

Location	Call	kHz	kW	Mode	Schedule
Arkhangelsk	RJH77	*25	300	CW	0706-0747
Khabarovsk	RAB99	**25	300	CW	0006-0040, 0406-0440
Krasnodar	RJH63	**25	300	+CW	0906-0940
N.Novgorod	RJH90	*25	300	CW	0606-0647

Key: *) :06-:25 on 25.0, :27-:30 on 25.1, :32-:35 on 25.5, :38-:41 on 23.0, :44-:47 on 20.5kHz; **) :06-:20 on 25.0, :21-23 on 25.1, :24-:26 on 25.5, :27-:31 on 23.0, :32-:40 on 20.5kHz; +) also in FSK mode :36-:40 on 20.5kHz.

✉ Main Metrological Center of the State Service for Time, Frequency and Earth rotation parameters determination (SSTF), National Research Institute for Physicotechnical and Radio Engineering Measurements (FSUE "VNIIFTRI"), Moscow Region, 141570 Mendeleevo, Russia ☎+7 495 5350836 🖷 +7 495 5350871 **E**: office@vniiftri.ru **W**: www.vniiftri.ru

Location	Call	kHz	kW	Mode	Schedule
Taldom	RBU	66.66	10	AM	24h
Taldom	RWM	4996	5	CW	24h
Taldom	RWM	9996	5	CW	24h
Taldom	RWM	14996	8	CW	24h

✉ East Siberian Branch of FSUE "VNIIFTR", 664056 Irkutsk, ul. Borodina 57, Russia ☎+7 3952 468303 🖷 +7 3952 463848 **E**: office@niiftri.irk.ru **W**: www.vniiftri-irk.ru

Location	Call	kHz	kW	Mode	Schedule
Angarsk	RTZ	50	10	CW	2000-1900

SPAIN

✉ Real Instituto y Observatorio de la Armada (ROA), Calle Cecilio Pujazón s/n, 11110 San Fernando ☎+34 956545590 🖷 +34 956599366 **W**: www.armada.mde.es

Location	Call	kHz	kW	Mode	Schedule
San Fernando	EBC	4998	10	CW	1030-1055 (MF)
		15006	10	CW	1000-1025 (MF)

NB: Service temporarily suspended.

TAIWAN

✉ National Time and Frequency Standard Laboratory, 12, Lane 551, Min-Tsu Road, Sec. 5, Yang-Mei, Taoyuan, 326, Rep. of China ☎+886 3 4244066 🖷 +886 3 4245474 **E**: linht@cht.com.tw **W**: www.stdtime.gov.tw

NB: Construction of a VLF time signal stn is projected near Lukang.

UNITED KINGDOM

✉ National Physical Laboratory, Hampton Road, Teddington, Middlesex, TW11 0LW, United Kingdom ☎ +44 20 89773222 🖷 +44 20 86140446 **E**: time@npl.co.uk **W**: www.npl.co.uk

Location	Call	kHz	kW	Mode	Schedule
Anthorn*	MSF	60	15	CW	24h
Droitwich**	(none)	198	400	PSK	24h
Burghead**	(none)	198	50	PSK	24h
Westerglen**	(none)	198	50	PSK	24h

Key: *) Tx is leased from Babcock; **) Txs are provided by Arqiva and carry the BBC Radio 4/BBCWS prgrs.

UNITED STATES OF AMERICA

✉ National Institute of Standards and Technology (NIST), Physical Masurement Laboratory, Time & Frequency Division, 325 Broadway, M/S 847, Boulder, CO 80305-3328, USA ☎ +1 303 4973295 🖷 +1 303 4976461 **E**: inquiries@nist.gov **W**: www.nist.gov

✉ NIST radio stations WWV/WWVB, 2000 East County Rd. 58, Ft. Collins, CO 80524 **E**: nist.radio@boulder.nist.gov

Location	Call	kHz	kW	Mode	Schedule
Ft. Collins, CO	WWVB	60	50	CW	24h
	WWV	2500	2.5	AM	24h
	WWV	5000	10	AM	24h
	WWV	10000	10	AM	24h
	WWV	15000	10	AM	24h
	WWV	20000	2.5	AM	24h

NB: WWV: Time announced in male voice. See also under Hawaii.

INTERNATIONAL ORGANISATIONS

ARAB STATES BROADCASTING UNION (ASBU)
CP 250, 1080 Tunis Cedex, Tunisia. Street address: Avenue Mohamed Ali Akid, Tunis, Tunisia
☎ +216 71849000 ▯ +216 71843054
E: asbu@asbu.nET **W:** www.asbu.net
L.P: Pres: Riyadh Kamal Najm; Vice Pres: Momtaz al-Skeikh

ASIA-PACIFIC BROADCASTING UNION (ABU)
P.O.Box 12287, 50772 Kuala Lumpur, Malaysia
☎ +60 3 22823592 ▯ +60 3 22825292
E: info@abu.org.my **W:** www.abu.org.my
LP: Pres: Kim In-Kyu; Secr. General: Javad Mottaghi

ASIA-PACIFIC INSTITUTE FOR BROADCASTING DEVELOPMENT (AIBD)
P.O.Box 12066, 50766 Kuala Lumpur, Malaysia. Street address: Angkasapuri, Jalan Pantai Dalam, 50614 Kuala Lumpur, Malaysia
☎ +60 3 22824618 ▯ +60 3 22822761
E: info@aibd.org.my **W:** www.aibd.org.my
L.P: Dir: Yang Binyuan

ASIA-PACIFIC SATELLITE COMMUNICATIONS COUNCIL (APSCC)
Suite T-1602 Poonglim Iwantplus, 255-1 Seohyun-dong, Bundang-gu, Seongnam, Kyungi-do 463-862, Republic of Korea
☎ +82 31 7836244 ▯ +82 31 7836249
E: info@apscc.or.kr **W:** www.apscc.or.kr
L.P: Pres: Yutaka Nagai

ASOCIACIÓN INTERNACIONAL DE RADIODIFUSIÓN (AIR)
Oficina Central, Carlos Quijano 1264, 11100 Montevideo, Uruguay ☎ +598 2 9011319 ▯ +598 2 9080458
E: mail@airiab.com **W:** www.airiab.com
L.P: Pres: Luís Pardo Sainz; DG: Héctor Oscar Amengual

CARIBBEAN BROADCASTING UNION (CBU)
CBU Secretariat, Suite 1B, Building #6A, Harbour Industrial Estate, Harbour Road, St. Michael, 11145, Barbados
☎ +1 246 4301006 ▯ +1 246 2289524
E: patrick.cozier@caribsurf.com **W:** www.caribunion.com
L.P: Secr. General: Patrick Cozier

COMMONWEALTH BROADCASTING ORGANISATION (CBA)
Secretariat, 17 Fleet Street, London EC4Y 1AA, United Kingdom
☎ +44 20 75835550 ▯ +44 20 75835549
E: cba@cba.org.uk **W:** www.cba.org.uk
L.P: Pres/GM: Moneeza Hashimi; Secr. General: Sally-Ann Wilson

DIGITAL RADIO MONDIALE (DRM)
DRM Project Office (London), c/o BBC World Service, Broadcasting House, Portland Place, London W1A 1AA, United Kingdom
☎ +44 20 75573271 ▯ +44 20 75570225
E: projectoffice@drm.org **W:** www.drm.org
L.P: Chmn (DRM Consortium)/Pres (DRM Association): Ruxandra Obeja

EUROPEAN BROADCASTING UNION (EBU)
L'Ancienne-Route 17A, CH-1218 Grand-Saconnex, Switzerland
☎ +41 22 7172111 ▯ +41 22 7474000
E: ebu@ebu.ch **W:** www.ebu.ch
L.P: Pres: Jean-Paul Philippot; DG: Ingrid Deltenre

HIGH FREQUENCY CO-ORDINATION CONFERENCE (HFCC)
Vinohradská 28, 12000 Praha 2, Czech Republic
☎ +420 91 0110774
E: info@hfcc.org **W:** www.hfcc.org
L.P: Chmn: Oldrich Cip

INTERNATIONAL INSTITUTE OF COMMUNICATIONS (IIC)
2 Printers Yard, 90a Broadway, London SW19 1RD, United Kingdom
☎ +44 20 84170600 ▯ +44 20 84170800
E: enquiries@iicom.org **W:** www.iicom.org
L.P: Pres: Fabio Colasanti

INTERNATIONAL TELECOMMUNICATIONS UNION (ITU)
Place des Nations, 1211 Genève 20, Switzerland
☎ +41 22 7305111 ▯ +41 22 7337256
E: itumail@itu.int **W:** www.itu.int
L.P: Secr. General: Hamadoun Touré; Deputy Secr. General: Houlin Zhao

ISLAMIC BROADCASTING UNION (IBU)
P.O.Box 6351, 21442 Jeddah, Saudi Arabia; Street address: 80 Rabita Islamia Street, Mushrafa, Jeddah, Saudi Arabia
☎ +966 2 6722269 ▯ +966 2 6722600
L.P: DG: Mohamedou Salem Ould Bouke

NORTH AMERICAN BROADCASTERS ASSOCIATION (NABA)
P.O.Box 500, Station A, Toronto, Ontario, M5W 1E6, Canada
☎ +1 416 5989877 ▯ +1 416 5989774
E: contact@nabanet.com **W:** www.nabanet.com
L.P: Pres: Robert Briskman; DG: Michael McEwen

SOUTHERN AFRICAN BROADCASTING ASSOCIATION (SABA)
Postnet Suite No. 210, Private Bag X9, Melville 2109, South Africa
☎ +27 11 8884472 ▯ +27 11 8884489
E: sabahq@telkomsa.net
L.P: Pres: Albertus Aochamub; Secr. General: Arlindo Lopez

UNION AFRICAINE DE RADIODIFFUSION (UAR)
BP 3237, Dakar, Senegal. Street address: 101 Rue Carnot, Dakar, Senegal
☎ +338211625 ▯ +221 338225113
W: www.aub-uar.org
L.P: Pres: Julien Pierre Akpaki; CEO: Lawrence Atiase

WORLD ASSOCIATION OF COMMUNITY RADIO BROADCASTERS (AMARC)
International Secretariat, 2 rue Sainte-Catherine Est, suite 102, Montréal, Quebec, H2X 1K4, Canada
☎ +1 514 9820351 ▯ +1 514 8497129
E: secretariat@si.amarc.org **W:** www.amarc.org
L.P: Pres: Maria Pia Matta; Secr. General: Marcelo Solervicens

WORLD DMB FORUM
WorldDMB Forum Project Office, 6th Floor, 55 New Oxford Street, London, WC1A 1BS, United Kingdom
☎ +44 20 70100742 ▯ +44 20 72884643
E: info@worlddab.org **W:** www.worlddab.org
L.P: Pres: Jørn Jensen

SELECTED INTERNET RESOURCES FOR DXERS & RADIO LISTENERS

GENERAL & LINK PAGES:

BCL News: bclnews.it
BCL News (Chinese): www.5bcl.com
Bruce's AM Log: bamlog.com
DX Information Centre: dxinfocentre.com
DXing.com: dxing.com
DXing.info: dxing.info
Dxingworld.com: dxingworld.com
DX Portal (Russian): dxing.ru
Canada's Original World Band Radio page: dxer.ca
Hard-Core-DX: hard-core-dx.com
History of SW: ontheshortwaves.com
History of WRTH: wrthhistory.com
Predavatel Europa: predavatel.eu
Radio Communication Archive: dokufunk.org
Radio Portal: radio portal.org
Radio Heritage Foundation: radioheritage.net
World of Radio: worldofradio.com

DATABASES & SCHEDULES:

ADDX Foreign Frequency List:
addx.de/Hfpdat/plaene.php
AM Query: fcc.gov/mb/audio/amq.html
Asian Broadcasting Institute: abiweb.jp
Bi Newsletter: geocities.jp/binewsjp
Broadcasting in South & SE Asia: asiawaves.net
Canada & US AM Station Info: topazdesigns.com/ambc
Combined HF Skeds: hfskeds.com/skeds
DXAsia: dxasia.info
EiBi Shortwave Schedules: eibi.de.vu
Euro-African Medium Wave Guide: emwg.info
FM List: fmlist.org
MW List: mwlist.org
KOJE-KOH-KOMEX: www.tapiokalmi.net/dx/koje
Pacific Asian Log: radioheritage.net/PAL_search.asp
Prime Time Shortwave: primetimeshortwave.com
Short-wave Info: short-wave.info
SW Radio Resource Center: shortwave.hfradio.org

NEWS SOURCES AND BULLETINS:

BC-DX Top News: wwdxc.de/topnews.htm
Diexman (Spanish): www.galeon.com/diexman
DX-Listening Digest: worldofradio.com/dxldmid.html
Electronic DX Press Radio Monitoring Association:
edxp.org
Shortwave Bulletin: hard-core-dx.com/swb
Ydun's Mediumwave Info: mediumwave.info

ONLINE RADIO:

mikesradioworld.com – live365.com – multilingualbooks.
com/online-radio.html –publicradiofan.com – radiobeta.
com –radiosure.com –radiotower.com – reciva.com

– shoutcast.com – tvradionetwork.com – web-radio.fm
– vtuner.com
Web DX-listening: globaltuners.com – onlinereceivers.
net – remotehams.com – sdrspace.com

RECEIVERS, ANTENNAS:

Dave's Radio Receiver page: n9ewo.angelfire.com
RF Circuit Building Blocks Page: qsl.net/wa1ion

STATION IDENTIFICATION:

Interval Signals Online: intervalsignals.net
National Anthems: national-anthems.net –
nationalanthems.info
Interval Signal Database: intervalsignals.org

PROPAGATION:

Solar Terrestrial Activity Report: solen.info/solar
Space Weather Prediction Center: swpc.noaa.gov

MAILING LISTS ETC:

A-DX Mailingliste (G): ratzer.at/A_DX_Info.php
Hard-Core-DX mailing list:
hard-core-dx.com/mailman/listinfo/hard-core-dx
IRC at irc.starchat.net: #mwdx & #swl
Radio Globe DX (French): rglobe.canalblog.com
Lists at ml.free.fr: Radio Globe DX (French): rglobe.canal-
blog.com & Euro Radio (Fr/Eng, eradio)
Google groups: groups.google.com/group/rus-radio-dx
(Ru) –groups.google.com/group/fr.rec.radio (F)
Lists at Mailman.qth.net: AMFMTVDX – SWL
Lists at Yahoogroups.com: ABDX – ASWLC – ausS-
WDXgroup – bangladx – bclnews (It.) – condiglist (S)
– conexiondigital (S) – cumbre_dx – dexismo (Port.)
– DRM-shortwave-dx – drmna – dxld – dxingwithcumbre
– dxplorer – dx_india – dx_rad (F) – dx_sasia – fmdxitalia
(I) – harmonics – LatinMWDX – longwaveradiostation-lis-
tening – media_dx (Ru.) – mwdx – mw-br (Port.) – NORDX
(Sw.) – NoticiasDX (S) – ondescourtes (F) – open_dx
(Ru.) – PakistanDXers – playdx2003 (I) – ptdx (Port.)
– RadioBroadcasting – radioescutas (Port.) – RealDX
– recradioshortwave – rusdx (Ru.) – SDRlist – shortwave
– ShortwaveBasics – shortwavedxing – shortwavelisten-
ing – ShortWaveRadio – ShortwaveRadios – shortwave-
radio – shortwaves – shortwavesites – Shortwave-SWL-
Antenna –skywavesdx – skywavesmw – soft_radio
– SWPirates – SWR-Wordwide – thebasicsofshortwave
– UDXF – webreceivers
Facebook.com: Cumbre DX – India DXing Cooperation
Forum – Indian DX Club International – No Mundo do
Dexismo (Port.) – Radio Listening Interest Group –
World DX

ADVERTISERS' INDEX

ADVERTISING SALES

Advertising sales manager:

Advertising Sales Manager
PO Box 290
Oxford OX2 7BG
UK
Tel: +44 1865 339355
Fax: +44 1865 339301
Email: wrth@wrth.com